MARYLAND 1850 CENSUS INDEX

EDITOR

Ronald Vern Jackson

Accelerated Indexing Systems, Inc.

Bountiful, Utah 84010

First printing 1976

ISBN 0-89593-065-X

Publisher

Accelerated Indexing Systems, Inc.®

Bountiful, Utah 84010

Made in the United States of America

PREFACE

THE COMPILATION OF A COMPLETE, CORRECT LISTING OF ALL PERSONS LISTED IN THIS CENSUS HAS BEEN A RATHER AWESOME TASK WITH THE VARIOUS TYPES OF HANDWRITING AND THE QUALITY OF THE MICROFILM COPY. EVERY EFFORT HAS BEEN MADE TO MAKE THIS VOLUME AS COMPLETE AND ACCURATE AS POSSIBLE, BUT SOME ERRORS OR OMISSIONS ARE INEVITABLE IN A WORK OF THIS TYPE. ACCELERATED INDEXING SYSTEMS EARNESTLY SOLICITS CORRECTIONS IN EXISTING OR OMITTED ENTRIES WITH CORRECTIONS NOTED. PLEASE SEND ALL SUCH INFORMATION TO A.I.S., 483 WEST 5300 SOUTH, SALT LAKE CITY, 84102.

ACCELERATED INDEXING SYSTEMS, INC. HAS AND IS PIONEERING THE WAY IN MERGING THE SCIENCES OF COMPUTER TECHNOLOGY AND GENEALOGY. THE USE OF COMPUTERS IN THE FIELD OF GENEALOGY HAS BROUGHT GENEALOGY FROM THE HUNT AND GUESS SYSTEM OF THE DARK AGES INTO THE WORLD OF SCIENTIFIC REALITY. ALTHOUGH COMPUTERS WERE ORIGINALLY DESIGNED WITH THE IDEA OF INDEXING SOME OF THE LATER UNITED STATES CENSUS RECORDS, IT WAS NEARLY THREE DECADES LATER (1967) WHEN ACCELERATED INDEXING SYSTEMS, INC. USED COMPUTER TECHNOLOGY TO REPRODUCE AND INDEX THE MASSIVE VOLUMES OF UNITED STATES CENSUS RECORDS.

OUR GOAL IS TO CREATE ONE "MASTER FILE" FOR THE UNITED STATES, CONTAINING ALL OF THE AMERICAN COLONIAL, CONTINENTAL, STATE AND FEDERAL CENSUS RECORDS WHICH EXIST UP TO AND INCLUDING THE 1880 FEDERAL CENSUS. THE WORK IS PROGRESSING IN AN ORDERLY, WELL ORGANIZED MANNER. THE ADVANTAGES OF INDEXING BY COMPUTER ARE MANY. HERE ARE JUST A FEW OF THE ADVANTAGES:

1. THE ENTIRE KNOWN CENSUS IS AVAILABLE IN A READABLE FORM (WHEN LEGIBLE ON THE FILM).
2. THE CENSUS CAN BE SEARCHED IN SECONDS, <u>NOT</u> DAYS, WEEKS OR MONTHS

3. NAMES OF PARTICULAR FAMILY MEMBERS ARE IN ONE PLACE.

4. THE INDEX LETS A RESEARCHER KNOW IF A PERSON IS OR IS NOT LISTED IN THE ORIGINAL TEXT.

5. ACCURACY IS INCREASED AND RESEARCH IS MADE EASIER.

SINCE 1900 THE COMPUTER HAS BEEN USED FOR THE PURPOSE OF COMPILING LARGE AMOUNTS OF DATA FROM CENSUS RECORDS. IT WAS SOME SEVENTY YEARS LATER BEFORE GENEALOGISTS WERE ABLE TO RECEIVE ANY DIRECT BENEFITS FROM ITS USE. THE MOST IMPORTANT BENEFIT IS THE NAME INDEX, WHICH, OF COURSE, DOES NOT SOLVE ALL OF OUR RESEARCH PROBLEMS. SUCH PROBLEMS AS SPELLING VARIATIONS, POOR WRITING. FAINT AND ILLEGIBLE FILMS, ETC., WILL REMAIN. DESPITE THESE PROBLEMS, A COMPLETE STATE INDEX WILL BE AN INDISPENSABLE RESEARCH TOOL.

THE UNITED STATES FEDERAL CENSUS IS CONSIDERED ONE OF THE MAIN STIMULANTS IN THE DEVELOPMENT OF THE COMPUTER. PUNCHED CARDS WERE FIRST CONSIDERED AS A MEANS OF PROCESSING LARGE AMOUNTS OF DATA WHEN SLOW MANUAL METHODS LED TO GREAT DELAYS IN THE TABULATION OF THE 1880 CENSUS ENUMERATION.

THE INVENTOR OF THE MODERN-DAY PUNCHED CARD WAS A STATISTICIAN BY THE NAME OF DR. HERMAN HOLLERITH. HE WAS HIRED BY THE CENSUS BUREAU TO ASSIST IN FINDING A SOLUTION TO THE CENSUS PROBLEM. IN 1887, HOLLERITH DEVELOPED THE CONCEPT OF A CARD, READABLE BY MACHINE, AND SUBSEQUENTLY DESIGNED A CARD SORTER KNOWN AS THE "CENSUS MACHINE."

TABULATING TIME WITH HOLLERITH'S MACHINE WAS GREATLY REDUCED, AND HIS METHODS WERE QUICKLY ADOPTED BY THE CENSUS BUREAU FOR USE IN THE 1890 CENSUS ENUMERATION. HIS MACHINE WAS CAPABLE OF PROCESSING UP TO 80 CARDS PER MINUTE, WHICH MEANT THAT THE 1890 ENUMERATION COULD BE COMPLETED IN LESS THAN THREE YEARS. WITHOUT HOLLERITH'S TECHNIQUES, THE COMPLETION OF THE 1890 CENSUS WOULD MOST LIKELY HAVE CON-

TINUED BEYOND 1900, VIOLATING THE CONSTITUTIONAL PROVISION THAT CONGRESSIONAL SEATS BE REAPPORTIONED EVERY TEN YEARS ON THE BASIS OF POPULATION RETURNS.

AFTER COMPLETING THE 1890 CENSUS, HOLLERITH BEGAN CONVERTING HIS MACHINE TO COMMERCIAL USE. IN 1896, HE FORMED THE TABULATION MACHINE COMPANY, WHICH LATER MERGED INTO WHAT BECAME THE INTERNATIONAL BUSINESS MACHINES CORPORATION (IBM). LATER, IN 1944, HARVARD PROFESSOR HOWARD AIKEN, WORKING IN CONNECTION WITH IBM ENGINEERS AND JAMES POWERS PRODUCED THE FIRST LARGE ELECTROMECHANICAL COMPUTER.

JAMES POWERS WAS A MAN WHO HAD FORMERLY BEEN EMPLOYED BY THE CENSUS BUREAU. HE WAS HIRED BY THE BUREAU FOR THE PURPOSE OF DEVELOPING ADDITIONAL MACHINERY FOR USE IN THE 1910 CENSUS ENUMERATION. HIS MACHINES WERE USED SO SUCCESSFULLY FOR THE 1910 ENUMERATION THAT IN 1911 HE FORMED THE POWERS ACCOUNTING MACHINE COMPANY. AFTER A LATER MERGER THIS BECAME THE REMINGTON RAND CORPORATION. IN 1951, AFTER MUCH PROGRESS, REMINGTON RAND PLACED THE FIRST COMMERCIALLY PRODUCED COMPUTER (UNIVERSAL AUTOMATIC COMPUTER, UNIVAC I) IN THE CENSUS BUREAU. THE UNIVAC I WAS A TOTALLY ELECTRONIC COMPUTER AND WAS USED BY THE CENSUS BUREAU WITH MUCH SUCCESS UNTIL IT WAS TRANSFERRED TO THE .SMITHSONIAN INSTITUTE IN 1963.

THERE WERE MANY MAJOR PROBLEMS WHICH CONFRONTED EARLY TABULATION EFFORTS; TABULATION OF DATA, ITS PRESENTATION IN GRAPHICAL OR PICTORIAL FORM, THE CALCULATION OF DESCRIPTIVE MEASURES, AND ITS STATISTICAL ANALYSIS WERE ONLY A FEW OF THE PROBLEMS. IT WAS DISCOVERED THAT THE COMPUTERS ARE BY FAR THE QUICKEST, MOST ACCURATE, AND ECONOMICAL WAY OF ACCOMPLISHING THESE TASKS.

FOR THE GENEALOGIST, THIS MEANS THAT CENSUS INDEXES CAN NOW BE PRODUCED IN RELATIVELY SHORT PERIODS OF TIME, WHEREAS BEFORE IT TOOK

MANY YEARS OF HARD, LABORIOUS WORK. ACCELERATED INDEXING SYSTEMS, INC., THE LEADER IN COMPUTERIZED GENEALOGY, HAS REALIZED THE GREAT IMPORTANCE THAT THE FEDERAL CENSUS PLAYS IN GENEALOGICAL RESEARCH, AND IS NOW ACTIVELY ENGAGED IN INDEXING, BY MODERN METHODS, THE CENSUS RECORDS OF THE 18TH AND 19TH CENTURIES.

THE ADVANTAGES OF USING THE COMPUTERIZED CENSUS INDEXES ARE MANY. FIRST, THE ORIGINAL RECORDS ARE READ BY PROFESSIONAL PEOPLE WHO ARE TRAINED IN PALEOGRAPHY; THE CHANCES FOR ERROR IN READING THE OLD WRITING ARE GREATLY REDUCED. SECOND, RESEARCH IS MADE EASIER AND MORE ACCURATE BECAUSE THE COMPUTER INDEX PUTS FAMILY NAMES IN ONE PLACE, IN A MORE READABLE FORM, WITH THE RESULT THAT A PERSON CAN KNOW IN A MATTER OF SECONDS WHETHER OR NOT A NAME IS LISTED IN THE ORIGINAL TEXT. GENEALOGICAL RESEARCH CAN NOW BE DONE IN LESS TIME, WITH GREATER REWARDS, WITH MORE ENJOYMENT, AND BY ANYONE WHO CAN PICK UP A BOOK AND READ THE TYPEWRITTEN PAGES. BOTH PROFESSIONAL AND LAY RESEARCHERS WILL FIND THE INDEXES VALUABLE TOOLS IN THEIR RESEARCH.

UNFORTUNATELY, CENSUS RECORDS ARE NOT PERFECT; TO OUR KNOWLEDGE, THERE DOES NOT EXIST TODAY ANY CENSUS RECORD THAT CAN BE CONSIDERED COMPLETE. OCCASIONALLY, PEOPLE KNOW OF AN ANCESTOR WHO LIVED IN A PARTICULAR PLACE, BUT THEY CANNOT FIND HIS NAME IN THE CENSUS RECORDS. TO HELP UNDERSTAND WHY A NAME MAY NOT BE FOUND, CONSIDER THE FOLLOWING FACTS:

1. ALL OF THE ORIGINAL CENSUS MANUSCRIPT OF A PARTICULAR STATE MAY BE MISSING. EXAMPLES: DELAWARE 1790, WASHINGTON D.C. 1810, GEORGIA 1790.

2. PARTS OF A CENSUS RECORD MAY BE MISSING FOR A PARTICULAR STATE OR COUNTY. EXAMPLES: TENNESSEE 1810, 1820; NORTH CAROLINA 1790; OHIO 1800,- 1810; AND GEORGIA 1800.

3. SOMETIMES THE CENSUS TAKER MISSED NAMES THROUGH NEGLECT, LAZINESS, OR DRUNKENESS. EXAMPLE: BALTIMORE CO., MARYLAND 1800.

4. NAMES WERE OMITTED IF PEOPLE WERE NOT HOME AT THE TIME THE CENSUS TAKER CAME. THIS IS PARTICULARLY TRUE IN THE LARGER CITIES.

5. PEOPLE WHO LIVED IN REMOTE RURAL AREAS WERE OCCASIONALLY NOT REACHED AND RECORDED.

6. MANY CENSUS TAKERS SPELLED NAMES PHONETICALLY AND NOT AS THEY WERE SPELLED BY THE FAMILY. FOR EXAMPLE: FISHER INSTEAD OF PHISHER OR PFISHER.

7. THE CENSUS TAKER MAY NOT HAVE KNOWN HOW TO SPELL THE NAME AT ALL, AND MAY HAVE GUESSED.

8. PEOPLE SEARCHING FOR A NAME ARE SOMETIMES NOT AWARE OF ALL THE SPELLING VARIATIONS THAT A NAME MAY HAVE. FOR EXAMPLE: WYATT, WIATT, VIATT, WYETT, ETC.

9. MANY ENUMERATORS WROTE POORLY OR USED THEIR OWN STYLE OF WRITING WHICH MAY BE IMPOSSIBLE TO READ.

10. NAMES MAY BE BLOCKED OUT OR LOST FROM THE ORIGINAL RECORD BY INK SMEARS, DAMAGED PAGES, TAPE REPAIRS, IMPROPER CUTTING, FAULTY BINDERY WORK, FADED INK, OR LOW QUALITY PHOTOGRAPHY.

11. NAMES MAY HAVE BEEN OMITTED WHEN THE CENSUS WORKERS MADE COPIES FOR THE STATE AND COUNTY GOVERNMENTS.

12. IN THE CASE OF THE CENSUS INDEX, THE INDEXER MAY NOT HAVE BEEN ABLE TO READ OR PERHAPS MISREAD THE NAME DUE TO SOME OF THE ABOVE REASONS. WHEN AN ERROR IS FOUND OF THIS TYPE, THE PUBLISHERS TAKE THE NECESSARY STEPS TO CORRECT IT.

DESPITE IMPERFECTIONS, CENSUSES REMAIN AN IMPORTANT AND VALUABLE GENEALOGICAL TOOL AND THE ADVENT OF THE COMPUTER HAS GREATLY ENHANCED THEIR USEFULNESS. AGAIN A.I.S. EARNESTLY SOLICITS CORRECTIONS FROM THE USERS OF OUR INDEXES.

INDEXES OF THE 1790, 1800, 1810, 1820, 1830, AND 1840 CENSUSES LIST ONLY THE "HEADS OF HOUSEHOLDS," THEREFORE OTHER SOURCES MUST BE CONSULTED TO DETERMINE THE OTHER MEMBERS OF THE HOUSEHOLD. THE EDITORS TRUST THAT THIS INDEX WILL BE HELPFUL IN CONDUCTING HISTORICAL RESEARCH IN THIS STATE. THE 1850 CENSUS INDEXES INCLUDE THE HEADS OF HOUSEHOLDS AND ANY OTHER SURNAME WITHIN THE HOUSE.

SINCERELY, THE EDITORS

INSTRUCTIONS TO THE CENSUS ENUMERATORS

WITHIN THE FOLLOWING PAGES ARE THE INSTRUCTIONS TO THE MARSHALL IN CHARGE OF TAKING THE CENSUS ENUMERATIONS. THESE INSTRUCTIONS ARE THOSE INSTITUTED BY CONGRESSIONAL LAW FROM 1789 TO 1850 INCLUSIVE.

EVEN THOUGH THIS PARTICULAR CENSUS INDEX COVERS ONLY ONE YEAR, A KNOWLEDGE OF WHAT WAS EXPECTED OF THE CENSUS ENUMERATOR FROM 1790 TO 1850 IS MOST HELPFUL. DURING THE MANY YEARS OF SERVING THE PUBLIC, WE HAVE CONSTANTLY RECEIVED LETTERS INQUIRING AS TO THE CONTENT OF THE VARIOUS CENSUS RECORDS.

IT SHOULD BE MADE CLEAR FROM THE BEGINNING THAT THE MARSHALL IN MANY CASES DID AS HE WELL PLEASED. MANY DISREGARDED THE INSTRUCTIONS AS SET FORTH BY CONGRESS AND EITHER SHORTENED HIS RESPONSIBILITIES BY TAKING SCANTY DATA OR BY TAKING OTHER LIBERTIES. HOWEVER, A FEW CENSUS ENUMERATORS WENT BEYOND THEIR CALL OF DUTY, GATHERED AND RECORDED ADDITIONAL INFORMATION, ETC.

ONE CENSUS ENUMERATOR IN THE 1800 MARYLAND CENSUS BECAME TOO DRUNK TO TAKE THE CENSUS---THEREFORE WE ARE MISSING BALTIMORE COUNTY 1800...WHILE THE CENSUS ENUMERATOR OF 1800 KENNEBEC COUNTY, MAINE, RECORDED THE DATE THE PERSON MOVED INTO THE COUNTY.

IN THE 1850 CENSUS ENUMERATIONS, SOME ENUMERATORS RECORDED FULL NAMES WHILE OTHERS RECORDED JUST THE INITIAL OF THE FIRST NAMES ALONG WITH THE LAST NAMES.

THE FOLLOWING DATA WILL BE MOST HELPFUL TO THE TRUE RESEARCHER.

INTRODUCTION

The First Census — 1790

The first United States Federal census was taken as the result of the Constitution, Article I, section 2 which states:

> Representatives and direct taxes shall be apportioned among the several States which may be included within this Union according to their respective numbers, which shall be determined by adding to the whole number of free persons, including those bound to service for a term of years, and excluding Indians not taxed, three-fifths of all other persons. The actual enumeration shall be made within three years after the first meeting of the Congress of the United States, and within every subsequent term of the years, in such manner as they shall be law direct.

With this provision the United States became the first country to have, by law, a periodic enumeration of its inhabitants. The Constitution did *not* provide for information beyond statistical data for each state.

Fortunately, the act which specifically called for a census enumeration went further. This act was approved 1 Mar 1790 during the second session of the First Congress.[1] It required that a marshal be appointed for each State, who was empowered to appoint as many assistants as necessary. By this act the Marshals were not only required to enumerate the number of inhabitants within each district but to distinguish the free population from the slave population, and to exclude Indians not taxed. This was sufficient information to meet the Constituttional requirements, but the act also required a distinction between sex, free persons of color, free males of 16 years and upward, and most importantly the names of the heads of each family.[2]

The task of taking the enumeration was to begin on the first Monday in August 1790 and close within nine months, at which time the marshals were to make their returns. To avoid the problems that airse from making an accurate count of a mobile population the act stated that each individual was to be enumerated in the home of "his usual place of abode"[3] on the first Monday in August 1790. In the case of persons having no settled place of residence the act stated that they should be listed in the division where they happened to be on the first day of August.

The act also stipulated that "each and every person more than 16 years of age, whether the head of a family or not, [was] to render a true account, to the best of his knowledge, of every person belonging to the family in which he usually resided, if so required by the assistant of his division, under penalty of forfeiting $20."[4]

Difficulty immediately came to the fore with the passage of this act. America was on the fringes of a vast wilderness and the great majority of the population lived in rural areas. Consequently, the assistants had to travel over long distances with few roads and bridges, in forests, swamps, etc. to make an accurate return. Often the population did not cooperate. Many people "imagined some scheme for increasing taxation, and were inclined to be cautious lest they should reveal too much of their own affairs."[5] There was opposition on religious grounds and it was feared that it would cause divine displeasure. Other problems were caused by the question of civil boundaries, and "even those of counties, were in many cases unknown or not defined at all." [6]

Each assistant was to make two additional copies of his return and post them in two public places for the inspection of the local inhabitants. He was then to forward the remaining copy to the respective marshal who was in turn to total each description of persons and send these totals (aggregate amounts) to the President.[7] The returns were then to be turned over to the clerks of the respective U.S. District Courts, who were directed to carefully preserve them.[8] It is assumed that these copies remained in the District Courts until a resolution, passed 28 May 1830, directed the District Court clerks to forward the returns to Washington.[9] "It is known that the 1790 schedules for Rhode Island were forwarded to Washington on June 22, 1830, as a result of the May 28 resolution. Presumably other extant population schedules, 1790-1820, were forwarded at about the same time, but no documentation of such action has been found."[10]

The size of sheets used to take this first census varied greatly as no forms were provided nor were instructions given concerning size, type of paper, etc. Usually the marshals and the assistants ruled columns in ink on each page and filled in the headings of each column. Apparently the only instructions the marshals were given were the following:

> Schedule of the whole number of persons within the
> Division allotted to
>
> Names of heads of families
> Free white males of 16 and upwards including heads of families
> Free white males under 16
> Free white females, including heads of families
> All other free persons
> Slaves [11]

Enumerations were taken in the thirteen original states *viz.:* Massachusetts, New Hampshire, Conneticut, Rhode Island, New York, New Jersey, Pennsylvania, Delaware, Maryland, Virginia, North Carolina, South Carolina, and Georgia.[12] Enumerations were also taken for Vermont which became a state in 1791; Maine which was a part of Massachusetts, Kentucky which was a part of Virginia, and the present states of Alabama and Mississippi which were parts of Georgia. There was also a census of the present state of Tennessee which was a part of North Carolina in 1790 but was organized as the Southwest Territory soon thereafter.[13]

The present state of Ohio, Indiana, Illinois, Michigan, and Wisconsin, as well as a part of Minnesota were known as the Northwest Territory, but there seems to have been little effort to take a census there.[14] In the printed enumeration totals, blanks were provided for the Northwest Territory but they were not filled in.[15]

By the act of 1 March 1790 the marshals were to transmit the aggregate amounts to the President on or before 1 Sept 1791; later legislation extended the time allowed to the states of Vermont and South Carolina. In the case of Vermont the enumeration was to begin the first Monday in Apr 1791 and close within five calendar months.[16] In the case of South Carolina the time of completion was extended to 1 March 1792.[17] Rhode Island, by the date of the act of 1 March 1790, had not accepted the Constitution, and thus was not a part of the Union. When she did accept the Constitution, legislation had to be enacted to take a census. This act was dated 5 July 1790.[18]

In the congressional appropriations bill for the year 1907 we find the following paragraphs:

> The Director of the Census is hereby authorized and directed to publish, in a permanent form, by counties and monor civil division, the names of the head of families returned at the First Census of the United States in seventeen hundred and ninety; and to sell said publications, the proceeds thereof to be covered into the treasury of the United States, to be deposited to the credit of miscellaneous receipts on account of proceeds of sales of Government property:
>
> *Provided,* that no expense shall be incurred hereunder additional to appropriations for the census office for printing....[19]

Printing began with the schedule of New Hampshire and we reproduce a portion of a page form the same.

The initial appropriations apparently were not enough to cover cost for printing all of the 1790 census[20] but in the next few years all known schedules were printed.

Unfortunately, some of the early census schedules had been lost or destroyed and could not be found by the Census Bureau in 1907. Those missing are for the states of Delaware, Georgia, Kentucky, New Jersey, Tennessee (Southwest Territory), and Virginia. In the introductory remarks of each printed 1790 census schedule is found the statement that the originals of the missing schedules were "destroyed when the British burned the Capitol at Washington during the War of 1812."[21] This is quite unlikely because the schedules most likely remained in the hands of the U.S. District Courts until the resolution of 28 March 1830.

For the states for which schedules are missing the government attempted to fill in with substitutes from state and county tax lists. This was done for the state of Virginia with some defects. The introduction of the 1908 publication entitled *Heads of Families at the first census-1790-Virginia states:*

> The loss of Virginia's original schedules for the First and Second censuses is so unfortunate that every endeavor has been made to secure date that would in some measure fill in the vacancy. The only records that could be secured were some manuscript lists of state enumerations made in the years 1782, 1783, 1784, and 1785; also the tax lists of Greenbrier county from 1783 to 1786. These documents were on file in the State Library and could not be removed therefrom. Through the courtesy of the State Librarian and the members of the Library Board, an act was passed by the legislature allowing the Census Office to withdraw the lists for the purpose of making copies and publishing the

names, in lieu of the Federal census returns. The counties for which the names of the heads of families are returned on the state census lists are 39 in number, and contain in 1790 a population of 370,000; 41 counties with 377,000 population are lacking; this publication covers therefore, only about one-half of the state.[22]

This Virginia tax lists publication was the only one undertaken by the Census Bureau. There have been publications that have also attempted to complete this project of supplying substitutes to the 1790 census through indexes to tax lists. These are probably not as complete as the censuses but are nonetheless helpful. For the missing portion of the state of Virginia there is *Virginia Tax Payers 1782-1784* by Augusta B. Fothergill and John Mark Naugle; For Kentucky there is *First Census of Kentucky 1790* compiled by Charles B. Heinemann. For Delaware a tax list of 1790 was compiled by Leon De Valinger and published in the "National Genealogical Society Quarterly" beginning in 1948, Vol 36 p. 95 and subsequent volumes. For Tennessee we have only a few good tax list available but those that are available are printed in Mary Barnett Curtis' *Early East Tennessee Tax Lists and Petitions* which covers the years 1778 through 1823 and in Pollyanna Creekmore's *Early East Tennessee Tax Payers.* The tax lists for Georgia are also very incomplete but some of those available are published in *Early Tax Digests of Georgia* by Ruth Blair. Only the state of New Jersey has no tax substitutes for the 1790 time period, but there is a military "census" which may be helpful. It is indexed in *Revolutionary Census of New Jersey 1773-1784,* by Kenn Stryker-Rodda.

As a final note, recently, a spanish census for 1790 for the New Mexico area has been found. The originals are located in the New Mexico State Record Center Historical Service Division in Santa Fe, and are published in *Spanish and Mexican Colonial Censuses of New Mexico: 1790, 1823, 1845,* translated and compiled by Virginia L. Olmsted. This find leads us to wonder if there are not censuses for the other Spanish Possessions in North America such as Louisiana, California, and Texas. If they do exist it is suspected that they will be found in the Church records of the various parishes.

Later Censuses — 1800-1840

Most of the legislation that brought about the taking of the later censuses was based upon the act of 1 Mar 1790. There was a gradual expansion of information required with each succeeding census. By 1810 there was an attempt to take a manufacturing census which was expanded in 1810. Included as a part of this introduction are the various acts and instructions to the marshals of the appropriate census year.

BIBLOGRAPHY

An Act for Apportioning Representatives Among the Several States, According to the First Enumeration. Statutes at Large, Vol 1 (1850).

An Act for Giving Effect to an Act Instituted "An Act Providing for the Enumeration of the Inhabitants of the United States," in respect to the State of Rhode Island and Providence Plantations. Statutes at Large, Vol I (1850).

An Act Giving Effect to the Laws of the United States within the State of Vermont. Statutes at Large, Vol I (1850).

An Act Granting Farther Time for Making Return of the Enumeration of the Inhabitants in the District of South Carolina. Statutes at Large, Vol I (1850).

An Act Providing for the Enumeration of the Inhabitants of the United States. Statutes at Large, Vol I (1850).

Davidson, Katherine H. and Charlotte M. Ashby. *Preliminary Inventory of the Records of the Bureau of the Census.* Washington, D.C. 1964.

Greenwood, Val D. *The Researcher's Guide to American Genealogy.* Baltimore: Genealogical Publishing Co., Inc. 1973.

Olmsted, Virginia L. *Spanish and Mexican Colonial Censuses of New Mexico: 1790, 1823, 1845.* Albuquerque, N.M.: New Mexico Genealogical Society Inc. 1975.

Return of the Whole Districts of the United States. Philadelphia: Child and Swaine, 1791.

U. S. Dpartment of Commerce. Bureau of the Census, *Historical Statistics of the United States Colonial Times to 1957.* Washington, D.C. 1960.

U. S. Department of Commerce and Labor. Bureau of the Census, *A Century of Population Growth From the First Census of the United States to the Twelfth 1790-1900.* Washington, D.C.: Government Printing Office 1909.

Washington, D.C.; Government Printing Office 1908.

U. S. Department of Commerce and Labor. Bureau of the Census, *Heads of Families at the First Census of the United States taken in the year 1790 South Carolina.* Washington, D.C.: Government Printing Office 1908.

Wright, Carroll D., and William C. Hunt. *The History and Growth of the United States Census.* Washington, D.C.: Government Printing Office, 1900.

U.S. Department of Commerce and Labor. Bureau of the Census, *Heads of Families at the First Census of the United States taken in the year 1790 Records of the State Enumerations: 1782 to 1785 Virginia.* Washington, D.C.: Government Printing Office 1908.

NOTES

1For more complete details about the political maneuvering preceding the act of 1 March 1790 see chapter III of U.S. Department of Commerce and Labor, Bureau of the Census, *A Century of Population Growth From the First Census of the United States to the Twelfth 1790-1900*. (Washington, DC: Government Printing Office 1909).

An Act Providing for the Enumeration of the Inhabitants of the United States, Statues at Large, I, Sec. I, 101 (1850).

3*Ibid.*, sec. 5.

4*Ibid.*, sec. 6.

5U. S., Department of Commerce and Labor, Bureau of the Census, *Heads of Families at the First Census of the United States Taken in the Year 1790 South Carolina*, 5.

6*Ibid.*

7*An Act Providing for the Enumeration of the Inhabitants of the United States*, sec. 7.

8Carroll D. Wright and William C. Hunt, *The History and Growth of the United States Census* (Washington, D.C.: Government Printing Office, 1900) pp. 14, 15.

9Statues at Large, IV, 430 (1850).

10Katherine H. Davidson and Charlotte M. Ashby, *Prelimary Inventory of the Records of the Bureau of the Census* (Washington, D.C. 1964) p. 94.

11Wright pp. 131, 132.

12*Return of the Whole Number of Persons within the Several Districts of the United States* (Philadelphia: Child and Swaine 1791) pp. 3-56

13*Heads of Families* p. 5.

14*Ibid.*

15*Return* pp. 3-56.

16*Statutes at Large*, I, Chap. XII. Sec. 5-7, 197-8.

17*Ibid.* Vol I, Chap. 1, 126.

18*Ibid.* Vol I, Chap. XXV, Sec 2, 129.

19*Ibid.* Vol XXXIV, Chap. 3914, 722.

20*Ibid.* Vol XXXV, 19.

21*Heads of Families* p. 3.

22U. S., Department of Commerce and Labor, Bureau of the Census, *Heads of Families at the First Census of the United States taken in the year 1790 Records of the State Enumerations: 1782 to 1785 Virginia* (Washington, D.C.: Government Printing Office, 1908) P.3.

ACT APPROVED MARCH 1, 1790.

AN ACT providing for the enumeration of the inhabitants of the United States.

SECTION 1. **Be it enacted by the Senate and House of Representatives of the United States of America in Congress assembled,** That the marshals of the several districts of the United States shall be, and they are hereby authorized and required to cause the number of the inhabitants within their respective districts to be taken; omitting in such enumeration Indians not taxed, and distinguishing free persons, including those bound to service for a term of years, from all others; distinguishing also the sexes and colours of free persons, and the free males of sixteen years and upwards from those under that age; for effecting which purpose the marshals shall have power to appoint as many assistants within their respective districts as to them shall appear necessary; assigning to each assistant a certain division of his district, which division shall consist of one or more counties, cities, towns, townships, hundreds or parishes, or of a territory plainly and distinctly bounded by water courses, mountains, or public roads. The marshals and their assistants shall respectively take an oath or affirmation, before some judge or justice of the peace, resident within their respective districts, previous to their entering on the discharge of the duties by this act required. The oath or affirmation of the marshals shall be, "I, A. B. marshal of the district of ———, do solemnly swear (or affirm) that I will well and truly cause to be made, a just and perfect enumeration and description of all persons resident within my district, and return the same to the President of the United States, agreeably to the directions of an act of Congress, intituled 'An act providing for the enumeration of the inhabitants of the United States, according to the best of my ability." The oath or affirmation of an assistant shall be, "I, A. B. do solemnly swear (or affirm) that I will make a just and perfect enumeration and description of all persons resident within the division assigned to me by the marshal of the district of ——— and make due return thereof to the said marshal, agreeably to the directions of an act of Congress, intituled 'An act providing for the enumeration of the inhabitants of the United States,' according to the best of my ability." The enumeration shall commence on the first Monday in August next, and shall close within nine calendar months thereafter. The several assistants shall, within the said nine mnths, transmit to the marshals by whom they shall be respectively appointed, accurate returns of all persons, except Indians not taxed, within their respective divisions, which returns shall be made in a schedule, distinguishing the several families by the name of their master, mistress, steward, overseer, or other principal person therein, in manner following, that is to say:

The number of persons within my division, consisting of ———, appears in a schedule hereto annexed, subscribed by me this —— day of ———. 179—.

A B, **assistant to the marshal of ———**

Schedule of the whole number of persons within the division allotted to A B.

Names of heads of families.	Free white males of 16 years and upwards, including heads of families.	Free white males under 16 years.	Free white females, including heads of families.	All other free persons.	Slaves.

SEC. 2. **And be it further enacted,** That every assistant failing to make return, or making a false return of the enumeration to the marshal, within the time by this act limited, shall forfeit the sum of two hundred dollars.

SEC. 3. **And be it further enacted,** That the marshals shall file the several returns aforesaid, with the clerks of their respective district courts, who are hereby directed to receive and carefully preserve the same: And the marshals respectively shall, on or before the first day of September, one thousand seven hundred and ninety-one, transmit to the President of the United States, the aggregate amount of each description of persons within their respective districts. An every marshal failing to file the returns of his assistants, or any of them, with the clerks of their respective district courts, or failing to return the aggregate amount of each description of persons in their respective districts, as the same shall appear from said returns, to the President of the United States, within the time limited by this act, shall, for every such offense, forfeit the sum of eight hundred dollars; all which forfeitures shall be recoverable in the courts of the districts where the offenses shall be committed, or in the circuit courts to be held within the same, by action of debt, information or indictment; the one half thereof to the use of the United States, and the other half to the informer; but where the prosection shall be first instituted on behalf of the United States, the whole shall accrue to their use. And for the more effectual discovery of offenses, the judges of the several district courts, at their next sessions to be held after the expiration of the time allowed for making the returns of the enumeration hereby directed, to the President of the United States, shall give this act in charge to the grand juries, in their respective courts, and shall cause the returns of the several assistants to be laid before them for their inspection.

SEC. 4. **And be it further enacted,** That every assistant shall receive at the rate of one dollar for every one hundred and fifty persons by him returned, where such persons reside in the country; and where such persons reside in a city, or town, containing more than five thousand persons, such assistant shall receive at the rate of one dollar for every three hundred persons; but where, from the dispersed situation of the inhabitants in some divisions, one dollar for every one hundred and fifty persons shall be insufficient, the marshals, with the approbation of the judges of their respective districts, may make such further allowance to the assistants in such divisions as shall be deemed an adequate compensation, provided the same does not exceed one dollar for every fifty persons by them returned. The several marshals shall receive as follows: The marshal of the district of Maine, two hundred dollars; the marshal of the district of New Hampshire, two hundred dollars; the marshal of the district of Massachusetts, three hundred dollars; the marshal of the district of Connecticut, two hundred dollars; the marshal of the district of New York, three hundred dollars; the marshal of the district of New Jersey, two hundred dollars; the marshal of the district of Pennsylvania, three hundred dollars; the marshal of the district of Delaware, one hundred dollars; the marshal of the district of Maryland, three hundred dollars; the marshal of the district of Virginia, five hundred dollars; the marshal of the district of Kentucky, two hundred and fifty dollars; the marshal of the district of North Carolina, three hundred and fifty dollars; the marshal of the district of South Carolina, three hundred dollars; the marshal of the district of Georgia, two hundred and fifty dollars. And to obviate all doubts which may arise respecting the persons to be returned, and the manner of making the returns,

SEC. 5. **Be it enacted,** That every person whose usual place of abode shall be in any family on the aforesaid first Monday in August next, shall be returned as of such family; and the name of every person, who shall be an inhabitant of any district, but without a settled place of residence, shall be inserted in the column of the aforesaid schedule, which is allotted for the heads of families, in that division where he or she shall be on the said first Monday in August next, and every person occasionally absent at the time of the enumeration, as belonging to that place in which he usually resides in the United States.

SEC. 6. **And be it further enacted,** That each and every person more than sixteen years of age, whether heads of families or not, belonging to any family within any division of a district made or established within the United States, shall be, and hereby is, obliged to render to such assistant of the division, a true account, if required, to the best of his or her knowledge, of all and every person belonging to such family respectively, according to the several descriptions aforesaid, on pain of forfeiting twenty dollars, to be sued for and recovered by such assistant, the one-half for his own use, and the other half for the use of the United States.

SEC. 7. **And be it further enacted,** That each assistant shall, previous to making his return to the marshal, cause a correct copy, signed by himself, of the schedule, containing the number of inhabitants within his division, to be set up at two of the most public places within the same, there to remain for the inspection of all concerned; for each of which copies the said assistant shall be entitled to receive two dollars, provided proof of a copy of the schedule having been so set up and suffered to remain, shall be transmitted to the marshal, with the return of the number of persons; and in case any assistant shall fail to make such proof to the marshal, he shall forfeit the compensation by this act allowed him.

Approved, March 1, 1790.

CHAPTER I. — **An Act granting farther Time for making Return of the Enumeration of the Inhabitants in the District of South Carolina.**

Be it enacted by the Senate and House of Representatives of the United State of America in Congress assembled, That it shall be lawful for the marshal of the district of South Carolina to complete and make return of the enumeration of the inhabitants of the said district, to the President of the United States, in the form and manner prescribed by the act, intituled "An act providing for the enumeration of the inhabitants of the United State," at any time on or before the first day of March next, any thing in the said act to the contrary notwithstanding.

APPROVED, November 8, 1791.

CHAP. XXV. — **An Act for giving effect to an act intituled "An act providing for the enumeration of the Inhabitants of the United States," in respect to the state of Rhode Island and Providence Plantations.**

SECTION 1. **Be it enacted by the Senate and House of Representatives of the United States of America in Congress assembled,** That the act passed the present session of Congress, intituled "An act providing for the enumeration of the inhabitants of the United States," shall be deemed to have the like force and operation within the state of Rhode Island and Providence Plantations, as elsewhere within the United States; and all the regulations, provisions, directions, authorities, penalties, and other matters whatsoever, contained or expressed in the said act, and which are not locally inapplicable, shall have the like force and effect within the said state, as if the same were repeated and re-enacted in and by this present act.

SEC. 2. **And be it further enacted,** That the marshal of the district of Rhode Island shall receive, in full compensation for the performance of all the duties and services confided to, and enjoined upon him by this act, one hundred dollars.

APPROVED, July 5, 1790.

CHAP. XII. — **An Act providing for the second Census or enumeration of the Inhabitants of the United States.**

SECTION 1. **Be it enacted by the Senate and House of Representatives of the United States of America in Congress assembled,** That the marshals of the several districts of the United States and the secretaries of the territory of the United States northwest of the river Ohio, and of the Mississippi territory, respectively, shall be, and they are hereby authorized and required, under the direction of the Secretary of State, and according to such instructions as he shall give pursuant to this act, to cause the number of the inhabitants within their respective districts and territories to be taken; omitting in such enumeration, Indians not taxed, and distinguishing free persons, including those bound to service for a term of years from all others; distinguishing also the sexes and colours of free persons and the free males under ten years of age; those of ten years and under sixteen; those of sixteen and under twenty-six; those of twenty-six and under forty-five; those of forty-five and upwards: and distinguishing free females under ten years of age; those of ten years and under sixteen; those of sixteen and under twenty-six; those of twenty-six and under forty-five; those of forty-five and upwards: for effecting which purpose, the marshals and secretaries aforesaid shall have power to appoint as many assistants within their respective districts and territories, as aforesaid, as to them shall appear necessary; assigning to each assistant a certain division of his district or territory, which division shall consist of one or more counties, cities, towns, townships, hundreds or parishes, or of a territory plainly and distincly bounded by water-courses, mountains or public roads. The marshals or secretaries, as the case may be, and their assistants, shall, respectively, taken an oath or affirmation, before some judge or justice of the peace, resident within their respective districts or terrirotires, previous to their entering on the discharge of the duties by this act required. The oath or affirmation of the marshal or secretary shall be,—"I, A.B., marshal of the district of (or secretary of the territory of as the case may be), do solemnly swear or affirm, that I will well and truly cause to be made, a just and perfect enumeration and description of all persons resident within my district or territory, and return the same to the Secretary of State, agreeably to the directions of an act of Congress, intituled 'an act providing for the enumeration of the inhabitants of the United States,' according to the best of my ability." The oath or affirmation of an assistant shall be,—"I, A.B., do solemnly swear, (or affirm) that I will make a just and perfect enumeration and description of all persons resident within the division assigned to me by the marshal of the district of (or the secretary of the territory of as the case may be), and make due return thereof to the said marshal, or secretary, agreeably to the directions of an act of Congress, intitutled 'an act providing for the enumeration of the inhabitants of the United States,' according to the best of my abilities." The enumeration shall commence on the first Monday of August next, and shall close within nine calendar months thereafter. The several assistants shall, within the said nine months, transmit to the marshal or secretaries, by whom they shall be respectively appointed, accurate returns of all persons, except Indians not taxed, within their respective divisions; which returns shall be made in a schedule, distinguishing in each county, parish, township, town or city, the several families, by the names of their master, mistress, steward, overseer or other principal person therein, in the manner following; that is to say: the number of persons within my division, consisting of appears in a schedule hereto annexed, subscribed by me this day of . A.B., assistant to the marshal of or to the secretary of

SCHEDULE of the whole number of persons within the division allotted to A. B.

Name of the county, parish, township, town or city where the family resides.	Names of head of family.	Free white males under ten years of age.	Free white males of ten, and under sixteen.	Free white males of sixteen, and under twenty-six, including heads of families.	Free white males of twenty-six, and under forty-five, including heads of families.	Free white males of forty-five and upwards, including heads of families.	Free white females under ten years of age.	Free white females of ten years, and under sixteen.	Free white females of sixteen, and under twenty-six, including heads of families.	Free white females of twenty-six, and under forty-five, including heads of families.	Free white females of forty-five and upwards, including heads of families.	All other free persons, except Indians, not taxed.	Slaves.

SEC. 2. **And be it further enacted,** That every assistant, failing to make a proper return, or making a false return of the enumeration to the marshal or the secretary (as the case may be) within the time by this act limited, shall forfeit the sum of two hundred dollars.

SEC. 3. **And be it further enacted,** That the marshal and secretaries shall file the several returns aforesaid, with the clerks of their respective district or superior courts (as the case may be) who are hereby directed to receive and carefully preserve the same: and the marshals, or secretaries, respectively, shall, on or before the first day of September, one thousand eight hundred and one, transmit to the Secretary of State, the aggregate amount of each description of persons within their respective district or territories. And every marshal or secretary failing to file the returns of his assistants or any of them, with the clerks of their respective courts as aforesaid, or failing to return the aggregate amount of each description of persons in their respective districts or territories, as the same shall appear from said returns, to the Secretary of State, within the time limited by this act, shall, for every such offence, forfeit the sum of eight hundred dollars; all which forfeitures shall be recoverable in the courts of the districts or territories where the offences shall be committed, or in the circuit courts to be held within the same, by action of debt, information or indictment; the one half thereof to the use of the United States, and the other half to the informer; but where the prosecution shall be first instituted on behalf of the United States, the whole shall accrue to their use. And for the more effectual discovery of offences, the judges of the several district courts in the several districts, and of the supreme courts, in the territories of the United States, as aforesaid, at their next sessions, to be held after the expiration of the time allowed for making the returns of the enumeration hereby directed, to the Secretary of State, shall give this act in charge to the grand juries, in their respective courts, and shall cause the returns of the several assitants to be laid before them for their inspection.

SEC. 4. **And be it further enacted,** That every assistant shall receive at the rate of one dollar, for every hundred persons by him returned, where such persons reside in the country, and where such persons reside in a city or town, containing more than three thousand persons, such assistant shall receive at the rate of one dollar for every three hundred persons, but where, from the dispersed situation of the inhabitants in some divisions, one dollar for every one hundred persons shall be insufficient, the marshals or secretaries, with the approbation of the judges of their respective districts or territories, may make such further allowance to the assistants in such divisions, as shall be deemed an adequate compensation: **Provided,** the same does not exceed one dollar for every fifty persons by them returned. The several marshals and secretaries shall receive as follows: The marshal of the district of Maine, two hundred dollars; the marshal of the district of New Hampshire, two hundred dollars; the marshal of the district of Massachusetts, three hundred dollars; the marshal of the district of Rhode Island, one hundred and fifty dollars; the marshal of the district of Connecticut, two hundred dollars; the marshal of the district of Vermont, two hundred dollars; the marshal of the district of New York, three hundred dollars; the marshal of the district of New Jersey, two hundred dollars; the marshal of the district of Pennsylvania, three hundred dollars; the marshal of Deleware, one hundred dollars; the marshal of the district of Maryland, three hundred dollars; the marshal of the district of Virginia, five hundred dollars; the marshal of the district of Kentucky, two hundred and fifty dollars; the marshal of the district of North Carolina, three hundred and fifty dollars; the marshal of the district of South Carolina, three hundred dollars; the marshal of the district of Georgia, two hundred and fifty dollars; the marshal of the district of Tennessee, two hundred dollars; the secretary of the territory of the United States northwest of the Ohio, two hundred dollars; the secretary of the Mississippi territory, one hundred dollars.

SEC. 5. **And be it further enacted,** That every person whose usualy place of abode shall be in any family on the aforesaid first Monday in August next. shall be returned as of such family, and the name of every person, who shall be an inhabitant of any district or territory, but without a settled place of residence, shall be inserted in the column of the aforesaid schedule, which is allotted for the heads of families in that division where he or she shall be, on the said first Monday in August next, and every person occasionally absent at the time of the enumeration, as belonging to that place in which he or she usually resides in the United States.

SEC. 6. **And be it further enacted,** That each and every free person, more than sixteen years of age, whether heads of families or not. belonging to any family within any division, district or territory made or established within the United States, shall be, and hereby is obliged to render to such assistant of the division, a true account, if required, to the best of his or her knowledge, of all and every person belonging to such family respectively, according to the several descriptions aforesaid, on pain of forfeiting twenty dollars, to be sued for and recovered by such assistant. the one half for his own use and the other half to the use of the United States.

SEC. 7. **And be it further enacted,** That each assistant shall, previous to making his returns to the marshal or secretary (as the case may be) cause a correct copy, signed by himself, of the schedule containing the number of inhabitants within his division, to be set up at two of the most public places within the same, there to remain for the inspection of all concerned, for each of which copies the said assistant shall be entitled to receive two dollars; provided, proof of the schedule having been so set up and suffered to remain, shall be transmitted to the marshal or secretary (as the case may be) with the return of the number of the persons, and in case any assistant shall fail to make such proof to the marshal or secretary, as aforesaid, he shall forfeit the compensation by this act allowed him.

SEC. 8. **And be it further enacted,** That the Secretary of State shall be, and hereby is authorized and required to transmit to the marshals of the several states and to the secretaries aforesaid, regulations and instructions pursuant to this act, for carrying the same into effect. and also the forms contained therein of schedule to be returned, and proper interrogatories to be administered by the several persons who shall be employed therein.

APPROVED, February 28, 1800.

CHAP. XXIII.—**An Act to alter the form of certain oaths and affirmations directed to be taken by the act intituled "An act providing for the second census or enumeration of the inhabitants of the United States."**

Be it enacted by the Senate and House of Representatives of the United States of America in Congress assembled, That so much of the first section of the act passed during the present session of Congress, intituled "An act providing for the second census or enumeration of the inhabitants of the United States," as relates to the form of the oaths or affirmations thereby directed to be taken by the marshals, secretaries, and assistants therein mentioned respectively, shall be, and hereby is repealed, and that the said oaths or affirmations shall be in the following form: that is to say: the marshals and secretaries' oath or affirmation in the form following: "I, A. B. marshal of the district of (or the secretary of the territory of as the case may be) do solemnly swear or affirm, that I will well and truly cause to be made a just and perfect enumeration and description of the persons resident within my district (or within the territory of as the case may be) and will return the same to the Secretary of State agreeably to the directions of an act of Congress, intituled 'An act providing for the second census or enumeration of the inhabitants of the United States,' according to the best of my ability." And the assistants' oath or affirmation in the form following: I, A. B. do solemnly swear (or affirm) that I will make a just and perfect enumeration and description of all persons resident within the division assigned to me by the marshal of the district of (or the secretary of the territory of as the case may be) and make due return thereeof to the said marshal (or secretary) agreeably to the directions of an Act of Congress, intituled "An Act providing for the second census or enumeration of the inhabitants of the United States," according to the best of my ability.

APPROVED, April 12, 1800.

INSTRUCTIONS TO MARSHALS — CENSUS OF 1820.

To the Marshal of the District of ———

DEPARTMENT OF STATE, **Washington, June 20, 1820.**

SIR: The "Act to provide for taking the fourth census or enumeration of the inhabitants of the United States, and for other purposes," copies of which are herewith inclosed, prescribes that this enumeration shall be taken, under the direction of the Secretary of State, and according to such instructions as he shall give, pursuant to the act: in obedience to the injunctions of which the following regulations and instructions are now transmitted to you, together with the forms of the schedule to be returned, and such others as may be necessary in carrying the act into execution, and proper interrogatories to be administered by the several persons to be employed in taking the enumeration.

The purposes of the legislature in this act, subsidiary to that of obtaining the aggregate amount of the population of the United States, are, to ascertain in detail the proportional numbers of which it is composed, according to the circumstances of sex, color, age, condition of life, as heads or members of families, as free or slaves, as citizens or foreigners, and particularly of the classes (including slaves) engaged in agriculture, commerce, and manufactures. And, also, to obtain an account of the manufacturing establishments, and their manufactures, throughout the United States.

The means provided by the legislature, in the act, for the attainment of these purposes, consist in the appointment of the marshals of the several districts, and of such assistants as they may select, for the accomplishment of the returns within the period prescribed by the law.

The importance of the duties assigned to these officers by the act, in the estimation of the legislature, is sufficiently indicated by the provisions, that every marshal and every assistant shall, before he enters on the duties required by the act, take an oath or affirmation for the faithful performance of them. And that after this performance, every assistant shall take a second oath, or affirmation, that he has faithfully performed these duties in the manner prescribed by the act. Blank forms of these oaths, numbered 2, 3, and 4, are herewith transmitted to you, in numbers sufficient to supply yourself and your assistants; and, for the sake of uniformity, the form of a certificate, to be subscribed by the magistrate who may administer the oath, is subjoined to it. For the security of the public, it is necessary that the evidence showing that these oaths have been taken, should be preserved. It is therfore recommended, that you should transmit to this department one copy of the certificate that you have, yourself, taken the oath required of the marshal; that you should require of all your assistants to deliver or transmit to you the certificates of their oaths, taken both before and after their returns, and that you should return them to this department, as they will be vouchers necessary for the settlement of your account.

It has already been suggested to you, and could not have escaped your observation upon perusal of the act, that much will depend for its execution in a manner which may correspond with the just expectations of the legislature, upon the judicious selection of your assistants. The duties to be performed by them, under the solemnities of an oath, both before and after their discharge, are such as will require assiduous industry, active intelligence, pure integrity, great facility and accuracy of computation; with an intimate knowledge of the division allotted to them respectively, and a faculty of discernment between the different classes of persons discriminated by the act, which will enable them readily to distinguish to which of the enumerated conditions of society each individual may, with the greatest propriety, be assigned. They must, by the letter of the act, be **residents** of the county or city for which they shall be appointed, and each division, though it may include one or more **towns**, townships, wards, hundreds, or parishes, plainly and distinctly bounded by water courses, mountains, public roads, or other monuments, must not consist of more than one county or city. The subdivisions of territory are known in different States by different denominations, and the same term of town, county, city, and parish, has a different idea annexed to it in the different parts of the Union. Hence it is that the act points to divisions bounded by water courses, mountains, public roads, or other monuments, to which you will duly attend, with reference to the particular territorial denominations known in your State, and with suitable precautions to aviod the assignment of the same portion of the population to more than one assistant, and the inconvenience that any two of them should interfere with each other.

A form of schedule (No. 1), such as is precribed by the act, is likewise inclosed. Your assistants will observe that the act expressly requires the enumeration to be made by an actual inquiry, at every dwelling house, or of the head of every family, **and not otherwise,** and that the oath or affirmation, to be taken by them, after their performance of the duty, and before they can receive compensation for the same, declares, expressly, that they have ascertained the numbers, **by such actual inquiry.**

The act requires that the enumeration should commence on the first Monday of August next, and should close within six clandar months thereafter. From the number and extent of the inquiries to made at every house, embracing many particulars, not required at any former census of the United States, it is obvious that the progress to be made by each assistant will be necessarily slow; and as it is extremely desirable that the enumeration should be completed within the time prescribed, you will perceive the necessity of appointing a number of assistants adequate to that result, as each assistant will be duly impressed with that of not losing a day in the performance of his task. And, I beg leave to suggest, as advisable, proper precautions, to meet the contingency that any of your assistants should be disabled by illness, or otherwise, from accomplishing his duties, and to supply immediately the places of such as may be vacated by death, or other casualty.

The interrogatories to be put at each dwelling house, or to the head of every family, are definitely marked in relation to the various classes of inhabitants discriminated in the several columns of the schedule, by the titles at the head of each column. That of the **name** of the head of each family, must indeed be varied according to its circumstances, as it may be that of a master, mistress, steward, overseer, or other principal person therein. The subsequent inquiries, How many free white males under 10 years there are in the family? How many of 10 and under 16? etc., will follow in the order of the columns. But, to facilitate the labor of your assistants, a printed list of all the interrogatories for enumeration, believed to be necessary, is inclosed; (No. 5) in which all the questions refer to the day when the enumeration is to commence; the first Monday in August next. Your assistants will thereby understand that they are to insert in their returns all the persons belonging to the family on the first Monday in August, even those who may be deceased at the time when they take the account; and, on the other hand, that they will not the legislature, as manifested by the clause providing that every person shall be recorded as of the family in which he or she shall reside on the first Monday in August.

shall reside on the first Monday in August.

It will be necessary to remember, that the numbers in the columns of free white males between 16 and 18 — foreigners not naturalized — persons engaged in agriculture — persons engaged in commerce — persons engaged in manufactures — must not be added to the general aggregates, of which the sum total is to be opposed. All the persons included within these columns must necessarily be included also in one of the other columns. Those, for instance, between 16 and 18, will all be repeated in the column of those between 16 and 26. The foreigners not naturalized, and those engaged in the three principal walks of life, will also be included in the columns embracing their respective ages. In the printed form of a schedule herewith inclosed, the description at the top of these columns is printed in italics, and the division lines between the columns themselves are double ruled, with a view to distinguish them from the other columns, the sums of which are to go to the general agregate. In preparing their schedules from this form, your assistants will find it useful, for convenience and accuracy, to distinguish those columns, by ruling them with red ink, or in some other manner, which may keep them separate from the others, by a sensible impression constantly operating upon the mind.

The discrimination between persons engaged in agriculture, commerce, and manufactures, will not be without it difficulties.

No inconsiderable portion of the population will probably be found, the individuals of which being asked, to which of those classes they belong, will answer, to all three. Yet, it is obviously not the intention of the legislature that any one individual should be included in more than one of them — or those whose occupations are exclusively agricultural or commerical, there can seldom arise a question, and in the column of manufactures will be included not only all the persons employed in what the act more specifically denominates manufacturing **establishments,** but all those artificers, handicraftsmen, and mechanics, whose labor is preeminently of the hand, and not upon the field.

By persons engaged in agriculture, commerce, or manufactures, your assistans will understand that they are to insert in those columns, not whole families, including infants and superannuated persons, but only those thus engaged by actual occupation. This construction is given to the act, because it is believed to be best adapted to fulfill the intentions of the legislature, and because, being susceptible of the other, it might be differently construed by different persons employed in the enumeration, and thus destroy the uniformity of returns, essential to a satisfactory result.

Besides this enumeration of manufactures, the marshals and their assistants are required, by the tenth section of the act to take an account of the several **manufacturing establishments and their manufactures,** within their several districts, territories, an divisions; and the meaning of the legislature, by this provision, is illustrated by the clause in the oaths of the marshals and assistants, that they will take an account of the manufactures, **except household manufactures,** from which it seems fairly deducible, that, in the intention of the legislature, persons employed only upon household manufactures are not to be included in the column of persons bearing that denomination, the occupation of manufacturing being, in such cases, only incidental, and not the profession properly marking the class of society to which such individual belongs.

This, then, offers a criterion by which your assistants may select the column of occupation to which each individual may be set down; namely, to that which is the principal and not the occasional, or incidental, occupation of his life.

The more particular the account of manufactures can be made, the more satisfactory will the returns prove. Among the papers inclosed is an alphabetical list of manufactures (No. 6), which may facilitate the labor of you assistants, but which they will not consider as complete. It is intended merely to give a direction to their inquiries, and each of them will add to it every manufacture not included in it and of which he takes an account within his division. A printed form (No. 7) is likewise inclosed, of inquiries to be made in relation to manufacturing establishments, on a sheet of paper, upon which the information requested may be written and returned. In every case when it can be conveniently done, your assistant will do well to give this form to some person principally concerned in the manufacturing establishment, requesting him to give the information desired himself.

The execution of the fifth section of the act requires the further interrogatories, whether any person, whose usual abode was in the family on the first Monday of August, 1820, be absent therefrom at the time of the inquiry made: and, if so, the sex, age, color, and condition, of such person are to be asked, and marked in the proper column, in the return of the family. It follows, of course, that any person who, at the time of taking the number of any family, has his usual abode in it, is nevertheless, not to be included in the return of that family, if his usual place of abode was, on the first Monday of August, in another family. The name of every person having no settled place of residence, is to be inserted in the column of the schedule allotted for the heads of families in the division where such person shall be on the first Monday of August.

Your assistants will be careful to observe, however, an important distinction between the inquiries directly necessary to the enumeration, and those relating to manufactures; they will **see**, that, by the sixth section of the act, each and every **free** person, more than 16 years of age, whether heads of families or not, belonging to any family within any division, district, or territory, is **obliged** to render the assistant of the division, if required, a true account, to the best of his or her knowledge, of every **person** belonging to such family respectively, according to the several descriptions in the schedule, upon a penalty of $20; but, as the act lays no positive injunction upon any individual to furnish information upon the situation of his property, or his private concerns, the answers to all inquiries of that character must be altogether voluntary, and every one, to whom they are put or addressed, will be at liberty to decline answering them at all. This has been a principal motive for putting the inquiries pointed to the two kinds of information to be required, into separate and distinct forms. It is to be expected that some individuals will feel reluctant to give all the information desired in relation to manufactures; but, as the views of Congress in directing the collection of this information, were undoubtedly views of kindness toward the manufacturing interest in general, it is hoped, that the general sentiment among the persons included in that highly important class of our population will incline them to give all the information relating to their condition, which may enable the legislature hereafter to promote their interests by measures conciliating with them those of the other great and leading classes of society.

By the seventh section of the act, every assistant, before making his return to you, is required to cause a correct copy, signed by himself, of the schedule containing the number of inhabitants within his division, to be set up at two of the most public places within the same, there to **remain** for the inspection of all concerned; proof of which is to be transmitted to you by each of your assistants, with the return of the number of persons — upon failure of which the assistant will forfeit the compensation allowed him by the act. The time during which the copy of the schedule must thus **remain** set up is not specified; but must be presumed a reasonable time for the purposes obviously intended by this provision, namely, for the detection of errors which may have happened in the names of the heads of families and numbers of persons to be returned; a time within which all the inhabitants recorded in the schedule may have had a sufficient opportunity for the inspection thus offered them, and to point out the errors in it, to be corrected. A form of a certificate, to be signed by two respectable witnesses, and annexed to the schedule No. 1, is inclosed, as a convenient mode of furnishing the proof required by the act.

The **returns of enumeration**, when received from all your assistants, are to be filed by you, together with an attested copy of the aggregate amount, to be made out by yourself, with the clerk of your district (or superior) court, who are directed to receive and carefully preserve them. And on or before the 1st day of April next, you are to transmit to this Department the aggregate amount of **each description of person** within your district (or territory): by which is to be understood, not merely the general aggregate amount of your whole district, but also the special aggregate of every subdivision, of counties, towns, townships, cities, boroughs, and parishes, and, in the principal cities, of their several wards.

The **return of manufactures** collected by yourself, and those made to you by your assistants, you are to transmit, together with abstracts of the same, to this Department, at the same time with the aggregate of the enumeration. The form of an abstract, corresponding with the questions on the blank sheet (No. 7) from the answers to which it is to be compiled, is herewith transmitted and numbered (9).

With the forms of return is inclosed that of the aggregates to be compiled by you (No. 8) from all the returns, and a specimen of the manner in which they may be most conveniently filled up by each of your assistants. By taking a quire of common paper, or as many sheets as his enumeration will require, and stitching them through at a proper fold, as a book, and prefixing the form of his return, to project beyond the edges of his book, he will always have under his eye the necessary guide to the proper columns in which entries are to be made, without being obliged to repeat the heading at the top of each sheet. Under the heading of each column, ciphered figures are also printed, denoting the different classes of persons, which, at a glance of the eye, will point to the column in which each entry is to be made.

For the purpose of uniformity in the mode of rendering the accounts of compensation for taking the census or enumeration of inhabitants, the following instructions on the point are added:

1. No payments will be made in advance from the Treasury for this object. On the rendering of the accounts by the marshals, the payments will be made at the Treasury; and the payment will be made, for the whole amount of compensation in each district or territory, to the marshal thereof. The assistants are to be apprised, that it is the marshal alone to whom they are to apply for their compensations.

2. As soon as the marshal has received the returns of all his assistants, he is to make out an abstract of their compensation in the form annexed (No. 10), adding at foot the amount of his own compensation, as fixed by the act of 14th of March, 1820.

3. If any of the assistants are allowed more than at the rate of $1 for every hundred persons enumerate 1, there must be annexed to the abstract the certificate of the district or territorial judge, approving such additional allowance.

4. The account of compensation is to be transmitted to this Department, at the same time with the returns of the census.

The column of compensation for taking account of manufactures must be left in blank; and the allowance will be a percentage, not exceeding 20 per cent on the amount allowed for the other services required by the act. This apportionment being subject to the direction of the Secretary of State, you will state in the column the amount of your claim for it; and if extending to, or approaching, the whole allowance within the limits of the act, you will assign the reasons upon which it may be allowed, by a justifiable exercise of the discretion authorized by the law.

Should any difficulty or obstacle occur to any of your assistants, in performing the duty assigned to him, it is expected that he will give you immediate notice of it, that you may take measures for removing it, if within your power. Should any such occur to yourself, for which it may be within the competency of this Department to provide a remedy, you are requested to give immediate communication of it, to me.

A number, believed to be competent, of copies of the act, of these instructions, and of the forms referred to in them, numbered as noted, is herewith furnished for the supply of yourself and your assistants, to whom they are supposed to be necessary. Should more be required, you will receive them, on giving notice of it by letter to this Department. You are requested, as soon as convenient, after the receipt of this letter, to acknowledge it.

I have the honor to be, with great respect, sir, your humble and obedient servant.

JOHN QUINCY ADAMS.

LIST OF PAPER INCLOSED.

Copeis of the act for taking the fourth census or enumeration.
Copies of these instructions.
Forms: [a]

1. Schedule of enumeration to be used by the assistants, and returned to the marshal, on or before the first Monday in February, 1821.
2. Oath or affirmation of the marshal, to be returned (certified by a judge or justice of the peace, resident within the district) to the Department of State.
3. Oath of the assistant, to be taken before entering on the duties required by the act, and by him returned, certified as aforesaid, to the marshal, and by the marshal to the Department of State.
4. Oath of the assistant, to be taken after completing his return, and transmitted with it certified as aforesaid, to the marshal, and by him to the Department of State.
5. Interrogatories of enumeration, to be used by the assistants.
6. Alphabetical list of manufactures, to be used by the assistants.
7. Questions concerning manufactures, to be answered on the same sheet; one to be used for each manufacturing establishment, and returned, with the answers, to the marshal, and by him to the Department of State.
8. Aggregate of enumeration, to be compiled by the marshal from the schedules returned by the assistants, and transmitted to the Department of State.
9. Abstract of manufactures, to be made by the marshal from the returns of the assistants, and transmitted with them by the marshal from the returns of the assistants, and transmitted with them to the Department of State.
10. Account of compensation, to be transmitted with the returns of the census by the marshal to the Department of State.

a Printed in full in Report on Census of 1820.

INSTRUCTIONS TO MARSHALS—CENSUS OF 1830.

DEPARTMENT OF STATE, **Washington, March 24, 1830.**

To the Marshal of the United States for the District of----

SIR: I herewith inclose a copy of "An act to provide for taking the fifth census, or enumeration of the inhabitants of the United States."

The instructions and regulations to be given in pursuance of this act, will be prepared as soon as possible, and transmitted to you, together with blank forms and interrogatories, and a sufficient number of those blanks for the use of the whole number of deputies in your district. This course is adopted, to produce a uniformity in all the official returns under the act referred to.

In the meantime, to avoid any unnecessary delay, and as the enumeration is to commence on the first day of June next, you will please make a selection of your assistants as soon as possible, and transmit to this Department a list of their names, and of the districts or divisions assigned to each.

On the persual of the act, you will see the necessity of your selecting persons of ability and intergrity, and possessing the additional qualification of diligent and industrious habits, and particularly those competent in accounts.

In order that I may form some estimate of the probable number of blanks that will be required in your district, be pleased to note on the list of assistants, the probable number of inhabitants in each assistant's division.

I will thank you to acknowledge this circular immediately, and to direct your answer to this, as well as all communications relating to the census, as follows:

"Department of State, Washington City, D.C.—Census."

And if it be practicable, it would conduce to the convenience of this Department, that you letters should be written upon paper of the dimensions of this sheet.

I am, sir, respectfully, your obedient servant.

M. VAN BUREN.

DEPARTMENT OF STATE, **Washington, April 15, 1830.**

To the Marshal of the United States for the District of----

SIR: The "Act to provide for taking the fifth census, or enumeration of the inhabitants of the United States," copies of which are herewith transmitted, prescribes, that this enumeration shall be taken under the direction of the Secretary of State, and according to such instructions as he shall give, pursuant to the act. In obedience to the injunctions therein contained, the following instructions are now transmitted to you.

The means provided by the legislature, in the act, for the attainment of the objects enumerated, are in the appointment of the marshals of the several districts, and of such assistants as they may select, for the accomplishment of the returns within the period prescribed by law.

The importance of the duties assigned to these officers, by the act, is sufficiently indicated by the provisions, that every marshal and every assistant, shall, before he enters on the duties required by the act, take an oath or affirmation for the faithful performance of them; and that, after this performance, every assistant shall take a second oath, or affirmation, that he has faithfully performed these duties in the manner prescribed by the act. Blank forms of these oaths, numbered 1, 2, and 7, are herewith transmitted to you, in numbers sufficient to supply yourself and your assistants, and, for the sake of uniformity, the form of a certificate, to be subscribed by the magistrate who may administer the oath, is subjoined to it. It is directed that you transmit to this Department one copy of the certificate that you have, yourself, taken the oath required of the marshal; that you should require of all your assistants to deliver, or transmit to you, the certificates of their oaths, taken both before and after their returns, and that you return them to this Department, as they will be vouchers necessary for the settlement of your account. Each **set** of oaths (or affirmations) to be immediately transmitted to the Department on receipt by the marshal.

The duties to be performed by your assistants, under the solemnities of an oath, are such as will require arduous industry, active intelligence, pure integrity, great facility and accuracy of computation, and an intimate knowledge of the division alloted to them respectively. They must, by the letter of the act, be **resideтns** of the county or city for which they shall be appointed, and each division may include one or more towns, townships, wards, hundreds, precincts, or parishes, which must be plainly and distinctly bounded; but a division mut, in no case, exceed one county. You will aso use all suitable precautions, to avoid the assignment of the same portion of the population, to more than one assistant, and the inconvenience that any two of them should interfere with each other.

Your assistants will observe, that the act expressly requires the enumeration to be made by an actual inquiry at every dwelling house, or by personal inquiry of the head of every family, **and not otherwise;** and that the oath or affirmation to be taken by them, after the performance of this duty, and before they can receive compensation for the same, declares, expressly, that they have ascertained the numbers **by such actual inquiry.**

The act requires that the enumeration shall commence on the 1st day of June next, and shall close within six calendar months thereafter, and that the said assistant shall, on or before the 1st day of December, 1830, deliver to the marshals by whom they shall have been appointed, respectively, two copies of the accurate returns of all persons (except Indians not taxed) enumerated as aforesaid, within their respective divisions. From the number of inquiries to be made at every house, it is obvious that the progress to be made by each assistant will be necessarily slow; and as it is required that the enumeration shall be completed within the time prescribed, you will perceive the necessity of appointing a number of assistants adequate to that result, and each assistant must be enjoined not to lose a day in the performance of his task. And I beg leave to suggest, as advisable, proper precautions to meet the contingency of any of your assistants being disabled by sickness, or otherwise, from accomplishing his duties, and to supply, immediately, the places of such as may be vacated by death, or other casualty.

To facilitate the labor of your assistants, a printed list of all the interrogatories for enumeration is inclosed (No. 3), in which all the questions refer to the day when the enumeration is to commence—the 1st day of next June. Your assistants will also bear in mind to include all persons of a family (except Indians not taxed) who were members thereof on the 1st day of June, 1830, whether present or not, and not to include any person whose usual abode was not in the family they are enumerating on the said 1st day of June. They will, of course, include such persons as may have deceased after that day, and will not include in it infants born after that day. This, though not prescribed in express terms by the act, is the undoubted intention of the legislature, as manifested by the clause, providing that every person shall be recorded as of the family in which he or she shall reside on the 1st day of June, 1830.

The execution of the fifth section of the act requires the further interrogatores, whether any person, whose usual abode was in the family on the 1st day of june, 1830, be absent therefrom at the time of making the inquiry, and if so, the sex, age, color, and condition, are to asked and marked in the proper column, in the return of the family. It follows, of course, that any person, who, at the time of taking the enumeration of any family, has his abode in it, is, nevertheless, not be included in the return of that family, **if his usual place of abode, was, on the 1st day of June, in another family.** The name of every person, having no settled place of residence, is to be inserted in the column of the schedule, allotted for the heads of families, in the division where such person shall be on the 1st day of June, and, of course, also in one of the other columns, according to the age and condition of such person.

You assistant will see, that, by the sixth section of the act, **each** and every **free** person, more than 16 years of age, whether heads of families or not, belonging to any family within any division, district, or territory, is **obliged** to render the assistant of the division, if required, a true account, to the best of his or her knowledge, of every person belonging to such family respectively, according to the several descriptions in the schedule, under a penalty of $20. They should, therefore, read that section to the person of whom they make the inquiry, whenever it may be found necessary.

By the seventh section of the act, every assistant, before making his return to you, is required to cause correct copies, signed by himself, of the schedule containing the number of inhabitants within his division, to be set up at two of the most public places within the same, for the inspection of all concerned; proof of which is to be transmitted to you by each of your assistants, and by you to the Department, with the return of the number of persons, upon failure of which, the assistant will forfeit the compensation allowed him by the act. A form of the certificate, to be written on the copy of the schedule No. 4, which is to be transmitted to the Department, signed by two respectable witnesses, is inclosed, as a convenient mode of furnishing the proof required by the act.

One copy of the returns of enumeration, when received from all your assistants, is to be filed by you, together with an attested copy of the aggregate amount, to be made out by yourself, with the clerk of your district (or superior) court, who is directed to receive, and carefully preserve them; and, on or before the 1st day of February, 1831, you are to transmit to this Department, one copy of the several returns received from each assistant, signed by each assistant respectively, and, also, by two respectable witnesses, that the same has been posted; and, also, one copy of the aggregate amount of each description of persons within your district: by which it is to be understood, not merely the general aggregate amount of yor whole district, but also the special aggregate of every subdivision of counties, cities, towns, townships, parishes, precincts, hundereds, and districts, and the several wards in the princioal cities.

For the purpose of uniformity in the mode of rendering accounts of compensation for taking the census, or enumeration of inhabitants, the following instructions on that point are added:

1. No payments will be made in advance for this object. Payment will be made, for the whole amount of compensation in each district, to the marshal thereof. The assistants are to be apprised that they are to apply to the marshal alone for their compensation.

2. As soon as the marshal has received the returns of all his assistants, he is to make out an abstract of their compensation, as in form No. 9, adding, at foot, the amount of his own compensation, as fixed by the act of 23d March, 1830.

3. If any of the assistants are allowed more than at the rate of $1.25 for every 100 persons enumerated, there must be annexed, to the abstract of the account, the certificate of the district or territorial judge of the United States approving such additional allowance.

4. The account of compensation is to be transmitted to this department, at the same time with the returns of the census.

5. The act provides for the payment to the marshals, of the amount of postage by them respectively paid, on letters relating to their duties under this act. The charges under this head must be accompanied with the receipt of the postmaster, to whom such postage has been paid.

Should any difficulty or obstacle occur to any of your assistants, in performing the duty assigned to him, it is directed that he give you immediate notice thereof, that you may take measures for removing it, if within you power. Should any such occur to yourself, you are requested to make immediate communication of it to me. A number, believed to be sufficient, of the copies of the act—of these instructions— and of the forms referred to in them :with the exception of Nos. 4, 8, and 9) is herewith transmitted, for the aupply of yourself and assistants. Should more be required, you will receive them on giving notice to this department.

The forms Nos. 4, and 8, in sufficient numbers for the enumeration of the whole of your district, and also a copy of No.9, will be forwarded by subsequent mails, as soon as they are prepared. You are requested to acknowledge this package immediately on receipt.

I am, sir, respectfully your obedient servant,

M. VAN BUREN.

LIST OF PAPERS INCLOSED.

Copies of the act for taking the fifth census, or enumeration of the inhabitants of the United States.
Copies of these instructions.
Blank forms:

1. Oath or affirmation of the marshal, to be returned to the Department of State.
2. Oath or affirmation of the assistant, to be taken before entering on the duties required by the act, and by him returned to the marshal, and by him returned to the marshal, and by the marshal to the Department of State.
3. Interrogatories to be used by the assistants.
5. Copy of a certificate of the assistant, to be written at the foot of schedule No. 4.
6. Copy of a certificate of two respectable inhabitants of the division, to be written at the foot of the schedule when returned by the assistant to the marshal.
7. Oath or affirmation of the assistant, to be taken after completing his return, and transmitted with it to the marshal, and by him to the Department of State.

TO BE HEREAFTER TRANSMITTED.

4. Schedule of enumeration to be used by the assistants, and returned to the marshal on or before the 1st day of December, 1830.
8. Aggregate of enumeration to be compiled by the marshal from the schedules returned by the assistants.
9. Account of compensation, to be transmitted with the returns of the census, by the marshal, to the Department of State.

INSTRUCTIONS TO MARSHALS, ETC.—CENSUS OF 1840.

SIR: I herewith inclose a copy of "an act to provide for taking the sixth census or enumeration of the inhabitants of the United States."

You will perceive a discrepancy in the dates named in the law for the commencing and completing the census; until further legislation, the Deepartment will construe the law to ordain, that the taking of the census or enumeration shall commence on the 1st day of June, 1840, and that it shall be completed and closed within ten calendar months thereafter (viz. April 1, 1841), and as nine months are given to the deputy marshals to make their returns to the marshals, the nine months will be held to terminate March 1, 1841.

The instructions and regulations to be given in pursuance of this act will be prepared in due season, and transmitted to you, together with blank forms and interrogatories, and a sufficient number of those blanks for the use of the whole number of deputies in your district. This course is adopted to produce a unformity in all the official returns under the act referred to.

In the meantime, as the enumeration is to commence on the 1st day of June, 1840, you will please made a selection of your assistants and transmit to this Department a list of their names, and of the districts or divisions assigned to each.

On the perusal of the act, you will see the strong necessity of your selecting persons of ability and integrity, and possessing the additional qualification of diligent and industrious habits, skilled in accounts, and in all cases a thorough knowledge and acquaintance with the district assigned them.

In order that I may form some estimate of the probable number of blanks that will be required in your district, be pleased to note, on your list of assistants, the probable number of inhabitants in each assistant's division.

I will thank you to acknowledge this circular immediately, and to direct your answer to this, as well as all communications relating to the census, as follows:

"Department of State, **Washington City**, D.C.—Census."

And if it be practible, it would conduce to the convenience of this Department that your letters should be written upon paper of the dimensions of this sheet.

SIR: I herewith inclose to you----copies of the interrogatories (No. 3).

An additional number of the above-mentioned form has been printed and distributed, in order to disseminate a more general knowledge of the subject among the people, and to facilitate the attaining the objects of the law by the assistants. Copies are forwarded to you to the extent of----for each assistant, with the request that they be given every possible publicity, unattended with expense.

On referring to the thirteenth section of the act, you will perceive the strong necessity for acquainting the people in advance with the nature of the inquiries to be made of them, and to give them time for preparation to answer the questions promptly. The act requires (in that section) the marshals and their assistants "to collect and return (in statistical tables, under proper heads, according to such forms as shall be furnished) all such information in relation to mines, agriculture, commerce, manufactures, and schools, as will exhibit a **full view** of the pursuits, industry, education, and resources of the country." All the questions which are to be asked upon those subjects are contained in No. 3. If they be made known and generally understood before the enumeration commences, the answers to the interrogatories will be prepared in time for the domiciliary visit of the assistant, and the responses promptly made.

In taking down the answers under the general heads in teh statistical tables (No. 10), great caution will be required in all cases of copartnership to avoid multiplying returns from the different partners in manufactories, commercial houses, and companies of every description. The assistant, in propounding the interrogatories, must inform himself of the fact whether the individual interrogated is sole owner or is a partner only of a company. In the latter case, one individual of the firm or company must answer for the whole.

It will be expected of the assistants in carrying into effect this portion of the act, that in its full and exact meaning the returns will exhibit a **full view** of the pursuits, industry, education, and resourses of the country. The inquiries must be carried home to every man: and it will require the utmost diligence to accomplish the object in the given period of time. When the importance of the subject is considered, and that no meager returns can be acceptable to the Government or the country, an assurance is felt by this Department that the duties will be faithfully performed.

An additional compensation to the assistants has been recommended to Congress by the Secretary of State, for the performance of this duty.

Objections, it has been suggested, may possibly arise on the part of some persons to give the statistical information required by the act, upon the ground of disinclination to expose their private affairs. Such, however, is not the intent, nor can be the effect, or answering ingenuously the interrogatores. On the statistical tables no name is inserted—the figures stand opposite no man's name; and therfore the objection can not apply. It is, morever, inculcated upon the assistant that he consider all communications made to him in the performance of this duty, relative to the business of the people, as strictly confidential.

SIR: The "act to provide for taking the sixth census or enumeration of the inhabitants of the United States," copies of which have been transmitted to you, prescribes that this census shall be taken under the direction of the Secretary of State, and according to such instructions as he shall give pursuant to the act. The following instructions are now, therefore, transmitted to you, and you careful attention to them required. To attain the objects in view, the legislature has directed the employment of the marshals of the several districts, and of such assistants as they may select, for the completion of the returns within the period prescribed by law.

The importance of the duties assigned to these officers is sufficiently indicated by the provisions of the act that every marshal and every assistant shall, before he enters upon them, take an oath or affirmation that he will faithfully perform them in the manner therein prescribed. Blank forms of these oaths, numbered 1, 2, and 7, have been transmitted to you in number sufficient to supply yourself and your assistants. Each set of oaths (or affirmations), after having been sworn to and duly authenticated, will be immediately returned to this Department on their receipt by the marshal.

The duties to be performed by your assistants, under the solemnity on an oath, are such as will require industry, intelligence, integrity, a facility and accuracy of computation, with an intimate knowledge of the division allotted to them respectively. They must, by the letter of the act, be **residents** of the county or city for which they shall be appointed, and each division may include one or more towns, townships, wards, hundreds, precincts, or parishes, which must be plainly and distinctly bounded; but a division must in no case exceed one county. You will carefully avoid the assignment of the same portion of the population to more than one assistant. Great inconvenience will be produced if there should be any interference by the assistants with each other.

Your assistants will observe that the act expressly requires the enumeration to be made by an actual inquiry at every **dwelling house**, or by **personal inquiry of the head of every family**, and **not otherwise**; and that the oath or affirmation, to be taken by them after the performance of this duty, and before they can receive compensation for the same, declares expressly that they have ascertained the numbers by **such actual inquiry**. The act requires that "the enumerations shall commence on the 1st day of June next, and close within ten calendar months thereafter; * * * and that the assistants shall, within nine months, or on or before the 1st day of October, 1840, deliver to the marshals, by whom they shall be appointed, respectively, two copies of the accurate returns of all persons, except Indians not taxed, to be enumerated as aforesaid, within their respective divisions." From the number of inquiries to be made at each house, it is obvious that the progress to be made by each assistant will be necessarily slow; and as there is a doubt, from the phraseology of the law, whether Congress did not intend that the enumeration should be completed by the 1st day of October, 1840, you will perceive the necessity of appointing a number of assistants adequate to effect that result, if the next Congress shall so determine. Each assistant must be enjoined not to lose a day in the performance of his task. I suggest, as advisable, proper precautions to meet the contingency of any of your assistants being disabled by sickness or otherwise from fulfilling his duties, and to supply immediately all places that may be vacated by any casualty.

To facilitate the labor of your assistants, a printed list of all the interrogatories for the enumeration of the people, and also the information required relative to mines, agriculture, commerce, manufactures, and schools, by the thirteenth section of the act, has been prepared and numbered 3 (No. 3), in which all the questions touching the enumeration (the answers to which are to be set down on schedule No. 4) refer to the 1st day of June, 1840, the day on which the enumeration is to commence. Your assistants will also bear in mind to include all persons of a family (except Indians not taxed) who were members thereof on the 1st day of June, whether present or not, and not include any person whose usual abode was not in the family they are enumerating on the said 1st day of June, 1840. They will, of course, include such persons as may have died after that day, and will not include in it infancts born after that day. This, though not prescribed in express terms by the act, is the undoubted intention of the legislature, as manifested by the clause providing that every person shall be recorded as of the family in which he or she shall reside on the 1st day of June, 1840.

The execution of the fifth section of the act requires the further interrogatories, whether any person, whose usual abode was in the family on the 1st day of June, 1840, be absent therefrom at the time of making the inquiry; and if so, the sex, age, color, and condition are to be asked for, and marked in the proper column in the return of the family. It follows, of course, that any person who, at the time of taking the enumeration of any family, has his abode in it, is, nevertheless, not to be included in the return of that family **if his usual place of abode was, on the 1st day of June, in another family**. The name of every person having no settled place of residence is to be inserted in the column of the schedule alloted for the heads of families, in the division where such person shall be on the 1st day of June, and proper insertions, also, in other columns, according to the age and condition of such person.

Your assistants will see that, by the sixth section of the act, each and every free person more than 16 years of age, whether heads of families or not, belonging to any family within any division, district, or Territory, is **obliged** to render the assistant of the division, if required, a true account, to the best of his or her knowledge, of every person belonging to such family respectively, according to the several descriptions in the schedule, under a penalty of $20. They should, therefore, read that section to the person of whom they make the inquiry whenever it may be found necessary.

By the seventh section of the act, every assistant, before making his return to you, is required to cause correct copies, signed by himself, of the schedule containing the number of inhabitants within his division, to be set up at two of the most public places within the same for the inspection of all concerned—proof of which is to be transmitted to you by each of your assistants, and by you to the Department of State, with the return of the number of persons—upon failure of which the assistant will forfeit the compensation allowed him by the act. A form of the certificate to be written on the copy of the schedule (no. 4), which is to be transmitted, signed by two respectable witnesses, to the Department of State, has been prepared as a convenient mode of furnishing the proof required by the act.

One copy of the returns of enumeration, when received from all your assistants, is to be filed by you, together with an attested copy of the aggregate amount, to be made out by yourself, with the clerk of your district or superior court, who is directed to receive and carefully preserve them; and on or before the 1st day of December, 1840, you are to transmit to this Department one copy of the several returns received from each assistant— signed by each assistant respectively, and also by two respectable witnesses, that the same has been posted—and also one copy of the aggregate amount of each description of persons within your district, by which is to be understood, not merely the general aggregate amount of your whole district, but also the special aggregate of every subdivision of counties, cities, towns, township, parishes, precincts, hundreds, and districts, and the several wards in principal cities—blanks for which are transmitted, numbered 8 and 9.

For the purpose of securing uniformity in the mode of rendering accounts of compensation for taking the census or enumeration of inhabitants, the following instructions on that point are added: No compensation will be made on account of enumeration until the whole of you district shall have been completed, and the returns made to this Department. When that shall have been done, you will make out an abstract of the compensation, payable to your assistants, on the blank forms (No. 11) transmitted to you for that purpose. This you will return in duplicate to this Department, accompanied by the necessary affidivits and certificates. For their amount, when found correct, a remittance will be made to you, with which you will be charged on the books of the Treasury. You will then, without delay, pay to each assistant the amount to which he is entitled, taking his receipt therefor. When the payments shall be completed you will transmit an account current with the United States for those payments—for any postages paid by you, and not before drawn for—and for your own compensation, as allowed by the act, you will credit in it the sums remitted to you. This account must be accompanied by the receipts of the assistants, and for postages charged therein. On its adjustment, the balance appearing due to you will be remitted. As it is intended to transmit to you all the blank forms necessary for your own use, as well as for that of your assistants, and as the law authorizes no allowances to marshals except those specified in the act for their services and postages, no charge can be allowed for stationery or other incidental expenses, or for commission for disbursements to assistants or postmasters.

The twelfth section of the act provides that there shall be allowed and paid to the marshal of the several states and territories, and the District of Columbia, the amount of postage by them respectively paid on letters relating to their duties under this act.

The intention of the section referred to appears to be, that the assistants as well as the marshals should be relieved from the expense of postage in performing their duties under the act. You will, therefore, apy the postage on all communications in relation to the census to, as well as from, your assistants, and charge the Department therewith.

It will, perhaps, be advisable for you to make an arrangement with the postmasters where you receive and mail your letters, etc., for the census, to keep an account of such postages, to be settled quarterly. His receipt therefor will be a coucher of your having made the payment. For its amount you may draw upon this Department, being careful that the postmaster's receipt either accompany or precede your draft. This latter precaution will be necessary to insure the payment of the draft. Blank forms of such receipts and drafts are prepared for the purpose.

Should any difficulty or obstacle occur to any of your assistants in performing the duty assigned to them, it is directed that they give you immediate notice thereof, that you may take measures for removing it, if within your power. Should any such occur to yourself, you are requested to make an immediate communication of it to me. Should a greater number of blank forms be required than have been transmitted to you, you will receive them on giving notice to this Department. You are requested to acknowledge promptly the receipt of every package or communication, and to be particularly attentive to direct your answers after the mode prescribed in the circular of the 5th of April.

I am, sir, your obedient servant, etc.

SEC. 7. **And be it further enacted,** That each and every assistant, previous to making his return to the marshal, shall cause a correct copy, signed by himself, of the schedule containing the number of inhabitants within his division, to be set up at two fo the most public places within the same, there to remain for the inspection of all concerned; for each of which copies, the said assistant shall be entitled to receive five dollars: **Provided,** proof of the schedule having been set up, shall be transmitted to the marshal, with the return of the number of persons; and, in case any assistant shall fail to make such proof to the marshal, with the return of the number of persons, as aforesaid, he shall forfeit the compensation allowed him by this act.

SEC. 8. **And be it further enacted,** That the Secretary of State shall be, and hereby is, authorized and required to transmit, to the marshals of the several districts and territories, regulations and instructions, pursuant to this act, for acrrying the same into effect; and, also, the forms contained therein, of the schedule to be returned, and such other forms as may be necessary in carrying this act into execution, and proper interrogatories, to be administered by the several persons to be employed in taking the enumeration.

SEC. 9. **And be it further enacted,** That those states composing two districts, and where a part of a county may be in each district, such county shall be considered as belonging to that district in which the courthouse of said county may be situate.

SEC. 10. **And be it further enacted,** That, in all cases where the superficial content of any county, or parish, shall exceed twenty miles square, and the number of inhabitants in said parish or county shall not exceed three thousand, the marshals or assistants shall be allowed, with the approbation of the judges of the respective districts or territories, such further compensation as shall be deemed reasonable: **Provided,** The same does not exceed four dollars for every fifty persons by them returned; and when any such county or parish shall exceed forty miles square, and the number of inhabitants in the same shall not exceed three thousand, a like allowance shall be made, not to exceed six dollars for every fifty persons so returned.

SEC. 11. **And be it further enacted,** That, when the aforesaid enumeration shall be completed, and returned to the office of the Secretary of State, by the marshals of the states and territories, he shall direct the printers to Congress to print, for the use of Congress, three thousand copies of the aggregate returns received for the marshals: **And provided,** That if any marshal, in any district within the United States or territories, shall, directly or indirectly, ask, demand or receive, or contract to receive, of any assistants to be appointed by him under this act, any fee, reward or compensation, for the appointment of such assistant to discharge the duties required of such assistant under this act, or shall retain from such assistant any portion of the compensation allowed to the assistant by this act, the said marshal shall be deemed guilty of a misdemeanor in office, and shall forfeit and pay the amount of five hundred dollars, for each offence, to be recovered by suit or indictment in any circuit or district court of the United States, or the territories thereof, one half to the use of the government, and the other half to the informer; and all contracts which may be made in violation of this law, shall be void, and all sums of money, or property, paid, may be recovered back by the party paying the same, in any court having jurisdiction of the same.

SEC. 12. **And be it further enacted,** That there shall be allowed and paid to the marshals of the several states, territories, and the District of Columbia, the amount of postage by them respectively paid on letters relating to their duties under this act.

SEC. 13. **And be it further enacted,** That the President of the United States is hereby authorized to cause to be made a careful revision of the statements heretofore transmitted to Congress, of all former enumerations of the population of the United States and their territories, and to cause an abstract of the aggregate amount of population in each state and territory, to be printed by the printer to Congress, (designating the number of inhabitants of each description, by counties or parishes,) to the number of two thousand copies, which said copies shall be distributed as Congress shall hereafter direct, and for that purpose, the sum of two thousand dollars is hereby appropriated, to be paid out of any money in the treasury, not otherwise appropriated.

APPROVED, March 23, 1830.

SCHEDULE of the whole number of persons within the division allotted to A. B. by the marshal of the district [or territory] of

FREE WHITE PERSONS, **SLAVES.** **FREE COLOURED PERSONS.**

(INCLUDING HEADS OF FAMILIES.)

MALES. FEMALES. MALES. FEMALES. MALES. FEMALES. TOTAL.

White persons included in the foregoing.

Slaves and coloured persons included in foregoing.

Who are blind.
Who are feaf and dumb of the age of twenty-five years and upwards.
Who are deaf and dumb of the age of fourteen and under twenty-five.
Who are deaf and dumb under fourteen years of age.

ALIENS—Foreigners not naturalized.
Who are blind.
Who are deaf and dumb of twenty-five years and upwards.
Who are deaf and dumb of the age of fourteen and under twenty-five.
Who are deaf and dumb under fourteen years of age.

Of one hundred and upwards.
Of fifty-five and under one hundred.
Of thirty-six and under fifty-five.
Of twenty-four and under thirty-six.
Of ten and under twenty-four.
Under ten years of age.

Of one hundred and upwards.
Of fifty-five and under one hundred.
Of thirty-six and under fifty-five.
Of twenty-four and under thirty-six.
Of ten and under twenty-four.
Under ten years of age.

Of one hundred and upwards.
Of fifty-five and under one hundred.
Of thirty-six and under fifty-five.
Of twenty-four and under thirty-six.
Of ten and under twenty-four.
Under ten years of age.

Of one hundred and upwards.
Of fifty-five and under one hundred.
Of thirty-six and under fifty-five.
Of twenty-four and under thirty-six.
Of ten and under twenty-four.
Under ten years of age.

Of one hundred and upwards.
Of ninety and under one hundred.
Of eighty and under ninety.
Of seventy and under eighty.
Of sixty and under seventy.
Of fifty and under sixty.
Of forty and under fifty.
Of thirty and under forty.
Of twenty and under thirty.
Of fifteen and under twenty.
Of ten and under fifteen.
Of five and under ten.
Under five years of age.

Of one hundred and upwards.
Of ninety and under one hundred.
Of eighty and under ninety.
Of seventy and under eighty.
Of sixty and under seventy.
Of fifty and under sixty.
Of forty and under fifty.
Of thirty and under forty.
Of twenty and under thirty.
Of fifteen and under twenty.
Of ten and under fifteen.
Of five and under ten.
Under five years of age.

Names of Heads of Families.
Name of County, City, Ward, Town, Townships, Parish, Precinct, Hundred, or District.

CHAP. XVII.—**An Act to amend the act for taking the fifth census.**

Be it enacted by the Senate and House of Representatives of the Unites States of America, in Congress assembled, That it shall and may be lawful for such of the assistants to the marshals in the respective states and territories, who have not, before the passage of this act, made their respective returns to such marshals, under the act hereby amended, to complete theri enumerations and make their returns under the said act, at any time before the first day of June, and for the marshals of such states and territories to make their returns to the Secretary of State of any time before the first day of August, one thousand eight hundred and thirty-one: **Provided,** That nothing herein contained shall be deemed to release such marshals and assistants from the penalties contained in the act aforesaid, unless their returns shall be made within the time prescribed in this act: **And provided further,** That no persons be included in the returns made under the present act, unless such persons shall have been inhabitants of the district for which such returns shall be made, on the first day of June, one thousand eight hundred and thirty.

SEC. 2. **And be it further enacted,** That the copies of returns and aggregate amounts directed to be filed by the marshals with the clerks of the several district courts, and supreme courts of the territories of the United States, shall be preserved by said clerks, and remain in their offices respectively; and so much of the act to which this is an amendment as requires that they shall be transmitted by said clerks to the Department of State, is hereby repealed.

SEC. 3. **And be it further enacted,** That it shall be the duty of the Secretary of State to note all the clerical errors in the returns of the marshals and assistants, whether in the additions, classification of inhabitants, or otherwise, and cause said notes to be printed with the aggregate returns of the marshals, for the use of Congress.

APPROVED, February 3, 1831.

CHAP. III.—**An Act further to amend the act entitled "An act to provide for taking the sixth census or enumeration of the inhabitants of the United States," approved March third, eighteen hundred and thirty-nine.**

Be it enacted by the Senate and House of Representatives of the United States of America in Congress assembled, That it shall and may be lawful for such of the assistants to the marshals, in the respective States and Territories, who have not, before the passage of this act, made their respective returns to such marshals under the act hereby amended, to complete their enumerations and make their returns, under the said act, at any time before the first day of May, eighteen hundred and forty-one, and for the marshals of such States and Territories to make their returns to the Secretary of State at any time before the first of June, eighteen hundred and forty-one; **Provided,** That nothing herein contained shall be deemed to release such marshals and assistants from the penalties contained in the act aforesaid, unless their returns shall be made within the time prescribed in this act: **And provided, further,** That no person be included in the returns made under the present act, unless such persons shall have been inhabitants of the district for which such returns shall be made, on the first day of June, one thousand eight hundred and forty.

SEC. 2. **And be it further enacted,** That so much of the eleventh section of the act for taking the sixth census as applies to the printing, under the direction of the Secretary of State, of the aggregate returns received from the marshals, be so construed as to apply equally to the census of pensioners, and the statistical aggregates returned by said marshals: **And be it further provided,** That for arranging and preparing the census of pensioners required by the thirteenth section of the act for taking the sixth census and for the compiling and supervision of the printing of the statistical returns taken under said act, there be allowed to the superinending clerk, upon the completion of the work, such compensation as the Secretary of State may deem just and equitable, not exceeding the rate heretofore allowed for compiling the statistics of the third census; and that an allowance be made to the disbursing agent of the Department of State for the extra duties which have been, or may be, imposed upon him on account of the sixth census, in relation to its preparatory measures, the accounts of the marshals, and the disbursements, at a rate not exceeding that allowed him for his services in relation to the fifth census, according to the time he shall have been engaged in such duties.

APPROVED January 14, 1841.

Be it enacted by the Senate and House of Representatives of the United States of America in Congress assembled, That it shall and may be lawful for the marshals of the respective States and Territories, who have not, before the passage of this act, completed their enumerations, and made their returns, under the acts hereby amended, to proceed personally and by their assistants to complete such enumerations, and make such returns under the said acts; and the said assistants shall be allowed until the first day of December, one thousand eight hundred and forty-one, to complete their enumerations, and make their returns to the marshals, and the said marshals shall be allowed to make their returns to the Secretary of State at any time before the first day of Januray, one thousand eight hundred and forty-two: **Provided,** That nothing herein contained shall be deemed to oath or affirmation, before some judge or justice of the peace, authorized to administer the same, to wit: "I, A. B., do solemnly swear (or affirm) that the number of persons set forth in the return made by me, agreeably to the provisions of the act, entitled 'An act to provide for taking the fifth census or enumeration of the inquiry at every dwelling-house, or a personal inquiry of the head of every family, in exact conformity with the provisions of said act; and that I have, in every respect, fulfilled the duties required of me by said act, to the best of my abilities; and that the return aforesaid is correct and true, according to the best of my knowledge and belief." The compensation of the several marshals shall be as follows:

The marshal of the district of Maine, three hundred dollars.
The marshal of the district of New Hampshire, three hundred dollars.
The marshal of the district of Massachusetts, three hundred and fifty dollars.
The marshal of the district of Rhode Island, two hundred dollars.
The marshal of the district of Vermont, three hundred dollars.
The marshal of the district of Connecticut, two hundred and fifty dollars.
The marshal of the southern district of New York, three hundred dollars.
The marshal of the northern district of New York, three hundred dollars.
The marshal of the district of New Jersey, two hundred and fifty dollars.
The marshal of the eastern district of Pennsylvania, three hundred dollars.
The marshal of the western district of Pennsylvania, three hundred dollars.
The marshal of the district of Delaware, one hundred and fifty dollars.
The marshal of the district of Maryland, three hundred and fifty dollars.
The marshal of the eastern district of Virginia, three hundred dollars.
The marshal of the western district of Virginia, three hundred dollars.
The marshal of the district of Kentucky, three hundred and fifty dollars.
The marshal of the district of North Carolina, three hundred and fifty dollars.
The marshal of the district of South Carolina, three hundred and fifty dollars.
The marshal of the district of Georgia, three hundred and fifty dollars.
The marshal of the district of east Tennessee, two hundred dollars.
The marshal of the district of west Tennessee, two hundred dollars.
The marshal of the district of Ohio, four hundred dollars.
The marshal of the district of Indiana, two hundred and fifty dollars.
The marshal of the district of Illinois, two hundred dollars.
The marshal of the district of Mississippi, two hundred dollars.
The marshals of the districts of Louisiana, one hundred and twenty-five dollars each.
The marshal of the district of Alabama, two hundred and fifty dollars.
The marshal of the district of Missouri, two hundred dollars.
The marshal of the district of Columbia, one hundred dollars.
The marshal of the Michigan Territory, one hundred and fifty dollars.
The marshal of the Arkansas Territory, one hundred and fifty dollars.
The marshals of the territory of Florida, respectively, one hundred dollars.

SEC. 5. **And be it further enacted,** That every person whose usual place of abode shall be in any family, on the said dirst day in June, one thousand eight hundred and thirty, shall be returned as of such family; and the name of every person who shall be an inhabitant of any district or territory, without a settled place of residence, shall be inserted in the column of the schedule which is allotted for the heads of families, in the division where he or she shall be, on the said first day in June; and every person occasionally absent at the time of enumeration, as belonging to the place in which he or she usually resides in the United States.

SEC. 6. **And be it further enacted,** That each and every free person, more than sixteen years of age, whether heads of families or not, belonging to the place in which he or she usually resides in the United States.

SEC. 6. **And be it further enacted,** 'That each and every free person, more than sixteen years of age, whether heads of families or not, belonging to any family within any division, district or territory, made or established within the United States, shall be, and hereby is, obliged to render to the assistant of the division if required, a true account to the best of his or her knowledge, of every person belonging to such family, respectively, according to the several descriptions aforesaid, on pain of forfeiting twenty dollars, to be sued for and recovered, in any action of debt, by such assistant: the one half to his own use, and the other half to the use of the United States.

INSTRUCTIONS TO MARSHALS AND ASSISTANT MARSHALS—CENSUS OF 1850.

To the Marshals:

Having appointed your assistants, and received a duplicate of the oath of office taken by each, pursuant to your instructions from this Department, of the 25th ultimo, you will proceed immediately to the further execution of your duty, as defined by the act. It is an important service, looked to in its results with much interest, and it is expected that you will use every effort to discharge it with promptness, efficiency, and exactness.

You will be immediately furnished, by express, with a portfolio for each of your assistants, and a sufficient number of blanks for each to commence work. The necessary additional blanks will be, in like manner, furnished you as soon as practicable.

As 160 names may be entered on one sheet of population returns, and as three copies altogether are required, it follows that, for 160 names, 3 sheets of schedule No. 1 will be needed; and that for a district of 20,000 free inhabitants, 375 sheets would be required. To the number, however, which is required, on an accurate calculation, an addition of 25 per cent should be made to cover possible errors, losses, etc.; so that for a population of 20,000 in any one district, there should be sent 470 sheets of population blanks, or schedule No. 1.

You will, accordingly, estimate the number of free persons in each assistant's district, and calculate thereon the number of this schedule (No. 1) which will be required; and you will apportion the other schedules according to the character of the district, whether it be agricultural, planting, mining, manufacturing, or mercantile. The portfolios and schedules are to be transmitted by your to your assistants by mail, pursuant to the seventeenth section of the act, unless a more eligible mode can be resorted to, without expense.

No. 2. Of schedule No. 2, **Slave Inhabitants,** the same number will be required for a slave population of 20,000 that would be required for the same number of free persons, as each sheet will include the same number of slaves that schedule No. 1 will of free population.

No. 3. No less than four copies of schedule No. 3 should be sent to each assistant, the fourth copy being sent to provide for loss or accident; and cases will not very frequently occur, except in populous districts, where more than that number will be necessary.

No. 4. Of the **Agricultural** schedule, you can be the only judge of what number will be requisite for a particular subdivision. Four sheets of schedule No. 4 should be sent for every eighty farm or plantation owners or occupiers.

No. 5. Of schedule No. 5, **Statistics of Industry,** there should be sent to the assistants about four sheets for each thirty manufacturers in his district; or forty, provided the manufactories are generally on a small scale. The statistics relating to **four** blacksmiths would not require more room than those relating to **one** woolen or cotton factory.

No. 6. Of schedule No. 6, **Social Statistics,** it is presumed that four sheets will be usfficient for most assistants, except in cities; and even there, unless the social statistics for a whole city should be taken by one individual.

If more than three copies of any schedule be required in a subdivision, six will be needed, as there must be **three copies** of every variety of statistics taken. You should use muct care in the distribution of the lanks, in order that the supply be not unnecessarily exhausted.

Having furnished your assistants with the blanks and instructions, you will direct them to inform you when they commence the enumeration of the district assigned, and at least once in every two weeks, where mail facilities exist, they should be required to inform you of the progress made in the work. Failing to get such information from any assistant, it will be your duty to make inquiries concerning the district, so as to be assured that the assistant is at work, and to take those efficient steps which the law provides, to remedy any evil or inattention which may exist. You have, at any time, for cause sufficient, the power to cancel the appointment of an assistant, and to appoint another for the district; and it is your duty to do so whenever the public interest suffers from the neglect or incompetency of any assistant.

2. By the seventh section of the above act, it is made your duty **"to keep an accurate record of the name, and area in sqare miles, of each subdivision,** and of each assistant within your district." The object of this proviso is to determine that rate of payment to be made to the assistants. It is supposed and believed that in all States the areas of the different subdivisions may be pretty accurately known. It should be ascertained with complete exactness when the means exist for doing so. Where the reputed or estimated area is upon data not **entirely reliable**, this fact whould be stated.

In the new States, where the county and town divisions are made by aprallel lines, little difficulty can occuur, and in the older States the gasetteers usually contain the required information; but, as they can not always be relied on, and counties have undergone change of character the information should be obtained from the county surveyor, or clerk, or other reliable source; and you should require each assistant to furnish you with a certificate, under the hand of some reliable person, of the number of square miles in his district.

You should consider this as one of your first duties, so that, if possible, it may be made known to the assistant, soon after his appointment, the area of his district, and thus prevent the occurrence of any subsequent dispute. You should arrange a book, in some convenient method, by which you can easily refer to the description of the district, the number of square miles therein, and the name of each assistant, and the state of the work in each subdivision.

Postmasters should be notified concerning the provision in the seventeenth section of the act, which authorizes you and your assistants to frank all census packages and letters.

3. By the fifth section it is also made your duty **"carefully to examine the returns of each assistant,** to see whether the work has been executed in a lawful manner."

You whould carefully examine the returns, to see that every part of the district embraced has been visited, and all the required information obtained, and the schedules filled up according to the instructions.

4. By the fifth section it is provided, that you shall transmit, forthwith, **"one set of the retums to the census office."** This set should be transmitted without any delay, and in convenient sized packages. You should keep an accurate account of returns forwarded to the census office, and of the date at which they were mailed; and if the receipt of them is not acknowledged in due course of mail, you should write and inquire whether they have been received. You are required, by the same section, to transmit the other copy thereof to the office of the secretary of State, or Territory, to which your district belongs.

5. You and your assistants are requested to obtain, if proacticable, and forward to the census office, copies of local printed reports of towns, counties, and States, relating to the expenditures, to schools, pauperism, crime, insanity, and other local matters which are required to be investigated by the schedules.

6. You should instruct your assistants, upon the receipt of the instructions and blanks, to commence immediately to discharge their duty, and use all exertions to have them performed during the earlier portion of the time allotted for the work, and not procrastinate, in the expectation of being able to prosecute the work during the latter portion of the period.

When such procrastination occurs, or other causes (which might by timely caution be avoided) operate to defeat the consummation of the duty, neither you nor your assistants will be entitled to compensation, but render yourselves liable to a penalty.

To the Assistant Marshals:

1. The assistant marshal, having been duly commissioned, will be provided with a portfolio, to be furnished with the schedules, of sufficient size to contain several sheets of the same without folding, that may be easily opened, and used for writing on, if necessary; and he should furnish himself with ink, blotting paper, and pens. Strings should be attached to the portfolio, to prevent the loss of any of its contents.

2. He is to approach every family and individual from whom he solicits information with civil and conciliatory manners, and adapt himself, as far as practicable, to the circumstances of each, to secure confidence and good will, as a means of obtaining the desired information with accuracy and despatch.

3. If any person, to whom application is made for information should refuse to give it, or should designedly give false information, the assistatn should inform him of the responsibility he thereby incurs, and that he renders himself liable to a penalty, according to the fifteenth section of the act of Congress.

4. The act provides that **"the assistant marshals shall make the enumeration by actual inquiry at every dwelling hourse, or by personal inquiry of the head of every family, and not otherwise."** This requirement must be strictly observed.

5. As soon as the schedules are filled up, and the information in relation to each family is obtained according to the instructions, the assistant should read over, and exhibit to the parties from whom he received the same, the record of the information obtained, and correct or supply any error or omission. The object of this rule is to prevent mistakes, and secure accuracy.

6. Each assistant is to complete the enumeration with as little delay as possible, after commencing it, and should inform the marshal, at least once in two weeks, of the progress he is making in his district.

7. On each page of the population and agricultural schedules is to be inserted the date when such page was **commenced**, although it may not have been completely filled up until the following day. When the whole enumeration in his district shall have been completed, two complete copies of all the pages are to be made. These are to be carefully read over, and each compared to see that it is correct and agrees with the original.

8. Each assistant is to sign his name on each page of the schedule, and certify, and make oath or affirmation, at the end of each set of returns, that they were made according to his oath and instructions, to the best of his knowledge and belief. Two of the sets are to be forwarded to the marshal of his district, and one filed with the clerk of the court for preservation with the county records; in proof of the filing of which he must procure, and forward to his marshal, the certificate of the clerk of the county.

Discretion as to what schedules will be needed by each assistant is lodged with the marshal, and is at all times to be used. In the free States schedule No. 2 will be omitted.

For the guidance of assistants, each will be furnished with a set of schedules filled up in the manner contemplated by the act of Congress and these instructions.

CIRCULAR TO MARSHALS, ETC—CENSUS OF 1850.

To the United States Marshals and Assistants:

Information has been received at this office that in some cases unnecessary exposure has been made by the assistant marshals with reference to the business and pursuits, and other facts relating to individuals, merely to gratify curiosity, or the facts applied to the private use or pecuniary advantage of the assistant, to the injury of others. Such a use of the returns was neither comtemplated by the act itself nor justified by the intentions and designs of those who enacted the law. No individual employed under sanction of the Government to obtain these facts has a right to promulgate or expose them without authority.

Although designed ultimately for the use of the people at large, the Department reserves to itself the privilege of examining into the correctness of the returns, and arranging them in proper form for publication by Congress before any other use shall be made thereof; and all marshals and assistants are expected to consider the facts instrusted to them as if obtained exclusively for the use of the Government, and not to be used in any way to the gratification of curiosity, the exposure of an man's business or pursuits, or for the private emolument of the marshal or assistants, who, while employed in this service, act as the agents of the Government in the most confidential capacity. When your original copies are filed with the clerks of the courts and secretary of your state, they will be under the control of those officers and subject to the usual regulations of the respective offices, and you can enjoy the same access to them which can be had by every citizen. To the publication of the mere aggregate number of persons in your district there can be no objection.

EXPLANATION OF SCHEDULE NO. 1.—FREE INHABITANTS.

This schedule is to be filled up in the following manner:

Insert in the heading the name or number of the district, town, or city of the county or parish, and of the state, and the day of the month upon which the enumeration was taken. This is to be attested on each page of each set, by the signature of the assistant.

The several columns are to be filled as follows:

1. Under heading 1, entitled **"Dwelling houses numbered in the order of visitation,"** insert the number of dwelling houses occupied by free inhabitants, as they are visited. The first house visited to be numbered 1; the second one visited, 2; the third one visited, 3; and so on to the last house visited in the subdivision. By a dwelling house is meant a separate inhabited tenement, containing one orm ore families under one roof. Where several tenements are in one block, with walls either of brick or wood to divide them, having separate entrances, they are each to be numbered as separate houses; but where not so divided, they are to be number as one house.

If a house is used partly for a store, shop, or for other purposes, and partly for a dwelling house, it is to be numbered as a dwelling house. Hotels, poorhouses, garrisons, hospitals, asylums, jails, penitentiaries, and other similar institutions, are each to be numbered as a dwelling house; where the house is of a public nature, as above, write perpendicularly under the number, in said column, the name or description, as "hotel," "poorhouse," etc.

2. Under heading 2, entitled **"Families numbered in the order of visitation,"** insert the number of the families of free persons, as they are visited. The first family visited by the assistant marshal is to be numbered 1; the second one visited, 2; and so on to the last one visited in his district.

By the term family is meant, either one person living separately in a house, or a part of a house, and providing for him or herself, or several persons living together in a house, or in part of a house, upon one common means of support, and separately from others in similar circumstances. A widow living alone and separately providing for herself, or 200 individuals living together and provided for by a common head, should each be numbered as one family.

The resident inmates of a hotel jail, garrison, hospital, an asylum, or other similar institution, should be reckoned as one family.

3. Under heading 3, entitled **"The name of every person whose usual place of abode on the 1st day of June, 1850, was in this family,"** insert the name of every free person in each family, of every age, including the names of those temporarily absent, as well as those that were at home on that day. The name of any member of a family who may have died **since the 1st day of June** is to be entered and described as if living, but the name of any person born since the 1st day of June is to be omitted. The names are to be written, beginning with the father and mother; or if either, or both, be dead, begin with some other ostensible head of the family; to be followed, as far as practicable, with the name of the oldest child residing at home, then the next oldest, and so on the youngest, then the other inmates, lodgers and boarders, laborers, domestics, and servants.

All landlords, jailors, superintendents of poorhouses, garrisons, hospitals, asylums, and other similar institutions, are to be considered as heads of their respective families, and the inmates under their care to be registered as members thereof, and the details concerning each designated in their proper columns.

Indians not taxed are not to be enumerated in this or any other schedule.

By place of abode is meant the house or usual lodging place of a person. Anyone who is temporarily absent on a journey, or for other purposes, without taking up his place of residence elsewhere, and with the intention of returning again, is to be considered a member of the family which the assistant marshal is enumerating.

Students in colleges, academies, or schools, when absent from the families to which they belong, are to be enumerated only as members of the family in which they usually boarded and lodged on the 1st day of June.

Assistant marshals are cirected to make inquiry at all stores, shops, eating houses, and other similar places, and take the name and description of every person who usually slept there, provided such person is not otherwise enumerated.

Inquiries are to be made at every dwelling house, or of the head of every family. Those only who belong to such family, and consider it their home or usual place of abode, whether present or temporarily absent on a visit, journey, or a voyage, are to be enumerated. Persons on board of vessels accidentally or temporarily in port, those whose only habitation was the vessel to which they belong, those who are temporarily boarding for a few days at a sailors' boarding or lodging house, if they belong to other places are not be enumerated as the population of a place.

The sailors and hands of a revenue cutter which belongs to a particular port should be enumerated as of such port. A similar rule will apply to those employed in the navigation of the lakes, rivers, and canals. All are to be taken at their homes or usual places of abode, whether present or absent; and if any live on board of vessels or boats who are not so enumerated, they are to be taken as of the place where the vessel or boat is owned, licensed, or registered. And the assistant marshals are to make inquiry at every vessel and boat employed in the internal navigation of the United States, and enumerated those who are not taken as belonging to a family on shore; and all persons of such description in any one vessel are to be considered as belonging to one family and the vessel their place of abode. The assistants in all seaports will apply at the proper office for lists of all persons on a voyage at sea and register all citizens of the United States who have not been registered as belonging to some family.

Errors necessarily occurred in the last census in enumerating those employed in navigation, because no uniform rule was adopted for the whole United States. Assistant marshals are required to be particular in following the above directions, that similar errors may now be avoided.

4. Under heading 4, entitled **"Age,"** insert in figures what was the specific age of each person at his or her last birthday previous to the 1st of June, opposite the name of such person. If the exact age in years can not be ascertained, insert a number which shall be the nearest approximation to it.

The age, either exact or estimated, or everyone, is to be inserted.

If the person be a child under 1 year old, the entry is to be made by the fractional parts of a year, thus: One month, one-twelfth; two months, two-twelfths; three months, three-twelfths, and so on to eleven months, eleven-twelfths.

5. Under heading 5, entitled **"Sex,"** insert the letter M for male, and F for female, opposite the name, in all cases, as the fact may be.

6. Under heading 6, entitled **"Color,"** in all cases where the person is white, leave the space blank; in all cases where the person is black, insert the letter B; if mulatto, insert M. It is very desirable that these particulars be carefully regarded.

7. Under head 7, entitled **"Profession, occupation, or trade of each person over 15 years of age,"** insert opposite the name of each male the specific profession, occupation, or trade which the said person is known and reputed to follow in the place where he resides—as clergyman, physician, lawyer, shoemaker, student, farmer, carpenter, laborer, tailor, boatman, sailor, or otherwise, as the fact may be. When more convenient, the name of the article he produces may be substituted.

When the individual is a clergyman, insert the initials of the denomination to which he belongs before his profession—as Meth. for Methodist, R. C. for Roman Catholic, O. S. P. for Old School Presbyterian, or other appropriate initials, as the fact may be. When a person follows several professions or occupations the name of the principal one only is to be give. If a person follows no particular occupation, the space is to be filled with the word "none."

8. Under heading 8 insert the value of real estate owned by each individual enumerated. You are to obtain the value of real estate by inquiry of each individual who is supposed to own real estate, be the same located where it may, and insert the amount in dollars. No abatement of the value is to be made on account of any lien or incumbrance thereon in the nature of debt.

9. Under heading 9, **"Place of birth."** The marshal should ask the place of birth of each person in the family. If born in the State or Territory where they reside, insert the name or initials of the State or Territory, or the name of the government or country if without the United States. The names of the several States may be abbreviated.

Where the place of birth is unknown, state "unknown."

10. Under No. 10 make a mark, or dash, opposite the name of each person married during the year previous to the 1st of June, whether male or female.

11. Under heading 11, entitled **"At school within the last year."** The marshal should ask what member of this family has been at school within the last year; he is to insert a mark, thus, (1), opposite the names of all those, whether male or female, who have been at educational institutions within that period. Sunday schools are not to be included.

12. Under heading 12, entitled **"Persons over 20 years of age who can not read and write."** The marshal should be careful to note all persons in each family, over 20 years of age, who can not read and write, nad opposite the name of each make a mark, thus, (1). The spaces opposite the names of those who can read and write are to be left blank. If the person can read and write a foreign language, he is to be considered as able to read and write.

13. Heading 13, entitled **"Deaf and dumb, blind, insane, idiotic, pauper, or convict."** The assistant marshal should ascertain if there by any person in the family deaf, dumb, idiotic, blind, insane, or pauper. If so, who? And insert the term "deaf and dumb," "blind," "insane," and "idiotic," opposite the name of such persons, as the fact may be. When persons who had been convicted of crime within the year reside in families on the 1st of June, the fact should be stated, as in the other cases of criminals; but, as the interrogatory might give offense, the assistants had better refer to the county record for information on this head, and not make the inquiry of any family. With the county record and his own knowledge he can seldom err.

Should a poorhouse, asylum for the blind, insane or idiotic, or other charitable institution, or a penitentiary, a jail, house of refuge, or other place of punishment, be visited by the assistant marshal, he must number such building in its regular order, and he must write after the number, an perpendicularly in the same column (No.1) the nature of such institution—that it is a penitentiary, jail, house of refuge, as the case may be; and in column 13, opposite the name of each person, he must state the character of the infirmity or misfortune, in the one case, and in the other he must state the crime for which each inmate is confined, and of which such person was convicted; and in column No. 3, with the name, give the year of conviction, and fill all the columns concerning age, sex, color, etc., with as much care as in the case of other individuals.

EXPLANATION OF SCHEDULE 2—SLAVE INHABITANTS.

This schedule is to be filled up in the following manner:

Insert in the heading the number or name of the district, town, city, and the county or parish, and of the state in which the slave inhabitants enumerated reside, and the day of the month upon which the enumeration was taken. This is to be attested on each page of each set, by the signature of the assistant marshal. The several columns are to be filled up as follows:

1. Under heading 1, entitled **"Name of slaveholders,"** insert, in proper order, the names of the owners of slaves. Where there are several owners to a slave, the name of the one only need be entered, or when owned by a corporation or trust estate, the name of the trustee or corporation.

2. Under heading 2, entitled **"Number of slaves,"** insert, in regular numerical order, the number of all the slaves of both sexes and of each age, belonging to such owners. In the case of slaves, numbers are to be substituted for names. The number of every slave who usually resides in the district enumerated is to be entered, although he may happen to be temporarily absent. The slaves of each owner re to be numbered separately, beginning at No. 1, and a separate description of each is to be give. The person in whose family, or on whose plantation, the slave is found to be employed, is to be considered the owner—the principal object being to get the number of slaves, and not that of masters or owners.

3. Under heading 3, entitled **"Age,"** insert, in figures, the specific age of each slave opposite the number of such slave. If the exact age can not be ascertained, insert a number which shall be the nearest approximation to it. The age of every slave, either exact or estimated, is to be inserted. If the slave be a child which, on the 1st of June, was under 1 year old, the entry is to be made by fractional parts of a year; thus, one month old, one-twelfth; two months, two twelfths, three months, three-twelfths; eleven months, eleven-twelfths; keeping ever in view, in all cases, that the age must be estimated at no later period than the 1st of June.

4. Under heading 4, entitled **"Sex"** insert the letter M for male, and F for female, opposite the number, in all cases, as the fact may be.

5. Under heading 5, entitled **"Color,"** insert, in all cases, when the slave is black, the letter B; when he or she is a mulatto, insert M. The color of all slaves should be noted.

6. Under heading 6 insert, in figures, opposite the name of the slave owner, the number of slaves who, having absconded within the year, have not been recovered.

7. In column 7, insert opposite the name of the former owner thereof, the number of slaves manumitted within the year. The name of the person is to be give, although at th time of the enumeration such person may not have held slaves on the 1st of June. In such case, no entry is to be made in column No. 2.

8. Under heading 8k entitled **"Deaf and dumb, blind, insane, or idiotic,"** the assistant should ascertain if any of these slaves be deaf and dumb, blind, insane, or idiotic; and if so, insert opposite the name or number of such slave, the term deaf and dumb, blind, insane, or idiotic, as the fact may be. If slaves be found imprisoned convicts, mention the crime in column 8, and the date of conviction before the number in the vacant space below the name of the owner. The convict slaves should be numbers with the other slaves of their proper owner.

[The explanations relating to the schedules of mortality, agriculture, products of industry, and social statistics follow the inquireis relating to these subjects under their respective heads.]

release such marshals and assistants from the penalties contained in the act aforesaid, unless their returns shall be made within the time prescribed in this act: **And provided further,** That no person be included in the returns made under the present act, unless such persons shall have been inhabitants of the district for which such returns shall be made on the first day of June, one thousand eight hundred and forty; and the Secretary of State be, and he is hereby, authorized to cause to be printed twenty thousand copies of the compendium or abridgment of the Sixth Census, by counties and principal towns, together with the tables of apportionment as prepared at the Department of State, for the use of Congress.

SEC. 2. **And be it further enacted,** That the Secretary of State is hereby authorized to have the Sixth Census documents bound in a plain and substantial manner, the cost of which shall not exceed fifty cents per volume; and that the amount thereof shall be paid out of any money in the Treasury not otherwise appropriated.

SEC. 3. **And be it further enacted,** That it shall and may be lawful for the marshal of the State of Maryland, and he is hereby required, under the direction of the Secretary of State, to cause the number of inhabitants within Montgomery county, in the State aforesaid, to be again taken according to the directions of the act to which this is a supplement, and the same to be returned before the first day of December next, and when so taken and returned shall be considered as the correct enumeration of the inhabitants of the said county: **Provided,** That nothing herein contained shall be deemed to release such marshal and his assistants from the penalities contained in the act aforesaid: **And provided further,** That no persons be included in the returns made under the present act, unless such persons shall have been inhabitants of the district for which such returns shall be made on the first day of June, one thousand eight hundred and forty: **And provided, also,** That the said corrected return shall not delay the printing of the Census: and that the said corrected return be printed by itself separately.

APPROVED, September 1, 1841.

CHAP. CXV.—**An Act to make Arrangements for taking the seventh Census.**

Be it enacted by the Senate and House of Representatives of the United States of America in Congress assembled, That the Secretary of State, the Attorney-General, and the Postmaster-General, shall constitute and be a board, to be styled in the Census Board; that it shall be the duty of the said board to prepare and cause to be printed such forms and schedules as may be necessary for the full enumeration of the inhabitants of the United States; and also proper forms and schedules for collecting in statistical tables, under proper heads, such information for collecting in statistical tables, under proper heads, such information as to mines, agriculture, commerce, manufactures, education, and other topics, as will exhibit a full view of the pursuits, industry, education, resources of the country; it being provided that the number of said inquiries, exclusive of the enumeration, shall not exceed one hundred, and that the expense incurred in preparing and printing said forms and schedules shall not exceed ten thousand dollars.

SEC. 2. **And be it further enacted,** That the said board shall have power to appoint a secretary, whose renumeration shall be determined by Congress, upon the completion of the duties assigned to the board.

APPROVED, March 3, 1849.

(No. 4.) **A Resolution in relation to the Census returns from the State of California.**

Resolved by the Senate and House of Representatives of the United States of America in Congress assembled, That the Secretary of the Interior be required to append the census returns of the State of California, made by that State, to the report thereof, now in course of preparation at the Census Office.

APPROVED, January 7, 1853.

The persons appointed by the governor to make an enumeration of inhabitants and qualified voters in the Territory having made their returns, the following table of inhabitants and qualified voters in the several districts is compiled therefrom.*

For discharging the expense of taking the fifth enumeration of the inhabitants of the United States, two hundred and fifty thousand dollars, in addition to the sum of three hundred and fifty thousand dollars, in addition to the sum of three hundred and fifty thousand dollars, appropriated for that purpose by the act of March second, one thousand eight hundred and twenty-nine.

CHAP. XL. — **An Act to procide for taking the fifth census or enumeration of the inhabitants of the United States.**

Be it enacted by the Senate and House of Representatives of the United States of America, in Congress assembled, That the marshals of the several districts of the United States, and of the District of Columbia, and of the territories of Michigan, Arkansas, and of Florida, respectively, shall be, and are hereby, required, under the direction of the Secretary of the Department of State, and according to such instructions as he shall give, pursuant to this act, to cause the number of the inhabitants within their respective districts and territories, (omitting, in such enumeration, Indians not taxed,) to be taken according to the directions of this act. The said enumeration shall distinguish the sexes of all free white persons, and ages of the free white males and females, respectively, under five years of age: those of five and under ten years of age; those of ten years and under fifteen; those of fifteen and under twenty; those of twenty and under thirty; those thirty and under forty; those of forty and under fifty; those of fifty and under sixty; those of sixty and under seventy; those of seventy and under eighty; those of eighty and under ninety; those of ninety and under one hundred; those of one hundred and upwards; and shall further distinguish the number of those free white persons included in such enumeration, who are deaf and dumb, under the age of fourteen years; and those of the age of fourteen years and under twenty-five, and of the age of twenty-five years and upwards; and shall further distinguish the number of those free white persons included in such enumeration, who are blind. The said enumeration shall distinguish the sexes of all free coloured persons, and of all other coloured persons bound to service for life, or fro a term of years, and the ages of such free and other coloured persons, respectively, of each sex, under ten years of age; those of ten and under twenty-four; those of twenty-four and under thirty-six; those of thirty-six and under fifty-five; those of fifty-five and under one hundred; and those of one hundred and upwards; and shall further distinguish the number of those free coloured and other coloured persons, included in the foregoing, who are deaf and dumb, without regard to age, and those who are blind. For effecting which, the marshals aforesaid shall have power, and are hereby required, to appoint one or more assistants in each city and county in their respective districts and territories, residents of such city or county for which they shall be appointed, and shall assign to each of the said assistants a certain division of territory, which division shall not consist, in any case, of more than one county, but may include one or more towns, townships, wards, hundreds, precincts, or parishes, and shall be plainly and distinctly bounded; the said enumeration shall be made by an actual inquiry by such marshals or assistants, at every dwelling-house, or by personal inquiry of the head of every family. The marshals and their assistants shall respectively, before entering on the performance of their futy under this act, take and subscribe an oath or affirmation, before some judge or justice of the peace, resident within their respective districts or territories, for the faithful performance of their duties. The oath or affirmation of the marshal shall be as follows: "I, A. B., marshal of the district (or territory) of , do solemnly swear, (or affirm,) that I will truly and faithfully cause to be made a full and perfect enumeration and description of all persons resident within my district, (or territory,) and return the same to the Secretary of State, agreeably to the directions of an act of Congress, entitled 'An act to provide for taking the fifth census, or enumeration of the inhabitants of the United States,' according to the best of my ability." The oath or affirmation of an assistant shall be as follows: "I, A. B., appointed an assistant to the marshal of the district (or territory) of , do solemnly swear, (or affirm,) that I will make a just, faithful, and perfect enumeration and description of all persons, resident within the division assigned to me for that purpose, by the marshal of the district, (or territory,) of , and make due return thereof to the said marshal, agreeably to the directions of an act of Congress, entitled 'An act to provide for the taking the fifth census or enumeration of the inhabitants of the United States,' according to the best of my ability, and that I will take the said enumeration and description, by actual inquiry at every dwelling-house within said division, or personal inquiry at every dwelling-house within said division, or personal inquiry of the head of every family, and not otherwise." The enumeration shall commence on the first day in June, in the year one thousand eight hundred and thirty, and shall be completed and closed within six calendar months thereafter; the several assistants shall, within the said six months, and on or before the first day of December, one thousand eight hundred and thirty, deliver to the marshals, by whom they shall be appointed, respectively, two copies of the accurate returns of all persons, except Indians not taxed, to be enumerated, as aforesaid, within their respective divisions; which returns shall be made in a schedule, the form of which is annexed to this act, and which shall distinguish, in each county, city, town, township, ward, precinct, hundred, district, or parish, according to the civil divisions of the states or territories, respectively, the several families, by the name of their master, mistress steward, overseer, or other principal persons therein.

SEC. 2. **And be it further enacted,** That every assistant failing or neglecting to make a proper return, or making a false return, of the enumeration, to the marshal, within the time limited by this act, shall forfeit the sum of two hundred dollars, recoverable in the manner pointed out in the next section of this act.

SEC. 3. **And be it further enacted,** That the marshal shall file one copy of each of the several returns aforesaid, and, also, an attested copy of the aggregate amount hereinafter directed, to be transmitted by them respectively, to the Secretary of State, with the clerks of their respective district or superior courts, as the case may be, who are hereby directed to receive, and carefully to preserve, the same: and the marshals, respectively, shall, on or before the first day of February, in the year one thousand eight hundred and thrity-one, transmit to the Secretary of State, one copy of the several returns received from each assistant, and, also, the aggregate amount of each description of persons within their respective districts or territories; and every marshal failing to file the returns of his assistants, or the returns of any of them, with the clerks of the respective courts, as aforesaid, or failing to return one copy of the several returns received from each assistant, and, also, the aggregate amount of each description of persons, in their respective districts or territories, as required by this act, and as the same shall appear from said returns, to the Secretary of State, within the time limited by this act, shall, for every such offence, forfeit the sum of one thousand dollars; which forfeiture shall be recoverable in the courts of the districts or territories where the offences shall be committed, or withinthe circuit courts held within the same, by action of debt, information, or indictment; the one half thereof to the use of the United States, and the other half to the informer; but, where the prosecution shall be first instituted on behalf of the United States, the whole shall accrue to their use, and, for the more effectual discovery of such offences, the judges of the several district courts, in the several districts, and of the Supreme Courts in the territories of the United States, as aforesaid, at their next session, to be held after the expiration of the time allowed for making the returns of the enumeration, hereby directed, to the Secretary of State, shall give this act in charge to the grand juries, in their respective courts, and shall cause the returns of the several assistants, and the said attested copy of the aggregate amount, to be laid before them for their inspection. And the respective clerks of the said courts shall, within thirty days after the said original returns shall have been laid before the grand juries aforesaid, transmit and deliver all such original returns, so filed, to the Department of State.

SEC. 4. **And be it further enacted,** That every assistant shall receive at the reate of one dollar and twenty-five cents for every hundred persons by him returned, where such persons reside in the country; and, where such persons reside in a city or town, containing more than three thousand persons, such assistant shall receive at the same rate for three thousand, and at the rate of one dollar and twenty-five cents for every three hundred persons over three thousand, residing in such city or twon, but where, from the dispersed situation of the inhabitants, in some divisions, one dollar and twenty-five cents will not be sufficient for one hundred persons, the marshals, with the approbation of the judges of their respective districts or territories, may make such further allowance to the assistants, in such divisions, as shall be deemed an adequate compensation; **Provided,** The same does not exceed one dollar and seventy-five cents for every fifty persons by them returned: **Provided, further,** That, before any assistant, as aforesaid, shall in any case, be entitled to receive said compensation, he shall take and subscribe the following

CHRONOLOGICAL LIST OF TERRITORIES:

Name of Territory	Date of Organic Act	Organic Act Effective	Admission as State	Years of Existence as Terr.	Number of Governors
Territory Northwest of R., Ohio	13 Jul 1787	No fixed date	1 Mar 1803[1]	15	1
Territory South of R., Ohio	26 May 1790	No fixed date	1 Jun 1796[2]	6	1
Mississippi	7 Apr 1798	7 Apr 1798	10 Dec 1817	19	4
Indiana	7 May 1800	4 Jul 1800	11 Dec 1816	16	2
Orleans	26 Mar 1804	1 Oct 1804	8 Apr 1812[3]	7	1
Michigan	11 Jan 1805	30 Jun 1805	26 Jan 1837	31	4
Louisiana-Missouri	3 Mar 1805[4]	4 Jul 1805	10 Aug 1821	16	4
Illinois	3 Feb 1809	1 Mar 1809	3 Dec 1818	9	1
Alabama	3 Mar 1817	10 Dec 1817	14 Dec 1819	2	1
Arkansas	2 Mar 1819	4 Jul 1819	15 Jun 1836	17	4
Florida	30 Mar 1822	30 Mar 1822	3 Mar 1845	23	5
Wisconsin	20 Apr 1836	3 Jul 1836	29 May 1848	12	3
Iowa	12 Jun 1838	3 Jul 1838	28 Dec 1846	7	3
Oregon	14 Aug 1848	14 Aug 1848	14 Feb 1859	10	4
Minnesota	3 Mar 1849	3 Mar 1849	11 May 1858	9	3
New Mexico	9 Sep 1850	9 Sep 1850	6 Jan 1912	61	18
Utah	9 Sep 1850	9 Sep 1850	4 Jan 1896	44	14
Washington	2 Mar 1853	2 Mar 1853	11 Nov 1889	36	13
Nebraska	30 May 1854	30 May 1854	9 Feb 1867	12	5
Kansas	30 May 1854	30 May 1854	29 Jan 1861	6	6
Colorado	28 Feb 1861	28 Feb 1861	1 Aug 1876	15	7
Nevada	2 Mar 1861	2 Mar 1861	31 Oct 1864	3	1
Dakota	2 Mar 1861	2 Mar 1861	2 Nov 1889	28	10
Arizona	24 Feb 1863	24 Feb 1863	14 Feb 1912	49	16
Idaho	3 Mar 1863	3 Mar 1863	3 Jul 1890	27	12
Montana	26 May 1864	26 May 1864	8 Nov 1889	25	9
Wyoming	25 Jul 1868	25 Jul 1868	10 Jul 1890	22	7
Oklahoma	2 May 1890	2 May 1890	16 Nov 1907	17	7
Alaska	6 Jan 1912	6 Jan 1912	3 Jan 1959	47	

[1] As the State of Ohio.
[2] As the State of Tennessee.
[3] As the State of Louisiana.

[4] The organic act for Missouri Territory, of 4 Jun 1812, became effective the first Monday in Dec (7th) 1812.

STATE	CAPITOL	AREA (SQ MI)	POPULATION (1960)	(1970)
Alabama	Montgomery	51,609	3,266,740	3,444,165
Alaska	Juneau	586,400	226,167	302,173
Arizona	Phoenix	113,909	1,302,161	1,772,482
Arkansas	Little Rock	53,102	1,786,272	1,923,295
California	Sacramento	158,693	15,717,204	19,953,134
Colorado	Denver	104,247	1,753,947	2,207,259
Connecticut	Hartford	5,009	2,535,234	3,032,217
Delaware	Dover	2,057	446,292	548,104
Florida	Tallahassee	58,560	4,951,560	6,789,443
Georgia	Atlanta	58,876	3,943,116	4,589,575
Hawaii	Honolulu	6,435	632,772	769,913
Idaho	Boise	83,557	667,191	713,008
Illinois	Springfield	56,400	10,081,158	11,113,976
Indiana	Indianapolis	36,291	4,662,498	5,193,669
Iowa	Des Moines	56,290	2,757,357	2,925,041
Kansas	Topeka	82,276	2,178,611	2,249,071
Kentucky	Frankfort	40,395	3,038,156	3,219,311
Louisiana	Baton Rouge	48,523	3,257,022	3,643,180
Maine	Augusta	33,215	969,265	993,663
Maryland	Annapolis	10,577	3,100,689	3,922,399
Massachusetts	Boston	8,257	5,148,578	5,689,170
Michigan	Lansing	58,216	7,823,194	8,875,083
Minnesota	St. Paul	84,068	3,413,864	3,805,069
Mississippi	Jackson	47,716	2,178,141	2,216,912
Missouri	Jefferson City	69,674	4,319,813	4,677,399
Montana	Helena	147,138	674,767	694,409
Nebraska	Lincoln	77,237	1,411,330	1,483,791

STATE	CAPITOL	AREA (SQ MI)	POPULATION (1960)	(1970)
Nevada	Carson City	110,540	285,278	488,738
New Hampshire	Concord	9,304	606,921	737,681
New Jersey	Trenton	7,836	6,066,782	7,168,164
New Mexico	Santa Fe	121,666	951,023	1,016,000
New York	Albany	49,576	16,782,304	18,190,740
North Carolina	Raleigh	52,712	4,556,155	5,082,059
North Dakota	Bismarck	70,665	632,446	617,761
Ohio	Columbus	41,222	9,706,397	10,652,017
Oklahoma	Oklahoma City	69,919	2,328,284	2,559,253
Oregon	Salem	96,981	1,768,687	2,091,385
Pennsylvania	Harrisburg	45,333	11,319,366	11,793,909
Rhode Island	Providence	1,214	859,488	949,723
South Carolina	Columbia	31,055	2,382,594	2,590,516
South Dakota	Pierre	77,047	680,514	666,257
Tennessee	Nashville	42,244	3,567,089	3,924,164
Texas	Austin	267,339	9,597,677	11,196,730
Utah	Salt Lake City	84,916	890,627	1,059,273
Vermont	Montpelier	9,609	389,881	444,732
Virginia	Richmond	40,815	3,966,949	4,648,494
Washington	Olympia	68,192	2,853,214	3,409,169
West Virginia	Charleston	24,181	1,860,421	1,744,237
Wisconsin	Madison	56,154	3,951,777	4,417,933
Wyoming	Cheyenne	97,014	330,066	332,416

The NATIONAL ARCHIVES and its Regional Centers:

National Archives & Record Service
National Archives Library
Pennsylvania Ave. at Eighth St. NW
Washington DC 20408

Regional Service Facility Centers:

address: Chief, Archives Branch
Federal Archives and Record Center

Boston:
380 Trapelo Road, Waltham MA 02154

New York:
Building 22--MOT Bayonne, Bayonne NJ 07702

Philadelphia:
5000 Wissahickon Ave., Philadelphia PA 19144

Atlanta:
1557 St. Joseph Ave., East Point GA 30344

Chicago:
7358 So. Pulaski Rd., Chicago IL 60629

Kansas City:
2306 E. Bannister Rd., Kansas City MO 64131

Fort Worth:
P. O. Box 6216, Fort Worth TX 76115

Denver:
Building 48, Denver Federal Center, Denver CO 80225

San Francisco:
100 Commodore Dr., San Bruno CA 94066

Los Angeles:
24000 Avila Rd., Laguna Niguel CA 92677

Seattle:
6125 Sand Point Way NE, Seattle WA 98115

STATE	SETTLED OR BECAME A TERRITORY	ADMISSION AS A STATE	YEARS AS A TERR.OR/ COLONY	ORDER OF ENTRY	AREA NAMES WHICH FORMED THE STATE
Alabama	3 Mar 1817	14 Dec 1819	2	22	Georgia, Mississippi Territories; South Carolina Cession
Alaska	6 Jan 1912	3 Jan 1959	47	49	Area purchased from Russia: 1867
Arizona	24 Feb 1863	14 Feb 1912	49	48	New Mexico Territory; Mexican Cession; Gadsden Purchase; Arizona Territory
Arkansas	2 Mar 1819	15 Jun 1836	17	25	Orleans Territory; Spanish Territory
California	1848	9 Sep 1850	2	31	Mexican Cession
Colorado	28 Feb 1861	1 Aug 1876	15	38	Missouri Territory; Indian Lands; Mexican Cession
Connecticut	1633	9 Jan 1788	155	5	English Colonial Lands
Delaware	1638	7 Dec 1787	149	1	English Colonial Lands
Florida	30 Mar 1822	3 Mar 1845	23	27	Spanish lands
Georgia	1732	2 Jan 1788	56	4	English Colonial Lands
Hawaii	1894	21 Aug 1959	65	50	Hawaiian Islands
Idaho	3 Mar 1863	3 Jul 1890	27	43	Oregon Territory; Indian Lands; Utah Territory; Northwest Territory
Illinois	3 Feb 1809	3 Dec 1818	9	21	Indiana Territory; Illinois Territory; Northwest Territory
Indiana	7 May 1800	11 Dec 1816	16	19	Indiana and Northwest Territories
Iowa	12 Jun 1838	28 Dec 1846	7	29	Indiana Territory; Missouri Territory; Iowa Territory
Kansas	30 May 1854	29 Jan 1861	6	34	Indian Lands; Iowa Territory; Missouri Territory
Kentucky	26 May 1790	1 Jun 1792	2	15	Virginia Lands
Louisiana Orleans	26 Mar 1804 3 Mar 1805	30 Apr 1812	8	18	Orleans Territory; Louisiana Territory
Maine	1625	15 Mar 1820	195	23	Massachusetts Lands; Canadian lands claimed by England
Maryland	1634	28 Apr 1788	154	7	Colonial Lands; Virginia Lands; Pennsylvania Lands
Massachusetts	1620	6 Feb 1788	168	6	Colonial Lands
Michigan	11 Jan 1805	26 Jan 1837	32	26	Northwest Territory; Indiana Territory; Illinois Territory; Michigan Territory
Minnesota	3 Mar 1849	11 May 1858	9	32	Minnesota Territory; Dakota Territory; Northwest Territory
Mississippi	7 Apr 1798	10 Dec 1817	19	20	Georgia Lands; Mississippi Territory
Missouri	4 Jun 1812	10 Aug 1821	9	24	Louisiana and Missouri Territories

State	Settled...	Admission...	Terr. Years-	State Order-	Area Names Which Formed the State
Montana	26 May 1864	8 Nov 1889	25	41	Dakota Territory; Washington Territory; Montana Territory
Nebraska	30 May 1854	1 Mar 1867	12	37	Dakota Territory; Indian Lands
Nevada	2 Mar 1861	31 Oct 1864	3	36	Utah Territory (State of Deseret); New Mexico Territory
New Hampshire	1623	21 Jun 1788	165	9	Massachusetts Lands
New Jersey	1624	18 Dec 1787	163	3	Colonial Lands
New Mexico	9 Sep 1850	6 Jan 1912	61	47	Mexican Cession; New Mexico Territory; Gadsden Purchase
New York	1624	26 Jul 1788	164	11	Colonial Lands
North Carolina	1653	21 Nov 1789	136	12	Colonial Lands
North Dakota	2 Mar 1861	2 Nov 1889	28	39	Minnesota and Dakota Territories
Ohio	13 Jul 1787	1 Mar 1803	15	17	Northwest Territory; Pennsylvania Lands; Virginia Lands; Massachusetts Lands; Connecticut Lands
Oklahoma	2 May 1890	16 Nov 1907	17	46	Arkansas Territory; Missouri Territory; Indian Territory; Oklahoma Territory
Oregon	14 Aug 1848	14 Feb 1859	10	33	Oregon Territory
Pennsylvania	1681	12 Dec 1787	106	2	Colonial Lands
Rhode Island	1636	24 May 1790	154	13	Colonial Lands
South Carolina	1670	23 May 1788	118	8	Colonial Lands
South Dakota	2 Mar 1861	2 Nov 1889	28	40	Dakota and Minnesota Territories
Tennessee	1769	1 Jun 1796	27	16	North Carolina Lands
Texas	1823	29 Dec 1845	22	28	Louisiana and Mexican Territories
Utah	9 Sep 1850	4 Jan 1896	45	45	Utah Territory (State of Deseret)
Vermont	1665	4 Mar 1791	126	14	Colonial Lands, claimed by New York
Virginia	1607	25 Jun 1788	181	10	Colonial Lands
Washington	2 Mar 1853	11 Nov 1889	36	42	Oregon and Washington Territories
West Virginia	11 Jun 1861	20 Jun 1863	2	35	Seceeded from Virginia
Wisconsin	20 Apr 1836	29 May 1848	12	30	Indian Territory; Northwest Territory; Michigan Territory; Wisconsin Territory
Wyoming	25 Jul 1868	10 Jul 1890	22	44	Indian Lands; Nebraska Territory; Dakota Territory; Wyoming Territory

WHERE TO WRITE FOR STATE VITAL RECORDS

STATE	ADDRESS	DATES AVAILABLE SINCE: (B=birth, M=marriage, D=death)	
Alabama	Bureau of Vital Statistics	B	1 Jan 1908
	State Department of Public Health	M	Aug 1936
	Montgomery AL 36104	D	1 Jan 1908
Alaska	Bureau of Vital Statistics	B	1913
	Dept. of Health and Welfare, Pouch H,	M	1913
	Juneau AK 99801	D	1913
American Samoa	Registrar of Vital Statistics	B	1900
	Pago Pago	M	1900
	American Samoa 96920	D	1900
Arizona	Division of Vital Records	B	1 Jul 1909
	State Department of Health	M	
	P.O.Box 6820, Phoenix AZ 85005	D	1 Jul 1909
	(marriage - Clerk of County Superior Court)		
Arkansas	Bureau of Vital Statistics	B	1 Feb 1914
	State Department of Health	M	1917
	Little Rock AR 72201	D	1 Feb 1914
California	Bureau of Vital Statistics	B	1 Jul 1905
	State Dept. of Public Health	M	
	744 "P" Street	D	1 Jul 1905
	Sacramento CA 95814		
Canal Zone	Vital Statistics Clerk	B	May 1904
	Health Bureau	M	
	Balboa Heights, Canal Zone	D	May 1904
Colorado	Records and Statistics Section	B	1 Jan 1907
	Colorado Department of Health	M	
	4210 East 11th Avenue	D	1 Jan 1907
	Denver CO 80220		
Connecticut	Public Health Statistics Section	B	1 Jul 1897
	State Department of Health	M	1 Jul 1897
	79 Elm Street	D	1 Jul 1897
	Hartford CT 06115		
Delaware	Bureau of Vital Statistics	B	1881
	State Board of Health	M	
	State Health Building	D	1881
	Dover DE 19901	(BD also 1861-3)	
District of	D.C. Department of Public Health	B	1871
	Vital Records Division, Room 1022	M	
	300 Indiana Avenue, N.W.	D	1855
	Washington, D.C. 20001		
Florida	Bureau of Vital Statistics	B	Jan 1917 (some Apr 1865)
	State Board of Health, P.O.Box 210	M	6 Jun 1927
	Jacksonville FL 32201	D	Jan 1917 (some Aug 1877)
Georgia	Vital Records Service	B	1 Jan 1919
	State Department of Public Health	M	9 Jun 1952 (centralized)
	47 Trinity Ave., S.W.	D	1 Jan 1919
	Atlanta GA 30334		

VITAL RECORDS - WHERE TO WRITE

Guam	Office of Vital and Health Statistics Dept. of Public Health & Social Services Government of Guam, P.O.Box 2816 Agana, Guam, M.I. 96910	B M D	26 Oct 1901 26 Oct 1901
Hawaii	Research and Statistics Office State Department of Health P.O.Box 3378 Honolulul HA 96801	B M D	1853 1853
Idaho	Bureau of Vital Statistics State Department of Health Boise ID 83701	B M D	1911 1947 1911
Illinois	Bureau of Statistics State Department of Public Health Springfield IL 62706	B M D	1 Jan 1916 1 Jan 1962 1 Jan 1916
Indiana	Division of Vital Records State Board of Health 1330 West Michigan Street Indianapolis IN 46206	B M D	1 Oct 1907 1958 1900
Iowa	Division of Records and Statistics State Department of Health Des Moines IA 50319	B M D	1 Jul 1880 1 Jul 1880
Kansas	Division of Vital Statistics State Department of Health Topeka KN 66612	B M D	1 Jul 1911 May 1913 1 Jul 1911
Kentucky	Office of Vital Statistics State Department of Health 275 East Main Street Frankfort KY 40601	B M D	1 Jan 1911 1 Jul 1958 1 Jan 1911
Louisiana (except New Orleans)	Division of Public Health Statistics State Board of Health, P.O.Box 60630 New Orleans LA 70160	B M D	1 Jul 1914 1946 1 Jul 1914
New Orleans LA	Bureau of Vital Statistics City Health Department 1W03 City Hall, Civic Center New Orleans LA 70112	B M D	1790 1803
Maine	Office of Vital Statistics State Dept. of Health and Welfare State House, Augusta ME 04330	B M D	1892 1892
Maryland (except Baltimore, B-D)	Division of Vital Records State Department of Health State Office Bldg, 301 W. Preston St. Baltimore MD 21201	B M D	1898 1 Jun 1951 1898
Baltimore MD	Bureau of Vital Records City Health Dept., Municipal Office Bldg Baltimore MD 21202	B M D	1 Jan 1875 1 Jan 1875
Massachusetts (except Boston, B-D)	Registrar of Vital Statistics 272 State House Boston MA 02133	B M D	1841 1841 1841
Boston MA	City Registrar, Registry Division Health Dept, Room 705, City Hall Annex Boston MA 02133	B M D	1639 1639

State	Address	Records
Michigan	Vital Records Section Michigan Department of Health 3500 North Logan Street Lansing MI 48914	B 1867 M Apr 1867 D 1867
Minnesota	Section of Vital Statistics State Department of Health 350 State Office Building St. Paul MN 55101	B Jan 1900 M Jan 1958 D Jan 1900
Mississippi	Division of Public Health Statistics State Board of Health, P.O.Box 1700 Jackson MS 39205	B 1 Nov 1912 M Jan 1926 D 1 Nov 1912
Missouri	Vital Records, Division of Health State Dept. of Public Health/Welfare Jefferson City MO 65101	B Jan 1910 M Jul 1948 D Jan 1910
Montana	Division of Records and Statistics State Department of Health Helena MT 59601	B late 1907 M Jul 1943 D late 1907
Nebraska	Bureau of Vital Statistics State Dept. of Health Lincoln Bldg., 1003 "O" Street Lincoln NB 68508	B late 1904 M Jan 1909 D late 1904
Nevada	Department of Health,Welfare, and Rehabilitation, Division of Health Section of Vital Statistics Carson City NV 89701	B 1 Jul 1911 M county D 1 Jul 1911
New Hampshire	Department of Health and Welfare Division of Public Health Bureau of Vital Statistics 61 South Spring Street Concord NH 03301	B M 1640 D
New Jersey	State Department of Health Bureau of Vital Statistics, Box 1540 Trenton NJ 08625	B May 1878 M May 1878 D May 1878
	Archives and History Bureau State Library Division State Department of Education Trenton NJ 08625	B May 1848-May 1878 M May 1848-May 1878 D May 1848-May 1878
New Mexico	Vital Records, New Mexico Health and Social Services Department PERA Building, Room 118 Santa Fe NM 87501	B M county D
New York (except New York City)	Bureau of Vital Records State Department of Health Albany NY 12208	B 1880 M Jan 1880* D 1880 *(1908-Apr 1915-M-county)
New York City Bronx Borough	Bureau of Records and Statistics Dept. of Health of New York City 1826 Arthur Avenue Bronx, NY 10457	B 1898 D 1898 (1866-1897 in Manhattan District)
	Office of City Clerk 1780 Grand Concourse, Bronx NY 10457	M (1908-1913 in Manhattan)

VITAL RECORDS - WHERE TO WRITE

Place	Address	Record	Date
New York City Brooklyn Borough	County Clerk, Kings County Historical Division, 360 Adams St. Brooklyn NY 11201	D	1847-1865
	Bureau of Records and Statistics Dept. of Health of New York City 295 Flatbush Ave. Ext. Brooklyn NY 11201	B D	1866 1866
	Office of City Clerk 208 Joralemon Street Brooklyn NY 11201	M	
New York City Manhattan	Bureau of Records and Statistics Dept. of Health of New York City 125 Worth Street, New York NY 10013	B D	1866 1866
	Office of City Clerk Chambers and Centre Streets New York NY 10007	M	
New York City Old City of New York-Manhattan and part of Bronx	Municipal Archives and Records Retention Center of the New York Public Library 238 William Street New York NY 10038	D	1847-1865
New York City Queens Borough	Bureau of Records and Statistics Dept. of Health of New York City 90-37 Parsons Blvd. Jamaica NY 11432	B D	1898 1898
	Office of City Clerk 120-55 Queens Blvd., Borough Hall Station Jamaica NY 11424	M	
New York City Richmond Borough	Bureau of Records and Statistics Dept. of Health of New York City 51 Stuyvesant Place St. George, Staten Island NY 10301	B D	1898 1898
	Office of City Clerk, Borough Hall St. George, Staten Island NY 10301	M	
North Carolina	Public Health Statistics Section State Board of Health, P.O.Box 2091 Raleigh NC 27602	B M D	1 Oct 1913 1 Jan 1962 1 Oct 1913
North Dakota	Division of Vital Statistics State Department of Health Bismarck ND 58501	B M D	1 Jul 1893 1 Jul 1925 1 Jul 1893 (1894-1920 incomplete)
Ohio	Division of Vital Statistics State Department of Health G-20 State Departments Building Columbus OH 43215	B M D	20 Dec 1908 Sep 1949 20 Dec 1908
Oklahoma	Divison of Statistics State Department of Health 3400 North Eastern Oklahoma City OK 73105	B M D	Oct 1908 county Oct 1908

VITAL RECORDS - WHERE TO WRITE

State	Address	Records
Oregon	Vital Statistics Section State Board of Health P.O. Box 231 Portland OR 97207	B Jul 1903 M Jan 1907 D Jul 1903
	Portland Bureau of Health 305 City Hall, Portland OR	(1903-1914 Portland)
Pennsylvania	Division of Vital Statistics State Department of Health Health and Welfare Bldg, P.O.Box 90 Harrisburg PA 17120	B 1 Jan 1906 M Jan 1941 D 1 Jan 1906
	Vital Statistics, Philadelphia Dept. of Public Health, City Hall Annex, Philadelphia PA 19107	B-D 1860-1915 Philadelphia
Puerto Rico	Divison of Demographic Registry and Vital Statistics, Dept. of Health San Juan, Puerto Rico 00908	B 22 Jul 1931 M D 22 Jul 1931
Rhode Island	Division of Vital Statistics State Department of Health State Office Building, Room 351 Providence RI 02903	B 1853 M Jan 1853 D 1853
South Carolina	Bureau of Vital Statistics State Board of Health, State Building Columbia SC 29201	B 1 Jan 1915 M 1 Jul 1950 D 1 Jan 1915
	Charleston - Charleston County Health Department	B 1877 D 1821
South Dakota	Divison of Public Health Statistics State Department of Health Pierre SD 57501	B 1 Jul 1905 M 1 Jul 1905 D 1 Jul 1905
Tennessee	Division of Vital Statistics State Department of Public Health Cordell Hull Building Nashville TN 37219	B 1 Jan 1914* M Jul 1945 D 1 Jan 1914*

*also:
B - Nashville - June 1881
B - Knoxville - July 1881
B - Chattanooga - Jan 1882
D - Nashville - July 1874
D - Knoxville - July 1887
D - Chattanooga - Mar 1872

State	Address	Records
Texas	Bureau of Vital Statistics State Department of Health 410 East 5th Street Austin TX 78701	B 1903 M county D 1903
Utah	Division of Vital Statistics Utah State Department of Health 44 Medical Drive Salt Lake City UT 84113	B 1905 M county D 1905
Vermont	Secretary of State Vital Records Department State House Montpelier VT 05602	B M 1857 D
	Town or City Clerk	B-D

VITAL RECORDS - WHERE TO WRITE

Virginia	Bureau of Vital Records and Statistics State Department of Health James Madison Bldg. (P.O.Box 1000) Richmond VA 05401	B M D B-D	4 Jun 1912 Jan 1853 4 Jun 1912 Jan 1858-Dec 1896
Virgin Islands (U.S.)			
St. Thomas	Registrar of Vital Statistics Charlotte Amalie St. Thomas, Virgin Islands 00802	B D	1 Jul 1906 1 Jan 1906
St. Thomas & St. John	Clerk of Municipal Court Municipal Court of the Virgin Islands Charlotte Amalie St. Thomas, Virgin Islands 00801	M	
St. Croix	Registrar of Vital Statistics Charles Harwood Memorial Hospital St. Croix, Virgin Islands 00820	B D	1840 1840
	Clerk of Municipal Court Municipal Court of the Virgin Islands Christiansted, St. Croix, Virgin Islands 00820	M	
Washington	Bureau of Vital Statistics State Department of Health Services P. O. Box 709 Olympia WA 98504	B M D	1 Jul 1907 1 Jan 1968 1 Jul 1907
West Virginia	Division of Vital Statistics State Department of Health State Office Building No. 3	B M D	Jan 1917 1921 Jan 1917
Wisconsin	Bureau of Health Statistics Wisconsin Division of Health P. O. Box 309 Madison WI 53701	B M D	1814 Apr 1835 1814 (early years incomplete)
Wyoming	Division of Vital Statistics State Department of Public Health State Office Building Cheyenne WY 82001	B M D	Jul 1909 May 1941 Jul 1909

NOTE: The above information on early vital statistics is not complete. Be sure to search the records of the various county offices, such as: Clerk, Recorder, or Judge of the following:

County Court	Circuit Court	Justices of the Peace
Probate Court	District Court	County Health Officer
Superior Court	Orphans Court	Recorder or Registrar of Deeds

Search city and town records (City or Town Clerk, Board of Health) for information if records are not available at county offices.

Be sure to check both marriage license and marriage records when writing for information.

The changing of county boundaries must be kept in mind when seeking information.

When writing your letter you may ask the clerk to direct you to where your particular records can be found if they are not available at his office.

Above information based on publications of the U.S. Department of Health, Education and Welfare: Where to Write for Birth and Death Records and Where to Write for Marriage Records, available from the U.S. Government Printing Office.

SELECTED MAJOR LIBRARIES, BY STATE, AND GENEALOGICAL COLLECTIONS IN THE U.S.

State		
Alabama	Alabama Dept. of Archives and History Library 624 Washington Avenue Montgomery AL 36104	Alabama Public Library Service 155 Administrative Bldg. 64 North Union Montgomery AL 36104
Alaska	Alaska Historical Library State Capitol Bldg. Pouch G Juneau AK 99801	Alaska Division of State Libraries State Capitol Bldg. Pouch G Juneau AK 99801
Arizona	Arizona State Department of Library & Archives Capitol Bldg, 3rd Floor Phoenix AZ 85007	Arizona Pioneers Historical Society Library 949 East Second Street Tucson AZ 85719
Arkansas	Arkansas History Commission Old State House, West Wing 300 West Markham Street Little Rock AR 72201	Little Rock Public Library (genealogy collection) 700 Louisiana Street Little Rock AR 72201
California	California State Library Courts Building; Box 2037 Sacramento CA 95809 CA Historical Society Library 2099 Pacific Avenue (mail: 2090 Jackson Street) San Francisco CA 94109	Los Angeles Public Library 630 West Fifth Street Los Angeles CA 90017
Colorado	Colorado State Library CO State Library Building 1362 Lincoln Street Denver CO 80203	Denver Public Library (genealogy collection) 1357 Broadway Denver CO 80203
Connecticut	Connecticut State Library 231 Capitol Avenue Hartford CT 06115	Connecticut Historical Society Library 1 Elizabeth Street Hartford CT 06105
Delaware	Delaware State Lib.Commission W. Loockerman St.; Box 635 Dover DE 19901	Historical Society of Delaware Library Old Town Hall; Sixth & Market Sts. Wilmington DE 19801
District of Columbia	Library of Congress Washington DC 29540 Daughters of the American Revolution Library 1776 "D" Street, N.W. Washington, D.C. 20006	National Archives & Record Service National Archives Library Pennsylvania Ave. at Eighth St, NW Washington, D.C. 20408
Florida	Florida State Library Supreme Court Bldg. Tallahassee FL 32304	St. Petersburg Historical Soc. Lib. 335 Second Avenue St. Petersburg FL 33706
Georgia	Georgia State Library 301 Judicial Building 40 Capitol Sq. SW Atlanta GA 30334 Washington Memorial Library, 1180 Washington Ave. & Middle Georgia Regional Library, 911 First St. Macon GA 31201. (genealogical department)	Georgia Dept. of Archives & History Search Room & Microfilm Library 330 Capitol Ave., SE Atlanta GA 30334

State		
Hawaii	Hawaii State Library System 478 South King Street Honolulu HA 96813	Hawaiian Historical Society Library 560 Kawaiahao St. (mail: Box 2596) Honolulu HA 96803
Idaho	Idaho State Library 517 Main St. Boise ID 83702	Idaho State Historical Soc. Libraries 61 0 N. Julia Davis Drive Boise ID 83706
Illinois	Illinois State Library Centennial Bldg. Springfield IL 62706	Illinois State Historical Library Centennial Bldg. Springfield IL 62706
	Newberry Library 60 W. Walton St. Chicago IL 60610	American Library Association Headquarters Library 50 E. Huron St. Chicago IL 60611
Indiana	Indiana State Library 140 N. Senate Ave. Indianapolis IN 46204	Indiana Historical Society 140 N. Senate Ave. Indianapolis IN 46204
Iowa	Iowa State Traveling Library Historical Building Des Moines IA 50319	State Historical Society of Iowa Library, Centennial Building Box 871, Iowa City IA 52204
Kansas	Kansas State Library State House Topeka KS 66612	Kansas State Historical Soc. Library 120 West Tenth Topeka KS 66612
Kentucky	Kentucky Historical Society Library, Old State House Box H Frankfurt KY 40601	Kentucky State Archives & Record Service Public Administration Library Division Capitol Annex, Box 537 Frankfurt KY 40601
Louisiana	Louisiana State Library Capitol Grounds Third St. (mail: Box 131) Baton Rouge LA 70821	Tulane University of Louisiana Howard-Tilton Memorial Library Audubon Pl. at Freret St. New Orleans LA 70118 (genealogy)
Maine	Bangor Public Library 145 Harlow St. (ME gen.) Bangor ME 04401	Maine Historical Society Library 485 Congress St. Portland ME 04111
Maryland	Maryland State Library Court of Appeals Bldg. Bladen St S & College Ave Box 191, Annapolis MD 21404	Maryland Historical Society Library 201 W. Monument St. Baltimore MD 21201
Massachusetts	Massachusetts State Library State House Boston MA 02133	Massachusetts Historical Society Library 1154 Boylston St. Boston MA 02215
	Boston Public Library & Eastern Massachusetts Regional Public Library System Copley Square (New England family genealogies) Boston MA 02117	
Michigan	Michigan State Library 735 E. Michigan Ave. Lansing MI 48913	Michigan Historical Commission State Archives Library 3405 N. Logan St. Lansing MI 48918

State	State Library	Other Collections
Minnesota	Minnesota Historical Society Library Cedar St. & Central Ave. St. Paul MN 55101	Macalester College Wayerhaeurser Library (MN hist.) Grand and Macalester Sts. St. Paul MN 55101
Mississippi	Mississippi Library Commission 405 State Office Bldg. Jackson MS 39201	Mississippi Dept. of Archives & History Library, War Memorial Bldg. N State St. (mail: Box 571) Jackson MS 39205
Missouri	Missouri State Library 308 E High St. Jefferson City MO 65101	Missouri Historical Soc. Library Jefferson Memorial Bldg. St. Louis MO 63112
	State Historical Society of Missouri Library Hitt & Lowry Sts., University of Missouri Library Columbia MO 65201	
Montana	Montana State Library 930 E Lyndale Ave. Helena MT 59601	Montana Historical Soc. Library Corner Sixth Ave & Roberts St. Helena MT 59601
Nebraska	Nebraska State Library 3rd Floor, State Capitol Lincoln NB 68509	Nebraska State Historical Soc. Library 1500 "R" Street Lincoln NB 68508
Nevada	Nevada State Library Carson City NV 89701	Nevada State Historical Soc. Library Box 1129 Reno NV 89504
New Hampshire	New Hampshire State Library 20 Park Street Concord NH 03301	New Hampshire Historical Soc. Library 30 Park Street Concord NH 03301
New Jersey	New Jersey State Library Department of Education 185 W. State St. Trenton NJ 08625	Atlantic City Free Public Library (New Jersey genealogy) Illinois & Pacific Aves. Atlantic City NJ 08401
New Mexico	New Mexico State Library 300 Don Gaspar St. (mail: Box 1629) Santa Fe NM 87501	Museum of New Mexico Historical Reference Library Palace of the Governors Santa Fe NM 87501
New York	New York State Library Education Building Albany NY 12224	New York Public Library Fifth Ave. & 42nd St. New York City NY 10018
	Holland Society of New York Library 122 E 58th St. New York City NY 10022	
North Carolina	North Carolina State Library Box 2889 Raleigh NC 27602	Rowan Public Library (NC hist-gen) 201 W. Fisher St. (mail: Box 1009) Salisbury NC 28144
North Dakota	North Dakota State Library Commission Liberty Memorial Building State Capitol Grounds Bismarck ND 58501	North Dakota State Historical Society Library Liberty Memorial Building Bismarck ND 58501

Ohio	Ohio Historical Soc. Library 1813 N High St. Columbus OH 43201	Western Reserve Historical Soc. Lib. 10825 East Blvd. Cleveland OH 44106
	State Library of Ohio 65 S Front St. Columbus OH 43215	
Oklahoma	Oklahoma Dept. of Libraries 109 State Capitol L (mail: Box 53344) Oklahoma City OK 73105	Oklahoma Historical Society Library Historical Building Oklahoma City OK 73105
Oregon	Oregon State Library State Library Building Salem OR 97301	Oregon Historical Soc. Library 1230 SW Park Ave. Portland OR 97205
Pennsylvania	Pennsylvania State Library Walnut St. & Commonwealth Ave. (mail: Box 1601) Harrisburg PA 17126	Historical Society of Pennsylvania Library 1300 Locust St. Philadelphia PA 19107
	Friends Historical Library of Swarthmore College Swarthmore PA 19081	
Rhode Island	Rhode Island State Library State House Providence RI 02903	Rhode Island Historical Soc. Library Hope & Power Sts. Providence RI 02903
South Carolina	South Carolina State Library 1001 Main St. Columbia SC 29201	South Carolina Historical Soc. Lib. Fireproof Bldg. at Chalmers St. Charleston SC 29401
South Dakota	South Dakota State Library 322 S Fort St. Pierre SD 57501	South Dakota Department of History Historical Society Library Memorial Bldg., Capitol Ave. Pierre SD 57501
Tennessee	Tennessee State Library & Archives Seventh Ave N. Nashville TN 37219	Public Library of Knoxville & Knox County (TN hist-gen) Lawson McGhee Library 217 Market St. Knoxville TN 27902
Texas	Texas State Library Texas Archives & Lib. Bldg. 1201 Brazos St. Drawer DD-Capitol Station Austin TX 78711	Dallas Public Library (genealogy) 1954 Commerce St. Dallas TX 75201 Fort Worth Public Library (gen.) Ninth & Throckmorton Sts. Ft. Worth TX 76102
Utah	Utah State Historical Society 603 E. South Temple Salt Lake City UT 84114	Brigham Young University Library Harold B. Lee Library Provo UT 84601
	Church of Jesus Christ of Latter-day Saints Genealogical Society Library 50 East North Temple Salt Lake City UT 84150	

Vermont	Vermont Historical Soc. Lib. State Administration Bldg. Montpelier VT 05602	Bennington Museum, Inc., Library W. Main St. (gen-fam.hist) Old Bennington VT 05201
Virginia	Virginia State Library Capitol St. Richmond VA 23219 Alexandria Library (gen,VA) 717 Queen St. Alexandria VA 23314	Virginia Historical Society Library 428 North Blvd. (mail: Box 7311) Richmond VA 23221
Washington	Washington State Library Olympia WA 98501 Spokane Public Library (gen) Comstock Bldg, W 906 Main Ave Spokane WA 99201	Washington State Historical Soc. Lib. State Historical Building 315 N. Stadium Way Tacoma WA 98403
West Virginia	West Virginia Lib. Commission 2004 Quarrier St. Charleston WV 25311	West Virginia Department of Archives & History Library State Capitol Bldg, Room E-400 Charleston WV 25305
Wisconsin	State Historical Society of Wisconsin Library 816 State St. Madison WI 53706	Division for Library Services Dept. of Public Instruction State of Wisconsin, Adm. Office, 126 Langdon St. Madison WI 53703
Wyoming	Wyoming State Library Supreme Court & State Library L-Bldg. Cheyenne WY 82001	Laramie County Library (gen and west hist) 2119 Capitol Ave. Cheyenne WY 82001

MARYLAND

COUNTY NAME	DATE ORGANIZED	PARENT COUNTY	MAP	PROGENY COUNTY
Allegany	25 Dec 1789	Washington	B-1	Garrett 1872
Ann Arundel[2]	9 Apr 1650	Colonial Lands	G-3	Howard 1851, Harford 1773
Baltimore[2,3]	12 Jan 1659	Colonial Lands	G-2	Galtimore City 1851, Carroll 1837, Cecil 1674, Harford 1773, Howard 1851
Baltimore City	13 May 1851	Baltimore(Functional as an independant city as early as 1729)		
Calvert[1]	30 Jul 1650	Old Charles	G-4	
Caroline	15 Jun 1773	Dorchester, Queen Anne's	H-3	
Carroll	19 Jan 1837	Baltimore, Frederick	F-1	
Cecil[3]	6 Jun 1674	Baltimore	H-1	
Charles[1]	3 Oct 1650	Colonial Lands	F-5	Calvert 1654, Prince George's 1695
Dorchester	27 May 1668	Colonial Lands	H-5	Carolina 1773
Frederick	10 Jun 1748	Prince George's	E-2	Carroll 1837, Montgomery 1776, Washington 1776
Garrett	4 Nov 1872	Allegany	A-1	
Harford	17 Dec 1773	Baltimore	G-1	
Howard[2]	13 May 1851	Baltimore, Anne Arundel	F-2	
Kent[3]	30 Dec 1637	Colonial Lands	H-2	Talbot 1661
Montgomery	6 Sep 1776	Frederick	E-3	
Patuxent[5]	3 Oct 1650	Colonial Lands		Worcester (old) 1669
Prince George's	3 Oct 1695	Charles, Calvert	F-4	Frederick 1748
Queen Anne's	9 Apr 1706	Talbot	H-3	Caroline 1773
Saint Mary's	24 Jan 1637	Colonial Lands	G-5	
Somerset	22 Aug 1666	Colonial Lands	I-5	Wicomico 1867, Worcester 1742
Talbot	19 Feb 1661	Kent	H-4	Queen Anne's 1706
Worcester	22 Oct 1742	Somerset	J-5	
Washington	6 Sep 1776	Frederick	D-1	
Wicomico	17 Aug 1867	Somerset, Worcester	J-5	
Worcester (Old)[5]	22 Oct 1669	Patuxent		
Worcester (New)[4]	22 Oct 1842	Somerset		Wicomico 1867

FOOTNOTES:

[1]Charles County was created 3 Oct 1650 and was discontinued 28 Sep 1653. Part of the area was incorporated into Calvert County. A new Charles County was created 13 April 1658.

[2]The present area of Howard County was originally a part of Anne Arundel County. In 1698 it was attached to Baltimore County. In 1727 the area was returned to Anne Arundel County. In 1838 it was made a separate county and named Howard County. Some lists show this county as being created in 1850, but that is the date that the Constitutional Convention formally recognized it as a new county. Many of the records date from the 1830's and 1840's.

[3]Most of the area comprizing present-day Cecil County was originally attached to Kent County until 1659 when it was attached to Baltimore County from which Cecil County was created in 1674.

[4]Worcester County was first established 22 Oct 1669 which layed claim to much of Delaware. By 1750 the Lords Proprietary abandoned the idea of the county. Morris L. Radoff states in The County Courthouses and Records of Maryland that there was no courthouse, pernaps no government and no records. Another Worcester County was formed in 1742 having no, or at least very little, relation with the "Old Worcester County".

[5]Patuxent County was created 3 Oct 1650 and was renamed Worcester County 22 Oct 1669.

SELECTED BIBLIOGRAPHY:

Radoff, Morris L., Skordas, G., and Jacobsen, P.R., The County Courthouses and Records of Maryland, 2 vol. Annapolis MD, 1960-63.

Bozman, John Leeds, History of Maryland, Baltimore MD, 1837.

Bozman, John Leeds, A Sketch of the History of Maryland, Baltimore MD, 1811.

Scharf, J. Thomas, History of Maryland, Hatboro PA, 1879.

McSherry, James, History of Maryland, Baltimore MD, 1849.

Walsh, Richard, and Fox, William Lloyd, (eds), Maryland: A History 1632-1974), Baltimore MD, 1974.

Wentz, Rev. Prof. Abdel Ross, Ph.D., History of the Maryland Synod, Harrisburg, 1920.

Passano, Eleanor P., An Index of the Source Records of Maryland: genealogical, historical, 1940, reprinted Baltimore, 1974.

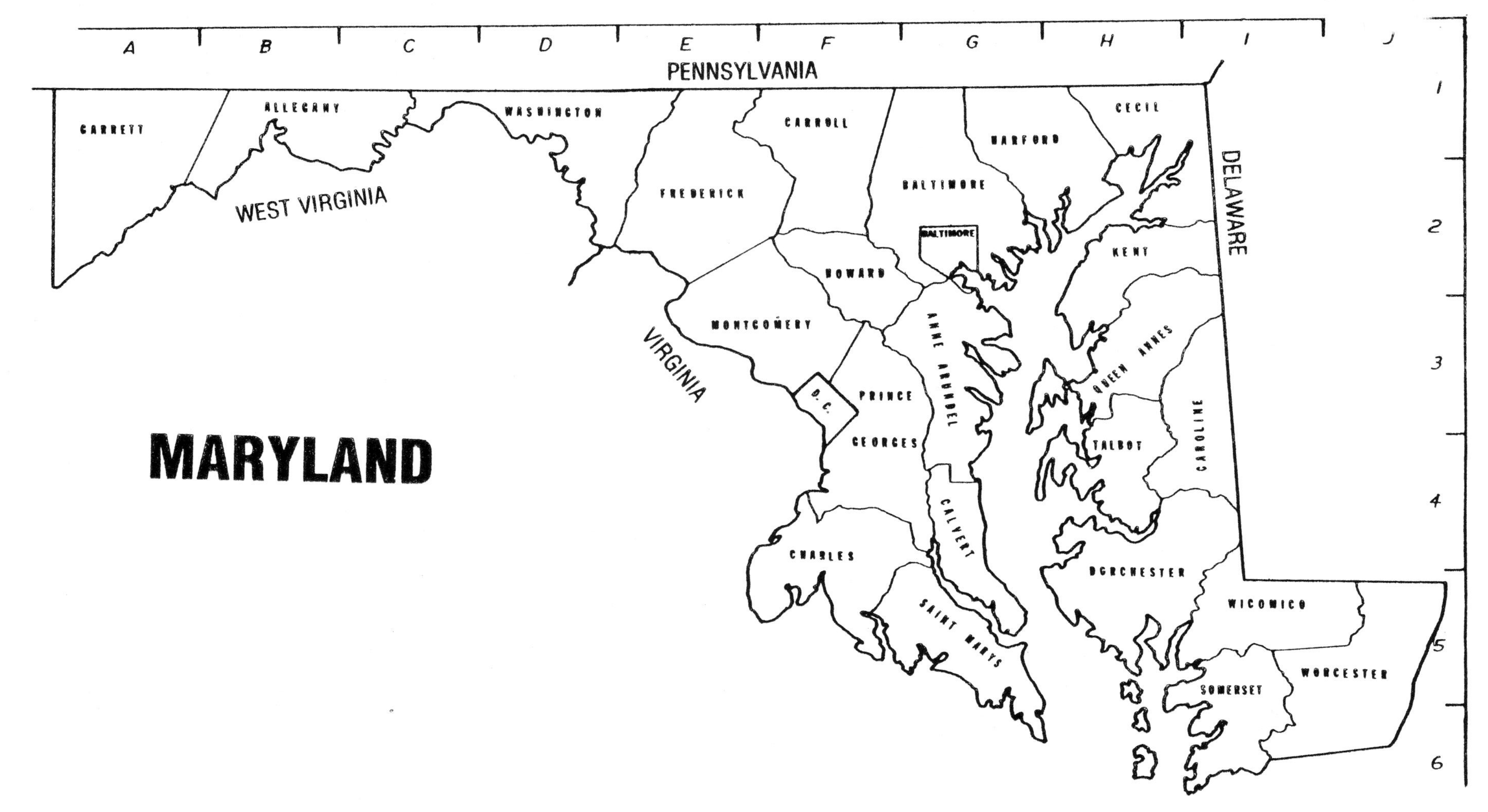
MARYLAND
A
B
C
D
E
F
G
H
I
J
1
2
3
4
5
6
PENNSYLVANIA
DELAWARE
WEST VIRGINIA
VIRGINIA
GARRETT
ALLEGANY
WASHINGTON
FREDERICK
CARROLL
BALTIMORE
BALTIMORE
HARFORD
CECIL
HOWARD
MONTGOMERY
D.C.
PRINCE GEORGES
ANNE ARUNDEL
KENT
QUEEN ANNES
TALBOT
CAROLINE
CALVERT
CHARLES
SAINT MARYS
DORCHESTER
WICOMICO
SOMERSET
WORCESTER

MARYLAND

MARYLAND

HOW TO USE THIS INDEX

THE INDEX TO THE 1850 FEDERAL CENSUS IS PRINTED IN FOUR COLUMNS. THE FOLLOWING PARAGRAPHS EXPLAIN THE MEANING OF EACH COLUMN WITH OTHER NECESSARY DETAILS FOR ITS USE.

COLUMN ONE

THE FIRST COLUMN LISTS IN ALPHABETICAL ORDER THE NAME OF THE INDIVIDUALS FOUND IN THE ORIGINAL CENSUS RECORD. IT SHOULD BE UNDERSTOOD THAT ALL OF THE NAMES ARE NOT INDEXED, BUT ONLY THOSE INDIVIDUALS WHO APPEAR AS THE HEAD OF A FAMILY, OR ANYONE LIVING WITHIN THE HOME WITH A DIFFERENT SURNAME. THE FOLLOWING EXAMPLES WILL ILLUSTRATE THIS. THOSE NAMES WHICH WOULD APPEAR IN THE INDEX ARE MARKED WITH AN ASTERISK (*).

FAMILY #1	JOHN SMITH*	43 M
	SALLY "	42 F
	JOHN " JR.	19 M
	SARAH "	15 F
	WILLIAM "	12 M
	JOHN THOMPSON*	23 M
	SALLY "	22 F
	WILLIAM SMITH	73 M
	FRANCES JONES*	70 F
FAMILY #2	JOHN WILLIAMS*	22 M
FAMILY #3	SAMUEL WILLIAMS*	29 M
	JANE "	30 F
	PHEBE "	15 F
	WILLIAM OLSON*	3/12 M

TWO OTHER POINTS OF IMPORTANCE SHOULD BE NOTED. FIRST, THE ASTERISK IN THE INDEX FOLLOWING A NAME INDICATES THAT THE SPELLING OF THE NAME IS IN QUESTION IN THE ORIGINAL TEXT. SECOND, WHEN GIVEN NAMES ARE ABBREVIATED IN THE CENSUS AND THE ABBREVIATION IS CLEARLY UNDERSTOOD, THE NAME IS WRITTEN OUT IN THE INDEX.

COLUMN TWO

COLUMN TWO CONTAINS A FOUR LETTER CODE WHICH PERTAINS TO THE COUNTIES. EACH CODE USES THE FIRST THREE LETTERS OF THE REGULAR SPELLING OF THE COUNTY; THUS PROV STANDS FOR PROVIDENCE COUNTY, NEWP STANDS FOR NEWPORT COUNTY, WASH STANDS FOR WASHINGTON COUNTY, KENT STANDS FOR KENT COUNTY, AND BRIS STANDS FOR BRISTOL COUNTY.

COLUMN THREE

THE THIRD COLUMN IS THE PAGE NUMBER ON THE MICROFILM. THE PAGE NUMBER IS LOCATED IN THE UPPER RIGHT-HAND CORNER OF THE CENSUS, AND IS THE STAMPED NUMBER. EVERY OTHER PAGE IS NUMBERED SO THAT EACH NUMBER REFERS TO THAT PAGE PLUS THE FOLLOWING PAGE. PAGES ON CERTAIN FILMS ARE NOT IN STRICT NUMERICAL ORDER, BUT MOST ARE. IF PAGES ARE FOUND TO BE OUR OF ORDER, A SEARCH FOR THE PROPER PAGE MAY BE NECESSARY.

COLUMN FOUR

THE FOURTH COLUMN GIVES THE FIRST EIGHT LETTERS (OR SPACES) OF THE CENSUS DIVISION WITHIN EACH COUNTY. THERE ARE NUMEROUS TYPES OF DIVISIONS WHICH INCLUDE TOWNSHIPS, CITIES, WARDS, DISTRICTS, TOWNS, ETC.

SUMMARY

THE FOLLOWING CHART SUMMARIZES THE FOUR COLUMNS ABOVE DESCRIBED:

NAME	COUNTY	PAGE #	CENSUS DIVISION
ALDERWICK, ANN	KENT	172	WARWICK
ALDRED, JAMES	NEWP	330	NEWPORT
ALDRICH, ABBY ANN	PROV	016	FOSTER T
ALDRICH, ADOCIA A.	PROV	153	GLOCESTE

Name	County	Page	Locality
A	FRE	197	5TH E DI
AACHENNAN, AARON	BAL	434	14TH WAR
AADLESPERGER, MAGDALENA'	CAR	241	TANEYTOW
AARON, CYRUS	BAL	218	17TH WAR
AARON, HANNAH	BAL	086	10TH WAR
AARON, JOHN	DOR	329	3RD DIVI
AARON, MARCELUS	DOR	329	3RD DIVI
AARON, MARCELUS	DOR	356	3RD DIVI
AARON, SAMUEL	DOR	360	3RD DIVI
AARONS, JOSPEH	BAL	048	9TH WARD
ABAM, JOHN *	BAL	262	2ND WARD
ABAUGH, ZACHARIAH	CAR	186	8TH DIST
ABB, CONROD	FRE	080	FREDERIC
ABB, JOHN	FRE	103	FREDERIC
ABB, MARGARET	FRE	032	FREDERIC
ABBARD, CHARLES	BAL	010	15TH WAR
ABBAUGH, CHRISTIAN	FRE	020	FREDERIC
ABBERT, CHARLES H.	WAS	003	WILLIAMS
ABBERTS, GEORGE	BAL	111	18TH WAR
ABBESS, FRANCIS	BAL	006	9TH WARD
ABBESS, JOHN	BAL	107	5TH WARD
ABBETT, ELIZABETH	CAR	150	NO TWP L
ABBEY, CHRISTOPHER	BAL	098	1ST WARD
ABBOT, DARIUS	BAL	046	15TH WAR
ABBOT, EDSON	BAL	402	1ST DIST
ABBOT, JEREMIAH	ALL	248	CUMBERLA
ABBOT, MICHAEL	ALL	243	CUMBERLA
ABBOT, SARAH	BAL	276	2ND WARD
ABBOT, WILLIAM	CAR	339	6TH DIST
ABBOTE, NOAH*	DOR	381	1ST DIST
ABBOTE, SARAH	DOR	383	1ST DIST
ABBOTT, ALEXANDER	SOM	504	SALISBUR
ABBOTT, DANIEL	TAL	055	EASTON D
ABBOTT, DAVID	BAL	276	2ND WARD
ABBOTT, DAVID	BAL	235	1ST DIST
ABBOTT, E.A.	BAL	183	2ND WARD
ABBOTT, EDUARD	FRE	014	FREDERIC
ABBOTT, ELIZABETH	BAL	334	13TH WAR
ABBOTT, ELIZABETH	BAL	385	3RD WARD
ABBOTT, ELIZABETH	SOM	480	TRAPP DI
ABBOTT, GEORGE	BAL	012	4TH WARD
ABBOTT, H.P.	BAL	244	12TH WAR
ABBOTT, HORACE	BAL	052	4TH WARD
ABBOTT, JABUS	SOM	451	DAMES QU
ABBOTT, JAMES	SOM	485	TRAPP DI
ABBOTT, JAMES	BAL	050	4TH WARD
ABBOTT, JAMES	BAL	162	1ST WARD
ABBOTT, JAMES	BAL	012	1ST WARD
ABBOTT, JAMES	BAL	180	2ND DIST
ABBOTT, JOHN	BAL	251	12TH WAR
ABBOTT, JOHN	BAL	068	2ND DIST
ABBOTT, JOHN	CAR	276	7TH DIST
ABBOTT, JOHN	CAR	276	7TH DIST
ABBOTT, JOHN E.	BAL	008	15TH WAR
ABBOTT, JULIA	FRE	020	FREDERIC
ABBOTT, LEAH	BAL	380	8TH WARD
ABBOTT, LEVI	SOM	404	BRINKLEY
ABBOTT, LLOYD	SOM	466	HANGARY
ABBOTT, MARIAH	TAL	055	EASTON D
ABBOTT, MARTIN	BAL	005	18TH WAR
ABBOTT, MARY	DOR	462	1ST DIST
ABBOTT, MASON	SOM	427	PRINCESS
ABBOTT, MATILDA	BAL	067	10TH WAR
ABBOTT, NOAH*	DOR	381	1ST DIST
ABBOTT, SAMUEL	DOR	402	1ST DIST
ABBOTT, SAMUEL	BAL	248	17TH WAR
ABBOTT, SAMUEL	BAL	069	15TH WAR
ABBOTT, SUSAN	SOM	466	HANGARY
ABBOTT, THOMAS	SOM	445	DAMES QU
ABBOTT, THOMAS M.	BAL	066	18TH WAR
ABBOTT, WILLIAM	DOR	352	3RD DIVI
ABBOTT, WILLIAM	SOM	474	TRAPPE D
ABBOTT, WILLIAM	BAL	012	1ST WARD
ABBOTT, WILLIAM C.	BAL	097	1ST WARD
ABBOTT, WILLIAM H.	BAL	242	17TH WAR
ABBOTTS, JAMES	BAL	383	8TH WARD
ABBOUGH, JAMES A.	ANN	507	HOWARD D
ABBS, HENRY	FRE	071	FREDERIC
ABBY, HARRIET	BAL	429	14TH WAR
ABDAIL, WILLIAM*	DOR	446	1ST DIST
ABDELL, MARY E.	SOM	512	BARREN C
ABDELL, ROBERT	SOM	496	SALISBUR
ABEL, CATHARINE	CAR	366	9TH DIST
ABEL, DANIEL	BAL	382	3RD WARD
ABEL, ELLEN	MGM	316	CRACKLIN
ABEL, EVELINE	BAL	354	3RD WARD
ABEL, MARY	BAL	382	3RD WARD
ABEL, THOMAS	BAL	182	19TH WAR
ABELBY, WILLIAM	BAL	359	1ST DIST
ABELIN, WILLAIM	BAL	227	19TH WAR
ABELL, ALEXANDER	ST	280	3RD E DI
ABELL, ANN	ST	286	2ND E DI
ABELL, B. J.	ST	255	3RD E DI
ABELL, CHRISTIAN	BAL	314	20TH WAR
ABELL, CLARA	ST	267	3RD E DI
ABELL, EDWARD B.	ST	254	3RD E DI
ABELL, ELIZABETH	BAL	062	15TH WAR
ABELL, FRANCIS J.	ST	348	5TH E DI
ABELL, GEORGE	ST	287	2ND E DI
ABELL, GEORGE W.	ST	256	3RD E DI
ABELL, HARRIET	ST	304	2ND E DI
ABELL, IGNATIUS	BAL	164	16TH WAR
ABELL, JAMES	BAL	266	17TH WAR
ABELL, JAMES F.	ST	254	3RD E DI
ABELL, JAMES L.	BAL	164	16TH WAR
ABELL, JOHN	ST	280	3RD E DI
ABELL, JOHN B.	ST	286	2ND E DI
ABELL, JOSEPH	ST	256	3RD E DI
ABELL, MARCELLUS D.	ST	280	3RD E DI
ABELL, MARY A.	ST	287	2ND E DI
ABELL, MARY A.	ST	267	3RD E DI
ABELL, MARY E.	ST	255	3RD E DI
ABELL, MILLY	ST	279	3RD E DI
ABELL, ROBERT	ST	279	3RD E DI
ABELL, SARAH	BAL	048	1ST WARD
ABELL, WILLIAM	ST	280	3RD E DI
ABELL, WILLIAM	BAL	078	18TH WAR
ABELL, WILLIAM C.	ST	286	2ND E DI
ABELL, WILLIAM E.	ST	281	3RD E DI
ABELL, WILLIAM L. L.	ST	284	2ND E DI
ABELL, WILLIAM L. L.	ST	285	2ND E DI
ABELLER, HENRY	BAL	178	2ND WARD
ABELS, FANNY	ANN	437	HOWARD D
ABENDSCHAN, CLEMENTS	BAL	040	15TH WAR
ABENDSHOEN, LEWIS	BAL	258	17TH WAR
ABENRY, BERNARD	BAL	086	1ST WARD
ABER, ALICE A.	BAL	182	19TH WAR
ABERCOMBIE, DAVID	BAL	195	6TH WARD
ABERCROMBIE, C. S.	BAL	332	1ST DIST
ABERCROMBIE, R.	WAS	021	2ND SUBD
ABERCROMBY, MARIA	PRI	003	BLADENSB
ABERLAIN, MICHAEL	BAL	227	2ND WARD
ABERLY, DANIEL	BAL	438	14TH WAR
ABERLY, FREDERICK	BAL	129	16TH WAR
ABERNATHEY, JAMES	ALL	127	4TH E.D.
ABERNATHY, J. WILLIAM	ALL	241	CUMBERLA
ABERT, ELIZABETH	BAL	447	8TH WARD
ABEY, JACOB	BAL	275	17TH WAR
ABEY, JOSEPH	BAL	272	17TH WAR
ABEY, PETER	BAL	275	17TH WAR
ABEY, WILLIAM H.	BAL	252	17TH WAR
ABIGAL, RICHARD	PRI	042	VANSVILL
ABIGAL, THOMAS	PRI	083	QUEEN AN
ABIGALL, RICHARD	ANN	415	HOWARD D
ABILE, HENRY	ST	256	3RD E DI
ABILE, JOHN L.	ST	266	3RD E DI
ABILL, ELIZABETH A.	ST	274	3RD E DI
ABLE, CHARLES	WAS	007	WILLIAMS
ABLE, DANIEL	WAS	244	SMITHSBU
ABLE, GEORGE	CAR	358	9TH DIST
ABLE, JOSHUA	BAL	035	4TH WARD
ABLE, LYDIA	FRE	427	8TH E DI
ABLE, MARY	CAR	268	WESTMINS
ABLE, SAMUEL J. B.	BAL	311	1ST DIST
ABLE, WILLIAM E.	BAL	311	1ST DIST
ABLETON, RACHEL	CEC	173	6TH E DI
ABOOK, WILLIAM	BAL	118	1ST WARD
ABOT, NANCY	CAR	190	4TH DIST
ABOTT, LUGHER*	DOR	338	3RD DIVI
ABOTT, THOMAS	DOR	365	3RD DIVI
ABOTT, THOMAS H.	DOR	369	3RD DIVI
ABOUGH, H.H.	BAL	233	1ST DIST
ABRAHAM, ELSY	BAL	250	20TH WAR
ABRAHAM, JAMES	BAL	062	1ST WARD
ABRAHAM, JOSEPH W.	CEC	147	PORT DUP
ABRAHAMS, CHARLES	BAL	083	1ST WARD
ABRAHAMS, HANNAH E.	BAL	058	10TH WAR
ABRAHAMS, HANNAH E.	CEC	147	PORT DUP
ABRAHAMS, HIRAM	CEC	191	5TH E DI
ABRAHAMS, JOHN	BAL	248	6TH WARD
ABRAHAMS, JOHN J.	BAL	363	3RD WARD
ABRAHAMS, RICHARD	CEC	140	5TH E DI
ABRAHAMS, WILLIAM	CEC	191	5TH E DI
ABRAHAMS, WOODWARD	BAL	360	3RD WARD
ABRAIS, JOHN *	BAL	325	12TH WAR
ABRAMS, JOHN	BAL	099	2ND DIST
ABRAMS, MARY A.	BAL	332	3RD WARD
ABRAMS, WASHINGTON	BAL	249	2ND WARD
ABRECHT, JOHN	FRE	003	FREDERIC
ABRECHT, WILLIAM	FRE	004	FREDERIC
ABRIDGET, BIDDY	BAL	079	15TH WAR
ABRY, CYRUS	ALL	221	CUMBERLA
ABSALUM, HENRY	SOM	539	TYASKIN
ABTEMAN, SARAH	CAR	094	NO TWP L
ABUM, JOHNSON	BAL	264	2ND WARD
ABY, ABRAHAM-BLACK	FRE	189	5TH E DI
ABY, DAVID	FRE	190	5TH E DI
ACELIGH, EARNEST	BAL	453	8TH WARD
ACERSON, FRANCIS	CEC	079	NORTHEAS
ACHE, MARY	BAL	382	8TH WARD
ACHE, REUBEN	ALL	199	CUMBERLA
ACHENBACH, H.	BAL	308	20TH WAR
ACHISON, ALICK	PRI	070	MARLBROU
ACHISON, ANN	PRI	072	MARLBROU
ACHISON, ELENOR	PRI	099	SPALDING
ACHISON, GEORGE G.	PRI	066	NOTTINGH
ACHISON, ROSILA	PRI	111	PISCATAW
ACHLEY, WILLIAM.	BAL	148	11TH WAR
ACHMAN, HENRY	BAL	221	19TH WAR
ACHO, MARIA-BLACK	QUE	188	3RD E DI
ACHRE, BARBARA	FRE	176	5TH E DI
ACHRE, HENRIETTA	FRE	172	5TH E DI
ACHRES, SARHA	BAL	416	8TH WARD
ACHROEDER, CHRISTIAN	BAL	415	14TH WAR
ACHY, FREDERICK	BAL	432	14TH WAR
ACK	CAR	085	NO TWP L
ACKELSON, ELIZABETH	BAL	262	12TH WAR
ACKEN, MARY	BAL	299	12TH WAR
ACKER, CATHARINE	CAR	306	1ST DIST
ACKER, GEORGE	BAL	120	1ST WARD
ACKER, JOSEPH	BAL	075	10TH WAR
ACKER, JOSEPH	CAR	301	1ST DIST
ACKERLY, ANN	BAL	077	4TH WARD
ACKERMAN, ALEXANDER F.	BAL	382	13TH WAR
ACKERMAN, ELIZABETH	BAL	275	17TH WAR
ACKERMAN, GEORGE A.	CAR	342	6TH DIST
ACKERMAN, J.	BAL	139	1ST WARD
ACKERMAN, MARY ANN	BAL	382	13TH WAR
ACKERMAN, WILLIAM	CAR	295	7TH DIST
ACKERMAN, SUENA	FRE	008	FREDERIC
ACKERS, ADRIAN	BAL	278	20TH WAR
ACKERT, WILLIAM	BAL	244	17TH WAR
ACKERWOOD, ELIZABETH	BAL	125	11TH WAR
ACKERWOOD, WILLIAM	BAL	128	11TH WAR
ACKHART, JOHN	BAL	073	2ND DIST
ACKINSON, SAAH	CAR	382	2ND DIST
ACKIS, MAIRAH	TAL	075	EASTON T
ACKLAND, JAMES	BAL	043	4TH WARD
ACKLAND, THOMAS	BAL	156	1ST WARD
ACKLER, JACOB B.	BAL	161	16TH WAR
ACKLER, MARY	BAL	162	16TH WAR
ACKLES, SAMUEL	ALL	150	6TH E.D.
ACKMAN, JAMES*	DOR	427	1ST DIST
ACKMAN, WILLIAM*	SOM	496	SALISBUR
ACKWORTH, A. E.	TAL	069	EASTON T
ACKWORTH, WILLIAM D.	DOR	446	1ST DIST
ACLERT, JOHN	BAL	133	16TH WAR
ACOEKER, GEORGE	BAL	275	17TH WAR
ACORN, HENRY	BAL	392	14TH WAR
ACOY, JOHN	KEN	308	3RD DIST
ACRABBS, EMILY	FRE	176	5TH E DI
ACRE, FRANK	ALL	220	CUMBERLA
ACRE, FREDERICA	ANN	424	HOWARD D
ACRE, HARMON	ANN	423	HOWARD D
ACRE, J.	BAL	166	1ST WARD
ACRES, ERMINA	HAR	193	3RD DIST
ACRES, ISAAC	HAR	118	2ND DIST
ACRES, JAMES	CAR	096	NO TWP L
ACRES, MARY	HAR	136	2ND DIST
ACRES, RUTHER A.*	TAL	020	EASTON D
ACRES, SALLY*	DOR	465	1ST DIST
ACRES, THOMAS	HAR	135	2ND DIST
ACRES, MARY-BLACK	QUE	147	1ST E DI
ACTON, ANN	CHA	291	MIDDLETO
ACTON, CHRISTIANNA	CHA	228	BOJANTOW
ACTON, EDWARD	ALL	129	4TH E.D.
ACTON, HANNIBAL	CHA	249	HILLTOP
ACTON, MARY A.	CHA	290	BOJANTOW
ACTON, WASHINGTON	CHA	292	BOJANTOW
ACTON, WILLIAM	CHA	266	MIDDLETO
ACTON, WILLIAM J.	CHA	251	MIDDLETO
ACWORTH, TRAIN	SOM	521	BARREN C
ACWORTH, W. T.	BAL	155	1ST WARD
ADAIR, JOHN	ANN	517	HOWARD D
ADAIR, ROBERT	BAL	270	2ND WARD
ADAIR, THOMAS	BAL	429	1ST DIST
ADALUM, ELIZABETH	FRE	024	FREDERIC
ADAM, ANDREW	FRE	038	FREDERIC
ADAM, GEORGE	BAL	453	14TH WAR
ADAM, JOHN	BAL	095	5TH WARD
ADAM, JOHN	BAL	280	2ND WARD
ADAM, JOSEPH	WOR	301	SNOW HIL
ADAM, JULIANN	ALL	199	CUMBERLA
ADAM, SAMUEL	ALL	168	6TH E.D.
ADAM, SARAH	BAL	096	5TH WARD
ADAM, TERESA	BAL	222	19TH WAR
ADAM, WILLIAM	FRE	019	FREDERIC
ADAMS, A. V.	ST	281	3RD E DI
ADAMS, AANN K.	CHA	269	ALLENS F
ADAMS, AARON	ANN	342	3RD DIST
ADAMS, ABRAHAM	FRE	084	FREDERIC
ADAMS, ABRAHAM	PRI	021	VANSVILL
ADAMS, ABRAHAM T.	FRE	019	FREDERIC
ADAMS, ADAM	FRE	268	NEW MARK
ADAMS, ADAM	BAL	157	6TH WARD
ADAMS, ADAM	BAL	318	7TH WARD
ADAMS, ADELIA	SOM	401	BRINKLEY
ADAMS, ADELINE	BAL	160	6TH WARD
ADAMS, ADELINE	ANN	448	HOWARD D
ADAMS, ALBERT	BAL	272	20TH WAR
ADAMS, ALEXANDER	ALL	254	CUMBERLA
ADAMS, ALEXANDER	ST	277	3RD E DI
ADAMS, ALFRED	BAL	454	8TH WARD
ADAMS, ALFRED	CHA	279	BOJANTOW
ADAMS, AMELIA	BAL	061	10TH WAR
ADAMS, AMOS	WAS	097	2ND DIST
ADAMS, ANDREW J.	ANN	479	HOWARD D
ADAMS, ANN	BAL	347	3RD WARD
ADAMS, ANN	ST	282	3RD E DI
ADAMS, ANN	TAL	060	EASTON D
ADAMS, ANN	CHA	235	HILLTOP
ADAMS, ANN	DOR	317	1ST DIST
ADAMS, ANN	BAL	188	19TH WAR
ADAMS, ANN M.	BAL	340	3RD WARD
ADAMS, ANN M.	BAL	115	15TH WAR
ADAMS, ARCHABALD	DOR	336	3RD DIVI
ADAMS, ARCHABALD	HAR	040	1ST DIST
ADAMS, ARNOLD	WAS	169	FUNKSTOW
ADAMS, ARNOLD S.	WAS	174	FUNKSTOW
ADAMS, BENJAMIN	ST	348	5TH E DI
ADAMS, BENJAMIN	BAL	141	16TH WAR
ADAMS, BENJAMIN	BAL	317	1ST DIST
ADAMS, BISCOE	ST	298	2ND E DI
ADAMS, C.	BAL	139	1ST WARD
ADAMS, C.	BAL	129	1ST WARD
ADAMS, CALEB	PRI	037	VANSVILL
ADAMS, CATHARINE	WAS	220	1ST DIST
ADAMS, CATHARINE	BAL	095	5TH WARD
ADAMS, CATHARINE A.	BAL	215	11TH WAR
ADAMS, CATHERINE	BAL	270	7TH WARD
ADAMS, CHARLES	BAL	272	1ST DIST
ADAMS, CHARLES	CHA	261	MIDDLETO
ADAMS, CHARLES	QUE	123	1ST E DI
ADAMS, CHARLES	FRE	161	EMMITTSB
ADAMS, CHARLES	BAL	118	18TH WAR
ADAMS, CHARLES	CEC	158	PORT DUP
ADAMS, CHARLES	ST	275	3RD E DI
ADAMS, CHARLES	WAS	073	2ND SUBD
ADAMS, CHARLES C.	TAL	047	EASTON T
ADAMS, CHARLES-BLACK	ST	320	4TH E DI
ADAMS, CHARLES-BLACK	CAR	163	NO TWP L
ADAMS, CHARLES-BLACK	CAR	145	NO TWP L
ADAMS, CHARLOTTE	BAL	189	19TH WAR
ADAMS, CHARLOTTE	BAL	057	15TH WAR
ADAMS, CHLOE A.	ST	264	3RD E DI
ADAMS, CLEMUEL	DOR	351	3RD DIVI
ADAMS, COLEMAN	SOM	391	BRINKLEY
ADAMS, CORNELIUS	ST	281	3RD E DI
ADAMS, DANIEL	WAS	220	1ST DIST
ADAMS, DANIEL-BLACK	CAR	157	NO TWP L
ADAMS, DAVID	BAL	035	4TH WARD
ADAMS, DAVID	BAL	133	1ST WARD
ADAMS, DAVID M.	BAL	380	13TH WAR
ADAMS, DENES*	DOR	330	3RD DIVI
ADAMS, DENSLOW	BAL	145	1ST WARD
ADAMS, DOUGLAS	PRI	078	MARLBROU
ADAMS, EDGAR	ST	349	5TH E DI
ADAMS, EDWARD	SOM	399	BRINKLEY
ADAMS, EDWARD	TAL	047	EASTON T
ADAMS, EDWARD	MGM	352	BERRYS D
ADAMS, EDWARD	SOM	404	BRINKLEY
ADAMS, EDWARD	BAL	084	18TH WAR
ADAMS, EDWARD M.	SOM	397	BRINKLEY
ADAMS, EDWIN	CHA	245	HILLTOP
ADAMS, ELEANOR	SOM	407	DUBLIN D
ADAMS, ELI	CEC	216	7TH E DI
ADAMS, ELIAS-BLACK	CAR	159	NO TWP L
ADAMS, ELIJAH	CAR	131	NO TWP L
ADAMS, ELIJAH	SOM	425	PRINCESS
ADAMS, ELIZA	CHA	217	ALLENS F
ADAMS, ELIZA	BAL	097	18TH WAR
ADAMS, ELIZA	FRE	159	EMMITTSB
ADAMS, ELIZA	BAL	201	19TH WAR
ADAMS, ELIZA A.	BAL	313	3RD WARD
ADAMS, ELIZABETH	BAL	368	8TH WARD
ADAMS, ELIZABETH	CEC	092	4TH E DI
ADAMS, ELIZABETH	CHA	245	HILLTOP
ADAMS, ELIZABETH	SOM	417	PRINCESS
ADAMS, ELIZABETH	CAR	122	NO TWP L
ADAMS, ELIZABETH	BAL	368	13TH WAR
ADAMS, ELIZABETH	BAL	268	17TH WAR
ADAMS, ELIZABETH	ST	268	3RD E DI
ADAMS, ELIZABETH	TAL	030	EASTON D
ADAMS, ELIZABETH	SOM	488	SALISBUR
ADAMS, ELIZABETH M.	BAL	385	13TH WAR
ADAMS, ELLEN	BAL	247	6TH WARD
ADAMS, ELLEN	ANN	441	HOWARD D
ADAMS, ELLEN A.	BAL	317	3RD WARD
ADAMS, ELZIABETH	CAR	390	2ND DIST
ADAMS, EMILY	BAL	195	11TH WAR
ADAMS, EMILY	PRI	033	VANSVILL
ADAMS, ESTER A.	BAL	345	3RD WARD
ADAMS, ESTHER	SOM	395	BRINKLEY
ADAMS, EUGENIA D.	BAL	016	4TH WARD
ADAMS, FRANCIS	BAL	408	14TH WAR
ADAMS, G. R.	BAL	148	1ST WARD
ADAMS, GEORGE	BAL	124	1ST WARD
ADAMS, GEORGE	CHA	251	MIDDLETO
ADAMS, GEORGE	FRE	429	8TH E DI
ADAMS, GEORGE	CHA	277	BOJANTOW

Name	County	Page	District
ADAMS, GEORGE	SOM	388	BRINKLEY
ADAMS, GEORGE	TAL	114	ST MICHA
ADAMS, GEORGE F.	CHA	283	BOJANTOW
ADAMS, GEORGE F.	BAL	346	3RD WARD
ADAMS, GEORGE M.	SOM	426	PRINCESS
ADAMS, GEORGE P.	BAL	189	2ND WARD
ADAMS, GEORGE R.-BLACK	ST	331	4TH E DI
ADAMS, GEORGE S.	WAS	220	1ST DIST
ADAMS, GEORGE-BLACK	CAR	164	NO TWP L
ADAMS, GEORGIANNA	PRI	048	AQUASCO
ADAMS, GILBERT	BAL	077	1ST WARD
ADAMS, GOERGE	BAL	131	2ND DIST
ADAMS, HANAH	BAL	333	7TH WARD
ADAMS, HANNAH	BAL	243	17TH WAR
ADAMS, HARRIET	CHA	218	ALLENS F
ADAMS, HEMSLEY	BAL	211	11TH WAR
ADAMS, HEMSLEY	BAL	146	11TH WAR
ADAMS, HENERETTA	SOM	484	TRAPP DI
ADAMS, HENRY	WAS	206	1ST DIST
ADAMS, HENRY	SOM	402	BRINKLEY
ADAMS, HENRY	WOR	332	1ST E DI
ADAMS, HENRY	CHA	258	MIDDLETO
ADAMS, HENRY	BAL	202	19TH WAR
ADAMS, HENRY	BAL	029	9TH WARD
ADAMS, HENRY J.	SOM	402	BRINKLEY
ADAMS, HESTER	BAL	227	6TH WARD
ADAMS, HESTER	BAL	021	4TH WARD
ADAMS, HESTOR	BAL	196	17TH WAR
ADAMS, ISAAC	BAL	255	12TH WAR
ADAMS, ISABELLA	BAL	090	1ST WARD
ADAMS, ISABELLA	HAR	198	3RD DIST
ADAMS, ISRIEL	BAL	439	1ST DIST
ADAMS, JACK	BAL	316	1ST DIST
ADAMS, JACOB	BAL	055	15TH WAR
ADAMS, JACOB	BAL	200	6TH WARD
ADAMS, JACOB	BAL	135	18TH WAR
ADAMS, JACOB	WAS	220	1ST DIST
ADAMS, JACOB	WAS	006	WILLIAMS
ADAMS, JAMES	SOM	396	BRINKLEY
ADAMS, JAMES	SOM	384	BRINKLEY
ADAMS, JAMES	SOM	485	TRAPP DI
ADAMS, JAMES	SOM	516	BARREN C
ADAMS, JAMES	SOM	514	BARREN C
ADAMS, JAMES	CHA	234	HILLTOP
ADAMS, JAMES	CAR	128	NO TWP L
ADAMS, JAMES	HAR	067	1ST DIST
ADAMS, JAMES	BAL	210	6TH WARD
ADAMS, JAMES	BAL	178	6TH WARD
ADAMS, JAMES	BAL	175	6TH WARD
ADAMS, JAMES	BAL	074	15TH WAR
ADAMS, JAMES	ANN	427	HOWARD D
ADAMS, JAMES	ALL	196	CUMBERLA
ADAMS, JAMES B.	TAL	104	ST MICHA
ADAMS, JAMES C.	BAL	437	14TH WAR
ADAMS, JAMES F.	SOM	395	BRINKLEY
ADAMS, JAMES O.	SOM	511	BARREN C
ADAMS, JAMES-BLACK	ST	330	4TH E DI
ADAMS, JAMES-BLACK	CAR	162	NO TWP L
ADAMS, JANE	BAL	125	11TH WAR
ADAMS, JANE	BAL	456	14TH WAR
ADAMS, JANE	CHA	250	MIDDLETO
ADAMS, JANE	ST	273	3RD E DI
ADAMS, JANE	ST	276	3RD E DI
ADAMS, JANE	TAL	077	EASTON T
ADAMS, JANE	BAL	006	9TH WARD
ADAMS, JANE	BAL	192	6TH WARD
ADAMS, JANE C.	ANN	520	HOWARD D
ADAMS, JANE E.	SOM	547	TYASKIN
ADAMS, JERRY	MGM	444	CLARKSTR
ADAMS, JIM	WAS	241	CAVETOWN
ADAMS, JOHN	WAS	252	1ST DIST
ADAMS, JOHN	ST	301	2ND E DI
ADAMS, JOHN	WAS	030	2ND SUBD
ADAMS, JOHN	SOM	536	TYASKIN
ADAMS, JOHN	WOR	238	6TH E DI
ADAMS, JOHN	SOM	398	BRINKLEY
ADAMS, JOHN	ST	282	3RD E DI
ADAMS, JOHN	BAL	319	1ST DIST
ADAMS, JOHN	BAL	350	1ST DIST
ADAMS, JOHN	BAL	379	1ST DIST
ADAMS, JOHN	BAL	160	6TH WARD
ADAMS, JOHN	BAL	164	1ST WARD
ADAMS, JOHN	BAL	218	12TH WAR
ADAMS, JOHN	ANN	273	ANNAPOLI
ADAMS, JOHN	ALL	068	5TH E.D.
ADAMS, JOHN	ANN	468	HOWARD D
ADAMS, JOHN	BAL	322	12TH WAR
ADAMS, JOHN	CHA	242	HILLTOP
ADAMS, JOHN	DOR	323	1ST DIST
ADAMS, JOHN	CAR	286	7TH DIST
ADAMS, JOHN	CEC	126	5TH E DI
ADAMS, JOHN	HAR	043	1ST DIST
ADAMS, JOHN	BAL	160	19TH WAR
ADAMS, JOHN	HAR	127	2ND DIST
ADAMS, JOHN	FRE	105	CREAGERS
ADAMS, JOHN	CAR	266	WESTMINS
ADAMS, JOHN A.	WAS	065	2ND SUBD
ADAMS, JOHN C.	TAL	002	EASTON D
ADAMS, JOHN E.	MGM	329	CRACKLIN
ADAMS, JOHN F.	BAL	129	16TH WAR
ADAMS, JOHN G.	BAL	209	6TH WARD
ADAMS, JOHN H.	SOM	417	PRINCESS
ADAMS, JOHN H.	WAS	272	RIDGEVIL
ADAMS, JOHN HENRY	SOM	488	SALISBUR
ADAMS, JOHN J.	WAS	207	1ST DIST
ADAMS, JOHN L.	BAL	002	EASTERN
ADAMS, JOHN Q.	BAL	104	10TH WAR
ADAMS, JOHN Q.	BAL	027	18TH WAR
ADAMS, JOHN T.	HAR	041	1ST DIST
ADAMS, JOHN T.	BAL	002	15TH WAR
ADAMS, JOHN-BLACK	QUE	189	3RD E DI
ADAMS, JOSEPH	PRI	013	BLADENSB
ADAMS, JOSEPH	BAL	051	15TH WAR
ADAMS, JOSEPH	BAL	055	15TH WAR
ADAMS, JOSEPH	BAL	267	12TH WAR
ADAMS, JOSEPH	DOR	329	3RD DIVI
ADAMS, JOSEPH JR.	BAL	055	15TH WAR
ADAMS, JOSEPH M.	CHA	268	BOJANTOW
ADAMS, JOSEPHINE	SOM	403	BRINKLEY
ADAMS, JOSHUA	BAL	298	7TH WARD
ADAMS, JOSHUA	TAL	062	EASTON D
ADAMS, JOSHUA-BLACK	CAR	141	NO TWP L
ADAMS, JOSHUA-BLACK	CAR	135	NO TWP L
ADAMS, JOSIAS	CHA	284	BOJANTOW
ADAMS, JULIA	BAL	192	6TH WARD
ADAMS, L.	BAL	053	4TH WARD
ADAMS, LAURA	ANN	466	HOWARD D
ADAMS, LEAH J.	SOM	417	PRINCESS
ADAMS, LEVEN	DOR	362	3RD DIVI
ADAMS, LEVI	CHA	250	MIDDLETO
ADAMS, LEVI	WOR	331	1ST E DI
ADAMS, LEVI	SOM	543	TYASKIN
ADAMS, LEVIN	SOM	399	BRINKLEY
ADAMS, LEVIN	SOM	395	BRINKLEY
ADAMS, LEVIN	DOR	336	3RD DIVI
ADAMS, LEWIS	ANN	349	3RD DIST
ADAMS, LEWIS	BAL	386	3RD WARD
ADAMS, LEWIS B.	CHA	276	ALLENS F
ADAMS, LITTLETON	SOM	398	BRINKLEY
ADAMS, LORENZO	DOR	338	3RD DIVI
ADAMS, LORENZO D.	ANN	446	HOWARD D
ADAMS, LOUISA	BAL	463	1ST DIST
ADAMS, LUDY	ALL	014	3RD E.D.
ADAMS, LYDIA	PRI	113	PISCATAW
ADAMS, MAHALA	WAS	194	1ST DIST
ADAMS, MALVINA	ANN	431	HOWARD D
ADAMS, MARGARET	ALL	196	CUMBERLA
ADAMS, MARGARET	BAL	364	3RD WARD
ADAMS, MARGARET	SOM	394	BRINKLEY
ADAMS, MARGARET	BAL	140	11TH WAR
ADAMS, MARGARET	BAL	200	19TH WAR
ADAMS, MARGARETT	DOR	297	1ST DIST
ADAMS, MARGRET	BAL	055	1ST WARD
ADAMS, MARIA	BAL	024	1ST WARD
ADAMS, MARIA	ANN	501	HOWARD D
ADAMS, MARIA	BAL	301	3RD WARD
ADAMS, MARIA	CAR	269	WESTMINS
ADAMS, MARIAH	SOM	481	TRAPP DI
ADAMS, MARTHA	BAL	387	13TH WAR
ADAMS, MARY	BAL	188	19TH WAR
ADAMS, MARY	CAR	194	4TH DIST
ADAMS, MARY	CHA	287	BOJANTOW
ADAMS, MARY	CHA	287	BOJANTOW
ADAMS, MARY	DOR	361	3RD DIVI
ADAMS, MARY	DOR	356	3RD DIVI
ADAMS, MARY	SOM	403	BRINKLEY
ADAMS, MARY	SOM	481	TRAPP DI
ADAMS, MARY	PRI	014	BLADENSB
ADAMS, MARY	PRI	014	BLADENSB
ADAMS, MARY	TAL	067	EASTON T
ADAMS, MARY	TAL	075	EASTON T
ADAMS, MARY	TAL	048	EASTON T
ADAMS, MARY	BAL	119	5TH WARD
ADAMS, MARY	ANN	480	HOWARD D
ADAMS, MARY	BAL	218	12TH WAR
ADAMS, MARY A.	BAL	171	6TH WARD
ADAMS, MARY B.	SOM	460	HANGARY
ADAMS, MARY J.	TAL	067	EASTON T
ADAMS, MARY J.	BAL	119	5TH WARD
ADAMS, MATHIAS	BAL	101	1ST WARD
ADAMS, MATILDA	PRI	031	VANSVILL
ADAMS, MATILDA	CHA	287	BOJANTOW
ADAMS, MATILDA-BLACK	ST	330	4TH E DI
ADAMS, MEDIA	SOM	428	PRINCESS
ADAMS, MENAMAR	DOR	329	3RD DIVI
ADAMS, MENAMAR SR.*	DOR	329	3RD DIVI
ADAMS, MILLY	BAL	058	4TH WARD
ADAMS, MORRIS H.	SOM	403	BRINKLEY
ADAMS, NATHAN	BAL	153	16TH WAR
ADAMS, NATHANIEL	WAS	097	2ND DIST
ADAMS, NATHANIEL	SOM	417	PRINCESS
ADAMS, NEAH	WOR	340	1ST E DI
ADAMS, NOAH-BLACK	CAR	145	NO TWP L
ADAMS, OLIVER	BAL	108	18TH WAR
ADAMS, P.J.	WAS	127	HAGERSTO
ADAMS, PERRY	BAL	099	15TH WAR
ADAMS, PERRY	BAL	227	6TH WARD
ADAMS, PHILIP	WAS	244	SMITHSBU
ADAMS, PRICILA	BAL	201	17TH WAR
ADAMS, PRISCILLA	BAL	034	15TH WAR
ADAMS, PRISILLA	TAL	099	ST MICHA
ADAMS, QUINCY	CAL	004	1ST DIST
ADAMS, RACHAEL	BAL	067	1ST WARD
ADAMS, RACHEL	BAL	320	1ST DIST
ADAMS, RACHELL	BAL	299	17TH WAR
ADAMS, REBECCA	FRE	164	EMMITTSB
ADAMS, REBECCA	BAL	190	11TH WAR
ADAMS, REBECCA-BLACK	CAR	120	NO TWP L
ADAMS, REMUS	BAL	320	1ST DIST
ADAMS, RICHARD	BAL	038	15TH WAR
ADAMS, RICHARD	CHA	276	ALLENS F
ADAMS, RICHARD H.	TAL	080	ST MICHA
ADAMS, ROBERT	TAL	114	ST MICHA
ADAMS, ROBERT	BAL	154	1ST WARD
ADAMS, ROBERT A.	BAL	323	3RD WARD
ADAMS, ROBERT W.	ANN	349	3RD DIST
ADAMS, RODGER	SOM	489	SALISBUR
ADAMS, ROSANNA	MGM	334	CRACKLIN
ADAMS, SALLY	CHA	287	BOJANTOW
ADAMS, SALONE	BAL	283	2ND WARD
ADAMS, SAMPSON	SOM	384	BRINKLEY
ADAMS, SAMUEL	SOM	390	BRINKLEY
ADAMS, SAMUEL	PRI	013	BLADENSB
ADAMS, SAMUEL	BAL	131	1ST WARD
ADAMS, SAMUEL	BAL	319	1ST DIST
ADAMS, SAMUEL	BAL	060	15TH WAR
ADAMS, SAMUEL	BAL	175	11TH WAR
ADAMS, SAMUEL	BAL	278	1ST DIST
ADAMS, SAMUEL	BAL	046	9TH WARD
ADAMS, SAMUEL	HAR	196	3RD DIST
ADAMS, SAMUEL	BAL	001	4TH WARD
ADAMS, SAMUEL H.	BAL	105	15TH WAR
ADAMS, SAMUEL S.	ST	348	5TH E DI
ADAMS, SAMUEL T.	SOM	392	BRINKLEY
ADAMS, SARAH	SOM	395	BRINKLEY
ADAMS, SARAH	SOM	399	BRINKLEY
ADAMS, SARAH	SOM	389	BRINKLEY
ADAMS, SARAH	BAL	343	3RD WARD
ADAMS, SARAH	BAL	102	5TH WARD
ADAMS, SARAH	CAR	119	NO TWP L
ADAMS, SARAH	SOM	417	PRINCESS
ADAMS, SARAH	BAL	048	18TH WAR
ADAMS, SARAH A.	BAL	290	3RD WARD
ADAMS, SELLY	CAR	119	NO TWP L
ADAMS, SEREMIA-BLACK	CAR	145	NO TWP L
ADAMS, SOPHY	ANN	358	3RD DIST
ADAMS, STEPHEN	BAL	048	1ST WARD
ADAMS, STEPHEN	FRE	165	EMMITTSB
ADAMS, STEPHEN	SOM	398	BRINKLEY
ADAMS, STEPHEN W.	ST	267	3RD E DI
ADAMS, SUSAN	SOM	395	BRINKLEY
ADAMS, SUSAN	BAL	060	10TH WAR
ADAMS, SUSAN	BAL	333	7TH WARD
ADAMS, SUSAN A.-BLACK	BAL	221	2ND WARD
ADAMS, SUSANNA	BAL	288	17TH WAR
ADAMS, THOMAS	CAR	128	NO TWP L
ADAMS, THOMAS	DOR	346	3RD DIVI
ADAMS, THOMAS	BAL	077	1ST WARD
ADAMS, THOMAS	SOM	396	BRINKLEY
ADAMS, THOMAS	SOM	488	SALISBUR
ADAMS, THOMAS B.	BAL	032	4TH WARD
ADAMS, THOMAS P.	SOM	385	BRINKLEY
ADAMS, URIAS	MGM	353	BERRYS D
ADAMS, UZACK	CHA	229	MIDDLETO
ADAMS, VALENTINE	FRE	069	FREDERIC
ADAMS, WALKER	HAR	012	1ST DIST
ADAMS, WESTLEY	DOR	332	3RD DIVI
ADAMS, WHITTINGHAM	BAL	288	7TH WARD
ADAMS, WILLIAM	BAL	135	1ST WARD
ADAMS, WILLIAM	BAL	060	1ST WARD
ADAMS, WILLIAM	ANN	448	HOWARD D
ADAMS, WILLIAM	DOR	338	3RD DIVI
ADAMS, WILLIAM	DOR	334	3RD DIVI
ADAMS, WILLIAM	HAR	029	1ST DIST
ADAMS, WILLIAM	HAR	011	1ST DIST
ADAMS, WILLIAM	HAR	119	2ND DIST
ADAMS, WILLIAM	CHA	289	BOJANTOW
ADAMS, WILLIAM	HAR	145	3RD DIST
ADAMS, WILLIAM	BAL	126	11TH WAR
ADAMS, WILLIAM	CAR	065	NO TWP L
ADAMS, WILLIAM	SOM	396	BRINKLEY
ADAMS, WILLIAM	SOM	395	BRINKLEY
ADAMS, WILLIAM	SOM	385	BRINKLEY
ADAMS, WILLIAM	WAS	246	SMITHSBU
ADAMS, WILLIAM	ST	302	2ND E DI
ADAMS, WILLIAM F.	PRI	114	PISCATAW
ADAMS, WILLIAM F.	BAL	262	6TH WARD
ADAMS, WILLIAM F.	ANN	520	HOWARD D
ADAMS, WILLIAM S.	SOM	399	BRINKLEY
ADAMS, WILLIAM W.	BAL	146	11TH WAR
ADAMS, WILLIAM*	CAR	112	NO TWP L
ADAMS, WILLIAM-BLACK	CAR	145	NO TWP L
ADAMS, WILLIAM-BLACK	CAR	141	NO TWP L
ADAMS, WILLIAMS L.	BAL	084	18TH WAR
ADAMS, MARY	ALL	257	CUMBERLA
ADAMS, RICHARD	CAR	381	2ND DIST
ADAMSON, BENJAMIN F.	MGM	368	BERRYS D
ADAMSON, JANE	MGM	367	BERRYS D
ADAMSON, SAMUEL	BAL	087	10TH WAR
ADAMSON, WALTER H.	MGM	374	ROCKERLE
ADAMSON, WASHINGTON	MGM	403	ROCKERLE
ADANS, ELISABETH	BAL	158	11TH WAR
ADANS, RATCHILL	HAR	196	3RD DIST
ADAY, CHARLES	CAR	123	NO TWP L
ADAY, JACKSON	CAR	123	NO TWP L
ADBINGTON, GEORGE G.	BAL	121	1ST WARD
ADDAMS, B.	BAL	074	10TH WAR
ADDAMS, CHARLES	BAL	291	7TH WARD
ADDER, JAMES F.	PRI	116	PISCATAW
ADDER, THOMAS	BAL	050	1ST WARD
ADDERSON, ELIZA	BAL	074	18TH WAR
ADDERSON, ELIZABETH	CAL	002	1ST DIST
ADDERSON, JOHN	CEC	057	1ST E DI
ADDINGTON, MARY	ANN	354	3RD DIST
ADDIS, JOHN	BAL	120	11TH WAR
ADDISON, ALFRED	PRI	013	BLADENSB
ADDISON, ALFRED	PRI	003	BLADENSB
ADDISON, ANN	BAL	205	11TH WAR
ADDISON, CATHARINE A.	BAL	387	13TH WAR
ADDISON, DENNIS	BAL	227	6TH WARD
ADDISON, E.	PRI	118	PISCATAW
ADDISON, EDWIN R.	BAL	314	7TH WARD
ADDISON, ELISABETH	ANN	369	4TH DIST
ADDISON, ELIZA	BAL	157	11TH WAR
ADDISON, ELIZABETH	BAL	172	16TH WAR
ADDISON, ELLEN E.	BAL	061	15TH WAR
ADDISON, EMILY J.	BAL	228	6TH WARD
ADDISON, EMMA	BAL	012	18TH WAR
ADDISON, FRANCIS	BAL	203	2ND WARD
ADDISON, GEORGE C.	BAL	110	15TH WAR
ADDISON, HENRY	BAL	083	4TH WARD
ADDISON, HENRY A.	BAL	338	3RD WARD
ADDISON, HETTY	BAL	188	19TH WAR
ADDISON, IGNATIUS	MGM	375	ROCKERLE
ADDISON, ISABELLA	BAL	151	5TH WARD
ADDISON, JAMES	ANN	463	HOWARD D
ADDISON, JAMES T.	PRI	094	SPALDING
ADDISON, JOHN	BAL	156	16TH WAR
ADDISON, JOHN	BAL	421	14TH WAR
ADDISON, JOHN	BAL	192	11TH WAR
ADDISON, JOHN W.	BAL	314	7TH WARD
ADDISON, LEVI	WAS	008	WILLIAMS
ADDISON, LOUISA	PRI	118	PISCATAW
ADDISON, MARGRET	BAL	001	18TH WAR
ADDISON, MARTHA	ANN	437	HOWARD D
ADDISON, MILLY	CAL	046	3RD DIST
ADDISON, MIXIUM	BAL	052	1ST WARD
ADDISON, NANCY	BAL	211	11TH WAR
ADDISON, PRISCILLA	BAL	232	6TH WARD
ADDISON, REBECCA	BAL	151	11TH WAR
ADDISON, SAMUEL L.	BAL	328	13TH WAR
ADDISON, SARAH	BAL	396	14TH WAR
ADDISON, SARAH-MULATTO	FRE	038	FREDERIC
ADDISON, SIDNEY	ANN	279	ANNAPOLI
ADDISON, THEADORE	BAL	320	7TH WARD
ADDISON, THOMAS	BAL	115	2ND DIST
ADDISON, WILLAIM	BAL	255	1ST DIST
ADDISON, WILLIAM	BAL	226	1ST DIST
ADDISON, WILLIAM	BAL	113	2ND DIST
ADDISON, WILLIAM H.	BAL	195	11TH WAR
ADDISON, MARY	CAL	046	3RD DIST
ADDISSON, WILLIAM	BAL	273	17TH WAR
ADDLEBERGER, MICHAE	ALL	204	CUMBERLA
ADDLEPERGER, REBECCA	WAS	139	HAGERSTO
ADDLESPERGER, ELIZABETH	CAR	270	WESTMINS
ADDLESPERGER, HARRIETT	CAR	303	1ST DIST
ADDLESPERGER, JAMES	CAR	242	TANEYTOW
ADDLESPERGER, JAMES W.	CAR	303	1ST DIST
ADDLESPERGER, JOHN	CAR	312	1ST DIST
ADDLESPERGER, JOSIAH	CAR	259	3RD DIST
ADDSBERGER, JOHN	FRE	163	EMMITTSB
ADELISON, SUSAN	BAL	314	12TH WAR
ADELSBERGER, JOSHUA	FRE	180	5TH E DI
ADELSBERGER, MARGARET	FRE	164	EMMITTSB
ADELSBERGER, MICHAEL	FRE	187	5TH E DI
ADELSBERGER, NICHOLAS	FRE	183	5TH E DI
ADELSBERGER, SEBASTIAN	FRE	168	EMMITTSB
ADELSHERGER, MICHAEL C.	FRE	161	EMMITTSB
ADEMY, HENRIETTA	BAL	158	19TH WAR
ADEN, ALFRED	MGM	425	MEDLEY 3
ADEN, JOHN B.	MGM	442	CLARKSTR
ADERSON, .	PRI	102	SPALDING
ADERSON, MARORA B.	FRE	399	JEFFERSO
ADERSON, T. W.	BAL	332	1ST DIST
ADESLUYS, CHARLES L.*	BAL	421	3RD WARD
ADGELLY, WILLIAM	BAL	121	11TH WAR
ADISON, JAMES	BAL	339	1ST DIST
ADISON, PACA	PRI	097	SPALDING
ADISON, SAMUEL R.	PRI	094	SPALDING
ADIZ, MARGARET	BAL	228	12TH WAR

Name	County	Page	District
ACKINS, ALFRED	BAL	172	1ST WARD
ACKINS, BARZILLAI	WOR	197	8TH E DI
ACKINS, EPHRAIM W.	WOR	219	4TH E DI
ACKINS, F.	BAL	166	1ST WARD
ADKINS, FRANCIS	WOR	219	4TH E DI
ACKINS, FRANKLIN	WOR	224	4TH E DI
ACKINS, FRNACIS T.	WOR	220	4TH E DI
ACKINS, GEORGE	FRE	080	FREDERIC
ADKINS, GEORGE D.	WOR	227	4TH E DI
ADKINS, HENRY W.	WOR	220	4TH E DI
ACKINS, ISABELLA	WOR	224	4TH E DI
ACKINS, JAMES	WOR	220	4TH E DI
ACKINS, JANE	WOR	220	4TH E DI
ACKINS, JOHN	WOR	222	4TH E DI
ACKINS, JOHN	WOR	237	6TH E DI
ADKINS, JOHN T.	WOR	225	4TH E DI
ADKINS, JONAHTAN	WOR	221	4TH E DI
ADKINS, JOSIAH A.	WOR	222	4TH E DI
ACKINS, LABAER	WOR	224	4TH E DI
ACKINS, LAMBERT	WOR	224	4TH E DI
ACKINS, MARTHA	WOR	291	9TH E DI
ACKINS, MARTHA C.	WOR	223	4TH E DI
ACKINS, MARY E.	WOR	240	6TH E DI
ACKINS, METILDA	BAL	128	11TH WAR
ACKINS, MIDDLETON	WOR	197	8TH E DI
ACKINS, MILBY JR.	WOR	222	4TH E DI
ADKINS, MILBY SR.	WOR	222	4TH E DI
ADKINS, NANCY	WOR	222	4TH E DI
ACKINS, NOAH	WOR	222	4TH E DI
ACKINS, PETER J.	WOR	223	4TH E DI
ACKINS, PRISCELLA	WOR	240	6TH E DI
ADKINS, R. REV.*	TAL	065	EASTON T
ACKINS, SAMPSON	WOR	226	4TH E DI
ACKINS, SAMUEL	FRE	210	BUCKEYST
ACKINS, STANTON	WOR	224	4TH E DI
ADKINS, STEPHEN	WOR	222	4TH E DI
ADKINS, WILLIAM	WOR	223	4TH E DI
ADKINS, WILLIAM J.	WOR	287	BERLIN I
ADKINS, WILLIAM S.	WOR	220	4TH E DI
ACKINS,ABRAHAM	FRE	217	BUCKEYST
ADKINSON, JOHN	WOR	321	1ST E DI
ADKINSON, JOHN	QUE	175	2ND E DI
ACKINSON, MARY S.	KEN	270	1ST DIST
ADKINSON, ROBERT	KEN	273	1ST DIST
ADKINSON, ROBERT	KEN	234	2ND DIST
ACKINSON, WILLIAM	KEN	249	2ND DIST
ACKINSON, WILLIAM	BAL	182	2ND WARD
ADKINSON, WILLIAM T.	KEN	232	2ND DIST
ADKY, BENJAMIN E. *	KEN	249	2ND DIST
ADLEMAN, LEWIS	BAL	212	19TH WAR
ADLEN, MARIA *	BAL	066	18TH WAR
ADLER, ADOLPH	BAL	317	12TH WAR
ACLER, FANNY	BAL	014	9TH WARD
ACLER, GEORGE	BAL	174	16TH WAR
ADLER, HENRY	BAL	138	1ST WARD
ACLER, JOHN	BAL	149	16TH WAR
ACLER, JOHN	ANN	402	8TH DIST
ADLER, JOSHUA	BAL	345	3RD WARD
ADLER, LEWIS H.	BAL	374	13TH WAR
ACLER, M.	BAL	319	12TH WAR
ADLER, MARIA *	BAL	066	18TH WAR
ADLER, MOSES	ANN	267	ANNAPOLI
ADLER, PHILIP	BAL	084	10TH WAR
ADLER, ULIAS	BAL	079	1ST WARD
ADLEY, CORBIN	WAS	200	1ST DIST
ADLEY, HORACE*	TAL	065	EASTON T
ADLEY, J.	BAL	152	1ST WARD
ADLUM, MLTIAM	CAR	327	1ST DIST
ADLUM, THOMAS	ALL	013	3RD E.D.
ADLY, CHARLES	WAS	059	2ND SUBD
ADLY, SAMUEL	WAS	026	2ND SUBD
ACLY, WASHINGTON	WAS	057	2ND SUBD
ADNERSON, HESTER	HAR	147	3RD DIST
ADNEY, CEASAR-BLACK	QUE	156	2ND E DI
ADNEY, SAMUEL-BLACK	QUE	179	2ND E DI
ADOLF, ABRAHAM	BAL	276	17TH WAR
ADOLPH, JOHN	BAL	284	2ND WARD
ADOLPH, WILLIAM	BAL	285	2ND WARD
ADOM, CARL	BAL	142	5TH WARD
ADOM, CATHERINE	CHA	262	MIDDLETO
ADOMS, CHARLES	BAL	300	17TH WAR
ADREON, CAROLINE A.	BAL	073	15TH WAR
ADREON, JOHN	BAL	203	2ND WARD
ADREON, PEARSON	BAL	395	3RD WARD
ADREON, WILLIAM	BAL	072	15TH WAR
ADRIAN, GEORGE	BAL	266	17TH WAR
ADRION, HANNAH	BAL	249	12TH WAR
ADRION, JOSEPH S.	WOR	339	1ST E DI
ADRON, HARRIETT	BAL	007	18TH WAR
ADSMS, ANN	BAL	127	11TH WAR
ACTUM, ANN	FRE	398	JEFFERSO
ACY, FRANCIS	BAL	064	2ND DIST
ADY, JAMES	BAL	228	12TH WAR
ACY, WILLAIM	WAS	301	1ST DIST
ACY, WILLIAM	HAR	139	2ND DIST
ACY, WILLIAM M.	HAR	006	1ST DIST
AEDELY, JANE	BAL	251	2ND WARD
AEFRIGHT, H. G.*	BAL	272	20TH WAR
AELL,SUSAN	ST	313	1ST E DI
AERHART, JOHN	ALL	147	6TH E.D.
AESUM, FREDERICK *	BAL	378	13TH WAR
AEWORTH, WILLIAM H.	SOM	528	QUANTICO
AFFAREAUX, MALANEY	BAL	163	16TH WAR
AFFAYROAX, WILLIAM	BAL	107	5TH WARD
AFFAYROUX, EPAULITE	BAL	209	6TH WARD
AFFLECK, JAMES	MGM	439	CLARKSTR
AFFLICIS, THOMPSON	BAL	474	14TH WAR
AFFULT, THORNTON	ALL	128	4TH E.D.
AFFUTT, DANIEL	ALL	126	4TH E.D.
AFFUTT, SUSSAN	ALL	092	5TH E.D.
AFLICK, JAMES	BAL	347	13TH WAR
AGAMISE, FREDERICK	ALL	260	CUMBERLA
AGAN, JOHN	ALL	226	CUMBERLA
AGAN, OWEN	BAL	445	1ST DIST
AGAN, PETGER	ALL	142	6TH E.D.
AGAN, THOAMS	ALL	078	5TH E.D.
AGAN, THOMAS	ALL	111	5TH E.D.
AGAR, ELIZABETH	BAL	290	20TH WAR
AGAR, MARY	BAL	319	20TH WAR
AGBORN, CALEB	FRE	241	NEW MARK
AGBORN, FUANE	FRE	241	NEW MARK
AGBORN, JOHN W.	FRE	264	NEW MARK
AGEN, MELISSA	CEC	196	6TH E DI
AGEN, VOLENTINE	CEC	196	6TH E DI
AGEN, WILLIAM	BAL	121	1ST WARD
AGENER, JACOB	BAL	049	18TH WAR
AGENGER, WILLIAM	BAL	327	13TH WAR
AGER, ALEXANDER	BAL	291	7TH WARD
AGER, ALICE	BAL	202	11TH WAR
AGER, ANN	BAL	167	11TH WAR
AGER, HENRY	BAL	245	20TH WAR
AGER, JAMES	BAL	202	11TH WAR
AGER, MATHEW	BAL	211	2ND WARD
AGER, MICHAEL	BAL	165	11TH WAR
AGER, ROBERT	BAL	123	5TH WARD
AGERA, ROSA	BAL	279	1ST DIST
AGLE, CAELINE R.	FRE	260	NEW MARK
AGLE, JOHN	BAL	315	7TH WARD
AGLE, RICHARD	FRE	264	NEW MARK
AGLE, SARAH	FRE	264	NEW MARK
AGNAN, GEORGE	BAL	254	2ND WARD
AGNEN, ROBERT	WOR	182	6TH E DI
AGNES, HENRY	BAL	185	11TH WAR
AGNES, MATHIAS	CEC	001	ELKTON 3
AGNEW, DAVID	FRE	160	EMMITTSB
AGNEW, HENRY	BAL	254	2ND WARD
AGNEW, J.P.	ALL	207	CUMBERLA
AGNEW, JOHN	FRE	166	EMMITTSB
AGNEW, JOHN L.	ALL	207	CUMBERLA
AGNEW, MARGARET	FRE	164	EMMITTSB
AGNEW, ROBERT	BAL	083	2ND DIST
AGNEW, SARAH J.	BAL	057	4TH WARD
AGNEW, SOPHIA	FRE	163	EMMITTSB
AGNEW, THOMAS	BAL	163	11TH WAR
AGNEW, THOMAS	WAS	093	2ND SUBD
AGNEW, WILLIAM	BAL	361	3RD WARD
AGON, ISABELLA	CEC	157	PORT DUP
AGRAW, CATHERINE	BAL	088	1ST WARD
AGUISHIE, ABSOLVE	BAL	050	1ST WARD
AGULAND, J. *	BAL	218	12TH WAR
AHALT, BARBARA	FRE	333	MIDDLETO
AHALT, DANIEL	FRE	330	MIDDLETO
AHALT, JACOB	FRE	330	MIDDLETO
AHALT, JACOB	FRE	404	JEFFERSO
AHALT, JOSHUA	FRE	327	MIDDLETO
AHALT, LYDIA	FRE	326	MIDDLETO
AHALT, MAGDALEN	FRE	330	MIDDLETO
AHALT, MAHALA	FRE	314	MIDDLETO
AHALT, MATTHIAS	FRE	325	MIDDLETO
AHALT, SAMUEL	FRE	325	MIDDLETO
AHE, JAMES	WOR	257	1ST CENS
AHELING, HENRY	BAL	011	9TH WARD
AHER, HENRY	BAL	150	2ND DIST
AHERN, CATHERINE	BAL	279	7TH WARD
AHL, MARY	ALL	146	6TH E.D.
AHL, WILLIAM	BAL	125	1ST WARD
AHL, WILLIAM	BAL	148	1ST WARD
AHLERS, MARY	BAL	109	5TH WARD
AHLL, CHARLOTTE W.	BAL	079	4TH WARD
AHLSBEGER, FREDERICK	BAL	127	16TH WAR
AHMAN, AMANDA	ALL	005	3RD E.D.
AHMAN, GEORGE	ALL	005	3RD E.D.
AHREAS, JOHN	BAL	253	2ND WARD
AHREN, JANE L.	BAL	003	9TH WARD
AHREN, JOHN	BAL	088	1ST WARD
AHREN, LAWRENCE	BAL	003	9TH WARD
AHREN, MICHAEL	BAL	088	1ST WARD
AHRENS, ADOLPH	BAL	105	10TH WAR
AHRENS, CHARLES	BAL	324	7TH WARD
AHRRIS, JOHN	TAL	095	ST MICHA
AHUSER, ADAM	ALL	061	10TH E.D
AIEN, RACHAEL-BLACK	BAL	224	2ND WARD
AIERY, JAMES	BAL	295	3RD WARD
AIGHMAN, JACOB	WAS	024	2ND SUBD
AIGNES, ELLEN	BAL	134	11TH WAR
AIKEN, ANDREW	BAL	128	1ST WARD
AIKEN, BETSEY	BAL	065	10TH WAR
AIKEN, ELIZA	BAL	096	18TH WAR
AIKEN, FRANCIS	BAL	173	11TH WAR
AIKEN, GEORGE B.	FRE	283	WOODSBOR
AIKEN, JOHN	CEC	083	CHARLEST
AIKEN, MARGARET	CEC	083	CHARLEST
AIKEN, MARY	FRE	066	FREDERIC
AIKEN, SAMUEL	CEC	188	7TH E DI
AIKEN, SAMUEL	CEC	185	7TH E DI
AIKEN, THOMAS	CEC	193	5TH E DI
AIKEN, WILLIAM E.A.	FRE	20	5TH E DI
AIKEN, WILLIAM G. A.	FRE	164	EMMITTSB
AIKER, GEORGE	HAR	126	2ND DIST
AIKER, MATTHEW K.	BAL	142	19TH WAR
AIKER, SARAH	BAL	142	19TH WAR
AIKINHURST, MARY	BAL	028	2ND DIST
AIKMAN, JAMES*	DOR	427	1ST DIST
AIKMAN, WILLIAM JR.	SOM	497	SALISBUR
AIKMAN, WILLIAM*	SOM	496	SALISBUR
AILER, ALLICE	BAL	093	18TH WAR
AILOR, ELIZABETH	CAR	066	NO TWP L
AILORS, ANN	BAL	068	1ST WARD
AILORS, HENRY	BAL	068	1ST WARD
AILY, ELIZABETH	ST	328	4TH E DI
AINENDER, G. P.	BAL	239	20TH WAR
AINET, SARAH	BAL	264	12TH WAR
AINPER, JOSEPH	HAR	085	2ND DIST
AINSWORTH, BARBARA	WAS	070	2ND SUBD
AINSWORTH, BENJAMIN	WAS	070	2ND SUBD
AINSWORTH, BENJAMIN	WAS	070	2ND SUBD
AINSWORTH, H.H.	ALL	239	CUMBERLA
AINSWORTH, JOHN P.	WAS	070	2ND SUBD
AINSWORTH, THOMAS	WAS	069	2ND SUBD
AINSWORTH, THOMAS	WAS	070	2ND SUBD
AINWATCHER, ADAM	BAL	120	18TH WAR
AIRD, THOMAS	ALL	088	5TH E.D.
AIRDEN, WILLIAM	BAL	001	1ST WARD
AIREY, FRANCIS A.	BAL	337	7TH WARD
AIRHART, ANNA	BAL	074	2ND DIST
AIRS, ASA	CAR	099	NO TWP L
AIRS, CATHARINE	BAL	254	1ST DIST
AIRS, ENOCH-BLACK	FRE	230	BUCKEYST
AIRS, JAMES	BAL	461	1ST DIST
AIRS, SARAH E.-BLACK	FRE	230	BUCKEYST
AIRS, SHARLOTT	CAR	099	NO TWP L
AIRS, WILLIAM	CAR	099	NO TWP L
AIRY, GEORGE	BAL	415	14TH WAR
AIRY, JEROME	BAL	192	19TH WAR
AIRY, JOHN	BAL	382	1ST DIST
AISA, MARGARETT *	BAL	027	18TH WAR
AITCHERSON, JOHN	PRI	034	VANSVILL
AITCHERSCN, PETER	PRI	034	VANSVILL
AITCHERSON, WILLIAM	PRI	034	VANSVILL
AITCHESON, ELISA	BAL	298	3RD WARD
AITKENS, ELIZA	BAL	093	5TH WARD
AITKENS, ELIZA	BAL	093	5TH WARD
AITKIN, JAMES	BAL	111	5TH WARD
AITKIN, REBECCA	BAL	024	4TH WARD
AKE, JAMES	WOR	257	1ST CENS
AKEHURST, CHARLES	BAL	407	1ST DIST
AKEHURST, SARAH J.	BAL	408	1ST DIST
AKEHURST, WILLIAM	BAL	179	2ND DIST
AKEISPEAR, CHARLES	BAL	245	20TH WAR
AKEMPLEIN, WILLIAM A.	BAL	122	1ST WARD
AKEN, THOMAS	BAL	459	1ST DIST
AKENBERGER, JACOB	ALL	015	3RD E.D.
AKER, JACOB	BAL	192	2ND WARD
AKERMAN, JOHN	BAL	136	1ST WARD
AKERS, DANIEL	BAL	293	17TH WAR
AKERS, EDWARD	BAL	158	16TH WAR
AKERSPEAR, ELIZABETH	BAL	245	20TH WAR
AKINS, HARRITT	HAR	191	3RD DIST
AKINS, HENRY	HAR	190	3RD DIST
ALAGOOD, PERRY	SOM	427	PRINCESS
ALAN, ETHAN A.	BAL	145	11TH WAR
ALARD, JOHN	BAL	400	14TH WAR
ALAWAY, MARTHA	BAL	368	8TH WARD
ALAWAYS, ELIZABETH	BAL	258	6TH WARD
ALBANY, HENRY	BAL	254	12TH WAR
ALBAUGH, ABRAHAM	ANN	483	HOWARD D
ALBAUGH, ABRAHAM	CAR	365	9TH DIST
ALBAUGH, ABSOLUM	FRE	022	FREDERIC
ALBAUGH, ADELINE	FRE	037	FREDERIC
ALBAUGH, ANDREW	FRE	282	WOODSBOR
ALBAUGH, CHARLES F.	FRE	037	FREDERIC
ALBAUGH, DANIEL	FRE	282	WOODSBOR
ALBAUGH, DANIEL	FRE	413	8TH E DI
ALBAUGH, DANIEL	ALL	172	7TH E.D.
ALBAUGH, DAVID	CAR	366	9TH DIST
ALBAUGH, DIANA	CAR	356	6TH DIST
ALBAUGH, EDWARD	FRE	006	FREDERIC
ALBAUGH, EDWARD	BAL	027	15TH WAR
ALBAUGH, ELIZA	ALL	207	CUMBERLA
ALBAUGH, ELLENORE	FRE	412	8TH E DI
ALBAUGH, EPRHAIM	FRE	448	8TH E DI
ALBAUGH, FRED	BAL	258	12TH WAR
ALBAUGH, GEORGE	BAL	294	20TH WAR
ALBAUGH, GRIFTEN	BAL	271	20TH WAR
ALBAUGH, ISAAC	FRE	128	CREAGERS
ALBAUGH, JOHN	CAR	331	MANCHEST
ALBAUGH, JOHN	CAR	356	6TH DIST
ALBAUGH, JOHN	FRE	287	WOODSBOR
ALBAUGH, JOHN	BAL	244	2ND WARD
ALBAUGH, JOHN W.	BAL	042	15TH WAR
ALBAUGH, JOHN W.	FRE	111	CREAGERS
ALBAUGH, LEWIS A.	FRE	446	8TH E DI
ALBAUGH, MARY S.	FRE	426	8TH E DI
ALBAUGH, SAMUEL	ALL	175	7TH E.D.
ALBAUGH, SOPHIAH	FRE	299	WOODSBOR
ALBAUGH, THEADORE T.	FRE	097	FREDERIC
ALBAUGH, THOMAS L.	FRE	445	8TH E DI
ALBAUGH, VALENTINE	FRE	096	FREDERIC
ALBAUGH, WILLIAM	BAL	300	20TH WAR
ALBAUGH, WILLIAM	CAR	356	6TH DIST
ALBAUGH, WILLIAM A.	FRE	295	WOODSBOR
ALBAUGH, WILLIAM H.	FRE	034	FREDERIC
ALBAUGH,BASIL H.	FRE	445	8TH E DI
ALBAUGH,HARRIET	FRE	049	FREDERIC
ALBAUGH,SINGLETON	FRE	396	PETERSVI
ALBAUGH,WILLIAM E.	FRE	417	8TH E DI
ALBAUGHN, HENRY	ALL	188	9TH E.D.
ALBERGER, ADAM	BAL	083	1ST WARD
ALBERGER, ALEXANDER	QUE	187	3RD E DI
ALBERGER, CAROLINE	QUE	207	3RD E DI
ALBERS, ANN D.	BAL	015	4TH WARD
ALBERS, ELIZABETH	BAL	094	5TH WARD
ALBERS, HENERY	DOR	361	3RD DIVI
ALBERS, HENRY	BAL	114	15TH WAR
ALBERS, JANE	BAL	303	7TH WARD
ALBERS, RUDOLP	ANN	489	HOWARD D
ALBERT, A.M.	WAS	003	WILLIAMS
ALBERT, ADAM	BAL	206	19TH WAR
ALBERT, ALEXANDER	CEC	025	ELKTON 3
ALBERT, ANN M.	WAS	181	BOONSBOR
ALBERT, AUGUSTAS J.	BAL	060	18TH WAR
ALBERT, AUGUSTAS J.	BAL	059	18TH WAR
ALBERT, CHARLES	CAR	269	WESTMINS
ALBERT, CORT	CAR	289	7TH DIST
ALBERT, DANIEL	BAL	083	10TH WAR
ALBERT, EDWARD	HAR	027	1ST DIST
ALBERT, GEORGE	CAR	272	WESTMINS
ALBERT, GEORGE	BAL	419	3RD WARD
ALBERT, GEORGE	WAS	150	HAGERSTO
ALBERT, GEORGE M.	WAS	137	HAGERSTO
ALBERT, HENRY	WAS	181	BOONSBOR
ALBERT, HENRY	BAL	401	8TH WARD
ALBERT, HY	BAL	211	6TH DIST
ALBERT, JACOB	WAS	181	BOONSBOR
ALBERT, JACOB	WAS	150	HAGERSTO
ALBERT, JACOB	BAL	141	11TH WAR
ALBERT, JOHN	BAL	457	14TH WAR
ALBERT, JOHN	CAR	410	2ND DIST
ALBERT, JOHN	WAS	137	HAGERSTO
ALBERT, JOHN	WAS	134	HAGERSTO
ALBERT, JOHN	WAS	027	2ND SUBD
ALBERT, JOHN	BAL	172	16TH WAR
ALBERT, JOHN	BAL	010	EASTERN
ALBERT, JOHN	BAL	192	2ND WARD
ALBERT, JOHN	BAL	221	2ND WARD
ALBERT, JOHN*	BAL	018	4TH WARD
ALBERT, LAWSON	WAS	181	BOONSBOR
ALBERT, LUIN	WAS	150	HAGERSTO
ALBERT, MOSES H.	BAL	129	16TH WAR
ALBERT, NICHOLAS	BAL	105	1ST WARD
ALBERT, THOMAS	CAR	364	9TH DIST
ALBERT, WILLIAM	BAL	054	18TH WAR
ALBERT, WILLIAM	HAR	029	1ST DIST
ALBERT, WILLIAM H.	WAS	134	HAGERSTO
ALBERT, WILLIAM J.	BAL	142	11TH WAR
ALBERTON, JACOB	ALL	184	9TH E.D.
ALBERTS, A.	WAS	005	WILLIAMS
ALBERTS, DANIEL	BAL	377	8TH WARD
ALBERTS, N.	BAL	117	1ST WARD
ALBERTSON, ANNA M.	CEC	162	6TH E DI
ALBERTSON, HARRIET	CEC	098	3RD E DI
ALBERTSON, JAMES	BAL	095	10TH WAR
ALBERTSON, JOHN	BAL	101	10TH WAR
ALBERTSON, JOHN	BAL	244	20TH WAR
ALBIN, FRANCES	BAL	204	5TH DIST
ALBIN, MORDECAI	BAL	204	6TH DIST
ALBIN, MORDECAI	BAL	209	5TH DIST
ALBIN, ZACH	BAL	204	5TH DIST
ALBIN, ZACHARIAH	BAL	219	6TH DIST
ALBINSON, JANE	MGM	320	CRACKLIN
ALBINSON, PETER	BAL	335	13TH WAR
ALBON, GEORGE	CAR	171	8TH DIST
ALBON, HENRY	CAR	172	8TH DIST
ALBON, LIHUE	CAR	173	8TH DIST
ALBON, MARY	CAR	171	8TH DIST
ALBORN, ELI	BAL	199	5TH DIST
ALBOT, RUFUS	WOR	341	1ST E DI
ALBRECHT, TIMOTHEUS	BAL	040	15TH WAR
ALBRIDGE, ELIZABETH	BAL	010	18TH WAR
ALBRIGHT, AUGUSTUS	CAR	173	8TH DIST

ALBRIGHT, DANIEL ALL 126 4TH E.D.
ALBRIGHT, FREDERICK BAL 267 1ST DIST
ALBRIGHT, HENRY BAL 371 8TH WARD
ALBRIGHT, HENRY CAR 188 4TH DIST
ALBRIGHT, JOHN BAL 068 4TH WARD
ALBRIGHT, MARY ALL 126 4TH E.D.
ALBRIGHT, SARAH ALL 229 CUMBERLA
ALBRIGHT, SUSAN ALL 095 5TH E.D.
ALBRIGHT, WILLIAM ALL 055 10TH E.D
ALBRIGHT, WILLIAM BAL 199 17TH WAR
ALBRIGHT, WILLIAM CAR 189 4TH DIST
ALBRUGH, DANIEL FRE 246 NEW MARK
ALBUE, C. BAL 163 1ST WARD
ALBUGAR, JACOB CAR 148 NO TWP L
ALBUGH, SOLOMON FRE 058 FREDERIC
ALBURGER, WILLIAM QUE 144 1ST E DI
ALBURGH, ABRAHAM A. FRE 298 WOODSBOR
ALBURN, FREDERICK WAS 216 1ST DIST
ALBY, CHARLES BAL 100 10TH WAR
ALBY, ELIZABETH MGM 374 ROCKERLE
ALCOCK, GEORGE FRE 001 FREDERIC
ALCOCK, M.H.D. BAL 212 19TH WAR
ALCOCK, MARGARET BAL 114 15TH WAR
ALCOCK, W. J. BAL 321 12TH WAR
ALCOCK, WILLIAM BAL 355 13TH WAR
ALCOMB, SARAH E. BAL 352 7TH WARD
ALCORD, JOHN BAL 002 EASTERN
ALCORN, PERRY BAL 167 16TH WAR
ALCOSE, REBECCA * BAL 380 13TH WAR
ALCOTT, MARY A. FRE 283 WOODSBOR
ALCOX, SARAH DOR 441 1ST DIST
ALCUM, ANN BAL 239 12TH WAR
ALDEL, HANNAH CEC 095 4TH E DI
ALDEN, B. F. BAL 281 2ND WARD
ALDEN, EBANEAZOR CEC 095 4TH E DI
ALDEN, FLORA BAL 360 3RD WARD
ALDEN, GEORGE CEC 095 4TH E DI
ALDEN, JOHN BAL 056 2ND DIST
ALDEN, LEWIS BAL 013 1ST WARD
ALDEN, MARGARET CEC 093 4TH E DI
ALDEN, MARY C. BAL 232 6TH WARD
ALDEN, SIMON BAL 126 5TH WARD
ALDENSON, C. J. BAL 282 2ND WARD
ALDER, DANIEL BAL 177 2ND DIST
ALDER, FRANCIS BAL 214 11TH WAR
ALDER, JAMES H. PRI 114 PISCATAW
ALDER, MICAHEL BAL 177 2ND DIST
ALDER, RACHEL S. BAL 178 2ND DIST
ALDER, ROSALDA BAL 093 10TH WAR
ALDER, WILLIAM BAL 442 1ST DIST
ALDERDICE, MARY BAL 184 16TH WAR
ALDERITE, MANUEL FRE 20 5TH E DI
ALDERSON, JAMES B. HAR 070 1ST DIST
ALDERSON, JOHN D. HAR 049 1ST DIST
ALDERSON, SARAH BAL 098 2ND DIST
ALDERSON, THOMAS HAR 068 1ST DIST
ALDERTON, LUKE ALL 184 9TH E.D.
ALDERTON, PETER ALL 177 7TH E.D.
ALDGMCOR, CONRAD BAL 226 2ND WARD
ALDIN, AMELD BAL 246 2ND WARD
ALDMAN, MARY BAL 049 18TH WAR
ALDREDGE, FREDERICK BAL 237 17TH WAR
ALDRIDGE, EDWARD W. BAL 004 EASTERN
ALDRIDGE, EVEN J. CAR 366 9TH DIST
ALDRIDGE, FREDUS CEC 002 ELKTON 3
ALDRIDGE, GEORGE W. FRE 423 8TH E DI
ALDRIDGE, JOHN CEC 002 ELKTON 3
ALDRIDGE, JOHN CEC 067 5TH E DI
ALDRIDGE, JOSEPH WAS 298 1ST DIST
ALDRIDGE, JOSHUA BAL 116 15TH WAR
ALDRIDGE, MARTHA PRI 037 VANSVILL
ALDRIDGE, OLIVER CAR 366 9TH DIST
ALDRIDGE, SAMUEL CEC 067 5TH E DI
ALDRIDGE, SARAH BAL 120 18TH WAR
ALDRIDGE, WASHINGTON PRI 020 VANSVILL
ALDRIGE, ALFRED ANN 510 HOWARD D
ALDRIGE, HANNAH ANN 461 HOWARD D
ALDRIGLE, ANDREW BAL 135 11TH WAR
ALDRIZE, LECNARD CAR 368 9TH DIST
ALE, DAVID FRE 404 JEFFERSO
ALE, JAMES BAL 139 1ST WARD
ALEC, WILLIAM H. PRI 032 VANSVILL
ALEN, ABRAM BAL 061 2ND DIST
ALEN, ANICE D. CHA 233 HILLTOP
ALEN, CHARLES CAR 212 5TH DIST
ALEN, FRANCIS CAR 233 5TH DIST
ALEN, GEORGE W. CAR 216 5TH DIST
ALEN, JANE * BAL 067 18TH WAR
ALENUTT, JAMES N. MGM 408 MEDLEY 3
ALENUTT, JAMES N. MGM 409 MEDLEY 3
ALER, CHRIS BAL 264 20TH WAR
ALER, ELIZABETH BAL 091 5TH WARD
ALER, GEORGE W. BAL 090 18TH WAR
ALER, H.D. BAL 129 1ST WARD
ALER, HENRY BAL 226 1ST DIST
ALER, J. BAL 052 18TH WAR
ALER, J. T. BAL 314 12TH WAR
ALER, JANE * BAL 067 18TH WAR
ALER, JOHN W. BAL 266 12TH WAR
ALER, MARTIN BAL 356 1ST DIST
ALER, MARY BAL 356 1ST DIST
ALER, NANCY BAL 091 5TH WARD
ALERBOUGH, AUGUSTINE BAL 350 3RD WARD
ALERS, HELEN BAL 070 15TH WAR
ALESXANDER, RUBEN CEC 174 6TH E DI
ALEVINS, PETER BAL 125 16TH WAR
ALEX, JOHN BAL 266 12TH WAR
ALEXANDER, AMOS BAL 152 2ND DIST
ALEXANDER, ANDREW BAL 020 18TH WAR
ALEXANDER, ANDREW CEC 010 ELKTON 3
ALEXANDER, ANN CEC 110 4TH E DI
ALEXANDER, ANN CEC 096 4TH E DI
ALEXANDER, ANN FRE 206 BUCKEYST
ALEXANDER, ANNA CEC 012 ELKTON 3
ALEXANDER, ARIANEA BAL 045 15TH WAR
ALEXANDER, ARMISTEAD FRE 321 MIDDLETO
ALEXANDER, ARTHUR CEC 088 4TH E DI
ALEXANDER, ASHTON BAL 063 10TH WAR
ALEXANDER, AUGUSTA BAL 038 18TH WAR
ALEXANDER, BENJAMIN BAL 020 15TH WAR
ALEXANDER, BENJAMIN T. CEC 211 7TH E DI
ALEXANDER, CATHARINE CEC 035 CHESAPEA
ALEXANDER, CATHRINE BAL 068 18TH WAR
ALEXANDER, CORNELIA FRE 322 MIDDLETO
ALEXANDER, DANIEL ALL 151 6TH E.D.
ALEXANDER, CAVID CEC 003 ELKTON 3
ALEXANDER, DONALD BAL 022 2ND DIST
ALEXANDER, EDWARD C. ANN 421 HOWARD D
ALEXANDER, ELISHA CEC 104 4TH E DI
ALEXANDER, ELIZA ALL 152 6TH E.D.

ALEXANDER, ELIZABETH FRE 321 MIDDLETO
ALEXANDER, EZEKIEL CEC 135 6TH E DI
ALEXANDER, FREDERICK FRE 332 MIDDLETO
ALEXANDER, GEORGE FRE 312 MIDDLETO
ALEXANDER, GEORGE CEC 104 4TH E DI
ALEXANDER, GEORGE CAR 320 1ST DIST
ALEXANDER, GEORGE CEC 011 ELKTON 3
ALEXANDER, GEORGE CEC 001 ELKTON 3
ALEXANDER, GEORGE FRE 394 PETERSVI
ALEXANDER, GEORGE BAL 327 13TH WAR
ALEXANDER, HANSON ALL 154 6TH E.D.
ALEXANDER, HARRIETT BAL 143 11TH WAR
ALEXANDER, HENERITTA BAL 319 12TH WAR
ALEXANDER, HENRY BAL 439 8TH WARD
ALEXANDER, HENRY ANN 499 HOWARD D
ALEXANDER, HENRY WAS 090 2ND SUBD
ALEXANDER, ISABELLA CEC 182 7TH E DI
ALEXANDER, JAMES BAL 008 18TH WAR
ALEXANDER, JAMES CEC 211 7TH E DI
ALEXANDER, JAMES CEC 191 5TH E DI
ALEXANDER, JAMES CEC 153 PORT DUP
ALEXANDER, JAMES CEC 144 PORT DUP
ALEXANDER, JAMES HAR 044 1ST DIST
ALEXANDER, JAMES BAL 110 2ND DIST
ALEXANDER, JAMES BAL 238 6TH WARD
ALEXANDER, JAMES A. CEC 140 5TH E DI
ALEXANDER, JAMES H. BAL 392 14TH WAR
ALEXANDER, JAMES T. CEC 096 4TH E DI
ALEXANDER, JANE BAL 303 12TH WAR
ALEXANDER, JOHN ALL 036 2ND E.D.
ALEXANDER, JOHN CEC 182 7TH E DI
ALEXANDER, JOHN BAL 074 18TH WAR
ALEXANDER, JOHN BAL 033 18TH WAR
ALEXANDER, JOHN CEC 091 4TH E DI
ALEXANDER, JOHN BAL 440 14TH WAR
ALEXANDER, JOHN CEC 039 CHESAPEA
ALEXANDER, JOHN FRE 328 MIDDLETO
ALEXANDER, JOHN FRE 315 MIDDLETO
ALEXANDER, JOHN FRE 316 MIDDLETO
ALEXANDER, JOHN KEN 286 3RD DIST
ALEXANDER, JOHN WAS 145 HAGERSTO
ALEXANDER, JOHN T. BAL 307 12TH WAR
ALEXANDER, JOSEPH ST 319 4TH E DI
ALEXANDER, JOSEPH FRE 326 MIDDLETO
ALEXANDER, JOSEPH CEC 168 6TH E DI
ALEXANDER, JOSEPH CEC 071 5TH E DI
ALEXANDER, JOSEPH CEC 095 4TH E DI
ALEXANDER, LARY V. HAR 154 3RD DIST
ALEXANDER, LAWSON FRE 316 MIDDLETO
ALEXANDER, LEVI BAL 130 2ND DIST
ALEXANDER, LIDDY BAL 071 18TH WAR
ALEXANDER, LOUISA ANN 277 ANNAPOLI
ALEXANDER, LUCY CHA 256 MIDDLETO
ALEXANDER, MARGARET BAL 392 14TH WAR
ALEXANDER, MARY CEC 195 6TH E DI
ALEXANDER, MARY FRE 321 MIDDLETO
ALEXANDER, MARY CEC 126 5TH E DI
ALEXANDER, MARY BAL 248 12TH WAR
ALEXANDER, MATILDA FRE 402 JEFFERSO
ALEXANDER, MILLICENT CEC 124 5TH E DI
ALEXANDER, MYER BAL 443 14TH WAR
ALEXANDER, NANCY CEC 211 7TH E DI
ALEXANDER, NATHAN CEC 179 7TH E DI
ALEXANDER, RAINY CEC 133 6TH E DI
ALEXANDER, REBECCA CEC 004 ELKTON 3
ALEXANDER, REBECCA ALL 139 6TH E.D.
ALEXANDER, REBECCA A. E. FRE 326 MIDDLETO
ALEXANDER, RICHARD BAL 067 10TH WAR
ALEXANDER, ROBERT FRE 331 MIDDLETO
ALEXANDER, ROBERT CEC 067 5TH E DI
ALEXANDER, ROBERT KEN 288 3RD DIST
ALEXANDER, RUBEN JR. CEC 174 6TH E DI
ALEXANDER, SAMUEL BAL 343 13TH WAR
ALEXANDER, SARAH BAL 243 17TH WAR
ALEXANDER, SUSAN ALL 243 CUMBERLA
ALEXANDER, TABITHA CEC 197 7TH E DI
ALEXANDER, THEOPHILUS BAL 027 15TH WAR
ALEXANDER, THOMAS BAL 246 17TH WAR
ALEXANDER, THOMAS CEC 113 4TH E DI
ALEXANDER, THOMAS S. BAL 107 10TH WAR
ALEXANDER, VALENTINE ALL 153 6TH E.D.
ALEXANDER, VALENTINE ALL 138 6TH E.D.
ALEXANDER, WARREN CEC 173 6TH E DI
ALEXANDER, WASHINGTON CEC 179 7TH E DI
ALEXANDER, WASHINGTON CEC 111 4TH E DI
ALEXANDER, WASHINGTON ANN 516 HOWARD D
ALEXANDER, WILLIAM ANN 266 ANNAPOLI
ALEXANDER, WILLIAM BAL 043 15TH WAR
ALEXANDER, WILLIAM ALL 227 CUMBERLA
ALEXANDER, WILLIAM BAL 260 1ST DIST
ALEXANDER, WILLIAM CEC 113 4TH E DI
ALEXANDER, WILLIAM CEC 149 PORT DUP
ALEXANDER, WILLIAM CEC 123 3RD E DI
ALEXANDER, WILLIAM CEC 211 7TH E DI
ALEXANDER, WILLIAM CEC 010 ELKTON 3
ALEXANDER, WILLIAM WAS 137 HAGERSTO
ALEXANDER, WILSON BAL 167 19TH WAR
ALEXANDER, WILLIAM HAR 037 1ST DIST
ALEXANORIA, EMELINE BAL 141 2ND DIST
ALEXINE, WILLIAM* BAL 369 3RD WARD
ALFA, MARY* SOM 520 BARREN C
ALFEDDER, LUTWICK BAL 307 7TH WARD
ALFERD, DAVID H. BAL 132 1ST WARD
ALFET, ELIZA BAL 249 20TH WAR
ALFLICK, THOMAS BAL 465 14TH WAR
ALFOLD, WILLIAM BAL 025 4TH WARD
ALFORD, ANN KEN 259 1ST DIST
ALFORD, GEORGE B. BAL 296 3RD WARD
ALFORD, JAMES E. BAL 296 3RD WARD
ALFORD, MARGARET BAL 225 6TH WARD
ALFORD, MARY A. C. KEN 260 1ST DIST
ALFORD, OWEN-BLACK FRE 430 8TH E DI
ALFORD, ROBERT ANN 488 HOWARD D
ALFRANDER, CONRAD BAL 256 2ND WARD
ALFRED, DANIEL DOR 322 1ST DIST
ALFRED, HENRY DOR 380 1ST DIST
ALFRED, JAMES QUE 125 1ST E DI
ALFRED, WILLIAM CAR 156 NO TWP L
ALFRED, MAHALY CAR 125 NO TWP L
ALFY, ELIZA CAR 095 NO TWP L
ALGEE, JAMES BAL 306 7TH WARD
ALGIER, GEORGE BAL 237 1ST DIST
ALGIER, JACOB BAL 237 1ST DIST
ALGIER, MELCHOR BAL 237 1ST DIST
ALGIRE, AMON CAR 189 4TH DIST
ALGIRE, JOSHUA CAR 176 8TH DIST
ALGIRE, JSOHUA F.C. CAR 178 8TH DIST
ALGIRE, MARY R. CAR 189 4TH DIST
ALGIRE, MELCHOR F. CAR 182 8TH DIST
ALGIRE, NICHOLAS CAR 182 8TH DIST

ALGIRE, REBECA CAR 187 4TH DIST
ALGOT, H. J. BAL 156 1ST WARD
ALHITON, WILLIAM CHA 276 ALLENS F
ALICE, EVAN ALL 119 5TH E.D.
ALICE, JACOB BAL 291 17TH WAR
ALICE, SUSAN CAR 379 2ND DIST
ALISON, ANN BAL 321 3RD WARD
ALISON, ELISABETH ALL 251 CUMBERLA
ALIX, JANE BAL 070 10TH WAR
ALKERE, HENRY ALL 163 6TH E.D.
ALKISE, JOHN ALL 171 7TH E.D.
ALL, RACHE BAL 294 12TH WAR
ALLABY, JOHN BAL 260 2ND WARD
ALLACE, LOUISA BAL 402 1ST DIST
ALLAN, JOHN HAR 137 2ND DIST
ALLAN, MARY BAL 458 14TH WAR
ALLAN, WILLIAM ANN 329 2ND DIST
ALLAN, WILLIAM BAL 083 1ST WARD
ALLANDE, WALTER * BAL 126 2ND DIST
ALLANDER, SARAH HAR 135 2ND DIST
ALLANSON, J. BAL 149 1ST WARD
ALLARD, JOSEPH BAL 233 6TH WARD
ALLARD, LOUISA R. BAL 189 6TH WARD
ALLARD, THOMAS B. BAL 188 6TH WARD
ALLARD, WILLIAM BAL 190 6TH WARD
ALLBAUGH, DANIEL WAS 199 1ST DIST
ALLBAUGH, GEORGE BAL 363 8TH WARD
ALLBAUGH, JOHN BAL 344 7TH WARD
ALLBAUGH, JOHN A. WAS 199 1ST DIST
ALLBAUGH, MARY WAS 166 1ST DIST
ALLBERGER, HENRY BAL 099 18TH WAR
ALLBRIGHT, JACOB ANN 520 HOWARD D
ALLBRIGHT, JESSE P. BAL 174 16TH WAR
ALLBRIGHT, JULIAN BAL 059 18TH WAR
ALLBRIGHT, OLIVIA M. BAL 174 16TH WAR
ALLCOM, GEORGE ANN 479 HOWARD D
ALLDING, ALBERT G. BAL 075 18TH WAR
ALLDRIDGE, JOHN BAL 349 1ST DIST
ALLDRIDGE, LOUISA BAL 349 1ST DIST
ALLEN, ABRAHAM CEC 194 7TH E DI
ALLEN, ABRAM BAL 062 2ND DIST
ALLEN, ADELINE HAR 114 2ND DIST
ALLEN, ALBERT BAL 134 2ND DIST
ALLEN, ALBERT WOR 297 9TH E DI
ALLEN, ALEXANDER BAL 448 8TH WARD
ALLEN, ALEXANDER-MULATTO BAL 224 2ND WARD
ALLEN, ALFRED PRI 088 SPALDING
ALLEN, AMOS BAL 113 15TH WAR
ALLEN, ANN KEN 293 3RD DIST
ALLEN, ANN CAL 016 1ST DIST
ALLEN, ANN BAL 149 11TH WAR
ALLEN, ANN E. BAL 315 1ST DIST
ALLEN, ARAMINTA PRI 092 MARLBROU
ALLEN, ARCHIBALD ALL 248 CUMBERLA
ALLEN, BARBARA ANN 270 ANNAPOLI
ALLEN, BENEDICT CEC 147 PORT DUP
ALLEN, BENJAMIN CEC 062 1ST E DI
ALLEN, BENJAMIN BAL 247 6TH WARD
ALLEN, BENN PRI 094 SPALDING
ALLEN, BENNETT TAL 009 EASTON D
ALLEN, BERY BAL 097 2ND DIST
ALLEN, CAROLINE SOM 425 PRINCESS
ALLEN, CATHARINE BAL 139 2ND DIST
ALLEN, CATHERINE CHA 242 HILLTOP
ALLEN, CHARLES MGM 393 ROCKERLE
ALLEN, CHARLES BAL 116 11TH WAR
ALLEN, CHARLES CEC 044 1ST E DI
ALLEN, CHARLES PRI 090 MARLBROU
ALLEN, CHARLOTT BAL 264 7TH WARD
ALLEN, CLARA KEN 211 2ND DIST
ALLEN, D.H. BAL 241 12TH WAR
ALLEN, DANIEL BAL 140 2ND DIST
ALLEN, DANIEL WOR 280 BERLIN 1
ALLEN, DAVID BAL 217 17TH WAR
ALLEN, DENAND-BLACK WOR 346 1ST E DI
ALLEN, DINAH CEC 141 6TH E DI
ALLEN, E.E. BAL 008 1ST WARD
ALLEN, EBENEZER WOR 182 6TH E DI
ALLEN, EBIN WOR 312 2ND E DI
ALLEN, EDITH DOR 378 1ST DIST
ALLEN, EDWARD BAL 205 17TH WAR
ALLEN, EDWARD C. BAL 189 6TH WARD
ALLEN, EDWARD H. HAR 030 1ST DIST
ALLEN, EDWARD-BLACK WOR 347 1ST E DI
ALLEN, ELI PRI 120 PISCATAW
ALLEN, ELIEL BAL 124 16TH WAR
ALLEN, ELIJAH PRI 098 SPALDING
ALLEN, ELIZA BAL 330 1ST DIST
ALLEN, ELIZA BAL 116 11TH WAR
ALLEN, ELIZABETH BAL 219 17TH WAR
ALLEN, ELIZABETH BAL 381 13TH WAR
ALLEN, ELIZABETH BAL 410 1ST DIST
ALLEN, ELIZABETH BAL 236 6TH WARD
ALLEN, ELIZABETH BAL 031 1ST WARD
ALLEN, ELIZABETH BAL 047 15TH WAR
ALLEN, ELIZABETH WOR 324 1ST E DI
ALLEN, ELIZABETH T. TAL 009 EASTON D
ALLEN, ELLEN ALL 249 CUMBERLA
ALLEN, ELLEN BAL 031 4TH WARD
ALLEN, EMILY CEC 014 ELKTON 3
ALLEN, EMILY BAL 126 2ND DIST
ALLEN, ETHAN BAL 241 1ST DIST
ALLEN, F. BAL 151 1ST WARD
ALLEN, F. BAL 160 1ST WARD
ALLEN, FANNY BAL 355 13TH WAR
ALLEN, FREDERICK ALL 173 7TH E.D.
ALLEN, FREEBORN SOM 484 TRAPP DI
ALLEN, GATTY WOR 292 9TH E DI
ALLEN, GEORGE PRI 076 MARLBROU
ALLEN, GEORGE BAL 373 1ST DIST
ALLEN, GEORGE BAL 315 12TH WAR
ALLEN, GEORGE CAR 275 7TH DIST
ALLEN, GEORGE CAL 017 1ST DIST
ALLEN, GEORGE F. BAL 023 1ST WARD
ALLEN, GEORGE S. BAL 234 6TH WARD
ALLEN, GEORGE W. ANN 285 ANNAPOLI
ALLEN, GOERGE E. PRI 098 SPALDING
ALLEN, HARIETT ANN 397 8TH DIST
ALLEN, HARRIET BAL 109 15TH WAR
ALLEN, HARRY DOR 458 1ST DIST
ALLEN, HAZEL ANN 349 3RD DIST
ALLEN, HENRIETTA-MULATTO CAR 138 NO TWP L
ALLEN, HENRY TAL 009 EASTON D
ALLEN, HENRY SOM 467 HANGARY
ALLEN, HENRY A. BAL 313 20TH WAR
ALLEN, HESTER CEC 008 ELKTON 3
ALLEN, HETLY CEC 135 6TH E DI
ALLEN, HIRAM BAL 041 9TH WARD
ALLEN, HUDRON BAL 126 2ND DIST
ALLEN, ISAAC BAL 015 1ST WARD

Name	County	Page	District
ALLEN, J.	BAL	167	1ST WARD
ALLEN, J. H.	BAL	101	10TH WAR
ALLEN, J.H.	WAS	139	HAGERSTO
ALLEN, JACOB	CEC	133	6TH E DI
ALLEN, JAMES	HAR	044	1ST DIST
ALLEN, JAMES	CEC	054	1ST E DI
ALLEN, JAMES	WAS	140	HAGERSTO
ALLEN, JAMES	WOR	315	2ND E DI
ALLEN, JAMES	WAS	002	WILLIAMS
ALLEN, JAMES	PRI	089	SPALDING
ALLEN, JAMES	PRI	097	SPALDING
ALLEN, JAMES	BAL	027	9TH WARD
ALLEN, JAMES	BAL	139	2ND DIST
ALLEN, JAMES	BAL	340	7TH WARD
ALLEN, JAMES	BAL	255	6TH WARD
ALLEN, JAMES B.	KEN	226	2ND DIST
ALLEN, JAMES W.	BAL	083	18TH WAR
ALLEN, JAMES W.	ANN	400	8TH DIST
ALLEN, JANE	BAL	320	7TH WARD
ALLEN, JANE	ANN	452	HOWARD O
ALLEN, JANE	BAL	295	1ST DIST
ALLEN, JANE	BAL	030	4TH WARD
ALLEN, JANE	CAL	054	3RD DIST
ALLEN, JEREMIAH	BAL	343	13TH WAR
ALLEN, JEREMIAH	BAL	185	6TH WARD
ALLEN, JOHN	BAL	165	1ST WARD
ALLEN, JOHN	BAL	120	1ST WARD
ALLEN, JOHN	BAL	012	9TH WARD
ALLEN, JOHN	ALL	196	CUMBERLA
ALLEN, JOHN	ANN	289	ANNAPOLI
ALLEN, JOHN	ALL	107	5TH E.D.
ALLEN, JOHN	BAL	282	2ND WARD
ALLEN, JOHN	BAL	144	16TH WAR
ALLEN, JOHN	BAL	363	1ST DIST
ALLEN, JCHN	CAR	141	NO TWP L
ALLEN, JOHN	BAL	454	14TH WAR
ALLEN, JOHN	CAR	097	NO TWP L
ALLEN, JOHN	CAR	281	7TH DIST
ALLEN, JOHN	BAL	078	18TH WAR
ALLEN, JOHN	BAL	303	17TH WAR
ALLEN, JOHN	BAL	271	20TH WAR
ALLEN, JOHN	PRI	099	SPALDING
ALLEN, JOHN	SOM	359	BRINKLEY
ALLEN, JOHN C.	BAL	051	9TH WARD
ALLEN, JOHN E.	BAL	292	3RD WARD
ALLEN, JOHN H.	TAL	039	EASTON O
ALLEN, JOHN L.	CAR	368	9TH DIST
ALLEN, JOHN W.	BAL	123	16TH WAR
ALLEN, JOHN W.	BAL	235	6TH WARD
ALLEN, JOHN-BLACK	WOR	322	1ST E DI
ALLEN, JOHN-MULATTO	QUE	160	2ND E DI
ALLEN, JOSEPH	PRI	013	BLADENSB
ALLEN, JOSEPH	BAL	158	16TH WAR
ALLEN, JOSEPH	BAL	128	1ST WARD
ALLEN, JUGH	BAL	308	20TH WAR
ALLEN, KETTA	HAR	156	3RD DIST
ALLEN, LETITIA R.	BAL	060	10TH WAR
ALLEN, LEVIN	CAR	146	NO TWP L
ALLEN, LEVIN	SOM	553	TYASKIN
ALLEN, LEVIN	WOR	292	9TH E DI
ALLEN, LEVIN-BLACK	WOR	336	1ST E DI
ALLEN, LEWIS	BAL	110	2ND DIST
ALLEN, LITTLETON	WOR	257	1ST CENS
ALLEN, LOUIS	BAL	325	1ST DIST
ALLEN, LYDIA	ANN	379	4TH DIST
ALLEN, MAJOR-BLACK	WOR	347	1ST E DI
ALLEN, MANUEL	SOM	467	HANGARY
ALLEN, MARGARET	SOM	533	QUANTICO
ALLEN, MARGARET	BAL	103	10TH WAR
ALLEN, MARGARET	BAL	172	6TH WARD
ALLEN, MARGARET	BAL	242	12TH WAR
ALLEN, MARGARETT	BAL	131	18TH WAR
ALLEN, MARIA	BAL	212	17TH WAR
ALLEN, MARTHA	BAL	403	14TH WAR
ALLEN, MARTHA	BAL	095	18TH WAR
ALLEN, MARTHA	CEC	196	6TH E DI
ALLEN, MARTIN	KEN	231	2ND DIST
ALLEN, MARY	BAL	131	5TH WARD
ALLEN, MARY	BAL	201	2ND WARD
ALLEN, MARY	ANN	324	2ND DIST
ALLEN, MARY	PRI	099	SPALDING
ALLEN, MARY	SOM	471	TRAPPE O
ALLEN, MARY A.	FRE	379	PETERSVI
ALLEN, MARY J.	SOM	478	TRAPP DI
ALLEN, MARY L.	BAL	058	18TH WAR
ALLEN, MERVIN	BAL	446	14TH WAR
ALLEN, MICHE	BAL	373	1ST DIST
ALLEN, MICHEL	BAL	268	7TH WARD
ALLEN, MINTY	CAL	051	3RD DIST
ALLEN, NANCY	BAL	351	1ST DIST
ALLEN, NANCY	PRI	103	SPALDING
ALLEN, NANCY	QUE	229	4TH E DI
ALLEN, NANNY	TAL	073	EASTON T
ALLEN, NATHANIEL	BAL	089	15TH WAR
ALLEN, NELSON-BLACK	CAR	111	NO TWP L
ALLEN, P.	BAL	332	1ST DIST
ALLEN, PHEBE	BAL	289	3RD WARD
ALLEN, PHILIP	BAL	325	1ST DIST
ALLEN, POLLY	MGM	363	BERRYS D
ALLEN, PRICILLA	BAL	379	8TH WARD
ALLEN, PRISCILLA	BAL	011	1ST WARD
ALLEN, PRISSY	DOR	417	1ST DIST
ALLEN, R. W.	BAL	039	4TH WARD
ALLEN, RACHEL	BAL	271	12TH WAR
ALLEN, REBECCA	BAL	072	10TH WAR
ALLEN, REBECCA	CEC	181	7TH E DI
ALLEN, REUBEN	MGM	404	ROCKERLE
ALLEN, ROBERT	CEC	200	7TH E DI
ALLEN, ROBERT	BAL	139	1ST WARD
ALLEN, ROBERT H.	BAL	180	2ND WARD
ALLEN, ROBERT T.	KEN	224	2ND DIST
ALLEN, SALLY	BAL	264	12TH WAR
ALLEN, SAMUEL	BAL	334	3RD WARD
ALLEN, SAMUEL	BAL	008	EASTERN
ALLEN, SAMUEL	FRE	042	FREDERIC
ALLEN, SAMUEL	CEC	044	CHESAPEA
ALLEN, SAMUEL	PRI	098	SPALDING
ALLEN, SAMUEL	PRI	098	SPALDING
ALLEN, SARAH	MGM	376	ROCKERLE
ALLEN, SARAH	ALL	255	CUMBERLA
ALLEN, SARAH	BAL	421	8TH WARD
ALLEN, SARAH	BAL	277	7TH WARD
ALLEN, SARAH G.	BAL	222	6TH WARD
ALLEN, SARAH J.	BAL	115	15TH WAR
ALLEN, SOLOMON	BAL	099	15TH WAR
ALLEN, STEPHEN	BAL	178	6TH WARD
ALLEN, SUSAN	QUE	250	5TH E DI
ALLEN, SUSANNAH	CEC	200	7TH E DI
ALLEN, SYLVESTER	BAL	101	10TH WAR
ALLEN, THADDEUS	FRE	048	FREDERIC
ALLEN, THOMAS	FRE	380	PETERSVI
ALLEN, THOMAS	BAL	155	1ST WARD
ALLEN, THOMAS	BAL	127	1ST WARD
ALLEN, THOMAS	ALL	224	CUMBERLA
ALLEN, THOMAS	BAL	295	3RD WARD
ALLEN, THOMAS	WAS	011	WILLIAMS
ALLEN, THOMAS	WAS	122	HAGERSTO
ALLEN, THOMAS S.	BAL	219	17TH WAR
ALLEN, THOMS	BAL	128	1ST WARD
ALLEN, WALTER	PRI	120	PISCATAW
ALLEN, WAPPING	BAL	222	1ST DIST
ALLEN, WILLAIM	PRI	098	SPALDING
ALLEN, WILLIAM	PRI	089	SPALDING
ALLEN, WILLIAM	QUE	246	5TH E DI
ALLEN, WILLIAM	BAL	123	1ST WARD
ALLEN, WILLIAM	BAL	129	2ND DIST
ALLEN, WILLIAM	ALL	260	CUMBERLA
ALLEN, WILLIAM	ANN	456	HOWARD O
ALLEN, WILLIAM	ANN	422	HOWARD O
ALLEN, WILLIAM	BAL	147	1ST WARD
ALLEN, WILLIAM	BAL	241	6TH WARD
ALLEN, WILLIAM	BAL	162	1ST WARD
ALLEN, WILLIAM	BAL	219	12TH WAR
ALLEN, WILLIAM	ANN	329	2ND DIST
ALLEN, WILLIAM	BAL	380	13TH WAR
ALLEN, WILLIAM	BAL	074	4TH WARD
ALLEN, WILLIAM	HAR	006	1ST DIST
ALLEN, WILLIAM	BAL	195	19TH WAR
ALLEN, WILLIAM	HAR	179	3RD DIST
ALLEN, WILLIAM	BAL	058	18TH WAR
ALLEN, WILLIAM	BAL	069	18TH WAR
ALLEN, WILLIAM H.	DOR	378	1ST DIST
ALLEN, WILLIAM H.	BAL	016	15TH WAR
ALLEN, WILLIAM M.	BAL	068	15TH WAR
ALLEN, WILLIAM M.	BAL	172	6TH WARD
ALLEN, WILLIAM W.	MGM	374	ROCKERLE
ALLEN, MARTHA	QUE	153	1ST E DI
ALLENBAUGH, JOHN O.	BAL	426	1ST DIST
ALLENBOCH, MERCY	BAL	280	12TH WAR
ALLENDER, ACHSALE	HAR	086	2ND DIST
ALLENDER, ELIZABETH	HAR	099	2ND DIST
ALLENDER, JAMES	BAL	095	2ND DIST
ALLENDER, JOHN	WAS	237	CAVETOWN
ALLENDER, JOSHUA	BAL	104	5TH WARD
ALLENDER, LORNIA	BAL	114	2ND DIST
ALLENDER, MARTHA	HAR	134	2ND DIST
ALLENDER, MARY	BAL	253	6TH WARD
ALLENDER, NICKOLAS	BAL	095	2ND DIST
ALLENDER, REBECCA	BAL	242	1ST DIST
ALLENDER, SUSAN E.	HAR	206	3RD DIST
ALLENDER, WILLIAM	BAL	242	1ST DIST
ALLENDER, WILLIAM	BAL	030	2ND DIST
ALLENS, ANDREW	BAL	041	1ST WARD
ALLENS, EVE	BAL	048	9TH WARD
ALLENS, ROBERT	BAL	003	18TH WAR
ALLENSWORTH, JAMES	BAL	159	1ST WARD
ALLER, JOHN A.	BAL	226	17TH WAR
ALLERMAN, WILLIAM	BAL	417	8TH WARD
ALLERS, CLOS.	ANN	419	HOWARD O
ALLERSON, ROBERT	CAL	013	1ST DIST
ALLERSON, WILLIAM S.	MGM	391	ROCKERLE
ALLEY, JAMES	BAL	160	1ST WARD
ALLEY, JOHN	QUE	124	1ST E DI
ALLEY, MARY W.	KEN	290	3RD DIST
ALLGOOD, SARAH E.-BLACK	BAL	217	2ND WARD
ALLICE, FRANCIS	BAL	291	17TH WAR
ALLICE, GEORGE	BAL	277	2ND WARD
ALLICE, TEMPERANCE	BAL	127	18TH WAR
ALLIE, WILLIAM	ALL	223	CUMBERLA
ALLIGOOD, WILLIAM	SOM	477	TRAPP DI
ALLIN, JOHN	ANN	280	ANNAPOLI
ALLIN, WILLIAM	HAR	005	1ST DIST
ALLISE, WILLIAM	BAL	008	9TH WARD
ALLISON, ANDREW	CEC	214	7TH E DI
ALLISON, ANN T.	BAL	011	4TH WARD
ALLISON, ANNA	BAL	383	1ST DIST
ALLISON, ELIZABETH	BAL	012	2ND DIST
ALLISON, ELIZABETH	BAL	297	20TH WAR
ALLISON, JAMES L.	BAL	406	8TH WARD
ALLISON, JOHN	PRI	109	PISCATAW
ALLISON, JOSEPH	BAL	014	2ND DIST
ALLISON, MATILDA	BAL	087	4TH WARD
ALLISON, ROBERT H.	BAL	360	3RD WARD
ALLISON, SAMUEL	BAL	413	8TH WARD
ALLISON, THOMAS	CAR	400	2ND DIST
ALLISON, WILLIAM	WAS	018	2ND SUBD
ALLISSON, GEORGE	BAL	197	17TH WAR
ALLISSON, ROBERT	FRE	173	5TH E DI
ALLISTON, JAMES H.	ST	317	4TH E DI
ALLITON, ELIZA	KEN	308	3RD DIST
ALLKETON, CHARLES	CHA	278	BOJANTOW
ALLKISE, SOLOMON	ALL	171	7TH E.D.
ALLMACK, GEORGE W.	BAL	135	18TH WAR
ALLMAN, JOHN	BAL	236	6TH WARD
ALLMAN, LEWIS	BAL	144	5TH WARD
ALLMAN, MARY	BAL	049	18TH WAR
ALLMAN, WILLIAM	BAL	430	8TH WARD
ALLNE, ELIZA	BAL	330	13TH WAR
ALLNE, ELIZABETH	BAL	319	12TH WAR
ALLNE, MARTHA	FRE	379	PETERSVI
ALLNE, SAMUE	WOR	292	9TH E DI
ALLNUT, ANN	CAL	052	3RD DIST
ALLNUTT, ADEN D.	MGM	324	CRACKLIN
ALLNUTT, BENONI	MGM	408	MEDLEY 3
ALLNUTT, GIDEON	CAL	036	2ND DIST
ALLNUTT, JOHN	MGM	324	CRACKLIN
ALLNUTT, MARGARET S.	BAL	114	15TH WAR
ALLNUTT, MARY M.	FRE	234	BUCKEYST
ALLNUTT, REBECCA F.	CAL	023	2ND DIST
ALLNUTT, WILLIAM P.	FRE	220	BUCKEYST
ALLOWAY, SUSAN	BAL	196	19TH WAR
ALLRICH, RODRICH	BAL	338	1ST DIST
ALLRICKER, JOHN	BAL	200	11TH WAR
ALLRIDGE, EMILY	BAL	010	18TH WAR
ALLRIDGE, JOHN	BAL	118	18TH WAR
ALLRUTT, JAMES J.	CAL	052	3RD DIST
ALLS, WILLIAM	CAR	068	NO TWP L
ALLSION, CHARLES N.	MGM	409	MEDLEY 3
ALLSION, SARAH T.	MGM	408	MEDLEY 3
ALLSTAN, JOHN J.	ST	318	4TH E DI
ALLSTAN, W ILLIAM	ST	318	4TH E DI
ALLSTON, L.JACKSON	ST	315	4TH E DI
ALLSUP, ELIZABETH	CAL	060	3RD DIST
ALLSUP, HEZEKIAH	WAS	227	1ST DIST
ALLSUP, JAMES	WAS	167	1ST DIST
ALLSUP, JOSEPH	WAS	227	1ST DIST
ALLWAYS, REACHEL	BAL	008	18TH WAR
ALLWELL, JOHN N.	BAL	350	7TH WARD
ALLWELL, STEPHEN D.	BAL	409	3RD WARD
ALLWINE, RICHARD	BAL	279	7TH WARD
ALLWISER, ANDREW	BAL	004	4TH WARD
ALLWOOD, GEORGE	CAR	353	6TH DIST
ALLYGOOD, LEONARD-BLACK	BAL	219	2ND WARD
ALLYN, MARGARET*	BAL	341	3RD WARD
ALMACK, DARBY	BAL	460	1ST DIST
ALMAN, HENRY	BAL	237	12TH WAR
ALMETT, JAMES W.	BAL	257	12TH WAR
ALMOND, WILLIAM	HAR	084	2ND DIST
ALMONEY, ROBERT	HAR	072	1ST DIST
ALMONY, ABRAHAM	HAR	021	1ST DIST
ALMONY, ANDREW B.	CAR	183	8TH DIST
ALMONY, AZARIAH	BAL	037	2ND DIST
ALMONY, BENJAMIN	HAR	021	1ST DIST
ALMONY, BENJAMIN	HAR	072	1ST DIST
ALMONY, ELIJAH	BAL	037	2ND DIST
ALMONY, ELIZABETH	HAR	022	1ST DIST
ALMONY, HERY T.	BAL	038	2ND DIST
ALMONY, JAMES	BAL	036	2ND DIST
ALMONY, JARRET	CAR	183	8TH DIST
ALMONY, JEFFESON	BAL	037	2ND DIST
ALMONY, JOHN G.	HAR	020	1ST DIST
ALMONY, WILLIAM	HAR	021	1ST DIST
ALMONY, WILLIAM	BAL	036	2ND DIST
ALMOT, ELIZABETH *	BAL	303	12TH WAR
ALNATT, NANCY	MGM	324	CRACKLIN
ALNUT, ELLEN	BAL	424	14TH WAR
ALNUTT, LUCUTIA C.	BAL	389	13TH WAR
ALNUTT, SARAH	BAL	104	15TH WAR
ALPHA, MITCHELL	SOM	521	BARREN C
ALRICKS, F. W.	BAL	190	11TH WAR
ALRICKS, LUCUS	KEN	226	2ND DIST
ALSER, DAVID	WAS	134	HAGERSTO
ALSOP, JACOB	WAS	079	2ND SUBD
ALSOP, JOHN	ANN	342	3RD DIST
ALSOP, RICHARD	ANN	405	8TH DIST
ALSOP, RICHARD	ANN	401	8TH DIST
ALSOP, SHARLOT	CAL	006	1ST DIST
ALSTED, AMINA	BAL	303	20TH WAR
ALSTON, JULIA	CHA	257	MIDDLETO
A_SUP, GUSTA	CAL	028	2ND DIST
ALSUP, HOLESWORTH	CAL	044	3RD DIST
ALSUP, ROSE	CAL	025	2ND DIST
ALTAMILLE, HARMON H.	WAS	291	1ST DIST
ALTEFANCK, AMELIA	BAL	067	1ST WARD
ALTEFANCK, FREDERICK	BAL	067	1ST WARD
ALTEN, SOLOMON	BAL	130	11TH WAR
ALTENHOFF, CHARLES	BAL	261	2ND WARD
ALTENMILLER, HENRY	WAS	153	HAGERSTO
ALTER, CATHARINE	WAS	232	1ST DIST
ALTER, FANNY	WAS	022	2ND SUBD
ALTER, JACOB	WAS	029	2ND SUBD
ALTER, JACOB	WAS	029	2ND SUBD
ALTER, ROZIR-MULATTO	FRE	394	PETERSVI
ALTER, SAMUEL	WAS	300	1ST DIST
ALTFEATHER, JACOB	BAL	392	8TH WARD
ALTHER, WILLIAM	BAL	170	2ND DIST
ALTHOFF, JOHN	CAR	301	1ST DIST
ALTHOOF, HENRY	FRE	184	5TH E DI
ALTMAN, JOHN	FRE	347	MIDDLETO
ALTMAN, JOHN	FRE	346	MIDDLETO
ALTON, CATHERINE	BAL	019	4TH WARD
ALTON, EDWARD	CAL	029	2ND DIST
ALTON, LEVRY*	BAL	061	4TH WARD
ALTON, SOPHIA	CAL	025	2ND DIST
ALTONS, CATHARINE E.	BAL	381	1ST DIST
ALTOYER, ELSY	BAL	209	19TH WAR
ALTRITH, CHRISTIAN	BAL	210	17TH WAR
ALTSTAN, ANN J.	ST	318	4TH E DI
ALTVATER, WILLIAM	BAL	294	3RD WARD
ALUBSON, CHARLES	QUE	245	5TH E DI
ALUM, J.	ANN	284	ANNAPOLI
ALVAY, MARY	BAL	002	1ST WARD
ALVERY, SUSAN C.	ST	273	3RD E DI
ALVEY, ANN	ST	330	4TH E DI
ALVEY, BASIL	ST	326	4TH E DI
ALVEY, DOMINICK	ST	342	5TH E DI
ALVEY, DORCAS	ST	332	4TH E DI
ALVEY, GEORGE N.P	ST	343	5TH E DI
ALVEY, JAME SH.	ST	343	5TH E DI
ALVEY, JAMES R.	ST	322	4TH E DI
ALVEY, JOEL	ST	270	3RD E DI
ALVEY, JOHN	PRI	046	AQUASCO
ALVEY, JOSHUA	ST	340	5TH E DI
ALVEY, MARGARET A.	ST	257	3RD E DI
ALVEY, MARY	ST	315	4TH E DI
ALVEY, MR-	BAL	058	15TH WAR
ALVEY, R.H.	WAS	136	HAGERSTO
ALVEY, REBECCA	PRI	006	BLADENSB
ALVEY, S.	BAL	151	1ST WARD
ALVEY, THOMAS	CAL	062	3RD DIST
ALVEY, THOMAS H.	ST	347	5TH E DI
ALVEY, WILLIAM	PRI	085	QUEEN AN
ALVEY, WILLIAM H.	ST	273	3RD E DI
ALVEY, WILLIAM T.	ST	322	4TH E DI
ALWAY, R.H.	WAS	154	HAGERSTO
AMBASH, WILLIAM	BAL	351	13TH WAR
AMBERS, SAMUEL	KEN	307	3RD DIST
AMBERSON, WILLIAM	BAL	415	14TH WAR
AMBRESTER, MARY	BAL	234	6TH WARD
AMBRISTER, CARL	BAL	221	19TH WAR
AMBROSE, ANN	BAL	194	11TH WAR
AMBROSE, CHARLOT	BAL	363	1ST DIST
AMBROSE, ELIZA A.	BAL	234	1ST DIST
AMBROSE, ELIZABETH	BAL	192	5TH DIST
AMBROSE, GEORGE	WAS	218	1ST DIST
AMBROSE, GEORGE W.	BAL	241	1ST DIST
AMBROSE, HENRY	WAS	092	2ND SUBD
AMBROSE, JACOB	FRE	340	MIDDLETO
AMBROSE, JAMES	BAL	241	1ST DIST
AMBROSE, JOHN	ALL	229	CUMBERLA
AMBROSE, JOHN	FRE	373	CATOCTIN
AMBROSE, JOHN T.	BAL	241	1ST DIST
AMBROSE, JOSHUA	BAL	200	5TH DIST
AMBROSE, JULIA A.	FRE	320	MIDDLETO
AMBROSE, MARY	FRE	341	MIDDLETO
AMBROSE, MARY	BAL	284	20TH WAR
AMBROSE, NANCY	FRE	071	FREDERIC
AMBROSE, ROBERT D.	BAL	244	1ST DIST
AMBROSE, ROSEANN	BAL	242	1ST DIST
AMBROSE, SALLY	WAS	155	HAGERSTO
AMBROSE, SARAH	WAS	187	BOONSBOR
AMBROSE, SARAH	WAS	181	BOONSBOR
AMBROSE, ZEAKEL	BAL	416	1ST DIST
AMBROSIA, GRACE A.	BAL	242	6TH WARD
AMBUSH, POLLY	WAS	133	2ND DIST
AMBY, CHARLES	BAL	336	3RD WARD
AMBY, J.	BAL	156	1ST WARD
AMBY, JOSEPH	BAL	005	1ST WARD
AMOUTTON, GEORGE	HAR	152	3RD DIST
AMEAN, LOUISA	BAL	164	11TH WAR

AMECK, WILLIAM	BAL	431	8TH WARD
AMEES, CORBIN	BAL	271	12TH WAR
AMELBURN, ALEXANDER	ST	289	2ND E DI
AMENS, NATHAN	BAL	052	1ST WARD
AMER, MARTIN	BAL	343	7TH WARD
AMER, MARTIN	BAL	222	17TH WAR
AMERICA, ANN	ALL	239	CUMBERLA
AMERICAN, ASHAEL	BAL	228	2ND WARD
AMERY, ELISA	BAL	115	18TH WAR
AMERY, PHILLIP	BAL	116	18TH WAR
AMERY, ROBERT L.	ST	337	4TH E DI
AMERY, WELSEY	BAL	412	14TH WAR
AMES, ANN	BAL	146	11TH WAR
AMES, CROBIN	BAL	146	19TH WAR
AMES, EMMERSON	BAL	079	15TH WAR
AMES, JOHN	BAL	079	15TH WAR
AMES, JOHN H.	BAL	237	12TH WAR
AMES, JOSHUA	BAL	160	19TH WAR
AMES, WILLIAM F.	BAL	245	20TH WAR
AMETION, -----*	BAL	026	4TH WARD
AMETTS, JAMES	HAR	090	2ND DIST
AMEY, GEORGE W.	BAL	116	18TH WAR
AMEY, JANE	BAL	293	12TH WAR
AMEY, JOHN	BAL	049	18TH WAR
AMEY, JOHN H.	BAL	234	12TH WAR
AMEY, MARY	BAL	152	11TH WAR
AMEY, PHIL	BAL	266	20TH WAR
AMEY, SAMUEL	BAL	109	18TH WAR
AMEY, SAMUEL	BAL	120	16TH WAR
AMEY, SARAH	BAL	285	20TH WAR
AMEY, TOBIAS	BAL	263	20TH WAR
AMEY, WILLIAM	BAL	292	17TH WAR
AMGNN, WILLIAM *	BAL	273	20TH WAR
AMICK, ELIZABETH	BAL	431	8TH WARD
AMILL, PETER	BAL	459	8TH WARD
AMINIE, JOHN*	SOM	364	BRINKLEY
AMINIE, NANCY*	SOM	364	BRINKLEY
AMLBRON, WILLIAM	BAL	301	12TH WAR
AMLIE, P. C.	BAL	218	12TH WAR
AMLKER, ELIZABETH	BAL	201	11TH WAR
AMMIKHOUSE, MALVINA	ALL	216	CUMBERLA
AMMIKHOUSE, MARY C.	ALL	216	CUMBERLA
AMMCND, GEORGE	BAL	361	13TH WAR
AMMCNS, GEORGE	CAR	065	NO TWP L
AMOM, GEORGE	BAL	211	17TH WAR
AMON, JAMES	BAL	168	2ND DIST
AMON, VALENTINE	BAL	225	2ND WARD
AMONS, ROBERT	HAR	039	1ST DIST
AMORY, RICHARD	BAL	058	2ND DIST
AMOS, ABRAHAM	HAR	066	1ST DIST
AMOS, ABRAHAM R.	HAR	064	1ST DIST
AMOS, ALEXANDER R.	HAR	049	1ST DIST
AMOS, AMANCA	BAL	437	1ST DIST
AMOS, ANN	HAR	067	1ST DIST
AMOS, AQUILA	BAL	072	18TH WAR
AMOS, BENJAMIN	HAR	009	1ST DIST
AMOS, BENJAMIN F.	BAL	450	8TH WARD
AMOS, BENJAMIN S.	HAR	050	1ST DIST
AMOS, CATHARINE	BAL	353	7TH WARD
AMOS, CHARLES	BAL	001	9TH WARD
AMOS, CHARLES	BAL	423	8TH WARD
AMOS, CHARLES	BAL	093	18TH WAR
AMOS, CHARLES H.	BAL	069	2ND DIST
AMOS, DANIEL	HAR	058	1ST DIST
AMOS, EDWARD	HAR	023	1ST DIST
AMOS, EDWARD	BAL	396	8TH WARD
AMOS, ELIZA	BAL	150	11TH WAR
AMOS, ELIZABETH	HAR	064	1ST DIST
AMOS, ELIZABETH	BAL	069	18TH WAR
AMOS, ELIZABETH	BAL	357	13TH WAR
AMOS, ELLEN	BAL	043	4TH WARD
AMOS, ELLIN	HAR	068	1ST DIST
AMOS, ELNORA	BAL	214	11TH WAR
AMOS, FREDERICK T.	HAR	047	1ST DIST
AMOS, GEORGE	HAR	048	1ST DIST
AMOS, GEORGE R.	HAR	139	2ND DIST
AMOS, HARRIET	BAL	250	12TH WAR
AMOS, HARRIET	BAL	248	1ST DIST
AMOS, HARRIETT	HAR	095	2ND DIST
AMOS, HENRY	HAR	058	1ST DIST
AMOS, HORACE	HAR	095	2ND DIST
AMOS, ISAAC	HAR	018	1ST DIST
AMOS, JAMES	HAR	066	1ST DIST
AMOS, JAMES	BAL	058	2ND DIST
AMOS, JAMES	BAL	312	3RD WARD
AMOS, JAMES	BAL	112	5TH WARD
AMOS, JAMES A.	HAR	094	2ND DIST
AMOS, JESSE J.	BAL	182	6TH WARD
AMOS, JOHN	BAL	040	4TH WARD
AMOS, JOHN A.	HAR	025	1ST DIST
AMOS, JOHN T.	HAR	062	1ST DIST
AMOS, JOHN T.	HAR	065	1ST DIST
AMOS, JOSEPH	BAL	271	20TH WAR
AMOS, JOSHUA	HAR	058	1ST DIST
AMOS, JOSHUA	BAL	027	2ND DIST
AMOS, JOSHUA M.	HAR	069	1ST DIST
AMOS, JULIA A.	BAL	402	8TH WARD
AMOS, LEMUEL	BAL	114	5TH WARD
AMOS, LEMUEL L.	HAR	140	2ND DIST
AMOS, LUTHER	BAL	213	6TH DIST
AMOS, LYDIA	BAL	039	4TH WARD
AMOS, MARTHA	HAR	058	1ST DIST
AMOS, MARTHA	HAR	062	1ST DIST
AMOS, MARY	BAL	049	9TH WARD
AMOS, MARY C.	HAR	048	1ST DIST
AMOS, MARY Q.	ALL	041	2ND E.D.
AMOS, MILTON	BAL	163	16TH WAR
AMOS, MRS.	BAL	114	5TH WARD
AMOS, OLIVER H.	HAR	078	2ND DIST
AMOS, PETER	BAL	077	1ST WARD
AMOS, PETER	BAL	353	3RD WARD
AMOS, PRISCILLA	HAR	095	2ND DIST
AMOS, RACHELL	BAL	154	5TH WARD
AMOS, REBECCA	BAL	200	6TH WARD
AMOS, REBECCA	BAL	364	8TH WARD
AMCS, ROBERT	HAR	087	2ND DIST
AMCS, ROBERT	BAL	214	11TH WAR
AMOS, SAMUEL	HAR	051	1ST DIST
AMOS, SAMUEL	HAR	051	1ST DIST
AMOS, SARAH	HAR	011	1ST DIST
AMOS, SUSAN	BAL	047	4TH WARD
AMOS, SUSAN	BAL	256	6TH WARD
AMOS, SUSANNA	HAR	070	1ST DIST
AMOS, WILLAIM	BAL	114	5TH WARD
AMOS, WILLIAM	BAL	160	2ND DIST
AMOS, WILLIAM	ALL	068	5TH E.D.
AMOS, WILLIAM	HAR	082	2ND DIST
AMOS, WILLIAM	HAR	025	1ST DIST
AMOS, WILLIAM	HAR	023	1ST DIST
AMOS, WILLIAM	HAR	018	1ST DIST
AMOS, WILLIAM	HAR	018	1ST DIST
AMOS, WILLIAM Y.	BAL	069	2ND DIST
AMOS,ARTHUR P.	BAL	074	2ND DIST
AMOS,FRANCIS	BAL	057	2ND DIST
AMOSS, WILLIAM L.	HAR	078	2ND DIST
AMOUR, HUGH	CEC	212	7TH E DI
AMOUS, DAVIS	BAL	092	2ND DIST
AMPRUSTY, REGANA	BAL	440	8TH WARD
AMPSTADDT, JACOB	MGM	437	CLARKSTR
AMREIN, GEORGE*	BAL	091	10TH WAR
AMSER, JACOB	FRE	159	EMMITTSB
AMY, HARRIET	BAL	213	19TH WAR
AMYLING, HENRY	BAL	010	9TH WARD
ANABA, ELLEN	WAS	127	HAGERSTO
ANABA, WILLIAM T.	WAS	281	LEITERSB
ANABY, ELIZABETH	WAS	126	HAGERSTO
ANABY, ISAIAH	WAS	126	HAGERSTO
ANADELL, WILLIAMD	ST	296	2ND E DI
ANCHER, MARY M.	BAL	389	8TH WARD
ANCHISE, ALEXANDER *	BAL	301	12TH WAR
ANCHOR, EDWARD	ANN	488	HOWARD D
ANCHOR, FRANCIS	BAL	198	6TH WARD
ANCHORS, ASCENATH	MGM	336	CRACKLIN
ANCHPASLER, MARY	BAL	438	14TH WAR
AND, ASA	MGM	411	MEDLEY 3
ANDAZO, ACHILLE	BAL	402	1ST DIST
ANDEN, HARRIET	CEC	032	CHESAPEA
ANDER, MARGARET*	TAL	031	EASTON D
ANDER, WILLIAM	CEC	032	CHESAPEA
ANDEROSN, BENJAMIN	QUE	235	4TH E DI
ANDERS, ABRAHAM	FRE	295	WOODSBOR
ANDERS, CORDELIA	BAL	362	1ST DIST
ANDERS, ELIZABETH	CAR	321	1ST DIST
ANDERS, GEORGE	FRE	296	WOODSBOR
ANDERS, GEORGE	FRE	233	BUCKEYST
ANDERS, HENRY	FRE	295	WOODSBOR
ANDERS, HERBERT	CAR	304	1ST DIST
ANDERS, JACOB	FRE	297	WOODSBOR
ANDERS, JESSE	CAR	382	2ND DIST
ANDERS, JOHN	CAR	325	1ST DIST
ANDERS, JOHN	FRE	294	WOODSBOR
ANDERS, JOHN	FRE	290	WOODSBOR
ANDERS, JOHN	HAR	135	2ND DIST
ANDERS, JOSHUA	CAR	325	1ST DIST
ANDERS, LUCENDA A.	FRE	281	WOODSBOR
ANDERS, LYDIA	CAR	236	UNION TO
ANDERS, MARY	FRE	280	WOODSBOR
ANDERS, MOSES	FRE	295	WOODSBOR
ANDERS, SAMUEL	CAR	317	1ST DIST
ANDERS, SAMUEL	CAR	383	2ND DIST
ANDERS, SARAH	CAR	413	2ND DIST
ANDERS, THOMAS	FRE	310	WOODSBOR
ANDERS, WILLIAM	FRE	139	CREAGERS
ANDERS, WILLIAM	FRE	139	CREAGERS
ANDERSN, R.	BAL	218	12TH WAR
ANDERSNO, ELIZA	BAL	424	14TH WAR
ANDERSNO, J.	BAL	154	1ST WARD
ANDERSON, A.	BAL	157	1ST WARD
ANDERSON, A.	BAL	148	1ST WARD
ANDERSON, A.	BAL	333	1ST DIST
ANDERSON, A.	BAL	139	1ST WARD
ANDERSON, A.B.	BAL	047	2ND DIST
ANDERSON, ABRAHAM	BAL	020	15TH WAR
ANDERSON, ABRAHAM	KEN	301	3RD DIST
ANDERSON, ABRAM	CEC	023	ELKTON 3
ANDERSON, ABSOLAM	ANN	328	2ND DIST
ANDERSON, ADAM	BAL	051	4TH WARD
ANDERSON, ADAM	SOM	452	DAMES QU
ANDERSON, ADAM *	FRE	270	NEW MARK
ANDERSON, ADELE	ANN	343	3RD DIST
ANDERSON, ADELINE M.	ST	320	4TH E DI
ANDERSON, AGNES	BAL	188	6TH WARD
ANDERSON, ALEXANDER	TAL	097	ST MICHA
ANDERSON, ALEXEAN	BAL	370	1ST DIST
ANDERSON, ALICE	CEC	085	5TH E DI
ANDERSON, ALLEN	CEC	146	PORT DUP
ANDERSON, AMANDA	BAL	454	1ST DIST
ANDERSON, AMOS	BAL	116	2ND DIST
ANDERSON, AMOS	BAL	118	2ND DIST
ANDERSON, AMOS	HAR	165	3RD DIST
ANDERSON, AMOS	QUE	235	4TH E DI
ANDERSON, AMRY	CAL	008	1ST DIST
ANDERSON, ANDREW	BAL	059	15TH WAR
ANDERSON, ANDREW	BAL	120	1ST WARD
ANDERSON, ANDREW T.	BAL	433	1ST DIST
ANDERSON, ANDREW W.	SOM	554	TYASKIN
ANDERSON, ANN	DOR	464	1ST DIST
ANDERSON, ANN	KEN	297	3RD DIST
ANDERSON, ANN	BAL	186	11TH WAR
ANDERSON, ANN	BAL	400	8TH WARD
ANDERSON, ANN	BAL	402	14TH WAR
ANDERSON, ANN	BAL	348	13TH WAR
ANDERSON, ANN	CEC	019	ELKTON 3
ANDERSON, ANN	HAR	056	1ST DIST
ANDERSON, ANN J.	FRE	204	BUCKEYST
ANDERSON, ANNA	BAL	220	6TH WARD
ANDERSON, ANNIE	BAL	352	3RD WARD
ANDERSON, BARBARA	BAL	003	1ST WARD
ANDERSON, BASEL	ALL	109	5TH E.D.
ANDERSON, BENJAMIN	HAR	065	1ST DIST
ANDERSON, BENJAMIN	BAL	395	14TH WAR
ANDERSON, BENJAMIN G.	HAR	017	1ST DIST
ANDERSON, BENJAMIN-BLACK	QUE	167	2ND E DI
ANDERSON, C. D.	BAL	282	2ND WARD
ANDERSON, CAROLINE	BAL	148	11TH WAR
ANDERSON, CATHARINE	BAL	335	13TH WAR
ANDERSON, CATHARINE	BAL	214	11TH WAR
ANDERSON, CATHARINE	BAL	377	1ST DIST
ANDERSON, CATHARINE	BAL	463	1ST DIST
ANDERSON, CATHERINE	BAL	143	11TH WAR
ANDERSON, CELESTE	BAL	160	19TH WAR
ANDERSON, CELIA	BAL	318	12TH WAR
ANDERSON, CHARLES	BAL	093	5TH WARD
ANDERSON, CHARLES	ANN	300	1ST DIST
ANDERSON, CHARLES	ANN	364	4TH DIST
ANDERSON, CHARLES	BAL	145	1ST WARD
ANDERSON, CHARLES	BAL	167	1ST WARD
ANDERSON, CHARLES	BAL	324	7TH WARD
ANDERSON, CHARLES	BAL	125	11TH WAR
ANDERSON, CHARLES	BAL	407	14TH WAR
ANDERSON, CHARLES	ST	334	4TH E DI
ANDERSON, CHARLES	QUE	223	4TH E DI
ANDERSON, CHARLES H.	QUE	190	3RD E DI
ANDERSON, CHARLES H.	MGM	368	BERRYS D
ANDERSON, CHARLES T.	MGM	437	CLARKSTR
ANDERSON, CHARLOTT	KEN	301	3RD DIST
ANDERSON, CHARLOTTE	BAL	154	11TH WAR
ANDERSON, CHRISTIAN	BAL	241	1ST DIST
ANDERSON, CLARA	TAL	036	EASTON D
ANDERSON, CLARE	BAL	212	11TH WAR
ANDERSON, CLINTON	BAL	197	11TH WAR
ANDERSON, CURTIS	DOR	374	1ST DIST
ANDERSON, DANIEL	HAR	131	2ND DIST
ANDERSON, DANIEL	KEN	212	2ND DIST
ANDERSON, DANIEL	BAL	155	5TH WARD
ANDERSON, DAVID	BAL	118	1ST WARD
ANDERSON, DAVID	ALL	090	5TH E.D.
ANDERSON, DAVID	BAL	126	16TH WAR
ANDERSON, DAVID	HAR	095	2ND DIST
ANDERSON, DAVID	CEC	043	CHESAPEA
ANDERSON, DAVID	WAS	102	2ND DIST
ANDERSON, DAVID	SOM	433	PRINCESS
ANDERSON, DEBORAH	CEC	065	1ST E DI
ANDERSON, DOROTHY	BAL	434	14TH WAR
ANDERSON, EDWARD	BAL	359	13TH WAR
ANDERSON, EDWARD	ANN	381	4TH DIST
ANDERSON, EDWARD	ANN	472	HOWARD D
ANDERSON, EDWIN	SOM	554	TYASKIN
ANDERSON, ELIJAH	BAL	428	14TH WAR
ANDERSON, ELIJAH	BAL	337	13TH WAR
ANDERSON, ELIJAH	CEC	140	6TH E DI
ANDERSON, ELIS	BAL	460	1ST DIST
ANDERSON, ELIZA	ANN	331	2ND DIST
ANDERSON, ELIZA	BAL	116	5TH WARD
ANDERSON, ELIZA	BAL	168	6TH WARD
ANDERSON, ELIZA	CEC	040	CHESAPEA
ANDERSON, ELIZA	CAR	195	4TH DIST
ANDERSON, ELIZA A.	BAL	138	11TH WAR
ANDERSON, ELIZABEH	QUE	238	5TH E DI
ANDERSON, ELIZABETH	HAR	109	2ND DIST
ANDERSON, ELIZABETH	HAR	031	1ST DIST
ANDERSON, ELIZABETH	KEN	220	2ND DIST
ANDERSON, ELIZABETH	BAL	416	1ST DIST
ANDERSON, ELIZABETH	BAL	424	1ST DIST
ANDERSON, ELIZABETH	ALL	114	5TH E.D.
ANDERSON, ELIZABETH	BAL	282	12TH WAR
ANDERSON, ELIZABETH	BAL	002	1ST WARD
ANDERSON, ELTON S.	SOM	472	TRAPPE D
ANDERSON, EMANUEL	BAL	353	3RD WARD
ANDERSON, EMILY	BAL	268	12TH WAR
ANDERSON, EMMA	BAL	182	11TH WAR
ANDERSON, EMORY	BAL	005	1ST WARD
ANDERSON, ERASTIS	CAR	098	NO TWP L
ANDERSON, ESTER	BAL	120	5TH WARD
ANDERSON, EVAN T.	MGM	437	CLARKSTR
ANDERSON, FRANCIS	PRI	041	VANSVILL
ANDERSON, FRANCIS	KEN	230	2ND DIST
ANDERSON, FRANCIS D.	HAR	116	2ND DIST
ANDERSON, FRANK-BLACK	QUE	165	2ND E DI
ANDERSON, FRANKLIN	BAL	233	1ST DIST
ANDERSON, GEORGE	BAL	351	1ST DIST
ANDERSON, GEORGE	BAL	265	12TH WAR
ANDERSON, GEORGE	BAL	159	1ST WARD
ANDERSON, GEORGE	ANN	422	HOWARD D
ANDERSON, GEORGE	BAL	279	2ND WARD
ANDERSON, GEORGE	KEN	297	3RD DIST
ANDERSON, GEORGE	QUE	207	3RD E DI
ANDERSON, GEORGE	KEN	259	1ST DIST
ANDERSON, GEORGE	HAR	119	2ND DIST
ANDERSON, GEORGE	HAR	159	3RD DIST
ANDERSON, GEORGE	KEN	246	2ND DIST
ANDERSON, GEORGE	FRE	243	NEW MARK
ANDERSON, GEORGE L.	BAL	447	1ST DIST
ANDERSON, GILLETT	SOM	469	TRAPPE D
ANDERSON, HANEY	BAL	229	12TH WAR
ANDERSON, HANNAH	HAR	095	2ND DIST
ANDERSON, HANNAH A.	BAL	239	5TH WARD
ANDERSON, HARIET	SOM	472	TRAPPE D
ANDERSON, HARRIET	KEN	215	2ND DIST
ANDERSON, HARRIET	CEC	028	CHESAPEA
ANDERSON, HARRIET	FRE	418	8TH E DI
ANDERSON, HARRIET A.	ANN	452	HOWARD D
ANDERSON, HENRY	BAL	223	12TH WAR
ANDERSON, HENRY	BAL	025	15TH WAR
ANDERSON, HENRY	ANN	331	2ND DIST
ANDERSON, HENRY	BAL	240	1ST DIST
ANDERSON, HENRY	CEC	024	ELKTON 3
ANDERSON, HENRY	SOM	452	DAMES QU
ANDERSON, HENRY	ST	340	5TH E DI
ANDERSON, HENRY M.	MGM	424	MEDLEY 3
ANDERSON, HENSON	BAL	205	11TH WAR
ANDERSON, HERIGON	CEC	066	1ST E DI
ANDERSON, HESTER A.	ANN	356	3RD DIST
ANDERSON, HETTA	CAL	016	1ST DIST
ANDERSON, HORACE	BAL	027	2ND DIST
ANDERSON, HORACE	ALL	182	8TH E.D.
ANDERSON, IRA	BAL	045	2ND DIST
ANDERSON, ISAAC	BAL	010	EASTERN
ANDERSON, ISAAC	BAL	206	6TH DIST
ANDERSON, ISAAC	KEN	215	2ND DIST
ANDERSON, ISAAC	SOM	453	DAMES QU
ANDERSON, ISAAC	SOM	474	TRAPPE D
ANDERSON, ISAAC	KEN	309	3RD DIST
ANDERSON, ISAAC C.	ANN	518	HOWARD D
ANDERSON, ISAAIAH	BAL	166	6TH WARD
ANDERSON, ISAIAH	CEC	051	1ST E DI
ANDERSON, ISRAEL	BAL	342	13TH WAR
ANDERSON, J.	BAL	228	19TH WAR
ANDERSON, J.	BAL	172	1ST WARD
ANDERSON, J.	BAL	117	1ST WARD
ANDERSON, J.	BAL	066	10TH WAR
ANDERSON, J. GEORGE	BAL	358	13TH WAR
ANDERSON, J.E.	BAL	173	1ST WARD
ANDERSON, J.E.	BAL	163	1ST WARD
ANDERSON, J.E.	BAL	129	1ST WARD
ANDERSON, J.F.	WAS	002	WILLIAMS
ANDERSON, JACOB	BAL	311	7TH WARD
ANDERSON, JACOB	BAL	093	15TH WAR
ANDERSON, JACOB	ALL	116	5TH E.D.
ANDERSON, JACOB	CEC	017	ELKTON 3
ANDERSON, JAMES	CEC	024	ELKTON 3
ANDERSON, JAMES	CEC	011	ELKTON 3
ANDERSON, JAMES	CEC	033	CHESAPEA
ANDERSON, JAMES	KEN	241	2ND DIST
ANDERSON, JAMES	BAL	103	18TH WAR
ANDERSON, JAMES	ALL	102	5TH E.D.
ANDERSON, JAMES	ALL	169	6TH E.D.
ANDERSON, JAMES	ANN	368	4TH DIST
ANDERSON, JAMES	BAL	264	7TH WARD
ANDERSON, JAMES	BAL	160	1ST WARD
ANDERSON, JAMES	BAL	135	5TH WARD
ANDERSON, JAMES	BAL	437	1ST DIST
ANDERSON, JAMES	ANN	441	HOWARD D
ANDERSON, JAMES	BAL	090	2ND DIST
ANDERSON, JAMES	WOR	259	BERLIN 1
ANDERSON, JAMES	QUE	168	2ND E DI
ANDERSON, JAMES	WAS	126	HAGERSTO
ANDERSON, JAMES M.	BAL	080	4TH WARD
ANDERSON, JAMES P.	TAL	072	EASTON T
ANDERSON, JAMES S.	SOM	471	TRAPPE D

Name	County	Page	District
ANDERSON, JAMES W.	MGM	402	ROCKERLE
ANDERSON, JAMES-BLACK	FRE	010	FREDERIC
ANDERSON, JAN	CEC	019	ELKTON 3
ANDERSON, JANE	BAL	192	11TH WAR
ANDERSON, JANE	WAS	161	HAGERSTO
ANDERSON, JEANETTE	BAL	238	6TH WARD
ANDERSON, JESSE	BAL	163	1ST WARD
ANDERSON, JESSE	PRI	101	SPALDING
ANDERSON, JESSE	BAL	126	11TH WAR
ANDERSON, JOHN	BAL	161	11TH WAR
ANDERSON, JOHN	BAL	451	14TH WAR
ANDERSON, JOHN	CEC	010	ELKTON 3
ANDERSON, JOHN	CEC	028	CHESAPEA
ANDERSON, JOHN	CEC	031	CHESAPEA
ANDERSON, JOHN	CEC	035	CHESAPEA
ANDERSON, JOHN	BAL	366	13TH WAR
ANDERSON, JOHN	KEN	236	2ND DIST
ANDERSON, JOHN	KEN	218	2ND DIST
ANDERSON, JOHN	HAR	135	2ND DIST
ANDERSON, JOHN	QUE	141	1ST E DI
ANDERSON, JOHN	PRI	002	BLADENSB
ANDERSON, JOHN	PRI	012	BLADENSB
ANDERSON, JOHN	SOM	533	QUANTICO
ANDERSON, JOHN	WAS	141	HAGERSTO
ANDERSON, JOHN	WAS	167	1ST DIST
ANDERSON, JOHN	QUE	176	2ND E DI
ANDERSON, JOHN	SOM	452	DAMES QU
ANDERSON, JOHN	WAS	105	2ND DIST
ANDERSON, JOHN	WOR	303	SNOW HIL
ANDERSON, JOHN	BAL	031	9TH WARD
ANDERSON, JOHN	BAL	200	6TH WARD
ANDERSON, JOHN	BAL	232	6TH WARD
ANDERSON, JOHN	BAL	154	1ST WARD
ANDERSON, JOHN	ANN	430	HOWARD D
ANDERSON, JOHN	BAL	046	2ND DIST
ANDERSON, JOHN	BAL	131	1ST WARD
ANDERSON, JOHN	BAL	128	1ST WARD
ANDERSON, JOHN	ALL	090	5TH E.D.
ANDERSON, JOHN	ALL	207	CUMBERLA
ANDERSON, JOHN	BAL	076	10TH WAR
ANDERSON, JOHN	BAL	042	9TH WARD
ANDERSON, JOHN	BAL	117	1ST WARD
ANDERSON, JOHN	BAL	106	1ST WARD
ANDERSON, JOHN	BAL	460	8TH WARD
ANDERSON, JOHN	BAL	002	9TH WARD
ANDERSON, JOHN	BAL	045	15TH WAR
ANDERSON, JOHN B.	KEN	243	2ND DIST
ANDERSON, JOHN B.	CAR	081	NO TWP L
ANDERSON, JOHN B.	CAR	081	NO TWP L
ANDERSON, JOHN D.	SOM	409	DUBLIN D
ANDERSON, JOHN E.	KEN	236	2ND DIST
ANDERSON, JOHN E.	BAL	167	1ST WARD
ANDERSON, JOHN G.	BAL	115	11TH WAR
ANDERSON, JOHN H.	BAL	024	9TH WARD
ANDERSON, JOHN H.	TAL	060	EASTON D
ANDERSON, JOHN J.	SOM	532	QUANTICO
ANDERSON, JOHN R.	FRE	275	NEW MARK
ANDERSON, JOHN W.	MGM	376	ROCKERLE
ANDERSON, JOHN W.	ANN	366	4TH DIST
ANDERSON, JOHN W. D.	SOM	540	TYASKIN
ANDERSON, JOHN-BLACK	QUE	169	2ND E DI
ANDERSON, JOSEPH	ST	257	3RD E DI
ANDERSON, JOSEPH	WAS	102	2ND DIST
ANDERSON, JOSEPH	MGM	437	CLARKSTR
ANDERSON, JOSEPH	ANN	519	HOWARD D
ANDERSON, JOSEPH	BAL	327	3RD WARD
ANDERSON, JOSEPH	BAL	059	18TH WAR
ANDERSON, JOSEPH C.	QUE	154	1ST E DI
ANDERSON, JOSEPH L.	BAL	167	6TH WARD
ANDERSON, JOSEPHINE	BAL	019	15TH WAR
ANDERSON, JOSEPHINE	MGM	320	CRACKLIN
ANDERSON, JOSEY*	BAL	338	3RD WARD
ANDERSON, JOSHUA	BAL	057	2ND DIST
ANDERSON, JOSHUA	ANN	430	HOWARD D
ANDERSON, JOSHUA	WAS	267	1ST DIST
ANDERSON, JULIA-BLACK	BAL	245	2ND WARD
ANDERSON, KELLIUM-MULATTO	WOR	323	1ST E DI
ANDERSON, L.B.	PRI	093	MARLBROU
ANDERSON, LAURANCE-BLACK	CAR	071	NO TWP L
ANDERSON, LAWRENCE	BAL	463	1ST DIST
ANDERSON, LENARD	BAL	027	2ND DIST
ANDERSON, LETICIA	KEN	291	3RD DIST
ANDERSON, LEVIN	SOM	488	SALISBUR
ANDERSON, LEVIN	TAL	036	EASTON D
ANDERSON, LEWIS T.	KEN	300	3RD DIST
ANDERSON, LOUIS	CEC	023	ELKTON 3
ANDERSON, LOUISA	CEC	041	CHESAPEA
ANDERSON, LOUISA	CEC	055	1ST E DI
ANDERSON, LOUISA	BAL	305	3RD WARD
ANDERSON, LOUISA	BAL	308	12TH WAR
ANDERSON, LUCIAN B.	CEC	090	4TH E DI
ANDERSON, LUCY	BAL	064	15TH WAR
ANDERSON, M.A.	PRI	085	QUEEN AN
ANDERSON, MARGARET	PRI	042	VANSVILL
ANDERSON, MARGARET	BAL	305	3RD WARD
ANDERSON, MARGARET A.	BAL	267	7TH WARD
ANDERSON, MARGARET L.	SOM	532	QUANTICO
ANDERSON, MARGERY B.	ANN	457	HOWARD D
ANDERSON, MARIA	BAL	403	1ST DIST
ANDERSON, MARIA	BAL	056	15TH WAR
ANDERSON, MARIA	KEN	296	3RD DIST
ANDERSON, MARIA-BLACK	QUE	180	2ND E DI
ANDERSON, MARIA-BLACK	QUE	164	2ND E DI
ANDERSON, MARIAH	SOM	554	TYASKIN
ANDERSON, MARION	CEC	114	3RD E DI
ANDERSON, MARTHA	HAR	096	2ND DIST
ANDERSON, MARTHA	BAL	193	17TH WAR
ANDERSON, MARTHA	BAL	236	6TH WARD
ANDERSON, MARTHA	BAL	099	1ST WARD
ANDERSON, MARY	BAL	016	9TH WARD
ANDERSON, MARY	BAL	458	8TH WARD
ANDERSON, MARY	ANN	482	HOWARD D
ANDERSON, MARY	BAL	128	2ND DIST
ANDERSON, MARY	CEC	061	1ST E DI
ANDERSON, MARY	CEC	066	1ST E DI
ANDERSON, MARY	BAL	027	18TH WAR
ANDERSON, MARY	CHA	281	BOJANTOW
ANDERSON, MARY	BAL	364	13TH WAR
ANDERSON, MARY	TAL	040	EASTON D
ANDERSON, MARY	QUE	176	2ND E DI
ANDERSON, MARY	QUE	215	3RD E DI
ANDERSON, MARY	QUE	230	4TH E DI
ANDERSON, MARY A.	PRI	030	VANSVILL
ANDERSON, MARY A.	BAL	035	15TH WAR
ANDERSON, MARY E.	ST	286	2ND E DI
ANDERSON, MARY E.	QUE	128	1ST E DI
ANDERSON, MARY-BLACK	FRE	215	BUCKEYST
ANDERSON, MATILDA	BAL	142	11TH WAR
ANDERSON, MATILDA	BAL	039	15TH WAR
ANDERSON, MATILDA	BAL	065	10TH WAR
ANDERSON, MICHAEL	CEC	044	CHESAPEA
ANDERSON, MILLA	BAL	240	1ST DIST
ANDERSON, MILLY	BAL	126	2ND DIST
ANDERSON, MILLY	BAL	046	18TH WAR
ANDERSON, MORGAN	CEC	039	CHESAPEA
ANDERSON, N.	BAL	153	1ST WARD
ANDERSON, NANCY	ANN	316	1ST DIST
ANDERSON, NANCY	CAL	041	3RD DIST
ANDERSON, NANCY	KEN	224	2ND DIST
ANDERSON, NANCY	QUE	207	3RD E DI
ANDERSON, NANCY	WAS	241	CAVETOWN
ANDERSON, NATHAN	CEC	092	4TH E DI
ANDERSON, NATHANIEL	BAL	243	20TH WAR
ANDERSON, NELLY	SOM	533	QUANTICO
ANDERSON, NOBLE	BAL	300	3RD WARD
ANDERSON, NORRIS	HAR	080	2ND DIST
ANDERSON, OLIVER	HAR	095	2ND DIST
ANDERSON, P.	BAL	167	1ST WARD
ANDERSON, P.	BAL	117	1ST WARD
ANDERSON, PERE	QUE	230	4TH E DI
ANDERSON, PETER	SOM	529	QUANTICO
ANDERSON, PETER	BAL	082	2ND DIST
ANDERSON, PETER	BAL	237	20TH WAR
ANDERSON, PHILIP	KEN	306	3RD DIST
ANDERSON, PHILLIS	KEN	288	3RD DIST
ANDERSON, PHOEBE	BAL	160	2ND DIST
ANDERSON, PIERRE	CEC	064	1ST E DI
ANDERSON, POLLY	SOM	490	SALISBUR
ANDERSON, POLLY	SOM	361	BRINKLEY
ANDERSON, PRASILAR	HAR	206	3RD DIST
ANDERSON, PRINCE	KEN	229	2ND DIST
ANDERSON, RACHAEL	BAL	131	11TH WAR
ANDERSON, RACHEL	CEC	105	3RD E DI
ANDERSON, RACHEL	CEC	015	ELKTON 3
ANDERSON, RACHEL A.	BAL	287	7TH WARD
ANDERSON, RACHIEL	HAR	044	1ST DIST
ANDERSON, REBECCA	KEN	230	2ND DIST
ANDERSON, REBECCA	BAL	251	6TH WARD
ANDERSON, REBECCA	ANN	456	HOWARD D
ANDERSON, REBECCA	BAL	110	10TH WAR
ANDERSON, RICHARD	BAL	397	1ST DIST
ANDERSON, RICHARD	ANN	331	2ND DIST
ANDERSON, RICHARD	ANN	399	8TH DIST
ANDERSON, RICHARD	FRE	231	BUCKEYST
ANDERSON, RICHARD M.D.	BAL	233	1ST DIST
ANDERSON, ROBERT	BAL	343	8TH WARD
ANDERSON, ROBERT	MGM	377	ROCKERLE
ANDERSON, ROBERT	CAR	154	NO TWP L
ANDERSON, ROBERT	BAL	339	13TH WAR
ANDERSON, ROBERT	WOR	229	6TH E DI
ANDERSON, ROBERT	QUE	177	2ND E DI
ANDERSON, ROBERT	QUE	164	2ND E DI
ANDERSON, ROBERT	WAS	002	WILLIAMS
ANDERSON, ROSANNA	BAL	035	15TH WAR
ANDERSON, ROSE-BLACK	QUE	163	2ND E DI
ANDERSON, ROSETTA	QUE	250	5TH E DI
ANDERSON, ROSETTA	BAL	193	6TH WARD
ANDERSON, SAM	ANN	328	2ND DIST
ANDERSON, SAMUEL	ANN	364	4TH DIST
ANDERSON, SAMUEL	ALL	203	CUMBERLA
ANDERSON, SAMUEL	BAL	170	6TH WARD
ANDERSON, SAMUEL	ANN	423	HOWARD D
ANDERSON, SAMUEL	BAL	227	17TH WAR
ANDERSON, SAMUEL	SOM	410	DUBLIN D
ANDERSON, SAMUEL	QUE	124	1ST E DI
ANDERSON, SAMUEL E.	PRI	041	VANSVILL
ANDERSON, SARAH	KEN	215	2ND DIST
ANDERSON, SARAH	KEN	239	2ND DIST
ANDERSON, SARAH	BAL	342	13TH WAR
ANDERSON, SARAH	CEC	012	ELKTON 3
ANDERSON, SARAH	BAL	017	15TH WAR
ANDERSON, SARAH	BAL	084	1ST WARD
ANDERSON, SARAH	BAL	065	10TH WAR
ANDERSON, SARAH	BAL	038	9TH WARD
ANDERSON, SARAH A.	KEN	217	2ND DIST
ANDERSON, SARAH A.	ST	320	4TH E DI
ANDERSON, SOLOMON	BAL	118	11TH WAR
ANDERSON, SOLOMON	BAL	118	11TH WAR
ANDERSON, SOPHIA	BAL	025	4TH WARD
ANDERSON, STEPHEN	SOM	459	HANGARY
ANDERSON, STEPHEN	WOR	260	BERLIN 1
ANDERSON, STEPHEN	ANN	487	HOWARD D
ANDERSON, SUSAN	ANN	438	HOWARD D
ANDERSON, SUSAN	ANN	362	4TH DIST
ANDERSON, SUSAN	BAL	410	8TH WARD
ANDERSON, SUSAN	SOM	545	TYASKIN
ANDERSON, SUSAN-BLACK	FRE	011	FREDERIC
ANDERSON, SYBELLA	BAL	232	2ND WARD
ANDERSON, THOASM	ST	265	3RD E DI
ANDERSON, THOMAS	QUE	252	5TH E DI
ANDERSON, THOMAS	SOM	519	BARREN C
ANDERSON, THOMAS	PRI	004	BLADENSB
ANDERSON, THOMAS	BAL	133	1ST WARD
ANDERSON, THOMAS	ANN	368	4TH DIST
ANDERSON, THOMAS	BAL	047	2ND DIST
ANDERSON, THOMAS	BAL	050	2ND DIST
ANDERSON, THOMAS	ALL	236	CUMBERLA
ANDERSON, THOMAS	ANN	518	HOWARD D
ANDERSON, THOMAS	ANN	331	2ND DIST
ANDERSON, THOMAS	BAL	086	15TH WAR
ANDERSON, THOMAS	BAL	178	11TH WAR
ANDERSON, THOMAS	BAL	226	6TH WARD
ANDERSON, THOMAS	CAL	055	3RD DIST
ANDERSON, THOMAS	HAR	157	3RD DIST
ANDERSON, THOMAS	CEC	116	3RD E DI
ANDERSON, THOMAS B.	BAL	446	1ST DIST
ANDERSON, THOMAS L.	CAL	026	2ND DIST
ANDERSON, THOMAS W.	DOR	374	1ST DIST
ANDERSON, THOMAS W.	ANN	363	4TH DIST
ANDERSON, THOMAS-BLACK	FRE	216	BUCKEYST
ANDERSON, THOMAS-BLACK	QUE	179	2ND E DI
ANDERSON, TOLBERT B.	FRE	231	BUCKEYST
ANDERSON, VIOLET	KEN	297	3RD DIST
ANDERSON, WILLAIM	WAS	284	1ST DIST
ANDERSON, WILLIAM	KEN	288	3RD DIST
ANDERSON, WILLIAM	QUE	177	2ND E DI
ANDERSON, WILLIAM	QUE	222	4TH E DI
ANDERSON, WILLIAM	PRI	044	VANSVILL
ANDERSON, WILLIAM	PRI	025	VANSVILL
ANDERSON, WILLIAM	SOM	488	SALISBUR
ANDERSON, WILLIAM	PRI	085	QUEEN AN
ANDERSON, WILLIAM	BAL	122	11TH WAR
ANDERSON, WILLIAM	CAR	098	NO TWP L
ANDERSON, WILLIAM	CEC	099	3RD E DI
ANDERSON, WILLIAM	KEN	241	2ND DIST
ANDERSON, WILLIAM	QUE	131	1ST E DI
ANDERSON, WILLIAM	BAL	275	20TH WAR
ANDERSON, WILLIAM	CEC	006	ELKTON 3
ANDERSON, WILLIAM	CEC	034	CHESAPEA
ANDERSON, WILLIAM	CEC	035	CHESAPEA
ANDERSON, WILLIAM	CEC	041	CHESAPEA
ANDERSON, WILLIAM	BAL	194	19TH WAR
ANDERSON, WILLIAM	BAL	346	13TH WAR
ANDERSON, WILLIAM	BAL	398	14TH WAR
ANDERSON, WILLIAM	SOM	405	DUBLIN D
ANDERSON, WILLIAM	HAR	017	1ST DIST
ANDERSON, WILLIAM	HAR	103	2ND DIST
ANDERSON, WILLIAM	FRE	040	FREDERIC
ANDERSON, WILLIAM	ANN	331	2ND DIST
ANDERSON, WILLIAM	BAL	112	5TH WARD
ANDERSON, WILLIAM	BAL	290	3RD WARD
ANDERSON, WILLIAM	BAL	165	1ST WARD
ANDERSON, WILLIAM	BAL	223	12TH WAR
ANDERSON, WILLIAM	BAL	057	2ND DIST
ANDERSON, WILLIAM	BAL	258	2ND WARD
ANDERSON, WILLIAM	BAL	383	3RD WARD
ANDERSON, WILLIAM	BAL	115	1ST WARD
ANDERSON, WILLIAM	BAL	073	1ST WARD
ANDERSON, WILLIAM B.-BLAC	QUE	164	2ND E DI
ANDERSON, WILLIAM C.	KEN	300	3RD DIST
ANDERSON, WILLIAM C.	KEN	275	1ST DIST
ANDERSON, WILLIAM H. F.	BAL	423	1ST DIST
ANDERSON, WILLIAM R.	FRE	270	NEW MARK
ANDERSON, WILLIAM-BLACK	QUE	201	3RD E DI
ANDERSON, ABSALOAM	FRE	239	NEW MARK
ANDERSON, JOHN	BAL	126	1ST WARD
ANDERSON, MANUEL-BLACK	QUE	149	1ST E DI
ANDERSON, MARY	BAL	005	EASTERN
ANDERSON, NEIL	BAL	118	1ST WARD
ANDERSON, PAUL	FRE	179	5TH E DI
ANDERSTON, HELENA A.	WAS	146	HAGERSTO
ANDERWS, ANN	BAL	355	13TH WAR
ANDES, WILLIAM	FRE	438	8TH E DI
ANDESON, AMRY	BAL	256	12TH WAR
ANDESON, WILLIAM	BAL	099	1ST WARD
ANDONBAUX, ADAM	BAL	375	8TH WARD
ANDRAE, CORNELIUS	PRI	019	BLADENSB
ANDRE, JAMES R. A.	TAL	017	EASTON D
ANDRE, SARAH	TAL	069	EASTON T
ANDRE, WILLIAM	BAL	363	3RD WARD
ANDREN, MARTHA A.	DOR	317	1ST DIST
ANDRES, JOHN T.	MGM	421	MEDLEY 3
ANDREW, ANN	CAR	130	NO TWP L
ANDREW, ANNE	CAR	132	NO TWP L
ANDREW, ARDILLE	CAR	124	NO TWP L
ANDREW, BARTENA	CAR	124	NO TWP L
ANDREW, CAPTAIN*	BAL	332	3RD WARD
ANDREW, CATHERINE	CAR	130	NO TWP L
ANDREW, CHARLES	BAL	356	13TH WAR
ANDREW, CHARLES P.	BAL	362	3RD WARD
ANDREW, CURTIS	CAR	135	NO TWP L
ANDREW, DANIEL B.	CAR	130	NO TWP L
ANDREW, DELIA	DOR	322	1ST DIST
ANDREW, EDWARD	CAR	121	NO TWP L
ANDREW, EDWARD	CAR	140	NO TWP L
ANDREW, ELISHA W.	CAR	122	NO TWP L
ANDREW, ELIZABETH	DOR	322	1ST DIST
ANDREW, ELIZABETH	DOR	301	1ST DIST
ANDREW, EUPHAMY	DOR	318	1ST DIST
ANDREW, GEORGE	CAR	120	NO TWP L
ANDREW, GEORGE	CAR	165	NO TWP L
ANDREW, HENRY	CAR	137	NO TWP L
ANDREW, ISAAC	CAR	155	NO TWP L
ANDREW, ISRAEL	CAR	165	NO TWP L
ANDREW, JACOB	BAL	384	13TH WAR
ANDREW, JACOB R.	CAR	136	NO TWP L
ANDREW, JAMES	CAR	144	NO TWP L
ANDREW, JOHN	DOR	300	1ST DIST
ANDREW, JOHN	ALL	095	5TH E.D.
ANDREW, JOHN W.	HAR	002	1ST DIST
ANDREW, JOSEPH	CAR	163	NO TWP L
ANDREW, JOSEPH	DOR	322	1ST DIST
ANDREW, LUCTIA	CAR	130	NO TWP L
ANDREW, MARGARET	HAR	020	1ST DIST
ANDREW, MARY	CAR	132	NO TWP L
ANDREW, MARY	CAR	107	NO TWP L
ANDREW, MARY	DOR	310	1ST DIST
ANDREW, MARY	DOR	322	1ST DIST
ANDREW, MARY C.	CAR	136	NO TWP L
ANDREW, MARY F.	CAR	161	NO TWP L
ANDREW, MELVIN	CAR	123	NO TWP L
ANDREW, MITCHEL	CAR	143	NO TWP L
ANDREW, MOSES-BLACK	CAR	162	NO TWP L
ANDREW, NEWTON	CAR	130	NO TWP L
ANDREW, NEWTON	CAR	130	NO TWP L
ANDREW, PETER	CAR	118	NO TWP L
ANDREW, PRICILLE	CAR	078	NO TWP L
ANDREW, REBECCA	CAR	234	UNION TO
ANDREW, RICHARD	CAR	135	NO TWP L
ANDREW, RICHARD	CAR	124	NO TWP L
ANDREW, RICHARD	CAR	139	NO TWP L
ANDREW, RICHARD	CAR	156	NO TWP L
ANDREW, ROBERT	BAL	062	2ND DIST
ANDREW, RUTH C.	HAR	167	3RD DIST
ANDREW, SELEY	CAR	127	NO TWP L
ANDREW, SELY	CAR	133	NO TWP L
ANDREW, SOPHIA	DOR	321	1ST DIST
ANDREW, SOPHIA	DOR	315	1ST DIST
ANDREW, STATON	CAR	121	NO TWP L
ANDREW, SYLVESTER	CAR	140	NO TWP L
ANDREW, TAMSY	CAR	108	NO TWP L
ANDREW, THOMAS	CAR	131	NO TWP L
ANDREW, THOMAS	CAR	130	NO TWP L
ANDREW, THOMAS	DOR	322	1ST DIST
ANDREW, TILGHMAN	DOR	307	1ST DIST
ANDREW, UPTON	FRE	109	CREAGERS
ANDREW, WILLIAM	CAR	110	NO TWP L
ANDREW, WILLIAM	CAR	156	NO TWP L
ANDREW, WILLIAM	CAR	067	NO TWP L
ANDREW, WILLIAM	HAR	021	1ST DIST
ANDREW, WILLIAM	BAL	170	1ST WARD
ANDREW, WILLIAM G.	CAR	118	NO TWP L
ANDREW, WILLIAM G.	HAR	188	3RD DIST
ANDREW, WILLIAM R.	CAR	137	NO TWP L
ANDREW, ZACHARIAH	CAR	154	NO TWP L
ANDREW, WESLEY	CAR	078	NO TWP L
ANDREWS, AARON	FRE	261	NEW MARK
ANDREWS, ABIGAIL	BAL	179	16TH WAR
ANDREWS, ABRAHAM	FRE	109	CREAGERS
ANDREWS, ALBEN	DOR	350	3RD DIVI
ANDREWS, ALIS	DOR	349	3RD DIVI
ANDREWS, AMOS	HAR	095	2ND DIST
ANDREWS, BETSEY	BAL	071	4TH WARD
ANDREWS, CHAPMAN	DOR	335	3RD DIVI
ANDREWS, CHARLES	CAR	117	NO TWP L
ANDREWS, CHARLES	BAL	043	18TH WAR
ANDREWS, CHARLES	DOR	456	1ST DIST
ANDREWS, CHRISTIANNA	WAS	161	2ND DIST
ANDREWS, CORNELIA	BAL	014	9TH WARD
ANDREWS, DAVID	BAL	257	2ND WARD

Name	County	Page	District
ANDREWS, DAVID	ANN	336	3RD DIST
ANDREWS, DAVID	CEC	032	CHESAPEA
ANDREWS, DEBORAH	CEC	041	CHESAPEA
ANDREWS, DELILA	MGM	421	MEDLEY 3
ANDREWS, EDWARD	CEC	041	CHESAPEA
ANDREWS, EDWARD	CEC	035	CHESAPEA
ANDREWS, EDWARD	BAL	471	14TH WAR
ANDREWS, ELIZA	CEC	039	CHESAPEA
ANDREWS, ELIZA	BAL	075	10TH WAR
ANDREWS, ELIZABETH	BAL	090	18TH WAR
ANDREWS, ELLEN	BAL	345	13TH WAR
ANDREWS, ELLISSON	BAL	262	17TH WAR
ANDREWS, EMILY	BAL	012	18TH WAR
ANDREWS, FLOUIDA	BAL	358	8TH WARD
ANDREWS, FRANCIS G.	CEC	169	6TH E DI
ANDREWS, GEORGE	CEC	039	CHESAPEA
ANDREWS, GUSTAV	BAL	012	15TH WAR
ANDREWS, H. W.	BAL	044	18TH WAR
ANDREWS, HANSON	MGM	444	CLARKSTR
ANDREWS, HESTOR	BAL	250	17TH WAR
ANDREWS, ISAAC	HAR	011	1ST DIST
ANDREWS, J.	BAL	147	1ST WARD
ANDREWS, JACOB	BAL	411	3RD WARD
ANDREWS, JACOB	TAL	036	EASTON D
ANDREWS, JAMES	MGM	444	CLARKSTR
ANDREWS, JAMES	BAL	058	18TH WAR
ANDREWS, JAMES	BAL	260	20TH WAR
ANDREWS, JAMES	BAL	151	19TH WAR
ANDREWS, JAMES	ANN	268	ANNAPOLI
ANDREWS, JANE	BAL	220	19TH WAR
ANDREWS, JANE	CEC	162	6TH E DI
ANDREWS, JEFFERSON	MGM	421	MEDLEY 3
ANDREWS, JOHN	BAL	075	18TH WAR
ANDREWS, JOHN	QUE	125	1ST E DI
ANDREWS, JOHN	HAR	132	2ND DIST
ANDREWS, JOHN	BAL	154	5TH WARD
ANDREWS, JOHN	BAL	383	8TH WARD
ANDREWS, JOHN	BAL	153	2ND DIST
ANDREWS, JOHN B.	BAL	020	1ST WARD
ANDREWS, JOHN P.	BAL	416	8TH WARD
ANDREWS, JOHN R.	DOR	350	3RD DIVI
ANDREWS, JOHN W.	BAL	279	2ND WARD
ANDREWS, LOUISA	BAL	352	7TH WARD
ANDREWS, MARGARET	BAL	220	19TH WAR
ANDREWS, MARGRETT	CAR	110	NO TWP L
ANDREWS, MARTHA	BAL	184	19TH WAR
ANDREWS, MARY	BAL	014	4TH WARD
ANDREWS, MARY	BAL	091	18TH WAR
ANDREWS, MARY	HAR	049	1ST DIST
ANDREWS, MARY	DOR	335	3RD DIVI
ANDREWS, MARY	DOR	336	3RD DIVI
ANDREWS, MARY	ST	281	3RD E DI
ANDREWS, MATILDA	MGM	439	CLARKSTR
ANDREWS, MISS E.	FRE	198	5TH E DI
ANDREWS, MISS P.	FRE	199	5TH E DI
ANDREWS, MISS V.	FRE	199	5TH E DI
ANDREWS, MOSES	BAL	162	6TH WARD
ANDREWS, MRS.	BAL	151	1ST WARD
ANDREWS, NANCY	BAL	447	14TH WAR
ANDREWS, RACHEL	CAR	385	2ND DIST
ANDREWS, RACHEL	CEC	036	CHESAPEX
ANDREWS, REBECCA	CEC	031	CHESAPEA
ANDREWS, RICHARD F.	MGM	421	MEDLEY 3
ANDREWS, ROBERT	BAL	391	14TH WAR
ANDREWS, ROBERT L.	BAL	074	10TH WAR
ANDREWS, SALLY A.	DOR	467	1ST DIST
ANDREWS, SAMUEL	DOR	349	3RD DIVI
ANDREWS, SAMUEL	BAL	250	17TH WAR
ANDREWS, SARAH	HAR	200	3RD DIST
ANDREWS, SARAH A.	HAR	133	2ND DIST
ANDREWS, SHARLOT	DOR	354	3RD DIVI
ANDREWS, SOPHIA	BAL	400	3RD WARD
ANDREWS, STEPHEN	CEC	036	CHESAPEA
ANDREWS, STEPHEN	BAL	090	18TH WAR
ANDREWS, STEPHEN	DOR	312	1ST DIST
ANDREWS, SUSAN J.	CEC	026	ELKTON 3
ANDREWS, SUSANNA	TAL	081	ST MICHA
ANDREWS, THOMAS	SOM	492	SALISBUR
ANDREWS, THOMAS	DOR	325	1ST DIST
ANDREWS, THOMAS	BAL	081	1ST WARD
ANDREWS, TILGHMAN	DOR	427	1ST DIST
ANDREWS, TIMOTHY P.	BAL	348	13TH WAR
ANDREWS, WILLIAM	FRE	276	NEW MARK
ANDREWS, WILLIAM	DOR	339	3RD DIVI
ANDREWS, WILLIAM	DOR	340	3RD DIVI
ANDREWS, WILLIAM	FRE	016	FREDERIC
ANDREWS, WILLIAM	HAR	143	2ND DIST
ANDREWS, WILLIAM	QUE	154	1ST E DI
ANDREWS, WILLIAM	BAL	232	6TH WARD
ANDREWS, WILLIAM	ALL	241	CUMBERLA
ANDREWS, WILLIAM H.	BAL	058	18TH WAR
ANDREWS, WILLIAM W.	DOR	350	3RD DIVI
ANDREWSON, JOHN	BAL	112	5TH WARD
ANDROSE, WILLIAM R.	BAL	134	18TH WAR
ANDRUS, ANN	FRE	220	BUCKEYST
ANDRUS, ANN-BLACK	CAR	145	NO TWP L
ANDRUS, ELIZABETH	CAR	150	NO TWP L
ANDRUS, HARRIETT	CAR	152	NO TWP L
ANDRUS, MARGRETT	CAR	145	NO TWP L
ANDRUS, WILLIS D.	CAR	150	NO TWP L
ANDUZE, ARCHILLE	BAL	384	13TH WAR
ANDY, CATHERINE	ALL	226	CUMBERLA
ANED, SAMUEL	BAL	033	1ST WARD
ANEL, JOHN	CAR	378	2ND DIST
ANELD, MOSES P.*	TAL	037	EASTON D
ANELIZ, FERNANDO	FRE	202	5TH E DI
ANEN, CATHARINE	BAL	048	1ST WARD
ANEY, WILLAIM	BAL	239	20TH WAR
ANGASS, THOMAS L.	BAL	419	14TH WAR
ANGEL, JACOB	FRE	264	NEW MARK
ANGEL, JOB	WAS	018	2ND SUBD
ANGEL, JOHN	CAR	316	1ST DIST
ANGEL, JOHN T.	BAL	395	8TH WARD
ANGEL, THOMAS	BAL	373	8TH WARD
ANGEL, WILLIAM	CAR	277	7TH DIST
ANGELBERGER, DAVID L.	FRE	085	FREDERIC
ANGELBURGER, JOHN	FRE	080	FREDERIC
ANGELL, ABRAHAM	CAR	322	1ST DIST
ANGELL, CHARLES	CAR	325	1ST DIST
ANGELL, DANIEL S.	CAR	319	1ST DIST
ANGELL, EPHRIAM	CAR	322	1ST DIST
ANGELL, GEORGE	CAR	324	1ST DIST
ANGELL, JOHN	CAR	315	1ST DIST
ANGELL, JOSEPH	CAR	298	1ST DIST
ANGELL, MARY	CAR	323	1ST DIST
ANGELL, SAMUEL	CAR	317	1ST DIST
ANGELL, THOMAS	CAR	321	1ST DIST
ANGHTERTBRIDGE, JAMES	BAL	161	1ST WARD
ANGILL, MARY	CAR	312	1ST DIST
ANGLE, ANN E.	ALL	201	CUMBERLA
ANGLE, HENRY	ALL	205	CUMBERLA
ANGLE, HENRY	WAS	102	2ND DIST
ANGLE, JACOB	WAS	286	1ST DIST
ANGLE, SUSAN	WAS	018	2ND SUBD
ANGLE, WILLIAM	CAR	380	2ND DIST
ANGLEBERGER, GEORGE W.	FRE	102	FREDERIC
ANGLEBERGER, JACOB	FRE	088	FREDERIC
ANGLEBERGER, JOSEPH	FRE	088	FREDERIC
ANGLEBERGER, JOYCE *	FRE	100	FREDERIC
ANGUS, MARIA	BAL	070	10TH WAR
ANI, AGNES	BAL	229	12TH WAR
ANIDALL, CHARLOTTE A.	ST	313	1ST E DI
ANIDER, JESSE	BAL	194	5TH DIST
ANISLAIR, THOMAS *	TAL	080	ST MICHA
ANJER, JOSIAH	ALL	250	CUMBERLA
ANKER, JOHN	BAL	097	5TH WARD
ANKER, JOHN J.	BAL	020	1ST WARD
ANKER, LEBANK	BAL	281	7TH WARD
ANKERMAN, JAMES	BAL	337	3RD WARD
ANKNEY, GEORGE	WAS	132	2ND DIST
ANKNEY, ISAAC	WAS	131	2ND DIST
ANKNEY, JOHN L.	WAS	128	2ND DIST
ANKNEY, SAMUEL	WAS	136	2ND DIST
ANKWARD, ELIJAH-BLACK	MGM	411	MEDLEY 3
ANNAN, ANDREW	FRE	167	EMMITTSB
ANNAN, JOHN	FRE	197	5TH E DI
ANNAN, ROBERT	FRE	190	5TH E DI
ANNAN, WILLIAM	FRE	149	10TH E D
ANNAN, WILLIAM	BAL	300	17TH WAR
ANNCHT, GEORGE H.	BAL	271	20TH WAR
ANNETT, HELLEN N.	BAL	445	8TH WARD
ANNIS, ZEBIDE	BAL	044	2ND DIST
ANNISEN, ELIZABETH	BAL	200	6TH WARD
ANNMUS, SOLOMON	TAL	096	ST MICHA
ANNON, J.R.	ALL	255	CUMBERLA
ANNON, JOHN	BAL	429	8TH WARD
ANNON, MARY	BAL	429	8TH WARD
ANNOR, LARENIA	BAL	217	6TH DIST
ANNOT, J. H.	BAL	283	20TH WAR
ANNOUN, JAMES	CEC	030	CHESAPEA
ANNWOOD, ELIZABETH	WOR	180	6TH E DI
ANNWOOD, FANNY	WOR	185	6TH E DI
ANNWOOD, LEVIN	WOR	185	6TH E DI
ANNWOOD, WESTLY	WOR	185	6TH E DI
ANOLD, JOHN	CAR	196	4TH DIST
ANSBERGER, HARRISON	WAS	196	1ST DIST
ANSEL, MYER	BAL	093	10TH WAR
ANSHELL, WILLAIM H.	BAL	345	7TH WARD
ANSLEY, MARY	BAL	321	3RD WARD
ANSON, C.	BAL	152	1ST WARD
ANSTADT, PETER	BAL	188	6TH WARD
ANSTEAD, MARIE	BAL	296	20TH WAR
ANSTIN, CHARLES	BAL	050	9TH WARD
ANSVANDER, RUDDEN	BAL	147	11TH WAR
ANSWOLD, FRANCIS	BAL	050	2ND DIST
ANTHANICA, FRANC	BAL	123	1ST WARD
ANTHONEY, EDWARD T.	TAL	067	EASTON T
ANTHONEY, JOHN	BAL	322	7TH WARD
ANTHONIA, FRANCIS	BAL	121	1ST WARD
ANTHONY, ANN L.	QUE	164	2ND E DI
ANTHONY, BENJAMIN	QUE	145	1ST E DI
ANTHONY, BROTHER	BAL	216	11TH WAR
ANTHONY, CHARLES-BLACK	QUE	179	2ND E DI
ANTHONY, CLAY	KEN	235	2ND DIST
ANTHONY, DANIEL	BAL	244	6TH WARD
ANTHONY, DAVID	BAL	278	2ND WARD
ANTHONY, ELIZA	DOR	464	1ST DIST
ANTHONY, ELIZABETH	BAL	032	4TH WARD
ANTHONY, GEORGE	BAL	367	3RD WARD
ANTHONY, GEORGE H.	BAL	243	6TH WARD
ANTHONY, HARRIET	BAL	321	20TH WAR
ANTHONY, HENRY	DOR	374	1ST DIST
ANTHONY, HENRY A.	BAL	206	19TH WAR
ANTHONY, HENRY-BLACK	QUE	180	2ND E DI
ANTHONY, HESTER	DOR	385	1ST DIST
ANTHONY, JAMES	QUE	215	3RD E DI
ANTHONY, JAMES	BAL	159	2ND DIST
ANTHONY, JAMES F.	BAL	328	7TH WARD
ANTHONY, JAMES T.	CAR	076	NO TWP L
ANTHONY, JOHN	CAR	092	NO TWP L
ANTHONY, JOHN	BAL	227	6TH WARD
ANTHONY, JOHN	ANN	471	HOWARD D
ANTHONY, JOHN	BAL	082	15TH WAR
ANTHONY, JOHN B.	CAR	113	NO TWP L
ANTHONY, JOHN T.	TAL	080	ST MICHA
ANTHONY, LACY	BAL	240	12TH WAR
ANTHONY, LEVI	ALL	081	5TH E.D.
ANTHONY, LEVIN	DOR	463	1ST DIST
ANTHONY, LIARA A.	KEN	290	3RD DIST
ANTHONY, MARGARET	BAL	359	3RD WARD
ANTHONY, MARY	BAL	038	15TH WAR
ANTHONY, MITCHELL	DOR	444	1ST DIST
ANTHONY, ROBERT	CAR	112	NO TWP L
ANTHONY, ROBERT E.	BAL	155	16TH WAR
ANTHONY, SAMUEL	BAL	275	12TH WAR
ANTHONY, SAMUEL	DOR	388	1ST DIST
ANTHONY, WAYN	KEN	294	3RD DIST
ANTHONY, WILLIAM	BAL	008	18TH WAR
ANTHONY, WILLIAM	BAL	007	18TH WAR
ANTHONY, WILLIAM	CAR	330	MANCHEST
ANTHONY, WILLIAM	BAL	423	8TH WARD
ANTHONY, WILLIAM	ALL	070	5TH E.D.
ANTHONY, WILLIAM-BLACK	QUE	164	2ND E DI
ANTINA, J.	BAL	147	1ST WARD
ANTOINIA, CHARLES	BAL	164	1ST WARD
ANTONE, HENRY	BAL	436	8TH WARD
ANTONEY, CONRAD	WAS	158	2ND DIST
ANTONIA, A.	BAL	170	1ST WARD
ANTONIA, J.	BAL	150	1ST WARD
ANTONIA, J.	BAL	142	1ST WARD
ANTONIA, P.	BAL	167	1ST WARD
ANTONUS, FRANCES	BAL	062	4TH WARD
ANTONY, CHRISTIANA	WAS	137	HAGERSTO
ANTONY, CONRAD	WAS	157	2ND DIST
ANTONY, ELIZABETH	WAS	157	2ND DIST
ANTONY, JOHN	BAL	407	14TH WAR
ANTONY, JOHN S.	BAL	008	4TH WARD
ANTONY, STEPHEN	BAL	257	2ND WARD
ANTS, JOHN	CAR	274	7TH DIST
ANVRIN, JOHN	ALL	228	CUMBERLA
ANYES, PATIENCE	BAL	193	11TH WAR
ANZMAN, JOSEPH	BAL	436	14TH WAR
AOURSPRING, MARY	BAL	276	1ST DIST
APER, P.	BAL	286	2ND WARD
APHOW, CHARLES	BAL	103	2ND DIST
APLEBY, SALLY	ANN	452	HOWARD D
APLEGARTH, JAMES	DOR	364	3RD DIVI
APLEGARTH, JOHN E.	DOR	332	3RD DIVI
APLEGARTH, JULIAN	DOR	365	3RD DIVI
APLIDO, JOHN	BAL	460	1ST DIST
APP, CARL	BAL	087	15TH WAR
APPEL, JOHN	BAL	170	2ND DIST
APPELBEE, WILLIAM	ANN	473	HOWARD D
APPELGAITT, N. *	BAL	281	20TH WAR
APPELLEE, MATHIAS*	TAL	004	EASTON D
APPELLER, MATHIAS*	TAL	004	EASTON D
APPENHEIMER, JACOB	CAR	342	6TH DIST
APPENHEIMER, L.	BAL	319	12TH WAR
APPLE, CHARLES	BAL	251	2ND WARD
APPLE, CHRISTIAN	BAL	442	14TH WAR
APPLE, GERTRUDE	ALL	180	8TH E.D.
APPLE, HENREITTA *	BAL	220	12TH WAR
APPLE, HENRY	BAL	264	12TH WAR
APPLE, HENRY	ALL	179	7TH E.D.
APPLE, HENRY	BAL	081	1ST WARD
APPLE, JOHN	BAL	106	5TH WARD
APPLE, JOSEPH	CAR	332	MANCHEST
APPLE, PETER	BAL	234	17TH WAR
APPLE, PETER	TAL	115	ST MICHA
APPLE, THEADORE	WAS	246	SMITHSBU
APPLE, THOMAS	BAL	297	1ST DIST
APPLE, THOMAS G.	WAS	246	SMITHSBU
APPLE, TRACY	FRE	044	FREDERIC
APPLE, WILLIAM	BAL	402	1ST DIST
APPLEBEE, WASHINGTON	CAR	224	5TH DIST
APPLEBY, ANDREW J.	BAL	127	1ST WARD
APPLEBY, ANN M.	ANN	509	HOWARD D
APPLEBY, BIGNAL	BAL	185	6TH WARD
APPLEBY, CHARLES	BAL	299	1ST DIST
APPLEBY, JAMES	ANN	437	HOWARD D
APPLEBY, JAMES C.	MGM	323	CRACKLIN
APPLEBY, JOHN L.	BAL	358	3RD WARD
APPLEBY, LEMUEL	BAL	298	1ST DIST
APPLEBY, PRISCILLA	MGM	333	CRACKLIN
APPLEBY, REBECCA	BAL	023	4TH WARD
APPLEBY, REZIN	BAL	136	16TH WAR
APPLEBY, ROSEANNA	BAL	344	1ST DIST
APPLEBY, SAMUEL	MGM	325	CRACKLIN
APPLEBY, WILLIAM	BAL	220	17TH WAR
APPLEGARTH, A.	BAL	272	20TH WAR
APPLEGARTH, ELIZABETH N.	BAL	087	15TH WAR
APPLEGARTH, GEORGE	DOR	402	1ST DIST
APPLEGARTH, GEORGE*	DOR	406	1ST DIST
APPLEGARTH, GRACE*	DOR	425	1ST DIST
APPLEGARTH, HENRY C.	BAL	262	17TH WAR
APPLEGARTH, JOHN A.	BAL	322	3RD WARD
APPLEGARTH, LAWSON	BAL	332	3RD WARD
APPLEGARTH, MARY A.	BAL	097	15TH WAR
APPLEGARTH, PEGGY	BAL	043	1ST WARD
APPLEGARTH, ROBERT	BAL	042	15TH WAR
APPLEGARTH, ROBET	BAL	100	15TH WAR
APPLEGARTH, THOMAS	DOR	402	1ST DIST
APPLEGRATH, MARY W.	BAL	136	11TH WAR
APPLEGRATH, THOMAS	SOM	523	BARREN C
APPLEH, WALTER	MGM	441	CLARKSTR
APPLEMAN, JACOB	FRE	316	MIDDLETO
APPLEMAN, JOHN	FRE	315	MIDDLETO
APPLEMAN, MARY	FRE	315	MIDDLETO
APPLER, ABRAM	CAR	386	2ND DIST
APPLER, AUGUST	BAL	272	12TH WAR
APPLER, DAVID	BAL	344	13TH WAR
APPLER, ISAAC	CAR	389	2ND DIST
APPLER, ISEBELLA	BAL	115	18TH WAR
APPLER, JESSE	BAL	114	18TH WAR
APPLER, JACOB	CAR	387	2ND DIST
APPLETGARTH, WILLIAM	BAL	183	2ND WARD
APPLETON, WILLIAM L.	BAL	147	11TH WAR
APPLETON, PETER	BAL	193	2ND WARD
APPOLD, ANDREW	BAL	311	20TH WAR
APPOLD, GEORGE	BAL	430	14TH WAR
APPOLD, GEORGE	BAL	184	11TH WAR
APPOLD, SAMUEL	BAL	209	11TH WAR
APPS, THOMAS	HAR	145	3RD DIST
APSLEY, J. W.	KEN	244	2ND DIST
APSLEY, MARTHA	KEN	210	2ND DIST
APSLEY, WILLIAM	KEN	271	1ST DIST
ARAH, ELXANDER *	HAR	194	3RD DIST
ARAL, HENRY	BAL	052	1ST WARD
ARANG, ROBERT W.	BAL	060	1ST WARD
ARBAUGH, BALTZER	CAR	268	WESTMINS
ARBAUGH, GEORGE	CAR	199	4TH DIST
ARBAUGH, JANE	HAR	075	BEL AIR
ARBAUGH, MARGARET	CAR	199	4TH DIST
ARBAUGH, WILLIAM	CAR	199	4TH DIST
ARBAUGH, WILLIAM H.	HAR	075	BEL AIR
ARCHABALD, EDWARD	FRE	039	FREDERIC
ARCHALD, WILLIAM	BAL	130	1ST WARD
ARCHE, ELIZABET	HAR	152	3RD DIST
ARCHER, CALEB G.	HAR	079	2ND DIST
ARCHER, CHARLES	BAL	102	10TH WAR
ARCHER, CORDELIA	BAL	325	12TH WAR
ARCHER, HENRY	HAR	049	1ST DIST
ARCHER, JAMES F.	HAR	142	2ND DIST
ARCHER, JAMES P.	BAL	065	10TH WAR
ARCHER, JANE	HAR	155	3RD DIST
ARCHER, JOHN	HAR	095	2ND DIST
ARCHER, JOHN	BAL	450	14TH WAR
ARCHER, JOHN T.	BAL	291	12TH WAR
ARCHER, ROBERT H.	BAL	097	10TH WAR
ARCHER, ROBERT H.	HAR	142	2ND DIST
ARCHER, STEVENSON	HAR	139	2ND DIST
ARCHER, THOMAS	HAR	092	2ND DIST
ARCHEY, MARY	BAL	341	7TH WARD
ARCHIBALD, DAVID	CEC	157	PORT DUP
ARCHIBALD, JAMES	ALL	051	10TH E.D
ARCHIBALD, W.	BAL	170	1ST WARD
ARCHIBALD, WILLIAM	BAL	171	1ST WARD
ARCHIBOLD, JAMES	ALL	153	6TH E.D.
ARCHIBOLD, SAMUEL	BAL	044	15TH WAR
ARCY, JOHN	ALL	252	CUMBERLA
ARD, JOHN	BAL	160	1ST WARD
ARD, JOHN	BAL	356	3RD WARD
ARDEL, PATRICK	BAL	025	18TH WAR
ARDEN, JANE	BAL	304	12TH WAR
ARDIN, JEAN F.	BAL	037	9TH WARD
ARDINGER, AMANDA	WAS	005	WILLIAMS
ARDINGER, CHARLES	WAS	018	2ND SUBD
ARDINGER, HANAH	WAS	010	WILLIAMS
ARDINGER, JACOB	WAS	137	HAGERSTO
ARDINGER, OWEN	WAS	007	WILLIAMS
ARDIS, AZARIAH	WOR	325	1ST E DI
ARDIS, GEORGE	WOR	325	1ST E DI
ARDIS, JAMES	WOR	347	1ST E DI
ARDIS, WILLIAM	WOR	347	1ST E DI
ARDISGER, JOHN	WAS	004	WILLIAMS
ARDLEMON, JOHN	BAL	057	1ST WARD
ARDMAN, FREDERICK	BAL	063	2ND DIST
ARDOIS, CLEMENT D.	BAL	313	12TH WAR
ARDREY, MARY	BAL	184	6TH WARD
ARENCE, GEORGE	WOR	320	1ST E DI

ARENDT, G. BAL 312 12TH WAR
ARENEDO, C. C. BAL 282 2ND WARD
ARENES, HENRY BAL 043 9TH WARD
ARES, MARY M. TAL 058 EASTON D
AREY, JOHN W. WAS 035 2ND SUBD
AREY, MICAHEL WAS 027 2ND SUBD
AREY, PHILIP * BAL 274 7TH WARD
AREY, THOMAS WAS 019 2ND SUBD
ARGARDINE, ISRAEL KEN 241 2ND DIST
ARGARBELLES, E. J. BAL 320 20TH WAR
ARGUTAY, JOHN FRE 365 CATOCTIN
ARINGDALE, THOMAS TAL 031 EASTON D
ARISTEAD, WALKER K. BAL 035 9TH WARD
ARKENFELDT, JOHN BAL 059 15TH WAR
ARKINS, JOSEPH ALL 262 CUMBERLA
ARKINSON, ANN BAL 033 18TH WAR
ARLETT, AARON M. QUE 182 3RD E DI
ARLEY, JOHN ALL 142 6TH E.D.
ARLINGTON, SALLIE ANN 317 1ST DIST
ARLOE, ANDREW BAL 274 7TH WARD
ARLOETTE, MARY M. BAL 356 13TH WAR
ARLY, NAPOLEON BAL 005 1ST WARD
ARM, TEMPY KEN 215 2ND DIST
ARMA, JAMES KEN 258 1ST DIST
ARMACAST, JOHN BAL 193 5TH DIST
ARMACOST, ACAM BAL 196 5TH DIST
ARMACOST, CALEB M. BAL 200 5TH DIST
ARMACOST, DAVID BAL 240 1ST DIST
ARMACOST, JOHN M. BAL 195 5TH DIST
ARMACOST, JOSEPH CAR 185 8TH DIST
ARMACOST, JOSHUA BAL 200 5TH DIST
ARMACOST, LUCY CAR 279 7TH DIST
ARMACOST, MELCHOR CAR 185 8TH DIST
ARMACOST, MELCHOR BAL 434 1ST DIST
ARMACOST, NICK BAL 020 2ND DIST
ARMACOST, RICHARD BAL 197 5TH DIST
ARMACOST, RICHARD BAL 196 5TH DIST
ARMACOST, RICHARD BAL 303 1ST DIST
ARMACOST, RUTH BAL 196 5TH DIST
ARMACOST, SUSANAH CAR 180 8TH DIST
ARMACOST, THOMAS BAL 444 1ST DIST
ARMACOST, WILLIAM BAL 444 1ST DIST
ARMAGER, ELIZA E. ANN 354 3RD DIST
ARMAGER, ELLEN ANN 337 3RD DIST
ARMAGER, HENRIETTA ANN 396 8TH DIST
ARMAGER, JESSE BAL 076 15TH WAR
ARMAGER, JESSE BAL 159 16TH WAR
ARMAGER, JOHN ANN 396 8TH DIST
ARMAGER, JOHN ANN 410 8TH DIST
ARMAGER, SARAH BAL 120 16TH WAR
ARMAGER, THOMAS ANN 396 8TH DIST
ARMAGOST, CORNEALOUS CAR 197 4TH DIST
ARMAGOST, DANIEL CAR 193 4TH DIST
ARMAGOST, JOHN CAR 191 4TH DIST
ARMAGOST, MARY F. CAR 191 4TH DIST
ARMALING, GEORGE BAL 264 2ND WARD
ARMAN, GEORGE W. FRE 293 WOODSBOR
ARMAT, MARY E. BAL 180 2ND DIST
ARMATAGE, JOHN BAL 363 1ST DIST
ARMBLISLER, WILLIAM ALL 251 CUMBERLA
ARMECAST, GEORGE BAL 154 5TH WARD
ARMER, DEWAL BAL 260 1ST DIST
ARMEY, CONRADT BAL 333 7TH WARD
ARMGER, MARGARET BAL 210 2ND WARD
ARMICORT, JABEZ BAL 192 5TH DIST
ARMICOST, JOSEPH BAL 169 2ND DIST
ARMIGER, ANN PRI 022 VANSVILL
ARMIGER, BENJAMIN BAL 158 6TH WARD
ARMIGER, BETSY ANN 307 1ST DIST
ARMIGER, JAMES R. BAL 249 6TH WARD
ARMIGER, JOHN BAL 092 5TH WARD
ARMIGER, JOHN F. BAL 391 8TH WARD
ARMIGER, JOHN H. BAL 284 7TH WARD
ARMIGER, JOHN S. CAL 029 2ND DIST
ARMIGER, JOSEPH BAL 325 7TH WARD
ARMIGER, SARAH A. BAL 197 6TH WARD
ARMIGER, WILLIAM ANN 304 1ST DIST
ARMIGER, WILLIAM ANN 370 4TH DIST
ARMIGER, WILLIAM ANN 352 3RD DIST
ARMIGORT, JACOB BAL 191 5TH DIST
ARMIGORT, JOSHUA BAL 184 5TH DIST
ARMIGOST, RACHAEL BAL 191 5TH DIST
ARMISTEAD, B. A. BAL 332 1ST DIST
ARMISTEAD, LEWIS BAL 036 4TH WARD
ARMITAGE, ANN BAL 383 13TH WAR
ARMITAGE, ANN E. BAL 182 19TH WAR
ARMITAGE, ELIZABETH BAL 095 10TH WAR
ARMITAGE, GEORGE T. BAL 097 18TH WAR
ARMITAGE, JAMES BAL 447 14TH WAR
ARMITAGE, JOSEPH ANN 439 HOWARD D
ARMITAGE, JULIANN BAL 240 17TH WAR
ARMIZORT, MICHAEL BAL 191 5TH DIST
ARMON, ANDREW BAL 200 2ND WARD
ARMON, WILLIAM BAL 265 2ND WARD
ARMONS, MARY A. BAL 191 6TH WARD
ARMOR, CHARLES M. BAL 141 1ST WARD
ARMOR, GEORGE F. BAL 174 16TH WAR
ARMOR, J. BAL 295 12TH WAR
ARMOR, JANE BAL 323 12TH WAR
ARMOR, JOHN BAL 137 18TH WAR
ARMOR, JOSEPH G. BAL 429 14TH WAR
ARMOR, WILLIAM BAL 300 12TH WAR
ARMOUR, CHARLES FRE 033 FREDERIC
ARMOUR, JOHN CEC 164 6TH E DI
ARMOUR, MARGE A. FRE 047 FREDERIC
ARMOUR, STEPHEN CEC 137 6TH E DI
ARMSTEAD, JOSEPH BAL 116 15TH WAR
ARMSTEAD, LOUISA BAL 151 11TH WAR
ARMSTEAD, T. BAL 282 2ND WARD
ARMSTON, ANDREW WAS 030 2ND SUBD
ARMSTONG, HENRIETA BAL 062 1ST WARD
ARMSTRONG, ABRAHAM CAR 345 6TH DIST
ARMSTRONG, ALBERT ST 297 2ND E DI
ARMSTRONG, ALEXANDER WAS 125 HAGERSTO
ARMSTRONG, ALFRED P. BAL 062 1ST WARD
ARMSTRONG, ALVIN HAR 146 3RD DIST
ARMSTRONG, AMELIA BAL 111 5TH WARD
ARMSTRONG, ANDREW BAL 274 2ND WARD
ARMSTRONG, ANDREW BAL 083 15TH WAR
ARMSTRONG, ANN BAL 232 12TH WAR
ARMSTRONG, ANN QUE 143 1ST E DI
ARMSTRONG, ANN WOR 255 1ST CENS
ARMSTRONG, ANNA D. CEC 111 4TH E DI
ARMSTRONG, ASA S. BAL 112 1ST WARD
ARMSTRONG, BENJAMIN BAL 058 18TH WAR
ARMSTRONG, BITSEY BAL 011 1ST WARD
ARMSTRONG, CATHARINE BAL 019 1ST WARD
ARMSTRONG, CATHARINE BAL 366 1ST DIST
ARMSTRONG, CHARLES BAL 099 1ST WARD
ARMSTRONG, CHARLOTT KEN 289 3RD DIST
ARMSTRONG, COMFORT WOR 237 6TH E DI
ARMSTRONG, COMFORT BAL 124 18TH WAR
ARMSTRONG, CYDNEY HAR 173 3RD DIST
ARMSTRONG, DANIEL BAL 366 1ST DIST
ARMSTRONG, DAVID T. ANN 305 1ST DIST
ARMSTRONG, DENNIS BAL 346 7TH WARD
ARMSTRONG, E.R. BAL 014 18TH WAR
ARMSTRONG, EDWARD BAL 475 14TH WAR
ARMSTRONG, ELIJAH-BLACK WOR 173 6TH E DI
ARMSTRONG, ELIZA WOR 183 6TH E DI
ARMSTRONG, ELIZA BAL 359 3RD WARD
ARMSTRONG, ELIZABETH BAL 385 3RD WARD
ARMSTRONG, ELIZABETH BAL 067 15TH WAR
ARMSTRONG, ELIZABETH BAL 215 11TH WAR
ARMSTRONG, EMELINE BAL 125 11TH WAR
ARMSTRONG, EMILY BAL 112 5TH WARD
ARMSTRONG, ESBRA BAL 316 3RD WARD
ARMSTRONG, ESTHER-BLACK WOR 166 6TH E DI
ARMSTRONG, GEORGE BAL 462 1ST DIST
ARMSTRONG, GEORGE BAL 430 14TH WAR
ARMSTRONG, GEORGE BAL 343 13TH WAR
ARMSTRONG, GEORGE W. CEC 129 6TH E DI
ARMSTRONG, GEORGE W. BAL 266 2ND WARD
ARMSTRONG, H. BAL 259 20TH WAR
ARMSTRONG, HANNAH BAL 032 4TH WARD
ARMSTRONG, HANNAH A. CEC 107 3RD E DI
ARMSTRONG, HENRIETTA BAL 218 6TH WARD
ARMSTRONG, HENRIETTA WOR 175 6TH E DI
ARMSTRONG, HENRY BAL 140 5TH WARD
ARMSTRONG, HENRY BAL 294 7TH WARD
ARMSTRONG, HENRY BAL 396 1ST DIST
ARMSTRONG, HENRY BAL 315 12TH WAR
ARMSTRONG, HENRY HAR 134 2ND DIST
ARMSTRONG, HESTER A. BAL 320 3RD WARD
ARMSTRONG, HORATIO BAL 075 2ND DIST
ARMSTRONG, HOSEA BAL 145 2ND DIST
ARMSTRONG, IRA BAL 086 4TH WARD
ARMSTRONG, ISAAC WOR 312 2ND E DI
ARMSTRONG, ISABELLA FRE 161 EMMITTSB
ARMSTRONG, ISABELLA BAL 184 2ND WARD
ARMSTRONG, ISHY * WOR 294 9TH E DI
ARMSTRONG, J. BAL 296 12TH WAR
ARMSTRONG, J. D. BAL 109 10TH WAR
ARMSTRONG, J. R. W. BAL 282 2ND WARD
ARMSTRONG, JACOB FRE 063 FREDERIC
ARMSTRONG, JAMES BAL 205 17TH WAR
ARMSTRONG, JAMES CEC 026 ELKTON 3
ARMSTRONG, JAMES BAL 460 8TH WARD
ARMSTRONG, JAMES BAL 173 1ST WARD
ARMSTRONG, JAMES BAL 226 6TH WARD
ARMSTRONG, JAMES BAL 004 EASTERN
ARMSTRONG, JAMES ST 308 1ST E DI
ARMSTRONG, JAMES WOR 214 4TH E DI
ARMSTRONG, JAMES D. ALL 091 5TH E.D.
ARMSTRONG, JAMES R. BAL 184 2ND WARD
ARMSTRONG, JAMES-BLACK ST 332 4TH E DI
ARMSTRONG, JAMESL. BAL 275 12TH WAR
ARMSTRONG, JANE BAL 254 6TH WARD
ARMSTRONG, JOHN BAL 100 10TH WAR
ARMSTRONG, JOHN BAL 162 1ST WARD
ARMSTRONG, JOHN BAL 110 1ST WARD
ARMSTRONG, JOHN BAL 254 1ST DIST
ARMSTRONG, JOHN WOR 291 9TH E DI
ARMSTRONG, JOHN WAS 022 2ND SUBD
ARMSTRONG, JOHN CEC 142 6TH E DI
ARMSTRONG, JOHN BAL 049 4TH WARD
ARMSTRONG, JOHN KEN 209 2ND DIST
ARMSTRONG, JOHN CEC 112 4TH E DI
ARMSTRONG, JOHN BAL 293 20TH WAR
ARMSTRONG, JOHN BAL 242 20TH WAR
ARMSTRONG, JOHN A. BAL 062 10TH WAR
ARMSTRONG, JOHN M. KEN 287 3RD DIST
ARMSTRONG, JOHN M. JR. KEN 287 3RD DIST
ARMSTRONG, JOHNS. BAL 192 19TH WAR
ARMSTRONG, JONATHAN BAL 053 4TH WARD
ARMSTRONG, JOSEHPINE BAL 263 2ND WARD
ARMSTRONG, JOSEPH FRE 096 FREDERIC
ARMSTRONG, JOSIAH BAL 336 3RD WARD
ARMSTRONG, LEWIS CEC 013 ELKTON 3
ARMSTRONG, LOTT WOR 301 SNOW HIL
ARMSTRONG, MARGARET CEC 135 6TH E DI
ARMSTRONG, MARGARET BAL 076 2ND DIST
ARMSTRONG, MARGARETT BAL 016 4TH WARD
ARMSTRONG, MARY CAR 273 WESTMINS
ARMSTRONG, MARY BAL 023 2ND DIST
ARMSTRONG, MARY BAL 320 3RD WARD
ARMSTRONG, MARY BAL 122 5TH WARD
ARMSTRONG, MARY ALL 091 5TH E.D.
ARMSTRONG, MARY BAL 167 11TH WAR
ARMSTRONG, MARY WAS 023 2ND SUBD
ARMSTRONG, MATILDA BAL 211 2ND WARD
ARMSTRONG, MATILDA BAL 424 14TH WAR
ARMSTRONG, MEARY A. BAL 108 1ST WARD
ARMSTRONG, PETER-BLACK WOR 176 6TH E DI
ARMSTRONG, PRISSY WOR 307 2ND E DI
ARMSTRONG, PURNELL WOR 316 2ND E DI
ARMSTRONG, Q. M. * ALL 054 10TH E.D
ARMSTRONG, RICHARD BAL 076 10TH WAR
ARMSTRONG, ROBERT G. BAL 324 12TH WAR
ARMSTRONG, SAMUEL KEN 292 3RD DIST
ARMSTRONG, SARAH BAL 332 3RD WARD
ARMSTRONG, SARAH BAL 192 19TH WAR
ARMSTRONG, SARAH L. BAL 099 1ST WARD
ARMSTRONG, SOLOMON BAL 017 1ST WARD
ARMSTRONG, SOLOMON BAL 026 2ND DIST
ARMSTRONG, SUSAN-BLACK FRE 052 FREDERIC
ARMSTRONG, THOMAS BAL 016 4TH WARD
ARMSTRONG, THOMAS BAL 372 13TH WAR
ARMSTRONG, THOMAS BAL 104 2ND DIST
ARMSTRONG, THOMAS BAL 039 1ST WARD
ARMSTRONG, THOMAS BAL 305 1ST DIST
ARMSTRONG, THOMAS BAL 102 5TH WARD
ARMSTRONG, THOMAS BAL 366 1ST DIST
ARMSTRONG, THOMAS BAL 328 13TH WAR
ARMSTRONG, THOMAS BAL 144 1ST WARD
ARMSTRONG, THOMAS H. ALL 055 10TH E.D
ARMSTRONG, VINA BAL 424 14TH WAR
ARMSTRONG, WALTER CEC 111 4TH E DI
ARMSTRONG, WILLIAM CEC 119 3RD E DI
ARMSTRONG, WILLIAM BAL 286 17TH WAR
ARMSTRONG, WILLIAM BAL 421 14TH WAR
ARMSTRONG, WILLIAM BAL 257 17TH WAR
ARMSTRONG, WILLIAM BAL 386 13TH WAR
ARMSTRONG, WILLIAM ALL 213 CUMBERLA
ARMSTRONG, WILLIAM BAL 058 1ST WARD
ARMSTRONG, WILLIAM BAL 160 2ND DIST
ARMSTRONG, WILLIAM WOR 219 4TH E DI
ARMSTRONG, WILLIAM G. KEN 310 3RD DIST
ARMSTRONG, WILLIAM J. WOR 216 4TH E DI
ARMSTRONG, WILLIAM P. QUE 153 1ST E DI
ARMSWORTH, MC KELVA ST 292 2ND E DI
ARMSWORTHY, ANN ST 303 2ND E DI
ARMSWORTHY, ANN ST 299 2ND E DI
ARMSWORTHY, ANN ST 287 2ND E DI
ARMSWORTHY, BENJAMIN ST 288 2ND E DI
ARMSWORTHY, CHARLES W. ST 288 2ND E DI
ARMSWORTHY, GEORGE ST 287 2ND E DI
ARMSWORTHY, THOMAS ST 287 2ND E DI
ARMWOOD, ARGO SOM 415 DUBLIN D
ARMWOOD, ELIZABETH WOR 184 6TH E DI
ARMWOOD, JAMES SOM 415 DUBLIN D
ARMWOOD, LEVI SOM 416 DUBLIN D
ARMWOOD, MARY-BLACK WOR 317 2ND E DI
ARMWOOD, RUTH SOM 459 HANGARY
ARMWOOD, SARAH SOM 421 PRINCESS
ARMWOOD, WHITTINGTON SOM 415 DUBLIN D
ARMWOOD, WHITTINGTON SOM 422 PRINCESS
ARMWOOD, WILLIAM SOM 433 PRINCESS
ARNATT, ELIZABETH BAL 089 10TH WAR
ARNBRUST, JACOB BAL 304 7TH WARD
ARNDER, LEWIS WAS 142 HAGERSTO
ARNDER, SOPHIA WAS 142 HAGERSTO
ARNOT, ANDREW ALL 011 3RD E.D.
ARNOT, JACOB ALL 011 3RD E.D.
ARNER, PHILIP BAL 117 18TH WAR
ARNES, WILLIAM CEC 031 CHESAPEA
ARNESS, SARAH CEC 018 ELKTON 3
ARNETE, JOSEPH DOR 393 1ST DIST
ARNETT, HENRY BAL 217 6TH WARD
ARNETT, JOHN DOR 313 1ST DIST
ARNETT, MARY A. DOR 394 1ST DIST
ARNETT, THOMAS DOR 308 1ST DIST
ARNETT, WILLIAM BAL 215 11TH WAR
ARNETT, WILLIAM H. BAL 256 6TH WARD
ARNEY, CHARLES CAR 145 NO TWP L
ARNEY, MARY CAR 153 NO TWP L
ARNNESS, JOHN CEC 029 CHESAPEA
ARNODL, ELMYRER WAS 215 1ST DIST
ARNOL, MARY A. CAR 210 5TH DIST
ARNOLD, ABRAHAM B. BAL 066 4TH WARD
ARNOLD, ALEXANDER BAL 393 1ST DIST
ARNOLD, ANN BAL 333 1ST DIST
ARNOLD, ANN FRE 033 FREDERIC
ARNOLD, ANN DOR 360 3RD DIVI
ARNOLD, ANTHONY CAR 195 4TH DIST
ARNOLD, AUTUSTUS CAR 306 1ST DIST
ARNOLD, BENJAMIN BAL 085 2ND DIST
ARNOLD, BETSY ANN 376 4TH DIST
ARNOLD, CAHRLES CAR 196 4TH DIST
ARNOLD, CATHARINE BAL 304 1ST DIST
ARNOLD, CHARLES BAL 085 2ND DIST
ARNOLD, CHARLES BAL 059 4TH WARD
ARNOLD, CLEMENT BAL 222 17TH WAR
ARNOLD, CLEMMONT BAL 055 18TH WAR
ARNOLD, CONRAD BAL 079 18TH WAR
ARNOLD, CONRAD BAL 018 9TH WARD
ARNOLD, CYRUS D. WAS 132 HAGERSTO
ARNOLD, DAVID BAL 125 18TH WAR
ARNOLD, DRUSELLA ALL 149 6TH E.D.
ARNOLD, EASTER CAR 282 7TH DIST
ARNOLD, EDWIN HAR 075 BEL AIR
ARNOLD, ELIJAH R. ANN 360 3RD DIST
ARNOLD, ELIZABETH BAL 188 6TH WARD
ARNOLD, ELIZABETH BAL 043 15TH WAR
ARNOLD, ELIZABETH BAL 009 4TH WARD
ARNOLD, ELIZABETH FRE 328 MIDDLETO
ARNOLD, ELIZABETH R. ANN 361 3RD DIST
ARNOLD, FRANCIS BAL 084 18TH WAR
ARNOLD, FRED BAL 296 17TH WAR
ARNOLD, GEORGE BAL 012 9TH WARD
ARNOLD, GEORGE BAL 259 12TH WAR
ARNOLD, GEORGE BAL 120 1ST WARD
ARNOLD, GEORGE W. BAL 337 13TH WAR
ARNOLD, HARRIET ANN 317 1ST DIST
ARNOLD, HEMEETTA * ALL 084 5TH E.D.
ARNOLD, HENRY MGM 428 CLARKSTR
ARNOLD, ISAAC BAL 266 7TH WARD
ARNOLD, ISAIAH ANN 388 4TH DIST
ARNOLD, JAMES ANN 376 4TH DIST
ARNOLD, JAMES BAL 174 16TH WAR
ARNOLD, JAMES CAR 211 5TH DIST
ARNOLD, JAMES WAS 216 1ST DIST
ARNOLD, JAMES E. BAL 365 3RD WARD
ARNOLD, JAMES M. FRE 005 FREDERIC
ARNOLD, JESSE ALL 101 5TH E.D.
ARNOLD, JESSE ALL 061 10TH E.D
ARNOLD, JOHN ALL 062 10TH E.D
ARNOLD, JOHN ALL 048 10TH E.D
ARNOLD, JOHN ANN 348 3RD DIST
ARNOLD, JOHN BAL 102 5TH WARD
ARNOLD, JOHN FRE 397 PETERSVI
ARNOLD, JOHN CAR 194 4TH DIST
ARNOLD, JOHN CAR 196 4TH DIST
ARNOLD, JOHN BAL 080 18TH WAR
ARNOLD, JOHN BAL 282 17TH WAR
ARNOLD, JOHN FRE 325 MIDDLETO
ARNOLD, JOHN PRI 095 SPALDING
ARNOLD, JONATHAN ALL 084 5TH E.D.
ARNOLD, JOSEPH ALL 148 6TH E.D.
ARNOLD, JOSEPH PRI 102 SPALDING
ARNOLD, JOSEPH PRI 095 SPALDING
ARNOLD, JOSEPH PRI 042 VANSVILL
ARNOLD, JOSEPH WAS 139 HAGERSTO
ARNOLD, JOSEPH CAR 200 4TH DIST
ARNOLD, JOSEPH CAR 315 1ST DIST
ARNOLD, JULIA A. ST 318 4TH E DI
ARNOLD, JULIANNA CEC 170 6TH E DI
ARNOLD, LAZARUS BAL 024 1ST WARD
ARNOLD, LYDDIA ALL 153 6TH E.D.
ARNOLD, MARGARET ALL 083 5TH E.D.
ARNOLD, MARGARET A. BAL 291 17TH WAR
ARNOLD, MARGARET R. CAR 211 5TH DIST
ARNOLD, MARTHA J. BAL 127 16TH WAR
ARNOLD, MARY BAL 462 1ST DIST
ARNOLD, MARY BAL 198 6TH WARD
ARNOLD, MARY CAR 300 1ST DIST
ARNOLD, MARY A. BAL 421 8TH WARD
ARNOLD, NATHANIEL ALL 087 5TH E.D.
ARNOLD, PEGGY BAL 333 1ST DIST
ARNOLD, PETER BAL 009 9TH WARD
ARNOLD, PETER FRE 327 MIDDLETO
ARNOLD, RACHAEL CAR 282 7TH DIST
ARNOLD, RICHARD BAL 343 13TH WAR
ARNOLD, RODRICK BAL 271 1ST DIST
ARNOLD, SAM C. B. BAL 177 2ND DIST
ARNOLD, SAMUEL ANN 391 4TH DIST
ARNOLD, SAMUEL PRI 095 SPALDING
ARNOLD, SARAH BAL 348 1ST DIST
ARNOLD, SARHA CAR 280 7TH DIST
ARNOLD, SIMON ALL 090 5TH E.D.

ARNOLD, SUSAN FRE 162 EMMITTSB
ARNOLD, SUSAN WAS 100 2ND DIST
ARNOLD, THOMAS DOR 357 3RD DIVI
ARNOLD, VALENTINE BAL 060 18TH WAR
ARNOLD, VICTORIA ANN 349 3RD DIST
ARNOLD, WILLIAM ANN 376 4TH DIST
ARNOLD, WILLIAM ALL 061 10TH E.D
ARNOLD, WILLIAM BAL 197 6TH WARD
ARNOLD, WILLIAM BAL 155 16TH WAR
ARNOLD, WILLIAM CEC 170 6TH E DI
ARNOLD, WILLIAM HAR 162 3RD DIST
ARNOLD, WILLIAM B. BAL 120 1ST WARD
ARNOLD, WILLIAM H. CAR 203 4TH DIST
ARNOLD,CAVID FRE 397 PETERSVI
ARNSPERGOR, WILLIAM FRE 145 10TH E D
ARNY, LETTY MGM 399 ROCKERLE
ARO, LEWIS BAL 234 17TH WAR
AROW, JOSEPH BAL 002 EASTERN
AROWELLER, ANN ALL 033 2ND E.D.
ARPREYS, LEWIS HAR 079 2ND DIST
ARREL, GEORGE WAS 231 1ST DIST
ARRENTS, WILLIAM CEC 073 5TH E DI
ARREY, ELIAS BAL 240 20TH WAR
ARRING, HENRY ALL 196 CUMBERLA
ARRINGDALE, EDWARD TAL 016 EASTON D
ARRINGDALE, JAMES TAL 032 EASTON D
ARRINGDALE, JOHN W. TAL 043 EASTON D
ARRINGDALE, THOMAS JR.* TAL 031 EASTON D
ARRINGDALE, WILLIAM TAL 020 EASTON D
ARRINGDALL, RICHARD JR. TAL 076 EASTON T
ARRINGTON, GRAFTON PRI 026 VANSVILL
ARRINGTON, MARY A. BAL 205 11TH WAR
ARROW, MATILDA BAL 191 2ND WARD
ARROWAY, JOHN BAL 162 16TH WAR
ARSBACK, ELIZA BAL 194 11TH WAR
ARSHIS, GEORGE W. WAS 109 2ND DIST
ARSMTRONG, HENRY CEC 107 3RD E DI
ARSON, JOHN CEC 078 NORTHEAS
ARTER, PHILIP CAR 248 3RD DIST
ARTER, SOLOMON CAR 248 3RD DIST
ARTERS, JOHN CAR 293 7TH DIST
ARTHER, BENJAMIN BAL 230 1ST DIST
ARTHER, CARMILLER * FRE 138 CREAGERS
ARTHER, FRANCES A. BAL 298 7TH WARD
ARTHER, JOHN FRE 129 CREAGERS
ARTHER, JOSIAH FRE 129 CREAGERS
ARTHER, MARGARET CAR 410 2ND DIST
ARTHUR, ANN BAL 151 11TH WAR
ARTHUR, ANN BAL 262 6TH WARD
ARTHUR, ANNE BAL 057 15TH WAR
ARTHUR, ANNY* BAL 342 3RD WARD
ARTHUR, AUSTIN BAL 258 1ST DIST
ARTHUR, CATHARINE CAR 403 2ND DIST
ARTHUR, CHARLES BAL 395 1ST DIST
ARTHUR, DAVID BAL 190 6TH WARD
ARTHUR, DAVID KEN 210 2ND DIST
ARTHUR, ELIZA HAR 068 1ST DIST
ARTHUR, ELIZA BAL 111 15TH WAR
ARTHUR, ELIZABETH CAR 291 7TH DIST
ARTHUR, ELLEN BAL 375 3RD WARD
ARTHUR, ESTHER BAL 316 20TH WAR
ARTHUR, GEORGE HAR 065 1ST DIST
ARTHUR, HUGH BAL 171 19TH WAR
ARTHUR, INDIANA BAL 092 10TH WAR
ARTHUR, JAMES PRI 022 VANSVILL
ARTHUR, JEREMIAH CAR 405 2ND DIST
ARTHUR, JOHN CAR 222 5TH DIST
ARTHUR, JOHN HAR 065 1ST DIST
ARTHUR, JOHN BAL 314 1ST DIST
ARTHUR, JOHN ALL 071 5TH E.D.
ARTHUR, JOSEPH CAR 412 2ND DIST
ARTHUR, MARY J. BAL 152 19TH WAR
ARTHUR, NELLY BAL 067 1ST WARD
ARTHUR, REBECCA BAL 152 11TH WAR
ARTHUR, ROBERT CAR 410 2ND DIST
ARTHUR, ROBERT HAR 065 1ST DIST
ARTHUR, SUSAN BAL 098 5TH WARD
ARTHUR, WILLIAM C. BAL 152 19TH WAR
ARTHUR,AGNES CAR 410 2ND DIST
ARTHUR,ANDREW CAR 410 2ND DIST
ARTHURS, MARK CEC 070 5TH E DI
ARTIS, CATHARINE ST 307 1ST E DI
ARTIS, JOHN C. ST 306 1ST E DI
ARTIS, JOSEPH T. ST 309 1ST E DI
ARTIS, MALACHI QUE 135 1ST E DI
ARTIS, MARGARET A.E. ST 314 1ST E DI
ARTMAN, ELIZABETH FRE 344 MIDDLETO
ARTON, CATHARINE WAS 194 1ST DIST
ARTQUIT, JOSEPHINE BAL 041 4TH WARD
ARTY, CORNELIUS WAS 128 HAGERSTO
ARTY, DAVID WAS 128 HAGERSTO
ARTZ, AUGUST BAL 275 17TH WAR
ARTZ, CATHARINE WAS 030 2ND SUBD
ARTZ, CHRISTIAN B. FRE 100 FREDERIC
ARTZ, ELIZA WAS 010 WILLIAMS
ARTZ, HENRY WAS 018 2ND SUBD
ARTZ, HENRY WAS 049 2ND SUBD
ARTZ, PETER WAS 050 2ND SUBD
ARTZ, RUE WAS 018 2ND SUBD
ARTZ, SMITH WAS 035 2ND SUBD
ARTZ, VINTON WAS 031 2ND SUBD
ARUTE, LEVI DOR 374 1ST DIST
ARVEY, GEORGE SOM 483 TRAPP DI
ARVEY, HESTER SOM 424 PRINCESS
ARVEY, LEVIN* SOM 525 QUANTICO
ARVINGDALE, RICHARD * TAL 072 EASTON T
ARWOOD, JANE ALL 190 9TH E.D.
ARWOOD, SUSAN BAL 353 1ST DIST
ARY, MINTY CAL 049 3RD DIST
ASA, BRIDGET BAL 325 1ST DIST
ASBERRY, FRANCIS WAS 199 1ST DIST
ASBINGER, JOHN BAL 194 2ND WARD
ASBORN, SAMUEL CEC 069 5TH E DI
ASBOURN, J.J. BAL 142 1ST WARD
ASBURY, ANDREW ANN 431 HOWARD D
ASCOM, GEORGE ST 345 5TH E DI
ASE, CHARLES ALL 073 5TH E.D.
ASGRIETT, ELSY* BAL 158 19TH WAR
ASGUITH, HENRY ANN 367 4TH DIST
ASH, ADALADE BAL 065 4TH WARD
ASH, AMANDA BAL 356 3RD WARD
ASH, CHARLES BAL 120 2ND DIST
ASH, CHARLES-BLACK CAR 079 NO TWP L
ASH, ELISABETH ALL 247 CUMBERLA
ASH, ELIZABETH BAL 135 16TH WAR
ASH, FRANCES CEC 024 ELKTON 3
ASH, FRANCIS BAL 021 1ST WARD
ASH, GEORGE T. TAL 007 EASTON D
ASH, GOERGE CEC 012 ELKTON 3
ASH, HANSON ALL 187 9TH E.D.
ASH, HENRY CEC 180 7TH E DI
ASH, ISRAEL BAL 134 16TH WAR
ASH, JACOB BAL 054 18TH WAR
ASH, JACOB CEC 015 ELKTON 3
ASH, JACOB G. CEC 004 ELKTON 3
ASH, JANE BAL 385 1ST DIST
ASH, JEREMIAH HAR 131 2ND DIST
ASH, JOHN CEC 197 7TH E DI
ASH, JOHN WAS 015 2ND SUBD
ASH, JOSHUA CEC 001 ELKTON 3
ASH, LOUIS BAL 117 15TH WAR
ASH, MARTHA BAL 311 3RD WARD
ASH, MARY-BLACK CAR 149 NO TWP L
ASH, MILES CEC 012 ELKTON 3
ASH, NICHOLAS BAL 417 3RD WARD
ASH, NICHOLAS BAL 054 18TH WAR
ASH, SAMUEL BAL 367 13TH WAR
ASH, THOASM BAL 469 14TH WAR
ASH, WILLIAM CAR 101 NO TWP L
ASH, WILLIAM CAR 101 NO TWP L
ASH, WILLIAM BAL 045 4TH WARD
ASH, WILSON BAL 227 6TH WARD
ASHAUPT, ALFRED BAL 068 1ST WARD
ASHBAUGH, AQUILLER FRE 282 WOODSBOR
ASHBAUGH, JOHN FRE 037 FREDERIC
ASHBAUGH, NIMROD WAS 277 LEITERSB
ASHBURN, WILLIAM BAL 245 17TH WAR
ASHBURNE, CHARLES H. BAL 022 2ND DIST
ASHBY, BYARD CEC 088 4TH E DI
ASHBY, JAMES R. BAL 120 5TH WARD
ASHBY, JESSE L. ALL 059 10TH E.D
ASHBY, WILLIAM ALL 059 10TH E.D
ASHBY, WILLIAM ALL 059 10TH E.D
ASHBY, WILLIAM W. ALL 059 10TH E.D
ASHCEM, THOMAS JR. QUE 184 3RD E DI
ASHCOM, ALEXANDER BAL 397 3RD WARD
ASHCOM, ANN B. ST 306 1ST E DI
ASHCOM, ELIZABETH ST 310 1ST E DI
ASHCOM, JAMES QUE 187 3RD E DI
ASHCOM, THOMAS QUE 190 3RD E DI
ASHCROFT, ROBERT BAL 007 1ST WARD
ASHCROFT, WELLS BAL 405 3RD WARD
ASHENBUNNER, BALTZER ALL 081 5TH E.D.
ASHER, RACHEL BAL 050 4TH WARD
ASHER, WILLIAM BAL 141 2ND DIST
ASHFORD, JOHN FRE 388 PETERSVI
ASHFORD, STEPHEN BAL 400 3RD WARD
ASHINS, HARRY TAL 101 ST MICHA
ASHINS, RICHARD* TAL 012 EASTON D
ASHINS, WILLIAM* TAL 012 EASTON D
ASHKELDE, ELIZABETH ALL 183 8TH E.D.
ASHLAND, CHARLOTTE-BLACK QUE 163 2ND E DI
ASHLAND, THOMAS BAL 126 16TH WAR
ASHLEY, ABRAHAM KEN 267 1ST DIST
ASHLEY, BENJAMIN KEN 239 2ND DIST
ASHLEY, BENJAMIN F. BAL 350 7TH WARD
ASHLEY, DAVID KEN 233 2ND DIST
ASHLEY, DAVID QUE 195 3RD E DI
ASHLEY, DAVID-BLACK QUE 166 2ND E DI
ASHLEY, DAVID-BLACK QUE 163 2ND E DI
ASHLEY, EMILY KEN 241 2ND DIST
ASHLEY, H. BAL 116 1ST WARD
ASHLEY, H. C. BAL 332 1ST DIST
ASHLEY, ISAIAH KEN 266 1ST DIST
ASHLEY, JOHN BAL 331 7TH WARD
ASHLEY, JOHN D. KEN 266 1ST DIST
ASHLEY, JOHN W. KEN 245 2ND DIST
ASHLEY, JOSEPH KEN 233 2ND DIST
ASHLEY, LEMUEL KEN 267 1ST DIST
ASHLEY, LEMUEL W. KEN 264 1ST DIST
ASHLEY, MARY KEN 218 2ND DIST
ASHLEY, MARY-BLACK QUE 166 2ND E DI
ASHLEY, RACHEL-BLACK QUE 167 2ND E DI
ASHLEY, THOMAS-BLACK QUE 170 2ND E DI
ASHLEY, WILLIAM H. ANN 336 3RD DIST
ASHMAN, ANN BAL 099 15TH WAR
ASHMAN, WILLIAM BAL 315 20TH WAR
ASHMEAD, JOSEPH R. SOM 466 DAMES QU
ASHMUN, WILLIAM BAL 100 5TH WARD
ASHTON, AGATHA BAL 406 14TH WAR
ASHTON, BASIL BAL 239 6TH WARD
ASHTON, CHRISTOPHER ALL 103 5TH E.D.
ASHTON, EDWARD HAR 051 1ST DIST
ASHTON, ELLEN BAL 126 11TH WAR
ASHTON, FREDRICK DOR 362 3RD DIVI
ASHTON, GEORGE BAL 262 2ND WARD
ASHTON, JAMES BAL 077 2ND DIST
ASHTON, JEMIMA CEC 098 3RD E DI
ASHTON, JOHN HAR 090 2ND DIST
ASHTON, JOHN BAL 018 4TH WARD
ASHTON, JOHN BAL 228 6TH WARD
ASHTON, JOSEPH HAR 066 1ST DIST
ASHTON, JOSEPH HAR 051 1ST DIST
ASHTON, M. BAL 127 11TH WAR
ASHTON, RICHARD HAR 051 1ST DIST
ASHTON, RICHARD BAL 227 19TH WAR
ASHTON, T. BAL 144 5TH WARD
ASHTON, THOAMS R. CAR 230 5TH DIST
ASHTON, THOMAS MGM 408 MEDLEY 3
ASHTON, THOMAS BAL 192 6TH WARD
ASHTON, WILLIAM BAL 378 8TH WARD
ASHTON, WILLIAM HAR 060 1ST DIST
ASHTON, WILLIAM R. BAL 151 16TH WAR
ASK, JOHN BAL 462 1ST DIST
ASKEN, CHARLES BAL 284 20TH WAR
ASKEN, JOHN V. B. MGM 353 BERRYS D
ASKENS, MARY BAL 079 15TH WAR
ASKETTLE, DAVID ALL 182 8TH E.D.
ASKEW, ELLEN BAL 448 8TH WARD
ASKEW, HANNAH W. CEC 129 6TH E DI
ASKEW, JOHN BAL 456 8TH WARD
ASKEY, A. BAL 138 1ST WARD
ASKEY, GEORGE BAL 339 1ST DIST
ASKEY, JAMES BAL 050 4TH WARD
ASKEY, JOHN ANN 457 HOWARD D
ASKEY, JOSHUA BAL 056 4TH WARD
ASKEY, MARGRET HAR 207 3RD DIST
ASKEY, ROBERT HAR 014 1ST DIST
ASKEY, SARAH E. BAL 050 4TH WARD
ASKEY, WILLIAM BAL 324 7TH WARD
ASKILL, THOMAS-BLACK BAL 222 2ND WARD
ASKIN, ANN E. BAL 279 20TH WAR
ASKINS, BLAIN BAL 300 3RD WARD
ASKINS, CHRISTOPHER BAL 089 15TH WAR
ASKINS, ELLEN BAL 194 11TH WAR
ASKINS, GEORGE MGM 321 CRACKLIN
ASKINS, HANNA TAL 046 EASTON T
ASKINS, JEMIMAH BAL 323 7TH WARD
ASKINS, JOBE TAL 021 EASTON D
ASKINS, JOSEPH TAL 015 EASTON D
ASKINS, JOSEPH* TAL 015 EASTON D
ASKINS, LEVIN DOR 401 1ST DIST
ASKINS, PHEBE BAL 194 11TH WAR
ASKINS, SAMUEL* TAL 037 EASTON D
ASKINS, THOMAS-MULATTO QUE 200 3RD E DI
ASKINS, WILLIAM* TAL 012 EASTON D
ASLAR, JOHN ANN 474 HOWARD D
ASLON, MARGARET BAL 156 2ND DIST
ASMUSS, HANS BAL 087 10TH WAR
ASPELMYER, FREDERICK BAL 087 10TH WAR
ASPLIN, HARIATT DOR 468 1ST DIST
ASQUITH, THOMAS BAL 262 6TH WARD
ASSEL, OTHO N. MGM 444 CLARKSTR
ASSEL, WILLIAM MGM 414 MEDLEY 3
ASSEY, WORTHINGTON ALL 221 CUMBERLA
ASSIESER, NICHOLAS * BAL 033 9TH WARD
ASTEN, ELIAS BAL 115 1ST WARD
ASTEN, JOSEPH ALL 109 5TH E.D.
ASTLIN, RICHARD MGM 410 MEDLEY 3
ASTON, ELIAS BAL 155 1ST WARD
ATANNET, JOSHUA CAL 028 2ND DIST
ATAR, GEORGE WAS 274 RIDGEVIL
ATAWOOD, ROSETTA KEN 278 1ST DIST
ATCHAISON, MARY CHA 253 MIDDLETO
ATCHER, JOHN BAL 020 9TH WARD
ATCHESON, WILLIAMSON ALL 154 6TH E.D.
ATCHINSON, ALEXANDER ALL 246 CUMBERLA
ATCHISON, ELISABETH ALL 247 CUMBERLA
ATCHISON, MARY J. BAL 031 9TH WARD
ATCHISON, WILLIAM BAL 459 8TH WARD
ATCHISON, WILLIAM WAS 049 2ND SUBD
ATCHISON, WILLIAM H. BAL 037 4TH WARD
ATCHKINSON, BEL BAL 153 11TH WAR
ATERBERT, JOHN BAL 237 12TH WAR
ATEVEK, JOHN D. * CAR 234 UNION TO
ATEWOOD, CATHARINE BAL 331 1ST DIST
ATHEY, CYRUS ALL 232 CUMBERLA
ATHEY, DEBRA ALL 177 7TH E.D.
ATHEY, ELIZABETH ALL 178 7TH E.D.
ATHEY, GEORGE ALL 177 7TH E.D.
ATHEY, JOHN T. ALL 208 CUMBERLA
ATHEY, MINERVA ALL 217 CUMBERLA
ATHEY, PRISLEY N. PRI 121 PISCATAW
ATHINSON, ANGLOE WOR 180 6TH E DI
ATHINSON, CHARLES WOR 182 6TH E DI
ATHROE, ELIZABETH* BAL 312 3RD WARD
ATHUR, JAMES KEN 209 2ND DIST
ATHY, MARY PRI 031 VANSVILL
ATINELL, MARGARET * BAL 392 1ST DIST
ATION, WILLIAM BAL 131 1ST WARD
ATKIN, BENJAMIN HAR 045 1ST DIST
ATKIN, CHARLOTT BAL 382 3RD WARD
ATKIN, CHARLOTTE ALL 170 7TH E.D.
ATKINS, ALFRED-BLACK BAL 208 2ND WARD
ATKINS, BENJAMIN FRE 085 FREDERIC
ATKINS, CHARLES FRE 083 FREDERIC
ATKINS, ELIZABETH FRE 130 CREAGERS
ATKINS, JACOB BAL 131 1ST WARD
ATKINS, JOHN DOR 373 1ST DIST
ATKINS, LEVIN* DOR 412 1ST DIST
ATKINS, WILLIAM ALL 073 5TH E.D.
ATKINS,MARY FRE 008 FREDERIC
ATKINSON, AARON WOR 186 7TH E DI
ATKINSON, ABRAHAM BAL 108 15TH WAR
ATKINSON, AGNES BAL 179 11TH WAR
ATKINSON, ALEXANDER BAL 114 1ST WARD
ATKINSON, ALFORD BAL 115 1ST WARD
ATKINSON, ALFRED BAL 160 1ST WARD
ATKINSON, ALGY DOR 425 1ST DIST
ATKINSON, ALLEN BAL 179 19TH WAR
ATKINSON, AMOS G. ANN 422 HOWARD D
ATKINSON, ANN BAL 408 14TH WAR
ATKINSON, BENJAMIN WOR 190 8TH E DI
ATKINSON, BULIA BAL 148 19TH WAR
ATKINSON, CLOE DOR 434 1ST DIST
ATKINSON, DAVID HAR 048 1ST DIST
ATKINSON, DAVID BAL 402 8TH WARD
ATKINSON, EDWARD CAR 112 NO TWP L
ATKINSON, ELISHA CEC 124 5TH E DI
ATKINSON, ELLEN BAL 151 19TH WAR
ATKINSON, GEORGE BAL 309 20TH WAR
ATKINSON, GEORGE S. SOM 431 PRINCESS
ATKINSON, HARIOTT DOR 443 1ST DIST
ATKINSON, HENRY BAL 190 19TH WAR
ATKINSON, HENRY BAL 190 19TH WAR
ATKINSON, HENRY CEC 199 7TH E DI
ATKINSON, HENRY B. BAL 014 2ND DIST
ATKINSON, ISAAC S. SOM 419 PRINCESS
ATKINSON, ISACK* TAL 006 EASTON D
ATKINSON, ISRAEL HAR 050 1ST DIST
ATKINSON, JAMES BAL 216 11TH WAR
ATKINSON, JAMES BAL 284 7TH WARD
ATKINSON, JOHN BAL 425 8TH WARD
ATKINSON, JOHN BAL 021 2ND DIST
ATKINSON, JOHN BAL 148 19TH WAR
ATKINSON, JOHN BAL 148 19TH WAR
ATKINSON, JOHN CEC 161 6TH E DI
ATKINSON, JOHN A. CEC 154 PORT DUP
ATKINSON, JOHN B. BAL 047 9TH WARD
ATKINSON, JOHN H. BAL 218 6TH WARD
ATKINSON, JOSEPH M. FRE 046 FREDERIC
ATKINSON, JOSEPH T. BAL 194 11TH WAR
ATKINSON, JOSHUA BAL 001 1ST WARD
ATKINSON, JOSHUA J. BAL 195 11TH WAR
ATKINSON, LATILLA E. ANN 521 HOWARD D
ATKINSON, LEAH DOR 434 1ST DIST
ATKINSON, LEVIN SOM 416 DUBLIN D
ATKINSON, LEVIN SOM 407 DUBLIN D
ATKINSON, LYDIA BAL 108 15TH WAR
ATKINSON, M. V. BAL 317 3RD WARD
ATKINSON, M. V. BAL 317 3RD WARD
ATKINSON, MAHLON HAR 086 2ND DIST
ATKINSON, MARGARET J. BAL 419 3RD WARD
ATKINSON, MARK HAR 051 1ST DIST
ATKINSON, MARTHA C. BAL 214 11TH WAR
ATKINSON, MARY DOR 434 1ST DIST
ATKINSON, MARY BAL 007 18TH WAR
ATKINSON, MARY BAL 318 1ST DIST
ATKINSON, MARY BAL 300 1ST DIST
ATKINSON, MARY BAL 233 6TH WARD
ATKINSON, MARY BAL 021 2ND DIST
ATKINSON, MARY BAL 264 12TH WAR
ATKINSON, MARY SOM 436 PRINCESS
ATKINSON, MARY E. DOR 432 1ST DIST
ATKINSON, MR.* DOR 377 1ST DIST
ATKINSON, PRITCHEL* DOR 432 1ST DIST
ATKINSON, ROBERT BAL 342 7TH WARD
ATKINSON, ROLLINS CEC 141 6TH E DI
ATKINSON, SAMUEL BAL 263 17TH WAR
ATKINSON, SAMUEL SOM 416 DUBLIN D

ATKINSON, SAMUEL BAL 337 7TH WARD
ATKINSON, SAMUEL C. BAL 226 19TH WAR
ATKINSON, SARAH BAL 126 2ND DIST
ATKINSON, SARAH J. BAL 347 7TH WARD
ATKINSON, STEPHEN CEC 126 5TH E DI
ATKINSON, SUSAN BAL 317 20TH WAR
ATKINSON, SUSAN BAL 287 3RD WARD
ATKINSON, SUSAN BAL 093 10TH WAR
ATKINSON, THOMAS BAL 227 19TH WAR
ATKINSON, THOMAS DOR 445 1ST DIST
ATKINSON, THOMAS BAL 150 19TH WAR
ATKINSON, THOMAS TAL 010 EASTON D
ATKINSON, THOMAS C. BAL 207 11TH WAR
ATKINSON, THOMAS REV. BAL 389 13TH WAR
ATKINSON, TISHA SOM 408 DUBLIN D
ATKINSON, WILLIAM SOM 426 PRINCESS
ATKINSON, WILLIAM BAL 302 20TH WAR
ATKINSON, WILLIAM ALL 249 CUMBERLA
ATKINSON, WILLIAM T. BAL 214 19TH WAR
ATKINSON,MATHEW BAL 067 1ST WARD
ATKINSON,T HOMAS CAR 112 NO TWP L
ATKISAW, CORDELIA BAL 227 6TH WARD
ATKISON, JAMES BAL 403 14TH WAR
ATKISON, JOSEPH BAL 446 14TH WAR
ATKISON, MARY BAL 410 14TH WAR
ATKISON, REBECCA BAL 455 14TH WAR
ATKISON, REBECCA BAL 455 14TH WAR
ATKISON, WILLIAM HAR 088 2ND DIST
ATKISSON, SARAH BAL 137 5TH WARD
ATLER, EDWARD ALL 232 CUMBERLA
ATLER, MARY BAL 138 16TH WAR
ATLEY, GEORGE BAL 280 2ND WARD
ATLEY, PRINLEY N. PRI 103 SPALDING
ATLICK, JOHN FRE 031 FREDERIC
ATLICKS, ADAM FRE 095 FREDERIC
ATLICKS, CONROD FRE 097 FREDERIC
ATMOOR, JOHN CEC 127 5TH E DI
ATMORE, JAMES CEC 100 3RD E DI
ATON, ELI BAL 426 8TH WARD
ATRINSON, EBVENEZER WOR 181 6TH E DI
ATTAFORD, WILLIAM * BAL 275 1ST DIST
ATTERAN, JOSPH ALL 136 4TH E.D.
ATTERFRITZ, MARYANN BAL 420 3RD WARD
ATTERWATER, ANN BAL 139 5TH WARD
ATTHOOF, AMBROSE FRE 178 5TH E DI
ATTICK, MOTELINE FRE 031 FREDERIC
ATTINZER, MYER BAL 213 2ND WARD
ATTIS, AMOS QUE 132 1ST E DI
ATTIS, JOSEPH QUE 132 1ST E DI
ATTLEBERG, CATHERINE ALL 206 CUMBERLA
ATTLEE, JAMES C. CAR 398 2ND DIST
ATTLEE, SAMUEL CAR 372 9TH DIST
ATTWATER, JAMES BAL 109 5TH WARD
ATTWATTERS, JOTHAN BAL 103 18TH WAR
ATTWELL, BENJAMIN JR. CAR 117 NO TWP L
ATTWELL, MARY A. BAL 117 18TH WAR
ATTWOOD, CATHARINE TAL 086 ST MICHA
ATWALTER, RYNER BAL 297 3RD WARD
ATWELL, ANN BAL 098 1ST WARD
ATWELL, ANNIE ANN 273 ANNAPOLI
ATWELL, BARBARA A. CAL 020 2ND DIST
ATWELL, BENJAMIN ANN 299 1ST DIST
ATWELL, BENJAMIN BAL 375 3RD WARD
ATWELL, BENJAMIN W. CAL 021 2ND DIST
ATWELL, EDWARD CEC 047 1ST E DI
ATWELL, EDWARD BAL 446 8TH WARD
ATWELL, ELIZABETH ANN 300 1ST DIST
ATWELL, HANNAH A. BAL 034 9TH WARD
ATWELL, HENRY BAL 031 2ND DIST
ATWELL, JOELL CAR 112 NO TWP L
ATWELL, JOSEPH ANN 308 1ST DIST
ATWELL, JOSEPH W. BAL 099 1ST WARD
ATWELL, MARGARET * BAL 392 1ST DIST
ATWELL, MISS- ANN 309 1ST DIST
ATWELL, NANCY ANN 277 ANNAPOLI
ATWELL, R. D. BAL 063 10TH WAR
ATWELL, ROBERT W. ANN 403 8TH DIST
ATWELL, SARAH E. BAL 075 1ST WARD
ATWELL, SUSAN BAL 075 1ST WARD
ATWELL, THOMAS ANN 410 8TH DIST
ATWELL, WASHINGTON CAR 116 NO TWP L
ATWELL, WILLIAM CAR 116 NO TWP L
ATWELL, WILLIAM BAL 172 1ST WARD
ATWELL,WILLIAM BAL 098 1ST WARD
ATWOD, HENY BAL 256 2ND WARD
ATWOOD, ANN E. MGM 377 ROCKERLE
ATWOOD, CAROLINE B. FRE 217 BUCKEYST
ATWOOC, GEORGE BAL 460 8TH WARD
ATWOOD, GEORGE P. MGM 399 ROCKERLE
ATWOOC, JANE BAL 454 8TH WARD
ATWOOD, JOHN BAL 454 8TH WARD
ATWUF, NATHANIEL BAL 098 1ST WARD
ATYRES, WILLIAM BAL 424 3RD WARD
AUBLE, JOHN BAL 324 1ST DIST
AUBORN, CATHARINE BAL 229 17TH WAR
AUCHHUTT, HENRY * BAL 276 1ST DIST
AUDO, WILLIAM J. ST 292 2ND E DI
AUDIN, LEWIS BAL 245 2ND WARD
AUDLAN, EDWARD ALL 213 CUMBERLA
AUER, ADOLPH BAL 369 13TH WAR
AUER, JOHN BAL 048 18TH WAR
AUEROCHS, DAVID BAL 166 16TH WAR
AUFORD, EMILY BAL 186 11TH WAR
AUG, JOHN ALL 006 3RD E.D.
AUG, JOSEPH ALL 006 3RD E.D.
AUGHINBAUGH, H.P. WAS 135 HAGERSTO
AUGHINHAUGH, GEORGE W. FRE 161 EMMITTSB
AUGLEY, JOHN BAL 143 11TH WAR
AUGSUT, MONTUR BAL 284 2ND WARD
AUGUST, CHARLES BAL 129 1ST WARD
AUGUST, GEORGE R. BAL 158 19TH WAR
AUGUST, MARTIN BAL 024 15TH WAR
AUGUST, THOMAS BAL 070 1ST WARD
AUGUSTA, CHARLES SOM 554 TYASKIN
AUGUSTA, FRED BAL 152 5TH WARD
AUGUSTA, MARY BAL 102 5TH WARD
AUGUSTA, SARAH BAL 332 13TH WAR
AUGUSTAS, AMELIA BAL 205 11TH WAR
AUGUSTAS, SARAH BAL 216 11TH WAR
AUGUSTINE, JOHN ALL 026 2ND E.D.
AUGUSTINE, WILLIAM BAL 326 3RD WARD
AUGUSTUS, ALONZO HAR 080 2ND DIST
AUGUSTUS, CHARLES QUE 205 3RD E DI
AUGUSTUS, JOHN H. BAL 116 15TH WAR
AUGUSTUS, MARTHA HAR 080 2ND DIST
AUGUSTUS, REBECCA BAL 127 16TH WAR
AUGUSTUS, THOMAS FRE 094 FREDERIC
AUGUSTUS, VICTORINE BAL 263 1ST DIST
AUGUSTUS, VINCENT BAL 050 1ST WARD
AUING, FREDERICK BAL 096 1ST WARD

BAL 095 1ST WARD
BAL 052 1ST WARD
A BAL 197 5TH DIST
AU BAL 196 5TH DIST
AUL BAL 408 14TH WAR
AULL BAL 075 15TH WAR
AULD, BAL 079 15TH WAR
AULD, BAL 043 9TH WARD
AULD, ...ES TAL 101 ST MICHA
AULD, JOHN BAL 067 1ST WARD
AULD, JOSEPH BAL 235 17TH WAR
AULD, MARY BAL 045 1ST WARD
AULD, SAMUEL BAL 034 1ST WARD
AULD, SARAH S. TAL 092 ST MICHA
AULD, THOMAS TAL 094 ST MICHA
AULD, THOMAS TAL 091 ST MICHA
AULD, THCMAS BAL 103 18TH WAR
AULDER, JOHN BAL 432 1ST DIST
AULDER, ROBERT BAL 413 1ST DIST
AULFANDER, JOHN BAL 018 9TH WARD
AULICK, JAMES BAL 048 18TH WAR
AULING, HENRY Z. BAL 041 1ST WARD
AULK, JOEL BAL 260 17TH WAR
AULL, JACOB BAL 166 2ND DIST
AULT, ADAM WAS 069 2ND SUBD
AULT, CONRAD WAS 069 2ND SUBD
AULT, GEORGE ALL 038 2ND E.D.
AULT, MARY ANN FRE 134 CREAGERS
AULT, SAMUEL BAL 235 6TH WARD
AULT, SAMUEL BAL 436 8TH WARD
AULT, SEBBEUS CAR 272 WESTMINS
AULT, WILLIAM WAS 069 2ND SUBD
AULWICK, JOHN BAL 368 1ST DIST
AULY, HESTER-BLACK BAL 203 2ND WARD
AUNOLD, NANCY BAL 396 8TH WARD
AUODOUN, OLIVER* BAL 389 3RD WARD
AUPERT, ALFRED FRE 054 FREDERIC
AURES, GUSTAVUS BAL 192 19TH WAR
AURING, EARNEST BAL 073 2ND DIST
AURMAN, JACOB BAL 050 18TH WAR
AURT, ELIZABETH * BAL 307 20TH WAR
AUSCHURST, CATHARINE BAL 199 2ND WARD
AUSCHUTZ, HENRY P. BAL 361 3RD WARD
AUSCHUTZ, MARTHA BAL 361 3RD WARD
AUSENDORF, CLEMENT BAL 111 10TH WAR
AUSHERMAN, DAVID FRE 327 MIDDLETO
AUSHERMAN, ELIZABETH FRE 325 MIDDLETO
AUSHERMAN, HENSON FRE 397 PETERSVI
AUSHERMAN, JOHN FRE 328 MIDDLETO
AUSHERMAN, LAWSON FRE 325 MIDDLETO
AUSHERMAN, SARAH WAS 050 2ND SUBD
AUSHERMAN, THOMAS WAS 050 2ND SUBD
AUSHERMAN,EZRA FRE 406 JEFFERSO
AUSKIN, JOHN ALL 105 5TH E.D.
AUSTAIN, JAMES TAL 073 EASTON T
AUSTAIN, JOHN C. TAL 038 EASTON D
AUSTAIN, WILLIAM TAL 065 EASTON T
AUSTEN, MARTHA MGM 394 ROCKERLE
AUSTEN, MARY ANN SOPHIA BAL 219 17TH WAR
AUSTEN, PHILIP H. BAL 389 13TH WAR
AUSTEN, SARAH BAL 351 3RD WARD
AUSTEN, THEODORE BAL 219 17TH WAR
AUSTERHUSS, MARGARET BAL 078 10TH WAR
AUSTHINE, HENRY BAL 126 2ND DIST
AUSTHINE, LAURA BAL 126 2ND DIST
AUSTIAN, C. BAL 239 2ND WARD
AUSTIN, A. H. BAL 315 12TH WAR
AUSTIN, ANA BAL 248 12TH WAR
AUSTIN, ANN BAL 263 1ST DIST
AUSTIN, CHARLES BAL 093 15TH WAR
AUSTIN, ELIZA BAL 242 2ND WARD
AUSTIN, ELIZABETH WAS 157 HAGERSTO
AUSTIN, FIELDER SOM 459 HANGARY
AUSTIN, FRANCIS BAL 345 7TH WARD
AUSTIN, FRANKLIN BAL 318 7TH WARD
AUSTIN, FREDERICK BAL 352 3RD WARD
AUSTIN, GEORGE BAL 170 16TH WAR
AUSTIN, GEORGE BAL 046 2ND DIST
AUSTIN, GEORGE BAL 153 1ST WARD
AUSTIN, GEORGE WOR 235 6TH E DI
AUSTIN, GEORGE E. SOM 533 QUANTICO
AUSTIN, HARRISON TAL 009 EASTON D
AUSTIN, JOHN SOM 440 DAMES QU
AUSTIN, JOHN BAL 104 1ST WARD
AUSTIN, JOHN H. MGM 419 MEDLEY 3
AUSTIN, JOHN T. BAL 215 11TH WAR
AUSTIN, JOSEPH BAL 166 19TH WAR
AUSTIN, LEAH SOM 536 TYASKIN
AUSTIN, LEAH J. SOM 462 HANGARY
AUSTIN, LEVINIA TAL 009 EASTON D
AUSTIN, MARTHA BAL 018 18TH WAR
AUSTIN, MARY CEC 206 7TH E DI
AUSTIN, MARY SOM 520 BARREN C
AUSTIN, MARY BAL 320 1ST DIST
AUSTIN, MARY E. QUE 205 3RD E DI
AUSTIN, NATHANIEL SOM 520 BARREN C
AUSTIN, SALLY CAL 046 3RD DIST
AUSTIN, SAMUEL FRE 333 MIDDLETO
AUSTIN, SAMUEL BAL 059 15TH WAR
AUSTIN, SARAH E. BAL 018 18TH WAR
AUSTIN, SARAH F. BAL 346 7TH WARD
AUSTIN, SARH QUE 206 3RD E DI
AUSTIN, SUSAN BAL 422 8TH WARD
AUSTIN, TAP-BLACK QUE 194 3RD E DI
AUSTIN, THOMAS TAL 003 EASTON D
AUSTIN, THOMAS J. MGM 432 CLARKSTR
AUSTIN, THOMAS L. BAL 337 7TH WARD
AUSTIN, WILLIAM BAL 076 1ST WARD
AUSTIN, WILLIAM A. MGM 374 ROCKERLE
AUSTIN, WILLIAM H. TAL 060 EASTON D
AUSTON, JAMES ALL 146 6TH E.D.
AUSTON, JOHN HAR 185 3RD DIST
AUTERWAN, FREDERICK BAL 065 2ND DIST
AUTHER, ANN BAL 146 11TH WAR
AUTHER, EASTHER BAL 315 7TH WARD
AUTHER, JOHN BAL 416 8TH WARD
AUTHER, JOHN BAL 297 7TH WARD
AUTHER, ROBERT BAL 314 7TH WARD
AUTIN, FERE BAL 237 1ST DIST
AVAN, WILLIAM BAL 021 9TH WARD
AVARUS, FRANCES HAR 174 3RD DIST
AVARUS, FRANCIS HAR 174 3RD DIST
AVELAY, JACOB BAL 267 1ST DIST
AVENLL, JOHN BAL 141 1ST WARD
AVEON, CHRISTINA BAL 203 2ND WARD
AVERY, ANDREW WAS 197 1ST DIST
AVERY, FRANK BAL 141 1ST WARD
AVERY, MARGARET WAS 083 2ND SUBD
AVERY, WILLIAM BAL 164 1ST WARD
AVES, DAVID CAL 011 1ST DIST

AVES, JAMES TAL 058 EASTON D
AVEY, ANDREW WAS 265 1ST DIST
AVEY, ELIZABETH WAS 208 1ST DIST
AVEY, ELIZABETH WAS 287 1ST DIST
AVEY, ELOLM WAS 210 1ST DIST
AVEY, HENRY WAS 208 1ST DIST
AVEY, JACOB WAS 047 2ND SUBD
AVEY, JACOB D. WAS 192 1ST DIST
AVEY, SAMUEL WAS 042 2ND SUBD
AVEY, SARAH WAS 170 FUNKSTOW
AVEY, SUSAN WAS 215 1ST DIST
AVEY, SUSANNA WAS 215 1ST DIST
AVILIS, JOSE FRE 202 5TH E DI
AVIS, ELIZABETH CAL 017 1ST DIST
AVIS, ELIZABETH CAL 017 1ST DIST
AVIS, WILLIAM CAR 168 NO TWP L
AVOY, JOHN BAL 019 9TH WARD
AVOYS, JOHN BAL 214 2ND WARD
AWATT, CASPER BAL 058 4TH WARD
AWAYS, ANDREW BAL 064 1ST WARD
AWAYS, ELIZA CAR 360 9TH DIST
AWEY, LEVIN* SOM 525 QUANTICO
AWINGS, SUSAN FRE 249 NEW MARK
AWKARD, HARRIET ANN 500 HOWARD D
AWKWARD, SAMUEL MGM 330 CRACKLIN
AWODOUN, OLIVER* BAL 389 3RD WARD
AXE, ANGELINA BAL 424 14TH WAR
AXE, JOHN CAR 340 6TH DIST
AXLEY, JOHN BAL 057 4TH WARD
AYD, JOHN BAL 428 8TH WARD
AYDELOTT, JOSIAH WOR 246 1ST CENS
AYDELOTT, PETER BAL 018 15TH WAR
AYDLETT, JOHN T. WOR 241 1ST CENS
AYDLLOTT, TABITHA WOR 249 1ST CENS
AYDLOTT, BENJAMIN WOR 326 1ST E DI
AYDLOTT, BENJAMIN T. WOR 326 1ST E DI
AYDLOTT, JAMES WOR 325 1ST E DI
AYDLOTT, JOHN WOR 326 1ST E DI
AYDLOTT, WILLIAM J. WOR 326 1ST E DI
AYDOLOTT, STEPHEN-MULATTO WOR 344 1ST E DI
AYER, THOMAS BAL 155 1ST WARD
AYERHART, HENRY BAL 076 2ND DIST
AYERS, CHARLES QUE 204 3RD E DI
AYERS, ELIZABETH BAL 084 1ST WARD
AYERS, ELLEN BAL 084 2ND DIST
AYERS, GEORGE BAL 283 2ND WARD
AYERS, JACOB BAL 209 17TH WAR
AYERS, JAMES BAL 202 17TH WAR
AYERS, JAMES BAL 012 9TH WARD
AYERS, JAMES-BLACK QUE 195 3RD E DI
AYERS, JONATHAN D. BAL 235 17TH WAR
AYERS, MOSES BAL 208 17TH WAR
AYERS, THOMAS HAR 072 1ST DIST
AYERS, WILLIAM HAR 049 1ST DIST
AYLER, MARTIN ANN 434 HOWARD D
AYLER, WILLIAM H. CAR 072 NO TWP L
AYLER,JOHN BAL 029 1ST WARD
AYRE, HENRIETTA BAL 157 11TH WAR
AYRES, AMELIA BAL 111 10TH WAR
AYRES, ANN BAL 226 6TH WARD
AYRES, ANNA-MULATTO FRE 241 NEW MARK
AYRES, BENJAMIN HAR 087 2ND DIST
AYRES, BORDEN WOR 298 9TH E DI
AYRES, CHARLES QUE 211 3RD E DI
AYRES, CHARLES HAR 065 1ST DIST
AYRES, CHARLES C. BAL 178 16TH WAR
AYRES, COMFORT WOR 261 BERLIN 1
AYRES, CORNELIUS ALL 114 5TH E.D.
AYRES, DAVID ALL 118 5TH E.D.
AYRES, ELIZA HAR 082 2ND DIST
AYRES, ELIZABETH HAR 072 1ST DIST
AYRES, ELIZABETH BAL 022 1ST WARD
AYRES, EMILINE BAL 205 11TH WAR
AYRES, EVILINE HAR 067 1ST DIST
AYRES, GEORGE WAS 018 2ND SUBD
AYRES, GEORGE W. ALL 034 2ND E.D.
AYRES, HANNAH BAL 337 13TH WAR
AYRES, HENERETTA SOM 524 BARREN C
AYRES, HENRY H. HAR 022 1ST DIST
AYRES, HENRY R. WOR 295 9TH E DI
AYRES, HESTER WOR 338 1ST E DI
AYRES, JAES WOR 262 BERLIN 1
AYRES, JAMES HAR 022 1ST DIST
AYRES, JAMES H. BAL 057 1ST WARD
AYRES, JOHN BAL 047 9TH WARD
AYRES, JOHN HAR 017 1ST DIST
AYRES, JOHN HAR 020 1ST DIST
AYRES, JOHN KEN 268 1ST DIST
AYRES, JOHN C. KEN 268 1ST DIST
AYRES, JOHN C. BAL 026 4TH WARD
AYRES, JOHN T. HAR 067 1ST DIST
AYRES, LAMBERT P. WOR 280 BERLIN 1
AYRES, LEMUEL KEN 269 1ST DIST
AYRES, LITTLETON BAL 070 15TH WAR
AYRES, M. BAL 230 19TH WAR
AYRES, MARGARET BAL 113 15TH WAR
AYRES, MARIA ALL 118 5TH E.D.
AYRES, MARIA E. HAR 082 2ND DIST
AYRES, MARY BAL 109 15TH WAR
AYRES, MARY A. TAL 058 EASTON D
AYRES, P. * BAL 305 12TH WAR
AYRES, REBECCA BAL 083 15TH WAR
AYRES, REBECCA BAL 084 15TH WAR
AYRES, SAMUEL BAL 005 1ST WARD
AYRES, SARAH-MULATTO FRE 241 NEW MARK
AYRES, THOMAS HAR 065 1ST DIST
AYRES, THOMAS K. KEN 268 1ST DIST
AYRES, WASHINGTON HAR 017 1ST DIST
AYRES, WILLIAM HAR 008 1ST DIST
AYRES, WILLIAM KEN 269 1ST DIST
AYRES, WILLIAM ALL 118 5TH E.D.
AYRS, BENJAMIN CAR 164 NO TWP L
AYRS, CAROLINE CAR 134 NO TWP L
AYRS, FRANCIS CAR 168 NO TWP L
AYTON, EPHRAIM B. MGM 324 CRACKLIN
AYTON, VICTORIA E. MGM 324 CRACKLIN
AZARES, MICHAEL BAL 021 1ST WARD
AZBASY, ANN LITTLE ALL 241 CUMBERLA
AZBASY, FRANCIS ALL 241 CUMBERLA
B BAL 128 1ST WARD
BAAR, WILLIAM H. BAL 237 12TH WAR
BAARTSCHEER, JOHN BAL 090 15TH WAR
BABCOCK, AARON BAL 169 1ST WARD
BABCOCK, AMELIA BAL 251 6TH WARD
BABCOCK, MARIA BAL 251 6TH WARD
BABE, HENRY BAL 150 1ST WARD
BABER, MARGRETT CAR 112 NO TWP L
BABES, ELIZABETH-BLACK CAR 069 NO TWP L
BABES, JOHN CAR 116 NO TWP L
BABES, JOHN-BLACK CAR 117 NO TWP L

Name	County	Page	Location
BABEY, JOS.	TAL	102	ST MICHA
BABEY, STEPHEN	WOR	301	SNOW HIL
BABINGTON, CHRISTIAN	BAL	075	2ND DIST
BABKER, MAURICE	BAL	267	1ST DIST
BABLETZ, PETER	CAR	337	6TH DIST
BABLITZ, ELIZABETH	BAL	202	6TH DIST
BABLITZ, MICHAEL	CAR	171	8TH DIST
BABSON, GEORGE	BAL	154	1ST WARD
BABTIST, FRANCES	CEC	214	7TH E DI
BABTIST, JOHN	BAL	127	1ST WARD
BABY, JOHN	BAL	009	1ST WARD
BABY, MAJOR-BLACK	WOR	332	1ST E DI
BABYLON, DAVID	CAR	412	2ND DIST
BABYLON, JACOB	CAR	403	2ND DIST
BABYLON, JAOCB	CAR	406	2ND DIST
BABYLON, JESSE	CAR	412	2ND DIST
BABYLON, JOHN	CAR	407	2ND DIST
BABYLON, JOHN	CAR	412	2ND DIST
BABYLON, JOSIAH	CAR	411	2ND DIST
BABYLON, MICHEAL	CAR	412	2ND DIST
BABYLON, PETER	CAR	409	2ND DIST
BABYLON, SAMUEL	CAR	314	1ST DIST
BABYLON, WILLIAM	CAR	411	2ND DIST
BABYLON, WILLIAM	CAR	412	2ND DIST
BACCHUS, WILLIAM	KEN	208	2ND DIST
BACCIGALUPPS, VINCENT	BAL	081	10TH WAR
BACEY, SAMUEL	ALL	163	6TH E.D.
BACH, JOHN	BAL	057	1ST WARD
BACH, PHILLIP	BAL	109	5TH WARD
BACHANAN, JANE	BAL	332	13TH WAR
BACHARACH, ABRAHAM	BAL	206	6TH WARD
BACHART, JACOB	BAL	224	2ND WARD
BACHEL, JOSEPH	WAS	144	2ND DIST
BACHEL, JOSEPH S.	WAS	110	2ND DIST
BACHELE, HARRIET	WAS	144	2ND DIST
BACHELLOR, PETER	DOR	463	1ST DIST
BACHELLOR, WILLIAM	DOR	445	1ST DIST
BACHELOR, ANDREW J.	BAL	016	1ST WARD
BACHELOR, GEORGE	BAL	067	2ND DIST
BACHELOR, JAMES	BAL	152	1ST WARD
BACHELOR, MARGARET	BAL	067	2ND DIST
BACHELOR, SUSAN	BAL	266	17TH WAR
BACHENHAUSEN, ANN	BAL	206	6TH WARD
BACHER, DANIEL	WAS	282	1ST DIST
BACHMAN, BENJAMIN	CAR	345	6TH DIST
BACHMAN, DAVID	CAR	350	6TH DIST
BACHMAN, FRANCIS	BAL	008	9TH WARD
BACHMAN, HENRY W.	BAL	125	16TH WAR
BACHMAN, JOHN	BAL	235	2ND WARD
BACHMAN, L.	BAL	044	9TH WARD
BACHMAN, LATITIA A.	BAL	164	16TH WAR
BACHMAN, MARGARET	BAL	235	2ND WARD
BACHMAN, MARY	BAL	084	10TH WAR
BACHMAN, SAMUEL	CAR	349	6TH DIST
BACHOLOR, WALLACE	BAL	211	17TH WAR
BACHRACH, SUSANNA	BAL	464	14TH WAR
BACHTEL, AARON	WAS	250	1ST DIST
BACHTEL, ANDREW	WAS	235	1ST DIST
BACHTEL, CATHARINE M.	WAS	231	1ST DIST
BACHTEL, DANIEL	WAS	234	1ST DIST
BACHTEL, DANIEL	WAS	236	CAVETOWN
BACHTEL, DANIEL	WAS	261	1ST DIST
BACHTEL, DAVID L.	WAS	254	1ST DIST
BACHTEL, ELIZABETH	WAS	250	1ST DIST
BACHTEL, GEORGE	WAS	240	CAVETOWN
BACHTEL, GEORGE B.	WAS	261	1ST DIST
BACHTEL, HENRY	WAS	267	1ST DIST
BACHTEL, HENRY	WAS	235	1ST DIST
BACHTEL, JACOB	WAS	234	1ST DIST
BACHTEL, JACOB	WAS	237	CAVETOWN
BACHTEL, JACOB L.	WAS	261	1ST DIST
BACHTEL, JACOB S.	WAS	252	1ST DIST
BACHTEL, JOHN	WAS	237	CAVETOWN
BACHTEL, JOHN B.	WAS	230	1ST DIST
BACHTEL, LYDIA A.	WAS	261	1ST DIST
BACHTEL, MARY E.	WAS	243	CAVETOWN
BACHTEL, SAMUEL	WAS	243	CAVETOWN
BACHTEL, SAMUEL	WAS	237	CAVETOWN
BACHTEL, SEPHRONA H.	WAS	237	CAVETOWN
BACHTELL, SAMUEL	WAS	235	1ST DIST
BACK, ADAM	BAL	446	8TH WARD
BACK, JACOB	BAL	228	1ST DIST
BACK, JOHN	BAL	138	1ST WARD
BACK, JOSEPH *	ANN	397	8TH DIST
BACK, JULIA	BAL	457	14TH WAR
BACK, LEANDER	BAL	102	1ST WARD
BACK, SARAH	BAL	056	4TH WARD
BACK, WILLIAM	FRE	291	WOODSBOR
BACK, WILLIAM	BAL	328	1ST DIST
BACKENHAM, GEORGE *	FRE	263	NEW MARK
BACKER, GEORGE M.	FRE	295	WOODSBOR
BACKER, HENRY	BAL	282	2ND WARD
BACKER, WILLIAM	BAL	134	1ST WARD
BACKERKOEN, JACOB	BAL	109	1ST WARD
BACKHEIMER, HENRY	BAL	039	9TH WARD
BACKHOLDER, CHRISTIAN	ALL	016	3RD E.D.
BACKINGER, CHRISTOPHER	ANN	517	HOWARD D
BACKLEY, MARY	BAL	119	11TH WAR
BACKLING, H.	BAL	152	1ST WARD
BACKMAN, DANIEL	FRE	363	CATOCTIN
BACKMAN, HENRY	CAR	219	5TH DIST
BACKMAN, JACOB	CAR	343	6TH DIST
BACKMAN, JOHN	BAL	236	2ND WARD
BACKMAN, JOSEPH	BAL	306	12TH WAR
BACKMAN, MARTHA	BAL	243	17TH WAR
BACKMAN, MARY	CAR	343	6TH DIST
BACKMAN, WILLIAM H.	BAL	351	13TH WAR
BACKNA, FREDERICK *	BAL	126	18TH WAR
BACKRACK, GETTA	BAL	230	2ND WARD
BACKS, JOSEPH	WAS	074	2ND SUBD
BACKSTER, JAMES	CHA	237	HILLTOP
BACKSTER, RUBIN	CHA	237	HILLTOP
BACKUS, JOHN C.	BAL	094	10TH WAR
BACKUS, MARY	BAL	395	14TH WAR
BACLKINUS, SOPHIA	BAL	229	2ND WARD
BACON, BARNEY	ANN	442	HOWARD D
BACON, BEN	ANN	374	4TH DIST
BACON, BENJAMIN	BAL	343	1ST DIST
BACON, CHLOE	ANN	454	HOWARD D
BACON, EDWARD	PRI	020	VANSVILL
BACON, ELIAS	BAL	447	1ST DIST
BACON, GEORGE	ANN	431	HOWARD D
BACON, HARRIET	BAL	127	16TH WAR
BACON, HENRY	FRE	067	FREDERIC
BACON, HENRY*	BAL	417	3RD WARD
BACON, JAMES	CEC	049	1ST E DI
BACON, JAMES	BAL	227	17TH WAR
BACON, JAMES	MGM	331	CRACKLIN
BACON, JAMES	BAL	388	1ST DIST
BACON, JAMES	BAL	156	1ST WARD
BACON, JAMES	WOR	180	6TH E DI
BACON, JEREMIAH	MGM	348	BERRYS D
BACON, JOHN	ANN	470	HOWARD D
BACON, JOHN	ANN	472	HOWARD D
BACON, JOHN	BAL	018	2ND DIST
BACON, JOHN C.	WOR	178	6TH E DI
BACON, JOHN T.	ANN	440	HOWARD D
BACON, MALINDA	BAL	322	1ST DIST
BACON, MARGRET	BAL	067	18TH WAR
BACON, MARTHA	BAL	049	18TH WAR
BACON, MARTHA	ANN	435	HOWARD D
BACON, MARY	BAL	074	18TH WAR
BACON, MARY	CAR	368	9TH DIST
BACON, SARAH	MGM	351	BERRYS D
BACON, SUSANNA	ANN	441	HOWARD D
BACON, TABITHA	WOR	178	6TH E DI
BACON, WILLIAM	SOM	516	BARREN C
BACON, WILLIAM	WOR	349	1ST E DI
BACON, WILLIAM	BAL	050	2ND DIST
BACON, WILLIAM G.	MGM	338	CRACKLIN
BACON, MARY-MULATTO	FRE	030	FREDERIC
BADARACK, DOMINIC	BAL	004	4TH WARD
BADARACK, ROSINA	BAL	004	4TH WARD
BADDEN, HARRIET A.	ST	282	3RD E DI
BADDEN, HENRY	BAL	377	3RD WARD
BADDEN, JOHN P.	BAL	054	2ND DIST
BADDER, CATHERINE	CEC	173	6TH E DI
BADDERS, ANGELINA	CEC	174	6TH E DI
BADDERS, JOHN	CEC	174	6TH E DI
BADDERS, JOHN	HAR	021	1ST DIST
BADDERS, PARY	HAR	050	1ST DIST
BADDLY, WILLIAM	BAL	053	2ND DIST
BADEN, BEN	PRI	055	AQUASCO
BADEN, CATHARINE	BAL	196	11TH WAR
BADEN, ELIZABETH	BAL	006	EASTERN
BADEN, ELIZABETH L.	ST	286	2ND E DI
BADEN, FANNY	BAL	389	13TH WAR
BADEN, JAMES	PRI	062	NOTTINGH
BADEN, JOHN R.	PRI	064	NOTTINGH
BADEN, JOSEPH N.	PRI	064	NOTTINGH
BADEN, MARGARET	PRI	064	NOTTINGH
BADEN, MARTHA	PRI	053	AQUASCO
BADEN, MARY	PRI	110	PISCATAW
BADEN, ROBERT W.G.	PRI	064	NOTTINGH
BADEN, SALLY B.	PRI	062	NOTTINGH
BADEN, THOMAS E.	PRI	041	VANSVILL
BADEN, THOMAS N.	PRI	064	NOTTINGH
BADEN, WILLIAM	PRI	056	AQUASCO
BADGER, ELISHA	BAL	143	16TH WAR
BADGER, ELLEN	BAL	210	11TH WAR
BADGER, FRANCIS	BAL	430	8TH WARD
BADGER, JARRET	BAL	143	16TH WAR
BADGER, JOHN	BAL	089	2ND DIST
BADGER, JOSEPH	BAL	060	15TH WAR
BADGER, JOSEPH	CEC	098	3RD E DI
BADGER, MARY	BAL	061	15TH WAR
BADGER, RICHARD	BAL	315	3RD WARD
BADHEIMER, PHILLIP	BAL	279	17TH WAR
BADLE, CONRAD	BAL	230	6TH WARD
BADLEY, AMANDA A.	WOR	229	6TH E DI
BADO, CHARLES	BAL	215	6TH WARD
BADO, ELIZABETH	BAL	215	6TH WARD
BADOR, BARBARA	FRE	161	EMMITTSB
BADTGER, EZEKIEL	BAL	328	13TH WAR
BAELY, SAMUEL	ALL	017	3RD E.D.
BAEN, RICHARD	BAL	034	1ST WARD
BAENS, WILLIAM	ALL	250	CUMBERLA
BAENTREE, HARVEY	WAS	021	2ND SUBD
BAER, AHROW*	BAL	304	3RD WARD
BAER, JACOB	FRE	312	MIDDLETO
BAER, JOHN	FRE	289	WOODSBOR
BAER, JOHN	BAL	088	1ST WARD
BAER, JOHN	ALL	146	6TH E.D.
BAER, JOHN	BAL	385	3RD WARD
BAER, LUCRETIA	FRE	408	JEFFERSO
BAER, SAMUEL	WAS	007	WILLIAMS
BAERER, F.	BAL	169	1ST WARD
BAFF, LETITIA	BAL	402	14TH WAR
BAFF, SISTER TERESA	FRE	198	5TH E DI
BAG, CATHERINE	BAL	421	3RD WARD
BAGAN, CATHERINE	BAL	074	4TH WARD
BAGER, TAWNEY	WAS	013	WILLIAMS
BAGFORD, CATHARINE	WAS	289	1ST DIST
BAGGE, THOMAS	BAL	046	9TH WARD
BAGGETT, MARY A.	ST	295	2ND E DI
BAGGS, ANDREW	CAR	076	NO TWP L
BAGGS, BENNETT	TAL	099	ST MICHA
BAGGS, JOSEPH	QUE	135	1ST E DI
BAGGS, MARY	QUE	141	1ST E DI
BAGGS, ANDREW	CAR	076	NO TWP L
BAGLEMAN, PETER	BAL	316	3RD WARD
BAGLEY, JOHN	MGM	399	ROCKERLE
BAGLEY, JOHN O.	HAR	081	2ND DIST
BAGLEY, PHILIP *	HAR	039	1ST DIST
BAGLEY, TIMOTHY	FRE	067	FREDERIC
BAGNAL, MARY	BAL	382	13TH WAR
BAGNELL, MICHAEL	BAL	271	17TH WAR
BAGNOL, JOHN	ALL	069	5TH E.D.
BAGS, ELIZABETH	CAR	098	NO TWP L
BAGS, SYLVESTER	CAR	100	NO TWP L
BAGUETT, JOHN	BAL	074	10TH WAR
BAGWELL, CATHERINE	BAL	401	3RD WARD
BAHAMEY, SALLY	BAL	273	17TH WAR
BAHNS, CAROLINE	BAL	263	1ST DIST
BAID, WILLIAM	BAL	030	1ST WARD
BAIE, REBECCA	CAR	365	9TH DIST
BAIFIELD, JAMES H.*	BAL	114	11TH WAR
BAILE, ABNER	CAR	365	9TH DIST
BAILE, ABRAHAM	CAR	393	2ND DIST
BAILE, HENRY	CAR	279	7TH DIST
BAILE, ISAAC	CAR	393	2ND DIST
BAILE, JESSE	CAR	358	9TH DIST
BAILE, JESSE	FRE	436	8TH E DI
BAILE, LEWIS N.	CAR	358	9TH DIST
BAILE, LUDWIG	CAR	392	2ND DIST
BAILE, MARY A.	CAR	358	9TH DIST
BAILE, PATRICK	BAL	269	1ST DIST
BAILE, PETER	CAR	392	2ND DIST
BAILE, PETER M.	CAR	281	7TH DIST
BAILE, SUSAN	CAR	358	9TH DIST
BAILE, WILLIAM	CAR	392	2ND DIST
BAILEE, CHARLES	CHA	225	ALLENS F
BAILEE, GEORGE	CHA	223	ALLENS F
BAILEE, HENRY	CHA	227	ALLENS F
BAILEE, JAMES	CHA	221	ALLENS F
BAILEE, JOSEPH	CHA	225	ALLENS F
BAILEE, M. D.	CHA	219	ALLENS F
BAILEE, MARIA	CHA	219	ALLENS F
BAILEE, ROBERT	CHA	282	BOJANTOW
BAILEI, RICHARD H.	CHA	232	HILLTOP
BAILEIE, ELIZA	CHA	223	ALLENS F
BAILER, ELIZABETH	BAL	134	18TH WAR
BAILEY, ADAM	BAL	433	1ST DIST
BAILEY, ALSEA	BAL	247	20TH WAR
BAILEY, ANDREW	BAL	440	1ST DIST
BAILEY, ANN M.	BAL	069	1ST WARD
BAILEY, ANTHONY	BAL	078	10TH WAR
BAILEY, CAROLINE	BAL	051	1ST WARD
BAILEY, CAROLINE	BAL	398	14TH WAR
BAILEY, CATHERINE	BAL	363	8TH WARD
BAILEY, CATHERINE A.	BAL	391	3RD WARD
BAILEY, CHARELS	FRE	095	FREDERIC
BAILEY, CHARLES	BAL	121	5TH WARD
BAILEY, CHARLES C.	ST	336	4TH E DI
BAILEY, CHARLOTT	BAL	224	17TH WAR
BAILEY, CHARLOTTE	BAL	344	13TH WAR
BAILEY, COMFORT	BAL	058	10TH WAR
BAILEY, DANIEL	KEN	275	1ST DIST
BAILEY, EDWARD P.	QUE	247	5TH E DI
BAILEY, EDWIN	BAL	204	11TH WAR
BAILEY, ELEANOR	BAL	084	15TH WAR
BAILEY, ELIJAH	BAL	197	17TH WAR
BAILEY, ELIZA	BAL	189	19TH WAR
BAILEY, ELIZABETH	BAL	278	20TH WAR
BAILEY, ELIZABETH	BAL	111	15TH WAR
BAILEY, ELIZABETH	BAL	373	1ST DIST
BAILEY, ELIZABETH	BAL	094	5TH WARD
BAILEY, EMILY	BAL	062	1ST WARD
BAILEY, FRANCIS	BAL	213	17TH WAR
BAILEY, G. W. W.	BAL	327	1ST DIST
BAILEY, GEORGE	BAL	394	3RD WARD
BAILEY, GEORGE	BAL	148	2ND DIST
BAILEY, GEORGE	BAL	049	15TH WAR
BAILEY, GEORGE	BAL	230	12TH WAR
BAILEY, GEORGE	BAL	380	13TH WAR
BAILEY, GEORGE	BAL	117	18TH WAR
BAILEY, GEORGE F.	ST	264	3RD E DI
BAILEY, GEORGE K.	BAL	383	1ST DIST
BAILEY, GRACEY A.	BAL	052	15TH WAR
BAILEY, HARRIET	BAL	363	13TH WAR
BAILEY, HARROLD	BAL	336	13TH WAR
BAILEY, HENRY	BAL	073	18TH WAR
BAILEY, HENRY	BAL	391	3RD WARD
BAILEY, HENRY	BAL	141	1ST WARD
BAILEY, HENRY	BAL	231	1ST DIST
BAILEY, HUGH	BAL	053	4TH WARD
BAILEY, ISAAC	CAR	092	NO TWP L
BAILEY, ISAAC	BAL	167	16TH WAR
BAILEY, JACOB	BAL	040	2ND DIST
BAILEY, JACOB	QUE	229	4TH E DI
BAILEY, JAMES	QUE	228	4TH E DI
BAILEY, JAMES	QUE	226	4TH E DI
BAILEY, JAMES	QUE	231	4TH E DI
BAILEY, JAMES	BAL	231	12TH WAR
BAILEY, JAMES	BAL	377	13TH WAR
BAILEY, JAMES	CEC	060	1ST E DI
BAILEY, JANE	BAL	231	12TH WAR
BAILEY, JANE	BAL	040	15TH WAR
BAILEY, JENKINS	BAL	154	11TH WAR
BAILEY, JEREMIAH	BAL	406	8TH WARD
BAILEY, JOHN	BAL	410	8TH WARD
BAILEY, JOHN	BAL	391	8TH WARD
BAILEY, JOHN	ANN	353	3RD DIST
BAILEY, JOHN	BAL	191	17TH WAR
BAILEY, JOHN	BAL	032	1ST WARD
BAILEY, JOHN	BAL	158	1ST WARD
BAILEY, JOHN	ALL	155	6TH E.D.
BAILEY, JOHN	BAL	115	11TH WAR
BAILEY, JOHN	BAL	045	4TH WARD
BAILEY, JOHN	BAL	212	17TH WAR
BAILEY, JOHN	FRE	272	NEW MARK
BAILEY, JOHN	BAL	177	19TH WAR
BAILEY, JOHN	HAR	120	2ND DIST
BAILEY, JOHN	QUE	228	4TH E DI
BAILEY, JOHN B.	ST	264	3RD E DI
BAILEY, JOHN B.	BAL	093	5TH WARD
BAILEY, JOHN G.	BAL	074	18TH WAR
BAILEY, JOHN L.	ST	309	1ST E DI
BAILEY, JOHN N.	BAL	048	1ST WARD
BAILEY, JOHN W.	BAL	353	7TH WARD
BAILEY, JOHN W.	QUE	125	1ST E DI
BAILEY, JOSEPH	BAL	220	17TH WAR
BAILEY, JOSEPH	BAL	048	1ST WARD
BAILEY, JOSEPH	QUE	238	5TH E DI
BAILEY, JOSEPH T.	MGM	384	ROCKERLE
BAILEY, LEWIS	BAL	387	13TH WAR
BAILEY, LLOYD	BAL	155	16TH WAR
BAILEY, LOUISA	BAL	103	15TH WAR
BAILEY, LOUISA	BAL	105	10TH WAR
BAILEY, LUCINDA	BAL	127	16TH WAR
BAILEY, LUSTRE	BAL	175	2ND WARD
BAILEY, MARGARET G.*	BAL	389	3RD WARD
BAILEY, MARIA	BAL	357	8TH WARD
BAILEY, MARTHA	BAL	236	12TH WAR
BAILEY, MARTHA R.	BAL	324	7TH WARD
BAILEY, MARY	BAL	302	12TH WAR
BAILEY, MARY	BAL	112	1ST WARD
BAILEY, MARY	BAL	153	11TH WAR
BAILEY, MARY A.	FRE	272	NEW MARK
BAILEY, MARY E.	BAL	111	15TH WAR
BAILEY, MARY J.	BAL	121	16TH WAR
BAILEY, MARY J.	BAL	046	4TH WARD
BAILEY, MARY J.	QUE	170	2ND E DI
BAILEY, MICHAEL	BAL	033	1ST WARD
BAILEY, MISS	BAL	205	11TH WAR
BAILEY, NEHEMIAH	QUE	186	3RD E DI
BAILEY, NOBLE	ALL	084	5TH E.D.
BAILEY, OSWALD	BAL	291	20TH WAR
BAILEY, OTHER	BAL	111	18TH WAR
BAILEY, PERE	QUE	235	4TH E DI
BAILEY, PETER	BAL	225	19TH WAR
BAILEY, PHILIS	BAL	128	11TH WAR
BAILEY, R. P.	BAL	074	10TH WAR
BAILEY, RICHARD	BAL	114	1ST WARD
BAILEY, RICHARD	BAL	363	13TH WAR
BAILEY, ROBERT M.	BAL	114	18TH WAR
BAILEY, RUTH	BAL	440	8TH WARD
BAILEY, SAMUEL	BAL	024	1ST WARD
BAILEY, SAMUEL	BAL	024	1ST WARD
BAILEY, SARAH	FRE	272	NEW MARK
BAILEY, SARAH	BAL	209	11TH WAR
BAILEY, SARAH	MGM	377	ROCKERLE
BAILEY, SARAH *	ANN	337	3RD DIST
BAILEY, SARAH A.	BAL	124	16TH WAR
BAILEY, SARAH A.	ST	328	4TH E DI
BAILEY, SHADERICK	HAR	133	2ND DIST
BAILEY, SHERKLIFF	ST	334	4TH E DI
BAILEY, SOLOMON	QUE	250	5TH E DI
BAILEY, SOLOMON	BAL	132	2ND DIST
BAILEY, SOPHIA	BAL	103	15TH WAR

Name	County	Page	District
BAILEY, STEPHEN	MGM	405	ROCKERLE
BAILEY, SUSAN	BAL	103	15TH WAR
BAILEY, SUSAN	BAL	375	1ST DIST
BAILEY, THOASM H.	ST	257	3RD E DI
BAILEY, THOMAS *	ANN	318	2ND DIST
BAILEY, THOMAS M.	BAL	009	15TH WAR
BAILEY, TOBIAS	BAL	155	5TH WARD
BAILEY, WASHINGTON	FRE	274	NEW MARK
BAILEY, WILLIAM	HAR	069	1ST DIST
BAILEY, WILLIAM	MGM	363	BERRYS D
BAILEY, WILLIAM	HAR	143	2ND DIST
BAILEY, WILLIAM	HAR	121	2ND DIST
BAILEY, WILLIAM	CAR	149	NO TWP L
BAILEY, WILLIAM	BAL	327	1ST DIST
BAILEY, WILLIAM	BAL	118	5TH WARD
BAILEY, WILLIAM	BAL	137	1ST WARD
BAILEY, WILLIAM H.	BAL	365	8TH WARD
BAILEY, WILLIAM J.	BAL	279	17TH WAR
BAILIE, ANN	CHA	226	ALLENS F
BAILIE, CORNELIUS	CHA	273	ALLENS F
BAILIE, FRANCIS	CHA	227	ALLENS F
BAILIE, IGNATIUS	CHA	227	ALLENS F
BAILIE, WILLIAM	BAL	008	1ST WARD
BAILING, SARAH	BAL	162	6TH WARD
BAILY, AGNESS	BAL	231	1ST DIST
BAILY, ALFRED	BAL	044	4TH WARD
BAILY, AQUILA	HAR	127	2ND DIST
BAILY, BENJAMIN	SOM	408	DUBLIN D
BAILY, CHARLOTTE	BAL	344	3RD WARD
BAILY, DRUSILLA *	FRE	247	NEW MARK
BAILY, EDWARD-BLACK	WOR	340	1ST E DI
BAILY, ELIZA	BAL	370	1ST DIST
BAILY, ELLINORA	BAL	066	18TH WAR
BAILY, ESMA C.	SOM	525	BARREN C
BAILY, FANNY-BLACK	WOR	348	1ST E DI
BAILY, GEORGE	BAL	301	1ST DIST
BAILY, GEORGE H.	BAL	394	14TH WAR
BAILY, HARRIET	BAL	453	14TH WAR
BAILY, HENRY	BAL	180	2ND WARD
BAILY, HENRY	BAL	399	3RD WARD
BAILY, HEZEKIAH	FRE	272	NEW MARK
BAILY, JAMES	SOM	461	HANGARY
BAILY, JOHN	CEC	180	7TH E DI
BAILY, JOHN	BAL	013	1ST WARD
BAILY, JOHN	BAL	363	1ST DIST
BAILY, JOHN	BAL	440	1ST DIST
BAILY, JOHN F.	CHA	269	ALLENS F
BAILY, MARY	BAL	027	1ST WARD
BAILY, MARY	BAL	210	2ND WARD
BAILY, MARY J.	BAL	046	18TH WAR
BAILY, MINTY	BAL	331	3RD WARD
BAILY, NOAH	ST	323	4TH E DI
BAILY, OBED-MULATTO	CAR	146	NO TWP L
BAILY, PEGGY	SOM	497	SALISBUR
BAILY, PETER	CAR	337	6TH DIST
BAILY, PRICELLA	BAL	316	3RD WARD
BAILY, ROSA	WOR	344	1ST E DI
BAILY, ROSANA	BAL	174	11TH WAR
BAILY, THOMAS C.	CAR	092	NO TWP L
BAILY,JAMES	CAR	101	NO TWP L
BAIM, WILLIAM	WAS	146	HAGERSTO
BAIN, ELLEN	BAL	066	2ND DIST
BAIN, GEORGE	BAL	079	2ND DIST
BAIN, JAMES	BAL	431	8TH WARD
BAIN, JOHN	BAL	080	2ND DIST
BAIN, JOHN	BAL	203	2ND WARD
BAIN, JOHN	WAS	143	2ND DIST
BAIN, JULIUS	BAL	463	14TH WAR
BAIN, LAURA	BAL	065	2ND DIST
BAIN, LUTHER*	DOR	395	1ST DIST
BAIN, MARY	BAL	293	12TH WAR
BAIN, MICHAEL	ANN	342	3RD DIST
BAIN, MICHAEL	BAL	042	18TH WAR
BAIN, THOMAS	BAL	066	2ND DIST
BAIN, THOMAS J.	BAL	007	1ST WARD
BAIN, WILLIAM	BAL	065	2ND DIST
BAIN, WILLIAM	BAL	081	2ND DIST
BAIN, WILLIAM	BAL	310	20TH WAR
BAINES, ANN	BAL	183	6TH WARD
BAINES, ASHAEL	BAL	022	9TH WARD
BAINES, JAMES A.	WOR	184	6TH E DI
BAINES, JOHN	BAL	120	2ND DIST
BAINES, SUSANAH	FRE	250	NEW MARK
BAINHEART, JENNY	ANN	503	HOWARD D
BAINHOUSE, JACOB	ALL	029	2ND E.D.
BAINKLEY, HENRY F.	WOR	339	1ST E DI
BAINS, GEORGE	BAL	180	2ND WARD
BAINS, JOHN	BAL	005	EASTERN
BAINS, T.*	DOR	409	1ST DIST
BAINS, TERREY.	BAL	381	8TH WARD
BAINS, WILLIAM-BLACK	ST	292	2ND E DI
BAIR, ANDREW	CAR	375	9TH DIST
BAIR, CHRISTIAN	WAS	144	2ND DIST
BAIR, GEORGE	CAR	375	9TH DIST
BAIR, HANORD	CAR	375	9TH DIST
BAIR, HENRY	BAL	014	9TH WARD
BAIR, ISAAC	WAS	145	2ND DIST
BAIR, LOUISA	CAR	341	6TH DIST
BAIR, PETER	ALL	083	5TH E.D.
BAIRD, JAMES	BAL	256	2ND WARD
BAIRD, SUSAN	ALL	138	6TH E.D.
BAIRD, THOMAS	KEN	229	2ND DIST
BAIRLEY, JOHN	BAL	419	14TH WAR
BAISCMAN, MARY	CAR	211	5TH DIST
BAISEMAN, JOSHUA	CAR	214	5TH DIST
BAIST, ELIZABETH	BAL	009	9TH WARD
BAIT, NATHAN	CAR	315	1ST DIST
BAITGES, MARGARET	FRE	059	FREDERIC
BAITMAN, SARAH*	BAL	312	3RD WARD
BAITZ, HENRY	BAL	252	2ND WARD
BAITZELL, GEORGE	BAL	131	18TH WAR
BAKE,R ANNA	ALL	213	CUMBERLA
BAKE,R SUSANN	FRE	447	8TH E DI
BAKEHOUSE, JOSEPH	ANN	384	4TH DIST
BAKEMAN, AGUSTUS	BAL	252	2ND WARD
BAKEMAN, HENRY	BAL	280	7TH WARD
BAKEMAN, PAMELIA	BAL	005	1ST WARD
BAKEMIRE, CATHERINE	BAL	278	20TH WAR
BAKEN, JOHN	BAL	094	2ND DIST
BAKER, A.H.	CAR	398	2ND DIST
BAKER, AARON	FRE	307	WOODSBOR
BAKER, ABRAHAM	HAR	066	1ST DIST
BAKER, ABRAHAM	HAR	162	3RD DIST
BAKER, ABSALOM	BAL	218	6TH DIST
BAKER, ADAM	FRE	284	WOODSBOR
BAKER, ADAZILLA	ANN	456	HOWARD D
BAKER, ALBERT W.	MGM	435	CLARKSTR
BAKER, ALEN	CAR	196	4TH DIST
BAKER, ALEXANDER	FRE	044	FREDERIC
BAKER, ALEXANDER	WOR	251	1ST CENS
BAKER, ALFRED	MGM	433	CLARKSTR
BAKER, ALFRED	BAL	234	17TH WAR
BAKER, ALFRED	BAL	160	1ST WARD
BAKER, ALICE	BAL	358	3RD WARD
BAKER, AMANDA	BAL	306	1ST DIST
BAKER, ANN	WAS	049	2ND SUBD
BAKER, ANN C.	PRI	036	VANSVILL
BAKER, ANN E.	CEC	179	7TH E DI
BAKER, ANNA	WOR	250	1ST CENS
BAKER, ANNA	WOR	253	1ST CENS
BAKER, ANNA	WOR	269	BERLIN 1
BAKER, ARTHUR	PRI	036	VANSVILL
BAKER, ARTHUR	ALL	069	5TH E.D.
BAKER, ASA	FRE	263	NEW MARK
BAKER, AUGUST	BAL	426	8TH WARD
BAKER, BASEL	FRE	286	WOODSBOR
BAKER, BENJAMIN	FRE	291	WOODSBOR
BAKER, BENJAMIN	BAL	240	12TH WAR
BAKER, BENJAMIN	TAL	055	EASTON D
BAKER, BROOK	FRE	283	WOODSBOR
BAKER, BURTON	WOR	270	BERLIN 1
BAKER, CAPTAIN	CEC	183	7TH E DI
BAKER, CAROLINE	CEC	131	6TH E DI
BAKER, CAROLINE	ANN	459	HOWARD D
BAKER, CATHARINE	BAL	297	12TH WAR
BAKER, CATHARINE H.	FRE	435	8TH E DI
BAKER, CATHERINE	FRE	060	FREDERIC
BAKER, CATHERINE	FRE	112	CREAGERS
BAKER, CATHRINE	BAL	052	18TH WAR
BAKER, CHARLES	BAL	037	18TH WAR
BAKER, CHARLES	HAR	165	3RD DIST
BAKER, CHARLES	BAL	089	10TH WAR
BAKER, CHARLES	BAL	284	1ST DIST
BAKER, CHARLES	BAL	377	3RD WARD
BAKER, CHARLES	BAL	280	2ND WARD
BAKER, CHARLES	BAL	293	3RD WARD
BAKER, CHARLES G.	HAR	180	3RD DIST
BAKER, CHARLES H.	MGM	384	ROCKERLE
BAKER, CHARLES J.	BAL	258	12TH WAR
BAKER, CHARLES L.	WAS	203	1ST DIST
BAKER, CHARLOTTE	BAL	047	15TH WAR
BAKER, CHLOE A.	BAL	269	20TH WAR
BAKER, CHRISTIAN	CEC	148	PORT DUP
BAKER, COLUMBUS	BAL	379	1ST DIST
BAKER, CONRAD	BAL	104	2ND DIST
BAKER, DANIEL	BAL	196	17TH WAR
BAKER, DANIEL	FRE	014	FREDERIC
BAKER, DANIEL	FRE	328	MIDDLETO
BAKER, DANIEL	FRE	338	MIDDLETO
BAKER, DAVID	FRE	204	BUCKEYST
BAKER, DAVID	FRE	171	5TH E DI
BAKER, DAVID	BAL	022	4TH WARD
BAKER, DAVID	WAS	274	RIDGEVIL
BAKER, DAVID	WAS	288	1ST DIST
BAKER, DAVID U.	FRE	109	CREAGERS
BAKER, EDMUND E.	MGM	364	BERRYS D
BAKER, EDWARD	CEC	024	ELKTON 3
BAKER, EDWARD	FRE	225	BUCKEYST
BAKER, EDWARD	BAL	465	14TH WAR
BAKER, EDWARD	BAL	314	1ST DIST
BAKER, EDWARD	BAL	054	15TH WAR
BAKER, ELIAS	WAS	060	2ND SUBD
BAKER, ELISABETH	ALL	245	CUMBERLA
BAKER, ELIZA	BAL	345	7TH WARD
BAKER, ELIZA	BAL	277	7TH WARD
BAKER, ELIZA	ALL	134	4TH E.D.
BAKER, ELIZA	CEC	186	7TH E DI
BAKER, ELIZABETH	BAL	211	11TH WAR
BAKER, ELIZABETH	FRE	267	NEW MARK
BAKER, ELIZABETH	CAR	204	4TH DIST
BAKER, ELIZABETH	HAR	115	2ND DIST
BAKER, ELIZABETH	HAR	207	3RD DIST
BAKER, ELIZABETH	BAL	254	12TH WAR
BAKER, ELIZABETH	ANN	431	HOWARD D
BAKER, ELIZABETH	BAL	189	2ND WARD
BAKER, ELIZABETH	BAL	206	2ND WARD
BAKER, ELIZABETH	BAL	169	6TH WARD
BAKER, ELIZABETH	WAS	153	HAGERSTO
BAKER, ELIZAH	WOR	205	4TH E DI
BAKER, ELLEN	WOR	204	4TH E DI
BAKER, ELZA J.	BAL	379	1ST DIST
BAKER, EMANUEL	BAL	380	8TH WARD
BAKER, EMELINE	ALL	147	6TH E.D.
BAKER, EMILY	CAR	335	6TH DIST
BAKER, EPHRAIM	SOM	497	SALISBUR
BAKER, EZRA	CAR	185	8TH DIST
BAKER, F. A.	WAS	188	1ST DIST
BAKER, FANNY	WAS	178	BOONSBOR
BAKER, FRANCIS	BAL	370	1ST DIST
BAKER, FRANCIS	BAL	370	1ST DIST
BAKER, FRANCIS	BAL	411	1ST DIST
BAKER, FRANCIS	ALL	200	CUMBERLA
BAKER, FRANCIS H.	TAL	049	EASTON T
BAKER, FRANCIS L.	BAL	338	13TH WAR
BAKER, FRANCIS M.	KEN	261	1ST DIST
BAKER, FRED	FRE	380	PETERSVI
BAKER, FREDERIC	BAL	180	2ND DIST
BAKER, FREDERICK	BAL	014	9TH WARD
BAKER, FREDERICK	BAL	353	3RD WARD
BAKER, FREDERICK	BAL	280	7TH WARD
BAKER, FREDERICK	BAL	390	3RD WARD
BAKER, FREDERICK	BAL	407	8TH WARD
BAKER, FREDERICK	BAL	203	2ND WARD
BAKER, FREDERICK S.	WAS	075	2ND SUBD
BAKER, GARRETTSON G.	BAL	023	9TH WARD
BAKER, GEORGE	WOR	205	4TH E DI
BAKER, GEORGE	BAL	396	8TH WARD
BAKER, GEORGE	BAL	246	2ND WARD
BAKER, GEORGE	BAL	213	6TH DIST
BAKER, GEORGE	BAL	236	1ST DIST
BAKER, GEORGE	BAL	077	1ST WARD
BAKER, GEORGE	BAL	459	8TH WARD
BAKER, GEORGE	ALL	087	5TH E.D.
BAKER, GEORGE	ALL	002	3RD E.D.
BAKER, GEORGE	BAL	037	18TH WAR
BAKER, GEORGE A.	TAL	095	ST MICHA
BAKER, GEORGE C.	BAL	271	2ND WARD
BAKER, GEORGE E.	FRE	229	BUCKEYST
BAKER, GEORGE W.	HAR	167	3RD DIST
BAKER, GEORGIAN	BAL	277	7TH WARD
BAKER, GODLIP	BAL	215	17TH WAR
BAKER, GOUDSBOROUGH	WOR	205	4TH E DI
BAKER, GRAFTON	HAR	158	3RD DIST
BAKER, GREENBERRY	MGM	435	CLARKSTR
BAKER, HANNAH	FRE	321	MIDDLETO
BAKER, HANNAH	CEC	002	ELKTON 3
BAKER, HARRIET	BAL	411	1ST DIST
BAKER, HARRIET	BAL	346	1ST DIST
BAKER, HENRY	BAL	278	7TH WARD
BAKER, HENRY	BAL	254	2ND WARD
BAKER, HENRY	BAL	136	1ST WARD
BAKER, HENRY	ALL	090	5TH E.D.
BAKER, HENRY	BAL	434	8TH WARD
BAKER, HENRY	BAL	225	1ST DIST
BAKER, HENRY	BAL	190	5TH DIST
BAKER, HENRY	BAL	091	1ST WARD
BAKER, HENRY	ANN	474	HOWARD D
BAKER, HENRY	BAL	229	19TH WAR
BAKER, HENRY	FRE	276	NEW MARK
BAKER, HENRY	HAR	150	3RD DIST
BAKER, HENRY	BAL	275	17TH WAR
BAKER, HENRY	CAR	390	2ND DIST
BAKER, HENRY	FRE	434	8TH E DI
BAKER, HENRY	FRE	447	8TH E DI
BAKER, HENRY	FRE	404	JEFFERSO
BAKER, HENRY	MGM	359	BERRYS D
BAKER, HENRY	CAR	134	NO TWP L
BAKER, HENRY	WOR	276	BERLIN 1
BAKER, HENRY	WAS	152	2ND DIST
BAKER, HETTY	WOR	286	BERLIN 1
BAKER, HEZAKIAH	CAR	379	2ND DIST
BAKER, HIRAM	FRE	362	CATOCTIN
BAKER, HIRAM	BAL	120	18TH WAR
BAKER, HULLY	BAL	288	20TH WAR
BAKER, HY	BAL	207	5TH DIST
BAKER, HY	BAL	211	6TH DIST
BAKER, ISAAC	BAL	045	1ST WARD
BAKER, ISAAC	BAL	240	12TH WAR
BAKER, ISAAC	BAL	311	1ST DIST
BAKER, ISAAH	FRE	033	FREDERIC
BAKER, ISAIAH	BAL	173	2ND DIST
BAKER, ISAIAH	WOR	207	4TH E DI
BAKER, J.L.W.	WAS	005	WILLIAMS
BAKER, JACOB	WAS	049	2ND SUBD
BAKER, JACOB	BAL	011	9TH WARD
BAKER, JACOB	ALL	057	10TH E.D
BAKER, JACOB	BAL	364	3RD WARD
BAKER, JACOB	CAR	377	2ND DIST
BAKER, JACOB	FRE	171	5TH E DI
BAKER, JACOB	HAR	080	2ND DIST
BAKER, JACOB	BAL	217	19TH WAR
BAKER, JAEMS	FRE	306	WOODSBOR
BAKER, JAMES	BAL	145	19TH WAR
BAKER, JAMES	CAR	203	4TH DIST
BAKER, JAMES	BAL	311	7TH WARD
BAKER, JAMES	ALL	069	5TH E.D.
BAKER, JAMES	BAL	001	15TH WAR
BAKER, JAMES	BAL	170	1ST WARD
BAKER, JAMES	WOR	205	4TH E DI
BAKER, JAMES B.	HAR	069	1ST DIST
BAKER, JAMES C.	BAL	019	1ST WARD
BAKER, JAMES H.	TAL	050	EASTON T
BAKER, JAMES M.	BAL	359	3RD WARD
BAKER, JANE	BAL	392	1ST DIST
BAKER, JANE F.	KEN	210	2ND DIST
BAKER, JESSA	WOR	245	1ST CENS
BAKER, JESSE	WOR	252	1ST CENS
BAKER, JESSE	CAR	206	4TH DIST
BAKER, JOH W.	BAL	419	14TH WAR
BAKER, JOHN	CEC	140	5TH E DI
BAKER, JOHN	CEC	166	6TH E DI
BAKER, JOHN	CAR	202	4TH DIST
BAKER, JOHN	FRE	266	NEW MARK
BAKER, JOHN	HAR	192	3RD DIST
BAKER, JOHN	BAL	035	18TH WAR
BAKER, JOHN	FRE	365	CATOCTIN
BAKER, JOHN	FRE	339	MIDDLETO
BAKER, JOHN	FRE	443	8TH E DI
BAKER, JOHN	DOR	325	1ST DIST
BAKER, JOHN	CAR	142	NO TWP L
BAKER, JOHN	CAR	134	NO TWP L
BAKER, JOHN	WAS	049	2ND SUBD
BAKER, JOHN	WAS	001	WILLIAMS
BAKER, JOHN	WAS	070	2ND SUBD
BAKER, JOHN	SOM	497	SALISBUR
BAKER, JOHN	WAS	192	1ST DIST
BAKER, JOHN	TAL	070	EASTON T
BAKER, JOHN	BAL	270	2ND WARD
BAKER, JOHN	BAL	267	2ND WARD
BAKER, JOHN	BAL	125	1ST WARD
BAKER, JOHN	BAL	027	1ST WARD
BAKER, JOHN	BAL	035	1ST WARD
BAKER, JOHN	BAL	104	1ST WARD
BAKER, JOHN	BAL	055	1ST WARD
BAKER, JOHN	BAL	124	1ST WARD
BAKER, JOHN	BAL	268	1ST DIST
BAKER, JOHN	ALL	001	3RD E.D.
BAKER, JOHN	ANN	409	8TH DIST
BAKER, JOHN	ANN	434	HOWARD D
BAKER, JOHN	ALL	246	CUMBERLA
BAKER, JOHN	ALL	251	CUMBERLA
BAKER, JOHN	BAL	012	2ND DIST
BAKER, JOHN *	BAL	288	1ST DIST
BAKER, JOHN A.	FRE	295	WOODSBOR
BAKER, JOHN C.	BAL	323	1ST DIST
BAKER, JOHN G.	BAL	048	1ST WARD
BAKER, JOHN G.	BAL	284	7TH WARD
BAKER, JOHN H.	BAL	065	18TH WAR
BAKER, JOHN H.	HAR	074	1ST DIST
BAKER, JOHN H.	TAL	070	EASTON T
BAKER, JOHN J.	BAL	198	11TH WAR
BAKER, JOHN J. G.	WOR	207	4TH E DI
BAKER, JOHN T.	MGM	355	BERRYS D
BAKER, JOHN T.	BAL	389	8TH WARD
BAKER, JOHN W.	BAL	351	1ST DIST
BAKER, JOHN W.	MGM	368	BERRYS D
BAKER, JOHN W.	BAL	471	14TH WAR
BAKER, JOHNATHAN	TAL	049	EASTON T
BAKER, JOHNATHAN	WOR	253	1ST CENS
BAKER, JONAS	WOR	272	BERLIN 1
BAKER, JOSEPH	BAL	231	1ST DIST
BAKER, JOSEPH	BAL	013	15TH WAR
BAKER, JOSEPH	WOR	252	1ST CENS
BAKER, JOSEPH	FRE	441	8TH E DI
BAKER, JOSEPH	BAL	217	19TH WAR
BAKER, JOSEPH C.	HAR	150	3RD DIST
BAKER, JOSHUA	WOR	269	BERLIN 1
BAKER, JOSHUA	BAL	223	12TH WAR
BAKER, JOSIAH	BAL	358	1ST DIST
BAKER, JOSIAH	BAL	352	1ST DIST
BAKER, JOSIAH	WOR	206	4TH E DI
BAKER, JOSIAH B.	BAL	412	3RD WARD
BAKER, JULIA	BAL	221	12TH WAR
BAKER, JULIA	BAL	058	2ND DIST
BAKER, KENNEDY	ALL	045	10TH E.D
BAKER, LANE	ANN	284	ANNAPOLI
BAKER, LEIWS	BAL	392	14TH WAR
BAKER, LEVI	WAS	224	1ST DIST
BAKER, LEVIN	WOR	268	BERLIN 1
BAKER, LEVIN	WOR	267	BERLIN 1

Name	County	Page	District
BAKER, LEVINA	BAL	356	1ST DIST
BAKER, LEVITT	ALL	161	6TH E.D.
BAKER, LEWIS	WAS	138	HAGERSTO
BAKER, LOUIS	ALL	055	10TH E.D
BAKER, LOUISEA	BAL	235	2ND WARD
BAKER, MADDEN	ALL	119	5TH E.D.
BAKER, MAGDALIN	FRE	328	MIDDLETO
BAKER, MAIRAH	FRE	283	WOODSBOR
BAKER, MALAN	ALL	064	10TH E.D
BAKER, MARGARET	BAL	287	3RD WARD
BAKER, MARGARET	BAL	044	15TH WAR
BAKER, MARGARET	BAL	024	9TH WARD
BAKER, MARIA	BAL	059	10TH WAR
BAKER, MARIA	WAS	267	1ST DIST
BAKER, MARIAH	CAR	155	NO TWP L
BAKER, MARY	BAL	141	11TH WAR
BAKER, MARY	CEC	045	1ST E DI
BAKER, MARY	BAL	303	20TH WAR
BAKER, MARY	BAL	288	20TH WAR
BAKER, MARY	BAL	311	20TH WAR
BAKER, MARY	BAL	042	4TH WARD
BAKER, MARY	WOR	269	BERLIN 1
BAKER, MARY	WOR	275	BERLIN 1
BAKER, MARY	SOM	525	QUANTICO
BAKER, MARY	BAL	024	9TH WARD
BAKER, MARY	BAL	236	12TH WAR
BAKER, MARY	BAL	341	7TH WARD
BAKER, MARY	BAL	463	1ST DIST
BAKER, MARY	BAL	300	1ST DIST
BAKER, MARY A.	QUE	136	1ST E DI
BAKER, MARY C.	BAL	265	20TH WAR
BAKER, MARY C.	WAS	189	1ST DIST
BAKER, MARY E.	CAR	072	NO TWP L
BAKER, MARY E.	ANN	279	ANNAPOLI
BAKER, MARY J.	BAL	027	1ST WARD
BAKER, MARY M.	FRE	113	CREAGERS
BAKER, MASHEK	FRE	242	NEW MARK
BAKER, MESHACH	CAR	375	9TH DIST
BAKER, MICHAEL	CAR	334	6TH DIST
BAKER, MICHAEL	BAL	075	10TH WAR
BAKER, MINTY	BAL	229	12TH WAR
BAKER, MOLLY	WOR	276	BERLIN 1
BAKER, MOSES	BAL	370	1ST DIST
BAKER, MURRY P.	BAL	268	12TH WAR
BAKER, NANCY	BAL	085	2ND DIST
BAKER, NANCY	CAR	213	5TH DIST
BAKER, NANCY C.	WOR	251	1ST CENS
BAKER, NAOMA	CAR	212	5TH DIST
BAKER, NATHAIEL	WOR	248	1ST CENS
BAKER, NATHAN	FRE	301	WOODSBOR
BAKER, NATHANIEL	CAL	005	1ST DIST
BAKER, NEEKY	BAL	317	12TH WAR
BAKER, NELSON	BAL	206	6TH DIST
BAKER, NELSON	ALL	045	10TH E.D
BAKER, NICHOLAS	ALL	057	10TH E.D
BAKER, NICHOLAS	BAL	293	17TH WAR
BAKER, NICHOLAS	HAR	135	2ND DIST
BAKER, NICHOLAS	BAL	070	4TH WARD
BAKER, OTHO	WAS	049	2ND SUBD
BAKER, PARKER	WOR	253	1ST CENS
BAKER, PEGGY	WOR	280	BERLIN 1
BAKER, PERRY	BAL	314	1ST DIST
BAKER, PETER	ALL	013	3RD E.D.
BAKER, PETER	BAL	085	2ND DIST
BAKER, PETER	BAL	199	2ND WARD
BAKER, PETER	WOR	203	4TH E DI
BAKER, PETER	CEC	094	4TH E DI
BAKER, PHILIP	FRE	401	JEFFERSO
BAKER, PULCHERIA	BAL	212	11TH WAR
BAKER, RACHEL	BAL	028	18TH WAR
BAKER, RACHEL	TAL	059	EASTON D
BAKER, RACHEL	BAL	247	6TH WARD
BAKER, REBECCA	CAR	143	NO TWP L
BAKER, REY	BAL	301	7TH WARD
BAKER, REZIN	CAR	193	4TH DIST
BAKER, RICHARD	BAL	330	1ST DIST
BAKER, RICHARD A.	CAR	143	NO TWP L
BAKER, ROBERT	CEC	045	1ST E DI
BAKER, ROBERT	BAL	372	1ST DIST
BAKER, ROBERT	ANN	444	HOWARD D
BAKER, ROBERT	WOR	273	BERLIN 1
BAKER, ROBERT B.	BAL	400	14TH WAR
BAKER, ROBERT E.	WOR	205	4TH E DI
BAKER, ROBERT M.	WOR	262	BERLIN 1
BAKER, ROSETTA	TAL	094	ST MICHA
BAKER, RUBEN	PRI	037	VANSVILL
BAKER, SAMPSON	CAL	034	2ND DIST
BAKER, SAMSON	CAL	027	2ND DIST
BAKER, SAMUEL	CAR	201	4TH DIST
BAKER, SAMUEL	CAR	367	9TH DIST
BAKER, SAMUEL	FRE	285	WOODSBOR
BAKER, SAMUEL	FRE	289	WOODSBOR
BAKER, SAMUEL	WOR	251	1ST CENS
BAKER, SAMUEL	WOR	252	1ST CENS
BAKER, SAMUEL	WOR	286	BERLIN 1
BAKER, SAMUEL	WAS	291	1ST DIST
BAKER, SAMUEL	WAS	200	1ST DIST
BAKER, SAMUEL	BAL	391	1ST DIST
BAKER, SAMUEL E.	KEN	252	1ST DIST
BAKER, SARAH	FRE	416	8TH E DI
BAKER, SARAH	HAR	070	1ST DIST
BAKER, SARAH	WAS	070	2ND SUBD
BAKER, SARAH A.	FRE	323	MIDDLETO
BAKER, SARAH C.	FRE	443	8TH E DI
BAKER, SARAH E.	BAL	277	7TH WARD
BAKER, SARAH J.	BAL	341	7TH WARD
BAKER, SETH	WOR	250	1ST CENS
BAKER, SOLOMON	WOR	281	BERLIN 1
BAKER, SOPHIA	WAS	186	BOONSBOR
BAKER, SOPHIA	MGM	400	ROCKERLE
BAKER, STEVEN	ALL	068	5TH E.D.
BAKER, SUSAN	BAL	201	6TH DIST
BAKER, SUSAN	BAL	053	1ST WARD
BAKER, SUSAN	KEN	246	2ND DIST
BAKER, T.	BAL	205	19TH WAR
BAKER, THEODORE	ALL	136	4TH E.D.
BAKER, THEODORE	BAL	220	6TH WARD
BAKER, THOASM	HAR	194	3RD DIST
BAKER, THOMAS	FRE	274	NEW MARK
BAKER, THOMAS	MGM	360	BERRYS D
BAKER, THOMAS	CAR	370	9TH DIST
BAKER, THOMAS	CEC	120	4TH E DI
BAKER, THOMAS	BAL	160	1ST WARD
BAKER, THOMAS	ALL	058	10TH E.D
BAKER, THOMAS	BAL	123	1ST WARD
BAKER, THOMAS	WOR	252	1ST CENS
BAKER, THOMAS	TAL	037	EASTON D
BAKER, THOMAS	MGM	444	CLARKSTR
BAKER, THOMAS	MGM	434	CLARKSTR
BAKER, THOMAS A.	FRE	229	BUCKEYST
BAKER, THOMAS M.	TAL	046	EASTON T
BAKER, THORTON	ALL	153	6TH E.D.
BAKER, TOHIAL B.*	BAL	386	3RD WARD
BAKER, W. E.	BAL	271	20TH WAR
BAKER, WILLAM	WOR	267	BERLIN 1
BAKER, WILLIA MA.	BAL	159	6TH WARD
BAKER, WILLIAM	BAL	029	9TH WARD
BAKER, WILLIAM	BAL	173	1ST WARD
BAKER, WILLIAM	BAL	123	5TH WARD
BAKER, WILLIAM	BAL	240	2ND WARD
BAKER, WILLIAM	BAL	228	2ND WARD
BAKER, WILLIAM	BAL	374	8TH WARD
BAKER, WILLIAM	BAL	136	1ST WARD
BAKER, WILLIAM	ALL	012	3RD E.D.
BAKER, WILLIAM	BAL	190	5TH DIST
BAKER, WILLIAM	BAL	416	1ST DIST
BAKER, WILLIAM	BAL	311	1ST DIST
BAKER, WILLIAM	BAL	325	1ST DIST
BAKER, WILLIAM	BAL	341	7TH WARD
BAKER, WILLIAM	BAL	458	8TH WARD
BAKER, WILLIAM	ANN	462	HOWARD D
BAKER, WILLIAM	BAL	041	9TH WARD
BAKER, WILLIAM	TAL	034	EASTON D
BAKER, WILLIAM	WOR	287	BERLIN 1
BAKER, WILLIAM	WOR	278	BERLIN 1
BAKER, WILLIAM	WOR	250	1ST CENS
BAKER, WILLIAM	TAL	117	ST MICHA
BAKER, WILLIAM	WAS	267	1ST DIST
BAKER, WILLIAM	BAL	303	20TH WAR
BAKER, WILLIAM	FRE	378	PETERSVI
BAKER, WILLIAM	FRE	014	FREDERIC
BAKER, WILLIAM	CHA	217	ALLENS F
BAKER, WILLIAM	CHA	245	HILLTOP
BAKER, WILLIAM	CEC	178	7TH E DI
BAKER, WILLIAM	CEC	185	7TH E DI
BAKER, WILLIAM	MGM	355	BERRYS D
BAKER, WILLIAM	MGM	377	ROCKERLE
BAKER, WILLIAM	BAL	229	19TH WAR
BAKER, WILLIAM	BAL	023	4TH WARD
BAKER, WILLIAM	BAL	048	4TH WARD
BAKER, WILLIAM	BAL	243	17TH WAR
BAKER, WILLIAM D.	HAR	069	1ST DIST
BAKER, WILLIAM D.	BAL	330	3RD WARD
BAKER, WILLIAM H.	CAR	212	5TH DIST
BAKER, WILLIAM H.	FRE	283	WOODSBOR
BAKER, WILLIAM H. H.	CAR	206	4TH DIST
BAKER, WILLIAM L.	BAL	127	1ST WARD
BAKER, WILLIAM T.	KEN	252	1ST DIST
BAKER, ZYLPHIA	SOM	525	BARREN C
BAKER,ELIZABETH	QUE	195	3RD E DI
BAKER,LEVI	ALL	204	CUMBERLA
BAKETS, HENRY	WOR	313	2ND E DI
BAKIN, HARRIETT	QUE	219	3RD E DI
BAKMAN, JOHN	BAL	071	1ST WARD
BAKNER, JOHN	BAL	225	2ND WARD
BAKON, JANE	BAL	387	1ST DIST
BAKRMAN, HIRAM	FRE	349	MIDDLETO
BAKS, SHADRACK	BAL	376	1ST DIST
BAL, MARY	ANN	295	1ST DIST
BALA, EDWARD	ALL	239	CUMBERLA
BALAHAN, PATRICK	BAL	448	1ST DIST
BALANO, MARY A.	BAL	053	4TH WARD
BALASH, SAMUEL	BAL	065	1ST WARD
BALASH, ZACARIAH	BAL	065	1ST WARD
BALBIRRICE, GEORGE	BAL	037	4TH WARD
BALCH, BENJAMIN S.	BAL	040	9TH WARD
BALCHAN, PATRICK	BAL	448	1ST DIST
BALCKESTON, NANCY	QUE	238	5TH E DI
BALCKSTON, LEWIS	QUE	252	5TH E DI
BALCKSTONE, HENRY	BAL	148	2ND DIST
BALD, AUGUSTA	BAL	225	12TH WAR
BALD, CATHARINE	BAL	238	17TH WAR
BALD, FREDERICK	BAL	225	12TH WAR
BALD, WALTER	BAL	242	12TH WAR
BALD, WILLIAM	BAL	237	17TH WAR
BALDANE, IRA	BAL	174	19TH WAR
BALDEN, JOHN	BAL	078	18TH WAR
BALDEN, JOHN	BAL	167	16TH WAR
BALDEN, MARY	BAL	351	1ST DIST
BALDEN, SARAH	BAL	167	16TH WAR
BALDEN,JESSE	CAR	151	NO TWP L
BALDENHOUSE, JOHN	BAL	130	1ST WARD
BALDERSON, JOHN	FRE	055	FREDERIC
BALDERSCN, JOHNSON	BAL	278	2ND WARD
BALDERSON, JOHNSON	BAL	286	2ND WARD
BALDERSCN, MARTHA	BAL	356	1ST DIST
BALDERSON, MARTHA	ANN	436	HOWARD D
BALDERSCN, STEPHEN	ANN	435	HOWARD D
BALDERSTON, DANIEL	BAL	129	5TH WARD
BALDERSTON, ISIAH	BAL	062	10TH WAR
BALDERSTON, ISIAH	BAL	117	5TH WARD
BALDERSTON, WILSON	BAL	067	15TH WAR
BALDES, THOMAS	WOR	302	SNOW HIL
BALDES, WILLIAM A.	WOR	298	9TH E DI
BALDGEN, HENRY	BAL	167	2ND DIST
BALDIN, CHARLES	ALL	055	10TH E.D
BALDIN, MARY	BAL	356	1ST DIST
BALDING, JOSEPH	BAL	135	18TH WAR
BALDING, LYDIA A.	FRE	094	FREDERIC
BALDIWN, GEORGE	BAL	235	12TH WAR
BALDNER, MICHAEL	FRE	410	8TH E DI
BALDOCK, GEORGE	BAL	168	1ST WARD
BALDUSTON, HUGH	BAL	331	13TH WAR
BALDUSTON, JACOB	BAL	332	13TH WAR
BALDWIN, ANDREW	BAL	032	18TH WAR
BALDWIN, ANGALINE	ANN	391	4TH DIST
BALDWIN, ANN	CEC	096	4TH E DI
BALDWIN, ARERIANTA	PRI	028	VANSVILL
BALDWIN, BENJAMIN	BAL	127	2ND DIST
BALDWIN, C. C.	BAL	465	14TH WAR
BALDWIN, CHARLOTT	HAR	048	1ST DIST
BALDWIN, CORNELIA	PRI	017	BLADENSB
BALDWIN, CORNELIA J.	CEC	085	5TH E DI
BALDWIN, DAVID	BAL	370	3RD WARD
BALDWIN, EDWARD	ANN	328	2ND DIST
BALDWIN, EDWARD C.	BAL	115	5TH WARD
BALDWIN, ELIZA	CEC	001	ELKTON 3
BALDWIN, ELIZABETH	PRI	004	BLADENSB
BALDWIN, EMILY	CEC	093	4TH E DI
BALDWIN, F.B.	BAL	126	1ST WARD
BALDWIN, GEORGE	HAR	137	2ND DIST
BALDWIN, GEORGE	PRI	030	VANSVILL
BALDWIN, GEORGE R.	BAL	162	19TH WAR
BALDWIN, GRACE	FRE	205	BUCKEYST
BALDWIN, HANNAH	BAL	008	18TH WAR
BALDWIN, HARRIETT E.	BAL	117	5TH WARD
BALDWIN, HENRY	ANN	354	3RD DIST
BALDWIN, HENRY N.	PRI	027	VANSVILL
BALDWIN, JAMES	BAL	168	1ST WARD
BALDWIN, JAMES	BAL	193	2ND WARD
BALDWIN, JAMES	HAR	050	1ST DIST
BALDWIN, JAMES	HAR	001	1ST DIST
BALDWIN, JAMES	HAR	037	1ST DIST
BALDWIN, JAMES F.	ANN	333	2ND DIST
BALDWIN, JOHN	BAL	089	2ND DIST
BALDWIN, JOHN	WAS	181	FORT EDW
BALDWIN, JOHN	CEC	144	PORT DUP
BALDWIN, JOHN A.	ANN	329	2ND DIST
BALDWIN, JOHN H.	BAL	363	3RD WARD
BALDWIN, JOHN N.	CEC	009	ELKTON 3
BALDWIN, JOHN P.	BAL	171	16TH WAR
BALDWIN, JOHN T.	BAL	092	5TH WARD
BALDWIN, JOSEPH J.	BAL	187	6TH WARD
BALDWIN, LEVI	PRI	027	VANSVILL
BALDWIN, LYDIA A.	FRE	205	BUCKEYST
BALDWIN, MARGARET	ANN	360	3RD DIST
BALDWIN, MARTHA	CEC	087	4TH E DI
BALDWIN, MARY	FRE	275	NEW MARK
BALDWIN, MARY	FRE	274	NEW MARK
BALDWIN, MARY	BAL	128	5TH WARD
BALDWIN, MARY	BAL	362	3RD WARD
BALDWIN, MARY	PRI	032	VANSVILL
BALDWIN, MARY	PRI	074	MARLBROU
BALDWIN, NATHAN	CEC	015	ELKTON 3
BALDWIN, NICHOLAS	BAL	389	1ST DIST
BALDWIN, RACHEL	PRI	020	VANSVILL
BALDWIN, REBECCA	BAL	071	15TH WAR
BALDWIN, ROBERT	BAL	055	15TH WAR
BALDWIN, ROBERT	CEC	111	4TH E DI
BALDWIN, ROBERT T.	BAL	167	16TH WAR
BALDWIN, RUTHA	ANN	354	3RD DIST
BALDWIN, SALLY	HAR	137	2ND DIST
BALDWIN, SAMUEL	HAR	132	2ND DIST
BALDWIN, SAMUEL	ANN	368	4TH DIST
BALDWIN, SAMUEL	ANN	378	4TH DIST
BALDWIN, SILAS	HAR	049	1ST DIST
BALDWIN, THOMAS	ANN	400	8TH DIST
BALDWIN, THOMAS	ANN	377	4TH DIST
BALDWIN, THOMAS	BAL	128	5TH WARD
BALDWIN, THOMAS	PRI	002	BLADENSB
BALDWIN, THOMAS	PRI	122	PISCATAW
BALDWIN, THOMAS C.	BAL	336	1ST DIST
BALDWIN, W. H.	BAL	469	14TH WAR
BALDWIN, WILLIAM	HAR	048	1ST DIST
BALDWIN, WILLIAM	HAR	089	2ND DIST
BALDWIN, WILLIAM	CEC	096	4TH E DI
BALDWIN, WILLIAM	ANN	419	HOWARD D
BALDWIN, WILLIAM H.	ANN	323	2ND DIST
BALDWIN, Z.	PRI	057	AQUASCO
BALDWIN, ZACHARIAH	PRI	121	PISCATAW
BALDWIN, ZACHARIAH	PRI	103	SPALDING
BALDWIN,LEMUEL R.	BAL	168	1ST WARD
BALDY, HENLY	WAS	021	2ND SUBD
BALE, CATHERINE	CEC	193	5TH E DI
BALE, J.*	DOR	425	1ST DIST
BALE, MATTHEW	CEC	040	CHESAPEA
BALE, NEWKIRD	CEC	193	5TH E DI
BALE, RACHEL*	DOR	424	1ST DIST
BALE, THOMAS J.*	DOR	448	1ST DIST
BALE, WALTER	BAL	242	12TH WAR
BALENGER, SAMUEL	BAL	085	18TH WAR
BALEY, BRIDGET	HAR	146	3RD DIST
BALEY, GATHARINE	DOR	300	1ST DIST
BALEY, CHRISTINA	BAL	371	1ST DIST
BALEY, EDWARD	BAL	130	1ST WARD
BALEY, FREDERICK	BAL	205	6TH DIST
BALEY, ISMA	WOR	221	4TH E DI
BALEY, JACOB	BAL	210	6TH DIST
BALEY, JIM-BLACK	WOR	332	1ST E DI
BALEY, JOHN C.	BAL	213	6TH DIST
BALEY, JOSEPH	KEN	303	3RD DIST
BALEY, LEVEN	CAL	017	1ST DIST
BALEY, RICHARD	KEN	302	3RD DIST
BALEY, URIAS	BAL	329	1ST DIST
BALEY, WALTER	BAL	029	2ND DIST
BALEY, WILLIAM	BAL	056	1ST WARD
BALK, STEPHEN	BAL	112	15TH WAR
BALK, STEPHEN JR.	BAL	109	15TH WAR
BALKE, CHARLOTTE	BAL	328	13TH WAR
BALKLEY, JOHN	BAL	098	2ND DIST
BALL, BARBARA	BAL	251	1ST DIST
BALL, BARNEY	BAL	447	8TH WARD
BALL, BOB*	DOR	423	1ST DIST
BALL, CAORLINE	BAL	044	1ST WARD
BALL, CAROLINE	BAL	054	15TH WAR
BALL, CHRISTOPHER	SOM	480	TRAPP DI
BALL, DABNEY REV.	CAR	268	WESTMINS
BALL, DANIEL M.	BAL	287	17TH WAR
BALL, DAVID	BAL	253	12TH WAR
BALL, DAVID	ANN	337	3RD DIST
BALL, DORCAS	PRI	101	SPALDING
BALL, E.	PRI	069	MARLBROU
BALL, ELIZABETH	BAL	471	14TH WAR
BALL, ELIZABETH	BAL	428	14TH WAR
BALL, ELLEN	BAL	340	3RD WARD
BALL, FRANCES E.	FRE	103	FREDERIC
BALL, GEORGE	BAL	119	1ST WARD
BALL, HENRY	BAL	340	3RD WARD
BALL, HENRY	ALL	149	6TH E.D.
BALL, HENRY J.	PRI	070	MARLBROU
BALL, HENRY W.	PRI	107	PISCATAW
BALL, HILEARY	MGM	391	ROCKERLE
BALL, HYRAM	HAR	060	1ST DIST
BALL, J.T.	ALL	252	CUMBERLA
BALL, JACOB	BAL	257	12TH WAR
BALL, JAMES	ALL	210	CUMBERLA
BALL, JAMES	BAL	042	4TH WARD
BALL, JAMES	PRI	071	MARLBROU
BALL, JAMES K.	ANN	324	2ND DIST
BALL, JAMES T.	ALL	221	CUMBERLA
BALL, JANE	BAL	030	15TH WAR
BALL, JOHN	BAL	041	2ND DIST
BALL, JOHN	ALL	108	5TH E.D.
BALL, JOHN	BAL	117	5TH WARD
BALL, JOHN	BAL	061	1ST WARD
BALL, JOHN	BAL	171	2ND DIST
BALL, JOHN	BAL	033	9TH WARD
BALL, JOHN	BAL	358	3RD WARD
BALL, JOHN	BAL	272	2ND WARD
BALL, JOHN	PRI	103	SPALDING
BALL, JOHN	PRI	102	SPALDING
BALL, JOHN	PRI	117	PISCATAW
BALL, JOHN	TAL	106	ST MICHA
BALL, JOHN	PRI	011	BLADENSB
BALL, JOHN	TAL	093	ST MICHA
BALL, JOHN	MGM	419	MEDLEY 3
BALL, JOHN	KEN	250	2ND DIST
BALL, JOHN H.	MGM	390	ROCKERLE
BALL, JOHN M.	BAL	249	20TH WAR
BALL, JOHN W.	BAL	275	12TH WAR

Name	County	Page	District
BALL, JOSEPH M.	FRE	021	FREDERIC
BALL, JULIA	BAL	456	14TH WAR
BALL, JULIA	BAL	229	19TH WAR
BALL, JULIA A.	TAL	109	ST MICHA
BALL, LEDIA	WOR	325	1ST E DI
BALL, LETHANNA	MGM	360	BERRYS D
BALL, LEWIS	MGM	382	ROCKERLE
BALL, MARTHA E.	BAL	251	6TH WARD
BALL, MARTIN	BAL	253	12TH WAR
BALL, MARY	BAL	030	15TH WAR
BALL, MARY	FRE	384	PETERSVI
BALL, PAMELA	BAL	058	10TH WAR
BALL, RACHAEL	BAL	267	7TH WARD
BALL, RACHEL	BAL	302	20TH WAR
BALL, RICHARD	BAL	182	2ND WARD
BALL, RICHARD D.	ANN	311	1ST DIST
BALL, ROBERT	BAL	251	2ND WARD
BALL, ROSE	BAL	430	8TH WARD
BALL, SAMUEL	BAL	244	12TH WAR
BALL, SAMUEL	WOR	325	1ST E DI
BALL, SARAH	PRI	099	SPALDING
BALL, SARAH	CAL	001	1ST DIST
BALL, SARAH	FRE	194	5TH E DI
BALL, SARAH A.	BAL	185	6TH WARD
BALL, SARAH J.	TAL	066	EASTON T
BALL, STEPHEN	ANN	435	HOWARD D
BALL, SUSAN A.	TAL	105	ST MICHA
BALL, THOMAS	PRI	072	MARLBROU
BALL, THOMAS	PRI	073	MARLBROU
BALL, THOMAS	PRI	071	MARLBROU
BALL, THOMAS	CAL	006	1ST DIST
BALL, THOMAS J.*	DOR	448	1ST DIST
BALL, WALTER	CAL	006	1ST DIST
BALL, WALTER	BAL	210	6TH WARD
BALL, WILLIAM	BAL	170	11TH WAR
BALL, WILLIAM	BAL	085	15TH WAR
BALL, WILLIAM	BAL	130	11TH WAR
BALL, WILLIAM	MGM	419	MEDLEY J
BALL, WILLIAM	BAL	428	14TH WAR
BALL, WILLIAM	TAL	002	EASTON D
BALL, WILLIAM A.	BAL	185	6TH WARD
BALL, WILLIAM S.	CAL	018	1ST DIST
BALLA, JOHN	BAL	284	17TH WAR
BALLAND, WILLIAM	CEC	043	CHESAPEA
BALLANTINE, ANNA	BAL	051	9TH WARD
BALLARD, ADAM	SOM	402	BRINKLEY
BALLARD, ANDREW	SOM	389	BRINKLEY
BALLARD, ARNOLD	BAL	413	14TH WAR
BALLARD, C. ADELINE	BAL	026	15TH WAR
BALLARD, CALEB	BAL	026	15TH WAR
BALLARD, CAROLINE	SOM	360	BRINKLEY
BALLARD, CATHARINE	SOM	415	DUBLIN D
BALLARD, DANIEL	SOM	554	TYASKIN
BALLARD, DANIEL	SOM	431	PRINCESS
BALLARD, DANIEL J.	SOM	352	BRINKLEY
BALLARD, DAVID	SOM	361	BRINKLEY
BALLARD, DAVID	SOM	436	PRINCESS
BALLARD, E. J.	BAL	097	16TH WAR
BALLARD, EDWARD	BAL	269	7TH WARD
BALLARD, ELIZABETH	BAL	040	9TH WARD
BALLARD, FRANCIS	BAL	451	8TH WARD
BALLARD, FREDERICK	BAL	001	EASTERN
BALLARD, GEORGE	BAL	250	2ND WARD
BALLARD, GEORGE	SOM	431	PRINCESS
BALLARD, GEORGE	SOM	460	HANGARY
BALLARD, GEORGE	SOM	408	DUBLIN D
BALLARD, GEORGE R.	SOM	431	PRINCESS
BALLARD, HANNAH	SOM	436	PRINCESS
BALLARD, HARIET	SOM	419	PRINCESS
BALLARD, HARRIET-BLACK	WOR	347	1ST E DI
BALLARD, HENRY	SOM	453	DAMES QU
BALLARD, HENRY	BAL	414	14TH WAR
BALLARD, HEY E. *	ANN	350	3RD DIST
BALLARD, ISAAC	SOM	419	PRINCESS
BALLARD, JAMES	BAL	254	17TH WAR
BALLARD, JAMES	BAL	198	11TH WAR
BALLARD, JEFFREY	WOR	185	6TH E DI
BALLARD, JOHN	SOM	415	DUBLIN D
BALLARD, LARCAS	WOR	326	1ST E DI
BALLARD, LEVIN	WOR	184	6TH E DI
BALLARD, LEVIN	SOM	482	TRAPP DI
BALLARD, LEVIN	SOM	431	PRINCESS
BALLARD, LEVIN	SOM	467	HANGARY
BALLARD, LEVIN	SOM	437	PRINCESS
BALLARD, LEVIN	SOM	404	BRINKLEY
BALLARD, LEVIN*	SOM	405	DUBLIN D
BALLARD, LEVINA	BAL	451	8TH WARD
BALLARD, MARGARET	SOM	419	PRINCESS
BALLARD, MARIAH-BLACK	WOR	340	1ST E DI
BALLARD, MARTHA	SOM	352	BRINKLEY
BALLARD, MARY	SOM	405	DUBLIN D
BALLARD, MARY	BAL	232	2ND WARD
BALLARD, N.	BAL	332	1ST DIST
BALLARD, NANCY	SOM	350	BRINKLEY
BALLARD, NATHAN	HAR	120	2ND DIST
BALLARD, NELLY	SOM	459	HANGARY
BALLARD, NOAH	SOM	453	DAMES QU
BALLARD, PRISSA-BLACK	WOR	346	1ST E DI
BALLARD, R.	BAL	147	1ST WARD
BALLARD, ROBERT	BAL	330	7TH WARD
BALLARD, ROBERT R.	SOM	360	BRINKLEY
BALLARD, SAMUEL	WOR	327	1ST E DI
BALLARD, SAMUEL	SOM	414	DUBLIN D
BALLARD, SARAH	SOM	437	PRINCESS
BALLARD, SARAH	SOM	460	HANGARY
BALLARD, SARAH	BAL	345	3RD WARD
BALLARD, SOMMERSETT	WAS	158	HAGERSTO
BALLARD, SOPHIA	SOM	436	PRINCESS
BALLARD, SOPHIA	SOM	533	QUANTICO
BALLARD, TABITHA	SOM	409	DUBLIN D
BALLARD, THOMAS	SOM	409	DUBLIN D
BALLARD, THOMAS E.	SOM	354	BRINKLEY
BALLARD, VIRGINIA	BAL	254	17TH WAR
BALLARD, WASHINGTON	SOM	529	QUANTICO
BALLARD, WILLIAM	SOM	530	QUANTICO
BALLARD, WILLIAM	WOR	328	1ST E DI
BALLARD, WILLIAM	SOM	459	HANGARY
BALLARD, WILLIAM J.	SOM	435	PRINCESS
BALLARD, ZEPORA	SOM	421	PRINCESS
BALLATES, PHILIMON	BAL	188	19TH WAR
BALLATUS, CACK	BAL	188	19TH WAR
BALLAUF, AUGUSTUS	BAL	087	10TH WAR
BALLE, LAURENCE	MGM	380	ROCKERLE
BALLET, ROBERT	BAL	026	15TH WAR
BALLHUS, JOHN	BAL	429	8TH WARD
BALLING, FREDERICK	BAL	464	14TH WAR
BALLMAN, HENRY	BAL	296	17TH WAR
BALLOCK, JAMES	BAL	042	4TH WARD
BALLON, JEREMIAH	CAR	198	4TH DIST
BALLONF, JOSEPHINE	BAL	109	10TH WAR
BALLOW, WILLIAM	BAL	476	14TH WAR
BALLREN, VALENTINE *	BAL	108	2ND DIST
BALLS, WILLIAM	BAL	465	14TH WAR
BALMAN, CHRISTIAN	BAL	253	2ND WARD
BALMER, THOMAS	BAL	174	1ST WARD
BALONE, PASQUAL	BAL	303	7TH WARD
BALOUS, WILLIAM H.	WAS	163	2ND DIST
BALSTER, JOHN C.	BAL	103	1ST WARD
BALTE, JOSHUA	BAL	078	2ND DIST
BALTEN, JOHN	BAL	146	2ND DIST
BALTER, JANE	BAL	178	11TH WAR
BALTIMORE, BASIL*	DOR	424	1ST DIST
BALTIMORE, JAMES	BAL	291	17TH WAR
BALTIMORE, LEVIN	BAL	413	14TH WAR
BALTIN, WILLIAM	BAL	077	1ST WARD
BALTMAN, FREDERICK	BAL	105	1ST WARD
BALTNER, ANN M.	CAR	261	3RD DIST
BALTON, JEREMIAH	CAR	198	4TH DIST
BALTZ, CATHARINE	WAS	127	2ND DIST
BALTZ, ELIZABETH	BAL	407	8TH WARD
BALTZ, HENRY	BAL	303	20TH WAR
BALTZ, JOHN	WAS	299	1ST DIST
BALTZALL, LAWRENCE	FRE	132	CREAGERS
BALTZELL, ALEXANDER	BAL	465	14TH WAR
BALTZELL, ANNE	BAL	143	11TH WAR
BALTZELL, ARON H.	FRE	111	CREAGERS
BALTZELL, C.	BAL	303	12TH WAR
BALTZELL, EDWARD	FRE	135	CREAGERS
BALTZELL, EDWARD B.	FRE	019	FREDERIC
BALTZELL, EMMA	BAL	369	8TH WARD
BALTZELL, GEORGE	FRE	033	FREDERIC
BALTZELL, HARRIETT	BAL	102	5TH WARD
BALTZELL, HENRY P.	BAL	198	11TH WAR
BALTZELL, JAMES	FRE	183	5TH E DI
BALTZELL, JOHN	FRE	039	FREDERIC
BALTZELL, JOHN J.	BAL	465	14TH WAR
BALTZELL, NOTLEY T.	FRE	136	CREAGERS
BALTZELL, PHILIP C.	BAL	385	13TH WAR
BALTZELL, WESTLEY	FRE	134	CREAGERS
BALTZELL, WILLIAM H.	BAL	070	15TH WAR
BALTZELL, MICHAEL	FRE	046	FREDERIC
BALWOWIN, JAMES A.	BAL	112	5TH WARD
BALWIN, JOHN	BAL	096	2ND DIST
BALY, CYRUS	DOR	383	1ST DIST
BALY, JOHN	DOR	380	1ST DIST
BALY, WILLIAM	SOM	459	HANGARY
BALZER, HENRY	BAL	201	2ND WARD
BAMACLOUD, JONATHAN	FRE	023	FREDERIC
BAMBARGER, JOHN *	BAL	043	18TH WAR
BAMBAUGH, ELIZABEHT	MGM	366	BERRYS D
BAMBER, JAMES	BAL	053	2ND DIST
BAMBER, WILLIAM	BAL	028	2ND DIST
BAMBERGER, ISAAC	BAL	060	15TH WAR
BAMBERGER, JAMES	BAL	054	1ST WARD
BAMBERGER, JOHN	BAL	008	EASTERN
BAMBERGER, JOHN H.	BAL	043	18TH WAR
BAMBERGER, JOSEPH	ANN	368	4TH DIST
BAMBERGER, SARAH	BAL	435	8TH WARD
BAMBERGER, WILLIAM H.	BAL	326	7TH WARD
BAMBLE, SERENA	BAL	129	11TH WAR
BAMBOROUGH, JOHN	QUE	245	5TH E DI
BAMBURGER, ABRAM	DOR	381	1ST DIST
BAMBURGER, ANN R.	DOR	382	1ST DIST
BAMELL, WASHINGTON	CAR	103	NO TWP L
BAMES, JONAS	HAR	016	1ST DIST
BAMEY, MINTA	BAL	290	17TH WAR
BAMFORD, ALEXANDER	BAL	101	2ND DIST
BAMFORD, HENRY	WAS	044	2ND SUBD
BAMFORTH, JOHN	BAL	187	6TH WARD
BAMICK, JOHN	QUE	191	3RD E DI
BAMMER, PATRICK	BAL	132	2ND DIST
BAMP, BETSEY *	BAL	065	15TH WAR
BAN, RICHARD	BAL	034	1ST WARD
BANAHAN, JOHN	BAL	448	1ST DIST
BANAN, JOHN	ALL	261	CUMBERLA
BANAND, JOHN	BAL	233	2ND WARD
BANARD, MARY R.	BAL	214	11TH WAR
BANARD, WILLIAM A.	ALL	002	3RD E.D.
BANAROUSE, ANTONIA	BAL	121	1ST WARD
BANAWITZ, THEODORE	BAL	142	16TH WAR
BANBIER, MARTHA	BAL	317	20TH WAR
BANBLITZ, CHRISTIAN	BAL	207	6TH DIST
BANBLITZ, GEORGE	BAL	219	6TH DIST
BANBRIDGE, JESSE	FRE	341	MIDDLETO
BANCKER, JOHN	BAL	070	1ST WARD
BANCROFT, GEORGE	WAS	130	HAGERSTO
BANCROFT, JOHN	BAL	042	4TH WARD
BAND, JACOB	BAL	258	20TH WAR
BAND, JULYA	HAR	157	3RD DIST
BAND, PRISCILLA	BAL	408	1ST DIST
BANDALL, HUGH	BAL	084	2ND DIST
BANDALL, JOHN	BAL	270	2ND WARD
BANDEL, HENRY *	BAL	258	6TH WARD
BANDEL, JANE	BAL	162	11TH WAR
BANDEL, JOHN M.	BAL	329	3RD WARD
BANDELL, ANDREW J.	BAL	408	3RD WARD
BANDERY, BIDDY	BAL	226	19TH WAR
BANDING, RACHAEL	BAL	057	15TH WAR
BANDLE, CHARLES	BAL	140	5TH WARD
BANDLE, GEORGE W.	BAL	351	7TH WARD
BANDLE, MARY	BAL	351	7TH WARD
BANDLE, WILLIAM	BAL	337	7TH WARD
BANDORF, JOHN	PRI	107	PISCATAW
BANDT, HENRY	BAL	290	12TH WAR
BANE, HARVEY	ALL	021	2ND E.D.
BANE, JOHN	ALL	049	10TH E.D
BANE, JOSEPHINE	MGM	319	CRACKLIN
BANE, JULIA	BAL	325	3RD WARD
BANE, WILLIAM	ALL	046	10TH E.D
BANER, GEORGE	WAS	069	2ND SUBD
BANES, ADAM	ALL	209	CUMBERLA
BANES, ARTHUR	ALL	172	7TH E.D.
BANES, MARTHA E.	FRE	431	8TH E DI
BANES, TIMOTHY	ALL	051	10TH E.D
BANES, VIRGINIA	BAL	424	3RD WARD
BANES, WILLIAM	BAL	129	1ST WARD
BANESTER, ABRAHAM	CAL	015	1ST DIST
BANETT, JOHN	BAL	113	1ST WARD
BANEY, ELIZABETH *	BAL	282	7TH WARD
BANG, GEORGE F.	BAL	144	16TH WAR
BANG, SIMON	CAR	397	2ND DIST
BANG, SISTER M.P.	FRE	198	5TH E DI
BANGARDNER, DANIEL	CAR	276	7TH DIST
BANGARTS, JOSEPH	BAL	106	1ST WARD
BANGE, JANE	HAR	185	3RD DIST
BANGER, THOMAS	FRE	389	PETERSVI
BANGHER, E. H.	BAL	469	14TH WAR
BANGLE, SARAH	BAL	317	20TH WAR
BANGS, CHARLES	BAL	286	17TH WAR
BANGS, CHARLES	BAL	382	3RD WARD
BANGS, CHARLES	BAL	234	6TH WARD
BANGS, JAMES H.	FRE	028	FREDERIC
BANGS, JEREMIAH	BAL	382	3RD WARD
BANGS, JOHN	BAL	129	16TH WAR
BANGS, MARY	BAL	303	12TH WAR
BANGS, MARY A.	BAL	259	6TH WARD
BANGS, MARY A.*	BAL	334	3RD WARD
BANGS, THROP*	BAL	335	3RD WARD
BANGS, WILLIAM	BAL	371	3RD WARD
BANGS, WILLIAM	BAL	460	8TH WARD
BANGS, WILLIAM H.	BAL	031	18TH WAR
BANHAN, RACHEL	BAL	434	1ST DIST
BANICKNAN, CATHARINE	BAL	185	2ND WARD
BANIE, LUCETTA	BAL	268	12TH WAR
BANIS, ARTHUR	BAL	039	1ST WARD
BANISTER, ANDREW W.	HAR	162	3RD DIST
BANISTER, GEORGETTA	BAL	391	1ST DIST
BANISTER, JAMES	BAL	391	1ST DIST
BANISTER, JAMES	BAL	007	EASTERN
BANISTER, WILLIAM	CEC	018	ELKTON 3
BANISTER, WILLIAM *	BAL	065	18TH WAR
BANK, BENJAMIN L.	HAR	063	1ST DIST
BANKAMP, ADAM	BAL	248	20TH WAR
BANKARD, ANTHONY	BAL	392	8TH WARD
BANKARD, D.H.	BAL	221	19TH WAR
BANKARD, JACOB	BAL	108	1ST WARD
BANKARD, JACOB J.	BAL	102	1ST WARD
BANKARD, JAMES	BAL	108	1ST WARD
BANKARD, RUDOLPH	BAL	283	7TH WARD
BANKARD, WILLIAM	BAL	107	1ST WARD
BANKERD, JOHN	FRE	427	8TH E DI
BANKERT, ABRAHAM	CAR	249	3RD DIST
BANKERT, ABRAHAM	CAR	383	2ND DIST
BANKERT, ABRAHAM	CAR	413	2ND DIST
BANKERT, BENJAMIN	CAR	245	3RD DIST
BANKERT, CATHARINE	CAR	384	2ND DIST
BANKERT, CHRISTIAN	CAR	248	3RD DIST
BANKERT, DANIEL	CAR	246	3RD DIST
BANKERT, DAVID	CAR	245	3RD DIST
BANKERT, DAVID	CAR	352	6TH DIST
BANKERT, ELIAS	CAR	254	3RD DIST
BANKERT, ELIZABETH	CAR	293	7TH DIST
BANKERT, FRANCIS	CAR	267	WESTMINS
BANKERT, HANAH	CAR	253	3RD DIST
BANKERT, HENRY	CAR	251	3RD DIST
BANKERT, HENRY	CAR	384	2ND DIST
BANKERT, ISAAC	CAR	249	3RD DIST
BANKERT, JACOB	CAR	380	2ND DIST
BANKERT, JACOB	CAR	275	7TH DIST
BANKERT, JAMES	CAR	251	3RD DIST
BANKERT, JOHN	CAR	246	3RD DIST
BANKERT, JOHN	CAR	278	7TH DIST
BANKERT, JOHN	CAR	271	WESTMINS
BANKERT, MARY	CAR	293	7TH DIST
BANKERT, MATILDA	CAR	289	7TH DIST
BANKERT, PETER	CAR	293	7TH DIST
BANKERT, QUEEN	CAR	294	7TH DIST
BANKERT, SUSAN	CAR	238	UNION TO
BANKERT, WILLIAM	CAR	294	7TH DIST
BANKERT, WILLIAM H.	CAR	381	2ND DIST
BANKHEAD, JOHN	HAR	023	1ST DIST
BANKHEAD, ROBERT	BAL	030	18TH WAR
BANKMAN, B.	BAL	139	1ST WARD
BANKROFT, MARY A.	BAL	445	8TH WARD
BANKS, ABRAM	BAL	134	2ND DIST
BANKS, ANN	BAL	182	6TH WARD
BANKS, ANN	DOR	416	1ST DIST
BANKS, ANN	DOR	452	1ST DIST
BANKS, ANNE	BAL	112	10TH WAR
BANKS, BENJAMIN	SOM	476	TRAPPE D
BANKS, CHARITY	BAL	325	7TH WARD
BANKS, CHARLES	HAR	137	2ND DIST
BANKS, DANIEL B.	BAL	324	12TH WAR
BANKS, DAVID	BAL	334	7TH WARD
BANKS, DAVID	DOR	425	1ST DIST
BANKS, ELEANORA	BAL	179	6TH WARD
BANKS, ELIZA	DOR	357	3RD DIVI
BANKS, ELIZABETH	SOM	474	TRAPPE D
BANKS, ELIZABETH A.	BAL	116	18TH WAR
BANKS, ELLEN	WAS	271	1ST DIST
BANKS, EMORY	SOM	479	TRAPP DI
BANKS, FRANCIS F.	BAL	369	13TH WAR
BANKS, FREDRICK	BAL	002	4TH WARD
BANKS, HARIAT	DOR	453	1ST DIST
BANKS, HARRETT	BAL	164	11TH WAR
BANKS, HARRIET	BAL	251	6TH WARD
BANKS, HENRIETTA	BAL	430	14TH WAR
BANKS, HENRY	BAL	323	7TH WARD
BANKS, HENRY	BAL	005	EASTERN
BANKS, HENRY	PRI	046	AQUASCO
BANKS, HENRY P.	QUE	186	3RD E DI
BANKS, HESTER	SOM	475	TRAPPE D
BANKS, HORACE	BAL	255	20TH WAR
BANKS, ISAAC	DOR	465	1ST DIST
BANKS, ISRAEL	BAL	475	14TH WAR
BANKS, J.	DOR	421	1ST DIST
BANKS, J.	BAL	138	1ST WARD
BANKS, J.	BAL	154	1ST WARD
BANKS, JACOB	BAL	327	1ST DIST
BANKS, JAMES	HAR	134	2ND DIST
BANKS, JANE	BAL	243	5TH WARD
BANKS, JESSE	WAS	050	2ND SUBD
BANKS, JOHN	TAL	053	EASTON D
BANKS, JOHN	BAL	130	2ND DIST
BANKS, JOHN	ANN	458	HOWARD D
BANKS, JOHN W.	BAL	346	13TH WAR
BANKS, JOSEPH	BAL	281	2ND WARD
BANKS, JOSEPH	BAL	459	8TH WARD
BANKS, JULIA	DOR	418	1ST DIST
BANKS, LEVI	BAL	369	1ST DIST
BANKS, LEWIS	BAL	115	18TH WAR
BANKS, MARGARET	DOR	421	1ST DIST
BANKS, MARGARET	FRE	057	FREDERIC
BANKS, MARGARET	BAL	002	1ST WARD
BANKS, MARY	BAL	277	1ST DIST
BANKS, MARY	TAL	074	EASTON T
BANKS, MORRISON	ANN	444	HOWARD D
BANKS, MOSES	DOR	418	1ST DIST
BANKS, MOSES	DOR	353	3RD DIVI
BANKS, NICY*	DOR	448	1ST DIST
BANKS, PETER	DOR	446	1ST DIST
BANKS, PETER	BAL	269	20TH WAR
BANKS, PHOEBE	BAL	250	17TH WAR
BANKS, REBECCA	SOM	470	TRAPPE D
BANKS, ROBERT	BAL	338	3RD WARD
BANKS, ROBERT T.	BAL	005	4TH WARD
BANKS, ROSE	DOR	432	1ST DIST
BANKS, SALLY	TAL	045	EASTON T
BANKS, SAMUEL	BAL	192	19TH WAR
BANKS, SAMUEL	BAL	168	6TH WARD

Name	County	Page	Location
BANKS, STEPHEN	SOM	481	TRAPP DI
BANKS, THOMAS	SOM	479	TRAPP DI
BANKS, WILLIAM	SOM	475	TRAPPE D
BANKS, WILLIAM	BAL	289	7TH WARD
BANKS, WILLIAM	BAL	293	7TH WARD
BANKS, WILLIAM	DOR	356	3RD DIVI
BANKS, WILLIAM	DOR	417	1ST DIST
BANKS, WILLIAM F.	BAL	396	1ST DIST
BANKSON, ELIZABETH	BAL	061	10TH WAR
BANKSON, ELIZABETH	BAL	061	10TH WAR
BANLLEY, JOSEPH	BAL	063	18TH WAR
BANMAN, PATRICK	BAL	158	11TH WAR
BANMERS, HERNY	BAL	103	1ST WARD
BANMILER, MARGARET	BAL	215	11TH WAR
BANN, ELLEN	BAL	308	12TH WAR
BANNAN, CHARLES	BAL	385	8TH WARD
BANNAN, HUGH	BAL	186	11TH WAR
BANNAN, MARGARET	ALL	181	8TH E.D.
BANNAN, PATRICK	BAL	022	9TH WARD
BANNARD, EDWARD D.	FRE	258	NEW MARK
BANNARD, MICHAEL	BAL	370	8TH WARD
BANNAWAY, ANN	ANN	336	3RD DIST
BANNEM, MARGARET	BAL	284	7TH WARD
BANNER, CHRISTOF	BAL	279	1ST DIST
BANNER, CHRISTOPHER	WAS	299	1ST DIST
BANNER, ELIZABETH	WAS	136	HAGERSTO
BANNER, HENRY	BAL	013	2ND DIST
BANNER, JACOB F.	WAS	174	FUNKSTOW
BANNER, MARCUS	WAS	175	FUNKSTOW
BANNER, MARGARET	BAL	243	12TH WAR
BANNER, MARY	BAL	091	5TH WARD
BANNER, MARY J.	WAS	159	2ND DIST
BANNERMAN, MARY A.	BAL	053	9TH WARD
BANNERMAN, SUSAN	BAL	207	2ND WARD
BANNERMAN, WILLIAM	BAL	054	9TH WARD
BANNERMAN, WILLIAM E.	BAL	054	9TH WARD
BANNESTER, EMELINE	BAL	300	7TH WARD
BANNESTER, WILLIAM	BAL	261	2ND WARD
BANNET, MARY	BAL	189	2ND WARD
BANNETT, SOLOMON	TAL	070	EASTON T
BANNEY, NICHOLAS	TAL	091	ST MICHA
BANNIG, ALEXANDER	TAL	096	ST MICHA
BANNING, C. E.	BAL	321	12TH WAR
BANNING, ELIZA A.	CAR	169	NO TWP L
BANNING, GREENBURY	TAL	114	ST MICHA
BANNING, JOHN	DOR	452	1ST DIST
BANNING, NELL	TAL	060	EASTON D
BANNING, NICHOLAS	TAL	055	EASTON D
BANNING, ROBERT	TAL	096	ST MICHA
BANNING, SUSAN	TAL	069	EASTON T
BANNING, THOMAS	TAL	105	ST MICHA
BANNING, THOMAS H.	BAL	024	15TH WAR
BANNING, WILLIAM	DOR	309	1ST DIST
BANNISTER, EMMA	BAL	235	12TH WAR
BANNISTER, JOHN	CEC	036	CHESAPEA
BANNISTER, MARGARET	BAL	180	19TH WAR
BANNON, JOHN	BAL	300	20TH WAR
BANNON, JOHN	BAL	409	14TH WAR
BANNON, LORENZ	BAL	299	20TH WAR
BANNON, PATRICK	BAL	181	16TH WAR
BANOLDS, SAMUEL J.	BAL	450	8TH WARD
BANOLL, MARY A.*	TAL	044	EASTON D
BANOLL, STEPHEN	TAL	045	EASTON T
BANON, ELIZABETH	BAL	107	2ND DIST
BANON, HENRY W.*	TAL	033	EASTON D
BANOTE, HENRY	ALL	047	10TH E.D
BANOTT, ANDREW	ALL	051	10TH E.D
BANRIEL, SARAH	QUE	249	5TH E DI
BANSNUR, WILLIAM	BAL	469	14TH WAR
BANTAIN, HENRY	BAL	277	20TH WAR
BANTAM, BENJAMIN	BAL	434	14TH WAR
BANTAM, JOHN	KEN	281	3RD DIST
BANTLE, JOHN *	WAS	166	HAGERSTO
BANTOM, MARY-BLACK	CAR	136	NO TWP L
BANTON, ALFRED	BAL	153	11TH WAR
BANTON, AMELIA	BAL	154	11TH WAR
BANTON, HARRIET-MULATTO	CAR	162	NO TWP L
BANTORN, JOHN-BLACK	CAR	084	NO TWP L
BANTUM, ADOLPHIAS	TAL	018	EASTON D
BANTUM, ANN M.	TAL	045	EASTON T
BANTUM, EDWARD	TAL	063	EASTON D
BANTUM, EMELINE	TAL	046	EASTON T
BANTUM, GEORGE	TAL	050	EASTON T
BANTUM, GEORGE	TAL	049	EASTON T
BANTUM, GEORGE	TAL	053	EASTON D
BANTUM, HARRIET	TAL	060	EASTON D
BANTUM, HARRIET	TAL	043	EASTON D
BANTUM, HARRISON	TAL	045	EASTON T
BANTUM, HENRY	TAL	048	EASTON T
BANTUM, HENRY	TAL	060	EASTON D
BANTUM, ISACK	TAL	043	EASTON D
BANTUM, JAMES	TAL	049	EASTON T
BANTUM, JAMES	TAL	098	ST MICHA
BANTUM, JOSEPH	TAL	074	EASTON T
BANTUM, LILLY	TAL	059	EASTON D
BANTUM, LILLY*	TAL	044	EASTON D
BANTUM, LOUISA	TAL	048	EASTON T
BANTUM, MARIAH	TAL	049	EASTON T
BANTUM, MARTHA	TAL	003	EASTON D
BANTUM, PERRY	BAL	100	15TH WAR
BANTUM, REBECCA	TAL	045	EASTON T
BANTUM, RICHARD	TAL	050	EASTON T
BANTUM, ROSE	TAL	043	EASTON D
BANTUM, SOPHIA	TAL	050	EASTON T
BANTUM, SUSAN*	DOR	460	1ST DIST
BANTUM, WILLIAM	TAL	063	EASTON D
BANTZ, GIDEON	FRE	014	FREDERIC
BANTZ, GIDEON SR.	FRE	031	FREDERIC
BANTZ, WILLIAM S.	FRE	030	FREDERIC
BANTZE, THEODORE	BAL	455	14TH WAR
BANUM, THOMAS	WAS	048	2ND SUBD
BANUN, MARY *	BAL	287	20TH WAR
BAON, HENRY*	BAL	417	3RD WARD
BAORD, CHARLES	HAR	202	3RD DIST
BAOUKE, JOHN	ALL	152	6TH E.D.
BAPFELER, J.	BAL	135	1ST WARD
BAPFORD, ALBERT E.	KEN	312	3RD DIST
BAPFORD, SARAH	KEN	312	3RD DIST
BAPIST, HENRY-BLACK	WOR	166	6TH E DI
BAPIST, MARIA-BLACK	WOR	166	6TH E DI
BAPP, ADAM	BAL	095	1ST WARD
BAPTIST, JOHN	HAR	093	2ND DIST
BAPTIST, LOUISA	HAR	032	1ST DIST
BAPTISTA, A. L.	BAL	357	3RD WARD
BAR, GEORGE	BAL	251	1ST DIST
BAR, JOHN	BAL	279	1ST DIST
BAR, ROBERT	ALL	208	CUMBERLA
BARACK, HENRIETTA	BAL	227	2ND WARD
BARAGARS, ADELE	BAL	455	14TH WAR
BARBACK, ELIZABETH	BAL	133	2ND DIST
BARBAR, JOHN	BAL	462	14TH WAR
BARBAR, JOHN	ST	337	4TH E DI
BARBAR, L.P. JR.	ST	335	4TH E DI
BARBAR, LUKE P.	ST	336	4TH E DI
BARBAR, REASON	ST	336	4TH E DI
BARBAR, THOMAS	ST	336	4TH E DI
BARBER, ALEXANDER	ALL	096	5TH E.D.
BARBER, ANN	ST	325	4TH E DI
BARBER, ANN	ST	282	3RD E DI
BARBER, BENJAMIN	PRI	063	NOTTINGH
BARBER, BENJAMIN	BAL	090	2ND DIST
BARBER, CATHARINE	ANN	292	ANNAPOLI
BARBER, CATHARINE	WAS	032	2ND SUBD
BARBER, DANIEL	BAL	075	2ND DIST
BARBER, EDWARD	BAL	084	2ND DIST
BARBER, ELIZABETH	MGM	336	CRACKLIN
BARBER, ELLICK	FRE	205	BUCKEYST
BARBER, GEORGE	CEC	016	ELKTON 3
BARBER, GEORGE	CAR	202	4TH DIST
BARBER, GEORGE	WAS	124	HAGERSTO
BARBER, GEORGE A.	ANN	331	2ND DIST
BARBER, GEORGE A. OR-	ANN	331	2ND DIST
BARBER, HANNAH	CEC	164	6TH E DI
BARBER, HENRY-BLACK	ST	333	4TH E DI
BARBER, HEZEKIAH	MGM	342	CLARKSBU
BARBER, IGNATIUS	WAS	195	1ST DIST
BARBER, IGNATIUS	WAS	171	FUNKSTOW
BARBER, J.	BAL	165	1ST WARD
BARBER, J.Y.	CAL	063	3RD DIST
BARBER, JOHN	BAL	451	1ST DIST
BARBER, JOHN	BAL	403	3RD WARD
BARBER, JOHN	WAS	127	HAGERSTO
BARBER, JOHN G.	BAL	004	15TH WAR
BARBER, JOHN T.	BAL	003	15TH WAR
BARBER, JOHN T. OF GEORGE	ANN	267	ANNAPOLI
BARBER, JOHN W.	BAL	191	5TH DIST
BARBER, JOHN W.	CAR	202	4TH DIST
BARBER, JOHNNY	FRE	242	NEW MARK
BARBER, JOSEPH N.	HAR	203	3RD DIST
BARBER, JOSIAH	BAL	062	2ND DIST
BARBER, LEWIS	MGM	323	CRACKLIN
BARBER, LOUISA	DOR	379	1ST DIST
BARBER, LOVERING	CAR	369	9TH DIST
BARBER, LOWSON *	FRE	313	MIDDLETO
BARBER, LUCY	ANN	269	ANNAPOLI
BARBER, M.	BAL	152	1ST WARD
BARBER, MARIA	ANN	288	ANNAPOLI
BARBER, MARTHA	MGM	333	CRACKLIN
BARBER, MARY	CEC	018	ELKTON 3
BARBER, MARY	BAL	090	2ND DIST
BARBER, MARY	WAS	141	HAGERSTO
BARBER, MARY E.	CEC	167	6TH E DI
BARBER, MATILDA	FRE	206	BUCKEYST
BARBER, MATILDA	FRE	207	BUCKEYST
BARBER, MERIDITH	BAL	458	8TH WARD
BARBER, MICHAEL	BAL	286	2ND WARD
BARBER, PHILIP	BAL	074	2ND DIST
BARBER, RHEUBEN	BAL	462	1ST DIST
BARBER, RUBEN	BAL	420	8TH WARD
BARBER, SAMUEL	WAS	009	WILLIAMS
BARBER, SAMUEL J.	FRE	067	FREDERIC
BARBER, SARAH	PRI	051	AQUASCO
BARBER, SUSAN	BAL	421	8TH WARD
BARBER, SUSANNAH	BAL	456	1ST DIST
BARBER, THEODROE P.	DOR	378	1ST DIST
BARBER, THOMAS	PRI	054	AQUASCO
BARBER, URIAH	BAL	069	18TH WAR
BARBER, W.M.	WAS	021	2ND SUBD
BARBER, WALTER	ST	335	4TH E DI
BARBER, WILLIAM	HAR	189	3RD DIST
BARBER, WILLIAM	BAL	190	5TH DIST
BARBER, WILLIAM H.	BAL	304	17TH WAR
BARBER, YATES	CHA	288	BOJANTOW
BARBER, ZADOK	MGM	344	CLARKSBU
BARBERS, MICHEL	BAL	327	3RD WARD
BARBIN, THOMAS	BAL	408	3RD WARD
BARBINE, ELIZABETH	BAL	006	15TH WAR
BARBINE, MARY R.	BAL	296	17TH WAR
BARBINES, CHARLES	BAL	294	17TH WAR
BARBON, MARY*	SOM	535	QUANTICO
BARBOUR, ELIZABETH	BAL	162	2ND DIST
BARBOUR, JOHN	ALL	106	5TH E.D.
BARBOURN, THOMAS	SOM	462	HANGARY
BARBRIDGE, JOHN	BAL	119	1ST WARD
BARCAY, JOSEPH	BAL	095	5TH WARD
BARCH, BENEDICT	CHA	274	ALLENS F
BARCHER, SUSAN	BAL	248	2ND WARD
BARCLAY, GERTRUDE	ANN	413	HOWARD D
BARCLAY, MARY	HAR	007	1ST DIST
BARCROFT, JOHN	MGM	352	BERRYS D
BARCUS, FRANCES A.	CAR	075	NO TWP L
BARCUS, HENRY	PRI	039	VANSVILL
BARCUS, JOHN	ALL	099	5TH E.D.
BARCUS, MARTHA	CAR	080	NO TWP L
BARCUS, WILLIAM	CAR	075	NO TWP L
BARD, E. R.*	BAL	101	10TH WAR
BARDEN, JACOB	BAL	399	1ST DIST
BARDEN, MARGARET	BAL	008	9TH WARD
BARDOLPH, JAMES	ALL	093	5TH E.D.
BARDWELL, JAMES R.	CAR	332	MANCHEST
BARE, ADAM	ALL	246	CUMBERLA
BARE, ANTHONY	HAR	016	1ST DIST
BARE, DAVID	FRE	288	WOODSBOR
BARE, ELIZABETH	BAL	462	8TH WARD
BARE, JACOB	CAR	411	2ND DIST
BARE, LYDIA	CAR	410	2ND DIST
BARE, MATTHEW	BAL	221	19TH WAR
BARE, MICHAEL	ANN	366	4TH DIST
BARE, SAMUEL	BAL	277	20TH WAR
BAREHAM, ALETHIA	BAL	043	2ND DIST
BARELS, WILLIAM	BAL	314	12TH WAR
BARENCE, JOHN	CEC	207	7TH E DI
BARENETT, ARTHUR *	CAR	215	5TH DIST
BARENGER, ANDREW	BAL	003	EASTERN
BARER, LAURENCE	BAL	225	2ND WARD
BARETT, SIRUS	BAL	270	1ST DIST
BAREUS, JOHN	CAR	096	NO TWP L
BAREY, NICHOLAS	HAR	074	1ST DIST
BARFIELD, JAMES H.*	BAL	114	11TH WAR
BARFORD, THOMAS	SOM	490	SALISBUR
BARG, CONRAD	ALL	198	CUMBERLA
BARGAIN, PADDY	BAL	039	2ND DIST
BARGANER, MICHAEL	BAL	460	1ST DIST
BARGARIST, SEPHORNIUS *	BAL	046	18TH WAR
BARGDALE, JONATHAN	ALL	153	6TH E.D.
BARGDOLL, DAVID	WAS	257	1ST DIST
BARGDOLL, ELIE	WAS	276	RIDGEVIL
BARGDOLL, GEORGE	WAS	277	RIDGEVIL
BARGDOLL, GEORGE	WAS	259	1ST DIST
BARGDOLL, HENRY	WAS	260	1ST DIST
BARGDOLL, HENRY	WAS	273	RIDGEVIL
BARGDOLL, JOHN	WAS	249	1ST DIST
BARGDOLL, JOHN	WAS	257	1ST DIST
BARGDOLL, NANCY	WAS	249	1ST DIST
BARGDOLL, NANCY	WAS	276	RIDGEVIL
BARGDOLL, PETER	WAS	272	RIDGEVIL
BARGDOLL, PETER	WAS	257	1ST DIST
BARGE, SARAH	ALL	162	6TH E.D.
BARGEE, MILE	FRE	275	NEW MARK
BARGER, CHARLES S.	FRE	401	JEFFERSO
BARGER, DEETER	BAL	144	11TH WAR
BARGER, FRANCIS B. T.	CHA	232	HILLTOP
BARGER, GEORGE W.	FRE	400	JEFFERSO
BARGER, HENRY	FRE	402	JEFFERSO
BARGER, JOSEPH	BAL	213	17TH WAR
BARGER, MARY	BAL	297	7TH WARD
BARGESEL, FREDERICK	BAL	267	2ND WARD
BARGLEY, AQUILOR	HAR	151	3RD DIST
BARGMAN, MARTIN	ALL	246	CUMBERLA
BARGUS, RUTH	BAL	473	14TH WAR
BARH, JOHN C.	QUE	239	5TH E DI
BARHAM, GEORGE T.	BAL	214	6TH DIST
BARHAN, ANGUS	ALL	154	6TH E.D.
BARHOSA, JUAN	FRE	20	5TH E DI
BARIER, HENRY	BAL	146	11TH WAR
BARINGER, JOHN	WAS	020	2ND SUBD
BARK, PETER	ALL	256	CUMBERLA
BARK, PHOEBE	BAL	143	5TH WARD
BARK, WILLIAM	ALL	050	10TH E.D
BARKE, JOHN H.	BAL	162	11TH WAR
BARKELEY, CHARLOTT	BAL	352	7TH WARD
BARKER, ADELINE	BAL	318	7TH WARD
BARKER, ALEXANDER	CAL	052	3RD DIST
BARKER, ALFRED	BAL	386	8TH WARD
BARKER, ALLY	PRI	078	MARLBROU
BARKER, ANN	BAL	166	19TH WAR
BARKER, ANN M.	CHA	238	HILLTOP
BARKER, CATHARINE	CAL	040	3RD DIST
BARKER, DEBY	BAL	254	17TH WAR
BARKER, E.	ANN	342	3RD DIST
BARKER, EDWARD	BAL	318	7TH WARD
BARKER, ELENORR	BAL	067	18TH WAR
BARKER, ELIZA	CEC	049	1ST E DI
BARKER, ELIZABETH	BAL	019	4TH WARD
BARKER, ELIZABETH A.	BAL	052	1ST WARD
BARKER, GIDEON	BAL	034	1ST WARD
BARKER, HARROTT A.	BAL	191	11TH WAR
BARKER, HAVANNA	CHA	236	HILLTOP
BARKER, HENRY	CAL	031	2ND DIST
BARKER, JAMES	BAL	172	1ST WARD
BARKER, JAMES E.	BAL	413	3RD WARD
BARKER, JOHN	BAL	180	11TH WAR
BARKER, JOHN	BAL	224	12TH WAR
BARKER, JOHN	BAL	247	2ND WARD
BARKER, JOHN *	BAL	288	1ST DIST
BARKER, JOSEPH	CHA	236	HILLTOP
BARKER, JOSEPH	ST	342	5TH E DI
BARKER, JOSEPH W.	BAL	318	7TH WARD
BARKER, JULIA	BAL	379	8TH WARD
BARKER, JULIA A.	BAL	193	11TH WAR
BARKER, LEFY	BAL	060	4TH WARD
BARKER, LUCY-BLACK	CAL	056	3RD DIST
BARKER, MARTHA A.	PRI	030	VANSVILL
BARKER, MARY	CHA	235	HILLTOP
BARKER, MARY	CHA	236	HILLTOP
BARKER, MARY	BAL	233	6TH WARD
BARKER, MARY E.	BAL	276	2ND WARD
BARKER, MARY G.	CHA	235	HILLTOP
BARKER, MARY J.	ANN	412	HOWARD D
BARKER, MATILDA	BAL	069	4TH WARD
BARKER, REBECCA	CHA	236	HILLTOP
BARKER, REBECCA	BAL	413	3RD WARD
BARKER, ROBERT	ALL	089	5TH E.D.
BARKER, SAMUEL D.	BAL	020	4TH WARD
BARKER, SUSAN	ALL	206	CUMBERLA
BARKER, WILLIAM K.	BAL	160	16TH WAR
BARKER, WILLIAM R.	PRI	056	AQUASCO
BARKER, REBECCA	CAL	057	3RD DIST
BARKERS, LEWIS	ANN	298	1ST DIST
BARKERT, HANNAH-MULATTO	FRE	450	8TH E DI
BARKHOLD, WILLIAM	ALL	010	3RD E.D.
BARKHOLDER, CHRISTINA	ALL	032	2ND E.D.
BARKHOLDER, GEORGE W.	ALL	040	2ND E.D.
BARKHOLDER, SMAUEL	ALL	040	2ND E.D.
BARKHOLDER, PHILLIP	ALL	016	3RD E.D.
BARKINS, GEORGE	BAL	249	20TH WAR
BARKINSON, MARY F.	BAL	214	11TH WAR
BARKLAID, BRIDGET	ALL	254	CUMBERLA
BARKLE, HENRY	BAL	354	13TH WAR
BARKLEY, SAMUEL	CHA	258	MIDDLETO
BARKLEY, CALEB	SOM	550	TYASKIN
BARKLEY, DIAH	DOR	335	3RD DIVI
BARKLEY, ELEN	DOR	348	3RD DIVI
BARKLEY, ELIZABETH	SOM	551	TYASKIN
BARKLEY, ESTHER	SOM	427	PRINCESS
BARKLEY, GEORGE	SOM	551	TYASKIN
BARKLEY, HANNAH	DOR	333	3RD DIVI
BARKLEY, HESTER	SOM	538	TYASKIN
BARKLEY, HUGH	BAL	362	8TH WARD
BARKLEY, ISAAC	SOM	545	TYASKIN
BARKLEY, ISMA	SOM	545	TYASKIN
BARKLEY, JANE	SOM	553	TYASKIN
BARKLEY, JEMIMA	SOM	536	TYASKIN
BARKLEY, JESSE	SOM	550	TYASKIN
BARKLEY, JOHN	SOM	551	TYASKIN
BARKLEY, JOHN	DOR	338	3RD DIVI
BARKLEY, JOSEPH	SOM	424	PRINCESS
BARKLEY, JOSEPH	SOM	484	TRAPP DI
BARKLEY, JOSHUA	SOM	543	TYASKIN
BARKLEY, MARGRETT	DOR	335	3RD DIVI
BARKLEY, MARY	SOM	551	TYASKIN
BARKLEY, MARY	BAL	184	16TH WAR
BARKLEY, NANCY *	SOM	429	PRINCESS
BARKLEY, ORLANDER	SOM	424	PRINCESS
BARKLEY, REBECCA A.	DOR	338	3RD DIVI
BARKLEY, SHEPPARD	DOR	335	3RD DIVI
BARKLEY, SYPHLET	SOM	551	TYASKIN
BARKLEY, WILLIAM	DOR	337	3RD DIVI
BARKLEY, WILLIAM	BAL	356	3RD WARD
BARKLY, E.	PRI	110	PISCATAW
BARKLY, GEORGE N.	CHA	257	MIDDLETO
BARKLY, WILLIAM	PRI	110	PISCATAW
BARKMAN, AMELIA	BAL	290	3RD WARD
BARKMAN, CATHARINE	WAS	097	2ND DIST
BARKMAN, CONRADT	BAL	395	8TH WARD
BARKMAN, DAVID	WAS	038	2ND SUBD
BARKMAN, DAVID	WAS	225	1ST DIST
BARKMAN, DAVID	FRE	361	CATOCTIN
BARKMAN, EVE	WAS	104	2ND DIST
BARKMAN, HENRY	WAS	183	BOONSBOR

BARKMAN, JACOB BAL 182 16TH WAR
BARKMAN, JOSEPH BAL 351 13TH WAR
BARKMAN, LEWIS WAS 152 HAGERSTO
BARKMAN, MARY A. BAL 076 4TH WARD
BARKMAN, SAMUEL WAS 125 HAGERSTO
BARKMAN, SOPHIA WAS 184 BOONSBOR
BARKMAN, SUSAN WAS 241 CAVETOWN
BARKMAN, WILLIAM WAS 224 1ST DIST
BARKS, JACOB WAS 057 2ND SUBD
BARKS, SAMUEL WAS 071 2ND SUBD
BARKUS, JOHN CEC 105 3RD E DI
BARKUS, OTHO G. ALL 097 5TH E.D.
BARLA, CHRISTIANA BAL 406 14TH WAR
BARLAGE, DIEDERICH BAL 165 16TH WAR
BARLAGE, HENRY BAL 291 17TH WAR
BARLET, FRANCIS BAL 002 15TH WAR
BARLEY, DORCAS BAL 222 12TH WAR
BARLIN, JAMES ST 299 2ND E DI
BARLINE, ACAM BAL 146 2ND DIST
BARLING, ADORN BAL 192 17TH WAR
BARLING, CHRISTIAN BAL 139 2ND DIST
BARLING, ELIZABETH BAL 080 4TH WARD
BARLING, JOSEPH BAL 111 5TH WARD
BARLLETT, JAMES JR. TAL 088 ST MICHA
BARLON, MARY* SOM 535 QUANTICO
BARLOW, GEORGE BAL 411 14TH WAR
BARLOW, JOSEPH BAL 269 12TH WAR
BARLOW, JOSHUA ANN 519 HOWARD D
BARLOW, JOSHUA JR. ANN 512 HOWARD D
BARLOW, RICHARD BAL 097 10TH WAR
BARLOW, WILLIAM BAL 221 6TH WARD
BARLUP, ANN WAS 260 1ST DIST
BARMAN, HENRY BAL 283 1ST DIST
BARMAN, MICHAEL BAL 108 10TH WAR
BARMGARTNER, PETER CAR 309 1ST DIST
BARNABY, ELIAS CEC 050 1ST E DI
BARNABY, JOHN J. MGM 322 CRACKLIN
BARNALLOWS, WILLIAM QUE 157 2ND E DI
BARNAN, A. BAL 155 1ST WARD
BARNARD, BROADUS BAL 119 15TH WAR
BARNARD, CATHERINE BAL 140 11TH WAR
BARNARD, EDWARD ALL 129 4TH E.D.
BARNARD, EDWARD ALL 130 4TH E.D.
BARNARD, ELIZABETH * TAL 076 EASTON T
BARNARD, GEORGE ALL 135 4TH E.D.
BARNARD, JOAB BAL 220 1ST DIST
BARNARD, JOHN ALL 130 4TH E.D.
BARNARD, JOHN ALL 260 CUMBERLA
BARNARD, MARY BAL 097 10TH WAR
BARNARD, MARY BAL 361 13TH WAR
BARNARD, SARAH BAL 169 16TH WAR
BARNARD, THOMAS ALL 087 5TH E.D.
BARNARD, WILLIAM H. ALL 129 4TH E.D.
BARNARDS, ALEXANDER ALL 243 CUMBERLA
BARNCAN, HENRY ALL 147 6TH E.D.
BARNE, FRANCES HAR 004 1ST DIST
BARNE.S BENJAMIN WOR 176 6TH E DI
BARNE.S HENRY CAR 375 9TH DIST
BARNECLAUS, RICHARD FRE 385 PETERSVI
BARNECLOE, ELIZABETH QUE 208 3RD E DI
BARNEHAN, JOHN BAL 451 14TH WAR
BARNEHART, MARY FRE 310 WOODSBOR
BARNER, ELLEN BAL 023 4TH WARD
BARNER, MARTHA BAL 323 12TH WAR
BARNER, PERGIN CHA 273 ALLENS F
BARNES, A. BAL 141 1ST WARD
BARNES, ABRAM WAS 104 2ND DIST
BARNES, ACAM CAR 211 5TH DIST
BARNES, ALCINA BAL 058 10TH WAR
BARNES, AMELIA KEN 298 3RD DIST
BARNES, AMERICA C. FRE 211 BUCKEYST
BARNES, AMOS HAR 156 3RD DIST
BARNES, ANCREW CAR 361 9TH DIST
BARNES, ANN CEC 091 4TH E DI
BARNES, ANN BAL 066 10TH WAR
BARNES, ANTHONY ALL 185 9TH E.D.
BARNES, ANY CAR 215 5TH DIST
BARNES, BAZZELL CAR 202 4TH DIST
BARNES, BENETT HAR 170 3RD DIST
BARNES, BENJAMIN CAR 207 4TH DIST
BARNES, BENJAMIN ANN 508 HOWARD D
BARNES, BENNETT HAR 203 3RD DIST
BARNES, C. BAL 162 1ST WARD
BARNES, CAROLINE HAR 170 3RD DIST
BARNES, CATHARINE FRE 182 5TH E DI
BARNES, CATHERINE ALL 240 CUMBERLA
BARNES, CHARELS WAS 157 HAGERSTO
BARNES, CHARLES BAL 132 1ST WARD
BARNES, CHARLES N. CHA 220 ALLENS F
BARNES, CHARLES W. CAR 228 5TH DIST
BARNES, CHRISTIAN R. BAL 344 3RD WARD
BARNES, DANIEL WAS 167 1ST DIST
BARNES, CAVID BAL 165 1ST WARD
BARNES, CAVID BAL 076 4TH WARD
BARNES, DAVIS H. FRE 252 NEW MARK
BARNES, DELILAH QUE 206 3RD E DI
BARNES, E.P. PRI 079 QUEEN AN
BARNES, EBEN ANN 466 HOWARD D
BARNES, EDWARD D. BAL 132 1ST WARD
BARNES, EDWARD-BLACK ST 335 4TH E DI
BARNES, EDWIN BAL 343 7TH WARD
BARNES, ELIAS CAR 210 5TH DIST
BARNES, ELISHA HAR 089 2ND DIST
BARNES, ELIZA FRE 062 FREDERIC
BARNES, ELIZA BAL 289 3RD WARD
BARNES, ELIZA BAL 074 10TH WAR
BARNES, ELIZABETH BAL 114 2ND DIST
BARNES, ELIZABETH CAR 221 5TH DIST
BARNES, ELIZABETH BAL 039 4TH WARD
BARNES, ELIZABETH CAR 361 9TH DIST
BARNES, ELIZABETH BAL 122 11TH WAR
BARNES, ELLEN BAL 117 18TH WAR
BARNES, ELLEN ALL 186 9TH E.D.
BARNES, ESTHER WOR 186 7TH E DI
BARNES, FLETCHER C. BAL 011 4TH WARD
BARNES, FRANCIS BAL 026 15TH WAR
BARNES, G.W. ALL 260 CUMBERLA
BARNES, GEORGE ANN 298 1ST DIST
BARNES, GEORGE ANN 513 HOWARD D
BARNES, GEORGE BAL 162 1ST WARD
BARNES, GEORGE BAL 475 14TH WAR
BARNES, GEORGE HAR 033 1ST DIST
BARNES, GEORGE DOR 339 3RD DIVI
BARNES, GEORGE W. HAR 152 3RD DIST
BARNES, GEROGE HAR 034 1ST DIST
BARNES, GUSTAVUS ANN 447 HOWARD D
BARNES, HARRIET TAL 055 EASTON D
BARNES, HENRY WOR 181 6TH E DI
BARNES, HENRY BAL 317 3RD WARD
BARNES, HENRY ALL 121 4TH E.D.
BARNES, HENRY BAL 032 15TH WAR
BARNES, HENRY HAR 146 3RD DIST
BARNES, HENRY FRE 248 NEW MARK
BARNES, HENRY FRE 262 NEW MARK
BARNES, HOZIER HAR 133 2ND DIST
BARNES, HUGH FRE 334 MIDDLETO
BARNES, ISAAC SOM 417 PRINCESS
BARNES, ISAAC BAL 021 9TH WARD
BARNES, J. BAL 148 1ST WARD
BARNES, JACOB WAS 198 1ST DIST
BARNES, JAMES WAS 066 2ND SUBD
BARNES, JAMES BAL 010 9TH WARD
BARNES, JAMES ANN 336 3RD DIST
BARNES, JAMES BAL 141 1ST WARD
BARNES, JAMES BAL 026 1ST WARD
BARNES, JAMES MGM 360 BERRYS D
BARNES, JAMES A. FRE 445 8TH E DI
BARNES, JAMES E. ANN 499 HOWARD D
BARNES, JAMES P. FRE 255 NEW MARK
BARNES, JAMES W. ANN 494 HOWARD D
BARNES, JANE BAL 037 9TH WARD
BARNES, JANE F. BAL 109 1ST WARD
BARNES, JEREMIAH BAL 348 3RD WARD
BARNES, JOHN BAL 130 1ST WARD
BARNES, JOHN BAL 144 1ST WARD
BARNES, JOHN BAL 145 1ST WARD
BARNES, JOHN ALL 123 4TH E.D.
BARNES, JOHN ALL 122 4TH E.D.
BARNES, JOHN ANN 453 HOWARD D
BARNES, JOHN BAL 110 18TH WAR
BARNES, JOHN CEC 196 6TH E DI
BARNES, JOHN MGM 361 BERRYS D
BARNES, JOHN HAR 120 2ND DIST
BARNES, JOHN MGM 356 BERRYS D
BARNES, JOHN HAR 161 3RD DIST
BARNES, JOHN TAL 009 EASTON D
BARNES, JOHN KEN 294 3RD DIST
BARNES, JOHN B. ALL 131 4TH E.D.
BARNES, JOHN D. ANN 471 HOWARD D
BARNES, JOHN H. BAL 123 16TH WAR
BARNES, JOHN H. CHA 239 HILLTOP
BARNES, JOHN M. BAL 361 8TH WARD
BARNES, JOSHUA FRE 430 8TH E DI
BARNES, JOSHUA CAR 195 4TH DIST
BARNES, JOSIAH CAR 218 5TH DIST
BARNES, JULIANN ALL 181 8TH E.D.
BARNES, KITTY BAL 150 5TH WARD
BARNES, KITTY BAL 451 14TH WAR
BARNES, LEAVEN ANN 502 HOWARD D
BARNES, LEVI F. FRE 431 8TH E DI
BARNES, LINDEL BAL 119 11TH WAR
BARNES, LOUISA BAL 118 11TH WAR
BARNES, LUCINDA CAR 182 8TH DIST
BARNES, MARGARET E. MGM 357 BERRYS D
BARNES, MARGARETT FRE 434 8TH E DI
BARNES, MARIA HAR 139 2ND DIST
BARNES, MARTHA A. ST 281 3RD E DI
BARNES, MARY WAS 089 2ND SUBD
BARNES, MARY CHA 289 MIDDLETO
BARNES, MARY BAL 153 11TH WAR
BARNES, MARY FRE 258 NEW MARK
BARNES, MARY BAL 446 1ST DIST
BARNES, MARY ALL 227 CUMBERLA
BARNES, MARY A. HAR 170 3RD DIST
BARNES, MARY A. FRE 092 FREDERIC
BARNES, MARY A. KEN 312 3RD DIST
BARNES, MARY-BLACK CAR 364 9TH DIST
BARNES, MATILDA BAL 038 15TH WAR
BARNES, MAY A. BAL 230 12TH WAR
BARNES, MILLA BAL 180 11TH WAR
BARNES, MORDICA HAR 166 3RD DIST
BARNES, MOSES CAR 206 4TH DIST
BARNES, MOSES CAR 207 4TH DIST
BARNES, N.P. ALL 172 7TH E.D.
BARNES, NANCY BAL 231 6TH WARD
BARNES, NANCY BAL 283 12TH WAR
BARNES, NATHANIEL CAR 224 5TH DIST
BARNES, PATTY HAR 139 2ND DIST
BARNES, PERRY CAR 206 4TH DIST
BARNES, PHEBE WAS 022 2ND SUBD
BARNES, PRIMUS-BLACK ST 338 4TH E DI
BARNES, RACHAEL CAR 364 9TH DIST
BARNES, RACHEL BAL 227 6TH WARD
BARNES, REAZIN CAR 210 5TH DIST
BARNES, REBECCA BAL 054 4TH WARD
BARNES, RICHARD HAR 169 3RD DIST
BARNES, RICHARD MGM 359 BERRYS D
BARNES, RICHARD CHA 241 HILLTOP
BARNES, RICHARD ST 343 5TH E DI
BARNES, RICHARD A. CAR 221 5TH DIST
BARNES, RICHARD A. CAR 233 5TH DIST
BARNES, ROBERT CAR 297 7TH DIST
BARNES, ROBERT DOR 358 3RD DIVI
BARNES, ROBERT A. HAR 131 2ND DIST
BARNES, ROBERT C. BAL 389 3RD WARD
BARNES, ROBERT M. CAR 212 5TH DIST
BARNES, ROSE BAL 342 3RD WARD
BARNES, ROSS BAL 170 11TH WAR
BARNES, RUFUS FRE 444 8TH E DI
BARNES, RUTH FRE 255 NEW MARK
BARNES, SAMUEL BAL 116 18TH WAR
BARNES, SAMUEL FRE 385 PETERSVI
BARNES, SAMUEL ANN 516 HOWARD D
BARNES, SAMUEL BAL 174 2ND DIST
BARNES, SAMUEL WAS 100 2ND DIST
BARNES, SAMUEL WAS 152 2ND DIST
BARNES, SAMUEL TAL 058 EASTON D
BARNES, SARAH BAL 170 11TH WAR
BARNES, SARAH BAL 287 12TH WAR
BARNES, SARAH BAL 014 4TH WARD
BARNES, SARAH E. BAL 031 4TH WARD
BARNES, SATTENA MGM 437 CLARKSTR
BARNES, SOLOMON ALL 236 CUMBERLA
BARNES, SUSAN CAR 177 8TH DIST
BARNES, SUSANA BAL 044 9TH WARD
BARNES, SUSANNAH HAR 169 3RD DIST
BARNES, THOMAS FRE 250 NEW MARK
BARNES, THOMAS CAR 230 5TH DIST
BARNES, THOMAS FRE 010 FREDERIC
BARNES, THOMAS ALL 239 CUMBERLA
BARNES, THOMAS ANN 426 HOWARD D
BARNES, TRUMAN ANN 504 HOWARD D
BARNES, UPTON S. FRE 211 BUCKEYST
BARNES, URETH CAR 365 9TH DIST
BARNES, WESLEY CAR 194 4TH DIST
BARNES, WHEATLEY D. HAR 107 2ND DIST
BARNES, WHEATLY SOM 402 BRINKLEY
BARNES, WILLIAM SOM 403 BRINKLEY
BARNES, WILLIAM KEN 297 3RD DIST
BARNES, WILLIAM CAR 361 9TH DIST
BARNES, WILLIAM DOR 359 3RD DIVI
BARNES, WILLIAM DOR 448 1ST DIST
BARNES, WILLIAM HAR 133 2ND DIST
BARNES, WILLIAM BAL 316 3RD WARD
BARNES, WILLIAM BAL 152 1ST WARD
BARNES, WILLIAM BAL 173 1ST WARD
BARNES, WILLIAM ALL 118 5TH E.D.
BARNES, WILLIAM C. CHA 230 MIDDLETO
BARNES, WILLIAM F. HAR 156 3RD DIST
BARNES, WILLIAM J. SOM 417 PRINCESS
BARNES,CATHARINE BAL 030 2ND DIST
BARNESTER, ISAAC CEC 039 CHESAPEA
BARNESTON, THOMAS BAL 469 14TH WAR
BARNET, ANN WAS 148 2ND DIST
BARNET, ANN E. BAL 028 15TH WAR
BARNET, ARA ANN 343 3RD DIST
BARNET, DAVID WAS 148 2ND DIST
BARNET, ELIZA* DOR 428 1ST DIST
BARNET, ELIZZBETH BAL 431 14TH WAR
BARNET, GEORGE HAR 002 1ST DIST
BARNET, HANNAH BAL 365 13TH WAR
BARNET, HENRY WAS 148 2ND DIST
BARNET, JACOB BAL 290 3RD WARD
BARNET, JAMES ALL 109 5TH E.D.
BARNET, JOHN BAL 040 15TH WAR
BARNET, JOSEPH ALL 103 5TH E.D.
BARNET, MARTHA A. BAL 028 15TH WAR
BARNET, MARTHA A. BAL 338 3RD WARD
BARNET, MATILDA BAL 094 10TH WAR
BARNET, NICHOLAS HAR 134 2ND DIST
BARNET, RAYMOND FRE 394 PETERSVI
BARNET, REESA HAR 160 3RD DIST
BARNET, ROBERT BAL 423 8TH WARD
BARNET, SARAH BAL 459 1ST DIST
BARNET, SARAH WAS 034 2ND SUBD
BARNET, SOLOMON CAL 058 3RD DIST
BARNET, THOMAS BAL 259 1ST DIST
BARNET, WILLIAM BAL 379 13TH WAR
BARNETS, ANDREW BAL 254 1ST DIST
BARNETT, ANN TAL 050 EASTON T
BARNETT, BENJAMIN TAL 005 EASTON D
BARNETT, BETSY BAL 216 17TH WAR
BARNETT, CHARLES * BAL 170 2ND DIST
BARNETT, ELIZABETH BAL 167 6TH WARD
BARNETT, ELIZABETH WAS 185 BOONSBOR
BARNETT, FRISBY BAL 317 3RD WARD
BARNETT, HARISON DOR 428 1ST DIST
BARNETT, HENRY CAL 041 3RD DIST
BARNETT, JAMES KEN 209 2ND DIST
BARNETT, JAMES TAL 025 EASTON D
BARNETT, JAMES E. TAL 067 EASTON T
BARNETT, JOHN BAL 295 20TH WAR
BARNETT, JOHN BAL 276 7TH WARD
BARNETT, JOHN ANN 401 8TH DIST
BARNETT, JOHN DR. TAL 091 ST MICHA
BARNETT, JOSEPH E.* TAL 001 EASTON D
BARNETT, LYDIA C. KEN 249 2ND DIST
BARNETT, MARIA WAS 097 2ND DIST
BARNETT, MARTHA HAR 006 1ST DIST
BARNETT, MARY A. BAL 121 16TH WAR
BARNETT, MARY* DOR 417 1ST DIST
BARNETT, MICHAEL J. ANN 461 HOWARD D
BARNETT, NANCY BAL 012 4TH WARD
BARNETT, OAKLEY BAL 167 6TH WARD
BARNETT, PERRY BAL 038 1ST WARD
BARNETT, RICHARD ANN 406 8TH DIST
BARNETT, RICHARD TAL 008 EASTON D
BARNETT, S. V. TAL 003 EASTON D
BARNETT, SAMUEL ANN 401 8TH DIST
BARNETT, SAMUEL ANN 403 8TH DIST
BARNETT, THOMAS ALL 129 4TH E.D.
BARNETT, THOMAS BAL 386 3RD WARD
BARNETT, THOMAS P. TAL 008 EASTON D
BARNETT, WASHINGTON BAL 303 17TH WAR
BARNETT, WILLIAM CAR 221 5TH DIST
BARNETT, WILLIAM BAL 135 18TH WAR
BARNETT, WILLIAM BAL 241 20TH WAR
BARNETT, WILLIAM BAL 121 11TH WAR
BARNETT, WILLIAM TAL 113 ST MICHA
BARNETT, WILLIAM BAL 154 16TH WAR
BARNETT, WILLIAM M. BAL 301 20TH WAR
BARNETT, WILLIAM P. DOR 373 1ST DIST
BARNETTS, LOUISA BAL 430 14TH WAR
BARNETZ, MICHAEL CAR 264 WESTMINS
BARNEY, A.J. BAL 229 1ST DIST
BARNEY, ABRAHAM BAL 398 1ST DIST
BARNEY, ALEXANDER FRE 032 FREDERIC
BARNEY, ANN L. BAL 140 11TH WAR
BARNEY, BEN-BLACK QUE 138 1ST E DI
BARNEY, BENJAMIN-BLACK QUE 128 1ST E DI
BARNEY, ELIZABETH HAR 191 3RD DIST
BARNEY, ELIZABETH-BLACK QUE 138 1ST E DI
BARNEY, EMMA BAL 111 5TH WARD
BARNEY, GEORGE BAL 457 8TH WARD
BARNEY, GEORGE CAR 217 5TH DIST
BARNEY, HARRIET CAL 054 3RD DIST
BARNEY, ISAAC ANN 309 1ST DIST
BARNEY, JAMES BAL 169 1ST WARD
BARNEY, JAMES BAL 216 17TH WAR
BARNEY, JANE BAL 136 5TH WARD
BARNEY, JEROME A. FRE 032 FREDERIC
BARNEY, JOHN CAR 215 5TH DIST
BARNEY, JOHN BAL 093 10TH WAR
BARNEY, JOHN* BAL 086 10TH WAR
BARNEY, MARY J. BAL 032 9TH WARD
BARNEY, PETER BAL 139 11TH WAR
BARNEY, PHILIP BAL 064 4TH WARD
BARNEY, ROBERT BAL 235 1ST DIST
BARNEY, S. A. BAL 092 10TH WAR
BARNEY, SMITH BAL 125 1ST WARD
BARNEY, WILLIAM BAL 197 17TH WAR
BARNEY, WILLIAM BAL 316 3RD WARD
BARNEY, WILLIAM BAL 256 17TH WAR
BARNEY, WILLIAM J. BAL 388 13TH WAR
BARNFIELD, HENRY BAL 243 17TH WAR
BARNHARD, J. CHARLES BAL 029 18TH WAR
BARNHARD, LEWIS BAL 289 17TH WAR
BARNHARDT, JACOB BAL 005 18TH WAR
BARNHARDT, JOHN BAL 041 18TH WAR
BARNHARDT, ABRAHAM WAS 095 2ND SUBD
BARNHART, ANDREW BAL 290 17TH WAR
BARNHART, BARBARA FRE 310 WOODSBOR
BARNHART, BARBARA A. WAS 301 1ST DIST
BARNHART, CATHERINE BAL 307 20TH WAR
BARNHART, DAVID CAR 308 1ST DIST
BARNHART, JOHN FRE 090 FREDERIC
BARNHART, JOHN CAR 401 2ND DIST
BARNHART, MARY FRE 289 WOODSBOR
BARNHART, RHODA BAL 026 2ND DIST
BARNHART, WILLIAM FRE 181 5TH E DI

NAME	CO.	PAGE	DISTRICT
BARNHART, WILLIAM	WAS	277	RIDGEVIL
BARNHEART, JACOB	WAS	274	RIDGEVIL
BARNHEART, SAMUEL	WAS	266	1ST DIST
BARNHOLF, EUGENE	ALL	044	10TH E.D
BARNHOUSE, MATTHEW P.	ALL	123	4TH E.D.
BARNICK, JOHN*	DOR	307	1ST DIST
BARNIE, R. J.	BAL	360	13TH WAR
BARNIN, MARIAH	FRE	264	NEW MARK
BARNING, CASSA	TAL	075	EASTON T
BARNING, MARY *	QUE	253	5TH E DI
BARNITS, WILLIAM*	BAL	082	10TH WAR
BARNITY, ALEXANDER	BAL	116	11TH WAR
BARNITZ, C. D.	BAL	321	20TH WAR
BARNITZ, LELIA	BAL	154	11TH WAR
BARNITZ, WILLIAM	BAL	297	1ST DIST
BARNITZ, WILLIAM*	BAL	082	10TH WAR
BARNMET, JAMES L.	BAL	011	9TH WARD
BARNOON, SARAH	ALL	147	6TH E.D.
BARNRRTT, ELIPHALET *	BAL	135	2ND DIST
BARNS, ABRAHAM	ST	279	3RD E DI
BARNS, ALEXANDER	ST	286	2ND E DI
BARNS, ALEXANDER-BARNS	ST	295	2ND E DI
BARNS, ALEXANDER-BLACK	ST	293	2ND E DI
BARNS, ALEXANDER-BLACK	ST	301	2ND E DI
BARNS, ALEXANDER-BLACK	ST	310	1ST E DI
BARNS, ANN	DOR	360	3RD DIVI
BARNS, ANN	BAL	084	18TH WAR
BARNS, ANN-BLACK	ST	310	1ST E DI
BARNS, ARIAL	BAL	463	1ST DIST
BARNS, BENJAMIN	HAR	118	2ND DIST
BARNS, BENJAMIN	BAL	205	17TH WAR
BARNS, CHARITY	DOR	411	1ST DIST
BARNS, CHARLE-SBLACK	ST	310	1ST E DI
BARNS, CHARLES	ST	266	3RD E DI
BARNS, CHARLES	WAS	157	HAGERSTO
BARNS, CHARLES	BAL	053	4TH WARD
BARNS, CHARLES-BLACK	ST	310	1ST E DI
BARNS, DANIEL	BAL	423	3RD WARD
BARNS, DAVID	CEC	193	5TH E DI
BARNS, DAVID	BAL	144	5TH WARD
BARNS, DEBORAH	BAL	353	1ST DIST
BARNS, DEBORAY	BAL	272	17TH WAR
BARNS, ELIJAH	WOR	304	SNOW HIL
BARNS, ELIZA-MULATTO	ST	294	2ND E DI
BARNS, ELIZABETH	ST	282	3RD E DI
BARNS, ELIZABETH	DOR	378	1ST DIST
BARNS, ELIZABETH	CAR	096	NO TWP L
BARNS, ELIZABETH	HAR	123	2ND DIST
BARNS, ELIZABETH-BLACK	ST	297	2ND E DI
BARNS, FREDERICK	ST	279	3RD E DI
BARNS, GARNER	ST	264	3RD E DI
BARNS, GEORGE	WAS	064	2ND SUBD
BARNS, GEORGE-BLACK	ST	310	1ST E DI
BARNS, GERALTIUS	ST	276	3RD E DI
BARNS, HANNAH	BAL	022	18TH WAR
BARNS, HANSON	ST	276	3RD E DI
BARNS, HARRIET A.	ST	288	2ND E DI
BARNS, HENRY E.E.-BLACK	ST	297	2ND E DI
BARNS, HENRY*	DOR	380	1ST DIST
BARNS, HENRY-BLACK	ST	301	2ND E DI
BARNS, ISAAC	ST	289	2ND E DI
BARNS, JACOB-BLACK	ST	301	2ND E DI
BARNS, JAMES	CEC	188	7TH E DI
BARNS, JAMES	BAL	139	2ND DIST
BARNS, JAMES	BAL	452	8TH WARD
BARNS, JAMES	BAL	065	1ST WARD
BARNS, JAMES T.	ST	259	3RD E DI
BARNS, JANE	ST	282	3RD E DI
BARNS, JOHN	ST	286	2ND E DI
BARNS, JOHN	DOR	337	3RD DIVI
BARNS, JOHN	CEC	041	CHESAPEA
BARNS, JOHN A.	ST	261	3RD E DI
BARNS, JOHN H.	BAL	419	3RD WARD
BARNS, JOHN-BLACK	ST	294	2ND E DI
BARNS, JOSEPH	DOR	423	1ST DIST
BARNS, JOSEPH	BAL	342	7TH WARD
BARNS, JOSEPH	BAL	107	2ND DIST
BARNS, JOSEPH L.	CEC	152	PORT DUP
BARNS, JOSEPH-BLACK	ST	300	2ND E DI
BARNS, JOSHUA	BAL	371	1ST DIST
BARNS, JOSHUA-BLACK	ST	301	2ND E DI
BARNS, JOSIAH	DOR	414	1ST DIST
BARNS, LEVI	CAR	373	9TH DIST
BARNS, LOUISA	BAL	363	3RD WARD
BARNS, LOUISA-BLACK	ST	293	2ND E DI
BARNS, MARTHA	ST	266	3RD E DI
BARNS, MARTHA	BAL	363	3RD WARD
BARNS, MARY	BAL	107	2ND DIST
BARNS, MARY	BAL	300	1ST DIST
BARNS, MARY A.	WAS	241	CAVETOWN
BARNS, MARY J.-BLACK	ST	301	2ND E DI
BARNS, MARY-BLACK	ST	296	2ND E DI
BARNS, MARY-MULATTO	ST	302	2ND E DI
BARNS, MONICHA	ST	275	3RD E DI
BARNS, PETER	ST	281	3RD E DI
BARNS, PHILIP-BLACK	ST	301	2ND E DI
BARNS, PLEANNA-BLACK	ST	298	2ND E DI
BARNS, RACHELL	BAL	224	17TH WAR
BARNS, RICHARD-BLACK	ST	293	2ND E DI
BARNS, RICHARD-BLACK	ST	301	2ND E DI
BARNS, RICHARD-BLACK	ST	294	2ND E DI
BARNS, ROBERT	ST	278	3RD E DI
BARNS, ROBERT	CAR	374	9TH DIST
BARNS, ROBERT S.	CAR	375	9TH DIST
BARNS, ROBERT-BLACK	ST	300	2ND E DI
BARNS, ROBERT-MULATTO	ST	297	2ND E DI
BARNS, ROSE	ST	298	2ND E DI
BARNS, SAMUEL	BAL	268	1ST DIST
BARNS, SARAH	BAL	348	1ST DIST
BARNS, STEPHEN	DOR	423	1ST DIST
BARNS, STEPHEN-BLACK	ST	298	2ND E DI
BARNS, STEPHEN-BLACK	ST	300	2ND E DI
BARNS, SYRUS-MULATTO	ST	300	2ND E DI
BARNS, THOMAS-BLACK	ST	301	2ND E DI
BARNS, WALTER	ST	282	3RD E DI
BARNS, WASHINGTON	ST	265	3RD E DI
BARNS, WASHINGTON	CAR	284	7TH DIST
BARNS, WILLIAM	DOR	371	3RD DIVI
BARNS, WILLIAM	BAL	289	17TH WAR
BARNS, WILLIAM	CEC	207	7TH E DI
BARNS, WILLIAM	ST	278	3RD E DI
BARNS, WILLIAM	ST	275	3RD E DI
BARNS, WILLIAM H.-BLACK	ST	300	2ND E DI
BARNS, WILLIAM-BLACK	ST	312	1ST E DI
BARNS, WILLIAM-MULATTO	ST	298	2ND E DI
BARNS.RACHIEL	CAR	161	NO TWP L
BARNSCHLAGLE, BALDHASEY	FRE	048	FREDERIC
BARNSLEY, JAMES F.	MGM	315	CRACKLIN
BARNSLEY, JOHNATHAN D.	MGM	315	CRACKLIN
BARNSLEY, MOSES	MGM	315	CRACKLIN
BARNSLY, THOAMS	BAL	029	18TH WAR
BARNUM, ANN K.	BAL	108	10TH WAR
BARNUM, JAMES	BAL	120	1ST WARD
BARNUM, JOHN	BAL	273	12TH WAR
BARNUM, LEVIN*	DOR	445	1ST DIST
BARNY, MARTIN	BAL	098	2ND DIST
BARNY, ROBERT	BAL	139	11TH WAR
BARNZOFT, WILLIAM	WAS	131	HAGERSTO
BARR, ANNA	WAS	124	HAGERSTO
BARR, BENJAMIN	WAS	151	HAGERSTO
BARR, BENJAMIN	BAL	440	1ST DIST
BARR, CATHARINE	BAL	389	1ST DIST
BARR, CHARLES G.	BAL	134	1ST WARD
BARR, CHRISTIAN	BAL	145	2ND DIST
BARR, CHRISTIAN	WAS	140	HAGERSTO
BARR, D. T.	BAL	281	2ND WARD
BARR, D.J.	WAS	127	HAGERSTO
BARR, DENNIS	BAL	281	2ND WARD
BARR, ELVINA	HAR	168	3RD DIST
BARR, ISAAC	WAS	114	2ND DIST
BARR, JAMES	HAR	205	3RD DIST
BARR, JOHN	CEC	196	6TH E DI
BARR, LEWIS K.	WAS	282	1ST DIST
BARR, MARY	BAL	230	19TH WAR
BARR, ROSEANNA	CEC	016	ELKTON 3
BARR,MARGARET	QUE	196	3RD E DI
BARRACKENAN, CHARLES W.	BAL	088	4TH WARD
BARRACKMAN, LEBAS	BAL	012	4TH WARD
BARRAM, MARY S.	BAL	456	1ST DIST
BARRATOLL, BARNEY H.	HAR	107	2ND DIST
BARRATT, ANDREW	CAR	117	NO TWP L
BARRECKMAN, ELLEN	HAR	198	3RD DIST
BARRELL, BENJAMIN	BAL	317	1ST DIST
BARRELL, GEORGE	BAL	143	1ST WARD
BARRELL, GEORGE *	KEN	244	2ND DIST
BARRELL, RICHARD *	KEN	221	2ND DIST
BARRELL, WILIAM B.	ALL	216	CUMBERLA
BARREN, CHRISTIAN	BAL	276	7TH WARD
BARREN, JOHN M.	HAR	196	3RD DIST
BARREN, SAMUEL H.	HAR	187	3RD DIST
BARRENGER, JOHN	BAL	003	EASTERN
BARRENGER, MARY	BAL	350	7TH WARD
BARRENGER, THOMAS F.	BAL	294	7TH WARD
BARRER, JOHN	HAR	040	1ST DIST
BARRET, ALEXANDER	CAR	223	5TH DIST
BARRET, ASA	BAL	431	14TH WAR
BARRET, BRIDGET	BAL	397	3RD WARD
BARRET, DANIEL	BAL	146	1ST WARD
BARRET, ELIZA	BAL	291	3RD WARD
BARRET, ELLEN	BAL	291	3RD WARD
BARRET, EMORY	BAL	475	14TH WAR
BARRET, JULIUS	CAR	232	5TH DIST
BARRET, LEVI	MGM	389	ROCKERLE
BARRET, MARIA	KEN	218	2ND DIST
BARRET, MICHAEL	BAL	372	3RD WARD
BARRET, SARAH	BAL	436	1ST DIST
BARRET, SARAH	BAL	420	1ST DIST
BARRET, THOMAS	ANN	471	HOWARD D
BARRET, WILLIAM	ANN	288	ANNAPOLI
BARRETT, ALEXANDER	KEN	220	2ND DIST
BARRETT, AMANDA	CEC	157	PORT DUP
BARRETT, ANDREW	CEC	067	5TH E DI
BARRETT, ANN	MGM	355	BERRYS D
BARRETT, ANTHONY	ALL	142	6TH E.D.
BARRETT, ANTHONY	BAL	400	1ST DIST
BARRETT, BENJAMIN	BAL	172	1ST WARD
BARRETT, BENJAMIN	MGM	352	BERRYS D
BARRETT, CAROLINE	BAL	161	6TH WARD
BARRETT, CASSANDRA	HAR	126	2ND DIST
BARRETT, CECELIA C.	BAL	404	8TH WARD
BARRETT, CORNELIUS	CEC	132	6TH E DI
BARRETT, EDWARD	ALL	076	5TH E.D.
BARRETT, ELIZA	BAL	038	9TH WARD
BARRETT, EMMA	BAL	222	6TH WARD
BARRETT, FLORA	ANN	431	HOWARD D
BARRETT, FRANCIS	BAL	356	3RD WARD
BARRETT, FRANCIS A.	BAL	405	8TH WARD
BARRETT, GREGORY	BAL	172	19TH WAR
BARRETT, HARRIET	BAL	174	2ND DIST
BARRETT, HENRY	ANN	455	HOWARD D
BARRETT, HENRY	CEC	208	7TH E DI
BARRETT, ISABELLA G.	BAL	043	15TH WAR
BARRETT, JAMES	ALL	140	6TH E.D.
BARRETT, JAMES	CEC	207	7TH E DI
BARRETT, JAMES	BAL	058	4TH WARD
BARRETT, JAMES	KEN	216	2ND DIST
BARRETT, JAMES	CEC	117	4TH E DI
BARRETT, JOHN	KEN	223	2ND DIST
BARRETT, JOHN	KEN	213	2ND DIST
BARRETT, JOHN	ALL	139	6TH E.D.
BARRETT, JOHN	ALL	076	5TH E.D.
BARRETT, JOHN	ALL	035	2ND E.D.
BARRETT, JOHN	BAL	371	3RD WARD
BARRETT, JOHN	BAL	441	1ST DIST
BARRETT, JOSEPH	BAL	100	18TH WAR
BARRETT, LORETTA	MGM	361	BERRYS D
BARRETT, LUCY	BAL	198	17TH WAR
BARRETT, MARCUS	BAL	107	5TH WARD
BARRETT, MARIA	ANN	378	4TH DIST
BARRETT, MARY	HAR	046	1ST DIST
BARRETT, MARY	BAL	281	17TH WAR
BARRETT, MARY	BAL	057	18TH WAR
BARRETT, MARY A.	KEN	216	2ND DIST
BARRETT, MILES	ALL	077	5TH E.D.
BARRETT, MR.	BAL	033	15TH WAR
BARRETT, NICHOLAS	ANN	378	4TH DIST
BARRETT, PATRICK	ALL	139	6TH E.D.
BARRETT, PATRICK	BAL	099	18TH WAR
BARRETT, PETER	DOR	469	1ST DIST
BARRETT, RICHARD	MGM	356	BERRYS D
BARRETT, ROBERT	ALL	142	6TH E.D.
BARRETT, ROBINSON	CEC	209	7TH E DI
BARRETT, ROSELLA	BAL	338	7TH WARD
BARRETT, SAMUEL	CEC	208	7TH E DI
BARRETT, THOMAS	CEC	201	6TH E DI
BARRETT, THOMAS	ALL	136	4TH E.D.
BARRETT, THOMAS	ALL	100	5TH E.D.
BARRETT, WILLIAM	ANN	468	HOWARD D
BARREY, ELIZABETH *	BAL	282	7TH WARD
BARREY, EMILY	BAL	460	8TH WARD
BARREY, RACHEL	BAL	337	7TH WARD
BARREY, RICHARD	BAL	308	7TH WARD
BARREY, WILLIAM H.	BAL	443	8TH WARD
BARRICK, BENJAMIN	FRE	283	WOODSBOR
BARRICK, CAROLINE	FRE	165	EMMITTSB
BARRICK, CATHERINE	ALL	235	CUMBERLA
BARRICK, CORNELIUS	FRE	141	CREAGERS
BARRICK, DANILE	FRE	138	CREAGERS
BARRICK, DR.	FRE	144	10TH E D
BARRICK, ELIZA	FRE	284	WOODSBOR
BARRICK, ELIZA E.	FRE	309	WOODSBOR
BARRICK, GEORGE	FRE	294	WOODSBOR
BARRICK, GEORGE	FRE	111	CREAGERS
BARRICK, GEORGE P.	FRE	295	WOODSBOR
BARRICK, HENRY	FRE	301	WOODSBOR
BARRICK, JACOB	FRE	309	WOODSBOR
BARRICK, JOHN	FRE	290	WOODSBOR
BARRICK, JOHN W.	FRE	294	WOODSBOR
BARRICK, JOSEPH	FRE	295	WOODSBOR
BARRICK, JULIA	BAL	266	17TH WAR
BARRICK, LEVI	FRE	285	WOODSBOR
BARRICK, LEVI	FRE	323	MIDDLETO
BARRICK, NOAH	FRE	310	WOODSBOR
BARRICK, PETER	FRE	204	BUCKEYST
BARRICK, RANDOLPH G.	FRE	284	WOODSBOR
BARRICK, SAMUEL	FRE	285	WOODSBOR
BARRICK, SOLOMON	FRE	295	WOODSBOR
BARRICK, SOLOMON	FRE	307	WOODSBOR
BARRICK, SOPHIA	CAR	325	1ST DIST
BARRICK, SOPHIAH	FRE	307	WOODSBOR
BARRICK, THEODORE	FRE	294	WOODSBOR
BARRICK, THOAMS	QUE	217	3RD E DI
BARRICK, WILLIAM	FRE	109	CREAGERS
BARRICK, WILLIAM	FRE	164	EMMITTSB
BARRICK, WILLIAM	FRE	087	FREDERIC
BARRICK, WILLIAM	FRE	355	MIDDLETO
BARRICKMAN, JACOB	BAL	347	7TH WARD
BARRICKMAN, JOHN	BAL	270	17TH WAR
BARRICKMAN, MARIETTA	BAL	251	6TH WARD
BARRICKMAN, MICHAEL	BAL	091	5TH WARD
BARRICT, SARHA *	TAL	077	EASTON T
BARRIER, ALFRED	CAR	359	9TH DIST
BARRIER, GEORGE	BAL	111	2ND DIST
BARRIER, JANE	BAL	112	5TH WARD
BARRIER, THERESA	BAL	111	5TH WARD
BARRIN, EMLAY	HAR	187	3RD DIST
BARRINGER, FRANCIS	PRI	095	SPALDING
BARRINGER, JAMES S.	BAL	349	7TH WARD
BARRINGER, JOHN A.	BAL	169	6TH WARD
BARRINGER, LEWIS L.B.	BAL	169	6TH WARD
BARRINGTON, CATHERINE	BAL	042	4TH WARD
BARRINGTON, EDWARD	BAL	408	3RD WARD
BARRINGTON, SOPHIA	BAL	103	10TH WAR
BARRIS, CAROLINE E.	BAL	075	1ST WARD
BARRIS, MARY E.	MGM	375	ROCKERLE
BARRIS, SAMUEL	WAS	158	2ND DIST
BARRIS, THOMAS	BAL	280	2ND WARD
BARRISS, ANN	MGM	315	CRACKLIN
BARRISS, HENRY	MGM	363	BERRYS D
BARRISTER, JAMES	CAL	391	1ST DIST
BARRISTER, MARY	CEC	121	4TH E DI
BARRISTER, WILLIAM *	BAL	065	18TH WAR
BARROETT, ANN M. *	TAL	085	ST MICHA
BARROL, WILLIAM H.	BAL	013	18TH WAR
BARROLL, GEORGE	KEN	267	1ST DIST
BARROLL, GRACE	KEN	285	3RD DIST
BARROLL, HARRISON*	TAL	048	EASTON T
BARROLL, JAMES E.	KEN	212	2ND DIST
BARROLL, JAMES W.	BAL	388	13TH WAR
BARROLL, MARY A.*	TAL	044	EASTON D
BARROLL, SARAH	KEN	291	3RD DIST
BARROLL, SARAH H.	KEN	216	2ND DIST
BARROLL, WILLIAM	TAL	052	EASTON D
BARRON, ALDRUF	CAR	184	9TH DIST
BARRON, BERNARD	BAL	275	7TH WARD
BARRON, HENRY W.*	TAL	033	EASTON D
BARRON, JAMES	BAL	123	11TH WAR
BARRON, JOHN	BAL	469	14TH WAR
BARRON, JOHN	BAL	187	16TH WAR
BARRON, JOHN	BAL	100	15TH WAR
BARRON, JOHN C.	BAL	143	16TH WAR
BARRON, JOSEPH	ALL	219	CUMBERLA
BARRON, SARAH F.	BAL	044	15TH WAR
BARRONN, CHARLOTTE*	BAL	066	4TH WARD
BARROT, MARY	TAL	069	EASTON T
BARROT, PATRICK	ALL	053	10TH E.D
BARROTT, ANTHONY	ALL	075	5TH E.D.
BARROTT, CHARLES	TAL	018	EASTON D
BARROTT, J.	BAL	151	1ST WARD
BARROTT, JAMES	ALL	075	5TH E.D.
BARROTT, JOHN	CAL	002	1ST DIST
BARROTT, MICHAEL	ALL	053	10TH E.D
BARROW, B.	WAS	021	2ND SUBD
BARROW, BARNEY	BAL	161	11TH WAR
BARROW, CATHARINE	BAL	251	1ST DIST
BARROW, CATHRINE	BAL	014	18TH WAR
BARROW, DANIEL	PRI	002	BLADENSB
BARROW, FRANCIS M.	PRI	003	BLADENSB
BARROW, HENRY	PRI	004	BLADENSB
BARROW, HENRY T.	BAL	049	4TH WARD
BARROW, JAMES	BAL	250	1ST DIST
BARROW, JAMES L.	HAR	109	2ND DIST
BARROW, JOHN	HAR	113	2ND DIST
BARROW, MARGARET	BAL	251	1ST DIST
BARROW, MARY	BAL	082	18TH WAR
BARROW, PAT	BAL	118	5TH WARD
BARROW, ROSE	TAL	073	EASTON T
BARROW, SARAH	BAL	066	4TH WARD
BARROW, THOMAS REV.	BAL	038	4TH WARD
BARROW, WILLIAM D.	DOR	466	1ST DIST
BARROWN, CHARLOTTE*	BAL	066	4TH WARD
BARROWS, ALEXANDER	BAL	033	4TH WARD
BARROWS, DENWOOD H.	BAL	044	4TH WARD
BARROWS, EBEN	KEN	218	2ND DIST
BARROWS, EDWARD	QUE	133	1ST E DI
BARROWS, ELIJAH	BAL	374	13TH WAR
BARROWS, GEORGE K.*	TAL	004	EASTON D
BARROWS, HENRY	BAL	045	4TH WARD
BARROWS, MICHAEL	BAL	045	4TH WARD
BARROWS, ZADOK	MGM	402	ROCKERLE
BARRS, ELIZABETH	DOR	378	1ST DIST
BARRS, HESTER*	DOR	435	1ST DIST
BARRS, JAMES*	DOR	466	1ST DIST
BARRS, PATIENCE*	DOR	448	1ST DIST
BARRS, PETER	DOR	425	1ST DIST
BARRS, ROSE A.*	DOR	375	1ST DIST
BARRUS, PERRY H.	HAR	152	3RD DIST
BARRY, AMOS D.	BAL	140	1ST WARD
BARRY, BASIL	MGM	375	ROCKERLE
BARRY, CAROLINE	BAL	029	9TH WARD
BARRY, CATHARINE	BAL	460	14TH WAR
BARRY, CECILIA	ALL	210	CUMBERLA
BARRY, CHARLES B.	BAL	381	13TH WAR
BARRY, DAVID	BAL	400	3RD WARD
BARRY, DAVID	WAS	026	2ND SUBD
BARRY, DAVID	PRI	089	SPALDING
BARRY, DAVIS	BAL	120	1ST WARD
BARRY, EDWARD	HAR	001	1ST DIST
BARRY, ELLEN R.	FRE	160	EMMITTSB
BARRY, ISA	CEC	156	PORT DUP

Name	Co.	Page	District
BARRY, JAMES	CEC	161	6TH E DI
BARRY, JAMES	BAL	176	11TH WAR
BARRY, JAMES	ALL	227	CUMBERLA
BARRY, JAMES C.	BAL	275	12TH WAR
BARRY, JOHN	BAL	270	1ST DIST
BARRY, JOHN	BAL	127	5TH WARD
BARRY, JOHN	FRE	159	EMMITTSB
BARRY, JOHN	CAR	100	NO TWP L
BARRY, JOHN L.	BAL	435	14TH WAR
BARRY, JOHN W.	BAL	441	14TH WAR
BARRY, JOSEPH	BAL	123	18TH WAR
BARRY, JOSEPH	ALL	241	CUMBERLA
BARRY, JOSEPHINE	BAL	212	11TH WAR
BARRY, LAURA V.	HAR	033	1ST DIST
BARRY, MARY	BAL	155	11TH WAR
BARRY, MARY	BAL	155	11TH WAR
BARRY, MARY	BAL	371	13TH WAR
BARRY, MARY	BAL	178	2ND DIST
BARRY, MARY A.	BAL	157	6TH WARD
BARRY, MARY E.	BAL	276	12TH WAR
BARRY, PHILIP	ALL	210	CUMBERLA
BARRY, SAMUEL M.	BAL	277	1ST DIST
BARRY, SETH	ANN	347	3RD DIST
BARRY, SUSAN	ANN	365	4TH DIST
BARRY, SUSAN	BAL	187	16TH WAR
BARRY, THOMAS L.	BAL	269	1ST DIST
BARRY, WASHINGTON L.	WAS	302	1ST DIST
BARRY, WILLIAM	BAL	426	14TH WAR
BARRY, WILLIAM	BAL	198	11TH WAR
BARRY, WILLIAM B.	BAL	270	1ST DIST
BARRY, WILLIAM F.	BAL	301	17TH WAR
BARRY, WILLIAM J.	BAL	447	14TH WAR
BARRYHMAN, GEORGE	BAL	314	12TH WAR
BARS, JEMIMA	BAL	213	11TH WAR
BARS, JESSE	CAR	375	9TH DIST
BARS, SAMUEL	KEN	284	3RD DIST
BARSELL, GEORGE	KEN	244	2ND DIST
BARSELL, RICHARD *	KEN	221	2ND DIST
BARSON, FANNY	BAL	020	2ND DIST
BARSON, R.	BAL	154	1ST WARD
BARSONS, THOMAS D.	WOR	180	6TH E DI
BARSTON, JOSLINA	BAL	254	12TH WAR
BART, E. R.*	BAL	101	10TH WAR
BART, JOHN	ALL	128	4TH E.D.
BART, JOHN	ALL	128	4TH E.D.
BART, JOSEPH	FRE	071	FREDERIC
BART, SOLOMON A.	FRE	070	FREDERIC
BART, SUSAN-BLACK	CAR	085	NO TWP L
BARTAS, SIDNEY	BAL	422	14TH WAR
BARTCHER, ANN	BAL	232	2ND WARD
BARTEL, ANN	BAL	042	18TH WAR
BARTEL, ELIZABETH	BAL	032	18TH WAR
BARTELL, HENRY	BAL	212	2ND WARD
BARTELLE, JOHN	ALL	052	10TH E.D
BARTELLO, B. F.	FRE	145	10TH E D
BARTELS, ANNE C.	BAL	146	16TH WAR
BARTELS, FREDERICK	FRE	359	CATOCTIN
BARTEN, JEFFERSON	BAL	322	3RD WARD
BARTEN, JOSHUA	BAL	210	11TH WAR
BARTER, SARAH	ANN	350	3RD DIST
BARTER, SOPHIA	BAL	161	16TH WAR
BARTES, HARNETT	BAL	137	11TH WAR
BARTGES, FRANK	FRE	086	FREDERIC
BARTGIS, GEORGE	FRE	053	FREDERIC
BARTGIS, HIRAM	FRE	014	FREDERIC
BARTGIS, JOHN M.	BAL	039	9TH WARD
BARTGIS, TITUS V.	FRE	102	FREDERIC
BARTGISS, ANDREW	WAS	180	BOONSBOR
BARTGISS, MARY	WAS	187	BOONSBOR
BARTH, ADAM	ALL	176	7TH E.O.
BARTH, CATHARINE	WAS	301	1ST DIST
BARTH, CHESTER	ALL	176	7TH E.D.
BARTH, CHRISTIAN	BAL	266	12TH WAR
BARTH, DANIEL	BAL	210	11TH WAR
BARTH, GODFRED	BAL	103	1ST WARD
BARTH, JOHN H.	BAL	090	5TH WARD
BARTH, SIMON	BAL	024	1ST WARD
BARTHEL, EDWARD	BAL	120	11TH WAR
BARTHELOW, GEORGE	FRE	251	NEW MARK
BARTHELOW, JOHN	FRE	247	NEW MARK
BARTHLOW, ELISHA	FRE	134	CREAGERS
BARTHLOW, HANSON	CAR	206	4TH DIST
BARTHLOW, MICHAEL	FRE	431	8TH E DI
BARTHOL, JAMES H.	BAL	010	4TH WARD
BARTHOLDT, AUGUST	BAL	333	13TH WAR
BARTHOLDT, JOHN F.	BAL	097	10TH WAR
BARTHOLEW, ADAM	BAL	090	18TH WAR
BARTHOLMA, FRANK	BAL	214	11TH WAR
BARTHOLMEW, ANN A.	BAL	215	11TH WAR
BARTHOLOMEW, AUGUST	BAL	390	3RD WARD
BARTHOLOMEW, GOTLIEHB	BAL	161	2ND DIST
BARTHOLOMEW, M. F.	BAL	311	1ST DIST
BARTHOLOMEW, MARY	BAL	235	20TH WAR
BARTHOLOMEW, WESLEY E. B.	BAL	454	8TH WARD
BARTHOLOW, E.	BAL	218	19TH WAR
BARTHOLOW, JOHN	BAL	217	19TH WAR
BARTHOLOW, S. J.	BAL	475	14TH WAR
BARTHOLOW, THOMAS	CAR	396	2ND DIST
BARTHOLOW, THOMAS	BAL	163	19TH WAR
BARTHOW, FREDERICK	BAL	112	5TH WARD
BARTHS, JAMES*	DOR	463	1ST DIST
BARTILL, DANIEL*	TAL	017	EASTON D
BARTIN, ELIZABETH	BAL	299	1ST DIST
BARTIN, NATHANIEL	BAL	067	1ST WARD
BARTINE, WILLIAM	DOR	301	1ST DIST
BARTING, GEORGE	BAL	185	5TH DIST
BARTINSLAGER, JOHN	BAL	430	8TH WARD
BARTLE, JOHN	WAS	121	2ND DIST
BARTLE, JOSEPHUS	WAS	133	2ND DIST
BARTLE, MARY	WAS	104	2ND DIST
BARTLE, WILLIAM	WAS	120	2ND DIST
BARTLER, HENRY	PRI	053	AQUASCO
BARTLER, SARAH	ALL	062	10TH E.D
BARTLES, ANN	WAS	100	2ND DIST
BARTLES, BENJAMIN	WAS	149	2ND DIST
BARTLES, LLOYD A.	WAS	149	2ND DIST
BARTLESON, MARY A.	BAL	068	10TH WAR
BARTLET, JAMES	BAL	392	3RD WARD
BARTLET, JOHN	BAL	313	1ST DIST
BARTLET, JOHN	BAL	312	1ST DIST
BARTLET, JOHN*	TAL	001	EASTON D
BARTLET, JOSEPH*	TAL	001	EASTON D
BARTLET, REBECCA	BAL	333	1ST DIST
BARTLETT, A.	BAL	281	2ND WARD
BARTLETT, ANTHONY	ALL	143	6TH E.D.
BARTLETT, DAVID L.	BAL	049	15TH WAR
BARTLETT, ELIZA	TAL	023	EASTON D
BARTLETT, ELIZABETH	TAL	001	EASTON D
BARTLETT, EMMA	WAS	020	2ND SUBD
BARTLETT, FRANCIS A.	TAL	024	EASTON D
BARTLETT, GEORGE	BAL	376	13TH WAR
BARTLETT, ISAAC	BAL	265	2ND WARD
BARTLETT, J.	BAL	302	20TH WAR
BARTLETT, JAEMS	TAL	098	ST MICHA
BARTLETT, JAMES	BAL	159	1ST WARD
BARTLETT, JAMES JR.	TAL	060	EASTON D
BARTLETT, JAMES R.	TAL	060	EASTON D
BARTLETT, JONATHAN	TAL	098	ST MICHA
BARTLETT, JOSEPH	TAL	057	EASTON D
BARTLETT, MICHAEL	ALL	047	10TH E.D
BARTLETT, SAMUEL	TAL	041	EASTON D
BARTLETT, SOPHIA	BAL	180	11TH WAR
BARTLETT, TENET*	TAL	041	EASTON D
BARTLETT, THOASM	BAL	286	7TH WARD
BARTLETT, THOMAS	TAL	057	EASTON D
BARTLETT, VINCENT P.	CAR	087	NO TWP L
BARTLETT, WILLIAM	CEC	046	1ST E DI
BARTLETT, WILLIAM	BAL	301	17TH WAR
BARTLETT, WILLIAM	BAL	106	1ST WARD
BARTLETT, WILLIAM A.	BAL	423	14TH WAR
BARTLETT, WILLIAM E.	BAL	134	16TH WAR
BARTLETT, WILLIAM E. JR.	BAL	470	14TH WAR
BARTLEY, C.	PRI	103	SPALDING
BARTLEY, HANNAH C.	BAL	371	3RD WARD
BARTLEY, JAMES	BAL	311	3RD WARD
BARTLEY, JOHN	PRI	014	BLADENSB
BARTLEY, KITTY	BAL	246	17TH WAR
BARTLEY, MARY	BAL	176	2ND DIST
BARTLEY, WILLIAM	PRI	010	BLADENSB
BARTLILOW, ROBERT *	CAR	183	8TH DIST
BARTLING, THOMAS E.	BAL	085	15TH WAR
BARTLITT, DANIEL*	TAL	017	EASTON D
BARTLY, JOHN	WAS	264	1ST DIST
BARTLY, JOHN	CEC	015	ELKTON 3
BARTLY, LETIA	CEC	004	ELKTON 3
BARTMAN, AARON	ANN	486	HOWARD D
BARTMAN, CHRISOPHER	BAL	251	2ND WARD
BARTMAN, CHRISTOPHER	BAL	251	2ND WARD
BARTMAN, PETER	BAL	221	2ND WARD
BARTMAN, SARAH*	BAL	312	3RD WARD
BARTOL, B.B.	HAR	155	3RD DIST
BARTOLD, CHRISTIAN	BAL	006	EASTERN
BARTOLE, VIRGINIA	BAL	383	13TH WAR
BARTOLL, MARY ANN	BAL	148	5TH WARD
BARTOLS, LUDWICK	BAL	416	14TH WAR
BARTON, A.	PRI	108	PISCATAW
BARTON, ANN	BAL	228	19TH WAR
BARTON, ANN	BAL	465	14TH WAR
BARTON, AQUILA	HAR	103	2ND DIST
BARTON, ASA	ALL	237	CUMBERLA
BARTON, CAROLINE	CAR	074	NO TWP L
BARTON, CHARLOTTE	DOR	320	1ST DIST
BARTON, ELIJAH	ANN	356	3RD DIST
BARTON, ELIZABETH	BAL	098	2ND DIST
BARTON, ELIZABETH	QUE	212	3RD E DI
BARTON, ELLEN	PRI	107	PISCATAW
BARTON, EMILY	HAR	073	1ST DIST
BARTON, FANNY	ALL	238	CUMBERLA
BARTON, FITTY	BAL	081	2ND DIST
BARTON, FRANCIS	BAL	013	4TH WARD
BARTON, GEORGE	BAL	357	13TH WAR
BARTON, GEORGE	KEN	218	2ND DIST
BARTON, HANNAH	BAL	281	7TH WARD
BARTON, HENRY	FRE	185	5TH E DI
BARTON, HENRY E.	BAL	220	17TH WAR
BARTON, HESTOR	BAL	013	4TH WARD
BARTON, IGNATIUS	BAL	126	5TH WARD
BARTON, ISAAC	MGM	350	BERRYS D
BARTON, ISAAC	BAL	105	18TH WAR
BARTON, ISAAC	WAS	213	1ST DIST
BARTON, J.	BAL	164	1ST WARD
BARTON, JAMES	FRE	261	NEW MARK
BARTON, JAMES	HAR	135	2ND DIST
BARTON, JAMES	BAL	414	3RD WARD
BARTON, JAMES	BAL	076	4TH WARD
BARTON, JAMES	BAL	093	18TH WAR
BARTON, JENNINGS	BAL	371	3RD WARD
BARTON, JOHN	BAL	315	3RD WARD
BARTON, JOHN	BAL	288	3RD WARD
BARTON, JOHN	BAL	106	5TH WARD
BARTON, JOHN	ANN	304	1ST DIST
BARTON, JOHN	FRE	141	CREAGERS
BARTON, JOHN	DOR	373	1ST DIST
BARTON, JOHN	HAR	024	1ST DIST
BARTON, JOHN T.*	BAL	416	3RD WARD
BARTON, JOSHUA	HAR	059	1ST DIST
BARTON, L. VIRGINIA	MGM	350	BERRYS D
BARTON, LAVINIA	PRI	111	PISCATAW
BARTON, LEVI	BAL	456	8TH WARD
BARTON, LEWIS	BAL	297	12TH WAR
BARTON, LEWIS	HAR	020	1ST DIST
BARTON, LOYD	BAL	116	2ND DIST
BARTON, MARGARET	BAL	292	7TH WARD
BARTON, MARTHA A.	HAR	068	1ST DIST
BARTON, MARY	HAR	010	1ST DIST
BARTON, MARY	FRE	179	5TH E DI
BARTON, MARY	BAL	027	4TH WARD
BARTON, MARY	BAL	179	11TH WAR
BARTON, MARY	BAL	267	12TH WAR
BARTON, MARY A.	BAL	026	2ND DIST
BARTON, NATHANIEL	BAL	107	18TH WAR
BARTON, PATIENCE	BAL	060	4TH WARD
BARTON, PERRY	BAL	177	11TH WAR
BARTON, PETER	BAL	292	3RD WARD
BARTON, PHILIP A.	HAR	029	1ST DIST
BARTON, REBECA	BAL	009	EASTERN
BARTON, REBECCA	ALL	222	CUMBERLA
BARTON, REBECCA	BAL	167	11TH WAR
BARTON, REBECCA	BAL	174	11TH WAR
BARTON, RHODA	QUE	212	3RD E DI
BARTON, ROBERT	BAL	127	18TH WAR
BARTON, ROSE	BAL	074	10TH WAR
BARTON, SAMUEL	ANN	306	1ST DIST
BARTON, SAMUEL	FRE	184	5TH E DI
BARTON, SAMUEL L.	BAL	435	8TH WARD
BARTON, SAMUEL T.	BAL	057	4TH WARD
BARTON, SARAH A.	BAL	172	6TH WARD
BARTON, STEPHEN	BAL	299	1ST DIST
BARTON, STEPHEN	HAR	062	1ST DIST
BARTON, SUAN	MGM	335	CRACKLIN
BARTON, THADDEUS J.	BAL	087	10TH WAR
BARTON, THOMAS	ALL	245	CUMBERLA
BARTON, THOMAS	ALL	250	CUMBERLA
BARTON, THOMAS	FRE	109	CREAGERS
BARTON, THOMAS	DOR	370	3RD DIVI
BARTON, WILLIA	BAL	183	11TH WAR
BARTON, WILLIAM	BAL	057	2ND DIST
BARTON, WILLIAM	BAL	131	16TH WAR
BARTON, WILLIAM	BAL	126	5TH WARD
BARTON, WILLIAM	ANN	359	3RD DIST
BARTON, WILLIAM	BAL	345	3RD WARD
BARTON, WILLIAM	HAR	143	2ND DIST
BARTON, WILLIAM	BAL	075	4TH WARD
BARTON, WILLIAM	CEC	153	PORT DUP
BARTON, WILLIAM	QUE	212	3RD E DI
BARTON, WILLIAM D.	ALL	210	CUMBERLA
BARTON, WILLIAM H.	DOR	373	1ST DIST
BARTON, ZEKIEL	BAL	389	13TH WAR
BARTON,JAMES	QUE	233	4TH E DI
BARTONVETLETT, LOUIS	BAL	456	1ST DIST
BARTOW, JAMES L.	BAL	476	14TH WAR
BARTOW, JOHN T.*	BAL	416	3RD WARD
BARTOW, MATILDA	BAL	088	4TH WARD
BARTRON, ISAAC	ALL	103	5TH E.D.
BARTS, MARTHA	BAL	462	1ST DIST
BARTTEN, JESSE	WOR	206	4TH E DI
BARTTLES, HENRY	WAS	142	2ND DIST
BARTUM, SALLY A.*	DOR	414	1ST DIST
BARTZER, IRONICA	FRE	084	FREDERIC
BARUM, MARY *	BAL	287	20TH WAR
BARWELL, JOHN	WAS	047	2ND SUBD
BARWICK, BARBARY	BAL	226	17TH WAR
BARWICK, EMILY	CEC	027	CHESAPEA
BARWICK, FRANCIS	QUE	157	2ND E DI
BARWICK, FRANCIS	QUE	159	2ND E DI
BARWICK, HARRY J.	CAR	090	NO TWP L
BARWICK, HENRY	QUE	173	2ND E DI
BARWICK, JAMES H.	CAR	066	NO TWP L
BARWICK, MAT.	QUE	208	3RD E DI
BARWICK, SAMUEL-BLACK	QUE	173	2ND E DI
BARWICK, WHITE	TAL	080	ST MICHA
BARWICK,MARY	QUE	199	3RD E DI
BARWISH, JOHN W.	TAL	086	ST MICHA
BARWISH, SHARLOTT	TAL	027	EASTON D
BARY, ELIZABETH	HAR	018	1ST DIST
BARY, ELY	HAR	019	1ST DIST
BARY, JOAN	HAR	022	1ST DIST
BARY, MARY	HAR	021	1ST DIST
BARY, MARY	BAL	145	11TH WAR
BARY, ROBERT C.	BAL	137	11TH WAR
BARZ, MARY *	HAR	021	1ST DIST
BARZE, JOHN	CAL	042	3RD DIST
BASALLE, LEWIS	BAL	012	4TH WARD
BASARED, JACOB *	WAS	051	2ND SUBD
BASCHLEY, MARY	BAL	357	8TH WARD
BASCROFT, GEROGE	BAL	380	13TH WAR
BASCSOME, ABRAHAM *	KEN	281	3RD DIST
BASE, ADAM	ALL	255	CUMBERLA
BASE, ANDREW	BAL	086	2ND DIST
BASE, CONRAD	ALL	262	CUMBERLA
BASE, JOHN	ALL	262	CUMBERLA
BASE, JOSEPH	BAL	086	2ND DIST
BASE, SOLOMON	ALL	244	CUMBERLA
BASECKE, BERUH	BAL	066	15TH WAR
BASEHAM, AQUILLA	BAL	215	6TH DIST
BASEHAM, BETSY	BAL	215	5TH DIST
BASEHAM, JOSHUA F.	BAL	207	6TH DIST
BASEHAM, NANCY	BAL	207	6TH DIST
BASEMAN, NIMROD	BAL	033	18TH WAR
BASEMAN, RBEECCA	CAR	369	9TH DIST
BASEMAN, SAMUEL	ANN	519	HOWARD D
BASET, JOSEPH	WAS	060	2ND SUBD
BASETER, JOHN	BAL	120	1ST WARD
BASFORCE, CAROLINE	MGM	438	CLARKSTR
BASFORD, ABRAHAM	FRE	232	BUCKEYST
BASFORD, ADAM	FRE	232	BUCKEYST
BASFORD, ALFRED	FRE	204	BUCKEYST
BASFORD, ALFRED	FRE	234	BUCKEYST
BASFORD, ALVERTUS	ANN	294	1ST DIST
BASFORD, GEORGE	FRE	232	BUCKEYST
BASFORD, HENRY	ANN	294	1ST DIST
BASFORD, HENRY	ANN	301	1ST DIST
BASFORD, HENRY	BAL	353	7TH WARD
BASFORD, ISAAC	FRE	227	BUCKEYST
BASFORD, JAMES	DOR	380	1ST DIST
BASFORD, JOHN T.	FRE	234	BUCKEYST
BASFORD, SARAH	PRI	044	VANSVILL
BASFORD, SUSANNAH	FRE	234	BUCKEYST
BASFORD, THOMAS	FRE	223	BUCKEYST
BASFORD, THOMAS	ANN	360	3RD DIST
BASFORD,ELENORE	FRE	234	BUCKEYST
BASFORT, J.	BAL	130	1ST WARD
BASH, ANN-BLACK	ST	336	4TH E DI
BASH, GEORGE	FRE	249	NEW MARK
BASH, J. H.	BAL	332	1ST DIST
BASHEARS, SAMUEL E.	CAR	363	9TH DIST
BASIL, HENRY	ANN	279	ANNAPOLI
BASIL, JOHN	ANN	291	ANNAPOLI
BASIL, MARTIN	ANN	386	4TH DIST
BASIL, MICHAEL	BAL	076	1ST WARD
BASIL, RALPH	ANN	319	2ND DIST
BASIL, RALPH	ANN	289	ANNAPOLI
BASIL, SALLY	ANN	277	ANNAPOLI
BASIL, W.D.	ANN	271	ANNAPOLI
BASIL, WILLIAM	ANN	289	ANNAPOLI
BASIL, WILLIAM	BAL	286	7TH WARD
BASILL, W.	ANN	286	ANNAPOLI
BASLEY, FANNY	BAL	145	5TH WARD
BASLEY, JOHN	BAL	436	1ST DIST
BASMAN, MARY*	SOM	353	BRINKLEY
BASMER, CAROLINE *	WAS	172	FUNKSTOW
BASMER, EDWARD	HAR	170	3RD DIST
BASON, ANN	ALL	210	CUMBERLA
BASON, GEORGE	BAL	281	2ND WARD
BASON, LYDIA	BAL	392	3RD WARD
BASORE, JOHN	WAS	112	2ND DIST
BASS, HENRY	BAL	329	3RD WARD
BASS, JOHN	BAL	226	17TH WAR
BASS, SIMON	BAL	391	3RD WARD
BASSARD, GEORGE	BAL	035	9TH WARD
BASSELL, JOHN	BAL	027	1ST WARD
BASSET, CATHERINE	ALL	261	CUMBERLA
BASSET, GEORGE	WAS	049	2ND SUBD
BASSET, HARIET	WAS	049	2ND SUBD
BASSET, JAMES	WAS	048	2ND SUBD
BASSETT, ANN	WAS	197	1ST DIST
BASSETT, BENJAMIN	WOR	170	6TH E DI
BASSETT, BENJAMIN	WOR	284	BERLIN 1
BASSETT, E.	BAL	142	5TH WARD
BASSETT, EMALINE	WOR	293	9TH E DI
BASSETT, FREEMAN	BAL	249	17TH WAR
BASSETT, JAMES	BAL	015	4TH WARD
BASSETT, JOHN	BAL	360	8TH WARD
BASSETT, JOSIAH	DOR	460	1ST DIST
BASSETT, MARTHA	WOR	289	9TH E DI
BASSETT, THOMAS	BAL	257	17TH WAR
BASSFORD, JOHN H.	CAL	024	2ND DIST
BASSFORD, JOHN W.	FRE	275	NEW MARK
BASSFORD, SARAH A.	CAL	024	2ND DIST
BASSFORD, THOMAS REV-	BAL	057	10TH WAR

BASSIT, LEVINIE	CAR	097	NO TWP L
BASSON, E.J.	BAL	115	1ST WARD
BASSON, EDWARD	BAL	115	1ST WARD
BASSON, SUSAN	BAL	200	5TH DIST
BASSOW, CHAELS	BAL	189	5TH DIST
BAST, CORNELIUS	FRE	389	PETERSVI
BAST, JOHN	FRE	213	BUCKEYST
BASTABLE, GILBERT M.	BAL	074	18TH WAR
BASTABLE, V.	BAL	073	18TH WAR
BASTAN, LORENZO	CHA	246	HILLTOP
BASTBRIDG, THOMAS*	DOR	351	3RD DIVI
BASTBRIDG, WILLIAM	DOR	351	3RD DIVI
BASTEIN, JOHN T.	CHA	246	HILLTOP
BASTER, JOHN G.	BAL	434	8TH WARD
BASTER, WILLIAM	BAL	128	2ND DIST
BASTIK, CHARLES	CEC	018	ELKTON 3
BASTON, CATHERINE	FRE	030	FREDERIC
BASTON, MARGRETT-BLACK	CAR	149	NO TWP L
BASTON, NELA	ALL	218	CUMBERLA
BASTON, RACHEL	BAL	413	1ST DIST
BASTOR, JACOB	HAR	180	3RD DIST
BASTOS, JUAN	FRE	202	5TH E DI
BASTUN, STENCER *	CHA	246	HILLTOP
BASTY, CATHARINE	BAL	199	2ND WARD
BASWELL, EDWARD	BAL	395	1ST DIST
BATCH, JOHN	BAL	457	8TH WARD
BATCHELDER, RICHARD	BAL	160	1ST WARD
BATCHELOR, DAVID	BAL	295	7TH WARD
BATCHELOR, EMILY	BAL	171	2ND DIST
BATCHELOR, JOSEPH	BAL	376	8TH WARD
BATCHELOR, LAURA	BAL	309	7TH WARD
BATCHELOR, NATHANIEL	BAL	297	3RD WARD
BATCHELOR, SAMUEL*	BAL	048	4TH WARD
BATCHELOR, WILLIAM	BAL	056	4TH WARD
BATCHER, ROBERT	FRE	211	BUCKEYST
BATCHER, THOMAS-BLACK	FRE	241	NEW MARK
BATCHLER, G.G.	BAL	161	1ST WARD
BATCHLOR, JACOB	BAL	391	14TH WAR
BATE, JOSEPH	BAL	412	1ST DIST
BATEHEIMER, CHARISANA	FRE	080	FREDERIC
BATEMAN, ALFRED W.	HAR	075	BEL AIR
BATEMAN, BENJAMIN T.	CHA	223	ALLENS F
BATEMAN, CATHARINE	ST	323	4TH E DI
BATEMAN, CATHERINE	BAL	311	3RD WARD
BATEMAN, CONSTANCE	BAL	255	17TH WAR
BATEMAN, EDWARD	BAL	342	7TH WARD
BATEMAN, ELIZA	BAL	032	15TH WAR
BATEMAN, ELKANNA	FRE	033	FREDERIC
BATEMAN, EMILY	CHA	223	ALLENS F
BATEMAN, EMLY	CHA	288	BOJANTOW
BATEMAN, GEORGE	CHA	227	ALLENS F
BATEMAN, H. G.	TAL	005	EASTON D
BATEMAN, JAMES	QUE	172	2ND E DI
BATEMAN, JAMES	BAL	336	1ST DIST
BATEMAN, JAMES D.	BAL	255	17TH WAR
BATEMAN, JOHN	BAL	413	3RD WARD
BATEMAN, JOHN	BAL	104	1ST WARD
BATEMAN, JOHN	QUE	167	2ND E DI
BATEMAN, JOHN R.	BAL	067	15TH WAR
BATEMAN, JOSEPH M.	HAR	104	2ND DIST
BATEMAN, JULIS A. R.	BAL	102	15TH WAR
BATEMAN, MARGARET	BAL	040	9TH WARD
BATEMAN, MARGARET	BAL	278	17TH WAR
BATEMAN, MARY	CEC	050	1ST E DI
BATEMAN, MARY	FRE	034	FREDERIC
BATEMAN, MISSY	CHA	289	BOJANTOW
BATEMAN, R. E.	CHA	236	HILLTOP
BATEMAN, REBECCA	CHA	221	ALLENS F
BATEMAN, REILY	BAL	162	11TH WAR
BATEMAN, ROSETTA	BAL	055	4TH WARD
BATEMAN, SAMUEL	BAL	278	17TH WAR
BATEMAN, SAMUEL	HAR	080	2ND DIST
BATEMAN, SAMUEL D.	BAL	022	15TH WAR
BATEMAN, SAMUEL-BLACK	QUE	163	2ND E DI
BATEMAN, SUSAN	CHA	227	ALLENS F
BATEMAN, WASHINGTON	CHA	290	BOJANTOW
BATEMAN, WILLIAM C.	ST	338	4TH E DI
BATEMAN, WILLIAM H.	BAL	400	8TH WARD
BATEMAN, WILLIAM L.	BAL	339	13TH WAR
BATEMAN, WILLIS	CEC	199	7TH E DI
BATEMEN, MARTHA	CHA	217	ALLENS F
BATEN, PHILIP	BAL	330	13TH WAR
BATENGER, HENRY	ALL	013	3RD E.D.
BATER, EVA	BAL	223	19TH WAR
BATERS, JULVER	BAL	282	12TH WAR
BATES, ANDREWS	BAL	183	19TH WAR
BATES, BENJAMIN	BAL	146	1ST WARD
BATES, BENJAMIN	ALL	262	CUMBERLA
BATES, CAROLINE	BAL	260	1ST DIST
BATES, CHARLES	BAL	361	3RD WARD
BATES, DEBORAH	CEC	206	7TH E DI
BATES, ELIZABETH	BAL	361	3RD WARD
BATES, FRANKLIN L.	BAL	361	3RD WARD
BATES, HENRY	BAL	258	1ST DIST
BATES, HENRY-BLACK	QUE	137	1ST E DI
BATES, JAMES	BAL	421	3RD WARD
BATES, JAMES	BAL	164	11TH WAR
BATES, JOHN	BAL	360	3RD WARD
BATES, JOHN	BAL	128	5TH WARD
BATES, JOHN H.	CAR	220	5TH DIST
BATES, JOHN M.	BAL	031	9TH WARD
BATES, JOSEPH	CAR	316	1ST DIST
BATES, LAWRENCE W.	BAL	425	14TH WAR
BATES, MARY	BAL	472	14TH WAR
BATES, MARY	ALL	229	CUMBERLA
BATES, REBECCA	BAL	370	8TH WARD
BATES, ROBERT	BAL	031	9TH WARD
BATES, SARAH	CEC	188	7TH E DI
BATES, THOMAS	ALL	261	CUMBERLA
BATES, WILLIAM	CEC	078	NORTHEAS
BATESEY, MARY	BAL	130	11TH WAR
BATEY, ETLICE *	BAL	024	18TH WAR
BATEZELL, JACOB	BAL	183	19TH WAR
BATGAR, HENRY	BAL	321	3RD WARD
BATH, J.	BAL	143	11TH WAR
BATHURT, JOHN G.	BAL	150	11TH WAR
BATHUS, ANNA	BAL	474	14TH WAR
BATK, JOSEPH	BAL	235	2ND WARD
BATLES, DANIEL	WAS	100	2ND DIST
BATMAN, THOMAS B.	HAR	202	3RD DIST
BATON, JOHN	BAL	115	18TH WAR
BATON,MARY	ALL	229	CUMBERLA
BATOSN, GEORGE	CAR	281	7TH DIST
BATS, NERUNE	ALL	261	CUMBERLA
BATSAOM, WESTLEY	ALL	103	5TH E.D.
BATSEN, MILLEY	BAL	426	8TH WARD
BATSON, BENJAMIN	FRE	034	FREDERIC
BATSON, CALEB	ANN	309	1ST DIST
BATSON, D.	PRI	111	PISCATAW
BATSON, DANIEL	CAR	198	4TH DIST
BATSON, GEROGE	BAL	420	14TH WAR
BATSON, HENRY T. *	ANN	424	HOWARD D
BATSON, JOHN D.	FRE	206	BUCKEYST
BATSON, LEONARD	ANN	485	HOWARD D
BATSON, MARTIN H.	ANN	485	HOWARD D
BATSON, MARY	PRI	058	NOTTINGH
BATSON, MARY L.	MGM	418	MEDLEY 3
BATSON, NANCY	PRI	113	PISCATAW
BATSON, R.W.	BAL	261	12TH WAR
BATSON, ROBERT	WOR	194	8TH E DI
BATSON, WILLIAM	ANN	312	1ST DIST
BATSON,SARAH	BAL	261	12TH WAR
BATT, MARGARET	BAL	213	11TH WAR
BATT, WILLIAM	MGM	365	BERRYS D
BATT,W ILLIAM	MGM	398	ROCKERLE
BATTA, LOUISA	BAL	457	1ST DIST
BATTEE, GEORGE	BAL	056	18TH WAR
BATTEE, JOHN	BAL	359	3RD WARD
BATTEE, MARY	BAL	216	6TH WARD
BATTEE, SOPHIA G.	BAL	031	15TH WAR
BATTELER, HENRY A.	CAR	185	8TH DIST
BATTELL, COR E.	WOR	259	BERLIN 1
BATTEN, CATHARINE	BAL	030	1ST WARD
BATTER, ANN-BLACK	ST	348	5TH E DI
BATTER, ELIZA	BAL	031	9TH WARD
BATTER, GOERGE	BAL	077	2ND DIST
BATTER, JOHN W.	TAL	095	ST MICHA
BATTER, JULIAN	BAL	060	4TH WARD
BATTERFIELD, CHRISTIAN	BAL	270	2ND WARD
BATTERMAN, ELIZABETH	CEC	041	CHESAPEA
BATTERSBY, FRANCIS	BAL	146	5TH WARD
BATTERSON, WILLIAM	BAL	041	2ND DIST
BATTES, SARAH J.*	BAL	398	3RD WARD
BATTESE, JOHN	ANN	273	ANNAPOLI
BATTEY, AUGUST	BAL	066	1ST WARD
BATTEY, MARY	TAL	092	ST MICHA
BATTICE, HENRY	BAL	446	1ST DIST
BATTIE, ISABELLA	BAL	010	EASTERN
BATTIE, SAMUEL	BAL	172	2ND DIST
BATTIE, SAMUEL	BAL	289	7TH WARD
BATTIS, SARAH J.*	BAL	398	3RD WARD
BATTISE, JOHN	BAL	039	9TH WARD
BATTISE, JOHN	BAL	299	17TH WAR
BATTISE, JOHN	QUE	130	1ST E DI
BATTLE, ALFRED	CHA	260	MIDDLETO
BATTLE, DENNIS	BAL	078	2ND DIST
BATTLE, JOE	BAL	234	1ST DIST
BATTON, ANN	BAL	462	1ST DIST
BATTON, JAMES	CEC	056	1ST E DI
BATTON, JAMES	HAR	079	2ND DIST
BATTON, LOUISA	CEC	030	CHESAPEA
BATTON, MAILAN	CEC	108	3RD E DI
BATTON, THOMAS	BAL	388	13TH WAR
BATTS, ELLEN	BAL	022	4TH WARD
BATTS, SARAH	BAL	346	1ST DIST
BATTS, THOMAS	SOM	503	SALISBUR
BATTUS, MARY	BAL	061	1ST WARD
BATTY, ANN P.	BAL	356	13TH WAR
BATTY, GEORGE A.	ST	288	2ND E DI
BATTY, GEORGE G.	ST	288	2ND E DI
BATTY, HANNAH	HAR	029	1ST DIST
BATTY, JANE	HAR	054	1ST DIST
BATTY, JOHN	WAS	071	2ND SUBD
BATTY, JOSEPH	BAL	190	2ND WARD
BATTY, SAMUEL	HAR	069	1ST DIST
BATTY, WILLIAM	HAR	054	1ST DIST
BATTZ, ANTON	BAL	245	2ND WARD
BATZOLD, WILLIAM	BAL	243	2ND WARD
BATZY, B.	ANN	345	3RD DIST
BAU, MICHAEL DR.	BAL	332	13TH WAR
BAUBEAR, SISTER M CELESTE	FRE	198	5TH E DI
BAUBLITZ, SAMUEL	BAL	219	6TH DIST
BAUCH, JOSEPH	BAL	196	6TH WARD
BAUCH, PHILI	BAL	433	8TH WARD
BAUCHANNAN, ELLEN	BAL	109	18TH WAR
BAUDELL, EMILY	BAL	069	10TH WAR
BAUDER, ISRAEL	CAL	029	2ND DIST
BAUER, GEORGE	BAL	223	6TH WARD
BAUER, JOHN	BAL	211	2ND WARD
BAUER, JOHN	BAL	370	13TH WAR
BAUER, JOSEPH	BAL	173	6TH WARD
BAUER, LEOPOLD	BAL	190	11TH WAR
BAUER, TH.	BAL	449	8TH WARD
BAUER, WILLIAM	BAL	207	2ND WARD
BAUERGELDT, CHARLES	BAL	223	6TH WARD
BAUGH, CAHTERINE	FRE	035	FREDERIC
BAUGH, LOUISA	ALL	091	5TH E.D.
BAUGH, PETER	ALL	035	2ND E.D.
BAUGHAN, ANN	BAL	021	4TH WARD
BAUGHER, ANN E.	FRE	042	FREDERIC
BAUGHER, CHARLES H.	FRE	164	EMMITTSB
BAUGHER, JAMES W.	FRE	164	EMMITTSB
BAUGHER, JOHN	FRE	308	WOODSBOR
BAUGHER, JOSEPH	BAL	418	14TH WAR
BAUGHER, JOSIAH S.	CAR	286	7TH DIST
BAUGHER, SAMUEL	FRE	305	WOODSBOR
BAUGHER, SUSANNA	FRE	078	FREDERIC
BAUGHINARD, ANN	BAL	277	20TH WAR
BAUGHMAN, ALACE	BAL	271	1ST DIST
BAUGHMAN, ALFRED	BAL	031	4TH WARD
BAUGHMAN, C. W.	BAL	294	20TH WAR
BAUGHMAN, DANIEL	BAL	270	1ST DIST
BAUGHMAN, ELIZA	BAL	410	1ST DIST
BAUGHMAN, ELIZABETH	CAR	274	7TH DIST
BAUGHMAN, F. M.	BAL	284	20TH WAR
BAUGHMAN, GEORGE	BAL	140	19TH WAR
BAUGHMAN, H. F.	BAL	284	20TH WAR
BAUGHMAN, JACOB	BAL	028	2ND DIST
BAUGHMAN, JOHN W.	FRE	044	FREDERIC
BAUGHMAN, LAVINIA	BAL	169	19TH WAR
BAUGHMAN, MARY	BAL	358	1ST DIST
BAUGHMAN, MICHAEL	CAR	264	WESTMINS
BAUGHMAN, WILLIAM	CAR	277	7TH DIST
BAUGHMARD, ANN *	BAL	277	20TH WAR
BAUGHMARD, SUSAN *	BAL	277	20TH WAR
BAUGHN, MARY	BAL	358	1ST DIST
BAUGMGARTNER, ALEXIUS *	CAR	312	1ST DIST
BAUGS, ISRAEL	KEN	275	1ST DIST
BAUGS, WILLIAM	KEN	274	1ST DIST
BAUHES, WILLIAM	BAL	136	11TH WAR
BAUHOLON, E. M. *	BAL	313	20TH WAR
BAUM, AMELIA	BAL	008	1ST WARD
BAUM, AMOS	CAR	349	6TH DIST
BAUM, HANNAH	BAL	394	14TH WAR
BAUM, HENRY	ALL	094	5TH E.D.
BAUM, JACOB	CAR	248	3RD DIST
BAUM, JOHN*	BAL	328	3RD WARD
BAUM, LEWIS	BAL	297	17TH WAR
BAUM, LEWIS E.	BAL	434	14TH WAR
BAUM, MARGARET E.	CAR	251	3RD DIST
BAUM, MARIA L.	BAL	435	14TH WAR
BAUM, MARY R.	BAL	156	11TH WAR
BAUM, WILLIAM	BAL	343	3RD WARD
BAUM, WILLIAM	BAL	266	7TH WARD
BAUMAGARDNER, CATHARINE	CAR	348	6TH DIST
BAUMAN, AARON	BAL	152	2ND DIST
BAUMAN, SUSAN	BAL	188	2ND WARD
BAUMANN, LOUISA	BAL	067	15TH WAR
BAUMBAUGH, SAMUE LD.	WAS	282	1ST DIST
BAUMBERGER, JAMES	BAL	162	11TH WAR
BAUMER, HENRY	BAL	232	17TH WAR
BAUMGARDNER, THOMAS	FRE	062	FREDERIC
BAUMGARTNER, ANDREW	BAL	025	4TH WARD
BAUMGARTNER, BARBARA	CAR	312	1ST DIST
BAUMGARTNER, ELIZABETH	CAR	246	3RD DIST
BAUMGARTNER, HENRY	CAR	250	3RD DIST
BAUMGARTNER, HENRY	CAR	309	1ST DIST
BAUMGARTNER, JACOB	CAR	249	3RD DIST
BAUMGARTNER, JOHN	CAR	250	3RD DIST
BAUMGARTNER, JOHN	CAR	270	WESTMINS
BAUMGARTNER, JOHN J.	CAR	270	WESTMINS
BAUMGARTNER, JOSIAH	CAR	312	1ST DIST
BAUMGARTNER, MARY M.	CAR	312	1ST DIST
BAUMHAUER, ROBERT	BAL	146	19TH WAR
BAUMMAN, WILLIAM	BAL	104	18TH WAR
BAUMONT, EDWARD	BAL	393	1ST DIST
BAUMSINGER, MICHAEL	BAL	127	18TH WAR
BAUMUTH, PHILIP	BAL	455	8TH WARD
BAUNAN, MARY	BAL	165	11TH WAR
BAUNDS, JOSHUA	BAL	365	1ST DIST
BAUNEGARDNER, HENRY	FRE	265	NEW MARK
BAUNEGARTNER, JOSHUA	CAR	277	7TH DIST
BAUNER, SUSANNAH	FRE	266	NEW MARK
BAUNGARDNER, JOHN	BAL	253	12TH WAR
BAUNHARON, EDWARD	BAL	146	19TH WAR
BAUNNER, JOHN J.	FRE	094	FREDERIC
BAURN, CHARLES	BAL	319	3RD WARD
BAUSMAN, ELIZABETH	BAL	226	1ST DIST
BAUSMAN, JOHN	BAL	249	1ST DIST
BAUSS, SAMUEL	ANN	497	HOWARD D
BAUST, CORNELIUS	CAR	404	2ND DIST
BAUST, JOSEPH	CAR	409	2ND DIST
BAUST, MARY A.	CAR	407	2ND DIST
BAUST, SIDNEY A.	CAR	279	7TH DIST
BAUTLE, JOHN *	WAS	166	HAGERSTO
BAUTLOOF, JOHN	BAL	199	2ND WARD
BAUTTS, JAMES*	DOR	463	1ST DIST
BAUVICK, THOMAS	BAL	133	11TH WAR
BAVENERE, GEORGE T.	BAL	181	2ND DIST
BAWARD, MARY	BAL	436	8TH WARD
BAWDEN, JOHN	BAL	332	3RD WARD
BAWDEN, JOHN H.	BAL	333	3RD WARD
BAWEN, RICHARD	BAL	313	1ST DIST
BAWERER, CAROLINE	WAS	172	FUNKSTOW
BAWERS, WILLIAM	BAL	303	1ST DIST
BAWITCH, ELLIS	BAL	023	9TH WARD
BAWLDEN, TIMOTHY	HAR	180	3RD DIST
BAWN, JOHN*	BAL	328	3RD WARD
BAWMON, JACOB	WAS	214	1ST DIST
BAWMONT, THOMAS *	BAL	291	1ST DIST
BAWSTICK, ANN-BLACK	FRE	419	8TH E DI
BAXLEY, CLAUD	BAL	262	1ST DIST
BAXLEY, ELIZA	BAL	406	8TH WARD
BAXLEY, HENRY WILLIS	BAL	456	14TH WAR
BAXLEY, J.	BAL	333	13TH WAR
BAXLEY, JAMES	BAL	296	7TH WARD
BAXLEY, JAMES	BAL	034	1ST WARD
BAXLEY, JAMES	ANN	490	HOWARD D
BAXLEY, JOSHUA D.	BAL	163	11TH WAR
BAXLEY, R. J.	BAL	142	11TH WAR
BAXLEY, SARAH	TAL	117	ST MICHA
BAXLEY, SUSAN G.	BAL	301	20TH WAR
BAXLEY, WILLIAM	BAL	419	14TH WAR
BAXR, CATHERINE	MGM	420	MEDLEY 3
BAXSOME, ABRAHAM *	KEN	281	3RD DIST
BAXTER, ALEXANDER	CEC	092	4TH E DI
BAXTER, ANDREW	WAS	152	2ND DIST
BAXTER, BARBARY	WAS	100	2ND DIST
BAXTER, BENJAMIN	BAL	234	1ST DIST
BAXTER, CHARLES	QUE	231	4TH E DI
BAXTER, CHRISTOPHER	QUE	156	2ND E DI
BAXTER, COMACK	FRE	127	CREAGERS
BAXTER, DAVID	WAS	161	2ND DIST
BAXTER, DAVID	ALL	219	CUMBERLA
BAXTER, DELIA	BAL	228	6TH WARD
BAXTER, E.T.	BAL	134	5TH WARD
BAXTER, ELIJAH	WAS	122	2ND DIST
BAXTER, ELIZA	BAL	246	6TH WARD
BAXTER, ELIZABETH	WAS	152	2ND DIST
BAXTER, ELLEN J.	WAS	153	2ND DIST
BAXTER, GEORGIANNA	QUE	216	3RD E DI
BAXTER, GREENBERRY	QUE	227	4TH E DI
BAXTER, HANNAH	WAS	110	2ND DIST
BAXTER, HESTER	BAL	086	4TH WARD
BAXTER, J.	BAL	135	1ST WARD
BAXTER, JACOB	QUE	232	4TH E DI
BAXTER, JAMES	WAS	161	2ND DIST
BAXTER, JAMES	TAL	014	EASTON D
BAXTER, JAMES	BAL	137	2ND DIST
BAXTER, JAMES	HAR	009	1ST DIST
BAXTER, JAMES S.	QUE	193	3RD E DI
BAXTER, JOHN	WAS	118	2ND DIST
BAXTER, JOHN	QUE	155	2ND E DI
BAXTER, JOHN	BAL	130	2ND E DI
BAXTER, JOHN	BAL	137	1ST WARD
BAXTER, JOHN A.	ST	308	1ST E DI
BAXTER, JOSHUA	WAS	150	2ND DIST
BAXTER, LEVI	QUE	158	2ND E DI
BAXTER, LEWIS	QUE	158	2ND E DI
BAXTER, LLOYD	WAS	152	2ND DIST
BAXTER, M.	BAL	282	2ND WARD
BAXTER, MARTHA J.	BAL	375	3RD WARD
BAXTER, MARY J.	CEC	092	4TH E DI
BAXTER, MICHAEL	BAL	163	2ND DIST
BAXTER, MICHAEL	ALL	098	5TH E.D.
BAXTER, PHILIP	TAL	012	EASTON D
BAXTER, REBECCA	BAL	329	13TH WAR
BAXTER, REBECCA	HAR	079	2ND DIST
BAXTER, SAMUEL	QUE	144	1ST E DI
BAXTER, SARAH	QUE	203	3RD E DI
BAXTER, THOMAS	QUE	232	4TH E DI
BAXTER, THOMAS	BAL	236	1ST DIST
BAXTER, THOMAS	BAL	031	15TH WAR
BAXTER, WILLIAM	QUE	208	3RD E DI
BAXTER, WILLIAM	HAR	055	1ST DIST
BAXTER, WILLIAM B.	ST	313	1ST E DI
BAXTON, JAEMS	BAL	114	2ND DIST
BAXTON, WILLIAM	ALL	221	CUMBERLA
BAXTON, WILLIAM	MGM	339	CLARKSBU
BAY, ARABELLA	HAR	037	1ST DIST

Name	County	Page	District
BAY, CATHARINE	BAL	236	12TH WAR
BAY, CANIEL	HAR	047	1ST DIST
BAY, HUGH	HAR	048	1ST DIST
BAY, HUGH	BAL	278	20TH WAR
BAY, IRA	BAL	189	19TH WAR
BAY, JAMES	BAL	337	13TH WAR
BAY, JAMES	BAL	164	2ND DIST
BAY, JOHN	HAR	057	1ST DIST
BAY, ROBERT	HAR	062	1ST DIST
BAY, THOMAS	HAR	057	1ST DIST
BAY, WILLIAM	HAR	047	1ST DIST
BAYARD, ROBERT	HAR	131	2ND DIST
BAYER, HENRY	FRE	232	BUCKEYST
BAYER, SARAH W.	BAL	344	3RD WARD
BAYFIELD, JAMES	BAL	314	12TH WAR
BAYFIELD, MARY	BAL	314	12TH WAR
BAYFORD, JAMES	CAL	005	1ST DIST
BAYFORD, MARY E.	CAL	011	1ST DIST
BAYFORD, REBECCA	CAL	017	1ST DIST
BAYFORD, RICHARD	CAL	015	1ST DIST
BAYFORD, THOMAS *	CAL	010	1ST DIST
BAYLE, JAMES	BAL	316	20TH WAR
BAYLE, SISTER M. GERTRUDE	FRE	197	5TH E DI
BAYLE, WILLIAM A.	HAR	152	3RD DIST
BAYLER, THOMAS	TAL	115	ST MICHA
BAYLESS HENRIETTA B.	BAL	073	10TH WAR
BAYLESS, ANN	BAL	054	2ND DIST
BAYLESS, ASEL B.	HAR	164	3RD DIST
BAYLESS, CHARLES F.	BAL	351	7TH WARD
BAYLESS, JAMES R.	BAL	145	19TH WAR
BAYLESS, MARY F.	HAR	171	3RD DIST
BAYLESS, SAMUEL	HAR	162	3RD DIST
BAYLESS, SAMUEL M.	HAR	129	2ND DIST
BAYLESS, THOMAS	BAL	441	8TH WARD
BAYLESS, WILLIAM T.	HAR	129	2ND DIST
BAYLESS, ZEPHINIA	HAR	129	2ND DIST
BAYLEY, ALBERT M.	WOR	166	6TH E DI
BAYLEY, ALEX	DOR	389	1ST DIST
BAYLEY, CHARLES	TAL	025	EASTON D
BAYLEY, DRAPER	BAL	231	6TH WARD
BAYLEY, ELIZA	BAL	078	15TH WAR
BAYLEY, ELIZABETH	BAL	032	9TH WARD
BAYLEY, GEDARD	HAR	160	3RD DIST
BAYLEY, GEORGE	BAL	264	20TH WAR
BAYLEY, GEORGE	TAL	045	EASTON T
BAYLEY, HENRY	TAL	001	EASTON D
BAYLEY, HENRY	BAL	025	9TH WARD
BAYLEY, J.	TAL	108	ST MICHA
BAYLEY, JAMES	TAL	106	ST MICHA
BAYLEY, JAMES	KEN	306	3RD DIST
BAYLEY, JAMES P.	BAL	291	12TH WAR
BAYLEY, JANE	BAL	167	6TH WARD
BAYLEY, JANE	TAL	108	ST MICHA
BAYLEY, JOHN	BAL	162	19TH WAR
BAYLEY, JOHN-BLACK	BAL	222	2ND WARD
BAYLEY, LITTLETON	WOR	176	6TH E DI
BAYLEY, MARY	BAL	247	20TH WAR
BAYLEY, NOAH	TAL	104	ST MICHA
BAYLEY, NOAH	TAL	107	ST MICHA
BAYLEY, PETER*	TAL	037	EASTON D
BAYLEY, PHILIP *	HAR	039	1ST DIST
BAYLEY, RACHEL A.	BAL	228	6TH WARD
BAYLEY, SALLY	WOR	222	4TH E DI
BAYLEY, SAMUEL	BAL	227	6TH WARD
BAYLEY, SAMUEL	BAL	057	1ST WARD
BAYLEY, SARAH	BAL	168	6TH WARD
BAYLEY, SARAH	TAL	041	EASTON D
BAYLEY, SARAH A.	BAL	072	1ST WARD
BAYLEY, SUSAN	TAL	010	EASTON D
BAYLEY, THOMAS C.	WOR	234	6TH E DI
BAYLEY, WILLIAM	BAL	186	19TH WAR
BAYLEY, WILLIAM S.	TAL	080	ST MICHA
BAYLIES, GEORGE H.	BAL	191	6TH WARD
BAYLIES, N.	BAL	074	4TH WARD
BAYLOR, BARTHOLAMEW	CAR	250	3RD DIST
BAYLY, ALEXANDER H.	DOR	377	1ST DIST
BAYLY, ANN H.	DOR	377	1ST DIST
BAYLY, BRIDGET	SOM	434	PRINCESS
BAYLY, CAROLINE	BAL	163	2ND DIST
BAYLY, DAVID	SOM	477	TRAPP DI
BAYLY, DINAH	DOR	384	1ST DIST
BAYLY, ELIAS	SOM	466	HANGARY
BAYLY, ELIJAH	SOM	535	QUANTICO
BAYLY, ELIZABETH	FRE	030	FREDERIC
BAYLY, ELLEN V.	BAL	020	18TH WAR
BAYLY, ENOCK	DOR	448	1ST DIST
BAYLY, FRANCIS	BAL	167	6TH WARD
BAYLY, GARDINER	DOR	381	1ST DIST
BAYLY, GEORGE W.	BAL	019	18TH WAR
BAYLY, HAMILTON J.	BAL	288	20TH WAR
BAYLY, HARRY	SOM	480	TRAPP DI
BAYLY, ISAAC	DOR	420	1ST DIST
BAYLY, JACOB	SOM	415	DUBLIN D
BAYLY, JEREMIAH	BAL	242	6TH WARD
BAYLY, JOHN	SOM	450	DAMES QU
BAYLY, JOHN W. H.	SOM	514	BARREN C
BAYLY, KATHLEEN A.	DOR	378	1ST DIST
BAYLY, LUCRETIA	BAL	175	19TH WAR
BAYLY, MARY	BAL	243	6TH WARD
BAYLY, MATILDA	BAL	289	20TH WAR
BAYLY, MITCHELL	DOR	388	1ST DIST
BAYLY, OSIRUS	SOM	515	BARREN C
BAYLY, PETER	DOR	443	1ST DIST
BAYLY, PHOEBE	SOM	495	SALISBUR
BAYLY, ROBERT	SOM	460	HANGARY
BAYLY, SALLY C.	SOM	506	BARREN C
BAYLY, STEPHEN T.	SOM	506	BARREN C
BAYLY, SUSAN	BAL	196	19TH WAR
BAYLY, TAMER	SOM	412	DUBLIN D
BAYLY, THOMAS D.	SOM	506	BARREN C
BAYLY, THOMAS J.	SOM	515	BARREN C
BAYLY, WILLIAM	SOM	476	TRAPPE D
BAYLY, WILLIAM	DOR	415	1ST DIST
BAYLY, WILLIAM	BAL	239	6TH WARD
BAYLY, WILLIAM	BAL	369	8TH WARD
BAYMONT, MIFLIN J.	HAR	082	2ND DIST
BAYMOUNT, EDWARD	HAR	078	2ND DIST
BAYNAR.D GOERG	CAR	065	NO TWP L
BAYNARD, AARON SR.-BLACK	CAR	110	NO TWP L
BAYNARD, AARON-BLACK	CAR	110	NO TWP L
BAYNARD, ANN	BAL	317	20TH WAR
BAYNARD, BENJAMIN	QUE	226	4TH E DI
BAYNARD, CHARLES-BLACK	QUE	146	1ST E DI
BAYNARD, CHARLOTTE ANN-BL	QUE	183	3RD E DI
BAYNARD, DEBORAH	QUE	209	3RD E DI
BAYNARD, EDWARD-BLACK	QUE	194	3RD E DI
BAYNARD, EEMELINE M.	TAL	110	ST MICHA
BAYNARD, ELDRIDGE-BLACK	CAR	095	NO TWP L
BAYNARD, ELIZA	BAL	108	10TH WAR
BAYNARD, ELIZABETH	CAR	105	NO TWP L
BAYNARD, EUGENE-BLACK	CAR	111	NO TWP L
BAYNARD, GEORGE-BLACK	QUE	135	1ST E DI
BAYNARD, HARRIETT	QUE	222	4TH E DI
BAYNARD, HARRIETT	QUE	215	3RD E DI
BAYNARD, JAMES S.	QUE	190	3RD E DI
BAYNARD, JAMES*	DOR	403	1ST DIST
BAYNARD, JOHN	CAR	103	NO TWP L
BAYNARD, JOHN	TAL	100	ST MICHA
BAYNARD, JOHN	TAL	019	EASTON D
BAYNARD, JOSEPH	BAL	157	6TH WARD
BAYNARD, LEVIN	CAR	103	NO TWP L
BAYNARD, LEVIN	CAR	105	NO TWP L
BAYNARD, LUCY A.	BAL	189	17TH WAR
BAYNARD, MARTHA-BLACK	CAR	111	NO TWP L
BAYNARD, MARY	QUE	213	3RD E DI
BAYNARD, PERRY-BLACK	CAR	104	NO TWP L
BAYNARD, PHILLIS	QUE	226	4TH E DI
BAYNARD, ROBERT	CAR	078	NO TWP L
BAYNARD, ROBERT J.H.	QUE	198	3RD E DI
BAYNARD, SAMUEL	QUE	210	3RD E DI
BAYNARD, SARAH	QUE	207	3RD E DI
BAYNARD, SARAH	QUE	206	3RD E DI
BAYNARD, SUSAN	ANN	350	3RD DIST
BAYNARD, THOMAS	ANN	350	3RD DIST
BAYNARD, WESLEY	ANN	356	3RD DIST
BAYNARD, WILLIAM	TAL	019	EASTON D
BAYNARD, WILLIAM H.	TAL	100	ST MICHA
BAYNARD, WILLIAM-BLACK	CAR	068	NO TWP L
BAYNAUSE, JOHN*	TAL	018	EASTON D
BAYNE, CAHRLES D.	BAL	439	8TH WARD
BAYNE, ELVIRA	ALL	021	2ND E.D.
BAYNE, FANNY	MGM	319	CRACKLIN
BAYNE, FREDERICK	BAL	374	8TH WARD
BAYNE, JAMES	DOR	301	1ST DIST
BAYNE, JAMES F.	BAL	097	1ST WARD
BAYNE, JOHN H.	PRI	088	SPALDING
BAYNE, JUDITH C.	PRI	089	SPALDING
BAYNE, L. P.	BAL	046	18TH WAR
BAYNE, S. C.	TAL	041	EASTON D
BAYNE, STEPHEN	BAL	321	7TH WARD
BAYNE, THOMAS REV.	TAL	039	EASTON D
BAYNE, WILLIAM	FRE	241	NEW MARK
BAYNE, WILLIAM C.	ST	306	1ST E DI
BAYNER, HENRY R.	BAL	129	16TH WAR
BAYNES, GEORGE B.	MGM	347	BERRYS D
BAYNES, JAMES	BAL	235	6TH WARD
BAYNES, JOSEPH P.	BAL	188	6TH WARD
BAYNUM, R. M.	WOR	260	BERLIN 1
BAYZANO, WILLIAM H.	BAL	182	6TH WARD
BAZELL, EASTHER	KEN	298	3RD DIST
BAZELL, WILLIAM	KEN	281	3RD DIST
BAZELL, WILLIAM	KEN	280	3RD DIST
BAZER, ISAAC	BAL	161	1ST WARD
BAZET, WASHINGTON	DOR	333	3RD DIVI
BAZIE, ROBERT	BAL	446	14TH WAR
BAZWEL, LOUISA	PRI	054	AQUASCO
BBING, JOHN *	KEN	257	1ST DIST
BEACH, CHARELS W.	BAL	442	14TH WAR
BEACH, CORNELEA	ALL	077	5TH E.D.
BEACH, E.	PRI	103	SPALDING
BEACH, ELIZA	BAL	297	12TH WAR
BEACH, H.	BAL	148	1ST WARD
BEACH, HUMPHREY	SOM	362	BRINKLEY
BEACH, NOEL	BAL	309	12TH WAR
BEACH, REBECCA	BAL	138	18TH WAR
BEACH, THEODORE	SOM	357	BRINKLEY
BEACH, THOMAS J.	BAL	308	12TH WAR
BEACH, WALDON	BAL	008	9TH WARD
BEACH, WILLIAM	BAL	008	9TH WARD
BEACH, WILLIAM	BAL	459	1ST DIST
BEACHAM, ANN	SOM	351	BRINKLEY
BEACHAM, BENJAMIN	SOM	410	DUBLIN D
BEACHAM, C.R.	BAL	225	19TH WAR
BEACHAM, EDWARD	SOM	350	BRINKLEY
BEACHAM, ELISHA	SOM	413	DUBLIN D
BEACHAM, ELIZABETH	BAL	171	11TH WAR
BEACHAM, ELIZABETH	BAL	158	6TH WARD
BEACHAM, ELIZABETH	BAL	251	1ST DIST
BEACHAM, ELLEN	SOM	490	SALISBUR
BEACHAM, GEORGE	SOM	362	BRINKLEY
BEACHAM, HENRY	SOM	401	BRINKLEY
BEACHAM, ISAAC T.	SOM	399	BRINKLEY
BEACHAM, JAMES	BAL	370	3RD WARD
BEACHAM, JESSE	SOM	407	DUBLIN D
BEACHAM, JOHN	BAL	127	11TH WAR
BEACHAM, JOHN	BAL	259	17TH WAR
BEACHAM, JOHN	BAL	127	1ST WARD
BEACHAM, JOHN	BAL	075	1ST WARD
BEACHAM, JOHN	SOM	389	BRINKLEY
BEACHAM, JOSEPH	SOM	449	DAMES QU
BEACHAM, LEAH	SOM	504	SALISBUR
BEACHAM, LEAH W.	SOM	430	PRINCESS
BEACHAM, LENOX	BAL	171	11TH WAR
BEACHAM, LEVIN	SOM	402	BRINKLEY
BEACHAM, LEVIN	SOM	409	DUBLIN D
BEACHAM, MARGARET	SOM	429	PRINCESS
BEACHAM, MARIAH	SOM	363	BRINKLEY
BEACHAM, MILLY	SOM	485	TRAPP DI
BEACHAM, ROBERT	SOM	351	BRINKLEY
BEACHAM, ROBERT	BAL	378	3RD WARD
BEACHAM, SALLY	BAL	126	11TH WAR
BEACHAM, SAMUEL	SOM	362	BRINKLEY
BEACHAM, SARAH	SOM	362	BRINKLEY
BEACHAM, SELBY	SOM	437	PRINCESS
BEACHAM, THOMAS	SOM	407	DUBLIN D
BEACHAM, THOMAS H.	SOM	401	BRINKLEY
BEACHAM, TUBMAN	SOM	414	DUBLIN D
BEACHAM, WILLIAM	SOM	436	PRINCESS
BEACHAM, WILLIAM	WOR	179	6TH E DI
BEACHAM, WILLIAM W.	SOM	429	PRINCESS
BEACHAMP, CURTIS	CAR	135	NO TWP L
BEACHAMP, ELIZA	CAR	133	NO TWP L
BEACHAMP, JEREMIAH	CAR	105	NO TWP L
BEACHAMP, JOHN E.	CAR	072	NO TWP L
BEACHAMP, RHODY	CAR	135	NO TWP L
BEACHAMP, THOMAS	CAR	113	NO TWP L
BEACHAMP, THOMAS	CAR	133	NO TWP L
BEACHAMP, WILLIAM	WOR	340	1ST E DI
BEACHAMP.LEVIN A.	CAR	139	NO TWP L
BEACHAN, SARAH	BAL	020	1ST WARD
BEACHAVE, WILLIAM	BAL	020	2ND DIST
BEACHBERD, MARGARET	WOR	350	1ST E DI
BEACHBORD, JAMES	WOR	300	SNOW HIL
BEACHEAM, CATHARINE	BAL	268	17TH WAR
BEACHEAM, JOHN	BAL	207	11TH WAR
BEACHEAN, SAMUEL	BAL	207	11TH WAR
BEACHER, ELISHA	SOM	386	BRINKLEY
BEACHER, ESTHER	SOM	407	DUBLIN D
BEACHER, WHITTY	SOM	389	BRINKLEY
BEACHEY, ABRAM	ALL	009	3RD E.D.
BEACHEY, CHRISTIAN	ALL	010	3RD E.D.
BEACHEY, DANIEL	ALL	039	2ND E.D.
BEACHEY, ELIZABETH	ALL	009	3RD E.D.
BEACHEY, EMANUEL	ALL	010	3RD E.D.
BEACHEY, SAMUEL	ALL	058	10TH E.D
BEACHFORD, ELIZABETH	BAL	178	2ND DIST
BEACHLEY, CONRAD	FRE	352	MIDDLETO
BEACHLEY, JOHN	FRE	324	MIDDLETO
BEACHLORD, WILLIAM	WOR	299	SNOW HIL
BEACHTREE, CATHERINE MRS-	BAL	315	20TH WAR
BEACHUM, JAMES	WOR	250	1ST CENS
BEACHUM, JANE	SOM	404	BRINKLEY
BEACHUM, MILBORN	WOR	250	1ST CENS
BEACHY, CHISTLEY	ALL	017	3RD E.D.
BEACHY, ELIAS	ALL	008	3RD E.D.
BEACHY, JOEL	ALL	014	3RD E.D.
BEACHY, JOHN	ALL	017	3RD E.D.
BEACK, W.J.	BAL	248	1ST DIST
BEACKAM, J. REBECCA	BAL	385	13TH WAR
BEACONCOFF, MARY	BAL	063	4TH WARD
BEACSLAND, MICHAEL	ALL	047	10TH E.D
BEACTLY, MARTIN	WAS	035	2ND SUBD
BEACULORD, WILLIAM*	SOM	400	BRINKLEY
BEAD, ELIZA	BAL	286	2ND WARD
BEADEL, JOHN DR. *	BAL	369	13TH WAR
BEADL, WILLAIM	ALL	160	6TH E.D.
BEADS, JOHN	BAL	118	2ND DIST
BEAGAN, PHILIP	BAL	367	8TH WARD
BEAGER, ANTON	BAL	229	2ND WARD
BEAGLE, JOHN	BAL	170	2ND DIST
BEAHR, ARMENIA	BAL	137	18TH WAR
BEAHR, LEWIS	BAL	137	18TH WAR
BEAHRENS, HENRY	BAL	219	17TH WAR
BEAK, JAMES	ALL	103	5TH E.D.
BEAKE, WILLIAM	ALL	102	5TH E.D.
BEAKEH, GEORGE	BAL	468	14TH WAR
BEAKEY, JOSEPH	FRE	165	EMMITTSB
BEAKLEY, JANE	QUE	220	3RD E DI
BEAL, ALEXANDER	BAL	072	4TH WARD
BEAL, ALPHEUS	ALL	239	CUMBERLA
BEAL, ANN M.-MULATTO	ST	303	2ND E DI
BEAL, CHALRES	BAL	037	18TH WAR
BEAL, CHARITY-BLACK	ST	303	2ND E DI
BEAL, DAVID	FRE	281	WOODSBOR
BEAL, EMILY MISS-	BAL	315	20TH WAR
BEAL, HENRY	BAL	413	1ST DIST
BEAL, HENRY-BLACK	ST	302	2ND E DI
BEAL, JACOB	FRE	281	WOODSBOR
BEAL, JEMIMA	ANN	490	HOWARD D
BEAL, JOHN	FRE	281	WOODSBOR
BEAL, LEWIS	FRE	300	WOODSBOR
BEAL, WILLIAM	CAR	311	1ST DIST
BEAL, WILLIAM E.	BAL	297	7TH WARD
BEAL, WILLIAM-BLACK	ST	302	2ND E DI
BEALE, BASIL	MGM	440	CLARKSTR
BEALE, BASIL	MGM	388	ROCKERLE
BEALE, BASIL M.	MGM	390	ROCKERLE
BEALE, GEORGE	ST	308	1ST E DI
BEALE, GEORGE-BLACK	ST	291	2ND E DI
BEALE, HORACE	MGM	441	CLARKSTR
BEALE, HORATIO	PRI	014	BLADENSB
BEALE, ISAAC	CAR	248	3RD DIST
BEALE, JAMES	ALL	112	5TH E.D.
BEALE, JAMES	ALL	122	4TH E.D.
BEALE, JAMES T.	MGM	436	CLARKSTR
BEALE, JOHN	QUE	208	3RD E DI
BEALE, JOHN W.	MGM	441	CLARKSTR
BEALE, MARIA T.	ST	307	1ST E DI
BEALE, RICHARD D.	MGM	383	ROCKERLE
BEALE, SAMUEL M.	MGM	386	ROCKERLE
BEALE, SERELA	MGM	389	ROCKERLE
BEALE, SOLON	BAL	214	6TH WARD
BEALE, THOMAS	BAL	262	2ND WARD
BEALE, WILLIAM S.	MGM	440	CLARKSTR
BEALL, ABSALOM	MGM	354	BERRYS D
BEALL, ALFORD	ALL	222	CUMBERLA
BEALL, ALPHEUS	PRI	081	QUEEN AN
BEALL, ALPHEUS B.	ALL	165	6TH E.D.
BEALL, AMANDA	BAL	357	13TH WAR
BEALL, AMELIA	PRI	006	BLADENSB
BEALL, ASA	ALL	165	6TH E.D.
BEALL, ASA	ALL	207	CUMBERLA
BEALL, ASA	ALL	210	CUMBERLA
BEALL, AVORY C.	MGM	416	MEDLEY 3
BEALL, AZEL	PRI	008	BLADENSB
BEALL, BARTHOLOMEW	FRE	058	FREDERIC
BEALL, BELINDA	FRE	244	NEW MARK
BEALL, BENJAMIN	PRI	036	VANSVILL
BEALL, BURIL	PRI	015	BLADENSB
BEALL, CHARITY	MGM	425	MEDLEY 3
BEALL, CHARLES	MGM	355	BERRYS D
BEALL, CHARLES	ALL	007	3RD E.D.
BEALL, CHARLES R.	PRI	115	PISCATAW
BEALL, CHARLES W.	MGM	351	BERRYS D
BEALL, DENNIS	PRI	073	MARLBROU
BEALL, E.M.	PRI	104	PISCATAW
BEALL, EDITHAL	ALL	238	CUMBERLA
BEALL, EDWN	MGM	369	BERRYS D
BEALL, ELISHA	MGM	433	CLARKSTR
BEALL, ELIZA	MGM	362	BERRYS D
BEALL, ELIZABETH	FRE	001	FREDERIC
BEALL, ELIZABETH	ALL	091	5TH E.D.
BEALL, EMMA	ALL	213	CUMBERLA
BEALL, EMORY M.	FRE	233	BUCKEYST
BEALL, ENOCH	FRE	452	8TH E DI
BEALL, FRANCIS	FRE	043	FREDERIC
BEALL, G.B.	PRI	076	MARLBROU
BEALL, GEORGE T.	PRI	015	BLADENSB
BEALL, GEORGE W.	PRI	004	BLADENSB
BEALL, GEORGE W.	PRI	076	MARLBROU
BEALL, GEORGE W.	FRE	274	NEW MARK
BEALL, GRACE C.	PRI	066	NOTTINGH
BEALL, GUSTAVUS	ALL	229	CUMBERLA
BEALL, HARRIET-BLACK	MGM	412	MEDLEY 3
BEALL, HARRIET-BLACK	MGM	408	MEDLEY 3
BEALL, HENRY T.	ALL	007	3RD E.D.
BEALL, HEZEKIAH	FRE	272	NEW MARK
BEALL, ISAIAH	MGM	369	BERRYS D
BEALL, JAMES	MGM	425	MEDLEY 3
BEALL, JAMES	ALL	092	5TH E.D.
BEALL, JAMES B.	MGM	401	ROCKERLE
BEALL, JOHN	ALL	146	6TH E.D.
BEALL, JOHN	ALL	235	CUMBERLA
BEALL, JOHN	ALL	225	CUMBERLA
BEALL, JOHN	PRI	091	MARLBROU
BEALL, JOHN	PRI	091	MARLBROU
BEALL, JOHN	PRI	039	VANSVILL
BEALL, JOHN A.	FRE	001	FREDERIC
BEALL, JOHN B.	PRI	045	VANSVILL
BEALL, JOHN D.	PRI	077	MARLBROU

BEALL, JOHN H. PRI 118 PISCATAW
BEALL, JOHN H. FRE 264 NEW MARK
BEALL, JOHN T.G. FRE 224 BUCKEYST
BEALL, JOHN V. PRI 081 QUEEN AN
BEALL, JOSEPHUS ALL 183 8TH E.D.
BEALL, JOSHUA PRI 009 BLADENSB
BEALL, JOSHUA FRE 256 NEW MARK
BEALL, JOSIAH MGM 351 BERRYS D
BEALL, LAVINA ALL 001 3RD E.D.
BEALL, LEMUEL MGM 415 MEDLEY 3
BEALL, LEONARD H. BAL 048 18TH WAR
BEALL, LEVEN C. FRE 223 BUCKEYST
BEALL, LOUISA MGM 382 ROCKERLE
BEALL, LUCRETIA R. MGM 367 BERRYS D
BEALL, LUCY ALL 246 CUMBERLA
BEALL, MARGARETT MGM 363 BERRYS D
BEALL, MARIA L. MGM 383 ROCKERLE
BEALL, MARK PRI 077 MARLBROU
BEALL, MARY PRI 091 MARLBROU
BEALL, MARY PRI 015 BLADENSB
BEALL, MARY PRI 015 BLADENSB
BEALL, MARY PRI 063 NOTTINGH
BEALL, MARY FRE 226 BUCKEYST
BEALL, MARY ALL 106 5TH E.D.
BEALL, MATILDA MGM 404 ROCKERLE
BEALL, NACE PRI 078 MARLBROU
BEALL, NANCY FRE 063 FREDERIC
BEALL, NATHAN MGM 351 BERRYS D
BEALL, NATHANIEL FRE 274 NEW MARK
BEALL, NELSON ALL 091 5TH E.D.
BEALL, NINIAN PRI 045 VANSVILL
BEALL, ORATIO BAL 084 18TH WAR
BEALL, OTHO B. PRI 014 BLADENSB
BEALL, OTHO-BLACK MGM 418 MEDLEY 3
BEALL, PHILLLIP PRI 106 PISCATAW
BEALL, R. B. BAL 279 20TH WAR
BEALL, R.H. PRI 121 PISCATAW
BEALL, R.H. PRI 068 NOTTINGH
BEALL, RACHEL BAL 357 13TH WAR
BEALL, RENNIS PRI 091 MARLBROU
BEALL, RICHARD PRI 010 BLADENSB
BEALL, RICHARD ALL 091 5TH E.D.
BEALL, RIZEN ALL 165 6TH E.D.
BEALL, ROBERTA MGM 320 CRACKLIN
BEALL, SAMUEL H. CHA 262 MIDDLETO
BEALL, SARAH FRE 033 FREDERIC
BEALL, SARAH JANE ALL 207 CUMBERLA
BEALL, SHADERICK PRI 036 VANSVILL
BEALL, SUSAN FRE 258 NEW MARK
BEALL, THEOPHILUS PRI 011 BLADENSB
BEALL, THOMAS PRI 039 VANSVILL
BEALL, THOMAS FRE 238 NEW MARK
BEALL, THOMAS MGM 368 BERRYS D
BEALL, THOMAS ALL 164 6TH E.D.
BEALL, THOMAS ALL 165 6TH E.D.
BEALL, THOMAS ALL 091 5TH E.D.
BEALL, THOMAS B. PRI 036 VANSVILL
BEALL, THOMAS L. PRI 065 NOTTINGH
BEALL, WASHINGTON J. PRI 076 MARLBROU
BEALL, WILLIAM PRI 083 QUEEN AN
BEALL, WILLIAM ALL 212 CUMBERLA
BEALL, WILLIAM ALL 135 4TH E.D.
BEALL, WILLIAM FRE 261 NEW MARK
BEALL, WILLIAM FRE 276 NEW MARK
BEALL, WILLIAM FRE 008 FREDERIC
BEALL, WILLIAM H. MGM 368 BERRYS D
BEALL, WILLIAM Z. PRI 073 MARLBROU
BEALL.ELEMA MGM 409 MEDLEY 3
BEALL.W ILLIAM R. FRE 233 BUCKEYST
BEALLE, ALVIN F. CHA 255 MIDDLETO
BEALLE, MARY MGM 379 ROCKERLE
BEALLE, PENELOPE A. CHA 254 MIDDLETO
BEALLE, PRISCILLA MGM 435 CLARKSTR
BEALLE, WILLIAM CHA 253 MIDDLETO
BEALLE, WILLIAM P. HAR 105 2ND DIST
BEALMEAR, THOMAS BAL 178 16TH WAR
BEALD, THOMAS ST 345 5TH E DI
BEALS, FREDERICK FRE 027 FREDERIC
BEALS, SARAH ALL 243 CUMBERLA
BEAM, ADELINE CAR 236 UNION TO
BEAM, ALEXANDER CEC 146 PORT DUP
BEAM, ANNA R. BAL 060 1ST WARD
BEAM, BARBARA BAL 251 1ST DIST
BEAM, BENJAMIN BAL 077 1ST WARD
BEAM, BENJAMIN BAL 059 1ST WARD
BEAM, CHRISTIANA BAL 003 1ST WARD
BEAM, DAVID BAL 352 13TH WAR
BEAM, ELIZABETH BAL 395 1ST DIST
BEAM, FANNY ALL 095 5TH E.D.
BEAM, HENRY BAL 253 1ST DIST
BEAM, HENRY BAL 203 19TH WAR
BEAM, HENRY C. BAL 268 1ST DIST
BEAM, JOHN ALL 223 CUMBERLA
BEAM, JOSEPH BAL 296 1ST DIST
BEAM, LYDIA M. WAS 286 1ST DIST
BEAM, MINERVA ALL 095 5TH E.D.
BEAM, SAMUEL BAL 268 1ST DIST
BEAM, SAMUEL FRE 162 EMMITTSB
BEAM, SIMEON BAL 060 1ST WARD
BEAM, STEPHEN J. CEC 153 PORT DUP
BEAM, WILLIAM BAL 325 1ST DIST
BEAM,S AMUEL ALL 236 CUMBERLA
BEAMDSBER, CHRISTIAN BAL 354 7TH WARD
BEAMER, HENRY BAL 236 1ST DIST
BEAMER, HENRY WAS 263 1ST DIST
BEAMONT, ISAAC BAL 466 14TH WAR
BEAMS, ANDREW BAL 382 1ST DIST
BEAMS, GEORGE ALL 103 5TH E.D.
BEAMS, NANCY BAL 120 18TH WAR
BEAMS, THOMAS BAL 082 2ND DIST
BEAMS, WILLIAM FRE 128 CREAGERS
BEAN, ADAM BAL 453 8TH WARD
BEAN, ADWAY ALL 221 CUMBERLA
BEAN, ALEXANDER H. MGM 395 ROCKERLE
BEAN, AMOS W. MGM 395 ROCKERLE
BEAN, ANN E. CHA 294 BOJANTOW
BEAN, ANN E. ST 310 1ST E DI
BEAN, BASIL MGM 402 ROCKERLE
BEAN, BENNETT ST 289 2ND E DI
BEAN, CATHARINE T.A. ST 303 2ND E DI
BEAN, CHARLES ANN 338 3RD DIST
BEAN, CHARLES* TAL 050 EASTON T
BEAN, CHARLOTTE ST 274 3RD E DI
BEAN, COLMORE MGM 355 BERRYS D
BEAN, DENNIS PRI 070 MARLBROU
BEAN, DORCAS ST 298 2ND E DI
BEAN, ELIZABETH MGM 403 ROCKERLE
BEAN, EMILY ST 307 1ST E DI
BEAN, FRANKLIN BAL 269 20TH WAR
BEAN, GEORGE ST 299 2ND E DI
BEAN, GEORGE PRI 079 MARLBROU
BEAN, GOERGE PRI 121 PISCATAW
BEAN, GRACE B. PRI 089 SPALDING
BEAN, H.E. PRI 114 PISCATAW
BEAN, HEZEKIAH H. CHA 276 ALLENS F
BEAN, HOPEWELL WAS 162 2ND DIST
BEAN, JAMES CAL 013 1ST DIST
BEAN, JOHN MGM 394 ROCKERLE
BEAN, JOHN MGM 403 ROCKERLE
BEAN, JOHN MGM 395 ROCKERLE
BEAN, JCHN MGM 364 BERRYS D
BEAN, JOHN BAL 032 1ST WARD
BEAN, JOHN C. MGM 364 BERRYS D
BEAN, JOHN H. CHA 251 MIDDLETO
BEAN, JOHN H. ST 297 2ND E DI
BEAN, JOHN L. ST 290 2ND E DI
BEAN, JOHN W. MGM 402 ROCKERLE
BEAN, JOSEPH BAL 269 20TH WAR
BEAN, JOSEPH A. ST 301 2ND E DI
BEAN, LEMUEL MGM 317 CRACKLIN
BEAN, MARIA ST 313 1ST E DI
BEAN, MARTHA MGM 404 ROCKERLE
BEAN, MARY ST 313 1ST E DI
BEAN, MARY ST 310 1ST E DI
BEAN, MILLEAR N. CHA 251 MIDDLETO
BEAN, PHELPS ALL 088 5TH E.D.
BEAN, RICHARD MGM 403 ROCKERLE
BEAN, ROBERT ST 310 1ST E DI
BEAN, ROBERT M. BAL 392 3RD WARD
BEAN, SALLY CHA 290 BOJANTOW
BEAN, SAMUEL CAR 408 2ND DIST
BEAN, SMUEL ALL 221 CUMBERLA
BEAN, STEPHEN L. ST 294 2ND E DI
BEAN, SUSAN PRI 099 SPALDING
BEAN, THOMAS PRI 072 MARLBROU
BEAN, THOMAS PRI 090 MARLBROU
BEAN, THOMAS WAS 126 2ND DIST
BEAN, THOMAS V. CHA 258 BOJANTOW
BEAN, VIRGINIA BAL 048 18TH WAR
BEANAN, JOHN BAL 358 13TH WAR
BEANCHAND, WILLIAM BAL 190 2ND WARD
BEANDENBURG, MAHALA FRE 353 MIDDLETO
BEANOR, THOMAS K. BAL 269 2ND WARD
BEANS, SALLIE BAL 142 11TH WAR
BEAR, ANNA C. FRE 166 EMMITTSB
BEAR, BETSY BAL 268 2ND WARD
BEAR, C. D. BAL 282 2ND WARD
BEAR, CATHERINE FRE 062 FREDERIC
BEAR, CHRISTOPHER BAL 070 1ST WARD
BEAR, DAN WAS 252 1ST DIST
BEAR, ELIZABETH WAS 097 2ND DIST
BEAR, ELLEN WAS 219 1ST DIST
BEAR, GEORGE WAS 097 2ND DIST
BEAR, GEORGE FRE 339 MIDDLETO
BEAR, GECRGE FRE 032 FREDERIC
BEAR, GEORGE FRE 312 MIDDLETO
BEAR, ISAAC WAS 299 1ST DIST
BEAR, JACOB WAS 275 RIDGEVIL
BEAR, JACOB WAS 217 1ST DIST
BEAR, JACOB WAS 219 1ST DIST
BEAR, JACOB FRE 222 BUCKEYST
BEAR, JACOB H. FRE 092 FREDERIC
BEAR, JOHN WAS 265 1ST DIST
BEAR, JOHN WAS 252 1ST DIST
BEAR, JOHN WAS 266 1ST DIST
BEAR, JOHN WAS 299 1ST DIST
BEAR, JOHN FRE 176 5TH E DI
BEAR, JOHN FRE 177 5TH E DI
BEAR, JOHN BAL 059 18TH WAR
BEAR, JOHN BAL 132 5TH WARD
BEAR, JOHN BAL 102 15TH WAR
BEAR, JOSEPH FRE 336 MIDDLETO
BEAR, MARGARET WAS 182 BOONSBOR
BEAR, MARGARET MISS- BAL 315 20TH WAR
BEAR, MARTIN WAS 299 1ST DIST
BEAR, MARY C. WAS 299 1ST DIST
BEAR, MATILDA FRE 222 BUCKEYST
BEAR, MEYER BAL 422 14TH WAR
BEAR, NIMROD BAL 033 18TH WAR
BEAR, PHILIP FRE 337 MIDDLETO
BEAR, SAMUEL WAS 258 1ST DIST
BEAR, WILLIAM CAR 231 5TH DIST
BEAR, WILLIAM G. FRE 332 MIDDLETO
BEARAN, THOMAS BAL 106 1ST WARD
BEARD, ADAM WAS 144 2ND DIST
BEARD, ANNA WAS 236 CAVETOWN
BEARD, BENIDICT BAL 423 1ST DIST
BEARD, CATHARIN FRE 213 BUCKEYST
BEARD, CATHARINE BAL 206 19TH WAR
BEARD, CATHARINE FRE 148 10TH E D
BEARD, CATHARINE WAS 179 BOONSBOR
BEARD, DANIEL WAS 241 CAVETOWN
BEARD, DENTON WAS 138 2ND DIST
BEARD, ELIZA BAL 224 6TH WARD
BEARD, ELIZA ANN 274 ANNAPOLI
BEARD, ELIZABETH WAS 245 SMITHSBU
BEARD, ELIZABETH WAS 262 1ST DIST
BEARD, ELIZABETH FRE 320 MIDDLETO
BEARD, ELLEN WAS 148 2ND DIST
BEARD, GEORGE WAS 157 2ND DIST
BEARD, GEORGE WAS 241 CAVETOWN
BEARD, GEORGE W. FRE 079 FREDERIC
BEARD, HANAH BAL 032 2ND DIST
BEARD, HENRY CAR 410 2ND DIST
BEARD, HIRAM WAS 039 2ND SUBD
BEARD, HUGH HAR 043 1ST DIST
BEARD, JACOB FRE 291 WOODSBOR
BEARD, JACOB JR. FRE 296 WOODSBOR
BEARD, JAMES BAL 216 11TH WAR
BEARD, JOHN CAR 284 7TH DIST
BEARD, JOHN CAR 202 4TH DIST
BEARD, JOHN FRE 296 WOODSBOR
BEARD, JOHN CAR 411 2ND DIST
BEARD, JOHN DOR 443 1ST DIST
BEARD, JOHN CAR 400 2ND DIST
BEARD, JOHN WAS 093 2ND SUBD
BEARD, JOHN WAS 251 1ST DIST
BEARD, JOHN WAS 217 1ST DIST
BEARD, JOHN WAS 163 2ND DIST
BEARD, JOHN ALL 060 10TH E.D
BEARD, JOHN ANN 326 2ND DIST
BEARD, JOHN BAL 423 1ST DIST
BEARD, JOHN BAL 072 15TH WAR
BEARD, JOHN BAL 047 15TH WAR
BEARD, JOHN D. FRE 273 NEW MARK
BEARD, JOHN HENRY FRE 196 5TH E DI
BEARD, JOSEPH FRE 073 FREDERIC
BEARD, JOSIAH BAL 427 1ST DIST
BEARD, JULIA A. CAR 411 2ND DIST
BEARD, LEWIS BAL 182 16TH WAR
BEARD, LEWIS WAS 148 2ND DIST
BEARD, LOUISA WAS 217 1ST DIST
BEARD, LYDIA WAS 117 2ND DIST
BEARD, MARCELLUS DOR 438 1ST DIST
BEARD, MARGARET BAL 273 20TH WAR
BEARD, MARGARET BAL 364 1ST DIST
BEARD, MARGARET E. WAS 246 SMITHSBU
BEARD, MARY FRE 313 MIDDLETO
BEARD, MARY FRE 194 5TH E DI
BEARD, MARY A. FRE 076 FREDERIC
BEARD, MARY A. WAS 109 2ND DIST
BEARD, MARY A. ANN 314 1ST DIST
BEARD, MARY A. BAL 222 6TH WARD
BEARD, MARY J. FRE 320 MIDDLETO
BEARD, MATHIAS FRE 296 WOODSBOR
BEARD, MICHAEL WAS 187 BOONSBOR
BEARD, NANCY DOR 443 1ST DIST
BEARD, NICHOLAS WAS 280 LEITERSB
BEARD, NICHOLAS WAS 234 1ST DIST
BEARD, PETER FRE 296 WOODSBOR
BEARD, PHILIP FRE 412 8TH E DI
BEARD, SAMUEL WAS 234 1ST DIST
BEARD, SAMUEL WAS 144 2ND DIST
BEARD, SOLOMON FRE 296 WOODSBOR
BEARD, STEPHEN JR. ANN 325 2ND DIST
BEARD, STEPHEN SR. ANN 325 2ND DIST
BEARD, SUSAN ANN 317 1ST DIST
BEARD, SUSANNA WAS 230 1ST DIST
BEARD, THOMAS R. ANN 326 2ND DIST
BEARD, THOMAS W. PRI 107 PISCATAW
BEARD, W. W. CAL 021 2ND DIST
BEARD, WILLIAM WAS 013 WILLIAMS
BEARD, WILLIAM ALL 241 CUMBERLA
BEARD, WILLIAM H. WAS 234 1ST DIST
BEARDLEY, MARGARET BAL 155 11TH WAR
BEARERMAN, WIHEMA BAL 152 11TH WAR
BEARHART, HENRY* BAL 178 2ND DIST
BEARIN, ISAAC BAL 157 1ST WARD
BEARINGER, HENRY ALL 148 6TH E.D.
BEARN, MARY A. BAL 170 19TH WAR
BEARN, WILLIAM J. BAL 170 19TH WAR
BEARNES, JOHN BAL 007 9TH WARD
BEARS, ELIZA BAL 142 16TH WAR
BEARS, WILLIAM BAL 150 2ND DIST
BEARSHEARS, MARY A. BAL 206 11TH WAR
BEARSNIDER, HENRY FRE 154 10TH E D
BEARSOCK, JOHN BAL 289 1ST DIST
BEARTON, THOMAS* TAL 067 EASTON T
BEASE, CHARLES* TAL 050 EASTON T
BEASEL, ELLEN BAL 382 8TH WARD
BEASEL, HENRY BAL 381 8TH WARD
BEASHEAR, ZACHARIAH FRE 250 NEW MARK
BEASLA, GEORGE BAL 338 1ST DIST
BEASLEY, NANCY BAL 036 15TH WAR
BEASMAN, JOHN BAL 357 1ST DIST
BEASMAN, LOYDE BAL 250 1ST DIST
BEASMAN, NIMROD BAL 362 1ST DIST
BEASMAN, SYLVESTER BAL 229 1ST DIST
BEASMAN, VACHIEL W. BAL 229 1ST DIST
BEASSMAN, WILLIAM BAL 135 5TH WARD
BEASTALL, MARGARET BAL 266 7TH WARD
BEASTEN, GEORGE J. BAL 175 16TH WAR
BEASTON, MARY S. KEN 296 3RD DIST
BEASTON, THOMAS* TAL 067 EASTON T
BEATE, WILLIAM CAR 191 4TH DIST
BEATEN, SOPHIA-BLACK ST 322 4TH E DI
BEATHAND, WILLIAM G. WOR 225 4TH E DI
BEATHARD, ADAM P. WOR 225 4TH E DI
BEATHARD, ISAAC WOR 286 BERLIN 1
BEATHARD, JAMES WOR 254 1ST CENS
BEATHARD, MARY J. WOR 226 4TH E DI
BEATHARD, RICHARDM. WOR 225 4TH E DI
BEATHARDS, SALLY C. WOR 255 1ST CENS
BEATIN, MATILDA-BLACK ST 333 4TH E DI
BEATIS, WILLIAM H. BAL 020 4TH WARD
BEATLE, JOHN TAL 067 EASTON T
BEATLY, CATHARINE FRE 146 10TH E D
BEATLY, GEORGE* BAL 313 3RD WARD
BEATLY, MARY E. FRE 137 CREAGERS
BEATLY, WILLAIM R. BAL 278 2ND WARD
BEATSON, JOHN BAL 067 10TH WAR
BEATTECOURT, WILLIAM H. WAS 021 2ND SUBD
BEATTEY, JOHN * WAS 055 2ND SUBD
BEATTIE, WILLAIM BAL 137 2ND DIST
BEATTY, ANN BAL 274 12TH WAR
BEATTY, CHARLES BAL 175 2ND DIST
BEATTY, CORNELIUS E. BAL 103 10TH WAR
BEATTY, EDWARD WAS 133 HAGERSTO
BEATTY, ELIE WAS 140 HAGERSTO
BEATTY, ELIZA G. BAL 061 10TH WAR
BEATTY, GEORGE BAL 127 1ST WARD
BEATTY, GEORGE BAL 132 1ST WARD
BEATTY, GEORGE J. WAS 132 HAGERSTO
BEATTY, GEORGE W. FRE 204 BUCKEYST
BEATTY, HENRIETTA BAL 274 12TH WAR
BEATTY, HENRY E. WAS 015 2ND SUBD
BEATTY, ISAIAH BAL 111 1ST WARD
BEATTY, J.G.T. WAS 124 HAGERSTO
BEATTY, JAMES BAL 218 6TH DIST
BEATTY, JAMES BAL 061 10TH WAR
BEATTY, JAMES JR. BAL 380 1ST DIST
BEATTY, LEWIS A. FRE 145 10TH E D
BEATTY, LEWIS H. QUE 145 1ST E DI
BEATTY, MARY A. CEC 164 6TH E DI
BEATTY, MICHAEL BAL 001 15TH WAR
BEATTY, ROBERT S. BAL 008 1ST WARD
BEATTY, ROSE CHA 226 ALLENS F
BEATTY, SARAH FRE 027 FREDERIC
BEATTY, SARAH BAL 262 2ND WARD
BEATTY, WILLIAM H.T. FRE 028 FREDERIC
BEATY, ARCHIBALD BAL 462 1ST DIST
BEATY, MARY BAL 440 14TH WAR
BEATY, SARAH A. BAL 083 15TH WAR
BEATY, SOPHIA BAL 347 3RD WARD
BEATY, WILLIAM H. BAL 155 11TH WAR
BEATZELL, JOHN H. BAL 077 18TH WAR
BEATZELL, MARTHA A. BAL 079 18TH WAR
BEAUCHAM, MARY A. BAL 180 19TH WAR
BEAUCHAMP, ELIZABETH BAL 006 15TH WAR
BEAUCHAMP, LEVIN W. WOR 184 6TH E DI
BEAUCHAMP, MARY BAL 006 15TH WAR
BEAUCHAMP, SUSAN WOR 200 3RD E DI
BEAUFIT, JAMES BAL 150 5TH WARD
BEAUMONT, A. BAL 063 10TH WAR
BEAUSEY, JAMES BAL 052 18TH WAR
BEAVAN, WALTER W. ST 344 5TH E DI
BEAVEN, JAMES PRI 102 SPALDING
BEAVER, ANDREW J. CAR 199 4TH DIST
BEAVER, BARBARA WAS 280 LEITERSB
BEAVER, F. PRI 088 SPALDING

BEAVER, JACOB CAR 272 WESTMINS
BEAVER, JOHN CAR 280 7TH DIST
BEAVER, MARGARET CAR 282 7TH DIST
BEAVER, MARGARET CEC 174 6TH E DI
BEAVER, ROBERT CHA 281 BOJANTOW
BEAVER, ROBERT PRI 069 MARLBROU
BEAVER, SUSAN CAR 282 7TH DIST
BEAVER, THOMAS QUE 185 3RD E DI
BEAVER, WILLIAM CAR 280 7TH DIST
BEAVIN, JOHN W. CHA 270 ALLENS F
BEAWNER, C. D. CHA 219 ALLENS F
BEAZLEY, CHRISTIAN BAL 246 6TH WARD
BEBA, TOBED CEC 035 CHESAPEA
BEBEE, JOHN S. BAL 182 16TH WAR
BEBEE, SAMUEL BAL 136 16TH WAR
BEBELL, JOHN BAL 236 20TH WAR
BEBIE, HENRY BAL 072 10TH WAR
BECAY, EDWARD ALL 162 6TH E.D.
BECCA, RACHEL FRE 107 CREAGERS
BECE, BARRY BAL 251 20TH WAR
BECHEL, LEWIS BAL 301 7TH WARD
BECHLER, CHARLOTTE M. BAL 335 13TH WAR
BECHLER, JULIA BAL 165 16TH WAR
BECHLY, JONATHAN FRE 352 MIDDLETO
BECHT, MARY A. FRE 286 WOODSBOR
BECHTEL, HENRY CAR 246 3RD DIST
BECHTEL, MARYANN FRE 428 8TH E DI
BECHTEL, MATILDA CAR 246 3RD DIST
BECHTIE, MARY BAL 258 12TH WAR
BECHTOL, DANIEL FRE 345 MIDDLETO
BECHTOL, JOHN FRE 078 FREDERIC
BECHTOL, SAMUEL HAR 062 1ST DIST
BECHTOL, SAMUEL CAR 253 3RD DIST
BECK, AARON FRE 304 WOODSBOR
BECK, ADAM BAL 275 20TH WAR
BECK, AJMES KEN 244 2ND DIST
BECK, ALEXANDER CEC 037 CHESAPEA
BECK, ANN QUE 153 1ST E DI
BECK, ANN BAL 145 19TH WAR
BECK, ANN BAL 035 18TH WAR
BECK, ANSEL BAL 201 19TH WAR
BECK, ARAMINTA KEN 241 2ND DIST
BECK, ARAMINTA BAL 159 6TH WARD
BECK, BARBARY BAL 034 18TH WAR
BECK, BENJAMIN R. KEN 262 1ST DIST
BECK, CAROLINE BAL 033 1ST WARD
BECK, CASPAR BAL 202 19TH WAR
BECK, CASPER BAL 458 8TH WARD
BECK, CHARLES BAL 167 1ST WARD
BECK, CHRISTIAN BAL 281 17TH WAR
BECK, DAVID CEC 096 4TH E DI
BECK, DAVID H. WAS 159 HAGERSTO
BECK, EDWARD KEN 265 1ST DIST
BECK, ELIZA KEN 291 3RD DIST
BECK, ELIZA BAL 045 18TH WAR
BECK, ELIZABETH KEN 253 1ST DIST
BECK, ELIZABETH FRE 286 WOODSBOR
BECK, ELIZABETH PRI 043 VANSVILL
BECK, EVE BAL 451 8TH WARD
BECK, F. BAL 166 1ST WARD
BECK, FRANCIS BAL 405 3RD WARD
BECK, FREDERICK BAL 295 7TH WARD
BECK, FREDERICK BAL 209 17TH WAR
BECK, GEORGE KEN 245 2ND DIST
BECK, GEORGE CAR 176 8TH DIST
BECK, GEORGE BAL 201 2ND WARD
BECK, GEORGE KEN 273 1ST DIST
BECK, HENRY BAL 217 19TH WAR
BECK, HORATIO KEN 262 1ST DIST
BECK, JACOB CAR 194 4TH DIST
BECK, JAMES FRE 303 WOODSBOR
BECK, JAMES WAS 068 2ND SUBD
BECK, JAMES BAL 240 12TH WAR
BECK, JEREMIAH CAR 382 2ND DIST
BECK, JOHN KEN 242 2ND DIST
BECK, JOHN BAL 242 20TH WAR
BECK, JOHN BAL 268 12TH WAR
BECK, JOHN BAL 010 15TH WAR
BECK, JOHN BAL 270 2ND WARD
BECK, JOHN BAL 165 16TH WAR
BECK, JOHN WAS 293 1ST DIST
BECK, JOHN QUE 172 2ND E DI
BECK, LAURA KEN 290 3RD DIST
BECK, LEMUEL KEN 233 2ND DIST
BECK, LIZZY BAL 306 3RD WARD
BECK, MALINDA WAS 292 1ST DIST
BECK, MARTHA KEN 291 3RD DIST
BECK, MARY A. FRE 305 WOODSBOR
BECK, MARY ANN BAL 237 17TH WAR
BECK, MATILDA KEN 270 1ST DIST
BECK, MAY KEN 244 2ND DIST
BECK, MICHAEL BAL 143 19TH WAR
BECK, MICHAEL-BLACK QUE 154 1ST E DI
BECK, MICHAEL-BLACK QUE 131 1ST E DI
BECK, MICHAL BAL 308 7TH WARD
BECK, NICHOLAS BAL 070 4TH WARD
BECK, NICHOLAS FRE 055 FREDERIC
BECK, OSBORN FRE 394 PETERSVI
BECK, PERRY R. BAL 237 17TH WAR
BECK, PHILIP WAS 261 CAVETOWN
BECK, REBECCA QUE 235 4TH E DI
BECK, SAMUEL CAR 194 4TH DIST
BECK, SARAH R. KEN 232 2ND DIST
BECK, SARAH R. KEN 281 3RD DIST
BECK, SUSAN WAS 128 HAGERSTO
BECK, SUSAN ANN 327 2ND DIST
BECK, THEADORE CEC 183 7TH E DI
BECK, THOMAS BAL 085 10TH WAR
BECK, UPTON CAR 176 8TH DIST
BECK, VIRGINIA BAL 049 4TH WARD
BECK, WANDLE ALL 202 CUMBERLA
BECK, WILLIAM CAR 327 1ST DIST
BECK, WILLIAM WAS 146 HAGERSTO
BECK, WILLIAM WAS 122 HAGERSTO
BECK, WILLIAM QUE 179 2ND E DI
BECK, WILLIAM H. QUE 167 2ND E DI
BECK, WILLIAM R. BAL 036 18TH WAR
BECK, WILLIAM R. BAL 171 6TH WARD
BECK, ZEBULON MGM 320 CRACKLIN
BECKENBAUGH, GEORGE FRE 027 FREDERIC
BECKENBAUGH, JOHN FRE 322 MIDDLETO
BECKENBAUGH, MICHAEL FRE 311 MIDDLETO
BECKENBAUGH, MICHAEL L. FRE 110 CREAGERS
BECKER, FERDINAND * BAL 367 1ST DIST
BECKER, GEORGE W. BAL 158 16TH WAR
BECKER, HAMILTON BAL 033 18TH WAR
BECKER, HENRY BAL 358 1ST DIST
BECKER, HENRY BAL 213 2ND WARD
BECKER, ITHO BAL 130 5TH WARD
BECKER, JOHN BAL 326 3RD WARD
BECKER, JOHN CAR 365 9TH DIST
BECKER, JOSEPH D. BAL 097 5TH WARD
BECKER, NICHOLAS BAL 025 15TH WAR
BECKER, NICHOLAS BAL 003 4TH WARD
BECKER, PETER BAL 037 15TH WAR
BECKER, POLLY FRE 178 5TH E DI
BECKER, WILLIAM F. BAL 032 9TH WARD
BECKER, WILLIAM S. CAR 088 NO TWP L
BECKERBOWER, GEORGE ALL 256 CUMBERLA
BECKERSINGER, WILLIAM BAL 295 12TH WAR
BECKET, ELIZABETH BAL 424 14TH WAR
BECKET, JSOIAH-BLACK BAL 238 2ND WARD
BECKET, MARIA ANN 363 4TH DIST
BECKET, SOLOMON BAL 337 3RD WARD
BECKETON, HESTER BAL 246 12TH WAR
BECKETS, GEORGE-BLACK WOR 335 1ST E DI
BECKETS, HARRIET-BLACK WOR 321 1ST E DI
BECKETS, ISAAC-BLACK WOR 335 1ST E DI
BECKETS, JOHN-BLACK WOR 335 1ST E DI
BECKETS, MATILDA BAL 373 13TH WAR
BECKETT, ALFRED PRI 042 VANSVILL
BECKETT, BENJAMIN PRI 041 VANSVILL
BECKETT, ELIZA BAL 207 17TH WAR
BECKETT, HENRY BAL 023 9TH WARD
BECKETT, HUMPHREY PRI 015 BLADENSB
BECKETT, JOHN PRI 030 VANSVILL
BECKETT, JOHN PRI 014 BLADENSB
BECKETT, LEVIN BAL 411 8TH WARD
BECKETT, MAHALA J. BAL 457 8TH WARD
BECKETT, MARGARET PRI 040 VANSVILL
BECKETT, MARY BAL 340 13TH WAR
BECKETT, MARY BAL 157 11TH WAR
BECKETT, NANCY BAL 207 17TH WAR
BECKETT, RICHARD CAL 029 2ND DIST
BECKETT, SUSAN M. CAL 036 2ND DIST
BECKETT, TERESA PRI 014 BLADENSB
BECKETT, THOMAS BAL 073 18TH WAR
BECKETT, WILLIAM BAL 258 17TH WAR
BECKETT, WILLIAM BAL 209 2ND WARD
BECKETT, WILLIAM BAL 113 15TH WAR
BECKEY, SARAH FRE 067 FREDERIC
BECKFORD, JOHN BAL 001 1ST WARD
BECKH, FREDERICK G. BAL 112 15TH WAR
BECKHAM, ELIZA BAL 352 3RD WARD
BECKINGBAUGH, CATHARIEN CAR 229 5TH DIST
BECKINHEIM, DAVID BAL 302 3RD WARD
BECKLEY, ANN BAL 430 14TH WAR
BECKLEY, EMELIA BAL 328 1ST DIST
BECKLEY, GABRIEL FRE 023 FREDERIC
BECKLEY, HENRY BAL 339 1ST DIST
BECKLEY, HENRY WAS 177 1ST DIST
BECKLEY, JACOB BAL 241 1ST DIST
BECKLEY, JACOB BAL 223 1ST DIST
BECKLEY, JAMES BAL 034 9TH WARD
BECKLEY, JESSE BAL 221 1ST DIST
BECKLEY, JOHN BAL 222 1ST DIST
BECKLEY, JOHN BAL 327 1ST DIST
BECKLEY, JOHN BAL 424 8TH WARD
BECKLEY, JOHN WAS 176 1ST DIST
BECKLEY, JOSHUA BAL 321 1ST DIST
BECKLEY, MARTHA CAR 187 4TH DIST
BECKLEY, MARY WAS 195 1ST DIST
BECKLEY, MATILDA BAL 223 1ST DIST
BECKLEY, NICHOLAS BAL 358 13TH WAR
BECKLEY, PHILIP BAL 222 1ST DIST
BECKLEY, SAMUEL ALL 041 2ND E.D.
BECKLEY, WILLIAM BAL 117 5TH WARD
BECKLY, DAVID WAS 019 2ND SUBD
BECKLY, JOHN WAS 019 2ND SUBD
BECKLY, MARGARET * WAS 055 2ND SUBD
BECKMAN, FRANK BAL 107 2ND DIST
BECKMAN, FRANK BAL 073 2ND DIST
BECKMAN, HENRY ALL 223 CUMBERLA
BECKMAN, MARY BAL 359 1ST DIST
BECKS, JOHN FRE 075 FREDERIC
BECKS, REBECCA* DOR 316 1ST DIST
BECKS, SAM** DOR 414 1ST DIST
BECKS, SUSAN PRI 079 QUEEN AN
BECKWARTH, CHARLES MGM 386 ROCKERLE
BECKWITH, AAKEA MGM 403 ROCKERLE
BECKWITH, ANN MGM 398 ROCKERLE
BECKWITH, ELBERT MGM 352 BERRYS D
BECKWITH, ELIZA MGM 403 ROCKERLE
BECKWITH, HENRY BAL 074 1ST WARD
BECKWITH, JAMES DOR 405 1ST DIST
BECKWITH, JANE DOR 405 1ST DIST
BECKWITH, JEREMIAH DOR 311 1ST DIST
BECKWITH, JOHN DOR 404 1ST DIST
BECKWITH, JOSHUA H. FRE 315 MIDDLETO
BECKWITH, LEAH C. DOR 451 1ST DIST
BECKWITH, MARY DOR 423 1ST DIST
BECKWITH, MARY BAL 002 15TH WAR
BECKWITH, NEHEMIAH DOR 404 1ST DIST
BECKWITH, RICHARD BAL 009 1ST WARD
BECKWITH, ROBERT O. MGM 325 CRACKLIN
BECKWITH, SAMUEL W. FRE 248 NEW MARK
BECKWITH, SARAH BAL 012 1ST WARD
BECKWITH, SINGLETON MGM 359 BERRYS D
BECKWITH, WILLIAM DOR 395 1ST DIST
BECKWITH, WILLIAM TAL 001 EASTON D
BECKWOOD, HENRY ANN 440 HOWARD D
BECKWORTH, HORACE BAL 028 4TH WARD
BECRAFT, ELIZ BAL 251 12TH WAR
BECRAFT, GEORGE BAL 164 11TH WAR
BECRAFT, GEORGE W. BAL 306 1ST DIST
BECRAFT, JAMES CAR 221 5TH DIST
BECRAFT, JULUT MGM 422 MEDLEY 3
BECRAFT, LUSIA CAR 202 4TH DIST
BECRAFT, MAHALA BAL 306 1ST DIST
BECRAFT, MARY A. ANN 493 HOWARD D
BECRAFT, PERRY ANN 493 HOWARD D
BECRAFT, PETER ANN 493 HOWARD D
BECRAFT, PETER BAL 306 1ST DIST
BECRAFT, WILLIAM ANN 493 HOWARD D
BECROFT, JAMES ANN 493 HOWARD D
BEDCOPH, MICHAEL BAL 103 5TH WARD
BEDDEO, WILLIAM CHA 277 BOJANTOW
BEDDER, A. PRI 057 AQUASCO
BEDDER, A. PRI 122 PISCATAW
BEDDER, ALLY PRI 070 MARLBROU
BEDDER, MARY PRI 052 AQUASCO
BEDEL, ADAM BAL 008 15TH WAR
BEDELY, HENRY-BLACK BAL 223 2ND WARD
BEDENCUP, CASPER BAL 381 3RD WARD
BEDERS, JOHN CAL 016 1ST DIST
BEDFORD, ALICE-MULATTO FRE 038 FREDERIC
BEDFORD, CATHARINE FRE 267 NEW MARK
BEDFORD, JOHN BAL 304 7TH WARD
BEDFORD, MARIA BAL 234 6TH WARD
BEDFORD, MARY-MULATTO FRE 038 FREDERIC
BEDFORD, OLIVIA BAL 102 15TH WAR
BEDFORD, WILLIAM BAL 140 2ND DIST
BEDICA, CHARLES BAL 227 17TH WAR
BEDIMARS, MRS. BAL 221 17TH WAR
BEDINGER, PETER BAL 025 4TH WARD
BEDINGER, PHILLIP FRE 298 WOODSBOR
BEDLICK, JAMES CEC 212 7TH E D
BEDMAN, FRANCAS BAL 212 2ND WARD
BEDRICK, AMANDA CEC 031 CHESAPEA
BEDSWORTH, ANN SOM 520 BARREN C
BEDSWORTH, BENJAMIN SOM 389 BRINKLEY
BEDSWORTH, JOHN H. SOM 382 BRINKLEY
BEDSWORTH, SALLY A. SOM 520 BARREN C
BEDSWORTH, TUBMAN SOM 519 BARREN C
BEDSWORTH, WHITTINGTON SOM 431 PRINCESS
BEDSWORTH, WILLIAMANNA* SOM 516 BARREN C
BEDWELL, ELIZABETH CEC 034 CHESAPEA
BEDWELL, GEORGE CAR 100 NO TWP L
BEDWELL, JAMES CAR 101 NO TWP L
BEDWELL, JAMES CEC 031 CHESAPEA
BEDWELL, MARY BAL 305 7TH WARD
BEDWICK, JACKSON CEC 035 CHESAPEA
BEEBE, J. T. BAL 361 13TH WAR
BEEBEE, ELIZABETH BAL 306 7TH WARD
BEECHAM, SALAS* BAL 049 4TH WARD
BEECHAM, TALAS* BAL 049 4TH WARD
BEECHELEY, BARBARA FRE 333 MIDDLETO
BEECHELY, PETER FRE 332 MIDDLETO
BEECHGOOD, AMELIA BAL 168 19TH WAR
BEECHLEY, DANIEL FRE 333 MIDDLETO
BEEDS, JESSE BAL 263 1ST DIST
BEEFEET, EDDY BAL 043 4TH WARD
BEEGHLEY, BENJAMIN ALL 035 2ND E.D.
BEEGHLEY, EMANUEL ALL 037 2ND E.D.
BEEGHLEY, EZIAS ALL 036 2ND E.D.
BEEGHLEY, JOSIAH ALL 035 2ND E.D.
BEEGHLEY, NICHOLAS K. ALL 036 2ND E.D.
BEEKER, ELIZABETH ALL 110 5TH E.D.
BEEKER, JOHN ALL 110 5TH E.D.
BEEKES, MARTHA CEC 055 1ST E DI
BEEKLEY, CATHARINE ALL 039 2ND E.D.
BEEKLEY, JACOB ALL 039 2ND E.D.
BEEKLY, ANN BAL 083 18TH WAR
BEEKLY, JOHN W. BAL 083 18TH WAR
BEEKMAN, HENRY ALL 049 10TH E.D
BEEKMAN, JOHN ALL 049 10TH E.D
BEELE, DAVID * ALL 165 6TH E.D.
BEELER, ANDREW WAS 284 1ST DIST
BEELER, CHRISTENA BAL 404 8TH WARD
BEELER, DAVID WAS 085 2ND SUBD
BEELER, DAVID WAS 221 1ST DIST
BEELER, DAVID WAS 213 1ST DIST
BEELER, HENRY L. BAL 055 4TH WARD
BEELER, JOSEPH WAS 197 1ST DIST
BEELER, LEWIS ALL 235 CUMBERLA
BEELER, PETER WAS 036 2ND SUBD
BEELER, SAMUEL WAS 083 2ND SUBD
BEELER, SAMUEL WAS 054 2ND SUBD
BEELER, SUSAN WAS 084 2ND SUBD
BEELFORD, MARY FRE 064 FREDERIC
BEELLER, JAMES W. WAS 197 1ST DIST
BEEM, JAMES W. BAL 030 18TH WAR
BEEM, MARY J. BAL 065 18TH WAR
BEEMAN, JOSEPH J. HAR 117 2ND DIST
BEEMAN, NANCY BAL 125 2ND DIST
BEEMFORD, GEORGE BAL 271 7TH WARD
BEEMILLER, ELIZABETH CAR 248 3RD DIST
BEEN, JOHN CEC 159 PORT DUP
BEENE, MARTHA KEN 217 2ND DIST
BEENGLE, CARLINE FRE 034 FREDERIC
BEENIS, GEORGE KEN 307 3RD DIST
BEENS, EDWORD HAR 200 3RD DIST
BEENS, ELIAS H. HAR 200 3RD DIST
BEER, JOSEPH BAL 063 15TH WAR
BEER, SARAH C. WAS 204 1ST DIST
BEERMAN, LOUISE BAL 182 16TH WAR
BEERRY, MARY PRI 010 BLADENSB
BEERS, CHARELS BAL 032 15TH WAR
BEERS, EDUARD BAL 256 2ND WARD
BEERS, JAMES CEC 098 4TH E DI
BEET, VIRGINIA BAL 277 20TH WAR
BEETLE, JOSHUA BAL 028 4TH WARD
BEETLE, RICHARD BAL 028 4TH WARD
BEEVER, FRANCIS FRE 281 WOODSBOR
BEEZE, EDWARD BAL 162 1ST WARD
BEFELT, MARY BAL 443 14TH WAR
BEGENHARD, CHARLES ALL 118 5TH E.D.
BEGENHARDT, CHARLES ALL 126 4TH E.D.
BEGGAR, HENRY BAL 170 2ND DIST
BEGGERICK, AARON BAL 391 3RD WARD
BEGGS, DORIAS PRI 098 SPALDING
BEGGS, JOHN CAR 293 7TH DIST
BEGGS, MARY CAR 295 7TH DIST
BEGGS, RICHARD CAR 293 7TH DIST
BEGGS, WILLIAM CAR 350 6TH DIST
BEGHOND, HENRY BAL 406 14TH WAR
BEGLEN, LARRY ALL 170 7TH E.D.
BEGLEY, DENNIS BAL 379 8TH WARD
BEGLEY, JULIA BAL 379 8TH WARD
BEHAMY, THOMAS HAR 182 3RD DIST
BEHICE, JOHN BAL 173 19TH WAR
BEHINE, JAMES BAL 237 2ND WARD
BEHIRE, ROSANNA BAL 172 19TH WAR
BEHLE, FREDERICK BAL 107 1ST WARD
BEHLER, FREDERICA BAL 106 1ST WARD
BEHLER, H. BAL 129 1ST WARD
BEHLER, PAUL BAL 105 1ST WARD
BEHO, BEALE CAR 266 WESTMINS
BEHO, LUCY CAR 267 WESTMINS
BEHO, WILLIAM BAL 250 1ST DIST
BEHOE, LYMUS BAL 124 16TH WAR
BEHOO, ROBERT ANN 506 HOWARD D
BEHRANS, JOHANNA FRE 019 FREDERIC
BEHRENDOS, CUSEL BAL 348 13TH WAR
BEHRENS, CONRAD BAL 048 15TH WAR
BEHRENS, JACOB BAL 107 5TH WARD
BEHRENS, WILLIAM BAL 247 17TH WAR
BEHREUS, WILLIAM H. BAL 247 17TH WAR
BEHRLEN, CHRISTIANA BAL 111 10TH WAR
BEICRAFT, MARGARET CAR 368 9TH DIST
BEIDEL, MARY FRE 153 10TH E D
BEIER, ELIZABETH P. BAL 037 15TH WAR
BEIGHLY, JOHN ALL 023 2ND E.D.
BEIN, HENRY BAL 045 15TH WAR
BEINHENER, L. BAL 319 12TH WAR
BEINTZ, MARY BAL 105 2ND DIST
BEIRLY, ALEXANDER BAL 459 1ST DIST
BEISSWANGER, JACOB BAL 238 6TH WARD
BEITZ, WILLIAM BAL 088 10TH WAR
BEITZEL, FRANKLIN FRE 159 EMMITTSB

Name	County	Page	District
BEITZEL, JOHNATHAN	CAR	326	1ST DIST
BEJAS, HENRY-BLACK	CAR	089	NO TWP L
BEKELY, JOHN	CAR	087	NO TWP L
BELCHAM, WILLIAM	BAL	286	2ND WARD
BELCHNER, GEORGE	BAL	267	17TH WAR
BELCHNER, LINHART	CAR	331	MANCHEST
BELDING, FRANCES MISS	PRI	047	AQUASCO
BELDING, SOPHRONA	BAL	378	1ST DIST
BELE, CYRUS*	DOR	456	1ST DIST
BELE, ELIZABETH*	DOR	414	1ST DIST
BELE, JOHN W.*	DOR	456	1ST DIST
BELE, SUSAN*	DOR	447	1ST DIST
BELFREY, JAMES	BAL	200	17TH WAR
BELHICK, PAUL	BAL	137	1ST WARD
BELHS, JOHN	BAL	073	1ST WARD
BELINGER, JOHN	BAL	206	6TH DIST
BELISON, RICHARD	CAR	209	5TH DIST
BELKE, E.	BAL	449	8TH WARD
BELKNAP, EBEN	BAL	035	9TH WARD
BELKNAP, JAMES	FRE	042	FREDERIC
BELKNER, ELY	BAL	261	20TH WAR
BELL, ABBE	ALL	241	CUMBERLA
BELL, ABRAHAM	BAL	307	7TH WARD
BELL, ABSOLOM	BAL	409	1ST DIST
BELL, ADAM	MGM	325	CRACKLIN
BELL, AGNESS	BAL	308	1ST DIST
BELL, AIRA A. *	BAL	414	1ST DIST
BELL, ALEXANDER	BAL	031	9TH WARD
BELL, ALFRED	BAL	365	1ST DIST
BELL, ALFRED	BAL	310	20TH WAR
BELL, ALFRED	CEC	150	PORT DUP
BELL, AMELIA	SOM	386	BRINKLEY
BELL, AMOS	CAR	340	6TH DIST
BELL, AMY	BAL	404	14TH WAR
BELL, ANN	DOR	466	1ST DIST
BELL, ANN	BAL	186	6TH WARD
BELL, ANN	BAL	252	6TH WARD
BELL, ANN	BAL	352	7TH WARD
BELL, ANN	BAL	351	3RD WARD
BELL, ANN M.	BAL	192	17TH WAR
BELL, ANN M.	WAS	147	HAGERSTO
BELL, ANTHONY	KEN	243	2ND DIST
BELL, ARAH	BAL	351	1ST DIST
BELL, ARTHUR	SOM	512	BARREN C
BELL, ATHELINDER	WAS	280	LEITERSB
BELL, BASIL	ANN	387	4TH DIST
BELL, BENJAMIN	ST	294	2ND E DI
BELL, BENJAMIN	BAL	439	14TH WAR
BELL, BENJAMIN	FRE	259	NEW MARK
BELL, CALEP	DOR	367	3RD DIVI
BELL, CASSANDA	BAL	159	2ND DIST
BELL, CATHARINE	BAL	440	14TH WAR
BELL, CATHRINE	BAL	093	18TH WAR
BELL, CHARLES	BAL	383	1ST DIST
BELL, CHARLOTTE	BAL	222	12TH WAR
BELL, CHONBY	BAL	435	14TH WAR
BELL, CLEM	DOR	334	3RD DIVI
BELL, CYRUS*	DOR	456	1ST DIST
BELL, DANIEL	WAS	275	RIDGEVIL
BELL, DANIEL	KEN	242	2ND DIST
BELL, CAVID	ANN	446	HOWARD D
BELL, DIVID	WAS	189	1ST DIST
BELL, EDWARD	WOR	303	SNOW HIL
BELL, ECWARD	BAL	101	2ND DIST
BELL, EDWARD	BAL	382	1ST DIST
BELL, EDWARD H.	BAL	060	4TH WARD
BELL, EDWARD T.	BAL	011	4TH WARD
BELL, ELEEN	BAL	379	13TH WAR
BELL, ELIZA ANN	BAL	295	17TH WAR
BELL, ELIZA J.	SOM	551	TYASKIN
BELL, ELIZABETH	WAS	280	LEITERSB
BELL, ELIZABETH	WAS	271	1ST DIST
BELL, ELIZABETH	BAL	365	1ST DIST
BELL, ELIZABETH	BAL	105	5TH WARD
BELL, ELIZABETH	BAL	259	6TH WARD
BELL, ELIZABETH	BAL	210	6TH WARD
BELL, ELIZABETH J.	BAL	267	7TH WARD
BELL, ELIZABETH*	DOR	414	1ST DIST
BELL, ELLEN	BAL	024	18TH WAR
BELL, ELLIN	HAR	067	1ST DIST
BELL, EMANUEL	ANN	488	HOWARD D
BELL, EMILY	BAL	298	20TH WAR
BELL, EPHRAIM	BAL	031	2ND DIST
BELL, EZEKIEL E.	ANN	374	4TH DIST
BELL, F.	BAL	152	1ST WARD
BELL, F. H.	BAL	154	1ST WARD
BELL, FRANCIS L.	MGM	325	CRACKLIN
BELL, FRANK	BAL	233	1ST DIST
BELL, FREDERICK	WAS	269	1ST DIST
BELL, G. F. M.	BAL	035	4TH WARD
BELL, GARRETT-BLACK	QUE	168	2ND E DI
BELL, GEORGE	WAS	275	RIDGEVIL
BELL, GEORGE	BAL	142	19TH WAR
BELL, GEORGE	BAL	402	14TH WAR
BELL, GEORGE	BAL	156	2ND DIST
BELL, GEORGE	BAL	154	1ST WARD
BELL, GEORGE	BAL	391	1ST DIST
BELL, GEORGE	BAL	413	1ST DIST
BELL, GEORGE H.	QUE	135	1ST E DI
BELL, GEORGE-BLACK	CAR	113	NO TWP L
BELL, HANNA, HUGH *	BAL	311	1ST DIST
BELL, HARIETT	DOR	339	3RD DIVI
BELL, HARRISON	BAL	307	12TH WAR
BELL, HENRY	BAL	007	15TH WAR
BELL, HENRY	FRE	313	MIDDLETO
BELL, HENRY	BAL	024	18TH WAR
BELL, HENRY	WAS	091	2ND SUBD
BELL, HENRY	WAS	131	HAGERSTO
BELL, HETTY	SOM	489	SALISBUR
BELL, ISAAC	WAS	269	1ST DIST
BELL, ISAAC	BAL	055	18TH WAR
BELL, ISAIAH	BAL	407	1ST DIST
BELL, J.	BAL	136	1ST WARD
BELL, JACOB	DOR	426	1ST DIST
BELL, JACOB	KEN	310	3RD DIST
BELL, JACOB	WOR	194	8TH E DI
BELL, JACOB	SOM	400	BRINKLEY
BELL, JACOB	TAL	058	EASTON D
BELL, JACOB E.	WAS	262	1ST DIST
BELL, JAMES	WOR	302	SNOW HIL
BELL, JAMES	BAL	137	1ST WARD
BELL, JAMES	BAL	089	5TH WARD
BELL, JAMES	BAL	367	1ST DIST
BELL, JAMES	BAL	244	12TH WAR
BELL, JAMES	BAL	051	9TH WARD
BELL, JAMES	BAL	025	1ST WARD
BELL, JAPHEAL	ALL	241	CUMBERLA
BELL, JEHU	BAL	079	18TH WAR
BELL, JEMIMA	BAL	201	6TH WARD
BELL, JESSE	BAL	171	2ND DIST

Name	County	Page	District
BELL, JOHN	BAL	174	1ST WARD
BELL, JOHN	ALL	241	CUMBERLA
BELL, JOHN	ANN	416	HOWARD D
BELL, JOHN	BAL	002	EASTERN
BELL, JOHN	BAL	403	1ST DIST
BELL, JOHN	BAL	131	1ST WARD
BELL, JOHN	BAL	136	1ST WARD
BELL, JOHN	FRE	259	NEW MARK
BELL, JOHN	BAL	304	20TH WAR
BELL, JOHN	QUE	128	1ST E DI
BELL, JOHN	BAL	212	17TH WAR
BELL, JOHN	BAL	203	19TH WAR
BELL, JOHN	BAL	313	20TH WAR
BELL, JOHN	WAS	170	FUNKSTOW
BELL, JOHN A.	WAS	269	1ST DIST
BELL, JOHN D.	WAS	198	1ST DIST
BELL, JOHN G.	DOR	358	3RD DIVI
BELL, JOHN H.	SOM	485	TRAPP DI
BELL, JOHN J.	SOM	389	BRINKLEY
BELL, JOHN W.	BAL	362	13TH WAR
BELL, JOHN W.	BAL	245	12TH WAR
BELL, JOHN W.*	DOR	456	1ST DIST
BELL, JOHN*	DOR	369	3RD DIVI
BELL, JONAS	WAS	251	1ST DIST
BELL, JOSEPH	HAR	098	2ND DIST
BELL, JOSEPH	BAL	306	12TH WAR
BELL, JOSEPH H.*	DOR	303	1ST DIST
BELL, JOSHUA	BAL	382	1ST DIST
BELL, JSOHUA-BLACK	CAR	128	NO TWP L
BELL, JULIA	BAL	077	10TH WAR
BELL, LAURA	BAL	171	11TH WAR
BELL, LAURA	WAS	012	WILLIAMS
BELL, LAVINA	BAL	004	15TH WAR
BELL, LAVINA	ALL	221	CUMBER_A
BELL, LEMUEL	DOR	337	3RD DIVI
BELL, LEVEN	DOR	334	3RD DIVI
BELL, LEVIN	ANN	379	4TH DIST
BELL, LEWIS	WAS	091	2ND SUBD
BELL, LLOYD	BAL	145	1ST WARD
BELL, LOUISA	BAL	287	12TH WAR
BELL, LUCY	BAL	239	6TH WARD
BELL, MANE	BAL	245	20TH WAR
BELL, MARGARET	BAL	150	16TH WAR
BELL, MARGARET	WOR	300	SNOW HIL
BELL, MARGARET	SOM	398	BRINKLEY
BELL, MARIA	BAL	069	10TH WAR
BELL, MARIA	ANN	432	HOWARD D
BELL, MARIA	BAL	400	3RD WARD
BELL, MARIA E.	FRE	337	MIDDLETO
BELL, MARTHA	BAL	282	12TH WAR
BELL, MARY	BAL	116	15TH WAR
BELL, MARY	ANN	447	HOWARD D
BELL, MARY	BAL	353	1ST DIST
BELL, MARY	HAR	017	1ST DIST
BELL, MARY	SOM	364	BRINKLEY
BELL, MARY	QUE	232	4TH E DI
BELL, MARY J.	DOR	423	1ST DIST
BELL, MARY R.A.	ANN	521	HOWARD D
BELL, MARY-BLACK	CAR	138	NO TWP L
BELL, MINGO	SOM	500	SALISBUR
BELL, MOSES	HAR	024	1ST DIST
BELL, NANCY	SOM	364	BRINKLEY
BELL, NATHANIEL J.	ST	291	2ND E DI
BELL, NETTA A.	WAS	172	FUNKSTOW
BELL, NICHOLAS	BAL	226	12TH WAR
BELL, NOAH	SOM	491	SALISBUR
BELL, PATRICK	BAL	036	9TH WARD
BELL, PETER	WAS	269	1ST DIST
BELL, PETGER	BAL	321	12TH WAR
BELL, PRICILLA	CHA	264	MIDDLETO
BELL, RANDOLPH	BAL	033	9TH WARD
BELL, REBECCA	FRE	262	NEW MARK
BELL, REBECCA C.	BAL	455	8TH WARD
BELL, RHODA	DOR	366	3RD DIVI
BELL, RICHARD	BAL	428	14TH WAR
BELL, RICHARD	BAL	121	5TH WARD
BELL, RICHARD	ANN	415	HOWARD D
BELL, RICHARD D.	BAL	109	5TH WARD
BELL, RICHARD H.	BAL	046	4TH WARD
BELL, ROBERT	DOR	378	1ST DIST
BELL, ROBERT	CEC	205	7TH E DI
BELL, ROBERT SR.	CAR	342	6TH DIST
BELL, ROSA	WOR	280	BERLIN 1
BELL, SALLY	WOR	326	1ST E DI
BELL, SAMUEL	WAS	087	2ND SUBD
BELL, SAMUEL	CAR	346	6TH DIST
BELL, SAMUEL	BAL	092	18TH WAR
BELL, SAMUEL	CHA	219	ALLENS F
BELL, SAMUEL	BAL	428	14TH WAR
BELL, SAMUEL	HAR	063	1ST DIST
BELL, SAMUEL	ANN	372	4TH DIST
BELL, SARAH	BAL	382	1ST DIST
BELL, SARAH	BAL	362	1ST DIST
BELL, SARAH	ANN	337	3RD DIST
BELL, SARAH	BAL	306	12TH WAR
BELL, SARAH	ANN	447	HOWARD D
BELL, SARAH	BAL	129	2ND DIST
BELL, SARAH	ALL	251	CUMBER_A
BELL, SARAH	BAL	038	2ND DIST
BELL, SARAH	BAL	426	14TH WAR
BELL, SARAH	BAL	024	18TH WAR
BELL, SARAH E.	BAL	409	1ST DIST
BELL, SENECA P.	BAL	181	16TH WAR
BELL, SHADARACK	CAL	057	3RD DIST
BELL, SHAFER	CAR	342	6TH DIST
BELL, SUSAN	BAL	284	20TH WAR
BELL, SUSAN	DOR	445	1ST DIST
BELL, SUSAN	BAL	321	12TH WAR
BELL, SUSAN	ANN	372	4TH DIST
BELL, SUSAN	BAL	251	6TH WARD
BELL, SUSAN D.	WAS	136	HAGERSTO
BELL, SUSAN*	DOR	447	1ST DIST
BELL, THOAMS	BAL	318	20TH WAR
BELL, THOAMS H.	KEN	230	2ND DIST
BELL, THOMAS	FRE	037	FREDERIC
BELL, THOMAS	DOR	320	1ST DIST
BELL, THOMAS	CAR	073	NO TWP L
BELL, THOMAS	SOM	400	BRINKLEY
BELL, THOMAS	WAS	157	2ND DIST
BELL, THOMAS	WAS	211	1ST DIST
BELL, THOMAS	SOM	536	TYASKIN
BELL, THOMAS	ANN	324	2ND DIST
BELL, THOMAS	BAL	364	1ST DIST
BELL, THOMAS	ANN	432	HOWARD D
BELL, THOMAS	ANN	432	HOWARD D
BELL, THOMAS	ANN	351	3RD DIST
BELL, THOMAS B.	BAL	290	3RD WARD
BELL, THOMAS H.*	DOR	377	1ST DIST
BELL, UPTON	WAS	280	LEITERSB
BELL, WALTER	BAL	132	16TH WAR

Name	County	Page	District
BELL, WASHINGTON	BAL	169	19TH WAR
BELL, WESLEY	BAL	283	12TH WAR
BELL, WILLIAM	BAL	391	1ST DIST
BELL, WILLIAM	BAL	112	2ND DIST
BELL, WILLIAM	BAL	254	6TH WARD
BELL, WILLIAM	BAL	046	15TH WAR
BELL, WILLIAM	BAL	165	1ST WARD
BELL, WILLIAM	FRE	330	MIDDLETO
BELL, WILLIAM	FRE	325	MIDDLETO
BELL, WILLIAM	HAR	017	1ST DIST
BELL, WILLIAM	FRE	194	5TH E DI
BELL, WILLIAM	BAL	185	19TH WAR
BELL, WILLIAM	WAS	241	CAVETOWN
BELL, WILLIAM	WOR	320	1ST E DI
BELL, WILLIAM A.	SOM	491	SALISBUR
BELL, WILLIAM B.	SOM	492	SALISBUR
BELL, WILLIAM E.-BLACK	CAR	383	2ND DIST
BELL, WILLIAM H.	BAL	411	1ST DIST
BELL, WILLIAM L.	BAL	385	13TH WAR
BELL, WILLIAM*	DOR	376	1ST DIST
BELL, ZADOC	BAL	154	2ND DIST
BELL, ZEAKLE	BAL	381	1ST DIST
BELL, ZEBEDEE	BAL	304	17TH WAR
BELL.LEWIS	CAR	373	9TH DIST
BELL.MARTHA A.	BAL	204	2ND WARD
BELL.RICHARD	BAL	048	1ST WARD
BELLE, ARA	BAL	069	18TH WAR
BELLE, FRANCIS	BAL	075	18TH WAR
BELLEE, ANDREW	ALL	056	10TH E.D
BELLENA, ABRAHAM	BAL	266	7TH WARD
BELLERMAN, ANTHONY	BAL	055	15TH WAR
BELLESON, GEORGE	FRE	410	8TH E DI
BELLFIELD, LUCY	BAL	134	11TH WAR
BELLINGER.ELSE	ALL	010	3RD E.D.
BELLINGHAM, WILLIAM	TAL	077	EASTON T
BELLINGS, E.	BAL	152	1ST WARD
BELLINGSLEY, DENTON	CAL	024	2ND DIST
BELLINGSLEY, WILLIAM	CAL	024	2ND DIST
BELLISON, RACHEAL	CAR	394	2ND DIST
BELLISON.MARY	BAL	247	12TH WAR
BELLMAN, HENRIETTA	WAS	140	HAGERSTO
BELLMEAN, CATHARINE	BAL	115	11TH WAR
BELLNAP, CRATON	BAL	298	1ST DIST
BELLOW, HENRY	ALL	200	CUMBERLA
BELLOWS, ISAAC	MGM	356	BERRYS D
BELLOWS, JOHN A.	MGM	364	BERRYS D
BELLOWS, JOSIAH	MGM	364	BERRYS D
BELLOWS, KITTY	MGM	351	BERRYS D
BELLS, HENRY	BAL	267	17TH WAR
BELLS, JOSHUA *	CAR	342	6TH DIST
BELLSTER, THOMAS *	BAL	285	20TH WAR
BELLWART, WILLIAM	BAL	066	1ST WARD
BELLWOOD, ANN	ST	314	1ST E DI
BELMAN, CHARLES	ALL	201	CUMBERLA
BELMEAR, ANN M.	ANN	363	4TH DIST
BELMEAR, JAMES	ANN	363	4TH DIST
BELMEAR, SAMUEL	ANN	363	4TH DIST
BELMIER, EVELINE	FRE	428	8TH E DI
BELMOST, SELINA	ALL	263	CUMBERLA
BELO, JOHN	BAL	324	12TH WAR
BELONGA, MARY	ANN	318	2ND DIST
BELRAROS, ADAM	BAL	326	3RD WARD
BELSHOOVER, SALLY	ALL	218	CUMBERLA
BELSKI, CASPER J.	FRE	20	5TH E DI
BELT, ADDISON	MGM	384	ROCKERLE
BELT, AMOS	BAL	337	1ST DIST
BELT, AMOS-MULATTO	FRE	044	FREDERIC
BELT, ANN	FRE	387	PETERSVI
BELT, ANN H.	BAL	127	18TH WAR
BELT, CAROLINE	CAR	174	8TH DIST
BELT, CHARLES	BAL	326	1ST DIST
BELT, DARBY	BAL	237	1ST DIST
BELT, DARBY	BAL	194	5TH DIST
BELT, DENNIS-BLACK	FRE	042	FREDERIC
BELT, EDWARD W.	WAS	021	2ND SUBD
BELT, ELEANOR	MGM	384	ROCKERLE
BELT, ELISHA	BAL	009	18TH WAR
BELT, ELIZABETH	BAL	226	2ND WARD
BELT, ELLEN	FRE	083	FREDERIC
BELT, ENOS W.	FRE	216	BUCKEYST
BELT, FRANCIS	BAL	061	2ND DIST
BELT, FREEMAN	BAL	195	11TH WAR
BELT, GEORGE	CAR	364	9TH DIST
BELT, HARRY	WAS	157	HAGERSTO
BELT, HICKMAN	BAL	015	18TH WAR
BELT, HUMPHREY	BAL	231	1ST DIST
BELT, JACKSON	CAR	186	8TH DIST
BELT, JAMES	FRE	234	BUCKEYST
BELT, JAMES	BAL	167	2ND DIST
BELT, JAMES B.	PRI	093	MARLBROU
BELT, JOHN	BAL	040	2ND DIST
BELT, JOHN	BAL	015	15TH WAR
BELT, JOHN B.	MGM	403	ROCKERLE
BELT, JOHN L.	FRE	234	BUCKEYST
BELT, JOHN R.	FRE	222	BUCKEYST
BELT, JOHN W.	MGM	325	CRACKLIN
BELT, JOHN W.	ANN	337	3RD DIST
BELT, JOHN-MULATTO	FRE	390	PETERSVI
BELT, JOSHUA	BAL	240	1ST DIST
BELT, JOSIAH	CAR	392	2ND DIST
BELT, JULIAN-BLACK	FRE	010	FREDERIC
BELT, KENGEY	BAL	017	2ND DIST
BELT, LENARD	CAR	173	8TH DIST
BELT, LIZZY*	BAL	039	4TH WARD
BELT, LLOYD A.	FRE	216	BUCKEYST
BELT, LOUISA A.	BAL	125	11TH WAR
BELT, LUCETTA	MGM	336	CRACKLIN
BELT, MARTHA A.C.	WAS	246	SMITHSBU
BELT, MARY	BAL	067	15TH WAR
BELT, MARY E.P.P	ST	305	2ND E DI
BELT, MOSES	BAL	060	2ND DIST
BELT, OTHO	ANN	429	HOWARD D
BELT, PHILIP T.	PRI	020	VANSVILL
BELT, RACHAEL	BAL	241	1ST DIST
BELT, RICHARD	BAL	240	1ST DIST
BELT, ROBERT B.	BAL	104	15TH WAR
BELT, SAMUEL	ANN	283	ANNAPOLI
BELT, SOLIMAN	ALL	217	CUMBERLA
BELT, STEPHEN	PRI	081	QUEEN AN
BELT, SUSAN	WAS	136	HAGERSTO
BELT, SUSANNNA	PRI	007	BLADENSB
BELT, THOMAS	BAL	193	5TH DIST
BELT, WALTER T.	PRI	021	VANSVILL
BELT, WILLAM	BAL	187	5TH DIST
BELT, WILLIAM	MGM	340	CLARKSBU
BELT, WILLIAM H.	BAL	171	1ST WARD
BELT, WILLIAM J.	PRI	082	QUEEN AN
BELT, WILLIAM T.	MGM	330	CRACKLIN
BELT.MARY	FRE	030	FREDERIC
BELTEHIMER, HENRY	WAS	138	HAGERSTO

Name	County	Page	District
BELTINGSTEN, ELIZABETH	ANN	277	ANNAPOLI
BELTON, TURBOTT	QUE	203	3RD E DI
BELTS, SAMUEL	QUE	176	2ND E DI
BELTY, THOMAS	CEC	068	5TH E DI
BELTZ, BARBARA	BAL	368	13TH WAR
BELTZ, ELIZABETH	BAL	212	6TH DIST
BELTZ, JACOB *	BAL	218	12TH WAR
BELTZ, WILLIAM	CAR	176	8TH DIST
BELTZE, CORNEILA	BAL	445	14TH WAR
BEMAJE, JAMES H.*	TAL	028	EASTON D
BEMCKER, CHARLES H.	BAL	131	1ST WARD
BEMER, NICHOLAS	BAL	066	1ST WARD
BEMETT, WESLEY	CAR	218	5TH DIST
BEMILLER, JOHN	CAR	248	3RD DIST
BEMILLER, MATILDA	CAR	261	3RD DIST
BEMMOT, HENRY *	BAL	313	20TH WAR
BEMS, EDWARD	BAL	106	1ST WARD
BEMY, MARY	BAL	067	1ST WARD
BEMY, SAMUEL	BAL	067	1ST WARD
BENA, ANNA-BLACK	FRE	011	FREDERIC
BENACICT, SUSAN	WAS	258	1ST DIST
BENAMON, B. E.	BAL	322	12TH WAR
BENANLY, ANN *	BAL	277	2ND WARD
BENARD, MARY A.	BAL	316	7TH WARD
BENBACK, ERNEST	BAL	059	1ST WARD
BENBERGH, ABRAHAM	BAL	215	2ND WARD
BENBURY, J. R.	BAL	332	1ST DIST
BENBURY, L. C.	BAL	333	1ST DIST
BENCH, AUGUSTEN D.	CHA	274	ALLENS F
BENCH, SAMUEL H.	WAS	010	WILLIAMS
BENCHAMP, J.M.	BAL	171	1ST WARD
BENCHANET, J.	BAL	148	1ST WARD
BENCHANT, CHARLES	BAL	221	2ND WARD
BENCHLEY, JOSEPH	TAL	035	EASTON D
BENCKER, WILLIAM *	BAL	055	15TH WAR
BENCY, BENJAMIN H.	BAL	186	2ND WARD
BEND, ROSE	BAL	069	4TH WARD
BEND, SAMUEL	ST	324	4TH E DI
BENDAWAULD, LEWIS	BAL	442	14TH WAR
BENDE, JAMES	BAL	078	1ST WARD
BENDELL, JUSTINA B.	BAL	187	2ND WARD
BENDEN, E.	BAL	154	1ST WARD
BENDEN, ELIZABETH	BAL	305	12TH WAR
BENDER, AUGUST	BAL	022	18TH WAR
BENDER, BARBARA	FRE	052	FREDERIC
BENDER, CATHARINE	CAR	249	3RD DIST
BENDER, CHARLES	BAL	256	20TH WAR
BENDER, CHRISTIAN	ALL	189	9TH E.D.
BENDER, DANIEL	BAL	095	10TH WAR
BENDER, DANIEL	CAR	289	7TH DIST
BENDER, CANIEL	WAS	055	2ND SUBD
BENDER, DAVID	ALL	189	9TH E.D.
BENDER, EDWARD	BAL	021	18TH WAR
BENDER, ELIAS	WAS	151	HAGERSTO
BENDER, ELIZA	BAL	016	4TH WARD
BENDER, EMILY	BAL	320	12TH WAR
BENDER, FREDERICK	FRE	025	FREDERIC
BENDER, G. A.	WAS	121	HAGERSTO
BENDER, GEORGE	BAL	266	20TH WAR
BENDER, JACOB	WAS	107	2ND DIST
BENDER, JACOB	WAS	107	2ND DIST
BENDER, JOHN	WAS	042	2ND SUBD
BENDER, JOHN	BAL	150	19TH WAR
BENDER, JOHN	BAL	199	6TH WARD
BENDER, JOHN W.	WAS	288	1ST DIST
BENDER, LEWIS	BAL	130	18TH WAR
BENDER, MARY	WAS	168	FUNKSTOW
BENDER, REBECCA	WAS	097	2ND DIST
BENDER, SAMUEL	WAS	006	WILLIAMS
BENDER, SAMUEL	WAS	044	2ND SUBD
BENDER, SAMUEL	BAL	265	20TH WAR
BENDER, SIMON	ANN	427	HOWARD D
BENDER, W ALTER	ALL	184	9TH E.D.
BENDETT, NETTEY	FRE	317	MIDDLETO
BENDETT, SIDNEY A.	FRE	255	NEW MARK
BENDING, GEORGE	CAR	137	NO TWP L
BENDING, JAMES	CAR	157	NO TWP L
BENDON, HARRISON	DOR	310	1ST DIST
BENDUM, HORACE	BAL	348	3RD WARD
BENEDICT, AUGUSTUS	BAL	166	11TH WAR
BENEDICT, HELEN M.	ANN	521	HOWARD D
BENEDICT, HENRIETTA	HAR	062	1ST DIST
BENEHENEL, EUGENE	CAR	096	NO TWP L
BENENBERG, FREDERICK	BAL	422	14TH WAR
BENER, CATHARINE	CAR	260	3RD DIST
BENESTIRD, FREDERICK	BAL	202	2ND WARD
BENET, MARY	BAL	228	12TH WAR
BENETES, JOHN	FRE	051	FREDERIC
BENFERT, SARAH	BAL	321	3RD WARD
BENFETTER, JOHN	BAL	185	2ND WARD
BENFORD, JOHNATHAN	ALL	233	CUMBERLA
BENFORD, MALVINA	ALL	233	CUMBERLA
BENGAR, GEORGE	BAL	272	12TH WAR
BENGEE, JOHN	CEC	104	4TH E DI
BENGER, F.	BAL	211	19TH WAR
BENGER, PHILLIP	FRE	082	FREDERIC
BENGUERAL, EUPHRENI	WAS	044	2ND SUBD
BENHAM, V.M.	BAL	117	1ST WARD
BENHANK, DAVER	BAL	251	12TH WAR
BENHOFF, FREDERICK	BAL	146	2ND DIST
BENIAGE, WILLIAM T.	TAL	058	EASTON D
BENILUNT, SOPHIA	BAL	333	1ST DIST
BENIS, MOSES-BLACK	BAL	219	2ND WARD
BENITT, ADAM	DOR	350	3RD DIVI
BENIX, ELLEN	BAL	361	1ST DIST
BENJAMIN, ALBERT	CEC	112	4TH E DI
BENJAMIN, ANN	HAR	156	3RD DIST
BENJAMIN, DAVID A.	KEN	214	2ND DIST
BENJAMIN, EVAN	CEC	160	PORT DUP
BENJAMIN, GEORGE	CEC	160	PORT DUP
BENJAMIN, GEORGE	CEC	178	7TH E DI
BENJAMIN, ISAAC	ANN	343	3RD DIST
BENJAMIN, JOHN L.	ANN	290	ANNAPOLI
BENJAMIN, JOSEPH	CEC	134	6TH E DI
BENJAMIN, LEVI	BAL	063	4TH WARD
BENJAMIN, NELSON	CEC	149	PORT DUP
BENJAMIN, SAMUEL	BAL	241	6TH WARD
BENJAMIN, SAMUEL	BAL	274	1ST DIST
BENJAMIN, SARAH C.	CEC	006	ELKTON 3
BENJAMIN, THOMAS	CEC	137	6TH E DI
BENJAMIN, WILLIAM	CEC	160	PORT DUP
BENJAMIN, WILLIAM	CEC	190	5TH E DI
BENJAMIN, WILLIAM T.	HAR	156	3RD DIST
BENJAMINE, ISARH *	TAL	071	EASTON T
BENKE, JOHN	BAL	353	13TH WAR
BENKE, LUKE	ALL	048	10TH E.D
BENKE, WILLIAM *	KEN	216	2ND DIST
BENKENS, LOUISA	BAL	327	13TH WAR
BENKHEIM, PHILIP	BAL	372	13TH WAR
BENKMAN, WILLIAM	ALL	180	8TH E.D.
BENLEER, B.	BAL	227	12TH WAR
BENLEY, JACOB	BAL	273	12TH WAR
BENLEY, MARY	BAL	233	20TH WAR
BENMAN, WILLIAM	BAL	308	12TH WAR
BENN, WILLIAM	BAL	119	1ST WARD
BENNALL, MARY *	BAL	298	12TH WAR
BENNANSON, JOHN	BAL	249	1ST DIST
BENNARD, MARY	BAL	144	19TH WAR
BENNATON, NEWTON	FRE	202	5TH E DI
BENNEL, DAVID	FRE	018	FREDERIC
BENNELL, HONOR	FRE	271	NEW MARK
BENNEMYER, JACOB	ALL	005	3RD E.D.
BENNER, AARON	BAL	038	9TH WARD
BENNER, ALBERT	BAL	249	17TH WAR
BENNER, CAROLINE	BAL	096	5TH WARD
BENNER, CATHARINE	WAS	135	HAGERSTO
BENNER, DANIEL	WAS	041	2ND SUBD
BENNER, ELIZA	BAL	040	4TH WARD
BENNER, GEORGE	BAL	266	2ND WARD
BENNER, HENRY	BAL	266	12TH WAR
BENNER, HENRY A.	BAL	339	7TH WARD
BENNER, JACOB	WAS	067	2ND SUBD
BENNER, JACOB	WAS	040	2ND SUBD
BENNER, JOHN	WAS	041	2ND SUBD
BENNER, JOSEPH	WAS	043	2ND SUBD
BENNER, MARY	FRE	322	MIDDLETO
BENNER, SAMUEL	BAL	250	17TH WAR
BENNER, SAMUEL	WAS	064	2ND SUBD
BENNER, SAMUEL	WAS	045	2ND SUBD
BENNER, THOMAS S.	BAL	209	6TH WARD
BENNERZETTE, GEORGE W.	BAL	241	6TH WARD
BENNET, ADOLPHUS	FRE	20	5TH E DI
BENNET, ALFRED	BAL	439	14TH WAR
BENNET, ANDREW M.	ANN	386	4TH DIST
BENNET, BENJAMIN	CAR	372	9TH DIST
BENNET, BENJAMIN B.	MGM	419	MEDLEY 3
BENNET, BENJAMIN W.	CAR	373	9TH DIST
BENNET, BRISCOE	ST	347	5TH E DI
BENNET, CHARLES	ALL	164	6TH E.D.
BENNET, CHARLOTT	FRE	047	FREDERIC
BENNET, COLUMBUS	BAL	126	2ND DIST
BENNET, DAVID	DOR	362	3RD DIVI
BENNET, EDWARD	BAL	345	7TH WARD
BENNET, ELIZA	ALL	208	CUMBERLA
BENNET, ELIZA	WAS	101	2ND DIST
BENNET, FRANCES	BAL	301	12TH WAR
BENNET, GARRISON	BAL	201	17TH WAR
BENNET, GEORGE	ST	341	5TH E DI
BENNET, HARIET*	BAL	420	3RD WARD
BENNET, HENRY	MGM	432	CLARKSTR
BENNET, JAMES	BAL	424	14TH WAR
BENNET, JAMES SR.	WOR	322	1ST E DI
BENNET, JESSE	BAL	324	1ST DIST
BENNET, JESSE F.	ANN	386	4TH DIST
BENNET, JOHN	BAL	110	2ND DIST
BENNET, JOHN	BAL	270	2ND WARD
BENNET, JOHN B.	ANN	336	3RD DIST
BENNET, JOHN W.	CAR	373	9TH DIST
BENNET, JOSEPH	BAL	330	13TH WAR
BENNET, LEWIS H.	FRE	017	FREDERIC
BENNET, LOUISA	BAL	331	3RD WARD
BENNET, MARGARET	BAL	030	1ST WARD
BENNET, MARIA	ST	340	5TH E DI
BENNET, MARY	ANN	386	4TH DIST
BENNET, MARY	BAL	150	11TH WAR
BENNET, NANCY	MGM	444	CLARKSTR
BENNET, NOAH	DOR	372	3RD DIVI
BENNET, REZIN	MGM	443	CLARKSTR
BENNET, ROBERT	WAS	162	2ND DIST
BENNET, ROBERT	CAR	373	9TH DIST
BENNET, ROBERT	BAL	131	1ST WARD
BENNET, ROBERT	ANN	453	HOWARD D
BENNET, RUTH	MGM	444	CLARKSTR
BENNET, RUTH	MGM	443	CLARKSTR
BENNET, STEPHEN	BAL	074	1ST WARD
BENNET, THOMAS	BAL	068	10TH WAR
BENNET, WESLEY	MGM	444	CLARKSTR
BENNET, WILLAIM	ANN	479	HOWARD D
BENNET, WILLIAM	WOR	350	1ST E DI
BENNET, WILLIAM	BAL	420	3RD WARD
BENNETE, THOMAS	DOR	406	1ST DIST
BENNETT, ABNER	BAL	253	12TH WAR
BENNETT, ABRAHAM	BAL	092	15TH WAR
BENNETT, ALEN	CAR	218	5TH DIST
BENNETT, ALEXANDER	BAL	343	3RD WARD
BENNETT, ALFRED	CEC	110	4TH E DI
BENNETT, AMIUL*	DOR	393	1ST DIST
BENNETT, ANDREW	BAL	245	12TH WAR
BENNETT, ANN E.	BAL	312	3RD WARD
BENNETT, ANNY*	TAL	031	EASTON D
BENNETT, ANTHONY	SOM	470	TRAPPE D
BENNETT, ANTHONY	SOM	424	PRINCESS
BENNETT, BARBARA	BAL	108	15TH WAR
BENNETT, BARZELEUS	FRE	228	BUCKEYST
BENNETT, BENJAMIN F.	BAL	105	15TH WAR
BENNETT, BERTUS	FRE	118	CREAGERS
BENNETT, CATHARINE	CAR	211	5TH DIST
BENNETT, CATHERINE	CEC	190	5TH E DI
BENNETT, CHARLES	CAR	188	4TH DIST
BENNETT, CHARLES	SOM	495	SALISBUR
BENNETT, CURTIS	BAL	394	8TH WARD
BENNETT, DANIEL H.	BAL	098	1ST WARD
BENNETT, DAVID	ANN	441	HOWARD D
BENNETT, DOUGLASS	BAL	106	15TH WAR
BENNETT, EBEN T.	SOM	507	BARREN C
BENNETT, EDWARD	BAL	042	1ST WARD
BENNETT, EDWARD	BAL	180	2ND DIST
BENNETT, EDWIN	BAL	381	3RD WARD
BENNETT, ELI	BAL	298	20TH WAR
BENNETT, ELIAS	BAL	314	3RD WARD
BENNETT, ELISHA	SOM	524	BARREN C
BENNETT, ELISHA JR.	SOM	524	BARREN C
BENNETT, ELIZA	KEN	219	2ND DIST
BENNETT, ELIZA *	BAL	036	15TH WAR
BENNETT, ELIZA L.-MULATTO	BAL	179	2ND WARD
BENNETT, ELIZABETH	KEN	214	2ND DIST
BENNETT, ELIZABETH	SOM	515	BARREN C
BENNETT, ELIZABETH	SOM	507	BARREN C
BENNETT, ELIZABETH W.	WOR	237	6TH E DI
BENNETT, ELLEN	BAL	244	12TH WAR
BENNETT, ELY	BAL	144	19TH WAR
BENNETT, ESTHER	SOM	468	TRAPPE D
BENNETT, FRANCIS W.	BAL	114	15TH WAR
BENNETT, GEORGE	BAL	358	3RD WARD
BENNETT, GEORGE	ALL	135	4TH E.D.
BENNETT, GEORGE	KEN	271	1ST DIST
BENNETT, GEORGE	SOM	510	BARREN C
BENNETT, GEORGE	SOM	510	BARREN C
BENNETT, GEORGE	KEN	208	2ND DIST
BENNETT, GEORGE	CEC	028	CHESAPEA
BENNETT, GEORGE H.	WOR	310	2ND E DI
BENNETT, GEORGE H.	BAL	144	1ST WARD
BENNETT, GEORGE W.	BAL	381	3RD WARD
BENNETT, GEORGE W.	WOR	317	2ND E DI
BENNETT, GEORGE W.	BAL	077	18TH WAR
BENNETT, GEORGIANA	BAL	224	6TH WARD
BENNETT, GORGE*	TAL	036	EASTON)
BENNETT, GRIFFITH	BAL	299	20TH WAR
BENNETT, HAMILTON B.	SOM	511	BARREN C
BENNETT, HENRIETTER	FRE	228	BUCKEYST
BENNETT, HENRY	CEC	007	ELKTON 3
BENNETT, HENRY	ANN	356	3RD DIST
BENNETT, HENRY P.	CEC	018	ELKTON 3
BENNETT, HUGH	BAL	234	17TH WAR
BENNETT, ISABELA J.	CAR	217	5TH DIST
BENNETT, J.	TAL	065	EASTON T
BENNETT, JACOB	CEC	110	4TH E DI
BENNETT, JAMES	SOM	519	BARREN C
BENNETT, JAMES	BAL	137	2ND DIST
BENNETT, JAMES	BAL	104	15TH WAR
BENNETT, JAMES C.	BAL	075	15TH WAR
BENNETT, JAMES L.	BAL	195	2ND WARD
BENNETT, JOEPH P.	ST	300	2ND E DI
BENNETT, JOHN	BAL	345	7TH WARD
BENNETT, JOHN	BAL	150	16TH WAR
BENNETT, JOHN	BAL	029	1ST WARD
BENNETT, JOHN	BAL	106	1ST WARD
BENNETT, JOHN	CEC	080	NORTHEAS
BENNETT, JOHN	CEC	009	ELKTON 3
BENNETT, JOHN	BAL	178	19TH WAR
BENNETT, JOHN	DOR	302	1ST DIST
BENNETT, JOHN B.	SOM	511	BARREN C
BENNETT, JOHN H.	SOM	531	QUANTICO
BENNETT, JOHN S.	BAL	177	6TH WARD
BENNETT, JOHN W.	ST	306	1ST E DI
BENNETT, JONATHAN	SOM	518	BARREN C
BENNETT, JONATHAN P.	SOM	512	BARREN C
BENNETT, JOSEPH	BAL	270	17TH WAR
BENNETT, JOSEPH S.	FRE	049	FREDERIC
BENNETT, JOSHUA	CAR	078	NO TWP L
BENNETT, JOSHUA	SOM	510	BARREN C
BENNETT, JOSHUA	BAL	359	8TH WARD
BENNETT, LAMBERT	SOM	522	BARREN C
BENNETT, LAURA A.	ST	303	2ND E DI
BENNETT, LEVI T.	CAR	209	5TH DIST
BENNETT, LEVIN	SOM	517	BARREN C
BENNETT, LEWIS	BAL	397	8TH WARD
BENNETT, LITTLETON	BAL	036	15TH WAR
BENNETT, LIVINGSTON M.	BAL	296	20TH WAR
BENNETT, MARY	BAL	342	7TH WARD
BENNETT, MARY	BAL	272	12TH WAR
BENNETT, MARY	BAL	261	6TH WARD
BENNETT, MARY	WOR	305	SNOW HIL
BENNETT, MARY E.	SOM	524	BARREN C
BENNETT, MICHAEL	BAL	299	20TH WAR
BENNETT, N.	BAL	114	1ST WARD
BENNETT, PEGGY	SOM	501	SALISBUR
BENNETT, PERRY	CAR	217	5TH DIST
BENNETT, PETER	WOR	313	2ND E DI
BENNETT, PHILIP	BAL	159	1ST WARD
BENNETT, R.	BAL	173	1ST WARD
BENNETT, RACHEL	CAR	209	5TH DIST
BENNETT, RACHEL	CAR	229	5TH DIST
BENNETT, RACHEL	CAR	078	NO TWP L
BENNETT, RACHEL	CEC	117	4TH E DI
BENNETT, REBECCA	BAL	138	2ND DIST
BENNETT, REUBEN	BAL	068	15TH WAR
BENNETT, RICHARD	BAL	244	12TH WAR
BENNETT, RICHARD H.	ST	307	1ST E DI
BENNETT, ROBERT	BAL	223	6TH WARD
BENNETT, ROBERT	BAL	116	1ST WARD
BENNETT, ROBERT	BAL	230	2ND WARD
BENNETT, ROBERT	BAL	170	16TH WAR
BENNETT, ROSE	DOR	423	1ST DIST
BENNETT, RUDOLPH	CEC	013	ELKTON 3
BENNETT, RUDOLPH	CEC	007	ELKTON 3
BENNETT, RUFUS	BAL	263	20TH WAR
BENNETT, RUTH	FRE	228	BUCKEYST
BENNETT, RUTH A.	BAL	228	6TH WARD
BENNETT, SAMUEL	BAL	127	1ST WARD
BENNETT, SAMUEL	CAR	216	5TH DIST
BENNETT, SAMUEL T.	FRE	229	BUCKEYST
BENNETT, SARAH	BAL	209	5TH WARD
BENNETT, SARAH	BAL	146	5TH WARD
BENNETT, SARAH	BAL	174	2ND DIST
BENNETT, SARAH A.	BAL	089	15TH WAR
BENNETT, SARAH A.	CAR	077	NO TWP L
BENNETT, SARRAH	SOM	526	QUANTICO
BENNETT, SELATHIEL	SOM	510	BARREN C
BENNETT, SILAS	BAL	318	12TH WAR
BENNETT, SYLVANUS	ALL	183	8TH E.D.
BENNETT, THOMAS	BAL	145	1ST WARD
BENNETT, THOMAS	BAL	402	8TH WARD
BENNETT, THOMAS	BAL	435	8TH WARD
BENNETT, THOMAS	KEN	209	2ND DIST
BENNETT, THOMAS G.	HAR	177	3RD DIST
BENNETT, THOMAS J.	ST	277	3RD E DI
BENNETT, THOMAS W.	ST	267	3RD E DI
BENNETT, TILGHMAN B.	FRE	260	NEW MARK
BENNETT, TILLY	TAL	027	EASTON D
BENNETT, URITH	BAL	439	8TH WARD
BENNETT, WASH A.	FRE	132	CREAGERS
BENNETT, WILLIAM	DOR	401	1ST DIST
BENNETT, WILLIAM	CEC	081	CHARLEST
BENNETT, WILLIAM	BAL	389	3RD WARD
BENNETT, WILLIAM	BAL	101	15TH WAR
BENNETT, WILLIAM	BAL	137	2ND DIST
BENNETT, WILLIAM	SOM	512	BARREN C
BENNETT, WILLIAM	SOM	518	BARREN C
BENNETT, WILLIAM D.	SOM	519	BARREN C
BENNETT, WILLIAM H.	SOM	518	BARREN C
BENNETT, WILLIAM J.	SOM	440	DAMES QU
BENNETT, WILLIAM R.	KEN	239	2ND DIST
BENNETT,N.F.	BAL	124	1ST WARD
BENNEY, JONATHAN	BAL	312	7TH WARD
BENNEY, JOSEPH	BAL	243	17TH WAR
BENNEY, MOSES	KEN	223	2ND DIST
BENNEY, RICHARD E.	QUE	242	5TH E DI
BENNING, W.	BAL	314	12TH WAR
BENNINGTON, JEREMIAH	HAR	046	1ST DIST
BENNINGTON, JOHN	HAR	042	1ST DIST
BENNINGTON, THOAMS	HAR	046	1ST DIST
BENNINGTON, WILLIAM	HAR	042	1ST DIST
BENNIS, FRANCIS	BAL	229	12TH WAR
BENNIS, JOSHUA	TAL	012	EASTON D
BENNIT, HARRIET	HAR	018	1ST DIST
BENNIT, JOHN	BAL	213	2ND WARD
BENNIX, HENRY	BAL	136	2ND DIST
BENNIX, JOHN	BAL	292	20TH WAR
BENNIX, MARY	BAL	278	20TH WAR

Name	County	Page	District
BENNIX, NATHAN	BAL	295	20TH WAR
BENNIX, WILLIAM	WAS	138	HAGERSTO
BENNNER, NANCY	WAS	046	2ND SUBD
BENNOCK, MARY A.	BAL	307	3RD WARD
BENNOCK, PETER	BAL	308	3RD WARD
BENNOCK, THOMAS	BAL	307	3RD WARD
BENNOW, PETER	BAL	139	2ND DIST
BENNS, GEROGE	KEN	285	3RD DIST
BENNY, ALICE	CEC	140	5TH E DI
BENNY, ANTHONY	KEN	237	2ND DIST
BENNY, AZARIH*	TAL	007	EASTON D
BENNY, BENJAMIN	BAL	010	1ST WARD
BENNY, CHARLES	CEC	004	ELKTON 3
BENNY, HENRY H.	TAL	054	EASTON D
BENNY, JAMES W.	TAL	004	EASTON D
BENNY, JANE	BAL	269	12TH WAR
BENNY, JONOTHAN	KEN	248	2ND DIST
BENNY, MARY	BAL	011	1ST WARD
BENNY, MARY A.	BAL	257	2ND WARD
BENNY, SAMUEL H.	TAL	076	EASTON T
BENNYMAN, DEBORAH	BAL	233	12TH WAR
BENOIST, SANGUINET	FRE	202	5TH E DI
BENOR, GEORGE	HAR	084	2ND DIST
BENOSN, ELIZA	BAL	195	5TH DIST
BENOSN, MARY E.	TAL	104	ST MICHA
BENOY, ELIZABETH	ANN	464	HOWARD D
BENRON, GEORGE	BAL	226	17TH WAR
BENSOLD, ANDREW	BAL	055	1ST WARD
BENSOM, BENJAMIN	BAL	195	2ND WARD
BENSON, -----	ANN	367	4TH DIST
BENSON, ALLEN M.	MGM	384	ROCKERLE
BENSON, AMOS	HAR	083	2ND DIST
BENSON, ANN	BAL	132	18TH WAR
BENSON, ANN	BAL	096	5TH WARD
BENSON, ANN	ANN	500	HOWARD D
BENSQN, ANN	TAL	055	EASTON D
BENSON, ANN	SOM	403	BRINKLEY
BENSON, BASIL	PRI	021	VANSVILL
BENSON, BASIL	ANN	377	4TH DIST
BENSON, BENJAMIN	BAL	188	5TH DIST
BENSON, BENJAMIN	HAR	140	2ND DIST
BENSON, BENJAMIN	CEC	047	1ST E DI
BENSON, BENJAMIN	CEC	106	3RD E DI
BENSON, BENJAMIN T.	BAL	002	4TH WARD
BENSON, C.R.	PRI	080	QUEEN AN
BENSON, CAHRITY	BAL	170	6TH WARD
BENSON, CARCLINE	BAL	200	6TH WARD
BENSON, CAROLINE	HAR	088	2ND DIST
BENSON, CATHERINE	MGM	321	CRACKLIN
BENSON, CATHERINE	BAL	344	3RD WARD
BENSON, CHARLES	TAL	083	ST MICHA
BENSON, CHARLOTTE L.	BAL	191	6TH WARD
BENSON, DANIEL	SOM	402	BRINKLEY
BENSON, DEBBY-BLACK	QUE	183	3RD E DI
BENSON, EDWARD	TAL	040	EASTON D
BENSON, EDWIN*	DOR	425	1ST DIST
BENSON, ELEANOR	BAL	184	5TH DIST
BENSON, ELISA	BAL	297	3RD WARD
BENSON, ELIZABETH	BAL	002	15TH WAR
BENSON, ELIZABETH	FRE	272	NEW MARK
BENSON, ELIZABETH	DOR	302	1ST DIST
BENSON, ELIZABETH C.	BAL	306	7TH WARD
BENSON, ELLICK	KEN	307	3RD DIST
BENSON, GEORGE	BAL	129	1ST WARD
BENSON, GEORGE	BAL	248	12TH WAR
BENSON, GEORGE	BAL	066	1ST WARD
BENSON, GEORGE	BAL	116	1ST WARD
BENSON, GEORGE	BAL	163	1ST WARD
BENSON, GEORGE A.	BAL	284	12TH WAR
BENSON, GEORGE H.	BAL	416	8TH WARD
BENSON, GILBERT	BAL	243	6TH WARD
BENSON, H.	BAL	150	1ST WARD
BENSON, HARRIET	ANN	367	4TH DIST
BENSON, HECTOR	BAL	002	15TH WAR
BENSON, HENRIETTA	BAL	175	6TH WARD
BENSON, HENRY	BAL	143	5TH WARD
BENSON, HENRY	BAL	220	2ND WARD
BENSON, HENRY	HAR	172	3RD DIST
BENSON, HENRY	HAR	188	3RD DIST
BENSON, HENRY C.	BAL	160	1ST WARD
BENSON, HYLAND	CEC	062	1ST E DI
BENSON, ISAAC-BLACK	QUE	181	2ND E DI
BENSON, J.W.	BAL	271	12TH WAR
BENSON, JAMES	BAL	458	8TH WARD
BENSON, JAMES	BAL	150	5TH WARD
BENSON, JAMES	BAL	139	1ST WARD
BENSON, JAMES	TAL	083	ST MICHA
BENSON, JAMES	SOM	428	PRINCESS
BENSON, JAMES	CEC	051	1ST E DI
BENSON, JAMES	CEC	051	1ST E DI
BENSON, JAMES	DOR	310	1ST DIST
BENSON, JAMES A.	MGM	406	MEDLEY 3
BENSON, JEREMIAH	TAL	003	EASTON D
BENSON, JOHN	PRI	037	VANSVILL
BENSON, JOHN	CEC	062	1ST E DI
BENSON, JOHN	BAL	228	17TH WAR
BENSON, JOHN	BAL	131	18TH WAR
BENSON, JOHN	BAL	133	1ST WARD
BENSON, JOHN	BAL	297	12TH WAR
BENSON, JOHN	BAL	228	1ST DIST
BENSON, JOHN	ANN	418	HOWARD D
BENSON, JOHN W.	SOM	510	BARREN C
BENSON, JOHNSON	MGM	339	CLARKSBU
BENSON, JONATHAN B.	MGM	413	MEDLEY 3
BENSON, JONATHAN B.	MGM	414	MEDLEY 3
BENSON, JOSEPH	CEC	050	1ST E DI
BENSON, JOSEPH	BAL	053	15TH WAR
BENSON, JOSEPH	ANN	392	4TH DIST
BENSON, JULIA A.	FRE	256	NEW MARK
BENSON, KETLURA	BAL	268	12TH WAR
BENSON, L.H.	BAL	141	1ST WARD
BENSON, LEWIN T.	MGM	413	MEDLEY 3
BENSON, LLOYD	BAL	160	19TH WAR
BENSON, LOUISA	ANN	352	3RD DIST
BENSON, MABLE	TAL	110	ST MICHA
BENSON, MARGARET	ANN	352	3RD DIST
BENSON, MARGARET	BAL	189	5TH DIST
BENSON, MARIA-BLACK	QUE	126	1ST E DI
BENSON, MARIAH R.	TAL	037	EASTON D
BENSON, MARTHA	BAL	051	4TH WARD
BENSON, MARTHA	BAL	176	6TH WARD
BENSON, MARY	BAL	192	6TH WARD
BENSON, MARY	TAL	049	EASTON T
BENSON, MARY	MGM	436	CLARKSTR
BENSON, MARY A	ANN	489	HOWARD D
BENSON, MARY J.	BAL	027	9TH WARD
BENSON, MARY M.	MGM	426	MEDLEY 3
BENSON, MORDECAI	BAL	188	5TH DIST
BENSON, MOSES	HAR	097	2ND DIST
BENSON, NANCY	TAL	036	EASTON D
BENSON, NATHAN	ANN	341	3RD DIST
BENSON, NICHOLAS	ANN	492	HOWARD D
BENSON, NICHOLAS	CEC	106	3RD E DI
BENSON, PAUL	BAL	388	3RD WARD
BENSON, PERRY*	TAL	036	EASTON D
BENSON, R.	ANN	346	3RD DIST
BENSON, REBECA	BAL	286	20TH WAR
BENSON, ROBERT	BAL	126	1ST WARD
BENSON, ROBERT F.	BAL	312	3RD WARD
BENSON, ROBERT F.	TAL	079	ST MICHA
BENSON, S.	ANN	346	3RD DIST
BENSON, SAMUEL	BAL	308	7TH WARD
BENSON, SAMUEL	BAL	276	2ND WARD
BENSON, SAMUEL	BAL	097	10TH WAR
BENSON, SAMUEL	DOR	428	1ST DIST
BENSON, SAMUEL	DOR	385	1ST DIST
BENSON, SERENA	BAL	150	5TH WARD
BENSON, SUSAN	BAL	105	15TH WAR
BENSON, THOMAS	CEC	059	1ST E DI
BENSON, THOMAS	TAL	110	ST MICHA
BENSON, THOMAS	TAL	110	ST MICHA
BENSON, THOMAS	PRI	037	VANSVILL
BENSON, THOMAS R.	ANN	446	HOWARD D
BENSON, WILLIAM	BAL	043	15TH WAR
BENSON, WILLIAM	TAL	048	EASTON T
BENSON, WILLIAM	MGM	429	CLARKSTR
BENSON, WILLIAM	HAR	152	3RD DIST
BENSON, WILLIAM *	BAL	296	20TH WAR
BENSON, WILLIAM A.	BAL	404	14TH WAR
BENSON, WILLIAM G.	BAL	459	8TH WARD
BENSON, WILLIAM H.	MGM	339	CLARKSBU
BENSON, WILLIAM K.	MGM	339	CLARKSBU
BENSON, WILLIAM R.	BAL	312	3RD WARD
BENSON, WILLIAM T.	ST	303	2ND E DI
BENSON, WILLIAMSOLER, JAC	BAL	128	1ST WARD
BENSON, ISAAC-BLACK	QUE	203	3RD E DI
BENSON, MATILDA	BAL	250	12TH WAR
BENSON, SOLOMON	BAL	008	EASTERN
BENSTEAD, SAMUEL	BAL	169	1ST WARD
BENSTON, ALFORD H.	WOR	341	1ST E DI
BENSTON, ELIAS	WOR	333	1ST E DI
BENSTON, JANE	WOR	212	4TH E DI
BENSTON, JESSE	WOR	329	1ST E DI
BENSTON, LEAH	WOR	210	4TH E DI
BENSTON, SAMUEL	WOR	184	6TH E DI
BENSTON, SAMUEL W.	WOR	329	1ST E DI
BENSTON, SARAH	WOR	319	1ST E DI
BENSTON, THOMAS	WOR	333	1ST E DI
BENSTON, WILLIAM	WOR	333	1ST E DI
BENSTON, WILLIAM F.	WOR	243	1ST CENS
BENSWAGER, SAMUEL	BAL	457	14TH WAR
BENSYL, GEORGE	BAL	463	1ST DIST
BENT, JANE	HAR	201	3RD DIST
BENT, REACHE	BAL	142	19TH WAR
BENTALL, JOHN	BAL	139	1ST WARD
BENTBY, GRAFTON	BAL	030	2ND DIST
BENTEEN, FRED D.	BAL	225	19TH WAR
BENTELE, M.	BAL	449	8TH WARD
BENTER, JOANNA	BAL	163	19TH WAR
BENTGRAFF, ADELINE	BAL	172	19TH WAR
BENTGRAFF, J.	BAL	172	19TH WAR
BENTHALL, JOHN D.	BAL	143	1ST WARD
BENTHALL, ROBERT	BAL	011	1ST WARD
BENTHOER, BERNARD	BAL	234	12TH WAR
BENTHOLM, JAMES G.G.	BAL	297	12TH WAR
BENTINN, ENNALS-MULATTO	BAL	214	2ND WARD
BENTLE, J.	BAL	138	5TH WARD
BENTLEY, ALICE A.	MGM	347	BERRYS D
BENTLEY, BAKER	BAL	072	18TH WAR
BENTLEY, CALEB	MGM	347	BERRYS D
BENTLEY, CHARLES H.	BAL	043	4TH WARD
BENTLEY, GEORGE	BAL	120	1ST WARD
BENTLEY, HENRY	TAL	011	EASTON D
BENTLEY, JACOB	BAL	318	1ST DIST
BENTLEY, JAMES	BAL	256	17TH WAR
BENTLEY, JOHN *	WAS	055	2ND SUBD
BENTLEY, LUCY	BAL	148	2ND DIST
BENTLEY, MARY CATHARINE	BAL	376	13TH WAR
BENTLEY, R.A.	BAL	015	1ST WARD
BENTLEY, SUSAN	TAL	007	EASTON D
BENTLEY, THOMAS	TAL	014	EASTON D
BENTLEY, WILLIAM	BAL	315	1ST DIST
BENTLY, ELIZABETH	BAL	258	6TH WARD
BENTLY, EMILA	BAL	319	1ST DIST
BENTLY, GEORGE	BAL	334	1ST DIST
BENTLY, JACOB	BAL	420	14TH WAR
BENTLY, JAMES-BLACK	CAR	386	2ND DIST
BENTLY, JOHN	KEN	243	2ND DIST
BENTLY, MARY	BAL	461	1ST DIST
BENTLY, THOMAS	BAL	134	18TH WAR
BENTON, AARON	BAL	228	17TH WAR
BENTON, ALEXANDER	SOM	449	DAMES QU
BENTON, BENJAMIN	BAL	008	18TH WAR
BENTON, BENJAMIN	BAL	076	2ND DIST
BENTON, BRIDGET	ALL	196	CUMBERLA
BENTON, F.	BAL	137	1ST WARD
BENTON, GEORGE	BAL	456	8TH WARD
BENTON, HORACE	MGM	386	ROCKERLE
BENTON, J.	BAL	149	1ST WARD
BENTON, J.	BAL	149	1ST WARD
BENTON, J.	BAL	154	1ST WARD
BENTON, JAMES	BAL	152	1ST WARD
BENTON, JAMES	BAL	121	2ND DIST
BENTON, JAMES	CHA	236	HILLTOP
BENTON, JAMES	QUE	235	4TH E DI
BENTON, JAMES M.	HAR	198	3RD DIST
BENTON, JOHN S.-BLACK	QUE	140	1ST E DI
BENTON, JOHN-BLACK	QUE	136	1ST E DI
BENTON, JOSEPH	BAL	117	2ND DIST
BENTON, LEMUEL C.	QUE	152	1ST E DI
BENTON, LEVER	ALL	181	8TH E.D.
BENTON, MARY A.	MGM	442	CLARKSTR
BENTON, MARY E.	KEN	264	1ST DIST
BENTON, MORDECCA	ALL	143	6TH E.D.
BENTON, NATHANIEL O.	MGM	382	ROCKERLE
BENTON, RICHARD	QUE	233	4TH E DI
BENTON, SAMUEL C.	HAR	198	3RD DIST
BENTON, SAMUEL S.	FRE	228	BUCKEYST
BENTON, SARAH E.	BAL	008	18TH WAR
BENTON, THOMAS	KEN	265	1ST DIST
BENTON, THOMAS	MGM	442	CLARKSTR
BENTON, THOMAS N.	BAL	183	19TH WAR
BENTON, THOSM H.	BAL	375	13TH WAR
BENTON, VINCENT	QUE	178	2ND E DI
BENTON, VINCENT F.	QUE	149	1ST E DI
BENTON, WILLIAM	CEC	155	PORT DUP
BENTON, WILLIAM	ALL	229	CUMBERLA
BENTON, WILLIAM W.	FRE	243	NEW MARK
BENTON, ELIJAH	QUE	178	2ND E DI
BENTON, MATHIAS	BAL	053	1ST WARD
BENTON, NATHAN	QUE	151	1ST E DI
BENTON, WILLIAM D.	FRE	229	BUCKEYST
BENTOR, MARY	BAL	076	2ND DIST
BENTS, JACOB	BAL	322	1ST DIST
BENTSHEY, CAROLINE H.	BAL	239	1ST DIST
BENTSON, MOSES	HAR	146	3RD DIST
BENTSON, RICHARD	HAR	152	3RD DIST
BENTY, ANDREW	BAL	185	19TH WAR
BENTY, CASPER	BAL	021	18TH WAR
BENTY, CATHARINE	BAL	185	19TH WAR
BENTY, ERNEST	BAL	214	19TH WAR
BENTY, LEONARD	BAL	121	18TH WAR
BENTZ, ANNA M.	FRE	045	FREDERIC
BENTZ, CAROLINE J.	WAS	187	BOONSBOR
BENTZ, CLAY	WAS	222	1ST DIST
BENTZ, CULLING E.	WAS	188	BOONSBOR
BENTZ, ELIZABETH	WAS	143	HAGERSTO
BENTZ, ELIZABETH	WAS	222	1ST DIST
BENTZ, ELIZABETH	FRE	065	FREDERIC
BENTZ, FREDERICK	BAL	420	14TH WAR
BENTZ, H.	BAL	252	2ND WARD
BENTZ, HENRY	WAS	221	1ST DIST
BENTZ, HORATIO	FRE	006	FREDERIC
BENTZ, JACOB M.	FRE	006	FREDERIC
BENTZ, LAURENCE	FRE	058	FREDERIC
BENTZ, LEWIS	FRE	103	FREDERIC
BENTZ, REBECCA	FRE	059	FREDERIC
BENTZ, SAMUEL	WAS	187	BOONSBOR
BENTZ, WILLIAM	FRE	006	FREDERIC
BENTZE, JOHN	CAR	185	8TH DIST
BENTZER, JOSEPH	BAL	215	2ND WARD
BENVARE, SUSAN	BAL	075	1ST WARD
BENYON, WILLIAM*	BAL	388	3RD WARD
BENZEON, FRANCIS	BAL	204	2ND WARD
BENZINGER, MATTHEWS	BAL	268	12TH WAR
BENZON, A.	BAL	161	1ST WARD
BEOHNOR, ELISABETH	ALL	252	CUMBERLA
BERAEIS, NATHAN*	BAL	239	12TH WAR
BERAGE, SOLOMON M.	CAR	166	NC TWP L
BERAGE, WASHINGTON-BLACK	CAR	126	NO TWP L
BERANE, ISAAC	BAL	164	1ST WARD
BERASTAL, JOHN	BAL	251	2ND WARD
BERAUS, PERRY-BLACK	BAL	253	2ND WARD
BERAY, JOHN W.	HAR	151	3RD DIST
BERBET, ELIZABETH	BAL	029	1ST WARD
BERCE, WILLIAM	BAL	119	1ST WARD
BERCH, CHRISTIAN	BAL	308	20TH WAR
BERCH, FREEMAN	BAL	157	1ST WARD
BERCH, JAMES	KEN	251	2ND DIST
BERCH, SAMUEL	BAL	385	13TH WAR
BERCH, SARAH	BAL	277	2ND WARD
BERCH, WILLIAM	BAL	308	20TH WAR
BERCHANAL, THOMAS*	TAL	008	EASTON D
BERCK, SIMON	BAL	042	9TH WARD
BERCKHEAD, JOHN	BAL	301	3RD WARD
BERCKHEAD, MARY A.	BAL	360	13TH WAR
BERDEP, ELIZA A.*	DOR	425	1ST DIST
BERDOCH, ROSE	BAL	063	15TH WAR
BEREN, JOSEPH	FRE	032	FREDERIC
BERERICKS, WILLIAM	KEN	251	1ST DIST
BERFOOT, MARGARET	ANN	430	HOWARD D
BERG, Q. H.	BAL	062	10TH WAR
BERG, TAMER	DOR	299	1ST DIST
BERGAGE, MARTHA	CAR	067	NO TWP L
BERGAN, ELIZABETH	BAL	074	2ND DIST
BERGAN, GEORGE	WAS	058	2ND SUBD
BERGE, HESTER	KEN	274	1ST DIST
BERGEE, NACE	WAS	122	2ND DIST
BERGEN, CAROLINE	BAL	214	11TH WAR
BERGEN, CATHERINE	FRE	051	FREDERIC
BERGEN, DAVID	BAL	010	EASTERN
BERGEN, JOSHUA	BAL	068	2ND DIST
BERGEN, SARAH	BAL	160	6TH WARD
BERGEN, SARAH	WAS	140	HAGERSTO
BERGEN, WILLIAM	BAL	335	7TH WARD
BERGENS, ANN	CEC	019	ELKTON 3
BERGER, ABRAHAM	FRE	385	PETERSVI
BERGER, ADAM	BAL	426	8TH WARD
BERGER, ADAM	BAL	284	2ND WARD
BERGER, C. H.	BAL	082	10TH WAR
BERGER, CHRISTIAN	BAL	010	15TH WAR
BERGER, CHRISTOPHER	BAL	002	9TH WARD
BERGER, CHRISTOPHER	FRE	055	FREDERIC
BERGER, CLEMENTS	BAL	170	19TH WAR
BERGER, DANIEL	BAL	126	16TH WAR
BERGER, DAVID	WAS	265	1ST DIST
BERGER, ELIZABETH	WAS	136	2ND DIST
BERGER, GEORGE	WAS	286	1ST DIST
BERGER, H.	BAL	109	10TH WAR
BERGER, HENRY	FRE	015	FREDERIC
BERGER, JOHN	BAL	275	7TH WARD
BERGER, JOHN	WAS	207	1ST DIST
BERGER, JOSEPH	BAL	412	8TH WARD
BERGER, MARY	BAL	220	6TH WARD
BERGER, MICHAEL	BAL	264	2ND WARD
BERGER, MORRIS	BAL	171	19TH WAR
BERGER, OBEDAH	WAS	111	2ND DIST
BERGER, SUSAN	WAS	266	1ST DIST
BERGER, WILLIAM	WAS	149	HAGERSTO
BERGES, GEORGE	BAL	183	16TH WAR
BERGHOFF, MARY	BAL	133	16TH WAR
BERGMAN, HESTER	ALL	252	CUMBERLA
BERGMAN, PHILIP	ALL	252	CUMBERLA
BERGMAN, WOLF	ALL	241	CUMBERLA
BERGMANN, ANDREW	BAL	081	10TH WAR
BERGOIN, JAMES	WAS	116	2ND DIST
BERGOLD, UPTON A.	WAS	102	2ND DIST
BERGUNDER, BENJAMIN	BAL	063	15TH WAR
BERGZINGER, CHRISTIAN	BAL	372	13TH WAR
BERHWITH, JOHN	TAL	076	EASTON T
BERICE, GEORGE	BAL	322	7TH WARD
BERINGER, HENRY	HAR	119	2ND DIST
BERISON, WILLIAM *	BAL	296	20TH WAR
BERK, GEORGE W.	TAL	072	EASTON T
BERK, JOHN	TAL	014	EASTON D
BERKELY, EDW.	BAL	300	20TH WAR
BERKENKOLL, JAMES	ALL	169	6TH E.D.
BERKERD, HUGH	BAL	040	1ST WARD
BERKET, JOHN	BAL	263	2ND WARD
BERKET, JOHN	BAL	263	2ND WARD
BERKETT, MARY	BAL	371	13TH WAR
BERKETT, MARY E. H.	BAL	126	11TH WAR
BERKHEAD, JACOB	CAL	041	3RD DIST
BERKHOLT, CHARLES	BAL	002	9TH WARD
BERKIRK, LORENZO*	BAL	271	20TH WAR
BERKISN, ADALINE	HAR	030	1ST DIST
BERKMAN, ANN M.	WAS	278	LEITERSB
BERKMAN, HENRY	BAL	214	2ND WARD
BERLANDIER, RAFAEL	FRE	20	5TH E DI
BERLIN, JAMES	CEC	151	PORT DUP

BERLINER, JOHN * WAS 093 2ND SUBD
BERLLY, JAMES BAL 163 1ST WARD
BERLON, SUSAN BAL 301 12TH WAR
BERLTA, JOSEPH BAL 031 1ST WARD
BERM, NICHOLAS BAL 248 2ND WARD
BERMAN, DANIEL WAS 040 2ND SUBD
BERMAN, HENRY BAL 060 1ST WARD
BERMANT, LOUISA WAS 142 HAGERSTO
BERMARD, JAMES BAL 087 2ND DIST
BERMINGHAM, MATTHEW BAL 037 2ND DIST
BERMONDEY, AUGUSTUS BAL 040 2ND DIST
BERMUTH, PETER BAL 456 8TH WARD
BERNAI, SOLOMON BAL 092 10TH WAR
BERNAJE, HUGH M. TAL 046 EASTON T
BERNAN, ALEX WAS 063 2ND SUBD
BERNARD, ANN BAL 010 9TH WARD
BERNARD, ANN BAL 016 9TH WARD
BERNARD, JAMES HAR 069 1ST DIST
BERNARD, JOHN BAL 452 8TH WARD
BERNARD, JOHN H. BAL 303 12TH WAR
BERNARD, JOHN H. HAR 060 1ST DIST
BERNARD, JOHN H. HAR 049 1ST DIST
BERNARD, JOHN P. BAL 150 1ST WARD
BERNARD, JOSEPH ALL 088 5TH E.D.
BERNARD, JOSEPH W. CAR 096 NO TWP L
BERNARD, LEWIS BAL 047 9TH WARD
BERNARD, LEWIS BAL 141 2ND DIST
BERNARD, LOUISA BAL 214 11TH WAR
BERNARD, M. BAL 071 4TH WARD
BERNARD, MARY ALL 123 4TH E.D.
BERNARD, PARKER BAL 415 3RD WARD
BERNARD, TERERSA P. BAL 210 19TH WAR
BERNARD, THOMAS P. BAL 410 3RD WARD
BERNARD, WILLIAM BAL 299 17TH WAR
BERNARD, WILLIAM BAL 100 2ND DIST
BERNCE, ELIZABETH BAL 251 2ND WARD
BERNE, ANN BAL 452 14TH WAR
BERNE, ELIZABETH BAL 266 2ND WARD
BERNEGER, LEONARD ALL 227 CUMBERLA
BERNER, JOHN BAL 220 2ND WARD
BERNET, J. ST 318 4TH E DI
BERNET, JOHN BAL 268 2ND WARD
BERNIE, CLOTWORTHY CAR 269 WESTMINS
BERNODAY, CHARLES BAL 040 2ND DIST
BERNS, SAMUEL KEN 305 3RD DIST
BERNWER, R. BAL 265 20TH WAR
BEROMGER, GEORGE BAL 159 19TH WAR
BEROYER, THEODORE BAL 076 2ND DIST
BERREY, JOHN BAL 363 8TH WARD
BERREY, JOHN BAL 316 7TH WARD
BERREY, RICHARD BAL 378 3RD WARD
BERRI, MISS L. FRE 200 5TH E DI
BERRIAGE, ELIZABETH TAL 057 EASTON D
BERRICK, GOOLIP BAL 270 17TH WAR
BERRIMAN, JOHN BAL 334 7TH WARD
BERRINGER, BODUS BAL 016 15TH WAR
BERRINGTON, ANDREW FRE 339 MIDDLETO
BERRIS, ELEAZER ALL 176 7TH E.D.
BERRRY, JOHN E. JR. PRI 012 BLADENSB
BERRSER, JOHN * KEN 213 2ND DIST
BERRY, ABRAHAM BAL 433 14TH WAR
BERRY, ABRAHAM BAL 434 14TH WAR
BERRY, ACENATH CHA 229 MIDDLETO
BERRY, ADALINE BAL 057 4TH WARD
BERRY, ALBERT P. PRI 011 BLADENSB
BERRY, ALBY CAL 035 2ND DIST
BERRY, ALEXANDER HAR 033 1ST DIST
BERRY, ALFRED PRI 075 MARLBROU
BERRY, ALLY CAL 030 2ND DIST
BERRY, ALONZO ALL 216 CUMBERLA
BERRY, ALVERCA M. BAL 321 20TH WAR
BERRY, AMANCA WAS 096 2ND SUBD
BERRY, AMELIA BAL 212 19TH WAR
BERRY, ANDERSON KEN 297 3RD DIST
BERRY, ANN BAL 026 2ND DIST
BERRY, ARMANTA BAL 273 2ND WARD
BERRY, ARTHUMUS BAL 153 5TH WARD
BERRY, BEN PRI 082 QUEEN AN
BERRY, BENJAMIN PRI 072 MARLBROU
BERRY, BENJAMIN FRE 253 NEW MARK
BERRY, BENJAMIN D. BAL 401 3RD WARD
BERRY, BETSY CEC 002 ELKTON 3
BERRY, CAROLINE WOR 277 BERLIN 1
BERRY, CATHARINE CEC 006 ELKTON 3
BERRY, CHARLES CHA 261 MIDDLETO
BERRY, CHARLES A. BAL 372 3RD WARD
BERRY, CHARLES C. CAR 369 9TH DIST
BERRY, CHRISTIAN BAL 147 2ND DIST
BERRY, CHRISTIANNA E. CHA 241 HILLTOP
BERRY, DANIEL TAL 045 EASTON T
BERRY, DEBORAH PRI 010 BLADENSB
BERRY, DIANNA BAL 154 5TH WARD
BERRY, E. M. CHA 252 BOJANTOW
BERRY, EDGAR BAL 370 13TH WAR
BERRY, ELIJA PRI 098 SPALDING
BERRY, ELIZA A. MRS- BAL 315 20TH WAR
BERRY, ELIZABETH CAR 148 NO TWP L
BERRY, ELIZABETH PRI 099 SPALDING
BERRY, ELLEN BAL 246 6TH WARD
BERRY, EMILY BAL 211 6TH DIST
BERRY, EMILY H. BAL 476 14TH WAR
BERRY, GABRIEL BAL 370 13TH WAR
BERRY, GEORGE CEC 131 6TH E DI
BERRY, GEORGE BAL 105 18TH WAR
BERRY, GEORGE BAL 105 18TH WAR
BERRY, GEORGE ANN 382 4TH DIST
BERRY, GEORGE BAL 105 5TH WARD
BERRY, GEORGE ST 335 4TH E DI
BERRY, GEORGE F. CHA 289 BOJANTOW
BERRY, GEORGE H. CHA 254 MIDDLETO
BERRY, GEORGE H. SOM 367 BRINKLEY
BERRY, GEORGE R. BAL 079 15TH WAR
BERRY, GEORGE W. BAL 226 6TH WARD
BERRY, GEORGE W. CHA 260 MIDDLETO
BERRY, HENRY CEC 065 1ST E DI
BERRY, HENRY B. CHA 255 MIDDLETO
BERRY, HORATIO BAL 407 14TH WAR
BERRY, HORATIO PRI 100 SPALDING
BERRY, IBBY HAR 071 1ST DIST
BERRY, JAMES FRE 096 FREDERIC
BERRY, JAMES CAR 230 5TH DIST
BERRY, JAMES BAL 155 1ST WARD
BERRY, JAMES BAL 087 15TH WAR
BERRY, JAMES BAL 337 3RD WARD
BERRY, JAMES BAL 257 1ST DIST
BERRY, JAMES BAL 257 2ND WARD
BERRY, JAMES H. WAS 170 FUNKSTOW
BERRY, JAMES W. BAL 046 15TH WAR
BERRY, JAMES-BLACK CAR 086 NO TWP L
BERRY, JANE BAL 269 17TH WAR
BERRY, JANE BAL 296 20TH WAR
BERRY, JANE BAL 028 1ST WARD
BERRY, JANE PRI 091 MARLBROU
BERRY, JERRY ANN 449 HOWARD D
BERRY, JOHN QUE 234 4TH E DI
BERRY, JOHN WAS 095 2ND SUBD
BERRY, JOHN BAL 292 20TH WAR
BERRY, JOHN CEC 215 7TH E DI
BERRY, JOHN CEC 149 PORT DUP
BERRY, JOHN BAL 318 20TH WAR
BERRY, JOHN E. PRI 011 BLADENSB
BERRY, JOHN H. BAL 098 15TH WAR
BERRY, JOHN T. PRI 063 NOTTINGH
BERRY, JOHN W. BAL 407 14TH WAR
BERRY, JOHN W. BAL 162 19TH WAR
BERRY, JOSEPH T. TAL 028 EASTON D
BERRY, JULIA BAL 318 20TH WAR
BERRY, JULIA A. BAL 106 15TH WAR
BERRY, JULIANN BAL 254 17TH WAR
BERRY, L. BAL 281 2ND WARD
BERRY, L. PRI 100 SPALDING
BERRY, LEAH BAL 396 14TH WAR
BERRY, LOUIS CEC 215 7TH E DI
BERRY, LUCRETIA BAL 108 15TH WAR
BERRY, MARGARET CHA 293 BOJANTOW
BERRY, MARGARETT A. BAL 023 18TH WAR
BERRY, MARGERY PRI 073 MARLBROU
BERRY, MARIA PRI 015 BLADENSB
BERRY, MARTHA BAL 144 5TH WARD
BERRY, MARTHA E. BAL 097 15TH WAR
BERRY, MARY BAL 229 12TH WAR
BERRY, MARY PRI 074 MARLBROU
BERRY, MARY CHA 293 BOJANTOW
BERRY, MARY BAL 192 19TH WAR
BERRY, MARY E. BAL 396 14TH WAR
BERRY, MARY E. PRI 082 QUEEN AN
BERRY, MARY P. CHA 253 MIDDLETO
BERRY, MARY R. WAS 121 HAGERSTO
BERRY, MARY V. BAL 097 15TH WAR
BERRY, MATILDA BAL 028 4TH WARD
BERRY, MILDRED CHA 250 MIDDLETO
BERRY, NATHAN BAL 101 2ND DIST
BERRY, NATHAN E. BAL 118 15TH WAR
BERRY, NICHOLAS BAL 162 19TH WAR
BERRY, RACHEL BAL 035 2ND DIST
BERRY, RACHEL-BLACK QUE 194 3RD E DI
BERRY, RACHEL-BLACK QUE 193 3RD E DI
BERRY, RBEECCA BAL 084 1ST WARD
BERRY, RICHARD BAL 158 2ND DIST
BERRY, ROBERT D. BAL 234 6TH WARD
BERRY, ROSE BAL 012 18TH WAR
BERRY, S. BAL 151 1ST WARD
BERRY, S. T. CHA 253 MIDDLETO
BERRY, SALLY WOR 277 BERLIN 1
BERRY, SAMUEL BAL 170 1ST WARD
BERRY, SAMUEL BAL 121 1ST WARD
BERRY, SAMUEL BAL 130 1ST WARD
BERRY, SAMUEL H. PRI 093 MARLBROU
BERRY, SARAH BAL 108 15TH WAR
BERRY, SARAH BAL 460 1ST DIST
BERRY, SARAH BAL 402 14TH WAR
BERRY, SARAH L. ANN 521 HOWARD D
BERRY, SARAH-BLACK CAR 071 NO TWP L
BERRY, SHARTOLE-BLACK CAR 084 NO TWP L
BERRY, SOLOMON W. BAL 040 9TH WARD
BERRY, STEPHEN BAL 463 1ST DIST
BERRY, SUSAN M. CHA 254 MIDDLETO
BERRY, THOMAS CEC 041 CHESAPEA
BERRY, THOMAS BAL 119 1ST WARD
BERRY, THOMAS BAL 043 1ST WARD
BERRY, THOMAS ALL 195 CUMBERLA
BERRY, THOMAS PRI 088 SPALDING
BERRY, THOMAS B. CHA 254 MIDDLETO
BERRY, THOMAS E. PRI 081 QUEEN AN
BERRY, TIMOTHY BAL 022 9TH WARD
BERRY, URAMINDA BAL 030 4TH WARD
BERRY, WALTER W. BAL 075 15TH WAR
BERRY, WILLIAM BAL 088 15TH WAR
BERRY, WILLIAM BAL 130 1ST WARD
BERRY, WILLIAM CHA 229 MIDDLETO
BERRY, WILLIAM CAR 114 NO TWP L
BERRY, WILLIAM BAL 248 17TH WAR
BERRY, WILLIAM CEC 155 PORT DUP
BERRY, WILLIAM CEC 149 PORT DUP
BERRY, WILLIAM BAL 105 18TH WAR
BERRY, WILLIAM A. WOR 320 1ST E DI
BERRY, WILLIAM H. ANN 443 HOWARD D
BERRY, WILLIAM J. BAL 064 15TH WAR
BERRY, WILLIAM J. PRI 082 QUEEN AN
BERRY, WILLIAM J. CAR 283 7TH DIST
BERRY, WILLIAM L. CHA 293 BOJANTOW
BERRY, ZACARIAH PRI 073 MARLBROU
BERRY, ZACHARIAH PRI 081 QUEEN AN
BERRY,ELIZABETH PRI 014 BLADENSB
BERRY,MARSHAL BAL 026 2ND DIST
BERRYMAN, CAROLINE-BLACK BAL 026 2ND DIST
BERRYMAN, CHARLES QUE 194 3RD E DI
BERRYMAN, EPHRAIM BAL 244 6TH WARD
BERRYMAN, FRAN BAL 222 1ST DIST
BERRYMAN, GEORGE BAL 212 11TH WAR
BERRYMAN, HANNAH KEN 231 2ND DIST
BERRYMAN, JAMES KEN 264 1ST DIST
BERRYMAN, JAMES KEN 261 1ST DIST
BERRYMAN, JOHN KEN 230 2ND DIST
BERRYMAN, JOHN KEN 270 1ST DIST
BERRYMAN, R. M. BAL 024 1ST WARD
BERRYMAN, WILLIAM BAL 232 1ST DIST
BERRYMAN, WILLIAM BAL 225 1ST DIST
BERSCH, HENRY CAR 207 4TH DIST
BERSEY, HENRY BAL 042 4TH WARD
BERSICK, MICHAEL MGM 387 ROCKERLE
BERT, AMELIA BAL 016 15TH WAR
BERT, DAVID WAS 108 2ND DIST
BERT, MARY FRE 069 FREDERIC
BERTAN, EMILY BAL 359 13TH WAR
BERTER, HENRY BAL 080 4TH WARD
BERTEY, GEORGE BAL 044 4TH WARD
BERTHA, JAMES BAL 219 2ND WARD
BERTHEW, HENRY FRE 389 PETERSVI
BERTHIAN, MARYANN BAL 460 1ST DIST
BERTICK, W. BAL 330 3RD WARD
BERTNER, HENRY BAL 318 12TH WAR
BERTPITCH, FRANCES* BAL 295 1ST DIST
BERTPITCH, JOSEPH* DOR 376 1ST DIST
BERTRAM, ANTHONY DOR 411 1ST DIST
BERTRAM, DAVID ALL 160 6TH E.D.
BERTRAM, JOHN J. BAL 207 2ND WARD
BERTRAN, THOMAS D. BAL 268 2ND WARD
BERTRANA, JOHN BAL 271 2ND WARD
BERTRAND, JOHN BAL 381 8TH WARD
BERTSCH, JACOB BAL 446 8TH WARD
BERTSH, LEWIS BAL 145 16TH WAR
BERTZ, CASPAR BAL 269 12TH WAR
BERVARD, JAMES BAL 275 20TH WAR
BERWAGER, FREDERIC HAR 006 1ST DIST
BERWAGER, JACOB CAR 340 6TH DIST
BERWAGER, JACOB F. CAR 340 6TH DIST
BERWAGER, LUCINDA CAR 345 6TH DIST
BERWICK, WILLIAM CAR 346 6TH DIST
BERY, JAMES QUE 141 1ST E DI
BERZ, WILLIAM BAL 329 1ST DIST
BESANT, JAMES H. BAL 180 5TH WARD
BESCOE, EMELINE FRE 223 BUCKEYST
BESEON, BYRON M. BAL 142 11TH WAR
BESERICK, ROBERT CAL 027 2ND DIST
BESERICKS, ELIZA KEN 249 2ND DIST
BESH, FREDERICK KEN 262 1ST DIST
BESHEARS, JOHN BAL 259 2ND WARD
BESHIRD, WILLIAM BAL 106 15TH WAR
BESHWITH, JOHN WAS 143 HAGERSTO
BESICKER, DANIE TAL 096 ST MICHA
BESICKER, FREDERICK WAS 017 2ND SUBD
BESICKS, MAY WAS 017 2ND SUBD
BESIGHT, FRANCIS BAL 071 15TH WAR
BESINCKS, EMORY * BAL 128 18TH WAR
BESINCKS, JERRY KEN 254 1ST DIST
BESINCKS, ROBERT * KEN 247 2ND DIST
BESING, FREDERICK KEN 254 1ST DIST
BESIRICKS, ROBERT * FRE 059 FREDERIC
BESLER, CHRISTIAN H. KEN 254 1ST DIST
BESLEY, JOSHUA HAR 068 1ST DIST
BESORE, JEREMIAH BAL 097 2ND DIST
BESORE, JOSEPH H. WAS 259 1ST DIST
BESORE, MARY WAS 276 RIDGEVIL
BESS, HENRY CAR 264 WESTMINS
BESS, THOMAS WAS 070 2ND SUBD
BESSENT, JOHN BAL 130 1ST WARD
BESSER, GEORGE BAL 164 1ST WARD
BESSER, WEMER BAL 267 2ND WARD
BESSEX, WILLIAM-BLACK BAL 272 2ND WARD
BESSEY, DANIEL W. CAR 076 NO TWP L
BESSICK, SAMUEL BAL 407 3RD WARD
BESSICKS, JOSHUA HAR 029 1ST DIST
BESSINCKS, PETER BAL 435 14TH WAR
BESSIRICK, MATILDA KEN 277 1ST DIST
BESSIX, JAMES KEN 261 1ST DIST
BEST, CATHARINE TAL 095 ST MICHA
BEST, CHARLES FRE 308 WOODSBOR
BEST, CHRISTIAN ALL 098 5TH E.D.
BEST, HEZEKIAH N. FRE 284 WOODSBOR
BEST, HEZEKIAH ANN 328 2ND DIST
BEST, JOHN ANN 327 2ND DIST
BEST, MATTHIAS BAL 213 6TH WARD
BEST, MICHAEL ANN 314 1ST DIST
BEST, UPTON BAL 011 15TH WAR
BEST, WILLIAM MGM 382 ROCKERLE
BESTALL, WILLIAM H. CEC 123 3RD E DI
BESTON, ANN BAL 321 12TH WAR
BESTON, JAMES BAL 321 12TH WAR
BESTON, JOHN BAL 163 19TH WAR
BESTON, SARAH CEC 035 CHESAPEA
BESTON, THOMAS CEC 030 CHESAPEA
BESTON, WILLIAM BAL 318 12TH WAR
BESTON, WILLIAM CEC 032 CHESAPEA
BESTOR, J. R. CEC 144 PORT DUP
BESTPITCH, FRANCES* BAL 023 4TH WARD
BESTPITCH, JOSEPH* DOR 376 1ST DIST
BESTPITCH, LEAH J. DOR 411 1ST DIST
BESTPITCH, THOMAS* DOR 468 1ST DIST
BESWELL, THOMAS DOR 442 1ST DIST
BESWICK, BENJAMIN FRE 342 MIDDLETO
BETEBENNER, CATHARIEN BAL 387 3RD WARD
BETEBENNER, GEORGE WAS 182 BOONSBOR
BETEBENNER, JOHN FRE 334 MIDDLETO
BETEELER, SARAH L. WAS 184 BOONSBOR
BETENKEEP, JOHN FRE 400 JEFFERSO
BETERBETTER, JOHN BAL 223 19TH WAR
BETES, JACOB FRE 394 PETERSVI
BETHANTON, ELIZABETH * ALL 088 5TH E.D.
BETHARDS, MARY BAL 373 1ST DIST
BETKINS, JOHN W. SOM 554 TYASKIN
BETRAM, ANN BAL 021 9TH WARD
BETRAM, JOHN H. BAL 356 8TH WARD
BETRAM, PETER * BAL 356 8TH WARD
BETS, JOHN ALL 159 6TH E.D.
BETS, WILLIAM WAS 138 HAGERSTO
BETSCHLER, MARTIN BAL 319 1ST DIST
BETSON, EMILY BAL 024 15TH WAR
BETSON, EMMA BAL 068 18TH WAR
BETSON, JOHN BAL 420 14TH WAR
BETSOW, REBECCA FRE 092 FREDERIC
BETSWELL, FREDERICK FRE 096 FREDERIC
BETSWORTH, ELIZABETH ALL 224 CUMBERLA
BETT, JOHN BAL 157 6TH WARD
BETT, JOHN-BLACK FRE 100 FREDERIC
BETT, LIZZY* FRE 225 BUCKEYST
BETT, MIDDLETON BAL 039 4TH WARD
BETT, RACHAEL PRI 042 VANSVILL
BETT, T. HANSON FRE 040 FREDERIC
BETT, THORNTON BAL 210 11TH WAR
BETT, TURNER CHA 236 HILLTOP
BETTE, HARRIET A. PRI 040 VANSVILL
BETTEN, SAMUEL CHA 239 HILLTOP
BETTER, CATHARINE QUE 179 2ND E DI
BETTER, JOHN BAL 160 19TH WAR
BETTER, MARY C. BAL 431 8TH WARD
BETTER, MIKE-BLACK KEN 259 1ST DIST
BETTET, WILIAM QUE 129 1ST E DI
BETTHOUSER, WILLIAM ALL 247 CUMBERLA
BETTIS, LUCY BAL 226 17TH WAR
BETTLE, REBECCA WAS 011 WILLIAMS
BETTON, HELEN QUE 169 2ND E DI
BETTON, JULIA BAL 148 16TH WAR
BETTON, MARY S. BAL 012 18TH WAR
BETTON, SAMUEL D. QUE 170 2ND E DI
BETTON, WILLIAM HENRY QUE 246 5TH E DI
BETTRANTON, ELIZABETH * QUE 203 3RD E DI
BETTRELL, ISAAC BAL 373 1ST DIST
BETTS, ADELAIDE BAL 162 2ND DIST
BETTS, ALEXANDER P.* KEN 260 1ST DIST
BETTS, ARMINTA BAL 342 3RD WARD
BETTS, CHRIST BAL 061 10TH WAR
BETTS, DANIEL WAS 297 1ST DIST
BETTS, EDARD BAL 122 1ST WARD
BETTS, EDWARDS SR. BAL 181 2ND DIST
BETTS, ELEANOR BAL 097 15TH WAR
BETTS, ELIZA WOR 211 4TH E DI
BETTS, ELIZABETH WAS 297 1ST DIST
BETTS, FREDERICK WAS 168 FUNKSTOW
WAS 180 BOONSBOR

BETTS, FREEBORN L. WOR 202 4TH E DI
BETTS, GUSTAVUS BAL 030 15TH WAR
BETTS, HENRY CAR 329 MANCHEST
BETTS, ISABELLA BAL 061 10TH WAR
BETTS, JACOB WAS 162 HAGERSTO
BETTS, JACOB WAS 213 1ST DIST
BETTS, JAMES BAL 165 1ST WARD
BETTS, JASPER WOR 202 4TH E DI
BETTS, JOHN WAS 243 CAVETOWN
BETTS, JOHN CEC 009 ELKTON 3
BETTS, JOHN T. ST 278 3RD E DI
BETTS, JOHN U. WAS 168 FUNKSTOW
BETTS, LUTHER D. WAS 230 1ST DIST
BETTS, LYDIA WAS 213 1ST DIST
BETTS, MARY BAL 329 3RD WARD
BETTS, MARY E. BAL 326 7TH WARD
BETTS, MARY J. ST 273 3RD E DI
BETTS, MATHISA J. WOR 203 4TH E DI
BETTS, ROBERT BAL 160 6TH WARD
BETTS, ROBERT O. BAL 160 6TH WARD
BETTS, ROYSTON BAL 046 9TH WARD
BETTS, S. BAL 228 19TH WAR
BETTS, SAMUEL WAS 186 BOONSBOR
BETTS, SOLOMON QUE 170 2ND E DI
BETTS, SUSAN BAL 077 4TH WARD
BETTS, THOMAS BAL 154 1ST WARD
BETTS, THOMAS W. BAL 045 9TH WARD
BETTS, W.W. ALL 217 CUMBERLA
BETTS, WILLIAM BAL 073 4TH WARD
BETTS, WILLIAM BAL 233 20TH WAR
BETTS, WILLIAM WAS 180 BOONSBOR
BETTY, JOHN BAL 190 19TH WAR
BETY, ANN WAS 083 2ND SUBD
BETY, DANIEL * WAS 082 2ND SUBD
BETZ, ADAM BAL 280 1ST DIST
BETZ, ANDREWS BAL 334 13TH WAR
BETZ, CHRISTOPHER BAL 086 1ST WARD
BETZ, DANIEL * WAS 082 2ND SUBD
BETZ, JANE BAL 390 1ST DIST
BETZ, JOHN BAL 377 1ST DIST
BETZ, JOHN BAL 086 1ST WARD
BETZ, JOHN BAL 349 13TH WAR
BETZ, JOHN GOLLIEB BAL 334 13TH WAR
BETZ, PHILIP BAL 062 15TH WAR
BETZ, ROBERT BAL 397 1ST DIST
BETZ, WILLIAM BAL 036 15TH WAR
BETZALL, ELISABETH ALL 248 CUMBERLA
BETZENBERGER, ALSA FRE 093 FREDERIC
BETZENBERGER, REBECCA FRE 098 FREDERIC
BETZENBERGER, WILLIAM FRE 092 FREDERIC
BETZER, AUGUST BAL 206 19TH WAR
BETZHOOVER, HENRY BAL 048 9TH WARD
BEUCHAMP, J.M. BAL 170 1ST WARD
BEUCKE, JOHN DR. BAL 373 13TH WAR
BEUCKER, WILLIAM * BAL 055 15TH WAR
BEUKEN, JACOB CEC 130 6TH E DI
BEUKEN, MARY CEC 131 6TH E DI
BEULIN, ISIAH M. CEC 156 PORT DUP
BEULL, DAVID R. * ALL 160 6TH E.D.
BEULL, WILLIAM ALL 164 6TH E.D.
BEULLESPACHER, FREDERICKA WAS 159 HAGERSTO
BEUMASTER, JOSEPH CAL 002 1ST DIST
BEURGEE, HANNAH WAS 102 2ND DIST
BEUSTON, LEVI WOR 182 6TH E DI
BEVAN, ANN BAL 257 12TH WAR
BEVAN, CHARLES F. BAL 278 20TH WAR
BEVAN, CORNELIA BAL 425 14TH WAR
BEVAN, DAVER BAL 270 12TH WAR
BEVAN, ELIZABETH BAL 304 20TH WAR
BEVAN, ELIZABETH MISS- BAL 315 20TH WAR
BEVAN, GALEN MGM 386 ROCKERLE
BEVAN, GEORGE BAL 153 16TH WAR
BEVAN, ISAAC BAL 171 1ST WARD
BEVAN, J. BAL 147 1ST WARD
BEVAN, JAMES BAL 197 11TH WAR
BEVAN, JOHN BAL 425 14TH WAR
BEVAN, JOHN PRI 066 NOTTINGH
BEVAN, JOHN H. FRE 253 NEW MARK
BEVAN, JOHN T. MGM 399 ROCKERLE
BEVAN, JOSHUA BAL 140 2ND DIST
BEVAN, LAURA BAL 403 14TH WAR
BEVAN, LAURA A. ANN 521 HOWARD D
BEVAN, MARTHA BAL 186 11TH WAR
BEVAN, MARY BAL 303 17TH WAR
BEVAN, MARY A. BAL 403 14TH WAR
BEVAN, PAMELIA BAL 141 2ND DIST
BEVAN, SAMUEL BAL 403 14TH WAR
BEVAN, SAMUEL BAL 142 11TH WAR
BEVAN, THOAMS H. * BAL 280 20TH WAR
BEVAN, THOMAS BAL 313 3RD WARD
BEVAN, WILLIAM BAL 186 11TH WAR
BEVAN, WILLIAM BAL 091 1ST WARD
BEVAN, WILLIAM BAL 298 20TH WAR
BEVAND, CHARLES BAL 125 2ND DIST
BEVANS, ANASTACIA BAL 250 6TH WARD
BEVANS, ANN E. BAL 351 7TH WARD
BEVANS, CATHARINE KEN 221 2ND DIST
BEVANS, DAVID ALL 135 4TH E.D.
BEVANS, ELLEN ALL 180 8TH E.D.
BEVANS, HANAH ANN 396 8TH DIST
BEVANS, HENRY BAL 452 8TH WARD
BEVANS, HOBEDEN-BLACK WOR 321 1ST E DI
BEVANS, JOHN SOM 361 BRINKLEY
BEVANS, JOHN ALL 264 CUMBERLA
BEVANS, JOHN ALL 263 CUMBERLA
BEVANS, JOHNS. ALL 094 5TH E.D.
BEVANS, JOSEPH BAL 062 1ST WARD
BEVANS, REUBEN A. L. BAL 359 3RD WARD
BEVANS, SUSAN J. BAL 282 7TH WARD
BEVANS, THOMAS WAS 163 2ND DIST
BEVANS, WALTER ALL 183 8TH E.D.
BEVANS, WILLIAM BAL 151 2ND DIST
BEVARD, GEORGE* HAR 003 1ST DIST
BEVARD, JAMES * BAL 125 2ND DIST
BEVEDES, MARY BAL 261 12TH WAR
BEVELY, ELBERT CAL 006 1ST DIST
BEVELY, ELIZABETH CAL 016 1ST DIST
BEVELY, SARHA CAL 016 1ST DIST
BEVEN, CHARLES H. CHA 277 BOJANTOW
BEVEN, GEORGE F. CHA 229 MIDDLETO
BEVEN, GOERGE F. CHA 277 BOJANTOW
BEVEN, JULIA CHA 286 BOJANTOW
BEVEN, THOMAS CHA 270 ALLENS F
BEVENS, CLOE WOR 178 6TH E DI
BEVENS, EBENEZER WOR 183 6TH E DI
BEVENS, ELIJAH WOR 201 3RD E DI
BEVENS, MARY WOR 185 6TH E DI
BEVENS, RACHEL WOR 182 6TH E DI
BEVERAGE, RESSELL ALL 105 5TH E.D.
BEVERIDGE, FRANCIS BAL 357 8TH WARD
BEVERLY, LOUISA D. ST 340 5TH E DI
BEVERS, JOHN L. WOR 177 6TH E DI
BEVERS, WILLIAM FRE 220 BUCKEYST
BEVINS, AGNESS WOR 179 6TH E DI
BEVINS, BARSHABA J. WOR 177 6TH E DI
BEVWENS, ROLAND E. WOR 182 6TH E DI
BEW, HENRY-BLACK QUE 127 1ST E DI
BEW, WILLIAM-BLACK QUE 127 1ST E DI
BEWARD, CHRISTINA CAR 175 8TH DIST
BEWARD, JAMES ANN 493 HOWARD D
BEWARD, JAMES * HAR 006 1ST DIST
BEWARD, JONATHAN ANN 493 HOWARD D
BEWARD, MARGARET CAR 176 8TH DIST
BEWE, ELIZA BAL 123 11TH WAR
BEWLEY, THOMAS QUE 180 2ND E DI
BEWLEY, WILLIAM C. QUE 160 2ND E DI
BEX, WILLIAM CAR 118 NO TWP L
BEXLEY, MARIA BAL 429 14TH WAR
BEYAN, MICAHEL ALL 075 5TH E.D.
BEYER, GEROGE BAL 220 6TH WARD
BEYER, LEWIS ALL 226 CUMBERLA
BEYER, REBECCA BAL 154 19TH WAR
BEYER, SUSAN FRE 035 FREDERIC
BEYERS, DAVID CAR 195 4TH DIST
BEZE, GEORGE * HAR 016 1ST DIST
BEZINGER, JULIA BAL 021 1ST WARD
BEZLER, MAGDALEN CAR 328 MANCHEST
BIALY, ELORA BAL 396 14TH WAR
BIAN, CATHERINE ALL 242 CUMBERLA
BIARD, CHALRES WAS 094 2ND SUBD
BIARD, FRANCIS CEC 099 3RD E DI
BIAS, CRARA ANN 336 3RD DIST
BIAS, DAVY CAL 046 3RD DIST
BIAS, DORCAS QUE 218 3RD E DI
BIAS, ELIZA ANN 304 1ST DIST
BIAS, ELSIE-BLACK QUE 181 2ND E DI
BIAS, FANNY CAL 053 3RD DIST
BIAS, HENRY ANN 337 3RD DIST
BIAS, JAMES QUE 215 3RD E DI
BIAS, JAMES WAS 107 2ND DIST
BIAS, MARIA ANN 300 1ST DIST
BIAS, MARY ANN 336 3RD DIST
BIAS, MARY E. BAL 419 14TH WAR
BIAS, MURRY FRE 029 FREDERIC
BIAS, RICHARD-BLACK QUE 196 3RD E DI
BIAS, ROBERT BAL 132 16TH WAR
BIAS, SAMUEL BAL 423 8TH WARD
BIAS, SARAH ANN 300 1ST DIST
BIAS, SCHADRACK BAL 057 1ST WARD
BIAS, WILLIAM WAS 155 HAGERSTO
BIAYS, MARGARETT WAS 107 2ND DIST
BIBB, AMANDA BAL 010 4TH WARD
BIBB, GECRGE M. MGM 428 CLARKSTR
BIBBINS, LITTLETON BAL 046 15TH WAR
BIBBY, HENERY DOR 354 3RD DIVI
BIBBY, JAMES DOR 350 3RD DIVI
BICATIN, ANN BAL 041 1ST WARD
BICE, DAVID CEC 125 5TH E DI
BICHL, GEORGE F. FRE 109 CREAGERS
BICKEL, MARY BAL 053 2ND DIST
BICKER, CONRAD BAL 274 1ST DIST
BICKER, SAMUEL * CAR 276 7TH DIST
BICKERO, DAVID BAL 297 3RD WARD
BICKERSTAFF, JOHN BAL 210 11TH WAR
BICKERSTETH, MARY BAL 059 10TH WAR
BICKERT, CHARLES BAL 120 1ST WARD
BICKERTON, C. BAL 021 9TH WARD
BICKERY, JAMES * BAL 125 2ND DIST
BICKETT, SOLOMON BAL 141 1ST WARD
BICKLEY, GEORGE BAL 198 5TH DIST
BICKLEY, SAMUEL BAL 026 4TH WARD
BICKMEYER, CAROLINE BAL 140 16TH WAR
BICKNER, PETER BAL 009 4TH WARD
BICOLE, JOHN BAL 129 1ST WARD
BICTORY, SOPHIA BAL 274 7TH WARD
BICTS, CHARLES BAL 133 1ST WARD
BIDAMER, ISAIAH WAS 151 2ND DIST
BIDDERSON, SALLY BAL 236 6TH WARD
BIDDINGER, ADAM FRE 445 8TH E DI
BIDDINGER, DANIEL FRE 432 8TH E DI
BIDDINGER, ONAIEL ALL 027 2ND E.D.
BIDDINGER, EPHRAIM FRE 446 8TH E DI
BIDDISON, ELIZABETH BAL 075 2ND DIST
BIDDISON, HANNAH BAL 053 15TH WAR
BIDDISON, HESTER A. BAL 328 7TH WARD
BIDDISON, JAMES BAL 336 7TH WARD
BIDDISON, SUSAN BAL 074 2ND DIST
BIDDISON, THOMAS BAL 153 2ND DIST
BIDDLE, ANDREW CEC 085 5TH E DI
BIDDLE, BENJAMIN F. HAR 063 1ST DIST
BIDDLE, BOULDEN CEC 018 ELKTON 3
BIDDLE, CHARLES CEC 019 ELKTON 3
BIDDLE, CHARLES BAL 005 EASTERN
BIDDLE, E. J. BAL 332 1ST DIST
BIDDLE, EDWARD CEC 085 5TH E DI
BIDDLE, EMMA CEC 085 5TH E DI
BIDDLE, FRANCINA CEC 018 ELKTON 3
BIDDLE, GEORGE CEC 096 4TH E DI
BIDDLE, GEORGE BAL 172 16TH WAR
BIDDLE, HANNAH CEC 033 CHESAPEA
BIDDLE, ISAAC BAL 254 6TH WARD
BIDDLE, J. BAL 332 1ST DIST
BIDDLE, JACKSON CEC 033 CHESAPEA
BIDDLE, JAMES H. BAL 173 16TH WAR
BIDDLE, JOHN BAL 139 1ST WARD
BIDDLE, JOHN CEC 033 CHESAPEA
BIDDLE, JOHN CEC 032 CHESAPEA
BIDDLE, JOHN CEC 026 ELKTON 3
BIDDLE, JOHN KEN 257 1ST DIST
BIDDLE, JOSEPH ALL 218 CUMBERLA
BIDDLE, JOSHUA KEN 280 3RD DIST
BIDDLE, KOBLE CEC 019 ELKTON 3
BIDDLE, LAMBERT W. CEC 036 CHESAPEA
BIDDLE, LEANDER CEC 035 CHESAPEA
BIDDLE, LORENZO CEC 034 CHESAPEA
BIDDLE, MALVINA BAL 028 15TH WAR
BIDDLE, MARGARET CEC 098 3RD E DI
BIDDLE, MARTHA CEC 030 CHESAPEA
BIDDLE, MARTHA BAL 022 4TH WARD
BIDDLE, MICHAEL CEC 085 5TH E DI
BIDDLE, MRTHA CEC 025 ELKTON 3
BIDDLE, PERRIGINE BAL 068 18TH WAR
BIDDLE, RICHARD CEC 028 CHESAPEA
BIDDLE, RICHARD CEC 024 ELKTON 3
BIDDLE, SALLY BAL 172 6TH WARD
BIDDLE, SAMUEL BAL 253 6TH WARD
BIDDLE, SAMUEL R. CEC 047 1ST E DI
BIDDLE, SAMUEL R. BAL 058 18TH WAR
BIDDLE, SARAH CEC 087 4TH E DI
BIDDLE, SARAH CEC 017 ELKTON 3
BIDDLE, STEPHEN KEN 245 2ND DIST
BIDDLE, SUSAN M. BAL 068 18TH WAR
BIDDLE, THOMAS CEC 025 ELKTON 3
BIDDLE, THOMAS A. HAR 175 3RD DIST
BIDDLE, TOBIAS R. CEC 125 5TH E DI
BIDDLE, W. S. BAL 332 1ST DIST
BIDDLE, WILLIAM BAL 177 16TH WAR
BIDDLE, WILLIAM CEC 026 ELKTON 3
BIDDLE, WILLIAM R. CEC 048 1ST E DI
BIDDLEMAN, JOHN BAL 265 7TH WARD
BIDELER, CHRISTOPHER FRE 347 MIDDLETO
BIDELISON, MASHAE BAL 112 2ND DIST
BIDEN, CHARLES BAL 310 1ST DIST
BIDEN, WILLIAM BAL 284 1ST DIST
BIDER, EMANUEL BAL 176 2ND DIST
BIDINGER, DAVID FRE 300 WOODSBOR
BIDINGER, JACOB FRE 303 WOODSBOR
BIDINGER, JULEAN FRE 307 WOODSBOR
BIDINGER, LEVI ANN 515 HOWARD D
BIDINGER, SUSAN FRE 304 WOODSBOR
BIDINKER, LORENZO BAL 029 15TH WAR
BIDLE, HENRY WAS 231 1ST DIST
BIDLER, JOHN FRE 299 WOODSBOR
BIENNED, WILLIAM BAL 057 1ST WARD
BIENS, JOHN W. CEC 149 PORT DUP
BIENT, JAMES W. CHA 231 HILLTOP
BIER, GEORGE BAL 158 11TH WAR
BIER, JACOB BAL 027 9TH WARD
BIERBOWER, LEMUEL BAL 100 15TH WAR
BIERCE, JOSEPH * BAL 288 7TH WARD
BIERD, JOSEPH BAL 288 7TH WARD
BIERD, JOSEPH * BAL 288 7TH WARD
BIERDSWALE, ADOLPH BAL 017 4TH WARD
BIERFISCHER, DOROTHY BAL 067 10TH WAR
BIERLAND, FREDERICK BAL 024 4TH WARD
BIERLY, GEORGE FRE 280 WOODSBOR
BIERS, MARY I. BAL 296 3RD WARD
BIERS, RICHARD ALL 245 CUMBERLA
BIERSHING, CATHARINE A. WAS 124 HAGERSTO
BIERSHING, GEORGE WAS 083 2ND SUBD
BIERSHING, JOHN WAS 084 2ND SUBD
BIERSHING, MARIA WAS 131 HAGERSTO
BIERSHING, WILLIAM WAS 124 HAGERSTO
BIERSHING, WILLIAM WAS 126 HAGERSTO
BIERSTAFF, CHARLES BAL 194 17TH WAR
BIERTY, JOHN ANN 426 HOWARD D
BIET, JAMES H. BAL 085 4TH WARD
BIGAGS, JANE C.T. MGM 398 ROCKERLE
BIGBEE, MARTIN BAL 132 2ND DIST
BIGBEE, THOMAS BAL 154 2ND DIST
BIGBY, CARY A. BAL 359 1ST DIST
BIGESS, DAVID-BLACK FRE 423 8TH E DI
BIGESS, JOHN-BLACK FRE 441 8TH E DI
BIGG, FRANCIS KEN 225 2ND DIST
BIGGERMAN, JOHN BAL 018 9TH WARD
BIGGESS, SOLOMON-BLACK FRE 443 8TH E DI
BIGGINS, JEMIMA FRE 096 FREDERIC
BIGGINS, WILLIAM H. BAL 096 5TH WARD
BIGGS, A.A. WAS 042 2ND SUBD
BIGGS, ABNER ALL 001 3RD E.D.
BIGGS, ALFRED E. PRI 098 SPALDING
BIGGS, ANN PRI 100 SPALDING
BIGGS, ANN WHITE ALL 064 10TH E.D
BIGGS, BASIL-BLACK CAR 398 2ND DIST
BIGGS, BENJAMIN FRE 179 5TH E DI
BIGGS, CATHARINE FRE 165 EMMITTSB
BIGGS, CATHARINE CAR 320 1ST DIST
BIGGS, DORCAS PRI 120 PISCATAW
BIGGS, ELIJAH FRE 285 WOODSBOR
BIGGS, FRANCES ALL 064 10TH E.D
BIGGS, GEORGE CEC 056 1ST E DI
BIGGS, JACOB FRE 180 5TH E DI
BIGGS, JAMES CEC 064 1ST E DI
BIGGS, JAMES BAL 315 20TH WAR
BIGGS, JAMES BAL 331 7TH WARD
BIGGS, JAMES W. FRE 285 WOODSBOR
BIGGS, JOHN KEN 288 3RD DIST
BIGGS, JOHN A. BAL 039 18TH WAR
BIGGS, JOHN C. ANN 382 4TH DIST
BIGGS, JOHN W. ANN 391 4TH DIST
BIGGS, JOSEPH BAL 299 7TH WARD
BIGGS, JOSEPH CEC 063 1ST E DI
BIGGS, JOSEPH FRE 125 CREAGERS
BIGGS, JOSEPH CAR 320 1ST DIST
BIGGS, JOSHUA FRE 112 CREAGERS
BIGGS, LEANDER FRE 179 5TH E DI
BIGGS, MARTHA A. MGM 382 ROCKERLE
BIGGS, MIDDLETON S. ALL 064 10TH E.D
BIGGS, RESIN-BLACK FRE 440 8TH E DI
BIGGS, SARAH FRE 112 CREAGERS
BIGGS, THOMAS PRI 087 SPALDING
BIGGS, WILLIAM FRE 179 5TH E DI
BIGGS, WILLIAM CEC 063 1ST E DI
BIGGS, WILLIAM ALL 064 10TH E.D
BIGGS, WILLIAM BAL 351 7TH WARD
BIGHAM, AGNUS L. WAS 248 SMITHSBU
BIGHAM, ALBERT WAS 276 RIDGEVIL
BIGHAM, ALFRED BAL 397 1ST DIST
BIGHAM, ELIZABETH WAS 252 1ST DIST
BIGHAM, ELIZABETH FRE 168 EMMITTSB
BIGHAM, HENRIETTA BAL 395 1ST DIST
BIGHAM, JOHN FRE 446 8TH E DI
BIGHAM, JOHN WAS 218 1ST DIST
BIGHAM, JOSEPH CAR 396 2ND DIST
BIGHAM, JOSEPH BAL 025 9TH WARD
BIGHAM, ROBERT BAL 397 1ST DIST
BIGHAM, SAMUEL WAS 276 RIDGEVIL
BIGHART, JOHN BAL 059 2ND DIST
BIGHORN, ELIZABETH BAL 268 12TH WAR
BIGLER, G.W. WAS 137 HAGERSTO
BIGLOW, ROBERT BAL 168 1ST WARD
BIGLOW, ROBERT BAL 138 1ST WARD
BIGLOW, T. BAL 138 1ST WARD
BIGMAN, WILLIAM BAL 323 3RD WARD
BIGOT, FRANCIS FRE 181 5TH E DI
BIGURS, THOMAS W. BAL 074 10TH WAR
BIJEAU, ADLINE* BAL 115 11TH WAR
BIKLE, CHRISTIAN WAS 247 SMITHSBU
BILD, RUDOLPH BAL 014 9TH WARD
BILERS, MARY BAL 292 20TH WAR
BILES, CHARLES CEC 117 4TH E DI
BILES, JOHN L. CEC 113 4TH E DI
BILES, SHARLOT TAL 012 EASTON D
BILES, WILLIAM B. SR. CEC 118 4TH E DI
BILETOR, MARY CAR 140 NO TWP L
BILINGER, JAMES BAL 205 6TH DIST
BILINGER, JOSEPH BAL 204 6TH DIST
BILL, JOHN* DOR 369 3RD DIVI
BILL, MARY BAL 271 1ST DIST
BILLINGER, HENRY BAL 074 4TH WARD

Name	County	Page	District
BILLINGER, JACOB	CAR	380	2ND DIST
BILLINGKAMP, JOHN	BAL	196	11TH WAR
BILLINGLEE, JOHN	BAL	058	2ND DIST
BILLINGLY, BENNTT M.	HAR	190	3RD DIST
BILLINGLY, SAMUEL	BAL	088	2ND DIST
BILLINGS, EDWARD	BAL	129	18TH WAR
BILLINGSBY, BARZILLA *	BAL	091	2ND DIST
BILLINGSBY, MARY E.	CAL	056	3RD DIST
BILLINGSBY, THOMAS B.	CAL	026	2ND DIST
BILLINGSLEA, CHARLES	HAR	027	1ST DIST
BILLINGSLEA, CHARLTON W.	HAR	144	2ND DIST
BILLINGSLEA, JAMES	HAR	016	1ST DIST
BILLINGSLEA, JAMES	HAR	017	2ND DIST
BILLINGSLEA, JOHN	HAR	016	1ST DIST
BILLINGSLEA, SAMUEL	BAL	057	2ND DIST
BILLINGSLEA, WALTER	HAR	113	2ND DIST
BILLINGSLED, CAROLINE	HAR	123	2ND DIST
BILLINGSLED, EMILY	HAR	123	2ND DIST
BILLINGSLED, JANE	HAR	088	2ND DIST
BILLINGSLED, JOHN	HAR	122	2ND DIST
BILLINGSLED, SAMUEL	HAR	134	2ND DIST
BILLINGSLED, WILLIAM	HAR	124	2ND DIST
BILLINGSLEE, G.	BAL	138	1ST WARD
BILLINGSLER, NICHOLAS	HAR	074	1ST DIST
BILLINGSLEY, CHAPMAN	ST	254	3RD E DI
BILLINGSLEY, CORDELIA	BAL	190	17TH WAR
BILLINGSLEY, JAMES	BAL	092	2ND DIST
BILLINGSLEY, MARTHA *	HAR	204	3RD DIST
BILLINGSLEY,WILLIAM	HAR	195	3RD DIST
BILLINGSLY, ELIZABETH	HAR	190	3RD DIST
BILLINGSLY, JAMES	HAR	190	3RD DIST
BILLINGSLY, RICHARD	CAL	037	2ND DIST
BILLINGTON, GOVARD	BAL	354	3RD WARD
BILLINGTON, JOHN J.	BAL	355	3RD WARD
BILLINGTON, LOUISA	CEC	116	3RD E DI
BILLIPS, WILLIAM	DOR	423	1ST DIST
BILLISON, GEORGE W.	CAR	374	9TH DIST
BILLISON, WILLIAM	CAR	374	9TH DIST
BILLIUPS, R.W.	BAL	173	1ST WARD
BILLMAN, GEORGE	BAL	298	17TH WAR
BILLMAN, THOMAS	BAL	381	8TH WARD
BILLMIRE, KATE S.	CAR	192	4TH DIST
BILLMYER, ALBERT	WAS	130	HAGERSTO
BILLMYER, DANIEL	CAR	269	WESTMINS
BILLMYER, GEORGE	WAS	129	HAGERSTO
BILLMYER, JACOB	BAL	385	8TH WARD
BILLMYER, JACOB	BAL	385	8TH WARD
BILLMYER, JOHN	CAR	389	2ND DIST
BILLMYER, MARTIN	CAR	236	UNION TO
BILLONS, JOSEPH	BAL	120	11TH WAR
BILLUP, STANILUS	BAL	212	11TH WAR
BILLUPS, B. W. S.	BAL	151	1ST WARD
BILLUPS, CHARLES L.	BAL	053	15TH WAR
BILLUPS, LOUISA MRS.	BAL	327	13TH WAR
BILLUPS, RICHARD	BAL	053	15TH WAR
BILMAN, SAMUEL	BAL	033	1ST WARD
BILMEAR, ELIZABETH	MGM	404	ROCKERLE
BILMOND, CATHARINE	BAL	344	13TH WAR
BILROFF, LINEHART	BAL	105	2ND DIST
BILSON, HENRY	BAL	087	18TH WAR
BILSON, SAMUEL	BAL	437	14TH WAR
BILSON, ZACHARY	BAL	139	5TH WARD
BILT, VIRGINIA *	BAL	277	20TH WAR
BILTZ, PETER	BAL	107	2ND DIST
BIM, JAMES	KEN	289	3RD DIST
BIMER, GEORGE C. *	BAL	282	20TH WAR
BINDER, ANN	WAS	161	HAGERSTO
BINDER, ELIZABETH	WAS	131	HAGERSTO
BINDING, ARTHUR	QUE	171	2ND E DI
BINDY, JAMES	BAL	047	1ST WARD
BINES, HARRIET	TAL	039	EASTON D
BINES, JOHN	BAL	026	15TH WAR
BINES, ROBERT	BAL	162	16TH WAR
BING, CONRAD	BAL	106	2ND DIST
BING, ELIZA	BAL	063	18TH WAR
BING, HENRIETTA	BAL	281	20TH WAR
BING, JOHN *	BAL	064	18TH WAR
BING, MARGARET	BAL	248	20TH WAR
BINGAY, ELIZA	BAL	275	2ND WARD
BINGER, E.	BAL	449	8TH WARD
BINGER, M.	BAL	449	8TH WARD
BINGHAM, JOHN	BAL	010	4TH WARD
BINGHAM, REBECCA	BAL	136	2ND DIST
BINGHAM, SAMUEL	CAR	219	5TH DIST
BINGHAM, SARAH A.	BAL	025	15TH WAR
BINGHAM, THOMAS	CAR	222	5TH DIST
BINGHAM, VINTON	MGM	319	CRACKLIN
BINGHAM,PHILIP	BAL	074	2ND DIST
BINGHMAN, ANN M.	BAL	104	1ST WARD
BINGHMAN, JOHN	BAL	103	1ST WARD
BINGLE, GEORGE	BAL	250	12TH WAR
BINIECK, PETER	BAL	421	1ST DIST
BININ, THOMAS	BAL	031	1ST WARD
BINIS, WILLIAM	BAL	159	11TH WAR
BINK, ANTHONY	BAL	217	2ND WARD
BINK, EDWARD	BAL	168	1ST WARD
BINK, JOSEPH	BAL	217	2ND WARD
BINKE, JACOB	BAL	271	20TH WAR
BINKHART, EZRA	FRE	103	FREDERIC
BINKLEY, A. O.	BAL	151	1ST WARD
BINKLEY, DANIEL	WAS	295	1ST DIST
BINKLEY, JOHN	WAS	296	1ST DIST
BINKLEY, PETER	WAS	286	1ST DIST
BINKLEY, URILLA	WAS	127	2ND DIST
BINKLY, ELIZABETH	WAS	060	2ND SUBD
BINKLY, JULIA A.	WAS	030	2ND SUBD
BINKNER, MARGARET	BAL	230	17TH WAR
BINLEY, J.	BAL	235	12TH WAR
BINNERMAN, JOHN	BAL	073	18TH WAR
BINNEX, WILLIAM	ANN	421	HOWARD D
BINNINY, SARAH	BAL	144	2ND DIST
BINNIX, GEORGE	BAL	093	18TH WAR
BINNIX, MARTHA	BAL	192	6TH WARD
BINNIX, PETER	BAL	059	18TH WAR
BINNOX, MARY E.	BAL	190	6TH WARD
BINNTON, L.	BAL	218	12TH WAR
BINNY, ELLEN	BAL	189	2ND WARD
BINS, HANNAH	BAL	003	9TH WARD
BINSWANGER, ELIZA	BAL	085	10TH WAR
BINSWANGER, EMANUEL	BAL	084	10TH WAR
BINYARD, JOHN	BAL	372	8TH WARD
BINYON, JOHN*	BAL	384	3RD WARD
BINYON, THOMAS W.*	BAL	384	3RD WARD
BINYON, WILLIAM*	BAL	388	3RD WARD
BINYOU, JOHN*	BAL	384	3RD WARD
BINYOU, THOMAS W.*	BAL	384	3RD WARD
BINZ, JOHN *	BAL	064	18TH WAR
BIRA, WILLIAM	CEC	035	CHESAPEA
BIRCBEL, URIAH S.	BAL	293	1ST DIST
BIRCH, CLARA	CEC	019	ELKTON 3
BIRCH, DAVID	KEN	270	1ST DIST
BIRCH, ELLEN	BAL	431	14TH WAR
BIRCH, EMMA	WOR	274	BERLIN 1
BIRCH, FRANCIS	BAL	386	3RD WARD
BIRCH, FRED	BAL	264	20TH WAR
BIRCH, HARRIET	MGM	354	BERRYS D
BIRCH, HOSEY	ST	342	5TH E DI
BIRCH, JAMES	WOR	274	BERLIN 1
BIRCH, JOHN	KEN	271	1ST DIST
BIRCH, JOHN G.	QUE	220	3RD E DI
BIRCH, JOSEPH	BAL	313	12TH WAR
BIRCH, LOUIS	BAL	260	12TH WAR
BIRCH, MICHAEL	BAL	277	20TH WAR
BIRCH, TEMPERANCE	BAL	171	16TH WAR
BIRCH, THOMAS	BAL	335	3RD WARD
BIRCH, THOMAS	FRE	138	CREAGERS
BIRCH, V. M.	BAL	471	14TH WAR
BIRCH, WILLIAM	QUE	200	3RD E DI
BIRCH, WILLIAM L.	BAL	456	8TH WARD
BIRCH,A NN	ST	259	3RD E DI
BIRCHALL, WILLIAM	BAL	033	18TH WAR
BIRCHLEAD, LENOX	BAL	116	2ND DIST
BIRCHWART, CONRAD	BAL	253	2ND WARD
BIRCK, JAMES	FRE	141	CREAGERS
BIRCKARD, N.	BAL	141	1ST WARD
BIRCKHARD, C.	BAL	153	1ST WARD
BIRCKHEAD, CHRISTOPHER	BAL	197	6TH WARD
BIRCKHEAD, ELIZA A.	BAL	197	6TH WARD
BIRCKHEAD, HANNAH	BAL	095	15TH WAR
BIRCKHEAD, ROBERT	ANN	400	8TH DIST
BIRCKHEAD, ROBERT	ANN	400	8TH DIST
BIRCKHEAD, W. N.	ANN	410	8TH DIST
BIRCKHEAD, WILLIAM	SOM	487	SALISBUR
BIRD, AMOS	WOR	292	9TH E DI
BIRD, ANN	BAL	237	12TH WAR
BIRD, BENJAMIN	CEC	044	1ST E DI
BIRD, BENJAMIN L.	ANN	306	1ST DIST
BIRD, CALVIN	BAL	404	3RD WARD
BIRD, CEZAR	WOR	293	9TH E DI
BIRD, COMFORT	WOR	291	9TH E DI
BIRD, EDWARD	BAL	266	17TH WAR
BIRD, ELIZA	HAR	001	1ST DIST
BIRD, EPRON	BAL	102	18TH WAR
BIRD, FORTUNE*	DOR	384	1ST DIST
BIRD, FRANK	BAL	041	18TH WAR
BIRD, GALTY	WOR	293	9TH E DI
BIRD, GEORGE H.	BAL	471	14TH WAR
BIRD, J.	BAL	296	20TH WAR
BIRD, JACOB W.	ANN	306	1ST DIST
BIRD, JAMES	ANN	407	8TH DIST
BIRD, JAMES	BAL	084	15TH WAR
BIRD, JAMES	BAL	148	1ST WARD
BIRD, JOHN F.	ANN	314	1ST DIST
BIRD, JOHN J.	HAR	033	1ST DIST
BIRD, JOSEPH	CEC	133	6TH E DI
BIRD, JOSEPH	BAL	106	10TH WAR
BIRD, JULIA A.	ANN	315	1ST DIST
BIRD, LIDDY A.	BAL	116	11TH WAR
BIRD, LUCY, J.	BAL	241	6TH WARD
BIRD, MARIA	DOR	384	1ST DIST
BIRD, MARY ANN	BAL	265	17TH WAR
BIRD, MARY ELIZA	DOR	384	1ST DIST
BIRD, ODION	BAL	258	17TH WAR
BIRD, REBECCA	ANN	305	1ST DIST
BIRD, RICHARD T.	BAL	334	13TH WAR
BIRD, S. L.	BAL	063	10TH WAR
BIRD, SARAH	BAL	265	17TH WAR
BIRD, T. EDWARD *	BAL	342	13TH WAR
BIRD, THOMAS	WAS	017	2ND SUBD
BIRD, THOMAS T.	ANN	305	1ST DIST
BIRD, TOBIAS	BAL	118	11TH WAR
BIRD, WILLIAM	BAL	094	18TH WAR
BIRD, WILLIAM H.	ANN	312	1ST DIST
BIRDEY,LEWIS	FRE	036	FREDERIC
BIRDITH, ASCENA	MGM	328	CRACKLIN
BIRDLEY, FRANCIS P.	BAL	269	20TH WAR
BIRDLEY, J. C.	BAL	269	20TH WAR
BIRDLEY, SARAH	BAL	221	12TH WAR
BIRDSALE, SAMUEL	BAL	083	2ND DIST
BIREAD, ANDREW *	BAL	044	18TH WAR
BIRELEY, CHARLOTT	FRE	054	FREDERIC
BIRELEY, VALENTINE	FRE	025	FREDERIC
BIRELS, ALFRED-BLACK	FRE	218	BUCKEYST
BIRELY, CHARLES	BAL	358	1ST DIST
BIRELY, DAVID	FRE	280	WOODSBOR
BIRELY, FREDERICK	FRE	287	WOODSBOR
BIRELY, JACOB	FRE	013	FREDERIC
BIRELY, JOHN	BAL	409	1ST DIST
BIRELY, JOHN G.	FRE	062	FREDERIC
BIRELY, JOHN W.	FRE	061	FREDERIC
BIRELY, LEWIS	CAR	319	1ST DIST
BIRELY, LEWIS A.	BAL	429	14TH WAR
BIRELY, PHILIP	BAL	359	1ST DIST
BIRELY, SAMUEL	FRE	280	WOODSBOR
BIREN, MARY	BAL	258	12TH WAR
BIRES, RACHEL	ALL	256	CUMBERLA
BIRGIN, HENRY	FRE	395	PETERSVI
BIRINGER, E.	BAL	449	8TH WARD
BIRINIE, ROGES	CAR	410	2ND DIST
BIRK, ANDREW	BAL	193	11TH WAR
BIRK, ELIZABETH	HAR	073	1ST DIST
BIRK, JAMES B.	ST	311	1ST E DI
BIRK, NELLY	BAL	017	1ST WARD
BIRKELD, WILLIAM	BAL	192	19TH WAR
BIRKETT, SAMUEL	HAR	196	3RD DIST
BIRKEY, THOMAS H.	BAL	065	15TH WAR
BIRKHEAD, CABOON	CAL	037	2ND DIST
BIRKHEAD, SAMUEL	CAL	041	3RD DIST
BIRKHEAD, WILLIAM	BAL	150	11TH WAR
BIRKINS, WILLIAM	BAL	062	18TH WAR
BIRKNER, JOHN	BAL	168	16TH WAR
BIRKWALD, SOLOMON	BAL	226	2ND WARD
BIRLEY, SAMUEL	BAL	065	1ST WARD
BIRMINGHAM, ANDREW	BAL	197	6TH WARD
BIRMINGHAM, C.	BAL	044	4TH WARD
BIRMINGHAM, CHARLES	BAL	285	12TH WAR
BIRMINGHAM, GEORGE F.	FRE	390	PETERSVI
BIRMINGHAM, JAMES	BAL	139	16TH WAR
BIRMINGHAM, JOHN	FRE	390	PETERSVI
BIRMINGHAM, JULIA	BAL	118	18TH WAR
BIRNES, ELIZA	TAL	022	EASTON D
BIRNEY, SUSAN	BAL	209	19TH WAR
BIRNEY, THOMAS A.	CEC	211	7TH E DI
BIRNISH, TEMSSA	BAL	460	14TH WAR
BIRON, MARY	BAL	266	2ND WARD
BIRS, DANIEL	BAL	309	12TH WAR
BIRSON, HARRIET	BAL	461	1ST DIST
BIRTE, BENNETT	HAR	198	3RD DIST
BIRTLER, MARTHA	BAL	162	19TH WAR
BIRTON, ELLEN	BAL	322	12TH WAR
BISCOE, ADALINE	ST	302	2ND E DI
BISCOE, ALBERT A.	QUE	188	3RD E DI
BISCOE, ANN	ST	313	1ST E DI
BISCOE, ANNA C.	BAL	068	15TH WAR
BISCOE, ELLENOR B.	ST	337	4TH E DI
BISCOE, ELVINA V.	ST	291	2ND E DI
BISCOE, GEORGE R.	ST	298	2ND E DI
BISCOE, JAMES	BAL	163	16TH WAR
BISCOE, JAMES L.	ST	291	2ND E DI
BISCOE, JOSIAH	ST	311	1ST E DI
BISCOE, ROBERT M.	ST	312	1ST E DI
BISCOE, ROUSBERRY-BLACK	ST	314	1ST E DI
BISCOE, SAMUEL*	BAL	389	3RD WARD
BISCOE, SARAH	ST	312	1ST E DI
BISCOE, SARAH	ST	308	1ST E DI
BISCOE, SARAH A.-MULATTO	ST	298	2ND E DI
BISCOE, THOAMS R.	ST	291	2ND E DI
BISCOE, WALTER	ST	311	1ST E DI
BISCOE, WILLIAM	ST	315	4TH E DI
BISCOE, WILLIAM	QUE	141	1ST E DI
BISCOE, WILLIAM B.	ST	300	2ND E DI
BISCOE, WILLIAM C.	ST	290	2ND E DI
BISCOE, WILLIAM L.	ST	304	2ND E DI
BISCOE, WILLIAM-MULATTO	QUE	188	3RD E DI
BISEE, COLUMBUS *	FRE	315	MIDDLETO
BISELEY, MARY	ALL	235	CUMBERLA
BISELEY, THEODORE *	FRE	057	FREDERIC
BISER, ADAM	FRE	352	MIDDLETO
BISER, ANN	FRE	347	MIDDLETO
BISER, DANIEL	FRE	345	MIDDLETO
BISER, DANIEL S.	FRE	394	PETERSVI
BISER, ENOS	FRE	345	MIDDLETO
BISER, FREDERICK	FRE	338	MIDDLETO
BISER, GEORGE C.	FRE	399	JEFFERSO
BISER, GEORGE K.	FRE	400	JEFFERSO
BISER, HENRY	FRE	336	MIDDLETO
BISER, HENRY H.	FRE	392	PETERSVI
BISER, JACOB	FRE	347	MIDDLETO
BISER, JACOB JR.	FRE	347	MIDDLETO
BISER, JOHN	FRE	318	MIDDLETO
BISER, JOHN	FRE	209	BUCKEYST
BISER, JOHN G.	FRE	396	PETERSVI
BISER, MAHLON K.	FRE	396	PETERSVI
BISER, PETER	FRE	344	MIDDLETO
BISER, PETER	FRE	347	MIDDLETO
BISER, SOPHIA	FRE	393	PETERSVI
BISER, SOPHIA	FRE	392	PETERSVI
BISER, THOMAS	FRE	396	PETERSVI
BISER, TILGHMAN	FRE	388	PETERSVI
BISH, ADAM	CAR	278	7TH DIST
BISH, DANIEL	CAR	249	3RD DIST
BISH, JACOB	CAR	249	3RD DIST
BISH, LEVI	CAR	250	3RD DIST
BISH, MARY	CAR	261	3RD DIST
BISH, WILLAIM	CAR	278	7TH DIST
BISH, WILLIAM	CAR	277	7TH DIST
BISHCOFF, ANN E.	BAL	133	16TH WAR
BISHELL, CATHERINE	BAL	032	9TH WARD
BISHOP, ADAM	BAL	010	15TH WAR
BISHOP, ANNA	FRE	039	FREDERIC
BISHOP, ANTHONY-BLACK	QUE	133	1ST E DI
BISHOP, BENJAMIN	WOR	309	2ND E DI
BISHOP, CALEB	CAR	180	8TH DIST
BISHOP, CASPER	BAL	428	8TH WARD
BISHOP, CHARLES	BAL	095	10TH WAR
BISHOP, CHARLES	BAL	105	18TH WAR
BISHOP, CHARLES	WOR	285	BERLIN 1
BISHOP, CHARLES	WOR	307	2ND E DI
BISHOP, CHARLES W.	WOR	320	1ST E DI
BISHOP, CHARLOTTE	BAL	083	15TH WAR
BISHOP, CHARLOTTE E.	WOR	246	1ST CENS
BISHOP, COMFORT W.	WOR	244	1ST CENS
BISHOP, DAVID	BAL	392	8TH WARD
BISHOP, DELIA	SOM	412	DUBLIN D
BISHOP, DETRICK	CAR	306	1ST DIST
BISHOP, EBI	WOR	242	1ST CENS
BISHOP, EBIN	WOR	307	2ND E DI
BISHOP, EBIN	WOR	307	2ND E DI
BISHOP, ELIAS	BAL	388	8TH WARD
BISHOP, ELIJAH	QUE	213	3RD E DI
BISHOP, ELIJAH	WAS	244	SMITHSBU
BISHOP, ELIJAH	BAL	168	19TH WAR
BISHOP, ELIZA	BAL	102	18TH WAR
BISHOP, ELIZABETH	BAL	071	1ST WARD
BISHOP, ELLEN	BAL	238	1ST DIST
BISHOP, ELLEN-BLACK	CAR	071	NO TWP L
BISHOP, ELLEN-BLACK	CAR	125	NO TWP L
BISHOP, EMMELINE	WOR	211	4TH E DI
BISHOP, FANNY	HAR	097	2ND DIST
BISHOP, FRANCIS E.	BAL	460	8TH WARD
BISHOP, FREDERICK	BAL	097	15TH WAR
BISHOP, GEORGE	BAL	077	2ND DIST
BISHOP, GEORGE	FRE	300	WOODSBOR
BISHOP, GEORGE	WOR	291	9TH E DI
BISHOP, GEORGE	WOR	307	2ND E DI
BISHOP, GEORGE	WOR	315	2ND E DI
BISHOP, GEORGE W.	BAL	112	1ST WARD
BISHOP, GEORGE W.	BAL	378	1ST DIST
BISHOP, GOTFRED	BAL	123	16TH WAR
BISHOP, HANNAH	KEN	301	3RD DIST
BISHOP, HARRIET	CAR	183	8TH DIST
BISHOP, HENRY	CAR	305	1ST DIST
BISHOP, HENRY	WAS	006	WILLIAMS
BISHOP, HENRY	BAL	313	1ST DIST
BISHOP, HENRY	BAL	213	6TH WARD
BISHOP, HICKS	DOR	329	3RD DIVI
BISHOP, HIRAM R.	BAL	001	9TH WARD
BISHOP, HORRICE	BAL	186	11TH WAR
BISHOP, ISAAC-BLACK	CAR	149	NO TWP L
BISHOP, ISABELLA	BAL	069	15TH WAR
BISHOP, JACOB	BAL	125	11TH WAR
BISHOP, JACOB	BAL	145	11TH WAR
BISHOP, JACOB	CAR	260	3RD DIST
BISHOP, JACOB	FRE	138	CREAGERS
BISHOP, JACOB	WOR	212	4TH E DI
BISHOP, JACOB H.	HAR	191	3RD DIST
BISHOP, JAMES	BAL	070	18TH WAR
BISHOP, JAMES	BAL	114	1ST WARD
BISHOP, JAMES E.	BAL	460	8TH WARD
BISHOP, JAMES E.	WOR	231	6TH E DI
BISHOP, JAMES H.	WOR	217	4TH E DI
BISHOP, JAMES-BLACK	WOR	349	1ST E DI
BISHOP, JAMIMA	BAL	304	17TH WAR
BISHOP, JANE	BAL	318	12TH WAR
BISHOP, JOHN	BAL	177	16TH WAR
BISHOP, JOHN	BAL	379	1ST DIST
BISHOP, JOHN	BAL	252	2ND WARD
BISHOP, JOHN	WOR	246	1ST CENS
BISHOP, JOHN	WOR	293	9TH E DI
BISHOP, JOHN	WOR	297	9TH E DI

NAME	COUNTY	PAGE	DISTRICT
BISHOP, JOHN H.	BAL	382	3RD WARD
BISHOP, JOHN H.	BAL	167	1ST WARD
BISHOP, JOHN L.	BAL	071	18TH WAR
BISHOP, JOHN S.	BAL	202	11TH WAR
BISHOP, JOSEPH	BAL	164	1ST WARD
BISHOP, JOSEPH	BAL	167	1ST WARD
BISHOP, JOSEPH	BAL	162	1ST WARD
BISHOP, JOSEPH	WOR	314	2ND E DI
BISHOP, JOSEPH-MULATTO	BAL	245	2ND WARD
BISHOP, JOSHUA	WOR	246	1ST CENS
BISHOP, L. R. JR.	WOR	243	1ST CENS
BISHOP, LELTLETON R. *	WOR	241	1ST CENS
BISHOP, LEVIN-BLACK	WOR	324	1ST E DI
BISHOP, MAJOR	BAL	138	5TH WARD
BISHOP, MAJOR	BAL	240	12TH WAR
BISHOP, MARIA	BAL	048	1ST WARD
BISHOP, MARIA	WOR	227	4TH E DI
BISHOP, MARK	FRE	063	FREDERIC
BISHOP, MARTHA	WOR	185	7TH E DI
BISHOP, MARTHA	BAL	353	7TH WARD
BISHOP, MARTHA H.	BAL	057	1ST WARD
BISHOP, MARY	BAL	077	1ST WARD
BISHOP, MARY	BAL	248	6TH WARD
BISHOP, MARY	ANN	417	HOWARD D
BISHOP, MARY	WOR	182	6TH E DI
BISHOP, MARY	WOR	262	BERLIN 1
BISHOP, MOSES	ANN	265	ANNAPOLI
BISHOP, N.	BAL	142	1ST WARD
BISHOP, NICHOLAS	BAL	117	2ND DIST
BISHOP, ORIN *	WOR	314	2ND E DI
BISHOP, PATRICK	BAL	183	16TH WAR
BISHOP, PERRY	CAR	111	NO TWP L
BISHOP, PETER W.	WOR	211	4TH E DI
BISHOP, RAUNEY	KEN	217	2ND DIST
BISHOP, RICHARD	CAR	100	NO TWP L
BISHOP, RICHARD	BAL	340	13TH WAR
BISHOP, RICHARD R.	BAL	076	1ST WARD
BISHOP, RICHARD W.	BAL	083	1ST WARD
BISHOP, ROBERT	BAL	193	19TH WAR
BISHOP, ROSETTA	WOR	185	6TH E DI
BISHOP, RUBIN	WOR	245	1ST CENS
BISHOP, SABRIA	WOR	301	SNOW HIL
BISHOP, SALLY W.	WOR	307	2ND E DI
BISHOP, SARAH	WAS	223	1ST DIST
BISHOP, SARAH	BAL	078	2ND DIST
BISHOP, SARAH-BLACK	CAR	158	NO TWP L
BISHOP, T.	BAL	172	1ST WARD
BISHOP, THOMAS H. J.	WOR	183	6TH E DI
BISHOP, THOMAS V.	CAR	146	NO TWP L
BISHOP, VALETTA	BAL	077	1ST WARD
BISHOP, WESLY	HAR	193	3RD DIST
BISHOP, WILLIAM	BAL	151	11TH WAR
BISHOP, WILLIAM	CAR	066	NO TWP L
BISHOP, WILLIAM	BAL	223	6TH WARD
BISHOP, WILLIAM	BAL	395	3RD WARD
BISHOP, WILLIAM	BAL	389	3RD WARD
BISHOP, WILLIAM	BAL	279	7TH WARD
BISHOP, WILLIAM	ANN	279	ANNAPOLI
BISHOP, WILLIAM	QUE	213	3RD E DI
BISHOP, WILLIAM	WOR	285	BERLIN 1
BISHOP, WILLIAM	WOR	309	2ND E DI
BISHOP, WILLIAM H.	ANN	414	HOWARD D
BISHOP, WILLIAM H.	BAL	348	3RD WARD
BISHOP, WILLIAM H.	BAL	060	15TH WAR
BISHOP,NICHOLAS	BAL	041	1ST WARD
BISHOP,SOPHIA	BAL	180	2ND WARD
BISHUP, JOHN	HAR	189	3RD DIST
BISKLY, MARGARET *	WAS	055	2ND SUBD
BISLEY, WILLIAM	BAL	308	20TH WAR
BISON, HOPEY-MULATTO	ST	320	4TH E DI
BISSEL, PHEBE	BAL	101	2ND DIST
BISSELL, ELIZABETH	HAR	141	2ND DIST
BISSELL, HARRIET L.	BAL	097	10TH WAR
BISSELL, MARGARET	HAR	140	2ND DIST
BISSELL, WILLIAM L.	HAR	141	2ND DIST
BISSEN, WILLIAM	BAL	148	1ST WARD
BISSEN, WILLIAM	BAL	104	1ST WARD
BISSET, CHARLES	BAL	121	1ST WARD
BISSETT, OWEN	WAS	095	2ND SUBD
BISSEX, MARY-BLACK	QUE	148	1ST E DI
BISSICK, FRANCIS	HAR	030	1ST DIST
BISSIEN, THEADORE	HAR	069	1ST DIST
BISSIER, ERMAN	BAL	308	20TH WAR
BISSOTT, THOMAS	BAL	115	18TH WAR
BISTICK, JACOB	CEC	041	CHESAPEA
BISTOL, JOHN	BAL	049	18TH WAR
BITCHEL, PHILIP	BAL	431	1ST DIST
BITCHEMAN, NICHOLAS	BAL	232	17TH WAR
BITELER, SAMUEL	FRE	115	CREAGERS
BITLER, ANN	FRE	304	WOODSBOR
BITNER, ANDREW	BAL	195	2ND WARD
BITNER, FREDERICK	BAL	089	1ST WARD
BITNER, JOHN	BAL	037	18TH WAR
BITNER, JOHN	WAS	111	2ND DIST
BITSER, JOHN	BAL	439	8TH WARD
BITTENAUGH, CATHERINE	BAL	043	1ST WARD
BITTERSON, CATHARINE	BAL	116	5TH WARD
BITTERSON, WILLIAM	BAL	089	18TH WAR
BITTINGER, CATHARINE	ALL	017	3RD E.D.
BITTINGER, ELSIABETH	ALL	016	3RD E.D.
BITTINGER, HENRY	ALL	017	3RD E.D.
BITTINGER, JOHN J.	BAL	252	12TH WAR
BITTINGER, JONATHAN	ALL	016	3RD E.D.
BITTINGER, JOSEPH	ALL	015	3RD E.D.
BITTINGER, LYDIA	ALL	015	3RD E.D.
BITTINGER, MARGARET	ALL	015	3RD E.D.
BITTINGER, PETER	ALL	015	3RD E.D.
BITTINGER, SOLOMON	ALL	016	3RD E.D.
BITTINGER, WILLIAM	ALL	017	3RD E.D.
BITTINGSLEY, MARTHA *	HAR	204	3RD DIST
BITTLE, DAVID	FRE	316	MIDDLETO
BITTLE, JONATHAN	FRE	340	MIDDLETO
BITTLE, PETER	CAR	255	3RD DIST
BITTLE, THOMAS	FRE	340	MIDDLETO
BITZEE, CHARLES	BAL	275	20TH WAR
BITZELL, MARGARET	BAL	260	1ST DIST
BITZENBERGER, SUSAN	WAS	263	1ST DIST
BITZENER, JOHN	BAL	359	1ST DIST
BITZENER, LAWRENCE	BAL	361	1ST DIST
BIVANS, AMANDA B.	WOR	300	SNOW HIL
BIVANS, ANNA	WOR	347	1ST E DI
BIVANS, CHARLOT	WOR	336	1ST E DI
BIVANS, JAMES	WOR	322	1ST E DI
BIVANS, POLLY	WOR	347	1ST E DI
BIVANS, SARAH R.	FRE	439	8TH E DI
BIVENS, ANN	WAS	140	2ND DIST
BIVENS, THOAMS	KEN	222	2ND DIST
BIVINS, MARY	BAL	150	19TH WAR
BIXBEY, SARHA	WOR	303	SNOW HIL
BIXBY, MARIA	WOR	264	BERLIN 1
BIXCHING, HENRY	BAL	116	1ST WARD
BIXCROFT, GEORGE	CAR	351	6TH DIST
BIXLEN, JES	BAL	234	12TH WAR
BIXLEN, LOUIS A.	BAL	121	11TH WAR
BIXLER, ABRAHAM	CAR	351	6TH DIST
BIXLER, ANDREW	BAL	009	15TH WAR
BIXLER, BARBARA	CAR	347	6TH DIST
BIXLER, CANIEL	CAR	345	6TH DIST
BIXLER, FREDERIC	CAR	345	6TH DIST
BIXLER, JACOB	CAR	266	WESTMINS
BIXLER, JOHN	CAR	277	7TH DIST
BIXLER, PETER	CAR	346	6TH DIST
BIXLER, PETER	CAR	350	6TH DIST
BIXLER, PRICILLA	CAR	347	6TH DIST
BIXLER, SARAH J.	CAR	351	6TH DIST
BIXLER, WILLIAM TELL	BAL	020	18TH WAR
BIXLY, DAVID	BAL	435	14TH WAR
BIXLY, MAGDALENA	BAL	435	14TH WAR
BIXLY, TGHOMAS	MGM	408	MEDLEY 3
BKAER, GEORGE	BAL	250	6TH WARD
BLACHER, JACOB	WAS	186	BOONSBOR
BLACK, ALEXANDER	ANN	376	4TH DIST
BLACK, ALEXANDER	BAL	279	17TH WAR
BLACK, AMELIA	CEC	174	6TH E DI
BLACK, AMELIA	BAL	394	14TH WAR
BLACK, ANN	HAR	082	2ND DIST
BLACK, ANN	HAR	100	2ND DIST
BLACK, ANN	BAL	213	11TH WAR
BLACK, ANNA	CAR	412	2ND DIST
BLACK, ARTHUR	BAL	398	1ST DIST
BLACK, BECKY	BAL	206	19TH WAR
BLACK, BENJAMIN	HAR	094	2ND DIST
BLACK, BENJAMIN	HAR	142	2ND DIST
BLACK, BENJAMIN-BLACK	CAR	402	2ND DIST
BLACK, BETTY	BAL	383	13TH WAR
BLACK, BETTY	BAL	149	2ND DIST
BLACK, CATHARINE	BAL	187	16TH WAR
BLACK, CATHARINE	HAR	139	2ND DIST
BLACK, CATHARINE	CAR	388	2ND DIST
BLACK, CATHRINE	BAL	025	18TH WAR
BLACK, CHARITY	HAR	139	2ND DIST
BLACK, CHARLES	HAR	138	2ND DIST
BLACK, CHARLES	HAR	105	2ND DIST
BLACK, CHARLES	BAL	134	1ST WARD
BLACK, CHARLOTTE	BAL	439	14TH WAR
BLACK, CHARLOTTE	SOM	501	SALISBUR
BLACK, CHRISTOPHER	KEN	276	1ST DIST
BLACK, CURTIS-BLACK	WOR	321	1ST E DI
BLACK, DANIEL	SOM	533	QUANTICO
BLACK, DANIEL	CAR	360	9TH DIST
BLACK, DANIEL-BLACK	CAR	115	NO TWP L
BLACK, DAVID	CAR	379	2ND DIST
BLACK, ELIJAH E.	CEC	107	3RD E DI
BLACK, ELISABETH	ANN	375	4TH DIST
BLACK, ELIZA	BAL	407	3RD WARD
BLACK, ELIZA	BAL	268	12TH WAR
BLACK, ELIZA	CAR	250	3RD DIST
BLACK, ELIZA	HAR	127	2ND DIST
BLACK, ELIZABETH	CAR	070	NO TWP L
BLACK, ELIZABETH	FRE	165	EMMITTSB
BLACK, ELLEN	ANN	348	3RD DIST
BLACK, ELLENER	BAL	009	18TH WAR
BLACK, EMELINE	BAL	102	10TH WAR
BLACK, EVERINE	WOR	178	6TH E DI
BLACK, FREDERICK	FRE	162	EMMITTSB
BLACK, G.	BAL	136	1ST WARD
BLACK, GEORGE	ANN	370	4TH DIST
BLACK, GEORGE	CAR	348	6TH DIST
BLACK, GEORGE	CEC	175	7TH E DI
BLACK, GEORGE	CAR	287	7TH DIST
BLACK, GEORGE	SOM	467	TRAPPE D
BLACK, GRANVILLE	CAR	234	UNION TO
BLACK, HANNAH	HAR	127	2ND DIST
BLACK, HANNAH	HAR	072	1ST DIST
BLACK, HANNAH	BAL	432	14TH WAR
BLACK, HANSON	CAR	303	1ST DIST
BLACK, HARMAN	BAL	398	8TH WARD
BLACK, HARRIET	BAL	300	3RD WARD
BLACK, HARRIET	HAR	097	2ND DIST
BLACK, HARRIETT	HAR	124	2ND DIST
BLACK, HENRETTA	BAL	112	18TH WAR
BLACK, HENRY	FRE	118	CREAGERS
BLACK, HENRY	BAL	189	19TH WAR
BLACK, HENRY	CAR	256	3RD DIST
BLACK, HENRY	CAR	115	NO TWP L
BLACK, HENRY	BAL	249	6TH WARD
BLACK, HENRY J.	CAR	296	7TH DIST
BLACK, HESTER*	SOM	477	TRAPP DI
BLACK, ISIBELLE	ALL	208	CUMBERLA
BLACK, JACOB	FRE	378	PETERSVI
BLACK, JAMES	HAR	138	2ND DIST
BLACK, JAMES	FRE	192	5TH E DI
BLACK, JAMES	ALL	195	CUMBERLA
BLACK, JAMES B.	BAL	017	1ST WARD
BLACK, JAMES F.	BAL	186	16TH WAR
BLACK, JAMS	BAL	122	1ST WARD
BLACK, JANE	HAR	141	2ND DIST
BLACK, JANE	HAR	132	2ND DIST
BLACK, JANE	HAR	102	2ND DIST
BLACK, JANE	SOM	478	TRAPP DI
BLACK, JEMIMA	BAL	012	2ND DIST
BLACK, JESSE-BLACK	CAR	117	NO TWP L
BLACK, JOHN	BAL	452	14TH WAR
BLACK, JOHN	HAR	142	2ND DIST
BLACK, JOHN	KEN	232	2ND DIST
BLACK, JOHN	CAR	299	1ST DIST
BLACK, JOHN	CEC	076	NORTHEAS
BLACK, JOHN	CAR	412	2ND DIST
BLACK, JOHN	BAL	164	19TH WAR
BLACK, JOHN	BAL	164	19TH WAR
BLACK, JOHN	BAL	062	4TH WARD
BLACK, JOHN	ALL	241	CUMBERLA
BLACK, JOHN	BAL	268	1ST DIST
BLACK, JOHN	BAL	312	12TH WAR
BLACK, JOHN	BAL	134	1ST WARD
BLACK, JOHN	BAL	291	3RD WARD
BLACK, JOHN	SOM	478	TRAPP DI
BLACK, JOHN F.	CAR	287	7TH DIST
BLACK, JOHN R.	BAL	165	19TH WAR
BLACK, KISSY-BLACK	CAR	117	NO TWP L
BLACK, LAURA	HAR	116	2ND DIST
BLACK, LEVIN	BAL	265	17TH WAR
BLACK, LEWIS	HAR	123	2ND DIST
BLACK, LEWIS	WAS	302	1ST DIST
BLACK, LONCENOA-BLACK	CAR	117	NO TWP L
BLACK, LOYD	BAL	069	2ND DIST
BLACK, LUCRETIA-BLACK	CAR	134	NO TWP L
BLACK, MARGARET	BAL	187	16TH WAR
BLACK, MARGARET	ANN	364	4TH DIST
BLACK, MARGRETT	BAL	106	18TH WAR
BLACK, MARIA	HAR	122	2ND DIST
BLACK, MARIA	HAR	099	2ND DIST
BLACK, MARIAH	CAR	072	NO TWP L
BLACK, MARIAH-BLACK	CAR	147	NO TWP L
BLACK, MARTHA	BAL	440	1ST DIST
BLACK, MARY	BAL	005	EASTERN
BLACK, MARY	BAL	396	3RD WARD
BLACK, MARY	BAL	383	3RD WARD
BLACK, MARY	BAL	459	8TH WARD
BLACK, MARY	BAL	202	11TH WAR
BLACK, MARY	HAR	087	2ND DIST
BLACK, MARY	HAR	133	2ND DIST
BLACK, MARY	HAR	142	2ND DIST
BLACK, MARY	CEC	187	7TH E DI
BLACK, MARY A.	BAL	452	14TH WAR
BLACK, MARY E.	BAL	029	15TH WAR
BLACK, MAY A.	CAR	380	2ND DIST
BLACK, MICHAEL	CAR	342	6TH DIST
BLACK, MICHAL M.	HAR	199	3RD DIST
BLACK, NANCY	CEC	081	CHARLEST
BLACK, NANCY	HAR	127	2ND DIST
BLACK, NOAH	CAR	070	NO TWP L
BLACK, NOAH-BLACK	CAR	117	NO TWP L
BLACK, PETER	BAL	134	1ST WARD
BLACK, PHEBE	HAR	096	2ND DIST
BLACK, PHILIP	CEC	208	7TH E DI
BLACK, RACHEL	HAR	083	2ND DIST
BLACK, RICHARD	BAL	296	1ST DIST
BLACK, ROSANNA	WAS	302	1ST DIST
BLACK, ROSE	BAL	420	1ST DIST
BLACK, RUBEN	BAL	288	1ST DIST
BLACK, SALLY	HAR	144	2ND DIST
BLACK, SAMUEL	BAL	200	19TH WAR
BLACK, SAMUEL	BAL	149	5TH WARD
BLACK, SAMUEL	SOM	470	TRAPPE D
BLACK, SAMUEL	KEN	277	1ST DIST
BLACK, SAMUEL	KEN	285	3RD DIST
BLACK, SARAH	WAS	161	2ND DIST
BLACK, SARAH	ANN	343	3RD DIST
BLACK, SARAH	BAL	290	20TH WAR
BLACK, SARAH	CEC	082	CHARLEST
BLACK, SARAH	CAR	399	2ND DIST
BLACK, SEVERN	SOM	470	TRAPPE D
BLACK, SHADRICK-BLACK	CAR	119	NO TWP L
BLACK, STEPHEN	CEC	204	6TH E DI
BLACK, SUSAN	KEN	312	3RD DIST
BLACK, SUSAN	BAL	379	3RD WARD
BLACK, SUSAN	BAL	369	3RD WARD
BLACK, THOMAS	BAL	178	2ND WARD
BLACK, THOMAS	BAL	470	14TH WAR
BLACK, WALTER	HAR	117	2ND DIST
BLACK, WASHINGTCN	CEC	081	CHARLEST
BLACK, WASHINGTON	BAL	054	9TH WARD
BLACK, WILIAM	BAL	117	1ST WARD
BLACK, WILLAIM	BAL	453	1ST DIST
BLACK, WILLIAM	BAL	318	1ST DIST
BLACK, WILLIAM	BAL	081	1ST WARD
BLACK, WILLIAM	BAL	069	2ND DIST
BLACK, WILLIAM	HAR	123	2ND DIST
BLACK, WILLIAM	FRE	181	5TH E DI
BLACK, WILLIAM	SOM	470	TRAPPE D
BLACK, WILLIAM B.	ANN	312	1ST DIST
BLACK, WILLIAM T.	FRE	191	5TH E DI
BLACK, WILLIS-BLACK	CAR	116	NO TWP L
BLACK,W ILLIAM	BAL	267	12TH WAR
BLACKBOURN, JANE	CEC	112	4TH E DI
BLACKBURN, BENJAMIN	CAL	002	1ST DIST
BLACKBURN, CATHERINE	BAL	180	11TH WAR
BLACKBURN, CROMWELL	CEC	169	6TH E DI
BLACKBURN, JABEZ	BAL	065	2ND DIST
BLACKBURN, JAMES W.	CAL	004	1ST DIST
BLACKBURN, JEHU	BAL	371	1ST DIST
BLACKBURN, JOHN A.	CAL	018	1ST DIST
BLACKBURN, JOHN C.	BAL	251	12TH WAR
BLACKBURN, JOSEPH	ALL	238	CUMBERLA
BLACKBURN, MANESSAH	CEC	169	6TH E DI
BLACKBURN, MARGARETT	BAL	012	4TH WARD
BLACKBURN, MARY	CEC	202	6TH E DI
BLACKBURN, MISS A.	FRE	199	5TH E DI
BLACKBURN, MISS E.	FRE	199	5TH E DI
BLACKBURN, MISS S.	FRE	199	5TH E DI
BLACKBURN, SAMUEL	BAL	288	20TH WAR
BLACKBURN, SARAH	BAL	038	9TH WARD
BLACKBURN, URANIA	BAL	082	2ND DIST
BLACKBURN, URIAH	BAL	371	1ST DIST
BLACKBURN, WILLIAM	ANN	489	HOWARD D
BLACKBURN, WILLIMA	CAL	004	1ST DIST
BLACKEEDE, GEORGE	WAS	160	2ND DIST
BLACKER, JACOB	ALL	059	1CTH E.D
BLACKESTIN, SUSAN	KEN	313	3RD DIST
BLACKESTON, BENJAMIN F.	KEN	311	3RD DIST
BLACKESTON, ELIZABETH	KEN	296	3RD DIST
BLACKESTON, JOHN	KEN	309	3RD DIST
BLACKESTON, LOEZA	KEN	295	3RD DIST
BLACKESTON, MARIA	BAL	223	6TH WARD
BLACKESTON, RACHEL	KEN	301	3RD DIST
BLACKESTON, RICHARD	KEN	300	3RD DIST
BLACKESTON, SAMUEL	KEN	311	3RD DIST
BLACKESTON, WILLIAM	KEN	293	3RD DIST
BLACKESTONE, GASTAVUS	BAL	364	13TH WAR
BLACKESTONE, PRSCILLA	BAL	364	13TH WAR
BLACKFORD, WILLIAM	WAS	055	2ND SUBD
BLACKISTER, DAVID C.	KEN	281	3RD DIST
BLACKISTER, DEMBY	KEN	285	3RD DIST
BLACKISTER, HENRY	KEN	264	1ST DIST
BLACKISTER, JAMES E.	KEN	232	2ND DIST
BLACKISTER, SARAH-BLACK	QUE	129	1ST E DI
BLACKISTER, THOMAS M.	KEN	229	2ND DIST
BLACKISTER, WILLIAM H.	KEN	281	3RD DIST
BLACKISTON, NANCY	KEN	288	3RD DIST
BLACKISTON, WILLIAM	CAR	383	2ND DIST
BLACKISTONE, JAMES	QUE	191	3RD E DI
BLACKISTONE, JOHN	QUE	165	2ND E DI
BLACKISTONE, JOHN	ANN	308	1ST DIST
BLACKLECK, CORNELIA B.	BAL	118	15TH WAR
BLACKLIN, SAMUEL	HAR	101	2ND DIST
BLACKLOCK, GOVID	BAL	063	2ND DIST
BLACKLOCK, N. F.	BAL	476	14TH WAR
BLACKLON, WILLIAM	BAL	127	1ST WARD
BLACKMILT, JULIA	BAL	016	2ND DIST
BLACKMORE, DANIEL	ALL	215	CUMBERLA
BLACKNELL, SARAH *	WAS	070	2ND SUBD
BLACKNER, E. S.	BAL	037	9TH WARD
BLACKNIGHT, PERRY	TAL	118	ST MICHA
BLACKS, SARAH	BAL	082	4TH WARD
BLACKSMITH, E.	BAL	260	20TH WAR
BLACKSON, ANN	BAL	323	7TH WARD
BLACKSON, HENRY	BAL	322	7TH WARD
BLACKSON, MILLY	BAL	104	15TH WAR
BLACKSON, ROBERT	ANN	319	2ND DIST

Name	Co.	Page	Location
BLACKSTIN, WILLIAM	ANN	266	ANNAPOLI
BLACKSTOCK, MIACEL *	CHA	273	ALLENS F
BLACKSTON, EBENEZER	BAL	353	7TH WARD
BLACKSTON, ELIZABETH	PRI	042	VANSVILL
BLACKSTON, ELLEN	QUE	251	5TH E DI
BLACKSTON, HANNAH	PRI	041	VANSVILL
BLACKSTON, JOHN	PRI	041	VANSVILL
BLACKSTON, JOHN	FRE	428	8TH E DI
BLACKSTON, JOHN B.	BAL	402	14TH WAR
BLACKSTON, REBECCA	FRE	428	8TH E DI
BLACKSTON, SAMUEL	QUE	216	3RD E DI
BLACKSTON, THEADORE	TAL	066	EASTON T
BLACKSTONE, ANN B.	ST	319	4TH E DI
BLACKSTONE, BENJAMIN	FRE	035	FREDERIC
BLACKSTONE, CLOWIE A.-BLA	ST	320	4TH E DI
BLACKSTONE, CORNELIUS	BAL	040	9TH WARD
BLACKSTONE, DELIA	BAL	429	14TH WAR
BLACKSTONE, ELIZABETH	BAL	291	17TH WAR
BLACKSTONE, GEORGE W.	ST	319	4TH E DI
BLACKSTONE, GEROGE	BAL	062	18TH WAR
BLACKSTONE, HARRIET	BAL	325	7TH WARD
BLACKSTONE, HENRY H.	ST	319	4TH E DI
BLACKSTONE, HERBERT	ST	330	4TH E DI
BLACKSTONE, JOHN	ST	330	4TH E DI
BLACKSTONE, JOHN	BAL	061	18TH WAR
BLACKSTONE, JOHN	CAR	386	2ND DIST
BLACKSTONE, JOHN P.	ALL	238	CUMBERLA
BLACKSTONE, M.T.	ST	329	4TH E DI
BLACKSTONE, R.P.	ST	319	4TH E DI
BLACKSTONE, REBECCA	ST	319	4TH E DI
BLACKSTONE, SALLY	ANN	269	ANNAPOLI
BLACKSTONE, SAMUEL-BLACK	QUE	163	2ND E DI
BLACKSTONE, THOMAS	BAL	036	4TH WARD
BLACKSTONE, THOMAS M.	QUE	134	1ST E DI
BLACKSTONE, WILLIAM	BAL	088	18TH WAR
BLACKSTONE, WILLIAM	QUE	211	3RD E DI
BLACKSTONE, WILLIAM	BAL	047	9TH WARD
BLACKSTONE, WILLIAM	BAL	175	6TH WARD
BLACKSTONE, WILLIAM C.	CEC	147	PORT DUP
BLACKSTONE, WILLIAM J.	ST	319	4TH E DI
BLACKSTORE, SAMUEL	BAL	151	5TH WARD
BLACKSTOW, CATHERINE	FRE	056	FREDERIC
BLACKUDE, SARAH	WAS	160	2ND DIST
BLACKWAY, JOHN	KEN	305	3RD DIST
BLACKWAY, MARY	KEN	290	3RD DIST
BLACKWAY, WILLIAM	BAL	288	17TH WAR
BLACKWELL, DAVID	BAL	146	16TH WAR
BLACKWELL, HELOT L.	WAS	162	2ND DIST
BLACKWELL, HENRY	FRE	153	10TH E D
BLACKWELL, J.	BAL	149	1ST WARD
BLACKWELL, MARGARET	WAS	159	2ND DIST
BLACKWELL, SARAH *	WAS	070	2ND SUBD
BLACKWELL, WILLIAM	ALL	216	CUMBERLA
BLADDER, FREDERICK	BAL	393	3RD WARD
BLADE, LEWIS	CAR	163	NO TWP L
BLADEN, ALFRED	BAL	232	12TH WAR
BLADEN, KITTY	BAL	263	1ST DIST
BLADEN, MILLY	BAL	159	16TH WAR
BLADEN, RICHARD	CEC	204	6TH E DI
BLADER, RACHIEL	CAR	153	NO TWP L
BLADES, ALEXANDER	TAL	031	EASTON D
BLADES, ANN	CAR	133	NO TWP L
BLADES, BENJAMIN	TAL	082	ST MICHA
BLADES, BENJAMIN	WOR	350	1ST E DI
BLADES, BENJAMIN H.	TAL	081	ST MICHA
BLADES, CHARLES	BAL	266	7TH WARD
BLADES, COLMORE	BAL	019	15TH WAR
BLADES, DAVID L.	WOR	345	1ST E DI
BLADES, ELIZA A.	CAR	162	NO TWP L
BLADES, ELIZABETH	WOR	342	1ST E DI
BLADES, ELLEN	TAL	075	EASTON T
BLADES, ELLEN	TAL	075	EASTON T
BLADES, ELLEN	TAL	027	EASTON D
BLADES, ELLEN	CAR	143	NO TWP L
BLADES, GEORGE	WOR	342	1ST E DI
BLADES, GEORGE W.	DOR	430	1ST DIST
BLADES, HULDA	WOR	243	1ST CENS
BLADES, ISAAH C.	CAR	144	NO TWP L
BLADES, ISAH*	TAL	022	EASTON D
BLADES, JACOB	WOR	166	6TH E DI
BLADES, JAMES	SOM	373	BRINKLEY
BLADES, JAMES	CAR	072	NO TWP L
BLADES, JAMES H.	TAL	012	EASTON D
BLADES, JAMES-BLACK	CAR	158	NO TWP L
BLADES, JANE	WOR	246	1ST CENS
BLADES, JESSE W.	CAR	158	NO TWP L
BLADES, JESSIE	WOR	346	1ST E DI
BLADES, JOHN	CAR	144	NO TWP L
BLADES, JOHN B.	TAL	051	EASTON D
BLADES, JOHN L.	TAL	081	ST MICHA
BLADES, JOHN S.	TAL	080	ST MICHA
BLADES, JOHN W.	TAL	081	ST MICHA
BLADES, JOSHUA H.	TAL	078	EASTON T
BLADES, JULIANA	TAL	082	ST MICHA
BLADES, LEAH	KEN	264	1ST DIST
BLADES, LOUISA	TAL	103	ST MICHA
BLADES, MARGARET	TAL	086	ST MICHA
BLADES, MARY	TAL	030	EASTON D
BLADES, MARY	ST	264	3RD E DI
BLADES, MARY A.	TAL	082	ST MICHA
BLADES, MARY A.	WOR	297	9TH E DI
BLADES, MARY E.	TAL	080	ST MICHA
BLADES, MARY J.	WOR	328	1ST E DI
BLADES, NICHOLAS C.	TAL	082	ST MICHA
BLADES, PERMELIA	WOR	345	1ST E DI
BLADES, PETER	WOR	301	SNOW HIL
BLADES, POLLY	WOR	335	1ST E DI
BLADES, RACHEL	WOR	346	1ST E DI
BLADES, SALLY	TAL	052	EASTON D
BLADES, SALLY	WOR	314	2ND E DI
BLADES, SAMUEL	WOR	346	1ST E DI
BLADES, SAMUEL A.	BAL	134	5TH WARD
BLADES, SAMUEL H.	TAL	083	ST MICHA
BLADES, SARAH	WOR	241	1ST CENS
BLADES, SARAH	QUE	187	3RD E DI
BLADES, SARAH	CAR	161	NO TWP L
BLADES, SETH	SOM	373	BRINKLEY
BLADES, STANTTY*	TAL	007	EASTON D
BLADES, STEPHEN	WOR	344	1ST E DI
BLADES, SUSAN	TAL	120	ST MICHA
BLADES, THOMAS	TAL	086	ST MICHA
BLADES, THOMAS	TAL	082	ST MICHA
BLADES, THOMAS	CAR	147	NO TWP L
BLADES, WILLIAM	CAR	163	NO TWP L
BLADES, WILLIAM	WOR	346	1ST E DI
BLADES, WILLIAM R.	ST	310	1ST E DI
BLADIN, JOHN	PRI	009	BLADENSB
BLAHER, JOSEPH	BAL	165	16TH WAR
BLAIL, JOSEPH *	BAL	278	20TH WAR
BLAIN, JOHN *	WAS	090	2ND SUBD
BLAIN, MARIAH-BLACK	WOR	341	1ST E DI
BLAIN, MOYT	BAL	128	11TH WAR
BLAIN, THOMAS J.	WOR	341	1ST E DI
BLAINE, WILLIAM	FRE	169	5TH E DI
BLAIR, ANDREW J.	WAS	121	2ND DIST
BLAIR, ANN E.	WAS	123	2ND DIST
BLAIR, DAVID G.	ALL	218	CUMBERLA
BLAIR, ELLEN	BAL	120	5TH WARD
BLAIR, EXPERENCE	WOR	303	SNOW HIL
BLAIR, FRANCIS A.	FRE	108	CREAGERS
BLAIR, FRANCIS P.	MGM	358	BERRYS D
BLAIR, GEORGE W.	BAL	158	19TH WAR
BLAIR, J. DOCTOR	SOM	400	BRINKLEY
BLAIR, J.G.	FRE	184	5TH E DI
BLAIR, JAMES	HAR	091	2ND DIST
BLAIR, JAMES	BAL	032	9TH WARD
BLAIR, JAMES	BAL	154	2ND DIST
BLAIR, JANE	BAL	212	19TH WAR
BLAIR, JESE	ST	330	4TH E DI
BLAIR, JESSE	WAS	123	2ND DIST
BLAIR, JOHN	WAS	135	HAGERSTO
BLAIR, JOHN	WAS	100	2ND DIST
BLAIR, JOHN	BAL	301	7TH WARD
BLAIR, MARY	WAS	113	2ND DIST
BLAIR, MICHAEL	BAL	201	11TH WAR
BLAIR, MOSES-BLACK	WOR	176	6TH E DI
BLAIR, NANCY	BAL	109	1ST WARD
BLAIR, SAMUEL	ST	276	3RD E DI
BLAIR, THOMAS	BAL	154	2ND DIST
BLAIR, THOMAS	ALL	093	5TH E.D.
BLAIR, WILLIAM	ANN	347	3RD DIST
BLAIR, WILLIAM	WAS	135	HAGERSTO
BLAIR, WILLIAM	ST	330	4TH E DI
BLAKC, HANNAH	CEC	174	6TH E DI
BLAKDES, JOHN	CAR	163	NO TWP L
BLAKE, AARON	ANN	409	8TH DIST
BLAKE, ABRAHAM	BAL	134	1ST WARD
BLAKE, ALEXANDER	CAR	134	NO TWP L
BLAKE, AMOS	CEC	096	4TH E DI
BLAKE, ANDREW	HAR	111	2ND DIST
BLAKE, ANDREW	BAL	107	18TH WAR
BLAKE, ANN	BAL	268	12TH WAR
BLAKE, ANN J.	BAL	036	15TH WAR
BLAKE, ANNE	BAL	034	18TH WAR
BLAKE, BEN	WOR	311	2ND E DI
BLAKE, BENAJMIN-BLACK	QUE	124	1ST E DI
BLAKE, BENJAMIN-BLACK	QUE	149	1ST E DI
BLAKE, BESTY	TAL	070	EASTON T
BLAKE, BILL-BLACK	WOR	338	1ST E DI
BLAKE, BRIDGET	BAL	032	1ST WARD
BLAKE, CATHARINE	HAR	105	2ND DIST
BLAKE, CATHARINE	FRE	168	EMMITTSB
BLAKE, CATO	KEN	255	1ST DIST
BLAKE, CATO	BAL	151	19TH WAR
BLAKE, CHARLES	KEN	208	2ND DIST
BLAKE, CHARLES	BAL	274	20TH WAR
BLAKE, CHARLES	BAL	247	6TH WARD
BLAKE, CHARLES-BLACK	WOR	234	6TH E DI
BLAKE, CHARLOTTE	QUE	155	2ND E DI
BLAKE, CHARLOTTE A.-BLACK	HAR	122	2ND DIST
BLAKE, DANIEL-BLACK	QUE	156	2ND E DI
BLAKE, DARKY	BAL	219	2ND WARD
BLAKE, DAVID	CAL	041	3RD DIST
BLAKE, DUNCAN	BAL	142	2ND DIST
BLAKE, EASTER	BAL	137	1ST WARD
BLAKE, EDWARD	WOR	312	2ND E DI
BLAKE, EDWARD	BAL	175	11TH WAR
BLAKE, ELEONRA	ANN	404	8TH DIST
BLAKE, ELEVEN	QUE	248	5TH E DI
BLAKE, ELIZA	BAL	329	7TH WARD
BLAKE, ELIZABETH	BAL	104	15TH WAR
BLAKE, ELIZABETH	BAL	183	16TH WAR
BLAKE, ELIZABETH	CAL	043	3RD DIST
BLAKE, ELIZABETH M.	HAR	122	2ND DIST
BLAKE, ELLEN	WOR	182	6TH E DI
BLAKE, EMILY	BAL	056	10TH WAR
BLAKE, EMMELINE	BAL	247	6TH WARD
BLAKE, GADDA	WOR	180	6TH E DI
BLAKE, GARRISON	BAL	183	16TH WAR
BLAKE, GEORGE	TAL	071	EASTON T
BLAKE, GEORGE	SOM	356	BRINKLEY
BLAKE, GEORGE	WOR	312	2ND E DI
BLAKE, GEORGE	BAL	079	15TH WAR
BLAKE, GEORGE	BAL	108	10TH WAR
BLAKE, GEORGE	BAL	151	19TH WAR
BLAKE, GEORGE W.	DOR	420	1ST DIST
BLAKE, GREENDERSON *	SOM	355	BRINKLEY
BLAKE, HARRIET	ST	286	2ND E DI
BLAKE, HARRIETT	BAL	320	7TH WARD
BLAKE, HARY	BAL	148	2ND DIST
BLAKE, HENRIETTA	DOR	437	1ST DIST
BLAKE, HENRY	WOR	232	6TH E DI
BLAKE, HENRY	KEN	215	2ND DIST
BLAKE, HENRY	KEN	253	1ST DIST
BLAKE, HESTER	CEC	136	6TH E DI
BLAKE, HESTER	DOR	424	1ST DIST
BLAKE, J.*	BAL	067	10TH WAR
BLAKE, JACOB-BLACK	DOR	408	1ST DIST
BLAKE, JAMES	WOR	337	1ST E DI
BLAKE, JAMES	WOR	179	6TH E DI
BLAKE, JAMES	WAS	010	WILLIAMS
BLAKE, JAMES	KEN	270	1ST DIST
BLAKE, JAMES	BAL	224	19TH WAR
BLAKE, JAMES	BAL	277	12TH WAR
BLAKE, JAMES	ALL	179	7TH E.D.
BLAKE, JAMES B.	BAL	031	1ST WARD
BLAKE, JAMES P.	KEN	269	1ST DIST
BLAKE, JANE	QUE	184	3RD E DI
BLAKE, JANE	WAS	010	WILLIAMS
BLAKE, JANE	WOR	305	2ND E DI
BLAKE, JANE	CEC	016	ELKTON 3
BLAKE, JANE-BLACK	KEN	235	2ND DIST
BLAKE, JERLY-MULATTO	BAL	188	2ND WARD
BLAKE, JIM-BLACK	CAR	069	NO TWP L
BLAKE, JIM-BLACK	WOR	329	1ST E DI
BLAKE, JOEL N.	WOR	332	1ST E DI
BLAKE, JOHN	BAL	326	12TH WAR
BLAKE, JOHN	BAL	280	12TH WAR
BLAKE, JOHN	BAL	242	6TH WARD
BLAKE, JOHN	BAL	244	6TH WARD
BLAKE, JOHN	BAL	151	2ND DIST
BLAKE, JOHN	BAL	424	8TH WARD
BLAKE, JOHN	BAL	310	3RD WARD
BLAKE, JOHN	WOR	308	2ND E DI
BLAKE, JOHN	KEN	272	1ST DIST
BLAKE, JOHN	WAS	123	HAGERSTO
BLAKE, JOHN	BAL	160	11TH WAR
BLAKE, JOHN	KEN	235	2ND DIST
BLAKE, JOHN	DOR	421	1ST DIST
BLAKE, JOHN	DOR	338	3RD DIVI
BLAKE, JOHN	HAR	119	2ND DIST
BLAKE, JOHN	HAR	075	BEL AIR
BLAKE, JOHN	SOM	416	DUBLIN D
BLAKE, JOHN	CEC	063	1ST E DI
BLAKE, JOHN E.	BAL	175	11TH WAR
BLAKE, JOHN R.	BAL	308	7TH WARD
BLAKE, JOHN W.	BAL	410	14TH WAR
BLAKE, JOHN-BLACK	QUE	179	2ND E DI
BLAKE, JOSEPH	WAS	007	WILLIAMS
BLAKE, JOSEPH	CAL	053	3RD DIST
BLAKE, JOSEPH	BAL	468	14TH WAR
BLAKE, JOSEPH	ALL	154	6TH E.D.
BLAKE, JULIA	BAL	175	6TH WARD
BLAKE, JULIAN	DOR	437	1ST DIST
BLAKE, KATE	WAS	124	HAGERSTO
BLAKE, L.	WAS	010	WILLIAMS
BLAKE, LEIGHER	DOR	342	3RD DIVI
BLAKE, LEMERY	CEC	036	CHESAPEA
BLAKE, LEVIN	WOR	183	6TH E DI
BLAKE, LEVIN*	DOR	434	1ST DIST
BLAKE, LEVIN-MULATTO	WOR	176	6TH E DI
BLAKE, LEWIS	CAL	014	1ST DIST
BLAKE, LIDIA	TAL	077	EASTON T
BLAKE, LORENZO	CEC	154	PORT DUP
BLAKE, LOTTY-BLACK	WOR	331	1ST E DI
BLAKE, LOUISA	KEN	218	2ND DIST
BLAKE, LOUISA	BAL	175	16TH WAR
BLAKE, MARGARET	BAL	420	14TH WAR
BLAKE, MARIA	WOR	177	6TH E DI
BLAKE, MARIA-BLACK	QUE	130	1ST E DI
BLAKE, MARTHA	BAL	075	2ND DIST
BLAKE, MARY	BAL	324	12TH WAR
BLAKE, MARY	ALL	103	5TH E.D.
BLAKE, MARY	BAL	153	2ND DIST
BLAKE, MARY	BAL	077	4TH WARD
BLAKE, MARY	BAL	062	18TH WAR
BLAKE, MARY	WOR	312	2ND E DI
BLAKE, MARY	WOR	312	2ND E DI
BLAKE, MARY A.	SOM	535	QUANTICO
BLAKE, MARY A.	BAL	158	11TH WAR
BLAKE, MARY ANN	BAL	376	13TH WAR
BLAKE, MATILDA	HAR	116	2ND DIST
BLAKE, MICHAEL	ALL	049	10TH E.D
BLAKE, MOLLY-BLACK	WOR	337	1ST E DI
BLAKE, MOSES	DOR	411	1ST DIST
BLAKE, NANCY	BAL	381	13TH WAR
BLAKE, NANCY	WOR	311	2ND E DI
BLAKE, NANCY	TAL	026	EASTON D
BLAKE, NELLY	HAR	123	2ND DIST
BLAKE, PAT	BAL	224	19TH WAR
BLAKE, PATTY-BLACK	WOR	336	1ST E DI
BLAKE, PERE F.	QUE	209	3RD E DI
BLAKE, PERRY	CEC	090	4TH E DI
BLAKE, PETER	DOR	385	1ST DIST
BLAKE, PHILLIS	HAR	134	2ND DIST
BLAKE, PHILLIS	BAL	069	15TH WAR
BLAKE, PURNELL	SOM	486	TRAPP DI
BLAKE, QUEILLA	BAL	218	12TH WAR
BLAKE, REBECCA	DOR	411	1ST DIST
BLAKE, REBECCA A.-BLACK	QUE	134	1ST E DI
BLAKE, REBECCA-BLACK	QUE	150	1ST E DI
BLAKE, RICHAD	BAL	095	5TH WARD
BLAKE, RICHARD	BAL	077	15TH WAR
BLAKE, ROBERT	WOR	195	8TH E DI
BLAKE, SAMUEL	SOM	496	SALISBUR
BLAKE, SAMUEL	TAL	033	EASTON D
BLAKE, SAMUEL	KEN	220	2ND DIST
BLAKE, SARAH	CAR	117	NO TWP L
BLAKE, SARAH	WOR	180	6TH E DI
BLAKE, SARAH	BAL	071	10TH WAR
BLAKE, SARAH	BAL	053	9TH WARD
BLAKE, SARAH	BAL	460	1ST DIST
BLAKE, SARAH A.	BAL	143	16TH WAR
BLAKE, SOLOMON	CEC	137	6TH E DI
BLAKE, SOPHIA	HAR	119	2ND DIST
BLAKE, SUSAN	CAL	014	1ST DIST
BLAKE, THOMAS	CAL	052	3RD DIST
BLAKE, THOMAS	CEC	097	4TH E DI
BLAKE, THOMAS	BAL	132	1ST WARD
BLAKE, THOMAS H.	TAL	037	EASTON D
BLAKE, THOMAS V.	CAL	063	3RD DIST
BLAKE, WASHINGTON	DOR	425	1ST DIST
BLAKE, WILLIAM	WOR	294	9TH E DI
BLAKE, WILLIAM	WOR	182	6TH E DI
BLAKE, WILLIAM	BAL	441	1ST DIST
BLAKE, WILLIAM	BAL	233	12TH WAR
BLAKE, WILLIAM	BAL	116	1ST WARD
BLAKE, WILLIAM	BAL	026	9TH WARD
BLAKE, WILLIAM-BLACK	WOR	332	1ST E DI
BLAKE, ZELPHA	WOR	312	2ND E DI
BLAKE, WILLIAM	FRE	205	BUCKEYST
BLAKELY, A. B.	BAL	075	10TH WAR
BLAKELY, CHRISTOPHER	ANN	510	HOWARD D
BLAKELY, GEORGE	BAL	102	2ND DIST
BLAKELY, JOHN	BAL	123	1ST WARD
BLAKELY, LEWIS	BAL	301	20TH WAR
BLAKELY, RICHARD	BAL	117	2ND DIST
BLAKELY, RICHARD	BAL	117	2ND DIST
BLAKELY, SUSAN	BAL	007	1ST WARD
BLAKEMAN, GEORGE B.	BAL	334	13TH WAR
BLAKEMAN, MARTHA	BAL	216	17TH WAR
BLAKENEY, ABEL R.	BAL	217	6TH WARD
BLAKENEY, REBECA	BAL	278	7TH WARD
BLAKENEY, SALUSTINE	BAL	209	6TH WARD
BLAKENEY, WILLIAM	BAL	195	6TH WARD
BLAKENY, JOHN	BAL	446	1ST DIST
BLAKER, WESLEY	CEC	191	5TH E DI
BLAKESTER, ABRAHAM	BAL	338	13TH WAR
BLAKESTINE, HENRIETTA	BAL	313	12TH WAR
BLAKESTONE, JAMES T.	ST	272	3RD E DI
BLAKISTONE, ANN B.	ST	307	1ST E DI
BLAKLAR, CHARLES	BAL	355	3RD WARD
BLAKLEY, JOHN	BAL	208	11TH WAR
BLAKLEY, JOSHUA	BAL	110	2ND DIST
BLAKLEY, SAMUEL H.	BAL	035	4TH WARD
BLALE, NINIAN	MGM	391	ROCKERLE
BLAM, MARGARET	WAS	130	HAGERSTO
BLAMMING, LEWIS	BAL	079	1ST WARD
BLAN, ROBERTA ANN*	BAL	406	3RD WARD
BLANAGHIN, JOHN S.	ST	317	4TH E DI
BLANAGIN, ELIZA	ST	316	4TH E DI
BLANCH, ELIZABETH	BAL	023	4TH WARD
BLANCH, ELLEN	BAL	259	7TH WARD
BLANCH, JAMES	BAL	268	7TH WARD
BLANCH, JAMES	HAR	049	1ST DIST
BLANCH, WILLIAM	CAR	147	NO TWP L
BLANCHARD, ELIZABETH	BAL	154	11TH WAR
BLANCHARD, GEORGE	BAL	131	1ST WARD
BLANCHARD, GEORGE W.	BAL	280	2ND WARD
BLANCHARD, J. H.	BAL	284	20TH WAR

BLANCHARD, THOMAS H. BAL 065 4TH WARD
BLANCHFIELD, JOHN WAS 055 2ND SUBD
BLANCHFIELD, SAMUEL KEN 295 3RD DIST
BLANCK, JEREMIAH BAL 306 7TH WARD
BLAND, DELILAH BAL 351 7TH WARD
BLAND, ELIZABETH CAR 142 NO TWP L
BLAND, JANE CAR 156 NO TWP L
BLAND, JOSEPH CAR 142 NO TWP L
BLAND, MARY BAL 005 EASTERN
BLAND, PHILIMON TAL 007 EASTON D
BLAND, ROBERT-BLACK CAR 155 NO TWP L
BLAND, SAMUEL BAL 270 12TH WAR
BLAND, SARAH BAL 347 13TH WAR
BLAND, WILLIAM J. BAL 259 1ST DIST
BLANDARD, B. F. CHA 255 MIDDLETO
BLANDY, ALFRED A. BAL 106 10TH WAR
BLANER, MARY ALL 084 5TH E.D.
BLANES, LIDIA TAL 082 ST MICHA
BLANEY, ALVERTE HAR 051 1ST DIST
BLANEY, ELIZA HAR 056 1ST DIST
BLANEY, ELLEN HAR 051 1ST DIST
BLANEY, JAMES W. BAL 137 18TH WAR
BLANEY, JOHN HAR 159 3RD DIST
BLANEY, MELISSA HAR 053 1ST DIST
BLANEY, SARAH BAL 416 8TH WARD
BLANEY, W.H. CAL 054 3RD DIST
BLANEY, WILLIAM HAR 053 1ST DIST
BLANEY, WILLIAM J. HAR 053 1ST DIST
BLANFORD, BENJAMIN CHA 255 MIDDLETO
BLANFORD, CHARLES B. CHA 255 MIDDLETO
BLANFORD, DAVID BAL 232 2ND WARD
BLANFORD, ELIZABETH A. BAL 013 1ST WARD
BLANFORD, ROBERT N. CAL 017 1ST DIST
BLANFORD, SARA CHA 251 MIDDLETO
BLANFORD, STANILAUS PRI 117 PISCATAW
BLANIGAN, JOHN HAR 157 3RD DIST
BLANK, JAMES A. BAL 238 17TH WAR
BLANK, JOHN FRE 080 FREDERIC
BLANK, NOAH QUE 250 5TH E DI
BLANK, S. BAL 148 1ST WARD
BLANKENSHIP, DANIEL BAL 011 15TH WAR
BLANKMAN, DORRITY BAL 288 17TH WAR
BLANSFERR, WALTER CHA 250 MIDDLETO
BLANSHFIELD, JAMES WAS 068 2ND SUBD
BLANY, JOHN HAR 152 3RD DIST
BLASDEN, MARY BAL 292 12TH WAR
BLASING, FREDERICK BAL 288 7TH WARD
BLASKNER, ELENORA ANN 268 ANNAPOLI
BLASS, MARTHA BAL 233 6TH WARD
BLASS, WILLIAM H. BAL 019 4TH WARD
BLASSITT, DAVID BAL 279 2ND WARD
BLATCHEY, ROBERT S. BAL 270 1ST DIST
BLATCHLEY, PETER BAL 177 2ND DIST
BLATEHLY, LYDIA BAL 177 2ND DIST
BLATHER, FREDERICK BAL 121 1ST WARD
BLATIS, FREDERICK BAL 264 2ND WARD
BLATTAN, CLARA BAL 357 3RD WARD
BLAU, ROBERTA ANN* BAL 406 3RD WARD
BLAVES, JOHN S. BAL 232 2ND WARD
BLAWOOD, H. R. CHA 259 MIDDLETO
BLAXTON, JESSE BAL 002 18TH WAR
BLAY, ADAM-BLACK CAR 161 NO TWP L
BLAYBOURN, GEORGE W. BAL 074 2ND DIST
BLAYLOCK, RICHARD HAR 155 3RD DIST
BLAZE, MARY E. FRE 333 MIDDLETO
BLEACK, CATHARINE BAL 141 19TH WAR
BLEAK, BRIDGET BAL 318 3RD WARD
BLEAK, GEORGE BAL 353 3RD WARD
BLEAK, MARTIN BAL 317 3RD WARD
BLEARDHAM, H. * BAL 310 12TH WAR
BLEAUFOOT, LEWIS BAL 352 13TH WAR
BLEEKEN, ISABEL BAL 209 19TH WAR
BLEENY, FREDERICK BAL 143 19TH WAR
BLEIMER, HENRY BAL 095 1ST WARD
BLEIR, WILLIAM * ANN 375 4TH DIST
BLEMCLURE, JOHN BAL 178 2ND WARD
BLEMELINE, ANN BAL 213 2ND WARD
BLENCAR, WASHINGTON ALL 188 9TH E.D.
BLENKENSOT, SISTER E. FRE 197 5TH E DI
BLENNIX, RICHARD BAL 045 15TH WAR
BLEPING, JOHN * WAS 086 2ND SUBD
BLESKEY, JOHNG. BAL 089 1ST WARD
BLESSING, ANN WAS 087 2ND SUBD
BLESSING, DAVID W. FRE 400 JEFFERSO
BLESSING, ELIZABETH FRE 389 PETERSVI
BLESSING, ELIZABETH BAL 323 3RD WARD
BLESSING, GEORGE FRE 369 CATOCTIN
BLESSING, GEORGE FRE 310 WOODSBOR
BLESSING, HENRY WAS 183 BOONSBOR
BLESSING, JOHN WAS 086 2ND SUBD
BLESSING, JOHN BAL 224 6TH WARD
BLESSING, MARY BAL 164 6TH WARD
BLESSING, MARY FRE 212 BUCKEYST
BLESSING, MARY E. FRE 380 PETERSVI
BLESSING, THOMA FRE 392 PETERSVI
BLESSING,E VE FRE 400 JEFFERSO
BLESSON, ELIZABETH ALL 203 CUMBERLA
BLETHEN, J. BAL 153 1ST WARD
BLETTENBERGEN, THOMAS BAL 022 2ND DIST
BLEU, WILLIAM * ANN 375 4TH DIST
BLEYS, JAMES CEC 048 1ST E DI
BLGER, ANN BAL 027 9TH WARD
BLICK, JAMES C. BAL 437 8TH WARD
BLICK, WILLIAM B. BAL 311 7TH WARD
BLICKENETGAFF, JOHN * FRE 369 CATOCTIN
BLICKENSTAFF, DANIEL FRE 362 CATOCTIN
BLICKENSTAFF, ELIAS FRE 366 CATOCTIN
BLICKENTROFF, LISETTE BAL 041 9TH WARD
BLIGH, ISIAH BAL 459 8TH WARD
BLIGHT, WILLIAM BAL 273 12TH WAR
BLIMLINE, HENRY BAL 334 3RD WARD
BLIMLINE, JOSEPH BAL 298 7TH WARD
BLINKERT, WILLIAM CAR 255 3RD DIST
BLINKHOUSE, ANDREW ANN 375 4TH DIST
BLINKSOP, WILLIAM ALL 112 5TH E.D.
BLINN, AMBROSE * BAL 354 1ST DIST
BLINN, JOHN * BAL 354 1ST DIST
BLINN, SARAH BAL 235 12TH WAR
BLINSINGER, GEORGE M. BAL 294 12TH WAR
BLINTSINGER, SAMUEL CAR 266 WESTMINS
BLISH, JAMES FRE 380 PETERSVI
BLISS, SUSAN BAL 388 3RD WARD
BLITHE, JAMES BAL 163 2ND DIST
BLITT, CHARLES BAL 217 17TH WAR
BLITT, CHRISTIAN BAL 168 6TH WARD
BLIZARD, JOHN BAL 078 2ND DIST
BLIZZARD, CALEB BAL 260 1ST DIST
BLIZZARD, CALEB BAL 227 1ST DIST
BLIZZARD, CHARLES BAL 233 1ST DIST
BLIZZARD, ELIJAH CAR 197 4TH DIST
BLIZZARD, GEORGE CAR 280 7TH DIST
BLIZZARD, HIANTHA CAR 200 4TH DIST
BLIZZARD, ISIAH CAR 198 4TH DIST
BLIZZARD, JAMES CAR 200 4TH DIST
BLIZZARD, JAMES CAR 287 7TH DIST
BLIZZARD, JOHN M. CAR 200 4TH DIST
BLIZZARD, MARGARET CAR 198 4TH DIST
BLIZZARD, MARGARET CAR 269 WESTMINS
BLIZZARD, RACHEL CAR 194 4TH DIST
BLIZZARD, RACHEL CAR 197 4TH DIST
BLIZZARD, REBECA CAR 200 4TH DIST
BLIZZARD, REBIE BAL 277 12TH WAR
BLIZZARD, SAMUEL CAR 201 4TH DIST
BLIZZARD, SARAH CAR 177 8TH DIST
BLIZZARD, STEPHEN BAL 364 3RD WARD
BLIZZARD, ZACHARIAH CAR 176 8TH DIST
BLL, SARAH BAL 218 12TH WAR
BLOCH, LEOPOLD BAL 183 6TH WARD
BLOCHER, JACOB WAS 186 BOONSBOR
BLOCK, BENJAMIN BAL 404 1ST DIST
BLOCK, GEORGE BAL 007 15TH WAR
BLOCK, HESTER* SOM 477 TRAPP DI
BLOCK, JOHN BAL 265 12TH WAR
BLOCK, LEWIS BAL 261 20TH WAR
BLOCK, MARGARET BAL 365 8TH WARD
BLOCK, SARAH BAL 286 1ST DIST
BLOCK, SIMON J. BAL 237 2ND WARD
BLOCKER, DANIEL ALL 220 CUMBERLA
BLOCKER, ELISABETH ALL 220 CUMBERLA
BLOCKER, ELISABETH ALL 220 CUMBERLA
BLOCKER, GEORGE ALL 220 CUMBERLA
BLOCKER, GEORGE M. ALL 221 CUMBERLA
BLOCKMIRE, AUGUST BAL 008 4TH WARD
BLOCKSON, KENDAL SOM 351 BRINKLEY
BLOCKWELL, THOMAS BAL 444 1ST DIST
BLODEN, HENRY BAL 234 1ST DIST
BLODSWORTH, MARGRETT DOR 341 3RD DIVI
BLOHORN, LUCRETIA BAL 273 17TH WAR
BLOID, AMANDA WOR 330 1ST E DI
BLOIS, MARY A. MGM 382 ROCKERLE
BLOKS, LAURENCE BAL 157 6TH WARD
BLOMAIER, H. BAL 449 8TH WARD
BLOME, JOHN BAL 223 6TH WARD
BLON, JOHN CEC 070 5TH E DI
BLOND, WILLIAM H.* TAL 041 EASTON D
BLONDEL, ANTHONY BAL 354 13TH WAR
BLONKER, ELIZABETH BAL 083 10TH WAR
BLONOWAY, JAMES BAL 047 1ST WARD
BLOODE, L.P. PRI 091 MARLBROU
BLOODSWORTH, JOHN DOR 342 3RD DIVI
BLOODSWORTH, MARGRETT DOR 342 3RD DIVI
BLOODSWORTH, WILLIAM DOR 342 3RD DIVI
BLOODWORTH, NATHAN TAL 082 ST MICHA
BLOOM, ADAM CAR 375 9TH DIST
BLOOM, AMBROSE ANN 444 HOWARD D
BLOOM, BARBARA BAL 334 3RD WARD
BLOOM, DAVID CAR 399 2ND DIST
BLOOM, ENOCH WAS 194 1ST DIST
BLOOM, GEORGE ALL 149 6TH E.D.
BLOOM, ISAAC BAL 343 3RD WARD
BLOOM, ISAAC CAR 379 2ND DIST
BLOOM, JACOB CAR 322 1ST DIST
BLOOM, JOHN CAR 389 2ND DIST
BLOOM, JOHN FRE 257 NEW MARK
BLOOM, JOSIAH WAS 195 1ST DIST
BLOOM, MARIAH WAS 030 2ND SUBD
BLOOM, MICHAEL FRE 253 NEW MARK
BLOOM, SAMUEL WAS 128 HAGERSTO
BLOOM, WILLIAM CAR 375 9TH DIST
BLOOMENAIN, GEORGE FRE 012 FREDERIC
BLOOMENAUR, CHARLES FRE 054 FREDERIC
BLOOMENCUR, HENRY FRE 021 FREDERIC
BLOOMER, ALBERT BAL 124 2ND DIST
BLOOMER, AUGSUT BAL 417 8TH WARD
BLOOMER, CHRISTIAN BAL 453 8TH WARD
BLOOMER, HARRIET C. BAL 056 10TH WAR
BLOOMER, JOHN W. BAL 068 10TH WAR
BLOOMER, LOUISA BAL 123 2ND DIST
BLOOMFIELD, FRANCIS CEC 098 3RD E DI
BLOOMINAUR, NICHOLAS FRE 026 FREDERIC
BLOOMINGHOUR, GEORGE WAS 181 BOONSBOR
BLOOMINGOUR, CHRIST. WAS 168 FUNKSTOW
BLOOMINGOUR, MICHAEL WAS 168 FUNKSTOW
BLOOMINGTON, JOHN BAL 164 1ST WARD
BLOOMONAUR, NICHOLAS FRE 053 FREDERIC
BLOOMS, FRANK BAL 131 1ST WARD
BLOONTHAL, LEVI BAL 103 1ST WARD
BLORGHTZ, ANN M. ALL 231 CUMBERLA
BLOSS, FRED ANN 419 HOWARD D
BLOSS, JOHN BAL 036 15TH WAR
BLOSSONR, JOAL FRE 093 FREDERIC
BLOT, JOHN BAL 383 1ST DIST
BLOTNER, CHRISTOPHER BAL 427 8TH WARD
BLOTTENBERGE,R JOSEPH BAL 019 2ND DIST
BLOTTENBERGER, PHILIP BAL 414 8TH WARD
BLOTTER, NICHOLAS BAL 015 15TH WAR
BLOTTON, MARY A. ANN 500 HOWARD D
BLOUGHSMAN, HANAH BAL 035 2ND DIST
BLOWBERRY, JOHN BAL 105 1ST WARD
BLOWER, ISAAC FRE 423 8TH E DI
BLOWERD, CAROLINE BAL 267 20TH WAR
BLOWERS, ANN ANN 483 HOWARD D
BLOWERS, BENJAMIN ANN 496 HOWARD D
BLOWERS, JONATHAN ANN 476 HOWARD D
BLOWERS, RICHARD FRE 037 FREDERIC
BLOXSOME, J. S. BAL 152 1ST WARD
BLOY, JAMES FRE 393 PETERSVI
BLOYER, JACOB WAS 299 1ST DIST
BLUBAUGH, ANDREW ALL 098 5TH E.D.
BLUBAUGH, GEORGE O. BAL 291 7TH WARD
BLUBAUGH, JACOB ALL 083 5TH E.D.
BLUBAUGH, SIMEON ALL 112 5TH E.D.
BLUDSWORTH, JANE SOM 461 HANGARY
BLUDSWORTH, LITTLETON SOM 463 HANGARY
BLUDSWORTH, RISDON SOM 457 DAMES QU
BLUDSWORTH, SARAH SOM 463 HANGARY
BLUE, DAVID ANN 420 HOWARD D
BLUE, DAVID ANN 416 HOWARD D
BLUE, FRANCES C. FRE 065 FREDERIC
BLUE, JOEL ANN 448 HOWARD D
BLUE, MARY G. BAL 121 16TH WAR
BLUEBAKER, JOHN C. BAL 095 5TH WARD
BLUEBANK, SAMUEL ANN 334 2ND DIST
BLUEMEYER, AMOS BAL 063 1ST WARD
BLUESKINS, SIDNEY ANN 267 ANNAPOLI
BLUFFORD, SARAH BAL 396 1ST DIST
BLUFFORD, WILLIAM BAL 458 8TH WARD
BLUHER, MARGARET WAS 078 2ND SUBD
BLUM, AMBROSE * BAL 354 1ST DIST
BLUM, CHRISTIAN ALL 252 CUMBERLA
BLUM, GEORGE BAL 004 15TH WAR
BLUM, GEORGE BAL 007 4TH WARD
BLUM, ISAAC BAL 232 2ND WARD
BLUM, JOHN BAL 354 1ST DIST
BLUM, JOSEPH BAL 367 1ST DIST
BLUM, LOUIS BAL 062 15TH WAR
BLUM, MICHAEL BAL 367 1ST DIST
BLUM, VALENTINE BAL 143 19TH WAR
BLUME, JOHN BAL 370 1ST DIST
BLUME, JOSEPH BAL 176 11TH WAR
BLUME, JOSEPH BAL 358 8TH WARD
BLUME, THEADORE FRE 203 5TH E DI
BLUMENAUER, HERNY BAL 371 13TH WAR
BLUMENAUR, HENRY * BAL 057 15TH WAR
BLUMENDUR, HENRY * BAL 057 15TH WAR
BLUMENOUR, MICHAEL FRE 050 FREDERIC
BLUMER, AGUST BAL 029 2ND DIST
BLUMER, JOHN ANN 336 3RD DIST
BLUMER, LEWIS BAL 382 8TH WARD
BLUMER, SARAH BAL 386 8TH WARD
BLUMET, JOHN CEC 215 7TH E DI
BLUMMAUR, HENRY * BAL 057 15TH WAR
BLUMMER, SOLOMAN ALL 241 CUMBERLA
BLUMMER, WILLIAM W. ANN 413 HOWARD D
BLUNDELL, A. BAL 318 12TH WAR
BLUNDELL, DENNIS BAL 321 12TH WAR
BLUNDELL, DENNIS BAL 292 12TH WAR
BLUNDELL, M. BAL 320 12TH WAR
BLUNDEN, ELIZABETH BAL 251 17TH WAR
BLUNDEN, SARAH BAL 088 15TH WAR
BLUNK, CHRISTIAN BAL 279 1ST DIST
BLUNK, JOHN D. BAL 255 1ST DIST
BLUNK, JOSEPH QUE 239 5TH E DI
BLUNK, ROBERT BAL 132 1ST WARD
BLUNKERT, JOSEPH CAR 255 3RD DIST
BLUNT, ALICE K. BAL 204 11TH WAR
BLUNT, ANN-BLACK CAR 075 NO TWP L
BLUNT, ANNE-BLACK QUE 160 2ND E DI
BLUNT, CHARLES B. TAL 103 ST MICHA
BLUNT, CHARLES F. TAL 103 ST MICHA
BLUNT, ELIZABETH BAL 081 18TH WAR
BLUNT, FREDERICK BAL 007 9TH WARD
BLUNT, JAMES E. CAL 015 1ST DIST
BLUNT, JAMES R. TAL 080 ST MICHA
BLUNT, LOUISA-BLACK QUE 140 1ST E DI
BLUNT, MARTHA QUE 241 5TH E DI
BLUNT, NELSON BAL 397 1ST DIST
BLUNT, PERRY ANN 361 3RD DIST
BLUNT, S.F. BAL 204 11TH WAR
BLUNT, SAMUEL MGM 339 CLARKSBU
BLUNT, SAMUEL BAL 398 14TH WAR
BLUNT, SARAH ANN 502 HOWARD D
BLUNT, SARAH JANE QUE 217 3RD E DI
BLUNTT, RICHARD CAL 038 2ND DIST
BLUTE, MARY BAL 052 15TH WAR
BLY, JAMES BAL 165 11TH WAR
BLYTHE, GEORGE BAL 166 11TH WAR
BLYTHE, JULIA CAR 396 2ND DIST
BNAKER, SAMUEL BAL 302 20TH WAR
BNAKERT, JOHN SR. CAR 246 3RD DIST
BNEDER, LYDIA WAS 099 2ND DIST
BNOSLEY, SUSAN BAL 057 2ND DIST
BOACH, JACOB * BAL 158 2ND DIST
BOADLY, WILLIAM BAL 403 3RD WARD
BOADWIN, JOSHUA CAR 152 NO TWP L
BOAK, CASPER BAL 209 2ND WARD
BOANNAN, COLUMBUS HAR 076 BEL AIR
BOANT, JOHN BAL 010 9TH WARD
BOARDING, MARTHA FRE 253 NEW MARK
BOARDLEY, ANANA BAL 435 14TH WAR
BOARDLEY, CALUMBS HAR 201 3RD DIST
BOARDLEY, CUFF KEN 261 1ST DIST
BOARDLEY, DANIEL BAL 434 14TH WAR
BOARDLEY, DANIEL BAL 038 15TH WAR
BOARDLEY, EDWARD HAR 206 3RD DIST
BOARDLEY, GEORGE BAL 034 9TH WARD
BOARDLEY, JOHN KEN 254 1ST DIST
BOARDLEY, SPENCE BAL 165 11TH WAR
BOARDLEY, WILLIAM BAL 167 1ST WARD
BOARDLY, HENRIETTA G. QUE 184 3RD E DI
BOARDLY, JOHN ANN 402 8TH DIST
BOARDLY, JOHN KEN 215 2ND DIST
BOARDLY, MARTHA A. KEN 265 1ST DIST
BOARDLY, MATILDA ANN 355 3RD DIST
BOARDLY, R. ANN 284 ANNAPOLI
BOARDLY, SUSAN ANN 366 4TH DIST
BOARDLY, THOMAS KEN 237 2ND DIST
BOARKE, ULRICH ALL 146 6TH E.D.
BOARMAN, BENJAMIN W. HAR 008 1ST DIST
BOARMAN, FRANCIS L. CHA 275 ALLENS F
BOARMAN, FRANKLIN HAR 088 2ND DIST
BOARMAN, GEORGE S. BAL 050 18TH WAR
BOARMAN, HARIET BAL 250 6TH WARD
BOARMAN, HENRY HAR 137 2ND DIST
BOARMAN, HENRY HAR 137 2ND DIST
BOARMAN, IDA CHA 274 ALLENS F
BOARMAN, JACK CHA 226 ALLENS F
BOARMAN, JOHN B. CHA 273 ALLENS F
BOARMAN, JOSEPH CHA 274 ALLENS F
BOARMAN, JOSEPH Z. CHA 274 ALLENS F
BOARMAN, M. JULIA BAL 212 11TH WAR
BOARMAN, MARTHA A. CHA 264 HILLTOP
BOARMAN, MARY CHA 280 BOJANTOW
BOARMAN, RAPHAEL CHA 275 ALLENS F
BOARMAN, ROBERT HAR 110 2ND DIST
BOARMAN, ROSE A. CHA 279 BOJANTOW
BOARMAN, SOPHA CHA 283 BOJANTOW
BOARMAN, THOMAS J. CHA 280 BOJANTOW
BOARMAN, WALTER F. CHA 293 BOJANTOW
BOASIUS, ELISA BAL 035 18TH WAR
BOASMAN, SOPHIA BAL 429 14TH WAR
BOAT, WILLIAM BAL 166 1ST WARD
BOATILER, ESROM BAL 126 1ST WARD
BOATMAN, BENJAMIN B. WAS 158 2ND DIST
BOATS, RHODA BAL 381 8TH WARD
BOAZ, JAMES BAL 022 15TH WAR
BOBART, MARY* BAL 339 3RD WARD
BOBBITS, GEORGE BAL 198 5TH DIST
BOBBITS, SARAH BAL 198 5TH DIST
BOBEE, JOSEPH F. BAL 007 15TH WAR
BOBEE, MARY BAL 007 15TH WAR
BOBERT, JOHN BAL 206 2ND WARD
BOBERT, JOHN D. BAL 133 16TH WAR
BOBI, ELIZABETH FRE 003 FREDERIC
BOBLITZ, CAROLINE CAR 173 8TH DIST
BOBLITZ, CATHARINE BAL 197 5TH DIST
BOBLITZ, CATHARINE BAL 191 5TH DIST
BOBLITZ, CATHERINE CAR 172 8TH DIST
BOBLITZ, CHRIS BAL 205 6TH DIST
BOBLITZ, DANIEL BAL 202 6TH DIST

Name	County	Page	District
BOBLITZ, JOHN F.	BAL	205	6TH DIST
BOBLITZ, JOHN J.	CAR	171	8TH DIST
BOBLITZ, LOUIS	BAL	205	6TH DIST
BOBLITZ, PETER	CAR	172	8TH DIST
BOBLITZ, RACHAEL	BAL	203	6TH DIST
BOBLITZ, SAMUEL	BAL	205	6TH DIST
BOBLITZ, SAVILIA J.	CAR	185	8TH DIST
BOBLITZ, WILLIAM	BAL	197	5TH DIST
BOCE, JAMES	BAL	411	3RD WARD
BOCH, JOHN	BAL	102	15TH WAR
BOCH, MARGARET	BAL	099	15TH WAR
BOCHENS, SAMUEL	BAL	381	1ST DIST
BOCHLET, FRANCIS *	BAL	158	2ND DIST
BOCHME, CHARLES L.	BAL	422	3RD WARD
BOCKELMANN, CONRAD H.	BAL	142	16TH WAR
BOCKELMANN, HENRY	BAL	142	16TH WAR
BOCKER, PHILIP	BAL	195	6TH WARD
BOCKHAUS, CHARLES	BAL	126	16TH WAR
BOCKHOUSE, LOUIS	BAL	459	1ST DIST
BOCKLEY, JOHN	BAL	288	12TH WAR
BOCKMAN, HENRY	BAL	214	2ND WARD
BOCKMAN, JASH	BAL	054	2ND DIST
BOCKNAN, JOSEPH	BAL	273	2ND WARD
BOCKWOOD, JIM	BAL	310	1ST DIST
BOCUEGAN, GOTLEIB	BAL	240	2ND WARD
BODDEKER, DARNS	BAL	464	14TH WAR
BODDENSICK, GEORGE	BAL	288	1ST DIST
BODDER, PETER	BAL	427	14TH WAR
BODDOWS, THOMAS	BAL	153	1ST WARD
BODDY, ADELINE	CEC	212	7TH E DI
BODDY, CATHERINE	CEC	214	7TH E DI
BODDY, CHARLES	CEC	215	7TH E DI
BODDY, CHARLOTTA	CEC	215	7TH E DI
BODDY, GEORGE	CEC	215	7TH E DI
BODDY, JAMES	CEC	211	7TH E DI
BODDY, MARY	CEC	210	7TH E DI
BODELY, DAVID	CAL	049	3RD DIST
BODELY, HARRIET	CAL	037	2ND DIST
BODEMAR, FRED J.	BAL	262	20TH WAR
BODEN, HESEKIAH	BAL	469	14TH WAR
BODEN, ISAAC	ALL	182	8TH E.D.
BODEN, WILLIAM	CAR	109	NO TWP L
BODEN, WILLIAM J.	CAR	138	NO TWP L
BODENSICK, M.	BAL	174	19TH WAR
BODER, LAMBERT	FRE	266	NEW MARK
BODER, WILLIAM G. M.D.	BAL	456	1ST DIST
BODEY, MARGARET	BAL	312	12TH WAR
BODEY, WILLIAM	BAL	311	12TH WAR
BODFIELD, MARY	BAL	224	6TH WARD
BODGE, DANIEL	BAL	458	14TH WAR
BODGE, FRANCIS	BAL	362	8TH WARD
BODGUET, FRANK	BAL	133	1ST WARD
BODLE, CHRIS	BAL	227	12TH WAR
BODLEY, AQUILA	HAR	183	3RD DIST
BODLEY, ARCHABLE	WOR	246	1ST CENS
BODLEY, CHARLES	BAL	246	20TH WAR
BODLEY, HANNAH	BAL	041	4TH WARD
BODLEY, PETER H.	HAR	181	3RD DIST
BODLEY, SOPHIA	BAL	357	1ST DIST
BODLEY, WILLIAM	WOR	247	1ST CENS
BODLING, SOLOMON	QUE	244	5TH E DI
BODLY, JOHN E.	HAR	201	3RD DIST
BODLY, JOSHUA	CEC	025	ELKTON 3
BODMAN, MISS V.	FRE	199	5TH E DI
BODMAN, SUSAN	WAS	141	HAGERSTO
BODMSICK, DAVID	BAL	198	19TH WAR
BODY, MATILDA	ANN	377	4TH DIST
BOE, ANDREW *	ANN	380	4TH DIST
BOECH, MARY *	WOR	305	SNOW HIL
BOEHERS, MATILDA	BAL	251	12TH WAR
BOEHM, CHARLES G.	BAL	057	15TH WAR
BOEHME, AUGUSTUS	BAL	073	15TH WAR
BOEHNER, LEWIS C.	ALL	255	CUMBERLA
BOEMAN, JOHN	ALL	114	5TH E.D.
BOEN, ANN	FRE	304	WOODSBOR
BOER, HENRY	BAL	294	12TH WAR
BOERS, JOHN	BAL	034	15TH WAR
BOES, CATHRIN	BAL	033	18TH WAR
BOESENBACH, HENRY	BAL	024	4TH WARD
BOFEP, SEB. *	BAL	306	12TH WAR
BOGAN, FREDERICK	ALL	084	5TH E.D.
BOGAN, SPENCER	CEC	046	1ST E DI
BOGANS, JANE	CEC	046	1ST E DI
BOGART, H.	BAL	292	12TH WAR
BOGART, PETER	PRI	023	VANSVILL
BOGENA, JOHN	FRE	343	MIDDLETO
BOGER, AIRY	KEN	211	2ND DIST
BOGER, ANNA	KEN	211	2ND DIST
BOGER, FRED *	KEN	263	1ST DIST
BOGER, ISAAC	KEN	211	2ND DIST
BOGER, JOHN	KEN	245	2ND DIST
BOGER, JOHN	BAL	306	12TH WAR
BOGER, MARYH	ALL	037	2ND E.D.
BOGER, PERRY *	KEN	246	2ND DIST
BOGERS, MILTON	WAS	274	RIDGEVIL
BOGERST, S.	BAL	235	20TH WAR
BOGG, JAMES	BAL	276	20TH WAR
BOGGS, ABRAHAM	BAL	122	1ST WARD
BOGGS, E. W.	BAL	332	1ST DIST
BOGGS, EDWARD	SOM	455	DAMES QU
BOGGS, FRANCIS M. K.	SOM	403	BRINKLEY
BOGGS, H.C.	BAL	166	1ST WARD
BOGGS, HARMANUS	BAL	065	10TH WAR
BOGGS, HIRAM	BAL	208	17TH WAR
BOGGS, JAMES	BAL	027	4TH WARD
BOGGS, JAMES	BAL	189	11TH WAR
BOGGS, JOHN	BAL	082	4TH WARD
BOGGS, JOHN	BAL	199	11TH WAR
BOGGS, JOHN	TAL	027	EASTON D
BOGGS, JOHN G.	BAL	040	4TH WARD
BOGGS, LEVIN	SOM	406	DUBLIN D
BOGGS, LEVIN	SOM	406	DUBLIN D
BOGGS, LITCHEY	SOM	359	BRINKLEY
BOGGS, M. M. D.	BAL	281	2ND WARD
BOGGS, MARGARET K.	ANN	521	HOWARD D
BOGGS, MARY A.	BAL	199	11TH WAR
BOGGS, NAT	SOM	352	BRINKLEY
BOGGS, SAMUEL	SOM	402	BRINKLEY
BOGGS, SAMUEL E.	WAS	162	2ND DIST
BOGGS, SARAH	BAL	021	4TH WARD
BOGGS, SIMON	BAL	085	4TH WARD
BOGGS, THOMAS	BAL	117	11TH WAR
BOGGS, W. A.	BAL	066	10TH WAR
BOGGS, WILLIAM	BAL	300	12TH WAR
BOGGS, WILLIAM	BAL	025	4TH WARD
BOGINA, ELIZABETH	FRE	341	MIDDLETO
BOGLE, JANE	BAL	334	7TH WARD
BOGLE, MITELDA	BAL	020	18TH WAR
BOGLE, ROBERT	ANN	461	HOWARD D
BOGLE, WILLIAM	MGM	422	MEDLEY 3

Name	County	Page	District
BOGLE, WILLIAM	MGM	422	MEDLEY 3
BOGLEMAN, CHRISTIAN	BAL	070	1ST WARD
BOGNE, HENRY	BAL	256	12TH WAR
BOGOW, MICHAEL	WAS	012	WILLIAMS
BOGS, JAMES	BAL	406	1ST DIST
BOGUE, CHARLES	FRE	065	FREDERIC
BOGUE, JAMES	BAL	048	9TH WARD
BOGUSCH, SIMON	BAL	429	8TH WARD
BOHAGER, THOMAS	BAL	198	2ND WARD
BOHAM, MAHALA	FRE	303	WOODSBOR
BOHAN, ANDREW	FRE	20	5TH E DI
BOHAN, ANNA	ALL	210	CUMBERLA
BOHANAN, IGNATIUS	ST	287	2ND E DI
BOHANAN, JOHN	ST	302	2ND E DI
BOHANAN, WILLIAM H.	ST	304	2ND E DI
BOHANON, JAMES F.	ST	287	2ND E DI
BOHEN, CAMILA	BAL	052	15TH WAR
BOHIM, MICHAEL	BAL	245	2ND WARD
BOHM, ADOLPH	BAL	025	15TH WAR
BOHN, CHRISTOPHER	BAL	046	1ST WARD
BOHN, ELIZA J.	WAS	125	HAGERSTO
BOHN, ERASMUS	BAL	036	9TH WARD
BOHN, JACOB	BAL	465	14TH WAR
BOHN, MARY	BAL	273	2ND WARD
BOHN, SARAH	WAS	183	BOONSBOR
BOHN, WALLENTINE	WAS	165	HAGERSTO
BOHNARD, M.	BAL	181	2ND WARD
BOHRER, B.F. M.D.	BAL	231	1ST DIST
BOHRER, CORNELIA L.	MGM	385	ROCKERLE
BOHRER, ELIZABETH	MGM	394	ROCKERLE
BOHRER, LUCINDA	MGM	359	BERRYS D
BOHUR, CASPER	BAL	024	4TH WARD
BOICE, GEORGE M.	BAL	269	1ST DIST
BOICE, HUGH	DOR	457	1ST DIST
BOICE, HUST*	DOR	456	1ST DIST
BOICE, ISACK*	TAL	057	EASTON D
BOICE, MARTHA	BAL	353	1ST DIST
BOICE, PERRY	TAL	057	EASTON D
BOICE, WESLEY	BAL	016	18TH WAR
BOICE, WILLIAM	CAR	104	NO TWP L
BOICE, WILLIAM*	TAL	053	EASTON D
BOICH, SALLY E.	WOR	315	2ND E DI
BOID, M. D.	CHA	219	ALLENS F
BOIEL, MARY	WOR	283	BERLIN 1
BOILDING, MARY	BAL	055	18TH WAR
BOILEAN, DAVID	FRE	313	MIDDLETO
BOILEN, LAWRENCE	ALL	141	6TH E.D.
BOILS, AMOS	CEC	119	3RD E DI
BOILS, ANNA	CEC	119	3RD E DI
BOILS, HENRY J.	CEC	011	ELKTON 3
BOILS, RACHEL	CEC	010	ELKTON 3
BOINS, EDWARD	FRE	257	NEW MARK
BOIS, LEWIS	BAL	433	14TH WAR
BOIS, LOUISA	BAL	316	12TH WAR
BOISANBIN, MARC	FRE	202	5TH E DI
BOISANHIN, EDWARD	FRE	202	5TH E DI
BOIST, ISRAEL	FRE	259	NEW MARK
BOIST, SUSANNAH	FRE	257	NEW MARK
BOKE, BERNA	BAL	209	2ND WARD
BOKEE, C.F.	BAL	090	5TH WARD
BOKEE, JOHN C.*	BAL	114	15TH WAR
BOKEL, ANTHONEY	BAL	427	8TH WARD
BOKEL, J. H.	BAL	133	11TH WAR
BOKEL, JOHANAH	BAL	428	8TH WARD
BOKEL, JOHN G.	BAL	180	6TH WARD
BOKHARRIS, PETER	BAL	316	12TH WAR
BOKMAN, RUDOLPH	BAL	038	18TH WAR
BOKOSS, A.	BAL	310	12TH WAR
BOLACK, JOSEPH	BAL	037	1ST WARD
BOLAM, ELLEN	BAL	296	12TH WAR
BOLAM, THOMAS	BAL	296	12TH WAR
BOLAN, BRIDGETT	BAL	035	4TH WARD
BOLAND, ELLEN	BAL	319	20TH WAR
BOLAND, GEORGE	CAR	350	6TH DIST
BOLAND, GEORGE	BAL	054	15TH WAR
BOLAND, JAMES	BAL	034	15TH WAR
BOLAND, JAMES	BAL	304	1ST DIST
BOLAND, MARY A.	SOM	494	SALISBUR
BOLAND, THOMAS	FRE	387	PETERSVI
BOLBBIN, ELIZABETH	ALL	008	3RD E.D.
BOLBKE, HENRY	BAL	334	13TH WAR
BOLCUS, JOSEPH	PRI	039	VANSVILL
BOLD, MARY	ANN	279	ANNAPOLI
BOLDEN, BRIDGET	BAL	078	18TH WAR
BOLDEN, CATHARINE	BAL	186	19TH WAR
BOLDEN, GEROGE	KEN	280	3RD DIST
BOLDEN, HESTER	CEC	090	4TH E DI
BOLDEN, JOHN	CEC	216	7TH E DI
BOLDEN, NELSON	CEC	180	7TH E DI
BOLDEN, RICHARD	BAL	280	12TH WAR
BOLDEN, RODNEY	BAL	077	18TH WAR
BOLDER, HENRY	ALL	218	CUMBERLA
BOLDERSON, LOYD	CEC	202	6TH E DI
BOLDIN, WILLAIM	BAL	098	18TH WAR
BOLDING, BENEDICT-BLACK	ST	320	4TH E DI
BOLDING, CHARLOTTE	QUE	212	3RD E DI
BOLDING, CHARLOTTE-BLACK	ST	300	2ND E DI
BOLDING, JAEMS	QUE	246	5TH E DI
BOLDING, JOSEPH	QUE	242	5TH E DI
BOLDING, LUCINDA	QUE	252	5TH E DI
BOLDING, MARY ANN	QUE	210	3RD E DI
BOLDING, MAVILL	BAL	128	11TH WAR
BOLDING, SAMUEL	QUE	205	3RD E DI
BOLDING, SOLOMON	QUE	250	5TH E DI
BOLDING, SOLOMON	QUE	241	5TH E DI
BOLDING, SPENCER	QUE	211	3RD E DI
BOLDING, WILLIAM	QUE	205	3RD E DI
BOLDINGER, JACOB	BAL	060	18TH WAR
BOLDLINGSHOLFER, GEROGE	BAL	334	13TH WAR
BOLDONEY, HENRY	CAR	173	8TH DIST
BOLDOSTON, JOHN J.	CEC	200	7TH E DI
BOLDOS, EUPHINIA *	WOR	260	BERLIN 1
BOLOSTON, WILLIAM	CEC	201	6TH E DI
BOLE, EVERHART	ALL	197	CUMBERLA
BOLELA, MENEWA *	FRE	258	NEW MARK
BOLEMAN, HENRY	BAL	285	17TH WAR
BOLEN, HENRY-BLACK	CAR	138	NO TWP L
BOLEN, PHILI	FRE	396	PETERSVI
BOLEN, THOMAS	ALL	143	6TH E.D.
BOLEY, BETSEY	BAL	132	5TH WARD
BOLEY, GEORGE H.	BAL	039	4TH WARD
BOLEY, LEIGHER	DOR	371	3RD DIVI
BOLEY, PETER	ALL	049	10TH E.D
BOLEY, RACHEL	ANN	343	3RD DIST
BOLEY, WILLIAM	BAL	425	1ST DIST
BOLF, JOSEPH	WAS	062	2ND SUBD
BOLGER, JAMES	BAL	207	6TH WARD
BOLGIANO, EDWARD G.	BAL	013	4TH WARD
BOLGIANO, JOHN	BAL	234	6TH WARD
BOLGIANO, JOHN	BAL	256	6TH WARD

Name	County	Page	District
BOLIN MARY	BAL	207	11TH WAR
BOLIN, EDWARD	ALL	220	CUMBERLA
BOLIN, JOHN	ALL	119	5TH E.D.
BOLIN, MARY	BAL	085	4TH WARD
BOLIN, PETER	CAR	096	NO TWP L
BOLINDER, DAVID	BAL	036	15TH WAR
BOLING, JOEPH	FRE	205	BUCKEYST
BOLING, PERE	QUE	242	5TH E DI
BOLINGER, GEORGE	WAS	042	2ND SUBD
BOLINGER, JACOB	WAS	149	HAGERSTO
BOLINGER, JACOB	BAL	209	6TH DIST
BOLINGER, JEFFERSON	BAL	206	6TH DIST
BOLINGER, JOHN	BAL	044	1ST WARD
BOLINGER, JOHN	WAS	042	2ND SUBD
BOLINGER, LYDIA	BAL	209	6TH DIST
BOLINGER, MATHIAS	BAL	197	5TH DIST
BOLK, JOHN	BAL	034	4TH WARD
BOLLA, FREDERICK	FRE	238	NEW MARK
BOLLAR, DANIEL	FRE	095	FREDERIC
BOLLARD, JOHN	FRE	114	CREAGERS
BOLLER, HARRIET	FRE	095	FREDERIC
BOLLETS, CARLINE	FRE	129	CREAGERS
BOLLINGER, CHRISTIAN	FRE	311	MIDDLETO
BOLLINGER, DANIEL	CAR	341	6TH DIST
BOLLINGER, EDWARD	CAR	350	6TH DIST
BOLLINGER, ELI	CAR	344	6TH DIST
BOLLINGER, JACOB M.	CAR	384	2ND DIST
BOLLINGER, LOUISA	CAR	346	6TH DIST
BOLLMAN, HENDELL	BAL	208	19TH WAR
BOLLMAN, HENRY	BAL	009	9TH WARD
BOLLMAN, HERMAN	BAL	036	15TH WAR
BOLLMAN, JOHN T.	BAL	136	16TH WAR
BOLMAN, HENRY	BAL	012	9TH WARD
BOLOS, CHARLES	ALL	109	5TH E.D.
BOLSTEN, CHARLES	BAL	344	3RD WARD
BOLSTEN, RICHARD	BAL	344	3RD WARD
BOLSTER, THOMAS E.	BAL	266	17TH WAR
BOLT, MATILDA	BAL	310	3RD WARD
BOLTER, CHRISTIAN	BAL	192	5TH DIST
BOLTON, AMELIA	CEC	085	5TH E DI
BOLTON, ANTHONY	BAL	014	15TH WAR
BOLTON, DANIEL	BAL	159	6TH WARD
BOLTON, GEORGE	HAR	078	2ND DIST
BOLTON, H.	BAL	141	1ST WARD
BOLTON, HENRY	BAL	074	4TH WARD
BOLTON, HUGH	BAL	128	5TH WARD
BOLTON, JAMES	CEC	085	5TH E DI
BOLTON, JAMES T.	BAL	159	6TH WARD
BOLTON, JULIA	BAL	054	9TH WARD
BOLTON, JULIA	BAL	054	9TH WARD
BOLTON, JULIA	BAL	054	9TH WARD
BOLTON, MARIA	BAL	160	6TH WARD
BOLTON, MARIA L.	BAL	128	5TH WARD
BOLTON, MARY	BAL	170	6TH WARD
BOLTON, MARY	CEC	085	5TH E DI
BOLTON, SARAH	BAL	140	11TH WAR
BOLTON, THOMAS	HAR	083	2ND DIST
BOLTON, WILLIAM	CEC	022	ELKTON 3
BOLTON, WILLIAM	BAL	347	3RD WARD
BOLTS, ALEXANDER P.*	BAL	342	3RD WARD
BOLUS, BENJAMIN	ANN	388	4TH DIST
BOLY, JACOB	ANN	380	4TH DIST
BOM, WILLIAM	ALL	240	CUMBERLA
BOMACK, ROSANN	BAL	103	2ND DIST
BOMAN, GEORGE W.	ALL	196	CUMBERLA
BOMAN, WILLIAM H.	FRE	280	WOODSBOR
BOMBARGER, HENRIETTA	BAL	084	4TH WARD
BOMBARGER, HENRY CLAY	BAL	184	6TH WARD
BOMBARGER, WILLIAM	BAL	179	6TH WARD
BOMBECK, FREDERICK	BAL	426	8TH WARD
BOMBERGER, BARBARA	BAL	338	7TH WARD
BOMBERGER, CATHARINE	WAS	214	1ST DIST
BOMBERGER, CATHARINE	WAS	223	1ST DIST
BOMBERGER, HENRY	WAS	021	2ND SUBD
BOMBERGER, JACOB	WAS	214	1ST DIST
BOMBERGER, JOHN	WAS	214	1ST DIST
BOMBERGER, JOHN	BAL	281	7TH WARD
BOMBERGER, JOHN W.	BAL	312	7TH WARD
BOMBERGER, JONAS	WAS	182	BOONSBOR
BOMBERGER, MOSES	WAS	181	BOONSBOR
BOMBERGER, NANCY	WAS	010	WILLIAMS
BOMBGARDNER, JOHN	WAS	253	1ST DIST
BOMDEL, HENRY *	BAL	258	6TH WARD
BOMGARDNER, JACOB	WAS	283	1ST DIST
BOMGARDNER, JOHN	BAL	333	7TH WARD
BOMHOUL, FREDERICK	FRE	338	MIDDLETO
BOMIUR, CHARRITY*	DOR	314	1ST DIST
BOMLINE, JOSEPH	BAL	401	8TH WARD
BOMRER, SAMUEL G.	DOR	315	1ST DIST
BOMRUR, CHARRITY*	DOR	314	1ST DIST
BOMSLEY, NELSON	BAL	215	6TH DIST
BONA, THOMAS	BAL	422	8TH WARD
BONAN, CHARLES	BAL	307	12TH WAR
BONAPARTE, J.W.	BAL	216	11TH WAR
BONAR, HENRY	ALL	225	CUMBERLA
BONAWELL, JAMES	SOM	406	DUBLIN D
BONAWILLE, HALL	CAR	143	NO TWP L
BONCE, JOHN	CEC	061	1ST E DI
BONCE, SARAH	ALL	249	CUMBERLA
BONCHELL, JOHN	CEC	037	CHESAPEA
BONCHOR, HENRY	BAL	469	14TH WAR
BOND, ALEXANDER	BAL	267	20TH WAR
BOND, ALICE	HAR	084	2ND DIST
BOND, ALONZO	HAR	113	2ND DIST
BOND, AMERICA	HAR	118	2ND DIST
BOND, AMERICA	BAL	077	2ND DIST
BOND, ANDREW	BAL	348	7TH WARD
BOND, ANDREW	BAL	311	1ST DIST
BOND, ANDREW	HAR	203	3RD DIST
BOND, ANDREW	HAR	139	2ND DIST
BOND, ANGELINE	BAL	211	6TH DIST
BOND, ANN C.	BAL	220	1ST DIST
BOND, ATAWAY	ST	272	3RD E DI
BOND, BASEL D.	CAL	010	1ST DIST
BOND, BASIL	MGM	326	CRACKLIN
BOND, BATTLE	FRE	378	PETERSVI
BOND, BELLEY-BLACK	ST	329	4TH E DI
BOND, BENEDICT	ST	311	1ST E DI
BOND, BENJAMIN	HAR	123	2ND DIST
BOND, BENJAMIN	HAR	079	2ND DIST
BOND, BENJAMIN	CAR	188	4TH DIST
BOND, BENJAMIN	BAL	409	1ST DIST
BOND, BENJAMINE	CAR	364	9TH DIST
BOND, BENSON	CAL	018	1ST DIST
BOND, BERNARD	BAL	158	11TH WAR
BOND, BRIDGET	HAR	124	2ND DIST
BOND, CAROLINE	HAR	076	BEL AIR
BOND, CAS	HAR	079	2ND DIST
BOND, CHARLES	HAR	137	2ND DIST
BOND, CHARLES M.	ST	262	3RD E DI

Name	County	Page	District
BOND, CORBIN	HAR	094	2ND DIST
BOND, CORNELIOUS	FRE	420	8TH E DI
BOND, D.	BAL	147	1ST WARD
BOND, DANIEL	MGM	321	CRACKLIN
BOND, EDWARD	HAR	096	2ND DIST
BOND, EDWARD	HAR	079	2ND DIST
BOND, EDWARD	CAR	195	4TH DIST
BOND, EDWARD	CEC	157	PORT DUP
BOND, EDWARD	BAL	234	1ST DIST
BOND, EDWARD	BAL	106	15TH WAR
BOND, EDWARD	TAL	115	ST MICHA
BOND, ELEANOR	BAL	226	6TH WARD
BOND, ELIJAH	KEN	229	2ND DIST
BOND, ELIJAH	KEN	236	2ND DIST
BOND, ELIJAH	CAR	392	2ND DIST
BOND, ELIJAH J.	HAR	076	BEL AIR
BOND, ELIZA	CEC	147	PORT DUP
BOND, ELIZA	BAL	365	8TH WARD
BOND, ELIZA J.	BAL	462	14TH WAR
BOND, ELIZA J.	TAL	069	EASTON T
BOND, ELIZABETH	BAL	043	4TH WARD
BOND, ELIZABETH	BAL	423	8TH WARD
BOND, ELIZABETH	BAL	180	6TH WARD
BOND, ELIZABETH	BAL	182	6TH WARD
BOND, ELIZABETH	BAL	055	9TH WARD
BOND, ELIZABETH	BAL	134	2ND DIST
BOND, ELIZABETH P.	MGM	388	ROCKERLE
BOND, EMERY	BAL	052	18TH WAR
BOND, EMORY	BAL	128	16TH WAR
BOND, EMORY	BAL	076	10TH WAR
BOND, FANNY	HAR	142	2ND DIST
BOND, FRANCIS	BAL	197	11TH WAR
BOND, FRANCIS	BAL	077	10TH WAR
BOND, FRANCIS H.	BAL	031	2ND DIST
BOND, FREEBORN	HAR	091	2ND DIST
BOND, GEORGE	HAR	078	2ND DIST
BOND, GEORGE	HAR	143	2ND DIST
BOND, GEORGE	BAL	213	17TH WAR
BOND, GEORGE	ANN	482	HOWARD D
BOND, GEORGE	ANN	455	HOWARD D
BOND, GEORGE	ANN	473	HOWARD D
BOND, GEORGE	BAL	057	2ND DIST
BOND, GEORGE M.	BAL	437	8TH WARD
BOND, GRACE	CEC	145	PORT DUP
BOND, H.	BAL	129	1ST WARD
BOND, HARRIETT	BAL	269	7TH WARD
BOND, HARRIETT A.	BAL	170	11TH WAR
BOND, HARRY	MGM	331	CRACKLIN
BOND, HEMSLEY	HAR	093	2ND DIST
BOND, HENRY	HAR	080	2ND DIST
BOND, HENRY	CEC	148	PORT DUP
BOND, HENRY	CAR	188	4TH DIST
BOND, HENRY	BAL	167	19TH WAR
BOND, HESTER	BAL	158	11TH WAR
BOND, HESTER	BAL	062	2ND DIST
BOND, HESTER	BAL	082	2ND DIST
BOND, ISAAC	MGM	347	BERRYS D
BOND, ISABEL	HAR	097	2ND DIST
BOND, JACKSON	CAR	188	4TH DIST
BOND, JACOB	BAL	113	1ST WARD
BOND, JAMES	BAL	034	2ND DIST
BOND, JAMES	BAL	165	6TH WARD
BOND, JAMES	BAL	166	1ST WARD
BOND, JAMES	BAL	424	3RD WARD
BOND, JAMES	TAL	092	ST MICHA
BOND, JAMES A.	CAL	001	1ST DIST
BOND, JAMES L.	MGM	355	BERRYS D
BOND, JAMES W.	BAL	095	10TH WAR
BOND, JANE E.	ST	262	3RD E DI
BOND, JEMIMAH	BAL	324	7TH WARD
BOND, JOHN	BAL	244	1ST DIST
BOND, JOHN	BAL	200	5TH DIST
BOND, JOHN	BAL	298	7TH WARD
BOND, JOHN	BAL	400	8TH WARD
BOND, JOHN	BAL	449	1ST DIST
BOND, JOHN	HAR	105	2ND DIST
BOND, JOHN	HAR	092	2ND DIST
BOND, JOHN	HAR	031	1ST DIST
BOND, JOHN	CAL	001	1ST DIST
BOND, JOHN	BAL	208	11TH WAR
BOND, JOHN	HAR	126	2ND DIST
BOND, JOHN	KEN	229	2ND DIST
BOND, JOHN	HAR	166	3RD DIST
BOND, JOHN	CHA	227	ALLENS F
BOND, JOHN W.	BAL	470	14TH WAR
BOND, JOSEPH	HAR	118	2ND DIST
BOND, JOSEPH	ALL	236	CUMBERLA
BOND, JOSHUA	BAL	438	1ST DIST
BOND, JOSHUA	PRI	024	VANSVILL
BOND, JULIA-BLACK	ST	329	4TH E DI
BOND, L.D.	ST	318	4TH E DI
BOND, LAMBERT W.	BAL	001	9TH WARD
BOND, LEONARD	BAL	040	4TH WARD
BOND, LIDIA	HAR	033	1ST DIST
BOND, LOUIS	MGM	322	CRACKLIN
BOND, LOYD	CEC	205	7TH E DI
BOND, MAND	BAL	243	20TH WAR
BOND, MARGARET	BAL	265	20TH WAR
BOND, MARGARET	KEN	254	1ST DIST
BOND, MARGARET	HAR	032	1ST DIST
BOND, MARIA	MGM	338	CRACKLIN
BOND, MARRETTA	BAL	328	13TH WAR
BOND, MARY	BAL	037	9TH WARD
BOND, MARY	BAL	353	1ST DIST
BOND, MARY	BAL	158	2ND DIST
BOND, MARY	MGM	347	BERRYS D
BOND, MARY	BAL	159	11TH WAR
BOND, MARY	CEC	150	PORT DUP
BOND, MARY E.	BAL	170	11TH WAR
BOND, MARY F.	BAL	310	7TH WARD
BOND, MARY M.	BAL	437	14TH WAR
BOND, MATHEW	KEN	275	1ST DIST
BOND, MATILDA	HAR	139	2ND DIST
BOND, MICHAEL	BAL	054	9TH WARD
BOND, MOSES	HAR	032	1ST DIST
BOND, NANCY	WAS	149	HAGERSTO
BOND, NATHAN	BAL	167	19TH WAR
BOND, NATHAN	BAL	108	10TH WAR
BOND, NICHOLAS M.	HAR	095	2ND DIST
BOND, PETER	FRE	414	8TH E DI
BOND, PETER P.	BAL	311	1ST DIST
BOND, PETERINA	HAR	076	BEL AIR
BOND, PHEBE	HAR	088	2ND DIST
BOND, PHEBE	HAR	088	2ND DIST
BOND, PHILIS	BAL	194	11TH WAR
BOND, PRISCILLA	CEC	148	PORT DUP
BOND, RACHAEL	BAL	326	12TH WAR
BOND, RACHAEL A.	BAL	138	11TH WAR
BOND, RACHEL	HAR	085	2ND DIST
BOND, RACHEL	BAL	163	19TH WAR
BOND, REZIN	ANN	497	HOWARD D
BOND, RICHARD	BAL	232	6TH WARD
BOND, RICHARD B.	HAR	085	2ND DIST
BOND, RICHARD G. B.	ST	262	3RD E DI
BOND, RICHARD H.	CHA	269	ALLENS F
BOND, ROBERT	WAS	124	2ND DIST
BOND, ROBERT	ANN	436	HOWARD D
BOND, ROSE	HAR	076	BEL AIR
BOND, ROSE	HAR	055	1ST DIST
BOND, RUSH	HAR	113	2ND DIST
BOND, RUTH	CAR	360	9TH DIST
BOND, SALLY	ST	336	4TH E DI
BOND, SAMUEL	ST	339	4TH E DI
BOND, SAMUEL	BAL	026	4TH WARD
BOND, SAMUEL	BAL	182	6TH WARD
BOND, SAMUEL	BAL	311	3RD WARD
BOND, SAMUEL	BAL	128	16TH WAR
BOND, SAMUEL	BAL	267	1ST DIST
BOND, SARAH	BAL	325	1ST DIST
BOND, SARAH	BAL	165	6TH WARD
BOND, SARAH E.	TAL	056	EASTON D
BOND, SARAH W.	ANN	521	HOWARD D
BOND, SHADE	BAL	190	5TH DIST
BOND, SHADERAC	BAL	016	2ND DIST
BOND, SOPHIA	BAL	023	2ND DIST
BOND, STEPHEN	BAL	107	10TH WAR
BOND, STEPHEN	HAR	097	2ND DIST
BOND, STEPHEN	HAR	201	3RD DIST
BOND, SUSAN	BAL	076	10TH WAR
BOND, THOAMS	HAR	031	1ST DIST
BOND, THOMAS	MGM	361	BERRYS D
BOND, THOMAS	CEC	041	CHESAPEA
BOND, THOMAS	BAL	186	19TH WAR
BOND, THOMAS	BAL	035	18TH WAR
BOND, THOMAS	CEC	152	PORT DUP
BOND, THOMAS	CEC	147	PORT DUP
BOND, THOMAS	BAL	134	2ND DIST
BOND, THOMAS	BAL	422	1ST DIST
BOND, THOMAS	BAL	454	8TH WARD
BOND, THOMAS	ST	320	4TH E DI
BOND, THOMAS E.	HAR	139	2ND DIST
BOND, THOMAS E. DR. JR.	BAL	332	13TH WAR
BOND, THOMAS J.	BAL	170	16TH WAR
BOND, THOMAS J.	BAL	246	1ST DIST
BOND, THOMAS S.	BAL	226	6TH WARD
BOND, THOMAS T.	HAR	084	2ND DIST
BOND, TOWER	HAR	157	3RD DIST
BOND, VIRGINIA	MGM	349	BERRYS D
BOND, VIRGINIA A.	ANN	507	HOWARD D
BOND, WESLEY	HAR	089	2ND DIST
BOND, WESLEY	HAR	083	2ND DIST
BOND, WESLEY	HAR	079	2ND DIST
BOND, WESLEY	HAR	093	2ND DIST
BOND, WESLEY	HAR	118	2ND DIST
BOND, WESLY	HAR	029	1ST DIST
BOND, WILLAIM	HAR	141	2ND DIST
BOND, WILLAIM	BAL	101	2ND DIST
BOND, WILLIAM	BAL	129	2ND DIST
BOND, WILLIAM	BAL	156	16TH WAR
BOND, WILLIAM	BAL	054	9TH WARD
BOND, WILLIAM	BAL	269	7TH WARD
BOND, WILLIAM	HAR	033	1ST DIST
BOND, WILLIAM	HAR	032	1ST DIST
BOND, WILLIAM	HAR	079	2ND DIST
BOND, WILLIAM	ST	261	3RD E DI
BOND, WILLIAM B.	HAR	075	BEL AIR
BOND, ZACHARIAH	CHA	270	ALLENS F
BOND, ZACHEUS O.	BAL	226	6TH WARD
BOND, ZELETA	CHA	223	ALLENS F
BOND,. ADAM	BAL	086	18TH WAR
BOND.ELISHA	BAL	057	2ND DIST
BONDERS, SUSAN	WOR	264	BERLIN 1
BONDES, ADAM	BAL	280	7TH WARD
BONDICE, JOHN	CAR	153	NO TWP L
BONDICE, LEANDER	CAR	155	NO TWP L
BONDLE, ELIZA	CAR	122	NO TWP L
BONDLE, HENRY	CAR	128	NO TWP L
BONDLE, RACHIEL	CAR	140	NO TWP L
BONDLE, WILLIAM	CAR	159	NO TWP L
BONDLLE, DANIL T.	CAR	122	NO TWP L
BONDS, MRS.	BAL	184	19TH WAR
BONDS, SAMUEL-BLACK	QUE	194	3RD E DI
BONDS, WILLIAM	BAL	064	10TH WAR
BONDWELL, ANDREW	SOM	414	DUBLIN D
BONE, CEMY B. *	CHA	270	ALLENS F
BONE, ELIJAH	BAL	170	11TH WAR
BONE, FLETCHER	BAL	040	1ST WARD
BONE, HARRIET	BAL	262	12TH WAR
BONE, HUGH	ANN	464	HOWARD D
BONE, HUGHE	BAL	356	1ST DIST
BONE, MARGARET	BAL	265	12TH WAR
BONE, RACHAEL-BLACK	FRE	015	FREDERIC
BONE, WILLIAM	ALL	119	5TH E.D.
BONEE, MARGARET	BAL	057	1ST WARD
BONEHER, ADELORD	FRE	202	5TH E DI
BONEHER, THEODORE	MGM	395	ROCKERLE
BONER, ALEXANDER	WAS	262	1ST DIST
BONER, BARBARA	WAS	279	LEITERSB
BONER, ELIZABETH	WAS	265	1ST DIST
BONER, FRISBY	CEC	063	1ST E DI
BONER, ISABELLA	BAL	072	4TH WARD
BONER, JAMES	WAS	276	RIDGEVIL
BONER, PETER	BAL	179	11TH WAR
BONES, SAMUEL	ALL	182	8TH E.D.
BONEWELL, JAMES	WOR	337	1ST E DI
BONEWELL, JOSEPH	SOM	411	DUBLIN D
BONEWELL, TUBMAN F.	SOM	412	DUBLIN D
BONFORD, VIRGINIA MISS-	BAL	315	20TH WAR
BONFRIES, JOHN	BAL	005	18TH WAR
BONGEN, SOPHIA	BAL	307	1ST DIST
BONGER, FRANCIS	CEC	057	1ST E DI
BONGINE, RESEN *	BAL	313	12TH WAR
BONGTON, CHARLOTTE	BAL	162	11TH WAR
BONHAM, RICHARD	FRE	440	8TH E DI
BONIFANT, MARY	MGM	366	BERRYS D
BONIFANT, WASHINGTON	MGM	358	BERRYS D
BONINGER, ARNOLD	BAL	382	13TH WAR
BONINGER, BICTORINE S.	BAL	078	15TH WAR
BONIS, STEPHEN	BAL	069	10TH WAR
BONMAN, ARON	WAS	034	2ND SUBD
BONMART, JOHN *	BAL	273	20TH WAR
BONN, ANTHONY	BAL	119	15TH WAR
BONN, FREDERIC	BAL	199	6TH WARD
BONN, HANNAH	BAL	169	16TH WAR
BONN, JOHN	BAL	110	5TH WARD
BONN, JOSEPH	BAL	168	16TH WAR
BONN, JULIA	BAL	121	16TH WAR
BONN, RICHARD	BAL	178	16TH WAR
BONN, UPTON	BAL	048	4TH WARD
BONN, WILLIAM	BAL	202	2ND WARD
BONNER, ELIJA	BAL	056	4TH WARD
BONNER, JOHN A.	BAL	253	20TH WAR
BONNER, JOHN*	DOR	311	1ST DIST
BONNER, MARY	BAL	086	15TH WAR
BONNER, MATTHIES*	DOR	380	1ST DIST
BONNER, WILLIAM A.	BAL	388	13TH WAR
BONNES, O.	BAL	156	1ST WARD
BONNETT, THOMAS	ALL	241	CUMBERLA
BONNEVILL, JAOCB	WOR	328	1ST E DI
BONNEWELL, JOHN	WOR	329	1ST E DI
BONNEY, ELIAS	BAL	408	3RD WARD
BONNEY.EDARD	BAL	125	1ST WARD
BONNINGER, MARGARET	BAL	131	16TH WAR
BONNKAMP, ANN	BAL	245	12TH WAR
BONNOR, JOHN*	DOR	311	1ST DIST
BONNUR, CHARRITY*	DOR	314	1ST DIST
BONS, THOMAS	ALL	102	5TH E.D.
BONSAL, JOHN	BAL	011	2ND DIST
BONSAL, LEWIS	BAL	081	4TH WARD
BONSAL, MARY	BAL	181	2ND DIST
BONSELL, HENRY	BAL	095	5TH WARD
BONSELL, S.S.	FRE	044	FREDERIC
BONSEY, PHILLIP	BAL	105	1ST WARD
BONSLAGER, GEORGE	BAL	255	17TH WAR
BONSOR, FRANCIS	KEN	212	2ND DIST
BONTON, FRANKLIN	QUE	222	4TH E DI
BONUS, MARY	ALL	182	8TH E.D.
BONY, ANN	BAL	089	5TH WARD
BONZER, ISAAC	BAL	157	1ST WARD
BOOBET, HERMAN	BAL	321	3RD WARD
BOODY, HENRY	WAS	064	2ND SUBD
BOOFETER, PRIS *	BAL	282	20TH WAR
BOOFLET, JOHN	BAL	354	3RD WARD
BOOFSTER, HANNAH	HAR	055	1ST DIST
BOOFSTER, THOMAS *	HAR	026	1ST DIST
BOOFTER, ELIJAH	BAL	282	20TH WAR
BOOG, JOSEPH	WAS	125	HAGERSTO
BUOGHER, ALLEN	FRE	272	NEW MARK
BOOK, WILLIAM	BAL	287	3RD WARD
BOOKE, JOHN	ALL	258	CUMBERLA
BOOKEN, JURLETT	QUE	239	5TH E DI
BOOKER, JAMES	QUE	160	2ND E DI
BOOKER, JAMES B.	QUE	203	3RD E DI
BOOKER, JAMES W.	QUE	144	1ST E DI
BOOKER, JOHN	BAL	216	19TH WAR
BOOKER, JOHN	BAL	219	19TH WAR
BOOKER, JOHN L.	BAL	289	12TH WAR
BOOKER, MARCELLUS	CAR	086	NO TWP L
BOOKER, RACHEAL	BAL	008	18TH WAR
BOOKER, RACHEL	CAR	077	NO TWP L
BOOKER, ROBERT	QUE	149	1ST E DI
BOOKER, THOMAS	CAR	077	NO TWP L
BOOKER, THOMAS B.	QUE	196	3RD E DI
BOOKER, WILLIAM	QUE	174	2ND E DI
BOOKER, WILLIAM G.	CAR	077	NO TWP L
BOOKER, WILLIAM H.	CAR	085	NO TWP L
BOOKER.LOUISA	QUE	173	2ND E DI
BOOKERD, JOSEPH	BAL	093	2ND DIST
BOOKFETTER, JOHN	FRE	060	FREDERIC
BOOKHEINER, GILBERT	BAL	176	2ND WARD
BOOKHEINER, JOHN	BAL	176	2ND WARD
BOOKHEMER, GEORGE	BAL	230	2ND WARD
BOOKHITE, PETER	BAL	280	17TH WAR
BOOKHOLTS, CRESTIAN	ALL	101	5TH E.D.
BOOKHULTY, GEORGE	BAL	122	18TH WAR
BOOKHULTZ, MARY	BAL	138	16TH WAR
BOOKHURST, FRANCIS	BAL	123	5TH WARD
BOOKMAN, ABRAHAM	CAR	179	8TH DIST
BOOKMAN, ELZY	BAL	222	19TH WAR
BOOKMAN, GEORGE A.	WAS	296	1ST DIST
BOOKMAN, GEORGE W.	BAL	037	4TH WARD
BOOKMAN, JACOB	BAL	221	19TH WAR
BOOKMAN, JACOB	CAR	341	6TH DIST
BOOKMAN, JOSEPH	BAL	384	1ST DIST
BOOKMAN, MICHEAL	CAR	179	8TH DIST
BOOKS, JANE	BAL	306	12TH WAR
BOOKS, SABARROW	FRE	262	NEW MARK
BOOL, AMINDA	BAL	181	19TH WAR
BOOL, BALZA	BAL	108	5TH WARD
BOOL, H. W.	BAL	074	10TH WAR
BOOLEY, HENRY	ALL	214	CUMBERLA
BUOM, COONROD	BAL	131	2ND DIST
BOOM, DAVID	BAL	088	2ND DIST
BOOM, EDWORD	HAR	197	3RD DIST
BOOM, ISAAH	HAR	189	3RD DIST
BOOM, JOHN *	ALL	161	6TH E.D.
BOOM, RIHCARD	HAR	201	3RD DIST
BOOM, ZACH.	CAL	028	2ND DIST
BOOME, DAVID	CAL	004	1ST DIST
BOOME, ELIZA	CAL	004	1ST DIST
BOOME, JOSEPH H.	BAL	361	3RD WARD
BOOME, MARY	CAL	002	1ST DIST
BOOME, THOMAS	CAL	003	1ST DIST
BOOMER, WILLIAM	DOR	325	1ST DIST
BOOMEVEL, SUSAN	TAL	091	ST MICHA
BOOMWELL, REBECCA	TAL	087	ST MICHA
BOOMWELL, THOMAS	TAL	114	ST MICHA
BOON, ADREAS	BAL	207	2ND WARD
BOON, ALEXANDER	CAR	311	1ST DIST
BOON, ANN	BAL	296	17TH WAR
BOON, ANN M.	FRE	298	WOODSBOR
BOON, BENJAMIN	BAL	128	2ND DIST
BOON, BENJAMIN	BAL	159	2ND DIST
BOON, BENJAMIN T.	BAL	037	15TH WAR
BOON, BYARD-BLACK	CAR	145	NO TWP L
BOON, CHARLE-BLACK	CAR	165	NO TWP L
BOON, CYRUS	WAS	218	1ST DIST
BOON, DANIEL	BAL	188	2ND WARD
BOON, DAVID	CAL	032	2ND DIST
BOON, DAVY	CAL	035	2ND DIST
BOON, DELIA	BAL	422	14TH WAR
BOON, ELIZA	BAL	272	1ST DIST
BOON, EMELINE	BAL	362	13TH WAR
BOON, FRANK	BAL	062	15TH WAR
BOON, GEORGANNA-BLACK	FRE	017	FREDERIC
BOON, H. G.	BAL	154	1ST WARD
BOON, HARRIET	BAL	228	17TH WAR
BOON, HARRIS	BAL	170	1ST WARD
BOON, HARRIS	BAL	160	1ST WARD
BOON, HELEN A.	QUE	130	1ST E DI
BOON, HENRIETTA-BLACK	CAR	068	NO TWP L
BOON, HENRIETTA-BLACK	CAR	164	NO TWP L
BOON, HENRY	BAL	282	17TH WAR
BOON, HESTER A.	TAL	039	EASTON D
BOON, HORACE	BAL	174	6TH WARD
BOON, HORAN	BAL	121	1ST WARD
BOON, HORIS	BAL	158	1ST WARD
BOON, ISAAAC	CAL	034	2ND DIST
BOON, ISAAC	CAL	036	2ND DIST
BOON, ISAAC	CAL	033	2ND DIST

BOON, JAMES-BLACK	CAR	085	NO TWP L
BOON, JOHN	CAL	035	2ND DIST
BOON, JOHN	CAL	030	2ND DIST
BOON, JOHN	ANN	454	HOWARD D
BOON, JOHN	BAL	127	16TH WAR
BOON, JOHN	BAL	047	9TH WARD
BOON, JOHN H.	CEC	075	NORTHEAS
BOON, JOSEPH	BAL	201	17TH WAR
BOON, JOSEPH H.	BAL	079	15TH WAR
BOON, LUCRETIA	ANN	351	3RD DIST
BOON, LYDIA	QUE	210	3RD E DI
BOON, M.	PRI	060	NOTTINGH
BOON, MARIA	BAL	026	15TH WAR
BOON, MARK-BLACK	CAR	133	NO TWP L
BOON, MARY	CAR	103	NO TWP L
BOON, MARY A.	ANN	501	HOWARD D
BOON, MARY C.	FRE	208	BUCKEYST
BOON, MARY E.	QUE	207	3RD E DI
BOON, MARY J.	CHA	253	MIDDLETO
BOON, MARY R.	BAL	385	3RD WARD
BOON, NANCY-BLACK	FRE	214	BUCKEYST
BOON, OWEN	TAL	010	EASTON D
BOON, PETER C.	CAR	073	NO TWP L
BOON, PRINCE	CAL	034	2ND DIST
BOON, REZIN	BAL	174	6TH WARD
BOON, REZIN	BAL	175	6TH WARD
BOON, ROBERT	BAL	385	3RD WARD
BOON, ROBERT	PRI	101	SPALDING
BOON, SAMSON	BAL	213	17TH WAR
BOON, SAMUEL	BAL	330	1ST DIST
BOON, SAMUEL	BAL	412	1ST DIST
BOON, SAMUEL	BAL	411	1ST DIST
BOON, SUSAN	WAS	218	1ST DIST
BOON, SYLVESTER	PRI	111	PISCATAW
BOON, THOMAS	BAL	194	17TH WAR
BOON, VACHEL	ANN	425	HOWARD D
BOON, VICE	ANN	414	HOWARD D
BOON, WILLIAM	BAL	190	17TH WAR
BOON, WILLIAM	BAL	317	1ST DIST
BOON, WILLIAM	BAL	122	1ST WARD
BOON, WILLIAM E.	TAL	011	EASTON D
BOON, WILLIAM M.	PRI	080	QUEEN AN
BOON, WILLIAM-BLACK	QUE	135	1ST E DI
BOON.JAMES	QUE	203	3RD E DI
BOOND, OLIVER	ALL	212	CUMBERLA
BOONE, ALFRED	MGM	332	CRACKLIN
BOONE, ANN	FRE	059	FREDERIC
BOONE, ANN M.	ANN	358	3RD DIST
BOONE, BENEDICT	FRE	387	PETERSVI
BOONE, BENJAMIN	BAL	114	2ND DIST
BOONE, CARLINE	FRE	023	FREDERIC
BOONE, CATHERINE	BAL	110	10TH WAR
BOONE, CHARLES	ANN	357	3RD DIST
BOONE, CHARLES	ANN	355	3RD DIST
BOONE, CHARLES F.	BAL	349	3RD WARD
BOONE, DAVID-MULATTO	FRE	028	FREDERIC
BOONE, DENNIS	FRE	418	8TH E DI
BOONE, EDWARD	FRE	064	FREDERIC
BOONE, EDWARD D.	CHA	290	BOJANTOW
BOONE, ELIZABETH	ANN	357	3RD DIST
BOONE, ELIZABETH	BAL	073	15TH WAR
BOONE, ELIZABETH-BLACK	FRE	033	FREDERIC
BOONE, EMANUEL	FRE	426	8TH E DI
BOONE, GEOGE	BAL	356	13TH WAR
BOONE, GEORGE	FRE	447	8TH E DI
BOONE, HANNAH	FRE	278	NEW MARK
BOONE, HARRIET	FRE	044	FREDERIC
BOONE, HARRIET	ANN	454	HOWARD D
BOONE, HENRY	FRE	416	8TH E DI
BOONE, ISAAC	MGM	370	BERRYS D
BOONE, JACOB	FRE	445	8TH E DI
BOONE, JAMES	FRE	071	FREDERIC
BOONE, JAMES	BAL	150	11TH WAR
BOONE, JENNINGHAM	FRE	029	FREDERIC
BOONE, JOHN H. D.	BAL	203	6TH WARD
BOONE, JOHN S.	ANN	355	3RD DIST
BOONE, JOHN W.	BAL	297	7TH WARD
BOONE, LYDIA	BAL	382	8TH WARD
BOONE, MARTHA	ANN	356	3RD DIST
BOONE, MARY	ANN	426	HOWARD D
BOONE, MARY M.	FRE	445	8TH E DI
BOONE, MARY-BLACK	FRE	010	FREDERIC
BOONE, MICHAEL	FRE	421	8TH E DI
BOONE, N.	BAL	154	1ST WARD
BOONE, NELLY	TAL	118	ST MICHA
BOONE, NICHOLAS	BAL	162	6TH WARD
BOONE, R.	PRI	101	SPALDING
BOONE, ROBERT	FRE	029	FREDERIC
BOONE, RUTH	BAL	004	9TH WARD
BOONE, SAMUEL	BAL	307	3RD WARD
BOONE, SIDNEY-MULATTO	FRE	045	FREDERIC
BOONE, SOLOMON	FRE	438	8TH E DI
BOONE, STEPHEN	BAL	155	2ND DIST
BOONE, THOMAS	BAL	349	3RD WARD
BOONE, THOMAS	BAL	004	9TH WARD
BOONE, THOMAS W.	FRE	447	8TH E DI
BOONEY, MARY	BAL	377	13TH WAR
BOONS, AMOS	CAR	339	6TH DIST
BOOP, PETER	BAL	313	1ST DIST
BOORIS, ALMIRA	BAL	034	9TH WARD
BOORKAMP, HERMNA	BAL	263	1ST DIST
BOORLAND, THOMAS	ANN	486	HOWARD D
BOOS, ADAM	BAL	147	5TH WARD
BOOSE, DANIEL	CAR	257	3RD DIST
BOOSE, DINAH-MULATTO	FRE	420	8TH E DI
BOOSE, JACOB	CAR	256	3RD DIST
BOOSE, JOHN	BAL	244	2ND WARD
BOOSE, THOMAS	BAL	110	1ST WARD
BOOSE,CAROLINE-BLACK	FRE	431	8TH E DI
BOOSEN, TONEY	CEC	184	7TH E DI
BOOSER, JERREMIAH	WAS	058	2ND SUBD
BOOSER, TERRY	WAS	049	2ND SUBD
BOOSSTER, THOMAS *	HAR	026	1ST DIST
BOOTES, JAMES	CEC	026	ELKTON 3
BOOTH, A. J.	BAL	332	13TH WAR
BOOTH, ALFRED	BAL	239	6TH WARD
BOOTH, ALICE	BAL	331	3RD WARD
BOOTH, ANTHONY	TAL	027	EASTON D
BOOTH, ARA	WAS	073	2ND SUBD
BOOTH, CAROLINE	BAL	244	12TH WAR
BOOTH, CHARLES	ANN	516	HOWARD D
BOOTH, CRISSEN	WOR	314	2ND E DI
BOOTH, DAVID	WAS	161	HAGERSTO
BOOTH, DAVID	BAL	125	11TH WAR
BOOTH, ELIAS	ST	275	3RD E DI
BOOTH, ELIJAH	BAL	210	17TH WAR
BOOTH, ELIZABETH	BAL	444	14TH WAR
BOOTH, ELIZABETH	BAL	463	14TH WAR
BOOTH, ELIZABETH	BAL	101	5TH WARD
BOOTH, EMELINE	BAL	320	3RD WARD
BOOTH, GEORGE	BAL	218	6TH WARD
BOOTH, GEORGE	CHA	293	BOJANTOW
BOOTH, GEORGE	BAL	005	EASTERN
BOOTH, HARIET	SOM	496	SALISBUR
BOOTH, HARRIET	BAL	003	18TH WAR
BOOTH, HARRIET	BAL	141	19TH WAR
BOOTH, HENRIETTA	BAL	190	11TH WAR
BOOTH, HENRY	BAL	137	5TH WARD
BOOTH, ISAAC	BAL	106	5TH WARD
BOOTH, J.M.	BAL	020	2ND DIST
BOOTH, JACOB	CEC	170	6TH E DI
BOOTH, JANE	BAL	002	EASTERN
BOOTH, JANE	BAL	119	2ND DIST
BOOTH, JOHN	BAL	239	12TH WAR
BOOTH, JOHN	WOR	234	6TH E DI
BOOTH, JOHN	WAS	302	1ST DIST
BOOTH, JOHN	ST	306	1ST E DI
BOOTH, JOHN R.	BAL	255	6TH WARD
BOOTH, JOHN W.	ST	294	2ND E DI
BOOTH, JOSEPH	ST	300	2ND E DI
BOOTH, JOSEPH	BAL	009	15TH WAR
BOOTH, JOSEPH	BAL	295	3RD WARD
BOOTH, JULIUS B.	BAL	133	5TH WARD
BOOTH, LAURA	BAL	067	10TH WAR
BOOTH, MARTHA	SOM	502	SALISBUR
BOOTH, MARY	BAL	318	12TH WAR
BOOTH, MARY	BAL	111	15TH WAR
BOOTH, MATHEW A.	BAL	050	4TH WARD
BOOTH, OLIVER	PRI	079	MARLBROU
BOOTH, OLIVIA	PRI	121	PISCATAW
BOOTH, RACHEL	BAL	060	10TH WAR
BOOTH, RICHARD	BAL	019	1ST WARD
BOOTH, RICHARD	CEC	016	ELKTON 3
BOOTH, RICHARD R.	CAR	273	WESTMINS
BOOTH, SAMUEL	BAL	164	11TH WAR
BOOTH, SAMUEL	ST	306	1ST E DI
BOOTH, SARAH	BAL	140	19TH WAR
BOOTH, SARAH A.	BAL	093	15TH WAR
BOOTH, STANISLANS	ST	274	3RD E DI
BOOTH, SUSAN	SOM	502	SALISBUR
BOOTH, SUSANNA	ST	271	3RD E DI
BOOTH, WAITMAN	DOR	419	1ST DIST
BOOTH, WALTER	BAL	087	2ND DIST
BOOTH, WILLIAM	BAL	144	1ST WARD
BOOTH, WILLIAM	BAL	407	3RD WARD
BOOTH, WILLIAM	BAL	216	17TH WAR
BOOTH, WILLIAM	BAL	470	14TH WAR
BOOTH, WILLIAM	WAS	198	1ST DIST
BOOTH, WILLIAM O. L.	BAL	049	4TH WARD
BOOTHE, ANN	PRI	065	NOTTINGH
BOOTHE, ELIJA-BLACK	CAL	056	3RD DIST
BOOTHE, FRANCIS	BAL	096	18TH WAR
BOOTHE, HELLEN	PRI	070	MARLBROU
BOOTHE, HENRY	PRI	110	PISCATAW
BOOTHE, JAMES	CAL	058	3RD DIST
BOOTHE, JAMES	BAL	119	11TH WAR
BOOTHE, JANE	CAL	058	3RD DIST
BOOTHE, JANE	BAL	458	1ST DIST
BOOTHE, MARGARET	PRI	065	NOTTINGH
BOOTHE, MARSHALL	PRI	065	NOTTINGH
BOOTHE, MISS M.	FRE	199	5TH E DI
BOOTHE, PRISCILLA	MGM	331	CRACKLIN
BOOTHE, SAMUEL	CAL	052	3RD DIST
BOOTHE, SMITH	PRI	104	PISCATAW
BOOTHE, STEPHEN	CAL	058	3RD DIST
BOOTHE, THOMAS	ANN	395	8TH DIST
BOOTHES, JOHN	CAL	054	3RD DIST
BOOTHS, JAMES	CAL	014	1ST DIST
BOOTHS, JOHN	WAS	303	1ST DIST
BOOTMAN, FRANCIS	WAS	158	2ND DIST
BOOTMAN, JOHN W.	WAS	157	2ND DIST
BOOTS, BENJAMIN	CEC	049	1ST E DI
BOOTS, ELIZABETH	QUE	136	1ST E DI
BOOTS, JAOCB	CAL	005	1ST DIST
BOOTS, JERE	CAL	030	2ND DIST
BOOTS, JERRY	CAL	015	1ST DIST
BOOTS, JOHN W.	KEN	221	2ND DIST
BOOTS, JOSEPH	CEC	049	1ST E DI
BOOTS, MARY	KEN	247	2ND DIST
BOOTS, SAMUEL	CAL	035	2ND DIST
BOOTTS, ISAL	ANN	441	HOWARD D
BOOZ, ANNE	BAL	146	16TH WAR
BOOZ, EMILY	BAL	202	6TH WARD
BOOZ, EMILY J.	BAL	077	15TH WAR
BOOZE, BARZILIA	DOR	367	3RD DIVI
BOOZE, BARZILIA	DOR	371	3RD DIVI
BOOZE, BENJAMIN	BAL	415	3RD WARD
BOOZE, DAVID	CAR	174	8TH DIST
BOOZE, ELIZA	DOR	362	3RD DIVI
BOOZE, ELIZA	BAL	103	10TH WAR
BOOZE, ELIZABETH	BAL	283	17TH WAR
BOOZE, GEORGE	DOR	353	3RD DIVI
BOOZE, GEORGE	DOR	350	3RD DIVI
BOOZE, HENRY	CAR	174	8TH DIST
BOOZE, JAMES	DOR	348	3RD DIVI
BOOZE, JAMES	DOR	348	3RD DIVI
BOOZE, JAMES	BAL	264	1ST DIST
BOOZE, JAMES W.	BAL	322	3RD WARD
BOOZE, JOHN	CAR	175	8TH DIST
BOOZE, JOHN	FRE	306	WOODSBOR
BOOZE, LEONARD	DOR	362	3RD DIVI
BOOZE, LILLEY	DOR	350	3RD DIVI
BOOZE, MARY A.	CAR	175	8TH DIST
BOOZE, PEGGY	FRE	164	EMMITTSB
BOOZE, REBECCA	DOR	331	3RD DIVI
BOOZE, THOMAS H.	BAL	127	1ST WARD
BOOZE, WILLIAM	BAL	135	1ST WARD
BOOZE, WILLIAM	DOR	330	3RD DIVI
BOOZE, WILLIAM	DOR	328	3RD DIVI
BOPP, BARBARA	BAL	394	14TH WAR
BOPP, CATHARINE	BAL	005	15TH WAR
BOPP, LAWRENCE	BAL	004	15TH WAR
BOPP, MARTIN	WAS	126	2ND DIST
BOPST, MARY	FRE	081	FREDERIC
BOPST, WILLIAM	FRE	052	FREDERIC
BORAN, JOSHUA	FRE	194	5TH E DI
BORBOUR, ALICE	ANN	391	4TH DIST
BORCHERDING, JOHN G.	BAL	341	13TH WAR
BORCHERDING, MARY	BAL	342	13TH WAR
BORD, JOHN	HAR	191	3RD DIST
BORD, ROSETTA	BAL	174	2ND DIST
BORDAN, MICHAEL	CEC	031	CHESAPEA
BORDATER, JOHN	WAS	293	1ST DIST
BORDEN, F.	BAL	117	1ST WARD
BORDEN, JULIA	BAL	022	4TH WARD
BORDEN, MARIA	ANN	495	HOWARD D
BORDEN, WILLIAM	ALL	012	3RD E.D.
BORDER, ELIZA	BAL	188	19TH WAR
BORDER, HENRIETTA	BAL	012	18TH WAR
BORDER, HENRIETTA	BAL	012	18TH WAR
BORDEY, MARTHA	BAL	142	5TH WARD
BORDIN, WILLIAM	BAL	135	1ST WARD
BORDLAY, JIM-BLACK	QUE	200	3RD E DI
BORDLEY, ANDREW	CEC	024	ELKTON 3
BORDLEY, ANN	QUE	232	4TH E DI
BORDLEY, ANN MARIA-BLACK	QUE	148	1ST E DI
BORDLEY, ANTHONY	BAL	396	14TH WAR
BORDLEY, ARTHUR-BLACK	QUE	126	1ST E DI
BORDLEY, CHARLES	QUE	228	4TH E DI
BORDLEY, CHARLES-BLACK	QUE	141	1ST E DI
BORDLEY, CHURSTINA	BAL	070	10TH WAR
BORDLEY, CREELY	ANN	448	HOWARD D
BORDLEY, CUFF	KEN	230	2ND DIST
BORDLEY, D. C. H.	BAL	066	10TH WAR
BORDLEY, DANIEL	BAL	109	10TH WAR
BORDLEY, FRISBY	BAL	203	11TH WAR
BORDLEY, HANNAH	BAL	089	2ND DIST
BORDLEY, HARRIET	BAL	020	1ST WARD
BORDLEY, HARRIETT	QUE	228	4TH E DI
BORDLEY, HENRY	QUE	226	4TH E DI
BORDLEY, HENRY-BLACK	QUE	127	1ST E DI
BORDLEY, HERNY	QUE	228	4TH E DI
BORDLEY, J.B.	ALL	049	10TH E.D
BORDLEY, JAMES	BAL	096	15TH WAR
BORDLEY, JAMES	QUE	223	4TH E DI
BORDLEY, JANE	BAL	169	6TH WARD
BORDLEY, JAOCB-BLACK	QUE	150	1ST E DI
BORDLEY, JOHN	CEC	026	ELKTON 3
BORDLEY, JOHN	BAL	084	2ND DIST
BORDLEY, JOHN-BLACK	QUE	141	1ST E DI
BORDLEY, LUCY	BAL	207	19TH WAR
BORDLEY, LUCY	BAL	082	18TH WAR
BORDLEY, MARGARETTA C.	BAL	357	13TH WAR
BORDLEY, MARY	WAS	139	HAGERSTO
BORDLEY, MARY A.	BAL	154	16TH WAR
BORDLEY, MOSES-BLACK	QUE	156	2ND E DI
BORDLEY, PERE	QUE	232	4TH E DI
BORDLEY, PRISCILLA	BAL	101	15TH WAR
BORDLEY, RICHARD	BAL	271	17TH WAR
BORDLEY, ROSANNA	BAL	370	13TH WAR
BORDLEY, SAMUEL C.	BAL	154	16TH WAR
BORDLEY, SARAH	KEN	302	3RD DIST
BORDLEY, SHARLOT	TAL	036	EASTON D
BORDLEY, SIMON-BLACK	QUE	145	1ST E DI
BORDLEY, SIMON-BLACK	QUE	140	1ST E DI
BORDLEY, SOPHIA	ANN	452	HOWARD D
BORDLEY, STEPHEN	BAL	167	16TH WAR
BORDLEY, THEADORE	KEN	299	3RD DIST
BORDLEY, THOMAS	QUE	206	3RD E DI
BORDLEY, WESLEY	HAR	144	2ND DIST
BORDLEY, WILLIAM	QUE	238	5TH E DI
BORDLEY, WILLIAM	BAL	148	16TH WAR
BORDLEY, WILLIAM C.	BAL	074	4TH WARD
BORDLEY,JAMES	BAL	275	12TH WAR
BORDLY, HESTEN M.	BAL	122	11TH WAR
BORDLY, PRISSILLA	BAL	132	18TH WAR
BORDLY, WILLIAM	BAL	461	1ST DIST
BORDRANS, FRANK	BAL	133	1ST WARD
BOREEL, HENRIETTA	CAR	236	UNION TO
BORELAND, SISTER M.C.	FRE	198	5TH E DI
BOREM, ABRAHAM	BAL	341	7TH WARD
BOREM, JESSE	CEC	034	CHESAPEA
BOREN, GEORGE	ALL	163	6TH E.D.
BOREN, JOHN H.	WAS	102	2ND DIST
BOREN, LEVI	FRE	194	5TH E DI
BOREN, SAMUEL	WAS	146	HAGERSTO
BORENNER, JOHN H.	FRE	095	FREDERIC
BORES, JOSHUA	CEC	023	ELKTON 3
BORES, P.	BAL	150	1ST WARD
BORG, LOUIS	BAL	445	1ST DIST
BORGADING, BERNARDINA	BAL	111	10TH WAR
BORGALL, SARAH	BAL	306	1ST DIST
BORGER, MARY E.	WAS	264	1ST DIST
BORGERDING, HENRY	BAL	198	6TH WARD
BORGES, CATHARINE	ALL	186	9TH E.D.
BORGETT, JACOB	BAL	214	17TH WAR
BORGMAN, C. T.	CHA	217	ALLENS F
BORGUST, D.	BAL	137	1ST WARD
BORHMAN, FREDERICK	BAL	469	14TH WAR
BORHNER, MARY	BAL	093	10TH WAR
BORING, BRYON	BAL	201	6TH DIST
BORING, ELIZABETH	CAR	214	5TH DIST
BORING, EZELIEL	CAR	340	6TH DIST
BORING, JACOB W.	CAR	333	MANCHEST
BORING, JOHN	CAR	297	7TH DIST
BORING, REBECCA	BAL	460	14TH WAR
BORING, SARAH	BAL	134	16TH WAR
BORINGE, JOSEPH	BAL	154	19TH WAR
BORK, A.	BAL	282	2ND WARD
BORKIN, ANTHONY	ALL	253	CUMBERLA
BORKMAN, HENRY	BAL	220	2ND WARD
BORLAN, THOMAS	CAR	230	5TH DIST
BORLAND, ABRAHAM	CEC	110	4TH E DI
BORLAND, JOHN	CEC	005	ELKTON 3
BORLAND, MARGARET A.	MGM	438	CLARKSTR
BORLAND, MATTHEW	CEC	110	4TH E DI
BORLAND, RISDIN*	TAL	009	EASTON D
BORLAND, THOAMS	BAL	316	20TH WAR
BORLAND, THOMAS	BAL	186	2ND WARD
BORLEY, JOSEPH	BAL	320	1ST DIST
BORMAN, ELIZABETH	BAL	001	EASTERN
BORMAN, WILLIAM J.	BAL	001	EASTERN
BORMAT, PHILIP	BAL	003	EASTERN
BORMEN, MATTHIES*	DOR	380	1ST DIST
BORN, HERMAN	BAL	199	6TH WARD
BORN, SANDY-BLACK	QUE	185	3RD E DI
BORNE, REBECCA	DOR	304	1ST DIST
BORNES, DAVID	CAR	174	8TH DIST
BORNETT, MARY*	DOR	417	1ST DIST
BORNEYMERE, FREDERICK	ALL	147	6TH E.D.
BORNIE, ROBERT E.	CAR	269	WESTMINS
BORNNA, MARY *	BAL	298	12TH WAR
BORNS, EMUND	CAR	350	6TH DIST
BOROHAN, FRANCIS M.	FRE	248	NEW MARK
BOROLUS, B.	BAL	288	20TH WAR
BOROUGH, JOHN J.	CEC	073	5TH E DI
BOROUGHS, ANNANDA	ST	307	1ST E DI
BOROUGHS, CHARLES D.	ST	260	3RD E DI
BOROUGHS, JESSE C.	ST	302	2ND E DI
BOROUGHS, JOHN W.	ST	255	3RD E DI
BOROUGHS, RUTHA A.	ST	257	3RD E DI
BOROUGHS, S.G.M.	ST	302	2ND E DI
BORRA, J.	BAL	100	10TH WAR
BORRA, JOSEPH	BAL	389	13TH WAR
BORRING, GREENBERRY	BAL	195	5TH DIST
BORRING, RICHARD	BAL	200	5TH DIST
BORRIS, HENRY	BAL	416	8TH WARD
BORRSER, JOHN *	KEN	213	2ND DIST
BORRWO, MARY	DOR	380	1ST DIST
BORSE, THOMAS	BAL	099	1ST WARD

Name	County	Page	District
BORSER, GEORGE	WAS	033	2ND SUBD
BORSER, MARY	CEC	074	NORTHEAS
BORT, ELIAS	FRE	079	FREDERIC
BORT, ISAAC	FRE	079	FREDERIC
BORTLE, HENRY	BAL	360	1ST DIST
BORTON, ELIZA ANN	BAL	375	13TH WAR
BORTON, HANNAH E.	FRE	273	NEW MARK
BORTON, SOLOMON*	DOR	448	1ST DIST
BORTON, WILLIAM-BLACK	CAR	092	NO TWP L
BORTVEN, ELIZABETH *	BAL	104	2ND DIST
BORVEN, EDW. *	BAL	302	20TH WAR
BORVERSOX, DAVID*	BAL	148	19TH WAR
BORWICK, P.	BAL	162	1ST WARD
BORWN, ELIZA	BAL	363	13TH WAR
BORWN, SARAH	BAL	148	11TH WAR
BORZ, ELIJAH	BAL	279	12TH WAR
BORZ, LAVALIN	BAL	279	12TH WAR
BOSAICK, JOHN LAWSON *	BAL	408	14TH WAR
BOSAY, SABASTIAN	BAL	429	8TH WARD
BOSCHELT, AMELIA	BAL	343	13TH WAR
BOSE, ELIZABETH	BAL	005	18TH WAR
BOSE, JANE	BAL	146	11TH WAR
BOSE, JESSE	CAR	343	6TH DIST
BOSE, LEWIS	BAL	050	18TH WAR
BOSE, LOUIS	BAL	269	1ST DIST
BOSE, MILTON	BAL	401	14TH WAR
BOSE, MITILDA	BAL	036	18TH WAR
BOSE, WILLIAM	BAL	056	10TH WAR
BOSEE, ALFRED	CEC	031	CHESAPEA
BOSH, JACOB	BAL	248	6TH WARD
BOSH, JOHN	BAL	230	6TH WARD
BOSHIP, SHADRICK *	CAL	010	1ST DIST
BOSKIN, CHARLES	BAL	433	1ST DIST
BOSLER, MARGARET	BAL	381	3RD WARD
BOSLER, SARAH	BAL	380	3RD WARD
BOSLEY, ABRAHAM	BAL	162	11TH WAR
BOSLEY, ALEXANDER	BAL	164	11TH WAR
BOSLEY, ALIJAH	CAR	335	6TH DIST
BOSLEY, ANN	BAL	058	2ND DIST
BOSLEY, BENJAMIN	BAL	044	2ND DIST
BOSLEY, C. N.	BAL	111	10TH WAR
BOSLEY, CATHARINE	BAL	115	11TH WAR
BOSLEY, CORNELIUS	BAL	443	1ST DIST
BOSLEY, DANIEL	BAL	427	1ST DIST
BOSLEY, DANIEL	BAL	423	1ST DIST
BOSLEY, DINAH	BAL	210	6TH WARD
BOSLEY, E.A.	BAL	451	1ST DIST
BOSLEY, EDWARD	BAL	111	18TH WAR
BOSLEY, ELIZABETH	BAL	030	2ND DIST
BOSLEY, ELIZABETH	BAL	157	16TH WAR
BOSLEY, EMELINE	BAL	055	2ND DIST
BOSLEY, FRANCES	SOM	552	TYASKIN
BOSLEY, FRANKLIN	BAL	112	18TH WAR
BOSLEY, GEORGE	BAL	219	6TH DIST
BOSLEY, GRAFTON	BAL	178	2ND DIST
BOSLEY, HANAH	BAL	042	2ND DIST
BOSLEY, HENRY	BAL	141	5TH WARD
BOSLEY, JAMES	ANN	462	HOWARD D
BOSLEY, JAMES	ANN	284	ANNAPOLI
BOSLEY, JOHN	BAL	030	2ND DIST
BOSLEY, JOHN	BAL	352	3RD WARD
BOSLEY, JOHN	BAL	201	6TH DIST
BOSLEY, JOHN	BAL	462	1ST DIST
BOSLEY, JOHN	BAL	318	3RD WARD
BOSLEY, JOHN	BAL	218	17TH WAR
BOSLEY, JOSEPH C.	HAR	073	1ST DIST
BOSLEY, JOSEPH H.	BAL	097	5TH WARD
BOSLEY, JOSHUA M.	BAL	450	1ST DIST
BOSLEY, JSOHUA	CAR	356	6TH DIST
BOSLEY, LAURA	BAL	111	5TH WARD
BOSLEY, MARCUS	ALL	157	6TH E.D.
BOSLEY, MARGARET A.	BAL	167	6TH WARD
BOSLEY, MARIA	BAL	161	11TH WAR
BOSLEY, MARIAH	CAR	182	8TH DIST
BOSLEY, MARIETTA	CAR	357	6TH DIST
BOSLEY, MARTHA	BAL	423	1ST DIST
BOSLEY, MARY	HAR	021	1ST DIST
BOSLEY, PETER	BAL	418	1ST DIST
BOSLEY, PHOEBE	BAL	141	5TH WARD
BOSLEY, RACHEL	ANN	508	HOWARD D
BOSLEY, REBECCA	BAL	108	15TH WAR
BOSLEY, SAMUEL	ALL	066	10TH E.D
BOSLEY, SAMUEL	BAL	058	2ND DIST
BOSLEY, SAMUEL	BAL	057	18TH WAR
BOSLEY, SARAH	BAL	340	13TH WAR
BOSLEY, TALBOT	BAL	073	4TH WARD
BOSLEY, THOMAS	CAR	356	6TH DIST
BOSLEY, THOMAS	ALL	060	10TH E.D
BOSLEY, THOMAS C.	BAL	422	1ST DIST
BOSLEY, VINCENT	HAR	073	1ST DIST
BOSLEY, WASHINGTON	BAL	349	3RD WARD
BOSLEY, WASHINGTON	BAL	292	7TH WARD
BOSLEY, WILLIAM OF JOHN	BAL	443	1ST DIST
BOSLEY, WILLIAM S.	BAL	030	2ND DIST
BOSMAN, ALFRED	SOM	440	DAMES QU
BOSMAN, BALLARD	SOM	419	PRINCESS
BOSMAN, BIDDY	SOM	442	DAMES QU
BOSMAN, CHARLES	BAL	076	18TH WAR
BOSMAN, EDWARD	BAL	371	8TH WARD
BOSMAN, ELIZABETH	SOM	440	DAMES QU
BOSMAN, ELIZABETH	SOM	437	DAMES QU
BOSMAN, ELIZABETH	SOM	361	BRINKLEY
BOSMAN, GEORGE	SOM	420	PRINCESS
BOSMAN, ISAAC	SOM	419	PRINCESS
BOSMAN, JOHN	CAR	121	NO TWP L
BOSMAN, JOHN	SOM	444	DAMES QU
BOSMAN, JOHN	SOM	440	DAMES QU
BOSMAN, MARY	SOM	444	DAMES QU
BOSMAN, MARY	SOM	419	PRINCESS
BOSMAN, MARY*	SOM	353	BRINKLEY
BOSMAN, ROBERT	SOM	441	DAMES QU
BOSMAN, SARAH	SOM	420	PRINCESS
BOSMAN, SUSAN	SOM	419	PRINCESS
BOSMAN, SUSAN	BAL	413	14TH WAR
BOSMAN, THOMAS	SOM	440	DAMES QU
BOSMAN, THOMAS	BAL	020	1ST WARD
BOSMAN, WILLIAM	BAL	041	15TH WAR
BOSMAN, WILLIAM	SOM	419	PRINCESS
BOSRE, MARY	BAL	203	2ND WARD
BOSS, ARTHUR	BAL	200	2ND WARD
BOSS, CATHARINE	WAS	040	2ND SUBD
BOSS, HENERY*	DOR	331	3RD DIVI
BOSS, JOHN	BAL	165	2ND DIST
BOSS, MARTHA*	BAL	003	4TH WARD
BOSS, MARY	BAL	023	9TH WARD
BOSS, SAMUEL	CEC	027	CHESAPEA
BOSS, WILLIAM	BAL	062	4TH WARD
BOSS, WILLIAM	CEC	055	1ST E DI
BOSSARD, MICHAEL	BAL	189	6TH WARD
BOSSE, ANDREAS	BAL	162	16TH WAR
BOSSE, REBECCA	BAL	249	17TH WAR
BOSSEE, JOHN	KEN	226	2ND DIST
BOSSICK, STEPHEN	BAL	266	2ND WARD
BOSSLE, CHARLES	BAL	001	4TH WARD
BOSSMAN, WILLIAM	BAL	199	17TH WAR
BOSSOM, EDITH	BAL	200	5TH DIST
BOSSON, RACHEL	BAL	016	1ST WARD
BOSSTS, DANIEL	FRE	205	BUCKEYST
BOST, ANDREW	FRE	403	JEFFERSO
BOST, SARAH	CAR	192	4TH DIST
BOSTER, LEREMY	BAL	231	19TH WAR
BOSTIAN, ISAAC	FRE	441	8TH E DI
BOSTIAN, SAMUEL	FRE	425	8TH E DI
BOSTIAN, SOLOMON	FRE	420	8TH E DI
BOSTIC, ELIZABETH	CEC	001	ELKTON 3
BOSTIC, MALINDA	CEC	092	4TH E DI
BOSTIC, WILLIAM H.	ALL	052	10TH E.D
BOSTICK, ANN	FRE	062	FREDERIC
BOSTICK, CATHARINE	CEC	026	ELKTON 3
BOSTICK, CATHARINE	CEC	008	ELKTON 3
BOSTICK, CHARLES	CEC	033	CHESAPEA
BOSTICK, CLEMENT	QUE	127	1ST E DI
BOSTICK, FRANCINA	CEC	004	ELKTON 3
BOSTICK, GEORGE	CEC	001	ELKTON 3
BOSTICK, HENRY	KEN	281	3RD DIST
BOSTICK, JOHN	CEC	015	ELKTON 3
BOSTICK, JOHN A.	CEC	010	ELKTON 3
BOSTICK, MARY E.	TAL	068	EASTON T
BOSTICK, MARY J.	CEC	005	ELKTON 3
BOSTICK, PETER	CEC	011	ELKTON 3
BOSTICK, PETER	CEC	016	ELKTON 3
BOSTICK, SAMUEL	QUE	166	2ND E DI
BOSTICK, SARAH A.	QUE	131	1ST E DI
BOSTICK, WILLIAM H.	TAL	068	EASTON T
BOSTICKS, MARY F.	FRE	304	WOODSBOR
BOSTICKS, ROBERT	FRE	281	WOODSBOR
BOSTIE, RICHARD	BAL	336	1ST DIST
BOSTION, ANDREW	CAR	379	2ND DIST
BOSTION, GEORGE	FRE	291	WOODSBOR
BOSTION, JOHN	FRE	297	WOODSBOR
BOSTON, ABRAM	BAL	263	12TH WAR
BOSTON, ALEXANDER	MGM	365	BERRYS D
BOSTON, ALFORD	BAL	091	18TH WAR
BOSTON, ALICE	BAL	208	17TH WAR
BOSTON, ANN	BAL	085	15TH WAR
BOSTON, ANN MARIA	BAL	203	17TH WAR
BOSTON, ANTHONY	ANN	309	1ST DIST
BOSTON, ANTHONY	ANN	315	1ST DIST
BOSTON, BARBARA	ANN	391	4TH DIST
BOSTON, CATHARINE A.	ANN	461	HOWARD D
BOSTON, CEASER	ANN	298	1ST DIST
BOSTON, CHARELS	BAL	167	6TH WARD
BOSTON, CHARLES	BAL	160	1ST WARD
BOSTON, CHARLES	BAL	289	3RD WARD
BOSTON, CHARLOTTE	BAL	001	15TH WAR
BOSTON, CLARA	ANN	330	2ND DIST
BOSTON, DANIEL	ANN	309	1ST DIST
BOSTON, DANIEL	ANN	315	1ST DIST
BOSTON, DANIEL	BAL	029	15TH WAR
BOSTON, DANIEL	BAL	306	3RD WARD
BOSTON, DANIEL	BAL	437	14TH WAR
BOSTON, DANIEL	BAL	247	20TH WAR
BOSTON, DANIEL	SOM	400	BRINKLEY
BOSTON, ELIZA	ANN	442	HOWARD D
BOSTON, ELIZABETH	BAL	024	1ST WARD
BOSTON, ELIZABETH	SOM	406	DUBLIN D
BOSTON, EPHRAIM-BLACK	CAR	114	NO TWP L
BOSTON, ESAU JR.	WOR	334	1ST E DI
BOSTON, ESAU SR.	WOR	328	1ST E DI
BOSTON, FRANCIS	BAL	243	17TH WAR
BOSTON, FRANCIS	BAL	247	6TH WARD
BOSTON, GEORGE	BAL	099	2ND DIST
BOSTON, GEORGE	SOM	406	DUBLIN D
BOSTON, GEORGE	BAL	101	18TH WAR
BOSTON, GEORGE	CEC	104	4TH E DI
BOSTON, HANNAH	BAL	179	19TH WAR
BOSTON, HANNAH	ANN	290	ANNAPOLI
BOSTON, HARRIET	BAL	094	10TH WAR
BOSTON, HENRY	BAL	086	4TH WARD
BOSTON, HENRY	WOR	283	BERLIN 1
BOSTON, HESTER	BAL	128	11TH WAR
BOSTON, HESTOR	BAL	221	17TH WAR
BOSTON, ISAAC	WOR	295	9TH E DI
BOSTON, ISEBELLA	BAL	126	18TH WAR
BOSTON, JACOB	WOR	325	1ST E DI
BOSTON, JACOB	BAL	043	9TH WARD
BOSTON, JAMES	ANN	434	HOWARD D
BOSTON, JAMES	BAL	143	11TH WAR
BOSTON, JOHN	ANN	430	HOWARD D
BOSTON, JOHN	ANN	296	1ST DIST
BOSTON, JOHN	ANN	391	4TH DIST
BOSTON, JOHN	BAL	344	3RD WARD
BOSTON, JOHN	WOR	331	1ST E DI
BOSTON, JOHN	SOM	550	TYASKIN
BOSTON, JOHN	SOM	435	PRINCESS
BOSTON, JOHN B.	BAL	419	3RD WARD
BOSTON, JOHN H.	ANN	291	ANNAPOLI
BOSTON, JOHN T.	MGM	366	BERRYS D
BOSTON, JOST	BAL	101	18TH WAR
BOSTON, LOUISA	BAL	106	15TH WAR
BOSTON, LUCY	BAL	153	16TH WAR
BOSTON, MARGARET	BAL	059	10TH WAR
BOSTON, MARGARET	BAL	461	14TH WAR
BOSTON, MARIA	MGM	370	BERRYS D
BOSTON, MARIAH	TAL	033	EASTON D
BOSTON, MARY	BAL	128	11TH WAR
BOSTON, MARY	BAL	310	3RD WARD
BOSTON, MARY A.	WOR	328	1ST E DI
BOSTON, MATILDA	ANN	431	HOWARD D
BOSTON, NACE	ANN	280	ANNAPOLI
BOSTON, NACE	SOM	417	PRINCESS
BOSTON, NICHOLAS	BAL	215	6TH WARD
BOSTON, PEGGY	SOM	410	DUBLIN D
BOSTON, PERRY	DOR	466	1ST DIST
BOSTON, PETER	BAL	084	15TH WAR
BOSTON, PHILIP	BAL	012	18TH WAR
BOSTON, RACHEL	ANN	436	HOWARD D
BOSTON, RACHEL	WOR	297	9TH E DI
BOSTON, RICHARD	ANN	463	HOWARD D
BOSTON, RICHARD	BAL	195	6TH WARD
BOSTON, RICHARD	ANN	318	2ND DIST
BOSTON, RICHARD	ANN	296	1ST DIST
BOSTON, RICHARD	BAL	251	20TH WAR
BOSTON, ROBERT	BAL	046	15TH WAR
BOSTON, ROBERT-BLACK	CAR	134	NO TWP L
BOSTON, ROSEANNA	BAL	195	17TH WAR
BOSTON, RUTH	BAL	419	3RD WARD
BOSTON, SALLY	WOR	292	9TH E DI
BOSTON, SAMUEL	SOM	406	DUBLIN D
BOSTON, SAMUEL A.	BAL	090	15TH WAR
BOSTON, SARAH	ANN	391	4TH DIST
BOSTON, SARAH	BAL	099	2ND DIST
BOSTON, SMITH	BAL	201	17TH WAR
BOSTON, SOLENA	BAL	462	14TH WAR
BOSTON, STEPHEN-BLACK	WOR	334	1ST E DI
BOSTON, SUSAN A.	BAL	100	15TH WAR
BOSTON, SUSAN-BLACK	BAL	221	2ND WARD
BOSTON, THOAMS	ANN	391	4TH DIST
BOSTON, THOMAS	BAL	173	11TH WAR
BOSTON, THOMAS	MGM	365	BERRYS D
BOSTON, VIOLETTA	BAL	097	15TH WAR
BOSTON, VIRGINIA	MGM	365	BERRYS D
BOSTON, WASHINGTON	BAL	179	19TH WAR
BOSTON, WILLIAM	BAL	411	14TH WAR
BOSTON, WILLIAM	BAL	227	12TH WAR
BOSTON, WILLIAM	BAL	033	1ST WARD
BOSTON, WILLIAM-BLACK	WOR	329	1ST E DI
BOSTON, WILLIMA	WOR	295	9TH E DI
BOSTRAN, JACOB	FRE	412	8TH E DI
BOSTRON, WILLIAM	FRE	288	WOODSBOR
BOSTWICK, ALEXANDER	QUE	133	1ST E DI
BOSTWICK, GEORGE	ANN	440	HOWARD D
BOSTWICK, JOHN	QUE	138	1ST E DI
BOSTWICK, JOSH	BAL	287	3RD WARD
BOSTWICK, WILLIAM T.	QUE	133	1ST E DI
BOSWELL, ALEXANDER	BAL	132	11TH WAR
BOSWELL, ALEXANDER F.	MGM	386	ROCKERLE
BOSWELL, AMY	WAS	162	HAGERSTO
BOSWELL, ANDREW J.	MGM	380	ROCKERLE
BOSWELL, ANGELINE	WAS	048	2ND SUBD
BOSWELL, ANN	PRI	028	VANSVILL
BOSWELL, BENJAMIN	BAL	399	14TH WAR
BOSWELL, CATHERINE	CHA	254	MIDDLETO
BOSWELL, CHARLES C.	PRI	059	NOTTINGH
BOSWELL, E.	PRI	112	PISCATAW
BOSWELL, E.	PRI	110	PISCATAW
BOSWELL, EDMUN DP.	CAL	027	2ND DIST
BOSWELL, ELIGA	CHA	245	HILLTOP
BOSWELL, GEORGE	FRE	363	CATOCTIN
BOSWELL, GEORGE	MGM	370	BERRYS D
BOSWELL, HENRY	CHA	267	MIDDLETO
BOSWELL, HENRY	ANN	298	1ST DIST
BOSWELL, J.	PRI	110	PISCATAW
BOSWELL, JAMES	BAL	419	3RD WARD
BOSWELL, JAMES	BAL	032	4TH WARD
BOSWELL, JAMES W.	MGM	382	ROCKERLE
BOSWELL, JETSON	ANN	469	HOWARD D
BOSWELL, JOHN	ANN	473	HOWARD D
BOSWELL, JOHN	MGM	404	ROCKERLE
BOSWELL, JOHN	CHA	250	MIDDLETO
BOSWELL, JOHN	BAL	120	18TH WAR
BOSWELL, JOHN	PRI	113	PISCATAW
BOSWELL, JOHN	WAS	047	2ND SUBD
BOSWELL, JOHN F.	CHA	232	HILLTOP
BOSWELL, JOHN H.	CHA	219	ALLENS F
BOSWELL, JOHN H.	MGM	401	ROCKERLE
BOSWELL, LEONARD	CHA	259	MIDDLETO
BOSWELL, LEONARD	PRI	059	NOTTINGH
BOSWELL, M.	PRI	112	PISCATAW
BOSWELL, MARGARET	ST	312	1ST E DI
BOSWELL, MARIA	CHA	267	MIDDLETO
BOSWELL, MARY	BAL	030	18TH WAR
BOSWELL, MARY J.	MGM	354	BERRYS D
BOSWELL, MATTHEW	CHA	255	MIDDLETO
BOSWELL, NICHOLASS	MGM	369	BERRYS D
BOSWELL, OTHO	MGM	383	ROCKERLE
BOSWELL, REZIN	CHA	266	MIDDLETO
BOSWELL, SAMUEL	WAS	068	2ND SUBD
BOSWELL, SARAH	PRI	059	NOTTINGH
BOSWELL, SUSANNA	CHA	263	MIDDLETO
BOSWELL, TERRESA	CHA	217	ALLENS F
BOSWELL, THOMAS	CHA	261	MIDDLETO
BOSWELL, THOMAS	MGM	348	BERRYS D
BOSWELL, TUBMAN	CHA	258	MIDDLETO
BOSWELL, WASHINGTON	PRI	057	NOTTINGH
BOSWELL, WILLIAM	CHA	219	ALLENS F
BOSWELL, WILLIAM	CHA	290	BOJANTOW
BOSWELL, WILLIAM	BAL	120	18TH WAR
BOSWELL, WILLIAM H.S.	CAL	060	3RD DIST
BOSWICK, CHARLES	BAL	471	14TH WAR
BOSWORTH, CISSAR	BAL	109	18TH WAR
BOSWORTH, DAVID	MGM	355	BERRYS D
BOSWORTH, HILLERY	PRI	024	VANSVILL
BOSWORTH, JULIAN	BAL	201	2ND WARD
BOSWORTH, THOMAS	BAL	201	2ND WARD
BOSWORTH, WILLIAM	PRI	024	VANSVILL
BOTARD, CHARLES	BAL	222	2ND WARD
BOTCHEE, LINGAN	FRE	314	MIDDLETO
BOTELER, AUGUSTUS	FRE	013	FREDERIC
BOTELER, BENJAMIN	FRE	230	BUCKEYST
BOTELER, EDWARD S.	FRE	382	PETERSVI
BOTELER, ELIZA	FRE	408	JEFFERSO
BOTELER, ELIZA J.	FRE	312	MIDDLETO
BOTELER, HENRY	FRE	012	FREDERIC
BOTELER, HEZEKIAH	WAS	096	2ND SUBD
BOTELER, JEREMIA	PRI	043	VANSVILL
BOTELER, JOHN D.	PRI	044	VANSVILL
BOTELER, JOHN-MULATTO	FRE	405	JEFFERSO
BOTELER, JOSEPH-BLACK	FRE	405	JEFFERSO
BOTELER, LEMUEL	PRI	045	VANSVILL
BOTELER, LINGAN	WAS	096	2ND SUBD
BOTELER, MARY	FRE	409	JEFFERSO
BOTELER, MARY	FRE	024	FREDERIC
BOTELER, MARY	FRE	230	BUCKEYST
BOTELER, THOMAS	WAS	091	2ND SUBD
BOTELER, VIOLETTA	FRE	380	PETERSVI
BOTELER, WILLIAM	FRE	401	JEFFERSO
BOTELER, WILLIAM	WAS	085	2ND SUBD
BOTELER, WILLIAM H.	FRE	409	JEFFERSO
BOTELER, WILLIAM-BLACK	FRE	008	FREDERIC
BOTELLER, SUSAN	PRI	001	BLADENSB
BOTHAM, LEWIS D.	DOR	383	1ST DIST
BOTHERER, ELIZABETH	BAL	264	12TH WAR
BOTHERER, JOHN	BAL	263	12TH WAR
BOTHMAN, COLUMBUS*	BAL	034	4TH WARD
BOTHMANN, AUGUST	BAL	088	15TH WAR
BOTHMANN, ERNEST F. C.	BAL	091	15TH WAR
BOTHMARD, FREDERICK	BAL	284	17TH WAR
BOTHUM, MARGARET	SOM	478	TRAPP DI
BOTHUM, VIRGINIA	SOM	478	TRAPP DI
BOTINGER, PETER	BAL	207	6TH DIST
BOTLE, MICHAEL	BAL	295	1ST DIST
BOTLER, BEVERLY W. *	BAL	067	18TH WAR
BOTSER, JOSEPH	BAL	434	8TH WARD
BOTSNER, GEORGE	BAL	444	8TH WARD
BOTTELER, JOHN H. A.	CAR	185	8TH DIST
BOTTELS, ANN E.	WAS	121	2ND DIST
BOTTELS, SUSAN	WAS	121	2ND DIST
BOTTENHOT, AMELIA	BAL	007	9TH WARD
BOTTER, BEVERLY W. *	BAL	067	18TH WAR

Name	County	Page	District
BOTTER, THOMAS	BAL	459	8TH WARD
BCTTERILE, THOMAS	ANN	478	HOWARD D
BOTTIMON, ROBERT	BAL	355	13TH WAR
BOTTIMORE, JANE	BAL	035	4TH WARD
BOTTLEMESS, PETER	ALL	232	CUMBERLA
BOTTLES, CATHERINE	BAL	336	3RD WARD
BOTTOMAR, MARY C.	BAL	262	20TH WAR
BOTTON, HANNAH	BAL	332	3RD WARD
BOTTCN, ROBERT W.	HAR	179	3RD DIST
BOTTRELL, WILLIAM	ANN	445	HOWARD D
BOTTRILL, ISABELLA	BAL	186	6TH WARD
BOTTS, ASEL	HAR	126	2ND DIST
BOTTS, AVERILLA	HAR	162	3RD DIST
BOTTS, GEORGE	CEC	151	PORT DUP
BOTTS, ISAAC	HAR	003	1ST DIST
BOTTS, JOHN	HAR	130	2ND DIST
BOTTS, JOHN	HAR	127	2ND DIST
BOTTS, JOHN B.	HAR	173	3RD DIST
BOTTS, SOPHIA	BAL	004	18TH WAR
BOTZLER, JOHN*	BAL	089	10TH WAR
BOUCHELL, EDWIN	BAL	028	15TH WAR
BOUCHELL, ELLA	CEC	042	CHESAPEA
BOUCHELL, HYLAND	CEC	036	CHESAPEA
BOUCHELL, ISAAC	CEC	041	CHESAPEA
BOUCHELL, MARY W.	CEC	033	CHESAPEA
BOUCHELL, PETER	BAL	027	15TH WAR
BOUCHER, ANDREW	ALL	049	10TH E.D
BOUCHER, EDWARD L.	PRI	107	PISCATAW
BOUCHER, JOHN	ALL	048	10TH E.D
BOUCHER, WILLIAM	BAL	301	3RD WARD
BOUCHER, WILLIAM	BAL	041	4TH WARD
BCUCHET, JOHN M.	BAL	372	8TH WARD
BOUCHET, MARY	BAL	088	10TH WAR
BCUDEN, HENRY	WOR	312	2ND E DI
BOUDEN, JAMES S.	WOR	243	1ST CENS
BOUDEN, LOTTA	WOR	316	2ND E DI
BOUE, MARY	BAL	026	2ND DIST
BOUEN, ELIZABETH	WAS	035	2ND SUBD
BCUER, MARGARET	BAL	469	14TH WAR
BOUER, RICHARD	WAS	154	HAGERSTO
BCUERY, THOMAS H.	FRE	069	FREDERIC
BOUEY, SINGLETON	FRE	093	FREDERIC
BOUG, JOHN	BAL	054	18TH WAR
BOUGE, HENRY	BAL	380	1ST DIST
BCUGE, MARIA	BAL	029	9TH WARD
BOUGHAN, J. H.	BAL	332	1ST DIST
BOUGHER, DANIEL	FRE	073	FREDERIC
BOUGHMAN, SAMUEL	WAS	123	HAGERSTO
BOUGHMAN, WILSON*	BAL	057	4TH WARD
BOUGHSTER, THOMAS	HAR	055	1ST DIST
BOUGHTWELL, SAMUEL*	BAL	399	3RD WARD
BOUIE, WILLIAM	CHA	235	HILLTOP
BOUIL, MARY	HAR	181	3RD DIST
BOUIS, EMMA J.	BAL	440	14TH WAR
BOUIS, HENRY	BAL	416	8TH WARD
BOUIS, JOHN	BAL	416	8TH WARD
BOUIS, JOHN	BAL	440	14TH WAR
BOUIS, ROBERT H. G.	BAL	069	10TH WAR
BOUKES, GEORGE	FRE	318	MIDDLETO
BCULBOCK, SAMUEL	BAL	120	1ST WARD
BOULBY, SARAH A. L.	BAL	379	8TH WARD
BOULD, HENRY	QUE	215	3RD E DI
BOULD, RICHARD	BAL	116	1ST WARD
BOULDAIR, DAVID P.	BAL	347	3RD WARD
BOULDAM, J.P.	BAL	020	2ND DIST
BOULDEN, ANN	CEC	119	3RD E DI
BCULDEN, CHALROTTE	BAL	023	2ND DIST
BCULDEN, CHARLES	CEC	015	ELKTON 3
BOULDEN, EMALINE	CEC	057	1ST E DI
BOULDEN, EZEKIEL	CEC	018	ELKTON 3
BOULDEN, GEORGE	CEC	025	ELKTON 3
BOULDEN, ISAAC	CEC	002	ELKTON 3
BOULDEN, JESSE	CEC	107	3RD E DI
BOULDEN, JOHN	CEC	119	3RD E DI
BOULDEN, JOHN N.	CEC	097	4TH E DI
BCULDEN, JOHNSON	CEC	107	3RD E DI
BOULDEN, LAMBERT	CEC	025	ELKTON 3
BOULDEN, LEVI	CEC	023	ELKTON 3
BOULDEN, LEVI	CEC	003	ELKTON 3
BOULDEN, LEVIN*	TAL	033	EASTON D
BOULDEN, LOUISA	CEC	022	ELKTON 3
BOULDEN, MARGARET	CEC	018	ELKTON 3
BOULDEN, MARGARET*	TAL	019	EASTON D
BOULDEN, MARTHA	BAL	076	10TH WAR
BOULDEN, MARY	CEC	017	ELKTON 3
BOULDEN, MARY W.	CEC	156	PORT DUP
BOULDEN, MILLICENT	CEC	021	ELKTON 3
BOULDEN, NANCY	BAL	424	14TH WAR
BCULDEN, RICHARD	CEC	024	ELKTON 3
BOULDEN, SAMUEL	CEC	070	5TH E DI
BOULDEN, SAMUEL	CEC	068	5TH E DI
BOULDEN, SARAH	CEC	070	5TH E DI
BOULDEN, SPENCER	BAL	175	6TH WARD
BOULDEN, THOMAS	CEC	015	ELKTON 3
BOULDEN, VIOLET	CEC	024	ELKTON 3
BOULDEN, WILLIAM	CEC	042	CHESAPEA
BOULDEN, WILLIAM	CEC	035	CHESAPEA
BOULDER, HARRIET	TAL	048	EASTON T
BOULDER, HELTY	BAL	122	2ND DIST
BOULDER, JACOB*	TAL	047	EASTON T
BOULDER, LEVIN*	TAL	033	EASTON D
BOULDER, MARGARET*	TAL	019	EASTON D
BOULDER, SUSAN	TAL	077	EASTON T
BOULDIN, ALEXANDER J.	BAL	220	6TH WARD
BOULDIN, CHARLES D.	HAR	076	BEL AIR
BOULDIN, ELLEN	BAL	051	9TH WARD
BOULDIN, HENRY	BAL	348	7TH WARD
BOULDIN, JAMES	BAL	060	2ND DIST
BOULDIN, JANE A.	BAL	348	7TH WARD
BOULDIN, JARRETT L.	HAR	163	3RD DIST
BOULDIN, OWEN	BAL	448	8TH WARD
BCULDIN, RADNOLPH J.	BAL	394	14TH WAR
BOULDIN, WASHINGTON	BAL	228	6TH WARD
BOULDIN, WILLAIM	HAR	076	BEL AIR
BOULDCN, ANN	CEC	013	ELKTON 3
BOULDS, THOMAS	WOR	260	BERLIN 1
BOULEY, ANN	DOR	369	3RD DIVI
BOULEY, BINER	DOR	368	3RD DIVI
BOULEY, HAGER	DOR	347	3RD DIVI
BOULEY, LUCY	DOR	361	3RD DIVI
BOULEYER, WARNER	MGM	413	MEDLEY 3
BOULLT, T.A.	WAS	122	HAGERSTO
BOULT, THOMAS H.	BAL	335	3RD WARD
BCULTON, CHARLES H.	BAL	379	8TH WARD
BOULTON, JAMES	KEN	265	1ST DIST
BOULTON, MARY	CEC	006	ELKTON 3
BCULUS, WILLIAM *	FRE	326	MIDDLETO
BCUMAN, GEORGE-BLACK	FRE	004	FREDERIC
BCUN, GEORGE	WAS	144	HAGERSTO
BOUN, JOHN	BAL	253	2ND WARD
BOUNASS, JOSEHP	BAL	059	18TH WAR
BOUND, JAMES R.	BAL	413	1ST DIST
BOUNDS, ELIZABETH	WOR	187	7TH E DI
BOUNDS, GEORGE	SOM	529	QUANTICO
BOUNDS, GEORGE W.	SOM	516	BARREN C
BOUNDS, HENRY J.	SOM	477	TRAPP DI
BOUNDS, JACOB	CAR	108	NO TWP L
BOUNDS, JAMES	SOM	529	QUANTICO
BOUNDS, JAMES H.	SOM	474	TRAPPE D
BOUNDS, JAMES R.*	SOM	527	QUANTICO
BOUNDS, JOHN	ANN	388	4TH DIST
BOUNDS, JOHN J.	SOM	535	QUANTICO
BCUNOS, RELZIN	ANN	433	HOWARD D
BOUNDS, RICHARD	SOM	474	TRAPPE D
BOUNDS, SAMUEL	SOM	531	QUANTICO
BOUNDS, SAMUEL	SOM	430	PRINCESS
BOUNDS, WILLIAM	SOM	474	TRAPPE D
BOUNDS, WILLIAM A. D.	SOM	462	HANGARY
BOUNDS, ZEPORA	SOM	516	BARREN C
BOUNES, THOMAS*	BAL	419	3RD WARD
BOUNKHARD, LUKE*	TAL	115	ST MICHA
BOURBERGER, C.	WAS	004	WILLIAMS
BOURES, ROBERT	CEC	074	5TH E DI
BOURGUET, FRANCES	BAL	079	4TH WARD
BOURING, J.	BAL	149	1ST WARD
BOURK, SABINA	ALL	253	CUMBERLA
BOURKE, EDWARD	ALL	128	4TH E.D.
BOURKE, EDWARD	ANN	337	3RD DIST
BOURKE, JOHN	ALL	130	4TH E.D.
BOURKE, LEMUEL	ANN	353	3RD DIST
BOURKE, MARTIN	ALL	128	4TH E.D.
BOURKE, MARY	QUE	193	3RD E DI
BOURKE, MICHAEL	ANN	451	HOWARD D
BOURMAN, FREDERICK	BAL	045	9TH WARD
BOURN, MARY	BAL	375	8TH WARD
BOURNAN, ELIZABETH *	WAS	168	FUNKSTOW
BOURNAN, ISAAC	WAS	209	1ST DIST
BOURNE, CORNILLA D.	CAL	011	1ST DIST
BOURNE, ELIZABETH	CAL	056	3RD DIST
BOURNE, EMILY M.	MGM	329	CRACKLIN
BOURNE, GEORGE	CAL	059	3RD DIST
BOURNE, GEORGE	BAL	185	16TH WAR
BOURNE, JAMES E.	CAL	007	1ST DIST
BOURNE, JAMES J.	CAL	013	1ST DIST
BOURNE, JOHN	CAL	058	3RD DIST
BOURNE, MARY A.	MGM	329	CRACKLIN
BOURNE, THOMAS B.	CAL	056	3RD DIST
BOURS, JOHN H.	BAL	393	8TH WARD
BOURSAND, AUGUSTUS	BAL	065	18TH WAR
BOURY, JOSEPH	BAL	086	4TH WARD
BOUSACK, NATHANIEL	CAR	291	7TH DIST
BOUSE, SOPHIA	BAL	255	12TH WAR
BOUSELL, MRS.	ANN	269	ANNAPOLI
BOUSEN, CASEY	CEC	155	PORT DUP
BOUSEN, HANNAH	CEC	150	PORT DUP
BOUSER, ALISER	HAR	153	3RD DIST
BOUSER, AQUILER S.	HAR	170	3RD DIST
BOUSER, CHARLES-BLACK	QUE	169	2ND E DI
BOUSER, ISAAC	QUE	236	4TH E DI
BOUSER, MARRIA	HAR	178	3RD DIST
BOUSER, MARY	HAR	170	3RD DIST
BOUSER, ROBERT	HAR	171	3RD DIST
BOUSER, WILLIAM	HAR	163	3RD DIST
BOUSTECKER, JOHN	BAL	214	19TH WAR
BOUTON, THOMS	BAL	125	1ST WARD
BOUTWELL, HENSEN	BAL	078	15TH WAR
BOVEY, ADAM	WAS	057	2ND SUBD
BOVEY, CATHARINE	WAS	289	1ST DIST
BOVEY, CATHARINE	WAS	274	RIDGEVIL
BOVEY, CHRISTIAN	WAS	285	1ST DIST
BOVEY, DAVID	WAS	252	1ST DIST
BOVEY, EMANUEL	WAS	300	1ST DIST
BOVEY, ENRY	WAS	232	1ST DIST
BOVEY, GEORGE	WAS	231	1ST DIST
BOVEY, JACOB	WAS	290	1ST DIST
BOVEY, LYDIA	WAS	057	2ND SUBD
BOVEY, ROSANNA	WAS	292	1ST DIST
BOVEY, SAMUEL	WAS	099	2ND DIST
BOVEY, SIMON	WAS	213	1ST DIST
BOVEY, SOLOMON	WAS	237	CAVETOWN
BOVEY, SUSAN	WAS	102	2ND DIST
BOW*ER, WILLIAM	WOR	289	9TH E DI
BOWAN, CHARLES	FRE	253	NEW MARK
BOWAN, WILLIAM E.	CAL	010	1ST DIST
BOWARD, ANDREW	WAS	160	HAGERSTO
BOWARD, ANDREW	WAS	160	HAGERSTO
BOWARD, ANDY J.	WAS	167	1ST DIST
BOWARD, ANN	WAS	137	HAGERSTO
BOWARD, DAVID	WAS	032	2ND SUBD
BOWARD, ELIZABETH	WAS	160	HAGERSTO
BOWARD, HENRY	WAS	160	HAGERSTO
BOWARD, JACOB	WAS	205	1ST DIST
BOWARD, MARY	WAS	160	HAGERSTO
BOWARD, MICHAEL	WAS	160	HAGERSTO
BOWARD, MICHAEL	WAS	160	HAGERSTO
BOWARD, WILLIAM	WAS	135	HAGERSTO
BOWARD, WILLIAM	WAS	135	HAGERSTO
BOWARDS, JACOB	WAS	156	HAGERSTO
BOWARDS, JOHN	WAS	128	2ND DIST
BOWARDS, LEVI	WAS	107	2ND DIST
BOWARDS, LUCRETIANNA	WAS	162	2ND DIST
BOWBY, D.	BAL	115	1ST WARD
BOWCHER, ADDAM	WAS	142	2ND DIST
BOWDEN, DECATER	WOR	294	9TH E DI
BOWDEN, EDWARD	BAL	156	1ST WARD
BOWDEN, EDWARD	BAL	162	1ST WARD
BOWDEN, GEORGE E.	BAL	194	11TH WAR
BOWDEN, GEORGE W.	WOR	297	9TH E DI
BOWDEN, JAMES	BAL	217	6TH WARD
BOWDEN, JOHN	BAL	356	3RD WARD
BOWDEN, JOSEPH	WOR	318	2ND E DI
BOWDEN, LOYD	BAL	210	11TH WAR
BOWDEN, MARY	PRI	120	PISCATAW
BOWDEN, NANCY	WOR	308	2ND E DI
BOWDEN, SAMUEL	ALL	162	6TH E.D.
BOWDEN, WILLIAM	BAL	203	6TH WARD
BOWDEN, WILLIAM	WOR	251	1ST CENS
BOWDEN, WILLIAM J.	WOR	299	SNOW HIL
BOWDEN, WILLIAM K.	BAL	314	7TH WARD
BOWDER, ADELINE	TAL	025	EASTON D
BOWDER, CHARLES H.	TAL	024	EASTON D
BOWDER, JAMES	TAL	011	EASTON D
BOWDER, JAMES	ALL	231	CUMBERLA
BOWDER, LOFTUS	TAL	051	EASTON D
BOWDER, NANCY*	TAL	048	EASTON T
BOWDER, SUSAN	WOR	264	BERLIN 1
BOWDERS, CHRISTIANNA	WOR	289	9TH E DI
BOWDIN, PETER	BAL	211	11TH WAR
BOWDIN, VIRGINIA A.	BAL	212	11TH WAR
BOWDLE, ALEXANDER	TAL	051	EASTON D
BOWDLE, AMES*	DOR	415	1ST DIST
BOWDLE, ANN E.*	TAL	054	EASTON D
BOWDLE, BENJAMIN M.	TAL	043	EASTON D
BOWDLE, CALEB	DOR	315	1ST DIST
BOWDLE, EDWARD T.*	TAL	050	EASTON T
BOWDLE, JOHN	DOR	318	1ST DIST
BOWDLE, JULIA A.	TAL	043	EASTON D
BOWDLE, MARIA	BAL	408	8TH WARD
BOWDLE, MARY	TAL	045	EASTON T
BOWDLE, NANCY*	TAL	048	EASTON T
BOWDLE, RACHEL J.	TAL	048	EASTON T
BOWDLE, SALLY	BAL	001	15TH WAR
BOWDLE, SARAH M.	TAL	047	EASTON T
BOWDLE, THOMAS	DOR	375	1ST DIST
BOWDLE, WILLIAM H.*	DOR	375	1ST DIST
BOWE, EDWARD	FRE	196	5TH E DI
BOWE, ISABELLA	TAL	056	EASTON D
BOWE, JAMES-BLACK	FRE	189	5TH E DI
BOWE, MARY	BAL	065	15TH WAR
BOWEDER, SAMUEL	WOR	297	9TH E DI
BOWELDEN, MARGARET	BAL	160	11TH WAR
BOWELL, WILLIAM	BAL	156	1ST WARD
BOWEN, ABRAM G.	CAL	032	2ND DIST
BOWEN, ALFRED	ANN	490	HOWARD D
BOWEN, ALPHONSA	BAL	395	1ST DIST
BOWEN, ALVIRA*	BAL	069	4TH WARD
BOWEN, AMELIA	BAL	255	17TH WAR
BOWEN, AMELIA	MGM	372	BERRYS D
BOWEN, ANDREW	BAL	407	1ST DIST
BOWEN, ANN	BAL	028	15TH WAR
BOWEN, ANN	BAL	148	11TH WAR
BOWEN, ANN R.	BAL	296	3RD WARD
BOWEN, AQUILLA G.	CAL	018	1ST DIST
BOWEN, AUGUSTUS	CAL	001	1ST DIST
BOWEN, BENJAMIN	BAL	417	1ST DIST
BOWEN, BENJAMIN	BAL	339	7TH WARD
BOWEN, BENJAMIN	BAL	172	2ND DIST
BOWEN, BENJAMIN SR.	CEC	088	4TH E DI
BOWEN, CASPER	BAL	278	2ND WARD
BOWEN, CATHARINE	BAL	109	5TH WARD
BOWEN, CHARLES	BAL	155	1ST WARD
BOWEN, CHARLES	BAL	210	2ND WARD
BOWEN, CHARLES	BAL	053	18TH WAR
BOWEN, CHARLES	MGM	349	BERRYS D
BOWEN, CHARLES	FRE	276	NEW MARK
BOWEN, CHARLES W.	CAL	001	1ST DIST
BOWEN, CORNELIUS	CAL	033	2ND DIST
BOWEN, CORNELIUS	BAL	168	2ND DIST
BOWEN, CORNELIUS	ANN	482	HOWARD D
BOWEN, CURYS	FRE	101	FREDERIC
BOWEN, DANIEL	CAL	028	2ND DIST
BOWEN, DANIEL	WAS	035	2ND SUBD
BOWEN, DAVID	BAL	347	1ST DIST
BOWEN, DORITHA	CAL	003	1ST DIST
BOWEN, E. J. H.	CAL	018	1ST DIST
BOWEN, EDWARD	BAL	389	13TH WAR
BOWEN, EDWARD	BAL	457	1ST DIST
BOWEN, EDWARD	BAL	078	10TH WAR
BOWEN, ELIAS	BAL	417	1ST DIST
BOWEN, ELIJAH	CAL	032	2ND DIST
BOWEN, ELIZA	BAL	212	17TH WAR
BOWEN, ELIZA	BAL	147	2ND DIST
BOWEN, ELIZA	BAL	344	7TH WARD
BOWEN, ELIZA	WOR	295	9TH E DI
BOWEN, ELIZABETH	CAL	032	2ND DIST
BOWEN, ELIZABETH	SOM	422	PRINCESS
BOWEN, ELLEN	BAL	387	13TH WAR
BOWEN, ELLEN	BAL	440	1ST DIST
BOWEN, ELLEN	BAL	093	5TH WARD
BOWEN, EMILY	BAL	100	5TH WARD
BOWEN, EMILY	BAL	028	15TH WAR
BOWEN, EMILY	BAL	131	11TH WAR
BOWEN, EPHRAIM	BAL	178	6TH WARD
BOWEN, FRANCES	BAL	008	EASTERN
BOWEN, FRANCIS	BAL	119	5TH WARD
BOWEN, FREDERICK	FRE	101	FREDERIC
BOWEN, G. W.	BAL	040	4TH WARD
BOWEN, GAMELIEB	CAL	010	1ST DIST
BOWEN, GEORGE	CAL	026	2ND DIST
BOWEN, GEORGE	BAL	229	2ND WARD
BOWEN, GEORGE	WOR	282	BERLIN 1
BOWEN, GEORGE C.	WOR	268	BERLIN 1
BOWEN, GEORGE W.	BAL	324	12TH WAR
BOWEN, GEORGE W.	CAL	006	1ST DIST
BOWEN, GEORGE Y.	CAL	005	1ST DIST
BOWEN, GILBERT S.	WOR	251	BERLIN 1
BOWEN, GRAFTON.	BAL	300	1ST DIST
BOWEN, GUSTAVUS	CAL	030	2ND DIST
BOWEN, HANDERSON	CAL	032	2ND DIST
BOWEN, HANNAH	BAL	067	10TH WAR
BOWEN, HARRIET	CAL	030	2ND DIST
BOWEN, HARRIET	MGM	367	BERRYS D
BOWEN, HENRIETTA	BAL	198	6TH WARD
BOWEN, HENRY	BAL	306	12TH WAR
BOWEN, HENSON	BAL	296	1ST DIST
BOWEN, HILLEARY	CAL	028	2ND DIST
BOWEN, HOLESWORTH	CAL	028	2ND DIST
BOWEN, ISAAC	CAL	027	2ND DIST
BOWEN, ISAAC	BAL	199	6TH WARD
BOWEN, IVEN	CHA	283	BOJANTOW
BOWEN, IWLLIAM	BAL	416	1ST DIST
BOWEN, JACBH	CAL	030	2ND DIST
BOWEN, JAEMS	WOR	250	1ST CENS
BOWEN, JAMES	WOR	264	BERLIN 1
BOWEN, JAMES	WOR	289	9TH E DI
BOWEN, JAMES	WOR	280	BERLIN 1
BOWEN, JAMES	MGM	317	CRACKLIN
BOWEN, JAMES	BAL	387	1ST DIST
BOWEN, JAMES	BAL	230	1ST DIST
BOWEN, JAMES	BAL	016	15TH WAR
BOWEN, JAMES	BAL	005	15TH WAR
BOWEN, JASPER Y.	CAL	001	1ST DIST
BOWEN, JESSE	BAL	338	7TH WARD
BOWEN, JOHN	BAL	246	1ST DIST
BOWEN, JOHN	BAL	011	2ND DIST
BOWEN, JOHN	ALL	243	CUMBERLA
BOWEN, JOHN	BAL	317	20TH WAR
BOWEN, JOHN	WOR	251	1ST CENS
BOWEN, JOHN A.	BAL	343	7TH WARD
BOWEN, JOHN T.	BAL	191	6TH WARD
BOWEN, JOHN W.	QUE	188	3RD E DI
BOWEN, JOSEPH	BAL	169	2ND DIST
BOWEN, JOSEPH	BAL	113	5TH WARD
BOWEN, JOSEPH	BAL	091	15TH WAR
BOWEN, JOSIAH	BAL	283	7TH WARD
BOWEN, JOSIAS	BAL	148	2ND DIST
BOWEN, JULIET A.	CAL	026	2ND DIST
BOWEN, KENDAL	WOR	258	1ST CENS
BOWEN, KENDAL	WOR	272	BERLIN 1
BOWEN, LEVI K.	BAL	018	2ND DIST

Name	County	Page	District
BOWEN, LEVI K.	BAL	111	5TH WARD
BOWEN, LOUISA	BAL	003	18TH WAR
BOWEN, MARGARET	ANN	472	HOWARD D
BOWEN, MARGARET D.	WOR	200	3RD E DI
BOWEN, MARGARET J.	CAL	024	2ND DIST
BOWEN, MARIA	WOR	306	2ND E DI
BOWEN, MARIAH	SOM	418	PRINCESS
BOWEN, MARTHA	WOR	263	BERLIN 1
BOWEN, MARY	CAL	031	2ND DIST
BOWEN, MARY	BAL	157	2ND DIST
BOWEN, MARY	BAL	149	5TH WARD
BOWEN, MARY	BAL	338	7TH WARD
BOWEN, MARY A.	BAL	149	5TH WARD
BOWEN, MARYLAND	CAL	029	2ND DIST
BOWEN, MATILDA	BAL	316	20TH WAR
BOWEN, MOSES	WOR	292	9TH E DI
BOWEN, MR-	BAL	038	15TH WAR
BOWEN, MRS. L.K.	BAL	112	5TH WARD
BOWEN, NATHANIEL C.	ANN	301	1ST DIST
BOWEN, NELLY	CAL	032	2ND DIST
BOWEN, OCTAVIUS W.	CAL	018	1ST DIST
BOWEN, OLIVER	WOR	316	2ND E DI
BOWEN, OSWALD	BAL	335	7TH WARD
BOWEN, PARKER	WOR	297	9TH E DI
BOWEN, PERE	CAL	031	2ND DIST
BOWEN, PERRY	BAL	189	17TH WAR
BOWEN, PETER	BAL	126	2ND DIST
BOWEN, PETER	WOR	292	9TH E DI
BOWEN, PHEBE	FRE	024	FREDERIC
BOWEN, PHILIP	BAL	158	2ND DIST
BOWEN, POLLY	MGM	326	CRACKLIN
BOWEN, POLLY	WOR	289	9TH E DI
BOWEN, REBECCA	CAL	001	1ST DIST
BOWEN, RICHARD	BAL	288	7TH WARD
BOWEN, ROANNA	CAL	028	2ND DIST
BOWEN, ROBERT	WOR	295	9TH E DI
BOWEN, ROBERT YU.	CAL	003	1ST DIST
BOWEN, SALLY	WOR	295	9TH E DI
BOWEN, SAMUEL	CAL	027	2ND DIST
BOWEN, SAMUEL	MGM	349	BERRYS D
BOWEN, SAMUEL A.	CAL	018	1ST DIST
BOWEN, SAMUEL C.	CAL	026	2ND DIST
BOWEN, SAMUEL W.	BAL	297	7TH WARD
BOWEN, SARAH	BAL	260	2ND WARD
BOWEN, SARAH	BAL	255	1ST DIST
BOWEN, SARAH	BAL	069	1ST WARD
BOWEN, SARAH	BAL	061	10TH WAR
BOWEN, SARAH	BAL	154	5TH WARD
BOWEN, SARAH	CAL	015	1ST DIST
BOWEN, SARAH	CAL	016	1ST DIST
BOWEN, SARAH	BAL	276	17TH WAR
BOWEN, SARAH	FRE	257	NEW MARK
BOWEN, SARAH A.	BAL	286	7TH WARD
BOWEN, SELBY	WOR	255	1ST CENS
BOWEN, SOLOMON	BAL	172	2ND DIST
BOWEN, SOPHIA-BLACK	FRE	190	5TH E DI
BOWEN, SYDNEY	BAL	200	6TH WARD
BOWEN, THADEUS	CAL	001	1ST DIST
BOWEN, THOAMS	BAL	309	20TH WAR
BOWEN, THOMAS	BAL	168	19TH WAR
BOWEN, THOMAS	BAL	169	2ND DIST
BOWEN, THOMAS	BAL	307	3RD WARD
BOWEN, WALTER J.	BAL	052	15TH WAR
BOWEN, WESLEY W.	CAL	031	2ND DIST
BOWEN, WILKS	BAL	287	1ST DIST
BOWEN, WILLIAM	BAL	172	2ND DIST
BOWEN, WILLIAM	BAL	338	7TH WARD
BOWEN, WILLIAM	BAL	388	1ST DIST
BOWEN, WILLIAM	BAL	453	1ST DIST
BOWEN, WILLIAM	BAL	200	2ND WARD
BOWEN, WILLIAM	BAL	011	2ND DIST
BOWEN, WILLIAM	ALL	089	5TH E.D.
BOWEN, WILLIAM	CAL	028	2ND DIST
BOWEN, WILLIAM	MGM	369	BERRYS D
BOWEN, WILLIAM	WOR	272	BERLIN 1
BOWEN, WILLIAM J.	CAL	025	2ND DIST
BOWEN, ZACHARIAH	WOR	290	9TH E DI
BOWEN, ZADOK W.	WOR	251	1ST CENS
BOWEN.JULIA	BAL	052	2ND DIST
BOWENS, CHARLES-MULATTO	FRE	016	FREDERIC
BOWENS, FRANCIS-BLACK	FRE	038	FREDERIC
BOWENS, FRANK	ALL	217	CUMBERLA
BOWENS, NATHANIEL	BAL	239	1-7TH WAR
BOWER, ADAM	FRE	170	5TH E DI
BOWER, ADAM	FRE	098	FREDERIC
BOWER, ADAM	BAL	122	18TH WAR
BOWER, ADAM	FRE	150	10TH E D
BOWER, ADAM	BAL	034	18TH WAR
BOWER, ALLICE	BAL	283	2ND WARD
BOWER, ANDREW	BAL	313	7TH WARD
BOWER, AQUILA	CAR	374	9TH DIST
BOWER, BARBARA	BAL	156	19TH WAR
BOWER, CASPER	BAL	207	2ND WARD
BOWER, CATHARINE	BAL	237	2ND WARD
BOWER, CATHARINE	BAL	210	19TH WAR
BOWER, CATHERINE	BAL	460	8TH WARD
BOWER, CATHERINE	ALL	241	CUMBERLA
BOWER, CHARLES H.	WOR	297	9TH E DI
BOWER, CHRISTINE	BAL	307	20TH WAR
BOWER, CHRISTOPHER	BAL	372	8TH WARD
BOWER, CONRAD	CAR	374	9TH DIST
BOWER, CONRAD	BAL	079	18TH WAR
BOWER, DAVID	WAS	259	1ST DIST
BOWER, ELIZA	WOR	257	1ST CENS
BOWER, ELIZABETH	WAS	173	FUNKSTOW
BOWER, ELIZABETH	BAL	428	8TH WARD
BOWER, ELIZABETH	BAL	165	2ND DIST
BOWER, ELIZABETH	BAL	124	16TH WAR
BOWER, EMILY	BAL	286	12TH WAR
BOWER, ESME L.	HAR	145	3RD DIST
BOWER, FRANCIS	BAL	411	14TH WAR
BOWER, FRANK	BAL	235	2ND WARD
BOWER, GEORGE	WAS	171	FUNKSTOW
BOWER, HENRY	BAL	140	5TH WARD
BOWER, HENRY	FRE	151	10TH E D
BOWER, HENRY	FRE	373	CATOCTIN
BOWER, ISAAC	WOR	298	9TH E DI
BOWER, JACOB	BAL	253	20TH WAR
BOWER, JOHN	BAL	241	20TH WAR
BOWER, JOHN	HAR	185	3RD DIST
BOWER, JOHN	BAL	307	20TH WAR
BOWER, JOHN	CAR	285	7TH DIST
BOWER, JOHN	WOR	287	BERLIN 1
BOWER, JOHN	BAL	253	6TH WARD
BOWER, JOHN	BAL	276	1ST DIST
BOWER, JOHN	BAL	051	1ST WARD
BOWER, JOHN	CAL	256	1ST DIST
BOWER, JOSHUA	WOR	297	9TH E DI
BOWER, LAWRENCE W.	FRE	170	5TH E DI
BOWER, LEWILLA	BAL	114	11TH WAR
BOWER, LITTLETON	WOR	271	BERLIN 1
BOWER, MARTHA	WOR	273	BERLIN 1
BOWER, MARY	WOR	257	1ST CENS
BOWER, MARY	WOR	258	1ST CENS
BOWER, MARY	BAL	072	4TH WARD
BOWER, MARY A.	WOR	289	9TH E DI
BOWER, MICHAEL	BAL	006	15TH WAR
BOWER, MICHAEL	BAL	006	15TH WAR
BOWER, NICHOLAS	BAL	280	7TH WARD
BOWER, RICHARD	WOR	257	1ST CENS
BOWER, RICHARD W.	PRI	045	VANSVILL
BOWER, ROBERT	WOR	270	BERLIN 1
BOWER, ROBERT	HAR	058	1ST DIST
BOWER, ROSE E.	WOR	297	9TH E DI
BOWER, RUFUS	BAL	273	12TH WAR
BOWER, SALLY	BAL	340	13TH WAR
BOWER, SAMUEL C.	CAR	241	TANEYTOW
BOWER, SY	BAL	257	1ST DIST
BOWER, TENANT	WOR	256	1ST CENS
BOWER, WILILAM	QUE	216	3RD E DI
BOWER, WILLIAM	WAS	016	2ND SUBD
BOWER, WILLIAM	BAL	283	2ND WARD
BOWER, WILLIAM	BAL	049	18TH WAR
BOWER, WILLIAM G.	CAR	324	1ST DIST
BOWER, ZACHEUS	WOR	263	BERLIN 1
BOWERMAN, HENRY	BAL	298	20TH WAR
BOWERMAN, MARGARET H.	BAL	111	15TH WAR
BOWERN, MARGS	BAL	146	11TH WAR
BOWERRSOX, EPHRAIM	CAR	391	2ND DIST
BOWERS, ABNER	BAL	228	1ST DIST
BOWERS, ADAM	CAR	244	3RD DIST
BOWERS, ADAM	FRE	438	8TH E DI
BOWERS, BARBARA	WAS	251	1ST DIST
BOWERS, BENJAMIN	KEN	284	3RD DIST
BOWERS, CATHARINE	WAS	235	1ST DIST
BOWERS, CATHARINE	WAS	287	1ST DIST
BOWERS, CATHARINE	FRE	338	MIDDLETO
BOWERS, CHARLES S.	WOR	292	9TH E DI
BOWERS, CLARA	BAL	156	19TH WAR
BOWERS, DANIEL	FRE	302	WOODSBOR
BOWERS, DANIEL	FRE	101	FREDERIC
BOWERS, DANIEL P.	TAL	043	EASTON D
BOWERS, DANIEL W.	FRE	304	WOODSBOR
BOWERS, DAVID	FRE	156	10TH E D
BOWERS, DAVID	WAS	228	1ST DIST
BOWERS, DAVID	WAS	194	1ST DIST
BOWERS, EDWARD	WOR	274	BERLIN 1
BOWERS, ELEXIUS	CAR	306	1ST DIST
BOWERS, ELIAS	BAL	280	12TH WAR
BOWERS, ELIZA J.	CAR	286	7TH DIST
BOWERS, ELIZABETH	BAL	091	15TH WAR
BOWERS, ELIZABETH	BAL	194	6TH WARD
BOWERS, ELLEN	BAL	193	6TH WARD
BOWERS, EMELINE	WAS	232	1ST DIST
BOWERS, EMELY	FRE	338	MIDDLETO
BOWERS, EMILY	BAL	051	18TH WAR
BOWERS, EPHRAIM	CAR	384	2ND DIST
BOWERS, FRANCES	WOR	290	9TH E DI
BOWERS, FRANCES	WAS	300	1ST DIST
BOWERS, FRANCIS	BAL	295	17TH WAR
BOWERS, FREDERICK	WAS	248	SMITHSBU
BOWERS, GEORGE	WAS	251	1ST DIST
BOWERS, GEORGE	WAS	064	2ND SUBD
BOWERS, GEORGE	WAS	063	2ND SUBD
BOWERS, GEORGE	CAR	261	3RD DIST
BOWERS, GEORGE	BAL	311	7TH WARD
BOWERS, GEORGE E.	BAL	173	16TH WAR
BOWERS, GEORGE W.	BAL	387	8TH WARD
BOWERS, H.H.	BAL	114	1ST WARD
BOWERS, HANDY	WOR	293	9TH E DI
BOWERS, HANNAH	FRE	172	5TH E DI
BOWERS, HENRIETTA	BAL	421	14TH WAR
BOWERS, HENRY	CAR	217	5TH DIST
BOWERS, HENRY	FRE	424	8TH E DI
BOWERS, HENRY	BAL	390	8TH WARD
BOWERS, HENRY	BAL	063	2ND DIST
BOWERS, HENRY F.	BAL	311	1ST DIST
BOWERS, HEZEKIAH-BLACK	FRE	038	FREDERIC
BOWERS, ISAAC	BAL	142	1ST WARD
BOWERS, ISACK	TAL	001	EASTON D
BOWERS, JACOB	WAS	041	2ND SUBD
BOWERS, JACOB	WAS	261	1ST DIST
BOWERS, JACOB	WAS	251	1ST DIST
BOWERS, JACOB	WAS	180	BOONSBOR
BOWERS, JACOB	WAS	168	FUNKSTOW
BOWERS, JACOB	KEN	235	2ND DIST
BOWERS, JACOB C.C.	WAS	230	1ST DIST
BOWERS, JACOB H.	WAS	245	SMITHSBU
BOWERS, JAMES	PRI	107	PISCATAW
BOWERS, JAMES	FRE	159	EMMITTSB
BOWERS, JAMES	BAL	289	20TH WAR
BOWERS, JAMES	BAL	396	14TH WAR
BOWERS, JAMES	FRE	268	NEW MARK
BOWERS, JAMES	BAL	136	2ND DIST
BOWERS, JAMES L.	KEN	245	2ND DIST
BOWERS, JANE	WAS	041	2ND SUBD
BOWERS, JANE	WAS	013	WILLIAMS
BOWERS, JOB	WAS	124	HAGERSTO
BOWERS, JOHN	WAS	240	CAVETOWN
BOWERS, JOHN	WAS	224	1ST DIST
BOWERS, JOHN	WAS	062	2ND SUBD
BOWERS, JOHN	WAS	073	2ND SUBD
BOWERS, JOHN	QUE	246	5TH E DI
BOWERS, JOHN	CEC	149	PORT DUP
BOWERS, JOHN	CAR	300	1ST DIST
BOWERS, JOHN	ALL	236	CUMBERLA
BOWERS, JOHN	BAL	090	1ST WARD
BOWERS, JOHN C.	WAS	161	HAGERSTO
BOWERS, JOHN C.	WAS	247	SMITHSBU
BOWERS, JOHN F.	BAL	030	18TH WAR
BOWERS, JOHN H.	CAR	285	7TH DIST
BOWERS, JOHN J.	BAL	156	19TH WAR
BOWERS, JOHN M.	CAR	376	9TH DIST
BOWERS, JONATHAN	FRE	135	CREAGERS
BOWERS, JOSEPH	CAR	384	2ND DIST
BOWERS, JOSEPH	BAL	052	18TH WAR
BOWERS, JOSEPH	CAR	240	TANEYTOW
BOWERS, JOSEPH	WAS	150	2ND DIST
BOWERS, JOSEPH	WAS	065	2ND SUBD
BOWERS, JOSEPH	WAS	045	2ND SUBD
BOWERS, JOSEPH	BAL	279	2ND WARD
BOWERS, LOUISA	BAL	316	12TH WAR
BOWERS, LUCY	BAL	286	12TH WAR
BOWERS, MALINDA	WAS	173	FUNKSTOW
BOWERS, MARGARET	WAS	240	CAVETOWN
BOWERS, MARGARET	BAL	251	6TH WARD
BOWERS, MARGARET	BAL	259	6TH WARD
BOWERS, MARIA L.	BAL	296	3RD WARD
BOWERS, MARY	BAL	284	7TH WARD
BOWERS, MARY	FRE	047	FREDERIC
BOWERS, MARY A.	KEN	246	2ND DIST
BOWERS, MARY ANN	FRE	134	CREAGERS
BOWERS, MARY E.	WAS	144	HAGERSTO
BOWERS, MOSES	ALL	200	CUMBERLA
BOWERS, MRS.	BAL	145	5TH WARD
BOWERS, NANCY	WAS	055	2ND SUBD
BOWERS, NATHAN	BAL	132	18TH WAR
BOWERS, PERRY	BAL	131	2ND DIST
BOWERS, PETER	CAR	306	1ST DIST
BOWERS, PETER	BAL	064	18TH WAR
BOWERS, RACHAEL-BLACK	FRE	048	FREDERIC
BOWERS, REBECA	CAR	202	4TH DIST
BOWERS, REBECCA	CAR	374	9TH DIST
BOWERS, ROBERT F.	WOR	281	BERLIN 1
BOWERS, ROSA	KEN	246	2ND DIST
BOWERS, ROSE	BAL	236	12TH WAR
BOWERS, SAMUEL	CAR	384	2ND DIST
BOWERS, SAMUEL	CAR	253	3RD DIST
BOWERS, SAMUEL	CAR	299	1ST DIST
BOWERS, SAMUEL	WAS	107	2ND DIST
BOWERS, SAMUEL	WAS	169	FUNKSTOW
BOWERS, SAMUEL	WAS	255	1ST DIST
BOWERS, SAMUEL-BLACK	FRE	195	5TH E DI
BOWERS, SARAH	WAS	001	WILLIAMS
BOWERS, SEBASTIAN	CAR	375	9TH DIST
BOWERS, STEPHEN	CAR	383	2ND DIST
BOWERS, STEPHEN JR.	CAR	387	2ND DIST
BOWERS, SYMON	BAL	327	3RD WARD
BOWERS, THOMAS	BAL	145	5TH WARD
BOWERS, WILLIAM	BAL	298	3RD WARD
BOWERS, WILLIAM	BAL	350	1ST DIST
BOWERS, WILLIAM	BAL	402	8TH WARD
BOWERS, WILLIAM	BAL	301	20TH WAR
BOWERS, WILLIAM	WAS	040	2ND SUBD
BOWERS, WILLIAM	WOR	256	1ST CENS
BOWERS, WILLIAM	WAS	243	CAVETOWN
BOWERS, WILLIAM E.	BAL	218	6TH WARD
BOWERS, WILLIAM J.	BAL	155	11TH WAR
BOWERS,RACHAEL	FRE	196	5TH E DI
BOWERSET, AUSTIN	HAR	200	3RD DIST
BOWERSIT, M.	BAL	160	19TH WAR
BOWERSMITH, PHILIP	BAL	274	7TH WARD
BOWERSOCK, CLARA	BAL	460	8TH WARD
BOWERSOCKS, JOHN	BAL	252	1ST DIST
BOWERSOCKS, LORA V.	BAL	253	1ST DIST
BOWERSON, GEORGE	FRE	321	MIDDLETO
BOWERSON, GEORGE	FRE	321	MIDDLETO
BOWERSOX, ANNA	CAR	391	2ND DIST
BOWERSOX, AUGUSTUS	BAL	309	2CTH WAR
BOWERSOX, AUGUSTUS	BAL	310	20TH WAR
BOWERSOX, BENAJMIN	CAR	393	2ND DIST
BOWERSOX, DANIEL	CAR	246	3RD DIST
BOWERSOX, GEORGE A. W.	CAR	266	WESTMINS
BOWERSOX, HENRY	FRE	108	CREAGERS
BOWERSOX, JERAMIAH	CAR	260	3RD DIST
BOWERSOX, LEVI	FRE	345	MIDDLETO
BOWERSOX, MARGARET A.	CAR	391	2ND DIST
BOWERSOX, VALENTEINE	FRE	106	CREAGERS
BOWES, JOHN L.	KEN	251	2ND DIST
BOWHAN, GEORGE	FRE	448	8TH E DI
BOWHAN, SUSANN	FRE	452	8TH E DI
BOWHANAN, LEVIN-BLACK	WOR	342	1ST E DI
BOWIE, A.M.	PRI	122	PISCATAW
BOWIE, A.M.	PRI	057	AQUASCO
BOWIE, ADA	PRI	085	QUEEN AN
BOWIE, ALICE	MGM	340	CLARKSBU
BOWIE, ALLEN P.	PRI	072	MARLBROU
BOWIE, ALONZO	PRI	073	MARLBROU
BOWIE, ANN	BAL	155	11TH WAR
BOWIE, ANTHONY	ANN	318	2ND DIST
BOWIE, B.	BAL	066	10TH WAR
BOWIE, CANTLER	FRE	379	PETERSVI
BOWIE, CAROLINE	BAL	155	11TH WAR
BOWIE, CAROLINE	ANN	274	ANNAPOLI
BOWIE, CATHARINE	PRI	067	NOTTINGH
BOWIE, CHARLES	PRI	005	BLADENSB
BOWIE, CHARLOTTE	MGM	319	CRACKLIN
BOWIE, DORATHY	CHA	242	HILLTOP
BOWIE, ELIZA	CAL	050	3RD DIST
BOWIE, ELIZABETH	CHA	234	HILLTOP
BOWIE, ELIZABETH	ANN	489	HOWARD D
BOWIE, F. F.	BAL	332	1ST DIST
BOWIE, FIELDER	PRI	063	NOTTINGH
BOWIE, FRANCIS	PRI	041	VANSVILL
BOWIE, FRANCIS	CHA	244	HILLTOP
BOWIE, FRANCIS M.	PRI	073	MARLBROU
BOWIE, GEORGE W.	PRI	078	MARLBROU
BOWIE, GEORGE W.	BAL	341	3RD WARD
BOWIE, HAGAR-MULATTO	FRE	440	8TH E DI
BOWIE, HANAH	BAL	270	7TH WARD
BOWIE, HESTER A.	BAL	121	16TH WAR
BOWIE, ISAAC	PRI	085	QUEEN AN
BOWIE, J.W.L.	PRI	057	AQUASCO
BOWIE, JAMES	BAL	340	3RD WARD
BOWIE, JAMES-BLACK	FRE	416	8TH E DI
BOWIE, JESSE-BLACK	FRE	433	8TH E DI
BOWIE, JOHN	CHA	244	HILLTOP
BOWIE, JOHN	BAL	121	16TH WAR
BOWIE, JOHN	BAL	102	15TH WAR
BOWIE, JOHN	PRI	073	MARLBROU
BOWIE, JOHN E.	CHA	234	HILLTOP
BOWIE, JOHN N.	PRI	007	BLADENSB
BOWIE, JOHN T.	BAL	040	15TH WAR
BOWIE, JOSEPH	CHA	246	HILLTOP
BOWIE, LEONARD O.	BAL	102	10TH WAR
BOWIE, LEVI	WAS	093	2ND SUBD
BOWIE, MARGARET	BAL	087	15TH WAR
BOWIE, MARGARET	MGM	316	CRACKLIN
BOWIE, MARIA	CHA	235	HILLTOP
BOWIE, MARIE	BAL	389	13TH WAR
BOWIE, MARTHA J.	BAL	049	15TH WAR
BOWIE, MARY	ANN	278	ANNAPOLI
BOWIE, MARY A.	PRI	079	MARLBROU
BOWIE, MRS.	ANN	265	ANNAPOLI
BOWIE, ODEN	PRI	083	QUEEN AN
BOWIE, OSWELL	CHA	247	HILLTOP
BOWIE, PHILBERT	CHA	237	HILLTOP
BOWIE, PHLENVY	CHA	234	HILLTOP
BOWIE, R. C.	BAL	101	10TH WAR
BOWIE, RACHEL	ANN	499	HOWARD D
BOWIE, RACHEL	MGM	339	CLARKSBU
BOWIE, RICHARD	FRE	411	8TH E DI
BOWIE, RICHARD	PRI	090	MARLBROU
BOWIE, RICHARD J.	MGM	374	ROCKERLE
BOWIE, ROBERT	PRI	064	NOTTINGH
BOWIE, RUBEN L.	BAL	377	8TH WARD
BOWIE, RUFUS A.	MGM	413	MEDLEY 3
BOWIE, SARAH H.	MGM	413	MEDLEY 3
BOWIE, SARAH M.	PRI	076	MARLBROU
BOWIE, SARAH M.L.	PRI	090	MARLBROU

Name	County	Page	District
BOWIE, SOLOMON	BAL	250	17TH WAR
BOWIE, THOMAS	CHA	278	BOJANTOW
BOWIE, THOMAS	BAL	159	16TH WAR
BOWIE, THOMAS F.	PRI	068	NOTTINGH
BOWIE, THOMAS F.	PRI	121	PISCATAW
BOWIE, THOMAS J.	MGM	315	CRACKLIN
BOWIE, WALTER W.W.	PRI	085	QUEEN AN
BOWIE, WILLAIM D.	PRI	085	QUEEN AN
BOWIE, WILLIAM	ANN	317	1ST DIST
BOWIE, WILLIAM	ANN	323	2ND DIST
BOWIE, WILLIAM B.	PRI	072	MARLBROU
BOWIE, WILLIAM D.	PRI	085	QUEEN AN
BOWIE, WILLIAM M.	PRI	073	MARLBROU
BOWIE, WILLIAM V.	MGM	375	ROCKERLE
BOWIE, ZACHARIAH	CHA	264	MIDDLETO
BOWIER, AMELIA	WOR	189	7TH E DI
BOWIER, SAMUEL-BLACK	CAR	080	NO TWP L
BOWIN, MARY	PRI	049	AQUASCO
BOWIN, MARY E.	CHA	283	BOJANTOW
BOWIN, TOM	PRI	051	AQUASCO
BOWING, JANE*	BAL	233	12TH WAR
BOWING, THOMAS	BAL	201	2ND WARD
BOWINGS, ELIZABETH-BLACK	FRE	023	FREDERIC
BOWINGS, SAMUEL*	BAL	103	10TH WAR
BOWITZ, GEORGE	BAL	035	9TH WARD
BOWLAN, MALINDA	BAL	397	8TH WARD
BOWLAN, MARY	BAL	065	18TH WAR
BOWLAN, PATRICK	BAL	419	1ST DIST
BOWLAND, CATHARINE	BAL	004	EASTERN
BOWLAND, JOHN	BAL	001	15TH WAR
BOWLAND, MICHAEL	BAL	109	18TH WAR
BOWLEES, SOPHIA	FRE	314	MIDDLETO
BOWLER, KITTY	BAL	220	19TH WAR
BOWLERS, BENS	WAS	227	1ST DIST
BOWLES, DOMENICK T.	ST	323	4TH E DI
BOWLES, ISAAC	FRE	314	MIDDLETO
BOWLES, ISLAND	ST	342	5TH E DI
BOWLES, JOHN H.	WAS	105	2ND DIST
BOWLES, JOHN J.	WAS	159	2ND DIST
BOWLES, JOHN S.	WAS	122	2ND DIST
BOWLES, MARTHA	WAS	161	2ND DIST
BOWLES, SAMUEL	FRE	320	MIDDLETO
BOWLES, SUSAN	ST	321	4TH E DI
BOWLES, WASHINGTON	ST	341	5TH E DI
BOWLES, WILLIAM S.	ST	323	4TH E DI
BOWLES,ELZIABETH	ST	327	4TH E DI
BOWLEY, BENJAMIN	BAL	206	17TH WAR
BOWLEY, CATHARINE	BAL	226	19TH WAR
BOWLEY, DANIEL	BAL	341	3RD WARD
BOWLEY, DESDEMONIA	BAL	341	3RD WARD
BOWLEY, ELIZABETH	BAL	424	1ST DIST
BOWLEY, GABLE	BAL	086	15TH WAR
BOWLEY, HENRY	BAL	084	15TH WAR
BOWLEY, JANE	BAL	080	4TH WARD
BOWLEY, RICHARD	BAL	343	3RD WARD
BOWLEY, SAMUEL H.	BAL	082	4TH WARD
BOWLEY, WILLIAM L.	BAL	353	7TH WARD
BOWLIN, CHAMBILIN*	DOR	406	1ST DIST
BOWLIN, JOHN	BAL	135	2ND DIST
BOWLIN, JOHN	BAL	015	1ST WARD
BOWLIN, LEVIN P.	SOM	412	DUBLIN D
BOWLING, ANN M.	CHA	252	BOJANTOW
BOWLING, CHARLES	ST	329	4TH E DI
BOWLING, D.	BAL	282	2ND WARD
BOWLING, CANIEL	BAL	123	1ST WARD
BOWLING, ECWARD	BAL	364	8TH WARD
BOWLING, EMILY	CHA	291	MIDDLETO
BOWLING, HENRY	CHA	283	BOJANTOW
BOWLING, HENRY	CHA	291	MIDDLETO
BOWLING, J.H.	PRI	117	PISCATAW
BOWLING, JANE V.	CHA	241	HILLTOP
BOWLING, JOHN D. COL.	PRI	046	AQUASCO
BOWLING, JOHN N.	SOM	427	PRINCESS
BOWLING, JOHN T.	CHA	254	MIDDLETO
BOWLING, MARY	PRI	051	AQUASCO
BOWLING, MARY A.	PRI	092	MARLBROU
BOWLING, RICHARD Q.	PRI	088	SPALDING
BOWLING, ROBERT	ANN	420	HOWARD D
BOWLING, SARA	CHA	293	BOJANTOW
BOWLING, SEPARAH	BAL	009	1ST WARD
BOWLING, SPENCER	BAL	118	11TH WAR
BOWLING, SYDNEY	SOM	428	PRINCESS
BOWLING, THOMAS	BAL	413	3RD WARD
BOWLING, THOMAS W.	CHA	252	BOJANTOW
BOWLING, WILLIAM F.	CHA	280	BOJANTOW
BOWLS, E.A.-MULATTO	BAL	214	2ND WARD
BOWLUS, ADAM	FRE	353	MIDDLETO
BOWLUS, ANN R.	FRE	344	MIDDLETO
BOWLUS, ASA	FRE	313	MIDDLETO
BOWLUS, BARBARA	FRE	311	MIDDLETO
BOWLUS, CORA G.	FRE	344	MIDDLETO
BOWLUS, JOSEPH	FRE	351	MIDDLETO
BOWLUS, SAMUEL H.	FRE	340	MIDDLETO
BOWLUS, STEVEN	FRE	335	MIDDLETO
BOWLUS, SUSAN	FRE	318	MIDDLETO
BOWLY, JANE	BAL	020	2ND DIST
BOWLY, RICHARD	DOR	380	1ST DIST
BOWLY, W.H.	BAL	004	EASTERN
BOWMAN, .	BAL	154	5TH WARD
BOWMAN, ADEN	MGM	344	CLARKSBU
BOWMAN, ALCINDA	MGM	336	CRACKLIN
BOWMAN, ALLAN	MGM	354	BERRYS D
BOWMAN, ALLEN	FRE	244	NEW MARK
BOWMAN, ANDREW	BAL	012	1ST WARD
BOWMAN, ANN	BAL	359	3RD WARD
BOWMAN, ANN	WAS	162	HAGERSTO
BOWMAN, BARBARY	WAS	163	HAGERSTO
BOWMAN, BETSEY	MGM	379	ROCKERLE
BOWMAN, BILLY	BAL	298	12TH WAR
BOWMAN, CATHARINE	BAL	207	6TH DIST
BOWMAN, CATHARINE	WAS	208	1ST DIST
BOWMAN, CHALRES	WAS	188	1ST DIST
BOWMAN, CHARLES	HAR	143	2ND DIST
BOWMAN, CHRISTIAN	BAL	232	1ST DIST
BOWMAN, CLEM	BAL	264	1ST DIST
BOWMAN, DANIEL	ALL	039	2ND E.D.
BOWMAN, DARIUS	PRI	007	BLADENSB
BOWMAN, CAVID	WAS	240	CAVETOWN
BOWMAN, DOROTHY	MGM	433	CLARKSTR
BOWMAN, EDWARD	BAL	450	14TH WAR
BOWMAN, EDWARD	BAL	173	2ND DIST
BOWMAN, ELEANOR	CHA	267	BOJANTOW
BOWMAN, ELIAS	FRE	128	CREAGERS
BOWMAN, ELIAS	WAS	220	1ST DIST
BOWMAN, ELIZABETH	WAS	168	FUNKSTOW
BOWMAN, ELIZABETH	CAR	378	2ND DIST
BOWMAN, ELLEN	FRE	003	FREDERIC
BOWMAN, EMANUEL	WAS	208	1ST DIST
BOWMAN, EVAN	MGM	317	CRACKLIN
BOWMAN, EVAN	MGM	344	CLARKSBU
BOWMAN, FREDERICK	FRE	025	FREDERIC
BOWMAN, FREDERICK	MGM	418	MEDLEY 3
BOWMAN, FREDERICK	CEC	170	6TH E DI
BOWMAN, GARRETT	BAL	286	17TH WAR
BOWMAN, GEORGE	CAR	246	3RD DIST
BOWMAN, GEORGE	FRE	067	FREDERIC
BOWMAN, GEORGE	CAR	207	4TH DIST
BOWMAN, GEORGE	WAS	247	SMITHSBU
BOWMAN, GEORGE	WAS	239	CAVETOWN
BOWMAN, GEORGE	WAS	154	HAGERSTO
BOWMAN, GEORGE	ALL	114	5TH E.D.
BOWMAN, GEORGE R.	WAS	149	HAGERSTO
BOWMAN, GEORGE W.	MGM	334	CRACKLIN
BOWMAN, GEORGIA*	BAL	318	3RD WARD
BOWMAN, HENRY	BAL	002	9TH WARD
BOWMAN, HENRY	WAS	118	2ND DIST
BOWMAN, HENRY	WAS	214	1ST DIST
BOWMAN, ISAAC	WAS	192	1ST DIST
BOWMAN, J.P.	WAS	021	2ND SUBD
BOWMAN, JACOB	WAS	173	FUNKSTOW
BOWMAN, JACOB	WAS	239	CAVETOWN
BOWMAN, JACOB	WAS	255	1ST DIST
BOWMAN, JACOB	CAR	341	6TH DIST
BOWMAN, JACOB	CAR	344	6TH DIST
BOWMAN, JACOB-MULATTO	FRE	429	8TH E DI
BOWMAN, JANE-BLACK	FRE	025	FREDERIC
BOWMAN, JEROME	CAR	305	1ST DIST
BOWMAN, JOHN	CAR	199	4TH DIST
BOWMAN, JOHN	CAR	345	6TH DIST
BOWMAN, JOHN	BAL	309	20TH WAR
BOWMAN, JOHN	BAL	458	14TH WAR
BOWMAN, JOHN	FRE	205	BUCKEYST
BOWMAN, JOHN	WAS	219	1ST DIST
BOWMAN, JOHN	WAS	219	1ST DIST
BOWMAN, JOHN	BAL	254	1ST DIST
BOWMAN, JOHN D.	CAR	378	2ND DIST
BOWMAN, JOHN D.	BAL	008	18TH WAR
BOWMAN, JOHN H.	KEN	228	2ND DIST
BOWMAN, JOHN W.	CHA	274	ALLENS F
BOWMAN, JOSEPH S.	CHA	293	BOJANTOW
BOWMAN, LUCY	BAL	114	15TH WAR
BOWMAN, MARGARET	WAS	098	2ND DIST
BOWMAN, MARY	WAS	194	1ST DIST
BOWMAN, MAY D.	KEN	286	3RD DIST
BOWMAN, MICHAEL	BAL	377	1ST DIST
BOWMAN, NACE-BLACK	FRE	387	PETERSVI
BOWMAN, NELIN	ANN	492	HOWARD D
BOWMAN, PERRY	MGM	335	CRACKLIN
BOWMAN, PETER	ALL	035	2ND E.D.
BOWMAN, PETER	WAS	256	1ST DIST
BOWMAN, PETER B.	WAS	256	1ST DIST
BOWMAN, PHILIP H.	BAL	352	3RD WARD
BOWMAN, PRISCILLA	CEC	013	ELKTON 3
BOWMAN, RAPHAEL	CHA	275	ALLENS F
BOWMAN, REBECCA	CHA	268	BOJANTOW
BOWMAN, SAMUEL	CEC	123	3RD E DI
BOWMAN, SAMUEL	BAL	011	1ST WARD
BOWMAN, SAMUEL	WAS	213	1ST DIST
BOWMAN, SAMUEL	WAS	225	1ST DIST
BOWMAN, SARAH	BAL	090	15TH WAR
BOWMAN, THOMAS	CEC	018	ELKTON 3
BOWMAN, THOMAS D.	CHA	291	MIDDLETO
BOWMAN, VOLENTINE	HAR	072	1ST DIST
BOWMAN, WILLIAM	FRE	155	10TH E D
BOWMAN, WILLIAM	CAR	247	3RD DIST
BOWMAN, WILLIAM C.	MGM	334	CRACKLIN
BOWMAN, WILLIAM H.	MGM	344	CLARKSBU
BOWMAN, WILLIAM H.	WAS	168	FUNKSTOW
BOWMAN, WILLIAM S.	HAR	120	2ND DIST
BOWMASTER, EASTER	WAS	193	1ST DIST
BOWMONT, JOHN *	BAL	273	20TH WAR
BOWN, ELIZABETH	HAR	184	3RD DIST
BOWN, JOSEPH	BAL	018	18TH WAR
BOWNE, CHARLES	BAL	167	1ST WARD
BOWNE, RANEY	MGM	379	ROCKERLE
BOWNES, VACHEL	QUE	208	3RD E DI
BOWNET, PETER	BAL	253	1ST DIST
BOWNLY, ANN	BAL	250	17TH WAR
BOWNSAN, MINA	BAL	263	1ST DIST
BOWRAKS, HENRY	HAR	197	3RD DIST
BOWRKE, FREDERICK *	ALL	129	4TH E.D.
BOWS, JOHN B.	ST	277	3RD E DI
BOWSEN, MARY	BAL	124	11TH WAR
BOWSER, ADAM	WAS	225	1ST DIST
BOWSER, ADRE S.	CAR	342	6TH DIST
BOWSER, ALFRED	BAL	425	8TH WARD
BOWSER, BARBARA	CAR	344	6TH DIST
BOWSER, BOLLEY	BAL	194	11TH WAR
BOWSER, DENNIS	PRI	083	QUEEN AN
BOWSER, DOLLY	QUE	250	5TH E DI
BOWSER, EDWARD	PRI	085	QUEEN AN
BOWSER, GABRIEL	ALL	010	3RD E.D.
BOWSER, GEORGE	CAR	344	6TH DIST
BOWSER, GEORGE H.	HAR	175	3RD DIST
BOWSER, HANNAH	BAL	314	3RD WARD
BOWSER, HARRIET	CAR	337	6TH DIST
BOWSER, HENRY	ALL	020	2ND E.D.
BOWSER, HENRY	WAS	174	FUNKSTOW
BOWSER, HENRY	TAL	012	EASTON D
BOWSER, ISAIAH	HAR	002	1ST DIST
BOWSER, JACOB	ALL	026	2ND E.D.
BOWSER, JAMES	BAL	152	16TH WAR
BOWSER, JAMES	BAL	335	13TH WAR
BOWSER, JAMES-BLACK	BAL	221	2ND WARD
BOWSER, JANE	BAL	335	3RD WARD
BOWSER, JOHN	BAL	230	17TH WAR
BOWSER, JONOTHAN	WAS	281	LEITERSB
BOWSER, JOSEP	CAR	357	6TH DIST
BOWSER, JOSEPH	BAL	271	7TH WARD
BOWSER, LYDIA	BAL	366	13TH WAR
BOWSER, MARGARET	BAL	168	6TH WARD
BOWSER, MARTHA	BAL	064	10TH WAR
BOWSER, MARY	PRI	081	QUEEN AN
BOWSER, MILLY	PRI	083	QUEEN AN
BOWSER, MOSES	TAL	069	EASTON T
BOWSER, NATHAN	PRI	083	QUEEN AN
BOWSER, RACHEL-MULATTO	BAL	223	2ND WARD
BOWSER, RICHARD	CEC	060	1ST E DI
BOWSER, ROBERT	KEN	239	2ND DIST
BOWSER, SARAH S.	ALL	021	2ND E.D.
BOWSER, WASHINGTON	BAL	403	3RD WARD
BOWSER, WASHINGTCN	BAL	020	1ST WARD
BOWSER, WASHINGTON	PRI	084	QUEEN AN
BOWSTICK, JAMES-BLACK	FRE	223	BUCKEYST
BOWTON, MARGARET	BAL	053	9TH WARD
BOWYER, ADAM	FRE	257	NEW MARK
BOWYER, GRACE	BAL	324	12TH WAR
BOWYER, JOHN	HAR	158	3RD DIST
BOWYER, JOHN H.	BAL	121	16TH WAR
BOWYER, JOSEPH	BAL	094	15TH WAR
BOWYER, LEVI	BAL	081	15TH WAR
BOWYER, PETER	FRE	258	NEW MARK
BOWYER, SAMUEL	CEC	109	3RD E DI
BOWYER, WILLIAM	FRE	274	NEW MARK
BOWZER, DANIEL	BAL	459	8TH WARD
BOXERS, DAVID	WAS	177	1ST DIST
BOXTER, MARGARET	WAS	150	2ND DIST
BOXWELL, LEON	BAL	109	18TH WAR
BOXWELL, WILLIAM	BAL	460	14TH WAR
BOY, JOHN	HAR	084	2ND DIST
BOYAN, HENRY	TAL	092	ST MICHA
BOYARD, R.	PRI	109	PISCATAW
BOYCE, ALBERT G.	BAL	363	3RD WARD
BOYCE, ANN	BAL	432	8TH WARD
BOYCE, CHRISTIAN	ALL	014	3RD E.D.
BOYCE, DANIEL	BAL	230	19TH WAR
BOYCE, DANIEL	BAL	230	19TH WAR
BOYCE, DAVID	FRE	103	FREDERIC
BOYCE, ELISABETH	ALL	022	2ND E.D.
BOYCE, ELIZA	ANN	442	HOWARD D
BOYCE, ELLEANORA	ALL	017	3RD E.D.
BOYCE, HEZEKIAH	ANN	522	HOWARD D
BOYCE, JAMES	BAL	038	9TH WARD
BOYCE, JAMES E.	ANN	425	HOWARD D
BOYCE, JOHN	BAL	038	9TH WARD
BOYCE, JOHN	BAL	182	16TH WAR
BOYCE, JOHN	ALL	019	2ND E.D.
BOYCE, JOHN	QUE	125	1ST E DI
BOYCE, MARY	ALL	034	2ND E.D.
BOYCE, MARY E.	BAL	363	3RD WARD
BOYCE, MICHAEL	ALL	034	2ND E.D.
BOYCE, SARAH	BAL	041	15TH WAR
BOYCE, SUTTON	BAL	038	15TH WAR
BOYCE, THOMAS	BAL	174	16TH WAR
BOYD, ALEXANDER	BAL	391	8TH WARD
BOYD, ALICE	HAR	147	3RD DIST
BOYD, ALICE A.	BAL	153	16TH WAR
BOYD, AMELIA	QUE	204	3RD E DI
BOYD, ANDREW	BAL	119	1ST WARD
BOYD, ANDREW	FRE	043	FREDERIC
BOYD, ANN	HAR	105	2ND DIST
BOYD, ANN	BAL	140	11TH WAR
BOYD, ANN E.	HAR	107	2ND DIST
BOYD, ASA	BAL	194	6TH WARD
BOYD, BRIDGET	BAL	133	18TH WAR
BOYD, CAROLINE	ANN	391	4TH DIST
BOYD, CATHARINE	BAL	212	11TH WAR
BOYD, CLARINDA	ALL	204	CUMBERLA
BOYD, CORNELIUS	BAL	164	16TH WAR
BOYD, DANIEL	CAL	041	3RD DIST
BOYD, DAVID	HAR	052	1ST DIST
BOYD, EDWARD	BAL	134	1ST WARD
BOYD, ELIZA	BAL	293	7TH WARD
BOYD, ELIZA	QUE	124	1ST E DI
BOYD, ELIZABETH A.	CAL	038	2ND DIST
BOYD, ELLEN	BAL	423	14TH WAR
BOYD, EMELINE	ANN	316	1ST DIST
BOYD, FRANCES	BAL	189	5TH DIST
BOYD, FRANCIS	CEC	102	4TH E DI
BOYD, FRANCIS	CEC	184	7TH E DI
BOYD, FREDERICK	BAL	122	18TH WAR
BOYD, GEORGE	WAS	099	2ND DIST
BOYD, GEORGE S.	BAL	262	6TH WARD
BOYD, GEORGE W.	CAL	005	1ST DIST
BOYD, H.	BAL	149	1ST WARD
BOYD, HARRIET	CEC	202	6TH E DI
BOYD, HENRIETTA	HAR	151	3RD DIST
BOYD, HENRIETTA-BLACK	FRE	017	FREDERIC
BOYD, HENRY	CEC	157	PORT DUP
BOYD, HENRY	HAR	070	1ST DIST
BOYD, HENRY	WAS	045	2ND SUBD
BOYD, HUGH	CEC	179	7TH E DI
BOYD, HUGH L.	BAL	306	7TH WARD
BOYD, ISAAC L.	QUE	204	3RD E DI
BOYD, J. EDWIN	WAS	125	HAGERSTO
BOYD, JACOB	BAL	405	14TH WAR
BOYD, JAMES	CEC	143	7TH E DI
BOYD, JAMES	CEC	182	7TH E DI
BOYD, JAMES	CEC	177	7TH E DI
BOYD, JAMES	CEC	098	3RD E DI
BOYD, JAMES	CEC	193	5TH E DI
BOYD, JAMES	CEC	027	CHESAPEA
BOYD, JAMES	BAL	180	19TH WAR
BOYD, JAMES	WAS	051	2ND SUBD
BOYD, JAMES	BAL	234	1ST DIST
BOYD, JAMES	ALL	215	CUMBERLA
BOYD, JAMES F.	BAL	413	8TH WARD
BOYD, JAMES H.	BAL	083	18TH WAR
BOYD, JAMES Y.	BAL	375	8TH WARD
BOYD, JANE	BAL	372	3RD WARD
BOYD, JARRETT	HAR	093	2ND DIST
BOYD, JOHN	HAR	063	1ST DIST
BOYD, JOHN	BAL	319	20TH WAR
BOYD, JOHN	CEC	201	5TH E DI
BOYD, JOHN	HAR	148	3RD DIST
BOYD, JOHN	HAR	158	3RD DIST
BOYD, JOHN	BAL	133	1ST WARD
BOYD, JOHN	BAL	167	1ST WARD
BOYD, JOHN	BAL	288	3RD WARD
BOYD, JOHN	WAS	045	2ND SUBD
BOYD, JOHN C.	BAL	099	5TH WARD
BOYD, JOHN J.	FRE	061	FREDERIC
BOYD, JOHN L.	BAL	413	8TH WARD
BOYD, JOHN T.	BAL	103	5TH WARD
BOYD, JOHN-BLACK	FRE	017	FREDERIC
BOYD, JOSEH	BAL	128	5TH WARD
BOYD, JOSEPH	BAL	157	6TH WARD
BOYD, JOSEPH	KEN	225	2ND DIST
BOYD, JOSEPH	CEC	186	7TH E DI
BOYD, JOSEPH	WAS	139	HAGERSTO
BOYD, JOSEPH C.	BAL	102	5TH WARD
BOYD, JOSEPHINE-BLACK	FRE	020	FREDERIC
BOYD, JOSHUA	CAL	040	3RD DIST
BOYD, JOSHUA H.	BAL	357	3RD WARD
BOYD, LOUISA	BAL	188	2ND WARD
BOYD, LUCY	MGM	318	CRACKLIN
BOYD, LUCY-BLACK	FRE	015	FREDERIC
BOYD, LYDIA	HAR	159	3RD DIST
BOYD, M.A.	WAS	122	HAGERSTO
BOYD, MARGARET	BAL	126	18TH WAR
BOYD, MARGARET A.	HAR	052	1ST DIST
BOYD, MARTHA C.	BAL	392	8TH WARD
BOYD, MARY	BAL	188	2ND WARD
BOYD, MARY	BAL	260	1ST DIST
BOYD, MARY	BAL	059	10TH WAR
BOYD, MARY	BAL	440	8TH WARD
BOYD, MARY A.	HAR	056	1ST DIST
BOYD, MARY J.	BAL	379	13TH WAR
BOYD, MARY J.	BAL	306	7TH WARD
BOYD, MATHEW	BAL	391	8TH WARD

BOYD, MICHAEL WAS 154 HAGERSTO
BOYD, MILCAH HAR 039 1ST DIST
BOYD, MILLICENT A. CEC 143 7TH E DI
BOYD, MIRANCA ALL 240 CUMBERLA
BOYD, NELSON CEC 189 7TH E DI
BOYD, PATRICK HAR 160 3RD DIST
BOYD, PHILIP D. BAL 034 4TH WARD
BOYD, ROBERT BAL 448 8TH WARD
BOYD, SAMUEL BAL 214 6TH WARD
BOYD, SAMUEL BAL 424 3RD WARD
BOYD, SAMUEL HAR 085 2ND DIST
BOYD, SAMUEL BAL 144 19TH WAR
BOYD, SAMUEL WAS 097 2ND DIST
BOYD, SARAH CAL 035 2ND DIST
BOYD, SARAH BAL 153 11TH WAR
BOYD, SARAH BAL 050 9TH WARD
BOYD, SOPHIA E. BAL 128 5TH WARD
BOYD, STEPHEN HAR 130 2ND DIST
BOYD, STEPHEN A. HAR 199 3RD DIST
BOYD, SUSAN C. BAL 423 14TH WAR
BOYD, SUSANNA CEC 049 1ST E DI
BOYD, THEADORE CEC 183 7TH E DI
BOYD, THOMAS HAR 158 3RD DIST
BOYD, THOMAS BAL 074 15TH WAR
BOYD, THOMAS WAS 124 HAGERSTO
BOYD, THOMAS W. BAL 290 1ST DIST
BOYD, WESTERN HAR 158 3RD DIST
BOYD, WILLIAM CEC 177 7TH E DI
BOYD, WILLIAM CEC 144 PORT DUP
BOYD, WILLIAM CEC 202 6TH E DI
BOYD, WILLIAM BAL 236 6TH WARD
BOYD, WILLIAM BAL 050 9TH WARD
BOYD, WILLIAM ANN 321 2ND DIST
BOYD, WILLIAM WAS 121 2ND DIST
BOYD, WILLIAM A. BAL 023 4TH WARD
BOYD, WILLIAM H. WAS 144 HAGERSTO
BOYD, WILLLIAM B. ANN 308 1ST DIST
BOYD, WILSON BAL 463 14TH WAR
BOYDE, CATHERINE CHA 292 BOJANTOW
BOYE, CAROLINE BAL 217 17TH WAR
BOYEL,PETER BAL 123 1ST WARD
BOYER, ADAM ALL 190 9TH E.D.
BOYER, ALBERT J. BAL 406 1ST DIST
BOYER, ANN ALL 035 2ND E.D.
BOYER, ANN BAL 228 6TH WARD
BOYER, ANN WOR 200 3RD E DI
BOYER, ANN M. FRE 051 FREDERIC
BOYER, ANNA KEN 216 2ND DIST
BOYER, BENJAMIN CEC 138 6TH E DI
BOYER, BENJAMIN-BLACK QUE 169 2ND E DI
BOYER, BILL HAR 099 2ND DIST
BOYER, CATHARINE WAS 091 2ND SUBD
BOYER, CATHARINE WAS 011 WILLIAMS
BOYER, CHRISTIAN FRE 369 CATOCTIN
BOYER, DANIEL FRE 369 CATOCTIN
BOYER, DANIEL ALL 218 CUMBERLA
BOYER, CANIEL-BLACK FRE 418 8TH E DI
BOYER, DAVID BAL 204 2ND WARD
BOYER, EDWARD KEN 284 3RD DIST
BOYER, EDWARD H. KEN 312 3RD DIST
BOYER, ELIZA CEC 011 ELKTON 3
BOYER, ELIZABETH FRE 369 CATOCTIN
BOYER, ELIZABETH CAR 335 6TH DIST
BOYER, ELIZABETH KEN 283 3RD DIST
BOYER, ELIZABETH MGM 434 CLARKSTR
BOYER, EMMA J. FRE 311 MIDDLETO
BOYER, FANNY KEN 301 3RD DIST
BOYER, FRANKLIN WAS 163 2ND DIST
BOYER, FREDERICK M.S. KEN 291 3RD DIST
BOYER, GEORGE CEC 050 1ST E DI
BOYER, HENRY FRE 311 MIDDLETO
BOYER, HENRY HAR 030 1ST DIST
BOYER, HENRY HAR 140 2ND DIST
BOYER, J.W. ALL 034 2ND E.D.
BOYER, JACOB ALL 188 9TH E.D.
BOYER, JAMES BAL 429 1ST DIST
BOYER, JAMES QUE 140 1ST E DI
BOYER, JAMES KEN 301 3RD DIST
BOYER, JAMES KEN 299 3RD DIST
BOYER, JAMES A. QUE 231 4TH E DI
BOYER, JESSE ANN 387 4TH DIST
BOYER, JESSE T. FRE 400 JEFFERSO
BOYER, JOHN HAR 143 2ND DIST
BOYER, JOHN KEN 245 2ND DIST
BOYER, JOHN FRE 318 MIDDLETO
BOYER, JOHN ALL 216 CUMBERLA
BOYER, JOHN BAL 094 1ST WARD
BOYER, JOHN QUE 236 4TH E DI
BOYER, JOHN WAS 221 1ST DIST
BOYER, JOHN A. CEC 008 ELKTON 3
BOYER, JOHN JR. MGM 434 CLARKSTR
BOYER, JOHN SR. MGM 434 CLARKSTR
BOYER, JOHN W. KEN 291 3RD DIST
BOYER, JOHN W. BAL 064 4TH WARD
BOYER, JOHN WILLIAM FRE 154 10TH E D
BOYER, JONATHAN FRE 369 CATOCTIN
BOYER, JONATHAN FRE 375 CATOCTIN
BOYER, JONATHAN WAS 039 2ND SUBD
BOYER, LARKIN BAL 286 1ST DIST
BOYER, LAWSON FRE 313 MIDDLETO
BOYER, LEVY BAL 202 17TH WAR
BOYER, MARGARET BAL 237 12TH WAR
BOYER, MARGARET WAS 065 2ND SUBD
BOYER, MARIA KEN 220 2ND DIST
BOYER, MARY ALL 188 9TH E.D.
BOYER, MARY R. BAL 431 14TH WAR
BOYER, MARY* BAL 078 10TH WAR
BOYER, MATHEW KEN 311 3RD DIST
BOYER, MICHAEL FRE 324 MIDDLETO
BOYER, PERE-BLACK QUE 142 1ST E DI
BOYER, PERRY KEN 258 1ST DIST
BOYER, PERRY * KEN 246 2ND DIST
BOYER, PETER CAR 404 2ND DIST
BOYER, PETER FRE 392 PETERSVI
BOYER, PETER FRE 062 FREDERIC
BOYER, PHILIP BAL 320 20TH WAR
BOYER, REZIN ANN 387 4TH DIST
BOYER, RICHARD T. KEN 282 3RD DIST
BOYER, ROSANNA E. FRE 081 FREDERIC
BOYER, SAMUEL CAR 339 6TH DIST
BOYER, SAMUEL QUE 175 2ND E DI
BOYER, SAMUEL WAS 050 2ND SUBD
BOYER, SARAH CEC 015 ELKTON 3
BOYER, SARAH BAL 178 6TH WARD
BOYER, SARAH W. BAL 295 7TH WARD
BOYER, SIMON W. KEN 283 3RD DIST
BOYER, STEPHEN KEN 282 3RD DIST
BOYER, STEPHEN CEC 011 ELKTON 3
BOYER, SUSAN BAL 170 11TH WAR
BOYER, THOMAS BAL 137 1ST WARD
BOYER, THOMAS FRE 081 FREDERIC
BOYER, WILLIAM BAL 255 17TH WAR
BOYER, WILLIAM BAL 107 1ST WARD
BOYER, WILLIAM R. KEN 301 3RD DIST
BOYERS, ANN WAS 044 2ND SUBD
BOYERS, HENRY WAS 025 2ND SUBD
BOYERS, JOHN WAS 068 2ND SUBD
BOYERS, JOSEPH WAS 003 WILLIAMS
BOYERS, MARTHA WAS 023 2ND SUBD
BOYERS, PETER WAS 014 2ND SUBD
BOYERS, SALLY WAS 165 HAGERSTO
BOYERS, SAMUEL WAS 070 2ND SUBD
BOYERS, SOLOMON WAS 043 2ND SUBD
BOYL, ANDREW HAR 040 1ST DIST
BOYLAND, JOHN F. BAL 215 2ND WARD
BOYLE, AGNES BAL 304 3RD WARD
BOYLE, AGNESS BAL 413 1ST DIST
BOYLE, ANN BAL 183 11TH WAR
BOYLE, BARNEY BAL 068 4TH WARD
BOYLE, BARTHOLOMEW ALL 057 10TH E.D
BOYLE, BERNARD BAL 313 12TH WAR
BOYLE, BERNARD ANN 418 HOWARD D
BOYLE, CATHARINE FRE 196 5TH E DI
BOYLE, CHARLES BAL 149 16TH WAR
BOYLE, EDWARD BAL 372 13TH WAR
BOYLE, ELIZABETH FRE 188 5TH E DI
BOYLE, ELIZABETH BAL 024 9TH WARD
BOYLE, EMILY BAL 276 17TH WAR
BOYLE, FRANCIS E. BAL 312 12TH WAR
BOYLE, GEORGE BAL 192 17TH WAR
BOYLE, HENRY BAL 291 12TH WAR
BOYLE, JAMES BAL 385 8TH WARD
BOYLE, JAMES FRE 095 FREDERIC
BOYLE, JAMES PRI 057 AQUASCO
BOYLE, JAMES SR. ANN 280 ANNAPOLI
BOYLE, JOHN A. TAL 051 EASTON D
BOYLE, JOHN B. CAR 270 WESTMINS
BOYLE, JOHN H. PRI 093 MARLBROU
BOYLE, JOHN J. BAL 394 14TH WAR
BOYLE, JOSEPH WAS 164 HAGERSTO
BOYLE, JOSEPH M. BAL 408 14TH WAR
BOYLE, MARGARET BAL 445 1ST DIST
BOYLE, MARTIN BAL 022 9TH WARD
BOYLE, MARY ANN 494 HOWARD D
BOYLE, MARY BAL 354 7TH WARD
BOYLE, MARY FRE 066 FREDERIC
BOYLE, MICHAEL BAL 005 18TH WAR
BOYLE, OWEN BAL 441 1ST DIST
BOYLE, OWEN BAL 021 2ND DIST
BOYLE, P. BAL 158 1ST WARD
BOYLE, PATRICK CEC 173 6TH E DI
BOYLE, PETER ALL 247 CUMBERLA
BOYLE, PHILIP CAR 413 2ND DIST
BOYLE, REBECCA BAL 226 19TH WAR
BOYLE, REBECCA BAL 226 19TH WAR
BOYLE, ROBERT BAL 001 15TH WAR
BOYLE, ROBERT BAL 041 9TH WARD
BOYLE, THOMAS BAL 447 1ST DIST
BOYLE, WILLIAM BAL 418 1ST DIST
BOYLE, WILLIAM H. BAL 191 17TH WAR
BOYLE, WILLIAM K. BAL 193 11TH WAR
BOYLE, WILLIAM O. BAL 394 8TH WARD
BOYLER, THOMAS BAL 025 9TH WARD
BOYLES, LAWRENCE BAL 171 11TH WAR
BOYLES, NATHANIEL BAL 459 8TH WARD
BOYLIS, JAMES BAL 420 3RD WARD
BOYNE, J. BAL 168 1ST WARD
BOYNE, JOHN BAL 243 12TH WAR
BOYNE, JOHN BAL 124 1ST WARD
BOYNE, THOMAS BAL 218 6TH WARD
BOYNES, JOHN ALL 104 5TH E.D.
BOYOER, ESAU BAL 293 1ST DIST
BOYOT, WILLIAM * WAS 064 2ND SUBD
BOYRISET, ANGUS BAL 018 4TH WARD
BOYRIST, GEORGE BAL 235 20TH WAR
BOYSWANGER, WILLIAM BAL 112 1ST WARD
BOZMAN, MARGARET TAL 029 EASTON D
BOZMAN, T. E. BAL 151 1ST WARD
BOZWEL, M. PRI 054 AQUASCO
BOZWELL, HENRY PRI 055 AQUASCO
BOZWELL, OTHO BAL 408 14TH WAR
BOZWELL, TRUEMAN PRI 054 AQUASCO
BRAADE, CHARLOTTE BAL 355 1ST DIST
BRABAKER, GEORGE BAL 193 2ND WARD
BRABECH, JACOB BAL 278 20TH WAR
BRABSTON, HENRY HAR 153 3RD DIST
BRABY, HENRY* BAL 069 4TH WARD
BRABY, JOSEPH BAL 143 1ST WARD
BRABY, MICHAEL BAL 005 EASTERN
BRACCE, BENNET BAL 063 4TH WARD
BRACCO, PHILIF-BLACK CAR 162 NO TWP L
BRACE, CHARLES ALL 254 CUMBERLA
BRACE, RUSSEL MGM 407 MEDLEY 3
BRACEN, JERRY-MULATTO FRE 434 8TH E DI
BRACES, MARIA-MULATTO QUE 185 3RD E DI
BRACH, RICHARD CEC 072 5TH E DI
BRACHEN, THOMAS C. FRE 247 NEW MARK
BRACHER, PARKER SOM 377 BRINKLEY
BRACHER, PETER FRE 339 MIDDLETO
BRACHMAN, CHARLES BAL 274 1ST DIST
BRACHMAN, THERESA BAL 087 10TH WAR
BRACK, ADELIA HAR 139 2ND DIST
BRACK, HENRIETTA HAR 140 2ND DIST
BRACK, MATILDA HAR 139 2ND DIST
BRACKEAN, ORBOM FRE 249 NEW MARK
BRACKEN, HENRY BAL 300 20TH WAR
BRACKEN, JAMES BAL 164 11TH WAR
BRACKEN, JOHN BAL 401 8TH WARD
BRACKEN, MARY BAL 407 8TH WARD
BRACKEN, MARY ANN BAL 001 15TH WAR
BRACKENRIDGE, ALLICE BAL 245 1ST DIST
BRACKENRIDGE, KITTY BAL 227 1ST DIST
BRACKENRIDGE, LATINA BAL 247 1ST DIST
BRACKER, JAMES QUE 249 5TH E DI
BRACKER, JOHN BAL 088 10TH WAR
BRACKER, LAURA L. BAL 079 10TH WAR
BRACKET, MARGARET * BAL 345 13TH WAR
BRACKS, RACHAEL BAL 141 11TH WAR
BRADBOURN, ISAAC A. BAL 285 7TH WARD
BRADBURN, EDWARD R. ST 269 3RD E DI
BRADBURN, EMILY J. BAL 266 7TH WARD
BRADBURN, JAMES ST 293 2ND E DI
BRADBURN, JOHN BAL 144 16TH WAR
BRADBURN, WILLIAM C. ST 316 4TH E DI
BRADBURN,ISAAC BAL 051 2ND DIST
BRADBURRY, ROBERT R. BAL 163 1ST WARD
BRADBURY, JOHN T. HAR 147 3RD DIST
BRADBURY, JOSEPH P. CEC 124 5TH E DI
BRADDE, HENRY * BAL 354 1ST DIST
BRADDECKS, HENRY BAL 351 13TH WAR
BRADDOCK, ELIZABETH MGM 376 ROCKERLE
BRADDOCK, GEORGE TAL 058 EASTON D
BRADDOCK, GEORGE R. MGM 375 ROCKERLE
BRADDOCK, JOHN MGM 375 ROCKERLE
BRADDOCK, JOHN JR. MGM 375 ROCKERLE
BRADDOCK, LAURA MGM 374 ROCKERLE
BRADDOCK, MICHAEL ALL 072 5TH E.D.
BRADDOCK, WILLIAM ALL 079 5TH E.D.
BRADDOCK, WILLIAM MGM 376 ROCKERLE
BRADDOCK, WILLIAMP. ST 343 5TH E DI
BRADDY, EDWARD HAR 170 3RD DIST
BRADDY, JOHN BAL 115 11TH WAR
BRADE, JOHN BAL 283 1ST DIST
BRADEE, M. BAL 227 19TH WAR
BRADEHWARD, JOHN BAL 198 11TH WAR
BRADEKAMP, HENRY PRI 007 BLADENSB
BRADEN, FRANCIS BAL 369 8TH WARD
BRADEN, JAMES BAL 158 11TH WAR
BRADEN, JOHN BAL 198 11TH WAR
BRADENBAUGH, DARCAS BAL 381 1ST DIST
BRADENBAUGH, JACOB ANN 452 HOWARD D
BRADENBAUGH, JOHN BAL 374 13TH WAR
BRADENBAUGH, THOMAS HAR 050 1ST DIST
BRADENBOUGH, JACOB HAR 017 1ST DIST
BRADENBOUGH, JACOB HAR 072 1ST DIST
BRADENBURGH, PRISCILLA BAL 269 12TH WAR
BRADENMINGER, LEWIS BAL 269 2ND WARD
BRADFIELD, BENJAMIN L. HAR 183 3RD DIST
BRADFIELD, FRANKLIN ALL 013 3RD E.D.
BRADFIELD, GEORGE HAR 173 3RD DIST
BRADFIELD, JAMES E. HAR 172 3RD DIST
BRADFIELD, SAMUEL HAR 186 3RD DIST
BRADFORD, A. W. BAL 181 2ND DIST
BRADFORD, ADAMS WOR 285 BERLIN 1
BRADFORD, ALEXANDER BAL 037 1ST WARD
BRADFORD, BENEDICT HAR 032 1ST DIST
BRADFORD, CHARLES H. BAL 250 6TH WARD
BRADFORD, ELIZA H. HAR 079 2ND DIST
BRADFORD, ELLEN BAL 158 11TH WAR
BRADFORD, EMELINE K. BAL 181 2ND DIST
BRADFORD, EMILY BAL 011 1ST WARD
BRADFORD, ESTHER WOR 263 BERLIN 1
BRADFORD, FANNY WOR 258 1ST CENS
BRADFORD, FLASKY CEC 200 7TH E DI
BRADFORD, G. W. BAL 356 13TH WAR
BRADFORD, GEORGE HAR 097 2ND DIST
BRADFORD, GEORGE HAR 001 1ST DIST
BRADFORD, GEORGE HAR 138 2ND DIST
BRADFORD, GEORGE BAL 132 18TH WAR
BRADFORD, GEORGE ANN 475 HOWARD D
BRADFORD, HANNAH BAL 333 3RD WARD
BRADFORD, HANNAH HAR 079 2ND DIST
BRADFORD, HANNAH BAL 376 13TH WAR
BRADFORD, JACOB BAL 224 17TH WAR
BRADFORD, JAMES HAR 206 3RD DIST
BRADFORD, JAMES BAL 092 2ND DIST
BRADFORD, JAMES BAL 065 1ST WARD
BRADFORD, JANE BAL 253 6TH WARD
BRADFORD, JOHN BAL 098 15TH WAR
BRADFORD, JOHN BAL 123 11TH WAR
BRADFORD, JOHN BAL 140 11TH WAR
BRADFORD, JOSEPH BAL 115 18TH WAR
BRADFORD, JOSEPH ANN 328 2ND DIST
BRADFORD, JULIA HAR 177 3RD DIST
BRADFORD, JULIA-BLACK BAL 216 2ND WARD
BRADFORD, M. * WOR 285 BERLIN 1
BRADFORD, MARY WOR 264 BERLIN 1
BRADFORD, MARY BAL 225 12TH WAR
BRADFORD, MARY J. BAL 053 15TH WAR
BRADFORD, NAOMI BAL 044 15TH WAR
BRADFORD, REBECA BAL 280 7TH WARD
BRADFORD, REBECCA BAL 101 15TH WAR
BRADFORD, RTHOMAS WOR 298 9TH E DI
BRADFORD, SAMPSON WOR 285 BERLIN 1
BRADFORD, SAMUEL WOR 265 BERLIN 1
BRADFORD, SARAH BAL 441 14TH WAR
BRADFORD, SELBY WOR 289 9TH E DI
BRADFORD, THOMAS CAR 115 NO TWP L
BRADFORD, THOMAS BAL 106 15TH WAR
BRADFORD, THOMAS BAL 065 1ST WARD
BRADFORD, WILLIAM BAL 293 1ST DIST
BRADFORD, WILLIAM BAL 189 2ND WARD
BRADFORD, WILLIAM ANN 363 4TH DIST
BRADFORD, WILLIAM BAL 402 1ST DIST
BRADFORD, WILLIAM BAL 133 11TH WAR
BRADFORD, WILLIAM CEC 004 ELKTON 3
BRADFORD, WILLIAM CEC 004 ELKTON 3
BRADFORD, WILLIAM WOR 291 9TH E DI
BRADFORD, WILLIAM WOR 294 9TH E DI
BRADFORD, WILLIAM W. HAR 206 3RD DIST
BRADGERS, JOSEPH BAL 164 2ND DIST
BRADLE, JOHN BAL 287 3RD WARD
BRADLE, WRILEY * HAR 204 3RD DIST
BRADLER, THOMAS BAL 122 2ND DIST
BRADLEY, AARON SOM 384 BRINKLEY
BRADLEY, ADELAIDE V. ANN 521 HOWARD D
BRADLEY, ALICE BAL 249 12TH WAR
BRADLEY, AMANDA SOM 506 BARREN C
BRADLEY, BENJAMIN SOM 507 BARREN C
BRADLEY, BYARD SOM 550 TYASKIN
BRADLEY, CASSIS BAL 197 19TH WAR
BRADLEY, CHARLES ALL 087 5TH E.D.
BRADLEY, CHARLES D. SOM 506 BARREN C
BRADLEY, CHARLES E. QUE 128 1ST E DI
BRADLEY, CHRISTOPHER C. SOM 513 BARREN C
BRADLEY, CLEMENT DOR 312 1ST DIST
BRADLEY, DARHIS* TAL 028 EASTON D
BRADLEY, DEBORA FRE 165 EMMITTSB
BRADLEY, E. B. BAL 470 14TH WAR
BRADLEY, ELIHU SOM 519 BARREN C
BRADLEY, ELIZA A. WOR 228 6TH E DI
BRADLEY, ELIZABETH SOM 518 BARREN C
BRADLEY, ELIZABETH E. SOM 518 BARREN C
BRADLEY, ELLEN BAL 046 4TH WARD
BRADLEY, ELLY DOR 306 1ST DIST
BRADLEY, ELY DOR 299 1ST DIST
BRADLEY, FRANCIS BAL 137 11TH WAR
BRADLEY, FRANKLIN FRE 178 5TH E DI
BRADLEY, GEORGE FRE 234 BUCKEYST
BRADLEY, GEORGE SOM 491 SALISBUR
BRADLEY, HANNAH SOM 518 BARREN C
BRADLEY, HARRIETT DOR 307 1ST DIST
BRADLEY, HENRY MGM 395 ROCKERLE
BRADLEY, HENRY E. KEN 247 2ND DIST
BRADLEY, HOOPER DOR 308 1ST DIST
BRADLEY, HUGH BAL 359 8TH WARD
BRADLEY, ISAAC ANN 316 1ST DIST
BRADLEY, ISABELA BAL 153 5TH WARD
BRADLEY, JACOB BAL 143 1ST WARD
BRADLEY, JAMES SOM 513 BARREN C

Name	County	Page	District
BRADLEY, JAMES	PRI	025	VANSVILL
BRADLEY, JAMES H.	BAL	080	10TH WAR
BRADLEY, JAMES H.	BAL	003	4TH WARD
BRADLEY, JAMES W.	SOM	509	BARREN C
BRADLEY, JASON	BAL	075	2ND DIST
BRADLEY, JEREMIAH	SOM	507	BARREN C
BRADLEY, JOE	BAL	358	13TH WAR
BRADLEY, JOHN	SOM	519	BARREN C
BRADLEY, JOHN	SOM	514	BARREN C
BRADLEY, JOHN	BAL	027	2ND DIST
BRADLEY, JOHN	BAL	185	2ND WARD
BRADLEY, JOHN	BAL	201	6TH WARD
BRADLEY, JOHN H.	BAL	153	5TH WARD
BRADLEY, JOHN W.	SOM	518	BARREN C
BRADLEY, JOHN W.	CAR	147	NO TWP L
BRADLEY, JOSEPHINE	BAL	077	10TH WAR
BRADLEY, MARGARET	BAL	193	11TH WAR
BRADLEY, MARGARET	BAL	193	19TH WAR
BRADLEY, MARY	BAL	138	11TH WAR
BRADLEY, MARY	HAR	078	2ND DIST
BRADLEY, MARY	ANN	472	HOWARD D
BRADLEY, MARY	BAL	302	3RD WARD
BRADLEY, MARY	WAS	150	2ND DIST
BRADLEY, MARY A.	ANN	522	HOWARD D
BRADLEY, MARY E.	SOM	507	BARREN C
BRADLEY, MATHEW M.	DOR	312	1ST DIST
BRADLEY, MEDFORD	QUE	191	3RD E DI
BRADLEY, MICHAEL	HAR	083	2ND DIST
BRADLEY, ORANGE	CAL	020	2ND DIST
BRADLEY, PATRICK	HAR	085	2ND DIST
BRADLEY, PATRICK	BAL	264	7TH WARD
BRADLEY, PERRY	SOM	493	SALISBUR
BRADLEY, PETER	ALL	149	6TH E.D.
BRADLEY, PRUSILA	SOM	499	SALISBUR
BRADLEY, PRUSILLA	SOM	514	BARREN C
BRADLEY, REBECCA	ANN	326	2ND DIST
BRADLEY, REBECCA	BAL	161	19TH WAR
BRADLEY, RESEDA *	BAL	220	12TH WAR
BRADLEY, RICHARD	ANN	408	8TH DIST
BRADLEY, RICHARD W.	PRI	016	BLADENSB
BRADLEY, ROBERT H.	BAL	025	4TH WARD
BRADLEY, ROZETTA	ST	345	5TH E DI
BRADLEY, SAMUEL	HAR	138	2ND DIST
BRADLEY, SAMUEL L.	BAL	196	19TH WAR
BRADLEY, SARAH	SOM	510	BARREN C
BRADLEY, SARAH A.	PRI	017	BLADENSB
BRADLEY, SENURA	PRI	025	VANSVILL
BRADLEY, SISTER HELLEN	FRE	198	5TH E DI
BRADLEY, STEPHEN J.	QUE	182	3RD E DI
BRADLEY, THOAMS	BAL	277	20TH WAR
BRADLEY, THOMAS	DOR	303	1ST DIST
BRADLEY, THOMAS	DOR	297	1ST DIST
BRADLEY, THOMAS	DOR	304	1ST DIST
BRADLEY, THOMAS	BAL	379	13TH WAR
BRADLEY, WILLIAM	SOM	531	QUANTICO
BRADLEY, WILLIAM	SOM	534	QUANTICO
BRADLEY, WILLIAM C.	DOR	312	1ST DIST
BRADLEY, WILLIAM C.	BAL	137	11TH WAR
BRADLEY, WILLIAM H.	SOM	507	BARREN C
BRADLING, JOHN	ALL	244	CUMBERLA
BRADLY, BETSY	ANN	328	2ND DIST
BRADLY, FRANCIS	CHA	231	HILLTOP
BRADLY, FRANCIS-BLACK	CAR	090	NO TWP L
BRADLY, HENRIETTA C.	CAR	132	NO TWP L
BRADLY, JAMES	DOR	448	1ST DIST
BRADLY, JAMES	SOM	518	BARREN C
BRADLY, JOHN	DOR	448	1ST DIST
BRADLY, JOHN	DOR	427	1ST DIST
BRADLY, JOHN	CAR	125	NO TWP L
BRADLY, JOHN	HAR	085	2ND DIST
BRADLY, JOHN	ALL	203	CUMBERLA
BRADLY, JOHN-BLACK	CAR	087	NO TWP L
BRADLY, JOSEPH	BAL	266	7TH WARD
BRADLY, MARGARET	BAL	166	11TH WAR
BRADLY, MARY C.	ST	339	4TH E DI
BRADLY, NANCY	DOR	450	1ST DIST
BRADLY, NANCY	CEC	106	3RD E DI
BRADLY, REBECCA	DOR	404	1ST DIST
BRADLY, ROBERT	CEC	106	3RD E DI
BRADLY, SAMUEL	SOM	515	BARREN C
BRADLY, SUSAN	HAR	083	2ND DIST
BRADLY, THOMAS	CAR	108	NO TWP L
BRADLY, THOMAS L.	DOR	449	1ST DIST
BRADLY, WILLIAM	DOR	455	1ST DIST
BRADLY, WILLIAM	DOR	422	1ST DIST
BRADS, JAMES	WAS	178	BOONSBOR
BRADSELL, JACOB	BAL	298	17TH WAR
BRADSHAW, ANDREW J.	DOR	342	3RD DIVI
BRADSHAW, ANN	TAL	113	ST MICHA
BRADSHAW, ANN M.	BAL	189	6TH WARD
BRADSHAW, BENJAMIN	SOM	456	DAMES QU
BRADSHAW, DAVID	SOM	455	DAMES QU
BRADSHAW, DEBORAH	KEN	310	3RD DIST
BRADSHAW, ELISHA	SOM	456	DAMES QU
BRADSHAW, ELIZA	DOR	327	3RD DIVI
BRADSHAW, HAMILTON	SOM	456	DAMES QU
BRADSHAW, HANEY	SOM	455	DAMES QU
BRADSHAW, JAMES	DOR	377	1ST DIST
BRADSHAW, JAMES-BLACK	QUE	180	2ND E DI
BRADSHAW, JOHN	TAL	038	EASTON D
BRADSHAW, JOHN	BAL	085	18TH WAR
BRADSHAW, JOHN J.	BAL	037	18TH WAR
BRADSHAW, JOHN*	DOR	377	1ST DIST
BRADSHAW, JOHN-BLACK	QUE	129	1ST E DI
BRADSHAW, JOSEPH	DOR	380	1ST DIST
BRADSHAW, JOSEPH	WAS	098	2ND DIST
BRADSHAW, LEVENIA	SOM	454	DAMES QU
BRADSHAW, LITTLETON	SOM	455	DAMES QU
BRADSHAW, MARGARET	FRE	018	FREDERIC
BRADSHAW, MARIA	BAL	339	7TH WARD
BRADSHAW, MARY	DOR	420	1ST DIST
BRADSHAW, MISS S.	FRE	199	5TH E DI
BRADSHAW, NATHANIEL	SOM	456	DAMES QU
BRADSHAW, OGLETON	CHA	245	HILLTOP
BRADSHAW, PHILLIS	KEN	293	3RD DIST
BRADSHAW, RICHARD	SOM	456	DAMES QU
BRADSHAW, RICHARD	SOM	454	DAMES QU
BRADSHAW, RICHARD	DOR	342	3RD DIVI
BRADSHAW, RICHARD	DOR	410	1ST DIST
BRADSHAW, S.	BAL	116	1ST WARD
BRADSHAW, SAMUEL	BAL	113	1ST WARD
BRADSHAW, SAMUEL	BAL	133	1ST WARD
BRADSHAW, SAMUEL	BAL	006	4TH WARD
BRADSHAW, SAMUEL	KEN	291	3RD DIST
BRADSHAW, SEVERN	SOM	454	DAMES QU
BRADSHAW, SOLOMON	SOM	366	BRINKLEY
BRADSHAW, TANER	BAL	144	1ST WARD
BRADSHAW, TEMPERANCE	KEN	214	2ND DIST
BRADSHAW, THOAMS	SOM	456	DAMES QU
BRADSHAW, THOMAS	SOM	457	DAMES QU
BRADSHAW, THOMAS	BAL	185	6TH WARD
BRADSHAW, WILLIAM	BAL	051	9TH WARD
BRADSHAW, WILLIAM	DOR	386	1ST DIST
BRADSON, STEPHEN	CEC	175	7TH E DI
BRADSTREET, MARY W.	WOR	264	BERLIN 1
BRADTHAMMER, AUGUSTUS	BAL	155	2ND DIST
BRADWATER, GEORGE	BAL	122	1ST WARD
BRADWATERS, ELLEN	ALL	004	3RD E.D.
BRADWELL, LOUIS	CEC	077	NORTHEAS
BRADWOOD, JOHN	BAL	115	18TH WAR
BRADY, AGNES	BAL	035	9TH WARD
BRADY, ALEXANDER	BAL	193	11TH WAR
BRADY, ANDREW	BAL	007	4TH WARD
BRADY, ANN	HAR	150	3RD DIST
BRADY, ANN	BAL	380	3RD WARD
BRADY, ANNE	BAL	116	15TH WAR
BRADY, BAKER	BAL	103	2ND DIST
BRADY, BASIL	PRI	077	MARLBROU
BRADY, BENJAMIN	BAL	414	1ST DIST
BRADY, BERNARD	BAL	033	15TH WAR
BRADY, BERNARD	BAL	272	17TH WAR
BRADY, BETHEL	CEC	044	1ST E DI
BRADY, BRIDGET	BAL	207	19TH WAR
BRADY, CAROLINE	HAR	075	BEL AIR
BRADY, CATHERINE	BAL	019	9TH WARD
BRADY, DELIA	ALL	241	CUMBERLA
BRADY, DENIS	BAL	046	1ST WARD
BRADY, EDWARD	WAS	158	2ND DIST
BRADY, EDWIN	BAL	306	3RD WARD
BRADY, ELIZABETH	ST	289	2ND E DI
BRADY, ELLEN	BAL	136	18TH WAR
BRADY, EMILY	BAL	051	15TH WAR
BRADY, FRANCIS	CAL	015	1ST DIST
BRADY, FRANK	HAR	076	BEL AIR
BRADY, G.W.	PRI	075	MARLBROU
BRADY, GEORGE	BAL	165	11TH WAR
BRADY, H.	PRI	081	QUEEN AN
BRADY, HENRY L.	FRE	312	MIDDLETO
BRADY, HENRY*	BAL	069	4TH WARD
BRADY, HUGH	BAL	132	11TH WAR
BRADY, HUGH	ALL	147	6TH E.D.
BRADY, ISAAC	BAL	224	17TH WAR
BRADY, JAMES	BAL	124	18TH WAR
BRADY, JAMES	CEC	012	ELKTON 3
BRADY, JAMES	CEC	085	5TH E DI
BRADY, JAMES	BAL	017	18TH WAR
BRADY, JAMES	BAL	010	18TH WAR
BRADY, JAMES	FRE	389	PETERSVI
BRADY, JAMES	BAL	002	9TH WARD
BRADY, JAMES	BAL	088	10TH WAR
BRADY, JAMES	PRI	074	MARLBROU
BRADY, JANE	WAS	153	HAGERSTO
BRADY, JOANNAH	ANN	277	ANNAPOLI
BRADY, JOHN	BAL	020	2ND DIST
BRADY, JOHN	BAL	155	5TH WARD
BRADY, JOHN	BAL	198	2ND WARD
BRADY, JOHN	WAS	163	2ND DIST
BRADY, JOHN	PRI	082	QUEEN AN
BRADY, JOHN	WAS	018	2ND SUBD
BRADY, JOHN	CEC	099	3RD E DI
BRADY, JOHN	HAR	159	3RD DIST
BRADY, JOHN	CHA	276	ALLENS F
BRADY, JOHN A.	WAS	163	2ND DIST
BRADY, JOHN JR.	ANN	277	ANNAPOLI
BRADY, JOHN P.	BAL	297	3RD WARD
BRADY, JOSHUA	WAS	163	2ND DIST
BRADY, JOSHUA	ST	290	2ND E DI
BRADY, KAET B.	FRE	065	FREDERIC
BRADY, L.C.	CEC	013	ELKTON 3
BRADY, LAWRENCE	BAL	445	8TH WARD
BRADY, LUCRETIA	SOM	528	QUANTICO
BRADY, M.	ALL	155	6TH E.D.
BRADY, MARGARET	BAL	298	3RD WARD
BRADY, MARGARET	BAL	316	20TH WAR
BRADY, MARGARETT	BAL	126	11TH WAR
BRADY, MARIA	FRE	314	MIDDLETO
BRADY, MARY	BAL	158	11TH WAR
BRADY, MARY	ALL	216	CUMBERLA
BRADY, MARY	BAL	187	6TH WARD
BRADY, MICHAEL	ANN	322	2ND DIST
BRADY, MICHAEL	ANN	330	2ND DIST
BRADY, MICHAEL	ALL	110	5TH E.D.
BRADY, MICHAEL	BAL	446	1ST DIST
BRADY, MICHAEL	BAL	281	12TH WAR
BRADY, MICHAEL	HAR	082	2ND DIST
BRADY, MICHAEL	BAL	259	20TH WAR
BRADY, NATHANIEL	PRI	102	SPALDING
BRADY, PATRICK	BAL	018	18TH WAR
BRADY, PATRICK	ALL	068	5TH E.D.
BRADY, PATRICK	ALL	077	5TH E.D.
BRADY, PATRICK	BAL	039	15TH WAR
BRADY, PATRICK	BAL	001	15TH WAR
BRADY, PATRICK O.	BAL	123	18TH WAR
BRADY, PETER	CEC	209	7TH E DI
BRADY, RANSOM	ALL	068	5TH E.D.
BRADY, S.	ANN	283	ANNAPOLI
BRADY, SAMUEL	BAL	293	3RD WARD
BRADY, SAMUEL	BAL	165	2ND DIST
BRADY, SAMUEL	BAL	371	3RD WARD
BRADY, SARAH	PRI	001	BLADENSB
BRADY, SARAH J.	BAL	122	16TH WAR
BRADY, SUSAN	BAL	061	10TH WAR
BRADY, THOMAS	BAL	315	7TH WARD
BRADY, THOMAS	WAS	177	1ST DIST
BRADY, THOMAS	BAL	372	13TH WAR
BRADY, WASHINGTON	BAL	376	3RD WARD
BRADY, WILLIAM	CAR	129	NO TWP L
BRADY, WILLIAM	CEC	008	ELKTON 3
BRADY, WILLIAM	WAS	155	2ND DIST
BRADY, WILLIAM	PRI	075	MARLBROU
BRADY,HENRY	PRI	078	MARLBROU
BRADYHOUSE, REIGINICA	BAL	266	2ND WARD
BRADYHOUSE, RICHARD	BAL	265	2ND WARD
BRADYHOUSE, THOMAS	BAL	029	1ST WARD
BRADYHOUSE, WILLIAM	BAL	058	1ST WARD
BRAED, ANN *	BAL	442	8TH WARD
BRAER, MARY *	BAL	304	20TH WAR
BRAERICK, MICHAEL	ALL	256	CUMBERLA
BRAFIELD, ELIAS	CHA	268	BOJANTOW
BRAFIELD, JOHN	CHA	276	ALLENS F
BRAFORD, MARY	BAL	461	14TH WAR
BRAGDEN, CHARLES	BAL	161	1ST WARD
BRAGDEN, JOHN	BAL	230	12TH WAR
BRAGDON, JAEMS B.	BAL	385	13TH WAR
BRAGG, FREDERICK A.	BAL	127	1ST WARD
BRAGHER, ISAAC F.	BAL	048	9TH WARD
BRAGHER, NICHOLAS	FRE	265	NEW MARK
BRAGHT, JOHN F.	BAL	092	1ST WARD
BRAGRIME, GREORGE *	WAS	124	2ND DIST
BRAGS, ELIZA	BAL	218	19TH WAR
BRAHEARS, GEORGE W.	PRI	003	BLADENSB
BRAHENS, PRISCILLA	FRE	240	NEW MARK
BRAHLER, WILLIAM	BAL	250	12TH WAR
BRAILER, CONRAD	BAL	284	2ND WARD
BRAIN, CATHERINE	FRE	082	FREDERIC
BRAIN, ELIZA	ALL	212	CUMBERLA
BRAIN, EZRA	FRE	336	MIDDLETO
BRAIN, GEORGE	FRE	081	FREDERIC
BRAIN, HENRY	FRE	078	FREDERIC
BRAIN, JOHN	FRE	081	FREDERIC
BRAIN, STEPHEN	BAL	273	12TH WAR
BRAINARD, BENJAMIN	BAL	074	2ND DIST
BRAINARD, JACOB	ANN	356	3RD DIST
BRAINARD, JESSE	ALL	020	2ND E.D.
BRAINCE, JOSEPH	BAL	005	EASTERN
BRAIND, HENRY	BAL	381	8TH WARD
BRAINTREE, ELLEN	WAS	076	2ND SUBD
BRAIR, JOHN	BAL	213	2ND WARD
BRAKCETT, J. T.	BAL	139	19TH WAR
BRAKE, CHARLOTTE	BAL	033	15TH WAR
BRAKE, JOHN	BAL	033	15TH WAR
BRAKEMAN, FRANK	ALL	257	CUMBERLA
BRAKEMAN, HENRY	ALL	198	CUMBERLA
BRAKEN, JOHN	BAL	049	18TH WAR
BRAKENBRIDGE, THOMAS	BAL	160	11TH WAR
BRAKER, ELLEN	HAR	092	2ND DIST
BRAKEY, MARGARET	ALL	251	CUMBERLA
BRAMAN, MARIA	BAL	416	1ST DIST
BRAMAN, MICHAEL	BAL	274	2ND WARD
BRAMBEL, JOHN	WAS	115	2ND DIST
BRAMBLE, AARON	DOR	439	1ST DIST
BRAMBLE, AARON	DOR	438	1ST DIST
BRAMBLE, ANDREW	KEN	223	2ND DIST
BRAMBLE, ANN	DOR	344	3RD DIVI
BRAMBLE, ANN	KEN	292	3RD DIST
BRAMBLE, BARZILIA*	DOR	343	3RD DIVI
BRAMBLE, CAROLINE	DOR	345	3RD DIVI
BRAMBLE, CATHARINE	TAL	096	ST MICHA
BRAMBLE, CLEMENT	DOR	343	3RD DIVI
BRAMBLE, CYRUS	DOR	380	1ST DIST
BRAMBLE, EDWARD	DOR	308	1ST DIST
BRAMBLE, ELIZABETH	KEN	285	3RD DIST
BRAMBLE, EMELINE*	DOR	435	1ST DIST
BRAMBLE, GEORGE	QUE	123	1ST E DI
BRAMBLE, HENRY	KEN	234	2ND DIST
BRAMBLE, HENRY J.	DOR	298	1ST DIST
BRAMBLE, HENRY T.	BAL	011	15TH WAR
BRAMBLE, HUDSON	DOR	344	3RD DIVI
BRAMBLE, HUTSON	DOR	439	1ST DIST
BRAMBLE, ISAACK	DOR	344	3RD DIVI
BRAMBLE, JAMES H.	DOR	299	1ST DIST
BRAMBLE, JEREMIAH	DOR	349	3RD DIVI
BRAMBLE, JEREMIAH	DOR	454	1ST DIST
BRAMBLE, JESE*	DOR	444	1ST DIST
BRAMBLE, JESE*	DOR	410	1ST DIST
BRAMBLE, JESE*	DOR	409	1ST DIST
BRAMBLE, JOHN	KEN	235	2ND DIST
BRAMBLE, JOHN	QUE	134	1ST E DI
BRAMBLE, JOHN	HAR	095	2ND DIST
BRAMBLE, JOHN	CEC	095	4TH E DI
BRAMBLE, JOHN	SOM	461	HANGARY
BRAMBLE, JOHN	SOM	463	HANGARY
BRAMBLE, JOHN H.	DOR	308	1ST DIST
BRAMBLE, LENIX	DOR	354	3RD DIVI
BRAMBLE, LINIE *	SOM	431	PRINCESS
BRAMBLE, LOUWA*	DOR	343	3RD DIVI
BRAMBLE, MARGARET	DOR	448	1ST DIST
BRAMBLE, MARY A.	KEN	235	2ND DIST
BRAMBLE, MARY E.	SOM	482	TRAPP DI
BRAMBLE, MATHEW	DOR	344	3RD DIVI
BRAMBLE, MESHACK	DOR	334	3RD DIVI
BRAMBLE, MINNY*	DOR	434	1ST DIST
BRAMBLE, MOSES	DOR	344	3RD DIVI
BRAMBLE, SARAH	KEN	290	3RD DIST
BRAMBLE, SARAH	BAL	149	5TH WARD
BRAMBLE, SERENE	DOR	350	3RD DIVI
BRAMBLE, 'STANSBURY	DOR	298	1ST DIST
BRAMBLE, SUSAN	DOR	428	1ST DIST
BRAMBLE, THOAMS	HAR	201	3RD DIST
BRAMBLE, THOMAS	KEN	285	3RD DIST
BRAMBLE, WASHINGTON	DOR	448	1ST DIST
BRAMBLE, WILLIAM	DOR	444	1ST DIST
BRAMBLE, WILLIAM	HAR	094	2ND DIST
BRAMBLE, WILLIAM	BAL	446	8TH WARD
BRAMBLEY, SARAH*	SOM	483	TRAPP DI
BRAMBLEY, WARREN	SOM	483	TRAPP DI
BRAMER, HELPHER	CAR	392	2ND DIST
BRAMWELL, GEORGE	CAR	193	4TH DIST
BRAMWELL, MARY	BAL	189	6TH WARD
BRAMWELL, MARY	BAL	016	9TH WARD
BRAMWELL, TYSON	BAL	175	6TH WARD
BRANA, MARY	BAL	427	8TH WARD
BRANABY, JOHN	BAL	149	16TH WAR
BRANAGAN, ELIZABETH E.	ST	328	4TH E DI
BRANAGAN, JAMES H.	ST	323	4TH E DI
BRANAGAN, JULIA A.	ST	328	4TH E DI
BRANAGON, MARY	BAL	318	1ST DIST
BRANAN, BRIDGET	BAL	104	1ST WARD
BRANAN, MARY	BAL	048	1ST WARD
BRANAN, THOMAS	BAL	279	2ND WARD
BRANARD, AMOS	WOR	248	1ST CENS
BRANARD, JAMES F.	WOR	260	BERLIN 1
BRANARD, STEPHEN	WOR	248	1ST CENS
BRANCH, DANIEL	BAL	156	1ST WARD
BRANCH, HENRY	BAL	128	1ST WARD
BRANCH, HENRY	BAL	132	1ST WARD
BRAND, ALEXANDER	BAL	102	5TH WARD
BRAND, BENJAMIN F.	BAL	133	16TH WAR
BRAND, CH.	BAL	449	8TH WARD
BRAND, CHRIST.	BAL	295	1ST DIST
BRAND, ELIZABETH	ALL	081	5TH E.D.
BRAND, GEORGE	BAL	297	17TH WAR
BRAND, JOHN	BAL	010	15TH WAR
BRAND, JOHN	BAL	126	16TH WAR
BRAND, MARTIN	ALL	231	CUMBERLA
BRAND, MATTHEW	BAL	159	1ST WARD
BRAND, MRS.	BAL	143	11TH WAR
BRAND, WILLIAM	CEC	041	CHESAPEA
BRAND, WILLIAM	BAL	134	1ST WARD
BRAND, WILLIAM F.	HAR	107	2ND DIST
BRAND, WILLY	BAL	323	12TH WAR
BRANDA, CHARLES	BAL	281	2ND WARD
BRANDA, EPHRIAM	BAL	296	1ST DIST
BRANDA, WILLIAM H.	ALL	215	CUMBERLA
BRANDAL, HENRY	BAL	278	1ST DIST
BRANDE, HENRY *	BAL	354	1ST DIST
BRANDELL, SARAH	BAL	092	18TH WAR
BRANDENBARG, JESSE	FRE	277	NEW MARK
BRANDENBERG, PETER	FRE	392	PETERSVI
BRANDENBRY, MARTIN	FRE	322	MIDDLETO

NAME	CO	PAGE	LOCALITY
BRANDENBURG, ELIZABETH	FRE	351	MIDDLETO
BRANDENBURG, GEORGE	ANN	497	HOWARD D
BRANDENBURG, HENRY	FRE	347	MIDDLETO
BRANDENBURG, ISAAC	FRE	336	MIDDLETO
BRANDENBURG, SAMUEL	FRE	277	NEW MARK
BRANDENBURG, SAMUEL	FRE	345	MIDDLETO
BRANDENBURG, SARAH	ANN	497	HOWARD D
BRANDENBURY, SAMUEL	FRE	363	CATOCTIN
BRANDENBUY, JOHNM.	FRE	338	MIDDLETO
BRANDENNA, WILLIAM	ALL	153	6TH E.D.
BRANDERBURY, DAVID	FRE	353	MIDDLETO
BRANDES, FREDRICK F.	BAL	008	4TH WARD
BRANDLE, FREDERICK	BAL	128	5TH WARD
BRANDLE, GEORGE	BAL	177	6TH WARD
BRANDLE, MICHAEL	BAL	315	20TH WAR
BRANDON, CHRISTINE	BAL	219	12TH WAR
BRANDON, JEBHARD	BAL	335	3RD WARD
BRANDOW, HERONE	BAL	284	1ST DIST
BRANDT, C.	FRE	200	5TH E DI
BRANDT, CHARLE	BAL	132	1ST WARD
BRANDT, DENNIS	ALL	164	6TH E.D.
BRANDT, FERDINAND	BAL	120	1ST WARD
BRANDT, FREDERIC	BAL	036	9TH WARD
BRANDT, J. SR.	BAL	094	10TH WAR
BRANDT, JOHN	ALL	164	6TH E.D.
BRANDUEL, GEORGE H.	BAL	218	12TH WAR
BRANE, MARGARET	HAR	145	3RD DIST
BRANE, MICHAEL	BAL	285	1ST DIST
BRANE, MICHAEL	BAL	133	1ST WARD
BRANENBURGH, WILLIAM	CAR	228	5TH DIST
BRANER, JOSEPH	MGM	410	MEDLEY 3
BRANFORD, HENRY	ANN	333	2ND DIST
BRANFORD, JANE	ANN	332	2ND DIST
BRANFORD, JOHN	ANN	332	2ND DIST
BRANFORD, WILLIAM	ANN	331	2ND DIST
BRANGAN, MICHAEL	BAL	262	20TH WAR
BRANGELL, ANN	ST	254	3RD E DI
BRANGER, JOHN	BAL	262	2ND WARD
BRANGLE, CHARLES	WAS	183	BOONSBOR
BRANICK, RACHEL	DOR	360	3RD DIVI
BRANIN, R.B.	HAR	165	3RD DIST
BRANINGTON, SARAH	BAL	053	9TH WARD
BRANMELL, CHRISTOVEL	BAL	169	16TH WAR
BRANNAGAN, EDWARD	ALL	256	CUMBERLA
BRANNAMAN, GEORGE	BAL	164	6TH WARD
BRANNAN, ANN*	BAL	048	4TH WARD
BRANNAN, BERNARD	BAL	270	7TH WARD
BRANNAN, BRIDGET	BAL	338	13TH WAR
BRANNAN, CATHARINE	BAL	210	6TH WARD
BRANNAN, CATHERINE	BAL	363	3RD WARD
BRANNAN, CHARLES	ALL	084	5TH E.D.
BRANNAN, ELLEN	BAL	304	12TH WAR
BRANNAN, ELLEN	BAL	051	15TH WAR
BRANNAN, EUKHEMIA B.	BAL	347	13TH WAR
BRANNAN, HUGH	BAL	161	11TH WAR
BRANNAN, JAMES	BAL	107	15TH WAR
BRANNAN, JAMES	ALL	112	5TH E.D.
BRANNAN, JAMES M.	BAL	327	13TH WAR
BRANNAN, JOHN	BAL	267	12TH WAR
BRANNAN, JOHN	ANN	429	HOWARD D
BRANNAN, JOHN	BAL	043	4TH WARD
BRANNAN, JOHN	BAL	420	14TH WAR
BRANNAN, MARY	BAL	367	8TH WARD
BRANNAN, PATRICK	BAL	012	1ST WARD
BRANNAN, PETER	BAL	001	9TH WARD
BRANNAN, SARAH	BAL	036	15TH WAR
BRANNAN, SARAH	BAL	325	3RD WARD
BRANNAN, SOPHIA	BAL	028	4TH WARD
BRANNAN, THOMAS	BAL	411	3RD WARD
BRANNAN, WILLIAM	BAL	311	1ST DIST
BRANNANN, OWEN	BAL	174	11TH WAR
BRANNARD, H.	BAL	117	1ST WARD
BRANNELL, THOMAS J.	BAL	206	2ND WARD
BRANNEN, MARY	BAL	076	15TH WAR
BRANNETT, ANNETTE	BAL	222	6TH WARD
BRANNICK, JANE	DOR	357	3RD DIVI
BRANNIF, MARY *	BAL	287	20TH WAR
BRANNOCH, JOHN	DOR	392	1ST DIST
BRANNOCK, ANNA E.	DOR	418	1ST DIST
BRANNOCK, FRANK*	DOR	405	1ST DIST
BRANNOCK, HENRIETTA	DOR	389	1ST DIST
BRANNOCK, HENRY	DOR	468	1ST DIST
BRANNOCK, JAMES	DOR	452	1ST DIST
BRANNOCK, JAMES	DOR	467	1ST DIST
BRANNOCK, JAMES	DOR	414	1ST DIST
BRANNOCK, JOHN H.	DOR	415	1ST DIST
BRANNOCK, SUSAN	DOR	424	1ST DIST
BRANNOCK, THOMAS	DOR	414	1ST DIST
BRANNOCK, WILLIS	DOR	391	1ST DIST
BRANNOCK, ZACHARIAH	DOR	417	1ST DIST
BRANNON, ANN	BAL	144	11TH WAR
BRANNON, CATHERINE	BAL	292	3RD WARD
BRANNON, ELIZA	BAL	353	3RD WARD
BRANNON, JAMES	BAL	278	1ST DIST
BRANNON, JAMES	ALL	052	10TH E.D
BRANNON, JOHN	BAL	476	14TH WAR
BRANNON, MARY	BAL	415	1ST DIST
BRANNON, MARY J.	HAR	120	2ND DIST
BRANNON, MICHAEL	ALL	050	10TH E.D
BRANNON, THOMAS	BAL	174	11TH WAR
BRANNON, WILLIAM	BAL	459	1ST DIST
BRANNON, WILLIAM	HAR	123	2ND DIST
BRANNS, JACOB	BAL	068	1ST WARD
BRANNSON, EDWARD	BAL	047	1ST WARD
BRANNT, JOHN	BAL	014	9TH WARD
BRANNY, MARGARET	BAL	372	13TH WAR
BRANNY, MARY *	BAL	287	20TH WAR
BRANNY, PATRICK	ANN	415	HOWARD D
BRANON, PATRICK	CAR	230	5TH DIST
BRANSBURY, CHARLES	BAL	154	16TH WAR
BRANSEL, GEORGE	ANN	278	ANNAPOLI
BRANSEL, JAMES	ANN	278	ANNAPOLI
BRANSON, CATHARINE	ST	285	2ND E DI
BRANSON, DAVID W.	MGM	347	BERRYS D
BRANSON, HERNY	BAL	281	2ND WARD
BRANSON, JAMES A.	ST	279	3RD E DI
BRANSON, JOHN	ST	269	3RD E DI
BRANSON, JOSEPH	BAL	458	1ST DIST
BRANSON, MARY	BAL	018	18TH WAR
BRANSON, ROSETTA	ANN	334	2ND DIST
BRANT, CRATON	BAL	108	5TH WARD
BRANT, DANIEL R.	ALL	055	10TH E.D
BRANT, ELISABETH	ALL	045	10TH E.D
BRANT, G.W.	PRI	105	PISCATAW
BRANT, GEORGE	ALL	166	6TH E.D.
BRANT, GEORGE	BAL	286	2ND WARD
BRANT, GEORGE JR.	ALL	166	6TH E.D.
BRANT, HENNERITTA	BAL	132	18TH WAR
BRANT, ISAAC	BAL	132	18TH WAR
BRANT, JAMES	ALL	166	6TH E.D.
BRANT, JANE	HAR	184	3RD DIST
BRANT, JOHN	ALL	165	6TH E.D.
BRANT, JOHN	BAL	010	9TH WARD
BRANT, JOSEPH	ALL	165	6TH E.D.
BRANT, MARGARET	ALL	202	CUMBERLA
BRANT, MARIANN	ALL	073	5TH E.D.
BRANT, MARY	FRE	318	MIDDLETO
BRANT, MARY ANN	ALL	248	CUMBERLA
BRANT, MARY-BLACK	CAR	123	NO TWP L
BRANT, MRS. HARRETT	BAL	009	18TH WAR
BRANT, ROBERT	BAL	007	9TH WARD
BRANT, S. L.	BAL	104	10TH WAR
BRANT, SARAH A.	ALL	166	6TH E.D.
BRANT, WILLIAM	ALL	204	CUMBERLA
BRANT, WILLIAM R.	ALL	166	6TH E.D.
BRANTER, JOHN	WAS	184	BOONSBOR
BRANTIGAN, MARTIN	BAL	221	6TH WARD
BRANTNER, JACOB	WAS	186	BOONSBOR
BRANTNER, JOHN	WAS	082	2ND SUBD
BRANTNER, SUSAN	WAS	082	2ND SUBD
BRANTON, MARY J.	BAL	121	5TH WARD
BRANWACK, JOHN	BAL	097	1ST WARD
BRART, JOSEPH *	BAL	126	18TH WAR
BRASAW, EMILY	BAL	331	3RD WARD
BRASHAW, WILLIAM	BAL	393	1ST DIST
BRASHEAR, CHRISTIAN	FRE	250	NEW MARK
BRASHEAR, ISABELLA	ANN	265	ANNAPOLI
BRASHEAR, JACCB	FRE	424	8TH E DI
BRASHEAR, JOSHUA	FRE	424	8TH E DI
BRASHEAR, OTHO	FRE	249	NEW MARK
BRASHEAR, RICHARD	FRE	424	8TH E DI
BRASHEARS, ANDREW J.	PRI	023	VANSVILL
BRASHEARS, BENEDICT	PRI	041	VANSVILL
BRASHEARS, CATHARIN A.	CAR	363	9TH DIST
BRASHEARS, CORNELIUS	CAR	363	9TH DIST
BRASHEARS, FRANCIS JR.*	ANN	316	1ST DIST
BRASHEARS, FRANCIS SR.	ANN	313	1ST DIST
BRASHEARS, GASSAWAYH	CAR	363	9TH DIST
BRASHEARS, GREEN	PRI	045	VANSVILL
BRASHEARS, J.	PRI	076	MARLBROU
BRASHEARS, JAMES	PRI	076	MARLBROU
BRASHEARS, JOHN T.	BAL	190	19TH WAR
BRASHEARS, JOSEPH P.	PRI	035	VANSVILL
BRASHEARS, POLLY	BAL	458	1ST DIST
BRASHEARS, RICHARD G.	PRI	034	VANSVILL
BRASHEARS, ROBERT J.	BAL	395	8TH WARD
BRASHEARS, SARAH	BAL	211	17TH WAR
BRASHEARS, THCMAS	BAL	462	1ST DIST
BRASHEARS, THOMAS	WAS	063	2ND SUBD
BRASHEARS, VAN	WAS	043	2ND SUBD
BRASHEARS, WILLIAM	WAS	036	2ND SUBD
BRASHEARS, WILLIAM	PRI	037	VANSVILL
BRASHEAY, CELIA	ALL	158	6TH E.D.
BRASHEMS, THOMAS	PRI	024	VANSVILL
BRASHEONES, CHRISTOPHER	PRI	003	BLADENSB
BRASHEORY, OTHRO	PRI	012	BLADENSB
BRASHER, ANN	HAR	200	3RD DIST
BRASHER, ROBERT	BAL	097	18TH WAR
BRASHERNS, MISS	ANN	281	ANNAPOLI
BRASHERS, ZADOCK	ALL	158	6TH E.D.
BRASHERT, JOHN B.	BAL	032	9TH WARD
BRASHIER, WILLIAM	BAL	242	17TH WAR
BRASHIERS, FRANCIS	BAL	428	14TH WAR
BRASHIERS, JOHN S.	BAL	198	17TH WAR
BRASHIERS, REBECCA L.	BAL	429	14TH WAR
BRASHIERS, WILLIAM	BAL	419	8TH WARD
BRASHIMS, JEREMIAH	PRI	011	BLADENSB
BRASS, JOSEPH	BAL	107	15TH WAR
BRASS, THOMAS	BAL	344	1ST DIST
BRASSEY, GEORGE	BAL	143	1ST WARD
BRASSEY, GEORGE	BAL	020	4TH WARD
BRASSON, JOHN	BAL	044	4TH WARD
BRAT, JOHN H.	BAL	094	18TH WAR
BRATEN, HENRY	BAL	132	11TH WAR
BRATHEARS, FRANCIS JR. *	ANN	316	1ST DIST
BRATHEAS, HANNAH	MGM	384	ROCKERLE
BRATHEAUS, JAMES *	MGM	383	ROCKERLE
BRATHER, RUGHT B.	WAS	102	2ND DIST
BRATT, JOHN	BAL	012	18TH WAR
BRATT, JOHN T.	MGM	347	BERRYS D
BRATT, MARY E.	BAL	270	1ST DIST
BRATT, NOAH	BAL	018	15TH WAR
BRATT, ROBERT	BAL	280	17TH WAR
BRATT, SARAH	BAL	280	17TH WAR
BRATT, THOAMS	BAL	110	18TH WAR
BRATT, WILLIAM	BAL	357	8TH WARD
BRATTAN, ALSEY	SOM	418	PRINCESS
BRATTAN, ANN M.	SOM	528	QUANTICO
BRATTAN, ELEANOR A.	SOM	516	BARREN C
BRATTAN, ELIJAH	SOM	403	BRINKLEY
BRATTAN, JOSEPH	SOM	516	BARREN C
BRATTAN, JOSEPH	SOM	402	BRINKLEY
BRATTAN, LEMUEL R.	SOM	515	BARREN C
BRATTAN, ROBERT	SOM	402	BRINKLEY
BRATTAN, SAMUEL	SOM	515	BARREN C
BRATTAN, SAMUEL C.	SOM	398	BRINKLEY
BRATTAN, SARAH	SOM	389	BRINKLEY
BRATTAN, WILIAM	WOR	254	1ST CENS
BRATTAN, WILLIAM S.	SOM	395	BRINKLEY
BRATTEN, CHARLES	WOR	312	2ND E DI
BRATTEN, ELEANOR*	SOM	402	BRINKLEY
BRATTEN, GEORGE	WOR	201	3RD E DI
BRATTEN, JAMES D.	WOR	236	6TH E DI
BRATTEN, JUSTUS M.	WOR	201	3RD E DI
BRATTEN, JUSUS M.	WOR	201	3RD E DI
BRATTEN, MARIA	WOR	201	3RD E DI
BRATTEN, MARY	WOR	304	SNOW HIL
BRATTEN, NOAH	WOR	185	6TH E DI
BRATTEN, SAMUEL T.	WOR	211	4TH E DI
BRATTEN, WILLIAM	SOM	483	TRAPP DI
BRATTIN, N.	WOR	314	2ND E DI
BRATTON, CATHERINE	CEC	207	7TH E DI
BRATTON, DAMUEL C.	WOR	269	BERLIN 1
BRATTON, DANIEL	CEC	004	ELKTON 3
BRATTON, ELIZABETH	WOR	308	2ND E DI
BRATTON, GEORGE	WOR	309	2ND E DI
BRATTON, GEORGE	WOR	307	2ND E DI
BRATTON, HENRY	WOR	320	1ST E DI
BRATTON, ISAAC	WOR	307	2ND E DI
BRATTON, MARY-BLACK	WOR	321	1ST E DI
BRATTON, NANCY	WOR	309	2ND E DI
BRATTON, WILLIAM	WOR	275	BERLIN 1
BRATTON, WILLIAM	WOR	301	SNOW HIL
BRATTON, WILLIAM	WOR	309	2ND E DI
BRATY, FRANKLIN	HAR	127	2ND DIST
BRAUGH, JOHN	BAL	226	2ND WARD
BRAUGH, SAMUEL	BAL	226	1ST DIST
BRAUM, ELIZABETH	BAL	249	1ST DIST
BRAUN, ELIZA	FRE	379	PETERSVI
BRAUNER, WILILAM T.	BAL	093	18TH WAR
BRAUNGERT, MARY A.	WAS	151	HAGERSTO
BRAUNS, EMMA J.	BAL	065	10TH WAR
BRAUNS, HARRIET	BAL	095	15TH WAR
BRAUTNER, JOHN *	WAS	082	2ND SUBD
BRAUTNER, MICHAEL	WAS	034	2ND SUBD
BRAUTNER, SUSAN *	WAS	082	2ND SUBD
BRAUTNER, WILLIAM	WAS	031	2ND SUBD
BRAVE, S.	BAL	142	1ST WARD
BRAVER, FRANCES	BAL	024	4TH WARD
BRAWHARON, ANN M.*	DOR	460	1ST DIST
BRAWNER, ANDREW	BAL	398	8TH WARD
BRAWNER, CATHARINE	BAL	470	14TH WAR
BRAWNER, EDGAR	CHA	259	MIDDLETO
BRAWNER, HARRIOT	CHA	263	MIDDLETO
BRAWNER, J. THADEUS	CHA	257	MIDDLETO
BRAWNER, JAMES	BAL	102	10TH WAR
BRAWNER, JOSEPH	FRE	200	5TH E DI
BRAWNER, MARY	FRE	188	5TH E DI
BRAWNER, SARAH	FRE	182	5TH E DI
BRAWNER, SUSAN	BAL	138	5TH WARD
BRAWNER, WILLIAM	FRE	193	5TH E DI
BRAWNER, WILLIAM	FRE	188	5TH E DI
BRAY, BENJAMIN	BAL	020	1ST WARD
BRAY, C.H.	BAL	140	1ST WARD
BRAY, HENRY	ALL	066	10TH E.D
BRAY, JOHN	ALL	066	10TH E.D
BRAY, JOHN	ALL	067	10TH E.D
BRAY, JOSEPH	ANN	342	3RD DIST
BRAY, MARY	ANN	348	3RD DIST
BRAY, MATILDA	ANN	342	3RD DIST
BRAY, SARAH L.	ANN	340	3RD DIST
BRAY, WILLIAM	ALL	120	5TH E.D.
BRAY, WILLIAM	BAL	130	11TH WAR
BRAYDEN, JANE	BAL	116	11TH WAR
BRAYDEN, ROBERT J.	BAL	116	11TH WAR
BRAYDEN, WILLIAM	BAL	115	11TH WAR
BRAYDEN, WILLIAM JR.	BAL	302	20TH WAR
BRAYLE, EZRA M.	FRE	264	NEW MARK
BRAYMAN, BOTINA	BAL	218	2ND WARD
BRAYONIER, ANN	WAS	038	2ND SUBD
BRAYSHAW, JAMES	BAL	343	1ST DIST
BRAYWOOD, CHARLES-BLACK	BAL	218	2ND WARD
BRAYWOOD, HENRY-BLACK	BAL	218	2ND WARD
BRAYWOOD, KATURAH-BLACK	BAL	219	2ND WARD
BRAZIER, JACOB	WOR	244	1ST CENS
BRAZIER, WILLIAM	WAS	139	HAGERSTO
BRAZIL, MITCHEAL	HAR	156	3RD DIST
BRAZY, WILIAM	ALL	247	CUMBERLA
BRDAGAN, CATHARINE	BAL	462	1ST DIST
BREACH, JAMES	BAL	377	8TH WARD
BREADEN, JACOB	CAL	011	1ST DIST
BREADEN, RICHARD A.	CAL	011	1ST DIST
BREADEN, RICHARD P.	CAL	011	1ST DIST
BREADEN, WILLIAM	CAL	012	1ST DIST
BREADY, DAVID	MGM	366	BERRYS D
BREADY, GEORGE A.	FRE	209	BUCKEYST
BREADY, JOHN W.	FRE	209	BUCKEYST
BREAGLE, JOHN G.	BAL	409	8TH WARD
BREAM, POWLES	BAL	299	17TH WAR
BREAN, CAROLINE	TAL	071	EASTON T
BREAN, MARGARET	BAL	404	1ST DIST
BREASENT, MILCHA A.	CEC	103	4TH E DI
BREASHEARS, JOHN H.	FRE	047	FREDERIC
BREATHED, JOHN W.	WAS	207	1ST DIST
BREBACK, JACOB	ALL	057	10TH E.D
BRECAID, JAMES	BAL	444	14TH WAR
BRECHT, CHARLES	BAL	334	7TH WARD
BRECHT, ELIZABETH	FRE	004	FREDERIC
BRECK, CAROLINE	BAL	053	4TH WARD
BRECK, JOSHUA	BAL	033	4TH WARD
BRECKER, WILLIAM	BAL	164	16TH WAR
BRECKERNAN, MARY	ALL	184	9TH E.D.
BRECKHN, WILLIAM	TAL	111	ST MICHA
BRECKINGE, P.*	BAL	293	12TH WAR
BRECKLEN, HENRY	BAL	033	4TH WARD
BREDAKAMP, JOHN	PRI	007	BLADENSB
BREDAKAMP, JOHN	PRI	007	BLADENSB
BREDDELL, MARY	WOR	171	6TH E DI
BREDEKAMP, HERMAN	BAL	284	17TH WAR
BREDEL, BERNAR	BAL	242	2ND WARD
BREDEMYER, LOUISA	BAL	105	10TH WAR
BREDEN, SIDNEY	BAL	294	12TH WAR
BREDGLE, JOHN	BAL	393	8TH WARD
BREDING, JOSEPH	ALL	234	CUMBERLA
BREED, MARY	BAL	046	9TH WARD
BREEDEN, SUSANNAH	BAL	062	15TH WAR
BREEDING, ELIZABETH-MULAT	CAR	092	NO TWP L
BREEDING, ELLEN	CAR	117	NO TWP L
BREEDING, ERMALS	CAR	108	NO TWP L
BREEDING, SARAH	CAR	092	NO TWP L
BREEDMILLER, LEWIS	ALL	224	CUMBERLA
BREEGAN, LAWRENCE	ALL	135	4TH E.D.
BREEN, FRANCIS P.	BAL	347	13TH WAR
BREEN, JOHN	BAL	126	1ST WARD
BREENS, JOHN	BAL	210	17TH WAR
BREERWOOD, ALLY*	DOR	416	1ST DIST
BREESH, JOHN	WAS	142	2ND DIST
BREEWOOD, CHARLES*	DOR	405	1ST DIST
BREGET, MISS	ANN	266	ANNAPOLI
BREGUET, GEORGE W.	BAL	098	15TH WAR
BREHARN, SEBASTIAN	BAL	420	14TH WAR
BREIGHNER, ANTHONY	FRE	195	5TH E DI
BREIGHNER, DANIEL	FRE	194	5TH E DI
BREIGHNER, HANNAH	FRE	195	5TH E DI
BREIGHNER, JERECME	FRE	163	EMMITTSB
BREISH, D. G.	WAS	184	BOONSBOR
BREISH, JOHN J.	WAS	139	HAGERSTO
BREITHOUGH, CHARLES *	FRE	304	WOODSBOR
BREKLE, HENRY	BAL	133	16TH WAR
BREL, MARY	BAL	357	13TH WAR
BRELER, THAD	BAL	265	12TH WAR
BRELHART, JONATHAN	CAR	330	MANCHEST
BREMAN, AMBROSE	BAL	212	11TH WAR
BREMER, GEORGE	BAL	275	7TH WARD
BREMER, HENRY	BAL	022	9TH WARD
BREMER, JOHN	BAL	323	3RD WARD
BREMMAR, JOHN	BAL	288	17TH WAR
BREMMER, ANTHONY	BAL	352	3RD WARD
BREMMON, BRIDGET	ALL	139	6TH E.D.
BRENALL, JOSEPH	BAL	269	2ND WARD
BRENAN, ALFRED	BAL	277	12TH WAR
BRENAN, EDWARD	BAL	120	5TH WARD
BRENAN, F. XAVIER	BAL	061	10TH WAR
BRENAN, FRANCES	BAL	098	15TH WAR
BRENAN, JOHN J. A.	BAL	089	10TH WAR
BRENAN, P. E.	BAL	072	10TH WAR
BREND, HENRY	BAL	248	6TH WARD
BRENDLE, DANIEL	WAS	024	2ND SUBD
BRENDLE, GEORGE	WAS	123	HAGERSTO
BRENDLE, HENRY	FRE	316	MIDDLETO

Name	County	Page	District
BRENGLE, CATHERINE	FRE	026	FREDERIC
BRENGLE, CHARLES W.	ALL	235	CUMBERLA
BRENGLE, CHRISTIAN	FRE	050	FREDERIC
BRENGLE, DANIEL	FRE	049	FREDERIC
BRENGLE, DAVID	ALL	222	CUMBERLA
BRENGLE, ELIZABETH	FRE	059	FREDERIC
BRENGLE, GEORGE L.	FRE	036	FREDERIC
BRENGLE, JACOB	ALL	211	CUMBERLA
BRENGLE, LAURENCE	FRE	039	FREDERIC
BRENGLE, LEWIS A.	FRE	059	FREDERIC
BRENGLE, MARIA	FRE	045	FREDERIC
BRENGLE, MARY	FRE	407	JEFFERSO
BRENGLE, MARY	FRE	264	NEW MARK
BRENGLE, MARY	FRE	099	FREDERIC
BRENGLE, NICHOLAS	FRE	008	FREDERIC
BRENHAL, PHILIP	BAL	035	1ST WARD
BRENING, SOLOMON	BAL	135	1ST WARD
BRENIZER, RETNER	FRE	123	CREAGERS
BRENKMAN, HENRY N.	CAR	333	MANCHEST
BRENMAN, JOSEPH	BAL	078	2ND DIST
BRENNALL, D.	BAL	116	1ST WARD
BRENNAN, PATRICK	ALL	100	5TH E.D.
BRENNAN, THOMAS	BAL	456	8TH WARD
BRENNEMAN, DANIEL	CAR	290	7TH DIST
BRENNEMAN, MARY	ALL	005	3RD E.D.
BRENNEMAN, SAMUEL	ALL	016	3RD E.D.
BRENNER, ANN	FRE	047	FREDERIC
BRENNER, GEORGE *	WAS	086	2ND SUBD
BRENNER, JOSEPH	FRE	022	FREDERIC
BRENNER, SOLOMON	BAL	334	3RD WARD
BRENNER, WILLIAM F.	FRE	049	FREDERIC
BRENNERMAN, FREDERIC	BAL	194	6TH WARD
BRENNON, B.	ALL	155	6TH E.D.
BRENNUM, JOHN	WAS	225	1ST DIST
BRENNUSEN, MARGARET	ANN	508	HOWARD D
BRENON, MARTHA E.	CHA	219	ALLENS F
BRENSEN, HIRONEMUS	FRE	439	8TH E DI
BRENSENDORF, CHARLES	ALL	038	2ND E.D.
BRENSTINE, HENRY	ALL	100	5TH E.D.
BRENT, CHRISTIAN	BAL	404	1ST DIST
BRENT, CHRISTOPHER	BAL	288	3RD WARD
BRENT, EMILY	CHA	225	ALLENS F
BRENT, GEORGE	CHA	294	BOJANTOW
BRENT, GEORGE	BAL	135	16TH WAR
BRENT, GEORGE	WAS	155	2ND DIST
BRENT, GEROGE	BAL	315	20TH WAR
BRENT, HENNERIETTA	BAL	156	11TH WAR
BRENT, JAMES	CHA	241	HILLTOP
BRENT, MATILDA	BAL	156	11TH WAR
BRENT, ROBERT Y.	MGM	360	BERRYS D
BRENTLER, NICHOLAS	ALL	199	CUMBERLA
BRENTLINGER, FREDERICK	FRE	256	NEW MARK
BRENTON, ALBIN H.	CEC	088	4TH E DI
BRENTZE, RACHEL	HAR	112	2ND DIST
BREPPY, JOHN	BAL	155	1ST WARD
BRERITT, BENEDICT *	KEN	268	1ST DIST
BRERME, ELIZABETH *	KEN	212	2ND DIST
BRERME, HENRY *	KEN	212	2ND DIST
BRESCUP, THOMAS JR.	BAL	298	7TH WARD
BRESHMILLER, CATHERINE	BAL	302	20TH WAR
BRESLER, CALEB	CEC	205	7TH E DI
BRESLIN, MICHAEL	FRE	378	PETERSVI
BRESLON, WILLIAM H.	ALL	252	CUMBERLA
BRESNAHAM, RICHARD	BAL	406	8TH WARD
BRESSHLER, HENRY	BAL	054	18TH WAR
BRETHED, JOHN	WAS	196	1ST DIST
BRETHOD, ISAAC	WAS	148	2ND DIST
BRETHOD, JAMES	WAS	154	2ND DIST
BRETT, ELIZABETH M.	BAL	404	1ST DIST
BRETT, MARTHA H.	ANN	521	HOWARD D
BRETT, SIRUS	BAL	270	1ST DIST
BRETTLEBANK, JULIUS	BAL	474	14TH WAR
BRETZFELDER, LENA	BAL	063	15TH WAR
BREUNER, GEORGE *	WAS	086	2ND SUBD
BREVITT, CHARITY S.	BAL	040	4TH WARD
BREWER, A.	ANN	272	ANNAPOLI
BREWER, ABRAM	BAL	223	12TH WAR
BREWER, ALEXANDER	ST	343	5TH E DI
BREWER, AMELIA	WAS	141	2ND DIST
BREWER, ANN E.	ST	280	3RD E DI
BREWER, BRICE JR.	ANN	272	ANNAPOLI
BREWER, CATHERINE	WAS	111	2ND DIST
BREWER, CHARLES	BAL	293	17TH WAR
BREWER, CHARLES	HAR	054	1ST DIST
BREWER, DANIEL	WAS	100	2ND DIST
BREWER, DAVID	WAS	135	2ND DIST
BREWER, DINAH	ANN	457	HOWARD D
BREWER, EDWARD	ANN	292	ANNAPOLI
BREWER, ELIAS	WAS	105	2ND DIST
BREWER, ELIZABETH	WAS	124	2ND DIST
BREWER, ELIZBETH	WAS	118	2ND DIST
BREWER, EMILY	WAS	256	1ST DIST
BREWER, EMMA	BAL	359	13TH WAR
BREWER, FRANCIS	BAL	294	17TH WAR
BREWER, GEORGE	BAL	218	17TH WAR
BREWER, GEORGE	MGM	422	MEDLEY 3
BREWER, GEORGE	WAS	120	2ND DIST
BREWER, GEORGE	WAS	136	2ND DIST
BREWER, GEORGE	BAL	329	13TH WAR
BREWER, GEORGE G.	ANN	292	ANNAPOLI
BREWER, HENRIETTA	BAL	023	4TH WARD
BREWER, HENRY	BAL	220	17TH WAR
BREWER, HENRY	WAS	026	2ND SUBD
BREWER, HENRY S.	WAS	107	2ND DIST
BREWER, JACOB	WAS	110	2ND DIST
BREWER, JACOB H.	WAS	110	2ND DIST
BREWER, JAMES B.	ANN	272	ANNAPOLI
BREWER, JAMES T.	ST	256	3RD E DI
BREWER, JOHN	WAS	026	2ND SUBD
BREWER, JOHN	BAL	173	16TH WAR
BREWER, JOHN	BAL	415	8TH WARD
BREWER, JOHN	MGM	376	ROCKERLE
BREWER, JOHN	CEC	098	3RD E DI
BREWER, JOHN A.	WAS	106	2ND DIST
BREWER, JOHN OF JOHN	ANN	269	ANNAPOLI
BREWER, JOSEPH	ALL	238	CUMBERLA
BREWER, JOSEPH	BAL	149	5TH WARD
BREWER, JOSEPH	WAS	141	2ND DIST
BREWER, JOSEPH	MGM	409	MEDLEY 3
BREWER, JOSEPH N.	ANN	310	1ST DIST
BREWER, JUDGE N.	ANN	287	ANNAPOLI
BREWER, LEUSE	ST	257	3RD E DI
BREWER, LEWIS	BAL	422	8TH WARD
BREWER, LLOYD A.	ST	280	3RD E DI
BREWER, LUCRETIA	FRE	039	FREDERIC
BREWER, MARY	WAS	153	2ND DIST
BREWER, MARY	ANN	286	ANNAPOLI
BREWER, MATHEW	ANN	325	2ND DIST
BREWER, NACE	ANN	331	2ND DIST
BREWER, NATHAN	ANN	369	4TH DIST
BREWER, NATHANIEL N.	ANN	310	1ST DIST
BREWER, NICHOLAS	ANN	289	ANNAPOLI
BREWER, NICHOLAS	MGM	412	MEDLEY 3
BREWER, NICHOLAS	BAL	064	4TH WARD
BREWER, NICK	ANN	325	2ND DIST
BREWER, PETER	WAS	128	2ND DIST
BREWER, PHILIP	BAL	017	4TH WARD
BREWER, RICHARD	BAL	333	3RD WARD
BREWER, RUTH	ANN	272	ANNAPOLI
BREWER, S.	ANN	283	ANNAPOLI
BREWER, SAMUEL	ALL	247	CUMBERLA
BREWER, SAMUEL	ALL	229	CUMBERLA
BREWER, THOMAS	ANN	286	ANNAPOLI
BREWER, VINCENT	MGM	341	CLARKSBU
BREWER, VIRGINIA	WAS	116	2ND DIST
BREWER, WILLAIM	ANN	272	ANNAPOLI
BREWER, WILLIAM	ANN	286	ANNAPOLI
BREWER, WILLIAM	ANN	280	ANNAPOLI
BREWER, WILLIAM	BAL	208	19TH WAR
BREWER, WILLIAM	MGM	426	MEDLEY 3
BREWER, WILLIAM	HAR	107	2ND DIST
BREWER, WILLIAM	HAR	091	2ND DIST
BREWER, ZACHARIAH	ST	256	3RD E DI
BREWERS, DANIEL	BAL	210	19TH WAR
BREWGLE, ALFRED F.	FRE	057	FREDERIC
BREWINGTON, ANN	WOR	239	6TH E DI
BREWINGTON, CAROLINE	SOM	470	TRAPPE D
BREWINGTON, CHARLOTTE	WOR	204	4TH E DI
BREWINGTON, DRUCILLA	WOR	240	6TH E DI
BREWINGTON, EBENEZER	WOR	228	6TH E DI
BREWINGTON, EDWARD	SOM	472	TRAPPE D
BREWINGTON, GEORGE	SOM	481	TRAPP DI
BREWINGTON, HANNAH *	WOR	210	4TH E DI
BREWINGTON, HENRY	WOR	239	6TH E DI
BREWINGTON, HENRY	SOM	488	SALISBUR
BREWINGTON, HENRY J.	SOM	490	SALISBUR
BREWINGTON, ISAAC	BAL	180	2ND DIST
BREWINGTON, JAMES	SOM	470	TRAPPE D
BREWINGTON, JAMES W.	WOR	232	6TH E DI
BREWINGTON, JOHN P.	SOM	482	TRAPP DI
BREWINGTON, LEAH	SOM	497	SALISBUR
BREWINGTON, MARY	SOM	481	TRAPP DI
BREWINGTON, MIRANDA	SOM	471	TRAPPE D
BREWINGTON, SCOTT	SOM	488	SALISBUR
BREWINGTON, THEODORE	SOM	497	SALISBUR
BREWNER, ELLEN	BAL	191	17TH WAR
BREWNER, LEONARD W.	BAL	300	17TH WAR
BREWS, MARY J.	BAL	216	17TH WAR
BREWSTER, JAOCB S.	QUE	132	1ST E DI
BREWWER, LURCELIA *	ST	258	3RD E DI
BREXSH, JOHN	WAS	142	2ND DIST
BRIAE, CHRISTOPHE *	BAL	067	18TH WAR
BRIAL, CHRISTOPER *	BAL	067	18TH WAR
BRIAN, ARTHIN	BAL	155	2ND DIST
BRIAN, BROOK	ALL	237	CUMBERLA
BRIAN, CATHARINE	HAR	169	3RD DIST
BRIAN, CATHARINE	BAL	401	14TH WAR
BRIAN, CHARLES	BAL	150	16TH WAR
BRIAN, EDWARD	BAL	107	5TH WARD
BRIAN, ELIZABETH	BAL	255	17TH WAR
BRIAN, ELIZABETH	HAR	032	1ST DIST
BRIAN, ELLEN	BAL	413	14TH WAR
BRIAN, ELLEN	ST	258	3RD E DI
BRIAN, ELLEN	ST	258	3RD E DI
BRIAN, HARRIET	BAL	168	2ND DIST
BRIAN, ISAIAH	BAL	401	3RD WARD
BRIAN, JAMES	BAL	168	2ND DIST
BRIAN, JAMES	ALL	241	CUMBERLA
BRIAN, JAMES	BAL	068	2ND DIST
BRIAN, JAMES C.	TAL	017	EASTON D
BRIAN, JOHN	BAL	018	2ND DIST
BRIAN, JOHN	BAL	175	2ND DIST
BRIAN, JOHN G.	BAL	094	5TH WARD
BRIAN, JOSEPH	BAL	048	2ND DIST
BRIAN, JULIA	BAL	142	11TH WAR
BRIAN, MARTIN	BAL	110	5TH WARD
BRIAN, NATHANIEL	ALL	241	CUMBERLA
BRIAN, NICHOLAS	BAL	068	2ND DIST
BRIAN, PATRICK	BAL	082	2ND DIST
BRIAN, PETER	FRE	087	FREDERIC
BRIAN, ROBERT	BAL	143	1ST WARD
BRIAN, SANTY	HAR	032	1ST DIST
BRIAN, SOLOMAN	TAL	042	EASTON D
BRIAN, WILLIAM	BAL	239	17TH WAR
BRIAN, WILLIAM	BAL	144	5TH WARD
BRIAN, WILLIAM A.	BAL	094	5TH WARD
BRIARTON, JOHN	BAL	343	13TH WAR
BRIBAK, FREDERICK	ALL	056	10TH E.D
BRICE, *	BAL	194	5TH DIST
BRICE, ANDREW	ALL	131	4TH E.D.
BRICE, ANN-BLACK	MGM	414	MEDLEY 3
BRICE, BENJAMIN	HAR	048	1ST DIST
BRICE, CHARLES C.	ANN	349	3RD DIST
BRICE, CHARLOTTE	KEN	266	1ST DIST
BRICE, CORNELIA	BAL	119	5TH WARD
BRICE, EDMUND	BAL	197	17TH WAR
BRICE, EDWARD	BAL	252	17TH WAR
BRICE, ELIZA	BAL	180	11TH WAR
BRICE, EPHRAIM	BAL	185	11TH WAR
BRICE, GEORGE P.D.	BAL	257	12TH WAR
BRICE, HARCULES	BAL	456	1ST DIST
BRICE, HARIET	BAL	271	20TH WAR
BRICE, HARKLEY	BAL	014	2ND DIST
BRICE, HENRY	BAL	430	8TH WARD
BRICE, HENRY	BAL	247	6TH WARD
BRICE, HESTER	BAL	211	11TH WAR
BRICE, ISACK*	TAL	020	EASTON D
BRICE, ISACK*	TAL	057	EASTON D
BRICE, IWLLIAM	ANN	320	2ND DIST
BRICE, JAMES	BAL	180	6TH WARD
BRICE, JAMES	BAL	240	6TH WARD
BRICE, JAMES	CAR	210	5TH DIST
BRICE, JAMES	CAR	209	5TH DIST
BRICE, JAMES*	TAL	042	EASTON D
BRICE, JOE	TAL	020	EASTON D
BRICE, JOHN	BAL	216	19TH WAR
BRICE, JOHN	ANN	266	ANNAPOLI
BRICE, JOHN	BAL	247	6TH WARD
BRICE, JOHN	ANN	340	3RD DIST
BRICE, JOHN	BAL	101	5TH WARD
BRICE, JOHN	BAL	283	12TH WAR
BRICE, JOHN H.	ANN	287	ANNAPOLI
BRICE, JOSEPH	QUE	167	2ND E DI
BRICE, JOSEPH H.	BAL	312	7TH WARD
BRICE, KINSAY	BAL	050	9TH WARD
BRICE, KINSEY	BAL	181	6TH WARD
BRICE, M. A.	BAL	105	10TH WAR
BRICE, MARTHA	KEN	215	2ND DIST
BRICE, MARY	CEC	029	CHESAPEA
BRICE, MARY	BAL	272	12TH WAR
BRICE, MARY J.	BAL	453	14TH WAR
BRICE, NICHOLIS	BAL	154	11TH WAR
BRICE, RICHARD	BAL	202	6TH WARD
BRICE, RICHARD T.	ANN	350	3RD DIST
BRICE, ROBERT	BAL	115	18TH WAR
BRICE, SALLY A.	TAL	020	EASTON D
BRICE, SARAH A.	HAR	015	1ST DIST
BRICE, SUSANNAH	BAL	094	15TH WAR
BRICE, THOMAS	BAL	322	3RD WARD
BRICE, THOMAS	BAL	006	4TH WARD
BRICE, THOMAS G.	ANN	303	1ST DIST
BRICE, WILLIAM	ANN	289	ANNAPOLI
BRICE, WILLIAM	BAL	421	14TH WAR
BRICE, WILLIAM A.	KEN	282	3RD DIST
BRICE, WILLIAM*	TAL	053	EASTON D
BRICELAND, JAMES	BAL	125	1ST WARD
BRICELAND, ROSE	BAL	424	1ST DIST
BRICHFIELD, JAMES	ALL	226	CUMBERLA
BRICK, ANN R.	ST	317	4TH E DI
BRICK, ANNA	BAL	067	4TH WARD
BRICK, JAEMS	BAL	395	14TH WAR
BRICK, JOHN C.	BAL	059	10TH WAR
BRICK, MARY E.-BLACK	CAR	397	2ND DIST
BRICK, RACHAEL	BAL	068	4TH WARD
BRICK, THOMAS	HAR	141	2ND DIST
BRICKARD, EMANUEL	BAL	447	1ST DIST
BRICKEL, NATHANIEL	DOR	466	1ST DIST
BRICKER, DORUS	BAL	233	17TH WAR
BRICKER, FRANKLIN	BAL	300	17TH WAR
BRICKERING, MARY C. F.	BAL	139	16TH WAR
BRICKHOUSE, PEGGY	BAL	200	17TH WAR
BRICKHOUSEN, SMITH L.	BAL	200	17TH WAR
BRICKLEY, ALEM	CEC	152	PORT DUP
BRICKLEY, IRACEN	CEC	195	6TH E DI
BRICKLEY, ISAIAH	DOR	392	1ST DIST
BRICKLEY, JOSEPH	BAL	426	8TH WARD
BRICKLEY, JOSHUA R.	BAL	060	4TH WARD
BRICKLEY, WILLIAM	CEC	137	6TH E DI
BRICKLY, HESTER	CEC	195	6TH E DI
BRICKLY, JOACEM	CEC	211	7TH E DI
BRICKLY, JULIA	CEC	132	6TH E DI
BRICKLY, MARGARET	CEC	195	6TH E DI
BRICKLY, MARY	CEC	195	6TH E DI
BRICKLY, SAMUEL	CEC	195	6TH E DI
BRICKLY, WILLIAM*	DOR	453	1ST DIST
BRICKMAN, CHARLES	BAL	457	14TH WAR
BRICKMAN, WILLIAM	HAR	107	2ND DIST
BRICKNER, GEORGE	BAL	279	17TH WAR
BRICKVADER, JOSEPH	BAL	290	17TH WAR
BRIDAL, SAMUEL	BAL	113	5TH WARD
BRIDDE, ADAM *	BAL	099	18TH WAR
BRIDDELL, AMY	WOR	276	BERLIN 1
BRIDDELL, BILL	WOR	272	BERLIN 1
BRIDDELL, DAVID	WOR	168	6TH E DI
BRIDDELL, HENRY	WOR	264	BERLIN 1
BRIDDELL, HET	WOR	281	BERLIN 1
BRIDDELL, JOSHUA	WOR	287	BERLIN 1
BRIDDELL, JULIA	WOR	273	BERLIN 1
BRIDDELL, KENDAL	WOR	272	BERLIN 1
BRIDDELL, MARIAH	WOR	287	BERLIN 1
BRIDDELL, MARIAH	WOR	330	1ST E DI
BRIDDELL, PATTY	WOR	279	BERLIN 1
BRIDDELL, ZEB	WOR	282	BERLIN 1
BRIDDEN, JESSE	BAL	193	17TH WAR
BRIDE, COTTER	BAL	355	13TH WAR
BRIDE, ELLEN	BAL	025	9TH WARD
BRIDE, GUSTAVUS	BAL	348	7TH WARD
BRIDE, JOHN	BAL	296	12TH WAR
BRIDE, PETER	BAL	384	8TH WARD
BRIDE, ROBERT	TAL	075	EASTON T
BRIDEGUM, FREDERICK	BAL	074	2ND DIST
BRIDELL, JOE	WOR	287	BERLIN 1
BRIDELL, JOSHUA	SOM	405	DUBLIN D
BRIDELL, LOUISA G.	BAL	071	15TH WAR
BRIDELL, MARGARET	WOR	262	BERLIN 1
BRIDELL, MARTHA	SOM	411	DUBLIN D
BRIDELL, THOAMS	WOR	301	SNOW HIL
BRIDEMAN, JACOB	BAL	407	8TH WARD
BRIDEN, WILLIAM	HAR	199	3RD DIST
BRIDENDALPH, ANTHONEY	WAS	134	2ND DIST
BRIDENER, JACOB	BAL	404	14TH WAR
BRIDENER, JOSEPH	KEN	216	2ND DIST
BRIDENHART, MARY	ALL	263	CUMBERLA
BRIDENHAUGH, JACOB	BAL	288	3RD WARD
BRIDENPH, WILLIAM	WAS	142	2ND DIST
BRIDENSFIELD, CAROLINE	BAL	010	4TH WARD
BRIDENSTINE, CASPER	BAL	279	17TH WAR
BRIDGE, ADOLPHUS	BAL	049	1ST WARD
BRIDGE, CATHARINE	WAS	293	1ST DIST
BRIDGE, ELIZA	BAL	079	10TH WAR
BRIDGE, J.	BAL	173	1ST WARD
BRIDGE, JACOB	WAS	143	HAGERSTO
BRIDGE, JOHN	BAL	129	1ST WARD
BRIDGE, STEPHEN	BAL	114	5TH WARD
BRIDGES, ANN M.	TAL	115	ST MICHA
BRIDGES, BETSEY	TAL	055	EASTON D
BRIDGES, DANIEL	TAL	106	ST MICHA
BRIDGES, HELEN	WAS	158	2ND DIST
BRIDGES, JAMES	TAL	107	ST MICHA
BRIDGES, JOHN	TAL	110	ST MICHA
BRIDGES, JOHN	BAL	423	8TH WARD
BRIDGES, JOHN	BAL	394	14TH WAR
BRIDGES, MRS. MARY	BAL	015	18TH WAR
BRIDGES, REBECCA	WAS	158	2ND DIST
BRIDGES, RICHARD	TAL	107	ST MICHA
BRIDGES, THOMAS	TAL	107	ST MICHA
BRIDGES, THOMAS	TAL	107	ST MICHA
BRIDGES, WILLIAM	BAL	335	13TH WAR
BRIDGES, WILLIAM H.	TAL	109	ST MICHA
BRIDGMAN, JAMES	CAR	079	NO TWP L
BRIDING, ERNEST W.	BAL	061	15TH WAR
BRIDINTON, MARY	BAL	336	3RD WARD
BRIDLES, EDWARD-BLACK	CAR	088	NO TWP L
BRIDLESPECKER, CHARLES	BAL	351	1ST DIST
BRIDLEY, SUSAN	BAL	272	12TH WAR
BRIDMAN, ANN J.	WAS	157	2ND DIST
BRIDNER, MARTIN	BAL	455	14TH WAR
BRIDNER, PHILIP	BAL	257	1ST DIST
BRIDRICK, THOMAS	ALL	155	6TH E.D.
BRIDWELL, ANN	PRI	026	VANSVILL
BRIDWELL, ANN	PRI	003	BLADENSB
BRIDWELL, WILLIAM	PRI	003	BLADENSB
BRIEL, AUGUST	BAL	372	13TH WAR
BRIEN, ANN H.	FRE	001	FREDERIC
BRIEN, CATHARIEN V.	BAL	464	14TH WAR
BRIEN, CATHARINE	BAL	253	2ND WARD
BRIEN, ELEN	CAR	194	4TH DIST
BRIEN, ELIZA	BAL	126	11TH WAR
BRIEN, GEORGE F.	BAL	120	1ST WARD
BRIEN, HARRIET-BLACK	FRE	452	8TH E DI

Name	County	Page	District
BRIEN, HARRIETT	ALL	134	4TH E.D.
BRIEN, ISAAC	CAR	214	5TH DIST
BRIEN, ISABELLA	WAS	062	2ND SUBD
BRIEN, J. MC P.	BAL	099	10TH WAR
BRIEN, JAEMS	CAR	201	4TH DIST
BRIEN, JOHN	BAL	253	2ND WARD
BRIEN, JOHN	BAL	142	2ND DIST
BRIEN, L. L.	BAL	142	11TH WAR
BRIEN, LUKE TIERNAN *	BAL	411	1ST DIST
BRIEN, MARY M.	FRE	450	8TH E DI
BRIEN, PHILIP	BAL	149	2ND DIST
BRIEN, SARAH	CAR	215	5TH DIST
BRIEN, SARAH	FRE	147	10TH E D
BRIEN, SUSAN	BAL	215	19TH WAR
BRIEN, WILLIAM-BLACK	FRE	451	8TH E DI
BRIENES, AUGUSTUS	BAL	444	14TH WAR
BRIENING, WILLIAM	WAS	156	HAGERSTO
BRIERLY, CORDELIA	HAR	070	1ST DIST
BRIERWOOD, JULIA	DOR	418	1ST DIST
BRIERWOOD, THOMAS	DOR	382	1ST DIST
BRIGEG, JOHN *	BAL	044	18TH WAR
BRIGES, GEORGE	BAL	262	1ST DIST
BRIGGMAN, WILLIAM	BAL	084	10TH WAR
BRIGGS, ANN	BAL	043	15TH WAR
BRIGGS, ANN	MGM	408	MEDLEY 3
BRIGGS, CALEB	ANN	369	4TH DIST
BRIGGS, CHARLES	BAL	340	7TH WARD
BRIGGS, HANNAH	MGM	347	BERRYS D
BRIGGS, JAMES	BAL	303	17TH WAR
BRIGGS, JAMES M.	BAL	226	2ND WARD
BRIGGS, MARY	BAL	057	4TH WARD
BRIGGS, SAMUEL S.	MGM	405	ROCKERLE
BRIGGS, SARAH	BAL	276	12TH WAR
BRIGGS, SARAH	BAL	216	6TH DIST
BRIGGS, SARAH J.	BAL	216	6TH DIST
BRIGGS, THOMAS	BAL	182	16TH WAR
BRIGGS, WILLIAM HENRY	MGM	347	BERRYS D
BRIGHAM, E. W.	BAL	337	13TH WAR
BRIGHAM, HENRY	BAL	036	9TH WARD
BRIGHAM, JOHN	BAL	051	9TH WARD
BRIGHAM, JOSIAH	BAL	026	9TH WARD
BRIGHT, AARON	KEN	243	2ND DIST
BRIGHT, ALFRED-BLACK	QUE	189	3RD E DI
BRIGHT, ANDREW	BAL	458	8TH WARD
BRIGHT, CLOUDSBERRY	BAL	369	3RD WARD
BRIGHT, EDWARD	MGM	328	CRACKLIN
BRIGHT, ELLEN	BAL	369	3RD WARD
BRIGHT, FRANKLIN	QUE	231	4TH E DI
BRIGHT, GARIETTSON*	DOR	363	3RD DIVI
BRIGHT, HAMUTAL	BAL	402	8TH WARD
BRIGHT, HERNY	BAL	288	7TH WARD
BRIGHT, JACOB	BAL	141	5TH WARD
BRIGHT, JAEMS	QUE	229	4TH E DI
BRIGHT, JOHN	BAL	096	2ND DIST
BRIGHT, JOHN	MGM	327	CRACKLIN
BRIGHT, JOHN H.	ANN	276	ANNAPOLI
BRIGHT, LUCRETIA	BAL	315	3RD WARD
BRIGHT, MARY A.	ANN	286	ANNAPOLI
BRIGHT, MOSES	DOR	333	3RD DIVI
BRIGHT, MOSES	DOR	336	3RD DIVI
BRIGHT, NATHANIEL	BAL	281	7TH WARD
BRIGHT, PHILIP	MGM	329	CRACKLIN
BRIGHT, RACHAEL-BLACK	FRE	421	8TH E DI
BRIGHT, RICHARD	BAL	405	1ST DIST
BRIGHT, ROBERT	MGM	328	CRACKLIN
BRIGHT, SARAH	BAL	240	12TH WAR
BRIGHT, SINAH*	BAL	083	4TH WARD
BRIGHT, SUSAN	BAL	129	16TH WAR
BRIGHT, THOMAS	BAL	411	8TH WARD
BRIGHT, WILLIAM J.	MGM	384	ROCKERLE
BRIGHT, WILLIB	BAL	242	6TH WARD
BRIGHT,ALEXANDER	CAR	102	NO TWP L
BRIGHTELL, THOMAS	FRE	251	NEW MARK
BRIGHTLINE, FATNA	BAL	088	15TH WAR
BRIGHTMAN, E.	BAL	146	11TH WAR
BRIGHTMAN, EDWARD	BAL	146	11TH WAR
BRIGHTMAN, GEORGE	CAR	273	WESTMINS
BRIGHTMAN, HENRY	BAL	396	14TH WAR
BRIGHTMAN, MARY A.	CAR	266	WESTMINS
BRIGHTMAN, SUSAN	BAL	134	11TH WAR
BRIGHTNELL, ELIZA	PRI	049	AQUASCO
BRIGHTON, ABRAHAM	BAL	305	12TH WAR
BRIGHTON, ANNA	FRE	067	FREDERIC
BRIGHTON, HARRIET-BLACK	FRE	048	FREDERIC
BRIGHTON, MARGARET-BLACK	FRE	048	FREDERIC
BRIGHTWELL, JOHN	FRE	449	8TH E DI
BRIGHTWELL, JOHNG	CAL	061	3RD DIST
BRIGHTWELL, JONATHAN H.	FRE	411	8TH E DI
BRIGHTWELL, MARIA	PRI	049	AQUASCO
BRIGHTWELL, P.	PRI	068	NOTTINGH
BRIGHTWELL, THOMAS	FRE	450	8TH E DI
BRIGHTWELL, WILLY	PRI	049	AQUASCO
BRIGLE, B.	WAS	010	WILLIAMS
BRIGY, JOHN *	BAL	044	18TH WAR
BRIKE, MARY ANN	ALL	011	3RD E.D.
BRIKHEAD, GEORGE	BAL	429	8TH WARD
BRIKHEAD, LOUISA	BAL	430	8TH WARD
BRILEY, ANN E.	BAL	157	19TH WAR
BRILEY, ANTONY	BAL	454	8TH WARD
BRILEY, LAURA	BAL	157	19TH WAR
BRILEY, THOMAS	DOR	304	1ST DIST
BRILHART, DAVID	CAR	334	6TH DIST
BRILHART, JOHN	CAR	351	6TH DIST
BRILL, ASA	BAL	392	8TH WARD
BRILL, CHARLES	BAL	361	1ST DIST
BRILL, WILLIAM	BAL	125	16TH WAR
BRILLA, JOSEPH	BAL	371	8TH WARD
BRILLE, ELIZABETH	BAL	035	15TH WAR
BRILLO, CHARLES	BAL	130	11TH WAR
BRIMAJON, JAMES	BAL	446	1ST DIST
BRIMAN, MARGARET O.	HAR	155	3RD DIST
BRIMER, CATHARIN	BAL	041	18TH WAR
BRIMER, WILLIAM	WOR	270	BERLIN 1
BRIMING, ANNE	BAL	224	12TH WAR
BRIMM, PATRICK	ALL	210	CUMBERLA
BRIMMAGREN, JAMES	ALL	257	CUMBERLA
BRIMMELL, ELIZABETH	CAR	112	NO TWP L
BRIMMER, CATHARINE	BAL	452	14TH WAR
BRIMMERMAN, ANTHONY	FRE	261	NEW MARK
BRIMMERMAN, FREDERICK	FRE	261	NEW MARK
BRIMS, MARY	BAL	200	19TH WAR
BRIMSTEAD, CATHARINE	BAL	202	19TH WAR
BRIN, MARY P.	BAL	215	11TH WAR
BRIN, MICHAEL	PRI	067	NOTTINGH
BRINAN, CASPER	BAL	213	2ND WARD
BRINAN, EDWARD	BAL	269	1ST DIST
BRINCEFIELD, WILLIAM J.	BAL	389	3RD WARD
BRINDA, AMANDA	BAL	156	11TH WAR
BRINDARILL, THOMAS	BAL	119	1ST WARD
BRINDLE, JAMES A.	DOR	374	1ST DIST
BRINDLE, JOHN	BAL	356	8TH WARD
BRINDLE, NATHANIEL	HAR	025	1ST DIST
BRINE, JOHN A.	CEC	210	7TH E DI
BRINE, ROBERT	ANN	280	ANNAPOLI
BRINE, THOMAS	WAS	159	2ND DIST
BRINE, WILLIAM	CEC	191	5TH E DI
BRINEN, WILLIAM	HAR	199	3RD DIST
BRINER, LEVI	WOR	278	BERLIN 1
BRINERY, JACOB	HAR	122	2ND DIST
BRINGER, MARY E.	BAL	210	17TH WAR
BRINGLE, BARBARA	FRE	057	FREDERIC
BRINGLE, NICHOLAS	BAL	109	18TH WAR
BRINGLE, WILLIAM H.	WAS	012	WILLIAMS
BRINGLY, JOSEPH	PRI	068	NOTTINGH
BRINGMAN, J. L. H.	CAR	266	WESTMINS
BRINHAM, WILLIAM P.	PRI	069	MARLBROU
BRINIE, MARGARET	CAR	410	2ND DIST
BRINIG, JOHN	BAL	096	15TH WAR
BRINING, ADAM	WAS	122	HAGERSTO
BRINING, F.W.	WAS	159	HAGERSTO
BRINING, HENRY	BAL	156	16TH WAR
BRINING, ROBERT	BAL	281	2ND WARD
BRINK, ANTHONY	BAL	330	3RD WARD
BRINKER, GEORGE	ALL	237	CUMBERLA
BRINKHENDT, ADAM	BAL	201	19TH WAR
BRINKLEY, BENJAMIN	SOM	386	BRINKLEY
BRINKLEY, BENJAMIN-BLACK	QUE	165	2ND E DI
BRINKLEY, CAROLINE	SOM	395	BRINKLEY
BRINKLEY, CLARISA	SOM	493	SALISBUR
BRINKLEY, GOERGE	BAL	193	17TH WAR
BRINKLEY, HESTER	SOM	394	BRINKLEY
BRINKLEY, HESTER	SOM	386	BRINKLEY
BRINKLEY, JOHN	SOM	481	TRAPP DI
BRINKLEY, SALLY	SOM	485	TRAPP DI
BRINKLEY, WILLIAM-BLACX	QUE	143	1ST E DI
BRINKLEY, WILSON-BLACK	QUE	168	2ND E DI
BRINKLEY, WILSCN-BLACK	QUE	169	2ND E DI
BRINKMAN, ADAM	WAS	268	1ST DIST
BRINKMAN, FREDERICK	ALL	183	8TH E.D.
BRINKMAN, FREDRICK	BAL	109	2ND DIST
BRINKMAN, HENRY	BAL	036	15TH WAR
BRINKMAN, MARY M.	WAS	268	1ST DIST
BRINKMEYER, CHARLES	BAL	012	9TH WARD
BRINKY, CASPER	ALL	201	CUMBERLA
BRINLING, J. C.	WAS	182	BOONSBOR
BRINN, ANDREW	BAL	089	18TH WAR
BRINN, ANN	ALL	243	CUMBERLA
BRINN, SISTER P.	FRE	198	5TH E DI
BRINNAN, ELIZA	BAL	004	1ST WARD
BRINNER, SALLY E.	WOR	295	9TH E DI
BRINSFIELD, ELIJAH	DOR	458	1ST DIST
BRINSFIELD, ELIJAH	DOR	456	1ST DIST
BRINSFIELD, ELIZABETH	DOR	459	1ST DIST
BRINSFIELD, EMILINE	BAL	247	17TH WAR
BRINSFIELD, GEORGE F.	TAL	026	EASTON D
BRINSFIELD, MARA	DOR	458	1ST DIST
BRINSFIELD, SARAH	DOR	313	1ST DIST
BRINSFIELD, THCMAS	TAL	058	EASTON D
BRINSFIELD, WILLIAM H.	DOR	300	1ST DIST
BRINTMAN, EDWARD	HAR	003	1ST DIST
BRINTMAN, JOHN J.	HAR	004	1ST DIST
BRINTON, ELLIS	CEC	208	7TH E DI
BRINTON, GARY	BAL	218	12TH WAR
BRINTON, JOSEPH	BAL	457	1ST DIST
BRINTON, LYDIA	CEC	209	7TH E DI
BRINTON, WELDON	BAL	094	2ND DIST
BRINTZE, LOUISA	HAR	101	2ND DIST
BRION, GARRISCN	DOR	314	1ST DIST
BRION, JAMES-BLACK	CAR	145	NO TWP L
BRION, PARCELLA	CAR	165	NO TWP L
BRION, WILLIAM	BAL	404	3RD WARD
BRION, WILLIAM-BLACK	CAR	142	NO TWP L
BRIRELY, JOHN	BAL	300	1ST DIST
BRISCALL, F.	BAL	148	1ST WARD
BRISCO, GEORGE	WAS	030	2ND SUBD
BRISCO, LEOARD	BAL	269	1ST DIST
BRISCO, MARGARET	BAL	329	7TH WARD
BRISCO, MARY	BAL	261	1ST DIST
BRISCOE, AGNES	BAL	343	13TH WAR
BRISCOE, APPELONA	ST	335	4TH E DI
BRISCOE, CHARITY	WAS	016	2ND SUBD
BRISCOE, CHARLES T. S.	CHA	222	ALLENS F
BRISCOE, EASTER	WAS	207	1ST DIST
BRISCOE, EDDY-BLACK	ST	337	4TH E DI
BRISCOE, EDMOND	PRI	115	PISCATAW
BRISCOE, EDWARD	CHA	259	MIDDLETO
BRISCOE, ELIZABETH B.	ST	264	3RD E DI
BRISCOE, ELIZABETH R.	CHA	270	ALLENS F
BRISCOE, FRANIS-BLACK	FRE	403	JEFFERSO
BRISCOE, GABRIEL	BAL	117	11TH WAR
BRISCOE, GASTAVUS B.	ST	349	5TH E DI
BRISCOE, GEORGE	FRE	132	CREAGERS
BRISCOE, GERARD-BLACK	ST	333	4TH E DI
BRISCOE, HENRIETTA	BAL	086	4TH WARD
BRISCOE, HENRIETTA H.	BAL	181	11TH WAR
BRISCOE, HONOR	CAR	268	WESTMINS
BRISCOE, ISABELLA	FRE	128	CREAGERS
BRISCOE, ISABELLA	KEN	222	2ND DIST
BRISCOE, JAMES	BAL	112	10TH WAR
BRISCOE, JAMES T.	CAL	025	2ND DIST
BRISCOE, JAMES-BLACK	FRE	197	5TH E DI
BRISCOE, JEREMIAH	FRE	132	CREAGERS
BRISCOE, JINNETT E.	ST	264	3RD E DI
BRISCOE, JOHN	WAS	020	2ND SUBD
BRISCOE, JOHN	BAL	117	11TH WAR
BRISCOE, JOHN	FRE	039	FREDERIC
BRISCOE, JOHN	BAL	191	11TH WAR
BRISCOE, JOHN C.	KEN	282	3RD DIST
BRISCOE, JOHN H.	BAL	061	10TH WAR
BRISCOE, JOHN T.	KEN	290	3RD DIST
BRISCOE, JOHN-BLACK	FRE	196	5TH E DI
BRISCOE, JOSEPH	MGM	372	BERRYS D
BRISCOE, JOSEPH-BLACK	FRE	010	FREDERIC
BRISCOE, LAURA	KEN	283	3RD DIST
BRISCOE, LEAH	BAL	178	11TH WAR
BRISCOE, LEWIS	BAL	267	20TH WAR
BRISCOE, LOTTY	MGM	361	BERRYS D
BRISCOE, M.	CHA	222	ALLENS F
BRISCOE, MARIA	ST	321	4TH E DI
BRISCOE, MARIA	PRI	051	AQUASCO
BRISCOE, MARY	BAL	039	4TH WARD
BRISCOE, MARY A.	CHA	256	MIDDLETO
BRISCOE, MARY E.	CHA	256	MIDDLETO
BRISCOE, MARY JANE-BLACK	FRE	197	5TH E DI
BRISCOE, NANCY	ALL	262	CUMBERLA
BRISCOE, RACHEAL	WAS	170	FUNKSTOW
BRISCOE, RACHEL A.	BAL	356	13TH WAR
BRISCOE, RASTUS	BAL	117	11TH WAR
BRISCOE, RICHARD	CEC	051	1ST E DI
BRISCOE, RICHARD	WAS	015	2ND SUBD
BRISCOE, SAAH A.	ST	348	5TH E DI
BRISCOE, SAMUEL E.	QUE	187	3RD E DI
BRISCOE, SAMUEL J.	CHA	270	ALLENS F
BRISCOE, SARAH A.	BAL	094	15TH WAR
BRISCOE, SUSAN	BAL	167	16TH WAR
BRISCOE, TAMASON	KEN	294	3RD DIST
BRISCOE, THOMAS	BAL	101	10TH WAR
BRISCOE, THOMAS	BAL	119	11TH WAR
BRISCOE, WALTER H.	ST	264	3RD E DI
BRISCOE, WILLIAM H.	BAL	038	15TH WAR
BRISCOE, WILLIAM T.	ST	348	5TH E DI
BRISCUE, JAMES A.	KEN	221	2ND DIST
BRISE, JAMES*	TAL	042	EASTON D
BRISEE, HENRYIETTA	CEC	165	6TH E DI
BRISER, MARY	BAL	257	1ST DIST
BRISFORD, DOLLY	PRI	029	VANSVILL
BRISGES, MARGARET	TAL	107	ST MICHA
BRISH, DAVID	FRE	003	FREDERIC
BRISH, ELIZA	FRE	103	FREDERIC
BRISHELL, THOMAS	WOR	234	6TH E DI
BRISLAND, ANN	BAL	122	2ND DIST
BRISON, ANN	BAL	135	5TH WARD
BRISON, GILBERT	ALL	127	4TH E.D.
BRISON, HARRIET	CEC	004	ELKTON 3
BRISON, JAMES	BAL	088	18TH WAR
BRISON, SAMUEL	BAL	016	18TH WAR
BRISON, THOMAS	CEC	021	ELKTON 3
BRISON, THOMAS	CEC	021	ELKTON 3
BRISON, WILLIAM	CEC	192	5TH E DI
BRISTA, LOUIS	CEC	032	CHESAPEA
BRISTE, HENRY	CEC	055	1ST E DI
BRISTE, LOUISA	CEC	031	CHESAPEA
BRISTE, RICHARD	CEC	072	5TH E DI
BRISTEE, EELIZABETH*	TAL	039	EASTON D
BRISTEE, MARY*	TAL	063	EASTON D
BRISTER, ELIZABETH	CEC	075	NORTHEAS
BRISTER, LOUIS	CEC	032	CHESAPEA
BRISTER, MARY*	TAL	063	EASTON D
BRISTER, WILLIAM	CEC	031	CHESAPEA
BRISTER, WILLIAM B.	CEC	032	CHESAPEA
BRISTO, JOHN	CEC	072	5TH E DI
BRISTO, WILLIAM	CEC	030	CHESAPEA
BRISTOE, SAMUEL	CAR	271	WESTMINS
BRISTOL, JAMES	FRE	073	FREDERIC
BRISTOL, WILLIAM-BLACK	BAL	217	2ND WARD
BRISTON, JOHN	CEC	029	CHESAPEA
BRISTON, RACHEL	CEC	067	5TH E DI
BRISTOR, SUSAN	BAL	140	5TH WARD
BRISTOR, WILLIAM B.	BAL	249	6TH WARD
BRIT, JOHN	CEC	038	CHESAPEA
BRIT, JOSHUA	WOR	181	6TH E DI
BRITAIN, MARY	BAL	152	2ND DIST
BRITAR, JACOB	BAL	239	20TH WAR
BRITEN, JOSEPH	WAS	134	2ND DIST
BRITIAN, FRANCIS	BAL	098	2ND DIST
BRITLARN, LEWIS	BAL	154	19TH WAR
BRITLEY, WILLIAM	PRI	014	BLADENSB
BRITSEL, WILLIAM	BAL	416	8TH WARD
BRITT, SEVCUM	BAL	225	12TH WAR
BRITT, THOMAS	BAL	077	18TH WAR
BRITT, WALTER	BAL	028	4TH WARD
BRITTAIN, CHAPMAN	HAR	060	1ST DIST
BRITTAIN, MARY	HAR	060	1ST DIST
BRITTEN, ANN C.	KEN	214	2ND DIST
BRITTINGHAM, ANN B.	WOR	184	6TH E DI
BRITTINGHAM, AZARIAH	WOR	209	4TH E DI
BRITTINGHAM, BENJAMIN	WOR	316	2ND E DI
BRITTINGHAM, BENJAMIN	WOR	252	1ST CENS
BRITTINGHAM, BETSY	WOR	217	4TH E DI
BRITTINGHAM, CATHARINE	BAL	340	13TH WAR
BRITTINGHAM, EASTHEN	WOR	332	1ST E DI
BRITTINGHAM, EDWARD	WOR	328	1ST E DI
BRITTINGHAM, EDWARD	SOM	490	SALISBUR
BRITTINGHAM, ELI	WOR	308	2ND E DI
BRITTINGHAM, ELIJAH M.	WOR	207	4TH E DI
BRITTINGHAM, ELIZA	WOR	265	BERLIN 1
BRITTINGHAM, ELIZABETH	WOR	275	BERLIN 1
BRITTINGHAM, EPHRAIM	WOR	254	1ST CENS
BRITTINGHAM, GEORGE	WOR	268	BERLIN 1
BRITTINGHAM, GECRGE	WOR	281	BERLIN 1
BRITTINGHAM, GEORGE B.	WOR	218	4TH E DI
BRITTINGHAM, ISAAC	WOR	217	4TH E DI
BRITTINGHAM, ISAAC S.	WOR	221	4TH E DI
BRITTINGHAM, JAMES	WOR	284	BERLIN 1
BRITTINGHAM, JAMES	WOR	261	BERLIN 1
BRITTINGHAM, JAMES	SOM	435	PRINCESS
BRITTINGHAM, JAMES	SOM	414	DUBLIN D
BRITTINGHAM, JOHN	WOR	230	6TH E DI
BRITTINGHAM, JOHN	WOR	332	1ST E DI
BRITTINGHAM, JOHN	BAL	013	15TH WAR
BRITTINGHAM, JOHN P.	WOR	213	4TH E DI
BRITTINGHAM, JOSEPH J.	WOR	210	4TH E DI
BRITTINGHAM, JOSEPH T.	WOR	222	4TH E DI
BRITTINGHAM, JOSIAH	WOR	177	6TH E DI
BRITTINGHAM, MAHALEA C.	WOR	268	BERLIN 1
BRITTINGHAM, MARGARET	WOR	257	1ST CENS
BRITTINGHAM, MARGARET E.	WOR	331	1ST E DI
BRITTINGHAM, MARY	WOR	218	4TH E DI
BRITTINGHAM, MARY A. E.	WOR	207	4TH E DI
BRITTINGHAM, MARY E.	WOR	178	6TH E DI
BRITTINGHAM, MATTHIAS	WOR	286	BERLIN 1
BRITTINGHAM, NATHANIEL	WOR	267	BERLIN 1
BRITTINGHAM, PETER	WOR	264	BERLIN 1
BRITTINGHAM, PRARCE	WOR	346	1ST E DI
BRITTINGHAM, PURNELL	WOR	346	1ST E DI
BRITTINGHAM, SAMUEL	WOR	350	1ST E DI
BRITTINGHAM, SAMUEL	BAL	013	15TH WAR
BRITTINGHAM, SARAH	WOR	274	BERLIN 1
BRITTINGHAM, SARAH	WOR	213	4TH E DI
BRITTINGHAM, SARAH E.	WOR	166	6TH E DI
BRITTINGHAM, THOMAS B.	WOR	207	4TH E DI
BRITTINGHAM, THOMAS M.	WOR	331	1ST E DI
BRITTINGHAM, WILLAIM	WOR	235	6TH E DI
BRITTINGHAM, WILLIAM	WOR	240	6TH E DI
BRITTINGHAM, WILLIAM	WOR	215	4TH E DI
BRITTINGHAM, WILLIAM	WOR	181	6TH E DI
BRITTINGHAM, WILLIAM	WOR	326	1ST E DI
BRITTINGHAM, WILLIAM	WOR	337	1ST E DI
BRITTINGHAM, WILLIAM	WOR	291	9TH E DI
BRITTINGHAM, WILLIAM -BLA	WOR	331	1ST E DI
BRITTINGHAM, WILLIAM H.	WOR	185	7TH E DI
BRITTINGHAM, WILLIAM H.	WOR	224	4TH E DI
BRITTINGHAM, WILLIAM J.	SOM	435	PRINCESS
BRITTINGHAM, ZADOCK H.	WOR	217	4TH E DI
BRITTINGHAM., HENNA	WOR	337	1ST E DI
BRITTINGHAN, JAMES M.	BAL	164	1ST WARD
BRITTINGHHAM, DIXON	WOR	328	1ST E DI
BRITTINGS, JOHN	BAL	116	1ST WARD
BRITTON, ANN E.	BAL	212	11TH WAR
BRITTON, CAROLINE	BAL	112	5TH WARD

Name	County	Page	District
BRITTON, CATHERINE J.	BAL	365	3RD WARD
BRITTON, CHARLES	BAL	142	1ST WARD
BRITTON, HANNAH	BAL	301	17TH WAR
BRITTON, JAMES	KEN	310	3RD DIST
BRITTON, JAMES L.	CEC	128	5TH E DI
BRITTON, JOHN	CAL	007	1ST DIST
BRITTON, LAVINIA	CEC	133	6TH E DI
BRITTON, MARY E.	QUE	130	1ST E DI
BRITTON, MARY E.	BAL	333	3RD WARD
BRITTON, THOMAS J.	QUE	124	1ST E DI
BRITTOON, JOHN	HAR	082	2ND DIST
BRIVER, HENRY	BAL	229	17TH WAR
BRIWINGTON, THOMAS A.	WOR	236	6TH E DI
BRIZAR, ELIZA	BAL	336	3RD WARD
BROABS, MICHAEL	BAL	090	1ST WARD
BROAD, JANE	BAL	097	15TH WAR
BROADAWAY, RICHARD	CAR	072	NO TWP L
BROADBECK, AMOS	BAL	187	6TH WARD
BROADBENT, FERDINAND	BAL	055	9TH WARD
BROADBENT, GERSHAM	BAL	387	13TH WAR
BROADBENT, STEPHEN	BAL	055	9TH WARD
BROADBENT, W.	BAL	063	10TH WAR
BROADEIS, FREDERICK	BAL	140	19TH WAR
BROADERS, JAMES	BAL	406	8TH WARD
BROADFOOT, CATHARINE	BAL	371	13TH WAR
BROADFOOT, JOSHUA	BAL	078	4TH WARD
BROADFORT, ANN LOUISA *	BAL	369	13TH WAR
BROADOUGH, CHARLES *	FRE	086	FREDERIC
BROADRUP, EDWARD	FRE	104	FREDERIC
BROADWATER, CHARLES	ALL	143	6TH E.D.
BROADWATER, ELIZABETH	ALL	145	6TH E.D.
BROADWATER, GEORGE	BAL	155	1ST WARD
BROADWATER, GUY	ALL	123	4TH E.D.
BROADWATER, F. G.	ALL	144	6TH E.D.
BROADWATER, HARRIETT *	ALL	118	5TH E.D.
BROADWATER, LEVIN J. M.	WOR	299	SNOW HIL
BROADWATER, MARY	WOR	179	6TH E DI
BROADWATER, MARY	BAL	242	17TH WAR
BROADWATER, MARY E.	ALL	145	6TH E.D.
BROADWATER, RICHARD	BAL	241	17TH WAR
BROADWATER, SAMUEL	ALL	121	4TH E.D.
BROADWATER, WILLIAM	ALL	144	6TH E.D.
BROADWATERS, CHARLES	ALL	144	6TH E.D.
BROADWATERS, JEFFERSON	ALL	016	3RD E.D.
BROADWATERS, ROBERT	ALL	002	3RD E.D.
BROADWATERS, WILLIAM	ALL	132	4TH E.D.
BROADWAY, EMELY D.	KEN	254	1ST DIST
BROADWAY, GEORGE-BLACK	QUE	197	3RD E DI
BROADWAY, JOHN	KEN	253	1ST DIST
BROADWAY, RICHARD	TAL	004	EASTON D
BROAN, JEREMIAH	FRE	264	NEW MARK
BROAX, WILLIAM	BAL	226	17TH WAR
BROBSON, JOHN	HAR	138	2ND DIST
BROBST, FREDERICK	FRE	004	FREDERIC
BROBST, JOHN	ALL	046	10TH E.D
BROCH, JOHN	BAL	099	15TH WAR
BROCHE, ELIZABETH	BAL	165	2ND DIST
BROCHT, LUKE	BAL	077	4TH WARD
BROCHURS, CHARLES	CEC	149	PORT DUP
BROCK, BURLIDGE	CEC	021	ELKTON 3
BROCK, CHRISTIAN	BAL	357	8TH WARD
BROCK, DORITY	BAL	358	8TH WARD
BROCK, HENRY	BAL	063	2ND DIST
BROCK, HETTY	BAL	166	19TH WAR
BROCK, MARGARET	BAL	351	3RD WARD
BROCK, PERREY	BAL	327	7TH WARD
BROCK, PERRY	BAL	097	10TH WAR
BROCK, SEDWICK	BAL	357	8TH WARD
BROCKEN, GEORGEANNA	CEC	158	PORT DUP
BROCKEN, HENRY B.	CEC	158	PORT DUP
BROCKER, GEORGE	BAL	164	11TH WAR
BROCKETT, JOSEPH	BAL	037	18TH WAR
BROCKEY, FREDERICK	FRE	305	WOODSBOR
BROCKFAGH, MARY *	BAL	104	2ND DIST
BROCKFOGU, ADAM	BAL	111	2ND DIST
BROCKMAN, PHILLIP	BAL	067	1ST WARD
BROCKMEYER, MARY	BAL	160	16TH WAR
BROCKRENS, ISAAC	BAL	158	2ND DIST
BROCKRES, MARY	BAL	101	2ND DIST
BROCTOR, SAMUEL	BAL	146	1ST WARD
BRODBECK, WILLIAM	BAL	378	13TH WAR
BRODD, DANIEL	ALL	086	5TH E.D.
BRODDERS, PATRICK	BAL	405	8TH WARD
BRODEN, ELIZA	BAL	005	15TH WAR
BRODEN, HANNAH	BAL	260	2ND WARD
BRODERICK, ANN	BAL	028	4TH WARD
BRODERICK, ELIZABETH	BAL	019	9TH WARD
BRODERICK, JOHN	ALL	048	10TH E.D
BRODERICK, JOHN	ALL	072	5TH E.D.
BRODERICK, JOSEPH	BAL	292	12TH WAR
BRODERICK, LAWRENCE	BAL	372	13TH WAR
BRODERICK, THOMAS	ALL	256	CUMBERLA
BRODERICK, WILLIAM	BAL	126	16TH WAR
BRODICK, MARY	FRE	066	FREDERIC
BRODIE, ALEXANDER	BAL	224	19TH WAR
BRODIE, EVA	BAL	224	19TH WAR
BRODIE, L.A.	PRI	083	QUEEN AN
BRODLEY, ROSE	BAL	139	11TH WAR
BRODMAKR, HENRY	ALL	167	6TH E.D.
BRODMARK, JAMES H.	ALL	165	6TH E.D.
BRODMARKE, JOHN	ALL	167	6TH E.D.
BRODMARKE, MICHAEL	ALL	166	6TH E.D.
BRODNOX, JOHN D.	BAL	287	1ST DIST
BRODRICK, ANN J.	BAL	220	1ST DIST
BRODRICK, DANIEL	BAL	169	11TH WAR
BRODRICK, MARY	BAL	169	11TH WAR
BRODRICK, PATRICK *	ALL	129	4TH E.D.
BRODRICK, WILLIAM	BAL	393	8TH WARD
BRODWATER, AMOS	ALL	145	6TH E.D.
BRODWATER, CALEB	SOM	420	PRINCESS
BRODWATERS, CHARLES	ALL	144	6TH E.D.
BRODY, SIMEON	BAL	379	13TH WAR
BROENING, CATHERINE N.	BAL	111	10TH WAR
BROFEE, ELIZABETH	BAL	389	1ST DIST
BROGAN, CATHARINE	BAL	014	15TH WAR
BROGAN, JAMES W.	BAL	148	11TH WAR
BROGAN, PATRICK	CAR	230	5TH DIST
BROGAN, PATRICK	WAS	163	2ND DIST
BROGAN, PHILIP	BAL	330	13TH WAR
BROGAN, ROSA MRS.	BAL	330	13TH WAR
BROGAN, WILLIAM	WAS	154	2ND DIST
BROGANIER, ELIZABETH	WAS	159	HAGERSTO
BROGAY, MARY	BAL	091	18TH WAR
BROGDEN, ABRAHAM	BAL	459	8TH WARD
BROGDEN, AUSTIN	BAL	221	12TH WAR
BROGDEN, CATHERINE	PRI	025	VANSVILL
BROGDEN, DANIEL	MGM	376	ROCKERLE
BROGDEN, DAVID W.	ANN	296	1ST DIST
BROGDEN, EMELINE	PRI	032	VANSVILL
BROGDEN, HENRY	ANN	331	2ND DIST
BROGDEN, JOHN	ANN	274	ANNAPOLI
BROGDEN, MARY	ANN	364	4TH DIST
BROGDEN, SAMUEL	BAL	453	14TH WAR
BROGDEN, THOMAS	ANN	328	2ND DIST
BROGDEN, WILLIAM	ANN	296	1ST DIST
BROGDEN, WILLIAM	ANN	449	HOWARD D
BROGDEN, WILLIAM	BAL	146	11TH WAR
BROGDEN, WILLIAM	BAL	126	18TH WAR
BROGDON, CHARLOTTE	ANN	289	ANNAPOLI
BROGDON, JOSEPHINE	BAL	170	16TH WAR
BROGDON, S.	ANN	290	ANNAPOLI
BROGER, RUTH	HAR	124	2ND DIST
BROGHTON, CELIA	BAL	467	14TH WAR
BROGIRNIER, JACOB	WAS	204	1ST DIST
BROGLY, SAMUEL	ANN	386	4TH DIST
BROGNARD, FERDINAND	BAL	094	2ND DIST
BROGONIER, ANN	ALL	213	CUMBERLA
BROGONIER, GEORGE H.	ALL	213	CUMBERLA
BROGONIER, JACOB	ALL	213	CUMBERLA
BROGONIER, JOHN	ALL	216	CUMBERLA
BROGUINER, DAVID	WAS	204	1ST DIST
BROGUNIER, DANIEL	WAS	300	1ST DIST
BROGUNIER, ELIZABETH	WAS	177	1ST DIST
BROGUNIER, JOHN	WAS	135	HAGERSTO
BROGUNIER, JONATHAN	WAS	125	HAGERSTO
BROGUNIER, LUTH	WAS	152	HAGERSTO
BROGUNIER, MARY	WAS	204	1ST DIST
BROGUNIER, SUSAN	WAS	135	HAGERSTO
BROGUNIER, UPTON	WAS	158	HAGERSTO
BROGUNIER, UPTON H.	WAS	300	1ST DIST
BROHAWN, ANN M.*	DOR	460	1ST DIST
BROHAWN, JOHN	DOR	326	3RD DIVI
BROHAWN, JOHN*	DOR	463	1ST DIST
BROHAWN, SAMUEL	DOR	327	3RD DIVI
BROHEE, THOMAS	BAL	255	1ST DIST
BROHOWN, PATRICK	BAL	018	15TH WAR
BROIDRICK, PATRICK	WAS	161	2ND DIST
BROILER, MARGARET	WAS	161	2ND DIST
BROIN, GEANDESON	FRE	103	FREDERIC
BROING, CALEB	CAR	297	7TH DIST
BROING, ELIZABETH	CAR	335	6TH DIST
BROKAW, CALEB	CEC	101	4TH E DI
BROKAW, JAMES	DOR	464	1ST DIST
BROKAW, SAMUEL	DOR	465	1ST DIST
BROKE, MICHAEL	ALL	143	6TH E.D.
BROKEE, BRIDGET	BAL	255	1ST DIST
BROKER, ELIZABETH	BAL	161	19TH WAR
BROKER, GARRET	ALL	176	7TH E.D.
BROKLMAN, FREDERICK	ALL	210	CUMBERLA
BROM, JANE	BAL	143	11TH WAR
BROMBAUM, JACOB	BAL	231	2ND WARD
BROMBLEY, GEORGE	WOR	320	1ST E DI
BROME, DARCUS R.*	BAL	347	3RD WARD
BROME, WILLIAM H.	BAL	347	3RD WARD
BROMER, WILLIAM	BAL	219	19TH WAR
BROMETT, MICHAEL	FRE	008	FREDERIC
BROMETT, SUSANNA	WAS	186	BOONSBOR
BROMLEY, ELIZABETH	BAL	023	9TH WARD
BROMLEY, JOHN N.	BAL	365	8TH WARD
BROMLEY, THOMAS J.	BAL	041	4TH WARD
BROMLY, ALFRED	BAL	294	17TH WAR
BROMLY, HEZEKIAH	BAL	002	EASTERN
BROMNEL, HENRY	BAL	116	15TH WAR
BROMOTT, JOHN T.	CHA	245	HILLTOP
BROMSHE, JOHN	BAL	146	19TH WAR
BROMWELL, ALFRED	BAL	319	7TH WARD
BROMWELL, AUGUST	BAL	292	12TH WAR
BROMWELL, ELIZA	BAL	205	17TH WAR
BROMWELL, GEORGE	BAL	393	3RD WARD
BROMWELL, GEORGE	BAL	394	3RD WARD
BROMWELL, HOSEA J.	FRE	243	NEW MARK
BROMWELL, ISAAC	BAL	460	8TH WARD
BROMWELL, J.E.	FRE	240	NEW MARK
BROMWELL, JACOB T.	TAL	037	EASTON D
BROMWELL, JAMES	BAL	374	3RD WARD
BROMWELL, JAMES D.	TAL	050	EASTON T
BROMWELL, JEREMIAH	TAL	041	EASTON D
BROMWELL, JOSIAH R.	BAL	136	11TH WAR
BROMWELL, LAURA	BAL	226	19TH WAR
BROMWELL, MARIA	BAL	340	13TH WAR
BROMWELL, ROBERT*	TAL	007	EASTON D
BROMWELL, SARAH	BAL	231	12TH WAR
BROMWELL, SUSAN	TAL	040	EASTON D
BROMWELL, THOMAS	TAL	046	EASTON T
BROMWELL, THOMAS	DOR	465	1ST DIST
BROMWELL, WILLIAM	TAL	107	ST MICHA
BROMWELL, WILLIAM H.	TAL	102	ST MICHA
BROMWELL, WILLIAM J.	TAL	030	EASTON D
BROMWELL, WILLIAM R.	TAL	107	ST MICHA
BRON, ANN	BAL	029	2ND DIST
BRON, JAMES	BAL	322	12TH WAR
BROND, ELIZABETH	BAL	214	19TH WAR
BRONDER, GEORGE	BAL	222	12TH WAR
BRONDOUR, JOHN *	BAL	322	1ST DIST
BRONDY, JOHN	BAL	162	1ST WARD
BRONE, ELIZABETH-BLACK	CAR	080	NO TWP L
BRONES, ELEN M.	CAR	174	8TH DIST
BRONGER, HETTA	WAS	159	2ND DIST
BRONGLE, SAMUEL T.	FRE	406	JEFFERSO
BRONNELL, ROBERT	CEC	156	PORT DUP
BRONNER, GEORGE	ALL	119	5TH E.D.
BRONNER, GEORGE	ALL	089	5TH E.D.
BRONON, WILLIAM *	CAR	195	4TH DIST
BRONS, JANE	BAL	408	14TH WAR
BRONSON, CHARLES	BAL	404	14TH WAR
BRONSON, MARGARET	BAL	404	14TH WAR
BRONSON, SIMEON	BAL	367	3RD WARD
BRONT, GODFRED	BAL	268	20TH WAR
BRONW, ADDLER	BAL	278	2ND WARD
BRONW, ANDREW	QUE	236	4TH E DI
BRONW, CHARLES	BAL	328	13TH WAR
BRONW, ELIZA J.	BAL	455	14TH WAR
BRONW, HENRY	CAR	273	WESTMINS
BRONW, ISAAC	BAL	151	2ND DIST
BRONW, J.	BAL	156	1ST WARD
BRONW, JAMES	BAL	282	2ND WARD
BRONW, JANE	CAR	183	8TH DIST
BRONW, JIM	BAL	067	4TH WARD
BRONW, JOHN	BAL	280	2ND WARD
BRONW, JOHN-BLACK	QUE	190	3RD E DI
BRONW, SARAH	BAL	301	12TH WAR
BRONWELL, JAMES	BAL	099	1ST WARD
BRONWELL, WILLIAM C.	CEC	129	6TH E DI
BRONZ, LOUISA	BAL	345	3RD WARD
BROOCKMAN, JOHN	BAL	104	2ND DIST
BROOF, JACOB	BAL	261	20TH WAR
BROOGHTON, AMANDA	ANN	269	ANNAPOLI
BROOHEART, CAPANDER *	BAL	088	2ND DIST
BROOK, ANN	ANN	439	HOWARD D
BROOK, DANIEL*	TAL	028	EASTON D
BROOK, ENLEP	HAR	078	2ND DIST
BROOK, GEORGE	WAS	197	1ST DIST
BROOK, JAMES	BAL	114	18TH WAR
BROOK, JAMES W.	HAR	175	3RD DIST
BROOK, JOHN	BAL	041	18TH WAR
BROOK, JOSEPH	BAL	025	1ST WARD
BROOK, LOUISA A.	BAL	158	6TH WARD
BROOK, MARY	BAL	213	2ND WARD
BROOK, SARAH	CAL	008	1ST DIST
BROOK, WILLIAM	BAL	205	2ND WARD
BROOKBANK, ANN	CHA	219	ALLENS F
BROOKBANK, ELIAS	ST	339	5TH E DI
BROOKBANK, JAMES	ST	335	4TH E DI
BROOKBANK, SAMUEL	ST	335	4TH E DI
BROOKBANK, WILLIAM	CHA	223	ALLENS F
BROOKE, ALTA	CAL	003	1ST DIST
BROCKE, B. F.	ANN	333	2ND DIST
BROOKE, CATHARINE	PRI	117	PISCATAW
BROOKE, CLEMENT H.	PRI	097	SPALDING
BROOKE, ELIJAH	BAL	047	1ST WARD
BROOKE, ELIZA	CAL	004	1ST DIST
BROOKE, ELIZA A.	CAL	013	1ST DIST
BROOKE, ELIZABETH	CAL	008	1ST DIST
BROOKE, GEORGE	FRE	316	MIDDLETO
BROOKE, HENRIETTA M.	MGM	390	ROCKERLE
BROOKE, HERY	PRI	075	MARLBROU
BROOKE, IGNATIUS	FRE	027	FREDERIC
BROOKE, JOHN B.	PRI	075	MARLBROU
BROOKE, JOHN R.	ALL	263	CUMBERLA
BROOKE, MARY	PRI	073	MARLBROU
BROOKE, MARY	MGM	349	BERRYS D
BROOKE, MARY B.	MGM	316	CRACKLIN
BROOKE, MICHAEL	WAS	008	WILLIAMS
BROOKE, MILLY	PRI	050	AQUASCO
BROOKE, NICHOLAS	PRI	097	SPALDING
BROOKE, NICHOLAS	MGM	416	MEDLEY 3
BROOKE, O. B.	ST	266	3RD E DI
BROOKE, PETER	CAL	013	1ST DIST
BROOKE, PETER	CAL	013	1ST DIST
BROOKE, RICHARD	MGM	316	CRACKLIN
BROOKE, ROBERT	PRI	010	BLADENSB
BROOKE, ROBERT C.	PRI	082	QUEEN AN
BROOKE, ROGER	MGM	321	CRACKLIN
BROOKE, ROGER	MGM	362	BERRYS D
BROOKE, SAMUEL L.	PRI	075	MARLBROU
BROOKE, THOMAS A.	MGM	391	ROCKERLE
BROOKE, THOMAS H.	BAL	068	10TH WAR
BROOKE, THOMAS R.	PRI	102	SPALDING
BROOKE, WALTER B.	PRI	088	SPALDING
BROOKE, WALTER B.	PRI	010	BLADENSB
BROOKE, WILLIAM	PRI	115	PISCATAW
BROOKER, BETSY	BAL	153	5TH WARD
BROOKES, CAPT. JOHN	PRI	090	MARLBROU
BROOKES, HAMILTON-BLACK	QUE	139	1ST E DI
BROOKES, ILZY*	BAL	310	3RD WARD
BROOKES, JAMES B.	ANN	465	HOWARD D
BROOKES, JAMES B.	PRI	080	QUEEN AN
BROOKES, JANE	PRI	061	NOTTINGH
BROOKES, MONICA	PRI	089	SPALDING
BROOKES, SAMUEL	PRI	076	MARLBROU
BROOKES, WILLIAM	BAL	103	18TH WAR
BROOKFIELD, ANNE-BLACK	CAR	121	NO TWP L
BROOKHART, JOHN	BAL	106	5TH WARD
BROOKHART, SOLOMAN	BAL	417	8TH WARD
BROOKHART, WILLIAM	BAL	416	8TH WARD
BROOKIN, CHARLES	FRE	317	MIDDLETO
BROOKING, JAMES	BAL	160	1ST WARD
BROOKINGS, CHARLES	CEC	187	7TH E DI
BROOKINGS, MARY	CEC	111	4TH E DI
BROOKINGS, MATILDA	BAL	146	5TH WARD
BROOKINGS, RICHARD	CEC	110	4TH E DI
BROOKINGS, ROBERT J.	BAL	297	7TH WARD
BROOKINS, RACHAEL	FRE	313	MIDDLETO
BROOKINS, RICHARD	BAL	067	4TH WARD
BROOKLIN, JAMES	PRI	115	PISCATAW
BROOKMAN, FREDERICK	BAL	471	14TH WAR
BROOKMAN, HENRY	BAL	120	2ND DIST
BROOKMEYER, WILLIAM	BAL	007	15TH WAR
BROOKMYER, HENRY	BAL	427	8TH WARD
BROOKMYER, RICHARD	BAL	429	8TH WARD
BROOKS, ABRAHAM	BAL	423	1ST DIST
BROOKS, ABRAHAM	QUE	241	5TH E DI
BROOKS, ALEX	BAL	230	12TH WAR
BROOKS, ALEXANDER	BAL	065	15TH WAR
BROOKS, ALLEN-BLACK	ST	346	5TH E DI
BROOKS, AMOS	CEC	023	ELKTON 3
BROOKS, ANDREW	BAL	107	18TH WAR
BROOKS, ANDREW	BAL	278	2ND WARD
BROOKS, ANN	BAL	298	7TH WARD
BROOKS, ANN	BAL	301	12TH WAR
BROOKS, ANN	BAL	036	4TH WARD
BROOKS, ANN	TAL	077	EASTON T
BROOKS, ANN E.	BAL	042	1ST WARD
BROOKS, ANNA	BAL	341	1ST DIST
BROOKS, ANNA M.	ANN	434	HOWARD D
BROOKS, ANTHONY	CEC	060	1ST E DI
BROOKS, ARAMINTA	KEN	227	2ND DIST
BROOKS, AUGUSTAS	BAL	048	18TH WAR
BROOKS, BASIL	MGM	349	BERRYS D
BROOKS, BASSLE	CHA	233	HILLTOP
BROOKS, BENEDICT	BAL	048	1ST WARD
BROOKS, BENJAMIN	ANN	473	HOWARD D
BROOKS, BETSEY	SOM	424	PRINCESS
BROOKS, BETTY	CHA	238	HILLTOP
BROOKS, CAESAR	CAL	034	2ND DIST
BROOKS, CAROLINE	BAL	462	14TH WAR
BROOKS, CAROLINE	BAL	127	11TH WAR
BROOKS, CATHARINE	ANN	431	HOWARD D
BROOKS, CATHARINE	BAL	150	16TH WAR
BROOKS, CHARLES	BAL	021	2ND DIST
BROOKS, CHARLES	ANN	358	3RD DIST
BROOKS, CHARLES	BAL	428	1ST DIST
BROOKS, CHARLES	BAL	452	1ST DIST
BROOKS, CHARLES	BAL	388	9TH WARD
BROOKS, CHARLES	BAL	224	12TH WAR
BROOKS, CHARLES	BAL	424	14TH WAR
BROOKS, CHARLOT	WAS	008	WILLIAMS
BROOKS, CHARLOTTE	BAL	036	4TH WARD
BROOKS, CHARLOTTE-BLACK	ST	299	2ND E DI
BROOKS, CHAUNCY	BAL	398	1ST DIST
BROOKS, CHRISTIANA-MULATT	FRE	031	FREDERIC
BROOKS, CHRISTY	BAL	469	14TH WAR
BROOKS, CURTIS	DOR	391	1ST DIST
BROOKS, DANIEL	BAL	175	6TH WARD
BROOKS, DAVID	BAL	459	8TH WARD
BROOKS, DAVID	ANN	451	HOWARD D
BROOKS, DAVID	BAL	217	17TH WAR
BROOKS, DAVID	TAL	061	EASTON D
BROOKS, DAVID	TAL	070	EASTON T
BROOKS, DELIA	PRI	064	NOTTINGH

BROOKS, DOLLY BAL 021 4TH WARD
BROOKS, DORCUS BAL 429 1ST DIST
BROOKS, EDWARD ANN 343 3RD DIST
BROOKS, EDWARD BAL 128 16TH WAR
BROOKS, EDWARD BAL 040 9TH WARD
BROOKS, ELEANOR BAL 321 1ST DIST
BROOKS, ELIAS-BLACK FRE 449 8TH E DI
BROOKS, ELISABETH ANN 391 4TH DIST
BROOKS, ELIZA BAL 075 10TH WAR
BROOKS, ELIZA WAS 153 HAGERSTO
BROOKS, ELIZA SOM 468 TRAPPE D
BROOKS, ELIZA J. SOM 467 TRAPPE D
BROOKS, ELIZABETH TAL 061 EASTON D
BROOKS, ELIZABETH BAL 094 10TH WAR
BROOKS, ELIZABETH ANN 275 ANNAPOLI
BROOKS, ELIZABETH BAL 041 2ND DIST
BROOKS, ELIZABETH BAL 170 6TH WARD
BROOKS, ELIZABETH CHA 233 HILLTOP
BROOKS, ELIZABETH DOR 360 3RD DIVI
BROOKS, ELIZABETH A. BAL 246 6TH WARD
BROOKS, ELLEN BAL 098 15TH WAR
BROOKS, ELLEN C.-MULATTO FRE 209 BUCKEYST
BROOKS, ENELS* BAL 378 3RD WARD
BROOKS, ESTER-BLACK ST 297 2ND E DI
BROOKS, F. BAL 332 1ST DIST
BROOKS, FLORA CHA 238 HILLTOP
BROOKS, FRANCIS A. TAL 049 EASTON T
BROOKS, FRANK-BLACK FRE 423 8TH E DI
BROOKS, FUTNAM BAL 042 1ST WARD
BROOKS, GEORGE BAL 353 1ST DIST
BROOKS, GEORGE ANN 365 4TH DIST
BROOKS, GEORGE BAL 422 3RD WARD
BROOKS, GEORGE TAL 045 EASTON T
BROOKS, GECRGE TAL 038 EASTON D
BROOKS, GEORGE TAL 031 EASTON D
BROOKS, GECRGE TAL 065 EASTON T
BROOKS, GEORGE W. BAL 197 6TH WARD
BROOKS, GEORGINANA BAL 452 14TH WAR
BROOKS, GRAFTON BAL 420 1ST DIST
BROOKS, GREENBURY BAL 366 1ST DIST
BROOKS, H. BAL 164 1ST WARD
BROOKS, HARY* DOR 411 1ST DIST
BROOKS, HENRY BAL 114 18TH WAR
BROOKS, HENRY BAL 471 14TH WAR
BROOKS, HENRY BAL 289 7TH WARD
BROOKS, HENRY TAL 063 EASTON D
BROOKS, HENRY WAS 008 WILLIAMS
BROOKS, HENRY KEN 267 1ST DIST
BROOKS, HESTER WAS 104 2ND DIST
BROOKS, HUGH BAL 346 3RD WARD
BROOKS, ISAAC BAL 090 5TH WARD
BROOKS, ISAAC BAL 014 9TH WARD
BROOKS, J. BAL 171 1ST WARD
BROOKS, J. BAL 160 1ST WARD
BROOKS, JACOB BAL 144 16TH WAR
BROOKS, JACOB ANN 459 HOWARD D
BROOKS, JAMES BAL 044 9TH WARD
BROOKS, JAMES BAL 003 15TH WAR
BROOKS, JAMES BAL 314 7TH WARD
BROOKS, JAMES BAL 124 18TH WAR
BROOKS, JAMES CEC 047 1ST E DI
BROOKS, JAMES HAR 127 2ND DIST
BROOKS, JAMES H. BAL 415 14TH WAR
BROOKS, JAMES-BLACK ST 299 2ND E DI
BROOKS, JAMES-BLACK QUE 177 2ND E DI
BROOKS, JANE KEN 233 2ND DIST
BROOKS, JANE BAL 192 11TH WAR
BROOKS, JANE BAL 362 8TH WARD
BROOKS, JENNY PRI 108 PISCATAW
BROOKS, JEREMIAH BAL 424 8TH WARD
BROOKS, JESSE BAL 116 15TH WAR
BROOKS, JOE TAL 030 EASTON D
BROOKS, JOHN TAL 043 EASTON D
BROOKS, JOHN BAL 058 10TH WAR
BROOKS, JOHN BAL 085 15TH WAR
BROOKS, JOHN BAL 104 10TH WAR
BROOKS, JOHN BAL 269 2ND WARD
BROOKS, JOHN BAL 032 9TH WARD
BROOKS, JOHN BAL 192 2ND WARD
BROOKS, JOHN ANN 496 HOWARD D
BROOKS, JOHN BAL 101 1ST WARD
BROOKS, JOHN BAL 180 2ND DIST
BROOKS, JOHN BAL 436 14TH WAR
BROOKS, JOHN BAL 083 4TH WARD
BROOKS, JOHN BAL 001 4TH WARD
BROOKS, JOHN FRE 424 8TH E DI
BROOKS, JOHN FRE 085 FREDERIC
BROOKS, JOHN CEC 094 4TH E DI
BROOKS, JOHN A.-BLACK FRE 052 FREDERIC
BROOKS, JOHN E. BAL 428 1ST DIST
BROOKS, JOHN H. BAL 379 13TH WAR
BROOKS, JOHN POPLAR MGM 361 BERRYS D
BROOKS, JOHN S. BAL 419 1ST DIST
BROOKS, JOSEPH BAL 076 2ND DIST
BROOKS, JOSEPH CEC 039 CHESAPEA
BROOKS, JOSEPH TAL 101 ST MICHA
BROOKS, JOSEPH TAL 104 ST MICHA
BROOKS, JOSEPH DOR 469 1ST DIST
BROOKS, JOSEPH C. BAL 334 1ST DIST
BROOKS, JOSEPH E. BAL 094 15TH WAR
BROOKS, JOSEPH R. BAL 024 9TH WARD
BROOKS, JOSEPHEAN BAL 335 1ST DIST
BROOKS, JOSHUA BAL 305 12TH WAR
BROOKS, JULIA A. BAL 116 15TH WAR
BROOKS, KITTY ANN 474 HOWARD D
BROOKS, L. PRI 094 SPALDING
BROOKS, LEE HAR 198 3RD DIST
BROOKS, LEWIS FRE 329 MIDDLETO
BROOKS, LEWIS BAL 256 6TH WARD
BROOKS, LIDDY BAL 083 4TH WARD
BROOKS, LIDIA BAL 276 1ST DIST
BROOKS, MARGARET BAL 282 7TH WARD
BROOKS, MARGARET BAL 213 6TH WARD
BROOKS, MARGARET FRE 066 FREDERIC
BROOKS, MARIA CEC 062 1ST E DI
BROOKS, MARY BAL 014 18TH WAR
BROOKS, MARY FRE 254 NEW MARK
BROOKS, MARY BAL 113 18TH WAR
BROOKS, MARY BAL 260 20TH WAR
BROOKS, MARY BAL 278 7TH WARD
BROOKS, MARY BAL 362 8TH WARD
BROOKS, MARY TAL 065 EASTON T
BROOKS, MARY WAS 114 2ND DIST
BROOKS, MARY C. BAL 366 1ST DIST
BROOKS, MARY E. BAL 419 1ST DIST
BROOKS, MARY E. TAL 052 EASTON D
BROOKS, MARY J. DOR 470 1ST DIST
BROOKS, MICHAEL ALL 152 6TH E.D.
BROOKS, MINTY* BAL 331 3RD WARD
BROOKS, NANCY TAL 031 EASTON D
BROOKS, NANCY SOM 473 TRAPPE D
BROOKS, NANCY CEC 139 6TH E DI
BROOKS, NECHOLAS TAL 077 EASTON T
BROOKS, NICK W. BAL 234 17TH WAR
BROOKS, ORANGE HAR 194 3RD DIST
BROOKS, PERRY BAL 365 13TH WAR
BROOKS, PERRY TAL 115 ST MICHA
BROOKS, PETER BAL 219 17TH WAR
BROOKS, PETER BOYER BAL 224 17TH WAR
BROOKS, PLATER BAL 126 18TH WAR
BROOKS, PRISCILLA BAL 432 14TH WAR
BROOKS, PRISCILLA BAL 173 2ND DIST
BROOKS, PRISCILLA ANN 356 3RD DIST
BROOKS, R. BAL 285 12TH WAR
BROOKS, RACHEL ANN 364 4TH DIST
BROOKS, RACHEL-BLACK CAR 092 NO TWP L
BROOKS, RALPH WAS 223 1ST DIST
BROOKS, RICHARD BAL 120 1ST WARD
BROOKS, RICHARD BAL 361 8TH WARD
BROOKS, RICHARD H. BAL 310 7TH WARD
BROOKS, ROBERT BAL 311 3RD WARD
BROOKS, ROBERT F. BAL 011 1ST WARD
BROOKS, ROBERT S. BAL 392 3RD WARD
BROOKS, RUBY-BLACK QUE 166 2ND E DI
BROOKS, SAMUEL WAS 155 HAGERSTO
BROOKS, SAMUEL ANN 370 4TH DIST
BROOKS, SAMUEL ANN 257 ANNAPOLI
BROOKS, SAMUEL BAL 413 14TH WAR
BROOKS, SAMUEL BAL 258 20TH WAR
BROOKS, SAMUEL BAL 302 20TH WAR
BROOKS, SAMUEL R. BAL 030 4TH WARD
BROOKS, SAMUEL-BLACK FRE 223 BUCKEYST
BROOKS, SANDY KEN 225 2ND DIST
BROOKS, SARAH BAL 430 14TH WAR
BROOKS, SARAH BAL 299 1ST DIST
BROOKS, SARAH BAL 183 6TH WARD
BROOKS, SARAH TAL 103 ST MICHA
BROOKS, SARAH A. BAL 369 1ST DIST
BROOKS, SHEDRACK BAL 074 4TH WARD
BROOKS, SILVIA PRI 094 SPALDING
BROOKS, SMAUEL BAL 074 1ST WARD
BROOKS, STEPHEN BAL 240 1ST DIST
BROOKS, STEPHEN QUE 207 3RD E DI
BROOKS, STEPHEN-BLACK FRE 427 8TH E DI
BROOKS, STEPHEN-BLACK FRE 017 FREDERIC
BROOKS, SUSAN FRE 254 NEW MARK
BROOKS, SUSAN BAL 346 1ST DIST
BROOKS, SUSAN A. TAL 075 EASTON T
BROOKS, TERESIA BAL 079 18TH WAR
BROOKS, THOAMS BAL 184 5TH DIST
BROOKS, THOMAS BAL 167 19TH WAR
BROOKS, THOMAS J. BAL 358 3RD WARD
BROOKS, THOMAS S. BAL 428 1ST DIST
BROOKS, THORNDIKE BAL 337 13TH WAR
BROOKS, THORNDIKE BAL 470 14TH WAR
BROOKS, TOM TAL 077 EASTON T
BROOKS, VAN WAS 017 2ND SUBD
BROOKS, WALTER B. BAL 471 14TH WAR
BROOKS, WALTER B. BAL 362 13TH WAR
BROOKS, WILLIAM BAL 204 17TH WAR
BROOKS, WILLIAM CEC 173 6TH E DI
BROOKS, WILLIAM BAL 199 19TH WAR
BROOKS, WILLIAM TAL 031 EASTON D
BROOKS, WILLIAM WAS 163 2ND DIST
BROOKS, WILLIAM QUE 233 4TH E DI
BROOKS, WILLIAM BAL 457 1ST DIST
BROOKS, WILLIAM BAL 420 1ST DIST
BROOKS, WILLIAM BAL 280 2ND WARD
BROOKS, WILLIAM BAL 130 1ST WARD
BROOKS, WILLIAM BAL 195 5TH DIST
BROOKS, WILLIAM BAL 177 2ND DIST
BROOKS, WILLIAM BAL 256 1ST DIST
BROOKS, WILLIAM BAL 246 6TH WARD
BROOKS, WILLIAM BAL 126 5TH WARD
BROOKS, WILLIAM ANN 365 4TH DIST
BROOKS, WILLIAM BAL 102 15TH WAR
BROOKS, WILLIAM BAL 149 16TH WAR
BROOKS, WILLIAM BAL 187 16TH WAR
BROOKS, WILLIAM BAL 439 8TH WARD
BROOKS, WILLIAM B. PRI 002 BLADENSB
BROOKS,ANDREW BAL 132 1ST WARD
BROOKS,ELIZA BAL 408 14TH WAR
BROOKS,HENRY WAS 008 WILLIAMS
BROOKS,RBEECCA BAL 042 1ST WARD
BROOKS,THOMAS J. BAL 142 1ST WARD
BROOKS,WILLIAM BAL 073 1ST WARD
BROOKSLEINE, JOEPH BAL 048 1ST WARD
BROOM, BETTY BAL 011 2ND DIST
BROOM, HENRIET BAL 223 12TH WAR
BROOM, HENRY BAL 405 1ST DIST
BROOM, JOHN BAL 181 2ND DIST
BROOM, KITTY * ANN 375 4TH DIST
BROOM, MAJOR BAL 040 15TH WAR
BROOM, PERRY CAL 020 2ND DIST
BROOM, SAMUEL WAS 241 CAVETOWN
BROOM, THOMAS BAL 079 15TH WAR
BROOM, WILLIAM SOM 456 DAMES QU
BROOME, JOHN M. ST 306 1ST E DI
BROOME, MICE BAL 250 20TH WAR
BROOME, NATHANIEL W. CAL 007 1ST DIST
BROOME, REBECCA ST 298 2ND E DI
BROOME, SARAH R. ST 306 1ST E DI
BROOME, THOMAS CAL 009 1ST DIST
BROOMFIELD, AUGUSTUS CEC 182 7TH E DI
BROOMFIELD, JOSEPH CEC 205 7TH E DI
BROOMFIELD, LYDIA CEC 149 PORT DUP
BROOMFIELD, MARY CEC 182 7TH E DI
BROOMIFIELD, JOHN CEC 077 NORTHEAS
BROOMW, MARY E. CAL 006 1ST DIST
BROOMWELL, JOHN TAL 092 ST MICHA
BROOMWELL, SAMUEL TAL 087 ST MICHA
BROON, ANN* BAL 385 3RD WARD
BROON, GEORGE H. BAL 201 17TH WAR
BROPHY, THOMAS ALL 226 CUMBERLA
BRORME, AARON * KEN 229 2ND DIST
BROSEN, MARY BAL 233 2ND WARD
BROSENON, FRANCIS ALL 241 CUMBERLA
BROSEUS, ELLEN ALL 259 CUMBERLA
BROSIAS, JOHN S. FRE 318 MIDDLETO
BROSIR, THOMAS HAR 199 3RD DIST
BROSIUS, DANIEL WAS 154 2ND DIST
BROSIUS, GEORGE WAS 161 2ND DIST
BROSIUS, JOHN WAS 161 2ND DIST
BROSIUS, JOHN J. WAS 155 2ND DIST
BROSIUS, MARY WAS 156 2ND DIST
BROSIUS, WILLIAM WAS 102 2ND DIST
BROSSEY, PATRICK BAL 159 11TH WAR
BROSSOM, MARY BAL 184 5TH DIST
BROTE, CHARLES ALL 111 5TH E.D.
BROTHER, WILLIAM BAL 167 19TH WAR
BROTHERS, BENJAMIN CAR 201 4TH DIST
BROTHERS, ELIAS CAR 196 4TH DIST
BROTHERS, FRANCIS CAR 201 4TH DIST
BROTHERS, FRANCIS ST 308 1ST E DI
BROTHERS, SAMUEL ANN 514 HOWARD D
BROTHERS, SOLOMON CAR 201 4TH DIST
BROTHERS, THOMAS CAR 203 4TH DIST
BROTHERTON, DAVID H. BAL 013 15TH WAR
BROTHERTON, JOHN A. J. BAL 255 6TH WARD
BROTHERTON, JOHN P. BAL 038 18TH WAR
BROTHERTON, THOMAS W. BAL 308 3RD WARD
BROTSON, ANN BAL 193 11TH WAR
BROTTEN, MARY ANN 506 HOWARD D
BROTTEN, SAMUEL BAL 116 15TH WAR
BROTTON, MARY CEC 104 4TH E DI
BROUCHER, JOSEPH BAL 099 18TH WAR
BROUDOUR, JOHN * BAL 322 1ST DIST
BROUGH, CHARLES J. BAL 362 8TH WARD
BROUGH, EMANUEL FRE 178 5TH E DI
BROUGH, JOHN BAL 321 7TH WARD
BROUGHAM, MARY MRS- BAL 315 20TH WAR
BROUGHBOY, ROBERT BAL 103 1ST WARD
BROUGHTON, BRIDGET BAL 010 4TH WARD
BROUGHTON, CECELIA BAL 153 16TH WAR
BROUGHTON, E. BAL 281 2ND WARD
BROUGHTON, HENRY BAL 337 3RD WARD
BROUGHTON, ISAAC BAL 118 18TH WAR
BROUGHTON, JAMES BAL 311 3RD WARD
BROUGHTON, JULIA A. BAL 463 14TH WAR
BROUGHTON, LETITIA BAL 030 9TH WARD
BROUGHTON, LOUISA BAL 107 15TH WAR
BROUND, CHARLES QUE 244 5TH E DI
BROUNITON, PATRICK WAS 162 2ND DIST
BROUNRODE, ELIZABETH BAL 448 14TH WAR
BROUNS, FERDINAND BAL 412 14TH WAR
BROUNSFIELD, SOLLOMON TAL 092 ST MICHA
BROUNSON, HENRY FRE 067 FREDERIC
BROUSHIREN, JOHN BAL 066 2ND DIST
BROW, HENRIETTA BAL 453 14TH WAR
BROW, JAMES ANN 272 ANNAPOLI
BROW, PHILLIP ALL 019 2ND E.D.
BROW, SUSAN ANN 286 ANNAPOLI
BROW, ZACHARIAH BAL 453 14TH WAR
BROWDEN, EDWARD BAL 164 1ST WARD
BROWDY, JOHN BAL 159 1ST WARD
BROWEL, JACOB * KEN 256 1ST DIST
BROWELL, HUS BAL 231 12TH WAR
BROWEN, JOHN M. ST 265 3RD E DI
BROWER, DAVID ALL 218 CUMBERLA
BROWER, JOHN WAS 127 2ND DIST
BROWER, MAHALA CAL 014 1ST DIST
BROWER, MARIAN H. * KEN 256 1ST DIST
BROWER, RICHARD ANN 272 ANNAPOLI
BROWER, STEPHEN * ANN 291 ANNAPOLI
BROWER, WILLIAM ALL 218 CUMBERLA
BROWING, JOHNATHAN FRE 447 8TH E DI
BROWM, JAMES BAL 161 1ST WARD
BROWN LAW, ROBERT * BAL 406 1ST DIST
BROWN, A. BAL 172 1ST WARD
BROWN, A. D. BAL 046 18TH WAR
BROWN, ABNER BAL 157 19TH WAR
BROWN, ABNER J. BAL 122 1ST WARD
BROWN, ABRAHAM BAL 452 1ST DIST
BROWN, ABRAHAM BAL 380 1ST DIST
BROWN, ABRAHAM ALL 219 CUMBERLA
BROWN, ABRAHAM FRE 254 NEW MARK
BROWN, ABRAHAM BAL 032 18TH WAR
BROWN, ABRAHAM HAR 183 3RD DIST
BROWN, ABRAHAM WAS 084 2ND SUBD
BROWN, ABRAHAM-BLACK FRE 222 BUCKEYST
BROWN, ABRAM CEC 089 4TH E DI
BROWN, ABRAM CEC 139 6TH E DI
BROWN, ABRAM BAL 066 2ND DIST
BROWN, ABRAM BAL 178 2ND DIST
BROWN, ADALINE ANN 364 4TH DIST
BROWN, ADAM FRE 340 MIDDLETO
BROWN, ADAM WAS 086 2ND SUBD
BRUWN, ADAM C. PRI 003 BLADENSB
BROWN, ADDISON BAL 456 8TH WARD
BROWN, AGNES FRE 163 EMMITTSB
BROWN, ALBERT ANN 284 ANNAPOLI
BROWN, ALEXANDER ANN 417 HOWARD D
BROWN, ALEXANDER BAL 029 2ND DIST
BROWN, ALEXANDER BAL 412 1ST DIST
BROWN, ALEXANDER BAL 167 1ST WARD
BROWN, ALEXANDER CEC 150 PORT DUP
BROWN, ALEXANDER BAL 213 17TH WAR
BROWN, ALEXANDER BAL 115 18TH WAR
BROWN, ALEXANDER CAL 057 3RD DIST
BROWN, ALEXANDER QUE 228 4TH E DI
BROWN, ALEXANDER D. BAL 453 1ST DIST
BROWN, ALEXANDER P. BAL 347 7TH WARD
BROWN, ALEXINA BAL 241 6TH WARD
BROWN, ALFRED BAL 144 5TH WARD
BROWN, ALFRED KEN 299 3RD DIST
BROWN, ALFRED BAL 388 13TH WAR
BROWN, ALFRED FRE 331 MIDDLETO
BROWN, ALFRED CEC 129 6TH E DI
BROWN, ALFRED MGM 337 CRACKLIN
BROWN, ALFRED-BLACK FRE 016 FREDERIC
BROWN, ALICE TAL 031 EASTON D
BROWN, ALICE M. CEC 082 CHARLEST
BROWN, ALLEN CEC 162 6TH E DI
BROWN, ALLEN BAL 134 1ST WARD
BROWN, ALONZO CEC 132 6TH E DI
BROWN, AMANDA BAL 221 17TH WAR
BROWN, AMBROSE BAL 081 2ND DIST
BROWN, AMELIA BAL 269 20TH WAR
BROWN, AMELIA J. BAL 121 16TH WAR
BROWN, AMOS CAL 023 2ND DIST
BROWN, ANDERSON BAL 108 18TH WAR
BROWN, ANDREW HAR 153 3RD DIST
BROWN, ANDREW MGM 361 BERRYS D
BROWN, ANDREW BAL 160 1ST WARD
BROWN, ANDREW BAL 161 1ST WARD
BROWN, ANDREW BAL 219 2ND WARD
BROWN, ANDREW BAL 001 1ST WARD
BROWN, ANDREW J. CAR 265 WESTMINS
BROWN, ANDRWE BAL 170 2ND DIST
BROWN, ANGELINA BAL 455 8TH WARD
BROWN, ANN BAL 340 7TH WARD
BROWN, ANN BAL 014 9TH WARD
BROWN, ANN BAL 147 16TH WAR
BROWN, ANN ANN 460 HOWARD D
BROWN, ANN BAL 029 2ND DIST
BROWN, ANN BAL 394 3RD WARD
BROWN, ANN BAL 294 7TH WARD
BROWN, ANN BAL 343 3RD WARD
BROWN, ANN ALL 052 10TH E.D
BROWN, ANN BAL 066 18TH WAR

Name	County	Page	District
BROWN, ANN	BAL	145	19TH WAR
BROWN, ANN	BAL	265	20TH WAR
BROWN, ANN	BAL	241	20TH WAR
BROWN, ANN	CAR	191	4TH DIST
BROWN, ANN	WAS	091	2ND SUBD
BROWN, ANN	KEN	311	3RD DIST
BROWN, ANN	KEN	283	3RD DIST
BROWN, ANN	QUE	219	3RD E DI
BROWN, ANN	TAL	053	EASTON D
BROWN, ANN B.	BAL	039	4TH WARD
BROWN, ANN M.	BAL	223	17TH WAR
BROWN, ANN M.	BAL	096	5TH WARD
BROWN, ANN P.	BAL	101	1ST WARD
BROWN, ANN R.	CAL	044	3RD DIST
BROWN, ANN W.	BAL	294	12TH WAR
BROWN, ANN-BLACK	QUE	184	3RD E DI
BROWN, ANNA	BAL	051	9TH WARD
BROWN, ANNA	BAL	266	12TH WAR
BROWN, ANNA	BAL	022	9TH WARD
BROWN, ANNA	CAL	035	2ND DIST
BROWN, ANNA	CAL	027	2ND DIST
BROWN, ANNY	BAL	034	4TH WARD
BROWN, ARIEL H.	BAL	230	6TH WARD
BROWN, ARMEAL	BAL	045	18TH WAR
BROWN, ARON	BAL	058	4TH WARD
BROWN, ARTHUR	CAR	209	5TH DIST
BROWN, ARTHUR	BAL	199	6TH WARD
BROWN, ARTHUR G.	BAL	216	11TH WAR
BROWN, ASARIAH	SOM	513	BARREN C
BROWN, AUGUST	BAL	393	14TH WAR
BROWN, AUGUSTUS	BAL	107	1ST WARD
BROWN, AULARY	BAL	013	9TH WARD
BROWN, B.	BAL	151	1ST WARD
BROWN, B.T.	BAL	135	5TH WARD
BROWN, BALTEMER-BLACK	CAR	074	NO TWP L
BROWN, BARBARA	CAR	368	9TH DIST
BROWN, BASEL	CAL	024	2ND DIST
BROWN, BASER	PRI	075	MARLBROU
BROWN, BASIL	PRI	089	SPALDING
BROWN, BASIL	PRI	097	SPALDING
BROWN, BASIL	ANN	327	2ND DIST
BROWN, BAZIL	QUE	214	3RD E DI
BROWN, BAZIL	QUE	213	3RD E DI
BROWN, BENEDICT	PRI	075	MARLBROU
BROWN, BENJAMIN	QUE	241	5TH E DI
BROWN, BENJAMIN	QUE	224	4TH E DI
BROWN, BENJAMIN	WAS	122	2ND DIST
BROWN, BENJAMIN	ANN	305	1ST DIST
BROWN, BENJAMIN	ALL	206	CUMBERLA
BROWN, BENJAMIN	BAL	152	5TH WARD
BROWN, BENJAMIN	BAL	332	7TH WARD
BROWN, BENJAMIN	BAL	192	5TH DIST
BROWN, BENJAMIN	BAL	152	2ND DIST
BROWN, BENJAMIN	CAL	045	3RD DIST
BROWN, BENJAMIN	CEC	179	7TH E DI
BROWN, BENJAMIN	CEC	175	7TH E DI
BROWN, BENJAMIN	BAL	009	18TH WAR
BROWN, BENJAMIN	BAL	237	20TH WAR
BROWN, BENJAMIN	BAL	203	17TH WAR
BROWN, BENJAMIN	CEC	143	7TH E DI
BROWN, BENJAMIN	BAL	115	18TH WAR
BROWN, BENJAMIN F.	CAR	236	UNION TO
BROWN, BENJAMIN F.	HAR	014	1ST DIST
BROWN, BENJAMIN O.	BAL	260	6TH WARD
BROWN, BENJAMIN-BLACK	QUE	180	2ND E DI
BROWN, BETSEY	TAL	111	ST MICHA
BROWN, BETSEY	BAL	056	10TH WAR
BROWN, BETSEY	BAL	084	4TH WARD
BROWN, BETSEY	CAL	029	2ND DIST
BROWN, BETSEY*	BAL	310	3RD WARD
BROWN, BETSY	BAL	133	5TH WARD
BROWN, BETSY-BROWN	FRE	407	JEFFERSO
BROWN, BEVERIDGE	ANN	317	1ST DIST
BROWN, BIDDY	SOM	517	BARREN C
BROWN, BRADFORD	QUE	207	3RD E DI
BROWN, BRIDGET	ANN	425	HOWARD D
BROWN, BYARD	SOM	513	BARREN C
BROWN, C.	BAL	148	1ST WARD
BROWN, C.	BAL	135	1ST WARD
BROWN, C.	BAL	241	20TH WAR
BROWN, C. GRAHAM	CHA	236	HILLTOP
BROWN, C. H.	BAL	150	1ST WARD
BROWN, CAFFEE*	DOR	409	1ST DIST
BROWN, CAHRLES	HAR	089	2ND DIST
BROWN, CALVERT	PRI	078	MARLBROU
BROWN, CALVERT	PRI	081	QUEEN AN
BROWN, CAROLINE	FRE	337	MIDDLETO
BROWN, CAROLINE	BAL	204	2ND WARD
BROWN, CAROLINE	BAL	395	8TH WARD
BROWN, CAROLINE	BAL	078	2ND DIST
BROWN, CAROLINE	ANN	433	HOWARD D
BROWN, CAROLINE	BAL	137	2ND DIST
BROWN, CASPER	ALL	168	6TH E.D.
BROWN, CASSANDRA	BAL	176	6TH WARD
BROWN, CASSANDRA	BAL	426	1ST DIST
BROWN, CASSY	MGM	354	BERRYS D
BROWN, CATHAIRNE	BAL	253	12TH WAR
BROWN, CATHARINE	BAL	237	12TH WAR
BROWN, CATHARINE	BAL	020	2ND DIST
BROWN, CATHARINE	BAL	227	2ND WARD
BROWN, CATHARINE	BAL	467	14TH WAR
BROWN, CATHARINE	BAL	462	14TH WAR
BROWN, CATHARINE	BAL	211	17TH WAR
BROWN, CATHARINE	BAL	223	19TH WAR
BROWN, CATHARINE	BAL	014	18TH WAR
BROWN, CATHARINE	BAL	032	18TH WAR
BROWN, CATHARINE	WAS	087	2ND SUBD
BROWN, CATHARINE A.	PRI	079	MARLBROU
BROWN, CATHERINE	QUE	229	4TH E DI
BROWN, CATHERINE	BAL	159	11TH WAR
BROWN, CATHERINE	BAL	141	11TH WAR
BROWN, CATHERINE	MGM	337	CRACKLIN
BROWN, CATHERINE	BAL	177	11TH WAR
BROWN, CATHERINE	ANN	377	4TH DIST
BROWN, CATHERINE M.	QUE	230	4TH E DI
BROWN, CECELIA	BAL	387	13TH WAR
BROWN, CECILIA	BAL	413	1ST DIST
BROWN, CECILIA MISS-	BAL	315	20TH WAR
BROWN, CHARELS	BAL	170	6TH WARD
BROWN, CHARELS	BAL	243	1ST DIST
BROWN, CHARLES	BAL	248	1ST DIST
BROWN, CHARLES	BAL	050	1ST WARD
BROWN, CHARLES	BAL	056	1ST WARD
BROWN, CHARLES	BAL	151	5TH WARD
BROWN, CHARLES	BAL	163	1ST WARD
BROWN, CHARLES	BAL	325	3RD WARD
BROWN, CHARLES	BAL	337	7TH WARD
BROWN, CHARLES	BAL	060	15TH WAR
BROWN, CHARLES	BAL	136	1ST WARD
BROWN, CHARLES	BAL	137	1ST WARD
BROWN, CHARLES	BAL	141	1ST WARD
BROWN, CHARLES	BAL	140	1ST WARD
BROWN, CHARLES	BAL	128	1ST WARD
BROWN, CHARLES	BAL	127	1ST WARD
BROWN, CHARLES	ANN	350	3RD DIST
BROWN, CHARLES	BAL	050	9TH WARD
BROWN, CHARLES	BAL	105	15TH WAR
BROWN, CHARLES	MGM	370	BERRYS D
BROWN, CHARLES	BAL	114	11TH WAR
BROWN, CHARLES	CAR	161	NO TWP L
BROWN, CHARLES	HAR	147	3RD DIST
BROWN, CHARLES	CAR	198	4TH DIST
BROWN, CHARLES	CEC	016	ELKTON 3
BROWN, CHARLES	CEC	013	ELKTON 3
BROWN, CHARLES	BAL	050	4TH WARD
BROWN, CHARLES	BAL	273	20TH WAR
BROWN, CHARLES	PRI	094	SPALDING
BROWN, CHARLES	PRI	031	VANSVILL
BROWN, CHARLES	WAS	005	WILLIAMS
BROWN, CHARLES	KEN	300	3RD DIST
BROWN, CHARLES C.	ANN	462	HOWARD D
BROWN, CHARLES H.	BAL	190	17TH WAR
BROWN, CHARLES H.	PRI	107	PISCATAW
BROWN, CHARLES H.	HAR	184	3RD DIST
BROWN, CHARLES H. H.	BAL	314	20TH WAR
BROWN, CHARLES W.	ANN	510	HOWARD D
BROWN, CHARLES-BLACK	QUE	148	1ST E DI
BROWN, CHARLOTTA	CEC	216	7TH E DI
BROWN, CHARLOTTE	MGM	355	BERRYS D
BROWN, CHARLOTTE	BAL	385	13TH WAR
BROWN, CHARLOTTE	BAL	128	16TH WAR
BROWN, CHARLOTTE	ANN	326	2ND DIST
BROWN, CHRIS	BAL	247	20TH WAR
BROWN, CHRISTIAN	BAL	184	5TH DIST
BROWN, CHRISTIAN H.	BAL	075	18TH WAR
BROWN, CLARISSA	BAL	356	13TH WAR
BROWN, CLARISSA	BAL	182	11TH WAR
BROWN, CLENENDY G.	HAR	160	3RD DIST
BROWN, CLOE	BAL	321	3RD WARD
BROWN, CLOWIE-BLACK	ST	323	4TH E DI
BROWN, COLLIN	BAL	049	1ST WARD
BROWN, CONRAD	BAL	220	19TH WAR
BROWN, CONROD	WAS	130	HAGERSTO
BROWN, CORA	KEN	313	3RD DIST
BROWN, CORNELIA	BAL	105	10TH WAR
BROWN, CORNELIUS	BAL	232	12TH WAR
BROWN, CORNELIUS	BAL	046	2ND DIST
BROWN, CORNELIUS	BAL	046	2ND DIST
BROWN, CORNELIUS E.	FRE	368	CATOCTIN
BROWN, CORNELIUS-BLACK	FRE	381	PETERSVI
BROWN, COSSEY*	BAL	061	4TH WARD
BROWN, D. U.	BAL	059	10TH WAR
BROWN, DAN	ANN	423	HOWARD D
BROWN, DANIEL	BAL	063	2ND DIST
BROWN, DANIEL	BAL	458	8TH WARD
BROWN, DANIEL	ALL	107	5TH E.D.
BROWN, DANIEL	BAL	200	6TH WARD
BROWN, DANIEL	CEC	140	6TH E DI
BROWN, DANIEL	FRE	340	MIDDLETO
BROWN, DANIEL	BAL	192	19TH WAR
BROWN, DANIEL	HAR	183	3RD DIST
BROWN, DANIEL	FRE	150	10TH E D
BROWN, DANIEL	WAS	239	CAVETOWN
BROWN, DANIEL	WAS	084	2ND SUBD
BROWN, DANIEL-BLACK	QUE	197	3RD E DI
BROWN, DARIAS	CAR	404	2ND DIST
BROWN, DARKNESS	BAL	118	11TH WAR
BROWN, CAVID	CAR	411	2ND DIST
BROWN, DAVID	CEC	171	6TH E DI
BROWN, DAVID	BAL	400	14TH WAR
BROWN, DAVID	BAL	414	14TH WAR
BROWN, DAVID	BAL	090	18TH WAR
BROWN, DAVID	CEC	174	6TH E DI
BROWN, DAVID	KEN	302	3RD DIST
BROWN, DAVID	WAS	086	2ND SUBD
BROWN, DAVID	WAS	063	2ND SUBD
BROWN, CAVID	BAL	171	1ST WARD
BROWN, DAVID	BAL	227	6TH WARD
BROWN, DAVID	BAL	333	7TH WARD
BROWN, DAVID	ANN	509	HOWARD D
BROWN, DEBORAH	ANN	355	3RD DIST
BROWN, DELIA	ANN	454	HOWARD D
BROWN, DELIA	BAL	245	6TH WARD
BROWN, DELILA	BAL	159	2ND DIST
BROWN, DENNIS	TAL	056	EASTON D
BROWN, DERAS	BAL	211	11TH WAR
BROWN, DIANA	BAL	269	20TH WAR
BROWN, DINAH	WAS	007	WILLIAMS
BROWN, DINAH	ANN	414	HOWARD D
BROWN, DIXON	BAL	049	2ND DIST
BROWN, DIXON	BAL	045	2ND DIST
BROWN, DOLLY	TAL	094	ST MICHA
BROWN, DORCUS	BAL	442	1ST DIST
BROWN, DORCUS	CAL	054	3RD DIST
BROWN, DOROTHY	ST	286	2ND E DI
BROWN, E.	ANN	285	ANNAPOLI
BROWN, E.	BAL	165	1ST WARD
BROWN, E.	BAL	171	1ST WARD
BROWN, E.	BAL	281	2ND WARD
BROWN, E. LINCOLN	CAR	397	2ND DIST
BROWN, EBENEZER	KEN	312	3RD DIST
BROWN, EDMOND	BAL	121	1ST WARD
BROWN, EDMUND JR.	CEC	007	ELKTON 3
BROWN, EDMUND SR.	CEC	006	ELKTON 3
BROWN, EDMUND*	DOR	383	1ST DIST
BROWN, EDW. *	BAL	302	20TH WAR
BROWN, EDWARD	BAL	128	18TH WAR
BROWN, EDWARD	BAL	200	11TH WAR
BROWN, EDWARD	BAL	343	13TH WAR
BROWN, EDWARD	HAR	087	2ND DIST
BROWN, EDWARD	FRE	060	FREDERIC
BROWN, EDWARD	BAL	155	2ND DIST
BROWN, EDWARD	BAL	280	2ND WARD
BROWN, EDWARD	BAL	266	2ND WARD
BROWN, EDWARD	BAL	270	2ND WARD
BROWN, EDWARD	BAL	130	1ST WARD
BROWN, EDWARD	BAL	257	2ND WARD
BROWN, EDWARD	BAL	157	1ST WARD
BROWN, EDWARD	BAL	152	1ST WARD
BROWN, EDWARD	BAL	146	1ST WARD
BROWN, EDWARD	ALL	112	5TH E.D.
BROWN, EDWARD	ANN	304	1ST DIST
BROWN, EDWARD	BAL	218	12TH WAR
BROWN, EDWARD	BAL	073	10TH WAR
BROWN, EDWARD	KEN	256	1ST DIST
BROWN, EDWARD C.	CAR	068	NO TWP L
BROWN, EDWARD H.	CEC	136	6TH E DI
BROWN, EDWARD N.	BAL	133	5TH WARD
BROWN, EDWARD-BLACK	CAR	404	2ND DIST
BROWN, EDWARD-BLACK	FRE	018	FREDERIC
BROWN, EDWIN	BAL	204	17TH WAR
BROWN, EDWIN J.	CEC	121	4TH E DI
BROWN, EJSSE	BAL	048	1ST WARD
BROWN, ELI	ANN	509	HOWARD D
BROWN, ELIAS	BAL	124	11TH WAR
BROWN, ELIAS	CAR	233	5TH DIST
BROWN, ELIJAH	BAL	159	6TH WARD
BROWN, ELIJAH	ANN	427	HOWARD D
BROWN, ELIPHALET-BLACK	QUE	192	3RD E DI
BROWN, ELISHA	ANN	478	HOWARD D
BROWN, ELISHA	BAL	217	6TH DIST
BROWN, ELISHA	BAL	236	1ST DIST
BROWN, ELISHA	BAL	193	5TH DIST
BROWN, ELISHA	CEC	131	6TH E DI
BROWN, ELISHA	CEC	156	PORT DUP
BROWN, ELISHA	CEC	161	6TH E DI
BROWN, ELISHA	CEC	101	4TH E DI
BROWN, ELISHA JR.	ANN	478	HOWARD D
BROWN, ELISHA-BLACK	WOR	346	1ST E DI
BROWN, ELIZA	PRI	074	MARLBROU
BROWN, ELIZA	BAL	166	6TH WARD
BROWN, ELIZA	ANN	509	HOWARD D
BROWN, ELIZA	BAL	093	5TH WARD
BROWN, ELIZA	BAL	072	10TH WAR
BROWN, ELIZA	BAL	124	16TH WAR
BROWN, ELIZA	BAL	296	12TH WAR
BROWN, ELIZA	BAL	242	12TH WAR
BROWN, ELIZA	BAL	455	8TH WARD
BROWN, ELIZA	ANN	326	2ND DIST
BROWN, ELIZA	BAL	246	20TH WAR
BROWN, ELIZA	HAR	147	3RD DIST
BROWN, ELIZA A.	WOR	303	SNOW HIL
BROWN, ELIZA S.	CHA	256	MIDDLETO
BROWN, ELIZABETH	HAR	151	3RD DIST
BROWN, ELIZABETH	HAR	167	3RD DIST
BROWN, ELIZABETH	FRE	151	10TH E D
BROWN, ELIZABETH	FRE	156	10TH E D
BROWN, ELIZABETH	FRE	156	10TH E D
BROWN, ELIZABETH	BAL	031	18TH WAR
BROWN, ELIZABETH	CEC	087	4TH E DI
BROWN, ELIZABETH	CEC	129	6TH E DI
BROWN, ELIZABETH	BAL	196	19TH WAR
BROWN, ELIZABETH	CAR	181	8TH DIST
BROWN, ELIZABETH	CAR	279	7TH DIST
BROWN, ELIZABETH	BAL	124	18TH WAR
BROWN, ELIZABETH	MGM	363	BERRYS D
BROWN, ELIZABETH	HAR	005	1ST DIST
BROWN, ELIZABETH	WAS	086	2ND SUBD
BROWN, ELIZABETH	QUE	169	2ND E DI
BROWN, ELIZABETH	KEN	294	3RD DIST
BROWN, ELIZABETH	SOM	441	DAMES QU
BROWN, ELIZABETH	SOM	441	DAMES QU
BROWN, ELIZABETH	ANN	287	ANNAPOLI
BROWN, ELIZABETH	ALL	009	3RD E.D.
BROWN, ELIZABETH	BAL	343	7TH WARD
BROWN, ELIZABETH	BAL	329	7TH WARD
BROWN, ELIZABETH	BAL	191	11TH WAR
BROWN, ELIZABETH	BAL	279	12TH WAR
BROWN, ELIZABETH	BAL	084	15TH WAR
BROWN, ELIZABETH	BAL	039	9TH WARD
BROWN, ELIZABETH	ANN	496	HOWARD D
BROWN, ELIZABETH	BAL	137	5TH WARD
BROWN, ELIZABETH	ANN	482	HOWARD D
BROWN, ELIZABETH	ANN	434	HOWARD D
BROWN, ELIZABETH	ANN	443	HOWARD D
BROWN, ELIZABETH	ANN	420	HOWARD D
BROWN, ELIZABETH	BAL	120	2ND DIST
BROWN, ELIZABETH	BAL	102	1ST WARD
BROWN, ELIZABETH	BAL	369	8TH WARD
BROWN, ELIZABETH	BAL	384	8TH WARD
BROWN, ELIZABETH	BAL	393	3RD WARD
BROWN, ELIZABETH	BAL	248	6TH WARD
BROWN, ELIZABETH	BAL	272	7TH WARD
BROWN, ELIZABETH	BAL	372	3RD WARD
BROWN, ELIZABETH A.	ANN	443	HOWARD D
BROWN, ELIZABETH M.	HAR	093	2ND DIST
BROWN, ELIZABETH R.	CEC	171	6TH E DI
BROWN, ELIZABETH W.	CEC	135	6TH E DI
BROWN, ELIZABETH-BLACK	CAR	375	9TH DIST
BROWN, ELIZABETH-BLACK	FRE	008	FREDERIC
BROWN, ELIZABETH-MULATTO	ST	331	4TH E DI
BROWN, ELLEN	BAL	341	13TH WAR
BROWN, ELLEN	BAL	422	3RD WARD
BROWN, ELLEN	BAL	260	6TH WARD
BROWN, ELLEN	BAL	226	1ST DIST
BROWN, ELLEN	BAL	049	1ST WARD
BROWN, ELLEN	BAL	243	6TH WARD
BROWN, ELLEN	BAL	110	10TH WAR
BROWN, ELLEN	BAL	248	12TH WAR
BROWN, ELLEN-BLACK	QUE	159	2ND E DI
BROWN, ELSIE-BLACK	QUE	180	2ND E DI
BROWN, EMELINE	BAL	232	6TH WARD
BROWN, EMELINE	BAL	152	2ND DIST
BROWN, EMILIA	BAL	265	1ST DIST
BROWN, EMILINE	BAL	119	5TH WARD
BROWN, EMILY	BAL	144	5TH WARD
BROWN, EMILY	KEN	301	3RD DIST
BROWN, EMILY	BAL	437	14TH WAR
BROWN, EMILY	CEC	104	4TH E DI
BROWN, EMMA	BAL	299	17TH WAR
BROWN, ENOCH	ANN	450	HOWARD D
BROWN, EPHRAIM	HAR	185	3RD DIST
BROWN, EPHRAIM	HAR	185	3RD DIST
BROWN, EPHRAIM	BAL	201	11TH WAR
BROWN, EPHRAIM W.	MGM	335	CRACKLIN
BROWN, ERAPMUS	BAL	315	20TH WAR
BROWN, EUGENE	CHA	264	HILLTOP
BROWN, EVE	CEC	206	7TH E DI
BROWN, EZECLE *	KEN	283	3RD DIST
BROWN, EZEKIEL	CEC	066	1ST E DI
BROWN, EZEKLE	KEN	291	3RD DIST
BROWN, F.	BAL	172	1ST WARD
BROWN, FANNY	BAL	138	5TH WARD
BROWN, FANNY	BAL	161	2ND DIST
BROWN, FANNY	BAL	223	12TH WAR
BROWN, FANNY	TAL	120	ST MICHA
BROWN, FANNY	BAL	281	17TH WAR
BROWN, FANNY-BLACK	QUE	129	1ST E DI
BROWN, FANNY-MULATTO	FRE	033	FREDERIC
BROWN, FENTON	HAR	136	2ND DIST
BROWN, FLORA	BAL	156	11TH WAR
BROWN, FLORA	BAL	348	1ST DIST
BROWN, FRANCES	BAL	369	3RD WARD
BROWN, FRANCES	CEC	146	PORT DUP
BROWN, FRANCES	BAL	062	4TH WARD
BROWN, FRANCES	QUE	211	3RD E DI
BROWN, FRANCIS	PRI	102	SPALDING
BROWN, FRANCIS	WAS	177	1ST DIST
BROWN, FRANCIS	HAR	157	3RD DIST
BROWN, FRANCIS	SOM	430	PRINCESS

Name	County	Page	District
BROWN, FRANCIS	BAL	134	1ST WARD
BROWN, FRANCIS	BAL	078	1ST WARD
BROWN, FRANCIS	BAL	114	1ST WARD
BROWN, FRANCIS	BAL	153	1ST WARD
BROWN, FRANCIS	BAL	004	EASTERN
BROWN, FRANCIS	BAL	003	EASTERN
BROWN, FRANCIS A.-BLACK	ST	337	4TH E DI
BROWN, FRANCIS-BLACK	CAR	392	2ND DIST
BROWN, FRANK	BAL	125	1ST WARD
BROWN, FRANKLIN	BAL	456	8TH WARD
BROWN, FRANKLIN	BAL	027	18TH WAR
BROWN, FREDERICK	BAL	234	17TH WAR
BROWN, FREDERICK	FRE	240	NEW MARK
BROWN, FREDERICK	BAL	062	15TH WAR
BROWN, FREDERICK S.	CHA	244	HILLTOP
BROWN, FREDERICK-BLACK	QUE	157	2ND E DI
BROWN, FRITZ	BAL	227	2ND WARD
BROWN, G.W.	BAL	230	1ST DIST
BROWN, GARRET	BAL	467	14TH WAR
BROWN, GEORGE	HAR	135	2ND DIST
BROWN, GEORGE	BAL	105	18TH WAR
BROWN, GEORGE	BAL	057	4TH WARD
BROWN, GEORGE	BAL	385	13TH WAR
BROWN, GEORGE	CEC	111	4TH E DI
BROWN, GEORGE	CAR	350	6TH DIST
BROWN, GEORGE	HAR	100	2ND DIST
BROWN, GEORGE	FRE	076	FREDERIC
BROWN, GEORGE	CAR	283	7TH DIST
BROWN, GEORGE	CAR	180	8TH DIST
BROWN, GEORGE	CEC	018	ELKTCN 3
BROWN, GEORGE	CEC	026	ELKTCN 3
BROWN, GEORGE	BAL	220	19TH WAR
BROWN, GEORGE	BAL	115	1ST WARD
BROWN, GEORGE	BAL	295	1ST DIST
BROWN, GEORGE	BAL	150	5TH WARD
BROWN, GEORGE	BAL	171	1ST WARD
BROWN, GEORGE	BAL	177	11TH WAR
BROWN, GEORGE	BAL	403	3RD WARD
BROWN, GEORGE	BAL	394	8TH WARD
BROWN, GEORGE	BAL	096	2ND DIST
BROWN, GEORGE	BAL	137	2ND DIST
BROWN, GEORGE	ALL	228	CUMBERLA
BROWN, GEORGE	BAL	189	17TH WAR
BROWN, GEORGE	ANN	284	ANNAPOLI
BROWN, GEORGE	QUE	215	3RD E DI
BROWN, GEORGE	TAL	109	ST MICHA
BROWN, GEORGE	WAS	046	2ND SUBD
BROWN, GEORGE	TAL	023	EASTON D
BROWN, GEORGE	TAL	021	EASTCN D
BROWN, GEORGE A.	BAL	299	20TH WAR
BROWN, GEORGE F.	BAL	398	3RD WARD
BROWN, GEORGE H.	BAL	180	6TH WARD
BROWN, GEORGE R.	PRI	012	BLADENSB
BROWN, GEORGE T.	WOR	194	8TH E DI
BROWN, GEORGE W.	WAS	086	2ND SUBD
BROWN, GEORGE W.	BAL	362	3RD WARD
BROWN, GEORGE W.	BAL	307	7TH WARD
BROWN, GEORGE W.	BAL	177	16TH WAR
BROWN, GEORGE W.	BAL	216	11TH WAR
BROWN, GEORGE W.	HAR	157	3RD DIST
BROWN, GEORGE-BLACK	QUE	147	1ST E DI
BROWN, GEORGE-BLACK	QUE	134	1ST E DI
BROWN, GEORGE-BLACK	QUE	191	3RD E DI
BROWN, GEORGIANNA	PRI	039	VANSVILL
BROWN, GIDEON	CEC	211	7TH E DI
BROWN, GODFREY	BAL	143	5TH WARD
BROWN, GOERGE	ALL	011	3RD E.D.
BROWN, GOERGE	ANN	452	HOWARD D
BROWN, GOERGE	CEC	018	ELKTCN 3
BROWN, GRACE	BAL	001	EASTERN
BROWN, GRANVILLE K.	CEC	132	6TH E DI
BROWN, GREENSBURY-BLACK	QUE	194	3RD E DI
BROWN, H.	BAL	135	1ST WARD
BROWN, H. F.	BAL	155	1ST WARD
BROWN, H.A.	BAL	140	5TH WARD
BROWN, HAGAR	BAL	192	6TH WARD
BROWN, HANNA	TAL	065	EASTON T
BROWN, HANNAH	BAL	376	1ST DIST
BROWN, HANNAH	HAR	032	1ST DIST
BROWN, HANNAH	BAL	152	11TH WAR
BROWN, HANNAH D.	ANN	521	HOWARD D
BROWN, HANNAH-MULATTO	FRE	411	8TH E DI
BROWN, HANSON	MGM	331	CRACKLIN
BROWN, HANSON	ALL	009	3RD E.D.
BROWN, HARRETT	BAL	014	18TH WAR
BROWN, HARRICK	WOR	193	8TH E DI
BROWN, HARRIET	CEC	090	4TH E DI
BROWN, HARRIET	MGM	332	CRACKLIN
BROWN, HARRIET	HAR	033	1ST DIST
BROWN, HARRIET	BAL	425	14TH WAR
BROWN, HARRIET	BAL	197	17TH WAR
BROWN, HARRIET	BAL	001	1ST WARD
BROWN, HARRIET B.	CEC	170	6TH E DI
BROWN, HARRIET-BLACK	FRE	017	FREDERIC
BROWN, HARRIET-BLACK	QUE	183	3RD E DI
BROWN, HARRIETT	KEN	311	3RD DIST
BROWN, HARRIETT	DOR	313	1ST DIST
BROWN, HARRIOTT	BAL	053	4TH WARD
BROWN, HARRIOTT	BAL	078	4TH WARD
BROWN, HARRISON	BAL	319	12TH WAR
BROWN, HATTON	MGM	424	MEDLEY 3
BROWN, HENREITTA	WOR	196	8TH E DI
BROWN, HENRIETTA	BAL	321	3RD WARD
BROWN, HENRIETTA	BAL	262	12TH WAR
BROWN, HENRIETTA-BLACK	QUE	140	1ST E DI
BROWN, HENRY	MGM	338	CRACKLIN
BROWN, HENRY	FRE	153	10TH E D
BROWN, HENRY	FRE	151	10TH E D
BROWN, HENRY	CEC	060	1ST E DI
BROWN, HENRY	CEC	079	NORTHEAS
BROWN, HENRY	CAR	369	9TH DIST
BROWN, HENRY	CAR	391	2ND DIST
BROWN, HENRY	CAR	257	3RD DIST
BROWN, HENRY	BAL	074	18TH WAR
BROWN, HENRY	CAL	037	2ND DIST
BROWN, HENRY	CEC	045	1ST E DI
BROWN, HENRY	CEC	045	1ST E DI
BROWN, HENRY	BAL	165	19TH WAR
BROWN, HENRY	FRE	337	MIDDLETO
BROWN, HENRY	BAL	120	5TH WARD
BROWN, HENRY	BAL	190	17TH WAR
BROWN, HENRY	BAL	199	17TH WAR
BROWN, HENRY	BAL	301	12TH WAR
BROWN, HENRY	BAL	167	2ND DIST
BROWN, HENRY	BAL	092	1ST WARD
BROWN, HENRY	BAL	237	1ST DIST
BROWN, HENRY	BAL	072	1ST WARD
BROWN, HENRY	BAL	119	1ST WARD
BROWN, HENRY	BAL	125	1ST WARD
BROWN, HENRY	BAL	124	1ST WARD
BROWN, HENRY	BAL	121	1ST WARD
BROWN, HENRY	BAL	122	1ST WARD
BROWN, HENRY	ALL	038	2ND E.D.
BROWN, HENRY	ALL	008	3RD E.D.
BROWN, HENRY	ANN	330	2ND DIST
BROWN, HENRY	BAL	167	1ST WARD
BROWN, HENRY	BAL	132	1ST WARD
BROWN, HENRY	BAL	227	2ND WARD
BROWN, HENRY	BAL	281	2ND WARD
BROWN, HENRY	QUE	185	3RD E DI
BROWN, HENRY	TAL	074	EASTON T
BROWN, HENRY	ST	262	3RD E DI
BROWN, HENRY	WAS	156	HAGERSTO
BROWN, HENRY A.	BAL	323	7TH WARD
BROWN, HENRY E.	ANN	303	1ST DIST
BROWN, HENRY G.	BAL	131	16TH WAR
BROWN, HENRY L.	BAL	237	1ST DIST
BROWN, HENRY T.	BAL	004	EASTERN
BROWN, HENRY-BLACK	QUE	180	2ND E DI
BROWN, HENRY-BLACK	CAR	085	NO TWP L
BROWN, HENRY-BLACK	QUE	141	1ST E DI
BROWN, HESIKIAH	BAL	296	17TH WAR
BROWN, HESTER	BAL	135	18TH WAR
BROWN, HESTER	BAL	424	14TH WAR
BROWN, HESTER	QUE	213	3RD E DI
BROWN, HESTER	WAS	254	1ST DIST
BROWN, HESTER	BAL	389	8TH WARD
BROWN, HETTY	BAL	162	19TH WAR
BROWN, HETTY	BAL	160	19TH WAR
BROWN, HEZEKIAH	CAL	053	3RD DIST
BROWN, HIRAM	CEC	136	6TH E DI
BROWN, HIRAM	KEN	209	2ND DIST
BROWN, HCNOR	BAL	290	1ST DIST
BROWN, HCNORE	ALL	149	6TH E.D.
BROWN, HCRACE	BAL	460	8TH WARD
BROWN, HCRACE	QUE	234	4TH E DI
BROWN, HUGH	CEC	074	NORTHEAS
BROWN, IGNATIUS	FRE	156	10TH E D
BROWN, IRA	BAL	357	13TH WAR
BROWN, ISAAC	CEC	161	6TH E DI
BROWN, ISAAC	BAL	051	4TH WARD
BROWN, ISAAC	HAR	179	3RD DIST
BROWN, ISAAC	HAR	186	3RD DIST
BROWN, ISAAC	BAL	129	11TH WAR
BROWN, ISAAC	BAL	201	11TH WAR
BROWN, ISAAC	CEC	009	ELKTON 3
BROWN, ISAAC	QUE	229	4TH E DI
BROWN, ISAAC	WAS	177	1ST DIST
BROWN, ISAAC	KEN	303	3RD DIST
BROWN, ISAAC	KEN	285	3RD DIST
BROWN, ISAAC	KEN	285	3RD DIST
BROWN, ISAAC	BAL	154	2ND DIST
BROWN, ISAAC	ANN	478	HOWARD D
BROWN, ISAAC	BAL	068	2ND DIST
BROWN, ISAAC	BAL	108	10TH WAR
BROWN, ISAAC	BAL	122	5TH WARD
BROWN, ISABEL	CAL	044	3RD DIST
BROWN, ISABEL	BAL	256	20TH WAR
BROWN, ISABELLA	BAL	344	1ST DIST
BROWN, ISAIAH	BAL	288	12TH WAR
BROWN, ISIAH	BAL	276	17TH WAR
BROWN, J.	BAL	147	1ST WARD
BROWN, J.	BAL	157	1ST WARD
BROWN, J.	BAL	117	1ST WARD
BROWN, J.	BAL	139	1ST WARD
BROWN, J.	BAL	141	1ST WARD
BROWN, J.	BAL	139	1ST WARD
BROWN, J. HARMAN	BAL	003	EASTERN
BROWN, J.C.	BAL	251	1ST DIST
BROWN, J.G.	WAS	234	1ST DIST
BROWN, JACKSON	BAL	106	18TH WAR
BROWN, JACOB	FRE	266	NEW MARK
BROWN, JACOB	HAR	200	3RD DIST
BROWN, JACOB	BAL	276	17TH WAR
BROWN, JACOB	BAL	350	13TH WAR
BROWN, JACOB	CEC	131	6TH E DI
BROWN, JACOB	BAL	229	17TH WAR
BROWN, JACOB	BAL	118	11TH WAR
BROWN, JACOB	CEC	012	ELKTON 3
BROWN, JACOB	BAL	092	1ST WARD
BROWN, JACOB	BAL	026	1ST WARD
BROWN, JACOB	BAL	130	2ND DIST
BROWN, JACOB	BAL	141	1ST WARD
BROWN, JACOB	BAL	169	1ST WARD
BROWN, JACOB	BAL	021	9TH WARD
BROWN, JACOB	BAL	122	16TH WAR
BROWN, JACOB	BAL	122	16TH WAR
BROWN, JACOB	BAL	195	17TH WAR
BROWN, JACOB	BAL	338	3RD WARD
BROWN, JACOB	BAL	459	1ST DIST
BROWN, JACOB	BAL	038	15TH WAR
BROWN, JACOB H.	HAR	188	3RD DIST
BROWN, JAEMS	BAL	451	8TH WARD
BROWN, JAEMS	BAL	184	5TH DIST
BROWN, JAMES	BAL	077	1ST WARD
BROWN, JAMES	BAL	415	1ST DIST
BROWN, JAMES	BAL	189	17TH WAR
BROWN, JAMES	BAL	304	12TH WAR
BROWN, JAMES	BAL	050	9TH WARD
BROWN, JAMES	BAL	020	9TH WARD
BROWN, JAMES	BAL	022	9TH WARD
BROWN, JAMES	BAL	149	1ST WARD
BROWN, JAMES	BAL	198	6TH WARD
BROWN, JAMES	BAL	132	1ST WARD
BROWN, JAMES	BAL	130	1ST WARD
BROWN, JAMES	BAL	385	8TH WARD
BROWN, JAMES	BAL	384	8TH WARD
BROWN, JAMES	BAL	281	2ND WARD
BROWN, JAMES	BAL	368	3RD WARD
BROWN, JAMES	ANN	345	3RD DIST
BROWN, JAMES	BAL	011	2ND DIST
BROWN, JAMES	ANN	467	HOWARD D
BROWN, JAMES	BAL	078	2ND DIST
BROWN, JAMES	ALL	050	10TH E.D
BROWN, JAMES	MGM	332	CRACKLIN
BROWN, JAMES	MGM	337	CRACKLIN
BROWN, JAMES	CEC	015	ELKTON 3
BROWN, JAMES	CAL	043	3RD DIST
BROWN, JAMES	BAL	136	11TH WAR
BROWN, JAMES	CAR	088	NO TWP L
BROWN, JAMES	BAL	446	14TH WAR
BROWN, JAMES	BAL	474	14TH WAR
BROWN, JAMES	CEC	164	6TH E DI
BROWN, JAMES	BAL	203	17TH WAR
BROWN, JAMES	DOR	434	1ST DIST
BROWN, JAMES	BAL	296	20TH WAR
BROWN, JAMES	BAL	294	20TH WAR
BROWN, JAMES	CEC	120	3RD E DI
BROWN, JAMES	CAR	394	2ND DIST
BROWN, JAMES	BAL	043	18TH WAR
BROWN, JAMES	HAR	075	BEL AIR
BROWN, JAMES	MGM	392	ROCKERLE
BROWN, JAMES	KEN	282	3RD DIST
BROWN, JAMES	KEN	284	3RD DIST
BROWN, JAMES	KEN	305	3RD DIST
BROWN, JAMES	QUE	227	4TH E DI
BROWN, JAMES	WAS	187	BCONSBOR
BROWN, JAMES	WAS	157	HAGERSTO
BROWN, JAMES	SOM	529	QUANTICO
BROWN, JAMES	SOM	508	BARREN C
BROWN, JAMES	TAL	038	EASTON D
BROWN, JAMES B.	KEN	292	3RD DIST
BROWN, JAMES E.	PRI	080	QUEEN AN
BROWN, JAMES E.	BAL	198	6TH WARD
BROWN, JAMES E.	BAL	303	3RD WARD
BROWN, JAMES F.	BAL	131	16TH WAR
BROWN, JAMES F.	PRI	100	SPALDING
BROWN, JAMES F.	PRI	012	BLADENSB
BROWN, JAMES H.	BAL	351	7TH WARD
BROWN, JAMES M.	BAL	178	16TH WAR
BROWN, JAMES M.	BAL	185	16TH WAR
BROWN, JAMES V.	BAL	221	6TH WARD
BROWN, JAMES-BLACK	QUE	203	3RD E DI
BROWN, JAMES-BLACK	FRE	419	8TH E DI
BROWN, JAMES-BLACK	CAR	079	NO TWP L
BROWN, JAMES-BLACK	QUE	158	2ND E DI
BROWN, JANE	BAL	201	11TH WAR
BROWN, JANE	BAL	200	11TH WAR
BROWN, JANE	BAL	279	17TH WAR
BROWN, JANE	BAL	038	18TH WAR
BROWN, JANE	DOR	374	1ST DIST
BROWN, JANE	CEC	017	ELKTON 3
BROWN, JANE	CEC	005	ELKTCN 3
BROWN, JANE	WAS	066	2ND SUBD
BROWN, JANE	BAL	132	5TH WARD
BROWN, JANE	BAL	141	16TH WAR
BROWN, JANE	BAL	170	11TH WAR
BROWN, JANE	BAL	105	5TH WARD
BROWN, JANE	BAL	081	2ND DIST
BROWN, JANE	BAL	137	2ND DIST
BROWN, JANE	BAL	370	3RD WARD
BROWN, JANE	BAL	238	1ST DIST
BROWN, JANE-BLACK	BAL	222	2ND WARD
BROWN, JANE-BLACK	QUE	139	1ST E DI
BROWN, JARRET	ANN	348	3RD DIST
BROWN, JASPER	BAL	121	18TH WAR
BROWN, JEANETTE	BAL	186	6TH WARD
BROWN, JEFFERSON	ANN	515	HOWARD D
BROWN, JEFFERSON	CAR	388	2ND DIST
BROWN, JENNEY	FRE	093	FREDERIC
BROWN, JEREMIAH	CEC	165	6TH E DI
BROWN, JEREMIAH	BAL	130	16TH WAR
BROWN, JEREMIAH	WAS	089	2ND SUBD
BROWN, JEROME	WAS	009	WILLIAMS
BROWN, JERRY	WAS	150	HAGERSTO
BROWN, JESSE	PRI	065	NOTTINGH
BROWN, JESSE	CEC	161	6TH E DI
BROWN, JESSE	CEC	069	5TH E DI
BROWN, JESSE	CAR	176	8TH DIST
BROWN, JIM	BAL	155	1ST WARD
BROWN, JIM	BAL	233	1ST DIST
BROWN, JOANNA	BAL	081	10TH WAR
BROWN, JOE	BAL	210	11TH WAR
BROWN, JOHN	BAL	207	11TH WAR
BROWN, JOHN	BAL	396	14TH WAR
BROWN, JOHN	CAL	051	3RD DIST
BROWN, JOHN	CAL	051	3RD DIST
BROWN, JOHN	CAL	022	2ND DIST
BROWN, JOHN	CAL	029	2ND DIST
BROWN, JOHN	BAL	028	4TH WARD
BROWN, JOHN	CAR	316	1ST DIST
BROWN, JOHN	BAL	422	3RD WARD
BROWN, JOHN	CAR	191	4TH DIST
BROWN, JOHN	CAR	381	2ND DIST
BROWN, JOHN	CAR	378	2ND DIST
BROWN, JOHN	CEC	103	4TH E DI
BROWN, JOHN	BAL	025	18TH WAR
BROWN, JOHN	BAL	025	18TH WAR
BROWN, JOHN	CEC	161	6TH E DI
BROWN, JOHN	BAL	202	17TH WAR
BROWN, JOHN	BAL	230	17TH WAR
BROWN, JOHN	BAL	268	17TH WAR
BROWN, JOHN	CEC	132	6TH E DI
BROWN, JOHN	DOR	298	1ST DIST
BROWN, JOHN	BAL	076	4TH WARD
BROWN, JOHN	BAL	062	4TH WARD
BROWN, JOHN	BAL	382	13TH WAR
BROWN, JOHN	MGM	393	ROCKERLE
BROWN, JOHN	HAR	024	1ST DIST
BROWN, JOHN	HAR	118	2ND DIST
BROWN, JOHN	HAR	199	3RD DIST
BROWN, JOHN	FRE	262	NEW MARK
BROWN, JOHN	DOR	408	1ST DIST
BROWN, JOHN	DOR	419	1ST DIST
BROWN, JOHN	HAR	185	3RD DIST
BROWN, JOHN	HAR	177	3RD DIST
BROWN, JOHN	FRE	151	10TH E D
BROWN, JOHN	HAR	160	3RD DIST
BROWN, JOHN	HAR	150	3RD DIST
BROWN, JOHN	CEC	201	6TH E DI
BROWN, JOHN	BAL	190	17TH WAR
BROWN, JOHN	BAL	145	16TH WAR
BROWN, JOHN	BAL	177	16TH WAR
BROWN, JOHN	BAL	069	1ST WARD
BROWN, JOHN	BAL	030	1ST WARD
BROWN, JOHN	BAL	114	1ST WARD
BROWN, JOHN	BAL	085	1ST WARD
BROWN, JOHN	BAL	107	1ST WARD
BROWN, JOHN	BAL	095	1ST WARD
BROWN, JOHN	BAL	121	1ST WARD
BROWN, JOHN	BAL	119	1ST WARD
BROWN, JOHN	BAL	124	1ST WARD
BROWN, JOHN	BAL	156	1ST WARD
BROWN, JOHN	BAL	159	1ST WARD
BROWN, JOHN	BAL	154	1ST WARD
BROWN, JOHN	BAL	151	1ST WARD
BROWN, JOHN	BAL	159	1ST WARD
BROWN, JOHN	BAL	145	1ST WARD
BROWN, JOHN	BAL	146	1ST WARD
BROWN, JOHN	BAL	146	1ST WARD
BROWN, JOHN	BAL	144	1ST WARD
BROWN, JOHN	BAL	129	5TH WARD
BROWN, JOHN	BAL	227	6TH WARD
BROWN, JOHN	BAL	223	6TH WARD
BROWN, JOHN	BAL	168	1ST WARD
BROWN, JOHN	BAL	170	1ST WARD
BROWN, JOHN	BAL	168	1ST WARD
BROWN, JOHN	BAL	160	1ST WARD
BROWN, JOHN	BAL	169	1ST WARD
BROWN, JOHN	BAL	163	1ST WARD

BROWN, JOHN BAL 205 2ND WARD
BROWN, JOHN BAL 173 1ST WARD
BROWN, JOHN ANN 496 HOWARD D
BROWN, JOHN BAL 095 5TH WARD
BROWN, JOHN BAL 459 1ST DIST
BROWN, JOHN BAL 350 1ST DIST
BROWN, JOHN ANN 356 3RD DIST
BROWN, JOHN ANN 359 3RD DIST
BROWN, JOHN ANN 481 HOWARD D
BROWN, JOHN BAL 073 2ND DIST
BROWN, JOHN ALL 229 CUMBERLA
BROWN, JOHN ALL 241 CUMBERLA
BROWN, JOHN BAL 281 2ND WARD
BROWN, JOHN BAL 281 2ND WARD
BROWN, JOHN BAL 138 1ST WARD
BROWN, JOHN BAL 137 1ST WARD
BROWN, JOHN BAL 138 1ST WARD
BROWN, JOHN BAL 134 1ST WARD
BROWN, JOHN BAL 139 1ST WARD
BROWN, JOHN BAL 136 1ST WARD
BROWN, JOHN BAL 142 1ST WARD
BROWN, JOHN BAL 141 1ST WARD
BROWN, JOHN BAL 135 1ST WARD
BROWN, JOHN BAL 401 3RD WARD
BROWN, JOHN BAL 398 3RD WARD
BROWN, JOHN BAL 126 1ST WARD
BROWN, JOHN BAL 125 1ST WARD
BROWN, JOHN BAL 402 8TH WARD
BROWN, JOHN BAL 126 1ST WARD
BROWN, JOHN BAL 169 11TH WAR
BROWN, JOHN BAL 187 11TH WAR
BROWN, JOHN BAL 170 11TH WAR
BROWN, JOHN BAL 459 8TH WARD
BROWN, JOHN BAL 051 15TH WAR
BROWN, JOHN BAL 346 7TH WARD
BROWN, JOHN ANN 317 1ST DIST
BROWN, JOHN ANN 273 ANNAPOLI
BROWN, JOHN ALL 107 5TH E.D.
BROWN, JOHN ANN 386 4TH DIST
BROWN, JOHN WOR 210 4TH E DI
BROWN, JOHN WAS 193 1ST DIST
BROWN, JOHN WAS 008 WILLIAMS
BROWN, JOHN WAS 285 1ST DIST
BROWN, JOHN WAS 087 2ND SUBD
BROWN, JOHN WAS 066 2ND SUBD
BROWN, JOHN PRI 002 BLADENSB
BROWN, JOHN TAL 027 EASTON D
BROWN, JOHN TAL 011 EASTON D
BROWN, JOHN QUE 170 2ND E DI
BROWN, JOHN KEN 300 3RD DIST
BROWN, JOHN KEN 281 3RD DIST
BROWN, JOHN KEN 285 3RD DIST
BROWN, JOHN WAS 216 1ST DIST
BROWN, JOHN WAS 222 1ST DIST
BROWN, JOHN WAS 255 1ST DIST
BROWN, JOHN A. QUE 166 2ND E DI
BROWN, JOHN A. BAL 361 3RD WARD
BROWN, JOHN A. CAR 352 6TH DIST
BROWN, JOHN C. BAL 110 5TH WARD
BROWN, JOHN C. BAL 098 10TH WAR
BROWN, JOHN E. CEC 003 ELKTON 3
BROWN, JOHN F. BAL 116 15TH WAR
BROWN, JOHN F. BAL 404 8TH WARD
BROWN, JOHN F. ST 320 4TH E DI
BROWN, JOHN F. WOR 196 8TH E DI
BROWN, JOHN G. BAL 121 18TH WAR
BROWN, JOHN H. BAL 408 8TH WARD
BROWN, JOHN H. ANN 324 2ND DIST
BROWN, JOHN J. BAL 317 12TH WAR
BROWN, JOHN J. CAR 182 8TH DIST
BROWN, JOHN JR. CAR 380 2ND DIST
BROWN, JOHN JR. BAL 196 6TH WARD
BROWN, JOHN M. BAL 130 18TH WAR
BROWN, JOHN M. CHA 256 MIDDLETO
BROWN, JOHN M. PRI 010 BLADENSB
BROWN, JOHN N. BAL 443 14TH WAR
BROWN, JOHN O. CAR 224 5TH DIST
BROWN, JOHN R. ST 295 2ND E DI
BROWN, JOHN R. ANN 452 HOWARD D
BROWN, JOHN S. BAL 037 9TH WARD
BROWN, JOHN S. BAL 094 1ST WARD
BROWN, JOHN S. BAL 291 1ST DIST
BROWN, JOHN S. CAR 221 5TH DIST
BROWN, JOHN S. BAL 284 17TH WAR
BROWN, JOHN T. FRE 041 FREDERIC
BROWN, JOHN T. BAL 093 5TH WARD
BROWN, JOHN T. ST 280 3RD E DI
BROWN, JOHN W. QUE 227 4TH E DI
BROWN, JOHN W. PRI 020 VANSVILL
BROWN, JOHN W. SOM 520 BARREN C
BROWN, JOHN W. BAL 096 5TH WARD
BROWN, JOHN W. CAR 233 5TH DIST
BROWN, JOHN W. CEC 167 6TH E DI
BROWN, JOHN-BLACK CAR 399 2ND DIST
BROWN, JOHN-BLACK QUE 146 1ST E DI
BROWN, JONAS BAL 305 20TH WAR
BROWN, JONATHAN CEC 131 6TH E DI
BROWN, JOSEPH BAL 415 14TH WAR
BROWN, JOSEPH FRE 342 MIDDLETO
BROWN, JOSEPH FRE 387 PETERSVI
BROWN, JOSEPH FRE 150 10TH E D
BROWN, JOSEPH FRE 121 CREAGERS
BROWN, JOSEPH FRE 102 FREDERIC
BROWN, JOSEPH DOR 385 1ST DIST
BROWN, JOSEPH CEC 019 ELKTON 3
BROWN, JOSEPH CEC 014 ELKTON 3
BROWN, JOSEPH BAL 206 19TH WAR
BROWN, JOSEPH FRE 055 FREDERIC
BROWN, JOSEPH FRE 084 FREDERIC
BROWN, JOSEPH CEC 109 3RD E DI
BROWN, JOSEPH BAL 284 17TH WAR
BROWN, JOSEPH CEC 099 3RD E DI
BROWN, JOSEPH CAR 395 2ND DIST
BROWN, JOSEPH CEC 060 1ST E DI
BROWN, JOSEPH CAR 255 3RD DIST
BROWN, JOSEPH BAL 344 3RD WARD
BROWN, JOSEPH ANN 483 HOWARD D
BROWN, JOSEPH BAL 146 1ST WARD
BROWN, JOSEPH ANN 366 4TH DIST
BROWN, JOSEPH BAL 412 8TH WARD
BROWN, JOSEPH BAL 129 1ST WARD
BROWN, JOSEPH ST 264 3RD E DI
BROWN, JOSEPH TAL 070 EASTON T
BROWN, JOSEPH KEN 306 3RD DIST
BROWN, JOSEPH WAS 044 2ND SUBD
BROWN, JOSEPH TAL 077 EASTON T
BROWN, JOSEPH T. CEC 090 4TH E DI
BROWN, JOSEPH W. ST 333 4TH E DI
BROWN, JOSEPH-BLACK QUE 148 1ST E DI
BROWN, JOSEPHINE BAL 158 6TH WARD
BROWN, JOSEPHINE BAL 267 12TH WAR
BROWN, JOSHUA BAL 247 6TH WARD
BROWN, JOSHUA ANN 277 ANNAPOLI
BROWN, JOSHUA ANN 423 HOWARD D
BROWN, JOSHUA MGM 337 CRACKLIN
BROWN, JOSHUA BAL 313 20TH WAR
BROWN, JOSHUA BAL 244 20TH WAR
BROWN, JOSHUA BAL 075 4TH WARD
BROWN, JOSHUA QUE 251 5TH E DI
BROWN, JOSHUA D. BAL 390 8TH WARD
BROWN, JOSHUA L. BAL 326 1ST DIST
BROWN, JOSHUA V. MGM 345 CLARKSBU
BROWN, JOSHUA-BLACK FRE 216 BUCKEYST
BROWN, JOSIAH BAL 220 17TH WAR
BROWN, JOSIAH CAR 221 5TH DIST
BROWN, JOSIAH C. WOR 194 8TH E DI
BROWN, JSOEPH BAL 092 15TH WAR
BROWN, JSOHUA BAL 172 1ST WARD
BROWN, JUDY WAS 148 HAGERSTO
BROWN, JULIA WAS 141 HAGERSTO
BROWN, JULIA BAL 280 7TH WARD
BROWN, JULIA BAL 254 12TH WAR
BROWN, JULIA BAL 260 12TH WAR
BROWN, JULIA MGM 324 CRACKLIN
BROWN, JULIA HAR 091 2ND DIST
BROWN, JULIA A. BAL 123 11TH WAR
BROWN, JULIA F. BAL 013 1ST WARD
BROWN, JULIA-BLACK WOR 322 1ST E DI
BROWN, KARFMAN BAL 432 8TH WARD
BROWN, KIBBLE J. WOR 227 4TH E DI
BROWN, KINSEY CAL 043 3RD DIST
BROWN, KIRK HAR 188 3RD DIST
BROWN, KITTY BAL 057 10TH WAR
BROWN, KITTY * ANN 375 4TH DIST
BROWN, L. BAL 148 1ST WARD
BROWN, L. BAL 154 1ST WARD
BROWN, LARKIN ANN 433 HOWARD D
BROWN, LARRNIA C. QUE 253 5TH E DI
BROWN, LAURA QUE 253 5TH E DI
BROWN, LAURA ANN 521 HOWARD D
BROWN, LAVINA CEC 206 7TH E DI
BROWN, LEAR-BLACK CAR 076 NO TWP L
BROWN, LEDIA T. BAL 382 1ST DIST
BROWN, LEONARD SOM 513 BARREN C
BROWN, LEVI CEC 213 7TH E DI
BROWN, LEVI CEC 131 6TH E DI
BROWN, LEVIN C. WOR 211 4TH E DI
BROWN, LEVINIA WAS 138 HAGERSTO
BROWN, LEWIS KEN 282 3RD DIST
BROWN, LEWIS WAS 025 2ND SUBD
BROWN, LEWIS BAL 369 13TH WAR
BROWN, LEWIS BAL 080 18TH WAR
BROWN, LEWIS BAL 078 2ND DIST
BROWN, LEWIS BAL 049 9TH WARD
BROWN, LEWIS BAL 008 9TH WARD
BROWN, LEWIS B. BAL 283 20TH WAR
BROWN, LEWIS H. CAR 219 5TH DIST
BROWN, LIDDY A. BAL 139 11TH WAR
BROWN, LISBON CAL 032 2ND DIST
BROWN, LLOYD CAR 222 5TH DIST
BROWN, LLOYD ANN 297 1ST DIST
BROWN, LLOYD-BLACK CAR 150 NO TWP L
BROWN, LLOYD-BLACK QUE 129 1ST E DI
BROWN, LOUIS CEC 210 7TH E DI
BROWN, LOUIS BAL 423 1ST DIST
BROWN, LOUISA ANN 517 HOWARD D
BROWN, LOUISA BAL 017 9TH WARD
BROWN, LOUISA BAL 202 6TH WARD
BROWN, LOUISA BAL 421 3RD WARD
BROWN, LOUISA MGM 361 BERRYS D
BROWN, LOUISA WAS 154 HAGERSTO
BROWN, LOUISA-BLACK FRE 397 PETERSVI
BROWN, LOUIZA BAL 144 5TH WARD
BROWN, LSIBON CAL 044 3RD DIST
BROWN, LUCINDA BAL 194 17TH WAR
BROWN, LUCY ALL 148 6TH E.D.
BROWN, LUCY CEC 018 ELKTON 3
BROWN, LUKE CEC 162 6TH E DI
BROWN, LUKE ALL 127 4TH E.D.
BROWN, LUSCITA * TAL 109 ST MICHA
BROWN, LYDIA BAL 111 15TH WAR
BROWN, M. BAL 130 11TH WAR
BROWN, MADISON TAL 011 EASTON D
BROWN, MADISON QUE 184 3RD E DI
BROWN, MAHALA-BLACK QUE 159 2ND E DI
BROWN, MAHALIA HAR 140 2ND DIST
BROWN, MAJOR CAL 042 3RD DIST
BROWN, MAR A. BAL 252 6TH WARD
BROWN, MARANDA CAR 360 9TH DIST
BROWN, MARCELLUS WOR 193 8TH E DI
BROWN, MAREN BAL 297 12TH WAR
BROWN, MARGARET BAL 398 3RD WARD
BROWN, MARGARET BAL 018 15TH WAR
BROWN, MARGARET BAL 268 12TH WAR
BROWN, MARGARET BAL 072 1ST WARD
BROWN, MARGARET PRI 015 BLADENSB
BROWN, MARGARET QUE 215 3RD E DI
BROWN, MARGARET CAR 385 2ND DIST
BROWN, MARGARET CAL 045 3RD DIST
BROWN, MARGARET CAR 182 8TH DIST
BROWN, MARGARET BAL 145 19TH WAR
BROWN, MARGARET A. BAL 279 17TH WAR
BROWN, MARGARET W. BAL 360 3RD WARD
BROWN, MARGARET-BLACK FRE 219 BUCKEYST
BROWN, MARGARETT BAL 133 18TH WAR
BROWN, MARGARETT BAL 185 11TH WAR
BROWN, MARGARETT A. BAL 010 18TH WAR
BROWN, MARGRET BAL 055 1ST WARD
BROWN, MARIA BAL 111 1ST WARD
BROWN, MARIA BAL 355 3RD WARD
BROWN, MARIA BAL 376 3RD WARD
BROWN, MARIA BAL 274 12TH WAR
BROWN, MARIA BAL 152 16TH WAR
BROWN, MARIA DOR 419 1ST DIST
BROWN, MARIA HAR 192 3RD DIST
BROWN, MARIA BAL 195 11TH WAR
BROWN, MARIA BAL 211 11TH WAR
BROWN, MARIA BAL 194 11TH WAR
BROWN, MARIA BAL 436 14TH WAR
BROWN, MARIA BAL 276 17TH WAR
BROWN, MARIA HAR 087 2ND DIST
BROWN, MARIA E. WAS 156 HAGERSTO
BROWN, MARIAH TAL 120 ST MICHA
BROWN, MARION H. KEN 256 1ST DIST
BROWN, MARK CEC 131 6TH E DI
BROWN, MARK BAL 150 2ND DIST
BROWN, MARK BAL 458 8TH WARD
BROWN, MARK-BLACK FRE 388 PETERSVI
BROWN, MARTHA BAL 157 11TH WAR
BROWN, MARTHA CAR 065 NO TWP L
BROWN, MARTHA FRE 234 BUCKEYST
BROWN, MARTHA BAL 204 19TH WAR
BROWN, MARTHA BAL 041 4TH WARD
BROWN, MARTHA BAL 190 17TH WAR
BROWN, MARTHA BAL 162 16TH WAR
BROWN, MARTHA BAL 344 3RD WARD
BROWN, MARTHA WAS 019 2ND SUBD
BROWN, MARTHA A. BAL 201 11TH WAR
BROWN, MARTHA A. CEC 136 6TH E DI
BROWN, MARTHA J. BAL 219 6TH WARD
BROWN, MARTIN S. BAL 231 12TH WAR
BROWN, MARY BAL 177 11TH WAR
BROWN, MARY BAL 248 12TH WAR
BROWN, MARY BAL 353 7TH WARD
BROWN, MARY BAL 013 15TH WAR
BROWN, MARY BAL 158 6TH WARD
BROWN, MARY BAL 176 6TH WARD
BROWN, MARY ANN 512 HOWARD D
BROWN, MARY ANN 496 HOWARD D
BROWN, MARY BAL 097 5TH WARD
BROWN, MARY BAL 462 1ST DIST
BROWN, MARY BAL 447 1ST DIST
BROWN, MARY BAL 290 3RD WARD
BROWN, MARY BAL 328 13TH WAR
BROWN, MARY BAL 118 15TH WAR
BROWN, MARY BAL 106 10TH WAR
BROWN, MARY BAL 227 1ST DIST
BROWN, MARY BAL 355 3RD WARD
BROWN, MARY BAL 094 1ST WARD
BROWN, MARY BAL 101 1ST WARD
BROWN, MARY BAL 061 1ST WARD
BROWN, MARY BAL 248 1ST DIST
BROWN, MARY BAL 273 2ND WARD
BROWN, MARY BAL 228 2ND WARD
BROWN, MARY ANN 333 2ND DIST
BROWN, MARY ALL 108 5TH E.D.
BROWN, MARY BAL 066 2ND DIST
BROWN, MARY BAL 101 2ND DIST
BROWN, MARY CEC 130 6TH E DI
BROWN, MARY BAL 355 13TH WAR
BROWN, MARY BAL 216 17TH WAR
BROWN, MARY BAL 079 4TH WARD
BROWN, MARY CAL 030 2ND DIST
BROWN, MARY CAR 154 NO TWP L
BROWN, MARY BAL 474 14TH WAR
BROWN, MARY BAL 038 4TH WARD
BROWN, MARY BAL 009 4TH WARD
BROWN, MARY BAL 006 4TH WARD
BROWN, MARY HAR 195 3RD DIST
BROWN, MARY BAL 139 19TH WAR
BROWN, MARY CEC 200 7TH E DI
BROWN, MARY BAL 318 20TH WAR
BROWN, MARY FRE 095 FREDERIC
BROWN, MARY BAL 006 18TH WAR
BROWN, MARY BAL 017 18TH WAR
BROWN, MARY BAL 082 18TH WAR
BROWN, MARY BAL 069 18TH WAR
BROWN, MARY BAL 032 18TH WAR
BROWN, MARY BAL 047 18TH WAR
BROWN, MARY HAR 166 3RD DIST
BROWN, MARY HAR 133 2ND DIST
BROWN, MARY KEN 281 3RD DIST
BROWN, MARY QUE 213 3RD E DI
BROWN, MARY WAS 255 1ST DIST
BROWN, MARY WAS 255 1ST DIST
BROWN, MARY KEN 300 3RD DIST
BROWN, MARY SOM 441 DAMES QU
BROWN, MARY PRI 102 SPALDING
BROWN, MARY QUE 241 5TH E DI
BROWN, MARY WAS 133 HAGERSTO
BROWN, MARY A. SOM 366 BRINKLEY
BROWN, MARY A. MGM 321 CRACKLIN
BROWN, MARY A. BAL 104 18TH WAR
BROWN, MARY A. CAR 196 4TH DIST
BROWN, MARY A. BAL 232 2ND WARD
BROWN, MARY A. BAL 101 10TH WAR
BROWN, MARY A. BAL 369 1ST DIST
BROWN, MARY C. FRE 173 5TH E DI
BROWN, MARY C. BAL 411 14TH WAR
BROWN, MARY C. QUE 207 3RD E DI
BROWN, MARY C. TAL 029 EASTON D
BROWN, MARY E. WAS 239 CAVETOWN
BROWN, MARY E. WAS 137 HAGERSTO
BROWN, MARY E. FRE 121 CREAGERS
BROWN, MARY E. BAL 281 20TH WAR
BROWN, MARY E. BAL 176 6TH WARD
BROWN, MARY E. BAL 176 6TH WARD
BROWN, MARY E. BAL 204 2ND WARD
BROWN, MARY H. DOR 316 1ST DIST
BROWN, MARY J. BAL 436 14TH WAR
BROWN, MARY J. BAL 260 17TH WAR
BROWN, MARY J. MGM 357 BERRYS D
BROWN, MARY J. PRI 098 SPALDING
BROWN, MARY M. BAL 022 1ST WARD
BROWN, MARY N. BAL 075 15TH WAR
BROWN, MARY P. WOR 201 3RD E DI
BROWN, MARY RIDDELL BAL 251 1ST DIST
BROWN, MARY-BLACK FRE 037 FREDERIC
BROWN, MARY-BLACK FRE 028 FREDERIC
BROWN, MASON MGM 365 BERRYS D
BROWN, MATHIAS BAL 047 9TH WARD
BROWN, MATILDA BAL 245 1ST DIST
BROWN, MATILDA BAL 302 7TH WARD
BROWN, MATILDA BAL 067 4TH WARD
BROWN, MATILDA BAL 397 14TH WAR
BROWN, MATILDA-BLACK QUE 201 3RD E DI
BROWN, MATTEST BAL 229 2ND WARD
BROWN, MATTHEW BAL 024 9TH WARD
BROWN, MATTHEW BAL 235 20TH WAR
BROWN, MAY BAL 130 11TH WAR
BROWN, MC LANE ANN 457 HOWARD D
BROWN, MELCHOR BAL 424 1ST DIST
BROWN, MELISCNET A. BAL 042 15TH WAR
BROWN, MELVIN O. BAL 122 1ST WARD
BROWN, MELVINA BAL 137 16TH WAR
BROWN, MERCE M. ANN 495 HOWARD D
BROWN, MICHAEL ANN 517 HOWARD D
BROWN, MICHAEL BAL 397 1ST DIST
BROWN, MICHAEL BAL 259 6TH WARD
BROWN, MICHAEL ALL 127 4TH E.D.
BROWN, MICHAEL ALL 051 10TH E.D
BROWN, MICHAEL CEC 038 CHESAPEA
BROWN, MICHAEL FRE 067 FREDERIC
BROWN, MICHAEL MGM 417 MEDLEY 3
BROWN, MICHAEL BAL 090 18TH WAR
BROWN, MICHAEL WAS 156 HAGERSTO
BROWN, MILES CEC 206 7TH E DI
BROWN, MILLIN HAR 183 3RD DIST
BROWN, MILLY ST 283 3RD E DI
BROWN, MILLY ST 284 2ND E DI

Name	County	Page	District
BROWN, MILLY	KEN	310	3RD DIST
BROWN, MONNOSE *	ALL	149	6TH E.D.
BROWN, MONTILLION	CEC	127	5TH E DI
BROWN, MORRIS	BAL	296	7TH WARD
BROWN, MOSES	BAL	296	7TH WARD
BROWN, MOSES	CEC	214	7TH E DI
BROWN, MOSES	CEC	213	7TH E DI
BROWN, N.	BAL	173	1ST WARD
BROWN, N.	BAL	153	1ST WARD
BROWN, N.	BAL	153	1ST WARD
BROWN, N.	BAL	153	1ST WARD
BROWN, NACE	CEC	135	6TH E DI
BROWN, NACKEY	BAL	353	1ST DIST
BROWN, NALL	CAL	008	1ST DIST
BROWN, NANCY	CAL	023	2ND DIST
BROWN, NANCY	CEC	160	6TH E DI
BROWN, NANCY	CEC	115	3RD E DI
BROWN, NANCY	BAL	416	1ST DIST
BROWN, NANCY	ANN	372	4TH DIST
BROWN, NANCY	BAL	262	12TH WAR
BROWN, NANCY	BAL	339	7TH WARD
BROWN, NANCY	ANN	479	HOWARD D
BROWN, NANCY H.	MGM	352	BERRYS D
BROWN, NAPOLEON	BAL	078	1ST WARD
BROWN, NATHAN	BAL	197	17TH WAR
BROWN, NATHAN	CAR	232	5TH DIST
BROWN, NATHAN-BLACK	QUE	186	3RD E DI
BROWN, NATHANIEL	QUE	237	4TH E DI
BROWN, NATHANIEL	CEC	113	4TH E DI
BROWN, NED-BLACK	QUE	192	3RD E DI
BROWN, NELSON	CAR	196	4TH DIST
BROWN, NEWTON	CEC	090	4TH E DI
BROWN, NICHOLAS	BAL	255	20TH WAR
BROWN, NICHOLAS	BAL	230	12TH WAR
BROWN, NICHOLAS L.	BAL	358	13TH WAR
BROWN, NOAH	CAR	181	8TH DIST
BROWN, NOAH	BAL	192	5TH DIST
BROWN, NORMAND	ALL	011	3RD E.D.
BROWN, OLIVER	WAS	086	2ND SUBD
BROWN, ORBERT	ANN	298	1ST DIST
BROWN, OSBOURN	PRI	033	VANSVILL
BROWN, OWEN	ANN	391	4TH DIST
BROWN, OWEN	MGM	345	CLARKSBU
BROWN, PARKER	HAR	015	1ST DIST
BROWN, PAT	BAL	260	20TH WAR
BROWN, PATIENCE	BAL	207	19TH WAR
BROWN, PATIENCE-BLACK	FRE	041	FREDERIC
BROWN, PATRICK	BAL	297	1ST DIST
BROWN, PATRICK	KEN	306	3RD DIST
BROWN, PATTSY	FRE	254	NEW MARK
BROWN, PERE-BLACK	QUE	123	1ST E DI
BROWN, PERRY	CAR	220	5TH DIST
BROWN, PERRY	BAL	076	18TH WAR
BROWN, PERRY	KEN	283	3RD DIST
BROWN, PERRY	BAL	039	15TH WAR
BROWN, PERRY	BAL	185	6TH WARD
BROWN, PETER	BAL	109	1ST WARD
BROWN, PETER	BAL	107	1ST WARD
BROWN, PETER	ALL	056	10TH E.D
BROWN, PETER	BAL	195	17TH WAR
BROWN, PETER	BAL	427	1ST DIST
BROWN, PETER	BAL	345	1ST DIST
BROWN, PETER	BAL	126	1ST WARD
BROWN, PETER	CAR	245	3RD DIST
BROWN, PETER	BAL	218	19TH WAR
BROWN, PETER	HAR	029	1ST DIST
BROWN, PETER	BAL	067	4TH WARD
BROWN, PETER A.	BAL	387	3RD WARD
BROWN, PETER-BLACK	FRE	197	5TH E DI
BROWN, PETER-BLACK	FRE	190	5TH E DI
BROWN, PHEEY	CEC	121	4TH E DI
BROWN, PHILIP	BAL	400	8TH WARD
BROWN, PHILIP	BAL	115	1ST WARD
BROWN, PHILIP	BAL	158	6TH WARD
BROWN, PHILIP	BAL	066	15TH WAR
BROWN, PHILIP	KEN	304	3RD DIST
BROWN, PHILIP	KEN	291	3RD DIST
BROWN, PHILIP	WAS	170	FUNKSTOW
BROWN, POMPEY-BLACK	QUE	195	3RD E DI
BROWN, PRESCILLA	BAL	057	10TH WAR
BROWN, PRISCILLA	BAL	249	2ND WARD
BROWN, PRISCILLA	CAR	374	9TH DIST
BROWN, PRISSILLA	WAS	104	2ND DIST
BROWN, PURNELL	BAL	096	15TH WAR
BROWN, R.	BAL	135	1ST WARD
BROWN, R.	ANN	338	3RD DIST
BROWN, RACHAEL	BAL	058	4TH WARD
BROWN, RACHAEL	FRE	099	FREDERIC
BROWN, RACHAEL	BAL	151	19TH WAR
BROWN, RACHAEL-MULATTO	FRE	024	FREDERIC
BROWN, RACHE	BAL	240	12TH WAR
BROWN, RACHEL	BAL	271	7TH WARD
BROWN, RACHEL	BAL	261	6TH WARD
BROWN, RACHEL	BAL	047	9TH WARD
BROWN, RACHEL	BAL	143	16TH WAR
BROWN, RACHEL	BAL	373	1ST DIST
BROWN, RACHEL	BAL	343	3RD WARD
BROWN, RACHEL	BAL	205	19TH WAR
BROWN, RACHEL	CAR	233	5TH DIST
BROWN, RACHEL	BAL	021	4TH WARD
BROWN, RACHEL A.	BAL	339	7TH WARD
BROWN, RACHEL J.	CEC	132	6TH E DI
BROWN, RACHIEL	HAR	004	1ST DIST
BROWN, RACHIEL-BLACK	CAR	071	NO TWP L
BROWN, RALEY	PRI	006	BLADENSB
BROWN, RANDOLPH	PRI	014	BLADENSB
BROWN, REBECCA	KEN	305	3RD DIST
BROWN, REBECCA	QUE	246	5TH E DI
BROWN, REBECCA	BAL	208	17TH WAR
BROWN, REBECCA	BAL	022	4TH WARD
BROWN, REBECCA	BAL	122	18TH WAR
BROWN, REBECCA	BAL	171	11TH WAR
BROWN, REBECCA	BAL	348	1ST DIST
BROWN, REBECCA	BAL	081	15TH WAR
BROWN, REBECCA	BAL	230	2ND WARD
BROWN, REMUS	MGM	326	CRACKLIN
BROWN, RESIN	BAL	226	1ST DIST
BROWN, REZIN	ANN	380	4TH DIST
BROWN, REZIN	MGM	316	CRACKLIN
BROWN, RICHARD	HAR	180	3RD DIST
BROWN, RICHARD	BAL	003	4TH WARD
BROWN, RICHARD	CEC	014	ELKTON 3
BROWN, RICHARD	MGM	364	BERRYS D
BROWN, RICHARD	ANN	334	2ND DIST
BROWN, RICHARD	ALL	143	6TH E.D.
BROWN, RICHARD	BAL	160	2ND DIST
BROWN, RICHARD	BAL	107	1ST WARD
BROWN, RICHARD	BAL	126	1ST WARD
BROWN, RICHARD	BAL	348	1ST DIST
BROWN, RICHARD	KEN	299	3RD DIST
BROWN, RICHARD	PRI	073	MARLBROU
BROWN, RICHARD H.	BAL	193	5TH DIST
BROWN, RICHARD H.-BLACK	FRE	022	FREDERIC
BROWN, RICHARD L.	ANN	495	HOWARD D
BROWN, RICHARD REV-	ANN	423	HOWARD D
BROWN, RICHARD-BLACK	QUE	178	2ND E DI
BROWN, ROBERT	SOM	520	BARREN C
BROWN, ROBERT	BAL	369	1ST DIST
BROWN, ROBERT	BAL	311	1ST DIST
BROWN, ROBERT	BAL	089	1ST WARD
BROWN, ROBERT	BAL	023	1ST WARD
BROWN, ROBERT	BAL	067	1ST WARD
BROWN, ROBERT	BAL	124	1ST WARD
BROWN, ROBERT	BAL	121	1ST WARD
BROWN, ROBERT	BAL	120	1ST WARD
BROWN, ROBERT	BAL	123	1ST WARD
BROWN, ROBERT	BAL	138	1ST WARD
BROWN, ROBERT	BAL	165	1ST WARD
BROWN, ROBERT	CEC	194	7TH E DI
BROWN, ROBERT	MGM	361	BERRYS D
BROWN, ROBERT	MGM	355	BERRYS D
BROWN, ROBERT	CEC	013	ELKTON 3
BROWN, ROBERT	HAR	180	3RD DIST
BROWN, ROBERT	MGM	337	CRACKLIN
BROWN, ROBERT	MGM	337	CRACKLIN
BROWN, ROBERT	BAL	137	18TH WAR
BROWN, ROBERT	CEC	128	5TH E DI
BROWN, ROBERT	BAL	337	13TH WAR
BROWN, ROBERT	CEC	161	6TH E DI
BROWN, ROBERT P.	BAL	105	10TH WAR
BROWN, ROSA	ST	265	3RD E DI
BROWN, ROSENA	BAL	207	19TH WAR
BROWN, ROSEY-BLACK	QUE	175	2ND E DI
BROWN, RUTH	HAR	152	3RD DIST
BROWN, RUTH A.	ANN	521	HOWARD D
BROWN, RUTH-BLACK	CAR	368	9TH DIST
BROWN, RUTHANNA	CEC	161	6TH E DI
BROWN, RUTHEY	BAL	121	18TH WAR
BROWN, SALLY	BAL	031	4TH WARD
BROWN, SALLY	CHA	224	ALLENS F
BROWN, SALLY	ANN	307	1ST DIST
BROWN, SAMSON	HAR	078	2ND DIST
BROWN, SAMUEL	BAL	296	20TH WAR
BROWN, SAMUEL	BAL	243	20TH WAR
BROWN, SAMUEL	CEC	025	ELKTON 3
BROWN, SAMUEL	BAL	133	18TH WAR
BROWN, SAMUEL	FRE	262	NEW MARK
BROWN, SAMUEL	CEC	161	6TH E DI
BROWN, SAMUEL	CEC	142	6TH E DI
BROWN, SAMUEL	CEC	160	6TH E DI
BROWN, SAMUEL	CAR	394	2ND DIST
BROWN, SAMUEL	CAR	392	2ND DIST
BROWN, SAMUEL	ANN	396	8TH DIST
BROWN, SAMUEL	ANN	520	HOWARD D
BROWN, SAMUEL	BAL	338	1ST DIST
BROWN, SAMUEL	BAL	163	6TH WARD
BROWN, SAMUEL	BAL	138	1ST WARD
BROWN, SAMUEL	BAL	281	2ND WARD
BROWN, SAMUEL	BAL	061	1ST WARD
BROWN, SAMUEL	SOM	522	BARREN C
BROWN, SAMUEL	WAS	087	2ND SUBD
BROWN, SAMUEL	WAS	086	2ND SUBD
BROWN, SAMUEL-BLACK	QUE	180	2ND E DI
BROWN, SAMUEL-BLACK	QUE	200	3RD E DI
BROWN, SAMUEL-BLACK	FRE	243	NEW MARK
BROWN, SAMUEL-MULATTO	FRE	429	8TH E DI
BROWN, SARAH	BAL	149	19TH WAR
BROWN, SARAH	BAL	140	19TH WAR
BROWN, SARAH	CEC	166	6TH E DI
BROWN, SARAH	BAL	428	14TH WAR
BROWN, SARAH	BAL	213	11TH WAR
BROWN, SARAH	CAR	273	WESTMINS
BROWN, SARAH	HAR	029	1ST DIST
BROWN, SARAH	MGM	395	ROCKERLE
BROWN, SARAH	QUE	151	1ST E DI
BROWN, SARAH	BAL	475	14TH WAR
BROWN, SARAH	CAL	008	1ST DIST
BROWN, SARAH	QUE	212	3RD E DI
BROWN, SARAH	PRI	074	MARLBROU
BROWN, SARAH	BAL	041	1ST WARD
BROWN, SARAH	BAL	264	2ND WARD
BROWN, SARAH	BAL	333	1ST DIST
BROWN, SARAH	ALL	013	3RD E.D.
BROWN, SARAH	BAL	147	16TH WAR
BROWN, SARAH	BAL	185	11TH WAR
BROWN, SARAH	BAL	332	7TH WARD
BROWN, SARAH	BAL	001	15TH WAR
BROWN, SARAH	BAL	013	9TH WARD
BROWN, SARAH A.	BAL	245	6TH WARD
BROWN, SARAH A.-MULATTO	FRE	429	8TH E DI
BROWN, SARAH B.	CAR	125	NO TWP L
BROWN, SARAH F.	BAL	186	16TH WAR
BROWN, SARAH J.	BAL	452	1ST DIST
BROWN, SARAH R.	MGM	327	CRACKLIN
BROWN, SARAH-BLACK	QUE	133	1ST E DI
BROWN, SARAH-BLACK	QUE	139	1ST E DI
BROWN, SARAH-BLACK	FRE	028	FREDERIC
BROWN, SARHA	BAL	250	12TH WAR
BROWN, SCOTT-BLACK	WOR	337	1ST E DI
BROWN, SELAR*	DOR	348	3RD DIVI
BROWN, SEVILLA	WAS	283	1ST DIST
BROWN, SILVIA	CEC	204	6TH E DI
BROWN, SIMON	DOR	385	1ST DIST
BROWN, SIMON	BAL	190	11TH WAR
BROWN, SISTER AMELIA	FRE	197	5TH E DI
BROWN, SISTER ELLEN	FRE	198	5TH E DI
BROWN, SOLOMON	BAL	168	19TH WAR
BROWN, SOLOMON	BAL	253	17TH WAR
BROWN, SOPHIA	BAL	168	19TH WAR
BROWN, SOPHIA	ANN	457	HOWARD D
BROWN, SOPHIA E.A.	BAL	024	15TH WAR
BROWN, STEPHEN	BAL	178	6TH WARD
BROWN, STEPHEN	BAL	072	1ST WARD
BROWN, STEPHEN	CAL	023	2ND DIST
BROWN, STEPHEN *	ANN	291	ANNAPOLI
BROWN, STEPHEN J.	CEC	156	PORT DUP
BROWN, STEPHEN-BLACK	CAR	068	NO TWP L
BROWN, STEPHEN-BLACK	QUE	139	1ST E DI
BROWN, STEVEN T.	CAR	221	5TH DIST
BROWN, STREET	CEC	167	6TH E DI
BROWN, SUSAN	CAR	291	7TH DIST
BROWN, SUSAN	CAR	234	UNION TO
BROWN, SUSAN	CAL	033	2ND DIST
BROWN, SUSAN	MGM	370	BERRYS D
BROWN, SUSAN	CAR	264	WESTMINS
BROWN, SUSAN	CEC	119	3RD E DI
BROWN, SUSAN	BAL	222	1ST DIST
BROWN, SUSAN	BAL	151	5TH WARD
BROWN, SUSAN	BAL	155	5TH WARD
BROWN, SUSAN	ANN	356	3RD DIST
BROWN, SUSAN	WAS	139	HAGERSTO
BROWN, SUSAN-BLACK	FRE	240	NEW MARK
BROWN, SUSANNA	BAL	247	6TH WARD
BROWN, SUSANNA	ANN	519	HOWARD D
BROWN, T. J.	BAL	006	10TH WAR
BROWN, TABITHA	BAL	281	20TH WAR
BROWN, TABITHA A.	MGM	338	CRACKLIN
BROWN, TAMER	BAL	065	2ND DIST
BROWN, TEENY	BAL	065	4TH WARD
BROWN, THEADORE	CAR	230	5TH DIST
BROWN, THOAMS	BAL	142	2ND DIST
BROWN, THOAMS	BAL	284	7TH WARD
BROWN, THOMAS	BAL	279	2ND WARD
BROWN, THOMAS	BAL	128	1ST WARD
BROWN, THOMAS	BAL	066	2ND DIST
BROWN, THOMAS	BAL	064	2ND DIST
BROWN, THOMAS	ANN	355	3RD DIST
BROWN, THOMAS	BAL	148	16TH WAR
BROWN, THOMAS	BAL	091	15TH WAR
BROWN, THOMAS	BAL	343	1ST DIST
BROWN, THOMAS	BAL	101	5TH WARD
BROWN, THOMAS	BAL	056	1ST WARD
BROWN, THOMAS	ANN	406	8TH DIST
BROWN, THOMAS	ALL	077	5TH E.D.
BROWN, THOMAS	BAL	339	7TH WARD
BROWN, THOMAS	BAL	218	12TH WAR
BROWN, THOMAS	BAL	240	12TH WAR
BROWN, THOMAS	BAL	286	2ND WARD
BROWN, THOMAS	BAL	457	8TH WARD
BROWN, THOMAS	BAL	020	4TH WARD
BROWN, THOMAS	CEC	021	ELKTON 3
BROWN, THOMAS	BAL	224	19TH WAR
BROWN, THOMAS	HAR	131	2ND DIST
BROWN, THOMAS	HAR	177	3RD DIST
BROWN, THOMAS	BAL	259	20TH WAR
BROWN, THOMAS	FRE	206	BUCKEYST
BROWN, THOMAS	CEC	114	3RD E DI
BROWN, THOMAS	CEC	075	NORTHEAS
BROWN, THOMAS	MGM	362	BERRYS D
BROWN, THOMAS	SOM	416	DUBLIN D
BROWN, THOMAS	CAL	008	1ST DIST
BROWN, THOMAS	PRI	004	BLADENSB
BROWN, THOMAS	PRI	077	MARLBROU
BROWN, THOMAS	WOR	196	8TH E DI
BROWN, THOMAS	TAL	105	ST MICHA
BROWN, THOMAS	ST	291	2ND E DI
BROWN, THOMAS	WAS	249	1ST DIST
BROWN, THOMAS	QUE	160	2ND E DI
BROWN, THOMAS	WAS	219	1ST DIST
BROWN, THOMAS C.	ANN	330	2ND DIST
BROWN, THOMAS C.	BAL	231	1ST DIST
BROWN, THOMAS D.	CAR	068	NO TWP L
BROWN, THOMAS S.	CAR	190	4TH DIST
BROWN, THOMAS-BLACK	FRE	017	FREDERIC
BROWN, THOMAS-BLACK	ST	333	4TH E DI
BROWN, THOMAS-MULATTO	FRE	415	8TH E DI
BROWN, THOMASY	BAL	012	1ST WARD
BROWN, TITUS	BAL	287	12TH WAR
BROWN, TOBIAS	WAS	086	2ND SUBD
BROWN, UPTON	FRE	299	WOODSBOR
BROWN, URIAS	ANN	486	HOWARD D
BROWN, URIAS	ANN	486	HOWARD D
BROWN, VACHEL	CAR	231	5TH DIST
BROWN, VINSENT	CAR	215	5TH DIST
BROWN, VIRGIL	CAL	042	3RD DIST
BROWN, VIRGINIA	SOM	425	PRINCESS
BROWN, W.	ANN	286	ANNAPOLI
BROWN, W.J.	BAL	173	1ST WARD
BROWN, WALTER	PRI	121	PISCATAW
BROWN, WALTER	PRI	082	QUEEN AN
BROWN, WALTERS	DOR	371	3RD DIVI
BROWN, WARNER	BAL	011	15TH WAR
BROWN, WASHINGTON	BAL	333	7TH WARD
BROWN, WASHINGTON	BAL	113	5TH WARD
BROWN, WASHINGTON	CEC	205	7TH E DI
BROWN, WASHINGTON	CAR	384	2ND DIST
BROWN, WASHINGTON	CHA	288	BOJANTOW
BROWN, WASHINGTON	CEC	135	6TH E DI
BROWN, WASHINGTON	KEN	300	3RD DIST
BROWN, WASHINGTON R.	FRE	412	8TH E DI
BROWN, WILIAM	FRE	344	MIDDLETO
BROWN, WILIAM	BAL	152	1ST WARD
BROWN, WILLAIM	BAL	156	1ST WARD
BROWN, WILLAIM	BAL	286	2ND WARD
BROWN, WILLAIM	BAL	151	2ND DIST
BROWN, WILLAIM	ANN	455	HOWARD D
BROWN, WILLAIM	BAL	102	2ND DIST
BROWN, WILLAIM	PRI	096	SPALDING
BROWN, WILLIA	BAL	172	1ST WARD
BROWN, WILLIA MF.	BAL	353	7TH WARD
BROWN, WILLIAM	BAL	012	15TH WAR
BROWN, WILLIAM	BAL	231	12TH WAR
BROWN, WILLIAM	BAL	317	7TH WARD
BROWN, WILLIAM	BAL	435	8TH WARD
BROWN, WILLIAM	BAL	432	8TH WARD
BROWN, WILLIAM	BAL	171	11TH WAR
BROWN, WILLIAM	BAL	163	1ST WARD
BROWN, WILLIAM	BAL	166	1ST WARD
BROWN, WILLIAM	BAL	166	1ST WARD
BROWN, WILLIAM	BAL	162	1ST WARD
BROWN, WILLIAM	BAL	168	1ST WARD
BROWN, WILLIAM	BAL	151	1ST WARD
BROWN, WILLIAM	BAL	150	1ST WARD
BROWN, WILLIAM	BAL	157	1ST WARD
BROWN, WILLIAM	BAL	155	1ST WARD
BROWN, WILLIAM	BAL	176	6TH WARD
BROWN, WILLIAM	BAL	143	5TH WARD
BROWN, WILLIAM	BAL	213	2ND WARD
BROWN, WILLIAM	BAL	138	5TH WARD
BROWN, WILLIAM	BAL	080	2ND DIST
BROWN, WILLIAM	ANN	475	HOWARD D
BROWN, WILLIAM	ANN	344	3RD DIST
BROWN, WILLIAM	BAL	141	2ND DIST
BROWN, WILLIAM	ANN	441	HOWARD D
BROWN, WILLIAM	ANN	434	HOWARD D
BROWN, WILLIAM	BAL	156	2ND DIST
BROWN, WILLIAM	BAL	009	1ST WARD
BROWN, WILLIAM	BAL	067	1ST WARD
BROWN, WILLIAM	BAL	046	1ST WARD
BROWN, WILLIAM	BAL	025	1ST WARD
BROWN, WILLIAM	BAL	305	1ST DIST
BROWN, WILLIAM	BAL	119	1ST WARD
BROWN, WILLIAM	BAL	118	1ST WARD
BROWN, WILLIAM	BAL	124	1ST WARD
BROWN, WILLIAM	BAL	107	1ST WARD
BROWN, WILLIAM	BAL	105	1ST WARD
BROWN, WILLIAM	BAL	160	2ND DIST
BROWN, WILLIAM	BAL	179	2ND DIST
BROWN, WILLIAM	BAL	331	3RD WARD
BROWN, WILLIAM	BAL	338	3RD WARD

BROWN, WILLIAM BAL 454 1ST DIST
BROWN, WILLIAM BAL 449 1ST DIST
BROWN, WILLIAM BAL 304 3RD WARD
BROWN, WILLIAM ANN 318 2ND DIST
BROWN, WILLIAM ANN 369 4TH DIST
BROWN, WILLIAM BAL 323 12TH WAR
BROWN, WILLIAM BAL 052 9TH WARD
BROWN, WILLIAM BAL 065 10TH WAR
BROWN, WILLIAM BAL 404 8TH WARD
BROWN, WILLIAM BAL 279 2ND WARD
BROWN, WILLIAM BAL 138 1ST WARD
BROWN, WILLIAM BAL 404 3RD WARD
BROWN, WILLIAM BAL 374 8TH WARD
BROWN, WILLIAM SOM 441 DAMES QU
BROWN, WILLIAM WAS 062 2ND SUBD
BROWN, WILLIAM WAS 148 HAGERSTO
BROWN, WILLIAM ST 259 3RD E DI
BROWN, WILLIAM ST 267 3RD E DI
BROWN, WILLIAM QUE 231 4TH E DI
BROWN, WILLIAM DOR 315 1ST DIST
BROWN, WILLIAM CEC 127 5TH E DI
BROWN, WILLIAM DOR 298 1ST DIST
BROWN, WILLIAM CEC 161 6TH E DI
BROWN, WILLIAM CEC 162 6TH E DI
BROWN, WILLIAM BAL 245 17TH WAR
BROWN, WILLIAM BAL 231 17TH WAR
BROWN, WILLIAM BAL 224 17TH WAR
BROWN, WILLIAM BAL 436 14TH WAR
BROWN, WILLIAM BAL 433 14TH WAR
BROWN, WILLIAM BAL 383 13TH WAR
BROWN, WILLIAM CHA 295 HILLTOP
BROWN, WILLIAM HAR 164 3RD DIST
BROWN, WILLIAM HAR 127 2ND DIST
BROWN, WILLIAM MGM 332 CRACKLIN
BROWN, WILLIAM MGM 353 BERRYS D
BROWN, WILLIAM QUE 124 1ST E DI
BROWN, WILLIAM FRE 153 10TH E D
BROWN, WILLIAM CAR 394 2ND DIST
BROWN, WILLIAM CEC 186 7TH E DI
BROWN, WILLIAM BAL 047 18TH WAR
BROWN, WILLIAM BAL 018 18TH WAR
BROWN, WILLIAM FRE 336 MIDDLETO
BROWN, WILLIAM HAR 120 2ND DIST
BROWN, WILLIAM MGM 354 BERRYS D
BROWN, WILLIAM HAR 051 1ST DIST
BROWN, WILLIAM FRE 069 FREDERIC
BROWN, WILLIAM CAL 024 2ND DIST
BROWN, WILLIAM CAL 042 3RD DIST
BROWN, WILLIAM BAL 119 11TH WAR
BROWN, WILLIAM . BAL 207 19TH WAR
BROWN, WILLIAM -BLCK FRE 384 PETERSVI
BROWN, WILLIAM A. BAL 137 18TH WAR
BROWN, WILLIAM B. FRE 155 10TH E D
BROWN, WILLIAM C. BAL 300 17TH WAR
BROWN, WILLIAM C. BAL 256 17TH WAR
BROWN, WILLIAM F. WOR 232 6TH E DI
BROWN, WILLIAM G. ST 345 5TH E DI
BROWN, WILLIAM G. BAL 093 18TH WAR
BROWN, WILLIAM H. CAR 412 2ND DIST
BROWN, WILLIAM H. QUE 231 4TH E DI
BROWN, WILLIAM H. ST 285 2ND E DI
BROWN, WILLIAM H. BAL 361 3RD WARD
BROWN, WILLIAM H. BAL 128 16TH WAR
BROWN, WILLIAM H. BAL 138 5TH WARD
BROWN, WILLIAM J WOR 236 6TH E DI
BROWN, WILLIAM JR. FRE 148 10TH E D
BROWN, WILLIAM L. CAR 271 WESTMINS
BROWN, WILLIAM M. BAL 013 18TH WAR
BROWN, WILLIAM N. CAL 041 3RD DIST
BROWN, WILLIAM S. FRE 013 FREDERIC
BROWN, WILLIAM S. BAL 204 2ND WARD
BROWN, WILLIAM SR. FRE 156 10TH E D
BROWN, WILLIAM T. BAL 171 16TH WAR
BROWN, WILLIAM T. WAS 155 HAGERSTO
BROWN, WILLIAM W. BAL 412 8TH WARD
BROWN, WILLIAM-BLACK WOR 321 1ST E DI
BROWN, WILLIAM-BLACK QUE 170 2ND E DI
BROWN, WILLIAM-BLACK QUE 176 2ND E DI
BROWN, WILLIAM-BLACK QUE 141 1ST E DI
BROWN, WILLIAM-BLACK QUE 133 1ST E DI
BROWN, WILLIAM-BLACK QUE 158 2ND E DI
BROWN, WILLIAM-BLACK FRE 215 BUCKEYST
BROWN, WILLIAM-BLACK FRE 051 FREDERIC
BROWN, WILLIAM-BLACK FRE 050 FREDERIC
BROWN, WILLIAM-MULATTO FRE 412 8TH E DI
BROWN, WILLIAM-MULATTO BAL 228 2ND WARD
BROWN, Z.R. BAL 141 1ST WARD
BROWN, ZACHAIRAH CAR 231 5TH DIST
BROWN, ZACHARIAH CAR 232 5TH DIST
BROWN, ZACHARIAH BAL 340 3RD WARD
BROWN, ZACHARIAH BAL 427 1ST DIST
BROWN, ZEPHERICH PRI 002 BLADENSB
BROWN,DENTON ALL 206 CUMBERLA
BROWN,E.M. BAL 130 1ST WARD
BROWN,EDWARD BAL 123 1ST WARD
BROWN,ELIJAH ALL 013 3RD E.D.
BROWN,EPHRAIM-BLACK CAR 384 2ND DIST
BROWN,H.F. BAL 170 1ST WARD
BROWN,HENRY BAL 079 1ST WARD
BROWN,HENRY-BLACK CAR 165 NO TWP L
BROWN,JAMES BAL 174 1ST WARD
BROWN,JOHN BAL 130 1ST WARD
BROWN,MARGARET-BLACK QUE 199 3RD E DI
BROWN,MARY ALL 013 3RD E.D.
BROWN,MARY BAL 003 EASTERN
BROWN,MATHEWS BAL 178 2ND WARD
BROWN,MICHAEL BAL 075 1ST WARD
BROWN,NANCY ALL 013 3RD E.D.
BROWN,NANCY-BLACK QUE 200 3RD E DI
BROWN,OTTO C. BAL 120 1ST WARD
BROWN,PHILLIP BAL 114 1ST WARD
BROWN,RACHAEL CAR 368 9TH DIST
BROWN,ROBERT BAL 162 1ST WARD
BROWN,SAMUEL BAL 011 2ND DIST
BROWN,SAMUEL QUE 165 2ND E DI
BROWN,THOMAS BAL 135 1ST WARD
BROWN,WILLIAM BAL 122 1ST WARD
BROWNBY, CATHARINE BAL 008 1ST WARD
BROWNO, EDWIN BAL 199 19TH WAR
BROWNE, AARON KEN 274 1ST DIST
BROWNE, AARON * KEN 229 2ND DIST
BROWNE, ABRAHAM KEN 239 2ND DIST
BROWNE, ABRAHAM KEN 278 1ST DIST
BROWNE, ALEXANDER KEN 261 1ST DIST
BROWNE, ALEXANDER KEN 235 2ND DIST
BROWNE, ALEXANDER KEN 241 2ND DIST
BROWNE, ALEXANDER MGM 383 ROCKERLE
BROWNE, AMILY KEN 232 2ND DIST
BROWNE, ANN E. KEN 272 1ST DIST
BROWNE, C. C. KEN 256 1ST DIST

BROWNE, CATHERINE CHA 231 HILLTOP
BROWNE, CHARLES KEN 211 2ND DIST
BROWNE, DANIEL BAL 079 2ND DIST
BROWNE, DAVID KEN 275 1ST DIST
BROWNE, EDWARD ANN 321 2ND DIST
BROWNE, EDWARD F. QUE 223 4TH E DI
BROWNE, EDWIN KEN 238 2ND DIST
BROWNE, ELIAS KEN 275 1ST DIST
BROWNE, ELIZA BAL 348 13TH WAR
BROWNE, ELIZABETH KEN 239 2ND DIST
BROWNE, ELIZABETH KEN 212 2ND DIST
BROWNE, FRANCES BAL 338 13TH WAR
BROWNE, FREDRICK KEN 263 1ST DIST
BROWNE, HAGER HAR 091 2ND DIST
BROWNE, HENRY KEN 237 2ND DIST
BROWNE, HENRY KEN 212 2ND DIST
BROWNE, HENRY KEN 256 1ST DIST
BROWNE, HENRY ANN 324 2ND DIST
BROWNE, JAEMS KEN 256 1ST DIST
BROWNE, JAMES KEN 256 1ST DIST
BROWNE, JAMES KEN 233 2ND DIST
BROWNE, JAMES T. CHA 231 HILLTOP
BROWNE, JAMES T. QUE 242 5TH E DI
BROWNE, JESS HAR 095 2ND DIST
BROWNE, JOHN H. ANN 324 2ND DIST
BROWNE, JOSEPH KEN 244 2ND DIST
BROWNE, MARGARET KEN 216 2ND DIST
BROWNE, MARGARET KEN 276 1ST DIST
BROWNE, MARTHA KEN 274 1ST DIST
BROWNE, MARTHA T. QUE 239 5TH E DI
BROWNE, MARY KEN 273 1ST DIST
BROWNE, MARY KEN 268 1ST DIST
BROWNE, MARY BAL 076 2ND DIST
BROWNE, MARY C. KEN 270 1ST DIST
BROWNE, MICHAEL KEN 276 1ST DIST
BROWNE, NICHOLAS V. BAL 031 9TH WARD
BROWNE, PERE QUE 242 5TH E DI
BROWNE, SAMEUL ANN 288 ANNAPOLI
BROWNE, SARAH KEN 252 1ST DIST
BROWNE, THOMAS R. KEN 231 2ND DIST
BROWNE, WILLIAM KEN 257 1ST DIST
BROWNE, WILLIAM KEN 262 1ST DIST
BROWNEA, CHARLES G. * BAL 144 1ST WARD
BROWNELL, BETSEY QUE 210 3RD E DI
BROWNER, CAMEL CHA 219 ALLENS F
BROWNER, CAROLINE BAL 098 5TH WARD
BROWNER, HEZEKIAH CHA 257 MIDDLETO
BROWNER, JOHN J. CHA 245 HILLTOP
BROWNER, JOHN S. CHA 247 HILLTOP
BROWNER, WILLIAM H. CHA 243 HILLTOP
BROWNEY, RICHARD FRE 277 NEW MARK
BROWNGANT, FRANCIS BAL 112 15TH WAR
BROWNGART, TRACEY BAL 112 15TH WAR
BROWNING, ANN S. FRE 097 FREDERIC
BROWNING, BENJAMIN BAL 024 1ST WARD
BROWNING, BENJAMIN MGM 439 CLARKSTR
BROWNING, BERSILLA BAL 318 7TH WARD
BROWNING, DRASILLA FRE 274 NEW MARK
BROWNING, EDMUND ALL 055 10TH E.D
BROWNING, EDWARD ANN 477 HOWARD D
BROWNING, EDWARD BAL 284 17TH WAR
BROWNING, EMELINE KEN 244 2ND DIST
BROWNING, EPHRAIM ALL 186 9TH E.D.
BROWNING, GEORGE R. ANN 438 HOWARD D
BROWNING, GEORGE W. ALL 042 10TH E.D
BROWNING, J. M. BAL 147 1ST WARD
BROWNING, J.F. ALL 043 10TH E.D
BROWNING, JAME SB. FRE 381 PETERSVI
BROWNING, JAMES BAL 274 17TH WAR
BROWNING, JAMES ALL 043 10TH E.D
BROWNING, JAMES ALL 053 10TH E.D
BROWNING, JAMES S. BAL 135 5TH WARD
BROWNING, JANE ALL 042 10TH E.D
BROWNING, JEREMIAH ALL 043 10TH E.D
BROWNING, JOHN L. ALL 044 10TH E.D
BROWNING, JOHN W. ALL 055 10TH E.D
BROWNING, JOHN W. KEN 282 3RD DIST
BROWNING, JOHN W. PRI 021 VANSVILL
BROWNING, JOHNATHAN FRE 417 8TH E DI
BROWNING, JOSEPH FRE 406 JEFFERSO
BROWNING, LUTHER MGM 435 CLARKSTR
BROWNING, MAHAL ALL 033 2ND E.D.
BROWNING, MAHLON MGM 425 MEDLEY 3
BROWNING, MARGARETT BAL 277 17TH WAR
BROWNING, MARIA ALL 043 10TH E.D
BROWNING, MARSLINE PRI 029 VANSVILL
BROWNING, MARY BAL 241 12TH WAR
BROWNING, MARY BAL 100 5TH WARD
BROWNING, MARY ANN ALL 040 2ND E.D.
BROWNING, MARY E. ANN 492 HOWARD D
BROWNING, MESHACK ALL 043 10TH E.D
BROWNING, PERRY MGM 437 CLARKSTR
BROWNING, RHODA MGM 436 CLARKSTR
BROWNING, RITSON BAL 292 3RD WARD
BROWNING, SAMUEL BAL 036 9TH WARD
BROWNING, SAMUEL D. BAL 318 7TH WARD
BROWNING, SILAS FRE 082 FREDERIC
BROWNING, SUSAN BAL 292 3RD WARD
BROWNING, THOMAS ALL 043 10TH E.D
BROWNING, WILLIAM ALL 042 10TH E.D
BROWNING, WILLIAM BAL 291 20TH WAR
BROWNING, WILLIAM MGM 436 CLARKSTR
BROWNING, WILLIAM E. BAL 027 15TH WAR
BROWNING, WILLIAM S. BAL 163 16TH WAR
BROWNING, ZALMON ALL 042 10TH E.D
BROWNING,HENRY BAL 135 1ST WARD
BROWNLAW, FOSTER BAL 113 1ST WARD
BROWNLEY, ANN BAL 222 17TH WAR
BROWNLEY, JAMES BAL 055 4TH WARD
BROWNLEY, JOHN BAL 285 20TH WAR
BROWNLEY, JOHN W. BAL 028 1ST WARD
BROWNLEY, JOSEPH L. BAL 040 1ST WARD
BROWNLEY, JOSHUA BAL 033 4TH WARD
BROWNLOW, FOSTER BAL 115 1ST WARD
BROWNMAN, ELIZABETH BAL 214 11TH WAR
BROWNS, JONES WOR 186 7TH E DI
BROWNS, SAMUEL BAL 135 11TH WAR
BROWNSON, ERASMUS BAL 280 1ST DIST
BROWNSON, HENRY BAL 141 1ST WARD
BROWNSON, JOHN BAL 141 1ST WARD
BROWNWOOD, JOHN BAL 060 15TH WAR
BROWSDISH, G.W. BAL 137 1ST WARD
BROXSON, JINNY BAL 383 1ST DIST
BROZENO, FREDERICK * BAL 355 1ST DIST
BROZIER, JACOB BAL 214 19TH WAR
BRUAN, FRANCIS BAL 343 3RD WARD
BRUAS, THOMAS* TAL 004 EASTON D
BRUBAKE, JOHN FRE 088 FREDERIC
BRUBAUGH, ELEANORA ALL 013 3RD E.D.
BRUBECKER, MARTIN BAL 419 1ST DIST

BRUC, AMELIA CEC 032 CHESAPEA
BRUCE, ANNA BAL 289 7TH WARD
BRUCE, CAHRLES H. BAL 466 14TH WAR
BRUCE, CELIA BAL 157 11TH WAR
BRUCE, EDWARD CEC 205 7TH E DI
BRUCE, GEORGE ALL 094 5TH E.D.
BRUCE, GEORGE R. ALL 014 3RD E.D.
BRUCE, GOERGE CAR 413 2ND DIST
BRUCE, HENRY ALL 009 3RD E.D.
BRUCE, HENRY ALL 255 CUMBERLA
BRUCE, HENRY ST 345 5TH E DI
BRUCE, ISAAC ALL 170 6TH E.D.
BRUCE, ISAAC CAR 288 7TH DIST
BRUCE, JACK PRI 093 MARLBROU
BRUCE, JAMES HAR 139 2ND DIST
BRUCE, JAMES A. BAL 249 17TH WAR
BRUCE, JANE CAR 297 7TH DIST
BRUCE, JEPTHA BAL 018 9TH WARD
BRUCE, JOHN R. ALL 013 3RD E.D.
BRUCE, LOUISA BAL 027 15TH WAR
BRUCE, MARY PRI 056 AQUASCO
BRUCE, MARY A. CEC 166 5TH E DI
BRUCE, MARY J. BAL 376 13TH WAR
BRUCE, NANCY BAL 031 15TH WAR
BRUCE, NORAN ALL 240 CUMBERLA
BRUCE, PETER BAL 140 11TH WAR
BRUCE, PHEBE CAR 273 WESTMINS
BRUCE, ROBERT BAL 130 11TH WAR
BRUCE, ROBERT ALL 212 CUMBERLA
BRUCE, ROBERT BAL 398 8TH WARD
BRUCE, ROBERT BAL 331 13TH WAR
BRUCE, SARAH BAL 172 11TH WAR
BRUCE, THOMAS BAL 283 7TH WARD
BRUCE, THOMAS PRI 075 MARLBROU
BRUCE, UPTON ALL 063 10TH E.D
BRUCE, VIRGINIA BAL 192 6TH WARD
BRUCE, WALTER ALL 254 CUMBERLA
BRUCE, WILLAIM W. BAL 114 2ND DIST
BRUCE, WILLIAM BAL 203 6TH WARD
BRUCE, WILLIAM BAL 045 9TH WARD
BRUCE, WILLIAM BAL 383 13TH WAR
BRUCE, WILLIAM A. ALL 150 6TH E.D.
BRUCH, HENRY M. BAL 125 16TH WAR
BRUCHE, JACOB FRE 053 FREDERIC
BRUCHE, WILLIAM FRE 053 FREDERIC
BRUCHEY, HENRY FRE 036 FREDERIC
BRUCHL, JUSTICE BAL 003 1ST WARD
BRUCHY, CATHARINE FRE 450 8TH E DI
BRUCKER, FREDERICK FRE 336 MIDDLETO
BRUCKEY, MARY FRE 301 WOODSBOR
BRUCKMAN, CHARLES BAL 369 1ST DIST
BRUCKMAN, JOHN BAL 121 1ST WARD
BRUCKNER, CATHERINE BAL 085 10TH WAR
BRUCKWEEDE, T. BAL 126 1ST WARD
BRUCY, WILLIAM CAR 196 4TH DIST
BRUDENBERGER, CAROLINE BAL 042 2ND DIST
BRUDING, JAMES CAR 115 NO TWP L
BRUDING, SARAH CAR 133 NO TWP L
BRUDING, WILLIAM CAR 115 NO TWP L
BRUDING, WILLIAM CAR 116 NO TWP L
BRUFF, ANN M. CAR 121 NO TWP L
BRUFF, E. J. WOR 284 BERLIN 1
BRUFF, HENRIETTA M. KEN 216 2ND DIST
BRUFF, J. R. KEN 264 1ST DIST
BRUFF, JAMES BAL 404 14TH WAR
BRUFF, JOHN TAL 085 ST MICHA
BRUFF, JOHN W. BAL 430 14TH WAR
BRUFF, JOSEPH TAL 109 ST MICHA
BRUFF, JOSEPH BAL 036 1ST WARD
BRUFF, JOSHUA D.* BAL 405 3RD WARD
BRUFF, MARY BAL 355 3RD WARD
BRUFF, RACHEL BAL 092 15TH WAR
BRUFF, SARAH WOR 263 BERLIN 1
BRUFF, THOMAS TAL 088 ST MICHA
BRUFF, THOMAS TAL 083 ST MICHA
BRUFF, THOMAS A. TAL 088 ST MICHA
BRUFF, WILLIAM T. SOM 371 BRINKLEY
BRUFF, WILLIAM W. TAL 099 ST MICHA
BRUFF, ZIPPORAH WOR 263 BERLIN 1
BRUGGY, JEREMIAH BAL 036 15TH WAR
BRUICE, ROBERT HAR 055 1ST DIST
BRUICE, ROBERT * HAR 014 1ST DIST
BRUINGOTN, SARAH BAL 331 13TH WAR
BRUINGTON, JENER* DOR 321 1ST DIST
BRUINGTON, LUKE DOR 323 1ST DIST
BRUITY, MARTHA BAL 435 8TH WARD
BRULEY, GRACEY BAL 241 20TH WAR
BRUM, RHEINHARDT BAL 189 6TH WARD
BRUMART, JOHN H. BAL 379 13TH WAR
BRUMBAUGH, DAVID WAS 299 1ST DIST
BRUMBAUGH, ELIAS WAS 286 1ST DIST
BRUMBAUGH, ELIZABETH WAS 286 1ST DIST
BRUMBAUGH, GEORGE WAS 293 1ST DIST
BRUMBAUGH, HENRY WAS 282 1ST DIST
BRUMBAUGH, JOSEPH WAS 286 1ST DIST
BRUMBAUGH, NATHAN WAS 286 1ST DIST
BRUMBLEY, BENJAMIN B. WOR 223 4TH E DI
BRUMBLEY, CHARLOTTE WOR 177 6TH E DI
BRUMBLEY, HENRY W. WOR 189 7TH E DI
BRUMBLEY, JOHN WOR 205 4TH E DI
BRUMBLEY, MARY WOR 186 7TH E DI
BRUMBLEY, NOAH WOR 203 4TH E DI
BRUMBLY, ABRAHM SOM 469 TRAPPE D
BRUMBLY, MARY SOM 423 PRINCESS
BRUMBY, LEAH* SOM 483 TRAPP DI
BRUMETT, NOAH WAS 108 2ND DIST
BRUMFIELD, HANNAH BAL 370 13TH WAR
BRUMLEY, WILLIAM WOR 251 1ST CENS
BRUMLY, PRISSY WOR 253 1ST CENS
BRUMMEL, ELIZABETH BAL 106 15TH WAR
BRUMMELL, DAVID CAR 174 8TH DIST
BRUMMELL, JOSEPH CAR 174 8TH DIST
BRUMMELL, JOSEPH CAR 187 4TH DIST
BRUMMER, CHARLES ALL 202 CUMBERLA
BRUMMER, MARY BAL 355 13TH WAR
BRUNNNINGS, HENRIETTA BAL 406 14TH WAR
BRUMWELL, JAMES DOR 365 3RD DIVI
BRUN, ADAM BAL 068 4TH WARD
BRUNAN, ROBERT BAL 006 1ST WARD
BRUNDAGE, THOMAS V. BAL 292 12TH WAR
BRUNDIGE, HANNAH BAL 058 10TH WAR
BRUNDIGE, JAMES BAL 058 10TH WAR
BRUNDIGE, KY DR. BAL 058 10TH WAR
BRUNDIGE, ROSETTA BAL 104 15TH WAR
BRUNDIGE, WILLIAM BAL 104 15TH WAR
BRUNDIGE, WILLIAM BAL 200 19TH WAR
BRUNE, ELLEN ANN BAL 067 10TH WAR
BRUNE, FREDRICK W. BAL 067 10TH WAR
BRUNE, GEORGE BAL 033 1ST WARD
BRUNE, JAMES BAL 065 1ST WARD

BRUNE, JOHN BAL 388 3RD WARD
BRUNE, JOHN BAL 388 3RD WARD
BRUNE, JOHN O. BAL 152 11TH WAR
BRUNE, JOHN W. BAL 148 11TH WAR
BRUNE, THOMAS O. BAL 001 15TH WAR
BRUNER, ABLE BAL 296 7TH WARD
BRUNER, ANDY-BLACK FRE 408 JEFFERSO
BRUNER, D. E. BAL 298 20TH WAR
BRUNER, GRAYNOR BAL 398 8TH WARD
BRUNER, JOHN BAL 161 16TH WAR
BRUNER, JOHN C. BAL 003 15TH WAR
BRUNER, JOSEPH WAS 090 2ND SUBD
BRUNER, LYDIA MGM 410 MEDLEY 3
BRUNER, S. FRE 154 10TH E D
BRUNES, HENRY BAL 095 15TH WAR
BRUNESTON, ISAAC B. BAL 471 14TH WAR
BRUNHAM, LUKE* TAL 115 ST MICHA
BRUNIN, DANIEL WAS 015 2ND SUBD
BRUNING, HARMAN H. BAL 139 16TH WAR
BRUNKLEY, GEORGE WOR 175 6TH E DI
BRUNNER, ANDREW BAL 435 14TH WAR
BRUNNER, BARBARA FRE 053 FREDERIC
BRUNNER, CATHARINE E. WAS 239 CAVETOWN
BRUNNER, CATHERINE FRE 095 FREDERIC
BRUNNER, DANIEL BAL 174 16TH WAR
BRUNNER, ELIZABETH FRE 024 FREDERIC
BRUNNER, ELLEN C. FRE 014 FREDERIC
BRUNNER, EMANUEL FRE 317 MIDDLETO
BRUNNER, HENRY FRE 096 FREDERIC
BRUNNER, ISAAC FRE 096 FREDERIC
BRUNNER, JACOB WAS 238 CAVETOWN
BRUNNER, JAMES FRE 056 FREDERIC
BRUNNER, JOHN L. BAL 016 9TH WARD
BRUNNER, JONATHAN FRE 097 FREDERIC
BRUNNER, LEWIS FRE 030 FREDERIC
BRUNNER, PETER FRE 099 FREDERIC
BRUNNER, PHILIP WAS 239 CAVETOWN
BRUNNER, POLLY BAL 031 18TH WAR
BRUNNER, ROSANA BAL 347 3RD WARD
BRUNNER, SOPHIA FRE 030 FREDERIC
BRUNNER, VAN ANTERN FRE 033 FREDERIC
BRUNRIDGE, PETER BAL 275 17TH WAR
BRUNS, BARNEY BAL 153 5TH WARD
BRUNT, ANN BAL 210 19TH WAR
BRUNT, RALPH BAL 210 19TH WAR
BRUNT, SARAH BAL 141 19TH WAR
BRUNT, WILLIAM BAL 210 19TH WAR
BRUNT, WILLIAM BAL 379 8TH WARD
BRUNTSH, ANDREW BAL 251 2ND WARD
BRUNTZ, CARLOS BAL 123 11TH WAR
BRUNTZ, HENRY BAL 440 14TH WAR
BRUSCASS, MARY BAL 284 2ND WARD
BRUSCUP, ALBERT BAL 328 7TH WARD
BRUSCUP, COLUMBUS BAL 357 3RD WARD
BRUSFIELD, JAMES TAL 093 ST MICHA
BRUSH, JOHN WAS 142 2ND DIST
BRUSHAM, HERMAN * BAL 158 2ND DIST
BRUSHAM, MARY BAL 019 9TH WARD
BRUSHEA, JOSEPH-MULATTO FRE 429 8TH E DI
BRUSHMILLER, WILLIAM BAL 389 8TH WARD
BRUSSER, WILLIAM * BAL 270 2ND WARD
BRUST, CASPAR FRE 007 FREDERIC
BRUSTER, JAMES CAR 273 WESTMINS
BRUSTER, MARY J. * BAL 186 6TH WARD
BRUSTIN, ELIZABETH-MULATT ST 319 4TH E DI
BRUTCHE, ELIZABETH FRE 063 FREDERIC
BRUTZMAN, FRANCIS C. BAL 368 13TH WAR
BRUY, PRESCELLA J. ALL 162 6TH E.D.
BRWON, CHARLES W. BAL 059 10TH WAR
BRWON, CHRISTIAN BAL 215 6TH DIST
BRWON, GEORGE BAL 143 5TH WARD
BRWON, HENRY CAR 220 5TH DIST
BRWON, LOYD CEC 215 7TH E DI
BRWON, MARY HAR 097 2ND DIST
BRWON, MARY BAL 053 9TH WARD
BRWON, SAMUEL BAL 153 11TH WAR
BRWON, SIMON HAR 029 1ST DIST
BRWON, STEPHEN BAL 451 1ST DIST
BRYAN, ACHSAH ANN 383 4TH DIST
BRYAN, AMELIA ANN 269 ANNAPOLI
BRYAN, ANN M. KEN 268 1ST DIST
BRYAN, ANNA BAL 168 6TH WARD
BRYAN, ARTHUR BAL 069 2ND DIST
BRYAN, ARTHUR QUE 243 5TH E DI
BRYAN, CHARLES DOR 412 1ST DIST
BRYAN, CHARLES J. QUE 243 5TH E DI
BRYAN, CHRISTOPHER BAL 134 16TH WAR
BRYAN, DEBORAH ANN 338 3RD DIST
BRYAN, DENNIS WAS 163 2ND DIST
BRYAN, DENWOOD* DOR 432 1ST DIST
BRYAN, EDWARD QUE 243 5TH E DI
BRYAN, EDWARD ANN 485 HOWARD D
BRYAN, ELIZA ANN 270 ANNAPOLI
BRYAN, ELIZA DOR 416 1ST DIST
BRYAN, ELIZABETH BAL 184 19TH WAR
BRYAN, ELIZABETH CEC 137 6TH E DI
BRYAN, ELIZABETH QUE 248 5TH E DI
BRYAN, FREDERICK WAS 291 1ST DIST
BRYAN, GEORGE CEC 037 CHESAPEA
BRYAN, GEORGE C. QUE 247 5TH E DI
BRYAN, HANNAH ANN 269 ANNAPOLI
BRYAN, HENRY QUE 207 3RD E DI
BRYAN, HENRY QUE 182 3RD E DI
BRYAN, JAMES QUE 251 5TH E DI
BRYAN, JAMES ANN 371 4TH DIST
BRYAN, JAMES BAL 380 13TH WAR
BRYAN, JAMES DOR 376 1ST DIST
BRYAN, JAMES A. ST 258 3RD E DI
BRYAN, JAMES DOCTOR* DOR 356 3RD DIVI
BRYAN, JAMES L. QUE 224 4TH E DI
BRYAN, JAMES L. BAL 108 10TH WAR
BRYAN, JAMES M. ANN 337 3RD DIST
BRYAN, JAMES M. QUE 231 4TH E DI
BRYAN, JAMES S. ANN 384 4TH DIST
BRYAN, JOAL CEC 038 CHESAPEA
BRYAN, JOE* DOR 427 1ST DIST
BRYAN, JOHN BAL 148 19TH WAR
BRYAN, JOHN ANN 426 HOWARD D
BRYAN, JOHN BAL 022 15TH WAR
BRYAN, JOHN ST 312 1ST E DI
BRYAN, JOHN KEN 304 3RD DIST
BRYAN, JOHN A. QUE 245 5TH E DI
BRYAN, JOHN C. QUE 230 4TH E DI
BRYAN, JOHN W. BAL 459 1ST DIST
BRYAN, JOHN-MULATTO ST 306 1ST E DI
BRYAN, JOSEPH PRI 112 PISCATAW
BRYAN, JOSEPH CEC 030 CHESAPEA
BRYAN, LEVIN DOR 462 1ST DIST
BRYAN, LEWIS QUE 224 4TH E DI
BRYAN, LEWIS BAL 115 1ST WARD
BRYAN, MARY ANN 425 HOWARD D
BRYAN, MARY BAL 179 16TH WAR
BRYAN, MARY ST 286 2ND E DI
BRYAN, MARY DOR 427 1ST DIST
BRYAN, MARY CEC 195 6TH E DI
BRYAN, MARY E. BAL 134 16TH WAR
BRYAN, MARY J. WAS 140 2ND DIST
BRYAN, MARY O. QUE 147 1ST E DI
BRYAN, MATTHEW KEN 278 1ST DIST
BRYAN, MRS. ANN 270 ANNAPOLI
BRYAN, O. N. CHA 256 MIDDLETO
BRYAN, R.T. ANN 269 ANNAPOLI
BRYAN, REBECCA A. CHA 292 BOJANTOW
BRYAN, RICHARD CEC 030 CHESAPEA
BRYAN, RICHARD WAS 162 2ND DIST
BRYAN, RICHARD PRI 097 SPALDING
BRYAN, RICHARD W. CHA 256 MIDDLETO
BRYAN, RICHARD-MULATTO ST 301 2ND E DI
BRYAN, ROBERT DOR 465 1ST DIST
BRYAN, ROBERT S. QUE 248 5TH E DI
BRYAN, SAMUEL QUE 247 5TH E DI
BRYAN, SAMUEL CEC 038 CHESAPEA
BRYAN, SAMUEL ANN 313 1ST DIST
BRYAN, SAMUEL BAL 023 15TH WAR
BRYAN, SARAH * QUE 224 4TH E DI
BRYAN, STEPHEN ANN 425 HOWARD D
BRYAN, STEPHEN W. QUE 230 4TH E DI
BRYAN, SUSAN BAL 220 1ST DIST
BRYAN, THOAMS ST 288 2ND E DI
BRYAN, THOMAS WAS 151 2ND DIST
BRYAN, THOMAS BAL 458 8TH WARD
BRYAN, W. DOR 426 1ST DIST
BRYAN, WALTER QUE 250 5TH E DI
BRYAN, WASHINGTON* DOR 428 1ST DIST
BRYAN, WESLEY BAL 226 17TH WAR
BRYAN, WILLIAM QUE 247 5TH E DI
BRYAN, WILLIAM QUE 253 5TH E DI
BRYAN, WILLIAM QUE 236 4TH E DI
BRYAN, WILLIAM PRI 117 PISCATAW
BRYAN, WILLIAM ANN 429 HOWARD D
BRYAN, WILLIAM ANN 324 2ND DIST
BRYAN, WILLIAM ANN 268 ANNAPOLI
BRYAN, WILLIAM ANN 381 4TH DIST
BRYAN, WILLIAM OF RICHARD PRI 116 PISCATAW
BRYAN, WILLIAM-MULATTO ST 292 2ND E DI
BRYAN, WILLIAM-MULATTO ST 299 2ND E DI
BRYANT, ANDREW J. FRE 202 5TH E DI
BRYANT, ELIJAH ANN 383 4TH DIST
BRYANT, ELIZABETH-MULATTO ST 293 2ND E DI
BRYANT, JEREMIAH BAL 337 7TH WARD
BRYANT, MARY BAL 250 12TH WAR
BRYANT, MARY R. ANN 521 HOWARD D
BRYANT, MRS. ANN 455 HOWARD D
BRYANT, REBECA BAL 317 7TH WARD
BRYANT, SAMUEL BAL 051 9TH WARD
BRYANT, SUSAN E. ANN 521 HOWARD D
BRYARD, JOHN BAL 211 2ND WARD
BRYARLY, ROBERT BAL 157 16TH WAR
BRYD, ELIZA QUE 131 1ST E DI
BRYDEN, ELIZABETH BAL 435 14TH WAR
BRYDEN, JAMES W. BAL 293 7TH WARD
BRYDSTONE, MARY ALL 239 CUMBERLA
BRYEN, MARGARET WAS 102 2ND DIST
BRYENT, JOSHWAY HAR 156 3RD DIST
BRYER, JOHN CEC 034 CHESAPEA
BRYLY, MANDA J.* DOR 301 1ST DIST
BRYLY, WILLIAM* DOR 301 1ST DIST
BRYN, FRANCIS P. BAL 124 5TH WARD
BRYNS, MARY BAL 258 12TH WAR
BRYON, JAMES CAR 111 NO TWP L
BRYON, MARGARETT DOR 296 1ST DIST
BRYON, MARY BAL 143 16TH WAR
BRYON, MARY A. CAR 123 NO TWP L
BRYON, ROBERT CAR 122 NO TWP L
BRYON, SARAH J. CAR 112 NO TWP L
BRYON, WILLIAM CAR 121 NO TWP L
BRYRON, CHARLES WAS 129 HAGERSTO
BRYSON, CHARLES BAL 334 7TH WARD
BRYSON, DANIEL M. BAL 292 3RD WARD
BRYSON, HUGH BAL 319 7TH WARD
BRYSON, IWLLIAM BAL 104 18TH WAR
BRYSON, JAMES BAL 261 6TH WARD
BRYSON, W. J. BAL 291 3RD WARD
BRYSON, ROBERT BAL 066 2ND DIST
BSOWELL, G OERGE H. MGM 406 MEDLEY 3
BSOWORTH, A.W. ALL 218 CUMBERLA
BTAIN, CATHERINE FRE 075 FREDERIC
BTUER, BATTSON * BAL 043 18TH WAR
BUALEY, PERRY * KEN 284 3RD DIST
BUANION, FREDERICK BAL 105 5TH WARD
BUANION, JOHN BAL 105 5TH WARD
BUARD, J.H.A. BAL 193 2ND WARD
BUAUL, SAMUEL * BAL 124 2ND DIST
BUBAND, JAOCB BAL 142 1ST WARD
BUBBART, JOHN BAL 386 1ST DIST
BUBERT, FRANCES BAL 234 12TH WAR
BUBERT, JOHN G. BAL 316 12TH WAR
BUBET, MARY * BAL 162 2ND DIST
BUCEY, BENJAMIN ALL 089 5TH E.D.
BUCEY, CHARLES ALL 189 9TH E.D.
BUCEY, DANIEL ALL 189 9TH E.D.
BUCEY, ELLEN ALL 057 10TH E.D
BUCEY, GEORGE ALL 162 6TH E.D.
BUCEY, HENRY ALL 189 9TH E.D.
BUCEY, MARGARETT BAL 087 4TH WARD
BUCEY, SAMUEL ALL 163 6TH E.D.
BUCEY, SARAH ALL 162 6TH E.D.
BUCH, ALBERT ST 317 4TH E DI
BUCH, JAMES ST 259 3RD E DI
BUCH, JAMES W. ST 325 4TH E DI
BUCH, WILLIAM ST 345 5TH E DI
BUCHAM, JAMES BAL 258 20TH WAR
BUCHAN, J.C. BAL 161 1ST WARD
BUCHANAN, ALEXANDER BAL 132 1ST WARD
BUCHANAN, ANN M. BAL 046 15TH WAR
BUCHANAN, CHARLES BAL 172 2ND DIST
BUCHANAN, CHARLOTTE BAL 253 6TH WARD
BUCHANAN, ELLEN WAS 036 2ND SUBD
BUCHANAN, HARIET WAS 027 2ND SUBD
BUCHANAN, J. M. ALL 147 6TH E.D.
BUCHANAN, JAMES BAL 258 12TH WAR
BUCHANAN, JAMES MGM 329 CRACKLIN
BUCHANAN, JAMES A. BAL 058 10TH WAR
BUCHANAN, JAMES M. BAL 177 2ND DIST
BUCHANAN, JANE BAL 243 20TH WAR
BUCHANAN, JOHN CEC 027 CHESAPEA
BUCHANAN, JOHN WAS 020 2ND SUBD
BUCHANAN, LEWIS CEC 009 ELKTON 3
BUCHANAN, MARGARET BAL 072 10TH WAR
BUCHANAN, MARY BAL 243 1ST DIST
BUCHANAN, MARY BAL 082 4TH WARD
BUCHANAN, MISS A. FRE 199 5TH E DI
BUCHANAN, MISS J. FRE 199 5TH E DI
BUCHANAN, MORIAH CAR 284 7TH DIST
BUCHANAN, SUSAN BAL 062 10TH WAR
BUCHANAN, THOMAS E. WAS 027 2ND SUBD
BUCHANAN, VICTORIA WAS 062 2ND SUBD
BUCHANAN, WILLIAM BAL 282 2ND WARD
BUCHANNA, HARRIET BAL 194 5TH DIST
BUCHANNAN, ANDREW BAL 027 9TH WARD
BUCHANNAN, ANN C. TAL 002 EASTON D
BUCHANNAN, ARAMINTA BAL 242 6TH WARD
BUCHANNAN, ELLEN TAL 002 EASTON D
BUCHANNAN, H.* TAL 003 EASTON D
BUCHANNAN, JARRET BAL 333 3RD WARD
BUCHANNAN, JOHN BAL 025 9TH WARD
BUCHANNAN, SAMUEL CEC 210 7TH E DI
BUCHANNAN, SAMUEL CEC 215 7TH E DI
BUCHANNON, R. H.* BAL 349 3RD WARD
BUCHANNOW, R. H.* BAL 349 3RD WARD
BUCHANON, HENRY BAL 318 1ST DIST
BUCHANON, TABITHA BAL 033 4TH WARD
BUCHANON, THOMAS BAL 201 11TH WAR
BUCHEIMER, CONRAD FRE 206 BUCKEYST
BUCHEN, ALBERT CAR 187 8TH DIST
BUCHEN, CATHARINE CAR 174 8TH DIST
BUCHEN, ELLEN BAL 242 1ST DIST
BUCHEN, HENRY Z. CAR 186 8TH DIST
BUCHEN, JOHN Z. CAR 185 8TH DIST
BUCHER, ADAM CAR 344 6TH DIST
BUCHER, JACOB WAS 171 FUNKSTOW
BUCHER, MICHAEL WAS 282 1ST DIST
BUCHER, NOAH BAL 237 1ST DIST
BUCHHIMER, PETER BAL 038 4TH WARD
BUCHINHAN, MARY BAL 114 18TH WAR
BUCHMAN, SAMUEL WAS 296 1ST DIST
BUCHNEB, JOHN BAL 426 8TH WARD
BUCHNER, CONRAD BAL 029 15TH WAR
BUCHSTON, WILLIAM WAS 072 2ND SUBD
BUCHT, SOPHIE BAL 238 12TH WAR
BUCHTA, JOHN BAL 088 10TH WAR
BUCHTENHAM, SARAH CEC 158 PORT DUP
BUCHWALTER, ABRAHAM BAL 052 15TH WAR
BUCK, AGNES BAL 447 14TH WAR
BUCK, ALEXANDER K. BAL 262 1ST DIST
BUCK, ALFRED BAL 447 14TH WAR
BUCK, ANDREW CEC 027 CHESAPEA
BUCK, ANGELINE CEC 028 CHESAPEA
BUCK, ANN CEC 010 ELKTON 3
BUCK, ANNA BAL 046 2ND DIST
BUCK, BENJAMIN BAL 277 2ND WARD
BUCK, BENJAMIN C. BAL 446 14TH WAR
BUCK, BENJAMIN G. BAL 021 18TH WAR
BUCK, BENJAMIN M. BAL 068 2ND DIST
BUCK, BENJAMIN-BLACK BAL 217 2ND WARD
BUCK, CATHARINE M. BAL 215 6TH WARD
BUCK, CHARLES HAR 141 2ND DIST
BUCK, CHARLES C. BAL 021 18TH WAR
BUCK, CHARLOTTE BAL 098 10TH WAR
BUCK, ELIZA J. BAL 176 16TH WAR
BUCK, F. BAL 165 1ST WARD
BUCK, FREDERICK BAL 071 1ST WARD
BUCK, GEORGE BAL 021 9TH WARD
BUCK, GEORGE WAS 142 HAGERSTO
BUCK, HENRY CAL 018 1ST DIST
BUCK, HIRAM WAS 074 2ND SUBD
BUCK, JAEMS A. ST 286 2ND E DI
BUCK, JAMES BAL 285 12TH WAR
BUCK, JAMES BAL 458 8TH WARD
BUCK, JAMES B. BAL 171 16TH WAR
BUCK, JOHN BAL 012 9TH WARD
BUCK, JOHN BAL 013 15TH WAR
BUCK, JOHN BAL 102 1ST WARD
BUCK, JOHN ANN 268 ANNAPOLI
BUCK, JOHN CAR 107 NO TWP L
BUCK, JOHN BAL 087 4TH WARD
BUCK, JOHN M. BAL 082 18TH WAR
BUCK, JOHN Q. BAL 093 18TH WAR
BUCK, JOHN SR. WAS 073 2ND SUBD
BUCK, JOHN 2ND WAS 073 2ND SUBD
BUCK, JOSEPH WAS 082 2ND SUBD
BUCK, JOSEPH A. BAL 030 15TH WAR
BUCK, JOSHUA BAL 012 4TH WARD
BUCK, JULIA BAL 346 3RD WARD
BUCK, LEWIS F. BAL 052 4TH WARD
BUCK, LOUIS BAL 116 5TH WARD
BUCK, MARGARETT BAL 065 4TH WARD
BUCK, MARIA BAL 004 1ST WARD
BUCK, MARY BAL 298 12TH WAR
BUCK, MARY BAL 031 9TH WARD
BUCK, MARY BAL 158 6TH WARD
BUCK, MARY BAL 429 14TH WAR
BUCK, MILES BAL 099 2ND DIST
BUCK, MRS. J. BAL 015 18TH WAR
BUCK, NANCY DOR 330 3RD DIVI
BUCK, NATHANIEL H. BAL 054 4TH WARD
BUCK, OLIVIA HAR 203 3RD DIST
BUCK, ROBERT BAL 122 18TH WAR
BUCK, SAMUEL BAL 339 3RD WARD
BUCK, SARAH BAL 012 1ST WARD
BUCK, SARAH BAL 005 15TH WAR
BUCK, SARAH-BLACK BAL 218 2ND WARD
BUCK, SOPHIA BAL 244 12TH WAR
BUCK, THOAMS BAL 346 13TH WAR
BUCK, THOMAS BAL 059 10TH WAR
BUCK, WILLIAM BAL 047 9TH WARD
BUCK, WILLIAM FRE 054 FREDERIC
BUCK, WILLIAM H. BAL 053 4TH WARD
BUCKALEW, JOHN HAR 046 1ST DIST
BUCKANAN, MATILDA * KEN 269 1ST DIST
BUCKANAN, SMAUEL BAL 073 2ND DIST
BUCKANAN, WILLIAM SOM 454 DAMES QU
BUCKANNAW, L. B. BAL 183 11TH WAR
BUCKARMAN, JAMES KEN 241 2ND DIST
BUCKELS, HENRY WAS 068 2ND SUBD
BUCKELS, MARY BAL 340 7TH WARD
BUCKEN, ULERICK Z. CAR 184 8TH DIST
BUCKENHAM, MARY FRE 378 PETERSVI
BUCKENHART, JACOB CEC 149 PORT DUP
BUCKENTRAN, N.G. HAR 155 3RD DIST
BUCKER, ABRAM BAL 006 EASTERN
BUCKER, BARNEY ALL 155 6TH E.D.
BUCKER, DAVID ALL 159 6TH E.D.
BUCKER, DAVID CAR 183 8TH DIST
BUCKER, GEORGE BAL 007 EASTERN
BUCKER, HENRY FRE 411 8TH E DI
BUCKER, JOHN ALL 179 7TH E.D.
BUCKER, JOHN S. FRE 002 FREDERIC
BUCKER, WILLIAM CEC 064 1ST E DI
BUCKERT, JOHN BAL 202 2ND WARD

BUCKERT, RICHARD-MULATTO FRE 418 8TH E DI
BUCKERYHAW, MATILDA FRE 266 NEW MARK
BUCKEY, ADMANA BAL 370 13TH WAR
BUCKEY, ADRIAN BAL 370 13TH WAR
BUCKEY, ANN BAL 264 12TH WAR
BUCKEY, CATHERINE FRE 060 FREDERIC
BUCKEY, CHARLOTT FRE 046 FREDERIC
BUCKEY, EDWARD FRE 075 FREDERIC
BUCKEY, ESRA FRE 432 8TH E DI
BUCKEY, JACOB M. FRE 207 BUCKEYST
BUCKEY, JAMES ALL 249 CUMBERLA
BUCKEY, JAOCB FRE 009 FREDERIC
BUCKEY, JULIAN FRE 264 NEW MARK
BUCKEY, JULIET WAS 036 2ND SUBD
BUCKEY, MARION E.H. FRE 045 FREDERIC
BUCKEY, MARY R. FRE 207 BUCKEYST
BUCKEY, SARAH ALL 222 CUMBERLA
BUCKEY, SARAH BAL 264 12TH WAR
BUCKEY, V.A. ALL 205 CUMBERLA
BUCKHAM, LOFIRE HAR 163 3RD DIST
BUCKHAN, GEORGE HAR 151 3RD DIST
BUCKHANAN, ABRAHAM HAR 024 1ST DIST
BUCKHANAN, EDWARD HAR 023 1ST DIST
BUCKHANAN, JOHN HAR 024 1ST DIST
BUCKHANAN, JOSHUA HAR 025 1ST DIST
BUCKHANON, GEORGE CAL 017 1ST DIST
BUCKHANON, LARKIN CAR 215 5TH DIST
BUCKHANON, OCTAVIS CAR 214 5TH DIST
BUCKHARDT, J. L. BAL 469 14TH WAR
BUCKHART, JOSEPH CEC 116 3RD E DI
BUCKHEAD, CHRISTOPHER BAL 013 1ST WARD
BUCKHEAD, HUGH BAL 389 13TH WAR
BUCKINGHA, THOMAS B. CAR 371 9TH DIST
BUCKINGHAM, ANNE BAL 054 15TH WAR
BUCKINGHAM, ARCHIBALD ANN 508 HOWARD D
BUCKINGHAM, BEAL CAR 371 9TH DIST
BUCKINGHAM, BRICE BAL 366 1ST DIST
BUCKINGHAM, CATHARINE CAR 389 2ND DIST
BUCKINGHAM, CATHARINE FRE 450 8TH E DI
BUCKINGHAM, CATHARINE FRE 441 8TH E DI
BUCKINGHAM, CHARLES E. BAL 181 16TH WAR
BUCKINGHAM, CORDELIA BAL 006 15TH WAR
BUCKINGHAM, CORDELIA BAL 006 15TH WAR
BUCKINGHAM, DAVID CAR 361 9TH DIST
BUCKINGHAM, ELIAS CAR 332 MANCHEST
BUCKINGHAM, ELISHA CAR 202 4TH DIST
BUCKINGHAM, ELIZA CAR 195 4TH DIST
BUCKINGHAM, ELIZA T. ANN 427 HOWARD D
BUCKINGHAM, ELIZABETH FRE 433 8TH E DI
BUCKINGHAM, ELIZABETH A. HAR 083 2ND DIST
BUCKINGHAM, EPHRAIM CAR 225 5TH DIST
BUCKINGHAM, GEORGE CAR 225 5TH DIST
BUCKINGHAM, GEORGE BAL 114 18TH WAR
BUCKINGHAM, GREENBURY BAL 366 1ST DIST
BUCKINGHAM, HARRIETT FRE 377 PETERSVI
BUCKINGHAM, HESTER V. BAL 269 7TH WARD
BUCKINGHAM, ISAIAH BAL 232 12TH WAR
BUCKINGHAM, JAMES BAL 186 6TH WARD
BUCKINGHAM, JESSE ANN 505 HOWARD D
BUCKINGHAM, JOHN CAR 280 7TH DIST
BUCKINGHAM, JOHN E. BAL 131 18TH WAR
BUCKINGHAM, JOHN W FRE 248 NEW MARK
BUCKINGHAM, JOHN W. ANN 508 HOWARD D
BUCKINGHAM, LAAH BAL 223 1ST DIST
BUCKINGHAM, LARKIN CAR 367 9TH DIST
BUCKINGHAM, LEMUAL CAR 232 5TH DIST
BUCKINGHAM, LEONARD J. CAR 360 9TH DIST
BUCKINGHAM, MARACA CAR 223 5TH DIST
BUCKINGHAM, MARY BAL 232 12TH WAR
BUCKINGHAM, MARY BAL 249 2ND WARD
BUCKINGHAM, MARY J. CAR 226 5TH DIST
BUCKINGHAM, MICHAEL ANN 426 HOWARD D
BUCKINGHAM, NICHOLAS CAR 202 4TH DIST
BUCKINGHAM, NIMROD CAR 366 9TH DIST
BUCKINGHAM, OBEDIAH CAR 211 5TH DIST
BUCKINGHAM, OBEDIAH CAR 194 4TH DIST
BUCKINGHAM, OLIVER P. CAR 214 5TH DIST
BUCKINGHAM, OLIVIA BAL 393 14TH WAR
BUCKINGHAM, OWEN CAR 195 4TH DIST
BUCKINGHAM, OWEN F. CAR 195 4TH DIST
BUCKINGHAM, PERSY G.* BAL 397 3RD WARD
BUCKINGHAM, THOMAS B. FRE 441 8TH E DI
BUCKINGHAM, VACHEL CAR 281 7TH DIST
BUCKINGHAM, WILLIAM CAR 204 4TH DIST
BUCKINGHAM, WILLIAM FRE 387 PETERSVI
BUCKINGHAM, WILLIAM FRE 406 JEFFERSO
BUCKINGHAM, WILLIAM CAR 413 2ND DIST
BUCKINGHAM, WILLIAM HAR 079 2ND DIST
BUCKINGHAM, WILLIAM H. BAL 314 7TH WARD
BUCKINHAM, JAMES R. BAL 124 11TH WAR
BUCKINTRAM, LANSON FRE 377 PETERSVI
BUCKL, WILLIAM F. CEC 137 6TH E DI
BUCKLE, CHARLES BAL 076 2ND DIST
BUCKLER, ALEXANDER ST 341 5TH E DI
BUCKLER, BENEDICT ST 270 3RD E DI
BUCKLER, CHRISTINA BAL 110 10TH WAR
BUCKLER, E. BAL 106 10TH WAR
BUCKLER, E. LOUISA ST 320 4TH E DI
BUCKLER, ELIZABETH BAL 056 18TH WAR
BUCKLER, ELZIABETH ST 334 4TH E DI
BUCKLER, GEORGE CAL 026 2ND DIST
BUCKLER, GEORGE W. ST 261 3RD E DI
BUCKLER, GEORGE W. L. ST 261 3RD E DI
BUCKLER, JAMES L. CAL 015 1ST DIST
BUCKLER, JOHN BAL 106 10TH WAR
BUCKLER, JOHN H. ST 325 4TH E DI
BUCKLER, LEONARD BAL 109 1ST WARD
BUCKLER, THOMAS CHA 283 BOJANTOW
BUCKLER, THOMAS H. BAL 109 10TH WAR
BUCKLESS, HENRY BAL 396 3RD WARD
BUCKLEY, ARNOLD* TAL 043 EASTON D
BUCKLEY, BENJAMIN C. CEC 154 PORT DUP
BUCKLEY, BENNETT TAL 066 EASTON T
BUCKLEY, CATHARINE BAL 292 7TH WARD
BUCKLEY, CATHERINE BAL 405 8TH WARD
BUCKLEY, CATHERINE BAL 053 4TH WARD
BUCKLEY, CHARLES TAL 005 EASTON D
BUCKLEY, CORNEALOUS CAR 195 4TH DIST
BUCKLEY, D. G. BAL 149 1ST WARD
BUCKLEY, D.G. BAL 123 1ST WARD
BUCKLEY, DANIEL BAL 010 9TH WARD
BUCKLEY, DANIEL BAL 445 1ST DIST
BUCKLEY, DAVID L. BAL 245 17TH WAR
BUCKLEY, DAVID T. BAL 219 17TH WAR
BUCKLEY, EDMOND BAL 445 1ST DIST
BUCKLEY, EDMUND BAL 179 2ND DIST
BUCKLEY, ELIJAH BAL 143 2ND DIST
BUCKLEY, FIDELUS BAL 145 5TH WARD
BUCKLEY, HANNA* TAL 053 EASTON D
BUCKLEY, HANNAH BAL 428 1ST DIST
BUCKLEY, HANNAH BAL 041 9TH WARD
BUCKLEY, JAMES E. CEC 129 6TH E DI
BUCKLEY, JOHN HAR 141 2ND DIST
BUCKLEY, JOHN BAL 449 1ST DIST
BUCKLEY, JOHN BAL 024 2ND DIST
BUCKLEY, JOHN BAL 425 8TH WARD
BUCKLEY, JOHN J. BAL 218 6TH WARD
BUCKLEY, MARGARET BAL 160 19TH WAR
BUCKLEY, MARGARET WAS 045 2ND SUBD
BUCKLEY, MARY BAL 016 4TH WARD
BUCKLEY, MARY BAL 341 7TH WARD
BUCKLEY, MICHAEL BAL 010 9TH WARD
BUCKLEY, NATHANIEL D. CEC 118 4TH E DI
BUCKLEY, PATRICK BAL 447 1ST DIST
BUCKLEY, ROBERT BAL 042 9TH WARD
BUCKLEY, SAMUEL BAL 001 EASTERN
BUCKLEY, SAMUEL CAR 158 NO TWP L
BUCKLEY, SUSANNA BAL 115 5TH WARD
BUCKLEY, THERESE BAL 218 6TH WARD
BUCKLEY, THOMAS BAL 226 6TH WARD
BUCKLEY, THOMAS BAL 120 1ST WARD
BUCKLEY, THOMS BAL 131 1ST WARD
BUCKLEY, TIMOTHY ALL 249 CUMBERLA
BUCKLEY, WILLIAM BAL 039 1ST WARD
BUCKLIN, EDWORD HAR 203 3RD DIST
BUCKLY, ANDREW CEC 195 6TH E DI
BUCKLY, ANN CEC 168 6TH E DI
BUCKLY, BENJAMIN P. CEC 166 6TH E DI
BUCKLY, GEORGE W. FRE 265 NEW MARK
BUCKLY, JAMES BAL 455 14TH WAR
BUCKLY, JOHN CEC 202 6TH E DI
BUCKLY, JOHN CEC 067 5TH E DI
BUCKLY, JOHN M. CEC 167 6TH E DI
BUCKLY, JOHN W. CEC 163 6TH E DI
BUCKLY, MARY ALL 234 CUMBERLA
BUCKLY, SAMUEL BAL 075 1ST WARD
BUCKLY, WILLIAM P. CEC 006 ELKTON 3
BUCKMAN, FRANCIS BAL 056 1ST WARD
BUCKMAN, GEORGE BAL 249 1ST DIST
BUCKMAN, JAMES E. BAL 116 18TH WAR
BUCKMAN, LOUISA BAL 387 13TH WAR
BUCKMAN, M. BAL 158 1ST WARD
BUCKMAN, MARY A. BAL 008 18TH WAR
BUCKMAN, SAMUEL BAL 010 EASTERN
BUCKMAN, SUSAN BAL 268 1ST DIST
BUCKMAN, THOMAS BAL 290 1ST DIST
BUCKMAN, WILLIAM P. BAL 373 1ST DIST
BUCKMASTER, ALEXANDER CAL 035 2ND DIST
BUCKMASTER, ELIZA BAL 129 16TH WAR
BUCKMASTER, ELIZABETH CAL 035 2ND DIST
BUCKMASTER, GUSTAVUS CAL 035 2ND DIST
BUCKMASTER, JAMES CAL 033 2ND DIST
BUCKMASTER, JAMES CAL 030 2ND DIST
BUCKMASTER, JOHN CAL 031 2ND DIST
BUCKMASTER, SAMUEL CAL 033 2ND DIST
BUCKMASTER, SEWYLEN CAL 027 2ND DIST
BUCKMASTER, WILLIAM CAL 026 2ND DIST
BUCKMILLER, REBECCA BAL 218 6TH WARD
BUCKMILLER, ROBERT S. BAL 206 11TH WAR
BUCKMILLER, WILLIAM BAL 397 8TH WARD
BUCKNER, JOSEPH BAL 071 2ND DIST
BUCKRIDGE, ALFRED CAR 336 6TH DIST
BUCKS, CHARLES W. BAL 011 4TH WARD
BUCKSBAUM, HENRY BAL 248 2ND WARD
BUCKSBAURN, J. BAL 247 2ND WARD
BUCKSEED, WILLIAM ALL 251 CUMBERLA
BUCKSMYER, MICHAEL BAL 287 1ST DIST
BUCKSON, THOMAS-BLACK CAR 136 NO TWP L
BUCKSTON, SUSAN BAL 361 8TH WARD
BUCKSTONE, BENJAMIN BAL 011 1ST WARD
BUCKWITH, CHARLES CEC 034 CHESAPEA
BUCKWITH, JOHN CEC 034 CHESAPEA
BUCKWITH, MARY CEC 068 5TH E DI
BUCKY, GEORGE P. FRE 265 NEW MARK
BUCLKER, ROBERT CAL 026 2ND DIST
BUCTA, CATHARINE W. BAL 098 5TH WARD
BUD, JAMES CHA 283 BOJANTOW
BUD, MARY BAL 232 1ST DIST
BUD, THOMAS J. BAL 232 1ST DIST
BUDD, ANTONY BAL 113 2ND DIST
BUDD, ARTAMACY CHA 238 HILLTOP
BUDD, CECELIA CHA 269 ALLENS F
BUDD, CHARLES MGM 321 CRACKLIN
BUDD, DANIEL MGM 332 CRACKLIN
BUDD, DANIEL MGM 327 CRACKLIN
BUDD, ELIZA MGM 316 CRACKLIN
BUDD, GEORGE MGM 331 CRACKLIN
BUDD, GEORGE MGM 370 BERRYS D
BUDD, GEORGE BAL 121 1ST WARD
BUDD, HAMILTON MGM 327 CRACKLIN
BUDD, HENRY FRE 027 FREDERIC
BUDD, JOHN R. BAL 039 1ST WARD
BUDD, JOHN T. CHA 269 ALLENS F
BUDD, MARY A. MGM 316 CRACKLIN
BUDD, MILCAH HAR 160 3RD DIST
BUDD, PERRY MGM 321 CRACKLIN
BUDDING, HENRY BAL 131 2ND DIST
BUDDY, LEWIS BAL 139 2ND DIST
BUDDY,PHILIP ALL 243 CUMBERLA
BUDENMEYER, WILLIAM BAL 063 1ST WARD
BUDGET, NIMRAD CAR 204 4TH DIST
BUDK, AGNESS BAL 378 1ST DIST
BUDLEY, PERRY BAL 241 20TH WAR
BUDNER, LEWIS BAL 081 1ST WARD
BUEE, WILLIAM D. BAL 304 12TH WAR
BUEHANECN, PHILIP FRE 202 5TH E DI
BUEHL, JOHN BAL 282 20TH WAR
BUEL, D.H. WAS 021 2ND SUBD
BUELER, OLIVER BAL 149 11TH WAR
BUELL, E.H. PRI 107 PISCATAW
BUEN, WILLIAM BAL 078 1ST WARD
BUER, JOHN ALL 111 5TH E.D.
BUERALL, ADAM FRE 253 NEW MARK
BUFELT, JAMES BAL 122 1ST WARD
BUFFIN, EDWARD FRE 305 WOODSBOR
BUFFINGTON, ABRAHAM CAR 324 1ST DIST
BUFFINGTON, ALEXANDER FRE 411 8TH E DI
BUFFINGTON, ALEXANDER FRE 426 8TH E DI
BUFFINGTON, ANN E. FRE 411 8TH E DI
BUFFINGTON, DAVID CAR 317 1ST DIST
BUFFINGTON, ISAAC FRE 288 WOODSBOR
BUFFINGTON, JESSEE CEC 103 4TH E DI
BUFFINGTON, LEVI CAR 241 TANEYTOW
BUFFINGTON, MARGARET FRE 425 8TH E DI
BUFFINGTON, SUSAN A. FRE 414 8TH E DI
BUFFINGTON, WILLIAM CAR 323 1ST DIST
BUFFORD, CHRISTIAN C.* BAL 397 3RD WARD
BUFFUS, ABRAHAM CAR 273 WESTMINS
BUGBY, EDWARD L. WAS 154 HAGERSTO
BUGBY, ELIJAH BAL 462 1ST DIST
BUGBY, JOSEPH A. BAL 293 3RD WARD
BUGEE, MATILDA BAL 306 1ST DIST
BUGER, ADAM FRE 354 MIDDLETO
BUGGS, ROBERT CEC 125 5TH E DI
BUGHMYER, CHRISTOPHER ALL 175 7TH E.D.
BUGLEY, YENCE BAL 307 12TH WAR
BUHANAN, ELIZABETH BAL 067 10TH WAR
BUHARD, W. BAL 138 1ST WARD
BUHL, HENRY BAL 386 13TH WAR
BUHOFF, GEORGE BAL 240 17TH WAR
BUHRE, ELIZABETH BAL 035 15TH WAR
BUHRMAN, CELIA A. FRE 154 10TH E D
BUHRMAN, CORNELIAN * FRE 151 10TH E D
BUHRMAN, DANIEL FRE 150 10TH E D
BUHRMAN, GEORGE FRE 153 10TH E D
BUHRMAN, HANNAH E. FRE 150 10TH E D
BUHRMAN, HENRY FRE 148 10TH E D
BUHRMAN, HENRY FRE 156 10TH E D
BUHRMAN, JACOB FRE 153 10TH E D
BUHRMAN, JACOB SR. FRE 156 10TH E D
BUHRMAN, JOHN FRE 154 10TH E D
BUICE, JAMES-MULATTO FRE 425 8TH E DI
BUICKET, MOSES BAL 102 2ND DIST
BUILER, WILLIAM BAL 300 17TH WAR
BUIN, PETER BAL 281 12TH WAR
BUIS, HANS ALL 244 CUMBERLA
BUJAC, JAMES BAL 331 1ST DIST
BUKAMP, FRANCIS BAL 293 12TH WAR
BUKENBAUGH, WILLIAM W. FRE 115 CREAGERS
BUKER,AARVA BAL 100 1ST WARD
BUKER,LEVI CAR 386 2ND DIST
BUKLEY, MARY BAL 449 1ST DIST
BULA, ELIZA BAL 317 1ST DIST
BULACK, JOSEPH BAL 328 13TH WAR
BULASH, ADELINE BAL 436 14TH WAR
BULB, HENRY ANN 332 2ND DIST
BULDING, MATILDA CAR 115 NO TWP L
BULEN, MARGARET BAL 307 12TH WAR
BULEN, MARY BAL 128 11TH WAR
BULER, CHARLES BAL 273 17TH WAR
BULER, ELIZABETH CEC 081 CHARLEST
BULER, SUSAN WAS 036 2ND SUBD
BULER, VINTON WAS 038 2ND SUBD
BULET, SAMUEL BAL 440 1ST DIST
BULETTE, WILLIAM A. BAL 180 6TH WARD
BULEY, GEORGE BAL 108 10TH WAR
BULEY, MARTHA A. BAL 374 3RD WARD
BULEY, PICKERING BAL 132 2ND DIST
BULGER, ELLEN CEC 016 ELKTON 3
BULGER, MICHAEL BAL 160 19TH WAR
BULGER, PATRICK BAL 386 8TH WARD
BULGINE, MARY BAL 360 3RD WARD
BULKLY, JOHN BAL 126 1ST WARD
BULL, AMANDA BAL 326 12TH WAR
BULL, AMBROSE BAL 199 5TH DIST
BULL, AMBROSE T. BAL 435 1ST DIST
BULL, ANN BAL 439 14TH WAR
BULL, ANN E. HAR 109 2ND DIST
BULL, BENNETT HAR 111 2ND DIST
BULL, CARRY ANN 288 ANNAPOLI
BULL, CHRISTOPHER BAL 216 6TH DIST
BULL, CHRISTOPHER BAL 218 6TH DIST
BULL, E. BAL 162 6TH WARD
BULL, EDMOND HAR 110 2ND DIST
BULL, EDMUND BAL 255 12TH WAR
BULL, EMANUEL BAL 009 EASTERN
BULL, G.H. BAL 133 1ST WARD
BULL, ISAAC BAL 334 3RD WARD
BULL, JACOB BAL 456 1ST DIST
BULL, JACOB H. BAL 198 5TH DIST
BULL, JAMES BAL 214 6TH DIST
BULL, JAMES HAR 111 2ND DIST
BULL, JAMES HAR 109 2ND DIST
BULL, JAMES MGM 391 ROCKERLE
BULL, JOHN HAR 111 2ND DIST
BULL, JOHN BAL 249 20TH WAR
BULL, JOHN B. BAL 435 1ST DIST
BULL, JOHN E. HAR 087 2ND DIST
BULL, JOHN OF NICHOLAS BAL 434 1ST DIST
BULL, JOSEPH BAL 208 6TH DIST
BULL, LODMAN BAL 025 2ND DIST
BULL, MARY BAL 278 7TH WARD
BULL, MARY BAL 297 12TH WAR
BULL, MARY HAR 069 1ST DIST
BULL, MARY MGM 392 ROCKERLE
BULL, MARY HAR 059 1ST DIST
BULL, MARY A. BAL 393 8TH WARD
BULL, MARY E. BAL 262 1ST DIST
BULL, MARY E. HAR 095 2ND DIST
BULL, NATHANIEL WOR 247 1ST CENS
BULL, NICHOLAS BAL 040 2ND DIST
BULL, NICHOLAS BAL 435 1ST DIST
BULL, NICHOLAS BAL 165 6TH WARD
BULL, NICHOLAS H. BAL 199 5TH DIST
BULL, PHILLIP BAL 263 2ND WARD
BULL, RUTH BAL 435 1ST DIST
BULL, SAMUEL BAL 213 6TH DIST
BULL, SARAH BAL 254 12TH WAR
BULL, SHADRACK BAL 303 12TH WAR
BULL, SUSAN HAR 111 2ND DIST
BULL, TEMPERANCE BAL 305 12TH WAR
BULL, THOMAS BAL 219 6TH DIST
BULL, V. E. BAL 328 13TH WAR
BULL, WASHINGTON BAL 009 EASTERN
BULL, WILLIAM BAL 040 2ND DIST
BULL, WILLIAM HAR 109 2ND DIST
BULL, WILLIAM HAR 111 2ND DIST
BULL, WILLIAM HAR 018 1ST DIST
BULLAN, JAMES BAL 305 20TH WAR
BULLANTYNE, GEORGE PRI 107 PISCATAW
BULLEN, ANN TAL 046 EASTON T
BULLEN, ANN* TAL 040 EASTON D
BULLEN, CHARLES BAL 171 16TH WAR
BULLEN, CHARLES BAL 171 16TH WAR
BULLEN, ELIZABETH QUE 225 4TH E DI
BULLEN, JESSE TAL 047 EASTON T
BULLEN, JOHN BAL 457 8TH WARD
BULLEN, JOHN CEC 136 6TH E DI
BULLEN, JOHN CEC 031 CHESAPEA
BULLEN, MARTHA A. BAL 212 6TH WARD
BULLEN, MARY F. BAL 215 11TH WAR
BULLEN, NOAH QUE 229 4TH E DI
BULLEN, WILLIAM CEC 097 4TH E DI
BULLEN, WILLIAM BAL 151 16TH WAR
BULLER, ANN* TAL 040 EASTON D
BULLER, CHARLES FRE 115 CREAGERS
BULLER, FRANCIS C. FRE 012 FREDERIC
BULLER, HENRY BAL 377 13TH WAR
BULLER, JACOB QUE 235 4TH E DI
BULLER, JAMES QUE 226 4TH E DI

Name	County	Page	District
BULLER, JESSE	CAR	110	NO TWP L
BULLER, WILLIAM	FRE	195	5TH E DI
BULLERS, MARY J.	BAL	119	2ND DIST
BULLIN, WILLIAM*	TAL	066	EASTON T
BULLING, C.	BAL	043	9TH WARD
BULLINGER, JACOB	FRE	172	5TH E DI
BULLOCH, MARY*	TAL	032	EASTON D
BULLOCK, FREDERICK	BAL	150	2ND DIST
BULLOCK, ISAAC	CEC	169	6TH E DI
BULLOCK, JACOB	CEC	078	NORTHEAS
BULLOCK, JOHN	BAL	123	18TH WAR
BULLOCK, JOHN	ST	276	3RD E DI
BULLOCK, JOHN W.	DOR	321	1ST DIST
BULLOCK, MARY	CEC	122	4TH E DI
BULLOCK, MARY*	TAL	032	EASTON D
BULLOCK, RICHARD	CAR	153	NO TWP L
BULLOCK, SOLOMON	BAL	127	2ND DIST
BULLOCK, THAY	BAL	127	18TH WAR
BULLOCK, THOMAS	CAR	105	NO TWP L
BULLOCK, THOMAS	CEC	121	4TH E DI
BULLOCK, WILLIAM J.	TAL	040	EASTON D
BULLOKC, EZRA	BAL	170	1ST WARD
BULLUCK, WILLIAM	BAL	256	1ST DIST
BULOC, MARY	BAL	055	9TH WARD
BULTON, ELIJAH	ANN	268	ANNAPOLI
BULTON, JOHN	BAL	108	2ND DIST
BULY, GABRIEL-BLACK	CAR	150	NO TWP L
BULY, LEMUEL	BAL	364	1ST DIST
BULY, SOLOMON-BLACK	CAR	150	NO TWP L
BUM, CHARLES	ANN	483	HOWARD D
BUM, MARY	BAL	021	4TH WARD
BUMBERGER, JOHN M.	WAS	213	1ST DIST
BUMBERGER, JOSEPH	WAS	213	1ST DIST
BUMENT, JULIUS	BAL	234	12TH WAR
BUMER, JACKSON	BAL	146	1ST WARD
BUMES, JANE *	BAL	092	18TH WAR
BUMGARDNER, ELIZABETH	FRE	115	CREAGERS
BUMISON, ISAAC	FRE	390	PETERSVI
BUMLES, ELEN	CHA	271	ALLENS F
BUMLEY, CHRISTOPHER	BAL	284	2ND WARD
BUMLEY, JOSEPH	BAL	284	2ND WARD
BUMMER, LAWRENCE	BAL	254	2ND WARD
BUMP, BETSEY *	BAL	065	15TH WAR
BUMP, MARGARET	BAL	184	19TH WAR
BUMS, MARY	WAS	001	WILLIAMS
BUNALL, JOHN	FRE	254	NEW MARK
BUNALL, SOLOMON	FRE	254	NEW MARK
BUNAN, IRA	BAL	243	12TH WAR
BUNBINDA, ANTONIA M. *	BAL	311	1ST DIST
BUNCAN, HIRAM B.	WOR	267	BERLIN 1
BUNCE, EDWARD	BAL	441	8TH WARD
BUNCE, JOHN	BAL	375	8TH WARD
BUNCE, JOHN W.	BAL	192	2ND WARD
BUNCE, REBECA	BAL	396	8TH WARD
BUNCE, RICHARD	WAS	067	2ND SUBD
BUNCE, ROBERT	BAL	267	7TH WARD
BUNCH, ELIZABETH	BAL	327	7TH WARD
BUNCH, ELLEN C.	BAL	331	7TH WARD
BUNCHAROT, W.	BAL	314	12TH WAR
BUNCHE, JAMES A.	BAL	008	1ST WARD
BUNCHNALE, MARY	BAL	435	8TH WARD
BUNDAY, WILLIAM A.	BAL	088	15TH WAR
BUNDICK, DAVID	SOM	554	TYASKIN
BUNDY, M.	BAL	269	20TH WAR
BUNDY, VICTORINE	BAL	169	6TH WARD
BUNE, HENRY	BAL	210	2ND WARD
BUNE, IRIS	BAL	223	19TH WAR
BUNEL, E. C.	BAL	322	12TH WAR
BUNER, GEORGE C.*	BAL	282	20TH WAR
BUNER, NICHOLAS	BAL	254	2ND WARD
BUNGAR, JOHN H.	BAL	314	3RD WARD
BUNGARD, BARBARA	BAL	392	8TH WARD
BUNGS, MARY A.*	BAL	334	3RD WARD
BUNHAM, JOHN	BAL	087	1ST WARD
BUNIS, PAT	BAL	293	12TH WAR
BUNKE, F.	BAL	147	1ST WARD
BUNKIR, JOHN	ANN	425	HOWARD D
BUNN, BRIDGET	BAL	195	2ND WARD
BUNN, E.	BAL	116	1ST WARD
BUNN, HENRY	BAL	087	15TH WAR
BUNN, JACOB	BAL	124	11TH WAR
BUNN, JOHN*	BAL	118	15TH WAR
BUNN, JOSEPH	BAL	082	15TH WAR
BUNN, THOMAS	BAL	213	2ND WARD
BUNNAN, ANN	BAL	352	7TH WARD
BUNNELS, WILLIAM	ANN	367	4TH DIST
BUNNER, PATRICK	ALL	260	CUMBERLA
BUNNILL, SAMUEL	CEC	188	7TH E DI
BUNOHAN, VIRGIL	BAL	051	1ST WARD
BUNORS, N.	BAL	129	1ST WARD
BUNOW, MARGARETT	FRE	405	JEFFERSO
BUNSMAN, ELIZABETH	BAL	214	2ND WARD
BUNSMAN, HENRY	BAL	213	2ND WARD
BUNTAGE, SOPHIA	WOR	285	BERLIN 1
BUNTING, CHARLES	MGM	360	BERRYS D
BUNTING, CHARLOTT E.	WOR	247	1ST CENS
BUNTING, DAVID	BAL	257	17TH WAR
BUNTING, JANE	BAL	193	6TH WARD
BUNTING, JOHN	BAL	407	3RD WARD
BUNTING, REBECCA	CEC	194	7TH E DI
BUNTING, S. K.	BAL	072	18TH WAR
BUNTING, WILLIAM	SOM	413	DUBLIN D
BUNTING, WILLIAM J.	BAL	359	13TH WAR
BUNTON, BROOK	FRE	246	NEW MARK
BUNTON, ELIZABETH*	BAL	053	4TH WARD
BUNTON, GATTY	WOR	243	1ST CENS
BUNTON, ISAAC	WOR	320	1ST E DI
BUNTON, ISAAC	WOR	325	1ST E DI
BUNTON, JOSEPH	WOR	247	1ST CENS
BUNTON, JOSIAH	WOR	247	1ST CENS
BUNTON, JOSIAH *	SOM	413	DUBLIN D
BUNTON, MARY E.	BAL	088	15TH WAR
BUNTON, MERCA	FRE	270	NEW MARK
BUNTON, SAMUEL T.	FRE	272	NEW MARK
BUNTRAM, BERNARD	BAL	078	1ST WARD
BUNTZ, BETSEY	BAL	453	8TH WARD
BUNTZ, JACOB	HAR	161	3RD DIST
BUNTZE, JOHN	HAR	087	2ND DIST
BUNYAN, EDWARD	ANN	498	HOWARD D
BUR, AARON	BAL	270	1ST DIST
BURAGAR, CHARLES	BAL	287	1ST DIST
BURALL, JOHN	ALL	214	CUMBERLA
BURALL, JOSEPH	FRE	279	WOODSBOR
BURALL, SAMUEL	FRE	422	8TH E DI
BURALL, OTHE	ALL	198	CUMBERLA
BURAN, E.	BAL	152	1ST WARD
BURBAGE, ELIJA	WOR	278	BERLIN 1
BURBAGE, ELIZA	WOR	295	9TH E DI
BURBAGE, ISAAC	WOR	216	4TH E DI
BURBAGE, JOHN	WOR	285	BERLIN 1
BURBAGE, JOSEPH	WOR	285	BERLIN 1
BURBAGE, MARGARET A.	WOR	286	BERLIN 1
BURBAGE, PETER	WOR	257	1ST CENS
BURBAGE, SAMPSON	WOR	240	6TH E DI
BURBAGE, WILLIAM	WOR	284	BERLIN 1
BURBAGE, WILLIAM	WOR	283	BERLIN 1
BURBANK, AUGUST	BAL	266	2ND WARD
BURBARD, WILLIAM	ALL	153	6TH E.D.
BURBLY, ALEXANDER	CEC	160	PORT DUP
BURBRIDGE, ELISABETH	ALL	234	CUMBERLA
BURCE, THOMAS	HAR	137	2ND DIST
BURCH, ALEXANDER	CAL	037	2ND DIST
BURCH, BENEDICT F.	CHA	277	BOJANTOW
BURCH, BUCK	PRI	049	AQUASCO
BURCH, COLUMBUS	BAL	013	15TH WAR
BURCH, ELIZABETH	BAL	177	11TH WAR
BURCH, ELIZABETH	CHA	281	BOJANTOW
BURCH, GEORGE	CHA	282	BOJANTOW
BURCH, H.D.	ST	297	2ND E DI
BURCH, ISABEL	CHA	280	BOJANTOW
BURCH, JAMES	MGM	376	ROCKERLE
BURCH, JAMES H.	CHA	231	HILLTOP
BURCH, JAMES M.	CHA	289	MIDDLETO
BURCH, JERRY	CHA	280	BOJANTOW
BURCH, JOHN T.	CHA	286	BOJANTOW
BURCH, LUCY	PRI	049	AQUASCO
BURCH, MARTHA	BAL	050	18TH WAR
BURCH, MARY E.	CHA	274	ALLENS F
BURCH, PHIL	PRI	049	AQUASCO
BURCH, ROBERT Z.	CHA	287	BOJANTOW
BURCH, SUSAN	BAL	206	6TH WARD
BURCH, THOMAS F.	CHA	283	BOJANTOW
BURCH, THOMAS F.	CHA	260	MIDDLETO
BURCH, WILLIAM N.	PRI	067	NOTTINGH
BURCHENAL, ANNA M.	BAL	049	15TH WAR
BURCHENAL, JEREMIAH	CAR	089	NO TWP L
BURCHENAL, WILILAM	QUE	218	3RD E DI
BURCHENAL, WILLIAM S.	CAR	137	NO TWP L
BURCHENEL, JAMES	CAR	096	NO TWP L
BURCHINA, MICHAEL	BAL	045	15TH WAR
BURCHNELL, JOHN	KEN	303	3RD DIST
BURCKHART, ELIZABETH	FRE	035	FREDERIC
BURCKHEART, MARTIN	WAS	289	1ST DIST
BURDAGE, JOHN	CEC	032	CHESAPEA
BURDELL, MILTON	CAR	368	9TH DIST
BURDEN, RHEUBEN	BAL	379	1ST DIST
BURDEN, RICHARD B.	BAL	296	1ST DIST
BURDENER, DAVID	BAL	239	20TH WAR
BURDET, ELIZABETH	MGM	443	CLARKSTR
BURDETT, DAVID	ANN	506	HOWARD D
BURDETT, HARRIET	ANN	509	HOWARD D
BURDETT, MARY A.	MGM	442	CLARKSTR
BURDETT, NICHOLAS	ANN	494	HOWARD D
BURDETT, PHILIP	ANN	493	HOWARD D
BURDETT, RICHARD H.	MGM	432	CLARKSTR
BURDETT, WILLIAM H.	ANN	507	HOWARD D
BURDICK, WILLIAM	BAL	136	1ST WARD
BURDICK, WILLIAM H.	BAL	065	10TH WAR
BURDING, GEORGE	BAL	225	2ND WARD
BURDIT, BENJAMIN	MGM	383	ROCKERLE
BURDIT, ELIZABETH	MGM	435	CLARKSTR
BURDIT, GREENBERRY	MGM	443	CLARKSTR
BURDIT, JAMES	MGM	443	CLARKSTR
BURDIT, LEWIS G.	MGM	436	CLARKSTR
BURDIT, NATHAN	MGM	435	CLARKSTR
BURDIT, SARH B.	MGM	437	CLARKSTR
BURDIT, WILLIAM	MGM	435	CLARKSTR
BURDIT, WLMAN G.	MGM	441	CLARKSTR
BURDIT, ZACHARIAS J. H.	MGM	437	CLARKSTR
BURDITT, ELIZABETH	MGM	341	CLARKSBU
BURDITT, ELIZABETH A.	MGM	332	CRACKLIN
BURDITT, HAMILTON	MGM	340	CLARKSBU
BURDITT, JOHN	MGM	344	CLARKSBU
BURDITT, WILLIAM H.	MGM	345	CLARKSBU
BURONIG, ARBANNA	CAR	137	NO TWP L
BUREALL, SOLOMON	FRE	252	NEW MARK
BUREL, MARY	WAS	129	HAGERSTO
BURFERT, JOHN *	BAL	282	1ST DIST
BURFORD, EDWARD	SOM	510	BARREN C
BURFORD, WILLIAM	MGM	351	BERRYS D
BURG, CATHARINE	BAL	108	5TH WARD
BURGAGE, JOHN	KEN	211	2ND DIST
BURGAIN, ZACHARIA	BAL	071	2ND DIST
BURGAN, CATHARINE	BAL	071	2ND DIST
BURGAN, DEBORAH	BAL	104	2ND DIST
BURGAN, JOHN	BAL	413	1ST DIST
BURGAN, JOSHUA	BAL	103	2ND DIST
BURGAN, NICHOLAS	WAS	159	2ND DIST
BURGAN, PATRICK	BAL	170	11TH WAR
BURGAN, SYLVINA	BAL	074	2ND DIST
BURGAN, THOMAS	BAL	075	2ND DIST
BURGAN, THOMAS	BAL	111	2ND DIST
BURGANE, HENRY	BAL	118	1ST WARD
BURGANTINE, JOHN	CEC	103	4TH E DI
BURGAR, CONROD	BAL	049	18TH WAR
BURGAR, WASH	BAL	271	20TH WAR
BURGATE, JOHN	TAL	107	ST MICHA
BURGDOLL, JOSEPH	WAS	242	CAVETOWN
BURGE, SINGLETON	BAL	300	1ST DIST
BURGEE, ABRAHAM-BLACK	FRE	418	8TH E DI
BURGEE, FREDERICK	FRE	276	NEW MARK
BURGEE, GRAFTON	FRE	276	NEW MARK
BURGEE, ISAAC-BLACK	FRE	419	8TH E DI
BURGEE, LEWIS-BLACK	FRE	048	FREDERIC
BURGEE, MARIAH	FRE	299	WOODSBOR
BURGEE, MARY	ANN	436	HOWARD D
BURGEE, THOMAS	ANN	438	HOWARD D
BURGEE, WILLIAM P.	ANN	435	HOWARD D
BURGELL, EMILINE	BAL	169	19TH WAR
BURGEN, PRICELLA	SOM	465	HANGARY
BURGER, ANN	WAS	242	CAVETOWN
BURGER, CHARLES	ALL	056	10TH E.D
BURGER, GEORGIANNA	BAL	142	11TH WAR
BURGER, HENRY	FRE	083	FREDERIC
BURGER, JACOB	FRE	014	FREDERIC
BURGER, MARY	WAS	277	RIDGEVIL
BURGER, MARY H.	FRE	024	FREDERIC
BURGER, NICHOLAS	BAL	291	17TH WAR
BURGER, THOMAS	ANN	325	2ND DIST
BURGER, WILLIAM	FRE	055	FREDERIC
BURGERS, JULIA	ANN	299	1ST DIST
BURGES, ALBERT	BAL	429	1ST DIST
BURGES, ASBURY	BAL	015	2ND DIST
BURGES, GEORGE	BAL	169	19TH WAR
BURGES, ISRIEL	BAL	427	1ST DIST
BURGES, ISRIEL	BAL	223	1ST DIST
BURGES, JOHN	CHA	246	HILLTOP
BURGES, JOSEPH	BAL	168	19TH WAR
BURGES, JOSEPHENE	BAL	359	3RD WARD
BURGES, LEVI	CEC	077	NORTHEAS
BURGES, MATILDA	PRI	070	MARLBROU
BURGES, NORDICIA	PRI	070	MARLBROU
BURGES, NATHAN	BAL	425	1ST DIST
BURGES, RACHEL	BAL	426	1ST DIST
BURGES, SAMUEL	CEC	077	NORTHEAS
BURGES, SARA	CHA	233	HILLTOP
BURGES, SARAH	BAL	300	1ST DIST
BURGES, SARAH	ANN	403	8TH DIST
BURGES, THOMAS	ANN	275	ANNAPOLI
BURGES, THOMAS	BAL	423	1ST DIST
BURGES, THOMAS V.	CHA	245	HILLTOP
BURGES, WILLIAM	CEC	056	1ST E DI
BURGESS, ABSOLEM	ANN	498	HOWARD D
BURGESS, ALEXANDER	BAL	152	5TH WARD
BURGESS, ALLEN	BAL	291	7TH WARD
BURGESS, ANN	CAL	059	3RD DIST
BURGESS, ANN	KEN	312	3RD DIST
BURGESS, ANN M.	BAL	175	16TH WAR
BURGESS, AQUILLA	FRE	096	FREDERIC
BURGESS, ASBURY	BAL	017	2ND DIST
BURGESS, BARNEY	BAL	334	7TH WARD
BURGESS, BAZEL	BAL	038	18TH WAR
BURGESS, BENJAMIN	BAL	098	18TH WAR
BURGESS, BETSY	BAL	112	5TH WARD
BURGESS, CALEB W.	BAL	234	6TH WARD
BURGESS, CALEB-BLACK	FRE	429	8TH E DI
BURGESS, CATHARINE	PRI	093	MARLBROU
BURGESS, CHARLES	PRI	070	MARLBROU
BURGESS, DEBORAH	MGM	362	BERRYS D
BURGESS, ELEANOR	MGM	393	ROCKERLE
BURGESS, ELIZA	BAL	011	1ST WARD
BURGESS, ELIZABETH	WAS	162	HAGERSTO
BURGESS, ELIZABETH	WAS	152	HAGERSTO
BURGESS, ENOCH M.	PRI	092	MARLBROU
BURGESS, EVAN	ANN	481	HOWARD D
BURGESS, GEORGE	ANN	452	HOWARD D
BURGESS, HANNAH A. S.	BAL	104	15TH WAR
BURGESS, HENREITTA	CAR	327	1ST DIST
BURGESS, HENRIETTA	BAL	444	8TH WARD
BURGESS, HENRY	ANN	434	HOWARD D
BURGESS, HENRY	BAL	162	2ND DIST
BURGESS, HENRY	PRI	003	BLADENSB
BURGESS, HENRY W.	MGM	389	ROCKERLE
BURGESS, JAMES	SOM	502	SALISBUR
BURGESS, JAMES	BAL	336	7TH WARD
BURGESS, JANE	FRE	273	NEW MARK
BURGESS, JEST	BAL	228	12TH WAR
BURGESS, JOHN	ANN	450	HOWARD D
BURGESS, JOHN	ANN	468	HOWARD D
BURGESS, JOHN	ALL	025	2ND E.D.
BURGESS, JOHN	TAL	084	ST MICHA
BURGESS, JOHN A.	PRI	009	BLADENSB
BURGESS, JOHN H.	MGM	390	ROCKERLE
BURGESS, JOHN J.	SOM	516	BARREN C
BURGESS, JOSEPH	PRI	109	PISCATAW
BURGESS, JOSHUA	ANN	508	HOWARD D
BURGESS, JOSIAH	ANN	274	ANNAPOLI
BURGESS, LOAMMI	BAL	073	1CTH WAR
BURGESS, LUCINDA	WAS	043	2ND SUBD
BURGESS, LUCY R.	KEN	210	2ND DIST
BURGESS, MAN	ANN	423	HOWARD D
BURGESS, MARY	ALL	027	2ND E.D.
BURGESS, MARY	PRI	117	PISCATAW
BURGESS, MARY	PRI	008	BLADENSB
BURGESS, MARY J.	TAL	066	EASTON T
BURGESS, MARY-MULATTO	FRE	218	BUCKEYST
BURGESS, NANCY	PRI	120	PISCATAW
BURGESS, NELSON	BAL	162	11TH WAR
BURGESS, OLIVER	BAL	020	2ND DIST
BURGESS, RACHAEL W.	FRE	411	8TH E DI
BURGESS, RACHEAL	FRE	410	8TH E DI
BURGESS, REUBEN	ANN	485	HOWARD D
BURGESS, RICHARD M.	PRI	004	BLADENSB
BURGESS, RODERICK	ANN	485	HOWARD D
BURGESS, SARAH	BAL	242	12TH WAR
BURGESS, SARAH A.	KEN	232	2ND DIST
BURGESS, SARAH J.	QUE	175	2ND E DI
BURGESS, SINGLETON-BLACK	CAR	398	2ND DIST
BURGESS, STEPHEN F.	BAL	351	7TH WARD
BURGESS, THOMAS	ANN	456	HOWARD D
BURGESS, THOMAS	BAL	067	10TH WAR
BURGESS, THOMAS	ANN	511	HOWARD D
BURGESS, THOMAS	PRI	005	BLADENSB
BURGESS, THOMAS D.	KEN	231	2ND DIST
BURGESS, WASHINGTON	FRE	243	NEW MARK
BURGESS, WILLIAM	PRI	002	BLADENSB
BURGESS, WILLIAM	ANN	450	HOWARD D
BURGESS, WILLIAM	BAL	242	12TH WAR
BURGESS, WILLIAM	ALL	054	10TH E.D
BURGESS, WILLIAM H.	BAL	296	7TH WARD
BURGESS, MARY	QUE	149	1ST E DI
BURGET, HENRY	BAL	100	2ND DIST
BURGETT, DANIEL-BLACK	QUE	201	3RD E DI
BURGETT, JOHN-BLACK	QUE	203	3RD E DI
BURGETT, SOLOMON-BLACK	QUE	201	3RD E DI
BURGIE, THOMAS	FRE	271	NEW MARK
BURGIS, CHALES	CAR	067	NO TWP L
BURGIS, ELIZABETH	BAL	195	19TH WAR
BURGISS, ELIZABETGH	BAL	310	12TH WAR
BURGISS, EVAN	MGM	349	BERRYS D
BURGISS, GEORGE T.	CAR	080	NO TWP L
BURGLESSER, DANIEL	WAS	244	SMITHSBU
BURGLESSER, GEORGE	WAS	269	1ST DIST
BURGMAN, FREDRICK	BAL	369	8TH WARD
BURGOIN, AUGUSTUS	BAL	248	5TH WARD
BURGOIN, CLARA	BAL	205	11TH WAR
BURGOON, FRANCIS	CAR	297	7TH DIST
BURGOON, WILLIAM	CAR	259	3RD DIST
BURGOT, ANTHONY	BAL	297	1ST DIST
BURGOT, WILHEMINA	BAL	298	1ST DIST
BURGOYNE, CYRUS R.	CEC	123	3RD E DI
BURGOYNE, ELIZABETH	CEC	106	3RD E DI
BURGOYNE, H.	BAL	142	1ST WARD
BURGOYNE, MARY E.	CEC	128	5TH E DI
BURGOYNE, REBECCA	CEC	197	7TH E DI
BURGOYNE, SARAH L.	CEC	125	5TH E DI
BURGOYNE, SCONIDAS R. *	CEC	126	5TH E DI
BURGUNDER, JOSEPH	ALL	241	CUMBERLA
BURGUNDER, SAMUEL	BAL	013	9TH WARD
BURHAM, CHRISTIAN *	ALL	154	6TH E.D.
BURHAM, DANIEL	BAL	210	11TH WAR
BURHROD, ISAAC *	ANN	304	1ST DIST
BURICE, ROBERT *	HAR	014	1ST DIST
BURICK, JOHN*	DOR	375	1ST DIST
BURICK, JOHN*	DOR	417	1ST DIST
BURICK, SARAH*	DOR	416	1ST DIST
BURIES, THOMAS	ANN	444	HOWARD D
BURIGES, JOHN	ALL	182	8TH E.D.
BURINE, THOMAS	BAL	092	2ND DIST
BURINGHAM, JAMES	BAL	274	2ND WARD

Name	County	Page	District
BURITT, BENEDICT *	KEN	268	1ST DIST
BURK, AMELIA	BAL	359	3RD WARD
BURK, ANDREW	BAL	236	1ST DIST
BURK, ANDREW J.	BAL	393	8TH WARD
BURK, ANN	BAL	383	8TH WARD
BURK, ANN	ALL	218	CUMBERLA
BURK, ANN	BAL	198	11TH WAR
BURK, BARTHOLEMEW	BAL	458	8TH WARD
BURK, BIDDY	BAL	028	4TH WARD
BURK, BIDDY	BAL	021	4TH WARD
BURK, BITTA-BLACK	BAL	220	2ND WARD
BURK, BRIDGET	BAL	027	1ST WARD
BURK, BRIDGET	BAL	012	1ST WARD
BURK, BRIDGET	BAL	098	5TH WARD
BURK, CAROLINE	BAL	423	3RD WARD
BURK, CARROLL	CEC	078	NORTHEAS
BURK, CATHARINE	BAL	133	5TH WARD
BURK, CHAPMAN	CHA	273	ALLENS F
BURK, DAVID	BAL	074	1ST WARD
BURK, DAVID*	BAL	420	3RD WARD
BURK, DOMINICK	BAL	359	8TH WARD
BURK, EDWARD	BAL	014	1ST WARD
BURK, ELISHA	BAL	017	4TH WARD
BURK, ELIZA	BAL	241	17TH WAR
BURK, ELIZA	BAL	153	5TH WARD
BURK, ELIZABETH	CEC	009	ELKTON 3
BURK, ELLEN	BAL	379	3RD WARD
BURK, ELLEN	BAL	406	1ST DIST
BURK, EVE ANN	FRE	277	NEW MARK
BURK, EZEKIEL	BAL	417	8TH WARD
BURK, FREDERICK	HAR	123	2ND DIST
BURK, GEORGE	HAR	175	3RD DIST
BURK, GEORGE W.	BAL	235	1ST DIST
BURK, HENRY	CHA	272	ALLENS F
BURK, ISAAC	FRE	244	NEW MARK
BURK, JACOB	BAL	121	1ST WARD
BURK, JACOB	BAL	387	1ST DIST
BURK, JACOB JR.	BAL	387	1ST DIST
BURK, JAMES	BAL	125	1ST WARD
BURK, JAMES	CAR	241	TANEYTOW
BURK, JAMES K.	WAS	283	1ST DIST
BURK, JAMES M.	BAL	353	7TH WARD
BURK, JESSE	CEC	152	PORT DUP
BURK, JOHANNA	BAL	002	9TH WARD
BURK, JOHN	BAL	457	8TH WARD
BURK, JOHN	BAL	368	3RD WARD
BURK, JOHN	BAL	400	3RD WARD
BURK, JOHN	BAL	398	3RD WARD
BURK, JOHN	BAL	390	1ST DIST
BURK, JOHN	BAL	463	1ST DIST
BURK, JOHN	BAL	462	1ST DIST
BURK, JOHN	BAL	185	6TH WARD
BURK, JOHN	BAL	216	2ND WARD
BURK, JOHN	BAL	037	2ND DIST
BURK, JOHN	BAL	067	4TH WARD
BURK, JOHN	BAL	415	14TH WAR
BURK, JOHN	BAL	198	11TH WAR
BURK, JOHN M.	BAL	457	1ST DIST
BURK, JOHN-BLACK	ST	337	4TH E DI
BURK, JOSEPH	FRE	010	FREDERIC
BURK, JOSEPH *	ANN	397	8TH DIST
BURK, JULIANN	BAL	254	17TH WAR
BURK, MARGARET	BAL	390	1ST DIST
BURK, MARGARET	WAS	212	1ST DIST
BURK, MARTHA	BAL	036	18TH WAR
BURK, MARTIN	BAL	103	18TH WAR
BURK, MARTIN	BAL	027	18TH WAR
BURK, MARTIN	BAL	124	18TH WAR
BURK, MARY	FRE	267	NEW MARK
BURK, MARY	CAR	243	TANEYTOW
BURK, MARY	CEC	072	5TH E DI
BURK, MARY	BAL	151	11TH WAR
BURK, MARY	BAL	151	11TH WAR
BURK, MARY	CHA	283	BOJANTOW
BURK, MARY	HAR	017	1ST DIST
BURK, MARY	BAL	285	7TH WARD
BURK, MARY A.	HAR	153	3RD DIST
BURK, MARY E.	BAL	398	3RD WARD
BURK, MATHEW	BAL	029	4TH WARD
BURK, MONTAGUE	BAL	286	2ND WARD
BURK, NANCY	BAL	074	1ST WARD
BURK, NICHOLAS	BAL	411	8TH WARD
BURK, NICK	BAL	121	5TH WARD
BURK, OWEN	BAL	406	1ST DIST
BURK, PATRICK	BAL	463	1ST DIST
BURK, PATRICK	BAL	409	14TH WAR
BURK, PETER	BAL	381	3RD WARD
BURK, PETER	BAL	187	2ND WARD
BURK, PHILLIP	FRE	009	FREDERIC
BURK, RICHARD	BAL	168	2ND DIST
BURK, SAMUEL	CEC	204	6TH E DI
BURK, SAMUEL	CHA	238	HILLTOP
BURK, SARAH	CEC	193	5TH E DI
BURK, SARAH	BAL	297	7TH WARD
BURK, SARAH	BAL	121	5TH WARD
BURK, STEVEN	WAS	092	2ND SUBD
BURK, STEWART	BAL	415	8TH WARD
BURK, SUSAN	BAL	406	3RD WARD
BURK, T. M.*	BAL	370	3RD WARD
BURK, THEADORE	FRE	003	FREDERIC
BURK, THOMAS	BAL	001	4TH WARD
BURK, THOMAS	CHA	270	ALLENS F
BURK, THOMAS	CEC	102	4TH E DI
BURK, THOMAS	BAL	398	3RD WARD
BURK, THOMAS	BAL	383	8TH WARD
BURK, THOMAS	BAL	037	15TH WAR
BURK, WILLAIM	BAL	154	1ST WARD
BURK, WILLIAM	BAL	418	8TH WARD
BURK, WILLIAM	BAL	406	1ST DIST
BURK, WILLIAM	BAL	444	1ST DIST
BURK, WILLIAM	BAL	387	1ST DIST
BURK, WILLIAM	CAR	240	TANEYTOW
BURK, WILLIAM B.	BAL	087	4TH WARD
BURK, WILLIAM J.	BAL	393	3RD WARD
BURK, ZEKEL	BAL	297	7TH WARD
BURK,RACHAEL-BLACK	BAL	223	2ND WARD
BURKE, ALTHRADE	BAL	076	1ST WARD
BURKE, ANN	ANN	464	HOWARD D
BURKE, CATHARINE	BAL	265	12TH WAR
BURKE, CATHERINE	BAL	172	11TH WAR
BURKE, CECELIA	BAL	219	6TH WARD
BURKE, CHARLES	BAL	010	EASTERN
BURKE, CHARLES	BAL	278	12TH WAR
BURKE, CORNELIUS	BAL	079	10TH WAR
BURKE, D.G.	WAS	021	2ND SUBD
BURKE, DEBORAH	BAL	263	12TH WAR
BURKE, EDWARD	BAL	001	15TH WAR
BURKE, ELIJAH	BAL	086	15TH WAR
BURKE, ELIZABETH	BAL	023	15TH WAR
BURKE, FRANCIS	BAL	248	12TH WAR
BURKE, FRANCIS	BAL	299	20TH WAR
BURKE, G.B.	WAS	021	2ND SUBD
BURKE, GEORGE	BAL	230	12TH WAR
BURKE, GEORGE W.	BAL	196	6TH WARD
BURKE, GEORGE W.	BAL	420	3RD WARD
BURKE, HENRY	PRI	115	PISCATAW
BURKE, HENRY	SOM	502	SALISBUR
BURKE, ISAAC	BAL	264	12TH WAR
BURKE, JAMES	ANN	463	HOWARD D
BURKE, JAMES	BAL	316	3RD WARD
BURKE, JAMES	CEC	043	CHESAPEA
BURKE, JAMES	BAL	041	18TH WAR
BURKE, JAMES	CAL	021	2ND DIST
BURKE, JAMES F.	WOR	197	8TH E DI
BURKE, JANE	BAL	071	15TH WAR
BURKE, JEROME	BAL	228	12TH WAR
BURKE, JIM	CAL	029	2ND DIST
BURKE, JOHN	BAL	402	14TH WAR
BURKE, JOHN	ALL	135	4TH E.D.
BURKE, JOHN	ALL	076	5TH E.D.
BURKE, JOHN	ALL	056	10TH E.D
BURKE, JOHN	PRI	057	NOTTINGH
BURKE, LUCINDA	BAL	312	20TH WAR
BURKE, MARGARET	BAL	226	12TH WAR
BURKE, MARGARET	BAL	255	12TH WAR
BURKE, MARSHALL	WOR	230	6TH E DI
BURKE, MARTIN	ALL	048	10TH E.D
BURKE, MARY	BAL	002	15TH WAR
BURKE, MARY	BAL	247	6TH WARD
BURKE, MARY	BAL	315	12TH WAR
BURKE, MARY	FRE	182	5TH E DI
BURKE, MARY	BAL	164	19TH WAR
BURKE, MATILDA	ANN	336	3RD DIST
BURKE, MICHAEL	ALL	050	10TH E.D
BURKE, NOAH	WOR	230	6TH E DI
BURKE, PATRICK	ALL	057	10TH E.D
BURKE, PATRICK	CAR	241	TANEYTOW
BURKE, PATRICK	BAL	026	18TH WAR
BURKE, PETER	ALL	049	10TH E.D
BURKE, PETER	ALL	119	5TH E.D.
BURKE, PETER	BAL	005	9TH WARD
BURKE, PHOEBE	BAL	237	20TH WAR
BURKE, RICHARD-BLACK	BAL	241	2ND WARD
BURKE, STEPHEN	BAL	126	1ST WARD
BURKE, THOMAS	BAL	220	6TH WARD
BURKE, THOMAS	BAL	025	18TH WAR
BURKE, THOMAS	BAL	159	19TH WAR
BURKE, THOMAS	BAL	419	14TH WAR
BURKE, WALTER L.	BAL	293	20TH WAR
BURKE, WESLEY	BAL	272	20TH WAR
BURKE, WILLIAM	BAL	283	20TH WAR
BURKE, WILLIAM	BAL	235	20TH WAR
BURKE, WILLIAM *	KEN	216	2ND DIST
BURKE, WILLIAM G.	HAR	077	BEL AIR
BURKE, WILLIAM R.	WAS	021	2ND SUBD
BURKE, WILLY	BAL	222	12TH WAR
BURKELIGHT, SUSANNA	FRE	150	10TH E D
BURKER, ANNA	BAL	448	14TH WAR
BURKER, MR.	ANN	284	ANNAPOLI
BURKERT, JOHN-MULATTO	FRE	418	8TH E DI
BURKES, STEPHEN	HAR	175	3RD DIST
BURKET, JANE	FRE	163	EMMITTSB
BURKET, MARTHA	BAL	025	2ND DIST
BURKET, WILLIAM	BAL	440	14TH WAR
BURKET, WILLIAM	FRE	225	BUCKEYST
BURKET,EDWARD	FRE	196	5TH E DI
BURKETT, CHARITY	SOM	530	QUANTICO
BURKETT, FRANK	BAL	140	11TH WAR
BURKETT, JOHN	SOM	532	QUANTICO
BURKETT, RICHARD	CAL	054	3RD DIST
BURKETT, SANDY	SOM	532	QUANTICO
BURKHART, CHARELS H.	FRE	085	FREDERIC
BURKHART, FREDERICK	ALL	189	9TH E.D.
BURKHART, JACOB	WAS	161	HAGERSTO
BURKHART, LEWIS	WAS	041	2ND SUBD
BURKHART, WILLIAM	WAS	279	LEITERSB
BURKHEART, CATHARINE	WAS	202	1ST DIST
BURKHEART, CATHARINE	WAS	205	1ST DIST
BURKHEART, DAVID	WAS	290	1ST DIST
BURKHEART, DAVID	WAS	285	1ST DIST
BURKHEART, ELIZABETH	WAS	126	HAGERSTO
BURKHEART, GEORGE	WAS	275	RIDGEVIL
BURKHEART, JACOB	WAS	278	LEITERSB
BURKHEART, JACOB	WAS	290	1ST DIST
BURKHEART, JACOB	WAS	237	CAVETOWN
BURKHEART, JOHN	WAS	284	1ST DIST
BURKHEART, LAURETTA	WAS	231	1ST DIST
BURKHEART, T. L.	WAS	182	BOONSBOR
BURKHEART, WASHINGTON	WAS	275	RIDGEVIL
BURKHOLDER, SIMON K.	BAL	083	15TH WAR
BURKINS, BALDERSON	HAR	010	1ST DIST
BURKINS, BALSON	HAR	006	1ST DIST
BURKINS, CHARLES	HAR	016	1ST DIST
BURKINS, ISAAC	HAR	034	1ST DIST
BURKINS, ISAAC	HAR	005	1ST DIST
BURKINS, JACOB	HAR	035	1ST DIST
BURKINS, JOHN	HAR	067	1ST DIST
BURKINS, JOSEPH	HAR	060	1ST DIST
BURKINS, JOSEPH E.	HAR	035	1ST DIST
BURKINS, MARTHA	CEC	214	7TH E DI
BURKINS, SARAH	CEC	176	7TH E DI
BURKIS, JAMES	HAR	198	3RD DIST
BURKITT, HENRY	FRE	393	PETERSVI
BURKLEY, ARNOLD*	TAL	043	EASTON D
BURKLEY, HANNA*	TAL	053	EASTON D
BURKLEY, NANCY *	SOM	429	PRINCESS
BURKLY, DANIEL G.	BAL	126	1ST WARD
BURKMAN, ADALINE	WAS	225	1ST DIST
BURKS, DANIEL	KEN	298	3RD DIST
BURKS, ELLEN	WAS	163	HAGERSTO
BURL, JOSAPHENE	WAS	165	HAGERSTO
BURLARGE, ELIZA	BAL	393	14TH WAR
BURLARK, PETER	BAL	037	1ST WARD
BURLES, MARY	BAL	186	11TH WAR
BURLEY, AMAND	BAL	389	1ST DIST
BURLEY, BENJAMIN	BAL	177	16TH WAR
BURLEY, ELSTAND	BAL	192	11TH WAR
BURLEY, GABE	ANN	331	2ND DIST
BURLEY, GABRIEL	ANN	385	4TH DIST
BURLEY, GARRISON	TAL	028	EASTON D
BURLEY, HARRIET	BAL	124	5TH WARD
BURLEY, HENRY	BAL	364	13TH WAR
BURLEY, HESTER	ANN	464	HOWARD D
BURLEY, ISAAC	BAL	244	6TH WARD
BURLEY, ISAAC	BAL	314	7TH WARD
BURLEY, JEREMIAH	BAL	242	6TH WARD
BURLEY, JIM	TAL	017	EASTON D
BURLEY, JOSEPH	ANN	365	4TH DIST
BURLEY, MARY	ST	268	3RD E DI
BURLEY, MARY E.	PRI	043	VANSVILL
BURLEY, MARY J.	BAL	192	11TH WAR
BURLEY, NELLY	ANN	363	4TH DIST
BURLEY, RACHEL	BAL	244	6TH WARD
BURLEY, REBECCA	TAL	017	EASTON D
BURLEY, SARAH *	ANN	337	3RD DIST
BURLEY, THOMAS	PRI	041	VANSVILL
BURLEY, THOMAS *	ANN	318	2ND DIST
BURLIN, JOHN	CEC	197	7TH E DI
BURLINGAME, WALTER	BAL	389	13TH WAR
BURLINS, HUGH F.	CEC	155	PORT DUP
BURLL, MARIAH	CAR	316	1ST DIST
BURLY, MARY A.	ANN	439	HOWARD D
BURM, JOHN	BAL	160	19TH WAR
BURMAKER, NATHAN T.	PRI	023	VANSVILL
BURMAN, BARB *	BAL	303	20TH WAR
BURMAN, FREDERICKA	BAL	009	9TH WARD
BURMAN, HENRY	BAL	133	11TH WAR
BURMAR, MARTIN	PRI	070	MARLBROU
BURMINGHAM, WILLIAM	ANN	402	8TH DIST
BURMINGTON, GEORGE *	WOR	237	6TH E DI
BURMONT, EVAN	CEC	183	7TH E DI
BURMONT, LOUISA	WAS	143	HAGERSTO
BURN, AMBROSE	ALL	109	5TH E.D.
BURN, ANN	BAL	183	2ND WARD
BURN, BRIDGET	BAL	313	1ST DIST
BURN, CATHARINE	BAL	097	5TH WARD
BURN, CATHARINE	CAR	328	MANCHEST
BURN, FRANCES-BLACK	BAL	245	2ND WARD
BURN, JOHN T.	CEC	138	6TH E DI
BURN, LOUISA	BAL	249	20TH WAR
BURN, MARAELUNE	BAL	281	12TH WAR
BURN, MARGARET	BAL	051	9TH WARD
BURN, PATRICK	BAL	048	1ST WARD
BURN, THOMAS H.	TAL	093	ST MICHA
BURN, WILLIAM	CAR	107	NO TWP L
BURN, WILLIAM A.	TAL	079	ST MICHA
BURNAM, EDWARD	BAL	452	1ST DIST
BURNAM, G. G. W.	BAL	372	1ST DIST
BURNAM, GEORGE	BAL	328	1ST DIST
BURNAM, JAMES	BAL	382	1ST DIST
BURNAM, JOHN	BAL	245	1ST DIST
BURNAM, JOHNSEY	BAL	453	1ST DIST
BURNAM, MARY A.	BAL	373	1ST DIST
BURNAM, NANCY	BAL	403	1ST DIST
BURNAM, THOMAS	BAL	142	16TH WAR
BURNAMAN, FRITZ	BAL	091	5TH WARD
BURNAP, ELIZABETH	BAL	319	3RD WARD
BURNAP, GEORGE W.	BAL	065	10TH WAR
BURNAP, NANCY W.	BAL	065	10TH WAR
BURNARD, R.	ALL	216	CUMBERLA
BURNE, BRIDGET	BAL	004	4TH WARD
BURNE, M.	BAL	162	1ST WARD
BURNE, SAMUEL	BAL	157	1ST WARD
BURNE, THOMAS	BAL	175	19TH WAR
BURNEISON, ISAAC	BAL	378	8TH WARD
BURNEL, RUBIN	PRI	074	MARLBROU
BURNELL, E.E.A.	PRI	053	AQUASCO
BURNELL, JAMES	BAL	141	1ST WARD
BURNELL, JOHN	WOR	181	6TH E DI
BURNELL, R.R.	PRI	053	AQUASCO
BURNER, JOHN	FRE	154	10TH E D
BURNER, LOUISA	BAL	291	17TH WAR
BURNES, EDWARD	BAL	108	18TH WAR
BURNES, ELLEN	BAL	114	18TH WAR
BURNES, GEORGE	FRE	154	10TH E D
BURNES, JOHN	WAS	164	2ND DIST
BURNES, JOHN	BAL	182	11TH WAR
BURNES, MICHAEL	BAL	020	9TH WARD
BURNES, MICHEAL	BAL	103	18TH WAR
BURNES, OWEN	BAL	017	1ST WARD
BURNES, WILLAIM	BAL	121	2ND DIST
BURNESTON, ISAAC	BAL	455	14TH WAR
BURNESTON, WILLIAM R.	BAL	398	1ST DIST
BURNET, ABNER	BAL	093	2ND DIST
BURNET, ARA	ANN	343	3RD DIST
BURNET, ELIZABETH	BAL	264	7TH WARD
BURNET, JOSEPH	BAL	011	2ND DIST
BURNET, PHILIP	BAL	133	1ST WARD
BURNETT, AMANDA	FRE	407	JEFFERSO
BURNETT, ASA	HAR	086	2ND DIST
BURNETT, B.F.	BAL	138	1ST WARD
BURNETT, EDETH	WOR	340	1ST E DI
BURNETT, ELIZA	BAL	036	15TH WAR
BURNETT, ELIZA J.	BAL	020	4TH WARD
BURNETT, F.	BAL	152	1ST WARD
BURNETT, GEORGE H.	HAR	087	2ND DIST
BURNETT, HENRY	BAL	346	7TH WARD
BURNETT, JAMES K.	CEC	091	4TH E DI
BURNETT, LEVI	KEN	211	2ND DIST
BURNETT, LUCRITTA	BAL	033	18TH WAR
BURNETT, MARY	SOM	394	BRINKLEY
BURNETT, SAMUEL	CEC	094	4TH E DI
BURNETT, SAMUEL	BAL	137	16TH WAR
BURNETT, SARAH	WOR	342	1ST E DI
BURNETT, WILLIAM	BAL	266	7TH WARD
BURNEY, GEORGE	BAL	051	18TH WAR
BURNEY, GEORGE	BAL	149	19TH WAR
BURNEY, JULIA	BAL	149	19TH WAR
BURNEY, NANCY	BAL	152	19TH WAR
BURNHAM, A.	BAL	170	1ST WARD
BURNHAM, ABSALOM	BAL	179	2ND DIST
BURNHAM, ANN	BAL	185	2ND WARD
BURNHAM, JAMES H.	BAL	353	3RD WARD
BURNHAM, JOHN H.	BAL	060	4TH WARD
BURNHAM, KEZIAH	BAL	195	6TH WARD
BURNHAM, MARY E.	BAL	055	4TH WARD
BURNHAM, WILLIAM	BAL	003	1ST WARD
BURNHEART, MARY E.	ALL	250	CUMBERLA
BURNIER, ABASALOM	FRE	417	8TH E DI
BURNINGHAM, MARY	BAL	171	11TH WAR
BURNINTON, MARY	BAL	133	11TH WAR
BURNIS, ELIZUR *	BAL	305	12TH WAR
BURNISTON, CATHERINE*	BAL	369	3RD WARD
BURNITE, EBAN	CEC	119	3RD E DI
BURNS, ABRAHAM	CAR	219	5TH DIST
BURNS, ABRAHAM	BAL	356	3RD WARD
BURNS, ADAM	CAR	330	MANCHEST
BURNS, AMANDA	BAL	094	5TH WARD
BURNS, ANDREW	BAL	198	2ND WARD
BURNS, ANDREW	BAL	200	2ND WARD
BURNS, ANDREW	BAL	170	19TH WAR
BURNS, ANDREW	WAS	087	2ND SUBD
BURNS, ANN	QUE	165	2ND E DI
BURNS, ANN	MGM	343	CLARKSBU
BURNS, ANN	BAL	173	11TH WAR
BURNS, ARTHUR	BAL	044	9TH WARD
BURNS, BARNARD	BAL	458	1ST DIST
BURNS, BARNEY	BAL	448	1ST DIST
BURNS, BENJAMN	BAL	408	14TH WAR
BURNS, BERNARD	ALL	135	4TH E.D.

Name	County	Page	District
BURNS, BRIDGET A.	BAL	454	8TH WARD
BURNS, CATHARINE	BAL	418	1ST DIST
BURNS, CATHARINE	BAL	234	6TH WARD
BURNS, CATHARINE	BAL	195	5TH DIST
BURNS, CATHERINE MRS-	BAL	315	20TH WAR
BURNS, CHARLES	BAL	446	8TH WARD
BURNS, CHARLES M.	BAL	172	16TH WAR
BURNS, CHARLES W.	FRE	101	FREDERIC
BURNS, CHARLOTTE	WOR	180	6TH E DI
BURNS, CHRISTIAN	CEC	041	CHESAPEA
BURNS, DAIVD	CAR	264	WESTMINS
BURNS, DANIEL	CAR	295	7TH DIST
BURNS, DANIEL	FRE	375	CATOCTIN
BURNS, DAVID W.	CAR	295	7TH DIST
BURNS, DENNIS	BAL	317	3RD WARD
BURNS, EDWARD	BAL	030	15TH WAR
BURNS, EDWARD	BAL	015	9TH WARD
BURNS, EDWARD	BAL	281	7TH WARD
BURNS, EDWARD	CAR	280	7TH DIST
BURNS, ELIZA	BAL	193	19TH WAR
BURNS, ELIZA	CAR	353	6TH DIST
BURNS, ELIZA	BAL	460	1ST DIST
BURNS, ELIZABETH	BAL	336	1ST DIST
BURNS, ELIZABETH E.	ALL	192	9TH E.D.
BURNS, EMANUEL	CAR	328	MANCHEST
BURNS, EMORY	WAS	087	2ND SUBD
BURNS, FINCLEY H.	MGM	347	BERRYS D
BURNS, FRANCIS	BAL	171	16TH WAR
BURNS, GEOREG	BAL	365	13TH WAR
BURNS, GEORGE	CEC	109	4TH E DI
BURNS, GEORGE P.	CAR	331	MANCHEST
BURNS, HANNAH	CAR	220	5TH DIST
BURNS, HENRIETTA	BAL	088	4TH WARD
BURNS, HENRY	CEC	160	PORT DUP
BURNS, HENRY	FRE	360	CATOCTIN
BURNS, HENRY	BAL	276	1ST DIST
BURNS, IWLLIAM	BAL	312	1ST DIST
BURNS, JACOB	WAS	113	2ND DIST
BURNS, JACOB	WAS	019	2ND SUBD
BURNS, JAMES	QUE	244	5TH E DI
BURNS, JAMES	BAL	408	1ST DIST
BURNS, JAMES	BAL	460	1ST DIST
BURNS, JAMES	BAL	118	1ST WARD
BURNS, JAMES	ALL	101	5TH E.D.
BURNS, JAMES	BAL	378	3RD WARD
BURNS, JAMES	BAL	372	3RD WARD
BURNS, JAMES	BAL	173	11TH WAR
BURNS, JAMES	BAL	160	1ST WARD
BURNS, JAMES	FRE	403	JEFFERSO
BURNS, JAMES	CEC	142	6TH E DI
BURNS, JAMES	BAL	401	14TH WAR
BURNS, JAMES	BAL	336	13TH WAR
BURNS, JAMES	BAL	443	14TH WAR
BURNS, JAMES N.	BAL	185	6TH WARD
BURNS, JANE	QUE	145	1ST E DI
BURNS, JAOCB	CAR	352	6TH DIST
BURNS, JOHN	CAR	357	6TH DIST
BURNS, JOHN	MGM	343	CLARKSBU
BURNS, JOHN	BAL	394	14TH WAR
BURNS, JOHN	FRE	359	CATOCTIN
BURNS, JOHN	CAR	189	4TH DIST
BURNS, JOHN	BAL	131	5TH WARD
BURNS, JOHN	BAL	005	15TH WAR
BURNS, JOHN	BAL	127	1ST WARD
BURNS, JOHN	BAL	410	8TH WARD
BURNS, JOHN	ALL	150	6TH E.D.
BURNS, JOHN	BAL	460	1ST DIST
BURNS, JOHN	BAL	171	16TH WAR
BURNS, JOHN	BAL	036	2ND DIST
BURNS, JOHN	BAL	014	2ND DIST
BURNS, JOHN	BAL	012	2ND DIST
BURNS, JOHN N.	BAL	265	20TH WAR
BURNS, JOHN T.	CAR	191	4TH DIST
BURNS, JOHN T.	BAL	309	7TH WARD
BURNS, JOHN W.	QUE	202	3RD E DI
BURNS, JOHN*	BAL	118	15TH WAR
BURNS, JONATHAN	CEC	160	6TH E DI
BURNS, JOSEPH	BAL	161	1ST WARD
BURNS, JOSEPH	BAL	225	6TH WARD
BURNS, L. *	BAL	132	2ND DIST
BURNS, LAWRENCE	BAL	165	11TH WAR
BURNS, LEWIS	WAS	249	1ST DIST
BURNS, LOUIS H.	BAL	142	16TH WAR
BURNS, LOURETTA	CAR	072	NO TWP L
BURNS, LYDIA	CAR	352	6TH DIST
BURNS, MARGARET	BAL	177	16TH WAR
BURNS, MARGARET	ALL	086	5TH E.D.
BURNS, MARY	ALL	081	5TH E.D.
BURNS, MARY	BAL	049	9TH WARD
BURNS, MARY	BAL	149	5TH WARD
BURNS, MARY	BAL	276	7TH WARD
BURNS, MARY	BAL	251	6TH WARD
BURNS, MARY	BAL	459	1ST DIST
BURNS, MARY	BAL	441	1ST DIST
BURNS, MARY	BAL	093	5TH WARD
BURNS, MARY	BAL	356	3RD WARD
BURNS, MARY	BAL	002	1ST WARD
BURNS, MARY	BAL	198	11TH WAR
BURNS, MARY	BAL	024	4TH WARD
BURNS, MARY	BAL	031	4TH WARD
BURNS, MARY	BAL	268	20TH WAR
BURNS, MARY	BAL	159	19TH WAR
BURNS, MARY	KEN	272	1ST DIST
BURNS, MARY	WAS	283	1ST DIST
BURNS, MARY	WAS	091	2ND SUBD
BURNS, MARY C.	BAL	379	8TH WARD
BURNS, MARY E.	BAL	119	15TH WAR
BURNS, MARY E.	BAL	015	9TH WARD
BURNS, MARY P.	FRE	065	FREDERIC
BURNS, MATHEWS	BAL	199	2ND WARD
BURNS, MATTHEW	CAL	024	2ND DIST
BURNS, MICHAEL	BAL	027	4TH WARD
BURNS, MICHAEL	CEC	045	1ST E DI
BURNS, MICHAEL	BAL	430	1ST DIST
BURNS, NELSON	MGM	343	CLARKSBU
BURNS, OWEN	MGM	341	CLARKSBU
BURNS, OWEN	BAL	200	2ND WARD
BURNS, P.	BAL	139	1ST WARD
BURNS, PATRICK	BAL	181	16TH WAR
BURNS, PATRICK	BAL	125	1ST WARD
BURNS, PATRICK	BAL	050	1ST WARD
BURNS, PATRICK	ALL	128	4TH E.D.
BURNS, PATRICK	BAL	097	2ND DIST
BURNS, PETER	BAL	331	3RD WARD
BURNS, PETTER	BAL	171	11TH WAR
BURNS, RACHEL	BAL	364	13TH WAR
BURNS, REBECCA A.	QUE	152	1ST E DI
BURNS, REBECCA A.	QUE	166	2ND E DI
BURNS, ROBERT	ANN	308	1ST DIST
BURNS, ROBERT D.	BAL	064	10TH WAR
BURNS, ROBERTG	BAL	049	1ST WARD
BURNS, ROYAN	CHA	269	ALLENS F
BURNS, SAMUEL	CEC	134	6TH E DI
BURNS, SAMUEL	BAL	443	14TH WAR
BURNS, SAMUEL	BAL	260	20TH WAR
BURNS, SAMUEL	BAL	131	5TH WARD
BURNS, SAMUEL	WAS	283	1ST DIST
BURNS, SARAH	BAL	255	20TH WAR
BURNS, SARAH J.	FRE	055	FREDERIC
BURNS, SARAH R.	BAL	290	7TH WARD
BURNS, SHADRICK	CAR	073	NO TWP L
BURNS, SUSAN	WAS	122	2ND DIST
BURNS, SUSAN *	WAS	099	2ND DIST
BURNS, TERRENCE	WAS	091	2ND SUBD
BURNS, THOMAS	QUE	165	2ND E DI
BURNS, THOMAS	BAL	083	4TH WARD
BURNS, THOMAS	CAR	398	2ND DIST
BURNS, THOMAS	BAL	384	3RD WARD
BURNS, THOMAS	BAL	456	1ST DIST
BURNS, THOMAS	BAL	100	2ND DIST
BURNS, THOMAS	BAL	134	2ND DIST
BURNS, THOMAS W.	FRE	403	JEFFERSO
BURNS, WILLIAM	CAR	397	2ND DIST
BURNS, WILLIAM	BAL	262	17TH WAR
BURNS, WILLIAM	MGM	342	CLARKSBU
BURNS, WILLIAM	BAL	120	2ND DIST
BURNS, WILLIAM	BAL	040	2ND DIST
BURNS, WILLIAM	BAL	248	6TH WARD
BURNS, WILLIAM	BAL	213	6TH WARD
BURNS, WILLIAM	BAL	174	2ND DIST
BURNS, WILLIAM	ANN	375	4TH DIST
BURNS, WILLIAM F.	BAL	119	15TH WAR
BURNS,NICHOLAS	BAL	113	1ST WARD
BURNS,RINNA	BAL	029	1ST WARD
BURNSIDE, HENRY	BAL	084	18TH WAR
BURNSIDES, THOMAS	CEC	082	CHARLEST
BURNUP, WILLIAM G.	BAL	241	17TH WAR
BURNUST, HENRY	BAL	197	2ND WARD
BURNY, MRS.	CEC	044	CHESAPEA
BURNY, NANCY	CEC	210	7TH E DI
BURO, JONAS-BLACK	CAR	387	2ND DIST
BUROTN, HORATIO *	BAL	116	2ND DIST
BUROUGH, JOHN A.	CHA	224	ALLENS F
BUROUGHS, HENRY	PRI	050	AQUASCO
BURP, REDMOND	BAL	121	1ST WARD
BURR, GEORGE	BAL	114	1ST WARD
BURR, HENRY	BAL	310	20TH WAR
BURRALL, JOHN	ALL	159	6TH E.D.
BURRALL, SUSAN	ALL	159	6TH E.D.
BURRARD, WILLIAM	FRE	359	CATOCTIN
BURREL, ELIZABETH	BAL	426	14TH WAR
BURREN, REUBEN T.	BAL	193	19TH WAR
BURRES, JANE *	BAL	092	18TH WAR
BURRESS, HILRA *	BAL	282	1ST DIST
BURRIER, DANIEL	FRE	304	WOODSBOR
BURRIER, ELI	FRE	299	WOODSBOR
BURRIER, JAOB	FRE	418	8TH E DI
BURRIER, JOHN	FRE	418	8TH E DI
BURRIER, JOHN	BAL	291	17TH WAR
BURRIER, JOHN	BAL	125	5TH WARD
BURRIER, JOHN O.	BAL	330	7TH WARD
BURRIER, RAYMOND	BAL	123	5TH WARD
BURRIER, SARAH J.	BAL	330	7TH WARD
BURRIER, SIMON W.	BAL	396	1ST DIST
BURRIER, SOLOMCN	BAL	395	1ST DIST
BURRIET, LAFAYETT	BAL	279	7TH WARD
BURRIFF, JOHN	BAL	011	15TH WAR
BURRIFF, THOMAS	BAL	011	15TH WAR
BURRIS, BARNY *	ANN	411	8TH DIST
BURRIS, EDWARD	BAL	200	19TH WAR
BURRIS, FRED	BAL	459	1ST DIST
BURRIS, HENRY M.	MGM	380	ROCKERLE
BURRIS, HETTY	BAL	002	9TH WARD
BURRIS, JAMES	ANN	347	3RD DIST
BURRIS, JAMES	QUE	130	1ST E DI
BURRIS, JAMES	QUE	205	3RD E DI
BURRIS, JAMES	WAS	158	2ND DIST
BURRIS, JOHN	ANN	347	3RD DIST
BURRIS, SUSAN	WAS	099	2ND DIST
BURRISS, CHARLES	MGM	367	BERRYS D
BURRISS, ELI	MGM	428	CLARKSTR
BURRISS, ELIZA	BAL	064	18TH WAR
BURRISS, JAMES	MGM	363	BERRYS D
BURRISS, JAMES	QUE	130	1ST E DI
BURRISS, JOHN	MGM	316	CRACKLIN
BURRISS, JOHN	BAL	001	9TH WARD
BURRISS, LEMUEL P.	MGM	319	CRACKLIN
BURRISS, RUTH E.	MGM	429	CLARKSTR
BURRISS, SAMUEL	MGM	365	BERRYS D
BURRISS, WILLIAM G.	MGM	362	BERRYS D
BURROUGH, HORACE	BAL	331	13TH WAR
BURROUGH, JACOB	BAL	330	13TH WAR
BURROUGH, JOHN H.	CHA	289	BOJANTOW
BURROUGH, ROBERT B.	CHA	288	BOJANTOW
BURROUGHS, ALEXANDER M.	ST	340	5TH E DI
BURROUGHS, ANN	BAL	303	12TH WAR
BURROUGHS, AQUILLA	ST	324	4TH E DI
BURROUGHS, CATHARINE	ST	346	5TH E DI
BURROUGHS, EDWARD	WOR	230	6TH E DI
BURROUGHS, ELLEN	BAL	198	6TH WARD
BURROUGHS, GEORGE	CEC	197	7TH E DI
BURROUGHS, GEORGE R.	HAR	053	1ST DIST
BURROUGHS, GEORGE T.	ST	342	5TH E DI
BURROUGHS, HEZEKIAH JR.	ST	348	5TH E DI
BURROUGHS, J.F.	PRI	064	NOTTINGH
BURROUGHS, JAMES	ST	342	5TH E DI
BURROUGHS, JOHN	CEC	208	7TH E DI
BURROUGHS, JOHN	CEC	185	7TH E DI
BURROUGHS, JOHN A.	ST	323	4TH E DI
BURROUGHS, LEVEN	CHA	285	BOJANTOW
BURROUGHS, MARY	CHA	223	ALLENS F
BURROUGHS, MARY	ST	345	5TH E DI
BURROUGHS, MARY S.	ST	343	5TH E DI
BURROUGHS, MILTON	WOR	193	8TH E DI
BURROUGHS, NANCY	CHA	224	ALLENS F
BURROUGHS, PHILIP H.	ST	330	4TH E DI
BURROUGHS, RICHARD D.	PRI	067	NOTTINGH
BURROUGHS, SAMUEL	ST	344	5TH E DI
BURROUGHS, WILLIAM	ST	346	5TH E DI
BURROWS, ANN	BAL	167	6TH WARD
BURROWS, ARON	MGM	389	ROCKERLE
BURROWS, BASIL	MGM	383	ROCKERLE
BURROWS, ELEANOR	MGM	410	MEDLEY 3
BURROWS, ELLEN	BAL	321	20TH WAR
BURROWS, GEORGE K.*	TAL	004	EASTON D
BURROWS, HENRIETTA	PRI	039	VANSVILL
BURROWS, HENRY	TAL	120	ST MICHA
BURROWS, JAMES	SOM	504	SALISBUR
BURROWS, JOHN	BAL	137	16TH WAR
BURROWS, LEVIN	SOM	509	BARREN C
BURROWS, LOYD	MGM	402	ROCKERLE
BURROWS, MARY A.	MGM	404	ROCKERLE
BURROWS, MILTON	SOM	468	TRAPPE D
BURROWS, NATHAN	ALL	263	CUMBERLA
BURROWS, NICHOLAS	MGM	386	ROCKERLE
BURROWS, RUFUS	SOM	467	HANGARY
BURROWS, RUTH A.	MGM	383	ROCKERLE
BURROWS, RUTH E.	ANN	437	HOWARD D
BURROWS, SARAH A.	TAL	115	ST MICHA
BURROWS, TAMER	SOM	469	TRAPPE D
BURROWS, WILLIAM	TAL	113	ST MICHA
BURRS, HESTER*	DOR	435	1ST DIST
BURRS, JAMES*	DOR	466	1ST DIST
BURRS, JOHN	BAL	196	2ND WARD
BURRS, MARY ANN	BAL	316	20TH WAR
BURRS, PATIENCE*	DOR	448	1ST DIST
BURRS, WILLIAM	BAL	377	3RD WARD
BURRY, CATHARINE	BAL	214	19TH WAR
BURRY, J.	BAL	151	1ST WARD
BURRY, JOHN	BAL	113	1ST WARD
BURS, SARAH R.	BAL	342	3RD WARD
BURSALL, MARY E.	FRE	253	NEW MARK
BURSALL, ROBERT	BAL	204	19TH WAR
BURSHNAHAM, JOHN	BAL	446	8TH WARD
BURSON, MARTIN	ALL	150	6TH E.D.
BURST, WILLIAM A.*	TAL	011	EASTON D
BURT, AMELIA	BAL	224	12TH WAR
BURT, ELIZA-MULATTO	FRE	038	FREDERIC
BURT, FENNY	CAR	085	NO TWP L
BURT, ISAAC	CAR	099	NO TWP L
BURT, SARAH-BLACK	CAR	081	NO TWP L
BURT, THOMAS	CAR	079	NO TWP L
BURT, THOMAS	BAL	127	16TH WAR
BURT, THOMAS	QUE	197	3RD E DI
BURT, WILLIAM	CAR	099	NO TWP L
BURTEAN, NICHOLAS	BAL	340	3RD WARD
BURTMYER, RICHARD	BAL	306	20TH WAR
BURTON, AMILIA	DOR	383	1ST DIST
BURTON, BASIL	MGM	337	CRACKLIN
BURTON, CATHARINE	DOR	361	3RD DIVI
BURTON, CATHARINE-BLACK	BAL	224	2ND WARD
BURTON, CLEMENT	DOR	339	3RD DIVI
BURTON, COLENS*	DOR	345	3RD DIVI
BURTON, DAVID	CEC	099	3RD E DI
BURTON, DAVID	BAL	269	17TH WAR
BURTON, E.	ANN	282	ANNAPOLI
BURTON, ELIJAH	BAL	070	2ND DIST
BURTON, GEORGE	ANN	483	HOWARD D
BURTON, GEORGE	QUE	168	2ND E DI
BURTON, HENRY	WOR	340	1ST E DI
BURTON, IRE	ALL	151	6TH E.D.
BURTON, ISAAC	MGM	350	BERRYS D
BURTON, J. W.	ALL	097	5TH E.D.
BURTON, JACOB	QUE	236	4TH E DI
BURTON, JAMES	ALL	012	3RD E.D.
BURTON, JAMES	BAL	091	2ND DIST
BURTON, JAMES	BAL	116	2ND DIST
BURTON, JAMES	DOR	363	3RD DIVI
BURTON, JAMES	FRE	259	NEW MARK
BURTON, JANE	WAS	101	2ND DIST
BURTON, JOHN	DOR	363	3RD DIVI
BURTON, JOHN	BAL	366	13TH WAR
BURTON, JOHN	BAL	117	2ND DIST
BURTON, JOHN	BAL	091	2ND DIST
BURTON, JOHN	BAL	091	2ND DIST
BURTON, JOHN	BAL	110	2ND DIST
BURTON, JOHN	BAL	455	1ST DIST
BURTON, JOHN W.	FRE	419	8TH E DI
BURTON, JOSHUA	BAL	123	2ND DIST
BURTON, JOSHUA	BAL	091	2ND DIST
BURTON, JOSIAH *	SOM	413	DUBLIN D
BURTON, LEVIN	SOM	416	DUBLIN D
BURTON, MARGARET	BAL	346	13TH WAR
BURTON, MARTHA	CEC	195	6TH E DI
BURTON, MATHEW	BAL	439	1ST DIST
BURTON, MATILDA	BAL	252	20TH WAR
BURTOM, NANCY	ALL	166	6TH E.D.
BURTON, OWEN	BAL	117	2ND DIST
BURTON, PERRY	TAL	111	ST MICHA
BURTON, ROBERT	DOR	326	3RD DIVI
BURTON, ROBERT	DOR	361	3RD DIVI
BURTON, ROBERT	DOR	376	1ST DIST
BURTON, SAMUEL	BAL	093	2ND DIST
BURTON, SAMUEL	BAL	071	10TH WAR
BURTON, SARAH	BAL	362	3RD WARD
BURTON, SHADRAC	WOR	166	6TH E DI
BURTON, WILLIAM	ANN	359	3RD DIST
BURTON, WILLIAM	DOR	437	1ST DIST
BURTON, WILLIAM A.	PRI	037	VANSVILL
BURTY, RACHEL	BAL	159	16TH WAR
BURTZ, SAMUEL	BAL	313	1ST DIST
BURWELL, MARY C.	BAL	139	16TH WAR
BUSARD, ELIZA	WAS	053	2ND SUBD
BUSARD, ELIZABETH	WAS	032	2ND SUBD
BUSARD, SAMUEL	WAS	052	2ND SUBD
BUSARED, JACOB *	WAS	051	2ND SUBD
BUSBY, ABRAHAM H.	CAR	269	WESTMINS
BUSBY, CATHARINE	CAR	331	MANCHEST
BUSBY, ZACHARIAH	CAR	195	4TH DIST
BUSCH, ABRAHAM	BAL	254	17TH WAR
BUSCH, CHRISTIAN	ANN	415	HOWARD D
BUSCH, DEDRICK	BAL	108	1ST WARD
BUSCH, GEORGE L.	BAL	280	7TH WARD
BUSCH, HENRY	BAL	027	1ST WARD
BUSCH, HENRY	BAL	254	17TH WAR
BUSCH, HENRY	BAL	276	17TH WAR
BUSCH, JOHN	BAL	004	9TH WARD
BUSCH, JULIA	BAL	381	13TH WAR
BUSCH, MARY	BAL	146	2ND DIST
BUSCH, MICHAEL	BAL	105	2ND DIST
BUSCH, MORICE	BAL	390	8TH WARD
BUSCH, NICKOLAS	BAL	101	2ND DIST
BUSCHMANN, CHRISTOPHER	BAL	064	15TH WAR
BUSCO, PHILIP	BAL	136	2ND DIST
BUSCOE, JOSEPH G.	KEN	301	3RD DIST
BUSCUE, BENJAMIN	KEN	295	3RD DIST
BUSEEK, ERNEST	BAL	274	1ST DIST
BUSEY, ANN	MGM	375	ROCKERLE
BUSEY, BENJAMIN	FRE	252	NEW MARK
BUSEY, CASSADRA	FRE	252	NEW MARK
BUSEY, HENRIETTA	BAL	215	11TH WAR
BUSEY, JOSEPH	ANN	306	1ST DIST
BUSEY, RICHARD	WAS	016	2ND SUBD
BUSFORD, HENRY	FRE	205	BUCKEYST
BUSH, A.L.	ALL	206	CUMBERLA
BUSH, ADAM	BAL	305	17TH WAR
BUSH, AMANDA	FRE	131	CREAGERS
BUSH, ANN	CHA	286	BOJANTOW
BUSH, BARNARD	BAL	322	7TH WARD
BUSH, BARNEY	BAL	442	8TH WARD

Name	County	Page	District
BUSH, BARNEY	BAL	074	2ND DIST
BUSH, BARNY	BAL	200	2ND WARD
BUSH, BENJAMIN	BAL	192	5TH DIST
BUSH, BENJAMIN	FRE	131	CREAGERS
BUSH, BILL	HAR	068	1ST DIST
BUSH, CAIN	BAL	371	3RD WARD
BUSH, CATHERINE	BAL	405	8TH WARD
BUSH, CATHERINE	ALL	252	CUMBERLA
BUSH, CECELIA-BLACK	ST	338	4TH E DI
BUSH, CHARLES	TAL	038	EASTON D
BUSH, CHARLOTTE	BAL	180	2ND DIST
BUSH, CHARLOTTE	BAL	144	11TH WAR
BUSH, CIRCELIA	ST	268	3RD E DI
BUSH, CANIEL	CAR	190	4TH DIST
BUSH, DEDRICK	BAL	333	7TH WARD
BUSH, DELILA	FRE	058	FREDERIC
BUSH, EASTER-BLACK	ST	338	4TH E DI
BUSH, EDWARD S.	BAL	062	1ST WARD
BUSH, ELIZABETH	FRE	249	NEW MARK
BUSH, GENEVA*	BAL	269	20TH WAR
BUSH, GEORGE	BAL	017	15TH WAR
BUSH, GOERGE H.C.J.	BAL	265	17TH WAR
BUSH, H. M.	BAL	143	11TH WAR
BUSH, HENRY	BAL	159	2ND DIST
BUSH, HENRY	ANN	280	ANNAPOLI
BUSH, HEZIAH	BAL	307	12TH WAR
BUSH, ISAACK	DOR	328	3RD DIVI
BUSH, JACOB	BAL	459	8TH WARD
BUSH, JAMES	BAL	095	2ND DIST
BUSH, JAMES	DOR	364	3RD DIVI
BUSH, JOHAMIAH	BAL	083	1ST WARD
BUSH, JOHN	BAL	429	8TH WARD
BUSH, JOHN	BAL	169	11TH WAR
BUSH, JOHN	BAL	138	1ST WARD
BUSH, JOHN	FRE	057	FREDERIC
BUSH, JOHN	CHA	286	BOJANTOW
BUSH, JOHN	PRI	039	VANSVILL
BUSH, JOHN W.-BLACK	ST	336	4TH E DI
BUSH, JOHN-BLACK	ST	345	5TH E DI
BUSH, JOHN-BLACK	ST	337	4TH E DI
BUSH, JOSEPH C.	SOM	493	SALISBUR
BUSH, JOSEPH E.	BAL	273	7TH WARD
BUSH, LAURENCE	BAL	224	6TH WARD
BUSH, LAWRENCE	BAL	106	5TH WARD
BUSH, LEWIS	BAL	268	2ND WARD
BUSH, LOUIS	ALL	066	10TH E.D
BUSH, LYDIA	BAL	273	7TH WARD
BUSH, MARGARET	CAR	289	7TH DIST
BUSH, MARGRET	BAL	178	2ND WARD
BUSH, MARY	BAL	265	7TH WARD
BUSH, MARY	BAL	306	1ST DIST
BUSH, MARY	DOR	367	3RD DIVI
BUSH, P.	BAL	148	1ST WARD
BUSH, RACHEL	BAL	315	1ST DIST
BUSH, RICHARD	BAL	273	7TH WARD
BUSH, ROBERT	FRE	205	BUCKEYST
BUSH, ROSA	BAL	297	3RD WARD
BUSH, SPENCER	DOR	321	1ST DIST
BUSH, THOMAS	BAL	335	1ST DIST
BUSH, FRANK	BAL	252	2ND WARD
BUSHAM, WILLIAM	BAL	129	1ST WARD
BUSHAW, JOHN	BAL	269	20TH WAR
BUSHBY, CLARA	BAL	219	12TH WAR
BUSHE, THOMAS	HAR	197	3RD DIST
BUSHEL, ROSANA	BAL	300	3RD WARD
BUSHELL, HEZEKIAH	FRE	248	NEW MARK
BUSHELL, JULIA	BAL	261	20TH WAR
BUSHER, HARMAN	PRI	008	BLADENSB
BUSHER, HENRY	PRI	008	BLADENSB
BUSHER, PHILIP	BAL	152	19TH WAR
BUSHER, WILLIAM	BAL	157	6TH WARD
BUSHEY, HENRY	BAL	234	1ST DIST
BUSHEY, ISAAC	BAL	276	17TH WAR
BUSHEY, WILLAIM H.	BAL	238	1ST DIST
BUSHFIELD, ABRAHAM	HAR	183	3RD DIST
BUSHHAM, FRANKLIN CAPTAIN	TAL	002	EASTON D
BUSHING, HENRICH	BAL	268	7TH WARD
BUSHKY, FYETT	BAL	191	2ND WARD
BUSHMAN, FREDERICK	BAL	250	17TH WAR
BUSHMAN, GEORGE	BAL	236	2ND WARD
BUSHMAN, HENRY	BAL	300	17TH WAR
BUSHMAN, JOHN	BAL	313	20TH WAR
BUSHMAN, JOHN	BAL	394	14TH WAR
BUSHMAN, JOSEPH	BAL	228	19TH WAR
BUSHMAN, SAMUEL	BAL	456	14TH WAR
BUSHMAN, THOMAS	FRE	162	EMMITTSB
BUSHOP, ABRAHAM	DOR	364	3RD DIVI
BUSIC, JOSHUA	BAL	206	6TH WARD
BUSICH, JOHN*	DOR	417	1ST DIST
BUSICK, AIRY N.	BAL	023	9TH WARD
BUSICK, JAMES	DOR	416	1ST DIST
BUSICK, JOHN*	DOR	417	1ST DIST
BUSICK, LOUISA	KEN	224	2ND DIST
BUSICK, SARAH*	DOR	416	1ST DIST
BUSICK, WILLIAM L.	QUE	174	2ND E DI
BUSIE, RICHARD	BAL	105	1ST WARD
BUSIE, THOMAS	BAL	272	7TH WARD
BUSING, ISAAC	FRE	375	CATOCTIN
BUSK, CATHARINE	BAL	254	12TH WAR
BUSK, DAVID*	BAL	420	3RD WARD
BUSK, HARRIET	BAL	264	1ST DIST
BUSK, JOHN	BAL	300	17TH WAR
BUSK, JOHN-MULATTO	BAL	217	2ND WARD
BUSK, MARY C.	BAL	264	1ST DIST
BUSK, T. M.*	BAL	370	3RD WARD
BUSK, THOMAS	BAL	074	1ST WARD
BUSKE, BING	BAL	084	2ND DIST
BUSKENY, ELISA	CEC	210	7TH E DI
BUSKIRK, EMILY	ALL	116	5TH E.D.
BUSKIRK, LEWIS	ALL	116	5TH E.D.
BUSKIRK, SAMUEL	ALL	116	5TH E.D.
BUSKIRK, THOMAS J.	CEC	030	CHESAPEA
BUSKIRK, WILLIAM	ALL	116	5TH E.D.
BUSKLY, JACOB M.	FRE	207	BUCKEYST
BUSKY, CONRAD	BAL	079	1ST WARD
BUSLEY, THOMAS	ALL	089	5TH E.D.
BUSMAN, WILLIAM	BAL	232	17TH WAR
BUSS, ANN	CAR	388	2ND DIST
BUSSALE, OLVER	FRE	242	NEW MARK
BUSSALL, THOMAS	FRE	254	NEW MARK
BUSSARD, ELIZA	FRE	299	WOODSBOR
BUSSARD, ENOS	FRE	106	CREAGERS
BUSSARD, JOHN W.	FRE	371	CATOCTIN
BUSSARD, LUTHER M.	BAL	085	18TH WAR
BUSSARD, MARSHALL L.	BAL	101	18TH WAR
BUSSARD, MATHEW	BAL	057	18TH WAR
BUSSARD, PETER	FRE	365	CATOCTIN
BUSSARD, PETER	FRE	081	FREDERIC
BUSSELL, MICHAEL	BAL	042	18TH WAR
BUSSELS, JAMES H.	WOR	195	8TH E DI
BUSSELS, MILTON	SOM	446	DAMES QU
BUSSEY, BENEDICT	HAR	114	2ND DIST
BUSSEY, CHARITY	FRE	272	NEW MARK
BUSSEY, ELIZABETH	HAR	113	2ND DIST
BUSSEY, HENRY	BAL	209	6TH WARD
BUSSEY, REBECCA	BAL	120	18TH WAR
BUSSEY, RICHARD	BAL	236	17TH WAR
BUSSMAN, ADELINE	BAL	040	15TH WAR
BUSSRARD, CATHARINE	FRE	370	CATOCTIN
BUSSU, FRANK *	ANN	426	HOWARD D
BUSSY, BENNETT H.	CEC	081	CHARLEST
BUST, DAVID	BAL	215	19TH WAR
BUSTER, SIYAN	BAL	243	12TH WAR
BUSTON, COLENS*	DOR	345	3RD DIVI
BUSTUO, WARNER R.	CAR	150	NO TWP L
BUSWARD, JOHN	WAS	091	2ND SUBD
BUSY, HENRY	WAS	156	2ND DIST
BUTCH, GEORGE	WOR	317	2ND E DI
BUTCH, SINAH	WOR	317	2ND E DI
BUTCHER, ALEXANDER	BAL	259	1ST DIST
BUTCHER, ANN	BAL	223	12TH WAR
BUTCHER, ANN-BLACK	FRE	397	PETERSVI
BUTCHER, BENJAMIN	BAL	226	12TH WAR
BUTCHER, CHARLES	BAL	261	1ST DIST
BUTCHER, EVERLINE	FRE	223	BUCKEYST
BUTCHER, FREDERICK	FRE	057	FREDERIC
BUTCHER, HENRY-MULATTO	FRE	419	8TH E DI
BUTCHER, JACOB	FRE	419	8TH E DI
BUTCHER, JULIA	KEN	307	3RD DIST
BUTCHER, MARGARET	BAL	190	19TH WAR
BUTCHER, MARTHEW-BLACK	FRE	022	FREDERIC
BUTCHER, MR.	BAL	213	17TH WAR
BUTCHER, PHILIP H.	FRE	223	BUCKEYST
BUTCHER, THOMAS	MGM	425	MEDLEY 3
BUTCHER, WILLIAM	CEC	054	1ST E DI
BUTCHER, WILLIAM	KEN	285	3RD DIST
BUTCHER, ZACHARIAH-MULATT	FRE	010	FREDERIC
BUTE, CAROLINE	BAL	266	12TH WAR
BUTELER, EDWARD L.	WAS	210	1ST DIST
BUTERBAUGH, STEPHEN	WAS	015	2ND SUBD
BUTGE, MARTIN	BAL	107	5TH WARD
BUTH, JAMES	CAR	316	1ST DIST
BUTHEN, T.	BAL	138	1ST WARD
BUTHER, HARRIET	BAL	234	20TH WAR
BUTHER, JAMES R.	BAL	196	2ND WARD
BUTHER, LUCRETIA	FRE	209	BUCKEYST
BUTHOOF, JACOB	BAL	239	17TH WAR
BUTLAR, CLARE-BLACK	ST	323	4TH E DI
BUTLER, AARON	KEN	275	1ST DIST
BUTLER, ABEL	BAL	364	1ST DIST
BUTLER, ABRAHAM	BAL	428	14TH WAR
BUTLER, ABRAHAM-BLACK	FRE	017	FREDERIC
BUTLER, ABRAM	KEN	257	1ST DIST
BUTLER, ADAM	FRE	379	PETERSVI
BUTLER, ALBERT	KEN	221	2ND DIST
BUTLER, ALBERT	KEN	259	1ST DIST
BUTLER, ALEXANDER	PRI	088	SPALDING
BUTLER, ALEXANDER	BAL	207	6TH WARD
BUTLER, ALEXANDER-MULATTO	ST	330	4TH E DI
BUTLER, ALEXANDRIA	BAL	072	1ST WARD
BUTLER, ALFRED	BAL	125	18TH WAR
BUTLER, ALLICE	WAS	095	2ND SUBD
BUTLER, ALLIS	FRE	206	BUCKEYST
BUTLER, AMANDA	MGM	436	CLARKSTR
BUTLER, AMOS	BAL	362	3RD WARD
BUTLER, AMY	ANN	300	1ST DIST
BUTLER, AMY *	FRE	251	NEW MARK
BUTLER, ANDREWS	ALL	062	10TH E.D
BUTLER, ANN	BAL	280	1ST DIST
BUTLER, ANN	BAL	259	12TH WAR
BUTLER, ANN	BAL	317	7TH WARD
BUTLER, ANN	CHA	286	BOJANTOW
BUTLER, ANN	DOR	318	1ST DIST
BUTLER, ANN	HAR	005	1ST DIST
BUTLER, ANN	BAL	149	11TH WAR
BUTLER, ANN	PRI	047	AQUASCO
BUTLER, ANN	ST	268	3RD E DI
BUTLER, ANN	ST	268	3RD E DI
BUTLER, ANN C.	CAR	108	NO TWP L
BUTLER, ANN E.	BAL	057	15TH WAR
BUTLER, ANN M.	BAL	032	18TH WAR
BUTLER, ANNE	BAL	124	18TH WAR
BUTLER, ANNIE	FRE	129	CREAGERS
BUTLER, ANNON *	WAS	094	2ND SUBD
BUTLER, ARMON *	WAS	094	2ND SUBD
BUTLER, AVA-MULATTO	FRE	245	NEW MARK
BUTLER, BARTON	WAS	091	2ND SUBD
BUTLER, BENEDICT-MULATTO	ST	317	4TH E DI
BUTLER, BETSEY	FRE	163	EMMITTSB
BUTLER, CATHARINE	BAL	065	15TH WAR
BUTLER, CATHARINE	BAL	409	8TH WARD
BUTLER, CATHARINE	BAL	287	12TH WAR
BUTLER, CATHERINE*	BAL	352	3RD WARD
BUTLER, CATHERINE*	BAL	352	3RD WARD
BUTLER, CHARLES	BAL	176	2ND DIST
BUTLER, CHARLES	BAL	164	16TH WAR
BUTLER, CHARLES	BAL	320	7TH WARD
BUTLER, CHARLES	BAL	237	12TH WAR
BUTLER, CHARLES	WAS	090	2ND SUBD
BUTLER, CHARLES	WOR	184	6TH E DI
BUTLER, CHARLES H.	CHA	257	MIDDLETO
BUTLER, CHARLES J.	BAL	164	16TH WAR
BUTLER, CHARLES-MULATTO	FRE	447	8TH E DI
BUTLER, CHARLOTTE	BAL	222	12TH WAR
BUTLER, CHARLOTTE-BLACK	ST	321	4TH E DI
BUTLER, CHRISTIAN	BAL	323	3RD WARD
BUTLER, CICELIA	ST	268	3RD E DI
BUTLER, CLARA	BAL	147	11TH WAR
BUTLER, CLEM-BLACK	ST	299	2ND E DI
BUTLER, CLEMENT	HAR	055	1ST DIST
BUTLER, COMFORT	WOR	199	8TH E DI
BUTLER, CORNELIUS	BAL	210	11TH WAR
BUTLER, COURTNEY A.	BAL	454	8TH WARD
BUTLER, DANIEL	KEN	233	2ND DIST
BUTLER, DANIEL	WOR	178	6TH E DI
BUTLER, DENNIS	CHA	264	MIDDLETO
BUTLER, E.-BLACK	FRE	200	5TH E DI
BUTLER, EDWARD	CHA	257	MIDDLETO
BUTLER, EDWARD	QUE	251	5TH E DI
BUTLER, EDWARD	WAS	157	HAGERSTO
BUTLER, EDWARD J.	ANN	299	1ST DIST
BUTLER, ELISHA	WAS	160	2ND DIST
BUTLER, ELIZA	PRI	110	PISCATAW
BUTLER, ELIZA	BAL	462	1ST DIST
BUTLER, ELIZA	BAL	300	12TH WAR
BUTLER, ELIZA	BAL	218	6TH WARD
BUTLER, ELIZA	BAL	132	2ND DIST
BUTLER, ELIZA	CHA	277	BOJANTOW
BUTLER, ELIZA	CEC	085	5TH E DI
BUTLER, ELIZA ELLEN	BAL	207	17TH WAR
BUTLER, ELIZABETH	BAL	057	4TH WARD
BUTLER, ELIZABETH	FRE	108	CREAGERS
BUTLER, ELIZABETH	CHA	257	MIDDLETO
BUTLER, ELIZABETH	BAL	151	11TH WAR
BUTLER, ELIZABETH	BAL	138	18TH WAR
BUTLER, ELIZABETH	BAL	443	1ST DIST
BUTLER, ELIZABETH-MULATTO	FRE	245	NEW MARK
BUTLER, ELIZABETH-MULATTO	WOR	321	1ST E DI
BUTLER, ELLEN	BAL	475	14TH WAR
BUTLER, ELLEN	BAL	461	1ST DIST
BUTLER, ELLEN	BAL	337	3RD WARD
BUTLER, ELLEN-BLACK	ST	316	4TH E DI
BUTLER, ELLEN-BLACK	ST	345	5TH E DI
BUTLER, EMELY J.	FRE	270	NEW MARK
BUTLER, F.	BAL	156	1ST WARD
BUTLER, FANNY	BAL	094	10TH WAR
BUTLER, FRANCIS	HAR	026	1ST DIST
BUTLER, FRANCIS	PRI	092	MARLBROU
BUTLER, FREDERICK	BAL	201	2ND WARD
BUTLER, GAITHER	FRE	439	8TH E DI
BUTLER, GEDEANNA	CHA	289	MIDDLETO
BUTLER, GEORGE	BAL	106	18TH WAR
BUTLER, GEORGE	BAL	166	6TH WARD
BUTLER, GEORGE	BAL	146	16TH WAR
BUTLER, GEORGE	ANN	327	2ND DIST
BUTLER, GEORGE	BAL	113	1ST WARD
BUTLER, GEORGE	BAL	281	7TH WARD
BUTLER, GEORGE	PRI	106	PISCATAW
BUTLER, GEORGE H.	BAL	317	7TH WARD
BUTLER, GEORGE L.	BAL	244	1ST DIST
BUTLER, GEORGE L.	BAL	244	1ST DIST
BUTLER, GEORGE S.	BAL	197	6TH WARD
BUTLER, GEORGE W.	BAL	170	6TH WARD
BUTLER, GEORGE-MULATTO	BAL	237	2ND WARD
BUTLER, GEROGE	HAR	033	1ST DIST
BUTLER, GOERGE	BAL	114	1ST WARD
BUTLER, GREST	FRE	162	EMMITTSB
BUTLER, HANNAH	BAL	381	13TH WAR
BUTLER, HANNAH	WAS	133	HAGERSTO
BUTLER, HARMAN	FRE	060	FREDERIC
BUTLER, HARRIET	BAL	413	14TH WAR
BUTLER, HARRIET	CHA	283	BOJANTOW
BUTLER, HARRIET	FRE	116	CREAGERS
BUTLER, HARRIET	ST	318	4TH E DI
BUTLER, HARRIET	BAL	399	8TH WARD
BUTLER, HARRIET	BAL	012	9TH WARD
BUTLER, HARRY	FRE	139	CREAGERS
BUTLER, HENERATTA T.	FRE	076	FREDERIC
BUTLER, HENRIETTA	BAL	249	6TH WARD
BUTLER, HENRY	BAL	201	6TH WARD
BUTLER, HENRY	BAL	450	1ST DIST
BUTLER, HENRY	KEN	211	2ND DIST
BUTLER, HENRY	BAL	377	13TH WAR
BUTLER, HENRY	BAL	123	18TH WAR
BUTLER, HENRY	CHA	256	MIDDLETO
BUTLER, HENRY	CHA	256	MIDDLETO
BUTLER, HENRY	CHA	240	HILLTOP
BUTLER, HENRY	CAL	050	3RD DIST
BUTLER, HENRY	ST	262	3RD E DI
BUTLER, HENRY	ST	258	3RD E DI
BUTLER, HENRY	WOR	186	7TH E DI
BUTLER, HENRY	PRI	054	AQUASCO
BUTLER, HENRY	PRI	047	AQUASCO
BUTLER, HENRY	WAS	005	WILLIAMS
BUTLER, HENRY D.	BAL	074	15TH WAR
BUTLER, HENRY-BLACK	ST	322	4TH E DI
BUTLER, HODENA	CHA	217	ALLENS F
BUTLER, HORATIO	BAL	037	4TH WARD
BUTLER, IGNATIOUS	CHA	287	BOJANTOW
BUTLER, IGNATIUS	MGM	372	BERRYS D
BUTLER, ISAAC	WOR	178	6TH E DI
BUTLER, ISAIAH	BAL	391	14TH WAR
BUTLER, J.H.	BAL	138	1ST WARD
BUTLER, JACKSON-BLACK	ST	318	4TH E DI
BUTLER, JACOB	CHA	252	BOJANTOW
BUTLER, JAMES	CAR	120	NO TWP L
BUTLER, JAMES	CAR	143	NO TWP L
BUTLER, JAMES	BAL	399	14TH WAR
BUTLER, JAMES	BAL	354	13TH WAR
BUTLER, JAMES	BAL	291	17TH WAR
BUTLER, JAMES	PRI	054	AQUASCO
BUTLER, JAMES	QUE	241	5TH E DI
BUTLER, JAMES	BAL	340	1ST DIST
BUTLER, JAMES	BAL	154	1ST WARD
BUTLER, JAMES	BAL	154	1ST WARD
BUTLER, JAMES	ANN	328	2ND DIST
BUTLER, JAMES	ALL	110	5TH E.D.
BUTLER, JAMES	BAL	100	2ND DIST
BUTLER, JAMES	BAL	100	2ND DIST
BUTLER, JAMES	ANN	342	3RD DIST
BUTLER, JAMES .S	CAR	074	NO TWP L
BUTLER, JAMES H.	BAL	142	1ST WARD
BUTLER, JAMES J.	QUE	242	5TH E DI
BUTLER, JAMES M.	BAL	124	18TH WAR
BUTLER, JAMES R.	PRI	046	AQUASCO
BUTLER, JAMES-BLACK	FRE	245	NEW MARK
BUTLER, JANE	CAR	108	NO TWP L
BUTLER, JANE	CHA	257	MIDDLETO
BUTLER, JANE	CHA	285	BOJANTOW
BUTLER, JANE	PRI	049	AQUASCO
BUTLER, JANE	PRI	053	AQUASCO
BUTLER, JANE	BAL	425	8TH WARD
BUTLER, JANE R.	BAL	227	6TH WARD
BUTLER, JARRET	BAL	130	16TH WAR
BUTLER, JEFF-BLACK	ST	320	4TH E DI
BUTLER, JEFFERSON	BAL	062	10TH WAR
BUTLER, JEFFERSON	KEN	233	2ND DIST
BUTLER, JEFFERSON	FRE	077	FREDERIC
BUTLER, JEFFERSON-BLACK	ST	340	5TH E DI
BUTLER, JEROME	BAL	323	12TH WAR
BUTLER, JERRY-BLACK	MGM	397	ROCKERLE
BUTLER, JESE	CAR	113	NO TWP L
BUTLER, JETSON	PRI	058	NOTTINGH
BUTLER, JOHN	PRI	053	AQUASCO
BUTLER, JOHN	WOR	180	6TH E DI
BUTLER, JOHN	PRI	047	AQUASCO
BUTLER, JOHN	PRI	112	PISCATAW
BUTLER, JOHN	KEN	273	1ST DIST
BUTLER, JOHN	ST	263	3RD E DI
BUTLER, JOHN	WAS	138	HAGERSTO
BUTLER, JOHN	CAR	116	NO TWP L
BUTLER, JOHN	CAL	051	3RD DIST
BUTLER, JOHN	HAR	055	1ST DIST
BUTLER, JOHN	CHA	264	MIDDLETO
BUTLER, JOHN	FRE	126	CREAGERS
BUTLER, JOHN	FRE	439	8TH E DI
BUTLER, JOHN	FRE	251	NEW MARK
BUTLER, JOHN	BAL	372	13TH WAR
BUTLER, JOHN	BAL	261	17TH WAR
BUTLER, JOHN	CEC	123	3RD E DI

Name	County	Page	District
BUTLER, JOHN	BAL	229	6TH WARD
BUTLER, JOHN	BAL	151	1ST WARD
BUTLER, JOHN	BAL	131	1ST WARD
BUTLER, JOHN	ANN	324	2ND DIST
BUTLER, JOHN	BAL	344	1ST DIST
BUTLER, JOHN	BAL	446	1ST DIST
BUTLER, JOHN	BAL	388	1ST DIST
BUTLER, JOHN	BAL	058	15TH WAR
BUTLER, JOHN	BAL	071	1ST WARD
BUTLER, JOHN H.	BAL	455	1ST DIST
BUTLER, JOHN H.	BAL	191	17TH WAR
BUTLER, JOHN JR.	CAR	117	NO TWP L
BUTLER, JOHN L.-BLACK	ST	333	4TH E DI
BUTLER, JOHN-BLACK	ST	318	4TH E DI
BUTLER, JOHN-BLACK	ST	302	2ND E DI
BUTLER, JOHN-MULATTO	ST	344	5TH E DI
BUTLER, JOHNA.	ST	268	3RD E DI
BUTLER, JONATHAN	CAR	134	NO TWP L
BUTLER, JOSEPH	BAL	428	14TH WAR
BUTLER, JOSEPH	CEC	160	6TH E DI
BUTLER, JOSEPH	BAL	101	18TH WAR
BUTLER, JOSEPH	ST	268	3RD E DI
BUTLER, JOSEPH-BLACK	FRE	018	FREDERIC
BUTLER, JOSEPH-MULATTO	ST	332	4TH E DI
BUTLER, JOSIA	CHA	274	ALLENS F
BUTLER, JOSIAH	BAL	407	14TH WAR
BUTLER, JOSIAH	BAL	405	14TH WAR
BUTLER, JOSIAS	CHA	293	BOJANTOW
BUTLER, KITTY	ANN	319	2ND DIST
BUTLER, LARKIN	BAL	310	1ST DIST
BUTLER, LCHOAS	CHA	289	MIDDLETO
BUTLER, LEVY	BAL	384	8TH WARD
BUTLER, LEWIS	BAL	412	14TH WAR
BUTLER, LEWIS	PRI	048	AQUASCO
BUTLER, LOUIS	CEC	211	7TH E DI
BUTLER, LOUIS-BLACK	BAL	222	2ND WARD
BUTLER, LOUISA	ANN	343	3RD DIST
BUTLER, LOUISA M.	BAL	342	3RD WARD
BUTLER, LUCY	FRE	288	WOODSBOR
BUTLER, LYDIA	BAL	129	2ND DIST
BUTLER, MANUEL*	DOR	314	1ST DIST
BUTLER, MARGARET	ANN	343	3RD DIST
BUTLER, MARGARET	BAL	191	6TH WARD
BUTLER, MARGARET	ANN	325	2ND DIST
BUTLER, MARGARET	BAL	107	15TH WAR
BUTLER, MARGARET	BAL	351	3RD WARD
BUTLER, MARIA	ST	261	3RD E DI
BUTLER, MARTHA	BAL	121	16TH WAR
BUTLER, MARTHA	BAL	345	1ST DIST
BUTLER, MARTHA	BAL	425	8TH WARD
BUTLER, MARTHY	HAR	176	3RD DIST
BUTLER, MARTIN	BAL	297	12TH WAR
BUTLER, MARTIN	BAL	067	1ST WARD
BUTLER, MARY	BAL	291	12TH WAR
BUTLER, MARY	ALL	150	6TH E.D.
BUTLER, MARY	CHA	275	ALLENS F
BUTLER, MARY	DOR	303	1ST DIST
BUTLER, MARY	DOR	301	1ST DIST
BUTLER, MARY	CAL	038	2ND DIST
BUTLER, MARY	BAL	149	11TH WAR
BUTLER, MARY	BAL	149	11TH WAR
BUTLER, MARY	PRI	113	PISCATAW
BUTLER, MARY A.	BAL	058	4TH WARD
BUTLER, MARY A.	BAL	257	1ST DIST
BUTLER, MARY A.	BAL	059	15TH WAR
BUTLER, MARY A.	BAL	163	6TH WARD
BUTLER, MARY B.	BAL	197	2ND WARD
BUTLER, MARY E.	FRE	021	FREDERIC
BUTLER, MARY E.	ST	267	3RD E DI
BUTLER, MARY F.	CHA	245	HILLTOP
BUTLER, MARY J.	WOR	179	6TH E DI
BUTLER, MARY J.	BAL	130	16TH WAR
BUTLER, MARY M.	BAL	183	2ND WARD
BUTLER, MARY S.	BAL	059	15TH WAR
BUTLER, MARY*	BAL	357	3RD WARD
BUTLER, MARY*	BAL	357	3RD WARD
BUTLER, MARY-BLACK	ST	330	4TH E DI
BUTLER, MARY-BLACK	ST	325	4TH E DI
BUTLER, MARY-BLACK	ST	302	2ND E DI
BUTLER, MATHEW	BAL	223	17TH WAR
BUTLER, MATILDA	CHA	221	ALLENS F
BUTLER, MATILDA	ST	269	3RD E DI
BUTLER, MATILDA	BAL	460	1ST DIST
BUTLER, MICHEAL	BAL	025	18TH WAR
BUTLER, MOSES	CAR	112	NO TWP L
BUTLER, MOSES	WAS	186	BOONSBOR
BUTLER, MUNCH	CHA	257	MIDDLETO
BUTLER, NANCY	CHA	278	BOJANTOW
BUTLER, NANCY	WOR	174	6TH E DI
BUTLER, NANCY	BAL	447	8TH WARD
BUTLER, NANCY L.	TAL	022	EASTON D
BUTLER, NOAH	BAL	447	8TH WARD
BUTLER, PATRICK	WAS	155	2ND DIST
BUTLER, PATRICK	BAL	104	18TH WAR
BUTLER, PAUL	ALL	150	6TH E.D.
BUTLER, PEGGY	BAL	094	10TH WAR
BUTLER, PEGGY	PRI	046	AQUASCO
BUTLER, PERMELIA-BLACK	ST	316	4TH E DI
BUTLER, PERRY-BLACK	ST	346	5TH E DI
BUTLER, PETER	BAL	065	15TH WAR
BUTLER, PETER-BLACK	ST	324	4TH E DI
BUTLER, PRISCILLA*	DOR	304	1ST DIST
BUTLER, R.	BAL	156	1ST WARD
BUTLER, R.	BAL	282	2ND WARD
BUTLER, R.-BLACK	FRE	200	5TH E DI
BUTLER, RACHEL	ANN	369	4TH DIST
BUTLER, RALPH	FRE	266	NEW MARK
BUTLER, REASON-BLACK	ST	327	4TH E DI
BUTLER, REBECCA	ST	269	3RD E DI
BUTLER, REBECCA	HAR	026	1ST DIST
BUTLER, RICHARD	BAL	088	18TH WAR
BUTLER, RICHARD	BAL	118	11TH WAR
BUTLER, RICHARD-BLACK	ST	345	5TH E DI
BUTLER, ROBERT	CAR	137	NO TWP L
BUTLER, ROBERT	MGM	376	ROCKERLE
BUTLER, ROBERT	BAL	410	8TH WARD
BUTLER, ROBERT	BAL	457	8TH WARD
BUTLER, ROBERT	BAL	050	1ST WARD
BUTLER, ROSANA	BAL	026	1ST WARD
BUTLER, ROSETTA	QUE	240	5TH E DI
BUTLER, SAMUEL	BAL	183	2ND WARD
BUTLER, SAMUEL	BAL	200	6TH WARD
BUTLER, SAMUEL	BAL	196	6TH WARD
BUTLER, SAMUEL	CEC	214	7TH E DI
BUTLER, SAMUEL-BLACK	CAR	158	NO TWP L
BUTLER, SANDY	BAL	126	2ND DIST
BUTLER, SARA	CHA	256	MIDDLETO
BUTLER, SARAH	FRE	288	WOODSBOR
BUTLER, SARAH	FRE	117	CREAGERS
BUTLER, SARAH	BAL	236	12TH WAR

Name	County	Page	District
BUTLER, SARAH-BLACK	FRE	027	FREDERIC
BUTLER, SHADRACH-BLACK	ST	328	4TH E DI
BUTLER, SHELDON	CEC	215	7TH E DI
BUTLER, SILAS	BAL	157	1ST WARD
BUTLER, STEPHEN	BAL	345	1ST DIST
BUTLER, SUSAN	ANN	317	1ST DIST
BUTLER, SUSAN	MGM	320	CRACKLIN
BUTLER, SUSAN	CAL	051	3RD DIST
BUTLER, SUSAN	KEN	284	3RD DIST
BUTLER, SUSAN-BLACK	ST	335	4TH E DI
BUTLER, SYLVANUS	ALL	018	3RD E.D.
BUTLER, SYLVESTER-BLACK	CAR	411	2ND DIST
BUTLER, THOMAS	CAL	036	2ND DIST
BUTLER, THOMAS	CAR	111	NO TWP L
BUTLER, THOMAS	FRE	023	FREDERIC
BUTLER, THOMAS	FRE	166	EMMITTSB
BUTLER, THOMAS	CEC	102	4TH E DI
BUTLER, THOMAS	BAL	065	15TH WAR
BUTLER, THOMAS	ANN	419	HOWARD D
BUTLER, THOMAS	BAL	130	1ST WARD
BUTLER, THOMAS	BAL	131	16TH WAR
BUTLER, THOMAS	KEN	301	3RD DIST
BUTLER, THOMAS A.	FRE	033	FREDERIC
BUTLER, THOMAS-BLACK	ST	292	2ND E DI
BUTLER, TOM	CHA	226	ALLENS F
BUTLER, WALTER	CHA	246	HILLTOP
BUTLER, WALTER	HAR	160	3RD DIST
BUTLER, WASHINGTON	CAR	119	NO TWP L
BUTLER, WENTWORTH S.	FRE	380	PETERSVI
BUTLER, WILLIAM	CAR	109	NO TWP L
BUTLER, WILLIAM	BAL	132	11TH WAR
BUTLER, WILLIAM	BAL	103	18TH WAR
BUTLER, WILLIAM	FRE	069	FREDERIC
BUTLER, WILLIAM	DOR	296	1ST DIST
BUTLER, WILLIAM	BAL	236	20TH WAR
BUTLER, WILLIAM	QUE	253	5TH E DI
BUTLER, WILLIAM	PRI	048	AQUASCO
BUTLER, WILLIAM	PRI	082	QUEEN AN
BUTLER, WILLIAM	BAL	130	16TH WAR
BUTLER, WILLIAM	BAL	164	16TH WAR
BUTLER, WILLIAM	BAL	101	2ND DIST
BUTLER, WILLIAM	BAL	134	2ND DIST
BUTLER, WILLIAM	BAL	001	9TH WARD
BUTLER, WILLIAM	ANN	325	2ND DIST
BUTLER, WILLIAM	BAL	374	1ST DIST
BUTLER, WILLIAM	BAL	168	2ND DIST
BUTLER, WILLIAM C.	BAL	287	12TH WAR
BUTLER, WILLIAM E.	CHA	280	BOJANTOW
BUTLER, WILLIAM H.	CHA	264	MIDDLETO
BUTLER, WILLIAM H.	BAL	100	18TH WAR
BUTLER, WILLIAM H.	BAL	136	18TH WAR
BUTLER, WILLIAM W.	CEC	133	6TH E DI
BUTLER, WILLIAM-BLACK	ST	322	4TH E DI
BUTLER,CATHERINE	ALL	235	CUMBERLA
BUTLER,CLOWEI-BLACK	ST	324	4TH E DI
BUTLER,FRED	BAL	250	12TH WAR
BUTLER,PETER	BAL	276	12TH WAR
BUTLER,RACHEL	ALL	236	CUMBERLA
BUTLERBAUGH, GOERGE	BAL	100	5TH WARD
BUTLIR, PRISCILLA*	DOR	304	1ST DIST
BUTNAM, JOHN H.	ALL	221	CUMBERLA
BUTNER, ANDREW	BAL	004	4TH WARD
BUTNER, MICHAEL R.	BAL	409	1ST DIST
BUTSCH, JOHN A.	BAL	017	4TH WARD
BUTSON, JOSEPH	BAL	292	12TH WAR
BUTT, CATHERINE	BAL	295	3RD WARD
BUTT, DE. DR- *	BAL	036	18TH WAR
BUTT, FRED	BAL	273	20TH WAR
BUTT, HAZLE	ALL	210	CUMBERLA
BUTT, HENRY	BAL	252	20TH WAR
BUTT, HENRY	BAL	183	19TH WAR
BUTT, IRA H.	BAL	183	19TH WAR
BUTT, ISAIAAH	FRE	326	MIDDLETO
BUTT, JOHN H.	BAL	015	9TH WARD
BUTT, JOHN-BLACK	FRE	437	8TH E DI
BUTT, JOSEPH	WAS	029	2ND SUBD
BUTT, LETITIA	BAL	183	19TH WAR
BUTT, MARGARETT	BAL	054	4TH WARD
BUTT, PEGGY	WAS	067	2ND SUBD
BUTT, RICHARD	PRI	034	VANSVILL
BUTT, RIGNAL	MGM	362	BERRYS D
BUTT, RUTH	WAS	162	2ND DIST
BUTT, WILLIAM	WAS	214	1ST DIST
BUTT, WILLIAM	ALL	223	CUMBERLA
BUTTE, LIDDY*	BAL	363	3RD WARD
BUTTE, RICHARD	CHA	288	BOJANTOW
BUTTER, A.C.	BAL	162	19TH WAR
BUTTER, ANN	HAR	179	3RD DIST
BUTTER, ANN	ST	343	5TH E DI
BUTTER, ELIZABETH	HAR	134	2ND DIST
BUTTER, EZEKIEL	WOR	178	6TH E DI
BUTTER, GRIFFIN	PRI	106	PISCATAW
BUTTER, HANNAH	ALL	208	CUMBERLA
BUTTER, HENRY	BAL	110	10TH WAR
BUTTER, HESTER	KEN	286	3RD DIST
BUTTER, JAMES	HAR	084	2ND DIST
BUTTER, JOHN-BLACK	CAR	142	NO TWP L
BUTTER, JOSEPH	HAR	134	2ND DIST
BUTTER, JOSEPH	ST	347	5TH E DI
BUTTER, M.	PRI	053	AQUASCO
BUTTER, MANUEL*	DOR	314	1ST DIST
BUTTER, RACHEL	BAL	337	13TH WAR
BUTTER, RACHEL	ANN	501	HOWARD D
BUTTER, SAMUEL	BAL	447	1ST DIST
BUTTER, SARAH	CEC	121	4TH E DI
BUTTER, SOLOMON	CAR	149	NO TWP L
BUTTER, STEPHEN *	BAL	345	1ST DIST
BUTTER, THOMAS	HAR	094	2ND DIST
BUTTER, THOMAS	HAR	055	1ST DIST
BUTTER, WILLAIM	PRI	092	MARLBROU
BUTTER, WILLIAM	HAR	107	2ND DIST
BUTTER, WILLIAM *X	BAL	103	18TH WAR
BUTTER, WILLIAM H.	BAL	446	1ST DIST
BUTTERLY, JAMES	BAL	163	2ND DIST
BUTTKISSER, BARNEY	BAL	210	17TH WAR
BUTTLE, SMITH	CHA	293	BOJANTOW
BUTTLE, E.	BAL	147	5TH WARD
BUTTLER, ELIJAH	BAL	241	17TH WAR
BUTTLER, ELIZABETH	BAL	051	2ND DIST
BUTTLER, JAMES	DOR	316	1ST DIST
BUTTLER, JOHN H.	BAL	192	17TH WAR
BUTTLER, NELSON	BAL	211	17TH WAR
BUTTLER, SILAS	DOR	346	3RD DIVI
BUTTLER, WILLIAM	BAL	056	2ND DIST
BUTTON, EMORY	ANN	291	ANNAPOLI
BUTTON, EMORY	KEN	274	1ST DIST
BUTTON, JACOB	BAL	169	2ND DIST
BUTTON, JACOB	BAL	160	2ND DIST
BUTTON, JAEMS	BAL	101	2ND DIST
BUTTON, SARA B.	CHA	220	ALLENS F

Name	County	Page	District
BUTTON, SUSAN	BAL	369	3RD WARD
BUTTRIL, ISABEL	BAL	012	2ND DIST
BUTTS, BAPTIST	ALL	218	CUMBERLA
BUTTS, CATHERINE	BAL	042	9TH WARD
BUTTS, JACOB	WAS	164	HAGERSTO
BUTTS, JOHN	ANN	324	2ND DIST
BUTTS, JOHN	ANN	322	2ND DIST
BUTTS, JOHN D.	FRE	119	CREAGERS
BUTTS, ROBERT W.	BAL	164	1ST WARD
BUTZ, ANDREW	BAL	031	15TH WAR
BUVALL, ELIZABETH	PRI	004	BLADENSB
BUXON, MARY A.	FRE	095	FREDERIC
BUXTON, JOHN W.	ANN	488	HOWARD D
BUXTON, JULIAN	FRE	382	PETERSVI
BUXTON, MARGARET E.	MGM	339	CLARKSBU
BUXTON, MARY M.	MGM	440	CLARKSTR
BUYERS, HENRYH.	BAL	218	12TH WAR
BUYERS, JOHN	BAL	078	4TH WARD
BUYES, TERRESA	CHA	232	HILLTOP
BUYWIN, CECILIA MISS-	BAL	315	20TH WAR
BUZARD, MARY M.	FRE	214	BUCKEYST
BUZZARD, CATHARINE	FRE	155	10TH E D
BUZZARD, CATHARINE	WAS	197	1ST DIST
BUZZARD, DAVID	CAR	368	9TH DIST
BUZZARD, HANSON	FRE	154	10TH E D
BUZZARD, JOHN	FRE	154	10TH E D
BUZZARD, MARTHA A.	WAS	245	SMITHSBU
BUZZARD, MARY	WAS	198	1ST DIST
BUZZARD, SARAH	FRE	448	8TH E DI
BVAER, MARTHA E.	FRE	402	JEFFERSO
BVENS, SAMUEL	FRE	310	WOODSBOR
BVLAURST, MARGARET	BAL	425	14TH WAR
BVUCKEY, MARY	FRE	047	FREDERIC
BWARP, SARAH*	DOR	411	1ST DIST
BYALL, GEORGE	BAL	230	17TH WAR
BYAN, MATHER	BAL	097	2ND DIST
BYAN, WILLIAM	BAL	155	1ST WARD
BYANE, MICHAEL	BAL	047	1ST WARD
BYARD, ANN	CEC	025	ELKTON 3
BYARD, ANN	CEC	034	CHESAPEA
BYARD, ANNA	CEC	065	1ST E DI
BYARD, CHARLES	CEC	036	CHESAPEA
BYARD, EDITH	CEC	074	5TH E DI
BYARD, EDWARD	CEC	013	ELKTON 3
BYARD, EZEKIEL	CEC	038	CHESAPEA
BYARD, HENRY	CEC	037	CHESAPEA
BYARD, ISAAC	CEC	013	ELKTON 3
BYARD, ISAAC	CEC	053	1ST E DI
BYARD, JAMES	CEC	057	1ST E DI
BYARD, JAMES	CEC	065	1ST E DI
BYARD, JAMES A. *	KEN	253	1ST DIST
BYARD, JAMES-BLACK	CAR	162	NO TWP L
BYARD, JOHN	BAL	092	1ST WARD
BYARD, JOHN R.	HAR	147	3RD DIST
BYARD, JOSEPH	CEC	026	ELKTON 3
BYARD, JULY ANN	HAR	147	3RD DIST
BYARD, MARY	CEC	036	CHESAPEA
BYARD, REBECCA	CEC	030	CHESAPEA
BYARD, SAMUEL	KEN	288	3RD DIST
BYARD, SARAH	CEC	017	ELKTON 3
BYARD, STEPHEN	CEC	024	ELKTON 3
BYARD, SYLVIA	CEC	025	ELKTON 3
BYARD, THOMAS	CEC	026	ELKTON 3
BYARD, THOMAS	CEC	037	CHESAPEA
BYARD, THOMAS	HAR	148	3RD DIST
BYARD, THOMAS	CEC	107	3RD E DI
BYARD, VIRGINIA	HAR	147	3RD DIST
BYAS, CITTY	BAL	286	1ST DIST
BYAS, STEPHEN	BAL	340	7TH WARD
BYDEN, JANE	BAL	284	1ST DIST
BYDEN, MARY	BAL	284	1ST DIST
BYDNE, WILLIAM	BAL	156	1ST WARD
BYEN, CHARLES	BAL	140	1ST WARD
BYEN, TOBY	BAL	458	8TH WARD
BYENS, JAMES	ALL	053	10TH E.D
BYER, ANDREAS	BAL	274	7TH WARD
BYER, CHARLES	BAL	125	1ST WARD
BYER, FRED	BAL	312	20TH WAR
BYER, GEORGE	BAL	283	1ST DIST
BYER, JOHN	BAL	252	1ST DIST
BYER, JOHN	BAL	377	8TH WARD
BYER, JOHN	BAL	071	2ND DIST
BYER, MARGARET	BAL	378	8TH WARD
BYER, MARY FREDOLINE SIS-	BAL	316	20TH WAR
BYER, PETER	BAL	429	8TH WARD
BYERLEY, GEORGE	FRE	148	10TH E D
BYERLEY, JACOB	WAS	170	FUNKSTOW
BYERLEY, SUSAN	FRE	148	10TH E D
BYERLY, CATHARINE	WAS	196	1ST DIST
BYERLY, EZRA	WAS	186	BOONSBOR
BYERLY, JACOB	BAL	236	1ST DIST
BYERLY, JACOB	BAL	192	5TH DIST
BYERLY, JOHN	FRE	144	10TH E D
BYERLY, PETER	BAL	265	1ST DIST
BYERLY, SUSAN	FRE	144	10TH E D
BYERLY, THOMAS	BAL	236	1ST DIST
BYERLY, WILLIAM	CAR	326	1ST DIST
BYERMAN, HY	BAL	209	6TH DIST
BYERMAN, ISAIAH	BAL	302	7TH WARD
BYERS, ALFRED	BAL	241	20TH WAR
BYERS, AMANDA	BAL	174	2ND DIST
BYERS, BARBARA	WAS	062	2ND SUBD
BYERS, BARBARY E.	BAL	069	18TH WAR
BYERS, BENJAMIN J.	WAS	288	1ST DIST
BYERS, CAPT.	WAS	132	HAGERSTO
BYERS, CAROLINE	BAL	203	19TH WAR
BYERS, CHARLES	DOR	383	1ST DIST
BYERS, EDWARD	CAR	209	5TH DIST
BYERS, ELIXIMIA*	DOR	415	1ST DIST
BYERS, ELIZABETH	CAR	293	7TH DIST
BYERS, ELLEN	CAR	293	7TH DIST
BYERS, FREDERICK	FRE	248	NEW MARK
BYERS, FREDERICK	BAL	410	1ST DIST
BYERS, GEORGE	ANN	389	4TH DIST
BYERS, GEORGE K.	WAS	270	1ST DIST
BYERS, HENRY	WAS	270	1ST DIST
BYERS, HENRY	ANN	389	4TH DIST
BYERS, HORACE	DOR	394	1ST DIST
BYERS, IRENE	BAL	157	16TH WAR
BYERS, ISRAEL	FRE	285	WOODSBOR
BYERS, JAMES	DOR	387	1ST DIST
BYERS, JOHN	DOR	415	1ST DIST
BYERS, JOHN	CAR	290	7TH DIST
BYERS, JOHN	WAS	125	HAGERSTO
BYERS, JOHN A.	WAS	158	2ND DIST
BYERS, JOHN J.	WAS	166	1ST DIST
BYERS, JOHN W.	DOR	413	1ST DIST
BYERS, JOSEPH H.	BAL	157	16TH WAR
BYERS, MICHAEL	CAR	295	7TH DIST
BYERS, MOSES	DOR	422	1ST DIST

NAME	CO	PAGE	DISTRICT
BYERS, MOSES-MULATTO	FRE	429	8TH E DI
BYERS, NANCY	WAS	279	LEITERSB
BYERS, NOAH A.	FRE	100	FREDERIC
BYERS, OLIVER	BAL	081	1ST WARD
BYERS, STEPHEN	DOR	406	1ST DIST
BYERS, SUSAN	WAS	149	HAGERSTO
BYERS, SUSANA	CAR	279	7TH DIST
BYERS, THOMAS	DOR	365	3RD DIVI
BYERS, THOMAS E.	FRE	248	NEW MARK
BYERS, THOMAS*	DOR	401	1ST DIST
BYERS, WILLIAM S.*	DOR	380	1ST DIST
BYES, ALEXANDER	BAL	076	2ND DIST
BYHAM, BERRY	BAL	161	19TH WAR
BYHAM, OLIVER	BAL	152	19TH WAR
BYID, LOUISA	BAL	210	11TH WAR
BYINE, EDWARD H.	BAL	403	8TH WARD
BYINE, HENRY F. *	TAL	107	ST MICHA
BYING, CELINDA J.	FRE	047	FREDERIC
BYLAND, ANDREW	ALL	032	2ND E.D.
BYLESS, ADVILLA	HAR	162	3RD DIST
BYMSLOW, HENRY	BAL	303	7TH WARD
BYNION, ANN	CAL	013	1ST DIST
BYNION, JOHN	CAL	018	1ST DIST
BYONS, THOMAS	BAL	067	4TH WARD
BYOUR, JANE	BAL	141	19TH WAR
BYRADES, JOHN	FRE	215	BUCKEYST
BYRAN, DANIEL J.	BAL	228	19TH WAR
BYRAN, GEORGE	BAL	143	2ND DIST
BYRAN, JOHN	KEN	269	1ST DIST
BYRAN, MATHEW	KEN	269	1ST DIST
BYRD, BENJAMIN H.	SOM	502	SALISBUR
BYRD, DAVID	SOM	381	BRINKLEY
BYRD, DAVID	SOM	379	BRINKLEY
BYRD, ELEXINE E.*	SOM	400	BRINKLEY
BYRD, ELIZABETH	SOM	419	PRINCESS
BYRD, ELLEN	SOM	379	BRINKLEY
BYRD, GEORGE	MGM	408	MEDLEY 3
BYRD, HENERETTA	SOM	506	BARREN C
BYRD, HENRY	SOM	381	BRINKLEY
BYRD, HENRY J.	SOM	504	SALISBUR
BYRD, JACOB	SOM	379	BRINKLEY
BYRD, JACOB	SOM	389	BRINKLEY
BYRD, JAEMS	SOM	428	PRINCESS
BYRD, JOHN	SOM	379	BRINKLEY
BYRD, JOHN	SOM	447	DAMES QU
BYRD, JOHN	SOM	443	DAMES QU
BYRD, JOHN	BAL	002	15TH WAR
BYRD, JOHN S.	SOM	523	BARREN C
BYRD, JOSEPH	SOM	378	BRINKLEY
BYRD, JOSHUA	SOM	519	BARREN C
BYRD, LEVI	SOM	383	BRINKLEY
BYRD, MARGARET	BAL	061	15TH WAR
BYRD, MARY	SOM	379	BRINKLEY
BYRD, MARY E.	BAL	002	15TH WAR
BYRD, RHODA	SOM	379	BRINKLEY
BYRD, SALLY A.	SOM	458	DAMES QU
BYRD, STEPHEN	SOM	379	BRINKLEY
BYRD, THOMAS	SOM	494	SALISBUR
BYRD, THOMAS J.	SOM	503	SALISBUR
BYRD, WILLIAM	SOM	379	BRINKLEY
BYRD, WILLIAM J.	SOM	426	PRINCESS
BYRD, WILLIAM R.	SOM	504	SALISBUR
BYREIN, SALLY	BAL	032	1ST WARD
BYRELY, MARGY A.	CAR	326	1ST DIST
BYREMAN, HENRY	FRE	387	PETERSVI
BYRN, BRIDGET	BAL	275	1ST DIST
BYRN, CHARLES	BAL	252	1ST DIST
BYRN, EDWARD	BAL	442	1ST DIST
BYRN, ELIZABETH	MGM	402	ROCKERLE
BYRN, GEORGE E.	BAL	052	15TH WAR
BYRN, JAMES	MGM	400	ROCKERLE
BYRN, LAWRENCE M.D.	BAL	252	1ST DIST
BYRN, MICHAEL	BAL	275	1ST DIST
BYRN, MICHAEL	BAL	453	1ST DIST
BYRN, WILLAIM	BAL	124	5TH WARD
BYRN, WILLIAM W.	BAL	051	15TH WAR
BYRNE, ANN	BAL	100	10TH WAR
BYRNE, ANN	BAL	030	4TH WARD
BYRNE, BRIDGET	BAL	399	14TH WAR
BYRNE, CANIEL	BAL	223	6TH WARD
BYRNE, ELIZA	BAL	212	11TH WAR
BYRNE, ELIZA A.	BAL	212	11TH WAR
BYRNE, ELLEN	BAL	353	13TH WAR
BYRNE, JAMES	BAL	148	1ST WARD
BYRNE, JAMES	BAL	028	9TH WARD
BYRNE, JAMES H.	FRE	065	FREDERIC
BYRNE, JEFFERSON	BAL	030	4TH WARD
BYRNE, JOHN	BAL	083	10TH WAR
BYRNE, JOHN E.	BAL	333	13TH WAR
BYRNE, JOHNB.P	FRE	20	5TH E DI
BYRNE, JOSEPH	BAL	051	2ND DIST
BYRNE, MARY S.	FRE	065	FREDERIC
BYRNE, NICHOLAS	FRE	20	5TH E DI
BYRNE, PIERCE	ALL	242	CUMBERLA
BYRNE, THOMAS	BAL	004	9TH WARD
BYRNE, THOMAS	BAL	472	14TH WAR
BYRNE, WILLIAM	WAS	096	2ND SUBD
BYRNE, WILLIAM H.	BAL	210	6TH WARD
BYRNES, CATHERINE	BAL	109	10TH WAR
BYRNES, E.	FRE	200	5TH E DI
BYRNS, FRANCIS	BAL	275	17TH WAR
BYROAD, JAMES	ALL	230	CUMBERLA
BYRODE, NANCY	FRE	259	NEW MARK
BYRODES, DANIEL	FRE	265	NEW MARK
BYRODES, PETER	FRE	265	NEW MARK
BYROM, CHARLES H.	BAL	137	16TH WAR
BYRON, JAMES	KEN	273	1ST DIST
BYRON, JAMES	BAL	169	1ST WARD
BYRON, PATRICK	WAS	069	2ND SUBD
BYROT, JOHN	BAL	131	16TH WAR
BYRUM, CHARLES	WAS	269	1ST DIST
BYRUM, ELIE	WAS	267	1ST DIST
BYRUN, THOMAS	BAL	424	1ST DIST
BYRUS, ELENORA	BAL	207	11TH WAR
BYRUS, MICHAEL	FRE	069	FREDERIC
BYRUS, ROSE	BAL	304	12TH WAR
BYUS, DELIA*	DOR	378	1ST DIST
BYUS, RACHEL*	BAL	074	10TH WAR
BYUS, THOMAS*	DOR	401	1ST DIST
BYUS, WILLIAM S.*	DOR	380	1ST DIST
BYWOOD, CAROLINE	BAL	073	4TH WARD
CAADOCM, JOHN *	ALL	068	5TH E.D.
CABACH, DANE	BAL	245	12TH WAR
CABBIN, MARY	BAL	392	1ST DIST
CABE, MICHAEL M.	BAL	413	8TH WARD
CABEE, SAMUEL W.	KEN	258	1ST DIST
CABEL, ANTHONY	ALL	202	CUMBERLA
CABELL, ROSE	ALL	234	CUMBERLA
CABEZAS, ISABEL	BAL	213	11TH WAR
CABINSS, MARY	BAL	050	9TH WARD
CABITT, SOPHIA	CEC	180	7TH E DI
CABLE, GEORGE	BAL	282	7TH WARD
CABLE, GEORGE	WOR	345	1ST E DI
CABLE, JAMES-BLACK	WOR	319	1ST E DI
CABLE, JOHN	WOR	326	1ST E DI
CABLE, JOHN	FRE	424	8TH E DI
CABLE, MARY J.	BAL	282	7TH WARD
CABLE, WILLIAM	BAL	072	18TH WAR
CABLE, WILLIAM-BLACK	WOR	320	1ST E DI
CABLES, FREDERICK	ANN	429	HOWARD D
CABLES, MARY	BAL	335	13TH WAR
CABNER, SARAH	CAR	124	NO TWP L
CABRIERE, FRANCIS *	BAL	410	14TH WAR
CACE, JOHN A.	BAL	009	1ST WARD
CACEY, FRANCIS R.	QUE	126	1ST E DI
CACINY, ROSINIA	BAL	248	20TH WAR
CACKE, W. E.	BAL	469	14TH WAR
CACY, CHARLES	KEN	266	1ST DIST
CACY, EDWARD	QUE	157	2ND E DI
CACY, GEORGE W.	KEN	310	3RD DIST
CACY, JOHNE .	KEN	310	3RD DIST
CACY, WILLIAM	KEN	284	3RD DIST
CADAY, ALFRED	BAL	240	6TH WARD
CADDEN, FRANCES	BAL	064	2ND DIST
CADDEN, FRANCIS	ST	284	2ND E DI
CADDEN, FRANCIS	ST	285	2ND E DI
CADDEN, JOSEPH	ANN	303	1ST DIST
CADDEN, PATRICK	BAL	441	1ST DIST
CADDER, ROBERT	BAL	064	2ND DIST
CADDGAN, ANN	BAL	050	9TH WARD
CADDICK, THOMAS	ANN	421	HOWARD D
CADDIN, FRANK	ST	272	3RD E DI
CADDIN, JOHN	ST	280	3RD E DI
CADDIN, JOHN	ST	274	3RD E DI
CADDIN, MARTHA A.	ST	273	3RD E DI
CADDIN, MARY	ST	282	3RD E DI
CADDIN, MITCHEL	ST	272	3RD E DI
CADDINGTCN, WILLIAM	ANN	447	HOWARD D
CADDY, CHARLOTT	HAR	045	1ST DIST
CADE, CHARLES N.	BAL	395	3RD WARD
CADE, ELIJAH	CAR	170	NO TWP L
CADE, ELIZABETH	BAL	012	9TH WARD
CADE, JAMES	ALL	013	3RD E.D.
CADE, NELSON	BAL	395	3RD WARD
CADE, SUSAN	CAR	133	NO TWP L
CADE,W ILLIAM	CAR	168	NO TWP L
CADEGAN, BRIDGET	CAR	193	4TH DIST
CADEL, SAMUEL	BAL	089	18TH WAR
CADEL, SAMUEL	BAL	371	3RD WARD
CADEM, ELIZA	ALL	088	5TH E.D.
CADENCE, JAMES	BAL	019	4TH WARD
CADETT, JOHN	BAL	394	3RD WARD
CADFLESSER, JOHN	WAS	162	HAGERSTO
CADIS, JAMES	BAL	354	7TH WARD
CADLE, ANN	ANN	323	2ND DIST
CADLE, ANN	ANN	346	3RD DIST
CADLE, HUMPHREY	PRI	006	BLADENSB
CADLE, JAMES	ANN	323	2ND DIST
CADLE, JAMES S.	PRI	118	PISCATAW
CADLE, MARY	WAS	180	BOONSBOR
CADLE, MARY	ANN	323	2ND DIST
CADLE, RICHARD	ANN	323	2ND DIST
CADLE, RUFUS W.	ANN	428	HOWARD D
CADLELER, GUTLIP	BAL	209	17TH WAR
CADOMORE, JOHN	BAL	075	1ST WARD
CADON, JAMES E.	BAL	161	19TH WAR
CADUC, MARY A.	BAL	069	15TH WAR
CADWALLADER, ABEL	BAL	174	19TH WAR
CADWALLADER, HANNAH	HAR	078	2ND DIST
CADY, ELISA	BAL	016	18TH WAR
CADY, JOHN	ANN	418	HOWARD D
CADY, JOHN	BAL	418	1ST DIST
CADY, MARY	BAL	431	14TH WAR
CADY, NANCY	MGM	398	ROCKERLE
CADY, WILLIAM A.	MGM	397	ROCKERLE
CAEN, JOSHUA	FRE	247	NEW MARK
CAFF, HANAH	WOR	220	4TH E DI
CAFF, THOMAS	ALL	050	10TH E.D
CAFF, THOMAS *	KEN	208	2ND DIST
CAFFERTY, ELIZABETH M.	BAL	119	15TH WAR
CAFFERTY, THOMAS	BAL	291	7TH WARD
CAFFEY, JAMES	BAL	160	1ST WARD
CAFFEY, WILLIAM	HAR	048	1ST DIST
CAFFREY, DONALDSON	BAL	312	12TH WAR
CAFFREY, HUGH	HAR	152	3RD DIST
CAFFREY, ROSA	BAL	073	10TH WAR
CAFFREY, SUSAN	BAL	259	12TH WAR
CAFNEIT, CONRAD	BAL	066	1ST WARD
CAFRAN, CATHARINE	BAL	333	13TH WAR
CAGE, ANDREW	ALL	160	6TH E.D.
CAGE, JAMES	HAR	191	3RD DIST
CAGE, JOHN	CHA	283	BOJANTOW
CAGE, JOHN	PRI	067	NOTTINGH
CAGE, T.T.	PRI	053	AQUASCO
CAGE, THOMAS J.	CHA	283	BOJANTOW
CAGE, WILLIAM	PRI	067	NOTTINGH
CAGER, GEORGE	ANN	445	HOWARD D
CAGER, JOHN	BAL	172	6TH WARD
CAGER, MARGARET	BAL	302	7TH WARD
CAGLE, ADAM	ALL	261	CUMBERLA
CAGLE, ADEN	ALL	226	CUMBERLA
CAGLE, GEORGE	ALL	261	CUMBERLA
CAGNIER, BARBARA	BAL	053	1ST WARD
CAGNIER, STEFFIN	BAL	053	1ST WARD
CAGWOOD, ALICE	PRI	113	PISCATAW
CAGY, CAROLINE	BAL	296	3RD WARD
CAGY, PETER	BAL	077	4TH WARD
CAHAL, ELIZABETH	TAL	027	EASTON D
CAHAL, EMELINE	TAL	072	EASTON T
CAHAL, MARGARET	TAL	082	ST MICHA
CAHAL, MARY C.	TAL	061	EASTON D
CAHALL, ALEXANDER	CAR	096	NO TWP L
CAHALL, ANN	CAR	095	NO TWP L
CAHALL, BAYARD	CAR	084	NO TWP L
CAHALL, MARIAH	CAR	094	NO TWP L
CAHALL, SOLOMON	CAR	112	NO TWP L
CAHALL, THOMAS	CAR	076	NO TWP L
CAHALL, WILLIAM	QUE	201	3RD E DI
CAHALL, WILLIAM H.	CAR	120	NO TWP L
CAHARTY, MARY F.	BAL	038	2ND DIST
CAHAUF, CHARLES	BAL	076	1ST WARD
CAHEIL, SARAH	ALL	252	CUMBERLA
CAHEL, JOHN	BAL	127	5TH WARD
CAHERTY, PATRICK	BAL	275	20TH WAR
CAHIL, JOHN	ALL	237	CUMBERLA
CAHILL, CATHARINE	WAS	279	LEITERSB
CAHILL, EDMUND	BAL	404	3RD WARD
CAHILL, ELIZABETH	BAL	012	15TH WAR
CAHILL, ELIZABETH	BAL	297	17TH WAR
CAHILL, JACOB	WAS	278	LEITERSB
CAHILL, JAMES	BAL	234	17TH WAR
CAHILL, JOHN W.	WAS	104	2ND DIST
CAHILL, MARGARET A.	BAL	213	11TH WAR
CAHILL, PATRICK	BAL	368	13TH WAR
CAHOE, MATHIAS	WAS	280	LEITERSB
CAHOE,MARTIN	FRE	390	PETERSVI
CAHOLE, PATRICK	CEC	174	6TH E DI
CAHOON, EMMA	SOM	393	BRINKLEY
CAHOON, JAMES	ALL	118	5TH E.D.
CAHOON, JOHN	BAL	055	2ND DIST
CAHSE, JOSEPH	BAL	201	11TH WAR
CAIBAN, REBECCA	BAL	252	2ND WARD
CAIG, JOHN	BAL	125	1ST WARD
CAIG, WESLY	BAL	160	2ND DIST
CAIHHBERY, JAACOB*	BAL	115	11TH WAR
CAILER, ANDREW	WAS	217	1ST DIST
CAILER, JOHN	WAS	217	1ST DIST
CAILOR, ANDREW	WAS	229	1ST DIST
CAILOR, JACOB	WAS	222	1ST DIST
CAIMS, JAMES	BAL	026	1ST WARD
CAIN, AARON	BAL	069	15TH WAR
CAIN, AARON	BAL	151	1ST WARD
CAIN, ALFRED	BAL	190	11TH WAR
CAIN, ALFRED	QUE	214	3RD E DI
CAIN, ANDREW	HAR	055	1ST DIST
CAIN, ANN-BLACK	CAR	359	9TH DIST
CAIN, ANTHONY	ALL	261	CUMBERLA
CAIN, BENJAMIN	FRE	252	NEW MARK
CAIN, BERNARD	CAR	244	3RD DIST
CAIN, CAMBERLIN	HAR	033	1ST DIST
CAIN, CATHARINE	BAL	187	16TH WAR
CAIN, CATHERINE	FRE	246	NEW MARK
CAIN, DANIEL	ALL	255	CUMBERLA
CAIN, DAVIS	BAL	100	2ND DIST
CAIN, DEBIE	ANN	317	1ST DIST
CAIN, EDWARD	BAL	286	2ND WARD
CAIN, ELIZABETH	FRE	265	NEW MARK
CAIN, ELLEN	BAL	319	20TH WAR
CAIN, FRANCES	WAS	148	HAGERSTO
CAIN, GEORGE	CAR	285	7TH DIST
CAIN, ISAAC	WAS	106	2ND DIST
CAIN, ISAAC	WAS	294	1ST DIST
CAIN, JACOB	BAL	043	9TH WARD
CAIN, JOHN	ALL	129	4TH E.D.
CAIN, JOHN	ALL	053	10TH E.D
CAIN, JOHN	ALL	052	10TH E.D
CAIN, JOHN	ALL	257	CUMBERLA
CAIN, JOHN	BAL	065	1ST WARD
CAIN, JOHN D.	FRE	248	NEW MARK
CAIN, JOSEPH	FRE	246	NEW MARK
CAIN, LEVI	WAS	164	HAGERSTO
CAIN, LEWIS	HAR	055	1ST DIST
CAIN, MARY	QUE	211	3RD E DI
CAIN, MARY A.	BAL	127	16TH WAR
CAIN, MATHEW	ALL	052	10TH E.D
CAIN, MATTHEW	HAR	103	2ND DIST
CAIN, MICHAEL	BAL	448	14TH WAR
CAIN, MICHAEL	ALL	257	CUMBERLA
CAIN, MICHAEL	BAL	021	15TH WAR
CAIN, PATRICK	ALL	255	CUMBERLA
CAIN, PATRICK	ALL	052	10TH E.D
CAIN, PATRICK	ALL	057	10TH E.D
CAIN, PATRICK	BAL	120	16TH WAR
CAIN, RICHARD	CAR	287	7TH DIST
CAIN, SARAH	FRE	252	NEW MARK
CAIN, SOLOMON	FRE	453	8TH E DI
CAIN, THOMAS	FRE	417	8TH E DI
CAIN, THOMAS	BAL	014	4TH WARD
CAIN, THOMAS	ALL	202	CUMBERLA
CAIN, THOMAS	WAS	164	HAGERSTO
CAIN, TILGHMAN	WAS	017	2ND SUBD
CAIN, TIMOTHY	ALL	048	10TH E.D
CAIN, WILLIAM	BAL	120	16TH WAR
CAIN, WILLIAM	FRE	252	NEW MARK
CAINE, BERNARD	BAL	149	5TH WARD
CAINE, W. JOSHUA	FRE	248	NEW MARK
CAINER, E.	BAL	139	1ST WARD
CAINES, MATTHEW	BAL	253	20TH WAR
CAINEY, ELIZABETH	BAL	038	1ST WARD
CAINS, ELLENORA	BAL	111	1ST WARD
CAINS, JOHN	BAL	073	1ST WARD
CAINS, JOHN	BAL	200	2ND WARD
CAIR, CHARLES	QUE	209	3RD E DI
CAIR, THOMAS	QUE	214	3RD E DI
CAIR, WILLIAM	BAL	446	8TH WARD
CAIRNES, C.	WAS	020	2ND SUBD
CAIRNES, MARY A.	HAR	006	1ST DIST
CAIRNES, WILLIAM	HAR	065	1ST DIST
CAIRNS, EDWARD	BAL	074	4TH WARD
CAIS, WILLIAM	CEC	024	ELKTON 3
CAIZAR, THOMAS C.	CEC	075	NORTHEAS
CAKER, JACOB	CAR	390	2ND DIST
CAKLES, JACOB	BAL	110	1ST WARD
CAKNER, CHARLES	BAL	219	19TH WAR
CALAHAN, JOHN	ALL	002	3RD E.D.
CALAHAN, JOHN	WOR	321	1ST E DI
CALAHAN, MARGARET	WAS	190	1ST DIST
CALAHAN, MARTHA	QUE	135	1ST E DI
CALAHAN, THOMAS	WAS	189	1ST DIST
CALAHAN, THOMAS	ALL	155	6TH E.D.
CALAHAN,W ILLIAM	BAL	053	2ND DIST
CALAMAN, WESLY	WAS	072	2ND SUBD
CALAMAR, JOHN	WAS	073	2ND SUBD
CALAMER, ROL	WAS	071	2ND SUBD
CALAMER, WILLIAM	WAS	071	2ND SUBD
CALARY, PETER	HAR	067	1ST DIST
CALASKY, CHARLES	ALL	249	CUMBERLA
CALAWAY, AARON H.	SOM	521	BARREN C
CALAWAY, BENJAMIN	SOM	496	SALISBUR
CALAWAY, CHARLES	DOR	301	1ST DIST
CALAWAY, CHARLES W.	SOM	506	BARREN C
CALAWAY, H. R.	SOM	494	SALISBUR
CALAWAY, JONATHAN	DOR	302	1ST DIST
CALAWAY, MARGARET	BAL	182	6TH WARD
CALAWAY, SAMUEL	DOR	301	1ST DIST
CALAWAY, STANSBERRY	SOM	541	TYASKIN
CALBECK, THOMAS	BAL	286	2ND WARD
CALBERT, ELIZABETH	BAL	351	1ST DIST
CALBERT, WILLIAM	BAL	406	1ST DIST
CALBERT, WILLIAM	WAS	158	2ND DIST
CALCHAN, MARTHA-BLACK	CAR	080	NO TWP L
CALDAN, JAMES	ALL	188	9TH E.D.
CALDAN, JOHN	ALL	053	10TH E.D
CALDER, HARRIET	ANN	274	ANNAPOLI
CALDER, JOSEPHUS	HAR	064	1ST DIST
CALDER, LLOYD	HAR	063	1ST DIST
CALDER, LLOYD	HAR	058	1ST DIST
CALDER, MARY E.	KEN	213	2ND DIST
CALDER, PRESTON M.	HAR	067	1ST DIST
CALDER, WILLIAM	BAL	304	20TH WAR

Name	County	Page	District
CALDWEL, MARY H.	BAL	198	11TH WAR
CALDWELE, JOSEPH*	DOR	379	1ST DIST
CALDWELL, BARBARA	BAL	477	14TH WAR
CALDWELL, BENJAMIN-BLACK	CAR	149	NO TWP L
CALDWELL, CATHERINE	BAL	025	1ST WARD
CALDWELL, CHARLE	BAL	020	2ND DIST
CALDWELL, CHARLES	BAL	024	1ST WARD
CALDWELL, CHARLES	BAL	304	17TH WAR
CALDWELL, DANIEL	BAL	166	11TH WAR
CALDWELL, DAVID S.	ANN	289	ANNAPOLI
CALDWELL, ELIJAH	BAL	198	11TH WAR
CALDWELL, ELIZABETH	CEC	194	7TH E DI
CALDWELL, ELLEN	CEC	203	6TH E DI
CALDWELL, FRANKLIN	FRE	174	5TH E DI
CALDWELL, GEORGE	BAL	125	5TH WARD
CALDWELL, GEORGE	BAL	165	16TH WAR
CALDWELL, HARRIET	CEC	145	PORT DUP
CALDWELL, J.	BAL	140	1ST WARD
CALDWELL, J.B.	BAL	114	1ST WARD
CALDWELL, JAMES	BAL	024	1ST WARD
CALDWELL, JAMES	BAL	035	9TH WARD
CALDWELL, JAMES	BAL	014	15TH WAR
CALDWELL, JAMES	ANN	418	HOWARD D
CALDWELL, JOHN	BAL	098	15TH WAR
CALDWELL, JOHN L.	MGM	382	ROCKERLE
CALDWELL, JOHN M.	MGM	409	MEDLEY 3
CALDWELL, JOHN W.	CEC	195	6TH E DI
CALDWELL, JOSEPH*	DOR	379	1ST DIST
CALDWELL, JOSIAH	CEC	186	7TH E DI
CALDWELL, JOSPEH	CAR	273	WESTMINS
CALDWELL, MARGARET	BAL	452	14TH WAR
CALDWELL, MARTHA	FRE	167	EMMITTSB
CALDWELL, MARY	FRE	169	5TH E DI
CALDWELL, MARY	FRE	170	5TH E DI
CALDWELL, MARY	HAR	078	2ND DIST
CALDWELL, MARY	WAS	065	2ND SUBD
CALDWELL, MARY A.	BAL	025	1ST WARD
CALDWELL, NICKERSON	BAL	198	11TH WAR
CALDWELL, ROBERT	BAL	009	18TH WAR
CALDWELL, SISTER M.E.	FRE	198	5TH E DI
CALDWELL, THOMAS	CEC	203	6TH E DI
CALDWELL, THOMAS	CEC	203	6TH E DI
CALDWELL, THOMAS	BAL	168	6TH WARD
CALDWELL, WILLIAM	BAL	170	1ST WARD
CALDWELL, WILLIAM	BAL	223	6TH WARD
CALDWELL, WILLIAM	BAL	221	12TH WAR
CALDWELL, WILLIAM	BAL	283	2ND WARD
CALDWELL, WILLIAM N.	MGM	408	MEDLEY 3
CALDWELL, WILLIAM Q.	BAL	452	14TH WAR
CALE, ELIZA	BAL	196	19TH WAR
CALE, GEORGE-BLACK	ST	333	4TH E DI
CALE, LAR	BAL	286	7TH WARD
CALE, WILLIAM-BLACK	ST	331	4TH E DI
CALEAL, BELINA	QUE	168	2ND E DI
CALEB, ANN	KEN	271	1ST DIST
CALEB, HARRIET-BLACK	FRE	409	JEFFERSO
CALEB, JOSEPH	WAS	008	WILLIAMS
CALEB, MARTHA-BLACK	FRE	409	JEFFERSO
CALEB, MARTHA-MULATTO	FRE	407	JEFFERSO
CALEB, SAMUEL W.	KEN	257	1ST DIST
CALEF, SARAH-BLACK	FRE	223	BUCKEYST
CALENDER, HENRY	DOR	370	3RD DIVI
CALES, HARBIN	ALL	236	CUMBERLA
CALFORD, THOMAS	BAL	066	2ND DIST
CALFREY, JOHN	BAL	091	1ST WARD
CALHOON, JOHN	BAL	352	13TH WAR
CALHOON, LYDIA	BAL	181	2ND DIST
CALHOUN, BENJAMIN	HAR	161	3RD DIST
CALHOUN, BENJAMIN C.	BAL	015	18TH WAR
CALHOUN, CHARLES	BAL	436	14TH WAR
CALHOUN, HENRY	BAL	436	14TH WAR
CALHOUN, SUSAN	ANN	453	HOWARD D
CALHOUN, WILLIAM	BAL	424	1ST DIST
CALHOUN, WILLIAM	WOR	262	BERLIN 1
CALIGAN, ANN	BAL	368	13TH WAR
CALIHAN, CAVID	WOR	302	SNOW HIL
CALIK, MARY	CEC	011	ELKTON 3
CALILE, WASHINGTON	HAR	190	3RD DIST
CALIP, ALLIS-BLACK	FRE	219	BUCKEYST
CALIP, ATHALA	WAS	026	2ND SUBD
CALISTER, MARY M.	WOR	262	BERLIN 1
CALK, HESTER A.	ANN	420	HOWARD D
CALK, JAMES	KEN	297	3RD DIST
CALK, JOHN	KEN	294	3RD DIST
CALKER, J.	BAL	285	12TH WAR
CALL, CATHARINE	BAL	309	12TH WAR
CALL, CATHARINE	FRE	203	5TH E DI
CALL, CHARITY	BAL	350	1ST DIST
CALL, HUGH	FRE	130	CREAGERS
CALL, LEWIS	BAL	125	1ST WARD
CALL, THOMAS	BAL	264	20TH WAR
CALL, D.	BAL	118	1ST WARD
CALLA, JOHN	BAL	439	1ST DIST
CALLAGFERLER, JAMES	BAL	100	1ST WARD
CALLAGHAN, CANIEL	BAL	300	3RD WARD
CALLAGHAN, WILIAM	ALL	050	10TH E.D
CALLAHAN, ALEXANDER	TAL	022	EASTON D
CALLAHAN, ANDREW	TAL	048	EASTON T
CALLAHAN, BRIDGET	BAL	107	5TH WARD
CALLAHAN, ELLEN	BAL	304	17TH WAR
CALLAHAN, FELIX	ALL	078	5TH E.D.
CALLAHAN, JAMES	BAL	458	1ST DIST
CALLAHAN, JAMES	TAL	023	EASTON D
CALLAHAN, JOHN	TAL	062	EASTON D
CALLAHAN, JOHN	ALL	056	10TH E.D
CALLAHAN, JOHN	MGM	389	ROCKERLE
CALLAHAN, ROBERT	QUE	191	3RD E DI
CALLAHAN, ROBERT H.	TAL	012	EASTON D
CALLAHAN, SAMUEL	TAL	021	EASTON D
CALLAHAN, SAMUEL G.	ST	343	5TH E DI
CALLAHAN, THOMAS	BAL	227	1ST DIST
CALLAHAN, THOMAS	ALL	237	CUMBERLA
CALLAHAN, THOMAS	BAL	253	12TH WAR
CALLAHAN, WILLIAM	QUE	215	3RD E DI
CALLAHAN, WILLIAM C.	TAL	022	EASTON D
CALLAHON, SUSAN	BAL	456	14TH WAR
CALLAMAN, THOMAS	FRE	267	NEW MARK
CALLAN, CATHERINE	BAL	127	11TH WAR
CALLAN, FRANCIS	BAL	141	5TH WARD
CALLAN, JAMES	BAL	044	9TH WARD
CALLAN, THOMAS	BAL	038	9TH WARD
CALLANA, JOHN	BAL	390	8TH WARD
CALLAR, DANIEL	HAR	061	1ST DIST
CALLAWAY, CHARLES D.	DOR	299	1ST DIST
CALLAWAY, GEORGE	BAL	085	15TH WAR
CALLBELL, JAMES R.	BAL	173	1ST WARD
CALLEGHAN, C. O.	BAL	152	1ST WARD
CALLEGHAN, THOMAS	BAL	358	13TH WAR
CALLEHAN, NANCY E.	BAL	262	17TH WAR
CALLEM, A.	BAL	140	1ST WARD
CALLEM, GEORGE *	BAL	043	18TH WAR
CALLEN, ANN	BAL	379	1ST DIST
CALLEN, BRIDGET	BAL	199	11TH WAR
CALLENBEYER, WILLIAM	BAL	205	19TH WAR
CALLENDER, ANN	ANN	463	HOWARD D
CALLENDER, S. N.	WAS	172	FUNKSTOW
CALLENDER, SARAH	BAL	013	15TH WAR
CALLENDER, SARAH	BAL	053	4TH WARD
CALLENDER, WILLIAM	BAL	249	6TH WARD
CALLENGERGER, S. A.	ANN	416	HOWARD D
CALLER, PATRICK	HAR	061	1ST DIST
CALLEY, EBEN	CEC	040	CHESAPEA
CALLEY, JERRY	BAL	286	20TH WAR
CALLEY, MARK	BAL	100	1ST WARD
CALLIHAN, MARGARET	FRE	194	5TH E DI
CALLIHAW, JAMES	FRE	182	5TH E DI
CALLIS, ALBERT	BAL	155	1ST WARD
CALLIS, GEORGE R.	BAL	290	3RD WARD
CALLIS, JAMES H.	BAL	290	3RD WARD
CALLISON, JOHN W.S.	ST	304	2ND E DI
CALLISON, SAMUEL	ST	304	2ND E DI
CALLISON, WELFORD-MULATTO	ST	312	1ST E DI
CALLMOER, ANN S.	BAL	007	1ST WARD
CALLOMAN, JOSEPH-BLACK	FRE	223	BUCKEYST
CALLOMAN, OTHC-MULATTO	FRE	234	BUCKEYST
CALLON, TIMOTHY	BAL	218	12TH WAR
CALLOW, ELIZABETH	BAL	303	12TH WAR
CALLOW, JOHN	BAL	278	20TH WAR
CALLOW, WILLIAM	BAL	409	14TH WAR
CALLOWAY, CHARLOTTE	WOR	239	6TH E DI
CALLOWAY, JACOB	QUE	155	2ND E DI
CALLOWAY, PERCY	WOR	195	8TH E DI
CALLOWAY, SARAH E.	QUE	187	3RD E DI
CALLOWAY, SARAH M.	QUE	187	3RD E DI
CALLOWAY, THOMAS	WOR	239	6TH E DI
CALLOWAY, WILLIAM L.	BAL	455	8TH WARD
CALLRIDER, JOHN	BAL	037	18TH WAR
CALLWELL, WILLIAM	BAL	273	17TH WAR
CALMARY, JAMES	CEC	030	CHESAPEA
CALOLES, CHARLES	BAL	401	8TH WARD
CALOLES, MARY	BAL	401	8TH WARD
CALOMAN, CHARLES W.	FRE	224	BUCKEYST
CALON, WILLIAM	BAL	011	2ND DIST
CALRK, C.E.	PRI	058	NOTTINGH
CALRK, SARAH	ALL	112	5TH E.D.
CALRKE, AMANDA	FRE	168	EMMITTSB
CALRKE, HARRIETT A.	BAL	215	11TH WAR
CALSERT, SYLVESTER	FRE	063	FREDERIC
CALTDRIDER, SARAH	BAL	210	6TH DIST
CALTRIDER, BARBARY	BAL	210	6TH DIST
CALTSCOTT, SLEVIN	CAR	114	NO TWP L
CALTZ, JAMES	BAL	177	19TH WAR
CALUSBY, MICHAEL	BAL	304	17TH WAR
CALVALAGA, MARY	BAL	033	15TH WAR
CALVENT, OPPER	BAL	175	11TH WAR
CALVER, CHARLOTTE A.	WOR	234	6TH E DI
CALVER, JAMES-MULATTO	BAL	224	2ND WARD
CALVERT, ALICE	CEC	082	CHARLEST
CALVERT, BIGGS	CAL	054	3RD DIST
CALVERT, BILL	ANN	300	1ST DIST
CALVERT, CASSANDRA	MGM	371	BERRYS D
CALVERT, CECILIA	BAL	141	11TH WAR
CALVERT, CHARELS F.	PRI	073	MARLBROU
CALVERT, CHARLES	BAL	128	11TH WAR
CALVERT, CHARLES B.	PRI	008	BLADENSB
CALVERT, EDWARD H.	PRI	068	NOTTINGH
CALVERT, G.	PRI	119	PISCATAW
CALVERT, GEORGE	WAS	022	2ND SUBD
CALVERT, GEORGE	ANN	300	1ST DIST
CALVERT, GEORGE	BAL	441	8TH WARD
CALVERT, HARRIET	BAL	249	20TH WAR
CALVERT, HENRY	BAL	300	17TH WAR
CALVERT, HENRY	ANN	363	4TH DIST
CALVERT, ISABELLA	BAL	411	1ST DIST
CALVERT, ISABELLA	CEC	184	7TH E DI
CALVERT, JACKSON	ANN	328	2ND DIST
CALVERT, JANE	BAL	387	13TH WAR
CALVERT, JOHN	CEC	187	7TH E DI
CALVERT, JOSEPH	BAL	355	1ST DIST
CALVERT, JULIA A.	BAL	353	7TH WARD
CALVERT, KITTY	ANN	362	4TH DIST
CALVERT, MR-	ANN	301	1ST DIST
CALVERT, MULKY	BAL	248	20TH WAR
CALVERT, ROBERT	BAL	283	2ND WARD
CALVERT, SARAH A.	BAL	137	16TH WAR
CALVERT, SUSAN-BLACK	FRE	182	5TH E DI
CALVERT, WILLIAM	CEC	083	CHARLEST
CALVERT, WILLIAM	BAL	334	7TH WARD
CALVERT, WILLIAM V.	BAL	133	11TH WAR
CALVERWELL, WILLIAM	BAL	266	2ND WARD
CALVEY, PATRICK	BAL	189	11TH WAR
CALVIMER, GEORGE*	BAL	304	3RD WARD
CALVIN, GEORGE	BAL	165	1ST WARD
CALVIN, GEORGE	BAL	172	1ST WARD
CALVIN, JOHN	CEC	060	1ST E DI
CALVIN, PATRICK	BAL	163	19TH WAR
CALVIN, RACHEL*	BAL	425	3RD WARD
CALVIN, RICHARD *	ANN	376	4TH DIST
CALVIN, WILLIAM	WAS	062	2ND SUBD
CALWELL, ANN	BAL	007	15TH WAR
CALWELL, ELIZABETH	BAL	070	15TH WAR
CALWELL, JOHN	BAL	216	6TH DIST
CALWELL, JOHN K.	BAL	068	15TH WAR
CALWELL, LUCIAN B.	BAL	066	15TH WAR
CALZAR, FOARD	CEC	021	ELKTON 3
CAMACK, HOSEY-MULATTO	BAL	223	2ND WARD
CAMALIER, JHN A.	ST	266	3RD E DI
CAMAN, PAT	BAL	258	20TH WAR
CAMBEL, ELLEN	BAL	251	1ST DIST
CAMBELL, ALEXANDRIA	FRE	384	PETERSVI
CAMBELL, ELIZABETH	BAL	231	2ND WARD
CAMBELL, JACOB	CAR	333	MANCHEST
CAMBELL, WASHINGTON L.	BAL	249	1ST DIST
CAMBEN, W.	ANN	282	ANNAPOLI
CAMBERLIN, WILLIAM J.	HAR	033	1ST DIST
CAMBERS, NED	ANN	288	ANNAPOLI
CAMBERS, PERRY	KEN	211	2ND DIST
CAMBERS, SAVERA	CAR	286	7TH DIST
CAMBEY, WILLIAM J.	CEC	202	6TH E DI
CAMBLE, ALLACE	BAL	443	1ST DIST
CAMBLE, JAMES	CAR	182	8TH DIST
CAMBLE, MARIA	CHA	224	ALLENS F
CAMBLE, MATHEW	CHA	288	BOJANTOW
CAMBLE, ROBERT	TAL	011	EASTON D
CAMBLE, SAMUEL	BAL	373	1ST DIST
CAMBPEE, WILLIAM	TAL	106	ST MICHA
CAMBPELL, ANN	BAL	375	13TH WAR
CAMBPELL, BARBARA	FRE	160	EMMITTSB
CAMBPELL, ISAIAH	WOR	250	1ST CENS
CAMBPELL, JANE E.	ST	277	3RD E DI
CAMBPELL, JOHN	BAL	281	2ND WARD
CAMBPELL, JOHN	BAL	441	8TH WARD
CAMBPELL, MARGARET	BAL	346	13TH WAR
CAMBPELL, THOMAS	BAL	145	1ST WARD
CAMBRIDGE, MARY	BAL	329	13TH WAR
CAMBRIDGET, JOHN M.	BAL	123	5TH WARD
CAMBRILL, JOHN G.	BAL	142	1ST WARD
CAMBROSE, JAMES	BAL	169	1ST WARD
CAMBURK, DIANNA-BLACK	FRE	017	FREDERIC
CAMBWELL, WILLIAM*	DOR	379	1ST DIST
CAMCO, GEORGE	CHA	280	BOJANTOW
CAMCO, THOMAS	CHA	280	BOJANTOW
CAMDEN, GEORGE H.	ANN	268	ANNAPOLI
CAMDEN, JOHN M.	BAL	187	2ND WARD
CAMDEN, MASON	ANN	324	2ND DIST
CAMDEN, THOMAS M.	ANN	330	2ND DIST
CAME, EDWARD	WAS	150	2ND DIST
CAMEFORD, JAMES	ALL	199	CUMBERLA
CAMEL, CATHARINE	BAL	280	1ST DIST
CAMEL, JAMES	CHA	257	MIDDLETO
CAMEL, MARTHA	PRI	108	PISCATAW
CAMEL, WILLIAM	HAR	191	3RD DIST
CAMELL, ANN	SOM	400	BRINKLEY
CAMELL, DISACK	BAL	376	1ST DIST
CAMELL, JOHN	BAL	099	2ND DIST
CAMELL, JOHN H.	SOM	506	BARREN C
CAMELLAIR, VINCENT	ST	254	3RD E DI
CAMER, EMORA *	KEN	253	1ST DIST
CAMERAN, JAMES	BAL	133	1ST WARD
CAMERE, ARCHIBALD	ALL	145	6TH E.D.
CAMERE, CASPAR	BAL	308	20TH WAR
CAMEPON, ALICE	CEC	138	6TH E DI
CAMERON, ALICE	BAL	012	9TH WARD
CAMERON, AMOS	CEC	137	6TH E DI
CAMERON, ANDREW	CEC	018	ELKTON 3
CAMERON, ANDREW M.	CEC	126	5TH E DI
CAMERON, ANN	BAL	325	12TH WAR
CAMERON, C. C.	WAS	178	BOONSBOR
CAMERON, CATHARINE	BAL	437	1ST DIST
CAMERON, ESTHER A.	WOR	309	2ND E DI
CAMERON, GEORGE W.	CEC	126	5TH E DI
CAMERON, HUGH	CEC	125	5TH E DI
CAMERON, HUGH	BAL	143	2ND DIST
CAMERON, HUGH	BAL	175	2ND WARD
CAMERON, JAMES N.	CEC	125	5TH E DI
CAMERON, JOHN	CEC	194	7TH E DI
CAMERON, JOHN	KEN	273	1ST DIST
CAMERON, JOHN C.	CEC	125	5TH E DI
CAMERON, JOSEPH	CEC	145	PORT DUP
CAMERON, JOSEPH	PR	107	PISCATAW
CAMERON, JOSEPH	BAL	005	9TH WARD
CAMERON, JOSIAH	CAR	164	NO TWP L
CAMERON, M.	BAL	159	1ST WARD
CAMERON, MARGARET	CEC	130	6TH E DI
CAMERON, RACHEL	BAL	206	6TH WARD
CAMERON, ROSE	BAL	046	9TH WARD
CAMERON, SAMUEL	CEC	194	7TH E DI
CAMERON, SARAH	BAL	264	17TH WAR
CAMERON, THOMAS	CEC	147	PORT DUP
CAMERON, WILLIAM	CEC	126	5TH E DI
CAMERON, WILLIAM	CEC	192	5TH E DI
CAMERON, WILLIAM	CEC	195	6TH E DI
CAMERON, WILLIAM	CEC	072	5TH E DI
CAMERSON, SARAH	BAL	276	17TH WAR
CAMES, MARGARET	CEC	194	7TH E DI
CAMESUAS, FREDERICK	CEC	148	PORT DUP
CAMFIELD, ADAM	BAL	041	18TH WAR
CAMICK, SARAH	BAL	227	19TH WAR
CAMIE, MARGARET	BAL	314	12TH WAR
CAMILL, MARGARET	BAL	361	1ST DIST
CAMINEHART, MARY	WAS	277	LEITERSB
CAML, ANN	BAL	036	1ST WARD
CAMMACK, MAITLEY	BAL	134	11TH WAR
CAMMAN, MARY *	BAL	149	2ND DIST
CAMMEL, ELLEN	FRE	301	WOODSBOR
CAMMEL, J.	PRI	118	PISCATAW
CAMMEL, JAMES	CAL	038	2ND DIST
CAMMEL, LEVIN H.	TAL	054	EASTON D
CAMMELL, CATHERINE	BAL	318	20TH WAR
CAMMELL, NATHAN.	BAL	330	1ST DIST
CAMMER, MARY A.	BAL	454	14TH WAR
CAMMILL, ELIZA-BLACK	FRE	038	FREDERIC
CAMNORD, LARY L.	HAR	154	3RD DIST
CAMP, ADAM	HAR	060	1ST DIST
CAMP, ALICE MRS-	BAL	315	20TH WAR
CAMP, E.S. SUMMER	ALL	216	CUMBERLA
CAMP, ELIJAH	ALL	011	3RD E.D.
CAMP, GEORGE W.	KEN	253	1ST DIST
CAMP, JAMES L.	BAL	131	16TH WAR
CAMP, JOSEPH	BAL	004	1ST WARD
CAMP, MARY	BAL	178	19TH WAR
CAMP, SARAH	BAL	029	9TH WARD
CAMP, VIRGINIA	KEN	295	3RD DIST
CAMP, WILLIAM	KEN	262	1ST DIST
CAMP, WILLIAM	ALL	179	7TH E.D.
CAMPARIO, JOHN	BAL	217	17TH WAR
CAMPBELE, LEVINA D.*	DOR	446	1ST DIST
CAMPBELL, A.	BAL	161	1ST WARD
CAMPBELL, A. P.	BAL	470	14TH WAR
CAMPBELL, ABNER	FRE	034	FREDERIC
CAMPBELL, ALEXANDER	CEC	111	4TH E DI
CAMPBELL, ALFRED	BAL	390	8TH WARD
CAMPBELL, ALLEN	HAR	155	3RD DIST
CAMPBELL, ANDREW	BAL	108	10TH WAR
CAMPBELL, ANN	BAL	299	17TH WAR
CAMPBELL, ANN	BAL	287	20TH WAR
CAMPBELL, ANN	BAL	234	20TH WAR
CAMPBELL, ANN	BAL	410	3RD WARD
CAMPBELL, ANN	WOR	315	2ND E DI
CAMPBELL, ANN H.	ST	255	3RD E DI
CAMPBELL, ANN P.	MGM	436	CLARKSTR
CAMPBELL, ANTHONY	WAS	155	HAGERSTO
CAMPBELL, ARCHIBALD	BAL	054	15TH WAR
CAMPBELL, ARTHUR	BAL	446	14TH WAR
CAMPBELL, ARTHUR J.A.	ANN	487	HOWARD D
CAMPBELL, B. M.	BAL	330	13TH WAR
CAMPBELL, BARBARA	FRE	285	WOODSBOR
CAMPBELL, BARNEY	ALL	074	5TH E.D.
CAMPBELL, BERNARD, U.	ANN	420	HOWARD D
CAMPBELL, BOLLY	ALL	255	CUMBERLA
CAMPBELL, C. M.	BAL	296	1ST DIST
CAMPBELL, CATHARINE	ALL	074	5TH E.D.
CAMPBELL, CATHARINE	BAL	175	19TH WAR
CAMPBELL, CHARLES	BAL	229	19TH WAR
CAMPBELL, CHARLES	FRE	238	NEW MARK
CAMPBELL, CHARLOTTE	ALL	233	CUMBERLA
CAMPBELL, CHARLOTTE	BAL	069	10TH WAR
CAMPBELL, CLENTON	FRE	288	WOODSBOR
CAMPBELL, CORNELIUS-BLACK	FRE	016	FREDERIC
CAMPBELL, DANIEL	BAL	253	20TH WAR

Name	Co.	Page	Location
CAMPBELL, DANIEL	BAL	026	15TH WAR
CAMPBELL, EDWARD	CEC	189	7TH E DI
CAMPBELL, EDWARD	BAL	469	14TH WAR
CAMPBELL, EDWARD	BAL	122	11TH WAR
CAMPBELL, EDWARD	BAL	195	11TH WAR
CAMPBELL, ELIZA	FRE	284	WOODSBOR
CAMPBELL, ELIZA	WOR	225	4TH E DI
CAMPBELL, ELIZABETH	MGM	355	BERRYS D
CAMPBELL, ELIZABETH	BAL	448	8TH WARD
CAMPBELL, ELIZABETH	BAL	329	3RD WARD
CAMPBELL, EMAL	FRE	287	WOODSBOR
CAMPBELL, ENOCH	PRI	059	NOTTINGH
CAMPBELL, ESTER	FRE	295	WOODSBOR
CAMPBELL, F.	BAL	161	1ST WARD
CAMPBELL, FRANCES	BAL	268	7TH WARD
CAMPBELL, FRANCIS	BAL	191	11TH WAR
CAMPBELL, FRANCIS	BAL	035	9TH WARD
CAMPBELL, FRANCIS	FRE	202	5TH E DI
CAMPBELL, GEORGE	CEC	016	ELKTON 3
CAMPBELL, GEORGE	BAL	437	14TH WAR
CAMPBELL, GEORGE	BAL	258	12TH WAR
CAMPBELL, GEORGE	BAL	131	1ST WARD
CAMPBELL, GEORGE	ST	306	1ST E DI
CAMPBELL, GEORGE R.	BAL	432	8TH WARD
CAMPBELL, HUGH	PRI	107	PISCATAW
CAMPBELL, ISABELL	BAL	255	12TH WAR
CAMPBELL, J. MASON	BAL	094	10TH WAR
CAMPBELL, JAMES	BAL	459	8TH WARD
CAMPBELL, JAMES	BAL	059	15TH WAR
CAMPBELL, JAMES	BAL	374	8TH WARD
CAMPBELL, JAMES	BAL	153	1ST WARD
CAMPBELL, JAMES	ALL	256	CUMBERLA
CAMPBELL, JAMES	ALL	205	CUMBERLA
CAMPBELL, JAMES	ANN	285	ANNAPOLI
CAMPBELL, JAMES	HAR	050	1ST DIST
CAMPBELL, JAMES	CEC	082	CHARLEST
CAMPBELL, JAMES E.	ST	255	3RD E DI
CAMPBELL, JAMES H.	BAL	266	20TH WAR
CAMPBELL, JAMES W.	MGM	377	ROCKERLE
CAMPBELL, JANE	CEC	111	4TH E DI
CAMPBELL, JANE	BAL	193	6TH WARD
CAMPBELL, JANE	BAL	070	10TH WAR
CAMPBELL, JOHN	BAL	099	10TH WAR
CAMPBELL, JOHN	BAL	162	1ST WARD
CAMPBELL, JOHN	BAL	194	2ND WARD
CAMPBELL, JOHN	BAL	296	7TH WARD
CAMPBELL, JOHN	BAL	120	5TH WARD
CAMPBELL, JOHN	BAL	097	5TH WARD
CAMPBELL, JOHN	BAL	171	2ND DIST
CAMPBELL, JOHN	CEC	108	3RD E DI
CAMPBELL, JOHN	CEC	114	3RD E DI
CAMPBELL, JOHN	CEC	086	4TH E DI
CAMPBELL, JOHN	HAR	052	1ST DIST
CAMPBELL, JOHN	BAL	398	14TH WAR
CAMPBELL, JOHN	CAR	085	NO TWP L
CAMPBELL, JOHN B.	CEC	189	7TH E DI
CAMPBELL, JOHN B.H.	ALL	234	CUMBERLA
CAMPBELL, JOHN J.	BAL	118	18TH WAR
CAMPBELL, JOHN W.	BAL	002	EASTERN
CAMPBELL, JOSEPH	BAL	057	10TH WAR
CAMPBELL, JOSEPH	WOR	249	1ST CENS
CAMPBELL, JOSEPH R.	BAL	294	7TH WARD
CAMPBELL, KITTY	BAL	439	14TH WAR
CAMPBELL, LEVINA D.*	DOR	446	1ST DIST
CAMPBELL, LEWIS	FRE	271	NEW MARK
CAMPBELL, LOUISA	BAL	196	11TH WAR
CAMPBELL, LYDIA D.	BAL	189	6TH WARD
CAMPBELL, MARGAERT	BAL	317	12TH WAR
CAMPBELL, MARGARET	BAL	234	6TH WARD
CAMPBELL, MARGARET	BAL	316	20TH WAR
CAMPBELL, MARGERY	MGM	385	ROCKERLE
CAMPBELL, MARY	BAL	141	11TH WAR
CAMPBELL, MARY	BAL	156	19TH WAR
CAMPBELL, MARY	BAL	377	13TH WAR
CAMPBELL, MARY	BAL	380	3RD WARD
CAMPBELL, MARY E.	BAL	353	7TH WARD
CAMPBELL, MATILDA	BAL	255	12TH WAR
CAMPBELL, MICHAEL	BAL	300	17TH WAR
CAMPBELL, MICHEAL	BAL	078	18TH WAR
CAMPBELL, NANCEY	BAL	093	15TH WAR
CAMPBELL, NANCY	BAL	006	1ST WARD
CAMPBELL, NANCY	WOR	250	1ST CENS
CAMPBELL, P.	BAL	204	11TH WAR
CAMPBELL, P. M.	ALL	074	5TH E.D.
CAMPBELL, PAT	BAL	142	5TH WARD
CAMPBELL, PATRICK	BAL	137	11TH WAR
CAMPBELL, PHILIP	ST	348	5TH E DI
CAMPBELL, RACHEL	BAL	090	5TH WARD
CAMPBELL, REBECCA	BAL	091	5TH WARD
CAMPBELL, RICHARD	BAL	054	9TH WARD
CAMPBELL, RICHARD	MGM	325	CRACKLIN
CAMPBELL, ROBERT	ALL	160	6TH E.D.
CAMPBELL, ROBERT	BAL	186	11TH WAR
CAMPBELL, ROBERT	WAS	132	HAGERSTO
CAMPBELL, ROBERT-BLACK	FRE	016	FREDERIC
CAMPBELL, ROSEL L.	BAL	004	18TH WAR
CAMPBELL, ROSS	BAL	151	11TH WAR
CAMPBELL, SAMUEL	CEC	164	6TH E DI
CAMPBELL, SAMUEL	BAL	171	2ND DIST
CAMPBELL, SARAH	BAL	099	15TH WAR
CAMPBELL, SARAH	BAL	108	10TH WAR
CAMPBELL, SARAH	BAL	295	3RD WARD
CAMPBELL, SARAH	BAL	207	6TH DIST
CAMPBELL, SARAH	BAL	196	11TH WAR
CAMPBELL, SARAH	BAL	248	20TH WAR
CAMPBELL, SARAH J.	ANN	459	HOWARD D
CAMPBELL, STEPHEN	BAL	336	3RD WARD
CAMPBELL, SUSAN	BAL	110	10TH WAR
CAMPBELL, SUSANNA	MGM	386	ROCKERLE
CAMPBELL, TEMPERANCE	WOR	222	4TH E DI
CAMPBELL, TERESA	BAL	151	19TH WAR
CAMPBELL, THOASM W.	WOR	218	4TH E DI
CAMPBELL, THOMAS	BAL	247	20TH WAR
CAMPBELL, THOMAS	BAL	421	8TH WARD
CAMPBELL, THOMAS	ALL	049	10TH E.D
CAMPBELL, THOMAS	BAL	160	1ST WARD
CAMPBELL, THOMAS	BAL	373	8TH WARD
CAMPBELL, THOMAS W.	BAL	135	16TH WAR
CAMPBELL, THOMAS-MULATTO	BAL	208	2ND WARD
CAMPBELL, WILLIAM	BAL	185	2ND WARD
CAMPBELL, WILLIAM	BAL	128	1ST WARD
CAMPBELL, WILLIAM	ALL	256	CUMBERLA
CAMPBELL, WILLIAM	BAL	067	2ND DIST
CAMPBELL, WILLIAM	BAL	263	20TH WAR
CAMPBELL, WILLIAM	CEC	101	4TH E DI
CAMPBELL, WILLIAM	CEC	114	3RD E DI
CAMPBELL, WILLIAM	MGM	344	CLARKSBU
CAMPBELL, WILLIAM G.	ALL	203	CUMBERLA
CAMPBELL, WILLIAM L.	BAL	004	18TH WAR
CAMPBELL, WILLIAM-MULATTO	FRE	418	8TH E DI

Name	Co.	Page	Location
CAMPBELL, MARTIN	BAL	057	1ST WARD
CAMPBELL, MARY	ALL	202	CUMBERLA
CAMPBEN, JOSEPH	TAL	107	ST MICHA
CAMPBILL, HUGH	BAL	169	1ST WARD
CAMPBILL, MARTIN H.	BAL	035	1ST WARD
CAMPBILL, ROBERT	BAL	056	1ST WARD
CAMPBILL, THOMAS	BAL	171	1ST WARD
CAMPBILL, THOMAS	BAL	166	1ST WARD
CAMPE, AARON*	DOR	409	1ST DIST
CAMPE, ISAAC*	DOR	445	1ST DIST
CAMPE, ISAIH*	DOR	433	1ST DIST
CAMPE, JOHN	DOR	432	1ST DIST
CAMPE, JULIA A.	DOR	431	1ST DIST
CAMPE, LOUIS*	DOR	443	1ST DIST
CAMPEE, MARTIN *	TAL	106	ST MICHA
CAMPELL, JOHN	HAR	154	3RD DIST
CAMPER, ABRAM*	DOR	444	1ST DIST
CAMPER, ANDREW	DOR	371	3RD DIVI
CAMPER, ANN	DOR	362	3RD DIVI
CAMPER, ANN	DOR	445	1ST DIST
CAMPER, ANN	DOR	315	1ST DIST
CAMPER, DENNIS	DOR	371	3RD DIVI
CAMPER, DENNIS	DOR	462	1ST DIST
CAMPER, DERIAS-MULATTO	CAR	126	NO TWP L
CAMPER, DRAPER*	DOR	462	1ST DIST
CAMPER, ELIZABETH	DOR	319	1ST DIST
CAMPER, ELIZABETH	BAL	190	6TH WARD
CAMPER, EMMA J.	DOR	425	1ST DIST
CAMPER, FRANCES A.	DOR	445	1ST DIST
CAMPER, HENRY	DOR	311	1ST DIST
CAMPER, HENRY	DOR	311	1ST DIST
CAMPER, HENRY	DOR	462	1ST DIST
CAMPER, HENRY	TAL	063	EASTON D
CAMPER, ISAAC	DOR	451	1ST DIST
CAMPER, ISAAC	SOM	506	BARREN C
CAMPER, ISAAC S.	BAL	279	7TH WARD
CAMPER, ISAAC*	DOR	445	1ST DIST
CAMPER, JACOB	DOR	383	1ST DIST
CAMPER, JACOB	TAL	057	EASTON D
CAMPER, JAMES	DOR	311	1ST DIST
CAMPER, JAMES	CAR	137	NO TWP L
CAMPER, JANE	DOR	412	1ST DIST
CAMPER, JANE	DOR	462	1ST DIST
CAMPER, JOHN	DOR	321	1ST DIST
CAMPER, JOHN	BAL	012	9TH WARD
CAMPER, JOHN H.	DOR	462	1ST DIST
CAMPER, LEVIN	DOR	419	1ST DIST
CAMPER, LEVIN*	DOR	445	1ST DIST
CAMPER, LOUIS*	DOR	443	1ST DIST
CAMPER, MARIA	DOR	426	1ST DIST
CAMPER, MARIA	BAL	198	17TH WAR
CAMPER, MARY	BAL	254	6TH WARD
CAMPER, MARY	DOR	322	1ST DIST
CAMPER, MARY	DOR	311	1ST DIST
CAMPER, MARY	CAR	125	NO TWP L
CAMPER, MARY	CAR	162	NO TWP L
CAMPER, MARY C.	BAL	344	7TH WARD
CAMPER, MILLA	DOR	368	3RD DIVI
CAMPER, MILLY	DOR	297	1ST DIST
CAMPER, NANCY	DOR	431	1ST DIST
CAMPER, NICKOLAS	BAL	098	5TH WARD
CAMPER, PETER	BAL	344	7TH WARD
CAMPER, SAMUEL	CAR	164	NO TWP L
CAMPER, SARAH	CAR	122	NO TWP L
CAMPER, STEPHEN	DOR	384	1ST DIST
CAMPER, STEPHEN	BAL	247	6TH WARD
CAMPER, THOMAS	DOR	412	1ST DIST
CAMPER, THOMAS	BAL	136	11TH WAR
CAMPER, VICTORIA	BAL	348	3RD WARD
CAMPER, WILEY	DOR	463	1ST DIST
CAMPER, WILLIAM	BAL	335	3RD WARD
CAMPER, WILLIAM*	DOR	445	1ST DIST
CAMPER, WILLIAM	BAL	124	1ST WARD
CAMPHER, AGNES	BAL	419	14TH WAR
CAMPHER, ANDREW	BAL	287	7TH WARD
CAMPHER, C.	BAL	161	1ST WARD
CAMPHER, MARGARET A.	BAL	399	8TH WARD
CAMPHER, MARY	ANN	291	ANNAPOLI
CAMPHER, MARY A.	BAL	044	4TH WARD
CAMPHER, MARY J.	BAL	065	15TH WAR
CAMPHOR, AGNESS	BAL	459	1ST DIST
CAMPHOR, ALLEN	BAL	101	15TH WAR
CAMPHOR, DENNIS	BAL	043	15TH WAR
CAMPHOR, JOHN	BAL	081	15TH WAR
CAMPHOR, PRISCILLA	BAL	436	14TH WAR
CAMPHOR, RICHARD	BAL	412	3RD WARD
CAMPHOR, WILLIAM	BAL	092	15TH WAR
CAMPION, SISTER M.	FRE	198	5TH E DI
CAMPLIN, HENRY	BAL	129	1ST WARD
CAMPTON, ELIZA	BAL	401	1ST DIST
CAMPTON, JAMES	BAL	392	1ST DIST
CAMPWELL, MATILDA*	DOR	379	1ST DIST
CAMRON, DANIEL	CAR	093	NO TWP L
CAMRON, GEORGE	CAR	125	NO TWP L
CAMRON, HUDSON	CAR	132	NO TWP L
CAMRON, JEREMIAH	CAR	124	NO TWP L
CAMRON, JOHN	QUE	132	1ST E DI
CAMRON, JOHN M.	CAR	086	NO TWP L
CAMRON, TABITHA	BAL	021	15TH WAR
CAMRON, WASHINGTON-BLACK	CAR	126	NO TWP L
CAMTWELL, JOHN	CEC	098	3RD E DI
CAMTWELL, JOSEPH P.	CEC	013	ELKTON 3
CAMTWELL, ROBERT	CEC	013	ELKTON 3
CAMTWELL, THOMAS	CEC	007	ELKTON 3
CAN, GEORGE-BLACK	WOR	332	1ST E DI
CAN, WILLIAM HY CLAY *	FRE	077	FREDERIC
CANABLE, JOHN	WAS	141	2ND DIST
CANADA, ALEXANDER	BAL	189	17TH WAR
CANADA, H.E.	ALL	216	CUMBERLA
CANADE, ANN	CEC	186	7TH E DI
CANADE, JOSEPH	ALL	094	5TH E.D.
CANADY, JOHN	HAR	081	2ND DIST
CANADY, PERRY-BLACK	CAR	069	NO TWP L
CANADY, PHILIP-BLACK	CAR	069	NO TWP L
CANADY, SAMUEL W.	KEN	208	2ND DIST
CANADY, WILLIAM	HAR	130	2ND DIST
CANAGHAN, JOHN	ALL	048	10TH E.D
CANAHAN, JOHN	BAL	091	10TH WAR
CANAL, PATRICK	ALL	100	5TH E.D.
CANAN, ELIZA	CEC	103	4TH E DI
CANAN, MICHAEL	CEC	142	6TH E DI
CANAP, HENRY	ALL	154	6TH E.D.
CANAP, JOHN	ALL	062	10TH E.D
CANAPP, HENRY	ALL	114	5TH E.D.
CANARE, PATRICK	ALL	202	CUMBERLA
CANAY, WILLIAM F.	BAL	054	1ST WARD
CANBER, BERNARD	BAL	091	1ST WARD
CANBIN, WILLIAM *	ANN	358	3RD DIST
CANBY, JAMES M.	BAL	285	7TH WARD
CANBY, MARY	MGM	336	CRACKLIN

Name	Co.	Page	Location
CANBY, SAMUEL	BAL	350	1ST DIST
CANBY, THOMAS	MGM	366	BERRYS D
CANBY, THOMAS Y.	BAL	114	15TH WAR
CANBY, WILLIAM	MGM	335	CRACKLIN
CANCY, ROSS	CAR	118	NO TWP L
CAND, GEORGE	BAL	250	12TH WAR
CANDEE, MARY	BAL	011	15TH WAR
CANDER, GEORGE	WAS	023	2ND SUBD
CANDLE, JOHN	FRE	002	FREDERIC
CANDLER, ANN E.	FRE	207	BUCKEYST
CANDLER, JOHN	BAL	136	1ST WARD
CANDLER, JOHN	ALL	052	10TH E.D
CANDLER, LEONARD W.	MGM	374	ROCKERLE
CANDLER, ROSETTA	MGM	375	ROCKERLE
CANDLER, SARAH	MGM	374	ROCKERLE
CANDLIS, DOUGLAS	BAL	179	19TH WAR
CANDON, JOHN H.	FRE	439	8TH E DI
CANDOR, SUSAN	FRE	040	FREDERIC
CANDROY, PATRICK	BAL	046	1ST WARD
CANDRY, REBECCA	DOR	372	3RD DIVI
CANDY, DANIEL-BLACK	CAR	131	NO TWP L
CANDY, ELIZABETH	DOR	364	3RD DIVI
CANDY, MARY	DOR	361	3RD DIVI
CANDY, WILLIAM H.	MGM	347	BERRYS D
CANE, ANTHONY	ALL	135	4TH E.D.
CANE, CATHRINE	BAL	206	11TH WAR
CANE, DENNIS	WAS	140	2ND DIST
CANE, ELIZA	TAL	046	EASTON T
CANE, FREDERICK	ALL	139	6TH E.D.
CANE, HARRIET	TAL	055	EASTON D
CANE, HENRY	HAR	173	3RD DIST
CANE, JANE	BAL	322	12TH WAR
CANE, JOHN	ALL	135	4TH E.D.
CANE, JOHN	ALL	142	6TH E.D.
CANE, JOHN	ALL	119	5TH E.D.
CANE, JOHN	BAL	350	1ST DIST
CANE, JOHN	BAL	418	3RD WARD
CANE, JOHN W.	BAL	410	3RD WARD
CANE, MARY	TAL	045	EASTON T
CANE, MARY C.	WAS	150	2ND DIST
CANE, PATERICK	CAR	230	5TH DIST
CANE, PETER	ALL	108	5TH E.D.
CANE, SALLY	WAS	126	2ND DIST
CANE, SARAH E.	FRE	091	FREDERIC
CANE, SOPHIA	HAR	122	2ND DIST
CANE, WILLIAM	BAL	110	10TH WAR
CANELLY, ELLEN	BAL	210	2ND WARD
CANEN, WILLIAM W.	BAL	139	1ST WARD
CANEROSS, JOHN	BAL	368	13TH WAR
CANES, CATHERINE	BAL	050	9TH WARD
CANESELL, JAMES	ALL	148	6TH E.D.
CANESS, MARY C.	ALL	244	CUMBERLA
CANETTEN, LUCY	BAL	130	5TH WARD
CANEY, ELIZABETH	HAR	051	1ST DIST
CANEY, JOHN	BAL	129	16TH WAR
CANFED, WINEFRED	BAL	361	1ST DIST
CANFEILD, CHARLES	BAL	052	18TH WAR
CANFIELD, BRIDGET	BAL	215	11TH WAR
CANFIELD, J. C.	BAL	057	10TH WAR
CANFIELD, LEVI	BAL	130	1ST WARD
CANFIELD, MARY	BAL	215	11TH WAR
CANFIELD, MARY	BAL	091	18TH WAR
CANFIELD, WILLIAM B.	BAL	256	12TH WAR
CANFRITE, ELISABETH	BAL	361	3RD WARD
CANGHEY, ELIZA J.	BAL	460	14TH WAR
CANGTON, EDWARD	BAL	011	15TH WAR
CANIBUS, LYDIA-MULATTO	FRE	429	8TH E DI
CANIPHER, ELIZABETH-BLACK	BAL	210	2ND WARD
CANISH, MARY	BAL	013	4TH WARD
CANISTER, ELLEN	BAL	450	8TH WARD
CANK, MARY	CEC	023	ELKTON 3
CANKER, WESLY*	DOR	431	1ST DIST
CANLAP, MARY M.	ALL	141	6TH E.D.
CANLY, BENJAMIN	BAL	182	19TH WAR
CANN, ALEXANDER	BAL	281	2ND WARD
CANN, EDWARD	BAL	243	2ND WARD
CANN, ELIZA	BAL	288	12TH WAR
CANN, FRANCIS	KEN	253	1ST DIST
CANN, HENRY M.	BAL	120	1ST WARD
CANN, HERMAN F.	BAL	262	2ND WARD
CANN, JAMES	BAL	179	19TH WAR
CANN, JAMES R.	BAL	089	15TH WAR
CANN, JOHN	BAL	180	2ND WARD
CANN, JOHN	CEC	103	4TH E DI
CANN, JOHN	CEC	112	4TH E DI
CANN, KATE	BAL	090	15TH WAR
CANN, MARY	BAL	244	2ND WARD
CANN, MARY	FRE	080	FREDERIC
CANN, PATRICK	CEC	177	7TH E DI
CANN, RICHARD	BAL	459	8TH WARD
CANN, THOMAS	BAL	108	5TH WARD
CANN, W.	BAL	117	1ST WARD
CANNADAY, DAVID	QUE	214	3RD E DI
CANNADY, PRECIOUS	FRE	233	BUCKEYST
CANNAGAN, MARY	BAL	380	1ST DIST
CANNAN, PATRICK	BAL	286	1ST DIST
CANNAUGHTON, MICHAEL	BAL	300	17TH WAR
CANNER, CHARLES	ALL	195	CUMBERLA
CANNER, JAMES W.	WAS	157	2ND DIST
CANNER, JOHN	WAS	157	2ND DIST
CANNER, THOMAS J.	BAL	271	2ND WARD
CANNESS, ELIZABETH	BAL	201	11TH WAR
CANNICLE, JAMES M.	BAL	132	1ST WARD
CANNING, JOHN	BAL	048	9TH WARD
CANNIO, AUGUST	BAL	004	4TH WARD
CANNIO, MANISO*	BAL	004	4TH WARD
CANNISON, EMILY	BAL	200	2ND WARD
CANNOLEY, CHARLES	BAL	274	20TH WAR
CANNON, AARON	DOR	344	3RD DIVI
CANNON, ANN	BAL	013	1ST WARD
CANNON, BARTINE A.	BAL	275	7TH WARD
CANNON, BENEDICT	FRE	067	FREDERIC
CANNON, BENJAMIN	SOM	408	DUBLIN D
CANNON, BURTON	BAL	061	15TH WAR
CANNON, CALEB	BAL	092	2ND DIST
CANNON, CATHERINE	BAL	161	11TH WAR
CANNON, CHARLES	CEC	155	PORT DEP
CANNON, CLEMENT	DOR	343	3RD DIVI
CANNON, COMFORT	DOR	344	3RD DIVI
CANNON, DANIEL	DOR	316	1ST DIST
CANNON, DRUCILLA	SOM	423	PRINCESS
CANNON, EBEN	SOM	409	DUBLIN D
CANNON, ELIZABETH	CAR	159	NO TWP L
CANNON, ELIZAH	BAL	094	2ND DIST
CANNON, FANNY	BAL	141	11TH WAR
CANNON, GEORGE	DOR	343	3RD DIVI
CANNON, H.*	TAL	032	EASTON D
CANNON, HUDSON*	DOR	344	3RD DIVI
CANNON, JACOB	FRE	084	FREDERIC
CANNON, JAMES	BAL	002	4TH WARD

Name	County	Page	District
CANNON, JAMES	SOM	468	TRAPPE D
CANNON, JENKINS	DOR	342	3RD DIVI
CANNON, JOHN	BAL	127	5TH WARD
CANNON, JOHN B.	BAL	336	13TH WAR
CANNON, JOHN E.	KEN	250	2ND DIST
CANNON, JOHN W.	HAR	185	3RD DIST
CANNON, LEAH	BAL	069	10TH WAR
CANNON, LEVIN	DOR	303	1ST DIST
CANNON, LEVIN	DOR	322	1ST DIST
CANNON, LOUISA H.	BAL	194	11TH WAR
CANNON, LUCINDA	FRE	072	FREDERIC
CANNON, MALINDA	BAL	321	3RD WARD
CANNON, MARY	BAL	465	14TH WAR
CANNON, MARY A.	BAL	181	6TH WARD
CANNON, MARY C.	BAL	194	11TH WAR
CANNON, MATTHEW	SOM	467	TRAPPE D
CANNON, MICHAEL	ALL	049	10TH E.D
CANNON, MILLY	SOM	511	BARREN C
CANNON, NOBLE	HAR	177	3RD DIST
CANNON, REBECCA	BAL	341	3RD WARD
CANNON, RENIS	DOR	338	3RD DIVI
CANNON, RHODY	CAR	148	NO TWP L
CANNON, RIO JANIRO*	BAL	318	3RD WARD
CANNON, RITTY*	DOR	304	1ST DIST
CANNCN, ROBERT	QUE	179	2ND E DI
CANNON, SAMUEL	DOR	334	3RD DIVI
CANNON, SARAH	CAR	157	NO TWP L
CANNON, SARAH	CEC	033	CHESAPEA
CANNON, SOPHIA	FRE	096	FREDERIC
CANNON, SUSAN	BAL	122	2ND DIST
CANNON, SUSAN J.	SOM	351	BRINKLEY
CANNON, THOMAS	QUE	133	1ST E DI
CANNON, THOMAS N.W.	WOR	166	6TH E DI
CANNON, VALENTINE	DOR	343	3RD DIVI
CANNON, WILLIAM	DOR	316	1ST DIST
CANNON, WILLIAM	FRE	322	MIDDLETO
CANNON, WILLIAM	BAL	142	16TH WAR
CANNON, WILLIAM B.	QUE	198	3RD E DI
CANNOWAY, JANE	CEC	097	4TH E DI
CANNY, SUSAN	CHA	292	BOJANTOW
CANOLES, CHALRES	BAL	064	2ND DIST
CANOLES, EDWIN C.	BAL	030	4TH WARD
CANOLES, RUTH	BAL	417	1ST DIST
CANOLES, WILLIAM	BAL	064	2ND DIST
CANOLL, JAMES	ALL	058	10TH E.D
CANON, GEORGE	DOR	344	3RD DIVI
CANON, JOSEPH	WOR	341	1ST E DI
CANON, MARY	DOR	345	3RD DIVI
CANON, MAXWELL	BAL	194	2ND WARD
CANOP, PETER	ALL	070	5TH E.D.
CANOPP, JOHN	ALL	119	5TH E.D.
CANOR, ELIZABETH C.	WOR	341	1ST E DI
CANOX, JOSEPH	BAL	266	12TH WAR
CANPBELL, SALLY	BAL	118	18TH WAR
CANPHER, RACHEL N.	BAL	011	1ST WARD
CANSBELL, MARY	WAS	133	HAGERSTO
CANSEY, ANN	CAR	144	NO TWP L
CANSEY, FOSTER-BLACK	CAR	154	NO TWP L
CANSEY, JACOB-BLACK	CAR	135	NO TWP L
CANSEY, JAMES *	BAL	064	15TH WAR
CANSEY, JOSIAH	WOR	192	8TH E DI
CANSEY, LOUIS	WOR	190	8TH E DI
CANSEY, MARTHA-BLACK	CAR	131	NO TWP L
CANSEY, PATRICK *	SOM	435	PRINCESS
CANSSEY, ANN M.	CAR	072	NO TWP L
CANSY, DARCUS-BLACK	CAR	131	NO TWP L
CANSY, SARAH	CAR	118	NO TWP L
CANT, HENRY-BLACK	QUE	161	2ND E DI
CANT, JOHN	QUE	214	3RD E DI
CANT, JOHN	KEN	263	1ST DIST
CANT, THOMAS	BAL	121	1ST WARD
CANTER, ANN	CHA	294	BOJANTOW
CANTER, CAROLINE-BLACK	QUE	202	3RD E DI
CANTER, FRANCIS	CHA	286	BOJANTOW
CANTER, HENRY	CHA	294	BOJANTOW
CANTER, JOSEPH	PRI	049	AQUASCO
CANTER, L. H.	CHA	281	BOJANTOW
CANTER, LEVEN	CHA	286	BOJANTOW
CANTER, LUCINDA	CHA	273	ALLENS F
CANTER, MARY	CHA	285	BOJANTOW
CANTER, THOMAS T.	CHA	277	BOJANTOW
CANTER, WILLIAM T.	CHA	284	BOJANTOW
CANTERBURY, BISHOP-MULATT	CAR	115	NO TWP L
CANTHWAIT, WILLIAM	BAL	099	2ND DIST
CANTIOUS, HARRIET	ANN	511	HOWARD D
CANTLER, HENRY	HAR	158	3RD DIST
CANTLER, MARY	HAR	157	3RD DIST
CANTLER, MARY E.	HAR	008	1ST DIST
CANTLER, ROBERT	HAR	008	1ST DIST
CANTLIN, MARY	HAR	084	2ND DIST
CANTMER, JOHN	BAL	059	2ND DIST
CANTON, EDWARD	BAL	171	11TH WAR
CANTON, HENRY	BAL	171	11TH WAR
CANTON, JOHN	BAL	025	18TH WAR
CANTON, MARY *	BAL	026	18TH WAR
CANTTER, WILLIAM	HAR	127	2ND DIST
CANTWELL, CALEB	CEC	005	ELKTON 3
CANTWELL, EDWARD	SOM	434	PRINCESS
CANTWELL, ELIZABETH	BAL	249	2ND WARD
CANTWELL, JOHN	WOR	228	6TH E DI
CANTWELL, JOSEPH	CEC	115	3RD E DI
CANTWELL, LEWIS	BAL	052	18TH WAR
CANTWELL, MATTHEW	CEC	005	ELKTON 3
CANTWELL, ROBERT	CEC	001	ELKTON 3
CANTWELL, SAMUEL	SOM	494	SALISBUR
CANTWELL, THOMAS	SOM	494	SALISBUR
CANTWORUTH, ELLENORA	BAL	183	2ND WARD
CANTZ, PATRICK	BAL	407	1ST DIST
CANTZ, SOLOMON	BAL	064	1ST WARD
CANTZ, WILLIAM	BAL	064	1ST WARD
CANULLAN, GEORGE	BAL	083	1ST WARD
CANUTHAS, EDORSUS*	BAL	010	4TH WARD
CANVAES, MARY	BAL	378	13TH WAR
CANVALIER, C.	BAL	112	10TH WAR
CANVERS, JOHN	BAL	402	1ST DIST
CANVING, HENRY	BAL	055	1ST WARD
CAONLY, BRANSON	WOR	324	1ST E DI
CAPARC, LEWIS	BAL	020	2ND DIST
CAPE, ALEXANDER	BAL	350	13TH WAR
CAPE, JOHN	BAL	162	1ST WARD
CAPE,JOHN COLE	BAL	107	10TH WAR
CAPELL, GEORGE	BAL	096	1ST WARD
CAPEY, GEORGE	BAL	121	1ST WARD
CAPHIL, PHILLIP	ALL	229	CUMBERLA
CAPHUS, LEVIN	DOR	411	1ST DIST
CAPILS, WILLIAM K.	BAL	282	20TH WAR
CAPITO, MARGARET	WAS	136	HAGERSTO
CAPITT, ELIZABETH	BAL	397	14TH WAR
CAPLER, LAURA	BAL	214	11TH WAR
CAPLER, MRS. L.	BAL	214	11TH WAR
CAPLES, ELLEN	ANN	376	4TH DIST
CAPLES, JACOB	BAL	110	1ST WARD
CAPLES, JACOB	CAR	207	4TH DIST
CAPLES, JACOB L.	BAL	183	5TH DIST
CAPLES, JAOCB	CAR	201	4TH DIST
CAPLES, JOHN	ANN	377	4TH DIST
CAPLES, MARY	ANN	376	4TH DIST
CAPLES, MARY	CAR	194	4TH DIST
CAPLES, WILLIAM	CAR	200	4TH DIST
CAPNELL, GEORGE	WAS	063	2ND SUBD
CAPON, GEORGE W.*	TAL	060	EASTON D
CAPON, JAMES W.	TAL	018	EASTON D
CAPON, THOMAS	TAL	066	EASTON T
CAPOOTE, MARY	FRE	183	5TH E DI
CAPPAGE, TRAVICE	ALL	246	CUMBER_A
CAPPAN, JOSEPH	BAL	110	5TH WARD
CAPPE.ALEXANDER	ALL	241	CUMBERLA
CAPPEAU, JOSEPH	BAL	220	12TH WAR
CAPPER, WILLIAM	BAL	123	1ST WARD
CAPPERS, JOHN	BAL	098	1ST WARD
CAPPERSMITH, ELIAS	CAR	400	2ND DIST
CAPPING, SARAH	BAL	294	3RD WARD
CAPPO, M.	BAL	162	1ST WARD
CAPPORILA, MAURICE	BAL	109	5TH WARD
CAPRETS, JAMES	ALL	217	CUMBERLA
CAPRIDGE, LUCINDA	ALL	223	CUMBERLA
CAPRIESE, JOSEPH	BAL	068	1ST WARD
CAPRIESE, JOSEPH	BAL	068	1ST WARD
CAPRON, ALBERT	BAL	402	1ST DIST
CAPRON, F. B.	BAL	469	14TH WAR
CAPRON, HARACE	BAL	402	1ST DIST
CAPRON, HORACE	PRI	026	VANSVILL
CAPRON, RICHARD J.	BAL	046	9TH WARD
CAPSEY, ANN	ST	342	5TH E DI
CAPSEY, ELIZABETH	ST	341	5TH E DI
CAPSEY, ELIZABETH	ST	342	5TH E DI
CAPSEY, JOHN	ST	341	5TH E DI
CAPTOR, JACOB F.	BAL	249	17TH WAR
CAR, JOHNATHAN	HAR	156	3RD DIST
CARAGAN, THOMAS	BAL	273	1ST DIST
CARAIY, GEORGE *	BAL	153	1ST WARD
CARANIER, JOSEPH	BAL	028	9TH WARD
CARAWAY, MARGARET	BAL	025	1ST WARD
CARBACK, DAVID L.	BAL	323	7TH WARD
CARBACK, E.	BAL	284	20TH WAR
CARBACK, JOHN	BAL	153	2ND DIST
CARBACK, JOHN	BAL	267	7TH WARD
CARBACK, MARGARET	BAL	401	3RD WARD
CARBACK, MARY	BAL	134	2ND DIST
CARBACK, REBECA	BAL	323	7TH WARD
CARBACK, SARAH	BAL	130	2ND DIST
CARBACK, SARAH	BAL	134	2ND DIST
CARBACK, SARAH	BAL	284	20TH WAR
CARBACK, WILLIAM	BAL	133	2ND DIST
CARBACK.JOHN	BAL	133	2ND DIST
CARBALEY, SAMUEL	ST	309	1ST E DI
CARBBELL, JAMES W.*	SOM	523	BARREN C
CARBELL, ANN	BAL	273	2ND WARD
CARBERRY, JAMESA .	ST	276	3RD E DI
CARBERRY, JOSEPH S.	HAR	199	3RD DIST
CARBERRY, MARY	BAL	250	6TH WARD
CARBINE, JOHN	ALL	155	6TH E.D.
CARBODY, MARY	BAL	247	17TH WAR
CARBOX, SAMUEL	CAR	192	4TH DIST
CARBOYNE, SYLVESTER	BAL	162	1ST WARD
CARBY, CHARLES W.	BAL	156	1ST WARD
CARCAND, DAVID	CAL	059	3RD DIST
CARCAND, WILLIAM	CAL	056	3RD DIST
CARCY, SARAH	BAL	258	17TH WAR
CARD, WILLIAM	BAL	079	15TH WAR
CARDELL, GEORGE	BAL	224	19TH WAR
CARDEN, THOMAS	BAL	449	1ST DIST
CARDER, GEORGE	ALL	172	7TH E.D.
CARDER, GEORGE	BAL	471	14TH WAR
CARDER, MARTHA	BAL	216	17TH WAR
CARDER, T.	BAL	135	1ST WARD
CARDERY, JAMES	BAL	057	2ND DIST
CARDES, WILLIAM*	BAL	329	3RD WARD
CARDLE, ROSE M.	BAL	456	14TH WAR
CARDLING, PETER	BAL	081	1ST WARD
CARDNEY, CURTIS	CEC	042	CHESAPEA
CARDON, NANCY	BAL	022	2ND DIST
CARDRAY, MATILDA	BAL	135	2ND DIST
CARDS, WILLIAM*	BAL	329	3RD WARD
CARDY, DANIEL	BAL	020	9TH WARD
CARELTON, OLIVER	BAL	281	7TH WARD
CARENCER, BRIDGETT	BAL	063	4TH WARD
CAREW, JOHN W.	SOM	442	DAMES QU
CAREW, RICHARD	SOM	458	DAMES QU
CAREY, ANN	SOM	472	TRAPPE D
CAREY, ANN	WOR	339	1ST E DI
CAREY, CATHARINE	BAL	344	7TH WARD
CAREY, DANIEL	BAL	062	2ND DIST
CAREY, CANIEL	ALL	003	3RD E.D.
CAREY, DAVID	SOM	468	TRAPPE D
CAREY, EBENEZER	WOR	199	8TH E DI
CAREY, EDWARD	ALL	140	6TH E.D.
CAREY, EDWARD	BAL	034	9TH WARD
CAREY, ELIJAH	WOR	191	8TH E DI
CAREY, ELISHA	WOR	321	1ST E DI
CAREY, ELIZABETH	WOR	194	8TH E DI
CAREY, ELJABETH	WOR	247	1ST CENS
CAREY, GEORGE	WOR	187	7TH E DI
CAREY, GEORGE	BAL	058	4TH WARD
CAREY, HENRY	WOR	248	1ST CENS
CAREY, HENRY	WOR	167	6TH E DI
CAREY, HENRY M.	WOR	194	8TH E DI
CAREY, J. A. *	BAL	298	12TH WAR
CAREY, JAMES	BAL	115	15TH WAR
CAREY, JAMES	BAL	144	2ND DIST
CAREY, JAMES	WOR	346	1ST E DI
CAREY, JOHN	WOR	188	7TH E DI
CAREY, JOHN	SOM	493	SALISBUR
CAREY, JOHN	BAL	144	2ND DIST
CAREY, JOHN	BAL	117	2ND DIST
CAREY, JOHN	BAL	243	6TH WARD
CAREY, JOHN	BAL	167	6TH WARD
CAREY, JOHN	BAL	172	11TH WAR
CAREY, JOHN	BAL	353	7TH WARD
CAREY, JOHN	FRE	212	BUCKEYST
CAREY, JOSEPH	MGM	375	ROCKER_E
CAREY, JOSEPH	WOR	251	1ST CENS
CAREY, JOSEPH	WAS	121	2ND DIST
CAREY, JOSEPH K.	TAL	054	EASTON D
CAREY, JOSHUA	WOR	195	8TH E DI
CAREY, JOSHUA M.	WOR	299	SNOW HIL
CAREY, JOSIAH H.	WOR	187	7TH E DI
CAREY, LEVIN	WOR	248	1ST CENS
CAREY, LEVIN J.	WOR	200	8TH E DI
CAREY, LCUISA	WAS	056	2ND SUBD
CAREY, LOUISA	BAL	330	13TH WAR
CAREY, MAHALAH E.	WOR	235	6TH E DI
CAREY, MARY	WOR	204	4TH E DI
CAREY, MARY	WOR	188	7TH E DI
CAREY, MARY	BAL	272	12TH WAR
CAREY, MARY A.	FRE	045	FREDERIC
CAREY, MICHAEL	HAR	093	2ND DIST
CAREY, MICHAEL	BAL	131	16TH WAR
CAREY, MICHAEL	BAL	305	12TH WAR
CAREY, MICHAEL	WOR	194	8TH E DI
CAREY, MISS A.	FRE	198	5TH E DI
CAREY, MOSES T.	BAL	001	15TH WAR
CAREY, NANCY	WOR	194	8TH E DI
CAREY, NANCY	WOR	235	5TH E DI
CAREY, NANCY T.	WOR	195	8TH E DI
CAREY, ROBERT	BAL	094	15TH WAR
CAREY, SALLY	WOR	340	1ST E DI
CAREY, SARAH M.	WOR	182	6TH E DI
CAREY, SOLOMON	WOR	260	BERLIN 1
CAREY, THOMAS	BAL	014	1ST WARD
CAREY, WALTON	WOR	168	6TH E DI
CAREY, WILLAIM	BAL	327	13TH WAR
CAREY, WILLIAM	WAS	163	2ND DIST
CAREY,JAMES	FRE	019	FREDERIC
CARFMAN, KEZIAH	FRE	363	CATOCTIN
CARHART, DANIEL	CEC	131	6TH E DI
CARHART, JOHN	CEC	130	6TH E DI
CARHART, MARY	CEC	131	6TH E DI
CARHART, SAMUEL	CEC	133	6TH E DI
CARHOFF, JOSHUA	BAL	024	4TH WARD
CARICK, JOHN	BAL	177	2ND DIST
CARICK, JOHN	ALL	048	10TH E.D
CARICK, WILLIAM	CHA	281	BOJANTOW
CARIDINE, CHRISTOPHER	CEC	084	CHARLEST
CARIENE, JOHN	BAL	183	11TH WAR
CARINE, ANDREW *	BAL	154	2ND DIST
CARINGHAM, PAT	ANN	347	3RD DIST
CARIRLL, EDMUND	QUE	225	4TH E DI
CARISS, ELIZABETH	BAL	073	10TH WAR
CARISS, MARGARET	BAL	162	16TH WAR
CARISS, SAMSON	BAL	072	10TH WAR
CARITHERS, ALEXANDER	HAR	051	1ST DIST
CARK, ELLIS	CEC	019	ELKTON 3
CARK, SUSAN	BAL	364	1ST DIST
CARKE, LINA	FRE	162	EMMITTSB
CARKY, MARY	WAS	147	HAGERSTO
CARL, CORNELIUS	BAL	444	1ST DIST
CARL, ELIZ	BAL	241	12TH WAR
CARL, ELLEN	BAL	110	5TH WARD
CARL, HENRY	BA.	038	18TH WAR
CARL, JOANA	BAL	449	1ST DIST
CARL, JOHN	CAR	331	MANCHEST
CARL, JOSEPH	BAL	254	12TH WAR
CARL, MARY	BAL	448	1ST DIST
CARL, PATRICK	BAL	169	16TH WAR
CARL, PATRICK	ALL	215	CUMBERLA
CARLAN, ELIZA	BAL	465	14TH WAR
CARLANE, JAMES	BAL	171	11TH WAR
CARLE, GEORGE	FRE	026	FREDERIC
CARLE, JOHN H.	BAL	413	1ST DIST
CARLE, JOHN M.	BAL	122	16TH WAR
CARLES, DAVID	WAS	108	2ND DIST
CARLES, M.	ANN	337	3RD DIST
CARLES, MARIA	CAL	042	3RD DIST
CARLES, WILLIAM *	ALL	135	4TH E.D.
CARLESTON, RUBEN	BAL	126	1ST WARD
CARLETON, ROBERT	BAL	039	1ST WARD
CARLETT, JAMES	BAL	173	11TH WAR
CARLETT, LEWIS G.*	BAL	044	4TH WARD
CARLEY, JAMES	ALL	243	CUMBERLA
CARLEY, JAMES	KEN	270	1ST DIST
CARLEY, JESSE	CAR	344	6TH DIST
CARLEY, JOHN	ALL	249	CUMBERLA
CARLEY, MARGARET	BAL	421	14TH WAR
CARLEY, OWEN	BAL	420	14TH WAR
CARLEY, RUBEN	FRE	129	CREAGERS
CARLEY.JOHN	BAL	120	1ST WARD
CARLI, JOHN C.	BAL	361	13TH WAR
CARLILE, JAMES H.	BAL	251	6TH WARD
CARLILE, JOHN	CAR	078	NO TWP L
CARLILE, MARIA	BAL	034	4TH WARD
CARLILE, MARY	CAR	078	NO TWP L
CARLILE, SAMUEL	CAR	082	NO TWP L
CARLILE, VALENTINE	CAR	078	NO TWP L
CARLILSE, ABDIL	CAR	390	2ND DIST
CARLIN, AGNESS	FRE	014	FREDERIC
CARLIN, ANNA P.	FRE	257	NEW MARK
CARLIN, DAVID	FRE	061	FREDERIC
CARLIN, FRANCIS	BAL	042	2ND DIST
CARLIN, FRANKLIN	ALL	074	5TH E.D.
CARLIN, HENRY	FRE	053	FREDERIC
CARLIN, JAMES	FRE	052	FREDERIC
CARLIN, JOHN	MGM	430	CLARKSTR
CARLIN, JOHN	CEC	177	7TH E DI
CARLIN, JOSEPH	FRE	054	FREDERIC
CARLIN, THOMAS	FRE	062	FREDERIC
CARLIN, THOMAS	FRE	054	FREDERIC
CARLIN.ELZIA	FRE	020	FREDERIC
CARLINE, JOHN	BAL	299	3RD WARD
CARLINE, THOMAS	BAL	120	5TH WARD
CARLING, MARY	BAL	083	18TH WAR
CARLIS, EDWARD	BAL	286	1ST DIST
CARLISLE, ALEXANDER	ALL	014	3RD E.D.
CARLISLE, AMOS	BAL	152	19TH WAR
CARLISLE, ANNA	CAR	389	2ND DIST
CARLISLE, BURLINGTON	BAL	453	1ST DIST
CARLISLE, CHARLES	FRE	383	PETERSVI
CARLISLE, CORNELIA	ALL	014	3RD E.D.
CARLISLE, DAVID	BAL	416	1ST DIST
CARLISLE, DAVID	FRE	395	PETERSVI
CARLISLE, DAVID	WAS	091	2ND SUBD
CARLISLE, DAVID R.	CAR	413	2ND DIST
CARLISLE, HARRIET	BAL	281	20TH WAR
CARLISLE, JAMES A.	MGM	423	MEDLEY 3
CARLISLE, JOHN	BAL	120	1ST WARD
CARLISLE, MARY	FRE	395	PETERSVI
CARLISLE, MICHAEL	PRI	036	VANSVILL
CARLISLE, SARAH	BAL	281	20TH WAR
CARLISLE, STEPHEN	WAS	063	2ND SUBD
CARLISLE, THOMAS	FRE	327	MIDDLETO
CARLISLE, WILLIAM	BAL	012	4TH WARD
CARLISNE, JOSEPH	BAL	311	1ST DIST
CARLKIN, JAMES	ALL	099	5TH E.D.
CARLON, ANN	BAL	036	2ND DIST
CARLON, ELIZABETH	HAR	072	1ST DIST
CARLON, JAMES	HAR	071	1ST DIST
CARLON, JOSIAH	HAR	072	1ST DIST
CARLON, SARAH	HAR	071	1ST DIST
CARLON, WILLIAM	BAL	041	2ND DIST
CARLOS, ANN	BAL	463	14TH WAR

Name	County	Page	District
CARLOS, PATRICK	ALL	242	CUMBERLA
CARLOTT, JOHN	BAL	184	11TH WAR
CARLOTT, JOHN	KEN	302	3RD DIST
CARLOW, BIDDY	BAL	069	10TH WAR
CARLTON, D.	BAL	141	1ST WARD
CARLTON, HENRY D.	ALL	213	CUMBERLA
CARLTON, HENRY L.	PRI	006	BLADENSB
CARLTON, JAMES P.	ALL	213	CUMBERLA
CARLTON, MARY	FRE	050	FREDERIC
CARLTY, ELIZAETH	BAL	195	11TH WAR
CARLY, JOHN	BAL	246	20TH WAR
CARLY, JOSEPH L.	FRE	020	FREDERIC
CARLYLE, GEORGE	BAL	006	18TH WAR
CARLYON, JAMES	CAR	222	5TH DIST
CARMACK, CATHARINE	FRE	410	8TH E DI
CARMACK, EDWARD	FRE	280	WOODSBOR
CARMACK, ELLEN	FRE	281	WOODSBOR
CARMACK, EMILY	ANN	437	HOWARD D
CARMACK, EPHRAHAM	FRE	131	CREAGERS
CARMACK, FRANCES	BAL	245	6TH WARD
CARMACK, HANSON	FRE	048	FREDERIC
CARMACK, JAMES	CAR	325	1ST DIST
CARMACK, JEHUE	BAL	322	7TH WARD
CARNACK, JOHN	FRE	137	CREAGERS
CARMACK, JOHN	WAS	131	HAGERSTO
CARMACK, JOHN L.	BAL	174	6TH WARD
CARMACK, MARY	FRE	011	FREDERIC
CARMACK, PAUL	FRE	284	WOODSBOR
CARMACK, SOLOME	FRE	028	FREDERIC
CARMACK, THOMAS	BAL	101	1ST WARD
CARMACK, WILLIAM	FRE	300	WOODSBOR
CARMACK, JOEL	BAL	398	14TH WAR
CARMAN, ANDREW	BAL	308	20TH WAR
CARMAN, ANN	BAL	020	4TH WARD
CARMAN, CATHARINE	BAL	217	6TH DIST
CARMAN, CATHARINE M.	BAL	033	2ND DIST
CARMAN, ELIJAH	BAL	094	2ND DIST
CARMAN, ELIZABETH	BAL	380	3RD WARD
CARMAN, FRANK	BAL	441	1ST DIST
CARMAN, GEORGE	SOM	416	DUBLIN D
CARMAN, HANNAH	BAL	060	4TH WARD
CARMAN, J.	BAL	082	4TH WARD
CARMAN, JACOB	BAL	197	11TH WAR
CARMAN, JAMES	BAL	266	17TH WAR
CARMAN, JOHN	CAR	159	NO TWP L
CARMAN, JOHN	BAL	202	6TH DIST
CARMAN, JOHN	ANN	461	HOWARD D
CARMAN, MARTHA	BAL	094	2ND DIST
CARMAN, MARY	BAL	294	3RD WARD
CARMAN, ROBERT	BAL	081	18TH WAR
CARMAN, SAMUEL	BAL	045	9TH WARD
CARMAN, SARAH	BAL	038	2ND DIST
CARMAN, WILLIAM	BAL	188	11TH WAR
CARMANY, C.	BAL	333	13TH WAR
CARMAUGH, DANIEL	BAL	472	14TH WAR
CARMEAN, EDWARD	CAR	119	NO TWP L
CARMEAN, JOSEPH W.	CAR	080	NO TWP L
CARMEAN, MARTHA	CAR	160	NO TWP L
CARMEAN, MARY A.	QUE	192	3RD E DI
CARMEAN, SARAH	CAR	160	NO TWP L
CARMEEN, ANN	BAL	126	11TH WAR
CARMEIN, WILLIAM	BAL	061	4TH WARD
CARMER, HENRY	CAR	250	3RD DIST
CARMER, WILLIAM	BAL	222	17TH WAR
CARMICHAEL, CHARLES	QUE	246	5TH E DI
CARMICHAEL, CHARLES-BLACK	QUE	194	3RD E DI
CARMICHAEL, HESTER	BAL	169	6TH WARD
CARMICHAEL, JAMES	BAL	385	13TH WAR
CARMICHAEL, JOHN	ANN	485	HOWARD D
CARMICHAEL, JOSEPH H.	BAL	179	19TH WAR
CARMICHAEL, PETER-BLACK	QUE	192	3RD E DI
CARMICHAEL, RICHARD B.	QUE	242	5TH E DI
CARMICHAEL, SIMON	KEN	256	1ST DIST
CARMICHAEL, WILLIAM	BAL	292	20TH WAR
CARMICHAEL, WILLIAM	BAL	272	12TH WAR
CARMICHAEL, WILLIAM	BAL	049	15TH WAR
CARMICHAEL, WILLIAM	BAL	004	9TH WARD
CARMICHAEL, WILLIAM	BAL	261	1ST DIST
CARMICHEAL, CHARLE-SBLACK	QUE	195	3RD E DI
CARMICHEL, BENJAMIN*	BAL	356	3RD WARD
CARMICHEL, ELIZABETH	BAL	073	10TH WAR
CARMINE, ANN	BAL	089	10TH WAR
CARMINE, CATHARINE	BAL	312	7TH WARD
CARMINE, ELIZABETH	SOM	528	QUANTICO
CARMINE, GEORGE	BAL	224	6TH WARD
CARMINE, JACOB L.	WOR	208	4TH E DI
CARMINE, JAMES	BAL	184	6TH WARD
CARMINE, JAMES	BAL	289	7TH WARD
CARMINE, JOSEPH W.	BAL	264	7TH WARD
CARMINE, LEVIN	WOR	292	9TH E DI
CARMINE, MARY	BAL	084	18TH WAR
CARMIRE, KENCH	WOR	238	6TH E DI
CARMOAN, CHARLES	CAR	163	NO TWP L
CARMOCK, WILLIAM	ALL	051	10TH E.D
CARMON, SARAH	BAL	160	11TH WAR
CARMON, THOMAS	HAR	056	1ST DIST
CARMPTON, JOHN W.	FRE	380	PETERSVI
CARN, FRANCIS	WAS	219	1ST DIST
CARN, FRANCIS	WAS	219	1ST DIST
CARN, JOHN	BAL	091	2ND DIST
CARN, JOHN	BAL	449	1ST DIST
CARN, SAMUEL	BAL	219	12TH WAR
CARN, SOLOMON	FRE	307	WOODSBOR
CARNAHAN, ELIZABETH *	FRE	254	NEW MARK
CARNAHAN, HENRY	BAL	469	14TH WAR
CARNAHAN, JANE	FRE	239	NEW MARK
CARNALL, JULIA	BAL	256	20TH WAR
CARNAMAN, EDWARD	CEC	063	1ST E DI
CARNAMAN, ELIZABETH	CEC	064	1ST E DI
CARNAN, ELLEN	BAL	075	15TH WAR
CARNAN, JOHN	CEC	046	1ST E DI
CARNARL, SIMON	BAL	270	2ND WARD
CARNAUER, PATRICK*	BAL	115	11TH WAR
CARNCK, VALENTINE	BAL	213	19TH WAR
CARNECE, RACHEL	CAR	214	5TH DIST
CARNELL, BARTHOLOMEW	HAR	154	3RD DIST
CARNELL, JACOB	CAR	299	1ST DIST
CARNELL, LEONARD	ALL	161	6TH E.D.
CARNELL, WILLIAM	ALL	146	6TH E.D.
CARNER, SOLOMON	BAL	287	3RD WARD
CARNES, DELILIA	WAS	199	1ST DIST
CARNES, FREDERICK	BAL	267	20TH WAR
CARNES, HENRY	FRE	060	FREDERIC
CARNES, ISAAC H.	HAR	065	1ST DIST
CARNES, JOHN	FRE	106	CREAGERS
CARNES, JOHN	FRE	217	BUCKEYST
CARNES, JOHN C.	BAL	264	7TH WARD
CARNES, JOHN D.	BAL	101	10TH WAR
CARNES, LYDIA	WAS	168	FUNKSTOW
CARNES, MARGARET	FRE	076	FREDERIC
CARNES, MARY	BAL	361	3RD WARD
CARNES, MARY M.	BAL	169	19TH WAR
CARNES, RACHELL	HAR	193	3RD DIST
CARNES, WILLIAM	BAL	168	11TH WAR
CARNEY, ALICE	BAL	195	11TH WAR
CARNEY, ANN G.	BAL	081	1ST WARD
CARNEY, CAROLINE	WAS	230	1ST DIST
CARNEY, CATHARINE	BAL	396	1ST DIST
CARNEY, CHARLES	BAL	298	1ST DIST
CARNEY, CHRISTOPHER	ALL	078	5TH E.D.
CARNEY, ELIZABETH	WAS	041	2ND SUBD
CARNEY, HENRY	BAL	460	8TH WARD
CARNEY, HUGH	HAR	042	1ST DIST
CARNEY, JAEMS	BAL	313	12TH WAR
CARNEY, JAMES	BAL	168	11TH WAR
CARNEY, JAMES	BAL	124	18TH WAR
CARNEY, JANE	ALL	078	5TH E.D.
CARNEY, JOHN	BAL	208	6TH DIST
CARMEY, JOHN	BAL	038	18TH WAR
CARNEY, JOHN	QUE	188	3RD E DI
CARNEY, JOHN	SOM	360	BRINKLEY
CARNEY, L.	BAL	308	12TH WAR
CARNEY, LOUISA	WAS	252	1ST DIST
CARNEY, MARGARET	WAS	148	2ND DIST
CARNEY, OWEN	BAL	275	1ST DIST
CARNEY, RAFA	BAL	342	7TH WARD
CARNEY, THOMAS-BLACK	CAR	092	NO TWP L
CARNEY, WILLIAM-BLACK	QUE	126	1ST E DI
CARNIFF, JOHN	CEC	202	6TH E DI
CARNIGON, SARAH	BAL	275	12TH WAR
CARNINE, REBBECCA	BAL	010	18TH WAR
CARNS, JOHN	BAL	299	7TH WARD
CARNS, MICHAEL	ALL	053	10TH E.D
CARNS, PATRICK	WAS	064	2ND SUBD
CARNWOOD, THOMAS	BAL	458	1ST DIST
CARNY, HENRY	CEC	039	CHESAPEA
CAROE, JOHN	CAR	214	5TH DIST
CAROL, PETER	HAR	197	3RD DIST
CAROLINE, L.	BAL	134	2ND DIST
CAROLL, ELIZABETH	BAL	395	1ST DIST
CAROLL, WILLIAM	PRI	087	SPALDING
CAROLOUS, BRIDGET	BAL	019	18TH WAR
CARON, ELIZA C.	ST	313	1ST E DI
CARON, HESTER A.*	TAL	049	EASTON T
CARON, PATRICK	ALL	072	5TH E.D.
CARONE, WILLIAM *	SOM	443	DAMES QU
CAROO, ANN	SOM	445	DAMES QU
CARORD, WILLIAM *	SOM	443	DAMES QU
CAROUE, WILLIAM *	SOM	443	DAMES QU
CAROY, ELIZABETH	ANN	448	HOWARD D
CARPENTER, ANN	BAL	259	1ST DIST
CARPENTER, ANN	CAR	066	NO TWP L
CARPENTER, ANN A.	ST	270	3RD E DI
CARPENTER, CHARLES	CEC	033	CHESAPEA
CARPENTER, CHARLOTTE	FRE	342	MIDDLETO
CARPENTER, ELI	BAL	414	14TH WAR
CARPENTER, ELIZABETH	BAL	093	15TH WAR
CARPENTER, GEORGE	ST	345	5TH E DI
CARPENTER, GEORGE A.	ST	337	4TH E DI
CARPENTER, GEORGE P.	CEC	047	1ST E DI
CARPENTER, GEORGE W.	CHA	246	HILLTOP
CARPENTER, GEORGE-MULATTO	ST	317	4TH E DI
CARPENTER, HENRY	WAS	176	1ST DIST
CARPENTER, HENRY	ANN	292	ANNAPOLI
CARPENTER, JAMES	BAL	414	14TH WAR
CARPENTER, JAMES B.	CHA	235	HILLTOP
CARPENTER, JAMES D.	CHA	244	HILLTOP
CARPENTER, JANE	CHA	235	HILLTOP
CARPENTER, JEREMIAH	WAS	290	1ST DIST
CARPENTER, JOHN	ST	266	3RD E DI
CARPENTER, JOHN E.	ST	297	2ND E DI
CARPENTER, JOSEPH	BAL	078	10TH WAR
CARPENTER, KATE	BAL	297	1ST DIST
CARPENTER, LOUIS	ST	268	3RD E DI
CARPENTER, M. D.	BAL	296	1ST DIST
CARPENTER, MARGARET	BAL	085	15TH WAR
CARPENTER, MARY	ST	317	4TH E DI
CARPENTER, MARY H.	BAL	087	4TH WARD
CARPENTER, MILLY	ST	276	3RD E DI
CARPENTER, NANCY	TAL	072	EASTON T
CARPENTER, NANCY	BAL	398	8TH WARD
CARPENTER, RACHEL	BAL	177	16TH WAR
CARPENTER, SAMUEL	BAL	213	19TH WAR
CARPENTER, SARA V.	CHA	235	HILLTOP
CARPENTER, SARAH E.	BAL	147	16TH WAR
CARPENTER, STEVEN	FRE	335	MIDDLETO
CARPENTER, SUSAN	BAL	097	10TH WAR
CARPENTER, THOMAS	ST	275	3RD E DI
CARPENTER, THOMAS	TAL	115	ST MICHA
CARPENTER, VIRGINIA	CHA	236	HILLTOP
CARPENTER, WILLIAM	BAL	211	6TH WARD
CARPENTER, WILLIAM B.	CHA	233	HILLTOP
CARPENTER, WILLIAM C.	BAL	082	15TH WAR
CARPENTER, WILLIAM H.	BAL	319	1ST DIST
CARPENTER, WILLIAM J.C.	HAR	072	1ST DIST
CARPER, J.	BAL	116	1ST WARD
CARPER, RACHAEL	BAL	066	15TH WAR
CARPETNER, SMAUEL	CAR	074	NO TWP L
CARPREN, MOSES	BAL	040	1ST WARD
CARR, ABEDNIGO	ANN	439	HOWARD D
CARR, ALEXANDER	CAR	375	9TH DIST
CARR, AMEAL	BAL	127	11TH WAR
CARR, AMY	BAL	328	1ST DIST
CARR, ANN	BAL	365	8TH WARD
CARR, ANN	ANN	400	8TH DIST
CARR, ANN	PRI	103	SPALDING
CARR, ANN	PRI	119	PISCATAW
CARR, ANN A.	BAL	440	8TH WARD
CARR, ANTOINETTE	MGM	350	BERRYS D
CARR, ARTRIDGE	ANN	303	1ST DIST
CARR, ASSILLA	CAR	221	5TH DIST
CARR, BEDDY	BAL	339	13TH WAR
CARR, BENJAMIN	CAL	059	3RD DIST
CARR, BENJAMIN	ANN	408	8TH DIST
CARR, BENJAMIN	SOM	477	TRAPP DI
CARR, BENJAMIN D.	MGM	350	BERRYS D
CARR, BENNJAMIN	MGM	350	BERRYS D
CARR, BETSEY	WOR	341	1ST E DI
CARR, BETSY	WAS	130	HAGERSTO
CARR, BRIDGET	BAL	031	15TH WAR
CARR, CATHERINE	BAL	350	3RD WARD
CARR, CATHERINE	BAL	138	11TH WAR
CARR, CHALRES	BAL	093	18TH WAR
CARR, CHARELS	ANN	481	HOWARD D
CARR, CHARLES	CAL	061	3RD DIST
CARR, CLARA	BAL	204	2ND WARD
CARR, DABNEY S.	BAL	058	10TH WAR
CARR, DAVID	ANN	362	4TH DIST
CARR, E.	FRE	200	5TH E DI
CARR, E. MRS-	ANN	319	2ND DIST
CARR, EDWARD	CEC	131	6TH E DI
CARR, EDWARD	WAS	233	1ST DIST
CARR, ELEANORA	BAL	183	6TH WARD
CARR, ELEXANDER	HAR	170	3RD DIST
CARR, ELIZA	BAL	299	20TH WAR
CARR, ELIZA	BAL	380	3RD WARD
CARR, ELIZA	WAS	154	HAGERSTO
CARR, ELIZA	PRI	065	NOTTINGH
CARR, ELIZABETH	BAL	281	20TH WAR
CARR, ELLEN	BAL	125	11TH WAR
CARR, ELLEN	HAR	118	2ND DIST
CARR, ELLEN	BAL	095	15TH WAR
CARR, ELLEN M.	FRE	451	8TH E DI
CARR, EMMANUEL N.	BAL	054	15TH WAR
CARR, FIELDER	ANN	405	8TH DIST
CARR, FRANCIS M.	BAL	146	1ST WARD
CARR, GEORGE	BAL	343	1ST DIST
CARR, HARRIET	BAL	064	10TH WAR
CARR, HENRY	BAL	033	4TH WARD
CARR, HENRY K.	BAL	033	9TH WARD
CARR, HESTER	BAL	121	16TH WAR
CARR, HUDAIS	CEC	137	6TH E DI
CARR, HUGH	BAL	457	8TH WARD
CARR, ISAAC	BAL	370	1ST DIST
CARR, J.	BAL	152	1ST WARD
CARR, JACOB	BAL	052	1ST WARD
CARR, JAEMS	CAL	022	2ND DIST
CARR, JAMES	BAL	117	11TH WAR
CARR, JAMES	BAL	198	11TH WAR
CARR, JAMES	CAR	280	7TH DIST
CARR, JAMES	BAL	328	1ST DIST
CARR, JAMES	BAL	345	3RD WARD
CARR, JAMES	BAL	177	16TH WAR
CARR, JAMES	BAL	309	12TH WAR
CARR, JAMES	ANN	400	8TH DIST
CARR, JAMES	BAL	384	8TH WARD
CARR, JAMES	ANN	438	HOWARD D
CARR, JAMES E.	CAL	060	3RD DIST
CARR, JANE	BAL	255	20TH WAR
CARR, JESSE	HAR	006	1ST DIST
CARR, JESSE	BAL	036	18TH WAR
CARR, JESSE	BAL	328	1ST DIST
CARR, JOHN	BAL	314	3RD WARD
CARR, JOHN	BAL	396	1ST DIST
CARR, JOHN	ANN	347	3RD DIST
CARR, JOHN	BAL	271	7TH WARD
CARR, JOHN	ANN	394	8TH DIST
CARR, JOHN	ANN	299	1ST DIST
CARR, JOHN	BAL	095	15TH WAR
CARR, JOHN	BAL	112	1ST WARD
CARR, JOHN	BAL	154	1ST WARD
CARR, JOHN	BAL	179	11TH WAR
CARR, JOHN	BAL	273	20TH WAR
CARR, JOHN	CAL	047	3RD DIST
CARR, JOHN	BAL	216	11TH WAR
CARR, JOHN	BAL	022	4TH WARD
CARR, JOHN	BAL	221	19TH WAR
CARR, JOHN	BAL	222	17TH WAR
CARR, JOHN	BAL	236	17TH WAR
CARR, JOHN	HAR	193	3RD DIST
CARR, JOHN	PRI	004	BLADENSB
CARR, JOHN H.	CAR	220	5TH DIST
CARR, JOHN K.	HAR	040	1ST DIST
CARR, JOSEPH	HAR	008	1ST DIST
CARR, JOSEPH	BAL	097	15TH WAR
CARR, JOSEPH	ANN	310	1ST DIST
CARR, LEWIS	ANN	411	8TH DIST
CARR, LEWIS	ANN	474	HOWARD D
CARR, LILY	ANN	457	HOWARD D
CARR, LOUIS	CEC	136	6TH E DI
CARR, LUCRETIA	BAL	073	10TH WAR
CARR, MARGARET	ANN	444	HOWARD D
CARR, MARGARET	BAL	221	19TH WAR
CARR, MARGARET	DOR	379	1ST DIST
CARR, MARY	BAL	453	8TH WARD
CARR, MARY A.	BAL	005	9TH WARD
CARR, MARY A.	BAL	211	11TH WAR
CARR, MARY A.	QUE	170	2ND E DI
CARR, MARY A.E.	CAL	051	3RD DIST
CARR, MATILDA	WAS	189	1ST DIST
CARR, NICHOLAS	BAL	124	11TH WAR
CARR, NICHOLAS	ANN	447	HOWARD D
CARR, OWEN	BAL	161	11TH WAR
CARR, P.	BAL	152	1ST WARD
CARR, PATRICK	BAL	128	5TH WARD
CARR, PATRICK	BAL	449	14TH WAR
CARR, PATRICK	BAL	469	14TH WAR
CARR, PEWELL	BAL	051	1ST WARD
CARR, PETER	BAL	201	6TH DIST
CARR, PHILIP D.	ANN	303	1ST DIST
CARR, REBECCA	ANN	482	HOWARD D
CARR, RICHARD	ANN	444	HOWARD D
CARR, RICHARD	PRI	019	VANSVILL
CARR, RICHARD T.	BAL	017	9TH WARD
CARR, ROBERT	ANN	300	1ST DIST
CARR, ROBERT	DOR	385	1ST DIST
CARR, ROBERT	CEC	135	6TH E DI
CARR, ROBERT	CEC	143	7TH E DI
CARR, ROBERT	HAR	040	1ST DIST
CARR, ROBERT H.	ANN	265	ANNAPOLI
CARR, ROSBURY	ALL	210	CUMBERLA
CARR, ROSE	BAL	297	3RD WARD
CARR, ROSEBY	BAL	280	1ST DIST
CARR, SAMUEL	ANN	299	1ST DIST
CARR, SAMUEL	CAR	201	4TH DIST
CARR, SAMUEL	BAL	078	18TH WAR
CARR, SAMUEL W.	ANN	405	8TH DIST
CARR, SARAH	BAL	121	5TH WARD
CARR, SARAH	BAL	005	9TH WARD
CARR, SARAH A.	BAL	357	1ST DIST
CARR, SOPHIA	DOR	466	1ST DIST
CARR, SUSAN	BAL	365	3RD WARD
CARR, SUSAN	BAL	213	11TH WAR
CARR, THOMAS	HAR	008	1ST DIST
CARR, THOMAS	CAL	053	3RD DIST
CARR, THOMAS	FRE	450	8TH E DI
CARR, THOMAS	BAL	364	8TH WARD
CARR, THOMAS	BAL	211	6TH WARD
CARR, WALTER	ANN	405	8TH DIST
CARR, WILLAIM	HAR	112	2ND DIST
CARR, WILLIAM	ANN	323	2ND DIST
CARR, WILLIAM	BAL	380	3RD WARD
CARR, WILLIAM	BAL	357	1ST DIST
CARR, WILLIAM	BAL	348	7TH WARD
CARR, WILLIAM	BAL	297	1ST DIST
CARR, WILLIAM	BAL	184	16TH WAR
CARRABY, JOHN	BAL	183	16TH WAR
CARRACK, ELIZA	BAL	292	1ST DIST
CARRACK, GEORGE	BAL	208	11TH WAR
CARRACK, WILLIAM	BAL	158	11TH WAR

Name	County	Page	District
CARRADY, JOSEPH	BAL	372	13TH WAR
CARRAL, MARY	CAR	121	NO TWP L
CARRALHO, D. N.	BAL	052	9TH WARD
CARRALL, A.	BAL	170	1ST WARD
CARRALL, WILLIAM	BAL	156	1ST WARD
CARRAN, FRANCIS	BAL	132	11TH WAR
CARRAN, WILLIAM	CEC	103	4TH E DI
CARREBE, CHARLES	BAL	155	11TH WAR
CARREGAN, TIMOTHY	ALL	142	6TH E.D.
CARRELL, ISAAC N.	HAR	167	3RD DIST
CARRELL, JOHN W.	HAR	166	3RD DIST
CARRELL, KATE	BAL	057	10TH WAR
CARRELL, WILLIAM	BAL	346	13TH WAR
CARREY, WILLIAM	HAR	064	1ST DIST
CARRICK, BENJAMIN	BAL	155	16TH WAR
CARRICK, BENJAMIN	ANN	294	1ST DIST
CARRICK, DORCUS	PRI	040	VANSVILL
CARRICK, HENRY	PRI	044	VANSVILL
CARRICK, JAMES	BAL	453	1ST DIST
CARRICK, JAMES	BAL	284	20TH WAR
CARRICK, JOHN	PRI	087	QUEEN AN
CARRICK, JOSIAH	ANN	372	4TH DIST
CARRICK, RICHARD	PRI	043	VANSVILL
CARRICK, STEPHEN	BAL	300	17TH WAR
CARRICK, WILLIAM	PRI	043	VANSVILL
CARRICK, WILLIAM	ANN	294	1ST DIST
CARRIE, REBECCA	ANN	287	ANNAPOLI
CARRIER, AMBROSE	BAL	467	14TH WAR
CARRIER, HARRIET M.	BAL	066	10TH WAR
CARRIER, JOHN M.	BAL	084	18TH WAR
CARRIER, JONATHAN	CEC	187	7TH E DI
CARRIER, WILIAM	BAL	443	14TH WAR
CARRIGAN, ANN	BAL	010	9TH WARD
CARRIGAN, BRIDGET	BAL	027	4TH WARD
CARRIGAN, JAMES	BAL	369	8TH WARD
CARRIGAN, JUDAH	BAL	026	18TH WAR
CARRIGAN, OWEN	BAL	027	4TH WARD
CARRIGAN, PATRICK	BAL	210	11TH WAR
CARRIGAN, SARAH	BAL	286	20TH WAR
CARRIGAN, WILLIAM J.	ANN	421	HOWARD D
CARRILL, JOHN R.	QUE	171	2ND E DI
CARRINGTON, BRIDGET	BAL	050	9TH WARD
CARRINGTON, JOHN	CHA	258	MIDDLETO
CARRINGTON, JOHN R.	HAR	080	2ND DIST
CARRINGTON, MARY	BAL	467	14TH WAR
CARRINGTON, MARY C.	CHA	266	MIDDLETO
CARRINGTON, SAMUEL	CHA	264	HILLTOP
CARRIS, CATHARINE	BAL	373	13TH WAR
CARRIVAN, PATRICK	BAL	011	9TH WARD
CARRLL, JAMES	BAL	174	11TH WAR
CARRLL, JOHN	HAR	197	3RD DIST
CARRLL, MARY	BAL	139	11TH WAR
CARROH, JOHN	CAR	166	NO TWP L
CARROL, ANN	CAR	151	NO TWP L
CARROL, BENJAMIN	BAL	327	3RD WARD
CARROL, CASSANDRA-BLACK	FRE	037	FREDERIC
CARROL, CHARLES	BAL	148	11TH WAR
CARROL, CHARLES	BAL	306	1ST DIST
CARROL, CORNELIUS	BAL	024	2ND DIST
CARROL, DINAH	BAL	188	11TH WAR
CARROL, ELIZABETH	CAR	094	NO TWP L
CARROL, HENRY-BLACK	FRE	038	FREDERIC
CARROL, JAMES	BAL	474	14TH WAR
CARROL, JAMES	BAL	126	18TH WAR
CARROL, JAMES	BAL	053	2ND DIST
CARROL, JAMES JR.	BAL	097	2ND DIST
CARROL, JOHN	BAL	170	11TH WAR
CARROL, JOHN	BAL	475	14TH WAR
CARROL, L. KING	BAL	187	11TH WAR
CARROL, LETITIA	CAR	161	NO TWP L
CARROL, LIBBY	ANN	346	3RD DIST
CARROL, MARGARET	BAL	145	11TH WAR
CARROL, MARGARET	PRI	045	VANSVILL
CARROL, REACHEL	BAL	186	11TH WAR
CARROL, SOPHIA	ANN	303	1ST DIST
CARROL, THOMAS	BAL	419	14TH WAR
CARROLE, GEORGE	DOR	407	1ST DIST
CARROLE, JOHN*	DOR	428	1ST DIST
CARROLER, FREDERICK	BAL	218	19TH WAR
CARROLL, ALEXANDER	CEC	174	6TH E DI
CARROLL, AMANDA	BAL	122	16TH WAR
CARROLL, ANN	BAL	450	1ST DIST
CARROLL, ANN	BAL	447	14TH WAR
CARROLL, ANN	MGM	359	BERRYS D
CARROLL, ANN E.	CAR	121	NO TWP L
CARROLL, ANN M.	FRE	100	FREDERIC
CARROLL, AQUILOR	HAR	168	3RD DIST
CARROLL, BEMAN	BAL	316	20TH WAR
CARROLL, BENJAMIN	BAL	256	20TH WAR
CARROLL, BENJAMIN F.	HAR	173	3RD DIST
CARROLL, BRIDGET	BAL	271	20TH WAR
CARROLL, CARLES	ANN	286	ANNAPOLI
CARROLL, CATHARINE	BAL	263	12TH WAR
CARROLL, CHARLES	ALL	154	6TH E.D.
CARROLL, CHARLES	BAL	087	2ND DIST
CARROLL, CHARLES	BAL	089	2ND DIST
CARROLL, CHARLES	ANN	470	HOWARD D
CARROLL, CHARLES	SOM	403	BRINKLEY
CARROLL, CHARLES	BAL	453	14TH WAR
CARROLL, CHARLES C.	BAL	205	6TH WARD
CARROLL, CHARLES R.	BAL	141	11TH WAR
CARROLL, CHARLES W.	DOR	320	1ST DIST
CARROLL, CAVID	BAL	308	1ST DIST
CARROLL, CAVID	PRI	005	BLADENSB
CARROLL, DENNARD*	DOR	307	1ST DIST
CARROLL, EDWARD	BAL	046	4TH WARD
CARROLL, EDWARD	BAL	400	3RD WARD
CARROLL, EDWARD*	DOR	464	1ST DIST
CARROLL, EILY	CAR	128	NO TWP L
CARROLL, ELENOR	BAL	194	19TH WAR
CARROLL, ELIZABETH	BAL	267	17TH WAR
CARROLL, ELIZABETH	KEN	219	2ND DIST
CARROLL, ELIZABETH	BAL	331	3RD WARD
CARROLL, ELIZABETH	BAL	208	6TH DIST
CARROLL, ELIZABETH*	DOR	418	1ST DIST
CARROLL, ELLEN	BAL	455	14TH WAR
CARROLL, ELLEN	BAL	394	8TH WARD
CARROLL, EUGENE	FRE	20	5TH E DI
CARROLL, FELIX	BAL	410	3RD WARD
CARROLL, GEORGE	DOR	458	1ST DIST
CARROLL, GEORGE	PRI	108	PISCATAW
CARROLL, GEORGIANN	BAL	096	18TH WAR
CARROLL, GLEN	ANN	375	4TH DIST
CARROLL, HAMILTON-BLACK	FRE	234	BUCKEYST
CARROLL, HANNAH	PRI	071	MARLBROU
CARROLL, HENRIETTA	BAL	040	9TH WARD
CARROLL, HENRY	BAL	077	10TH WAR
CARROLL, HENRY	PRI	057	AQUASCO
CARROLL, HENRY	FRE	202	5TH E DI
CARROLL, HENRY	CAL	026	2ND DIST

Name	County	Page	District
CARROLL, HENRY J.	ST	304	2ND E DI
CARROLL, HENRY JR.	BAL	045	2ND DIST
CARROLL, HORATIO	PRI	083	QUEEN AN
CARROLL, HUGH	BAL	133	2ND DIST
CARROLL, ISABEL J.	BAL	443	8TH WARD
CARROLL, J.	BAL	286	2ND WARD
CARROLL, J.J.	BAL	247	12TH WAR
CARROLL, JAMES	ANN	367	4TH DIST
CARROLL, JAMES	BAL	405	8TH WARD
CARROLL, JAMES	BAL	449	1ST DIST
CARROLL, JAMES	PRI	078	MARLBROU
CARROLL, JAMES	PRI	112	PISCATAW
CARROLL, JAMES	BAL	469	14TH WAR
CARROLL, JAMES	CEC	175	7TH E DI
CARROLL, JAMES	DOR	324	1ST DIST
CARROLL, JAMES	CHA	255	MIDDLETO
CARROLL, JAMES	HAR	084	2ND DIST
CARROLL, JAMES A.	DOR	430	1ST DIST
CARROLL, JAMES M.	DOR	320	1ST DIST
CARROLL, JESSE	ANN	362	4TH DIST
CARROLL, JOHN	ANN	345	3RD DIST
CARROLL, JOHN	BAL	109	2ND DIST
CARROLL, JOHN	BAL	204	6TH DIST
CARROLL, JOHN	ANN	514	HOWARD D
CARROLL, JOHN	BAL	363	3RD WARD
CARROLL, JOHN	ANN	413	HOWARD D
CARROLL, JOHN	ALL	100	5TH E.D.
CARROLL, JOHN	BAL	183	11TH WAR
CARROLL, JOHN	BAL	166	11TH WAR
CARROLL, JOHN	BAL	007	15TH WAR
CARROLL, JOHN	BAL	006	15TH WAR
CARROLL, JOHN	BAL	189	17TH WAR
CARROLL, JOHN	BAL	203	6TH WARD
CARROLL, JOHN	BAL	151	1ST WARD
CARROLL, JOHN	BAL	146	1ST WARD
CARROLL, JOHN	KEN	220	2ND DIST
CARROLL, JOHN	BAL	037	4TH WARD
CARROLL, JOHN	PRI	104	PISCATAW
CARROLL, JOHN B.	BAL	442	8TH WARD
CARROLL, JOHN E.	BAL	143	1ST WARD
CARROLL, JOHN F.	PRI	122	PISCATAW
CARROLL, JOHN H.	PRI	115	PISCATAW
CARROLL, JOHN H.	BAL	246	1ST DIST
CARROLL, JOHN J.	ST	255	3RD E DI
CARROLL, JOHN K.	BAL	037	9TH WARD
CARROLL, JOHN R.	BAL	016	15TH WAR
CARROLL, JOHN W.	KEN	208	2ND DIST
CARROLL, JOHN*	DOR	428	1ST DIST
CARROLL, JOHN-BLACK	FRE	246	NEW MARK
CARROLL, JOSIAH	DOR	430	1ST DIST
CARROLL, JSOEPH	BAL	316	7TH WARD
CARROLL, JUDITH C.	BAL	104	10TH WAR
CARROLL, JULIA*	BAL	073	10TH WAR
CARROLL, KATE	BAL	280	20TH WAR
CARROLL, KATE	BAL	200	11TH WAR
CARROLL, KITTY	DOR	381	1ST DIST
CARROLL, KITTY	MGM	379	ROCKERLE
CARROLL, LEWIS	BAL	118	1ST WARD
CARROLL, LOUISA	BAL	049	1ST WARD
CARROLL, MARGAERT	BAL	029	9TH WARD
CARROLL, MARGARET	BAL	310	12TH WAR
CARROLL, MARGARET	BAL	033	15TH WAR
CARROLL, MARGARETT	DOR	321	1ST DIST
CARROLL, MARIA	BAL	370	13TH WAR
CARROLL, MARIA	ANN	515	HOWARD D
CARROLL, MARY	ANN	500	HOWARD D
CARROLL, MARY	ANN	515	HOWARD D
CARROLL, MARY	BAL	342	1ST DIST
CARROLL, MARY	BAL	175	6TH WARD
CARROLL, MARY	BAL	403	8TH WARD
CARROLL, MARY	BAL	272	2ND WARD
CARROLL, MARY	ALL	170	6TH E.D.
CARROLL, MARY	CEC	173	6TH E DI
CARROLL, MARY	CHA	260	MIDDLETO
CARROLL, MARY	FRE	308	WOODSBOR
CARROLL, MARY	MGM	339	CLARKSBU
CARROLL, MARY	BAL	193	19TH WAR
CARROLL, MARY A.	BAL	413	1ST DIST
CARROLL, MARY A.	BAL	263	1ST DIST
CARROLL, MARY E.	BAL	295	3RD WARD
CARROLL, MARY J.	BAL	166	16TH WAR
CARROLL, MATTHIAS	FRE	278	NEW MARK
CARROLL, MICHAEL	BAL	203	6TH WARD
CARROLL, MICHAEL B.	PRI	068	NOTTINGH
CARROLL, MILEY J.*	DOR	463	1ST DIST
CARROLL, MINA	ANN	355	3RD DIST
CARROLL, MOSES	BAL	387	1ST DIST
CARROLL, MRS.	ANN	270	ANNAPOLI
CARROLL, NANCY	MGM	378	ROCKERLE
CARROLL, NICHOLAS	BAL	336	1ST DIST
CARROLL, NICHOLAS	BAL	460	1ST DIST
CARROLL, OWEN	FRE	069	FREDERIC
CARROLL, OWEN	PRI	036	VANSVILL
CARROLL, PAELY	BAL	222	12TH WAR
CARROLL, PATRICK	BAL	119	2ND DIST
CARROLL, PATRICK	BAL	393	8TH WARD
CARROLL, PATRICK	BAL	366	8TH WARD
CARROLL, PATRICK	WAS	055	2ND SUBD
CARROLL, PATRICK	BAL	016	4TH WARD
CARROLL, PATRICK	BAL	469	14TH WAR
CARROLL, PATRICK J.	BAL	017	4TH WARD
CARROLL, PETER	DOR	463	1ST DIST
CARROLL, PHIL	KEN	242	2ND DIST
CARROLL, PHILIP	ST	304	2ND E DI
CARROLL, PHILIP	ALL	146	6TH E.D.
CARROLL, PHILLIP	BAL	118	1ST WARD
CARROLL, RACHEL	ANN	511	HOWARD D
CARROLL, REBECCA	ANN	458	HOWARD D
CARROLL, RICHARD-BLACK	FRE	005	FREDERIC
CARROLL, SALLY	SOM	403	BRINKLEY
CARROLL, SAMUEL	BAL	096	15TH WAR
CARROLL, SAMUEL	PRI	032	VANSVILL
CARROLL, SAMUEL S.	BAL	107	10TH WAR
CARROLL, SARAH	BAL	189	17TH WAR
CARROLL, SARAH	HAR	131	2ND DIST
CARROLL, SARAH	BAL	215	11TH WAR
CARROLL, SARAH C.	BAL	006	15TH WAR
CARROLL, SILUS*	DOR	462	1ST DIST
CARROLL, SUSAN	ST	292	2ND E DI
CARROLL, SUSAN	BAL	106	15TH WAR
CARROLL, SUSANNAH	BAL	295	3RD WARD
CARROLL, TERRESA	CHA	254	MIDDLETO
CARROLL, THOMAS	FRE	380	PETERSVI
CARROLL, THOMAS	FRE	393	PETERSVI
CARROLL, THOMAS	HAR	137	2ND DIST
CARROLL, THOMAS	MGM	379	ROCKERLE
CARROLL, THOMAS	BAL	051	15TH WAR
CARROLL, THOMAS	ANN	482	HOWARD D
CARROLL, THOMAS	BAL	034	9TH WARD
CARROLL, THOMAS	DOR	464	1ST DIST

Name	County	Page	District
CARROLL, THOMAS J.	KEN	213	2ND DIST
CARROLL, WALTER	MGM	386	ROCKERLE
CARROLL, WASHINGTON	PRI	097	SPALDING
CARROLL, WILLIAM	TAL	109	ST MICHA
CARROLL, WILLIAM	HAR	062	1ST DIST
CARROLL, WILLIAM	FRE	065	FREDERIC
CARROLL, WILLIAM	DOR	320	1ST DIST
CARROLL, WILLIAM	BAL	364	13TH WAR
CARROLL, WILLIAM	BAL	023	9TH WARD
CARROLL, WILLIAM	BAL	113	2ND DIST
CARROLL, WILLIAM	BAL	092	2ND DIST
CARROLL, WILLIAM	BAL	003	EASTERN
CARROLL, WILLIAM	BAL	155	11TH WAR
CARROLL, WILLIAM	BAL	259	12TH WAR
CARROLL, WILLIAM	BAL	336	1ST DIST
CARROLL, WILLIAM	BAL	271	1ST DIST
CARROLL, WILLIAM S.	BAL	391	8TH WARD
CARROLL, WILLIAM W.	BAL	017	9TH WARD
CARROLL, WILLIAM W.	BAL	017	9TH WARD
CARROLL, WILLIAM-BLACK	FRE	212	BUCKEYST
CARROLL,MARTHA	BAL	051	2ND DIST
CARROLTON, THOMAS	BAL	168	1ST WARD
CARRON, ALJERMON*	DOR	320	1ST DIST
CARRON, JERRY	BAL	449	1ST DIST
CARRON, JOSEPH W.	KEN	251	2ND DIST
CARRON, PATRICK	BAL	250	1ST DIST
CARRONERS, JAMES *	WAS	159	2ND DIST
CARROW, JOHN	KEN	291	3RD DIST
CARRS, MIMA	BAL	410	3RD WARD
CARRY, BENJAMIN *	ANN	343	3RD DIST
CARRY, JOHN L.	BAL	470	14TH WAR
CARRY, JOHN T.	ANN	303	1ST DIST
CARRY, JOHN W.	BAL	120	2ND DIST
CARRY, JOSEPH	DOR	369	3RD DIVI
CARRY, LOUIZA	BAL	127	5TH WARD
CARRY, RESIN *	BAL	347	1ST DIST
CARSCAN, MICHAEL	FRE	067	FREDERIC
CARSEY, JESSE	WAS	282	1ST DIST
CARSEY, M.R.	PRI	077	MARLBROU
CARSLY, MARY	WOR	328	1ST E DI
CARSON, CATHARINE	WAS	285	1ST DIST
CARSON, DAVID	BAL	133	18TH WAR
CARSON, EDWARD C.	BAL	462	14TH WAR
CARSON, ELIJAH	BAL	451	14TH WAR
CARSON, ELIZA	BAL	462	14TH WAR
CARSON, ELIZABETH	WAS	228	1ST DIST
CARSON, FRANCIS	BAL	043	1ST WARD
CARSON, GEORGE	WAS	169	FUNKSTOW
CARSON, GEORGE	BAL	130	18TH WAR
CARSON, GEORGE	CAR	396	2ND DIST
CARSON, GEORGE	BAL	007	18TH WAR
CARSON, GEORGE	CAR	335	6TH DIST
CARSON, HANNAH	WAS	146	HAGERSTO
CARSON, HEMSLEY-BLACK	QUE	145	1ST E DI
CARSON, J.C.	BAL	129	1ST WARD
CARSON, JAME	BAL	050	1ST WARD
CARSON, JOHN	BAL	115	1ST WARD
CARSON, JOHN	BAL	155	1ST WARD
CARSON, JOHN	BAL	002	15TH WAR
CARSON, JOHN	CEC	156	PORT DUP
CARSON, JONOTHAN	BAL	160	19TH WAR
CARSON, JOSEPH H.	BAL	200	19TH WAR
CARSON, JOSEPH M.*	TAL	015	EASTON D
CARSON, LAURANA	CAR	083	NO TWP L
CARSON, LEVI-BLACK	QUE	165	2ND E DI
CARSON, MARGARET	WAS	228	1ST DIST
CARSON, MARGARET	BAL	317	7TH WARD
CARSON, MARTHA A.	BAL	023	4TH WARD
CARSON, MARY A.	BAL	477	14TH WAR
CARSON, NATHANIEL R.	CEC	156	PORT DUP
CARSON, OLUMBUS	BAL	208	11TH WAR
CARSON, PETER	BAL	450	14TH WAR
CARSON, PETER	BAL	457	8TH WARD
CARSON, RACHEL J.-BLACK	QUE	144	1ST E DI
CARSON, ROBERT	BAL	273	1ST DIST
CARSON, ROBERT E.-BLACK	QUE	145	1ST E DI
CARSON, ROBERT-MULATTO	CAR	166	NO TWP L
CARSON, SAMUEL	CEC	155	PORT DUP
CARSON, SAMUEL	ALL	182	8TH E.D.
CARSON, SARAH	BAL	032	9TH WARD
CARSON, SARAH J.	BAL	023	4TH WARD
CARSON, SARAH R.	CEC	158	PORT DUP
CARSON, SUSAN	FRE	114	CREAGERS
CARSON, SUSAN-BLACK	CAR	097	NO TWP L
CARSON, THOMAS J.	BAL	314	20TH WAR
CARSON, WASHINGTON R.	BAL	476	14TH WAR
CARSON, WILLIAM	BAL	042	18TH WAR
CARSON, WILLIAM	BAL	274	1ST DIST
CARSON,AMANDA	FRE	051	FREDERIC
CARSON,PETER	BAL	105	1ST WARD
CARSONS, ANN	HAR	134	2ND DIST
CARSONS, GEORGE	BAL	170	1ST WARD
CARSONS, HEMSLEY	QUE	218	3RD E DI
CARSONS, JOHN	BAL	116	1ST WARD
CARSONS, JOSEPH M.	QUE	166	2ND E DI
CARSONS, JOSEPHA	QUE	136	1ST E DI
CARSONS, ROSE	QUE	218	3RD E DI
CARSONS, WILLIAM	QUE	136	1ST E DI
CARSTE, ELIZA C.	QUE	154	1ST E DI
CARSWELL, JOHN S.	BAL	262	2ND WARD
CART, ANN	BAL	444	1ST DIST
CART, EMANUEL	CAR	250	3RD DIST
CARTAIN, MARY	BAL	333	13TH WAR
CARTELL, WOOLFROM	BAL	279	1ST DIST
CARTELLS, PATRICK *	BAL	472	14TH WAR
CARTER, JOHN C.	WOR	167	6TH E DI
CARTER, ADAM	BAL	166	16TH WAR
CARTER, ALEXANDER	ALL	009	3RD E.D.
CARTER, ALEXANDER M.	BAL	114	15TH WAR
CARTER, ALICE	ANN	460	HOWARD D
CARTER, ANN	FRE	309	WOODSBOR
CARTER, ANN AH.	ANN	521	HOWARD D
CARTER, ANN-BLACK	CAR	398	2ND DIST
CARTER, ANNA	QUE	161	2ND E DI
CARTER, ARTHUR	ANN	290	ANNAPOLI
CARTER, ASBURY	BAL	428	14TH WAR
CARTER, AUGUSTUS R.	BAL	084	15TH WAR
CARTER, BERNARD	WAS	021	2ND SUBD
CARTER, BRIDGET	BAL	208	11TH WAR
CARTER, CAROLIEN	WAS	155	2ND DIST
CARTER, CATHERINE	ALL	216	CUMBERLA
CARTER, CATHERINE	BAL	163	11TH WAR
CARTER, CECLIA A.-BLACK	ST	329	4TH E DI
CARTER, CHARELS	ALL	072	5TH E.D.
CARTER, CHARELS	BAL	203	17TH WAR
CARTER, CHARLES	BAL	148	11TH WAR
CARTER, CHARLES	BAL	276	7TH WARD
CARTER, CHARLES	TAL	019	EASTON D
CARTER, CHARLES H.	PRI	081	QUEEN AN
CARTER, CHARLOTTE	ALL	091	5TH E.D.

Name	County	Page	District
CARTER, CLEMENT	BAL	126	5TH WARD
CARTER, CLOUD	CEC	090	4TH E DI
CARTER, DANIEL	BAL	223	12TH WAR
CARTER, DANIEL JR.	CEC	128	5TH E DI
CARTER, DANIEL SR.	CEC	131	6TH E DI
CARTER, DELILIA	CHA	234	HILLTOP
CARTER, DENNIS	BAL	090	2ND DIST
CARTER, DENNIS	BAL	095	2ND DIST
CARTER, DURUS *	BAL	186	6TH WARD
CARTER, EDMOND	BAL	460	1ST DIST
CARTER, EDMUND	BAL	049	9TH WARD
CARTER, EDWARD	ANN	267	ANNAPOLI
CARTER, EDWARD	ANN	267	ANNAPOLI
CARTER, EDWARD	ANN	329	2ND DIST
CARTER, EDWARD	CAL	050	3RD DIST
CARTER, EDWARD	TAL	024	EASTON D
CARTER, EDWARD F.	BAL	064	4TH WARD
CARTER, ELEANOR	CHA	287	BOJANTOW
CARTER, ELIABETH	BAL	061	10TH WAR
CARTER, ELIJAH	CAL	053	3RD DIST
CARTER, ELIZA	BAL	181	2ND DIST
CARTER, ELIZABETH	ANN	275	ANNAPOLI
CARTER, ELIZABETH	BAL	183	6TH WARD
CARTER, ELIZABETH	FRE	398	JEFFERSO
CARTER, ELIZABETH	BAL	295	20TH WAR
CARTER, ELLEN E.	ALL	054	10TH E.D
CARTER, FRANCES	CEC	083	CHARLEST
CARTER, FRANCES A.	CAR	075	NO TWP L
CARTER, FRANCIS	BAL	121	5TH WARD
CARTER, FRANCIS A.	BAL	182	19TH WAR
CARTER, GEORGE	CEC	195	6TH E DI
CARTER, GEORGE	BAL	119	1ST WARD
CARTER, GEORGE	BAL	315	1ST DIST
CARTER, GEORGE	ANN	339	3RD DIST
CARTER, GEORGE W.	FRE	395	PETERSVI
CARTER, GEORGE W.	BAL	428	14TH WAR
CARTER, HARRIET	BAL	110	15TH WAR
CARTER, HARRIET-BLACK	FRE	051	FREDERIC
CARTER, HENNETTA	BAL	450	8TH WARD
CARTER, HENRY	ALL	233	CUMBERLA
CARTER, HENRY	BAL	457	1ST DIST
CARTER, HENRY	BAL	303	3RD WARD
CARTER, HENRY	CHA	220	ALLENS F
CARTER, HENRY	MGM	333	CRACKLIN
CARTER, HENRY-MULATTO	ST	324	4TH E DI
CARTER, HETTY	BAL	104	10TH WAR
CARTER, HORATIO	ST	348	5TH E DI
CARTER, IGNATIUS	ST	259	3RD E DI
CARTER, ISAAC	BAL	383	3RD WARD
CARTER, J. M.	BAL	154	1ST WARD
CARTER, J.H.	BAL	233	20TH WAR
CARTER, JACOB	BAL	222	12TH WAR
CARTER, JACOB	QUE	231	4TH E DI
CARTER, JACOB D.	ALL	145	6TH E.D.
CARTER, JAEMS H.	BAL	446	14TH WAR
CARTER, JAMES	BAL	115	11TH WAR
CARTER, JAMES	CHA	275	ALLENS F
CARTER, JAMES-BLACK	CAR	083	NO TWP L
CARTER, JAMES-BLACK	FRE	435	8TH E DI
CARTER, JAMES-BLACK	ST	327	4TH E DI
CARTER, JAMES-BLACK	ST	330	4TH E DI
CARTER, JAMES-MULATTO	CAR	077	NO TWP L
CARTER, JAMES-MULATTO	CAR	074	NO TWP L
CARTER, JANE	CAL	050	3RD DIST
CARTER, JESSEE	BAL	449	8TH WARD
CARTER, JOEL	HAR	097	2ND DIST
CARTER, JOHN	QUE	155	2ND E DI
CARTER, JOHN	BAL	027	4TH WARD
CARTER, JOHN	CAR	219	5TH DIST
CARTER, JOHN	BAL	003	18TH WAR
CARTER, JOHN	ALL	150	6TH E.D.
CARTER, JOHN	BAL	131	1ST WARD
CARTER, JOHN G.	BAL	416	3RD WARD
CARTER, JOHN H.	BAL	175	11TH WAR
CARTER, JOHN P. REV.	ANN	460	HOWARD D
CARTER, JOHN W.	BAL	176	16TH WAR
CARTER, JOHN-BLACK	CAR	373	9TH DIST
CARTER, JOHN-BLACK	ST	330	4TH E DI
CARTER, JOSEPH	QUE	160	2ND E DI
CARTER, JOSEPH	QUE	211	3RD E DI
CARTER, JOSEPH	QUE	212	3RD E DI
CARTER, JOSEPH	BAL	046	18TH WAR
CARTER, JOSEPH	BAL	289	17TH WAR
CARTER, JOSEPH	BAL	261	17TH WAR
CARTER, JOSHUA	BAL	037	4TH WARD
CARTER, JOSHUA	BAL	095	2ND DIST
CARTER, JOSHUA	ANN	333	2ND DIST
CARTER, JOSIAH	BAL	051	2ND DIST
CARTER, JULIANN	CAR	107	NO TWP L
CARTER, LEAH	BAL	349	13TH WAR
CARTER, LETTY	CAL	044	3RD DIST
CARTER, LEWER	ALL	158	6TH E.D.
CARTER, LEWIS	ANN	337	3RD DIST
CARTER, LEWIS	BAL	136	1ST WARD
CARTER, LIDDY	BAL	135	11TH WAR
CARTER, LIZZY	BAL	207	17TH WAR
CARTER, LOUISA	BAL	086	4TH WARD
CARTER, MARGARET	CEC	016	ELKTON 3
CARTER, MARGARET	ALL	085	5TH E.D.
CARTER, MARTHA	BAL	476	14TH WAR
CARTER, MARTHA	WAS	157	HAGERSTO
CARTER, MARY	KEN	292	3RD DIST
CARTER, MARY	BAL	131	11TH WAR
CARTER, MARY	BAL	127	11TH WAR
CARTER, MARY	CAR	216	5TH DIST
CARTER, MARY	CEC	123	3RD E DI
CARTER, MARY	CHA	269	ALLENS F
CARTER, MARY	FRE	184	5TH E DI
CARTER, MARY	BAL	290	7TH WARD
CARTER, MARY	BAL	229	12TH WAR
CARTER, MARY A.	ALL	145	6TH E.D.
CARTER, MARY E.	QUE	198	3RD E DI
CARTER, MARY M.	BAL	085	15TH WAR
CARTER, MARYANN	BAL	375	3RD WARD
CARTER, MATHEW	BAL	376	3RD WARD
CARTER, MATILDA	BAL	167	16TH WAR
CARTER, MATILDA	BAL	361	13TH WAR
CARTER, MATILDA	CEC	104	4TH E DI
CARTER, MATTHEW	BAL	136	1ST WARD
CARTER, MATTHEW	BAL	125	1ST WARD
CARTER, METILDA	BAL	118	11TH WAR
CARTER, MICHAEL	BAL	420	8TH WARD
CARTER, MOSES	BAL	259	12TH WAR
CARTER, NANCY	BAL	463	1ST DIST
CARTER, NELSON	CEC	215	7TH E DI
CARTER, NICHOLAS	BAL	122	11TH WAR
CARTER, NICHOLAS	BAL	123	11TH WAR
CARTER, NICHOLAS	BAL	457	1ST DIST
CARTER, NIMROD	BAL	123	16TH WAR
CARTER, OWNEY	BAL	025	18TH WAR

Name	County	Page	District
CARTER, PERE	QUE	210	3RD E DI
CARTER, R.	ALL	217	CUMBERLA
CARTER, RAHAH	ALL	111	5TH E.D.
CARTER, REBECA	BAL	267	7TH WARD
CARTER, REBECCA	BAL	291	3RD WARD
CARTER, RICHARD	ALL	084	5TH E.D.
CARTER, RICHARD	QUE	240	5TH E DI
CARTER, RICHARD C.	CAR	092	NO TWP L
CARTER, RICHARD D.	BAL	151	19TH WAR
CARTER, RICHARD F.	QUE	143	1ST E DI
CARTER, RICHARD J.	QUE	197	3RD E DI
CARTER, ROBERT	CEC	108	3RD E DI
CARTER, ROBERT	CEC	090	4TH E DI
CARTER, ROBERT	ALL	111	5TH E.D.
CARTER, ROBERT E.	BAL	075	15TH WAR
CARTER, ROBERT SR.	CEC	122	4TH E DI
CARTER, ROBERT W.	MGM	376	ROCKERLE
CARTER, ROBERT-MULATTO	ST	317	4TH E DI
CARTER, SAMUEL	QUE	229	4TH E DI
CARTER, SAMUEL	SOM	405	DUBLIN D
CARTER, SAMUEL	BAL	040	18TH WAR
CARTER, SARAH J.	CEC	111	4TH E DI
CARTER, SARAH-BLACK	ST	328	4TH E DI
CARTER, SEUGAN *	BAL	128	2ND DIST
CARTER, SILAS	CEC	131	6TH E DI
CARTER, SOPHIA	ANN	337	3RD DIST
CARTER, TEENEY	QUE	214	3RD E DI
CARTER, THOMAS	QUE	228	4TH E DI
CARTER, THOMAS	ST	259	3RD E DI
CARTER, THOMAS	WAS	149	2ND DIST
CARTER, THOMAS A.-BLACK	ST	319	4TH E DI
CARTER, THOMAS J.	CAR	216	5TH DIST
CARTER, THOMAS-MULATTO	ST	329	4TH E DI
CARTER, TILLISTON	CEC	167	6TH E DI
CARTER, UPTON-MULATTO	FRE	038	FREDERIC
CARTER, URIAH	BAL	080	2ND DIST
CARTER, VALENTINE	BAL	366	13TH WAR
CARTER, VALENTINE	CAR	105	NO TWP L
CARTER, VIOLETTA	BAL	415	1ST DIST
CARTER, WILLIAM	BAL	335	3RD WARD
CARTER, WILLIAM	BAL	091	2ND DIST
CARTER, WILLIAM	ALL	084	5TH E.D.
CARTER, WILLIAM	BAL	068	15TH WAR
CARTER, WILLIAM	BAL	032	15TH WAR
CARTER, WILLIAM	BAL	134	1ST WARD
CARTER, WILLIAM	BAL	262	2ND WARD
CARTER, WILLIAM	BAL	163	16TH WAR
CARTER, WILLIAM	BAL	129	5TH WARD
CARTER, WILLIAM	BAL	130	11TH WAR
CARTER, WILLIAM	BAL	127	11TH WAR
CARTER, WILLIAM	CAL	012	1ST DIST
CARTER, WILLIAM	CAL	055	3RD DIST
CARTER, WILLIAM	CEC	129	6TH E DI
CARTER, WILLIAM	KEN	306	3RD DIST
CARTER, WILLIAM	WOR	199	8TH E DI
CARTER, WILLIAM A.	CAL	013	1ST DIST
CARTER, WILLIAM G.	CAR	108	NO TWP L
CARTER, WILLIAM G.	BAL	067	15TH WAR
CARTER, WILLIAM H.	ANN	329	2ND DIST
CARTER, WILLIAM S.	BAL	353	7TH WARD
CARTER, WILLIAM-MULATTO	ST	316	4TH E DI
CARTERY, WILLIAM	CAR	077	NO TWP L
CARTES, ARAMURTE	CAR	108	NO TWP L
CARTEY, ELIZABETH	BAL	179	6TH WARD
CARTEY, JAMES	HAR	205	3RD DIST
CARTEY, JOHN	HAR	205	3RD DIST
CARTHUN, MARGARET A.	HAR	117	2ND DIST
CARTICE, MARY J.-BLACK	ST	338	4TH E DI
CARTIS, PETER *	BAL	104	18TH WAR
CARTITH, EDWARD	BAL	272	1ST DIST
CARTLE, DANIEL	FRE	332	MIDDLETO
CARTNAIL, LOUISA	FRE	354	MIDDLETO
CARTNEY, JOHN	WAS	141	2ND DIST
CARTNEY, SARAH	CEC	007	ELKTON 3
CARTR, HENRY	CAR	210	5TH DIST
CARTRIGHT, KITTY	CHA	272	ALLENS F
CARTRIGHT, MARIA	CHA	272	ALLENS F
CARTRIGHT, WILLIAM J.	ST	341	5TH E DI
CARTWELE, THOMAS*	DOR	403	1ST DIST
CARTWELL, JOSIAH	DOR	395	1ST DIST
CARTWELL, MILLY	DOR	394	1ST DIST
CARTWRIGHT, ELIZA	ST	345	5TH E DI
CARTWRIGHT, ELIZABETH L.	ANN	521	HOWARD D
CARTWRIGHT, RACHEL	PRI	002	BLADENSB
CARTWRIGHT,A L.	BAL	130	1ST WARD
CARTY, ANDREW	BAL	169	2ND DIST
CARTY, BARNEY	WAS	140	2ND DIST
CARTY, CATHARINE M.	WAS	140	2ND DIST
CARTY, CONELIUS	WAS	062	2ND SUBD
CARTY, EDWARD	KEN	217	2ND DIST
CARTY, EDWARD	CAR	085	NO TWP L
CARTY, GEORGE	WAS	032	2ND SUBD
CARTY, JACOB	WAS	061	2ND SUBD
CARTY, JACOB	WAS	071	2ND SUBD
CARTY, JOHN W.	CAR	077	NO TWP L
CARTY, MARY	HAR	146	3RD DIST
CARTY, MARY	WAS	140	2ND DIST
CARTY, MICHAEL	WAS	071	2ND SUBD
CARTY, SAMUEL	WAS	196	1ST DIST
CARTY, SARAH	WAS	033	2ND SUBD
CARTY, SARAH	CAR	086	NO TWP L
CARTY, WILLIAM	HAR	146	3RD DIST
CARTY, WILLIAM	HAR	102	2ND DIST
CARTZ, JOHN	ALL	242	CUMBERLA
CARTZDAFNER, EDMOND	FRE	406	JEFFERSO
CARTZDAFNER, MARGARET	FRE	403	JEFFERSO
CARTZDAFNER, MICHAEL	FRE	404	JEFFERSO
CARTZENDAFNE, DAVID	FRE	386	PETERSVI
CARTZENDAFNE, SOPHIA	FRE	381	PETERSVI
CARTZENDAFNER, GEORGE	FRE	391	PETERSVI
CARTZENDAFNER, JOSEPH	FRE	406	JEFFERSO
CARUTHER, ANDREW	BAL	007	EASTERN
CARUTHERS, WILLIAM	HAR	050	1ST DIST
CARVALER, TOBIAS	BAL	229	17TH WAR
CARVALHO, DAVID N.	BAL	052	9TH WARD
CARVELL, ANNE	BAL	106	18TH WAR
CARVER, DANIEL	WAS	126	HAGERSTO
CARVER, FRANCIS F.	BAL	162	19TH WAR
CARVER, HENRY	HAR	155	3RD DIST
CARVER, JAMES	SOM	405	DUBLIN D
CARVER, JOHN	SOM	364	BRINKLEY
CARVER, JOHN W.	HAR	109	2ND DIST
CARVER, JOHN W.	HAR	155	3RD DIST
CARVER, JONAS	BAL	279	1ST DIST
CARVER, JOSEPH	CEC	150	PORT DEP
CARVER, JOSEPH C.	HAR	154	3RD DIST
CARVER, MARY	BAL	341	3RD WARD
CARVER, PETER	SOM	401	BRINKLEY
CARVER, WILLIAM	BAL	451	1ST DIST

Name	County	Page	District
CARVEY, MICHAEL	ALL	047	10TH E.D
CARVILL, THOMAS	QUE	228	4TH E DI
CARVILL, WILLAIM	BAL	185	16TH WAR
CARVILLE, EDWIN *	KEN	237	2ND DIST
CARVILLE, WILLIAM	QUE	247	5TH E DI
CARVILLO, EMANUEL	BAL	051	9TH WARD
CARVIN, ELLIOTT	SOM	461	HANGARY
CARVINGER, STEVEN	ALL	050	10TH E.D
CARVINS, JAMES	WAS	132	HAGERSTO
CARWEL, CHARLES	BAL	076	2ND DIST
CARWER, GEORGE	BAL	076	2ND DIST
CARWIE, ELIZA	BAL	268	12TH WAR
CARWIN, JAMES H.	SOM	482	TRAPP DI
CARWNERS, JAMES *	WAS	159	2ND DIST
CARWOOD, ALEXANDER	CHA	286	BOJANTOW
CARY, ADAL	BAL	114	18TH WAR
CARY, ARCHIBALD	ALL	253	CUMBERLA
CARY, CHARLOTT*	BAL	351	3RD WARD
CARY, EDWARD	BAL	005	18TH WAR
CARY, ELIZABETH	BAL	459	14TH WAR
CARY, FRANCIS	BAL	177	2ND WARD
CARY, GEORGE	BAL	134	11TH WAR
CARY, HENRY	SOM	393	BRINKLEY
CARY, JAMES	BAL	012	1ST WARD
CARY, JANE	ALL	254	CUMBERLA
CARY, JANE M.	BAL	058	10TH WAR
CARY, JOHN	BAL	336	1ST DIST
CARY, LAWRENCE	FRE	386	PETERSVI
CARY, LYDIA-BLACK	CAR	158	NO TWP L
CARY, MARTIN	ALL	050	10TH E.D
CARY, MARY	BAL	192	17TH WAR
CARY, PETER	BAL	393	1ST DIST
CARY, REUBEN	ANN	519	HOWARD D
CARY, THOMAS	QUE	133	1ST E DI
CARY, THOMAS W.	DOR	373	1ST DIST
CARY, W. F.	BAL	069	10TH WAR
CARY, WILLIAM	BAL	382	1ST DIST
CARY, WILLIAM	SOM	393	BRINKLEY
CARYHBERY, JAACOB*	BAL	115	11TH WAR
CARYLINN, ANN	BAL	132	11TH WAR
CASA, BENJAMIN	BAL	365	1ST DIST
CASADAY, JACOB	WAS	146	2ND DIST
CASBER, MARY T.	BAL	171	11TH WAR
CASBERY, NOLAN	BAL	171	11TH WAR
CASBURY, JOSEPH	BAL	169	11TH WAR
CASCUM, CASPER	ALL	184	9TH E.D.
CASE, ABEL	BAL	269	12TH WAR
CASE, ALBERT	FRE	275	NEW MARK
CASE, BENJAMIN	BAL	251	20TH WAR
CASE, BENJAMIN	MGM	437	CLARKSTR
CASE, CARVIN	BAL	345	1ST DIST
CASE, CHRISTIAN	HAR	150	3RD DIST
CASE, DANIEL	TAL	017	EASTON D
CASE, DAVID O.	MGM	381	ROCKERLE
CASE, ELIZABETH	FRE	184	5TH E DI
CASE, ELIZABETH	CEC	201	5TH E DI
CASE, FREDERICK T.	MGM	387	ROCKERLE
CASE, GEORGE W.	MGM	396	ROCKERLE
CASE, HENRY	MGM	401	ROCKERLE
CASE, ISRAEL	MGM	443	CLARKSTR
CASE, JOHN T.	MGM	430	CLARKSTR
CASE, MARTHA	MGM	316	CRACKLIN
CASE, MARY	MGM	316	CRACKLIN
CASE, MOUNTGUE	MGM	396	ROCKERLE
CASE, RACHAL *	KEN	251	2ND DIST
CASE, REBECCA	MGM	372	BERRYS D
CASE, RICHARD	BAL	173	2ND DIST
CASE, ROBERT	FRE	227	BUCKEYST
CASE, SAMUEL	FRE	170	5TH E DI
CASE, SARAH C.	TAL	054	EASTON D
CASE, SARAH V.	MGM	379	ROCKERLE
CASE, SARHA L.	FRE	275	NEW MARK
CASE, SIMON	ANN	478	HOWARD D
CASE, THOMAS D.	CAR	138	NO TWP L
CASE, VIRGINIA	MGM	361	BERRYS D
CASE, WILLIAM	MGM	443	CLARKSTR
CASE, WILLIAM W.	MGM	387	ROCKERLE
CASE, ZADOK	MGM	417	MEDLEY 3
CASEE, JOHN	ALL	150	6TH E.D.
CASENBROOK, FREDERICK	BAL	215	19TH WAR
CASENBROOK, J.	BAL	215	19TH WAR
CASER, GEORGE	ALL	071	5TH E.D.
CASERES, ELIZABETH	BAL	040	4TH WARD
CASES, HENRY	ALL	258	CUMBERLA
CASET, CATHARIEN	HAR	031	1ST DIST
CASEY, ABRAHAM	BAL	005	15TH WAR
CASEY, CON	BAL	275	1ST DIST
CASEY, ELIZABETH	BAL	215	6TH WARD
CASEY, ELLIN	BAL	015	9TH WARD
CASEY, HENRIETTA SIS-	BAL	316	20TH WAR
CASEY, J.A.P.	BAL	116	1ST WARD
CASEY, JAMES	BAL	144	1ST WARD
CASEY, JANE	KEN	267	1ST DIST
CASEY, JOHN	BAL	363	8TH WARD
CASEY, JOHN	BAL	068	2ND DIST
CASEY, JOHN T.	FRE	077	FREDERIC
CASEY, JOSEPH	BAL	189	19TH WAR
CASEY, MARGARET	BAL	214	11TH WAR
CASEY, PATRICK	BAL	084	1ST WARD
CASEY, RICHARD	WAS	055	2ND SUBD
CASEY, ROSE	BAL	404	3RD WARD
CASEY, SALLIE	BAL	156	19TH WAR
CASEY, SARAH	BAL	005	15TH WAR
CASEY, THOMAS	BAL	394	8TH WARD
CASEY, THOMAS	BAL	305	20TH WAR
CASEY, WILLIAM	BAL	363	8TH WARD
CASEY, WILLIAM	BAL	368	8TH WARD
CASH, ANTHONY	FRE	281	WOODSBOR
CASH, DAVID	CAR	317	1ST DIST
CASH, HENRY	BAL	136	1ST WARD
CASH, JOHN	BAL	114	11TH WAR
CASH, OLIVER W.	BAL	257	1ST DIST
CASHARM, PETER	FRE	412	8TH E DI
CASHAUN, MARGARETT E.	FRE	440	8TH E DI
CASHAUN, WILLIAM	FRE	446	8TH E DI
CASHAUR, JACOB	FRE	423	8TH E DI
CASHCART, ROBERT*	BAL	392	3RD WARD
CASHELL, ANGELINE	MGM	361	BERRYS D
CASHELL, GEORGE	MGM	369	BERRYS D
CASHELL, GEORGE W.	MGM	315	CRACKLIN
CASHELL, HAZEL B.	MGM	315	CRACKLIN
CASHELL, JAMES W.	MGM	317	CRACKLIN
CASHELL, RICHARD H.	MGM	360	BERRYS D
CASHELL, SAMUEL	MGM	367	BERRYS D
CASHEY, MARY	BAL	222	19TH WAR
CASHMAN, PAT	BAL	264	20TH WAR
CASHMAN, WILLIAM	BAL	087	10TH WAR
CASHMIRE, PETER	BAL	031	4TH WARD
CASHO, ANN	CEC	015	ELKTON 3
CASHO, JACOB	CEC	001	ELKTON 3

CASHOUR, HEZEKIAH CAR 360 9TH DIST
CASHOUR, JOHN FRE 296 WOODSBOR
CASIDLE, LOUISTIA BAL 215 11TH WAR
CASIRE, MARY BAL 320 12TH WAR
CASKEE, ROBERT BAL 297 12TH WAR
CASKEY, JOHN W. BAL 260 17TH WAR
CASKEY, ROBERT HAR 011 1ST DIST
CASKEY, SUSAN FRE 171 5TH E DI
CASKIL, JOSEPH BAL 290 20TH WAR
CASKINS, SUSAN WOR 350 1ST E DI
CASLAND, DAVID ALL 014 3RD E.D.
CASLER, MARIA BAL 352 1ST DIST
CASLEY, CATHARINE BAL 015 1ST WARD
CASNER, CASPER BAL 200 2ND WARD
CASNER, DAVID CEC 208 7TH E DI
CASNEY, JAMES * BAL 143 1ST WARD
CASON, HESTER A.* TAL 049 EASTON T
CASON, SAMUEL TAL 062 EASTON D
CASPAIR, CHARLES* BAL 075 10TH WAR
CASPAN, CHARLES* BAL 075 10TH WAR
CASPAR, ELIZABETH BAL 180 2ND DIST
CASPAR, JOHN BAL 180 2ND DIST
CASPARIE, CASPAR BAL 182 19TH WAR
CASPBERY, FERDINAN BAL 004 18TH WAR
CASPBERY, HARRETT BAL 003 18TH WAR
CASPER, ABRAHAM ALL 218 CUMBERLA
CASPER, ISAIH BAL 031 1ST WARD
CASPER, J. BAL 168 1ST WARD
CASPER, J.J. BAL 117 1ST WARD
CASPER, WILLIAM ANN 514 HOWARD D
CASPERIA, WILLIAM BAL 130 5TH WARD
CASS, LEWIS CAR 381 2ND DIST
CASS, LOUIS KEN 268 1ST DIST
CASS, THOMAS BAL 119 1ST WARD
CASSA, THOAMS ALL 056 10TH E.D
CASSADA, MICHEAL ALL 170 6TH E.D.
CASSADAY, CHARLES FRE 388 PETERSVI
CASSADEY, JOHN J. FRE 053 FREDERIC
CASSADY, BRIDGET ANN 418 HOWARD D
CASSADY, ELLEN BAL 287 3RD WARD
CASSADY, FRANKLIN MGM 320 CRACKLIN
CASSADY, JOHN ANN 267 ANNAPOLI
CASSADY, JULIANNA ANN 418 HOWARD D
CASSADY, MARGARETT BAL 073 4TH WARD
CASSADY, THOMAS HAR 040 1ST DIST
CASSADY, THOMAS BAL 101 2ND DIST
CASSAMAZOR, HENRY FRE 202 5TH E DI
CASSAN, MARGURITE FRE 066 FREDERIC
CASSARD, GEORGE BAL 080 4TH WARD
CASSARD, GILBERT BAL 074 18TH WAR
CASSARD, GILBERT BAL 105 5TH WARD
CASSARD, MARIA BAL 356 8TH WARD
CASSDY, THOMAS ALL 081 5TH E.D.
CASSEDY, CHARLOT BAL 357 1ST DIST
CASSEDY, JOHN BAL 114 11TH WAR
CASSEL, ABRAHAM CAR 394 2ND DIST
CASSEL, ANN BAL 397 14TH WAR
CASSEL, CHARY BAL 440 14TH WAR
CASSEL, FITZY BAL 276 17TH WAR
CASSEL, JAMES BAL 080 18TH WAR
CASSEL, JOSEPH CAR 393 2ND DIST
CASSEL, OTHO FRE 300 WOODSBOR
CASSEL, SAMUEL QUE 173 2ND E DI
CASSELL, ABRAHAM BAL 113 18TH WAR
CASSELL, ABRAHAM CAR 286 7TH DIST
CASSELL, CATHARINE-MULATT FRE 009 FREDERIC
CASSELL, CATHERINE-MULATT FRE 018 FREDERIC
CASSELL, CHRISTOPHER BAL 067 4TH WARD
CASSELL, DAVID CAR 286 7TH DIST
CASSELL, EDWARD A. BAL 248 20TH WAR
CASSELL, ELIZABETH FRE 018 FREDERIC
CASSELL, ELIZABETH BAL 010 4TH WARD
CASSELL, GEORGE CAR 287 7TH DIST
CASSELL, GOERGE BAL 248 20TH WAR
CASSELL, HENRY P. BAL 164 19TH WAR
CASSELL, J. BAL 249 12TH WAR
CASSELL, JACOB CAR 287 7TH DIST
CASSELL, JAMES FRE 074 FREDERIC
CASSELL, JOHN BAL 221 12TH WAR
CASSELL, JOSEPH BAL 140 19TH WAR
CASSELL, LUMAN BAL 258 20TH WAR
CASSELL, MARGARET F. QUE 173 2ND E DI
CASSELL, MARIN BAL 249 12TH WAR
CASSELL, MARY BAL 288 7TH WARD
CASSELL, REUBEN CAR 287 7TH DIST
CASSELL, WILLIAM BAL 065 1ST WARD
CASSELLO, L. BAL 163 1ST WARD
CASSELLS, BENJAMIN BAL 211 17TH WAR
CASSELLS, HENRY BAL 211 17TH WAR
CASSEN, SRAH BAL 266 17TH WAR
CASSEY, JOHN BAL 127 5TH WARD
CASSEY, MARY BAL 299 17TH WAR
CASSIDAY, ANN BAL 147 11TH WAR
CASSIDAY, BARNARD BAL 414 8TH WARD
CASSIDAY, JAMES BAL 021 9TH WARD
CASSIDAY, MARY BAL 352 7TH WARD
CASSIDAY, MICHAEL ANN 402 8TH DIST
CASSIDY, BART BAL 165 19TH WAR
CASSIDY, EDWARD ALL 170 6TH E.D.
CASSIDY, ELIZABETH BAL 070 4TH WARD
CASSIDY, GEORGE BAL 229 12TH WAR
CASSIDY, JAMES CEC 087 4TH E DI
CASSIDY, JAMES E. ANN 452 HOWARD D
CASSIDY, JOHN ALL 240 CUMBERLA
CASSIDY, JOHN BAL 197 2ND WARD
CASSIDY, LUKE BAL 395 8TH WARD
CASSIDY, OWEN BAL 229 12TH WAR
CASSIDY, PAT BAL 257 12TH WAR
CASSIDY, PATRICK BAL 279 12TH WAR
CASSIDY, SALLY BAL 223 17TH WAR
CASSIDY, THOMAS ALL 053 10TH E.D
CASSIDY, WILLIAM BAL 138 2ND DIST
CASSILLY, THOMAS BAL 317 3RD WARD
CASSIN, EVELINA BAL 396 14TH WAR
CASSIN, MARGARET BAL 431 14TH WAR
CASSIN, THOMAS WAS 022 2ND SUBD
CASSIN, WILLIAM D. ALL 122 4TH E.D.
CASSIUS, HENRY ANN 486 HOWARD D
CASSLE, ELISABETH BAL 114 2ND DIST
CASSOLL, D. T. D. * BAL 082 2ND DIST
CASSON, BILL TAL 094 ST MICHA
CASSON, GEORGE WAS 225 1ST DIST
CASSON, GEORGE BAL 209 6TH DIST
CASSON, GEORGE BAL 274 2ND WARD
CASSON, GEORGE W.* TAL 060 EASTON D
CASSON, MARY TAL 093 ST MICHA
CASSON, RICHARD WAS 225 1ST DIST
CASSOUR, ELIZABETH BAL 082 15TH WAR
CASSUE, EMILY FRE 278 NEW MARK
CASSY, MARY BAL 041 18TH WAR

CASTEEL, ARCHIBALD ALL 043 10TH E.D
CASTEEL, JESSE ALL 032 2ND E.D.
CASTEEL, MESHACK ALL 041 2ND E.D.
CASTEEL, NATHANIEL ALL 042 10TH E.D
CASTEEL, NATHANIEL ALL 041 2ND E.D.
CASTEEL, OLIPHANT ALL 037 2ND E.D.
CASTEEL, SARAH ALL 032 2ND E.D.
CASTEEL, THOMAS ALL 043 10TH E.D
CASTEEL, THOMAS ALL 042 10TH E.D
CASTEEL, THOMAS ALL 034 2ND E.D.
CASTEEL, WILLIAM ALL 034 2ND E.D.
CASTEEL, NATHAN ALL 034 2ND E.D.
CASTEL, SOPHIA BAL 413 1ST DIST
CASTELL, GEORGE L. WAS 134 2ND DIST
CASTELLMAN, J. J. BAL 312 12TH WAR
CASTELLO, JAMES ALL 135 4TH E.D.
CASTELLO, MICHAEL ALL 049 10TH E.D
CASTELLO, PETER ALL 136 4TH E.D.
CASTELLO, THOMAS ALL 051 10TH E.D
CASTELLO, WILLIAM ALL 018 3RD E.D.
CASTELLO, WINEFRED BAL 384 13TH WAR
CASTEN, JANE BAL 280 20TH WAR
CASTENE, AN. BAL 164 1ST WARD
CASTER, JANE E. CAL 011 1ST DIST
CASTER, JOHN F. BAL 145 2ND DIST
CASTER, NICHOLAS PRI 069 MARLBROU
CASTIGAN, SYLVESTER J. ST 260 3RD E DI
CASTILLO, MARY BAL 249 2ND WARD
CASTING, MENA BAL 426 8TH WARD
CASTING, NOAH WOR 233 6TH E DI
CASTINGS, JOSEPH ALL 062 10TH E.D
CASTINOLINE, JOHN CEC 186 7TH E DI
CASTISON, GEORGE BAL 299 17TH WAR
CASTLE, ABRAHAM H. FRE 219 BUCKEYST
CASTLE, AMANDA BAL 156 11TH WAR
CASTLE, AMOS WAS 192 1ST DIST
CASTLE, ANN A. FRE 210 BUCKEYST
CASTLE, ANN R. FRE 321 MIDDLETO
CASTLE, CATHARINE B. FRE 213 BUCKEYST
CASTLE, CHARLES BAL 165 19TH WAR
CASTLE, CHRIS BAL 142 11TH WAR
CASTLE, CORNELIUS WAS 179 BOONSBOR
CASTLE, DANIEL WAS 011 WILLIAMS
CASTLE, DANIEL FRE 333 MIDDLETO
CASTLE, EDWARD BAL 077 18TH WAR
CASTLE, ELIE WAS 086 2ND SUBD
CASTLE, ELIZABETH FRE 354 MIDDLETO
CASTLE, FANNY J. FRE 409 JEFFERSO
CASTLE, HENRY FRE 354 MIDDLETO
CASTLE, HENRY L. WAS 002 WILLIAMS
CASTLE, ISRAEL WAS 004 WILLIAMS
CASTLE, JAMES BAL 299 20TH WAR
CASTLE, JOHN BAL 030 18TH WAR
CASTLE, JOHN FRE 329 MIDDLETO
CASTLE, JOHN WAS 179 BOONSBOR
CASTLE, JOHN ALL 095 5TH E.D.
CASTLE, JOHN A. FRE 385 PETERSVI
CASTLE, JOSEPH FRE 357 CATOCTIN
CASTLE, JOSEPH BAL 118 11TH WAR
CASTLE, JOSEPHUS FRE 405 JEFFERSO
CASTLE, MADEAS ALL 168 6TH E.D.
CASTLE, MAHLON FRE 354 MIDDLETO
CASTLE, MARTHA E. FRE 320 MIDDLETO
CASTLE, MARY FRE 321 MIDDLETO
CASTLE, PETER ALL 226 CUMBERLA
CASTLE, R. FRE 325 MIDDLETO
CASTLE, WILLIAM BAL 236 20TH WAR
CASTLE, WILLIAM BAL 251 12TH WAR
CASTLE, WILLIAM BAL 102 10TH WAR
CASTLE, CARLILA FRE 002 FREDERIC
CASTLER, LOUISA BAL 158 2ND DIST
CASTON, CAROLINE BAL 045 4TH WARD
CASTON, CHARLES BAL 131 5TH WARD
CASTOR, CRISTIAN DOR 468 1ST DIST
CASTOR, JAMES BAL 141 16TH WAR
CASTOR, JANE BAL 107 15TH WAR
CASTOR, NAPOLEON BAL 459 8TH WARD
CASTOR, PETER BAL 092 15TH WAR
CASTORS, MARGARET BAL 131 5TH WARD
CASTUCK, BETTY BAL 241 2ND WARD
CASWARE, ANN CEC 042 CHESAPEA
CASWELL, MARY J. BAL 363 1ST DIST
CASY, ELIZ BAL 247 12TH WAR
CASY, JOHN BAL 247 1ST DIST
CASY, MARY BAL 227 1ST DIST
CASY, THOMAS BAL 247 1ST DIST
CASY, WILLIAM BAL 339 1ST DIST
CATALINE, JAMES * WOR 183 6TH E DI
CATCHOT, GABRIEL * BAL 427 8TH WARD
CATE, AMMON BAL 334 13TH WAR
CATE, EBENEZER BAL 135 16TH WAR
CATELL, JOHN ALL 110 5TH E.D.
CATEMON, ALEXANDER BAL 169 11TH WAR
CATEN, CHARLOTTE CHA 236 HILLTOP
CATEN, JOSEPH CHA 219 ALLENS F
CATEN, SCPHA CHA 239 HILLTOP
CATER, ALFRED BAL 119 1ST WARD
CATER, BETSY CHA 292 BOJANTOW
CATER, CATHERINA CHA 236 HILLTOP
CATER, JAMES BAL 398 3RD WARD
CATER, THOMAS G. PRI 010 BLADENSB
CATER, WILLIAM A. PRI 011 BLADENSB
CATER, WILLIAM E. BAL 115 1ST WARD
CATES, GEORGE BAL 443 8TH WARD
CATES, WILLIAM BAL 266 2ND WARD
CATHALL, PRISCILLA* BAL 073 4TH WARD
CATHALL, SARAH A. BAL 074 4TH WARD
CATHARINE, WILLIAM WAS 092 2ND SUBD
CATHART, HANNAH BAL 014 2ND DIST
CATHCART, BENJAMIN HAR 016 1ST DIST
CATHCART, GEORGE H. BAL 011 2ND DIST
CATHCART, JOHN P. HAR 022 1ST DIST
CATHCART, JOSEPH HAR 021 1ST DIST
CATHCART, ROBERT* BAL 392 3RD WARD
CATHCART, RUTH HAR 074 1ST DIST
CATHCART, THOMAS M. HAR 062 1ST DIST
CATHCART, WILLIAM H. BAL 394 3RD WARD
CATHEL, JOSEPH BAL 112 1ST WARD
CATHEL, MARGARET A. ANN 307 1ST DIST
CATHELL, ALEXANDER T. WOR 226 4TH E DI
CATHELL, ANN WOR 237 6TH E DI
CATHELL, CHARLES SOM 489 SALISBUR
CATHELL, CHARLES BAL 419 8TH WARD
CATHELL, HENRY WOR 232 6TH E DI
CATHELL, JAMES SOM 503 SALISBUR
CATHELL, JAMES M. WOR 192 8TH E DI
CATHELL, MARY SOM 425 PRINCESS
CATHELL, MITCHEL BAL 419 8TH WARD
CATHELL, SALLY SOM 496 SALISBUR
CATHENS, CHARLES BAL 267 12TH WAR

CATHER, DAVID HAR 125 2ND DIST
CATHER, MARY CEC 167 6TH E DI
CATHER, ROBERT BAL 080 15TH WAR
CATHER, SARAH CEC 165 6TH E DI
CATHER, SARAH HAR 126 2ND DIST
CATHERS, ANN E. CEC 149 PORT DUP
CATHERS, MARTHA CEC 087 4TH E DI
CATHERS, MARY CEC 100 3RD E DI
CATHERS, MARY BAL 146 5TH WARD
CATHERS, REBECCA CEC 104 4TH E DI
CATHERS, ROBERT CEC 193 5TH E DI
CATHERS, WILLIAM CEC 150 PORT DUP
CATHGART, CATHARINE BAL 106 5TH WARD
CATHILL, JAMS WOR 275 BERLIN I
CATHILL, JOHN WOR 273 BERLIN I
CATHILL, NANCY WOR 279 BERLIN I
CATHRELL, EMELY BAL 264 2ND WARD
CATIN, WILLIAM BAL 109 18TH WAR
CATING, MARY BAL 358 8TH WARD
CATINS, BARTOLS BAL 060 10TH WAR
CATLERS, JOHN BAL 054 9TH WARD
CATLETT, CHARLES W. MGM 377 ROCKERLE
CATLETT, EMILY MGM 378 ROCKERLE
CATLETT, MARY MGM 319 CRACKLIN
CATLETT, RACHAEL WAS 162 2ND DIST
CATLIN, BETSEY SOM 433 PRINCESS
CATLIN, JOHN SOM 535 QUANTICO
CATLIN, JOHN SOM 410 DUBLIN D
CATLIN, JOHN C. W. SOM 553 TYASKIN
CATLIN, JOSEPH QUE 169 2ND E DI
CATLIN, JOSEPH A. QUE 169 2ND E DI
CATLIN, THOMAS G. SOM 549 TYASKIN
CATLIN, WILLIAM SOM 539 TYASKIN
CATLIN, WILLIAM SR. SOM 539 TYASKIN
CATLING, EDWARD SOM 361 BRINKLEY
CATLING, FRANCIS WOR 346 1ST E DI
CATLING, HENRY SOM 360 BRINKLEY
CATLING, NELLY SOM 420 PRINCESS
CATLING, WESLEY SOM 403 BRINKLEY
CATMEN, GEORGE CEC 031 CHESAPEA
CATO, THOMAS CEC 142 6TH E DI
CATOLTA, EZRA FRE 307 WOODSBOR
CATON, EDWARD REV. ANN 469 HOWARD D
CATON, ELIZA ALL 094 5TH E.D.
CATON, HONORA BAL 162 16TH WAR
CATON, JOHN ALL 018 3RD E.D.
CATON, JOHN ALL 004 3RD E.D.
CATON, JOHN ALL 006 3RD E.D.
CATON, MARY A. BAL 033 4TH WARD
CATON, MICHAEL ALL 150 6TH E.D.
CATON, ROBERT ALL 262 CUMBERLA
CATON, SARAH* BAL 383 3RD WARD
CATON, WILLIAM BAL 399 8TH WARD
CATOR, ABEL DOR 358 3RD DIVI
CATOR, ELIZABETH BAL 104 15TH WAR
CATOR, GEORGE PRI 063 NOTTINGH
CATOR, HANAH E. G. DOR 390 1ST DIST
CATOR, JOSEPH HAR 205 3RD DIST
CATOR, JOSEPH BAL 108 15TH WAR
CATOR, LOUISA PRI 103 SPALDING
CATOR, SAMUEL MGM 407 MEDLEY J
CATOR, THOMAS DOR 357 3RD DIVI
CATOR, THOMAS PRI 100 SPALDING
CATOR, WILLIAM H. BAL 286 2ND WARD
CATRAGAN, ELIZABETH BAL 454 14TH WAR
CATRISS, HENRY TAL 070 EASTON T
CATRO, SAMUEL WAS 055 2ND SUBD
CATROP, J. BAL 161 1ST WARD
CATROUP, ELIZABETH TAL 090 ST MICHA
CATRUP, ANN TAL 028 EASTON D
CATRUP, CAROLINE* TAL 004 EASTON D
CATRUP, JOHN TAL 030 EASTON D
CATRUP, JOHN W. TAL 022 EASTON D
CATRUP, MARY TAL 068 EASTON T
CATRUP, SAMUEL H. BAL 336 7TH WARD
CATSAEL, SARAH FRE 252 NEW MARK
CATSAIL, ANN J. FRE 087 FREDERIC
CATSEBAUGH, MARY BAL 251 17TH WAR
CATSENSTINE, MOSES BAL 248 6TH WARD
CATSUP, JEROME CAR 091 NO TWP L
CATTE, CLARISSA BAL 460 14TH WAR
CATTELE, MARGARET BAL 058 1ST WARD
CATTELL, MARIA BAL 181 2ND DIST
CATTERTON, CHARLES O. CAL 016 1ST DIST
CATTERTON, JAMS CAL 021 2ND DIST
CATTERTON, JOHN CAL 016 1ST DIST
CATTERTON, JOHN CAL 026 2ND DIST
CATTERTON, MALACHI CAL 046 3RD DIST
CATTERTON, SAMUEL CAL 020 2ND DIST
CATTERTON, WILLIAM BAL 032 15TH WAR
CATTERTON, WILLIAM W. CAL 019 1ST DIST
CATTING, ELEANOR WOR 344 1ST E DI
CATTON, THOMAS BAL 445 1ST DIST
CATTRIDER, DANIEL CAR 340 6TH DIST
CATTRIDER, DANIEL CAR 335 6TH DIST
CATTRIDER, HENRY CAR 342 6TH DIST
CATTRIDER, JOSEPH CAR 342 6TH DIST
CAUBIN, HARRIET ANN 359 3RD DIST
CAUBIN, WILLIAM * ANN 358 3RD DIST
CAUBY, A. M. BAL 154 1ST WARD
CAUDRICKS, JOHN WAS 147 2ND DIST
CAUDRY, ELIZABETH SOM 540 TYASKIN
CAUDRY, FRANCES SOM 499 SALISBUR
CAUDRY, GEORGE W. SOM 540 TYASKIN
CAUDRY, JAMES SOM 489 SALISBUR
CAUDRY, JOHN* SOM 493 SALISBUR
CAUDRY, SAMPSON SOM 540 TYASKIN
CAUDRY, SAMUEL SOM 517 BARREN C
CAUFFIELD, MARGARET BAL 213 11TH WAR
CAUFFMAN, JOHN CAR 364 9TH DIST
CAUFMAN, WILLIAM WAS 031 2ND SUBD
CAUGH, MICHAEL BAL 216 2ND WARD
CAUGHEY, ANN BAL 261 12TH WAR
CAUGHEY, ELIZABETH ANN 504 HOWARD D
CAUGHEY, JOHN ANN 504 HOWARD D
CAUGHEY, MICHAEL BAL 251 6TH WARD
CAUGHEY, PATRICK BAL 260 12TH WAR
CAUGHEY, SAMUEL BAL 131 5TH WARD
CAUGHEY, SAMUEL H. BAL 076 4TH WARD
CAUGHLIN, CATHERINE BAL 119 2ND DIST
CAUGHLIN, SISTER F.A. FRE 198 5TH E DI
CAUGHSON, JAMES ALL 049 10TH E.D
CAUGHY, JOHN H. BAL 252 6TH WARD
CAULB, ANN TAL 105 ST MICHA
CAULB, CHARELS TAL 097 ST MICHA
CAULB, DAWSON TAL 081 ST MICHA
CAULB, JAMES TAL 084 ST MICHA
CAULB, JOHN D. TAL 080 ST MICHA
CAULB, JOHN H. TAL 105 ST MICHA
CAULB, JOHN H. TAL 105 ST MICHA

Name	Co.	Page	Location
CAULB, JOHN R.	TAL	101	ST MICHA
CAULB, KEMP R.	TAL	103	ST MICHA
CAULB, SUSAN A.	TAL	096	ST MICHA
CAULB, WILLIAM	TAL	096	ST MICHA
CAULB, WILLIAM	TAL	108	ST MICHA
CAULBECK, ANN	BAL	388	3RD WARD
CAULDER, ANN	TAL	065	EASTON T
CAULDER, BENJMAIN F.	KEN	217	2ND DIST
CAULEY, CHARLES M.	BAL	414	8TH WARD
CAULEY, MATILDA	KEN	221	2ND DIST
CAULGVIN, WILLIAM*	TAL	007	EASTON D
CAULIFLOWER, JAMES	FRE	394	PETERSVI
CAULK, ALEXANDER	CEC	031	CHESAPEA
CAULK, ALONZA	BAL	145	1ST WARD
CAULK, ELI	BAL	313	7TH WARD
CAULK, ELIZABETH	BAL	325	3RD WARD
CAULK, ERMINA R.	TAL	120	ST MICHA
CAULK, FANNY	ANN	265	ANNAPOLI
CAULK, HENRY	BAL	070	1ST WARD
CAULK, HENRY	BAL	422	3RD WARD
CAULK, JACOB	CEC	043	CHESAPEA
CAULK, JAMES	BAL	263	17TH WAR
CAULK, JAMES M.	BAL	325	3RD WARD
CAULK, JOHN	BAL	178	2ND WARD
CAULK, JOHN	CEC	067	5TH E DI
CAULK, JOHN	CEC	068	5TH E DI
CAULK, JOSEPH	TAL	042	EASTON D
CAULK, MARTHA	BAL	330	7TH WARD
CAULK, MARY ANN	BAL	237	17TH WAR
CAULK, MARY I.	BAL	294	3RD WARD
CAULK, PRISCILLA	DOR	317	1ST DIST
CAULK, THOMAS	BAL	077	10TH WAR
CAULK, VIRGINIA	BAL	325	3RD WARD
CAULK, WILLIAM	BAL	129	16TH WAR
CAULK, WILLIAM	CEC	043	CHESAPEA
CAULKE, DANIEL	ANN	265	ANNAPOLI
CAULTE, ELIZA	TAL	080	ST MICHA
CAULY, SUSAN	SOM	398	BRINKLEY
CAUN, JAMES	BAL	220	19TH WAR
CAUN, SOPHIA	BAL	197	11TH WAR
CAUN, SOPHIA	BAL	197	11TH WAR
CAUSA, WILLIAM	ALL	197	CUMBERLA
CAUSDEN, GEORGE	CEC	012	ELKTON 3
CAUSDEN, JOHN	CEC	012	ELKTON 3
CAUSEY, AMANDA E.	SOM	436	PRINCESS
CAUSEY, FRANKLIN	WOR	198	8TH E DI
CAUSEY, JAMES	WOR	190	8TH E DI
CAUSEY, JAMES *	BAL	064	15TH WAR
CAUSEY, JOHN	WOR	190	8TH E DI
CAUSEY, LEVIN	WOR	191	8TH E DI
CAUSEY, MARGARET	SOM	449	DAMES QU
CAUSEY, MARY	WOR	196	8TH E DI
CAUSEY, MARY	SOM	408	DUBLIN D
CAUSEY, MARY-BLACK	CAR	167	NO TWP L
CAUSEY, PATRICK *	SOM	435	PRINCESS
CAUSEY, PRICELLA	SOM	485	TRAPP DI
CAUSEY, URIAH F.	BAL	250	6TH WARD
CAUSTIGAN, WILLIAM	BAL	373	3RD WARD
CAUSTIN, SUSAN	BAL	031	9TH WARD
CAUSY, CHARLES	CAR	129	NO TWP L
CAUSY, HARRISON-BLACK	CAR	134	NO TWP L
CAUT, JOHN *	KEN	263	1ST DIST
CAUTH, JOHN	TAL	106	ST MICHA
CAUTHERS, FRANCIS	BAL	055	1ST WARD
CAUTION, ELIJAH	WAS	104	2ND DIST
CAUTION, JAMES	BAL	427	1ST DIST
CAUTION, JOHN	BAL	423	1ST DIST
CAUTION, LUKE	BAL	424	1ST DIST
CAUTION, MARY	WAS	116	2ND DIST
CAUTION, SAMUEL	WAS	137	2ND DIST
CAUTON, JOHN *	BAL	025	18TH WAR
CAUTON, MARY *	BAL	026	18TH WAR
CAUXSON, CHARLES	BAL	207	11TH WAR
CAVANAUGH, MICHAEL	BAL	300	17TH WAR
CAVE, CHARLES	BAL	115	5TH WARD
CAVE, JOHN W.	BAL	116	5TH WARD
CAVE, MARY	BAL	095	18TH WAR
CAVEN, ELIZA	BAL	358	8TH WARD
CAVEN, RUTH	BAL	282	1ST DIST
CAVENAUGH, ELIZABETH	BAL	033	18TH WAR
CAVENAUGH, GEORGE	BAL	033	18TH WAR
CAVENAUGH, JOHN	BAL	054	18TH WAR
CAVENAUGH, JOHN	FRE	067	FREDERIC
CAVENAUGH, JULIA	BAL	463	1ST DIST
CAVENAUGH, MARIA	BAL	172	11TH WAR
CAVENAUGH, PATRICK	BAL	126	5TH WARD
CAVENAUGH, TREASEA C.	BAL	172	11TH WAR
CAVENDER, JAMES	HAR	009	1ST DIST
CAVENDER, JAMES	CEC	199	7TH E DI
CAVENDER, JULIAN	BAL	205	2ND WARD
CAVENDER, MARIA	CEC	038	CHESAPEA
CAVENDER, NICOLAS	KEN	272	1ST DIST
CAVENDER, WILLIAM	HAR	032	1ST DIST
CAVENER, ISAAC	ALL	119	5TH E.D.
CAVENER, MARY	ALL	119	5TH E.D.
CAVENER, MICHAEL	BAL	180	2ND WARD
CAVENER, NICHOLAS	BAL	036	9TH WARD
CAVENEY, MICHAEL	ALL	050	10TH E.D
CAVENNER, ROGER	BAL	271	20TH WAR
CAVENY, PETER	BAL	382	1ST DIST
CAVEOUGH, JAMES	BAL	415	14TH WAR
CAVEY, HENRY	BAL	265	1ST DIST
CAVEY, JOSEPH	ANN	462	HOWARD D
CAVIER, SOPHIA	FRE	056	FREDERIC
CAVIN, JOHN	BAL	151	2ND DIST
CAVNER, DENIS	BAL	444	1ST DIST
CAVNER, LEWIS	BAL	006	18TH WAR
CAVNOR, ANN	BAL	008	18TH WAR
CAVON, AARON	HAR	155	3RD DIST
CAVY, BASIL	BAL	352	1ST DIST
CAVY, BEAL	ANN	519	HOWARD D
CAVY, BRICE	ANN	520	HOWARD D
CAVY, CORNELIUS	BAL	350	1ST DIST
CAVY, HENRY	ANN	420	HOWARD D
CAVY, JANE	BAL	352	1ST DIST
CAVY, LOUISA	BAL	352	1ST DIST
CAVY, RESIN *	BAL	347	1ST DIST
CAWAN, JAMES	BAL	281	2ND WARD
CAWIN, ELLIOTT *	SOM	461	HANGARY
CAWKINS, JAMES F.	ANN	320	2ND DIST
CAWL, RUTH	BAL	227	1ST DIST
CAWLEY, RODERIC	BAL	281	1ST DIST
CAWLY, CATHARINE	BAL	281	1ST DIST
CAWLY, WILLIAM D.	ANN	328	2ND DIST
CAWMAN, JOSEPH	BAL	214	17TH WAR
CAWMAN, MARY J.	BAL	213	17TH WAR
CAWNON, THOMAS B.	WAS	020	2ND SUBD
CAWOOD, ALEXANDER	ST	274	3RD E DI
CAWOOD, HENRY B.	ST	276	3RD E DI
CAWOOD, HEZEKIAH	ST	270	3RD E DI
CAWOOD, MARY	ST	345	5TH E DI
CAWTION, SAMUEL	BAL	178	6TH WARD
CAWTON, JOHN	WAS	108	2ND DIST
CAYGROVE, HARRIET B.	FRE	055	FREDERIC
CAYLOR, ABRAHAM	CAR	389	2ND DIST
CAYLOR, AMOS	CAR	401	2ND DIST
CAYMAN, WILLIAM W.	WOR	197	8TH E DI
CAYNOR, BRIDGET	BAL	192	11TH WAR
CAYTON, JOHN	WOR	345	1ST E DI
CAYWOOD, J.B.L.	PRI	113	PISCATAW
CAYWOOD, ROBERT	BAL	406	8TH WARD
CAYWOOD, THOMAS	PRI	114	PISCATAW
CAZIRE, JANE D.	TAL	103	ST MICHA
CCARTY, F	BAL	152	1ST WARD
CCLOOLEY, ANNE	BAL	359	13TH WAR
CEANE, MICHAEL	ALL	052	10TH E.D
CEAPHUS, HARRISON	DOR	296	1ST DIST
CEAPHUS, HENERITTA	DOR	308	1ST DIST
CEAPHUS, WILLIAM	DOR	316	1ST DIST
CEARS, MARY	FRE	230	BUCKEYST
CEBSER, AUGUSTUS REV.	BAL	381	13TH WAR
CECERSE, JAMES P.	KEN	254	1ST DIST
CECIL, AMRY	QUE	202	3RD E DI
CECIL, BARTHOLOMEW	BAL	221	2ND WARD
CECIL, ELIZABETH	BAL	396	3RD WARD
CECIL, JAMES	ANN	324	2ND DIST
CECIL, JOHN	QUE	188	3RD E DI
CECIL, MORTON	QUE	202	3RD E DI
CECIL, OWEN	ANN	368	4TH DIST
CECIL, SAMEUL	ANN	391	4TH DIST
CECIL, SARAH A. MISS-	BAL	315	20TH WAR
CECIL, SUSAN J.	HAR	044	1ST DIST
CECIL, THOMAS	MGM	355	BERRYS D
CECIL, THOMAS L.	KEN	311	3RD DIST
CECIL, WALPOLE	FRE	202	5TH E DI
CECIL, WILLIAM	FRE	210	BUCKEYST
CECIL, WILLIAM	ANN	419	HOWARD D
CECIL, MARGARET	ALL	045	10TH E.D
CECILL, CECELIA	FRE	228	BUCKEYST
CECILL, SAMUEL	FRE	229	BUCKEYST
CECKEY, EDWARD	BAL	144	11TH WAR
CECTSAIL, BENJAMIN	FRE	084	FREDERIC
CEDERS, ELIZABETH ANN	BAL	197	17TH WAR
CEE, HESTER A.*	DOR	436	1ST DIST
CEFFEE, MARY	ALL	255	CUMBERLA
CEFUS, DANIEL-BLACK	CAR	150	NO TWP L
CEFUS, DERIAS-BLACK	CAR	150	NO TWP L
CEHUS, RICHARD*	TAL	020	EASTON D
CELANDER, GEORGE*	BAL	391	3RD WARD
CELBUT, HARRISCN*	TAL	044	EASTON D
CELLAR, GEORGE	ALL	203	CUMBERLA
CELLERY, GEORGE	CEC	072	5TH E DI
CELTY, MARY	CEC	071	5TH E DI
CELWELL, JOHN	CEC	056	1ST E DI
CELY, JOHN	BAL	384	1ST DIST
CEMARSEN, WILLIAM *	BAL	237	6TH WARD
CEMBLY, PRICILLA	CHA	285	BOJANTOW
CEMMER, JOHN S.	ALL	247	CUMBERLA
CENA, ELIZA	BAL	459	1ST DIST
CENBS, HENRY	BAL	079	1ST WARD
CENOIS, CHARLOTTE	BAL	231	12TH WAR
CENES, HENRY	ALL	222	CUMBERLA
CENEY, ANNA	BAL	260	12TH WAR
CENEY, ISABEL	BAL	304	20TH WAR
CENLIN, M.	BAL	239	20TH WAR
CENNEY, MOSES	BAL	211	17TH WAR
CENREL, JOHN	FRE	212	BUCKEYST
CENSIL, MARTIN	WAS	022	2ND SUBD
CENSON, DEROW	BAL	304	12TH WAR
CENSON, JOSHUA	BAL	304	12TH WAR
CENTER, JOHN	BAL	284	12TH WAR
CENTER, SARAH	BAL	155	11TH WAR
CENTER, WILLIAM	BAL	126	1ST WARD
CENTER, LEWIS	BAL	134	1ST WARD
CENTERS, HENRY	ALL	224	CUMBERLA
CEORPLES, ADDISON *	BAL	130	2ND DIST
CEPHAS, CHARELS W.	BAL	174	6TH WARD
CEPHAS, ELIZA	BAL	387	13TH WAR
CEPHAS, JAMES	QUE	233	4TH E DI
CEPHAS, JANE	DOR	434	1ST DIST
CEPHAS, JOHN W.	BAL	180	6TH WARD
CEPHAS, JOSEPH	BAL	227	6TH WARD
CEPHAS, JOSEPHUS	BAL	174	6TH WARD
CEPHASBOOK, MARY SIS-	BAL	316	20TH WAR
CEPHUS, ALEY*	DOR	439	1ST DIST
CEPHUS, ANN E.	DOR	465	1ST DIST
CEPHUS, HANNON	ALL	198	CUMBERLA
CEPHUS, JAMES	DOR	460	1ST DIST
CEPHUS, JOE	DOR	460	1ST DIST
CEPHUS, JOE	DOR	431	1ST DIST
CEPHUS, JOSEPH	DOR	457	1ST DIST
CEPHUS, MARGARET	DOR	440	1ST DIST
CEPHUS, MITILDY*	DOR	411	1ST DIST
CEPHUS, RIDY	BAL	013	4TH WARD
CEPHUS, SOPHIA	DOR	431	1ST DIST
CEPHUS, WILLIAM	DOR	455	1ST DIST
CEPHUS, WILLIAM*	DOR	465	1ST DIST
CEPPERMAN, NICHOLAS	FRE	037	FREDERIC
CEPUTY, JOSHIA *	KEN	280	3RD DIST
CERARD, MARY*	BAL	322	12TH WAR
CERE, MARY	WAS	065	2ND SUBD
CERES, JOSEPH	HAR	002	1ST DIST
CERKCAN, DAVID *	BAL	275	20TH WAR
CERMAND, CATHARINE	CAR	223	5TH DIST
CERNT, ISABEL*	BAL	233	12TH WAR
CEROTTEY, DAVID	BAL	352	7TH WARD
CERSE, ELIZABETH	KEN	214	2ND DIST
CERSE, HENRY DE *	KEN	216	2ND DIST
CERSE, MARY	KEN	246	2ND DIST
CERSE, RACHAL *	KEN	251	2ND DIST
CERTAIN, MARIA	ANN	446	HOWARD D
CERTEL, GEORGE *	WAS	185	BOONSBOR
CESAR, MARK	BAL	457	8TH WARD
CESEL, PHILIP	ALL	151	6TH E.D.
CESNA, CHARLES	ALL	214	CUMBERLA
CESPER, ESRIL	BAL	125	1ST WARD
CESS, FRANCIS	BAL	317	7TH WARD
CESSARA, HENRIETTA	ALL	254	CUMBERLA
CESSEL, MARY A.	MGM	431	CLARKSTR
CESSEL, WILLIAMS H.	MGM	444	CLARKSTR
CESSELL, JOSEPH T.	ST	292	2ND E DI
CESSEX, MARY*	BAL	001	4TH WARD
CESSLER, SAMUEL JR.	ALL	030	2ND E.D.
CESSLER, SMAUEL	ALL	030	2ND E.D.
CETHER, MARY S.*	BAL	375	3RD WARD
CETLEY, JONAH	CEC	078	NORTHEAS
CEZAR, HENRY-MULATTO	FRE	234	BUCKEYST
CH---, PATRICK	ANN	296	1ST DIST
CHABER, CONRAD O.	BAL	139	5TH WARD
CHACE, ABRAHAM	DOR	320	1ST DIST
CHACE, SALLY	CHA	222	ALLENS F
CHACE, VINA	CHA	240	HILLTOP
CHACKESTER, GEORGE	BAL	425	8TH WARD
CHAD, JANE	BAL	048	1ST WARD
CHADBURN, JOHN	BAL	238	17TH WAR
CHADBURN, THOMAS	BAL	005	EASTERN
CHADWICK, ELIZABETH	ALL	109	5TH E.D.
CHADWICK, JOHN	BAL	070	4TH WARD
CHADWICK, THOMAS	WOR	273	BERLIN 1
CHAEK, LEVI *	BAL	296	20TH WAR
CHAFEMAN, MARIA	BAL	304	17TH WAR
CHAFFAREH, DANIEL	CAR	116	NO TWP L
CHAFFENCH, HALL	CAR	133	NO TWP L
CHAFFENCH, SARAH	DOR	382	1ST DIST
CHAFFENCH, WILLIAM	CAR	131	NO TWP L
CHAFFIMER, WILLIAM*	DOR	381	1ST DIST
CHAFFIN, CATHARINE	TAL	051	EASTON D
CHAFFINCH, AZEL	TAL	042	EASTON D
CHAFFINCH, ELISHA	DOR	382	1ST DIST
CHAFFINCH, ELIZABETH	TAL	031	EASTON D
CHAFFINCH, LEWIS	CAR	134	NO TWP L
CHAFFINS, ANN C.*	TAL	056	EASTON D
CHAFFURCH, SAMUEL	CAR	116	NO TWP L
CHAFITCH, ELIZABETH	BAL	462	1ST DIST
CHAFLING, JOHN	BAL	325	3RD WARD
CHAFNEY, CHARLES	BAL	138	1ST WARD
CHAGAHISE, MICHAEL	WAS	126	2ND DIST
CHAILLON, STANISLAUS	BAL	124	16TH WAR
CHAING, THOMAS	CHA	225	ALLENS F
CHAIRS, EDWARD	ANN	347	3RD DIST
CHAIRS, FRANKLIN	ANN	344	3RD DIST
CHAIRS, GEORGE	QUE	205	3RD E DI
CHAIRS, JANE F.	QUE	164	2ND E DI
CHAIRS, JOHN	QUE	194	3RD E DI
CHAIRS, JOHN-BLACK	QUE	171	2ND E DI
CHAIRS, MARIA	QUE	216	3RD E DI
CHAIRS, MARY	QUE	195	3RD E DI
CHAIRS, NATHANIEL	QUE	163	2ND E DI
CHAIRS, R.	ANN	346	3RD DIST
CHAIRS, R.	ANN	347	3RD DIST
CHAIRS, ROBERT	BAL	248	17TH WAR
CHAIRS, THOMAS	QUE	167	2ND E DI
CHAIRS, TONEY	QUE	206	3RD E DI
CHAIRS, EDWARD-BLACK	QUE	198	3RD E DI
CHAISTREE, JAMES H.	HAR	101	2ND DIST
CHAISTY, E.J.	BAL	237	12TH WAR
CHALESKY, V.	BAL	286	12TH WAR
CHALFMAN, HY.	BAL	287	1ST DIST
CHALK, ELIAS	BAL	401	1ST DIST
CHALK, ELIZA	BAL	162	11TH WAR
CHALK, ELIZABETH	BAL	088	2ND DIST
CHALK, GILES	BAL	416	3RD WARD
CHALK, HARRISON	HAR	038	1ST DIST
CHALK, J.	BAL	163	1ST WARD
CHALK, JOHN	BAL	300	1ST DIST
CHALK, JOSEPH	BAL	172	1ST WARD
CHALK, JOSHUA	BAL	165	1ST WARD
CHALK, REBECCA	BAL	382	3RD WARD
CHALK, SAMUEL	HAR	049	1ST DIST
CHALLION, STANILAUS	BAL	110	10TH WAR
CHALMER, JAMES M.	BAL	440	8TH WARD
CHALMER, PERRY	BAL	174	11TH WAR
CHALMERS, GEORGE	BAL	174	11TH WAR
CHALMERS, SARAH	BAL	174	11TH WAR
CHALMES, JAMES	BAL	194	19TH WAR
CHALMEY, P.S.	BAL	239	20TH WAR
CHALTON, ABSOLUM	CAL	014	1ST DIST
CHAMBER, JOANA	WAS	182	BOONSBOR
CHAMBERES, JOHN	QUE	238	5TH E DI
CHAMBERES, WILLIAM	FRE	055	FREDERIC
CHAMBERLAIN, ANN M.	TAL	039	EASTON D
CHAMBERLAIN, CHARLES	WOR	228	6TH E DI
CHAMBERLAIN, EASTER	DOR	308	1ST DIST
CHAMBERLAIN, EMILY	DOR	308	1ST DIST
CHAMBERLAIN, FERNANDO	BAL	253	6TH WARD
CHAMBERLAIN, H.	BAL	260	12TH WAR
CHAMBERLAIN, HANNAH	CEC	149	PORT DUP
CHAMBERLAIN, HANNAH	CEC	143	7TH E DI
CHAMBERLAIN, HENRY	CEC	212	7TH E DI
CHAMBERLAIN, JAMES	FRE	447	8TH E DI
CHAMBERLAIN, JAMES	HAR	113	2ND DIST
CHAMBERLAIN, JAMES	FRE	312	MIDDLETO
CHAMBERLAIN, JOB C. M.	TAL	066	EASTON T
CHAMBERLAIN, JOHN	CEC	184	7TH E DI
CHAMBERLAIN, JOHN	BAL	129	16TH WAR
CHAMBERLAIN, JOHN	BAL	169	6TH WARD
CHAMBERLAIN, JOHN JR.	BAL	129	16TH WAR
CHAMBERLAIN, JOSEPH	QUE	214	3RD E DI
CHAMBERLAIN, JOSEPHINE	BAL	170	6TH WARD
CHAMBERLAIN, LOUISA	BAL	396	3RD WARD
CHAMBERLAIN, MARGARET	BAL	253	6TH WARD
CHAMBERLAIN, NICHOLAS H.	TAL	039	EASTON D
CHAMBERLAIN, PHILIP	BAL	196	6TH WARD
CHAMBERLAIN, REUBEN	BAL	252	6TH WARD
CHAMBERLAIN, SAMUEL	TAL	043	EASTON D
CHAMBERLAIN, WILLIAM	BAL	326	1ST DIST
CHAMBERLAIN, WILLIAM M.	TAL	043	EASTON D
CHAMBERLAINE, MARY A.	BAL	460	14TH WAR
CHAMBERLAND, FREEMAN	KEN	289	3RD DIST
CHAMBERLIN, ANN	BAL	357	1ST DIST
CHAMBERLIN, GEORGE	DOR	308	1ST DIST
CHAMBERLIN, JOHN	BAL	122	18TH WAR
CHAMBERLIN, JOHN E.	BAL	279	7TH WARD
CHAMBERLIN, MARIAT	CAR	092	NO TWP L
CHAMBERLIN, REBECCA	BAL	023	1ST WARD
CHAMBERS, AGNES	BAL	151	19TH WAR
CHAMBERS, AMELIA	BAL	309	3RD WARD
CHAMBERS, ANN A.	BAL	149	11TH WAR
CHAMBERS, ANN M.	BAL	454	8TH WARD
CHAMBERS, ANNA	BAL	144	5TH WARD
CHAMBERS, ANTHONY-BLACK	CAR	158	NO TWP L
CHAMBERS, ASBERRY	FRE	294	WOODSBOR
CHAMBERS, B.B.	PRI	092	MARLBROU
CHAMBERS, BENJAMIN	CEC	022	ELKTON 3
CHAMBERS, BENJAMIN C.	PRI	002	BLADENSB
CHAMBERS, BETSEY	BAL	314	3RD WARD
CHAMBERS, CAROLINE L.	BAL	395	3RD WARD
CHAMBERS, CHARLES	CAR	390	2ND DIST
CHAMBERS, CHARLOTTE	BAL	032	18TH WAR
CHAMBERS, CHRISTIANA	CAL	035	2ND DIST
CHAMBERS, CHRLES	CAL	024	2ND DIST
CHAMBERS, COLLIN	CAL	063	3RD DIST
CHAMBERS, CORNELIA	BAL	100	10TH WAR
CHAMBERS, DANIEL	BAL	010	4TH WARD
CHAMBERS, DAVID	BAL	375	13TH WAR
CHAMBERS, DAVID	ALL	059	10TH E.D
CHAMBERS, ELI	BAL	096	10TH WAR
CHAMBERS, ELIZA	KEN	263	1ST DIST
CHAMBERS, ELIZABETH	WAS	071	2ND SUBD
CHAMBERS, ELIZABETH	BAL	326	3RD WARD

CHAMBERS, ELLEN WAS 097 2ND DIST
CHAMBERS, ELLEN M. BAL 396 14TH WAR
CHAMBERS, EMMA CEC 202 6TH E DI
CHAMBERS, EZEKIEL F. KEN 217 2ND DIST
CHAMBERS, FRANCIS KEN 220 2ND DIST
CHAMBERS, FREDERICK KEN 270 1ST DIST
CHAMBERS, GEORGE CAL 022 2ND DIST
CHAMBERS, GEORGE CEC 141 6TH E DI
CHAMBERS, GEORGE W. CEC 148 PORT DUP
CHAMBERS, GEORGE W. BAL 003 9TH WARD
CHAMBERS, HARRIET CEC 129 6TH E DI
CHAMBERS, HENRIETTA BAL 039 4TH WARD
CHAMBERS, HENRIETTA BAL 183 16TH WAR
CHAMBERS, HENRY CAR 391 2ND DIST
CHAMBERS, HENRY KEN 270 1ST DIST
CHAMBERS, HENRY WAS 162 HAGERSTO
CHAMBERS, HORACE HAR 100 2ND DIST
CHAMBERS, ISABELLA HAR 155 3RD DIST
CHAMBERS, J. BAL 142 1ST WARD
CHAMBERS, J. BAL 136 1ST WARD
CHAMBERS, JAMES HAR 142 2ND DIST
CHAMBERS, JAMES KEN 211 2ND DIST
CHAMBERS, JAMES KEN 250 2ND DIST
CHAMBERS, JAMES QUE 155 2ND E DI
CHAMBERS, JAMES BAL 278 17TH WAR
CHAMBERS, JAMES WAS 182 BOONSBOR
CHAMBERS, JAMES TAL 028 EASTON D
CHAMBERS, JAMES B. BAL 097 1ST WARD
CHAMBERS, JANE ANN 432 HOWARD D
CHAMBERS, JANE KEN 308 3RD DIST
CHAMBERS, JANE BAL 306 20TH WAR
CHAMBERS, JANE BAL 197 11TH WAR
CHAMBERS, JOSEPHINE * BAL 221 12TH WAR
CHAMBERS, JOHN BAL 431 8TH WARD
CHAMBERS, JOHN ANN 363 4TH DIST
CHAMBERS, JOHN BAL 022 2ND DIST
CHAMBERS, JOHN BAL 124 1ST WARD
CHAMBERS, JOHN BAL 142 1ST WARD
CHAMBERS, JOHN BAL 374 3RD WARD
CHAMBERS, JOHN BAL 197 17TH WAR
CHAMBERS, JOHN BAL 461 1ST DIST
CHAMBERS, JOHN CAL 043 3RD DIST
CHAMBERS, JOHN KEN 273 1ST DIST
CHAMBERS, JOHN S. BAL 152 19TH WAR
CHAMBERS, JOHN T. BAL 235 12TH WAR
CHAMBERS, JOHN W. BAL 396 14TH WAR
CHAMBERS, JOHN W. CEC 095 4TH E DI
CHAMBERS, JOHN W. QUE 188 3RD E DI
CHAMBERS, KETTY BAL 381 13TH WAR
CHAMBERS, LAURA CEC 197 7TH E DI
CHAMBERS, LAURA L. FRE 056 FREDERIC
CHAMBERS, LEVI ANN 510 HOWARD D
CHAMBERS, LOUISA ANN 272 ANNAPOLI
CHAMBERS, LOUISIA-BLACK BAL 219 2ND WARD
CHAMBERS, LUKEY BAL 439 1ST DIST
CHAMBERS, M.F. PRI 092 MARLBROU
CHAMBERS, MARGARET CEC 064 1ST E DI
CHAMBERS, MARGARETA BAL 393 8TH WARD
CHAMBERS, MARIA BAL 157 11TH WAR
CHAMBERS, MARTHA BAL 340 13TH WAR
CHAMBERS, MARTHA BAL 266 1ST DIST
CHAMBERS, MARY BAL 312 7TH WARD
CHAMBERS, MARY BAL 460 1ST DIST
CHAMBERS, MARY BAL 151 5TH WARD
CHAMBERS, MARY ANN BAL 392 14TH WAR
CHAMBERS, MARY F. PRI 002 BLADENSB
CHAMBERS, PERE QUE 219 3RD E DI
CHAMBERS, PERE KEN 224 2ND DIST
CHAMBERS, PEREGRIN BAL 459 8TH WARD
CHAMBERS, PERRY BAL 126 18TH WAR
CHAMBERS, PHINEAS CEC 094 4TH E DI
CHAMBERS, RACHEAL-BLACK CAR 391 2ND DIST
CHAMBERS, ROBERT BAL 258 17TH WAR
CHAMBERS, ROBERT BAL 406 14TH WAR
CHAMBERS, ROBERT BAL 406 14TH WAR
CHAMBERS, ROSANNA WAS 296 1ST DIST
CHAMBERS, RUTH BAL 322 3RD WARD
CHAMBERS, SAMUEL BAL 152 5TH WARD
CHAMBERS, SAMUEL BAL 169 1ST WARD
CHAMBERS, SAMUEL BAL 273 7TH WARD
CHAMBERS, SAMUEL BAL 397 8TH WARD
CHAMBERS, SAMUEL BAL 282 2ND WARD
CHAMBERS, SAMUEL KEN 308 3RD DIST
CHAMBERS, SAMUEL W. KEN 255 1ST DIST
CHAMBERS, SAMUEL-BLACK FRE 390 PETERSVI
CHAMBERS, SARAH KEN 219 2ND DIST
CHAMBERS, SOPHIA CEC 054 1ST E DI
CHAMBERS, STEPHEN BAL 177 16TH WAR
CHAMBERS, SUSAN BAL 075 18TH WAR
CHAMBERS, SUSAN CAR 099 NO TWP L
CHAMBERS, THOMAS ANN 431 HOWARD D
CHAMBERS, THOMAS ANN 477 HOWARD D
CHAMBERS, THOMAS QUE 199 3RD E DI
CHAMBERS, THOMAS WAS 093 2ND SUBD
CHAMBERS, W. BAL 075 18TH WAR
CHAMBERS, W.H. WAS 021 2ND SUBD
CHAMBERS, WILIAM CAR 138 NO TWP L
CHAMBERS, WILKY BAL 157 2ND DIST
CHAMBERS, WILLIAM BAL 003 9TH WARD
CHAMBERS, WILLIAM CAL 055 3RD DIST
CHAMBERS, WILLIAM CAL 044 3RD DIST
CHAMBERS, WILLIAM CAL 061 3RD DIST
CHAMBERS, WILLIAM CEC 083 CHARLEST
CHAMBERS, WILLIAM QUE 203 3RD E DI
CHAMBERS, WILLIAM QUE 246 5TH E DI
CHAMBERS, WILLIAM H. BAL 143 16TH WAR
CHAMBERS, WILLIAM* TAL 016 EASTON D
CHAMBERS,R.D. FRE 239 NEW MARK
CHAMBUS, CHARLES TAL 023 EASTON D
CHAMBUS, DANIEL HAR 175 3RD DIST
CHAMBUS, WILLIAM* TAL 016 EASTON D
CHAMFOR, PRISCILLA BAL 459 1ST DIST
CHAMLERNS, WILLIAM * BAL 402 1ST DIST
CHAMLESTON, JAMES BAL 113 2ND DIST
CHAMLIN, NAPOLIAN CAR 219 5TH DIST
CHAMLUNS, WILLIAM BAL 402 1ST DIST
CHAMOMILE, JANE CEC 128 5TH E DI
CHAMPAIGM, JOHN BAL 246 17TH WAR
CHAMPANE, MARIAN R. BAL 352 1ST DIST
CHAMPANE, RACHEL BAL 352 1ST DIST
CHAMPANE, WILLIAM R. BAL 198 19TH WAR
CHAMPHER, CHARLES BAL 113 1ST WARD
CHAMPION, JAMES CEC 120 4TH E DI
CHAMPION, JAMES PRI 107 PISCATAW
CHAMPION, WILLIAM BAL 404 3RD WARD
CHAMYTON, GEORGE BAL 166 2ND DIST
CHAN, CHLOE WAS 104 2ND DIST
CHANAN, FRIDAY BAL 168 11TH WAR
CHANCE, ANN QUE 208 3RD E DI
CHANCE, DANIEL TAL 015 EASTON D
CHANCE, EDWARD L. QUE 219 3RD E DI
CHANCE, ELI CAR 170 NO TWP L
CHANCE, ELI* TAL 029 EASTON D
CHANCE, ELIJAH KEN 313 3RD DIST
CHANCE, ELIJAH QUE 241 5TH E DI
CHANCE, ELIZA BAL 214 11TH WAR
CHANCE, EMILY BAL 128 11TH WAR
CHANCE, FRANCES A. QUE 141 1ST E DI
CHANCE, GEORGE W.* TAL 006 EASTON D
CHANCE, HENRY TAL 006 EASTON D
CHANCE, JAMES CAR 074 NO TWP L
CHANCE, JAMES R. BAL 356 13TH WAR
CHANCE, JOHN QUE 137 1ST E DI
CHANCE, JOHN PRI 122 PISCATAW
CHANCE, JOHN PRI 057 AQUASCO
CHANCE, JOHN BAL 161 1ST WARD
CHANCE, JOSHUA QUE 207 3RD E DI
CHANCE, JOSHUA L. QUE 212 3RD E DI
CHANCE, JULIANN QUE 197 3RD E DI
CHANCE, MARY BAL 356 13TH WAR
CHANCE, NATHAN TAL 031 EASTON D
CHANCE, SAMUEL BAL 297 1ST DIST
CHANCE, SUSAN* TAL 061 EASTON D
CHANCE, TILGHMANN.* TAL 029 EASTON D
CHANCE, WILLIAM TAL 009 EASTON D
CHANCE, WILLIAM E. CAR 090 NO TWP L
CHANCE, WILLIAM J. BAL 164 11TH WAR
CHANCE,CLEM QUE 182 3RD E DI
CHANCEAULME, MARTIN BAL 157 6TH WARD
CHANCEY, BENJAMIN HAR 174 3RD DIST
CHANCEY, BERARD PRI 107 PISCATAW
CHANCEY, SARAH B. HAR 174 3RD DIST
CHANCULME, WILLIAM BAL 293 7TH WARD
CHANCY, BENJAMIN HAR 174 3RD DIST
CHANCY, JAMES BAL 245 17TH WAR
CHANCY, MARION TAL 067 EASTON T
CHANCY, SARAH KEN 251 2ND DIST
CHANCY, SARAH B. HAR 174 3RD DIST
CHANCY, VINA* TAL 046 EASTON T
CHANDLEE, MAHLON MGM 348 BERRYS D
CHANDLER, ABRAM CEC 006 ELKTON 3
CHANDLER, CAROLINE BAL 283 7TH WARD
CHANDLER, DAVID BAL 356 13TH WAR
CHANDLER, E. BAL 132 5TH WARD
CHANDLER, EDWARD BAL 136 1ST WARD
CHANDLER, EDWIN BAL 334 13TH WAR
CHANDLER, ELIZA A. BAL 194 6TH WARD
CHANDLER, ELIZABETH BAL 059 15TH WAR
CHANDLER, ELLIS B. CEC 136 6TH E DI
CHANDLER, GEORGE W. BAL 284 17TH WAR
CHANDLER, H.J. REV. BAL 431 1ST DIST
CHANDLER, HARRIET BAL 366 3RD WARD
CHANDLER, HARRIET BAL 425 3RD WARD
CHANDLER, JAMES BAL 044 1ST WARD
CHANDLER, JAMES WOR 244 1ST CENS
CHANDLER, JOHN WOR 245 1ST CENS
CHANDLER, JOHN BAL 383 1ST DIST
CHANDLER, JOHN BAL 341 7TH WARD
CHANDLER, JOHN CEC 031 CHESAPEA
CHANDLER, JOHN B. CEC 136 6TH E DI
CHANDLER, JULIAN BAL 408 3RD WARD
CHANDLER, JULIANA BAL 070 15TH WAR
CHANDLER, MARY WAS 140 HAGERSTO
CHANDLER, MILLICANT CEC 137 6TH E DI
CHANDLER, MR. BAL 092 5TH WARD
CHANDLER, NANCY A. BAL 328 7TH WARD
CHANDLER, PRESEY WOR 241 1ST CENS
CHANDLER, RICHARD BAL 434 14TH WAR
CHANDLER, SARAH BAL 112 15TH WAR
CHANDLER, THOMAS J BAL 341 7TH WARD
CHANDLER, WILLIAM SOM 424 PRINCESS
CHANDLEY, MARY BAL 245 12TH WAR
CHANE, JOHN BAL 075 1ST WARD
CHANE, JOHN HAR 157 3RD DIST
CHANECELLEMY, R. P. BAL 330 13TH WAR
CHANES, JAMES* TAL 040 EASTON D
CHANEY, ALEXANDER KEN 250 2ND DIST
CHANEY, AMELIA WAS 196 1ST DIST
CHANEY, ANDREW W. BAL 111 5TH WARD
CHANEY, ANN ANN 348 3RD DIST
CHANEY, ANN ANN 357 3RD DIST
CHANEY, ANN WOR 217 4TH E DI
CHANEY, ANN PRI 080 QUEEN AN
CHANEY, ANNA BAL 401 14TH WAR
CHANEY, BNEJAMIN BAL 087 18TH WAR
CHANEY, CAROLINE BAL 458 8TH WARD
CHANEY, CATHARINE BAL 086 1ST WARD
CHANEY, CORNELIUS BAL 212 6TH WARD
CHANEY, EDITH BAL 381 13TH WAR
CHANEY, EDWARD ANN 363 4TH DIST
CHANEY, ELIAS WAS 173 FUNKSTOW
CHANEY, ELISABETH ANN 373 4TH DIST
CHANEY, ELIZA BAL 314 3RD WARD
CHANEY, ELIZA BAL 108 18TH WAR
CHANEY, ELIZABETH ANN 373 4TH DIST
CHANEY, FLOYD BAL 050 15TH WAR
CHANEY, GEORGIANNA ANN 370 4TH DIST
CHANEY, HARRIET TAL 061 EASTON D
CHANEY, HENRY FRE 251 NEW MARK
CHANEY, HEZEKIAH WAS 196 1ST DIST
CHANEY, ISAAC ANN 373 4TH DIST
CHANEY, ISAAC ANN 362 4TH DIST
CHANEY, ISAIAH BAL 440 14TH WAR
CHANEY, JACOB CAL 047 3RD DIST
CHANEY, JACOB C. BAL 143 1ST WARD
CHANEY, JACOB C. BAL 277 7TH WARD
CHANEY, JAMES BAL 011 1ST WARD
CHANEY, JAMES TAL 041 EASTON D
CHANEY, JAMES T. CAL 049 3RD DIST
CHANEY, JAMES* TAL 040 EASTON D
CHANEY, JANE TAL 040 EASTON D
CHANEY, JEHU ANN 363 4TH DIST
CHANEY, JOHN ANN 411 8TH DIST
CHANEY, JOHN BAL 458 8TH WARD
CHANEY, JOHN BAL 120 18TH WAR
CHANEY, JOSEPH CAL 054 3RD DIST
CHANEY, JOSEPH ANN 396 8TH DIST
CHANEY, JOSHUA B. ANN 362 4TH DIST
CHANEY, LEWIS CAL 049 3RD DIST
CHANEY, LEWIS FRE 249 NEW MARK
CHANEY, LEWIS PRI 033 VANSVILL
CHANEY, NED ANN 409 8TH DIST
CHANEY, NELSON PRI 084 QUEEN AN
CHANEY, REBECCA BAL 159 11TH WAR
CHANEY, REBECCA BAL 215 11TH WAR
CHANEY, REZIN ANN 363 4TH DIST
CHANEY, RICHARD ANN 358 3RD DIST
CHANEY, RICHARD ANN 391 4TH DIST
CHANEY, SAMUEL ANN 380 4TH DIST
CHANEY, SAMUEL ANN 373 4TH DIST
CHANEY, SAMUEL ANN 328 2ND DIST
CHANEY, SARAH BAL 304 1ST DIST
CHANEY, SARAH KEN 252 1ST DIST
CHANEY, SOLOMON G. ANN 312 1ST DIST
CHANEY, STEPHEN W. BAL 047 9TH WARD
CHANEY, THOMAS ANN 378 4TH DIST
CHANEY, THOMAS BAL 003 9TH WARD
CHANEY, THOMAS BAL 357 8TH WARD
CHANEY, VIOLETTA ANN 427 HOWARD D
CHANEY, WILLIAM ANN 295 1ST DIST
CHANEY,MICHAEL BAL 059 1ST WARD
CHANG, THOMAS CHA 225 ALLENS F
CHANGLEY, JAMES C. HAR 151 3RD DIST
CHANICK, WILLIAM SOM 375 BRINKLEY
CHANLEE, WILLIAM ANN 452 HOWARD D
CHANLY, CATHARINE CAR 366 9TH DIST
CHANNEL , MADILON BAL 120 11TH WAR
CHANOUSE, WILLIAM BAL 008 9TH WARD
CHANPIN, JULIA BAL 054 9TH WARD
CHANSE, ELI* TAL 029 EASTON D
CHANSE, GEORGE W.* TAL 006 EASTON D
CHANTAN, SOLOMON BAL 226 2ND WARD
CHANTICE, WORLEY J. CAR 257 3RD DIST
CHANY, ANDREW ANN 374 4TH DIST
CHANY, FRANCIS FRE 249 NEW MARK
CHANY, JANE CAR 363 9TH DIST
CHANY, JANE KEN 251 2ND DIST
CHANY, LUCY ANN FRE 253 NEW MARK
CHANY, NOAH TAL 040 EASTON D
CHANY, THOMAS WOR 259 BERLIN 1
CHANY, THOMAS H. ALL 224 CUMBERLA
CHANY, VINA* TAL 046 EASTON T
CHANY,NICHOLAS BAL 087 1ST WARD
CHAPEE, C. H. BAL 389 13TH WAR
CHAPELL, RICHARD BAL 453 8TH WARD
CHAPIN, CHARLES ANN 386 4TH DIST
CHAPIN, HERMAN BAL 042 15TH WAR
CHAPIN, PHILIP BAL 041 15TH WAR
CHAPKUM, CATHARINE BAL 164 6TH WARD
CHAPLAIN, DANIEL BAL 070 15TH WAR
CHAPLAIN, DAVID TAL 048 EASTON T
CHAPLAIN, ELIZA S. TAL 048 EASTON T
CHAPLAIN, ELIZABETH TAL 055 EASTON D
CHAPLAIN, J. BOND BAL 108 10TH WAR
CHAPLAIN, JAMES TAL 047 EASTON T
CHAPLAIN, JAMES L. BAL 388 13TH WAR
CHAPLAIN, MARIAH R. TAL 048 EASTON T
CHAPLAIN, THOMAS J. TAL 051 EASTON D
CHAPLE, REUBEN BAL 130 11TH WAR
CHAPLIN, CATHARINE WAS 073 2ND SUBD
CHAPLIN, DAVID BAL 168 1ST WARD
CHAPLIN, JOSEPH BAL 374 3RD WARD
CHAPLIN, PERRY BAL 154 11TH WAR
CHAPLIN, WILLIAM BAL 140 1ST WARD
CHAPLIN, WILLIAM ALL 254 CUMBERLA
CHAPLIN, WILLIAM WAS 073 2ND SUBD
CHAPMAHN, JANE BAL 078 4TH WARD
CHAPMAN, ALLAN BAL 213 19TH WAR
CHAPMAN, ANDERSON BAL 152 5TH WARD
CHAPMAN, ANN B. BAL 284 7TH WARD
CHAPMAN, ANN E. BAL 429 14TH WAR
CHAPMAN, C. PRI 105 PISCATAW
CHAPMAN, CAROLINE J. CEC 004 ELKTON 3
CHAPMAN, CATHARINE BAL 248 20TH WAR
CHAPMAN, CECELIA CHA 257 MIDDLETO
CHAPMAN, CHARLES BAL 227 19TH WAR
CHAPMAN, CHARLES PRI 105 PISCATAW
CHAPMAN, DANIEL BAL 330 3RD WARD
CHAPMAN, DEBORA TAL 071 EASTON T
CHAPMAN, ELIZABETH BAL 010 18TH WAR
CHAPMAN, FRANCIS R. TAL 032 EASTON D
CHAPMAN, GEORGE S. ANN 265 ANNAPOLI
CHAPMAN, GREENBERY BAL 102 18TH WAR
CHAPMAN, HENRIETTA TAL 065 EASTON T
CHAPMAN, HENRY BAL 291 7TH WARD
CHAPMAN, HENRY BAL 170 1ST WARD
CHAPMAN, HESTER J. BAL 353 13TH WAR
CHAPMAN, JAMES BAL 282 2ND WARD
CHAPMAN, JAMES B. BAL 367 3RD WARD
CHAPMAN, JESSE ALL 165 6TH E.D.
CHAPMAN, JOHN G. CHA 217 ALLENS F
CHAPMAN, JOHN L. BAL 015 4TH WARD
CHAPMAN, JONATHAN J. BAL 077 4TH WARD
CHAPMAN, JOSEPH BAL 143 1ST WARD
CHAPMAN, JOSEPH BAL 115 2ND DIST
CHAPMAN, LITTLETON WOR 328 1ST E DI
CHAPMAN, MARIA QUE 187 3RD E DI
CHAPMAN, MARY BAL 101 5TH WARD
CHAPMAN, MARY BAL 216 17TH WAR
CHAPMAN, MARY E. BAL 326 1ST DIST
CHAPMAN, NANCY QUE 217 3RD E DI
CHAPMAN, NIMROD BAL 286 12TH WAR
CHAPMAN, PERRY BAL 370 13TH WAR
CHAPMAN, RACHEL CAR 200 4TH DIST
CHAPMAN, REBECCA BAL 249 12TH WAR
CHAPMAN, ROSE BAL 330 3RD WARD
CHAPMAN, SARAH PRI 026 VANSVILL
CHAPMAN, SUSAN BAL 130 11TH WAR
CHAPMAN, SUSAN DOR 438 1ST DIST
CHAPMAN, THOMAS BAL 384 13TH WAR
CHAPMAN, THOMAS HAR 155 3RD DIST
CHAPMAN, THOMAS H. BAL 409 3RD WARD
CHAPMAN, THOMAS S. BAL 069 10TH WAR
CHAPMAN, W. P. TAL 032 EASTON D
CHAPMAN, WILLIAM BAL 326 1ST DIST
CHAPMAN, WILLIAM BAL 211 17TH WAR
CHAPMAN, WILLIAM CEC 109 4TH E DI
CHAPPEL, NATHAN BAL 342 7TH WARD
CHAPPEL, PATTENCE BAL 397 14TH WAR
CHAPPELE, REBECCA ST 345 5TH E DI
CHAPPELL, ANN T. L. BAL 219 6TH WARD
CHAPPELL, ELIZABETH BAL 202 19TH WAR
CHAPPELL, JOHN BAL 343 13TH WAR
CHAPPELL, JOHN G. BAL 052 15TH WAR
CHAPPELL, P. S. BAL 320 20TH WAR
CHAPPELL, WILLIAM O. MGM 375 ROCKERLE
CHAPPLE, ANN HAR 065 1ST DIST
CHAPPLEAR, GEORGE ST 344 5TH E DI
CHARARD, JANE M. BAL 356 13TH WAR
CHARD, ANN R. BAL 402 8TH WARD
CHARD, HENRIETTA BAL 164 6TH WARD
CHARELS, JACOB BAL 113 2ND DIST
CHARLES BAL 171 1ST WARD
CHARLES, ANDREW BAL 304 17TH WAR
CHARLES, BENJAMIN BAL 399 3RD WARD
CHARLES, CAIN CHA 285 BOJANTOW
CHARLES, CANNON CAR 121 NO TWP L
CHARLES, EDWARD BAL 181 6TH WARD
CHARLES, F.M. WAS 021 2ND SUBD
CHARLES, JAOCB CAR 125 NO TWP L

Name	County	Page	District
CHARLES, JOEL	WAS	142	2ND DIST
CHARLES, JOHN	BAL	281	12TH WAR
CHARLES, JOHN	BAL	154	2ND DIST
CHARLES, JOHN-BLACK	QUE	194	3RD E DI
CHARLES, JOSEPH	WAS	111	2ND DIST
CHARLES, JOSIAH	DOR	321	1ST DIST
CHARLES, LEVINA	BAL	154	2ND DIST
CHARLES, LOUISA	BAL	058	15TH WAR
CHARLES, MARGARET	BAL	314	12TH WAR
CHARLES, MARGARET	ALL	254	CUMBERLA
CHARLES, MARY	BAL	265	17TH WAR
CHARLES, MICHAEL	DOR	314	1ST DIST
CHARLES, SAMUEL-BLACK	QUE	147	1ST E DI
CHARLES, SIMON PETER	DOR	322	1ST DIST
CHARLES, THEODORE	BAL	277	2ND WARD
CHARLES, WILLIAM	DOR	311	1ST DIST
CHARLES, WILLIAM	QUE	210	3RD E DI
CHARLES, WILLIAM H.	CAR	126	NO TWP L
CHARLES, WILLIS	CAR	125	NO TWP L
CHARLES,MARY	CAR	110	NO TWP L
CHARLESTON, LEWIS	HAR	009	1ST DIST
CHARLS, CHARLES	BAL	054	9TH WARD
CHARLTON, BENJAMIN	ALL	143	6TH E.D.
CHARLTON, CATHARINE	HAR	060	1ST DIST
CHARLTON, ELIZABETH	CAL	005	1ST DIST
CHARLTON, INA	WAS	012	WILLIAMS
CHARLTON, JAMES	CAL	007	1ST DIST
CHARLTON, JOHN	BAL	336	7TH WARD
CHARLTON, JOHN W.	FRE	407	JEFFERSO
CHARLTON, MARY A.	WAS	013	WILLIAMS
CHARLTON, MILLY	ALL	090	5TH E.D.
CHARLTON, THOMAS	WAS	006	WILLIAMS
CHARLTON, WESLEY	ALL	051	10TH E.D
CHARLTON,HARIET	BAL	048	2ND DIST
CHARMS, ABRAHAM	BAL	456	1ST DIST
CHARMS, JARRETT	BAL	111	18TH WAR
CHARMS, JOSEPH	BAL	255	20TH WAR
CHARSHE, CLARISSA A.	BAL	406	3RD WARD
CHARSHE, JOHN C.	BAL	405	3RD WARD
CHARSHEE, EDWARD	HAR	131	2ND DIST
CHASE, A.G.	BAL	193	11TH WAR
CHASE, ABRAHAM-BLACK	CAR	134	NO TWP L
CHASE, ABSALOM	BAL	452	14TH WAR
CHASE, ALEXANDER	ANN	358	3RD DIST
CHASE, ALLEN	BAL	344	3RD WARD
CHASE, AMELIA	BAL	184	19TH WAR
CHASE, ANDREW	BAL	273	7TH WARD
CHASE, ANN	BAL	150	11TH WAR
CHASE, ANN M.	WAS	121	HAGERSTO
CHASE, ANTHONY	FRE	367	CATOCTIN
CHASE, ARCHIBALD*	DOR	438	1ST DIST
CHASE, ARNEAL	BAL	121	11TH WAR
CHASE, ARTHUR	KEN	216	2ND DIST
CHASE, BENJAMIN	BAL	101	10TH WAR
CHASE, CHARITY-MULATTO	FRE	240	NEW MARK
CHASE, CHARLES	CAR	237	UNION TO
CHASE, CHARLES H.	BAL	083	4TH WARD
CHASE, CLEM	TAL	058	EASTON D
CHASE, COMFORT	FRE	208	BUCKEYST
CHASE, D.	BAL	280	20TH WAR
CHASE, DANIEL	ANN	378	4TH DIST
CHASE, DAVID	BAL	320	7TH WARD
CHASE, DENNIS	CAR	234	UNION TO
CHASE, ELIZA	BAL	344	7TH WARD
CHASE, ELIZA	BAL	243	6TH WARD
CHASE, ELIZABETH	WAS	163	HAGERSTO
CHASE, ELIZABETH A.	BAL	036	1ST WARD
CHASE, ELLEN	WAS	123	HAGERSTO
CHASE, ELLEN	WAS	011	WILLIAMS
CHASE, EMILY	BAL	201	6TH WARD
CHASE, EMORY-BLACK	QUE	151	1ST E DI
CHASE, FANNY	CAL	020	2ND DIST
CHASE, FRANCES	MGM	351	BERRYS D
CHASE, FRANCIS	BAL	032	1ST WARD
CHASE, FRANCIS	BAL	346	7TH WARD
CHASE, GEORGE	BAL	249	6TH WARD
CHASE, GEORGE	WAS	121	2ND DIST
CHASE, GEORGE W.	FRE	435	8TH E DI
CHASE, HANNA	BAL	069	4TH WARD
CHASE, HANNAH	KEN	216	2ND DIST
CHASE, HANNIBAL H.	BAL	159	16TH WAR
CHASE, HARRIET	ANN	435	HOWARD D
CHASE, HARRISON	BAL	128	16TH WAR
CHASE, HENRY	BAL	152	16TH WAR
CHASE, HENRY	BAL	242	6TH WARD
CHASE, HENRY	BAL	413	14TH WAR
CHASE, HENRY	CAL	040	3RD DIST
CHASE, HENRY	TAL	058	EASTON D
CHASE, HENRY-BLACK	CAR	160	NO TWP L
CHASE, HESTER	ALL	244	CUMBERLA
CHASE, HEZEKIAH-BLACK	CAR	161	NO TWP L
CHASE, ISAAC H.	BAL	279	20TH WAR
CHASE, ISABELLA	BAL	083	4TH WARD
CHASE, JAMES	CAL	022	2ND DIST
CHASE, JAMES	CAL	040	3RD DIST
CHASE, JAMES	CAL	006	1ST DIST
CHASE, JAMES	BAL	095	2ND DIST
CHASE, JAMES	BAL	026	9TH WARD
CHASE, JAMES	QUE	232	4TH E DI
CHASE, JAMES-BLACK	CAR	161	NO TWP L
CHASE, JANE	ALL	263	CUMBERLA
CHASE, JENNY	WAS	020	2ND SUBD
CHASE, JEREMIAH-BLACK	BAL	224	2ND WARD
CHASE, JERRY	TAL	090	ST MICHA
CHASE, JOHN	WAS	015	2ND SUBD
CHASE, JOHN	WAS	027	2ND SUBD
CHASE, JOHN	PRI	084	QUEEN AN
CHASE, JOHN	ANN	421	HOWARD D
CHASE, JOHN J.	BAL	274	2ND WARD
CHASE, JOHN-BLACK	CAR	136	NO TWP L
CHASE, JOHN-BLACK	QUE	137	1ST E DI
CHASE, JOSEPH-BLACK	CAR	138	NO TWP L
CHASE, JOSHUA	BAL	124	1ST WARD
CHASE, LEVI	BAL	239	6TH WARD
CHASE, LEWIS	ANN	320	2ND DIST
CHASE, LEWIS	ANN	320	2ND DIST
CHASE, LUCINDA	BAL	459	8TH WARD
CHASE, LUCRETIA	CAR	284	7TH DIST
CHASE, LYDIA	ANN	355	3RD DIST
CHASE, MARGARET	BAL	041	9TH WARD
CHASE, MARGARET J.	BAL	110	15TH WAR
CHASE, MARY	BAL	042	9TH WARD
CHASE, MARY	BAL	098	10TH WAR
CHASE, MARY	BAL	451	14TH WAR
CHASE, MARY	BAL	299	20TH WAR
CHASE, MARY	FRE	098	FREDERIC
CHASE, MARY A.	BAL	274	2ND WARD
CHASE, MARY ANN	BAL	092	10TH WAR
CHASE, MARY E.	WAS	020	2ND SUBD
CHASE, MILLY	ST	279	3RD E DI
CHASE, MILLY	DOR	438	1ST DIST
CHASE, MOSES	ALL	220	CUMBERLA
CHASE, NANCY	BAL	108	5TH WARD
CHASE, NANCY	BAL	376	1ST DIST
CHASE, PERRY	ST	278	3RD E DI
CHASE, PERRY	TAL	034	EASTON D
CHASE, PERRY*	TAL	005	EASTON D
CHASE, PHIL	BAL	296	20TH WAR
CHASE, RACHEL *	BAL	301	20TH WAR
CHASE, REBECCA	WAS	014	2ND SUBD
CHASE, REBECCA	QUE	224	4TH E DI
CHASE, RICHARD	CAL	023	2ND DIST
CHASE, RICHARD	ANN	448	HOWARD D
CHASE, RICHARD	BAL	306	12TH WAR
CHASE, RICHARD M.	BAL	235	6TH WARD
CHASE, ROBERT	BAL	227	17TH WAR
CHASE, SAMUEL	BAL	229	6TH WARD
CHASE, SAMUEL	BAL	202	6TH WARD
CHASE, SAMUEL	BAL	089	15TH WAR
CHASE, SAMUEL	ANN	432	HOWARD D
CHASE, SAMUEL	ALL	229	CUMBERLA
CHASE, SAMUEL	ANN	346	3RD DIST
CHASE, SAMUEL	BAL	239	12TH WAR
CHASE, SAMUEL	TAL	051	EASTON D
CHASE, SAMUEL	PRI	005	BLADENSB
CHASE, SAMUEL	SOM	551	TYASKIN
CHASE, SAMUEL W.	BAL	424	8TH WARD
CHASE, SAMUEL-BLACK	BAL	219	2ND WARD
CHASE, SAMUEL-BLACK	CAR	156	NO TWP L
CHASE, SAMUEL-BLACK	CAR	161	NO TWP L
CHASE, SARAH	BAL	087	2ND DIST
CHASE, SARAH	WAS	121	2ND DIST
CHASE, SARAH	PRI	079	QUEEN AM
CHASE, SARAH	PRI	080	QUEEN AN
CHASE, SARAH-BLACK	BAL	219	2ND WARD
CHASE, SHARLOTT	TAL	024	EASTON D
CHASE, SOPHIA	BAL	080	15TH WAR
CHASE, SOPHIA	BAL	294	3RD WARD
CHASE, STEPHEN	BAL	392	3RD WARD
CHASE, TABITHA A.	BAL	429	14TH WAR
CHASE, THOMAS	BAL	175	11TH WAR
CHASE, THOMAS	PRI	080	QUEEN AN
CHASE, THORNDICK*	BAL	372	3RD WARD
CHASE, THORNDIEK*	BAL	372	3RD WARD
CHASE, W. HENRY	MGM	350	BERRYS D
CHASE, WELLS	BAL	160	16TH WAR
CHASE, WILLIAM	BAL	100	5TH WARD
CHASE, WILLIAM	BAL	192	6TH WARD
CHASE, WILLIAM	BAL	153	1ST WARD
CHASE, WILLIAM	ANN	352	3RD DIST
CHASE, WILLIAM	BAL	083	4TH WARD
CHASE, WILLIAM	BAL	352	13TH WAR
CHASE, WILLIAM	CAR	235	UNION TO
CHASE, WILLIAM	BAL	154	11TH WAR
CHASE, WILLIAM	DOR	416	1ST DIST
CHASE, WILLIAM	DOR	419	1ST DIST
CHASE, WILLIAM	PRI	055	AQUASCO
CHASE, WILLIAM F.-BLACK	CAR	160	NO TWP L
CHASE, YOUNG	CAL	036	2ND DIST
CHASEN, H.	BAL	157	1ST WARD
CHASER, WILLIAM-BLACK	CAR	129	NO TWP L
CHASES, CHARLES	BAL	338	13TH WAR
CHASEY, B.	BAL	116	1ST WARD
CHASEY, RICHARD	BAL	146	1ST WARD
CHASMAN, ELIZABETH	CAR	163	NO TWP L
CHASMAN, JAMES	CAR	163	NO TWP L
CHASMAN, JOHN	CAR	163	NO TWP L
CHASMAN, LEVIN L.	CAR	163	NO TWP L
CHASMAN, THOMAS	CAR	162	NO TWP L
CHASSING, PAMYRA	BAL	200	11TH WAR
CHASTEAR, LEWIS	BAL	014	4TH WARD
CHASTHER, BENET	HAR	148	3RD DIST
CHASUM, MARY	CAR	142	NO TWP L
CHATARD, FERDINAND E.	BAL	388	13TH WAR
CHATARD, FRANCIS	FRE	202	5TH E DI
CHATARD, FREDERICK	BAL	201	11TH WAR
CHATARD, LUKE T.	FRE	202	5TH E DI
CHATARD, MISS J.	FRE	199	5TH E DI
CHATARD, PIERRE	FRE	202	5TH E DI
CHATARD, SILAS M.	FRE	202	5TH E DI
CHATFAN, WILLIAM	BAL	084	2ND DIST
CHATHAM, CHARLES	WOR	196	8TH E DI
CHATHAM, GEORGE	KEN	236	2ND DIST
CHATHAM, JOHN B.	WOR	188	7TH E DI
CHATHAM, JOSIAH F.	WOR	184	6TH E DI
CHATING, EDUARD	BAL	195	2ND WARD
CHATMAN, ELIZA	QUE	208	3RD E DI
CHATMAN, JOHN	WOR	322	1ST E DI
CHATMAN, MARY	BAL	398	1ST DIST
CHATTAM, ELIJAH	SOM	473	TRAPPE D
CHATTAM, FRANCIS	SOM	425	PRINCESS
CHATTAM, HARVEY	SOM	473	TRAPPE D
CHATTAM, JOHN	SOM	473	TRAPPE D
CHATTAM, JOHN	SOM	476	TRAPPE D
CHATTEL, JOHN	MGM	389	ROCKERLE
CHATTIEMBER, WILLIAM-BLAC	ST	315	4TH E DI
CHAULK, ABRAHAM	PRI	026	VANSVILL
CHAULK, BENNETT H.	HAR	107	2ND DIST
CHAULK, JAMES	PRI	032	VANSVILL
CHAULK, KESIAH	PRI	026	VANSVILL
CHAULK, MARY A.	PRI	027	VANSVILL
CHAUNCEY, ANN	HAR	157	3RD DIST
CHAUTICE, PETER	BAL	176	16TH WAR
CHAVES, WILLIAM	CEC	050	1ST E DI
CHAYFOR, ANDREW	BAL	047	1ST WARD
CHAZLE, WILLIAM D.	BAL	167	1ST WARD
CHEEKS, JOSEPH	CEC	023	ELKTON 3
CHEES, RICHARD*	TAL	020	EASTON D
CHEESBOUROUGH, R.	BAL	154	5TH WARD
CHEESEMAN, SARAH J.*	DOR	440	1ST DIST
CHEESMAN, JOHN	CAR	133	NO TWP L
CHEESMAN, RICHARD	CAR	135	NO TWP L
CHEESMAN, SAMUEL-BLACK	CAR	159	NO TWP L
CHEESMAN, WILLIAM	CAR	159	NO TWP L
CHEESMAN, WILLIAM	CAR	151	NO TWP L
CHEESZUM, THOMAS	DOR	446	1ST DIST
CHEESZUM, TILGHMAN	DOR	452	1ST DIST
CHEEZEMAN, DANIEL R. D.*	TAL	003	EASTON D
CHEEZEMAN, MARY	DOR	325	1ST DIST
CHEEZUM, ANN	TAL	047	EASTON T
CHEEZUM, DANIEL R. D.	TAL	003	EASTON D
CHEEZUM, JOHN W.	TAL	003	EASTON D
CHEFFINS, ANN	TAL	032	EASTON D
CHEIS, A. M. *	TAL	085	ST MICHA
CHELTON, FLEET C.	SOM	364	BRINKLEY
CHELTON, FLEET J.	SOM	364	BRINKLEY
CHELTON, HENRY F.	SOM	364	BRINKLEY
CHELTON, JAMES W.	SOM	362	BRINKLEY
CHELTON, SARAH	SOM	364	BRINKLEY
CHEMOUR, THOMAS	BAL	451	8TH WARD
CHEN, HENRY B.	BAL	081	2ND DIST
CHENAN, ELIZABETH	BAL	229	19TH WAR
CHENBOL, FRANCIS O.	BAL	160	19TH WAR
CHENE, NATHANIEL	HAR	156	3RD DIST
CHENEWORTH, THOMAS	BAL	151	5TH WARD
CHENEY, DAVID	ALL	191	9TH E.D.
CHENEY, GELY	WAS	178	BOONSBOR
CHENEY, GEORGE	BAL	236	12TH WAR
CHENEY, HENRY	ALL	212	CUMBERLA
CHENEY, J.W.	WAS	006	WILLIAMS
CHENEY, JOHN	WAS	006	WILLIAMS
CHENEY, JOHN	ALL	004	3RD E.D.
CHENEY, JOHNSON	ALL	179	7TH E.D.
CHENEY, LEWIS	WAS	006	WILLIAMS
CHENEY, MARGARET	ALL	186	9TH E.D.
CHENEY, MARY	ALL	186	9TH E.D.
CHENEY, REVERDY	BAL	228	6TH WARD
CHENEY, SAMUEL	WAS	196	1ST DIST
CHENEY, SAMUEL	BAL	189	19TH WAR
CHENEY, THOMAS	WAS	196	1ST DIST
CHENEY, WILLIAM	BAL	258	12TH WAR
CHENEY, WILLIAM B.	WAS	141	HAGERSTO
CHENEY, ZACHARIAH	ALL	191	9TH E.D.
CHENG, ELLEN W.	BAL	058	1ST WARD
CHENNETT, JOHN	HAR	059	1ST DIST
CHENNOWETH, A.	BAL	204	19TH WAR
CHENNOWETH, CATHARINE	BAL	264	20TH WAR
CHENNVETT, HARRIS	BAL	205	19TH WAR
CHENOTH, BRADFORD	BAL	137	2ND DIST
CHENOWETH, BENJAMIN	BAL	030	4TH WARD
CHENOWETH, JAMES B.	BAL	030	4TH WARD
CHENOWETH, JOHN B.	CAR	182	8TH DIST
CHENOWETH, JULIA A.	BAL	136	16TH WAR
CHENOWETH, RICHARD	BAL	299	20TH WAR
CHENOWETH, SARAH J.	CAR	182	8TH DIST
CHENOWITH, ALEXANDER	BAL	246	6TH WARD
CHENOWITH, AMELIA J.	BAL	224	6TH WARD
CHENOWITH, ELIZABETH	BAL	220	6TH WARD
CHENOWITH, G.D.	BAL	202	11TH WAR
CHENOWITH, GEORGE D.	BAL	245	6TH WARD
CHENOWITH, MARY	BAL	214	6TH WARD
CHENOWITH, RICHARD B.	BAL	224	6TH WARD
CHENOWITT, KEZIAH	BAL	127	2ND DIST
CHENOWORTH, BRADFORD	BAL	129	2ND DIST
CHENOWORTH, MARY	BAL	472	14TH WAR
CHENOWORTH, RICHARD	BAL	301	17TH WAR
CHENOWORTH, THOMAS	BAL	244	17TH WAR
CHENRY, ANN	BAL	162	19TH WAR
CHENWITH, CECELIA	BAL	213	11TH WAR
CHENWITH, DINAH	BAL	191	11TH WAR
CHEPCHASE, JAMES	ST	342	5TH E DI
CHERBONIER, CORNINNE	BAL	476	14TH WAR
CHERBONIER, PETER	BAL	476	14TH WAR
CHERBONINA, PETER O.	CAR	149	NO TWP L
CHERBY, RICHARD	CAR	222	5TH DIST
CHERDON, MICHAEL*	BAL	409	3RD WARD
CHERDOW, MICHAEL*	BAL	409	3RD WARD
CHERGREEN, WILLIAM	BAL	116	11TH WAR
CHERICK, JAMES	WOR	336	1ST E DI
CHERICKS, DAVID	WOR	324	1ST E DI
CHERICKS, PURNELL	WOR	297	9TH E DI
CHERICKS, SALLY	WOR	321	1ST E DI
CHERICKS, SALLY A. M. C.	WOR	315	2ND E DI
CHERLEY, CATHARINE	CAR	221	5TH DIST
CHERNOITT, THOMAS	BAL	098	2ND DIST
CHERO, BENJAMIN-BLACK	QUE	200	3RD E DI
CHERREY, WILLIAM J.	BAL	352	7TH WARD
CHERRICKS, CHARLOTT	WOR	312	2ND E DI
CHERRICKS, JOHN	WOR	316	2ND E DI
CHERRY, ABRAHAM P.	BAL	239	20TH WAR
CHERRY, CHARLES	BAL	159	1ST WARD
CHERRY, EDWARD	BAL	441	14TH WAR
CHERRY, JAMES W.	BAL	028	18TH WAR
CHERRY, JEROME	BAL	058	15TH WAR
CHERRY, NANCY	BAL	027	18TH WAR
CHERRY, PALMADGE F.	BAL	370	13TH WAR
CHERS, WILLIAM	BAL	097	15TH WAR
CHERV, THOMA SJ.	CAL	043	3RD DIST
CHERWITH, THOMAS *	BAL	092	2ND DIST
CHERWURTH, HARRIET	BAL	124	2ND DIST
CHESE, MARGARET	BAL	240	12TH WAR
CHESEBROUGH, ROBERT	BAL	186	2ND WARD
CHESELDINE, BISCCE	ST	320	4TH E DI
CHESELDINE, ELLENOR	ST	334	4TH E DI
CHESELDINE, GERARD	ST	318	4TH E DI
CHESELDINE, JAMES H.	ST	318	4TH E DI
CHESELDINE, JOHN	ST	330	4TH E DI
CHESELDINE, RICHARD	ST	319	4TH E DI
CHESELDINE, WILLIAM C.	ST	333	4TH E DI
CHESELDINE,WILLIAM H.	ST	320	4TH E DI
CHESGRIEN, WILLIAM	BAL	232	12TH WAR
CHESGRIER, CHARLES	BAL	159	11TH WAR
CHESHE, ANN	HAR	166	3RD DIST
CHESHER, SUSAN	WAS	126	HAGERSTO
CHESLEY, GRACE A.	BAL	202	6TH WARD
CHESLEY, JAEMS A.	CAL	001	1ST DIST
CHESLEY, JOHN	PRI	121	PISCATAW
CHESLEY, JOHN F.	PRI	104	PISCATAW
CHESLEY, NATHANIEL	ANN	395	8TH DIST
CHESLEY, PAUL	ANN	396	8TH DIST
CHESLEY, SUSAN	PRI	121	PISCATAW
CHESLEY, ZEDOCK	PRI	072	MARLBROU
CHESLY, RACHEL	BAL	399	14TH WAR
CHESNEY, BENJAMINE	BAL	271	7TH WARD
CHESNEY, DANIEL B.	HAR	186	3RD DIST
CHESNEY, HARRIET T.	BAL	439	8TH WARD
CHESNEY, JAMES	HAR	178	3RD DIST
CHESNEY, JESSE F.	HAR	150	3RD DIST
CHESNEY, LEWIS A.	BAL	439	8TH WARD
CHESNEY, THOMAS	BAL	130	1ST WARD
CHESNEY, THOMAS	BAL	201	6TH WARD
CHESNEY, WILLAIM	HAR	117	2ND DIST
CHESNEY, WILLIAM	HAR	131	2ND DIST
CHESNEY, WILLIAM	BAL	377	8TH WARD
CHESNEY, WILLIAM L.	HAR	163	3RD DIST
CHESNUT, GERARD	BAL	347	3RD WARD
CHESNUT, HUGH	BAL	348	7TH WARD
CHESNUT, SAMUEL	BAL	313	3RD WARD
CHESNUT, WILLIAM	BAL	082	4TH WARD
CHESSER, PURNEL	ANN	314	1ST DIST
CHESSER, WALTER	QUE	237	4TH E DI
CHESTER, FRED	KEN	282	3RD DIST
CHESTER, JAMES	DOR	327	3RD DIVI
CHESTER, JEREMIAH	BAL	011	1ST WARD
CHESTER, MARTHA	BAL	098	2ND DIST
CHESTER, MICHAEL	BAL	098	2ND DIST
CHESTER, MICHAEL	BAL	428	8TH WARD
CHESTER, PATIENCE	DOR	326	3RD DIVI
CHESTER, SOLOMON	BAL	152	5TH WARD
CHESTER, STEPHEN	BAL	330	3RD WARD

CHESTER, STEPHEN-BLACK BAL 224 2ND WARD
CHESTER, SUSAN A. BAL 086 4TH WARD
CHESTER, WILLIAM QUE 205 3RD E DI
CHESTER, WILLIAM-BLACK BAL 224 2ND WARD
CHESTERS, WILLIAM BAL 174 11TH WAR
CHESTNER, BONAPART BAL 176 2ND WARD
CHESTNUT, CHARLES BAL 334 3RD WARD
CHESTON, GALLAWAY BAL 381 13TH WAR
CHESTON, GALOWAY WAS 151 HAGERSTO
CHESTON, JAMES DR- ANN 315 1ST DIST
CHESTON, MARY ANN 302 1ST DIST
CHESWELL, WILLIAM PRI 107 PISCATAW
CHETCOAT, MARGARET BAL 169 16TH WAR
CHEVER, BELINDA BAL 369 13TH WAR
CHEVERAL, JAMES BAL 051 1ST WARD
CHEVERAL, VIRGINIA BAL 183 2ND WARD
CHEW, ADELINE BAL 352 3RD WARD
CHEW, ALEXANDER KEN 223 2ND DIST
CHEW, CAROLINE BAL 116 5TH WARD
CHEW, CHARLES BAL 127 16TH WAR
CHEW, CYRUS BAL 180 2ND DIST
CHEW, DIANAH ANN 279 ANNAPOLI
CHEW, EDWARD M. HAR 027 1ST DIST
CHEW, ELIZA C. HAR 122 2ND DIST
CHEW, ELIZA F. BAL 353 3RD WARD
CHEW, ELIZABETH CAL 008 1ST DIST
CHEW, ELIZABETH CAL 059 3RD DIST
CHEW, ELIZABETH BAL 140 19TH WAR
CHEW, ELIZABETH A. BAL 093 15TH WAR
CHEW, EMERLINE R. HAR 151 3RD DIST
CHEW, FANNEY HAR 034 1ST DIST
CHEW, FANNY-BLACK QUE 201 3RD E DI
CHEW, GEORGIANA BAL 099 10TH WAR
CHEW, HENRIETTA BAL 092 15TH WAR
CHEW, HENRY M. PRI 064 NOTTINGH
CHEW, JAMES J. PRI 092 MARLBROU
CHEW, JAMES W. BAL 269 12TH WAR
CHEW, JANE BAL 189 17TH WAR
CHEW, JOH BAL 383 13TH WAR
CHEW, JOHN CAL 014 1ST DIST
CHEW, JOHN BAL 100 18TH WAR
CHEW, JOHN BAL 167 16TH WAR
CHEW, JOHN A. HAR 151 3RD DIST
CHEW, JOHN H. CAR 207 4TH DIST
CHEW, JOHN H. ST 329 4TH E DI
CHEW, JOHN W. ANN 302 1ST DIST
CHEW, JULIA HAR 117 2ND DIST
CHEW, LAURA CAR 394 2ND DIST
CHEW, LEONARD H. PRI 093 MARLBROU
CHEW, LIGHE WAS 104 2ND DIST
CHEW, LOWMAN BAL 315 20TH WAR
CHEW, MARGARET BAL 342 7TH WARD
CHEW, MARGRET ANN 271 ANNAPOLI
CHEW, MARTHA ANN 305 1ST DIST
CHEW, MARTHA J. PRI 009 BLADENSB
CHEW, MILLY BAL 109 10TH WAR
CHEW, PERRY BAL 204 17TH WAR
CHEW, REBECCA BAL 356 3RD WARD
CHEW, RICHARD B.B. PRI 093 MARLBROU
CHEW, ROBERT B. CAL 059 3RD DIST
CHEW, ROBERT W. BAL 090 15TH WAR
CHEW, SAMUEL BAL 154 5TH WARD
CHEW, SAMUEL BAL 154 5TH WARD
CHEW, SAMUEL BAL 228 17TH WAR
CHEW, SAMUEL BAL 039 4TH WARD
CHEW, SAMUEL M. DR. BAL 135 11TH WAR
CHEW, STEPHEN HAR 029 1ST DIST
CHEW, STEPHEN BAL 075 15TH WAR
CHEW, STEPHEN-BLACK FRE 223 BUCKEYST
CHEW, THOMAS CAL 060 3RD DIST
CHEW, THOMAS ANN 302 1ST DIST
CHEW, WAS. P. HAR 159 3RD DIST
CHEW, WILLIAM BAL 073 18TH WAR
CHEW, WILLIAM H. CAR 394 2ND DIST
CHEW, WILLIAM S. HAR 156 3RD DIST
CHEWS, LOWMAN QUE 226 4TH E DI
CHEYNEY, JESSE PRI 085 QUEEN AN
CHEYNEY, SARAH PRI 084 QUEEN AN
CHICHESTER, WASHINGTON B. MGM 316 CRACKLIN
CHICKER, JOHN HAR 070 1ST DIST
CHICKET, JOHN HAR 070 1ST DIST
CHICKY, JOSEPH CEC 037 CHESAPEA
CHICN, JOHN BAL 110 1ST WARD
CHIESTLEN, H. C. BAL 282 2ND WARD
CHIEZER, JOHN F. BAL 209 6TH WARD
CHIFFELLE, MRS. H. BAL 137 11TH WAR
CHIFFELLE, THOMAS K. BAL 061 10TH WAR
CHIGATE, H.J. PRI 104 PISCATAW
CHILCOAT, ABRAM BAL 057 2ND DIST
CHILCOAT, ANN BAL 341 13TH WAR
CHILCOAT, ELIJAH BAL 057 2ND DIST
CHILCOAT, RICHARD FRE 406 JEFFERSO
CHILCOT, GOERGE BAL 428 1ST DIST
CHILCOTE, ENSOR BAL 430 1ST DIST
CHILCOTE, GEORGE BAL 418 1ST DIST
CHILCOTE, JOHN BAL 430 1ST DIST
CHILCOTE, JOHN BAL 430 1ST DIST
CHILCOTE, JOHN CAR 137 NO TWP L
CHILCOTE, RACHEL BAL 418 1ST DIST
CHILD, S.G. BAL 262 12TH WAR
CHILD, W. BAL 063 10TH WAR
CHILDERS, SARAH E. ANN 444 HOWARD D
CHILDERS, SPITSWOOD BAL 016 2ND DIST
CHILDERSON, MARGARET BAL 078 15TH WAR
CHILDES, ENOS BAL 049 4TH WARD
CHILDRIS, BENJAMIN BAL 336 1ST DIST
CHILDS, ANN BAL 001 18TH WAR
CHILDS, ANN E. BAL 245 6TH WARD
CHILDS, BRIGADEER GENERAL BAL 302 17TH WAR
CHILDS, CHARLES BAL 190 19TH WAR
CHILDS, CHARLES D. BAL 222 6TH WARD
CHILDS, CHARLOTTE BAL 387 3RD WARD
CHILDS, DANIEL BAL 421 1ST DIST
CHILDS, ELIZABETH BAL 408 14TH WAR
CHILDS, ELLEN BAL 111 1ST WARD
CHILDS, F.S. WAS 021 2ND SUBD
CHILDS, GEORGE BAL 421 1ST DIST
CHILDS, GEORGE BAL 100 10TH WAR
CHILDS, GRIFFITH ALL 090 5TH E.D.
CHILDS, HILLEARY CAL 047 3RD DIST
CHILDS, J. D. ANN 403 8TH DIST
CHILDS, JAMES R. TAL 069 EASTON T
CHILDS, JOHN PRI 112 PISCATAW
CHILDS, JOHN C. BAL 163 19TH WAR
CHILDS, JOHN D. BAL 222 6TH WARD
CHILDS, JOSEPH BAL 476 14TH WAR
CHILDS, LEVI BAL 297 1ST DIST
CHILDS, MARIA BAL 242 12TH WAR
CHILDS, MARTHA BAL 072 2ND DIST
CHILDS, MARTHA A. BAL 391 1ST DIST

CHILDS, MARY BAL 266 1ST DIST
CHILDS, MARY BAL 071 10TH WAR
CHILDS, MATILDA BAL 277 1ST DIST
CHILDS, NATHAN ANN 479 HOWARD D
CHILDS, SAMUEL BAL 135 5TH WARD
CHILDS, SARAH E. BAL 336 1ST DIST
CHILDS, SINGLETON CAL 051 3RD DIST
CHILDS, SOPHIA BAL 179 16TH WAR
CHILDS, SOPHIA ANN 403 8TH DIST
CHILDS, STEPHEN D. MGM 325 CRACKLIN
CHILDS, SUSAN ANN 297 1ST DIST
CHILDS, WILLIAM BAL 390 1ST DIST
CHILDS, WILLIAM C. ANN 401 8TH DIST
CHILDS, WILLIAM J. CHA 243 HILLTOP
CHILDS, WILLIAM P. CAL 044 3RD DIST
CHILDS, ZACHERIAN BAL 337 7TH WARD
CHILENG, JOHN C. ALL 257 CUMBERLA
CHILES, MARY BAL 189 19TH WAR
CHILEULT, JOHN* TAL 008 EASTON D
CHILLING, GEORGE BAL 191 19TH WAR
CHILLING, PAUL BAL 194 6TH WARD
CHILPANT, JOSEPH CEC 200 7TH E DI
CHILTON, CAROLINE SOM 364 BRINKLEY
CHILTON, MATHEW CAR 116 NO TWP L
CHILTON, WILLIAM F. CAR 109 NO TWP L
CHILTON, WILLIAM H. SOM 364 BRINKLEY
CHIN, ADDISON BAL 101 15TH WAR
CHIN, CHARLES BAL 045 15TH WAR
CHIN, GERARD ST 337 4TH E DI
CHIN, JOHN ST 336 4TH E DI
CHIND, LAURA BAL 025 1ST WARD
CHINE, JAMES BAL 141 5TH WARD
CHINERWORTH, ASBURY BAL 151 5TH WARD
CHINETT, ELIZABETH HAR 050 1ST DIST
CHINHNZER, AUGUSTAS * BAL 029 18TH WAR
CHINIBUTT, WILLIAM ALL 127 4TH E.D.
CHINOMELT, WILLAIM BAL 114 2ND DIST
CHINOWETH, ARTHUR BAL 263 1ST DIST
CHINOWETH, CHARLES BAL 301 1ST DIST
CHINOWETH, ELLEN BAL 298 1ST DIST
CHINOWETH, GEORGE BAL 248 1ST DIST
CHINOWETH, JOHN BAL 416 1ST DIST
CHINOWETH, JOHN H. BAL 242 1ST DIST
CHINOWETH, ROBERT BAL 374 1ST DIST
CHINOWETH, SUSAN BAL 299 1ST DIST
CHINOWETH, WILLIAM BAL 237 1ST DIST
CHINOWITH, JSOEPH BAL 237 1ST DIST
CHINOWITH, WASHINGTON HAR 110 2ND DIST
CHIONOWETH, WILLIAM BAL 414 1ST DIST
CHIPMAN, DANIEL HAR 075 BEL AIR
CHIPMAN, EMANUEL HAR 004 1ST DIST
CHIPMAN, JOHN HAR 008 1ST DIST
CHIPMAN, MARY HAR 015 1ST DIST
CHIPMAN, THOMSA H. WOR 266 BERLIN 1
CHIPPY, ELIZBAETH CAR 090 NO TWP L
CHIPPY, FRANCIS CAR 097 NO TWP L
CHIRE, BECKY BAL 071 4TH WARD
CHISEDINE, WILLIAM E. ST 316 4TH E DI
CHISELDINE, CHARLES ST 318 4TH E DI
CHISELDINE, ELIJAH ST 317 4TH E DI
CHISELDINE, KENEDLAR ST 317 4TH E DI
CHISELDINE, KENELM G. ST 316 4TH E DI
CHISELTINE, TRESA CHA 246 HILLTOP
CHISELY, DIANA BAL 246 20TH WAR
CHISENN, ANN E. BAL 242 2ND WARD
CHISHOLM, ARCHIBALD ALL 058 10TH E.D
CHISHOLM, CHARLES HAR 204 3RD DIST
CHISHOLM, HENRY BAL 031 15TH WAR
CHISHOLM, JAMES ALL 063 10TH E.D
CHISHOLM, URIAH SOM 489 SALISBUR
CHISHOLM, WILLIAM ALL 058 10TH E.D
CHISHOME, JOHN HAR 195 3RD DIST
CHISHUM, BRIDGE BAL 012 1ST WARD
CHISLEY, HENRY WAS 108 2ND DIST
CHISLY, JACOB WAS 008 WILLIAMS
CHISLY, ROBERT BAL 459 1ST DIST
CHISMAN, CHRISTINA BAL 257 2ND WARD
CHISSELL, J. BAL 138 1ST WARD
CHISSINGER, EMREL WAS 144 HAGERSTO
CHISTRE, JANE BAL 147 11TH WAR
CHISWELL, GEORGE W. MGM 410 MEDLEY 3
CHISWELL, JOHN A. MGM 409 MEDLEY 3
CHISWELL, JOSEPH N. FRE 218 BUCKEYST
CHISWELL, THOMAS F. MGM 410 MEDLEY 3
CHISWELL, WILLIAM MGM 411 MEDLEY 3
CHISWELL, WILLIAM A. MGM 410 MEDLEY 3
CHISWICK, WILLAIM BAL 032 15TH WAR
CHITTENDEN, CATHARINE BAL 109 1ST WARD
CHITTENDEN, JOHN A. CAR 368 9TH DIST
CHITTON, ELIZA BAL 460 1ST DIST
CHITTOTSON, MARGARET DOR 403 1ST DIST
CHITTY, MOSES CEC 199 7TH E DI
CHITTY, SARAH BAL 204 2ND WARD
CHIVERAL, ALEXANDER B. BAL 170 6TH WARD
CHIVERAL, HOPEWELL BAL 221 6TH WARD
CHIZLEY, HENRY BAL 168 1ST WARD
CHOANS, CHARLES BAL 025 15TH WAR
CHOAT, AMY BAL 224 1ST DIST
CHOAT, SOLOMON BAL 223 1ST DIST
CHOATE, CHARLES P. BAL 088 15TH WAR
CHOATE, EDWARD BAL 087 15TH WAR
CHOATE, ELIZABETH BAL 327 1ST DIST
CHOATE, HELAND BAL 229 1ST DIST
CHOATE, HEROD BAL 231 1ST DIST
CHOATE, RICHARD BAL 266 1ST DIST
CHOATE, SAMUEL CAR 372 9TH DIST
CHOCK, ANN M. HAR 060 1ST DIST
CHOCK, AQUILLA HAR 045 1ST DIST
CHOCK, ELIZABETH HAR 058 1ST DIST
CHOCK, GEORGE HAR 058 1ST DIST
CHOCK, HANNAH HAR 058 1ST DIST
CHOCK, HENDON HAR 059 1ST DIST
CHOCK, IGNATIUS HAR 058 1ST DIST
CHOCK, JOHN H. HAR 063 1ST DIST
CHOCK, SAMUEL HAR 009 1ST DIST
CHOCKRAN, MICHAEL BAL 461 1ST DIST
CHOFIELD, GUSTAVUS CEC 060 1ST E DI
CHOFIPELL, HORNENCE J. * BAL 311 1ST DIST
CHOOMASH, HENRY CEC 181 7TH E DI
CHOPP, BETSEY BAL 369 8TH WARD
CHORD, A. BAL 118 1ST WARD
CHORE, ANN BAL 174 19TH WAR
CHORNON, JOHN B. BAL 325 12TH WAR
CHRESMAN, RUEANN WAS 049 2ND SUBD
CHRESS, DULANA CAR 272 WESTMINS
CHRETUN, LUCY MISS- BAL 315 20TH WAR
CHRISFIELD, JOHN W. SOM 434 PRINCESS
CHRISINGER, SAMUEL WAS 126 HAGERSTO
CHRISMAN, JACOB ALL 188 9TH E.D.
CHRISMAN, JAMES BAL 195 17TH WAR

CHRISMAN, MICHAEL WAS 026 2ND SUBD
CHRISMAN, RUEANA * WAS 049 2ND SUBD
CHRISMAN, WILLIAM BAL 080 1ST WARD
CHRISMER, M. FRE 200 5TH E DI
CHRISON, SARAH BAL 196 17TH WAR
CHRISRIAL, FREDERICK BAL 458 8TH WARD
CHRISSINGER, GEORGE WAS 164 HAGERSTO
CHRISSINGER, GEORGE H. L. WAS 127 HAGERSTO
CHRIST, ADAM WAS 130 2ND DIST
CHRIST, CHRISTIAN WAS 237 CAVETOWN
CHRIST, CHRISTOPHER WAS 212 1ST DIST
CHRIST, DAVID WAS 149 HAGERSTO
CHRIST, EPHRAIM FRE 086 FREDERIC
CHRIST, FREDERICK FRE 027 FREDERIC
CHRIST, GEORGE CAR 274 7TH DIST
CHRIST, IZREAL * FRE 110 CREAGERS
CHRIST, JACOB CAR 238 UNION TO
CHRIST, JACOB BAL 288 3RD WARD
CHRIST, LYDIA CAR 264 WESTMINS
CHRIST, PETER CAR 234 UNION TO
CHRIST, PETER WAS 129 2ND DIST
CHRIST, PHILLIP BAL 264 2ND WARD
CHRIST, URIAH CAR 238 UNION TO
CHRIST, WILLIAM CAR 394 2ND DIST
CHRISTA, EMILY BAL 257 20TH WAR
CHRISTAIN, WILLMER WOR 311 2ND E DI
CHRISTE, MATILDA BAL 457 14TH WAR
CHRISTE, THOMAS* DOR 454 1ST DIST
CHRISTER, ANN ST 257 3RD E DI
CHRISTEY, CHARLES BAL 352 7TH WARD
CHRISTEY, J. M. BAL 147 1ST WARD
CHRISTFIELD, ALFRED KEN 286 3RD DIST
CHRISTFIELD, GEORGE W. KEN 286 3RD DIST
CHRISTFIELD, JAMES G. KEN 306 3RD DIST
CHRISTHELF, HENRY BAL 259 12TH WAR
CHRISTHILL, GEORGE A. BAL 360 13TH WAR
CHRISTHILL, SUSANNAH BAL 360 13TH WAR
CHRISTIAN, ELLEN WOR 322 1ST E DI
CHRISTIAN, FITE BAL 111 2ND DIST
CHRISTIAN, GEORGE E. WAS 028 2ND SUBD
CHRISTIAN, MARY BAL 187 2ND WARD
CHRISTIAN, THOMAS BAL 066 2ND DIST
CHRISTAIN,E LIZABETH BAL 291 12TH WAR
CHRISTIE, CHARELS BAL 384 13TH WAR
CHRISTIE, DAVID BAL 021 2ND DIST
CHRISTIE, JOHN ALL 157 6TH E.D.
CHRISTIE, JOHN HAR 124 2ND DIST
CHRISTIE, MARGARETT HAR 137 2ND DIST
CHRISTIE, MARY HAR 126 2ND DIST
CHRISTIE, ROBEWRT ALL 157 6TH E.D.
CHRISTMAS, ADAM CEC 018 ELKTON 3
CHRISTMAS, JAMES BAL 228 6TH WARD
CHRISTMAS, NICHOLAS BAL 227 6TH WARD
CHRISTON, DINIAH * BAL 068 18TH WAR
CHRISTON, T. BAL 138 1ST WARD
CHRISTON, WILLIAM BAL 182 11TH WAR
CHRISTOPHER, ANN SOM 495 SALISBUR
CHRISTOPHER, ELIZABETH WOR 277 BERLIN 1
CHRISTOPHER, ELIZABETH R. BAL 345 13TH WAR
CHRISTOPHER, ESTHER WOR 190 8TH E DI
CHRISTOPHER, GEORGE BAL 169 1ST WARD
CHRISTOPHER, HARRIET BAL 308 3RD WARD
CHRISTOPHER, HENRY ALL 164 6TH E.D.
CHRISTOPHER, JAMES BAL 071 2ND DIST
CHRISTOPHER, JANE BAL 177 11TH WAR
CHRISTOPHER, JOHN CAR 112 NO TWP L
CHRISTOPHER, JOSIAH BAL 257 6TH WARD
CHRISTOPHER, JULIA BAL 189 2ND WARD
CHRISTOPHER, MARGARET SOM 472 TRAPPE D
CHRISTOPHER, MARTIN BAL 466 14TH WAR
CHRISTOPHER, MARY BAL 041 9TH WARD
CHRISTOPHER, MICHAEL BAL 102 18TH WAR
CHRISTOPHER, MILTON BAL 282 7TH WARD
CHRISTOPHER, N. BAL 242 2ND WARD
CHRISTOPHER, NOBLE WOR 250 1ST CENS
CHRISTOPHER, PEGGY SOM 437 PRINCESS
CHRISTOPHER, THOMAS SOM 548 TYASKIN
CHRISTOPHER, THOMAS BAL 140 2ND DIST
CHRISTOPHER, THOMAS BAL 136 2ND DIST
CHRISTOPHER, WILLIAM BAL 064 2ND DIST
CHRISTOPHER, WILLIAM CAR 136 NO TWP L
CHRISTOPHER, WILLIAM BAL 345 13TH WAR
CHRISTOPHER, WILLIAM L. CAR 151 NO TWP L
CHRISTPHOR, JOSEPH BAL 027 18TH WAR
CHRISTY, CHARLES CEC 027 CHESAPEA
CHRISTY, CHARLES HAR 123 2ND DIST
CHRISTY, DAVID BAL 025 2ND DIST
CHRISTY, GABRIEL HAR 170 3RD DIST
CHRISTY, HENRY M. BAL 263 20TH WAR
CHRISTY, JAMES HAR 101 2ND DIST
CHRISTY, JOHN CEC 216 7TH E DI
CHRISTY, JOSEPH BAL 125 1ST WARD
CHRISTY, MARIA BAL 353 3RD WARD
CHRISTY, MARTIN HAR 088 2ND DIST
CHRISTY, MICHAEL BAL 151 19TH WAR
CHRISTY, RACHEL BAL 080 4TH WARD
CHRISTY, ROBERT CEC 103 4TH E DI
CHRISTY, ROBERT PRI 030 VANSVILL
CHROMPER, CATHEINE ALL 231 CUMBERLA
CHRYSTAL, JOHN BAL 217 5TH WARD
CHRYSTOM, LISTER BAL 472 14TH WAR
CHSE, D.A. BAL 115 1ST WARD
CHUBB, EMILY W. BAL 108 10TH WAR
CHUBB, JOHN PRI 060 NOTTINGH
CHUCK, LEVI * BAL 296 20TH WAR
CHUCK, LORRAINE * BAL 297 20TH WAR
CHUM, DAVID PRI 115 PISCATAW
CHUNCK, ELIZABETH A. BAL 029 2ND DIST
CHUNN, HENRY ST 320 4TH E DI
CHUNN, JULIANN ST 321 4TH E DI
CHUNN, MARK B. ST 327 4TH E DI
CHUNY, JAMES W. ALL 218 CUMBERLA
CHURCH, A. BAL 265 20TH WAR
CHURCH, ABRAHAM DOR 370 3RD DIVI
CHURCH, ANN BAL 342 13TH WAR
CHURCH, CHARLOTTE BAL 177 11TH WAR
CHURCH, EDWARD SOM 530 QUANTICO
CHURCH, EDWARD J. BAL 234 6TH WARD
CHURCH, EDWARD J. BAL 186 6TH WARD
CHURCH, ELEAZER F. BAL 201 6TH WARD
CHURCH, FANNY SOM 402 BRINKLEY
CHURCH, ISRAEL WAS 070 2ND SUBD
CHURCH, JAMES BAL 401 3RD WARD
CHURCH, JAMES SOM 404 BRINKLEY
CHURCH, JAMES* BAL 344 3RD WARD
CHURCH, JANE BAL 187 6TH WARD
CHURCH, JOHN BAL 377 3RD WARD
CHURCH, JOHN SOM 529 QUANTICO
CHURCH, MARY QUE 180 2ND E DI
CHURCH, RICHARD BAL 236 17TH WAR

CHURCH, ROYALL BAL 342 13TH WAR
CHURCH, SAMUEL T. ANN 338 3RD DIST
CHURCH, SAMUEL T. BAL 106 10TH WAR
CHURCH, THOMAS BAL 186 6TH WARD
CHURCH, WILLIAM BAL 208 6TH WARD
CHURCHILL, EMELINE CHA 234 HILLTOP
CHURCHMAN, CAVID CEC 210 7TH E DI
CHURCHMAN, FRANCES BAL 054 15TH WAR
CHURCHMAN, MASSY CEC 131 6TH E DI
CHURCHMAN, REBECCA CEC 204 6TH E DI
CHURCHWELL, SMAUEL BAL 171 1ST WARD
CHURCHWELL, H.E. BAL 141 1ST WARD
CHURCHWILL, H. C. BAL 151 1ST WARD
CHURRALL, JAMES ST 297 2ND E DI
CHURRICKS, PETER WOR 313 2ND E DI
CHURSTOPHER, EDWARD V. DOR 308 1ST DIST
CHURSTOPHER, LEVIN* DOR 458 1ST DIST
CHUSKEN, WILLIAM ANN 499 HOWARD D
CHUSTEL, JOSEPHINE BAL 031 1ST WARD
CHUSTY, JOHN * BAL 145 2ND DIST
CHUSTY, PRESCILLA BAL 325 12TH WAR
CIAMPI, ANTHONY FRE 067 FREDERIC
CIBISON, MAGNESS BAL 472 14TH WAR
CICEL, IGNATIUS ST 285 2ND E DI
CIGLER, MARGARETT BAL 002 4TH WARD
CILL, EDWARD KEN 303 3RD DIST
CILLY, JOEL BAL 184 2ND WARD
CILMORE, MATILDA CEC 114 3RD E DI
CIMBELL, MATTHEW CEC 216 7TH E DI
CIMMERLY, JOHN WAS 133 2ND DIST
CINCANNON, MICHAEL BAL 291 20TH WAR
CINCK, LEWIS BAL 116 1ST WARD
CINCLEN, MARTIN BAL 133 11TH WAR
CINEGARD, JAMES BAL 165 19TH WAR
CINNAMOND, GEORGE R. BAL 065 10TH WAR
CINNAMOND, MOORHEAD BAL 350 13TH WAR
CINNINYS, SARAH BAL 139 11TH WAR
CIRAM, WILLIAM H. * BAL 294 20TH WAR
CIRCLE, DAVID CAR 262 3RD DIST
CIRCLE, LYDIA CAR 262 3RD DIST
CIRE, SUSAN BAL 223 12TH WAR
CIREL, WILLIAM S. TAL 082 ST MICHA
CIRK, ISAAC KEN 225 2ND DIST
CIRK, JOSHUA KEN 225 2ND DIST
CIRK, NOAH KEN 225 2ND DIST
CIRLCE, JACOB CAR 409 2ND DIST
CIROS, THOMAS BAL 091 18TH WAR
CIRSING, CAROLINE BAL 458 1ST DIST
CIRTIS, LORETTA HAR 183 3RD DIST
CIRTLAND, WILLIAM TAL 012 EASTON D
CIRTON, MARSH BAL 226 19TH WAR
CIRTS, GEORGE BAL 201 19TH WAR
CISCER, GEORGE* KEN 281 3RD DIST
CISSEL, BENJAMIN G. ANN 479 HOWARD D
CISSEL, ISABEL MGM 351 BERRYS D
CISSEL, JAMES MGM 349 BERRYS D
CISSEL, PHILIP ANN 480 HOWARD D
CISSEL, RICHARD MGM 369 BERRYS D
CISSEL, SAMUEL ANN 479 HOWARD D
CISSEL, ZEPHANIAH ANN 483 HOWARD D
CISSELL, JEREMIAH ST 311 1ST E DI
CISSELL, JOHN B. ST 286 2ND E DI
CISTER, JOHN WAS 137 2ND DIST
CITY, BILL HAR 075 BEL AIR
CITY, MARGARETT HAR 075 BEL AIR
CITY, MILK HAR 076 BEL AIR
CITY, ROBERT HAR 079 2ND DIST
CITY, THOMAS HAR 078 2ND DIST
CIVALEY, CATHERINE PRI 002 BLADENSB
CIVEL, HENRY TAL 068 EASTON T
CK CAR 114 NO TWP L
CLABAUGH, E.A. ALL 263 CUMBERLA
CLABAUGH, ELIZABETH CAR 315 1ST DIST
CLABAUGH, HANSON CAR 326 1ST DIST
CLABAUGH, JAEMS CAR 326 1ST DIST
CLABAUGH, JAMES CAR 306 1ST DIST
CLABAUGH, JOHN CAR 327 1ST DIST
CLABAUGH, JONES FRE 059 FREDERIC
CLABAUGH, MARY WAS 243 CAVETOWN
CLABAUGH, MARY E. WAS 162 2ND DIST
CLABAUGH, NORMAN B. FRE 070 FREDERIC
CLABAUGH, NULL FRE 173 5TH E DI
CLABAUGH, SARAH CAR 301 1ST DIST
CLABAUGH, THOMAS FRE 176 5TH E DI
CLABAUGH, THOMAS SR. FRE 177 5TH E DI
CLABAUGH, TILLY E. CAR 306 1ST DIST
CLABAUGH, WILLIAM FRE 177 5TH E DI
CLABAUGH, N.N. FRE 222 BUCKEYST
CLABORNE, CAROLINE BAL 103 5TH WARD
CLABOUGH, JOHN CAR 302 1ST DIST
CLABOUGH, JOHN CAR 240 TANEYTOW
CLACKNER, GEANVILLE F. BAL 420 3RD WARD
CLACKNER, JAMES BAL 046 2ND DIST
CLACKNER, JOSEPH BAL 162 6TH WARD
CLACKNER, MATTHEW BAL 162 6TH WARD
CLADER, JOSEPH BAL 027 1ST WARD
CLADWELL, EDWARD CAR 380 2ND DIST
CLADWELL, WILLIAM Q. BAL 452 14TH WAR
CLAFFY, PAT BAL 460 1ST DIST
CLAFIELD, WINFIELD CEC 031 CHESAPEA
CLAGET, HEZEKIAH WAS 031 2ND SUBD
CLAGET, MARY BAL 039 4TH WARD
CLAGETE, JOHN W. MGM 385 ROCKERLE
CLAGETE, ORATIO MGM 385 ROCKERLE
CLAGETT, ALFRED WAS 084 2ND SUBD
CLAGETT, BETTIE ANN 294 1ST DIST
CLAGETT, CHARLES PRI 076 MARLBROU
CLAGETT, DAN * BAL 105 2ND DIST
CLAGETT, ELIZA B. BAL 097 10TH WAR
CLAGETT, ELIZABETH MGM 397 ROCKERLE
CLAGETT, ELIZABETH BAL 394 14TH WAR
CLAGETT, ELIZABETH CHA 288 BOJANTOW
CLAGETT, GEORGE T. PRI 113 PISCATAW
CLAGETT, GRAFTON FRE 396 PETERSVI
CLAGETT, HENRY BAL 067 10TH WAR
CLAGETT, HORATIO WAS 085 2ND SUBD
CLAGETT, J. W. ANN 326 2ND DIST
CLAGETT, JAME SH. MGM 401 ROCKERLE
CLAGETT, JAMES MGM 381 ROCKERLE
CLAGETT, JAMES H. WAS 086 2ND SUBD
CLAGETT, JANE M. MGM 400 ROCKERLE
CLAGETT, JANE T. MGM 342 CLARKSBU
CLAGETT, JOHN MGM 346 CLARKSBU
CLAGETT, JOHN H. MGM 402 ROCKERLE
CLAGETT, JOHN H. PRI 114 PISCATAW
CLAGETT, JOSEPH B. MGM 402 ROCKERLE
CLAGETT, LUCY MGM 328 CRACKLIN
CLAGETT, MARGARET MGM 327 CRACKLIN
CLAGETT, MARTHA FRE 066 FREDERIC
CLAGETT, MATILDA WAS 085 2ND SUBD

CLAGETT, MISS M. FRE 199 5TH E DI
CLAGETT, NATHANIEL R. MGM 397 ROCKERLE
CLAGETT, RICHARD H. PRI 077 MARLBROU
CLAGETT, ROBERT FRE 396 PETERSVI
CLAGETT, ROBERT A. PRI 076 MARLBROU
CLAGETT, SALLY D. FRE 066 FREDERIC
CLAGETT, SAMUEL WAS 088 2ND SUBD
CLAGETT, SAMUEL WAS 194 1ST DIST
CLAGETT, SAMUEL ANN 295 1ST DIST
CLAGETT, SAMUEL A. ANN 326 2ND DIST
CLAGETT, SARAH A. MGM 424 MEDLEY 3
CLAGETT, SARAH E. MGM 402 ROCKERLE
CLAGETT, SOPHIA FRE 386 PETERSVI
CLAGETT, THOMAS MGM 396 ROCKERLE
CLAGETT, THOMAS BAL 352 3RD WARD
CLAGETT, THOMAS PRI 091 MARLBROU
CLAGETT, WILLIAM BAL 026 4TH WARD
CLAGETT, WILLIAM BAL 005 4TH WARD
CLAGETT, WILLIAM D. PRI 079 QUEEN AN
CLAGETT, WILLIAM O. M. MGM 345 CLARKSBU
CLAGETT, Z.G. WAS 133 HAGERSTO
CLAGETTT, HENRY MGM 322 CRACKLIN
CLAGGELL, THOMAS FRE 271 NEW MARK
CLAGGETT, MARY A. ANN 421 HOWARD D
CLAGGETT, NATHAN FRE 077 FREDERIC
CLAGGETT, THOMAS J. BAL 132 5TH WARD
CLAGGETT, WILLIAM H. CHA 256 MIDDLETO
CLAGILT, THOMAS D. CHA 256 MIDDLETO
CLAGITT, SAMUEL WAS 021 2ND SUBD
CLAGNER, CONRAD BAL 074 1ST WARD
CLAHAN, LAWRENCE BAL 446 14TH WAR
CLAIBORNE, BOBENET MISS- BAL 315 20TH WAR
CLAIBORNE, CAROLINE BAL 250 12TH WAR
CLAID, CHARLES BAL 123 1ST WARD
CLAIM, ANTON BAL 105 1ST WARD
CLAINA, ELIJAH FRE 424 8TH E DI
CLAIR, ELLEN S. BAL 388 13TH WAR
CLAIR, NICHOLAS S. ALL 249 CUMBERLA
CLAISON, OCELL BAL 266 2ND WARD
CLALAND, MARY BAL 184 2ND WARD
CLAM, ASBURY BAL 085 4TH WARD
CLAMAN, FREDERICK BAL 244 12TH WAR
CLAMAN, PETER WAS 155 2ND DIST
CLAMPETT, ELIAS BAL 145 5TH WARD
CLANAN, BRIDGETY * BAL 275 1ST DIST
CLANCY, PATRICK BAL 012 2ND DIST
CLANDENY, THOMAS CAR 081 NO TWP L
CLANDER, DENNIS JR. ANN 270 ANNAPOLI
CLANEL, PETER WOR 337 1ST E DI
CLANEY, EDWARD BAL 051 1ST WARD
CLANNAHAN, ELIZABETH QUE 187 3RD E DI
CLANNAHAN, JOHN QUE 251 5TH E DI
CLANNAHAN, JOHN T. TAL 014 EASTON D
CLANSY, JOHN BAL 012 2ND DIST
CLANTICE, CATHARINE BAL 261 20TH WAR
CLANTICE, FRANCIS * BAL 217 6TH WARD
CLANTICE, GEORGE * BAL 303 20TH WAR
CLANTICE, HENRY BAL 389 8TH WARD
CLANTICE, JOHN BAL 389 8TH WARD
CLANTON, J. REV. BAL 330 13TH WAR
CLANTZ, SARAH FRE 296 WOODSBOR
CLANUG, SARAH E. BAL 207 2ND WARD
CLAPAFURGER, ADAM BAL 036 1ST WARD
CLAPER, CATHARINE WAS 084 2ND SUBD
CLAPER, JOHN WAS 083 2ND SUBD
CLAPER, JOHN SR. WAS 083 2ND SUBD
CLAPER, JOSEPH WAS 074 2ND SUBD
CLAPER, JOSHUA WAS 082 2ND SUBD
CLAPER, WILLIAM WAS 083 2ND SUBD
CLAPHAN, ANN C. BAL 211 11TH WAR
CLAPP, GEORGE BAL 100 5TH WARD
CLAPP, LAURA B. BAL 102 5TH WARD
CLAPP, MARY BAL 201 11TH WAR
CLAPP, MRS. BAL 093 5TH WARD
CLAPPER, AMELIA BAL 325 12TH WAR
CLAPPER, J. BAL 273 12TH WAR
CLAPPER, LETITIA BAL 417 3RD WARD
CLAPPER, WILLIAM BAL 170 1ST WARD
CLAPPLER, HARMAN WAS 075 2ND SUBD
CLAPSADDLE, MICHAEL CAR 240 TANEYTOW
CLAPSLANDER, FRANKLIN BAL 068 18TH WAR
CLAPTER, JOSEPH BAL 118 2ND DIST
CLARA, MARY BAL 213 11TH WAR
CLARADY, JOHN BAL 244 17TH WAR
CLARANCE, BRIDGET BAL 335 7TH WARD
CLARANCE, MICHAEL BAL 158 11TH WAR
CLARCK, CAROLINE BAL 271 2ND WARD
CLARCK, CHARLES BAL 106 1ST WARD
CLARCK, CONILY BAL 258 2ND WARD
CLARCK, HESTER A. BAL 080 1ST WARD
CLARCK, J. BAL 117 1ST WARD
CLARCK, JAEMS BAL 271 2ND WARD
CLARCK, JAMES A. BAL 016 1ST WARD
CLARCK, JOHN BAL 013 1ST WARD
CLARCK, JOHN BAL 055 1ST WARD
CLARCK, JOHN BAL 034 1ST WARD
CLARCK, JOHN BAL 170 1ST WARD
CLARCK, JOHN S. BAL 062 1ST WARD
CLARCK, MARGARET BAL 108 1ST WARD
CLARCK, MARTIN BAL 055 1ST WARD
CLARCK, ROSE-BLACK BAL 222 2ND WARD
CLARCK, WILLIAM BAL 128 1ST WARD
CLARCK, WILLIAM F. BAL 276 2ND WARD
CLARCK, ZACK BAL 011 1ST WARD
CLARE, CHARLOTTE BAL 219 17TH WAR
CLARE, ELIZABETH M. CAL 036 2ND DIST
CLARE, GEORGE BAL 334 7TH WARD
CLARE, GUSTAVIS B. BAL 082 18TH WAR
CLARE, ISAAC BAL 076 15TH WAR
CLARE, MARY BAL 071 2ND DIST
CLARE, MARY-BLACK ST 317 4TH E DI
CLARE, THOMAS BAL 155 1ST WARD
CLARE, THOMAS J. BAL 082 18TH WAR
CLAREAGE, JAMES* DOR 370 3RD DIVI
CLAREAGE, SARRAH* DOR 357 3RD DIVI
CLAREL, JOSHUA WOR 292 9TH E DI
CLARELY, MARY BAL 321 20TH WAR
CLARETON, JOEL BAL 104 5TH WARD
CLAREY, JESSE T. FRE 424 8TH E DI
CLARIAGE, WILLIAM* DOR 367 3RD DIVI
CLARIDGE, ASH A. BAL 244 17TH WAR
CLARIDGE, HENRY BAL 145 1ST WARD
CLARIDGE, JAMES DOR 399 1ST DIST
CLARIDGE, JAMES* DOR 370 3RD DIVI
CLARIDGE, JOHN H. BAL 298 3RD WARD
CLARIDGE, LLOYD BAL 036 15TH WAR
CLARIDGE, MARY DOR 357 3RD DIVI
CLARIDGE, SARRAH* DOR 357 3RD DIVI
CLARIDGE, W. H. DOR 393 1ST DIST
CLARIDGE, WILLIAM* DOR 367 3RD DIVI

CLARINCER, THOMAS M. BAL 168 11TH WAR
CLARINS, EMILY BAL 010 EASTERN
CLARK, AARON FRE 442 8TH E DI
CLARK, ABLE TAL 054 EASTON D
CLARK, ABRAHAM ANN 340 3RD DIST
CLARK, ABREHAM CEC 023 ELKTON 3
CLARK, ADAM CEC 122 4TH E DI
CLARK, AGNES MGM 357 BERRYS D
CLARK, ALBERT H. BAL 392 1ST DIST
CLARK, ALEXANDER CAR 073 NO TWP L
CLARK, ALFRED ANN 343 3RD DIST
CLARK, AMBROSE BAL 126 1ST WARD
CLARK, AMEY-MULATTO CAR 165 NO TWP L
CLARK, AMOS ANN 391 4TH DIST
CLARK, AMRBSOE BAL 120 1ST WARD
CLARK, ANDREW BAL 279 1ST DIST
CLARK, ANGELIN BAL 152 11TH WAR
CLARK, ANGELINA BAL 404 3RD WARD
CLARK, ANN ALL 214 CUMBERLA
CLARK, ANN ANN 447 HOWARD D
CLARK, ANN ALL 217 CUMBERLA
CLARK, ANN BAL 349 1ST DIST
CLARK, ANN MGM 357 BERRYS D
CLARK, ANN BAL 334 13TH WAR
CLARK, ANN KEN 281 3RD DIST
CLARK, ANNA WAS 162 HAGERSTO
CLARK, ANNA BAL 056 18TH WAR
CLARK, ASBURY HAR 101 2ND DIST
CLARK, ASBURY HAR 099 2ND DIST
CLARK, AUGUSTUS BAL 116 2ND DIST
CLARK, BARNET HAR 108 2ND DIST
CLARK, BECCA BAL 257 1ST DIST
CLARK, BENJAMIN F. BAL 077 18TH WAR
CLARK, BENJAMIN J. BAL 339 7TH WARD
CLARK, BETSEY BAL 107 18TH WAR
CLARK, BETTY A. CHA 250 MIDDLETO
CLARK, BIDDY BAL 123 11TH WAR
CLARK, BRIDGET BAL 204 11TH WAR
CLARK, BRIDGET BAL 099 1ST WARD
CLARK, BRIDGETT BAL 034 4TH WARD
CLARK, BRIDGETT BAL 019 4TH WARD
CLARK, CAIN M. BAL 020 15TH WAR
CLARK, CALEB ANN 433 HOWARD D
CLARK, CAROLINE BAL 240 1ST DIST
CLARK, CAROLINE * BAL 315 1ST DIST
CLARK, CATHARIEN BAL 353 7TH WARD
CLARK, CATHARINE BAL 108 2ND DIST
CLARK, CATHARINE ALL 180 8TH E.D.
CLARK, CATHARINE WAS 169 FUNKSTOW
CLARK, CATHERINE M. BAL 268 7TH WARD
CLARK, CATHERINE-BLACK FRE 021 FREDERIC
CLARK, CHALRES BAL 088 18TH WAR
CLARK, CHARITY HAR 092 2ND DIST
CLARK, CHARITY HAR 092 2ND DIST
CLARK, CHARLES HAR 101 2ND DIST
CLARK, CHARLES BAL 036 18TH WAR
CLARK, CHARLES CAR 117 NO TWP L
CLARK, CHARLES BAL 135 1ST WARD
CLARK, CHARLES ALL 172 7TH E.D.
CLARK, CHARLES BAL 121 1ST WARD
CLARK, CHARLES WOR 279 BERLIN 1
CLARK, CHARLES H. TAL 076 EASTON T
CLARK, CHARLES H. BAL 279 20TH WAR
CLARK, CHARLOTT BAL 026 4TH WARD
CLARK, CHARLOTTE BAL 475 14TH WAR
CLARK, CHARLOTTE-BLACK QUE 171 2ND E DI
CLARK, CHRISTOPHER BAL 010 1ST WARD
CLARK, CLARANCE BAL 030 18TH WAR
CLARK, CLEMET S.* TAL 016 EASTON D
CLARK, CLOWDSBERRY H. TAL 001 EASTON D
CLARK, DANIEL PRI 085 QUEEN AN
CLARK, DANIEL BAL 104 18TH WAR
CLARK, DANIEL ALL 132 4TH E.D.
CLARK, DANIEL ANN 435 HOWARD D
CLARK, DANIEL ANN 340 3RD DIST
CLARK, DANIEL H. BAL 236 6TH WARD
CLARK, DANIEL H. BAL 296 17TH WAR
CLARK, DAVID ANN 494 HOWARD D
CLARK, DAVID WAS 287 1ST DIST
CLARK, DENNIS ALL 139 6TH E.D.
CLARK, DENWOOD DOR 410 1ST DIST
CLARK, EDMUND MGM 356 BERRYS D
CLARK, EDWARD-BLACK QUE 167 2ND E DI
CLARK, EDWIN CEC 197 7TH E DI
CLARK, ELINOR PRI 072 MARLBROU
CLARK, ELISA BAL 014 18TH WAR
CLARK, ELISABETH ANN 349 3RD DIST
CLARK, ELIZA ANN 268 ANNAPOLI
CLARK, ELIZABETH ALL 132 4TH E.D.
CLARK, ELIZABETH ANN 422 HOWARD D
CLARK, ELIZABETH BAL 187 2ND WARD
CLARK, ELIZABETH BAL 102 1ST WARD
CLARK, ELIZABETH BAL 363 3RD WARD
CLARK, ELIZABETH BAL 298 7TH WARD
CLARK, ELIZABETH HAR 109 2ND DIST
CLARK, ELIZABETH MGM 390 ROCKERLE
CLARK, ELIZABETH BAL 388 13TH WAR
CLARK, ELIZABETH BAL 467 14TH WAR
CLARK, ELIZABETH CEC 045 1ST E DI
CLARK, ELIZABETH MGM 337 CRACKLIN
CLARK, ELIZABETH KEN 216 2ND DIST
CLARK, ELIZABETH TAL 070 EASTON T
CLARK, ELIZABETH A.L. QUE 187 3RD E DI
CLARK, ELLEN WAS 114 2ND DIST
CLARK, ELLEN BAL 366 3RD WARD
CLARK, ELLEN BAL 339 3RD WARD
CLARK, ELLY BAL 280 17TH WAR
CLARK, EMILINE CAR 136 NO TWP L
CLARK, EMILY ALL 212 CUMBERLA
CLARK, FRANCES CEC 207 7TH E DI
CLARK, FRANCIS HAR 099 2ND DIST
CLARK, FRANCIS PRI 081 QUEEN AN
CLARK, FREEBORN HAR 187 3RD DIST
CLARK, GARRET ALL 007 3RD E.D.
CLARK, GEORGE ALL 220 CUMBERLA
CLARK, GEORGE ALL 218 CUMBERLA
CLARK, GEORGE CAR 154 NO TWP L
CLARK, GEORGE WAS 175 1ST DIST
CLARK, GEORGE WAS 136 2ND DIST
CLARK, GEORGE W. FRE 288 WOODSBOR
CLARK, GEORGE W. BAL 073 2ND DIST
CLARK, GEROGE SOM 424 PRINCESS
CLARK, GILES BAL 126 1ST WARD
CLARK, GUNY BAL 249 2ND WARD
CLARK, HACKY V. BAL 038 18TH WAR
CLARK, HAGAR HAR 123 2ND DIST
CLARK, HANNAH HAR 035 1ST DIST
CLARK, HANNAH BAL 174 11TH WAR
CLARK, HARIETT* BAL 019 4TH WARD
CLARK, HARMAN BAL 078 2ND DIST

CLARK, HARRIET ANN 352 3RD DIST
CLARK, HARRIET BAL 269 12TH WAR
CLARK, HELLEN ANN 303 1ST DIST
CLARK, HENRIETTA BAL 228 17TH WAR
CLARK, HENRY MGM 357 BERRYS D
CLARK, HENRY HAR 115 2ND DIST
CLARK, HENRY HAR 116 2ND DIST
CLARK, HENRY HAR 056 1ST DIST
CLARK, HENRY BAL 373 1ST DIST
CLARK, HENRY BAL 225 1ST DIST
CLARK, HENRY BAL 156 1ST WARD
CLARK, HENRY WOR 272 BERLIN 1
CLARK, HENRY-BLACK QUE 163 2ND E DI
CLARK, HENRY-BLACK FRE 038 FREDERIC
CLARK, HEROD BAL 151 16TH WAR
CLARK, HEZEKIAH MGM 350 BERRYS D
CLARK, IDA D. BAL 341 7TH WARD
CLARK, IRA QUE 170 2ND E DI
CLARK, ISAAC ALL 210 CUMBERLA
CLARK, ISAAC ANN 386 4TH DIST
CLARK, ISAAC HAR 033 1ST DIST
CLARK, ISAAC FRE 034 FREDERIC
CLARK, ISAAC * BAL 315 1ST DIST
CLARK, J. BAL 147 1ST WARD
CLARK, JACOB CEC 061 1ST E DI
CLARK, JAMES CEC 070 5TH E DI
CLARK, JAMES CEC 181 7TH E DI
CLARK, JAMES BAL 308 20TH WAR
CLARK, JAMES BAL 338 13TH WAR
CLARK, JAMES CEC 041 CHESAPEA
CLARK, JAMES DOR 421 1ST DIST
CLARK, JAMES BAL 106 5TH WARD
CLARK, JAMES ALL 214 CUMBERLA
CLARK, JAMES ALL 134 4TH E.D.
CLARK, JAMES BAL 015 15TH WAR
CLARK, JAMES BAL 022 1ST WARD
CLARK, JAMES BAL 001 1ST WARD
CLARK, JAMES BAL 187 5TH DIST
CLARK, JAMES ANN 450 HOWARD D
CLARK, JAMES ANN 475 HOWARD D
CLARK, JAMES BAL 139 1ST WARD
CLARK, JAMES BAL 136 1ST WARD
CLARK, JAMES QUE 179 2ND E DI
CLARK, JAMES SOM 446 DAMES QU
CLARK, JAMES PRI 081 QUEEN AN
CLARK, JAMES G. BAL 021 4TH WARD
CLARK, JAMES M. ANN 347 3RD DIST
CLARK, JAMES T. CAR 071 NO TWP L
CLARK, JAMS KEN 258 1ST DIST
CLARK, JANE BAL 357 13TH WAR
CLARK, JANE HAR 101 2ND DIST
CLARK, JANE ANN 444 HOWARD D
CLARK, JANE BAL 360 8TH WARD
CLARK, JEMINA BAL 351 1ST DIST
CLARK, JESSE QUE 183 3RD E DI
CLARK, JESTER BAL 020 18TH WAR
CLARK, JETSCN PRI 086 QUEEN AN
CLARK, JIM-BLACK QUE 193 3RD E DI
CLARK, JOHANNA FRE 241 NEW MARK
CLARK, JOHN HAR 038 1ST DIST
CLARK, JOHN HAR 037 1ST DIST
CLARK, JOHN FRE 064 FREDERIC
CLARK, JOHN BAL 443 14TH WAR
CLARK, JOHN CAR 118 NO TWP L
CLARK, JOHN BAL 389 13TH WAR
CLARK, JOHN CEC 030 CHESAPEA
CLARK, JOHN BAL 414 3RD WARD
CLARK, JOHN BAL 302 20TH WAR
CLARK, JOHN HAR 121 2ND DIST
CLARK, JOHN WAS 216 1ST DIST
CLARK, JOHN WAS 026 2ND SUBD
CLARK, JOHN WAS 106 2ND DIST
CLARK, JOHN TAL 090 ST MICHA
CLARK, JOHN TAL 046 EASTON T
CLARK, JOHN WOR 339 1ST E DI
CLARK, JOHN BAL 093 5TH WARD
CLARK, JOHN BAL 447 1ST DIST
CLARK, JOHN BAL 355 8TH WARD
CLARK, JOHN BAL 397 8TH WARD
CLARK, JOHN ANN 340 3RD DIST
CLARK, JOHN BAL 137 2ND DIST
CLARK, JOHN ALL 217 CUMBERLA
CLARK, JOHN ALL 218 CUMBERLA
CLARK, JOHN ALL 233 CUMBERLA
CLARK, JOHN BAL 022 1ST WARD
CLARK, JOHN BAL 255 1ST DIST
CLARK, JOHN BAL 358 3RD WARD
CLARK, JOHN BAL 016 15TH WAR
CLARK, JOHN BAL 002 15TH WAR
CLARK, JOHN BAL 253 12TH WAR
CLARK, JOHN BAL 183 11TH WAR
CLARK, JOHN BAL 174 1ST WARD
CLARK, JOHN BAL 153 5TH WARD
CLARK, JOHN BAL 150 5TH WARD
CLARK, JOHN BAL 199 17TH WAR
CLARK, JOHN BAL 107 10TH WAR
CLARK, JOHN BAL 188 16TH WAR
CLARK, JOHN BAL 275 12TH WAR
CLARK, JOHN A. BAL 222 6TH WARD
CLARK, JOHN D. BAL 027 18TH WAR
CLARK, JOHN G. CEC 082 CHARLEST
CLARK, JOHN H. ALL 246 CUMBERLA
CLARK, JOHN H. BAL 393 3RD WARD
CLARK, JOHN M. BAL 142 16TH WAR
CLARK, JOHN P. BAL 414 3RD WARD
CLARK, JOHN W. BAL 038 18TH WAR
CLARK, JOHN W. ANN 422 HOWARD D
CLARK, JOHN W. ANN 460 HOWARD D
CLARK, JOHNATHAN BAL 247 17TH WAR
CLARK, JOSEPH BAL 090 18TH WAR
CLARK, JOSEPH BAL 359 8TH WARD
CLARK, JOSEPH WAS 145 2ND DIST
CLARK, JOSEPH H. BAL 356 13TH WAR
CLARK, JOSEPH J. ANN 383 4TH DIST
CLARK, JOSEPH-BLACK CAR 068 NO TWP L
CLARK, JOSEPHINE BAL 444 14TH WAR
CLARK, JOSEPHINE BAL 018 18TH WAR
CLARK, JOSHUA KEN 226 2ND DIST
CLARK, JOSHUA T. PRI 087 QUEEN AN
CLARK, JOSHUA T. PRI 087 QUEEN AN
CLARK, JOSIAH ANN 383 4TH DIST
CLARK, JOSIAH BAL 101 15TH WAR
CLARK, JULIA BAL 406 3RD WARD
CLARK, JULIA BAL 392 14TH WAR
CLARK, JULIA CAR 287 7TH DIST
CLARK, KANE TAL 043 EASTON D
CLARK, LARKIN CAR 285 7TH DIST
CLARK, LAWRENCE BAL 160 11TH WAR
CLARK, LAWSCN ANN 379 4TH DIST
CLARK, LAWSON A. PRI 058 NOTTINGH
CLARK, LEAH TAL 075 EASTON T
CLARK, LESTER BAL 256 6TH WARD
CLARK, LESTER BAL 174 2ND DIST
CLARK, LEVI ALL 132 4TH E.D.
CLARK, LEVI BAL 355 1ST DIST
CLARK, LEVI BAL 352 1ST DIST
CLARK, LEVI DOR 402 1ST DIST
CLARK, LEVI DOR 401 1ST DIST
CLARK, LEWIS BAL 366 13TH WAR
CLARK, LEWIS BAL 169 1ST WARD
CLARK, LEWIS B. BAL 136 5TH WARD
CLARK, LLOYD ALL 116 5TH E.D.
CLARK, LUCY BAL 317 3RD WARD
CLARK, MARGARET BAL 137 5TH WARD
CLARK, MARGARET BAL 019 15TH WAR
CLARK, MARGARET WAS 194 1ST DIST
CLARK, MARGARET A. BAL 317 3RD WARD
CLARK, MARGARET A. BAL 416 3RD WARD
CLARK, MARGARET C. BAL 169 16TH WAR
CLARK, MARIA BAL 304 7TH WARD
CLARK, MARIA ANN 461 HOWARD D
CLARK, MARIA MGM 354 BERRYS D
CLARK, MARIAN QUE 135 1ST E DI
CLARK, MARTHA CEC 072 5TH E DI
CLARK, MARTHA A. CAR 167 NO TWP L
CLARK, MARTIN BAL 318 3RD WARD
CLARK, MARTIN BAL 363 13TH WAR
CLARK, MARTIN BAL 441 1ST DIST
CLARK, MARTIN BAL 400 1ST DIST
CLARK, MARY BAL 003 EASTERN
CLARK, MARY BAL 046 2ND DIST
CLARK, MARY BAL 299 7TH WARD
CLARK, MARY BAL 071 10TH WAR
CLARK, MARY BAL 181 11TH WAR
CLARK, MARY ANN 369 4TH DIST
CLARK, MARY BAL 003 1ST WARD
CLARK, MARY CEC 018 ELKTON 3
CLARK, MARY BAL 194 19TH WAR
CLARK, MARY BAL 048 18TH WAR
CLARK, MARY BAL 114 11TH WAR
CLARK, MARY BAL 466 14TH WAR
CLARK, MARY CAR 100 NO TWP L
CLARK, MARY QUE 170 2ND E DI
CLARK, MARY A. BAL 446 14TH WAR
CLARK, MARY A. BAL 075 18TH WAR
CLARK, MARY A. CEC 174 6TH E DI
CLARK, MARY A. QUE 135 1ST E DI
CLARK, MARY C. ALL 134 4TH E.D.
CLARK, MARY E. BAL 403 3RD WARD
CLARK, MARY J. BAL 003 1ST WARD
CLARK, MATHEW BAL 014 18TH WAR
CLARK, MATILDA CEC 025 ELKTON 3
CLARK, MATILDA BAL 016 4TH WARD
CLARK, MATTHEW HAR 056 1ST DIST
CLARK, MATTHEW BAL 001 15TH WAR
CLARK, MATTHEW WAS 168 FUNKSTOW
CLARK, MICHAEL FRE 386 PETERSVI
CLARK, MILTON BAL 121 1ST WARD
CLARK, MOSES MGM 317 CRACKLIN
CLARK, N. H. KEN 218 2ND DIST
CLARK, NATHAN CAR 213 5TH DIST
CLARK, NATHAN-BLACK CAR 071 NO TWP L
CLARK, NEHEMIAH FRE 016 FREDERIC
CLARK, NEHEMIAH H. KEN 218 2ND DIST
CLARK, NICHOLAS CEC 070 5TH E DI
CLARK, NOAH ANN 382 4TH DIST
CLARK, ORPHY ANN 467 HOWARD D
CLARK, OWEN BAL 139 16TH WAR
CLARK, P. R. BAL 271 20TH WAR
CLARK, PATIENCE * ANN 340 3RD DIST
CLARK, PATRICK BAL 036 9TH WARD
CLARK, PATRICK ALL 180 8TH E.D.
CLARK, PATRICK BAL 410 8TH WARD
CLARK, PATRICK BAL 462 1ST DIST
CLARK, PATRICK HAR 145 3RD DIST
CLARK, PATRICK HAR 101 2ND DIST
CLARK, PERE-BLACK QUE 158 2ND E DI
CLARK, PERREY BAL 329 7TH WARD
CLARK, PERRY CAL 023 2ND DIST
CLARK, PETER FRE 378 PETERSVI
CLARK, PETER CAR 206 4TH DIST
CLARK, PHILIP FRE 390 PETERSVI
CLARK, PHILLIP FRE 009 FREDERIC
CLARK, PHILLIP BAL 139 2ND DIST
CLARK, PRISCELLA BAL 316 12TH WAR
CLARK, R. BAL 163 1ST WARD
CLARK, RACHEL ANN 484 HOWARD D
CLARK, RACHEL DOR 432 1ST DIST
CLARK, RALPH HAR 081 2ND DIST
CLARK, REBECCA WAS 018 2ND SUBD
CLARK, REBECCA M. BAL 084 15TH WAR
CLARK, RICHARD BAL 446 1ST DIST
CLARK, RICHARD TAL 061 EASTON D
CLARK, RILLA HAR 041 1ST DIST
CLARK, ROBERT HAR 024 1ST DIST
CLARK, ROBERT WAS 123 HAGERSTO
CLARK, ROBERT BAL 459 1ST DIST
CLARK, ROBINSGN BAL 247 6TH WARD
CLARK, ROSA-BLACK QUE 185 3RD E DI
CLARK, RUBEN F. BAL 341 7TH WARD
CLARK, S.* BAL 109 10TH WAR
CLARK, SALLY ANN 452 HOWARD D
CLARK, SAMUEL BAL 043 2ND DIST
CLARK, SAMUEL BAL 093 5TH WARD
CLARK, SAMUEL KEN 256 1ST DIST
CLARK, SAMUEL WAS 276 RIDGEVIL
CLARK, SAMUEL PRI 121 PISCATAW
CLARK, SAMUEL CAR 104 NO TWP L
CLARK, SAMUEL CEC 186 7TH E DI
CLARK, SAMUEL BAL 236 17TH WAR
CLARK, SAMUEL J. CAR 096 NO TWP L
CLARK, SAMUEL P. WAS 027 2ND SUBD
CLARK, SARAH BAL 427 14TH WAR
CLARK, SARAH SOM 424 PRINCESS
CLARK, SARAH KEN 215 2ND DIST
CLARK, SARAH BAL 332 3RD WARD
CLARK, SARAH BAL 160 2ND DIST
CLARK, SARAH BAL 232 1ST DIST
CLARK, SARAH E. BAL 427 14TH WAR
CLARK, SARAH F. BAL 017 15TH WAR
CLARK, SHELBY PRI 092 MARLBROU
CLARK, SCLOMON HAR 113 2ND DIST
CLARK, SCPHIA H. BAL 342 1ST DIST
CLARK, STEPHEN HAR 101 2ND DIST
CLARK, STEPHEN BAL 002 18TH WAR
CLARK, SUMMERVILLE BAL 337 1ST DIST
CLARK, SUSAN BAL 315 3RD WARD
CLARK, SUSAN ANN 460 HOWARD D
CLARK, SUSAN KEN 226 2ND DIST
CLARK, THADDEUS T. ANN 471 HOWARD D
CLARK, THEODORE BAL 082 15TH WAR
CLARK, THOMAS BAL 135 16TH WAR
CLARK, THOMAS BAL 003 EASTERN
CLARK, THOMAS BAL 090 2ND DIST
CLARK, THOMAS BAL 141 1ST WARD
CLARK, THOMAS BAL 145 1ST WARD
CLARK, THOMAS BAL 175 2ND WARD
CLARK, THOMAS HAR 160 3RD DIST
CLARK, THOMAS BAL 046 4TH WARD
CLARK, THOMAS CEC 197 7TH E DI
CLARK, THOMAS SOM 533 QUANTICO
CLARK, THOMAS B. WAS 263 1ST DIST
CLARK, THOMAS J. TAL 069 EASTON T
CLARK, THOMAS K. BAL 164 11TH WAR
CLARK, THOMAS S. QUE 135 1ST E DI
CLARK, TIMOTHY BAL 442 1ST DIST
CLARK, URILLA WAS 282 1ST DIST
CLARK, VIRGINIA ALL 239 CUMBERLA
CLARK, W. A. BAL 355 1ST DIST
CLARK, WALTER BAL 155 16TH WAR
CLARK, WASHINGTON ANN 387 4TH DIST
CLARK, WASHINGTON BAL 120 11TH WAR
CLARK, WASHINGTON-BLACK CAR 116 NO TWP L
CLARK, WESLEY-BLACK CAR 069 NO TWP L
CLARK, WESTLEY ALL 137 4TH E.D.
CLARK, WHEELER ANN 457 HOWARD D
CLARK, WILLAIM BAL 122 5TH WARD
CLARK, WILLAIM BAL 256 1ST DIST
CLARK, WILLIAM BAL 296 1ST DIST
CLARK, WILLIAM BAL 172 1ST WARD
CLARK, WILLIAM BAL 167 1ST WARD
CLARK, WILLIAM ANN 484 HOWARD D
CLARK, WILLIAM ANN 457 HOWARD D
CLARK, WILLIAM ANN 434 HOWARD D
CLARK, WILLIAM ANN 435 HOWARD D
CLARK, WILLIAM ALL 073 5TH E.D.
CLARK, WILLIAM BAL 155 16TH WAR
CLARK, WILLIAM BAL 098 10TH WAR
CLARK, WILLIAM BAL 352 1ST DIST
CLARK, WILLIAM BAL 091 5TH WARD
CLARK, WILLIAM BAL 139 1ST WARD
CLARK, WILLIAM BAL 268 7TH WARD
CLARK, WILLIAM CAR 139 NO TWP L
CLARK, WILLIAM CEC 190 5TH E DI
CLARK, WILLIAM BAL 217 17TH WAR
CLARK, WILLIAM CEC 125 5TH E DI
CLARK, WILLIAM CEC 081 CHARLEST
CLARK, WILLIAM FRE 067 FREDERIC
CLARK, WILLIAM MGM 381 ROCKERLE
CLARK, WILLIAM HAR 191 3RD DIST
CLARK, WILLIAM WOR 265 BERLIN 1
CLARK, WILLIAM TAL 040 EASTON D
CLARK, WILLIAM QUE 225 4TH E DI
CLARK, WILLIAM WAS 137 2ND DIST
CLARK, WILLIAM PRI 080 QUEEN AN
CLARK, WILLIAM SOM 505 SALISBUR
CLARK, WILLIAM B. TAL 078 EASTON T
CLARK, WILLIAM G. BAL 207 11TH WAR
CLARK, WILLIAM H. BAL 467 14TH WAR
CLARK, WILLIAM H. BAL 218 6TH WARD
CLARK, WILLIAM J.S. WOR 341 1ST E DI
CLARK, WILLIAM P. ALL 122 4TH E.D.
CLARK, WILLIAM S. BAL 249 12TH WAR
CLARK, WILLIAM T. BAL 088 15TH WAR
CLARK, WILLLIAM BAL 175 11TH WAR
CLARK, WINFORD BAL 068 18TH WAR
CLARK, WRIGHTSON TAL 061 EASTON D
CLARK, Z.B. WAS 141 HAGERSTO
CLARK, ZEDOC ALL 248 CUMBERLA
CLARKE, A. BAL 239 20TH WAR
CLARKE, ALBERT BAL 169 19TH WAR
CLARKE, ALEXANDER ST 313 1ST E DI
CLARKE, AUGNITHA PRI 045 VANSVILL
CLARKE, BENJAMIN BAL 147 19TH WAR
CLARKE, BENJAMIN ANN 374 4TH DIST
CLARKE, BERNHARD BAL 081 4TH WARD
CLARKE, CAROLIEN ST 312 1ST E DI
CLARKE, CHARLES WAS 151 2ND DIST
CLARKE, CHARLES H. WOR 218 4TH E DI
CLARKE, CLARA FRE 159 EMMITTSB
CLARKE, D. WAS 021 2ND SUBD
CLARKE, DANIEL DOR 365 3RD DIVI
CLARKE, DARCHUS ST 306 1ST E DI
CLARKE, E. B. BAL 074 10TH WAR
CLARKE, EDWARD ST 254 3RD E DI
CLARKE, EDWIN SOM 355 BRINKLEY
CLARKE, ELEANOR ST 280 3RD E DI
CLARKE, ELENER BAL 239 20TH WAR
CLARKE, ELIZABETH BAL 225 19TH WAR
CLARKE, ELIZABETH PRI 040 VANSVILL
CLARKE, ELIZABETH BAL 292 12TH WAR
CLARKE, ELIZABETH B. BAL 218 6TH WARD
CLARKE, EMMA FRE 066 FREDERIC
CLARKE, GABRIEL D. BAL 101 10TH WAR
CLARKE, GEORGE A. ST 291 2ND E DI
CLARKE, GEORGE A. D. PRI 017 BLADENSB
CLARKE, GEORGE B. BAL 047 15TH WAR
CLARKE, HATSELL F. BAL 200 19TH WAR
CLARKE, HENRIETTA WOR 216 4TH E DI
CLARKE, HENRY BAL 252 20TH WAR
CLARKE, HESTER SOM 467 HANGARY
CLARKE, IGNATIUS ST 299 2ND E DI
CLARKE, J. ANN 347 3RD DIST
CLARKE, JAMES BAL 110 10TH WAR
CLARKE, JAMES WOR 222 4TH E DI
CLARKE, JAMES WOR 177 6TH E DI
CLARKE, JAMES BAL 169 19TH WAR
CLARKE, JAMES-MULATTO FRE 197 5TH E DI
CLARKE, JOHN WOR 184 6TH E DI
CLARKE, JOHN BAL 279 12TH WAR
CLARKE, JOHN BAL 149 1ST WARD
CLARKE, JOHN BAL 152 1ST WARD
CLARKE, JOHN BAL 155 1ST WARD
CLARKE, JOHN ANN 292 ANNAPOLI
CLARKE, JOHN A. BAL 112 10TH WAR
CLARKE, JOHN F. PRI 011 BLADENSB
CLARKE, JOHN T. ST 287 2ND E DI
CLARKE, JOSEPH BAL 157 19TH WAR
CLARKE, LEVI C. CEC 148 PORT DUP
CLARKE, LOUISA M. ST 278 3RD E DI
CLARKE, LUCINDA M. ST 291 2ND E DI
CLARKE, LUCY CAL 038 2ND DIST
CLARKE, LUCY CAL 032 2ND DIST
CLARKE, LUCY FRE 160 EMMITTSB
CLARKE, M. FRE 200 5TH E DI
CLARKE, MARGARET ANN 378 4TH DIST
CLARKE, MARGARET BAL 226 6TH WARD
CLARKE, MARGARET BAL 064 10TH WAR
CLARKE, MARIA BAL 067 10TH WAR
CLARKE, MARIA L. ST 311 1ST E DI

CLARKE, MARTIN ALL 072 5TH E.D.
CLARKE, MARY ANN 343 3RD DIST
CLARKE, MARY FRE 162 EMMITTSB
CLARKE, MARY A. BAL 290 20TH WAR
CLARKE, MARY A. SOM 472 TRAPPE D
CLARKE, MARY S. BAL 165 19TH WAR
CLARKE, MATILDA ST 278 3RD E DI
CLARKE, MATTHEW BAL 268 12TH WAR
CLARKE, NANCY A. PRI 044 VANSVILL
CLARKE, NELSON BAL 056 10TH WAR
CLARKE, NELSON B. ST 305 1ST E DI
CLARKE, P. C. BAL 305 20TH WAR
CLARKE, PATRICK BAL 277 20TH WAR
CLARKE, PATRICK BAL 349 13TH WAR
CLARKE, PEARSON CAL 040 3RD DIST
CLARKE, PETER FRE 168 EMMITTSB
CLARKE, PHILIP ST 286 2ND E DI
CLARKE, PHILIP-BLACK FRE 196 5TH E DI
CLARKE, RICHARD ST 310 1ST E DI
CLARKE, ROBERT ST 314 1ST E DI
CLARKE, ROBERT PRI 007 BLADENSB
CLARKE, ROBERT BAL 317 20TH WAR
CLARKE, ROBERT BAL 279 20TH WAR
CLARKE, ROBERT BAL 293 20TH WAR
CLARKE, ROBERT A. BAL 088 10TH WAR
CLARKE, ROBERT L. CAL 005 1ST DIST
CLARKE, SAMUEL CEC 089 4TH E DI
CLARKE, SAMUEL-BLACK FRE 176 5TH E DI
CLARKE, SARAH C. ANN 436 HOWARD D
CLARKE, SARRAH DOR 363 3RD DIVI
CLARKE, SISTER GERTRUDE FRE 197 5TH E DI
CLARKE, SISTER M.R. FRE 197 5TH E DI
CLARKE, SUSAN SOM 467 HANGARY
CLARKE, SYLVESTER ANN 375 4TH DIST
CLARKE, THOMAS BAL 156 1ST WARD
CLARKE, THOMAS ST 299 2ND E DI
CLARKE, W.D. WAS 021 2ND SUBD
CLARKE, WILLIAM ST 273 3RD E DI
CLARKE, WILLIAM WOR 192 8TH E DI
CLARKE, WILLIAM ALL 248 CUMBERLA
CLARKE, WILLIAM BAL 290 20TH WAR
CLARKE, WILLIAM B. WAS 164 HAGERSTO
CLARKE, WILLIAM D. PRI 044 VANSVILL
CLARKE, WILLIAM F. BAL 111 15TH WAR
CLARKE, WILLIAM H. BAL 246 12TH WAR
CLARKE, WILLIAM H.REV. ANN 522 HOWARD D
CLARKEN, RHODA BAL 169 16TH WAR
CLARKER, SOPHIA * BAL 115 2ND DIST
CLARKSON, AMANDA KEN 239 2ND DIST
CLARKSON, ANN BAL 321 12TH WAR
CLARKSON, CATHERINE PRI 006 BLADENSB
CLARKSON, ELIZA-BLACK CAR 115 NO TWP L
CLARKSON, ELIZABETH CEC 012 ELKTON 3
CLARKSON, ELIZABETH BAL 312 1ST DIST
CLARKSON, F.L. WAS 021 2ND SUBD
CLARKSON, GEORGE BAL 170 6TH WARD
CLARKSON, HENRY KEN 239 2ND DIST
CLARKSON, J.T. WAS 021 2ND SUBD
CLARKSON, JOSEPH BAL 187 6TH WARD
CLARKSON, JOSEPH P. WAS 021 2ND SUBD
CLARKSON, M.C. WAS 018 2ND SUBD
CLARKSON, MARY-BLACK CAR 115 NO TWP L
CLARKSON, MARY-MULATTO CAR 150 NO TWP L
CLARKSON, WESLEY SOM 512 BARREN C
CLARNES, GEORGE HAR 065 1ST DIST
CLARRITON, GEORGIANNE BAL 104 5TH WARD
CLARRO, HARRIET WOR 341 1ST E DI
CLARRO, WILLIAM WOR 341 1ST E DI
CLARRY, EDWARD BAL 145 2ND DIST
CLARTHE, AMOS HAR 159 3RD DIST
CLARY, ADEN ALL 095 5TH E.D.
CLARY, BARNEY ALL 143 6TH E.D.
CLARY, BURGESS N. FRE 303 WOODSBOR
CLARY, CATHARINE BAL 001 EASTERN
CLARY, CORNELIUS FRE 244 NEW MARK
CLARY, ELLEN BAL 397 3RD WARD
CLARY, EUGENIA FRE 252 NEW MARK
CLARY, GERARD ALL 109 5TH E.D.
CLARY, HANSON FRE 251 NEW MARK
CLARY, HENRY FRE 444 8TH E DI
CLARY, JAMES TAL 106 ST MICHA
CLARY, JAMES H. FRE 412 8TH E DI
CLARY, JOANNA FRE 445 8TH E DI
CLARY, MARTIN ALL 169 6TH E.D.
CLARY, NATHAN FRE 249 NEW MARK
CLARY, NATHANIEL ANN 509 HOWARD D
CLARY, PHILIP CAR 281 7TH DIST
CLARY, SAMUEL CAR 369 9TH DIST
CLARY, SARAH FRE 249 NEW MARK
CLARY, SARAH FRE 249 NEW MARK
CLARY, SOLOMON FRE 251 NEW MARK
CLARY, THEODORE FRE 254 NEW MARK
CLARY, TIMOTHY ALL 201 CUMBERLA
CLARY, WILLIAM BAL 373 1ST DIST
CLARYMIRE, HENRY BAL 214 19TH WAR
CLASE, JOHN H. ALL 085 5TH E.D.
CLASEY, HARRIET H. BAL 209 2ND WARD
CLASH, CLONCSBOROUGH CAR 065 NO TWP L
CLASH, ELIZA BAL 370 1ST DIST
CLASH, GARRETTSON KEN 253 1ST DIST
CLASH, JAMES DOR 420 1ST DIST
CLASH, MARIA BAL 063 18TH WAR
CLASH, STEPHEN DOR 430 1ST DIST
CLASHINGER, JOSEPH BAL 323 3RD WARD
CLASKEY, SAMUEL BAL 260 17TH WAR
CLASSEN, HARMAN BAL 083 15TH WAR
CLASSEY, WILLIAM BAL 456 8TH WARD
CLASTERMAN, JOHN B. ALL 257 CUMBERLA
CLATHEM, HERMAN BAL 079 1ST WARD
CLATON, JESSY BAL 011 1ST WARD
CLAUDE, DENNIS ANN 265 ANNAPOLI
CLAUDE, DENNIS JR. ANN 271 ANNAPOLI
CLAUDGE, JOHN W. BAL 145 1ST WARD
CLAUGHLEY, WILLIAM BAL 016 4TH WARD
CLAUNAHAN, ELIZABETH C. BAL 165 11TH WAR
CLAUSON, AUGUST BAL 386 13TH WAR
CLAUSON, WILIAM BAL 169 1ST WARD
CLAUTIA, W. A. BAL 033 9TH WARD
CLAUTICE, FRANCIS * BAL 217 6TH WARD
CLAVEL, JAMES WOR 306 2ND E DI
CLAVEL, WILLIAM WOR 306 2ND E DI
CLAVERT, GEORGE BAL 312 1ST DIST
CLAVERT, JOHN BAL 109 18TH WAR
CLAVIL, JOHN WOR 290 9TH E DI
CLAVIL, MATILDA WOR 291 9TH E DI
CLAVILL, MOSES WOR 298 9TH E DI
CLAVILLE, CAROLINE BAL 321 3RD WARD
CLAVILLE, EDWARD BAL 152 1ST WARD
CLAVILLE, JOHN A. BAL 322 3RD WARD
CLAWSON, LAWRENCE BAL 404 1ST DIST

CLAXTON, JOHN ST 260 3RD E DI
CLAY, ADAM FRE 267 NEW MARK
CLAY, ADAM W. FRE 267 NEW MARK
CLAY, ARTEMESA FRE 241 NEW MARK
CLAY, CATHARINE BAL 359 1ST DIST
CLAY, CHARLES H. QUE 196 3RD E DI
CLAY, ELIZA BAL 442 14TH WAR
CLAY, ELIZABETH FRE 245 NEW MARK
CLAY, FRANK WAS 145 HAGERSTO
CLAY, GEORGE FRE 245 NEW MARK
CLAY, GEORGE W. BAL 111 18TH WAR
CLAY, H. BAL 158 19TH WAR
CLAY, HANSON QUE 174 2ND E DI
CLAY, HARRY C. BAL 262 1ST DIST
CLAY, HENRIETTA BAL 206 11TH WAR
CLAY, HENRY CAR 141 NO TWP L
CLAY, HENRY CAR 133 NO TWP L
CLAY, HENRY CAR 124 NO TWP L
CLAY, HENRY CAR 120 NO TWP L
CLAY, HENRY CAR 147 NO TWP L
CLAY, HENRY BAL 094 18TH WAR
CLAY, HENRY BAL 001 18TH WAR
CLAY, HENRY FRE 380 PETERSVI
CLAY, HENRY BAL 032 1ST WARD
CLAY, HENRY BAL 032 1ST WARD
CLAY, HENRY BAL 440 1ST DIST
CLAY, JACOB WAS 150 2ND DIST
CLAY, JAMES BAL 373 1ST DIST
CLAY, JAMES BAL 114 11TH WAR
CLAY, LUCINDA A. CHA 270 ALLENS F
CLAY, MARY B. FRE 267 NEW MARK
CLAY, NATHANIEL H. FRE 251 NEW MARK
CLAY, PETER FRE 251 NEW MARK
CLAY, RANDOLPH FRE 245 NEW MARK
CLAY, VIRGINIA BAL 319 20TH WAR
CLAY, WILLIAM WAS 151 2ND DIST
CLAY, WILLIAM GEORGE FRE 267 NEW MARK
CLAY, YOCTLEB BAL 154 19TH WAR
CLAY.HENRY QUE 126 1ST E DI
CLAYBAUGH, G.W. ALL 212 CUMBERLA
CLAYBOURNE, HENRIETTA BAL 245 2ND WARD
CLAYBURN, T.S.B. WAS 017 2ND SUBD
CLAYERT, THOMAS BAL 250 12TH WAR
CLAYETT, THOMAS JR. MGM 399 ROCKERLE
CLAYHING, CHARLES BAL 256 2ND WARD
CLAYLAND, ELISA P. BAL 039 18TH WAR
CLAYLAND, SAMUEL R. BAL 037 18TH WAR
CLAYNEY, JANE ANN 466 HOWARD D
CLAYPOOLE, JOHN BAL 186 6TH WARD
CLAYPOOLE, SEPTIMUS BAL 209 6TH WARD
CLAYRILL, MAJOR WOR 306 2ND E DI
CLAYTON, CAROLINE-BLACK CAR 074 NO TWP L
CLAYTON, CAROLINE-MULATTO BAL 248 2ND WARD
CLAYTON, CHARLES QUE 226 4TH E DI
CLAYTON, E. BAL 225 19TH WAR
CLAYTON, EDWARD BAL 094 2ND DIST
CLAYTON, EDWARD BAL 073 15TH WAR
CLAYTON, ELIJAH BAL 093 2ND DIST
CLAYTON, ELIZABETH-BLACK QUE 189 3RD E DI
CLAYTON, G. ANN 281 ANNAPOLI
CLAYTON, G. BAL 320 12TH WAR
CLAYTON, GEORGE D. ANN 299 1ST DIST
CLAYTON, HANNAH QUE 228 4TH E DI
CLAYTON, ISAAC KEN 284 3RD DIST
CLAYTON, JACOB KEN 293 3RD DIST
CLAYTON, JAMES WAS 047 2ND SUBD
CLAYTON, JAMES-BLACK QUE 187 3RD E DI
CLAYTON, JOHN QUE 180 2ND E DI
CLAYTON, JOHN BAL 118 2ND DIST
CLAYTON, JOHN BAL 193 6TH WARD
CLAYTON, JOHN L. CEC 023 ELKTON 3
CLAYTON, JOSEPH BAL 118 2ND DIST
CLAYTON, LEVI BAL 098 15TH WAR
CLAYTON, LEWIS ANN 281 ANNAPOLI
CLAYTON, MAHALA-BLACK QUE 155 2ND E DI
CLAYTON, MARY ANN 297 1ST DIST
CLAYTON, MARY QUE 224 4TH E DI
CLAYTON, NANCY-BLACK QUE 187 3RD E DI
CLAYTON, NANCY-BLACK QUE 132 1ST E DI
CLAYTON, PERRY KEN 242 2ND DIST
CLAYTON, PERRY TAL 071 EASTON T
CLAYTON, PHILLIP ANN 271 ANNAPOLI
CLAYTON, PHILLIP ANN 281 ANNAPOLI
CLAYTON, RICHARD E. QUE 204 3RD E DI
CLAYTON, RICHARD-BLACK QUE 176 2ND E DI
CLAYTON, ROSANA-MULATTO BAL 214 2ND WARD
CLAYTON, SALLY ANN-BLACK QUE 187 3RD E DI
CLAYTON, SAMUEL KEN 293 3RD DIST
CLAYTON, SAMUEL BAL 109 15TH WAR
CLAYTON, SAMUEL BAL 007 9TH WARD
CLAYTON, SAMUEL BAL 008 9TH WARD
CLAYTON, SAMUEL S. BAL 112 15TH WAR
CLAYTON, SARAH BAL 118 2ND DIST
CLAYTON, SARAH QUE 230 4TH E DI
CLAYTON, SARAH BAL 377 13TH WAR
CLAYTON, SARAH A. KEN 225 2ND DIST
CLAYTON, SIMON-BLACK CAR 074 NO TWP L
CLAYTON, SUSAN BAL 245 6TH WARD
CLAYTON, THOMAS BAL 128 2ND DIST
CLAYTON, THOMAS CEC 043 CHESAPEA
CLAYTON, THOMAS D. CEC 162 6TH E DI
CLAYTON, WALTER J. QUE 167 2ND E DI
CLAYTON, WELLS BAL 097 2ND DIST
CLAYTON, WILLIAM CEC 129 6TH E DI
CLAYTON, WILLIAM L. ANN 278 ANNAPOLI
CLAYTON, WILLIAM* TAL 058 EASTON D
CLAYTON.WILLIAM-BLACK CAR 100 NO TWP L
CLAYVEL, WILLIAM WOR 305 SNOW HIL
CLAYWELL, ELI WOR 200 3RD E DI
CLAYWELL, JAMES F. WOR 169 6TH E DI
CLAYWELL, JOHN WOR 315 2ND E DI
CLAYWELL, LITTLETON SOM 527 QUANTICO
CLAYWELL, ROBERT SOM 489 SALISBUR
CLAZEY, GOERGE BAL 287 17TH WAR
CLCOKER, JOHN B. ST 304 2ND E DI
CLEADE, JOHNAN BAL 053 1ST WARD
CLEAR, ALEXANDER ALL 263 CUMBERLA
CLEAR, THOMAS ALL 262 CUMBERLA
CLEARY, EDWARD BAL 145 2ND DIST
CLEARY, JOHANNA BAL 401 3RD WARD
CLEARY, JOHN BAL 145 2ND DIST
CLEARY, JOHN BAL 083 4TH WARD
CLEAVELAND, A. J. BAL 137 11TH WAR
CLEAVES, ANN BAL 325 12TH WAR
CLEAVES, JOHN C. CEC 012 ELKTON 3
CLEAVLAND, JOSHUA L.* BAL 407 3RD WARD
CLECK, BEDA* BAL 037 4TH WARD
CLECKNER, PETER ANN 386 4TH DIST
CLEDON, GEORGE CEC 101 4TH E DI
CLEEK, BEDA* BAL 037 4TH WARD

CLEERY, MAURICE BAL 028 4TH WARD
CLEFF, ARNOLD BAL 369 8TH WARD
CLEFF, FRANCIS A. QUE 135 1ST E DI
CLEFFORD, AUSTIN BAL 187 16TH WAR
CLEFFORD, SYLVETER BAL 187 16TH WAR
CLEGETT, JOHN WAS 195 1ST DIST
CLEGETT, SALLY WAS 128 HAGERSTO
CLEGGET, HENRY WAS 159 2ND DIST
CLEGLE, LEWIS FRE 379 PETERSVI
CLELAND, JOHN BAL 061 10TH WAR
CLELY, PETER BAL 310 20TH WAR
CLEM, BARBARA FRE 106 CREAGERS
CLEM, ENOS FRE 106 CREAGERS
CLEM, EVE FRE 063 FREDERIC
CLEM, GEORGE FRE 130 CREAGERS
CLEM, GEORGE A. FRE 141 CREAGERS
CLEM, HARRIET M.E. FRE 013 FREDERIC
CLEM, JACOB FRE 094 FREDERIC
CLEM, JOHN FRE 105 CREAGERS
CLEM, JOSEPH M. FRE 130 CREAGERS
CLEM, MARGARET W. BAL 050 1ST WARD
CLEM, MARY A. FRE 105 CREAGERS
CLEM, PHILLIP FRE 305 WOODSBOR
CLEM, SAMUEL FRE 105 CREAGERS
CLEMANCE, C.A. BAL 165 1ST WARD
CLEMANIE, RACHEL CAR 210 5TH DIST
CLEMANT, DAVID KEN 295 3RD DIST
CLEMANT, MARY A. CEC 120 4TH E DI
CLEMANT, SAMUEL CEC 120 4TH E DI
CLEMARS, JOHN BAL 034 1ST WARD
CLEMEM, WILLIAM BAL 050 1ST WARD
CLEMEN, WILLIAM T. D. BAL 346 3RD WARD
CLEMENCE, MARY S. CHA 265 MIDDLETO
CLEMENCY, CHARLES TAL 056 EASTON D
CLEMENCY, HENRY TAL 052 EASTON D
CLEMENCY, HERRIET TAL 068 EASTON T
CLEMENCY, THOMAS H. TAL 052 EASTON D
CLEMENNS, SUSANNA J. CHA 253 MIDDLETO
CLEMENS, ANN BAL 241 12TH WAR
CLEMENS, GEORGE W. CHA 289 BOJANTOW
CLEMENS, GREEN CHA 266 MIDDLETO
CLEMENS, ISABELLA MGM 321 CRACKLIN
CLEMENS, JAMES R. CHA 261 MIDDLETO
CLEMENS, JOSEPH CHA 260 MIDDLETO
CLEMENS, JOSEPH MGM 320 CRACKLIN
CLEMENS, JUDSON CHA 253 MIDDLETO
CLEMENS, LEONARD A. CHA 266 MIDDLETO
CLEMENS, LOUISA WAS 126 HAGERSTO
CLEMENS, MARTHA CHA 253 MIDDLETO
CLEMENS, MARY CHA 264 HILLTOP
CLEMENS, TERSA CHA 251 MIDDLETO
CLEMENS, THOMAS CHA 263 MIDDLETO
CLEMENT, ANN BAL 132 11TH WAR
CLEMENT, JEMIMA ANN 521 HOWARD D
CLEMENT, JOHN KEN 305 3RD DIST
CLEMENT, THOAMS HAR 007 1ST DIST
CLEMENT, WILLIAM M. TAL 021 EASTON D
CLEMENTS, ANN E. BAL 192 19TH WAR
CLEMENTS, ARTHUR ANN 413 HOWARD D
CLEMENTS, CHARLES S. QUE 191 3RD E DI
CLEMENTS, ELIZA A. MGM 418 MEDLEY 3
CLEMENTS, ELIZABETH BAL 192 19TH WAR
CLEMENTS, FERDNAND CHA 229 MIDDLETO
CLEMENTS, GEORGE BAL 170 1ST WARD
CLEMENTS, HENRIETTA BAL 065 10TH WAR
CLEMENTS, HENRY MGM 404 ROCKERLE
CLEMENTS, HOWARD MGM 417 MEDLEY 3
CLEMENTS, J. M. BAL 154 1ST WARD
CLEMENTS, JAMES H. BAL 017 15TH WAR
CLEMENTS, JAMES H. CAR 099 NO TWP L
CLEMENTS, JOEL QUE 174 2ND E DI
CLEMENTS, JOHN CHA 233 HILLTOP
CLEMENTS, JOHN BAL 394 3RD WARD
CLEMENTS, JOHN F. BAL 189 11TH WAR
CLEMENTS, JOHN W. BAL 244 12TH WAR
CLEMENTS, JUPTON BAL 079 18TH WAR
CLEMENTS, LEMUEL MGM 401 ROCKERLE
CLEMENTS, PETER H. MGM 378 ROCKERLE
CLEMENTS, THOMAS DOR 376 1ST DIST
CLEMENTS, THOMAS QUE 208 3RD E DI
CLEMENTS, VALENTINE QUE 247 5TH E DI
CLEMENTS, WALTER ANN 424 HOWARD D
CLEMENTS, WESLEY QUE 170 2ND E DI
CLEMENTS, WILLIAM MGM 384 ROCKERLE
CLEMERCY, WILLIAM DOR 412 1ST DIST
CLEMINGS, JOHN M. CAR 217 5TH DIST
CLEMINGS, MARY A. CAR 217 5TH DIST
CLEMM, JOHN BAL 157 6TH WARD
CLEMM, JOHN BAL 050 1ST WARD
CLEMM, MARIA BAL 095 10TH WAR
CLEMM, WILLIAM E. BAL 057 4TH WARD
CLEMMENS, ALEXANDER* BAL 055 4TH WARD
CLEMMENS, JOHN DOR 300 1ST DIST
CLEMMENS, MAGDELINE BAL 356 13TH WAR
CLEMMENT, JOHN S. BAL 181 6TH WARD
CLEMMENTS, JAMES B. BAL 079 18TH WAR
CLEMMENTS, JAMES P. BAL 040 9TH WARD
CLEMMENTS, JOHN BAL 256 20TH WAR
CLEMMER, JACOB ALL 024 3RD E.D.
CLEMMING, WILLIAM BAL 218 12TH WAR
CLEMMM, ADAM BAL 048 1ST WARD
CLEMMONS, ALEXANDER* BAL 055 4TH WARD
CLEMMONS, ANN BAL 168 6TH WARD
CLEMMONS, AUGUSTUS BAL 132 5TH WARD
CLEMMONS, ELIZABETH BAL 356 1ST DIST
CLEMMONS, JOHN D. BAL 277 7TH WARD
CLEMMONS, JOHN W. BAL 388 8TH WARD
CLEMMONS, JOHN W. ST 298 2ND E DI
CLEMMONS, JOSHUA BAL 353 1ST DIST
CLEMMONS, MARIA ST 301 2ND E DI
CLEMMONS, MARY BAL 279 17TH WAR
CLEMMONS, RACHEL BAL 168 6TH WARD
CLEMMONS, SETH BAL 388 8TH WARD
CLEMMONS, WILLIAM BAL 353 1ST DIST
CLEMMONS, WILLIAM BAL 353 7TH WARD
CLEMMONS, WILLIAMS BAL 106 15TH WAR
CLEMMORE, JAMES BAL 230 17TH WAR
CLEMON, ADAM BAL 071 1ST WARD
CLEMONCY, CHARLES H. TAL 024 EASTON D
CLEMONS, BENNET T. PRI 112 PISCATAW
CLEMONS, JOSIAH PRI 112 PISCATAW
CLEMONS, MARCELLUS PRI 110 PISCATAW
CLEMONS, THOMAS CAL 027 2ND DIST
CLEMONTS, HENRY BAL 224 19TH WAR
CLEMSON, DENNIS FRE 428 8TH E DI
CLEMSON, HARIS F. FRE 427 8TH E DI
CLEMSON, JOHN FRE 428 8TH E DI
CLEMSON, JOHN D. FRE 433 8TH E DI
CLEMSON, WILLIAM BAL 171 1ST WARD
CLEMY, REACHEL A. BAL 300 11TH WAR

Name	Co.	Page	District
CLEN, JOHN *	KEN	237	2ND DIST
CLENDEMING, ROBERT	CAR	079	NO TWP L
CLENDENAN, DANIEL	CEC	202	6TH E DI
CLENDENEN, ARTHUR	BAL	350	1ST DIST
CLENDENIA, ROBERT	BAL	343	13TH WAR
CLENDENIN, ELLEN	HAR	109	2ND DIST
CLENDENNAN, CATHERINE	CEC	202	6TH E DI
CLENDENNAN, MARIE	CEC	201	6TH E DI
CLENDENNAN, MARY	CEC	197	7TH E DI
CLENDINEN, JANE	BAL	317	20TH WAR
CLENDINEN, JOSEPH	BAL	237	6TH WARD
CLENDINEN, MARY M.*	BAL	098	10TH WAR
CLENDINEN, WILLIAM	BAL	317	20TH WAR
CLENDINNAM, ALEXANDER	BAL	086	4TH WARD
CLENEN, THOMAS	WAS	201	1ST DIST
CLENNEY, JOHN	BAL	304	7TH WARD
CLENS, WILLIAM	QUE	127	1ST E DI
CLENSMITH, VALENTINE	BAL	125	2ND DIST
CLENSTENING, LETITIA	QUE	146	1ST E DI
CLER, JOSEPH	BAL	292	12TH WAR
CLERICE, LEWIS	BAL	046	9TH WARD
CLERK, HENRY H.	BAL	073	4TH WARD
CLERSEY, DANIEL	ALL	013	3RD E.D.
CLERY, AARON	BAL	285	7TH WARD
CLESLER, WILLIAM	HAR	065	1ST DIST
CLETY, ANDREW	ALL	161	6TH E.D.
CLETZ, WILLIAM A.	ALL	162	6TH E.D.
CLEVEL, HENRY	WOR	302	SNOW HIL
CLEVELAND, A. J.	BAL	101	10TH WAR
CLEVELAND, CHARLES	BAL	121	1ST WARD
CLEVELAND, D. C.	BAL	427	14TH WAR
CLEVELAND, GEORGE	BAL	256	17TH WAR
CLEVELAND, J. A.	BAL	101	10TH WAR
CLEVELAND, SYLVESTER	BAL	071	10TH WAR
CLEVER, CHARLES	BAL	403	8TH WARD
CLEVER, PETER	BAL	357	8TH WARD
CLEVER, PETER	CEC	023	ELKTON 3
CLEVER, WILLIAM	BAL	349	13TH WAR
CLEVETT, LOUISA	WAS	153	2ND DIST
CLEVIDENCE, DAVID	WAS	223	1ST DIST
CLEVIDENCE, GEORGE	WAS	227	1ST DIST
CLEVIDENCE, GEORGE	WAS	228	1ST DIST
CLEVIDENCE, JOHN	WAS	226	1ST DIST
CLEVIDENCE, LEAH	WAS	245	SMITHSBU
CLEVIDENCE, SAMUEL	WAS	229	1ST DIST
CLEVISON, GEORGE	WAS	274	RIDGEVIL
CLEYETT, OTHO	BAL	098	2ND DIST
CLEZY, GEORGE	BAL	022	15TH WAR
CLGETT, E.	PRI	112	PISCATAW
CLICK, BENS	WAS	202	1ST DIST
CLICK, CASPER	BAL	429	8TH WARD
CLICK, CHARLES	BAL	039	9TH WARD
CLICK, CONRADT	BAL	423	8TH WARD
CLICKNER, SAMUEL A.	BAL	044	9TH WARD
CLIFF, ABRAHAM	BAL	380	8TH WARD
CLIFF, JOHN	CHA	229	MIDDLETO
CLIFFE, GEORGE	BAL	111	15TH WAR
CLIFFE, HENRY	BAL	047	15TH WAR
CLIFFORD, CAR	BAL	461	1ST DIST
CLIFFORD, EDWARD	BAL	037	1ST WARD
CLIFFORD, ELIZA	BAL	110	5TH WARD
CLIFFORD, HANAH	WAS	036	2ND SUBD
CLIFFORD, HANNAH	BAL	408	14TH WAR
CLIFFORD, JAMES	ALL	143	6TH E.D.
CLIFFORD, JOHN JR.	BAL	030	4TH WARD
CLIFFORD, MARGARET	BAL	419	14TH WAR
CLIFFORD, MARGARETT	BAL	026	4TH WARD
CLIFFORD, MARY	BAL	460	1ST DIST
CLIFFORD, MARY	BAL	406	3RD WARD
CLIFFORD, MICHAEL	BAL	348	7TH WARD
CLIFFORD, S.	BAL	232	12TH WAR
CLIFFORD, SAMUEL	BAL	428	14TH WAR
CLIFFORD, SARAH A.	BAL	324	7TH WARD
CLIFFORD, WILLIAM	BAL	110	5TH WARD
CLIFT, DEBORAH	BAL	018	15TH WAR
CLIFT, GEORGE	CAR	216	5TH DIST
CLIFT, JOHN W.	BAL	221	17TH WAR
CLIFT, THOMAS H.	BAL	222	17TH WAR
CLIFTON, ALPHONSO	BAL	387	13TH WAR
CLIFTON, D.	BAL	171	1ST WARD
CLIFTON, EMILY	DOR	307	1ST DIST
CLIFTON, FEBY	CAR	089	NO TWP L
CLIFTON, FRANCIS	DOR	453	1ST DIST
CLIFTON, JANE	BAL	364	3RD WARD
CLIFTON, JOHN	ALL	238	CUMBERLA
CLIFTON, JOHN M.	BAL	111	15TH WAR
CLIFTON, LEANDER	WOR	259	BERLIN 1
CLIFTON, THOMAS	DOR	300	1ST DIST
CLIFTON, VIRGINIA	BAL	369	8TH WARD
CLIFTON, WILLIAM	DOR	466	1ST DIST
CLIFTON, WILLIAM W.*	DOR	447	1ST DIST
CLIMANCE, CHARLES A.	BAL	115	1ST WARD
CLIMENTS, THOMAS	PRI	002	BLADENSB
CLINE, ALPHEUS	ALL	216	CUMBERLA
CLINE, ANNA M.	BAL	062	1ST WARD
CLINE, ANTHONY	BAL	062	1ST WARD
CLINE, CASPER	FRE	037	FREDERIC
CLINE, CATHARINE	BAL	245	2ND WARD
CLINE, CATHERINE	BAL	039	9TH WARD
CLINE, DANIEL	FRE	010	FREDERIC
CLINE, ELIZABETH	BAL	263	2ND WARD
CLINE, EMMA	BAL	021	1ST WARD
CLINE, FREDERICK	FRE	424	8TH E DI
CLINE, GEORGE	FRE	439	8TH E DI
CLINE, GEORGE	FRE	005	FREDERIC
CLINE, HENRY	HAR	199	3RD DIST
CLINE, HENRY	BAL	045	1ST WARD
CLINE, J.D.	WAS	125	HAGERSTO
CLINE, JACOB C.	BAL	017	15TH WAR
CLINE, JAMES	BAL	156	1ST WARD
CLINE, JOHN	ANN	417	HOWARD D
CLINE, JOHN	WAS	065	2ND SUBD
CLINE, JOHN	BAL	223	19TH WAR
CLINE, JONATHAN	FRE	081	FREDERIC
CLINE, LEVI	HAR	145	3RD DIST
CLINE, MARIA	BAL	045	1ST WARD
CLINE, MICHAEL B.	BAL	314	1ST DIST
CLINE, MOSES	WAS	066	2ND SUBD
CLINE, R.	WAS	021	2ND SUBD
CLINE, RACHAL	WAS	099	2ND DIST
CLINE, SUSAN	FRE	022	FREDERIC
CLINE, WILLIAM	BAL	119	15TH WAR
CLINER, ANDREW	HAR	119	2ND DIST
CLINGAN, JOHN	CAR	380	2ND DIST
CLINGAN, SAMUEL	CAR	298	1ST DIST
CLINGAN, WILLIAM T.	CAR	378	2ND DIST
CLINGAN, WINCHESTER	FRE	059	FREDERIC
CLINGEN, JOHN	FRE	069	FREDERIC
CLINGER, CHARLES	BAL	201	19TH WAR
CLINGER, HENZER	BAL	202	2ND WARD
CLINGMAN, E. M.	BAL	075	18TH WAR
CLININGHAFFER, JOHN	BAL	050	1ST WARD
CLINK, ANDREW	ALL	111	5TH E.D.
CLINK, BARBARA	ALL	111	5TH E.D.
CLINK, FERDIANO *	ALL	126	4TH E.D.
CLINKER, BILLEY	BAL	137	5TH WARD
CLINTON, ALEXANDER	ALL	152	6TH E.D.
CLINTON, ANN	BAL	393	14TH WAR
CLINTON, CASSA	CAL	053	3RD DIST
CLINTON, DAVID	BAL	024	1ST WARD
CLINTON, DEWIT	BAL	237	6TH WARD
CLINTON, WILLIAM	ALL	085	5TH E.D.
CLINTON,WARTON	ALL	203	CUMBERLA
CLINY, NICHOLAS	ALL	169	6TH E.D.
CLIPP, JOHN	FRE	080	FREDERIC
CLIPPER, CASPER	BAL	295	17TH WAR
CLIPPER, GEORGE	BAL	296	17TH WAR
CLISE, JANE	ALL	238	CUMBERLA
CLISHEM, MICHAEL	BAL	358	8TH WARD
CLISHEN, PETER	BAL	361	8TH WARD
CLISHLEY, WILLIAM	BAL	414	8TH WARD
CLISHMAN, WILLIAM	BAL	085	10TH WAR
CLISTER, HENRY ARM	ALL	251	CUMBERLA
CLITPENGER, VALENTINE	ALL	251	CUMBERLA
CLITZ, DAVID	ALL	165	6TH E.D.
CLITZ, JOHN M. B.	MGM	359	BERRYS D
CLOBILL, ALLICE	WAS	242	CAVETOWN
CLOCKER, ELIZABETH	ST	309	1ST E DI
CLOCKER, JOHNH.	ST	299	2ND E DI
CLOCKER, WILLIAM	ST	303	2ND E DI
CLOCKNER, MATHEW	BAL	068	4TH WARD
CLOCKSTONE, JOHN-BLACK	QUE	175	2ND E DI
CLOCKSTONE, JONAS-BLACK	QUE	175	2ND E DI
CLOCKWORTHEY, WILIAM	BAL	416	8TH WARD
CLODFETTY, ALEXANDER	ALL	010	3RD E.D.
CLOGG, EMMELINE	WOR	185	7TH E DI
CLOGG, GEORGE S.	BAL	131	16TH WAR
CLOGG, GEORGE S.	BAL	112	10TH WAR
CLOGG, JAMES	WOR	179	6TH E DI
CLOGG, SALLY	WOR	179	6TH E DI
CLOGG, WILLIAM H.	WOR	181	6TH E DI
CLOGH, PETER	MGM	381	ROCKERLE
CLOLFELTY, JOSEPH	ALL	012	3RD E.D.
CLOMAN, EDWARD	HAR	008	1ST DIST
CLOMON, GEORGE	HAR	010	1ST DIST
CLONDSLEY, JOH H. *	ANN	342	3RD DIST
CLONINGER, HENRY	WAS	139	2ND DIST
CLOONAN, TIMOTHY	BAL	409	3RD WARD
CLOOS, JOHN	BAL	127	1ST WARD
CLOPER, JACOB	WAS	078	2ND SUBD
CLOPER, SAMUEL	WAS	078	2ND SUBD
CLOPPER, FRANCES C.	MGM	402	ROCKERLE
CLOPPER, FRANCIS	BAL	315	20TH WAR
CLOPPER, GEORGE	BAL	470	14TH WAR
CLOPPER, HENRY	WAS	190	1ST DIST
CLOPPER, HENRY	WAS	242	CAVETOWN
CLOPPER, HENRY	WAS	268	1ST DIST
CLOPPER, JOHN	WAS	264	1ST DIST
CLOPPER, JOHN	WAS	242	CAVETOWN
CLOPPER, SAMUEL	WAS	283	1ST DIST
CLOSE, ANDREW J.M.	BAL	122	1ST WARD
CLOSE, CHRISTIAN	ANN	495	HOWARD D
CLOSE, EDWARD	BAL	123	1ST WARD
CLOSE, ELIJAH	FRE	177	5TH E DI
CLOSE, JESSE	FRE	177	5TH E DI
CLOSE, JOHN	BAL	032	4TH WARD
CLOSE, NICHOLAS	BAL	329	3RD WARD
CLOSE, RACHEL *	BAL	301	20TH WAR
CLOSE, ROBERT	BAL	059	10TH WAR
CLOSE, WILLIAM	ALL	122	4TH E.D.
CLOSKER, JOHN W.	KEN	300	3RD DIST
CLOSNYER, JOHN *	BAL	122	2ND DIST
CLOSSBRONNER, ELIZABETH	WAS	253	1ST DIST
CLOTFELTY, EDWIN	ALL	013	3RD E.D.
CLOTFELTY, WILLIAM	ALL	017	3RD E.D.
CLOTHER, SARAH	KEN	291	3RD DIST
CLOTHIER, SARAH J.	QUE	126	1ST E DI
CLOTHIER, WILLIAM	QUE	126	1ST E DI
CLOTIS, HENRY	BAL	151	2ND DIST
CLOTWORTHY, ALEXANDER	BAL	358	13TH WAR
CLOUCH, JAMES T.	BAL	349	3RD WARD
CLOUD, BENJAMIN	BAL	188	6TH WARD
CLOUD, CHARLES F.	BAL	096	10TH WAR
CLOUD, DANIEL	BAL	470	14TH WAR
CLOUD, ELIZA JANE	BAL	188	6TH WARD
CLOUD, JESSE	BAL	250	12TH WAR
CLOUD, JOSEPH	PRI	002	BLADENSB
CLOUD, JOSEPHINE	BAL	135	11TH WAR
CLOUD, LAURA	BAL	421	3RD WARD
CLOUD, NATHAN	BAL	427	1ST DIST
CLOUD, ROBERT	BAL	164	6TH WARD
CLOUDERLEY, JANE	BAL	182	19TH WAR
CLOUDSLEY, JOHN H. *	ANN	342	3RD DIST
CLOUGH, CHRISTA A.	PRI	027	VANSVILL
CLOUGH, DAVID	CEC	109	4TH E DI
CLOUGH, JAMES	TAL	040	EASTON D
CLOUGH, JOHN A.	TAL	037	EASTON D
CLOUGH, JOHN A.JR.	CAR	170	NO TWP L
CLOUGH, SAMUEL	ANN	460	HOWARD D
CLOUGH, THOMAS	PRI	026	VANSVILL
CLOUGH, WILLIAM	BAL	022	4TH WARD
CLOUSE, GEORGE	ALL	123	4TH E.D.
CLOUSE, HENRY	BAL	181	19TH WAR
CLOUTIEN, FRANK E.	BAL	191	11TH WAR
CLOW, AMELIA	QUE	138	1ST E DI
CLOW, CHANA	QUE	137	1ST E DI
CLOW, ISAIAH	QUE	138	1ST E DI
CLOW, JAMES	QUE	129	1ST E DI
CLOW, MARTHA	QUE	135	1ST E DI
CLOW, NOAH	QUE	138	1ST E DI
CLOW, REBECCA	QUE	152	1ST E DI
CLOW, SARAH	KEN	305	3RD DIST
CLOW, WASHINGTON	QUE	155	2ND E DI
CLOWMAN, ELIZA	BAL	121	2ND DIST
CLRK, EDARD	BAL	114	1ST WARD
CLRK, JAMES	BAL	355	8TH WARD
CLUB, JOHN	ANN	409	8TH DIST
CLUBB, HORATIO	PRI	070	MARLBROU
CLUBB, JOHN	PRI	061	NOTTINGH
CLUBB, MRS.	PRI	075	MARLBROU
CLUCH, JOHN B.	BAL	187	11TH WAR
CLUE, JOHN *	KEN	237	2ND DIST
CLUFF, DANIEL-BLACK	WOR	332	1ST E DI
CLUFF, EDWARD	SOM	396	BRINKLEY
CLUFF, LITTLETON	WOR	325	1ST E DI
CLUFF, MICHAEL	SOM	396	BRINKLEY
CLUFF, PHILLIP	SOM	466	HANGARY
CLUFF, ROBERT W.	SOM	401	BRINKLEY
CLUFF, SALLY	WOR	324	1ST E DI
CLUFF, WHITTINGTON	SOM	395	BRINKLEY
CLUGH, CAROLINE	BAL	221	17TH WAR
CLUGH, JOHN	BAL	221	17TH WAR
CLUNET, VICTOR	BAL	039	9TH WARD
CLUNG, EDWARD	CEC	054	1ST E DI
CLURVINGER, SAMUEL	BAL	266	2ND WARD
CLUSTER, PETER M.	WAS	140	2ND DIST
CLUSTINE, FRANCIS	BAL	083	1ST WARD
CLUTS, ELI	FRE	164	EMMITTSB
CLUTTS, JACOB	CAR	319	1ST DIST
CLUTY, VALENTINE	WAS	016	2ND SUBD
CLYCE, ENOCH	ALL	091	5TH E.D.
CLYCE, GEORGE	ALL	112	5TH E.D.
CLYCE, GEORGE	ALL	148	6TH E.D.
CLYNCH, SYLVESTER	BAL	145	1ST WARD
CLYNTON, THOMAS	QUE	135	1ST E DI
CM CALL, PETER	BAL	172	2ND DIST
CM CAULEY, JOHN	FRE	119	CREAGERS
COAD, CECELIA	ST	307	1ST E DI
COAD, GEORGE D.	ST	301	2ND E DI
COAD, J. EDWIN	ST	297	2ND E DI
COAD, WILLIAM	ST	297	2ND E DI
COAH, WILLIAM	BAL	160	1ST WARD
COAHLER, JAMES	BAL	058	2ND DIST
COAK, CHRISTOPHER	BAL	301	7TH WARD
COAKLEY, ELIZA	BAL	385	13TH WAR
COAKLUG, G.H.	BAL	164	1ST WARD
COAKLY, GEORGE W.	WAS	021	2ND SUBD
COAL, FRANCES	WAS	158	HAGERSTO
COAL, JAMES M.	FRE	029	FREDERIC
COAL, PHILLIP	ALL	230	CUMBERLA
COALE, ABRAM	BAL	245	20TH WAR
COALE, ALFRED	ANN	447	HOWARD D
COALE, ANN	ANN	447	HOWARD D
COALE, CHARLES	BAL	002	1ST WARD
COALE, E. P.	BAL	350	13TH WAR
COALE, EDWARD	BAL	233	12TH WAR
COALE, ELEANA	BAL	233	12TH WAR
COALE, ELIZABETH	BAL	214	11TH WAR
COALE, HARRIET-MULATTO	FRE	434	8TH E DI
COALE, HETTY	BAL	220	6TH WARD
COALE, ISAAC M.	HAR	118	2ND DIST
COALE, JAMES	BAL	325	1ST DIST
COALE, JAMES C.	BAL	315	1ST DIST
COALE, JOHN A.	ANN	448	HOWARD D
COALE, JOHN C.	HAR	118	2ND DIST
COALE, JOHN T.	BAL	184	5TH DIST
COALE, JOSEPH R.	HAR	116	2ND DIST
COALE, MARY	BAL	381	13TH WAR
COALE, MARY A.	BAL	140	11TH WAR
COALE, NACKEY	BAL	318	1ST DIST
COALE, NATHAN	BAL	232	12TH WAR
COALE, RACHEL*	BAL	104	10TH WAR
COALE, RICHAD	FRE	449	8TH E DI
COALE, SAMUEL C.	HAR	118	2ND DIST
COALE, SUSAN H.	BAL	315	1ST DIST
COALE, THEODORE-MULATTO	FRE	429	8TH E DI
COALE, THOMAS	BAL	322	1ST DIST
COALE, WILLIAM	BAL	333	1ST DIST
COALE, WILLIAM E.	BAL	315	1ST DIST
COALE, WILLIAM E. JR.	BAL	315	1ST DIST
COALE, WILLIAM M.	BAL	158	1ST WARD
COALHUNT, ELLEN	BAL	161	19TH WAR
COALL, SAMUEL	BAL	221	19TH WAR
COALS, JOHN	CEC	042	CHESAPEA
COALTON, ALEXANDER	BAL	023	9TH WARD
COANILLEY, JOHN F.	MGM	411	MEDLEY 3
COANSLEMAN, SARAH	BAL	018	18TH WAR
COAR, MARGARET	BAL	110	5TH WARD
COARD, CHARLES	WOR	244	1ST CENS
COARKLEY, THOMAS	BAL	018	2ND DIST
COARLEY, REBECCA	BAL	415	1ST DIST
COARROLL, JOHN	BAL	267	1ST DIST
COARSE, ELIZABETH	HAR	027	1ST DIST
COARST, WILLIAM	BAL	103	1ST WARD
COARTS, JOHN	BAL	090	18TH WAR
COAT, JOHN	BAL	147	2ND DIST
COATE, MARY	BAL	074	10TH WAR
COATES, AGNES	BAL	292	20TH WAR
COATES, ANDREW	BAL	208	19TH WAR
COATES, DELITHA	PRI	010	BLADENSB
COATES, FANNY	BAL	008	9TH WARD
COATES, HENRY	FRE	252	NEW MARK
COATES, ISAAC-BLACK	FRE	445	8TH E DI
COATES, JOHN	BAL	412	14TH WAR
COATES, JOHN	BAL	089	1ST WARD
COATES, JOSIAH	BAL	216	6TH WARD
COATES, LEMUEL	BAL	237	20TH WAR
COATES, LEONARD	BAL	094	10TH WAR
COATES, M.-BLACK	FRE	200	5TH E DI
COATES, MARGARET-BLACK	FRE	197	5TH E DI
COATES, MARY	BAL	219	6TH WARD
COATES, MARY A.	BAL	237	20TH WAR
COATES, MATT	BAL	141	19TH WAR
COATES, SAMUEL	BAL	044	15TH WAR
COATES, SARAH-BLACK	FRE	196	5TH E DI
COATES, SUSAN	BAL	357	13TH WAR
COATES, THOMAS KELLY-BLAC	FRE	197	5TH E DI
COATH, THOMAS J.	BAL	304	3RD WARD
COATH, WILLIAM S.	BAL	052	4TH WARD
COATHS, MARY J.	BAL	057	18TH WAR
COATHS, ROBERT E.	BAL	078	18TH WAR
COATLIFF, JOHN	BAL	207	11TH WAR
COATNEY, ROBERT	ST	306	1ST E DI
COATS, AUGUSTUS	CAR	312	1ST DIST
COATS, BEN	ANN	323	2ND DIST
COATS, BETSY	ANN	396	8TH DIST
COATS, CAROLINE	BAL	337	7TH WARD
COATS, CATHERINE	ALL	240	CUMBERLA
COATS, CATO	ANN	304	1ST DIST
COATS, CHARLES	ANN	295	1ST DIST
COATS, CLEM	BAL	165	19TH WAR
COATS, DARKY	CAL	040	3RD DIST
COATS, DEMBY	CAL	022	2ND DIST
COATS, ELIJAH	CAL	052	3RD DIST
COATS, ELIZABETH	BAL	407	1ST DIST
COATS, ELIZABETH	BAL	408	8TH WARD
COATS, GEORGE W.	CAL	001	1ST DIST
COATS, HENRY	CAL	052	3RD DIST
COATS, ISAAC H.	ALL	251	CUMBERLA
COATS, JACOB	CEC	038	CHESAPEA
COATS, JAMES	CAR	307	1ST DIST
COATS, JARRET	CAL	036	2ND DIST
COATS, JOHN	CAR	240	TANEYTOW
COATS, JOHN	ANN	304	1ST DIST
COATS, JOHN	ANN	304	1ST DIST
COATS, LOYD-BLACK	CAR	381	2ND DIST
COATS, MARY Y.	BAL	155	11TH WAR
COATS, NANCY	PRI	109	PISCATAW
COATS, RICHARD	CAL	036	2ND DIST
COATS, RICHARD	HAR	047	1ST DIST

COATS, SARAH BAL 057 15TH WAR
COATS, SMAUEL BAL 005 EASTERN
COATS, SUSAN CAL 036 2ND DIST
COATS, WILLIAM ANN 397 8TH DIST
COATS, WILLIAM PRI 014 BLADENSB
COATS, WILLIAM-BLACK CAR 381 2ND DIST
COBB, CHARLES H. BAL 235 12TH WAR
COBB, EDWARD MGM 319 CRACKLIN
COBB, ELIZA BAL 326 12TH WAR
COBB, HIRAM CAR 308 1ST DIST
COBB, JAMES BAL 282 2ND WARD
COBB, JOSIAH BAL 373 13TH WAR
COBB, RUTH BAL 341 13TH WAR
COBB, SARAH ANN 437 HOWARD D
COBBAGE, HARRIET E. ALL 221 CUMBERLA
COBBERT, ARCHIBALD WAS 157 2ND DIST
COBBINER, GILBERT T. ANN 281 ANNAPOLI
COBBITT, HENRY BAL 115 1ST WARD
COBBUTZ, ELIZABETH FRE 318 MIDDLETO
COBBY, CHAELS B. BAL 157 1ST WARD
COBEIN, JOHN BAL 059 15TH WAR
COBELING, JANE-MULATTO FRE 009 FREDERIC
COBER, JOHN BAL 341 7TH WARD
COBERTH, LLOYD BAL 078 15TH WAR
COBERTH, MARGARET CAL 026 2ND DIST
COBISN, LEAH* DOR 411 1ST DIST
COBLENTS, PHILIP FRE 319 MIDDLETO
COBLENTY, ANN FRE 318 MIDDLETO
COBLENTZ, DAVID FRE 402 JEFFERSO
COBLENTZ, HENRY FRE 336 MIDDLETO
COBLENTZ, HENRY FRE 336 MIDDLETO
COBLENTZ, JOHN FRE 319 MIDDLETO
COBLENTZ, JOHN B. FRE 336 MIDDLETO
COBLENTZ, OLIVER P. FRE 319 MIDDLETO
COBOURN, BENJAMIN F. BAL 292 7TH WARD
COBOURN, GEORGE BAL 370 8TH WARD
COBOURN, HARRIET BAL 045 1ST WARD
COBOURN, HENRY BAL 396 8TH WARD
COBOURN, JOHN BAL 282 7TH WARD
COBOURN, THOMAS BAL 370 8TH WARD
COBOURN, WILLIAM H. BAL 292 7TH WARD
COBURN, CALEB ANN 359 3RD DIST
COBURN, JAMES BAL 072 10TH WAR
COBURN, LAMBERT* TAL 067 EASTON T
COBURN, N. BAL 281 2ND WARD
COBURN, SOLLOMAN TAL 047 EASTON T
COBURN, THOMAS DOR 376 1ST DIST
COBURN, W. DOR 389 1ST DIST
COBURN, WILLIAM BAL 445 14TH WAR
COBURN, WILLIAM BAL 445 14TH WAR
COBURTH, HESTER W. ANN 282 ANNAPOLI
COBY, CATHERINE C. CHA 248 HILLTOP
COBY, HEZEKIAH CHA 259 MIDDLETO
COBY, JANE BAL 240 1ST DIST
COBY, JOHN T. CHA 239 HILLTOP
COBY, THOMAS BAL 234 1ST DIST
COCCONIA, DANIEL HAR 061 1ST DIST
COCHARNE, ALEXANDER ALL 127 4TH E.D.
COCHENOUR, DANIEL WAS 142 HAGERSTO
COCHER, CONROD M. WAS 160 HAGERSTO
COCHLAN, MICHAEL BAL 275 1ST DIST
COCHLIN, PATRICK BAL 285 1ST DIST
COCHORAN, JULIA BAL 299 17TH WAR
COCHRAIN, DAVID CEC 129 6TH E DI
COCHRAIN, JOSEPH CEC 177 7TH E DI
COCHRAN, ANTHONY CEC 110 4TH E DI
COCHRAN, CORNELIUS FRE 407 JEFFERSO
COCHRAN, DAVID WAS 229 1ST DIST
COCHRAN, ELIZA KEN 290 3RD DIST
COCHRAN, ELIZABETH FRE 392 PETERSVI
COCHRAN, FRAMES CAR 137 NO TWP L
COCHRAN, FREDERICK A. BAL 058 15TH WAR
COCHRAN, HENRY FRE 403 JEFFERSO
COCHRAN, HESTER KEN 267 1ST DIST
COCHRAN, JAMES HAR 190 3RD DIST
COCHRAN, JAMES BAL 457 8TH WARD
COCHRAN, JAMES E. BAL 164 6TH WARD
COCHRAN, JOHN BAL 457 8TH WARD
COCHRAN, JOHN FRE 440 8TH E DI
COCHRAN, JOHN BAL 018 4TH WARD
COCHRAN, JOHN BAL 026 4TH WARD
COCHRAN, JOHN W. FRE 441 8TH E DI
COCHRAN, MARY BAL 069 15TH WAR
COCHRAN, RICHARD BAL 292 12TH WAR
COCHRANE, INA WAS 034 2ND SUBD
COCHRANE, MARTIN BAL 348 7TH WARD
COCHRANE, WILLIAM ANN 312 1ST DIST
COCHRIAN, CHARLOTT HAR 160 3RD DIST
COCK, JENNY BAL 217 19TH WAR
COCK, N.J.A. BAL 248 20TH WAR
COCK, WILLIAM BAL 248 20TH WAR
COCKER, JOHN BAL 100 2ND DIST
COCKER, MARGARET BAL 007 1ST WARD
COCKERELL, WILLIAM BAL 156 1ST WARD
COCKES, BENJAMIN CEC 047 1ST E DI
COCKES, ELIZABETH CEC 071 5TH E DI
COCKES, GEORGE CEC 060 1ST E DI
COCKES, WILLIAM CEC 071 5TH E DI
COCKEY, AMANDA QUE 229 4TH E DI
COCKEY, ANNA BAL 249 1ST DIST
COCKEY, AUGUSTA BAL 447 14TH WAR
COCKEY, CATO BAL 222 1ST DIST
COCKEY, CHARLES T. BAL 416 1ST DIST
COCKEY, EDWARD QUE 227 4TH E DI
COCKEY, ELIZABETH S. BAL 024 2ND DIST
COCKEY, ELLEN M. BAL 441 1ST DIST
COCKEY, HENRIETTA CAR 264 WESTMINS
COCKEY, HENRIETTA O. BAL 472 14TH WAR
COCKEY, JACOB BAL 243 20TH WAR
COCKEY, JAMES QUE 229 4TH E DI
COCKEY, JOHN QUE 227 4TH E DI
COCKEY, JOHN E. QUE 228 4TH E DI
COCKEY, JOHN G. BAL 163 16TH WAR
COCKEY, JOHN JR. BAL 464 1ST DIST
COCKEY, JOHN P. BAL 032 4TH WARD
COCKEY, JOHN R. BAL 242 1ST DIST
COCKEY, JOHN SR. BAL 464 1ST DIST
COCKEY, JOSHUA BAL 115 11TH WAR
COCKEY, JOSHUA F. BAL 021 2ND DIST
COCKEY, MARION FRE 066 FREDERIC
COCKEY, MARY BAL 090 5TH WARD
COCKEY, MARY BAL 263 1ST DIST
COCKEY, MARY QUE 227 4TH E DI
COCKEY, MORDICA G. CAR 193 4TH DIST
COCKEY, PETER F. BAL 021 2ND DIST
COCKEY, RACHEL BAL 472 14TH WAR
COCKEY, RACHEL BAL 408 14TH WAR
COCKEY, ROBERT BAL 077 1ST WARD
COCKEY, S. G. FRE 309 WOODSBOR
COCKEY, SAMUEL BAL 453 1ST DIST
COCKEY, SARAH BAL 228 6TH WARD
COCKEY, SEBASTIAN G. FRE 273 NEW MARK
COCKEY, SUSAN BAL 029 9TH WARD
COCKEY, THEADORE FRE 033 FREDERIC
COCKEY, THOMAS FRE 044 FREDERIC
COCKEY, THOMAS BAL 439 1ST DIST
COCKEY, THOMAS QUE 228 4TH E DI
COCKEY, THOMAS B. BAL 403 1ST DIST
COCKEY, THOMAS B. BAL 281 7TH WARD
COCKEY, THOMAS D. BAL 449 1ST DIST
COCKEY, THOMAS D. BAL 448 1ST DIST
COCKEY, WILLIAM H. BAL 249 12TH WAR
COCKEY, WILLIAM HENRY QUE 228 4TH E DI
COCKLAN, ANN BAL 189 11TH WAR
COCKLAND, MARY BAL 149 19TH WAR
COCKLIN, BRIDGET ALL 215 CUMBERLA
COCKLIN, JAMES CAR 262 3RD DIST
COCKLIN, JOHN S. BAL 124 1ST WARD
COCKRAN, ANN M. CAR 155 NO TWP L
COCKRAN, BRIDGET BAL 199 11TH WAR
COCKRAN, CAROLINE BAL 052 15TH WAR
COCKRAN, CHARLES BAL 052 15TH WAR
COCKRAN, CHARLES CAR 139 NO TWP L
COCKRAN, CHARLES T. FRE 320 MIDDLETO
COCKRAN, DAVID CAR 282 7TH DIST
COCKRAN, ELISHA CAR 154 NO TWP L
COCKRAN, J. BAL 161 1ST WARD
COCKRAN, JACOB FRE 323 MIDDLETO
COCKRAN, JAMES CAR 139 NO TWP L
COCKRAN, JAMES CAL 003 1ST DIST
COCKRAN, JANE CAR 086 NO TWP L
COCKRAN, JOHN DOR 430 1ST DIST
COCKRAN, JOSIAH CAR 164 NO TWP L
COCKRAN, MARGARET BAL 317 20TH WAR
COCKRAN, RACHAEL J. * BAL 080 15TH WAR
COCKRAN, SELY CAR 145 NO TWP L
COCKRAN, THOMAS BAL 181 2ND WARD
COCKRAN, WILLIAM CAL 003 1ST DIST
COCKRAN, WILLIAM BAL 155 19TH WAR
COCKRAN, WILLIAM * BAL 079 15TH WAR
COCKRANE, ALEXANDER ALL 135 4TH E.D.
COCKRANE, ALICE BAL 445 8TH WARD
COCKRANE, ANN BAL 420 8TH WARD
COCKRANE, ANTHONY ALL 135 4TH E.D.
COCKRANE, JOHN ALL 135 4TH E.D.
COCKRANE, L. MORRIS BAL 381 13TH WAR
COCKRANE, THOMAS BAL 458 8TH WARD
COCKRILL, JAMES J. BAL 062 1ST WARD
COCKRILL, JANE BAL 419 3RD WARD
COCKRILL, REBECCA BAL 278 2ND WARD
COCKRILL, SOPHIA BAL 420 3RD WARD
COCKS, ELIZABETH CEC 045 1ST E DI
COCKS, JANE CEC 060 1ST E DI
COCLITAN, BRIDGET * BAL 275 1ST DIST
COCO, PHILIP-BLACK BAL 214 2ND WARD
COCORAN, JOHN ST 348 5TH E DI
COCTER, GRIFFIN CHA 219 ALLENS F
COCTILL, JAMES W. * BAL 289 20TH WAR
CODD, ELIZA A. BAL 370 3RD WARD
CODD, PELKINGTON BAL 410 3RD WARD
CODDINGTON, JONATHAN ALL 025 2ND E.D.
CODDINGTON, JOSEPH ALL 023 2ND E.D.
CODDINGTON,W ILLIAM ALL 026 2ND E.D.
CODE, PETER HAR 172 3RD DIST
CODE, PHILLIP BAL 097 1ST WARD
CODET, J. R. BAL 102 10TH WAR
CODEY, ROSANNA BAL 143 11TH WAR
CODILL, JAMES W. * BAL 289 20TH WAR
CODLIN, SARAH BAL 387 1ST DIST
CODMAN, FREDERICK BAL 291 12TH WAR
CODWAY, WILLIAM D.* DOR 447 1ST DIST
CODY, EDWARD BAL 157 1ST WARD
CODY, MICHAEL MGM 391 ROCKERLE
COE, CHARLES CEC 107 3RD E DI
COE, FRISBY TAL 061 EASTON D
COE, GEORGE G. PRI 115 PISCATAW
COE, JOSEPH CAR 409 2ND DIST
COE, JULIA A. BAL 034 2ND DIST
COE, KENSEY J. PRI 053 AQUASCO
COE, MARY PRI 115 PISCATAW
COE, REBECCA BAL 185 6TH WARD
COE, SAMUEL PRI 104 PISCATAW
COE, SARAH BAL 014 2ND DIST
COE, WILLIAM BAL 127 2ND DIST
COE, WILLIAM BAL 171 2ND DIST
COE, WILLIAM G. BAL 235 12TH WAR
COE, WILLIAM H. BAL 021 9TH WARD
COEHM, E. W. BAL 471 14TH WAR
COEL, TOM ANN 420 HOWARD D
COELMAN, BERNARD ALL 243 CUMBERLA
COELMAN, JAMES BAL 291 12TH WAR
COELMAN, JAMES BAL 102 5TH WARD
COELMAN, JOHN W. FRE 202 5TH E DI
COELMAN, NOAH BAL 325 7TH WARD
COELMANN, PRUDENCE FRE 447 8TH E DI
COEN, JOHN HAR 169 3RD DIST
COEW, TIMOTHY WAS 052 2ND SUBD
COEY, ELISHA CAR 156 NO TWP L
COEY, ELIZA CAR 167 NO TWP L
COEY, GOREY CAR 121 NO TWP L
COEY, LEVIN CAR 122 NO TWP L
COEY, MARY CAR 132 NO TWP L
COEY, WILLIAM CAR 110 NO TWP L
COFER, FRANCIS CHA 237 HILLTOP
COFER, JOHN CHA 223 ALLENS F
COFF, LAURENA * ALL 141 6TH E.D.
COFF, LEWIS BAL 310 12TH WAR
COFF, PATRICK ALL 050 10TH E.D
COFFEE, ANN CHA 238 HILLTOP
COFFEE, B. FRE 200 5TH E DI
COFFEE, C. FRE 200 5TH E DI
COFFEE, FANNY BAL 089 5TH WARD
COFFEE, JOHN ALL 155 6TH E.D.
COFFEE, MARTIN ALL 050 10TH E.D
COFFEE, MATHEW ALL 227 CUMBERLA
COFFEE, PATRICK HAR 145 3RD DIST
COFFEE, STEPHEN WAS 212 1ST DIST
COFFEY, MICHAEL FRE 161 EMMITTSB
COFFEY, ROBERT BAL 168 2ND DIST
COFFIELD, BRIDGET BAL 353 7TH WARD
COFFIELD, GEORGE C. R. BAL 339 13TH WAR
COFFIELD, HUGH BAL 080 18TH WAR
COFFIELD, JEREMIAH BAL 145 16TH WAR
COFFIELD, JOHN BAL 080 18TH WAR
COFFIELD, JOSEPH BAL 212 11TH WAR
COFFIER, JANE BAL 257 12TH WAR
COFFIN, CHARLES E. BAL 272 2ND WARD
COFFIN, DAVID WOR 274 BERLIN I
COFFIN, GEORGE BAL 312 3RD WARD
COFFIN, ISAAC WOR 257 1ST CENS
COFFIN, JAEMS WOR 271 BERLIN I
COFFIN, JOEL WOR 274 BERLIN I
COFFIN, JOHN L. BAL 083 18TH WAR
COFFIN, MAJOR WOR 279 BERLIN I
COFFIN, O. M. BAL 151 1ST WARD
COFFIN, SAUL WOR 280 BERLIN I
COFFIN, WILLIAM G. BAL 248 2ND WARD
COFFINBAGGER, JACOB BAL 009 4TH WARD
COFFINE, OBED M.* BAL 341 3RD WARD
COFFIT, MARY ALL 242 CUMBERLA
COFFMAN, ANDREW FRE 143 10TH E D
COFFMAN, DAVID WAS 019 2ND SUBD
COFFMAN, FANNY BAL 268 12TH WAR
COFFMAN, HENRY WAS 076 2ND SUBD
COFFMAN, HENRY FRE 150 10TH E D
COFFMAN, JACOB WAS 035 2ND SUBD
COFFMAN, JULIA A. FRE 157 10TH E D
COFFMAN, LAVINA WAS 036 2ND SUBD
COFFMAN, SIMON WAS 042 2ND SUBD
COFFMAN, WASH FRE 164 EMMITTSB
COFFRAN, JAMES BAL 085 18TH WAR
COFFRON, THOMAS PRI 065 NOTTINGH
COFINBERGER, PETER WAS 256 1ST DIST
COFRAN, FRANCIS PRI 068 NOTTINGH
COGAN, ANN ANN 418 HOWARD D
COGAN, JOHN ALL 128 4TH E.D.
COGATE, SUSAN* TAL 044 EASTON D
COGE, GEORGE-BLACK CAR 088 NO TWP L
COGE, ROBERT-BLACK QUE 129 1ST E DI
COGER, GUSTY PRI 109 PISCATAW
COGGIN, MARGARET BAL 045 2ND DIST
COGGINS, ANNA M. FRE 041 FREDERIC
COGGINS, CHARLES BAL 083 10TH WAR
COGGINS, GEORGE BAL 411 8TH WARD
COGGINS, JAMES BAL 411 8TH WARD
COGGINS, JOHN BAL 411 8TH WARD
COGGINS, WILLIAM BAL 411 8TH WARD
COGHLAN, EDWARD FRE 380 PETERSVI
COGHLAN, JOHNP. FRE 397 PETERSVI
COGHLAN,RICHARD FRE 389 PETERSVI
COGHLIN, JOHN BAL 124 1ST WARD
COGLE, MARY BAL 465 14TH WAR
COGLER, MARY WAS 256 1ST DIST
COGLES, MARTHA BAL 416 8TH WARD
COGSWELL, GEORGE ALL 220 CUMBERLA
COGSWELL, GEORGE BAL 254 12TH WAR
COGSWELL, JAMES BAL 292 7TH WARD
COGSWELL, LYDIA BAL 244 12TH WAR
COGSWELL, MARY E. BAL 150 16TH WAR
COGSWELL, NATHANIEL BAL 149 16TH WAR
COGSWELL, WILLIAM ALL 220 CUMBERLA
COHAGEN, ANN G. CHA 220 ALLENS F
COHAGEN, LOUISA BAL 013 9TH WARD
COHANNAX, JOHN BAL 038 18TH WAR
COHE, MARGARET CEC 063 1ST E DI
COHEE, ANN BAL 056 18TH WAR
COHEE, HENRY KEN 242 2ND DIST
COHEE, SARAH DOR 321 1ST DIST
COHEE, WILLIAM * KEN 242 2ND DIST
COHELASURE, FANNY FRE 273 NEW MARK
COHEN, ADOLPH BAL 028 1ST WARD
COHEN, ARNOLDINA BAL 166 16TH WAR
COHEN, BERRY BAL 317 12TH WAR
COHEN, CELIA E. BAL 201 11TH WAR
COHEN, CHARITY BAL 200 6TH WARD
COHEN, DAVID BAL 334 7TH WARD
COHEN, DEBY BAL 125 11TH WAR
COHEN, E. R.* BAL 093 10TH WAR
COHEN, ELLEN BAL 351 13TH WAR
COHEN, GEORGE BAL 461 1ST DIST
COHEN, GERSON BAL 014 9TH WARD
COHEN, HENRIETTA BAL 022 4TH WARD
COHEN, ISRAEL BAL 201 11TH WAR
COHEN, J. J. JR. BAL 149 11TH WAR
COHEN, MARGARET MGM 337 CRACKLIN
COHEN, MARY BAL 321 7TH WARD
COHEN, MATILDA BAL 079 1ST WARD
COHEN, MOSES BAL 184 6TH WARD
COHEN, NATHAN BAL 298 3RD WARD
COHEN, RACHEL BAL 334 7TH WARD
COHEN, ROSA BAL 090 10TH WAR
COHENBERG, ALFONSO BAL 321 7TH WARD
COHER, ELIZABETH KEN 305 3RD DIST
COHER, WILLIAM KEN 242 2ND DIST
COHILL, E. PRI 113 PISCATAW
COHN, JAMES* TAL 022 EASTON D
COHN, WILLIAM C.* TAL 023 EASTON D
COHU, JAMES* TAL 022 EASTON D
COHU, JAMES* TAL 022 EASTON D
COHU, WILLIAM C.* TAL 023 EASTON D
COIL, GOSPEL BAL 139 2ND DIST
COIL, MARGARET BAL 232 17TH WAR
COILS, JAMES FRE 288 WOODSBOR
COILSTON, SAMUEL BAL 148 11TH WAR
COIN, JULIAN BAL 068 2ND DIST
COIN, MARY HAR 041 1ST DIST
COINER, SARAH* BAL 078 4TH WARD
COING, WILLIAM-BLACK BAL 216 2ND WARD
COINTOISE, SOPHIA M. FRE 039 FREDERIC
COIT, J.H. WAS 021 2ND SUBD
COKE, JAMES BAL 364 3RD WARD
COKE, LOUISA BAL 384 13TH WAR
COKE, NATHAN-BLACK CAR 168 NO TWP L
COKELY, PHILIPP BAL 059 2ND DIST
COKELY, THOMAS BAL 233 1ST DIST
COKEN, MESEY BAL 317 12TH WAR
COKER, ABNER-MULATTO CAR 106 NO TWP L
COKER, CHRISTIAN BAL 038 9TH WARD
COKER, FRANCES BAL 041 15TH WAR
COKER, HENRY-BLACK CAR 094 NO TWP L
COKER, JOHN CAR 244 3RD DIST
COKER, JOHN W. CAR 294 7TH DIST
COKER, LEVIN* TAL 022 EASTON D
COKER, MISS BAL 143 5TH WARD
COKER, MOSES-MULATTO CAR 105 NO TWP L
COKER, PHILIP BAL 373 3RD WARD
COKER, SUSAN CAR 279 7TH DIST
COKER, WILLIAM QUE 213 3RD E DI
COKES, CATHARINE CEC 064 1ST E DI
COKY, BRIDGET BAL 285 12TH WAR
COLADAY, JOSEPH A. BAL 020 18TH WAR
COLADY, CHARLES BAL 019 18TH WAR
COLAFLOWER, CATHARINE WAS 228 1ST DIST
COLAFLOWER, HENRY WAS 236 CAVETOWN
COLAFLOWER, JOHN WAS 228 1ST DIST
COLAHON, JOHN BAL 445 14TH WAR
COLAMER, ARTHER FRE 123 CREAGERS
COLAMER, ROLA WAS 086 2ND SUBD
COLAMER, SALLY WAS 073 2ND SUBD
COLAMER, SUSAN WAS 073 2ND SUBD

Name	County	Page	District
COLAMER, THOMAS	WAS	085	2ND SUBD
COLAN, JOHN	BAL	142	16TH WAR
COLAN, JOHN	ALL	253	CUMBERLA
COLAN, JOHN	BAL	453	1ST DIST
COLARD, THOMPSON	CEC	169	6TH E DI
COLBAUGH, ZEDWICK W.	ALL	130	4TH E.D.
COLBERN, E.	ANN	281	ANNAPOLI
COLBERT, ANNA	ANN	353	3RD DIST
COLBERT, CHARLES	WAS	156	HAGERSTO
COLBERT, DIANA	BAL	176	6TH WARD
COLBERT, ELIZABETH	BAL	100	15TH WAR
COLBERT, FRANCIS	WAS	158	HAGERSTO
COLBERT, FRANCIS	FRE	219	BUCKEYST
COLBERT, JAMES	WAS	094	2ND SUBD
COLBERT, JERRY	WAS	009	WILLIAMS
COLBERT, JOHN	BAL	048	9TH WARD
COLBERT, JOSEPH	FRE	250	NEW MARK
COLBERT, LEVIN	SOM	350	BRINKLEY
COLBERT, LEWIN A.	BAL	303	17TH WAR
COLBERT, MARY A.	BAL	245	17TH WAR
COLBERT, MATTHIAS	BAL	077	15TH WAR
COLBERT, NATHAN	FRE	125	CREAGERS
COLBERT, SUSAN	WAS	009	WILLIAMS
COLBERT, WESLEY	WAS	154	HAGERSTO
COLBERT, WHITTY	SOM	352	BRINKLEY
COLBERT, WILLIAM	WAS	156	HAGERSTO
COLBERT, WILLIAM	FRE	219	BUCKEYST
COLBERTT, HORACE	MGM	408	MEDLEY 3
COLBET, CLARN	BAL	242	12TH WAR
COLBITT, MARTIN	WAS	264	1ST DIST
COLBORNE, ELIZABETH	SOM	360	BRINKLEY
COLBORNE, JAMES F.	SOM	386	BRINKLEY
COLBORNE, MARY	SOM	385	BRINKLEY
COLBORNE, MARY	SOM	403	BRINKLEY
COLBORNE, STEPHEN	SOM	400	BRINKLEY
COLBORNE, THOMAS L.	SOM	386	BRINKLEY
COLBORNE, WILLIAM	SOM	360	BRINKLEY
COLBOURN, BENJAMIN	SOM	365	BRINKLEY
COLBOURN, SAMUEL	SOM	396	BRINKLEY
COLBOURN, WILLIAM	SOM	365	BRINKLEY
COLBOURNE, CRIPPEN	SOM	365	BRINKLEY
COLBOURNE, JOHN J.D.	WOR	174	6TH E DI
COLBOURNE, WILLIAM W.	SOM	366	BRINKLEY
COLBUM, ELIJAH	DOR	318	1ST DIST
COLBUM, MICHAEL	DOR	296	1ST DIST
COLBURN, BETHANY	DOR	324	1ST DIST
COLBURN, DANIEL	DOR	324	1ST DIST
COLBURN, DE HERVEY	BAL	357	13TH WAR
COLBURN, E.A.	WAS	021	2ND SUBD
COLBURN, JOEL	BAL	088	18TH WAR
COLBURN, JOSEPH	TAL	020	EASTON D
COLBURN, MARIA	ANN	363	4TH DIST
COLBURN, WILLIAM	TAL	011	EASTON D
COLBURN, WILLIAM	WOR	348	1ST E DI
COLBURN, WINDEE*	TAL	011	EASTON D
COLBY, WILLIAM	CHA	249	HILLTOP
COLDAT, JAMES	BAL	341	1ST DIST
COLDEN, CALEB	BAL	293	3RD WARD
COLDEN, SAMUEL	BAL	145	11TH WAR
COLDER, FRANKLIN	HAR	083	2ND DIST
COLDER, JAMES	HAR	083	2ND DIST
COLDER, MARTIN	HAR	066	1ST DIST
COLDER, ROSANA	BAL	204	2ND WARD
COLDWELL, EELIZA	TAL	116	ST MICHA
COLDWELL, HARRISON	TAL	110	ST MICHA
COLDWELL, JAMES	TAL	118	ST MICHA
COLDWELL, JOSEPH	TAL	103	ST MICHA
COLDWELL, MARY	TAL	111	ST MICHA
COLE MEYER, HENRY	BAL	459	14TH WAR
COLE, ABIGAS	BAL	193	5TH DIST
COLE, ABRAHAM	HAR	192	3RD DIST
COLE, ABRAHAM G.	BAL	462	14TH WAR
COLE, AJMS	BAL	286	20TH WAR
COLE, ALANSON	BAL	110	2ND DIST
COLE, ALEXANDER	PRI	029	VANSVILL
COLE, ALEXANDER	ST	265	3RD E DI
COLE, ALFRED	BAL	353	1ST DIST
COLE, ALFRED	ANN	399	8TH DIST
COLE, ALFRED	CAR	334	6TH DIST
COLE, ALFRED C.	CEC	011	ELKTON 3
COLE, ALLEY	ST	335	4TH E DI
COLE, AMELIA	BAL	359	13TH WAR
COLE, AMRY	BAL	074	15TH WAR
COLE, ANN	BAL	356	8TH WARD
COLE, ANN L.	BAL	424	8TH WARD
COLE, ANSON	TAL	045	EASTON T
COLE, AUGUSTUS	BAL	192	6TH WARD
COLE, B.	BAL	162	1ST WARD
COLE, BENEDICT	ST	265	3RD E DI
COLE, BENJAMIN	BAL	066	2ND DIST
COLE, BENJAMIN	HAR	167	3RD DIST
COLE, BEVI	BAL	165	2ND DIST
COLE, CARNLIA A.	HAR	147	3RD DIST
COLE, CAROLINE-BLACK	CAR	159	NO TWP L
COLE, CASIAK	BAL	422	1ST DIST
COLE, CATHARINE	BAL	012	15TH WAR
COLE, CATHARINE	BAL	114	15TH WAR
COLE, CATHERINE	FRE	030	FREDERIC
COLE, CHARLES.A.	BAL	216	11TH WAR
COLE, CHARLES T.	HAR	156	3RD DIST
COLE, CHARLES-BLACK	ST	297	2ND E DI
COLE, CORNELIOUS	HAR	177	3RD DIST
COLE, CORNELIUS H.	BAL	179	16TH WAR
COLE, CORNELIUS M.	BAL	146	5TH WARD
COLE, CRAVIN	CAR	171	8TH DIST
COLE, DANIEL	BAL	091	2ND DIST
COLE, DANIEL	QUE	194	3RD E DI
COLE, E.H.	HAR	179	3RD DIST
COLE, EDWARD	BAL	072	2ND DIST
COLE, ELI	BAL	190	5TH DIST
COLE, ELIAS	BAL	269	1ST DIST
COLE, ELIAS	QUE	179	2ND E DI
COLE, ELIAS	ST	272	3RD E DI
COLE, ELIZA	BAL	438	14TH WAR
COLE, ELIZABETH	BAL	091	2ND DIST
COLE, ELIZABETH	BAL	016	2ND DIST
COLE, ELIZABETH	BAL	055	9TH WARD
COLE, ELIZABETH	BAL	325	7TH WARD
COLE, ELIZABETH	BAL	444	8TH WARD
COLE, ELIZABETH	BAL	282	7TH WARD
COLE, ELLEN	BAL	234	12TH WAR
COLE, ELLEN J.	BAL	137	5TH WARD
COLE, EMILINE-MULATTO	ST	339	4TH E DI
COLE, ERNESTUS	BAL	183	5TH DIST
COLE, EZEKIEL	HAR	163	3RD DIST
COLE, F.	BAL	230	1ST DIST
COLE, FLORA	CEC	153	PORT DUP
COLE, GEORGE	CEC	158	PORT DUP
COLE, GEORGE	CEC	011	ELKTON 3
COLE, GEORGE	ST	299	2ND E DI
COLE, GEORGE A.	FRE	035	FREDERIC
COLE, GEORGE H.	BAL	030	2ND DIST
COLE, GEORGE W.	ANN	484	HOWARD D
COLE, H.	BAL	152	1ST WARD
COLE, HANAH	BAL	404	8TH WARD
COLE, HANNA	BAL	015	4TH WARD
COLE, HARRISON	BAL	460	8TH WARD
COLE, HENRIETTA-BLACK	ST	301	2ND E DI
COLE, HENRY	BAL	153	1ST WARD
COLE, HENRY	BAL	188	6TH WARD
COLE, HENRY M.	HAR	178	3RD DIST
COLE, HENRY-BLACK	QUE	192	3RD E DI
COLE, HESEKIAH H.	BAL	279	7TH WARD
COLE, HINSON	QUE	153	1ST E DI
COLE, HINSON W.	BAL	088	4TH WARD
COLE, HUGH	WAS	027	2ND SUBD
COLE, HYRIM	HAR	189	3RD DIST
COLE, ISAAC	WAS	148	2ND DIST
COLE, ISAAC	BAL	455	1ST DIST
COLE, ISAAC JR.	BAL	470	14TH WAR
COLE, ISAAC M.D.	BAL	244	1ST DIST
COLE, ISABAELLA	BAL	406	14TH WAR
COLE, ISAIAH	PRI	031	VANSVILL
COLE, J. H.	BAL	470	14TH WAR
COLE, J. W.	BAL	282	2ND WARD
COLE, JACOB	BAL	095	10TH WAR
COLE, JAMES	BAL	034	1ST WARD
COLE, JAMES	BAL	028	1ST WARD
COLE, JAMES	BAL	125	1ST WARD
COLE, JAMES	BAL	346	3RD WARD
COLE, JAMES	ANN	399	8TH DIST
COLE, JAMES	CAL	047	3RD DIST
COLE, JAMES	BAL	252	17TH WAR
COLE, JAMES	HAR	173	3RD DIST
COLE, JAMES	HAR	027	1ST DIST
COLE, JAMES	WAS	028	2ND SUBD
COLE, JAMES	TAL	091	ST MICHA
COLE, JAMES C.	HAR	163	3RD DIST
COLE, JAMES H.	ANN	409	8TH DIST
COLE, JAMES W.	QUE	203	3RD E DI
COLE, JANE A.	BAL	034	1ST WARD
COLE, JANE-BLACK	QUE	150	1ST E DI
COLE, JARET	BAL	423	1ST DIST
COLE, JARRETT	HAR	120	2ND DIST
COLE, JARRETT	BAL	046	4TH WARD
COLE, JEMIMA	BAL	184	5TH DIST
COLE, JEREMIAH	BAL	423	8TH WARD
COLE, JERRY	PRI	050	AQUASCO
COLE, JIM	TAL	012	EASTON D
COLE, JOHN	TAL	095	ST MICHA
COLE, JOHN	QUE	191	3RD E DI
COLE, JOHN	QUE	168	2ND E DI
COLE, JOHN	BAL	264	1ST DIST
COLE, JOHN	BAL	390	1ST DIST
COLE, JOHN	ANN	304	1ST DIST
COLE, JOHN	BAL	450	8TH WARD
COLE, JOHN	ANN	481	HOWARD D
COLE, JOHN	BAL	020	2ND DIST
COLE, JOHN	BAL	093	2ND DIST
COLE, JOHN	CEC	147	PORT DUP
COLE, JOHN	MGM	375	ROCKERLE
COLE, JOHN	BAL	156	11TH WAR
COLE, JOHN	FRE	003	FREDERIC
COLE, JOHN A.	ST	273	3RD E DI
COLE, JOHN F.	ST	287	2ND E DI
COLE, JOHN H.	BAL	231	6TH WARD
COLE, JOHN R.	BAL	263	12TH WAR
COLE, JOHN-BLACK	CAR	159	NO TWP L
COLE, JONAS H	HAR	162	3RD DIST
COLE, JORDAN	BAL	188	5TH DIST
COLE, JOSEPH	BAL	420	1ST DIST
COLE, JOSEPH	BAL	100	5TH WARD
COLE, JOSEPH	BAL	295	12TH WAR
COLE, JOSEPH	HAR	184	3RD DIST
COLE, JOSEPH	BAL	273	20TH WAR
COLE, JOSEPH-BLACK	CAR	159	NO TWP L
COLE, JOSHUA	BAL	162	19TH WAR
COLE, JOSHUA	BAL	077	2ND DIST
COLE, JOSHUA B.	BAL	366	3RD WARD
COLE, JULIA	BAL	253	6TH WARD
COLE, JULIA	CAR	289	7TH DIST
COLE, JULIA A.	BAL	241	6TH WARD
COLE, JULIANA	BAL	453	14TH WAR
COLE, KITTY	ANN	419	HOWARD D
COLE, L.	BAL	152	1ST WARD
COLE, LEWIS	BAL	288	12TH WAR
COLE, LEWIS	BAL	130	18TH WAR
COLE, LIZZA	BAL	353	1ST DIST
COLE, LOUIS M.	BAL	114	15TH WAR
COLE, LOUIS R.	BAL	428	1ST DIST
COLE, LOUISA	BAL	194	5TH DIST
COLE, LOUISA A.	BAL	022	18TH WAR
COLE, LUCINDA	BAL	244	1ST DIST
COLE, MARGARET	ANN	437	HOWARD D
COLE, MARGARET	HAR	058	1ST DIST
COLE, MARGARET	MGM	439	CLARKSTR
COLE, MARGARET S.	BAL	088	1ST WARD
COLE, MARGARETT	BAL	060	4TH WARD
COLE, MARGARETT A.	BAL	012	4TH WARD
COLE, MARIA	BAL	474	14TH WAR
COLE, MARIA	BAL	311	12TH WAR
COLE, MARTHA	BAL	185	16TH WAR
COLE, MARTHA E.	BAL	429	1ST DIST
COLE, MARY	BAL	454	1ST DIST
COLE, MARY	BAL	325	7TH WARD
COLE, MARY	CEC	011	ELKTON 3
COLE, MARY	BAL	336	13TH WAR
COLE, MARY	HAR	093	2ND DIST
COLE, MARY	CEC	215	7TH E DI
COLE, MARY	WAS	026	2ND SUBD
COLE, MARY A.	WAS	157	HAGERSTO
COLE, MARY E.	ANN	385	4TH DIST
COLE, MARY J.	BAL	271	17TH WAR
COLE, MARY-BLACK	QUE	183	3RD E DI
COLE, MARY-BLACK	ST	301	2ND E DI
COLE, MARY-MULATTO	ST	336	4TH E DI
COLE, MATILDA	CAR	282	7TH DIST
COLE, MERRYMAN	BAL	145	5TH WARD
COLE, MICHAEL	BAL	077	18TH WAR
COLE, MICHAEL	HAR	162	3RD DIST
COLE, MINTY-BLACK	ST	310	1ST E DI
COLE, NANCY	DOR	421	1ST DIST
COLE, NEWTON	BAL	135	1ST WARD
COLE, NICHOLUS	TAL	017	EASTON D
COLE, NICKLAUS	BAL	007	15TH WAR
COLE, PHILIP	BAL	331	3RD WARD
COLE, PRISCILLA	ANN	433	HOWARD D
COLE, RACHEAL	BAL	037	18TH WAR
COLE, RACHEL	BAL	398	14TH WAR
COLE, RACHEL	CAL	061	3RD DIST
COLE, RACHEL	BAL	110	2ND DIST
COLE, RACHEL	BAL	316	1ST DIST
COLE, RACHEL	BAL	199	6TH WARD
COLE, RACHEL	ANN	385	4TH DIST
COLE, RACHIEL	BAL	254	1ST DIST
COLE, REBECA	TAL	097	ST MICHA
COLE, REBECCA	ANN	480	HOWARD D
COLE, REBECCA	BAL	404	3RD WARD
COLE, RICHARD	BAL	257	6TH WARD
COLE, RICHARD	BAL	051	18TH WAR
COLE, ROBERT	CEC	209	7TH E DI
COLE, ROSE A.	BAL	151	11TH WAR
COLE, SAMUEL	MGM	315	CRACKLIN
COLE, SAMUEL	BAL	309	7TH WARD
COLE, SAMUEL	BAL	176	2ND DIST
COLE, SAMUEL	BAL	177	6TH WARD
COLE, SAMUEL	BAL	097	5TH WARD
COLE, SAMUEL W.	QUE	131	1ST E DI
COLE, SARAH	BAL	144	11TH WAR
COLE, SARAH	ANN	474	HOWARD D
COLE, SARAH	BAL	274	12TH WAR
COLE, SARAH	QUE	208	3RD E DI
COLE, SARAH A.	ST	268	3RD E DI
COLE, SARAH E.	MGM	370	BERRYS D
COLE, SELAH	BAL	192	6TH WARD
COLE, SLATHEL	BAL	422	1ST DIST
COLE, SLATHEL B.	BAL	429	1ST DIST
COLE, SOPHIA	BAL	193	5TH DIST
COLE, SOPHIA	MGM	369	BERRYS D
COLE, STEPHEN	BAL	388	8TH WARD
COLE, SUSAN	BAL	064	2ND DIST
COLE, SUSAN	FRE	060	FREDERIC
COLE, SUSANA	HAR	151	3RD DIST
COLE, SUSANNA-BLACK	ST	301	2ND E DI
COLE, T.	BAL	138	1ST WARD
COLE, THOMAS	ANN	432	HOWARD D
COLE, THOMAS	BAL	300	1ST DIST
COLE, THOMAS	BAL	214	6TH WARD
COLE, THOMAS	ST	255	3RD E DI
COLE, THOMAS	ST	275	3RD E DI
COLE, THOMAS	TAL	096	ST MICHA
COLE, THOMAS	BAL	078	4TH WARD
COLE, THOMAS B.	ANN	432	HOWARD D
COLE, THOMAS W.	ANN	385	4TH DIST
COLE, THOMS	BAL	126	1ST WARD
COLE, WATT-MULATTO	ST	339	4TH E DI
COLE, WESLEY	BAL	112	1ST WARD
COLE, WILLIAM	BAL	289	1ST DIST
COLE, WILLIAM	BAL	263	1ST DIST
COLE, WILLIAM	ANN	453	HOWARD D
COLE, WILLIAM	BAL	065	2ND DIST
COLE, WILLIAM	BAL	110	2ND DIST
COLE, WILLIAM	BAL	236	6TH WARD
COLE, WILLIAM	BAL	178	6TH WARD
COLE, WILLIAM	BAL	015	9TH WARD
COLE, WILLIAM	QUE	166	2ND E DI
COLE, WILLIAM	TAL	084	ST MICHA
COLE, WILLIAM	PRI	015	BLADENSB
COLE, WILLIAM	DOR	306	1ST DIST
COLE, WILLIAM	MGM	387	ROCKERLE
COLE, WILLIAM	CEC	199	7TH E DI
COLE, WILLIAM	BAL	301	17TH WAR
COLE, WILLIAM A.	ST	280	3RD E DI
COLE, WILLIAM C.-MULATTO	ST	341	5TH E DI
COLE, WILLIAM E.	ST	299	2ND E DI
COLE, WILLIAM E.	BAL	069	15TH WAR
COLE, WILLIAM G.	FRE	021	FREDERIC
COLE, WILLIAM H.	BAL	295	20TH WAR
COLE, WILLIAM H.	BAL	086	4TH WARD
COLE, WILLIAM H.	QUE	153	1ST E DI
COLE, WILLIAM H.	BAL	033	9TH WARD
COLE, WILLIAM H.	BAL	018	2ND DIST
COLE, WILLIAM H.	ST	269	3RD E DI
COLE, WILLIAM L.	BAL	455	8TH WARD
COLE, WILLIAM M.	BAL	256	12TH WAR
COLE, WILLIAM M.	BAL	153	1ST WARD
COLE, WILLIAM N.	BAL	171	1ST WARD
COLE, WILLIAM P.	BAL	093	5TH WARD
COLE, WILLIAM V.	BAL	198	11TH WAR
COLE, WILLIAM W.	ANN	394	8TH DIST
COLE, WILLIAM W.	ST	269	3RD E DI
COLE, ZACHARIAH	BAL	432	1ST DIST
COLE, ZILA-BLACK	QUE	150	1ST E DI
COLE,CHARLES	FRE	017	FREDERIC
COLE,MALINDA	BAL	030	1ST WARD
COLE,WILLIAM	BAL	124	1ST WARD
COLEBERRY, ELIZABETH	FRE	043	FREDERIC
COLEBRAKER, JOHN	WAS	253	1ST DIST
COLEBURN, JOHN*	DOR	427	1ST DIST
COLEBURN, MADISON	DOR	458	1ST DIST
COLEBURN, SARAH	DOR	460	1ST DIST
COLEFLOUER, MICHAEL	FRE	127	CREAGERS
COLEFLOWER, BARNEY	FRE	116	CREAGERS
COLEFLOWER, JOHN	FRE	126	CREAGERS
COLEGATE, EDWARD	FRE	216	BUCKEYST
COLEHOUR, FREDERICK J.	BAL	348	1ST DIST
COLEHOUR, JOHN	CAR	190	4TH DIST
COLEHOUSE, WILLIAM H.	BAL	097	10TH WAR
COLELOYZER, THOMAS F.	DOR	375	1ST DIST
COLEMAN, ALEXANDER	BAL	231	17TH WAR
COLEMAN, ALTON	ALL	124	4TH E.D.
COLEMAN, ANDREW	BAL	132	18TH WAR
COLEMAN, ANN	BAL	019	4TH WARD
COLEMAN, ANN	BAL	329	7TH WARD
COLEMAN, ANN E.	KEN	238	2ND DIST
COLEMAN, BARNEY	ALL	243	CUMBERLA
COLEMAN, BENJAMIN	ALL	116	5TH E.D.
COLEMAN, CALETA	ALL	117	5TH E.D.
COLEMAN, CATHARINE	ANN	431	HOWARD D
COLEMAN, CATHARINE E.	DOR	445	1ST DIST
COLEMAN, CATHERINE A.	FRE	065	FREDERIC
COLEMAN, CHARLES	HAR	204	3RD DIST
COLEMAN, CHARLES	BAL	142	1ST WARD
COLEMAN, CHARLES R.	BAL	099	15TH WAR
COLEMAN, CHARLES W.	BAL	198	6TH WARD
COLEMAN, DENNIS	BAL	008	1ST WARD
COLEMAN, DOROTHY	BAL	454	14TH WAR
COLEMAN, DR. E.F.	BAL	012	18TH WAR
COLEMAN, EDWARD	BAL	384	3RD WARD
COLEMAN, EDWARD B.	BAL	184	11TH WAR
COLEMAN, EDWARD W.	BAL	117	11TH WAR
COLEMAN, EDWIN S.	BAL	290	3RD WARD
COLEMAN, ELIZA	BAL	347	1ST DIST
COLEMAN, ELIZA	BAL	104	10TH WAR
COLEMAN, ELIZA J.	BAL	058	10TH WAR
COLEMAN, ELIZABETH	BAL	095	5TH WARD
COLEMAN, ELIZABETH	BAL	321	7TH WARD
COLEMAN, ELIZABETH	BAL	259	2ND WARD
COLEMAN, ELLEN	BAL	442	1ST DIST
COLEMAN, EMERY-BLACK	QUE	199	3RD E DI

Name	County	Page	District
COLEMAN, EVAN	BAL	262	6TH WARD
COLEMAN, FRANCES	QUE	152	1ST E DI
COLEMAN, GEORGE	DOR	433	1ST DIST
COLEMAN, GEORGE	BAL	204	19TH WAR
COLEMAN, GIDEON	ALL	133	4TH E.D.
COLEMAN, HARMON	ALL	039	2ND E.D.
COLEMAN, HARRIET C.	BAL	249	2ND WARD
COLEMAN, HOOPER	DOR	444	1ST DIST
COLEMAN, ISRAIL	HAR	195	3RD DIST
COLEMAN, J.	BAL	293	12TH WAR
COLEMAN, JACKSON	KEN	216	2ND DIST
COLEMAN, JACOB	FRE	280	WOODSBOR
COLEMAN, JACOB	BAL	354	1ST DIST
COLEMAN, JAMES	BAL	168	11TH WAR
COLEMAN, JAMES	BAL	439	8TH WARD
COLEMAN, JAMES	BAL	171	6TH WARD
COLEMAN, JAMES	HAR	204	3RD DIST
COLEMAN, JAMES	KEN	243	2ND DIST
COLEMAN, JAMES	BAL	086	18TH WAR
COLEMAN, JAMES	QUE	162	2ND E DI
COLEMAN, JAMES	QUE	166	2ND E DI
COLEMAN, JAMES	KEN	268	1ST DIST
COLEMAN, JAMES	DOR	457	1ST DIST
COLEMAN, JANE	QUE	191	3RD E DI
COLEMAN, JANE	DOR	431	1ST DIST
COLEMAN, JANE	BAL	019	9TH WARD
COLEMAN, JEREMIAH	ALL	122	4TH E.D.
COLEMAN, JOHANA	ALL	155	6TH E.D.
COLEMAN, JOHN	BAL	309	12TH WAR
COLEMAN, JOHN	BAL	290	7TH WARD
COLEMAN, JOHN	BAL	356	3RD WARD
COLEMAN, JOHN	CAR	279	7TH DIST
COLEMAN, JOHN	BAL	306	20TH WAR
COLEMAN, JOHN	KEN	273	1ST DIST
COLEMAN, JOHN H.	CEC	057	1ST E DI
COLEMAN, JOHN H.	BAL	077	15TH WAR
COLEMAN, JOHN T.	BAL	013	15TH WAR
COLEMAN, JOHN W.	KEN	243	2ND DIST
COLEMAN, JOSEPH	BAL	347	1ST DIST
COLEMAN, JOSEPH	BAL	290	3RD WARD
COLEMAN, JOSEPH G.	BAL	131	18TH WAR
COLEMAN, JULIA	BAL	248	2ND WARD
COLEMAN, JULIA A.	BAL	014	15TH WAR
COLEMAN, KENNARD	DOR	461	1ST DIST
COLEMAN, LIVE	QUE	151	1ST E DI
COLEMAN, LOUISA	QUE	164	2ND E DI
COLEMAN, MARGARET	BAL	178	11TH WAR
COLEMAN, MARK	ALL	142	6TH E.D.
COLEMAN, MARTHA A.	QUE	162	2ND E DI
COLEMAN, MARY	PRI	030	VANSVILL
COLEMAN, MARY	ALL	133	4TH E.D.
COLEMAN, MARY	BAL	457	8TH WARD
COLEMAN, MARY	BAL	316	12TH WAR
COLEMAN, MARY	ALL	253	CUMBERLA
COLEMAN, MARY	BAL	027	18TH WAR
COLEMAN, MARY	BAL	027	4TH WARD
COLEMAN, MARY	BAL	270	17TH WAR
COLEMAN, MARY	BAL	378	13TH WAR
COLEMAN, MARY A.	QUE	162	2ND E DI
COLEMAN, MARY J.	ANN	521	HOWARD D
COLEMAN, MARY N.	BAL	063	18TH WAR
COLEMAN, MICHAEL	ALL	236	CUMBERLA
COLEMAN, MICHALE	ALL	154	6TH E.D.
COLEMAN, MORGAN	BAL	469	14TH WAR
COLEMAN, NANCY	BAL	239	6TH WARD
COLEMAN, NANCY	DOR	453	1ST DIST
COLEMAN, NATHAN	BAL	152	16TH WAR
COLEMAN, NOAH	QUE	164	2ND E DI
COLEMAN, OTHO	ALL	132	4TH E.D.
COLEMAN, P.	BAL	028	18TH WAR
COLEMAN, PATRICK	ALL	067	10TH E.D
COLEMAN, PATRICK	BAL	441	1ST DIST
COLEMAN, PETER	ALL	119	5TH E.D.
COLEMAN, PETER	BAL	280	2ND WARD
COLEMAN, PHEBE	KEN	292	3RD DIST
COLEMAN, PRISSY	DOR	456	1ST DIST
COLEMAN, RACHEL	BAL	103	15TH WAR
COLEMAN, RICHARD	BAL	007	9TH WARD
COLEMAN, RICHARD	QUE	165	2ND E DI
COLEMAN, RICHARD	KEN	264	1ST DIST
COLEMAN, ROBERT H.	BAL	362	13TH WAR
COLEMAN, SALESBERY	BAL	209	11TH WAR
COLEMAN, SAMUEL	KEN	236	2ND DIST
COLEMAN, SAMUEL	BAL	286	20TH WAR
COLEMAN, SAMUEL	BAL	044	1ST WARD
COLEMAN, SAMUEL J.	KEN	235	2ND DIST
COLEMAN, SARAH	CEC	163	6TH E DI
COLEMAN, SARAH	ALL	117	5TH E.D.
COLEMAN, SARAH A.	BAL	158	6TH WARD
COLEMAN, SILAS	BAL	127	11TH WAR
COLEMAN, SUMER	ANN	374	4TH DIST
COLEMAN, THOMAS	BAL	279	2ND WARD
COLEMAN, THOMAS	BAL	407	3RD WARD
COLEMAN, TILEY*	DOR	463	1ST DIST
COLEMAN, URIAH	BAL	282	7TH WARD
COLEMAN, WALTER	KEN	238	2ND DIST
COLEMAN, WILLAIM	ALL	055	10TH E.D
COLEMAN, WILLIAM	ALL	133	4TH E.D.
COLEMAN, WILLIAM	BAL	292	7TH WARD
COLEMAN, WILLIAM	BAL	385	3RD WARD
COLEMAN, WILLIAM	BAL	138	1ST WARD
COLEMAN, WILLIAM	BAL	027	1ST WARD
COLEMAN, WILLIAM	BAL	348	7TH WARD
COLEMAN, WILLIAM	BAL	088	18TH WAR
COLEMAN, WILLIAM	KEN	264	1ST DIST
COLEMAN, WILLIAM	QUE	170	2ND E DI
COLEMAN, WILLIAM H.	KEN	269	1ST DIST
COLEMAN, WILLIAM H.	KEN	232	2ND DIST
COLEMAN, WILLIAM P.	ALL	124	4TH E.D.
COLEMAN, ZEBULON S.	QUE	169	2ND E DI
COLEMER, GRAFTON	WAS	073	2ND SUBD
COLEN	BAL	253	12TH WAR
COLENS, EPHRAIM	FRE	446	8TH E DI
COLENSURGH, THEODORE	BAL	006	1ST WARD
COLER, GEORGE	WAS	270	1ST DIST
COLER, JONAS	WAS	270	1ST DIST
COLERAINE, NANCY	HAR	141	2ND DIST
COLERTSON, MOSES	WAS	074	2ND SUBD
COLES, DANIEL B.	BAL	122	1ST WARD
COLES, JERAMIAH	CEC	099	3RD E DI
COLES, JOHN	ALL	104	5TH E.D.
COLES, LYDIA	CAR	235	UNION TO
COLES, MARY E.	BAL	074	10TH WAR
COLES, WILLIAM	BAL	074	10TH WAR
COLESTEAD, ANN	BAL	336	7TH WARD
COLEY, GODFREY	BAL	440	8TH WARD
COLEY, RACHEL	BAL	343	3RD WARD
COLFELTY, AUGUSTUS	ALL	012	3RD E.D.
COLFER, THOMAS	BAL	086	2ND DIST
COLFLECH, GEORGE B.	BAL	176	16TH WAR

Name	County	Page	District
COLFLESH, CASH	BAL	269	20TH WAR
COLGAN, ELIZABETH	CAR	075	NO TWP L
COLGAN, FRANCES	QUE	174	2ND E DI
COLGAN, HANNAH	CAR	071	NO TWP L
COLGAN, HCARLES	BAL	051	15TH WAR
COLGAN, JAMES	FRE	168	EMMITTSB
COLGAN, JANE	QUE	147	1ST E DI
COLGAN, MARGARET	BAL	466	14TH WAR
COLGAN, MARY M.	QUE	161	2ND E DI
COLGAN, SAMUEL	CAR	074	NO TWP L
COLGAR, BENONI	QUE	157	2ND E DI
COLGATE, H.	BAL	156	1ST WARD
COLGATE, MARGRETT	BAL	112	18TH WAR
COLGERHOHOUN, COLLINS	BAL	216	11TH WAR
COLGLOYZER, HENRY*	DOR	375	1ST DIST
COLHAM, JOHN	ALL	203	CUMBERLA
COLHEISTINE, CHRISTINA	BAL	030	1ST WARD
COLHOUN, MAHALA	BAL	159	19TH WAR
COLHOUN, MARGARET	BAL	362	13TH WAR
COLHOUN, PETER	BAL	159	19TH WAR
COLICE, RICHARD S.	TAL	006	EASTON D
COLICK, ISRAEL	SOM	482	TRAPP DI
COLIER, HARRIET	TAL	015	EASTON D
COLIER, JOHN C.	WAS	011	WILLIAMS
COLIFLOUER, SUSAN	FRE	128	CREAGERS
COLIFLOWER, GEORGE M.	FRE	137	CREAGERS
COLIHOUR, GEORGE	BAL	336	1ST DIST
COLINS, ANN	BAL	405	8TH WARD
COLINS, MARY A.	BAL	155	11TH WAR
COLINS, MARY J.	BAL	192	2ND WARD
COLIP, JOHN	BAL	353	7TH WARD
COLISCART, SARAH	BAL	053	9TH WARD
COLISHA, ANN	BAL	152	11TH WAR
COLISON, MARGARETT	DOR	309	1ST DIST
COLKLESSER, MARY E.	WAS	123	HAGERSTO
COLKLESSER, SOLOMON	WAS	122	HAGERSTO
COLLAGAR, JOHN	BAL	294	1ST DIST
COLLAGHAN, CATHERINE	BAL	004	4TH WARD
COLLAION, JOHN W.	HAR	161	3RD DIST
COLLAMER, DORTHA	BAL	055	1ST WARD
COLLAY, PATRICK	ALL	052	10TH E.D
COLLAY, THOMAS	ALL	053	10TH E.D
COLLEGE, JAMES	ALL	257	CUMBERLA
COLLEGE, JAMES POLK	ALL	258	CUMBERLA
COLLEM, GEORGE *	BAL	043	18TH WAR
COLLENBERG, HENRY	BAL	255	2ND WARD
COLLENBERGER, ISRAEL	FRE	449	8TH E DI
COLLENBERGER, JACOB	FRE	450	8TH E DI
COLLENDER, ROBERT*	DOR	406	1ST DIST
COLLENS, MARGARET A.	BAL	329	13TH WAR
COLLEPAUSAYER, MARGARET	BAL	050	1ST WARD
COLLER, CONRADT	BAL	272	7TH WARD
COLLERD, ELIZABETH	ANN	269	ANNAPOLI
COLLET, ELIZABETH	BAL	017	2ND DIST
COLLET, J.	BAL	165	1ST WARD
COLLET, JEMIMA	BAL	035	2ND DIST
COLLET, JOHN	BAL	040	2ND DIST
COLLET, MOSES	BAL	039	2ND DIST
COLLET, WILLIAM	BAL	039	2ND DIST
COLLETT, SUSANAH	BAL	115	11TH WAR
COLLETT, WILLIAM	BAL	410	1ST DIST
COLLEY, ALEXANDER	BAL	218	19TH WAR
COLLEY, AMANDA M.	BAL	211	17TH WAR
COLLEY, ANN	BAL	048	18TH WAR
COLLEY, CONRAD	BAL	300	7TH WARD
COLLEY, JOHN W.	BAL	031	18TH WAR
COLLGAN, REBECCA	QUE	126	1ST E DI
COLLICK, ANN	WOR	314	2ND E DI
COLLICK, HARRIET A.	WOR	189	7TH E DI
COLLICK, RHODA	WOR	201	3RD E DI
COLLICK, RILEY	WOR	316	2ND E DI
COLLICK, WILLIAM	WOR	312	2ND E DI
COLLIDAY, MARY	BAL	314	20TH WAR
COLLIEN, MARY	BAL	457	1ST DIST
COLLIER, B.	BAL	137	1ST WARD
COLLIER, B.	BAL	124	1ST WARD
COLLIER, CHANA	SOM	536	TYASKIN
COLLIER, CHARLES E.	BAL	461	14TH WAR
COLLIER, CLONDSBERRY	QUE	249	5TH E DI
COLLIER, E.	BAL	160	1ST WARD
COLLIER, EBENEZER	BAL	161	1ST WARD
COLLIER, EBENEZER	BAL	006	4TH WARD
COLLIER, ELEANOR	SOM	529	QUANTICO
COLLIER, EZRA	HAR	147	3RD DIST
COLLIER, GEORGE E. R. J.	SOM	541	TYASKIN
COLLIER, GEORGE R.	WOR	230	6TH E DI
COLLIER, GRACE	HAR	180	3RD DIST
COLLIER, HENRY	BAL	099	2ND DIST
COLLIER, HENRY	ANN	352	3RD DIST
COLLIER, JACKSON	BAL	064	10TH WAR
COLLIER, JOHN	ANN	451	HOWARD D
COLLIER, JOHN	ALL	059	10TH E.D
COLLIER, JOHN	QUE	193	3RD E DI
COLLIER, JOHN	KEN	268	1ST DIST
COLLIER, JOHN F.	SOM	528	QUANTICO
COLLIER, JOSEPH	QUE	248	5TH E DI
COLLIER, JULIA A.	SOM	427	PRINCESS
COLLIER, LEVIN	SOM	536	TYASKIN
COLLIER, LYDIA	BAL	160	19TH WAR
COLLIER, MARTCN	HAR	199	3RD DIST
COLLIER, MARY E.	BAL	112	18TH WAR
COLLIER, MICHAEL	BAL	036	4TH WARD
COLLIER, PITT	SOM	533	QUANTICO
COLLIER, RALP	ANN	444	HOWARD D
COLLIER, ROBERT	QUE	250	5TH E DI
COLLIER, SARAH	BAL	274	1ST DIST
COLLIER, STEPHEN B.	SOM	488	SALISBUR
COLLIER, VALARIOUS F.	SOM	529	QUANTICO
COLLIER, W. JAMES	BAL	056	18TH WAR
COLLIER, WILLIAM	QUE	251	5TH E DI
COLLIER, WILLIAM	BAL	127	1ST WARD
COLLIER, WILLIAM F.	SOM	536	TYASKIN
COLLIFLOUR, LEWIS	FRE	148	10TH E D
COLLIFLOWER, JOHN C.	MGM	335	CRACKLIN
COLLIFLOWER, LOYD C.	FRE	135	CREAGERS
COLLIFLOWER, WILLIAM F.	CAR	332	MANCHEST
COLLIGAN, BRIDGETT	BAL	031	4TH WARD
COLLIN, CHARLES	BAL	009	9TH WARD
COLLIN, HENRY W.	SOM	488	SALISBUR
COLLIN, JAMES	BAL	131	1ST WARD
COLLIN, JOHN	BAL	308	20TH WAR
COLLIN, LEVIN D.	SOM	491	SALISBUR
COLLIN, RENNA*	TAL	029	EASTON D
COLLIN, RICHARD	BAL	428	14TH WAR
COLLIN, WILLIAM	CHA	230	BOJANTOW
COLLINGHEAD, RACHEL	PRI	037	VANSVILL
COLLINGTON, ELIJAH	BAL	351	13TH WAR
COLLINGWOOD, DRUSILLA	PRI	020	VANSVILL
COLLINGWOOD, WILLIAM	BAL	281	2ND WARD
COLLINS, ----*	TAL	049	EASTON T

Name	County	Page	District
COLLINS, ABRAHAM	CAR	133	NO TWP L
COLLINS, ABRAHAM-BLACK	CAR	151	NO TWP L
COLLINS, ABROSE	SOM	415	DUBLIN D
COLLINS, ALAN	CAR	216	5TH DIST
COLLINS, AMANDA	CEC	098	4TH E DI
COLLINS, AMELIA	SOM	485	TRAPP DI
COLLINS, ANDREW-BLACK	CAR	092	NO TWP L
COLLINS, ANN	BAL	216	11TH WAR
COLLINS, ANN	SOM	490	SALISBUR
COLLINS, ANN	WOR	293	9TH E DI
COLLINS, ANN	BAL	384	8TH WARD
COLLINS, ANN	BAL	013	2ND DIST
COLLINS, ANN	BAL	145	5TH WARD
COLLINS, ANNA	BAL	315	1ST DIST
COLLINS, ASA	WOR	316	2ND E DI
COLLINS, B.	BAL	171	1ST WARD
COLLINS, B.	BAL	163	1ST WARD
COLLINS, BENJAMIN F.	BAL	012	15TH WAR
COLLINS, BETSEY	BAL	135	2ND DIST
COLLINS, BUSHRAD	DOR	309	1ST DIST
COLLINS, C.	BAL	150	1ST WARD
COLLINS, CALEB	SOM	414	DUBLIN D
COLLINS, CAROLIEN	BAL	111	18TH WAR
COLLINS, CAROLINE	BAL	110	18TH WAR
COLLINS, CAROLINE	PRI	113	PISCATAW
COLLINS, CATHARINE	DOR	440	1ST DIST
COLLINS, CATHARINE	BAL	259	17TH WAR
COLLINS, CATHARINE	BAL	257	6TH WARD
COLLINS, CATHERINE	ALL	241	CUMBERLA
COLLINS, CATHERINE	BAL	021	4TH WARD
COLLINS, CECHLIN *	BAL	139	19TH WAR
COLLINS, CHARITY	BAL	215	6TH WARD
COLLINS, CHARLES	BAL	374	3RD WARD
COLLINS, CHARLES	BAL	272	1ST DIST
COLLINS, CHARLES	WOR	314	2ND E DI
COLLINS, CHARLES	WOR	296	9TH E DI
COLLINS, CHARLES S.	BAL	176	16TH WAR
COLLINS, CHARLOT .	BAL	325	1ST DIST
COLLINS, DANIEL	TAL	030	EASTON D
COLLINS, DANIEL	MGM	379	ROCKEPLE
COLLINS, DANIEL *	KEN	210	2ND DIST
COLLINS, DARIEL *	KEN	210	2ND DIST
COLLINS, DAVID	CEC	002	ELKTON 3
COLLINS, DELPHI	BAL	042	15TH WAR
COLLINS, DENNIS B.	BAL	098	15TH WAR
COLLINS, DIAMA*	DOR	317	1ST DIST
COLLINS, DICK	ANN	443	HOWARD D
COLLINS, EDWARD	SOM	412	DUBLIN D
COLLINS, EDWARD	WOR	184	6TH E DI
COLLINS, EIZABETH G.	CAR	164	NO TWP L
COLLINS, ELEANOR	WOR	293	9TH E DI
COLLINS, ELGY-BLACK	WOR	321	1ST E DI
COLLINS, ELI	WOR	318	2ND E DI
COLLINS, ELIJAH	WOR	272	BERLIN 1
COLLINS, ELIJAH	FRE	046	FREDERIC
COLLINS, ELIJAH	ALL	103	5TH E.D.
COLLINS, ELIJAH	ALL	153	6TH E.D.
COLLINS, ELISHA	WOR	246	1ST CENS
COLLINS, ELISHA D.	DOR	447	1ST DIST
COLLINS, ELIZA	BAL	316	20TH WAR
COLLINS, ELIZA	WOR	325	1ST E DI
COLLINS, ELIZA-BLACK	CAR	152	NO TWP L
COLLINS, ELIZABETH	BAL	158	11TH WAR
COLLINS, ELIZABETH	CHA	256	MIDDLETO
COLLINS, ELIZABETH	BAL	253	17TH WAR
COLLINS, ELIZABETH	BAL	218	17TH WAR
COLLINS, ELIZABETH	BAL	061	15TH WAR
COLLINS, ELIZABETH	BAL	023	15TH WAR
COLLINS, ELIZABETH	BAL	023	15TH WAR
COLLINS, ELIZABETH	BAL	302	1ST DIST
COLLINS, ELIZABETH	BAL	205	2ND WARD
COLLINS, ELIZABETH E.	CHA	222	ALLENS F
COLLINS, ELLEN	BAL	154	11TH WAR
COLLINS, ELLEN	BAL	111	10TH WAR
COLLINS, ELLEN	BAL	386	1ST DIST
COLLINS, EMALINE	WOR	261	BERLIN 1
COLLINS, EMILY	BAL	139	5TH WARD
COLLINS, EMILY J.	CAR	150	NO TWP L
COLLINS, EMMA	WOR	303	SNOW HIL
COLLINS, EPHRAIM	SOM	514	BARREN C
COLLINS, FRANCE	BAL	013	2ND DIST
COLLINS, FRANCES J.	DOR	315	1ST DIST
COLLINS, FRANCIS-BLACK	WOR	320	1ST E DI
COLLINS, GEORGE	WOR	280	BERLIN 1
COLLINS, GEORGE	BAL	145	2ND DIST
COLLINS, GEORGE	BAL	153	1ST WARD
COLLINS, GEORGE	BAL	398	1ST DIST
COLLINS, GEORGE	BAL	106	1ST WARD
COLLINS, GEORGE C.	BAL	005	15TH WAR
COLLINS, GEORGE H. J.	WOR	186	7TH E DI
COLLINS, GEORGE R.	BAL	086	1ST WARD
COLLINS, GEORGE T.	BAL	313	12TH WAR
COLLINS, GEORGE W.	BAL	277	7TH WARD
COLLINS, GEORGE W.	CAR	132	NO TWP L
COLLINS, GEORGE W.	KEN	254	1ST DIST
COLLINS, HANDY	SOM	415	DUBLIN D
COLLINS, HANNAH	DOR	304	1ST DIST
COLLINS, HANNAH	QUE	180	2ND E DI
COLLINS, HARRIET	BAL	315	1ST DIST
COLLINS, HARRIETT	BAL	130	11TH WAR
COLLINS, HENRIETTA	WOR	256	1ST CENS
COLLINS, HENRY	SOM	472	TRAPPE D
COLLINS, HENRY	PRI	113	PISCATAW
COLLINS, HENRY	DOR	466	1ST DIST
COLLINS, HENRY	BAL	277	17TH WAR
COLLINS, HENRY	CHA	222	ALLENS F
COLLINS, HENRY	BAL	192	19TH WAR
COLLINS, HENRY	BAL	290	17TH WAR
COLLINS, HENRY	BAL	455	8TH WARD
COLLINS, HESTER	BAL	085	1ST WARD
COLLINS, HUGH	SOM	512	BARREN C
COLLINS, IDELET	BAL	375	3RD WARD
COLLINS, IMMANUEL-MULATTO	CAR	125	NO TWP L
COLLINS, ISAAC	SOM	409	DUBLIN D
COLLINS, ISAAC	BAL	075	2ND DIST
COLLINS, ISAAC	SOM	509	BARREN C
COLLINS, ISAAC	WOR	243	1ST CENS
COLLINS, ISRA	CAR	131	NO TWP L
COLLINS, ISRAEL-BLACK	CAR	150	NO TWP L
COLLINS, JACOB-BLACK	WOR	325	1ST E DI
COLLINS, JAME	BAL	292	12TH WAR
COLLINS, JAME SB.	WOR	171	6TH E DI
COLLINS, JAMES	KEN	259	1ST DIST
COLLINS, JAMES	SOM	476	TRAPPE D
COLLINS, JAMES	WOR	336	1ST E DI
COLLINS, JAMES	WOR	347	1ST E DI
COLLINS, JAMES	WOR	246	1ST CENS
COLLINS, JAMES	SOM	491	SALISBUR
COLLINS, JAMES	WOR	308	2ND E DI
COLLINS, JAMES	BAL	139	2ND DIST

Name	County	Page	District
COLLINS, JAMES	BAL	292	1ST DIST
COLLINS, JAMES	BAL	007	1ST WARD
COLLINS, JAMES	ANN	317	1ST DIST
COLLINS, JAMES	BAL	104	18TH WAR
COLLINS, JAMES	BAL	038	4TH WARD
COLLINS, JAMES	BAL	439	14TH WAR
COLLINS, JAMES	CEC	154	PORT DUP
COLLINS, JAMES A.	MGM	357	BERRYS D
COLLINS, JAMES E.	BAL	262	2ND WARD
COLLINS, JAMES H.	WOR	180	6TH E DI
COLLINS, JAMES L.	BAL	175	16TH WAR
COLLINS, JAMES P.	WOR	222	4TH E DI
COLLINS, JANE	BAL	151	16TH WAR
COLLINS, JANE	BAL	242	17TH WAR
COLLINS, JANE	CAR	222	5TH DIST
COLLINS, JANE	BAL	139	11TH WAR
COLLINS, JANE	CHA	223	ALLENS F
COLLINS, JANE-BLACK	ST	335	4TH E DI
COLLINS, JERRY*	DOR	310	1ST DIST
COLLINS, JIM	WOR	244	1ST CENS
COLLINS, JIM	TAL	004	EASTON D
COLLINS, JIM	WOR	346	1ST E DI
COLLINS, JOHANNA	BAL	091	1ST WARD
COLLINS, JOHN	BAL	293	1ST DIST
COLLINS, JOHN	BAL	389	3RD WARD
COLLINS, JOHN	BAL	273	7TH WARD
COLLINS, JOHN	BAL	400	1ST DIST
COLLINS, JOHN	BAL	092	5TH WARD
COLLINS, JOHN	SOM	362	BRINKLEY
COLLINS, JOHN	WAS	188	1ST DIST
COLLINS, JOHN	WOR	201	3RD E DI
COLLINS, JOHN	BAL	244	20TH WAR
COLLINS, JOHN	CAR	151	NO TWP L
COLLINS, JOHN	CAR	130	NO TWP L
COLLINS, JOHN	BAL	219	19TH WAR
COLLINS, JOHN	CEC	028	CHESAPEA
COLLINS, JOHN	HAR	129	2ND DIST
COLLINS, JOHN	BAL	109	18TH WAR
COLLINS, JOHN A.	BAL	030	9TH WARD
COLLINS, JOHN M.	QUE	171	2ND E DI
COLLINS, JOHN T.	BAL	034	15TH WAR
COLLINS, JOHN W.	BAL	277	2ND WARD
COLLINS, JOSANNA	WOR	244	1ST CENS
COLLINS, JOSEPH	WOR	243	1ST CENS
COLLINS, JOSEPH	DOR	455	1ST DIST
COLLINS, JOSEPH	TAL	051	EASTON D
COLLINS, JOSEPH	DOR	448	1ST DIST
COLLINS, JOSEPH	HAR	130	2ND DIST
COLLINS, JOSEPH	HAR	126	2ND DIST
COLLINS, JOSEPH	HAR	127	2ND DIST
COLLINS, JOSEPH	CEC	204	6TH E DI
COLLINS, JOSEPH	BAL	063	18TH WAR
COLLINS, JOSEPH C.	SOM	494	SALISBUR
COLLINS, JOSEPH R.	WOR	227	4TH E DI
COLLINS, JOSEPH W.	ANN	304	1ST DIST
COLLINS, JOSEPH-BLACK	ST	331	4TH E DI
COLLINS, JOSHUA-BLACK	WOR	348	1ST E DI
COLLINS, JOSIAH	WOR	294	9TH E DI
COLLINS, JOSPEH-BLACK	ST	325	4TH E DI
COLLINS, JSOHUA-BLACK	WOR	348	1ST E DI
COLLINS, JULIA	ALL	214	CUMBERLA
COLLINS, JULIE-BLACK	CAR	109	NO TWP L
COLLINS, JULIUS	BAL	172	6TH WARD
COLLINS, KENDAL	WOR	284	BERLIN 1
COLLINS, KITTY	ANN	317	1ST DIST
COLLINS, LEAH	BAL	023	15TH WAR
COLLINS, LEE	BAL	116	18TH WAR
COLLINS, LEONARD	BAL	025	15TH WAR
COLLINS, LEVIN-BLACK	CAR	151	NO TWP L
COLLINS, LEVIN-BLACK	CAR	152	NO TWP L
COLLINS, LEVY	BAL	063	18TH WAR
COLLINS, LITTLETON	SOM	415	DUBLIN D
COLLINS, LOUIS	BAL	315	1ST DIST
COLLINS, LOUISA	WOR	303	SNOW HIL
COLLINS, MAHALA	DOR	430	1ST DIST
COLLINS, MAJOR	SOM	351	BRINKLEY
COLLINS, MARCELLES	CAR	118	NO TWP L
COLLINS, MARGARET	ANN	508	HOWARD D
COLLINS, MARGARET	BAL	082	1ST WARD
COLLINS, MARGARET	BAL	075	10TH WAR
COLLINS, MARGARETTA	BAL	321	7TH WARD
COLLINS, MARIA	CEC	214	7TH E DI
COLLINS, MARTHA	WOR	326	1ST E DI
COLLINS, MARTHA	ST	269	3RD E DI
COLLINS, MARTHA	WOR	289	9TH E DI
COLLINS, MARTHA	SOM	531	QUANTICO
COLLINS, MARY	SOM	497	SALISBUR
COLLINS, MARY	PRI	113	PISCATAW
COLLINS, MARY	TAL	030	EASTON D
COLLINS, MARY	WOR	270	BERLIN 1
COLLINS, MARY	SOM	395	BRINKLEY
COLLINS, MARY	CAR	129	NO TWP L
COLLINS, MARY	BAL	398	14TH WAR
COLLINS, MARY A.	BAL	377	13TH WAR
COLLINS, MARY A.-BLACK	ST	324	4TH E DI
COLLINS, MARY E.	SOM	511	BARREN C
COLLINS, MATILDA	WOR	263	BERLIN 1
COLLINS, MATILDA-BLACK	ST	333	4TH E DI
COLLINS, MICHAEL	BAL	204	2ND WARD
COLLINS, MICHEAL	BAL	023	18TH WAR
COLLINS, MILLY	SOM	410	DUBLIN D
COLLINS, MOSES	WAS	010	WILLIAMS
COLLINS, NANCY	PRI	055	AQUASCO
COLLINS, NANCY	DOR	297	1ST DIST
COLLINS, NOAH	SOM	416	DUBLIN D
COLLINS, NOAH	CAR	216	5TH DIST
COLLINS, NOAH	WAS	148	HAGERSTO
COLLINS, NOAH R.	BAL	037	9TH WARD
COLLINS, ORLANDO	ANN	467	HOWARD D
COLLINS, PAT	BAL	219	19TH WAR
COLLINS, PATRICK	BAL	088	18TH WAR
COLLINS, PATRICK	BAL	003	EASTERN
COLLINS, PATRICK	BAL	086	10TH WAR
COLLINS, PATRICK	BAL	087	10TH WAR
COLLINS, PATRICK	BAL	196	2ND WARD
COLLINS, PATRICK	BAL	171	6TH WARD
COLLINS, PATRICK	BAL	025	9TH WARD
COLLINS, PATRICK	BAL	169	11TH WAR
COLLINS, PATRICK	BAL	164	2ND DIST
COLLINS, PATRICK	BAL	440	1ST DIST
COLLINS, PATRICK	ALL	082	5TH E.D.
COLLINS, PATRICK	ALL	057	10TH E.D
COLLINS, PATRICK	ALL	082	5TH E.D.
COLLINS, PATRICK	KEN	304	3RD DIST
COLLINS, PERRY*	DOR	310	1ST DIST
COLLINS, PETER	SOM	431	PRINCESS
COLLINS, PETER	CAR	139	NO TWP L
COLLINS, PETER	BAL	087	10TH WAR
COLLINS, RACHEL	ANN	349	3RD DIST
COLLINS, RACHEL	WOR	244	1ST CENS
COLLINS, RACHEL	WOR	292	9TH E DI
COLLINS, REBECCA	DOR	297	1ST DIST
COLLINS, REBECCA	BAL	345	13TH WAR
COLLINS, RICHARD	BAL	146	11TH WAR
COLLINS, RICHARD	WOR	312	2ND E DI
COLLINS, RICHARD	BAL	106	2ND DIST
COLLINS, RICHARDSON	BAL	143	2ND DIST
COLLINS, ROBERT	BAL	225	12TH WAR
COLLINS, ROBERT	BAL	378	13TH WAR
COLLINS, ROBERT-BLACK	WOR	348	1ST E DI
COLLINS, RUBEN	BAL	314	7TH WARD
COLLINS, SALLY	DOR	314	1ST DIST
COLLINS, SAMUEL	CHA	256	MIDDLETO
COLLINS, SAMUEL	CAR	129	NO TWP L
COLLINS, SAMUEL	CAR	146	NO TWP L
COLLINS, SAMUEL	SOM	414	DUBLIN D
COLLINS, SAMUEL	BAL	249	6TH WARD
COLLINS, SAMUEL	SOM	353	BRINKLEY
COLLINS, SAMUEL	DOR	454	1ST DIST
COLLINS, SAMUEL	WOR	290	9TH E DI
COLLINS, SAMUEL S.	DOR	311	1ST DIST
COLLINS, SARAH	DOR	324	1ST DIST
COLLINS, SARAH	BAL	389	13TH WAR
COLLINS, SARAH	BAL	049	4TH WARD
COLLINS, SARAH	CAR	215	5TH DIST
COLLINS, SARAH	BAL	215	11TH WAR
COLLINS, SARAH	DOR	455	1ST DIST
COLLINS, SARAH	SOM	366	BRINKLEY
COLLINS, SARAH	SOM	498	SALISBUR
COLLINS, SARAH	ANN	292	ANNAPOLI
COLLINS, SARAH	BAL	434	1ST DIST
COLLINS, SARHA	BAL	278	2ND WARD
COLLINS, SARRAH A.	DOR	329	3RD DIVI
COLLINS, SENE	TAL	001	EASTON D
COLLINS, SEVIN	WOR	254	1ST CENS
COLLINS, SEYMOUR	ANN	317	1ST DIST
COLLINS, SILAS	DOR	454	1ST DIST
COLLINS, SINDALOW	TAL	074	EASTON T
COLLINS, SOLOMON	BAL	216	17TH WAR
COLLINS, STEPHEN	WOR	181	6TH E DI
COLLINS, STEPHEN B.	WOR	293	9TH E DI
COLLINS, STEPHEN-MULATTO	WOR	176	6TH E DI
COLLINS, SUSAN	SOM	353	BRINKLEY
COLLINS, SUSAN	BAL	038	15TH WAR
COLLINS, SUSAN L.	BAL	130	5TH WARD
COLLINS, SUSANNAH	BAL	120	2ND DIST
COLLINS, TABITHA	FRE	013	FREDERIC
COLLINS, TAMSEY	CAR	131	NO TWP L
COLLINS, THOMAS	CAR	131	NO TWP L
COLLINS, THOMAS	BAL	174	19TH WAR
COLLINS, THOMAS	HAR	026	1ST DIST
COLLINS, THOMAS	ALL	034	2ND E.D.
COLLINS, THOMAS	BAL	128	1ST WARD
COLLINS, THOMAS	BAL	272	1ST DIST
COLLINS, THOMAS	WOR	245	1ST CENS
COLLINS, THOMAS F.	BAL	456	8TH WARD
COLLINS, THOMAS S.	BAL	114	1ST WARD
COLLINS, THOMS	WOR	304	SNOW HIL
COLLINS, THOMSA	ANN	317	1ST DIST
COLLINS, TILGHMAN	CAR	119	NO TWP L
COLLINS, W.	WAS	022	2ND SUBD
COLLINS, WILLIAM	TAL	044	EASTON D
COLLINS, WILLIAM	WOR	179	6TH E DI
COLLINS, WILLIAM	WOR	181	6TH E DI
COLLINS, WILLIAM	SOM	536	TYASKIN
COLLINS, WILLIAM	SOM	354	BRINKLEY
COLLINS, WILLIAM	ST	269	3RD E DI
COLLINS, WILLIAM	ST	271	3RD E DI
COLLINS, WILLIAM	CAR	121	NO TWP L
COLLINS, WILLIAM	SOM	425	PRINCESS
COLLINS, WILLIAM	CAR	203	4TH DIST
COLLINS, WILLIAM	CAR	170	NO TWP L
COLLINS, WILLIAM	DOR	324	1ST DIST
COLLINS, WILLIAM	BAL	106	18TH WAR
COLLINS, WILLIAM	DOR	409	1ST DIST
COLLINS, WILLIAM	BAL	164	2ND DIST
COLLINS, WILLIAM	BAL	126	1ST WARD
COLLINS, WILLIAM H.	BAL	302	7TH WARD
COLLINS, WILLIAM H.	BAL	306	3RD WARD
COLLINS, WILLIAM H.	BAL	094	10TH WAR
COLLINS, WILLIAM J.	WOR	228	6TH E DI
COLLINS, WILLIAM W.	BAL	307	3RD WARD
COLLINS.BARNEY	BAL	133	1ST WARD
COLLINS.FREDERICK	BAL	055	2ND DIST
COLLINS.JENNETT	CAR	116	NO TWP L
COLLINS.JIM	WOR	293	9TH E DI
COLLINS.MARGARET	FRE	390	PETERSVI
COLLINS.MARY	CAR	129	NO TWP L
COLLINS.MARY E.	CAR	108	NO TWP L
COLLINSON, EDWARD	ANN	310	1ST DIST
COLLINSON, JOHN	ANN	311	1ST DIST
COLLINSON, JOHN	CAR	109	NO TWP L
COLLINSON, JOSEPH	ANN	311	1ST DIST
COLLINSON, THOMAS W.	ANN	309	1ST DIST
COLLIOUS, CATRHINE	BAL	019	18TH WAR
COLLIS, ELY-BLACK	FRE	231	BUCKEYSTU
COLLIS, HENRY A.	PRI	094	SPALDING
COLLIS, THOMAS-BLACK	FRE	231	BUCKEYST
COLLISN, LEVIN	WOR	241	1ST CENS
COLLISON, ANDREW	TAL	019	EASTON D
COLLISON, CATHARINE	TAL	117	ST MICHA
COLLISON, CHARLES W.	BAL	006	4TH WARD
COLLISON, DAVID	BAL	107	1ST WARD
COLLISON, EDWARD	TAL	039	EASTON D
COLLISON, EDWARD F.	TAL	107	ST MICHA
COLLISON, FEBS*	TAL	018	EASTON D
COLLISON, GEORGE W.	CAR	168	NO TWP L
COLLISON, GOERGE W.	BAL	299	17TH WAR
COLLISON, HENRY	TAL	043	EASTON D
COLLISON, JAMES	TAL	116	ST MICHA
COLLISON, JAMES	BAL	249	20TH WAR
COLLISON, JAMES	BAL	019	15TH WAR
COLLISON, JOHN	BAL	359	3RD WARD
COLLISON, LEAH	DOR	411	1ST DIST
COLLISON, LEAH	DOR	431	1ST DIST
COLLISON, LEVIN R.	DOR	310	1ST DIST
COLLISON, LUCY	BAL	458	1ST DIST
COLLISON, MAHALY	CAR	095	NO TWP L
COLLISON, MARGARET	DOR	417	1ST DIST
COLLISON, MARY	CAR	089	NO TWP L
COLLISON, NOAH	BAL	249	20TH WAR
COLLISON, PERRY	BAL	059	1ST WARD
COLLISON, RICHEL	TAL	093	ST MICHA
COLLISON, ROBERT H.	CAR	168	NO TWP L
COLLISON, ROBERT K.	CAR	167	NO TWP L
COLLISON, THOMAS	DOR	449	1ST DIST
COLLISON, THOMAS W.	BAL	049	1ST WARD
COLLISON, WILLIAM	BAL	174	16TH WAR
COLLISON, WILLIAM	TAL	072	EASTON T
COLLISON, WILLIAM	DOR	415	1ST DIST
COLLISON, WILLIAM J.	BAL	019	15TH WAR
COLLISON,ELI	CAR	147	NO TWP L
COLLISTER, WILLIAM H.	BAL	305	7TH WARD
COLLIT, MARGARET	BAL	033	2ND DIST
COLLIT, SARAH	BAL	034	2ND DIST
COLLITT,MRS.	BAL	034	2ND DIST
COLLITY, POLLY	BAL	459	1ST DIST
COLLIVER, PETER	BAL	129	18TH WAR
COLLMUS, LEVI	BAL	260	6TH WARD
COLLMUS, SOLOMON	BAL	114	5TH WARD
COLLNGWOOD, WILLIAM	BAL	123	1ST WARD
COLLNIET, EUGENE	BAL	301	20TH WAR
COLLOCK, ARA	WOR	307	2ND E DI
COLLOCK, JOHN	WOR	310	2ND E DI
COLLOCK, LEMUEL	WOR	298	9TH E DI
COLLODAY, MARY	BAL	282	12TH WAR
COLLOK, ARALANTO	WOR	310	2ND E DI
COLLON, MARGARET	BAL	098	10TH WAR
COLLOP, JOHN	BAL	402	1ST DIST
COLLOWAY, NANCY	WOR	234	6TH E DI
COLLUM,.C.H.	ALL	033	2ND E.D.
COLLWELL, GEORGE	BAL	115	1ST WARD
COLLY, ANNA B.	BAL	092	15TH WAR
COLLY, EVA	BAL	109	15TH WAR
COLLY, JANE	BAL	261	1ST DIST
COLLY, JOHN	BAL	232	1ST DIST
COLLY, SARAH A.	BAL	281	20TH WAR
COLLY, THOMAS	ALL	055	10TH E.D
COLLYER, JAMES	WOR	284	BERLIN 1
COLLYER, JOSHUA	WOR	279	BERLIN 1
COLLYER, MARIAH	WOR	271	BERLIN 1
COLLYER, MARY	WOR	293	9TH E DI
COLLYER, PETER	WOR	265	BERLIN 1
COLLYER, SALLY	WOR	271	BERLIN 1
COLLYER, WILLIAM	WOR	270	BERLIN 1
COLMAN, ELIZA	BAL	040	1ST WARD
COLMAN, HENRY	BAL	040	1ST WARD
COLMAN, OTHO-MULATTO	FRE	409	JEFFERSO
COLMAN, RODY	DOR	450	1ST DIST
COLMAN, THOMAS	DOR	358	3RD DIVI
COLMARY, BUSKIRCK	CEC	030	CHESAPEA
COLMARY, JAMES	CEC	096	4TH E DI
COLMARY, RACHEL	CEC	105	3RD E DI
COLON, WILLIAM	BAL	176	2ND DIST
COLP, CASPER	BAL	198	5TH DIST
COLP, JY	BAL	198	5TH DIST
COLPEN, MARTIN	ALL	142	6TH E.D.
COLSBURN, ADORA	CAL	015	1ST DIST
COLSON, J.	BAL	152	1ST WARD
COLSON, JOSEPH	ST	299	2ND E DI
COLSTON, CELIA	DOR	468	1ST DIST
COLSTON, CHARLES	BAL	068	4TH WARD
COLSTON, ELIZA A.	TAL	005	EASTON D
COLSTON, GLADSTON	DOR	419	1ST DIST
COLSTON, JAMES*	DOR	412	1ST DIST
COLSTON, M. C.	TAL	095	ST MICHA
COLSTON, RICHARD	DOR	420	1ST DIST
COLT, CHARLES	BAL	354	3RD WARD
COLT, ELIZABETH	BAL	241	17TH WAR
COLT, RICHARD*	TAL	022	EASTON D
COLTORIDER, DANIEL	BAL	208	6TH DIST
COLTEHUSAYER, CHARLOTTE	BAL	051	1ST WARD
COLTEN, ELLEN M.	BAL	138	11TH WAR
COLTER, GEORGE	BAL	128	1ST WARD
COLTER, JOHN	BAL	258	2ND WARD
COLTER, JOHN	BAL	154	11TH WAR
COLTER, JOHN	BAL	129	18TH WAR
COLTER, MARY	BAL	181	11TH WAR
COLTER, PHILIP	BAL	157	1ST WARD
COLTER, ROSANNA	BAL	180	11TH WAR
COLTER, WILLIAM	BAL	171	1ST WARD
COLTHRUST, HENRY	BAL	167	1ST WARD
COLTMAN, GOERGE S.	BAL	002	15TH WAR
COLTMAN, JAMES S.	BAL	195	11TH WAR
COLTMIER, WILLIAM	BAL	025	4TH WARD
COLTMUTH, EDWARD	BAL	313	12TH WAR
COLTON, ASA S.	FRE	226	BUCKEYST
COLTON, GEORGE	ANN	296	1ST DIST
COLTON, JOHN L.	CHA	289	BOJANTOW
COLTON, MARTHA	BAL	226	12TH WAR
COLTON, WILLIAM	BAL	078	1ST WARD
COLTRIDER, ADALINE	BAL	210	5TH DIST
COLTRIDER, FREDERIC	CAR	295	7TH DIST
COLTRIDER, GEORGE	CAR	173	8TH DIST
COLTRIDER, JACOB	CAR	173	8TH DIST
COLTRIDER, JACOB	BAL	207	6TH DIST
COLTRIDER, JOHN	BAL	210	5TH DIST
COLTRIDER, JOSHUA	CAR	171	8TH DIST
COLTRIDER, NOAH C.	CAR	173	8TH DIST
COLTRIDER, SUSANNAH	CAR	171	8TH DIST
COLTRIDGER, HENRY	BAL	210	6TH DIST
COLTS, CHRISTENA	BAL	372	8TH WARD
COLTZ, EDWARD	BAL	169	19TH WAR
COLTZ, JACOB GREEN	CAR	382	2ND DIST
COLTZHYER, ANN R.	BAL	216	19TH WAR
COLUM, AUGUSTUS	WAS	044	2ND SUBD
COLUMBUS, NORRIS	CAR	391	2ND DIST
COLVILL, CAROLINE	ST	340	5TH E DI
COLVILLE, W.	BAL	063	10TH WAR
COLVIN, ELLEN	ALL	242	CUMBERLA
COLVIN, ENALS	BAL	373	3RD WARD
COLVIN, JOHN	ALL	167	6TH E.D.
COLVIN, RACHEL*	BAL	425	3RD WARD
COLVIN, WILLIAM	BAL	192	11TH WAR
COLWELL, ANN	QUE	208	3RD E DI
COLWELL, CAROLINE	BAL	001	4TH WARD
COLWELL, EDWARD	BAL	270	12TH WAR
COLWELL, EDWARD-BLACK	CAR	068	NO TWP L
COLWELL, ELIZA	BAL	270	12TH WAR
COLWELL, ELIZA	BAL	460	1ST DIST
COLWELL, J.	BAL	158	1ST WARD
COLWELL, JAMES	BAL	289	20TH WAR
COLWELL, JOHN	ALL	109	5TH E.D.
COLWELL, JOHN C.	BAL	332	3RD WARD
COLWELL, JOSEP	WAS	262	1ST DIST
COLWELL, JOSEPHENE	DOR	379	1ST DIST
COLWELL, JOSHUA	BAL	154	1ST WARD
COLWELL, MARGARET	BAL	332	3RD WARD
COLWELL, MARY	BAL	216	6TH DIST
COLWELL, NANCY	BAL	083	4TH WARD
COLWELL, RACHEL	KEN	291	3RD DIST
COLWELL, WESLEY	BAL	196	19TH WAR
COLWELL, WILLIAM	BAL	135	1ST WARD
COLY, CHARLES	DOR	437	1ST DIST
COLYER, HENRY	BAL	070	18TH WAR
COLYER, JOHN	BAL	423	8TH WARD
COMAR, MARGO	ALL	047	10TH E.D
COMARD, JOHN	CEC	073	5TH E DI
COMAS, JANE	KEN	253	1ST DIST
COMAS, TERRA	BAL	280	12TH WAR

Name	County	Page	District
COMB, ALEXANDER	BAL	396	3RD WARD
COMB, CHARLES A.	BAL	458	14TH WAR
COMB, WILLIAM A.	BAL	458	14TH WAR
COMBA, JOHN	ALL	092	5TH E.D.
COMBACK, MICHEAL	BAL	130	18TH WAR
COMBER, ANN	BAL	258	20TH WAR
COMBER, BERARD	BAL	151	2ND DIST
COMBS, ALEXANDER	ST	272	3RD E DI
COMBS, CHARLOTTE	ST	278	3RD E DI
COMBS, CHARLOTTE M.	ST	292	2ND E DI
COMBS, CORNELIUS	ST	299	2ND E DI
COMBS, EDWARD P.	ST	313	1ST E DI
COMBS, ELISHA	ALL	115	5TH E.D.
COMBS, ELIZABETH	BAL	463	1ST DIST
COMBS, FRANCES E.	BAL	161	6TH WARD
COMBS, GEORGE	ST	273	3RD E DI
COMBS, HENRIETTA	WAS	293	1ST DIST
COMBS, IGNAUIUS	ST	276	3RD E DI
COMBS, JAMES	ST	283	3RD E DI
COMBS, JAMES N.	ST	287	2ND E DI
COMBS, JESSEE	WAS	281	1ST DIST
COMBS, JOHN	ALL	130	4TH E.D.
COMBS, JOHN C.	ST	273	3RD E DI
COMBS, LOUIS T.	ST	281	3RD E DI
COMBS, LOUISA	FRE	062	FREDERIC
COMBS, MARY A.	FRE	065	FREDERIC
COMBS, MARY O.	ST	273	3RD E DI
COMBS, MARY J.	ST	281	3RD E DI
COMBS, MARY M.	ST	291	2ND E DI
COMBS, MARY S.	BAL	289	3RD WARD
COMBS, NANNA	ST	273	3RD E DI
COMBS, NICHOLAS	ST	282	3RD E DI
COMBS, PERRY	ST	299	2ND E DI
COMBS, PETER	BAL	258	1ST DIST
COMBS, PHILIP T.	ST	304	2ND E DI
COMBS, RACHEL	BAL	182	6TH WARD
COMBS, ROBERT L.	ST	282	3RD E DI
COMBS, THOAMS	BAL	406	1ST DIST
COMBS, THOMAS	WAS	193	1ST DIST
COMBS, THOMAS	ST	299	2ND E DI
COMBS, WILLAM	ALL	127	4TH E.D.
COMBS, WILLIAM A.	ST	285	2ND E DI
COMBS, WILLIAM A.	ST	284	2ND E DI
COMEGEG, J.	BAL	295	12TH WAR
COMEGES, RICHARD	CAR	083	NO TWP L
COMEGES, WILLIAM	CAR	094	NO TWP L
COMEGEY, ABRIHAM	BAL	195	17TH WAR
COMEGEY, JOHN W.	TAL	092	ST MICHA
COMEGEY, MARY E.	BAL	195	17TH WAR
COMEGEYS, EVERLINE M.	BAL	379	1ST DIST
COMEGEYS, KATE	BAL	378	1ST DIST
COMEGGS, ANN	KEN	230	2ND DIST
COMEGGS, ARAMINTA	KEN	216	2ND DIST
COMEGGS, BARTUS *	BAL	139	19TH WAR
COMEGGS, BENJAMIN	KEN	229	2ND DIST
COMEGGS, BENJAMIN	KEN	283	3RD DIST
COMEGGS, EDWARD	KEN	255	1ST DIST
COMEGGS, HARRIET A.	KEN	216	2ND DIST
COMEGGS, HENRY	KEN	296	3RD DIST
COMEGGS, ISAAC	KEN	238	2ND DIST
COMEGGS, JONOTHAN	KEN	255	1ST DIST
COMEGYS, CLARISSA *	BAL	299	1ST DIST
COMEGYS, CORNELIUS	QUE	150	1ST E DI
COMEGYS, CORNELIUS-BLACK	QUE	155	2ND E DI
COMEGYS, ELIAS	BAL	294	3RD WARD
COMEGYS, ELIJAH	QUE	142	1ST E DI
COMEGYS, HENRY F.	KEN	298	3RD DIST
COMEGYS, JOHN M.	KEN	298	3RD DIST
COMEGYS, REBECCA	QUE	197	3RD E DI
COMEGYS, SAMUEL	KEN	298	3RD DIST
COMEGYS, SAMUEL W.	KEN	305	3RD DIST
COMEGYS, SAMUEL-BLACK	QUE	199	3RD E DI
COMEGYS, SARAH	QUE	142	1ST E DI
COMEGYS, THOMAS	QUE	173	2ND E DI
COMEGYS, WILLIAM	QUE	161	2ND E DI
COMER, ANNA	BAL	198	19TH WAR
COMER, HENRY	BAL	304	20TH WAR
COMER, ISAAC	BAL	272	17TH WAR
COMER, JOHN T.	CEC	194	7TH E DI
COMER, PETER	BAL	197	19TH WAR
COMER, W.	BAL	138	1ST WARD
COMERL, WILLIAM	BAL	426	1ST DIST
COMERY, BRIDGET	BAL	026	9TH WARD
COMFORT, ABRAHAM	FRE	150	10TH E D
COMFORT, CATHERINE	BAL	042	4TH WARD
COMICK, JOSHUA	FRE	313	MIDDLETO
COMIGES, MATILDA	CAR	079	NO TWP L
COMIGES, PERRY-BLACK	CAR	078	NO TWP L
COMIGGS, LEMUEL *	BAL	298	1ST DIST
COMINGS, FRANCIS	BAL	173	11TH WAR
COMINS, WILLIAM	HAR	168	3RD DIST
COMLY, BIDDY	BAL	319	20TH WAR
COMLY, JAMES	BAL	284	20TH WAR
COMLY, JAMES	BAL	267	12TH WAR
COMLY, LOUISA	BAL	285	20TH WAR
COMLY, SETH J.	BAL	062	15TH WAR
COMMANDER, MARY A.	FRE	108	CREAGERS
COMMANDRICK, J.	BAL	142	1ST WARD
COMMEGER, GEORGE	BAL	382	8TH WARD
COMMELL, NOTLEY	BAL	250	1ST DIST
COMMELL, PETER	CAR	230	5TH DIST
COMMER, CATHARINE	CAL	016	1ST DIST
COMMERMAN, CHARLES	MGM	391	ROCKERLE
COMMODORE, ANN	BAL	399	14TH WAR
COMMODORE, HARRIET	CAL	063	3RD DIST
COMMON, ELIZABETH	CAR	154	NO TWP L
COMMONDORE, JOHN	CAL	032	2ND DIST
COMMONS, GARRISON	TAL	056	EASTON D
COMMONS, HARRISON	BAL	365	3RD WARD
COMNEGRESS, S.	BAL	063	10TH WAR
COMFELTON, RACHAEL	BAL	119	11TH WAR
COMPLE, NANCY L.	BAL	356	13TH WAR
COMPTON, BUEL	CHA	257	MIDDLETO
COMPTON, DAVID	ALL	020	2ND E.D.
COMPTON, ELIZA T.	PRI	046	AQUASCO
COMPTON, JEHU	PRI	036	VANSVILL
COMPTON, MRS-	ANN	408	8TH DIST
COMPTON, REBECCA	WAS	006	WILLIAMS
COMPTON, WILLIAM	CHA	270	ALLENS F
COMPTON,MARY	PRI	036	VANSVILL
COMRIL, WILLIAM*	TAL	026	EASTON D
COMRON, DANIEL	BAL	437	1ST DIST
COMSTOCK, GEORGE J.	BAL	250	12TH WAR
COMSTOCK, W.B.	BAL	169	1ST WARD
COMTE, ANN	BAL	010	4TH WARD
COMTHINTER, DEBORAH *	BAL	099	2ND DIST
COMTHWAIT, JOHN O.	BAL	163	6TH WARD
COMTHWAIT, ROBERT*	BAL	385	3RD WARD
CON, HARRIET	FRE	265	NEW MARK
CON, THOMAS	WAS	067	2ND SUBD
CONA, BARTARA	ALL	014	3RD E.D.
CONACHAN, BRIDGET	BAL	082	10TH WAR
CONAIN, LOUIS	BAL	053	4TH WARD
CONALY, PATRICK	BAL	414	8TH WARD
CONANT, ANDREW W.	BAL	005	15TH WAR
CONANT, SAMUEL W.	BAL	195	6TH WARD
CONARAY, JOHN	BAL	272	7TH WARD
CONARD, EDWARD	CEC	061	1ST E DI
CONARD, JAMES	CEC	177	7TH E DI
CONARD, JAMES M.	CEC	179	7TH E DI
CONARD, JESSE	CEC	203	6TH E DI
CONARD, JOSEPH B.	CEC	179	7TH E DI
CONART, CLARISA	DOR	355	3RD DIVI
CONARY, JOHN P.	BAL	273	7TH WARD
CONAUGHT, WILLIAM	FRE	173	5TH E DI
CONAUGHTON, BRYAN	BAL	275	1ST DIST
CONAWAY, AMELIA	CAR	224	5TH DIST
CONAWAY, CARVILL	BAL	006	4TH WARD
CONAWAY, CHARLES	CAR	214	5TH DIST
CONAWAY, CHARLES H.	CAR	215	5TH DIST
CONAWAY, EDWARD	BAL	211	6TH WARD
CONAWAY, ELIZABETH	BAL	307	1ST DIST
CONAWAY, FRANCES A.	BAL	397	8TH WARD
CONAWAY, HENRY	FRE	297	WOODSBOR
CONAWAY, ISAAC	BAL	160	1ST WARD
CONAWAY, JAMES	BAL	006	4TH WARD
CONAWAY, JANE	DOR	316	1ST DIST
CONAWAY, JOHANNA	BAL	384	3RD WARD
CONAWAY, JOHN	ALL	060	10TH E.D
CONAWAY, JOHN W.	CAR	095	NO TWP L
CONAWAY, MARTIN	ALL	119	5TH E.D.
CONAWAY, MARY	CAR	099	NO TWP L
CONAWAY, MINOS*	DOR	312	1ST DIST
CONAWAY, NATHAN	BAL	324	1ST DIST
CONAWAY, PATRICK	ALL	031	2ND E.D.
CONAWAY, PAUL	DOR	316	1ST DIST
CONAWAY, RICHARD	BAL	155	1ST WARD
CONAWAY, RUBEN	CAR	223	5TH DIST
CONAWAY, SOLOMON F.	FRE	304	WOODSBOR
CONAWAY, THOMAS	CAR	214	5TH DIST
CONAWAY, THOMAS	WOR	338	1ST E DI
CONAWAY, WILLIAM	DOR	312	1ST DIST
CONCANNON,MARY	BAL	023	2ND DIST
CONCHE, ANN M.*	DOR	431	1ST DIST
CONCHLAN, JOSEPH	BAL	067	1ST WARD
CONCHMAN, GEORG	BAL	108	1ST WARD
CONCKLING, RICHARD	BAL	265	2ND WARD
CONDEAN, HENRY	BAL	038	9TH WARD
CONDER, EDWARD	BAL	173	1ST WARD
CONDER, RIGGA	BAL	081	1ST WARD
CONDIFF, HENRY	SOM	461	HANGARY
CONDIN, EDWARD	ALL	197	CUMBERLA
CONDING, WILLIAM	BAL	257	12TH WAR
CONDLIN, ANN	BAL	321	20TH WAR
CONDOLL, JOSEPH	BAL	135	16TH WAR
CONDON, ALFRED	BAL	115	1ST WARD
CONDON, AMELIA	CAR	372	9TH DIST
CONDON, CAHRINE	FRE	424	8TH E DI
CONDON, ELIZA C.	CAR	366	9TH DIST
CONDON, ELIZA E.	FRE	431	8TH E DI
CONDON, HARRIET	FRE	425	8TH E DI
CONDON, HENRY*	DOR	461	1ST DIST
CONDON, ISABELLA	BAL	035	9TH WARD
CONDON, JANE	BAL	061	10TH WAR
CONDON, JOHN	DOR	433	1ST DIST
CONDON, JOHN R.	BAL	386	13TH WAR
CONDON, MARGARET P.	DOR	454	1ST DIST
CONDON, NIMROD	FRE	425	8TH E DI
CONDON, PERRY	FRE	425	8TH E DI
CONDON, RACHAEL E.	CAR	372	9TH DIST
CONDON, RICHARD	TAL	011	EASTON D
CONDON, RICHARD W.	CAR	371	9TH DIST
CONDON, THOMAS	CAR	366	9TH DIST
CONDON, WESLEY	CAR	395	2ND DIST
CONDON, WILLIAM	FRE	425	8TH E DI
CONDON, WILLIAM H.	BAL	049	9TH WARD
CONDON,LEVI Z.	CAR	361	9TH DIST
CONDOR, ELAM	DOR	466	1ST DIST
CONDOR, HENRY*	DOR	461	1ST DIST
CONDOR, MARY*	BAL	400	3RD WARD
CONDORS, MARY*	BAL	400	3RD WARD
CONDOW, MARY*	BAL	400	3RD WARD
CONDRA, DANIEL	BAL	236	12TH WAR
CONDRY, WILLIAM	BAL	383	3RD WARD
CONDRY,JOHN	FRE	206	BUCKEYST
CONDWICK, JOSEPH	BAL	128	1ST WARD
CONDY, MICHAEL	ALL	139	6TH E.D.
CONE, JOHN	ALL	051	10TH E.D
CONE, MARY	ALL	148	6TH E.D.
CONE, MARY	ALL	147	6TH E.D.
CONE, WILLIAM	ALL	051	10TH E.D
CONEGAN, PATRICK	BAL	032	1ST WARD
CONEGES, LUIS	TAL	081	ST MICHA
CONEGYS, JOHN	QUE	124	1ST E DI
CONEGYS, SAMUEL	QUE	146	1ST E DI
CONELLY, JOHN	ALL	082	5TH E.D.
CONELLY, MARGARET	BAL	449	1ST DIST
CONELLY, MARY	BAL	070	10TH WAR
CONELLY, S.K.	BAL	198	2ND WARD
CONELLY, THOMAS	MGM	365	BERRYS D
CONELY, JOHN	BAL	043	1ST WARD
CONER, AMELIA C.	HAR	145	3RD DIST
CONER, CONELIUS	WAS	064	2ND SUBD
CONER, MARGARET	BAL	449	1ST DIST
CONERA, WILLIAM	BAL	115	1ST WARD
CONERS, MARGARET	BAL	110	1ST WARD
CONES, JOHN W.	FRE	266	NEW MARK
CONETIR, ALEXANDER	BAL	305	20TH WAR
CONEY, BRIDGET	ALL	238	CUMBERLA
CONEY, ELIZABETH	BAL	231	19TH WAR
CONEY, JOHN	ALL	143	6TH E.D.
CONEY, JOHN	ALL	047	10TH E.D
CONEY, JOSEPH	WAS	292	1ST DIST
CONEY, MARY	BAL	274	12TH WAR
CONEY, MICHAEL	ANN	464	HOWARD D
CONEY, PARKER	SOM	392	BRINKLEY
CONEY,MICHAEL	ALL	227	CUMBERLA
CONGAN, ELLEN	BAL	080	4TH WARD
CONGAN, MICHAEL	KEN	222	2ND DIST
CONGAUL, PATRICK	BAL	032	1ST WARD
CONGER, WILLIAM	KEN	209	2ND DIST
CONGLAN, CORNELIUS	BAL	197	2ND WARD
CONGO, WILLIAM	BAL	083	4TH WARD
CONIGAN, GEORGE	CEC	043	CHESAPEA
CONIGAN, PATRICK	BAL	199	2ND WARD
CONIKIN, MELISSA	BAL	458	14TH WAR
CONINE, W. C.	BAL	084	10TH WAR
CONING, JANE	ANN	454	HOWARD D
CONISH, SUSANER	HAR	151	3RD DIST
CONIWAY, OSBURN	ANN	331	2ND DIST
CONKER, ANN M.*	DOR	431	1ST DIST
CONKER, PETER M.	BAL	328	7TH WARD
CONKEY, JAMES	BAL	155	1ST WARD
CONKLIN, DANIEL	ALL	023	2ND E.D.
CONKLIN, GEORGE	BAL	154	1ST WARD
CONKLIN, JULIUS	BAL	084	4TH WARD
CONKLIN, MICHAEL	BAL	266	17TH WAR
CONKLIN, SARAH	BAL	463	1ST DIST
CONKLIN, THOMAS	BAL	114	1ST WARD
CONKLIN, WILLIAM	ALL	023	2ND E.D.
CONKLING, ANN	BAL	129	5TH WARD
CONKLING, CAROLINE	BAL	188	11TH WAR
CONKLING, ELIZABETH	BAL	212	19TH WAR
CONKLING, ISAIAH B.	BAL	171	16TH WAR
CONKLING, JOHN	BAL	104	1ST WARD
CONKLING, M.J.	BAL	162	19TH WAR
CONKLING, OLIVER	BAL	212	19TH WAR
CONKLING, WILLIAM	BAL	407	3RD WARD
CONKLING, WILLIAM H.	BAL	165	1ST WARD
CONKLING, WILLIAM H.	BAL	241	2ND WARD
CONLAN, JAMES	BAL	077	10TH WAR
CONLAN, MARGARET	BAL	247	12TH WAR
CONLANA, JAMES	BAL	355	8TH WARD
CONLAY, BENNY	BAL	298	12TH WAR
CONLEHAN, THOMAS	ALL	244	CUMBERLA
CONLEHAN, THOMAS	ALL	244	CUMBERLA
CONLEY, CATHARINE	BAL	347	1ST DIST
CONLEY, CATHARINE	WAS	219	1ST DIST
CONLEY, CHARLES O.	BAL	457	1ST DIST
CONLEY, DONNATIUS	HAR	002	1ST DIST
CONLEY, FRANCES	QUE	170	2ND E DI
CONLEY, H.	ANN	336	3RD DIST
CONLEY, HARRISON	FRE	026	FREDERIC
CONLEY, IGNATIUS	HAR	014	1ST DIST
CONLEY, JAMES B.	HAR	082	2ND DIST
CONLEY, JOHN	ALL	141	6TH E.D.
CONLEY, JOHN	ALL	200	CUMBERLA
CONLEY, JOHN	BAL	379	1ST DIST
CONLEY, JOHN	BAL	154	1ST WARD
CONLEY, JOHN SR.	BAL	005	18TH WAR
CONLEY, MARTHA M.	ANN	437	HOWARD D
CONLEY, MARY	MGM	324	CRACKLIN
CONLEY, MICHAEL	FRE	217	BUCKEYST
CONLEY, SAMUEL	BAL	134	18TH WAR
CONLEY, SAMUEL	WOR	285	BERLIN 1
CONLEY, SARAH	BAL	134	18TH WAR
CONLEY, THOMAS Y.	MGM	351	BERRYS D
CONLEY, WATT	HAR	006	1ST DIST
CONLIN, ANDREW	BAL	281	17TH WAR
CONLIN, DANIEL	BAL	286	17TH WAR
CONLIN, JOHN	CAR	230	5TH DIST
CONLIN, MICHAEL	ALL	074	5TH E.D.
CONLSON, ELIZABETH	BAL	337	13TH WAR
CONLTER, J.	BAL	282	2ND WARD
CONLY, JAMES	ALL	076	5TH E.D.
CONLY, JAMES	BAL	461	1ST DIST
CONLY, JAMES H.	BAL	012	4TH WARD
CONLY, JOHN	ALL	050	10TH E.D
CONLY, MARGARET	BAL	262	12TH WAR
CONLY, PATRICK	BAL	263	12TH WAR
CONLY, PATRICK	MGM	396	ROCKERLE
CONN, BRIDGET	BAL	357	3RD WARD
CONN, CHARLES B.	KEN	299	3RD DIST
CONN, HENRY	BAL	431	1ST DIST
CONN, JACOB S.	BAL	267	7TH WARD
CONN, JAMES C.	BAL	225	1ST DIST
CONN, M.	BAL	258	12TH WAR
CONN, MARTHA	BAL	016	2ND DIST
CONN, MARY E.	BAL	212	11TH WAR
CONN, REBECCA	ALL	084	5TH E.D.
CONN, SILAS E.	BAL	050	9TH WARD
CONN, THOMAS O.	ANN	368	4TH DIST
CONN, WILLIAM R.	BAL	178	19TH WAR
CONN, WIN	BAL	135	2ND DIST
CONNALEMAN, CHARLES	BAL	018	18TH WAR
CONNALINE, MICHAEL	BAL	144	1ST WARD
CONNAWAY, JAMES	BAL	043	1ST WARD
CONNAWAY, JINCEY*	DOR	317	1ST DIST
CONNAUAY, MARY	DOR	373	1ST DIST
CONNDY, NANCY	BAL	124	11TH WAR
CONNDY, PATRICK	BAL	368	8TH WARD
CONNEL, CHARLES	BAL	175	2ND DIST
CONNELL, AGNES	MGM	330	CRACKLIN
CONNELL, ANN	BAL	120	11TH WAR
CONNELL, CORNELIUS	BAL	079	4TH WARD
CONNELL, HENORA	BAL	079	4TH WARD
CONNELL, JAMS	MGM	320	CRACKLIN
CONNELL, JOHN	MGM	320	CRACKLIN
CONNELL, JOHN	BAL	118	1ST WARD
CONNELL, MARGARETT	BAL	078	4TH WARD
CONNELL, MARGARETT	BAL	078	4TH WARD
CONNELL, MARY	CEC	031	CHESAPEA
CONNELL, MARY J.	CHA	292	BOJANTOW
CONNELL, OSBURN	CHA	234	HILLTOP
CONNELL, PHILIP	MGM	384	ROCKERLE
CONNELL, PPHILIP J.	MGM	375	ROCKERLE
CONNELL, ROBERT	MGM	386	ROCKERLE
CONNELL, RUTH P.	BAL	247	12TH WAR
CONNELL, SAMUEL	MGM	384	ROCKERLE
CONNELL, SARAH	BAL	125	18TH WAR
CONNELL, THOMAS	ALL	155	6TH E.D.
CONNELL, WILLIAM	MGM	387	ROCKERLE
CONNELLER, JOHN T.	ST	289	2ND E DI
CONNELLEY, BRIDGET	MGM	395	ROCKERLE
CONNELLEY, SARAH A.	MGM	411	MEDLEY 3
CONNELLY, ANN	BAL	088	4TH WARD
CONNELLY, ANN	CAR	133	NO TWP L
CONNELLY, ANN	QUE	184	3RD E DI
CONNELLY, ANN	BAL	130	11TH WAR
CONNELLY, ANN J.	BAL	165	11TH WAR
CONNELLY, ARDRUY	BAL	202	6TH WARD
CONNELLY, BARBARA	MGM	411	MEDLEY 3
CONNELLY, BARTH	BAL	173	11TH WAR
CONNELLY, BERNARD	BAL	369	8TH WARD
CONNELLY, BIDDY	BAL	193	11TH WAR
CONNELLY, CALEB	CAR	157	NO TWP L
CONNELLY, CALEB	CAR	159	NO TWP L
CONNELLY, CATHARINE	BAL	212	11TH WAR
CONNELLY, CATHERINE	BAL	066	4TH WARD
CONNELLY, CHARLES	DOR	314	1ST DIST
CONNELLY, CHARLES	BAL	036	18TH WAR
CONNELLY, DAVID	CEC	128	5TH E DI
CONNELLY, DENNIS	CEC	028	CHESAPEA
CONNELLY, EDWARD	BAL	122	11TH WAR
CONNELLY, EDWARD	ALL	141	6TH E.D.
CONNELLY, EDWARD	BAL	036	9TH WARD
CONNELLY, EDWARD *	BAL	199	6TH WARD
CONNELLY, ELEANORA	BAL	029	4TH WARD
CONNELLY, ELIZA	BAL	294	20TH WAR
CONNELLY, ELIZA	BAL	002	1ST WARD

Name	County	Page	District
CONNELLY. ELIZABETH	BAL	110	10TH WAR
CONNELLY. ELIZABETH	SOM	511	BARREN C
CONNELLY. ELLEN	BAL	033	4TH WARD
CONNELLY. ELLEN	BAL	147	11TH WAR
CONNELLY. EPHRAIM	BAL	379	3RD WARD
CONNELLY. F.	BAL	123	1ST WARD
CONNELLY. FRANCIS E.	BAL	440	8TH WARD
CONNELLY. GEORGE	BAL	196	2ND WARD
CONNELLY. HENRY	CAR	077	NO TWP L
CONNELLY. HENRY	SOM	504	SALISBUR
CONNELLY. HUGH	ANN	520	HOWARD D
CONNELLY. J.	BAL	050	18TH WAR
CONNELLY. JAMES	CAR	152	NO TWP L
CONNELLY. JAMES	BAL	276	2ND WARD
CONNELLY. JANE	BAL	117	11TH WAR
CONNELLY. JANE	CEC	155	PORT DUP
CONNELLY. JAOCB	CAR	119	NO TWP L
CONNELLY. JOHN	CEC	128	5TH E DI
CONNELLY. JOHN	BAL	177	11TH WAR
CONNELLY. JOHN	BAL	162	11TH WAR
CONNELLY. JOHN	ALL	128	4TH E.D.
CONNELLY. JOHN	ANN	450	HOWARD D
CONNELLY. JOHN	SOM	504	SALISBUR
CONNELLY. JOHN	WAS	010	WILLIAMS
CONNELLY. JOHN F.	BAL	455	8TH WARD
CONNELLY. JOHN R.	ANN	469	HOWARD D
CONNELLY. JOHN W.	QUE	211	3RD E DI
CONNELLY. JOHN W.	CAR	168	NO TWP L
CONNELLY. LEWIS	BAL	001	1ST WARD
CONNELLY. LOVICE	CAR	156	NO TWP L
CONNELLY. MARGARET	BAL	332	13TH WAR
CONNELLY. MARTHA E.	SOM	514	BARREN C
CONNELLY. MARY	BAL	055	9TH WARD
CONNELLY. MARY	BAL	379	3RD WARD
CONNELLY. MARY	BAL	399	3RD WARD
CONNELLY. MARY	BAL	305	3RD WARD
CONNELLY. MARY	BAL	184	2ND WARD
CONNELLY. MARY J.	BAL	398	8TH WARD
CONNELLY. MICHAEL	ANN	454	HOWARD D
CONNELLY. MICHAEL	ANN	426	HOWARD D
CONNELLY. MICHAEL	ALL	135	4TH E.D.
CONNELLY. MICHAEL	MGM	365	BERRYS D
CONNELLY. MITCHEL	CAR	130	NO TWP L
CONNELLY. MOSES	SOM	512	BARREN C
CONNELLY. PATRICK	BAL	360	8TH WARD
CONNELLY. PATRICK	BAL	328	13TH WAR
CONNELLY. PATRICK	BAL	189	11TH WAR
CONNELLY. RBEECCA	CAR	144	NO TWP L
CONNELLY. RICHARD	BAL	210	11TH WAR
CONNELLY. RICHARD	BAL	034	4TH WARD
CONNELLY. RICHARD	ALL	073	5TH E.D.
CONNELLY. SAMUEL	BAL	213	2ND WARD
CONNELLY. SARAH	CAR	091	NO TWP L
CONNELLY. SARAH	BAL	006	18TH WAR
CONNELLY. SARAH C.	BAL	072	18TH WAR
CONNELLY. SISTER M.	FRE	198	5TH E DI
CONNELLY. SUSAN	QUE	211	3RD E DI
CONNELLY. THOMAS	HAR	091	2ND DIST
CONNELLY. THOMAS	BAL	398	8TH WARD
CONNELLY. TIMOTHY	BAL	176	11TH WAR
CONNELLY. WILLIAM	BAL	176	11TH WAR
CONNELLY. WILLIAM	BAL	161	1ST WARD
CONNELLY. WILLIAM	BAL	221	6TH WARD
CONNELLY. WILLIAM	CAR	145	NO TWP L
CONNELLY. WILLIAM	CAR	067	NO TWP L
CONNELLY. WILLIAM	CEC	047	1ST E DI
CONNELLY. WILLIAM	CEC	140	5TH E DI
CONNELLY.DANIEL	CAR	145	NO TWP L
CONNELLY.NATHAN	CAR	145	NO TWP L
CONNELLY.OWEN	CAR	156	NO TWP L
CONNELY. MARY	BAL	241	2ND WARD
CONNELY. THOMAS	ALL	053	10TH E.D
CONNER. ADAM	BAL	268	2ND WARD
CONNER. ALBERT	WOR	307	2ND E DI
CONNER. AMOS	ALL	167	6TH E.D.
CONNER. B.M	BAL	194	11TH WAR
CONNER. BARTLEY	BAL	406	8TH WARD
CONNER. BENJAMIN	QUE	206	3RD E DI
CONNER. BENJAMIN	KEN	305	3RD DIST
CONNER. BENJAMIN	KEN	305	3RD DIST
CONNER. BENJAMIN	CAR	104	NO TWP L
CONNER. BENJAMIN H.	QUE	190	3RD E DI
CONNER. BRIDGET	CEC	010	ELKTON 3
CONNER. BRIDGET	BAL	142	19TH WAR
CONNER. BRIGIT O.	BAL	090	5TH WARD
CONNER. CATHARINE	BAL	186	16TH WAR
CONNER. CATHERINE	QUE	131	1ST E DI
CONNER. CHARLOTTA	CEC	212	7TH E DI
CONNER. CLEMET M.*	TAL	011	EASTON D
CONNER. CORNELIUS	ALL	232	CUMBERLA
CONNER. CORNELIUS	BAL	042	1ST WARD
CONNER. DANIEL	BAL	100	10TH WAR
CONNER. CANUEL	WAS	115	2ND DIST
CONNER. EDWARD	WOR	328	1ST E DI
CONNER. EDWARD	BAL	085	15TH WAR
CONNER. ELIZA	BAL	403	8TH WARD
CONNER. ELIZABETH	BAL	166	16TH WAR
CONNER. ELLEN	BAL	079	4TH WARD
CONNER. EMILY	ANN	320	2ND DIST
CONNER. FRANCES	BAL	379	13TH WAR
CONNER. FREDERICK	BAL	150	19TH WAR
CONNER. FRENETTA*	SOM	388	BRINKLEY
CONNER. HENRITTA	QUE	252	5TH E DI
CONNER. HENRY	SOM	394	BRINKLEY
CONNER. HUGH	BAL	043	1ST WARD
CONNER. JACOB	ALL	237	CUMBERLA
CONNER. JAMES	CAL	038	2ND DIST
CONNER. JAMES W.	DOR	381	1ST DIST
CONNER. JOHN	BAL	014	1ST WARD
CONNER. JOHN	ALL	081	5TH E.D.
CONNER. JOHN	BAL	095	10TH WAR
CONNER. JOHN	BAL	179	11TH WAR
CONNER. JOHN	BAL	169	11TH WAR
CONNER. JOHN	SOM	393	BRINKLEY
CONNER. JOHN	WOR	178	6TH E DI
CONNER. JOHN H.	WAS	226	1ST DIST
CONNER. JOHN O.	BAL	174	11TH WAR
CONNER. LAWRENCE	ALL	155	6TH E.D.
CONNER. LAWRENCE	BAL	449	1ST DIST
CONNER. LEVI	ALL	020	2ND E.D.
CONNER. LEVIN	SOM	386	BRINKLEY
CONNER. LUTHER W.	SOM	364	BRINKLEY
CONNER. M.W.	ANN	274	ANNAPOLI
CONNER. MAHALA	SOM	381	BRINKLEY
CONNER. MARGARET	BAL	001	1ST WARD
CONNER. MARGARET	CAL	038	2ND DIST
CONNER. MARGARET	CAL	024	2ND DIST
CONNER. MARGARET	BAL	392	14TH WAR
CONNER. MARGARET	BAL	283	20TH WAR
CONNER. MARY	FRE	306	WOODSBOR
CONNER. MARY	BAL	359	13TH WAR
CONNER. MARY	ANN	407	8TH DIST
CONNER. MARY	BAL	007	EASTERN
CONNER. MARY	BAL	286	7TH WARD
CONNER. MARY	QUE	240	5TH E DI
CONNER. MARY A.	BAL	210	2ND WARD
CONNER. MATTHEW	ALL	129	4TH E.D.
CONNER. MICHAEL	ALL	056	10TH E.D
CONNER. MICHAEL	BAL	210	2ND WARD
CONNER. MRS.	PRI	080	QUEEN AN
CONNER. NATHANIEL	SOM	393	BRINKLEY
CONNER. PATRICK	ALL	047	10TH E.D
CONNER. PATRICK	BAL	247	2ND WARD
CONNER. PATRICK	BAL	449	1ST DIST
CONNER. PATRICK	BAL	445	14TH WAR
CONNER. PETER	BAL	445	1ST DIST
CONNER. PETER	BAL	018	1ST WARD
CONNER. ROBERT	ALL	231	CUMBERLA
CONNER. RODGER C.	BAL	209	2ND WARD
CONNER. SAMUEL	KEN	305	3RD DIST
CONNER. SAMUEL C.J.	WOR	331	1ST E DI
CONNER. SARAH C.	WAS	149	2ND DIST
CONNER. STEPHEN	SOM	388	BRINKLEY
CONNER. SUSAN	ALL	162	6TH E.D.
CONNER. SUSAN O.	BAL	341	3RD WARD
CONNER. THOMAS	ALL	246	CUMBERLA
CONNER. THOMAS	BAL	315	7TH WARD
CONNER. THOMAS	SOM	376	BRINKLEY
CONNER. THOMAS	FRE	018	FREDERIC
CONNER. TIMOTHY	FRE	410	8TH E DI
CONNER. VALENTINE	QUE	188	3RD E DI
CONNER. WILLIAM	WOR	168	6TH E DI
CONNER. WILLIAM F.	BAL	263	12TH WAR
CONNERS. JAMES	CEC	200	7TH E DI
CONNERS. JANE	BAL	334	3RD WARD
CONNERS. JOHN W.	BAL	120	1ST WARD
CONNERS. MICHAEL	BAL	063	1ST WARD
CONNERS. PATRICK	BAL	192	11TH WAR
CONNERY. JOHN	BAL	442	8TH WARD
CONNET. H.	BAL	168	1ST WARD
CONNEY. JARED	BAL	176	2ND DIST
CONNICE. DELIA	QUE	227	4TH E DI
CONNICK. BETTY	CAL	052	3RD DIST
CONNICK. C.R.	PRI	050	AQUASCO
CONNICK. DANIEL	PRI	051	AQUASCO
CONNICK. ELIJA	PRI	053	AQUASCO
CONNICK. JAMES W.	BAL	118	11TH WAR
CONNICK. WILLIAM H.	BAL	127	1ST WARD
CONNIER. CHARLES-BLACK	QUE	193	3RD E DI
CONNIER. SAM-BLACK	QUE	194	3RD E DI
CONNIGAN. THOMAS	CEC	043	CHESAPEA
CONNIGER. JOHN T.	CAR	078	NO TWP L
CONNIKEN. HANNAH	BAL	134	16TH WAR
CONNING. MICHAEL	CEC	200	7TH E DI
CONNIOR. STFANIS	BAL	004	4TH WARD
CONNISE. GEORGE W.*	TAL	034	EASTON D
CONNISH. ANNE*	BAL	109	10TH WAR
CONNOLING. GEORGE	BAL	270	2ND WARD
CONNOLLEY. WILLIAM A.	QUE	236	4TH E DI
CONNOLLY. ANN	CAR	155	NO TWP L
CONNOLLY. ANN M.	BAL	062	18TH WAR
CONNOLLY. BRIDGET	BAL	365	8TH WARD
CONNOLLY. BRIDGET	BAL	313	3RD WARD
CONNOLLY. CATHARINE	BAL	129	5TH WARD
CONNOLLY. HANNAH	BAL	118	18TH WAR
CONNOLLY. JAMES	BAL	139	5TH WARD
CONNOLLY. JEREMIAH	BAL	302	17TH WAR
CONNOLLY. JOHN	BAL	145	19TH WAR
CONNOLLY. MARCELLA	BAL	244	20TH WAR
CONNOLLY. MARIA A.	BAL	061	18TH WAR
CONNOLLY. MARY	BAL	121	11TH WAR
CONNOLLY. MICHAEL	BAL	175	2ND WARD
CONNOLLY. MICHEAL	BAL	072	18TH WAR
CONNOLLY. NICHOLAS	BAL	090	1ST WARD
CONNOLLY. PATRICK	BAL	184	16TH WAR
CONNOLLY. PETER	BAL	001	9TH WARD
CONNOLLY. WILLIAM	HAR	001	1ST DIST
CONNOLY. ALPHCNA	BAL	212	11TH WAR
CONNOLY. CARROLINE	TAL	058	EASTON D
CONNOLY. DENNIS	BAL	026	15TH WAR
CONNOLY. HENRY	BAL	060	15TH WAR
CONNOLY. OWEN	BAL	005	9TH WARD
CONNOLY. SAMUEL	TAL	049	EASTON T
CONNOLY. TIMOTHY	BAL	058	15TH WAR
CONNON. ASBURY	BAL	115	1ST WARD
CONNON. ASBURY	BAL	123	1ST WARD
CONNON. AUGUSTUS*	DOR	340	3RD DIVI
CONNON. HUDSON*	DOR	344	3RD DIVI
CONNON. MICHEL	BAL	089	2ND DIST
CONNOR. ANN	BAL	363	3RD WARD
CONNOR. AUGUSTUS*	DOR	340	3RD DIVI
CONNOR. BERNARD	BAL	388	3RD WARD
CONNOR. BRIDGET	BAL	384	3RD WARD
CONNOR. BRIDGET	BAL	259	6TH WARD
CONNOR. BRIDGET	BAL	041	9TH WARD
CONNOR. BRIDGETT	BAL	012	4TH WARD
CONNOR. CHARLES	BAL	153	16TH WAR
CONNOR. DOMINICK	BAL	209	11TH WAR
CONNOR. ELLEN	BAL	257	12TH WAR
CONNOR. HANNA	BAL	038	4TH WARD
CONNOR. HANNAH	BAL	108	1ST WARD
CONNOR. HENRIETTA	BAL	366	3RD WARD
CONNOR. J.	BAL	165	1ST WARD
CONNOR. JAMES	BAL	075	10TH WAR
CONNOR. JOHN	BAL	117	1ST WARD
CONNOR. JOHN	BAL	004	9TH WARD
CONNOR. JOHN	BAL	002	9TH WARD
CONNOR. JOHN	ANN	453	HOWARD D
CONNOR. JOHN	BAL	023	2ND DIST
CONNOR. JOHN*	BAL	372	3RD WARD
CONNOR. LYDIA A.	FRE	249	NEW MARK
CONNOR. M.	BAL	169	1ST WARD
CONNOR. MARGARET	BAL	343	3RD WARD
CONNOR. MARGRET	BAL	097	1ST WARD
CONNOR. MARTIN	BAL	152	16TH WAR
CONNOR. MARY	BAL	059	18TH WAR
CONNOR. OWEN	BAL	270	12TH WAR
CONNOR. ROBERT	MGM	381	ROCKERLE
CONNOR. ROSANNA	ANN	414	HOWARD D
CONNOR. SARAH	ANN	461	HOWARD D
CONNOR. THOMAS	BAL	134	2ND DIST
CONNOR. THOMAS	BAL	139	2ND DIST
CONNOR. THOMAS	BAL	351	3RD WARD
CONNOR. THOMAS	BAL	020	9TH WARD
CONNOR. THOMAS	BAL	245	6TH WARD
CONNOR. THOMAS	BAL	211	11TH WAR
CONNOR. THOMAS W.	BAL	040	18TH WAR
CONNOR. WILLIAM	BAL	031	18TH WAR
CONNOR. WILLIAM P.	BAL	333	3RD WARD
CONNORS. JAMES	PRI	107	PISCATAW
CONNOWAY. GARRETT	BAL	121	11TH WAR
CONNOWAY. JOHN	BAL	165	1ST WARD
CONNS. GEROGE *	HAR	191	3RD DIST
CONNUDIN. GOERGE	BAL	235	20TH WAR
CONOLE. CHARLES	BAL	458	8TH WARD
CONOLL. MARGARET	BAL	363	8TH WARD
CONOLLY. CATHARINE	BAL	168	2ND DIST
CONOLLY. CATHARINE	BAL	400	14TH WAR
CONOLLY. DIXON	BAL	084	2ND DIST
CONOLLY. HENRY	BAL	134	2ND DIST
CONOLLY. JOHN	BAL	270	12TH WAR
CONOLLY. MICHAEL	BAL	276	12TH WAR
CONOLLY. THOMAS	BAL	312	12TH WAR
CONOLLY. THOMAS	BAL	167	2ND DIST
CONOLLY. W.	BAL	312	12TH WAR
CONOLY. JOHN	BAL	069	2ND DIST
CONOLY. JOHN	BAL	414	14TH WAR
CONOLY. SARAH	BAL	331	7TH WARD
CONOR. ALLEN	BAL	445	1ST DIST
CONOR. MARTIN	BAL	445	1ST DIST
CONOWAY. CHARLES	BAL	204	6TH WARD
CONOWAY. GEORGE	BAL	037	1ST WARD
CONOWAY. HENRY J.	BAL	066	1ST WARD
CONOWAY. JOHN	BAL	100	1ST WARD
CONOWAY. MARY	BAL	208	11TH WAR
CONOWAY. MARY	BAL	054	18TH WAR
CONOWAY. PATRICK	BAL	023	18TH WAR
CONOWAY. PATRICK	ALL	141	6TH E.D.
CONOWAY. PATRICK	ALL	119	5TH E.D.
CONOWAY. SOLOMON	BAL	039	18TH WAR
CONOWAY. SOPHIA	BAL	127	2ND DIST
CONOWAY. THOMAS	BAL	064	1ST WARD
CONOWAY.LAURENCE	BAL	247	2ND WARD
CONOWAY.PATRICK	BAL	247	2ND WARD
CONRAD. AMELIA	BAL	143	19TH WAR
CONRAD. ARMSTEAD M.	BAL	371	13TH WAR
CONRAD. AUGUST	BAL	405	14TH WAR
CONRAD. CHRISTIAN	WAS	134	2ND DIST
CONRAD. DANIEL	ALL	111	5TH E.D.
CONRAD. F. W.	WAS	164	HAGERSTO
CONRAD. GEORGE	WAS	171	FUNKSTOW
CONRAD. HENRY	BAL	381	3RD WARD
CONRAD. JACOB	ALL	090	5TH E.D.
CONRAD. JAMES	FRE	053	FREDERIC
CONRAD. JOHN	FRE	053	FREDERIC
CONRAD. JOHN	BAL	259	12TH WAR
CONRAD. JOHN	WAS	160	2ND DIST
CONRAD. JOSEPH	BAL	024	2ND DIST
CONRAD. LEVI	BAL	163	19TH WAR
CONRAD. LEWIS	BAL	209	17TH WAR
CONRAD. MARGARET	BAL	163	19TH WAR
CONRAD. MARGARET	BAL	380	1ST DIST
CONRAD. PHILIP	BAL	087	15TH WAR
CONRAD. SAMUEL	WAS	272	RIDGEVIL
CONRAD. SARAH	WAS	192	1ST DIST
CONRAD. SOLOMON	CAR	332	MANCHEST
CONRAD. THOAMS	ALL	095	5TH E.D.
CONRAD. WILLIAM	ALL	111	5TH E.D.
CONRAD. WILLIAM	BAL	144	19TH WAR
CONRADT. ELIZABETH	WAS	155	HAGERSTO
CONRADT. EUNICE	BAL	249	12TH WAR
CONRADT. G. T.	BAL	335	13TH WAR
CONRADT. GEORGE	BAL	240	17TH WAR
CONRADT. JACOB	BAL	303	20TH WAR
CONRAY. FRANCES	ALL	136	4TH E.D.
CONRAY. JOHN	BAL	275	1ST DIST
CONRAY. MARY	BAL	276	1ST DIST
CONRAY. PATRICK	BAL	276	1ST DIST
CONRAY. PATRICK	BAL	447	8TH WARD
CONRAY. PETER	BAL	275	1ST DIST
CONRAY. PETER	BAL	384	1ST DIST
CONREY. SAMUEL	BAL	330	1ST DIST
CONROD. ALICE V.	FRE	053	FREDERIC
CONROD. CASMEN	BAL	133	11TH WAR
CONROD. GEORGE M.	BAL	045	4TH WARD
CONROD. JOSEPH	FRE	053	FREDERIC
CONROD. JULIA	FRE	095	FREDERIC
CONROD. MARGARET	FRE	053	FREDERIC
CONRODBOCHER. GEORGE	WAS	146	2ND DIST
CONRONG. PAT *	BAL	146	2ND DIST
CONROY. CATHERINE	BAL	046	1ST WARD
CONROY. NANCY	FRE	062	FREDERIC
CONRY. MARCILLA	BAL	357	13TH WAR
CONRY. MICHAEL	ALL	136	4TH E.D.
CONSANT. JOANNA	BAL	268	12TH WAR
CONSELER. JAMES*	TAL	003	EASTON D
CONSELL. SARAH *	ANN	340	3RD DIST
CONSEY. MICHAEL	BAL	409	8TH WARD
CONSEY. RICHARD L.	CAR	231	5TH DIST
CONSIANCE. PHOEBE	BAL	119	5TH WARD
CONSIDINE. JOHN	BAL	064	15TH WAR
CONSIDINE. JOHN	BAL	213	11TH WAR
CONSIN. G.	BAL	157	1ST WARD
CONSLE. THOMAS R.	DOR	417	1ST DIST
CONSLOW. ELIZABETH	CEC	178	7TH E DI
CONSON. A.	BAL	216	19TH WAR
CONSOR. AMELIA	FRE	100	FREDERIC
CONSTABLE. ALBERT	CEC	216	7TH E DI
CONSTABLE. ANN	BAL	128	11TH WAR
CONSTABLE. BENJAMIN	BAL	127	16TH WAR
CONSTABLE. CHARLES	BAL	081	4TH WARD
CONSTABLE. ELIZABETH	BAL	257	12TH WAR
CONSTABLE. JESSE LEE	BAL	400	14TH WAR
CONSTABLE. JOHN S.	KEN	268	1ST DIST
CONSTABLE. JULIA	KEN	215	2ND DIST
CONSTABLE. LINNY ANN	MGM	444	CLARKSTR
CONSTABLE. WILLIAM S.	KEN	234	2ND DIST
CONSTAILD. ARON	BAL	209	2ND WARD
CONSTANCE. JULIA	BAL	037	15TH WAR
CONSTANDT. EMILY	FRE	164	EMMITTSB
CONSTANT. EDWARD	BAL	265	1ST DIST
CONSTANT. HARRIET-BLACK	FRE	179	5TH E DI
CONSTANT. JOHN	BAL	081	10TH WAR
CONSTANT. JOSEPH	BAL	363	13TH WAR
CONSTANT. SAMUEL	BAL	265	1ST DIST
CONSTANTINE. DANIEL	BAL	099	1ST WARD
CONSTANTINE. MARY A.	BAL	202	11TH WAR
CONSTANTINE. MICHAEL	BAL	411	14TH WAR
CONSULMAN. JOHN	CEC	148	PORT DUP
CONTE. ELIZABETH	BAL	110	15TH WAR
CONTE. PHILIP	BAL	040	15TH WAR
CONTE. PHILIP	BAL	005	15TH WAR
CONTEE. CASSY	MGM	367	BERRYS D
CONTEE. CESAR	MGM	368	BERRYS D
CONTEE. MARY	FRE	278	NEW MARK
CONTEE. MELVILLE	BAL	103	15TH WAR
CONTEE. MIRANDA	MGM	326	CRACKLIN
CONTEE. R.	BAL	332	1ST DIST
CONTER. ANN L.	PRI	021	VANSVILL
CONTER. JOHN	PRI	083	QUEEN AN

Name	County	Page	Location
CONTES, CHARLOTTE	ANN	265	ANNAPOLI
CONTHER, JOHN	BAL	281	2ND WARD
CONVERSE, EMILY	ANN	292	ANNAPOLI
CONVEY, BRIDGET	BAL	300	1ST DIST
CONVOY, JAMES	BAL	385	13TH WAR
CONWAY, ALBERT	BAL	183	19TH WAR
CONWAY, BETSEY	SOM	537	TYASKIN
CONWAY, BETSY	BAL	376	13TH WAR
CONWAY, BRIDGET	BAL	085	10TH WAR
CONWAY, CATHARINE	BAL	377	13TH WAR
CONWAY, CATHRINE	BAL	025	18TH WAR
CONWAY, ELIZABETH	SOM	470	TRAPPE D
CONWAY, FANNY	SOM	537	TYASKIN
CONWAY, FRANCES	SOM	545	TYASKIN
CONWAY, HENRY	BAL	122	5TH WARD
CONWAY, ISAAC	BAL	030	4TH WARD
CONWAY, JAMES	BAL	293	17TH WAR
CONWAY, JAMES	BAL	024	9TH WARD
CONWAY, JAMES R. W.	SOM	553	TYASKIN
CONWAY, JEMIMA	ANN	520	HOWARD D
CONWAY, JESSE	ANN	376	4TH DIST
CONWAY, JOHN	ANN	369	4TH DIST
CONWAY, JOHN	BAL	273	1ST DIST
CONWAY, JOHN	BAL	287	17TH WAR
CONWAY, JOHN R.	BAL	083	15TH WAR
CONWAY, LARINA	BAL	274	2ND WARD
CONWAY, MARGARET	BAL	116	5TH WARD
CONWAY, MARY	BAL	083	15TH WAR
CONWAY, MARY	BAL	195	6TH WARD
CONWAY, MARY	HAR	140	2ND DIST
CONWAY, MICHAEL	BAL	409	3RD WARD
CONWAY, MOSES	SOM	535	QUANTICO
CONWAY, MOSES	SOM	539	TYASKIN
CONWAY, NANCY	SOM	538	TYASKIN
CONWAY, OSBORNE	ANN	448	HOWARD D
CONWAY, PATRICK	BAL	102	2ND DIST
CONWAY, PATRICK	ALL	079	5TH E.D.
CONWAY, PATRICK	MGM	375	ROCKERLE
CONWAY, PERRY	BAL	293	17TH WAR
CONWAY, RICHARD	ANN	448	HOWARD D
CONWAY, ROBERT	BAL	224	2ND WARD
CONWAY, ROBERT	BAL	247	12TH WAR
CONWAY, SAMUEL	BAL	289	17TH WAR
CONWAY, SAMUEL	SOM	538	TYASKIN
CONWAY, SARAH	SOM	538	TYASKIN
CONWAY, SARAH	SOM	538	TYASKIN
CONWAY, SARAH	BAL	055	15TH WAR
CONWAY, THOMAS	BAL	280	2ND WARD
CONWAY, WILLIAM	BAL	044	9TH WARD
CONWAY, WILLIAM	BAL	093	5TH WARD
CONWAY, WILLIAM	SOM	553	TYASKIN
CONWAY, WILLIAM	BAL	183	19TH WAR
CONWAY, WILLIAM B.	ANN	447	HOWARD D
CONWELE, JOEL*	DOR	447	1ST DIST
CONWELL, WILLIAM	BAL	309	12TH WAR
CONWIN, JOHN	CAR	230	5TH DIST
CONWOWAY, WILLIAM	BAL	070	18TH WAR
CONY, REGIS	BAL	212	11TH WAR
COOCH, ZEBULON F.	BAL	108	10TH WAR
COOCK, JOEL M.	HAR	190	3RD DIST
COOCKERLY, ANN	WAS	056	2ND SUBD
COOFERTY, JOHN	ALL	138	6TH E.D.
COOGAN, ANDREW	BAL	086	18TH WAR
COOGAN, LIDIA*	TAL	008	EASTON D
COOGLE, JOHN	BAL	072	2ND DIST
COOGLE, JOHN	BAL	359	1ST DIST
COOK, ABBE	BAL	260	12TH WAR
COOK, ABRAHAM	FRE	302	WOODSBOR
COOK, ABRAM	CAL	063	3RD DIST
COOK, ADDISON S.	BAL	292	1ST DIST
COOK, ALBERT	ANN	360	3RD DIST
COOK, ALEXANDER	BAL	205	6TH WARD
COOK, ALEXANDER	PRI	095	SPALDING
COOK, ALEXANDER-BLACK	CAR	068	NO TWP L
COOK, ALICE	BAL	198	6TH WARD
COOK, ANDREW	BAL	135	18TH WAR
COOK, ANDREW	BAL	062	4TH WARD
COOK, ANDREW J.	BAL	292	20TH WAR
COOK, ANN	BAL	143	5TH WARD
COOK, ANN	BAL	229	1ST DIST
COOK, ANN E.	BAL	349	3RD WARD
COOK, ANN-MULATTO	CAR	364	9TH DIST
COOK, ANNA	DOR	423	1ST DIST
COOK, ANNA	WAS	115	2ND DIST
COOK, ANTHONY	BAL	004	18TH WAR
COOK, BARTHOLOMEW	FRE	405	JEFFERSO
COOK, BEN	MGM	372	BERRYS D
COOK, BENJAMIN	KEN	303	3RD DIST
COOK, BENJAMIN	BAL	297	1ST DIST
COOK, BENJAMIN	BAL	320	7TH WARD
COOK, BENJAMIN	BAL	337	1ST DIST
COOK, BENJAMIN	ANN	382	4TH DIST
COOK, BENJAMIN M.	BAL	319	7TH WARD
COOK, BETSY	BAL	012	18TH WAR
COOK, BETTY	BAL	388	13TH WAR
COOK, BYARD	SOM	552	TYASKIN
COOK, C.	HAR	155	3RD DIST
COOK, C.	BAL	307	12TH WAR
COOK, C. SHAFER	WAS	127	HAGERSTO
COOK, C.H.	BAL	171	1ST WARD
COOK, CAROLINE	BAL	108	2ND DIST
COOK, CAROLINE	BAL	386	8TH WARD
COOK, CATHAIRNE	BAL	340	13TH WAR
COOK, CATHARINE	BAL	392	14TH WAR
COOK, CATHARINE	ALL	150	6TH E.D.
COOK, CATHARINE	WAS	097	2ND DIST
COOK, CATHARINE	TAL	056	EASTON D
COOK, CHARLES	BAL	174	1ST WARD
COOK, CHARLES	BAL	329	7TH WARD
COOK, CHARLES	BAL	311	1ST DIST
COOK, CHARLES	BAL	338	3RD WARD
COOK, CHARLES H.	BAL	135	1ST WARD
COOK, CHRISTIAN	BAL	237	17TH WAR
COOK, CLARA	BAL	224	12TH WAR
COOK, CLARA	BAL	148	5TH WARD
COOK, CLARA	BAL	105	1ST WARD
COOK, CLARISSA	BAL	274	2ND WARD
COOK, CLINTON	BAL	166	11TH WAR
COOK, CLINTON	QUE	187	3RD E DI
COOK, CODELIA	BAL	230	17TH WAR
COOK, COLUMBUS E.	BAL	251	6TH WARD
COOK, CORDELIA	BAL	291	12TH WAR
COOK, CORNELIAS	BAL	229	1ST DIST
COOK, DAVID	BAL	400	8TH WARD
COOK, DEALLY	BAL	247	1ST DIST
COOK, DELINA	BAL	129	11TH WAR
COOK, DINAH	MGM	379	ROCKERLE
COOK, DOROTHEA	BAL	156	19TH WAR
COOK, EBER F.	BAL	451	8TH WARD
COOK, EDWARD	ANN	289	ANNAPOLI
COOK, EDWARD	BAL	236	20TH WAR
COOK, EDWARD E.	DOR	357	3RD DIVI
COOK, EDWARD H.	DOR	427	1ST DIST
COOK, ELENARA	BAL	369	8TH WARD
COOK, ELENORE	BAL	369	8TH WARD
COOK, ELISHA	HAR	119	2ND DIST
COOK, ELIZA	BAL	196	2ND WARD
COOK, ELIZABETH	BAL	194	11TH WAR
COOK, ELIZABETH	BAL	155	16TH WAR
COOK, ELIZABETH	CAR	212	5TH DIST
COOK, ELIZABETH	BAL	005	4TH WARD
COOK, ELIZABETH	BAL	143	11TH WAR
COOK, ELIZABETH-BLACK	CAR	113	NO TWP L
COOK, ELLEN	ANN	485	HOWARD D
COOK, EMILY	PRI	089	SPALDING
COOK, EPHRAIM	CAR	209	5TH DIST
COOK, F.	BAL	139	1ST WARD
COOK, FRANANA H.	CAR	272	WESTMINS
COOK, FRANK	BAL	126	1ST WARD
COOK, FRANK F.	CHA	288	BOJANTOW
COOK, FREDERICK	BAL	080	18TH WAR
COOK, FREDERICK	BAL	220	17TH WAR
COOK, FREDERICK	BAL	220	17TH WAR
COOK, FREDERICK	BAL	134	1ST WARD
COOK, FREDERICK	WAS	139	HAGERSTO
COOK, GEORGE	WAS	169	FUNKSTOW
COOK, GEORGE	WAS	010	WILLIAMS
COOK, GEORGE	ANN	463	HOWARD D
COOK, GEORGE	ALL	141	6TH E.D.
COOK, GEORGE	ANN	336	3RD DIST
COOK, GEORGE	BAL	319	3RD WARD
COOK, GEORGE	BAL	315	3RD WARD
COOK, GEORGE	BAL	373	13TH WAR
COOK, GEORGE A.	BAL	125	5TH WARD
COOK, GEORGE E.	FRE	213	BUCKEYST
COOK, GECRGE P.	HAR	140	2ND DIST
COOK, GEORGE R.	BAL	274	2ND WARD
COOK, GECRGE W.	BAL	403	8TH WARD
COOK, GECRGE W.	BAL	096	1ST WARD
COOK, GEORGE-BLACK	CAR	131	NO TWP L
COOK, GEORT H.	PRI	111	PISCATAW
COOK, GREENBURY W.	CAR	210	5TH DIST
COOK, HANNAH	BAL	050	4TH WARD
COOK, HARISON	DOR	436	1ST DIST
COOK, HENERY	HAR	202	3RD DIST
COOK, HENERY	HAR	202	3RD DIST
COOK, HENRIETTA	BAL	454	8TH WARD
COOK, HENRY	BAL	229	12TH WAR
COOK, HENRY	BAL	036	15TH WAR
COOK, HENRY	BAL	271	1ST DIST
COOK, HENRY	BAL	362	8TH WARD
COOK, HENRY	BAL	094	5TH WARD
COOK, HENRY	BAL	148	2ND DIST
COOK, HENRY	BAL	075	10TH WAR
COOK, HENRY	BAL	279	12TH WAR
COOK, HENRY	DOR	397	1ST DIST
COOK, HENRY	PRI	062	NOTTINGH
COOK, HENRY F.	BAL	069	10TH WAR
COOK, HENRY W.	BAL	187	16TH WAR
COOK, HESTER	BAL	228	19TH WAR
COOK, ISAAC	CAR	281	7TH DIST
COOK, ISAAC	CAR	374	9TH DIST
COOK, ISAAC	BAL	327	1ST DIST
COOK, ISAAC *	KEN	225	2ND DIST
COOK, ISAAC P. REV.	BAL	069	10TH WAR
COOK, ISRIEL	BAL	278	1ST DIST
COOK, J.	BAL	135	1ST WARD
COOK, J.	BAL	286	2ND WARD
COOK, J.	BAL	153	1ST WARD
COOK, J. M.	BAL	051	4TH WARD
COOK, J.C.	ALL	049	10TH E.D
COOK, JACOB	ANN	269	ANNAPOLI
COOK, JACOB	BAL	156	5TH WARD
COOK, JACOB	BAL	247	2ND WARD
COOK, JACOB	BAL	290	12TH WAR
COOK, JAMES	BAL	130	1ST WARD
COOK, JAMES	BAL	148	5TH WARD
COOK, JAMES	ALL	231	CUMBEPLA
COOK, JAMES	CEC	153	PORT DUP
COOK, JAMES	CEC	022	ELKTON 3
COOK, JAMES	BAL	198	11TH WAR
COOK, JAMES	TAL	069	EASTON T
COOK, JAMES	QUE	251	5TH E DI
COOK, JAMES	ST	325	4TH E DI
COOK, JAMES	QUE	219	3RD E DI
COOK, JAMES B.J.	BAL	121	1ST WARD
COOK, JAMES-MULATTO	FRE	415	8TH E DI
COOK, JANE	BAL	203	11TH WAR
COOK, JANE	BAL	056	4TH WARD
COOK, JANE	BAL	058	4TH WARD
COOK, JANE	BAL	408	14TH WAR
COOK, JANE B.	WAS	157	HAGERSTO
COOK, JASPER	BAL	240	17TH WAR
COOK, JEREMIAH	BAL	229	1ST DIST
COOK, JOEL	HAR	121	2ND DIST
COOK, JOHN	BAL	398	14TH WAR
COOK, JOHN	BAL	284	20TH WAR
COOK, JOHN	CAR	203	4TH DIST
COOK, JOHN	CAR	210	5TH DIST
COOK, JOHN	BAL	006	18TH WAR
COOK, JOHN	DOR	398	1ST DIST
COOK, JOHN	FRE	214	BUCKEYST
COOK, JOHN	BAL	126	18TH WAR
COOK, JOHN	BAL	030	1ST WARD
COOK, JOHN	BAL	084	1ST WARD
COOK, JOHN	BAL	063	1ST WARD
COOK, JOHN	BAL	085	1ST WARD
COOK, JOHN	BAL	059	2ND DIST
COOK, JOHN	ALL	260	CUMBER_A
COOK, JOHN	ALL	240	CUMBERLA
COOK, JOHN	BAL	191	17TH WAR
COOK, JOHN	BAL	131	16TH WAR
COOK, JOHN	BAL	091	15TH WAR
COOK, JOHN	BAL	227	12TH WAR
COOK, JOHN	BAL	323	3RD WARD
COOK, JOHN	WAS	158	HAGERSTO
COOK, JOHN	WAS	150	HAGERSTO
COOK, JOHN	WAS	130	2ND DIST
COOK, JOHN	QUE	225	4TH E DI
COOK, JOHN	SOM	506	BARREN C
COOK, JOHN	SOM	507	BARREN C
COOK, JOHN	WAS	099	2ND DIST
COOK, JOHN A.	BAL	049	15TH WAR
COOK, JOHN D.	BAL	435	8TH WARD
COOK, JOHN F.	BAL	358	3RD WARD
COOK, JOHN F.	BAL	217	6TH WARD
COOK, JOHN F.	BAL	053	18TH WAR
COOK, JOHN H.	BAL	050	18TH WAR
COOK, JOHN H.	BAL	202	11TH WAR
COOK, JOHN H.	BAL	112	5TH WARD
COOK, JOHN H.	WAS	171	FUNKSTOW
COOK, JOHN J.	BAL	137	1ST WARD
COOK, JOHN J.	BAL	024	18TH WAR
COOK, JOHN S.	BAL	148	2ND DIST
COOK, JOHN T.	BAL	325	1ST DIST
COOK, JOSEPH	BAL	081	10TH WAR
COOK, JOSEPH	BAL	079	18TH WAR
COOK, JOSEPH K.	QUE	208	3RD E DI
COOK, JOSEPH L.	QUE	173	2ND E DI
COOK, JOSEPH M.	BAL	188	16TH WAR
COOK, JULIA	ANN	499	HOWARD D
COOK, JULIA	DOR	378	1ST DIST
COOK, JULIA-BLACK	FRE	238	NEW MARK
COOK, KITTY	ANN	285	ANNAPOLI
COOK, LARKIN	CAR	221	5TH DIST
COOK, LARKIN G.	WAS	230	1ST DIST
COOK, LAURA M.	BAL	069	10TH WAR
COOK, LENOARD	BAL	035	18TH WAR
COOK, LEVIN P.	DOR	404	1ST DIST
COOK, LEVINA	BAL	365	3RD WARD
COOK, LEWIS-BLACK	CAR	132	NO TWP L
COOK, LIDIA	BAL	461	1ST DIST
COOK, LIDIA	TAL	042	EASTON D
COOK, LUTHER E.	FRE	452	8TH E DI
COOK, MARGARET	BAL	357	13TH WAR
COOK, MARGARETT	WAS	108	2ND DIST
COOK, MARGARETT	BAL	458	1ST DIST
COOK, MARIA	BAL	317	1ST DIST
COOK, MARIA	ANN	285	ANNAPOLI
COOK, MARIA	ANN	484	HOWARD D
COOK, MARIA	BAL	435	14TH WAR
COOK, MARK	DOR	391	1ST DIST
COOK, MARTHA	BAL	183	2ND WARD
COOK, MARTHA	PRI	071	MARLBROU
COOK, MARTIN	BAL	146	19TH WAR
COOK, MARY	FRE	270	NEW MARK
COOK, MARY	BAL	125	11TH WAR
COOK, MARY	BAL	057	18TH WAR
COOK, MARY	BAL	057	18TH WAR
COOK, MARY	BAL	010	4TH WARD
COOK, MARY	HAR	083	2ND DIST
COOK, MARY	BAL	150	5TH WARD
COOK, MARY	BAL	301	7TH WARD
COOK, MARY	BAL	060	10TH WAR
COOK, MARY	BAL	327	7TH WARD
COOK, MARY A.	BAL	027	18TH WAR
COOK, MARY A.	CAL	052	3RD DIST
COOK, MARY L.	BAL	363	8TH WARD
COOK, MARY S.	BAL	075	10TH WAR
COOK, MARY SIENNE SIS-	BAL	316	20TH WAR
COOK, MATILDA	BAL	167	19TH WAR
COOK, MATTHEW	BAL	314	20TH WAR
COOK, MIMMA	BAL	057	18TH WAR
COOK, MITCHELL-BLACK	CAR	149	NO TWP L
COOK, NANCY	CAR	272	WESTMINS
COOK, NANCY	CAR	202	4TH DIST
COOK, NATHAN	BAL	301	12TH WAR
COOK, NATHAN.	DOR	430	1ST DIST
COOK, NICHOLAS	BAL	453	8TH WARD
COOK, OTHO T.	FRE	275	NEW MARK
COOK, PATIENCE	ANN	454	HOWARD D
COOK, PETER	BAL	217	2ND WARD
COOK, PETER	ANN	392	4TH DIST
COOK, PETER	CAR	364	9TH DIST
COOK, PETER S.	DOR	424	1ST DIST
COOK, PHIL	ANN	338	3RD DIST
COOK, PHILENA T.	QUE	219	3RD E DI
COOK, PRISCILLA	BAL	475	14TH WAR
COOK, R.E.	WAS	037	2ND SUBD
COOK, RACHAEL	BAL	025	15TH WAR
COOK, RACHEL	BAL	457	1ST DIST
COOK, RASAN R.	WAS	163	2ND DIST
COOK, RICHARD	CHA	291	MIDDLETO
COOK, RICHARD L.	FRE	397	PETERSVI
COOK, RICHARD R.	PRI	056	AQUASCO
COOK, ROBERT	QUE	151	1ST E DI
COOK, ROBERT	DOR	400	1ST DIST
COOK, ROBERT	BAL	003	9TH WARD
COOK, ROBERT	BAL	191	17TH WAR
COOK, ROBERT	BAL	090	10TH WAR
COOK, ROBERT H.	BAL	094	5TH WARD
COOK, ROSE	DOR	461	1ST DIST
COOK, SARAH	QUE	206	3RD E DI
COOK, SARAH	BAL	373	1ST DIST
COOK, SARAH	BAL	126	5TH WARD
COOK, SARAH	BAL	155	11TH WAR
COOK, SARAH-MULATTO	BAL	223	2ND WARD
COOK, SOPHIA	BAL	204	11TH WAR
COOK, SOPHIA	BAL	455	14TH WAR
COOK, STEPHEN	SOM	514	BARREN C
COOK, SUAN	BAL	008	15TH WAR
COOK, SUSAN	BAL	454	8TH WARD
COOK, SUSAN	PRI	117	PISCATAW
COOK, SUSAN	QUE	190	3RD E DI
COOK, SUSAN	QUE	161	2ND E DI
COOK, SUSANER	HAR	148	3RD DIST
COOK, T.	BAL	261	12TH WAR
COOK, TEMPY*	SOM	551	TYASKIN
COOK, THEREZA	HAR	120	2ND DIST
COOK, THOMAS	BAL	398	14TH WAR
COOK, THOMAS	DOR	375	1ST DIST
COOK, THOMAS	DOR	378	1ST DIST
COOK, THOMAS	CAR	315	1ST DIST
COOK, THOMAS	BAL	439	14TH WAR
COOK, THOMAS	BAL	421	14TH WAR
COOK, THOMAS	QUE	170	2ND E DI
COOK, THOMAS	QUE	186	3RD E DI
COOK, THOMAS	QUE	207	3RD E DI
COOK, THOMAS	PRI	068	NOTTINGH
COOK, THOMAS	PRI	097	SPALDING
COOK, THOMAS	BAL	162	1ST WARD
COOK, THOMAS	ANN	497	HOWARD D
COOK, THOMAS	BAL	311	12TH WAR
COOK, THOMAS	BAL	306	12TH WAR
COOK, THOMAS	BAL	056	10TH WAR
COOK, THOMAS	BAL	034	1ST WARD
COOK, THOMAS A.	KEN	312	3RD DIST
COOK, THOMAS JR.	CAR	364	9TH DIST
COOK, THOMAS SR.	CAR	364	9TH DIST
COOK, THOMSA	ALL	052	10TH E.D
COOK, WARNER	MGM	370	BERRYS D
COOK, WILIAM	BAL	266	2ND WARD
COOK, WILLAIN	PRI	054	AQUASCO
COOK, WILLIAM	SOM	508	BARREN C
COOK, WILLIAM	WAS	172	FUNKSTOW
COOK, WILLIAM	ANN	273	ANNAPOLI
COOK, WILLIAM	ANN	327	2ND DIST
COOK, WILLIAM	ALL	150	6TH E.D.
COOK, WILLIAM	BAL	131	16TH WAR
COOK, WILLIAM	BAL	383	1ST DIST

COOK, WILLIAM BAL 112 5TH WARD
COOK, WILLIAM BAL 008 9TH WARD
COOK, WILLIAM BAL 009 9TH WARD
COOK, WILLIAM ANN 352 3RD DIST
COOK, WILLIAM BAL 252 17TH WAR
COOK, WILLIAM CAR 214 5TH DIST
COOK, WILLIAM CEC 014 ELKTON 3
COOK, WILLIAM HAR 191 3RD DIST
COOK, WILLIAM HAR 196 3RD DIST
COOK, WILLIAM BAL 136 18TH WAR
COOK, WILLIAM CHA 286 BOJANTOW
COOK, WILLIAM F. FRE 20 5TH E DI
COOK, WILLIAM H. BAL 135 18TH WAR
COOK, WILLIAM H. BAL 044 15TH WAR
COOK, WILLIAM H. BAL 326 1ST DIST
COOK, WILLIAM H. BAL 106 15TH WAR
COOK, WILLIAM H. BAL 138 5TH WARD
COOK, WILLIAM H. PRI 054 AQUASCO
COOK, WILLIAM L. BAL 229 1ST DIST
COOK, WILLIAM S. WAS 117 2ND DIST
COOK, WILLIAM S. DOR 398 1ST DIST
COOK, WILLIAM S.-BLACK MGM 402 ROCKERLE
COOK, WILLIAM T. PRI 056 AQUASCO
COOK, WILLIAM-BLACK CAR 158 NO TWP L
COOK,DANIEL FRE 428 8TH E DI
COOK,ELISHA J. CAR 398 2ND DIST
COOK,ELIZA CAR 383 2ND DIST
COOK,F. BAL 118 1ST WARD
COOK,LUCY FRE 396 PETERSVI
COOKAN, , PATRICK * BAL 274 1ST DIST
COOKE, ANGELINA BAL 273 20TH WAR
COOKE, ANN BAL 318 20TH WAR
COOKE, CATH BAL 221 12TH WAR
COOKE, DANE BAL 227 12TH WAR
COOKE, ELIZABETH BAL 043 15TH WAR
COOKE, ELLEN A. ANN 412 HOWARD D
COOKE, GRACE CAL 015 1ST DIST
COOKE, HENRY W. BAL 074 15TH WAR
COOKE, J. BAL 148 1ST WARD
COOKE, JAMES PRI 016 BLADENSB
COOKE, JOHN BAL 288 20TH WAR
COOKE, JOHN BAL 240 20TH WAR
COOKE, JOSEPH BAL 281 2ND WARD
COOKE, MARTHA A. ANN 462 HOWARD D
COOKE, MARY BAL 269 12TH WAR
COOKE, MARY BAL 319 20TH WAR
COOKE, MATILDA ANN 474 HOWARD D
COOKE, NATHAN MGM 318 CRACKLIN
COOKE, NICHOLAS PRI 016 BLADENSB
COOKE, REBECCA D. MGM 318 CRACKLIN
COOKE, SAMUEL DOR 430 1ST DIST
COOKE, SARAH BAL 293 12TH WAR
COOKE, SEPTEMUS J. PRI 045 VANSVILL
COOKE, WILLIAM BAL 289 12TH WAR
COOKE, WILLIAM BAL 293 12TH WAR
COOKE, WILLIAM ANN 431 HOWARD D
COOKE, WILLIAM BAL 149 11TH WAR
COOKE, WILLIAM T. ANN 431 HOWARD D
COOKE, WINFIELD BAL 289 20TH WAR
COOKEILY, MICHAEL FRE 250 NEW MARK
COOKER, MARY C. TAL 076 EASTON T
COOKER, SARAH QUE 215 3RD E DI
COOKER, WILLIAM QUE 204 3RD E DI
COOKERLY, BENJAMIN WAS 042 2ND SUBD
COOKERLY, ELIZABETH FRE 250 NEW MARK
COOKERLY, GEORGE FRE 261 NEW MARK
COOKERLY, LEWIS C. FRE 367 CATOCTIN
COOKERLY, SARAH FRE 315 MIDDLETC
COOKERLY, VIRGENIA * FRE 262 NEW MARK
COOKERLY, WILLIAM FRE 012 FREDERIC
COOKERY, JACOB FRE 315 MIDDLETC
COOKLEY, JAMES BAL 292 12TH WAR
COOKRAL, THOMAS* TAL 017 EASTON D
COOKS, CHARLES BAL 218 17TH WAR
COOKSELL, GEORGE BAL 269 2ND WARD
COOKSEY, ALBERT G. ANN 323 2ND DIST
COOKSEY, AMELIA CHA 272 ALLENS F
COOKSEY, CATHERINE CHA 277 BOJANTOW
COOKSEY, CHRISTIAN K. BAL 357 3RD WARD
COOKSEY, JAMES PRI 054 AQUASCO
COOKSEY, JOSEPH H. CHA 264 HILLTOP
COOKSEY, MATHIAS CHA 268 BOJANTOW
COOKSEY, NATHAN CHA 277 BOJANTOW
COOKSEY, REBECCA SOM 478 TRAPP DI
COOKSEY, SALLY SOM 474 TRAPPE D
COOKSEY, SOMERSET CHA 220 ALLENS F
COOKSEY, TERRESA CHA 268 BOJANTOW
COOKSEY, WILLIAM BAL 068 1ST WARD
COOKSEY, WILLIAM W. ANN 323 2ND DIST
COOKSON, DENNIS CAR 403 2ND DIST
COOKSON, JESSEE WAS 276 RIDGEVIL
COOKSON, JOHNC. CAR 403 2ND DIST
COOKSON,RACHEAL CAR 403 2ND DIST
COOKSY, SARA A. CHA 294 BOJANTOW
COOLAN, BENNONA CEC 179 7TH E DI
COOLAN, SUSAN BAL 195 11TH WAR
COOLE, RACHEL* BAL 104 10TH WAR
COOLER, JAMES MGM 334 CRACKLIN
COOLER, JAMES MGM 331 CRACKLIN
COOLER, JAMES MGM 372 BERRYS D
COOLER, REZIN MGM 320 CRACKLIN
COOLER, ROBERT MGM 372 BERRYS D
COOLEY, ALMIRA BAL 033 15TH WAR
COOLEY, ANN MGM 426 MEDLEY 3
COOLEY, BENJAMIN MGM 413 MEDLEY 3
COOLEY, DANIEL M HAR 130 2ND DIST
COOLEY, EDWARD BAL 144 1ST WARD
COOLEY, ELIZABETH J. HAR 077 BEL AIR
COOLEY, HENRY MGM 418 MEDLEY 3
COOLEY, JOHN FRE 233 BUCKEYST
COOLEY, JOHN CEC 003 ELKTON 3
COOLEY, LUCINGUS MGM 387 ROCKERLE
COOLEY, LUCY MGM 387 ROCKERLE
COOLEY, ROBERT T. MGM 427 MEDLEY 3
COOLEY, SAMUEL ANN 478 HOWARD D
COOLEY, THOMAS MGM 430 CLARKSTR
COOLEY, WILLIAM H. BAL 004 9TH WARD
COOLIDGE, BELT PRI 071 MARLBROU
COOLIDGE, ELIZA PRI 071 MARLBROU
COOLIN, JOHN ANN 462 HOWARD D
COOLIN, REBECCA CEC 082 CHARLEST
COOLIN, WILLIAM CEC 077 NORTHEAS
COOLING, HANNAH BAL 030 15TH WAR
COOLLEY, EDWARD MGM 419 MEDLEY 3
COOLY, COOVILLE CEC 207 7TH E DI
COOMAN, JOHN ANN 469 HOWARD D
COOMAN, PATRICK* BAL 404 3RD WARD
COOMASH, LORENZO CEC 181 7TH E DI
COOMBS, JOHN KEN 278 1ST DIST
COOMBS, MARIA ALL 127 4TH E.D.
COOMBS, MARY BAL 322 3RD WARD
COOMBS, MARY MGM 320 CRACKLIN
COOMENE, FRANCIS * TAL 082 ST MICHA
COOMES, JOSEPH R. MGM 330 CRACKLIN
COOMHEAN, GEORGE BAL 121 1ST WARD
COOMS, FALLONUS CHA 261 MIDDLETO
COOMS, GEORGE W. CHA 261 MIDDLETO
COOMS, HENRY TAL 023 EASTON D
COOMS, JOSIAS W. CHA 261 MIDDLETO
COOMS, RAPHAEL FRE 417 8TH E DI
COOMS, SIMON FRE 306 WOODSBOR
COOMS, TERRESA V. CHA 260 MIDDLETO
COOMS, WILLIAM CHA 280 BOJANTOW
COOMS, WILLIAM F. CHA 250 MIDDLETO
COOMS, WILLIAM W. CHA 270 ALLENS F
COON, BILL WOR 282 BERLIN 1
COON, EDWARD ALL 258 CUMBERLA
COON, ELIZABETH CAR 258 3RD DIST
COON, ELIZABETH BAL 365 13TH WAR
COON, HY BAL 215 6TH DIST
COON, JAMES WAS 144 HAGERSTO
COON, JIM TAL 024 EASTON D
COON, JOHN BAL 215 6TH DIST
COON, JOHN B. WAS 041 2ND SUBD
COON, JOHN W. FRE 145 10TH E D
COON, JOSEPH FRE 126 CREAGERS
COON, RACHEL WOR 258 1ST CENS
COON, WILLIAM WAS 294 1ST DIST
COONAN, ANNA BAL 169 6TH WARD
COONAN, DANIEL BAL 016 9TH WARD
COONAN, MICHAEL BAL 016 9TH WARD
COONAN, PATRICK* BAL 404 3RD WARD
COONBOY, ANDRWE ALL 050 10TH E.D
COONER, WILLIAM BAL 411 8TH WARD
COONEY, BRIDGET ALL 243 CUMBERLA
COONEY, CATHERINE MISS- BAL 315 20TH WAR
COONEY, CHRISTOPHER BAL 157 6TH WARD
COONEY, EDWARD ALL 242 CUMBERLA
COONEY, LAWRENCE BAL 040 18TH WAR
COONEY, MARY BAL 419 8TH WARD
COONEY, MICHAEL BAL 361 3RD WARD
COONEY, MICHAEL ALL 128 4TH E.D.
COONEY, SARAH CAL 016 1ST DIST
COONEY, WILLIAM BAL 060 10TH WAR
COONN, ELIZA BAL 203 2ND WARD
COONROD, JAOCB BAL 131 2ND DIST
COONRODE, LUTHER HAR 197 3RD DIST
COONS, JOHN BAL 131 2ND DIST
COONS, MICHAEL BAL 401 1ST DIST
COONS, NANCY * BAL 320 20TH WAR
COONS, SUSAN BAL 153 11TH WAR
COONS, WILLIAM BAL 126 2ND DIST
COONWELL, WILLIAM H. ANN 446 HOWARD D
COOP, GEORGEANA BAL 302 7TH WARD
COOPER, ABRAHAM HAR 093 2ND DIST
COOPER, ABRAHAM CAR 334 MANCHEST
COOPER, ALEXANDER BAL 269 7TH WARD
COOPER, ALEXANDER BAL 159 1ST WARD
COOPER, ALEXANDER BAL 286 2ND WARD
COOPER, ALEXANDER ST 270 3RD E DI
COOPER, ALEXANDER-BLACK ST 337 4TH E DI
COOPER, AMANDA BAL 187 11TH WAR
COOPER, AMELIA BAL 378 3RD WARD
COOPER, AMOS G. CEC 113 4TH E DI
COOPER, ANESTECIA BAL 358 1ST DIST
COOPER, ANN ALL 122 4TH E.D.
COOPER, ANN BAL 152 11TH WAR
COOPER, ANN ST 268 3RD E DI
COOPER, ANN ST 259 3RD E DI
COOPER, ANNA-BLACK ST 334 4TH E DI
COOPER, ANNA-BLACK QUE 142 1ST E DI
COOPER, ANNY BAL 021 4TH WARD
COOPER, ANTHONY BAL 181 16TH WAR
COOPER, BARBANY BAL 198 5TH DIST
COOPER, BENJAMIN TAL 061 EASTON D
COOPER, BENJAMIN TAL 101 ST MICHA
COOPER, BENJAMIN WOR 242 1ST CENS
COOPER, BETSEY BAL 300 3RD WARD
COOPER, CAROLINE CAR 092 NO TWP L
COOPER, CARVILLE HAR 128 2ND DIST
COOPER, CASSA* TAL 055 EASTON D
COOPER, CATHARINE CEC 108 3RD E DI
COOPER, CATHERINE ANN 369 4TH DIST
COOPER, CHARLES BAL 133 1ST WARD
COOPER, CHARLES BAL 167 11TH WAR
COOPER, CHARLES BAL 435 8TH WARD
COOPER, CHARLES BAL 180 2ND WARD
COOPER, CHARLES BAL 021 9TH WARD
COOPER, CHARLES BAL 170 1ST WARD
COOPER, CHARLES CEC 117 4TH E DI
COOPER, CHARLES MGM 360 BERRYS D
COOPER, CHARLES MGM 359 BERRYS D
COOPER, CHARLOTTE BAL 157 11TH WAR
COOPER, CHARLOTTE BAL 146 16TH WAR
COOPER, CHARLOTTE ST 271 3RD E DI
COOPER, DANIEL TAL 100 ST MICHA
COOPER, DANIEL CAR 338 6TH DIST
COOPER, DIANAH BAL 024 1ST WARD
COOPER, DORCAS BAL 244 6TH WARD
COOPER, DOROTHY TAL 112 ST MICHA
COOPER, EBANEZER CEC 069 5TH E DI
COOPER, EDWARD HAR 100 2ND DIST
COOPER, EDWARD CEC 040 CHESAPEA
COOPER, EDWARD BAL 241 20TH WAR
COOPER, EDWARD J. BAL 349 3RD WARD
COOPER, EDWARD O. BAL 422 3RD WARD
COOPER, EHRNY BAL 421 1ST DIST
COOPER, ELIJAH W. WOR 215 4TH E DI
COOPER, ELISHA BAL 263 2ND WARD
COOPER, ELIZA-BLACK CAR 074 NO TWP L
COOPER, ELIZA-BLACK CAR 068 NO TWP L
COOPER, ELIZABETH V. BAL 392 3RD WARD
COOPER, ELLEN BAL 215 6TH DIST
COOPER, ELLEN BAL 374 13TH WAR
COOPER, ELLEN J. BAL 399 3RD WARD
COOPER, ELSBURY BAL 403 3RD WARD
COOPER, EMANUEL BAL 205 6TH DIST
COOPER, EMANUEL-BLACK FRE 435 8TH E DI
COOPER, EMELINA BAL 204 11TH WAR
COOPER, EMELINE BAL 273 12TH WAR
COOPER, ERNEST BAL 241 20TH WAR
COOPER, ERVIN BAL 383 1ST DIST
COOPER, EZEKIEL CAR 068 NO TWP L
COOPER, EZEKIEL QUE 210 3RD E DI
COOPER, FIBE BAL 262 2ND WARD
COOPER, FRANCIS S. TAL 112 ST MICHA
COOPER, FRANCIS-BLACK BAL 245 2ND WARD
COOPER, FRANKLIN BAL 315 1ST DIST
COOPER, GARRISON-BLACK CAR 073 NO TWP L
COOPER, GEORGE BAL 030 18TH WAR
COOPER, GEORGE HAR 126 2ND DIST
COOPER, GEORGE BAL 097 1ST WARD
COOPER, GEORGE WOR 271 BERLIN 1
COOPER, GEORGE TAL 001 EASTON D
COOPER, GEORGE TAL 055 EASTON D
COOPER, GEORGE TAL 058 EASTON D
COOPER, GEORGE WAS 185 BOONSBOR
COOPER, GEORGE E. BAL 291 3RD WARD
COOPER, GEORGE E. BAL 206 2ND WARD
COOPER, GEORGE H. HAR 137 2ND DIST
COOPER, GEORGE W. DOR 371 3RD DIVI
COOPER, GEORGE W. BAL 291 3RD WARD
COOPER, GEORGE* TAL 035 EASTON D
COOPER, GUSTENIA TAL 053 EASTON D
COOPER, HADDAMAN * TAL 079 ST MICHA
COOPER, HAMILTON BAL 403 3RD WARD
COOPER, HANNIBLE BAL 152 5TH WARD
COOPER, HARIOTT BAL 069 4TH WARD
COOPER, HARRIET CEC 053 1ST E DI
COOPER, HARRIET BAL 036 1ST WARD
COOPER, HARRIET BAL 085 15TH WAR
COOPER, HARRIETT BAL 240 20TH WAR
COOPER, HARRISON TAL 042 EASTON D
COOPER, HELLEN-BLACK ST 315 4TH E DI
COOPER, HENRY TAL 042 EASTON D
COOPER, HENRY TAL 001 EASTON D
COOPER, HENRY WOR 266 BERLIN 1
COOPER, HENRY BAL 298 17TH WAR
COOPER, HENRY BAL 227 17TH WAR
COOPER, HENRY CEC 043 CHESAPEA
COOPER, HENRY BAL 086 15TH WAR
COOPER, HENRY BAL 168 2ND DIST
COOPER, HENRY J. BAL 183 16TH WAR
COOPER, HENRY R. CAR 085 NO TWP L
COOPER, HESTER ALL 235 CUMBERLA
COOPER, HY BAL 197 5TH DIST
COOPER, HYRAM B. SOM 511 BARREN C
COOPER, ISAAC WOR 296 9TH E DI
COOPER, ISAAC QUE 242 5TH E DI
COOPER, ISAAC CEC 141 6TH E DI
COOPER, ISAAC CEC 059 1ST E DI
COOPER, ISAAC J. SOM 474 TRAPPE D
COOPER, J. BAL 163 1ST WARD
COOPER, JACOB CAR 085 NO TWP L
COOPER, JAKE KEN 223 2ND DIST
COOPER, JAMES BAL 014 18TH WAR
COOPER, JAMES BAL 028 18TH WAR
COOPER, JAMES BAL 071 18TH WAR
COOPER, JAMES DOR 354 3RD DIVI
COOPER, JAMES BAL 036 1ST WARD
COOPER, JAMES BAL 047 9TH WARD
COOPER, JAMES BAL 001 9TH WARD
COOPER, JAMES BAL 069 15TH WAR
COOPER, JAMES TAL 051 EASTON D
COOPER, JAMES TAL 037 EASTON D
COOPER, JAMES E. CEC 153 PORT DUP
COOPER, JAMES H. TAL 114 ST MICHA
COOPER, JANE TAL 053 EASTON D
COOPER, JANE CEC 053 1ST E DI
COOPER, JANE CEC 179 7TH E DI
COOPER, JANE CEC 040 CHESAPEA
COOPER, JEFFERSON-BLACK QUE 152 1ST E DI
COOPER, JEFFERSON-BLACK QUE 175 2ND E DI
COOPER, JOHN QUE 206 3RD E DI
COOPER, JOHN QUE 212 3RD E DI
COOPER, JOHN ST 263 3RD E DI
COOPER, JOHN SOM 511 BARREN C
COOPER, JOHN PRI 017 BLADENSB
COOPER, JOHN WOR 265 BERLIN 1
COOPER, JOHN FRE 181 5TH E DI
COOPER, JOHN BAL 415 3RD WARD
COOPER, JOHN CEC 064 1ST E DI
COOPER, JOHN BAL 044 4TH WARD
COOPER, JOHN CAR 107 NO TWP L
COOPER, JOHN DOR 388 1ST DIST
COOPER, JOHN HAR 100 2ND DIST
COOPER, JOHN HAR 038 1ST DIST
COOPER, JOHN BAL 007 9TH WARD
COOPER, JOHN BAL 301 1ST DIST
COOPER, JOHN BAL 219 5TH DIST
COOPER, JOHN BAL 120 1ST WARD
COOPER, JOHN BAL 198 2ND WARD
COOPER, JOHN BAL 160 1ST WARD
COOPER, JOHN BAL 266 2ND WARD
COOPER, JOHN BAL 291 3RD WARD
COOPER, JOHN BAL 436 1ST DIST
COOPER, JOHN C. CAR 066 NO TWP L
COOPER, JOHN H. BAL 408 3RD WARD
COOPER, JOHN L. QUE 218 3RD E DI
COOPER, JOHN N. TAL 111 ST MICHA
COOPER, JOHN W. QUE 187 3RD E DI
COOPER, JOHN-BLACK ST 331 4TH E DI
COOPER, JOHN-BLACK QUE 164 2ND E DI
COOPER, JOHN-BLACK CAR 071 NO TWP L
COOPER, JOHN-BLACK QUE 144 1ST E DI
COOPER, JONAS BAL 246 17TH WAR
COOPER, JONATHAN SOM 511 BARREN C
COOPER, JOSEPH TAL 038 EASTON D
COOPER, JOSEPH BAL 051 15TH WAR
COOPER, JOSEPH BAL 170 16TH WAR
COOPER, JOSEPH ALL 093 5TH E.D.
COOPER, JOSIAH K. CEC 166 6TH E DI
COOPER, JULIA BAL 194 11TH WAR
COOPER, JULIANNA ANN 431 HOWARD D
COOPER, KEVIN CAR 105 NO TWP L
COOPER, KINSEY TAL 104 ST MICHA
COOPER, LAURA BAL 299 20TH WAR
COOPER, LEVIN SOM 507 BARREN C
COOPER, LEVIN BAL 155 1ST WARD
COOPER, LEVIN* TAL 053 EASTON D
COOPER, LEVINIA TAL 057 EASTON D
COOPER, LOUISA BAL 038 1ST WARD
COOPER, LUCRETIA BAL 025 1ST WARD
COOPER, LUCRETIA BAL 290 3RD WARD
COOPER, LUCY BAL 072 15TH WAR
COOPER, LYDIA-BLACK ST 329 4TH E DI
COOPER, MADISON BAL 076 4TH WARD
COOPER, MAHALY CAR 091 NO TWP L
COOPER, MANSFIELD BAL 379 8TH WARD
COOPER, MARGARET BAL 400 3RD WARD
COOPER, MARGARET BAL 403 3RD WARD
COOPER, MARGARET BAL 383 3RD WARD
COOPER, MARGARET BAL 098 10TH WAR
COOPER, MARGARET BAL 030 18TH WAR
COOPER, MARGARET SOM 514 BARREN C
COOPER, MARGARET A. BAL 028 1ST WARD
COOPER, MARIAH TAL 054 EASTON D
COOPER, MARTHA TAL 071 EASTON T
COOPER, MARTHA TAL 042 EASTON D
COOPER, MARTHA BAL 124 16TH WAR

Name	County	Page	District
COOPER, MARTHA	BAL	474	14TH WAR
COOPER, MARY	KEN	253	1ST DIST
COOPER, MARY	HAR	031	1ST DIST
COOPER, MARY	BAL	040	1ST WARD
COOPER, MARY	BAL	380	8TH WARD
COOPER, MARY	BAL	358	1ST DIST
COOPER, MARY	TAL	116	ST MICHA
COOPER, MARY	WOR	239	6TH E DI
COOPER, MARY A.	TAL	116	ST MICHA
COOPER, MARY A.	BAL	037	15TH WAR
COOPER, MARY A.	BAL	325	7TH WARD
COOPER, MARY E.	BAL	346	3RD WARD
COOPER, MARY F.-BLACK	ST	326	4TH E DI
COOPER, MARY-BLACK	ST	338	4TH E DI
COOPER, MATHEW H.	BAL	393	3RD WARD
COOPER, MATILDA	BAL	334	7TH WARD
COOPER, MICAJAI	BAL	215	6TH DIST
COOPER, MICHAEL	BAL	247	2ND WARD
COOPER, MICHAEL	BAL	408	1ST DIST
COOPER, MICHAEL-BLACK	QUE	175	2ND E DI
COOPER, MILLY	ST	269	3RD E DI
COOPER, MINOSOTO A.	FRE	069	FREDERIC
COOPER, MOSES	CEC	045	1ST E DI
COOPER, NANCY	WAS	008	WILLIAMS
COOPER, NANCY	BAL	227	2ND WARD
COOPER, NANCY	BAL	225	2ND WARD
COOPER, NANNIE-BLACK	QUE	202	3RD E DI
COOPER, NELL	TAL	004	EASTON D
COOPER, NELSON	BAL	011	2ND DIST
COOPER, OLIVER-BLACK	CAR	138	NO TWP L
COOPER, PENECELA	BAL	228	12TH WAR
COOPER, PERRY	BAL	007	1ST WARD
COOPER, PERRY	FRE	075	FREDERIC
COOPER, PERRY	CEC	185	7TH E DI
COOPER, PERRY	CEC	198	7TH E DI
COOPER, PERRY-BLACK	CAR	076	NO TWP L
COOPER, PETER	TAL	060	EASTON D
COOPER, PHEBE	BAL	230	6TH WARD
COOPER, PHILIS	BAL	076	4TH WARD
COOPER, PILL	KEN	253	1ST DIST
COOPER, POSTERLAND	BAL	445	8TH WARD
COOPER, PURNEL	BAL	382	3RD WARD
COOPER, RACHEL	BAL	380	1ST DIST
COOPER, RACHEL	CEC	159	PORT DUP
COOPER, RACHEL	TAL	053	EASTON D
COOPER, RACHEL	TAL	009	EASTON D
COOPER, RICHARD	TAL	058	EASTON D
COOPER, RICHARD W.	TAL	105	ST MICHA
COOPER, ROBERT	SOM	508	BARREN C
COOPER, ROBERT	QUE	203	3RD E DI
COOPER, ROBERT	HAR	039	1ST DIST
COOPER, ROBERT	BAL	031	1ST WARD
COOPER, ROBERT-BLACK	BAL	224	2ND WARD
COOPER, ROSABELLA	BAL	058	10TH WAR
COOPER, RUTH	BAL	389	3RD WARD
COOPER, SAMEUL	BAL	273	17TH WAR
COOPER, SAMUEL	CAR	106	NO TWP L
COOPER, SAMUEL	CAR	093	NO TWP L
COOPER, SAMUEL	BAL	457	14TH WAR
COOPER, SAMUEL	FRE	405	JEFFERSO
COOPER, SAMUEL	BAL	260	20TH WAR
COOPER, SAMUEL	BAL	298	17TH WAR
COOPER, SAMUEL	BAL	377	3RD WARD
COOPER, SAMUEL	BAL	166	11TH WAR
COOPER, SAMUEL	WOR	214	4TH E DI
COOPER, SAMUEL	TAL	060	EASTON D
COOPER, SAMUEL	TAL	041	EASTON D
COOPER, SAMUEL W.	QUE	244	5TH E DI
COOPER, SAMUEL-BLACK	QUE	188	3RD E DI
COOPER, SARAH	SOM	473	TRAPPE D
COOPER, SARAH	ANN	454	HOWARD D
COOPER, SARAH	BAL	453	14TH WAR
COOPER, SARAH	BAL	351	13TH WAR
COOPER, SARAH E.	QUE	201	3RD E DI
COOPER, SEVERN	SOM	514	BARREN C
COOPER, SOLOMAN	WAS	143	2ND DIST
COOPER, SOLOMON M.	CAR	165	NO TWP L
COOPER, SUSAN	BAL	253	17TH WAR
COOPER, SUSAN	QUE	234	4TH E DI
COOPER, SUSAN J.	CEC	117	4TH E DI
COOPER, TEGO	BAL	434	1ST DIST
COOPER, TERRY	WAS	020	2ND SUBD
COOPER, THEODORE-BLACK	QUE	152	1ST E DI
COOPER, THOMAS	BAL	365	13TH WAR
COOPER, THOMAS	BAL	253	20TH WAR
COOPER, THOMAS	TAL	093	ST MICHA
COOPER, THOMAS	TAL	107	ST MICHA
COOPER, THOMAS	SOM	514	BARREN C
COOPER, THOMAS	WOR	195	8TH E DI
COOPER, THOMAS	BAL	434	1ST DIST
COOPER, THOMAS	BAL	457	8TH WARD
COOPER, THOMAS	BAL	035	1ST WARD
COOPER, THOMAS	BAL	269	1ST DIST
COOPER, THOMAS A.	QUE	135	1ST E DI
COOPER, THOMAS A.	BAL	455	14TH WAR
COOPER, THOMAS C.	BAL	109	10TH WAR
COOPER, THOMAS J.	TAL	118	ST MICHA
COOPER, THOMAS-BLACK	ST	308	1ST E DI
COOPER, THOMAS-BLACK	BAL	223	2ND WARD
COOPER, THOMAS-MULATTO	FRE	039	FREDERIC
COOPER, TOBIAS	BAL	276	2ND WARD
COOPER, VIRGINA	BAL	299	12TH WAR
COOPER, WELLS	BAL	371	13TH WAR
COOPER, WESLEY	CAR	103	NO TWP L
COOPER, WILLIAM	QUE	141	1ST E DI
COOPER, WILLIAM	DOR	385	1ST DIST
COOPER, WILLIAM	BAL	289	12TH WAR
COOPER, WILLIAM	BAL	140	1ST WARD
COOPER, WILLIAM	BAL	222	6TH WARD
COOPER, WILLIAM	BAL	035	1ST WARD
COOPER, WILLIAM	BAL	188	11TH WAR
COOPER, WILLIAM	ALL	224	CUMBERLA
COOPER, WILLIAM	WAS	229	1ST DIST
COOPER, WILLIAM	TAL	118	ST MICHA
COOPER, WILLIAM	TAL	118	ST MICHA
COOPER, WILLIAM	WAS	006	WILLIAMS
COOPER, WILLIAM	TAL	049	EASTON T
COOPER, WILLIAM	WAS	170	FUNKSTOW
COOPER, WILLIAM B.	WOR	215	4TH E DI
COOPER, WILLIAM H.	TAL	050	EASTON T
COOPER, WILLIAM H.	BAL	344	13TH WAR
COOPER, WILLIAM O.	DOR	350	3RD DIVI
COOPER, WILLIAM-BLACK	ST	323	4TH E DI
COOPER, WILLIMA B.	BAL	178	16TH WAR
COOPER,EMANUEL-MULATTO	FRE	429	8TH E DI
COOPER,GIDEON	CAR	104	NO TWP L
COOPER,JACOB-MULATTO	CAR	091	NO TWP L
COOPER,JOSEPH	BAL	005	1ST WARD
COOPER,LEVIN	BAL	123	1ST WARD
COOPER,MARTIN	BAL	244	2ND WARD
COOPER,PERRY	BAL	031	1ST WARD
COOPER,ROBERT-BLACK	CAR	095	NO TWP L
COOPPER, FANNY	WOR	282	BERLIN 1
COOPPER, GEORGE	WOR	256	1ST CENS
COOPPER, GEORGE	CAL	002	1ST DIST
COOPPER, JULIA	WOR	249	1ST CENS
COOPPER, NANCY	WOR	282	BERLIN 1
COOPWA, SARAH*	TAL	018	EASTON D
COOSEY, ALLEN	TAL	107	ST MICHA
COOSEY, LUCRETIA	BAL	151	5TH WARD
COOSEY, NICHOLAS	CAR	358	9TH DIST
COOTE, SARAH	FRE	165	EMMITTSB
COOVER, WILLIAM	FRE	125	CREAGERS
COPE, CHARLES	BAL	302	12TH WAR
COPE, VINCENT	BAL	294	3RD WARD
COPELAND, GOERGE W.	FRE	224	BUCKEYST
COPELAND, JAMES	BAL	282	2ND WARD
COPELAND, JANE	FRE	195	5TH E DI
COPELAND, JOSEPH W.	BAL	187	16TH WAR
COPELAND, RICHARD	BAL	386	8TH WARD
COPELAND, ROBERT	BAL	443	1ST DIST
COPELAND, STEPHEN	BAL	137	1ST WARD
COPELAND, STEPHEN	BAL	123	1ST WARD
COPENHAM, CATHARINE	BAL	092	2ND DIST
COPENHAVEN, AUGUSTUS	BAL	033	1ST WARD
COPENHAVER, ISAIAH	CAR	262	3RD DIST
COPENHAVER, WILLIAM	CAR	260	3RD DIST
COPERSMITH, PETER	BAL	216	6TH DIST
COPES, WILLIAM	BAL	015	15TH WAR
COPEY, ANN	TAL	008	EASTON D
COPHER, CHRIS	ALL	171	7TH E.D.
COPLES, WILLIAM	CAR	177	8TH DIST
COPLES, WILLIAM H.	CAR	195	4TH DIST
COPNER, JOHN	BAL	181	2ND WARD
COPP, THEODORE	FRE	313	MIDDLETO
COPPAGE, BENJAMIN	QUE	134	1ST E DI
COPPAGE, HENRIETTA	QUE	134	1ST E DI
COPPAGE, HENRIETTA	QUE	128	1ST E DI
COPPAGE, JOHN	QUE	130	1ST E DI
COPPAGE, JOHN F.	QUE	129	1ST E DI
COPPAGE, RUTHA-BLACK	QUE	139	1ST E DI
COPPAGE, RUTHY-BLACK	QUE	134	1ST E DI
COPPE,R JOHN	BAL	266	12TH WAR
COPPENHAVER, MATHIAS	CAR	406	2ND DIST
COPPER, ABRAHAM	BAL	097	15TH WAR
COPPER, ABSALOM	BAL	035	15TH WAR
COPPER, AMANDA	KEN	257	1ST DIST
COPPER, CYRUS	KEN	278	1ST DIST
COPPER, DOUGLAS C.	MGM	429	CLARKSTR
COPPER, GEORGE	KEN	244	2ND DIST
COPPER, GEORGE	KEN	263	1ST DIST
COPPER, GEORGE T.	KEN	264	1ST DIST
COPPER, HARRIET	KEN	257	1ST DIST
COPPER, HENRY	KEN	264	1ST DIST
COPPER, HENRY	KEN	232	2ND DIST
COPPER, JAMES	BAL	125	1ST WARD
COPPER, JOHN	KEN	244	2ND DIST
COPPER, JOHN	BAL	144	11TH WAR
COPPER, JOSHUA	KEN	250	2ND DIST
COPPER, JOSHUA	BAL	077	18TH WAR
COPPER, JOSHUA T.	KEN	225	2ND DIST
COPPER, KENNARD	KEN	250	2ND DIST
COPPER, MARY M.	KEN	219	2ND DIST
COPPER, PERE-BLACK	QUE	179	2ND E DI
COPPER, PRICILLA	BAL	285	7TH WARD
COPPER, SAMUEL G.	KEN	268	1ST DIST
COPPER, SAMUEL N.	BAL	161	6TH WARD
COPPER, SARAH A.	BAL	092	5TH WARD
COPPER, THOMAS	KEN	250	2ND DIST
COPPER, WILLIAM	BAL	271	1ST DIST
COPPER, WILLIAM	KEN	268	1ST DIST
COPPERHAND, ELIZABETH	CAR	404	2ND DIST
COPPERMSITH, AZENETH	CAR	383	2ND DIST
COPPERSMITH, DAVID	CAR	184	8TH DIST
COPPERSMITH, ERRA S.	CAR	184	8TH DIST
COPPERSMITH, JACOB	CAR	382	2ND DIST
COPPERSMITH, KEEFER	CAR	178	8TH DIST
COPPERSMITH, LEWIS	FRE	042	FREDERIC
COPPERSMITH, MAGOULINE	FRE	107	CREAGERS
COPPERSMITH, MARY ANN	BAL	402	14TH WAR
COPPERSMITH, PARMENUS	CAR	187	4TH DIST
COPPERSMITH, ROSE L.	BAL	237	1ST DIST
COPPERTHWAIT, FRANKLIN	BAL	280	2ND WARD
COPPLEMAN, JOHN G.	BAL	078	10TH WAR
COPPUCK, JAMES	BAL	020	4TH WARD
COPSEY, ELIZABETH	ST	328	4TH E DI
COPSEY, ENOCH S.	ST	342	5TH E DI
COR, MARY A.	BAL	020	9TH WARD
COR, WILLIAM	BAL	164	1ST WARD
CORAIN, JERRY	KEN	301	3RD DIST
CORAL, FREDERICK	FRE	241	NEW MARK
CORAM, ANN	BAL	149	16TH WAR
CORAM, JOSEPH	BAL	147	16TH WAR
CORAM, MARY J.	BAL	178	16TH WAR
CORAN, JOHN	QUE	245	5TH E DI
CORAY, WILLIAM	FRE	374	CATOCTIN
CORB, JOHN	BAL	373	3RD WARD
CORBALL, WILLIAM	BAL	290	3RD WARD
CORBAN, CHARLOTTE	SOM	399	BRINKLEY
CORBE, HARVEY	BAL	216	19TH WAR
CORBEL, LOUISA	BAL	087	10TH WAR
CORBELL, PETER	BAL	091	10TH WAR
CORBERT, SARAH	BAL	204	6TH WARD
CORBET, BARTLEY	ALL	141	6TH E.D.
CORBET, EMMANUEL	BAL	009	15TH WAR
CORBET, MARGARET	BAL	017	1ST WARD
CORBET, WILLIAM	WAS	157	2ND DIST
CORBETT, GEORGE	BAL	022	4TH WARD
CORBEY, SISTER A.E.	FRE	197	5TH E DI
CORBIN, ANN	WOR	324	1ST E DI
CORBIN, ANNA M.	MGM	442	CLARKSTR
CORBIN, JAMES	BAL	385	13TH WAR
CORBIN, JOHN	SOM	411	DUBLIN D
CORBIN, JOHN	WOR	178	6TH E DI
CORBIN, JOHN O.	CAR	290	7TH DIST
CORBIN, JOSHUA	CAR	291	7TH DIST
CORBIN, LEVIN	SOM	419	PRINCESS
CORBIN, MARGARET A.	WOR	185	6TH E DI
CORBIN, MARTIN	BAL	037	9TH WARD
CORBIN, MATILDA	BAL	080	2ND DIST
CORBIN, NATHAN	BAL	117	2ND DIST
CORBIN, PETER	WOR	344	1ST E DI
CORBIN, RALPH	SOM	418	PRINCESS
CORBIN, ROBERT	SOM	408	DUBLIN D
CORBIN, SARAH	SOM	377	BRINKLEY
CORBIN, SARAH	BAL	081	2ND DIST
CORBIN, SAVIN	WOR	319	1ST E DI
CORBIN, WILLIAM	WOR	324	1ST E DI
CORBIN, WILLIAM	BAL	079	2ND DIST
CORBIN, WILLIAM	BAL	419	1ST DIST
CORBIN, WILLIAM	CAR	176	8TH DIST
CORBINS, ANN	ALL	122	4TH E.D.
CORBIT, AMELIA	WAS	155	2ND DIST
CORBIT, JANE	BAL	444	14TH WAR
CORBIT, JOHN	BAL	285	17TH WAR
CORBIT, JOHN	WAS	163	2ND DIST
CORBIT, MARY	WAS	157	2ND DIST
CORBIT, THOMAS	ALL	069	5TH E.D.
CORBIT, WILLIAM	BAL	431	1ST DIST
CORBITT, ELIZA	BAL	026	9TH WARD
CORBITT, ISAAC	BAL	025	9TH WARD
CORBITT, LUCEY J.	WAS	141	2ND DIST
CORBITT, PETER	WAS	141	2ND DIST
CORBITT, REBECCA	BAL	062	10TH WAR
CORBLEY, RICHARD	KEN	305	3RD DIST
CORBLEY, RICHARD	KEN	293	3RD DIST
CORBY, MARIOTT H.*	DOR	448	1ST DIST
CORBY, JOHN	WAS	003	WILLIAMS
CORBY, JOHN W.	WAS	007	WILLIAMS
CORBY, WILLIAM	WAS	007	WILLIAMS
CORCORAN, FRANCIS	BAL	043	2ND DIST
CORCORAN, PAT	BAL	015	2ND DIST
CORD, CATHERINE	BAL	279	7TH WARD
CORD, EPHRAIM	BAL	202	19TH WAR
CORD, JOHN	HAR	176	3RD DIST
CORD, JOHN	BAL	107	1ST WARD
CORD, JOHN R.	WOR	256	1ST CENS
CORD, JOHN R.	WOR	261	BERLIN 1
CORD, MARY A.	BAL	108	1ST WARD
CORD, SARAH	BAL	216	11TH WAR
CORD, THOMAS	HAR	178	3RD DIST
CORD, WILLIAM B.	WOR	280	BERLIN 1
CORDAZ, FRITZ	BAL	268	2ND WARD
CORDE, MARY	ST	328	4TH E DI
CORDE, MARY	CEC	194	7TH E DI
CORDELL, BENJAMIN	BAL	053	1ST WARD
CORDELL, JOSEPH	WAS	003	WILLIAMS
CORDELL, WILLIA	BAL	053	1ST WARD
CORDEMAN, MARGARET	WAS	293	1ST DIST
CORDEMAN, MATHIAS	WAS	292	1ST DIST
CORDEMAN, SAMUEL	WAS	299	1ST DIST
CORDER, ANDREW J.	BAL	214	17TH WAR
CORDER, JOHN	BAL	215	17TH WAR
CORDERAY, ANN R.	BAL	251	17TH WAR
CORDERRY, PHILIP	HAR	020	1ST DIST
CORDERY, GEORGE	BAL	457	8TH WARD
CORDERY, MARIA	BAL	342	3RD WARD
CORDEY, HENRY G.	BAL	238	12TH WAR
CORDIMAN, MICHAL	WAS	132	2ND DIST
CORDIN, COMEGGS	KEN	302	3RD DIST
CORDRAY, ISAAC	KEN	270	1ST DIST
CORDREY, WILLIAM	BAL	093	10TH WAR
CORDRY, JOHN	WOR	238	6TH E DI
CORDSAY, JOHN	BAL	134	2ND DIST
CORDSEY, ASBURY	WOR	229	5TH E DI
CORE, HARMAN	BAL	104	2ND DIST
CORE, MARION	BAL	309	12TH WAR
CORE, MARY *	BAL	103	2ND DIST
CORE, MOLLY	BAL	027	9TH WARD
CORE, ROBERT M.*	TAL	038	EASTON D
COREAL, BRIDGET	ALL	069	5TH E.D.
CORELL, RICHARD	BAL	006	15TH WAR
COREY, BENJAMIN J.	BAL	308	12TH WAR
COREY, ELIZY J.*	DOR	322	1ST DIST
COREY, MICHAEL	BAL	356	8TH WARD
COREY, PARNELE B.*	DOR	373	1ST DIST
COREY, URIAH	CAR	117	NO TWP L
CORGAN, ANN	BAL	149	5TH WARD
CORGAN, OWEN	WAS	151	2ND DIST
CORGE, JOHN	BAL	085	15TH WAR
CORGE, SIMON	BAL	085	15TH WAR
CORGIN, JOHN	SOM	434	PRINCESS
CORGIN, JOSEPH	SOM	425	PRINCESS
CORIE, DANIEL	BAL	174	1ST WARD
CORK, ABRAM	CEC	019	ELKTON 3
CORK, FRANCES	BAL	306	20TH WAR
CORK, FREDERICK	BAL	376	1ST DIST
CORK, ISAAC *	KEN	225	2ND DIST
CORK, JACOB	KEN	248	2ND DIST
CORK, JAMES	CEC	031	CHESAPEA
CORK, JANE	KEN	300	3RD DIST
CORK, JOHN	KEN	296	3RD DIST
CORK, JOHN	CAR	154	NO TWP L
CORK, MOSES	DOR	390	1ST DIST
CORK, MOSES	KEN	313	3RD DIST
CORK, WILLIAM F.	CEC	031	CHESAPEA
CORKADALE, JOHN	CEC	117	4TH E DI
CORKAN, PATRICK *	BAL	274	1ST DIST
CORKEL, TIMOTHY	BAL	253	1ST DIST
CORKES, ELIZABETH	TAL	079	ST MICHA
CORKLAND, KATE	BAL	149	19TH WAR
CORKLAND, MARY	BAL	451	14TH WAR
CORKLAND, SARAH C.	BAL	164	19TH WAR
CORKLEY, JOHN	HAR	060	1ST DIST
CORKRAL, THOMAS*	TAL	017	EASTON D
CORKRALL, WILLIAM*	TAL	007	EASTON D
CORKRAN, CHARLES	DOR	382	1ST DIST
CORKRAN, CLEMENTINE	CAR	154	NO TWP L
CORKRAN, CYRUS	DOR	425	1ST DIST
CORKRAN, DANIL E.	DOR	461	1ST DIST
CORKRAN, DAVID M.	DOR	407	1ST DIST
CORKRAN, FRANCIS S.	BAL	180	16TH WAR
CORKRAN, HENRY	CAR	159	NO TWP L
CORKRAN, IRA R.	DOR	446	1ST DIST
CORKRAN, JOHN	DOR	460	1ST DIST
CORKRAN, MARY	DOR	450	1ST DIST
CORKRAN, MARY C.	DOR	426	1ST DIST
CORKRAN, NATHAN	CAR	154	NO TWP L
CORKRAN, PETER	DOR	312	1ST DIST
CORKRAN, RACHAEL J *	BAL	080	15TH WAR
CORKRAN, THOMAS	BAL	188	2ND WARD
CORKRAN, WILLIAM	DOR	422	1ST DIST
CORKRAN, WILLIAM *	BAL	079	15TH WAR
CORKRAN, WILLIS	CAR	154	NO TWP L
CORKRAN,WILLIAM H.	BAL	183	2ND WARD
CORKRAR, ELIZABETH	DOR	391	1ST DIST
CORKRAR, JOHN B.*	DOR	321	1ST DIST
CORKRON, MARTHA A.	DOR	322	1ST DIST
CORKRON, JOHN B.	DOR	311	1ST DIST
CORKRON, PRICE*	DOR	324	1ST DIST
CORKRON, SOPHIA*	DOR	316	1ST DIST
CORKRON, THOMAS	DOR	309	1ST DIST
CORKSON, MARY*	DOR	313	1ST DIST
CORKSON, PRICE*	DOR	324	1ST DIST
CORKSON, SOPHIA*	DOR	316	1ST DIST
CORKSRAN, ALLISON	CAR	159	NO TWP L
CORLES, MARGARET	BAL	080	1ST WARD
CORLETTA, ELIZA	BAL	225	2ND WARD
CORLIN, SUSANAH	BAL	414	1ST DIST
CORLIN, WILLIAM	BAL	079	2ND DIST

CORLITTER, JOSEPH	BAL	147	1ST WARD
CORLOCK, WILLIAM D.	CEC	102	4TH E DI
CORMACK, JAMES D.	BAL	111	5TH WARD
CORMACK, WILLIAM T.	ALL	142	6TH E.D.
CORMAN, WILLIAM	BAL	285	1ST DIST
CORMELL, MARY MAGDALEN SI	BAL	316	20TH WAR
CORMEOT, RACHEL*	DOR	371	3RD DIVI
CORMICK, JAMES H.	CAR	118	NO TWP L
CORMICK, JAMES W.	PRI	061	NOTTINGH
CORMICK, JOHN	BAL	281	2ND WARD
CORMICK, JOSEPH	CAR	118	NO TWP L
CORMICK, MARION E.	CAR	103	NO TWP L
CORMISH, JOHN	BAL	286	2ND WARD
CORMMISH, HENRY	BAL	119	11TH WAR
CORN, ABRAHAM	CEC	177	7TH E DI
CORN, AMELIA	BAL	116	5TH WARD
CORN, CHARLES	BAL	173	1ST WARD
CORN, MARY	HAR	191	3RD DIST
CORN, RACHEL	BAL	113	15TH WAR
CORN, WILLIAM	HAR	191	3RD DIST
CORNAND, MICHAEL	BAL	255	2ND WARD
CORNE, SAMUEL	DOR	403	1ST DIST
CORNEAL, ANN	BAL	062	18TH WAR
CORNEALE, M.	ANN	347	3RD DIST
CORNEGGS, ARAMINTA	KEN	216	2ND DIST
CORNEGRESS, ANN	BAL	157	2ND DIST
CORNEGYS, CLARISSA *	BAL	299	1ST DIST
CORNELALOUS, SAMUEL	CAR	192	4TH DIST
CORNELIA, MARGARET	BAL	204	2ND WARD
CORNELIA, MARY	ALL	196	CUMBERLA
CORNELIA, MARY	BAL	459	14TH WAR
CORNELIUS, CATHERINE	BAL	052	4TH WARD
CORNELIUS, EDWARD	BAL	310	7TH WARD
CORNELIUS, JAMES	BAL	282	7TH WARD
CORNELIUS, JANE	BAL	465	14TH WAR
CORNELIUS, JOHN	BAL	009	EASTERN
CORNELIUS, JOHN W.	BAL	100	15TH WAR
CORNELIUS, NICHOLAS	BAL	392	8TH WARD
CORNELIUS, NICHOLAS	BAL	387	8TH WARD
CORNELIUS, RICHARD	BAL	141	16TH WAR
CORNELIUS, SAMUEL	MGM	442	CLARKSTR
CORNELIUS, SARAH J.	BAL	388	8TH WARD
CORNELIUS, SUSAN	BAL	196	19TH WAR
CORNELIUS, THOMAS	BAL	157	1ST WARD
CORNELIUS, THOMAS	ST	338	4TH E DI
CORNELIUS, WILLIAM	QUE	162	2ND E DI
CORNELL, ALEXANDER	WAS	153	2ND DIST
CORNELL, JACKSON	PRI	036	VANSVILL
CORNELL, JAMES	CAR	303	1ST DIST
CORNELL, JAOCB	CAR	302	1ST DIST
CORNELL, JESSE	CAR	299	1ST DIST
CORNELL, MARGARET	CAR	299	1ST DIST
CORNELL, MICHAEL	BAL	196	19TH WAR
CORNELL, WILLIAM	WOR	260	BERLIN 1
CORNELUS, GEORGE	BAL	300	1ST DIST
CORNEN, JOHN	CEC	034	CHESAPEA
CORNER, CHARLES	BAL	444	8TH WARD
CORNER, GEORGE	BAL	077	1ST WARD
CORNER, GEORGE W.	BAL	357	3RD WARD
CORNER, JAMES	BAL	469	14TH WAR
CORNER, JAMES	CEC	083	CHARLEST
CORNER, JERISHA	PRI	031	VANSVILL
CORNER, JOHN	BAL	262	2ND WARD
CORNER, MARGARET	BAL	226	19TH WAR
CORNER, S.	BAL	063	10TH WAR
CORNER, SARAH*	BAL	078	4TH WARD
CORNER, SOLOMON	BAL	078	4TH WARD
CORNER, WILLIAM	BAL	149	1ST WARD
CORNESH, ANICH	BAL	280	7TH WARD
CORNEY, ALEXANDER	BAL	025	1ST WARD
CORNEY, MARY	ALL	196	CUMBERLA
CORNIAS, SERALPHA	BAL	212	11TH WAR
CORNICH, MARIAH	DOR	360	3RD DIVI
CORNICK, ANDREW	FRE	326	MIDDLETO
CORNICK, THOMAS	CAR	213	5TH DIST
CORNIER, HOWARD	BAL	382	13TH WAR
CORNIN, WILLIAM H.	HAR	007	1ST DIST
CORNING, GEORGE	BAL	280	2ND WARD
CORNING, JOHN	BAL	050	9TH WARD
CORNISH, -----*	DOR	413	1ST DIST
CORNISH, ABRAM	DOR	388	1ST DIST
CORNISH, ADAM	BAL	101	15TH WAR
CORNISH, ANN	BAL	094	5TH WARD
CORNISH, ANN	DOR	413	1ST DIST
CORNISH, ANNAH.	BAL	463	14TH WAR
CORNISH, ANNE*	BAL	109	10TH WAR
CORNISH, CAROLINE	BAL	154	11TH WAR
CORNISH, CATHARINE	BAL	054	15TH WAR
CORNISH, CELESTA	DOR	363	3RD DIVI
CORNISH, CHARLES	DOR	372	3RD DIVI
CORNISH, CHARLES	CEC	124	5TH E DI
CORNISH, CHARLES	BAL	190	17TH WAR
CORNISH, CHARLES	SOM	480	TRAPP DI
CORNISH, CHARLES-BLACK	CAR	150	NO TWP L
CORNISH, COLUMBUS	DOR	469	1ST DIST
CORNISH, DAVID	BAL	036	4TH WARD
CORNISH, DENNIS	BAL	098	15TH WAR
CORNISH, DENNIS	BAL	053	15TH WAR
CORNISH, DIANNA	BAL	276	17TH WAR
CORNISH, EDWARD	DOR	415	1ST DIST
CORNISH, EDWARD	TAL	060	EASTON D
CORNISH, ELIZA	DOR	385	1ST DIST
CORNISH, ELIZA	DOR	435	1ST DIST
CORNISH, ELIZA	DOR	310	1ST DIST
CORNISH, ELIZA	BAL	003	15TH WAR
CORNISH, ELIZA	BAL	124	16TH WAR
CORNISH, ELIZABETH	BAL	095	15TH WAR
CORNISH, ELIZABETH	DOR	360	3RD DIVI
CORNISH, ELIZABETH	CEC	125	5TH E DI
CORNISH, ELLEN	BAL	199	11TH WAR
CORNISH, EPHRAIM	CEC	148	PORT DUP
CORNISH, EVANSH*	DOR	467	1ST DIST
CORNISH, FRANCIS C.	BAL	139	11TH WAR
CORNISH, GEORGE	DOR	421	1ST DIST
CORNISH, GEORGE	SOM	434	PRINCESS
CORNISH, GRIFFIN	TAL	004	EASTON D
CORNISH, GUMER*	DOR	367	3RD DIVI
CORNISH, H. M.*	TAL	022	EASTON D
CORNISH, HARRIETT	BAL	349	13TH WAR
CORNISH, HARY	DOR	400	1ST DIST
CORNISH, HENRY	BAL	086	4TH WARD
CORNISH, HENRY	BAL	201	17TH WAR
CORNISH, HENRY	BAL	210	11TH WAR
CORNISH, HENRY	TAL	012	EASTON D
CORNISH, HESTER A.	BAL	337	3RD WARD
CORNISH, HETTY	BAL	196	19TH WAR
CORNISH, J.	BAL	136	1ST WARD
CORNISH, JACOB	DOR	463	1ST DIST
CORNISH, JAMES	BAL	337	3RD WARD
CORNISH, JOHN	BAL	168	1ST WARD
CORNISH, JOHN	BAL	167	1ST WARD
CORNISH, JOHN	BAL	239	6TH WARD
CORNISH, JOHN	DOR	467	1ST DIST
CORNISH, JOHN	SOM	460	HANGARY
CORNISH, JOHN	SOM	467	TRAPPE D
CORNISH, JOHN	BAL	456	14TH WAR
CORNISH, JOHN	CEC	145	PORT DUP
CORNISH, JOHN	DOR	391	1ST DIST
CORNISH, JOHN	DOR	387	1ST DIST
CORNISH, JOHN	DOR	367	3RD DIVI
CORNISH, JOHN	CEC	110	4TH E DI
CORNISH, JOSEPH	BAL	167	19TH WAR
CORNISH, JOSEPH	CEC	146	PORT DUP
CORNISH, JOSEPH	SOM	433	PRINCESS
CORNISH, KITTY	TAL	096	ST MICHA
CORNISH, LEVI	BAL	046	15TH WAR
CORNISH, LEVICY	DOR	423	1ST DIST
CORNISH, LOUISA	BAL	206	17TH WAR
CORNISH, LOUISANDER	BAL	138	11TH WAR
CORNISH, LUCY	BAL	154	11TH WAR
CORNISH, LUCY	BAL	399	14TH WAR
CORNISH, LYBERIA	BAL	203	17TH WAR
CORNISH, MARGARET	BAL	189	17TH WAR
CORNISH, MARGARET	TAL	093	ST MICHA
CORNISH, MARGARET	TAL	063	EASTON D
CORNISH, MARIAH	TAL	017	EASTON D
CORNISH, MARIAH	DOR	360	3RD DIVI
CORNISH, MARK	TAL	033	EASTON D
CORNISH, MARTHA	BAL	309	3RD WARD
CORNISH, MARY	BAL	092	15TH WAR
CORNISH, MARY	TAL	080	ST MICHA
CORNISH, MARY	DOR	427	1ST DIST
CORNISH, MARY	DOR	336	3RD DIVI
CORNISH, MARY A.	BAL	023	4TH WARD
CORNISH, MARY A.	BAL	053	15TH WAR
CORNISH, MARY J.	HAR	179	3RD DIST
CORNISH, MARY-BLACK	BAL	179	2ND WARD
CORNISH, MATILDA	TAL	045	EASTON T
CORNISH, MOSIS*	TAL	006	EASTON D
CORNISH, NACE	DOR	427	1ST DIST
CORNISH, NANCY	BAL	196	19TH WAR
CORNISH, NATHAN	CEC	103	4TH E DI
CORNISH, PARTY*	TAL	039	EASTON D
CORNISH, PHILLIS	DOR	424	1ST DIST
CORNISH, PRICELLA*	DOR	358	3RD DIVI
CORNISH, PRISSY	DOR	384	1ST DIST
CORNISH, RACHEL	DOR	366	3RD DIVI
CORNISH, RACHEL	DOR	469	1ST DIST
CORNISH, REBECCA	DOR	362	3RD DIVI
CORNISH, RITEY	DOR	388	1ST DIST
CORNISH, RUTH	DOR	468	1ST DIST
CORNISH, SAM	DOR	421	1ST DIST
CORNISH, SAMUEL	DOR	358	3RD DIVI
CORNISH, SAMUEL	CEC	145	PORT DUP
CORNISH, SAMUEL	BAL	095	15TH WAR
CORNISH, SAMUEL	BAL	148	2ND DIST
CORNISH, SARAH A.	BAL	206	11TH WAR
CORNISH, SELA	DOR	371	3RD DIVI
CORNISH, SOL.*	DOR	469	1ST DIST
CORNISH, SOLOMON	TAL	015	EASTON D
CORNISH, SUSAN	DOR	357	3RD DIVI
CORNISH, THENA	BAL	075	15TH WAR
CORNISH, THOMAS	DOR	407	1ST DIST
CORNISH, THOMAS	BAL	207	17TH WAR
CORNISH, THOMAS	TAL	019	EASTON D
CORNISH, THOMSA	TAL	097	ST MICHA
CORNISH, TRIFFE	DOR	366	3RD DIVI
CORNISH, VIRGINIA	BAL	174	11TH WAR
CORNISH, WILL	DOR	457	1ST DIST
CORNISH, WILLIAM	SOM	499	SALISBUR
CORNISH, WILLIAM	BAL	287	12TH WAR
CORNISH, WILLIAM	CAR	107	NO TWP L
CORNISH, WILLIAM	BAL	036	4TH WARD
CORNISH, WILLIAM H.	BAL	138	11TH WAR
CORNISH, WILLIAM JR.	SOM	503	SALISBUR
CORNISH, WILLIAM-BLACK	CAR	093	NO TWP L
CORNISSA, JOHN	DOR	307	1ST DIST
CORNOR, JOHN*	BAL	372	3RD WARD
CORNOR, WILLIAM	BAL	076	18TH WAR
CORNPROBST, BENARD	BAL	264	17TH WAR
CORNS, DECATUR	HAR	047	1ST DIST
CORNS, JACOB	BAL	049	18TH WAR
CORNS, MARTHA A.	BAL	050	18TH WAR
CORNS, RUTH	BAL	138	2ND DIST
CORNSEY, MARY D. *	BAL	245	6TH WARD
CORNTHWAIT, JOHN	BAL	389	3RD WARD
CORNTHWAIT, MARY	BAL	389	3RD WARD
CORNTHWAITE, WILSON	BAL	061	2ND DIST
CORNTHWART, JAMES	BAL	106	2ND DIST
CORNWALL, CARCLINE	ANN	521	HOWARD D
CORNWELE JOEL*	DOR	447	1ST DIST
CORNWELE, THOMAS*	DOR	376	1ST DIST
CORNWELL, ALPHONSE	BAL	256	20TH WAR
CORNWELL, EMILY R.	BAL	182	6TH WARD
CORNWELL, JEREMIAH	HAR	055	1ST DIST
CORNWELL, JOANA	SOM	519	BARREN C
CORNWELL, JOHN	DOR	447	1ST DIST
CORDICKS, JOHN M.	FRE	402	JEFFERSO
CORDMER, LOUIS	BAL	288	1ST DIST
CORPIN, WILLIAM	BAL	149	1ST WARD
CORRALL, THOMAS	ALL	243	CUMBER_A
CORRAN, SUSANNA	BAL	473	14TH WAR
CORRELL, CHRISTIAN	FRE	173	5TH E DI
CORREW, JANE	FRE	161	EMMITTSB
CORRIE, CATHARINE	BAL	381	13TH WAR
CORRIGAN, BARTHOLOMEW	BAL	265	2ND WARD
CORRIGAN, JAMES	HAR	029	1ST DIST
CORRIGAN, JOHN	BAL	027	4TH WARD
CORRIGAN, MARY	BAL	031	4TH WARD
CORRIGAN, MARY	BAL	088	10TH WAR
CORRIGAN, MICHAEL	FRE	166	EMMITTSB
CORRIGAN, PATRICK	BAL	172	6TH WARD
CORRIGAN, WILLIAM	HAR	035	1ST DIST
CORRIN, MARY	BAL	279	20TH WAR
CORRY, JANE	ALL	196	CUMBERLA
CORRY, PATRICK	FRE	20	5TH E DI
CORSE, JAMES	HAR	027	1ST DIST
CORSE, WILLIAM	BAL	099	2ND DIST
CORSEY, A.	ANN	296	1ST DIST
CORSEY, CHARLES	BAL	111	5TH WARD
CORSEY, DAVIS	BAL	175	11TH WAR
CORSEY, ELIZABETH	DOR	342	3RD DIVI
CORSEY, JANE	WAS	282	1ST DIST
CORSEY, KISSIAH	SOM	449	DAMES QU
CORSEY, MARY	CAR	297	7TH DIST
CORSEY, PATRICK	BAL	094	1ST WARD
CORSEY, PRICELLA	DOR	344	3RD DIVI
CORSEY, SHARLOTT	DOR	339	3RD DIVI
CORSEY, THOMAS	DOR	467	1ST DIST
CORSEY, WILLIAM	BAL	011	15TH WAR
CORSEY, WILLIAM	BAL	154	1ST WARD
CORSON, ANN E.	BAL	382	1ST DIST
CORT, BENEDICTINE	FRE	399	JEFFERSO
CORT, HENRY	FRE	406	JEFFERSO
CORTEL, MARY	BAL	062	2ND DIST
CORTES, MARGARET	BAL	080	1ST WARD
CORTIN, SALLY H.	WOR	201	3RD E DI
CORTLAND, JAMES JR.	BAL	145	5TH WARD
CORTLETT, PATRICK	BAL	233	1ST DIST
CORTOMAN, JAMES	BAL	267	20TH WAR
CORTS, JACOB	ALL	176	7TH E.D.
CORTS, MARTHA-MULATTO	FRE	434	8TH E DI
CORTY, JEFFERSON	ALL	220	CUMBERLA
CORUTHWAIT, WILLIAM P.	BAL	129	5TH WARD
CORVAN, J.	BAL	228	19TH WAR
CORVAN, MARGARET	BAL	228	19TH WAR
CORVILLE, MARCY	BAL	232	12TH WAR
CORVIN, ELLIOTT *	SOM	461	HANGARY
CORVIN, JAMES	BAL	257	12TH WAR
CORWIN, ELIZABETH	BAL	393	8TH WARD
CORWIN, MARY E.	FRE	182	5TH E DI
CORWIN, SUSAN	SOM	461	HANGARY
CORY, JOHN	CAR	118	NO TWP L
CORYNE, JEROME	BAL	140	11TH WAR
COSCAM, HENRY	ALL	184	9TH E.D.
COSDEN, BENJAMIN	QUE	162	2ND E DI
COSDEN, BENJAMIN	QUE	163	2ND E DI
COSDEN, FRANCES	QUE	172	2ND E DI
COSDEN, JAMES	QUE	162	2ND E DI
COSDEN, JOHN	QUE	163	2ND E DI
COSDEN, JOSHUA S.	QUE	169	2ND E DI
COSDEN, SAMUEL	QUE	164	2ND E DI
COSDEN, SARAH ANN	QUE	194	3RD E DI
COSDIN, WILLIAM	KEN	283	3RD DIST
COSE, HENRY	CEC	042	CHESAPEA
COSEN, LUCRETIA	BAL	151	11TH WAR
COSEY, ANN M.	BAL	081	15TH WAR
COSEY, DANIEL	WAS	293	1ST DIST
COSEY, ELIZY J.*	DOR	322	1ST DIST
COSEY, THOMAS	CAR	223	5TH DIST
COSEY, WILLIAM	WAS	296	1ST DIST
COSGROSE, JOHN	FRE	023	FREDERIC
COSGROVE, EDWARD	ALL	254	CUMBERLA
COSGROVE, JAMES	BAL	008	EASTERN
COSGROVE, PATRICK	BAL	184	2ND WARD
COSGROVE, PATRICK	BAL	035	1ST WARD
COSGROVE, PATRICK	BAL	348	13TH WAR
COSGROVE, PETER	BAL	226	17TH WAR
COSGROVE, SARH ANN	BAL	351	13TH WAR
COSGROVE, THOMAS	ALL	155	6TH E.D.
COSGROVES, PATRICK	ANN	415	HOWARD D
COSGRUE, MARGARET	BAL	271	1ST DIST
COSLEW, MARGARET	BAL	405	14TH WAR
COSLEY, DANIEL-MULATTO	FRE	452	8TH E DI
COSLEY, H. N. F.	BAL	058	10TH WAR
COSLEY, JAMES-MULATTO	FRE	436	8TH E DI
COSLEY, SOLOMON-MULATO	FRE	446	8TH E DI
COSLEY, SUSAN L.-MULATTO	FRE	418	8TH E DI
COSLEY, WILLIAM-MULATTO	FRE	452	8TH E DI
COSLEY, WILLIAM-MULATTO	FRE	015	FREDERIC
COSLUFF, MARGARET	BAL	379	1ST DIST
COSNTANT, FRANK H.	FRE	178	5TH E DI
COSRICK, MARY *	BAL	277	20TH WAR
COSS, JOHN	WAS	240	CAVETOWN
COSS, PETER	WAS	282	1ST DIST
COSSELL, ELIZABETH-MULATT	FRE	030	FREDERIC
COSSER, LYDIA G.	FRE	170	5TH E DI
COSSLEMAN, GEORGE	BAL	308	12TH WAR
COSSLY, SALLY	ALL	242	CUMBERLA
COSSMAN, JACOB	BAL	138	1ST WARD
COST, ANDREW	WAS	229	1ST DIST
COST, CATHARINE	WAS	182	BOONSBOR
COST, ELIZABETH	FRE	327	MIDDLETO
COST, EVE	WAS	075	2ND SUBD
COST, EZRA	FRE	342	MIDDLETO
COST, FREDERICK	BAL	209	2ND WARD
COST, JACOB	WAS	190	1ST DIST
COST, JOHN	WAS	183	BOONSBOR
COST, SAMUEL	WAS	075	2ND SUBD
COST, SAMUEL	WAS	251	1ST DIST
COST, SAMUEL W.	WAS	082	2ND SUBD
COST, WILLIAM	WAS	183	BOONSBOR
COST, WILLIAM	MGM	344	CLARKSBU
COST, WILLIAM JR.	FRE	362	CATOCTIN
COST, WILLIAM SR.	FRE	362	CATOCTIN
COSTA, CHARLES	BAL	113	1ST WARD
COSTALOE, JOHN	BAL	104	18TH WAR
COSTAR, JULIA A.	BAL	035	9TH WARD
COSTELLA, MAY A.	BAL	213	11TH WAR
COSTELLAY, EDW. *	BAL	273	20TH WAR
COSTELLO, ANN	BAL	059	15TH WAR
COSTELLO, CATHARINE	BAL	099	2ND DIST
COSTELLO, JAEMS	BAL	152	2ND DIST
COSTELLO, JAMES	BAL	116	5TH WARD
COSTELLO, JAMES	BAL	459	1ST DIST
COSTELLO, JOHN	BAL	294	3RD WARD
COSTELLO, MARK	BAL	140	1ST WARD
COSTELOY, ROSE E.	BAL	063	18TH WAR
COSTENBEDER, JOHN B.	WAS	124	HAGERSTO
COSTER, JOSEPH	BAL	311	7TH WARD
COSTER, LAURA	BAL	065	10TH WAR
COSTER, THOMAS	BAL	034	9TH WARD
COSTGROVE, H. B.	BAL	148	11TH WAR
COSTIGAN, ELIZA	BAL	252	6TH WARD
COSTIGAN, PAT	BAL	211	19TH WAR
COSTIGAN, PAT	BAL	230	19TH WAR
COSTILLO, SIS. M DECHANTE	FRE	198	5TH E DI
COSTIN, EDITHA	QUE	189	3RD E DI
COSTIN, JAMES	QUE	195	3RD E DI
COSTIN, RICHARD	QUE	189	3RD E DI
COSTLEMAN, DAVID	CHA	288	BOJANTOW
COSTLER, JOHN	BAL	001	1ST WARD
COSTLEY, GRAFTON	FRE	418	8TH E DI
COSTLEY, JOHN-MULATTO	FRE	005	FREDERIC
COSTLEY, MARY-BLACK	FRE	450	8TH E DI
COSTLEY, MARY-MULATTO	FRE	451	8TH E DI
COSTLEY, PATRICK	BAL	181	2ND DIST
COSTLEY, THOMAS J.	WAS	104	2ND DIST
COSTLEY, WILLIAM B.-BLACK	FRE	418	8TH E DI
COSTLY, WILLIAM	FRE	266	NEW MARK
COSTOLAY, MARY	BAL	183	6TH WARD
COSTON, ANN-BLACK	WOR	344	1ST E DI
COSTON, CHARLES	BAL	229	6TH WARD
COSTON, ELEANOR A.	SOM	523	BARREN C
COSTON, EZEKIEL	WOR	350	1ST E DI
COSTON, FRANCIS-MULATTO	CAR	069	NO TWP L
COSTON, HENRY	WOR	195	8TH E DI
COSTON, HENRY T.	WOR	325	1ST E DI
COSTON, HESTER-MULATTO	CAR	069	NO TWP L
COSTON, JAMES	SOM	433	PRINCESS

Name	County	Page	District
COSTON, LOPER-BLACK	WOR	330	1ST E DI
COSTON, MARGARET	BAL	186	11TH WAR
COSTON, MARY-BLACK	WOR	329	1ST E DI
COSTON, MAZY-MULATTO	CAR	069	NO TWP L
COSTON, MITCHEL-BLACK	WOR	337	1ST E DI
COSTON, NANCY	WOR	280	BERLIN I
COSTON, PARKER-BLACK	WOR	338	1ST E DI
COSTON, PETER	WOR	313	2ND E DI
COSTON, SAM-BLACK	WOR	338	1ST E DI
COSTON, SAMUEL	SOM	408	DUBLIN D
COSTON, THOMAS	SOM	414	DUBLIN D
COSTON, WILLIAM	BAL	123	1ST WARD
COSTON, WILLIAM N.	SOM	413	DUBLIN D
COSTON, WILLIAM SR.	SOM	414	DUBLIN D
COSTOR, SAMUEL-BLACK	WOR	321	1ST E DI
COSTOW, CEORGE-BLACK	WOR	321	1ST E DI
COSTOW, HENRY	WOR	312	2ND E DI
COSXO, MICHAEL	ALL	075	5TH E.D.
COTACT, GEORGE	BAL	302	12TH WAR
COTE, EMILY	BAL	008	4TH WARD
COTEMAN, LYNDA A.	SOM	404	BRINKLEY
COTES, WILLIAM	CEC	058	1ST E DI
COTFELTY, MARY	ALL	018	3RD E.D.
COTHER, SAMUEL	BAL	306	12TH WAR
COTHER, WILLIAM	HAR	134	2ND DIST
COTINGHAM, PRUDENCE	SOM	385	BRINKLEY
COTINSTINE, MICHAEL	BAL	193	2ND WARD
COTLER, SYLVIA	BAL	139	19TH WAR
COTLINGER, E.	BAL	125	11TH WAR
COTMAN, HENRY	SOM	411	DUBLIN D
COTMAN, LITTLETON	SOM	408	DUBLIN D
COTREE, PATRICK	HAR	053	1ST DIST
COTRILL, LEVI	BAL	266	1ST DIST
COTT, CHARLES	BAL	291	3RD WARD
COTT, SARAH S.	CAR	099	NO TWP L
COTTEN, RICHARDS	BAL	136	11TH WAR
COTTEN, SAMUEL	KEN	211	2ND DIST
COTTER, A.	BAL	138	1ST WARD
COTTER, JAMES	BAL	071	10TH WAR
COTTER, L. M.	BAL	088	10TH WAR
COTTER, MARIA *	KEN	270	1ST DIST
COTTER, RICHARD	BAL	426	14TH WAR
COTTING, ANN	BAL	243	17TH WAR
COTTINGHAM, EDWARD	WOR	176	6TH E DI
COTTINGHAM, EMILY	BAL	215	11TH WAR
COTTINGHAM, JEFFREY	SOM	391	BRINKLEY
COTTINGHAM, JOHN	SOM	390	BRINKLEY
COTTINGHAM, JOHNATHAN	WOR	313	2ND E DI
COTTINGHAM, JOSHUA-BLACK	WOR	172	6TH E DI
COTTINGHAM, LEAH	WOR	180	6TH E DI
COTTINGHAM, LUTHER A.	SOM	406	DUBLIN D
COTTINGHAM, MARY	WOR	180	6TH E DI
COTTINGHAM, PETER	WOR	300	SNOW HIL
COTTINGHAM, PURNELL	SOM	411	DUBLIN D
COTTINGHAM, R. J.	BAL	075	10TH WAR
COTTINGHAM, SALLY	WOR	171	6TH E DI
COTTINGHAM, SAMUEL	BAL	259	17TH WAR
COTTINGHAM, THOMAS	BAL	264	17TH WAR
COTTMAN, DANIEL	BAL	228	17TH WAR
COTTMAN, JANE	SOM	459	HANGARY
COTTMAN, JOSEPH S.	SOM	476	TRAPPE D
COTTMAN, LYDIA	SOM	473	TRAPPE D
COTTMAN, NELSON	SOM	441	DAMES QU
COTTMAN, PURCILLA	SOM	487	SALISBUR
COTTMAN, STEPHEN	SOM	459	HANGARY
COTTMAN, WILLIAM T.	WOR	200	3RD E DI
COTTON, CHARLES H.	KEN	253	1ST DIST
COTTON, DANIEL	BAL	068	15TH WAR
COTTON, ELLEN	KEN	258	1ST DIST
COTTON, GEORGE	KEN	261	1ST DIST
COTTON, HENRY	KEN	248	2ND DIST
COTTON, ISAAC	KEN	258	1ST DIST
COTTON, ISAAC	KEN	299	3RD DIST
COTTON, JOHN	BAL	143	16TH WAR
COTTON, JOHNSTON	ST	344	5TH E DI
COTTON, LERRA D.	BAL	378	1ST DIST
COTTON, MARIS	KEN	270	1ST DIST
COTTON, PERRY	KEN	257	1ST DIST
COTTON, RICHARD	ST	315	4TH E DI
COTTON, SARAH	KEN	244	2ND DIST
COTTON, SARAH A.	BAL	086	15TH WAR
COTTON, WILLIAM H.	BAL	073	2ND DIST
COTTREL, HENRY	CAR	372	9TH DIST
COTTRELL, CATHARINE	BAL	107	15TH WAR
COTTRELL, CLARK	BAL	010	15TH WAR
COTTRELL, DANIEL	BAL	011	15TH WAR
COTTRELL, ELIZABETH	BAL	286	20TH WAR
COTTRELL, HENRY W.	BAL	030	15TH WAR
COTTRELL, SARAH	BAL	286	20TH WAR
COTTS, LOUISA	BAL	072	2ND DIST
COTTSON, JOSEPH	HAR	046	1ST DIST
COUB, SARAH	FRE	054	FREDERIC
COUCH, ELIZA	BAL	367	3RD WARD
COUCH, TEMPERANCE	ANN	420	HOWARD D
COUCHERNOUR, FRANCES	BAL	099	15TH WAR
COUCHMAN, KEZIAH	BAL	237	6TH WARD
COUCIL, JOHN	QUE	192	3RD E DI
COUD, VICTOIRA	ST	274	3RD E DI
COUDAN, JOSEPH	CEC	143	7TH E DI
COUDIG, PITTY*	BAL	354	3RD WARD
COUDY, MICHAEL	BAL	139	2ND DIST
COUESEY, SARAH D.	BAL	324	12TH WAR
COUFMAN, MYER	HAR	145	3RD DIST
COUGHLAN, ELIZABETH	BAL	194	2ND WARD
COUGHLAN, PATRICK	BAL	197	2ND WARD
COUGHLAN, WILLIAM H.	BAL	194	2ND WARD
COUGHLAN, JOHANNA	BAL	197	2ND WARD
COUGHLIN, JAMES	BAL	109	10TH WAR
COUGHRAN, THOMAS	BAL	285	1ST DIST
COUGIE, MARIA	BAL	051	4TH WARD
COUGNET, EMILY	BAL	037	9TH WARD
COUKEY, WILLIAM	BAL	084	2ND DIST
COUKLEY, PHIL G.	BAL	292	12TH WAR
COULBEAM, HENRY	WOR	219	4TH E DI
COULBEM, ELIJAH P.	WOR	199	8TH E DI
COULBERN, ELIJAH	WOR	198	8TH E DI
COULBERN, HESTER	WOR	166	6TH E DI
COULBONE, MARY	CAR	124	NO TWP L
COULBONS, JAMES	CAR	115	NO TWP L
COULBORN, JOSEPH S.	BAL	232	17TH WAR
COULBORN, THOMAS	CAR	115	NO TWP L
COULBORNE, BETSEY	SOM	391	BRINKLEY
COULBORNE, ISAAC	SOM	366	BRINKLEY
COULBORNE, LEAH	SOM	391	BRINKLEY
COULBORNE, MARGARET	SOM	364	BRINKLEY
COULBORNE, MARY E.	SOM	429	PRINCESS
COULBORNE, WILLIAM*	SOM	365	BRINKLEY
COULBOURN, STEPHEN C.	BAL	371	13TH WAR
COULBOURNE, SAMPSON	WOR	174	6TH E DI
COULBOURNE, THERIPE	CAR	124	NO TWP L
COULBOURNE, WILLIAM*	SOM	366	BRINKLEY
COULBRINE, WILLIAM H.	WOR	166	6TH E DI
COULBURN, JOH	WOR	170	6TH E DI
COULBURN, JOSEPH	TAL	020	EASTON D
COULBURN, NANCY	DOR	301	1ST DIST
COULBURN, SHADY	WOR	231	6TH E DI
COULEN, MARYANN	ALL	084	5TH E.D.
COULHAN, MICHAEL *	BAL	143	1ST WARD
COULK, OGRATHA	BAL	212	2ND WARD
COULON, THOMAS	ALL	108	5TH E.D.
COULP, JOHN	BAL	038	4TH WARD
COULSEN, JESSE R.	CEC	155	PORT DUP
COULSON, ABNER O.	CEC	161	6TH E DI
COULSON, ANDREW	BAL	082	1ST WARD
COULSON, ARAMINTA	BAL	201	6TH WARD
COULSON, ELI	CEC	143	7TH E DI
COULSON, ELIZA	BAL	068	2ND DIST
COULSON, FREDERICK	BAL	083	1ST WARD
COULSON, GEORGE P.A.	BAL	226	12TH WAR
COULSON, JAMES	BAL	004	EASTERN
COULSON, JOHN	BAL	308	20TH WAR
COULSON, JOSEPH	BAL	112	5TH WARD
COULSON, M.	BAL	168	1ST WARD
COULSON, MAHALA	BAL	045	15TH WAR
COULSON, MARY	BAL	317	12TH WAR
COULSON, RICHARD	BAL	342	1ST DIST
COULSON, SAMUEL	BAL	343	1ST DIST
COULSON, SARAH A.	CEC	161	6TH E DI
COULSON, THOMAS H.	BAL	054	4TH WARD
COULSON, WILLIAM	BAL	060	4TH WARD
COULSON, WILLIAM	BAL	227	19TH WAR
COULSON, WILLIAM	BAL	296	17TH WAR
COULSTEL, ANN*	BAL	416	3RD WARD
COULSTON, ELI	CEC	200	7TH E DI
COULSTON, FRANCIS	BAL	272	7TH WARD
COULSTON, HENRY C.	CEC	169	6TH E DI
COULSTON, JAMES	CEC	168	6TH E DI
COULSTON, JOHN	CEC	168	6TH E DI
COULSTON, LOUIS	CEC	198	7TH E DI
COULTER, ANN	BAL	272	7TH WARD
COULTER, CHRISTOPHER	BAL	341	1ST DIST
COULTER, ELLEN M.	BAL	305	20TH WAR
COULTER, ESTHER	BAL	078	15TH WAR
COULTER, HENRY	ANN	279	ANNAPOLI
COULTER, JAMES S.	BAL	311	1ST DIST
COULTER, JOHN	BAL	110	5TH WARD
COULTER, JOHN	BAL	305	20TH WAR
COULTER, JOHN	BAL	265	17TH WAR
COULTER, LAVINIA	BAL	214	17TH WAR
COULTER, LEONARDUS	ANN	266	ANNAPOLI
COULTER, MARY	BAL	076	4TH WARD
COULTER, MOSES	QUE	252	5TH E DI
COULTER, SARAH A.	BAL	089	5TH WARD
COULTER, THOMAS	BAL	026	9TH WARD
COULTER, THOMAS	CAR	396	2ND DIST
COULTHURS, J. B. *	BAL	154	1ST WARD
COULTNEY, ELLEN	BAL	449	14TH WAR
COULTON, JOHN	BAL	358	8TH WARD
COUN, MARTER	BAL	021	2ND DIST
COUNALL, FRANCIS	QUE	198	3RD E DI
COUNALL, SARAH M.	QUE	198	3RD E DI
COUNAUGHT, ELLEN	BAL	082	18TH WAR
COUNCEL, GEORRGE	QUE	213	3RD E DI
COUNCELMAN, RACHAEL C.	BAL	312	1ST DIST
COUNCELMAN, SAMUEL	BAL	311	1ST DIST
COUNCIL, JOSEPH	TAL	070	EASTON T
COUNCIL, MR.	DOR	375	1ST DIST
COUNCIL, THOMAS	QUE	220	3RD E DI
COUNCIL, THOMAS	BAL	458	8TH WARD
COUNCIL, WILLIAM H.	QUE	135	1ST E DI
COUNCILE, SAMUEL	CAR	095	NO TWP L
COUNCILMAN, CHARLES	MGM	391	ROCKERLE
COUNCILMAN, JOHN T.	ANN	402	8TH DIST
COUND, C. G. *	BAL	045	18TH WAR
COUNELL, JOHN	ALL	155	6TH E.D.
COUNELLY, EDWARD	BAL	199	6TH WARD
COUNGER, WILLIAM	CAR	075	NO TWP L
COUNNELL, HONORE	FRE	066	FREDERIC
COUNSALMAN, GEORGE	BAL	107	2ND DIST
COUNSEL, JOHN	BAL	091	2ND DIST
COUNSELLER, CHARLES	BAL	206	2ND WARD
COUNSELLER, CHRISTRIA	BAL	206	2ND WARD
COUNSELMAN, HANNAH E.	MGM	392	ROCKERLE
COUNSELMAN, JACOB	BAL	432	14TH WAR
COUNSELMAN, JOHN	MGM	392	ROCKERLE
COUNSELMAN, LAWRENCE	BAL	136	18TH WAR
COUNSELMAN, WILLIAM	MGM	392	ROCKERLE
COUNSELMAN, WILLIAM	BAL	251	1ST DIST
COUNSELMAN, WILLIAM H.	BAL	092	18TH WAR
COUNSIL, RICHARD H.	TAL	067	EASTON T
COUNSIL, WILLIAM H.	TAL	067	EASTON T
COUNSLEMAN, GEORGE	BAL	092	18TH WAR
COUNT, JANE	BAL	386	8TH WARD
COUNT, MACY	CAL	031	2ND DIST
COUNT, MARGARET	BAL	229	19TH WAR
COUNTEE, CAROLINE	MGM	348	BERRYS D
COUNTEE, HENRY-BLACK	FRE	224	BUCKEYST
COUNTEE, JOHN-BLACK	FRE	230	BUCKEYST
COUNTEE, MATILDA	BAL	189	19TH WAR
COUNTEE, SOLLOMAN-BLACK	FRE	233	BUCKEYST
COUNTER, ALLEN	BAL	173	2ND DIST
COUNTER, ERASMUS-BLACK	CAL	056	3RD DIST
COUNTESS, JOSEPH	BAL	131	18TH WAR
COUNTICE, SARAH	CAR	075	NO TWP L
COUNTIE, SAMUEL	FRE	253	NEW MARK
COUNTISS, ELIZABETH	BAL	133	18TH WAR
COUNTREY, GEORGE W.	HAR	150	3RD DIST
COUNTRY, CYRUS	HAR	157	3RD DIST
COUNTRY, PHILIP	CHA	292	BOJANTOW
COUNTY, BENJAMIN T.	HAR	187	3RD DIST
COUNTY, HENRY	HAR	167	3RD DIST
COUNTY, HOLAS	HAR	150	3RD DIST
COUP, CATHARINE	WAS	029	2ND SUBD
COUP, ELIZABETH	WAS	105	2ND DIST
COUP, HESTER	BAL	302	3RD WARD
COUP, JACOB	WAS	029	2ND SUBD
COUPLAND, WILLIAM	BAL	222	6TH WARD
COUPLAND, WILLIAM G.	BAL	031	18TH WAR
COUPLES, THOMAS	ANN	416	HOWARD D
COURCEY, ANNE	BAL	134	16TH WAR
COURCEY, MARY	BAL	160	16TH WAR
COUREY, JAMES H.	CAR	085	NO TWP L
COUREY, LEMUEL	CAR	096	NO TWP L
COURG, MARY	BAL	253	20TH WAR
COURMAN, ANN	BAL	461	14TH WAR
COURN, WILLIAM	WAS	243	CAVETOWN
COUROY, MARGARET	FRE	062	FREDERIC
COURSE, AMELIA	BAL	424	3RD WARD
COURSELL, FANELLE*	BAL	053	4TH WARD
COURSEY, ALEXANDER	PRI	080	QUEEN AN
COURSEY, ANN	CAR	076	NO TWP L
COURSEY, ANN	BAL	099	10TH WAR
COURSEY, BENJAMIN F.	BAL	027	15TH WAR
COURSEY, CHARLES	QUE	210	3RD E DI
COURSEY, CHARLOTTE	QUE	211	3RD E DI
COURSEY, CHRISTOPHER	QUE	249	5TH E DI
COURSEY, EDWARD	QUE	250	5TH E DI
COURSEY, EDWARD	BAL	281	1ST DIST
COURSEY, EDWARD H.	QUE	250	5TH E DI
COURSEY, HENRY-BLACK	QUE	148	1ST E DI
COURSEY, HESTER-BLACK	QUE	177	2ND E DI
COURSEY, ISAAC	QUE	204	3RD E DI
COURSEY, JAMES	QUE	142	1ST E DI
COURSEY, JOHN D.	BAL	114	1ST WARD
COURSEY, JOHN F.	QUE	160	2ND E DI
COURSEY, JOHN H.	QUE	160	2ND E DI
COURSEY, JOHN-BLACK	QUE	129	1ST E DI
COURSEY, JOHN-BLACK	QUE	148	1ST E DI
COURSEY, JOSEPH	QUE	195	3RD E DI
COURSEY, MARIA	BAL	134	11TH WAR
COURSEY, MARY	QUE	160	2ND E DI
COURSEY, MARY	QUE	239	5TH E DI
COURSEY, MARY D. *	BAL	245	6TH WARD
COURSEY, MICHAEL	BAL	016	1ST WARD
COURSEY, SAMUEL	QUE	173	2ND E DI
COURSEY, SAMUEL D.	QUE	232	4TH E DI
COURSEY, THOMAS-BLACK	QUE	172	2ND E DI
COURSEY, WESLY	BAL	282	1ST DIST
COURSEY, WILLIAM	BAL	038	9TH WARD
COURSEY, WILLIAM	QUE	212	3RD E DI
COURSEY, WILLIAM	KEN	266	1ST DIST
COURSEY, WILLIAM H. D.	QUE	242	5TH E DI
COURSEY, RACHEL J.-BLACK	QUE	148	1ST E DI
COURT, JOHN	BAL	450	14TH WAR
COURT, WILLIAM	BAL	415	3RD WARD
COURTLAN, JAMES	BAL	086	4TH WARD
COURTLY, ELIZA	BAL	162	2ND DIST
COURTNEY, ABRAHAM	HAR	181	3RD DIST
COURTNEY, ANN J.	BAL	306	7TH WARD
COURTNEY, ANNE E.	BAL	441	8TH WARD
COURTNEY, DAVID L.	BAL	346	13TH WAR
COURTNEY, E. S.	BAL	106	10TH WAR
COURTNEY, FRANCIS	BAL	038	2ND DIST
COURTNEY, HENRY	BAL	076	2ND DIST
COURTNEY, JAMES	BAL	171	11TH WAR
COURTNEY, JAMES	BAL	171	11TH WAR
COURTNEY, JAMES	BAL	364	3RD WARD
COURTNEY, JOHN	BAL	315	7TH WARD
COURTNEY, JOSEPH	BAL	456	8TH WARD
COURTNEY, MARY	BAL	053	9TH WARD
COURTNEY, MARY	BAL	239	6TH WARD
COURTNEY, SARAH	BAL	257	6TH WARD
COURTNEY, SUSAN	BAL	411	8TH WARD
COURTNEY, SUSAN	BAL	237	6TH WARD
COURTNEY, THEODOTIUS	ST	308	1ST E DI
COURTNEY, THOMAS	BAL	154	2ND DIST
COURTNEY, W.H.	HAR	171	3RD DIST
COURTNEY, WILLIAM A.	HAR	164	3RD DIST
COURTNY, THOMAS	HAR	171	3RD DIST
COURTOISE, CLEMENTINE	FRE	040	FREDERIC
COURTRY, FRANCIS	HAR	163	3RD DIST
COURTRY, GEORGE	HAR	182	3RD DIST
COURTS, BENJAMIN	ALL	221	CUMBERLA
COURTS, MAJOR	PRI	065	NOTTINGH
COURTS, MARY	BAL	441	14TH WAR
COUSELL, SARAH *	ANN	340	3RD DIST
COUSEY, NOTLEY H. R.	QUE	242	5TH E DI
COUSIL, SARAH	BAL	069	2ND DIST
COUSINS, ELIZABETH	BAL	226	2ND WARD
COUSINS, JOHN	BAL	289	3RD WARD
COUSINS, JULIA	BAL	013	1ST WARD
COUSINS, STEPHEN	BAL	006	15TH WAR
COUSINS, WILLIAM	ALL	098	5TH E.D.
COUSMAN, JOHN*	BAL	369	3RD WARD
COUSON, MARGARET C.	BAL	408	3RD WARD
COUSTABLE, ELIZABETH	BAL	168	2ND DIST
COUSTANAT, MARIA	FRE	162	EMMITTSB
COUSTON, JOHN	CEC	198	7TH E DI
COUSWICK, DAVID	ALL	196	CUMBERLA
COUTE, FREDERICK	BAL	110	2ND DIST
COUTER, GEORGE	WAS	011	WILLIAMS
COUTER, GEORGE	WAS	011	WILLIAMS
COUTES, JOHN H.	BAL	266	20TH WAR
COUTIE, BENJAMIN	BAL	375	13TH WAR
COUTON, ARTHUR	ALL	216	CUMBERLA
COUTON, GEORGE	ALL	247	CUMBERLA
COUTTS, ANDREW	BAL	020	9TH WARD
COUTTS, HANSON-BLACK	FRE	387	PETERSVI
COUTZ, CASPER	CAR	214	5TH DIST
COUTZ, NANCY	CAR	181	8TH DIST
COUZENS, STEPHEN	BAL	367	13TH WAR
COVAL, JONATHAN F.	FRE	259	NEW MARK
COVAL, JOSHUA	FRE	260	NEW MARK
COVE, HENRY C.	CHA	272	ALLENS F
COVE, MARGARET	PRI	002	BLADENSB
COVEE, JEROME	BAL	331	3RD WARD
COVENTON, HEMMERITT A.	BAL	188	11TH WAR
COVENTON, NATHANIEL	BAL	039	18TH WAR
COVENTON, PHILLIP	DOR	352	3RD DIVI
COVENTRY, JAMES	BAL	124	1ST WARD
COVER, AMANDA J.	CAR	191	4TH DIST
COVER, EDWARD	CAR	369	9TH DIST
COVER, ELIZABETH	CAR	326	1ST DIST
COVER, ELIZABETH J.	FRE	435	8TH E DI
COVER, ENOS	FRE	129	CREAGERS
COVER, EPHRAIM	CAR	377	2ND DIST
COVER, EPHRIAM	CAR	325	1ST DIST
COVER, FREDERICK	FRE	115	CREAGERS
COVER, HENRY	CAR	372	9TH DIST
COVER, JEROME	FRE	137	CREAGERS
COVER, JOHN	CAR	325	1ST DIST
COVER, JOHN	FRE	435	8TH E DI
COVER, JOSIAH S.	CAR	372	9TH DIST
COVER, MARGARET	CAR	377	2ND DIST
COVER, MARGARET	FRE	125	CREAGERS
COVER, MARGARETT	WAS	256	1ST DIST
COVER, RACHAEL	FRE	095	FREDERIC
COVER, SAMUEL P.	CAR	247	3RD DIST
COVER, SOPHIA	FRE	091	FREDERIC
COVER, TOBIAS	CAR	377	2ND DIST
COVERN, MARY	CEC	190	5TH E DI
COVEY, ANDREW	CAR	152	NO TWP L
COVEY, BAYARD	CAR	134	NO TWP L
COVEY, CHARLES-BLACK	CAR	073	NO TWP L
COVEY, DARAH C.	DOR	324	1ST DIST
COVEY, EDWARD	TAL	120	ST MICHA
COVEY, ELLEN	TAL	060	EASTON D
COVEY, GREER	DOR	428	1ST DIST
COVEY, HENRY	TAL	032	EASTON D
COVEY, HEZEKIAH	CAR	154	NO TWP L

Name	County	Page	District
COVEY, HUTTEN	CAR	132	NO TWP L
COVEY, JACOB	CAR	156	NO TWP L
COVEY, JACOB	CAR	154	NO TWP L
COVEY, MARY	CAR	156	NO TWP L
COVEY, MARY	QUE	157	2ND E DI
COVEY, MARY	BAL	098	5TH WARD
COVEY, MATHEW M.	CAR	143	NO TWP L
COVEY, MITCHEL	CAR	154	NO TWP L
COVEY, PETER	CAR	155	NO TWP L
COVEY, SARAH	CAR	125	NO TWP L
COVEY, THOMAS	CAR	155	NO TWP L
COVEY, THOMAS	CAR	164	NO TWP L
COVEY, THOMAS	TAL	029	EASTON D
COVEY, WILLIAM	CAR	154	NO TWP L
COVEY, WILLIAM	CAR	135	NO TWP L
COVINGTON, AMELIA	WOR	262	BERLIN I
COVINGTON, ANN M.	BAL	191	6TH WARD
COVINGTON, BENJAMIN	CAR	097	NO TWP L
COVINGTON, CLARA	BAL	133	5TH WARD
COVINGTON, EBEN M.	QUE	201	3RD E DI
COVINGTON, ELIZABETH	SOM	506	BARREN C
COVINGTON, ELIZABETH W.	SOM	510	BARREN C
COVINGTON, GEORGE W.	BAL	003	15TH WAR
COVINGTON, HARRIET	QUE	204	3RD E DI
COVINGTON, HENRY	BAL	210	6TH WARD
COVINGTON, ISAAC	SOM	458	DAMES QU
COVINGTON, ISAAC P.	SOM	459	HANGARY
COVINGTON, ISABELLA	BAL	187	2ND WARD
COVINGTON, JAMES	QUE	209	3RD E DI
COVINGTON, JAMES	SOM	505	SALISBUR
COVINGTON, JOHN	SOM	460	HANGARY
COVINGTON, JOHN H.	QUE	156	2ND E DI
COVINGTON, JOHN R.	SOM	544	TYASKIN
COVINGTON, JOHN T.	SOM	510	BARREN C
COVINGTON, JOSEPH	BAL	112	10TH WAR
COVINGTON, MARTHA W.	SOM	543	TYASKIN
COVINGTON, NANCY	BAL	078	4TH WARD
COVINGTON, PHIL*	DOR	442	1ST DIST
COVINGTON, PHILIP	SOM	543	TYASKIN
COVINGTON, ROYSTON	SOM	523	BARREN C
COVINGTON, SAMUEL	KEN	293	3RD DIST
COVINGTON, SARAH A.	QUE	191	3RD E DI
COVINGTON, THOMAS S.	QUE	166	2ND E DI
COVINGTON, WASHINGTON	SOM	503	SALISBUR
COVINGTON, WILLIAM W.	SOM	547	TYASKIN
COVINGTON,ELIJAH	QUE	188	3RD E DI
COWAN, AGNES	ALL	106	5TH E.D.
COWAN, BENJAMIN	CEC	092	4TH E DI
COWAN, CATHARINE M.	BAL	230	6TH WARD
COWAN, CHARLES	ALL	105	5TH E.D.
COWAN, J.	BAL	148	1ST WARD
COWAN, JOHN	ALL	105	5TH E.D.
COWAN, JOSHUA	BAL	250	1ST DIST
COWAN, MARY	BAL	011	1ST WARD
COWAN, S.	ANN	271	ANNAPOLI
COWAN, SAMUEL	HAR	082	2ND DIST
COWAN, WILLIAM H.	BAL	230	6TH WARD
COWAN, WILLIAM L.	BAL	331	13TH WAR
COWARD, ANN	BAL	060	4TH WARD
COWARD, JOHN	DOR	336	3RD DIVI
COWARD, MEDORA	BAL	052	18TH WAR
COWARD, SOLOMON	TAL	092	ST MICHA
COWARD, THOMAS	BAL	391	14TH WAR
COWARD, W.	BAL	156	1ST WARD
COWARD, W.	BAL	151	1ST WARD
COWARD, WASHINGTON	BAL	026	1ST WARD
COWART, LAVINIA S.	BAL	104	15TH WAR
COWART, VIRGINIA	BAL	080	15TH WAR
COWDEN, WILLIAM	HAR	073	1ST DIST
COWDER, JANE	BAL	180	19TH WAR
COWDY, JAMES	WAS	156	2ND DIST
COWEL, ELLEN	BAL	043	2ND DIST
COWELL, BENJAMIN J.	BAL	144	1ST WARD
COWELL, G.	BAL	117	1ST WARD
COWELL, HARRIET	BAL	043	2ND DIST
COWELL, JAMES	CEC	204	6TH E DI
COWELL, RICHARD	BAL	143	1ST WARD
COWEN, CAVALIER	BAL	027	15TH WAR
COWEN, ELIZABETH	FRE	277	NEW MARK
COWEN, JOHN	HAR	173	3RD DIST
COWEN, JOHN	PRI	107	PISCATAW
COWEN, JOSEPH	HAR	082	2ND DIST
COWICK, MARY	BAL	321	7TH WARD
COWIN, WILLIAM	BAL	027	15TH WAR
COWL, ALBERTUS	ALL	184	9TH E.D.
COWLE, HENRY	BAL	008	EASTERN
COWLER, ANN ELIZA	BAL	080	18TH WAR
COWLER, GREENBERY	BAL	080	18TH WAR
COWLES, HENRY W.	BAL	070	2ND DIST
COWLES, THOMAS	BAL	078	2ND DIST
COWLES, WELSEY	BAL	182	11TH WAR
COWLEY, COMFORT	BAL	041	18TH WAR
COWLEY, JAMES	BAL	133	2ND DIST
COWLEY, JOSEPH	QUE	241	5TH E DI
COWLEY, JOSEPH	QUE	250	5TH E DI
COWLEY, ROSE	BAL	097	5TH WARD
COWLEY, THOMAS J. C.	QUE	250	5TH E DI
COWMAN, EDWARD	ANN	365	4TH DIST
COWMAN, ELLEND	BAL	172	16TH WAR
COWMAN, HENRIETTA	BAL	097	10TH WAR
COWMAN, JOHN T.	PRI	079	QUEEN AN
COWMAN, JOSEPH	ANN	364	4TH DIST
COWMAN, M.E.	ANN	271	ANNAPOLI
COWMAN, MARY A.	PRI	028	VANSVILL
COWMAN, MATILDA	ANN	280	ANNAPOLI
COWMAN, PHILIP E.	BAL	294	3RD WARD
COWMAN, PHILIP P.	ANN	307	1ST DIST
COWMAN, R.J.	ANN	279	ANNAPOLI
COWMAN, RICHARD	BAL	293	3RD WARD
COWMAN, RICHARD	BAL	330	13TH WAR
COWMAN, SAMUEL	BAL	460	14TH WAR
COWNEY, JANE	BAL	408	1ST DIST
COWNOVER, JOHN	CAR	301	1ST DIST
COWPER, JANE C.	CEC	080	NORTHEAS
COWPLAND, WILLIAM S.	BAL	370	3RD WARD
COWSAY, PERE	QUE	241	5TH E DI
COWSIER, CATHERINE J.	WOR	173	6TH E DI
COX, AARON W.	SOM	496	SALISBUR
COX, ABRAM	BAL	243	1ST DIST
COX, ADA	BAL	185	19TH WAR
COX, ADELINE-BLACK	QUE	141	1ST E DI
COX, ALFRED	CHA	247	HILLTOP
COX, AMMI M.	BAL	185	19TH WAR
COX, AMOS A.	BAL	255	1ST DIST
COX, ANDREW	WAS	229	1ST DIST
COX, ANN	WOR	178	6TH E DI
COX, ANN	CHA	261	MIDDLETO
COX, ANN C.	WAS	230	1ST DIST
COX, ANN E.	HAR	032	1ST DIST
COX, ANNS	CHA	289	MIDDLETO
COX, BENJAMIN	SOM	384	BRINKLEY
COX, BENJAMIN T.	KEN	284	3RD DIST
COX, BINAH	BAL	247	6TH WARD
COX, BRIDGET	BAL	176	11TH WAR
COX, C. C. DR.	TAL	073	EASTON T
COX, C.E.	PRI	117	PISCATAW
COX, CAROLINE	BAL	268	7TH WARD
COX, CHARLES	BAL	248	6TH WARD
COX, CHARLES	TAL	077	EASTON T
COX, COTLY	SOM	498	SALISBUR
COX, DANIEL	TAL	080	ST MICHA
COX, DANIEL	BAL	437	8TH WARD
COX, DANIEL	BAL	437	1ST DIST
COX, E. GOVER	CAR	194	4TH DIST
COX, ELEANOR	SOM	549	TYASKIN
COX, ELI	SOM	354	BRINKLEY
COX, ELIAS	CAR	159	NO TWP L
COX, ELIAS	BAL	395	3RD WARD
COX, ELIJAH	SOM	354	BRINKLEY
COX, ELISHA	BAL	380	3RD WARD
COX, ELIZA	CAR	236	UNION TO
COX, ELIZABETH	CAR	185	8TH DIST
COX, ELIZABETH	CAR	117	NO TWP L
COX, ELIZABETH	CAL	040	3RD DIST
COX, ELIZABETH	CHA	274	ALLENS F
COX, ELLEN	CAL	058	3RD DIST
COX, ELLEN	BAL	072	18TH WAR
COX, ELY	BAL	200	19TH WAR
COX, EMANUEL	CAR	184	8TH DIST
COX, EMILY	BAL	378	3RD WARD
COX, EMMA	BAL	118	5TH WARD
COX, EPHRAIM	BAL	433	1ST DIST
COX, ESSOR	BAL	121	18TH WAR
COX, GEORGE	FRE	414	8TH E DI
COX, GEORGE	BAL	258	6TH WARD
COX, GEORGE	BAL	282	2ND WARD
COX, GEORGE	BAL	048	9TH WARD
COX, GEORGE	BAL	291	12TH WAR
COX, GEORGE	SOM	357	BRINKLEY
COX, GEORGE	PRI	117	PISCATAW
COX, GEORGE	WAS	215	1ST DIST
COX, GEORGE	ST	300	2ND E DI
COX, GEORGE A.	SOM	396	BRINKLEY
COX, GEORGE W.	BAL	470	14TH WAR
COX, GULIELINA*	BAL	309	3RD WARD
COX, GUSTY	PRI	089	SPALDING
COX, HACHLESS*	TAL	063	EASTON D
COX, HENRY	TAL	097	ST MICHA
COX, HENRY	HAR	033	1ST DIST
COX, HESTER	TAL	047	EASTON T
COX, ISABELLA	CAL	021	2ND DIST
COX, ISABELLA	BAL	113	5TH WARD
COX, ISACK P.*	TAL	001	EASTON D
COX, JAMES	TAL	097	ST MICHA
COX, JAMES	PRI	094	SPALDING
COX, JAMES	CAL	061	3RD DIST
COX, JAMES	CAL	029	2ND DIST
COX, JAMES	BAL	229	19TH WAR
COX, JAMES	BAL	022	18TH WAR
COX, JAMES G.	BAL	264	1ST DIST
COX, JAMES H.	BAL	025	9TH WARD
COX, JAMES L.	BAL	313	7TH WARD
COX, JAMES T.	ST	338	4TH E DI
COX, JESSE	BAL	050	2ND DIST
COX, JOHN	BAL	038	2ND DIST
COX, JOHN	BAL	077	15TH WAR
COX, JOHN	BAL	279	2ND WARD
COX, JOHN	BAL	309	7TH WARD
COX, JOHN	SOM	388	BRINKLEY
COX, JOHN	BAL	282	17TH WAR
COX, JOHN	HAR	075	BEL AIR
COX, JOHN	CHA	259	MIDDLETO
COX, JOHN	CEC	144	PORT DUP
COX, JOHN	CAL	030	2ND DIST
COX, JOHN A.	BAL	455	8TH WARD
COX, JOHN H.	WAS	120	2ND DIST
COX, JOHN J.	SOM	383	BRINKLEY
COX, JOHN T.	ST	261	3RD E DI
COX, JOHN T.	FRE	420	8TH E DI
COX, JOHN-MULATTO	FRE	031	FREDERIC
COX, JOHN-MULATTO	BAL	246	1ST DIST
COX, JOSEPH	ALL	241	CUMBERLA
COX, JOSEPH H.	FRE	299	WOODSBOR
COX, JOSHUA	PRI	089	SPALDING
COX, LEONARD	WAS	133	2ND DIST
COX, LEVI	BAL	303	12TH WAR
COX, LOUISA	TAL	036	EASTON D
COX, LUTHER J.	BAL	067	10TH WAR
COX, LUTHER J. JR.	BAL	143	11TH WAR
COX, LYCD	BAL	035	2ND DIST
COX, MARCELLUS	CAR	184	8TH DIST
COX, MARGARET	TAL	033	EASTON D
COX, MARGARET	SOM	365	BRINKLEY
COX, MARGARET	ANN	343	3RD DIST
COX, MARIA	FRE	036	FREDERIC
COX, MARIA S.	BAL	107	5TH WARD
COX, MARION	BAL	452	1ST DIST
COX, MARY	BAL	146	16TH WAR
COX, MARY	BAL	176	2ND DIST
COX, MARY	DOR	381	1ST DIST
COX, MARY	MGM	319	CRACKLIN
COX, MARY	SOM	391	BRINKLEY
COX, MARY	PRI	094	SPALDING
COX, MARY E.	BAL	214	6TH WARD
COX, MELCHNER	BAL	152	19TH WAR
COX, MICHAEL	BAL	176	11TH WAR
COX, MILLY	SOM	381	BRINKLEY
COX, MISS M.	FRE	199	5TH E DI
COX, MOSES	WAS	052	2ND SUBD
COX, NATHANIEL	BAL	184	19TH WAR
COX, NED	ANN	343	3RD DIST
COX, NICHOLAS	BAL	401	1ST DIST
COX, PETER	WAS	217	1ST DIST
COX, PETER	SOM	473	TRAPPE D
COX, PHEBE	BAL	153	11TH WAR
COX, PRICE	KEN	281	3RD DIST
COX, PRUSILLA	SOM	553	TYASKIN
COX, RACHEAL	CAR	396	2ND DIST
COX, RACHIEL	HAR	007	1ST DIST
COX, REBECCA	BAL	048	2ND DIST
COX, RICHARD	QUE	149	1ST E DI
COX, ROBERT	CHA	220	ALLENS F
COX, SALLY	SOM	395	BRINKLEY
COX, SAMUEL	CHA	217	ALLENS F
COX, SAMUEL G.	SOM	551	TYASKIN
COX, SAMUEL H.	CHA	263	MIDDLETO
COX, SAMUEL*	TAL	061	EASTON D
COX, SARAH	SOM	365	BRINKLEY
COX, SARAH A.	SOM	550	TYASKIN
COX, SARAH E.	FRE	041	FREDERIC
COX, SELLMAN	BAL	038	2ND DIST
COX, SHELBY	BAL	471	14TH WAR
COX, SHELLY	BAL	370	13TH WAR
COX, SOPHIA	BAL	056	10TH WAR
COX, STEPHEN	SOM	377	BRINKLEY
COX, STEPHEN G.	BAL	308	7TH WARD
COX, STEPHEN S.	ALL	001	3RD E.D.
COX, SUSAN	WAS	211	1ST DIST
COX, SUSAN	CHA	259	MIDDLETO
COX, SUSANNA M.	CHA	263	MIDDLETO
COX, SUSANNAH	BAL	097	15TH WAR
COX, TABITHA	BAL	439	1ST DIST
COX, THOMAS	BAL	373	1ST DIST
COX, THOMAS	BAL	195	5TH DIST
COX, THOMAS	BAL	230	1ST DIST
COX, THOMAS	QUE	142	1ST E DI
COX, TRISTRAM	TAL	096	ST MICHA
COX, URIAH	BAL	451	1ST DIST
COX, W.	BAL	312	12TH WAR
COX, WALTER	CAL	042	3RD DIST
COX, WHITTINGTON	TAL	075	EASTON T
COX, WILLIAM	ST	295	2ND E DI
COX, WILLIAM	PRI	099	SPALDING
COX, WILLIAM	PRI	099	SPALDING
COX, WILLIAM	CAL	061	3RD DIST
COX, WILLIAM	CHA	236	HILLTOP
COX, WILLIAM	HAR	044	1ST DIST
COX, WILLIAM	CEC	055	1ST E DI
COX, WILLIAM	BAL	291	7TH WARD
COX, WILLIAM	BAL	265	7TH WARD
COX, WILLIAM	BAL	398	8TH WARD
COX, WILLIAM A.	TAL	098	ST MICHA
COX, WILLIAM B.	BAL	290	7TH WARD
COX, WILLIAM G.	FRE	415	8TH E DI
COX, WILLIAM H.	BAL	137	18TH WAR
COX, WILLIAM H.-MULATTO	FRE	010	FREDERIC
COX, WILLIAM J.	BAL	378	3RD WARD
COX, WILLIAM O.	WAS	052	2ND SUBD
COX, WILLIAM W.	CHA	263	MIDDLETO
COX, YOST	WAS	211	1ST DIST
COX, ZENIS	FRE	305	WOODSBOR
COXEN, CORNELIA	WAS	123	HAGERSTO
COXEN, IGNATIUS	MGM	429	CLARKSTR
COXEN, JAMES C.	WAS	125	HAGERSTO
COXEN, ROBERT	PRI	098	SPALDING
COXEN, SARAH	MGM	355	BERRYS D
COXEN, W.	PRI	102	SPALDING
COXIE, MORRIS	ALL	155	6TH E.D.
COXIN, THOMAS	PRI	089	SPALDING
COXON, JOHN	BAL	266	12TH WAR
COY, CHRISTIAN	WAS	275	RIDGEVIL
COY, CHRISTIAN	WAS	272	RIDGEVIL
COY, ELIZABETH A.	BAL	194	19TH WAR
COY, JACOB	WAS	234	1ST DIST
COY, PERE B.	KEN	216	2ND DIST
COY, WALLENTINE	WAS	267	1ST DIST
COY, WILLIAM	KEN	216	2ND DIST
COYCE, WILLIAM*	TAL	057	EASTON D
COYL, RANODLPH	ALL	215	CUMBERLA
COYLE, ANTHONY	BAL	058	15TH WAR
COYLE, BENJAMIN	BAL	067	1ST WARD
COYLE, BERNARD	BAL	231	19TH WAR
COYLE, BRIDGET	BAL	075	15TH WAR
COYLE, CHARLES	BAL	040	18TH WAR
COYLE, DANIEL	BAL	198	11TH WAR
COYLE, EDWARD	WAS	240	CAVETOWN
COYLE, EDWARD	WAS	238	CAVETOWN
COYLE, H.	BAL	295	1ST DIST
COYLE, JAMES	BAL	295	1ST DIST
COYLE, JOHN	BAL	176	11TH WAR
COYLE, JOHN	WAS	238	CAVETOWN
COYLE, JOHN	BAL	286	17TH WAR
COYLE, MARY	BAL	022	18TH WAR
COYLE, MARY	WAS	249	1ST DIST
COYLE, MARY	WAS	285	1ST DIST
COYLE, MARY	BAL	056	1ST WARD
COYLE, NANCY	BAL	385	13TH WAR
COYLE, PETER	BAL	354	13TH WAR
COYLE, TERENCE P.	BAL	094	10TH WAR
COYNE, EDWARD	BAL	461	1ST DIST
COYNEA, ROSINA	BAL	175	11TH WAR
COYSTER, JOHN J.	WAS	281	LEITERSB
COZERS, J.H.	BAL	139	1ST WARD
COZINE, MARY A.	BAL	168	19TH WAR
COZY, JOHN	PRI	109	PISCATAW
CRAB, DANIEL	ANN	429	HOWARD D
CRABB, CATHARINE	FRE	238	NEW MARK
CRABB, R.J.	ANN	282	ANNAPOLI
CRABBIN, BENJAMIN	BAL	288	17TH WAR
CRABBS, ANN F.	FRE	203	5TH E DI
CRABBS, CHARLES E.	CAR	323	1ST DIST
CRABBS, FRANKLIN	FRE	177	5TH E DI
CRABBS, FREDERIC	CAR	268	WESTMINS
CRABBS, FREDERICK	CAR	322	1ST DIST
CRABBS, FREDERICK	FRE	177	5TH E DI
CRABBS, FREDERICK W.	FRE	164	EMMITTSB
CRABBS, GEORGE	CAR	322	1ST DIST
CRABBS, JOHN	FRE	109	CREAGERS
CRABBS, JOSHUA	FRE	105	CREAGERS
CRABBS, LOUISA	CAR	278	7TH DIST
CRABBS, MICHAEL	CAR	336	6TH DIST
CRABBS, NATHAN	CAR	364	9TH DIST
CRABBS, SARAH	CAR	379	2ND DIST
CRABBS, WILLIAM	CAR	363	9TH DIST
CRABREE, ELIAS	ALL	178	7TH E.D.
CRABSLER, SUSAN	CAR	241	TANEYTOW
CRABSTER, GUSTAVUS W.	CAR	323	1ST DIST
CRABSTER, JOHN	CAR	241	TANEYTOW
CRABTREE, ABEL	ALL	175	7TH E.D.
CRABTREE, ANN	ALL	175	7TH E.D.
CRABTREE, BENJAMIN	ALL	176	7TH E.D.
CRABTREE, DANIEL	ALL	178	7TH E.D.
CRABTREE, GEORGE H.	ALL	175	7TH E.D.
CRABTREE, HANNAH	ALL	175	7TH E.D.
CRABTREE, JAMES	ALL	172	7TH E.D.
CRABTREE, LEWIS	ALL	175	7TH E.D.
CRABTREE, LEWIS	ALL	175	7TH E.D.
CRABTREE, LUCY	ALL	172	7TH E.D.
CRABTREE, MINA	ALL	175	7TH E.D.
CRABTREE, REZIR	ALL	178	7TH E.D.
CRABTREE, WILLIAM	ALL	174	7TH E.D.
CRACK, CHARLOTTE	PRI	093	MARLBROU
CRACK, LOUISIANA	PRI	093	MARLBROU
CRACKLIN, ELIZABETH	CAL	056	3RD DIST
CRACKLINE, WILLIAM	CAR	138	NO TWP L
CRADOCK, THOMAS	KEN	297	3RD DIST
CRAEMER, CHARLES	BAL	075	10TH WAR
CRAFONE, DANIEL *	BAL	171	2ND DIST
CRAFT, ANDREW	BAL	176	19TH WAR
CRAFT, CHRISTIAN	BAL	412	8TH WARD

Name	County	Page	District
CRAFT, CHRISTIAN	BAL	460	8TH WARD
CRAFT, CONRAD	BAL	080	1ST WARD
CRAFT, DANIEL P.	BAL	425	8TH WARD
CRAFT, ELIZABETH	TAL	044	EASTON D
CRAFT, ELIZABETH	TAL	050	EASTON T
CRAFT, FRED	BAL	240	20TH WAR
CRAFT, GEORGE	BAL	225	17TH WAR
CRAFT, GEORGE	BAL	187	11TH WAR
CRAFT, JACOB	BAL	171	6TH WARD
CRAFT, JOHN	BAL	410	14TH WAR
CRAFT, JOSEPH	BAL	270	2ND WARD
CRAFT, LEMUEL	TAL	049	EASTON T
CRAFT, LEVI	DOR	429	1ST DIST
CRAFT, MARGARET	BAL	154	5TH WARD
CRAFT, MARY	ALL	090	5TH E.D.
CRAFT, MARY	DOR	309	1ST DIST
CRAFT, MARY A.	BAL	181	19TH WAR
CRAFT, NANCY	CAR	333	MANCHEST
CRAFT, REBECCA	DOR	301	1ST DIST
CRAFT, REUBIN	HAR	025	1ST DIST
CRAFT, RICHARD O.	BAL	402	8TH WARD
CRAFT, SIMON	BAL	284	2ND WARD
CRAFT, SIMON	BAL	190	2ND WARD
CRAFT, SOPHIA	BAL	095	18TH WAR
CRAFT, THERESA	BAL	270	2ND WARD
CRAFT, THOMAS	DOR	457	1ST DIST
CRAFT, WILLIAM GEORGE	BAL	073	10TH WAR
CRAFTON, CHRISTOPHER	BAL	127	1ST WARD
CRAG, SUSAN	CHA	219	ALLENS F
CRAGE, ANN E.	HAR	152	3RD DIST
CRAGE, ROBERT	BAL	458	1ST DIST
CRAGER, CHRISTIAN	BAL	202	2ND WARD
CRAGG, BENJAMIN	BAL	459	8TH WARD
CRAGG, HENRY	BAL	396	8TH WARD
CRAGG, JOHN	ALL	053	10TH E.D
CRAGG, JOHN	BAL	144	2ND DIST
CRAGG, WILLIAM	BAL	459	8TH WARD
CRAGGS, CAROLINE	BAL	416	3RD WARD
CRAGGS, FRANCIS	BAL	424	3RD WARD
CRAGGS, FRANCIS	BAL	195	2ND WARD
CRAGGS, JOSEPH	ANN	376	4TH DIST
CRAGGS, WILLIAM	BAL	189	19TH WAR
CRAGHTON, WILLIAM	BAL	053	1ST WARD
CRAHAM, THOMAS	BAL	243	1ST DIST
CRAHAN, PATRICK	BAL	448	1ST DIST
CRAIG, AMANDA	ALL	134	4TH E.D.
CRAIG, AMY	CEC	177	7TH E DI
CRAIG, ANN E.	DOR	377	1ST DIST
CRAIG, ANNA	CEC	079	NORTHEAS
CRAIG, BENJAMIN	CEC	039	CHESAPEA
CRAIG, BENJAMIN	CEC	021	ELKTON 3
CRAIG, BRIDGET	ALL	129	4TH E.D.
CRAIG, CATHARINE	WAS	154	HAGERSTO
CRAIG, D.	BAL	267	20TH WAR
CRAIG, DAVID	BAL	159	2ND DIST
CRAIG, E.	BAL	170	1ST WARD
CRAIG, E.	BAL	172	1ST WARD
CRAIG, E.	BAL	165	1ST WARD
CRAIG, EBENEZER	BAL	168	1ST WARD
CRAIG, EDWARD	ALL	129	4TH E.D.
CRAIG, ELEN A.	BAL	242	2ND WARD
CRAIG, ELIZABETH A.	BAL	444	14TH WAR
CRAIG, EMPSON	CEC	039	CHESAPEA
CRAIG, FRANCIS E.	CEC	039	CHESAPEA
CRAIG, HENRY	BAL	130	11TH WAR
CRAIG, HENRY	WAS	045	2ND SUBD
CRAIG, HORATIO E.	BAL	319	20TH WAR
CRAIG, HUGH M.	BAL	457	14TH WAR
CRAIG, IRA	WAS	154	2ND DIST
CRAIG, J.	BAL	155	1ST WARD
CRAIG, JACOB	WAS	155	2ND DIST
CRAIG, JAMES	ANN	330	2ND DIST
CRAIG, JAMES	BAL	100	2ND DIST
CRAIG, JAMES	CEC	078	NORTHEAS
CRAIG, JAMES L.	CEC	040	CHESAPEA
CRAIG, JOHN	BAL	003	EASTERN
CRAIG, JOHN	ANN	331	2ND DIST
CRAIG, JOHN	BAL	097	5TH WARD
CRAIG, JOHN	BAL	283	12TH WAR
CRAIG, JOHN A.	BAL	062	10TH WAR
CRAIG, JOHN H.	CEC	084	CHARLEST
CRAIG, LEVIN	BAL	219	17TH WAR
CRAIG, LILLY	BAL	090	18TH WAR
CRAIG, MARGARET	BAL	245	6TH WARD
CRAIG, MORELL	BAL	014	9TH WARD
CRAIG, NICHOLAS	CEC	038	CHESAPEA
CRAIG, REBECCA	BAL	336	13TH WAR
CRAIG, RICHARD	CEC	026	ELKTON 3
CRAIG, RICHARD	CEC	037	CHESAPEA
CRAIG, RICHARD	CEC	084	CHARLEST
CRAIG, ROBERT	BAL	013	9TH WARD
CRAIG, SAMUEL	ALL	134	4TH E.D.
CRAIG, SAMUEL	DOR	364	3RD DIVI
CRAIG, SAMUEL	WAS	044	2ND SUBD
CRAIG, SUSAN	BAL	219	17TH WAR
CRAIG, THOMAS	BAL	210	6TH WARD
CRAIG, TINEY	CEC	008	ELKTON 3
CRAIG, WILLIAM	BAL	023	4TH WARD
CRAIG, WILLIAM	CEC	185	7TH E DI
CRAIG, WILLIAM	BAL	202	2ND WARD
CRAIG, WILLIAM *	BAL	097	18TH WAR
CRAIG,ROBERT	BAL	115	1ST WARD
CRAIGER, ANDREW	BAL	285	17TH WAR
CRAIGER, BARNEY	BAL	285	17TH WAR
CRAIGGS, ELLEN	ALL	205	CUMBERLA
CRAIGS, SUSAN	BAL	111	5TH WARD
CRAIN, FREDERICK	KEN	289	3RD DIST
CRAIN, JOSEPH	KEN	293	3RD DIST
CRAIN, PETER M.	CHA	221	ALLENS F
CRAIN, THOMAS	KEN	293	3RD DIST
CRAIN, THOMAS H.	KEN	293	3RD DIST
CRAIN, WILLIAM B.	KEN	310	3RD DIST
CRAINER, JOHN	BAL	303	17TH WAR
CRAINER, MARIA	QUE	124	1ST E DI
CRAITER, WILLIAM	BAL	297	12TH WAR
CRAITON, WILLIAM	BAL	123	5TH WARD
CRAKE, EMILY	SOM	355	BRINKLEY
CRAKE, WILLIAM	SOM	355	BRINKLEY
CRALBE, WILLIAM	ANN	433	HOWARD D
CRALEY, SAMUEL	WAS	206	1ST DIST
CRALL, ERNIST	ALL	217	CUMBERLA
CRALY, THOMAS	HAR	151	3RD DIST
CRAM, CHARLES-MULATTO	FRE	246	NEW MARK
CRAM, HETTY	FRE	265	NEW MARK
CRAMAR, CASPER	BAL	201	2ND WARD
CRAMER, ABSALOM	FRE	393	PETERSVI
CRAMER, AMOS	FRE	093	FREDERIC
CRAMER, ANN	FRE	327	MIDDLETO
CRAMER, ANN C.	FRE	325	MIDDLETO
CRAMER, AUGUSTUS	FRE	049	FREDERIC
CRAMER, BARBARA	FRE	310	WOODSBOR
CRAMER, CATHARINE	FRE	397	PETERSVI
CRAMER, CORNELIUS	FRE	307	WOODSBOR
CRAMER, DANIEL	WAS	217	1ST DIST
CRAMER, DANIEL	WAS	160	HAGERSTO
CRAMER, DAVID	WAS	217	1ST DIST
CRAMER, DAVID	WAS	042	2ND SUBD
CRAMER, EDON	FRE	304	WOODSBOR
CRAMER, ELI	FRE	106	CREAGERS
CRAMER, ELIZABETH	BAL	104	15TH WAR
CRAMER, EPHRAIM	FRE	404	JEFFERSO
CRAMER, EVE C.	FRE	140	CREAGERS
CRAMER, EZRA	FRE	284	WOODSBOR
CRAMER, FREDERICK	FRE	408	JEFFERSO
CRAMER, FREDERICK	BAL	271	17TH WAR
CRAMER, GEORGE	FRE	305	WOODSBOR
CRAMER, GEORGE	BAL	202	19TH WAR
CRAMER, GEORGE	WAS	254	1ST DIST
CRAMER, HENERETTA M.	FRE	106	CREAGERS
CRAMER, J. H.	FRE	297	WOODSBOR
CRAMER, JACOB	FRE	299	WOODSBOR
CRAMER, JESSE R.	CAR	392	2ND DIST
CRAMER, JOHN	FRE	308	WOODSBOR
CRAMER, JOHN	BAL	466	14TH WAR
CRAMER, JOHN	WAS	155	HAGERSTO
CRAMER, JOHN	ALL	052	10TH E.D
CRAMER, JOHN D.	FRE	309	WOODSBOR
CRAMER, JONATHAN H.	WAS	128	HAGERSTO
CRAMER, JOSEPH	FRE	298	WOODSBOR
CRAMER, JOSEPH	ALL	056	10TH E.D
CRAMER, LEWIS	BAL	220	17TH WAR
CRAMER, MARGARET	FRE	048	FREDERIC
CRAMER, MARY M.	FRE	106	CREAGERS
CRAMER, MOSES	FRE	106	CREAGERS
CRAMER, NATHAN J.	BAL	365	8TH WARD
CRAMER, NOAH	FRE	310	WOODSBOR
CRAMER, OLIVER	FRE	393	PETERSVI
CRAMER, PETER	FRE	301	WOODSBOR
CRAMER, PHILIP H.	FRE	061	FREDERIC
CRAMER, PHILLIP	FRE	295	WOODSBOR
CRAMER, SAMUEL	FRE	294	WOODSBOR
CRAMER, SAMUEL	QUE	132	1ST E DI
CRAMER, SAMUEL	WAS	034	2ND SUBD
CRAMER, SAMUEL H.	FRE	210	BUCKEYST
CRAMER, SARAH	FRE	393	PETERSVI
CRAMER, SOPHIA	BAL	220	17TH WAR
CRAMER, SUSANNA	WAS	217	1ST DIST
CRAMER, WILLIAM	WAS	155	HAGERSTO
CRAMLET, THOMAS	BAL	350	1ST DIST
CRAMMER, ENOTEN	BAL	097	1ST WARD
CRAMMER, FREDERICK	BAL	288	1ST DIST
CRAMMER, JACOB	BAL	438	1ST DIST
CRAMMER, JOSEPH	BAL	219	17TH WAR
CRAMPHIEN, AIRY	PRI	007	BLADENSB
CRAMPTON, ANN	FRE	379	PETERSVI
CRAMPTON, ELIE	WAS	084	2ND SUBD
CRAMPTON, ELIZABETH	WAS	201	1ST DIST
CRAMPTON, ELIZABETH	FRE	401	JEFFERSO
CRAMPTON, HARMON	FRE	401	JEFFERSO
CRAMPTON, JESSE	FRE	378	PETERSVI
CRAMPTON, JOHN	WAS	084	2ND SUBD
CRAMPTON, JOSIAH	WAS	061	2ND SUBD
CRAMPTON, O.S.	ALL	254	CUMBERLA
CRAMPTON, THOMAS	FRE	379	PETERSVI
CRAMPTON, THOMAS H.	WAS	084	2ND SUBD
CRANCK, MARY	BAL	099	1ST WARD
CRANDALL, JOSEPH	ANN	309	1ST DIST
CRANDALL, ROBERT	ANN	308	1ST DIST
CRANDALL, SARAH	BAL	093	10TH WAR
CRANDALL, SUSAN	ANN	315	1ST DIST
CRANDALL, WILLIAM	MGM	358	BERRYS D
CRANDELL, CLINTON	CEC	151	PORT DUP
CRANDELL, FRANK	ANN	409	8TH DIST
CRANDELL, JAMES F.	ANN	408	8TH DIST
CRANDELL, JOHN	ANN	409	8TH DIST
CRANDELL, JOHN F.	ANN	411	8TH DIST
CRANDELL, MARIA SR.	CEC	151	PORT DUP
CRANDELL, RICHARD	ANN	410	8TH DIST
CRANDLE, JAMES	PRI	092	MARLBROU
CRANDLE, JAMES A.	MGM	424	MEDLEY 3
CRANDLE, JOHN	ANN	407	8TH DIST
CRANDLE, JOHN	ANN	407	8TH DIST
CRANDLE, PRISCILLA	PRI	082	QUEEN AN
CRANDLE, THOMAS	ANN	407	8TH DIST
CRANDLE, THOMAS	ANN	323	2ND DIST
CRANDLEMINE, HENRY	ALL	133	4TH E.D.
CRANDOLL, F. M.	BAL	332	1ST DIST
CRANE, A. D.	BAL	475	14TH WAR
CRANE, ANDREW F.	BAL	419	14TH WAR
CRANE, ANN	CHA	219	ALLENS F
CRANE, ANNA	BAL	429	1ST DIST
CRANE, BENJAMIN	BAL	266	12TH WAR
CRANE, CATHARINE	BAL	339	13TH WAR
CRANE, CHARLES	BAL	015	9TH WARD
CRANE, DAVID H.	QUE	164	2ND E DI
CRANE, E.	BAL	146	5TH WARD
CRANE, EDWARD H.	CAL	032	2ND DIST
CRANE, ELLEN	BAL	004	9TH WARD
CRANE, GEORGE H.	BAL	349	3RD WARD
CRANE, GRACE	ST	311	1ST E DI
CRANE, HARRIET	FRE	114	CREAGERS
CRANE, HENRY	ALL	052	10TH E.D
CRANE, JAME SP.	ST	303	2ND E DI
CRANE, JHAMES E.	ST	298	2ND E DI
CRANE, JOHN	BAL	429	1ST DIST
CRANE, JOHN A.	ST	309	1ST E DI
CRANE, JONATHAN	QUE	178	2ND E DI
CRANE, JULIA	ST	311	1ST E DI
CRANE, MARY	BAL	035	9TH WARD
CRANE, MARY	BAL	329	13TH WAR
CRANE, MARY	CAL	051	3RD DIST
CRANE, MARY	CHA	218	ALLENS F
CRANE, MARY A.	ST	305	2ND E DI
CRANE, MICHAEL	ALL	141	6TH E.D.
CRANE, MINERVA-BLACK	FRE	242	NEW MARK
CRANE, NANNIE	PRI	056	AQUASCO
CRANE, PHILIP M.	BAL	237	6TH WARD
CRANE, REBECCA	PRI	092	MARLBROU
CRANE, ROBERT	ST	304	2ND E DI
CRANE, SARAH A.	ST	290	2ND E DI
CRANE, STEPHEN S.	QUE	156	2ND E DI
CRANE, THOMA	BAL	381	13TH WAR
CRANE, THOMAS	BAL	291	17TH WAR
CRANE, THOMAS	BAL	331	7TH WARD
CRANE, TIMOTHY	CAR	192	4TH DIST
CRANE, WILLIAM	BAL	095	10TH WAR
CRANEBLITE, FRANCIS	BAL	110	1ST WARD
CRANEN, NANTZY	BAL	001	4TH WARD
CRANER, ANTONY	BAL	265	7TH WARD
CRANER, DORATHA	BAL	089	1ST WARD
CRANER, JULIUS	BAL	268	2ND WARD
CRANER, MATTANE	CAR	179	8TH DIST
CRANER, SOLOMON D.	CAR	107	NO TWP L
CRANER, VALENTINE	BAL	089	1ST WARD
CRANESBECK, HENRY	BAL	200	17TH WAR
CRANEY, THOMAS	BAL	355	13TH WAR
CRANFAD, SAMUEL	FRE	267	NEW MARK
CRANFORD, GEORGE R.	CAL	022	2ND DIST
CRANFORD, JOHN	CAL	055	3RD DIST
CRANFORD, SAMUEL	CAL	021	2ND DIST
CRANGLE, JAMES E.	BAL	120	18TH WAR
CRANGLE, JOHN	BAL	132	16TH WAR
CRANK, SUSAN	BAL	186	2ND WARD
CRANLETO, LOUISA	BAL	271	2ND WARD
CRANLETO, STEPHEN *	BAL	271	2ND WARD
CRANOR, MARIA	QUE	175	2ND E DI
CRANPTON, JOHN	WAS	059	2ND SUBD
CRANPTON, SAPPINGTON, W.	HAR	192	3RD DIST
CRANSE, GEORGE	BAL	146	1ST WARD
CRANSMAN, FRANCES	BAL	050	1ST WARD
CRANTSON, MARY	HAR	046	1ST DIST
CRANWELL, CHARLES	WAS	125	HAGERSTO
CRANY, WILLIAM	BAL	190	5TH DIST
CRAP, T.	BAL	130	1ST WARD
CRAPETER, BASIL	ANN	498	HOWARD D
CRAPIN, SAMUEL	BAL	267	7TH WARD
CRAPPELTON, LITLONTAR	BAL	119	11TH WAR
CRAPPLE, WILLIAM H.	CAR	330	MANCHEST
CRAPSTER, ABRAHAM	FRE	177	5TH E DI
CRAPSTER, ELIZABETH H.	ANN	490	HOWARD D
CRAPSTER, JOHN G.	ANN	490	HOWARD D
CRAPSTER, WILLIAM T.	ANN	511	HOWARD D
CRAPTER, MILTON	BAL	173	2ND DIST
CRARES, ANDREW	BAL	059	1ST WARD
CRAROFT, MARGARET	BAL	330	1ST DIST
CRASER, ANN M. *	FRE	129	CREAGERS
CRASER, ELIZABETH	FRE	137	CREAGERS
CRASER, JOHN	FRE	120	CREAGERS
CRASER, PETER	FRE	090	FREDERIC
CRASFORD, WILLIAM	ALL	138	6TH E.D.
CRASGREY, FRANCIS	HAR	052	1ST DIST
CRASH, HENRY	BAL	003	4TH WARD
CRASMAS, THEADORE	CEC	034	CHESAPEA
CRASSH, JONATHAN	BAL	378	1ST DIST
CRASWELL, ELIZABETH	SOM	371	BRINKLEY
CRASWELL, JAMES	SOM	367	BRINKLEY
CRASWELL, SEVERN*	SOM	356	BRINKLEY
CRASWELL, SEVERN*	SOM	386	BRINKLEY
CRASWELL, STOCKLEY*	SOM	386	BRINKLEY
CRATER, FREDERICK	BAL	197	17TH WAR
CRATER, JUSTINA	BAL	058	1ST WARD
CRATON, HENRY	BAL	416	8TH WARD
CRATON, MARY	FRE	115	CREAGERS
CRATON, NANCY	FRE	298	WOODSBOR
CRATZ, EMELY	BAL	323	12TH WAR
CRATZIER, LUDWIG	BAL	253	12TH WAR
CRAUCH, CHRISTOPHER	BAL	199	2ND WARD
CRAUGH, JOHN	BAL	002	1ST WARD
CRAUGH, JOHN	BAL	002	1ST WARD
CRAUMER, JACOB	CAR	255	3RD DIST
CRAUSO, SARAH A.	BAL	057	4TH WARD
CRAVEN, CATHERINE A.	PRI	007	BLADENSB
CRAVEN, CATHERINE A.	PRI	007	BLADENSB
CRAVEN, JAMES	BAL	395	3RD WARD
CRAVEN, JOHN	FRE	362	CATOCTIN
CRAVEN, LIST	ANN	293	ANNAPOLI
CRAVER, AARON	FRE	364	CATOCTIN
CRAVER, GEORGE W.	FRE	093	FREDERIC
CRAVER, IGNATIOUS	BAL	451	1ST DIST
CRAVER, JOHN	BAL	353	7TH WARD
CRAVER, JOHN S.	BAL	200	19TH WAR
CRAVER, JOSHUA	FRE	093	FREDERIC
CRAVER, PETER	FRE	145	10TH E D
CRAVER, WILLIAM	ANN	468	HOWARD D
CRAW, CATHARINE	BAL	315	1ST DIST
CRAWFORD, A.	BAL	136	1ST WARD
CRAWFORD, ACHSAH	CAR	194	4TH DIST
CRAWFORD, ALEX	BAL	183	11TH WAR
CRAWFORD, ALEXANDER	BAL	077	15TH WAR
CRAWFORD, ALFRED	BAL	024	4TH WARD
CRAWFORD, ANDREW	BAL	064	18TH WAR
CRAWFORD, ANDREW	BAL	056	15TH WAR
CRAWFORD, ANDREW	SOM	528	QUANTICO
CRAWFORD, ANN	TAL	056	EASTON D
CRAWFORD, ANN	CAR	396	2ND DIST
CRAWFORD, ANN	FRE	103	FREDERIC
CRAWFORD, ANN E.	BAL	043	4TH WARD
CRAWFORD, ARABELLA	ANN	473	HOWARD D
CRAWFORD, BETSEY	WAS	174	FUNKSTOW
CRAWFORD, BRATTON	CEC	135	5TH E DI
CRAWFORD, CANIFELD	BAL	075	18TH WAR
CRAWFORD, CAROLINE	BAL	121	16TH WAR
CRAWFORD, CHARLES	BAL	078	18TH WAR
CRAWFORD, CHARLES	CAR	324	1ST DIST
CRAWFORD, CHARLOTT	BAL	129	11TH WAR
CRAWFORD, CHARLOTTE	BAL	043	4TH WARD
CRAWFORD, CLARINDA F.	WAS	170	FUNKSTOW
CRAWFORD, DARKY	BAL	396	14TH WAR
CRAWFORD, DAVID	PRI	014	BLADENSB
CRAWFORD, DICKSON	BAL	164	11TH WAR
CRAWFORD, ELIZABETH	BAL	319	3RD WARD
CRAWFORD, ELIZABETH	PRI	014	BLADENSB
CRAWFORD, ELIZABETH	WAS	154	HAGERSTO
CRAWFORD, ELIZABETH	CAR	358	9TH DIST
CRAWFORD, ELIZABETH	CAR	277	7TH DIST
CRAWFORD, EVAN	CAR	372	9TH DIST
CRAWFORD, FRANCIS J.	CAR	372	9TH DIST
CRAWFORD, GEORGE	PRI	013	BLADENSB
CRAWFORD, GEORGE	PRI	091	MARLBROU
CRAWFORD, GEORGE	WAS	052	2ND SUBD
CRAWFORD, GEORGE	BAL	375	1ST DIST
CRAWFORD, GEORGE	BAL	224	1ST DIST
CRAWFORD, HAMILTON	MGM	339	CLARKSBU
CRAWFORD, HENRY	BAL	170	2ND DIST
CRAWFORD, HORATIO	ANN	491	HOWARD D
CRAWFORD, HORATIO N.	SOM	535	QUANTICO
CRAWFORD, HUGH	CEC	146	PORT DUP
CRAWFORD, ISABEL	BAL	370	8TH WARD
CRAWFORD, JACOB	BAL	169	16TH WAR
CRAWFORD, JACOB	WAS	288	1ST DIST
CRAWFORD, JAEMS	BAL	191	2ND WARD
CRAWFORD, JAMES	BAL	138	1ST WARD
CRAWFORD, JAMES	BAL	376	1ST DIST
CRAWFORD, JAMES	BAL	311	1ST DIST
CRAWFORD, JAMES	BAL	358	3RD WARD
CRAWFORD, JAMES	BAL	185	11TH WAR
CRAWFORD, JAMES	ANN	475	HOWARD D
CRAWFORD, JAMES	ALL	192	9TH E.D.
CRAWFORD, JAMES	PRI	012	BLADENSB
CRAWFORD, JAMES	PRI	015	BLADENSB

NAME	CO.	PAGE	DISTRICT
CRAWFORD, JAMES	CEC	155	PORT DUP
CRAWFORD, JAMES	MGM	354	BERRYS D
CRAWFORD, JAMES H.	FRE	229	BUCKEYST
CRAWFORD, JAMES S.	CEC	090	4TH E DI
CRAWFORD, JAMES SR.	CEC	135	6TH E DI
CRAWFORD, JAMES W.	BAL	300	7TH WARD
CRAWFORD, JANE	CAR	278	7TH DIST
CRAWFORD, JANE	CEC	024	ELKTON 3
CRAWFORD, JOHN	MGM	339	CLARKSBU
CRAWFORD, JOHN	BAL	280	2ND WARD
CRAWFORD, JOHN	BAL	002	1ST WARD
CRAWFORD, JOHN	DOR	467	1ST DIST
CRAWFORD, JOHN A.	BAL	027	1ST WARD
CRAWFORD, JOSEPH	BAL	189	19TH WAR
CRAWFORD, JOSHUA	MGM	324	CRACKLIN
CRAWFORD, JOSHUA	CAR	407	2ND DIST
CRAWFCRD, LEWIS	FRE	149	10TH E D
CRAWFORD, LEWIS	BAL	069	18TH WAR
CRAWFORD, LUCINDA	WAS	275	RIDGEVIL
CRAWFORD, MARGARET	FRE	149	10TH E D
CRAWFORD, MARGARET	CEC	042	CHESAPEA
CRAWFORD, MARGARET	BAL	352	7TH WARD
CRAWFORD, MARGARET A.	FRE	040	FREDERIC
CRAWFORD, MARIA	BAL	083	15TH WAR
CRAWFORD, MARTHA	BAL	311	7TH WARD
CRAWFORD, MARTHA J.	BAL	297	3RD WARD
CRAWFORD, MARY	BAL	004	15TH WAR
CRAWFORD, MARY	FRE	028	FREDERIC
CRAWFORD, NANCY	HAR	034	1ST DIST
CRAWFORD, OSBORN	MGM	354	BERRYS D
CRAWFORD, PATRICK	BAL	025	18TH WAR
CRAWFORD, PATTY	BAL	027	2ND DIST
CRAWFORD, PHILIP	BAL	149	11TH WAR
CRAWFORD, RACHAEL	BAL	152	11TH WAR
CRAWFORD, RICHARD	BAL	252	6TH WARD
CRAWFORD, RICHARD	BAL	098	15TH WAR
CRAWFORD, ROBERT	BAL	243	2ND WARD
CRAWFORD, ROBERT	BAL	121	1ST WARD
CRAWFORD, ROBERT	CAR	249	3RD DIST
CRAWFORD, ROBERT K.	BAL	205	6TH WARD
CRAWFORD, ROSSAN	WAS	162	HAGERSTO
CRAWFORD, SALLY	WAS	170	FUNKSTOW
CRAWFORD, SAMUEL	BAL	021	1ST WARD
CRAWFORD, SAMUEL C.	PRI	005	BLADENSB
CRAWFORD, SARAH ANN	BAL	120	5TH WARD
CRAWFORD, SARAH J.	PRI	014	BLADENSB
CRAWFORD, SUSAN	BAL	230	1ST DIST
CRAWFORD, TERESA	WAS	227	1ST DIST
CRAWFORD, THOMAS	BAL	045	1ST WARD
CRAWFORD, THOMAS	ANN	436	HOWARD D
CRAWFORD, TILGHMAN	ANN	297	1ST DIST
CRAWFORD, VIRGINAIA	FRE	066	FREDERIC
CRAWFORD, WILLIAM	BAL	234	20TH WAR
CRAWFORD, WILLIAM	DOR	381	1ST DIST
CRAWFORD, WILLIAM	BAL	138	18TH WAR
CRAWFORD, WILLIAM	BAL	067	4TH WARD
CRAWFORD, WILLIAM	BAL	358	3RD WARD
CRAWFORD, WILLIAM	BAL	308	3RD WARD
CRAWFORD, WILLIAM	BAL	372	1ST DIST
CRAWFORD, WILLIAM	BAL	408	1ST DIST
CRAWFORD, WILLIAM	BAL	098	15TH WAR
CRAWFORD, WILLIAM	BAL	180	16TH WAR
CRAWFORD, WILLIAM J.	BAL	214	11TH WAR
CRAWFORD, WILLIAM W.	DOR	467	1ST DIST
CRAWFORD, WILLIMA	ANN	469	HOWARD D
CRAWLEY, ELIZA-BLACK	ST	329	4TH E DI
CRAWLEY, JANE-BLACK	ST	319	4TH E DI
CRAWLEY, MARIA	BAL	353	7TH WARD
CRAWLEY, MARY	BAL	360	8TH WARD
CRAWLEY, MARY-BLACK	ST	316	4TH E DI
CRAWLEY, MERIT-MULATTO	ST	294	2ND E DI
CRAWLEY, WILLIAM	BAL	155	2ND DIST
CRAWLEY, WILLIAM-MULATTO	ST	307	1ST E DI
CRAWMER, JOHN	BAL	459	1ST DIST
CRAWMER, LEVI	FRE	436	8TH E DI
CRAWMER, MARYANN	FRE	436	8TH E DI
CRAWN, ANNA	BAL	285	1ST DIST
CRAWPHIN, MATILDA	PRI	036	VANSVILL
CRAY, CHARLES P.	TAL	051	EASTON D
CRAY, ISAAC B.	DOR	310	1ST DIST
CRAY, RICHARD	QUE	229	4TH E DI
CRAYCROFT, AARON	MGM	367	BERRYS D
CRAYCROFT, JOHN	MGM	367	BERRYS D
CRAYCROFT, MARGARET	ANN	444	HOWARD D
CRAYCROFT, PERRIE	PRI	048	AQUASCO
CRAYCROFT, THOMAS B.	PRI	049	AQUASCO
CRAYON, MARTIN	ALL	049	10TH E.D
CRAYTON, CHARLES	ALL	216	CUMBERLA
CRAYTON, CANIEL	BAL	093	15TH WAR
CRAYTON, SARAH	BAL	343	13TH WAR
CRAZEN, EDWARD	BAL	087	18TH WAR
CRAZIER, LEWIS	BAL	086	1ST WARD
CREAGER, ABRAHAM	FRE	375	CATOCTIN
CREAGER, ADAM	FRE	307	WOODSBOR
CREAGER, AUGUSTUS	FRE	187	5TH E DI
CREAGER, BARBARY	WAS	161	HAGERSTO
CREAGER, CATHARINE	WAS	241	CAVETOWN
CREAGER, CATHERINE	FRE	027	FREDERIC
CREAGER, CANIEL	FRE	299	WOODSBOR
CREAGER, CANIEL	WAS	158	HAGERSTO
CREAGER, CAVID	WAS	272	RIDGEVIL
CREAGER, CAVID	WAS	291	1ST DIST
CREAGER, ELIZABETH	FRE	433	8TH E DI
CREAGER, EPHRAIM	FRE	299	WOODSBOR
CREAGER, GEORGE W.	FRE	109	CREAGERS
CREAGER, HENRY	WAS	143	HAGERSTO
CREAGER, HENRY	WAS	135	HAGERSTO
CREAGER, HERNY	FRE	086	FREDERIC
CREAGER, JAMES	FRE	125	CREAGERS
CREAGER, JOHN	FRE	126	CREAGERS
CREAGER, JOHN	WAS	290	1ST DIST
CREAGER, JOHN	WAS	251	1ST DIST
CREAGER, JOHNW.	FRE	088	FREDERIC
CREAGER, JONATHAN P.	CAR	272	WESTMINS
CREAGER, JOSEPH	BAL	291	20TH WAR
CREAGER, JOSEPH	BAL	290	20TH WAR
CREAGER, JOSEPH	BAL	184	19TH WAR
CREAGER, JOSEPH	CAR	306	1ST DIST
CREAGER, JOSEPH	WAS	300	1ST DIST
CREAGER, LUCINDA	WAS	125	HAGERSTO
CREAGER, MARY	FRE	315	MIDDLETO
CREAGER, MARY A.	FRE	116	CREAGERS
CREAGER, SAMUEL	WAS	241	CAVETOWN
CREAGER, SOLOMON	FRE	149	10TH E D
CREAGER, SUSAN	FRE	134	CREAGERS
CREAGER, WILLIAM	FRE	130	CREAGERS
CREAGER, WILLIAM H.	FRE	303	WOODSBOR
CREAGH, ELIZABETH	BAL	066	4TH WARD
CREAGH, GEORGE W.	BAL	040	1ST WARD
CREAGH, JOHN	BAL	316	20TH WAR
CREAGH, MICHAEL	BAL	372	3RD WARD
CREAGH, THOMAS	BAL	019	1ST WARD
CREAMBARN, REBECCA	BAL	115	5TH WARD
CREAMER, A.M.C.	ALL	238	CUMBERLA
CREAMER, ALEXANDER	BAL	254	6TH WARD
CREAMER, CAROLINE	BAL	303	20TH WAR
CREAMER, CHRISTIANA	BAL	227	6TH WARD
CREAMER, DAVID	BAL	388	8TH WARD
CREAMER, DAVID	CAR	360	9TH DIST
CREAMER, GEORGE	BAL	020	2ND DIST
CREAMER, HENRY	BAL	294	17TH WAR
CREAMER, JACOB	BAL	027	9TH WARD
CREAMER, JOHN	BAL	390	8TH WARD
CREAMER, JOHN	BAL	294	17TH WAR
CREAMER, JOHN	MGM	385	ROCKERLE
CREAMER, JOHN P.	CAR	303	1ST DIST
CREAMER, JOSEPHINE T.	BAL	218	6TH WARD
CREAMER, JOSHUA	BAL	115	5TH WARD
CREAMER, JOSHUA	BAL	210	17TH WAR
CREAMER, LOUISA	HAR	092	2ND DIST
CREAMER, MARY	BAL	161	6TH WARD
CREAMER, NICHOLAS	BAL	248	20TH WAR
CREAMER, PETER	MGM	379	ROCKERLE
CREAMER, SARAH	BAL	115	5TH WARD
CREAMER, THOMAS	BAL	182	2ND WARD
CREANEY, MARGARET	BAL	281	12TH WAR
CREARNE, JACOB	HAR	063	1ST DIST
CREARY, HENRY	BAL	018	9TH WARD
CREARY, WILLIAM	WAS	299	1ST DIST
CREASAMER, CATHARINE	CAR	324	1ST DIST
CREATE, EDWARD	BAL	268	2ND WARD
CREATER, GEORGE	BAL	005	9TH WARD
CREATIN, ALEXIUS	FRE	185	5TH E DI
CREATIN, JAMES	FRE	184	5TH E DI
CREATIN, JAMES JR.	FRE	181	5TH E DI
CREATIN, JOHN	FRE	184	5TH E DI
CREATIN, MARCELLUS	FRE	159	EMMITTSB
CREAZER, JACOB	WAS	264	1ST DIST
CREBBLE, DOWETY	BAL	192	2ND WARD
CREBS, ELLEN	WAS	210	1ST DIST
CRECK, GEORGE	ALL	183	8TH E.D.
CREDER, MARIA	BAL	447	14TH WAR
CREDERICK, MARY	CEC	066	1ST E DI
CREDICK, JOHN	CEC	065	1ST E DI
CREDICK, JOSEPH	CEC	056	1ST E DI
CREDICK, THOMAS	BAL	249	1ST DIST
CREDICK, WILLIAM	CEC	056	1ST E DI
CREDLY, MARY E. M. *	ANN	304	1ST DIST
CREED, PATRICK	BAL	300	17TH WAR
CREEDY, MARY E. M. *	ANN	304	1ST DIST
CREEGER, WILLIAM	FRE	115	CREAGERS
CREEK, CHARLES	ANN	304	1ST DIST
CREEK, JACOB	ALL	183	8TH E.D.
CREEK, JOHN WILLIAM	BAL	388	13TH WAR
CREEK, MARGARET	WAS	232	1ST DIST
CREEK, MARY	WAS	241	CAVETOWN
CREEK, MARY J. H.	BAL	116	15TH WAR
CREEK, PHILIP	BAL	412	14TH WAR
CREEK, POMPEY	ANN	395	8TH DIST
CREENY, WILLIAM R.	BAL	323	12TH WAR
CREEP, JACOB	ALL	041	2ND E.D.
CREERY, BERNARD	BAL	233	1ST DIST
CREERY, CATHERINE	BAL	042	4TH WARD
CREG, JAMES	DOR	366	3RD DIVI
CREG, LEVEN	DOR	365	3RD DIVI
CREG, SAMUEL	DOR	366	3RD DIVI
CREGAN, MICHAEL	ALL	156	6TH E.D.
CREGER, JOSHUA	WAS	161	2ND DIST
CREGER, WILLIAM	WAS	162	2ND DIST
CREGER, WILLIAM	BAL	259	1ST DIST
CREGG, BENJAMIN	ANN	397	8TH DIST
CREGG, NANCY	ANN	397	8TH DIST
CREHEE, BRIDGET *	BAL	065	15TH WAR
CREHORE, BENJAMIN F.	BAL	057	10TH WAR
CREIG, HENERY	DOR	365	3RD DIVI
CREIGH, ADAM	PRI	039	VANSVILL
CREIGH, JOSEPH	PRI	039	VANSVILL
CREIGHAN, MARY	BAL	183	11TH WAR
CREIGHTON, ANN	DOR	356	3RD DIVI
CREIGHTON, AUGUSTUS	BAL	054	15TH WAR
CREIGHTON, CATHARINE	DOR	348	3RD DIVI
CREIGHTON, CHARLES	BAL	213	17TH WAR
CREIGHTON, CHARLES N.	DOR	377	1ST DIST
CREIGHTCN, DOROTHY	BAL	183	6TH WARD
CREIGHTCN, DRAPER	DOR	358	3RD DIVI
CREIGHTON, DRAPER	DOR	357	3RD DIVI
CREIGHTCN, EASTER	DOR	345	3RD DIVI
CREIGHTON, ELMIRA	BAL	213	17TH WAR
CREIGHTCN, EMILY	BAL	462	14TH WAR
CREIGHTCN, HENERY	DOR	327	3RD DIVI
CREIGHTON, HENRY	BAL	273	17TH WAR
CREIGHTCN, JAMES	BAL	263	17TH WAR
CREIGHTON, JAMES A.	BAL	046	4TH WARD
CREIGHTCN, JANE	DOR	366	3RD DIVI
CREIGHTON, JOHN	DOR	387	1ST DIST
CREIGHTON, JOHN	DOR	328	3RD DIVI
CREIGHTON, LETTITIA	DOR	328	3RD DIVI
CREIGHTON, PERMELIA	DOR	328	3RD DIVI
CREIGHTCN, ROBERT	DOR	326	3RD DIVI
CREIGHTON, ROBERT	DOR	329	3RD DIVI
CREIGHTON, SAMUEL	BAL	249	17TH WAR
CREIGHTON, SARAH A.	BAL	342	3RD WARD
CREIGHTCN, THCMAS	DOR	347	3RD DIVI
CREIGHTON, THOMAS	DOR	329	3RD DIVI
CREIGHTCN, WILLIAM	BAL	242	17TH WAR
CREIGHTCN, WILLIAM	DOR	377	1ST DIST
CREIGHTON, WILLIAM	DOR	418	1ST DIST
CREIGHTCN, WILLIAM	BAL	029	4TH WARD
CREIGHTCN, CONRAD	BAL	010	1ST WARD
CREISMAN, PHLIP	BAL	204	19TH WAR
CREISNER, JACOB	BAL	083	1ST WARD
CREMENT, GEORGE	PRI	012	BLADENSB
CREMER, CATHARINE	BAL	222	19TH WAR
CREMER, PETER	ANN	376	4TH DIST
CREMER, SAMUEL	WAS	037	2ND SUBD
CREMIRE, AUGUST	BAL	375	3RD WARD
CRENDOFF, HENRY	CAR	222	5TH DIST
CREOGER, SOLOMON	FRE	303	WOODSBOR
CREQUE, JACOB	BAL	247	1ST DIST
CRERT, SABELLA	BAL	364	13TH WAR
CRESAP, CANIEL	ALL	138	6TH E.D.
CRESAP, CANIEL H.	ALL	163	6TH E.D.
CRESAP, ELIZABETH	ALL	154	6TH E.D.
CRESAP, ISABELLA	ALL	014	3RD E.D.
CRESAP, SUSAN	ALL	154	6TH E.D.
CRESAP, WILLIAM	ALL	124	4TH E.D.
CRESBY, JOSIAS	CAL	050	3RD DIST
CRESHAW, CLINTON	ALL	200	CUMBERLA
CRESO, JONAS J.	HAR	185	3RD DIST
CRESS, JOHN	ALL	251	CUMBERLA
CRESS, MARY	BAL	299	3RD WARD
CRESS, MICHEAL *	BAL	062	18TH WAR
CRESSAP, EMILY	ALL	207	CUMBERLA
CRESSNER, GEORGE	ALL	232	CUMBERLA
CRESSUP, E.L.M.	ALL	172	7TH E.D.
CRESTVERTINE, RICHARD *	BAL	163	2ND DIST
CRESUP, HANSON	ALL	148	6TH E.D.
CRESWELL, JEREMIAH	CEC	135	6TH E DI
CRESWELL, JOHN G.	CEC	154	PORT DUP
CRESWELL, JOSEPH	WAS	187	BOONSBOR
CRESWELL, MARTHA J.	CEC	176	7TH E DI
CRESWELL, MARY E.	WAS	290	1ST DIST
CRESWELL, REBECCA E.	CEC	147	PORT DUP
CRESWELL, WIRGINIA	BAL	371	13TH WAR
CRETA, CHARLES	BAL	309	12TH WAR
CRETON, MARY	FRE	029	FREDERIC
CREUSMAN, MARY	BAL	050	1ST WARD
CREVENSON, JACOB H.	HAR	109	2ND DIST
CREVISTON, GEORGE B.	HAR	177	3RD DIST
CREW—LL, WILLIAM *	KEN	237	2ND DIST
CREW, ALEXANDER	KEN	244	2ND DIST
CREW, ANDREW	BAL	422	8TH WARD
CREW, ANN	BAL	255	17TH WAR
CREW, ASBURY	BAL	428	14TH WAR
CREW, CHARLES	HAR	119	2ND DIST
CREW, CHARLES	HAR	038	1ST DIST
CREW, DELILA	BAL	186	16TH WAR
CREW, EDWARD	BAL	192	17TH WAR
CREW, FRANCIS	KEN	249	2ND DIST
CREW, HANSON	BAL	363	3RD WARD
CREW, JAMES	CEC	016	ELKTON 3
CREW, JAMES E.	KEN	249	2ND DIST
CREW, JOHN	HAR	119	2ND DIST
CREW, MARTHA A.	BAL	363	3RD WARD
CREW, MARY	BAL	252	20TH WAR
CREW, MARY M.	HAR	038	1ST DIST
CREW, RICHARD	BAL	093	15TH WAR
CREW, RICHARD	BAL	269	12TH WAR
CREW, THOMAS J.	HAR	037	1ST DIST
CREWS, BENJAMIN W.	BAL	132	1ST WARD
CREY, CHARLES	BAL	439	14TH WAR
CREY, FREDERICK	BAL	369	8TH WARD
CREY, FREDERICK	BAL	312	12TH WAR
CREY, HENRY	BAL	399	8TH WARD
CREY, LOUISA	BAL	086	10TH WAR
CREY, SUSAN	BAL	442	14TH WAR
CREYLE, JANE	BAL	266	12TH WAR
CRICARD, JAMES	BAL	026	18TH WAR
CRICE, HENRY	TAL	115	ST MICHA
CRICHARDT, DANIEL JR.	WAS	028	2ND SUBD
CRICHTON, MALCOM	BAL	263	1ST DIST
CRICK, FRANCIS	WAS	100	2ND DIST
CRICK, RICHARD	BAL	366	8TH WARD
CRICKEY, ANTHONY	BAL	240	20TH WAR
CRICWISE, THEADORE	CEC	040	CHESAPEA
CRIDER, EDWARD	BAL	455	14TH WAR
CRIDER, JOHN	WAS	283	1ST DIST
CRIDER, REBECCA	WAS	284	1ST DIST
CRIDLER, HARRIET P.	BAL	454	14TH WAR
CRIDLER, PETER	CAR	348	6TH DIST
CRIFIELD, SARAH E.	CEC	140	5TH E DI
CRIGG, JANE	BAL	256	12TH WAR
CRIGHTJON, ROBERT H.	DOR	328	3RD DIVI
CRIGUI, FERDINAND	BAL	130	16TH WAR
CRILLY, SAMUEL	WAS	025	2ND SUBD
CRIM, MARGARET *	BAL	298	20TH WAR
CRIM, TEMPERANCE	BAL	217	19TH WAR
CRIMENS, PATRICK	ANN	350	3RD DIST
CRIMMION, TIMOTHE *	BAL	041	18TH WAR
CRIMMONS, PATRICK	BAL	022	9TH WARD
CRIMP, EVELINA	BAL	057	1ST WARD
CRINCH, MARGARET E.	KEN	212	2ND DIST
CRINER, GEROGE	WAS	255	1ST DIST
CRINER, MICHAEL	WAS	275	RIDGEVIL
CRINER, SARAH*	BAL	078	4TH WARD
CRINER, VALLENTINE	WAS	275	RIDGEVIL
CRIP, CARTER	BAL	081	2ND DIST
CRIPPETTON, JOHN	BAL	120	11TH WAR
CRIPPIN, HENRIETTA	BAL	111	15TH WAR
CRIPPS, BENJAMIN	CEC	115	3RD E DI
CRIPPS, JOHN	BAL	120	1ST WARD
CRIPPS, JOHN	BAL	171	6TH WARD
CRIPPS, THOMAS	BAL	171	6TH WARD
CRIPS, GEORGE HENRY	BAL	311	1ST DIST
CRIPS, ISAAC	CEC	088	4TH E DI
CRIPS, WILLIAM B.	CEC	098	4TH E DI
CRISALL, JOHN	BAL	251	17TH WAR
CRISBALL, CHRISTIAN	BAL	086	1ST WARD
CRISE, BARBARA	CAR	241	TANEYTOW
CRISE, DANIEL	ALL	028	2ND E.D.
CRISE, DAVID G.	FRE	450	8TH E DI
CRISE, HENRY	FRE	292	WOODSBOR
CRISE, J. L.	BAL	284	20TH WAR
CRISE, JACOB	FRE	111	CREAGERS
CRISE, MARGARET	FRE	112	CREAGERS
CRISE, MARGARET	CAR	257	3RD DIST
CRISE, SAMUEL	FRE	292	WOODSBOR
CRISE, SUSAN	WAS	263	1ST DIST
CRISE, WILLIAM	FRE	111	CREAGERS
CRISEMAN, CATHARINE	ST	338	4TH E DI
CRISFRANCE, MARGARETTA	BAL	257	17TH WAR
CRISHMER, JOSEPH	BAL	388	8TH WARD
CRISLEY, ANN E.	BAL	316	20TH WAR
CRISON, GERHARDT	BAL	105	1ST WARD
CRISP, CHARLES F.	BAL	032	1ST WARD
CRISP, ELIJAH	BAL	271	12TH WAR
CRISP, JACOB	BAL	357	13TH WAR
CRISP, JOSEPH	BAL	032	1ST WARD
CRISP, MARY	QUE	167	2ND E DI
CRISP, MARY A.	ANN	336	3RD DIST
CRISP, MARY P.	SOM	549	TYASKIN
CRISP, SHADRACK	BAL	200	2ND WARD
CRISPIN, PETER	BAL	026	15TH WAR
CRISPINS, MARGARET	BAL	010	15TH WAR
CRISS, JAMES E.	BAL	473	14TH WAR
CRISS, JOHN	BAL	185	2ND WARD
CRISS, LOUISA	BAL	224	19TH WAR
CRISS, MICHEAL *	BAL	062	18TH WAR
CRISS, PETER	BAL	285	2ND WARD
CRISSMAN, ISAAC	BAL	141	1ST WARD
CRISSWELL, JEMIMA	BAL	178	2ND DIST
CRIST, DANIEL	FRE	383	PETERSVI
CRIST, ELIZABETH	WAS	155	HAGERSTO
CRIST, J.P.	WAS	131	HAGERSTO
CRIST, JACOB	FRE	211	BUCKEYST
CRIST, JACOB	BAL	247	2ND WARD
CRIST, JOSEPH	FRE	234	BUCKEYST
CRIST, MAGDALINE	BAL	398	8TH WARD
CRIST, SARAH	FRE	215	BUCKEYST
CRIST, SOPHIA	FRE	317	MIDDLETO

Name	County	Page	District
CRIST, WILLIAM	BAL	203	6TH WARD
CRISTA, LYNCA	HAR	163	3RD DIST
CRISTEY, JOSEPH	HAR	146	3RD DIST
CRISTFIELD, ARTHUR	DOR	378	1ST DIST
CRISTIAN, CHARLES	TAL	016	EASTON D
CRISTIAN, JOHN	TAL	030	EASTON D
CRISTIAN, JOHN	TAL	010	EASTON D
CRISTIAN, MARY	TAL	010	EASTON D
CRISTIAN, SALLA A.*	TAL	018	EASTON D
CRISTIAN, SAMUEL W.	BAL	235	17TH WAR
CRISTIE, ELIZABETH	BAL	373	3RD WARD
CRISTIE, HAZZARD	BAL	368	3RD WARD
CRISTIE, ISAAC	BAL	309	3RD WARD
CRISTIN, PETER	CAR	065	NO TWP L
CRISTMAN, JEMIMA	CAR	171	8TH DIST
CRISTMAN, ROSETTA	BAL	246	17TH WAR
CRISTMAN, WILLIAM	CAR	192	4TH DIST
CRISTMOND, JOHN	CHA	269	ALLENS F
CRISTOPHER, CDWARD*	DOR	415	1ST DIST
CRISTOPHER, JAMES	DOR	416	1ST DIST
CRISTOPHER, JAMES C.	BAL	123	1ST WARD
CRISTOPHER, JAMS	BAL	123	1ST WARD
CRISTOPHER, JOHN	DOR	414	1ST DIST
CRISTOPHER, RHODA	DOR	372	3RD DIVI
CRISTOPHER, ROSE	DOR	458	1ST DIST
CRISTOPHER, ROSE A.	DOR	365	3RD DIVI
CRISTOPHER, SAMUEL*	DOR	414	1ST DIST
CRISTOPHER, THOMAS	DOR	431	1ST DIST
CRISTOPHER, WILLIAM	DOR	454	1ST DIST
CRISTOPHER, WILLIAM*	DOR	414	1ST DIST
CRISTOPHIN, SAMUEL*	DOR	414	1ST DIST
CRISTY, ALBERT	HAR	015	1ST DIST
CRISTY, BEN	BAL	223	12TH WAR
CRISTY, GEORGE	BAL	300	3RD WARD
CRISTY, HARRIETT	HAR	187	3RD DIST
CRISTY, JAMES	HAR	184	3RD DIST
CRISTY, JAMES	HAR	183	3RD DIST
CRISTY, JOHN	HAR	184	3RD DIST
CRISTY, JCHN	BAL	112	18TH WAR
CRISTY, LOUIS	HAR	182	3RD DIST
CRISTY, MICHI	BAL	138	19TH WAR
CRISTY, PHILIS	HAR	029	1ST DIST
CRISTY, WILLIAM	HAR	187	3RD DIST
CRISWELL, ANN	HAR	098	2ND DIST
CRISWELL, CHARLES	HAR	097	2ND DIST
CRISWELL, ELIJAH	CAR	200	4TH DIST
CRISWELL, HANNAH	CAR	212	5TH DIST
CRISWELL, JAMES	CAR	211	5TH DIST
CRISWELL, JOHN	HAR	107	2ND DIST
CRISWELL, JOHN W.	CAR	209	5TH DIST
CRISWELL, JOHN W.	WAS	127	HAGERSTO
CRISWELL, NICHOLAS	ANN	500	HOWARD D
CRISWELL, SARHA	BAL	358	13TH WAR
CRISWELL, WILLIAM	HAR	097	2ND DIST
CRISWILL, JAMES	HAR	202	3RD DIST
CRITCHETT, MARY	SOM	492	SALISBUR
CRITFIELD, ROBERT	CEC	033	CHESAPEA
CRITZE, JOSEPH	FRE	188	5TH E DI
CRITZER, PETER	WAS	053	2ND SUBD
CRITZER, SAMUEL	WAS	053	2ND SUBD
CRIVESTON, GEORGE	HAR	180	3RD DIST
CRNISE, CHARLES	WAS	200	1ST DIST
CRNNAVALLY, ANTHONY*	BAL	031	4TH WARD
CROAIN, JOHN	BAL	133	1ST WARD
CROBLER, JACOB	BAL	043	2ND DIST
CROBSON, JOHN	HAR	206	3RD DIST
CROBSTER, JESSE A.	CAR	195	4TH DIST
CROBSTER, JOSEPHINE	CAR	196	4TH DIST
CROCK, DAVID	ALL	188	9TH E.D.
CROCK, RAGEN	ALL	193	9TH E.D.
CROCKER, EMANUEL	BAL	042	4TH WARD
CROCKER, JAMES	BAL	093	18TH WAR
CROCKER, JAMES A.	BAL	435	8TH WARD
CROCKER, JAMES J.	BAL	154	19TH WAR
CROCKER, JOHN	BAL	047	9TH WARD
CROCKER, ZACHARIAH	BAL	071	4TH WARD
CROCKERD, JOHN	BAL	191	19TH WAR
CROCKET, BENTON H.	DOR	376	1ST DIST
CROCKET, HUGH G.	CAR	220	5TH DIST
CROCKET, JAMES	CAR	310	1ST DIST
CROCKET, JAMES	WAS	157	2ND DIST
CROCKET, MARTHA-MULATTO	FRE	023	FREDERIC
CROCKET, VIRGINIA A.	DOR	376	1ST DIST
CROCKET, WILLIAM	DOR	446	1ST DIST
CROCKETT, ANN	BAL	129	5TH WARD
CROCKETT, CHARLES V.	SOM	549	TYASKIN
CROCKETT, CLOUD	CEC	177	7TH E DI
CROCKETT, CANIEL J.	SOM	419	PRINCESS
CROCKETT, HARIET	SOM	550	TYASKIN
CROCKETT, HENRY	MGM	321	CRACKLIN
CROCKETT, HESTER	SOM	515	BARREN C
CROCKETT, ISAIAH	WAS	156	2ND DIST
CROCKETT, JAMES	SOM	496	SALISBUR
CROCKETT, JENNY	SOM	547	TYASKIN
CROCKETT, JOHN	SOM	480	TRAPP DI
CROCKETT, JOHN	SOM	496	SALISBUR
CROCKETT, JOHN S.	SOM	514	BARREN C
CROCKETT, JOHN W.	SOM	449	DAMES QU
CROCKETT, JOSIAH	SOM	535	QUANTICO
CROCKETT, JOSIAH S.	SOM	425	PRINCESS
CROCKETT, JULIA	SOM	449	DAMES QU
CROCKETT, MARY	SOM	377	BRINKLEY
CROCKETT, N.	BAL	304	12TH WAR
CROCKETT, RACHAEL	SOM	455	DAMES QU
CROCKETT, ROBERT	SOM	441	DAMES QU
CROCKETT, SARAH D.	SOM	505	SALISBUR
CROCKETT, WALTER	BAL	304	12TH WAR
CROCKETT, WILLIAM	ANN	505	HOWARD D
CROCKETT, WILLIAM	SOM	505	SALISBUR
CROCKETT, WILLIAM	SOM	459	HANGARY
CROCKETT, WILLIAM	SOM	355	BRINKLEY
CROCKETT, WILLIAM B.	SOM	483	TRAPP DI
CROCKWELL, MARSHALL	BAL	269	17TH WAR
CROES, J.R.	WAS	021	2ND SUBD
CROFET, JACOB	WAS	124	2ND DIST
CROFFEUS, DANIEL	ALL	175	7TH E.D.
CROFFORD, THOMAS	BAL	454	1ST DIST
CROFFS, JEREMIAH	CAR	375	9TH DIST
CROFIT, SAMUEL*	DOR	446	1ST DIST
CROFT, CATHARINE	BAL	378	1ST DIST
CROFT, GEORGE	CAR	177	8TH DIST
CROFT, JOHN	BAL	175	2ND DIST
CROFT, MARTHA	CAR	177	8TH DIST
CROFT, MARTIN	BAL	444	1ST DIST
CROFT, MATILDA	CAR	178	8TH DIST
CROFT, SAMUEL*	DOR	446	1ST DIST
CROGAN, EEZEKIEL	TAL	008	EASTON D
CROGAN, MARGARET	BAL	336	7TH WARD
CROGAN, RACHEL	TAL	072	EASTON T
CROGAN, THOMAS	ALL	048	10TH E.D
CROGHAN, JOHN	BAL	028	9TH WARD
CROIN, GEORGE	MGM	380	ROCKER_E
CROIZER, MICHAEL	BAL	101	5TH WARD
CROIZER, WILLIAM	BAL	122	5TH WARD
CRCKER, ABRAHAM	BAL	435	8TH WARD
CROKER, DEBORAH	BAL	283	7TH WARD
CROLL, ELIZABETH	CAR	393	2ND DIST
CROLL, HENRY	CAR	393	2ND DIST
CROM, DANIEL	BAL	138	5TH WARD
CROM, SARAH	FRE	118	CREAGERS
CROM, SUSANNA	FRE	187	5TH E DI
CROM, WILLIAM	FRE	118	CREAGERS
CROMALL, RICHARD	BAL	149	11TH WAR
CROMAN, CHARLES	BAL	208	2ND WARD
CROMAULE, SHADRACK	DOR	408	1ST DIST
CROMBY, E.	FRE	200	5TH E DI
CRCMELL, JOHN	BAL	381	1ST DIST
CROMER, CHARLES	BAL	438	1ST DIST
CROMER, CHARLOTTE	BAL	212	6TH DIST
CROMER, ELEMENTINE	CAR	310	1ST DIST
CROMER, ELIZ	BAL	241	12TH WAR
CROMER, GEORGE	BAL	275	17TH WAR
CROMER, GEORGE	WAS	131	2ND DIST
CROMER, GEORGE W.	WAS	131	2ND DIST
CROMER, MARGARET	BAL	443	14TH WAR
CROMER, SOLOMAN *	BAL	295	20TH WAR
CROMER, SUSAN	BAL	124	18TH WAR
CROMER, THCMAS	BAL	266	20TH WAR
CROMER, THOMAS	BAL	266	20TH WAR
CROMER, WILLIAM	CEC	137	6TH E DI
CROMISE, ISAAC	FRE	308	WOODSBOR
CROMLEY, JAMES	BAL	298	12TH WAR
CROMLY, HENRY	FRE	121	CREAGERS
CROMMELL, B. F.	BAL	150	1ST WARD
CROMPTON, BRIDGET	BAL	443	14TH WAR
CRCMPTON, THOMAS	BAL	227	19TH WAR
CROMVELL, JOHN*	DOR	408	1ST DIST
CROMVELT, RICHARD	BAL	064	2ND DIST
CROMWELL, ABEL	DOR	421	1ST DIST
CRCMWELL, CAROLINE	BAL	091	5TH WARD
CROMWELL, CAROLINE R.	FRE	207	BUCKEYST
CROMWELL, CATHERIN M.	FRE	047	FREDERIC
CROMWELL, CEBELIA	BAL	408	14TH WAR
CROMWELL, CHARLES	ANN	354	3RD DIST
CROMWELL, DAVID	BAL	031	2ND DIST
CROMWELL, DEBCRAH	BAL	024	9TH WARD
CROMWELL, DORCAS	BAL	192	19TH WAR
CROMWELL, E. A.	ANN	342	3RD DIST
CROMWELL, ELEN	FRE	025	FREDERIC
CROMWELL, ELIZA	BAL	084	15TH WAR
CROMWELL, ELIZABETH	ANN	341	3RD DIST
CROMWELL, ELIZABETH	BAL	385	13TH WAR
CROMWELL, ELIZABETH	BAL	455	14TH WAR
CROMWELL, ELIZABETH-MULAT	FRE	038	FREDERIC
CROMWELL, ELLEN	BAL	368	1ST DIST
CRCMWELL, FANNY	BAL	274	1ST DIST
CROMWELL, FRANCIS	BAL	377	13TH WAR
CROMWELL, GABE	BAL	029	2ND DIST
CROMWELL, GARRETSON	BAL	096	15TH WAR
CROMWELL, GARRETSON	BAL	291	17TH WAR
CROMWELL, GEORGE	BAL	124	16TH WAR
CROMWELL, GEORGE	BAL	283	1ST DIST
CROMWELL, GEORGE H.	FRE	020	FREDERIC
CROMWELL, HARIET	BAL	029	2ND DIST
CROMWELL, HESTER A.	BAL	073	10TH WAR
CROMWELL, ISAAC	BAL	196	17TH WAR
CROMWELL, JACOB	ALL	220	CUMBERLA
CROMWELL, JACOB	BAL	314	1ST DIST
CROMWELL, JACCB	BAL	295	20TH WAR
CROMWELL, JACCB	WAS	154	HAGERSTO
CROMWELL, JACCB T.	BAL	192	19TH WAR
CRCMWELL, JAMES	ANN	342	3RD DIST
CROMWELL, JANE	BAL	057	10TH WAR
CROMWELL, JERRY	BAL	255	1ST DIST
CROMWELL, JESSE	CAR	283	7TH DIST
CROMWELL, JILES	ANN	341	3RD DIST
CROMWELL, JOE	ANN	338	3RD DIST
CROMWELL, JOHN	ANN	340	3RD DIST
CROMWELL, JOHN	ALL	228	CUMBERLA
CROMWELL, JOHN	BAL	147	16TH WAR
CROMWELL, JOHN	BAL	377	1ST DIST
CROMWELL, JOHN	BAL	243	6TH WARD
CROMWELL, JOHN	BAL	303	17TH WAR
CROMWELL, JOHN	FRE	106	CREAGERS
CROMWELL, JOHN F.	BAL	167	1ST WARD
CROMWELL, JOHN W.	BAL	193	17TH WAR
CROMWELL, JONAS-BLACK	FRE	209	BUCKEYST
CRCMWELL, JOSEPH	BAL	167	19TH WAR
CROMWELL, JOSEPH	BAL	282	12TH WAR
CROMWELL, JOSEPH W.	FRE	042	FREDERIC
CROMWELL, JOSHUA	BAL	393	3RD WARD
CROMWELL, LEINA	BAL	222	6TH WARD
CROMWELL, LOUISA	BAL	232	1ST DIST
CROMWELL, LOUIZA	BAL	112	5TH WARD
CRCMWELL, MARTHA	BAL	402	3RD WARD
CRCMWELL, MARTHA-BLACK	FRE	038	FREDERIC
CRCMWELL, MARY	BAL	416	3RD WARD
CRCMWELL, MARY	BAL	096	5TH WARD
CROMWELL, MARY	BAL	032	2ND DIST
CRCMWELL, MATILDA	FRE	014	FREDERIC
CRCMWELL, N.	BAL	225	19TH WAR
CROMWELL, NANCY	ALL	229	CUMBERLA
CROMWELL, MATHANIEL	BAL	228	1ST DIST
CRCMWELL, NICHOLAS	FRE	216	BUCKEYST
CROMWELL, NICHOLAS*	BAL	310	3RD WARD
CROMWELL, NIMROD	BAL	042	4TH WARD
CROMWELL, OLIVER	ANN	340	3RD DIST
CROMWELL, OLIVER	BAL	403	8TH WARD
CROMWELL, OLOVER	BAL	350	1ST DIST
CROMWELL, ORRA	FRE	305	WOODSBOR
CROMWELL, PHILCMON	FRE	306	WOODSBOR
CROMWELL, POLLY	ANN	369	4TH DIST
CROMWELL, RACHEL C.	BAL	333	3RD WARD
CROMWELL, RANDOLPH	ANN	342	3RD DIST
CROMWELL, RICHARD	ANN	336	3RD DIST
CROMWELL, RICHARD	BAL	274	12TH WAR
CROMWELL, RICHARD	FRE	208	BUCKEYST
CROMWELL, RICHARD	MGM	417	MEDLEY 3
CROMWELL, ROBERT	BAL	236	20TH WAR
CRCMWELL, SAIHRAH A.	BAL	289	3RD WARD
CROMWELL, SARAH	BAL	199	17TH WAR
CROMWELL, SARAH	BAL	108	15TH WAR
CROMWELL, SARAH	BAL	232	1ST DIST
CROMWELL, SARAH M.	BAL	422	3RD WARD
CROMWELL, THOMAS	BAL	422	3RD WARD
CROMWELL, THOMAS	FRE	309	WOODSBOR
CROMWELL, THOMAS	BAL	113	18TH WAR
CROMWELL, THOMAS	ANN	369	4TH DIST
CROMWELL, THOMAS-MULATTO	FRE	219	BUCKEYST
CROMWELL, TREASA	FRE	066	FREDERIC
CROMWELL, WILLIAM	BAL	282	17TH WAR
CROMWELL, WILLIAM	BAL	083	4TH WARD
CROMWELL, WILLIAM	ANN	340	3RD DIST
CROMWELL, WILLIAM	BAL	388	3RD WARD
CROMWELL, MARTHA	BAL	259	12TH WAR
CROMWLL, NICHOLAS*	BAL	310	3RD WARD
CROMY, FRANCES	CEC	137	6TH E DI
CRONALL, HENERITTA	BAL	149	11TH WAR
CRONALL, RICHARD	BAL	149	11TH WAR
CRONAN, JOHN	BAL	430	1ST DIST
CRONAN, WILLIAM	WAS	163	2ND DIST
CRONANS, MARGARET	BAL	263	20TH WAR
CRONCH, ANN E.	KEN	236	2ND DIST
CRONCH, GEORGE E.	KEN	254	1ST DIST
CRONCH, JAMES	KEN	233	2ND DIST
CRONCH, SAMUEL *	KEN	219	2ND DIST
CRONCH, SARAH A.	KEN	227	2ND DIST
CRONDLE, NELLY	PRI	103	SPALDING
CRONE, ------ *	BAL	369	8TH WARD
CRONE, CANROD	FRE	320	MIDDLETO
CRONE, GEORGIANA	BAL	255	5TH WARD
CRONE, HENRY	FRE	348	MIDDLETO
CRONE, JACOB	FRE	348	MIDDLETO
CRONE, JOHN	FRE	355	MIDDLETO
CRONE, MARGARET	FRE	048	FREDERIC
CRONE, VIRGINIA	BAL	012	9TH WARD
CRONEBERRY, JOHN	BAL	212	19TH WAR
CRONEHART, HENRY	BAL	246	1ST DIST
CRONENBERGER, FRANCIS	BAL	137	11TH WAR
CRONER, HENRY	BAL	146	1ST WARD
CRONER, MARY	BAL	035	18TH WAR
CRONER, MARY	TAL	069	EASTON T
CROWER, NANCY	CEC	185	7TH E DI
CRONER, ROBERT-BLACK	CAR	091	NO TWP L
CRONETHERS, DAVID*	BAL	311	3RD WARD
CRONETON, WESTLEY	ALL	143	6TH E.D.
CRONEY, CONRAD	BAL	205	2ND WARD
CRONEY, JOHN W.	BAL	241	2ND WARD
CRONHARDT, JOHN H.	BAL	444	8TH WARD
CRONHERTT, JOHN	BAL	221	5TH WARD
CRONIEN, MARY	BAL	187	2ND WARD
CRONIMBERGER, ADAM	BAL	013	2ND DIST
CRONIN, BENJAMIN F.	HAR	167	3RD DIST
CRONIN, ELLEN	BAL	204	19TH WAR
CRONIN, PATRICK	BAL	454	8TH WARD
CRONIRE, HANNAH L.	FRE	134	CREAGERS
CRONISE, FREDERICK	FRE	134	CREAGERS
CRONISE, GEORGE	WAS	040	2ND SUBD
CRONISE, JACBO	FRE	134	CREAGERS
CRONISE, JOSEPH	FRE	099	FREDERIC
CRONISE, SAMUEL	FRE	069	FREDERIC
CRONISE, SIMON	FRE	069	FREDERIC
CRONK, JULIAN	BAL	170	19TH WAR
CRONMILLER, ELIZABETH	BAL	073	15TH WAR
CRONMILLER, JACOB *	BAL	059	18TH WAR
CRONMILLER, JOHN	ANN	438	HOWARD D
CRONMILLER, MARY J.	ANN	438	HOWARD D
CRONNER, JERS.	WAS	222	1ST DIST
CRONOLY, CATHERINE	BAL	166	11TH WAR
CRONS, MARGARET	BAL	380	8TH WARD
CRONSENP, CATHARINE	BAL	192	2ND WARD
CRONSH, CHARLES*	SOM	480	TRAPP DI
CRONWELL, J. J.	BAL	157	1ST WARD
CROOK, ACHSAH	BAL	166	19TH WAR
CROOK, BERNARD	BAL	308	3RD WARD
CROOK, CHARLES	ANN	375	4TH DIST
CROOK, CHARLES	PRI	063	NOTTINGH
CROOK, CHARLOTTE	BAL	298	20TH WAR
CROOK, DANIEL	FRE	012	FREDERIC
CROOK, DANIEL	BAL	403	8TH WARD
CROOK, F. A.	BAL	301	20TH WAR
CROOK, FRANCIS	BAL	175	19TH WAR
CROOK, JAMES	BAL	075	4TH WARD
CROOK, JAMES	BAL	126	1ST WARD
CROOK, JAMES	BAL	280	2ND WARD
CROOK, JOHN	ANN	495	HOWARD D
CROOK, JOHN E.	BAL	061	1ST WARD
CROOK, JUL	ANN	341	3RD DIST
CROOK, L.	BAL	154	1ST WARD
CROOK, LAINHARAT	BAL	285	2ND WARD
CROOK, LEWIS	BAL	206	19TH WAR
CROOK, RICHARD	PRI	086	QUEEN AN
CROOK, SAMUEL	BAL	301	12TH WAR
CROOK, SARAH	PRI	063	NOTTINGH
CROOK, T.M.	BAL	114	1ST WARD
CROOK, VICTOR	BAL	113	1ST WARD
CROOK, VICTOR	BAL	169	1ST WARD
CROOK, WALTER	BAL	059	10TH WAR
CROOK, WILLIAM	BAL	158	1ST WARD
CROOK, WILLIAM	BAL	313	3RD WARD
CROOK, WILSON B.	BAL	412	14TH WAR
CROOKMAN, HENRY	ALL	219	CUMBERLA
CROOKS, DANIEL	CAR	256	3RD DIST
CROOKS, DANIEL T.	CAR	257	3RD DIST
CROOKS, ELIZA	BAL	296	1ST DIST
CROOKS, ELIZABETH	BAL	296	1ST DIST
CROOKS, HENRY	CAR	201	4TH DIST
CROOKS, ISRIEL O.	BAL	277	1ST DIST
CROOKS, JOHN	BAL	266	1ST DIST
CROOKS, JOSEPH	WAS	279	LEITERSB
CROOKS, RACHEL	CAR	221	5TH DIST
CROOKS, RESIN H.	BAL	427	14TH WAR
CROOKS, RICHARD	BAL	328	1ST DIST
CROOKS, ROBERT	FRE	193	5TH E DI
CROOKS, SAMUEL W.	BAL	330	1ST DIST
CROOKS, WILLIAM	BAL	292	3RD WARD
CROOKS, WILLIAM	BAL	374	1ST DIST
CROOKSHANK, FRANCIS B.	CEC	052	1ST E DI
CROOKSHANK, MARGARET	CEC	009	ELKTON 3
CROOKSHANKS, CHARLES	BAL	020	4TH WARD
CROOKSHANKS, JOHN	BAL	104	15TH WAR
CROOKSHANKS, THOMAS C.	CEC	064	1ST E DI
CROOKSHANKS, WILLIAM	CEC	004	ELKTON 3
CROOKSHAMT, WILLIAM	CEC	114	3RD E DI
CROOPLEY, NATHANIEL	KEN	306	3RD DIST
CROOSE, MARY	BAL	458	1ST DIST
CROP, AMELINE*	TAL	014	EASTON D
CROPER, HENRY	CEC	044	1ST E DI
CROPER, WILLIAM H-BLACK	CAR	088	NO TWP L
CROPLEY, ANN	KEN	292	3RD DIST
CROPLEY, JOSEPH	KEN	296	3RD DIST
CROPLEY, MOSES	KEN	299	3RD DIST
CROPLY, CRANCES E.	MGM	420	MEDLEY 3
CROPP, JOHN	BAL	303	7TH WARD
CROPP, R EGANA	BAL	303	7TH WARD
CROPPER, A. C.	WOR	258	1ST CENS
CROPPER, ANN	CEC	031	CHESAPEA
CROPPER, ELIZABETH	BAL	263	17TH WAR
CROPPER, ELIZABETH H.	WOR	302	SNOW HIL
CROPPER, HANNAH	BAL	014	9TH WARD

Name	County	Page	District
CROPPER, JOHN	BAL	303	7TH WARD
CROPPER, JOSIAH	WOR	306	2ND E DI
CROPPER, JULIA	SOM	400	BRINKLEY
CROPPER, KENCAL	WOR	289	9TH E DI
CROPPER, LEVIN	WOR	271	BERLIN 1
CROPPER, LYTTLETON	CEC	029	CHESAPEA
CROPPER, MARY	CEC	029	CHESAPEA
CROPPER, MARY J.	WOR	256	1ST CENS
CROPPER, PRINCE	WOR	271	BERLIN 1
CROPPER, R.H.	CEC	030	CHESAPEA
CROPPER, RICHARD	WOR	260	BERLIN 1
CROPPER, ROBERT	WOR	307	2ND E DI
CROPPER, SALLY	WOR	278	BERLIN 1
CROPPER, SAMUEL	WOR	293	9TH E DI
CROPPER, STEPHEN	WOR	281	BERLIN 1
CROPPER, STEPHEN	BAL	305	17TH WAR
CROPPER, WILLAIM	WOR	302	SNOW HIL
CROPPER, WILLIAM B.	BAL	168	1ST WARD
CROPPER, WILLIAM M.	WOR	264	BERLIN 1
CROPPER, WILLIAM M.	WOR	264	BERLIN 1
CROPPER, WILLIAM P.	CEC	029	CHESAPEA
CROPPER, ZORAH	BAL	019	4TH WARD
CROPPETT, BENJAMIN M.	CEC	043	CHESAPEA
CROPPURH, WILLIAM	TAL	110	ST MICHA
CROPSON, ANN	HAR	192	3RD DIST
CROS, FIELDER	PRI	085	QUEEN AN
CROSBEN, EDUARD	BAL	177	2ND WARD
CROSBY, DANIEL	CAL	062	3RD DIST
CROSBY, FRANCIS	BAL	410	8TH WARD
CROSBY, GEORGE	CAL	051	3RD DIST
CROSBY, HENRY *	CAR	237	UNION TO
CROSBY, JOHN	BAL	032	4TH WARD
CROSBY, JOHN	ANN	411	8TH DIST
CROSBY, JOHN P.	BAL	393	14TH WAR
CROSBY, JOHN V.	KEN	265	1ST DIST
CROSBY, JOSEPH	BAL	425	14TH WAR
CROSBY, JOSEPH	BAL	381	1ST DIST
CROSBY, LAVILLA	CAL	061	3RD DIST
CROSBY, MARTHA	BAL	346	1ST DIST
CROSBY, MARY	CAL	010	1ST DIST
CROSBY, MR.	BAL	127	5TH WARD
CROSBY, MRS.	DOR	455	1ST DIST
CROSBY, REBECCA	ANN	402	8TH DIST
CROSBY, RICHARD	CAL	047	3RD DIST
CROSBY, SAMUE, R	BAL	425	14TH WAR
CROSBY, SAMUEL	BAL	415	8TH WARD
CROSBY, SAMUEL	SOM	506	BARREN C
CROSBY, SUSAN	ALL	118	5TH E.D.
CROSBY, THOMAS	BAL	369	3RD WARD
CROSBY, WALTER	CAL	058	3RD DIST
CROSDALE, EDMOND	SOM	433	PRINCESS
CROSDALE, JOHN	WOR	341	1ST E DI
CROSDALE, MARY	SOM	426	PRINCESS
CROSDELL, KISSIAH	SOM	364	BRINKLEY
CROSE, CHARLES	KEN	297	3RD DIST
CROSERY, FELIX S. OR- *	BAL	387	1ST DIST
CROSEY, WILLIAM	BAL	101	18TH WAR
CROSGREY, FRANCIS	HAR	046	1ST DIST
CROSGROVE, JOHN	BAL	078	18TH WAR
CROSHAW, WILLIAM	BAL	394	8TH WARD
CROSIER, MARIA	BAL	342	3RD WARD
CROSLEY, CATHRINE	PRI	049	AQUASCO
CROSLEY, MARY	BAL	393	14TH WAR
CROSLEY, RISDON	QUE	139	1ST E DI
CROSLEY, SAMUEL	QUE	200	3RD E DI
CROSLEY, SARAH	KEN	300	3RD DIST
CROSLEY, WILLIAM A.	MGM	360	BERRYS D
CROSLY, JOHN	QUE	132	1ST E DI
CROSS, ALLEN	ANN	477	HOWARD D
CROSS, AMELINE*	TAL	014	EASTON D
CROSS, AMOS	BAL	215	6TH DIST
CROSS, ANDREW	BAL	279	7TH WARD
CROSS, ANDREW B.	BAL	230	6TH WARD
CROSS, ANN	ANN	477	HOWARD D
CROSS, BARTON	ANN	477	HOWARD D
CROSS, CAMILLA	PRI	015	BLADENSB
CROSS, CATHARINE	BAL	240	2ND WARD
CROSS, CATHARINE	ALL	155	6TH E.D.
CROSS, CELIA	PRI	041	VANSVILL
CROSS, DANIEL	PRI	003	BLADENSB
CROSS, DAVID	BAL	211	6TH WARD
CROSS, DAVID	BAL	374	1ST DIST
CROSS, DEMPSEY	ANN	485	HOWARD D
CROSS, DENNIS B.	PRI	092	MARLBROU
CROSS, EDWARD	BAL	106	1ST WARD
CROSS, ELIZA	ANN	477	HOWARD D
CROSS, ELIZA	BAL	304	12TH WAR
CROSS, ELIZA	WAS	180	BOONSBOR
CROSS, ELIZABETH	WAS	195	1ST DIST
CROSS, ELIZABETH	BAL	216	6TH DIST
CROSS, ELIZABETH	BAL	435	1ST DIST
CROSS, ELIZABETH	BAL	166	11TH WAR
CROSS, ELLINOR	ANN	477	HOWARD D
CROSS, ENOCH-BLACK	CAR	402	2ND DIST
CROSS, HANNAH	BAL	152	19TH WAR
CROSS, HANSON-BLACK	FRE	046	FREDERIC
CROSS, HARRIET	ANN	436	HOWARD D
CROSS, HENRY	FRE	087	FREDERIC
CROSS, HENRY	FRE	321	MIDDLETO
CROSS, HENRY	WAS	215	1ST DIST
CROSS, HOWERTON	PRI	004	BLADENSB
CROSS, ISAIAH	ANN	477	HOWARD D
CROSS, J. W.	WAS	183	BOONSBOR
CROSS, JACOB	WAS	294	1ST DIST
CROSS, JANE	BAL	379	1ST DIST
CROSS, JEMIMA	BAL	196	6TH WARD
CROSS, JEREMIAH	ANN	477	HOWARD D
CROSS, JOHN	BAL	435	1ST DIST
CROSS, JOHN	BAL	203	6TH DIST
CROSS, JOHN	WAS	149	HAGERSTO
CROSS, JOHN	PRI	051	AQUASCO
CROSS, JOHN	MGM	411	MEDLEY 3
CROSS, JOHN	CAL	061	3RD DIST
CROSS, JOHN H.	BAL	397	8TH WARD
CROSS, JONCTHAN	WAS	302	1ST DIST
CROSS, JOSEPH	PRI	057	AQUASCO
CROSS, JOSEPH	BAL	383	8TH WARD
CROSS, JOSHUA	BAL	013	2ND DIST
CROSS, JOSHUA H.	ANN	501	HOWARD D
CROSS, JOSPEH	ST	327	4TH E DI
CROSS, KEZIAH	BAL	405	8TH WARD
CROSS, LEMUEL	ALL	007	3RD E.D.
CROSS, LEWIS	BAL	085	1ST WARD
CROSS, MARGARET	ALL	186	9TH E.D.
CROSS, MARTHA	PRI	004	BLADENSB
CROSS, MARY	WAS	023	2ND SUBD
CROSS, MARY	FRE	065	FREDERIC
CROSS, MARY A.	BAL	292	7TH WARD
CROSS, MARY J.	BAL	226	1ST DIST
CROSS, MARY MISS	ANN	285	ANNAPOLI
CROSS, MARY-BLACK	FRE	018	FREDERIC
CROSS, MATILDA	PRI	024	VANSVILL
CROSS, MRS.	ANN	448	HOWARD D
CROSS, NANTZY	BAL	378	3RD WARD
CROSS, NOTE	BAL	434	1ST DIST
CROSS, PATHA	BAL	129	5TH WARD
CROSS, PHILEMON	BAL	195	6TH WARD
CROSS, R.	BAL	170	1ST WARD
CROSS, RACHEL	BAL	457	1ST DIST
CROSS, REUBEN	WAS	196	1ST DIST
CROSS, RICHARD	BAL	129	5TH WARD
CROSS, ROBERT	BAL	013	2ND DIST
CROSS, ROBERT	BAL	225	1ST DIST
CROSS, ROBERT C.	WAS	213	1ST DIST
CROSS, ROBERT JR.	WAS	203	1ST DIST
CROSS, ROBERT SR.	WAS	202	1ST DIST
CROSS, SAMUEL B.	BAL	166	16TH WAR
CROSS, SANDY	BAL	177	16TH WAR
CROSS, SARAH	ANN	330	2ND DIST
CROSS, SARAH E.	ANN	441	HOWARD D
CROSS, SERENDUS	BAL	203	6TH DIST
CROSS, TABITHA	ANN	436	HOWARD D
CROSS, THOAMS	BAL	315	20TH WAR
CROSS, THOMAS	BAL	013	2ND DIST
CROSS, THOMAS	ANN	484	HOWARD D
CROSS, THOMAS	ALL	136	4TH E.D.
CROSS, THOMAS	ALL	100	5TH E.D.
CROSS, THOMAS	ALL	098	5TH E.D.
CROSS, TILGHMAN	ANN	449	HOWARD D
CROSS, TRUEMAN	ANN	475	HOWARD D
CROSS, TRUMAN	BAL	467	14TH WAR
CROSS, TRUMAN D.	BAL	113	15TH WAR
CROSS, VALENTINE	BAL	023	2ND DIST
CROSS, W.	BAL	153	1ST WARD
CROSS, WALTER	BAL	379	8TH WARD
CROSS, WILLAIM	CAL	030	2ND DIST
CROSS, WILLIAM	BAL	152	19TH WAR
CROSS, WILLIAM	ALL	034	2ND E.D.
CROSS, WILLIAM	BAL	457	1ST DIST
CROSS, WILLIAM	BAL	454	1ST DIST
CROSS, WILLIAM	WAS	198	1ST DIST
CROSS, WILLIAM	PRI	047	AQUASCO
CROSS, WILLIAM O.	BAL	050	1ST WARD
CROSSBY, JAMES	BAL	410	8TH WARD
CROSSBY, MARK	ALL	057	10TH E.D
CROSSBY, SAMUEL K.	BAL	377	1ST DIST
CROSSER, J.	BAL	162	1ST WARD
CROSSEY, GEORGE	BAL	146	2ND DIST
CROSSFIELD, GEORGE	BAL	003	15TH WAR
CROSSGROVER, JESSE	WAS	268	1ST DIST
CROSSING, BERNARD M.	ANN	480	HOWARD D
CROSSLEY, ELIJAH	KEN	221	2ND DIST
CROSSLEY, EVAN	KEN	227	2ND DIST
CROSSLEY, THOMAS	BAL	028	2ND DIST
CROSSMAN, F.	BAL	152	1ST WARD
CROSSMAN, F.	BAL	124	1ST WARD
CROSSMAN, GOLISS	PRI	107	PISCATAW
CROSSMAN, JOHN N.	WAS	175	FUNKSTOW
CROSSMORE, JOHN	CEC	094	4TH E DI
CROSSMORE, OLIVER	BAL	137	2ND DIST
CROSSMORE, THEODORE	BAL	133	2ND DIST
CROSSMORE, WILLIAM	BAL	139	2ND DIST
CROST, JAEMS T.	BAL	452	8TH WARD
CROSTON, MARY A.	BAL	274	2ND WARD
CROSWEL, HENRY S.	SOM	364	BRINKLEY
CROSWELL, ELIZABETH	SOM	371	BRINKLEY
CROSWELL, SETH	SOM	386	BRINKLEY
CROSWELL, STOCKLEY*	SOM	386	BRINKLEY
CROSWELL, THOMAS	SOM	365	BRINKLEY
CROTHCERS, MILTON	MGM	425	MEDLEY 3
CROTHER, ELI	BAL	195	5TH DIST
CROTHER, JOHN	BAL	335	13TH WAR
CROTHERS, ILLINOIS	BAL	332	3RD WARD
CROTHERS, MARY	BAL	041	4TH WARD
CROTHERS, WILLIAM	BAL	033	18TH WAR
CROTHY, JULIA	BAL	333	13TH WAR
CROUATHERS, DAVID*	BAL	311	3RD WARD
CROUCH, ALEXANDER	BAL	286	7TH WARD
CROUCH, ANDREW	BAL	003	1ST WARD
CROUCH, ANTHONY	SOM	487	SALISBUR
CROUCH, BENJAMIN	CEC	071	5TH E DI
CROUCH, CHARLES	CEC	001	ELKTON 3
CROUCH, CHARLES C.	MGM	347	BERRYS D
CROUCH, CHARLES*	SOM	480	TRAPP DI
CROUCH, CLARISA	SOM	489	SALISBUR
CROUCH, D.	BAL	125	11TH WAR
CROUCH, DAVID	BAL	249	17TH WAR
CROUCH, DUDLEY	KEN	304	3RD DIST
CROUCH, EDWIN	KEN	284	3RD DIST
CROUCH, ELIJAH	CEC	030	CHESAPEA
CROUCH, ELIZABETH	BAL	049	9TH WARD
CROUCH, FRANCIS	CEC	029	CHESAPEA
CROUCH, GEORGE W.	BAL	273	17TH WAR
CROUCH, ISAAC	SOM	481	TRAPP DI
CROUCH, ISAAC	SOM	487	SALISBUR
CROUCH, JANE	CEC	069	5TH E DI
CROUCH, JOHN	BAL	268	17TH WAR
CROUCH, JOHN E.	KEN	287	3RD DIST
CROUCH, JOHN W.	KEN	298	3RD DIST
CROUCH, JOSEPH	CEC	063	1ST E DI
CROUCH, JOSHUA	SOM	481	TRAPP DI
CROUCH, LAURA	KEN	291	3RD DIST
CROUCH, LENSEA*	SOM	484	TRAPP DI
CROUCH, LEVI	CEC	069	5TH E DI
CROUCH, LIDIA	TAL	020	EASTON D
CROUCH, LOUISA	ANN	479	HOWARD D
CROUCH, LUCRETIA	WOR	228	6TH E DI
CROUCH, MARY	CEC	070	5TH E DI
CROUCH, MARY	CEC	014	ELKTON 3
CROUCH, PHILIP	ANN	478	HOWARD D
CROUCH, POLLY	SOM	423	PRINCESS
CROUCH, REBECCA	CEC	070	5TH E DI
CROUCH, REBECCA	BAL	187	2ND WARD
CROUCH, RICHARD	KEN	236	2ND DIST
CROUCH, ROBERT	CEC	031	CHESAPEA
CROUCH, SAMUEL	BAL	118	11TH WAR
CROUCH, SAMUEL *	KEN	219	2ND DIST
CROUCH, SARAH	CEC	111	4TH E DI
CROUCH, SARAH	CEC	214	7TH E DI
CROUCH, STEPHEN	CEC	070	5TH E DI
CROUCH, STEWART	BAL	141	16TH WAR
CROUCH, THOMAS C.	CEC	004	ELKTON 3
CROUCH, THOMAS E.	CEC	071	5TH E DI
CROUCH, THOMAS M.	ANN	312	1ST DIST
CROUCH, WILLIAM	CEC	066	1ST E DI
CROUCH, WILLIAM	CEC	029	CHESAPEA
CROUCH, WILLIAM J.	KEN	296	3RD DIST
CROUCK, WILLIAM	CEC	011	ELKTON 3
CROUDER, JACOB	BAL	221	17TH WAR
CROUGH, MARY	BAL	056	1ST WARD
CROUGHAN, PATRICK	BAL	001	9TH WARD
CROUGHEN, HUGHEY	BAL	275	1ST DIST
CROUISE, JACOB	FRE	243	NEW MARK
CROUMILELR, JACOB *	BAL	059	18TH WAR
CROUNER, HENRIETTA	QUE	230	4TH E DI
CROUNER, HENRY	QUE	230	4TH E DI
CROUSAY, AUGUST	ALL	011	3RD E.D.
CROUSE, ARTHUR	ALL	108	5TH E.D.
CROUSE, BARBARA	CAR	240	TANEYTOW
CROUSE, BARBARA	FRE	175	5TH E DI
CROUSE, CHARLES	CAR	315	1ST DIST
CROUSE, CHRISTIAN	CAR	296	7TH DIST
CROUSE, DANIEL	CAR	307	1ST DIST
CROUSE, DAVID	CAR	255	3RD DIST
CROUSE, ELIZABETH	CAR	353	6TH DIST
CROUSE, ELIZABETH C.	WAS	250	1ST DIST
CROUSE, EPHRAIM	FRE	185	5TH E DI
CROUSE, FREDERICK	FRE	173	5TH E DI
CROUSE, GEORGE	CAR	353	6TH DIST
CROUSE, GEORGE	ALL	206	CUMBERLA
CROUSE, GEORGE W.	FRE	311	MIDDLETO
CROUSE, IRA E.	CAR	267	WESTMINS
CROUSE, ISAAC	CAR	240	TANEYTOW
CROUSE, JACOB	WAS	250	1ST DIST
CROUSE, JAMES	CAR	304	1ST DIST
CROUSE, JOHN	CAR	254	3RD DIST
CROUSE, JOHN	CAR	264	WESTMINS
CROUSE, JOHN	CAR	410	2ND DIST
CROUSE, JOHN	FRE	177	5TH E DI
CROUSE, JOHN	FRE	186	5TH E DI
CROUSE, JOHN T.	CAR	254	3RD DIST
CROUSE, MARCELLUS	FRE	142	CREAGERS
CROUSE, MARY JANE	ALL	230	CUMBERLA
CROUSE, MICHAEL	BAL	216	2ND WARD
CROUSE, MICHAEL	FRE	185	5TH E DI
CROUSE, REBECCA	FRE	174	5TH E DI
CROUSE, SAMUEL	CAR	241	TANEYTOW
CROUSE, WILLIAM	CAR	254	3RD DIST
CROUSE, WILLIAM	CAR	265	WESTMINS
CROUSE, WILLIAM A.	BAL	296	12TH WAR
CROUT, H.	BAL	249	20TH WAR
CROUT, JOHN	HAR	167	3RD DIST
CROUT, RACHAEL	CAR	269	WESTMINS
CROUTHER, JOHN	BAL	227	12TH WAR
CROUTHERS, BETTE	BAL	192	11TH WAR
CROUTWERST, TROWCUTTER	BAL	073	2ND DIST
CROW, ANDREW	CEC	057	1ST E DI
CROW, ASA	ALL	117	5TH E.D.
CROW, BENJAMIN	WAS	017	2ND SUBD
CROW, ELEANOR	ALL	108	5TH E.D.
CROW, ELIZABETH	BAL	331	7TH WARD
CROW, ELLEN J.	BAL	269	17TH WAR
CROW, FRANCIS	BAL	374	8TH WARD
CROW, FREDERICK	ALL	113	5TH E.D.
CROW, GEORGE	ALL	093	5TH E.D.
CROW, GEORGE C.	QUE	180	2ND E DI
CROW, HENRY	ALL	010	3RD E.D.
CROW, JACOB	ALL	003	3RD E.D.
CROW, JAMES	CEC	025	ELKTON 3
CROW, JOHN	BAL	071	18TH WAR
CROW, JOHN	ALL	003	3RD E.D.
CROW, JOHN	ALL	086	5TH E.D.
CROW, JOHN	WAS	008	WILLIAMS
CROW, JOHN	PRI	009	BLADENSB
CROW, JOHN T.	BAL	063	10TH WAR
CROW, LOUISA	ALL	096	5TH E.D.
CROW, LOUISA	CEC	194	7TH E DI
CROW, MARY J.	BAL	293	7TH WARD
CROW, MARYANN	ALL	115	5TH E.D.
CROW, MICHAEL	BAL	051	15TH WAR
CROW, NATHANIEL T.	BAL	358	8TH WARD
CROW, PERRY	BAL	122	16TH WAR
CROW, SUSANNAH	BAL	358	8TH WARD
CROW, THOMAS A.	BAL	269	17TH WAR
CROW, THORNTON	ALL	096	5TH E.D.
CROW, WILLIAM	BAL	110	2ND DIST
CROW, WILLIAM	CEC	063	1ST E DI
CROW, WILLIAM	CEC	035	CHESAPEA
CROWDEN, ANTHONY	BAL	252	20TH WAR
CROWDY, MICHAEL	BAL	190	5TH DIST
CROWE, JOHN	BAL	230	19TH WAR
CROWE, MARY J.	ANN	521	HOWARD D
CROWELL, CAROLINE	BAL	195	11TH WAR
CROWELL, DENBY	HAR	074	1ST DIST
CROWELL, HENRY	FRE	357	CATOCTIN
CROWELL, PARKER-BLACK	WOR	345	1ST E DI
CROWELL, WILLIAM J.	BAL	409	8TH WARD
CROWFORD, G. J.	BAL	332	1ST DIST
CROWFORD, THOMAS	KEN	219	2ND DIST
CROWL, DAVID	CAR	279	7TH DIST
CROWL, DAVID	CAR	278	7TH DIST
CROWL, ELIAS	CAR	290	7TH DIST
CROWL, EMELINE	CAR	279	7TH DIST
CROWL, GEORGE	CAR	276	7TH DIST
CROWL, HEZEKIAH	CAR	279	7TH DIST
CROWL, JACOB	CAR	284	7TH DIST
CROWL, JESSE	CAR	411	2ND DIST
CROWL, LUCINDA	CAR	276	7TH DIST
CROWLE, DAVID	BAL	008	EASTERN
CROWLE, EDWARD *	BAL	222	6TH WARD
CROWLE, JOHN D.	BAL	002	15TH WAR
CROWLE, MISS C.	FRE	199	5TH E DI
CROWLETT, BRIDGET	BAL	183	6TH WARD
CROWLEY, ANN B.	BAL	371	13TH WAR
CROWLEY, BRIDGE	ALL	214	CUMBERLA
CROWLEY, CHARLES	BAL	309	3RD WARD
CROWLEY, DELPHA A.	BAL	379	3RD WARD
CROWLEY, ELIZA	ALL	254	CUMBERLA
CROWLEY, FREDERICK	BAL	191	2ND WARD
CROWLEY, GEORGE H.	BAL	199	6TH WARD
CROWLEY, JAMES	ALL	083	5TH E.D.
CROWLEY, JANE	BAL	102	5TH WARD
CROWLEY, JANE	BAL	074	4TH WARD
CROWLEY, JEREMIAH	ALL	185	9TH E.D.
CROWLEY, JOHN	BAL	348	3RD WARD
CROWLEY, JOHN	BAL	410	3RD WARD
CROWLEY, JULIA	BAL	317	3RD WARD
CROWLEY, MARY	BAL	155	19TH WAR
CROWLEY, PATRICK	BAL	339	3RD WARD
CROWLEY, PETER	BAL	055	1ST WARD
CROWLEY, RACHEL	BAL	108	10TH WAR
CROWLEY, SAMUEL	BAL	300	17TH WAR
CROWLEY, WILLIAM	BAL	104	18TH WAR
CROWLEY, WILLIAM T.	BAL	072	4TH WARD
CROWLING, FREDERICK	BAL	276	2ND WARD
CROWLING, JOHN	BAL	394	1ST DIST
CROWLLE, JOHN	FRE	20	5TH E DI
CROWLY, JOHN	WAS	095	2ND SUBD
CROWMER, ANDREW	BAL	279	1ST DIST
CROWMWELL, CURTLS	FRE	029	FREDERIC

CROWN, FREDERICK WAS 246 SMITHSBU
CROWN, HENRIETTA WAS 246 SMITHSBU
CROWN, HEZEKIAH MGM 357 BERRYS D
CROWN, JACOB FRE 261 NEW MARK
CROWN, JAMES T. MGM 393 ROCKERLE
CROWN, JOHN MGM 400 ROCKERLE
CROWN, JOHN O. WAS 259 1ST DIST
CROWN, JOSEPH MGM 378 ROCKERLE
CROWN, PATRICK M. BAL 379 13TH WAR
CROWN, SAMUEL MGM 384 ROCKERLE
CROWN, SAMUEL B. MGM 384 ROCKERLE
CROWN, STEVEN WAS 027 2ND SUBD
CROWN, THMAS ANN 330 2ND DIST
CROWN, THOMAS MGM 404 ROCKERLE
CROWN, THOMAS MGM 384 ROCKERLE
CROWN, WILLIAM T. FRE 014 FREDERIC
CROWN,MATILCA FRE 234 BUCKEYST
CROWNER, CHARLES ANN 429 HOWARD D
CROWNER, HARRY ANN 353 3RD DIST
CROWNER, JAMES ANN 428 HOWARD D
CROWNER, JOHN ANN 429 HOWARD D
CROWNFIELD, ANN J. BAL 085 10TH WAR
CROWNOVER, GAYNOR ANN 425 HOWARD D
CROWRY, JOHN Y. BAL 163 19TH WAR
CROWSER, JOSEPH BAL 378 8TH WARD
CROWTHER, ANN M. BAL 156 19TH WAR
CROWTHER, BENJAMIN BAL 256 1ST DIST.
CROWTHER, MARY A. BAL 256 1ST DIST
CROWTHER, MATILDA BAL 189 5TH DIST
CROWTLEW, WILLIAM BAL 271 2ND WARD
CROWW, RICHARD G. PRI 015 BLADENSB
CROXALL, ROBERT M. BAL 095 18TH WAR
CROXEALL, THOAMS BAL 095 18TH WAR
CROZIER, MARY A. BAL 336 3RD WARD
CROZIER, THOMAS BAL 305 3RD WARD
CRUCE, IES* BAL 234 12TH WAR
CRUCIFER, SIMON SOM 476 TRAPPE D
CRUCKER, MARY BAL 043 18TH WAR
CRUCKLEY, RACHAL FRE 305 WOODSBOR
CRUCLE, JOHN WAS 127 2ND DIST
CRUCY, RACHEL CAR 197 4TH DIST
CRUDER, JOSEPH BAL 138 2ND DIST
CRUDEY, MARY BAL 318 20TH WAR
CRUDRICKS, JOHN WAS 147 2ND DIST
CRUETT, LOUIS BAL 180 19TH WAR
CRUETT, MITILDA BAL 208 11TH WAR
CRUETT, WILLIAM BAL 202 11TH WAR
CRUGTON, MICHAEL BAL 004 9TH WARD
CRUICKSHANKS, ANDREW KEN 208 2ND DIST
CRUICKSHANKS, ANN KEN 231 2ND DIST
CRUICKSHANKS, DELIA KEN 211 2ND DIST
CRUICKSHANKS, GUILFORD D. KEN 261 1ST DIST
CRUICKSHANKS, JOHN D. KEN 269 1ST DIST
CRUICKSHANKS, LAURENCE KEN 209 2ND DIST
CRUIE, ELIZABETH BAL 418 8TH WARD
CRUIKSHANK, MARY A. QUE 164 2ND E DI
CRUIS, WILLIAM BAL 422 8TH WARD
CRULL, SYLVESTER BAL 206 6TH DIST
CRUM, ADAM FRE 298 WOODSBOR
CRUM, CASPAR FRE 005 FREDERIC
CRUM, CATHARINE FRE 263 NEW MARK
CRUM, CATHARINE A. FRE 303 WOODSBOR
CRUM, DAVID FRE 322 MIDDLETO
CRUM, DEBANY WAS 130 2ND DIST
CRUM, ELIZABRYH FRE 099 FREDERIC
CRUM, EVE FRE 303 WOODSBOR
CRUM, FRANCIS M. FRE 027 FREDERIC
CRUM, FREDERICK FRE 297 WOODSBOR
CRUM, HANSON FRE 099 FREDERIC
CRUM, HARRIET FRE 037 FREDERIC
CRUM, ISAAC FRE 263 NEW MARK
CRUM, ISAAC B. FRE 020 FREDERIC
CRUM, JACOB FRE 382 PETERSVI
CRUM, JEREMIAH FRE 386 PETERSVI
CRUM, JOHN FRE 418 8TH E DI
CRUM, JONATHAN W. FRE 379 PETERSVI
CRUM, LOUISA FRE 386 PETERSVI
CRUM, MARGARETT FRE 398 JEFFERSO
CRUM, MARTHA FRE 224 BUCKEYST
CRUM, MARY BAL 271 20TH WAR
CRUM, MARY ANN FRE 398 JEFFERSO
CRUM, REBECCA WAS 189 1ST DIST
CRUM, SIMON FRE 285 WOODSBOR
CRUM, SOLOMON FRE 306 WOODSBOR
CRUM, WILLIAM FRE 225 BUCKEYST
CRUM, WILLIAM FRE 391 PETERSVI
CRUMBACKER, DAVID CAR 377 2ND DIST
CRUMBACKER, EPHRAIM BAL 016 18TH WAR
CRUMBACKER, NATHAN CAR 377 2ND DIST
CRUMBAUGH, CATHARINE FRE 426 8TH E DI
CRUMBAUGH, GIDEON D. FRE 284 WOODSBOR
CRUMBAUGH, JOHN D. FRE 310 WOODSBOR
CRUMBECKER, WILLIAM CAR 386 2ND DIST
CRUMER, FRANCIS HAR 172 3RD DIST
CRUMMEL, MARGARET-BLACK CAR 402 2ND DIST
CRUMMELL, SOPHIA CAR 241 TANEYTOW
CRUMMER, CATHERNINE BAL 403 8TH WARD
CRUMMER, EDWARD BAL 403 8TH WARD
CRUMMER, JAMES L. BAL 183 6TH WARD
CRUMMER, STEPHEN BAL 407 8TH WARD
CRUMMER, THOMAS BAL 435 8TH WARD
CRUMMINS, IRA BAL 207 19TH WAR
CRUMMON, FREDERICK * ALL 168 6TH E.D.
CRUMPTON, ANN CAR 107 NO TWP L
CRUMRINE, DANIEL CAR 349 6TH DIST
CRUMRINE, HENRY CAR 350 6TH DIST
CRUMRINE, PHILIP CAR 345 6TH DIST
CRUMRINE, WILLIAM CAR 329 MANCHEST
CRUMRINE, WILLIAM CAR 252 3RD DIST
CRUNAVALLY, ANTHONY* BAL 031 4TH WARD
CRUNBAUGH, PHEBE FRE 284 WOODSBOR
CRUNBER, SARAH BAL 079 4TH WARD
CRURHON, ABRAHAM FRE 080 FREDERIC
CRURY, GEORGE SOM 425 PRINCESS
CRURY, SARAH ANN 407 8TH DIST
CRUSCAN, RENALDER-BLACK ST 308 1ST E DI
CRUSE, CHARLES BAL 014 1ST WARD
CRUSE, ELIZABETH BAL 036 1ST WARD
CRUSE, HENRY BAL 329 7TH WARD
CRUSE, ISAAC BAL 190 11TH WAR
CRUSE, JOHN BAL 096 1ST WARD
CRUSE, JOHN HAR 123 2ND DIST
CRUSE, MARIA BAL 382 13TH WAR
CRUSE, MARIA BAL 003 4TH WARD
CRUSE, MATILDA CAL 063 3RD DIST
CRUSE, MATILDA BAL 089 1ST WARD
CRUSE, WILLIAM BAL 378 8TH WARD
CRUSE, WILLIAM T. BAL 128 1ST WARD
CRUSENBARGE, WILLIAM ALL 138 6TH E.D.
CRUSER, ELIZABETH-MULATTO FRE 208 BUCKEYST

CRUSER, ISAAC BAL 041 15TH WAR
CRUSER, MARY BAL 461 14TH WAR
CRUSLEY, U. R BAL 322 12TH WAR
CRUSO, ELLEN HAR 093 2ND DIST
CRUSSELL, MARY L. BAL 353 7TH WARD
CRUTCHER, JOHN BAL 141 5TH WARD
CRUTCHLEY, ELIZABETH BAL 329 3RD WARD
CRUTCHLEY, NAT ANN 411 8TH DIST
CRUTHER, ISAAC BAL 302 1ST DIST
CRUTHERS, ALEXANDER CEC 086 4TH E DI
CRUTHERS, ATTHEWS CEC 170 6TH E DI
CRUTHERS, ELIZABETH CEC 170 6TH E DI
CRUTHERS, ELIZABETH W. CEC 171 6TH E DI
CRUTHERS, JAMES CEC 170 6TH E DI
CRUTHERS, JAMES CEC 133 6TH E DI
CRUTHERS, SAMUEL CEC 133 6TH E DI
CRUTHERS, WALTER CEC 104 4TH E DI
CRUVILL, DAVID BAL 422 8TH WARD
CRY, JOHN BAL 459 1ST DIST
CRYCE, JOBE* TAL 051 EASTON D
CRYCE, ROBERT TAL 057 EASTON D
CRYER, CORNELIA ST 254 3RD E DI
CRYER, ELIZABETH TAL 055 EASTON D
CRYER, JACOB BAL 261 1ST DIST
CRYER, JESSE* TAL 051 EASTON D
CRYER, MARY BAL 262 1ST DIST
CRYER, WILLIAM H. ST 276 3RD E DI
CSATINO, N. BAL 157 1ST WARD
CTERNER, MARIAH C. ALL 090 5TH E.D.
CUAGER, MARY FRE 241 NEW MARK
CUBBAGE, WILLIAM CAR 131 NO TWP L
CUBBY, SAMUEL BAL 122 1ST WARD
CUBLEY, JOHN KEN 306 3RD DIST
CUBRA, MARGARET BAL 290 1ST DIST
CUCHER, BARNEY BAL 073 18TH WAR
CUCHER, FRANCIS BAL 056 18TH WAR
CUCHER, WILLIAM BAL 026 18TH WAR
CUCLE, MARY CAR 406 2ND DIST
CUCTEN, JOSEPH BAL 363 8TH WARD
CUDDY, ELISHA BAL 044 2ND DIST
CUDDY, ISAAC BAL 444 1ST DIST
CUDDY, JOHN BAL 042 2ND DIST
CUDDY, LAWSON BAL 044 2ND DIST
CUDISH, ELLEN BAL 230 19TH WAR
CUEGA, MANASSAH FRE 255 NEW MARK
CUERA, MARY CEC 041 CHESAPEA
CUETZ, JOHN BAL 293 12TH WAR
CUFF, ANDREW WOR 167 6TH E DI
CUFF, BILL TAL 008 EASTON D
CUFF, GEORGE BAL 156 16TH WAR
CUFF, HENRY WOR 227 4TH E DI
CUFF, HORRACE TAL 032 EASTON D
CUFF, JAMES WOR 222 4TH E DI
CUFF, JIM-BLACK QUE 188 3RD E DI
CUFF, MARY WOR 215 4TH E DI
CUFF, MARY-BLACK QUE 189 3RD E DI
CUFF, MARY-BLACK CAR 071 NO TWP L
CUFF, MENTY KEN 290 3RD DIST
CUFF, NANCY-BLACK CAR 076 NO TWP L
CUFF, PATRICK MGM 348 BERRYS D
CUFF, PETER WOR 224 4TH E DI
CUFF, THOMAS BAL 127 11TH WAR
CUFF, THOMAS BAL 448 1ST DIST
CUFF, THOMAS * KEN 208 2ND DIST
CUFF, WILLIAM-BLACK QUE 160 2ND E DI
CUFFEY, JAMES BAL 120 1ST WARD
CUFFRY, MILLY-BLACK BAL 216 2ND WARD
CUFMAN, MARTH ST 289 2ND E DI
CUGAN, ELLEN ANN 413 HOWARD D
CUGAN, PATRICK BAL 361 8TH WARD
CUGAN,PATRICK ALL 247 CUMBERLA
CUGLE, BARTHOLOMEW BAL 348 13TH WAR
CUGLE, HENRIETTA* BAL 094 10TH WAR
CUGLE, JOHN BAL 273 12TH WAR
CUGLE, NICHOLAS ANN 412 HOWARD D
CUIN, MARGARET * BAL 298 20TH WAR
CUKE, MICHAEL BAL 256 20TH WAR
CULB, JOHN BAL 136 1ST WARD
CULBER, WILLIAM MGM 353 BERRYS D
CULBERTSON, CHARLES CEC 171 6TH E DI
CULBERTSON, CYRUS D. BAL 387 13TH WAR
CULBERTSON, ISABELLA BAL 212 6TH WARD
CULBERTSON, JOSEPH FRE 169 5TH E DI
CULBERTSON, ROBERT FRE 169 5TH E DI
CULBERTSON, SAMUEL WAS 003 WILLIAMS
CULBERTSON, SUSAN BAL 352 13TH WAR
CULBOOTH, CRAWFORD * TAL 071 EASTON T
CULBRETH, ROBERT B. CAR 085 NO TWP L
CULBUIN, DORCAS BAL 256 12TH WAR
CULF, GEORGE WAS 022 2ND SUBD
CULINA, BARTHOLOMEW BAL 048 9TH WARD
CULISON, MERRET BAL 034 1ST WARD
CULISON, WASHINGTON CAR 240 TANEYTOW
CULLAN, JANE L. WAS 181 BOONSBOR
CULLAY, ANN BAL 275 2ND WARD
CULLEN, EDWARD SOM 425 PRINCESS
CULLEN, ISAAC W. SOM 379 BRINKLEY
CULLEN, JAMES WAS 164 2ND DIST
CULLEN, JAMES BAL 237 6TH WARD
CULLEN, JULIA BAL 062 2ND DIST
CULLEN, KITTY SOM 378 BRINKLEY
CULLEN, MICHAEL BAL 099 1ST WARD
CULLEN, PATRICK BAL 223 6TH WARD
CULLEN, SEVERN SOM 367 BRINKLEY
CULLEN, TRAVIS SOM 379 BRINKLEY
CULLER, C. C. WAS 179 BOONSBOR
CULLER, DANIEL FRE 401 JEFFERSO
CULLER, HENRY FRE 398 JEFFERSO
CULLER, JACOB FRE 315 MIDDLETO
CULLER, JOHN FRE 402 JEFFERSO
CULLER, MICHAEL FRE 408 JEFFERSO
CULLER, PETER FRE 401 JEFFERSO
CULLER, PHILLIP FRE 071 FREDERIC
CULLER.HENRY JR. FRE 408 JEFFERSO
CULLERSON, WESLEY BAL 162 2ND DIST
CULLESON, LOUIS ST 285 2ND E DI
CULLEY, ELIZABETH BAL 015 15TH WAR
CULLEY, EMILY J. BAL 263 17TH WAR
CULLEY, LANGLY B. BAL 264 17TH WAR
CULLEY, ROBERT BAL 263 17TH WAR
CULLEY, WESLEY P. BAL 159 1ST WARD
CULLIMORE, JOHN BAL 408 3RD WARD
CULLIMORE, SARAH BAL 317 20TH WAR
CULLIN, ADALINE BAL 392 3RD WARD
CULLIN, JAMES WAS 123 2ND DIST
CULLIN, JOHN SOM 384 BRINKLEY
CULLIN, JOHN SOM 382 BRINKLEY
CULLIN, MARIA BAL 420 1ST DIST
CULLIN, MARY BAL 363 3RD WARD
CULLIN, THOMAS BAL 357 3RD WARD

CULLING, ISAAC SOM 374 BRINKLEY
CULLINGS, ISABEL BAL 402 3RD WARD
CULLINGS, JEREMIAH CAR 184 8TH DIST
CULLINGS, NELSON BAL 215 6TH DIST
CULLINS, CALEB BAL 206 6TH DIST
CULLINS, CALVERT ST 281 3RD E DI
CULLINS, GEORGE ST 296 2ND E DI
CULLINS, JAMSE BAL 208 6TH DIST
CULLINS, MATILDA ST 325 4TH E DI
CULLISON, ANDREW CAR 183 8TH DIST
CULLISON, ANN CAR 202 4TH DIST
CULLISON, ANN-BLACK ST 309 1ST E DI
CULLISON, ELIJAH CAR 189 4TH DIST
CULLISON, ENOCH CAR 201 4TH DIST
CULLISON, GEORGE H. ST 313 1ST E DI
CULLISON, JANE BAL 204 6TH DIST
CULLISON, JESSE BAL 194 5TH DIST
CULLISON, JESSE M. BAL 265 12TH WAR
CULLISON, JESSE M. BAL 022 2ND DIST
CULLISON, JOHN H. ST 332 4TH E DI
CULLISON, JOHN W. BAL 400 1ST DIST
CULLISON, JOSHUA BAL 194 5TH DIST
CULLISON, MARGARET BAL 200 5TH DIST
CULLISON, MICAJA BAL 207 6TH DIST
CULLISON, MICAJAH CAR 356 6TH DIST
CULLISON, MOSES FRE 355 MIDDLETO
CULLISON, MOSES BAL 200 5TH DIST
CULLISON, RICHARD BAL 223 1ST DIST
CULLISON, RUTH BAL 224 1ST DIST
CULLISON, THOMAS CAR 284 7TH DIST
CULLISON,WELFORD ST 309 1ST E DI
CULLISONS, GEORGE W. BAL 413 3RD WARD
CULLRETH, SAMUEL CAR 085 NO TWP L
CULLUM, EDWARD BAL 306 7TH WARD
CULLUM, EMMA J. BAL 183 16TH WAR
CULLUM, GEORGE HAR 135 2ND DIST
CULLUM, GEORGE L. HAR 135 2ND DIST
CULLUM, JESSE HAR 135 2ND DIST
CULLUM, JOHN BAL 415 8TH WARD
CULLUM, JOHN B. BAL 183 16TH WAR
CULLUM, MARY BAL 416 8TH WARD
CULLUM, MARY HAR 143 2ND DIST
CULLUM, NELSON BAL 219 6TH WARD
CULLUM, WILLAM HAR 135 2ND DIST
CULLUM, WILLIAM BAL 422 8TH WARD
CULLUMBER, BROOLIN CAL 003 1ST DIST
CULLUMBER, CATHARIEN CAL 014 1ST DIST
CULLUMBER, JOSHUA ST 290 2ND E DI
CULLUMBER, THOMAS CAL 017 1ST DIST
CULLY, ARCHABALD HAR 056 1ST DIST
CULLY, GEORGE T. CEC 176 7TH E DI
CULLY, JAMES CEC 108 3RD E DI
CULLY, JOHN CEC 061 1ST E DI
CULLY, MARY BAL 070 2ND DIST
CULLY, ROBERT A. CEC 175 7TH E DI
CULLY, SAMUEL CEC 187 7TH E DI
CULLY, THOMAS CEC 046 1ST E DI
CULNAN, GEORGE BAL 193 6TH WARD
CULNAN, GEORGE BAL 198 6TH WARD
CULNAN, SAMUEL BAL 197 6TH WARD
CULP, ALFRED BAL 290 1ST DIST
CULP, CHRISTINA BAL 070 1ST WARD
CULP, CHRISTOPHER BAL 024 4TH WARD
CULP, JACOB BAL 164 1ST WARD
CULP, JACOB BAL 165 1ST WARD
CULP, JACOB BAL 172 1ST WARD
CULP, JOHN ALL 242 CUMBERLA
CULP, JOHN A. ALL 242 CUMBERLA
CULP, RAHCAEL WAS 154 2ND DIST
CULP, SAMUEL WAS 119 2ND DIST
CULPERCE, ANDREW BAL 219 2ND WARD
CULPP, CHARLES BAL 070 1ST WARD
CULTHRETH, THOMAS B. CAR 082 NO TWP L
CULUM, RUTH BAL 391 3RD WARD
CULVER, C. BAL 151 1ST WARD
CULVER, CAROLINE SOM 499 SALISBUR
CULVER, ELIJAH SOM 531 QUANTICO
CULVER, GEORGE WOR 238 6TH E DI
CULVER, GEORGEAN BAL 267 7TH WARD
CULVER, HEMAN BAL 058 15TH WAR
CULVER, JOHN BAL 303 3RD WARD
CULVER, JOHN SOM 528 QUANTICO
CULVER, JOHN MGM 353 BERRYS D
CULVER, JOHN DOR 447 1ST DIST
CULVER, LEAH SOM 534 QUANTICO
CULVER, LEVIN SOM 487 SALISBUR
CULVER, LOVEY SOM 512 BARREN C
CULVER, LURANIA * BAL 285 7TH WARD
CULVER, MARGARET MGM 353 BERRYS D
CULVER, MARY MGM 379 ROCKERLE
CULVER, P.R. BAL 170 1ST WARD
CULVER, REBECCA MGM 365 BERRYS D
CULVER, SAMUEL CAR 097 NO TWP L
CULVER, SAMUEL CAR 098 NO TWP L
CULVER, SARAH E. BAL 148 16TH WAR
CULVER, WILLIAM MGM 370 BERRYS D
CULVER, WILLIAM T. BAL 147 16TH WAR
CULVERSON, BETSY BAL 107 1ST WARD
CULVERWELL, STEPHEN BAL 324 3RD WARD
CULVIMER, GEORGE* BAL 304 3RD WARD
CULY, ROBERT HAR 151 3RD DIST
CULY, THOMAS CEC 046 1ST E DI
CUMBASH, JOHN-BLACK FRE 049 FREDERIC
CUMBERLAINE, HESTOR BAL 089 5TH WARD
CUMBLEY, MARGARET BAL 107 2ND DIST
CUMBURH, TYLER FRE 098 FREDERIC
CUMERNER, MARGARETTA BAL 386 1ST DIST
CUMERY, JOHN DOR 367 3RD DIVI
CUMINGHAM, PATRICK BAL 032 1ST WARD
CUMINGS, DANIEL BAL 242 1ST DIST
CUMINGS, TIMOTHY BAL 301 1ST DIST
CUMINS, MICHAEL BAL 199 2ND WARD
CUMMCIONE, JAMES * BAL 139 19TH WAR
CUMMER, ANDREW BAL 235 20TH WAR
CUMMER, CAROLINE MGM 337 CRACKLIN
CUMMER, HENRY BAL 234 20TH WAR
CUMMERS, JAMES MGM 392 ROCKERLE
CUMMERVILLE, FRANCIS BAL 300 7TH WARD
CUMMIGS, JOSEPH H. TAL 115 ST MICHA
CUMMING, WILLIAM H. TAL 112 ST MICHA
CUMMING.S ANN L. MGM 442 CLARKSTR
CUMMINGHAM, J. FRE 196 5TH E DI
CUMMINGHAM, JAMES BAL 313 12TH WAR
CUMMINGHAM, JOHN BAL 161 2ND DIST
CUMMINGHAM, LYDIA CEC 182 7TH E DI
CUMMINGHAM, STEPHEN BAL 221 12TH WAR
CUMMINGHAM, THOMAS * BAL 104 2ND DIST
CUMMINGS, ANN E. TAL 117 ST MICHA
CUMMINGS, AUGUSTUS J. FRE 061 FREDERIC
CUMMINGS, BARNEY TAL 118 ST MICHA

Name	County	Page	District
CUMMINGS, C.	BAL	149	1ST WARD
CUMMINGS, CHRISTOFER	CAR	394	2ND DIST
CUMMINGS, CORNELIA	BAL	401	8TH WARD
CUMMINGS, ELIZABETH	CAR	341	6TH DIST
CUMMINGS, ELIZABETH	TAL	061	EASTON D
CUMMINGS, FREDERIC	CAR	335	6TH DIST
CUMMINGS, H.	TAL	107	ST MICHA
CUMMINGS, HENRY	CAR	297	7TH DIST
CUMMINGS, ISAAC	BAL	211	17TH WAR
CUMMINGS, J.C.	BAL	158	1ST WARD
CUMMINGS, JACOB	BAL	386	1ST DIST
CUMMINGS, JAMES	BAL	156	1ST WARD
CUMMINGS, JAMES	BAL	059	4TH WARD
CUMMINGS, JANE	QUE	160	2ND E DI
CUMMINGS, JANE P.	BAL	405	8TH WARD
CUMMINGS, JOHN	BAL	189	2ND WARD
CUMMINGS, JOHN	BAL	189	2ND WARD
CUMMINGS, JOHN	BAL	353	7TH WARD
CUMMINGS, JOHN	CAR	332	MANCHEST
CUMMINGS, JOHN G.	BAL	458	8TH WARD
CUMMINGS, LARRIMORE	TAL	113	ST MICHA
CUMMINGS, LAVINIA	BAL	475	14TH WAR
CUMMINGS, LEVENIA	BAL	373	3RD WARD
CUMMINGS, LEWIS	TAL	118	ST MICHA
CUMMINGS, LOUISA	BAL	391	8TH WARD
CUMMINGS, MARGARET	BAL	405	3RD WARD
CUMMINGS, MARGARET	BAL	346	13TH WAR
CUMMINGS, MARY	BAL	306	3RD WARD
CUMMINGS, MARY E.	BAL	262	1ST DIST
CUMMINGS, MICHAL	TAL	111	ST MICHA
CUMMINGS, NANCY	TAL	118	ST MICHA
CUMMINGS, NANCY	BAL	039	2ND DIST
CUMMINGS, NICHOLAS	TAL	114	ST MICHA
CUMMINGS, OAKLEY	TAL	118	ST MICHA
CUMMINGS, ROSE	TAL	084	ST MICHA
CUMMINGS, SARAH	BAL	043	4TH WARD
CUMMINGS, SARAH J.	TAL	117	ST MICHA
CUMMINGS, SHARLOTT	CAR	065	NO TWP L
CUMMINGS, SIMON	BAL	088	4TH WARD
CUMMINGS, THOMAS	BAL	364	3RD WARD
CUMMINGS, WILLIAM	BAL	349	7TH WARD
CUMMINGS, WILLIAM	TAL	108	ST MICHA
CUMMINS, ALEXANDER	BAL	312	3RD WARD
CUMMINS, ALEXANDER	BAL	182	19TH WAR
CUMMINS, BRIDGET	BAL	420	3RD WARD
CUMMINS, CASPER H.	WAS	256	1ST DIST
CUMMINS, CHARLOTTE	BAL	163	6TH WARD
CUMMINS, ELIZABETH	BAL	083	2ND DIST
CUMMINS, ELIZABETH	MGM	442	CLARKSTR
CUMMINS, ENOCH	BAL	374	3RD WARD
CUMMINS, HORACE	BAL	316	3RD WARD
CUMMINS, JOHN	BAL	035	4TH WARD
CUMMINS, JOHN H.	KEN	284	3RD DIST
CUMMINS, LEWIS	ANN	336	3RD DIST
CUMMINS, MARGARETT	BAL	077	4TH WARD
CUMMINS, MARIA	DOR	417	1ST DIST
CUMMINS, MARY	BAL	187	19TH WAR
CUMMINS, MARY	BAL	163	6TH WARD
CUMMINS, MARY A.	CEC	168	6TH E DI
CUMMINS, MARY JANE	BAL	404	14TH WAR
CUMMINS, MORRIS	BAL	315	7TH WARD
CUMMINS, ROBERT	BAL	101	2ND DIST
CUMMINS, ROBERT	BAL	350	3RD WARD
CUMMINS, SAMUEL	DOR	417	1ST DIST
CUMMINS, SARAH A.	BAL	316	3RD WARD
CUMMINS, SIMON	BAL	158	6TH WARD
CUMMINS, THOMAS	BAL	082	2ND DIST
CUMMINS, THOMAS	ALL	048	10TH E.D
CUMMINS, WILLIAM	MGM	377	ROCKERLE
CUMMINS,NANCY	BAL	048	2ND DIST
CUMMINS,PETER	BAL	205	2ND WARD
CUMMINS,ROBERT	CAR	400	2ND DIST
CUMMISKEY, CHARLES	BAL	302	12TH WAR
CUMMISKEY, J.	BAL	320	20TH WAR
CUMPBELL, N.	BAL	307	12TH WAR
CUMPHREY, JOHN	BAL	366	13TH WAR
CUMPMON, JOHN *	BAL	399	1ST DIST
CUMY, JAMES	BAL	114	1ST WARD
CUNALES, MAHALA*	DOR	425	1ST DIST
CUNAN, MICHAEL	BAL	180	2ND DIST
CUNAN, THOMAS	BAL	087	10TH WAR
CUNBELL, CATHERINE	BAL	139	11TH WAR
CUNBURLY, DAVID	SOM	357	BRINKLEY
CUNE, SARAH	BAL	193	19TH WAR
CUNGHAM, JOHN	BAL	049	2ND DIST
CUNINGHAM, ANDREW	BAL	285	7TH WARD
CUNINGHAM, CECELIA	BAL	328	7TH WARD
CUNINGHAM, ELEXANDER	HAR	168	3RD DIST
CUNINGHAM, ELLEN	BAL	418	8TH WARD
CUNINGHAM, FANNEY	BAL	265	7TH WARD
CUNINGHAM, GEORGE	BAL	031	2ND DIST
CUNINGHAM, J.B.	HAR	168	3RD DIST
CUNINGHAM, JAMES	BAL	327	7TH WARD
CUNINGHAM, JOHN	BAL	386	8TH WARD
CUNINGHAM, JOHN	BAL	369	8TH WARD
CUNINGHAM, JOHN	WAS	295	1ST DIST
CUNINGHAM, JOHN A.	HAR	189	3RD DIST
CUNINGHAM, JOSEPH	WAS	295	1ST DIST
CUNINGHAM, MARY E.	BAL	278	7TH WARD
CUNINGHAM, SAMUEL	BAL	417	8TH WARD
CUNINGHAM, SARAH C.	WAS	295	1ST DIST
CUNINGHAM, THOMAS	CEC	096	4TH E DI
CUNINGHAM, WARREN	BAL	271	1ST DIST
CUNINGHAM, WILLIAM A.	BAL	320	7TH WARD
CUNINGHAM, WILLIAM C.	BAL	282	7TH WARD
CUNMMINGHAM, THOMAS	CEC	172	6TH E DI
CUNN, THOMAS	BAL	273	1ST DIST
CUNNIFF, JAMES	CEC	154	PORT DUP
CUNNIGAM, HENRY	BAL	033	4TH WARD
CUNNIGAN, JAMES	PRI	039	VANSVILL
CUNNINE, JAMES	WOR	210	4TH E DI
CUNNINE, WILLIAM	WOR	210	4TH E DI
CUNNING, JOHN	WAS	039	2ND SUBD
CUNNINGAN, MERIC	HAR	077	BEL AIR
CUNNINGHA, MICHAEL	BAL	131	1ST WARD
CUNNINGHAM, ANDREW	HAR	039	1ST DIST
CUNNINGHAM, ANN	BAL	042	4TH WARD
CUNNINGHAM, ANN	BAL	061	18TH WAR
CUNNINGHAM, ANN	BAL	001	1ST WARD
CUNNINGHAM, ANN	BAL	331	13TH WAR
CUNNINGHAM, B.A.	FRE	211	BUCKEYST
CUNNINGHAM, B.C.W.	HAR	052	1ST DIST
CUNNINGHAM, CAROLINE	HAR	098	2ND DIST
CUNNINGHAM, CATHARINE	BAL	288	1ST DIST
CUNNINGHAM, CECELIA	BAL	382	13TH WAR
CUNNINGHAM, CHARLES	BAL	067	2ND DIST
CUNNINGHAM, CHARLES R.	BAL	191	6TH WARD
CUNNINGHAM, DANIEL	HAR	202	3RD DIST
CUNNINGHAM, DAVID	CEC	209	7TH E DI
CUNNINGHAM, EDWARD	BAL	187	19TH WAR
CUNNINGHAM, ELENOR	HAR	041	1ST DIST
CUNNINGHAM, ELISHA B.	BAL	253	6TH WARD
CUNNINGHAM, ELIZA	BAL	280	20TH WAR
CUNNINGHAM, ELIZABETH	BAL	171	11TH WAR
CUNNINGHAM, ELIZABETH	BAL	169	11TH WAR
CUNNINGHAM, ELIZABETH	BAL	345	3RD WARD
CUNNINGHAM, ELIZABETH	WAS	103	2ND DIST
CUNNINGHAM, ELLEN	BAL	384	13TH WAR
CUNNINGHAM, G. S.	BAL	082	18TH WAR
CUNNINGHAM, GEORGE	BAL	030	4TH WARD
CUNNINGHAM, GEORGE W.	BAL	398	1ST DIST
CUNNINGHAM, HENRY W.	BAL	042	9TH WARD
CUNNINGHAM, HUGH	BAL	168	11TH WAR
CUNNINGHAM, HUGH	HAR	046	1ST DIST
CUNNINGHAM, ISAAC H.	BAL	127	1ST WARD
CUNNINGHAM, ISABELLA	WAS	151	HAGERSTO
CUNNINGHAM, JAMES	BAL	437	8TH WARD
CUNNINGHAM, JAMES	BAL	050	9TH WARD
CUNNINGHAM, JAMES	ANN	425	HOWARD D
CUNNINGHAM, JAMES	ALL	107	5TH E.D.
CUNNINGHAM, JAMES	CEC	189	7TH E DI
CUNNINGHAM, JAMES M.	HAR	039	1ST DIST
CUNNINGHAM, JANET	BAL	402	14TH WAR
CUNNINGHAM, JOHN	CEC	085	5TH E DI
CUNNINGHAM, JOHN	HAR	198	3RD DIST
CUNNINGHAM, JOHN	BAL	159	19TH WAR
CUNNINGHAM, JOHN	ALL	173	7TH E.D.
CUNNINGHAM, JOHN	BAL	067	2ND DIST
CUNNINGHAM, JOHN	BAL	316	7TH WARD
CUNNINGHAM, JOHN	BAL	430	8TH WARD
CUNNINGHAM, JOHN	BAL	107	5TH WARD
CUNNINGHAM, JOHN	BAL	323	1ST DIST
CUNNINGHAM, JOHN	BAL	038	1ST WARD
CUNNINGHAM, JOHN	WAS	156	2ND DIST
CUNNINGHAM, JOHN M.	BAL	185	19TH WAR
CUNNINGHAM, JONATHAN	CAR	240	TANEYTOW
CUNNINGHAM, JOSEPH	BAL	051	9TH WARD
CUNNINGHAM, JULIA A.	BAL	018	18TH WAR
CUNNINGHAM, JULIANNA	MGM	363	BERRYS D
CUNNINGHAM, LEVINIA	BAL	380	3RD WARD
CUNNINGHAM, MARGARET	BAL	261	6TH WARD
CUNNINGHAM, MARGARET	BAL	274	2ND WARD
CUNNINGHAM, MARGARET	BAL	105	15TH WAR
CUNNINGHAM, MARGARET	BAL	004	EASTERN
CUNNINGHAM, MARGARET	CEC	208	7TH E DI
CUNNINGHAM, MARY	BAL	292	20TH WAR
CUNNINGHAM, MARY	BAL	348	13TH WAR
CUNNINGHAM, MARY	BAL	127	11TH WAR
CUNNINGHAM, MARY	ALL	231	CUMBERLA
CUNNINGHAM, MARY	ALL	118	5TH E.D.
CUNNINGHAM, MARY A.	WAS	160	HAGERSTO
CUNNINGHAM, MARY J.	BAL	025	9TH WARD
CUNNINGHAM, MICHAEL	WAS	173	FUNKSTOW
CUNNINGHAM, MORTIMER	BAL	086	4TH WARD
CUNNINGHAM, NICHOLAS	ANN	424	HOWARD D
CUNNINGHAM, NICHOLAS	BAL	099	10TH WAR
CUNNINGHAM, PATRICK	BAL	099	1ST WARD
CUNNINGHAM, REBECA	BAL	059	18TH WAR
CUNNINGHAM, REBECCA	BAL	169	11TH WAR
CUNNINGHAM, RESESE	HAR	202	3RD DIST
CUNNINGHAM, ROSANA	BAL	213	11TH WAR
CUNNINGHAM, S.S.	WAS	002	WILLIAMS
CUNNINGHAM, SAMUEL	BAL	003	EASTERN
CUNNINGHAM, SHAYT	ALL	018	3RD E.D.
CUNNINGHAM, SUSAN T.	BAL	087	4TH WARD
CUNNINGHAM, T.	BAL	282	2ND WARD
CUNNINGHAM, THOMAS	ALL	108	5TH E.D.
CUNNINGHAM, THOMAS	ALL	071	5TH E.D.
CUNNINGHAM, THOMAS	BAL	099	2ND DIST
CUNNINGHAM, THOMAS	BAL	016	15TH WAR
CUNNINGHAM, THOMAS W.	BAL	046	9TH WARD
CUNNINGHAM, WALTER	HAR	029	1ST DIST
CUNNINGHAM, WALTER	HAR	093	2ND DIST
CUNNINGHAM, WILLIAM	HAR	015	1ST DIST
CUNNINGHAM, WILLIAM	BAL	056	15TH WAR
CUNNINGHAM, WILLIAM	BAL	140	1ST WARD
CUNNINGHAM, WILLIAM	BAL	161	1ST WARD
CUNNINGHAM, WILLIAM	BAL	344	3RD WARD
CUNNINGHAM, WILLIAM	WAS	252	1ST DIST
CUNNINGHAM, WILLIAM C.	ALL	017	3RD E.D.
CUNNINGHAM, WILLIAM F.	MGM	319	CRACKLIN
CUNNINGHAM, WILLIAM H.	ANN	402	8TH DIST
CUNNINGHAM, WILLIAM H.	BAL	219	6TH WARD
CUNNINGHAM, WILLIAM W.	HAR	141	2ND DIST
CUNNINGHAM,MARY A.	BAL	003	1ST WARD
CUNNINGHAN, MARTHA	BAL	399	1ST DIST
CUNNINGS, MARY	BAL	007	4TH WARD
CUNNNINGHAM, JOHN	CEC	188	7TH E DI
CUPP, JOHN	ALL	036	2ND E.D.
CUPP, PERRY-BLACK	CAR	105	NO TWP L
CUPP, SENA	ALL	044	10TH E.D
CUPPISH, FREDERICK	WAS	265	1ST DIST
CURBY, JOSHUA	CAR	215	5TH DIST
CURBY, KERN	ALL	196	CUMBERLA
CURBY, THOMAS	BAL	281	1ST DIST
CURCHEVILLE, TALBOT	WAS	063	2ND SUBD
CURCHEVILLE, WILLIAM	WAS	062	2ND SUBD
CURD, SAMUEL	CEC	177	7TH E DI
CURDS, JOSEPH	CEC	155	PORT DUP
CURDY, CATHERINE	BAL	024	9TH WARD
CURE, RACHEL	BAL	058	10TH WAR
CUREN, JOHN P.	BAL	221	19TH WAR
CUREY, ANN	ALL	102	5TH E.D.
CURFMAN, HARRIET	FRE	154	10TH E D
CURFMAN, SARAH	FRE	367	CATOCTIN
CURFMAN, SARAH A.	FRE	040	FREDERIC
CURFMAN, WILLIAM	WAS	028	2ND SUBD
CURIANS, ELIJAH	CAR	302	1ST DIST
CURINGA, RICHARD	CEC	181	7TH E DI
CURITY, EMILY	BAL	215	11TH WAR
CURLETT, EDWARD	BAL	096	1ST WARD
CURLETT, ELIZABETH	BAL	259	6TH WARD
CURLETT, JOHN *	BAL	293	20TH WAR
CURLETT, LEWIS G.*	BAL	044	4TH WARD
CURLETT, LUCY	BAL	376	8TH WARD
CURLETT, LUCY W.*	BAL	413	3RD WARD
CURLETT, MARY	BAL	306	7TH WARD
CURLEY, BRIDGET	BAL	356	3RD WARD
CURLEY, CAHTERINE	BAL	055	9TH WARD
CURLEY, CATHARINE	BAL	313	12TH WAR
CURLEY, DAVID	WAS	130	2ND DIST
CURLEY, ELLEN	BAL	137	11TH WAR
CURLEY, EMELINE	FRE	065	FREDERIC
CURLEY, GEORGE	WAS	297	1ST DIST
CURLEY, HENRY	BAL	374	1ST DIST
CURLEY, HENRY R.	BAL	145	11TH WAR
CURLEY, J.M.	BAL	281	2ND WARD
CURLEY, JAMES	BAL	144	11TH WAR
CURLEY, JAMES	BAL	135	11TH WAR
CURLEY, JAMES	PRI	028	VANSVILL
CURLEY, JAMES W.	BAL	340	13TH WAR
CURLEY, JANE	BAL	440	14TH WAR
CURLEY, JOSEPH	ANN	330	2ND DIST
CURLEY, MARIA	PRI	030	VANSVILL
CURLEY, MARY	WAS	159	2ND DIST
CURLEY, MARY	BAL	046	15TH WAR
CURLEY, MARY	BAL	465	14TH WAR
CURLEY, RISE	BAL	264	12TH WAR
CURLEY, SUSAN	BAL	078	10TH WAR
CURLEY, THOMAS	ANN	429	HOWARD D
CURLEY, WILLIAM	BAL	078	10TH WAR
CURLEY, WILLIAM	BAL	389	8TH WARD
CURLEY, WILLIAM	BAL	137	11TH WAR
CURLEY, WILLIAM	BAL	096	18TH WAR
CURLL, PEARCE	ANN	424	HOWARD D
CURLOTT, JAMES	KEN	294	3RD DIST
CURMANE, WILLIAM	CAR	343	6TH DIST
CURMLET, THOMAS	BAL	161	19TH WAR
CURN, ALEXANDER	BAL	295	12TH WAR
CURNAUER, PATRICK*	BAL	115	11TH WAR
CURNER, JOSHUA	BAL	182	19TH WAR
CURNES, WILLIAM	BAL	271	12TH WAR
CURNEY, JAMES	BAL	021	1ST WARD
CURNNINGHAM, JOHN	ALL	080	5TH E.D.
CURNS, MICHAEL	ALL	056	10TH E.D
CURNY, JOHN	BAL	021	1ST WARD
CURNY, WILLIAM	CEC	014	ELKTON 3
CURRAM, ANN *	BAL	023	18TH WAR
CURRAN, DENNIS	MGM	381	ROCKERLE
CURRAN, JAMES	BAL	105	15TH WAR
CURRAN, JAMES	ANN	422	HOWARD D
CURRAN, JOHN	BAL	112	15TH WAR
CURRAN, JOHN	BAL	001	9TH WARD
CURRAN, JOHN	BAL	206	6TH WARD
CURRAN, MARY	BAL	305	3RD WARD
CURRAN, MARY A.	BAL	281	7TH WARD
CURRAN, MARY A.	BAL	259	6TH WARD
CURRAN, MICHAEL	BAL	418	8TH WARD
CURRAN, MICHAEL	BAL	273	1ST DIST
CURRAN, PATRICK	PRI	038	VANSVILL
CURRAN, STEPHEN	BAL	385	8TH WARD
CURRAN, THOMAS*	BAL	088	10TH WAR
CURRAN, WILLIAM	MGM	380	ROCKERLE
CURRANS, AMELIA	CAR	241	TANEYTOW
CURRANS, ELIJAH	CAR	240	TANEYTOW
CURRAY, SARAH	CAR	396	2ND DIST
CURREER, SAMUEL	ALL	111	5TH E.D.
CURREL, ANN M.	ST	300	2ND E DI
CURREL, DAVID	BAL	362	13TH WAR
CURREN, MARY	BAL	104	5TH WARD
CURREN, MARY A.	BAL	440	14TH WAR
CURRENS, MARGARET	FRE	178	5TH E DI
CURRENS, WILLIAM	FRE	118	CREAGERS
CURREY, ANN	HAR	013	1ST DIST
CURREY, HENRY	FRE	427	8TH E DI
CURREY, JOHN	HAR	006	1ST DIST
CURREY, JOHN-BLACK	FRE	425	8TH E DI
CURREY, LIDDY	BAL	037	4TH WARD
CURREY, SAMUEL P.	BAL	282	7TH WARD
CURREY,W ILLIAM-BLACK	FRE	433	8TH E DI
CURRIGAN, CATHARINE	BAL	204	11TH WAR
CURRIN, THOMAS	BAL	127	5TH WARD
CURROCK, AMOS	PRI	034	VANSVILL
CURRON, JANE	BAL	388	13TH WAR
CURRY, ADALINE A.	ST	261	3RD E DI
CURRY, ALEXANDER	CEC	015	ELKTON 3
CURRY, ARTHER	HAR	051	1ST DIST
CURRY, ARTHUR M.	ANN	288	ANNAPOLI
CURRY, CATHARINE	BAL	150	5TH WARD
CURRY, CATHARINE	BAL	150	5TH WARD
CURRY, DELILAH	BAL	034	2ND DIST
CURRY, EDWARD T.	BAL	158	19TH WAR
CURRY, EFFY	HAR	089	2ND DIST
CURRY, ELIZA	CEC	135	6TH E DI
CURRY, ELLEN	ANN	345	3RD DIST
CURRY, FRANCIS	BAL	149	2ND DIST
CURRY, HANNAH	BAL	119	2ND DIST
CURRY, HANNAH	HAR	026	1ST DIST
CURRY, HANNAH	HAR	115	2ND DIST
CURRY, HAXDEL	BAL	073	2ND DIST
CURRY, ISAAC	BAL	071	1ST WARD
CURRY, ISRAEL	BAL	047	2ND DIST
CURRY, JACKSON	HAR	087	2ND DIST
CURRY, JAMES	BAL	110	2ND DIST
CURRY, JAMES H.	CAR	397	2ND DIST
CURRY, JANE	ST	340	5TH E DI
CURRY, JOHN	ST	341	5TH E DI
CURRY, JOHN	KEN	256	1ST DIST
CURRY, JOHN	WAS	152	HAGERSTO
CURRY, JOHN	HAR	083	2ND DIST
CURRY, JOHN	CEC	135	6TH E DI
CURRY, JOHN	ANN	299	1ST DIST
CURRY, JOHN	BAL	104	5TH WARD
CURRY, JOHN W.	CHA	273	ALLENS F
CURRY, JOSEPH	ST	346	5TH E DI
CURRY, KEENE	BAL	038	2ND DIST
CURRY, LEVI H.	BAL	032	4TH WARD
CURRY, M.	BAL	166	1ST WARD
CURRY, MARTHA	CAR	234	UNION TO
CURRY, MARY	CEC	179	7TH E DI
CURRY, MARY	BAL	150	2ND DIST
CURRY, MARY	ST	340	5TH E DI
CURRY, MARY E.	HAR	083	2ND DIST
CURRY, NORMAN B.	BAL	278	20TH WAR
CURRY, REBECCA	CHA	275	ALLENS F
CURRY, RICHARD	CEC	067	5TH E DI
CURRY, ROBERT	ANN	359	3RD DIST
CURRY, ROSETTA	BAL	117	15TH WAR
CURRY, RUTH	BAL	440	1ST DIST
CURRY, SOPHIA	HAR	058	1ST DIST
CURRY, THOMAS	BAL	131	1ST WARD
CURRY, WILLIAM	CEC	190	5TH E DI
CURRY, WILLIAM	BAL	227	19TH WAR
CURRY, WILLIAM	BAL	123	11TH WAR
CURSE, JAMES	BAL	036	1ST WARD
CURSELL, JOHN	CEC	180	7TH E DI
CURSON, JOSEPH	BAL	403	14TH WAR
CURSTIS, ANN L.	WAS	133	HAGERSTO
CURTAIN, GEORGE	BAL	053	9TH WARD
CURTAIN, HENRY	BAL	003	EASTERN
CURTAIN, JAMES	BAL	002	EASTERN
CURTAIN, MARGARET	BAL	254	6TH WARD
CURTAIN, MARY	BAL	149	11TH WAR
CURTAIN, MARY	BAL	149	11TH WAR
CURTAIN, ROBERT	BAL	305	7TH WARD
CURTAIN, ROBERT	BAL	458	8TH WARD
CURTAIN, SAMUEL	BAL	358	3RD WARD
CURTAIN, TIMOTHY	ALL	013	3RD E.D.
CURTIAN, SUSAN	BAL	333	13TH WAR
CURTIAN, THOMAS	BAL	035	18TH WAR

CURTIC.E CHARLES-MULATTO ST 340 5TH E DI
CURTICE, ALEXANDER-BLACK ST 344 5TH E DI
CURTICE, ANN-BLACK ST 346 5TH E DI
CURTICE, CHARLES ST 324 4TH E DI
CURTICE, CHARLOTTE-BLACK ST 346 5TH E DI
CURTICE, CORNELIUS-BLACK ST 320 4TH E DI
CURTICE, ELIZA-BLACK ST 344 5TH E DI
CURTICE, ELIZABETH E.-BLA ST 344 5TH E DI
CURTICE, ELIZABETH-BLACK ST 338 4TH E DI
CURTICE, GEORGE ST 338 4TH E DI
CURTICE, GOERGE-BLACK ST 346 5TH E DI
CURTICE, GUSTY-BLACK ST 323 4TH E DI
CURTICE, HENRIETTA-MULATT ST 322 4TH E DI
CURTICE, HENRY-BLACK ST 338 4TH E DI
CURTICE, IGNATIUS H.-BLAC ST 347 5TH E DI
CURTICE, JAMES-BLACK ST 346 5TH E DI
CURTICE, JOHN L.-BLACK ST 333 4TH E DI
CURTICE, JOHN-BLACK ST 345 5TH E DI
CURTICE, JOSEPH-BLACK ST 322 4TH E DI
CURTICE, LOUIS-BLACK ST 332 4TH E DI
CURTICE, MARGARET ST 343 5TH E DI
CURTICE, MARTHA A.-BLACK ST 344 5TH E DI
CURTICE, MASHACK-BLACK ST 348 5TH E DI
CURTICE, MATILDA-MULATTO ST 321 4TH E DI
CURTICE, MOSES-BLACK ST 327 4TH E DI
CURTICE, REBECCA-BLACK ST 326 4TH E DI
CURTICE, REBECCA-BLACK ST 347 5TH E DI
CURTICE, SARAH-BLACK ST 320 4TH E DI
CURTICE, SARAH-BLACK ST 320 4TH E DI
CURTICE, VINCENT-BLACK ST 327 4TH E DI
CURTICE, WILLIAM-BLACK ST 342 5TH E DI
CURTIE, P. BAL 165 1ST WARD
CURTIN, DENNIS PRI 054 AQUASCO
CURTIN, ELIZABETH PRI 057 NOTTINGH
CURTIN, HEZEKIAH PRI 060 NOTTINGH
CURTIN, JAMES PRI 057 NOTTINGH
CURTIN, LEONE PRI 054 AQUASCO
CURTIN, MRS. PRI 093 MARLBROU
CURTIN, PATRICK BAL 051 15TH WAR
CURTIN, RICHEL PRI 061 NOTTINGH
CURTIN, ROZELLA PRI 060 NOTTINGH
CURTIN, WILLIAM PRI 057 NOTTINGH
CURTIN, WILLIAM PRI 049 AQUASCO
CURTIS, ABEDNEGO * BAL 441 8TH WARD
CURTIS, ACEEY BAL 098 18TH WAR
CURTIS, ADLINE CHA 288 BOJANTOW
CURTIS, ALEXANDER-BLACK ST 304 2ND E DI
CURTIS, ALFRED A. SOM 390 BRINKLEY
CURTIS, ANN BAL 441 8TH WARD
CURTIS, ANN M.-BLACK ST 295 2ND E DI
CURTIS, BENJAMIN BAL 023 9TH WARD
CURTIS, CHRISTIE BAL 452 8TH WARD
CURTIS, CLARA BAL 082 15TH WAR
CURTIS, CANIEL BAL 140 1ST WARD
CURTIS, DAVID BAL 251 1ST DIST
CURTIS, CAVID BAL 404 1ST DIST
CURTIS, EASTER-BLACK CAR 073 NO TWP L
CURTIS, EDWARD SOM 404 BRINKLEY
CURTIS, EDWARD SOM 466 HANGARY
CURTIS, ELIZABETH Y. CHA 283 BOJANTOW
CURTIS, ELLEN BAL 028 15TH WAR
CURTIS, ELLEN ALL 226 CUMBERLA
CURTIS, EMELINE ST 290 2ND E DI
CURTIS, FRANCES BAL 177 16TH WAR
CURTIS, FRANCIS BAL 266 20TH WAR
CURTIS, GEORGE ANN 438 HOWARD D
CURTIS, GEORGE BAL 257 1ST DIST
CURTIS, GEORGE ST 271 3RD E DI
CURTIS, GEORGE PRI 111 PISCATAW
CURTIS, GEORGE W. ST 270 3RD E DI
CURTIS, HAGNE A. BAL 051 18TH WAR
CURTIS, HELLARY ST 260 3RD E DI
CURTIS, HENRY ST 259 3RD E DI
CURTIS, HENRY ST 262 3RD E DI
CURTIS, HENRY-BLACK ST 304 2ND E DI
CURTIS, JACOB BAL 022 18TH WAR
CURTIS, JAEMS H. ST 257 3RD E DI
CURTIS, JAMES ST 268 3RD E DI
CURTIS, JAMES ST 258 3RD E DI
CURTIS, JAMES WOR 349 1ST E DI
CURTIS, JAMES BAL 155 1ST WARD
CURTIS, JANE BAL 340 1ST DIST
CURTIS, JANE BAL 400 14TH WAR
CURTIS, JANE M. FRE 445 8TH E DI
CURTIS, JESSE BAL 022 9TH WARD
CURTIS, JOHANNA BAL 207 2ND WARD
CURTIS, JOHN BAL 154 2ND DIST
CURTIS, JOHN BAL 170 2ND DIST
CURTIS, JOHN BAL 050 2ND DIST
CURTIS, JOHN BAL 025 15TH WAR
CURTIS, JOHN ALL 013 3RD E.D.
CURTIS, JOHN SOM 412 DUBLIN D
CURTIS, JOHN BAL 137 18TH WAR
CURTIS, JOHN SOM 361 BRINKLEY
CURTIS, JOHN SOM 485 TRAPP DI
CURTIS, JOHN H. BAL 196 19TH WAR
CURTIS, JOHN H. BAL 264 2ND WARD
CURTIS, JOHN-BLACK ST 294 2ND E DI
CURTIS, JOSEPH PRI 073 MARLBROU
CURTIS, JOSEPH BAL 057 2ND DIST
CURTIS, JUDSON M. QUE 209 3RD E DI
CURTIS, LEN-BLACK ST 313 1ST E DI
CURTIS, LEVIN SOM 458 DAMES QU
CURTIS, LEVY BAL 045 2ND DIST
CURTIS, LLEWELLEN * ST 258 3RD E DI
CURTIS, LOUISA J. WOR 182 6TH E DI
CURTIS, LUCIEN BAL 096 2ND DIST
CURTIS, LUCINDA BAL 235 6TH WARD
CURTIS, MAHALA * BAL 098 18TH WAR
CURTIS, MARGARET ANN 431 HOWARD D
CURTIS, MARGARET BAL 105 5TH WARD
CURTIS, MARTHA BAL 389 3RD WARD
CURTIS, MARY BAL 341 1ST DIST
CURTIS, MARY BAL 032 2ND DIST
CURTIS, MARY BAL 055 15TH WAR
CURTIS, MARY BAL 055 1ST WARD
CURTIS, MARY CHA 282 BOJANTOW
CURTIS, MARY ST 269 3RD E DI
CURTIS, MARY SOM 402 BRINKLEY
CURTIS, MARY E. BAL 023 9TH WARD
CURTIS, MATILDA CHA 281 BOJANTOW
CURTIS, MITILDA PRI 048 AQUASCO
CURTIS, MOSES ST 261 3RD E DI
CURTIS, NESSEY-BLACK CAR 080 NO TWP L
CURTIS, NICHOLAS BAL 154 2ND DIST
CURTIS, P. BAL 171 1ST WARD
CURTIS, PEGGY SOM 421 PRINCESS
CURTIS, PERRY-BLACK ST 291 2ND E DI
CURTIS, PETER BAL 162 1ST WARD
CURTIS, PETER BAL 262 2ND WARD

CURTIS, PETER * BAL 104 18TH WAR
CURTIS, PETGER BAL 143 1ST WARD
CURTIS, PHILIP-BLACK ST 310 1ST E DI
CURTIS, PRISCILLA ST 269 3RD E DI
CURTIS, PRISCILLA-BLACK CAR 073 NO TWP L
CURTIS, REVERDY J. ALL 220 CUMBERLA
CURTIS, ROBERT WAS 158 HAGERSTO
CURTIS, SALLIE M. ANN 521 HOWARD D
CURTIS, SARAH BAL 307 12TH WAR
CURTIS, SARAH PRI 026 VANSVILL
CURTIS, SUSAN CAL 025 2ND DIST
CURTIS, THOMAS WAS 133 HAGERSTO
CURTIS, THOMAS SOM 393 BRINKLEY
CURTIS, THOMAS BAL 193 5TH DIST
CURTIS, THOMAS BAL 452 8TH WARD
CURTIS, THOMAS H. WOR 331 1ST E DI
CURTIS, WILLIAM WAS 288 1ST DIST
CURTIS, WILLIAM BAL 193 5TH DIST
CURTIS, WILLIAM BAL 098 15TH WAR
CURTIS, WILLIAM CHA 282 BOJANTOW
CURTIS, WILLIAM A. ST 270 3RD E DI
CURTIS, WILLIAM-BLACK ST 303 2ND E DI
CURTIS,W ILLIAM BAL 045 2ND DIST
CURTROID, GILBERT P. BAL 253 12TH WAR
CURTUS, JOHN FRE 108 CREAGERS
CURTZ, JAMES BAL 168 1ST WARD
CURVEL, ALVINA BAL 296 20TH WAR
CURVEL, JOHN BAL 295 20TH WAR
CURVENT, SARAH CEC 030 CHESAPEA
CURVIL, MARGARET BAL 422 8TH WARD
CURWELL, GEORGE BAL 369 3RD WARD
CURY, RICHARD PRI 107 PISCATAW
CURZE, A. BAL 166 1ST WARD
CUSACK, PAT BAL 460 1ST DIST
CUSACK, THOMAS BAL 268 1ST DIST
CUSBACK, ELISHA BAL 133 2ND DIST
CUSE, BARBARA ALL 029 2ND E.D.
CUSE, J. L. * BAL 284 20TH WAR
CUSE, PAUL CAR 312 1ST DIST
CUSER, JANE BAL 292 12TH WAR
CUSER, MARY CEC 181 7TH E DI
CUSEY, DELIA WOR 316 2ND E DI
CUSEY, SAMUEL BAL 294 12TH WAR
CUSHEROWL, JACOB * BAL 108 2ND DIST
CUSHING, DAVID BAL 461 14TH WAR
CUSHING, H. B. BAL 106 10TH WAR
CUSHING, JOHN BAL 426 14TH WAR
CUSHING, JOSEPH CAR 284 7TH DIST
CUSHING, JOSEPH BAL 131 16TH WAR
CUSHING, JOSEPH BAL 344 7TH WARD
CUSHING, JOSEPH JR. BAL 339 13TH WAR
CUSHING, LOREZYG CAR 375 9TH DIST
CUSHING, ROBERT WAS 089 2ND SUBD
CUSHING, SUSAN CAR 371 9TH DIST
CUSHING, THOMAS CAR 371 9TH DIST
CUSHLEY, WILLIAM BAL 352 3RD WARD
CUSHNER, WILLIAM WAS 101 2ND DIST
CUSHUA, BEN H. WAS 135 2ND DIST
CUSHUA, CATHARINE WAS 131 2ND DIST
CUSHUA, DAVID WAS 131 2ND DIST
CUSHUA, ISAAC WAS 134 2ND DIST
CUSHUA, JOHN S. WAS 135 2ND DIST
CUSHWA, SARAH WAS 169 FUNKSTOW
CUSHWA, WILLIAM * WAS 101 2ND DIST
CUSHWER, ABRAHAM WAS 146 HAGERSTO
CUSIC, MARGRET BAL 181 2ND WARD
CUSICK, ALOYSIUS ST 257 3RD E DI
CUSICK, ANN E. ST 270 3RD E DI
CUSICK, AUSTIN CHA 285 BOJANTOW
CUSICK, EDWARD BAL 282 7TH WARD
CUSIER, ANTON BAL 105 1ST WARD
CUSLA, JOSEPH ALL 227 CUMBERLA
CUSLEY, ANN E. * BAL 316 20TH WAR
CUSMAN, JOHN BAL 285 2ND WARD
CUSMOWL, ALBRETCH BAL 108 2ND DIST
CUSON, BEN ANN 370 4TH DIST
CUSON, DAVID BAL 248 12TH WAR
CUSSAY, THOMAS ALL 056 10TH E.D
CUSSELL, JOHN J. BAL 190 19TH WAR
CUSSELL, JOSEPH BAL 267 20TH WAR
CUSSEY, GEORGE H. BAL 122 11TH WAR
CUSSIDY, MARY BAL 324 12TH WAR
CUSTAEL, JOHN FRE 249 NEW MARK
CUSTAIL, GEORGE W. FRE 087 FREDERIC
CUSTARD, ADAM FRE 001 FREDERIC
CUSTARD, PETER ALL 009 3RD E.D.
CUSTAS, LEAH BAL 195 11TH WAR
CUSTER, ADAM ALL 015 3RD E.D.
CUSTER, JOHN ALL 015 3RD E.D.
CUSTER, MICHAEL HAR 175 3RD DIST
CUSTER, SAMUEL ALL 009 3RD E.D.
CUSTIGAN, MARY BAL 162 19TH WAR
CUSTIS, CHARLES SOM 436 PRINCESS
CUSTIS, MAHALA * BAL 098 18TH WAR
CUSTMAN, CAROLINE BAL 269 12TH WAR
CUSTO, BRIDGET BAL 310 1ST DIST
CUSTRO, VIRGINIA* BAL 307 3RD WARD
CUSTRUS, JOHN CEC 203 6TH E DI
CUSTUS, GEORGE BAL 420 14TH WAR
CUSTY, LOUIZA KEN 290 3RD DIST
CUTCHALL, SOLOMAN WAS 145 2ND DIST
CUTER, ROBERT WAS 150 2ND DIST
CUTERMAN, JACOB BAL 181 19TH WAR
CUTERUFF, ANN BAL 287 1ST DIST
CUTHBERT, AGNES BAL 107 10TH WAR
CUTLER, ALEXANDER CEC 006 ELKTON 3
CUTLER, DAVID QUE 246 5TH E DI
CUTLER, DAVID QUE 246 5TH E DI
CUTLER, HARRIET BAL 042 9TH WARD
CUTLER, J.C. BAL 282 12TH WAR
CUTLER, JAMES WOR 251 1ST CENS
CUTLER, NANCY BAL 403 1ST DIST
CUTLIPP, BENJAMIN BAL 206 11TH WAR
CUTNAM, ELLEN BAL 037 9TH WARD
CUTSAGLE, MARY CAR 366 9TH DIST
CUTSAIL, JOHN FRE 103 FREDERIC
CUTSHALL, PHELLIPS FRE 292 WOODSBOR
CUTTER, HENRY ALL 121 4TH E.D.
CUTTER, JOSEPH P. CEC 171 6TH E DI
CUTTER, RACHEL BAL 178 16TH WAR
CUTTER, SCHOCKLY B. CEC 174 6TH E DI
CUTTLE, GEORGE BAL 263 12TH WAR
CUTTLE, JOHN BAL 263 12TH WAR
CUVALL, HENRY A. PRI 029 VANSVILL
CUYME, PETER BAL 200 19TH WAR
CUYMI, WILLIAM BAL 236 20TH WAR
CVISTIAN, MARGARET TAL 090 ST MICHA
CYLE, RACHAEL BAL 270 1ST DIST
CYOTT, MARTHA J. BAL 181 6TH WARD
CYPEE, MARY ALL 203 CUMBERLA

CYPHER, GEORGE ALL 155 6TH E.D.
CYPHER, MARY * ALL 146 6TH E.D.
CYPLES, TIGHLMAN ANN 320 2ND DIST
CYPOLE, DURILLA ALL 229 CUMBERLA
CYPRESS, CLARA QUE 250 5TH E DI
CYRIAX, E. C. BERNARD* BAL 085 10TH WAR
CYRUS, GEORGE P. FRE 007 FREDERIC
CYSER, THOMAS WAS 256 1ST DIST
DAARREY, IGNATIUS CHA 269 ALLENS F
DABBLE, SARAH WAS 206 1ST DIST
DABBS, ANN BAL 126 16TH WAR
DABBS, JOSHUA ANN 520 HOWARD D
DABLIN, DIANA BAL 295 3RD WARD
DABS, JOHN BAL 366 1ST DIST
DABSON, EDWARD CAR 168 NO TWP L
DABSON, ELIZABETH CAR 170 NO TWP L
DABSON, JAMES-BLACK CAR 164 NO TWP L
DABSON, MATHEN CAR 167 NO TWP L
DABUS, HENRY WAS 294 1ST DIST
DABUS, MAURITZ BAL 072 4TH WARD
DABUTTS, WILLY FRE 043 FREDERIC
DACEY, MARY BAL 027 9TH WARD
DACHE, MAY BAL 116 11TH WAR
DACKETT, MARSHALL MGM 320 CRACKLIN
DACON, GEORGE DOR 386 1ST DIST
DACON, LEVIN* DOR 469 1ST DIST
DACORRMON, LOUIS * KEN 213 2ND DIST
DACRE, JOHN H. HAR 097 2ND DIST
DACY, MARTIN BAL 409 3RD WARD
DADDS, ALEXANDER W.* TAL 035 EASTON D
DADDS, CHARLES ANN 292 ANNAPOLI
DADDS, MARY ANN 322 2ND DIST
DADDS, MARY BAL 214 17TH WAR
DADDS, WILLAIM ANN 281 ANNAPOLI
DADE, L. BAL 164 1ST WARD
DADE, L. BAL 172 1ST WARD
DADE, LANZY BAL 006 4TH WARD
DADE, ROBERT CAR 369 9TH DIST
DADE, ROBERT T. MGM 410 MEDLEY 3
DADE, WILLIAM CAR 369 9TH DIST
DADEL, WARREN* TAL 008 EASTON D
DADEY, JOHN FRE 165 EMMITTSB
DADISMAN, CATHERINE FRE 061 FREDERIC
DADS, MRS. ANN 270 ANNAPOLI
DADY, DANIEL BAL 298 3RD WARD
DADY, WASHINGTON BAL 299 3RD WARD
DAFFIN, BENJAMIN BAL 121 5TH WARD
DAFFIN, THOMAS J. TAL 008 EASTON D
DAFFIN, THOMAS* TAL 023 EASTON D
DAFFLER, JACOB BAL 339 7TH WARD
DAFFLER, JOHN CAR 295 7TH DIST
DAFFNEY, JOE ANN 338 3RD DIST
DAFFY, JAMES BAL 420 14TH WAR
DAFFY, JOHN B. BAL 147 11TH WAR
DAGAN, FRANCIS BAL 128 11TH WAR
DAGAN, JULIA-BLACK FRE 017 FREDERIC
DAGAN, LOUISA BAL 329 13TH WAR
DAGAN, MC CEARY PRI 037 VANSVILL
DAGAN, MICHAL WAS 130 2ND DIST
DAGAN, THOMAS BAL 143 1ST WARD
DAGEN, SUSAN BAL 129 11TH WAR
DAGENHARD, FRED BAL 199 2ND WARD
DAGENHARD, PHILIP BAL 401 8TH WARD
DAGENHEART, CHRIST. WAS 179 BOONSBOR
DAGENHEART, EMANUEL WAS 180 BOONSBOR
DAGENHEART, JOHN WAS 179 BOONSBOR
DAGENHEART, JOHN WAS 179 BOONSBOR
DAGENHEART, MARY WAS 179 BOONSBOR
DAGENHEART, SAMUEL WAS 179 BOONSBOR
DAGERT, EDWRD CEC 059 1ST E DI
DAGERTY, MR- BAL 077 15TH WAR
DAGHURTZ, MICHAEL BAL 096 1ST WARD
DAGINET, CATHERINE BAL 285 7TH WARD
DAGINET, ELIZABETH BAL 285 7TH WARD
DAGNAN, PATRICK CEC 064 1ST E DI
DAGNER, SAUEL BAL 219 2ND WARD
DAGOTT, MICHAEL BAL 183 11TH WAR
DAHAMEL,ALFRED A. QUE 191 3RD E DI
DAHL, CHRISTIAN F. BAL 012 9TH WARD
DAHLE, JOHN H.C. BAL 108 5TH WARD
DAHLER, GEORGE BAL 133 16TH WAR
DAHOFF, JACOB BAL 187 5TH DIST
DAHOFF, JOHN WAS 235 1ST DIST
DAHOON, JOHN FRE 264 NEW MARK
DAIGEN, JAMES BAL 300 17TH WAR
DAIGER, CHARLES H. BAL 105 15TH WAR
DAIGER, FREDERICK BAL 058 1ST WARD
DAIGER, JACOB BAL 058 1ST WARD
DAIGER, JAMES BAL 185 2ND WARD
DAIGER, JOSEPH BAL 181 6TH WARD
DAIGER, LUCY A. BAL 397 14TH WAR
DAIGER, MATTHIAS A. BAL 225 2ND WARD
DAIGNIN, JEROME BAL 158 6TH WARD
DAIL, ELIZABETH DOR 390 1ST DIST
DAIL, EMILY DOR 391 1ST DIST
DAIL, JOHN DOR 390 1ST DIST
DAIL, JOHN W. DOR 391 1ST DIST
DAIL, JOSEPH DOR 390 1ST DIST
DAIL, JOSIAH DOR 413 1ST DIST
DAIL, OLERIA BAL 184 2ND WARD
DAIL, OLIVIA DOR 377 1ST DIST
DAIL, ROSSY* DOR 391 1ST DIST
DAIL, THOMAS DOR 373 1ST DIST
DAIL, THOMAS J. DOR 373 1ST DIST
DAIL, THOMAS J. DOR 391 1ST DIST
DAIL, WILLIAM B. DOR 391 1ST DIST
DAILEY, AGNES BAL 301 17TH WAR
DAILEY, BARTHOLOMEW BAL 014 2ND DIST
DAILEY, ELIZABETH BAL 393 8TH WARD
DAILEY, EPHRAIM BAL 386 8TH WARD
DAILEY, HUGH FRE 159 EMMITTSB
DAILEY, J.E. BAL 138 1ST WARD
DAILEY, JACOB JR. BAL 264 7TH WARD
DAILEY, JAMES SOM 487 SALISBUR
DAILEY, JOHN ST 289 2ND E DI
DAILEY, JOHN BAL 340 7TH WARD
DAILEY, JOHN BAL 133 18TH WAR
DAILEY, JOHN C. BAL 177 2ND WARD
DAILEY, MARGARET ALL 255 CUMBERLA
DAILEY, MARTHA BAL 035 2ND DIST
DAILEY, MARY BAL 286 7TH WARD
DAILEY, MARY ALL 198 CUMBERLA
DAILEY, MARY FRE 103 FREDERIC
DAILEY, MARY BAL 387 13TH WAR
DAILEY, MARY J. ST 306 1ST E DI
DAILEY, OWEN BAL 056 15TH WAR
DAILEY, PATRICK ALL 202 CUMBERLA
DAILEY, PATRICK BAL 367 8TH WARD
DAILEY, PATRICK ALL 252 CUMBERLA
DAILEY, SAMUEL M. BAL 398 14TH WAR

Name	Co.	Page	District
DAILEY, THOMAS	ALL	250	CUMBERLA
DAILEY, THOMAS	BAL	182	11TH WAR
DAILEY, WILLIAM	SOM	487	SALISBUR
DAILEY,BARTLEY	ALL	226	CUMBERLA
DAILEY,BRYAN	FRE	218	BUCKEYST
DAILL, H.	BAL	281	2ND WARD
DAILY, CORNELIUS	BAL	014	2ND DIST
DAILY, DANIEL	ST	305	1ST E DI
DAILY, DELA	ANN	429	HOWARD D
DAILY, EDWARD D.	CAR	157	NO TWP L
DAILY, EDWIN N.	MGM	443	CLARKSTR
DAILY, ELIZABETH	CHA	289	BOJANTOW
DAILY, EZEKIEL	BAL	038	2ND DIST
DAILY, FRANCIS M.	MGM	405	ROCKERLE
DAILY, GEORGE	MGM	408	MEDLEY 3
DAILY, HENRY	BAL	164	2ND DIST
DAILY, ISAIAH	HAR	055	1ST DIST
DAILY, JESSE	HAR	037	1ST DIST
DAILY, JOHN	BAL	119	15TH WAR
DAILY, JOHN	BAL	459	1ST DIST
DAILY, JOHN	WAS	159	2ND DIST
DAILY, JOHN W.	MGM	321	CRACKLIN
DAILY, PATRICK	ALL	068	5TH E.D.
DAILY, RACHEL	BAL	033	2ND DIST
DAILY, SAMUEL	SOM	490	SALISBUR
DAILY, SARAH	SOM	489	SALISBUR
DAILY, SETH	BAL	435	1ST DIST
DAILY, SOPHIA	BAL	046	18TH WAR
DAILY, THOMAS	WAS	125	2ND DIST
DAILY, THOMAS	ST	274	3RD E DI
DAILY, THOMAS O.	CHA	289	BOJANTOW
DAILY, THOMAS S.	WAS	124	2ND DIST
DAILY,MARGARET	ALL	206	CUMBERLA
DAINA, CHARLES S.	BAL	187	19TH WAR
DAINALL, FIELDA	MGM	412	MEDLEY 3
DAINALL, THOMAS L.	MGM	407	MEDLEY 3
DAINE, ELIZABETH	MGM	382	ROCKERLE
DAINER, CHRISTIAN	BAL	084	1ST WARD
DAINER, JOHN	FRE	321	MIDDLETO
DAINTEL, LEWIS *	BAL	280	7TH WARD
DAINY, JULIA	BAL	119	11TH WAR
DAIRS, HENRIETTA	MGM	434	CLARKSTR
DAIRS, JOSHUA	MGM	375	ROCKERLE
DAIRS, REBECCA	QUE	197	3RD E DI
DAIRS, SALLY	MGM	379	ROCKERLE
DAIRS, WILLIAM	MGM	375	ROCKERLE
DAIRY, DAVID	BAL	417	14TH WAR
DAIRY, ELIZA C.	WAS	139	HAGERSTO
DAIRY, MANUEL	BAL	107	10TH WAR
DAIRY, MATHIAS	BAL	217	11TH WAR
DAIRY, SAMUEL	BAL	179	6TH WARD
DAISEY, MARY	BAL	035	1ST WARD
DAITFIELD, FREDERICK	BAL	275	2ND WARD
DAIVDSON, PHILIP T.	QUE	219	3RD E DI
DAIVS, CAROLINE	WOR	245	1ST CENS
DAIVS, CHARELS	WOR	279	BERLIN 1
DAIVS, ELIZABETH	WOR	252	1ST CENS
DAIVS, F. C.	BAL	151	1ST WARD
DAIVS, GEORGE A.	BAL	419	14TH WAR
DAIVS, ISAAC	FRE	230	BUCKEYST
DAIVS, ISAC	WOR	252	1ST CENS
DAIVS, ISHMAEL	WOR	265	BERLIN 1
DAIVS, ISMA	WOR	293	9TH E DI
DAIVS, JOHN	WOR	251	1ST CENS
DAIVS, JOSEPH M.	WOR	267	BERLIN 1
DAIVS, LORENZO D.	WOR	251	1ST CENS
DAIVS, MARY A.	WOR	299	SNOW HIL
DAIVS, SIMPSON	WOR	279	BERLIN 1
DAIVS, THOMAS	WOR	281	BERLIN 1
DAIVS, THOMAS	ALL	128	4TH E.D.
DAIVS, WILLIAM	WOR	293	9TH E DI
DAIVS, WILLIAM A.	WOR	294	9TH E DI
DAIVS, WILLIAM P.	WOR	260	BERLIN 1
DAIVS, ZACHARIAH H.	ANN	507	HOWARD D
DAKERS, JAMES	BAL	184	11TH WAR
DAKINS, CESAR	HAR	067	1ST DIST
DAKINS, SARAH-BLACK	MGM	424	MEDLEY 3
DAKINS, STEPHEN	HAR	072	1ST DIST
DALAMORE, PETER	BAL	025	9TH WARD
DALANDS, JOHN	BAL	270	2ND WARD
DALANEY, MARGARET	FRE	243	NEW MARK
DALANTRE, JOHN	BAL	278	17TH WAR
DALANY, WILLIAM	BAL	467	14TH WAR
DALASMAN, WILLIAM	ALL	251	CUMBERLA
DALBICH, CONRAD	BAL	089	10TH WAR
DALD, LEWIS	BAL	059	18TH WAR
DALE, CHARLES G.	WOR	176	6TH E DI
DALE, E.	ANN	303	1ST DIST
DALE, ELI	WOR	266	BERLIN 1
DALE, ELLEN	BAL	078	1ST WARD
DALE, HENRY	BAL	375	3RD WARD
DALE, ISAAC M.	WOR	213	4TH E DI
DALE, JAMES	WOR	268	BERLIN 1
DALE, JOHN	WOR	175	6TH E DI
DALE, JOHN M.	WOR	266	BERLIN 1
DALE, LAWRENCE	ALL	155	6TH E.D.
DALE, MARY	WOR	266	BERLIN 1
DALE, MARY	WOR	281	BERLIN 1
DALE, MARY	WOR	304	SNOW HIL
DALE, R.	BAL	227	19TH WAR
DALE, ROBERT G.	BAL	207	11TH WAR
DALE, SAMUEL	BAL	413	14TH WAR
DALE, WILLIAM J.M.	WOR	172	6TH E DI
DALECOUR, J. P.	BAL	456	8TH WARD
DALES, ELIZABETH	BAL	179	19TH WAR
DALEY, ANDREW	BAL	067	1ST WARD
DALEY, ANN	BAL	340	13TH WAR
DALEY, ANTHONY	BAL	207	6TH WARD
DALEY, BRIDGET	BAL	037	1ST WARD
DALEY, BRIDGET	BAL	176	11TH WAR
DALEY, BRIDGET	BAL	413	1ST DIST
DALEY, BRIDGET	BAL	333	3RD WARD
DALEY, CAROLINE B.	BAL	311	3RD WARD
DALEY, CATHARINE	BAL	291	12TH WAR
DALEY, CATHERINE	BAL	330	3RD WARD
DALEY, CATHRINE	BAL	019	18TH WAR
DALEY, CORNELIUS	BAL	042	9TH WARD
DALEY, CRILIN	BAL	138	11TH WAR
DALEY, EDMUND	MGM	331	CRACKLIN
DALEY, ELIJAH	BAL	256	6TH WARD
DALEY, ELIZA	BAL	388	3RD WARD
DALEY, ELIZABETH	BAL	210	6TH WARD
DALEY, ELIZABETH	MGM	402	ROCKERLE
DALEY, ELLEN	BAL	044	4TH WARD
DALEY, FRANCES	BAL	054	9TH WARD
DALEY, HANNAH	BAL	035	15TH WAR
DALEY, HELEN	BAL	054	9TH WARD
DALEY, HENRY B.	MGM	315	CRACKLIN
DALEY, JAMES	BAL	020	18TH WAR
DALEY, JAMES H.	QUE	177	2ND E DI
DALEY, JESSE	BAL	216	6TH DIST
DALEY, JOHN	BAL	103	1ST WARD
DALEY, JOHN	BAL	039	15TH WAR
DALEY, JOHN	BAL	262	12TH WAR
DALEY, JOHN	BAL	233	12TH WAR
DALEY, JOSEPH W.	BAL	159	6TH WARD
DALEY, JULIA	BAL	316	12TH WAR
DALEY, KATE	BAL	053	9TH WARD
DALEY, MARGARET Y.	MGM	315	CRACKLIN
DALEY, MARY	BAL	347	13TH WAR
DALEY, MARY	BAL	159	16TH WAR
DALEY, MARY	BAL	010	9TH WARD
DALEY, MARY	BAL	241	2ND WARD
DALEY, MARY E.	QUE	178	2ND E DI
DALEY, MICHAEL	BAL	166	11TH WAR
DALEY, MICHAEL	BAL	168	11TH WAR
DALEY, NANCY	BAL	021	9TH WARD
DALEY, OWEN	BAL	079	10TH WAR
DALEY, PATRICK	BAL	195	2ND WARD
DALEY, PATRICK	BAL	444	1ST DIST
DALEY, PETER	BAL	020	9TH WARD
DALEY, PETER	BAL	170	1ST WARD
DALEY, PETER	BAL	116	1ST WARD
DALEY, ROSE	BAL	050	9TH WARD
DALEY, SAMUEL	BAL	169	19TH WAR
DALEY, SARAH	BAL	064	4TH WARD
DALEY, THOMAS	BAL	043	1ST WARD
DALEY, THOMAS	BAL	180	11TH WAR
DALEY, WILLIAM	BAL	257	6TH WARD
DALEY, WILLIAM L.	MGM	390	ROCKERLE
DALEY, WILLIAM P.	BAL	074	18TH WAR
DALIN, ROSE	MGM	381	ROCKERLE
DALL, AUSTIN	BAL	094	10TH WAR
DALL, JAMES	BAL	262	1ST DIST
DALL, JOSEP	BAL	395	14TH WAR
DALL, WILLIAM	BAL	062	10TH WAR
DALLAM, EVEREST	BAL	191	11TH WAR
DALLAM, FRANCIS	BAL	364	13TH WAR
DALLAM, JAMES	HAR	100	2ND DIST
DALLAM, JOHN	BAL	154	11TH WAR
DALLAM, JOHN S.	HAR	075	BEL AIR
DALLAM, RICHARD	HAR	090	2ND DIST
DALLAM, THOMAS J.	BAL	398	8TH WARD
DALLAM, WILLIAM	HAR	100	2ND DIST
DALLAS, G.	BAL	173	1ST WARD
DALLAS, GEORGE	BAL	117	1ST WARD
DALLAS, JOHN	BAL	104	18TH WAR
DALLENGER, ANDREW	ST	298	2ND E DI
DALLWIN, EDW. B. *	BAL	314	20TH WAR
DALPHIRE, FRANK	BAL	197	17TH WAR
DALRIMPLE, JOHN	BAL	364	8TH WARD
DALRIMPLE, MARGARET	BAL	354	7TH WARD
DALRYMPLE, A.P.	PRI	094	SPALDING
DALRYMPLE, ALEXANDER P.	BAL	049	15TH WAR
DALRYMPLE, CHALRES W.	BAL	030	18TH WAR
DALRYMPLE, EIZIN	BAL	020	2ND DIST
DALRYMPLE, ELIZABETH	BAL	030	18TH WAR
DALRYMPLE, JESSIE J.	CAL	033	2ND DIST
DALRYMPLE, JOHN	BAL	087	15TH WAR
DALRYMPLE, MARY E.	CAL	033	2ND DIST
DALRYMPLE, REECCA	CAL	037	2ND DIST
DALRYMPLE, THOMAS	BAL	211	6TH WARD
DALRYMPLE, THOMAS	WAS	018	2ND SUBD
DALRYMPLE, VIRGIL B.	CAL	026	2ND DIST
DALRYMPLE, WILLIAM	CAL	041	3RD DIST
DALRYNPLE, REBECCA	CAL	030	2ND DIST
DALRYRIMPLE, JOSEPH	BAL	008	9TH WARD
DALTON, CATHARINE	BAL	143	5TH WARD
DALTON, CATHERINE	BAL	064	10TH WAR
DALTON, CHARLES F.	BAL	027	18TH WAR
DALTON, EDWARD	BAL	087	10TH WAR
DALTON, JOHN B.	BAL	134	5TH WARD
DALTON, MR.	PRI	105	PISCATAW
DALTON, WINNY*	BAL	012	4TH WARD
DALVYMPLE, CHRISTIAN A.	CAL	007	1ST DIST
DALWEG, CHARLES	BAL	029	2ND DIST
DALWICK, FREDERICKA	BAL	381	13TH WAR
DALY, ANTHONY	BAL	445	1ST DIST
DALY, CATHERINE	BAL	354	3RD WARD
DALY, GRAFTON	MGM	381	ROCKERLE
DALY, JAMES	FRE	384	PETERSVI
DALY, JOHN	BAL	120	1ST WARD
DALY, JOHN	BAL	444	1ST DIST
DALY, JOHN	BAL	459	1ST DIST
DALY, MARGARET	BAL	354	3RD WARD
DALY, MARIA	BAL	032	4TH WARD
DALY, MARTIN	BAL	421	1ST DIST
DALY, MICHIEL	BAL	220	1ST DIST
DALY, ZETH	BAL	439	1ST DIST
DALYRIMPLE, ELIZABETH	BAL	009	9TH WARD
DALZELE, ROBERT	MGM	390	ROCKERLE
DALZELL, JAMES	MGM	390	ROCKERLE
DALZELL, WILLIAM	MGM	408	MEDLEY 3
DAMA, SEBASTIAN	BAL	187	19TH WAR
DAMAN, SIMON	BAL	050	1ST WARD
DAMANUS, J. MRS-	BAL	289	1ST DIST
DAMEITH, DAVID	FRE	118	CREAGERS
DAMERON, JEMIMA	BAL	175	6TH WARD
DAMEROW, MARY	BAL	406	3RD WARD
DAMERSON, WILLIAM	BAL	130	1ST WARD
DAMERSON, WILLIAM	BAL	041	4TH WARD
DAMES, AUGUSTUS	BAL	007	EASTERN
DAMES, FRANCIS	BAL	222	17TH WAR
DAMES, WILLIAM	BAL	005	EASTERN
DAMLEY,RACHAEL	FRE	030	FREDERIC
DAMMAN, CATHARINE	BAL	379	13TH WAR
DAMMAN, L.	BAL	121	18TH WAR
DAMME,ADOLPH	BAL	049	1ST WARD
DAMMOND, MARY	BAL	191	11TH WAR
DAMON, SARAH	BAL	269	1ST DIST
DAMON, SARAH	BAL	015	2ND DIST
DAMORINE, WILLAIM	BAL	230	17TH WAR
DAMPHOUX, EDWARD	BAL	370	8TH WARD
DAMRON, WILLIAM	BAL	125	1ST WARD
DAMRY, N. J.	BAL	150	1ST WARD
DAMULL, RICHARD	CAL	044	3RD DIST
DAMUTH, HENRY	FRE	187	5TH E DI
DAMUTH, HENRY	FRE	186	5TH E DI
DAMUTH, JACOB	FRE	185	5TH E DI
DAMUTH, JAYSON	FRE	186	5TH E DI
DANA, MATHA	ALL	229	CUMBERLA
DANAGH, ANN	BAL	007	15TH WAR
DANBY, PERRY	BAL	459	8TH WARD
DANCAN, MARY	WOR	210	4TH E DI
DANCE, JESSE G.	HAR	076	BEL AIR
DANCE, JOSEPH G.	BAL	086	2ND DIST
DANCE, MARGARET	BAL	006	1ST WARD
DANCE, SUSAN A.	CEC	128	5TH E DI
DANCIN, ANN	HAR	173	3RD DIST
DANCIN, THOMAS	HAR	159	3RD DIST
DANDING, BARB	BAL	271	12TH WAR
DANDON, JOHN G.	BAL	273	2ND WARD
DANDRICK, PATRICK	BAL	449	14TH WAR
DANDS, SAMUEL	BAL	295	12TH WAR
DANDULET, FRANCIS *	BAL	301	20TH WAR
DANDY, GREGORY	BAL	310	1ST DIST
DANE, CATHARINE	BAL	177	19TH WAR
DANE, CATHARINE	BAL	215	19TH WAR
DANERVAN, MARY	BAL	028	1ST WARD
DANES, TYLER	FRE	270	NEW MARK
DANES, WILLIAM	FRE	270	NEW MARK
DANET, ALICE	ANN	269	ANNAPOLI
DANFMAN, ELHAMAN	BAL	092	2ND DIST
DANFMAN, WILLIAM	BAL	092	2ND DIST
DANFORTH, AMBROSE N.	WAS	150	2ND DIST
DANGAN, EMLEY	BAL	346	13TH WAR
DANGERFIELD, D.	BAL	305	12TH WAR
DANGERFIELD, LIDDY	BAL	064	4TH WARD
DANGERFIELD, WILLIAM H.	PRI	119	PISCATAW
DANGHERTY, JOSIAH	WOR	188	7TH E DI
DANIEL, ANN E.	BAL	018	15TH WAR
DANIEL, BILL-BLACK	QUE	155	2ND E DI
DANIEL, GEORGE-BLACK	QUE	141	1ST E DI
DANIEL, JOE M.*	TAL	059	EASTON D
DANIEL, JOHN-BLACK	QUE	140	1ST E DI
DANIEL, NOAH-BLACK	QUE	142	1ST E DI
DANIEL, NOBLE	CEC	021	ELKTON 3
DANIEL, ROBERT	BAL	105	10TH WAR
DANIEL, SARAH-BLACK	QUE	141	1ST E DI
DANIEL, SIMEON-BLACK	QUE	141	1ST E DI
DANIEL, THOMAS	BAL	281	2ND WARD
DANIEL, TRAVERS	SOM	453	DAMES QU
DANIEL,PERE-BLACK	QUE	148	1ST E DI
DANIELL, ELIZABETH	FRE	039	FREDERIC
DANIELS, BOLIVER D.	BAL	016	4TH WARD
DANIELS, CHARLES	BAL	128	1ST WARD
DANIELS, CHARLOTTE	BAL	017	1ST WARD
DANIELS, EDWARD	BAL	114	1ST WARD
DANIELS, ELIZABETH	MGM	377	ROCKERLE
DANIELS, FANNY	BAL	081	2ND DIST
DANIELS, GEORGE-BLACK	QUE	129	1ST E DI
DANIELS, GILES	BAL	163	16TH WAR
DANIELS, ISAAC	ALL	037	2ND E.D.
DANIELS, J.D.	BAL	167	1ST WARD
DANIELS, JAMES	BAL	122	1ST WARD
DANIELS, JOHN	ALL	170	7TH E.D.
DANIELS, JOHN	BAL	131	1ST WARD
DANIELS, JOHN	CAR	218	5TH DIST
DANIELS, JOHN D.	BAL	016	4TH WARD
DANIELS, JOHN D. SR.	BAL	016	4TH WARD
DANIELS, LEWIS-BLACK	QUE	123	1ST E DI
DANIELS, MARY	BAL	003	4TH WARD
DANIELS, PHILIP	BAL	087	2ND DIST
DANIELS, SETH	BAL	122	1ST WARD
DANIELS, SETH	BAL	123	1ST WARD
DANIELS, THOMAS	ALL	135	4TH E.D.
DANIELS, WALTER	BAL	417	8TH WARD
DANIELS, WILLIAM C.	BAL	164	1ST WARD
DANIELSON, WILLIAM	ALL	222	CUMBERLA
DANILE, THOMAS	BAL	167	1ST WARD
DANILL, MARY	BAL	086	2ND DIST
DANISON, CAROLINE	ANN	365	4TH DIST
DANITEL, LEWIS *	BAL	280	7TH WARD
DANKE, HENRY	BAL	313	12TH WAR
DANKS, SAMUEL	ALL	074	5TH E.D.
DANLEY, BRIDGET	BAL	038	9TH WARD
DANNELL, ELIZABETH	BAL	252	6TH WARD
DANNENBERG, ISAAC	ANN	451	HOWARD D
DANNENBERG, LOUISA	BAL	360	13TH WAR
DANNER, ABRAHAM	CAR	389	2ND DIST
DANNER, ADAM	CAR	234	UNION TO
DANNER, ANDREW	WAS	209	1ST DIST
DANNER, CLINTON D.	WAS	099	2ND DIST
DANNER, DANIEL	FRE	428	8TH E DI
DANNER, DAVID W.	FRE	442	8TH E DI
DANNER, DEBORAH	FRE	429	8TH E DI
DANNER, EZRA	CAR	390	2ND DIST
DANNER, GEORGE	FRE	405	JEFFERSO
DANNER, JOHN	FRE	435	8TH E DI
DANNER, JOSEPH	WAS	179	BOONSBOR
DANNER, MARTHA	FRE	162	EMMITTSB
DANNER, MARTIN	FRE	403	JEFFERSO
DANNER, PUTNAM	FRE	141	CREAGERS
DANNER, WARREN	FRE	197	5TH E DI
DANNIKER, HENRY	BAL	249	17TH WAR
DANNIKER, JOHN J.	BAL	257	17TH WAR
DANNISON, WINNA	PRI	040	VANSVILL
DANNJCK, JOHN	DOR	327	3RD DIVI
DANNOCK, RACHEL	DOR	355	3RD DIVI
DANNOCK, SAMUEL	DOR	347	3RD DIVI
DANNOCK, SAMUEL R.*	DOR	334	3RD DIVI
DANNOCK, SARRAH B.	DOR	326	3RD DIVI
DANOHUAGH, JAMES	BAL	444	1ST DIST
DANPIE, PETER	ALL	104	5TH E.D.
DANPLIN, WILLIAM	BAL	166	1ST WARD
DANSBROOK, SCIPIO	BAL	122	16TH WAR
DANSBURY, JAMES	BAL	342	7TH WARD
DANSBURY, RIGHTSON	BAL	342	7TH WARD
DANSIER, DEWIT C.	FRE	205	BUCKEYST
DANSKINS, WASHINGTON	BAL	418	14TH WAR
DANSON, WILLIAM	ALL	088	5TH E.D.
DANT, ELEANOR	PRI	041	VANSVILL
DANTON, HESTER A.	BAL	027	1ST WARD
DANVEN, RICHARD	BAL	131	1ST WARD
DANZBERGER, MATTHIAS	BAL	421	14TH WAR
DANZINGER, JOSEPH	BAL	269	7TH WARD
DAPLE, CORNELIUS	FRE	366	CATOCTIN
DAPPELL, ADALADE	BAL	020	4TH WARD
DARBEY, JOHN	BAL	228	17TH WAR
DARBY, ADEN	MGM	343	CLARKSBU
DARBY, DARIUS	MGM	343	CLARKSBU
DARBY, EDWARD	MGM	350	BERRYS D
DARBY, EDWARD	ALL	102	5TH E.D.
DARBY, ELIZA	ANN	457	HOWARD D
DARBY, EMILY J.	MGM	432	CLARKSTR
DARBY, GRAFTON	BAL	109	18TH WAR
DARBY, GRASFTON	FRE	391	PETERSVI
DARBY, HARRISON	MGM	344	CLARKSBU
DARBY, JOHN	FRE	202	5TH E DI
DARBY, JOHN	PRI	026	VANSVILL
DARBY, JOHN T.	SOM	533	QUANTICO
DARBY, JOHN W.	MGM	321	CRACKLIN
DARBY, MAJOR	BAL	248	17TH WAR
DARBY, MOUNT	BAL	087	18TH WAR
DARBY, NICHOLAS	MGM	343	CLARKSBU
DARBY, REZIN W.	MGM	351	BERRYS D
DARBY, RICHARD P.	SOM	508	BARREN C
DARBY, SAMUEL	SOM	397	BRINKLEY
DARBY, SAMUEL*	DOR	451	1ST DIST
DARBY, SARAH	FRE	061	FREDERIC

Name	County	Page	District
DARBY, SOLOMON	DOR	306	1ST DIST
DARBY, STEPHEN	BAL	190	17TH WAR
DARBY, WILLIAM	MGM	333	CRACKLIN
DARBY, WILLIAM	SOM	518	BARREN C
DARCH, ARNST	BAL	039	15TH WAR
DARCUS, DAVID	FRE	300	WOODSBOR
DARCUS, WILLIAM	BAL	328	7TH WARD
DARCY, AMELIA M.	BAL	152	11TH WAR
DARCY, JOHN	MGM	419	MEDLEY 3
DARDEN, ELIZABETH	BAL	272	2ND WARD
DARDEN, STEFEN	TAL	069	EASTON T
DARE, ADAM	BAL	439	14TH WAR
DARE, CATHARINE	BAL	080	15TH WAR
DARE, GEORGE	CAL	037	2ND DIST
DARE, JAMES	CAL	040	3RD DIST
DARE, JAMES THOMAS	CAL	040	3RD DIST
DARE, JOHN	FRE	400	JEFFERSO
DARE, JOHN	PRI	046	AQUASCO
DARE, JOHN G.	CAL	036	2ND DIST
DARE, MARGARET	CAL	025	2ND DIST
DARE, MARGARET	BAL	050	15TH WAR
DARE, RICHARD	CAL	036	2ND DIST
DARE, SAMUEL	CAL	040	3RD DIST
DARE, SAMUEL	BAL	023	15TH WAR
DARE, SARAH A.A.	BAL	333	7TH WARD
DARE, WILIAM	CAL	024	2ND DIST
DAREFLER, MARTIN	BAL	199	2ND WARD
DARGAN, GEORGE	BAL	146	5TH WARD
DARGER, FREDERICK	BAL	410	14TH WAR
DARHIELL, JOSIAH	WOR	230	6TH E DI
DARIDGE, CHARLES	BAL	043	15TH WAR
DARIEN, ELIAS	WAS	092	2ND SUBD
DARING, GEORGE A.	BAL	389	8TH WARD
DARITER, WILLIAM	BAL	284	12TH WAR
DARK, FREDERICK	ALL	229	CUMBERLA
DARKET, JOHN	CAR	279	7TH DIST
DARKET, MARY A.	CAR	279	7TH DIST
DARKEY, JAMES	ALL	214	CUMBERLA
DARKEY, JAMS	ALL	240	CUMBERLA
DARKINS, MARY	BAL	253	17TH WAR
DARKINS, ROBERT	BAL	014	4TH WARD
DARKLINS, ELIZABETH*	BAL	413	3RD WARD
DARKNEY, JOANNAH	BAL	041	4TH WARD
DARKS, THOMAS	WAS	158	HAGERSTO
DARKY, FRANCIS	ANN	292	ANNAPOLI
DARLIN, ISAAC	BAL	204	6TH WARD
DARLING, GEORGE	BAL	132	1ST WARD
DARLING, ISABELLA	BAL	107	10TH WAR
DARLING, J. MRS-	BAL	381	1ST DIST
DARLING, JAMES	BAL	213	6TH WARD
DARLING, JAMES	BAL	209	6TH WARD
DARLING, JOHN	BAL	303	7TH WARD
DARLING, JOSEPH	MGM	368	BERRYS D
DARLING, LEWIS	BAL	032	4TH WARD
DARLING, SARAH	BAL	005	9TH WARD
DARLINGSPUN, BENJAMIN	CEC	204	6TH E DI
DARLINGTON, SARAH	BAL	292	20TH WAR
DARLY, ELEANOR R.	MGM	410	MEDLEY 3
DARLY, GEORGE W.	MGM	410	MEDLEY 3
DARLY, GEORGE W.	MGM	432	CLARKSTR
DARLY, JOHN	MGM	410	MEDLEY 3
DARLY, LAWRENCE	MGM	408	MEDLEY 3
DARMAN, MICHAEL	HAR	063	1ST DIST
DARMAW, JAME G.*	BAL	015	4TH WARD
DARMER, HENRY	CAR	398	2ND DIST
DARMON, CHARLOTTE	BAL	295	12TH WAR
DARNABY, JOHN	BAL	141	2ND DIST
DARNAL, THOMAS	FRE	234	BUCKEYST
DARNALD, WILLIAM	FRE	223	BUCKEYST
DARNALL, CHARLES	CAL	013	1ST DIST
DARNALL, RICHARD	ANN	407	8TH DIST
DARNCAN, DANIEL	ALL	227	CUMBERLA
DARNE, ALEXANDER C.H.	MGM	426	MEDLEY 3
DARNEC, JAMES	BAL	136	11TH WAR
DARNELL, CHARLES R.	BAL	281	2ND WARD
DARNELL, FRANCIS L.	PRI	008	BLADENSB
DARNELL, HENRY	ANN	407	8TH DIST
DARNELL, JAMES	ANN	284	ANNAPOLI
DARNELL, JAMES-BLACK	CAR	100	NO TWP L
DARNELL, MARY C.	FRE	065	FREDERIC
DARNELL, NICHOLAS	ANN	407	8TH DIST
DARNELL, RICHARD N.	PRI	013	BLADENSB
DARNER, JOSEPH	FRE	320	MIDDLETO
DARNER, WILLIAM	FRE	321	MIDDLETO
DARNES, CADDY *	ST	255	3RD E DI
DARNEY, JOHN	BAL	281	1ST DIST
DARNING, CATHERINE	FRE	058	FREDERIC
DARNNANE, JOHN W.	BAL	100	5TH WARD
DARR, WILLIAM	BAL	216	6TH DIST
DARRAM, CATHARINE	BAL	122	5TH WARD
DARRAUGH, DANIEL	BAL	411	3RD WARD
DARREN, JAMES	BAL	130	1ST WARD
DARRIN, ELIAS *	WAS	092	2ND SUBD
DARRIN, JOHN *	WAS	066	2ND SUBD
DARRINGTON, WILLIAM	BAL	004	9TH WARD
DARROW, SAMUEL	BAL	076	10TH WAR
DARRVAN, STEWART	BAL	026	9TH WARD
DARRY, EDWARD G.*	BAL	397	3RD WARD
DARSEY, JAMES	WAS	197	1ST DIST
DARSEY, WILLIAM E.	PRI	008	BLADENSB
DART, BENJAMIN	WAS	157	HAGERSTO
DART, JOHN	ALL	162	6TH E.D.
DARTAN, GEORGE	BAL	017	2ND DIST
DARTZBAUGH, GEORGE	FRE	047	FREDERIC
DARTZBAUGH, GEORGE W.	FRE	053	FREDERIC
DARTZBAUGH, JOHN W.	FRE	064	FREDERIC
DARVEY, BENJAMIN	BAL	012	18TH WAR
DARVIS, RICHARD*	DOR	456	1ST DIST
DARWERN, MARY *	BAL	283	1ST DIST
DARY, MILLS *	TAL	084	ST MICHA
DARY, WILLIAM	BAL	226	2ND WARD
DARY, M.	BAL	284	12TH WAR
DASCH, ANTHONY*	BAL	400	3RD WARD
DASCH, HENRY	BAL	308	20TH WAR
DASEX, HENRY *	FRE	359	CATOCTIN
DASEY, CATHARINE	BAL	229	12TH WAR
DASEY, ISAAC	HAR	146	3RD DIST
DASEY, JOHN	BAL	080	18TH WAR
DASH, C. *	ALL	130	4TH E.D.
DASH, CATHRINE	BAL	060	18TH WAR
DASH, GEORGE	BAL	060	18TH WAR
DASH, JOHN A.	BAL	045	18TH WAR
DASH, JOHN P.	BAL	444	14TH WAR
DASH, MARGARET	BAL	045	18TH WAR
DASH, MARY	BAL	071	15TH WAR
DASHEAL, JAMES	BAL	326	3RD WARD
DASHEAL, PRISCILLA	BAL	069	4TH WARD
DASHEIL, SAMUEL K.	ANN	440	HOWARD D
DASHER, CHRISTIANA	WAS	126	HAGERSTO
DASHIEL, JACK*	DOR	379	1ST DIST
DASHIEL, MILCAH	ANN	440	HOWARD D
DASHIEL, ROBERT	BAL	086	4TH WARD
DASHIELD, COLUMBUS W.	BAL	402	14TH WAR
DASHIELD, ELIZA A.	BAL	045	15TH WAR
DASHIELD, JOHN	BAL	045	15TH WAR
DASHIELD, JULIUS M.	WAS	020	2ND SUBD
DASHIELDS, CAROLINE	BAL	207	2ND WARD
DASHIELDS, CHARLOTTE	BAL	045	15TH WAR
DASHIELDS, HENRY	BAL	021	15TH WAR
DASHIELDS, LEVIN	BAL	013	1ST WARD
DASHIELDS, LOUISE	BAL	079	15TH WAR
DASHIELDS, MARIA	BAL	101	15TH WAR
DASHIELDS, WILLIAM	BAL	170	16TH WAR
DASHIELL, ALFRED	SOM	550	TYASKIN
DASHIELL, ALGERNON S.	SOM	540	TYASKIN
DASHIELL, ANN	SOM	435	PRINCESS
DASHIELL, ASA	SOM	491	SALISBUR
DASHIELL, BENJAMIN	SOM	367	BRINKLEY
DASHIELL, BIDDY	SOM	536	TYASKIN
DASHIELL, CADMUS	SOM	550	TYASKIN
DASHIELL, CHAPMAN	SOM	500	SALISBUR
DASHIELL, CHARLES	SOM	494	SALISBUR
DASHIELL, CHARLES	SOM	530	QUANTICO
DASHIELL, CHARLES	SOM	522	BARREN C
DASHIELL, CHARLOTTE	SOM	548	TYASKIN
DASHIELL, CLARA M.	SOM	490	SALISBUR
DASHIELL, DANIEL J.	SOM	549	TYASKIN
DASHIELL, EDGAR	SOM	549	TYASKIN
DASHIELL, EDWARD	SOM	527	QUANTICO
DASHIELL, EDWIN	SOM	525	BARREN C
DASHIELL, EDWIN	SOM	522	BARREN C
DASHIELL, ELIZA	SOM	534	QUANTICO
DASHIELL, ELIZABETH	SOM	493	SALISBUR
DASHIELL, ELIZABETH	SOM	441	DAMES QU
DASHIELL, ELLEN	SOM	504	SALISBUR
DASHIELL, FEIFIG	SOM	485	TRAPP DI
DASHIELL, FLORA	SOM	495	SALISBUR
DASHIELL, GEORGE	SOM	490	SALISBUR
DASHIELL, GEORGE	SOM	502	SALISBUR
DASHIELL, GEORGE W.	SOM	428	PRINCESS
DASHIELL, GLASGO	SOM	467	TRAPPE D
DASHIELL, HAMPDEN	SOM	529	QUANTICO
DASHIELL, HASTE W.	SOM	530	QUANTICO
DASHIELL, HENRY J.	SOM	515	BARREN C
DASHIELL, HENRY J.	SOM	477	TRAPPE D
DASHIELL, ISAAC	SOM	362	BRINKLEY
DASHIELL, ISMA*	SOM	496	SALISBUR
DASHIELL, JAMES	SOM	515	BARREN C
DASHIELL, JAMES A.	SOM	399	BRINKLEY
DASHIELL, JANE	SOM	503	SALISBUR
DASHIELL, JANE	SOM	492	SALISBUR
DASHIELL, JANE	SOM	551	TYASKIN
DASHIELL, JOHN	SOM	477	TRAPP DI
DASHIELL, JOHN	SOM	473	TRAPPE D
DASHIELL, JOHN	SOM	404	BRINKLEY
DASHIELL, JOHN H.	BAL	177	2ND DIST
DASHIELL, JOHN J.	SOM	500	SALISBUR
DASHIELL, JOHN W.	SOM	428	PRINCESS
DASHIELL, LAMBERT H.	SOM	536	TYASKIN
DASHIELL, LEVIN	SOM	493	SALISBUR
DASHIELL, LEVIN	SOM	471	TRAPPE D
DASHIELL, LEVIN	SOM	470	TRAPPE D
DASHIELL, LEVIN M.	SOM	470	TRAPPE D
DASHIELL, LEVIN W.	SOM	526	QUANTICO
DASHIELL, LEVINA	SOM	496	SALISBUR
DASHIELL, LOVEY	SOM	425	PRINCESS
DASHIELL, MARCELLUS	SOM	545	TYASKIN
DASHIELL, MARY	SOM	535	QUANTICO
DASHIELL, MARY	SOM	543	TYASKIN
DASHIELL, MARY	SOM	490	SALISBUR
DASHIELL, MARY	BAL	066	10TH WAR
DASHIELL, MATILDA	SOM	505	SALISBUR
DASHIELL, MATILDA	SOM	523	BARREN C
DASHIELL, MATTHIAS	SOM	532	QUANTICO
DASHIELL, MERCER	SOM	534	QUANTICO
DASHIELL, NANCY	SOM	462	HANGARY
DASHIELL, NOAH	SOM	530	QUANTICO
DASHIELL, PETER	SOM	439	DAMES QU
DASHIELL, PETER	SOM	404	BRINKLEY
DASHIELL, ROBERT	SOM	547	TYASKIN
DASHIELL, ROBERT K. W.	SOM	432	PRINCESS
DASHIELL, SAMUEL	SOM	421	PRINCESS
DASHIELL, SAMUEL	SOM	527	QUANTICO
DASHIELL, SAMUEL	SOM	463	HANGARY
DASHIELL, SETH B.	SOM	425	PRINCESS
DASHIELL, TAMAR	SOM	538	TYASKIN
DASHIELL, THEODORE G.	SOM	426	PRINCESS
DASHIELL, THOMAS	SOM	510	BARREN C
DASHIELL, THOMAS W.	SOM	471	TRAPPE D
DASHIELL, WILLIAM	SOM	476	TRAPPE D
DASHIELL, WILLIAM	SOM	477	TRAPP DI
DASHIELL, WILLIAM	SOM	534	QUANTICO
DASHIELL, WILLIAM	SOM	548	TYASKIN
DASHIELL, WILLIAM S.	SOM	528	QUANTICO
DASHIELS, JACOB*	BAL	414	3RD WARD
DASHILL, ELIZABETH	BAL	148	11TH WAR
DASHILL, ERASTUS	CAL	018	1ST DIST
DASHIRLDS, MARY	BAL	019	1ST WARD
DASHNER, MARTIN	CEC	177	7TH E DI
DASHULDO, SALLY	BAL	207	2ND WARD
DASHULDS, MARY	BAL	248	2ND WARD
DASIY, JACOB	FRE	358	CATOCTIN
DASKINS, HENRY	BAL	339	7TH WARD
DASLIPLEEPLE, W. DR.	BAL	135	11TH WAR
DASPER, WILLIAM	CAR	322	1ST DIST
DASS, JOHN	BAL	154	1ST WARD
DATERS, BERNARD	BAL	290	17TH WAR
DATES, ELIZABETH	BAL	359	3RD WARD
DATIS, LOUIS	CEC	098	3RD E DI
DATON, WILLIAM	DOR	351	3RD DIVI
DATRO, GEORGE	FRE	304	WOODSBOR
DATROW, JOHN S.	FRE	211	BUCKEYST
DATROW, MARCUS	FRE	319	MIDDLETO
DATROW, SUSANANA	FRE	134	CREAGERS
DATTEN, RUTH	BAL	023	2ND DIST
DATUN, JOHN *	ANN	359	3RD DIST
DAUB, ADAM	BAL	097	18TH WAR
DAUB, JOEL	WAS	234	1ST DIST
DAUB, JOHN	WAS	219	1ST DIST
DAUB, JONATHAN	WAS	222	1ST DIST
DAUB, JONOTHAN F.	WAS	252	1ST DIST
DAUB, SAMUEL	WAS	201	1ST DIST
DAUCIN, JAMES H.	HAR	193	3RD DIST
DAUFMAN, WILLIAM	BAL	092	2ND DIST
DAUGAN, ELMIRA	MGM	319	CRACKLIN
DAUGHADAY, JOSEPH	FRE	033	FREDERIC
DAUGHADAY, JOSHUA	BAL	347	3RD WARD
DAUGHADAY, MARY	BAL	208	6TH WARD
DAUGHADAY, SAMUEL	BAL	251	6TH WARD
DAUGHADEY, JOHN	BAL	063	2ND DIST
DAUGHERTY, CATE	BAL	008	EASTERN
DAUGHERTY, CATHARINE	BAL	116	5TH WARD
DAUGHERTY, CATHARINE	HAR	004	1ST DIST
DAUGHERTY, CATHARINE	WAS	047	2ND SUBD
DAUGHERTY, FRANCES	BAL	226	1ST DIST
DAUGHERTY, HETTY	SOM	545	TYASKIN
DAUGHERTY, J. W.	BAL	230	6TH WARD
DAUGHERTY, JAMES	BAL	097	2ND DIST
DAUGHERTY, JAMES M.	BAL	213	6TH WARD
DAUGHERTY, JANE	BAL	284	12TH WAR
DAUGHERTY, JANE	SOM	504	SALISBUR
DAUGHERTY, JOHN	SOM	517	BARREN C
DAUGHERTY, JOHN	HAR	004	1ST DIST
DAUGHERTY, JOHN	SOM	425	PRINCESS
DAUGHERTY, JOHN	HAR	135	2ND DIST
DAUGHERTY, JULIA	BAL	025	2ND DIST
DAUGHERTY, MARGARETT	HAR	137	2ND DIST
DAUGHERTY, MARGEY	CAR	257	3RD DIST
DAUGHERTY, MARY	BAL	097	2ND DIST
DAUGHERTY, MARY	BAL	016	9TH WARD
DAUGHERTY, MARY	WAS	094	2ND SUBD
DAUGHERTY, MICHAEL	HAR	126	2ND DIST
DAUGHERTY, RACHAL	HAR	004	1ST DIST
DAUGHERTY, THOMAS H.	SOM	524	BARREN C
DAUGHERTY, WILLIAM	BAL	039	2ND DIST
DAUGHERTY, WILLIAM	BAL	040	2ND DIST
DAUGHETY, PETER	BAL	421	1ST DIST
DAUGHTERS, ISAIAH	SOM	500	SALISBUR
DAUGHTERS, JOSHUA	BAL	309	7TH WARD
DAUGHTERS, SAMUEL	WOR	230	6TH E DI
DAUGHTON, ANN	BAL	005	1ST WARD
DAUGHTON, ANN	HAR	044	1ST DIST
DAUGHTON, CATHARINE	BAL	448	1ST DIST
DAUGHTON, DANIEL	HAR	009	1ST DIST
DAUGHTON, HEZEKIAH	HAR	025	1ST DIST
DAUGHTON, JOHN	BAL	448	1ST DIST
DAUGHTON, JOHN	BAL	448	1ST DIST
DAUGHTON, JOHNSEY	HAR	025	1ST DIST
DAUGHTY, JAMES	BAL	168	2ND DIST
DAUGHTY, KITTY	BAL	155	11TH WAR
DAUGTON, DANIEL	HAR	035	1ST DIST
DAUKER, MATILDA	BAL	245	2ND WARD
DAUKINS, YOUNG P.	ST	288	2ND E DI
DAUNEY, ALBERT	HAR	196	3RD DIST
DAUNEY, JACKSON	HAR	204	3RD DIST
DAUNEY, WASHINGTON	HAR	206	3RD DIST
DAUNING, JOHN	BAL	170	2ND DIST
DAUNY, AMANDA R.	HAR	190	3RD DIST
DAUNY, PERY	HAR	185	3RD DIST
DAUNY, WILLIAM W.	HAR	190	3RD DIST
DAURTY, ANN	HAR	186	3RD DIST
DAUS, MARGRET*	DOR	348	3RD DIVI
DAUSE, JOHN L.	BAL	310	7TH WARD
DAUSH, MICHAEL	ANN	469	HOWARD D
DAUSON, ISAAC	DOR	363	3RD DIVI
DAUTERS, GILLIS	WOR	250	1ST CENS
DAUTRICH, JOHN	BAL	298	3RD WARD
DAVAGE, CHARLES	BAL	399	8TH WARD
DAVAGE, REBECCA	HAR	180	3RD DIST
DAVAGE, SYDNEY	BAL	026	9TH WARD
DAVALL, CHARLES	BAL	030	4TH WARD
DAVALL, ELDRIDGE	BAL	380	13TH WAR
DAVANETT, FREDERICK	BAL	109	2ND DIST
DAVENPORT, ANN	BAL	247	5TH WARD
DAVENPORT, G.H.	BAL	125	1ST WARD
DAVENPORT, JOSEPH	BAL	124	5TH WARD
DAVENPORT, LYDIA	WAS	160	2ND DIST
DAVENPORT, SAMUEL	BAL	384	13TH WAR
DAVENPORT, SUSANNA	BAL	451	14TH WAR
DAVES, JAMES	CEC	018	ELKTON 3
DAVES, MARY	CEC	021	ELKTON 3
DAVES, SAMUEL	CEC	082	CHARLEST
DAVEY, ELIZABETH	BAL	400	3RD WARD
DAVEY, HUGH	BAL	406	3RD WARD
DAVEY, JONATHAN	WAS	159	2ND DIST
DAVEY, MARY	BAL	187	19TH WAR
DAVEY, SAM	BAL	166	11TH WAR
DAVID, ABIGAIL	WAS	051	2ND SUBD
DAVID, CURTIS	BAL	064	15TH WAR
DAVID, JOHN	BAL	236	6TH WARD
DAVID, JOHN F.	BAL	156	16TH WAR
DAVID, JOSIAH	WAS	048	2ND SUBD
DAVID, LOYD	WAS	049	2ND SUBD
DAVID, MARGARETT	BAL	028	4TH WARD
DAVID, PETER	BAL	114	1ST WARD
DAVID, R.	BAL	150	1ST WARD
DAVID, REBECCA	MGM	385	ROCKERLE
DAVID, THOMAS	BAL	261	20TH WAR
DAVIDGE, AMELIA	BAL	109	10TH WAR
DAVIDGE, AMIEL	BAL	189	6TH WARD
DAVIDGE, EMMILE	BAL	169	16TH WAR
DAVIDGE, FRANCES A.S.	BAL	133	16TH WAR
DAVIDGE, JOHN	BAL	244	20TH WAR
DAVIDGE, KITTY	ANN	287	ANNAPOLI
DAVIDGE, MARY	BAL	093	5TH WARD
DAVIDGE, MARY J.	BAL	363	13TH WAR
DAVIDGE, SUSAN	ANN	464	HOWARD D
DAVIDS, RACHEL D.	BAL	240	6TH WARD
DAVIDSN, SOLOMON R.	BAL	386	13TH WAR
DAVIDSON, A. B.	BAL	342	13TH WAR
DAVIDSON, A. S.	BAL	308	1ST DIST
DAVIDSON, ALFRED N	BAL	273	17TH WAR
DAVIDSON, ARY	BAL	449	14TH WAR
DAVIDSON, CAHRLES A.	BAL	013	18TH WAR
DAVIDSON, CHARLES C.	BAL	290	12TH WAR
DAVIDSON, D.G.	BAL	117	1ST WARD
DAVIDSON, DANIEL D.	MGM	356	BERRYS D
DAVIDSON, DAVID	WOR	246	1ST CENS
DAVIDSON, EDWARD	CEC	134	6TH E DI
DAVIDSON, ELIZABETH	BAL	069	10TH WAR
DAVIDSON, ELIZABETH SR.	CEC	091	4TH E DI
DAVIDSON, ELLEN	BAL	157	11TH WAR
DAVIDSON, EZEKIEL	ANN	381	4TH DIST
DAVIDSON, FRANCIS	BAL	274	7TH WARD
DAVIDSON, G.	BAL	138	1ST WARD
DAVIDSON, GEORGE	BAL	135	1ST WARD
DAVIDSON, GEORGE	BAL	132	1ST WARD
DAVIDSON, GEORGE	CEC	143	7TH E DI
DAVIDSON, GEORGE	HAR	192	3RD DIST
DAVIDSON, GEORGE	WOR	272	BERLIN I
DAVIDSON, J. P. C.	BAL	332	1ST DIST
DAVIDSON, JAMES	ALL	170	6TH E.D.
DAVIDSON, JAMES	QUE	246	5TH E DI
DAVIDSON, JAMES	CAR	409	2ND DIST
DAVIDSON, JAMES	DOR	427	1ST DIST
DAVIDSON, JAMES	CEC	090	4TH E DI
DAVIDSON, JAMES	BAL	001	4TH WARD
DAVIDSON, JEANETTE	BAL	255	6TH WARD
DAVIDSON, JOHN	ALL	110	5TH E.D.
DAVIDSON, JOHN	BAL	070	10TH WAR

Name	County	Page	Location
DAVIDSON, JOHN	BAL	222	12TH WAR
DAVIDSON, JOHN	CEC	108	3RD E DI
DAVIDSON, JOHN	CAR	409	2ND DIST
DAVIDSON, JOHN	CEC	124	5TH E DI
DAVIDSON, JOHN	CEC	123	3RD E DI
DAVIDSON, JOHN	MGM	392	ROCKERLE
DAVIDSON, JOHN E.	BAL	215	17TH WAR
DAVIDSON, JOHN H.	BAL	172	1ST WARD
DAVIDSON, JULIA	BAL	392	8TH WARD
DAVIDSON, LEVIN	WOR	268	BERLIN 1
DAVIDSON, LEWIS	ALL	158	6TH E.D.
DAVIDSON, M.O.	ALL	263	CUMBERLA
DAVIDSON, MARGARET E.	CEC	115	3RD E DI
DAVIDSON, MARTHA	CEC	108	3RD E DI
DAVIDSON, MARY	FRE	059	FREDERIC
DAVIDSON, MARY	HAR	100	2ND DIST
DAVIDSON, MARY	FRE	160	EMMITTSB
DAVIDSON, MARY J.	CEC	016	ELKTON 3
DAVIDSON, NELSON	BAL	370	13TH WAR
DAVIDSON, P.	ANN	295	1ST DIST
DAVIDSON, POLLY	WOR	252	1ST CENS
DAVIDSON, ROBERT	BAL	154	19TH WAR
DAVIDSON, ROBERT G.	MGM	389	ROCKERLE
DAVIDSON, SAMUEL	ANN	287	ANNAPOLI
DAVIDSON, SAMUEL	ALL	159	6TH E.D.
DAVIDSON, SAMUEL A.	BAL	040	9TH WARD
DAVIDSON, SAMUEL G.	BAL	440	8TH WARD
DAVIDSON, SARAH	BAL	111	5TH WARD
DAVIDSON, SARAH	BAL	295	3RD WARD
DAVIDSON, SARAH A.	BAL	289	7TH WARD
DAVIDSON, SUSANNAH	BAL	375	13TH WAR
DAVIDSON, THOMAS	BAL	005	4TH WARD
DAVIDSON, THOMAS	ANN	295	1ST DIST
DAVIDSON, THOMAS	ALL	056	10TH E.D
DAVIDSON, THOMAS	BAL	145	1ST WARD
DAVIDSON, THOMAS M.	BAL	112	15TH WAR
DAVIDSON, WILLIA MT.	ANN	278	ANNAPOLI
DAVIDSON, WILLIAM	DOR	428	1ST DIST
DAVIDSON, WILLIAM B.	CEC	108	3RD E DI
DAVIDSON,J.	BAL	135	1ST WARD
DAVIE, JACOB	BAL	168	1ST WARD
DAVIE, RANDOLPH	CHA	267	MIDDLETO
DAVIES, JACOB G.	BAL	067	10TH WAR
DAVIES, WILLIAM	QUE	204	3RD E DI
DAVILL, MICHAEL	BAL	271	17TH WAR
DAVIM, JOHN *	WAS	066	2ND SUBD
DAVIN, MICHAEL	ALL	052	10TH E.D
DAVINSON, DAVID	HAR	006	1ST DIST
DAVINSON, GEORGE H.	BAL	293	7TH WARD
DAVINSON, JOHN S.	HAR	203	3RD DIST
DAVIS, AARON	WAS	087	2ND SUBD
DAVIS, ABGERT	HAR	160	3RD DIST
DAVIS, ADAM	DOR	309	1ST DIST
DAVIS, ADELINE	BAL	443	14TH WAR
DAVIS, ALBERT	CAR	124	NO TWP L
DAVIS, ALBION-BLACK	FRE	431	8TH E DI
DAVIS, ALEXANDER	ALL	116	5TH E.D.
DAVIS, ALEXANDER	BAL	163	2ND DIST
DAVIS, ALEXANDER MC D.*	BAL	086	4TH WARD
DAVIS, ALFRED	CAR	124	NO TWP L
DAVIS, ALLEN	BAL	052	18TH WAR
DAVIS, ALLEN B.	MGM	337	CRACKLIN
DAVIS, AMANDA	ANN	459	HOWARD D
DAVIS, AMELIA C.	ANN	509	HOWARD D
DAVIS, AMOS	BAL	379	1ST DIST
DAVIS, AMOS	BAL	101	2ND DIST
DAVIS, AMOS	CAR	366	9TH DIST
DAVIS, ANDREW	TAL	031	EASTON D
DAVIS, ANDREW	WOR	169	6TH E DI
DAVIS, ANN	WOR	267	BERLIN 1
DAVIS, ANN	ST	256	3RD E DI
DAVIS, ANN	CAR	124	NO TWP L
DAVIS, ANN	BAL	154	11TH WAR
DAVIS, ANN	BAL	392	14TH WAR
DAVIS, ANN	BAL	221	17TH WAR
DAVIS, ANN	CHA	238	HILLTOP
DAVIS, ANN	BAL	192	5TH DIST
DAVIS, ANN	BAL	271	2ND WARD
DAVIS, ANN	BAL	026	9TH WARD
DAVIS, ANN C.	BAL	319	3RD WARD
DAVIS, ANN C.	ST	283	3RD E DI
DAVIS, ANN E.	ST	284	2ND E DI
DAVIS, ANN E.	BAL	135	11TH WAR
DAVIS, ANN M.	FRE	390	PETERSVI
DAVIS, ANN M.	FRE	226	BUCKEYST
DAVIS, ANN M.	WAS	200	1ST DIST
DAVIS, ANN M.	BAL	405	3RD WARD
DAVIS, ANN O.	BAL	211	6TH WARD
DAVIS, AQUILA	HAR	091	2ND DIST
DAVIS, ARAMENTA	FRE	449	8TH E DI
DAVIS, ARCHIBALD	BAL	172	2ND DIST
DAVIS, ARHTUR	SOM	445	DAMES QU
DAVIS, ARMON	HAR	150	3RD DIST
DAVIS, AUGUSTUS	BAL	017	15TH WAR
DAVIS, BARBARA	BAL	007	EASTERN
DAVIS, BAYARD	CAR	105	NO TWP L
DAVIS, BENEDICT	CEC	210	7TH E DI
DAVIS, BENJAMIN	BAL	112	10TH WAR
DAVIS, BENJAMIN	MGM	342	CLARKSBU
DAVIS, BENJAMIN	CEC	151	PORT DUP
DAVIS, BENJAMIN	BAL	041	18TH WAR
DAVIS, BENJAMIN	CEC	022	ELKTON 3
DAVIS, BENJAMIN	CAR	283	7TH DIST
DAVIS, BENJAMIN	BAL	021	2ND DIST
DAVIS, BENJAMIN	BAL	106	1ST WARD
DAVIS, BENJAMIN	BAL	155	5TH WARD
DAVIS, BENJAMIN	ALL	066	10TH E.D
DAVIS, BENJAMIN	ALL	158	6TH E.D.
DAVIS, BENJAMIN	SOM	536	TYASKIN
DAVIS, BENJAMIN	WOR	177	6TH E DI
DAVIS, BRADFORD A.	BAL	422	3RD WARD
DAVIS, CALEB	FRE	260	NEW MARK
DAVIS, CALEB	WOR	255	1ST CENS
DAVIS, CALEB	ANN	461	HOWARD D
DAVIS, CALEB-BLACK	WOR	167	6TH E DI
DAVIS, CAROLINE	QUE	182	3RD E DI
DAVIS, CAROLINE	WOR	339	1ST E DI
DAVIS, CAROLINE	BAL	167	11TH WAR
DAVIS, CAROLINE	BAL	422	1ST DIST
DAVIS, CAROLINE	BAL	293	12TH WAR
DAVIS, CAROLINE	BAL	066	4TH WARD
DAVIS, CAROLINE	BAL	131	11TH WAR
DAVIS, CATHARINE	BAL	255	17TH WAR
DAVIS, CATHARINE	BAL	151	19TH WAR
DAVIS, CATHARINE	BAL	185	19TH WAR
DAVIS, CATHARINE	HAR	181	3RD DIST
DAVIS, CATHARINE	BAL	070	15TH WAR
DAVIS, CATHARINE	ANN	437	HOWARD D
DAVIS, CATHARINE	WAS	145	HAGERSTO
DAVIS, CATHARINE	ST	321	4TH E DI
DAVIS, CATHARINE A.	BAL	303	7TH WARD
DAVIS, CATHARINE A.	FRE	448	8TH E DI
DAVIS, CATHARINE E.	BAL	298	7TH WARD
DAVIS, CATHARINE R.	FRE	205	BUCKEYST
DAVIS, CATHERINE	CHA	239	HILLTOP
DAVIS, CATHERINE	BAL	296	3RD WARD
DAVIS, CATHERINE	QUE	226	4TH E DI
DAVIS, CECILIA A.	CHA	276	ALLENS F
DAVIS, CHARLES	KEN	212	2ND DIST
DAVIS, CHARLES	CEC	191	5TH E DI
DAVIS, CHARLES	FRE	378	PETERSVI
DAVIS, CHARLES	CAR	333	MANCHEST
DAVIS, CHARLES	BAL	013	18TH WAR
DAVIS, CHARLES	BAL	072	18TH WAR
DAVIS, CHARLES	TAL	059	EASTON D
DAVIS, CHARLES	WOR	267	BERLIN 1
DAVIS, CHARLES	WOR	291	9TH E DI
DAVIS, CHARLES	SOM	496	SALISBUR
DAVIS, CHARLES	BAL	133	1ST WARD
DAVIS, CHARLES	BAL	168	16TH WAR
DAVIS, CHARLES	BAL	238	1ST DIST
DAVIS, CHARLES	BAL	122	1ST WARD
DAVIS, CHARLES	BAL	016	1ST WARD
DAVIS, CHARLES F.	BAL	294	20TH WAR
DAVIS, CHARLES H.	BAL	203	17TH WAR
DAVIS, CHARLES L.	BAL	038	4TH WARD
DAVIS, CHARLES T.	WOR	180	6TH E DI
DAVIS, CHARLES W.	BAL	298	7TH WARD
DAVIS, CHARLES-BLACK	ST	295	2ND E DI
DAVIS, CHARLOTT	BAL	119	11TH WAR
DAVIS, CHARLOTT-MULATTO	BAL	182	2ND WARD
DAVIS, CHRISTOPHER	BAL	147	2ND DIST
DAVIS, CORDELIA	CAR	367	9TH DIST
DAVIS, CORNELIUS	WAS	074	2ND SUBD
DAVIS, CURTIS	CAR	124	NO TWP L
DAVIS, DAFF	WOR	266	BERLIN 1
DAVIS, DANIEL	SOM	492	SALISBUR
DAVIS, DANIEL	BAL	145	11TH WAR
DAVIS, DANIEL	BAL	143	2ND DIST
DAVIS, DANIEL	BAL	156	2ND DIST
DAVIS, DANIEL	BAL	050	9TH WARD
DAVIS, DANIEL	BAL	006	9TH WARD
DAVIS, DANIEL	ALL	071	5TH E.D.
DAVIS, DAVID	ALL	158	6TH E.D.
DAVIS, DAVID	BAL	298	1ST DIST
DAVIS, DAVID	BAL	276	7TH WARD
DAVIS, DAVID	CEC	060	1ST E DI
DAVIS, DAVID	HAR	087	2ND DIST
DAVIS, DAVID	HAR	084	2ND DIST
DAVIS, DAVID	PRI	048	AQUASCO
DAVIS, DAVID D.	WOR	328	1ST E DI
DAVIS, DAVID J.	CEC	062	1ST E DI
DAVIS, DENARD	WOR	281	BERLIN 1
DAVIS, DENNIS	BAL	196	11TH WAR
DAVIS, DENNIS	BAL	162	11TH WAR
DAVIS, DINAH	BAL	064	4TH WARD
DAVIS, DOLOMON	WAS	095	2ND SUBD
DAVIS, DORCAS	BAL	460	14TH WAR
DAVIS, E. C.	KEN	217	2ND DIST
DAVIS, E.A.	ANN	272	ANNAPOLI
DAVIS, E.C.	WAS	140	HAGERSTO
DAVIS, EASTHER	KEN	291	3RD DIST
DAVIS, ED	BAL	159	1ST WARD
DAVIS, EDITHA	QUE	156	2ND E DI
DAVIS, EDNIAS	DOR	430	1ST DIST
DAVIS, EDWARD	BAL	303	17TH WAR
DAVIS, EDWARD	BAL	199	19TH WAR
DAVIS, EDWARD	BAL	192	19TH WAR
DAVIS, EDWARD	BAL	226	19TH WAR
DAVIS, EDWARD	ANN	465	HOWARD D
DAVIS, EDWARD	BAL	330	3RD WARD
DAVIS, EDWARD	BAL	343	1ST DIST
DAVIS, EDWARD	WAS	178	BOONSBOR
DAVIS, EDWARD	WOR	295	9TH E DI
DAVIS, EDWARD	SOM	490	SALISBUR
DAVIS, EDWARD W.	BAL	325	7TH WARD
DAVIS, EDWARD Y.	TAL	020	EASTON D
DAVIS, ELIAS	WAS	182	BOONSBOR
DAVIS, ELIC-BLACK	FRE	240	NEW MARK
DAVIS, ELIE	FRE	268	NEW MARK
DAVIS, ELIE	FRE	248	NEW MARK
DAVIS, ELIJAH	WOR	167	6TH E DI
DAVIS, ELIJAH	BAL	201	6TH WARD
DAVIS, ELISA	BAL	024	18TH WAR
DAVIS, ELISABETH	ALL	067	10TH E.D
DAVIS, ELISABETH P.	ANN	327	2ND DIST
DAVIS, ELISHA	HAR	043	1ST DIST
DAVIS, ELISHA	WOR	239	6TH E DI
DAVIS, ELIZA	BAL	196	19TH WAR
DAVIS, ELIZA	CEC	009	ELKTON 3
DAVIS, ELIZA	HAR	145	3RD DIST
DAVIS, ELIZA	BAL	453	14TH WAR
DAVIS, ELIZA	BAL	180	11TH WAR
DAVIS, ELIZA	BAL	459	1ST DIST
DAVIS, ELIZA A.	CAR	096	NO TWP L
DAVIS, ELIZABERTH	BAL	411	14TH WAR
DAVIS, ELIZABETH	BAL	207	17TH WAR
DAVIS, ELIZABETH	BAL	265	17TH WAR
DAVIS, ELIZABETH	BAL	472	14TH WAR
DAVIS, ELIZABETH	KEN	216	2ND DIST
DAVIS, ELIZABETH	CHA	294	BOJANTOW
DAVIS, ELIZABETH	FRE	177	5TH E DI
DAVIS, ELIZABETH	FRE	260	NEW MARK
DAVIS, ELIZABETH	CHA	241	HILLTOP
DAVIS, ELIZABETH	CHA	230	BOJANTOW
DAVIS, ELIZABETH	BAL	116	5TH WARD
DAVIS, ELIZABETH	ALL	170	6TH E.D.
DAVIS, ELIZABETH	BAL	385	3RD WARD
DAVIS, ELIZABETH	BAL	082	15TH WAR
DAVIS, ELIZABETH	PRI	049	AQUASCO
DAVIS, ELIZABETH	WOR	260	BERLIN 1
DAVIS, ELIZABETH	WOR	257	1ST CENS
DAVIS, ELIZABETH	WOR	254	1ST CENS
DAVIS, ELIZAVBETH	FRE	254	NEW MARK
DAVIS, ELKANAH	ST	336	4TH E DI
DAVIS, ELLEN	FRE	216	BUCKEYST
DAVIS, ELLEN	BAL	026	18TH WAR
DAVIS, ELLEN	BAL	099	5TH WARD
DAVIS, ELMA	CEC	025	ELKTON 3
DAVIS, EMILY	BAL	369	3RD WARD
DAVIS, EMMA	BAL	200	2ND WARD
DAVIS, ENOCH	CAR	285	7TH DIST
DAVIS, EPHRAIM	FRE	276	NEW MARK
DAVIS, EUGENE	BAL	144	16TH WAR
DAVIS, EVAN	BAL	184	5TH DIST
DAVIS, EZEKIEL	BAL	371	8TH WARD
DAVIS, EZRA	ANN	509	HOWARD D
DAVIS, FANNY	BAL	154	5TH WARD
DAVIS, FANNY	BAL	246	17TH WAR
DAVIS, FANNY	BAL	412	14TH WAR
DAVIS, FRANCES	BAL	184	5TH DIST
DAVIS, FRANCES	QUE	173	2ND E DI
DAVIS, FRANCIS	PRI	024	VANSVILL
DAVIS, FRANCIS	BAL	114	1ST WARD
DAVIS, FRANCIS	BAL	155	1ST WARD
DAVIS, FRANCIS	BAL	030	9TH WARD
DAVIS, FRANCIS A.	CAR	361	9TH DIST
DAVIS, FRANCIS F.	CAR	369	9TH DIST
DAVIS, FREDERICK	BAL	111	10TH WAR
DAVIS, FREDERICK	WAS	140	HAGERSTO
DAVIS, FRY	ANN	463	HOWARD D
DAVIS, G.	BAL	151	1ST WARD
DAVIS, G. G.	CHA	294	BOJANTOW
DAVIS, GAITHER	ANN	465	HOWARD D.
DAVIS, GEIFFETH C.	HAR	046	1ST DIST
DAVIS, GENEVA	BAL	232	1ST DIST
DAVIS, GEORG EH.	CAR	369	9TH DIST
DAVIS, GEORGE	CEC	086	4TH E DI
DAVIS, GEORGE	CHA	267	BOJANTOW
DAVIS, GEORGE	BAL	445	14TH WAR
DAVIS, GEORGE	BAL	276	17TH WAR
DAVIS, GEORGE	FRE	217	BUCKEYST
DAVIS, GEORGE	CEC	025	ELKTON 3
DAVIS, GEORGE	BAL	420	3RD WARD
DAVIS, GEORGE	CAR	223	5TH DIST
DAVIS, GEORGE	DOR	334	3RD DIVI
DAVIS, GEORGE	BAL	097	1ST WARD
DAVIS, GEORGE	BAL	123	1ST WARD
DAVIS, GEORGE	BAL	151	1ST WARD
DAVIS, GEORGE	BAL	149	1ST WARD
DAVIS, GEORGE	BAL	240	6TH WARD
DAVIS, GEORGE	BAL	129	5TH WARD
DAVIS, GEORGE	BAL	081	15TH WAR
DAVIS, GEORGE	BAL	298	12TH WAR
DAVIS, GEORGE	BAL	261	12TH WAR
DAVIS, GEORGE	WAS	125	HAGERSTO
DAVIS, GEORGE C.	HAR	118	2ND DIST
DAVIS, GEORGE D.	QUE	161	2ND E DI
DAVIS, GEORGE H.	BAL	475	14TH WAR
DAVIS, GEORGE L.	BAL	374	13TH WAR
DAVIS, GEORGE W.	HAR	071	1ST DIST
DAVIS, GEORGE W.	BAL	451	8TH WARD
DAVIS, GEORGE-BLACK	FRE	019	FREDERIC
DAVIS, GEORGIANNA	BAL	205	11TH WAR
DAVIS, GEROGE	KEN	252	1ST DIST
DAVIS, GEROGE T.	HAR	003	1ST DIST
DAVIS, GILLY	SOM	498	SALISBUR
DAVIS, GOERGE W.	ANN	277	ANNAPOLI
DAVIS, GRIFFIN	ST	254	3RD E DI
DAVIS, H. WINTER	BAL	112	10TH WAR
DAVIS, HANSON	CAR	206	4TH DIST
DAVIS, HARRIET	HAR	003	1ST DIST
DAVIS, HARRIET	BAL	452	8TH WARD
DAVIS, HARRIET	BAL	298	1ST DIST
DAVIS, HARRIET B.	CHA	271	ALLENS F
DAVIS, HARRISON	BAL	085	15TH WAR
DAVIS, HENNETTA	BAL	363	13TH WAR
DAVIS, HENRIETTA	BAL	083	4TH WARD
DAVIS, HENRIETTA-BLACK	WOR	169	6TH E DI
DAVIS, HENRY	SOM	358	BRINKLEY
DAVIS, HENRY	WOR	225	4TH E DI
DAVIS, HENRY	TAL	014	EASTON D
DAVIS, HENRY	WOR	297	9TH E DI
DAVIS, HENRY	PRI	004	BLADENSB
DAVIS, HENRY	CEC	008	ELKTON 3
DAVIS, HENRY	BAL	040	4TH WARD
DAVIS, HENRY	CAR	159	NO TWP L
DAVIS, HENRY	CHA	230	BOJANTOW
DAVIS, HENRY	CAR	350	6TH DIST
DAVIS, HENRY	BAL	024	18TH WAR
DAVIS, HENRY	BAL	170	1ST WARD
DAVIS, HENRY	BAL	050	2ND DIST
DAVIS, HENRY	BAL	350	1ST DIST
DAVIS, HENRY B.	WOR	269	BERLIN 1
DAVIS, HENRY C.	BAL	053	9TH WARD
DAVIS, HENRY S.	WOR	165	6TH E DI
DAVIS, HENRY S.	CAR	369	9TH DIST
DAVIS, HENRY W.	KEN	263	1ST DIST
DAVIS, HENRY-BLACK	MGM	429	CLARKSTR
DAVIS, HESTER	WOR	261	BERLIN 1
DAVIS, HESTER A.E.	MGM	418	MEDLEY 3
DAVIS, HESTER-BLACK	CAR	098	NO TWP L
DAVIS, HEZAKIAH	WOR	166	6TH E DI
DAVIS, HEZEKIAH	MGM	357	BERRYS D
DAVIS, HIRAM	CAR	389	2ND DIST
DAVIS, HORATIO	BAL	109	1ST WARD
DAVIS, HOWARD	CEC	002	ELKTON 3
DAVIS, HUGH	ALL	087	5TH E.D.
DAVIS, HUMPHREY	CHA	234	HILLTOP
DAVIS, ISAAC	DOR	299	1ST DIST
DAVIS, ISAAC	BAL	422	14TH WAR
DAVIS, ISAAC	BAL	203	17TH WAR
DAVIS, ISAAC	ALL	158	6TH E.D.
DAVIS, ISAAC	ALL	157	6TH E.D.
DAVIS, ISAAC	BAL	239	1ST DIST
DAVIS, ISAAC	BAL	088	2ND DIST
DAVIS, ISAAC	WOR	166	6TH E DI
DAVIS, ISAAC	WAS	029	2ND SUBD
DAVIS, ISAAC	WOR	337	1ST E DI
DAVIS, ISAAC G.	WAS	236	CAVETOWN
DAVIS, ISAACK	DOR	359	3RD DIVI
DAVIS, ISABELLA	BAL	343	1ST DIST
DAVIS, ISAIAH	WAS	026	2ND SUBD
DAVIS, ISHMAEL	WOR	217	4TH E DI
DAVIS, J. H.	BAL	150	1ST WARD
DAVIS, J.B.	BAL	130	1ST WARD
DAVIS, J.C.	PRI	107	PISCATAW
DAVIS, JACOB	BAL	271	7TH WARD
DAVIS, JACOB	BAL	223	1ST DIST
DAVIS, JACOB	BAL	122	16TH WAR
DAVIS, JACOB	CEC	112	4TH E DI
DAVIS, JACOB C.	BAL	088	18TH WAR
DAVIS, JACOB T.	BAL	190	19TH WAR
DAVIS, JAMES	CAR	178	8TH DIST
DAVIS, JAMES	CEC	057	1ST E DI
DAVIS, JAMES	HAR	199	3RD DIST
DAVIS, JAMES	BAL	371	13TH WAR
DAVIS, JAMES	CEC	150	PORT DUP
DAVIS, JAMES	DOR	325	1ST DIST
DAVIS, JAMES	HAR	031	1ST DIST
DAVIS, JAMES	CAR	096	NO TWP L
DAVIS, JAMES	KEN	232	2ND DIST
DAVIS, JAMES	FRE	102	FREDERIC
DAVIS, JAMES	FRE	120	CREAGERS
DAVIS, JAMES	BAL	122	16TH WAR
DAVIS, JAMES	BAL	077	10TH WAR
DAVIS, JAMES	BAL	234	1ST DIST
DAVIS, JAMES	BAL	134	1ST WARD
DAVIS, JAMES	BAL	166	1ST WARD
DAVIS, JAMES	BAL	181	2ND WARD

DAVIS, JAMES BAL 116 2ND DIST
DAVIS, JAMES WOR 207 4TH E DI
DAVIS, JAMES WOR 240 6TH E DI
DAVIS, JAMES WOR 282 BERLIN 1
DAVIS, JAMES WOR 293 9TH E DI
DAVIS, JAMES TAL 095 ST MICHA
DAVIS, JAMES WAS 117 2ND DIST
DAVIS, JAMES SOM 397 BRINKLEY
DAVIS, JAMES A. ST 338 4TH E DI
DAVIS, JAMES C. BAL 399 3RD WARD
DAVIS, JAMES C. BAL 140 16TH WAR
DAVIS, JAMES C. BAL 289 3RD WARD
DAVIS, JAMES C. HAR 076 BEL AIR
DAVIS, JAMES E. BAL 191 19TH WAR
DAVIS, JAMES E. WOR 251 1ST CENS
DAVIS, JAMES H. BAL 378 8TH WARD
DAVIS, JAMES H. BAL 059 1ST WARD
DAVIS, JAMES L. KEN 299 3RD DIST
DAVIS, JAMES L. FRE 205 BUCKEYST
DAVIS, JAMES R. PRI 080 QUEEN AN
DAVIS, JAMES S. WOR 272 BERLIN 1
DAVIS, JAMESM. BAL 004 EASTERN
DAVIS, JAMS QUE 186 3RD E DI
DAVIS, JANE SOM 508 BARREN C
DAVIS, JANE ST 254 3RD E DI
DAVIS, JANE BAL 150 11TH WAR
DAVIS, JANE-BLACK WOR 166 6TH E DI
DAVIS, JEREMIAH WAS 124 2ND DIST
DAVIS, JEROME BAL 132 1ST WARD
DAVIS, JEROME BAL 143 1ST WARD
DAVIS, JERRY MGM 323 CRACKLIN
DAVIS, JERRY CHA 240 HILLTOP
DAVIS, JERRY CHA 240 HILLTOP
DAVIS, JESSA WOR 248 1ST CENS
DAVIS, JESSE WOR 237 6TH E DI
DAVIS, JIM WOR 305 2ND E DI
DAVIS, JOEL BAL 143 1ST WARD
DAVIS, JOEL BAL 145 1ST WARD
DAVIS, JOHN BAL 126 5TH WARD
DAVIS, JOHN BAL 206 2ND WARD
DAVIS, JOHN BAL 205 2ND WARD
DAVIS, JOHN BAL 168 1ST WARD
DAVIS, JOHN BAL 210 6TH WARD
DAVIS, JOHN BAL 133 1ST WARD
DAVIS, JOHN BAL 138 1ST WARD
DAVIS, JOHN BAL 371 8TH WARD
DAVIS, JOHN BAL 127 1ST WARD
DAVIS, JOHN BAL 137 2ND DIST
DAVIS, JOHN BAL 163 2ND DIST
DAVIS, JOHN BAL 099 1ST WARD
DAVIS, JOHN BAL 091 1ST WARD
DAVIS, JOHN BAL 118 1ST WARD
DAVIS, JOHN BAL 121 1ST WARD
DAVIS, JOHN BAL 247 1ST DIST
DAVIS, JOHN BAL 048 1ST WARD
DAVIS, JOHN BAL 326 3RD WARD
DAVIS, JOHN BAL 091 15TH WAR
DAVIS, JOHN BAL 085 15TH WAR
DAVIS, JOHN BAL 110 10TH WAR
DAVIS, JOHN ALL 151 6TH E.D.
DAVIS, JOHN ALL 158 6TH E.D.
DAVIS, JOHN ALL 157 6TH E.D.
DAVIS, JOHN ALL 157 6TH E.D.
DAVIS, JOHN ALL 134 4TH E.D.
DAVIS, JOHN ALL 188 9TH E.D.
DAVIS, JOHN ALL 065 10TH E.D
DAVIS, JOHN ALL 003 3RD E.D.
DAVIS, JOHN BAL 345 7TH WARD
DAVIS, JOHN WOR 297 9TH E DI
DAVIS, JOHN WOR 267 BERLIN 1
DAVIS, JOHN WAS 025 2ND SUBD
DAVIS, JOHN SOM 552 TYASKIN
DAVIS, JOHN WAS 044 2ND SUBD
DAVIS, JOHN WAS 014 2ND SUBD
DAVIS, JOHN WOR 177 6TH E DI
DAVIS, JOHN WAS 141 HAGERSTO
DAVIS, JOHN WOR 323 1ST E DI
DAVIS, JOHN QUE 191 3RD E DI
DAVIS, JOHN WAS 200 1ST DIST
DAVIS, JOHN WAS 255 1ST DIST
DAVIS, JOHN BAL 252 20TH WAR
DAVIS, JOHN KEN 228 2ND DIST
DAVIS, JOHN FRE 20 5TH E DI
DAVIS, JOHN BAL 127 11TH WAR
DAVIS, JOHN BAL 463 14TH WAR
DAVIS, JOHN FRE 269 NEW MARK
DAVIS, JOHN BAL 125 18TH WAR
DAVIS, JOHN FRE 249 NEW MARK
DAVIS, JOHN CEC 014 ELKTON 3
DAVIS, JOHN CAR 216 5TH DIST
DAVIS, JOHN CAR 204 4TH DIST
DAVIS, JOHN HAR 102 2ND DIST
DAVIS, JOHN HAR 098 2ND DIST
DAVIS, JOHN SOM 426 PRINCESS
DAVIS, JOHN SOM 412 DUBLIN D
DAVIS, JOHN BAL 403 14TH WAR
DAVIS, JOHN BAL 261 17TH WAR
DAVIS, JOHN CEC 099 3RD E DI
DAVIS, JOHN A. CHA 289 BOJANTOW
DAVIS, JOHN A. FRE 160 EMMITTSB
DAVIS, JOHN B. MGM 357 BERRYS D
DAVIS, JOHN B. PRI 009 BLADENSB
DAVIS, JOHN B. ALL 066 10TH E.D
DAVIS, JOHN C. BAL 098 18TH WAR
DAVIS, JOHN D.-MULATTO FRE 218 BUCKEYST
DAVIS, JOHN E. BAL 180 19TH WAR
DAVIS, JOHN E. DOR 324 1ST DIST
DAVIS, JOHN F. PRI 111 PISCATAW
DAVIS, JOHN G. WAS 134 HAGERSTO
DAVIS, JOHN G. BAL 242 17TH WAR
DAVIS, JOHN H. ST 269 3RD E DI
DAVIS, JOHN L. CHA 238 HILLTOP
DAVIS, JOHN M. QUE 141 1ST E DI
DAVIS, JOHN M. QUE 128 1ST E DI
DAVIS, JOHN M. ANN 266 ANNAPOLI
DAVIS, JOHN N. CEC 057 1ST E DI
DAVIS, JOHN T. HAR 003 1ST DIST
DAVIS, JOHN T. BAL 041 15TH WAR
DAVIS, JOHN T. BAL 401 3RD WARD
DAVIS, JOHN W. BAL 258 12TH WAR
DAVIS, JOHN W. BAL 349 3RD WARD
DAVIS, JOHN W. BAL 232 17TH WAR
DAVIS, JOHN W. CAR 300 1ST DIST
DAVIS, JOHN W. FRE 226 BUCKEYST
DAVIS, JOHN-BLACK FRE 189 5TH E DI
DAVIS, JOHN-BLACK CAR 145 NO TWP L
DAVIS, JOHNSON H. WOR 216 4TH E DI
DAVIS, JOICE B. WOR 204 4TH E DI
DAVIS, JONAS WAS 182 BOONSBOR
DAVIS, JONATHAN CEC 083 CHARLEST
DAVIS, JONATHAN ALL 068 5TH E.D.
DAVIS, JONATHAN ALL 065 10TH E.D
DAVIS, JONATHAN BAL 136 2ND DIST
DAVIS, JONOTHAN WAS 203 1ST DIST
DAVIS, JOSE ST 340 5TH E DI
DAVIS, JOSEPH KEN 306 3RD DIST
DAVIS, JOSEPH WAS 120 2ND DIST
DAVIS, JOSEPH WOR 294 9TH E DI
DAVIS, JOSEPH ANN 438 HOWARD D
DAVIS, JOSEPH BAL 104 1ST WARD
DAVIS, JOSEPH BAL 200 2ND WARD
DAVIS, JOSEPH CAR 323 1ST DIST
DAVIS, JOSEPH FRE 267 NEW MARK
DAVIS, JOSEPH CEC 015 ELKTON 3
DAVIS, JOSEPH DOR 299 1ST DIST
DAVIS, JOSEPH BAL 341 13TH WAR
DAVIS, JOSEPH FRE 031 FREDERIC
DAVIS, JOSEPH CEC 192 5TH E DI
DAVIS, JOSEPH CEC 191 5TH E DI
DAVIS, JOSEPH BAL 256 20TH WAR
DAVIS, JOSEPH B. ST 289 2ND E DI
DAVIS, JOSEPH E. QUE 128 1ST E DI
DAVIS, JOSHUA CEC 065 1ST E DI
DAVIS, JOSHUA FRE 076 FREDERIC
DAVIS, JOSHUA WOR 213 4TH E DI
DAVIS, JOSHUA ANN 462 HOWARD D
DAVIS, JOSHUA BAL 211 6TH DIST
DAVIS, JOSHUA B. ANN 435 HOWARD D
DAVIS, JOSIAH PRI 053 AQUASCO
DAVIS, JOSIAH WOR 255 1ST CENS
DAVIS, JOSIAH SOM 446 DAMES QU
DAVIS, JULIA FRE 131 CREAGERS
DAVIS, JULIA BAL 003 9TH WARD
DAVIS, JULIAN BAL 324 1ST DIST
DAVIS, JULYAME-BLACK CAR 085 NO TWP L
DAVIS, KATE BAL 099 10TH WAR
DAVIS, KEL W. CHA 271 ALLENS F
DAVIS, KENDAL WOR 296 9TH E DI
DAVIS, KENLE B. WOR 338 1ST E DI
DAVIS, L. BAL 099 10TH WAR
DAVIS, LAKE FRE 250 NEW MARK
DAVIS, LARKIN HAR 077 BEL AIR
DAVIS, LEAH WOR 282 BERLIN 1
DAVIS, LEMUEL ALL 092 5TH E.D.
DAVIS, LEONARD PRI 069 MARLBROU
DAVIS, LEVEN-BLACK FRE 234 BUCKEYST
DAVIS, LEVIN WOR 168 6TH E DI
DAVIS, LEVIN WOR 169 6TH E DI
DAVIS, LEVIN H. C. DOR 428 1ST DIST
DAVIS, LEVIN R. WOR 199 8TH E DI
DAVIS, LEWILLEN ST 337 4TH E DI
DAVIS, LEWIS BAL 089 18TH WAR
DAVIS, LITTLETON WOR 269 BERLIN 1
DAVIS, LODAWICK F. WOR 217 4TH E DI
DAVIS, LORETTA BAL 212 11TH WAR
DAVIS, LOUEZA DOR 300 1ST DIST
DAVIS, LOUIS J. BAL 229 1ST DIST
DAVIS, LOUISA ANN 520 HOWARD D
DAVIS, LOUISA BAL 414 14TH WAR
DAVIS, LOUISA WAS 108 2ND DIST
DAVIS, LOUISA-BLACK FRE 449 8TH E DI
DAVIS, LOUISA-BLACK FRE 452 8TH E DI
DAVIS, LUCRETIA A. MGM 330 CRACKLIN
DAVIS, LYDIA BAL 287 20TH WAR
DAVIS, LYDIA BAL 239 17TH WAR
DAVIS, LYDIA CAR 351 6TH DIST
DAVIS, LYDIA BAL 309 20TH WAR
DAVIS, LYDIA CEC 024 ELKTON 3
DAVIS, LYDIA BAL 223 19TH WAR
DAVIS, MAHLEN SR. FRE 450 8TH E DI
DAVIS, MAHLON JR. FRE 450 8TH E DI
DAVIS, MANE E. BAL 233 2ND WARD
DAVIS, MANSFIELD BAL 044 4TH WARD
DAVIS, MARANDA BAL 229 1ST DIST
DAVIS, MARGARET ANN 463 HOWARD D
DAVIS, MARGARET BAL 029 9TH WARD
DAVIS, MARGARET CEC 147 PORT DUP
DAVIS, MARGARET BAL 256 20TH WAR
DAVIS, MARGARET BAL 220 19TH WAR
DAVIS, MARGARET HAR 025 1ST DIST
DAVIS, MARGARET WAS 023 2ND SUBD
DAVIS, MARGARET WAS 142 HAGERSTO
DAVIS, MARGARET A. WAS 154 HAGERSTO
DAVIS, MARGARET A. BAL 364 3RD WARD
DAVIS, MARGARET J. WOR 207 4TH E DI
DAVIS, MARGARETT KEN 306 3RD DIST
DAVIS, MARGARETT DOR 297 1ST DIST
DAVIS, MARIA FRE 103 FREDERIC
DAVIS, MARIA BAL 151 11TH WAR
DAVIS, MARIA ALL 170 6TH E.D.
DAVIS, MARIA BAL 332 13TH WAR
DAVIS, MARIA BAL 172 16TH WAR
DAVIS, MARTHA BAL 025 1ST WARD
DAVIS, MARTHA BAL 115 5TH WARD
DAVIS, MARTHA HAR 029 1ST DIST
DAVIS, MARTHA FRE 079 FREDERIC
DAVIS, MARTHA CEC 025 ELKTON 3
DAVIS, MARTHA BAL 299 20TH WAR
DAVIS, MARTHA WAS 017 2ND SUBD
DAVIS, MARTHA WOR 269 BERLIN 1
DAVIS, MARTHA WOR 269 BERLIN 1
DAVIS, MARTHA A. BAL 378 8TH WARD
DAVIS, MARTHA B. ANN 521 HOWARD D
DAVIS, MARTHA W. SOM 528 QUANTICO
DAVIS, MARTIN WAS 136 HAGERSTO
DAVIS, MARTIN ALL 048 10TH E.D
DAVIS, MARTIN-BLACK QUE 140 1ST E DI
DAVIS, MARY CHA 294 BOJANTOW
DAVIS, MARY CEC 014 ELKTON 3
DAVIS, MARY HAR 004 1ST DIST
DAVIS, MARY HAR 065 1ST DIST
DAVIS, MARY SOM 412 DUBLIN D
DAVIS, MARY CAR 125 NO TWP L
DAVIS, MARY ALL 157 6TH E.D.
DAVIS, MARY BAL 315 1ST DIST
DAVIS, MARY BAL 312 3RD WARD
DAVIS, MARY BAL 248 2ND WARD
DAVIS, MARY BAL 359 3RD WARD
DAVIS, MARY BAL 169 16TH WAR
DAVIS, MARY BAL 170 15TH WAR
DAVIS, MARY BAL 026 9TH WARD
DAVIS, MARY BAL 187 6TH WARD
DAVIS, MARY BAL 339 7TH WARD
DAVIS, MARY WAS 143 2ND DIST
DAVIS, MARY WOR 258 1ST CENS
DAVIS, MARY WOR 255 1ST CENS
DAVIS, MARY WAS 122 HAGERSTO
DAVIS, MARY ST 345 5TH E DI
DAVIS, MARY A. BAL 321 7TH WARD
DAVIS, MARY A. BAL 205 6TH WARD
DAVIS, MARY A.-BLACK FRE 016 FREDERIC
DAVIS, MARY A.-MULATTO FRE 242 NEW MARK
DAVIS, MARY E. FRE 056 FREDERIC
DAVIS, MARY E. QUE 218 3RD E DI
DAVIS, MARY E. WOR 272 BERLIN 1
DAVIS, MARY F. BAL 098 15TH WAR
DAVIS, MARY J. CHA 247 HILLTOP
DAVIS, MARY J. CAR 301 1ST DIST
DAVIS, MARY J.A. BAL 052 1ST WARD
DAVIS, MARY JANE ANN 285 ANNAPOLI
DAVIS, MARY M. BAL 074 10TH WAR
DAVIS, MARY S. ALL 196 CUMBERLA
DAVIS, MARY W. ST 275 3RD E DI
DAVIS, MATILDA ANN 345 3RD DIST
DAVIS, MEREDITH FRE 224 BUCKEYST
DAVIS, MICHAEL ALL 075 5TH E.D.
DAVIS, MICHAEL BAL 345 1ST DIST
DAVIS, MILES BAL 209 5TH DIST
DAVIS, MISS DOR 453 1ST DIST
DAVIS, MOSESX BAL 299 12TH WAR
DAVIS, MR. BAL 207 17TH WAR
DAVIS, NANCY BAL 093 5TH WARD
DAVIS, NANCY WOR 343 1ST E DI
DAVIS, NANCY WOR 323 1ST E DI
DAVIS, NANCY WAS 159 2ND DIST
DAVIS, NANCY WOR 202 4TH E DI
DAVIS, NATHAN FRE 205 BUCKEYST
DAVIS, NATHAN W. TAL 026 EASTON D
DAVIS, NATHANIEL WOR 239 6TH E DI
DAVIS, NATHANIEL CAR 123 NO TWP L
DAVIS, NATHANIEL ANN 442 HOWARD D
DAVIS, NELLY ANN 291 ANNAPOLI
DAVIS, NELSON FRE 262 NEW MARK
DAVIS, NELSON CEC 072 5TH E DI
DAVIS, NERI ALL 158 6TH E.D.
DAVIS, NICHOLAS FRE 101 FREDERIC
DAVIS, NICHOLAS-BLACK FRE 016 FREDERIC
DAVIS, NIMROD MGM 330 CRACKLIN
DAVIS, OPHELIA BAL 452 8TH WARD
DAVIS, OWEN ST 347 5TH E DI
DAVIS, P. CHA 219 ALLENS F
DAVIS, PATRICK ALL 227 CUMBERLA
DAVIS, PETER BAL 307 12TH WAR
DAVIS, PETER BAL 047 9TH WARD
DAVIS, PETER CHA 267 MIDDLETO
DAVIS, PETER CEC 009 ELKTON 3
DAVIS, PETER CEC 050 1ST E DI
DAVIS, PETER KEN 292 3RD DIST
DAVIS, PETER WOR 286 BERLIN 1
DAVIS, PETER C. WOR 267 BERLIN 1
DAVIS, PETER S. WOR 256 BERLIN 1
DAVIS, PETER W. WOR 344 1ST E DI
DAVIS, PHILIP BAL 102 2ND DIST
DAVIS, PHILIP ANN 408 8TH DIST
DAVIS, PHILIP R. HAR 203 3RD DIST
DAVIS, PHILLIP ALL 066 10TH E.D
DAVIS, PRICILLA A. BAL 043 1ST WARD
DAVIS, PRISCELLA WOR 201 3RD E DI
DAVIS, PRISCILLA F. DOR 325 1ST DIST
DAVIS, PURNELL WOR 211 4TH E DI
DAVIS, R. BAL 148 1ST WARD
DAVIS, R. P. BAL 041 4TH WARD
DAVIS, RACHAEL BAL 088 4TH WARD
DAVIS, RACHEL BAL 430 14TH WAR
DAVIS, RACHEL CEC 017 ELKTON 3
DAVIS, RACHEL BAL 070 2ND DIST
DAVIS, RACHEL KEN 306 3RD DIST
DAVIS, RACHEL A. BAL 169 5TH WARD
DAVIS, RACHEL A. BAL 103 15TH WAR
DAVIS, RAMOND W. ST 255 3RD E DI
DAVIS, REBECCA BAL 056 10TH WAR
DAVIS, REBECCA QUE 129 1ST E DI
DAVIS, REESE HAR 203 3RD DIST
DAVIS, REESE W. ANN 450 HOWARD D
DAVIS, REGIN FRE 252 NEW MARK
DAVIS, RESIN CHA 281 BOJANTOW
DAVIS, RHODA CEC 056 1ST E DI
DAVIS, RICHARD CEC 072 5TH E DI
DAVIS, RICHARD DOR 429 1ST DIST
DAVIS, RICHARD ANN 468 HOWARD D
DAVIS, RICHARD BAL 217 6TH WARD
DAVIS, RICHARD BAL 162 2ND DIST
DAVIS, RICHARD WAS 146 HAGERSTO
DAVIS, RICHARD WAS 026 2ND SUBD
DAVIS, RICHARD T. BAL 082 15TH WAR
DAVIS, RION-BLACK WOR 165 6TH E DI
DAVIS, RISDON * SOM 445 DAMES QU
DAVIS, RISSA BAL 455 1ST DIST
DAVIS, ROBERT ANN 411 8TH DIST
DAVIS, ROBERT ANN 272 ANNAPOLI
DAVIS, ROBERT BAL 248 12TH WAR
DAVIS, ROBERT ST 335 4TH E DI
DAVIS, ROBERT CHA 244 HILLTOP
DAVIS, ROBERT CHA 231 HILLTOP
DAVIS, ROBERT BAL 209 11TH WAR
DAVIS, ROBERT BAL 130 11TH WAR
DAVIS, ROBERT C. BAL 146 16TH WAR
DAVIS, ROBERT E. ANN 309 1ST DIST
DAVIS, ROBERT M. WOR 219 4TH E DI
DAVIS, ROBERT W. CAR 095 NO TWP L
DAVIS, ROSEANN BAL 245 17TH WAR
DAVIS, ROSEANNA BAL 198 17TH WAR
DAVIS, ROSETTA ANN 290 ANNAPOLI
DAVIS, ROSINIA WOR 337 1ST E DI
DAVIS, RUBEN ALL 090 5TH E.D.
DAVIS, SALLY SOM 492 SALISBUR
DAVIS, SALLY CHA 247 HILLTOP
DAVIS, SAMEUL BAL 187 16TH WAR
DAVIS, SAMPSON WOR 206 4TH E DI
DAVIS, SAMUEL WOR 199 8TH E DI
DAVIS, SAMUEL SOM 438 DAMES QU
DAVIS, SAMUEL KEN 292 3RD DIST
DAVIS, SAMUEL TAL 031 EASTON D
DAVIS, SAMUEL ANN 269 ANNAPOLI
DAVIS, SAMUEL ANN 319 2ND DIST
DAVIS, SAMUEL BAL 407 1ST DIST
DAVIS, SAMUEL ANN 345 3RD DIST
DAVIS, SAMUEL CEC 199 7TH E DI
DAVIS, SAMUEL BAL 208 11TH WAR
DAVIS, SAMUEL CAR 409 2ND DIST
DAVIS, SAMUEL FRE 191 5TH E DI
DAVIS, SAMUEL C. REV. CAR 273 WESTMINS
DAVIS, SAMUEL G. CAR 370 9TH DIST
DAVIS, SAMUEL S. SOM 398 BRINKLEY
DAVIS, SAMUEL-BLACK WOR 166 6TH E DI
DAVIS, SARA J. CHA 294 BOJANTOW
DAVIS, SARAH BAL 130 18TH WAR
DAVIS, SARAH HAR 196 3RD DIST
DAVIS, SARAH BAL 129 11TH WAR
DAVIS, SARAH CAR 124 NO TWP L

DAVIS, SARAH QUE 229 4TH E DI
DAVIS, SARAH WOR 266 BERLIN 1
DAVIS, SARAH BAL 306 1ST DIST
DAVIS, SARAH ALL 212 CUMBERLA
DAVIS, SARAH ANN 379 4TH DIST
DAVIS, SARAH BAL 351 7TH WARD
DAVIS, SARAH A. BAL 058 15TH WAR
DAVIS, SARAH A. BAL 330 13TH WAR
DAVIS, SARAH A. BAL 446 14TH WAR
DAVIS, SARAH A. BAL 098 18TH WAR
DAVIS, SARAH G. ST 335 4TH E DI
DAVIS, SARAH L. BAL 300 3RD WARD
DAVIS, SARAH-BLACK FRE 039 FREDERIC
DAVIS, SEN-BLACK ST 324 4TH E DI
DAVIS, SEPTUMUST HAR 167 3RD DIST
DAVIS, SINGLETON WOR 248 1ST CENS
DAVIS, SISTER AMELIA FRE 197 5TH E DI
DAVIS, SOLOMON DOR 426 1ST DIST
DAVIS, SOLOMON WAS 182 BOONSBOR
DAVIS, SOPHIA ALL 196 CUMBERLA
DAVIS, SOPHIA-BLACK BAL 225 2ND WARD
DAVIS, SPENCER WOR 190 8TH E DI
DAVIS, ST. ANNA-BLACK BAL 216 2ND WARD
DAVIS, STEPHEN-BLACK FRE 009 FREDERIC
DAVIS, STEVEN ALL 057 10TH E.D
DAVIS, SUSAN CHA 244 HILLTOP
DAVIS, SUSAN BAL 420 14TH WAR
DAVIS, SUSAN QUE 225 4TH E DI
DAVIS, SUSAN WOR 326 1ST E DI
DAVIS, SUSAN WAS 203 1ST DIST
DAVIS, SUSAN WAS 033 2ND SUBD
DAVIS, SUSANER HAR 147 3RD DIST
DAVIS, THEODORE QUE 226 4TH E DI
DAVIS, THMAS BAL 394 14TH WAR
DAVIS, THOAMS BAL 455 14TH WAR
DAVIS, THOMAS CAR 148 NO TWP L
DAVIS, THOMAS HAR 148 3RD DIST
DAVIS, THOMAS CHA 228 ALLENS F
DAVIS, THOMAS CHA 240 HILLTOP
DAVIS, THOMAS FRE 313 MIDDLETO
DAVIS, THOMAS BAL 040 18TH WAR
DAVIS, THOMAS BAL 300 17TH WAR
DAVIS, THOMAS WOR 340 1ST E DI
DAVIS, THOMAS WAS 237 CAVETOWN
DAVIS, THOMAS ST 339 5TH E DI
DAVIS, THOMAS SOM 439 DAMES QU
DAVIS, THOMAS WOR 213 4TH E DI
DAVIS, THOMAS ALL 082 5TH E.D.
DAVIS, THOMAS ALL 201 CUMBERLA
DAVIS, THOMAS ALL 194 9TH E.D.
DAVIS, THOMAS ALL 167 6TH E.D.
DAVIS, THOMAS BAL 206 6TH WARD
DAVIS, THOMAS BAL 141 5TH WARD
DAVIS, THOMAS BAL 145 16TH WAR
DAVIS, THOMAS BAL 457 8TH WARD
DAVIS, THOMAS BAL 017 15TH WAR
DAVIS, THOMAS BAL 245 12TH WAR
DAVIS, THOMAS ANN 466 HOWARD D
DAVIS, THOMAS ANN 466 HOWARD D
DAVIS, THOMAS BAL 151 2ND DIST
DAVIS, THOMAS BAL 091 1ST WARD
DAVIS, THOMAS BAL 091 1ST WARD
DAVIS, THOMAS BAL 130 1ST WARD
DAVIS, THOMAS BAL 279 2ND WARD
DAVIS, THOMAS D. ALL 213 CUMBERLA
DAVIS, THOMAS D. BAL 413 3RD WARD
DAVIS, THOMAS G. ANN 442 HOWARD D
DAVIS, THOMAS L. BAL 409 3RD WARD
DAVIS, THOMAS L. BAL 079 18TH WAR
DAVIS, THOMAS L. ST 334 4TH E DI
DAVIS, THOMAS P. KEN 290 3RD DIST
DAVIS, THOMAS R. TAL 039 EASTON D
DAVIS, TIMOTHY BAL 116 1ST WARD
DAVIS, TRUSTIN H. DOR 325 1ST DIST
DAVIS, VERCHE BAL 255 20TH WAR
DAVIS, VERLINDA CHA 228 ALLENS F
DAVIS, VICOTRINE PRI 056 AQUASCO
DAVIS, VINCENT WAS 203 1ST DIST
DAVIS, W. S. BAL 066 18TH WAR
DAVIS, WASHINGTON CEC 150 PORT DUP
DAVIS, WASHINGTON ANN 467 HOWARD D
DAVIS, WILLAIM PRI 106 PISCATAW
DAVIS, WILLAIM PRI 103 SPALDING
DAVIS, WILLIAM WOR 221 4TH E DI
DAVIS, WILLIAM KEN 288 3RD DIST
DAVIS, WILLIAM KEN 306 3RD DIST
DAVIS, WILLIAM WAS 124 HAGERSTO
DAVIS, WILLIAM QUE 222 4TH E DI
DAVIS, WILLIAM WAS 016 2ND SUBD
DAVIS, WILLIAM WAS 051 2ND SUBD
DAVIS, WILLIAM TAL 092 ST MICHA
DAVIS, WILLIAM WAS 155 HAGERSTO
DAVIS, WILLIAM WAS 120 2ND DIST
DAVIS, WILLIAM ANN 450 HOWARD D
DAVIS, WILLIAM BAL 105 1ST WARD
DAVIS, WILLIAM BAL 152 2ND DIST
DAVIS, WILLIAM BAL 122 1ST WARD
DAVIS, WILLIAM BAL 075 1ST WARD
DAVIS, WILLIAM ALL 080 5TH E.D.
DAVIS, WILLIAM ALL 095 5TH E.D.
DAVIS, WILLIAM BAL 129 1ST WARD
DAVIS, WILLIAM BAL 129 1ST WARD
DAVIS, WILLIAM BAL 404 3RD WARD
DAVIS, WILLIAM BAL 139 1ST WARD
DAVIS, WILLIAM BAL 147 16TH WAR
DAVIS, WILLIAM BAL 192 17TH WAR
DAVIS, WILLIAM BAL 054 9TH WARD
DAVIS, WILLIAM BAL 166 1ST WARD
DAVIS, WILLIAM BAL 168 1ST WARD
DAVIS, WILLIAM BAL 153 1ST WARD
DAVIS, WILLIAM BAL 211 6TH DIST
DAVIS, WILLIAM BAL 341 1ST DIST
DAVIS, WILLIAM ANN 490 HOWARD D
DAVIS, WILLIAM BAL 252 17TH WAR
DAVIS, WILLIAM BAL 224 17TH WAR
DAVIS, WILLIAM BAL 071 18TH WAR
DAVIS, WILLIAM CEC 101 4TH E DI
DAVIS, WILLIAM CEC 093 4TH E DI
DAVIS, WILLIAM BAL 160 19TH WAR
DAVIS, WILLIAM CHA 271 ALLENS F
DAVIS, WILLIAM FRE 202 5TH E DI
DAVIS, WILLIAM CAR 124 NO TWP L
DAVIS, WILLIAM SOM 408 DUBLIN D
DAVIS, WILLIAM A. ST 335 4TH E DI
DAVIS, WILLIAM B. BAL 086 18TH WAR
DAVIS, WILLIAM C. CHA 274 ALLENS F
DAVIS, WILLIAM E. WAS 182 BOONSBOR
DAVIS, WILLIAM H. BAL 059 10TH WAR
DAVIS, WILLIAM H. BAL 099 1ST WARD
DAVIS, WILLIAM H. BAL 067 15TH WAR
DAVIS, WILLIAM J. WOR 169 6TH E DI
DAVIS, WILLIAM J. CAR 147 NO TWP L
DAVIS, WILLIAM M. BAL 053 18TH WAR
DAVIS, WILLIAM M. BAL 112 15TH WAR
DAVIS, WILLIAM M. ANN 450 HOWARD D
DAVIS, WILLIAM P. CAR 367 9TH DIST
DAVIS, WILLIAM R. ALL 199 CUMBERLA
DAVIS, WILLIAM R. ALL 199 CUMBERLA
DAVIS, WILLIAM R. PRI 064 NOTTINGH
DAVIS, WILLIAM T. BAL 329 13TH WAR
DAVIS, WILLIAM-BLACK BAL 231 2ND WARD
DAVIS, WILLIAMM. WOR 168 6TH E DI
DAVIS, WILSON WOR 210 4TH E DI
DAVIS, WILSON WAS 105 2ND DIST
DAVIS, ZACHARIAH BAL 190 19TH WAR
DAVIS, ZACHARIAH J. MGM 348 BERRYS D
DAVIS, ZACHERIAS WAS 123 2ND DIST
DAVIS, ZACKAY BAL 052 18TH WAR
DAVIS.MARY BAL 096 1ST WARD
DAVISON, CAROLINE ANN 371 4TH DIST
DAVISON, DEBORAH BAL 155 19TH WAR
DAVISON, JOHN CAR 181 8TH DIST
DAVISON, JOHN A. ANN 511 HOWARD D
DAVISON, MARTHA M. WAS 162 2ND DIST
DAVISON, ROBERT BAL 175 19TH WAR
DAVISON, SARAH J. CAR 399 2ND DIST
DAVISON, WILLIAM BAL 048 15TH WAR
DAVISS, AMANDA BAL 295 3RD WARD
DAVISS, JOHN BAL 106 10TH WAR
DAVISSON, THOMAS L. HAR 203 3RD DIST
DAVOE, OLIVER BAL 292 12TH WAR
DAVRAGE, HELEN HAR 180 3RD DIST
DAVY, CATHARINE SOM 358 BRINKLEY
DAVY, GEORGE SOM 454 DAMES QU
DAVY, GEORGE* SOM 358 BRINKLEY
DAVY, HENRY SOM 362 BRINKLEY
DAVY, JAMES BAL 064 10TH WAR
DAVY, JOSEPH CHA 286 BOJANTOW
DAVY, MARY S. SOM 360 BRINKLEY
DAVY, ROBERT SOM 377 BRINKLEY
DAVY, TITUS SOM 378 BRINKLEY
DAVY, WILLIAM SOM 371 BRINKLEY
DAVYS, RICHARD DOR 469 1ST DIST
DAVYS, WILLIAM J. DOR 404 1ST DIST
DAWDALL, ARMINIUS BAL 163 1ST WARD
DAWDEL, ISAIAH BAL 458 8TH WARD
DAWDEN, JULIA A. MGM 393 ROCKERLE
DAWER, JOHN C. BAL 138 18TH WAR
DAWERN, MARY * BAL 283 1ST DIST
DAWES, EDWARD MGM 364 BERRYS D
DAWES, EDWARD BAL 070 4TH WARD
DAWES, ELIZABETH BAL 070 4TH WARD
DAWES, HENRY BAL 089 18TH WAR
DAWES, JOSEPH MGM 343 CLARKSBU
DAWES, MELVIN ANN 266 ANNAPOLI
DAWES, RICHARD* DOR 456 1ST DIST
DAWIS, RICHARD* DOR 456 1ST DIST
DAWIS, SOLOMON WAS 051 2ND SUBD
DAWKINS, ANN CAL 009 1ST DIST
DAWKINS, HARRY CAL 035 2ND DIST
DAWKINS, MARIAH CAL 009 1ST DIST
DAWKINS, SARAH CAL 010 1ST DIST
DAWLING, TAYLOR BAL 388 8TH WARD
DAWNEY, ELIZABETH BAL 360 1ST DIST
DAWNEY, GOERGE BAL 352 1ST DIST
DAWNEY, HUGH BAL 360 1ST DIST
DAWNEY, ISABELLA HAR 007 1ST DIST
DAWNEY, MARGARETT BAL 353 1ST DIST
DAWNEY, SARAH HAR 105 2ND DIST
DAWNEY, VACHEL BAL 366 1ST DIST
DAWOSN, ANN BAL 446 14TH WAR
DAWS, CHARLES HAR 092 2ND DIST
DAWS, ELIZABETH BAL 025 4TH WARD
DAWS, FRANCIS BAL 461 14TH WAR
DAWS, LOUISA BAL 354 7TH WARD
DAWS, MARGRET* DOR 348 3RD DIVI
DAWS, SETH DOR 335 3RD DIVI
DAWSEN, THOMAS K. BAL 046 9TH WARD
DAWSER, CHARLES J. BAL 132 1ST WARD
DAWSEY, ALLEN BAL 313 1ST DIST
DAWSEY, BENJAMIN BAL 354 1ST DIST
DAWSEY, BRIDGET BAL 263 1ST DIST
DAWSEY, ELIZABETH BAL 374 1ST DIST
DAWSEY, FRANCIS BAL 374 1ST DIST
DAWSEY, HENRY BAL 405 1ST DIST
DAWSEY, ISAIAH BAL 404 1ST DIST
DAWSEY, REBECCA BAL 330 1ST DIST
DAWSEY, ROBERT BAL 384 1ST DIST
DAWSEY, ROBERT E. DR- BAL 285 1ST DIST
DAWSEY, SAMUEL BAL 377 1ST DIST
DAWSEY, SARAH BAL 379 1ST DIST
DAWSON, ABRAM ALL 134 4TH E.D.
DAWSON, ALCADE CAR 123 NO TWP L
DAWSON, ANANCY BAL 383 13TH WAR
DAWSON, ANN BAL 460 14TH WAR
DAWSON, ANN CEC 016 ELKTON 3
DAWSON, ANN M. CAR 072 NO TWP L
DAWSON, AURELIA CEC 168 6TH E DI
DAWSON, BENJAMIN B. ALL 132 4TH E.D.
DAWSON, BENONI MGM 412 MEDLEY 3
DAWSON, CATHARINE TAL 112 ST MICHA
DAWSON, CHARLES BAL 031 9TH WARD
DAWSON, CHARLOTTE ALL 112 5TH E.D.
DAWSON, DANIEL BAL 311 1ST DIST
DAWSON, DANIEL DOR 382 1ST DIST
DAWSON, DAVID BAL 265 1ST DIST
DAWSON, EDITH TAL 069 EASTON T
DAWSON, EDWARD ALL 105 5TH E.D.
DAWSON, EDWARD M. TAL 003 EASTON D
DAWSON, ELE ALL 135 4TH E.D.
DAWSON, ELIZA ALL 137 4TH E.D.
DAWSON, ELIZA DOR 393 1ST DIST
DAWSON, ELIZABETH ALL 091 5TH E.D.
DAWSON, ELIZABETH TAL 086 ST MICHA
DAWSON, ELLEN TAL 095 ST MICHA
DAWSON, ELLEN G. TAL 066 EASTON T
DAWSON, ELLEN* BAL 045 4TH WARD
DAWSON, EMILY ALL 138 6TH E.D.
DAWSON, EMILY A. MGM 412 MEDLEY 3
DAWSON, EMILY A.* TAL 068 EASTON T
DAWSON, FRAM R. ALL 127 4TH E.D.
DAWSON, FRANCIS BAL 010 1ST WARD
DAWSON, FREDERICK BAL 273 1ST DIST
DAWSON, GEORGE DOR 360 3RD DIVI
DAWSON, GEORGE H. TAL 057 EASTON D
DAWSON, HANNAH ALL 135 4TH E.D.
DAWSON, HENRIETTA MGM 406 MEDLEY 3
DAWSON, HENRIETTA MGM 320 CRACKLIN
DAWSON, HUGH TAL 081 ST MICHA
DAWSON, ISAAC DOR 363 3RD DIVI
DAWSON, ISAAC-BLACK CAR 136 NO TWP L
DAWSON, JACOB CEC 121 4TH E DI
DAWSON, JAMES MGM 409 MEDLEY 3
DAWSON, JAMES TAL 112 ST MICHA
DAWSON, JAMES TAL 104 ST MICHA
DAWSON, JAMES ALL 135 4TH E.D.
DAWSON, JAMES ALL 137 4TH E.D.
DAWSON, JAMES BAL 282 2ND WARD
DAWSON, JAMES BAL 157 16TH WAR
DAWSON, JAMES N. DOR 393 1ST DIST
DAWSON, JANE-BLACK CAR 094 NO TWP L
DAWSON, JEREMIAH ALL 137 4TH E.D.
DAWSON, JOHN ALL 137 4TH E.D.
DAWSON, JOHN ALL 095 5TH E.D.
DAWSON, JOHN MGM 409 MEDLEY 3
DAWSON, JOHN CEC 136 6TH E DI
DAWSON, JOHN TAL 098 ST MICHA
DAWSON, JOHN WAS 045 2ND SUBD
DAWSON, JOHN DOR 454 1ST DIST
DAWSON, JOHN JR. TAL 038 EASTON D
DAWSON, JOSEPH DOR 379 1ST DIST
DAWSON, JOSEPH ALL 136 4TH E.D.
DAWSON, JOSEPH N. MGM 406 MEDLEY 3
DAWSON, KESSANDRA BAL 009 4TH WARD
DAWSON, KESSIAH-BLACK CAR 096 NO TWP L
DAWSON, LAWRENCE A. MGM 374 ROCKERLE
DAWSON, LEWIS BAL 143 1ST WARD
DAWSON, LEWIS WAS 094 2ND SUBD
DAWSON, LOUIS BAL 447 1ST DIST
DAWSON, LOVARAN S.* DOR 319 1ST DIST
DAWSON, LUCY ANN ALL 134 4TH E.D.
DAWSON, LUCY-BLACK QUE 183 3RD E DI
DAWSON, MARGARET BAL 289 17TH WAR
DAWSON, MARIA QUE 187 3RD E DI
DAWSON, MARIAH-BLACK CAR 071 NO TWP L
DAWSON, MARIAN DOR 300 1ST DIST
DAWSON, MARY CEC 129 6TH E DI
DAWSON, MARY ALL 092 5TH E.D.
DAWSON, MARY JANE BAL 439 14TH WAR
DAWSON, MARY L. BAL 012 1ST WARD
DAWSON, MATILDA H. BAL 455 1ST DIST
DAWSON, MORDICA M. TAL 067 EASTON T
DAWSON, NANCY ALL 156 6TH E.D.
DAWSON, NAT* TAL 062 EASTON D
DAWSON, PENELOPE ALL 127 4TH E.D.
DAWSON, PHILIP T. BAL 218 6TH WARD
DAWSON, RACHEL CAR 095 NO TWP L
DAWSON, RALPH TAL 112 ST MICHA
DAWSON, REBECCA ALL 137 4TH E.D.
DAWSON, REBECCA BAL 317 1ST DIST
DAWSON, RICHARD BAL 090 5TH WARD
DAWSON, RICHARD L. QUE 186 3RD E DI
DAWSON, ROBERT CEC 077 NORTHEAS
DAWSON, ROBERT S. TAL 082 ST MICHA
DAWSON, ROBERT S. TAL 093 ST MICHA
DAWSON, RUTH ALL 134 4TH E.D.
DAWSON, SOPHIA ANN 313 1ST DIST
DAWSON, SOPHIA BAL 053 1ST WARD
DAWSON, SUSANA ALL 137 4TH E.D.
DAWSON, THEODORE W. ALL 133 4TH E.D.
DAWSON, THOMAS CAR 100 NO TWP L
DAWSON, THOMAS B. TAL 111 ST MICHA
DAWSON, THOMAS R. BAL 355 3RD WARD
DAWSON, THOMAS R. BAL 064 10TH WAR
DAWSON, THOMAS V. TAL 103 ST MICHA
DAWSON, THOMAS W. ALL 136 4TH E.D.
DAWSON, VINCENT BAL 454 1ST DIST
DAWSON, WILLIAM BAL 069 1ST WARD
DAWSON, WILLIAM TAL 111 ST MICHA
DAWSON, WILLIAM CEC 206 7TH E DI
DAWSON, WILLIAM N. ANN 313 1ST DIST
DAWSON,Z ENAS QUE 157 2ND E DI
DAWSY, SARAH BAL 266 1ST DIST
DAWTON, AQUILLA BAL 430 1ST DIST
DAWTON, JAMES BAL 306 7TH WARD
DAWTON, SHADRACK BAL 422 1ST DIST
DAY, AARON R. BAL 046 9TH WARD
DAY, ALEXANDER BAL 038 1ST WARD
DAY, ALFRED BAL 239 6TH WARD
DAY, AMELIA A. BAL 420 3RD WARD
DAY, AMOS HAR 024 1ST DIST
DAY, ANN CHA 238 HILLTOP
DAY, ANN P. MGM 436 CLARKSTR
DAY, AQUIER CAR 226 5TH DIST
DAY, ASA BAL 335 3RD WARD
DAY, BENJAMIN ANN 425 HOWARD D
DAY, BURGESS HAR 038 1ST DIST
DAY, C. BAL 057 1ST WARD
DAY, CAROLINE ANN 360 3RD DIST
DAY, CAROLINE ST 330 4TH E DI
DAY, CATHARINE FRE 297 WOODSBOR
DAY, DANIEL HAR 050 1ST DIST
DAY, E. W. CHA 219 ALLENS F
DAY, EDWARD HAR 063 1ST DIST
DAY, EDWARD ANN 486 HOWARD D
DAY, EDWARD W. HAR 079 2ND DIST
DAY, ELEANOR BAL 337 1ST DIST
DAY, ELIZABETH BAL 114 15TH WAR
DAY, ELIZABETH BAL 036 4TH WARD
DAY, ELLINOR ANN 459 HOWARD D
DAY, ELLIS W. HAR 158 3RD DIST
DAY, ENOCH G. CAR 368 9TH DIST
DAY, FANNY BAL 165 16TH WAR
DAY, FIELDER PRI 094 SPALDING
DAY, FRANCIS CHA 295 HILLTOP
DAY, FRANCIS A. ANN 459 HOWARD D
DAY, GEOERGE BAL 277 17TH WAR
DAY, HENRY CHA 263 MIDDLETO
DAY, HENRY CHA 256 MIDDLETO
DAY, HENRY L. BAL 119 1ST WARD
DAY, HONNE BAL 246 12TH WAR
DAY, ISAIAH BAL 377 3RD WARD
DAY, ISHMAEL BAL 114 2ND DIST
DAY, ISRAEL HAR 158 3RD DIST
DAY, JACOB MGM 322 CRACKLIN
DAY, JACOB MGM 322 CRACKLIN
DAY, JACOB BAL 297 7TH WARD
DAY, JAMES CEC 102 4TH E DI
DAY, JAMES WOR 246 1ST CENS
DAY, JAMES F. BAL 354 3RD WARD
DAY, JAMES T. FRE 205 BUCKEYST
DAY, JANE BAL 139 2ND DIST
DAY, JEFFERSON MGM 434 CLARKSTR
DAY, JOHN PRI 095 SPALDING
DAY, JOHN ANN 455 HOWARD D
DAY, JOHN CAR 231 5TH DIST
DAY, JOHN D. ANN 484 HOWARD D
DAY, JOHN D. ANN 496 HOWARD D
DAY, JOHN Z. BAL 119 2ND DIST
DAY, JULIA BAL 235 12TH WAR

Name	County	Page	District
DAY, JULIA	QUE	228	4TH E DI
DAY, LAURA V.	CAR	232	5TH DIST
DAY, LAWSON	MGM	322	CRACKLIN
DAY, LETITIA	BAL	072	10TH WAR
DAY, LEUTICIA	BAL	323	7TH WARD
DAY, LOUISA	BAL	149	16TH WAR
DAY, LOUISA	BAL	114	2ND DIST
DAY, LUTHER	BAL	095	2ND DIST
DAY, MARGARET	CAL	011	1ST DIST
DAY, MARIA	BAL	378	13TH WAR
DAY, MARIA	BAL	088	2ND DIST
DAY, MARIA	BAL	401	8TH WARD
DAY, MARY	BAL	365	8TH WARD
DAY, MILTON	CAR	229	5TH DIST
DAY, NATHANIEL	ANN	380	4TH DIST
DAY, NICHOLAS	BAL	005	18TH WAR
DAY, OWEN D.	CAR	232	5TH DIST
DAY, PATRICK O.	BAL	147	2ND DIST
DAY, PHILIP	ANN	343	3RD DIST
DAY, RALPH	CHA	238	HILLTOP
DAY, REBECCA	BAL	077	10TH WAR
DAY, RICHARD	ANN	499	HOWARD D
DAY, ROBERT W.	ANN	494	HOWARD D
DAY, RUFUS R.	MGM	436	CLARKSTR
DAY, SAMUEL	ANN	503	HOWARD D
DAY, SAMUEL	ANN	348	3RD DIST
DAY, SAMUEL	ANN	380	4TH DIST
DAY, SAMUEL	HAR	031	1ST DIST
DAY, SARAH	MGM	435	CLARKSTR
DAY, SUSAN	ANN	376	4TH DIST
DAY, TACY A.	CEC	102	4TH E DI
DAY, THOMAS	CHA	238	HILLTOP
DAY, THOMAS	ALL	219	CUMBERLA
DAY, THOMAS	MGM	433	CLARKSTR
DAY, THOMAS	PRI	111	PISCATAW
DAY, THOMAS	PRI	087	SPALDING
DAY, TOM	CHA	240	HILLTOP
DAY, URBAN W.	MGM	320	CRACKLIN
DAY, WARREN	ANN	518	HOWARD D
DAY, WASHINGTON	CHA	264	MIDDLETO
DAY, WESLEY	CAR	232	5TH DIST
DAY, WILLIAM	ANN	504	HOWARD D
DAY, WILLIAM	BAL	120	2ND DIST
DAY, WILLIAM	BAL	280	2ND WARD
DAY, WILLIAM B.	HAR	043	1ST DIST
DAY, WILLIAM G.	HAR	038	1ST DIST
DAY, WILLIAM-BLACK	QUE	167	2ND E DI
DAY,LADER L.	BAL	031	2ND DIST
DAY,MARY	FRE	245	NEW MARK
DAY,W ILLIAM M.	CAR	076	NO TWP L
DAYE, JOHN	PRI	102	SPALDING
DAYEY, WILLIAM *	WOR	253	1ST CENS
DAYHOFE, ELIZABETH	FRE	299	WOODSBOR
DAYHOFF, CHRISTIAN	CAR	305	1ST DIST
DAYHOFF, DANIEL	CAR	411	2ND DIST
DAYHOFF, ELIAS	CAR	326	1ST DIST
DAYHOFF, ELIZABETH	CAR	314	1ST DIST
DAYHOFF, GEORGE	CAR	410	2ND DIST
DAYHOFF, JACOB	CAR	407	2ND DIST
DAYHOFF, JACOB	CAR	317	1ST DIST
DAYHOFF, JAMES	FRE	018	FREDERIC
DAYHOFF, JAMES M.	FRE	101	FREDERIC
DAYHOFF, JOHN SR.	CAR	407	2ND DIST
DAYHOFF, JOSEPH	CAR	325	1ST DIST
DAYHOFF, JOSEPH	CAR	325	1ST DIST
DAYHOFF, JOSHUA	FRE	005	FREDERIC
DAYHOFF, JOSIAH	FRE	063	FREDERIC
DAYHOFF, MARY	CAR	326	1ST DIST
DAYLEY, BRUTUS	ANN	431	HOWARD D
DAYLEY, CATHARINE	BAL	462	14TH WAR
DAYLEY, GUSTAVUS	ANN	440	HOWARD D
DAYLEY, MATTHEW	ANN	469	HOWARD D
DAYLEY, NACE	ANN	432	HOWARD D
DAYLEY, PLUMMER	ANN	432	HOWARD D
DAYLEY, WESLEY	ANN	440	HOWARD D
DAYLY, ELIJAH	KEN	210	2ND DIST
DAYMON, CATHARINE	CAR	252	3RD DIST
DAYS, L.	PRI	120	PISCATAW
DAYTON, ABRAM	ALL	134	4TH E.D.
DAYTON, ELIZA	ALL	141	6TH E.D.
DAYTON, ELIZABETH	ALL	006	3RD E.D.
DAYTON, ELLEN	ALL	128	4TH E.D.
DAYTON, ISAAC	ALL	134	4TH E.D.
DAYTON, JAMES	BAL	300	17TH WAR
DAYTON, JAMES	DOR	352	3RD DIVI
DAYTON, KITTARA	DOR	352	3RD DIVI
DAYTON, OLIVER	ALL	134	4TH E.D.
DAYTON, PATRICK	ALL	140	6TH E.D.
DAYTON, PATRICK	ALL	127	4TH E.D.
DAYTON, RICAHRD	BAL	469	14TH WAR
DAYTON, ROSE A.	DOR	352	3RD DIVI
DAYTON, WILLIAM	ALL	128	4TH E.D.
DAYTON, WILLIAM MC LEAN	ALL	134	4TH E.D.
DAYUATT, NANCEY	WAS	109	2ND DIST
DAYWALT, CHRISTOPHER	BAL	263	17TH WAR
DAZEY, EMALINE	WOR	259	BERLIN 1
DAZY, JAMES	WOR	243	1ST CENS
DAZYE, BETSY	WOR	286	BERLIN 1
DCLOZIER, JOHN *	CHA	261	MIDDLETO
DCLPLY, MARGARET	CAR	234	UNION TO
DDE, PETER	BAL	021	9TH WARD
DE AHL, BERNARD	BAL	052	1ST WARD
DE BAUFRE, ANN	BAL	069	2ND DIST
DE BEET, AGNES	BAL	043	4TH WARD
DE BLANE, CESAIRE	FRE	202	5TH E DI
DE BLANE, EMANUEL	FRE	20	5TH E DI
DE BLANE, EMILE	FRE	202	5TH E DI
DE BLANE, LEWIS	FRE	20	5TH E DI
DE BOSS, SOPHIA	BAL	067	15TH WAR
DE BUTT, DR- *	BAL	036	18TH WAR
DE CANSEY, MARGARET A.	CEC	154	PORT DUP
DE CAVERGNE, JOHN A.	MGM	362	BERRYS D
DE CERSE, HENRY	KEN	216	2ND DIST
DE CONINCK, MISS A.	FRE	199	5TH E DI
DE CORMICK, MISS M.	FRE	199	5TH E DI
DE CORSEY, JAMES	PRI	039	VANSVILL
DE COUCEY, ELIZA B.	BAL	388	13TH WAR
DE COURSAY, HENRY	BAL	098	1ST WARD
DE COURSEY, MAJOR	BAL	037	9TH WARD
DE COURSEY, MARGARET	BAL	101	2ND DIST
DE COURSEY, ROSETTA	BAL	086	4TH WARD
DE COURSEY, SARAH	QUE	184	3RD E DI
DE COURSEY, SOLOMON	BAL	179	11TH WAR
DE COURSEY, SUSANNA	BAL	377	8TH WARD
DE COURSEY, WILLIAM	BAL	330	7TH WARD
DE COURSEY, WILLIAM	QUE	197	3RD E DI
DE CRAFT, MAHALA	CAR	363	9TH DIST
DE CROSEY, THOMAS	BAL	019	1ST WARD
DE CROW, MARY	BAL	359	8TH WARD
DE FORD, CHARELS	QUE	243	5TH E DI
DE FORD, RICHARD	BAL	042	4TH WARD
DE GILVIN, JOHN	BAL	029	1ST WARD
DE GOEY, MARY	BAL	044	4TH WARD
DE GRAFF, F.	BAL	104	1ST WARD
DE GRAUFT, ISAAC	CAR	260	3RD DIST
DE GROUCHEY, JOHN	BAL	076	4TH WARD
DE HAVEN, SARAH	BAL	294	20TH WAR
DE LACOUR, J.P.	BAL	238	12TH WAR
DE LAUGHREY, EDWARD	BAL	045	4TH WARD
DE LAW, BARRON *L	BAL	074	18TH WAR
DE LOUGHREY, CATHERINE	BAL	045	4TH WARD
DE RANEERAY, MARGARETT*	BAL	005	4TH WARD
DE SA, ALBANO	FRE	202	5TH E DI
DE SERRA, MARY	BAL	099	5TH WARD
DE SHIELDS, EMMA C.	BAL	124	5TH WARD
DE SHIELDS, JESSE D.	BAL	122	5TH WARD
DE SHIELDS, JOHN W.	BAL	310	7TH WARD
DE SHIELDS, MISS Z.	FRE	199	5TH E DI
DE SHIELDS,MISS M.	FRE	200	5TH E DI
DE SHON, CHRISTOPHER	BAL	230	19TH WAR
DE SPEDA, CHARLES	BAL	050	4TH WARD
DE SPEDA, VIRGINIA	BAL	050	4TH WARD
DE VALENGER, FRANCIS	CEC	029	CHESAPEA
DE VALLENGER, MARTHA	CEC	006	ELKTON 3
DE VEERGEY, FREDERICK	BAL	207	19TH WAR
DE VOO, MARY	CEC	098	3RD E DI
DE WARD, HENRY-MULATTO	BAL	218	2ND WARD
DE WITT, ABRAHAM	CEC	117	4TH E DI
DE WITT, CATHERINE	BAL	290	3RD WARD
DE YOUNG, ANNA	BAL	377	8TH WARD
DE YOUNG, MARY	BAL	380	8TH WARD
DEXVLIN, PATRICK	BAL	091	1ST WARD
DEA, NANCY	BAL	248	12TH WAR
DEACHEL, JOHN	BAL	059	18TH WAR
DEACHIE, JOHNM	BAL	047	1ST WARD
DEACONS, FRANCIS-BLACK	FRE	049	FREDERIC
DEACONS, HENRY	BAL	351	1ST DIST
DEAD, RACHEL J.*	BAL	043	4TH WARD
DEADER, ELIZABETH	BAL	054	18TH WAR
DEADER, PETER	BAL	054	18TH WAR
DEADER, PHILIP	BAL	054	18TH WAR
DEADY, RACHEL J.*	BAL	043	4TH WARD
DEAER, FREDERICK	BAL	123	18TH WAR
DEAFENBAUCHER, EVE	WAS	263	1ST DIST
DEAFENBAUGHER, EVE M.	WAS	254	1ST DIST
DEAFENDOLL, SAMUEL	FRE	145	10TH E D
DEAFFENDAFFER, JOHN	FRE	164	EMMITTSB
DEAGAN, VINTON	BAL	019	1ST WARD
DEAGMAN, JOHN	ALL	079	5TH E.D.
DEAH, JOHN	BAL	020	9TH WARD
DEAHOFF, SAMUEL	CAR	186	8TH DIST
DEAK, LITTLE	BAL	469	14TH WAR
DEAKANS, RAGAN	CHA	243	HILLTOP
DEAKEL, AMANDA	BAL	035	18TH WAR
DEAKEN, ANN E.	CHA	283	BOJANTOW
DEAKINS, MARGARET-MULATTO	FRE	385	PETERSVI
DEAKINS, NANCY-BLACK	MGM	424	MEDLEY 3
DEAKINS, ROBERT	PRI	115	PISCATAW
DEAKINS, WILLIAM F.	PRI	008	BLADENSB
DEAL, ALLICE	BAL	286	2ND WARD
DEAL, ANN	BAL	185	5TH DIST
DEAL, ANNA	CEC	037	CHESAPEA
DEAL, BALTZER	ALL	036	2ND E.D.
DEAL, CASPER	ALL	038	2ND E.D.
DEAL, CATHARINE	BAL	063	2ND DIST
DEAL, CATHARINE	BAL	132	16TH WAR
DEAL, CONRAD	ALL	035	2ND E.D.
DEAL, CONRAD	ALL	026	2ND E.D.
DEAL, ELISABETH	ALL	036	2ND E.D.
DEAL, ELISABETH	ALL	019	2ND E.D.
DEAL, ELIZA	ANN	410	8TH DIST
DEAL, ELIZABETH	FRE	057	FREDERIC
DEAL, ELIZABETH	WAS	130	2ND DIST
DEAL, ELLEN	BAL	257	2ND WARD
DEAL, FRANK	ANN	409	8TH DIST
DEAL, FRISBY	KEN	266	1ST DIST
DEAL, GEORGE J.	BAL	302	20TH WAR
DEAL, GEORGE W.	BAL	257	2ND WARD
DEAL, HENRY	BAL	238	2ND WARD
DEAL, HENRY	ALL	037	2ND E.D.
DEAL, JAEMS	KEN	273	1ST DIST
DEAL, JAMES	ANN	410	8TH DIST
DEAL, JAMES	BAL	122	1ST WARD
DEAL, JOHN	BAL	079	1ST WARD
DEAL, JOHN	ALL	054	10TH E.D
DEAL, JOHN	ANN	319	2ND DIST
DEAL, JOHN	BAL	330	7TH WARD
DEAL, JOHN	BAL	158	1ST WARD
DEAL, JOHN	KEN	271	1ST DIST
DEAL, JOHN H.	BAL	093	15TH WAR
DEAL, JONAH	CAR	181	8TH DIST
DEAL, JONAS	ALL	189	9TH E.D.
DEAL, JUSTENA	ALL	054	10TH E.D
DEAL, LEMUEL	BAL	228	6TH WARD
DEAL, LOUIS	BAL	081	15TH WAR
DEAL, LUCY	BAL	425	1ST DIST
DEAL, MARTIN	ALL	037	2ND E.D.
DEAL, MARTIN	ALL	020	2ND E.D.
DEAL, MARY	BAL	374	8TH WARD
DEAL, MARY A.	BAL	305	7TH WARD
DEAL, MARY A.	BAL	132	16TH WAR
DEAL, MICHAEL	BAL	368	1ST DIST
DEAL, RACHAL	ANN	410	8TH DIST
DEAL, ROBERT	BAL	132	1ST WARD
DEAL, SAMUEL	BAL	134	1ST WARD
DEAL, SARAH A.	BAL	100	15TH WAR
DEAL, WILLIAM	BAL	374	8TH WARD
DEALE, ANDREW	ALL	019	2ND E.D.
DEALE, BENJAMIN	CAL	042	3RD DIST
DEALE, OTHO	WAS	257	1ST DIST
DEALE, RICHARD	CAL	038	2ND DIST
DEALE, THOMAS	CAL	056	3RD DIST
DEALER, FRANK	BAL	416	14TH WAR
DEALLER, LEWIS	BAL	036	18TH WAR
DEALMAN, HENRY C.	FRE	182	5TH E DI
DEALMAN, MISS M.	FRE	199	5TH E DI
DEALMAN, MISS R.	FRE	199	5TH E DI
DEALY, CHARLES	BAL	227	1ST DIST
DEAN, ANN	BAL	353	7TH WARD
DEAN, ANN	DOR	338	3RD DIVI
DEAN, ASBERRY	DOR	306	1ST DIST
DEAN, BENJAMIN	FRE	206	BUCKEYST
DEAN, BENNETT	CAR	152	NO TWP L
DEAN, CATHARINE	DOR	343	3RD DIVI
DEAN, CHARLES	DOR	354	3RD DIVI
DEAN, CHARLES	CAR	066	NO TWP L
DEAN, CHARLES	CAR	124	NO TWP L
DEAN, CHARLES	ST	320	4TH E DI
DEAN, CHARLES	DOR	466	1ST DIST
DEAN, CORDELA	BAL	057	18TH WAR
DEAN, DANIEL	CAR	123	NO TWP L
DEAN, DAUL	BAL	248	5TH WARD
DEAN, DOROTHEY	DOR	338	3RD DIVI
DEAN, E.F.	ALL	185	9TH E.D.
DEAN, EDWARD-BLACK	FRE	216	BUCKEYST
DEAN, ELI-BLACK	CAR	138	NO TWP L
DEAN, ELIJAH	CAR	145	NO TWP L
DEAN, ELIZABETH	FRE	260	NEW MARK
DEAN, ELIZABETH	DOR	354	3RD DIVI
DEAN, ELIZABETH	FRE	092	FREDERIC
DEAN, ELIZABETH	ANN	472	HOWARD D
DEAN, ELIZABETH-BLACK	CAR	149	NO TWP L
DEAN, EZEKIEL	CAR	067	NO TWP L
DEAN, FRANCIS	ALL	083	5TH E.D.
DEAN, FRANCIS WILLIAM	ALL	218	CUMBERLA
DEAN, GEORGE	WAS	124	2ND DIST
DEAN, GEORGE W.	BAL	020	15TH WAR
DEAN, GEORGE W.	ANN	518	HOWARD D
DEAN, HANAH	BAL	347	7TH WARD
DEAN, HARIOT	DOR	455	1ST DIST
DEAN, HARRIET A.	BAL	277	7TH WARD
DEAN, HENRY	ALL	154	6TH E.D.
DEAN, HENRY	DOR	320	1ST DIST
DEAN, HENRY T.	CAR	090	NO TWP L
DEAN, HESTER A.	CAR	115	NO TWP L
DEAN, HORATIO	CAR	114	NO TWP L
DEAN, IGNATIUS	FRE	218	BUCKEYST
DEAN, JACOB	FRE	326	MIDDLETO
DEAN, JAMES	DOR	319	1ST DIST
DEAN, JAMES	DOR	465	1ST DIST
DEAN, JAMES	SOM	513	BARREN C
DEAN, JAMES K.	ST	259	3RD E DI
DEAN, JAMES W.	MGM	391	ROCKERLE
DEAN, JOHN	DOR	345	3RD DIVI
DEAN, JOHN	FRE	263	NEW MARK
DEAN, JOHN	DOR	362	3RD DIVI
DEAN, JOHN	DOR	425	1ST DIST
DEAN, JOHN	CAR	139	NO TWP L
DEAN, JOHN	CAR	103	NO TWP L
DEAN, JOHN	CEC	086	4TH E DI
DEAN, JOHN	DOR	454	1ST DIST
DEAN, JOHN	ST	315	4TH E DI
DEAN, JOHN	QUE	215	3RD E DI
DEAN, JOHN	BAL	110	10TH WAR
DEAN, JOHN B.	DOR	447	1ST DIST
DEAN, JOHN H.	ST	346	5TH E DI
DEAN, JOHN N.T.	ST	321	4TH E DI
DEAN, JOHN P.	BAL	224	1ST DIST
DEAN, JOHN T. W.	PRI	002	BLADENSB
DEAN, JOHN W.	DOR	312	1ST DIST
DEAN, JOSEPH	ALL	178	7TH E.D.
DEAN, JOSEPH	ALL	178	7TH E.D.
DEAN, JOSEPH	ALL	192	9TH E.D.
DEAN, L.	ALL	007	3RD E.D.
DEAN, LEONEDAY	ALL	102	5TH E.D.
DEAN, LEVI	ST	321	4TH E DI
DEAN, MARGARET	SOM	512	BARREN C
DEAN, MARTHA	BAL	458	1ST DIST
DEAN, MARTHA	FRE	395	PETERSVI
DEAN, MARY	DOR	340	3RD DIVI
DEAN, MARY	DOR	342	3RD DIVI
DEAN, MARY	DOR	446	1ST DIST
DEAN, MARY	FRE	218	BUCKEYST
DEAN, MARY	FRE	060	FREDERIC
DEAN, MARY	BAL	384	13TH WAR
DEAN, MARY	BAL	332	3RD WARD
DEAN, MARY A.	CHA	248	HILLTOP
DEAN, MARY J.	BAL	398	8TH WARD
DEAN, MARY O.	ALL	243	CUMBERLA
DEAN, MATTHEW G.	ALL	191	9TH E.D.
DEAN, MICHAEL	BAL	315	7TH WARD
DEAN, MICHAEL-BLACK	CAR	141	NO TWP L
DEAN, PETER	CAR	126	NO TWP L
DEAN, PRUDE	CAR	112	NO TWP L
DEAN, REBECCA	BAL	432	14TH WAR
DEAN, RICHARD	BAL	034	9TH WARD
DEAN, RITEY	DOR	441	1ST DIST
DEAN, ROBERT	CAR	144	NO TWP L
DEAN, ROBERT	PRI	072	MARLBROU
DEAN, SALLY A.	DOR	458	1ST DIST
DEAN, SAMUEL	CAR	157	NO TWP L
DEAN, SARAH	CEC	086	4TH E DI
DEAN, SOLOMON	CAR	117	NO TWP L
DEAN, SOPHIA	DOR	439	1ST DIST
DEAN, SUSAN	DOR	338	3RD DIVI
DEAN, SUSANNA	ST	322	4TH E DI
DEAN, THOMAS	ST	322	4TH E DI
DEAN, THOMAS	DOR	461	1ST DIST
DEAN, THOMAS	DOR	465	1ST DIST
DEAN, THOMAS	DOR	336	3RD DIVI
DEAN, THOMAS	BAL	196	19TH WAR
DEAN, W.	DOR	448	1ST DIST
DEAN, WILLIAM	FRE	263	NEW MARK
DEAN, WILLIAM	BAL	207	19TH WAR
DEAN, WILLIAM	DOR	354	3RD DIVI
DEAN, WILLIAM	DOR	312	1ST DIST
DEAN, WILLIAM	CAR	119	NO TWP L
DEAN, WILLIAM	CEC	096	4TH E DI
DEAN, WILLIAM	BAL	384	13TH WAR
DEAN, WILLIAM	ALL	178	7TH E.D.
DEAN, WILLIAM	ANN	514	HOWARD D
DEAN, WILLIAM	BAL	226	12TH WAR
DEAN, WILLIAM H.	ST	323	4TH E DI
DEAN, WILLIAM J.	DOR	306	1ST DIST
DEAN, WILLIAM N.	BAL	045	1ST WARD
DEAN, WILLIAM N.	BAL	353	1ST DIST
DEAN, Z.	TAL	004	EASTON D
DEAN, ZACHARIAH-BLACK	FRE	216	BUCKEYST
DEAN,PARNELL	CAR	118	NO TWP L
DEANE, JAMES	CEC	021	ELKTON 3
DEANE, NATHAN	HAR	089	2ND DIST
DEANE, RIDGAWAY	TAL	007	EASTON D
DEANER, CHRISTIAN	WAS	189	1ST DIST
DEANER, SAMUEL	WAS	189	1ST DIST
DEANS, THOAMS	WAS	162	HAGERSTO
DEANY, MICHAEL *	BAL	275	20TH WAR
DEAR, ELIJAH O. *	SOM	410	DUBLIN D
DEAR, MARY	BAL	042	15TH WAR
DEAR, RICHARD	CEC	085	4TH E DI
DEAR, SAMUEL	BAL	256	17TH WAR
DEAR, SARAH	BAL	268	17TH WAR
DEARBEAR, CHRISTIAN	BAL	193	17TH WAR
DEARBEAR, MARY L.	BAL	193	17TH WAR
DEARBER, JOHN	BAL	201	17TH WAR
DEARBONR, C.	BAL	172	1ST WARD
DEARBORN, OCEANA	BAL	160	5TH WARD
DEARBRUN, OCEANA	BAL	302	3RD WARD
DEARDUFF, DANIEL	WAS	130	2ND DIST
DEARDUFF, PETER N.	WAS	130	2ND DIST
DEARER, DAVID *	WAS	125	2ND DIST

Name	County	Page	District
DEARER, LEWIS A.	BAL	083	18TH WAR
DEARER, OTHO *	WAS	125	2ND DIST
DEARHALT, RICHARD	BAL	178	2ND DIST
DEARHART, JOHN	HAR	150	3RD DIST
DEARKSON, ANN	BAL	264	1ST DIST
DEAS, FRANCES	BAL	155	1ST WARD
DEASER, JOHN	BAL	054	1ST WARD
DEASON, JONATHAN	ALL	192	9TH E.D.
DEATH, JOSEPH	CEC	176	7TH E DI
DEATH, JOSEPH	CEC	206	7TH E DI
DEATS, GEORGE	BAL	309	1ST DIST
DEATY, ELIZABETH	BAL	143	11TH WAR
DEAUMAS, LOUIS	BAL	356	13TH WAR
DEAVER, ANN	BAL	351	13TH WAR
DEAVER, CHARELS	BAL	174	6TH WARD
DEAVER, DAVID *	WAS	125	2ND DIST
DEAVER, EDWARD	HAR	158	3RD DIST
DEAVER, ELIZABETH	BAL	265	17TH WAR
DEAVER, ELIZABETH	WAS	102	2ND DIST
DEAVER, FERDINAND	HAR	190	3RD DIST
DEAVER, GEORGE	HAR	099	2ND DIST
DEAVER, GEORGE	HAR	024	1ST DIST
DEAVER, GEROGE	HAR	037	1ST DIST
DEAVER, HENRY S.	FRE	378	PETERSVI
DEAVER, HUGH J.	HAR	116	2ND DIST
DEAVER, JAMES	HAR	011	1ST DIST
DEAVER, JAMES	HAR	173	3RD DIST
DEAVER, JAMES	BAL	232	6TH WARD
DEAVER, JOHN	HAR	158	3RD DIST
DEAVER, JOHN	HAR	123	2ND DIST
DEAVER, JOHN	HAR	040	1ST DIST
DEAVER, JOHN	BAL	097	18TH WAR
DEAVER, JOSEPH	HAR	085	2ND DIST
DEAVER, MARY ANN	BAL	090	5TH WARD
DEAVER, MATTHEW	HAR	194	3RD DIST
DEAVER, MISS L.	FRE	199	5TH E DI
DEAVER, OTHO,*	WAS	125	2ND DIST
DEAVER, RICHARD	HAR	184	3RD DIST
DEAVER, RICHARD	HAR	037	1ST DIST
DEAVER, SARAH	HAR	128	2ND DIST
DEAVER, STEPHEN	BAL	133	18TH WAR
DEAVER, WILLIAM	HAR	124	2ND DIST
DEAVON, CHARLES	BAL	165	1ST WARD
DEAVOR, ELIZA	BAL	279	20TH WAR
DEAVORAUX, JOHN	BAL	097	5TH WARD
DEBAUFRE, WILLIAM	BAL	240	6TH WARD
DEBAUGH, MARIAMA	BAL	173	2ND DIST
DEBAUGH, MARY J.	BAL	051	18TH WAR
DEBAUGH, PHILIP	BAL	172	2ND DIST
DEBELCH, JULIA	BAL	205	11TH WAR
DEBELL, JOHN	BAL	047	18TH WAR
DEBENING, G.T.	BAL	293	12TH WAR
DEBERBY, THOMAS	WOR	330	1ST E DI
DEBERING, ANTHONY	BAL	285	20TH WAR
DEBERING, JOHN	BAL	293	12TH WAR
DEBERRY, JOHN	FRE	174	5TH E DI
DEBERRY, MARGARET	FRE	133	CREAGERS
DEBERRY, WILLIAM	FRE	114	CREAGERS
DEBERT, FRANCIS	BAL	153	19TH WAR
DEBERT, JOSEPH	BAL	403	14TH WAR
DEBORHOUSE, JOHN	BAL	068	4TH WARD
DEBOS, CATHARINE	BAL	415	1ST DIST
DEBOULER, WILLIAM G. *	HAR	207	3RD DIST
DEBOW, ADAM	BAL	056	18TH WAR
DEBOW, GEORGE	BAL	056	18TH WAR
DEBOW, JOHN JR.	BAL	291	1ST DIST
DEBOW, LEMUEL	BAL	302	20TH WAR
DEBOW, MAHOLAN	BAL	159	11TH WAR
DEBOW, SARAH A.	BAL	160	11TH WAR
DEBRINE, GEORGE	BAL	059	1ST WARD
DEBRUBER, THOMAS W. *	HAR	192	3RD DIST
DEBRULER, BENJAMIN	BAL	093	18TH WAR
DEBRULER, MARY	FRE	032	FREDERIC
DEBRYMPLE, WILLIAM	BAL	423	14TH WAR
DEBT, JOSHUA	BAL	298	1ST DIST
DEBTOR, FREDERICK	MGM	356	BERRYS D
DEBTOR, ISAIAH A.	MGM	369	BERRYS D
DEBULER, THOMAS *	BAL	125	2ND DIST
DEBUT, CAROLINE	BAL	155	11TH WAR
DEBVERRY, JOHN	FRE	137	CREAGERS
DEBYNS, JAMES	BAL	127	1ST WARD
DECATER, WILLIAM H.	ST	300	2ND E DI
DECAUCRA, AUGUSTUS	BAL	255	17TH WAR
DECERSE, BARNEY	KEN	254	1ST DIST
DECERSE, WILLIAM	KEN	254	1ST DIST
DECHANT, E.	BAL	449	8TH WARD
DECISAN, MELSY-BLACK	ST	317	4TH E DI
DECK, GEORGE	WAS	214	1ST DIST
DECK, JOHN	BAL	268	12TH WAR
DECK, JOSEPH	FRE	031	FREDERIC
DECK, MARTIN	ANN	463	HOWARD D
DECK, SAM	BAL	186	19TH WAR
DECKARD, JOHN	BAL	085	1ST WARD
DECKELMAN, JOHN	BAL	162	19TH WAR
DECKELMAYER, F. X.	FRE	159	EMMITTSB
DECKEN, ALICE	ALL	164	6TH E.D.
DECKER, ADDISON	BAL	075	18TH WAR
DECKER, BARBARA	BAL	312	12TH WAR
DECKER, ELIZA	BAL	125	16TH WAR
DECKER, FRANCIS	BAL	373	3RD WARD
DECKER, FRANCIS	BAL	196	6TH WARD
DECKER, GEORGE	BAL	425	8TH WARD
DECKER, HENRY	BAL	263	2ND WARD
DECKER, HENRY	BAL	154	5TH WARD
DECKER, JACOB F.	BAL	340	13TH WAR
DECKER, JOHN	HAR	090	2ND DIST
DECKER, JOHN	BAL	263	2ND WARD
DECKER, JOHN	BAL	131	2ND DIST
DECKER, JOHN	PRI	005	BLADENSB
DECKER, LORIN N.	BAL	203	6TH WARD
DECKER, MAR	WAS	018	2ND SUBD
DECKER, MARY	BAL	125	11TH WAR
DECKER, PECAN	BAL	246	2ND WARD
DECKER, SUSAN	BAL	085	4TH WARD
DECKER, UPTON	CAR	403	2ND DIST
DECKERBAUGH, JOHN	CAR	213	5TH DIST
DECKERT, PAUL	WAS	140	HAGERSTO
DECKEY, PERRY-BLACK	CAR	083	NO TWP L
DECKMAN, HENRY	HAR	006	1ST DIST
DECKMAN, MARY J.	HAR	007	1ST DIST
DECKMAN, PETER	HAR	006	1ST DIST
DECKNER, AGNES	BAL	063	15TH WAR
DECKUS, ANNA	WAS	151	HAGERSTO
DECOMICK, FRANCIS	BAL	003	EASTERN
DECORMIS, SARAH C.	BAL	067	15TH WAR
DECORSE, AMANDA	BAL	388	13TH WAR
DECOUCY, ISAIAH	HAR	148	3RD DIST
DECOUNT, CHARLES	QUE	166	2ND E DI
DECOURCEY, HENRY	BAL	157	2ND DIST
DECOURCY, THOMAS	BAL	133	16TH WAR
DECOURSEY, ELIZABETH	BAL	220	1ST DIST
DECUIR, TENON	FRE	202	5TH E DI
DEDERICK, CASPER	BAL	291	17TH WAR
DEDERICK, CRISTOPHER	BAL	292	17TH WAR
DEDIAS, EUSEBE	BAL	186	2ND WARD
DEDLEY, EDWARD	BAL	061	18TH WAR
DEDREY, HENRIETTA	BAL	100	5TH WARD
DEE, DAVID	BAL	447	1ST DIST
DEECKE, CHRISTIAN	BAL	067	15TH WAR
DEEDS, HENRY	BAL	345	13TH WAR
DEEK, ROBERT	ALL	109	5TH E.D.
DEELIN, GEORGE	CEC	166	6TH E DI
DEEM, JOHN	BAL	136	16TH WAR
DEEMS, ADAM	BAL	110	18TH WAR
DEEMS, EDWARD	BAL	182	16TH WAR
DEEMS, JACOB	BAL	180	16TH WAR
DEEMS, JACOB	BAL	149	16TH WAR
DEEMS, JACOB	BAL	065	18TH WAR
DEEMS, JACOB	BAL	061	18TH WAR
DEEMS, JAMES	FRE	143	10TH E D
DEEMS, LAURA V.	BAL	181	16TH WAR
DEEMY, MARY C.	WAS	122	2ND DIST
DEEN, JACOB	DOR	458	1ST DIST
DEEN, JOSHUA	BAL	463	14TH WAR
DEEN, NATHAN	TAL	001	EASTON D
DEENS, LOUISA	BAL	180	11TH WAR
DEEPAWE, JOSEPH P.*	TAL	037	EASTON D
DEEPO, JOSPEH	BAL	358	13TH WAR
DEER, CONRADT	BAL	407	8TH WARD
DEER, FERDINAN	BAL	024	18TH WAR
DEER, MARGARET*	BAL	383	3RD WARD
DEER, MARY	CEC	012	ELKTON 3
DEER, WILLIAM	BAL	013	18TH WAR
DEER, WILLIAM H.	BAL	092	18TH WAR
DEERANGE, JOHN	FRE	213	BUCKEYST
DEERHOLT, GEORGE W.	BAL	401	1ST DIST
DEERHOLT, WILLIAM	BAL	401	1ST DIST
DEETER, ALEXANDER	FRE	056	FREDERIC
DEETER, CHARLES	BAL	374	3RD WARD
DEETRICK, PHILIP	BAL	020	18TH WAR
DEETS, ELIZA	BAL	088	2ND DIST
DEETS, FREDERICK	HAR	068	1ST DIST
DEETS, FREDERICK	HAR	068	1ST DIST
DEETS, GEORGE	BAL	406	8TH WARD
DEETS, GEORGE	BAL	458	8TH WARD
DEETS, GEORGE	BAL	332	7TH WARD
DEETS, GEORGE	BAL	161	2ND DIST
DEETS, ISABELLA	ALL	237	CUMBERLA
DEETS, JACOB	BAL	331	7TH WARD
DEETS, JOHN	ALL	237	CUMBERLA
DEETS, JOHN	BAL	393	8TH WARD
DEETS, JOHN	ALL	196	CUMBERLA
DEETS, JOHN	HAR	070	1ST DIST
DEETS, LANDRUM	BAL	332	7TH WARD
DEETS, MARGARETA	BAL	319	3RD WARD
DEETS, MARY	ALL	235	CUMBERLA
DEETS, RACHEL	BAL	205	6TH WARD
DEETS, SAMUEL	ALL	236	CUMBERLA
DEETZ, JOHN	ALL	238	CUMBERLA
DEFERESE, ABERT *	BAL	131	2ND DIST
DEFFENBARGH, BENJAMIN	ALL	175	7TH E.D.
DEFFENBARGH, DANIEL	ALL	175	7TH E.D.
DEFFENBARGH, JOHN	ALL	175	7TH E.D.
DEFFENBAUGH, ALEXANDER	ALL	178	7TH E.D.
DEFFENBAUGH, PETER	ALL	176	7TH E.D.
DEFFENBAUGH, RICHARD	ALL	178	7TH E.D.
DEFFENBOUGH, JOHN	CAR	238	UNION TO
DEFFENDAFFER, JOHN	BAL	429	1ST DIST
DEFFENDOOL, JOHN	CAR	324	1ST DIST
DEFFENDOLL, SAMUEL	CAR	325	1ST DIST
DEFFENDORFFER, JOHN	CAR	411	2ND DIST
DEFFONBAUGH, BARBARA	WAS	114	2ND DIST
DEFKER, HENRY	BAL	367	1ST DIST
DEFLER, MARGARET	BAL	465	14TH WAR
DEFLEY, MICHAEL	BAL	174	11TH WAR
DEFORD, BENJAMIN	BAL	380	13TH WAR
DEFORD, EDWAD	QUE	200	3RD E DI
DEFORD, HENRY-BLACK	QUE	201	3RD E DI
DEFORD, JAMES	KEN	228	2ND DIST
DEFORD, JOHN	CAR	095	NO TWP L
DEFORD, LEVI R.	QUE	156	2ND E DI
DEFORD, MARTHA A.	PRI	026	VANSVILL
DEFORD, MARY	KEN	253	1ST DIST
DEFORD, THOMAS	BAL	013	18TH WAR
DEFORREST, MARGARET	BAL	325	7TH WARD
DEFRANK, PETER	BAL	292	7TH WARD
DEFRIES, FREDERICK	BAL	304	3RD WARD
DEGAN, BRIDGET	BAL	088	1ST WARD
DEGAN, CECELIA	BAL	348	7TH WARD
DEGAN, JOSEPH	BAL	415	8TH WARD
DEGAN, THOMAS	BAL	088	1ST WARD
DEGAN, WILLIAM J.	BAL	105	10TH WAR
DEGAN, TIMOTHY	BAL	046	1ST WARD
DEGANHARDT, CHARLES	BAL	078	1ST WARD
DEGENESS, FREDERIC	WAS	158	2ND DIST
DEGENHARD, DENA	BAL	429	8TH WARD
DEGENHARDT, CHARLES	BAL	270	2ND WARD
DEGEOY, WILLIAM *	BAL	328	13TH WAR
DEGEUNGER, JOHN A.	FRE	072	FREDERIC
DEGGIS, CHARLES	BAL	166	19TH WAR
DEGLMAN, CONRAD	BAL	231	2ND WARD
DEGNAN, ELLEN	BAL	390	8TH WARD
DEGRAFF, ABHRAM	BAL	058	18TH WAR
DEGRAFT, JOHN	BAL	277	17TH WAR
DEGRAN, PATRICK	ALL	156	6TH E.D.
DEGRANGE, PETER	FRE	141	CREAGERS
DEGRAUSS, EDWARD	BAL	262	2ND WARD
DEGRAUT, ANNETT	BAL	263	2ND WARD
DEGRAW, THOMAS	BAL	025	18TH WAR
DEGROFF, LEWIS	BAL	337	1ST DIST
DEGUIRE, ELIZABETH	BAL	012	1ST WARD
DEHADAWAY, LEWIS	CAR	133	NO TWP L
DEHAVEN, SAMUEL	CEC	007	ELKTON 3
DEHAVEN, WILLIAM	ALL	018	3RD E.D.
DEHAVINE, JESSE *	BAL	115	2ND DIST
DEHINY, ROBERT	BAL	148	19TH WAR
DEHN, THEODORE	BAL	112	15TH WAR
DEHOFF, HENRY	WAS	237	CAVETOWN
DEHOFF, JOSHUA	WAS	250	1ST DIST
DEHOFF, JOSHUA	WAS	191	BOONSBOR
DEHOFF, LOUIS	BAL	416	1ST DIST
DEHOFF, LOUIS A.	BAL	451	1ST DIST
DEHOFF, MARGARET	BAL	007	18TH WAR
DEHOFF, MARGARETT C.	BAL	007	18TH WAR
DEHOFF, SAMUEL	WAS	271	1ST DIST
DEHOUN, ROSE ANN	BAL	416	14TH WAR
DEHUFF, MARY	BAL	438	1ST DIST
DEHUHN, REBECCA	WAS	141	HAGERSTO
DEHUS, HENRY	BAL	252	1ST DIST
DEIBBEN, JOHN	BAL	029	1ST WARD
DEIBEL, PETER	BAL	048	18TH WAR
DEIBERT, JACOB	WAS	235	1ST DIST
DEIBERT, NANCY	WAS	065	2ND SUBD
DEIBERT, SUSAN	WAS	235	1ST DIST
DEIDER, JOSEPHINE	BAL	086	18TH WAR
DEIDS, MARY	BAL	186	19TH WAR
DEIGHTON, J.	BAL	135	1ST WARD
DEIGHTON, JOHN	BAL	114	1ST WARD
DEIHEN, ANDREW	BAL	114	11TH WAR
DEIHEN, MARY	BAL	114	11TH WAR
DEIHL, ANDREW	ALL	020	2ND E.D.
DEIHL, DANIEL	CAR	247	3RD DIST
DEIHL, ELIZABETH	CAR	393	2ND DIST
DEIHL, ELIZABETH	WAS	150	HAGERSTO
DEIHL, GEORGE	WAS	127	HAGERSTO
DEIHL, JOHN	CAR	359	9TH DIST
DEIHM, JOHN P.	BAL	066	15TH WAR
DEIILMAN, MARGARET	CAR	388	2ND DIST
DEILMAN, ELIZABETH	BAL	089	1ST WARD
DEILMAN, LOUIS	CAR	398	2ND DIST
DEINTY, ELIZABETH	BAL	078	1ST WARD
DEISLER, JULIA A.	BAL	062	1ST WARD
DEISLER, M.	BAL	241	20TH WAR
DEISSON, WILLIAM Y.*	BAL	045	9TH WARD
DEIST, WILLIAM	BAL	093	18TH WAR
DEIT, JACOB	BAL	471	14TH WAR
DEIT, NICHOLAS	BAL	215	17TH WAR
DEITER, JACOB	BAL	460	14TH WAR
DEITER, JACOB	WAS	204	1ST DIST
DEITER, VALENTINE	BAL	037	18TH WAR
DEITERICH, FRANCES	WAS	142	HAGERSTO
DEITERLY, CHARLES*	BAL	080	10TH WAR
DEITHRICK, ADAM	BAL	448	14TH WAR
DEITMAN, FREDERICK	BAL	250	2ND WARD
DEITRICH, ELIZABETH	WAS	055	2ND SUBD
DEITRICH, JOHN	BAL	050	18TH WAR
DEITRICK, GEORGE	WAS	174	FUNKSTOW
DEITRICK, HENRY	WAS	199	1ST DIST
DEITRICK, HENRY H.	WAS	284	1ST DIST
DEITRICK, JOHN	BAL	266	2ND WARD
DEITRICK, MARGARET	WAS	175	FUNKSTOW
DEITRICK, NANCY	WAS	212	1ST DIST
DEITZ, ADAM	BAL	271	7TH WARD
DEITZ, CAROLINE	BAL	082	1ST WARD
DEITZ, CHRISTOPHER	CAR	333	MANCHEST
DEITZ, JACOB	CAR	250	3RD DIST
DEITZ, JOHN	CAR	352	6TH DIST
DEITZ, JOHN	BAL	081	1ST WARD
DEITZ, JOSEPH	BAL	103	1ST WARD
DEITZ, MICHAEL	CAR	348	6TH DIST
DEITZ, PHILIP	CAR	348	6TH DIST
DEITZ, PHILIP	MGM	388	ROCKERLE
DEITZLER, JOHN	BAL	235	2ND WARD
DEIVES, THOMAS	BAL	165	1ST WARD
DEKERO, HENRY	BAL	109	2ND DIST
DELA ROCHE, W.F.	BAL	292	12TH WAR
DELACOUR, DAVID	BAL	372	13TH WAR
DELACOUR, JOHN	BAL	283	7TH WARD
DELACOUR, MARY	BAL	109	10TH WAR
DELAERIA, MORRIS	BAL	124	1ST WARD
DELAHAY, WILLIAM	CAR	094	NO TWP L
DELAHUNT, GEORGE W.	WAS	017	2ND SUBD
DELAHUNT, L.	PRI	094	SPALDING
DELALVIN, MARY	WOR	338	1ST E DI
DELANDER, CATHARINE	FRE	369	CATOCTIN
DELANDER, DAVID	FRE	368	CATOCTIN
DELANDER, DAVID JR.	FRE	382	PETERSVI
DELANDER, ELI	FRE	343	MIDDLETO
DELANDER, EMALINE	FRE	369	CATOCTIN
DELANDER, FREDERICK	FRE	372	CATOCTIN
DELANDER, GEORGE	FRE	369	CATOCTIN
DELANDER, GEORGE	FRE	372	CATOCTIN
DELANDER, HENRY	FRE	368	CATOCTIN
DELANDER, JOHN	FRE	322	MIDDLETO
DELANDER, JOSHUA	FRE	366	CATOCTIN
DELANDER, REBECCA	FRE	370	CATOCTIN
DELANDER, SAMUEL	FRE	323	MIDDLETO
DELANEY, GEORGE E.	BAL	304	3RD WARD
DELANEY, HANNAH	BAL	289	12TH WAR
DELANEY, ISAAC	BAL	007	1ST WARD
DELANEY, ISAAC H.A.	BAL	248	2ND WARD
DELANEY, J.	FRE	200	5TH E DI
DELANEY, JOHN	BAL	168	2ND DIST
DELANEY, MARGARET	BAL	368	3RD WARD
DELANEY, MARGARET	BAL	296	12TH WAR
DELANEY, MARTIN	BAL	235	6TH WARD
DELANEY, MARY	BAL	025	9TH WARD
DELANEY, MISS V.	FRE	200	5TH E DI
DELANEY, ROBERT	BAL	019	9TH WARD
DELANEY, WILLIAM	BAL	281	12TH WAR
DELANGHDER, CALVIN	FRE	015	FREDERIC
DELANO, JOHN	HAR	087	2ND DIST
DELANTY, WILLIAM	BAL	241	17TH WAR
DELANY, BENJAMIN	CEC	131	6TH E DI
DELANY, CATHERINE	BAL	158	11TH WAR
DELANY, CHARLES	BAL	181	19TH WAR
DELANY, DANIEL	CEC	071	5TH E DI
DELANY, JOHN	BAL	158	11TH WAR
DELANY, JOHN	BAL	384	3RD WARD
DELANY, JOSEPH	BAL	111	2ND DIST
DELANY, M.	BAL	170	1ST WARD
DELAPLAIN, ELIZABETH	FRE	176	5TH E DI
DELAPLAIN, FRANCES	WAS	148	2ND DIST
DELAPLANE, EPHARAIM	FRE	107	CREAGERS
DELAPLANE, HESEKIAH	FRE	107	CREAGERS
DELAPLANE, JOHN	FRE	175	5TH E DI
DELAPLANE, JOHN	CAR	327	1ST DIST
DELAPLANE, JOSEPH	FRE	292	WOODSBOR
DELAPLANE, JOSHUA	FRE	292	WOODSBOR
DELAPLANE, MARY	FRE	127	CREAGERS
DELAPLANE, SOPHIA	FRE	293	WOODSBOR
DELAPLANE, THEODORE C.	FRE	026	FREDERIC
DELAPLANE, WESLEY	FRE	115	CREAGERS
DELAPLANE, WILLAIM	FRE	288	WOODSBOR
DELAPLANE, WILLIAM	FRE	292	WOODSBOR
DELAPORT, SAMUEL L.	WAS	264	1ST DIST
DELARNE, ANN	BAL	225	12TH WAR
DELARY, MARY	ALL	252	CUMBERLA
DELASCHELLE, ALELE H.	BAL	268	7TH WARD
DELASHMUTT, A.	FRE	212	BUCKEYST
DELASHMUTT, ANDREW	FRE	012	FREDERIC
DELASHMUTT, ANN	FRE	447	8TH E DI
DELASHMUTT, ELIAS L.	FRE	102	FREDERIC
DELASHRUTTE, ESTHER	MGM	444	CLARKSTR
DELATEY, RHODA	BAL	291	20TH WAR
DELAUDER, DAVID SR.	FRE	377	PETERSVI
DELAUGHTER, ELIZABETH	FRE	040	FREDERIC
DELAWARE, ELLEN	BAL	090	15TH WAR
DELAWAY, THOMAS	BAL	262	20TH WAR
DELAWDER, ADAM	ANN	509	HOWARD D

DELAWDER, LOYD ANN 507 HOWARD D
DELAY, DENTON BAL 104 18TH WAR
DELAY, DNETON BAL 105 18TH WAR
DELBAY, VINCENT ALL 224 CUMBERLA
DELBREWER, WILLIAM ALL 168 6TH E.D.
DELCAMP, JOHN HAR 062 1ST DIST
DELCHER, EDWARD BAL 279 7TH WARD
DELCHER, ELIZABETH BAL 415 8TH WARD
DELCHER, JOHN BAL 185 16TH WAR
DELCHER, JOHN T. BAL 390 8TH WARD
DELCHER, JOHN W. BAL 298 7TH WARD
DELCHER, LAURA BAL 298 7TH WARD
DELCHER, WILLIAM G. BAL 296 7TH WARD
DELCHER, WILLIAM J. BAL 358 3RD WARD
DELEGRAPH, MICHAEL BAL 245 1ST DIST
DELEHAY, JAMES TAL 058 EASTON D
DELEHAY, JEREMIAH TAL 041 EASTON D
DELEHAY, JESSE TAL 040 EASTON D
DELEIZIE, JOHN F. WAS 007 WILLIAMS
DELES, CHUSLEAN BAL 384 13TH WAR
DELEVAT, JAMES BAL 379 8TH WARD
DELEVETT, AMANDA BAL 030 9TH WARD
DELFETTER, JOHN BAL 264 1ST DIST
DELHAY, JAMES C. BAL 302 12TH WAR
DELIHAY, MARY A. DOR 424 1ST DIST
DELIHAY, ROBERT DOR 445 1ST DIST
DELIHAY, SARRAH DOR 432 1ST DIST
DELIHAY, WILLIAM DOR 446 1ST DIST
DELINER, ALEXANDER BAL 239 12TH WAR
DELINGER, CHARLES WAS 018 2ND SUBD
DELINGER, JACOB WAS 020 2ND SUBD
DELINGER, LEWIS WAS 020 2ND SUBD
DELINGER, LEWIS BAL 091 5TH WARD
DELIUS, WILLIAM BAL 351 7TH WARD
DELIVIE, SAMUEL BAL 009 9TH WARD
DELKEN, WILLIAM BAL 126 1ST WARD
DELL, CHARLES L. BAL 340 3RD WARD
DELL, CHRISTIAN BAL 237 17TH WAR
DELL, ELIZA A. CAR 224 5TH DIST
DELL, FRANCES M. BAL 362 13TH WAR
DELL, GEORGE, B. BAL 325 12TH WAR
DELL, HARRIET CAR 287 7TH DIST
DELL, HARRIET CAR 280 7TH DIST
DELL, HENRY BAL 074 2ND DIST
DELL, HENRY W. CAR 398 2ND DIST
DELL, JOHN CAR 372 9TH DIST
DELL, JOHN K. CAR 280 7TH DIST
DELL, JOHN T. BAL 019 18TH WAR
DELL, LEONARD A. ALL 185 9TH E.D.
DELL, LEONARD A. ALL 186 9TH E.D.
DELL, MARGARET BAL 019 18TH WAR
DELL, MARY CAR 412 2ND DIST
DELL, MARY A. CAR 269 WESTMINS
DELL, MARYANN E. BAL 380 3RD WARD
DELL, NICHOLAS BAL 324 1ST DIST
DELL, PRUDENCE P. CAR 204 4TH DIST
DELL, RACHAEL CAR 273 WESTMINS
DELL, RACHAEL CAR 374 9TH DIST
DELL, STATES M. CAR 202 4TH DIST
DELL, THOMAS E. BAL 085 4TH WARD
DELL, WILLIAM BAL 404 14TH WAR
DELLA, JARRET BAL 006 15TH WAR
DELLA, PETER BAL 143 16TH WAR
DELLAHAY, HENRY TAL 066 EASTON T
DELLAHAY, JAMES H.* TAL 040 EASTON D
DELLAHAY, JANE BAL 068 10TH WAR
DELLAHAY, MARGARET A.* TAL 048 EASTON T
DELLAHAY, WILLIAM BAL 433 8TH WARD
DELLANE, MARY HAR 206 3RD DIST
DELLANO, PHILIP BAL 018 18TH WAR
DELLANY, CHARLES V. ALL 224 CUMBERLA
DELLAY, SUSAN BAL 305 17TH WAR
DELLEHAY, MARGARET A.* TAL 048 EASTON T
DELLEN, MARGARET CEC 196 6TH E DI
DELLEN, SUSANER HAR 177 3RD DIST
DELLENOUGH, WILLIAM BAL 392 3RD WARD
DELLERIE, HESTER* BAL 090 10TH WAR
DELLERIE, SOLOMON* BAL 090 10TH WAR
DELLEVIE, HESTER* BAL 090 10TH WAR
DELLEVIE, SOLOMON* BAL 090 10TH WAR
DELLEY, JOHN ALL 127 4TH E.D.
DELLEY, JOSEPH ALL 145 6TH E.D.
DELLICH, PHILIP BAL 321 20TH WAR
DELLINGER, FREDRICK WAS 137 2ND DIST
DELLINGER, HENRY W. WAS 103 2ND DIST
DELLINGER, WILLIAM WAS 135 2ND DIST
DELLON, EDWARD ALL 091 5TH E.D.
DELLON, JAMES ALL 111 5TH E.D.
DELLON, MARTHETT * HAR 197 3RD DIST
DELLOW, COMFORT BAL 342 7TH WARD
DELLOW, PETER ALL 136 4TH E.D.
DELLUM, B. RUSH HAR 180 3RD DIST
DELLUM, CAROLINE HAR 191 3RD DIST
DELLUM, MARY HAR 185 3RD DIST
DELMAS, AMELIA BAL 080 4TH WARD
DELMAS, FANNY E. BAL 215 11TH WAR
DELMAS, THEADORE HAR 188 3RD DIST
DELMSLEY, WILLIAM BAL 356 3RD WARD
DELOB, MORRIS BAL 160 11TH WAR
DELOM, MARY HAR 027 1ST DIST
DELOM, THOAMS HAR 030 1ST DIST
DELON, MORDICA CEC 060 1ST E DI
DELONE, SISTER CATHARINE FRE 198 5TH E DI
DELONEY, ELIZA WAS 042 2ND SUBD
DELONEY, JOHN WAS 041 2ND SUBD
DELONG, JEREMIAH BAL 385 13TH WAR
DELOP, MARGRET CAR 306 1ST DIST
DELOSHER, THOMAS BAL 038 18TH WAR
DELOSIER, A. PRI 105 PISCATAW
DELOSIER, THOMAS CHA 236 HILLTOP
DELOSTE, FRANCES BAL 041 4TH WARD
DELOSURE, JACKSON WAS 257 1ST DIST
DELOSURE, JOHN WAS 249 1ST DIST
DELOSURE, MARGARET WAS 246 SMITHSBU
DELOSURE, WILLIAM WAS 259 1ST DIST
DELOTER, HENRY WAS 034 2ND SUBD
DELPHY, ANN M. CAR 316 1ST DIST
DELPHY, GEORGE CAR 398 2ND DIST
DELPHY, JOHN CAR 315 1ST DIST
DELPHY, WILLIAM CAR 396 2ND DIST
DELUGER, ISRAEL FRE 368 CATOCTIN
DELUM, HARRIETT HAR 153 3RD DIST
DELUM, WILLIAM M. HAR 184 3RD DIST
DELUSHMATT, ANN FRE 204 BUCKEYST
DELUSHMUTT, SARAH FRE 205 BUCKEYST
DELVALLIE, VIRGINIA BAL 069 4TH WARD
DELVER, HENRY ALL 112 5TH E.D.
DELWITZ, MARY BAL 125 5TH WARD
DEMAHUE, JAMES BAL 207 2ND WARD
DEMAN, DANIEL KEN 307 3RD DIST
DEMAN, HENRY BAL 417 3RD WARD
DEMAN, JULIA CHA 285 BOJANTOW
DEMAN, MARY BAL 225 12TH WAR
DEMANGUT, ALEXANDER BAL 226 2ND WARD
DEMAR, CATHARINE BAL 283 17TH WAR
DEMAR, JOHN CHA 285 BOJANTOW
DEMAR, PAUL BAL 277 17TH WAR
DEMARAN, JOHN H. O. BAL 143 11TH WAR
DEMARR, CHARLES PRI 047 AQUASCO
DEMAWAY, THOMAS FRE 095 FREDERIC
DEMAY, CHARLES BAL 458 8TH WARD
DEMBEY, ----- * BAL 122 11TH WAR
DEMBEY, ELEANORA BAL 241 6TH WARD
DEMBS, DOLLY* TAL 038 EASTON D
DEMBS, JIM TAL 075 EASTON T
DEMBY, ANN BAL 190 11TH WAR
DEMBY, ANNA-BLACK QUE 185 3RD E DI
DEMBY, AUSTIN BAL 094 15TH WAR
DEMBY, CHARLES H. BAL 071 4TH WARD
DEMBY, DOLLY* TAL 038 EASTON D
DEMBY, ELIZABETH QUE 251 5TH E DI
DEMBY, JAMES CEC 060 1ST E DI
DEMBY, JOHN QUE 211 3RD E DI
DEMBY, JOSHUA CEC 065 1ST E DI
DEMBY, JOSHUA CEC 065 1ST E DI
DEMBY, MARY J. ANN 425 HOWARD D
DEMBY, PHILIP BAL 204 11TH WAR
DEMBY, SAMUEL* TAL 005 EASTON D
DEMBY, THOMAS TAL 110 ST MICHA
DEMBY, TITUS QUE 182 3RD E DI
DEMBY, WASINGTON KEN 289 3RD DIST
DEMBY, WILLIAM KEN 272 1ST DIST
DEMELMAN, JOSHUA* BAL 307 3RD WARD
DEMELMAN, WILLIAM BAL 307 3RD WARD
DEMEN, RACHAEL BAL 027 2ND DIST
DEMENT, CHARLES T. PRI 113 PISCATAW
DEMENT, ELIJAH ST 312 1ST E DI
DEMENT, ELIZABETH PRI 089 SPALDING
DEMENT, ELIZABETH V. CHA 258 MIDDLETO
DEMENT, JANE PRI 112 PISCATAW
DEMENT, RICHARD CHA 258 MIDDLETO
DEMENT, WILLIAM CHA 255 MIDDLETO
DEMENT, WILLIAM S. CHA 258 MIDDLETO
DEMER, JOHN BAL 006 EASTERN
DEMET, MABERA BAL 144 19TH WAR
DEMFORD, MARY BAL 101 18TH WAR
DEMICK, MARY F. BAL 215 11TH WAR
DEMINT, HEZEKIAH CHA 295 HILLTOP
DEMIRES, SAMUEL ALL 252 CUMBERLA
DEMISH, JAMES QUE 182 3RD E DI
DEMIT, CLARISSA ALL 132 4TH E.D.
DEMLEY, MARK KEN 288 3RD DIST
DEMMAN, FRANCIS BAL 426 14TH WAR
DEMMEAD, ISAAC BAL 162 11TH WAR
DEMMET, HENRY FRE 425 8TH E DI
DEMMET, REBECCA BAL 326 1ST DIST
DEMMETT, JOHN H. BAL 266 1ST DIST
DEMMING, JOHN BAL 129 1ST WARD
DEMMINK, JOHN BAL 320 1ST DIST
DEMMITT, DALILAH BAL 433 14TH WAR
DEMODY, WALTER MGM 317 CRACKLIN
DEMORE, JAMES A. PRI 048 AQUASCO
DEMORSE, JOSHUA BAL 119 2ND DIST
DEMOSS, DAVID HAR 042 1ST DIST
DEMOSS, JOHN BAL 129 2ND DIST
DEMOSS, JOHN BAL 129 2ND DIST
DEMOSS, THOMAS CAR 193 4TH DIST
DEMPATER, WILLIAM ALL 086 5TH E.D.
DEMPHY, WILLIAM BAL 028 9TH WARD
DEMPSEY, ANN FRE 063 FREDERIC
DEMPSEY, BETSY BAL 118 5TH WARD
DEMPSEY, HUGH PRI 104 PISCATAW
DEMPSEY, MARGARET BAL 013 9TH WARD
DEMPSEY, MARY BAL 103 1ST WARD
DEMPSEY, OWEN BAL 134 11TH WAR
DEMPSEY, THOMAS ANN 509 HOWARD D
DEMPSEY, TIMOTHY BAL 145 5TH WARD
DEMPSEY, WARNER FRE 252 NEW MARK
DEMPSEY, WILLIAM BAL 170 11TH WAR
DEMPSEY, WILLIAM BAL 170 11TH WAR
DEMPSON, SARAH BAL 204 2ND WARD
DEMPSON, WILLIAM BAL 045 1ST WARD
DEMPSTER, J. C. BAL 157 1ST WARD
DEMPSTER, JAMES BAL 289 17TH WAR
DEMPSTER, JOHN BAL 290 17TH WAR
DEMPSTER, JOHN BAL 245 17TH WAR
DEMPSTER, SARAH E. BAL 133 11TH WAR
DEMSBY, WILLIAM CEC 175 7TH E DI
DEMSEY, FREDERICK CAR 370 9TH DIST
DEMSEY, JOHN CEC 034 CHESAPEA
DEMUSTO, AMANDA CAR 303 1ST DIST
DEMUTT, JOHN BAL 145 19TH WAR
DEMUTT, JOHN H. BAL 145 19TH WAR
DEN, DENNIS * KEN 213 2ND DIST
DEN, MARGARET* BAL 383 3RD WARD
DENAHAY, PATRICK FRE 182 5TH E DI
DENAHON, CATHARINE BAL 012 2ND DIST
DENAVAN, MARY A. HAR 183 3RD DIST
DENBAR, HARRIET BAL 251 12TH WAR
DENBOE, THOMAS HAR 083 2ND DIST
DENBOER, JULIA A. BAL 119 15TH WAR
DENBOER, JULIA G. BAL 215 6TH WARD
DENBOW, GABRIEL HAR 058 1ST DIST
DENBOW, JOHN HAR 057 1ST DIST
DENBY, HENRY-BLACK QUE 157 2ND E DI
DENBY, JOHN KEN 236 2ND DIST
DENBY, JOHN KEN 229 2ND DIST
DENBY, JOHN QUE 210 3RD E DI
DENBY, JULIA QUE 249 5TH E DI
DENBY, JULIA BAL 065 10TH WAR
DENBY, PERRY BAL 280 12TH WAR
DENBY, REBECA BAL 309 20TH WAR
DENBY, RICHARD QUE 213 3RD E DI
DENBY, ROBERT QUE 249 5TH E DI
DENBY, SAMUEL* DOR 451 1ST DIST
DENBY, SARAH BAL 145 5TH WARD
DENBY, THOMAS QUE 209 3RD E DI
DENBY, THOMAS H.-BLACK QUE 157 2ND E DI
DENBY, TITUS QUE 213 3RD E DI
DENBY, WILLIAM BAL 225 19TH WAR
DENCAN, JACOB ALL 167 6TH E.D.
DENCH, GEORGE BAL 201 2ND WARD
DENCKSON, MARGARET WOR 246 1ST CENS
DENDON, L. BAL 172 1ST WARD
DENEAD, EDWARD BAL 402 1ST DIST
DENEAN, WILLIAM * ALL 167 6TH E.D.
DENEEN, SAMUEL ALL 182 8TH E.D.
DENEFRIG, JANE BAL 215 11TH WAR
DENER, MARY WAS 092 2ND SUBD
DENER, SAMUEL WAS 087 2ND SUBD
DENESEY, THOMAS ALL 077 5TH E.D.
DENEY, WILLIAM BAL 038 1ST WARD
DENGER, CAROLINE BAL 123 11TH WAR
DENGLE, GEORGE BAL 043 1ST WARD
DENGLER, BARBARA BAL 064 15TH WAR
DENGLER, JOHN ALL 234 CUMBERLA
DENHARDT, HENRY BAL 007 18TH WAR
DENHART, HENRY BAL 131 5TH WARD
DENHOLM, CHARLES WAS 248 1ST DIST
DENIE, THOASM ANN 327 2ND DIST
DENIES, ELIZABETH* DOR 447 1ST DIST
DENIG, HANNAH BAL 110 1ST WARD
DENIGAN, PATRICK BAL 029 1ST WARD
DENIGLE, JOHN BAL 361 13TH WAR
DENIKER, ALMOR A. BAL 377 8TH WARD
DENING, MARGARET CAR 373 9TH DIST
DENINGER, MARY BAL 236 20TH WAR
DENIS, JOHN WOR 210 4TH E DI
DENIS, JOHN P. BAL 074 10TH WAR
DENIS, NARCISSA E. WOR 205 4TH E DI
DENISLHAN, M. BAL 166 1ST WARD
DENISON, ANN E. BAL 273 7TH WARD
DENISON, MARCUS BAL 023 9TH WARD
DENISON, MARY BAL 462 1ST DIST
DENISON, ROBERT M. BAL 413 1ST DIST
DENISON, SAMUEL BAL 009 1ST WARD
DENISTON, J. V. BAL 307 20TH WAR
DENKEL, HENRY BAL 036 15TH WAR
DENKEL, JACOB BAL 037 15TH WAR
DENKINS, JAMES MGM 383 ROCKERLE
DENLE, JOSEPH CAL 060 3RD DIST
DENMAN, MARANDA FRE 377 PETERSVI
DENMARK, JOE ELLEN-MULATT FRE 242 NEW MARK
DENMARK, JOHN T. MGM 317 CRACKLIN
DENMARK, PETER ANN 444 HOWARD D
DENMARK, THOMAS FRE 270 NEW MARK
DENMARK, LORETTA-MULATTO FRE 009 FREDERIC
DENMEAD, ADAM BAL 452 8TH WARD
DENMEAD, BENJAMIN BAL 059 2ND DIST
DENMEAD, MARY ANN 477 HOWARD D
DENMEAD, WILLIAM BAL 115 11TH WAR
DENN, MARY BAL 449 1ST DIST
DENNELL, DAWSON ANN 279 ANNAPOLI
DENNER, SARAH BAL 008 EASTERN
DENNER, SARAH WAS 091 2ND SUBD
DENNER, WILLIAM WAS 089 2ND SUBD
DENNETT, ENOCH ALL 114 5TH E.D.
DENNEY, FREDERICK BAL 038 1ST WARD
DENNEY, JAMES KEN 231 2ND DIST
DENNEY, JOHN FRE 095 FREDERIC
DENNEY, JOHN KEN 264 1ST DIST
DENNEY, THOMAS QUE 181 2ND E DI
DENNEY, WILLIAM KEN 266 1ST DIST
DENNEY, WILLIAM BAL 134 5TH WARD
DENNIE, WILLIAM BAL 286 2ND WARD
DENNIER, WILLIAM CEC 177 7TH E DI
DENNIGLE, ELISABETH ALL 044 10TH E.D
DENNILTTA, BEDDA BAL 458 1ST DIST
DENNIMORE, NANCY ALL 023 2ND E.D.
DENNING, ANN BAL 408 14TH WAR
DENNING, CHARLES CAR 358 9TH DIST
DENNING, CHARLES F. CEC 029 CHESAPEA
DENNING, CLEM BAL 233 20TH WAR
DENNING, DAVID BAL 233 20TH WAR
DENNING, ELIZA KEN 241 2ND DIST
DENNING, GEORGE KEN 240 2ND DIST
DENNING, GEORGE S. BAL 233 20TH WAR
DENNING, J.S. BAL 233 20TH WAR
DENNING, JAMES BAL 006 1ST WARD
DENNING, JOHN N. BAL 025 9TH WARD
DENNING, LOUISANA CAR 355 9TH DIST
DENNING, MARIA CAR 281 7TH DIST
DENNING, MARY BAL 233 20TH WAR
DENNING, MARY E. BAL 233 20TH WAR
DENNING, MATHEW CAR 373 9TH DIST
DENNINGTON, HANNAH HAR 018 1ST DIST
DENNIS, AMELA WOR 302 SNOW HIL
DENNIS, ANANIAS WOR 219 4TH E DI
DENNIS, ANDREW BAL 150 19TH WAR
DENNIS, ANN M. WOR 166 6TH E DI
DENNIS, BENJAMIN WOR 301 SNOW HIL
DENNIS, BENJAMIN M. BAL 150 19TH WAR
DENNIS, BENJAMIN-BLACK WOR 336 1ST E DI
DENNIS, BRIDGET BAL 339 3RD WARD
DENNIS, BRIDGET BAL 182 11TH WAR
DENNIS, CAROLINE BAL 175 16TH WAR
DENNIS, CATHARINE BAL 123 5TH WARD
DENNIS, CATHARINE TAL 092 ST MICHA
DENNIS, CATHARINE-BLACK WOR 333 1ST E DI
DENNIS, CHARLES BAL 125 1ST WARD
DENNIS, CHARLES A. BAL 238 17TH WAR
DENNIS, COUNCEL BAL 141 2ND DIST
DENNIS, DAID ALL 201 CUMBERLA
DENNIS, DANIEL BAL 092 1ST WARD
DENNIS, DANIEL J. WOR 213 4TH E DI
DENNIS, DAVID WAS 128 2ND DIST
DENNIS, EDWARD SOM 428 PRINCESS
DENNIS, ELIJAH SOM 520 BARREN C
DENNIS, ELIJAH M. WOR 202 4TH E DI
DENNIS, ELIZABETH SOM 550 TYASKIN
DENNIS, ELIZABETH BAL 325 12TH WAR
DENNIS, ELLEN BAL 420 8TH WARD
DENNIS, EMALINE SOM 554 TYASKIN
DENNIS, EMMA ALL 200 CUMBERLA
DENNIS, EVE CAR 336 6TH DIST
DENNIS, GEORGE DOR 313 1ST DIST
DENNIS, GEORGE BAL 031 9TH WARD
DENNIS, GEORGE R. SOM 362 BRINKLEY
DENNIS, GEORGE R. SOM 401 BRINKLEY
DENNIS, GILBERT BAL 161 1ST WARD
DENNIS, HANNAH BAL 259 20TH WAR
DENNIS, HENRY BAL 098 5TH WARD
DENNIS, HENRY WOR 301 SNOW HIL
DENNIS, HESTER BAL 376 13TH WAR
DENNIS, ISAAC WOR 303 SNOW HIL
DENNIS, J. ALL 143 6TH E.D.
DENNIS, JAMES BAL 324 7TH WARD
DENNIS, JAMES WOR 313 2ND E DI
DENNIS, JAMES SOM 475 TRAPPE D
DENNIS, JAMES P. WOR 222 4TH E DI
DENNIS, JANE WOR 331 1ST E DI
DENNIS, JANE SOM 406 DUBLIN D
DENNIS, JESSE WOR 292 9TH E DI
DENNIS, JIM WOR 286 BERLIN 1
DENNIS, JIM ANN 338 3RD DIST
DENNIS, JOHN WOR 215 4TH E DI
DENNIS, JOHN SOM 428 PRINCESS
DENNIS, JOHN DOR 313 1ST DIST
DENNIS, JOHN H. WOR 331 1ST E DI
DENNIS, JOHN W. WOR 331 1ST E DI

Name	County	Page	District
DENNIS, JOHN W.	WOR	214	4TH E DI
DENNIS, JOHN W.	WOR	206	4TH E DI
DENNIS, JOHN W.L.	BAL	206	17TH WAR
DENNIS, JOHNP.	WOR	165	6TH E DI
DENNIS, JOHNSON	WOR	206	4TH E DI
DENNIS, JOHNW.	WOR	220	4TH E DI
DENNIS, JOSEPH	WOR	202	4TH E DI
DENNIS, JOSEPH M.*	SOM	402	BRINKLEY
DENNIS, JOSEPH-BLACK	WOR	349	1ST E DI
DENNIS, JOSH	BAL	102	2ND DIST
DENNIS, JOSHUA	BAL	337	3RD WARD
DENNIS, L.	BAL	305	12TH WAR
DENNIS, LEVIN	WOR	219	4TH E DI
DENNIS, LEWIS	BAL	206	17TH WAR
DENNIS, LITTLETON	BAL	155	11TH WAR
DENNIS, LITTLETON	BAL	155	11TH WAR
DENNIS, LITTLETON	WOR	220	4TH E DI
DENNIS, MARGARET	BAL	366	8TH WARD
DENNIS, MARGARET A.	WOR	221	4TH E DI
DENNIS, MARIAH	SOM	402	BRINKLEY
DENNIS, MARY	BAL	265	12TH WAR
DENNIS, MARY	BAL	298	20TH WAR
DENNIS, MARY A.	BAL	008	9TH WARD
DENNIS, MARY-BLACK	WOR	333	1ST E DI
DENNIS, MILEY*	DOR	444	1ST DIST
DENNIS, NANCY	WOR	203	4TH E DI
DENNIS, NANCY	SOM	475	TRAPPE D
DENNIS, NELSON	SOM	385	BRINKLEY
DENNIS, PETER	BAL	338	3RD WARD
DENNIS, PRUNELL J.	WOR	217	4TH E DI
DENNIS, REEECCA	CEC	031	CHESAPEA
DENNIS, RICHARD J.	TAL	093	ST MICHA
DENNIS, ROBERT	BAL	118	11TH WAR
DENNIS, ROBERT	SOM	428	PRINCESS
DENNIS, ROBERT	BAL	070	10TH WAR
DENNIS, ROBERT H.	WOR	342	1ST E DI
DENNIS, SAMPSON D.	WOR	186	7TH E DI
DENNIS, SAMUEL	WAS	127	2ND DIST
DENNIS, SARAH	TAL	092	ST MICHA
DENNIS, SARAH	SOM	410	DUBLIN D
DENNIS, SARAH-BLACK	WOR	320	1ST E DI
DENNIS, SEABURY	BAL	336	3RD WARD
DENNIS, SEREPTA CAROLINE	SOM	554	TYASKIN
DENNIS, SPHRAIM W.	WOR	221	4TH E DI
DENNIS, STEPHEN	TAL	094	ST MICHA
DENNIS, STEWARD	BAL	276	2ND WARD
DENNIS, THOASM H.	WOR	204	4TH E DI
DENNIS, THOMAS	WOR	203	4TH E DI
DENNIS, THOMAS	WOR	215	4TH E DI
DENNIS, THOMAS H.	WOR	214	4TH E DI
DENNIS, THOMAS S.	BAL	150	19TH WAR
DENNIS, TOBIA-BLACK	WOR	337	1ST E DI
DENNIS, TOLBERT-BLACK	WOR	166	6TH E DI
DENNIS, WASHINGTON	SOM	488	SALISBUR
DENNIS, WILLIAM	WOR	204	4TH E DI
DENNIS, WILLIAM	BAL	150	19TH WAR
DENNIS, WILLIAM	BAL	158	16TH WAR
DENNIS, WILLIAM	ALL	118	5TH E.D.
DENNIS, WILLIAM H.	WOR	221	4TH E DI
DENNIS,LITTLETON Q.	WOR	165	6TH E DI
DENNISON, AERAHAM	WAS	207	1ST DIST
DENNISON, AMELIA	BAL	459	14TH WAR
DENNISON, ANN	BAL	011	9TH WARD
DENNISON, ELISHA	ALL	189	9TH E.D.
DENNISON, HEZEKIAH	WAS	207	1ST DIST
DENNISON, JOHN	BAL	272	7TH WARD
DENNISON, JOSEPH	ALL	191	9TH E.D.
DENNISON, JOSEPH	CEC	170	6TH E DI
DENNISON, MARGARET	CEC	185	7TH E DI
DENNISCN, ROBERT	ALL	191	9TH E.D.
DENNISON, ROBERT	ALL	191	9TH E.D.
DENNISON, SAMUEL	HAR	196	3RD DIST
DENNISON, SARAH	BAL	297	20TH WAR
DENNISON, THOMAS	BAL	018	9TH WARD
DENNISON, WILLIAM	CEC	191	5TH E DI
DENNISON, WILLIAM	CEC	185	7TH E DI
DENNISON, WILLIAM	MGM	392	ROCKERLE
DENNIST, MARY	ALL	250	CUMBERLA
DENNOTT, MARY	BAL	262	12TH WAR
DENNSER, JOSEPH	BAL	264	12TH WAR
DENNY, ARIANNA	QUE	224	4TH E DI
DENNY, CHARLES F.	BAL	329	1ST DIST
DENNY, CHARLOTTE A.	BAL	113	1ST WARD
DENNY, CLINTON	TAL	019	EASTON D
DENNY, DANIEL	CEC	140	6TH E DI
DENNY, ELIZA	BAL	144	11TH WAR
DENNY, ELIZA C.	BAL	342	3RD WARD
DENNY, ELIZABETH T.	BAL	290	3RD WARD
DENNY, EUGENE	BAL	384	3RD WARD
DENNY, FRANCIS*	BAL	384	3RD WARD
DENNY, GEORGE	BAL	303	17TH WAR
DENNY, GEORGE	DOR	339	3RD DIVI
DENNY, GEORGE	CEC	010	ELKTCN 3
DENNY, JACOB T.	QUE	222	4TH E DI
DENNY, JAMES	TAL	093	ST MICHA
DENNY, JAMES	QUE	225	4TH E DI
DENNY, JAMES	CEC	004	ELKTON 3
DENNY, JAMES	BAL	232	2ND WARD
DENNY, JOHN	BAL	019	15TH WAR
DENNY, JOHN	BAL	196	17TH WAR
DENNY, JOHN	DOR	339	3RD DIVI
DENNY, JOHN	QUE	224	4TH E DI
DENNY, MARGARET	TAL	088	ST MICHA
DENNY, MARIA	BAL	094	15TH WAR
DENNY, MARY	BAL	238	6TH WARD
DENNY, MARY	BAL	055	4TH WARD
DENNY, MARY A.	BAL	086	4TH WARD
DENNY, PAT	BAL	009	9TH WARD
DENNY, RICHARD	ANN	340	3RD DIST
DENNY, SAMUEL	CAR	065	NO TWP L
DENNY, SARAH E.	QUE	223	4TH E DI
DENNY, THOMAS	BAL	183	2ND WARD
DENNY, WILLIAM	ANN	458	HOWARD D
DENNY, WILLIAM	BAL	455	8TH WARD
DENNY, WILLIAM	ANN	280	ANNAPOLI
DENNY, WILLIAM	QUE	229	4TH E DI
DENOE, THOMAS	BAL	040	18TH WAR
DENOHUE, MARY	BAL	273	12TH WAR
DENP, RICHARD	BAL	025	1ST WARD
DENPKINS, HERNY	BAL	076	1ST WARD
DENSBY, REBECCA	HAR	155	3RD DIST
DENSER, WILLIAM	WAS	266	1ST DIST
DENSLEY, ELIZABETH	HAR	155	3RD DIST
DENSLEY, GEORGE E.	HAR	155	3RD DIST
DENSON, CHARLES J.	BAL	169	1ST WARD
DENSON, ELIZA	SOM	489	SALISBUR
DENSON, ELIZABETH	SOM	416	DUBLIN D
DENSON, GOTTEIB	BAL	245	2ND WARD
DENSON, HESTER	SOM	490	SALISBUR
DENSON, ISAAC	SOM	476	TRAPPE D
DENSON, ISAAC M.	BAL	457	8TH WARD
DENSON, J.	BAL	153	1ST WARD
DENSON, JAMES	SOM	477	TRAPPE D
DENSON, JESSE T.	SOM	537	TYASKIN
DENSON, JOHN	BAL	451	14TH WAR
DENSON, MARIA	BAL	063	18TH WAR
DENSON, RACHEL	CEC	196	6TH E DI
DENSON, SARAH	SOM	537	TYASKIN
DENSON, SARAH J.	SOM	477	TRAPPE D
DENSON, WESLEY A.	SOM	482	TRAPP DI
DENSON,ROSINA	BAL	245	2ND WARD
DENSSON, CHARLES	HAR	182	3RD DIST
DENSTING, JULIAN	FRE	027	FREDERIC
DENSTON, BENJAMIN	WOR	186	7TH E DI
DENSTON, GATTY	WOR	228	6TH E DI
DENSTON, LEVIN	WOR	180	6TH E DI
DENSTON, SAMUEL J. M.	WOR	184	6TH E DI
DENSTON, SARAH*	SOM	478	TRAPP DI
DENT, ALEXANDER	MGM	387	ROCKERLE
DENT, AMELIA V.	CHA	280	BOJANTOW
DENT, B.F.	PRI	111	PISCATAW
DENT, BENJAMIN	CHA	268	BOJANTOW
DENT, BENJAMIN F.	CHA	275	ALLENS F
DENT, CATHERINE	CHA	292	BOJANTOW
DENT, CHARLES H.	CHA	244	HILLTOP
DENT, CHARLES H.	CHA	248	HILLTOP
DENT, ELIZABETH	CHA	288	BOJANTOW
DENT, GEORGE	CHA	287	BOJANTOW
DENT, HENRY S.	CHA	247	HILLTOP
DENT, HEZEKIAH	ST	292	2ND E DI
DENT, JAMES	BAL	084	1ST WARD
DENT, JENNY	MGM	329	CRACKLIN
DENT, JOHN B.	CHA	268	BOJANTOW
DENT, JOHN F.	ST	318	4TH E DI
DENT, JOHN K.	BAL	003	15TH WAR
DENT, KITTY	CHA	245	HILLTOP
DENT, LEANNA	ANN	485	HOWARD D
DENT, LOUISA	CHA	242	HILLTOP
DENT, MARY B.	FRE	065	FREDERIC
DENT, MARY P.	CHA	258	MIDDLETO
DENT, MOSES	ANN	485	HOWARD D
DENT, NATHAN C.	MGM	388	ROCKERLE
DENT, SOPHIA	BAL	020	4TH WARD
DENT, STOUTEN W.	CHA	273	ALLENS F
DENT, SUSAN	ANN	490	HOWARD D
DENT, THEOPHILAS	CHA	264	HILLTOP
DENT, THEOPHILES	CHA	275	ALLENS F
DENT, THOMAS E.	ST	285	2ND E DI
DENT, VULINDIA	ST	307	1ST E DI
DENT, WALTER B.	ST	333	4TH E DI
DENT, WALTER C.	ST	335	4TH E DI
DENT, WALTER Z.	CHA	280	BOJANTOW
DENT, WESLEY	ANN	470	HOWARD D
DENT, WLLIAM	ST	290	2ND E DI
DENTER, FRANCIS	BAL	269	12TH WAR
DENTLEY, MARY	BAL	407	8TH WARD
DENTLEY, WILLIAM	BAL	407	8TH WARD
DENTO, JOSEPH P.	ALL	219	CUMBERLA
DENTON, ANN	BAL	142	5TH WARD
DENTON, BENJAMIN	CAL	025	2ND DIST
DENTON, ELIZABETH	CAL	035	2ND DIST
DENTON, GEORGE	CAL	010	1ST DIST
DENTON, JAEMS D.	CAL	007	1ST DIST
DENTON, JAMES	CAL	004	1ST DIST
DENTON, JOHN	BAL	154	2ND DIST
DENTON, JOSEPH T.	CAL	003	1ST DIST
DENTON, LOUIS	BAL	024	15TH WAR
DENTON, MARGARET	ANN	314	1ST DIST
DENTON, MARIA	WAS	121	HAGERSTO
DENTON, MARY	CAL	038	2ND DIST
DENTON, MORDICA F.	CAL	007	1ST DIST
DENTPHY, JOHN	BAL	165	11TH WAR
DENTS, ELIZA	BAL	145	11TH WAR
DENVAN, E.	ANN	271	ANNAPOLI
DENVER, ANDREW	BAL	128	1ST WARD
DENVER, MARY J.	BAL	279	20TH WAR
DENWOOD, LYDIA	DOR	422	1ST DIST
DENWOOD, MARY A.*	DOR	434	1ST DIST
DENWOOD, MARY-BLACK	CAR	161	NO TWP L
DENYER, CAROLINE	BAL	215	11TH WAR
DEOKENS, RUTH A.	CHA	287	BOJANTOW
DEONARD, GEORGE	BAL	289	1ST DIST
DEONIN, JAMES *	BAL	065	18TH WAR
DEOTT, GABRIEL T.	CEC	169	6TH E DI
DEPALPO, JOHN	BAL	172	1ST WARD
DEPER, CHRISTIAN	BAL	379	8TH WARD
DEPERN, FRED	BAL	110	5TH WARD
DEPETER, MARGARET	BAL	055	15TH WAR
DEPEW, JOHN	BAL	107	1ST WARD
DEPKEY, MARY	BAL	346	3RD WARD
DEPPER, MICHAEL	BAL	378	8TH WARD
DEPPERT, JOSEPH	BAL	118	15TH WAR
DEPPISH, BARBARA	BAL	395	8TH WARD
DEPPISH, ELIZA	BAL	091	5TH WARD
DEPPISH, HENRY	BAL	404	8TH WARD
DEPRING, CALEB	BAL	114	1ST WARD
DEPRY, CHARLES	BAL	252	2ND WARD
DEPRY, MARY	BAL	252	2ND WARD
DEPRYE, CASPER	BAL	237	2ND WARD
DEPSEY, CAROLINE	BAL	270	2ND WARD
DEPSEY, CASPER	BAL	269	2ND WARD
DER CARPENTER, BARTEN	CEC	031	CHESAPEA
DERALLAN, JANE	BAL	210	2ND WARD
DERAMORE, ABRAM	ALL	004	3RD E.D.
DERAN, CECILIA	BAL	080	2ND DIST
DERBERT, JACKSON	WAS	236	CAVETOWN
DERBERT, LENAH	WAS	243	CAVETOWN
DERBIN, HANNAH	ALL	221	CUMBERLA
DERBY, PRISCILLA	ALL	263	CUMBERLA
DEREBLISS, ISAIAH	FRE	136	CREAGERS
DERENBEYE, JACOB	BAL	256	20TH WAR
DERGNON, THOMAS *	ALL	082	5TH E.D.
DERGRANGE, JOHN S.	FRE	061	FREDERIC
DERGZEN, F.	BAL	150	1ST WARD
DERICK, JOSHUA	BAL	241	1ST DIST
DERICK, RICH	BAL	240	1ST DIST
DERICKS, GEORGE	BAL	241	1ST DIST
DERICKS, JOSHUA	BAL	243	1ST DIST
DERICKS, MARTHA A.	CAR	187	4TH DIST
DERICKS, SUSAN	BAL	241	1ST DIST
DERICKSON, ANN	WOR	245	1ST CENS
DERICKSON, BIL	WOR	300	SNOW HIL
DERICKSON, DANIEL-BLACK	WOR	348	1ST E DI
DERICKSON, ELIZABETH	BAL	100	15TH WAR
DERICKSON, JACOB	CEC	096	4TH E DI
DERICKSON, JAMES	WOR	256	1ST CENS
DERICKSON, JAMES	WOR	259	BERLIN 1
DERICKSON, JOHN	WOR	256	1ST CENS
DERICKSON, JOHN C.	WOR	260	BERLIN 1
DERICKSON, LEVIN	WOR	257	1ST CENS
DERICKSON, MARY	WOR	245	1ST CENS
DERIGE, LEWIS C.	BAL	303	12TH WAR
DERILBISS, REBECCA *	FRE	139	CREAGERS
DERILBISS, THOMAS	FRE	095	FREDERIC
DERIMAN, T.	BAL	135	1ST WARD
DERINE, JOHN	BAL	277	2ND WARD
DERING, JOHN S.	BAL	025	18TH WAR
DERIS, THOMAS *	BAL	154	2ND DIST
DERISSON, JOHN	HAR	185	3RD DIST
DERIX, RACHEL	BAL	439	1ST DIST
DERK, P.M.	BAL	141	1ST WARD
DERKIN, CHARLES	ALL	225	CUMBERLA
DERL, AUGUSTUS	ALL	247	CUMBERLA
DERLAN, SUSAN	BAL	213	11TH WAR
DERMEY, JAMES	HAR	186	3RD DIST
DERMMAN, CATHARINE	BAL	290	12TH WAR
DERMON, WILLIAM	ALL	088	5TH E.D.
DERMOT, HANNAH	BAL	324	12TH WAR
DERN, FREDERICK	CAR	325	1ST DIST
DERN, FREDERICK	CAR	388	2ND DIST
DERN, GEORGE F.	CAR	378	2ND DIST
DERN, HERNY C.	CAR	266	WESTMINS
DERN, ISAAC	CAR	324	1ST DIST
DERN, ISAAC	FRE	427	8TH E DI
DERN, MARY	FRE	280	WOODSBOR
DERNENN, ANN	BAL	121	11TH WAR
DERNING, MARY J.	BAL	349	1ST DIST
DEROCHBRENCE, THOMAS	CAR	074	NO TWP L
DEROCHBRUNE, PHILIP	CAR	168	NO TWP L
DEROCKLRUNE, GEORGE	QUE	186	3RD E DI
DERORLY, MARY	BAL	459	1ST DIST
DEROT, ELIZA	PRI	111	PISCATAW
DERR, ABRAHAM	FRE	296	WOODSBOR
DERR, ABRAHAM S.	FRE	192	5TH E DI
DERR, ADISON	FRE	406	JEFFERSO
DERR, ANN M.	FRE	348	MIDDLETO
DERR, CATHERINE	FRE	138	CREAGERS
DERR, CATHERINE	FRE	057	FREDERIC
DERR, DANIEL	FRE	347	MIDDLETO
DERR, DANIEL	FRE	005	FREDERIC
DERR, DAVID	FRE	072	FREDERIC
DERR, ELIZABETH	FRE	094	FREDERIC
DERR, EZRA	FRE	331	MIDDLETO
DERR, FREDERICK	FRE	134	CREAGERS
DERR, GEORGE	BAL	141	19TH WAR
DERR, GEORGE	CAR	177	8TH DIST
DERR, GEORGE W.	FRE	014	FREDERIC
DERR, HENRY	FRE	331	MIDDLETO
DERR, HENRY	FRE	135	CREAGERS
DERR, ISRAEL	CAR	241	TANEYTOW
DERR, JACOB	FRE	135	CREAGERS
DERR, JACOB	FRE	373	CATOCTIN
DERR, JAMES	BAL	141	19TH WAR
DERR, JOHN	FRE	346	MIDDLETO
DERR, JOHN	FRE	138	CREAGERS
DERR, JOHN	CAR	235	UNION TO
DERR, JOHN	FRE	094	FREDERIC
DERR, JOHN	WAS	241	CAVETOWN
DERR, JOHN A.	FRE	072	FREDERIC
DERR, LEWIS	BAL	397	14TH WAR
DERR, MANDY	CAR	177	8TH DIST
DERR, MARTHA T.	FRE	286	WOODSBOR
DERR, MARY	CAR	308	1ST DIST
DERR, MARY	BAL	273	20TH WAR
DERR, PHILIP	FRE	348	MIDDLETO
DERR, SAMUEL	FRE	348	MIDDLETO
DERR, SARAH	CAR	297	7TH DIST
DERR, SOLOMON	FRE	283	WOODSBOR
DERR, WILLIAM H.	FRE	045	FREDERIC
DERREN, EDWARD	BAL	257	20TH WAR
DERRICK, JIM	BAL	244	1ST DIST
DERRICK, JOHN	BAL	291	17TH WAR
DERRICKS, CHARLOTTE	BAL	103	15TH WAR
DERRICKSON, MARGARET	BAL	030	15TH WAR
DERRIGH, SARAH E.	BAL	345	13TH WAR
DERRIS, JOHN	BAL	367	8TH WARD
DERRISS, DANIEL	KEN	253	1ST DIST
DERROUGH, JAMES	BAL	215	2ND WARD
DERRUM, PARKER	BAL	054	2ND DIST
DERRY, ELIZABETH-BLACK	QUE	172	2ND E DI
DERRY, HENRY E.	BAL	144	5TH WARD
DERRY, JAMES	KEN	255	1ST DIST
DERRY, RICHARD	BAL	128	16TH WAR
DERRY, SALLY	BAL	354	1ST DIST
DERRY, SAMUEL	KEN	255	1ST DIST
DERRY, WILLIAM	BAL	175	6TH WARD
DERSEY, CHARLES	KEN	224	2ND DIST
DERSEY, LUCINDA	ALL	007	3RD E.D.
DERSEY, NICHOLAS	BAL	045	2ND DIST
DERSEY, W.M.	BAL	261	12TH WAR
DERSEY, WILLIAM	BAL	247	12TH WAR
DERSIVAL, DAVID M.	BAL	388	13TH WAR
DERTS, JOHN	BAL	268	20TH WAR
DERUGAN, PATRICK *	BAL	150	2ND DIST
DERUM, JOHN	SOM	463	HANGARY
DERVALL, JOHN	MGM	404	ROCKERLE
DERVSIN, LYDIA	BAL	205	11TH WAR
DESA, JOSE	FRE	202	5TH E DI
DESAGE, CATHERINE J.	QUE	166	2ND E DI
DESAGE, NANCY	QUE	166	2ND E DI
DESAGE, ROBERT	QUE	165	2ND E DI
DESAGE, WILLIAM	QUE	166	2ND E DI
DESANG, ADAM	BAL	239	2ND WARD
DESBINGER, MARTIN	BAL	170	2ND DIST
DESCH, JOHN M.	BAL	323	3RD WARD
DESCHIELDS, HARMAN	BAL	290	7TH WARD
DESELLAN, JOHNT.	MGM	403	ROCKERLE
DESHA, ELLEN	WAS	280	LEITERSB
DESHA, MARY	WAS	265	1ST DIST
DESHANE, SAMUEL J.	CEC	035	CHESAPEA
DESHAR,MARY	BAL	236	12TH WAR
DESHEALDS, JAMES	ANN	280	ANNAPOLI
DESHEALS, ROBERT	DOR	352	3RD DIVI
DESHIELD, ROBERT	BAL	429	1ST DIST
DESHIELDS, MATILDA-MULATT	BAL	212	2ND WARD
DESHIELDS, NICHOLAS	BAL	255	2ND WARD
DESHIELDS, SUSAN	BAL	167	11TH WAR
DESILBESS, THOMAS	FRE	117	CREAGERS
DESILBISS, CARLINE	FRE	106	CREAGERS
DESILBISS, JOHN	FRE	137	CREAGERS
DESILBISS, JOSHUA	FRE	142	CREAGERS
DESILSER, CAROLINE E.	BAL	212	11TH WAR
DESITT, DAVID B.	FRE	023	FREDERIC
DESK, JOHN	BAL	353	3RD WARD
DESMOYERS, MISS E.	FRE	200	5TH E DI
DESMUTT, DAVID	BAL	277	12TH WAR
DESON, MARY	BAL	352	1ST DIST
DESPALATACK, M.	BAL	162	1ST WARD
DESPANS, B.	BAL	168	1ST WARD
DESPAPH, JOHN	BAL	058	1ST WARD

Name	County	Page	District
DESPAR, ELIZA	BAL	010	1ST WARD
DESPAUX, HENRY J.	BAL	424	3RD WARD
DESPAUX, JOHN J.	BAL	334	3RD WARD
DESPAW, ANTHONY	BAL	286	2ND WARD
DESPREY, WILLIAM	BAL	286	2ND WARD
DESSEZ, GEORGE	ALL	240	CUMBERLA
DESSIN, HENRY	BAL	018	4TH WARD
DESSOP, JEMIMA	BAL	291	12TH WAR
DESWAN, MARGRETT	HAR	132	2ND DIST
DESWANN, CHRISTOHPER	HAR	132	2ND DIST
DET, EMELINE	BAL	232	1ST DIST
DET, ISAAC	BAL	240	1ST DIST
DET, NELSON	BAL	222	1ST DIST
DET, ROBERT	BAL	240	1ST DIST
DETA, MARGARET	BAL	422	3RD WARD
DETEMOL, ABRAHAM	BAL	247	20TH WAR
DETER, MARY	BAL	292	12TH WAR
DETERING, TERARD *	BAL	334	13TH WAR
DETERMAN, MARY A.	BAL	100	18TH WAR
DETMAR, COLUMBUS	BAL	383	1ST DIST
DETMAR, HENRY	BAL	383	1ST DIST
DETMOLD, WILLIAM	ALL	028	2ND E.D.
DETMORE, HENRY	BAL	010	9TH WARD
DETRAAP, JOSEPH	BAL	114	1ST WARD
DETRICHS, HENRY	BAL	155	11TH WAR
DETRICK, DAVID	WAS	280	LEITERSB
DETRICK, FREDERICK	WAS	254	1ST DIST.
DETRICK, JOHN H.	FRE	305	WOODSBOR
DETRICK, PHILLIP	FRE	305	WOODSBOR
DETRICK, SUSAN	WAS	215	1ST DIST
DETROP, JOSEPH	BAL	171	1ST WARD
DETWELLER, ANN E.	BAL	068	2ND DIST
DETWILER, JACOB	WAS	189	1ST DIST
DETZY, CHRISTTIANA*	BAL	054	4TH WARD
DEUCE, CHARLES	CAR	251	3RD DIST
DEVAGE, KITTY	ANN	280	ANNAPOLI
DEVALIN, E.	BAL	114	1ST WARD
DEVALIN, FELIX	BAL	401	8TH WARD
DEVALIN, HUGH	BAL	125	5TH WARD
DEVALIN, MARY	BAL	117	5TH WARD
DEVALIN, WILLIAM H.	BAL	122	1ST WARD
DEVALT, MARLIN	WAS	129	HAGERSTO
DEVALT, SIDNEY	WAS	298	1ST DIST
DEVAN, DANIEL-MULATTO	FRE	409	JEFFERSO
DEVAN, HALLY	MGM	408	MEDLEY 3
DEVAN, JOSE	BAL	285	20TH WAR
DEVAN, WILLIAM	BAL	033	4TH WARD
DEVANANCH, NICHOLAS	BAL	213	2ND WARD
DEVANDER, MATILDA	SOM	410	DUBLIN D
DEVANS, EDWARD R.	FRE	241	NEW MARK
DEVANS, SARAH A.	BAL	056	1ST WARD
DEVAREUX, JOSEPH	BAL	011	9TH WARD
DEVATIER, ALEXANDER	BAL	169	16TH WAR
DEVATIER, SUSANNAH	BAL	170	16TH WAR
DEVAUGHN, THOMAS	BAL	318	3RD WARD
DEVAUX, J.J.	BAL	127	5TH WARD
DEVE, ABRAHAM	ALL	004	3RD E.D.
DEVECMON, ELLEN *	ALL	055	10TH E.D
DEVECMON, GEORGE W.	ALL	256	CUMBERLA
DEVELAND, EDWRD	BAL	154	1ST WARD
DEVELBISS, CHARLES W.	FRE	307	WOODSBOR
DEVELBISS, DAVID	FRE	308	WOODSBOR
DEVELBISS, GEORGE	FRE	303	WOODSBOR
DEVELBISS, GEORGE C.	FRE	279	WOODSBOR
DEVELBISS, DAVID	FRE	443	8TH E DI
DEVELIN, HENRY	BAL	261	20TH WAR
DEVELIN, JAMES	BAL	201	6TH WARD
DEVELIN, JOHN	BAL	200	6TH WARD
DEVELINE, CHARLES *	BAL	280	2ND WARD
DEVELLING, HENRY	BAL	170	19TH WAR
DEVENEY, CALIB D. *	BAL	338	1ST DIST
DEVENPORT, F. E.	TAL	074	EASTON T
DEVENS, HENRY	BAL	402	3RD WARD
DEVENY, ANN	BAL	244	20TH WAR
DEVER, HENRIETTA	BAL	381	3RD WARD
DEVER, JAMES	BAL	337	13TH WAR
DEVER, JOSHUA	BAL	240	1ST DIST
DEVER, MARGARET	BAL	364	8TH WARD
DEVERACK, JAMES *	HAR	206	3RD DIST
DEVERACK, MICHAL	HAR	200	3RD DIST
DEVERAUX, BENJAMIN	QUE	173	2ND E DI
DEVERAUX, MARY	QUE	172	2ND E DI
DEVERAUX, ROBERT-BLACK	QUE	138	1ST E DI
DEVERE, JAMES	BAL	404	8TH WARD
DEVERE, PETER	BAL	161	6TH WARD
DEVERE, SARAH	BAL	403	8TH WARD
DEVERE, WILLIAM	BAL	338	7TH WARD
DEVERE, WILLIAM O.	BAL	404	8TH WARD
DEVEREAU, JAMES	ANN	416	HOWARD D
DEVEREAUX, SARAH A.	WOR	201	3RD E DI
DEVEREUX, ELLEN	BAL	204	11TH WAR
DEVERISH, THOMAS	QUE	178	2ND E DI
DEVERIX, JAMES	WOR	316	2ND E DI
DEVERS, GEORGE	WAS	169	FUNKSTOW
DEVERS, SARAH	WAS	172	FUNKSTOW
DEVESHAR, M.	BAL	116	1ST WARD
DEVETIER, JAMES	BAL	130	16TH WAR
DEVETIER, JANE	BAL	130	16TH WAR
DEVETIER, SARAH J.	BAL	130	16TH WAR
DEVIES, JACOB	BAL	390	1ST DIST
DEVIES, JOHN	BAL	230	1ST DIST
DEVILBISS, ADAM	WAS	197	1ST DIST
DEVILBISS, ADAM	FRE	421	8TH E DI
DEVILBISS, ADAM W.	FRE	421	8TH E DI
DEVILBISS, ANN A.	FRE	452	8TH E DI
DEVILBISS, ANNA	FRE	422	8TH E DI
DEVILBISS, CASPER	FRE	430	8TH E DI
DEVILBISS, CHARLES	CAR	405	2ND DIST
DEVILBISS, CHARLES W.	FRE	024	FREDERIC
DEVILBISS, GEORGE W.	FRE	412	8TH E DI
DEVILBISS, JAMES	CAR	395	2ND DIST
DEVILBISS, LEVI	FRE	430	8TH E DI
DEVILBISS, REUBEN	FRE	425	8TH E DI
DEVILBISS, RUFUS W.	FRE	412	8TH E DI
DEVILBISS, SAMUEL	CAR	274	7TH DIST
DEVILBISS, SAMUEL	FRE	309	WOODSBOR
DEVILBISS, THOMAS	FRE	430	8TH E DI
DEVILBISS, WILLIAM	CAR	406	2ND DIST
DEVILBISS, EDARD	CAR	411	2ND DIST
DEVILIN, FELIX P.	BAL	104	5TH WARD
DEVILLAN, THOMAS	CEC	092	4TH E DI
DEVILLE, FRANCIS	BAL	067	10TH WAR
DEVILLISS, CHARLES S.	CAR	234	UNION TO
DEVILLISS, FREDERICK *	CAR	235	UNION TO
DEVIN, ELIZABETH	CEC	096	4TH E DI
DEVINE, CATHARIEN	BAL	038	15TH WAR
DEVINE, CATHARINE	BAL	038	15TH WAR
DEVINE, CATHARINE	BAL	059	15TH WAR
DEVINE, ELLEN	BAL	385	8TH WARD
DEVINE, HENRIETTA	WAS	266	1ST DIST
DEVINE, HENRY	DOR	307	1ST DIST
DEVINE, JOHN	BAL	109	18TH WAR
DEVINE, JOHN	BAL	399	8TH WARD
DEVINE, JOHN *	BAL	218	12TH WAR
DEVINE, MARGARET	BAL	421	8TH WARD
DEVINE, MARY	BAL	360	8TH WARD
DEVINE, MARY	BAL	063	10TH WAR
DEVINE, MARY	CEC	096	4TH E DI
DEVINE, MARY	BAL	151	11TH WAR
DEVINE, MARY E.	FRE	066	FREDERIC
DEVINE, PATRICK	BAL	091	1ST WARD
DEVINE, THOMAS	BAL	109	5TH WARD
DEVINE, WILLIAM	BAL	369	8TH WARD
DEVINEY, HENRY E.	BAL	410	8TH WARD
DEVINNEY, WILLIAM	BAL	145	1ST WARD
DEVINNY, JOHN	CEC	089	4TH E DI
DEVINPORT, F. S.	TAL	066	EASTON T
DEVINS, THOMAS	BAL	318	20TH WAR
DEVINS, WILIAM	BAL	298	12TH WAR
DEVITT, HARRIET	BAL	123	16TH WAR
DEVITT, JOHN*	BAL	317	3RD WARD
DEVIVAN, ED.	BAL	272	20TH WAR
DEVLETT, LEWIS	BAL	345	7TH WARD
DEVO, ABRAM	ALL	007	3RD E.D.
DEVOE, JOHN	HAR	044	1ST DIST
DEVOE, SUSAN M.	ALL	172	7TH E.D.
DEVON, CARLOT	CAR	214	5TH DIST
DEVON, JESSE	HAR	096	2ND DIST
DEVON, PATRICK	BAL	143	2ND DIST
DEVONE, JAMES	HAR	091	2ND DIST
DEVONGES, A.	BAL	054	9TH WARD
DEVONS, VIOLET	BAL	178	19TH WAR
DEVOR, GEORGE	HAR	176	3RD DIST
DEVORE, JACOB	ALL	145	6TH E.D.
DEVORE, JOHN	HAR	090	2ND DIST
DEVORE, THOMAS	HAR	090	2ND DIST
DEVORRUE, JOHN	HAR	203	3RD DIST
DEVOUR, WILLIAM	BAL	122	1ST WARD
DEVOX, MARY	BAL	104	18TH WAR
DEVRIES, CHRISTAIN	CAR	220	5TH DIST
DEVRIES, ELIZA J.	BAL	246	1ST DIST
DEVRIES, HENRY	CAR	220	5TH DIST
DEVRIES, HENRY O.	BAL	221	1ST DIST
DEVRIES, JOHN	CAR	220	5TH DIST
DEVRIES, JOHN B.	CAR	220	5TH DIST
DEVRIES, SAIL	CAR	220	5TH DIST
DEVRIES, W. R.	BAL	333	1ST DIST
DEVRIES, WILLIAM	BAL	245	1ST DIST
DEVRIX, CHARLOTE	WOR	317	2ND E DI
DEVYER, EMULY	BAL	334	13TH WAR
DEW, GEORGE M.	CAL	051	3RD DIST
DEW, JOSEPH	BAL	134	2ND DIST
DEW, MARY	CAL	048	3RD DIST
DEWALL, REBECCA	BAL	436	14TH WAR
DEWALL, WILLIAM L.	ALL	057	10TH E.D
DEWALOD, ADAM	BAL	065	2ND DIST
DEWALT, ELIZABETH	WAS	146	HAGERSTO
DEWALT, MARY	WAS	296	1ST DIST
DEWALT, MRS.	WAS	147	HAGERSTO
DEWBY, NATHANIEL	QUE	208	3RD E DI
DEWEES, MARY A.	BAL	035	15TH WAR
DEWER, JOHN	BAL	130	18TH WAR
DEWER, SOPHIA	BAL	458	14TH WAR
DEWERSES, AMANDA	BAL	076	1ST WARD
DEWES, GARRET	BAL	171	2ND DIST
DEWES, JOSEPH	BAL	171	2ND DIST
DEWEY, C.	BAL	149	1ST WARD
DEWEY, SANFORD	ALL	185	9TH E.D.
DEWINE, CATHARINE	BAL	283	17TH WAR
DEWINE, THOMAS	BAL	097	5TH WARD
DEWINE, TIMOTHY	ALL	136	4TH E.D.
DEWIT, JOHN O.	ALL	177	7TH E.D.
DEWITT, JOHN	ALL	046	10TH E.D
DEWITT, JOHN	ALL	041	2ND E.D.
DEWITT, JOHN	ALL	041	2ND E.D.
DEWITT, JOSEPH	ALL	043	10TH E.D
DEWITT, JOSEPH	ALL	045	10TH E.D
DEWITT, PETER	ALL	031	2ND E.D.
DEWITT, PETER	ALL	031	2ND E.D.
DEWITT, SARAH	ALL	031	2ND E.D.
DEWITT, WILLIAM H.	ALL	043	10TH E.D
DEWOLF, BENJAMIN	BAL	090	10TH WAR
DEWOLF, JACOB	BAL	090	10TH WAR
DEWWES, GARRET	BAL	014	2ND DIST
DEWYER, PETER	BAL	064	18TH WAR
DEWYRE, ELIZEBETH *	HAR	204	3RD DIST
DEX, ISABELLA	BAL	357	13TH WAR
DEXCKER, JEREMIAH	CAR	196	4TH DIST
DEXTER, CHARLES H.	BAL	225	2ND WARD
DEXTER, ELIZABETH	BAL	222	2ND WARD
DEXTER, J.	BAL	117	1ST WARD
DEXTER, MARY	BAL	079	15TH WAR
DEXTER, SAMUEL	BAL	124	1ST WARD
DEY, BRADLY	PRI	098	SPALDING
DEYER, ALLICE	BAL	058	1ST WARD
DEYER, ANN	BAL	036	18TH WAR
DEYER, HENRITTA	BAL	036	18TH WAR
DEYER, JOHN	KEN	245	2ND DIST
DEYER, JOHN	KEN	210	2ND DIST
DEYER, MARY	BAL	047	1ST WARD
DEYER, RACHEL	KEN	215	2ND DIST
DGNER, SARAH	BAL	288	7TH WARD
DHIELE, HENRY	BAL	066	15TH WAR
DIAM, J.	FRE	200	5TH E DI
DIAMOND, JOHN	WAS	247	SMITHSBU
DIAMOND, MARY	BAL	099	10TH WAR
DIAMOND, MARY A.	ANN	424	HOWARD D
DIAMOND, NANCY	WAS	245	SMITHSBU
DIAMOND, PATRICK	CEC	155	PORT DUP
DIANE, MARION	ALL	042	10TH E.D
DIANSON, ROBERT	ALL	080	5TH E.D.
DIATTER, CHARLOTT	BAL	263	1ST DIST
DIBB, JAMES	BAL	055	18TH WAR
DIBELL, ELIZABETH	BAL	049	18TH WAR
DIBERT, ELIZABETH	WAS	238	CAVETOWN
DIBILRON, CALENAT *	BAL	126	18TH WAR
DIBLIN, REBECCA	BAL	463	1ST DIST
DIBSON, THOMAS	BAL	134	16TH WAR
DICAS, ELIZABETH	FRE	363	CATOCTIN
DICE, ANDREW	CAR	345	6TH DIST
DICE, CONRAD	BAL	238	12TH WAR
DICE, JOHN	ALL	050	10TH E.D
DICE, JOHN	BAL	065	2ND DIST
DICE, JOHN	BAL	300	17TH WAR
DICE, JOHN	HAR	196	3RD DIST
DICE, JOSEPH	BAL	116	1ST WARD
DICER, CHARLES	HAR	202	3RD DIST
DICK, ABRAM	BAL	437	1ST DIST
DICK, CATHARINE	WAS	163	2ND DIST
DICK, CHARLES	HAR	013	1ST DIST
DICK, DELILA	BAL	217	6TH DIST
DICK, FRANCES M. E.	ST	260	3RD E DI
DICK, HENRY	WAS	093	2ND SUBD
DICK, J. T.	BAL	470	14TH WAR
DICK, JACOB	WAS	093	2ND SUBD
DICK, JACOB	ALL	060	10TH E.D
DICK, JAMES	CEC	060	1ST E DI
DICK, JAMES	HAR	136	2ND DIST
DICK, JAMES L.	HAR	143	2ND DIST
DICK, JOHN	BAL	210	6TH DIST
DICK, JOHN	WAS	153	2ND DIST
DICK, LYDIA	ALL	043	10TH E.D
DICK, MARTHA A.	HAR	008	1ST DIST
DICK, MARY	FRE	175	5TH E DI
DICK, MARY	HAR	060	1ST DIST
DICK, MASON	WAS	049	2ND SUBD
DICK, RICHARD	ST	316	4TH E DI
DICK, SAMUEL	HAR	173	3RD DIST
DICK, WILLAIM	BAL	186	19TH WAR
DICK, WILLIAM	CEC	119	3RD E DI
DICKARSON, WILLIAM T.	WOR	171	6TH E DI
DICKEHUT, HANNAH	BAL	119	5TH WARD
DICKEL, CHARLES	BAL	041	9TH WARD
DICKEL, ELISABETH	ALL	244	CUMBERLA
DICKEL, HENRY	BAL	336	7TH WARD
DICKELL, JOHN H.	BAL	146	1ST WARD
DICKELLS, GEORGE H.	BAL	235	17TH WAR
DICKENS, CHARLES	ALL	215	CUMBERLA
DICKENS, ELOISE K.	BAL	338	13TH WAR
DICKENSHEETS, FREDERIC	CAR	292	7TH DIST
DICKENSHEETS, JOHN *	CAR	292	7TH DIST
DICKENSON, A. M.*	TAL	057	EASTON D
DICKENSON, CHARLES	QUE	219	3RD E DI
DICKENSON, DANIEL	TAL	058	EASTON D
DICKENSON, DAVID A.	CAR	220	5TH DIST
DICKENSON, GEORGE W.	BAL	074	10TH WAR
DICKENSON, HENRY	TAL	059	EASTON D
DICKENSON, HENRY E.	BAL	073	10TH WAR
DICKENSON, JAMES	BAL	194	17TH WAR
DICKENSON, JAMES	TAL	031	EASTON D
DICKENSON, JAMES	BAL	226	17TH WAR
DICKEMSON, JANE	TAL	062	EASTON D
DICKENSON, JOHN A.	BAL	003	18TH WAR
DICKENSON, MARIAH	TAL	047	EASTON T
DICKENSON, MOSIS	TAL	057	EASTON D
DICKENSON, PERRY	TAL	054	EASTON D
DICKENSON, PRUDY	WAS	152	HAGERSTO
DICKENSON, SAMUEL T.	TAL	050	EASTON T
DICKENSON, SAMUEL*	TAL	050	EASTON T
DICKENSON, WEST	TAL	007	EASTON D
DICKENSON, WILLIAM	TAL	042	EASTON D
DICKER, GEORGE	BAL	027	2ND DIST
DICKER, JOHN	BAL	370	13TH WAR
DICKERFOFF, DAVID	WAS	142	2ND DIST
DICKERHOFF, MARY	WAS	151	2ND DIST
DICKERHOOF, ANDREW	WAS	138	2ND DIST
DICKERHOOF, CHARLES F.	WAS	153	2ND DIST
DICKERHOOF, DAVID	WAS	144	2ND DIST
DICKERHOOF, GEORGE	WAS	109	2ND DIST
DICKERHOOF, GEORGE	ALL	004	3RD E.D.
DICKERHOOF, JOHN	WAS	138	2ND DIST
DICKERHOOF, WILLIAM	WAS	139	2ND DIST
DICKERSON, ABEL	SOM	545	TYASKIN
DICKERSON, ALEXANDER	BAL	199	17TH WAR
DICKERSON, ALFRED	BAL	146	16TH WAR
DICKERSON, AMY	DOR	324	1ST DIST
DICKERSON, ANN	BAL	066	18TH WAR
DICKERSON, ANN	WOR	312	2ND E DI
DICKERSON, ANN M.	BAL	199	17TH WAR
DICKERSON, ANN V.	SOM	551	TYASKIN
DICKERSON, BIDDY	SOM	540	TYASKIN
DICKERSON, CHARLES	BAL	036	4TH WARD
DICKERSON, COMFORT	WOR	174	6TH E DI
DICKERSON, COTHA	SOM	511	BARREN C
DICKERSON, CYRUS	DOR	322	1ST DIST
DICKERSON, EDWARD	SOM	425	PRINCESS
DICKERSON, ELIZA	DOR	422	1ST DIST
DICKERSON, ELIZA A.	KEN	252	1ST DIST
DICKERSON, ELIZABETH	KEN	217	2ND DIST
DICKERSON, FHILAMON	KEN	254	1ST DIST
DICKERSON, GEORGE	BAL	383	3RD WARD
DICKERSON, GIDEON	BAL	085	18TH WAR
DICKERSON, GRACE	BAL	175	11TH WAR
DICKERSON, HENRIETTA	BAL	424	14TH WAR
DICKERSON, HENRY	WOR	180	6TH E DI
DICKERSON, JAMES	DOR	308	1ST DIST
DICKERSON, JAMES M.	WOR	170	6TH E DI
DICKERSON, JAMES SR.	WOR	189	7TH E DI
DICKERSON, JOHN SR.	WOR	176	6TH E DI
DICKERSON, JOHN-MULATTO	FRE	415	8TH E DI
DICKERSON, LEMUEL	SOM	410	DUBLIN D
DICKERSON, MARIA-BLACK	QUE	160	2ND E DI
DICKERSON, MARTHA	BAL	312	7TH WARD
DICKERSON, MARTHY*	DOR	426	1ST DIST
DICKERSON, MARY A.M.	FRE	424	8TH E DI
DICKERSON, NATHAN	MGM	322	CRACKLIN
DICKERSON, NATHAN C.	MGM	322	CRACKLIN
DICKERSON, PETER	BAL	083	18TH WAR
DICKERSON, REBECCA	SOM	385	BRINKLEY
DICKERSON, RICHARD	BAL	241	6TH WARD
DICKERSON, SIAAC W.	WOR	175	6TH E DI
DICKERSON, SILAS	BAL	203	11TH WAR
DICKERSON, WASHINGTON	ALL	217	CUMBERLA
DICKERSON, WILLIAM	DOR	303	1ST DIST
DICKERSON, WILLIAM	SOM	540	TYASKIN
DICKERSON, ZADOCK	BAL	170	16TH WAR
DICKESHUTE, NANCY	CAR	237	UNION TO
DICKEY, BENJAMKN	BAL	126	2ND DIST
DICKEY, GEORGE S.	BAL	088	15TH WAR
DICKEY, JOHN	BAL	270	17TH WAR
DICKEY, JOHN	BAL	004	18TH WAR
DICKEY, JOHN	WAS	093	2ND SUBD
DICKEY, PATRICK	BAL	151	19TH WAR
DICKEY, SARAH J.	BAL	175	19TH WAR
DICKEY, WILLIAM J.	BAL	176	19TH WAR
DICKHAUS, FRANK	BAL	041	1ST WARD
DICKING, HENRY	CAR	307	1ST DIST
DICKINSON, ABRAHAM	BAL	151	5TH WARD
DICKINSON, CHARLES-BLACK	CAR	151	NO TWP L
DICKINSON, CLOA*	TAL	030	EASTON D
DICKINSON, ELI	CAR	154	NO TWP L
DICKINSON, ELISHA	BAL	292	17TH WAR
DICKINSON, EMEALS-BLACK	CAR	151	NO TWP L
DICKINSON, EMMERY-BLACK	CAR	136	NO TWP L
DICKINSON, FRANSINA-MULAT	CAR	384	2ND DIST
DICKINSON, HARRIET-BLACK	CAR	151	NO TWP L
DICKINSON, ISAAC	BAL	294	17TH WAR
DICKINSON, JAMES	BAL	239	6TH WARD
DICKINSON, JAMES-BLACK	CAR	127	NO TWP L
DICKINSON, JAMES-BLACK	CAR	152	NO TWP L

Name	County	Page	District
DICKINSON, JANE	TAL	055	EASTON D
DICKINSON, JOHN	TAL	004	EASTON D
DICKINSON, JOHN	DOR	321	1ST DIST
DICKINSON, JOHN	BAL	063	10TH WAR
DICKINSON, JOSEPH	BAL	179	11TH WAR
DICKINSON, JOSHUA	BAL	045	15TH WAR
DICKINSON, LEVIN-BLACK	CAR	135	NO TWP L
DICKINSON, LINIS*	TAL	012	EASTON D
DICKINSON, MARIA	CAR	113	NO TWP L
DICKINSON, MARSELLUS	TAL	035	EASTON D
DICKINSON, MARY	BAL	167	6TH WARD
DICKINSON, PRISCILLA H.	BAL	046	15TH WAR
DICKINSON, SAMUEL	BAL	174	6TH WARD
DICKINSON, SOLOMON-BLACK	CAR	068	NO TWP L
DICKINSON, THOMAS	BAL	097	5TH WARD
DICKINSON, WILLIAM	BAL	316	3RD WARD
DICKINSON, WILLIAM	BAL	476	14TH WAR
DICKINSON, WILLIAM T.	BAL	111	15TH WAR
DICKINSON,W ILLIAM	CAR	151	NO TWP L
DICKISON, ALFORD	WOR	329	1ST E DI
DICKISON, EDWARD	WOR	309	2ND E DI
DICKISON, MARGARET H.	WOR	309	2ND E DI
DICKISON, MARIAH	WOR	298	9TH E DI
DICKISON, MERRILL	WOR	345	1ST E DI
DICKISON, PETER	WOR	313	2ND E DI
DICKMAN, ANN	BAL	071	2ND DIST
DICKMAN, HENRY	BAL	110	15TH WAR
DICKS, AMY	SOM	399	BRINKLEY
DICKS, JOSEPH	BAL	319	20TH WAR
DICKS, MARTHA E.	CAR	225	5TH DIST
DICKS, MARY	CEC	208	7TH E DI
DICKS, PRESTON	BAL	090	15TH WAR
DICKS, WILLIAM	SOM	435	PRINCESS
DICKSON, AMRY	BAL	124	18TH WAR
DICKSON, ANN	CHA	227	ALLENS F
DICKSON, CAROLINE	DOR	370	3RD DIVI
DICKSON, DELA	BAL	157	11TH WAR
DICKSON, EDITH	BAL	330	13TH WAR
DICKSON, EDWARD	DOR	389	1ST DIST
DICKSON, ELIJAH	BAL	222	12TH WAR
DICKSON, ELIZA C.	BAL	267	20TH WAR
DICKSON, ELIZABETH	BAL	189	11TH WAR
DICKSON, ELIZABETH	TAL	040	EASTON D
DICKSON, ELLEN	BAL	252	6TH WARD
DICKSON, EMALINE	DOR	371	3RD DIVI
DICKSON, EMILY J.	BAL	225	6TH WARD
DICKSON, GANETT	ALL	052	10TH E.D
DICKSON, GEORGE	BAL	262	2ND WARD
DICKSON, GEORGE	CAR	227	5TH DIST
DICKSON, GEORGE	CEC	072	5TH E DI
DICKSON, HAGAR	BAL	069	15TH WAR
DICKSON, HENRY	CHA	227	ALLENS F
DICKSON, HESEKIAH	WAS	118	2ND DIST
DICKSON, ISAAC N.	BAL	457	14TH WAR
DICKSON, J.H.	BAL	239	12TH WAR
DICKSON, JACOB	DOR	371	3RD DIVI
DICKSON, JAMES	BAL	225	6TH WARD
DICKSON, JAMES T.	WOR	341	1ST E DI
DICKSON, JEREMIAH	BAL	164	6TH WARD
DICKSON, JOHN	BAL	193	5TH DIST
DICKSON, JOHN	BAL	161	19TH WAR
DICKSON, JOHN	CEC	080	NORTHEAS
DICKSON, JOHN	CAR	227	5TH DIST
DICKSON, LOFIRE *	HAR	192	3RD DIST
DICKSON, LOUIS	CEC	053	1ST E DI
DICKSON, LOUISA	BAL	161	19TH WAR
DICKSON, LUCRETIA	BAL	276	20TH WAR
DICKSON, MARGARET	CEC	055	1ST E DI
DICKSON, MARY	DOR	364	3RD DIVI
DICKSON, MARY	BAL	430	14TH WAR
DICKSON, MARY	BAL	183	5TH DIST
DICKSON, NOBLE	CHA	257	MIDDLETO
DICKSON, PEREGRINE	BAL	132	16TH WAR
DICKSON, PETER-BLACK	WOR	344	1ST E DI
DICKSON, REBECCA	BAL	124	18TH WAR
DICKSON, SARAH	BAL	252	20TH WAR
DICKSON, SUSAN	BAL	165	16TH WAR
DICKSON, THEODORE	BAL	036	18TH WAR
DICKSON, THOMAS	CEC	056	1ST E DI
DICKSON, WILLAIM	BAL	252	20TH WAR
DICKSON, WILLIAM	CHA	241	HILLTOP
DICKSON, WILLIAM	BAL	471	14TH WAR
DICKSON, WILLIAM	WAS	118	2ND DIST
DICKSON, WILLIAM	WOR	295	9TH E DI
DICKSON, WILLIAM H.	FRE	405	JEFFERSO
DICKSON, WILLIAM H.	HAR	193	3RD DIST
DICKSON,JANE	BAL	297	12TH WAR
DICKWORTH, SARAH	ALL	117	5TH E.D.
DICKY, JOSEPH R.	BAL	028	1ST WARD
DICKYON, ANNA*	BAL	236	12TH WAR
DICUS, GEORGE	CAR	210	5TH DIST
DICUS, MARY	CAR	217	5TH DIST
DICUS, MARY	CAR	213	5TH DIST
DICUS, MARY	FRE	289	WOODSBOR
DICUS, THOMAS	CAR	214	5TH DIST
DICUS, WILLIAM	PRI	042	VANSVILL
DIDDIER, JULIA A.	BAL	072	4TH WARD
DIDENHAER, WILLIAM	BAL	397	1ST DIST
DIDENHOVER, ROBERT L.	MGM	354	BERRYS D
DIDIER, ALEXANDER	BAL	099	5TH WARD
DIDIER, EDWARD	BAL	203	11TH WAR
DIDIER, THOMAS	BAL	079	15TH WAR
DIDO, JOHN	ALL	056	10TH E.D
DIDTER, CAROLINE	BAL	084	4TH WARD
DIE, ANN	BAL	083	15TH WAR
DIEBBING, AUGUSTUS L.	BAL	350	7TH WARD
DIECKMAN, HENRY	BAL	022	9TH WARD
DIEHL, ABRAHAM G.	FRE	413	8TH E DI
DIEHL, ELIZABETH	FRE	414	8TH E DI
DIEHL, FRANCES	WAS	240	CAVETOWN
DIEHL, JACOB	BAL	177	19TH WAR
DIEHL, MOSES	FRE	282	WOODSBOR
DIEHL, WILLIAM	FRE	432	8TH E DI
DIEL, CHRISTIAN	BAL	221	6TH WARD
DIEL, EDWARD	BAL	190	19TH WAR
DIEMER, JOSEPH	BAL	256	6TH WARD
DIER, ANN	BAL	392	1ST DIST
DIER, PERMETIAN	BAL	387	1ST DIST
DIERING, FREDERIC	BAL	037	9TH WARD
DIERKER, HENRY	BAL	034	15TH WAR
DIES, ANN	BAL	341	1ST DIST
DIES, ELIZABETH	BAL	341	1ST DIST
DIES, JACOB	BAL	340	1ST DIST
DIES, SALLY	WOR	257	1ST CENS
DIESERLY, BARBARA	BAL	251	2ND WARD
DIESEY, HARRIET	BAL	188	19TH WAR
DIESHONGUE, JOHN	WAS	200	1ST DIST
DIET, MAJOR	BAL	094	15TH WAR
DIET, WILLIAM	BAL	210	11TH WAR
DIETER, DANIEL	BAL	059	18TH WAR
DIETERICH, LANEHART	BAL	165	16TH WAR
DIETERICK, HENRY	BAL	010	15TH WAR
DIETERLY, JOHN	BAL	306	20TH WAR
DIETRICH, ADAM	BAL	238	20TH WAR
DIETRICH, HENRY	BAL	267	20TH WAR
DIETRICH, J. STULL	FRE	243	NEW MARK
DIETRICH, JOHN	BAL	212	19TH WAR
DIETRICH, JOHN H.	BAL	277	12TH WAR
DIETRICH, PHILIP	BAL	019	18TH WAR
DIETRING, MARY	BAL	043	9TH WARD
DIETS, MARY	BAL	213	19TH WAR
DIETSH, FREDERICK	BAL	298	12TH WAR
DIETZ, GEORGE	BAL	385	3RD WARD
DIETZ, HENRY	BAL	089	10TH WAR
DIETZ, JOHN	BAL	270	12TH WAR
DIETZ, JOHN B.	BAL	125	16TH WAR
DIETZ, LORENTZ	BAL	099	15TH WAR
DIETZ, LOUISA	BAL	125	16TH WAR
DIFER, ADAM	HAR	061	1ST DIST
DIFFEE, VICTOR	BAL	366	1ST DIST
DIFFEN, ALEXANDER	BAL	367	1ST DIST
DIFFENBAUGH, JOHN Y.	CAR	267	WESTMINS
DIFFENDAFFER, CHARLOTT	BAL	090	5TH WARD
DIFFENDAFFER, RICHARD	BAL	090	5TH WARD
DIFFENDAL, MARY	FRE	288	WOODSBOR
DIFFENDAL, SAMUEL	FRE	281	WOODSBOR
DIFFENDEEFFER, M.	BAL	332	1ST DIST
DIFFENDEFER, JOHN L.	ANN	287	ANNAPOLI
DIFFENDERFER, H.	BAL	063	10TH WAR
DIFFENDERFFER, C. R.	BAL	040	4TH WARD
DIFFENDERFFER, CHARLES	BAL	044	4TH WARD
DIFFENDERFFER, GEORGE	BAL	228	6TH WARD
DIFFENDERFFER, JOHN	CAR	287	7TH DIST
DIFFENDERFFER, JOHN A.	BAL	055	9TH WARD
DIFFENDERFFER, MARIA	BAL	430	14TH WAR
DIFFENDREFFER, MICHAEL	BAL	085	4TH WARD
DIFFER, JOHN	ALL	224	CUMBERLA
DIFFEY, ALEXANDER	BAL	088	18TH WAR
DIFFEY, MARY	BAL	106	18TH WAR
DIFFEY, OWEN	BAL	397	8TH WARD
DIFFEY, OWEN	BAL	354	3RD WARD
DIFFINBAUGH, JOHN H.	CAR	291	7TH DIST
DIFFINDAL, MARY	FRE	289	WOODSBOR
DIFFLY, JOHN	BAL	350	3RD WARD
DIFFUDALFF, WILLIAM L. *	BAL	299	12TH WAR
DIGAR, NICHOALS	BAL	322	1ST DIST
DIGBY, GEORGE	CEC	144	PORT DUP
DIGENHARA, ANTHONY	BAL	427	8TH WARD
DIGG, EDWARD	BAL	178	2ND DIST
DIGGES, CHARLES	PRI	007	BLADENSB
DIGGES, FRANCIS H.	CHA	289	BOJANTOW
DIGGES, GREENBERRY	FRE	254	NEW MARK
DIGGES, MALINDA	FRE	265	NEW MARK
DIGGES, NORAH	PRI	007	BLADENSB
DIGGIN, ELIZABETH	BAL	300	17TH WAR
DIGGINS, ANN M.	CAR	076	NO TWP L
DIGGINS, CATHARINE*	TAL	019	EASTON D
DIGGINS, DANIEL	QUE	156	2ND E DI
DIGGINS, FLOYD	TAL	102	ST MICHA
DIGGINS, HENRY	TAL	022	EASTON D
DIGGINS, HENRY	BAL	282	17TH WAR
DIGGINS, JOHN F.	CAR	098	NO TWP L
DIGGINS, JOHNL	TAL	022	EASTON D
DIGGINS, JULIA	BAL	086	15TH WAR
DIGGINS, SARAH	CAR	130	NO TWP L
DIGGINS, THOMAS	CAR	070	NO TWP L
DIGGINS, THOMAS	TAL	021	EASTON D
DIGGINS, THOMAS	QUE	196	3RD E DI
DIGGINS, TOY-BLACK	CAR	129	NO TWP L
DIGGINS, TOY-BLACK	CAR	146	NO TWP L
DIGGINS, WILLIAM	CAR	098	NO TWP L
DIGGIS, VIRGINIA	WAS	178	BOONSBOR
DIGGS, AMBROSE	WAS	158	HAGERSTO
DIGGS, BENJAMIN	BAL	178	6TH WARD
DIGGS, BEVERLY	BAL	012	4TH WARD
DIGGS, CHARLES F.	BAL	042	4TH WARD
DIGGS, CLARISSA	MGM	434	CLARKSTR
DIGGS, DANIEL C.	PRI	093	MARLBROU
DIGGS, CARCUS S.-BLACK	FRE	234	BUCKEYST
DIGGS, EDWARD	BAL	174	2ND DIST
DIGGS, ELIZA	BAL	191	5TH DIST
DIGGS, ELIZABETH	PRI	053	AQUASCO
DIGGS, ELLEN	BAL	136	18TH WAR
DIGGS, ELZIABETH-BLACK	FRE	008	FREDERIC
DIGGS, EMANUEL	BAL	195	5TH DIST
DIGGS, FANNY	ANN	326	2ND DIST
DIGGS, FRANK	BAL	458	8TH WARD
DIGGS, FRANK	CHA	217	ALLENS F
DIGGS, GEORGE	BAL	007	18TH WAR
DIGGS, GIDEON	BAL	024	15TH WAR
DIGGS, HENRY	BAL	292	3RD WARD
DIGGS, ISAAC	BAL	124	18TH WAR
DIGGS, ISAAC	WAS	059	2ND SUBD
DIGGS, J.H.	WAS	002	WILLIAMS
DIGGS, JACOB	WAS	161	HAGERSTO
DIGGS, JAMES	FRE	205	BUCKEYST
DIGGS, JAMES	ANN	300	1ST DIST
DIGGS, JAMES	ANN	410	8TH DIST
DIGGS, JAMES	BAL	038	1ST WARD
DIGGS, JAMES	BAL	111	1ST WARD
DIGGS, JOHN	ANN	369	4TH DIST
DIGGS, JOHN	BAL	404	1ST DIST
DIGGS, JOHN	WAS	166	1ST DIST
DIGGS, JOHN H.	CHA	224	ALLENS F
DIGGS, JOHN M.	FRE	087	FREDERIC
DIGGS, JOHN-BLACK	FRE	221	BUCKEYST
DIGGS, MARGARET	ANN	300	1ST DIST
DIGGS, MARY J.	BAL	222	1ST DIST
DIGGS, MRS.	BAL	126	5TH WARD
DIGGS, NACE	ANN	296	1ST DIST
DIGGS, NATHAN	ANN	326	2ND DIST
DIGGS, NELLY	ANN	290	ANNAPOLI
DIGGS, PERRY	CAL	038	2ND DIST
DIGGS, PERRY	WAS	068	2ND SUBD
DIGGS, RICHARD H.	BAL	373	3RD WARD
DIGGS, ROBERT	CHA	219	ALLENS F
DIGGS, ROBERT	CHA	218	ALLENS F
DIGGS, ROBERT-BLACK	FRE	234	BUCKEYST
DIGGS, SALLY	BAL	086	15TH WAR
DIGGS, SILAS	BAL	364	8TH WARD
DIGGS, SOLOMON	WAS	166	1ST DIST
DIGGS, SUSAN-BLACK	FRE	029	FREDERIC
DIGGS, TANY	FRE	029	FREDERIC
DIGGS, THOMAS	WAS	242	CAVETOWN
DIGGS, THOMAS	BAL	138	1ST WARD
DIGGS, THOMAS	ANN	295	1ST DIST
DIGGS, THOMAS-BLACK	FRE	012	FREDERIC
DIGGS, VERONICA	FRE	162	EMMITTSB
DIGGS, WILLIAM	ANN	370	4TH DIST
DIGGS, WILLIAM	BAL	388	1ST DIST
DIGGS, WILLIAM	BAL	273	12TH WAR
DIGLER, MARTHA A.	ALL	123	4TH E.D.
DIGMAN, CATHARINE	BAL	[illegible]	5TH WARD
DIGMAN, JOHN	BAL	109	5TH WARD
DIGMAN, JOHN	BAL	041	4TH WARD
DIGMAN, MRS.	BAL	150	5TH WARD
DIGMER, JOHN	BAL	082	2ND DIST
DIGNAM, JOHN	BAL	420	8TH WARD
DIGNAN, BYRN	BAL	344	1ST DIST
DIGNAN, ELLEN	BAL	183	11TH WAR
DIGNAN, LUKE	BAL	420	8TH WARD
DIGNAN, MARY	BAL	199	11TH WAR
DIGNER, HESH*	BAL	417	3RD WARD
DIGNER, LOUISA	BAL	006	4TH WARD
DIGNEY, CATHARINE	BAL	257	5TH WARD
DIGS, ANNA M.	BAL	240	1ST DIST
DIGS, BOSE	BAL	237	1ST DIST
DIGS, EMANUEL	BAL	236	1ST DIST
DIGS, HENRY	CAR	188	4TH DIST
DIGS, JULIA	BAL	234	1ST DIST
DIGS, MARY	BAL	234	1ST DIST
DIIER, J.	BAL	258	12TH WAR
DIKES, WILLIAM	BAL	424	14TH WAR
DIKXON, JOHN-BLACK	WOR	170	6TH E DI
DILAHAY, AMANDA	BAL	317	20TH WAR
DILAHAY, MARY	BAL	317	20TH WAR
DILAHEY, JESE	BAL	317	20TH WAR
DILAHUNT, ARABELLA V.	BAL	454	14TH WAR
DILAHUNT, JAMES	WAS	150	HAGERSTO
DILAHUNT, JOHN	WAS	131	HAGERSTO
DILAHUNT, SOLOMON S.	BAL	454	14TH WAR
DILANOR, MICHAEL	BAL	111	2ND DIST
DILAWAY, BENJAMIN	CEC	026	ELKTON 3
DILE, JAMES	ANN	485	HOWARD D
DILEHUNT, ANN J.	WAS	269	1ST DIST
DILEHUNT, ROSE	BAL	317	20TH WAR
DILEN, JOHN	BAL	133	1ST WARD
DILEN, JOHN*	DOR	414	1ST DIST
DILER, JOHN*	DOR	428	1ST DIST
DILER, JOHN*	DOR	416	1ST DIST
DILING, JOHN	HAR	197	3RD DIST
DILINGER, MARGARET	BAL	315	12TH WAR
DILL, CATHARINE	BAL	291	12TH WAR
DILL, EZRA	BAL	017	18TH WAR
DILL, FREDERICK	BAL	087	15TH WAR
DILL, HENRY	HAR	022	1ST DIST
DILL, JACOB P.	BAL	087	15TH WAR
DILL, JAMES	QUE	139	1ST E DI
DILL, JOHN	HAR	060	1ST DIST
DILL, JOHN	HAR	062	1ST DIST
DILL, JOHN	BAL	240	17TH WAR
DILL, JOHN	BAL	245	20TH WAR
DILL, JOHN F.	FRE	215	BUCKEYST
DILL, JOSHUA	FRE	055	FREDERIC
DILL, LEWIS H.	FRE	050	FREDERIC
DILL, PETER	BAL	448	14TH WAR
DILL, PHILIPINE	FRE	023	FREDERIC
DILL, WILLIAM H.	CAR	105	NO TWP L
DILL, WILLIAM H.	BAL	094	18TH WAR
DILL,ABNER	CAR	105	NO TWP L
DILL,LAINHAD	BAL	087	1ST WARD
DILL,SALOME	QUE	161	2ND E DI
DILLAHAY, EDWARD	BAL	126	16TH WAR
DILLAHAY, ELIZA	BAL	290	3RD WARD
DILLAHAY, JANE	TAL	048	EASTON T
DILLAHAY, JOHN	BAL	005	4TH WARD
DILLAHUNT, WILLIAM	BAL	237	6TH WARD
DILLAN, EDWARD	ALL	071	5TH E.D.
DILLAN, JOHN	BAL	114	1ST WARD
DILLARD, DRURY	BAL	287	1ST DIST
DILLAS, CHARLES	BAL	466	14TH WAR
DILLAY, FRANCIS	BAL	291	12TH WAR
DILLE, MITCHELL	DOR	430	1ST DIST
DILLEHAY, JAMES	BAL	196	17TH WAR
DILLEHAY, JESSE S.	TAL	076	EASTON T
DILLEHAY, WILFRED	MGM	444	CLARKSTR
DILLEHUNT, MARY	KEN	225	2ND DIST
DILLEHUNT, WILLIAM	BAL	021	15TH WAR
DILLEN, ELIZABETH	WAS	042	2ND SUBD
DILLEN, ELLEN	CAR	158	NO TWP L
DILLEN, JAMES	BAL	452	8TH WARD
DILLEN, JAMES E.	QUE	182	3RD E DI
DILLEN, JOHN	CAR	160	NO TWP L
DILLEN, JOHN	CAR	169	NO TWP L
DILLEN, JOHN A.	CAR	157	NO TWP L
DILLEN, MARTIN	FRE	420	8TH E DI
DILLEN, MARY	CAR	107	NO TWP L
DILLEN, SARAH	BAL	424	8TH WARD
DILLEN, SUSAN	QUE	157	2ND E DI
DILLEN, THOMAS	CAR	159	NO TWP L
DILLEN, WILLIAM	CAR	158	NO TWP L
DILLER, CON	BAL	459	1ST DIST
DILLER, JACOB	FRE	419	8TH E DI
DILLER, JOHN	BAL	274	20TH WAR
DILLER, JOHN	FRE	421	8TH E DI
DILLER, JOHN	QUE	207	3RD E DI
DILLER, NANCY	BAL	425	14TH WAR
DILLEY, JOHN F.	ALL	263	CUMBERLA
DILLIARD, SARAH	BAL	325	3RD WARD
DILLIHAY, JUDITH L.	ST	267	3RD E DI
DILLIHUNT, DANIEL	KEN	293	3RD DIST
DILLING, HENRY	BAL	138	2ND DIST
DILLING, HENRY	HAR	198	3RD DIST
DILLINGER, LOUISA	BAL	289	1ST DIST
DILLINGTY, GEORGE	CEC	196	6TH E DI
DILLIWAY, JOHN	BAL	071	18TH WAR
DILLMAN, JOHN H.	BAL	011	9TH WARD
DILLMARD, LEWIS	WAS	188	BOONSBOR
DILLON, CHRISTOPHER	BAL	048	9TH WARD
DILLON, CHRISTOPHER	BAL	427	14TH WAR
DILLON, DAVID	ALL	200	CUMBERLA
DILLON, EDWARD	BAL	034	15TH WAR
DILLON, ELLEN	BAL	118	2ND DIST
DILLON, J.	BAL	153	1ST WARD
DILLON, MARGARETT	BAL	082	4TH WARD
DILLON, MICHAEL	BAL	029	4TH WARD
DILLON, MICHAEL	BAL	403	3RD WARD
DILLON, THOMAS	ST	273	3RD E DI
DILLON, WILLAIM	BAL	222	19TH WAR
DILLONS, MARTHA	HAR	140	2ND DIST
DILLOW, WILLIAM	QUE	207	3RD E DI
DILLWATER, GEORGE WASH	FRE	151	10TH E D
DILMAN, C.	BAL	274	20TH WAR
DILO, JOHN T.	CAR	103	NO TWP L
DILPETER, D.	BAL	225	19TH WAR
DILTLEBAUGH, SIMON	WAS	128	HAGERSTO
DILWORTH, AMOS	WAS	278	LEITERSB
DILWORTH, MARY	BAL	096	10TH WAR
DILWORTH, OLIVER	BAL	283	7TH WARD
DILWORTH, SARAH	BAL	115	2ND DIST

DIMENBURG, HENRY FRE 226 BUCKEYST
DIMENT, AMERICA E. ST 312 1ST E DI
DIMENT, MARTHA A. ST 255 3RD E DI
DIMENT, MERIT ST 287 2ND E DI
DIMICK, SEBASTIAN BAL 099 15TH WAR
DIMMETT, NICHOLAS BAL 193 19TH WAR
DIMMICK, MICHAEL FRE 007 FREDERIC
DIMMICK, NICHOLAS BAL 008 15TH WAR
DIMMIT, C. EDWARD* BAL 084 10TH WAR
DIMMIT, JOHN BAL 448 14TH WAR
DIMMITT, ANN E. BAL 332 3RD WARD
DIMMITZ, CHARLES H. BAL 037 15TH WAR
DIMOND, CAROLINE BAL 261 1ST DIST
DIMOND, ELIZABETH BAL 261 1ST DIST
DIMOND, JOHN FRE 390 PETERSVI
DIMOND, MARY QUE 223 4TH E DI
DIMOND, MARY A. KEN 227 2ND DIST
DIMOND, MARY* TAL 017 EASTON D
DIMOND, REBECCA A. QUE 236 4TH E DI
DIMONT, AGNES BAL 002 15TH WAR
DIMTZ, CHARLES BAL 011 1ST WARD
DINAN, PATRICK HAR 001 1ST DIST
DINAN, WILILAM BAL 146 1ST WARD
DINDRICK, HENRY BAL 010 1ST WARD
DINELLY, ANN BAL 112 1ST WARD
DINER, JAMES FRE 189 5TH E DI
DINER, MARY ANN FRE 189 5TH E DI.
DINERY, THOMAS BAL 020 2ND DIST
DINESSON, PETER HAR 181 3RD DIST
DING, JAMES WAS 010 WILLIAMS
DINGE, EDWAC BAL 081 1ST WARD
DINGER, JOHN-BLACK QUE 196 3RD E DI
DINGFELDER, PETER BAL 181 16TH WAR
DINGLE, JACOB R. BAL 384 3RD WARD
DINGLE, JOHN BAL 234 17TH WAR
DINGLE, PHILLIP BAL 147 5TH WARD
DINGLEMAN, HENRY BAL 202 17TH WAR
DINGREFEET, A. * BAL 282 20TH WAR
DINION, SARAH * BAL 172 2ND DIST
DINISCH, JOHN BAL 072 1ST WARD
DINKS, MARIA ANN 329 2ND DIST
DINNEMON, EELIZABETH* TAL 023 EASTON D
DINNEY, BRIDGET ALL 142 6TH E.D.
DINNIE, SARAH L. BAL 469 14TH WAR
DINNIE, THOMAS BAL 469 14TH WAR
DINNY, WILLIAM H. BAL 112 1ST WARD
DINON, JOSHUA FRE 262 NEW MARK
DINSCALL, ELIZA BAL 001 1ST WARD
DINSEE, L. BAL 141 19TH WAR
DINSMAN, J.C. BAL 115 1ST WARD
DINSMORE, ALEXANDER WAS 226 1ST DIST
DINSMORE, C. BAL 165 1ST WARD
DINSMORE, DAVID BAL 151 2ND DIST
DINSMORE, ELIZA BAL 027 1ST WARD
DINSMORE, LOUISA HAR 172 3RD DIST
DINSMORE, MARGARET BAL 072 15TH WAR
DINSMORE, PATRICK BAL 120 11TH WAR
DINSMORE, SAMUEL BAL 071 18TH WAR
DINSMORE, SAMUEL BAL 057 18TH WAR
DINSMORE, THOMAS BAL 001 4TH WARD
DINSMORE, WILILAM BAL 286 2ND WARD
DINSMORE, WILLIAM HAR 172 3RD DIST
DINSSAN, MARGARET HAR 181 3RD DIST
DINST, ANTHONY BAL 210 6TH DIST
DINTARY, JAMES BAL 229 19TH WAR
DINTEM, HANNAH D. BAL 459 14TH WAR
DINTERMAN, GEORGE FRE 298 WOODSBOR
DINTON, GEORGE ANN 377 4TH DIST
DINTUMERS, CORNELIUS FRE 336 MIDDLETO
DINUSE, HENRY BAL 313 7TH WARD
DION, JOHN BAL 273 20TH WAR
DIPP, MARY ANN BAL 338 13TH WAR
DIPPEE, ELY BAL 170 19TH WAR
DIRAN, ELLEN BAL 065 4TH WARD
DIRDEN, JAMES WOR 296 9TH E DI
DIRFLY, JOSEPH BAL 210 19TH WAR
DIRESTER, MRS. BAL 148 11TH WAR
DIRKER, PHILIP BAL 411 14TH WAR
DIRNS, JOHN ST 254 3RD E DI
DIROIR, JOHN H. WOR 313 2ND E DI
DIRTH, LOVINA ALL 219 CUMBERLA
DIRUM, JOHN SOM 461 HANGARY
DIRVIN, HARRIET BAL 302 20TH WAR
DIRVIN, JAMES * BAL 301 20TH WAR
DISACT, REBECCA BAL 137 11TH WAR
DISCHEL, WILLIAM BAL 107 1ST WARD
DISCON, DENNIS B. CAL 027 2ND DIST
DISCON, JOHN CAL 030 2ND DIST
DISCON, JOHN BAL 458 8TH WARD
DISCON, JOSEPH BAL 146 1ST WARD
DISCUS, JOHN ANN 385 4TH DIST
DISE, ANNANIAS SOM 369 BRINKLEY
DISE, EPHRAIM SOM 442 DAMES QU
DISE, GEORGE SOM 369 BRINKLEY
DISE, GEORGE T. SOM 444 DAMES QU
DISE, HENRY SOM 373 BRINKLEY
DISE, HYRAM SOM 370 BRINKLEY
DISE, JANE SOM 485 TRAPP DI
DISE, JOHN SOM 368 BRINKLEY
DISE, LEVIN SOM 355 BRINKLEY
DISE, LEWIS SOM 368 BRINKLEY
DISE, MARY SOM 368 BRINKLEY
DISE, MORDECA SOM 370 BRINKLEY
DISE, PHELAN SOM 372 BRINKLEY
DISE, RICHARDSON SOM 353 BRINKLEY
DISE, SEVERN SOM 363 BRINKLEY
DISE, THOMAS SOM 370 BRINKLEY
DISE, TRIFFER SOM 355 BRINKLEY
DISE, VICEY SOM 367 BRINKLEY
DISE, WILLIAM SOM 391 BRINKLEY
DISE, WILLIAM SOM 441 DAMES QU
DISEN, GERARD F.G. ST 322 4TH E DI
DISHAROON, CALEB SOM 470 TRAPPE D
DISHAROON, EBENEZER WOR 194 8TH E DI
DISHAROON, ELIZABETH SOM 503 SALISBUR
DISHAROON, EMILY E. SOM 489 SALISBUR
DISHAROON, ISAAC WOR 195 8TH E DI
DISHAROON, JAMES SOM 468 TRAPPE D
DISHAROON, JAMES * WOR 195 8TH E DI
DISHAROON, JOHN WOR 195 8TH E DI
DISHAROON, MATTHIAS SOM 505 SALISBUR
DISHAROON, ROBERT SOM 477 TRAPP DI
DISHAROON, SARAH A. SOM 482 TRAPP DI
DISHAROON, THOMAS SOM 501 SALISBUR
DISHAROON, URSULA SOM 483 TRAPP DI
DISHAROON, WESLEY SOM 505 SALISBUR
DISHAROON, WILLIAM SOM 468 TRAPPE D
DISHAROON, WILLIAM W. SOM 477 TRAPP DI
DISHAROON, WINDER SOM 488 SALISBUR
DISHAWON, LEVIN WOR 172 5TH E DI
DISHENSON, ANN M. TAL 070 EASTON T
DISHENSON, HELTZ TAL 071 EASTON T
DISHENSON, LOUISA TAL 071 EASTON T
DISHENSON, POLLARD TAL 077 EASTON T
DISHMAN, JOHN BAL 084 18TH WAR
DISHMAN, SAMUEL BAL 059 18TH WAR
DISHMART, SAMUEL CHA 228 ALLENS F
DISILBISS, SAMUEL FRE 135 CREAGERS
DISMAN, CORNELIUS BAL 042 1ST WARD
DISMAY, RACHEL PRI 030 VANSVILL
DISNEY, AARON BAL 269 1ST DIST
DISNEY, ALFRED BAL 259 1ST DIST
DISNEY, AMELIA BAL 335 1ST DIST
DISNEY, ANN BAL 410 1ST DIST
DISNEY, BENAJMIN BAL 110 1ST WARD
DISNEY, BENJAMIN BAL 456 8TH WARD
DISNEY, BENJAMIN F. ANN 373 4TH DIST
DISNEY, DEBORAH ANN 455 HOWARD D
DISNEY, EDWARD W. BAL 145 1ST WARD
DISNEY, GEORGE BAL 033 1ST WARD
DISNEY, GEORGE BAL 272 7TH WARD
DISNEY, ISABEL BAL 258 1ST DIST
DISNEY, JAMES BAL 257 6TH WARD
DISNEY, JANE BAL 153 16TH WAR
DISNEY, JOHN BAL 146 16TH WAR
DISNEY, JOHN ANN 390 4TH DIST
DISNEY, JOHN W. BAL 136 16TH WAR
DISNEY, JOHN W. BAL 203 6TH WARD
DISNEY, JOSHUA BAL 130 2ND DIST
DISNEY, JOSHUA ANN 475 HOWARD D
DISNEY, JULIA A. ANN 386 4TH DIST
DISNEY, LEWIS ANN 338 3RD DIST
DISNEY, LOYD ANN 373 4TH DIST
DISNEY, MARY BAL 159 16TH WAR
DISNEY, MARY A. BAL 406 1ST DIST
DISNEY, NICHOLAS ANN 340 3RD DIST
DISNEY, OLIVER BAL 145 16TH WAR
DISNEY, OWEN ANN 388 4TH DIST
DISNEY, OWEN A. ANN 382 4TH DIST
DISNEY, PHILIP ANN 387 4TH DIST
DISNEY, PHILLIP BAL 092 5TH WARD
DISNEY, RICHARD BAL 335 1ST DIST
DISNEY, RICHARD ANN 390 4TH DIST
DISNEY, RICHARD ANN 340 3RD DIST
DISNEY, RICHARD J. BAL 410 1ST DIST
DISNEY, SAMUEL BAL 052 15TH WAR
DISNEY, SNOWDEN BAL 258 1ST DIST
DISNEY, SOLOMON BAL 015 1ST WARD
DISNEY, THEODORE BAL 278 2ND WARD
DISNEY, THOMAS S. ANN 383 4TH DIST
DISNEY, W. ANN 341 3RD DIST
DISNEY, WESLEY ANN 380 4TH DIST
DISNEY, WESLEY BAL 378 1ST DIST
DISNEY, WILLIAM ANN 387 4TH DIST
DISNEY, WILLIAM A. BAL 278 20TH WAR
DISON, ALICE MGM 344 CLARKSBU
DISON, HENRIETTA BAL 365 8TH WARD
DISSON, NANCY ALL 066 10TH E.D
DISTANCE, CHARLES BAL 342 7TH WARD
DISTANCE, EMELINE BAL 440 8TH WARD
DISTANCE, JOSIAH HAR 051 1ST DIST
DISTANCE, MARGARET BAL 447 8TH WARD
DITA, SARAH WAS 011 WILLIAMS
DITCH, HENRY WAS 273 RIDGEVIL
DITE, TERESA-BLACK ST 316 4TH E DI
DITER, DARCUS-BLACK CAR 096 NO TWP L
DITMAN, EMILY BAL 286 20TH WAR
DITMAN, GEORGE BAL 450 14TH WAR
DITMAN, HENRY CAR 278 7TH DIST
DITMAN, MARGARET CAR 278 7TH DIST
DITMAN, NELSON BAL 422 8TH WARD
DITMAN, RACHEL BAL 425 8TH WARD
DITMAN, THOMAS BAL 282 7TH WARD
DITMAN, WILLIAM H. BAL 215 6TH WARD
DITMER, ELIZABETH BAL 091 15TH WAR
DITNER, HERMAN* BAL 112 10TH WAR
DITTER, GOTLUD * BAL 165 2ND DIST
DITTMAN, JOHNS BAL 037 9TH WARD
DITTMER, HERMAN* BAL 112 10TH WAR
DITTO, WILLIAM WAS 126 2ND DIST
DITTON, GEORGIANNA BAL 213 11TH WAR
DITTUS, FRANCIS BAL 312 1ST DIST
DITTY, H. MR- ANN 306 1ST DIST
DITTY, HARRIET ANN 316 1ST DIST
DITTY, THOMAS N. ANN 294 1ST DIST
DITZ, NANCY BAL 182 11TH WAR
DITZELL, FREDERICK BAL 055 15TH WAR
DITZER, REBEC BAL 218 12TH WAR
DITZLER, GEORGE WAS 109 2ND DIST
DITZLER, JACOB CAR 345 6TH DIST
DITZLER, WILLIAM CAR 245 3RD DIST
DIVAN, JOHN BAL 186 5TH DIST
DIVARS, JOHN HAR 112 2ND DIST
DIVEL, JACOB WAS 099 2ND DIST
DIVELY, EDWARD ALL 011 3RD E.D.
DIVEMILLER, HENRY ANN 423 HOWARD D
DIVEN, ELIZA R. BAL 080 18TH WAR
DIVEN, JOHN BAL 064 18TH WAR
DIVENY, PETER ALL 051 10TH E.D
DIVER, CHRISTIAN WAS 047 2ND SUBD
DIVER, JAMES B. WOR 194 8TH E DI
DIVER, JOHN FRE 196 5TH E DI
DIVER, RICHARD PRI 039 VANSVILL
DIVERS, ANANIAS HAR 049 1ST DIST
DIVERS, HOLLAND HAR 136 2ND DIST
DIVERS, JOSEPH BAL 084 2ND DIST
DIVERS, SARAH HAR 102 2ND DIST
DIVIDARY, MARY A. BAL 056 10TH WAR
DIVIDSON, ISABELLA R. BAL 234 2ND WARD
DIVIN, A. FRE 200 5TH E DI
DIVIN, SISTER M. FRE 198 5TH E DI
DIVINE, ANN BAL 077 2ND DIST
DIVINE, BRIDGET BAL 423 3RD WARD
DIVINE, FRANCES BAL 028 4TH WARD
DIVINE, FRANCES BAL 029 4TH WARD
DIVINE, HUGH BAL 252 20TH WAR
DIVINE, JOHN DOR 421 1ST DIST
DIVINE, PATRICK BAL 047 1ST WARD
DIVINE, SOPHIA WAS 003 WILLIAMS
DIVINE, BRIDGET BAL 066 2ND DIST
DIVINEY, ANNA BAL 060 4TH WARD
DIVINY, PATRICK ALL 051 10TH E.D
DIVROX, EMORY-BLACK CAR 093 NO TWP L
DIWIN, JAMES * BAL 301 20TH WAR
DIX, ANN R. BAL 214 11TH WAR
DIX, CATHARINE BAL 413 8TH WARD
DIX, EUPHRASIA SIS- BAL 316 20TH WAR
DIX, ISAAC HAR 096 2ND DIST
DIX, JOHN BAL 083 2ND DIST
DIX, JOHN SOM 436 PRINCESS
DIX, JOHN H. WOR 320 1ST E DI
DIX, JOSEPH BAL 387 13TH WAR
DIX, LEVI SOM 398 BRINKLEY
DIX, LITTLETON-BLACK WOR 339 1ST E DI
DIX, MARGARET BAL 385 13TH WAR
DIX, NANCY WOR 272 BERLIN !
DIX, SOLOMON-BLACK WOR 332 1ST E DI
DIX, STEPHEN SOM 363 BRINKLEY
DIX, STEPHEN SOM 429 PRINCESS
DIX, STEPHEN-BLACK WOR 329 1ST E DI
DIX, WILLIAM BAL 007 EASTERN
DIXE, WILLOUBY W. BAL 279 2ND WARD
DIXESON, GILBB-BLACK WOR 332 1ST E DI
DIXION, MARY M. WAS 119 2ND DIST
DIXKSON, ELIJAH BAL 468 14TH WAR
DIXLER, GEORGE BAL 235 20TH WAR
DIXLER, HENRY BAL 007 EASTERN
DIXON, AMBROSE SOM 404 BRINKLEY
DIXON, AMOS A. CAR 165 NO TWP L
DIXON, ANN BAL 013 15TH WAR
DIXON, AUGUSTUS BAL 399 14TH WAR
DIXON, B. BAL 179 19TH WAR
DIXON, BEGEBAL ALL 152 6TH E.D.
DIXON, BENJAMIN ANN 429 HOWARD D
DIXON, BENJAMIN CAL 036 2ND DIST
DIXON, BENJAMIN KEN 253 1ST DIST
DIXON, BENJAMIN K. WAS 119 2ND DIST
DIXON, BETTY BAL 108 10TH WAR
DIXON, CALEB BAL 183 16TH WAR
DIXON, CASSY MGM 325 CRACKLIN
DIXON, CATHARINE BAL 218 19TH WAR
DIXON, CHARLES BAL 293 12TH WAR
DIXON, CURTIS WOR 218 4TH E DI
DIXON, CYNTHIA BAL 005 EASTERN
DIXON, DANIEL ANN 428 HOWARD D
DIXON, DANIEL BAL 121 16TH WAR
DIXON, DAVID BAL 011 2ND DIST
DIXON, DAVID CAR 090 NO TWP L
DIXON, DAVID HAR 027 1ST DIST
DIXON, DAVID-BLACK WOR 334 1ST E DI
DIXON, DINAH DOR 390 1ST DIST
DIXON, E. PRI 118 PISCATAW
DIXON, ELISABETH ALL 061 10TH E.D
DIXON, ELIZA BAL 106 10TH WAR
DIXON, ELIZA BAL 309 3RD WARD
DIXON, ELIZA BAL 154 11TH WAR
DIXON, ELIZABETH CAL 003 1ST DIST
DIXON, ELIZABETH BAL 400 3RD WARD
DIXON, ELIZABETH D. ST 336 4TH E DI
DIXON, ELIZABETH T. BAL 039 4TH WARD
DIXON, EMANUEL FRE 378 PETERSVI
DIXON, FRANCIS MGM 325 CRACKLIN
DIXON, G.L. PRI 053 AQUASCO
DIXON, GATTY WOR 237 5TH E DI
DIXON, GEORGE WOR 239 5TH E DI
DIXON, GEORGE WOR 233 6TH E DI
DIXON, GEORGE PRI 108 PISCATAW
DIXON, GEORGE KEN 281 3RD DIST
DIXON, GEORGE WAS 057 2ND SUBD
DIXON, GEORGE DR- SOM 424 PRINCESS
DIXON, GEORGE E. PRI 105 PISCATAW
DIXON, GEORGE W. WAS 029 2ND SUBD
DIXON, HARNES FRE 307 WOODSBOR
DIXON, HARRIET BAL 392 3RD WARD
DIXON, HENRY CAR 109 NO TWP L
DIXON, HUGH SOM 497 SALISBUR
DIXON, ISAAC BAL 145 16TH WAR
DIXON, ISAAC L. HAR 080 2ND DIST
DIXON, ISAIH * TAL 070 EASTON T
DIXON, J. BAL 135 1ST WARD
DIXON, J.B. BAL 223 19TH WAR
DIXON, JAMES CAR 150 NO TWP L
DIXON, JAMES FRE 234 BUCKEYST
DIXON, JAMES DOR 374 1ST DIST
DIXON, JAMES BAL 048 1ST WARD
DIXON, JAMES BAL 033 9TH WARD
DIXON, JAMES TAL 001 EASTON D
DIXON, JAMES WAS 093 2ND SUBD
DIXON, JAMES KEN 294 3RD DIST
DIXON, JAMES P. FRE 045 FREDERIC
DIXON, JAMES-BLACK CAR 104 NO TWP L
DIXON, JANE BAL 110 15TH WAR
DIXON, JANE BAL 344 7TH WARD
DIXON, JEREMIAH BAL 227 5TH WARD
DIXON, JOHN BAL 036 15TH WAR
DIXON, JOHN BAL 125 2ND DIST
DIXON, JOHN DOR 417 1ST DIST
DIXON, JOHN BAL 064 4TH WARD
DIXON, JOHN BAL 275 17TH WAR
DIXON, JOHN WOR 319 1ST E DI
DIXON, JOHN PRI 115 PISCATAW
DIXON, JOHN SOM 532 QUANTICO
DIXON, JOHN F. DOR 421 1ST DIST
DIXON, JOHN H. FRE 234 BUCKEYST
DIXON, JOHN H. BAL 167 19TH WAR
DIXON, JOHN H. BAL 108 15TH WAR
DIXON, JOHN JR. FRE 234 BUCKEYST
DIXON, JOHN S.-BLACK FRE 225 BUCKEYST
DIXON, JOHN W. FRE 234 BUCKEYST
DIXON, JOHN W. BAL 027 1ST WARD
DIXON, JOSEPH A. FRE 210 BUCKEYST
DIXON, JOSHUA WOR 223 4TH E DI
DIXON, JOSIAH PRI 115 PISCATAW
DIXON, LEAH A. WOR 254 1ST CENS
DIXON, LEVIN WOR 237 6TH E DI
DIXON, LOUIS L. M.D. BAL 222 1ST DIST
DIXON, LUCRETIA WOR 197 8TH E DI
DIXON, LUCY MGM 337 CRACKLIN
DIXON, LYDIA BAL 309 7TH WARD
DIXON, LYDIA A. BAL 378 3RD WARD
DIXON, MARGARET BAL 347 1ST DIST
DIXON, MARGARET M. FRE 233 BUCKEYST
DIXON, MARIA BAL 087 4TH WARD
DIXON, MARY BAL 075 4TH WARD
DIXON, MARY CAL 004 1ST DIST
DIXON, MARY HAR 099 2ND DIST
DIXON, MARY BAL 310 3RD WARD
DIXON, MARY BAL 177 16TH WAR
DIXON, MARY ANN 419 HOWARD D
DIXON, MARY ANN 416 HOWARD D
DIXON, MARY C. ST 261 3RD E DI
DIXON, MARY C. ST 261 3RD E DI
DIXON, MARY C.-BLACK BAL 224 2ND WARD
DIXON, MARY E. BAL 253 6TH WARD
DIXON, MARY E. TAL 120 ST MICHA
DIXON, MATTHEW DOR 469 1ST DIST
DIXON, NANCY-BLACK BAL 198 2ND WARD
DIXON, NATHAN CEC 028 CHESAPEA
DIXON, NATHANIEL SOM 420 PRINCESS
DIXON, NATHANIEL SOM 364 BRINKLEY

NAME	CO.	PAGE	DISTRICT
DIXON, PATRICK	ALL	129	4TH E.D.
DIXON, PETER	BAL	107	15TH WAR
DIXON, PRISCILLA	ANN	399	8TH DIST
DIXON, REBECCA	BAL	116	15TH WAR
DIXON, REBECCA	CAL	048	3RD DIST
DIXON, RICHARD F.	FRE	210	BUCKEYST
DIXON, ROBERT	ANN	451	HOWARD D
DIXON, ROSA	WOR	343	1ST E DI
DIXON, SALLEY	BAL	444	8TH WARD
DIXON, SALLY S.	CAL	011	1ST DIST
DIXON, SALLY*	DOR	415	1ST DIST
DIXON, SAMPSON	WOR	224	4TH E DI
DIXON, SAMUEL	WOR	228	6TH E DI
DIXON, SAMUEL	FRE	233	BUCKEYST
DIXON, SARAH	BAL	399	14TH WAR
DIXON, SARAH	CAR	165	NO TWP L
DIXON, SARAH	WAS	123	2ND DIST
DIXON, SARAH	ANN	437	HOWARD D
DIXON, SARAH	BAL	005	EASTERN
DIXON, SARAH	BAL	076	10TH WAR
DIXON, SARAH	BAL	401	1ST DIST
DIXON, SARAH	BAL	462	1ST DIST
DIXON, SARAH	BAL	099	1ST WARD
DIXON, SARAH A.	FRE	217	BUCKEYST
DIXON, SARAH-BLACK	FRE	232	BUCKEYST
DIXON, SOPHIA	BAL	086	4TH WARD
DIXON, SOPHIER	FRE	210	BUCKEYST
DIXON, STEVNE-BLACK	CAR	132	NO TWP L
DIXON, SUSAN	BAL	130	2ND DIST
DIXON, SUSAN B.	PRI	115	PISCATAW
DIXON, THOMAS	WOR	199	8TH E DI
DIXON, THOMAS	SOM	497	SALISBUR
DIXON, THOMAS	BAL	263	1ST DIST
DIXON, THOMAS	ALL	076	5TH E.D.
DIXON, THOMAS	FRE	217	BUCKEYST
DIXON, THOMAS	FRE	273	NEW MARK
DIXON, THOMAS	BAL	016	18TH WAR
DIXON, WESLEY	WOR	254	1ST CENS
DIXON, WILLAIM	BAL	125	2ND DIST
DIXON, WILLIAM	ALL	104	5TH E.D.
DIXON, WILLIAM	BAL	157	2ND DIST
DIXON, WILLIAM	BAL	349	7TH WARD
DIXON, WILLIAM	WOR	197	8TH E DI
DIXON, WILLIAM	ST	259	3RD E DI
DIXON, WILLIAM	CAL	030	2ND DIST
DIXON, WILLIAM	FRE	093	FREDERIC
DIXON, WILLIAM P.	WOR	234	6TH E DI
DIXON,HENRY-BLACK	CAR	110	NO TWP L
DIXS, RACHEL	ALL	245	CUMBERLA
DIXSON, ANNA-BLACK	FRE	441	8TH E DI
DIXSON, CHARLES	WOR	249	1ST CENS
DIXSON, ELISH	WOR	245	1ST CENS
DIXSON, ELIZABETH	WOR	263	BERLIN 1
DIXSON, HUDLY	WOR	302	SNOW HIL
DIXSON, JESSA	WOR	249	1ST CENS
DIXSON, JOHN A.	FRE	407	JEFFERSO
DIXSON, JULIE	FRE	297	WOODSBOR
DIXSON, RENA	WOR	245	1ST CENS
DIXSON, SALLY*	DOR	415	1ST DIST
DIXSON, THOMAS J.	SOM	364	BRINKLEY
DIXTROW, GEORGE	FRE	318	MIDDLETO
DIZENNY, SARAH	CEC	147	PORT DUP
DIZNEY, HENRY	CEC	155	PORT DUP
DLAPLANE, GEORGE W.	FRE	272	NEW MARK
DLEAP, NANCY	CAR	308	1ST DIST
DLEYENSTUEUBER, F. H.	BAL	075	10TH WAR
DMER, JOHN *	BAL	325	12TH WAR
DOAN, ANN	CAR	091	NO TWP L
DOANE, BRIDGET	BAL	334	13TH WAR
DOANNE, SUSANA	BAL	405	3RD WARD
DOAR, ANDREW	MGM	391	ROCKERLE
DOAS, HENRY	ALL	197	CUMBERLA
DOBB, JOHN	BAL	423	8TH WARD
DOBB, JOSEPH	BAL	290	12TH WAR
DOBBIN, ALEXANDER	BAL	400	14TH WAR
DOBBIN, ANNA	BAL	305	7TH WARD
DOBBIN, CATHERINE	BAL	046	4TH WARD
DOBBIN, CLARRA	BAL	104	1ST WARD
DOBBIN, GEORGE W.	ANN	418	HOWARD D
DOBBIN, HENRY	BAL	164	1ST WARD
DOBBIN, JAMES	BAL	164	1ST WARD
DOBBIN, JOHN	BAL	121	5TH WARD
DOBBIN, SUSANNAH	BAL	142	16TH WAR
DOBBINS, APPY	BAL	219	12TH WAR
DOBBINS, EMILY	BAL	291	17TH WAR
DOBBINS, FRANCIS	BAL	408	14TH WAR
DOBBINS, SARAH	BAL	080	15TH WAR
DOBBS, ABRAHAM	CEC	111	4TH E DI
DOBBS, JOHN	BAL	414	1ST DIST
DOBECKER, ADAM	BAL	119	18TH WAR
DOBERER, JOHN	BAL	258	12TH WAR
DOBERER, JOHN	BAL	259	12TH WAR
DOBLER, DAVID	BAL	317	7TH WARD
DOBLER, GEORGE	BAL	297	3RD WARD
DOBLER, MAGDELINE	BAL	373	8TH WARD
DOBLER, MARIA	BAL	380	8TH WARD
DOBLER, MEDORA	BAL	010	18TH WAR
DOBSON, AMANDA J.	BAL	131	16TH WAR
DOBSON, CHARLES*	DOR	413	1ST DIST
DOBSON, DEBORA	BAL	032	4TH WARD
DOBSON, DELIA	DOR	422	1ST DIST
DOBSON, ELIZA A.	TAL	025	EASTON D
DOBSON, ELIZABETH	BAL	093	10TH WAR
DOBSON, ELLEN	TAL	032	EASTON D
DOBSON, ELLEN	QUE	248	5TH E DI
DOBSON, EMMA	BAL	036	4TH WARD
DOBSON, FRANCES A.	BAL	158	6TH WARD
DOBSON, FRANCIS	BAL	332	13TH WAR
DOBSON, HENRY	BAL	130	11TH WAR
DOBSON, HENRY	TAL	012	EASTON D
DOBSON, HORACE	DOR	460	1ST DIST
DOBSON, ISAAC	BAL	115	2ND DIST
DOBSON, JACOB	QUE	240	5TH E DI
DOBSON, JAEMS	TAL	100	ST MICHA
DOBSON, JAMES	BAL	071	4TH WARD
DOBSON, JAMES H.	TAL	062	EASTON D
DOBSON, JESSE	TAL	088	ST MICHA
DOBSON, JOHN	TAL	035	EASTON D
DOBSON, JOHN	TAL	062	EASTON D
DOBSON, JOHN	TAL	060	EASTON D
DOBSON, JOHN	TAL	059	EASTON D
DOBSON, JOHN	TAL	078	EASTON T
DOBSON, JOHN	TAL	078	EASTON T
DOBSON, JOHN	BAL	363	3RD WARD
DOBSON, JOHN S.	TAL	067	EASTON T
DOBSON, JOSEPH	QUE	216	3RD E DI
DOBSON, JOSIAH	TAL	036	EASTON D
DOBSON, MARTHA A.	BAL	130	11TH WAR
DOBSON, PERRY	BAL	149	5TH WARD
DOBSON, RACHEL A.	TAL	003	EASTON D
DOBSON, REBECA	BAL	286	20TH WAR
DOBSON, ROBERT	BAL	152	5TH WARD
DOBSON, SAMUEL	ANN	339	3RD DIST
DOBSON, SAMUEL	TAL	016	EASTON D
DOBSON, SARAH	BAL	265	7TH WARD
DOBSON, SARAH A.	HAR	156	3RD DIST
DOBSON, SUSAN	BAL	158	6TH WARD
DOBSON, WILLIAM	BAL	314	7TH WARD
DOBSON, WILLIAM	TAL	008	EASTON D
DOBSON, WILLIAM	TAL	027	EASTON D
DOBSON, WILLIAM	TAL	034	EASTON D
DOCENY, THOMAS	ALL	082	5TH E.D.
DOCHERTY, ANN	BAL	352	7TH WARD
DOCHERTY, BOYER	ALL	077	5TH E.D.
DOCHERTY, MARY	ALL	077	5TH E.D.
DOCHERTY, THOMAS	ALL	052	10TH E.D
DOCK, JOHN	BAL	189	19TH WAR
DOCKERTY, JOHN	BAL	277	2ND WARD
DOCKERTY, MARTIN	ALL	082	5TH E.D.
DOCKERTY, OWEN	ALL	071	5TH E.D.
DOCKET, JOHN	ANN	367	4TH DIST
DOCKETT, L.	PRI	067	NOTTINGH
DOCKEY, CAROLINE	BAL	097	5TH WARD
DOCKINS, CHARLES	BAL	082	15TH WAR
DOCKINS, CHARLES H.	DOR	448	1ST DIST
DOCKINS, JAMES	BAL	101	15TH WAR
DOCKINS, JULIAN	DOR	448	1ST DIST
DOCKINS, MARY	DOR	436	1ST DIST
DOCKINS, PETER	DOR	466	1ST DIST
DOCKINS, SARAH	BAL	095	15TH WAR
DOCKMAN, ELIZABETH	CEC	123	3RD E DI
DOCRA, EDWIN	BAL	397	14TH WAR
DOD,DANIEL	BAL	092	1ST WARD
DODBSON, CHARLES	TAL	071	EASTON T
DODD, ALEXANDER	TAL	072	EASTON T
DODD, ALEXANDER	TAL	066	EASTON T
DODD, ANN-BLACK	QUE	159	2ND E DI
DODD, CATHARINE	TAL	073	EASTON T
DODD, DEBBY	QUE	219	3RD E DI
DODD, GEORGE E.	BAL	298	7TH WARD
DODD, HANNAH	BAL	195	11TH WAR
DODD, HENRY	QUE	244	5TH E DI
DODD, ISAAC	WAS	019	2ND SUBD
DODD, JAMES	TAL	020	EASTON D
DODD, JANE	BAL	298	7TH WARD
DODD, JOHN	QUE	162	2ND E DI
DODD, JOHN T.	KEN	220	2ND DIST
DODD, MARK-BLACK	QUE	195	3RD E DI
DODD, MARTHA-BLACK	QUE	190	3RD E DI
DODD, MISS E.	FRE	198	5TH E DI
DODD, NANCY	CAR	168	NO TWP L
DODD, RASHEL	TAL	077	EASTON T
DODD, SAMUEL	WAS	136	2ND DIST
DODD, THOMAS	QUE	244	5TH E DI
DODD, THOMAS	KEN	290	3RD DIST
DODD, THOMAS	WAS	092	2ND SUBD
DODD, WILLIAM	TAL	022	EASTON D
DODDERILL, JAMES H.	HAR	122	2ND DIST
DODDLE, ALICE	BAL	314	20TH WAR
DODDS, JOHN W.	QUE	251	5TH E DI
DODDS, MARGARET	CAR	396	2ND DIST
DODE, MILANNAH	BAL	021	9TH WARD
DODEBILH, CAROLINE	BAL	013	1ST WARD
DODGE, DANIEL	ALL	057	10TH E.D
DODGE, ELIZA	BAL	388	13TH WAR
DODGE, GEORGE R.	BAL	245	20TH WAR
DODGE, WILLIAM	WAS	136	2ND DIST
DODGES, HANNAH	BAL	432	14TH WAR
DODS, WILLIAM	BAL	156	2ND DIST
DODS, ELIZABETH	BAL	375	13TH WAR
DODSON, EDWARD	DOR	313	1ST DIST
DODSON, EDWARD	DOR	319	1ST DIST
DODSON, EDWARD	TAL	083	ST MICHA
DODSON, HARRIET	BAL	227	1ST DIST
DODSON, HENNY	ANN	381	4TH DIST
DODSON, JESSE	QUE	166	2ND E DI
DODSON, LEONARD	TAL	079	ST MICHA
DODSON, LOUISA	TAL	079	ST MICHA
DODSON, MARY J.	BAL	187	16TH WAR
DODSON, MATTHEW	BAL	023	9TH WARD
DODSON, PETER	BAL	194	17TH WAR
DODSON, ROBERT A.	TAL	085	ST MICHA
DODSON, ROBERT A. JR.	TAL	086	ST MICHA
DODSON, ROBERT M.	ANN	309	1ST DIST
DODSON, SAMUEL	ANN	317	1ST DIST
DODSON, SAMUEL	BAL	428	14TH WAR
DODSON, SUSAN	BAL	273	7TH WARD
DODSON, WALTER	ANN	394	8TH DIST
DODSON, WILLIAM H.	QUE	247	5TH E DI
DOEINGS, HENRY	BAL	123	16TH WAR
DOEL, DANIEL	BAL	184	2ND WARD
DOENGES, CONRAD	BAL	257	1ST DIST
DOESEY, JAMES E.	FRE	270	NEW MARK
DOFER, BARBARA	BAL	093	2ND DIST
DOFFIN, CHARLES C. D.	BAL	297	20TH WAR
DOFFY, JOHN	BAL	252	20TH WAR
DOFT, GEORGE	BAL	385	8TH WARD
DOGAN, ANDREW	ALL	052	10TH E.D
DOGAN, FRENCIS	ALL	051	10TH E.D
DOGAN, JOHN	ALL	051	10TH E.D
DOGAN, WILLIAM	ALL	047	10TH E.D
DOGANS, HENRY	BAL	211	11TH WAR
DOGANSHICN, HARRIET	CEC	212	7TH E DI
DOGAUS, ARMIE	BAL	204	11TH WAR
DOGODGE, MARY	MGM	379	ROCKERLE
DOGED, WILLIAM C.	BAL	220	6TH WARD
DOGGED, MARTIN	BAL	305	7TH WARD
DOGHERTY, ELLEN	BAL	213	11TH WAR
DOGHERTY, JAMES	BAL	063	18TH WAR
DOGLE, THOAMS	ALL	079	5TH E.D.
DOGMAN, MALRY	BAL	185	11TH WAR
DOGNAN, MARGARET	BAL	182	11TH WAR
DOHAMMER, RACHEL	BAL	302	3RD WARD
DOHE, JACOB	BAL	255	20TH WAR
DOHERTON, CATHERINE	BAL	403	3RD WARD
DOHERTY, CATHERINE	BAL	071	4TH WARD
DOHERTY, ELIZABETH	BAL	006	4TH WARD
DOHERTY, EMELINE	BAL	404	3RD WARD
DOHERTY, JAMES	HAR	050	1ST DIST
DOHERTY, PHILIP	ANN	340	3RD DIST
DOHERTY, THOMAS	BAL	304	3RD WARD
DOHERTY, WILLIAM	BAL	155	16TH WAR
DOHN, FRANKLIN	BAL	460	14TH WAR
DOHOLLY, NANCY	BAL	161	11TH WAR
DOHVOYNCT, JOSEPH	BAL	029	18TH WAR
DOIL, MARY E.	FRE	234	BUCKEYST
DOISEY, LOUISA	ALL	257	CUMBERLA
DOITEE, CAROLINE	BAL	010	4TH WARD
DOLAN, ANN	BAL	213	11TH WAR
DOLAN, ANN	BAL	110	10TH WAR
DOLAN, ANN	BAL	398	1ST DIST
DOLAN, ELIZA	BAL	078	4TH WARD
DOLAN, ELLEN	CEC	164	6TH E DI
DOLAN, FRANK	ALL	052	10TH E.D
DOLAN, HENRY	BAL	424	8TH WARD
DOLAN, JACOB	BAL	010	EASTERN
DOLAN, JAMES	BAL	001	EASTERN
DOLAN, JAMES	ALL	239	CUMBERLA
DOLAN, JAMES	ANN	460	HOWARD D
DOLAN, JAMES	BAL	384	3RD WARD
DOLAN, JAMES	ALL	186	9TH E.D.
DOLAN, JOHN	ALL	049	10TH E.D
DOLAN, JOHN	BAL	210	2ND WARD
DOLAN, JOHN	BAL	031	4TH WARD
DOLAN, JOHN	HAR	058	1ST DIST
DOLAN, JOHN H.	HAR	156	3RD DIST
DOLAN, JOSEPH	BAL	081	2ND DIST
DOLAN, MARGARETT	BAL	187	11TH WAR
DOLAN, MARGRET	HAR	134	3RD DIST
DOLAN, MARIA	BAL	213	11TH WAR
DOLAN, MARY	BAL	002	15TH WAR
DOLAN, MARY	BAL	398	1ST DIST
DOLAN, MARY	BAL	310	12TH WAR
DOLAN, MARY	WAS	135	HAGERSTO
DOLAN, MARY A.	BAL	109	18TH WAR
DOLAN, MICHAEL	ALL	237	CUMBERLA
DOLAN, PATRICK	BAL	043	2ND DIST
DOLAN, PATRICK	BAL	407	8TH WARD
DOLAN, PATRICK	BAL	163	2ND DIST
DOLAN, PATRICK	BAL	411	14TH WAR
DOLAN, ROSE	BAL	268	20TH WAR
DOLAN, THOMAS	BAL	185	2ND WARD
DOLAN, VALENTINE	BAL	179	2ND DIST
DOLAN, WATSON	ALL	077	5TH E.D.
DOLAN, WILLIAM	BAL	079	19TH WAR
DOLAND, JOHN	BAL	285	7TH WARD
DOLAND, THOMAS	BAL	275	1ST DIST
DOLAND, WILLIAM	BAL	315	7TH WARD
DOLAND, WILLIMA	BAL	460	1ST DIST
DOLBY, EDWARD	BAL	319	3RD WARD
DOLE, A. G.	WAS	181	BOONSBOR
DOLE, JOHN R.	WAS	056	2ND SUBD
DOLE, MARY	FRE	342	MIDDLETO
DOLE, SALLY	WOR	206	4TH E DI
DOLEMAN, CHARLES	CEC	066	1ST E DI
DOLEN, BURGES	CAR	192	4TH DIST
DOLEN, PATRICK	FRE	120	CREAGERS
DOLEN, RACHEL	CAR	204	4TH DIST
DOLEN, WILLIAM	BAL	286	2ND WARD
DOLFIR, JACOB	FRE	030	FREDERIC
DOLIN, CATHERINE J.	CEC	164	6TH E DI
DOLINGER, CHARLES	BAL	369	13TH WAR
DOLINGER, PETER	BAL	010	EASTERN
DOLINSON, ELLEN	KEN	263	1ST DIST
DOLK, JOHN C.	BAL	213	19TH WAR
DOLL, ANNIE M.	BAL	400	3RD WARD
DOLL, CHRISTIANA	BAL	044	15TH WAR
DOLL, DANIEL	BAL	114	18TH WAR
DOLL, EDWARD	FRE	050	FREDERIC
DOLL, ELIZABETH	FRE	351	MIDDLETO
DOLL, GEORGE W.	FRE	348	MIDDLETO
DOLL, HARRIET	FRE	043	FREDERIC
DOLL, JACOB	BAL	178	5TH WARD
DOLL, JOHN	FRE	033	FREDERIC
DOLL, JOSHUA J.	FRE	224	BUCKEYST
DOLL, MARY	FRE	032	FREDERIC
DOLL, MARY	FRE	448	8TH E DI
DOLL, SARAH	FRE	324	MIDDLETO
DOLL, WILLIAM	FRE	062	FREDERIC
DOLL, WILLIAM	BAL	185	19TH WAR
DOLL,LEWIS	FRE	022	FREDERIC
DOLLAN, JOHN	BAL	393	1ST WARD
DOLLAR, JOSEPH	BAL	181	19TH WAR
DOLLAR, LAURENCE	BAL	180	19TH WAR
DOLLARS, P.	BAL	220	17TH WAR
DOLLEHUNT, ALEXANDER	WAS	108	2ND DIST
DOLLERER, FREDERICK	CAR	254	3RD DIST
DOLLERER, GEORGE	CAR	258	3RD DIST
DOLLERER, JAMES	CAR	260	3RD DIST
DOLLEY, CATHARINE	BAL	030	18TH WAR
DOLLEY, FRANCIS	BAL	121	11TH WAR
DOLLEY,EMILY	BAL	292	12TH WAR
DOLLING, FREDERICK	BAL	210	2ND WARD
DOLON, JULEN	BAL	293	12TH WAR
DOLON, PHILIP	WAS	122	2ND DIST
DOLPHIN, JAMES	BAL	168	11TH WAR
DOLPHIN, THOMAS	ALL	049	10TH E.D
DOLPLIN, FRANCIS	BAL	235	12TH WAR
DOLSON, GEORGE	BAL	230	12TH WAR
DOLVAN, PATRICK *	ALL	136	4TH E.D.
DOMAN, ABRAHAM	KEN	310	3RD DIST
DOMAN, DANIEL	BAL	207	17TH WAR
DOMAN, ELIZABETH	BAL	155	11TH WAR
DOMAN, ELIZABETH	BAL	335	3RD WARD
DOMAN, GEORGE	CEC	122	4TH E DI
DOMAN, HENRIETTA	BAL	401	14TH WAR
DOMAN, JAMES	KEN	304	3RD DIST
DOMAN, JOHN	BAL	268	1ST DIST
DOMAN, JOSEPH	KEN	299	3RD DIST
DOMAN, MILLEY	BAL	207	17TH WAR
DOMAN, SAMUEL	KEN	298	3RD DIST
DOMAN, WILLIAM	KEN	306	3RD DIST
DOMAN, WILLIAM	BAL	207	17TH WAR
DOMBRY, ISAAC	CEC	022	ELKTON 3
DOME, MARTIN	WAS	104	2ND DIST
DOMER, DAVID	FRE	139	CREAGERS
DOMER, ELIZABETH C.	FRE	140	CREAGERS
DOMER, JACOB	WAS	059	2ND SUBD
DOMER, MARY EVE	FRE	139	CREAGERS
DOMER, ROLLA	WAS	059	2ND SUBD
DOMER, ROSANA	WAS	059	2ND SUBD
DOMEY, JAMES	BAL	140	1ST WARD
DOMINGER, CHARLES	BAL	404	14TH WAR
DOMINIS, HENRY	BAL	031	9TH WARD
DOMMAN, JOHN H.	WOR	177	6TH E DI
DOMMEL, MATHIAS	WAS	237	CAVETOWN
DOMUS, HANNAH	BAL	380	1ST DIST
DONAGAN, THOMAS	WAS	151	2ND DIST
DONAHEW, JANE	ALL	249	CUMBERLA
DONAHO, JOHN	CEC	141	6TH E DI
DONAHO, MATTHEW	MGM	395	ROCKERLE
DONAHOE, ANDREW	BAL	115	2ND DIST
DONAHOE, ELLEN	BAL	169	11TH WAR
DONAHOE, HENRY	ALL	110	5TH E.D.
DONAHOE, JAMES	ALL	110	5TH E.D.
DONAHOE, JOHN	ALL	056	10TH E.D
DONAHOE, JOHN	HAR	117	2ND DIST
DONAHOE, MARTIN	ALL	049	10TH E.D
DONAHOE, MICHAEL	ALL	129	4TH E.D.
DONAHOE, PETER	ALL	150	5TH E.D.

DONAHOE, THOMAS BAL 164 11TH WAR
DONAHOE, THOMAS BAL 115 2ND DIST
DONAHOO, PATRICK MGM 332 CRACKLIN
DONAHOO, REBECCA ALL 084 5TH E.D.
DONAHUE, ASSANA BAL 196 2ND WARD
DONAHUE, DANIEL BAL 105 1ST WARD
DONAHUE, EDWARD BAL 210 2ND WARD
DONAHUE, JOHN ALL 053 10TH E.D
DONAHUE, JOHN BAL 054 9TH WARD
DONAHUE, JOHN BAL 038 9TH WARD
DONAHUE, LYDIA WAS 289 1ST DIST
DONAHUE, MARY BAL 259 2ND WARD
DONAHUE, MARY BAL 257 17TH WAR
DONAHUE, MARY B. FRE 065 FREDERIC
DONAHUE, MICHAEL BAL 286 17TH WAR
DONAHUE, PATRICK ALL 051 10TH E.D
DONAHUE, THOMAS BAL 184 6TH WARD
DONALD, EUGENE BAL 154 11TH WAR
DONALD, JAMES W. BAL 313 3RD WARD
DONALD, MRS- BAL 334 1ST DIST
DONALD, PATRICK O. BAL 172 11TH WAR
DONALD, SON, MARY BAL 253 6TH WARD
DONALD, SUSAN BAL 313 12TH WAR
DONALDOSN, MARIA BAL 358 13TH WAR
DONALDSON, AMY FRE 145 10TH E D
DONALDSON, ANNE BAL 364 13TH WAR
DONALDSON, ARON BAL 016 4TH WARD
DONALDSON, CATHERINE BAL 148 11TH WAR
DONALDSON, CHARLOTTE BAL 388 13TH WAR
DONALDSON, DANIEL BAL 199 19TH WAR
DONALDSON, DAVID BAL 339 7TH WARD
DONALDSON, EDWARD ANN 304 1ST DIST
DONALDSON, ELIJAH ANN 467 HOWARD D
DONALDSON, GEORGE BAL 411 8TH WARD
DONALDSON, GEORGE E. BAL 070 10TH WAR
DONALDSON, GEORGE TL. PRI 035 VANSVILL
DONALDSON, J. BAL 301 20TH WAR
DONALDSON, JOHN BAL 010 4TH WARD
DONALDSON, JOHN WAS 090 2ND SUBD
DONALDSON, JOHN BAL 143 1ST WARD
DONALDSON, JOHN ANN 372 4TH DIST
DONALDSON, JOHN J. BAL 407 14TH WAR
DONALDSON, JOHN J. BAL 197 11TH WAR
DONALDSON, MARY A. BAL 365 1ST DIST
DONALDSON, MOSES ANN 366 4TH DIST
DONALDSON, MR. BAL 006 15TH WAR
DONALDSON, NOAH BAL 104 5TH WARD
DONALDSON, REBECA CEC 012 ELKTON 3
DONALDSON, RICHARD ANN 352 4TH DIST
DONALDSON, SAMUEL J. BAL 060 10TH WAR
DONALDSON, SHADY M. BAL 419 3RD WARD
DONALDSON, SIDNOR BAL 300 7TH WARD
DONALDSON, STEPHEN BAL 018 4TH WARD
DONALDSON, THOMAS BAL 198 19TH WAR
DONALDSON, VINIFRED BAL 056 15TH WAR
DONALDSON, WILHELMENIA BAL 004 1ST WARD
DONALDSON, WILLIAM BAL 124 1ST WARD
DONALOWON, THOMAS W. BAL 011 4TH WARD
DONALLSON, PRISCELLOR BAL 169 19TH WAR
DONALLY, HONORA CAR 242 TANEYTOW
DONALLY, JAMES BAL 359 8TH WARD
DONALLY, MARY BAL 358 8TH WARD
DONALNER, PLUMER * BAL 163 2ND DIST
DONALSON, ALEXANDER BAL 195 2ND WARD
DONALSON, JIMMINA BAL 298 3RD WARD
DONALSON, JOSEPH ALL 171 7TH E.D.
DONALSON, THOMAS ANN 413 HOWARD D
DONALY, PATRICK BAL 425 8TH WARD
DONAN, JOHN ALL 155 6TH E.D.
DONANCE, JANE BAL 008 4TH WARD
DONARD, ANN BAL 092 1ST WARD
DONARD, CATHARINE BAL 161 2ND DIST
DONARD, JACOB BAL 092 1ST WARD
DONATEL, MARY M. BAL 139 16TH WAR
DONAUGHEARRICK, JOSEPH BAL 330 7TH WARD
DONAVAN, HONORA BAL 345 7TH WARD
DONAVAN, JOHN BAL 143 1ST WARD
DONAVAN, MARY ALL 253 CUMBERLA
DONDLY, MATHEW WAS 034 2ND SUBD
DONDON, NICHOLAS BAL 061 2ND DIST
DONE, CHARLES SOM 420 PRINCESS
DONE, CHARLOTTE* SOM 484 TRAPP DI
DONE, D. BAL 138 1ST WARD
DONE, EDWARD SOM 484 TRAPP DI
DONE, ELIJAH SOM 420 PRINCESS
DONE, HARRIET BAL 241 12TH WAR
DONE, JOHN H. SOM 435 PRINCESS
DONE, JOHN-BLACK CAR 091 NO TWP L
DONE, LAURA BAL 298 20TH WAR
DONE, MARY BAL 178 11TH WAR
DONE, RACHAEL SOM 484 TRAPP DI
DONE, STEVIN-BLACK CAR 075 NO TWP L
DONE, WILLIAM-BLACK CAR 166 NO TWP L
DONEEN, GEORGE ALL 167 6TH E.D.
DONEHO, ANN BAL 398 14TH WAR
DONEHUE, ELLEN BAL 267 7TH WARD
DONEHUE, HANAH BAL 381 8TH WARD
DONEHUE, JAMES BAL 385 8TH WARD
DONEHUE, JOHN BAL 396 8TH WARD
DONEHUE, PATRICK BAL 418 8TH WARD
DONEL, JOHN BAL 458 8TH WARD
DONELL, JAMES O. BAL 175 11TH WAR
DONELLY, DANIEL WAS 016 2ND SUBD
DONELLY, EDWARD WAS 026 2ND SUBD
DONELLY, ELIZA BAL 011 2ND DIST
DONELLY, HANAH BAL 424 8TH WARD
DONELLY, JAMES BAL 104 18TH WAR
DONELLY, LOUISA WAS 002 WILLIAMS
DONELLY, MARGARET WAS 001 WILLIAMS
DONELLY, MARGARET BAL 265 20TH WAR
DONELLY, MARGARET BAL 332 13TH WAR
DONELLY, MARY BAL 169 11TH WAR
DONELSON, JAMES L. BAL 270 7TH WARD
DONELY, D. BAL 153 1ST WARD
DONELY, JOHN BAL 155 2ND DIST
DONENFELLER, JOHN BAL 042 1ST WARD
DONER, HUGH BAL 380 1ST DIST
DONER, WILLIAM WAS 196 1ST DIST
DONES, ROBERT QUE 233 4TH E DI
DONEVAN, DENNIS BAL 420 8TH WARD
DONEVAN, E.J. BAL 223 19TH WAR
DONEVAN, JOHN TAL 066 EASTON T
DONEVAN, JOSEPH J. BAL 352 7TH WARD
DONEWE, THOMAS BAL 301 17TH WAR
DONEY, ANN BAL 290 12TH WAR
DONEY, MARY E. QUE 202 3RD E DI
DONEY, MILLY BAL 229 12TH WAR
DONGAN, JAMES BAL 136 1ST WARD
DONGHERTY, BERNARD H. ALL 219 CUMBERLA
DONIAWIN, DENIS * HAR 199 3RD DIST

DONIGAN, OWEN BAL 359 8TH WARD
DONILAN, ELIZA BAL 213 11TH WAR
DONILLISS, LUTHER * FRE 254 NEW MARK
DONILY, JAMES ALL 219 CUMBERLA
DONITEE, ANDREW BAL 005 9TH WARD
DONITEE, CHARLES * BAL 265 7TH WARD
DONITZ, DANIEL BAL 110 1ST WARD
DONIZ, HENRY BAL 257 2ND WARD
DONLAHAN, PETER HAR 198 3RD DIST
DONLAN, BARTLEY CAR 230 5TH DIST
DONLAN, JOHN P. BAL 119 5TH WARD
DONLESON, JAMES BAL 063 18TH WAR
DONLEVY, DENNIS HAR 079 2ND DIST
DONLEY, CHARLES BAL 350 1ST DIST
DONLEY, GEORGE E. BAL 162 19TH WAR
DONLEY, JAMES BAL 253 20TH WAR
DONLEY, JOHN BAL 342 1ST DIST
DONLEY, JOHN BAL 363 1ST DIST
DONLEY, JOHN BAL 449 1ST DIST
DONLEY, MARKEY CAR 230 5TH DIST
DONLEY, MARY * BAL 307 1ST DIST
DONLIN, JAMES BAL 099 5TH WARD
DONLIN, WILLIAM HAR 157 3RD DIST
DONLY, HEUGH HAR 198 3RD DIST
DONN, JEN BAL 227 12TH WAR
DONN, JOHN M. PRI 008 BLADENSB
DONNAHO, MARY A. CEC 030 CHESAPEA
DONNALLY, AUGUSTUS BAL 037 9TH WARD
DONNALLY, MARGARET BAL 362 8TH WARD
DONNE, S. BAL 199 2ND WARD
DONNEGAN, JOHN F. BAL 299 3RD WARD
DONNEL, JAMES ANN 469 HOWARD D
DONNEL, SARAH CEC 028 CHESAPEA
DONNEL, SARAH J. BAL 381 3RD WARD
DONNELL, EDWARD ANN 517 HOWARD D
DONNELL, ELLEN C. BAL 300 12TH WAR
DONNELL, HENRY C. BAL 175 11TH WAR
DONNELL, JAMES BAL 129 1ST WARD
DONNELL, JAMES BAL 029 1ST WARD
DONNELL, JOHN BAL 145 11TH WAR
DONNELL, JOHN S. BAL 111 18TH WAR
DONNELL, LEWIS O. MGM 319 CRACKLIN
DONNELL, MARGARET BAL 345 3RD WARD
DONNELL, PETER BAL 163 19TH WAR
DONNELLY, AUGUSTA A. BAL 038 9TH WARD
DONNELLY, BANARD BAL 135 5TH WARD
DONNELLY, BERNARD BAL 203 6TH WARD
DONNELLY, CHARLES BAL 329 13TH WAR
DONNELLY, CHARLES FRE 168 EMMITTSB
DONNELLY, DANIEL BAL 179 19TH WAR
DONNELLY, ELIZA BAL 191 11TH WAR
DONNELLY, ELIZABETH BAL 203 6TH WARD
DONNELLY, ELIZABETH BAL 199 2ND WARD
DONNELLY, HENRY ALL 232 CUMBERLA
DONNELLY, HUGH BAL 362 8TH WARD
DONNELLY, JAMES BAL 250 2ND WARD
DONNELLY, JAMES ALL 239 CUMBERLA
DONNELLY, JAMES HAR 120 2ND DIST
DONNELLY, JOHN FRE 184 5TH E DI
DONNELLY, JOHN FRE 202 5TH E DI
DONNELLY, JOHN BAL 369 3RD WARD
DONNELLY, MARY BAL 064 2ND DIST
DONNELLY, MARY BAL 029 9TH WARD
DONNELLY, MARY BAL 171 19TH WAR
DONNELLY, MARY A. FRE 065 FREDERIC
DONNELLY, MARY A. L. BAL 161 11TH WAR
DONNELLY, MICHAEL BAL 071 4TH WARD
DONNELLY, MICHAEL ALL 051 10TH E.D
DONNELLY, MISS A. FRE 199 5TH E DI
DONNELLY, MISS C. FRE 199 5TH E DI
DONNELLY, MISS M. FRE 199 5TH E DI
DONNELLY, MISS R. FRE 199 5TH E DI
DONNELLY, MORRIS BAL 385 8TH WARD
DONNELLY, OWEN ANN 460 HOWARD D
DONNELLY, OWEN BAL 316 20TH WAR
DONNELLY, PATRICK FRE 040 FREDERIC
DONNELLY, PATRICK HAR 137 2ND DIST
DONNELLY, PETER BAL 170 2ND DIST
DONNELLY, RAMEY BAL 146 1ST WARD
DONNELLY, REGINA BAL 212 11TH WAR
DONNELLY, RICHARD CEC 154 PORT DUP
DONNELLY, SISTER M.M. FRE 197 5TH E DI
DONNELLY, SUSAN BAL 164 19TH WAR
DONNELLY, THOMAS ALL 237 CUMBERLA
DONNELLY, THOMAS BAL 169 11TH WAR
DONNELLY, WILLIAM BAL 162 11TH WAR
DONNELLY, WILLIAM BAL 132 1ST WARD
DONNELLY, A. BAL 161 1ST WARD
DONNELSON, HOMERD ANN 441 HOWARD D
DONNELSON, REBECCA CEC 036 CHESAPEA
DONNELSON, WILLIAM CEC 027 CHESAPEA
DONNELY, FRANCIS ALL 219 CUMBERLA
DONNELY, JAMES WAS 156 2ND DIST
DONNELY, MARGARET ALL 209 CUMBERLA
DONNEMAN, ELVIRA BAL 060 10TH WAR
DONNER, JOHN FRE 386 PETERSVI
DONNES, EDWARD QUE 240 5TH E DI
DONNES, WILLIAM T.-BLACK QUE 172 2ND E DI
DONNEY, A.J. WAS 135 HAGERSTO
DONNEY, HADASSAH WAS 017 2ND SUBD
DONNEY, JAMES KEN 231 2ND DIST
DONNEY, WILLIAM KEN 231 2ND DIST
DONNEY, WILLIAM BAL 153 1ST WARD
DONNINS, JAMES BAL 142 1ST WARD
DONNIS, PHILLIP FRE 074 FREDERIC
DONNOLL, COLUMBUS BAL 149 11TH WAR
DONOGHUE, EMILY BAL 037 4TH WARD
DONOGHUE, JOHN O. PRI 107 PISCATAW
DONOHAW, JOHN HAR 170 3RD DIST
DONOHO, ALEXANDER SOM 553 TYASKIN
DONOHO, ANN BAL 445 14TH WAR
DONOHO, C. P. DOR 443 1ST DIST
DONOHO, CAROLINE BAL 409 14TH WAR
DONOHO, CHRISTOPHER C. SOM 551 TYASKIN
DONOHO, ELIZABETH W. DOR 444 1ST DIST
DONOHO, JAMES R. DOR 443 1ST DIST
DONOHO, MICHAEL MGM 327 CRACKLIN
DONOHO, PRUCILLA SOM 411 DUBLIN D
DONOHO, WILLIAM SOM 531 QUANTICO
DONOHO, WILLIAM A. SOM 551 TYASKIN
DONOHO, WILLIAM O. SOM 523 BARREN C
DONOHOE, HUGH ANN 441 HOWARD D
DONOHOE, JOHN BAL 150 11TH WAR
DONOHOE, MARGARET BAL 199 11TH WAR
DONOHOE, MARGARET BAL 092 2ND DIST
DONOHOE, MICHAL HAR 203 3RD DIST
DONOHOE, PATRICK H. BAL 158 11TH WAR
DONOHOE, PHILIP ALL 135 6TH E.D.
DONOHOE, SISTER M.T. FRE 198 5TH E DI
DONOHOO, HUGH BAL 135 16TH WAR

DONOHOO, JOHN HAR 199 3RD DIST
DONOHOO, MARY HAR 164 3RD DIST
DONOHUE, CATHRINE CAR 408 2ND DIST
DONOHUE, ELIZABETH BAL 317 20TH WAR
DONOHUE, ELLEN BAL 286 20TH WAR
DONOHUE, GEORGE BAL 294 12TH WAR
DONOHUE, MARGARET BAL 075 10TH WAR
DONOHUE, PATRICK BAL 019 9TH WARD
DONOKO, CATHARINE BAL 462 14TH WAR
DONOLLY, ROSINA BAL 457 14TH WAR
DONORAN, D. BAL 150 1ST WARD
DONOUGHO, JOHN MGM 363 BERRYS D
DONOVAN, ANN BAL 318 12TH WAR
DONOVAN, CATHERINE BAL 029 9TH WARD
DONOVAN, DAVID ANN 469 HOWARD D
DONOVAN, ELLEN BAL 220 6TH WARD
DONOVAN, ELLEN ALL 201 CUMBERLA
DONOVAN, ELLEN BAL 311 20TH WAR
DONOVAN, ELLEN BAL 043 4TH WARD
DONOVAN, G. BAL 311 20TH WAR
DONOVAN, J. BAL 157 1ST WARD
DONOVAN, JAENS BAL 132 2ND DIST
DONOVAN, JAMES FRE 20 5TH E DI
DONOVAN, JOHN BAL 105 18TH WAR
DONOVAN, JULIA A. BAL 197 6TH WARD
DONOVAN, OLIVER BAL 078 2ND DIST
DONOVAN, RICHARD BAL 265 12TH WAR
DONOVAN, TIMOTHY BAL 247 6TH WARD
DONOVON, JOSEPH S. BAL 002 15TH WAR
DONRINEN, FREDERICK * BAL 076 18TH WAR
DONSHOE, RICHARD BAL 124 11TH WAR
DONSIFE, HENRY C. FRE 284 WOODSBOR
DONSTON, MARIA FRE 345 MIDDLETO
DOOBY, WILLIAM CEC 135 6TH E DI
DOOD, C.M. PRI 061 NOTTINGH
DOOD, DANIEL HAR 096 2ND DIST
DOODLING, MARIA BAL 349 13TH WAR
DOOGAN, ELIZA FRE 203 5TH E DI
DOOGAN, L.-BLACK FRE 200 5TH E DI
DOOGAN, LIKIA C.* TAL 008 EASTON D
DOOGAN, POLLY FRE 159 EMMITTSB
DOOGAN, VILOET FRE 162 EMMITTSB
DOOK, CAROLINE BAL 225 12TH WAR
DOOLAN, MICHAEL ALL 079 5TH E.D.
DOOLEG, WILLAIM ALL 136 4TH E.D.
DOOLEY, JEREMIAH ALL 224 CUMBERLA
DOOLEY, JOHN ALL 128 4TH E.D.
DOOLIN, JOHN HAR 058 1ST DIST
DOOLINS, WILLIAM B. CEC 206 7TH E DI
DOON, ALICE BAL 048 15TH WAR
DOONER, JAMES* BAL 081 10TH WAR
DOOR, ANN BAL 025 1ST WARD
DOOR, HENRY BAL 153 5TH WARD
DOOR, HESTER BAL 015 18TH WAR
DOOR, SARAH BAL 015 18TH WAR
DOOVE, THOMAS TAL 111 ST MICHA
DOPKE, MARY BAL 142 2ND DIST
DOPNER, H. BAL 270 2ND WARD
DOPNER, JOHN BAL 206 19TH WAR
DOR OTY, CATHERINE ALL 234 CUMBERLA
DOR OTY, HUGH ALL 234 CUMBERLA
DORAM, HANNAH QUE 244 5TH E DI
DORAM, JAMES HAR 198 3RD DIST
DORAN, CATHARINE BAL 162 2ND DIST
DORAN, HILDELIGHT HAR 074 1ST DIST
DORAN, JOHN BAL 460 8TH WARD
DORAN, MICHAEL BAL 372 3RD WARD
DORAN, PATRICK FRE 248 NEW MARK
DORAN, WILLAIM BAL 152 1ST WARD
DORANCIS, ELIZABETH BAL 092 1ST WARD
DORATALD, ANNA ALL 261 CUMBERLA
DORATHY, DAVID SOM 369 BRINKLEY
DORATHY, KENNY SOM 387 BRINKLEY
DORBAKER, WILLIAM BAL 132 16TH WAR
DORBAKER, WILLIAM H. BAL 182 16TH WAR
DORBY, MICHAEL BAL 299 17TH WAR
DORCAS, ANDREW BAL 056 1ST WARD
DORCEY, JOHN PRI 097 SPALDING
DORDEY, JOSEPH BAL 011 1ST WARD
DORE, AMANDA SOM 425 PRINCESS
DORE, EDMUND BAL 444 1ST DIST
DORE, LEWIS BAL 298 7TH WARD
DORE, ROBERT BAL 331 1ST DIST
DORE, SINGLETON CAR 198 4TH DIST
DORE, VACHEL CAR 197 4TH DIST
DOREMUS, SUSAN R. PRI 046 AQUASCO
DORENBERG, JOHN D. BAL 155 16TH WAR
DORENBERGER, WILLIAM WAS 057 2ND SUBD
DORERY, ELLEN BAL 152 11TH WAR
DORETHY, ELIZABETH BAL 065 1ST WARD
DORETT, REBECCA BAL 030 4TH WARD
DOREFF, MARY FRE 020 FREDERIC
DORGAN, ELIZABETH BAL 321 3RD WARD
DORGAN, GUSTAVUS BAL 019 1ST WARD
DORGAN, MARGARET BAL 058 15TH WAR
DORGES, MARY BAL 003 4TH WARD
DORGHTY, JAMES BAL 208 6TH DIST
DORHERTY, JOHN ANN 330 2ND DIST
DORING, CONRAD BAL 086 1ST WARD
DORITES, PELIA BAL 432 1ST DIST
DORITY, HUGH BAL 443 1ST DIST
DORITY, MARY BAL 361 8TH WARD
DORITY, WILLIAM BAL 154 2ND DIST
DORKLINS, ELIZABETH* BAL 413 3RD WARD
DORMAN, ALEXANDER BAL 059 10TH WAR
DORMAN, ANN SOM 477 TRAPP DI
DORMAN, ANN SOM 445 DAMES QU
DORMAN, CAROLINE SOM 473 TRAPPE D
DORMAN, D. BAL 150 1ST WARD
DORMAN, DANIEL HAR 062 1ST DIST
DORMAN, DENARD SOM 471 TRAPPE D
DORMAN, DENARD SOM 471 TRAPPE D
DORMAN, ELEANOR SOM 523 BARREN C
DORMAN, ELIZA SOM 430 PRINCESS
DORMAN, F.B. BAL 135 1ST WARD
DORMAN, FRANKLIN* BAL 015 4TH WARD
DORMAN, GEORGE SOM 443 DAMES QU
DORMAN, GEORGE SOM 440 DAMES QU
DORMAN, GEORGE SOM 442 DAMES QU
DORMAN, HANSON SOM 439 DAMES QU
DORMAN, HENRY SOM 450 DAMES QU
DORMAN, HETTY SOM 396 BRINKLEY
DORMAN, HETTY BAL 235 6TH WARD
DORMAN, J. BAL 136 1ST WARD
DORMAN, JAME G.* BAL 015 4TH WARD
DORMAN, JAMES BAL 058 1ST WARD
DORMAN, JAMES SOM 440 DAMES QU
DORMAN, JAMES SOM 467 TRAPPE D
DORMAN, JAMES WOR 181 6TH E DI
DORMAN, JAMES WOR 234 6TH E DI

Name	County	Page	District
DORMAN, JOHN	BAL	063	1ST WARD
DORMAN, JOHN	BAL	414	8TH WARD
DORMAN, JOSEPH	SOM	434	PRINCESS
DORMAN, JOSEPH	CEC	150	PORT DUP
DORMAN, LEVIN	WOR	194	8TH E DI
DORMAN, LEVIN	SOM	498	SALISBUR
DORMAN, MARIAH	WOR	340	1ST E DI
DORMAN, MARIAH	SOM	429	PRINCESS
DORMAN, MARTHA A.	SOM	443	DAMES QU
DORMAN, MATILDA	BAL	204	2ND WARD
DORMAN, MATTHIAS	SOM	527	QUANTICO
DORMAN, NELLY	SOM	472	TRAPPE D
DORMAN, NEMIAH O.	WOR	315	2ND E DI
DORMAN, REBECCA	SOM	443	DAMES QU
DORMAN, REBECCA	SOM	452	DAMES QU
DORMAN, ROBERT	SOM	523	BARREN C
DORMAN, SALLY	SOM	471	TRAPPE D
DORMAN, SOPHIA	MGM	320	CRACKLIN
DORMAN, THOMAS	BAL	020	4TH WARD
DORMAN, THOMAS	BAL	139	19TH WAR
DORMAN, THOMAS	SOM	482	TRAPP DI
DORMAN, WILLIAM	SOM	481	TRAPP DI
DORMAN, WILLIAM	SOM	440	DAMES QU
DORMAN, WILLIAM	WOR	167	6TH E DI
DORMAN, WILLIAM	CAR	223	5TH DIST
DORMAN, WILLIAM	MGM	320	CRACKLIN
DORMAN, ROONEY	BAL	116	1ST WARD
DORN, JOHN	BAL	373	13TH WAR
DORN, JOHN	BAL	296	17TH WAR
DORN, JOSEPH	BAL	258	6TH WARD
DORN, MARGARET	BAL	230	17TH WAR
DORNA, JOHN *	BAL	397	1ST DIST
DORNAN, RACHEL A.	BAL	103	10TH WAR
DORNBERT, LEANDER	BAL	082	10TH WAR
DORNEY, B.	BAL	292	12TH WAR
DORNEY, ISABELLA	BAL	029	4TH WARD
DORNEY, JOHN *	BAL	315	20TH WAR
DORNEY, JOSEPH	CAR	243	TANEYTOW
DORNEY, RICHARD	BAL	404	3RD WARD
DORNEY, THOAMS	BAL	315	20TH WAR
DORNIN, ANN	BAL	470	14TH WAR
DORNINGE, JOHN	FRE	384	PETERSVI
DORNN, CATHERINE	BAL	163	11TH WAR
DOROFELTER, JOHN *	BAL	165	2ND DIST
DOROLINGER, EVA	BAL	275	20TH WAR
DOROLINGER, PETER	BAL	275	20TH WAR
DOROTHY, ANDREW	BAL	415	14TH WAR
DOROTHY, ANNE	SOM	368	BRINKLEY
DOROTHY, BANJAMIN	SOM	369	BRINKLEY
DOROTHY, CHARLES M.	BAL	433	14TH WAR
DOROTHY, CHRISTIANA	SOM	386	BRINKLEY
DOROTHY, DENNIS	CAL	050	3RD DIST
DOROTHY, DICKERSON	SOM	369	BRINKLEY
DOROTHY, ELIJAH	SOM	392	BRINKLEY
DOROTHY, EMALINE	SOM	371	BRINKLEY
DOROTHY, ESTER	SOM	370	BRINKLEY
DOROTHY, GILLY	SOM	373	BRINKLEY
DOROTHY, HENRY	SOM	370	BRINKLEY
DOROTHY, ISAAC	SOM	363	BRINKLEY
DOROTHY, JACOB	SOM	369	BRINKLEY
DOROTHY, JAMES	SOM	407	DUBLIN D
DOROTHY, JEMIMA	SOM	373	BRINKLEY
DOROTHY, JESSE	SOM	368	BRINKLEY
DOROTHY, JOHN	SOM	372	BRINKLEY
DOROTHY, JOHN S.*	SOM	368	BRINKLEY
DOROTHY, LEVI	SOM	369	BRINKLEY
DOROTHY, MARY	SOM	372	BRINKLEY
DOROTHY, MARY	SOM	368	BRINKLEY
DOROTHY, NATHANIEL	SOM	369	BRINKLEY
DOROTHY, PATTY	SOM	371	BRINKLEY
DOROTHY, PATTY A.	SOM	373	BRINKLEY
DOROTHY, POLLY	SOM	369	BRINKLEY
DOROTHY, RACHAEL	SOM	368	BRINKLEY
DOROTHY, RESER*	SOM	383	BRINKLEY
DOROTHY, SARAH A.	ANN	437	HOWARD D
DOROTHY, SEVERN	SOM	369	BRINKLEY
DOROTHY, THOMAS	SOM	367	BRINKLEY
DOROTHY, THOMAS	SOM	385	BRINKLEY
DOROTHY, THOMAS W.	SOM	383	BRINKLEY
DOROTHY, VALRIAH	SOM	420	PRINCESS
DOROTHY, WILLIAM	SOM	370	BRINKLEY
DOROUGETY, MICHAEL	ST	276	3RD E DI
DORR, CASPER	BAL	214	17TH WAR
DORR, ELIZABETH	BAL	466	14TH WAR
DORR, GEORGE	BAL	313	7TH WARD
DORR, HENRY A.	CAR	215	5TH DIST
DORR, LEONARD	BAL	191	6TH WARD
DORRANCE, JAMES	WAS	101	2ND DIST
DORRANCY, GEORGE	BAL	092	1ST WARD
DORRELL, JAMES	BAL	143	16TH WAR
DORRELL, MARTHA	BAL	205	11TH WAR
DORRELL, NATHANIEL	BAL	204	6TH WARD
DORRELL, SUSAN A.	BAL	060	10TH WAR
DORRETY, ANN-BLACK	BAL	223	2ND WARD
DORRETY,ARRETTA E.	BAL	099	1ST WARD
DORRINGTON, LAURA	BAL	369	3RD WARD
DORRITEE, CHARLES *	BAL	265	7TH WARD
DORRITEE, JOHN T.	BAL	268	7TH WARD
DORRITEE, MARGARET A.	BAL	362	3RD WARD
DORRITEN, INTEN	BAL	269	20TH WAR
DORRITIE, MARY	BAL	191	6TH WARD
DORRITTY, PHILLIP	BAL	151	5TH WARD
DORRITY, MARY	BAL	103	5TH WARD
DORRITY, MARY	BAL	106	5TH WARD
DORRITY, WILLIAM	BAL	010	15TH WAR
DORROW, J.	BAL	118	1ST WARD
DORRSEY, JOHN *	BAL	315	20TH WAR
DORRY, FANNY	BAL	397	3RD WARD
DORRY, MARRY	BAL	040	1ST WARD
DORSCH, GOERGE	BAL	143	16TH WAR
DORSELY, SARAH	BAL	310	3RD WARD
DORSERS, ANN	BAL	009	EASTERN
DORSET, JOB	BAL	221	12TH WAR
DORSETT, H. MRS-	ANN	296	1ST DIST
DORSETT, J. HAWKINS	BAL	383	13TH WAR
DORSETT, NANNIE	PRI	056	AQUASCO
DORSETT, PATRICK	ALL	141	6TH E.D.
DORSETT, SAMUEL H.	ANN	296	1ST DIST
DORSETT, SUSAN	PRI	064	NOTTINGH
DORSETT, WILLIAM N.	PRI	066	NOTTINGH
DORSEY, A. E.	CAR	223	5TH DIST
DORSEY, AARON	KEN	249	2ND DIST
DORSEY, AARON	KEN	250	2ND DIST
DORSEY, ABRAHAM	ANN	474	HOWARD D
DORSEY, ABRAM	BAL	255	12TH WAR
DORSEY, ABRAM	ANN	518	HOWARD D
DORSEY, ADELINE	ANN	455	HOWARD D
DORSEY, ALEX	BAL	172	11TH WAR
DORSEY, ALEXANDER	BAL	370	3RD WARD
DORSEY, ALEXANDER	CAL	005	1ST DIST
DORSEY, ALEXANDER W.	CAR	273	WESTMINS
DORSEY, ALFRED	WAS	020	2ND SUBD
DORSEY, ALLEN	ANN	423	HOWARD D
DORSEY, ALLEN	ANN	507	HOWARD D
DORSEY, AMANDA	BAL	230	12TH WAR
DORSEY, AMELIA M.	BAL	168	16TH WAR
DORSEY, AMOS	ANN	474	HOWARD D
DORSEY, AMOS	MGM	345	CLARKSBU
DORSEY, ANDREW	ANN	520	HOWARD D
DORSEY, ANDREW	BAL	143	1ST WARD
DORSEY, ANDREW	BAL	064	1ST WARD
DORSEY, ANDREW-BLACK	FRE	197	5TH E DI
DORSEY, ANN	ANN	509	HOWARD D
DORSEY, ANN	BAL	160	6TH WARD
DORSEY, ANN M.	BAL	142	16TH WAR
DORSEY, ANN M.	BAL	126	18TH WAR
DORSEY, ANN MISS-	BAL	315	20TH WAR
DORSEY, ANN S.	CAR	229	5TH DIST
DORSEY, ANNE	BAL	100	10TH WAR
DORSEY, ASBERRY	FRE	101	FREDERIC
DORSEY, ASHSAH	CAR	203	4TH DIST
DORSEY, AUGUSTA	BAL	139	5TH WARD
DORSEY, AUTHER	BAL	293	7TH WARD
DORSEY, AXIA	MGM	377	ROCKERLE
DORSEY, BARBARY B.	ST	288	2ND E DI
DORSEY, BASIL-BLACK	FRE	431	8TH E DI
DORSEY, BAZZELL E.	CAR	229	5TH DIST
DORSEY, BEN H.	ANN	447	HOWARD D
DORSEY, BEN W.	PRI	095	SPALDING
DORSEY, BENJAMIN	WAS	004	WILLIAMS
DORSEY, BENJAMIN H.	ANN	412	HOWARD D
DORSEY, CABEL	ANN	465	HOWARD D
DORSEY, CALEB	BAL	063	10TH WAR
DORSEY, CALEB	ANN	496	HOWARD D
DORSEY, CALEB	ANN	504	HOWARD D
DORSEY, CALEB-MULATTO	FRE	438	8TH E DI
DORSEY, CAROLINE	HAR	077	BEL AIR
DORSEY, CAROLINE	BAL	267	12TH WAR
DORSEY, CAROLINE-MULATTO	FRE	049	FREDERIC
DORSEY, CASSANDA-BLACK	FRE	226	BUCKEYST
DORSEY, CASSEY	BAL	058	15TH WAR
DORSEY, CATHARINE	ANN	515	HOWARD D
DORSEY, CATHARINE	ANN	486	HOWARD D
DORSEY, CATHARINE	CAR	227	5TH DIST
DORSEY, CATHARINE	CAR	281	7TH DIST
DORSEY, CATHARINE	BAL	368	13TH WAR
DORSEY, CATHARINE C.	ANN	497	HOWARD D
DORSEY, CECELIA	BAL	180	16TH WAR
DORSEY, CECELIA	BAL	238	6TH WARD
DORSEY, CECELIA-BLACK	ST	320	4TH E DI
DORSEY, CHARITY	WAS	135	HAGERSTO
DORSEY, CHARLES	ANN	514	HOWARD D
DORSEY, CHARLES	ANN	471	HOWARD D
DORSEY, CHARLES	BAL	201	19TH WAR
DORSEY, CHARLES	BAL	201	19TH WAR
DORSEY, CHARLES	FRE	243	NEW MARK
DORSEY, CHARLES	FRE	268	NEW MARK
DORSEY, CHARLES W.	ANN	465	HOWARD D
DORSEY, CHARLES-MULATTO	FRE	438	8TH E DI
DORSEY, CHARLOTTE	ANN	506	HOWARD D
DORSEY, CHARLOTTE A.	ANN	456	HOWARD D
DORSEY, CHLOE	WAS	157	HAGERSTO
DORSEY, CLEGGETT	FRE	439	8TH E DI
DORSEY, CLEMENT	CAL	025	2ND DIST
DORSEY, CLEMENT	WAS	056	2ND SUBD
DORSEY, CLEMENT H.	CAL	006	1ST DIST
DORSEY, COMFORT W.	BAL	111	10TH WAR
DORSEY, CORNEALUS	BAL	373	1ST DIST
DORSEY, DANIEL	ANN	518	HOWARD D
DORSEY, DANIEL	BAL	045	9TH WARD
DORSEY, DAVID	ANN	498	HOWARD D
DORSEY, DAVID	ANN	430	HOWARD D
DORSEY, DAVID	BAL	227	6TH WARD
DORSEY, DAVID	CAL	015	1ST DIST
DORSEY, DAVID A.	CAR	230	5TH DIST
DORSEY, DAVID L.	FRE	076	FREDERIC
DORSEY, DENIS	CAR	215	5TH DIST
DORSEY, DINAH	ANN	329	2ND DIST
DORSEY, E.	BAL	130	1ST WARD
DORSEY, EDWARD	ANN	320	2ND DIST
DORSEY, EDWARD	BAL	151	1ST WARD
DORSEY, EDWARD	ANN	462	HOWARD D
DORSEY, EDWARD	BAL	180	16TH WAR
DORSEY, EDWARD	BAL	249	1ST DIST
DORSEY, EDWARD	BAL	193	19TH WAR
DORSEY, EDWARD	WAS	156	HAGERSTO
DORSEY, EDWARD H.	BAL	029	9TH WARD
DORSEY, EDWARD L.	PRI	073	MARLBROU
DORSEY, EDWIN	BAL	038	9TH WARD
DORSEY, EDWIN	ANN	431	HOWARD D
DORSEY, ELICK	BAL	157	2ND DIST
DORSEY, ELIZA	WAS	003	WILLIAMS
DORSEY, ELIZA	BAL	216	11TH WAR
DORSEY, ELIZA A.	ANN	486	HOWARD D
DORSEY, ELIZA D.	BAL	032	18TH WAR
DORSEY, ELIZABETH	HAR	100	2ND DIST
DORSEY, ELIZABETH	FRE	446	8TH E DI
DORSEY, ELIZABETH	BAL	267	20TH WAR
DORSEY, ELIZABETH	MGM	351	BERRYS D
DORSEY, ELIZABETH	FRE	168	EMMITTSB
DORSEY, ELIZABETH	BAL	300	12TH WAR
DORSEY, ELIZABETH	BAL	343	3RD WARD
DORSEY, ELIZABETH	BAL	112	5TH WARD
DORSEY, ELIZABETH	BAL	459	8TH WARD
DORSEY, ELLEN	BAL	189	11TH WAR
DORSEY, ELLEN	BAL	342	7TH WARD
DORSEY, ELLEN	BAL	086	2ND DIST
DORSEY, ELLEN	ANN	462	HOWARD D
DORSEY, ELLEN	BAL	254	1ST DIST
DORSEY, ELLEN	BAL	087	18TH WAR
DORSEY, ELLEN	BAL	197	11TH WAR
DORSEY, EMILY	BAL	343	13TH WAR
DORSEY, EMILY L.	BAL	061	4TH WARD
DORSEY, EMMA	FRE	424	8TH E DI
DORSEY, EMMA	BAL	211	6TH WARD
DORSEY, EMMA C.	ANN	373	4TH DIST
DORSEY, EMORY	BAL	120	1ST WARD
DORSEY, ENOCH	BAL	212	6TH WARD
DORSEY, EPHRAIM	MGM	348	BERRYS D
DORSEY, ESSEX	ANN	324	2ND DIST
DORSEY, EZRA	BAL	186	11TH WAR
DORSEY, F.	WAS	021	2ND SUBD
DORSEY, FERDINAND	CAR	229	5TH DIST
DORSEY, FRANCES	BAL	073	15TH WAR
DORSEY, FRANCIS	BAL	280	2ND WARD
DORSEY, FRANK	BAL	093	10TH WAR
DORSEY, FREDERICK	CAR	320	1ST DIST
DORSEY, FREDERICK	WAS	132	HAGERSTO
DORSEY, G. P.	BAL	372	1ST DIST
DORSEY, GEORGE	BAL	157	2ND DIST
DORSEY, GEORGE	BAL	227	6TH WARD
DORSEY, GEORGE	BAL	128	2ND DIST
DORSEY, GEORGE	FRE	120	CREAGERS
DORSEY, GEORGE A.	CAR	230	5TH DIST
DORSEY, GEORGE W.	CAL	001	1ST DIST
DORSEY, GEORGE W.	CAL	038	2ND DIST
DORSEY, GEORGE W.	BAL	402	1ST DIST
DORSEY, GEORGE-BLACK	CAR	397	2ND DIST
DORSEY, GOERGE	ANN	437	HOWARD D
DORSEY, GRACE	PRI	074	MARLBROU
DORSEY, GRACEY	BAL	132	16TH WAR
DORSEY, GUSTAVUS	CAR	369	9TH DIST
DORSEY, H.	BAL	311	20TH WAR
DORSEY, H.	BAL	316	12TH WAR
DORSEY, HAGAR	FRE	255	NEW MARK
DORSEY, HAGAR	FRE	430	8TH E DI
DORSEY, HAMMOND	ANN	438	HOWARD D
DORSEY, HANANH A.	CAL	029	2ND DIST
DORSEY, HANNAH	FRE	028	FREDERIC
DORSEY, HANNAH	BAL	246	20TH WAR
DORSEY, HANNAH	BAL	283	12TH WAR
DORSEY, HANNAH	WAS	154	HAGERSTO
DORSEY, HARRIET	PRI	095	SPALDING
DORSEY, HARRIET-BLACK	FRE	447	8TH E DI
DORSEY, HARRIETT	BAL	125	11TH WAR
DORSEY, HARRIETT	HAR	077	BEL AIR
DORSEY, HARRISON	BAL	230	12TH WAR
DORSEY, HARRY W.	FRE	248	NEW MARK
DORSEY, HENRY	BAL	262	20TH WAR
DORSEY, HENRY	BAL	434	14TH WAR
DORSEY, HENRY	BAL	407	14TH WAR
DORSEY, HENRY	BAL	257	12TH WAR
DORSEY, HENRY	BAL	267	12TH WAR
DORSEY, HENRY	BAL	289	12TH WAR
DORSEY, HENRY C.	MGM	362	BERRYS D
DORSEY, HENRY L.	SOM	352	BRINKLEY
DORSEY, HENSON	MGM	370	BERRYS D
DORSEY, HESTER	BAL	357	13TH WAR
DORSEY, HESTER	BAL	053	15TH WAR
DORSEY, HESTER	ANN	501	HOWARD D
DORSEY, HETTY	BAL	277	20TH WAR
DORSEY, HILLEARY	CAL	031	2ND DIST
DORSEY, HORACE	BAL	205	19TH WAR
DORSEY, HUMPHREY	ANN	497	HOWARD D
DORSEY, ISAAC H.	SOM	404	BRINKLEY
DORSEY, ISAAH	BAL	255	1ST DIST
DORSEY, ISABELLA	BAL	065	4TH WARD
DORSEY, ISABELLA H.	FRE	448	8TH E DI
DORSEY, J. E.	BAL	332	1ST DIST
DORSEY, J.C.	WAS	136	HAGERSTO
DORSEY, JACKSON	BAL	074	10TH WAR
DORSEY, JACKSON	CAR	230	5TH DIST
DORSEY, JACOB	BAL	216	11TH WAR
DORSEY, JACOB	BAL	056	10TH WAR
DORSEY, JACOB	BAL	238	12TH WAR
DORSEY, JACOB	BAL	335	7TH WARD
DORSEY, JAEMS	BAL	368	13TH WAR
DORSEY, JAMES	BAL	233	20TH WAR
DORSEY, JAMES	MGM	368	BERRYS D
DORSEY, JAMES	CAL	045	3RD DIST
DORSEY, JAMES	BAL	177	16TH WAR
DORSEY, JAMES	ALL	156	6TH E.D.
DORSEY, JAMES	WAS	154	HAGERSTO
DORSEY, JAMES B.	BAL	243	2ND WARD
DORSEY, JAMES B.	BAL	428	14TH WAR
DORSEY, JAMES E.	BAL	380	1ST DIST
DORSEY, JAMES L.	BAL	049	15TH WAR
DORSEY, JAMES O.	BAL	406	8TH WARD
DORSEY, JAMES Y.	CAL	032	2ND DIST
DORSEY, JAMES-MULATTO	CAR	362	9TH DIST
DORSEY, JANE	BAL	358	13TH WAR
DORSEY, JANE	BAL	255	17TH WAR
DORSEY, JARRETT	WAS	156	HAGERSTO
DORSEY, JASON R.	MGM	320	CRACKLIN
DORSEY, JENET	CAR	367	9TH DIST
DORSEY, JENNEY	MGM	368	BERRYS D
DORSEY, JERRE S.	BAL	334	13TH WAR
DORSEY, JESSE	FRE	114	CREAGERS
DORSEY, JOHN	MGM	331	CRACKLIN
DORSEY, JOHN	FRE	180	5TH E DI
DORSEY, JOHN	HAR	001	1ST DIST
DORSEY, JOHN	HAR	035	1ST DIST
DORSEY, JOHN	CAR	366	9TH DIST
DORSEY, JOHN	CAL	021	2ND DIST
DORSEY, JOHN	BAL	160	11TH WAR
DORSEY, JOHN	BAL	207	19TH WAR
DORSEY, JOHN	CAR	229	5TH DIST
DORSEY, JOHN	FRE	262	NEW MARK
DORSEY, JOHN	FRE	275	NEW MARK
DORSEY, JOHN	DOR	413	1ST DIST
DORSEY, JOHN	BAL	168	11TH WAR
DORSEY, JOHN	ANN	506	HOWARD D
DORSEY, JOHN	ANN	499	HOWARD D
DORSEY, JOHN	BAL	460	1ST DIST
DORSEY, JOHN	BAL	092	15TH WAR
DORSEY, JOHN	BAL	286	1ST DIST
DORSEY, JOHN	BAL	076	2ND DIST
DORSEY, JOHN A.	ANN	516	HOWARD D
DORSEY, JOHN G.	ANN	496	HOWARD D
DORSEY, JOHN H.	BAL	175	6TH WARD
DORSEY, JOHN R.	ANN	435	HOWARD D
DORSEY, JOHN T.	BAL	159	16TH WAR
DORSEY, JOHN T.	CAL	038	2ND DIST
DORSEY, JOHN T.	BAL	446	14TH WAR
DORSEY, JOHN T.B.	ANN	458	HOWARD D
DORSEY, JOHN T.W.	ANN	466	HOWARD D
DORSEY, JOHN W.	BAL	465	14TH WAR
DORSEY, JOHN W.	FRE	449	8TH E DI
DORSEY, JOHNANNAH	CAR	215	5TH DIST
DORSEY, JOHNATHAN	CAR	230	5TH DIST
DORSEY, JOSEPH J.	BAL	157	19TH WAR
DORSEY, JOSHUA	CAR	228	5TH DIST
DORSEY, JOSHUA	BAL	407	14TH WAR
DORSEY, JOSHUA	BAL	436	1ST DIST
DORSEY, JOSHUA W.	ANN	448	HOWARD D
DORSEY, JOSHUA W.	MGM	325	CRACKLIN
DORSEY, JUDITH MRS-	ANN	300	1ST DIST
DORSEY, JUDY	ANN	512	HOWARD D
DORSEY, JULIA	BAL	148	2ND DIST
DORSEY, JULIA	MGM	327	CRACKLIN
DORSEY, JULIA	FRE	066	FREDERIC
DORSEY, KIT-BLACK	ST	309	1ST E DI
DORSEY, KITTY	BAL	449	14TH WAR
DORSEY, LANCELOT D.	ANN	496	HOWARD D
DORSEY, LEMUEL	BAL	302	7TH WARD
DORSEY, LEVI	BAL	042	9TH WARD
DORSEY, LEVI-BLACK	FRE	428	8TH E DI
DORSEY, LEVIN H.	CAR	362	9TH DIST
DORSEY, LEWIS	HAR	033	1ST DIST
DORSEY, LEWIS	ANN	491	HOWARD D

Name	County	Page	District
DORSEY, LITTLETON	SOM	353	BRINKLEY
DORSEY, LLOYD	BAL	100	5TH WARD
DORSEY, LLOYD	MGM	318	CRACKLIN
DORSEY, LORENZO	BAL	377	13TH WAR
DORSEY, LOT	FRE	097	FREDERIC
DORSEY, LOUISA	HAR	119	2ND DIST
DORSEY, LOUISA	BAL	002	18TH WAR
DORSEY, LOUISA	BAL	273	12TH WAR
DORSEY, LOUISA-MULATO	FRE	437	8TH E DI
DORSEY, LOUIZA	BAL	120	5TH WARD
DORSEY, LOYD	FRE	058	FREDERIC
DORSEY, LUCY	FRE	057	FREDERIC
DORSEY, LUCY	BAL	475	14TH WAR
DORSEY, LUCY	FRE	271	NEW MARK
DORSEY, LUCY	BAL	059	10TH WAR
DORSEY, LUCY	BAL	076	2ND DIST
DORSEY, LUTHER	ANN	472	HOWARD D
DORSEY, LYDIA	ANN	484	HOWARD D
DORSEY, LYCIA-BLACK	FRE	438	8TH E DI
DORSEY, MALINDA	KEN	301	3RD DIST
DORSEY, MARCILLINA	BAL	215	11TH WAR
DORSEY, MARGARET	CAR	189	4TH DIST
DORSEY, MARGARET	BAL	421	14TH WAR
DORSEY, MARGARET	BAL	378	1ST DIST
DORSEY, MARGARET	ANN	277	ANNAPOLI
DORSEY, MARGARET A.	ANN	522	HOWARD D
DORSEY, MARGARETT A.	BAL	129	11TH WAR
DORSEY, MARIA	BAL	105	5TH WARD
DORSEY, MARIA	ANN	487	HOWARD D
DORSEY, MARIA	ANN	485	HOWARD D
DORSEY, MARIA	BAL	311	12TH WAR
DORSEY, MARIA A.	BAL	321	3RD WARD
DORSEY, MARTHA	BAL	302	12TH WAR
DORSEY, MARTHA	BAL	172	11TH WAR
DORSEY, MARTHA	CAL	030	2ND DIST
DORSEY, MARTHA	MGM	331	CRACKLIN
DORSEY, MARY	MGM	337	CRACKLIN
DORSEY, MARY	MGM	347	BERRYS D
DORSEY, MARY	BAL	355	13TH WAR
DORSEY, MARY	FRE	006	FREDERIC
DORSEY, MARY	BAL	114	15TH WAR
DORSEY, MARY	BAL	113	15TH WAR
DORSEY, MARY	ANN	496	HOWARD D
DORSEY, MARY	ANN	416	HOWARD D
DORSEY, MARY	ANN	381	4TH DIST
DORSEY, MARY	BAL	216	6TH DIST
DORSEY, MARY	PRI	026	VANSVILL
DORSEY, MARY A.	ANN	443	HOWARD D
DORSEY, MARY A.	BAL	081	15TH WAR
DORSEY, MARY A.	BAL	121	16TH WAR
DORSEY, MARY A.	BAL	074	18TH WAR
DORSEY, MARY ANN	ALL	220	CUMBERLA
DORSEY, MARY C.	BAL	261	6TH WARD
DORSEY, MARY E.	CEC	175	7TH E DI
DORSEY, MARY E.	FRE	273	NEW MARK
DORSEY, MARY E.	SOM	352	BRINKLEY
DORSEY, MARY J.	BAL	316	20TH WAR
DORSEY, MARY J.	ALL	212	CUMBERLA
DORSEY, MARY P.	ANN	443	HOWARD D
DORSEY, MARY-BLACK	FRE	044	FREDERIC
DORSEY, MARY-BLACK	CAR	398	2ND DIST
DORSEY, MATHEW	BAL	291	3RD WARD
DORSEY, MATILDA	ANN	518	HOWARD D
DORSEY, MATILDA	BAL	116	15TH WAR
DORSEY, MATILDA	BAL	348	13TH WAR
DORSEY, MATTHEW	BAL	415	14TH WAR
DORSEY, MOORA ANN	CAL	022	2ND DIST
DORSEY, MECHAEL	BAL	459	1ST DIST
DORSEY, MECME	BAL	300	1ST DIST
DORSEY, MICAHEL	FRE	125	CREAGERS
DORSEY, MICHAEL	CAL	031	2ND DIST
DORSEY, MICHAEL	BAL	019	1ST WARD
DORSEY, MICHAEL	BAL	120	16TH WAR
DORSEY, MICHAEL	BAL	301	12TH WAR
DORSEY, MICHAEL G.	ANN	472	HOWARD D
DORSEY, MILLIA	BAL	153	11TH WAR
DORSEY, MINNA	ANN	466	HOWARD D
DORSEY, MORTIMER	ANN	487	HOWARD D
DORSEY, NANCY	BAL	140	11TH WAR
DORSEY, NATHAN	ANN	442	HOWARD D
DORSEY, NATHAN	BAL	110	15TH WAR
DORSEY, NATHAN	WAS	205	1ST DIST
DORSEY, NATHAN	TAL	007	EASTON D
DORSEY, NATHANIEL	CEC	173	6TH E DI
DORSEY, NELLY-BLACK	FRE	018	FREDERIC
DORSEY, NICHOLAS	FRE	445	8TH E DI
DORSEY, NICHOLAS	CAR	219	5TH DIST
DORSEY, NICHOLAS	ANN	472	HOWARD D
DORSEY, NICHOLAS B.	ANN	485	HOWARD D
DORSEY, NICHOLAS O.	CAR	215	5TH DIST
DORSEY, NOAH	ANN	373	4TH DIST
DORSEY, OWEN	FRE	133	CREAGERS
DORSEY, OWEN	MGM	336	CRACKLIN
DORSEY, PATRICK	CAR	374	9TH DIST
DORSEY, PERRY	BAL	289	17TH WAR
DORSEY, PETER	BAL	459	8TH WARD
DORSEY, PETER	PRI	039	VANSVILL
DORSEY, PHILEMON	ANN	487	HOWARD D
DORSEY, PHILIP	ANN	472	HOWARD D
DORSEY, PHILIP	ANN	350	3RD DIST
DORSEY, PHILIP	ANN	355	3RD DIST
DORSEY, PHOEBE	ANN	454	HOWARD D
DORSEY, PHOEBE	ANN	491	HOWARD D
DORSEY, POLLY	BAL	211	6TH DIST
DORSEY, POTTINGER	FRE	249	NEW MARK
DORSEY, PRISCILLA	BAL	089	15TH WAR
DORSEY, PRISCILLA-MULATTO	FRE	436	8TH E DI
DORSEY, R. W.	BAL	332	1ST DIST
DORSEY, R.J.	BAL	244	12TH WAR
DORSEY, RACHAEL	FRE	448	8TH E DI
DORSEY, REESE-BLACK	CAR	383	2ND DIST
DORSEY, REMUS	MGM	318	CRACKLIN
DORSEY, REUBEN M.	ANN	469	HOWARD D
DORSEY, RICHARD	BAL	439	8TH WARD
DORSEY, RICHARD	BAL	314	1ST DIST
DORSEY, RICHARD	BAL	094	15TH WAR
DORSEY, RICHARD	CAR	400	2ND DIST
DORSEY, RICHARD	BAL	153	11TH WAR
DORSEY, RICHARD	FRE	046	FREDERIC
DORSEY, RICHARD B.	BAL	196	11TH WAR
DORSEY, RICHARD H.	BAL	211	6TH WARD
DORSEY, ROBERT H.	SOM	356	BRINKLEY
DORSEY, ROBERT L.	CAL	006	1ST DIST
DORSEY, ROBY-MULATTO	FRE	438	8TH E DI
DORSEY, RODERICK	FRE	248	NEW MARK
DORSEY, RODERICK	ANN	507	HOWARD D
DORSEY, RODERICK-BLACK	FRE	189	5TH E DI
DORSEY, ROSE	BAL	160	6TH WARD
DORSEY, RUBEN	ANN	498	HOWARD D
DORSEY, RUBEN	ANN	457	HOWARD D
DORSEY, RUTH	ANN	496	HOWARD D
DORSEY, SALLEY A.	BAL	379	1ST DIST
DORSEY, SAMUEL	ANN	518	HOWARD D
DORSEY, SAMUEL	ANN	447	HOWARD D
DORSEY, SAMUEL	BAL	144	1ST WARD
DORSEY, SAMUEL	FRE	254	NEW MARK
DORSEY, SAMUEL	CAR	228	5TH DIST
DORSEY, SAMUEL O.	MGM	332	CRACKLIN
DORSEY, SAMUEL S.	ANN	473	HOWARD D
DORSEY, SAMUEL Y.	CAL	042	3RD DIST
DORSEY, SAMUEL Y.	CAL	035	2ND DIST
DORSEY, SARAH	BAL	141	11TH WAR
DORSEY, SARAH	MGM	332	CRACKLIN
DORSEY, SARAH	FRE	270	NEW MARK
DORSEY, SARAH	HAR	075	BEL AIR
DORSEY, SARAH	BAL	436	14TH WAR
DORSEY, SARAH	BAL	439	14TH WAR
DORSEY, SARAH	BAL	016	9TH WARD
DORSEY, SARAH	BAL	190	11TH WAR
DORSEY, SARAH	BAL	157	16TH WAR
DORSEY, SARAH	BAL	164	16TH WAR
DORSEY, SCIPIO	WAS	157	HAGERSTO
DORSEY, SCOTT	FRE	100	FREDERIC
DORSEY, SERENA	BAL	173	15TH WAR
DORSEY, SERENE	FRE	108	CREAGERS
DORSEY, SIDNEY	FRE	130	CREAGERS
DORSEY, SOLOMON	ANN	492	HOWARD D
DORSEY, SOPHIA	BAL	070	10TH WAR
DORSEY, STEPHEN	ANN	430	HOWARD D
DORSEY, STEPHEN B.	ANN	494	HOWARD D
DORSEY, STEWART	BAL	036	1ST WARD
DORSEY, SUSAN	BAL	212	6TH DIST
DORSEY, SUSAN	BAL	186	11TH WAR
DORSEY, SUSAN	BAL	274	7TH WARD
DORSEY, SUSAN	ANN	291	ANNAPOLI
DORSEY, SUSAN	BAL	147	11TH WAR
DORSEY, SUSAN	BAL	460	14TH WAR
DORSEY, SUSAN	WAS	136	HAGERSTO
DORSEY, SUSAN-BLACK	CAR	372	9TH DIST
DORSEY, SUSANER	HAR	172	3RD DIST
DORSEY, SUSANNA	ANN	457	HOWARD D
DORSEY, TABY	SOM	427	PRINCESS
DORSEY, THOMAS	BAL	404	14TH WAR
DORSEY, THOMAS	BAL	259	20TH WAR
DORSEY, THOMAS	ALL	052	10TH E.D
DORSEY, THOMAS	BAL	092	5TH WARD
DORSEY, THOMAS	BAL	304	12TH WAR
DORSEY, THOMAS	WAS	133	HAGERSTO
DORSEY, THOMAS	WAS	154	HAGERSTO
DORSEY, THOMAS	WAS	027	2ND SUBD
DORSEY, THOMAS B.	ANN	470	HOWARD D
DORSEY, THOMAS H.	ANN	321	2ND DIST
DORSEY, THORNTON	CAL	039	2ND DIST
DORSEY, TRUMAN	BAL	102	10TH WAR
DORSEY, UPTON	ANN	482	HOWARD D
DORSEY, VACHEL	ANN	435	HOWARD D
DORSEY, VIOLET	BAL	121	2ND DIST
DORSEY, VIRGIL	HAR	138	2ND DIST
DORSEY, VIRGINIA	BAL	359	13TH WAR
DORSEY, W. H. E.	BAL	112	10TH WAR
DORSEY, WALTER	ANN	303	1ST DIST
DORSEY, WALTER	ANN	500	HOWARD D
DORSEY, WASH	BAL	297	1ST DIST
DORSEY, WASHINGTON	BAL	333	13TH WAR
DORSEY, WASHINGTON	HAR	033	1ST DIST
DORSEY, WILLAIM	HAR	100	2ND DIST
DORSEY, WILLAIM	CAL	026	2ND DIST
DORSEY, WILLAIM	FRE	273	NEW MARK
DORSEY, WILLIAM	FRE	274	NEW MARK
DORSEY, WILLIAM	CAL	057	3RD DIST
DORSEY, WILLIAM	BAL	435	14TH WAR
DORSEY, WILLIAM	HAR	124	2ND DIST
DORSEY, WILLIAM	CAR	228	5TH DIST
DORSEY, WILLIAM	CAR	200	4TH DIST
DORSEY, WILLIAM	BAL	218	6TH DIST
DORSEY, WILLIAM	ANN	285	ANNAPOLI
DORSEY, WILLIAM	BAL	127	1ST WARD
DORSEY, WILLIAM	BAL	456	8TH WARD
DORSEY, WILLIAM	SOM	352	BRINKLEY
DORSEY, WILLIAM	PRI	027	VANSVILL
DORSEY, WILLIAM -BLACK	FRE	221	BUCKEYST
DORSEY, WILLIAM A.	FRE	423	8TH E DI
DORSEY, WILLIAM B.	ANN	437	HOWARD D
DORSEY, WILLIAM H.	ANN	376	4TH DIST
DORSEY, WILLIAM H.	BAL	093	1ST WARD
DORSEY, WILLIAM H.	BAL	142	16TH WAR
DORSEY, WILLIAM N.	ANN	391	4TH DIST
DORSEY, WILLIAM-MULATTO	BAL	176	2ND WARD
DORSEY, WILLIAM-MULATTO	FRE	435	8TH E DI
DORSEY, WILLIAM-MULATTO	FRE	438	8TH E DI
DORSEY, WOLHAM	FRE	269	NEW MARK
DORSEY, ZULICKA	BAL	097	10TH WAR
DORSEY,ALICE	BAL	066	2ND DIST
DORSEY,E.	BAL	114	1ST WARD
DORSEY,MATILDA-MULATTO	FRE	438	8TH E DI
DORSH, WILLIAM	WAS	126	HAGERSTO
DORSIN, ELLEN	WAS	095	2ND SUBD
DORSON, THOMAS	HAR	180	3RD DIST
DORST, MICHAEL	BAL	203	2ND WARD
DORSY, GEORGE	FRE	249	NEW MARK
DORSY, JOHN	CEC	174	6TH E DI
DORSY, JOHN	CEC	064	1ST E DI
DORSY, LEWIS E.	CEC	149	PORT DUP
DORSY, MARY	CEC	173	5TH E DI
DORSY, SAMUEL A.	CEC	154	PORT DUP
DORSY, TOBIAS	CEC	039	CHESAPEA
DORTHY, JOHN	CHA	257	MIDDLETO
DORTON, JAMES	ALL	051	10TH E.D
DORY, BENJAMIN B.	BAL	335	3RD WARD
DORYHURTZ, CHARLES	BAL	117	11TH WAR
DORYLURS, JOSEPH	BAL	238	20TH WAR
DOSCH, ANTHONY*	BAL	400	3RD WARD
DOSE, JOHN	BAL	416	14TH WAR
DOSEAN, MADAM	BAL	364	13TH WAR
DOSEY, JOSEPH	BAL	009	1ST WARD
DOSH, MICHAEL	BAL	373	13TH WAR
DOSHELD, BENMAMIN D.	DOR	374	1ST DIST
DOSSAGE, SAMUEL	ALL	184	9TH E.D.
DOSTIGAN, ANN	BAL	076	4TH WARD
DOTCHERMANN, CONRAD	BAL	007	15TH WAR
DOTE, JOHN	FRE	167	EMMITTSB
DOTHARD, JAMES	KEN	311	3RD DIST
DOTSON, ELIZABETH	CAL	012	1ST DIST
DOTSON, ELLEN	PRI	101	SPALDING
DOTSON, HEMRY	ANN	337	3RD DIST
DOTSON, JOHN	PRI	049	AQUASCO
DOTSON, JOHN	BAL	135	18TH WAR
DOTSON, JOHN H.	ANN	308	1ST DIST
DOTSON, JSOEPH	BAL	093	15TH WAR
DOTSON, LETITIA	CHA	228	ALLENS F
DOTSON, THOMAS	ANN	342	3RD DIST
DOTSON, ZECK	ANN	491	HOWARD D
DOTSY, CHLOE	BAL	062	2ND DIST
DOTTEIER, JOSEPH	CAR	258	3RD DIST
DOTTEN, JOSEPH	BAL	169	2ND DIST
DOTTERER, HENRY	CAR	259	3RD DIST
DOTTERER, JOHN	CAR	294	7TH DIST
DOTTERER, JOHN	CAR	319	1ST DIST
DOTTERER, JOSHUA	CAR	287	7TH DIST
DOTY, JOHN	FRE	248	NEW MARK
DOTZHOUR, MICHEAL	CAR	412	2ND DIST
DOUB, ABRAHAM	FRE	341	MIDDLETO
DOUB, CATHARINE	FRE	374	CATOCTIN
DOUB, CATHERINE	FRE	073	FREDERIC
DOUB, DAVID	FRE	341	MIDDLETO
DOUB, ENOS	FRE	347	MIDDLETO
DOUB, ESTHER	FRE	059	FREDERIC
DOUB, EZRA	FRE	059	FREDERIC
DOUB, EZRA	WAS	192	1ST DIST
DOUBER, JOHN	ALL	225	CUMBERLA
DOUBLE, ANDREW	WAS	193	1ST DIST
DOUBLE, JACOB	WAS	031	2ND SUBD
DOUBLE, JACOB	FRE	399	JEFFERSO
DOUBLE, JONATHAN	WAS	149	HAGERSTO
DOUBLE, LAURA	FRE	399	JEFFERSO
DOUBLE, MARIAH	WAS	059	2ND SUBD
DOUBLE, MARY C.	FRE	400	JEFFERSO
DOUBLE, RUAN	WAS	208	1ST DIST
DOUCEY, SHADRICK	HAR	146	3RD DIST
DOUCK, MARY J.	BAL	028	2ND DIST
DOUCK, RUTH	BAL	028	2ND DIST
DOUD, CHARLOTTE	BAL	173	19TH WAR
DOUD, F.A.	ALL	256	CUMBERLA
DOUD, JOHN	BAL	040	2ND DIST
DOUD, JOHN	MGM	382	ROCKERLE
DOUD, JOSEPH	BAL	182	19TH WAR
DOUD, MARIE L.	BAL	174	19TH WAR
DOUD, THOMAS	BAL	336	13TH WAR
DOUDEN, SANTE	CEC	072	5TH E DI
DOUDLE, ISAAC	BAL	399	14TH WAR
DOUDOF, BALLY *	ANN	376	4TH DIST
DOUDY, MARY-BLACK	BAL	184	2ND WARD
DOUELY, JOHN *	BAL	163	2ND DIST
DOUFFSTATER, LAWRENCE	BAL	106	2ND DIST
DOUGAN, BARNEY	WAS	162	HAGERSTO
DOUGAN, EDWARD	BAL	150	2ND DIST
DOUGAN, ELIZABETH	ALL	103	5TH E.D.
DOUGAN, MARY	ALL	215	CUMBERLA
DOUGAN, PHILLIP	KEN	238	2ND DIST
DOUGAN, WILLIAM	ALL	022	2ND E.D.
DOUGHARTY, FRANCIS	CEC	117	4TH E DI
DOUGHER, MARGARET	BAL	409	3RD WARD
DOUGHERITY, HETTY	BAL	022	18TH WAR
DOUGHERTY, AMRTIN	BAL	408	14TH WAR
DOUGHERTY, ANN	BAL	168	11TH WAR
DOUGHERTY, BARNEY	BAL	145	1ST WARD
DOUGHERTY, BIDDY	BAL	470	14TH WAR
DOUGHERTY, CATHERINE	ALL	072	5TH E.D.
DOUGHERTY, CATHERINE	BAL	304	7TH WARD
DOUGHERTY, CHARLES	BAL	175	11TH WAR
DOUGHERTY, CHARLES M.	BAL	470	14TH WAR
DOUGHERTY, CONSTANTINE	BAL	287	7TH WARD
DOUGHERTY, DANIEL	CEC	038	CHESAPEA
DOUGHERTY, DENNIS	ALL	141	6TH E.D.
DOUGHERTY, EDWARD H.	BAL	408	3RD WARD
DOUGHERTY, ELIZABETH	BAL	357	1ST DIST
DOUGHERTY, H.	BAL	060	10TH WAR
DOUGHERTY, HUGH	BAL	408	3RD WARD
DOUGHERTY, J.	BAL	060	10TH WAR
DOUGHERTY, J.	BAL	117	1ST WARD
DOUGHERTY, JAMES	BAL	358	3RD WARD
DOUGHERTY, JAMES	WAS	033	2ND SUBD
DOUGHERTY, JANE	FRE	128	CREAGERS
DOUGHERTY, JOHN	BAL	235	20TH WAR
DOUGHERTY, JOHN	BAL	043	9TH WARD
DOUGHERTY, JOHN	BAL	313	12TH WAR
DOUGHERTY, JOHN	BAL	461	1ST DIST
DOUGHERTY, JOHN	ANN	324	2ND DIST
DOUGHERTY, JOHN	ANN	450	HOWARD D
DOUGHERTY, JULIA	BAL	341	13TH WAR
DOUGHERTY, MARGARET	BAL	319	20TH WAR
DOUGHERTY, MARY	BAL	126	11TH WAR
DOUGHERTY, MARY	ALL	076	5TH E.D.
DOUGHERTY, MARY A.	BAL	215	11TH WAR
DOUGHERTY, RICHARD	CEC	037	CHESAPEA
DOUGHERTY, SARAH	ALL	219	CUMBERLA
DOUGHERTY, SISTER ANNA	FRE	198	5TH E DI
DOUGHERTY, SISTER M.P.	FRE	197	5TH E DI
DOUGHERTY, THOMAS	BAL	041	4TH WARD
DOUGHERTY, THOMAS	CEC	088	4TH E DI
DOUGHERTY, THOMAS	BAL	331	3RD WARD
DOUGHERTY, THOMAS	BAL	127	5TH WARD
DOUGHERTY, THOMAS	ST	333	4TH E DI
DOUGHERTY, THOMAS D.	CAR	398	2ND DIST
DOUGHERTY, WILLIAM	CEC	148	PORT DUP
DOUGHERTY,MARY	ALL	217	CUMBERLA
DOUGHERY, ANN	FRE	175	5TH E DI
DOUGHITY, ELIZABETH	BAL	200	11TH WAR
DOUGHLAS, ROBERT	CEC	100	3RD E DI
DOUGHTY, JULIAN	BAL	132	1ST WARD
DOUGLAS, ANN	BAL	405	14TH WAR
DOUGLAS, ANN L.	BAL	396	14TH WAR
DOUGLAS, ARNOLD B.	BAL	207	2ND WARD
DOUGLAS, CHRISTIAN A.	BAL	475	14TH WAR
DOUGLAS, ELIZABETH	BAL	273	17TH WAR
DOUGLAS, GEORGE	BAL	251	20TH WAR
DOUGLAS, JANE	BAL	061	2ND DIST
DOUGLAS, JESSE	BAL	160	1ST WARD
DOUGLAS, LETITIA	ANN	465	HOWARD D
DOUGLAS, LETITIA G.	BAL	358	13TH WAR
DOUGLAS, MAN	MGM	417	MEDLEY 3
DOUGLAS, ROB	BAL	130	1ST WARD
DOUGLAS, ROBERT	BAL	394	1ST DIST
DOUGLAS, ROBERT	BAL	124	1ST WARD
DOUGLAS, THOMAS	BAL	131	18TH WAR
DOUGLAS, WILLIAM	FRE	221	BUCKEYST
DOUGLAS.S JAMES	BAL	129	1ST WARD
DOUGLASS, A.O.	ALL	206	CUMBERLA
DOUGLASS, ANNA	BAL	001	1ST WARD
DOUGLASS, CHARLES	BAL	095	10TH WAR
DOUGLASS, CHARLOTTE	DOR	296	1ST DIST
DOUGLASS, CLARYCY A.	BAL	305	7TH WARD
DOUGLASS, D. G. G.	BAL	150	1ST WARD
DOUGLASS, DAVID	BAL	179	5TH WARD
DOUGLASS, DAVID	ALL	208	CUMBERLA
DOUGLASS, ELIZABETH	BAL	138	11TH WAR
DOUGLASS, EMANUEL	WAS	191	1ST DIST
DOUGLASS, EPHRAIM	SOM	454	DAMES QU
DOUGLASS, FRANCIS	BAL	175	11TH WAR
DOUGLASS, GEORGE	BAL	099	10TH WAR

DOUGLASS, GEORGE T. SOM 544 TYASKIN
DOUGLASS, GEROGE WAS 193 1ST DIST
DOUGLASS, HENRY WAS 182 BOONSBOR
DOUGLASS, HENRY BAL 168 19TH WAR
DOUGLASS, JAMES BAL 042 15TH WAR
DOUGLASS, JAMES BAL 146 1ST WARD
DOUGLASS, JAMES B. BAL 018 18TH WAR
DOUGLASS, JAMES E. DOR 299 1ST DIST
DOUGLASS, JAMES R. SOM 546 TYASKIN
DOUGLASS, JANE BAL 264 20TH WAR
DOUGLASS, JESSE BAL 022 1ST WARD
DOUGLASS, JOANNA CHA 285 BOJANTOW
DOUGLASS, JOHN BAL 154 11TH WAR
DOUGLASS, JOHN BAL 048 9TH WARD
DOUGLASS, JOHN T. BAL 094 10TH WAR
DOUGLASS, JULIA A. BAL 147 11TH WAR
DOUGLASS, LEWIS J. BAL 264 7TH WARD
DOUGLASS, MARY CEC 214 7TH E DI
DOUGLASS, MARY JANE BAL 023 18TH WAR
DOUGLASS, NANCY DOR 456 1ST DIST
DOUGLASS, NEAMIAH SOM 544 TYASKIN
DOUGLASS, NICY SOM 537 TYASKIN
DOUGLASS, PATSY BAL 206 17TH WAR
DOUGLASS, PATTY SOM 547 TYASKIN
DOUGLASS, RICY CEC 090 4TH E DI
DOUGLASS, ROBERT CEC 094 4TH E DI
DOUGLASS, ROBERT BAL 265 17TH WAR
DOUGLASS, SAMUEL WAS 208 1ST DIST
DOUGLASS, SAMUEL BAL 155 1ST WARD
DOUGLASS, SARAH CEC 172 5TH E DI
DOUGLASS, SOLOMON BAL 056 10TH WAR
DOUGLASS, THOMAS BAL 028 18TH WAR
DOUGLASS, WARD SOM 551 TYASKIN
DOUGLASS, WILLIAM SOM 547 TYASKIN
DOUGLASS, WILLIAM WAS 193 1ST DIST
DOUGLASS, WILLIAM BAL 047 18TH WAR
DOUGLASS, WILLIAM BAL 206 17TH WAR
DOUGLASS, WILLIAM BAL 175 11TH WAR
DOUGLASS, WILLIAM BAL 212 6TH DIST
DOUGLASS, WILLIAM W. DOR 305 1ST DIST
DOUITEE, JOHN T. * BAL 268 7TH WARD
DOUITEE, RICHARD BAL 389 8TH WARD
DOUL, MARMACUKE * HAR 204 3RD DIST
DOULEY, MARY BAL 307 1ST DIST
DOUMEYER, THEODORE BAL 092 18TH WAR
DOUNENFELTER, MARTIN BAL 042 1ST WARD
DOUNER, JOHN BAL 190 11TH WAR
DOUNES, AMANDA-BLACK QUE 128 1ST E DI
DOUNES, BENNETT QUE 146 1ST E DI
DOUNES, JAMES QUE 206 3RD E DI
DOUNES, JONATHAN QUE 124 1ST E DI
DOUNES, JOSEPH QUE 206 3RD E DI
DOUPLETON, H. BAL 251 20TH WAR
DOUR IES, RICHARD E.C. QUE 180 2ND E DI
DOURINEN, FREDERICK * BAL 076 18TH WAR
DOURY, THOMAS BAL 126 1ST WARD
DOUSE, LOUISA HAR 055 1ST DIST
DOUSK, RACHE BAL 252 12TH WAR
DOUTRY, HENRY CEC 151 PORT DUP
DOUTTS, JOSEPH BAL 164 6TH WARD
DOUTY, JAMES CAR 363 9TH DIST
DOVE, ADAM BAL 056 1ST WARD
DOVE, ANN PRI 037 VANSVILL
DOVE, BENJAMIN SOM 472 TRAPPE D
DOVE, BENJAMIN BAL 105 18TH WAR
DOVE, CHARLES CAL 041 3RD DIST
DOVE, EDWARD ANN 403 8TH DIST
DOVE, ELIJAH ANN 396 8TH DIST
DOVE, ELIJAH BAL 296 20TH WAR
DOVE, ELIZABETH BAL 351 1ST DIST
DOVE, ELLEN ANN 403 8TH DIST
DOVE, EMMELINE WOR 198 8TH E DI
DOVE, ENOCH MGM 397 ROCKERLE
DOVE, GEORGE MGM 397 ROCKERLE
DOVE, JAMES SOM 472 TRAPPE D
DOVE, JAMES SOM 472 TRAPPE D
DOVE, JOHN SOM 468 TRAPPE D
DOVE, JOHN CAL 060 3RD DIST
DOVE, JOHN W. SOM 472 TRAPPE D
DOVE, JOSEPH CAL 061 3RD DIST
DOVE, LEVI MGM 318 CRACKLIN
DOVE, MARMACUKE * HAR 204 3RD DIST
DOVE, MARY A. ANN 420 HOWARD D
DOVE, MILKY SOM 429 PRINCESS
DOVE, MILTON MGM 430 CLARKSTR
DOVE, RICHARD PRI 121 PISCATAW
DOVE, SAMUEL ANN 399 8TH DIST
DOVE, SARAH WOR 190 8TH E DI
DOVE, WEBSTER MGM 429 CLARKSTR
DOVE, WESLEY SOM 476 TRAPPE D
DOVE, WILLIAM PRI 016 BLADENSB
DOVENBERGER, JOHN WAS 056 2ND SUBD
DOVER, BENJAMIN WAS 208 1ST DIST
DOVER, C. BAL 138 5TH WARD
DOVER, CHRISTOPHER BAL 168 16TH WAR
DOVER, JOHN BAL 150 16TH WAR
DOVER, NELSON CEC 213 7TH E DI
DOVER, THOMAS BAL 341 1ST DIST
DOVIS, JOHN L. PRI 112 PISCATAW
DOW, DENNIS * KEN 213 2ND DIST
DOW, LORENZO BAL 111 10TH WAR
DOW, LORENZO BAL 460 8TH WARD
DOW, MARY BAL 001 EASTERN
DOW, MARY WAS 062 2ND SUBD
DOW, MICHAEL BAL 415 8TH WARD
DOW, WILLIAM BAL 281 7TH WARD
DOW, WILLIAM T. BAL 281 7TH WARD
DOWALL, LEMUEL BAL 233 12TH WAR
DOWD, TARANCE CAR 231 5TH DIST
DOWDEN, ABRAHAM BAL 128 11TH WAR
DOWDEN, ADAM BAL 447 8TH WARD
DOWDEN, ADAM BAL 446 8TH WARD
DOWDEN, ASHTON ALL 103 5TH E.D.
DOWDEN, CATHARINE BAL 206 6TH WARD
DOWDEN, GEORGE ALL 232 CUMBERLA
DOWDEN, JAMES H. MGM 396 ROCKERLE
DOWDEN, L. BAL 136 5TH WARD
DOWDEN, MARY BAL 377 3RD WARD
DOWDEN, MARY BAL 115 15TH WAR
DOWDEN, PERRY BAL 238 6TH WARD
DOWDEN, RAYMOND P. PRI 001 BLADENSB
DOWDEN, SAMUEL BAL 378 13TH WAR
DOWDEN, SOLOMAN BAL 280 7TH WARD
DOWDEN, SOLOMON MGM 328 CRACKLIN
DOWDEN, THOMAS P. ALL 205 CUMBERLA
DOWDEN, WILLIAM ALL 236 CUMBERLA
DOWDIN, FLORA A.-BLACK BAL 216 2ND WARD
DOWDON, ISAAC BAL 048 2ND DIST
DOWED, BARTLEY BAL 273 1ST DIST
DOWEL, CATHERINE QUE 204 3RD E DI
DOWEL, CHARLOTT BAL 425 1ST DIST
DOWEL, LOUISA QUE 204 3RD E DI
DOWELL, BENJAMIN CAL 059 3RD DIST
DOWELL, CHARLES CAL 048 3RD DIST
DOWELL, GEORGE W. CAL 026 2ND DIST
DOWELL, ISAIAH CAL 056 3RD DIST
DOWELL, JAEMS J. CAL 011 1ST DIST
DOWELL, JOEL P. ANN 400 8TH DIST
DOWELL, JOHN BAL 255 6TH WARD
DOWELL, JOHN J. CAL 011 1ST DIST
DOWELL, JOHN S. CAL 059 3RD DIST
DOWELL, MARY ANN 304 1ST DIST
DOWELL, PETER BAL 462 1ST DIST
DOWELL, RICHARD CAL 057 3RD DIST
DOWELL, RICHARD H. CAL 045 3RD DIST
DOWELL, WILLIAM BAL 282 2ND WARD
DOWELL,DANIEL BAL 129 1ST WARD
DOWER, MARY WAS 272 RIDGEVIL
DOWER, WALLACE WAS 272 RIDGEVIL
DOWERA, THOMAS BAL 099 5TH WARD
DOWERY, JOHN BAL 418 8TH WARD
DOWERY, SARAH E. BAL 418 8TH WARD
DOWETY, JAMES QUE 213 3RD E DI
DOWEY, ANN M.-BLACK FRE 047 FREDERIC
DOWHARD, JOHN BAL 257 2ND WARD
DOWIE, ESTHER BAL 109 10TH WAR
DOWIN, EDWAD BAL 123 1ST WARD
DOWING, SUSAN BAL 095 5TH WARD
DOWLER, JAMES WAS 142 2ND DIST
DOWLER, MARTHA BAL 204 11TH WAR
DOWLEY, BARNEY ANN 336 3RD DIST
DOWLIN, JAMES KEN 230 2ND DIST
DOWLIN, JAMES KEN 259 1ST DIST
DOWLIN, MARY BAL 207 11TH WAR
DOWLIN, PATRICK BAL 133 2ND DIST
DOWLIN, WILLIAM BAL 125 2ND DIST
DOWLING, BRIDGET ANN 470 HOWARD D
DOWLING, EDWARD BAL 048 9TH WARD
DOWLING, EDWARD BAL 059 15TH WAR
DOWLING, ELIZA BAL 439 14TH WAR
DOWLING, FRANCIS BAL 252 1ST DIST
DOWLING, GEORGE HAR 091 2ND DIST
DOWLING, HEZEKIAH KEN 258 1ST DIST
DOWLING, JAMES HAR 114 2ND DIST
DOWLING, JAMES HAR 104 2ND DIST
DOWLING, JOHN BAL 404 3RD WARD
DOWLING, MARGARET ALL 203 CUMBERLA
DOWLING, MARY BAL 297 7TH WARD
DOWLING, MARY A. BAL 023 15TH WAR
DOWLING, NANCY BAL 295 12TH WAR
DOWLING, RICHARD KEN 258 1ST DIST
DOWN, ANTHONY CAL 023 2ND DIST
DOWN, ARAMINT BAL 243 20TH WAR
DOWN, BIDDY BAL 174 11TH WAR
DOWN, GEORGE BAL 281 2ND WARD
DOWNELL, JOHN ANN 284 ANNAPOLI
DOWNER, MABLE* TAL 030 EASTON D
DOWNES, BENNETT R. QUE 214 3RD E DI
DOWNES, CHARLES QUE 223 4TH E DI
DOWNES, CHARLES BAL 036 9TH WARD
DOWNES, EDWARD TAL 061 EASTON D
DOWNES, ELY BAL 212 19TH WAR
DOWNES, HARRIETT QUE 214 3RD E DI
DOWNES, HENRY TAL 022 EASTON D
DOWNES, HERTON TAL 091 ST MICHA
DOWNES, ISAIAH BAL 339 7TH WARD
DOWNES, JAMES TAL 035 EASTON D
DOWNES, JOHN TAL 037 EASTON D
DOWNES, JOHN H. QUE 202 3RD E DI
DOWNES, JOHN W. QUE 134 1ST E DI
DOWNES, JONATHAN QUE 231 4TH E DI
DOWNES, MABLE* TAL 030 EASTON D
DOWNES, MARIA QUE 206 3RD E DI
DOWNES, MARTHA QUE 214 3RD E DI
DOWNES, MILLY QUE 219 3RD E DI
DOWNES, PARRIS TAL 097 ST MICHA
DOWNES, RICHARD BAL 220 12TH WAR
DOWNES, ROBERT BAL 041 15TH WAR
DOWNES, SAMUEL T. QUE 247 5TH E DI
DOWNES, SARAH QUE 248 5TH E DI
DOWNES, SARAH QUE 215 3RD E DI
DOWNES, SHARLOTT TAL 077 EASTON T
DOWNES, THOMAS TAL 061 EASTON D
DOWNES, WASHINGTON TAL 016 EASTON D
DOWNES, WILLIAM H. QUE 211 3RD E DI
DOWNEY, ANN C. WAS 135 2ND DIST
DOWNEY, CATHARINE WAS 135 HAGERSTO
DOWNEY, EDMUND BAL 052 4TH WARD
DOWNEY, ELLEN ALL 259 CUMBERLA
DOWNEY, GEORGE BAL 230 19TH WAR
DOWNEY, HOWELL BAL 157 19TH WAR
DOWNEY, JACOB KEN 267 1ST DIST
DOWNEY, JACOB WAS 289 1ST DIST
DOWNEY, JACOB WAS 295 1ST DIST
DOWNEY, JAMES KEN 269 1ST DIST
DOWNEY, JAMES WAS 129 2ND DIST
DOWNEY, JAMES ALL 108 5TH E.D.
DOWNEY, JAMES M. WAS 108 2ND DIST
DOWNEY, JOHN KEN 266 1ST DIST
DOWNEY, JOHN BAL 252 12TH WAR
DOWNEY, JOHN BAL 271 17TH WAR
DOWNEY, JOHN FRE 437 8TH E DI
DOWNEY, MARY BAL 380 13TH WAR
DOWNEY, MARY BAL 401 14TH WAR
DOWNEY, MARY BAL 121 2ND DIST
DOWNEY, MARY BAL 311 12TH WAR
DOWNEY, MARY WAS 295 1ST DIST
DOWNEY, MARY A. KEN 268 1ST DIST
DOWNEY, MARY E. BAL 228 6TH WARD
DOWNEY, OTHO WAS 020 2ND SUBD
DOWNEY, OWEN D. ALL 128 4TH E.D.
DOWNEY, PATRICK H. BAL 157 16TH WAR
DOWNEY, PETER WAS 060 2ND SUBD
DOWNEY, REBECCA FRE 416 8TH E DI
DOWNEY, RICHARD BAL 003 1ST WARD
DOWNEY, ROSANNA WAS 257 1ST DIST
DOWNEY, SARAH A. BAL 385 8TH WARD
DOWNEY, SARAH J. BAL 261 17TH WAR
DOWNEY, THOMAS ALL 258 CUMBERLA
DOWNEY, THOMAS BAL 218 12TH WAR
DOWNEY, THOMAS WAS 025 2ND SUBD
DOWNEY, WILLIAM BAL 130 2ND DIST
DOWNEY, WILLIAM BAL 370 8TH WARD
DOWNEY, WILLIAM BAL 449 14TH WAR
DOWNEY, WILLIAM BAL 035 18TH WAR
DOWNEY, WILLIAM T. BAL 055 18TH WAR
DOWNFIELD, GEORGE HAR 160 3RD DIST
DOWNHART, JOHN MGM 367 BERRYS D
DOWNIN, LINA WAS 274 RIDGEVIL
DOWNING, AMANDA QUE 208 3RD E DI
DOWNING, ANNA CHA 293 BOJANTOW
DOWNING, DEBORA CHA 292 BOJANTOW
DOWNING, DRUCILLA BAL 130 2ND DIST
DOWNING, ELEN CHA 292 BOJANTOW
DOWNING, ELLEN PRI 067 NOTTINGH
DOWNING, GEORGE A. WOR 253 1ST CENS
DOWNING, GEORGE A. WOR 253 1ST CENS
DOWNING, GEORGE H. SOM 550 TYASKIN
DOWNING, JAMES W. WOR 212 4TH E DI
DOWNING, JANE SOM 488 SALISBUR
DOWNING, JOHN F. CHA 277 BOJANTOW
DOWNING, JOHN H. CHA 278 BOJANTOW
DOWNING, JOHN R. WOR 239 6TH E DI
DOWNING, JOHN-BLACK WOR 320 1ST E DI
DOWNING, LAVINIA A. E. WOR 240 6TH E DI
DOWNING, MARY BAL 075 4TH WARD
DOWNING, NANCY SOM 401 BRINKLEY
DOWNING, NANCY WOR 277 BERLIN I
DOWNING, NANCY QUE 208 3RD E DI
DOWNING, NATHAN BAL 017 18TH WAR
DOWNING, POWELL WOR 274 BERLIN I
DOWNING, RICHARD D. KEN 305 3RD DIST
DOWNING, SAMUEL WAS 293 1ST DIST
DOWNING, SAMUEL BAL 043 15TH WAR
DOWNING, SOBENIA BAL 139 11TH WAR
DOWNING, WILLIAM J. WOR 212 4TH E DI
DOWNS, -----* TAL 046 EASTON T
DOWNS, ABRA BAL 435 1ST DIST
DOWNS, ALEXANDER BAL 183 16TH WAR
DOWNS, ANN CAR 068 NO TWP L
DOWNS, ANN M. MGM 352 BERRYS D
DOWNS, ANN-BLACK QUE 179 2ND E DI
DOWNS, ARABELLA BAL 122 11TH WAR
DOWNS, BENJAMIN BAL 273 17TH WAR
DOWNS, BENJAMIN MGM 371 BERRYS D
DOWNS, BENJAMIN BAL 130 16TH WAR
DOWNS, BENJAMIN-BLACK CAR 165 NO TWP L
DOWNS, BETSY BAL 458 1ST DIST
DOWNS, BILEY ST 282 3RD E DI
DOWNS, BRIDGET BAL 053 9TH WARD
DOWNS, CHARLES G. WAS 015 2ND SUBD
DOWNS, CHARLES W. BAL 367 3RD WARD
DOWNS, CHARLES-MULATTO CAR 068 NO TWP L
DOWMS, CHRISTOPHER WAS 015 2ND SUBD
DOWNS, CIVILLA ST 278 3RD E DI
DOWNS, CORNELIUS ST 275 3RD E DI
DOWNS, DANIEL WOR 204 4TH E DI
DOWNS, DION BAL 177 6TH WARD
DOWNS, ELISABETH BAL 362 3RD WARD
DOWNS, ELIZA BAL 463 1ST DIST
DOWNS, ELIZABETH BAL 201 6TH WARD
DOWNS, ELIZABETH BAL 029 2ND DIST
DOWNS, ELIZABETH WAS 031 2ND SUBD
DOWNS, ELIZABETH BAL 374 13TH WAR
DOWNS, ELIZABETH BAL 122 18TH WAR
DOWNS, EMILY BAL 249 12TH WAR
DOWNS, FRANCIUS BAL 164 1ST WARD
DOWNS, FRED WAS 022 2ND SUBD
DOWNS, FREDELIA WAS 198 1ST DIST
DOWNS, GALTY WOR 204 4TH E DI
DOWNS, H. BAL 080 4TH WARD
DOWNS, HENRY BAL 455 8TH WARD
DOWNS, HENRY ANN 356 3RD DIST
DOWNS, HENRY BAL 111 1ST WARD
DOWNS, HESTER WOR 204 4TH E DI
DOWNS, HORACE T. BAL 320 7TH WARD
DOWNS, ISAAC BAL 204 19TH WAR
DOWNS, ISAAC BAL 006 18TH WAR
DOWNS, ISAAC T. WOR 205 4TH E DI
DOWNS, ISAAC-BLACK CAR 076 NO TWP L
DOWNS, ISABELLA ST 292 2ND E DI
DOWNS, ISAIAH BAL 338 3RD WARD
DOWNS, JAMES BAL 141 16TH WAR
DOWNS, JAMES WOR 208 4TH E DI
DOWNS, JAMES F. ST 295 2ND E DI
DOWNS, JAMES M. BAL 150 19TH WAR
DOWNS, JEFFERSON BAL 183 16TH WAR
DOWNS, JOHN BAL 169 2ND DIST
DOWNS, JOHN BAL 242 2ND WARD
DOWNS, JOHN MGM 351 BERRYS D
DOWNS, JOHN BAL 258 20TH WAR
DOWNS, JOHN WOR 206 4TH E DI
DOWNS, JOSEPH ST 282 3RD E DI
DOWNS, JOSEPH BAL 112 1ST WARD
DOWNS, JOSEPH BAL 379 1ST DIST
DOWNS, LUCY BAL 067 1ST WARD
DOWNS, LUCY BAL 252 20TH WAR
DOWNS, MARGARET TAL 104 ST MICHA
DOWNS, MARIA L. BAL 275 7TH WARD
DOWNS, MARTHA S. CHA 258 MIDDLETO
DOWNS, MARY BAL 205 19TH WAR
DOWNS, MATILDA QUE 185 3RD E DI
DOWNS, MAY CHA 258 MIDDLETO
DOWNS, MONTGOMERY-BLACK CAR 097 NO TWP L
DOWNS, NANCY MGM 358 BERRYS D
DOWNS, NANCY WOR 207 4TH E DI
DOWNS, NOAH ST 281 3RD E DI
DOWNS, PAMS-BLACK FRE 017 FREDERIC
DOWNS, RACHEL BAL 189 19TH WAR
DOWNS, RACHEL ANN 458 HOWARD D
DOWNS, RICHARD M. ANN 487 HOWARD D
DOWNS, ROBERT ANN 367 4TH DIST
DOWNS, ROBERT BAL 199 17TH WAR
DOWNS, SAMUEL QUE 218 3RD E DI
DOWNS, SARAH BAL 191 19TH WAR
DOWNS, SOLOMON BAL 163 6TH WARD
DOWNS, THOMAS BAL 145 19TH WAR
DOWNS, THOMAS S. WOR 219 4TH E DI
DOWNS, WILLIAM HAR 099 2ND DIST
DOWNS, WILLIAM BAL 073 10TH WAR
DOWNS, WILLIAM BAL 389 1ST DIST
DOWNS, WILLIAM BAL 013 1ST WARD
DOWNS, WILLIAM ANN 390 4TH DIST
DOWNS, WILLIAM H. CAR 077 NO TWP L
DOWNS, WILLIAM H. CAR 078 NO TWP L
DOWNS, WILLIAM L. WOR 204 4TH E DI
DOWNS, WILLSON-BLACK CAR 071 NO TWP L
DOWNS, WILLSON-MULATTO CAR 118 NO TWP L
DOWNS, WILOT BAL 130 16TH WAR
DOWNY, ANN M. BAL 107 5TH WARD
DOWNY, EDWARD BAL 164 2ND DIST
DOWNY, MARY CEC 004 ELKTON 3
DOWNY, NANCY CEC 015 ELKTON 3
DOWNY, WILLIAM CEC 005 ELKTON 3
DOWOVAN, CORNELIUS BAL 085 2ND DIST
DOWS, MARY ANN BAL 334 13TH WAR
DOWSEN, JOHN ANN 412 HOWARD D
DOWSEY, LOUIS BAL 232 1ST DIST
DOWSEY, WILLIAM FRE 239 NEW MARK
DOWSON, ELLEN* BAL 045 4TH WARD

Name	County	Page	District
DOXEN, ANN	BAL	098	2ND DIST
DOXEN, ELIZABETH	HAR	104	2ND DIST
DOXEN, JACOB	HAR	104	2ND DIST
DOXEN, JOHN	BAL	303	1ST DIST
DOXEY, JOSEPH	BAL	155	1ST WARD
DOXON, GEORGE	BAL	403	1ST DIST
DOXON, MARY	BAL	115	5TH WARD
DOYCE, JOHN	BAL	199	2ND WARD
DOYHERTY, JOSEPH	BAL	126	11TH WAR
DOYLE, ANN	BAL	263	2ND WARD
DOYLE, ANNA	WAS	262	1ST DIST
DOYLE, BARNEY	ALL	050	10TH E.D
DOYLE, BENJAMIND F.	WAS	208	1ST DIST
DOYLE, BERNARD	BAL	171	16TH WAR
DOYLE, BRIDGET	BAL	379	13TH WAR
DOYLE, BRIDGET	BAL	226	19TH WAR
DOYLE, CATHARINE	BAL	367	13TH WAR
DOYLE, CATHARINE	BAL	233	6TH WARD
DOYLE, CATHARINE	BAL	193	11TH WAR
DOYLE, CATHERINE	BAL	062	10TH WAR
DOYLE, CATHERINE	FRE	268	NEW MARK
DOYLE, CATHRINE	BAL	003	18TH WAR
DOYLE, DANIEL	BAL	097	2ND DIST
DOYLE, DAVID	BAL	066	15TH WAR
DOYLE, EDWARD	ALL	253	CUMBERLA
DOYLE, ELIZABETH	WAS	282	1ST DIST
DOYLE, ELLEN	BAL	015	4TH WARD
DOYLE, HANNAH	BAL	415	14TH WAR
DOYLE, HARRIET	BAL	242	12TH WAR
DOYLE, HENRY	FRE	006	FREDERIC
DOYLE, HERNY	FRE	022	FREDERIC
DOYLE, HESTER	BAL	395	14TH WAR
DOYLE, JACOB	WAS	218	1ST DIST
DOYLE, JACOB	WAS	223	1ST DIST
DOYLE, JAMES	WAS	150	2ND DIST
DOYLE, JAMES	CAR	270	WESTMINS
DOYLE, JAMES	BAL	458	8TH WARD
DOYLE, JAMES	BAL	004	9TH WARD
DOYLE, JAMES	BAL	372	3RD WARD
DOYLE, JAMES	BAL	037	1ST WARD
DOYLE, JAMES	BAL	257	1ST DIST
DOYLE, JAMES	BAL	119	1ST WARD
DOYLE, JANE G.	BAL	031	9TH WARD
DOYLE, JOHN	BAL	297	1ST DIST
DOYLE, JOHN	BAL	003	9TH WARD
DOYLE, JOHN	BAL	001	9TH WARD
DOYLE, JOHN	ALL	180	8TH E.D.
DOYLE, JOHN	ALL	140	6TH E.D.
DOYLE, JOHN	BAL	463	1ST DIST
DOYLE, JOHN	BAL	268	17TH WAR
DOYLE, JOHN	WAS	150	2ND DIST
DOYLE, JOHN L.	ANN	469	HOWARD D
DOYLE, LETITIA	BAL	245	20TH WAR
DOYLE, LUKE	BAL	358	8TH WARD
DOYLE, MARY	BAL	093	2ND DIST
DOYLE, MARY	BAL	003	9TH WARD
DOYLE, MARY	BAL	299	20TH WAR
DOYLE, MARY	BAL	201	11TH WAR
DOYLE, MARY	BAL	024	4TH WARD
DOYLE, MARY	BAL	319	20TH WAR
DOYLE, MATTHEW	ALL	107	5TH E.D.
DOYLE, MICHAEL	BAL	115	2ND DIST
DOYLE, MICHAEL	BAL	089	5TH WARD
DOYLE, PATRICK	BAL	413	1ST DIST
DOYLE, PATRICK	BAL	186	11TH WAR
DOYLE, PATRICK	BAL	427	8TH WARD
DOYLE, PATRICK	BAL	040	1ST WARD
DOYLE, PATRICK	BAL	168	2ND DIST
DOYLE, PATRICK	BAL	024	4TH WARD
DOYLE, PATRICK	CEC	152	PORT DUP
DOYLE, PETER	BAL	039	9TH WARD
DOYLE, RICHARD	ANN	454	HOWARD D
DOYLE, RICHARD	BAL	395	14TH WAR
DOYLE, SARAH	FRE	035	FREDERIC
DOYLE, SARAH	ALL	140	6TH E.D.
DOYLE, SARAH A.	BAL	357	8TH WARD
DOYLE, SISTER C.	FRE	198	5TH E DI
DOYLE, SUSAN	BAL	177	11TH WAR
DOYLE, TARANCE	CAR	194	4TH DIST
DOYLE, THOMAS	FRE	264	NEW MARK
DOYLE, THOMAS	BAL	423	8TH WARD
DOYLE, THOMAS	ALL	139	6TH E.D.
DOYLE, THOMAS	BAL	031	9TH WARD
DOYLE, WILLAIM	BAL	148	19TH WAR
DOYLE, WILLIAM	MGM	325	CRACKLIN
DOYLE, WILLIAM	BAL	365	13TH WAR
DOYLE, WILLIAM	BAL	346	13TH WAR
DOYLE, WILLIAM E.	WAS	132	HAGERSTO
DOYLE.EDWARD	BAL	128	1ST WARD
DOYLE.THOMAS	BAL	064	1ST WARD
DOYLES, JOHN	BAL	026	18TH WAR
DOZE, MOSES G.	BAL	134	1ST WARD
DOZIER, S.	BAL	117	1ST WARD
DOZLE, MICKY	BAL	199	2ND WARD
DOZUR, S.	BAL	141	1ST WARD
DRABANE, HENRY	BAL	072	10TH WAR
DRACH, HENRY	CAR	358	9TH DIST
DRACK, HANSON M.	CAR	183	8TH DIST
DRAIN, JAMES	BAL	049	9TH WARD
DRAIN, JOHN M.	HAR	084	2ND DIST
DRAIN, MARY*	DOR	377	1ST DIST
DRAKBUS, HENRY	BAL	075	1ST WARD
DRAKE, BIDDY	BAL	212	19TH WAR
DRAKE, DAVID	ALL	165	6TH E.D.
DRAKE, EDWARD	ALL	163	6TH E.D.
DRAKE, ELIZABETH	BAL	109	5TH WARD
DRAKE, GEORGE	BAL	275	2ND WARD
DRAKE, ISAAC	ALL	186	9TH E.D.
DRAKE, MARY AE.	FRE	389	PETERSVI
DRAKE, MATTHEW	BAL	131	1ST WARD
DRAKE, MATTHEW	BAL	168	16TH WAR
DRAKE, PUSSY	BAL	284	12TH WAR
DRAKE, SUSAN	ANN	522	HOWARD D
DRAKE, SUSAN	PRI	103	SPALDING
DRAKLEY, H.W.	BAL	012	18TH WAR
DRAMER, ELIZA	BAL	152	11TH WAR
DRAMMEN,F.	BAL	138	1ST WARD
DRAMOND, WILLIAM	MGM	402	ROCKERLE
DRANE, ALFRED	MGM	358	BERRYS D
DRANE, H.M.	WAS	021	2ND SUBD
DRANE, HENERITTA	DOR	304	1ST DIST
DRANE, JOHN	BAL	352	3RD WARD
DRANE, MARTHA A.	BAL	352	3RD WARD
DRANZ, GEORGE	BAL	278	20TH WAR
DRAPER, A.*	TAL	026	EASTON D
DRAPER, ANDREW	FRE	365	CATOCTIN
DRAPER, DANIEL	BAL	186	11TH WAR
DRAPER, DAVID	FRE	364	CATOCTIN
DRAPER, ELIZABETH P.	WAS	141	HAGERSTO
DRAPER, ELLEN	FRE	052	FREDERIC

Name	County	Page	District
DRAPER, GARRISON	BAL	386	8TH WARD
DRAPER, GIDEON	MGM	384	ROCKERLE
DRAPER, ISAAC	FRE	151	10TH E D
DRAPER, JAMES M.	TAL	061	EASTON D
DRAPER, JAMES S.	WAS	106	2ND DIST
DRAPER, JOHN	WAS	133	2ND DIST
DRAPER, JOHN	CAR	105	NO TWP L
DRAPER, MARANDA	BAL	083	18TH WAR
DRAPER, MARGARET	BAL	278	20TH WAR
DRAPER, MARGARET	WAS	233	1ST DIST
DRAPER, MARGARET	BAL	233	12TH WAR
DRAPER, PETER	CAR	169	NO TWP L
DRAPER, RICHARD J.	CAR	084	NO TWP L
DRAPER, SARAH	BAL	136	5TH WARD
DRAPER, SARAH	QUE	243	5TH E DI
DRAPER, THOMAS	WAS	137	2ND DIST
DRAPER, WILLIAM	TAL	025	EASTON D
DRAPER, WILLIAM	FRE	365	CATOCTIN
DRAPER, WILLIAM	FRE	152	10TH E D
DRAPP, JUSTIAN	BAL	318	3RD WARD
DRASCH, CHARLES	BAL	276	17TH WAR
DRAWBAUGH, GEORGE	ALL	093	5TH E.D.
DRAYN, SARAH	PRI	101	SPALDING
DRAYON, RICHARD	BAL	006	9TH WARD
DREDING, BARNEY	BAL	298	12TH WAR
DREER, ANN	BAL	107	18TH WAR
DREHER, ANDREW	FRE	367	CATOCTIN
DREING, LEWIS	BAL	037	9TH WARD
DRELS, DANIEL*	BAL	272	20TH WAR
DREMER, WILLAIM	BAL	221	19TH WAR
DREMK, ADAM *	BAL	150	2ND DIST
DRENAR, SUSAN	BAL	242	20TH WAR
DRENEN, THOMAS	WAS	116	2ND DIST
DRENENBURG, JACOB	FRE	226	BUCKEYST
DRENER, SAMUEL *	WAS	057	2ND SUBD
DRENNARD, SAMUEL	CEC	100	3RD E DI
DRENNEN, MARY	WAS	116	2ND DIST
DRENNER, JEREMIAH	WAS	264	1ST DIST
DRENNER, JOSEPH	WAS	225	1ST DIST
DRENNER, JOSEPH	WAS	225	1ST DIST
DRESHER, CHARLES	BAL	415	1ST DIST
DRESKELE, TIMOTHY	ALL	082	5TH E.D.
DRESSEL, CATHARINE	BAL	199	6TH WARD
DRESSEL, ELIZABETH*	BAL	109	10TH WAR
DRESSEL, JOHN	BAL	198	6TH WARD
DRESSEL, WERNER	BAL	412	14TH WAR
DRESSELL, MARY	BAL	220	12TH WAR
DRESSLER, JOHN	CAR	264	WESTMINS
DRESSLER, PETER	BAL	306	20TH WAR
DRESSMAN, GEORGE	ALL	233	CUMBERLA
DRESSNON, HENRY	ALL	205	CUMBERLA
DREUER, SAMUEL *	WAS	057	2ND SUBD
DREUX, MADAME	FRE	164	EMMITTSB
DREVIN, JESE*	DOR	436	1ST DIST
DREW, E.	BAL	085	4TH WARD
DREW, J.	BAL	085	4TH WARD
DREW, JACOB	BAL	118	1ST WARD
DREW, MARY	HAR	153	3RD DIST
DREW, MARY H.	BAL	264	7TH WARD
DREW, SAMUEL	CEC	215	7TH E DI
DREW, THOMAS	CEC	215	7TH E DI
DREWERY, THEODOSIA SIS-	BAL	316	20TH WAR
DREY, THEODORE	BAL	089	15TH WAR
DREYER, DENNIS	BAL	466	14TH WAR
DREYER, DOLAS	BAL	194	11TH WAR
DREYER, HAMMOND	BAL	459	14TH WAR
DREYER, HENRY*	BAL	089	10TH WAR
DREYER, JOHN	BAL	466	14TH WAR
DREYER, MARY*	BAL	089	10TH WAR
DRIBECK, CHARLES	ALL	254	CUMBERLA
DRIBEN, SILIAS *	BAL	124	18TH WAR
DRICKER, AUGUST	BAL	282	17TH WAR
DRICKSON, DAVID	CEC	109	3RD E DI
DRICY, RICHARD JR.*	TAL	025	EASTON D
DRIDEN, ELIZABETH	WOR	289	9TH E DI
DRIDEN, PETER	WOR	293	9TH E DI
DRIDER, SUSAN	WOR	344	1ST E DI
DRIDERS, JAMES	WOR	289	9TH E DI
DRIDING, JOSEPH	BAL	036	15TH WAR
DRIEDT, EARNEST	BAL	335	1ST DIST
DRIER, CREDERICK	BAL	107	18TH WAR
DRIER, JACOB	BAL	354	3RD WARD
DRIESADERF, JACOB	BAL	078	1ST WARD
DRIGE, CATHARINE	BAL	141	19TH WAR
DRIGE, MARY A.	BAL	142	19TH WAR
DRIGER, FRANCIS H. *	BAL	070	18TH WAR
DRIGGUS, WILLIAM	CAR	110	NO TWP L
DRIKEL, AUGUST	BAL	033	15TH WAR
DRILEY, MARK	BAL	161	11TH WAR
DRILL, HENRY	FRE	355	MIDDLETU
DRILL, JAMES M.	FRE	391	PETERSVI
DRILL, JANE	FRE	395	PETERSVI
DRIME, PATRICK	BAL	109	5TH WARD
DRINEN, JOSEPH	WAS	116	2ND DIST
DRINER, JOHN *	WAS	058	2ND SUBD
DRINKALE, JEREMIAH	WAS	029	2ND SUBD
DRINKHAUS, NICHOLAS	BAL	307	20TH WAR
DRINKS, CONRAD	HAR	132	2ND DIST
DRIPLE, REBECCA *	BAL	116	2ND DIST
DRISCOLL, CORNELIUS	BAL	197	6TH WARD
DRISCOLL, JOHN	BAL	300	17TH WAR
DRISCOLL, JOHN	BAL	299	17TH WAR
DRISCOLL, LEAH	BAL	325	7TH WARD
DRISCOLL, POLYCARP O.	BAL	145	5TH WARD
DRISFORD, MARGRETT	CAR	121	NO TWP L
DRISHELL, BENJAMIN	WOR	198	8TH E DI
DRISHELL, JOHN	WOR	167	6TH E DI
DRISHELL, JOSHUA	WOR	223	4TH E DI
DRISHELL, PURNELL	WOR	234	6TH E DI
DRISHELL, SHEPPARD	WOR	223	4TH E DI
DRISHELL, THOMAS	WOR	233	6TH E DI
DRISHELL, THOMAS	WOR	199	8TH E DI
DRISHELL, WILLIAM	WOR	235	6TH E DI
DRISKELL, MARGARET	WAS	114	2ND DIST
DRISKLE, CARLIN	WAS	114	2ND DIST
DRISSE, ERNEST	BAL	147	16TH WAR
DRISSELL, MARY	BAL	025	1ST WARD
DRIT, JAMES	CHA	242	HILLTOP
DRITERLY, CHARLES*	BAL	080	10TH WAR
DRIUT, WILLIAM	BAL	377	13TH WAR
DRIVER, ANNA M.	QUE	203	3RD E DI
DRIVER, DENTON	ANN	510	HOWARD D
DRIVER, EASTER-BLACK	CAR	092	NO TWP L
DRIVER, EDWARD	BAL	276	17TH WAR
DRIVER, EDWARD	CEC	148	PORT DUP
DRIVER, GEORGE W.	ANN	510	HOWARD D
DRIVER, HENRY	BAL	300	17TH WAR
DRIVER, HENRY	QUE	217	3RD E DI
DRIVER, HESTER	BAL	114	15TH WAR
DRIVER, JOSEPH-BLACK	CAR	164	NO TWP L

Name	County	Page	District
DRIVER, MARY	QUE	212	3RD E DI
DRIVER, MATHEW	TAL	007	EASTON D
DRIVER, MOSES	BAL	097	15TH WAR
DRIVER, N.*	DOR	413	1ST DIST
DRIVER, ROBERT	BAL	160	1ST WARD
DRIVER, THOMAS	WAS	101	2ND DIST
DRIVER, WILLIAM	BAL	457	8TH WARD
DRIVER, WILLIAM	BAL	123	18TH WAR
DRIVERS, HESTER	BAL	383	3RD WARD
DRIZE, HENRY	BAL	195	19TH WAR
DROBLER, CATHRINE	BAL	064	18TH WAR
DROGER, HENRY	BAL	433	14TH WAR
DROHAN, THOMAS	BAL	117	11TH WAR
DROKE, HENRY P.	BAL	336	1ST DIST
DROMER, HENRY	WAS	059	2ND SUBD
DROMER, OTHER	WAS	059	2ND SUBD
DRONEBERGER, JOHN	CAR	336	2ND DIST
DRONENBERG, HIRAM	FRE	395	PETERSVI
DRONENBRIG, WILLIAM J.	MGM	442	CLARKSTR
DRONENBURG, MARY	FRE	276	NEW MARK
DRONENBURG, MARY M.	FRE	227	BUCKEYST
DRONENTON, CHARLES F.	MGM	438	CLARKSTR
DRONENTON, CORNELIA	MGM	438	CLARKSTR
DRONENTON, JOHN H.	MGM	438	CLARKSTR
DROSTE, JOHN H.	BAL	088	15TH WAR
DROTA, JOHN H.	BAL	036	9TH WARD
DROUDNEY, MARGARET	BAL	434	8TH WARD
DROUGHT GEORGE	BAL	083	10TH WAR
DROUTFELLER, JOHN	BAL	178	2ND WARD
DROZLER, PATRICK	BAL	004	18TH WAR
DRUCK, E.	BAL	449	8TH WARD
DRUDGE, WILLIAM	MGM	368	BERRYS D
DRUENBERG, HENRY	BAL	172	1ST WARD
DRUIT, SUSAN	BAL	406	14TH WAR
DRULY, ELIZABETH	BAL	351	3RD WARD
DRUM, JAMES	FRE	095	FREDERIC
DRUMBOLTON, GEORGE	BAL	094	5TH WARD
DRUMIDA, CHARLES	BAL	262	20TH WAR
DRUMMER, SAMUEL	BAL	082	2ND DIST
DRUMMER, SAMUEL	BAL	081	2ND DIST
DRUMMOND, ALFRED T.	WOR	329	1ST E DI
DRUMMOND, CHARLES J.	BAL	172	6TH WARD
DRUMMOND, DAVID	WOR	337	1ST E DI
DRUMMOND, EMALINE	CEC	006	ELKTON 3
DRUMMOND, EVAN	BAL	413	14TH WAR
DRUMMOND, JAMES H.L.	CEC	097	4TH E DI
DRUMMOND, KERSY	CEC	129	6TH E DI
DRUMMOND, LEVEN J.*	BAL	034	4TH WARD
DRUMMOND, LOUISA	BAL	415	14TH WAR
DRUMMOND, MARTHA M	CEC	103	4TH E DI
DRUMMOND, MATHEW	CEC	106	3RD E DI
DRUMMOND, SAMUEL	BAL	050	9TH WARD
DRUMMOND, WASHINGTON S.	BAL	278	7TH WARD
DRUMMOND, WILLIAM M.	CEC	110	4TH E DI
DRUMOND, HENRY	PRI	025	VANSVILL
DRUNK, SUSAN	BAL	125	5TH WARD
DRUNPTENAN, CAROLINE	BAL	227	12TH WAR
DRUNPTENAN, CHRIS	BAL	227	12TH WAR
DRURA, ELIZABETH	DOR	305	1ST DIST
DRURA, WILLIAM S.	DOR	305	1ST DIST
DRURY, ANN	BAL	035	15TH WAR
DRURY, CHARLES H.	BAL	098	15TH WAR
DRURY, CORDELIA	ANN	401	8TH DIST
DRURY, CORNELIUS	ST	308	1ST E DI
DRURY, EGNIDOUS	WAS	133	2ND DIST
DRURY, ELIZABETH	BAL	080	4TH WARD
DRURY, HENRY	ANN	395	8TH DIST
DRURY, HENRY	ANN	399	8TH DIST
DRURY, HENRY C.	ANN	398	8TH DIST
DRURY, JAMES H.	ST	335	4TH E DI
DRURY, JANE M.	ST	268	3RD E DI
DRURY, JOHN H.	ANN	398	8TH DIST
DRURY, JOHN L.	ST	254	3RD E DI
DRURY, JOSEPH	ST	347	5TH E DI
DRURY, MARY	ST	273	3RD E DI
DRURY, PLUMMER J.	ANN	300	1ST DIST
DRURY, STEPHEN	SOM	472	TRAPPE D
DRURY, T.T.	ST	309	1ST E DI
DRURY, WILLIAM	ANN	398	8TH DIST
DRURY, WILLIAM	BAL	142	16TH WAR
DRURY, WILLIAM	ANN	450	HOWARD D
DRURY, WILLIAM A.	ST	322	4TH E DI
DRURY, WILLIAM H.	ST	282	3RD E DI
DRURY, WILLIAM H.	BAL	188	6TH WARD
DRUST, HERMAN	BAL	051	18TH WAR
DRYDEN, BENJAMIN	WOR	187	7TH E DI
DRYDEN, BETSEY	SOM	410	DUBLIN D
DRYDEN, C. P.	BAL	150	1ST WARD
DRYDEN, CHARLES	BAL	097	5TH WARD
DRYDEN, DAVID	SOM	406	DUBLIN D
DRYDEN, EDWARD	SOM	414	DUBLIN D
DRYDEN, ELIZA	WOR	179	6TH E DI
DRYDEN, ELIZABETH	SOM	417	PRINCESS
DRYDEN, GEORGE	SOM	386	BRINKLEY
DRYDEN, HANNAH	WOR	350	1ST E DI
DRYDEN, HARRIETT	BAL	184	11TH WAR
DRYDEN, HENRY	WOR	184	6TH E DI
DRYDEN, HENRY	SOM	413	DUBLIN D
DRYDEN, HENRY	SOM	411	DUBLIN D
DRYDEN, ISAAC	SOM	421	PRINCESS
DRYDEN, ISAAC	SOM	405	DUBLIN D
DRYDEN, ISAAC	BAL	073	15TH WAR
DRYDEN, JAEMS M.	SOM	417	PRINCESS
DRYDEN, JAMES	SOM	409	DUBLIN D
DRYDEN, JAMES	SOM	403	BRINKLEY
DRYDEN, JAMES	SOM	351	BRINKLEY
DRYDEN, JAMES P.	WOR	187	7TH E DI
DRYDEN, JANE A.	BAL	449	14TH WAR
DRYDEN, JOHN	SOM	406	DUBLIN D
DRYDEN, JOHN	WOR	187	7TH E DI
DRYDEN, JOHN	SOM	533	QUANTICO
DRYDEN, JOHN H.	BAL	117	15TH WAR
DRYDEN, JOHN N.	WOR	171	6TH E DI
DRYDEN, JOHN S. JR.	SOM	407	DUBLIN D
DRYDEN, JOHN W.	SOM	417	PRINCESS
DRYDEN, JOSHUA	BAL	142	19TH WAR
DRYDEN, JOSHUA	WOR	180	5TH E DI
DRYDEN, JOSHUA R.	BAL	105	15TH WAR
DRYDEN, LEMUEL	SOM	386	BRINKLEY
DRYDEN, LEVIN	SOM	482	TRAPP DI
DRYDEN, LITTLETON	SOM	405	DUBLIN D
DRYDEN, LOYUISA	WOR	345	1ST E DI
DRYDEN, MARY W.	SOM	417	PRINCESS
DRYDEN, NOBLE	WOR	350	1ST E DI
DRYDEN, PHILLES	WOR	198	8TH E DI
DRYDEN, PRISCILLA H.	WOR	187	7TH E DI
DRYDEN, PURNELL	SOM	410	DUBLIN D
DRYDEN, ROBERT	WOR	306	2ND E DI
DRYDEN, ROBERT M.	BAL	256	5TH WARD
DRYDEN, ROBERT W.	BAL	044	9TH WARD

DRYDEN, RUTH	BAL	204	6TH WARD
DRYDEN, SAMUEL	WOR	181	6TH E DI
DRYDEN, SAMUEL	BAL	205	17TH WAR
DRYDEN, SAMUEL	BAL	372	13TH WAR
DRYDEN, SARAH	SOM	418	PRINCESS
DRYDEN, THOMAS	SOM	397	BRINKLEY
DRYDEN, THOMAS A.	SOM	365	BRINKLEY
DRYDEN, WILLIAM	SOM	364	BRINKLEY
DRYDEN, WILLIAM	WOR	185	7TH E DI
DRYDEN, WILLIAM	SOM	407	DUBLIN D
DRYER, CHARLES	ALL	103	5TH E.D.
DRYER, CHARLES	ALL	149	6TH E.D.
DRYER, EMILY	BAL	078	4TH WARD
DRYER, ERNEST	BAL	265	20TH WAR
DRYER, HENRY	BAL	282	17TH WAR
DRYER, MARY	BAL	087	4TH WARD
DRYER, WILLIAM	BAL	092	5TH WARD
DRYLAN, NICHOLAS	BAL	291	1ST DIST
DUAMY, CONRAD	BAL	148	19TH WAR
DUANT, ELIZABETH	BAL	108	1ST WARD
DUBALL, DINAH	BAL	032	18TH WAR
DUBALL, ELEANOR	MGM	344	CLARKSBU
DUBALL, HENRY C.	FRE	383	PETERSVI
DUBALL, OCRTAVELD	BAL	187	11TH WAR
DUBB, THOMAS	BAL	058	1ST WARD
DUBBOROW, SARAH	ANN	427	HOWARD D
DUBEL, JAMES A.	BAL	376	3RD WARD
DUBELDA, CHARLOTTE	BAL	128	18TH WAR
DUBELDA, SAMUEL	BAL	128	18TH WAR
DUBITCH, JOHANNA	BAL	339	13TH WAR
DUBLEY, WILLIAM	WOR	319	1ST E DI
DUBLIN, JOSEPH	KEN	233	2ND DIST
DUBLIN, SIDNEY	BAL	179	16TH WAR
DUBOIS, A.	BAL	191	11TH WAR
DUBOIS, CHARLES A.	ANN	291	ANNAPOLI
DUBOIS, E.C.	WAS	011	WILLIAMS
DUBOIS, ED	BAL	137	11TH WAR
DUBOIS, EDWARD	ANN	291	ANNAPOLI
DUBOIS, PHILOMENA	BAL	205	11TH WAR
DUBREE, REBECCA	BAL	089	10TH WAR
DUBRET, DOMINIC	BAL	006	15TH WAR
DUBUYS, SCOCORDE	BAL	177	2ND WARD
DUBYTE, JOHN	BAL	035	9TH WARD
DUCAN, EDWARD M.	BAL	140	11TH WAR
DUCAN, JAMES	FRE	155	10TH E D
DUCAS, SOPHIA	BAL	361	8TH WARD
DUCATEL, GOANNA	BAL	461	14TH WAR
DUCATELE, HAPPOLYTE G.*	BAL	080	4TH WARD
DUCE, JOHN	BAL	244	1ST DIST
DUCE, JOHN	BAL	243	1ST DIST
DUCHEAT, JUDSON	BAL	092	2ND DIST
DUCK, CONSTANCE	BAL	261	1ST DIST
DUCK, JACOB	ALL	056	10TH E.D
DUCKE, S.	BAL	093	10TH WAR
DUCKER, EPHRAIM	BAL	291	12TH WAR
DUCKER, FANNY	MGM	321	CRACKLIN
DUCKER, HENRY H.	BAL	224	1ST DIST
DUCKER, JEREMIAH	BAL	233	1ST DIST
DUCKER, NATHANIEL	ALL	093	5TH E.D.
DUCKET, ISAAC	ANN	330	2ND DIST
DUCKET, JOHN	WAS	062	2ND SUBD
DUCKET, JOHN	WAS	086	2ND SUBD
DUCKETT, BASEL	PRI	118	PISCATAW
DUCKETT, BEN M.	PRI	085	QUEEN AN
DUCKETT, CAROLINE	PRI	053	AQUASCO
DUCKETT, ELIZABETH	BAL	255	12TH WAR
DUCKETT, FRANK	PRI	091	MARLBROU
DUCKETT, HENRY	BAL	240	12TH WAR
DUCKETT, ISAAC	BAL	240	12TH WAR
DUCKETT, JAMES	PRI	091	MARLBROU
DUCKETT, JAMES M.	PRI	010	BLADENSB
DUCKETT, JOHN	BAL	255	12TH WAR
DUCKETT, JOHN	ANN	317	1ST DIST
DUCKETT, LUCY	BAL	287	12TH WAR
DUCKETT, MARGARET	PRI	089	SPALDING
DUCKETT, MARIA	PRI	076	MARLBROU
DUCKETT, KARY	BAL	252	20TH WAR
DUCKETT, R.	PRI	086	QUEEN AN
DUCKETT, R.	WAS	021	2ND SUBD
DUCKETT, RICHARD	BAL	191	11TH WAR
DUCKETT, SARAH	PRI	072	MARLBROU
DUCKETT, T.B.	WAS	274	RIDGEVIL
DUCKETT, THOMAAS S.	PRI	017	BLADENSB
DUCKETT, THOMAS	WAS	090	2ND SUBD
DUCKEY, JAMES	CAR	101	NO TWP L
DUCKHART, JOHN	BAL	129	5TH WARD
DUCKLE, GEORGE	BAL	241	12TH WAR
DUCKREY, JAMES	BAL	106	15TH WAR
DUCKUSON, GEORGE W. *	ALL	086	5TH E.D.
DUCKWORTH, AARON	ALL	124	4TH E.D.
DUCKWORTH, ASHFORD	ALL	124	4TH E.D.
DUCKWORTH, CHARLES W.	ALL	088	5TH E.D.
DUCKWORTH, EZEKIEL	ALL	118	5TH E.D.
DUCKWORTH, GEORGE	ALL	133	4TH E.D.
DUCKWORTH, HIRAM	ALL	144	6TH E.D.
DUCKWORTH, ISRAEL	ALL	133	4TH E.D.
DUCKWORTH, JOHN	ALL	153	6TH E.D.
DUCKWORTH, JOHN	ALL	155	6TH E.D.
DUCKWORTH, LEWIS J.	ALL	131	4TH E.D.
DUCKWORTH, LYODEA	ALL	124	4TH E.D.
DUCKWORTH, MAHALA *	ALL	089	5TH E.D.
DUCKWORTH, PETER	ALL	130	4TH E.D.
DUCKWORTH, URIAH	ALL	131	4TH E.D.
DUCKWORTH, URIAH	ALL	133	4TH E.D.
DUCKWORTH, WILLIAM	ALL	131	4TH E.D.
DUCKWORTH, WILLIAM	ALL	143	6TH E.D.
DUCORNMON, LOUIS *	KEN	213	2ND DIST
DUCTER, K.M.	BAL	115	1ST WARD
DUCUS, MARY	CAR	210	5TH DIST
DUCY, RACHEL	BAL	231	12TH WAR
DUCY, WILLIAM	KEN	308	3RD DIST
DUDDERAN, JOHN F.	FRE	434	8TH E DI
DUDDERAR, COONRAD	FRE	230	BUCKEYST
DUDDERAR, ELIZABETH	FRE	230	BUCKEYST
DUDDERAR, FRANCIS W.	FRE	439	8TH E DI
DUDDERAR, GEORGE W.	FRE	438	8TH E DI
DUDDERAR, JOHN W.	FRE	229	BUCKEYST
DUDDEREAN, DAVID	FRE	434	8TH E DI
DUDDEREN, BENJAMIN	FRE	429	8TH E DI
DUDDEROW, WILLIAM	FRE	108	CREAGERS
DUDDY, WILLIAM	BAL	007	18TH WAR
DUDE, DAUGHTY	ALL	020	2ND E.D.
DUDE, FREDERICK	BAL	268	7TH WARD
DUDING, EDUARD	BAL	188	2ND WARD
DUDKEN, ANN	BAL	229	1ST DIST
DUDLEY, ALEXANDER C.	TAL	056	EASTON D
DUDLEY, BENJAMIN	KEN	311	3RD DIST
DUDLEY, ELIZA A.	QUE	145	1ST E DI
DUDLEY, ELIZA R.	BAL	332	3RD WARD
DUDLEY, ELIZABETH	TAL	107	ST MICHA
DUDLEY, EMELINE	KEN	215	2ND DIST
DUDLEY, FRANCIS A.	BAL	023	4TH WARD
DUDLEY, HANNA	TAL	030	EASTON D
DUDLEY, ISAAC	ANN	334	2ND DIST
DUDLEY, JAMES P.	QUE	175	2ND E DI
DUDLEY, JOHN	ALL	108	5TH E.D.
DUDLEY, JOHN	BAL	097	1ST WARD
DUDLEY, JOHN	KEN	234	2ND DIST
DUDLEY, JOSEPH	BAL	147	5TH WARD
DUDLEY, M.S.	BAL	154	1ST WARD
DUDLEY, MARIA	BAL	353	7TH WARD
DUDLEY, MARY	BAL	402	8TH WARD
DUDLEY, MARY	TAL	010	EASTON D
DUDLEY, MRS. J.L.	BAL	296	17TH WAR
DUDLEY, NANTRY*	BAL	057	4TH WARD
DUDLEY, NATHAN	ALL	108	5TH E.D.
DUDLEY, RICHARD	KEN	269	1ST DIST
DUDLEY, SALMON	BAL	067	4TH WARD
DUDLEY, SARAH E.	QUE	124	1ST E DI
DUDLEY, SARAH E.	KEN	285	3RD DIST
DUDLEY, SOPHIA	KEN	271	1ST DIST
DUDLEY, SOPHIA	BAL	445	14TH WAR
DUDLEY, SUSAN	KEN	295	3RD DIST
DUDLEY, WILLIAM	KEN	312	3RD DIST
DUDLEY, WILLIAM	QUE	154	1ST E DI
DUDLIN, LOUISA	BAL	397	14TH WAR
DUDLY, ELLEN	BAL	043	18TH WAR
DUDLY, MARY	BAL	090	2ND DIST
DUDMAN, WILLIAM	BAL	121	1ST WARD
DUDRAR, JOHN	FRE	310	WOODSBOR
DUDRO, ELIZABETH	FRE	310	WOODSBOR
DUDROW, JACOB	FRE	418	8TH E DI
DUDROW, RANDOLPH	FRE	309	WOODSBOR
DUE, ENOCH-BLACK	CAR	083	NO TWP L
DUEGAN, JOHN	BAL	366	13TH WAR
DUEPHT, DORIETY	BAL	079	18TH WAR
DUER, CHARLES	BAL	084	2ND DIST
DUER, ISAAC	SOM	408	DUBLIN D
DUER, JOHN	FRE	202	5TH E DI
DUER, JOHN JR.	BAL	381	13TH WAR
DUER, LAURA	BAL	085	2ND DIST
DUER, LITTLETON	WOR	339	1ST E DI
DUER, NANCY	SOM	408	DUBLIN D
DUER, REBECCA	HAR	079	2ND DIST
DUER, SAMUEL	BAL	131	16TH WAR
DUER, WILLIAM	SOM	408	DUBLIN D
DUER, WILLIAM	FRE	202	5TH E DI
DUFEE, BRIDGET	ALL	253	CUMBERLA
DUFEY, THOMAS	BAL	143	1ST WARD
DUFF, ANN	SOM	490	SALISBUR
DUFF, ANN G.	HAR	056	1ST DIST
DUFF, CHARLES	BAL	133	1ST WARD
DUFF, CHARLES J.	BAL	114	1ST WARD
DUFF, CHARLOTT	CEC	049	1ST E DI
DUFF, GEORGE	BAL	040	15TH WAR
DUFF, GORGE	BAL	029	2ND DIST
DUFF, HARRIET	HAR	065	1ST DIST
DUFF, HENRY	BAL	074	4TH WARD
DUFF, HENRY	BAL	278	7TH WARD
DUFF, JAMES	BAL	089	2ND DIST
DUFF, JAMES	ALL	207	CUMBERLA
DUFF, JOHN	BAL	314	20TH WAR
DUFF, LOUISA	BAL	204	6TH WARD
DUFF, MARTIN	BAL	097	1ST WARD
DUFF, MARY	BAL	059	10TH WAR
DUFF, MARY A.	BAL	355	13TH WAR
DUFF, SAUL	SOM	549	TYASKIN
DUFF, THOMAS	HAR	116	2ND DIST
DUFF, THOMAS	CEC	093	4TH E DI
DUFF, THOMAS	BAL	189	17TH WAR
DUFF, WILLIAM	BAL	028	9TH WARD
DUFFEE, BRIDGET	BAL	445	1ST DIST
DUFFEE, JOHN H.	FRE	065	FREDERIC
DUFFEE, THOMAS	FRE	064	FREDERIC
DUFFEE, THOMAS	WOR	307	2ND E DI
DUFFEE, WILLIAM	WOR	176	6TH E DI
DUFFEN, ELIJAH-BLACK	FRE	226	BUCKEYST
DUFFENBERGER, ADAM	WAS	249	1ST DIST
DUFFEY, CATHARINE	FRE	182	5TH E DI
DUFFEY, ELIZA	BAL	054	4TH WARD
DUFFEY, ELLEN	BAL	041	1ST WARD
DUFFEY, EMMA	BAL	419	3RD WARD
DUFFEY, JOHN	BAL	211	11TH WAR
DUFFEY, JOHN	BAL	424	8TH WARD
DUFFEY, MARGARET	FRE	161	EMMITTSB
DUFFEY, MICHEL	BAL	299	7TH WARD
DUFFEY, NANCY	SOM	425	PRINCESS
DUFFEY, THOMAS	MGM	400	ROCKERLE
DUFFEY, THOMAS	CAR	219	5TH DIST
DUFFEY, WILLIAM	MGM	400	ROCKERLE
DUFFIE, CHARLES	BAL	126	2ND DIST
DUFFIE, JAOCB-BLACK	WOR	172	6TH E DI
DUFFIELD, EDWRD	WOR	299	SNOW HIL
DUFFIELD, GEORGE	WAS	124	2ND DIST
DUFFIN, BASIL	BAL	041	2ND DIST
DUFFIN, GEORGE	WAS	170	FUNKSTOW
DUFFIN, JOSEPH-BLACK	FRE	382	PETERSVI
DUFFIN, MOSES	BAL	168	16TH WAR
DUFFIN, SAMUEL	WAS	161	HAGERSTO
DUFFREY, JOHN	BAL	143	1ST WARD
DUFFY, BERNARD	BAL	268	20TH WAR
DUFFY, BIDDY	SOM	482	TRAPP DI
DUFFY, BRIDGET	BAL	321	20TH WAR
DUFFY, CATHARINE	BAL	299	12TH WAR
DUFFY, CATHERINE	BAL	158	11TH WAR
DUFFY, CATHERINE	BAL	158	11TH WAR
DUFFY, CATHERINE	BAL	152	11TH WAR
DUFFY, D. J.	BAL	147	1ST WARD
DUFFY, DAVID	SOM	434	PRINCESS
DUFFY, GEORGE	SOM	429	PRINCESS
DUFFY, HUGH	CHA	241	HILLTOP
DUFFY, HUGH	BAL	298	20TH WAR
DUFFY, HUGH	BAL	187	6TH WARD
DUFFY, JAMES	BAL	023	9TH WARD
DUFFY, JAMES	ALL	051	10TH E.D
DUFFY, JOHN	ALL	155	6TH E.D.
DUFFY, JOHN	BAL	142	1ST WARD
DUFFY, JOHN	SOM	435	PRINCESS
DUFFY, MARK	MGM	381	ROCKERLE
DUFFY, MARY	CHA	260	MIDDLETO
DUFFY, MARY	BAL	152	11TH WAR
DUFFY, MARY	BAL	145	5TH WARD
DUFFY, MARY	BAL	119	15TH WAR
DUFFY, MARY	BAL	110	10TH WAR
DUFFY, MARY	SOM	460	HANGARY
DUFFY, MICHAEL	BAL	293	12TH WAR
DUFFY, MICHAEL	HAR	146	3RD DIST
DUFFY, MIHAEL	ALL	136	4TH E.D.
DUFFY, OWEN	BAL	445	14TH WAR
DUFFY, PETER	BAL	254	20TH WAR
DUFFY, PETER	BAL	189	5TH DIST
DUFFY, PHILIP	BAL	469	14TH WAR
DUFFY, SALLY	SOM	485	TRAPP DI
DUFFY, SARAH	HAR	088	2ND DIST
DUFFY, TERENCE	ALL	056	10TH E.D
DUFFY, THOMAS	ALL	155	6TH E.D.
DUFFY, THOMAS	BAL	190	5TH DIST
DUFFY, THOMAS	ALL	246	CUMBERLA
DUFFY, THOMAS	ANN	422	HOWARD D
DUFFY, THOMAS	BAL	202	17TH WAR
DUFFY, WILLIAM	WAS	205	1ST DIST
DUFFY, RACHEL	BAL	289	12TH WAR
DUFILHO, ALFRED	FRE	202	5TH E DI
DUFREST, B. *	BAL	298	12TH WAR
DUFRON, HENRY	BAL	127	5TH WARD
DUFUR, ORLANDO	BAL	184	16TH WAR
DUGAN, ANNA	ALL	238	CUMBERLA
DUGAN, CATHERINE	BAL	357	8TH WARD
DUGAN, CHARLES	HAR	152	3RD DIST
DUGAN, DANIEL	BAL	011	9TH WARD
DUGAN, FREDERIC J.	BAL	039	9TH WARD
DUGAN, FREDERICK	BAL	315	20TH WAR
DUGAN, JAMES	BAL	318	1ST DIST
DUGAN, JANE	BAL	201	19TH WAR
DUGAN, JOHN	FRE	224	BUCKEYST
DUGAN, JOHN	BAL	430	1ST DIST
DUGAN, JOSEPH D.	BAL	110	5TH WARD
DUGAN, JOSHUA	BAL	446	14TH WAR
DUGAN, MARIA	MGM	378	ROCKERLE
DUGAN, MARTIN	ANN	413	HOWARD D
DUGAN, MARY	BAL	203	6TH WARD
DUGAN, MATTHEW	CHA	252	BOJANTOW
DUGAN, ROBERT	KEN	222	2ND DIST
DUGAN, ROBERT W.	BAL	279	2ND WARD
DUGAN, SARAH	BAL	315	1ST DIST
DUGAN, SSUAN	FRE	004	FREDERIC
DUGAN, SUSAN	PRI	037	VANSVILL
DUGAN, THOMAS	KEN	209	2ND DIST
DUGAN, WILLIAM	FRE	099	FREDERIC
DUGAN, WILLIAM W.	KEN	208	2ND DIST
DUGBY, PLENDENKS	CEC	037	CHESAPEA
DUGEN, HENRY	BAL	111	2ND DIST
DUGEN, NABBIE	BAL	274	20TH WAR
DUGENBARDT, ANTHONY	BAL	094	1ST WARD
DUGENT, ELI	BAL	413	3RD WARD
DUGENT, FRANCIS	BAL	415	3RD WARD
DUGENT, FRANCIS	BAL	413	3RD WARD
DUGER, MICHAEL	BAL	444	14TH WAR
DUGHERTY, ELLA ROSE SIS-	BAL	316	20TH WAR
DUGION, ELLEN	HAR	151	3RD DIST
DUGLAS, JOSEPH	CHA	252	BOJANTOW
DUGLAS, ROBERT	FRE	398	JEFFERSO
DUGLASS, ELIZAVETH	CHA	228	ALLENS F
DUGLASS, JAMES-BLACK	WOR	325	1ST E DI
DUGLASS, PRISCILLA	ALL	207	CUMBERLA
DUGLASS, WILLIAM H.	BAL	029	18TH WAR
DUGNON, THOMAS	ALL	248	CUMBERLA
DUGUESNE, PETER	BAL	011	18TH WAR
DUHADAWAY, THOMAS	CAR	134	NO TWP L
DUHAMEL, ANN M.	BAL	032	15TH WAR
DUHAMEL, JAMES	BAL	272	12TH WAR
DUHAN, MALACHI	WAS	150	2ND DIST
DUHANEL, RACHEL-BLACK	QUE	147	1ST E DI
DUHERST, CASIRE	BAL	174	19TH WAR
DUHURST, GREENBEY	BAL	123	11TH WAR
DUHURST, H.	BAL	141	1ST WARD
DUHURST, MARY	BAL	074	10TH WAR
DUIAN, FELIX	BAL	252	12TH WAR
DUICKETT, ROBERT S.	BAL	445	8TH WARD
DUIFFEY, ANN	BAL	262	2ND WARD
DUIN, ELIZA J.	BAL	063	1ST WARD
DUKAMEL, SAMUEL L.	QUE	124	1ST E DI
DUKE, ALEXANDER B.	CAL	006	1ST DIST
DUKE, ANN	WAS	156	2ND DIST
DUKE, C.	BAL	167	1ST WARD
DUKE, GREEN H.	FRE	031	FREDERIC
DUKE, HESTER	CEC	009	ELKTON 3
DUKE, JAMES	BAL	191	6TH WARD
DUKE, JAMES	ST	344	5TH E DI
DUKE, JOHN	BAL	299	20TH WAR
DUKE, MARK A.	BAL	164	16TH WAR
DUKE, MARY	BAL	138	5TH WARD
DUKE, MARY A.	WOR	188	7TH E DI
DUKE, MELAIN *	ALL	100	5TH E.D.
DUKE, MICHAEL	BAL	446	1ST DIST
DUKE, NATHANIEL	CAL	031	2ND DIST
DUKE, PHILIP	HAR	124	2ND DIST
DUKE, REBECCA	BAL	348	3RD WARD
DUKE, WILLIAM	BAL	126	16TH WAR
DUKE, WILLIAM	WAS	144	2ND DIST
DUKE, WILLIAM T.	BAL	197	6TH WARD
DUKEHART, ADAM	BAL	181	2ND WARD
DUKEHART, BALDERSTON	BAL	176	16TH WAR
DUKEHART, EDWARD W.	BAL	079	15TH WAR
DUKEHART, ELIZABETH	BAL	102	2ND DIST
DUKEHART, FRANCIS	BAL	143	16TH WAR
DUKEHART, HENRY	FRE	189	5TH E DI
DUKEHART, JACOB	ALL	095	5TH E.D.
DUKEHART, JOSEPH	BAL	230	6TH WARD
DUKEHART, ROBERT W.	BAL	073	4TH WARD
DUKEHART, WILLIAM	BAL	364	8TH WARD
DUKEHEART, HENRY	BAL	064	10TH WAR
DUKEHEART, MAN	BAL	084	4TH WARD
DUKEHEART, SAMUEL M.*	BAL	051	4TH WARD
DUKEHEART, V.	BAL	101	10TH WAR
DUKENS, THOMAS	WAS	225	1ST DIST
DUKER, JOHN H.	CAR	073	NO TWP L
DUKES, CHARLES	CAR	119	NO TWP L
DUKES, CHARLES	CAR	129	NO TWP L
DUKES, DENNY	WOR	320	1ST E DI
DUKES, ELIZA	WOR	314	2ND E DI
DUKES, ELIZABETH	WOR	261	BERLIN 1
DUKES, ISAAC	DOR	434	1ST DIST
DUKES, JAMES	CAR	120	NO TWP L
DUKES, JAMES	WOR	319	1ST E DI
DUKES, JEREMIAH	CAR	151	NO TWP L
DUKES, LEMUEL	WOR	247	1ST CENS
DUKES, LEVI	CAR	169	NO TWP L
DUKES, LEVIN	BAL	069	4TH WARD
DUKES, LEVIN G.	DOR	320	1ST DIST
DUKES, LITTLETON	WOR	349	1ST E DI
DUKES, MARY A.	ST	287	2ND E DI
DUKES, PRISCILLA	ST	274	3RD E DI
DUKES, ROBERT P.	WOR	183	6TH E DI
DUKES, SARAH	CAR	146	NO TWP L
DUKES, THOMAS	CAR	143	NO TWP L
DUKES, THOMAS	WOR	338	1ST E DI
DUKES, THOMAS	WOR	319	1ST E DI
DUKES, WILLIAM	BAL	103	18TH WAR
DUKES, WSILLSON	CAR	068	NO TWP L

DUKES.LEVIN T.	CAR	165	NO TWP L
DUKES.MARY	CAR	092	NO TWP L
DUKEY,NANCY	ALL	233	CUMBERLA
DUKRON, A.	BAL	282	2ND WARD
DUKS. FREDERIC	WOR	322	1ST E DI
DULACK, JOSEPH	BAL	403	8TH WARD
DULAN, JAMES P.	BAL	169	1ST WARD
DULAN, MARY	BAL	448	1ST DIST
DULANEY, ELIZA	BAL	341	7TH WARD
DULANEY, ISABELL	BAL	300	7TH WARD
DULANEY, JOHN	PRI	114	PISCATAW
DULANEY, LUCINDA	BAL	300	7TH WARD
DULANEY, MARY	BAL	447	8TH WARD
DULANEY, MATHEW	BAL	110	10TH WAR
DULANEY, PETER	BAL	046	1ST WARD
DULANEY, SARAH	BAL	292	12TH WAR
DULANY, ANN M.	SOM	532	QUANTICO
DULANY, BLADEN	BAL	116	18TH WAR
DULANY, G. L.	BAL	190	11TH WAR
DULANY, HENRY	SOM	492	SALISBUR
DULANY, HENRY R.	BAL	190	11TH WAR
DULANY, JAMES	BAL	124	18TH WAR
DULANY, JOHN	BAL	191	11TH WAR
DULANY, JOSHUA H.	KEN	243	2ND DIST
DULANY, LUCY	PRI	048	AQUASCO
DULANY, MARY	PRI	047	AQUASCO
DULANY, PATRICK	BAL	179	11TH WAR
DULANY, RACHEAL	BAL	024	18TH WAR
DULANY, RACHEL	PRI	048	AQUASCO
DULANY, S.	BAL	191	11TH WAR
DULANY, THOMAS	SOM	530	QUANTICO
DULANY, THOMAS	FRE	238	NEW MARK
DULANY, WILLIAM	BAL	182	19TH WAR
DULANY, WILLIAM	PRI	047	AQUASCO
DULE, MARGARET	BAL	261	12TH WAR
DULEN, ALEXANDER A. DR.	BAL	387	13TH WAR
DULEN, DANIEL	CAR	170	NO TWP L
DULEN, JOHN	KEN	313	3RD DIST
DULEN, WILLIAM	KEN	311	3RD DIST
DULEX, MARY*	BAL	093	10TH WAR
DULEY, DANE	BAL	225	12TH WAR
DULEY, ELIZA	MGM	338	CRACKLIN
DULEY, ELIZABETH	MGM	405	ROCKERLE
DULEY, ELSY	BAL	267	20TH WAR
DULEY, JOHN	BAL	153	19TH WAR
DULEY, JONATHAN	MGM	321	CRACKLIN
DULEY, MARY*	BAL	093	10TH WAR
DULEY, SARAH	BAL	294	12TH WAR
DULEY, THOMAS J.	PRI	011	BLADENSB
DULEY, WESLEY	MGM	338	CRACKLIN
DULIN, ANN M.	TAL	044	EASTON D
DULIN, ELIZA	QUE	139	1ST E DI
DULIN, ELIZABETH	BAL	030	9TH WARD
DULIN, HANNAH	QUE	204	3RD E DI
DULIN, HENRY	QUE	235	4TH E DI
DULIN, JINNET	TAL	024	EASTON D
DULIN, JOHN T.	TAL	026	EASTON D
DULIN, LEVI	TAL	015	EASTON D
DULIN, MARY	TAL	044	EASTON D
DULIN, MARY	BAL	129	5TH WARD
DULIN, MARY	BAL	242	17TH WAR
DULIN, MRS.	BAL	218	17TH WAR
DULIN, REBECCA	BAL	071	15TH WAR
DULIN, RUBEN	TAL	041	EASTON D
DULIN, SALLY	TAL	018	EASTON D
DULIN, SAMUEL	TAL	022	EASTON D
DULIN, SUSAN A.	TAL	042	EASTON D
DULIN, THOMAS W.	CEC	070	5TH E DI
DULING, JAMES	BAL	260	2ND WARD
DULING, JOHN	TAL	096	ST MICHA
DULKER, GEORGE	BAL	077	4TH WARD
DULL, CATHARINE	BAL	233	17TH WAR
DULL, CATHARINE	BAL	320	1ST DIST
DULL, DAVID	ALL	187	9TH E.D.
DULL, HANNAH	WAS	125	2ND DIST
DULL, JAMES	BAL	396	3RD WARD
DULL, JOHN	BAL	377	3RD WARD
DULL, RUTH	BAL	394	3RD WARD
DULL, WILLIAM	BAL	054	1ST WARD
DULLHUFF, JOHN	BAL	369	1ST DIST
DULLY, THOMAS	MGM	386	ROCKERLE
DULOIS, NATHAN	BAL	240	12TH WAR
DULOP, JOHN	BAL	075	18TH WAR
DULS, DANIEL*	BAL	272	20TH WAR
DULUYS, AMEAL	BAL	177	2ND WARD
DULY, JOHN	BAL	127	5TH WARD
DULY, JOSEPH E.	CHA	273	ALLENS F
DULY, MARY	CHA	269	ALLENS F
DUM, BRIDGET	BAL	314	20TH WAR
DUM, JAMES	SOM	444	DAMES QU
DUMARAS, EMILY	BAL	148	5TH WARD
DUMAS, ELIZA A.	BAL	007	9TH WARD
DUMAX, MARY	BAL	245	12TH WAR
DUMAX, SARAH	BAL	245	12TH WAR
DUMB, MARY	WAS	204	1ST DIST
DUMBAUGH, JACOB	WAS	215	1ST DIST
DUMBAUGH, JACOB	WAS	215	1ST DIST
DUMBOTTON, JAMES A.	BAL	094	5TH WARD
DUMBRACE, JAMES	QUE	188	3RD E DI
DUMBUSKER, HENRY	ALL	101	5TH E.D.
DUMES, CHRISTINA	BAL	165	2ND DIST
DUMES, JULIA	BAL	065	18TH WAR
DUMFREY, ELIZABETH	ANN	518	HOWARD D
DUMFRIES, RICHARD	BAL	174	2ND DIST
DUMFRIES, RICHARD	BAL	178	2ND DIST
DUMFRIES, SARAH	BAL	179	2ND DIST
DUMHEART, ANDREW	ANN	482	HOWARD D
DUMING, MARTHA	BAL	166	6TH WARD
DUMM, JOHN W.*	SOM	356	BRINKLEY
DUMMAN, BASIL	WAS	144	HAGERSTO
DUMMINS, ISABELLA	BAL	368	8TH WARD
DUMMORE, AMOS	CEC	148	PORT DUP
DUMMORE, WILLIAM	WAS	287	1ST DIST
DUMNUTH, CAROLINE	BAL	026	18TH WAR
DUMOND, WILLIAM	TAL	020	EASTON D
DUMONT, THOMAS	CEC	156	PORT DUP
DUMPEY, CATHERINE	BAL	400	8TH WARD
DUMPFRIES, JAMES	BAL	174	2ND DIST
DUMPHREY, ANN	CAR	220	5TH DIST
DUMPHY, JOHN S.	BAL	200	11TH WAR
DUMPHY, MARY	BAL	012	2ND DIST
DUMPSON, HESTER	BAL	134	16TH WAR
DUMPSON, MARIA	CEC	012	ELKTON 3
DUMPSON, RANSOR	CEC	048	1ST E DI
DUMSON, JAMES	CEC	059	1ST E DI
DUMSON, MARTHA	CEC	049	1ST E DI
DUMSON, REBECCA	CEC	036	CHESAPEA
DUN, JOHN	ST	311	1ST E DI
DUN, SUSAN	ST	312	1ST E DI
DUN, THOMAS H.	BAL	472	14TH WAR

DUNAGAN, PATRICK	BAL	448	1ST DIST
DUNAGAN, WILLIAM	BAL	396	1ST DIST
DUNAGE, LAURENCE	ALL	143	6TH E.D.
DUNAHM, CIRGINAI A.	BAL	418	14TH WAR
DUNAHUE, THOMAS	BAL	334	3RD WARD
DUNAKER, CONRAD V.	BAL	192	19TH WAR
DUNALLEN, ANDREW	BAL	284	17TH WAR
DUNAN, ALFRED	BAL	273	2ND WARD
DUNAN, GUSTAVUS J.	BAL	061	15TH WAR
DUNAN, HAZLET	BAL	081	4TH WARD
DUNAVAN, D	BAL	153	1ST WARD
DUNAVAN.D.	BAL	137	1ST WARD
DUNAVAST, WILLIAM P.	BAL	145	19TH WAR
DUNAWAY, HENRY	WOR	252	1ST CENS
DUNAWAY, ISAAC	WOR	252	1ST CENS
DUNAWAY, JAMES	WOR	252	1ST CENS
DUNAWAY, JOHN	WOR	252	1ST CENS
DUNAWAY, JOSEPH	WOR	252	1ST CENS
DUNAWAY, L. H. B.	WOR	252	1ST CENS
DUNAWAY, MORDICA	WOR	252	1ST CENS
DUNAWAY, OHN	WOR	205	4TH E DI
DUNAWAY, RODAH	WOR	250	1ST CENS
DUNAWAY, SOPHIAH	WOR	247	1ST CENS
DUNAWAY, THOMAS	WOR	252	1ST CENS
DUNAWAY, WILLIAM	WOR	252	1ST CENS
DUNAWAY, WILLIAM	ST	304	2ND E DI
DUNAX, BENJAMIN	BAL	243	2ND WARD
DUNBACCO, WILLIAM	QUE	174	2ND E DI
DUNBAR, ANTHONY	ALL	142	6TH E.D.
DUNBAR, BALDWIN	ALL	053	10TH E.D
DUNBAR, CHARLES	CEC	144	PORT DUP
DUNBAR, CORA A.	ST	324	4TH E DI
DUNBAR, ELIZABETH	ANN	352	3RD DIST
DUNBAR, GEORGE	BAL	247	6TH WARD
DUNBAR, GEORGE	BAL	118	1ST WARD
DUNBAR, HENRITTA	ANN	269	ANNAPOLI
DUNBAR, HENRY C.	ANN	351	3RD DIST
DUNBAR, HENRY F.	ANN	352	3RD DIST
DUNBAR, JAMES A.	ST	312	1ST E DI
DUNBAR, JOHN	CEC	012	ELKTON 3
DUNBAR, JOHN H.	BAL	154	1ST WARD
DUNBAR, JOHN R.	ST	311	1ST E DI
DUNBAR, JOHN R. DR.	BAL	382	13TH WAR
DUNBAR, JOHNA.	ST	306	1ST E DI
DUNBAR, JOSEPH JR.	ST	323	4TH E DI
DUNBAR, JOSEPH SR.	ST	324	4TH E DI
DUNBAR, JULIA A.	ST	275	3RD E DI
DUNBAR, MARY	ST	314	1ST E DI
DUNBAR, MARY	CEC	056	1ST E DI
DUNBAR, MORRIS	HAR	175	3RD DIST
DUNBAR, SARAH	ST	270	3RD E DI
DUNBAR, WILLIAM	CEC	010	ELKTON 3
DUNBOUNY, FANNY	BAL	069	4TH WARD
DUNBRACCC, MARY E.	QUE	174	2ND E DI
DUNBRACE, ELIZABETH B.	QUE	180	2ND E DI
DUNCAN, ADAM	BAL	329	13TH WAR
DUNCAN, ALEXANDER	BAL	169	19TH WAR
DUNCAN, ALEXANDER	BAL	141	19TH WAR
DUNCAN, AMELIA	WOR	222	4TH E DI
DUNCAN, ANN E.	WOR	285	BERLIN 1
DUNCAN, ASBURY	SOM	466	HANGARY
DUNCAN, BENJAMIN	SOM	465	HANGARY
DUNCAN, BENJAMIN	HAR	128	2ND DIST
DUNCAN, BENJAMIN	FRE	152	10TH E D
DUNCAN, CAROLINE	WOR	244	1ST CENS
DUNCAN, CASTRANDA	BAL	208	11TH WAR
DUNCAN, CATHARINE	WOR	308	2ND E DI
DUNCAN, CATHRINE	BAL	091	18TH WAR
DUNCAN, CHRISTIAN	BAL	208	19TH WAR
DUNCAN, ELIZA	BAL	019	4TH WARD
DUNCAN, ELIZA	BAL	029	9TH WARD
DUNCAN, ELIZA J.	BAL	200	11TH WAR
DUNCAN, FRANCES	BAL	224	6TH WARD
DUNCAN, GALTY	WOR	266	BERLIN 1
DUNCAN, GI *	BAL	153	1ST WARD
DUNCAN, HARRISON W.	BAL	397	14TH WAR
DUNCAN, HENRY	HAR	021	1ST DIST
DUNCAN, HIRAM K.	WOR	206	4TH E DI
DUNCAN, ISABELL	ALL	235	CUMBERLA
DUNCAN, JAMES	WOR	240	6TH E DI
DUNCAN, JAMES	WOR	166	6TH E DI
DUNCAN, JAMES	HAR	021	1ST DIST
DUNCAN, JAMES	HAR	024	1ST DIST
DUNCAN, JAMES	HAR	019	1ST DIST
DUNCAN, JAMES	BAL	161	19TH WAR
DUNCAN, JAMES W.	BAL	364	3RD WARD
DUNCAN, JANE	BAL	438	14TH WAR
DUNCAN, JOHN	BAL	214	11TH WAR
DUNCAN, JOHN	BAL	131	1ST WARD
DUNCAN, JOHN	BAL	128	1ST WARD
DUNCAN, JOHN	BAL	151	1ST WARD
DUNCAN, JOHN M.	BAL	062	10TH WAR
DUNCAN, JOHN M.	BAL	204	11TH WAR
DUNCAN, JOSEPH	HAR	021	1ST DIST
DUNCAN, JOSEPH	BAL	031	9TH WARD
DUNCAN, MARIA	BAL	159	11TH WAR
DUNCAN, MARTHA	WOR	271	BERLIN 1
DUNCAN, MARY	WOR	210	4TH E DI
DUNCAN, MARY	BAL	036	9TH WARD
DUNCAN, MARY	BAL	324	12TH WAR
DUNCAN, MARY	BAL	059	15TH WAR
DUNCAN, NANCY	WOR	272	BERLIN 1
DUNCAN, ROBERT	BAL	069	18TH WAR
DUNCAN, SAMPSON S.	HAR	021	1ST DIST
DUNCAN, SARAH M.	WOR	267	BERLIN 1
DUNCAN, THOMAS	CAR	369	9TH DIST
DUNCAN, THOMAS	ANN	493	HOWARD D
DUNCAN, WILLIAM	BAL	029	9TH WARD
DUNCAN, WILLIAM	BAL	166	6TH WARD
DUNCAN, WILLIAM	WOR	270	BERLIN 1
DUNCAN, WILLIAM	KEN	264	1ST DIST
DUNCAN, WILLIAM	WAS	115	2ND DIST
DUNCAN, WMILBY	WOR	166	6TH E DI
DUND, ANDREW J.	BAL	156	1ST WARD
DUNDAULF, JACOB	BAL	240	2ND WARD
DUNDELL, JOHN	ALL	143	6TH E.D.
DUNDON, HENRY	BAL	025	1ST WARD
DUNDORE, JOHN	BAL	152	19TH WAR
DUNDY, LEWIS	ANN	349	3RD DIST
DUNEMITT, REBECCA	BAL	121	2ND DIST
DUNER, J.	BAL	449	8TH WARD
DUNER, JOSEPH	ALL	251	CUMBERLA
DUNFF, ELIZABETH	BAL	192	2ND WARD
DUNFIELD, JACOB	BAL	079	1ST WARD
DUNGAN, CATHARINE H.	BAL	419	14TH WAR
DUNGAN, FRANCIS T.	BAL	012	18TH WAR
DUNGAN, FRANK W.	BAL	012	18TH WAR
DUNGAN, HOPE	BAL	068	18TH WAR
DUNGAN, JANE	BAL	388	1ST DIST
DUNGAN, JANE *	BAL	099	2ND DIST

DUNGAN, JESSE	BAL	388	1ST DIST
DUNGAN, M.W.	BAL	020	18TH WAR
DUNGAN, MARY E.	BAL	020	18TH WAR
DUNGAN, STEVENSON	BAL	085	4TH WARD
DUNGAN, WILLIAM	FRE	053	FREDERIC
DUNGAN, WILLIAM	BAL	326	1ST DIST
DUNGE, WILLIAM	CEC	170	6TH E DI
DUNGEE, WILLIAM W.	BAL	246	6TH WARD
DUNGEN, JANE	BAL	411	1ST DIST
DUNHAM, CATHERINE	BAL	158	11TH WAR
DUNHAM, ELIZABETH	ANN	265	ANNAPOLI
DUNHAM, ELIZABETH	BAL	386	3RD WARD
DUNHAM, HARRIETT	BAL	136	5TH WARD
DUNHAM, JACOB	BAL	009	4TH WARD
DUNHAM, JAMES	WAS	068	2ND SUBD
DUNHAM, SMITH	BAL	122	1ST WARD
DUNHAM, THORNTON C.	BAL	418	14TH WAR
DUNHAM, WILLIAM	BAL	114	1ST WARD
DUNHAM, WILLIAM	ALL	236	CUMBERLA
DUNIGAN, ELLEN	BAL	210	2ND WARD
DUNINGSON, WILLIAM	BAL	004	1ST WARD
DUNINGTON, ELIZABETH C.	CHA	245	HILLTOP
DUNINGTON, ELUZA P.	CHA	235	HILLTOP
DUNINGTON, FRANCIS E.	CHA	240	HILLTOP
DUNINGTON, JAMES	CHA	248	HILLTOP
DUNINGTON, JONATHAN	CHA	243	HILLTOP
DUNINGTON, NATHAN	CHA	249	HILLTOP
DUNIVAN, JOHN	BAL	194	2ND WARD
DUNIVAN, MICHAEL	WAS	026	2ND SUBD
DUNKAN, GEORGE	BAL	289	1ST DIST
DUNKAN, GEORGE	BAL	312	1ST DIST
DUNKAN, JOHN	BAL	252	1ST DIST
DUNKAN, JOHNSEY	BAL	238	1ST DIST
DUNKAN, JULIA A.	BAL	239	1ST DIST
DUNKAN, LEVINA	BAL	228	1ST DIST
DUNKAN, WILLIAM	BAL	249	1ST DIST
DUNKAN, WILLIAM	BAL	446	1ST DIST
DUNKAS, HENRY	BAL	116	1ST WARD
DUNKEART, HANNAH	PRI	029	VANSVILL
DUNKELL, G. B.	BAL	305	20TH WAR
DUNKEN, GEORGE	MGM	381	ROCKERLE
DUNKEN, MARGARET S.	BAL	379	1ST DIST
DUNKEN, PATRICK	BAL	299	7TH WARD
DUNKER, HENRY	ANN	266	ANNAPOLI
DUNKERLY, RICHARD	BAL	112	18TH WAR
DUNKHURST, DORUS	FRE	034	FREDERIC
DUNKHURST, HENRY	FRE	015	FREDERIC
DUNKHURST, SOPHIA	FRE	012	FREDERIC
DUNKIN, JOHN	BAL	029	1ST WARD
DUNKIN, LEWIN H.	BAL	260	1ST DIST
DUNKINS, LEWIS	DOR	342	3RD DIVI
DUNKINSON, WILLIAM H.	ST	311	1ST E DI
DUNKMON, AUGUSTUS	BAL	115	11TH WAR
DUNLAP, ADELINE	BAL	241	6TH WARD
DUNLAP, CHARLES	BAL	325	12TH WAR
DUNLAP, HENRY	FRE	379	PETERSVI
DUNLAP, HUGH	BAL	228	19TH WAR
DUNLAP, JOHN	FRE	090	FREDERIC
DUNLAP, JOHN	BAL	240	17TH WAR
DUNLAP, JOHN	BAL	271	1ST DIST
DUNLAP, MARGARET	BAL	381	13TH WAR
DUNLAP, MARGARET	BAL	004	18TH WAR
DUNLAP, THOMAS	BAL	004	18TH WAR
DUNLAP, WILLIAM	FRE	136	CREAGERS
DUNLIN, THOMAS	BAL	238	17TH WAR
DUNLIN, THOMAS	BAL	144	1ST WARD
DUNLING, THOMAS C.	BAL	077	4TH WARD
DUNLOP, GEORGE	FRE	380	PETERSVI
DUNLOP, HENRIETTA	MGM	400	ROCKERLE
DUNLOP, ROBERT P.	MGM	392	ROCKERLE
DUNLOP, WILLIAM	MGM	362	BERRYS D
DUNMORE, CHARLES	CEC	144	PORT DUP
DUNMORE, EDWARD	CEC	176	7TH E DI
DUNMORE, ELIZA	CEC	073	5TH E DI
DUNMORE, HANNAH	CEC	156	PORT DUP
DUNMORE, HARRIET	CEC	201	6TH E DI
DUNMORE, HENRY	WAS	232	1ST DIST
DUNMORE, ISAAC	CEC	207	7TH E DI
DUNMORE, ISAAC	CEC	148	PORT DUP
DUNMORE, ISAAC	CEC	183	7TH E DI
DUNMORE, JOHN H.	BAL	355	3RD WARD
DUNMORE, LAVINIA	WAS	287	1ST DIST
DUNMORE, SQUIRE	CEC	155	PORT DUP.
DUNN, ALEXANDER	BAL	375	8TH WARD
DUNN, ALFRED	BAL	038	1ST WARD
DUNN, ANDREW	BAL	070	4TH WARD
DUNN, ANDREW	BAL	441	14TH WAR
DUNN, ANN	BAL	049	9TH WARD
DUNN, ANN	BAL	181	11TH WAR
DUNN, ANNA	BAL	008	4TH WARD
DUNN, ANTHONY*	DOR	421	1ST DIST
DUNN, BARNEY	BAL	123	11TH WAR
DUNN, BENJAMIN	SOM	541	TYASKIN
DUNN, BENJAMIN	WOR	329	1ST E DI
DUNN, C.	BAL	127	5TH WARD
DUNN, CATHERINE	BAL	025	4TH WARD
DUNN, CHARLES	BAL	231	6TH WARD
DUNN, CHARLES	BAL	257	12TH WAR
DUNN, CHARLES	QUE	234	4TH E DI
DUNN, CONRAD	BAL	260	2ND WARD
DUNN, DANIEL	BAL	174	6TH WARD
DUNN, CANIEL	BAL	444	1ST DIST
DUNN, DANIEL	WAS	299	1ST DIST
DUNN, DARL	BAL	024	2ND DIST
DUNN, E.	ANN	272	ANNAPOLI
DUNN, EDWARD	BAL	448	1ST DIST
DUNN, EDWARD	BAL	175	11TH WAR
DUNN, EDWARD	WAS	026	2ND SUBD
DUNN, EDWARD	BAL	104	18TH WAR
DUNN, ELIJAH	SOM	540	TYASKIN
DUNN, ELIZA	BAL	119	5TH WARD
DUNN, ELIZABETH	BAL	384	1ST DIST
DUNN, EMILY	CEC	120	4TH E DI
DUNN, FRANCIS	BAL	154	16TH WAR
DUNN, FRANK	BAL	037	2ND DIST
DUNN, GEORGE	BAL	401	8TH WARD
DUNN, GEORGE	DOR	450	1ST DIST
DUNN, GEORGE B.	SOM	543	TYASKIN
DUNN, HANAH	BAL	411	8TH WARD
DUNN, HELTY	BAL	043	1ST WARD
DUNN, HENERETTA	SOM	541	TYASKIN
DUNN, HENRY	BAL	146	1ST WARD
DUNN, HENRY L.	CEC	098	4TH E DI
DUNN, HESTER	BAL	363	8TH WARD
DUNN, ISAAC R.	SOM	541	TYASKIN
DUNN, JAMES	BAL	195	17TH WAR
DUNN, JAMES	BAL	169	16TH WAR
DUNN, JAMES	BAL	408	1ST DIST
DUNN, JAMES	BAL	035	4TH WARD
DUNN, JAMES	MGM	320	CRACKLIN

DUNN, JAMES * BAL 042 9TH WARD
DUNN, JANE BAL 033 18TH WAR
DUNN, JANE WAS 140 2ND DIST
DUNN, JOHN BAL 103 18TH WAR
DUNN, JOHN SOM 435 PRINCESS
DUNN, JOHN BAL 187 16TH WAR
DUNN, JOHN BAL 096 15TH WAR
DUNN, JOHN BAL 385 1ST DIST
DUNN, JOHN BAL 444 1ST DIST
DUNN, JOHN BAL 446 1ST DIST
DUNN, JOHN BAL 042 1ST WARD
DUNN, JOHN BAL 279 1ST DIST
DUNN, JOHN BAL 163 2ND DIST
DUNN, JOHN BAL 005 15TH WAR
DUNN, JOHN C. BAL 116 18TH WAR
DUNN, JOHN SR. BAL 175 2ND WARD
DUNN, JOHN SR. ANN 273 ANNAPOLI
DUNN, JOHN W. PRI 009 BLADENSB
DUNN, JOSEPH SOM 542 TYASKIN
DUNN, L. BAL 154 1ST WARD
DUNN, LAWRENCE WAS 055 2ND SUBD
DUNN, LEONARD ALL 001 3RD E.D.
DUNN, LEWIS ALL 241 CUMBERLA
DUNN, M. ANN 272 ANNAPOLI
DUNN, M. BAL 063 10TH WAR
DUNN, MARCUS A. BAL 354 7TH WARD
DUNN, MARGARET BAL 065 15TH WAR
DUNN, MARGARET SOM 542 TYASKIN
DUNN, MARSHALL P. BAL 151 16TH WAR
DUNN, MARY BAL 090 15TH WAR
DUNN, MARY WAS 024 2ND SUBD
DUNN, MARY ANN ALL 260 CUMBERLA
DUNN, MARY J. BAL 267 7TH WARD
DUNN, MICHAEL BAL 151 16TH WAR
DUNN, MICHAEL BAL 130 5TH WARD
DUNN, MICHAEL BAL 032 1ST WARD
DUNN, N.* DOR 413 1ST DIST
DUNN, OWEN BAL 197 2ND WARD
DUNN, PATRICK BAL 011 9TH WARD
DUNN, PATRICK ALL 202 CUMBERLA
DUNN, PATRICK BAL 342 1ST DIST
DUNN, PAUL BAL 005 1ST WARD
DUNN, PAUL BAL 384 3RD WARD
DUNN, R.P. BAL 171 19TH WAR
DUNN, REBECCA H. BAL 144 19TH WAR
DUNN, RICHARD QUE 234 4TH E DI
DUNN, ROSE BAL 159 19TH WAR
DUNN, SAMUEL WAS 024 2ND SUBD
DUNN, SARAH WAS 004 WILLIAMS
DUNN, SARAH BAL 333 3RD WARD
DUNN, SARAH ALL 221 CUMBERLA
DUNN, SUSAN BAL 238 12TH WAR
DUNN, SUSANNA BAL 265 17TH WAR
DUNN, TABITHA SOM 541 TYASKIN
DUNN, THOMAS SOM 541 TYASKIN
DUNN, THOMAS SOM 424 PRINCESS
DUNN, WASHINGTON BAL 260 17TH WAR
DUNN, WILLIAM KEN 220 2ND DIST
DUNN, WILLIAM SOM 542 TYASKIN
DUNN, WILLIAM DOR 450 1ST DIST
DUNN, WILLIAM BAL 032 2ND DIST
DUNN, WILLIAM BAL 387 1ST DIST
DUNN, WILLIAM BAL 373 8TH WARD
DUNN, WILLIAM BAL 282 1ST DIST
DUNN, WILLIAM M. BAL 402 3RD WARD
DUNN, LAMRINA BAL 167 1ST WARD
DUNNEGAN, WILLIAM BAL 444 14TH WAR
DUNNELL, JAMES BAL 028 1ST WARD
DUNNEMACKER, SAMUEL WAS 146 HAGERSTO
DUNNER, JOHN ALL 260 CUMBERLA
DUNNHAM, ISAAC ALL 203 CUMBERLA
DUNNIG, THOMAS BAL 106 1ST WARD
DUNNIG, WILLIAM BAL 106 1ST WARD
DUNNIN, PATRICK MGM 399 ROCKERLE
DUNNIN, SAMUEL BAL 445 8TH WARD
DUNNIN, WILLIAM BAL 445 8TH WARD
DUNNING, CHARLES BAL 074 10TH WAR
DUNNING, CHARLES A. BAL 458 8TH WARD
DUNNING, ELIZABETH BAL 059 18TH WAR
DUNNING, GEORGE BAL 268 1ST DIST
DUNNING, GEORGE F. TAL 076 EASTON T
DUNNING, J. W. BAL 075 10TH WAR
DUNNING, JOHN BAL 355 8TH WARD
DUNNING, JOHN TAL 088 ST MICHA
DUNNING, MARY BAL 166 6TH WARD
DUNNING, MARY A. BAL 446 8TH WARD
DUNNINGER, HENRY ALL 042 10TH E.D
DUNNINGHAM, ELLEN ANN 413 HOWARD D
DUNNINGTON, ELIZABETH BAL 401 14TH WAR
DUNNINGTON, FRANCIS CHA 242 HILLTOP
DUNNINGTON, GEORGE CHA 238 HILLTOP
DUNNINGTON, HENRY BAL 075 4TH WARD
DUNNINGTON, THOMAS BAL 002 4TH WARD
DUNNINGTON, WILLIAM A. BAL 111 15TH WAR
DUNNINGTONE, THOMAS* BAL 074 4TH WARD
DUNNISON, THOMAS R. PRI 032 VANSVILL
DUNNOCK, DOROTHEY DOR 326 3RD DIVI
DUNNOCK, DOROTHEY* DOR 363 3RD DIVI
DUNNOCK, JOHN DOR 326 3RD DIVI
DUNNOCK, JOHN BAL 131 1ST WARD
DUNNOCK, JOSPHIA FRE 066 FREDERIC
DUNNOCK, LEVIN DOR 327 3RD DIVI
DUNNOCK, NOD DOR 419 1ST DIST
DUNNOCK, SAMUEL R.* DOR 334 3RD DIVI
DUNNOG, HALL J. CEC 062 1ST E DI
DUNNS, MARGARET BAL 286 7TH WARD
DUNOR, BRIDGET BAL 278 1ST DIST
DUNOVAN, JAMES WAS 094 2ND SUBD
DUNOVAN, MARY ALL 206 CUMBERLA
DUNOVAN, TIMOTHY WAS 094 2ND SUBD
DUNRIDER, FREDERICK WAS 180 BOONSBOR
DUNS, CATHARINE BAL 151 16TH WAR
DUNSAIN, CATHERINE * FRE 263 NEW MARK
DUNSMIRE, MARY BAL 283 20TH WAR
DUNSON, BARNEY BAL 365 13TH WAR
DUNSON, NANCY BAL 049 15TH WAR
DUNSTAN, THOMAS-BLACK FRE 427 8TH E DI
DUNSTER, BENJAMIN-MULATTO CAR 383 2ND DIST
DUNSTER, JOSEPH-BLACK CAR 382 2ND DIST
DUNSTON, HENRIETTA FRE 163 EMMITTSB
DUNSTON, HENRY FRE 162 EMMITTSB
DUNSTON, THOMAS FRE 164 EMMITTSB
DUNSTON, WILLIAM H. BAL 002 4TH WARD
DUNSTUN, BARNEY CAR 377 2ND DIST
DUNSTUN, DACUS CAR 377 2ND DIST
DUNTAN, FANNY BAL 156 11TH WAR
DUNTY, WILLIAM BAL 097 2ND DIST
DUNWANE, MARY CEC 044 CHESAPEA
DUNWANE, MOSES CEC 044 CHESAPEA
DUNWORTH, CATHARINE BAL 352 7TH WARD
DUOL, ELIZABETH BAL 436 14TH WAR
DUOVAN, MARY ALL 255 CUMBERLA
DUPEE, SARAH E. MGM 322 CRACKLIN
DUPENIER, FREDERICK FRE 202 5TH E DI
DUPEW, AUGUSTUS BAL 107 1ST WARD
DUPHORN, BARBARA FRE 167 EMMITTSB
DUPHORN, IMAGINE FRE 168 EMMITTSB
DUPHORN, JACOB FRE 167 EMMITTSB
DUPHORN, SAMUEL FRE 197 5TH E DI
DUPLE, JOHN FRE 361 CATOCTIN
DUPLEX, CLARA BAL 067 10TH WAR
DUPNY, PEGGY BAL 438 14TH WAR
DUPOYS, JOHN BAL 218 2ND WARD
DUPPELL, ADALADE BAL 020 4TH WARD
DUPPELL, GEORGE BAL 020 4TH WARD
DUPPEY, ABRAHAM BAL 302 7TH WARD
DUPPINS, MARIA CAL 057 3RD DIST
DUPUI, CHARLES H. BAL 356 3RD WARD
DURALL, GEORGE FRE 014 FREDERIC
DURALL, JOHN CAR 369 9TH DIST
DURALL, LOYD T. FRE 033 FREDERIC
DURALL, WILLIAM T. FRE 026 FREDERIC
DURAM, ALLACE BAL 409 1ST DIST
DURAN, WILLIAM BAL 172 1ST WARD
DURAND, ANN E. BAL 181 6TH WARD
DURAND, E. BAL 150 1ST WARD
DURAND, JAMES BAL 033 9TH WARD
DURAND, MARY CEC 116 3RD E DI
DURAND, WASHINGTON BAL 146 1ST WARD
DURANG, ALICE BAL 001 EASTERN
DURANG, FRANK BAL 178 2ND DIST
DURANT, CLARK J. ST 273 3RD E DI
DURANT, FRANCIS ANN 359 3RD DIST
DURANT, JAMES ANN 359 3RD DIST
DURANT, MARTHA D. ST 292 2ND E DI
DURANT, NATHANIEL BAL 430 8TH WARD
DURATT, JOHN ANN 271 ANNAPOLI
DURBAN, GEORGE ALL 082 5TH E.D.
DURBEN, HENRIETTA WAS 218 1ST DIST
DURBEN, MICHAEL ALL 142 6TH E.D.
DURBEN, WILLIAM WAS 218 1ST DIST
DURBIN, A. REESE CAR 289 7TH DIST
DURBIN, ANN BAL 019 4TH WARD
DURBIN, CATHARINE CAR 279 7TH DIST
DURBIN, CHRISTIAN HAR 098 2ND DIST
DURBIN, COMFORT CAR 282 7TH DIST
DURBIN, EDWARD BAL 060 4TH WARD
DURBIN, HARRIETT HAR 172 3RD DIST
DURBIN, JESSE CAR 268 WESTMINS
DURBIN, JOHN HAR 130 2ND DIST
DURBIN, JOHN HAR 126 2ND DIST
DURBIN, JOHN W. CAR 267 WESTMINS
DURBIN, JOHN W. CAR 398 2ND DIST
DURBIN, NICHOLAS CAR 289 7TH DIST
DURBIN, STEPHEN HAR 130 2ND DIST
DURBIN, SUSAN CAR 289 7TH DIST
DURBIN, SUSANA ALL 004 3RD E.D.
DURBIN, THOMAS W. CAR 288 7TH DIST
DURBOROLL, REBECCA BAL 048 18TH WAR
DURBOROW, HAMMOND BAL 086 4TH WARD
DURBURG, UNDORS BAL 003 4TH WARD
DURCHAUSEN, H. C. BAL 326 12TH WAR
DURDINE, THOMAS BAL 279 2ND WARD
DURDING, A. M. BAL 059 4TH WARD
DURDING, JOHN BAL 254 17TH WAR
DURE, EDWARD WOR 341 1ST E DI
DURE, POLLY WOR 303 SNOW HIL
DURELL, GERTRUDE* BAL 115 15TH WAR
DURETTE, MATILDA BAL 111 10TH WAR
DURETY, WILLIAM HAR 198 3RD DIST
DUREY, CATHRIN BAL 065 18TH WAR
DUREY, CATHRINE BAL 062 18TH WAR
DURF, OTHO WAS 041 2ND SUBD
DURFEY, WILLIAM HAR 060 1ST DIST
DURFEY, WILLIAM BAL 356 3RD WARD
DURFFLER, CALEB BAL 199 2ND WARD
DURFLER, GEORGE BAL 117 5TH WARD
DURGIN, HENRY ANN 377 4TH DIST
DURGNER, GEORGE BAL 204 2ND WARD
DURHAM, ABEL HAR 051 1ST DIST
DURHAM, ABRAHAM HAR 057 1ST DIST
DURHAM, ABRAHAM HAR 065 1ST DIST
DURHAM, C. P. BAL 106 10TH WAR
DURHAM, CAROLINE CEC 148 PORT DUP
DURHAM, CHARLES M. BAL 185 19TH WAR
DURHAM, DAVID HAR 065 1ST DIST
DURHAM, E.G. BAL 163 1ST WARD
DURHAM, EDWARD BAL 157 1ST WARD
DURHAM, EDWARD BAL 355 8TH WARD
DURHAM, EDWIN BAL 164 1ST WARD
DURHAM, FRANCIS WAS 009 WILLIAMS
DURHAM, J. H. BAL 148 1ST WARD
DURHAM, JOHN BAL 058 15TH WAR
DURHAM, JOHN WAS 005 WILLIAMS
DURHAM, JOHN BAL 170 19TH WAR
DURHAM, JOHN KEN 243 2ND DIST
DURHAM, JULIANA WAS 007 WILLIAMS
DURHAM, LLOYD BAL 164 16TH WAR
DURHAM, MARY BAL 296 7TH WARD
DURHAM, MATILDA BAL 200 6TH WARD
DURHAM, NATHAN BAL 191 11TH WAR
DURHAM, SAMUEL BAL 144 5TH WARD
DURHAM, SMITH BAL 144 1ST WARD
DURHAM, UNITY CEC 147 PORT DUP
DURHAM, WILLIAM BAL 241 17TH WAR
DURHAM, WILLIAM BAL 200 19TH WAR
DURHAM, WILLIAM SOM 488 SALISBUR
DURHAM, WILLIAM JR. BAL 272 17TH WAR
DURHAM, ZACHEOUS BAL 401 1ST DIST
DURHAM, ZACHIEUS BAL 377 8TH WARD
DURHMAM, THOMAS BAL 263 1ST DIST
DURINGTON, MARY A. BAL 242 2ND WARD
DURITY, JOSEPHINE BAL 181 6TH WARD
DURITZ, JOHN W. BAL 127 1ST WARD
DURKEE, JANE M. BAL 264 7TH WARD
DURKEE, LOUISA BAL 261 6TH WARD
DURKEN, THOMAS BAL 410 3RD WARD
DURKIN, MARY BAL 168 2ND DIST
DURKINS, ANN BAL 303 3RD WARD
DURKINS, JANE BAL 167 16TH WAR
DURKINS, JOHN BAL 213 11TH WAR
DURKINS, MARY BAL 213 11TH WAR
DURLING, MARIA BAL 206 2ND WARD
DURMER, JOHN BAL 104 1ST WARD
DURMIN, JAMES * SOM 432 PRINCESS
DURMING, PATRICK ANN 472 HOWARD D
DURNE, JOHN BAL 134 1ST WARD
DURNER, JAMES ANN 384 4TH DIST
DURNEY, RICHARD WAS 101 2ND DIST
DURR, BENJAMIN WOR 314 2ND E DI
DURSELL, REBECCA BAL 163 19TH WAR
DURST, ADAM ALL 004 3RD E.D.
DURST, BARBARA ALL 010 3RD E.D.
DURST, CHRISTLEY ALL 015 3RD E.D.
DURST, DANIEL ALL 004 3RD E.D.
DURST, ELIZA ALL 014 3RD E.D.
DURST, FRANCES BAL 044 15TH WAR
DURST, H. ALL 014 3RD E.D.
DURST, H.ANNA ALL 017 3RD E.D.
DURST, HANSON ALL 010 3RD E.D.
DURST, HENRY ALL 011 3RD E.D.
DURST, JEREMIAH ALL 006 3RD E.D.
DURST, JEREMIAH ALL 008 3RD E.D.
DURST, JOHN ALL 015 3RD E.D.
DURST, JOHN ALL 006 3RD E.D.
DURST, JOHN ALL 006 3RD E.D.
DURST, JOHN ALL 017 3RD E.D.
DURST, JOHN W. BAL 044 15TH WAR
DURST, JONES BAL 119 15TH WAR
DURST, JOSIAH ALL 010 3RD E.D.
DURST, LYDDIA ALL 009 3RD E.D.
DURST, MARY BAL 006 EASTERN
DURST, MARY ANN ALL 015 3RD E.D.
DURST, MARY ANN ALL 015 3RD E.D.
DURST, MICHAEL ALL 009 3RD E.D.
DURST, PHILIP ALL 009 3RD E.D.
DURST, SALMON ALL 006 3RD E.D.
DURST, SARAH ALL 004 3RD E.D.
DURST, SUSANNAH BAL 045 15TH WAR
DURST, WILLIAM ALL 144 6TH E.D.
DURST.S AMUEL ALL 005 3RD E.D.
DURSTOFF, HENRY ALL 006 3RD E.D.
DURT, HANNAH * BAL 099 2ND DIST
DURT.CASPER ALL 011 3RD E.D.
DURTST, ELISHA ALL 006 3RD E.D.
DURTST, MICHAEL ALL 006 3RD E.D.
DURUM, HENRY SOM 477 TRAPP DI
DURWIN, JAMES * SOM 432 PRINCESS
DURWOOD, MARY A.* DOR 434 1ST DIST
DURY, BENJAMIN BAL 456 8TH WARD
DUSALL, JOHN FRE 020 FREDERIC
DUSAND, JOHN H. BAL 439 8TH WARD
DUSBY, PATRICK CHA 217 ALLENS F
DUSELL, JOHN BAL 427 8TH WARD
DUSEN, HENRITTA * BAL 378 13TH WAR
DUSENBERRY, MARY B. BAL 468 14TH WAR
DUSENBERY, SAMUEL B. BAL 468 14TH WAR
DUSEY, ELIZABETH BAL 166 19TH WAR
DUSEY, MATILDA BAL 300 12TH WAR
DUSHAND, MARY BAL 221 12TH WAR
DUSHANE, CAROLINE V. BAL 118 15TH WAR
DUSHANE, CONDIUS BAL 085 18TH WAR
DUSHANE, JOHN BAL 195 19TH WAR
DUSHANE, JOHN BAL 117 15TH WAR
DUSHANE, NATHANIEL T. BAL 245 20TH WAR
DUSING, DANIEL FRE 373 CATOCTIN
DUSING, HENRY WAS 175 1ST DIST
DUSING, ISAAC WAS 168 FUNKSTOW
DUSING, JOHN WAS 125 HAGERSTO
DUSING, MARIA FRE 341 MIDDLETO
DUSING, PETER WAS 208 1ST DIST
DUSING, PHILIP FRE 359 CATOCTIN
DUSIX, ELIAS FRE 359 CATOCTIN
DUSKEY, CHARLES WOR 311 2ND E DI
DUSKEY, JOSHUA WOR 311 2ND E DI
DUSSEL, ELIZABETH* BAL 109 10TH WAR
DUST, MARTIN BAL 434 14TH WAR
DUSTIN, ROBERT B. ANN 448 HOWARD D
DUTCH, CAROLINE BAL 074 2ND DIST
DUTCH, ELIZABETH BAL 350 1ST DIST
DUTCH, GEORGE ALL 150 6TH E.D.
DUTCH, HENRY ALL 127 4TH E.D.
DUTCH, JOSHUA ANN 336 3RD DIST
DUTCH, MARY ALL 215 CUMBERLA
DUTCH, MARY BAL 173 19TH WAR
DUTCH, WILLIAM BAL 290 12TH WAR
DUTCHESS, MARGARET ALL 218 CUMBERLA
DUTCHMAN, JOHN BAL 165 2ND DIST
DUTCHMAN, WALER HAR 064 1ST DIST
DUTCHNER, J.E. BAL 140 5TH WARD
DUTE, WILLIAM BAL 147 19TH WAR
DUTISS, FREDERICK BAL 261 1ST DIST
DUTREINE, JOSEPH SAMUEL * BAL 313 12TH WAR
DUTRERE, DAVID FRE 210 BUCKEYST
DUTRO, JACOB WAS 209 1ST DIST
DUTRO, OBEDIAH FRE 309 WOODSBOR
DUTRO, ROBERT BAL 080 18TH WAR
DUTRON, ELIZABETH FRE 215 BUCKEYST
DUTRON, GEORGE * BAL 140 19TH WAR
DUTROW, BENJAMIN FRE 227 BUCKEYST
DUTROW, CATHARINE FRE 334 MIDDLETO
DUTROW, DANIEL FRE 350 MIDDLETO
DUTROW, ELIZABETH FRE 353 MIDDLETO
DUTROW, GEORGE FRE 350 MIDDLETO
DUTROW, JACOB FRE 335 MIDDLETO
DUTROW, MARY FRE 341 MIDDLETO
DUTROW, R.P.T. FRE 219 BUCKEYST
DUTROW, RICHARD FRE 040 FREDERIC
DUTROW, SAMUEL FRE 214 BUCKEYST
DUTROW, SAMUEL FRE 352 MIDDLETO
DUTROW, SUSAN FRE 350 MIDDLETO
DUTSO, ANDREW FRE 304 WOODSBOR
DUTSOUE, JAMES FRE 090 FREDERIC
DUTTEN, DANIEL-BLACK CAR 133 NO TWP L
DUTTERER, MARY CAR 320 1ST DIST
DUTTEROW, HEZEKIAH FRE 177 5TH E DI
DUTTEROW, JOHN FRE 138 CREAGERS
DUTTERWICK, JOHN BAL 224 1ST DIST
DUTTERWICK, MARIA BAL 224 1ST DIST
DUTTON, ANDRED HAR 165 3RD DIST
DUTTON, ATALINE SOM 538 TYASKIN
DUTTON, CAROLINE BAL 127 11TH WAR
DUTTON, CHARLES DOR 465 1ST DIST
DUTTON, DAVID CEC 026 ELKTON 3
DUTTON, FRANCIS CAR 221 5TH DIST
DUTTON, GEORGE SOM 478 TRAPP DI
DUTTON, GEORGE H. BAL 429 14TH WAR
DUTTON, GEORGE W. HAR 168 3RD DIST
DUTTON, JAMES CHA 224 ALLENS F
DUTTON, JOHN SOM 428 PRINCESS
DUTTON, JOHN SOM 472 TRAPPE D
DUTTON, JOHN BAL 322 3RD WARD
DUTTON, JOHN R. BAL 322 3RD WARD
DUTTON, JOSHUA CEC 031 CHESAPEA
DUTTON, LEVINA BAL 048 2ND DIST
DUTTON, LLOYD BAL 206 17TH WAR
DUTTON, MARGARET HAR 015 1ST DIST
DUTTON, MARY BAL 225 17TH WAR
DUTTON, MARY CHA 259 MIDDLETO
DUTTON, N. N. CHA 222 ALLENS F

DUTTON, NICHOLAS BAL 376 13TH WAR
DUTTON, NOAH CAR 216 5TH DIST
DUTTON, NOAH-BLACK FRE 009 FREDERIC
DUTTON, NOTLEY CHA 222 ALLENS F
DUTTON, POLLY SOM 480 TRAPP DI
DUTTON, RACHEL L. CAR 214 5TH DIST
DUTTON, RICHARD HAR 014 1ST DIST
DUTTON, ROBERT BAL 234 2ND WARD
DUTTON, ROGER SOM 472 TRAPPE D
DUTTON, SARAH BAL 243 6TH WARD
DUTTON, STEPHEN SOM 535 QUANTICO
DUTTON, SUSAN SOM 488 SALISBUR
DUTTON, SYLVIA DOR 465 1ST DIST
DUTTON, TIMOTHY BAL 018 2ND DIST
DUTTON, WILLIAM HAR 030 1ST DIST
DUTTON,LEVI BAL 040 2ND DIST
DUVAL, BENJAMIN BAL 081 18TH WAR
DUVAL, MARIA BAL 128 18TH WAR
DUVAL, MARY E. BAL 373 1ST DIST
DUVAL, MARY U. BAL 082 18TH WAR
DUVAL, RICHARD BAL 032 18TH WAR
DUVALL, ABRAHAM CAR 308 1ST DIST
DUVALL, ABRAM ANN 329 2ND DIST
DUVALL, ALFRED BAL 039 4TH WARD
DUVALL, AMELIA ANN 327 2ND DIST
DUVALL, ANDREW J. ANN 449 HOWARD D
DUVALL, ANN BAL 431 14TH WAR
DUVALL, ANN PRI 083 QUEEN AN
DUVALL, ANN E. ANN 280 ANNAPOLI
DUVALL, AQUILA MGM 337 CRACKLIN
DUVALL, ARCHIBALD ANN 435 HOWARD D
DUVALL, BARTON ANN 333 2ND DIST
DUVALL, BASIL ANN 489 HOWARD D
DUVALL, BEAL BAL 376 1ST DIST
DUVALL, BEAL ANN 465 HOWARD D
DUVALL, BEALL FRE 424 8TH E DI
DUVALL, BENJAMIN CAR 215 5TH DIST
DUVALL, BENJAMIN MGM 400 ROCKERLE
DUVALL, BENJAMIN PRI 069 MARLBROU
DUVALL, BENJIMON HAR 200 3RD DIST
DUVALL, CATHARINE CAR 307 1ST DIST
DUVALL, CHARLES CAR 223 5TH DIST
DUVALL, CHARLES PRI 040 VANSVILL
DUVALL, CHARLES BAL 113 15TH WAR
DUVALL, CHARLES J. PRI 034 VANSVILL
DUVALL, CHARLES L. ANN 439 HOWARD D
DUVALL, CHARLES R. ANN 373 4TH DIST
DUVALL, CHARLES T. FRE 421 8TH E DI
DUVALL, CHRISTY PRI 015 BLADENSB
DUVALL, CLEORA MGM 371 BERRYS D
DUVALL, COMFORT FRE 234 BUCKEYST
DUVALL, CYNTHIA FRE 239 NEW MARK
DUVALL, DEBORAH MGM 366 BERRYS D
DUVALL, DENNIS PRI 085 QUEEN AN
DUVALL, DINAH BAL 196 11TH WAR
DUVALL, DNAIEL ANN 321 2ND DIST
DUVALL, E. PRI 102 SPALDING
DUVALL, EDMUND B. PRI 042 VANSVILL
DUVALL, EDWARD ANN 324 2ND DIST
DUVALL, EDWARD BAL 179 16TH WAR
DUVALL, EDWARD B. PRI 021 VANSVILL
DUVALL, EDWARD W. PRI 003 BLADENSB
DUVALL, EDWIN A. ANN 283 ANNAPOLI
DUVALL, ELIJAH A. PRI 016 BLADENSB
DUVALL, ELISHA PRI 086 QUEEN AN
DUVALL, ELIZA PRI 003 BLADENSB
DUVALL, ELIZABETH PRI 033 VANSVILL
DUVALL, ELIZABETH BAL 373 1ST DIST
DUVALL, ELIZABETH ANN 514 HOWARD D
DUVALL, ELLEN M. PRI 020 VANSVILL
DUVALL, EMELINE BAL 362 8TH WARD
DUVALL, EMMA PRI 020 VANSVILL
DUVALL, ENOCH ANN 316 1ST DIST
DUVALL, FLAVILLA BAL 359 1ST DIST
DUVALL, FLAVILLA BAL 145 16TH WAR
DUVALL, FRANCIS C. MGM 343 CLARKSBU
DUVALL, FREDERIC MGM 328 CRACKLIN
DUVALL, GABRIEL ANN 368 4TH DIST
DUVALL, GABRIEL H. ANN 318 2ND DIST
DUVALL, GABRILLA PRI 042 VANSVILL
DUVALL, GEORGE BAL 351 1ST DIST
DUVALL, GEORGE W. PRI 042 VANSVILL
DUVALL, GEORGE W. FRE 424 8TH E DI
DUVALL, GEORGE W. BAL 357 13TH WAR
DUVALL, GEORGE W. BAL 030 18TH WAR
DUVALL, GEORGE W. BAL 393 14TH WAR
DUVALL, GRAFTON MGM 344 CLARKSBU
DUVALL, GRAFTON ANN 350 3RD DIST
DUVALL, HARRIET MGM 343 CLARKSBU
DUVALL, HARRIETT WAS 141 HAGERSTO
DUVALL, HENRY BAL 098 15TH WAR
DUVALL, HOWARD M. ANN 315 1ST DIST
DUVALL, HOWARD M. ANN 316 1ST DIST
DUVALL, ISAAC ANN 340 3RD DIST
DUVALL, ISAAC BAL 070 18TH WAR
DUVALL, ISREAL ANN 488 HOWARD D
DUVALL, JACOB ANN 439 HOWARD D
DUVALL, JAMES BAL 374 8TH WARD
DUVALL, JAMES PRI 059 NOTTINGH
DUVALL, JAMES T. BAL 128 5TH WARD
DUVALL, JEMIMA A. FRE 204 BUCKEYST
DUVALL, JESSE H. PRI 015 BLADENSB
DUVALL, JOHN PRI 055 AQUASCO
DUVALL, JOHN PRI 071 MARLBROU
DUVALL, JOHN FRE 447 8TH E DI
DUVALL, JOHN ANN 445 HOWARD D
DUVALL, JOHN H. BAL 402 1ST DIST
DUVALL, JOHN H. BAL 187 11TH WAR
DUVALL, JOHN M. ANN 328 2ND DIST
DUVALL, JOSEPH J. PRI 080 QUEEN AN
DUVALL, JOSHUA MGM 344 CLARKSBU
DUVALL, KITTY ANN 319 2ND DIST
DUVALL, L. C. BAL 148 11TH WAR
DUVALL, LEWIS MGM 344 CLARKSBU
DUVALL, LEWIS H. MGM 329 CRACKLIN
DUVALL, LEWIS H. PRI 021 VANSVILL
DUVALL, LLOYD MGM 334 CRACKLIN
DUVALL, LOUIS BAL 336 1ST DIST
DUVALL, M. H. ANN 339 3RD DIST
DUVALL, M.E. PRI 116 PISCATAW
DUVALL, MADISON MGM 333 CRACKLIN
DUVALL, MARCELLA BAL 137 2ND DIST
DUVALL, MARCUS PRI 042 VANSVILL
DUVALL, MARGARET ANN 350 3RD DIST
DUVALL, MARIA ANN 316 1ST DIST
DUVALL, MARIA BAL 044 15TH WAR
DUVALL, MARIA PRI 032 VANSVILL
DUVALL, MARIA PRI 084 QUEEN AN
DUVALL, MARK PRI 038 VANSVILL
DUVALL, MARTHA ANN 421 HOWARD D
DUVALL, MARY ANN 421 HOWARD D
DUVALL, MARY ANN 355 3RD DIST
DUVALL, MARY ANN 414 HOWARD D
DUVALL, MARY A. MGM 333 CRACKLIN
DUVALL, MARY E. FRE 448 8TH E DI
DUVALL, MARY E. BAL 036 18TH WAR
DUVALL, MARY E. ANN 274 ANNAPOLI
DUVALL, MARY E. PRI 024 VANSVILL
DUVALL, MARY L. BAL 356 1ST DIST
DUVALL, MR. H. ANN 489 HOWARD D
DUVALL, MRS. BAL 002 18TH WAR
DUVALL, NICHOLAS C. ANN 295 1ST DIST
DUVALL, NICHOLAS D. ANN 295 1ST DIST
DUVALL, OTHO MGM 328 CRACKLIN
DUVALL, P.B. PRI 121 PISCATAW
DUVALL, PAULINA MGM 337 CRACKLIN
DUVALL, PHILIP MGM 329 CRACKLIN
DUVALL, RACHAEL BAL 043 18TH WAR
DUVALL, RACHELL BAL 101 5TH WARD
DUVALL, REZIN MGM 343 CLARKSBU
DUVALL, REZIN MGM 327 CRACKLIN
DUVALL, RICHARD BAL 026 18TH WAR
DUVALL, RICHARD BAL 456 8TH WARD
DUVALL, RICHARD PRI 084 QUEEN AN
DUVALL, RICHARD H. PRI 019 VANSVILL
DUVALL, RICHARD J. ANN 380 4TH DIST
DUVALL, RICHARD M. PRI 029 VANSVILL
DUVALL, RIDGELY BAL 402 1ST DIST
DUVALL, ROBERT E. ST 296 2ND E DI
DUVALL, S. ANN 290 ANNAPOLI
DUVALL, SAMUEL E. ANN 319 2ND DIST
DUVALL, SARAH ANN 436 HOWARD D
DUVALL, SARAH A. PRI 076 MARLBROU
DUVALL, THOMAS ANN 488 HOWARD D
DUVALL, THOMAS BAL 327 7TH WARD
DUVALL, THOMAS CAR 366 9TH DIST
DUVALL, THOMAS FRE 269 NEW MARK
DUVALL, THOMAS B. BAL 365 1ST DIST
DUVALL, THOMAS B. ANN 333 2ND DIST
DUVALL, TOBIAS H. PRI 084 QUEEN AN
DUVALL, WASHINGTON MGM 353 BERRYS D
DUVALL, WASHINGTON P. MGM 329 CRACKLIN
DUVALL, WILLIAM PRI 101 SPALDING
DUVALL, WILLIAM BAL 246 20TH WAR
DUVALL, WILLIAM B. BAL 144 11TH WAR
DUVALL, WILLIAM J. PRI 015 BLADENSB
DUVALL, WILLIAM L. ANN 441 HOWARD D
DUVALL, WILLIAM R. ANN 474 HOWARD D
DUVALL, WILLIAM T. FRE 248 NEW MARK
DUVALL,ELLENOR FRE 238 NEW MARK
DUVALLE, JOHN MGM 344 CLARKSBU
DUVALLS, AMOS ANN 488 HOWARD D
DUVANT, SAMUEL BAL 213 17TH WAR
DUVELL, GERTRUDE* BAL 115 15TH WAR
DUVON, JOHN T. QUE 187 3RD E DI
DUVOND, JAMES PRI 058 NOTTINGH
DUVOND, JOSEPHUS PRI 059 NOTTINGH
DUXLER, JOHN F. BAL 001 4TH WARD
DUYDEN, ALEXANDER BAL 318 12TH WAR
DUYER, BENJAMIN KEN 209 2ND DIST
DUYER, HENRY* BAL 089 10TH WAR
DUYER, MARY* BAL 089 10TH WAR
DUYER, THOMAS KEN 209 2ND DIST
DUYSER, LUKE BAL 052 2ND DIST
DUZELL, MARY BAL 175 11TH WAR
DUZESSE, JOHN BAL 004 1ST WARD
DVERACLK, JAMES * HAR 206 3RD DIST
DWALL, LEONELAS * ALL 118 5TH E.D.
DWAN, MARY BAL 072 10TH WAR
DWENN, LAWRENCE FRE 159 EMMITTSB
DWIGHT, HANNAH BAL 279 20TH WAR
DWIGHT, MARY BAL 298 12TH WAR
DWINN, JAMES * BAL 065 18TH WAR
DWWNEY, GEORGE BAL 069 10TH WAR
DWYER, CATHERINE BAL 059 10TH WAR
DWYER, ELIZABETH BAL 286 17TH WAR
DWYER, ELLEN BAL 461 1ST DIST
DWYER, HENRY MGM 327 CRACKLIN
DWYER, JAMES MGM 327 CRACKLIN
DWYER, JAMES MGM 335 CRACKLIN
DWYER, JESSE C. BAL 258 1ST DIST
DWYER, JOHN MGM 338 CRACKLIN
DWYER, MATHEW BAL 339 7TH WARD
DWYER, RICHARD CAR 368 9TH DIST
DWYER, WILLIAM MGM 330 CRACKLIN
DWYER, WILLIAM BAL 223 1ST DIST
DWYRE, MARY A. * KEN 282 3RD DIST
DYCKMAN, JOHN BAL 113 15TH WAR
DYCUS, JANE-BLACK CAR 398 2ND DIST
DYCUS, WILLIAM CAR 373 9TH DIST
DYE, DANIEL FRE 304 WOODSBOR
DYE, ELLEN BAL 321 3RD WARD
DYE, JAMES ALL 117 5TH E.D.
DYE, JAMES WAS 064 2ND SUBD
DYE, MARY WAS 064 2ND SUBD
DYE, MARY E. ALL 117 5TH E.D.
DYE, PHEBE BAL 084 2ND DIST
DYE, RUTH WAS 061 2ND SUBD
DYEDEN, THOMAS T. * TAL 090 ST MICHA
DYER, AJCOB BAL 132 18TH WAR
DYER, ANN M. ST 292 2ND E DI
DYER, DANIEL R. PRI 105 PISCATAW
DYER, E. PRI 118 PISCATAW
DYER, E.J. PRI 092 MARLBROU
DYER, ELIZABETH BAL 430 14TH WAR
DYER, GEORGE FRE 067 FREDERIC
DYER, GEORGE A. CHA 294 BOJANTOW
DYER, HENRY TAL 027 EASTON D
DYER, HENRY-BLACK CAR 092 NO TWP L
DYER, HORATIO PRI 089 SPALDING
DYER, ISAAC BAL 197 11TH WAR
DYER, IZEKIAH ST 284 2ND E DI
DYER, IZEKIAH * ST 283 3RD E DI
DYER, JACOB HAR 082 2ND DIST
DYER, JAMES C. PRI 103 SPALDING
DYER, JAMES C. PRI 121 PISCATAW
DYER, JAMES H. ST 282 3RD E DI
DYER, JERRY CHA 292 BOJANTOW
DYER, JOHN BAL 457 14TH WAR
DYER, JOHN ST 282 3RD E DI
DYER, JOHN BAL 174 11TH WAR
DYER, JOHN V. CHA 252 BOJANTOW
DYER, JOHN-MULATTO CAR 146 NO TWP L
DYER, JOSEPH ST 292 2ND E DI
DYER, JOSEPH A. ST 282 3RD E DI
DYER, LEON BAL 181 6TH WARD
DYER, LEOPOLD BAL 017 4TH WARD
DYER, LEVIN BAL 199 17TH WAR
DYER, MARTHA BAL 308 3RD WARD
DYER, MARY BAL 123 5TH WARD
DYER, MARY BAL 248 12TH WAR
DYER, MINTY BAL 202 17TH WAR
DYER, MRS. BAL 031 15TH WAR
DYER, NANCY BAL 130 18TH WAR
DYER, PAMELIA BAL 120 16TH WAR
DYER, RICHARD BAL 199 17TH WAR
DYER, RICHARD CHA 292 BOJANTOW
DYER, S. BAL 166 1ST WARD
DYER, SAMUEL BAL 115 1ST WARD
DYER, SARAH CAR 131 NO TWP L
DYER, SISTER M.J. FRE 198 5TH E DI
DYER, STEPHEN CAR 065 NO TWP L
DYER, STEPHEN QUE 214 3RD E DI
DYER, SUM BAL 172 1ST WARD
DYER, SUSANA BAL 285 7TH WARD
DYER, THOMAS BAL 065 15TH WAR
DYER, THOMAS G. PRI 105 PISCATAW
DYER, THOMAS-MULATTO CAR 092 NO TWP L
DYER, WALTER BAL 245 2ND WARD
DYER, WILLIAM C. CHA 285 BOJANTOW
DYER, WILLIAM L. ST 281 3RD E DI
DYES, HENRY SOM 456 DAMES QU
DYGES, HENRY BAL 225 19TH WAR
DYHUE, CHARLES ALL 143 6TH E.D.
DYKES, ALEXANDER BAL 071 18TH WAR
DYKES, BENJAMIN SOM 423 PRINCESS
DYKES, CATHARINE BAL 353 7TH WARD
DYKES, EBENEZER WOR 191 8TH E DI
DYKES, ELIZABETH BAL 126 13TH WAR
DYKES, ELLEN BAL 417 8TH WARD
DYKES, GEORGE WOR 190 8TH E DI
DYKES, JAMES WOR 195 8TH E DI
DYKES, JAMES BAL 069 18TH WAR
DYKES, JOHN BAL 002 18TH WAR
DYKES, JOHN SOM 480 TRAPP DI
DYKES, JULIA A. BAL 002 18TH WAR
DYKES, KELLUM WOR 199 8TH E DI
DYKES, PETER WOR 191 8TH E DI
DYKES, SELBY WOR 191 8TH E DI
DYKES, STEPHEN WOR 194 8TH E DI
DYKES, THOMAS SOM 416 DUBLIN D
DYMACK, EDWARD WOR 300 SNOW HIL
DYMACK, MARIAH WOR 300 SNOW HIL
DYMAN, HARRIET BAL 234 20TH WAR
DYMOCK, MARY WOR 179 6TH E DI
DYNON, THOMAS CHA 272 ALLENS F
DYONS, JOHN BAL 342 13TH WAR
DYOTT, AARON TAL 082 ST MICHA
DYOTT, ALEXANDER TAL 034 EASTON D
DYOTT, ANN QUE 218 3RD E DI
DYOTT, ANN* TAL 022 EASTON D
DYOTT, CHARLES BAL 183 11TH WAR
DYOTT, EDWARD QUE 182 3RD E DI
DYOTT, JOHN QUE 209 3RD E DI
DYOTT, JOHN C. BAL 066 18TH WAR
DYOTT, JULIA A. BAL 072 10TH WAR
DYOTT, LUTHER TAL 023 EASTON D
DYOTT, RICHARD TAL 023 EASTON D
DYOTT, SAMUEL* TAL 010 EASTON D
DYOTT, THOMAS TAL 083 ST MICHA
DYOTT, WILLIAM TAL 056 EASTON D
DYOTT, WILLIAM H. QUE 192 3RD E DI
DYPSEY, BRIDGET BAL 186 11TH WAR
DYRE, MATILDA BAL 246 2ND WARD
DYRERS, ANDREW ALL 051 10TH E.D
DYSART, CATHARINE CEC 093 4TH E DI
DYSART, MOSES A. BAL 225 6TH WARD
DYSART, SARAH CEC 015 ELKTON 3
DYSE, BETSEY SOM 367 BRINKLEY
DYSE, EPHRAIM SOM 371 BRINKLEY
DYSE, NOAH SOM 456 DAMES QU
DYSE, SAMUEL SOM 441 DAMES QU
DYSE, SMITH SOM 372 BRINKLEY
DYSEN, EDY ANN 422 HOWARD D
DYSEN, PRISCILLA ANN 463 HOWARD D
DYSEN, RUTH ANN 463 HOWARD D
DYSERT, ANN BAL 226 6TH WARD
DYSERT, LEVI CEC 093 4TH E DI
DYSIN, JACOB ANN 463 HOWARD D
DYSO, WESLEY SOM 381 BRINKLEY
DYSON, ALEXANDER CHA 276 ALLENS F
DYSON, ANTONY CHA 289 BOJANTOW
DYSON, BENNETT CHA 244 HILLTOP
DYSON, CATHARINE BAL 179 16TH WAR
DYSON, CHANEY BAL 148 16TH WAR
DYSON, ELIZABETH BAL 375 13TH WAR
DYSON, FRANCES S. BAL 135 16TH WAR
DYSON, JAMES L. CHA 248 HILLTOP
DYSON, JOHN BAL 189 17TH WAR
DYSON, JOHN BAL 102 15TH WAR
DYSON, MANDY CHA 224 ALLENS F
DYSON, MARGARET CHA 248 HILLTOP
DYSON, MARGARET CHA 272 ALLENS F
DYSON, MARY CHA 289 BOJANTOW
DYSON, MARY CHA 217 ALLENS F
DYSON, OSEN H. CHA 282 BOJANTOW
DYSON, OSWELL CHA 275 ALLENS F
DYSON, ROBERT CHA 294 BOJANTOW
DYSON, ROBERTS BAL 458 8TH WARD
DYSON, S. WASHINGTON CHA 276 ALLENS F
DYSON, TAPHENES MGM 308 MEDLEY 3
DYTHAN, AGUSTUS C. BAL 260 2ND WARD
DZIEROZINSKI, FRANCIS FRE 055 FREDERIC
EAB, ELIZABETH CAR 258 3RD DIST
EABBLER, FREDERICK BAL 073 1ST WARD
EACHUS, JANE BAL 185 16TH WAR
EADA, HENRY BAL 132 7TH WARD
EADAY, ROBERT CAR 193 4TH DIST
EADER, EDUARD FRE 006 FREDERIC
EADER, JONATHAN FRE 040 FREDERIC
EADER, LAZARUS FRE 385 PETERSVI
EADER, LEWIS B. FRE 037 FREDERIC
EADER, MARGARET FRE 041 FREDERIC
EADER, MARIA L. FRE 041 FREDERIC
EADER, WILLIAM FRE 103 FREDERIC
EADOR, FRANCES FRE 272 NEW MARK
EADOR, LEWIS A. FRE 271 NEW MARK
EADOR, MANASSEH FRE 258 NEW MARK
EAGAN, ELIZABETH CEC 198 7TH E DI
EAGAN, MARGARET CEC 196 6TH E DI
EAGAN, MARY CEC 004 ELKTON 3
EAGAN, RACHEL CEC 165 6TH E DI
EAGAN, SARAH CEC 165 6TH E DI
EAGAN, WOOLFORD DOR 434 1ST DIST
EAGAR, WILLIAM J. DOR 437 1ST DIST
EAGAR, WILLIAM* DOR 436 1ST DIST
EAGER, ALEXANDER BAL 353 3RD WARD
EAGER, FRANCES DOR 352 3RD DIVI
EAGER, JAMES BAL 353 3RD WARD
EAGER, JOHN BAL 181 2ND WARD

EAGER, LEVENIA BAL 070 18TH WAR
EAGER, WILLIAM* DOR 436 1ST DIST
EAGLE, CATHRINE BAL 034 18TH WAR
EAGLE, ELIJAH FRE 222 BUCKEYST
EAGLE, ELIZA J. BAL 137 11TH WAR
EAGLE, JULIA BAL 039 9TH WARD
EAGLE, LYCURGUS MGM 427 MEDLEY 3
EAGLE, NOAH K. KEN 292 3RD DIST
EAGLE, SOLOMON KEN 265 1ST DIST
EAGLE, WILLIAM FRE 222 BUCKEYST
EAGLER, KITTY ANN 325 2ND DIST
EAGLESTON, DANIEL BAL 153 2ND DIST
EAGLESTON, HARRIOTT BAL 332 3RD WARD
EAGLESTON, ISAIAH BAL 402 3RD WARD
EAGLESTON, JOHN BAL 138 2ND DIST
EAGLESTON, JOSEPH M. BAL 163 19TH WAR
EAGLESTON, JOSHUA BAL 139 2ND DIST
EAGNER, JOHN CEC 085 5TH E DI
EAGNER, JOHN W. CEC 090 4TH E DI
EAGON, ELIZABETH CEC 199 7TH E DI
EAGUM, JOHN ALL 203 CUMBERLA
EAKERS, JOHN BAL 250 2ND WARD
EAKLE, ABSALOM WAS 083 2ND SUBD
EAKLE, AMOS WAS 177 1ST DIST
EAKLE, BENJAMIN WAS 287 1ST DIST
EAKLE, ELIAS WAS 050 2ND SUBD
EAKLE, ELIAS WAS 178 BOONSBOR
EAKLE, ELIZABETH J. WAS 279 LEITERSB
EAKLE, GEORGE WAS 295 1ST DIST
EAKLE, HENRY WAS 203 1ST DIST
EAKLE, ISABELLA WAS 170 FUNKSTOW
EAKLE, JACOB WAS 176 1ST DIST
EAKLE, JOHN WAS 051 2ND SUBD
EAKLE, JOHN D. WAS 273 RIDGEVIL
EAKLE, JOSIAH WAS 275 RIDGEVIL
EAKLE, MARTIN WAS 072 2ND SUBD
EAKLE, THOMAS WAS 090 2ND SUBD
EAKLE, WASHINGTON WAS 244 SMITHSBU
EAKS, TOBIAS BAL 030 1ST WARD
EALEY, WILLIAM H. BAL 387 3RD WARD
EALL, JOHN BAL 152 2ND DIST
EALLER, GEORGE FRE 085 FREDERIC
EALON, PHILIP BAL 319 12TH WAR
EALY, JACOB BAL 066 2ND DIST
EAMBLETON, JAMES BAL 118 1ST WARD
EAMES, NATHAN* BAL 419 3RD WARD
EAMPS, JOHN HAR 059 1ST DIST
EANOS, PETER CAR 223 5TH DIST
EANSI, JOHN E. ALL 145 6TH E.D.
EARCKSON, B. H. BAL 157 1ST WARD
EARE, WILLIAM P. BAL 243 20TH WAR
EARECKSON, ROBERT BAL 061 4TH WARD
EARECKSON, THOMAS BAL 290 3RD WARD
EARHARD, GEORGE BAL 072 2ND DIST
EARHART, ANDREW WAS 151 HAGERSTO
EARHART, CATHARINE CAR 249 3RD DIST
EARHART, DAVID B. CAR 248 3RD DIST
EARHART, GEORGE CAR 397 2ND DIST
EARHART, JACOB CAR 245 3RD DIST
EARHART, JACOB CAR 245 3RD DIST
EARHART, JOHN WAS 162 2ND DIST
EARHART, JOHN BAL 166 6TH WARD
EARHART, JOHN N. FRE 122 CREAGERS
EARHRENBEFORD, WILLIAM * BAL 459 14TH WAR
EARICKSON, BENJAMIN W. QUE 227 4TH E DI
EARICKSON, EDWIN BAL 317 3RD WARD
EARICKSON, MARGARET QUE 227 4TH E DI
EARICKSON, RHODERICK QUE 226 4TH E DI
EARICKSON, RHODERICK QUE 227 4TH E DI
EARICKSON, WILLIAM QUE 227 4TH E DI
EARKSON, THOMAS J. CAR 096 NO TWP L
EARL, CHARLES DOR 430 1ST DIST
EARL, ISAAC-BLACK CAR 069 NO TWP L
EARL, J. M. BAL 153 1ST WARD
EARL, JACOB-BLACK CAR 076 NO TWP L
EARL, JOHN H.-BLACK CAR 163 NO TWP L
EARL, JOHN L. BAL 220 19TH WAR
EARL, JOSEPH W. BAL 133 2ND DIST
EARL, RICHARD PRI 101 SPALDING
EARL, SARAH TAL 115 ST MICHA
EARL, SYLVESTER-BLACK CAR 161 NO TWP L
EARL, WILLIAM R. QUE 230 4TH E DI
EARLAND, FRANCES BAL 042 15TH WAR
EARLE, ANN C. QUE 190 3RD E DI
EARLE, ANNA KEN 213 2ND DIST
EARLE, DANIEL F.* DOR 434 1ST DIST
EARLE, DAVID CAL 055 3RD DIST
EARLE, GEORGE CEC 004 ELKTON 3
EARLE, JAMES ANN 499 HOWARD D
EARLE, JOHN QUE 250 5TH E DI
EARLE, JOHN C. QUE 190 3RD E DI
EARLE, KATE D. ANN 521 HOWARD D
EARLE, RICHARD BAL 151 16TH WAR
EARLE, RICHARD T. QUE 206 3RD E DI
EARLE, SAMUEL T. QUE 205 3RD E DI
EARLE, SUSAN F. QUE 184 3RD E DI
EARLE, WILLIAM ANN 287 ANNAPOLI
EARLES, ELLEN BAL 057 10TH WAR
EARLES, JAMES BAL 259 12TH WAR
EARLES, LOUISA BAL 057 10TH WAR
EARLES, SAMUEL BAL 074 18TH WAR
EARLES, WILLIAMS BAL 125 18TH WAR
EARLEY, JAMES A. BAL 171 16TH WAR
EARLEY, JOHN WAS 205 1ST DIST
EARLEY, MARY ALL 047 10TH E.D
EARLEY, THOMAS BAL 373 8TH WARD
EARLEY,MARY BAL 250 6TH WARD
EARLING, DENNIS BAL 158 1ST WARD
EARLING, WILLIAM BAL 066 1ST WARD
EARLIS, JAMES CEC 179 7TH E DI
EARLOCKER, BERNETTA BAL 369 8TH WARD
EARLOCKER, FRANCIS BAL 350 1ST DIST
EARLOCKER, MARY WAS 041 2ND SUBD
EARLOUGHER, HENSON BAL 100 1ST WARD
EARLOUGHER, MARY BAL 277 7TH WARD
EARLOUGHER, REBECCA ANN 456 HOWARD D
EARLOUGHER, SARAH ANN 455 HOWARD D
EARLY, EDWARD CEC 187 7TH E DI
EARLY, HENRY BAL 092 5TH WARD
EARLY, HUGH ALL 139 6TH E.D.
EARLY, JAMES WAS 044 2ND SUBD
EARLY, JOHN D. BAL 445 14TH WAR
EARLY, JOSEPH FRE 369 CATOCTIN
EARLY, L.H. PRI 058 NOTTINGH
EARLY, MALVINA PRI 058 NOTTINGH
EARLY, SIBBY BAL 046 9TH WARD
EARLY, THOMAS BAL 275 2ND WARD
EARLY, THOMAS R. PRI 058 NOTTINGH
EARLY, WILLIAM BAL 169 2ND DIST
EARLY, WILLIAM H. PRI 058 NOTTINGH
EARNES, NATHAN* BAL 419 3RD WARD
EARNEST, DANIEL ALL 250 CUMBERLA
EARNEST, ELIJAH CEC 009 ELKTON 3
EARNEST, ELIZABETH BAL 437 14TH WAR
EARNEST, FAGAN CEC 008 ELKTON 3
EARNEST, HENRY W. KEN 216 2ND DIST
EARNEST, LOUISA QUE 124 1ST E DI
EARNEST, MARY BAL 149 11TH WAR
EARNEST, WILLIAM BAL 092 10TH WAR
EARNSHAW, BENJAMIN ANN 330 2ND DIST
EARNSHAW, WILLIAM ANN 462 HOWARD D
EARNST, HANNAH FRE 424 8TH E DI
EARNST, HENRY BAL 461 1ST DIST
EARNST, SOLOMON FRE 412 8TH E DI
EARON, JINNY* TAL 037 EASTON D
EAROUGH, MARGARET BAL 453 8TH WARD
EARP, AMOS ANN 461 HOWARD D
EARP, ANNIS BAL 209 19TH WAR
EARP, BENJAMIN ANN 424 HOWARD D
EARP, ELIZABETH MGM 419 MEDLEY 3
EARP, JAMES BAL 338 1ST DIST
EARP, JAMES BAL 285 1ST DIST
EARP, JOSEPH BAL 335 1ST DIST
EARP, KITTURAH BAL 285 1ST DIST
EARP, WALTER MGM 418 MEDLEY 3
EARP, WILLIAM MGM 336 CRACKLIN
EARP, WILLIAM B. MGM 419 MEDLEY 3
EARP, WILLIAM P. BAL 336 1ST DIST
EARP,W ILSON MGM 419 MEDLEY 3
EARPS, JAMES BAL 335 1ST DIST
EARTEN, SAMUEL CEC 053 1ST E DI
EASE, DAVID DOR 388 1ST DIST
EASE, MARY DOR 371 3RD DIVI
EASE, SALEY A. DOR 436 1ST DIST
EASE, SAMUEL DOR 421 1ST DIST
EASLEY, ELLENORA BAL 022 1ST WARD
EASON, JINNY* TAL 037 EASTON D
EASON, SAMUEL TAL 091 ST MICHA
EASON, THOMAS TAL 032 EASTON D
EASON, WILLIAM TAL 067 EASTON T
EASSING, HENRY BAL 143 5TH WARD
EAST, ADAM PRI 065 NOTTINGH
EAST, CHARLES BAL 145 1ST WARD
EAST, HENRY BAL 408 8TH WARD
EAST, RODA BAL 385 8TH WARD
EASTAS, CHARLES CEC 005 ELKTON 3
EASTELL, ANDREW BAL 251 2ND WARD
EASTEN, SIDNEY BAL 143 1ST WARD
EASTER, DAVID DOR 370 3RD DIVI
EASTER, EMANUEL ALL 251 CUMBERLA
EASTER, HAMILTON BAL 282 12TH WAR
EASTER, HESTER ANN 424 HOWARD D
EASTER, JACOB ALL 163 6TH E.D.
EASTER, JOHN BAL 232 17TH WAR
EASTER, JOHN BAL 381 13TH WAR
EASTER, JOHN BAL 414 14TH WAR
EASTER, JOHN BAL 425 14TH WAR
EASTER, MILLY BAL 310 3RD WARD
EASTER, THOMAS BAL 132 5TH WARD
EASTER, WILLIAM HAR 100 2ND DIST
EASTERBY, MARY BAL 007 4TH WARD
EASTERBY, SARAH BAL 312 7TH WARD
EASTERDAY, CATHARINE M. WAS 210 1ST DIST
EASTERDAY, CHRISTIAN WAS 210 1ST DIST
EASTERDAY, DANIEL WAS 209 1ST DIST
EASTERDAY, DANIEL FRE 319 MIDDLETO
EASTERDAY, ELIZABETH FRE 391 PETERSVI
EASTERDAY, GEORGE WAS 210 1ST DIST
EASTERDAY, GEORGE W. FRE 391 PETERSVI
EASTERDAY, GEROGE FRE 398 JEFFERSO
EASTERDAY, JACOB WAS 209 1ST DIST
EASTERDAY, JOHN WAS 200 1ST DIST
EASTERDAY, JOSEPH FRE 404 JEFFERSO
EASTERDAY, LAWRENCE FRE 375 CATOCTIN
EASTERDAY, LEWIS A. FRE 382 PETERSVI
EASTERDAY, MARY FRE 403 JEFFERSU
EASTERDAY, POLLY FRE 400 JEFFERSO
EASTERDAY, REBECCA FRE 362 CATOCTIN
EASTERDAY, SAMUEL WAS 209 1ST DIST
EASTERDAY, SUSAN WAS 210 1ST DIST
EASTERDY, MARY WAS 128 HAGERSTO
EASTMAN, EICHBOLD BAL 048 18TH WAR
EASTMAN, ELIZABETH BAL 047 9TH WARD
EASTMAN, GILES ANN 453 HOWARD D
EASTMAN, JONATHAN L. BAL 384 13TH WAR
EASTMAN, MARIA BAL 188 11TH WAR
EASTMAN, MATILDA E. BAL 048 18TH WAR
EASTMAN, RUTH BAL 177 11TH WAR
EASTMAN, SIMEON C. ALL 192 9TH E.D.
EASTMAN, TIMOTHY BAL 134 1ST WARD
EASTMAN, TIMOTHY BAL 171 1ST WARD
EASTMIN, F. BAL 147 1ST WARD
EASTNER, CATHEIRNE BAL 066 1ST WARD
EASTO, JANE ANN 455 HOWARD D
EASTON, ------* MGM 336 CRACKLIN
EASTON, ABRAHAM BAL 143 16TH WAR
EASTON, BENJAMIN MGM 402 ROCKERLE
EASTON, D. PRI 078 MARLBROU
EASTON, ELISHA WAS 080 2ND SUBD
EASTON, HEZEKIAH WAS 223 1ST DIST
EASTON, HILLEARY MGM 319 CRACKLIN
EASTON, J. BAL 138 1ST WARD
EASTON, JACKSON CAR 213 5TH DIST
EASTON, JAMES FRE 217 BUCKEYST
EASTON, JANE BAL 270 2ND WARD
EASTON, JEFFERY MGM 323 CRACKLIN
EASTON, JOHN W. MGM 322 CRACKLIN
EASTON, LEVIS WAS 132 HAGERSTO
EASTON, LOUIS BAL 361 1ST DIST
EASTON, MARGARET A. ANN 424 HOWARD D
EASTON, MARTHA BAL 361 1ST DIST
EASTON, MARTHA BAL 203 2ND WARD
EASTON, REBECCA ANN 495 HOWARD D
EASTON, ROBERT BAL 299 17TH WAR
EASTON, SARAH BAL 299 17TH WAR
EASTON, WALTER BAL 099 2ND DIST
EASTON, WILLIAM CAR 212 5TH DIST
EASTON, WILLIAM WAS 079 2ND SUBD
EASTON, WILLIAM WAS 078 2ND SUBD
EASTON,ROBEY MGM 402 ROCKERLE
EASTWOOD, JAMES BAL 048 4TH WARD
EASTWOOD, NOEL BAL 359 8TH WARD
EASWICKER, J.S. BAL 138 1ST WARD
EATEN, ALBERT W. QUE 156 2ND E DI
EATON, ALVIN BAL 330 1ST DIST
EATON, ANN BAL 101 10TH WAR
EATON, ANN BAL 291 12TH WAR
EATON, ANN BAL 011 15TH WAR
EATON, ASENATH BAL 021 2ND DIST
EATON, CALEB BAL 050 9TH WARD
EATON, CELEB CAR 140 NO TWP L
EATON, CHARLES J. M. BAL 167 11TH WAR
EATON, CLEMENT CAR 096 NO TWP L
EATON, DANIEL DOR 321 1ST DIST
EATON, EDWARD DOR 296 1ST DIST
EATON, EDWARD TAL 084 ST MICHA
EATON, ELEANOR BAL 400 3RD WARD
EATON, ELIJAH BAL 003 1ST WARD
EATON, ELISHA CAR 145 NO TWP L
EATON, EZEKIEL CAR 119 NO TWP L
EATON, GEORGE CAR 065 NO TWP L
EATON, GEORGE DOR 323 1ST DIST
EATON, GEORGE A. BAL 134 11TH WAR
EATON, HELENA BAL 242 12TH WAR
EATON, HENRY BAL 067 2ND DIST
EATON, HENRY CAR 133 NO TWP L
EATON, HENRY QUE 156 2ND E DI
EATON, HENRY FRE 138 CREAGERS
EATON, HIRAM BAL 217 6TH DIST
EATON, ISOM BAL 264 17TH WAR
EATON, JAMES QUE 250 5TH E DI
EATON, JOHN TAL 077 EASTON T
EATON, JOHN TAL 006 EASTON D
EATON, JOHN QUE 203 3RD E DI
EATON, JOHN BAL 079 13TH WAR
EATON, JOHN BAL 217 6TH DIST
EATON, JOSEPH BAL 218 6TH DIST
EATON, JOSEPH BAL 174 2ND DIST
EATON, JOSEPH BAL 460 8TH WARD
EATON, MARY FRE 113 CREAGERS
EATON, MARY DOR 315 1ST DIST
EATON, MARY A. DOR 321 1ST DIST
EATON, MARY JANE BAL 210 17TH WAR
EATON, MARY-BLACK CAR 118 NO TWP L
EATON, MASHELLUM BAL 330 1ST DIST
EATON, OWEN-BLACK CAR 070 NO TWP L
EATON, REBECCA CAR 138 NO TWP L
EATON, REBECCA CAR 134 NO TWP L
EATON, REBECCA BAL 403 1ST DIST
EATON, RICHARD TAL 084 ST MICHA
EATON, ROBINSON T. BAL 010 1ST WARD
EATON, SAMUEL BAL 034 2ND DIST
EATON, SARAH BAL 010 1ST WARD
EATON, SARAH CAR 165 NO TWP L
EATON, SARAH-MULATTO CAR 146 NO TWP L
EATON, SAULSBURY CAR 137 NO TWP L
EATON, SILAS CAR 131 NO TWP L
EATON, SUSAN CAR 136 NO TWP L
EATON, SUSAN BAL 016 4TH WARD
EATON, THOMAS C R 111 NO TWP L
EATON, THOMAS DOR 321 1ST DIST
EATON, WILLAIM BAL 217 6TH DIST
EATON, WILLIAM DOR 322 1ST DIST
EATON, WILLIAM E. DOR 312 1ST DIST
EATON, WILLIS TAL 069 EASTON T
EAVES, JOHN FRE 417 8TH E DI
EAVES, MARY F. FRE 417 8TH E DI
EAVES, PETER FRE 423 8TH E DI
EAVES, WILLIAM FRE 416 8TH E DI
EAVSLEY, THOMAS ANN 488 HOWARD D
EAWARD, JAMES* DOR 409 1ST DIST
EBANATHER, JAMES CEC 103 4TH E DI
EBAUGH, ADAM CAR 184 8TH DIST
EBAUGH, AMOS BAL 195 5TH DIST
EBAUGH, ANN BAL 271 1ST DIST
EBAUGH, CORNEALOUS CAR 206 4TH DIST
EBAUGH, DAVID CAR 184 8TH DIST
EBAUGH, ELIAS CAR 177 8TH DIST
EBAUGH, ELIAS K. CAR 177 8TH DIST
EBAUGH, ELIZABETH CAR 173 8TH DIST
EBAUGH, ELIZABETH C. CAR 287 7TH DIST
EBAUGH, GEORGE BAL 243 1ST DIST
EBAUGH, HENRY BAL 110 5TH WARD
EBAUGH, HENRY R. CAR 176 8TH DIST
EBAUGH, HY H. BAL 201 6TH DIST
EBAUGH, JEROME BAL 236 1ST DIST
EBAUGH, JESSE CAR 184 8TH DIST
EBAUGH, JOSEPH CAR 183 8TH DIST
EBAUGH, MARY CAR 175 8TH DIST
EBAUGH, MARY S. BAL 237 1ST DIST
EBAUGH, SARAH BAL 201 6TH DIST
EBAUGH, SAVANAH CAR 172 8TH DIST
EBAUGH, THOMAS CAR 275 7TH DIST
EBAUGH, WILLIAM CAR 175 8TH DIST
EBAUGH, WILLIAM K. BAL 244 1ST DIST
EBAUGH, ZACHARIAH CAR 178 8TH DIST
EBB, JOHN WAS 224 1ST DIST
EBB, MARRY WAS 054 2ND SUBD
EBB, WILLIAM WAS 054 2ND SUBD
EBB, WILLIAM BAL 331 1ST DIST
EBBEATH, ERNEST HAR 203 3RD DIST
EBBERT, ADAM BAL 113 18TH WAR
EBBERT, ADAM FRE 035 FREDERIC
EBBERT, BENJAMIN FRE 002 FREDERIC
EBBERT, CHARLOTT C. FRE 030 FREDERIC
EBBERT, ELI WAS 117 2ND DIST
EBBERT, ELIZABETH M. FRE 030 FREDERIC
EBBERT, JOHN FRE 027 FREDERIC
EBBERT, JOHN FRE 002 FREDERIC
EBBERT, JOHN WAS 118 2ND DIST
EBBERT, MARY C. FRE 399 JEFFERSO
EBBERT, VALERIOUS FRE 030 FREDERIC
EBBERTS, ELIZA CAR 382 2ND DIST
EBBERTS, ELIZABETH FRE 037 FREDERIC
EBBERTS, JOSEPH M. FRE 008 FREDERIC
EBBERTS, MICHAEL FRE 061 FREDERIC
EBBERTS, WILLIAM FRE 019 FREDERIC
EBBS, EDWARD ANN 508 HOWARD D
EBBS, HENRIETTA ANN 508 HOWARD D
EBEL, JOSEPH FRE 081 FREDERIC
EBELEY, FREDERICK BAL 318 3RD WARD
EBENEGANE, THOMAS J. CAR 132 NO TWP L
EBER, JOHN WAS 122 HAGERSTO
EBER, JOHN W. BAL 258 2ND WARD
EBERHART, CONRAD BAL 182 19TH WAR
EBERHART, JOHN BAL 240 12TH WAR
EBERHART, JOSEPH A. BAL 431 8TH WARD
EBERHART, LOUISA BAL 432 8TH WARD
EBERHART, MARGARET BAL 410 14TH WAR
EBERHEARD, ALLEN K. BAL 474 14TH WAR
EBERLY, FREDERICK E. BAL 424 3RD WARD
EBERLY, JACOB E. FRE 414 8TH E DI
EBERLY, SUSANNA FRE 439 8TH E DI
EBERNS, LEMUEL BAL 073 18TH WAR
EBSRT, CATHARINE BAL 022 2ND DIST
EBERT, GODFRED BAL 003 EASTERN
EBERT, JACOB FRE 302 WOODSBOR
EBERT, JOHN CAR 196 4TH DIST
EBERT, JOHN WAS 144 HAGERSTO
EBERT, THOMAS BAL 410 1ST DIST

EBERTS, JOSEPH HAR 044 1ST DIST
EBERTS, MARY A. FRE 310 WOODSBOR
EBERTS, MICHAEL FRE 293 WOODSBOR
EBERVIEN, SAMUEL BAL 311 1ST DIST
EBGRECHT, WILLIAM WAS 151 HAGERSTO
EBNER, MARTIN BAL 045 4TH WARD
EBURGH, JOHN CAR 173 8TH DIST
EBY, CHRISTIAN FRE 116 CREAGERS
EBY, EMANUEL FRE 302 WOODSBOR
EBY, GEORGE FRE 163 EMMITTSB
EBY, SUSAN FRE 127 CREAGERS
ECAVAILLE, JOSEPH B. BAL 031 9TH WARD
ECCLESON, BENJAMINE BAL 277 1ST DIST
ECCLESTON, BENJAMIN BAL 276 20TH WAR
ECCLESTON, DOROTHY A. DOR 376 1ST DIST
ECCLESTON, ELIZABETH BAL 066 15TH WAR
ECCLESTON, ESAN QUE 216 3RD E DI
ECCLESTON, ESAU-BLACK QUE 192 3RD E DI
ECCLESTON, JOHN B. KEN 214 2ND DIST
ECCLESTON, JOSEPH R. DOR 426 1ST DIST
ECCLESTON, MARY A. DOR 387 1ST DIST
ECCLESTON, SOPHIA DOR 379 1ST DIST
ECCLESTON, SUSAN DOR 452 1ST DIST
ECCLESTON, THOMAS J. H. DOR 409 1ST DIST
ECK, ANN MISS BAL 315 20TH WAR
ECK, ANN MRS- BAL 315 20TH WAR
ECK, JOHN WAS 221 1ST DIST
ECK, JOSEPH CAR 313 1ST DIST
ECK, PAUL CAR 259 3RD DIST
ECK, SAMUEL CAR 298 1ST DIST
ECKABERGER, PETER WAS 248 1ST DIST
ECKARD, HENRIETTA BAL 398 1ST DIST
ECKART, BALLSHASER * BAL 424 8TH WARD
ECKART, BALTSHASER BAL 424 8TH WARD
ECKART, FREDERICK FRE 365 CATOCTIN
ECKART, GEORGE BAL 442 1ST DIST
ECKART, HAMMOND BAL 050 18TH WAR
ECKART, WILLIAM BAL 209 6TH DIST
ECKE, CECELIA FRE 191 5TH E DI
ECKEL, HENRY M. BAL 024 9TH WARD
ECKEL, MARY BAL 403 8TH WARD
ECKEL, WILLLIAM J. BAL 193 6TH WARD
ECKELLS, JOHN ALL 238 CUMBERLA
ECKENBRODE, DANIEL FRE 187 5TH E DI
ECKENRODE, ELIJAH CAR 313 1ST DIST
ECKENRODE, JACOB CAR 299 1ST DIST
ECKENRODE, JACOB CAR 312 1ST DIST
ECKENRODE, JAMES FRE 184 5TH E DI
ECKENRODE, JERAMIAW * CAR 312 1ST DIST
ECKENRODE, JOHN FRE 186 5TH E DI
ECKER, BENJAMIN FRE 416 8TH E DI
ECKER, DAVID FRE 443 8TH E DI
ECKER, DAVID W. FRE 432 8TH E DI
ECKER, ELIZABETH FRE 416 8TH E DI
ECKER, FRANCIS M. CAR 391 2ND DIST
ECKER, FREDERICK FRE 430 8TH E DI
ECKER, HANNAH CAR 363 9TH DIST
ECKER, JACOB FRE 112 CREAGERS
ECKER, JOHN WAS 058 2ND SUBD
ECKER, LOUIS BAL 076 10TH WAR
ECKER, MARGARET L. CAR 391 2ND DIST
ECKER, PETER FRE 430 8TH E DI
ECKER, REUBEN FRE 410 8TH E DI
ECKER, SAMUEL FRE 423 8TH E DI
ECKER, SAMUEL CAR 391 2ND DIST
ECKER, SARAH FRE 429 8TH E DI
ECKER, WILLIAM CAR 391 2ND DIST
ECKER.T THOMAS CAR 413 2ND DIST
ECKERMAN, HERMAN BAL 278 20TH WAR
ECKERS, HENRY BAL 226 2ND WARD
ECKERS, WILLIAM BAL 441 1ST DIST
ECKERT, A. BAL 104 10TH WAR
ECKERT, DANIEL CAR 404 2ND DIST
ECKERT, GEORGE W. BAL 270 12TH WAR
ECKERT, HENRY BAL 081 10TH WAR
ECKERT, HENRY CAR 259 3RD DIST
ECKERT, JACOB CAR 413 2ND DIST
ECKERT, JACOB CAR 406 2ND DIST
ECKERT, JESSE CAR 291 7TH DIST
ECKERT, JOHN CAR 379 2ND DIST
ECKERT, MARY CAR 237 UNION TO
ECKERT, NOAH FRE 366 CATOCTIN
ECKERT, SARAH CAR 237 UNION TO
ECKERT, WILLIAM BAL 276 20TH WAR
ECKERTS, LEAR BAL 288 12TH WAR
ECKES, CHARLE BAL 292 12TH WAR
ECKHARDT, CRISTIAN BAL 038 18TH WAR
ECKHART, CHRISTIAN ALL 056 10TH E.D
ECKHART, JOHN ALL 102 5TH E.D.
ECKHART, JOHN BAL 008 EASTERN
ECKHART, JOHN C. BAL 391 8TH WARD
ECKHART, RICHARD ALL 227 CUMBERLA
ECKHOLTZ, JOHN FRE 127 CREAGERS
ECKINWAE, SUSAN CAR 320 1ST DIST
ECKLAND, JOSHUA CEC 135 6TH E DI
ECKLEMAN, HEMAN R. BAL 005 9TH WARD
ECKLER, ELIZABETH CAR 264 WESTMINS
ECKLER, RACHAEL CAR 266 WESTMINS
ECKLER, VALENTINE ALL 096 5TH E.D.
ECKLES, WILLIM ALL 103 5TH E.D.
ECKMAN, BENJAMIN BAL 122 16TH WAR
ECKMAN, DANIEL FRE 138 CREAGERS
ECKMAN, DANIEL L. FRE 136 CREAGERS
ECKMAN, EDITH CAR 383 2ND DIST
ECKMAN, ELIAS CAR 401 2ND DIST
ECKMAN, ELIE WAS 219 1ST DIST
ECKMAN, ELIZABETH CAR 396 2ND DIST
ECKMAN, ELIZABETH BAL 406 14TH WAR
ECKMAN, GEORGE CAR 407 2ND DIST
ECKMAN, HENRY B. FRE 057 FREDERIC
ECKMAN, JACOB CAR 328 MANCHEST
ECKMAN, JACOB BAL 229 1ST DIST
ECKMAN, MARGARET A. BAL 234 1ST DIST
ECKMAN, MARTHA J. WAS 194 1ST DIST
ECKMAN, WILLIAM BAL 451 1ST DIST
ECKR, JONAS CAR 396 2ND DIST
ECKS, LEWIS CAR 173 8TH DIST
ECKSTEIN, CHARLES BAL 222 19TH WAR
ECKSTEIN, JACOB WAS 292 1ST DIST
ECKSTEIN, JOHN WAS 274 RIDGEVIL
ECKSTIEN, JOHN WAS 148 HAGERSTO
ECKUS, CHRISTIAN FRE 049 FREDERIC
ECLER, WILLIAM ALL 149 6TH E.D.
ECLOFFSTEINER, J. BAL 177 2ND WARD
ECULBORNE, LEAH SOM 453 DAMES QU
ECWORTH, WILLIAM BAL 310 3RD WARD
EDA, AMANCA BAL 448 8TH WARD
EDA, EDWARD BAL 447 1ST DIST
EDA, WILLIAM BAL 448 8TH WARD
EDAMY, HARIET WAS 092 2ND SUBD

EDANY, JAMES WAS 089 2ND SUBD
EDDA, JOHN WAS 022 2ND SUBD
EDDAY, DAVID CAR 193 4TH DIST
EDDEN, ALEXANDER BAL 281 17TH WAR
EDDEN, FRANCIS PRI 087 SPALDING
EDDEN, GEORGE T. PRI 109 PISCATAW
EDDEN, J.B. PRI 104 PISCATAW
EDDEN, JOHN L. PRI 104 PISCATAW
EDDEN, PHILIP PRI 104 PISCATAW
EDDER, JARRET BAL 129 16TH WAR
EDDICKS, ELLEN BAL 172 11TH WAR
EDDICKS, JARRED BAL 381 13TH WAR
EDDY, JAEMS BAL 151 1ST WARD
EDDY, JARRET BAL 125 16TH WAR
EDDY, O T. BAL 287 12TH WAR
EDEL, JOSIAH BAL 399 8TH WARD
EDELEN, A. PRI 115 PISCATAW
EDELEN, ANN ST 265 3RD E DI
EDELEN, C. PRI 118 PISCATAW
EDELEN, CHARITY PRI 110 PISCATAW
EDELEN, CLARA ST 265 3RD E DI
EDELEN, E. H. CHA 218 ALLENS F
EDELEN, EDWARD CHA 272 ALLENS F
EDELEN, EDWARD V. CHA 274 ALLENS F
EDELEN, ELIZA BAL 422 14TH WAR
EDELEN, ELIZABETH BAL 212 11TH WAR
EDELEN, EMELINE CHA 277 BOJANTOW
EDELEN, EMILY PRI 109 PISCATAW
EDELEN, F.HOSTEN CHA 268 BOJANTOW
EDELEN, FRANCIS CHA 256 MIDDLETO
EDELEN, GEORGE CHA 279 BOJANTOW
EDELEN, H.D. PRI 116 PISCATAW
EDELEN, HENRY F. CHA 268 BOJANTOW
EDELEN, HORACE PRI 115 PISCATAW
EDELEN, JAMES PRI 091 MARLBROU
EDELEN, JAMES MGM 426 MEDLEY 3
EDELEN, JANE CHA 275 ALLENS F
EDELEN, JOHN CHA 230 BOJANTOW
EDELEN, JOHN D. PRI 104 PISCATAW
EDELEN, JOHN R. CHA 293 BOJANTOW
EDELEN, JOSEPH CHA 274 ALLENS F
EDELEN, JULIA CHA 226 ALLENS F
EDELEN, M. PRI 083 QUEEN AN
EDELEN, MARY PRI 109 PISCATAW
EDELEN, MARY CHA 254 MIDDLETO
EDELEN, MARY V. CHA 292 BOJANTOW
EDELEN, RAPHAEL C. PRI 119 PISCATAW
EDELEN, RICHARD PRI 105 PISCATAW
EDELEN, THOMAS PRI 066 NOTTINGH
EDELEN, THOMAS H. CHA 255 MIDDLETO
EDELEN, WILLIAM W. PRI 091 MARLBROU
EDELEN, WILLIAM J. PRI 104 PISCATAW
EDELEN, WILLIAM J. ST 277 3RD E DI
EDELER, WILLIAM BAL 217 6TH WARD
EDELIN, ALFRED CAL 051 3RD DIST
EDELIN, CLARINDA PRI 106 PISCATAW
EDELIN, LEONARD C. CHA 284 BOJANTOW
EDELIN, MARY E. ANN 518 HOWARD D
EDELIN, MARY E. ANN 420 HOWARD D
EDELIN, OLIVIA ANN 478 HOWARD D
EDELIN, THOMAS PRI 054 AQUASCO
EDELIN, WILLIAM M. CAL 058 3RD DIST
EDELINE, ELLEN BAL 213 11TH WAR
EDELIX, DOLLY BAL 256 12TH WAR
EDELL, ANDREW BAL 278 2ND WARD
EDEN, HENRY C. FRE 034 FREDERIC
EDEN, RACHAEL BAL 261 1ST DIST
EDEN, SARAH BAL 221 19TH WAR
EDEN, VIRGINIA BAL 087 4TH WARD
EDEN, VIRGINIA BAL 159 19TH WAR
EDEN, WILLIAM BAL 310 20TH WAR
EDENBAUGH, JOHN MGM 375 ROCKERLE
EDEPS, ANN BAL 453 14TH WAR
EDER, FREDERIC BAL 166 6TH WARD
EDER, SALLY E. BAL 249 1ST DIST
EDES, CATHARINE BAL 439 14TH WAR
EDES, GEORGE * KEN 267 1ST DIST
EDES, ISAAC CAL 063 3RD DIST
EDES, JAMES H. * KEN 267 1ST DIST
EDES, MARY A. BAL 438 14TH WAR
EDES, SAMUEL C. BAL 108 10TH WAR
EDGAR, ANN M. QUE 182 3RD E DI
EDGAR, AUGUSTINA BAL 048 4TH WARD
EDGAR, DULSENNA DOR 353 3RD DIVI
EDGAR, E. A. BAL 155 11TH WAR
EDGAR, E. A. BAL 155 11TH WAR
EDGAR, ELIZABETH CEC 098 3RD E DI
EDGAR, H. L. R. BAL 155 11TH WAR
EDGAR, HENRY BAL 048 4TH WARD
EDGAR, JOHN BAL 152 11TH WAR
EDGAR, JOHN DOR 335 3RD DIVI
EDGAR, JOHN ALL 045 10TH E.D
EDGAR, JOHN M. BAL 059 10TH WAR
EDGAR, JOSEPH DOR 337 3RD DIVI
EDGAR, RACHEL DOR 326 3RD DIVI
EDGAR, SAMUEL DOR 340 3RD DIVI
EDGAR, WILLIAM DOR 340 3RD DIVI
EDGAR, WILLIAM BAL 083 15TH WAR
EDGAR, WILLIAM H. BAL 037 15TH WAR
EDGEAR, ELIZABETH TAL 106 ST MICHA
EDGEAR, THOMAS C.* TAL 032 EASTON D
EDGEL, LEVI S. TAL 020 EASTON D
EDGEL, MATILDA TAL 030 EASTON D
EDGEL, ROALLY* TAL 032 EASTON D
EDGEL, T. J.* TAL 018 EASTON D
EDGEL, THOMAS TAL 067 EASTON T
EDGEL, THOMAS A.* TAL 024 EASTON D
EDGELL, MARY CAR 136 NO TWP L
EDGENTON, ANN BAL 195 2ND WARD
EDGER, ZIPPORA BAL 018 15TH WAR
EDGERS, HENRY BAL 220 17TH WAR
EDGERS, MARTIN * BAL 157 2ND DIST
EDGERSON, JOHN BAL 210 11TH WAR
EDGERTON, CHARLES C. BAL 306 7TH WARD
EDGERTON, JAMES H. BAL 392 8TH WARD
EDGERTON, MARY N. BAL 040 1ST WARD
EDGERTON, MICHAEL ALL 073 5TH E.D.
EDGERTON, PHILLIP A. BAL 133 5TH WARD
EDGES, JANE BAL 203 11TH WAR
EDGGY, THOMAS BAL 050 4TH WARD
EDGIN, ELIZABETH DOR 306 1ST DIST
EDGING, ANN CAR 162 NO TWP L
EDGING, MARTHA CAR 160 NO TWP L
EDGING, ROBERT CAR 131 NO TWP L
EDICKS, HOSEY BAL 296 1ST DIST
EDIE, ARTHOR S. CEC 096 4TH E DI
EDILEN, HORACE PRI 115 PISCATAW
EDINGER, ANN M. WAS 024 2ND SUBD
EDINGER, JOSEPH S. WAS 028 2ND SUBD
EDIX, AMELIA CEC 075 NORTHEAS

EDKERT, LOUIS BAL 333 13TH WAR
EDKINS, JOSEPH BAL 267 2ND WARD
EDLE, HENRY BAL 239 2ND WARD
EDLEMAN, VALENTINE BAL 299 3RD WARD
EDLEN, CHARLES WAS 101 2ND DIST
EDLER, GEORGE BAL 422 14TH WAR
EDLIN, ALICE ST 307 1ST E DI
EDLIN, ARAMINTA BAL 250 6TH WARD
EDLINE, AMOS BAL 328 1ST DIST
EDLING, JOHN BAL 035 18TH WAR
EDMAN, NATHAN BAL 141 2ND DIST
EDMEAL, AJMES KEN 265 1ST DIST
EDMINSTON, ANN BAL 339 13TH WAR
EDMINSTON, JOHN P. PRI 033 VANSVILL
EDMINSTON, SARAH PRI 035 VANSVILL
EDMOND, SALLY BAL 167 2ND DIST
EDMOND, SAMUEL BAL 248 12TH WAR
EDMONDS, BENJAMIN WAS 038 2ND SUBD
EDMONDS, CHARELS CAL 003 1ST DIST
EDMONDS, CHARLES BAL 131 1ST WARD
EDMONDS, GEORGE ALL 068 5TH E.D.
EDMONDS, JAMES FRE 403 JEFFERSO
EDMONDS, JANE BAL 020 4TH WARD
EDMONDS, REBECCA PRI 005 BLADENSB
EDMONDS, SARAH A. ANN 522 HOWARD D
EDMONDSON, DEBORAH ANN 504 HOWARD D
EDMONDSON, GEORGE BAL 190 6TH WARD
EDMONDSON, H. L. TAL 070 EASTON T
EDMONDSON, HARRIET BAL 393 1ST DIST
EDMONDSON, JAMES BAL 164 16TH WAR
EDMONDSON, LEONIDAS A. BAL 189 6TH WARD
EDMONDSON, MARGARET E. BAL 083 15TH WAR
EDMONDSON, MOSES L. BAL 164 16TH WAR
EDMONDSON, SHARLOTTE TAL 035 EASTON D
EDMONDSON, THOMAS G. BAL 059 10TH WAR
EDMONDSON, VIRGINIA BAL 287 17TH WAR
EDMONDSON, WILLIAM ST 308 1ST E DI
EDMONDSTONE, SUSAN* BAL 084 4TH WARD
EDMONSON, ANTHONY MGM 368 BERRYS D
EDMONSON, EDWARD O. MGM 378 ROCKERLE
EDMONSON, GEORGE W. BAL 238 17TH WAR
EDMONSON, JAMES CAR 209 5TH DIST
EDMONSON, JAMES DOR 358 3RD DIVI
EDMONSON, JOHN BAL 238 17TH WAR
EDMONSON, LOUISA MGM 368 BERRYS D
EDMONSON, MINGO* DOR 470 1ST DIST
EDMONSON, OWEN J. MGM 320 CRACKLIN
EDMONSON, PAUL MGM 368 BERRYS D
EDMONSON, ROBERT A. FRE 231 BUCKEYST
EDMONSON, SARRAH DOR 356 3RD DIVI
EDMONSON, SUSAN K. BAL 134 16TH WAR
EDMONSON, THOMAS BAL 229 19TH WAR
EDMONSON, WILLIAM V. M.* DOR 454 1ST DIST
EDMONSTON, EDWARD ALL 127 4TH E.D.
EDMONSTON, THOMAS B. ALL 187 9TH E.D.
EDMUNDS, JOHN W. FRE 334 MIDDLETO
EDMUNDS, NATHAN FRE 354 MIDDLETO
EDMUNDSON, CALEB CEC 194 7TH E DI
EDMUNDSON, ELIZA CEC 195 6TH E DI
EDMUNDSTON, ISABELLA BAL 032 4TH WARD
EDMUNSTON, HANNAH BAL 333 3RD WARD
EDON, MARTHA BAL 190 6TH WARD
EDUNGFIELAR, THOMAS CEC 056 1ST E DI
EDW, JAMES MGM 320 CRACKLIN
EDWADS, HARRISON ST 345 5TH E DI
EDWARD, ARM BAL 324 12TH WAR
EDWARD, CEASER ANN 343 3RD DIST
EDWARD, CHARLES QUE 199 3RD E DI
EDWARD, ELI P. BAL 443 8TH WARD
EDWARD, ELIZABETH BAL 422 8TH WARD
EDWARD, GEORGE ST 301 2ND E DI
EDWARD, GEORGE CAR 270 WESTMINS
EDWARD, JAMES* DOR 409 1ST DIST
EDWARD, JOHN QUE 140 1ST E DI
EDWARD, JOHN BAL 150 11TH WAR
EDWARD, MARGARET A. BAL 273 17TH WAR
EDWARD, MICHAEL BAL 198 11TH WAR
EDWARD, THOMAS BAL 242 17TH WAR
EDWARD, WILLIAM QUE 212 3RD E DI
EDWARD, WILLIAM-BLACK QUE 202 3RD E DI
EDWARDS, ABRAHAM WAS 298 1ST DIST
EDWARDS, AMANDA BAL 208 6TH WARD
EDWARDS, ANN BAL 279 20TH WAR
EDWARDS, ANN R. BAL 266 7TH WARD
EDWARDS, AQUILLA ANN 336 3RD DIST
EDWARDS, AVERILLA BAL 400 3RD WARD
EDWARDS, BENJAMIN BAL 021 1ST WARD
EDWARDS, BERTHA BAL 332 7TH WARD
EDWARDS, CAHRELS BAL 113 5TH WARD
EDWARDS, CAROLINE BAL 005 18TH WAR
EDWARDS, CATHARINE BAL 222 1ST DIST
EDWARDS, CHARELS BAL 147 1ST WARD
EDWARDS, CHARLOTTE BAL 405 14TH WAR
EDWARDS, EDWARD WAS 298 1ST DIST
EDWARDS, ELIZA BAL 025 4TH WARD
EDWARDS, ELIZA ANN 289 ANNAPOLI
EDWARDS, ELIZABETH BAL 023 15TH WAR
EDWARDS, ELIZABETH CHA 281 BOJANTOW
EDWARDS, ELIZABETH CHA 286 BOJANTOW
EDWARDS, ELIZABETH M. ST 347 5TH E DI
EDWARDS, ELKANAH ST 345 5TH E DI
EDWARDS, ELLEN BAL 162 19TH WAR
EDWARDS, EMILY A. QUE 178 2ND E DI
EDWARDS, EMORY WAS 087 2ND SUBD
EDWARDS, ERVIN WAS 089 2ND SUBD
EDWARDS, FRANCIS BAL 168 1ST WARD
EDWARDS, FRANCIS BAL 280 2ND WARD
EDWARDS, GARRETSON ANN 351 3RD DIST
EDWARDS, HAGAR ANN 351 3RD DIST
EDWARDS, HENRY BAL 375 3RD WARD
EDWARDS, HENRY S. ST 326 4TH E DI
EDWARDS, HENRY W. FRE 389 PETERSVI
EDWARDS, HIRAM BAL 242 17TH WAR
EDWARDS, ISAAC FRE 103 FREDERIC
EDWARDS, JAMES BAL 279 20TH WAR
EDWARDS, JAMES BAL 102 18TH WAR
EDWARDS, JAMES MGM 395 ROCKERLE
EDWARDS, JAMES WAS 065 2ND SUBD
EDWARDS, JAMES BAL 158 1ST WARD
EDWARDS, JAMES BAL 154 1ST WARD
EDWARDS, JAMES ALL 031 2ND E.D.
EDWARDS, JAMES BAL 043 9TH WARD
EDWARDS, JAMES A. KEN 311 3RD DIST
EDWARDS, JAMES B. BAL 032 4TH WARD
EDWARDS, JAMES C. BAL 006 15TH WAR
EDWARDS, JOHN ANN 387 4TH DIST
EDWARDS, JOHN BAL 155 1ST WARD
EDWARDS, JOHN BAL 083 2ND DIST
EDWARDS, JOHN BAL 330 1ST WARD
EDWARDS, JOHN KEN 232 2ND DIST

Name	County	Page	District
EDWARDS, JOHN	BAL	401	14TH WAR
EDWARDS, JOHN	ST	326	4TH E DI
EDWARDS, JOHN	KEN	273	1ST DIST
EDWARDS, JOHN F.	ALL	260	CUMBERLA
EDWARDS, JOHN H.	KEN	242	2ND DIST
EDWARDS, JOSEPH	FRE	262	NEW MARK
EDWARDS, JOSEPH	BAL	047	9TH WARD
EDWARDS, JOSEPH G.	KEN	245	2ND DIST
EDWARDS, JULIA A.	BAL	228	6TH WARD
EDWARDS, LARA	BAL	251	17TH WAR
EDWARDS, LETTECIA	BAL	293	7TH WARD
EDWARDS, LEWIS	ANN	353	3RD DIST
EDWARDS, LOUIS	ANN	352	3RD DIST
EDWARDS, LOUISA	BAL	337	7TH WARD
EDWARDS, MARIA	BAL	236	6TH WARD
EDWARDS, MARIA	MGM	369	BERRYS D
EDWARDS, MARRY	WAS	047	2ND SUBD
EDWARDS, MARY	ALL	238	CUMBERLA
EDWARDS, MARY	BAL	405	8TH WARD
EDWARDS, MARY A.	ANN	416	HOWARD D
EDWARDS, MARY E.	BAL	180	2ND DIST
EDWARDS, MARY J.	BAL	377	3RD WARD
EDWARDS, MILTON	FRE	097	FREDERIC
EDWARDS, MOSES	BAL	380	1ST DIST
EDWARDS, NOAH	ANN	340	3RD DIST
EDWARDS, PETER	BAL	159	2ND DIST
EDWARDS, RICHARD	BAL	004	EASTERN
EDWARDS, RICHARD	BAL	383	3RD WARD
EDWARDS, RICHARD	BAL	002	18TH WAR
EDWARDS, RICHARD B.	CHA	286	BOJANTOW
EDWARDS, ROBERT	BAL	304	7TH WARD
EDWARDS, ROBERT	ANN	318	2ND DIST
EDWARDS, S.	BAL	135	1ST WARD
EDWARDS, SALLY	ANN	520	HOWARD D
EDWARDS, SAMUEL	KEN	236	2ND DIST
EDWARDS, SAMUEL	BAL	242	17TH WAR
EDWARDS, SAMUEL H.	BAL	009	4TH WARD
EDWARDS, SARAH	MGM	323	CRACKLIN
EDWARDS, SARAH	ANN	369	4TH DIST
EDWARDS, SARH	BAL	283	2ND WARD
EDWARDS, SILVESTA	WAS	155	2ND DIST
EDWARDS, SOLOMON	ANN	351	3RD DIST
EDWARDS, STANTON	ST	325	4TH E DI
EDWARDS, SUSAN	FRE	077	FREDERIC
EDWARDS, T.	BAL	130	1ST WARD
EDWARDS, THOMAS	BAL	163	1ST WARD
EDWARDS, THOMAS	FRE	422	8TH E DI
EDWARDS, THOMAS	KEN	273	1ST DIST
EDWARDS, THOMAS W.	BAL	395	3RD WARD
EDWARDS, THOS	BAL	284	20TH WAR
EDWARDS, WILLIAM	BAL	279	20TH WAR
EDWARDS, WILLIAM	BAL	289	20TH WAR
EDWARDS, WILLIAM	BAL	285	20TH WAR
EDWARDS, WILLIAM	KEN	217	2ND DIST
EDWARDS, WILLIAM	BAL	006	18TH WAR
EDWARDS, WILLIAM	BAL	105	18TH WAR
EDWARDS, WILLIAM	BAL	131	1ST WARD
EDWARDS, WILLIAM	BAL	295	12TH WAR
EDWARDS, WILLIAM	WAS	155	2ND DIST
EDWARDS, WILLIAM P.	HAR	046	1ST DIST
EDWARDS, WILLIAM V.	BAL	105	1ST WARD
EDWIN, H.	BAL	153	1ST WARD
EDWIN, N.	ANN	460	HOWARD D
EDWRADS, CHARLES	BAL	323	7TH WARD
EDWRADS, ELIZABETH	BAL	263	17TH WAR
EDWRDS, REZAN	BAL	059	1ST WARD
EDY, CASSANDRA	HAR	108	2ND DIST
EDY, JANE	BAL	188	6TH WARD
EDY, JOHN	ALL	086	5TH E.D.
EDY, LEONARD	HAR	108	2ND DIST
EDY, ROBERT	BAL	224	1ST DIST
EECKEL, ANTHONY	BAL	114	11TH WAR
EELLIOTT, ENNALS	TAL	072	EASTON T
EELMON, LEWIS W.	BAL	108	1ST WARD
EERSVILLE, T.B.	BAL	129	1ST WARD
EFFENSTEINE, JAMES	BAL	129	5TH WARD
EFFERT, CATHARINE	BAL	165	16TH WAR
EFFERT, PETER	BAL	136	18TH WAR
EFFERT, THOMAS	BAL	280	1ST DIST
EFFILOT, MARY	BAL	025	9TH WARD
EFFINGER, ARNOLD	BAL	102	10TH WAR
EFFORT, WILLIAM	BAL	190	17TH WAR
EFFORT, WILLIAM	BAL	275	1ST DIST
EGA, MICHAEL	HAR	155	3RD DIST
EGAD, JOHN	BAL	350	7TH WARD
EGAN, ANN	BAL	124	16TH WAR
EGAN, JAMES	BAL	108	18TH WAR
EGAN, JOHN	BAL	028	9TH WARD
EGAN, JOHN T.	BAL	048	9TH WARD
EGAN, JULIA	BAL	333	13TH WAR
EGAN, JULIA ANN	FRE	160	EMMITTSB
EGAN, MARY	BAL	263	12TH WAR
EGAN, MARY	BAL	262	12TH WAR
EGAN, MICHEAL	BAL	112	18TH WAR
EGAN, OWEN	BAL	158	1ST WARD
EGAN, THOMAS	BAL	009	9TH WARD
EGAN, WILLIAM	BAL	002	9TH WARD
EGAN, WILLIAM	BAL	155	19TH WAR
EGBERT, JAMES M.	BAL	090	15TH WAR
EGE, ANDREW	CAR	327	1ST DIST
EGEBERT, DANIEL	BAL	192	11TH WAR
EGEL, IRA	BAL	206	19TH WAR
EGELSTON, ELIZABETH	BAL	013	1ST WARD
EGELSTON, JAMES	BAL	198	5TH DIST
EGENTER, MARGARET	BAL	158	19TH WAR
EGER, ELIZABETH	BAL	046	9TH WARD
EGER, ELLEN	BAL	046	9TH WARD
EGERTON, A. D.	BAL	037	9TH WARD
EGERTON, ANN	BAL	424	3RD WARD
EGERTON, CHARLES C. SR.	BAL	037	9TH WARD
EGERTON, CHARLES*	BAL	078	4TH WARD
EGERTON, ELIZABETH B.	BAL	037	9TH WARD
EGERTON, ISABELLA	BAL	080	4TH WARD
EGERTON, ISABELLA	BAL	078	4TH WARD
EGERTON, JOHN B.	BAL	080	4TH WARD
EGERTON, WILLIAMA E.*	BAL	078	4TH WARD
EGET, CLEMENT	BAL	171	19TH WAR
EGGERS, MARGARET	BAL	085	10TH WAR
EGGSHAW, RACHEL	ALL	192	9TH E.D.
EGHERINGTON, SARAH	BAL	449	8TH WARD
EGLASTON, CHARLES	BAL	107	1ST WARD
EGLEFITZ, JOHN	BAL	291	3RD WARD
EGLEHEART, GEORGE T.	BAL	468	14TH WAR
EGLESTON, ABRAHAM	BAL	042	18TH WAR
EGLESTON, JOHN	BAL	106	2ND DIST
EGLESTON, SUSAN-BLACK	BAL	178	2ND WARD
EGLESTON, WESLEY	QUE	214	3RD E DI
EGLETON, JOHN	WAS	092	2ND SUBD
EGNO, JHN	HAR	145	3RD DIST
EGO, MICHAEL	ANN	429	HOWARD D
EGR, MARGARET ANN	CAR	327	1ST DIST
EGRHAN, MARY	ALL	187	9TH E.D.
EGULF, ELVINA	CAR	173	8TH DIST
EHADLINE, JOHN J.	BAL	067	2ND DIST
EHARTE, MARY	BAL	209	2ND WARD
EHIMAN, SUSAN	BAL	084	1ST WARD
EHIRTH, MARTHA *	BAL	155	2ND DIST
EHITAKER, ABRAHAM	CEC	182	7TH E DI
EHLEN, JOHN H.	BAL	271	12TH WAR
EHLEN, OLIVIA	BAL	271	12TH WAR
EHLER, GEORGE	BAL	459	8TH WARD
EHLER, GEORGE	BAL	459	1ST DIST
EHLER, JOHN	BAL	123	18TH WAR
EHLER, LEWIS	BAL	121	18TH WAR
EHLERS, AARON	BAL	229	6TH WARD
EHLERS, HENRY	BAL	087	10TH WAR
EHOWARD, WILLIAM	ALL	212	CUMBERLA
EHRALT, WILLIAM	BAL	278	2ND WARD
EHRHAN, ALBERT	BAL	247	12TH WAR
EHRHARDT, FREDERICK	BAL	126	16TH WAR
EHRHARDT, GEORGE	BAL	125	16TH WAR
EHRING, CATHERINE	BAL	085	10TH WAR
EHRMAN, G.	BAL	251	2ND WARD
EHRMAN, JOHN	BAL	006	4TH WARD
EHRMAN, JOHN	BAL	222	19TH WAR
EHRMAN, JOHN J.	BAL	178	2ND WARD
EHRMAN, MARY	BAL	222	19TH WAR
EHRMANN, G. A.	BAL	092	10TH WAR
EICETERUER, MARY A. *	BAL	115	18TH WAR
EICHEBERGER, CATHARINE	BAL	258	1ST DIST
EICHELBERGER, AARON	WAS	129	2ND DIST
EICHELBERGER, CATHARINE	WAS	163	2ND DIST
EICHELBERGER, CHARLES W.	BAL	235	12TH WAR
EICHELBERGER, CHARLES D.	FRE	167	EMMITTSB
EICHELBERGER, ELIZA	BAL	408	14TH WAR
EICHELBERGER, ELIZABETH	BAL	096	10TH WAR
EICHELBERGER, EMMANUEL	BAL	160	16TH WAR
EICHELBERGER, GEORGE	WAS	140	2ND DIST
EICHELBERGER, GEORGE M.	FRE	028	FREDERIC
EICHELBERGER, GRAYSON	FRE	031	FREDERIC
EICHELBERGER, HAMET	WAS	063	2ND SUBD
EICHELBERGER, HAMILTON	WAS	124	2ND DIST
EICHELBERGER, HARVEY	BAL	423	14TH WAR
EICHELBERGER, HELEN	FRE	066	FREDERIC
EICHELBERGER, HENRY	FRE	217	BUCKEYST
EICHELBERGER, J.M.	BAL	238	12TH WAR
EICHELBERGER, JACOB	WAS	132	2ND DIST
EICHELBERGER, JAMES W.	FRE	167	EMMITTSB
EICHELBERGER, JOB D.	FRE	225	BUCKEYST
EICHELBERGER, JOHN	BAL	217	11TH WAR
EICHELBERGER, JOHN	WAS	138	2ND DIST
EICHELBERGER, JOHN	WAS	097	2ND DIST
EICHELBERGER, JOHN L.	WAS	097	2ND DIST
EICHELBERGER, JOHN L.	ANN	451	HOWARD D
EICHELBERGER, JOSEPH	WAS	144	2ND DIST
EICHELBERGER, JOSEPH	FRE	107	CREAGERS
EICHELBERGER, LAURA	BAL	006	18TH WAR
EICHELBERGER, P.J.	WAS	139	HAGERSTO
EICHELBERGER, PETER	WAS	159	HAGERSTO
EICHELBERGER, SAMUEL	WAS	165	HAGERSTO
EICHELBERGER, SAMUEL	FRE	113	CREAGERS
EICHELBERGER, SARAH	BAL	193	19TH WAR
EICHELBERGER, WILLIAM	BAL	006	18TH WAR
EICHELBERGER, WILLIAM A.	WAS	130	2ND DIST
EICHELBUGER, HENRIETTA M.	BAL	011	2ND DIST
EICHELMAN, CASPER	BAL	279	1ST DIST
EICHER, SAMUEL	ALL	006	3RD E.D.
EICHERT, ELIZABETH	BAL	055	18TH WAR
EICHILBERGER, MARY E.	MGM	416	MEDLEY 3
EICKELBERGER, EMMA L.	BAL	408	14TH WAR
EICKELBERGER, MARY	FRE	058	FREDERIC
EICKENS, MARTIN	BAL	109	1ST WARD
EICKLE, JOHN	BAL	068	1ST WARD
EIDEL, ELIZABETH	BAL	029	15TH WAR
EIDEL, JACOB	BAL	029	15TH WAR
EIDEL, PHILIP	BAL	194	6TH WARD
EIDER, HENRY	BAL	010	9TH WARD
EIDER, JOHN	CEC	120	3RD E DI
EIDER, WILLIAM	CEC	001	ELKTON 3
EIDLE, PHILIP	BAL	231	17TH WAR
EIDLER, HENRY	BAL	013	9TH WARD
EIGEL, CUNEGUNDA	BAL	082	10TH WAR
EIGELSTON, AMANDA	BAL	058	18TH WAR
EIGELSTON, ARMINTA	BAL	033	18TH WAR
EIGEN, HENRY	BAL	099	2ND DIST
EIGENBRADE, HENRY	BAL	169	6TH WARD
EIGLESON, RICHARD	BAL	253	17TH WAR
EIGUBRUT, CHRISTIAN	BAL	102	15TH WAR
EIKER, SARAH	FRE	128	CREAGERS
EIKHOLTZ, SAMUEL	FRE	127	CREAGERS
EIKLEMANN, E.	BAL	071	10TH WAR
EILBECHER, BARNADINA	BAL	036	15TH WAR
EILBECHER, JOHN	BAL	036	15TH WAR
EILER, JOHN	FRE	288	WOODSBOR
EILER, JOHN	FRE	288	WOODSBOR
EILIP, CHARLES	BAL	295	20TH WAR
EIMER, WILLIAM	BAL	369	1ST DIST
EINDRODER, CHARLES	BAL	189	6TH WARD
EINERVA, HENRIETTA	BAL	120	11TH WAR
EINHNER, ANDREW	BAL	095	18TH WAR
EINMAN, JACOB	BAL	216	19TH WAR
EINSBIEN, HENRY	WAS	129	HAGERSTO
EINWATCHER, ALEXANDER	BAL	119	18TH WAR
EIR, W.	BAL	148	1ST WARD
EISEMAN, MOXES	BAL	015	9TH WARD
EISENBRANDT, C. H.	BAL	094	10TH WAR
EISENBRANDT, HENRIETTA	BAL	095	10TH WAR
EISENHAUER, EADAM	BAL	235	2ND WARD
EISENHOUR, FRANCIS	BAL	313	7TH WARD
EISLER, JOHN	BAL	137	5TH WARD
EITON, WILLAIM	WAS	038	2ND SUBD
EIVAE, LYFELL	WOR	227	4TH E DI
EIVER, MINA	BAL	013	9TH WARD
EKE, HENRY	BAL	257	2ND WARD
EKHART, FREDERICK	BAL	220	19TH WAR
EKHART, JOHN	BAL	220	19TH WAR
EKLI, PETER	BAL	092	10TH WAR
EKOFF, SAMUEL	HAR	090	2ND DIST
EKPHART, GEORGE	FRE	234	BUCKEYST
EKSTERN, GEORGE	BAL	217	19TH WAR
ELAGLOBY, WILLIAM	BAL	137	11TH WAR
ELANORA	BAL	317	1ST DIST
ELAR, GEROGE	BAL	304	20TH WAR
ELAR, MARY	BAL	304	20TH WAR
ELAS, DEBORAH A.	BAL	019	18TH WAR
ELBEN, HENRY	ALL	194	9TH E.D.
ELBEN, REUBEN	ALL	187	9TH E.D.
ELBEN, WILLIAM	ALL	187	9TH E.D.
ELBERFELT, ANNA	BAL	306	3RD WARD
ELBERN, JOHN	QUE	131	1ST E DI
ELBERT, ALEXANDER *	BAL	079	19TH WAR
ELBERT, ANN M.	BAL	387	8TH WARD
ELBERT, ARAMINTA	KEN	298	3RD DIST
ELBERT, EDWARD	QUE	206	3RD E DI
ELBERT, ELIZABETH	BAL	103	10TH WAR
ELBERT, HARRIETT	BAL	062	18TH WAR
ELBERT, HENRY	BAL	245	6TH WARD
ELBERT, ISAAC	KEN	298	3RD DIST
ELBERT, JAMES	KEN	233	2ND DIST
ELBERT, JAMES	DOR	425	1ST DIST
ELBERT, LAWRANCE	BAL	386	8TH WARD
ELBERT, LYDIA	BAL	226	17TH WAR
ELBERT, OCTAVUS	BAL	463	14TH WAR
ELBERT, PHILEMON	BAL	224	19TH WAR
ELBERT, RACHEL	KEN	303	3RD DIST
ELBERT, SOPHIA	BAL	260	5TH WARD
ELBERT, THOMAS	KEN	299	3RD DIST
ELBERT, WILLIAM H.	TAL	092	ST MICHA
ELBIL, AGUSTAVES	BAL	209	11TH WAR
ELBORN, WILLIAM	KEN	269	1ST DIST
ELBRUN, EDWARD *	KEN	263	1ST DIST
ELBUM, THOMAS W.	KEN	218	2ND DIST
ELDAGGNER, CHARLES	BAL	127	1ST WARD
ELDER, ALEXERIS J.	BAL	312	12TH WAR
ELDER, ALLEN	BAL	300	7TH WARD
ELDER, AMRY	CAR	293	7TH DIST
ELDER, ANN U.	CAR	268	WESTMINS
ELDER, BASIL S.	BAL	260	12TH WAR
ELDER, BASIL Y.	BAL	147	11TH WAR
ELDER, CAROLINE	BAL	101	5TH WARD
ELDER, CATHARINE	ANN	424	HOWARD D
ELDER, CATHARINE	FRE	159	EMMITTSB
ELDER, ELIZA JEY	FRE	066	FREDERIC
ELDER, ELIZABETH	MGM	402	ROCKERLE
ELDER, ELIZABETH	ANN	514	HOWARD D
ELDER, ELIZABETH	BAL	173	16TH WAR
ELDER, FRANKLIN	BAL	101	5TH WARD
ELDER, GEORGE H.	BAL	249	1ST DIST
ELDER, HENRY	BAL	245	20TH WAR
ELDER, HERTER	BAL	375	13TH WAR
ELDER, JAMES	FRE	159	EMMITTSB
ELDER, JAMES	BAL	147	1ST WARD
ELDER, JAKES	BAL	149	1ST WARD
ELDER, JEREMIAH	BAL	364	8TH WARD
ELDER, JOACHIN	FRE	159	EMMITTSB
ELDER, JOHN	ANN	486	HOWARD D
ELDER, JOHN	BAL	233	12TH WAR
ELDER, JOHN F.	FRE	180	5TH E DI
ELDER, JOHN G.	BAL	258	20TH WAR
ELDER, JOHN T.	ANN	499	HOWARD D
ELDER, JOSEPH	BAL	151	2ND DIST
ELDER, LEVI	CAR	213	5TH DIST
ELDER, LEWIS	FRE	184	5TH E DI
ELDER, LEWIS	BAL	167	2ND DIST
ELDER, LUCY A.	BAL	006	1ST WARD
ELDER, MANUS	BAL	223	2ND WARD
ELDER, MARTHA	FRE	054	FREDERIC
ELDER, MARTHA E.	CAR	214	5TH DIST
ELDER, MARY A.	FRE	065	FREDERIC
ELDER, MARY WILLIAM SIS-	BAL	316	20TH WAR
ELDER, MICHAEL	BAL	177	2ND DIST
ELDER, OWEN	CAR	220	5TH DIST
ELDER, REBECCA	CAR	267	WESTMINS
ELDER, SAMUEL	BAL	114	11TH WAR
ELDER, SARAH	ANN	366	4TH DIST
ELDER, SISTER HILLENA	FRE	197	5TH E DI
ELDER, THOMAS	FRE	115	CREAGERS
ELDER, WILLIAM	FRE	187	5TH E DI
ELDER, WILLIAM H.	FRE	20	5TH E DI
ELDER, WILLIAM H. J.	BAL	290	20TH WAR
ELDERDICE, JOHN	WAS	005	WILLIAMS
ELDERKIN, JAES K.	BAL	182	2ND WARD
ELDERKIN, WILLIAM G.	BAL	182	2ND WARD
ELDRED, ANDREW	FRE	341	MIDDLETO
ELDRED, CATHERINE	ALL	235	CUMBERLA
ELDRED, HENRY	ALL	235	CUMBERLA
ELDRIC, MRY *	BAL	266	2ND WARD
ELDRIDGE, ABRAHAM	BAL	460	8TH WARD
ELDRIDGE, CHARLES	BAL	140	1ST WARD
ELDRIDGE, CLARK	MGM	405	MEDLEY 3
ELDRIDGE, GEORGE M.	CEC	080	NORTHEAS
ELDRIDGE, GEORGE M.	CEC	079	NORTHEAS
ELDRIDGE, JOB	CEC	163	6TH E DI
ELDRIDGE, JOSEPH	CEC	059	1ST E DI
ELDRIDGE, ROBERT	BAL	032	4TH WARD
ELDRIDGE, WILSON	BAL	181	6TH WARD
ELDRIGE, MARY	WAS	249	1ST DIST
ELDRIGH, HENRY	BAL	123	1ST WARD
ELDRIX, JOHN	ALL	211	CUMBERLA
ELEANORA, M.	BAL	296	1ST DIST
ELEASON, ELLIN	KEN	282	3RD DIST
ELEHESEN, THOMAS H.	FRE	239	NEW MARK
ELENDER, CAROLINE	BAL	464	14TH WAR
ELERN, MARGARET	DOR	414	1ST DIST
ELERY, ANN	BAL	408	14TH WAR
ELESILORE, SUSAN	CAR	403	2ND DIST
ELESLER, MARGARET	BAL	345	7TH WARD
ELEVERT, MARTIN	BAL	012	9TH WARD
ELEY, ELISABETH	ALL	059	10TH E.D
ELFANEY, WILLIAM H.	BAL	281	12TH WAR
ELFREY, JOHN	BAL	220	19TH WAR
ELGAN, JOHN	BAL	043	4TH WARD
ELGAR, JOHN	BAL	381	13TH WAR
ELGAR, ROSINA	BAL	042	4TH WARD
ELGENFRITZ, THOMAS	BAL	324	7TH WARD
ELGIN, CHARLES	WAS	092	2ND SUBD
ELGIN, JAMES	WAS	092	2ND SUBD
ELGIN, JAMES H.	WAS	092	2ND SUBD
ELGIN, WILLIAM	WAS	095	2ND SUBD
ELI, GEORGE	BAL	420	14TH WAR
ELIAN, JOHN	BAL	204	19TH WAR
ELIAS, JAMES	BAL	246	20TH WAR
ELIAS, SAMUEL	BAL	221	6TH WARD
ELIAS, SARAH	BAL	239	20TH WAR
ELIAS, VIOLET	BAL	177	19TH WAR
ELIASON, ERIC	BAL	438	14TH WAR
ELIASON, THOMAS W.	KEN	214	2ND DIST
ELICKS, ELIZABETH	BAL	419	14TH WAR
ELICOTT, EDWARD T.	BAL	333	1ST DIST
ELIEFRITY, BARNEY	WAS	164	HAGERSTO
ELIEFRITY, MARTIN	WAS	164	HAGERSTO
ELIEN, JOHN	BAL	086	1ST WARD
ELIET, BURNICE	HAR	193	3RD DIST
ELIGEER, ADAM	ALL	252	CUMBERLA
ELIGIN, GEORGE L.	WAS	084	2ND SUBD
ELIN, MARGARET	BAL	173	19TH WAR
ELINE, FRANCIS	CAR	301	1ST DIST
ELINE, LEOCADIN	FRE	203	5TH E DI
ELINE, SAMUEL P.	CAR	299	1ST DIST
ELINE, SOPHIA	FRE	177	5TH E DI

ELION, COATLEAP	TAL	100	ST MICHA
ELIOT, ARY	CAR	223	5TH DIST
ELIOT, JAMES	BAL	460	1ST DIST
ELIOT, JOHN	CAL	013	1ST DIST
ELIOT, SAMUEL	WAS	003	WILLIAMS
ELIOTT, ELIZABETH	DOR	341	3RD DIVI
ELIOTT, GEHEW	DOR	352	3RD DIVI
ELIOTT, HENERY	DOR	352	3RD DIVI
ELIOTT, HENRY	TAL	092	ST MICHA
ELIOTT, JOHN	DOR	345	3RD DIVI
ELIOTT, JOHN	DOR	340	3RD DIVI
ELIOTT, JOSEPH	BAL	189	11TH WAR
ELIOTT, PHEBY	DOR	352	3RD DIVI
ELIOTT, RACHEL	DOR	346	3RD DIVI
ELIOTT, WILLIAM	DOR	352	3RD DIVI
ELIOTT, WILLIAM	DOR	352	3RD DIVI
ELIS, FOUNTAIN	HAR	148	3RD DIST
ELIS, THOMAS	DOR	363	3RD DIVI
ELISHA, CAVID	BAL	303	17TH WAR
ELISHA, JAMES	QUE	169	2ND E DI
ELISHA, MATTHEW	BAL	303	17TH WAR
ELISHA, MATTHEW	BAL	303	17TH WAR
ELISHA, THOMAS	BAL	303	17TH WAR
ELISON, KITURAH	CAR	208	5TH DIST
ELISS, NEARCE	DOR	362	3RD DIVI
ELIZABETH	BAL	407	1ST DIST
ELIZABETH, MARY*	DOR	379	1ST DIST
ELKHORNE, EDWARD	MGM	361	BERRYS D
ELKIN, MARY	BAL	284	1ST DIST
ELKINGTON, J. C.	BAL	157	1ST WARD
ELKINS, JESSE	FRE	014	FREDERIC
ELKINS, JOSEPH	FRE	064	FREDERIC
ELKINS, WILLIAM	CHA	226	ALLENS F
ELKRIDGE, JAMES	BAL	106	5TH WARD
ELLAM, GEORGE	BAL	122	1ST WARD
ELLCOTT, THOMAS	BAL	021	1ST WARD
ELLECAMP, GEORGE	ALL	168	6TH E.D.
ELLEDER, FREDERICK	BAL	447	8TH WARD
ELLEN, EPHE	ALL	086	5TH E.D.
ELLEN, MARGARET A.	BAL	089	15TH WAR
ELLEN, MARY	ALL	176	7TH E.D.
ELLEN, MARY	QUE	199	3RD E DI
ELLEN, NANCY	BAL	217	6TH DIST
ELLEN, SARAH	ALL	134	4TH E.D.
ELLEN,RICHARD W.	MGM	430	CLARKSTR
ELLENBRICK, FRECRICK	BAL	060	18TH WAR
ELLENDER, CAROLINE V.	BAL	448	8TH WARD
ELLENDER, CHARITY	BAL	236	6TH WARD
ELLENDER, FREDERICK	BAL	313	7TH WARD
ELLENGER, JACOB	BAL	345	7TH WARD
ELLENGER, SAMUEL	BAL	343	7TH WARD
ELLER, BENJAMIN	MGM	401	ROCKERLE
ELLER, JOHN F.	MGM	376	ROCKERLE
ELLERMAN, ELIZABETH	BAL	179	16TH WAR
ELLERMAN, JOHN F.	BAL	440	8TH WARD
ELLERS, JAMES	QUE	219	3RD E DI
ELLERS, LEWIS	BAL	227	17TH WAR
ELLERS, MARGARET	BAL	264	20TH WAR
ELLE.Y, P. AUGUSTUS	BAL	061	15TH WAR
ELLERY, SARAH	BAL	242	20TH WAR
ELLES, EATHOLOMEW	BAL	404	1ST DIST
ELLES, GEORGE *	KEN	267	1ST DIST
ELLES, JAMES H. *	KEN	267	1ST DIST
ELLESS, JULIA A.	WOR	174	6TH E DI
ELLET, ELISABETH	ANN	341	3RD DIST
ELLETT, GRAYSON	HAR	112	2ND DIST
ELLETT, JANE	HAR	078	2ND DIST
ELLETT, JOHN	HAR	077	2ND DIST
ELLETT, JOHN	SOM	423	PRINCESS
ELLETT, MARTHA	HAR	084	2ND DIST
ELLICANT, HENRY	ALL	127	4TH E.D.
ELLICE, ANN	ST	317	4TH E DI
ELLICE, CHARLES	ST	319	4TH E DI
ELLICE, ELISABETH	ANN	323	2ND DIST
ELLICE, ELIZA C.	ST	319	4TH E DI
ELLICE, HENRY	ST	329	4TH E DI
ELLICE, JOHN	ST	330	4TH E DI
ELLICE, MARIA	ST	320	4TH E DI
ELLICE, SUSAN	ST	329	4TH E DI
ELLICK, JOHN	BAL	155	2ND DIST
ELLICOT, ELIZABETH	BAL	352	1ST DIST
ELLICCT, ELIZABETH	BAL	352	1ST DIST
ELLICOTT, ANDREW	BAL	067	15TH WAR
ELLICOTT, BERRY	BAL	259	12TH WAR
ELLICOTT, ELIAS	ANN	449	HOWARD D
ELLICOTT, GEORGE	ANN	463	HOWARD D
ELLICOTT, JOHN	ALL	127	4TH E.D.
ELLICOTT, JOHN	BAL	469	14TH WAR
ELLICOTT, L.	BAL	103	10TH WAR
ELLICOTT, M.	BAL	139	1ST WARD
ELLICOTT, MARGARET	BAL	462	14TH WAR
ELLICOTT, MARY A. T.	ANN	425	HOWARD D
ELLICOTT, MARY S.	ANN	413	HOWARD D
ELLICOTT, MARYAN	BAL	378	1ST DIST
ELLICOTT, SAMUEL	MGM	331	CRACKLIN
ELLICOTT, WILLIAM M.	BAL	067	10TH WAR
ELLIDISS, FREDERICK	HAR	080	2ND DIST
ELLIGOOD, ROBERT H.	SOM	492	SALISBUR
ELLIM, SALLY	BAL	005	1ST WARD
ELLIN, SARAH	ALL	211	CUMBERLA
ELLINCER, CHARLES	BAL	253	12TH WAR
ELLINGSWORTH, JOSIAH	SOM	505	SALISBUR
ELLINGSWORTH, WILLIAM	BAL	369	3RD WARD
ELLINSWORTH, JANE	WOR	261	BERLIN 1
ELLINSWORTH, WILLIAM	WOR	268	BERLIN 1
ELLIOCTT, PATTY T.	ANN	463	HOWARD D
ELLIOT, AMELIA	CEC	033	CHESAPEA
ELLIOT, ANN	BAL	004	9TH WARD
ELLIOT, ARMSTRONG	CEC	087	4TH E DI
ELLIOT, ELIZA	BAL	110	10TH WAR
ELLIOT, ELIZABETH	PRI	014	BLADENSB
ELLIOT, GEORGE	ALL	196	CUMBERLA
ELLIOT, GEORGE	HAR	035	1ST DIST
ELLIOT, GEORGE	QUE	156	2ND E DI
ELLIOT, HENRY C.	DOR	397	1ST DIST
ELLIOT, JAMES	CEC	035	CHESAPEA
ELLIOT, LEVI	CEC	032	CHESAPEA
ELLIOT, MARY A.	CEC	087	4TH E DI
ELLIOT, ROBERT	BAL	108	1ST WARD
ELLIOT, RUTH	ALL	222	CUMBERLA
ELLIOT, THOMAS	BAL	158	19TH WAR
ELLIOT, WILLIAM	FRE	377	PETERSVI
ELLIOTT, ABEL	DOR	352	3RD DIVI
ELLIOTT, ADAM	ALL	151	6TH E.D.
ELLIOTT, AMANDA	BAL	096	5TH WARD
ELLIOTT, AMELIA A.	ANN	292	ANNAPOLI
ELLIOTT, ANN	BAL	006	18TH WAR
ELLIOTT, ANN M.	BAL	125	11TH WAR
ELLIOTT, ANN M.	SOM	530	QUANTICO
ELLIOTT, ANNA	FRE	241	NEW MARK

ELLIOTT, BENJAMIN	BAL	322	3RD WARD
ELLIOTT, BENJAMIN	BAL	327	7TH WARD
ELLIOTT, BENJAMIN B.	CAL	062	3RD DIST
ELLIOTT, BENJAMIN J.	BAL	051	18TH WAR
ELLIOTT, BENJIMAN	HAR	159	3RD DIST
ELLIOTT, BETSY	ANN	376	4TH DIST
ELLIOTT, CHARLES	ANN	376	4TH DIST
ELLIOTT, CHARLES W.	BAL	278	17TH WAR
ELLIOTT, COLUMBUS	TAL	067	EASTON T
ELLIOTT, COMFORT	BAL	044	2ND DIST
ELLIOTT, DANIEL S.	BAL	278	17TH WAR
ELLIOTT, E.T.	BAL	206	11TH WAR
ELLIOTT, ELIZABETH	FRE	241	NEW MARK
ELLIOTT, ELIZABETH	BAL	347	7TH WARD
ELLIOTT, ELIZABETH	BAL	048	15TH WAR
ELLIOTT, ELIZABETH	BAL	222	6TH WARD
ELLIOTT, ELLEN H.J.	BAL	022	1ST WARD
ELLIOTT, ELSY	BAL	250	20TH WAR
ELLIOTT, GEORGE	FRE	240	NEW MARK
ELLIOTT, GEORGE	HAR	119	2ND DIST
ELLIOTT, GEORGE	BAL	403	14TH WAR
ELLIOTT, GEORGE	BAL	155	2ND DIST
ELLIOTT, GEORGE	BAL	135	5TH WARD
ELLIOTT, GEORGE	BAL	319	7TH WARD
ELLIOTT, HENRY	BAL	377	13TH WAR
ELLIOTT, HOOPER	BAL	196	2ND WARD
ELLIOTT, HUBBARD	BAL	293	17TH WAR
ELLIOTT, HUDSON	SOM	520	BARREN C
ELLIOTT, ISEBELLA	BAL	019	18TH WAR
ELLIOTT, JACOB T.	WOR	210	4TH E DI
ELLIOTT, JAMES	QUE	218	3RD E DI
ELLIOTT, JAMES	QUE	175	2ND E DI
ELLIOTT, JAMES	FRE	040	FREDERIC
ELLIOTT, JAMES	ANN	362	4TH DIST
ELLIOTT, JAMES	ALL	167	6TH E.D.
ELLIOTT, JAMES	BAL	289	3RD WARD
ELLIOTT, JAMES	BAL	303	7TH WARD
ELLIOTT, JAMES H.	BAL	278	17TH WAR
ELLIOTT, JAMES K.	SOM	529	QUANTICO
ELLIOTT, JANE	BAL	153	11TH WAR
ELLIOTT, JEHU	BAL	071	15TH WAR
ELLIOTT, JOHN	BAL	318	7TH WARD
ELLIOTT, JOHN	BAL	180	11TH WAR
ELLIOTT, JOHN	BAL	146	2ND DIST
ELLIOTT, JOHN	BAL	297	12TH WAR
ELLIOTT, JOHN	CAR	126	NO TWP L
ELLIOTT, JOHN	CEC	088	4TH E DI
ELLIOTT, JOHN	BAL	273	17TH WAR
ELLIOTT, JOHN	BAL	271	17TH WAR
ELLIOTT, JOHN	FRE	220	BUCKEYST
ELLIOTT, JOHN	DOR	395	1ST DIST
ELLIOTT, JOHN D.	QUE	159	2ND E DI
ELLIOTT, JOHN E.	BAL	183	6TH WARD
ELLIOTT, JOHN F.	CAR	125	NO TWP L
ELLIOTT, JOHN J.	QUE	182	3RD E DI
ELLIOTT, JOHN S.	BAL	258	6TH WARD
ELLIOTT, JOSEPH	BAL	231	6TH WARD
ELLIOTT, JOSEPH	BAL	310	3RD WARD
ELLIOTT, JOSEPH	BAL	338	13TH WAR
ELLIOTT, JOSEPH	BAL	027	18TH WAR
ELLIOTT, LAVINIA	BAL	231	6TH WARD
ELLIOTT, MARIAH	SOM	488	SALISBUR
ELLIOTT, MARY	SOM	542	TYASKIN
ELLIOTT, MARY	BAL	042	2ND DIST
ELLIOTT, MARY	BAL	007	15TH WAR
ELLIOTT, MARY	BAL	002	18TH WAR
ELLIOTT, MARY	BAL	122	11TH WAR
ELLIOTT, MARY A.	BAL	080	4TH WARD
ELLIOTT, MARY C.	TAL	067	EASTON T
ELLIOTT, MARY E.	ANN	415	HOWARD D
ELLIOTT, MATILDA	BAL	150	5TH WARD
ELLIOTT, MATILDA	FRE	218	BUCKEYST
ELLIOTT, MICHAEL	ALL	150	6TH E.D.
ELLIOTT, MISS M.	FRE	200	5TH E DI
ELLIOTT, NATHANIEL J.	BAL	348	3RD WARD
ELLIOTT, NOAH	ANN	382	4TH DIST
ELLIOTT, OLIVER	QUE	222	4TH E DI
ELLIOTT, PERE-BLACK	QUE	163	2ND E DI
ELLIOTT, PLUMMER	ANN	381	4TH DIST
ELLIOTT, RACHEL	BAL	121	11TH WAR
ELLIOTT, REBECCA	ALL	043	10TH E.D
ELLIOTT, REUBEN	ANN	391	4TH DIST
ELLIOTT, REUBEN	ANN	379	4TH DIST
ELLIOTT, RICHARD	ANN	309	1ST DIST
ELLIOTT, ROBERT	BAL	208	6TH WARD
ELLIOTT, ROBERT	BAL	042	2ND DIST
ELLIOTT, ROBERT	BAL	286	7TH WARD
ELLIOTT, ROBERT	BAL	130	11TH WAR
ELLIOTT, ROBERT	BAL	111	10TH WAR
ELLIOTT, ROBERT	BAL	006	4TH WARD
ELLIOTT, ROBERT O.	BAL	208	6TH WARD
ELLIOTT, SAMUEL	BAL	334	7TH WARD
ELLIOTT, SAMUEL*	BAL	051	4TH WARD
ELLIOTT, SARAH C.	DOR	396	1ST DIST
ELLIOTT, SEWALL-BLACK	QUE	154	1ST E DI
ELLIOTT, SISTER ELIZA	FRE	198	5TH E DI
ELLIOTT, SOLOMON	BAL	154	5TH WARD
ELLIOTT, SUSAN	ANN	294	1ST DIST
ELLIOTT, SUSAN W.	DOR	353	3RD DIVI
ELLIOTT, THOMAS	BAL	280	17TH WAR
ELLIOTT, THOMAS	SOM	415	DUBLIN D
ELLIOTT, THOMAS	BAL	326	7TH WARD
ELLIOTT, THOMAS	BAL	287	7TH WARD
ELLIOTT, THOMAS	BAL	344	1ST DIST
ELLIOTT, THOMAS	TAL	093	ST MICHA
ELLIOTT, THOMAS C.	ANN	346	3RD DIST
ELLIOTT, TOM	ANN	298	1ST DIST
ELLIOTT, WASHINGTON	ANN	272	ANNAPOLI
ELLIOTT, WILLIAM	BAL	276	7TH WARD
ELLIOTT, WILLIAM	BAL	208	6TH WARD
ELLIOTT, WILLIAM	BAL	193	6TH WARD
ELLIOTT, WILLIAM	BAL	193	5TH WARD
ELLIOTT, WILLIAM	BAL	187	6TH WARD
ELLIOTT, WILLIAM	QUE	161	2ND E DI
ELLIOTT, WILLIAM	KEN	298	3RD DIST
ELLIOTT, WILLIAM	TAL	065	EASTON T
ELLIOTT, WILLIAM	SOM	516	BARREN C
ELLIOTT, WILLIAM	SOM	488	SALISBUR
ELLIOTT, WILLIAM	SOM	511	BARREN C
ELLIOTT, WILLIAM	PRI	078	MARLBROU
ELLIOTT, WILLIAM	BAL	033	18TH WAR
ELLIOTT, WILLIAM	FRE	202	5TH E DI
ELLIOTT, WILLIAM	BAL	167	19TH WAR
ELLIOTT, WILLIAM	BAL	116	18TH WAR
ELLIOTT, WILLIAM H.	BAL	014	4TH WARD
ELLIOTT, WILLIAM S.	BAL	273	17TH WAR
ELLIOTT, WILLIAM T.	TAL	031	EASTON D
ELLIOTT, WILLIAM W.	ANN	382	4TH DIST
ELLIOTT, WILLIAM*	DOR	467	1ST DIST
ELLIOTT,ABRAM	BAL	042	2ND DIST

ELLIOTT,JOHN S.	QUE	152	1ST E DI
ELLIOTT,MARY A.	CAR	074	NO TWP L
ELLIS, ABRAHAM-BLACK	BAL	223	2ND WARD
ELLIS, BARSEY	DOR	372	3RD DIVI
ELLIS, BENJAMIN	BAL	334	3RD WARD
ELLIS, BISIA	DOR	362	3RD DIVI
ELLIS, C.K.	BAL	130	5TH WARD
ELLIS, CATHARINE	BAL	115	11TH WAR
ELLIS, CIPIO	BAL	058	4TH WARD
ELLIS, DANIEL	FRE	095	FREDERIC
ELLIS, DANIEL	FRE	081	FREDERIC
ELLIS, DANIEL	BAL	135	1ST WARD
ELLIS, DAVID	BAL	295	3RD WARD
ELLIS, DAVID	ALL	176	7TH E.D.
ELLIS, EDWARD	KEN	299	3RD DIST
ELLIS, ELIZABETH	BAL	356	8TH WARD
ELLIS, ELIZABETH A.	BAL	378	8TH WARD
ELLIS, EMMA J.	BAL	378	8TH WARD
ELLIS, ESTER	WOR	344	1ST E DI
ELLIS, FRANCES A.	CEC	013	ELKTON 3
ELLIS, GEORGE	DOR	362	3RD DIVI
ELLIS, GEORGE	WOR	346	1ST E DI
ELLIS, GEORGE	DOR	470	1ST DIST
ELLIS, GEORGE	SOM	502	SALISBUR
ELLIS, GEORGE	BAL	324	1ST DIST
ELLIS, GEORGE W.	BAL	297	7TH WARD
ELLIS, HENRY	BAL	132	16TH WAR
ELLIS, HENRY	DOR	469	1ST DIST
ELLIS, HENRY	BAL	277	17TH WAR
ELLIS, HIRAM	ALL	175	7TH E.D.
ELLIS, HUMPHREY	BAL	159	1ST WARD
ELLIS, IBBA-BLACK	WOR	345	1ST E DI
ELLIS, JAMES	KEN	292	3RD DIST
ELLIS, JAMES	BAL	261	20TH WAR
ELLIS, JANE	BAL	087	4TH WARD
ELLIS, JANE	BAL	091	5TH WARD
ELLIS, JESSIE	WOR	345	1ST E DI
ELLIS, JOHN	WOR	346	1ST E DI
ELLIS, JOHN	ANN	368	4TH DIST
ELLIS, JOHN	BAL	026	15TH WAR
ELLIS, JOHN C. H.	BAL	266	20TH WAR
ELLIS, JOSEPH	DOR	362	3RD DIVI
ELLIS, JOSEPH	MGM	440	CLARKSTR
ELLIS, JOSHUA	BAL	015	4TH WARD
ELLIS, LEAH	DOR	303	1ST DIST
ELLIS, LLOYD	DOR	469	1ST DIST
ELLIS, LOUISA	BAL	067	4TH WARD
ELLIS, LOUISA	BAL	062	4TH WARD
ELLIS, MARTHA R.	CEC	014	ELKTON 3
ELLIS, MARTIN	SOM	500	SALISBUR
ELLIS, MARY	BAL	001	18TH WAR
ELLIS, MARY	BAL	094	5TH WARD
ELLIS, MARY	BAL	205	6TH WARD
ELLIS, MARY	BAL	234	2ND WARD
ELLIS, MARY A.	BAL	023	15TH WAR
ELLIS, MARY E.	SOM	490	SALISBUR
ELLIS, POLLY	DOR	456	1ST DIST
ELLIS, REBECCA	BAL	070	4TH WARD
ELLIS, RICHARD	KEN	306	3RD DIST
ELLIS, SARAH E.-BLACK	BAL	216	2ND WARD
ELLIS, SOLOMON	DOR	302	1ST DIST
ELLIS, SOPHIAH	WOR	311	2ND E DI
ELLIS, THOMAS	BAL	029	9TH WARD
ELLIS, WILLIAM	BAL	309	7TH WARD
ELLIS, WILLIAM	BAL	359	8TH WARD
ELLIS, WILLIAM	BAL	125	1ST WARD
ELLIS, WILLIAM	BAL	004	EASTERN
ELLIS, WILLIAM	BAL	002	EASTERN
ELLIS, WILLIAM	KEN	291	3RD DIST
ELLIS, WILLIAM	BAL	093	18TH WAR
ELLIS, WILLIAM R.	SOM	499	SALISBUR
ELLISM JOHN	BAL	193	6TH WARD
ELLISON, FANNY	BAL	023	18TH WAR
ELLISON, LOUIS	CEC	038	CHESAPEA
ELLISON, MARGARET	BAL	276	2ND WARD
ELLISON, MARY	BAL	294	7TH WARD
ELLISON, MARY A.	BAL	287	3RD WARD
ELLISON, THOMAS	BAL	239	12TH WAR
ELLISS, CHARELS	WOR	240	6TH E DI
ELLISS, GEORGE	BAL	206	17TH WAR
ELLISS, JAME SM.	WOR	171	6TH E DI
ELLISS, JAMES	WOR	165	6TH E DI
ELLISS, JOHN	BAL	206	17TH WAR
ELLISS, JOSEPH A.	WOR	178	6TH E DI
ELLISS, JOSHUA	WOR	228	6TH E DI
ELLISS, LEAH J.	WOR	228	6TH E DI
ELLISS, LEVEN	DOR	362	3RD DIVI
ELLISS, WILLIAM	WOR	175	6TH E DI
ELLISSON, BETSEY	FRE	162	EMMITTSB
ELLIT, GEORGE	HAR	041	1ST DIST
ELLIT, JOHN	HAR	013	1ST DIST
ELLIT, MARY	HAR	046	1ST DIST
ELLIT, SAMUEL	HAR	013	1ST DIST
ELLITT, WILLIAM T.	SOM	413	DUBLIN D
ELLMAN, GEORGE E.	BAL	351	3RD WARD
ELLOTT, THOMAS M.	HAR	149	3RD DIST
ELLOWN, JOHN	BAL	265	1ST DIST
ELLRIDGE, WARREN	HAR	131	2ND DIST
ELLSLER, HENRY	BAL	216	6TH WARD
ELLSWORTH, F. T.	BAL	083	10TH WAR
ELLWOOD, JOHN	CEC	174	5TH E DI
ELLY, PIERSON	CEC	128	5TH E DI
ELLZEN, JOHN*	BAL	114	11TH WAR
ELLZER, JOHN*	BAL	114	11TH WAR
ELMAMS, JOHN	BAL	250	2ND WARD
ELMER, CHARLES	BAL	158	1ST WARD
ELMER, CHARLES	BAL	168	1ST WARD
ELMES, MARY E.	BAL	298	7TH WARD
ELMIRE, CHARLES	BAL	302	20TH WAR
ELMORE, JAMES	BAL	112	1ST WARD
ELMORE, VIRGINIA	WAS	093	2ND SUBD
ELMS, ANN	BAL	358	1ST DIST
ELMS, ANN	MGM	379	ROCKERLE
ELMS, ASENATH	MGM	337	CRACKLIN
ELMS, JAMES	MGM	378	ROCKERLE
ELMS, JEMIMA	BAL	134	2ND DIST
ELMS, WILLIAM	CAR	225	5TH DIST
ELOUGH, MARGARET	BAL	063	10TH WAR
ELOYATE, WILLIAM*	BAL	111	10TH WAR
ELRIDGE, LOUISA	DOR	365	3RD DIVI
ELROALL, JOHN	BAL	030	18TH WAR
ELSBA, THOMAS	DOR	324	1ST DIST
ELSBURY, NEHEMIAH	CAR	122	NO TWP L
ELSCROAD, CATHARINE	CAR	137	4TH DIST
ELSEROAD, FRANCIS	BAL	129	18TH WAR
ELSEROAD, GEORGE W.	ANN	464	HOWARD D
ELSEROAD, JOHN	CAR	137	4TH DIST
ELSEROOD, JOHN	ANN	428	HOWARD D
ELSEY, ADALINE	SOM	425	PRINCESS
ELSEY, ANDA GREEN	SOM	451	DAMES QU

Name	County	Page	District
ELSEY, ANGELINA R.	BAL	332	3RD WARD
ELSEY, CHARLES	SOM	510	BARREN C
ELSEY, CHARLOTTE	SOM	361	BRINKLEY
ELSEY, CROCKETT	SOM	522	BARREN C
ELSEY, DENNIS	SOM	457	DAMES QU
ELSEY, EDWARD	SOM	383	BRINKLEY
ELSEY, ELLEN MRS.	BAL	195	11TH WAR
ELSEY, GABRIEL	SOM	450	DAMES QU
ELSEY, GEORGE	SOM	465	TRAPP DI
ELSEY, GEORGE	SOM	435	PRINCESS
ELSEY, HENERETTA	SOM	426	PRINCESS
ELSEY, JAMES	SOM	545	TYASKIN
ELSEY, JOHN	SOM	430	PRINCESS
ELSEY, LEVIN	SOM	436	PRINCESS
ELSEY, MARGARET	SOM	550	TYASKIN
ELSEY, MATILDA	SOM	425	PRINCESS
ELSEY, MILLY	BAL	232	6TH WARD
ELSEY, MINGO K.	BAL	085	15TH WAR
ELSEY, NATHAN	SOM	447	DAMES QU
ELSEY, POLLY	SOM	546	TYASKIN
ELSEY, SAMUEL	SOM	546	TYASKIN
ELSEY, SAMUEL JR.	SOM	546	TYASKIN
ELSEY, THOMAS	SOM	550	TYASKIN
ELSEY, WILLIAM	SOM	510	BARREN C
ELSHLEY, JOHN	ALL	104	5TH E.D.
ELSLER, EDWARD	BAL	102	2ND DIST
ELSROAD, ELIZABERTH	FRE	131	CREAGERS
ELSROAD, JESSE	BAL	409	14TH WAR
ELSROADE, GEORGE	BAL	346	1ST DIST
ELSRODE, MELINDA	BAL	295	20TH WAR
ELSRODE, MICHAEL	BAL	175	2ND DIST
ELSTON, GEORGE	BAL	408	8TH WARD
ELSTON, ISAAC N.	DOR	377	1ST DIST
ELSY, LYDIA	DOR	377	1ST DIST
ELTERMAN, GOTTLIEB	BAL	070	2ND DIST
ELTHIEL, SEMON	ST	296	2ND E DI
ELTON, CHARLES W.	BAL	416	3RD WARD
ELTON, MARY	BAL	112	15TH WAR
ELTON, WILLIAM	SOM	373	BRINKLEY
ELTONHEAD, ARNOLD	BAL	155	5TH WARD
ELTONHEAD, SARAH	BAL	037	4TH WARD
ELTS, LOUISA A.	BAL	288	3RD WARD
ELUMAN, WILLIAM	BAL	025	9TH WARD
ELUPHUS, JAMES	DOR	466	1ST DIST
ELVANS, JOHN	FRE	377	PETERSVI
ELVEN, METILDA	BAL	131	11TH WAR
ELVERTS, JULIA	BAL	291	12TH WAR
ELWALT, BASIL	BAL	458	8TH WARD
ELWELL, ABERT G.*	BAL	413	3RD WARD
ELWELL, ALBERT G.*	BAL	413	3RD WARD
ELWELL, JOHN	QUE	154	1ST E DI
ELWELL, WILLIAM	BAL	141	1ST WARD
ELWOOD, ELLEN	BAL	443	1ST DIST
ELWOOD, FRANCAS	BAL	093	1ST WARD
ELWOOD, JOSEPH	BAL	302	12TH WAR
ELWOOD, LYCIA	PRI	101	SPALDING
ELWOOD, SAM	PRI	100	SPALDING
ELWOOD, THOMAS	BAL	443	1ST DIST
ELY, ANN	BAL	116	15TH WAR
ELY, ASHER	BAL	372	1ST DIST
ELY, CAROLINE	BAL	422	3RD WARD
ELY, CHARLES	BAL	101	1ST WARD
ELY, DAVID	FRE	053	FREDERIC
ELY, DAVID B.	HAR	051	1ST DIST
ELY, ELIZABETH	HAR	051	1ST DIST
ELY, EZRA	FRE	052	FREDERIC
ELY, HANNAH	HAR	084	2ND DIST
ELY, HANNAH	HAR	089	2ND DIST
ELY, JACOB	BAL	259	6TH WARD
ELY, JACOB	CAR	173	8TH DIST
ELY, JESSE F.	BAL	031	4TH WARD
ELY, JOHN	HAR	108	2ND DIST
ELY, JOHN	BAL	224	1ST DIST
ELY, JOHN C.	BAL	027	1ST WARD
ELY, JOHN E.-BLACK	FRE	421	8TH E DI
ELY, JOHN N.	BAL	008	1ST WARD
ELY, JOSEPH	BAL	375	1ST DIST
ELY, MAHLON	BAL	099	5TH WARD
ELY, MAHON	WAS	126	2ND DIST
ELY, SAMUEL	BAL	149	1ST WARD
ELY, SARAH	FRE	061	FREDERIC
ELY, SARAH	HAR	001	1ST DIST
ELY, SARAH N.	CEC	115	3RD E DI
ELY, SOLOMON	BAL	287	3RD WARD
ELY, SOPHIA	FRE	062	FREDERIC
ELY, THOMAS	HAR	002	1ST DIST
ELY, THOMAS J.	HAR	058	1ST DIST
ELY, WILLIAM	HAR	002	1ST DIST
ELY, WILLIAM	BAL	006	1ST WARD
ELZEY, LETITIA	BAL	031	9TH WARD
ELZEY, MARIA H.	BAL	032	9TH WARD
EMACK, ELBERT G.	PRI	020	VANSVILL
EMACK, MARY P.	BAL	382	13TH WAR
EMACK, WILLIAM A.	BAL	383	13TH WAR
EMATTHEWS, WILLIAM	BAL	118	1ST WARD
EMBECK, MARY L.	QUE	247	5TH E DI
EMBERT, ANDREW	BAL	280	1ST DIST
EMBERT, CHRISTIANA	QUE	247	5TH E DI
EMBERT, HENRY	QUE	193	3RD E DI
EMBERT, JAMES	CAR	086	NO TWP L
EMBERT, JHON	QUE	248	5TH E DI
EMBERT, JOHN	CAR	079	NO TWP L
EMBERT, WILLIAM	TAL	026	EASTON D
EMBERT, WILLIAM J.	QUE	230	4TH E DI
EMBERTON, SAMUEL	HAR	050	1ST DIST
EMBLY, THOMAS-MULATTO	BAL	208	2ND WARD
EMBSON, MARY	BAL	083	1ST WARD
EMDONDSON, SARAH	BAL	215	2ND WARD
EMEALS, JOHN	CAR	166	NO TWP L
EMERICH, CHRISTIAN	WAS	152	2ND DIST
EMERICH, JOHN	BAL	021	15TH WAR
EMERICH, JOHN W.	BAL	102	18TH WAR
EMERICK, CONRADT	BAL	400	8TH WARD
EMERICK, DAVID	BAL	302	20TH WAR
EMERICK, FREDERICK	CAR	255	3RD DIST
EMERICK, JOHN	BAL	338	7TH WARD
EMERICK, JOHN	BAL	264	12TH WAR
EMERICK, LOUISA	BAL	062	15TH WAR
EMERICK, PHILIP	BAL	023	9TH WARD
EMERICK, WIEGAND	BAL	117	15TH WAR
EMERINA, JOHN	BAL	059	2ND DIST
EMERINE, HENRY	BAL	085	2ND DIST
EMERING, CARL	BAL	105	1ST WARD
EMERSON, G.	BAL	101	10TH WAR
EMERSON, HARRIET	BAL	207	2ND WARD
EMERSON, ISABEL	BAL	100	2ND DIST
EMERSON, JAMES	CAR	079	NO TWP L
EMERSON, JOHN	BAL	115	1ST WARD
EMERSON, JOSHUA	BAL	131	2ND DIST
EMERSON, MARY	BAL	226	2ND WARD

Name	County	Page	District
EMERSON, ROBERT K.	CAR	168	NO TWP L
EMERSON, SAMUEL	BAL	121	1ST WARD
EMERSON, SAMUEL	TAL	040	EASTON D
EMERSON, WILLIAM	TAL	061	EASTON D
EMERSON, WILLIAM	BAL	011	15TH WAR
EMERSON, WILLIAM	BAL	047	4TH WARD
EMERSON, WILLIAM C.	BAL	150	16TH WAR
EMERY, CATHRINE	BAL	112	18TH WAR
EMERY, CONRAD	BAL	239	2ND WARD
EMERY, FANNY	BAL	022	4TH WARD
EMERY, GOERGE	BAL	120	5TH WARD
EMERY, J. W.	BAL	147	1ST WARD
EMERY, J. W.	BAL	147	1ST WARD
EMERY, JOHN B.	BAL	179	16TH WAR
EMERY, MARY J.-BLACK	CAR	080	NO TWP L
EMERY, ROBERT	HAR	188	3RD DIST
EMERY, SAMUEL	BAL	066	18TH WAR
EMERY, SAMUEL G.	BAL	019	4TH WARD
EMERY, WILLIAM J.	BAL	119	1ST WARD
EMEST, ADELE	BAL	386	13TH WAR
EMGELMYER, MATTHEW	BAL	155	19TH WAR
EMHOFFER, HENRY	BAL	036	9TH WARD
EMHUYSER, PETER	HAR	064	1ST DIST
EMICH, ANDREW	BAL	031	18TH WAR
EMICH, JOHN *	BAL	097	15TH WAR
EMICH, JOHN V.	BAL	081	18TH WAR
EMICK, DANIEL	BAL	015	18TH WAR
EMICK, GOERGE	BAL	461	1ST DIST
EMICK, MARY	BAL	384	1ST DIST
EMICK, MATILDA	BAL	232	1ST DIST
EMICK, MATILDA	BAL	233	1ST DIST
EMICK, PETER	BAL	056	18TH WAR
EMIDDLESON, MARY*	BAL	022	1ST WARD
EMILY, ELIZABETH	WAS	285	1ST DIST
EMINBURG, GEORGE	MGM	417	MEDLEY 3
EMINGER, JACOB	BAL	324	12TH WAR
EMINSTER, ROBERT D.	PRI	033	VANSVILL
EMIRNA, MARY	BAL	088	2ND DIST
EMIS, JOSEPH	BAL	027	1ST WARD
EMIS, WILLIAM B.	BAL	028	1ST WARD
EMKOFF, LORENZO	ANN	513	HOWARD D
EMLEN, CALEB	HAR	002	1ST DIST
EMLEN, JOHN	ANN	349	3RD DIST
EMLER, CHARLES	BAL	157	1ST WARD
EMLING, AUGUSTUS	BAL	104	5TH WARD
EMMA, GEORGE	BAL	201	19TH WAR
EMMA, PETER	BAL	436	8TH WARD
EMMACK, C.	BAL	326	12TH WAR
EMMALLS, JOHN	BAL	256	12TH WAR
EMMART, ADOLPH	BAL	302	12TH WAR
EMMART, DAVID	BAL	271	12TH WAR
EMMART, GEORGE	BAL	255	1ST DIST
EMMART, GEORGE F.	BAL	278	7TH WARD
EMMART, HARRIET	BAL	272	12TH WAR
EMMART, JOSEPH	BAL	259	12TH WAR
EMMART, MARGARET	BAL	302	12TH WAR
EMMART, MICHAEL	BAL	278	7TH WARD
EMMART, SAMUEL	BAL	036	1ST WARD
EMMART, WILLIAM	BAL	258	6TH WARD
EMMARY, JANE	BAL	253	17TH WAR
EMMEL, JOHN	BAL	408	3RD WARD
EMMELS,JOSEPH	ALL	225	CUMBERLA
EMMERSON, ALEXANDER	CAR	138	NO TWP L
EMMERSON, ELIZA J.	BAL	294	7TH WARD
EMMERSON, ELIZABETH J.	CAR	083	NO TWP L
EMMERSON, ELLENORA	BAL	294	7TH WARD
EMMERSON, GOERGE	CAR	164	NO TWP L
EMMERSON, HENRY	PRI	045	VANSVILL
EMMERSON, JAMES	BAL	352	13TH WAR
EMMERSON, OWEN	BAL	190	17TH WAR
EMMERSON, RACHEAL	WAS	200	1ST DIST
EMMERSON, SAMUEL	TAL	047	EASTON T
EMMERSON,S AMUEL	CAR	084	NO TWP L
EMMERT, ANDREW	WAS	216	1ST DIST
EMMERT, BENJAMIN	WAS	192	1ST DIST
EMMERT, DANIEL	WAS	034	2ND SUBD
EMMERT, HENRY	BAL	317	1ST DIST
EMMERT, JACOB	WAS	035	2ND SUBD
EMMERT, JARRETT	BAL	375	1ST DIST
EMMERT, JOHN	WAS	214	1ST DIST
EMMERT, JOHN	WAS	198	1ST DIST
EMMERT, JOSEPH	WAS	267	1ST DIST
EMMERT, JOSHUA	WAS	300	1ST DIST
EMMERT, LEONARD	WAS	196	1ST DIST
EMMERT, MARTIN	WAS	198	1ST DIST
EMMERT, MARY	WAS	129	2ND DIST
EMMERT, MICHAEL	WAS	198	1ST DIST
EMMERT, PHILIP	BAL	376	1ST DIST
EMMERT, SAMUEL	WAS	194	1ST DIST
EMMERT, SARAH	WAS	243	CAVETOWN
EMMERT, SARAH	BAL	378	1ST DIST
EMMERT, SARAH	BAL	376	1ST DIST
EMMERT, SUSAN	WAS	197	1ST DIST
EMMERT, SUSAN	MGM	420	MEDLEY 3
EMMERY, EDWARD	DOR	301	1ST DIST
EMMET, CHRISTOPHER	ANN	463	HOWARD D
EMMET, FRANCIS	BAL	193	2ND WARD
EMMET, PETER	ANN	462	HOWARD D
EMMETT, SARAH	WAS	279	LEITERSB
EMMETT, WILLIAM	QUE	130	1ST E DI
EMMIET, LUDING	BAL	275	20TH WAR
EMMINGTON, JOSEPH	ALL	153	6TH E.D.
EMMIS, AUGUSTUS	BAL	116	1ST WARD
EMMIS, ELIZABETH	WOR	196	8TH E DI
EMMONS, CATHERINE	CEC	023	ELKTON 3
EMMONS, FRANCES ANTONY	BAL	446	14TH WAR
EMMONS, HENRIETTA	BAL	207	6TH DIST
EMMONS, JOHN	CEC	080	NORTHEAS
EMMONS, PARSONS	BAL	041	9TH WARD
EMMORY JOHN	BAL	217	17TH WAR
EMMORY, ELIZA H.	BAL	136	11TH WAR
EMMORY, JOHN	FRE	021	FREDERIC
EMMORY, SOL*	DOR	461	1ST DIST
EMMORY, SOLOMON	DOR	431	1ST DIST
EMMOT, MICHAEL	WAS	198	1ST DIST
EMMY, THOAMS	BAL	404	14TH WAR
EMONDSON, JOHN	BAL	234	1ST DIST
EMONS, ANN	CEC	027	CHESAPEA
EMONS, MARY C.	BAL	100	5TH WARD
EMOOLTA, MARGARET	BAL	353	13TH WAR
EMOREY, C. NORTH	TAL	067	EASTON T
EMORING, ITHYAND	BAL	410	14TH WAR
EMORY, ALBERT T.	QUE	188	3RD E DI
EMORY, ANN	KEN	293	3RD DIST
EMORY, ANN	QUE	156	2ND E DI
EMORY, ANN	CHA	276	ALLENS F
EMORY, ANN ELIZABETH-BLAC	QUE	130	1ST E DI
EMORY, ARTHUR	BAL	166	16TH WAR
EMORY, AUGUSTUS	BAL	472	14TH WAR
EMORY, AUGUSTUS	BAL	316	20TH WAR

Name	County	Page	District
EMORY, AUTHUR	QUE	219	3RD E DI
EMORY, C. L.	BAL	083	18TH WAR
EMORY, CATHARINE D.	BAL	176	16TH WAR
EMORY, CHARLES	CEC	041	CHESAPEA
EMORY, D. C. H.	BAL	319	1ST DIST
EMORY, DANIEL C. H.	CEC	147	PORT DUP
EMORY, DANIEL G.	BAL	136	11TH WAR
EMORY, EDWARD	QUE	205	3RD E DI
EMORY, ELIJAH	CAR	397	2ND DIST
EMORY, ELISABETH B.	ANN	363	4TH DIST
EMORY, EMILY A.	TAL	019	EASTON D
EMORY, ENOCH	BAL	122	11TH WAR
EMORY, FANNY	BAL	334	13TH WAR
EMORY, FANNY	TAL	009	EASTON D
EMORY, FRISBY	BAL	026	15TH WAR
EMORY, HEMSLEY	KEN	293	3RD DIST
EMORY, HESTOR ANN	BAL	211	17TH WAR
EMORY, ISACK*	TAL	008	EASTON D
EMORY, J.K.B.	CEC	004	ELKTON 3
EMORY, JACOB	BAL	122	11TH WAR
EMORY, JAMES	BAL	147	2ND DIST
EMORY, JANE-BLACK	CAR	165	NO TWP L
EMORY, JANE-MULATTO	QUE	185	3RD E DI
EMORY, JOHN	KEN	295	3RD DIST
EMORY, JOHN	BAL	436	14TH WAR
EMORY, JOHN	HAR	102	2ND DIST
EMORY, JOHN	QUE	129	1ST E DI
EMORY, JOHN	BAL	123	2ND DIST
EMORY, JOHN	BAL	019	1ST WARD
EMORY, JOHN R.	QUE	193	3RD E DI
EMORY, LEVIN W.	TAL	006	EASTON D
EMORY, LIDDY	BAL	088	18TH WAR
EMORY, LYDIA-BLACK	QUE	202	3RD E DI
EMORY, MAIRA	QUE	250	5TH E DI
EMORY, MARGARET	QUE	163	2ND E DI
EMORY, MARIA	QUE	216	3RD E DI
EMORY, MARIA	KEN	268	1ST DIST
EMORY, MARIAH S.	SOM	395	BRINKLEY
EMORY, MARY-BLACK	QUE	200	3RD E DI
EMORY, MOSES	BAL	172	16TH WAR
EMORY, NANCY-BLACK	QUE	199	3RD E DI
EMORY, RICHARD	BAL	058	2ND DIST
EMORY, RICHARD H.	BAL	046	15TH WAR
EMORY, ROBERT	BAL	159	1ST WARD
EMORY, ROBERT	KEN	309	3RD DIST
EMORY, ROBERT	BAL	115	18TH WAR
EMORY, SAMUEL	BAL	351	7TH WARD
EMORY, SAMUEL	BAL	051	9TH WARD
EMORY, SAMUEL-BLACK	QUE	135	1ST E DI
EMORY, SAMUEL-BLACK	QUE	129	1ST E DI
EMORY, SARAH E.	QUE	245	5TH E DI
EMORY, STEPHEN	CEC	038	CHESAPEA
EMORY, STEWART R.	QUE	193	3RD E DI
EMORY, TEMPY-BLACK	QUE	148	1ST E DI
EMORY, THOMAS A.	TAL	005	EASTON D
EMORY, WASHINGTON J.	BAL	145	1ST WARD
EMORY, WASHINGTON J.	BAL	145	1ST WARD
EMORY, WILLIAM	QUE	186	3RD E DI
EMORY, WILLIAM	QUE	193	3RD E DI
EMORY, WILLIAM	QUE	130	1ST E DI
EMORY, WILLIAM	QUE	133	1ST E DI
EMORY, WILLIAM H.	BAL	195	11TH WAR
EMORY, WILLIAM J.	BAL	065	10TH WAR
EMORY, WILLIAM-BLACK	QUE	129	1ST E DI
EMOVEY, CHARLES *	TAL	075	EASTON T
EMPFIELD, PETER	BAL	160	1ST WARD
EMPS, D.	BAL	138	5TH WARD
EMPSON, ALEXANDER	CEC	049	1ST E DI
EMRICK, JOHN	BAL	249	20TH WAR
EMRICK, MARGARETT	BAL	257	1ST DIST
EMRON, JOSEPH	FRE	005	FREDERIC
EMSININGER, CHRISTIAN *	WAS	162	HAGERSTO
EMSININGER, CHRISTIAN	WAS	162	HAGERSTO
EMSLIE, S.	BAL	153	1ST WARD
EMSOL, CATHARINE A.	CAR	377	2ND DIST
EMSON, WILLIAM H.	CEC	048	1ST E DI
EMSOR, JAMES	BAL	210	6TH DIST
ENALS, ADAM	DOR	334	3RD DIVI
ENALS, CAROLINE	DOR	360	3RD DIVI
ENALS, CHARIETY	DOR	338	3RD DIVI
ENALS, JOSEPH	DOR	369	3RD DIVI
ENALS, MATILDA	DOR	328	3RD DIVI
ENALS, MATILDA	DOR	338	3RD DIVI
ENALS, SHARLOTT	DOR	338	3RD DIVI
ENANS, THOMAS	BAL	313	1ST DIST
ENARES, CHARLES	BAL	127	1ST WARD
ENAS, ANN	BAL	036	4TH WARD
ENBAULT, JOHN	BAL	199	2ND WARD
ENCHO, ELIZA	CEC	036	CHESAPEA
ENCK, MARY	BAL	083	15TH WAR
ENCSY, MARY	BAL	137	11TH WAR
ENDENON, GEORGE	CEC	042	CHESAPEA
ENDERSON, JOHN	BAL	049	2ND DIST
ENDRASS, JACOB	CEC	005	ELKTON 3
ENDRES, MARTIN	BAL	084	1ST WARD
ENERSON, JOSEPHINE	FRE	289	WOODSBOR
ENERY, HANNAH	BAL	064	18TH WAR
ENEST, WILLIAM	ALL	216	CUMBERLA
ENEY, JOHN	BAL	163	19TH WAR
ENEY, JULY A. *	BAL	063	18TH WAR
ENEY, OLIVER N.	BAL	064	18TH WAR
ENFIELD, JACOB	HAR	043	1ST DIST
ENGARD, CASPER	BAL	212	2ND WARD
ENGAS, ANDREW	BAL	258	2ND WARD
ENGEL, JOHN	FRE	433	8TH E DI
ENGELBACH, ROSANNA	BAL	091	10TH WAR
ENGELHARDT, C.	BAL	224	19TH WAR
ENGELHART, AUGUST	BAL	156	16TH WAR
ENGELHART, HENRY	BAL	156	16TH WAR
ENGELMEYER, JOSEPH W.	BAL	194	6TH WARD
ENGELMYER, MATHEW	BAL	177	19TH WAR
ENGERSON, SARAH	SOM	469	TRAPPE D
ENGERSON, THOMAS	SOM	459	HANGARY
ENGERT, JOHN A.	WAS	209	1ST DIST
ENGLAND, ABRAM	ANN	509	HOWARD D
ENGLAND, ANN	BAL	228	12TH WAR
ENGLAND, CHARLES	KEN	307	3RD DIST
ENGLAND, ELISHA	HAR	052	1ST DIST
ENGLAND, ELISHA B.	CEC	142	6TH E DI
ENGLAND, ELISHA H.	CEC	141	6TH E DI
ENGLAND, ELIZABETH	CEC	132	6TH E DI
ENGLAND, ELIZABETH	CEC	055	1ST E DI
ENGLAND, FRANCIS W.*	BAL	386	3RD WARD
ENGLAND, GEORGE	CEC	137	6TH E DI
ENGLAND, HARRIET	FRE	449	8TH E DI
ENGLAND, ISAAC	CEC	133	6TH E DI
ENGLAND, JOB	CEC	156	PORT DUP
ENGLAND, JOHN	CEC	132	6TH E DI
ENGLAND, JOHN	BAL	095	18TH WAR
ENGLAND, JOHN	HAR	090	2ND DIST

Name	County	Page	District
ENGLAND, JOHN	MGM	375	ROCKERLE
ENGLAND, JOHN	BAL	353	7TH WARD
ENGLAND, JOSEPH	CEC	142	6TH E DI
ENGLAND, JOSEPH T.	CEC	133	6TH E DI
ENGLAND, JOSEPH T.	BAL	057	15TH WAR
ENGLAND, KIRK	CEC	132	6TH E DI
ENGLAND, LUCINDA	CEC	132	6TH E DI
ENGLAND, MARY	HAR	052	1ST DIST
ENGLAND, MARY	BAL	139	5TH WARD
ENGLAND, MARY	BAL	139	5TH WARD
ENGLAND, MARY A.	FRE	049	FREDERIC
ENGLAND, MARY E.	CEC	004	ELKTON 3
ENGLAND, MAY	BAL	096	18TH WAR
ENGLAND, NATHAN	ANN	509	HOWARD D
ENGLAND, RACHAEL	FRE	189	5TH E DI
ENGLAND, ROBERT K.	CEC	132	6TH E DI
ENGLAND, SAMUEL	CEC	142	6TH E DI
ENGLAND, SARAH	CEC	057	1ST E DI
ENGLAND, W.	BAL	296	20TH WAR
ENGLAND, WILLIAM	BAL	148	1ST WARD
ENGLAND, WILLIAM	BAL	062	1ST WARD
ENGLAND, WILLIAM	BAL	021	1ST WARD
ENGLAND, WILLIAM E.	SOM	351	BRINKLEY
ENGLAND,SAMUEL	CAR	367	9TH DIST
ENGLAR, ABRAHAM	CAR	382	2ND DIST
ENGLAR, DAVID	CAR	287	7TH DIST
ENGLAR, ELIZA J.	CAR	395	2ND DIST
ENGLAR, ELIZABETH	CAR	413	2ND DIST
ENGLAR, EPHRAIM	CAR	399	2ND DIST
ENGLAR, FREDERICK	CAR	385	2ND DIST
ENGLAR, HANNAH	CAR	381	2ND DIST
ENGLAR, HENRY	CAR	380	2ND DIST
ENGLAR, JOHN	CAR	276	7TH DIST
ENGLAR, JOHN	CAR	286	7TH DIST
ENGLAR, JOHN	FRE	429	8TH E DI
ENGLAR, JONAS	CAR	390	2ND DIST
ENGLAR, JOSEPH	CAR	400	2ND DIST
ENGLAR, LEVI	CAR	384	2ND DIST
ENGLAR, MARY	CAR	386	2ND DIST
ENGLAR, MARY	CAR	385	2ND DIST
ENGLAR, MARY	FRE	413	8TH E DI
ENGLAR, MORDECIA	CAR	390	2ND DIST
ENGLAR, NATHAN	FRE	425	8TH E DI
ENGLAR, PHILIP	CAR	390	2ND DIST
ENGLAR, SARAH	CAR	386	2ND DIST
ENGLAR, WILLIAM	CAR	377	2ND DIST
ENGLAR,STINAM	CAR	390	2ND DIST
ENGLE, ABRAHAM	FRE	289	WOODSBOR
ENGLE, ALBERT	ALL	010	3RD E.D.
ENGLE, ANN	BAL	087	1ST WARD
ENGLE, ASA	BAL	151	2ND DIST
ENGLE, C.	BAL	270	12TH WAR
ENGLE, DANIEL	CAR	395	2ND DIST
ENGLE, DANIEL	FRE	111	CREAGERS
ENGLE, DAVID	CAR	363	9TH DIST
ENGLE, DAVID	CAR	359	9TH DIST
ENGLE, DAVID	ALL	015	3RD E.D.
ENGLE, ELI	ALL	015	3RD E.D.
ENGLE, ELIZABETH	ALL	006	3RD E.D.
ENGLE, EZRA	FRE	095	FREDERIC
ENGLE, GEORGE	FRE	082	FREDERIC
ENGLE, GEORGE	BAL	405	14TH WAR
ENGLE, GEORGE	BAL	070	1ST WARD
ENGLE, GOTTEIB	BAL	006	EASTERN
ENGLE, HANNAH	CAR	359	9TH DIST
ENGLE, HENRY	BAL	049	1ST WARD
ENGLE, HENRY	BAL	326	7TH WARD
ENGLE, JACOB	FRE	246	NEW MARK
ENGLE, JAMES	ALL	112	5TH E.D.
ENGLE, JOHN	BAL	127	1ST WARD
ENGLE, JOHN	FRE	083	FREDERIC
ENGLE, JOHN W.	FRE	245	NEW MARK
ENGLE, NICHOLAS	FRE	133	CREAGERS
ENGLE, PETER	CAR	359	9TH DIST
ENGLE, PHILIP	BAL	458	14TH WAR
ENGLE, REUBEN	FRE	289	WOODSBOR
ENGLE, SAMUEL	FRE	175	5TH E DI
ENGLE, SAMUEL	BAL	151	2ND DIST
ENGLE, SMAUEL	ALL	010	3RD E.D.
ENGLE, SOPHIA	BAL	081	10TH WAR
ENGLE, SUSAN	FRE	095	FREDERIC
ENGLE, TEZANIS	BAL	220	2ND WARD
ENGLE, WILLIAM	ALL	010	3RD E.D.
ENGLE, WILLIAM	BAL	294	1ST DIST
ENGLEBRECHT, GEORGE	FRE	039	FREDERIC
ENGLEBRECHT, JAOCB	FRE	027	FREDERIC
ENGLEBRECHT, JOHN A.	FRE	002	FREDERIC
ENGLEBRECHT, MARGARET	FRE	024	FREDERIC
ENGLEBRECHT, MICHAEL	FRE	043	FREDERIC
ENGLEBRECHT, SUSAN	FRE	044	FREDERIC
ENGLEBRECHT,LUTHER M.	FRE	020	FREDERIC
ENGLEBRIGHT, MARGARET	WAS	154	HAGERSTO
ENGLEBUCHT, FREDERICK	FRE	101	FREDERIC
ENGLEFELTER, JOHN	BAL	112	10TH WAR
ENGLEFUTZ, JOHN	BAL	206	2ND WARD
ENGLEHARD, EDWARD	BAL	084	10TH WAR
ENGLEHARDT, MARGARET	BAL	048	9TH WARD
ENGLEHART, BEN	BAL	211	17TH WAR
ENGLEHART, EDWARD	BAL	188	2ND WARD
ENGLEHART, WILLIAM	ALL	039	2ND E.D.
ENGLEHAUSEN, HENRY	BAL	135	11TH WAR
ENGLEHUTH, GEORGE *	FRE	096	FREDERIC
ENGLEKART, MICHAEL	ALL	038	2ND E.D.
ENGLEMAN, ELIZABETH	CAR	389	2ND DIST
ENGLEMAN, EMILY	CAR	384	2ND DIST
ENGLEMAN, HARRETT	CAR	403	2ND DIST
ENGLEMAN, JOHN	CAR	398	2ND DIST
ENGLEMAN, JOSIAH	CAR	296	7TH DIST
ENGLEMAN, LEWIS	CAR	402	2ND DIST
ENGLEMAN, MARY	CAR	386	2ND DIST
ENGLEMAN, MARY	FRE	426	8TH E DI
ENGLEMAN, PALMER	CAR	395	2ND DIST
ENGLEMAN, WILLIAM	CAR	389	2ND DIST
ENGLER, AGUSUTS	FRE	109	CREAGERS
ENGLES, WILLIAM A.	BAL	394	8TH WARD
ENGLIE, PETER	FRE	107	CREAGERS
ENGLIN, JOHN	BAL	263	20TH WAR
ENGLINGS, ADAM	BAL	259	20TH WAR
ENGLISH, ALFRED	SOM	517	BARREN C
ENGLISH, ELIZABETH	BAL	406	1ST DIST
ENGLISH, HANSON T.	CAR	360	9TH DIST
ENGLISH, HARRIET B.	BAL	419	3RD WARD
ENGLISH, HENRY	BAL	435	8TH WARD
ENGLISH, JAMES J.	FRE	055	FREDERIC
ENGLISH, JANE	BAL	339	3RD WARD
ENGLISH, JOHN	BAL	005	4TH WARD
ENGLISH, JOHN	CAR	358	9TH DIST
ENGLISH, JONATHAN B.	FRE	367	CATOCTIN
ENGLISH, JUDAH	BAL	164	11TH WAR
ENGLISH, LEVIN	SOM	508	BARREN C
ENGLISH, MARSHALL	WAS	215	1ST DIST
ENGLISH, MARSHALL	BAL	407	1ST DIST
ENGLISH, MARY	BAL	322	12TH WAR
ENGLISH, MARY	ALL	243	CUMBERLA
ENGLISH, MARY A.	FRE	055	FREDERIC
ENGLISH, MARY E.	MGM	428	CLARKSTR
ENGLISH, PATRICK	BAL	023	1ST WARD
ENGLISH, RICHARD	BAL	127	1ST WARD
ENGLISH, SAMUEL S.	SOM	509	BARREN C
ENGLISH, THOMAS	SOM	517	BARREN C
ENGLISH, THOMAS	BAL	286	2ND WARD
ENGLISH, THOMAS	MGM	429	CLARKSTR
ENGLISHMAN, JOHN	HAR	051	1ST DIST
ENGLISHMAN, NANCY	HAR	051	1ST DIST
ENGMAN, MARY	ALL	046	10TH E.D
ENHEIM, TERESA	BAL	172	19TH WAR
ENHEIN, ADAM	BAL	172	19TH WAR
ENICK, C.	BAL	138	1ST WARD
ENICKSON, ENICH	BAL	026	1ST WARD
ENIELY, MARY*	DOR	411	1ST DIST
ENIS, JOHN C.	BAL	423	1ST DIST
ENISINGER, GEORGE	BAL	428	8TH WARD
ENISTINE, JOSEPH	ALL	248	CUMBERLA
ENISUS, WILLIAM	CAL	044	3RD DIST
ENKERD, HENRY	BAL	111	2ND DIST
ENLOES, MARY ANN	QUE	252	5TH E DI
ENLOW, JEREMIAH	ALL	042	10TH E.D
ENLOW, WILLIAM	ALL	034	2ND E.D.
ENLOWS, JOHN	HAR	086	2ND DIST
ENLOWS, REBECCA	HAR	086	2ND DIST
ENMART, CATHARINE *	BAL	097	18TH WAR
ENNAL, JOHN	BAL	265	2ND WARD
ENNALES, ARCH*	DOR	439	1ST DIST
ENNALES, GARRETSON	DOR	423	1ST DIST
ENNALES, HARIATE	DOR	425	1ST DIST
ENNALES, MARGARETT	DOR	403	1ST DIST
ENNALES, MARY	DOR	378	1ST DIST
ENNALLS, JACOB	BAL	225	19TH WAR
ENNALLS, JOSEPH	BAL	294	7TH WARD
ENNALLS, KITT	BAL	459	8TH WARD
ENNALLS, MARGARET	BAL	029	9TH WARD
ENNALS, ELIZA	DOR	370	3RD DIVI
ENNALS, HENERY	DOR	361	3RD DIVI
ENNALS, MAHALA	DOR	360	3RD DIVI
ENNALS, SUSAN	BAL	145	11TH WAR
ENNALZ, TERRY*	DOR	327	3RD DIVI
ENNAR, MARY	BAL	090	15TH WAR
ENNEL, PHILIP	BAL	224	19TH WAR
ENNELL, JANE	CEC	053	1ST E DI
ENNELS, LEVI	CEC	036	CHESAPEA
ENNESS, JOHN	BAL	113	5TH WARD
ENNIE, C.	BAL	293	12TH WAR
ENNIS, ARTHUR	SOM	489	SALISBUR
ENNIS, AUGUSTUS	BAL	115	1ST WARD
ENNIS, CAROLIEN	WOR	175	6TH E DI
ENNIS, CATHARINE E.	FRE	388	PETERSVI
ENNIS, CHARLES	WOR	294	9TH E DI
ENNIS, COVINGTON	WOR	175	6TH E DI
ENNIS, DAVID	BAL	207	17TH WAR
ENNIS, ELIJAH	SOM	496	SALISBUR
ENNIS, ELIZABETH	BAL	408	14TH WAR
ENNIS, ELLEN C.	BAL	119	18TH WAR
ENNIS, GEORGE A.	BAL	177	6TH WARD
ENNIS, GILBERT	SOM	496	SALISBUR
ENNIS, GILLA	WOR	303	SNOW HIL
ENNIS, HARRIET	BAL	005	9TH WARD
ENNIS, HARRIET	BAL	412	14TH WAR
ENNIS, HARRIET R.	WOR	270	BERLIN 1
ENNIS, HESTER A.	BAL	155	16TH WAR
ENNIS, HOUSTON	WOR	304	SNOW HIL
ENNIS, ISAAC	WOR	311	2ND E DI
ENNIS, J.A.	BAL	170	1ST WARD
ENNIS, JAMES	BAL	210	2ND WARD
ENNIS, JAMES	WOR	304	SNOW HIL
ENNIS, JAMES	WOR	253	1ST CENS
ENNIS, JAMES	CAL	020	2ND DIST
ENNIS, JAMES	SOM	406	DUBLIN D
ENNIS, JOHN	BAL	119	11TH WAR
ENNIS, JOHN	FRE	381	PETERSVI
ENNIS, JOHN	WOR	296	9TH E DI
ENNIS, JOHN	BAL	307	12TH WAR
ENNIS, JOHN-BLACK	QUE	194	3RD E DI
ENNIS, JOSEPH	WOR	291	9TH E DI
ENNIS, JOSEPH	WOR	286	BERLIN 1
ENNIS, JOSEPH	BAL	210	2ND WARD
ENNIS, KITTY	ANN	404	8TH DIST
ENNIS, MARGARET	BAL	172	6TH WARD
ENNIS, MARGARET	BAL	353	3RD WARD
ENNIS, MARY	BAL	013	15TH WAR
ENNIS, MARY	WOR	251	1ST CENS
ENNIS, MARY	SOM	496	SALISBUR
ENNIS, MARY A.	BAL	177	6TH WARD
ENNIS, MARY ANN-BLACK	QUE	193	3RD E DI
ENNIS, MELLVILLE	BAL	029	9TH WARD
ENNIS, NANCY	WOR	330	1ST E DI
ENNIS, NANCY	BAL	427	14TH WAR
ENNIS, PETER	BAL	206	19TH WAR
ENNIS, PETER	QUE	188	3RD E DI
ENNIS, RUFUS	SOM	496	SALISBUR
ENNIS, SAMUEL R.	WOR	251	BERLIN 1
ENNIS, SPENCER	BAL	167	2ND DIST
ENNIS, STEPHEN	WOR	330	1ST E DI
ENNIS, THOMAS	BAL	208	17TH WAR
ENNIS, THOMAS	CAL	044	3RD DIST
ENNIS, WACK	BAL	208	17TH WAR
ENNIS, WESLEY	BAL	080	15TH WAR
ENNIS, WILLIAM	BAL	026	9TH WARD
ENNIS, WILLIAM	WOR	265	BERLIN 1
ENNIS, WILLIAM H.	SOM	413	DUBLIN D
ENNISO, GEORGE	FRE	395	PETERSVI
ENNISS, ELIJAH	WOR	231	6TH E DI
ENNISS, HESTER	WOR	212	4TH E DI
ENNISS, JAMES C.	WOR	227	4TH E DI
ENNISS, LEVIN	WOR	196	8TH E DI
ENNISS, RUFUS W. F.	WOR	226	4TH E DI
ENNISS, SAMUEL T. H.	WOR	204	4TH E DI
ENNISS, ZEADOCK	WOR	196	8TH E DI
ENNS, JAMES	BAL	264	1ST DIST
ENO, RICHARD	BAL	266	7TH WARD
ENOCH, WILLIAM W.	CHA	258	MIDDLETO
ENOCKS, CHARLES	WAS	133	HAGERSTO
ENONS, WILLIMA H.	BAL	098	5TH WARD
ENOS, ABRAHAM	KEN	312	3RD DIST
ENOS, HANNAH	CEC	002	ELKTON 3
ENOS, JAMES	ANN	459	HOWARD D
ENOS, JOSEPH	WAS	010	WILLIAMS
ENRICH, JOHN *	BAL	097	15TH WAR
ENSEL, MITCHEL	BAL	123	16TH WAR
ENSEMINGER, EVE	WAS	194	1ST DIST
ENSEMINGER, MARTIN	WAS	009	WILLIAMS
ENSEY, BENJAMIN	BAL	028	15TH WAR
ENSEY, CATHERINE	BAL	132	11TH WAR
ENSEY, ELIZABETH	BAL	297	7TH WARD
ENSEY, JOHN	BAL	042	18TH WAR
ENSEY, LOT	BAL	012	18TH WAR
ENSEY, RACHEL	CAR	223	5TH DIST
ENSEY, WILLIAM	BAL	180	16TH WAR
ENSINGER, JOHN	BAL	147	19TH WAR
ENSLER, JEMIMA	BAL	172	19TH WAR
ENSLEY, KISSIAH	SOM	550	TYASKIN
ENSMINGER, JOHN	WAS	002	WILLIAMS
ENSMINGER, MARGARET	WAS	011	WILLIAMS
ENSOM, ELIZA J.	BAL	137	2ND DIST
ENSOM, SUSAN	BAL	137	2ND DIST
ENSON, FANNY	BAL	243	20TH WAR
ENSON, MATISDA	BAL	141	2ND DIST
ENSOR, ABRA	BAL	428	1ST DIST
ENSOR, AGUSTUS	CAR	399	2ND DIST
ENSOR, ANN E.	BAL	429	1ST DIST
ENSOR, ANSON	BAL	141	5TH WARD
ENSOR, ARABELL	BAL	142	5TH WARD
ENSOR, DANIEL	BAL	259	1ST DIST
ENSOR, DARBY	BAL	427	1ST DIST
ENSOR, DARBY	BAL	432	1ST DIST
ENSOR, EDWARD	BAL	275	7TH WARD
ENSOR, FRANCIS	BAL	317	7TH WARD
ENSOR, FRANKLIN	BAL	428	1ST DIST
ENSOR, GEORGE	BAL	184	5TH DIST
ENSOR, GEORGE	BAL	185	5TH DIST
ENSOR, GEORGE	BAL	393	14TH WAR
ENSOR, GEORGE O.	BAL	430	1ST DIST
ENSOR, JAMES	BAL	074	10TH WAR
ENSOR, JOHN	BAL	420	1ST DIST
ENSOR, JOHN	BAL	283	7TH WARD
ENSOR, JOHN B.	BAL	428	1ST DIST
ENSOR, JOHN C.	BAL	430	1ST DIST
ENSOR, JOHN H.	BAL	430	1ST DIST
ENSOR, JOHN H.	BAL	401	14TH WAR
ENSOR, JOHN S.	BAL	430	1ST DIST
ENSOR, JOHN T.	BAL	427	1ST DIST
ENSOR, JOSEPH	BAL	199	5TH DIST
ENSOR, LUKE B.	BAL	428	1ST DIST
ENSOR, LUKE G.	BAL	430	1ST DIST
ENSOR, NATAN	BAL	431	1ST DIST
ENSOR, NATHAN	BAL	185	5TH DIST
ENSOR, NICHOLAS	BAL	199	5TH DIST
ENSOR, RACHEL	BAL	430	1ST DIST
ENSOR, REBECCA	BAL	430	1ST DIST
ENSOR, REBECCA	BAL	169	6TH WARD
ENSOR, REBECCA F.	BAL	429	1ST DIST
ENSOR, SARAH	BAL	420	1ST DIST
ENSOR, WILLIAM	BAL	161	6TH WARD
ENSOR, WILLIAM	CAR	184	8TH DIST
ENSOR, WILLIAM C.	BAL	428	1ST DIST
ENSOY, PERRY G.	CAR	223	5TH DIST
ENT, CHARLES	BAL	198	19TH WAR
ENT, GEORGE W.	FRE	014	FREDERIC
ENT, OTHO G.	FRE	020	FREDERIC
ENTENZA, GABRIEL	FRE	202	5TH E DI
ENTENZA, RAPHAEL	FRE	202	5TH E DI
ENTER, ADAM	BAL	243	2ND WARD
ENTIVISEL, CATHERINE	BAL	429	8TH WARD
ENTLER, AMELIA	BAL	273	7TH WARD
ENTLER, CATHARINE	BAL	391	14TH WAR
ENTLEY, EDWARD	BAL	201	17TH WAR
ENTLEY, WILLIAM	ALL	178	7TH E.D.
ENTON, MARY	BAL	242	12TH WAR
ENTRICKERS, ABIAH	BAL	155	2ND DIST
ENTY, FRED	BAL	131	2ND DIST
ENTZE, HENRIETTA	BAL	399	14TH WAR
ENVOY, TIMOHY	ALL	226	CUMBERLA
ENWRIGHT, BRIDGET	BAL	235	6TH WARD
ENY, JEREMIAH	BAL	291	1ST DIST
EOCKEY, SAMUEL	BAL	377	13TH WAR
EOLITT, LANA H.	HAR	192	3RD DIST
EOLITT, WILLIAM M.	HAR	192	3RD DIST
EPAUGH, HANNAH	BAL	054	2ND DIST
EPEX, R.	BAL	169	1ST WARD
EPHALINE, JAMES	BAL	423	14TH WAR
EPLER, CHARLES	BAL	392	8TH WARD
EPLER, CHARLES	BAL	392	8TH WARD
EPPE, PETER	BAL	066	2ND DIST
EPPE, THOMAS	BAL	117	18TH WAR
EPPING, JOHN	BAL	082	1ST WARD
EPPLER, JOHN	SOM	399	BRINKLEY
EPPLEY, SAMUEL O.	FRE	446	8TH E DI
EPPLY, REBECCA	FRE	447	8TH E DI
EPPOLD, GEORGE	BAL	072	2ND DIST
EPPOLD, MARGARET	BAL	072	2ND DIST
EPRON, LEWIS	BAL	110	5TH WARD
EPRON, MARY	BAL	106	1ST WARD
EPRON, PETER	BAL	275	7TH WARD
EPSERBY, MARY	HAR	085	2ND DIST
ERAELL, JOHN *	WOR	316	2ND E DI
ERAUS, BISHOP B. *	KEN	217	2ND DIST
ERB, CHARLES	CAR	258	3RD DIST
ERB, ELI	CAR	258	3RD DIST
ERB, JACOB	CAR	408	2ND DIST
ERB, JOHN	CAR	261	3RD DIST
ERB, JOSEPH	CAR	244	3RD DIST
ERB, PETER	CAR	258	3RD DIST
ERB, WILLIAM	CAR	261	3RD DIST
ERBACK, WILLIAM	BAL	207	19TH WAR
ERCHNER, LUTHER	BAL	139	1ST WARD
ERDMAN, BARBARA	BAL	073	2ND DIST
ERDMAN, BARBARA	BAL	043	15TH WAR
ERDMAN, CHARLES	BAL	182	16TH WAR
ERDMAN, FRANCIS	BAL	075	2ND DIST
ERDMAN, GOTLIEB	BAL	105	2ND DIST
ERDMAN, JOHN	BAL	060	2ND DIST
ERDMAN, MATHIAS	BAL	181	2ND DIST
ERDMAN, PETER	BAL	105	2ND DIST
ERDMAN,ANDREW	BAL	073	2ND DIST
EREK, HENRY	BAL	003	15TH WAR
EREK, ROSINA G.	BAL	107	15TH WAR
EREK, WILLIAM H.	BAL	107	15TH WAR
ERENHOUS, THEODORE	BAL	310	20TH WAR
ERENS, QUEEN	FRE	103	FREDERIC
ERGLE, HENRY	BAL	227	2ND WARD
ERGLER, HENRY	BAL	230	2ND WARD
ERGO, EMILY	BAL	199	19TH WAR
ERGOOD, JACOB	HAR	155	3RD DIST
ERHART, GEORGE	BAL	209	2ND WARD
ERHART, JACOB	BAL	309	20TH WAR
ERHEART, AUGUST	BAL	416	14TH WAR
ERHMAN, JACOB	BAL	443	14TH WAR
ERHMAN, PETER	BAL	217	2ND WARD
ERHMAN, PRISCILLA	BAL	443	14TH WAR
ERICK, E.	BAL	173	1ST WARD
ERICK, SARAH B.	BAL	059	4TH WARD

Name	Co.	Page	District
ERICKSON, EDWARD	TAL	040	EASTON D
ERINGTON, JOSEPH	ALL	051	10TH E.D
ERIS, ELI	WAS	109	2ND DIST
ERL, CATHARINE *	CAR	250	3RD DIST
ERL, O.	BAL	449	8TH WARD
ERLL, MARY A.	BAL	056	18TH WAR
ERLORRIE, ACASIA	WOR	301	SNOW HIL
ERMAN, PHILIP	BAL	308	20TH WAR
ERMEST, J. E.	BAL	153	1ST WARD
ERMEY, MICHAEL	BAL	262	12TH WAR
ERMY, MARY ANN	BAL	295	17TH WAR
ERNEST, FRANCIS	BAL	237	6TH WARD
ERNEST, U.J.	BAL	168	1ST WARD
ERNEST, U.J.	BAL	142	1ST WARD
ERNET, JACOB	BAL	252	20TH WAR
ERNIST, GEORGE	BAL	182	11TH WAR
ERNOLD, GEORGE	BAL	165	16TH WAR
ERNOLD, JOHN	BAL	261	20TH WAR
ERNST, GEORGE	WAS	120	2ND DIST
ERNST, JOHN	WAS	136	2ND DIST
ERNST, OCTAVIA	BAL	070	15TH WAR
ERNSTSIN, SAMUEL	FRE	028	FREDERIC
ERNY, WYLIE	BAL	433	14TH WAR
ERRANT, HENRY	BAL	060	18TH WAR
ERRICK, HELEN M.	WAS	180	BOONSBOR
ERRICK, JACOB	WAS	174	FUNKSTOW
ERRICK, JOHN	BAL	187	19TH WAR
ERRICK, JOHN H.	WAS	174	FUNKSTOW
ERRICK, SUSAN	WAS	174	FUNKSTOW
ERRICKSON, TERRILL	BAL	338	7TH WARD
ERRILL, E.C.	BAL	123	1ST WARD
ERRIST, SHARLOTT	HAR	202	3RD DIST
ERRMAN, JOHN	BAL	308	20TH WAR
ERRNST, GEROGE	WAS	120	2ND DIST
ERSENT, G.	BAL	185	19TH WAR
ERSKIN, ELIZABETH	BAL	117	5TH WARD
ERSLIGLE, MICHAEL	BAL	218	17TH WAR
ERTAGE, ANN	BAL	207	2ND WARD
ERTOSE, M.L.	BAL	165	1ST WARD
ERVA, JAMES	WOR	222	4TH E DI
ERVA, JOHN	WOR	224	4TH E DI
ERVA, LEVI D.	WOR	221	4TH E DI
ERVEN, JAMES	BAL	254	1ST DIST
ERVIN, JAMES	HAR	179	3RD DIST
ERVIN, JOHN	HAR	037	1ST DIST
ERVIN, JOHN	FRE	399	JEFFERSO
ERVIN, JOHN J.	FRE	398	JEFFERSO
ERVIN, SAMUEL	MGM	395	ROCKERLE
ERVING, JOHN	ALL	206	CUMBERLA
ERVINS, JESY	HAR	153	3RD DIST
ERWIN, GEORG EH.	BAL	132	1ST WARD
ERWIN, LAURENCE	BAL	456	1ST DIST
ERWIN, LEVI	CEC	117	4TH E DI
ERWIN, THOMAS	FRE	243	NEW MARK
ERWIN, WILLIAM S.	FRE	312	MIDDLETO
ERYLAND, MITHEA *	FRE	265	NEW MARK
ESCABAR, RICHARD	BAL	312	12TH WAR
ESCHBACH, ELIZABETH	BAL	061	15TH WAR
ESCHBACK, JOHN	BAL	190	11TH WAR
ESCRIDGE, WOLFORD	BAL	310	3RD WARD
ESELER, JOHN	BAL	155	19TH WAR
ESENBURY, PETER	KEN	260	1ST DIST
ESENDER, JAMES	BAL	441	14TH WAR
ESENDER, THEODORE	BAL	080	4TH WARD
ESENDER, THOMAS	BAL	070	18TH WAR
ESEX, EDWARD	BAL	278	17TH WAR
ESEX, WILLIAM	BAL	277	17TH WAR
ESGATE, THOMAS D.	DOR	413	1ST DIST
ESGATE, THOMAS*	DOR	413	1ST DIST
ESH, WILLIAM S.	BAL	072	1ST WARD
ESHAM, FRANCES	BAL	193	19TH WAR
ESHAM, JAMES	SOM	476	TRAPPE D
ESHELMAN, CHRISTIAN	WAS	293	1ST DIST
ESHELMAN, JOSEPH	WAS	268	1ST DIST
ESHELMAN, PETER	WAS	268	1ST DIST
ESHERICK, THOMAS	BAL	342	3RD WARD
ESHFIELD, JOHN	BAL	238	20TH WAR
ESHINE, SAMUEL	BAL	109	2ND DIST
ESHLEMAN, WILLIAM B. *	HAR	040	1ST DIST
ESHOM, MARY	WOR	193	8TH E DI
ESHOM, MUSSY	WOR	197	8TH E DI
ESHOM, RHODA J.	WOR	175	6TH E DI
ESHOM, ROBERT	WOR	174	6TH E DI
ESHOM, ROBERT H.	WOR	175	6TH E DI
ESHRISH, GEORGE	BAL	287	1ST DIST
ESHUSEN, W.N.	BAL	274	12TH WAR
ESKOM, HAMBLETON	WOR	189	7TH E DI
ESLAUGHER, SARAH	BAL	339	1ST DIST
ESLEN, ELIZABETH	BAL	229	17TH WAR
ESLEP, LUCY M.	CAL	050	3RD DIST
ESLER, FREDERICKER	BAL	136	11TH WAR
ESLEY, ROBERT	HAR	141	2ND DIST
ESLINE, SOLOMON	WAS	153	2ND DIST
ESLINGER, CHRISTIAN	BAL	324	3RD WARD
ESLINGER, FREDERICK	BAL	003	4TH WARD
ESMBREY, CHARLES	WAS	003	WILLIAMS
ESNART, J. F.	ALL	095	5TH E.D.
ESPENBECK, F.	BAL	213	2ND WARD
ESPEY, JOHN	BAL	330	7TH WARD
ESPEY, JOHN	BAL	181	2ND DIST
ESPEY, MARGARY	BAL	311	7TH WARD
ESPREM, WILLIAM	BAL	125	1ST WARD
ESPREY, SAMUEL B.	ANN	465	HOWARD D
ESPY, HANNAH	BAL	394	14TH WAR
ESRICH, AUGUST	BAL	081	1ST WARD
ESSECK, ANDREW	BAL	060	2ND DIST
ESSEDIN, F.M.	BAL	259	20TH WAR
ESSENBANNER, OLE	ANN	418	HOWARD D
ESSENDER, CATHARINE	BAL	216	11TH WAR
ESSENDER, JAMES	BAL	078	1ST WARD
ESSENDER, LEWIS	BAL	450	14TH WAR
ESSENDER, MARY	BAL	432	8TH WARD
ESSER, E.R.	BAL	169	1ST WARD
ESSERYER, JOHN *	BAL	302	20TH WAR
ESSEX, JOHN T.	WAS	050	2ND SUBD
ESSEX, MICHAEL	BAL	313	20TH WAR
ESSEX, MILEY	CAL	042	3RD DIST
ESSEX, ROBERT	CAL	022	2ND DIST
ESSEX, SALINA	BAL	067	15TH WAR
ESSEX, SAMUEL	CAL	024	2ND DIST
ESSEX, SUSAN	CAL	031	2ND DIST
ESSICK, ADAM	CAR	352	6TH DIST
ESSICK, BARBARA	CAR	352	6TH DIST
ESSIL, RHODA E.	MGM	384	ROCKERLE
ESSLER, FREDERICK	BAL	007	18TH WAR
ESSLER, JOHN	ANN	483	HOWARD D
ESSLER, SAMUEL	ANN	483	HOWARD D
ESTAS, SAMUEL	CEC	009	ELKTON 3
ESTEP, DNAIEL	BAL	092	15TH WAR
ESTEP, HENRY	BAL	092	15TH WAR
ESTEP, HENRY JR.	ANN	406	8TH DIST
ESTEP, JOHN C.	ST	347	5TH E DI
ESTEP, JOSHUA T.	ST	347	5TH E DI
ESTEP, REZIN	MGM	365	BERRYS D
ESTEP, RICHARD	ANN	406	8TH DIST
ESTER, ANDREW	HAR	199	3RD DIST
ESTERBROOK, ENOGE	BAL	384	13TH WAR
ESTERBY, ELIZABETH	BAL	317	20TH WAR
ESTERLEY, GEORGE	FRE	053	FREDERIC
ESTERLY, GEORGE	BAL	018	9TH WARD
ESTES, JEROME	BAL	170	1ST WARD
ESTES, JEROME	BAL	158	1ST WARD
ESTES, JOHN J.	MGM	319	CRACKLIN
ESTESS, JOHN L.	PRI	049	AQUASCO
ESTESS, THOMAS B.	PRI	048	AQUASCO
ESTHER, MARIA	BAL	182	11TH WAR
ESTLACK, HIRAM	BAL	324	7TH WARD
ESTOWMA, WILLIAM	CEC	126	5TH E DI
ESTRIM, MARGARET	BAL	013	9TH WARD
ESWORTHY, JAMES	FRE	258	NEW MARK
ESWORTHY, JONATHAN	FRE	259	NEW MARK
ESWORTHY, JOSEPH	FRE	259	NEW MARK
ETCHBERGER, JAMES	BAL	320	3RD WARD
ETCHBERGER, RALPH	BAL	412	3RD WARD
ETCHERSON, HENRY	CHA	254	MIDDLETO
ETCHINSON, ASBARRY	MGM	344	CLARKSBU
ETCHINSON, ELIJAH P.	MGM	345	CLARKSBU
ETCHINSON, ELISHA	MGM	345	CLARKSBU
ETCHINSON, FLAVILLA	MGM	329	CRACKLIN
ETCHINSON, JOHN W.	MGM	328	CRACKLIN
ETCHINSON, PERRY G.	MGM	328	CRACKLIN
ETCHINSON, RUTH	MGM	329	CRACKLIN
ETCHINSON, WILLIAM	MGM	329	CRACKLIN
ETCHISON, CHARLES	ANN	470	HOWARD D
ETCHISON, CHRISTIAN	FRE	400	JEFFERSO
ETCHISON, GREEN S.	MGM	432	CLARKSTR
ETCHISON, JAMES M.	MGM	433	CLARKSTR
ETCHISON, JOHN G.	FRE	400	JEFFERSO
ETCHISON, MAHLON A.	ANN	508	HOWARD D
ETCHUSON, JAMES	BAL	296	20TH WAR
ETENEGER, SAMUEL	WAS	254	1ST DIST
ETENEYER, DANIEL	WAS	183	BOONSBOR
ETENEYER, EMANUEL	WAS	214	1ST DIST
ETENEYER, HENRY	WAS	209	1ST DIST
ETENEYER, JOSHUA	WAS	209	1ST DIST
ETENEYER, WILLIAM	WAS	211	1ST DIST
ETENYER, ELIZABETH	WAS	208	1ST DIST
ETHART, HENRY	CEC	052	1ST E DI
ETHCESON, FREDERICK	FRE	047	FREDERIC
ETHERINGTON, J.	BAL	171	1ST WARD
ETHERSON, JOSIA	CHA	260	MIDDLETO
ETHESTON, TEMPERANCE	BAL	169	2ND DIST
ETINEYER, GEORGE	WAS	210	1ST DIST
ETMAN, FALDEN	BAL	113	2ND DIST
ETMAN, WILLIAM	BAL	004	EASTERN
ETON, ELIZA	BAL	042	2ND DIST
ETON, ISAAC	BAL	042	2ND DIST
ETSCH, CHARLES H.	BAL	034	18TH WAR
ETSON, HENRY	BAL	089	1ST WARD
ETTENEYER, GEORGE	WAS	215	1ST DIST
ETTER, JACOB	BAL	112	18TH WAR
ETTERMAN, FREDERICK	BAL	069	10TH WAR
ETTERNAN, PHILIP	BAL	071	2ND DIST
ETTICKS, HENRIETTE	BAL	363	13TH WAR
ETTING, RICHARD	BAL	392	14TH WAR
ETTING, SALLY	BAL	392	14TH WAR
ETTING, SAMUEL	BAL	456	14TH WAR
ETTINGER, JOHN	BAL	194	2ND WARD
ETTNER, ANDREW	BAL	082	10TH WAR
ETYNGE, FRANCES	BAL	460	14TH WAR
ETYNGE, SAMUEL	BAL	459	14TH WAR
ETYNGE, SOLOMON	BAL	066	4TH WARD
ETYTRINGE, SIMON	BAL	447	14TH WAR
ETZLER, DANIEL	FRE	417	8TH E DI
ETZLER, DANIEL	FRE	445	8TH E DI
ETZLER, DENNIS	FRE	448	8TH E DI
ETZLER, EZRA	FRE	442	8TH E DI
ETZLER, GEORGE	FRE	296	WOODSBOR
ETZLER, JOEL	FRE	453	8TH E DI
ETZLER, JOSEPH	FRE	450	8TH E DI
ETZLER, MALACHA	FRE	300	WOODSBOR
ETZLER, MARY C.	FRE	450	8TH E DI
ETZLER, WILLIAM H.	FRE	449	8TH E DI
EUBANKS, M.	KEN	222	2ND DIST
EUBERT, ADAM	BAL	194	6TH WARD
EUCLE, DANIEL F.*	DOR	434	1ST DIST
EUIN, JOHN	BAL	271	2ND WARD
EULER, ERNST	BAL	199	6TH WARD
EULER, JOHN	BAL	021	18TH WAR
EULL, GEORGE	BAL	109	15TH WAR
EULL, JOHN	BAL	328	13TH WAR
EULRICK, FRED W.	BAL	166	11TH WAR
EUMERICH, CRISTIAN	BAL	102	18TH WAR
EUNICE, HENRY	ALL	252	CUMBERLA
EUNICK, THOMAS	DOR	380	1ST DIST
EUREY, JAMES S.	BAL	206	6TH WARD
EURSCH, CATHARINE	BAL	219	19TH WAR
EURY, SAMUEL	FRE	440	8TH E DI
EUSTACE, WILLAIM	BAL	280	2ND WARD
EUTLER, GEORGE	WAS	055	2ND SUBD
EUTSEY, ANN	ALL	005	3RD E.D.
EVALINE, SARAH	BAL	111	5TH WARD
EVAN, REBECCA	BAL	459	1ST DIST
EVAND, GEORGE	BAL	088	4TH WARD
EVANFORD, MICHAEL	ALL	135	4TH E.D.
EVANS, ABBY	BAL	064	2ND DIST
EVANS, ABRAM	CEC	008	ELKTON 3
EVANS, ALBERT J.	WOR	207	4TH E DI
EVANS, ALEXANDER	CAR	147	NO TWP L
EVANS, ALEXANDER	ANN	289	ANNAPOLI
EVANS, ALEXANDER S.	SOM	529	QUANTICO
EVANS, ALFRED	BAL	386	8TH WARD
EVANS, AMOS	CAR	199	4TH DIST
EVANS, AMOS	HAR	035	1ST DIST
EVANS, AMOS H.	CEC	091	4TH E DI
EVANS, ANDERSON	CEC	035	CHESAPEA
EVANS, ANDREW	BAL	412	3RD WARD
EVANS, ANN	BAL	409	3RD WARD
EVANS, ANN	CEC	087	4TH E DI
EVANS, ANN	CAL	031	2ND DIST
EVANS, ANN	DOR	443	1ST DIST
EVANS, ANN	BAL	454	8TH WARD
EVANS, ANN E.	BAL	256	2ND WARD
EVANS, ANN L.	DOR	350	3RD DIVI
EVANS, ANN-MULATTO	BAL	219	2ND WARD
EVANS, ANNA	BAL	272	2ND WARD
EVANS, ANNE	ANN	278	ANNAPOLI
EVANS, BARZELIA JR.*	DOR	352	3RD DIVI
EVANS, BARZILIA	DOR	352	3RD DIVI
EVANS, BASEL	CAL	005	1ST DIST
EVANS, BENJAMIN	SOM	456	DAMES QU
EVANS, BENJAMIN	SOM	455	DAMES QU
EVANS, BENJAMIN NF.	WOR	327	1ST E DI
EVANS, BISHOP B. *	KEN	217	2ND DIST
EVANS, BYHEW	DOR	342	3RD DIVI
EVANS, CAROLINE	BAL	201	6TH WARD
EVANS, CASSA-BLACK	FRE	406	JEFFERSO
EVANS, CATHARINE	BAL	014	18TH WAR
EVANS, CERINDA	SOM	538	TYASKIN
EVANS, CHARLES	SOM	497	SALISBUR
EVANS, CHARLES	BAL	156	1ST WARD
EVANS, CHARLES	BAL	084	2ND DIST
EVANS, CHARLES	BAL	355	3RD WARD
EVANS, CHARLES W.	BAL	138	5TH WARD
EVANS, CHARLOTT	BAL	357	3RD WARD
EVANS, CHARLOTTE	WOR	205	4TH E DI
EVANS, CHARLOTTE	BAL	210	11TH WAR
EVANS, CHARLOTTE	BAL	409	3RD WARD
EVANS, CINA	SOM	457	DAMES QU
EVANS, CURRILLA	FRE	037	FREDERIC
EVANS, CYRUS	SOM	399	BRINKLEY
EVANS, DANIEL	BAL	234	2ND WARD
EVANS, DANIEL	BAL	330	1ST DIST
EVANS, DAVID	BAL	400	3RD WARD
EVANS, DAVID	BAL	138	5TH WARD
EVANS, DAVID	BAL	171	1ST WARD
EVANS, DAVID	ALL	074	5TH E.D.
EVANS, DAVID	QUE	251	5TH E DI
EVANS, DAVID	CAR	136	NO TWP L
EVANS, DAVID	FRE	430	8TH E DI
EVANS, DELILA	QUE	250	5TH E DI
EVANS, DENARD	SOM	453	DAMES QU
EVANS, DENNIS	KEN	288	3RD DIST
EVANS, DSZVID M.	ALL	071	5TH E.D.
EVANS, EDWARD	SOM	545	TYASKIN
EVANS, EDWARD A.	BAL	098	18TH WAR
EVANS, ELEANOR E.	BAL	081	4TH WARD
EVANS, ELIJAH	SOM	454	DAMES QU
EVANS, ELIJAH	SOM	455	DAMES QU
EVANS, ELIZA	BAL	081	15TH WAR
EVANS, ELIZA	BAL	109	10TH WAR
EVANS, ELIZA A.	BAL	193	11TH WAR
EVANS, ELIZA A.	CAR	227	5TH DIST
EVANS, ELIZABETH	BAL	077	18TH WAR
EVANS, ELIZABETH	BAL	200	11TH WAR
EVANS, ELIZABETH	BAL	152	19TH WAR
EVANS, ELSEY	SOM	465	HANGARY
EVANS, ELSEY	SOM	457	DAMES QU
EVANS, EMELY J.	SOM	359	BRINKLEY
EVANS, EVEN	KEN	284	3RD DIST
EVANS, FRANCES	BAL	091	1ST WARD
EVANS, FRANCIS	DOR	350	3RD DIVI
EVANS, FRANCIS	BAL	364	13TH WAR
EVANS, FRANCIS B.	BAL	458	8TH WARD
EVANS, FREDERICK	BAL	138	16TH WAR
EVANS, FREDERICK	BAL	303	17TH WAR
EVANS, FRISBY	BAL	044	18TH WAR
EVANS, GABRIEL	CEC	012	ELKTON 3
EVANS, GAMAGE	ANN	311	1ST DIST
EVANS, GEORGE	WOR	249	1ST CENS
EVANS, GEORGE	SOM	375	BRINKLEY
EVANS, GEORGE	SOM	375	BRINKLEY
EVANS, GEORGE	BAL	372	8TH WARD
EVANS, GEORGE	BAL	134	2ND DIST
EVANS, GEORGE	BAL	140	2ND DIST
EVANS, GEORGE	CEC	102	4TH E DI
EVANS, GEORGE P.	BAL	279	2ND WARD
EVANS, GEORGE S.	ALL	095	5TH E.D.
EVANS, GEORGE T.	WOR	249	1ST CENS
EVANS, GEORGE W.	SOM	443	DAMES QU
EVANS, GEORGE W.	BAL	262	6TH WARD
EVANS, GEORGE W.	BAL	383	3RD WARD
EVANS, GEORGE W.	BAL	082	18TH WAR
EVANS, GEROGE	BAL	440	14TH WAR
EVANS, GILBERT	CEC	004	ELKTON 3
EVANS, HANAH	DOR	466	1ST DIST
EVANS, HANNAH	CEC	097	4TH E DI
EVANS, HARRIET	BAL	101	2ND DIST
EVANS, HARRIET	BAL	228	6TH WARD
EVANS, HENRIETTA	QUE	125	1ST E DI
EVANS, HENRIETTA	SOM	355	BRINKLEY
EVANS, HENRY	WOR	243	1ST CENS
EVANS, HENRY	SOM	545	TYASKIN
EVANS, HENRY	CAR	363	9TH DIST
EVANS, HENRY	BAL	153	1ST WARD
EVANS, HENRY	BAL	042	9TH WARD
EVANS, HENRY	BAL	397	1ST DIST
EVANS, HENRY T.	SOM	530	QUANTICO
EVANS, HOOPER	BAL	036	4TH WARD
EVANS, HUGH D.	BAL	372	13TH WAR
EVANS, HUGH W.	BAL	447	14TH WAR
EVANS, ICHABOD	SOM	521	BARREN C
EVANS, ISAAC	SOM	454	DAMES QU
EVANS, ISAAC	WOR	266	BERLIN 1
EVANS, ISAAC	BAL	081	4TH WARD
EVANS, ISAAC	BAL	081	4TH WARD
EVANS, ISAAC L.	DOR	447	1ST DIST
EVANS, ISAAC W.	WOR	206	4TH E DI
EVANS, ISABELLA	BAL	454	8TH WARD
EVANS, JAEMS	BAL	411	8TH WARD
EVANS, JAMES	BAL	140	1ST WARD
EVANS, JAMES	BAL	208	6TH DIST
EVANS, JAMES	BAL	099	15TH WAR
EVANS, JAMES	BAL	149	1ST WARD
EVANS, JAMES	BAL	177	6TH WARD
EVANS, JAMES	BAL	128	2ND DIST
EVANS, JAMES	BAL	091	1ST WARD
EVANS, JAMES	ST	285	2ND E DI
EVANS, JAMES	CEC	159	PORT DUP
EVANS, JAMES	CEC	169	6TH E DI
EVANS, JAMES	CEC	214	7TH E DI
EVANS, JAMES	CEC	192	5TH E DI
EVANS, JAMES R.	WOR	282	BERLIN 1
EVANS, JASPER	SOM	535	QUANTICO
EVANS, JESSEE	BAL	084	2ND DIST
EVANS, JESSEE	ANN	395	8TH DIST
EVANS, JOB	BAL	299	12TH WAR
EVANS, JOB	SOM	464	HANGARY
EVANS, JOHN	SOM	455	DAMES QU
EVANS, JOHN	KEN	291	3RD DIST
EVANS, JOHN	WOR	256	1ST CENS
EVANS, JOHN	WOR	349	1ST E DI
EVANS, JOHN	BAL	315	12TH WAR
EVANS, JOHN	BAL	107	15TH WAR
EVANS, JOHN	ALL	079	5TH E.D.
EVANS, JOHN	BAL	120	2ND DIST
EVANS, JOHN	ALL	250	CUMBERLA
EVANS, JOHN	BAL	148	1ST WARD
EVANS, JOHN	BAL	300	3RD WARD
EVANS, JOHN	BAL	135	11TH WAR

Name	County	Page	District
EVANS, JOHN	CAR	199	4TH DIST
EVANS, JOHN	BAL	409	3RD WARD
EVANS, JOHN	CEC	092	4TH E DI
EVANS, JOHN	CAR	370	9TH DIST
EVANS, JOHN	SOM	412	DUBLIN D
EVANS, JOHN H.	BAL	068	10TH WAR
EVANS, JOHN H.	QUE	184	3RD E DI
EVANS, JOHN H.	SOM	537	TYASKIN
EVANS, JOHN J.	WOR	204	4TH E DI
EVANS, JOHN P.	CEC	168	6TH E DI
EVANS, JOHN R.	CEC	141	6TH E DI
EVANS, JOHN R.	ST	287	2ND E DI
EVANS, JOHN S.	SOM	540	TYASKIN
EVANS, JOHN S.	SOM	537	TYASKIN
EVANS, JOHN S.	WOR	249	1ST CENS
EVANS, JOHN T.	BAL	286	7TH WARD
EVANS, JOHN W.	QUE	135	1ST E DI
EVANS, JOHNSON	SOM	455	DAMES QU
EVANS, JOSEPH	KEN	284	3RD DIST
EVANS, JOSEPH	BAL	209	17TH WAR
EVANS, JOSEPH	CAR	372	9TH DIST
EVANS, JOSEPH	BAL	392	3RD WARD
EVANS, JOSEPH	BAL	315	1ST DIST
EVANS, JOSEPH	BAL	173	11TH WAR
EVANS, JOSEPH	BAL	022	15TH WAR
EVANS, JOSEPHENE	SOM	457	DAMES QU
EVANS, JULIA	SOM	456	DAMES QU
EVANS, JULIA	BAL	321	20TH WAR
EVANS, KATE W.	BAL	336	13TH WAR
EVANS, KEZIAH	CAR	191	4TH DIST
EVANS, KIZZA-BLACK	FRE	392	PETERSVI
EVANS, LABEN	SOM	456	DAMES QU
EVANS, LAPE *	BAL	318	20TH WAR
EVANS, LEVEN	DOR	349	3RD DIVI
EVANS, LEVI H.	CEC	178	7TH E DI
EVANS, LEVINA	SOM	443	DAMES QU
EVANS, LEWIS	SOM	453	DAMES QU
EVANS, LEWIS	CAR	192	4TH DIST
EVANS, LILBURN	BAL	128	2ND DIST
EVANS, LLYDIA B. V. S.	BAL	262	2ND WARD
EVANS, LOTTA	WOR	250	1ST CENS
EVANS, LOTTA	WOR	242	1ST CENS
EVANS, LOTTY	WOR	280	BERLIN 1
EVANS, LYDIA	BAL	156	2ND DIST
EVANS, MALVINA	BAL	157	6TH WARD
EVANS, MARCELLUS	SOM	544	TYASKIN
EVANS, MARGARET	BAL	275	17TH WAR
EVANS, MARGARET E.	WAS	214	1ST DIST
EVANS, MARTHA	SOM	537	TYASKIN
EVANS, MARY	WOR	262	BERLIN 1
EVANS, MARY	CEC	006	ELKTON 3
EVANS, MARY	HAR	117	2ND DIST
EVANS, MARY	BAL	063	18TH WAR
EVANS, MARY	BAL	392	14TH WAR
EVANS, MARY	BAL	195	2ND WARD
EVANS, MARY	BAL	367	3RD WARD
EVANS, MARY	BAL	346	3RD WARD
EVANS, MARY	BAL	340	3RD WARD
EVANS, MARY	BAL	078	15TH WAR
EVANS, MARY A.	BAL	392	8TH WARD
EVANS, MARY J.	CEC	129	6TH E DI
EVANS, MARY J.	SOM	550	TYASKIN
EVANS, MARY JANE	BAL	341	13TH WAR
EVANS, MASON	SOM	454	DAMES QU
EVANS, MICHAEL	BAL	042	1ST WARD
EVANS, MITCHEL	SOM	455	DAMES QU
EVANS, MITCHELL	SOM	453	DAMES QU
EVANS, MITCHELL	SOM	368	BRINKLEY
EVANS, MITCHELL	ANN	313	1ST DIST
EVANS, MITCHELL SR.	SOM	454	DAMES QU
EVANS, MOSES	SOM	540	TYASKIN
EVANS, MURGROM	BAL	298	12TH WAR
EVANS, NANCY	SOM	456	DAMES QU
EVANS, NANCY	SOM	456	DAMES QU
EVANS, NELSON	ST	309	1ST E DI
EVANS, NELSON	BAL	047	4TH WARD
EVANS, OBY	BAL	117	1ST WARD
EVANS, OGDEN	BAL	091	2ND DIST
EVANS, PETER	SOM	456	DAMES QU
EVANS, PETER	SOM	355	BRINKLEY
EVANS, PETER W.	WOR	205	4TH E DI
EVANS, RACHIEL	HAR	070	1ST DIST
EVANS, REASE	BAL	188	11TH WAR
EVANS, REBECCA	BAL	117	2ND DIST
EVANS, REBECCA	BAL	120	16TH WAR
EVANS, REBECCA	BAL	196	6TH WARD
EVANS, RESBEE	BAL	209	17TH WAR
EVANS, RICHARD	BAL	454	8TH WARD
EVANS, RICHARD	BAL	276	2ND WARD
EVANS, RICHARD	ST	265	3RD E DI
EVANS, RICHARD JR.	BAL	454	8TH WARD
EVANS, RITTY	SOM	455	DAMES QU
EVANS, ROBERT	SOM	449	DAMES QU
EVANS, ROBERT	CEC	169	6TH E DI
EVANS, ROBERT	CEC	097	4TH E DI
EVANS, RUFUS W.	WOR	205	4TH E DI
EVANS, RUTH	FRE	435	8TH E DI
EVANS, SALLY	SOM	536	TYASKIN
EVANS, SALLY	SOM	450	DAMES QU
EVANS, SALLY A.	SOM	454	DAMES QU
EVANS, SAMUEL	CEC	021	ELKTON 3
EVANS, SAMUEL	BAL	092	2ND DIST
EVANS, SAMUEL	ANN	292	ANNAPOLI
EVANS, SARAH	BAL	399	3RD WARD
EVANS, SARAH	WOR	287	BERLIN 1
EVANS, SARAH A.	BAL	084	1ST WARD
EVANS, SARAH A.	BAL	289	3RD WARD
EVANS, SEVERN	SOM	375	BRINKLEY
EVANS, SIDNEY	ST	311	1ST E DI
EVANS, SOLOMON	SOM	454	DAMES QU
EVANS, SOLOMON JR.	SOM	454	DAMES QU
EVANS, SUSAN	SOM	449	DAMES QU
EVANS, SUSAN	SOM	354	BRINKLEY
EVANS, SUSAN	SOM	497	SALISBUR
EVANS, TEAGLE	SOM	374	BRINKLEY
EVANS, TEAGLE	SOM	374	BRINKLEY
EVANS, THOAMS	SOM	444	DAMES QU
EVANS, THOAMS	BAL	213	6TH WARD
EVANS, THOAMS	BAL	098	18TH WAR
EVANS, THOAMS	BAL	086	18TH WAR
EVANS, THOMAS	DOR	350	3RD DIVI
EVANS, THOMAS	SOM	426	PRINCESS
EVANS, THOMAS	BAL	076	1ST WARD
EVANS, THOMAS	BAL	261	6TH WARD
EVANS, THOMAS	BAL	399	3RD WARD
EVANS, THOMAS	ALL	120	5TH E.D.
EVANS, THOMAS	BAL	104	15TH WAR
EVANS, THOMAS	BAL	164	16TH WAR
EVANS, THOMAS	SOM	375	BRINKLEY
EVANS, THOMAS	SOM	376	BRINKLEY

Name	County	Page	District
EVANS, THOMAS D.	WOR	179	6TH E DI
EVANS, THOMAS H.	KEN	283	3RD DIST
EVANS, THORNTON	BAL	095	15TH WAR
EVANS, TUBAMN	SOM	456	DAMES QU
EVANS, WILLAIM	CAR	229	5TH DIST
EVANS, WILLIAM	HAR	117	2ND DIST
EVANS, WILLIAM	BAL	273	17TH WAR
EVANS, WILLIAM	QUE	123	1ST E DI
EVANS, WILLIAM	SOM	455	DAMES QU
EVANS, WILLIAM	SOM	455	DAMES QU
EVANS, WILLIAM	SOM	453	DAMES QU
EVANS, WILLIAM	SOM	537	TYASKIN
EVANS, WILLIAM	WOR	228	6TH E DI
EVANS, WILLIAM	WOR	246	1ST CENS
EVANS, WILLIAM	SOM	368	BRINKLEY
EVANS, WILLIAM	BAL	214	6TH WARD
EVANS, WILLIAM	BAL	024	9TH WARD
EVANS, WILLIAM	BAL	017	15TH WAR
EVANS, WILLIAM *	BAL	116	2ND DIST
EVANS, WILLIAM F.	BAL	334	7TH WARD
EVANS, WILLIAM H.	BAL	135	5TH WARD
EVANS, WILLIAM H.	BAL	152	19TH WAR
EVANS, WILLIAM L.	ST	289	2ND E DI
EVANS, WILLIAM M.	SOM	457	DAMES QU
EVANS, WILLIAM S.	WOR	251	BERLIN 1
EVANS, WILLIAM W.	SOM	449	DAMES QU
EVANS, WILSON	BAL	035	18TH WAR
EVANS, ZEDEKIAH	DOR	352	3RD DIVI
EVANS.DEBBY	QUE	189	3RD E DI
EVANS,MARY H.	BAL	003	EASTERN
EVANS,S AMUEL	CAR	373	9TH DIST
EVANSA, J.	BAL	157	1ST WARD
EVANSHART, MICHAEL	ALL	134	4TH E.D.
EVANSMEYER, HENRY	BAL	142	2ND DIST
EVANSTINE, MARY C.	ALL	149	6TH E.D.
EVAR, MALINA	BAL	045	9TH WARD
EVATT, COLUMBUS	BAL	362	13TH WAR
EVATT, EDWARD	BAL	038	9TH WARD
EVATT, ELLEN*	BAL	095	10TH WAR
EVATT, MARGARET E.	BAL	362	13TH WAR
EVE, MALVIA	BAL	255	17TH WAR
EVE, MARIA	FRE	058	FREDERIC
EVELINE, MATTHEWS	ALL	095	5TH E.D.
EVELINK, SOPHIA	BAL	270	2ND WARD
EVELLS, JONATHAN	CAR	116	NO TWP L
EVELS, WILLIAM	MGM	398	ROCKERLE
EVELY, ELIZABETH	MGM	335	CRACKLIN
EVELY, JOHN	MGM	328	CRACKLIN
EVEMS, J.	BAL	174	1ST WARD
EVEN, ELIZABETH	BAL	451	1ST DIST
EVENEGARN, WILLIAM	CAR	157	NO TWP L
EVENS, E.A.	ALL	218	CUMBERLA
EVENS, J. WASHINGTON	ALL	218	CUMBERLA
EVENS, JAMES	ALL	218	CUMBERLA
EVENS, JAMES	FRE	307	WOODSBOR
EVENS, JOHN W.	DOR	382	1ST DIST
EVENS, WIDOW	BAL	182	2ND WARD
EVENS,PATRICK	ALL	239	CUMBERLA
EVEREDD, CHRISTINA	BAL	071	1ST WARD
EVERELLA, CAROLINE	BAL	215	11TH WAR
EVEREST, FRANCES A.	BAL	402	3RD WARD
EVEREST, HESTER A.	BAL	287	3RD WARD
EVEREST, JAMES	BAL	386	3RD WARD
EVEREST, JAMES	HAR	167	3RD DIST
EVEREST, JOB	BAL	402	3RD WARD
EVEREST, JOH M.	BAL	278	7TH WARD
EVEREST, JOHN	BAL	386	3RC WARD
EVEREST, THOMAS	HAR	167	3RD DIST
EVEREST, THOMAS B.	HAR	174	3RD DIST
EVEREST, THOMAS B.	HAR	174	3RD DIST
EVERET, HEZEKIAH	BAL	002	15TH WAR
EVERET, ISABELLA	BAL	405	1ST DIST
EVERET, MARGARET	BAL	399	3RD WARD
EVERET, SAMUEL	BAL	006	15TH WAR
EVERET, THOMAS	BAL	386	3RD WARD
EVERET, THOMAS	BAL	111	15TH WAR
EVERET, WILLAIM	BAL	005	15TH WAR
EVERETT, ANGENIA	KEN	249	2ND DIST
EVERETT, ANN	QUE	130	1ST E DI
EVERETT, BENJAMIN	QUE	138	1ST E DI
EVERETT, EDWARD	QUE	138	1ST E DI
EVERETT, ELIZA	BAL	366	3RD WARD
EVERETT, HARRIET	QUE	138	1ST E DI
EVERETT, HARRIET	QUE	134	1ST E DI
EVERETT, ISAAC	QUE	168	2ND E DI
EVERETT, J.W.	BAL	139	1ST WARD
EVERETT, J.W.	BAL	166	1ST WARD
EVERETT, JAMES	BAL	335	3RD WARD
EVERETT, JAMES	BAL	125	1ST WARD
EVERETT, JOHN	BAL	173	1ST WARD
EVERETT, JOHN	ALL	263	CUMBERLA
EVERETT, JOHN	BAL	022	2ND DIST
EVERETT, JOHN W.	BAL	125	1ST WARD
EVERETT, JOSEPH	BAL	202	6TH WARD
EVERETT, LENA	BAL	123	2ND DIST
EVERETT, MARY A.	BAL	020	9TH WARD
EVERETT, SAMUEL	BAL	279	2ND WARD
EVERETT, SISTER R.G.	FRE	198	5TH E DI
EVERETT, THOMAS	BAL	028	9TH WARD
EVERETT, THOMAS S.	BAL	276	20TH WAR
EVERETT, WILLIAM K.	KEN	248	2ND DIST
EVERETTS, GEORGE	ALL	002	3RD E.D.
EVERHARDT, HENRY	BAL	117	18TH WAR
EVERHARDT, MOWERS	BAL	109	1ST WARD
EVERHART, ELIZABETH	FRE	334	MIDDLETO
EVERHART, FREDERICK	BAL	015	15TH WAR
EVERHART, G.W.	BAL	294	12TH WAR
EVERHART, GEORGE	BAL	121	5TH WARD
EVERHART, GEORGE	BAL	263	17TH WAR
EVERHART, GEORGE	CAR	332	MANCHEST
EVERHART, GEORGE SR.	CAR	350	6TH DIST
EVERHART, GEORGE W.	BAL	294	12TH WAR
EVERHART, HY	BAL	206	6TH DIST
EVERHART, JACOB	BAL	306	12TH WAR
EVERHART, JACOB	CAR	264	WESTMINS
EVERHART, JAMES G.	BAL	212	6TH WARD
EVERHART, JOHN	CAR	278	7TH DIST
EVERHART, JOHN	CAR	328	MANCHEST
EVERHART, LEWIS	BAL	451	8TH WARD
EVERHART, M.	WAS	022	2ND SUBD
EVERHART, MARTIN	BAL	117	15TH WAR
EVERHART, MARY ANN	CAR	271	WESTMINS
EVERHART, WILLIAM G.	QUE	187	3RD E DI
EVERHEART, EMILY	WAS	152	HAGERSTO
EVERHEART, HANSON	WAS	180	BOONSBOR
EVERHEART, WILLIAM	BAL	471	14TH WAR
EVERINDGE, CATHARINE	BAL	110	1ST WARD
EVERISHMAN, JOHN	SOM	554	TYASKIN
EVERIST, JAMES	HAR	132	2ND DIST
EVERIST, JOSEPH	BAL	435	8TH WARD

Name	County	Page	District
EVERIST, JOSEPH J.	BAL	435	8TH WARD
EVERITT, AMOS	HAR	093	2ND DIST
EVERITT, ANN J.	BAL	401	8TH WARD
EVERITT, MARY	HAR	094	2ND DIST
EVERLEE, JOSEPH	BAL	170	6TH WARD
EVERLY, CHARLOTTE	WAS	174	FUNKSTOW
EVERLY, DAVID	CAR	276	7TH DIST
EVERLY, ELLEN	CAR	276	7TH DIST
EVERLY, JOSEPH	CAR	276	7TH DIST
EVERLY, MAGDALINE	BAL	462	1ST DIST
EVERLY, MARTIN	WAS	028	2ND SUBD
EVERLY, MARY	ALL	158	6TH E.D.
EVERLY, MARY A.	CAR	307	1ST DIST
EVERLY, REBECCA	CAR	411	2ND DIST
EVERLY, THEOPHILAS	WAS	015	2ND SUBD
EVERMANSE, GARRETT	BAL	238	17TH WAR
EVERNGAN, PETER	QUE	191	3RD E DI
EVERRETT, EYLVESTER	BAL	073	18TH WAR
EVERS, HENRY	BAL	001	4TH WARD
EVERS, JOHN	BAL	268	2ND WARD
EVERSBERGER, CHRISTIAN	BAL	055	1ST WARD
EVERSFIELD, EDWARD	PRI	116	PISCATAW
EVERSFIELD, JOHN	PRI	035	VANSVILL
EVERSFIELD, JOHN S.	PRI	041	VANSVILL
EVERSFIELD, JOHN T.	PRI	063	NOTTINGH
EVERSFIELD, PERRIE	MGM	319	CRACKLIN
EVERSMAN, FREDERICK	BAL	236	2ND WARD
EVERSOLE, JOSEPH	WAS	028	2ND SUBD
EVERSON, ABIGALE	BAL	131	11TH WAR
EVERSON, GEORGE	BAL	108	5TH WARD
EVERSON, JAMES	ALL	135	4TH E.D.
EVERSON, LEANDER	BAL	304	20TH WAR
EVERSON, LUDIVA *	BAL	304	20TH WAR
EVERSOUL, ABRAHAM	WAS	291	1ST DIST
EVERST, JOHN W.	HAR	160	3RD DIST
EVERT, FRISBY-BLACK	QUE	201	3RD E DI
EVERT, GEORGE	CAR	396	2ND DIST
EVERTS, ADAM	ALL	090	5TH E.D.
EVERTS, THOMAS	ALL	172	7TH E.D.
EVERVINE, MARGRETT	BAL	077	18TH WAR
EVERWINE, CHRISTIAN	BAL	305	20TH WAR
EVERWINE, WILLIAM	BAL	051	18TH WAR
EVERY, JAMES	BAL	294	17TH WAR
EVES, BASEL	FRE	301	WOODSBOR
EVES, THOMAS	BAL	131	1ST WARD
EVESLINE, ANDREW	ALL	081	5TH E.D.
EVEST, JONATHAN	ALL	168	6TH E.D.
EVET, FRED	BAL	441	1ST DIST
EVET, GEORGE	BAL	252	1ST DIST
EVETT, E.	BAL	141	1ST WARD
EVETTS, SETHEL H.	CAR	115	NO TWP L
EVEY, ELLEN	BAL	394	3RD WARD
EVEY, JULY A. *	BAL	063	18TH WAR
EVIL, SOFRER	ALL	246	CUMBERLA
EVILL, JOHN	BAL	251	2ND WARD
EVING, JEMIMA	CEC	036	CHESAPEA
EVING, JOHN R.	BAL	322	3RD WARD
EVINGTON, LORENZO	QUE	212	3RD E DI
EVINGTON, WILLIAM	QUE	212	3RD E DI
EVINS, EDWARD	WAS	091	2ND SUBD
EVINS, JOHN T.	HAR	151	3RD DIST
EVITH, FRANCIS A.	TAL	034	EASTON D
EVITT, MARY	FRE	041	FREDERIC
EVITTS, JOSEPH	CAR	165	NO TWP L
EVUST, JAMES	HAR	201	3RD DIST
EWALD, PHILIP	BAL	299	3RD WARD
EWALL, FORTHLAND	BAL	100	18TH WAR
EWALT, ANN	BAL	250	20TH WAR
EWALT, AUGUSTUS	BAL	250	20TH WAR
EWALT, CASPER	BAL	057	4TH WARD
EWALT, JOHN	BAL	288	3RD WARD
EWALT, SAMUEL A.	BAL	022	18TH WAR
EWART, DOROTHEA	BAL	250	20TH WAR
EWEEN, ANN	BAL	234	20TH WAR
EWEL, JOHN	DOR	351	3RD DIVI
EWELE, SYLVESTER S.*	DOR	456	1ST DIST
EWELL, ANN	PRI	022	VANSVILL
EWELL, ELIZABETH	PRI	093	MARLBROU
EWELL, ELIZABETH	WOR	320	1ST E DI
EWELL, HENRY	SOM	398	BRINKLEY
EWELL, JOHN Y.	MGM	364	BERRYS D
EWELL, MARY	QUE	218	3RD E DI
EWELL, SAMUEL	SOM	392	BRINKLEY
EWELL, SYLVESTER S.*	DOR	456	1ST DIST
EWELL, THOMAS H.	WOR	185	6TH E DI
EWEN, JACOB	BAL	452	1ST DIST
EWEN, JOHN	BAL	445	1ST DIST
EWIG, JOHN	BAL	372	13TH WAR
EWIN, WILLIAM H.	HAR	168	3RD DIST
EWING, ALEXANDER	CEC	209	7TH E DI
EWING, AMOS	CEC	198	7TH E DI
EWING, C. H. REV.	BAL	334	13TH WAR
EWING, CHARLES	CEC	024	ELKTON 3
EWING, EDWARD	BAL	356	8TH WARD
EWING, EDWIN	HAR	166	3RD DIST
EWING, ELI E.	CEC	172	6TH E DI
EWING, ESTHER	CEC	198	7TH E DI
EWING, GERDGE W.	HAR	003	1ST DIST
EWING, HANNAH	CEC	200	7TH E DI
EWING, HENRY	CEC	216	7TH E DI
EWING, HENRY	CEC	035	CHESAPEA
EWING, HENRY	BAL	007	EASTERN
EWING, HENRY J.	CEC	100	3RD E DI
EWING, JAMES	CEC	016	ELKTON 3
EWING, JAMES	CEC	202	6TH E DI
EWING, JAMES	CEC	152	PORT DUP
EWING, JAMES W.	HAR	166	3RD DIST
EWING, JOHN	CEC	112	4TH E DI
EWING, JOHN	CEC	117	4TH E DI
EWING, JOHN	BAL	409	8TH WARD
EWING, JOHN E.	HAR	168	3RD DIST
EWING, JOHN F.	CEC	172	6TH E DI
EWING, JOSEPH	CEC	152	PORT DUP
EWING, LOUISA	CEC	216	7TH E DI
EWING, LYDIA	BAL	005	EASTERN
EWING, MARGARET A.	CEC	113	4TH E DI
EWING, MARTHY A.	HAR	153	3RD DIST
EWING, MARTHY M	HAR	162	3RD DIST
EWING, MARY	CEC	113	4TH E DI
EWING, MARY	CAR	089	NO TWP L
EWING, MARY	ALL	238	CUMBERLA
EWING, MARY C.	CEC	170	6TH E DI
EWING, MARY M.	BAL	100	10TH WAR
EWING, MICHAEL	CEC	202	6TH E DI
EWING, PATRICK	CEC	213	7TH E DI
EWING, PATRICK	CEC	202	6TH E DI
EWING, PINKNEY	CEC	003	ELKTON 3
EWING, RACHEL	CEC	201	5TH E DI
EWING, ROBERT	BAL	116	1ST WARD
EWING, ROBERT	BAL	171	1ST WARD

Name	County	Page	District
EWING, ROBERT	PRI	024	VANSVILL
EWING, SAMUEL	ALL	249	CUMBERLA
EWING, SAMUEL	BAL	433	8TH WARD
EWING, SAMUEL L. C.	QUE	217	3RD E DI
EWING, SARAH A.	CEC	122	4TH E DI
EWING, THOMAS	CEC	200	7TH E DI
EWING, THOMAS	BAL	031	15TH WAR
EWING, THOMAS	BAL	289	7TH WARD
EWING, WILLIAM	BAL	282	1ST DIST
EWING, WILLIAM	CEC	216	7TH E DI
EWING, WILLIAM	HAR	121	2ND DIST
EWING, WILLIAM	BAL	129	18TH WAR
EWING, WILLIAM	FRE	239	NEW MARK
EWINGS, GEORGE	BAL	217	11TH WAR
EWOOD, MICHAEL	BAL	448	1ST DIST
EWORTHY, JAEMS A.	FRE	262	NEW MARK
EWRY, WILLIAM	FRE	443	8TH E DI
EX, ELIZABETH	BAL	413	8TH WARD
EXANS, LEVI *	CAR	268	WESTMINS
EXLINE, SOLOMON	WAS	153	2ND DIST
EXLY, BERNARD	BAL	188	11TH WAR
EXTINE, WILLIAM	BAL	398	1ST DIST
EXUM, MARY T.	ANN	521	HOWARD D
EY, ADAM	CAR	228	5TH DIST
EYER, HENRY	WAS	106	2ND DIST
EYERLY, HENRY	WAS	167	1ST DIST
EYERLY, WILLIAM	WAS	220	1ST DIST
EYLER, AARON	FRE	195	5TH E DI
EYLER, ADAM	FRE	143	10TH E D
EYLER, ALFRED	FRE	195	5TH E DI
EYLER, BENJAMIN	FRE	194	5TH E DI
EYLER, DAVID	FRE	186	5TH E DI
EYLER, EZRA	FRE	186	5TH E DI
EYLER, GEORGE	FRE	195	5TH E DI
EYLER, JOHN	FRE	195	5TH E DI
EYLER, JOHN	FRE	192	5TH E DI
EYLER, JOHN	FRE	143	10TH E D
EYLER, JOHN	FRE	157	10TH E D
EYLER, JOSEPH	FRE	118	CREAGERS
EYLER, PERRY	FRE	131	CREAGERS
EYLER, SARAH	FRE	149	10TH E D
EYLER, SIMON	FRE	178	5TH E DI
EYLER, THEADORE	FRE	133	CREAGERS
EYSENDER, CATHARINE	BAL	261	20TH WAR
EYSER, EMANUEL	FRE	173	5TH E DI
EYSER, HENRY	FRE	148	10TH E D
EYSER, JACOB	WAS	256	1ST DIST
EYSER, MATTHIAS	FRE	191	5TH E DI
EYSER, THOMAS	FRE	148	10TH E D
EYSTER, ANDREW	FRE	163	EMMITTSB
EYSTER, DANIEL	WAS	256	1ST DIST
EZEKIEL, BROTHER	BAL	216	11TH WAR
EZRA, DAVID	CAR	402	2ND DIST
EZRA, LEWIS	ANN	477	HOWARD D
FAAGY, MICHAEL	ALL	155	6TH E.D.
FABER, CONRAD	BAL	408	3RD WARD
FABER, HENRY J.	BAL	359	13TH WAR
FABER, JOHN	BAL	408	3RD WARD
FABER, JOHN	BAL	147	11TH WAR
FABER, WILLIAM	BAL	190	19TH WAR
FABLE, JOHN J.*	DOR	382	1ST DIST
FABLE, JOHN*	DOR	382	1ST DIST
FABLE, MAGDELINE	BAL	374	8TH WARD
FABLER, GEORGE	BAL	009	9TH WARD
FABRAN, THOMAS C.	BAL	158	1ST WARD
FABS, JAMES G.*	BAL	392	3RD WARD
FACE, ELLEN	BAL	433	1ST DIST
FACHEY, MARTIN	ALL	049	10TH E.D
FACHEY, MICHAEL	ALL	049	10TH E.D
FACHMAN, JACOB	BAL	279	1ST DIST
FACHTIG, LEVI R.	ALL	226	CUMBERLA
FAD, MARTHA	CHA	234	HILLTOP
FADCALL, CATHARINE	BAL	105	15TH WAR
FADDEMAN, MARGARET E.	QUE	184	3RD E DI
FADDON, MATILDA M.	BAL	438	8TH WARD
FADGEN, THOMAS	BAL	022	9TH WARD
FAELON, BENJAMIN	WOR	199	8TH E DI
FAFFY, JAMES	BAL	294	1ST DIST
FAGAN, ANN	BAL	123	18TH WAR
FAGAN, ARTHUR	BAL	028	18TH WAR
FAGAN, CORNELIUS	BAL	401	14TH WAR
FAGAN, GEORGE	FRE	003	FREDERIC
FAGAN, JOHN	BAL	121	18TH WAR
FAGAN, JOSEPH	BAL	005	18TH WAR
FAGAN, JOSEPHINE	FRE	003	FREDERIC
FAGAN, MARGARET O.	BAL	455	8TH WARD
FAGAN, MATHEW	ALL	083	5TH E.D.
FAGAN, MATHEW	BAL	027	4TH WARD
FAGAN, OWEN	BAL	133	5TH WARD
FAGAN, ROBERT	BAL	123	18TH WAR
FAGAN, SOPHIA	BAL	005	18TH WAR
FAGAN, THOMAS	FRE	003	FREDERIC
FAGART, WILLIAM	BAL	298	3RD WARD
FAGEL, JOHN C.	FRE	439	8TH E DI
FAGENBAKER, WILLIAM	ALL	124	4TH E.D.
FAGER, CONRAD	ALL	120	5TH E.D.
FAGERT, MARGARETT*	BAL	068	4TH WARD
FAGLE, ANDREW	FRE	426	8TH E DI
FAGLE, JACOB	FRE	432	8TH E DI
FAGLE, SMAUEL	FRE	414	8TH E DI
FAGON, FRANCES	BAL	249	1ST DIST
FAGRET, ANAISE	BAL	037	9TH WARD
FAGRET, FRANCIS	BAL	037	9TH WARD
FAGUE, JOHN	WAS	186	BOONSBOR
FAHA, JOHN	BAL	449	1ST DIST
FAHALY, PATRICK	ALL	050	10TH E.D
FAHAN, WILLIAM	BAL	127	5TH WARD
FAHAY, DANIEL	BAL	146	1ST WARD
FAHAY, ELIZA	BAL	005	9TH WARD
FAHAY, MARGARET	BAL	111	15TH WAR
FAHER, SARAH C.	BAL	362	13TH WAR
FAHER, THOMAS	BAL	437	8TH WARD
FAHERTY, JOHN	BAL	196	19TH WAR
FAHEY, JEMIMA	BAL	189	6TH WARD
FAHEY, JOSEPH	BAL	409	14TH WAR
FAHEY, MARY	BAL	213	11TH WAR
FAHEY, PATRICK	BAL	092	10TH WAR
FAHIM, CATHARINE	BAL	256	1ST DIST
FAHNESTOCK, PRESCILLA	BAL	362	13TH WAR
FAHNEY, NICHOLAS	WAS	214	1ST DIST
FAHNEY, PETER	WAS	214	1ST DIST
FAHORNEY, DAVID	WAS	216	1ST DIST
FAHRNEY, DANIEL	WAS	215	1ST DIST
FAHRNEY, DANIEL P.	WAS	216	1ST DIST
FAHRNEY, JACOB	WAS	223	1ST DIST
FAHRNEY, PETER	WAS	223	1ST DIST
FAHRNEY, SALLY	WAS	214	1ST DIST
FAHRNEY, SAMUEL	WAS	217	1ST DIST
FAHRNEY, SAMUEL	WAS	219	1ST DIST
FAHS, AMELIA	BAL	159	6TH WARD

Name	County	Page	District
FAHS, CATHARINE	BAL	159	6TH WARD
FAHS, LOUISA S.	BAL	110	15TH WAR
FAHY, ANN	BAL	052	4TH WARD
FAIRANKS, MARY*	DOR	404	1ST DIST
FAIGLER, HENRY	BAL	033	9TH WARD
FAILEY, H.	BAL	170	1ST WARD
FAILY, MICHAEL	CEC	142	6TH E DI
FAILY, SAMUEL	BAL	077	2ND DIST
FAINER, PETER	BAL	056	1ST WARD
FAINEY, CHARLES	BAL	132	1ST WARD
FAINFRUCK, ANN	WAS	124	HAGERSTO
FAIR, CHARLES	CAR	299	1ST DIST
FAIR, GEORGE H.	CAR	315	1ST DIST
FAIR, HENRY	CAR	338	6TH DIST
FAIR, HENRY JR.	CAR	337	6TH DIST
FAIR, HY	BAL	196	5TH DIST
FAIR, HY.	BAL	197	5TH DIST
FAIR, JACOB	CAR	338	6TH DIST
FAIR, JOHN	CAR	338	6TH DIST
FAIR, JOHN	CAR	241	TANEYTOW
FAIR, JOSIAH	CAR	340	6TH DIST
FAIR, LEVI	CAR	338	6TH DIST
FAIR, MARY	BAL	009	15TH WAR
FAIR, PETER	CAR	338	6TH DIST
FAIR, SAMUEL	BAL	196	5TH DIST
FAIR, SAMUEL	BAL	197	5TH DIST
FAIR, T.G.	WAS	021	2ND SUBD
FAIR, WILLIAM	CAR	337	6TH DIST
FAIRALL, ALEXZENA	PRI	022	VANSVILL
FAIRALL, ALFRED	PRI	022	VANSVILL
FAIRALL, GEORGE	BAL	114	18TH WAR
FAIRALL, JOHN	CAL	053	3RD DIST
FAIRALL, JOHN	ALL	018	3RD E.D.
FAIRALL, MARTHA	ALL	035	2ND E.D.
FAIRALL, RICHARD	ALL	035	2ND E.D.
FAIRALL, RICHARD	ANN	376	4TH DIST
FAIRALL, RICHARD	ANN	377	4TH DIST
FAIRALL, STEPHEN	ANN	374	4TH DIST
FAIRALL, SUSAN	CAL	054	3RD DIST
FAIRALL, TRUEMAN	ALL	020	2ND E.D.
FAIRALL, WILLIAM	ANN	468	HOWARD D
FAIRALL, WILLIAM H.	BAL	113	18TH WAR
FAIRBANK, ANDREW J	BAL	115	18TH WAR
FAIRBANK, CHARITY	ANN	417	HOWARD D
FAIRBANK, CHRISTOPHER	BAL	066	4TH WARD
FAIRBANK, EDWARD	TAL	113	ST MICHA
FAIRBANK, HENRY	BAL	081	18TH WAR
FAIRBANK, JAMES	TAL	113	ST MICHA
FAIRBANK, JAMES	BAL	258	2ND WARD
FAIRBANK, JOHN	TAL	106	ST MICHA
FAIRBANK, JOHN	BAL	084	18TH WAR
FAIRBANK, JOSIAH	TAL	094	ST MICHA
FAIRBANK, PETER H.	TAL	042	EASTON D
FAIRBANK, ROBERT	TAL	116	ST MICHA
FAIRBANK, ROBERT E.	TAL	094	ST MICHA
FAIRBANK, SARAH	TAL	107	ST MICHA
FAIRBANK, SARAH H.	TAL	108	ST MICHA
FAIRBANK, WRIGHTSON	TAL	080	ST MICHA
FAIRBANKS, CHARLES	BAL	084	18TH WAR
FAIRBANKS, DAVID	BAL	117	5TH WARD
FAIRBANKS, DEBBY	TAL	082	ST MICHA
FAIRBANKS, ED	BAL	079	1ST WARD
FAIRBANKS, ELIZA A.	BAL	117	18TH WAR
FAIRBANKS, ELIZABETH	BAL	022	18TH WAR
FAIRBANKS, GEORGE	BAL	132	1ST WARD
FAIRBANKS, GEORGE W.	BAL	105	18TH WAR
FAIRBANKS, H. F.	BAL	285	20TH WAR
FAIRBANKS, HANSON	TAL	115	ST MICHA
FAIRBANKS, HENRY	BAL	013	1ST WARD
FAIRBANKS, JAEMS H.	TAL	087	ST MICHA
FAIRBANKS, JAES	BAL	155	1ST WARD
FAIRBANKS, JAMES	BAL	174	1ST WARD
FAIRBANKS, JAMES	BAL	044	1ST WARD
FAIRBANKS, JAMES	BAL	044	1ST WARD
FAIRBANKS, JAMES	BAL	094	18TH WAR
FAIRBANKS, JOEL O.	BAL	108	10TH WAR
FAIRBANKS, MARY A.	TAL	072	EASTON T
FAIRBANKS, MARY*	DOR	404	1ST DIST
FAIRBANKS, NANCY	TAL	100	ST MICHA
FAIRBANKS, NEAH	BAL	019	4TH WARD
FAIRBANKS, NOAH	BAL	021	18TH WAR
FAIRBANKS, ROBERT	BAL	332	3RD WARD
FAIRBANKS, SUSAN	TAL	108	ST MICHA
FAIRBANKS, THOMAS	TAL	080	ST MICHA
FAIRBAUCH, DAVID	TAL	107	ST MICHA
FAIRBURN, JOHN	BAL	008	4TH WARD
FAIRCHILD, WILLIAM	BAL	188	6TH WARD
FAIRCHILD, WILLIAM	BAL	197	6TH WARD
FAIRFAX, JAMES	BAL	456	14TH WAR
FAIRFAX, JOHN	BAL	421	1ST DIST
FAIRFAX, RALPH	MGM	434	CLARKSTR
FAIRFIELD, LACMI	ANN	342	3RD DIST
FAIRMBUGH, HENRY	BAL	253	2ND WARD
FAIT, JOHN	WAS	153	2ND DIST
FAITH, ADAM	WAS	104	2ND DIST
FAITHERS, BEALE	WAS	158	2ND DIST
FAITHFUL, HENRY	ALL	218	CUMBERLA
FAITHFUL, HENRY	BAL	212	19TH WAR
FAITHFUL, LYDIA	BAL	160	19TH WAR
FAITHFUL, W. E. B.	BAL	319	12TH WAR
FAITHFUL, WILLAM	BAL	212	19TH WAR
FAITHPEL, JOSEPH	BAL	322	12TH WAR
FAITZ, ELIZABETH	BAL	229	2ND WARD
FAITZ, HENRY	BAL	229	2ND WARD
FAITZ, JOHN	BAL	048	1ST WARD
FAITZ, WILLIAM	BAL	229	2ND WARD
FAKEY, DAVID	ALL	239	CUMBERLA
FALBERT, HENRY	WAS	195	1ST DIST
FALBY, MICHAEL	BAL	413	8TH WARD
FALCK, CATHARINE	BAL	032	15TH WAR
FALCONAR, JONATHAN	BAL	069	15TH WAR
FALCONER, GEORGE	BAL	352	7TH WARD
FALCONER, JOHN	BAL	392	14TH WAR
FALCONER, REUBEN	FRE	238	NEW MARK
FALDA, DENIS	BAL	393	1ST DIST
FALDER, DANIEL	WAS	224	1ST DIST
FALDER, JOHN	WAS	217	1ST DIST
FALDER, JOSIAH	WAS	197	1ST DIST
FALDER, NANCY	WAS	219	1ST DIST
FALDER, PETER	WAS	217	1ST DIST
FALDERS, MARY	WAS	219	1ST DIST
FALDERS, SAMUEL	WAS	225	1ST DIST
FALE, RACHEL	CEC	063	1ST E DI
FALES, ANN C.	BAL	076	15TH WAR
FALES, MISS A.	FRE	200	5TH E DI
FALES, SAMUEL M.	BAL	090	5TH WARD
FALISTER, JAMES	SOM	483	TRAPP DI
FALK, RACHEL	ALL	092	5TH E.D.
FALKENSTEIN, FRANCIS	CAR	405	2ND DIST
FALKENSTEIN, HOVENS	CAR	336	6TH DIST

Name	County	Page	District
FALKENSTEIN, PETER	BAL	072	4TH WARD
FALKENSTEINE, SAMUEL	CAR	339	6TH DIST
FALKENSTINE, HENRY	CAR	336	6TH DIST
FALKER, HARMAN H.	BAL	139	16TH WAR
FALKER, JOHN	BAL	283	1ST DIST
FALKESTEINE, GEORGE	CAR	343	6TH DIST
FALKLER, GEORGE	WAS	218	1ST DIST
FALKLER, JACOB	WAS	240	CAVETOWN
FALKLER, JOHN	WAS	238	CAVETOWN
FALKLER, MARY	WAS	269	1ST DIST
FALKLER, MARY C.	WAS	236	CAVETOWN
FALKLER, PETER	WAS	237	CAVETOWN
FALKNER, ANNA	BAL	378	1ST DIST
FALKNER, E.	ANN	422	HOWARD D
FALKNER, ELIZABETH	CEC	053	1ST E DI
FALKNER, MARY	BAL	378	1ST DIST
FALKNER, SALLY	BAL	378	1ST DIST
FALKNER, THOMAS	TAL	120	ST MICHA
FALKUM, ELIZABETH	BAL	361	13TH WAR
FALL, BENJAMIN	FRE	255	NEW MARK
FALL, ELIZABETH*	DOR	368	3RD DIVI
FALL, JAMES*	BAL	313	3RD WARD
FALL, JULIA A.	BAL	054	1ST WARD
FALL, SAMUEL M.	BAL	128	1ST WARD
FALL, WILLIAM	WAS	242	CAVETOWN
FALLAM, JOHN	BAL	151	5TH WARD
FALLAN, PATRICK	BAL	095	5TH WARD
FALLAN, PATRICK	BAL	281	17TH WAR
FALLAN, THOMAS	ALL	050	10TH E.D
FALLEN, DENNIS	WAS	124	2ND DIST
FALLEN, JOHN	FRE	064	FREDERIC
FALLEN, MARTHA	BAL	057	4TH WARD
FALLEN, MARY	BAL	423	3RD WARD
FALLEN, PATRICK	ALL	075	5TH E.D.
FALLEN, SAMUEL	ALL	072	5TH E.D.
FALLEN, THOMAS	ALL	050	10TH E.D
FALLETT, JOHN	BAL	388	8TH WARD
FALLGAN, JOHN	CEC	034	CHESAPEA
FALLON, BARNARD	ALL	136	4TH E.D.
FALLON, BERNARD	BAL	369	8TH WARD
FALLON, EDWARD	MGM	407	MEDLEY 3
FALLON, JOANNA	ANN	430	HOWARD D
FALLON, MARY	BAL	262	12TH WAR
FALLON, PATRICK	BAL	005	EASTERN
FALLOW, MICHAEL	ALL	128	4TH E.D.
FALLOW, PETER	ALL	141	6TH E.D.
FALLOW, RACHAEL	ALL	069	5TH E.D.
FALLOWFIELD, ANN ELIZABET	QUE	144	1ST E DI
FALLOWFIELD, MARY	QUE	177	2ND E DI
FALLS, ELIJAH	CEC	160	6TH E DI
FALLS, ISAAC C.	BAL	107	15TH WAR
FALLS, M N.	BAL	099	10TH WAR
FALLS, MOOR	ANN	460	HOWARD D
FALLS, R.W.	BAL	161	1ST WARD
FALLS, ROBERT M.	BAL	164	1ST WARD
FALLS, SARAH	BAL	230	19TH WAR
FALLS, STEPHEN	BAL	121	2ND DIST
FALLS, WILLIAM	CEC	146	PORT DEP
FALT, PATRICK	BAL	409	3RD WARD
FALT, ROBERT	BAL	278	2ND WARD
FALTER, JOHN	BAL	209	6TH WARD
FALUSKER, HENRY	HAR	152	3RD DIST
FAMANDIS, SAMUEL	HAR	101	2ND DIST
FAMER, REZIN	ALL	067	10TH E.D
FAMNER, JAMES	ALL	052	10TH E.D
FAMOELL, JACOB	CAR	235	UNION TO
FAMOUS, SAMUEL R.	HAR	007	1ST DIST
FAMWALT, SOLOMON	CAR	413	2ND DIST
FAN, HENRY-BLACK	QUE	125	1ST E DI
FANAF, PHILLIP	BAL	290	17TH WAR
FANAHER, MARTS	ALL	049	10TH E.D
FANAN, HENRY A.	BAL	449	8TH WARD
FANAN, JOHN	BAL	313	12TH WAR
FANASTOCK, SARAH	BAL	012	18TH WAR
FANBLE, LEVI	BAL	263	20TH WAR
FANBURG, GEORGE	BAL	217	17TH WAR
FANCHNER, THOMAS M.*	TAL	035	EASTON D
FANCHOOFER, PETER	BAL	135	5TH WARD
FANCUM, ELIZA	KEN	308	3RD DIST
FANCZAHGY, MICHAEL	ALL	136	4TH E.D.
FANDESON, HENRY	BAL	040	1ST WARD
FANE, WILLIAM L.	MGM	352	BERRYS D
FANEL, ANDREW	BAL	228	2ND WARD
FANEN, CATHERINE	BAL	406	8TH WARD
FANEN, MARY	BAL	159	19TH WAR
FANESTOCK, DANIEL F.	BAL	397	14TH WAR
FANESTOCK, JESSE	BAL	407	14TH WAR
FANHIDEL, JOHN	BAL	428	8TH WARD
FANK, HENRY	BAL	118	1ST WARD
FANLEY, JOHN	ALL	082	5TH E.D.
FANLKNESS, WILLIAM H.	QUE	215	3RD E DI
FANLY, ROBERT	BAL	275	1ST DIST
FANN, FISHER	BAL	169	11TH WAR
FANN, PAT.	BAL	151	2ND DIST
FANNEHILL, SUSAN	BAL	217	19TH WAR
FANNELL, C.	BAL	162	1ST WARD
FANNELL, SARAH A.M.	BAL	180	2ND WARD
FANNER, MATHEW	BAL	271	20TH WAR
FANNERIN, JAMES	ALL	073	5TH E.D.
FANNERS, GEORGE J.*	BAL	349	3RD WARD
FANNING, ELLEN	BAL	147	16TH WAR
FANNING, JAMES	BAL	279	2ND WARD
FANNING, JOHN	BAL	128	1ST WARD
FANNING, JOHN	BAL	144	1ST WARD
FANNING, JOHN	BAL	304	3RD WARD
FANNING, LUKE	BAL	410	8TH WARD
FANNING, MARGARET	BAL	423	3RD WARD
FANNING, PATRICK	ALL	055	10TH E.D
FANNY, ANN	ST	325	4TH E DI
FANNY, FRANCES	BAL	031	4TH WARD
FANSK, HINSEN	BAL	103	1ST WARD
FANSTOCK, MARY	BAL	013	18TH WAR
FANT, EDWARD L.	BAL	385	13TH WAR
FANTHAN, JOSHUA M. *	TAL	070	EASTON T
FANTON, CATHERINE	BAL	349	3RD WARD
FANTUM, NATHAN A.	BAL	324	7TH WARD
FANY, DANIEL *	WAS	077	2ND SUBD
FAOMME, FREDERICK	BAL	341	3RD WARD
FAR, HERNIETTA-MULATTO	ST	347	5TH E DI
FARADAY, JANE	BAL	096	10TH WAR
FARAGER, TAMAR *	BAL	242	6TH WARD
FARAHTY, BIDDY	BAL	443	14TH WAR
FARARO, ALEXANDER	SOM	513	BARREN C
FARAYER, TAMAR *	BAL	242	6TH WARD
FARBAR, JOHN	BAL	453	8TH WARD
FARBAR, JOHN	BAL	044	18TH WAR
FARBER, HENRY	ALL	191	8TH E.D.
FARBOM, ELIZABETH	BAL	018	1ST WARD
FARCBRINGER, ANN	BAL	281	17TH WAR
FARCULL, MITCHEL	BAL	115	1ST WARD

FARDWELL, ELIZA	BAL	319	3RD WARD
FARDY, JOHN	BAL	028	15TH WAR
FAREWEATHER, CHARLOTT	BAL	310	7TH WARD
FAREWELL, LYDIA	QUE	205	3RD E DI
FAREWELL, RHODA	QUE	206	3RD E DI
FARGEUITT, DOMNICK *	BAL	051	18TH WAR
FARGUAHER, JOHN	FRE	243	NEW MARK
FARGUAH, JOEL	CAR	383	2ND DIST
FARGUHAR, E. W.	ANN	408	8TH DIST
FARGUHARSON, CHARLES	BAL	067	10TH WAR
FARGUSHAR, MARY	FRE	277	NEW MARK
FARGUSON, ISAAC	ANN	337	3RD DIST
FARGUSON, MARY	BAL	053	15TH WAR
FARGUSSON, ALEXANDER	ALL	104	5TH E.D.
FARHEY, DANILE	WOR	213	4TH E DI
FARHEY, THOMAS	WOR	211	4TH E DI
FARHNEY, ANDREW	WAS	216	1ST DIST
FARIBANKS, JAMES	TAL	076	EASTON T
FARIBANKS, WILLIAM F.	TAL	091	ST MICHA
FARINGEN, BENJAMIN	BAL	355	3RD WARD
FARJUSON, J. R.	BAL	120	11TH WAR
FARKEY, JAMES	WOR	213	4TH E DI
FARKEY, SALLY	WOR	213	4TH E DI
FARL, ANN	BAL	034	15TH WAR
FARLAN, JOHN	WAS	067	2ND SUBD
FARLAN, LANY	WAS	067	2ND SUBD
FARLAN, MARRY	WAS	067	2ND SUBD
FARLAND, A.M.	PRI	107	PISCATAW
FARLAND, CATHARINE	BAL	291	1ST DIST
FARLAND, ELIZABETH	BAL	212	11TH WAR
FARLAND, ELLEN	BAL	447	1ST DIST
FARLAND, JOSEPH	HAR	140	2ND DIST
FARLAND, MARY N.	BAL	081	1ST WARD
FARLAND, ROBERT	BAL	046	4TH WARD
FARLAND, WILLIAM	BAL	280	2ND WARD
FARLEN, JULIA	ALL	262	CUMBERLA
FARLEY, BRIDGET	BAL	062	10TH WAR
FARLEY, JAMES	WAS	246	SMITHSBU
FARLEY, MARY X.	FRE	065	FREDERIC
FARLEY, MICHAEL	CEC	178	7TH E DI
FARLEY, PATRICK	HAR	101	2ND DIST
FARLEY, PATRICK	BAL	382	1ST DIST
FARLEY, PETER	BAL	110	10TH WAR
FARLEY, THOMAS	ALL	080	5TH E.D.
FARLIE, THOMAS	BAL	423	8TH WARD
FARLING, JOHN	BAL	047	4TH WARD
FARLON, GEORRGE R.	WOR	203	4TH E DI
FARLON, JOHN	WOR	204	4TH E DI
FARLON, MARTHA	WOR	203	4TH E DI
FARLONG, DAVID	WAS	016	2ND SUBD
FARLONG, MOSES	BAL	043	2ND DIST
FARLOW, BENJAMIN	WOR	210	4TH E DI
FARLOW, BILLY F.	WOR	208	4TH E DI
FARLOW, DANIEL J.	WOR	210	4TH E DI
FARLOW, ELIZABETH	WOR	210	4TH E DI
FARLOW, GEORCE	WOR	210	4TH E DI
FARLOW, JOHN	BAL	004	1ST WARD
FARLOW, JONATHAN S.	WOR	236	6TH E DI
FARLOW, SARHA	WOR	208	4TH E DI
FARMAN, JAMES	BAL	275	1ST DIST
FARMAN, JOHN	BAL	381	1ST DIST
FARMAN, JOHN	CHA	286	BOJANTOW
FARMAN, JOHN J.	BAL	399	1ST DIST
FARMAN, MELVINA	CHA	286	BOJANTOW
FARMAR, JAMES A.	BAL	043	15TH WAR
FARMAR, PHILIP	BAL	464	14TH WAR
FARMER, ANDREW	BAL	130	18TH WAR
FARMER, BRIDGET	ALL	215	CUMBERLA
FARMER, ELIZABETH	BAL	126	18TH WAR
FARMER, GEORGE	WAS	004	WILLIAMS
FARMER, JERRY	WAS	285	1ST DIST
FARMER, JIM	TAL	112	ST MICHA
FARMER, JOHN	BAL	254	2ND WARD
FARMER, MARY	BAL	050	9TH WARD
FARMER, ROBERT-MULATTO	FRE	209	BUCKEYST
FARMER, ROSANNA	BAL	367	13TH WAR
FARMER, TERRENCE	BAL	235	6TH WARD
FARMER, THOMAS	CEC	211	7TH E DI
FARMER, WILLIAM	HAR	124	2ND DIST
FARMER, WILLIAM	ALL	154	6TH E.D.
FARNANDA, JOHN	BAL	031	1ST WARD
FARNANDIS, HENRY D.	HAR	093	2ND DIST
FARNANDIS, SAMUEL	BAL	068	15TH WAR
FARNANDIS, WALTER	BAL	389	13TH WAR
FARNANDIS, WILLIAM	HAR	093	2ND DIST
FARNELL, WILLIAM	BAL	181	19TH WAR
FARNER, CASANOSA	FRE	292	WOODSBOR
FARNER, FRANCIS	BAL	214	11TH WAR
FARNER, WILLIAM H.	BAL	351	1ST DIST
FARNEY, PERSAN	PRI	012	BLADENSB
FARNEY, PHILIP	PRI	012	BLADENSB
FARNHAM, WILLIAM H.*	TAL	054	EASTON D
FARNHUFF, LUDWIG	BAL	191	2ND WARD
FARNK, A. J.	BAL	152	1ST WARD
FARNLL, EDWARD	BAL	133	1ST WARD
FARNNEY, DANIEL	FRE	413	8TH E DI
FARNOW, JOHN	BAL	326	3RD WARD
FARNSON, HENRY	BAL	326	1ST DIST
FARNSWORTH, JOHN	BAL	006	9TH WARD
FARNTON, ANN	CEC	087	4TH E DI
FARO, MARY	WAS	012	WILLIAMS
FARO, NATHAN	WAS	012	WILLIAMS
FAROICLE, GEORGE *	FRE	115	CREAGERS
FAROUIETT, FREDERICK	FRE	131	CREAGERS
FAROURET, SAMUEL *	FRE	140	CREAGERS
FAROURITE, MARY	FRE	112	CREAGERS
FAROUSETE, DAYTON	FRE	108	CREAGERS
FARQAHARSON, THOMAS	BAL	034	9TH WARD
FARQUAR, JOSEPH	CAR	383	2ND DIST
FARQUARSON, JOHN J.	DOR	373	1ST DIST
FARQUHAR, SARAH B.	MGM	315	CRACKLIN
FARQUHAR, WILLIAM H.	MGM	347	BERRYS D
FARQUHARSON, JAMES	BAL	422	3RD WARD
FARR, ANN M.	CHA	270	ALLENS F
FARR, CATHARINE	CAR	332	MANCHEST
FARR, CATHERINE	BAL	004	9TH WARD
FARR, HARRISON H.	BAL	437	8TH WARD
FARR, JAMES	BAL	279	2ND WARD
FARR, JAMES	BAL	119	1ST WARD
FARR, JAMES	WAS	012	WILLIAMS
FARR, JONATHAN	TAL	002	EASTON D
FARR, JOSEPH	WOR	201	3RD E DI
FARR, MARIA	PRI	037	VANSVILL
FARR, SAMUEL	BAL	421	8TH WARD
FARR, WILLAIM	TAL	082	ST MICHA
FARR, WILLIAM	QUE	238	5TH E DI
FARRAL, ROBERT	ANN	517	HOWARD D
FARRALL, A.	BAL	150	1ST WARD
FARRALL, ALFRED	ANN	367	4TH DIST
FARRALL, ALFRED	PRI	022	VANSVILL
FARRALL, ISAAC	BAL	168	1ST WARD
FARRALL, JOHN	BAL	153	1ST WARD
FARRAN, BRINE	BAL	382	1ST DIST
FARRAN, DENNIS	ALL	049	10TH E.D
FARRAN, HONER	BAL	392	1ST DIST
FARRAN, PRISCILLA M.	WAS	154	2ND DIST
FARRAN,C.	BAL	157	1ST WARD
FARRAN,JAMES	BAL	157	1ST WARD
FARRANS, JANE R.	ST	348	5TH E DI
FARREL, ASHTON	MGM	389	ROCKERLE
FARREL, JOHN	QUE	156	2ND E DI
FARREL, LEWIS-BLACK	QUE	171	2ND E DI
FARREL, MARY	QUE	175	2ND E DI
FARREL, SALLY	WOR	279	BERLIN 1
FARREL, SAMUEL	QUE	164	2ND E DI
FARRELL, BRIDGET	BAL	206	6TH WARD
FARRELL, BRIDGET	BAL	331	7TH WARD
FARRELL, C.	BAL	151	1ST WARD
FARRELL, ELIZABETH	WOR	272	BERLIN 1
FARRELL, FANNY	BAL	095	1ST WARD
FARRELL, HENRY	BAL	248	2ND WARD
FARRELL, JAMES L.	BAL	397	8TH WARD
FARRELL, JOHN	BAL	275	7TH WARD
FARRELL, JOHN	BAL	119	1ST WARD
FARRELL, JOHN	ALL	095	5TH E.D.
FARRELL, JOHN G.	BAL	248	2ND WARD
FARRELL, JOSEPH	BAL	098	18TH WAR
FARRELL, LEONARD	CHA	232	HILLTOP
FARRELL, LIDIA	WOR	279	BERLIN 1
FARRELL, MARGARET	BAL	003	9TH WARD
FARRELL, MARGARET	BAL	056	10TH WAR
FARRELL, MARY	FRE	056	FREDERIC
FARRELL, MICHAEL	FRE	056	FREDERIC
FARRELL, MICHAEL	FRE	067	FREDERIC
FARRELL, MICHAEL	BAL	002	9TH WARD
FARRELL, NICHOLAS	BAL	021	15TH WAR
FARRELL, PATRICK	ALL	087	5TH E.D.
FARRELL, PATRICK	ALL	052	10TH E.D
FARRELL, PATRICK	BAL	029	4TH WARD
FARRELL, PETER	BAL	094	1ST WARD
FARRELL, SARAH	BAL	117	18TH WAR
FARRELL, SARAH	BAL	081	4TH WARD
FARRELL, WESTLEY	ALL	095	5TH E.D.
FARRELL, WILLIAM	ALL	147	6TH E.D.
FARRELL, WILLIAM	BAL	169	2ND DIST
FARRELL,AUGUSTUS	FRE	018	FREDERIC
FARREN, ANAS	BAL	212	11TH WAR
FARREN, MICHAEL	ALL	214	CUMBERLA
FARREN, MICHAEL	BAL	143	2ND DIST
FARREN, WILLIAM	BAL	117	1ST WARD
FARRENGER, CATHERINE	BAL	289	7TH WARD
FARRER, JOSEPH	BAL	159	19TH WAR
FARRER, REBECCA	BAL	212	11TH WAR
FARRIELL, MARY	BAL	156	11TH WAR
FARRIL, JAMES	MGM	381	ROCKERLE
FARRILL, LUKE	HAR	092	2ND DIST
FARRING, ELLEN	BAL	202	19TH WAR
FARRING, LEWIS H.	BAL	338	7TH WARD
FARRINGER, CHRISTIAN	BAL	098	5TH WARD
FARRINGER, JOHN G.	BAL	145	5TH WARD
FARRINGTON, GRACE	SOM	529	QUANTICO
FARRINGTON, JAMES	BAL	198	6TH WARD
FARRINGTON, WILLIAM H.	SOM	527	QUANTICO
FARRIS, JOHN B.	PRI	078	MARLBROU
FARRIS, ROBERT	CAR	096	NO TWP L
FARRLEY, ALICIA	BAL	083	10TH WAR
FARRO, ELIZA*	DOR	444	1ST DIST
FARRO, WILLAIM	WAS	012	WILLIAMS
FARROLL, NICHOLAS	BAL	456	8TH WARD
FARRON, LAMTSON	BAL	158	19TH WAR
FARRON, LARUA	BAL	158	19TH WAR
FARROW, HARRY	DOR	464	1ST DIST
FARROW, ISAAC	BAL	158	1ST WARD
FARROW, ISAAC	BAL	154	1ST WARD
FARROW, JOHN	WAS	111	2ND DIST
FARROW, JOSEPH	DOR	425	1ST DIST
FARROW, JOSEPH	BAL	048	18TH WAR
FARROW, LEVEN	BAL	315	3RD WARD
FARROW, LEVIN	SOM	427	PRINCESS
FARROW, LEVIN	SOM	465	HANGARY
FARROW, MARRY E.	BAL	048	18TH WAR
FARROW, MARGARET	BAL	440	14TH WAR
FARROW, MARGARET	WAS	111	2ND DIST
FARROW, MARY	WOR	287	BERLIN 1
FARROW, MARY	WAS	122	2ND DIST
FARROW, WILLIAM H.	WOR	305	SNOW HIL
FARROWS, KISSY*	DOR	407	1ST DIST
FARRY, SIMON	WAS	131	HAGERSTO
FARS, WILLIAM	BAL	367	13TH WAR
FARSCH, MITCHEL	BAL	139	16TH WAR
FARTHMAN, JOHN	WAS	121	HAGERSTO
FARTMAN, BARNEY	BAL	229	17TH WAR
FARVAN, THOMAS	BAL	448	1ST DIST
FARVER, ELIZABETH	ANN	513	HOWARD D
FARVER, ERASMUS	CAR	380	2ND DIST
FARVER, JACOB	CAR	375	9TH DIST
FARVLER, J.	BAL	323	12TH WAR
FARWOOD, GEORGE	BAL	269	12TH WAR
FARYHAM, GEORGE A.	BAL	246	12TH WAR
FASE, ANN	BAL	243	1ST DIST
FASE, PHILIP	CAR	252	3RD DIST
FASE, RICHARD	CAR	356	6TH DIST
FASE, SUSAN	CAR	348	6TH DIST
FASH, CATHARINE	CAR	342	6TH DIST
FASH, MARGARETT*	BAL	082	4TH WARD
FASHBENDER, CHARLES P.	BAL	410	14TH WAR
FASHER, SARAH	BAL	034	9TH WARD
FASHOCK, GEORGE ANNE *	ANN	348	3RD DIST
FASKEY, ELIJAH C.	WOR	213	4TH E DI
FASDINETE, ANDREW	FRE	140	CREAGERS
FASSE, DEALIA *	HAR	202	3RD DIST
FASSEL, PHILLAN	BAL	249	2ND WARD
FASSETT, CHARLOTTE	BAL	083	15TH WAR
FASSETT, LAMBERT*	SOM	502	SALISBUR
FASSITT, BETTS	WOR	315	2ND E DI
FASSITT, CHARLES	WOR	300	SNOW HIL
FASSITT, CORNELIUS	WOR	257	1ST CENS
FASSITT, HENRY	WOR	259	BERLIN 1
FASSITT, JAMES	WOR	268	BERLIN 1
FASSITT, JAMES	WOR	255	1ST CENS
FASSITT, NANCY	WOR	256	1ST CENS
FASSITT, WILLIAM	WOR	274	BERLIN 1
FASSITT, WILLIAM	WOR	220	4TH E DI
FAST, JACOB	ALL	197	CUMBERLA
FASTER, ANTHONY	BAL	380	1ST DIST
FASTER, MARY E.	FRE	402	JEFFERSO
FASTER, WILLIAM	BAL	146	1ST WARD
FASTIE, GEORGE	BAL	092	5TH WARD
FASTIN, JOHN	HAR	197	3RD DIST
FASTNACHT, CLARA M.	WAS	215	1ST DIST
FASTNACHT, HENRY	WAS	209	1ST DIST
FASTNACHT, HENRY	WAS	208	1ST DIST
FASTNACHT, JOHN	WAS	208	1ST DIST
FASTNACHT, JOSEPH	WAS	215	1ST DIST
FASTNACHT, MARY	WAS	215	1ST DIST
FASTNACT, BARBARY	WAS	181	BOONSBOR
FATH, HANNAH	BAL	288	17TH WAR
FATHERSON, BARNHARD	BAL	449	14TH WAR
FATING, LOUISA	BAL	215	19TH WAR
FATTE, JOHN	BAL	161	2ND DIST
FATTE, JOHN	BAL	161	2ND DIST
FAUBEL, HENRY	FRE	374	PETERSVI
FAUBEL,JOHN	FRE	001	FREDERIC
FAUBER, ELIJAH	FRE	337	MIDDLETO
FAUBLE, ALICE H.	FRE	007	FREDERIC
FAUBLE, DANIEL F.A.	FRE	006	FREDERIC
FAUBLE, JAOCB	FRE	007	FREDERIC
FAUBLE, JOHN	BAL	147	5TH WARD
FAUBLE, JOSEPH D.	FRE	007	FREDERIC
FAUBLE, JOSEPH M. *	BAL	418	1ST DIST
FAUBLE, MARGARET	FRE	038	FREDERIC
FAUBLE, SOLOMON	FRE	335	MIDDLETO
FAUCETT, JOHN	BAL	225	6TH WARD
FAUCETT, RICHARD	BAL	029	2ND DIST
FAUGE, CATHARIEN	WAS	186	BOONSBOR
FAUGERIER, THOMAS	BAL	001	15TH WAR
FAUGHER, JOHN	WAS	224	1ST DIST
FAUKNER, JACOB	CAR	080	NO TWP L
FAUKNER, JOHN	CAR	080	NO TWP L
FAUKNER, JOHN	CAR	091	NO TWP L
FAUKNER, MARGRETT	CAR	079	NO TWP L.
FAUKNER, WESLEY	CAR	084	NO TWP L
FAUKNER.ELIZABETH	CAR	103	NO TWP L
FAUL, AUGUSTUS*	BAL	085	10TH WAR
FAUL, GUSTOW	BAL	297	3RD WARD
FAULAS, ANTHONY	BAL	421	3RD WARD
FAULBERG, THEODORE	BAL	015	9TH WARD
FAULHANER, JOHN *	TAL	113	ST MICHA
FAULKMEYER, FREDERIC	BAL	230	6TH WARD
FAULKNER, A. M. G.	TAL	078	EASTON T
FAULKNER, ABSALOME*	TAL	015	EASTON D
FAULKNER, ANDREW	CAR	102	NO TWP L
FAULKNER, ANN	TAL	037	EASTON D
FAULKNER, ANN R.	QUE	252	5TH E DI
FAULKNER, BALINDA	BAL	347	3RD WARD
FAULKNER, CAROLINE G. W.	DOR	374	1ST DIST
FAULKNER, CORNELIUS	CAR	103	NO TWP L
FAULKNER, DANIEL	QUE	217	3RD E DI
FAULKNER, ELIZABETH	TAL	105	ST MICHA
FAULKNER, ELIZABETH	BAL	371	3RD WARD
FAULKNER, ELLEN	BAL	094	10TH WAR
FAULKNER, FREDERICK	CAR	139	NO TWP L
FAULKNER, GEORGE	CAR	139	NO TWP L
FAULKNER, GRANBERRY	CAR	103	NO TWP L
FAULKNER, HESTER A.	QUE	141	1ST E DI
FAULKNER, JAMES	CAR	168	NO TWP L
FAULKNER, JOHN G.	CAR	107	NO TWP L
FAULKNER, JONATHAN	SOM	527	QUANTICO
FAULKNER, LOUZA	CAR	092	NO TWP L
FAULKNER, M. A.	TAL	069	EASTON T
FAULKNER, MALON	ANN	458	HOWARD D
FAULKNER, MARGARET	BAL	070	15TH WAR
FAULKNER, MARGARETT	HAR	081	2ND DIST
FAULKNER, MARGRETT	CAR	081	NO TWP L
FAULKNER, MARY	TAL	054	EASTON D
FAULKNER, PRIDA	CAR	092	NO TWP L
FAULKNER, RICHARD	CAR	168	NO TWP L
FAULKNER, ROBERT	CAR	136	NO TWP L
FAULKNER, RUBEN M.	TAL	105	ST MICHA
FAULKNER, SARAH A.	BAL	277	2ND WARD
FAULKNER, SHARTOTE	CAR	167	NO TWP L
FAULKNER, WESLEY	CAR	105	NO TWP L
FAULKNER, WILLIAM	QUE	125	1ST E DI
FAULKNER, WILLIAM	BAL	193	2ND WARD
FAULKNER, WILLIAM B.	TAL	068	EASTON T
FAULKNER, WILLIAM H.	TAL	054	EASTON D
FAULKNER, WILLIAM H.	TAL	077	EASTON T
FAULKNER.EDWARD W.	CAR	097	NO TWP L
FAUNBAUGH, -----*	BAL	114	11TH WAR
FAUNTLEROY, LUCY	BAL	175	6TH WARD
FAUSK, HINSEN	BAL	103	1ST WARD
FAUSNACH, SARAH	WAS	061	2ND SUBD
FAUST, HUGO	BAL	039	15TH WAR
FAUST, JOHN	BAL	374	13TH WAR
FAUST, MARIA C.	CAR	405	2ND DIST
FAUSTEL, BALET	BAL	209	6TH WARD
FAUSTER, ANN M.	FRE	401	JEFFERSO
FAUSTER, HARRIETT J.	HAR	150	3RD DIST
FAUSTOCK, PETER	BAL	012	18TH WAR
FAUTH, FREDERICK	BAL	331	1ST DIST
FAUTH, GEORGE	BAL	331	1ST DIST
FAUX, ELIZABETH	CEC	210	7TH E DI
FAUX, JOHN	CEC	210	7TH E DI
FAVER, JOHN C.	BAL	145	1ST WARD
FAVER, JOSEPH	FRE	348	MIDDLETO
FAVER, LOUISA	BAL	356	13TH WAR
FAVIER, PETER N.	BAL	035	9TH WARD
FAVOR, MATTHIAS	CEC	175	7TH E DI
FAVORITE, ARTHUR	FRE	179	5TH E DI
FAVORITE, CASANDRA	WAS	041	2ND SUBD
FAVORITE, JACOB	FRE	162	EMMITTSB
FAVORITE, JEFFERSON	FRE	164	EMMITTSB
FAVORITE, JEREMIAH	FRE	169	5TH E DI
FAVORITE, JOHN	FRE	168	EMMITTSB
FAVORITE, MINERVA	FRE	160	EMMITTSB
FAVORITE, THOMAS	FRE	161	EMMITTSB
FAWCET, FRANCIS C.	BAL	298	1ST DIST
FAWCETT, ANN	BAL	459	1ST DIST
FAWCETT, BENJAMIN	MGM	353	BERRYS D
FAWCETT, DAVID	MGM	353	BERRYS D
FAWCETT, JOSEPH	MGM	353	BERRYS D
FAWCETT, THOMAS	MGM	353	BERRYS D
FAWCUS, JOHN W.	BAL	155	6TH WARD
FAWCUS, ROBERT	BAL	165	6TH WARD
FAWLY, SUSAN	BAL	273	1ST DIST
FAWN, WILLIAM	BAL	262	1ST DIST
FAWNER, ISACK C.	BAL	268	7TH WARD
FAWNSWORTH, LUCIAN	BAL	131	16TH WAR
FAX, CHANCE	BAL	421	1ST DIST
FAX, JESSE	BAL	247	1ST DIST
FAX, JOSEPH	BAL	440	1ST DIST
FAX, MICHAEL	BAL	418	3RD WARD
FAXTER, EBENEZER	BAL	332	13TH WAR
FAY, CATHARINE	BAL	011	18TH WAR
FAY, CATHARINE	CAL	054	3RD DIST
FAY, CHARLES	BAL	378	8TH WARD
FAY, FORDICE	BAL	129	5TH WARD
FAY, GERTRUDE	BAL	195	11TH WAR
FAY, HENRY	BAL	015	9TH WARD
FAY, JAMES	BAL	178	11TH WAR

Name	County	Page	District
FAY, JAMES	BAL	461	1ST DIST
FAY, JAMES	HAR	086	2ND DIST
FAY, JAMES C.	BAL	020	18TH WAR
FAY, JANE	BAL	015	18TH WAR
FAY, JOHN	BAL	232	17TH WAR
FAY, JOHN	BAL	445	1ST DIST
FAY, JOHN	BAL	446	8TH WARD
FAY, JOSEPH	WAS	100	2ND DIST
FAY, LAWRENCE	BAL	263	1ST DIST
FAY, MARGARET	BAL	276	20TH WAR
FAY, THOMAS	BAL	191	2ND WARD
FAY, W.	BAL	099	10TH WAR
FAY,MARTIN	BAL	026	1ST WARD
FAY,TOBITHA	BAL	006	1ST WARD
FAYAN, GEORGE JR.	FRE	015	FREDERIC
FAYAUX, GEORGE	BAL	101	10TH WAR
FAYHEY, JOHN	ANN	454	HOWARD D
FAYMOOD, WILLIAM	CAR	249	3RD DIST
FAYRON, N.	BAL	115	1ST WARD
FAYTHORN, W.	BAL	173	1ST WARD
FAZENBAKER, ANDREW J.	ALL	003	3RD E.D.
FAZENBAKER, ELIZABETH A.	ALL	110	5TH E.D.
FAZENBAKER, GEORGE	ALL	121	4TH E.D.
FAZENBAKER, GEORGE	ALL	144	6TH E.D.
FAZENBAKER, GOOFREY	ALL	123	4TH E.D.
FAZENBAKER, JACOB	ALL	144	6TH E.D.
FAZENBAKER, JOHN	ALL	144	6TH E.D.
FAZENBAKER, MARCEY	ALL	125	4TH E.D.
FAZENBAKER, MARIA	ALL	124	4TH E.D.
FAZENBAKER, MARY	ALL	144	6TH E.D.
FAZENBAKER, S.E.	ALL	003	3RD E.D.
FAZENBAKER, WILLIAM	ALL	003	3RD E.D.
FEADE, SOPHIA	DOR	414	1ST DIST
FEADER, GEORGE	BAL	360	1ST DIST
FEAGA, WILLIAM M.	FRE	088	FREDERIC
FEAGER, REBECCA	FRE	064	FREDERIC
FEAGLER, JOSEPH	FRE	382	PETERSVI
FEAGU, GEORGE	FRE	088	FREDERIC
FEANNY, MARY	BAL	194	19TH WAR
FEAR, B.C.	ALL	036	2ND E.D.
FEARER, GEORGE	ALL	025	2ND E.D.
FEARIS, JOHN	BAL	201	2ND WARD
FEARN, MARIA E.	ANN	521	HOWARD D
FEARNALD, MARY E.	BAL	020	4TH WARD
FEARNY, MICHAEL	BAL	271	1ST DIST
FEARSON, HANNAH	BAL	031	4TH WARD
FEARSON, HENRY	ST	336	4TH E DI
FEARSON, JOHN	ST	337	4TH E DI
FEASEN, ADAM	FRE	428	8TH E DI
FEASEN, DANIEL	FRE	428	8TH E DI
FEASER, MARY	FRE	115	CREAGERS
FEAST, MARY	BAL	340	3RD WARD
FEAST, SAMUEL	BAL	228	19TH WAR
FEASTER, DANIEL F.	FRE	406	JEFFERSO
FEASTER, ELIZABETH	WAS	162	HAGERSTO
FEASTER, HENRY	FRE	409	JEFFERSO
FEASTER, JACOB	FRE	399	JEFFERSO
FEASTER, JACOB SR.	FRE	402	JEFFERSO
FEASTER, JOHN	FRE	396	PETERSVI
FEASTER, JOHN SR.	FRE	398	JEFFERSO
FEASTER, JOHNATHAN	FRE	383	PETERSVI
FEATHER, JACOB	CAR	336	6TH DIST
FEATHER, JOHN	BAL	208	6TH DIST
FEATHER, JOHN	BAL	207	6TH DIST
FEATHER, JOHN S.	ALL	057	10TH E.D
FEATHERS, DELILAH	BAL	348	1ST DIST
FEATHERS, ELMIRA	BAL	347	1ST DIST
FEATHERS, KINSEY	BAL	348	1ST DIST
FEATHERS, SUAN	ALL	006	3RD E.D.
FEATHERS, SUSAN	ALL	250	CUMBERLA
FEATHERS, THOAMS	BAL	369	1ST DIST
FEATHERSPOON, J.	BAL	244	12TH WAR
FEATHERSTON, EVERD M.*	BAL	372	13TH WAR
FEBUSH, JOHN	BAL	305	17TH WAR
FECAN, HUGH	CEC	035	CHESAPEA
FECHLIG, GEORGE	WAS	131	HAGERSTO
FECHLIG, ISABELLA	WAS	140	HAGERSTO
FECHLIG, L.R.	WAS	126	HAGERSTO
FECHLIG, SARAH A.	WAS	126	HAGERSTO
FECHTIG, JAMES J.	WAS	150	HAGERSTO
FECK, JULIA	BAL	103	10TH WAR
FECLYMER, FRANCIS *	BAL	339	1ST DIST
FEDDEERMAN, MARY T.	QUE	199	3RD E DI
FEDDER, LAURENCE	BAL	163	6TH WARD
FEDDIMAN, LEVIN	WOR	304	SNOW HIL
FEDDIMAN, OLIVER	WOR	328	1ST E DI
FEDLINE, JAMES	MGM	359	BERRYS D
FEDOLPH, CHRISTIAN	BAL	263	2ND WARD
FEDON, FRANCIS	BAL	444	14TH WAR
FEE, JACOB	BAL	405	1ST DIST
FEE, JAMES	BAL	005	18TH WAR
FEE, MARGARET	BAL	005	18TH WAR
FEE, MARY	BAL	462	1ST DIST
FEEAN, BENJAMIN	KEN	292	3RD DIST
FEEDS, MARY	CEC	064	1ST E DI
FEEGS, JOHN	FRE	116	CREAGERS
FEEHAGAN, THOMAS	BAL	379	3RD WARD
FEEK, JOHN	ALL	045	10TH E.D
FEELER, CHRISTIAN	BAL	226	17TH WAR
FEELMYER, DAVID *	ANN	422	HOWARD D
FEELY, GEORGE	QUE	196	3RD E DI
FEELY, TEDDY	BAL	024	2ND DIST
FEELY, TIMOTHY	BAL	447	1ST DIST
FEELYMER, FRANCIS *	BAL	339	1ST DIST
FEEN, JOHN	ALL	050	10TH E.D
FEENEY, MARTIN	ALL	050	10TH E.D
FEESER, ADAM W.	CAR	295	7TH DIST
FEESER, ANGELINA	CAR	253	3RD DIST
FEESER, BENJAMIN	CAR	299	1ST DIST
FEESER, DAVID	CAR	253	3RD DIST
FEESER, HERNY	CAR	251	3RD DIST
FEESER, JAMES	CAR	301	1ST DIST
FEESER, JOHN	CAR	378	2ND DIST
FEESER, SAMUEL	CAR	248	3RD DIST
FEESER, SUSAN	CAR	296	7TH DIST
FEESER, WASHINGTON	CAR	249	3RD DIST
FEESER, WILLIAM J.	CAR	253	3RD DIST
FEESHOUR, GEORGE W.	FRE	138	CREAGERS
FEETE, ELIZABETH	FRE	316	MIDDLETO
FEETE, HARRISON	FRE	318	MIDDLETO
FEEZER, AMANDA	FRE	170	5TH E DI
FEEZER, EMANUEL	FRE	139	CREAGERS
FEEZER, JACOB	FRE	169	5TH E DI
FEEZER, LEVI	FRE	128	CREAGERS
FEEZER, SUSAN	FRE	139	CREAGERS
FEFEL, JOHN	BAL	073	18TH WAR
FEFEL, JOSEPH	BAL	051	18TH WAR
FEFLEN, MARY	BAL	121	2ND DIST
FEHAN, JOHN	BAL	210	2ND WARD
FEHEAR, J.	BAL	067	18TH WAR
FEHELY, MICHAEL	ALL	080	5TH E.D.
FEHLMYER, DAVID *	ANN	422	HOWARD D
FEHRING, ADAM	BAL	167	15TH WAR
FEI, CONRADT	WAS	151	HAGERSTO
FEICHER, SISTER M.	FRE	198	5TH E DI
FEICKETEL, JOHN	BAL	254	2ND WARD
FEIDT, GEORGE	WAS	115	2ND DIST
FEIDT, GEORGE	WAS	115	2ND DIST
FEIDT, JOHN	WAS	120	2ND DIST
FEIFELL, JOHN	BAL	239	17TH WAR
FEIG, ANDREW	BAL	349	3RD WARD
FEIGH, HENRY	ALL	038	2ND E.D.
FEIGHT, JOHN	ALL	036	2ND E.D.
FEIGLER, HENRY	BAL	086	10TH WAR
FEIGLEY, PETER	WAS	285	1ST DIST
FEIGLY, ANN	WAS	130	HAGERSTO
FEIGLY, CHARLES W.	WAS	131	HAGERSTO
FEIGLY, DANIEL	WAS	131	HAGERSTO
FEIGLY, ELIZABETH	WAS	145	HAGERSTO
FEIGLY, GEORGE	WAS	145	HAGERSTO
FEIGLY, HENRY	WAS	139	HAGERSTO
FEIGLY, JOHN	WAS	145	HAGERSTO
FEIK, CONRAD	ALL	040	2ND E.D.
FEILAS, ELLEN*	TAL	120	ST MICHA
FEILDS, CATHERINE	BAL	333	3RD WARD
FEILE, MARY	BAL	211	2ND WARD
FEINDOLLAR, CARMENIAS	FRE	128	CREAGERS
FEIRHAWK, ADOLPHUS	FRE	035	FREDERIC
FEISCHER, JACOB	WAS	289	1ST DIST
FEISER, DAVID	CAR	259	3RD DIST
FEISTER, FERDINAND	BAL	252	17TH WAR
FEISTER, L.	BAL	224	19TH WAR
FEITZ, CHARLES	BAL	267	2ND WARD
FEIZEL, PHILIP	BAL	406	3RD WARD
FELAMSER, CHARLES	CAR	065	NO TWP L
FELAMYRE, JOSEPH	BAL	256	1ST DIST
FELANAGHAN, TERESA	BAL	213	11TH WAR
FELCHNER, WILLIAM	BAL	398	1ST DIST
FELDA, GEORGE	BAL	289	1ST DIST
FELDER, JACOB	BAL	032	15TH WAR
FELDHOUS, BERNARD	BAL	173	6TH WARD
FELDHOWS, AUGUSTUS	BAL	294	3RD WARD
FELDMAN, DANIEL	BAL	107	1ST WARD
FELER, HENRY *	WAS	064	2ND SUBD
FELICITY, MARY A.	BAL	040	4TH WARD
FELIUS, JACOB	PRI	012	BLADENSB
FELIX, SISTER BEATRIX	FRE	198	5TH E DI
FELKER, ABRAHAM	WAS	298	1ST DIST
FELKER, ESREY	WAS	106	2ND DIST
FELKER, JACOB	WAS	296	1ST DIST
FELKER, JOHN	WAS	105	2ND DIST
FELKER, SARAH	WAS	140	HAGERSTO
FELKURNCY, R. C. *	BAL	286	1ST DIST
FELL, ANN	BAL	428	14TH WAR
FELL, BELINDA	BAL	129	2ND DIST
FELL, CASPAR	BAL	421	14TH WAR
FELL, CHARLES	BAL	128	2ND DIST
FELL, ESIA	ANN	452	HOWARD D
FELL, HENRY R.	BAL	448	1ST DIST
FELL, J.S.	ALL	216	CUMBERLA
FELL, JOHN	BAL	130	2ND DIST
FELL, JOHN	BAL	258	6TH WARD
FELL, LAURA	BAL	130	2ND DIST
FELL, SARAH	BAL	128	2ND DIST
FELL, STEPHEN	BAL	445	8TH WARD
FELL,PHILLIP S.	BAL	084	1ST WARD
FELLER, AMOS	BAL	122	2ND DIST
FELLER, CHARLES	BAL	178	2ND WARD
FELLER, JOHN *	BAL	306	20TH WAR
FELLER, VANSANT	BAL	174	2ND DIST
FELLERLNIG, JOHN M.	FRE	298	WOODSBOR
FELLING, FREDERICK	BAL	416	14TH WAR
FELLING, HENRY	BAL	416	14TH WAR
FELLING, JOHN H.	BAL	416	14TH WAR
FELLINGER, CATHARINE	BAL	261	20TH WAR
FELLINGER, FREDERICK	WAS	112	2ND DIST
FELLINGER, VALENTINE	HAR	199	3RD DIST
FELLMAN, MARY	ANN	278	ANNAPOLI
FELLMYER, PAUL	BAL	261	20TH WAR
FELLON, LOYD	CEC	097	4TH E DI
FELLON, MARY	BAL	361	8TH WARD
FELLON, WILLIAM	CEC	097	4TH E DI
FELLS, CATHARINE	BAL	101	2ND DIST
FELMAN, ROSS	WAS	127	2ND DIST
FELONONA, ANNA	WAS	216	1ST DIST
FELPS, JOHN	HAR	058	1ST DIST
FELPS, SARAH	HAR	051	1ST DIST
FELRURNOY, R. C. *	BAL	286	1ST DIST
FELTHOUSEN, HENRY	BAL	286	17TH WAR
FELTMAN, ELIZABETH	WAS	132	HAGERSTO
FELTMAN, JOHN	BAL	034	15TH WAR
FELTNER, HANNAH	BAL	003	EASTERN
FELTPUSH, MARY E.	BAL	407	8TH WARD
FELWINGER, ADAM	BAL	102	15TH WAR
FEMEYER, FREDERICK	BAL	192	19TH WAR
FEMIMAN, DEDERICK *	BAL	063	18TH WAR
FEMING, CHARLES *	BAL	150	1ST WARD
FEMORCK, ELIZA	BAL	256	20TH WAR
FEMORE, SAMUEL	CEC	029	CHESAPEA
FEN, THOMAS	BAL	268	1ST DIST
FENAN, J.J.	BAL	258	12TH WAR
FENANDINE, CIPRIANS	BAL	060	10TH WAR
FENBY, REBECCA	BAL	087	4TH WARD
FENBY, SAMUEL	BAL	086	4TH WARD
FENCE, JOHN	BAL	045	15TH WAR
FENCH, OTHO	BAL	151	2ND DIST
FENCH, WILLIAM	CEC	023	ELKTON 3
FENDAL, BENJAMIN P. P.	CHA	223	ALLENS F
FENDAL, M.	PRI	116	PISCATAW
FENDALE, SARHA E.	BAL	375	13TH WAR
FENDALL, FRANCIS	BAL	144	11TH WAR
FENDALL, JOHN	BAL	192	2ND WARD
FENDALL, M.F.S.	PRI	116	PISCATAW
FENDALL, PENELOPE	BAL	172	2ND DIST
FENDALL, WILLIAM S.	BAL	178	2ND DIST
FENDELUT, CHRISTOPHER	BAL	302	3RD WARD
FENDER, ELIZABETH	BAL	157	2ND DIST
FENDER, GASSAWAY	ANN	507	HOWARD D
FENDER, JOHN	CEC	039	CHESAPEA
FENDERICK, RUDOLPHUS	BAL	032	15TH WAR
FENDLEY, JAMES	BAL	153	19TH WAR
FENDLEY, MARY	BAL	154	19TH WAR
FENDRICH, CHARLES	BAL	254	6TH WARD
FENDRICH, JOSEPH	BAL	254	6TH WARD
FENEGAN, HENRY	BAL	401	14TH WAR
FENEN, WILLIAM	ALL	017	3RD E.D.
FENENT, JAMES	BAL	264	2ND WARD
FENER, FREE*	WAS	124	HAGERSTO
FENERTY, ELLEN	BAL	392	3RD WARD
FENERTY, JOHN	BAL	259	1ST DIST
FENEY, DANIEL	BAL	002	EASTERN
FENEY, PATRICK	BAL	038	15TH WAR
FENEY, WILLIAM	BAL	157	19TH WAR
FENHAGAN, CATHARIEN	ST	288	2ND E DI
FENKE, ANTHONY	ALL	055	10TH E.D
FENLEY, EDWARD	ALL	007	3RD E.D.
FENLEY, THERESA	BAL	112	5TH WARD
FENLY, PETER	BAL	109	2ND DIST
FENN, EMILY	BAL	051	9TH WARD
FENN, MARY	BAL	361	8TH WARD
FENNA, ANNA	CHA	248	HILLTOP
FENNAN, PATRICK	BAL	203	6TH WARD
FENNATE, MR.	BAL	191	11TH WAR
FENNEL, SAMUEL	CAL	025	2ND DIST
FENNELL, ALICE	BAL	237	6TH WARD
FENNELL, ANN	BAL	234	20TH WAR
FENNELL, JAMES	BAL	166	19TH WAR
FENNELL, KITTY A. *	ANN	403	8TH DIST
FENNELL, MAJOR	ANN	405	8TH DIST
FENNELL, MARY	BAL	470	14TH WAR
FENNELL, MAURICE	BAL	181	16TH WAR
FENNELL, THOMAS	BAL	237	6TH WARD
FENNELL, VIRGINIA	CEC	076	NORTHEAS
FENNEN, MICHAEL	WAS	163	HAGERSTO
FENNENER, FORTZIME	BAL	259	2ND WARD
FENNER, HENRY	BAL	138	16TH WAR
FENNER, RICHARD	BAL	013	4TH WARD
FENNER, WILLIAM	BAL	237	20TH WAR
FENNER, WILLIAM	BAL	075	2ND DIST
FENNERTY, MARGARET	BAL	360	13TH WAR
FENNIGAN, GEORGE	CEC	067	5TH E DI
FENNIGAN, MARY	BAL	406	8TH WARD
FENNMAN, DEDERICK *	BAL	063	18TH WAR
FENNY, JOHN	BAL	177	11TH WAR
FENNY,MARY	CAL	033	2ND DIST
FENOTY, JAMES	ALL	053	10TH E.D
FENOTY, JOHN	ALL	053	10TH E.D
FENSELY, WILLIAM	BAL	004	1ST WARD
FENSER, MAGDULENE	FRE	107	CREAGERS
FENSHTER, BALTZER	CAR	356	6TH DIST
FENSHTER, JOHN	CAR	357	6TH DIST
FENTAR, HENRY	BAL	285	12TH WAR
FENTEN, SEWALL	CEC	068	5TH E DI
FENTMYER, WASHINGTON	BAL	207	11TH WAR
FENTON, ------*	BAL	129	11TH WAR
FENTON, AARON	BAL	019	18TH WAR
FENTON, ANDREW	WAS	074	2ND SUBD
FENTON, ANN	BAL	150	2ND DIST
FENTON, BLAKELY A.	BAL	445	14TH WAR
FENTON, BLAKELY A.	BAL	445	14TH WAR
FENTON, CHARLES N.	BAL	280	2ND WARD
FENTON, ELIZABETH	BAL	329	1ST DIST
FENTON, ELIZABETH	BAL	128	18TH WAR
FENTON, FRANCIS	BAL	129	18TH WAR
FENTON, JOHN	BAL	349	3RD WARD
FENTON, JOSIHA J.	ALL	070	5TH E.D.
FENTON, MALIND	BAL	329	1ST DIST
FENTON, MARY	BAL	151	2ND DIST
FENTON, SAMUEL	BAL	121	11TH WAR
FENTON, SARAH	BAL	014	9TH WARD
FENTRESS, BENNETT	BAL	027	15TH WAR
FENWAKER, HENRY	BAL	075	1ST WARD
FENWELL, BIDDY	BAL	470	14TH WAR
FENWICK, A. F.	ST	281	3RD E DI
FENWICK, ANN	BAL	313	7TH WARD
FENWICK, BENNETT	ST	286	2ND E DI
FENWICK, DAVID	BAL	392	8TH WARD
FENWICK, ELIZABETH	ST	304	2ND E DI
FENWICK, HENRY	BAL	167	11TH WAR
FENWICK, JOHN NM.	ST	285	2ND E DI
FENWICK, MARTIN	ANN	304	1ST DIST
FENWICK, MARY A.	CHA	275	ALLENS F
FENWICK, WILLIAM	ST	303	2ND E DI
FENWICK, WILLIAM H.	ST	287	2ND E DI
FERAMAN, WILLIAM *	BAL	304	20TH WAR
FERAND, DANIEL	BAL	117	1ST WARD
FERANDIS, J.	BAL	165	1ST WARD
FERBUSH, SUSAN A.	QUE	146	1ST E DI
FERBUSH,JOSEPH	QUE	153	1ST E DI
FERDINAND, M. J.	BAL	133	11TH WAR
FEREL, JOSHUA	CEC	059	1ST E DI
FEREMAN,ISAAC	BAL	008	EASTERN
FERER, GEORGE	BAL	126	1ST WARD
FERGASON, MARGARET	CEC	120	4TH E DI
FERGASON, ROBERT	CHA	234	HILLTOP
FERGASON, SUSAN	BAL	044	9TH WARD
FERGASSON, FRANCES A.	BAL	102	15TH WAR
FERGHLINE, JOSEPH	BAL	338	7TH WARD
FERGOSON, ELIZA	BAL	343	7TH WARD
FERGUS, LOUIS	BAL	061	15TH WAR
FERGUSON, ALEXANDER	BAL	267	7TH WARD
FERGUSON, ANN	BAL	262	12TH WAR
FERGUSON, ANNA	ANN	434	HOWARD D
FERGUSON, ANNA	KEN	211	2ND DIST
FERGUSON, BENJAMIN	BAL	084	15TH WAR
FERGUSON, BENJAMIN F.	BAL	286	20TH WAR
FERGUSON, CATHERINE-BLACK	FRE	049	FREDERIC
FERGUSON, DANIEL	QUE	175	2ND E DI
FERGUSON, DAVID R.	BAL	324	12TH WAR
FERGUSON, EDWARD	CEC	048	1ST E DI
FERGUSON, ELIZABETH	CHA	295	HILLTOP
FERGUSON, ELIZABETH	BAL	420	14TH WAR
FERGUSON, ELIZABETH	PRI	100	SPALDING
FERGUSON, GEORGE	CEC	124	5TH E DI
FERGUSON, GEORGE	BAL	075	15TH WAR
FERGUSON, GEORGE	BAL	286	2ND WARD
FERGUSON, HANNAH	CEC	162	6TH E DI
FERGUSON, HENRY	BAL	331	1ST DIST
FERGUSON, HENRY	QUE	213	3RD E DI
FERGUSON, J. B.	CHA	245	HILLTOP
FERGUSON, JAMES	CHA	234	HILLTOP
FERGUSON, JAMES	CEC	195	6TH E DI
FERGUSON, JAMES	CEC	195	6TH E DI
FERGUSON, JAMES	CEC	165	6TH E DI
FERGUSON, JAMES	CEC	097	4TH E DI
FERGUSON, JAMES	ALL	211	CUMBERLA
FERGUSON, JOHN	BAL	117	15TH WAR
FERGUSON, JOHN	CEC	088	4TH E DI
FERGUSON, JOHN	CEC	170	6TH E DI
FERGUSON, JOHN	CEC	165	6TH E DI
FERGUSON, JOHN J.	BAL	124	2ND DIST
FERGUSON, JOHN W.	CAR	235	UNION TO
FERGUSON, JOHN R.	CHA	294	BOJANTOW
FERGUSON, JOHN W.	QUE	186	3RD E DI
FERGUSON, LEVI	BAL	083	2ND DIST
FERGUSON, LYDIA	ANN	441	HOWARD D
FERGUSON, MARGARET J.	BAL	027	15TH WAR
FERGUSON, MARSHAL	BAL	350	1ST DIST
FERGUSON, MARY	BAL	072	10TH WAR
FERGUSON, O. A.	CHA	219	ALLENS F

Name	County	Page	District
FERGUSON, PHEBY A.	CEC	124	5TH E DI
FERGUSON, RICHARD G.	BAL	290	20TH WAR
FERGUSON, ROBERT	CEC	169	6TH E DI
FERGUSCN, ROBERT	CEC	026	ELKTON 3
FERGUSON, ROBERT	BAL	286	12TH WAR
FERGUSON, RONALD	PRI	107	PISCATAW
FERGUSON, SAMUEL	ALL	040	2ND E.D.
FERGUSON, SARAH	ANN	438	HOWARD D
FERGUSON, THEODRICK	BAL	196	6TH WARD
FERGUSON, THOMAS	BAL	093	10TH WAR
FERGUSON, THOMAS L.	PRI	090	MARLBROU
FERGUSON, WILLIAM	BAL	262	12TH WAR
FERGUSON, WILLIAM	CHA	294	BOJANTOW
FERGUSSON, CATHARINE	BAL	067	15TH WAR
FERGUSSON, CATHERINE B.	BAL	034	4TH WARD
FERGUSSON, CELESTIA A.	BAL	104	15TH WAR
FERGUSSON, CHARLES	BAL	012	15TH WAR
FERGUSSON, E.	BAL	153	5TH WARD
FERGUSSON, ELI	FRE	193	5TH E DI
FERGUSSON, HUGH	FRE	192	5TH E DI
FERGUSSON, JOHN	BAL	149	16TH WAR
FERGUSSON, JOHN	ALL	107	5TH E.D.
FERGUSSON, JOHN	ALL	105	5TH E.D.
FERICK, MICHAEL *	BAL	275	1ST DIST
FERIVER, DAVID	BAL	193	19TH WAR
FERKE, JOHN*	BAL	087	10TH WAR
FERLONG, WILLIAM	WAS	133	2ND DIST
FERMER, FREDERICK	HAR	057	1ST DIST
FERNAN, JULIANA	BAL	067	10TH WAR
FERNANDIS, CATHARINE	BAL	080	2ND DIST
FERNANDIS, J.	BAL	157	1ST WARD
FERNAR, BARBARA	BAL	195	6TH WARD
FERNAR, BERNARD	BAL	194	6TH WARD
FERNARD, BERNARD	BAL	109	1ST WARD
FERNAUER, ALBERT	BAL	038	15TH WAR
FERNDENBERG, CATHERINE	FRE	420	8TH E DI
FERNELL, EDWARD	QUE	132	1ST E DI
FERNER, REBECCA	BAL	242	6TH WARD
FERNEY, CATHERINE	BAL	280	20TH WAR
FERNEY, JOHN	WAS	161	2ND DIST
FERNLY, THOMAS A.	CEC	014	ELKTON 3
FERNSTEN, VALENTINE	BAL	454	14TH WAR
FEROGA, MARIA	BAL	458	14TH WAR
FEROR, BENJAMIN	FRE	128	CREAGERS
FERRAL, DENNIS W.	PRI	003	BLADENSB
FERRAL, ELIZABETH	PRI	005	BLADENSB
FERRAL, THOMAS S.	PRI	007	BLADENSB
FERRALL, JOHN C.	ST	328	4TH E DI
FERRALL, NOBLE	ST	328	4TH E DI
FERRALL, RICHARD	CHA	281	BOJANTOW
FERRALL, THOMAS	ST	327	4TH E DI
FERRE, AMSY	BAL	185	19TH WAR
FERREL, ADAM-BLACK	QUE	140	1ST E DI
FERREL, JOSEPH-BLACK	CAR	100	NO TWP L
FERREL, MARGARETT	FRE	381	PETERSVI
FERREL, MICHAEL F.	BAL	292	3RD WARD
FERRELL, ANN E.	CHA	255	MIDDLETO
FERRELL, BETTY	CHA	250	MIDDLETO
FERRELL, CHARLES	CHA	230	BOJANTOW
FERRELL, ELISHA	BAL	098	18TH WAR
FERRELL, ELLEN	CHA	230	BOJANTOW
FERRELL, ELLY	CHA	231	HILLTOP
FERRELL, GRANDISON	CHA	235	HILLTOP
FERRELL, HENRY	CHA	249	MIDDLETO
FERRELL, HOLLY	CHA	241	HILLTOP
FERRELL, J.	BAL	286	2ND WARD
FERRELL, JAMES	CHA	278	BOJANTOW
FERRELL, JANE	CHA	241	HILLTOP
FERRELL, JOHN	CHA	274	ALLENS F
FERRELL, JOHN	CHA	284	BOJANTOW
FERRELL, JOSHUA	BAL	053	1ST WARD
FERRELL, JOSHUA	KEN	280	3RD DIST
FERRELL, MARY C.	CHA	284	BOJANTOW
FERRELL, MATHEW	ALL	072	5TH E.D.
FERRELL, NANCY	ALL	019	2ND E.D.
FERRELL, OLIVIA V.	CHA	284	BOJANTOW
FERRELL, PAT	ANN	281	ANNAPOLI
FERRELL, S.	CHA	220	ALLENS F
FERRELL, THOMAS	CHA	232	HILLTOP
FERRELL, WILLIAM	CHA	278	BOJANTOW
FERREN, JOHN	ALL	223	CUMBERLA
FERREN, SAMUEL	ALL	038	2ND E.D.
FERRETO, JOHN A.	BAL	041	4TH WARD
FERRIL, JAMES	FRE	389	PETERSVI
FERRIL, RICHARD	FRE	217	BUCKEYST
FERRILL, M.	ANN	281	ANNAPOLI
FERRILL, PETER	ANN	281	ANNAPOLI
FERRIS, BALDWIN	BAL	365	8TH WARD
FERRIS, DAVID	HAR	085	2ND DIST
FERRIS, JOHN	BAL	219	19TH WAR
FERRIS, WILLIAM	HAR	078	2ND DIST
FERRIS, WILLIAM	BAL	279	12TH WAR
FERRMAN, OLIVE	BAL	304	20TH WAR
FERRY, DAN	HAR	009	1ST DIST
FERRY, DANIEL	BAL	106	18TH WAR
FERRY, DENNIS	BAL	179	16TH WAR
FERRY, DENNIS O.	CEC	093	4TH E DI
FERRY, H. G.	BAL	333	1ST DIST
FERRY, HANNAH	CEC	093	4TH E DI
FERRY, J.	BAL	173	1ST WARD
FERRY, JOHN	BAL	027	15TH WAR
FERRY, MRS.	BAL	150	2ND DIST
FERRY, THOMAS	QUE	169	2ND E DI
FERRY, UPTON	CEC	161	6TH E DI
FERTENEY, SAMUEL	WAS	162	2ND DIST
FERTNEY, DAVID	WAS	160	2ND DIST
FERTNEY, SAMUEL	WAS	160	2ND DIST
FERUGSON, COLIN R.	QUE	185	3RD E DI
FERUGSON, JAMES	BAL	109	1ST WARD
FERUGUSSON, JAMES	FRE	193	5TH E DI
FESH, MARGARETT*	BAL	082	4TH WARD
FESHER, CHARLES W.	BAL	117	11TH WAR
FESLER, PHILIP	ANN	491	HOWARD D
FESSLER, ANDREW	WAS	255	1ST DIST
FESSLER, CORNELIA A.	WAS	255	1ST DIST
FESSLER, DAVID	WAS	255	1ST DIST
FESSLER, HENRY B.	FRE	035	FREDERIC
FESSLER, JACOB	WAS	238	CAVETOWN
FESSLER, JOHN	WAS	247	SMITHSBU
FESSLER, JOHN	FRE	035	FREDERIC
FESTER, BENJAMIN	FRE	402	JEFFERSO
FESTER, CHARLES	BAL	304	20TH WAR
FESTER, HENRY B.	BAL	244	12TH WAR
FESTER, JOSEPHINE	BAL	195	19TH WAR
FESTER, VULANT	BAL	237	20TH WAR
FETCH, JAMES	CEC	059	1ST E DI
FETCH, JOHN	BAL	218	17TH WAR
FETE, JOHN	BAL	254	12TH WAR
FETHIAN, WILLIAM	KEN	289	3RD DIST
FETKE, JOHN*	BAL	087	10TH WAR
FETLER, JOHN *	BAL	306	20TH WAR
FETREL, GEORGE	BAL	048	18TH WAR
FETSER, PEGGY	BAL	208	6TH DIST
FETTER, GEORGE	BAL	221	6TH WARD
FETTERLING, CATHARINE	CAR	279	7TH DIST
FETTING, JOHN	BAL	307	3RD WARD
FETTON, SARAH	KEN	312	3RD DIST
FETTS, GEORGE*	BAL	350	3RD WARD
FETTZ, GEORGE*	BAL	350	3RD WARD
FETUS, MARGRET	ANN	279	ANNAPOLI
FETZEMER, JOHN F.	BAL	378	13TH WAR
FETZHUGH, H. G.	ALL	094	5TH E.D.
FEUNELL, KITTY A. *	ANN	400	8TH DIST
FEUSS, F. H.	BAL	092	10TH WAR
FEUST, JOHN	BAL	139	19TH WAR
FEVER, JOHN	CEC	042	CHESAPEA
FEW, ESTHER	MGM	315	CRACKLIN
FEW, GEORGE W.	HAR	005	1ST DIST
FEW, JAMES C.	CAR	406	2ND DIST
FEX, CONRAD	BAL	259	2ND WARD
FEY, EMILY	WAS	192	1ST DIST
FEY, PATRICK	ALL	255	CUMBERLA
FEZERAN, FERDRIA	BAL	253	2ND WARD
FICHER, CATHARINE	FRE	407	JEFFERSO
FICHER, CHARLES-BLACK	FRE	399	JEFFERSO
FICHMIRE, CASPER	ALL	164	6TH E.D.
FICK, AUGUST	BAL	450	14TH WAR
FICK, CHARLES*	BAL	407	3RD WARD
FICK, FERDINAND	BAL	450	14TH WAR
FICK, MARGARET	BAL	030	1ST WARD
FICKER, MICHAEL	BAL	042	9TH WARD
FICKEY, CAROLINE A.	QUE	192	3RD E DI
FICKEY, CAROLINE V.	BAL	375	13TH WAR
FICKEY, FREDERICK	BAL	375	13TH WAR
FICKEY, FREDERICK	BAL	013	4TH WARD
FICKEY, HARMAN	BAL	348	7TH WARD
FICKEY, HENRY	BAL	352	13TH WAR
FICKEY, JAMES	QUE	236	4TH E DI
FICKEY, SARAH A.	QUE	186	3RD E DI
FICKLE, CAROLINE-BLACK	CAR	383	2ND DIST
FICKLE, ELI	BAL	245	6TH WARD
FICKLE, ELIZABETH	CAR	237	UNION TO
FICKLE, ISAAC	CAR	237	UNION TO
FICKNER, S.	BAL	137	1ST WARD
FIDDEMAN, JANE	TAL	011	EASTON D
FIDDEN, MARY*	BAL	351	3RD WARD
FIDDIS, BENJAMIN	KEN	210	2ND DIST
FIDDIS, LEVI	KEN	209	2ND DIST
FIDLE, JOHN	DOR	380	1ST DIST
FIDLE, JOHN	DOR	380	1ST DIST
FIE, JOHN	WAS	022	2ND SUBD
FIEK, CHARLES*	BAL	407	3RD WARD
FIELD, CAROLINE	BAL	412	3RD WARD
FIELD, DAVID	BAL	217	6TH WARD
FIELD, ELLEN	BAL	034	4TH WARD
FIELD, JAMES	BAL	295	7TH WARD
FIELD, JONAS	BAL	015	9TH WARD
FIELD, SARAH	BAL	133	11TH WAR
FIELDE, CATHARINE	BAL	373	13TH WAR
FIELDHOUSE, F. A.	BAL	095	10TH WAR
FIELDING, JOSEPHINE	BAL	346	13TH WAR
FIELDINGS, DAVID	BAL	089	2ND DIST
FIELDS, ALLEN	BAL	343	7TH WARD
FIELDS, ALTHEA	BAL	419	14TH WAR
FIELDS, ANNA T.	BAL	340	3RD WARD
FIELDS, ANTHONY B.	BAL	351	3RD WARD
FIELDS, DEILA	BAL	151	11TH WAR
FIELDS, EDWARD	BAL	238	6TH WARD
FIELDS, EDWARD	TAL	090	ST MICHA
FIELDS, ELIZABETH	BAL	342	3RD WARD
FIELDS, ELLEN	BAL	196	17TH WAR
FIELDS, ELLEN	ALL	169	6TH E.D.
FIELDS, GEORGE	SOM	480	TRAPP DI
FIELDS, HARRISON	TAL	101	ST MICHA
FIELDS, HARRISON	BAL	380	1ST DIST
FIELDS, HENRY	QUE	136	1ST E DI
FIELDS, J.	BAL	153	1ST WARD
FIELDS, JAMES	BAL	307	3RD WARD
FIELDS, JAMES	BAL	404	3RD WARD
FIELDS, JAMES	BAL	382	8TH WARD
FIELDS, JAMES	BAL	208	11TH WAR
FIELDS, JOHN	CEC	076	NORTHEAS
FIELDS, JOHN	MGM	380	ROCKERLE
FIELDS, JOHN	BAL	391	3RD WARD
FIELDS, JOHN	BAL	164	1ST WARD
FIELDS, JOHN	SOM	483	TRAPP DI
FIELDS, JOHN	SOM	479	TRAPP DI
FIELDS, JOHN	SOM	469	TRAPPE D
FIELDS, JOHN B.	BAL	351	3RD WARD
FIELDS, JONATHAN W.	MGM	385	ROCKERLE
FIELDS, LAVINIA	BAL	392	14TH WAR
FIELDS, LAVINIA	BAL	419	14TH WAR
FIELDS, LETETIA	FRE	035	FREDERIC
FIELDS, LEVI	SOM	479	TRAPP DI
FIELDS, LEVIN	TAL	095	ST MICHA
FIELDS, LORA	BAL	458	1ST DIST
FIELDS, LOUISA-BLACK	FRE	049	FREDERIC
FIELDS, LUKE	BAL	014	2ND DIST
FIELDS, MARGARET	MGM	374	ROCKERLE
FIELDS, MARIA	HAR	099	2ND DIST
FIELDS, MARTHA	BAL	228	17TH WAR
FIELDS, MARY	CEC	077	NORTHEAS
FIELDS, MARY	CEC	060	1ST E DI
FIELDS, MARY	BAL	458	1ST DIST
FIELDS, MARY	BAL	156	2ND DIST
FIELDS, MATTHEW	MGM	374	ROCKERLE
FIELDS, MOSES-BLACK	FRE	009	FREDERIC
FIELDS, NARCINE	BAL	289	20TH WAR
FIELDS, RICHARD	HAR	088	2ND DIST
FIELDS, RICHARD R.	BAL	362	3RD WARD
FIELDS, ROBERT C.	MGM	385	ROCKERLE
FIELDS, RUFUS	SOM	472	TRAPPE D
FIELDS, SARAH	BAL	289	12TH WAR
FIELDS, STEPHEN	SOM	492	SALISBUR
FIELDS, SUSAN	ST	306	1ST E DI
FIELDS, THOMAS	SOM	480	TRAPP DI
FIELDS, THOMAS	QUE	136	1ST E DI
FIELDS, VALENTINE	BAL	408	1ST DIST
FIELDS, WILLIAM	BAL	316	7TH WARD
FIELDS, WILLIAM	BAL	170	16TH WAR
FIELDS, WILLIAM	ANN	446	HOWARD D
FIELDS, WILLIAM	BAL	342	7TH WARD
FIELDS, WILLIAM	BAL	266	20TH WAR
FIELDS, WILLIAM	SOM	465	HANGARY
FIELDS, WILLIAM H.	BAL	131	18TH WAR
FIELDS, WINNY	BAL	416	3RD WARD
FIELDSTICK, PETER	BAL	193	2ND WARD
FIEND, PETER	BAL	013	2ND DIST
FIER, CHARLES	BAL	001	9TH WARD
FIERBACHER, POWELL	BAL	081	10TH WAR
FIERLDER, HENRY *	BAL	214	6TH WARD
FIERNAN, PATRICK	BAL	197	19TH WAR
FIERNY, PATRICK	BAL	444	1ST DIST
FIERRY, JOHN *	WAS	168	FUNKSTOW
FIERSTONE, HENRY M.	FRE	208	BUCKEYST
FIERY, BENJAMIN F.	WAS	175	1ST DIST
FIERY, HENRY	WAS	132	2ND DIST
FIERY, JACOB	WAS	176	1ST DIST
FIERY, JOHN	WAS	132	2ND DIST
FIERY, JOSEPH	WAS	152	HAGERSTO
FIERY, JOSEPH	WAS	167	1ST DIST
FIERY, SOLOMAN	WAS	130	2ND DIST
FIERY, SUSAN	WAS	140	HAGERSTO
FIERY, URILLA	WAS	124	HAGERSTO
FIERY, WILLIAM H.	WAS	167	1ST DIST
FIETLER, CHARLES	BAL	018	9TH WARD
FIFE, ANN	HAR	025	1ST DIST
FIFE, BARBARA	BAL	122	2ND DIST
FIFE, CHARLES	BAL	138	5TH WARD
FIFE, ELIZA	BAL	249	1ST DIST
FIFE, ELIZABETH	HAR	024	1ST DIST
FIFE, JACOB	BAL	137	5TH WARD
FIFE, ROBERT	BAL	388	8TH WARD
FIFER, CHRISTOPHER	BAL	200	11TH WAR
FIFER, DOHUT *	BAL	319	20TH WAR
FIFER, EDWARD *	BAL	144	1ST WARD
FIFER, ELIZABETH	BAL	358	13TH WAR
FIFER, GEORGE	BAL	119	11TH WAR
FIFER, JOHN	BAL	197	17TH WAR
FIFER, LOUISA	BAL	467	14TH WAR
FIFER, LOUISA	BAL	466	14TH WAR
FIFTH, SAMUEL	BAL	142	1ST WARD
FIG, JOHN	FRE	281	WOODSBOR
FIGGS, BENJAMIN	WOR	209	4TH E DI
FIGGS, GILLISS	WOR	225	4TH E DI
FIGGS, JESSE	WOR	173	6TH E DI
FIGGS, LEVIN W.	WOR	225	4TH E DI
FIGGS, THOMAS A.	WOR	212	4TH E DI
FIGGS, WILLIAM F.	DOR	400	1ST DIST
FIGHE, JAMES	BAL	418	3RD WARD
FIGHT, CHARLES	BAL	265	2ND WARD
FIGHT, MICHELL	HAR	193	3RD DIST
FIGHTS, ULA	WAS	043	2ND SUBD
FIGUS, BENJAMIN	WAS	138	2ND DIST
FIHNER, ISAAC	BAL	010	9TH WARD
FIHY, CATHARINE	BAL	001	EASTERN
FIKE, ABRAHAM	ALL	024	3RD E.D.
FIKE, ABRAHAM	ALL	024	3RD E.D.
FIKE, CHRISTIAN	ALL	023	2ND E.D.
FIKE, JACKSON	ALL	023	2ND E.D.
FIKE, JACOB B.	ALL	029	2ND E.D.
FIKE, JOHN	ALL	023	2ND E.D.
FIKE, JOHN	ALL	029	2ND E.D.
FIKE, LYDIA	ALL	042	10TH E.D
FIKE, MORRIS	ALL	103	5TH E.D.
FIKE, PETER	ALL	037	2ND E.D.
FIKEY, LEWIS*	BAL	013	4TH WARD
FILAND, LAWRANCE	ALL	056	10TH E.D
FILBERT, HANNAH	BAL	406	14TH WAR
FILCH, FREDERICK	BAL	175	2ND WARD
FILDEN, JOSEPH	CEC	004	ELKTON 3
FILE, AUGUST	BAL	275	17TH WAR
FILE, ELIZABETH	WAS	166	1ST DIST
FILED, JOHN A.	BAL	342	13TH WAR
FILENS, MARGARET	HAR	146	3RD DIST
FILERSON, CHESTER	HAR	204	3RD DIST
FILES, CHARLES	BAL	099	1ST WARD
FILES, MATILDA	BAL	102	1ST WARD
FILES, SAMUEL	CAR	404	2ND DIST
FILES, WILLIAM	BAL	099	1ST WARD
FILGHMAN, HARRIET	BAL	338	3RD WARD
FILGMAN, LYNE	BAL	339	7TH WARD
FILHEY, SAMUEL	FRE	164	EMMITTSB
FILINGER, MICHAEL	FRE	296	WOODSBOR
FILKER, HENRY	ANN	391	4TH DIST
FILKNEAR, CHRISTOPHER	BAL	270	17TH WAR
FILKNER, CATHARINE	ANN	391	4TH DIST
FILL, JOHN	BAL	096	1ST WARD
FILLASON, PERRY	KEN	280	3RD DIST
FILLEHET, D.	BAL	149	1ST WARD
FILLER, CASPER	BAL	314	1ST DIST
FILLER, DANIEL H.	FRE	412	8TH E DI
FILLER, ELIZABETH	FRE	303	WOODSBOR
FILLER, MICHAEL	BAL	312	12TH WAR
FILLER, REBECCA	FRE	304	WOODSBOR
FILLER, SOLOMON	FRE	412	8TH E DI
FILLIGAL, JOHN	BAL	283	1ST DIST
FILLIGAN, HANNAH	BAL	381	1ST DIST
FILLINGER, JOHN	BAL	171	16TH WAR
FILLINGER, JULIA	FRE	410	8TH E DI
FILLINGER, MARY	FRE	426	8TH E DI
FILLINGER, SUSAN	FRE	425	8TH E DI
FILLINGER, VICTORIA	FRE	410	8TH E DI
FILLINGSTEIN, FRANCES	HAR	193	3RD DIST
FILLINSER, ELIZABETH	FRE	420	8TH E DI
FILLIUS, THOMAS H.	BAL	309	7TH WARD
FILLMAN, BARNEY	BAL	004	4TH WARD
FILLMAN, HARRIET*	BAL	312	3RD WARD
FILLMORE, T.M.	BAL	158	1ST WARD
FILLMORE, WILLIAM H.	ANN	479	HOWARD D
FILLTER, JOHN	BAL	404	8TH WARD
FILSISCH, NICHOLAS	BAL	175	2ND WARD
FILSON, DAVID	WAS	256	1ST DIST
FILSTUES, SAMUEL	CEC	214	7TH E DI
FIN, ANN	BAL	259	1ST DIST
FIN, JAMES	BAL	291	1ST DIST
FIN, THOMAS *	BAL	258	1ST DIST
FINAFROCK, DANIEL	WAS	030	2ND SUBD
FINAMUS, ELSA *	BAL	022	18TH WAR
FINAPOCK, ROSANA	WAS	074	2ND SUBD
FINCH, JAMES	BAL	327	7TH WARD
FINCH, JOHN	BAL	005	18TH WAR
FINCH, JOHN	FRE	389	PETERSVI
FINCH, JOHN	FRE	053	FREDERIC
FINCH, MARY	BAL	327	7TH WARD
FINCH, MR. E.	BAL	352	7TH WARD
FINCH, R. F.	BAL	123	11TH WAR
FINCH, ROBERT	BAL	004	18TH WAR
FINCH, WILLIAM	BAL	004	18TH WAR
FINCHAUSEN, JOHN	BAL	063	1ST WARD
FINCHER, BENJAMIN	BAL	200	11TH WAR
FINCHI, ELIZABETH	BAL	196	6TH WARD
FINCKEL, JOHN	WAS	039	2ND SUBD
FINDA, JOHN *	BAL	088	2ND DIST
FINDEVER, JOHN	BAL	162	19TH WAR
FINDEWAULD, CATHARINE	BAL	442	14TH WAR
FINDLEY, JOHN	BAL	302	1ST DIST
FINDLEY, MARY	BAL	333	1ST DIST
FINDLY, SOPHIA V.L.	WAS	024	2ND SUBD
FINE, MARY	FRE	413	8TH E DI

FINEFROCK, PETER CAR 338 6TH DIST
FINEGAN, PATRICIUS ALL 214 CUMBERLA
FINEGAN, PATRICK ALL 102 5TH E.D.
FINEGAN, THOMAS WAS 125 HAGERSTO
FINEGAN, THOMAS ST 308 1ST E DI
FINEGAN, WINFORD BAL 370 8TH WARD
FINEHOUR, JOSEPHINE BAL 372 8TH WARD
FINELAN, MARY N. BAL 038 1ST WARD
FINELTY, MARGARET BAL 358 1ST DIST
FINEPOCK, SAMUEL WAS 058 2ND SUBD
FINES, CLEMENT F. * KEN 250 2ND DIST
FINESTY, MARY BAL 429 14TH WAR
FINETY, CELIA BAL 449 1ST DIST
FINETY, JAMES BAL 449 1ST DIST
FINETY, MARGARET BAL 449 1ST DIST
FINETY, MICHAEL BAL 449 1ST DIST
FINEY, THOMAS CEC 184 7TH E DI
FINFROCK, ELIAS WAS 198 1ST DIST
FINGER, AMELIA M. WAS 161 HAGERSTO
FINGER, DAVID F. FRE 057 FREDERIC
FINGER, SUSAN CAR 309 1ST DIST
FINHAGAN, EDWARD ST 288 2ND E DI
FINHEY, WILLIAM ALL 080 5TH E.D.
FINIGAN, CATHERINE PRI 030 VANSVILL
FINIGAN, JAMES P. PRI 031 VANSVILL
FINIX, JOSEPH WAS 055 2ND SUBD
FINK, A. BAL 118 1ST WARD
FINK, ALBERT BAL 208 19TH WAR
FINK, CONRAD BAL 369 1ST DIST
FINK, EDMUND BAL 187 6TH WARD
FINK, EMANUEL FRE 393 PETERSVI
FINK, FREDERICK BAL 416 14TH WAR
FINK, GEORGE BAL 200 2ND WARD
FINK, HENRY BAL 287 1ST DIST
FINK, JACOB BAL 247 20TH WAR
FINK, JACOB WAS 118 2ND DIST
FINK, JACOB WAS 137 2ND DIST
FINK, JAMES FRE 202 5TH E DI
FINK, JOHN FRE 395 PETERSVI
FINK, JOHN BAL 084 4TH WARD
FINK, JOHN FRE 315 MIDDLETO
FINK, JOHN WAS 118 2ND DIST
FINK, JOHN BAL 087 1ST WARD
FINK, JOHN BAL 087 1ST WARD
FINK, JOSEPH ALL 073 5TH E.D.
FINK, JOSEPH BAL 267 12TH WAR
FINK, LEAH FRE 395 PETERSVI
FINK, MARY BAL 200 19TH WAR
FINK, MARY BAL 088 1ST WARD
FINK, MARY WAS 180 BOONSBOR
FINK, MICHAEL WAS 016 2ND SUBD
FINK, NANCY FRE 326 MIDDLETO
FINK, ROSS ALL 215 CUMBERLA
FINK, SARAH FRE 393 PETERSVI
FINK, SIDNEY CAR 243 TANEYTOW
FINK, WILLIAM FRE 202 5TH E DI
FINKDYER, HENRY BAL 303 20TH WAR
FINKER, FREDERICK A. BAL 385 3RD WARD
FINKLE, CHRISTOPHER CAR 353 6TH DIST
FINKLE, SAMUEL ALL 201 CUMBERLA
FINKOUR, JOHN BAL 049 18TH WAR
FINLAY, CATHARINE BAL 060 15TH WAR
FINLAY, JANE BAL 255 6TH WARD
FINLAY, JOHN BAL 076 10TH WAR
FINLAY, MARY E. BAL 207 6TH WARD
FINLAY, THOMAS BAL 207 6TH WARD
FINLAYSON, ----* BAL 105 10TH WAR
FINLE, RICHARD BAL 167 2ND DIST
FINLEY, ALEXANDER ALL 019 2ND E.D.
FINLEY, BERNARD BAL 172 11TH WAR
FINLEY, CAROLINE BAL 093 15TH WAR
FINLEY, CATHERINE BAL 155 11TH WAR
FINLEY, CATHERINE BAL 155 11TH WAR
FINLEY, CHARLES MGM 380 ROCKERLE
FINLEY, ELIZA BAL 124 5TH WARD
FINLEY, GEORGE QUE 178 2ND E DI
FINLEY, J. BAL 319 20TH WAR
FINLEY, JACOB BAL 113 15TH WAR
FINLEY, JAMES HAR 040 1ST DIST
FINLEY, JOSEPH BAL 124 1ST WARD
FINLEY, LERY B. BAL 077 2ND DIST
FINLEY, LIDDY BAL 193 11TH WAR
FINLEY, MARGARET BAL 098 15TH WAR
FINLEY, MARY ALL 229 CUMBERLA
FINLEY, MICHAEL BAL 412 8TH WARD
FINLEY, ROSANA ALL 005 3RD E.D.
FINLEY, SALLY BAL 046 9TH WARD
FINLEY, SARAH BAL 125 11TH WAR
FINLEY, SISTER M.A. FRE 198 5TH E DI
FINLEY, TERENCE ALL 243 CUMBERLA
FINLEY, THOMAS BAL 455 8TH WARD
FINLEY, THOMAS CEC 102 4TH E DI
FINLEY, THOMAS BAL 342 13TH WAR
FINLEY, WASHINGTON QUE 178 2ND E DI
FINLY, MARGARET BAL 233 20TH WAR
FINN, DAVID BAL 202 17TH WAR
FINN, JERRY BAL 197 2ND WARD
FINN, JOHN CEC 179 7TH E DI
FINN, JOHN G. A. BAL 285 7TH.WARD
FINN, MICHAEL BAL 197 2ND WARD
FINNARYDER, JAMES WAS 022 2ND SUBD
FINNAUGH, ADAM BAL 204 2ND WARD
FINNAY, THOMAS MGM 375 ROCKERLE
FINNE, BERNARD BAL 427 8TH WARD
FINNEGAN, ANN BAL 055 9TH WARD
FINNEGAN, ANN E. BAL 251 2ND WARD
FINNEGAN, BARNEY PRI 039 VANSVILL
FINNEGAN, GEORGE CEC 067 5TH E DI
FINNEGAN, JOHN BAL 263 20TH WAR
FINNEGAN, MICHAEL HAR 085 2ND DIST
FINNEGAN, NATHANIEL ALL 213 CUMBERLA
FINNEGAN, NICHOLAS BAL 172 2ND DIST
FINNEGAN, PATRICK ALL 056 10TH E.D
FINNEGAN, WINIFRIED BAL 188 6TH WARD
FINNEHAN, BRIDGET ANN 475 HOWARD D
FINNERN, BRIDGET BAL 006 15TH WAR
FINNEY, ALVIN H. BAL 413 3RD WARD
FINNEY, ANN BAL 110 10TH WAR
FINNEY, CATHERINE BAL 110 10TH WAR
FINNEY, CATHERINE BAL 015 4TH WARD
FINNEY, CHARLES M. BAL 230 6TH WARD
FINNEY, FRANCIS BAL 019 4TH WARD
FINNEY, JAMES BAL 353 7TH WARD
FINNEY, JAMES BAL 132 1ST WARD
FINNEY, JOHN BAL 458 8TH WARD
FINNEY, JOHN BAL 098 1ST WARD
FINNEY, PAT BAL 099 5TH WARD
FINNEY, WILLIAM CEC 006 ELKTON 3
FINNEY, WILLIAM HAR 117 2ND DIST
FINNEY.JAMES FRE 207 BUCKEYST

FINNICKS, LAVINIA BAL 241 6TH WARD
FINNIGAN, HENRY BAL 103 18TH WAR
FINNIGAN, LAWRENCE BAL 178 11TH WAR
FINNIGAN, MARGARET ANN 471 HOWARD D
FINNIGAN, THOMAS PRI 039 VANSVILL
FINNIGAN, WILLIAMS BAL 383 3RD WARD
FINNIGEN, JOHN BAL 097 18TH WAR
FINNINGAN, HARRITTA BAL 103 18TH WAR
FINNINGAN, MARY BAL 055 18TH WAR
FINNINGHAN, OWEN BAL 179 11TH WAR
FINNIS, JOHN BAL 255 20TH WAR
FINNISTER, RHODA BAL 462 14TH WAR
FINNRAN, MARGARETT BAL 014 4TH WARD
FINOTTE, JOSEPH FRE 067 FREDERIC
FINOUR, ROBERT BAL 090 18TH WAR
FINSBY, JAMES-BLACK QUE 132 1ST E DI
FINSTER, JOHN CAR 171 8TH DIST
FINTON, HOWARD BAL 275 2ND WARD
FINZE, EVELINE * BAL 317 20TH WAR
FIONOUR, THOMAS * BAL 037 18TH WAR
FIOUOUR, THOMAS * BAL 037 18TH WAR
FIPPS, MARY BAL 050 15TH WAR
FIREPEAL, SIMON BAL 165 1ST WARD
FIRESTONE, FREDERICK FRE 024 FREDERIC
FIRESTONE, JOSHUA FRE 086 FREDERIC
FIREY, JOH S. * WAS 115 2ND DIST
FIRGO, REBECCA DOR 381 1ST DIST
FIRLEY, EDWARD TAL 012 EASTON D
FIRMAN, SALLY WOR 208 4TH E DI
FIRMEION, ELIZABETH BAL 275 1ST DIST
FIROIS, SUSAN CHA 261 MIDDLETO
FIRON, BENJAMIN FRE 133 CREAGERS
FIROR, DANIEL FRE 127 CREAGERS
FIROR, JACOB L. FRE 127 CREAGERS
FIROR, JOHN FRE 127 CREAGERS
FIRSDLAY, CHARLES BAL 379 13TH WAR
FIRSTER, MARY BAL 224 19TH WAR
FISCEL, HENRY BAL 317 1ST DIST
FISCHER, ADOLPH BAL 283 2ND WARD
FISCHER, ANDREW BAL 284 2ND WARD
FISCHER, CAROLINE BAL 114 15TH WAR
FISCHER, DOROTHA-BLACK FRE 241 NEW MARK
FISCHER, GEORGE J. FRE 017 FREDERIC
FISCHER, HENRY BAL 010 15TH WAR
FISCHER, J. BAL 158 1ST WARD
FISCHER, JOHN D. WAS 171 FUNKSTOW
FISCHER, JOSEPH BAL 194 6TH WARD
FISCHER, MARIA-MULATTO FRE 239 NEW MARK
FISCHER, SOPHIA BAL 073 1ST WARD
FISCHER, WILLIAM BAL 132 16TH WAR
FISCO, EDWARD BAL 167 1ST WARD
FISEHAUCH, ELIZA WAS 263 1ST DIST
FISENER, HENRY BAL 355 1ST DIST
FISH, A. BAL 135 1ST WARD
FISH, ALLEN BAL 139 1ST WARD
FISH, ALLEN BAL 126 1ST WARD
FISH, ANN BAL 320 3RD WARD
FISH, ANN M. BAL 385 3RD WARD
FISH, GEORGE W. BAL 320 3RD WARD
FISH, MARTHA A. BAL 279 7TH WARD
FISH, MARY WOR 229 6TH E DI
FISH, MARY MGM 340 CLARKSBU
FISH, MARY E. WAS 185 BOONSBOR
FISH, REBECCA BAL 390 1ST DIST
FISH, ROBERT WAS 185 BOONSBOR
FISH, ROBERT TAL 014 EASTON D
FISH, ROBERT MGM 333 CRACKLIN
FISH, SARAH BAL 303 7TH WARD
FISH, WILLIAM WAS 184 BOONSBOR
FISHACK, CATHARINE BAL 410 14TH WAR
FISHACK, WILLIAM ANN 348 3RD DIST
FISHAUCH, GEORGE WAS 258 1ST DIST
FISHAUCH, HENRY WAS 258 1ST DIST
FISHAUCH, JOHN WAS 270 1ST DIST
FISHAUCH, LYDIA WAS 249 1ST DIST
FISHAUCH, POLLY WAS 258 1ST DIST
FISHAUCK, GEORGE R. WAS 258 1ST DIST
FISHBARGH, HENRY BAL 284 12TH WAR
FISHBAUCK, HARMAN FRE 015 FREDERIC
FISHBAUGH, ANN BAL 208 11TH WAR
FISHBECK, CAROLINE BAL 110 10TH WAR
FISHCER, CHARLES BAL 172 1ST WARD
FISHCER, ELLEN-MULATTO FRE 242 NEW MARK
FISHE,R MATILDA WOR 276 BERLIN 1
FISHER, A. BAL 147 1ST WARD
FISHER, ABRAM BAL 163 19TH WAR
FISHER, ADAM CAR 067 NO TWP L
FISHER, ADAM BAL 289 1ST DIST
FISHER, ADAM BAL 218 12TH WAR
FISHER, ADAM-BLACK QUE 172 2ND E DI
FISHER, AEBASTIAN BAL 111 2ND DIST
FISHER, ALEXANDER BAL 101 10TH WAR
FISHER, ALLY A.B. QUE 191 3RD E DI
FISHER, ALMIRA CAL 044 3RD DIST
FISHER, ALMIRA BAL 311 20TH WAR
FISHER, AMIEL BAL 012 9TH WARD
FISHER, AMY C. MGM 387 ROCKERLE
FISHER, ANDREW CEC 193 5TH E DI
FISHER, ANDREW CEC 197 7TH E DI
FISHER, ANDREW BAL 104 2ND DIST
FISHER, ANDREW ALL 037 2ND E.D.
FISHER, ANDREW PRI 094 SPALDING
FISHER, ANN BAL 461 1ST DIST
FISHER, ANN E. BAL 381 8TH WARD
FISHER, ANN E. BAL 252 17TH WAR
FISHER, ANN M. MGM 385 ROCKERLE
FISHER, ANN M. ALL 230 CUMBERLA
FISHER, ANN-BLACK BAL 224 2ND WARD
FISHER, ANNA ANN 398 8TH DIST
FISHER, ANTHONY W. HAR 062 1ST DIST
FISHER, AQUILA MGM 396 ROCKERLE
FISHER, AUGUSTUS FRE 20 5TH E DI
FISHER, AUGUSTUS BAL 109 1ST WARD
FISHER, AUGUSTUS BAL 155 2ND DIST
FISHER, BARBARY BAL 075 18TH WAR
FISHER, BARNARD BAL 287 1ST DIST
FISHER, BARNEY FRE 026 FREDERIC
FISHER, BENJAMIN BAL 301 7TH WARD
FISHER, BETSEY DOR 457 1ST DIST
FISHER, CAROLINE BAL 374 3RD WARD
FISHER, CAROLINE BAL 438 8TH WARD
FISHER, CAROLINE BAL 376 13TH WAR
FISHER, CASANDREW CAR 403 2ND DIST
FISHER, CASPAR BAL 150 2ND DIST
FISHER, CASPER BAL 216 2ND WARD
FISHER, CASSANDRA BAL 299 1ST DIST
FISHER, CATHARINE BAL 283 12TH WAR
FISHER, CATHARINE FRE 337 MIDDLETO
FISHER, CATHERINE FRE 100 FREDERIC
FISHER, CATHERINE FRE 084 FREDERIC

FISHER, CATHERINE FRE 060 FREDERIC
FISHER, CELIA A. MGM 418 MEDLEY 3
FISHER, CHARLES MGM 324 CRACKLIN
FISHER, CHARLES BAL 105 1ST WARD
FISHER, CHARLES BAL 154 1ST WARD
FISHER, CHARLES BAL 167 1ST WARD
FISHER, CHARLES BAL 451 8TH WARD
FISHER, CHARLES BAL 257 5TH WARD
FISHER, CHARLES ALL 169 6TH E.D.
FISHER, CHARLES F. ANN 266 ANNAPOLI
FISHER, CHARLES F. TAL 020 EASTON D
FISHER, CHARLES D. BAL 269 1ST DIST
FISHER, CHARLES-BLACK BAL 224 2ND WARD
FISHER, CHARLES-BLACK FRE 434 8TH E DI
FISHER, CHRISTIAN BAL 396 1ST DIST
FISHER, CONRADDL BAL 146 2ND DIST
FISHER, DANIEL BAL 401 14TH WAR
FISHER, DAPNY CAR 067 NO TWP L
FISHER, DAVID FRE 140 CREAGERS
FISHER, DENWOOD CAR 093 NO TWP L
FISHER, DICK BAL 202 17TH WAR
FISHER, DINIST HAR 202 3RD DIST
FISHER, EDWARD HAR 067 1ST DIST
FISHER, EDWARD ANN 415 HOWARD D
FISHER, ELETT BAL 111 2ND DIST
FISHER, ELIAAS FRE 077 FREDERIC
FISHER, ELISABETH ALL 261 CUMBERLA
FISHER, ELISABETH ANN 382 4TH DIST
FISHER, ELIZA MGM 413 MEDLEY 3
FISHER, ELIZABETH FRE 036 FREDERIC
FISHER, ELIZABETH CAR 199 4TH DIST
FISHER, ELIZABETH ANN 505 HOWARD D
FISHER, ELIZABETH SOM 487 SALISBUR
FISHER, ELIZABETH DOR 449 1ST DIST
FISHER, ELLEN ALL 162 6TH E.D.
FISHER, ELLEN ALL 162 6TH E.D.
FISHER, ELLEN BAL 245 5TH WARD
FISHER, EMANUEL CAR 338 6TH DIST
FISHER, EMILY FRE 095 FREDERIC
FISHER, EMILY BAL 374 3RD WARD
FISHER, ERNEST BAL 032 9TH WARD
FISHER, EVERARD G. MGM 385 ROCKERLE
FISHER, F. BAL 225 19TH WAR
FISHER, F. BAL 080 10TH WAR
FISHER, F. A. BAL 469 14TH WAR
FISHER, FRANCES A. BAL 231 6TH WARD
FISHER, FRANCIS ANN 443 HOWARD D
FISHER, FRANCIS BAL 147 11TH WAR
FISHER, FRANCIS E. ANN 289 ANNAPOLI
FISHER, FRANCIS M. BAL 006 9TH WARD
FISHER, FRANKLIN CAR 250 3RD DIST
FISHER, FREDERICK BAL 278 17TH WAR
FISHER, FREDERICK TAL 043 EASTON D
FISHER, G. BAL 148 1ST WARD
FISHER, G.W. BAL 206 11TH WAR
FISHER, GAINES FRE 174 5TH E DI
FISHER, GEORGE BAL 443 14TH WAR
FISHER, GEORGE BAL 135 11TH WAR
FISHER, GEORGE BAL 122 11TH WAR
FISHER, GEORGE BAL 061 4TH WARD
FISHER, GEORGE FRE 216 BUCKEYST
FISHER, GEORGE BAL 022 15TH WAR
FISHER, GEORGE BAL 218 12TH WAR
FISHER, GEORGE ANN 430 HOWARD D
FISHER, GEORGE WAS 171 FUNKSTOW
FISHER, GEORGE WAS 151 2ND DIST
FISHER, GEORGE W. BAL 089 15TH WAR
FISHER, GEORGE W. BAL 221 1ST DIST
FISHER, GEORGIANA BAL 214 11TH WAR
FISHER, GERDGE HAR 035 1ST DIST
FISHER, GOERG EW. BAL 147 19TH WAR
FISHER, GOERGE CAR 165 NO TWP L
FISHER, GOERGE F. BAL 427 1ST DIST
FISHER, GOFRIED BAL 293 3RD WARD
FISHER, HANNAH BAL 353 3RD WARD
FISHER, HANNAH ALL 079 5TH E.D.
FISHER, HANNAH CEC 184 7TH E DI
FISHER, HANNAH BAL 030 18TH WAR
FISHER, HENRIETTA BAL 381 13TH WAR
FISHER, HENRIETTA BAL 362 3RD WARD
FISHER, HENRIETTA-BLACK FRE 042 FREDERIC
FISHER, HENRY FRE 060 FREDERIC
FISHER, HENRY CAR 364 9TH DIST
FISHER, HENRY BAL 322 1ST DIST
FISHER, HENRY BAL 300 7TH WARD
FISHER, HERNY FRE 369 CATOCTIN
FISHER, HESTER BAL 329 3RD WARD
FISHER, HESTER A. BAL 373 3RD WARD
FISHER, HESTER-BLACK WOR 347 1ST E DI
FISHER, HIRAM BAL 157 2ND DIST
FISHER, HORACE F. BAL 090 18TH WAR
FISHER, HUGH CAR 368 9TH DIST
FISHER, HY BAL 212 6TH DIST
FISHER, ISAAC ANN 419 HOWARD D
FISHER, ISAAC BAL 086 2ND DIST
FISHER, ISAAC FRE 170 5TH E DI
FISHER, ISAIH DOR 466 1ST DIST
FISHER, J. BAL 117 1ST WARD
FISHER, JACOB BAL 368 3RD WARD
FISHER, JACOB WAS 138 HAGERSTO
FISHER, JACOB KEN 236 2ND DIST
FISHER, JACOB CEC 207 7TH E DI
FISHER, JAMES CEC 128 5TH E DI
FISHER, JAMES QUE 190 3RD E DI
FISHER, JAMES ANN 423 HOWARD D
FISHER, JAMES ALL 163 6TH E.D.
FISHER, JAMES A. TAL 035 EASTON D
FISHER, JAMES B. BAL 019 15TH WAR
FISHER, JAMES J. BAL 103 10TH WAR
FISHER, JAMES P. CAR 363 9TH DIST
FISHER, JANE BAL 179 16TH WAR
FISHER, JANE* DOR 310 1ST DIST
FISHER, JADR WOR 327 1ST E DI
FISHER, JEFFERSCN WAS 152 2ND DIST
FISHER, JEREMIAH BAL 438 14TH WAR
FISHER, JERRY ANN 428 HOWARD D
FISHER, JESSE QUE 151 1ST E DI
FISHER, JOHN BAL 218 17TH WAR
FISHER, JOHN CEC 137 6TH E DI
FISHER, JOHN BAL 409 14TH WAR
FISHER, JOHN CEC 157 PORT DUP
FISHER, JOHN CEC 157 PORT DUP
FISHER, JOHN CEC 184 7TH E DI
FISHER, JOHN CAR 271 WESTMINS
FISHER, JOHN HAR 060 1ST DIST
FISHER, JOHN MGM 371 BERRYS D
FISHER, JOHN FRE 335 MIDDLETO
FISHER, JOHN BAL 109 18TH WAR
FISHER, JOHN ANN 420 HOWARD D
FISHER, JOHN BAL 088 2ND DIST

FISHER, JOHN ALL 222 CUMBERLA
FISHER, JOHN ALL 225 CUMBERLA
FISHER, JOHN BAL 364 8TH WARD
FISHER, JOHN BAL 281 1ST DIST
FISHER, JOHN BAL 037 1ST WARD
FISHER, JOHN ANN 505 HOWARD D
FISHER, JOHN BAL 022 9TH WARD
FISHER, JOHN TAL 016 EASTON D
FISHER, JOHN WOR 274 BERLIN 1
FISHER, JOHN WAS 038 2ND SUBD
FISHER, JOHN WAS 245 SMITHSBU
FISHER, JOHN A. BAL 241 6TH WARD
FISHER, JOHN A. FRE 101 FREDERIC
FISHER, JOHN B. BAL 258 1ST DIST
FISHER, JOHN H. SOM 435 PRINCESS
FISHER, JOHN H. BAL 205 11TH WAR
FISHER, JOHN J. BAL 388 1ST DIST
FISHER, JOHN-BLACK WOR 327 1ST E DI
FISHER, JOHN-MULATTO BAL 218 2ND WARD
FISHER, JOSEPH BAL 118 1ST WARD
FISHER, JOSEPH BAL 163 2ND DIST
FISHER, JOSEPH BAL 022 15TH WAR
FISHER, JOSEPH ALL 079 5TH E.D.
FISHER, JOSEPH CAR 321 1ST DIST
FISHER, JOSEPH R. MGM 416 MEDLEY 3
FISHER, JOSIAH BAL 368 3RD WARD
FISHER, JULIETTA BAL 374 13TH WAR
FISHER, LARKIN ANN 513 HOWARD D
FISHER, LAVINA CAR 286 7TH DIST
FISHER, LEMULE W. ANN 505 HOWARD D
FISHER, LEVEM T. DOCTOR DOR 337 3RD DIVI
FISHER, LEWIS FRE 026 FREDERIC
FISHER, LEWIS BAL 041 4TH WARD
FISHER, LEWIS FRE 317 MIDDLETO
FISHER, LEWIS ANN 290 ANNAPOLI
FISHER, LEWIS ALL 127 4TH E.D.
FISHER, LEWIS BAL 085 1ST WARD
FISHER, LOUISA ANN 290 ANNAPOLI
FISHER, M.J.M. BAL 197 19TH WAR
FISHER, MADISON HAR 015 1ST DIST
FISHER, MACISON FRE 190 5TH E DI
FISHER, MARGARET CEC 006 ELKTON 3
FISHER, MARGARET BAL 256 20TH WAR
FISHER, MARGARET BAL 399 1ST DIST
FISHER, MARGARET A. BAL 118 15TH WAR
FISHER, MARGARET M. BAL 213 19TH WAR
FISHER, MARIA FRE 043 FREDERIC
FISHER, MARIA BAL 118 11TH WAR
FISHER, MARIA BAL 151 11TH WAR
FISHER, MARIA PRI 024 VANSVILL
FISHER, MARTHA BAL 299 1ST DIST
FISHER, MARTHA BAL 039 15TH WAR
FISHER, MARY BAL 028 15TH WAR
FISHER, MARY BAL 269 1ST DIST
FISHER, MARY BAL 299 1ST DIST
FISHER, MARY BAL 298 12TH WAR
FISHER, MARY BAL 344 3RD WARD
FISHER, MARY BAL 192 6TH WARD
FISHER, MARY BAL 034 9TH WARD
FISHER, MARY ALL 218 CUMBERLA
FISHER, MARY QUE 169 2ND E DI
FISHER, MARY SOM 422 PRINCESS
FISHER, MARY CEC 203 6TH E DI
FISHER, MARY FRE 336 MIDDLETO
FISHER, MARY DOR 428 1ST DIST
FISHER, MARY BAL 059 18TH WAR
FISHER, MARY A. CAL 055 3RD DIST
FISHER, MARY E. FRE 415 8TH E DI
FISHER, MARY E. FRE 161 EMMITTSB
FISHER, MARY J. BAL 020 15TH WAR
FISHER, MATHIAS BAL 360 1ST DIST
FISHER, MATILDA BAL 247 12TH WAR
FISHER, NANCY CAR 313 1ST DIST
FISHER, NANCY SOM 465 HANGARY
FISHER, NANCY SOM 485 TRAPP DI
FISHER, NANCY-BLACK QUE 183 3RD E DI
FISHER, NATHAN FRE 266 NEW MARK
FISHER, NATHANIEL FRE 185 5TH E DI
FISHER, NORA ALL 256 CUMBERLA
FISHER, PETER BAL 433 8TH WARD
FISHER, PHILIP WAS 160 HAGERSTO
FISHER, PRICELLA SOM 425 PRINCESS
FISHER, RACHEL A. BAL 156 16TH WAR
FISHER, RICHARD BAL 053 2ND DIST
FISHER, ROBERT CEC 184 7TH E DI
FISHER, ROBERT PRI 108 PISCATAW
FISHER, ROBERT J. FRE 055 FREDERIC
FISHER, RYE ANN 430 HOWARD D
FISHER, SALLY ANN 289 ANNAPOLI
FISHER, SAMUEL BAL 399 1ST DIST
FISHER, SAMUEL BAL 231 1ST DIST
FISHER, SAMUEL DOR 300 1ST DIST
FISHER, SAMUEL QUE 168 2ND E DI
FISHER, SAMUEL G KEN 237 2ND DIST
FISHER, SAMUEL T. CEC 188 7TH E DI
FISHER, SAMUEL W. MGM 387 ROCKERLE
FISHER, SARAH SOM 414 DUBLIN D
FISHER, SARAH BAL 141 11TH WAR
FISHER, SARAH ANN 504 HOWARD D
FISHER, SARAH BAL 205 6TH DIST
FISHER, SARAH ANN BAL 252 17TH WAR
FISHER, SETH CAR 388 2ND DIST
FISHER, SHERMIGER KEN 257 1ST DIST
FISHER, SIMON BAL 302 20TH WAR
FISHER, STEPHEN WOR 279 BERLIN 1
FISHER, STEPHEN ANN 375 4TH DIST
FISHER, STEPHEN SR. WOR 279 BERLIN 1
FISHER, SUSAN WAS 025 2ND SUBD
FISHER, SUSAN KEN 270 1ST DIST
FISHER, SUSNA CAL 052 3RD DIST
FISHER, TEMPERANCE BAL 145 2ND DIST
FISHER, THOMAS ANN 275 ANNAPOLI
FISHER, THOMAS BAL 351 1ST DIST
FISHER, THOMAS BAL 035 9TH WARD
FISHER, THOMAS DOR 316 1ST DIST
FISHER, THOMAS DOR 315 1ST DIST
FISHER, THOMAS CEC 187 7TH E DI
FISHER, THOMAS CEC 160 6TH E DI
FISHER, THOMAS BAL 432 14TH WAR
FISHER, THOMAS FRE 113 CREAGERS
FISHER, THOMAS CAR 171 8TH DIST
FISHER, THOMAS WAS 059 2ND SUBD
FISHER, WILHELMINA BAL 012 9TH WARD
FISHER, WILLAIM BAL 154 2ND DIST
FISHER, WILLIAM BAL 043 15TH WAR
FISHER, WILLIAM BAL 351 1ST DIST
FISHER, WILLIAM ANN 489 HOWARD D
FISHER, WILLIAM ANN 398 8TH DIST
FISHER, WILLIAM ANN 311 1ST DIST
FISHER, WILLIAM ALL 253 CUMBERLA

FISHER, WILLIAM BAL 056 10TH WAR
FISHER, WILLIAM WOR 279 BERLIN 1
FISHER, WILLIAM TAL 042 EASTON D
FISHER, WILLIAM FRE 128 CREAGERS
FISHER, WILLIAM BAL 260 17TH WAR
FISHER, WILLIAM CAR 372 9TH DIST
FISHER, WILLIAM CAR 243 TANEYTOW
FISHER, WILLIAM BAL 303 20TH WAR
FISHER, WILLIAM BAL 288 20TH WAR
FISHER, WILLIAM BAL 306 20TH WAR
FISHER, WILLIAM FRE 252 NEW MARK
FISHER, WILLIAM F. BAL 209 19TH WAR
FISHER, WILLIAM H. SOM 424 PRINCESS
FISHER, WILLIAM H. BAL 234 12TH WAR
FISHER, WILLIAM H. L. MGM 387 ROCKERLE
FISHER, WILLIAM J. BAL 414 1ST DIST
FISHER, WILLIAM T. MGM 387 ROCKERLE
FISHER, WILLIAM-BLACK BAL 224 2ND WARD
FISHER, WILLIAM-BLACK WOR 342 1ST E DI
FISHER, ZOTT FRE 305 WOODSBOR
FISHER,ELIZABETH CAR 409 2ND DIST
FISHER,ELIZABETH BAL 283 12TH WAR
FISHER.SUSNA FRE 217 BUCKEYST
FISHER.WILLIAM MGM 415 MEDLEY 3
FISHER.WILLIAM BAL 067 2ND DIST
FISHMAN, FREDERICKA BAL 464 14TH WAR
FISHPAUGH, THOAMS BAL 326 1ST DIST
FISHPAW, AQUILLA BAL 326 1ST DIST
FISHPAW, ASBURY BAL 371 1ST DIST
FISHPAW, CALIB BAL 396 1ST DIST
FISHPAW, ELIJAH BAL 179 2ND DIST
FISHPAW, JAMES BAL 408 1ST DIST
FISHPAW, JOSEPH BAL 416 1ST DIST
FISHPAW, LOUIS BAL 297 1ST DIST
FISHPAW, MARGARET BAL 355 1ST DIST
FISHPAW, MARY A. BAL 397 1ST DIST
FISHPAW, RICHARD BAL 330 1ST DIST
FISK, CHARLE SB. ALL 215 CUMBERLA
FISK, GEORGE A. BAL 291 17TH WAR
FISK, JAMES BAL 053 9TH WARD
FISK, JOSEPH BAL 300 17TH WAR
FISK, LEANDER ALL 208 CUMBERLA
FISK, ROBERT WAS 185 BOONSBOR
FISK, WILBUR CEC 145 PORT DUP
FISLAGE, GEORGE BAL 181 16TH WAR
FISLER, D. JACOB D. CEC 094 4TH E DI
FISTER, ANREAS BAL 161 16TH WAR
FISTER, JACOB MGM 431 CLARKSTR
FISTUR, JANE* DOR 310 1ST DIST
FITALLS, BENJAMIN BAL 218 2ND WARD
FITCH, ANN BAL 369 13TH WAR
FITCH, DORCAS BAL 208 6TH WARD
FITCH, ELIZABETH BAL 329 3RD WARD
FITCH, EMMA BAL 174 2ND DIST
FITCH, GABRIEL MGM 423 MEDLEY 3
FITCH, HANNAH BAL 234 6TH WARD
FITCH, HENRY L. BAL 173 2ND DIST
FITCH, J. BAL 156 1ST WARD
FITCH, JAMES BAL 175 2ND DIST
FITCH, JAMES MGM 415 MEDLEY 3
FITCH, JAMES FRE 230 BUCKEYST
FITCH, JANE BAL 369 13TH WAR
FITCH, JOHN FRE 258 NEW MARK
FITCH, JOHN BAL 158 2ND DIST
FITCH, JOHN BAL 108 2ND DIST
FITCH, JOHN BAL 274 12TH WAR
FITCH, JOHN W. BAL 021 1ST WARD
FITCH, L. BAL 228 19TH WAR
FITCH, MARY CHA 231 HILLTOP
FITCH, MARY BAL 113 2ND DIST
FITCH, MORTIMER FRE 419 8TH E DI
FITCH, ROBERT BAL 068 2ND DIST
FITCH, SMAUEL BAL 129 1ST WARD
FITCHCKER, JOHN CEC 061 1ST E DI
FITCHELL, MARY WOR 271 BERLIN 1
FITCHPATRICK, THIMOTHY BAL 408 1ST DIST
FITE, C. R. BAL 140 11TH WAR
FITE, HENRY BAL 277 1ST DIST
FITE, JACOB FRE 049 FREDERIC
FITE, JOHN M. CAR 219 5TH DIST
FITE, MARTIN BAL 274 7TH WARD
FITE, SARAH BAL 463 1ST DIST
FITE, WILLIAM BAL 328 1ST DIST
FITES, ANDREW FRE 180 5TH E DI
FITES, GEORGE CAR 296 7TH DIST
FITES, SAVILIA CAR 175 8TH DIST
FITES, THOMAS FRE 179 5TH E DI
FITES.EDWARD FRE 179 5TH E DI
FITESHEW, CATHERINE FRE 007 FREDERIC
FITEZ, DAVID FRE 289 WOODSBOR
FITEZ, HENRY FRE 290 WOODSBOR
FITGERALD, HENRY BAL 102 18TH WAR
FITHEN, ------- * BAL 369 8TH WARD
FITLAS, MARY C. BAL 058 1ST WARD
FITMAN, JAMES WOR 329 1ST E DI
FITSGERRALD, MARGARETT BAL 065 18TH WAR
FITSIMMCNS, JOHANNES BAL 469 14TH WAR
FITSIMMCNS, PETER BAL 103 2ND DIST
FITSIMON, PHILIP HAR 061 1ST DIST
FITSPATRICK, DANIEL BAL 289 1ST DIST
FITSPATRICK, JOHN BAL 462 1ST DIST
FITSPATRICK, MARY BAL 363 8TH WARD
FITSPATRICK, MORRIS BAL 173 2ND DIST
FITTERBUG, JACOB FRE 433 8TH E DI
FITTERLING, RASS FRE 426 8TH E DI
FITTS, BENJAMIN * KEN 219 2ND DIST
FITZ PATRICK, DENNIS BAL 195 2ND WARD
FITZ, DAVID WAS 074 2ND SUBD
FITZ, JOHN BAL 150 11TH WAR
FITZ, RUDOLPH BAL 007 EASTERN
FITZ, SALLY BAL 257 1ST DIST
FITZBERGER, HENRY BAL 162 19TH WAR
FITZER, EDWARD BAL 004 15TH WAR
FITZGARALD, ELLEN BAL 343 7TH WARD
FITZGARALD, GUSTAVUS BAL 451 1ST DIST
FITZGARALD, HENRY BAL 342 1ST DIST
FITZGARALD, HENRY BAL 341 1ST DIST
FITZGARLAND, JOHN BAL 458 1ST DIST
FITZGERALD, ANN SOM 473 TRAPPE D
FITZGERALD, BRIDGET BAL 059 18TH WAR
FITZGERALD, CHARLES BAL 046 9TH WARD
FITZGERALD, CHARLES G. BAL 324 12TH WAR
FITZGERALD, CHRISTOPHER BAL 159 11TH WAR
FITZGERALD, DANIEL BAL 183 16TH WAR
FITZGERALD, DAVID BAL 208 11TH WAR
FITZGERALD, EDWARD F. FRE 423 8TH E DI
FITZGERALD, ELIZA BAL 187 2ND WARD
FITZGERALD, ELIZA J. BAL 354 7TH WARD
FITZGERALD, ELIZABETH G. BAL 175 16TH WAR
FITZGERALD, FLORENCE BAL 149 5TH WARD

FITZGERALD, GARRET BAL 186 16TH WAR
FITZGERALD, GEORGE BAL 119 1ST WARD
FITZGERALD, GEORGE BAL 283 17TH WAR
FITZGERALD, HENRY BAL 179 19TH WAR
FITZGERALD, J. BAL 147 1ST WARD
FITZGERALD, J. BAL 147 1ST WARD
FITZGERALD, J.K. BAL 249 12TH WAR
FITZGERALD, JAMES BAL 009 18TH WAR
FITZGERALD, JANE BAL 376 3RD WARD
FITZGERALD, JESSE SOM 418 PRINCESS
FITZGERALD, JOHN BAL 129 1ST WARD
FITZGERALD, JOHN BAL 186 16TH WAR
FITZGERALD, JOHN BAL 026 2ND DIST
FITZGERALD, M. BAL 173 1ST WARD
FITZGERALD, M. BAL 199 19TH WAR
FITZGERALD, MARGARET BAL 273 12TH WAR
FITZGERALD, MARIA BAL 352 7TH WARD
FITZGERALD, MICHAEL BAL 049 2ND DIST
FITZGERALD, MICHAEL BAL 086 2ND DIST
FITZGERALD, MICHAEL BAL 093 18TH WAR
FITZGERALD, MICHEAL BAL 060 18TH WAR
FITZGERALD, P. BAL 149 1ST WARD
FITZGERALD, PATRICK BAL 182 11TH WAR
FITZGERALD, R.B. BAL 236 12TH WAR
FITZGERALD, RICHARD BAL 158 1ST WARD
FITZGERALD, RICHARD BAL 144 1ST WARD
FITZGERALD, ROBERT SOM 473 TRAPPE D
FITZGERALD, SARAH HAR 095 2ND DIST
FITZGERALD, SISTER LEOCAD FRE 197 5TH E DI
FITZGERALD, THOMAS FRE 202 5TH E DI
FITZGERALD, WILLIAM BAL 065 4TH WARD
FITZGERALD.MARIE BAL 234 12TH WAR
FITZGERLAD, WILLIAM BAL 338 13TH WAR
FITZGERLAD, WILLIAM BAL 471 14TH WAR
FITZGERRALD, JAMES BAL 278 17TH WAR
FITZGRANDY, ELIZA CEC 020 ELKTON 3
FITZHET, WILLIAM A. BAL 306 3RD WARD
FITZHUGH, BENJAMIN FRE 141 CREAGERS
FITZHUGH, DANIEL BAL 103 10TH WAR
FITZHUGH, HARRY M. BAL 019 2ND DIST
FITZHUGH, MARY BAL 086 2ND DIST
FITZHUGH, MARY BAL 087 2ND DIST
FITZHUGH, PERRIGRINE FRE 124 CREAGERS
FITZHUGH, THOMAS BAL 085 15TH WAR
FITZHUGH, WILLIAM H. WAS 241 CAVETOWN
FITZIMMON, MICHAEL BAL 459 14TH WAR
FITZIMMONS, NICHOLAS FRE 227 BUCKEYST
FITZIMMOSN, MICHAEL BAL 469 14TH WAR
FITZIMMSON, JAMES BAL 279 2ND WARD
FITZJANAL, CHARLES C.* TAL 017 EASTON D
FITZJAREL, JOHN TAL 023 EASTON D
FITZJARELL, BERTON TAL 007 EASTON D
FITZJARELL, JAMES* TAL 007 EASTON D
FITZJORDAN, BRIGET BAL 090 5TH WARD
FITZMAN, CHARLES BAL 150 11TH WAR
FITZMAURICE, ELLEN BAL 034 9TH WARD
FITZMILLER, HANSON ALL 052 10TH E.D
FITZMORRIS, BRIDGET BAL 418 3RD WARD
FITZMORRIS, CECELIA BAL 381 13TH WAR
FITZMORRIS, CELIA BAL 429 14TH WAR
FITZMORRIS, LUKE ALL 136 4TH E.D.
FITZMORRIS, MARIA BAL 213 11TH WAR
FITZMORRIS, MARY BAL 447 14TH WAR
FITZOSBOURM, HENRY BAL 145 1ST WARD
FITZPARTICK, JOHANNA* BAL 028 4TH WARD
FITZPATRICK, ANN BAL 038 15TH WAR
FITZPATRICK, BRIDGET BAL 153 11TH WAR
FITZPATRICK, BRIDGET BAL 153 11TH WAR
FITZPATRICK, CAROLINE BAL 171 11TH WAR
FITZPATRICK, CECILIA BAL 043 15TH WAR
FITZPATRICK, CHARLES BAL 145 19TH WAR
FITZPATRICK, CORNELIUS FRE 20 5TH E DI
FITZPATRICK, DANIEL BAL 027 4TH WARD
FITZPATRICK, DANIEL BAL 127 5TH WARD
FITZPATRICK, ELIZABETH BAL 042 15TH WAR
FITZPATRICK, ELIZABETH BAL 379 13TH WAR
FITZPATRICK, ELLEN BAL 051 15TH WAR
FITZPATRICK, EMILY BAL 213 11TH WAR
FITZPATRICK, HENRY BAL 402 14TH WAR
FITZPATRICK, HUGH BAL 267 17TH WAR
FITZPATRICK, HUGH ALL 226 CUMBERLA
FITZPATRICK, HUGH WAS 034 2ND SUBD
FITZPATRICK, JAMES BAL 202 11TH WAR
FITZPATRICK, JAMES BAL 105 18TH WAR
FITZPATRICK, JANE BAL 385 13TH WAR
FITZPATRICK, JERRY BAL 145 19TH WAR
FITZPATRICK, JOHANNA* BAL 028 4TH WARD
FITZPATRICK, JOHN BAL 256 17TH WAR
FITZPATRICK, JOHN BAL 273 17TH WAR
FITZPATRICK, JOHN BAL 034 2ND DIST
FITZPATRICK, JOHN ALL 204 CUMBERLA
FITZPATRICK, JOHN M. BAL 019 9TH WARD
FITZPATRICK, JOHN* BAL 039 2ND DIST
FITZPATRICK, M. BAL 155 11TH WAR
FITZPATRICK, MARGARET BAL 468 14TH WAR
FITZPATRICK, MARGARETT BAL 038 18TH WAR
FITZPATRICK, MARY BAL 066 4TH WARD
FITZPATRICK, MARY BAL 215 11TH WAR
FITZPATRICK, MARY ANN 412 HOWARD D
FITZPATRICK, MARY BAL 055 15TH WAR
FITZPATRICK, MARY E. BAL 019 9TH WARD
FITZPATRICK, PATRICK BAL 027 4TH WARD
FITZPATRICK, PATRICK* BAL 414 3RD WARD
FITZPATRICK, REBECCA WAS 133 HAGERSTO
FITZPATRICK, RICHAD BAL 116 1ST WARD
FITZPATRICK, SISTER M.L. FRE 198 5TH E DI
FITZPATRICK, SUSAN CEC 097 4TH E DI
FITZPATRICK, THOMAS BAL 231 19TH WAR
FITZPATRICK, THOMAS BAL 042 4TH WARD
FITZPATRICK, THOMAS BAL 145 19TH WAR
FITZPATRICK, THOMAS BAL 012 15TH WAR
FITZPATRICK, WILLIAM BAL 422 14TH WAR
FITZPATRICK, WILLIAM BAL 291 17TH WAR
FITZPATRICK.MARY BAL 018 2ND DIST
FITZSIMMON, PATRICK BAL 084 2ND DIST
FITZSIMMONDS, C. BAL 085 18TH WAR
FITZSIMMONS, DANIEL BAL 289 12TH WAR
FITZSIMMONS, EDMUND BAL 175 19TH WAR
FITZSIMMONS, HUGH BAL 022 9TH WARD
FITZSIMONS, AMELIA J. BAL 450 1ST DIST
FITZTGERALD, MARY BAL 286 12TH WAR
FITZWATERS, SILAS ALL 046 10TH E.D
FITZWATES,NELSON ALL 046 10TH E.D
FITZZGERALD, E. FRE 200 5TH E DI
FIX, ANDREW BAL 349 13TH WAR
FIX, ZADOK WOR 274 BERLIN 1
FLABAN, THOMAS BAL 421 1ST DIST
FLABER, ANDREW WAS 169 FUNKSTOW
FLACK, FRANCIS MGM 394 ROCKERLE
FLACK, GEORGE W. BAL 162 6TH WARD

Name	County	Page	District
FLACK, GEORGE W.	BAL	162	6TH WARD
FLACK, JACOB	BAL	066	15TH WAR
FLACK, MATILDA	BAL	239	20TH WAR
FLACK, RACHEL	BAL	461	14TH WAR
FLACK, THOMAS J.	BAL	056	15TH WAR
FLADDEN, JESSE	TAL	096	ST MICHA
FLADEN, PHILIP	BAL	339	7TH WARD
FLADRING, MARTIN	BAL	301	7TH WARD
FLAGERS, FREDERICK	BAL	246	2ND WARD
FLAGERTY, CORNELIUS	BAL	399	1ST DIST
FLAGESTINE, JOHN	BAL	267	2ND WARD
FLAGG, SISTER A.	FRE	198	5TH E DI
FLAGG, WILLIAM C.	BAL	443	14TH WAR
FLAGHERTY, ELIZABETH	BAL	215	11TH WAR
FLAGHERTY, MARIA	BAL	215	11TH WAR
FLAHAN, JERENIA	HAR	160	3RD DIST
FLAHART, SARAH J.	HAR	013	1ST DIST
FLAHART, WILLIAM	HAR	045	1ST DIST
FLAHARTES, JOSHUA	FRE	125	CREAGERS
FLAHARTY, ALICE	DOR	423	1ST DIST
FLAHARTY, JAEMS E.	FRE	132	CREAGERS
FLAHARTY, JAMES	FRE	131	CREAGERS
FLAHARTY, JOHN	FRE	122	CREAGERS
FLAHARTY, JOSHUA	FRE	090	FREDERIC
FLAHARTY, SAMUEL T.*	DOR	317	1ST DIST
FLAHARTY, THOMAS C.	HAR	063	1ST DIST
FLAHARTY, THOMAS C.	HAR	006	1ST DIST
FLAHARTY, WILLIAM	FRE	450	8TH E DI
FLAHARTY, WILLIAM N.	FRE	132	CREAGERS
FLAHERTY, ANN	BAL	413	3RD WARD
FLAHERTY, ANN	BAL	052	4TH WARD
FLAHERTY, CHARLES	BAL	347	7TH WARD
FLAHERTY, EDWARD	BAL	395	3RD WARD
FLAHERTY, EDWARD	BAL	009	4TH WARD
FLAHERTY, FANN	BAL	242	20TH WAR
FLAHERTY, JOHN	BAL	258	20TH WAR
FLAHERTY, MARY	BAL	468	14TH WAR
FLAHERTY, MARY	BAL	472	14TH WAR
FLAHERTY, MARY	BAL	397	3RD WARD
FLAHERTY, MARY	BAL	001	15TH WAR
FLAHERTY, MICHAEL	ALL	141	6TH E.D.
FLAHERTY, MICHAEL	ANN	426	HOWARD D
FLAHERTY, MICHAEL	BAL	044	1ST WARD
FLAHERTY, MICHAEL	BAL	407	3RD WARD
FLAHERTY, MORGAN	BAL	300	20TH WAR
FLAHERTY, PATRICK	ALL	067	10TH E.D
FLAHERTY, SARAH	BAL	408	3RD WARD
FLAIM, LOUISA	BAL	170	19TH WAR
FLAITZ, JOHN	BAL	279	2ND WARD
FLAKE, JOHN	ALL	188	9TH E.D.
FLAKNER, JOHN	BAL	456	14TH WAR
FLAMA, MARIAH*	TAL	023	EASTON D
FLAMER, ADELINE	TAL	027	EASTON D
FLAMER, GEORGE	TAL	023	EASTON D
FLAMER, JOHN*	TAL	012	EASTON D
FLAMER, JOHN-BLACK	CAR	091	NO TWP L
FLAMER, JOSEPH	CAR	067	NO TWP L
FLAMER, MARY	BAL	396	3RD WARD
FLAMER, NICHOLAS	BAL	164	2ND DIST
FLAMER, REBECCA	TAL	015	EASTON D
FLAMER, REVECCA	BAL	200	6TH WARD
FLAMER, SHERRY	BAL	024	15TH WAR
FLAMER, SOLOMON*	TAL	008	EASTON D
FLAMES, MARY *	BAL	279	20TH WAR
FLAMM, PETER	BAL	019	9TH WARD
FLAMMER, FRANCIS	BAL	161	11TH WAR
FLAMMER, H.	BAL	143	5TH WARD
FLAMMER, JOHN	BAL	456	14TH WAR
FLAMMER, JOHN	BAL	412	14TH WAR
FLAMU, JOHN*	TAL	012	EASTON D
FLANAGAN, ANDREW	BAL	402	1ST DIST
FLANAGAN, CATHERINE	BAL	028	9TH WARD
FLANAGAN, DANIEL	BAL	406	8TH WARD
FLANAGAN, DANIEL	ALL	154	6TH E.D.
FLANAGAN, JANE	BAL	387	1ST DIST
FLANAGAN, JOHN	FRE	024	FREDERIC
FLANAGAN, JOHN-MULATTO	FRE	444	8TH E DI
FLANAGAN, LEMUEL	BAL	402	1ST DIST
FLANAGAN, MARY	BAL	173	11TH WAR
FLANAGAN, MICHAEL	BAL	127	5TH WARD
FLANAGAN, THOMAS	FRE	037	FREDERIC
FLANEGAN, C. *	ALL	154	6TH E.D.
FLANEGAN, CHARLOTTE	CHA	270	ALLENS F
FLANEGAN, JOHN	ALL	155	6TH E.D.
FLANEGAN, MARY	PRI	081	QUEEN AN
FLANEGAN, MICHAEL	ALL	155	6TH E.D.
FLANEGAN, PATRICK	BAL	127	5TH WARD
FLANETY, THOMAS	BAL	241	2ND WARD
FLANGAN, ELIZABETH	BAL	213	11TH WAR
FLANGEANT, WILHELMINA	BAL	271	2ND WARD
FLANIGAN, AIRY-BLACK	CAR	359	9TH DIST
FLANIGAN, ANDREW	BAL	021	4TH WARD
FLANIGAN, ANDREW	BAL	023	15TH WAR
FLANIGAN, BETSEY	FRE	162	EMMITTSB
FLANIGAN, CATHERINE	BAL	028	9TH WARD
FLANIGAN, JAMES	BAL	008	EASTERN
FLANIGAN, JOHN	BAL	361	8TH WARD
FLANIGAN, LUKE	BAL	364	8TH WARD
FLANIGAN, MARY	BAL	178	11TH WAR
FLANIGAN, MARY	BAL	278	20TH WAR
FLANIGAN, PATRICK	BAL	003	4TH WARD
FLANIGAN, PATRICK	BAL	360	8TH WARD
FLANIGAN, ROSE	BAL	083	10TH WAR
FLANIGAN, ROSE	HAR	048	1ST DIST
FLANIGAN, SUSAN A.	BAL	022	15TH WAR
FLANIGAN, WILLIAM	BAL	130	16TH WAR
FLANINGEN, MARGARET	BAL	079	1ST WARD
FLANK, LUCY	BAL	133	5TH WARD
FLANNAGAN, BRIDGET	BAL	336	13TH WAR
FLANNAGAN, JAMES	BAL	114	1ST WARD
FLANNAGAN, WILLIAM	ALL	051	10TH E.D
FLANNAGAN, ANDREW A.	BAL	297	3RD WARD
FLANNEGAN, BIDDY	BAL	021	4TH WARD
FLANNEGAN, MARIA	BAL	371	13TH WAR
FLANNER, MARTHY	TAL	022	EASTON D
FLANNERY, JULIA	BAL	325	12TH WAR
FLANNEY, HAMMOSA	BAL	348	13TH WAR
FLANNIGAN, B.F.	BAL	169	1ST WARD
FLANNIGAN, JOEPH	ALL	241	CUMBERLA
FLANNIGAN, LYDIA	BAL	039	9TH WARD
FLANNIGAN, MARY	BAL	021	9TH WARD
FLANNIGAN, MARY	BAL	166	11TH WAR
FLANRY, THOMAS	BAL	366	8TH WARD
FLANTT, GEORGE	FRE	147	10TH E D
FLARADY, PHILIP	BAL	260	1ST DIST
FLARE, PETER	FRE	086	FREDERIC
FLARETY, BIREDGET	BAL	241	2ND WARD
FLARETY, MARGARET	BAL	154	11TH WAR
FLARETY, PATRICK	ANN	424	HOWARD D
FLAREY, MICHAEL	BAL	077	18TH WAR
FLARITY, ANTHONY	BAL	208	11TH WAR
FLARITY, CATHARINE	BAL	204	2ND WARD
FLARITY, CORNELIUS	BAL	208	11TH WAR
FLARITY, MARY	BAL	013	18TH WAR
FLARITY, MATHIAS	BAL	010	18TH WAR
FLARITY, SARAH	BAL	250	6TH WARD
FLARNER, FRANKLIN	ALL	089	5TH E.D.
FLARRITY, JAMES	BAL	001	1ST WARD
FLARRITY, MARGARET	BAL	004	1ST WARD
FLARRITY, MARY	BAL	211	2ND WARD
FLARRITY, PATRICK	BAL	001	1ST WARD
FLASBI, GEORGE A.	BAL	304	20TH WAR
FLASBI, JOHN H. *	BAL	304	20TH WAR
FLASCOURT, W. C.	BAL	070	18TH WAR
FLASH, MARIA	BAL	082	18TH WAR
FLASHMAN, JOSEPH	HAR	197	3RD DIST
FLASKLEY, BRIDGET	BAL	383	1ST DIST
FLASKMAN, CARL *	BAL	220	12TH WAR
FLATCHER, LARY E.	HAR	163	3RD DIST
FLATER, ELISHA	CAR	191	4TH DIST
FLATER, JACOB	CAR	190	4TH DIST
FLATER, JESSE	CAR	190	4TH DIST
FLATER, JOHN	CAR	189	4TH DIST
FLATER, PETER	CAR	189	4TH DIST
FLATER, PETER	CAR	190	4TH DIST
FLATER, PHILIP	CAR	189	4TH DIST
FLATER, WILLIAM	CAR	200	4TH DIST
FLATHERS, JOHN	ANN	515	HOWARD D
FLATHEY, JOSEPH M.	BAL	199	19TH WAR
FLATLY, JOHN	ALL	129	4TH E.D.
FLATOR, SAMUEL	BAL	357	8TH WARD
FLATTY, BRIDGET	BAL	317	1ST DIST
FLAUB, JOSEPH	CHA	232	HILLTOP
FLAUTT, GEORGE	WAS	230	1ST DIST
FLAUTT, JACOB	FRE	150	10TH E D
FLAUTT, JOSEPH	WAS	255	1ST DIST
FLAUTT, SAMUEL	FRE	163	EMMITTSB
FLAVIETY, PATRICK	BAL	172	11TH WAR
FLAX, JOSEPH	BAL	439	1ST DIST
FLAXCLOE, WILLIAM	BAL	045	18TH WAR
FLAYHART, ANN	BAL	029	2ND DIST
FLAYMAN, NICHOLAS	BAL	160	11TH WAR
FLEAGLE, BENJAMIN	CAR	321	1ST DIST
FLEAGLE, BENJAMIN	CAR	405	2ND DIST
FLEAGLE, DANIEL	CAR	321	1ST DIST
FLEAGLE, DANIEL	CAR	321	1ST DIST
FLEAGLE, DAVID	CAR	323	1ST DIST
FLEAGLE, EMANUEL	FRE	192	5TH E DI
FLEAGLE, GEORGE	CAR	405	2ND DIST
FLEAGLE, HENRY	CAR	405	2ND DIST
FLEAGLE, JEREMIAH	CAR	322	1ST DIST
FLEAGLE, JESSE	CAR	406	2ND DIST
FLEAGLE, JOHN	CAR	406	2ND DIST
FLEAGLE, JOHN	CAR	380	2ND DIST
FLEAGLE, JOHN	FRE	175	5TH E DI
FLEAGLE, JOSEPH T.	CAR	407	2ND DIST
FLEAGLE, LEVI	CAR	407	2ND DIST
FLEAGLE, PETER	CAR	322	1ST DIST
FLEAGLE, SAMUEL	CAR	321	1ST DIST
FLEAGLE, SAMUEL	FRE	175	5TH E DI
FLEAGLE, SAMUEL	FRE	192	5TH E DI
FLEAGLE, WILLIAM	CAR	412	2ND DIST
FLEAGLE, URIAH	CAR	412	2ND DIST
FLEAWHERT, GEORGE	BAL	068	1ST WARD
FLECHER, FRANCIS	HAR	166	3RD DIST
FLECHER, PHILIP	BAL	126	1ST WARD
FLECHER, SAMUEL	HAR	166	3RD DIST
FLECK, ANDREW	BAL	253	2ND WARD
FLECKENSTEIN, GEORGE	BAL	234	17TH WAR
FLECKINSTINE, PETER	BAL	205	2ND WARD
FLEDDEN, AMELIA	BAL	463	1ST DIST
FLEDDERMAN, J. M.	BAL	310	12TH WAR
FLEER, SARAH LA	BAL	346	13TH WAR
FLEETWOOD, AVRICK	BAL	263	1ST DIST
FLEETWOOD, CHARLES	BAL	162	11TH WAR
FLEETWOOD, CHARLES	BAL	152	11TH WAR
FLEETWOOD, ISAAC	DOR	306	1ST DIST
FLEETWOOD, ISAAC	ANN	360	3RD DIST
FLEETWOOD, JENNY	ANN	350	3RD DIST
FLEETWOOD, MARIAH	DOR	306	1ST DIST
FLEGLE, CONRAD	BAL	211	17TH WAR
FLEGLE, ELIJAH	CAR	242	TANEYTOW
FLEGLE, GEORGE W.	CAR	319	1ST DIST
FLEGLE, MARY J.	CAR	243	TANEYTOW
FLEGLE, SARAH ANN	CAR	297	7TH DIST
FLEHARTY, FRANCES M.	DOR	317	1ST DIST
FLEHARTY, GEORGE	TAL	005	EASTON D
FLEHARTY, JAMES	CAR	141	NO TWP L
FLEHARTY, JANE	TAL	012	EASTON D
FLEHARTY, JOHN	CAR	160	NO TWP L
FLEHARTY, JOHN	CAR	163	NO TWP L
FLEHARTY, JOSEPH	CAR	159	NO TWP L
FLEHARTY, JOSEPH	CAR	150	NO TWP L
FLEHARTY, MARGRETE	CAR	140	NO TWP L
FLEHARTY, MARY	CAR	162	NO TWP L
FLEHARTY, SAMUEL	CAR	164	NO TWP L
FLEHARTY, SAMUEL	CAR	141	NO TWP L
FLEHARTY, SAMUEL T.*	DOR	317	1ST DIST
FLEHARTY, SARAH	CAR	160	NO TWP L
FLEHARTY, SUSAN	CAR	159	NO TWP L
FLEHARTY, WILLIAM H.	TAL	058	EASTON D
FLEHARTY, RICHARD	CAR	160	NO TWP L
FLEICHANT, HENRY	BAL	237	2ND WARD
FLEIGHLE, ISAAC	ALL	008	3RD E.D.
FLEISCHMAN, HESTER	BAL	058	1ST WARD
FLEISCHMAN, SOLOMON	BAL	057	1ST WARD
FLEISCHMANN, JOHN	BAL	030	15TH WAR
FLEISER, JOHN	BAL	105	1ST WARD
FLEISHELL, JACOB	BAL	196	19TH WAR
FLEISHELL, MARY	BAL	145	16TH WAR
FLEISHMAN, FREDERICK	CAR	405	2ND DIST
FLEISHMAN, MOSES	BAL	245	2ND WARD
FLEITMAN, HESS	BAL	035	1ST WARD
FLEM, BRIDGET	BAL	449	14TH WAR
FLEM, PETER	ALL	050	10TH E.D
FLEMER, ARY	TAL	014	EASTON D
FLEMING, ALFRED	SOM	527	QUANTICO
FLEMING, ANN *	BAL	132	2ND DIST
FLEMING, ARTHUR A.	FRE	283	WOODSBOR
FLEMING, CATHERINE M.	FRE	098	FREDERIC
FLEMING, CHARLES	BAL	110	5TH WARD
FLEMING, ELIZA	WOR	304	SNOW HIL
FLEMING, FRANK	BAL	275	17TH WAR
FLEMING, GEORGE	BAL	113	2ND DIST
FLEMING, HARRIET	FRE	047	FREDERIC
FLEMING, HENRY	BAL	411	1ST DIST
FLEMING, HENRY	BAL	264	1ST DIST
FLEMING, HENRY C.	BAL	311	20TH WAR
FLEMING, J.P.	BAL	146	5TH WARD
FLEMING, JAMES	BAL	275	12TH WAR
FLEMING, JAMES	BAL	146	5TH WARD
FLEMING, JAMES	BAL	110	5TH WARD
FLEMING, JAMES	TAL	039	EASTON D
FLEMING, JOHN	WAS	170	FUNKSTOW
FLEMING, JOHN	WAS	263	1ST DIST
FLEMING, JOHN	BAL	406	1ST DIST
FLEMING, JOHN	BAL	181	2ND DIST
FLEMING, JOHN	SOM	429	PRINCESS
FLEMING, JOHN F.	FRE	119	CREAGERS
FLEMING, JOHN F.	FRE	246	NEW MARK
FLEMING, JOHN G.	SOM	402	BRINKLEY
FLEMING, JOSEPH P.	BAL	111	10TH WAR
FLEMING, LAURA	FRE	078	FREDERIC
FLEMING, LAURA J.-MULATTO	FRE	119	CREAGERS
FLEMING, LUCINDY	FRE	010	FREDERIC
FLEMING, MARGARET	DOR	465	1ST DIST
FLEMING, MATHEW	BAL	406	1ST DIST
FLEMING, NEIL	BAL	455	1ST DIST
FLEMING, PATRICK	BAL	132	2ND DIST
FLEMING, REUBEN	BAL	021	9TH WARD
FLEMING, ROBERT	FRE	172	5TH E DI
FLEMING, ROBERT	FRE	173	5TH E DI
FLEMING, SARAH	CAR	101	NO TWP L
FLEMING, SILAS*	TAL	051	EASTON D
FLEMING, THOMAS	DOR	463	1ST DIST
FLEMING, WILLIAM	WAS	175	FUNKSTOW
FLEMING, WILLIAM	SOM	415	DUBLIN D
FLEMING, WILLIAM A. C.	BAL	120	5TH WARD
FLEMING, WILLIAM H.	SOM	350	BRINKLEY
FLEMING, WILLIAM R.	CAR	102	NO TWP L
FLEMINGS, ANDREW	FRE	101	FREDERIC
FLEMINGS, HENRY	BAL	100	18TH WAR
FLEMINS, JOHN	BAL	360	8TH WARD
FLEMINS, MATTHEW	BAL	092	1ST WARD
FLEMIST, JOHN	FRE	250	NEW MARK
FLEMM, GEORGE	CEC	214	7TH E DI
FLEMM, GEORGE	BAL	164	6TH WARD
FLEMMER, WILLIAM S.	BAL	163	6TH WARD
FLEMMING, ANN	BAL	323	12TH WAR
FLEMMING, ANN M.	BAL	416	3RD WARD
FLEMMING, CATHERINE	BAL	247	6TH WARD
FLEMMING, CHARLES F.	BAL	015	4TH WARD
FLEMMING, EMANUEL	CAR	371	9TH DIST
FLEMMING, FREDERICK A.	BAL	450	14TH WAR
FLEMMING, JOHN	BAL	293	3RD WARD
FLEMMING, JOHN	CAR	370	9TH DIST
FLEMMING, MARGARET	SOM	350	BRINKLEY
FLEMMING, MARY	BAL	078	15TH WAR
FLEMMING, NANCY	BAL	013	15TH WAR
FLEMMING, OTHO	CAR	371	9TH DIST
FLEMMING, ROBERT	ANN	492	HOWARD D
FLEMMING, SAMUEL	WOR	189	7TH E DI
FLEMMING, SAMUEL B.	FRE	295	WOODSBOR
FLEMMING, SARAH	BAL	126	11TH WAR
FLEMMING, SARAH A.	FRE	301	WOODSBOR
FLEMMING, STEPHEN K.	BAL	013	15TH WAR
FLEMMING, THOMAS	BAL	128	16TH WAR
FLEMMING, THOMAS	CAR	370	9TH DIST
FLEMMING, LAVINIA	CAR	369	9TH DIST
FLEMMING, WILLIAM	BAL	198	2ND WARD
FLEMMINGS, JAMES	BAL	117	1ST WARD
FLEMMINGS, MARY	BAL	183	5TH DIST
FLEMMINGS, WILLIAM	BAL	319	7TH WARD
FLEMMONS, CHARLES	BAL	424	8TH WARD
FLEMMONS, MARY A.	TAL	038	EASTON D
FLEMMONS, NICHOLAS T.	TAL	038	EASTON D
FLEMMONS, THOMAS	TAL	038	EASTON D
FLENN, THOMAS	TAL	038	EASTON D
FLENNEN, WILLIAM	BAL	445	14TH WAR
FLENNIX, AMANDA	CEC	034	CHESAPEA
FLERSHMAN, SIMON	BAL	445	8TH WARD
FLERSIER, MOSES	BAL	269	2ND WARD
FLESHMAN, HENRY	WAS	118	2ND DIST
FLESHMAN, PHILLIP	BAL	320	12TH WAR
FLETCER, WILLIAM	BAL	098	1ST WARD
FLETCHALL, ELEANOR W.	PRI	107	PISCATAW
FLETCHALL, SARAH N.	MGM	409	MEDLEY 3
FLETCHER, A.	MGM	410	MEDLEY 3
FLETCHER, ANN	BAL	172	1ST WARD
FLETCHER, ANN M.	CEC	124	5TH E DI
FLETCHER, ARCHABALD	SOM	521	BARREN C
FLETCHER, BARBARA	HAR	022	1ST DIST
FLETCHER, CHARELS	FRE	011	FREDERIC
FLETCHER, CHARLES	WOR	233	6TH E DI
FLETCHER, CHARLES-MULATTO	DOR	311	1ST DIST
FLETCHER, DAVID	FRE	383	PETERSVI
FLETCHER, EDA	ALL	188	9TH E.D.
FLETCHER, EDWARD	KEN	239	2ND DIST
FLETCHER, ELIZABETH	BAL	094	2ND DIST
FLETCHER, ELIZABETH	HAR	169	3RD DIST
FLETCHER, ELIZABETH	BAL	050	4TH WARD
FLETCHER, ELIZABETH	WOR	229	6TH E DI
FLETCHER, ELIZABETH	SOM	533	QUANTICO
FLETCHER, GEORGE	WAS	287	1ST DIST
FLETCHER, GEORGE	SOM	526	QUANTICO
FLETCHER, GEORGE	DOR	463	1ST DIST
FLETCHER, HARRIETT	DOR	455	1ST DIST
FLETCHER, ISAAC	DOR	324	1ST DIST
FLETCHER, ISACK A.	HAR	169	3RD DIST
FLETCHER, IWLLIAM	TAL	046	EASTON T
FLETCHER, JAMES	WAS	156	2ND DIST
FLETCHER, JAMES	SOM	471	TRAPPE D
FLETCHER, JAMES	BAL	079	4TH WARD
FLETCHER, JAMES H.-BLACK	HAR	074	1ST DIST
FLETCHER, JANE	BAL	245	2ND WARD
FLETCHER, JANE	BAL	442	8TH WARD
FLETCHER, JEREMIAH H.	DOR	311	1ST DIST
FLETCHER, JERRY	BAL	216	6TH WARD
FLETCHER, JOHN	SOM	531	QUANTICO
FLETCHER, JOHN	BAL	002	9TH WARD
FLETCHER, JOHN	BAL	362	8TH WARD
FLETCHER, JOHN	ALL	187	9TH E.D.
FLETCHER, JOHN	HAR	019	1ST DIST
FLETCHER, JOHN	CEC	124	5TH E DI
FLETCHER, JOHN H.	BAL	292	17TH WAR
FLETCHER, JOHN W.	DOR	462	1ST DIST
FLETCHER, JOSEPH	SOM	528	QUANTICO
FLETCHER, KILBY*	DOR	315	1ST DIST
FLETCHER, LEVIN	DOR	461	1ST DIST
FLETCHER, LEVIN	SOM	467	TRAPPE D
FLETCHER, LEWIS	DOR	310	1ST DIST
FLETCHER, LOUISA	WAS	178	BOONSBOR
FLETCHER, M.	BAL	122	16TH WAR
FLETCHER, MARGARET	TAL	072	EASTON T
FLETCHER, MARGARET	SOM	478	TRAPP DI
FLETCHER, MARGARET E.	CEC	086	4TH E DI
FLETCHER, MARY	SOM	521	BARREN C
FLETCHER, MARY	DOR	306	1ST DIST
FLETCHER, NATHAN	BAL	366	8TH WARD
	BAL	316	1ST DIST

NAME	CO	PAGE	DISTRICT
FLETCHER, OTTIS	BAL	076	18TH WAR
FLETCHER, PETER	DOR	421	1ST DIST
FLETCHER, PHILIP	ALL	187	9TH E.D.
FLETCHER, PRISCELLA	DOR	300	1ST DIST
FLETCHER, SAMUEL	BAL	079	4TH WARD
FLETCHER, SAMUEL	BAL	386	1ST DIST
FLETCHER, SARAH	KEN	307	3RD DIST
FLETCHER, SEPTIMUS	HAR	163	3RD DIST
FLETCHER, SUSAN-BLACK	BAL	245	2ND WARD
FLETCHER, TAMER	SOM	506	BARREN C
FLETCHER, THOMAS W.	SOM	535	QUANTICO
FLETCHER, WALTER	HAR	022	1ST DIST
FLETCHER, WILLIAM	HAR	160	3RD DIST
FLETCHER, WILLIAM	BAL	274	17TH WAR
FLETCHER, WILLIAM	SOM	480	TRAPP DI
FLETCHER, WILLIAM	WAS	136	BOONSBOR
FLETCHER, WILLIAM	BAL	442	8TH WARD
FLETCHER, WILLIAM E.	BAL	165	19TH WAR
FLETCHER,MARIA	BAL	190	2ND WARD
FLETCHER,PHILIP	BAL	102	1ST WARD
FLETHARTY, SUSAN	CAR	159	NO TWP L
FLEWHART, JOHN	ANN	509	HOWARD D
FLEXER, DANIEL	FRE	371	CATOCTIN
FLEZER, ELIZABETH	FRE	176	5TH E DI
FLIBBER, WILLIAM*	TAL	047	EASTON T
FLICK, ANN	BAL	120	11TH WAR
FLICK, CHRISTOPHER	BAL	217	19TH WAR
FLICK, GODPED	BAL	244	2ND WARD
FLICK, JOHN	BAL	244	2ND WARD
FLICKER, JOHN	BAL	191	11TH WAR
FLICKINGER, DAVID	CAR	261	3RD DIST
FLICKINGER, JOHN	CAR	261	3RD DIST
FLICKINGER, JOHN SR.	CAR	261	3RD DIST
FLICKINGER, JULIAN	CAR	392	2ND DIST
FLICKINGER, WILLIAM	CAR	258	3RD DIST
FLICKS, FLORENCE	BAL	240	20TH WAR
FLICKS,MARY	BAL	246	12TH WAR
FLIDERMAN, HENRY	BAL	372	8TH WARD
FLIES, HESTON ANN*	BAL	096	5TH WARD
FLIESELSMAN, MARY	BAL	048	1ST WARD
FLIM, CATHARINE	BAL	249	12TH WAR
FLIMI, REBECCA	BAL	095	5TH WARD
FLIMM, FREDERICK E.	BAL	312	7TH WARD
FLIMMS, SARAH	BAL	092	1ST WARD
FLIMSBAUGH, MATILDA	BAL	033	2ND DIST
FLIN, SUSAN C.	WAS	029	2ND SUBD
FLINCHAM, MARY	BAL	360	1ST DIST
FLING, JAMES W.	MGM	361	BERRYS D
FLING, THOMAS	FRE	408	JEFFERSO
FLINN, ANN	BAL	129	11TH WAR
FLINN, ANN	BAL	293	7TH WARD
FLINN, ANNA M.	HAR	115	2ND DIST
FLINN, ANTHONY	BAL	243	2ND WARD
FLINN, BARNEY	ALL	050	10TH E.D
FLINN, DAVID	BAL	158	11TH WAR
FLINN, EDWARD	CAR	091	NO TWP L
FLINN, J. W.	BAL	150	1ST WARD
FLINN, JOHN	BAL	447	1ST DIST
FLINN, MARY	ALL	075	5TH E.D.
FLINN, MICHAEL	BAL	123	18TH WAR
FLINN, MICHEAL	WAS	162	HAGERSTO
FLINN, PATRICK	BAL	176	11TH WAR
FLINN, SARAH	WAS	195	1ST DIST
FLINN, THOMAS	BAL	026	18TH WAR
FLINNM, GOERGE	CEC	056	1ST E DI
FLINSPACH, ELLEN	BAL	132	16TH WAR
FLINSPACH, FERDINAND	BAL	132	16TH WAR
FLINT, ALLAN	HAR	129	2ND DIST
FLINT, EDWARD	BAL	180	16TH WAR
FLINT, ISAAC S.	HAR	172	3RD DIST
FLINT, IWLLIAM	BAL	311	1ST DIST
FLINT, JOSEPH	DOR	381	1ST DIST
FLINT, JULIA	BAL	090	15TH WAR
FLINT, LUTHER	HAR	172	3RD DIST
FLINT, MARY A.	BAL	085	18TH WAR
FLINT, NANCY	CAL	036	2ND DIST
FLINT, ROBERT	ANN	375	4TH DIST
FLINT, SARAH A.	BAL	300	20TH WAR
FLINT, THOMAS	BAL	404	1ST DIST
FLINT, THOMAS M.	DOR	452	1ST DIST
FLINTEM, JOHN	CEC	066	1ST E DI
FLINTEM, WILLIAM	CEC	042	CHESAPEA
FLIPPER, ISABELLA*	BAL	307	3RD WARD
FLIPPER, LEVEN	DOR	369	3RD DIVI
FLIPPER, WILLIAM*	TAL	047	EASTON T
FLISHER, ANDREW	BAL	288	1ST DIST
FLISHER, FREDERICK	BAL	288	1ST DIST
FLITCHER, BENNETT	HAR	173	3RD DIST
FLITCHER, HIRAM-BLACK	CAR	157	NO TWP L
FLITCHEW, BENJAMIN*	DOR	326	3RD DIVI
FLITCHEW, EZEKIEL	DOR	334	3RD DIVI
FLITCHEW, HENRY	DOR	365	3RD DIVI
FLITCHEW, ZIKIL	DOR	334	3RD DIVI
FLITCHOFF, JOHN	MGM	353	BERRYS D
FLOGER, LISCITTA	BAL	006	EASTERN
FLOHARTY, WILLIAM	HAR	041	1ST DIST
FLOHR, PETER	FRE	153	10TH E D
FLOID, JOHN	WOR	316	2ND E DI
FLOID, WILLIAM	WOR	249	1ST CENS
FLOKE, ANTON	BAL	442	14TH WAR
FLOKEN, MICHAEL	SOM	399	BRINKLEY
FLOMON, PETER	CEC	014	ELKTON 3
FLOOD, ANN	BAL	067	10TH WAR
FLOOD, ANNIE	BAL	207	11TH WAR
FLOOD, BARNARD	BAL	446	1ST DIST
FLOOD, ELIZABETH	BAL	447	1ST DIST
FLOOD, ELIZABETH	BAL	102	5TH WARD
FLOOD, HENSON	MGM	331	CRACKLIN
FLOOD, JAMES	ANN	415	HOWARD D
FLOOD, JERNAH	HAR	198	3RD DIST
FLOOD, MARGARET	BAL	082	15TH WAR
FLOOD, MARGARET	BAL	383	3RD WARD
FLOOD, MARIA	BAL	195	11TH WAR
FLOOD, MARY	BAL	213	11TH WAR
FLOOD, MARY E.	BAL	202	11TH WAR
FLOOD, PHILIP	BAL	319	1ST DIST
FLOOD, PHILIP	ANN	490	HOWARD D
FLOOD, ROSE	BAL	057	10TH WAR
FLOOD, SISTER MELITA	FRE	198	5TH E DI
FLOOD, THOMAS	BAL	037	18TH WAR
FLOOD, WILLIAM	ANN	462	HOWARD D
FLOOK, AMANDA	FRE	400	JEFFERSO
FLOOK, DANIEL	FRE	326	MIDDLETO
FLOOK, DANIEL	FRE	335	MIDDLETO
FLOOK, DANIEL B.	FRE	326	MIDDLETO
FLOOK, DAWSON F.	FRE	333	MIDDLETO
FLOOK, HENRY	FRE	322	MIDDLETO
FLOOK, JACOB	FRE	326	MIDDLETO
FLOOK, JACOB C.	FRE	329	MIDDLETO
FLOOK, JACOB	FRE	400	JEFFERSO
FLOOK, JOHN	FRE	326	MIDDLETO
FLOOK, JOHN M.	FRE	333	MIDDLETO
FLOOK, JOHN P.	FRE	353	MIDDLETO
FLOOK, MARRY	WAS	075	2ND SUBD
FLOOR, GEORGE W.	BAL	259	1ST DIST
FLORA, ANN	WAS	254	1ST DIST
FLORA, ANN	WAS	247	SMITHSBU
FLORA, BENS	WAS	226	1ST DIST
FLORA, BERLIN	WAS	275	RIDGEVIL
FLORA, DAVID OF P.	WAS	244	SMITHSBU
FLORA, HENRY	ALL	214	CUMBERLA
FLORA, ISABELLA	WAS	244	SMITHSBU
FLORA, JAMES	WAS	230	1ST DIST
FLORA, JOHN	WAS	261	1ST DIST
FLORA, JOHN	WAS	269	1ST DIST
FLORA, JOHN C.	WAS	261	1ST DIST
FLORA, JOHN OF B.	WAS	259	1ST DIST
FLORA, MARGARET	WAS	259	1ST DIST
FLORA, MARY A.	WAS	245	SMITHSBU
FLORA, SUSAN	WAS	227	1ST DIST
FLORENCE, SEBASTIAN	FRE	196	5TH E DI
FLORENCE, SEBASTIAN	FRE	196	5TH E DI
FLORENERS, WILLIAM	BAL	097	2ND DIST
FLORERY, FRED	BAL	224	19TH WAR
FLORIA, ELIZABETH	WAS	259	1ST DIST
FLORIN, JOHN	ALL	217	CUMBERLA
FLORRIN, MARY	BAL	150	16TH WAR
FLORY, ALEXANDER	WAS	102	2ND DIST
FLORY, DANIEL	WAS	099	2ND DIST
FLORY, THOMAS	BAL	313	1ST DIST
FLOSBERGER, H.H.	BAL	461	1ST DIST
FLOSS, WILLIAM	BAL	079	1ST WARD
FLOUNDERS, NATHANIEL	CEC	104	4TH E DI
FLOURES, OWEN*	DOR	302	1ST DIST
FLOWER, JOHN B.	ST	310	1ST E DI
FLOWER, MARY	ST	308	1ST E DI
FLOWER, SOLOMON	FRE	071	FREDERIC
FLOWER, THOMAS	FRE	247	NEW MARK
FLOWERS, BENJAMIN C.	FRE	138	CREAGERS
FLOWERS, BLANCH	HAR	004	1ST DIST
FLOWERS, CHARLES	DOR	329	3RD DIVI
FLOWERS, DAVID	HAR	139	2ND DIST
FLOWERS, DAVID	BAL	137	18TH WAR
FLOWERS, ELIZABETH	CAR	162	NO TWP L
FLOWERS, JAMES	CAR	132	NO TWP L
FLOWERS, JERREMIAH	DOR	329	3RD DIVI
FLOWERS, M. REV.	WOR	302	SNOW HIL
FLOWERS, MARY E.	BAL	139	16TH WAR
FLOWERS, MICHAEL	FRE	011	FREDERIC
FLOWERS, PARKER	BAL	118	2ND DIST
FLOWERS, PERRY	DOR	318	1ST DIST
FLOWERS, ROBERT	HAR	106	2ND DIST
FLOWERS, RODY	HAR	106	2ND DIST
FLOWERS, WILLIAM	CAR	134	NO TWP L
FLOWERS, WILLIAM P.	CHA	222	ALLENS F
FLOWN, WILLIAM H.-BLACK	ST	294	2ND E DI
FLOWRS, WILLIS	CAR	156	NO TWP L
FLOYD, ANN	BAL	243	6TH WARD
FLOYD, CATHARIEN	BAL	389	13TH WAR
FLOYD, CHARLES	BAL	204	6TH WARD
FLOYD, CLEMENT	BAL	037	1ST WARD
FLOYD, ELLEN	BAL	061	15TH WAR
FLOYD, GEORGE W.	ST	281	3RD E DI
FLOYD, HEZEKIAH	FRE	354	MIDDLETO
FLOYD, IDA	BAL	271	1ST DIST
FLOYD, JAMES	BAL	340	3RD WARD
FLOYD, JAMES	BAL	270	7TH WARD
FLOYD, JAMES	QUE	182	3RD E DI
FLOYD, JAMES L.	TAL	006	EASTON D
FLOYD, JAMES R.	ST	258	3RD E DI
FLOYD, JOHN	BAL	292	17TH WAR
FLOYD, JOSEPH	ST	279	3RD E DI
FLOYD, JOSEPH	BAL	014	15TH WAR
FLOYD, MARGARET	BAL	297	3RD WARD
FLOYD, MARGARET E.	ST	259	3RD E DI
FLOYD, MARY	QUE	239	5TH E DI
FLOYD, MARY	BAL	201	11TH WAR
FLOYD, NANCY	BAL	061	2ND DIST
FLOYD, PASSEY *	TAL	097	ST MICHA
FLOYD, RACHEL R.	BAL	430	14TH WAR
FLOYD, ROBERT	QUE	189	3RD E DI
FLOYD, SARAH	CHA	294	BOJANTOW
FLOYD, THOMAS	BAL	159	2ND DIST
FLOYD, WILLIAM	BAL	123	1ST WARD
FLOYD, WILLIAM	ST	258	3RD E DI
FLOYD,MARY	ST	292	2ND E DI
FLOYOD, DAVIS O.*	BAL	364	3RD WARD
FLOYDE, PHILIP	TAL	067	EASTON T
FLUART, LEVIN	SOM	454	DAMES QU
FLUART, MARGARET	SOM	453	DAMES QU
FLUCH, THOMAS	WAS	039	2ND SUBD
FLUCK, CAROLINE	WAS	196	1ST DIST
FLUCK, DANIEL	WAS	196	1ST DIST
FLUCK, GEORGE C.	WAS	266	1ST DIST
FLUHARTY, JAMES	DOR	374	1ST DIST
FLUHARTY, JENETT*	DOR	319	1ST DIST
FLUMES, THOMAS SR.	BAL	095	5TH WARD
FLURRY, SUSANNAH	BAL	188	16TH WAR
FLURRY, WARREN	BAL	140	16TH WAR
FLURSHULTZ, JOHN	ALL	240	CUMBERLA
FLUSHMAN, SIMON	CAR	355	6TH DIST
FLUSTER, NANCY	BAL	460	1ST DIST
FLUSTMAN, JACOB	BAL	196	2ND WARD
FLWGEL, CHARELS	BAL	353	13TH WAR
FLYMMER, PIERCE	BAL	096	10TH WAR
FLYNN, ANN	BAL	298	20TH WAR
FLYNN, BERNARD	BAL	065	13TH WAR
FLYNN, DANIEL F.	BAL	017	9TH WARD
FLYNN, JAMES	BAL	046	1ST WARD
FLYNN, JAMES	BAL	180	2ND DIST
FLYNN, JAMES	BAL	394	8TH WARD
FLYNN, JAMES	BAL	298	20TH WAR
FLYNN, JOHN A.	BAL	150	16TH WAR
FLYNN, JOHN W.	BAL	238	20TH WAR
FLYNN, LAURENCE	BAL	047	1ST WARD
FLYNN, MARGARET	BAL	027	1ST WARD
FLYNN, MARGARET	BAL	115	15TH WAR
FLYNN, MARGARET	BAL	398	3RD WARD
FLYNN, MARY	BAL	110	10TH WAR
FLYNN, MARY	BAL	008	1ST WARD
FLYNN, MARY	BAL	134	5TH WARD
FLYNN, MATHEW	BAL	146	2ND DIST
FLYNN, MATTHEW	BAL	046	1ST WARD
FLYNN, PATRICK	BAL	387	3RD WARD
FLYNN, PATRICK	BAL	079	4TH WARD
FLYNN, PATRICK	MGM	397	ROCKERLE
FLYNN, PATRICK	MGM	381	ROCKERLE
FLYNN, SARAH	BAL	047	1ST WARD
FLYNN, SISTER M. KOSTKA	FRE	197	5TH E DI
FLYNN, THOMAS	BAL	451	14TH WAR
FOAK, JACOB	ALL	164	6TH E.D.
FOALDES, JANE	CEC	063	1ST E DI
FOALLA, MAJAH *	HAR	198	3RD DIST
FOALLD, MAJAH *	HAR	198	3RD DIST
FOARD, ARAMINTA	CEC	004	ELKTON 3
FOARD, CASANDER	HAR	067	1ST DIST
FOARD, CATHARINE	CEC	074	5TH E DI
FOARD, EDWRAD B.	CEC	051	1ST E DI
FOARD, FRANCIS A.	HAR	082	2ND DIST
FOARD, GEORGE	CEC	052	1ST E DI
FOARD, HEZEKIAH	CEC	010	ELKTON 3
FOARD, JACOB	CEC	138	6TH E DI
FOARD, JAMES	CEC	052	1ST E DI
FOARD, JAMES L.	CEC	009	ELKTON 3
FOARD, JOHN	CEC	074	5TH E DI
FOARD, JOHN A.	MGM	410	MEDLEY 3
FOARD, JOHN W.	CEC	045	1ST E DI
FOARD, KITTY	BAL	053	15TH WAR
FOARD, LAMBERT	CEC	021	ELKTON 3
FOARD, MARY	CEC	074	5TH E DI
FOARD, RICHARD J.	CEC	036	CHESAPEA
FOARD, SEWAL	CEC	004	ELKTON 3
FOARD, SOPHIA	CEC	021	ELKTON 3
FOARD, WILLIAM	CEC	006	ELKTON 3
FOARN, JAMES	BAL	106	5TH WARD
FOATZ, MORRISS *	ALL	092	5TH E.D.
FOBAT, ANN	BAL	063	16TH WAR
FOBLE, JOHN J.*	DOR	382	1ST DIST
FOBLE, JOHN*	DOR	382	1ST DIST
FOBRI, GOERGE	WAS	022	2ND SUBD
FOBS, JOHN C.	WAS	159	2ND DIST
FOBY, JONATHAN	FRE	327	MIDDLETO
FOCHE, AUGUSTUS	BAL	386	8TH WARD
FOCHIE, HENRIETTA	BAL	386	8TH WARD
FOCHT, GEORGE	BAL	070	15TH WAR
FOCK, JOHN	BAL	200	17TH WAR
FOCKE, FREDERICK	BAL	265	20TH WAR
FOCLE, JOHN	BAL	107	1ST WARD
FODDERS, CATHRIEN	WOR	311	2ND E DI
FODS, FRANCIS G.	BAL	219	19TH WAR
FOEGLE, CONRAD	BAL	267	2ND WARD
FOGAL, HENRY	BAL	013	18TH WAR
FOGAL, HENRY	BAL	011	18TH WAR
FOGAL, HENRY	BAL	013	18TH WAR
FOGARTY, PHEBE	BAL	132	16TH WAR
FOGARTY, THOMAS	BAL	079	10TH WAR
FOGEL, GOTLIEB	BAL	018	9TH WARD
FOGELER, JOHN	BAL	244	17TH WAR
FOGELL, CHALRES	BAL	035	18TH WAR
FOGERTY, LAVINA	ALL	216	CUMBERLA
FOGG, HORACE	BAL	123	1ST WARD
FOGINE, JACOB *	BAL	312	20TH WAR
FOGLE, ABRAHAM	CAR	305	1ST DIST
FOGLE, ADAM	WAS	245	SMITHSBU
FOGLE, BALTZA	FRE	112	CREAGERS
FOGLE, BALTZER	FRE	279	WOODSBOR
FOGLE, CHARLES	BAL	092	5TH WARD
FOGLE, CHRISTIAN	WAS	270	1ST DIST
FOGLE, CONRAD	BAL	161	2ND DIST
FOGLE, CONRADT	BAL	428	8TH WARD
FOGLE, DAVID	FRE	288	WOODSBOR
FOGLE, DAVID	CAR	322	1ST DIST
FOGLE, ELI	FRE	298	WOODSBOR
FOGLE, FRANCIS	CAR	319	1ST DIST
FOGLE, FREDERICK	FRE	290	WOODSBOR
FOGLE, GEORGE	FRE	288	WOODSBOR
FOGLE, HENRY	FRE	287	WOODSBOR
FOGLE, HENRY	FRE	421	8TH E DI
FOGLE, HEZAKIAH	FRE	109	CREAGERS
FOGLE, HORATIO	FRE	287	WOODSBOR
FOGLE, JACOB	FRE	310	WOODSBOR
FOGLE, JACOB	FRE	439	8TH E DI
FOGLE, JOHN	FRE	290	WOODSBOR
FOGLE, JOHN	FRE	281	WOODSBOR
FOGLE, JOHN	FRE	289	WOODSBOR
FOGLE, JOHN	FRE	254	NEW MARK
FOGLE, JOHN	CAR	304	1ST DIST
FOGLE, JOHN	BAL	339	3RD WARD
FOGLE, JOHN	ALL	083	5TH E.D.
FOGLE, JOHN	BAL	139	2ND DIST
FOGLE, JOHN M.	FRE	291	WOODSBOR
FOGLE, JOSEPH	CAR	308	1ST DIST
FOGLE, JOSEPH	FRE	179	5TH E DI
FOGLE, LAINHARDT	BAL	008	9TH WARD
FOGLE, LEVI	FRE	291	WOODSBOR
FOGLE, MARGARET	FRE	290	WOODSBOR
FOGLE, MARGARET	FRE	292	WOODSBOR
FOGLE, MARY	BAL	455	14TH WAR
FOGLE, MARY A.	CAR	322	1ST DIST
FOGLE, NICHOLAS	FRE	291	WOODSBOR
FOGLE, PETER	FRE	283	WOODSBOR
FOGLE, PETER	FRE	108	CREAGERS
FOGLE, PHILLIP	FRE	291	WOODSBOR
FOGLE, SOLOMON	FRE	291	WOODSBOR
FOGLE, SUSAN	FRE	301	WOODSBOR
FOGLE, SUSAN	FRE	432	8TH E DI
FOGLE, WESLEY	FRE	426	8TH E DI
FOGLE, WILIAM H.	FRE	448	8TH E DI
FOGLE, WILLIAM	FRE	452	8TH E DI
FOGLE, WILLIAM	FRE	417	8TH E DI
FOGLE, WILLIAM	FRE	303	WOODSBOR
FOGLELEAR, HENRY	BAL	270	17TH WAR
FOGLEMAN, GOERGE	BAL	147	5TH WARD
FOGLEMAN, LEWIS	BAL	243	17TH WAR
FOGLEMAN, RACHELL	BAL	391	17TH WAR
FOGLEPOLER, RUDOLPH	ALL	168	6TH E.D.
FOGLER, GEORGE	WAS	248	1ST DIST
FOGLER, HENRY	WAS	263	1ST DIST
FOGLER, JACOB	WAS	244	SMITHSBU
FOGLER, JOHN	WAS	244	SMITHSBU
FOGLER, LUTHER	WAS	248	SMITHSBU
FOGLER, MARGARET	FRE	053	FREDERIC
FOGLER, MARY	WAS	282	1ST DIST
FOGLER, REBECCA-BLACK	FRE	224	BUCKEYST
FOGLERN, HENRY	BAL	215	2ND WARD
FOGLESON, JOHN	BAL	073	2ND DIST
FOGLESONG, JACOB	CAR	409	2ND DIST
FOGSWELL, HARRIET	CAR	097	NO TWP L
FOGWELL, ANDY	QUE	129	1ST E DI
FOGWELL, AQUILLA	QUE	139	1ST E DI
FOGWELL, CLINTON	QUE	133	1ST E DI
FOGWELL, ELIZA	QUE	133	1ST E DI
FOGWELL, ELIZABETH-BLACK	QUE	134	1ST E DI
FOGWELL, EMORY-BLACK	QUE	128	1ST E DI
FOGWELL, OTHO	KEN	309	3RD DIST
FOGWELL, REBECA	WAS	114	2ND DIST
FOGWELL, SARAH C.	QUE	151	1ST E DI
FOGWELL, WILLIAM W.	WAS	114	2ND DIST
FOHN, ADAM	BAL	043	18TH WAR
FOIS, JOHN	BAL	187	19TH WAR

Name	County	Page	District
FOISE, FRANCES T. *	BAL	276	20TH WAR
FOIT, JOHN	BAL	272	17TH WAR
FOX, JOHN	BAL	156	2ND DIST
FOKELER, JOHN	BAL	377	8TH WARD
FOKLE, JOHN	BAL	060	2ND DIST
FOKS, JOSEPHINE	ANN	279	ANNAPOLI
FOLA, WILLAIM	BAL	463	1ST DIST
FOLACK, MARIA	BAL	450	8TH WARD
FOLAN, WILLIAM	ALL	249	CUMBERLA
FOLAND, SUSAN	BAL	396	3RD WARD
FOLAND, THOMAS	ANN	426	HOWARD D
FOLCK, DANIEL	ALL	164	6TH E.D.
FOLCK, JOHN	ALL	160	6TH E.D.
FOLD, HANNAH	HAR	201	3RD DIST
FOLEN, PATRICK	ANN	424	HOWARD D
FOLEN, WILLIAM*	DOR	340	3RD DIVI
FOLER, F.	BAL	165	1ST WARD
FOLET, JOHN	BAL	105	2ND DIST
FOLEY, ANN	BAL	172	6TH WARD
FOLEY, ANN	BAL	195	11TH WAR
FOLEY, ANN S.	BAL	063	1ST WARD
FOLEY, BRIDGET	BAL	380	13TH WAR
FOLEY, ELLEN	BAL	064	15TH WAR
FOLEY, HESTER	BAL	383	13TH WAR
FOLEY, JAMES	HAR	121	2ND DIST
FOLEY, JAMES	BAL	355	8TH WARD
FOLEY, JOHN	BAL	370	3RD WARD
FOLEY, JOHN	CAR	230	5TH DIST
FOLEY, LUKE	HAR	121	2ND DIST
FOLEY, MARY	HAR	154	3RD DIST
FOLEY, MARY	BAL	110	10TH WAR
FOLEY, MATTHEW	BAL	323	12TH WAR
FOLEY, PATRICK	BAL	361	8TH WARD
FOLEY, PATRICK	BAL	111	2ND DIST
FOLEY, RICHARD	HAR	200	3RD DIST
FOLEY, ROSE	HAR	154	3RD DIST
FOLEY, THOMAS P.	BAL	148	11TH WAR
FOLEY, WILLIAMC	BAL	159	1ST WARD
FOLEY,MICHAEL	ALL	229	CUMBERLA
FOLGER, R.	BAL	281	2ND WARD
FOLIA, LUKE	HAR	160	3RD DIST
FOLIGUS, BARBARA	BAL	104	1ST WARD
FOLIPES, THOMAS L.	CEC	081	CHARLEST
FOLK, ARCHIBALD W.	HAR	075	BEL AIR
FOLK, BOLLES	BAL	035	15TH WAR
FOLK, GEORGE	BAL	035	15TH WAR
FOLK, GEORGE	HAR	077	BEL AIR
FOLK, JACOB	CAR	347	6TH DIST
FOLK, JACOB *	ALL	101	5TH E.D.
FOLK, JOHN	BAL	284	2ND WARD
FOLK, JOHN M.	BAL	416	14TH WAR
FOLK, PENELOPE	ALL	229	CUMBERLA
FOLKE, CHARLES W.	BAL	009	4TH WARD
FOLKE, TECICKE	BAL	412	14TH WAR
FOLKES, MARGARETT	BAL	051	18TH WAR
FOLKNER, THOMAS	ALL	243	CUMBERLA
FOLKS, ALAXANDER	WAS	159	2ND DIST
FOLKS, ALCINDA	BAL	453	14TH WAR
FOLKS, GEORGE H.	BAL	145	16TH WAR
FOLKS, GOERCE F.	BAL	336	7TH WARD
FOLKS, MARY	BAL	145	16TH WAR
FOLKWINE, JOHN	CAR	355	6TH DIST
FOLL, MARGARET	FRE	025	FREDERIC
FOLLAND, HENRY	BAL	014	9TH WARD
FOLLEN, ELIZA	BAL	003	1ST WARD
FOLLEN, GREENBURY	SOM	358	BRINKLEY
FOLLEN, HENERY	DOR	340	3RD DIVI
FOLLEY, ELIZA	BAL	383	3RD WARD
FOLLEY, THOMAS	BAL	325	3RD WARD
FOLLEY, THOMAS	BAL	128	18TH WAR
FOLLIBUS, JOHN	QUE	176	2ND E DI
FOLLIN, DANIEL	BAL	262	17TH WAR
FOLLON, DOMINICK	BAL	161	2ND DIST
FOLLOW, GEORGE	CEC	207	7TH E DI
FOLLSON, SOPHIA-BLACK	CAR	075	NO TWP L
FOLLTEY, SARAH	BAL	165	11TH WAR
FOLMAN, CHARLES	BAL	160	1ST WARD
FOLOWERS, WILLIAM	WOR	329	1ST E DI
FOLSOM, JOHN	BAL	184	2ND WARD
FOLSTAFF, MARY	BAL	368	3RD WARD
FOLTON, ANNA	ALL	203	CUMBERLA
FOLTSON, HENRIETTA-BLACK	CAR	076	NO TWP L
FOLTZ, FELIX	CAR	309	1ST DIST
FOLTZ, JOHN	CAR	350	6TH DIST
FOLWER, PETER	BAL	258	1ST DIST
FOLY, TIMOTHY	BAL	413	1ST DIST
FOMAN, THOMAS-BLACK	FRE	222	BUCKEYST
FONATTA, HENRY	BAL	383	1ST DIST
FONCE, GOERGE	BAL	198	17TH WAR
FONCE, JACOB	BAL	198	17TH WAR
FONCE, JACOB	BAL	282	17TH WAR
FONCH, JOHATHAN	FRE	389	PETERSVI
FOND, FREEBORN	BAL	170	11TH WAR
FOND, JOHN	BAL	076	2ND DIST
FONDER, JACOB	BAL	454	8TH WARD
FONDER, RICHARD	BAL	326	7TH WARD
FONDERHEIDER, HEMAN	BAL	005	9TH WARD
FONERDON, JOHN	BAL	352	7TH WARD
FONGE, S. D. *	BAL	303	1ST DIST
FONKE, AUGUSTUS	FRE	041	FREDERIC
FONNAN, ISAAC	HAR	179	3RD DIST
FONT, MARGARET	FRE	040	FREDERIC
FONTAIN, MRS.	BAL	352	7TH WARD
FONTEMAN, THOMAS	CEC	045	1ST E DI
FONTERCREAM, WOLFGONG	BAL	436	8TH WARD
FONTS, JOHN	ALL	020	2ND E.D.
FONTZ, DAVID	WAS	088	2ND SUBD
FONUM, JOHN	BAL	066	4TH WARD
FOOBS, WILLIAM	BAL	116	1ST WARD
FOOHS, EBENEZER	WOR	207	4TH E DI
FOOHS, EBENEZER	WOR	196	8TH E DI
FOOHS, EBENEZER H.	WOR	226	4TH E DI
FOOHS, ISAAC	WOR	180	6TH E DI
FOOHS, JACOB	WOR	203	4TH E DI
FOOHS, JAMES	WOR	202	4TH E DI
FOOHS, JAMES M.	WOR	203	4TH E DI
FOOHS, JOHN	WOR	256	1ST CENS
FOOHS, MARIAH	WOR	219	4TH E DI
FOOHS, MARY	WOR	197	8TH E DI
FOOHS, MARY J.	WOR	218	4TH E DI
FOOHS, NOAH	WOR	257	1ST CENS
FOOHS, PAUL *	WOR	184	6TH E DI
FOOHS, RICHIE	WOR	211	4TH E DI
FOOHS, WILLIAM	WOR	196	8TH E DI
FOOKES, ANTHONY	SOM	424	PRINCESS
FOOKES, EBEN	SOM	428	PRINCESS
FOOKES, ELIZABETH	SOM	480	TRAPP DI
FOOKES, HENRY	SOM	411	DUBLIN D
FOOKES, JOHN	SOM	428	PRINCESS
FOOKES, LATITIA	SOM	472	TRAPPE D
FOOKES, LEAH	SOM	466	HANGARY
FOOKES, MARIAH	SOM	465	HANGARY
FOOKS, AMOS	SOM	517	BARREN C
FOOKS, ANN E.	WOR	193	8TH E DI
FOOKS, BAGH*	DOR	375	1ST DIST
FOOKS, BAYN*	DOR	375	1ST DIST
FOOKS, DE WITT C.	WOR	168	6TH E DI
FOOKS, ELIZABETH	WOR	269	BERLIN 1
FOOKS, ELIZABETH	DOR	416	1ST DIST
FOOKS, EMALINE	SOM	425	PRINCESS
FOOKS, GEORGE	WOR	195	8TH E DI
FOOKS, HENRY	WOR	192	8TH E DI
FOOKS, HESTER	WOR	195	8TH E DI
FOOKS, HULDA	WOR	299	SNOW HIL
FOOKS, ISAAC	WOR	272	BERLIN 1
FOOKS, ISAAC	WOR	268	BERLIN 1
FOOKS, JAMES*	DOR	414	1ST DIST
FOOKS, JOHN	SOM	424	PRINCESS
FOOKS, JOHN	WOR	256	1ST CENS
FOOKS, JOHN W.*	TAL	054	EASTON D
FOOKS, JOSIAH W.	WOR	186	7TH E DI
FOOKS, LEAH	SOM	489	SALISBUR
FOOKS, LEAH	SOM	465	HANGARY
FOOKS, LEVIN S.	DOR	416	1ST DIST
FOOKS, RENOLE*	DOR	412	1ST DIST
FOOKS, ROBERT	WOR	268	BERLIN 1
FOOKS, SARAH	WOR	269	BERLIN 1
FOOKS, URIAH	WOR	190	8TH E DI
FOOKS, ZACHARIA*	DOR	445	1ST DIST
FOOLE, MARY O.*	BAL	404	3RD WARD
FOOS, DANIEL	BAL	176	2ND DIST
FOOS, GEORGE	BAL	094	18TH WAR
FOOS, JOHN	BAL	180	16TH WAR
FOOS, THOMAS	BAL	406	3RD WARD
FOOSE, EDWIN A.	BAL	400	3RD WARD
FOOSE, ELIZABETH	CAR	343	6TH DIST
FOOSE, HENRY	BAL	154	5TH WARD
FOOSE, SARAH A.	BAL	074	4TH WARD
FOOSE, WILLIAM	CAR	396	2ND DIST
FOOT, AMILEA	BAL	389	13TH WAR
FOOT, BASIL	BAL	443	1ST DIST
FOOT, CHARLES	BAL	440	8TH WARD
FOOT, CHARLES	BAL	056	2ND DIST
FOOT, CHRISTAIN	KEN	282	3RD DIST
FOOT, ELIZABETH	BAL	286	7TH WARD
FOOT, JACOB	BAL	442	1ST DIST
FOOTE, ANNA	BAL	242	6TH WARD
FOOTE, ASA	BAL	123	1ST WARD
FOOTE, DANIEL	BAL	089	2ND DIST
FOOTE, ELIZA	BAL	251	6TH WARD
FOOTE, HENRY	BAL	181	6TH WARD
FOOTE, JAMES	BAL	154	1ST WARD
FOOTE, JAMES	BAL	127	1ST WARD
FOOTE, JOHN	BAL	263	12TH WAR
FOOTE, LEWIS H.	BAL	197	6TH WARD
FOOTE, PEGGY	BAL	234	20TH WAR
FOOTELL, ELIZABETH*	BAL	319	3RD WARD
FOOTMAN, NOAH	WAS	037	2ND SUBD
FOOTS, ISAAC	CAL	015	1ST DIST
FOOWLER, DEBORAH	PRI	065	NOTTINGH
FOR.D JOHN	TAL	087	ST MICHA
FORACRES, DANIEL	CEC	078	NORTHEAS
FORAN, P.	BAL	153	1ST WARD
FORBER, JULIANN	ALL	231	CUMBERLA
FORBES, ALEXANDER	BAL	149	19TH WAR
FORBES, CHARLES P.*	BAL	088	10TH WAR
FORBES, GEORGE	PRI	050	AQUASCO
FORBES, HARRIET	BAL	392	3RD WARD
FORBES, HENRIETTA	BAL	007	9TH WARD
FORBES, JOSEPH H.	HAR	079	2ND DIST
FORBES, W.L.	BAL	050	2ND DIST
FORBS, JAMES J.	ST	300	2ND E DI
FORBUSH, GEORGE	SOM	553	TYASKIN
FORBUSH, KITURA	SOM	553	TYASKIN
FORBUSH, WASHINGTON	SOM	552	TYASKIN
FORBUSH, WILLIAM A.	SOM	553	TYASKIN
FORCE, SARAH A.	WAS	165	HAGERSTO
FORCE, WILLIAM	WAS	129	HAGERSTO
FORD, AARON	SOM	384	BRINKLEY
FORD, ABIJAH	WAS	209	1ST DIST
FORD, ACSHE	BAL	427	1ST DIST
FORD, ANN	BAL	098	2ND DIST
FORD, ANN	BAL	325	7TH WARD
FORD, ANN	BAL	199	11TH WAR
FORD, ANN	BAL	008	1ST WARD
FORD, ANN	SOM	369	BRINKLEY
FORD, ANN	CHA	278	BOJANTOW
FORD, ANNA	CEC	191	5TH E DI
FORD, ARABELLA	CEC	053	1ST E DI
FORD, AUGUSTUS	SOM	409	DUBLIN D
FORD, BASIL	BAL	202	17TH WAR
FORD, BASIL	BAL	166	16TH WAR
FORD, BENJAMIN C.	BAL	353	7TH WARD
FORD, BETSEY	BAL	222	12TH WAR
FORD, BETSY	CHA	261	MIDDLETO
FORD, BIDDY	BAL	149	2ND DIST
FORD, BOYD	BAL	118	2ND DIST
FORD, BRICE	FRE	358	CATOCTIN
FORD, BRIDGET	BAL	378	1ST DIST
FORD, CAROLINE	BAL	353	7TH WARD
FORD, CAROLINE	BAL	034	4TH WARD
FORD, CAROLINE	TAL	085	ST MICHA
FORD, CASPER W.	BAL	222	17TH WAR
FORD, CASSANDRA	BAL	456	1ST DIST
FORD, CATHARINE	BAL	250	6TH WARD
FORD, CATHARINE	KEN	213	2ND DIST
FORD, CATHARINE	BAL	460	14TH WAR
FORD, CATHERINE	BAL	409	8TH WARD
FORD, CHARLES	FRE	270	NEW MARK
FORD, CHARLES F.	SOM	357	BRINKLEY
FORD, CHARLES T.	BAL	219	17TH WAR
FORD, CHLOE	PRI	057	AQUASCO
FORD, DANIEL	SOM	356	BRINKLEY
FORD, DANIEL	SOM	356	BRINKLEY
FORD, DANIEL	CAR	221	5TH DIST
FORD, DANIEL	SOM	408	DUBLIN D
FORD, DAVID	BAL	305	1ST DIST
FORD, DAVID-BLACK	QUE	200	3RD E DI
FORD, EDWARD	SOM	443	DAMES QU
FORD, EDWARD	BAL	040	9TH WARD
FORD, EDWARD	BAL	290	12TH WAR
FORD, EDWARD	ALL	056	10TH E.D
FORD, EDWARD	ALL	053	10TH E.D
FORD, EDWARD	ANN	394	8TH DIST
FORD, EDWARD	BAL	133	18TH WAR
FORD, EDWARD *	BAL	302	12TH WAR
FORD, ELEANOR	SOM	445	DAMES QU
FORD, ELIAS	BAL	256	12TH WAR
FORD, ELIZA	BAL	224	17TH WAR
FORD, ELIZA	BAL	029	18TH WAR
FORD, ELIZABETH	BAL	028	4TH WARD
FORD, ELIZABETH	CEC	038	CHESAPEA
FORD, ELIZABETH	BAL	011	1ST WARD
FORD, ELSEY	SOM	404	BRINKLEY
FORD, ENOCH	ALL	073	5TH E.D.
FORD, FARL	BAL	278	1ST DIST
FORD, FRANK	BAL	259	12TH WAR
FORD, FRANK	BAL	244	20TH WAR
FORD, G.F.	BAL	162	1ST WARD
FORD, GEORGE	BAL	321	7TH WARD
FORD, GEORGE	BAL	370	1ST DIST
FORD, GEORGE	CEC	045	1ST E DI
FORD, GEORGE	KEN	259	1ST DIST
FORD, GEORGE B.	KEN	252	1ST DIST
FORD, GEORGE E.	HAR	189	3RD DIST
FORD, GEORGE W.	BAL	045	18TH WAR
FORD, GEORGE W.	BAL	173	5TH WARD
FORD, GUSTAVUS	TAL	087	ST MICHA
FORD, HANNAH	BAL	215	6TH WARD
FORD, HANNAH	BAL	269	20TH WAR
FORD, HARRIET-BLACK	BAL	198	2ND WARD
FORD, HARRIETT	BAL	039	4TH WARD
FORD, HENRY	CEC	019	ELKTON 3
FORD, HENRY	BAL	244	20TH WAR
FORD, HENRY	DOR	426	1ST DIST
FORD, HENRY	CHA	278	BOJANTOW
FORD, HENRY	SOM	404	BRINKLEY
FORD, HENRY	BAL	256	17TH WAR
FORD, HENRY	BAL	118	5TH WARD
FORD, HENRY	BAL	034	15TH WAR
FORD, HENRY	ANN	411	8TH DIST
FORD, HENRY	SOM	445	DAMES QU
FORD, HENRY	KEN	307	3RD DIST
FORD, HENRY A.	ST	281	3RD E DI
FORD, HESTER	SOM	357	BRINKLEY
FORD, HESTER	BAL	196	19TH WAR
FORD, HILLARY	BAL	066	15TH WAR
FORD, HOPEWELL	QUE	187	3RD E DI
FORD, HUGH	SOM	360	BRINKLEY
FORD, ISAAC	BAL	096	2ND DIST
FORD, ISAAC	CAR	219	5TH DIST
FORD, ISAAC	KEN	251	2ND DIST
FORD, ISABEL	BAL	058	15TH WAR
FORD, J. D.	KEN	218	2ND DIST
FORD, JAMES	HAR	195	3RD DIST
FORD, JAMES	BAL	407	1ST DIST
FORD, JAMES	SOM	377	BRINKLEY
FORD, JAMES	PRI	065	NOTTINGH
FORD, JAMES C.	BAL	016	2ND DIST
FORD, JAMES E.	BAL	291	12TH WAR
FORD, JAMES H.	SOM	358	BRINKLEY
FORD, JAMES M.	ALL	066	10TH E.D
FORD, JAMES P.	FRE	209	BUCKEYST
FORD, JAMES W.	BAL	433	14TH WAR
FORD, JAMES-BLACK	ST	347	5TH E DI
FORD, JANE	BAL	305	3RD WARD
FORD, JANE	BAL	273	12TH WAR
FORD, JANE A.	ST	281	3RD E DI
FORD, JERAMIAH	CEC	070	5TH E DI
FORD, JEREMIAH	ALL	071	5TH E.D.
FORD, JESTON	ALL	120	5TH E.D.
FORD, JOHANNA	BAL	062	1ST WARD
FORD, JOHN	BAL	231	1ST DIST
FORD, JOHN	ALL	053	10TH E.D
FORD, JOHN	ANN	351	3RD DIST
FORD, JOHN	BAL	021	9TH WARD
FORD, JOHN	BAL	055	18TH WAR
FORD, JOHN	CEC	058	1ST E DI
FORD, JOHN	HAR	003	1ST DIST
FORD, JOHN	BAL	301	20TH WAR
FORD, JOHN	ST	279	3RD E DI
FORD, JOHN	WAS	228	1ST DIST
FORD, JOHN A.	ST	307	1ST E DI
FORD, JOHN B.	HAR	041	1ST DIST
FORD, JOHN B.	FRE	204	BUCKEYST
FORD, JOHN F.	TAL	086	ST MICHA
FORD, JOHN T.	BAL	232	1ST DIST
FORD, JOHN W.	BAL	185	6TH WARD
FORD, JOHN W.	WAS	124	2ND DIST
FORD, JOHN W.	BAL	396	14TH WAR
FORD, JOSEPH	FRE	232	BUCKEYST
FORD, JOSEPH	BAL	065	18TH WAR
FORD, JOSEPH	BAL	073	18TH WAR
FORD, JOSEPH	ANN	302	1ST DIST
FORD, JOSEPH L.	ST	254	3RD E DI
FORD, JOSHUA	WAS	209	1ST DIST
FORD, JOSHUA	FRE	368	CATOCTIN
FORD, JOSIAH	FRE	204	BUCKEYST
FORD, JOSIAS	BAL	363	8TH WARD
FORD, KITTY	CHA	288	BOJANTOW
FORD, LITTLETON D.	TAL	086	ST MICHA
FORD, LOVEY	BAL	332	7TH WARD
FORD, LUCRETIA	ST	277	3RD E DI
FORD, LYDIA	BAL	169	19TH WAR
FORD, LYLOUS	SOM	437	DAMES QU
FORD, M.	ANN	401	8TH DIST
FORD, M. L.	BAL	155	11TH WAR
FORD, MARGARET	BAL	357	13TH WAR
FORD, MARGARET	ALL	090	5TH E.D.
FORD, MARGARET	BAL	072	15TH WAR
FORD, MARGARET	BAL	133	5TH WARD
FORD, MARGARET	SOM	354	BRINKLEY
FORD, MARTHA	BAL	091	15TH WAR
FORD, MARTHA	CHA	278	BOJANTOW
FORD, MARTHA	CHA	277	BOJANTOW
FORD, MARY	BAL	154	11TH WAR
FORD, MARY	BAL	188	19TH WAR
FORD, MARY	BAL	140	16TH WAR
FORD, MARY	BAL	103	10TH WAR
FORD, MARY	BAL	189	6TH WARD
FORD, MARY	BAL	455	8TH WARD
FORD, MARY	ANN	406	8TH DIST
FORD, MARY	SOM	361	BRINKLEY
FORD, MARY	SOM	359	BRINKLEY
FORD, MARY	ST	284	2ND E DI
FORD, MARY	ST	310	1ST E DI
FORD, MARY A.	ST	292	2ND E DI
FORD, MARY A. F.	ST	254	3RD E DI
FORD, MARY ANN	SOM	357	BRINKLEY
FORD, MARY B.	ST	308	1ST E DI
FORD, MARY H.	BAL	466	14TH WAR
FORD, MARY J.	BAL	230	6TH WARD
FORD, MRS.	BAL	132	5TH WARD
FORD, N.	PRI	067	NOTTINGH
FORD, NANCY	SOM	485	TRAPP DI
FORD, NANCY	SOM	404	BRINKLEY
FORD, NELLY	SOM	360	BRINKLEY
FORD, NICHOLAS	BAL	303	12TH WAR
FORD, PATRICK	ALL	143	6TH E.D.
FORD, PATRICK	BAL	058	15TH WAR

FORD, PETER	BAL	287	1ST DIST
FORD, PRICE	WAS	209	1ST DIST
FORD, PRICEY-BLACK	FRE	017	FREDERIC
FORD, PRISCILLA	ST	291	2ND E DI
FORD, REBECCA	PRI	062	NOTTINGH
FORD, REBECCA	CHA	295	BOJANTOW
FORD, REBECCA	BAL	125	2ND DIST
FORD, REBECCA A.	QUE	150	1ST E DI
FORD, ROBERT	BAL	119	2ND DIST
FORD, ROBERT	BAL	169	11TH WAR
FORD, ROBERT	ST	313	1ST E DI
FORD, ROBERT	ST	254	3RD E DI
FORD, ROBERT T.	BAL	196	19TH WAR
FORD, ROBERT-BLACK	FRE	048	FREDERIC
FORD, ROSA	BAL	155	11TH WAR
FORD, ROSE E.	WAS	137	HAGERSTO
FORD, ROSINA	BAL	325	7TH WARD
FORD, RUTH	BAL	256	17TH WAR
FORD, RUTH A.	CEC	034	CHESAPEA
FORD, SAMUEL	BAL	154	11TH WAR
FORD, SAMUEL	BAL	048	2ND DIST
FORD, SAMUEL	SOM	357	BRINKLEY
FORD, SAMUEL B.	CEC	024	ELKTON 3
FORD, SARAH	CEC	039	CHESAPEA
FORD, SARAH	SOM	359	BRINKLEY
FORD, SARAH	BAL	145	5TH WARD
FORD, STEPHEN	CEC	042	CHESAPEA
FORD, STEPHEN H.	CEC	049	1ST E DI
FORD, SUSAN	SOM	438	DAMES QU
FORD, SUSANER	HAR	185	3RD DIST
FORD, SYLVESTER	BAL	094	2ND DIST
FORD, TERESE	ST	267	3RD E DI
FORD, THOMAS	SOM	363	BRINKLEY
FORD, THOMAS	SOM	355	BRINKLEY
FORD, THOMAS	WAS	210	1ST DIST
FORD, THOMAS	BAL	116	2ND DIST
FORD, THOMAS	BAL	159	1ST WARD
FORD, THOMAS	BAL	321	7TH WARD
FORD, THOMAS	BAL	445	8TH WARD
FORD, THOMAS	BAL	125	1ST WARD
FORD, THOMAS	BAL	176	2ND DIST
FORD, THOMAS	ANN	305	1ST DIST
FORD, THOMAS	FRE	058	FREDERIC
FORD, THOMAS C.	BAL	214	6TH WARD
FORD, THOMAS H.	QUE	192	3RD E DI
FORD, URIAH	BAL	458	8TH WARD
FORD, W. F.	BAL	336	13TH WAR
FORD, WALTER	ST	291	2ND E DI
FORD, WESLEY	BAL	123	2ND DIST
FORD, WILLIAM	BAL	116	2ND DIST
FORD, WILLIAM	BAL	156	1ST WARD
FORD, WILLIAM	BAL	164	1ST WARD
FORD, WILLIAM	BAL	170	1ST WARD
FORD, WILLIAM	BAL	171	1ST WARD
FORD, WILLIAM	BAL	252	1ST DIST
FORD, WILLIAM	BAL	052	1ST WARD
FORD, WILLIAM	BAL	053	1ST WARD
FORD, WILLIAM	BAL	067	10TH WAR
FORD, WILLIAM	BAL	138	1ST WARD
FORD, WILLIAM	SOM	354	BRINKLEY
FORD, WILLIAM	WAS	124	2ND DIST
FORD, WILLIAM	BAL	358	13TH WAR
FORD, WILLIAM	HAR	082	2ND DIST
FORD, WILLIAM	BAL	150	11TH WAR
FORD, WILLIAM	BAL	460	14TH WAR
FORD, WILLIAM	BAL	398	14TH WAR
FORD, WILLIAM A.	CAR	170	NO TWP L
FORD, WILLIAM E.	SOM	358	BRINKLEY
FORD, WILLIAM E.	BAL	015	15TH WAR
FORD, WILLIAM F.	BAL	192	17TH WAR
FORD, WILLIAM H.	BAL	050	9TH WARD
FORD, WILLIAM H.	ST	306	1ST E DI
FORD, WILLIAM J.	QUE	251	5TH E DI
FORD, WILLIAM JR.	SOM	358	BRINKLEY
FORD, WILLIAM T.	CHA	288	BOJANTOW
FORD,SAMUEL	FRE	228	BUCKEYST
FOROCRES, ROBERTH	CEC	079	NORTHEAS
FORDE, GUSTAVUS M.	BAL	185	16TH WAR
FORDE, MICHAEL	FRE	20	5TH E DI
FOROMAN, WILLIAM	QUE	240	5TH E DI
FORDCN, HENRY	BAL	355	13TH WAR
FCRDROUGH, MILES	BAL	007	1ST WARD
FOREACRE, ANN E.	CEC	103	4TH E DI
FOREACRE, ROBERT	CEC	102	4TH E DI
FOREL, THOMAS	BAL	205	2ND WARD
FOREMAN, ACAM	CAR	373	9TH DIST
FOREMAN, ALBERT	FRE	129	CREAGERS
FOREMAN, ALPHEUS	CAR	250	3RD DIST
FOREMAN, ANN	BAL	375	1ST DIST
FOREMAN, ANTHONY	BAL	357	8TH WARD
FOREMAN, AUGUSTIN	TAL	025	EASTON D
FOREMAN, BENJAMIN	CAR	387	2ND DIST
FOREMAN, CAROLINE	BAL	152	11TH WAR
FOREMAN, CARTER	CEC	059	1ST E DI
FOREMAN, CATHARINE	BAL	331	7TH WARD
FOREMAN, CATHERINE	BAL	423	8TH WARD
FOREMAN, DAVID	CAR	379	2ND DIST
FOREMAN, DAVID	CAR	360	9TH DIST
FOREMAN, ELIZABETH	CAR	247	3RD DIST
FOREMAN, ELLIS	CEC	204	6TH E DI
FOREMAN, EMELY J.	TAL	095	ST MICHA
FOREMAN, FRANCIS E.	BAL	435	8TH WARD
FOREMAN, FREEMAN	CEC	066	1ST E DI
FOREMAN, GEORGE W.	FRE	129	CREAGERS
FOREMAN, GLASGOW	MGM	362	BERRYS D
FOREMAN, GUDEIN *	KEN	242	2ND DIST
FOREMAN, HANAH	BAL	321	7TH WARD
FOREMAN, HENRIETTA	BAL	344	3RD WARD
FOREMAN, HENRIETTA	BAL	038	4TH WARD
FOREMAN, HENRY	BAL	348	7TH WARD
FOREMAN, ISAAC W.	SOM	547	TYASKIN
FOREMAN, JACOB	CAR	410	2ND DIST
FOREMAN, JAMES	CAR	379	2ND DIST
FOREMAN, JAMES	BAL	384	1ST DIST
FOREMAN, JAMES	BAL	134	1ST WARD
FOREMAN, JOHN	BAL	202	19TH WAR
FOREMAN, JOHN	MGM	342	CLARKSBU
FOREMAN, JOHN	MGM	362	BERRYS D
FOREMAN, JOHN	WOR	263	BERLIN 1
FOREMAN, JOSEPH	BAL	181	19TH WAR
FOREMAN, JOSEPH E.	BAL	340	7TH WARD
FOREMAN, JOSEPH R.	BAL	416	8TH WARD
FOREMAN, JOSHUA	CEC	205	7TH E DI
FOREMAN, LEONARD	ANN	357	3RD DIST
FOREMAN, LOUISA	CAR	411	2ND DIST
FOREMAN, MARY	BAL	070	4TH WARD
FOREMAN, MARY	BAL	253	6TH WARD
FOREMAN, MARY J.	BAL	340	7TH WARD
FOREMAN, MILTY	BAL	344	3RD WARD
FOREMAN, NOAH	TAL	037	EASTON D
FOREMAN, PETER	BAL	357	8TH WARD
FOREMAN, REBECCA	CAR	373	9TH DIST
FOREMAN, RICHARD	TAL	095	ST MICHA
FOREMAN, RON *	BAL	306	12TH WAR
FOREMAN, SAMUEL	BAL	205	6TH DIST
FOREMAN, SAMUEL	ANN	359	3RD DIST
FOREMAN, SAVILLA	CAR	265	WESTMINS
FOREMAN, STEPHEN	CAR	329	MANCHEST
FOREMAN, SUSAN	CAR	366	9TH DIST
FOREMAN, SUSAN	WAS	012	WILLIAMS
FOREMAN, THOMAS	BAL	284	7TH WARD
FOREMAN, THOMS	CEC	058	1ST E DI
FOREMAN, VALENT	BAL	245	20TH WAR
FOREMAN, VALENTINE	FRE	175	5TH E DI
FORES, WILLIAM	BAL	324	7TH WARD
FOREST, AQUILLA	ANN	383	4TH DIST
FOREST, FRANCIS A.	BAL	090	18TH WAR
FOREST, JOHN	ANN	383	4TH DIST
FORESTER, NANCY	ANN	367	4TH DIST
FORESTER, WILLIAM	BAL	393	8TH WARD
FORESYTHE, FRANCIS	BAL	439	8TH WARD
FORESYTHE, JAMES	BAL	327	7TH WARD
FOREY, JOHN S. *	WAS	115	2ND DIST
FORGAL, CASEMAN	BAL	132	18TH WAR
FORGATH, AUGUSTU	BAL	386	13TH WAR
FORGE, HELENA	BAL	288	17TH WAR
FORGETY, ANDY	BAL	454	14TH WAR
FORGOOD, MARY	BAL	066	4TH WARD
FORGUSON, DARCUS	HAR	055	1ST DIST
FORGUSON, DAVID	HAR	056	1ST DIST
FORKLIEN, ANDREW	BAL	240	2ND WARD
FORKNER, HIRAM	ALL	031	2ND E.D.
FORKNER, JAMES	ALL	030	2ND E.D.
FORKS, JAMES*	DOR	414	1ST DIST
FORKS, JOHNATHAN	WOR	261	BERLIN 1
FORLEY, WILLIAM	WAS	258	1ST DIST
FORLK, WILLIAM	BAL	052	1ST WARD
FORMAN, ALEXANDER D.	BAL	020	18TH WAR
FORMAN, AUTHOR	CAR	074	NO TWP L
FORMAN, CEZER	HAR	181	3RD DIST
FORMAN, CHARLOTTE	BAL	107	10TH WAR
FORMAN, CAVID	BAL	297	17TH WAR
FORMAN, ELIZABETH	BAL	069	10TH WAR
FORMAN, EVAN M.	BAL	162	6TH WARD
FORMAN, FRANCIS	BAL	168	6TH WARD
FORMAN, FRANCIS	BAL	443	14TH WAR
FORMAN, HENRY	KEN	301	3RD DIST
FORMAN, HENRY A.	QUE	164	2ND E DI
FORMAN, JACOB	HAR	109	2ND DIST
FORMAN, JOHN	BAL	444	14TH WAR
FORMAN, JOHN	HAR	164	3RD DIST
FORMAN, JOHN	BAL	250	17TH WAR
FORMAN, JOHN D.	BAL	331	7TH WARD
FORMAN, JOSHUA	BAL	329	7TH WARD
FORMAN, KAVEY	BAL	311	7TH WARD
FORMAN, MARIA	BAL	064	10TH WAR
FORMAN, MARY	QUE	236	4TH E DI
FORMAN, MARY	QUE	236	4TH E DI
FORMAN, MELISSA-BLACK	QUE	193	3RD E DI
FORMAN, PRISCILLA	BAL	070	10TH WAR
FORMAN, RACHAEL	BAL	115	11TH WAR
FORMAN, RACHAEL A.	BAL	063	18TH WAR
FORMAN, SARAH A.	BAL	077	10TH WAR
FORMAN, SOPHIA	BAL	380	1ST DIST
FORMAN, WILLIAM	CEC	026	ELKTON 3
FORMAN, WILLIAM R.	KEN	301	3RD DIST
FORMAN, WILLIAM W.	BAL	311	1ST DIST
FORMER, MARY	MGM	346	CLARKSBU
FORMHAL, LEWIS	BAL	255	2ND WARD
FORMON, JOHN	WOR	289	9TH E DI
FORMSHALL, JOHN	BAL	388	8TH WARD
FORN, SUSAN *	BAL	305	20TH WAR
FORNEL, MARY	BAL	046	1ST WARD
FORNEY, ABRAHAM	FRE	118	CREAGERS
FORNEY, ABRAHAM	FRE	172	5TH E DI
FORNEY, ANTHONY	CEC	205	7TH E DI
FORNEY, ANTHONY	CEC	205	7TH E DI
FORNEY, CATHERINE	PRI	009	BLADENSB
FORNEY, HENRY	BAL	253	17TH WAR
FORNEY, JACOB	CAR	316	1ST DIST
FORNEY, JACOB S.	BAL	222	1ST DIST
FORNEY, JAMES H.	FRE	279	WOODSBOR
FORNEY, MICHAEL	BAL	283	17TH WAR
FORNEY, SARAH J.	CAR	389	2ND DIST
FORNEY, SUSAN	CAR	303	1ST DIST
FORNEY, WILLIAM	CAR	388	2ND DIST
FORNEY, WILLIAM	BAL	084	10TH WAR
FORNKAMP, ANG*	BAL	294	12TH WAR
FORNTON, GEORGE	ALL	205	CUMBERLA
FORRACE, AMY	WAS	164	2ND DIST
FORRDCIET, PETER *	BAL	219	12TH WAR
FORRE, FRANCES T. *	BAL	276	20TH WAR
FORRE, PHILA *	BAL	276	20TH WAR
FORRED, WILLIAM L.	HAR	194	3RD DIST
FORREDS, HENRY W.	HAR	177	3RD DIST
FORREL, JAMES	FRE	380	PETERSVI
FORREST, ABRAHAM-BLACK	ST	296	2ND E DI
FORREST, ANNA M.S.	MGM	404	ROCKERLE
FORREST, BETSY	BAL	447	14TH WAR
FORREST, CATHERINE	FRE	086	FREDERIC
FORREST, DAVID	FRE	153	10TH E D
FORREST, DAVID C.	BAL	173	1ST WARD
FORREST, HESTER	BAL	244	17TH WAR
FORREST, JACOB	FRE	145	10TH E D
FORREST, JAMES	BAL	254	17TH WAR
FORREST, JAMES	BAL	069	4TH WARD
FORREST, JAMES P.	ST	310	1ST E DI
FORREST, JEREMIAH	FRE	153	10TH E D
FORREST, JOHN	FRE	152	10TH E D
FORREST, JOHN	BAL	292	20TH WAR
FORREST, JOHN	ANN	455	HOWARD D
FORREST, JOHN F.	BAL	131	16TH WAR
FORREST, JOHN W.	ST	305	1ST E DI
FORREST, JOSEPH	ST	280	3RD E DI
FORREST, JULIA	BAL	032	15TH WAR
FORREST, JULIA	BAL	164	2ND DIST
FORREST, LEONARD	BAL	254	17TH WAR
FORREST, MARY	ANN	455	HOWARD D
FORREST, MARY J.	BAL	111	1ST WARD
FORREST, MICHAEL	BAL	361	3RD WARD
FORREST, MOREAN	BAL	467	14TH WAR
FORREST, NELSON	CAR	285	7TH DIST
FORREST, NICHOLAS	BAL	252	17TH WAR
FORREST, SAMUEL	FRE	364	CATOCTIN
FORREST, SARAH	CAR	284	7TH DIST
FORREST, SARAH A.	BAL	191	6TH WARD
FORREST, SOLOMON	FRE	364	CATOCTIN
FORREST, SUSAN	ST	307	1ST E DI
FORREST, TALITHA*	BAL	347	3RD WARD
FORREST, THOMAS	BAL	010	1ST WARD
FORREST, THOMAS J.	BAL	108	15TH WAR
FORREST, URIAH	MGM	374	ROCKERLE
FORREST, WESLEY	FRE	364	CATOCTIN
FORREST, WILLIAM	BAL	193	17TH WAR
FORREST, WILLIAM	ALL	106	5TH E.D.
FORREST, WILLIAM A.	BAL	272	17TH WAR
FORRESTER, BENJAMIN	BAL	233	12TH WAR
FORRESTER, FRANCIS	BAL	137	2ND DIST
FORRESTER, GEORGE	BAL	250	17TH WAR
FORRESTER, JAMES	BAL	060	15TH WAR
FORRESTER, JAMES	BAL	286	7TH WARD
FORRESTER, JOHN	ANN	418	HOWARD D
FORRESTER, JOSEPH	BAL	105	2ND DIST
FORRESTER, OHN G.	BAL	047	1ST WARD
FORRESTER, RACHEL	BAL	106	2ND DIST
FORRESTER, ROBERT	BAL	029	15TH WAR
FORRISTER, THOMAS	HAR	140	2ND DIST
FORRSEY, DAVID	CAR	306	1ST DIST
FORSCER, HENRY	BAL	175	19TH WAR
FORSCHALL, JAMES	BAL	200	2ND WARD
FORSCHITE, ALEXANDER	BAL	118	1ST WARD
FORSETT, LEVY	BAL	122	11TH WAR
FORSEYTH, ALEXANDER	BAL	164	11TH WAR
FORSEYTH, BARNEY	BAL	040	16TH WAR
FORSEYTH, MARY	BAL	053	18TH WAR
FORST, DORCAS	ANN	433	HOWARD D
FORSTER, DANIEL H.	BAL	316	3RD WARD
FORSTER, FRANCIS	BAL	024	9TH WARD
FORSTER, JACOB	BAL	354	3RD WARD
FORSTER, JANE	BAL	055	4TH WARD
FORSTER, LEONARD	BAL	354	3RD WARD
FORSTER, PERRY	BAL	192	11TH WAR
FORSTER, WILLIAM	BAL	002	9TH WARD
FORSYTH, ALEXANDER	BAL	132	1ST WARD
FORSYTH, ALEXANDER	BAL	308	20TH WAR
FORSYTH, ANDREW	BAL	161	6TH WARD
FORSYTH, DAVID	BAL	302	20TH WAR
FORSYTH, EDWARD	BAL	338	13TH WAR
FORSYTH, EMANUEL	BAL	297	20TH WAR
FORSYTH, GEORGE W.	BAL	148	19TH WAR
FORSYTH, HENRY	ANN	515	HOWARD D
FORSYTH, JAMES	ALL	235	CUMBERLA
FORSYTH, JAMES	CAL	046	3RD DIST
FORSYTH, JOHN	ANN	515	HOWARD D
FORSYTH, JULIA	BAL	142	19TH WAR
FORSYTH, LEMUEL	BAL	194	6TH WARD
FORSYTH, MATILDA	BAL	132	5TH WARD
FORSYTH, PETER	CAR	298	1ST DIST
FORSYTH, RAYMOND	BAL	313	20TH WAR
FORSYTH, SARAH E.	BAL	006	16TH WAR
FORSYTH, THOMA	BAL	125	2ND DIST
FORSYTH, WILLIAM	BAL	024	2ND DIST
FORSYTH, WILLIAM	BAL	025	15TH WAR
FORSYTH, WILLIAM	ALL	215	CUMBERLA
FORSYTH, WILLIAM	BAL	183	19TH WAR
FORSYTH, WILLIAM	BAL	173	19TH WAR
FORSYTHE, BARNEY	BAL	101	18TH WAR
FORSYTHE, CATHARINE	ALL	040	2ND E.D.
FORSYTHE, ELSANDER J.	HAR	154	3RD DIST
FORSYTHE, GABRIEL	ALL	033	2ND E.D.
FORSYTHE, GEORGE	HAR	015	1ST DIST
FORSYTHE, GEORGE H.	CAR	277	7TH DIST
FORSYTHE, JACOB	WAS	114	2ND DIST
FORSYTHE, JAMES	BAL	348	1ST DIST
FORSYTHE, JOHN	ALL	035	2ND E.D.
FORSYTHE, JOSEPH	BAL	388	1ST DIST
FORSYTHE, SAMUEL	HAR	030	1ST DIST
FORSYTHE, SAMUEL	HAR	168	3RD DIST
FORSYTHE, SAMUEL	HAR	155	3RD DIST
FORSYTHE, SARAH	BAL	233	1ST DIST
FORSYTHE, SUSANA	CAR	249	3RD DIST
FORSYTHE, WILLIAM	HAR	030	1ST DIST
FORSYTHE, WILLIAM A.	HAR	030	1ST DIST
FORT, ANN	BAL	244	12TH WAR
FORT, BERNARD	ANN	457	HOWARD D
FORT, CATHARINE	BAL	229	1ST DIST
FORT, LEANDER A.	BAL	461	14TH WAR
FORT, MARTHA	BAL	152	19TH WAR
FORT, MARY C.	BAL	462	14TH WAR
FORT, THOMAS	BAL	239	20TH WAR
FORT, THOMAS	WAS	154	2ND DIST
FORT, WILLIAM	ANN	452	HOWARD D
FORTAIN, HENRY	BAL	250	2ND WARD
FORTENET, JONATHAN	CEC	045	1ST E DI
FORTHMAN, FERDINAND	WAS	131	HAGERSTO
FORTHMAN, FREDERICK	WAS	135	HAGERSTO
FORTHSYTH, DAVID	WAS	141	2ND DIST
FORTHSYTH, JACOB	WAS	141	2ND DIST
FORTHSYTHE, ABRAHAM	WAS	142	2ND DIST
FORTHSYTHE, DENTON	WAS	142	2ND DIST
FORTHSYTHE, JOHN	WAS	141	2ND DIST
FORTHSYTHE, JOHN	WAS	142	2ND DIST
FORTHSYTHE, JOHN	WAS	141	2ND DIST
FORTHYSE, JACOB	WAS	139	2ND DIST
FORTIA, HENRY *	BAL	245	5TH WARD
FORTIA, JOHN	BAL	245	5TH WARD
FORTIA, LEWIS R.	BAL	245	5TH WARD
FORTIE, GEORGE	BAL	395	14TH WAR
FORTIE, JANE R.	BAL	271	7TH WARD
FORTIE, JOHN	BAL	392	14TH WAR
FORTIE, JOHN C.	BAL	271	7TH WARD
FORTIE, MARY J.	BAL	069	10TH WAR
FORTIME, THOMAS	BAL	449	1ST DIST
FORTINNE, JOHN	BAL	210	2ND WARD
FORTLAND, LEVI	BAL	169	19TH WAR
FORTLING, HENRY	BAL	164	19TH WAR
FORTMAN, ADOLPHUS	BAL	128	1ST WARD
FORTMAN, JOHN	BAL	126	18TH WAR
FORTMAN, MARY	BAL	352	13TH WAR
FORTMAN, MINARD	BAL	135	11TH WAR
FORTNER, HEZEKIAH	FRE	155	10TH E D
FORTNER, HTOMAS	ANN	346	3RD DIST
FORTNER, REBECCA	ANN	346	3RD DIST
FORTNET, CHARLES	CEC	063	1ST E DI
FORTNEY, DAVID	FRE	072	FREDERIC
FORTNEY, THEODORE	BAL	227	1ST DIST
FORTUNE, ANN R.	BAL	057	10TH WAR
FORTUNE, COLUMBUS	BAL	029	4TH WARD
FORTUNE, GEORGE	BAL	035	1ST WARD
FORTUNE, JAMES	CEC	152	PORT DEP
FORTUNE, JOHN A.	BAL	057	10TH WAR
FORTUNE, MARY	BAL	361	13TH WAR
FORTUNE, SUSAN	BAL	317	3RD WARD
FORTY, ANN	BAL	151	11TH WAR
FORTY, DANIEL	BAL	152	5TH WARD
FORTY, GEORGIANNA	BAL	340	13TH WAR
FORTY, ROGER	ALL	139	6TH E.D.
FORTZER, CHARLES	BAL	135	1ST WARD
FORWARD, CHAUNCEY	ALL	096	5TH E.D.
FORWAY, JOSEPH	BAL	225	2ND WARD

Name	County	Page	District
FORWOOD, EDWARD	HAR	092	2ND DIST
FORWOOD, HENRY	HAR	077	BEL AIR
FORWOOD, JACOB	HAR	036	1ST DIST
FORWOOD, JACOB	HAR	112	2ND DIST
FORWOOD, JAMES	HAR	109	2ND DIST
FORWOOD, JAMES	HAR	034	1ST DIST
FORWOOD, JOHN	HAR	013	1ST DIST
FORWOOD, JONATHAN	HAR	083	2ND DIST
FORWOOD, MARY E.	HAR	036	1ST DIST
FORWOOD, PARKER	HAR	008	1ST DIST
FORWOOD, PARKER	HAR	109	2ND DIST
FORWOOD, SAMUEL W.	HAR	094	2ND DIST
FORWOOD, WILLIAM	HAR	094	2ND DIST
FOSBENNER, DANIEL	BAL	078	15TH WAR
FOSBENNER, WILLIAM	BAL	047	15TH WAR
FOSBORB, JOHN H.	BAL	383	8TH WARD
FOSCHT, MARGARET	FRE	155	10TH E D
FOSCHT, SAMUEL	FRE	153	10TH E D
FOSET, ISAAC	CAR	228	5TH DIST
FOSET, JOHN	CAR	228	5TH DIST
FOSETH, AMELIA	CAR	231	5TH DIST
FOSEY, CATHRENE	BAL	189	11TH WAR
FOSEY, HENRIETTA	BAL	048	15TH WAR
FOSHOT, NANCY	FRE	195	5TH E DI
FOSHER, CHARELS	BAL	286	2ND WARD
FOSLER, JOB	BAL	370	3RD WARD
FOSLER, MARY	BAL	371	3RD WARD
FOSOLET, BARBARA	BAL	436	8TH WARD
FOSS, CHARLES M.	BAL	083	1ST WARD
FOSS, CHRISTINA	BAL	154	16TH WAR
FOSS, HENRY	BAL	075	10TH WAR
FOSS, LAURA	BAL	465	14TH WAR
FOSS, LAURA M.	BAL	083	1ST WARD
FOSS, MARY	MGM	359	BERRYS D
FOSS, MATILDA	BAL	315	7TH WARD
FOSS, WILLIAM	BAL	457	14TH WAR
FOSSED, MARGARET	ANN	497	HOWARD D
FOSSETT, EDWARD	WOR	287	BERLIN 1
FOSSETT, H.	BAL	149	1ST WARD
FOSSETT, JAMES	PRI	033	VANSVILL
FOSSETT, JANE	BAL	415	8TH WARD
FOSSETT, JOHN	BAL	325	3RD WARD
FOSSETT, LAMBERT*	SOM	502	SALISBUR
FOSSETT, MICHAEL	BAL	278	7TH WARD
FOSSETT, THOMAS	SOM	488	SALISBUR
FOSSETT, THOMAS	CAR	373	9TH DIST
FOSSIT, GEORGE	WOR	271	BERLIN 1
FOSSITT, EBEN	WOR	294	9TH E DI
FOSSITT, JOHN	WOR	293	9TH E DI
FOSSITT, MARY	BAL	204	11TH WAR
FOSSITT, STEPHEN	WOR	293	9TH E DI
FOSTBINER, DANIEL	BAL	120	1ST WARD
FOSTCHER, JOSEPH	BAL	061	1ST WARD
FOSTEHER, MARGARET	BAL	061	1ST WARD
FOSTER, ANGELINE	FRE	108	CREAGERS
FOSTER, ANNA	BAL	150	5TH WARD
FOSTER, ARTHUR	BAL	260	6TH WARD
FOSTER, B.	BAL	154	1ST WARD
FOSTER, BETSY	DOR	448	1ST DIST
FOSTER, CATHARINE	BAL	204	11TH WAR
FOSTER, CATHARINE	ANN	515	HOWARD D
FOSTER, CHARLES	CEC	075	NORTHEAS
FOSTER, CHARLES	BAL	214	17TH WAR
FOSTER, CHRISTIAN	ALL	227	CUMBERLA
FOSTER, DAIVD	WOR	264	BERLIN 1
FOSTER, DANIEL	DOR	462	1ST DIST
FOSTER, DAVID	WAS	070	2ND SUBD
FOSTER, DAVID	BAL	434	1ST DIST
FOSTER, DIAH*	DOR	354	3RD DIVI
FOSTER, ELISHA	CEC	068	5TH E DI
FOSTER, ELIZABETH	CEC	067	5TH E DI
FOSTER, ELIZABETH	BAL	054	9TH WARD
FOSTER, EMEALS-BLACK	CAR	140	NO TWP L
FOSTER, FRANCIS	CEC	075	NORTHEAS
FOSTER, FRANCIS S.	BAL	039	1ST WARD
FOSTER, FRANK	BAL	264	7TH WARD
FOSTER, GEORGE	CEC	004	ELKTON 3
FOSTER, GEORGE	CAR	183	8TH DIST
FOSTER, GEORGE	SOM	397	BRINKLEY
FOSTER, GEORGE S.*	BAL	321	3RD WARD
FOSTER, GEORGE W.	QUE	123	1ST E DI
FOSTER, GEROCE	WAS	160	2ND DIST
FOSTER, HENRY	HAR	157	3RD DIST
FOSTER, HIRAM	BAL	090	5TH WARD
FOSTER, J.	BAL	152	1ST WARD
FOSTER, JACOB W.	ANN	514	HOWARD D
FOSTER, JAMES	BAL	134	1ST WARD
FOSTER, JAMES	BAL	121	1ST WARD
FOSTER, JAMES	BAL	156	16TH WAR
FOSTER, JAMES	BAL	049	15TH WAR
FOSTER, JAMES	FRE	123	CREAGERS
FOSTER, JAMES	CEC	029	CHESAPEA
FOSTER, JAMES G.	BAL	046	9TH WARD
FOSTER, JAMES J.	BAL	140	1ST WARD
FOSTER, JAMES K.	BAL	258	17TH WAR
FOSTER, JAMES M.	BAL	059	1ST WARD
FOSTER, JEFFERSON	CEC	078	NORTHEAS
FOSTER, JOHN	CEC	079	NORTHEAS
FOSTER, JOHN	CAR	140	NO TWP L
FOSTER, JOHN	CEC	193	5TH E DI
FOSTER, JOHN	BAL	134	1ST WARD
FOSTER, JOHN	BAL	123	2ND DIST
FOSTER, JOHN	WAS	162	2ND DIST
FOSTER, JOHN	KEN	306	3RD DIST
FOSTER, JOHN	ST	338	4TH E DI
FOSTER, JOSEPH	BAL	129	5TH WARD
FOSTER, JOSEPHINE	BAL	269	2ND WARD
FOSTER, JOSHUA	CEC	080	NORTHEAS
FOSTER, JULIANN	WAS	157	2ND DIST
FOSTER, KENNY	BAL	269	2ND WARD
FOSTER, LEMUEL	ALL	248	CUMBERLA
FOSTER, LUCIRA	BAL	040	1ST WARD
FOSTER, LUCY	DOR	416	1ST DIST
FOSTER, MALAN	BAL	442	8TH WARD
FOSTER, MARGARET	ALL	159	6TH E.D.
FOSTER, MARIA	CEC	020	ELKTON 3
FOSTER, MARY	BAL	113	18TH WAR
FOSTER, MARY	BAL	100	18TH WAR
FOSTER, MARY	BAL	154	2ND DIST
FOSTER, MARY A.	BAL	096	15TH WAR
FOSTER, MARY J.	CEC	079	NORTHEAS
FOSTER, N.	BAL	136	1ST WARD
FOSTER, NANCY	BAL	301	1ST DIST
FOSTER, NANCY	BAL	012	18TH WAR
FOSTER, NICHOLAS	BAL	015	2ND DIST
FOSTER, NICHOLAS	BAL	432	1ST DIST
FOSTER, PATRICK	BAL	163	2ND DIST
FOSTER, PERRY	BAL	281	2ND WARD
FOSTER, PRUDENCE	CEC	193	5TH E DI
FOSTER, REBECCA	CEC	021	ELKTON 3
FOSTER, ROBERT	BAL	258	6TH WARD
FOSTER, SAMUEL	BAL	089	18TH WAR
FOSTER, SAMUEL	CEC	187	7TH E DI
FOSTER, SAMUEL	BAL	131	18TH WAR
FOSTER, SAMUEL-BLACK	CAL	056	3RD DIST
FOSTER, SARAH	BAL	054	9TH WARD
FOSTER, SARAH	BAL	134	5TH WARD
FOSTER, SARAH P.	HAR	156	3RD DIST
FOSTER, SUSAN	KEN	233	2ND DIST
FOSTER, THOMAS	CEC	168	6TH E DI
FOSTER, THOMAS	BAL	171	1ST WARD
FOSTER, THOMAS	BAL	164	1ST WARD
FOSTER, THOMAS	ANN	435	HOWARD D
FOSTER, THOMAS	ST	339	5TH E DI
FOSTER, THOMAS R.	ANN	446	HOWARD D
FOSTER, THOMPSON	ANN	337	3RD DIST
FOSTER, WALTER A.	BAL	165	1ST WARD
FOSTER, WILLIAM	BAL	015	2ND DIST
FOSTER, WILLIAM	BAL	258	17TH WAR
FOSTER, WILLIAM	BAL	452	14TH WAR
FOSTER, WILLIAM	DOR	415	1ST DIST
FOSTER, WILLIAM H.	QUE	128	1ST E DI
FOSTER, WILLIAM H.D.	QUE	128	1ST E DI
FOSTER, WILLIAM J.	BAL	328	3RD WARD
FOSTER, WILLIAM T.	BAL	309	3RD WARD
FOSTER, WILLIAM-BLACK	CAR	140	NO TWP L
FOSTER, WINTHROP F.	BAL	376	3RD WARD
FOSTIE, GEORGE J.	BAL	092	5TH WARD
FOSWARD, MARY	BAL	119	2ND DIST
FOSYTH, LYDIA	BAL	307	12TH WAR
FOTEZ, TOBEAS	ALL	133	4TH E.D.
FOTHERGILL, ELIZA	BAL	045	1ST WARD
FOTNER, JOHN	BAL	068	1ST WARD
FOUBLE, CONRAD	BAL	283	1ST DIST
FOUCH, DAVID	WAS	293	1ST DIST
FOUCH, JOHN W.	BAL	415	14TH WAR
FOUCHILL, ANN	BAL	103	5TH WARD
FOUGE, RICHARD HENRY	BAL	304	1ST DIST
FOUGE, S. D.	BAL	303	1ST DIST
FOUGHT, JOHN	BAL	230	1ST DIST
FOUGHT, JOSEPH	BAL	150	11TH WAR
FOUK, GEORGE	WAS	294	1ST DIST
FOUK, GEORGE	WAS	162	HAGERSTO
FOUK, HARRIET	WAS	162	HAGERSTO
FOUK, HENRY	WAS	294	1ST DIST
FOUK, MARY E.	WAS	164	HAGERSTO
FOUKS, JANE	BAL	361	3RD WARD
FOUKS, JOHN	BAL	428	8TH WARD
FOUKS, JOHN-MULATTO	BAL	223	2ND WARD
FOULDS, JAMES H.	BAL	366	3RD WARD
FOULK, ELIZA	BAL	408	8TH WARD
FOULK, ROSA	BAL	287	3RD WARD
FOULKE, JOHN	BAL	108	2ND DIST
FOULKS, GEORGE	CEC	028	CHESAPEA
FOULL, MATTHEW	PRI	107	PISCATAW
FOULLEN, HENRY	CEC	025	ELKTON 3
FOULLEN, HENRY	CEC	026	ELKTON 3
FOULLON, SUSAN J.	CEC	026	ELKTON 3
FOULTON, CATHARINE	BAL	353	7TH WARD
FOULTON, HANNAH	CEC	023	ELKTON 3
FOUMAN, JACOB	FRE	099	FREDERIC
FOUND, MOSES	FRE	279	WOODSBOR
FOUNK, HENRY	BAL	125	1ST WARD
FOUNTAIN, ALBERT	BAL	208	17TH WAR
FOUNTAIN, ALFRED	BAL	211	17TH WAR
FOUNTAIN, BERTHA A.-BLACK	CAR	147	NO TWP L
FOUNTAIN, CHARLES	BAL	290	7TH WARD
FOUNTAIN, EDUARD	BAL	188	2ND WARD
FOUNTAIN, EDWARD B.A.	CAR	068	NO TWP L
FOUNTAIN, ELIZABETH-BLACK	CAR	167	NO TWP L
FOUNTAIN, ELLEN	CEC	004	ELKTON 3
FOUNTAIN, ESAU	BAL	160	2ND DIST
FOUNTAIN, FENDER-MULATTO	CAR	148	NO TWP L
FOUNTAIN, GEORGE	BAL	185	16TH WAR
FOUNTAIN, HARRIET	TAL	070	EASTON T
FOUNTAIN, HENNY*	TAL	024	EASTON D
FOUNTAIN, HENRY	BAL	462	14TH WAR
FOUNTAIN, HESTER	CAR	092	NO TWP L
FOUNTAIN, HESTER	BAL	246	6TH WARD
FOUNTAIN, IMANUEL	CEC	021	ELKTON 3
FOUNTAIN, JAMES	BAL	160	1ST WARD
FOUNTAIN, JAMES H.	CAR	169	NO TWP L
FOUNTAIN, JAMES M. C. R.	SOM	554	TYASKIN
FOUNTAIN, JOHN	BAL	408	14TH WAR
FOUNTAIN, JOHN A.	BAL	101	18TH WAR
FOUNTAIN, JOHN C.	QUE	245	5TH E DI
FOUNTAIN, JOHN R.	CAR	148	NO TWP L
FOUNTAIN, JOHN W.	TAL	092	ST MICHA
FOUNTAIN, JOHN-BLACK	CAR	091	NO TWP L
FOUNTAIN, JOHN-BLACK	QUE	159	2ND E DI
FOUNTAIN, JOSEPH-BLACK	CAR	131	NO TWP L
FOUNTAIN, JOSIAH	TAL	050	EASTON T
FOUNTAIN, LEVENIA	TAL	065	EASTON T
FOUNTAIN, LOUISA	BAL	121	16TH WAR
FOUNTAIN, LYDIA	CAR	147	NO TWP L
FOUNTAIN, MARCY	BAL	440	14TH WAR
FOUNTAIN, MARY	CEC	009	ELKTON 3
FOUNTAIN, MARY	WOR	189	7TH E DI
FOUNTAIN, MARY E.-BLACK	QUE	199	3RD E DI
FOUNTAIN, MARY JANE	BAL	211	17TH WAR
FOUNTAIN, MARY S.	WOR	307	2ND E DI
FOUNTAIN, NEHEMIAH	CAR	146	NO TWP L
FOUNTAIN, PATTY	TAL	029	EASTON D
FOUNTAIN, PETER	BAL	078	15TH WAR
FOUNTAIN, REBECA	CEC	019	ELKTON 3
FOUNTAIN, REBECCA	TAL	065	EASTON T
FOUNTAIN, ROSE-BLACK	QUE	125	1ST E DI
FOUNTAIN, SARAH	BAL	441	14TH WAR
FOUNTAIN, SOLOMON	BAL	167	16TH WAR
FOUNTAIN, SOTTY	WOR	343	1ST E DI
FOUNTAIN, STEPHEN	BAL	207	17TH WAR
FOUNTAIN, TABDIAL	CAR	165	NO TWP L
FOUNTAIN, WESLEY	CEC	068	5TH E DI
FOUNTAIN, WESTLEY	TAL	045	EASTON T
FOUNTAIN, WILLABY*	TAL	046	EASTON T
FOUNTAIN, WILLIAM	TAL	072	EASTON T
FOUNTAIN, WILLIAM	CAR	115	NO TWP L
FOUNTAIN, WILLIAM	BAL	119	11TH WAR
FOUNTAIN, WILLIAM	BAL	110	2ND DIST
FOUNTAINE, BENJAMIN	SOM	350	BRINKLEY
FOUNTAINE, CHARLES G.	SOM	350	BRINKLEY
FOUNTAINE, EDWARD	SOM	351	BRINKLEY
FOUNTAINE, ESTER	SOM	360	BRINKLEY
FOUNTAINE, JOHN E.	SOM	436	PRINCESS
FOUNTAINE, JOHN T.	SOM	418	PRINCESS
FOUNTAINE, LEAH	SOM	351	BRINKLEY
FOUNTAINE, LEVIN J.	SOM	520	BARREN C
FOUNTAINE, MARY	SOM	351	BRINKLEY
FOUNTAINE, WHITTY	SOM	351	BRINKLEY
FOUNTAN, LAZERIOUS	BAL	107	18TH WAR
FOURZE, JACOB	BAL	023	15TH WAR
FOUS, SAMEUL *	BAL	289	7TH WARD
FOUSCHILD, JAMES	BAL	113	5TH WARD
FOUSE, CATHARINE	BAL	346	7TH WARD
FOUSE, ELLENDER	BAL	018	1ST WARD
FOUSE, JAMES	BAL	017	1ST WARD
FOUSE, SUSAN	BAL	226	6TH WARD
FOUSE, WILLIAM	BAL	077	1ST WARD
FOUSKIS, THOMAS	BAL	137	1ST WARD
FOUST, JOHN	CAL	048	3RD DIST
FOUSTER, NICHOLAS	BAL	063	1ST WARD
FOUT, BARBARA	FRE	058	FREDERIC
FOUT, CHARLES	FRE	085	FREDERIC
FOUT, CHARLOT	FRE	014	FREDERIC
FOUT, GEORGE	FRE	077	FREDERIC
FOUT, GRAFTON	FRE	070	FREDERIC
FOUT, GREENBURY	FRE	070	FREDERIC
FOUT, HENRY	FRE	015	FREDERIC
FOUT, JOHNH.	FRE	098	FREDERIC
FOUT, LEWIS	FRE	070	FREDERIC
FOUT, MAGDALENE	FRE	069	FREDERIC
FOUT, MICHAEL W.	FRE	377	PETERSVI
FOUT, PETER L.	FRE	070	FREDERIC
FOUT, SUSAN C.	FRE	070	FREDERIC
FOUTCH, WILLIAM	WAS	134	2ND DIST
FOUTRY, MARY	CEC	210	7TH E DI
FOUTTS, SUSAN	CEC	156	6TH E DI
FOUTZ, DAVID	FRE	279	WOODSBOR
FOUTZ, ELIZABETH	CAR	381	2ND DIST
FOUTZ, ELIZABETH	WAS	106	2ND DIST
FOUTZ, HENRY	WAS	099	2ND DIST
FOUTZ, JACOB	CAR	389	2ND DIST
FOUTZ, JOSEPH	CAR	379	2ND DIST
FOUTZ, MARY	ALL	097	5TH E.D.
FOUTZ, RICHARD B.	CAR	383	2ND DIST
FOW, WASHINGTON	WAS	074	2ND SUBD
FOWARD, SARAH	CEC	172	6TH E DI
FOWBLE, ABRAHAM	BAL	394	14TH WAR
FOWBLE, ARASBUS	CAR	182	8TH DIST
FOWBLE, DAVID	CAR	174	8TH DIST
FOWBLE, DELIA	BAL	069	2ND DIST
FOWBLE, DINAH	BAL	190	5TH DIST
FOWBLE, ELIZABETH	BAL	283	7TH WARD
FOWBLE, HENRY	CAR	174	8TH DIST
FOWBLE, IRENA	BAL	197	5TH DIST
FOWBLE, JACOB	BAL	197	5TH DIST
FOWBLE, MICHAEL	CAR	174	8TH DIST
FOWBLE, PETER	CAR	330	MANCHEST
FOWBLE, PETER	BAL	197	5TH DIST
FOWBLE, PETER	BAL	190	5TH DIST
FOWBLE, PETER	BAL	196	5TH DIST
FOWBLE, RICHARD B.	BAL	183	5TH DIST
FOWBLE, SARAH	BAL	237	1ST DIST
FOWBLE, THOMAS	BAL	029	18TH WAR
FOWBLE, THOMAS	CAR	184	8TH DIST
FOWBLE, WILLIAM	BAL	432	1ST DIST
FOWBLE, WILLIAM A.	CAR	185	8TH DIST
FOWBLE, WILLIAM J.	CAR	182	8TH DIST
FOWBLES, FREDERICK	BAL	237	1ST DIST
FOWDRANE, DEDRICK	BAL	276	2ND WARD
FOWDRY, WILLIAM	BAL	014	2ND DIST
FOWELL, AMELIA	BAL	207	2ND WARD
FOWELL, MARY	BAL	290	12TH WAR
FOWL, ROBERT	BAL	240	17TH WAR
FOWLE, MELCHER	BAL	189	5TH DIST
FOWLER, ALEXANDER	KEN	210	2ND DIST
FOWLER, ALEXANDER C.	CAL	035	2ND DIST
FOWLER, ALICE	FRE	022	FREDERIC
FOWLER, ANN	ST	345	5TH E DI
FOWLER, ANN S.	CHA	221	ALLENS F
FOWLER, AQUILLA	BAL	069	2ND DIST
FOWLER, BARBARA	CAL	038	2ND DIST
FOWLER, BENEDICT	PRI	071	MARLBROU
FOWLER, BENJAMIN	CAR	282	7TH DIST
FOWLER, BENJAMIN	FRE	037	FREDERIC
FOWLER, BENJAMIN	BAL	209	2ND WARD
FOWLER, BIRDJELL	KEN	219	2ND DIST
FOWLER, CATHERINE	BAL	076	4TH WARD
FOWLER, CLEMENT	CAR	095	NO TWP L
FOWLER, CYRILUIS	CAL	028	2ND DIST
FOWLER, DANIEL	PRI	065	NOTTINGH
FOWLER, DAVID	BAL	013	1ST WARD
FOWLER, DAVID A.	BAL	281	20TH WAR
FOWLER, E.H.	BAL	003	18TH WAR
FOWLER, EDWARD	CAR	282	7TH DIST
FOWLER, EDWARD	SOM	499	SALISBUR
FOWLER, EDWARD JR.	CAR	282	7TH DIST
FOWLER, EDWIN	HAR	091	2ND DIST
FOWLER, ELISTH	BAL	134	2ND DIST
FOWLER, ELIZABETH	CEC	027	CHESAPEA
FOWLER, ELIZABETH	CAL	012	1ST DIST
FOWLER, ELIZABETH	PRI	100	SPALDING
FOWLER, ELIZABETH	ST	346	5TH E DI
FOWLER, ELIZABETH	ST	322	4TH E DI
FOWLER, ELIZABETH J.	BAL	081	4TH WARD
FOWLER, ELIZABETH S.	KEN	208	2ND DIST
FOWLER, ELLEN	FRE	043	FREDERIC
FOWLER, ELLEN	ANN	311	1ST DIST
FOWLER, EVAN M.	QUE	123	1ST E DI
FOWLER, FAMILIA	BAL	044	4TH WARD
FOWLER, FRANCES	BAL	087	4TH WARD
FOWLER, FRANCES	BAL	264	2ND WARD
FOWLER, FRANCIS	BAL	435	14TH WAR
FOWLER, FREDERICK	WAS	287	1ST DIST
FOWLER, GEORGE A.	CAR	282	7TH DIST
FOWLER, GEORGE B. V.	CAR	283	7TH DIST
FOWLER, GEORGE SR.	CAR	283	7TH DIST
FOWLER, GEORGE W.	CAL	043	3RD DIST
FOWLER, GUSTAVUS	CHA	246	HILLTOP
FOWLER, HARRY	MGM	379	ROCKERLE
FOWLER, HENRY	ST	343	5TH E DI
FOWLER, HENRY	BAL	108	2ND DIST
FOWLER, HENRY	ANN	357	3RD DIST
FOWLER, HENSON	BAL	289	7TH WARD
FOWLER, ISAAC	BAL	190	6TH WARD
FOWLER, ISAAC	CAL	002	1ST DIST
FOWLER, ISAAC J.	BAL	076	4TH WARD
FOWLER, J.	BAL	158	1ST WARD
FOWLER, JAMES	BAL	076	2ND DIST
FOWLER, JAMES	BAL	022	2ND DIST
FOWLER, JAMES H.	BAL	005	18TH WAR
FOWLER, JAMES H.	PRI	014	BLADENSB
FOWLER, JAMES W.	ANN	295	1ST DIST
FOWLER, JANE F.	ST	322	4TH E DI
FOWLER, JOHN	ST	348	5TH E DI
FOWLER, JOHN	ANN	300	1ST DIST
FOWLER, JOHN	BAL	156	1ST WARD
FOWLER, JOHN	BAL	260	2ND WARD
FOWLER, JOHN	BAL	141	1ST WARD
FOWLER, JOHN	BAL	399	3RD WARD

Name	County	Page	District
FOWLER, JOHN	BAL	259	1ST DIST
FOWLER, JOHN	BAL	099	15TH WAR
FOWLER, JOHN	BAL	352	7TH WARD
FOWLER, JOHN	CAR	267	WESTMINS
FOWLER, JOHN	CAL	033	2ND DIST
FOWLER, JOHN	MGM	391	ROCKERLE
FOWLER, JOHN	CHA	246	HILLTOP
FOWLER, JOHN A.	PRI	101	SPALDING
FOWLER, JOHN D.	PRI	052	AQUASCO
FOWLER, JOHN E.	SOM	490	SALISBUR
FOWLER, JOHN H.	MGM	359	BERRYS D
FOWLER, JOHN W.	KEN	308	3RD DIST
FOWLER, JOSEPH	WAS	160	2ND DIST
FOWLER, JOSEPH	CHA	222	ALLENS F
FOWLER, JOSEPH	FRE	180	5TH E DI
FOWLER, JOSEPH	ANN	397	8TH DIST
FOWLER, JOSEPH H.	ST	324	4TH E DI
FOWLER, JOSEPH O.	CAL	049	3RD DIST
FOWLER, JOSHUA	BAL	133	2ND DIST
FOWLER, JOSHUA U.	BAL	191	5TH DIST
FOWLER, LEMUEL G.	CAL	053	3RD DIST
FOWLER, LEONARD	BAL	296	17TH WAR
FOWLER, LEWIS	CAR	397	2ND DIST
FOWLER, LLOYD	BAL	225	19TH WAR
FOWLER, LOUISA	BAL	200	5TH DIST
FOWLER, M.	PRI	117	PISCATAW
FOWLER, MARGARET	BAL	162	6TH WARD
FOWLER, MARGARET	BAL	305	3RD WARD
FOWLER, MARGARET A.	CAL	024	2ND DIST
FOWLER, MARGARET B.	PRI	065	NOTTINGH
FOWLER, MARGARETT	BAL	085	4TH WARD
FOWLER, MARIA	BAL	115	5TH WARD
FOWLER, MARIA	BAL	206	2ND WARD
FOWLER, MARTHA	BAL	004	4TH WARD
FOWLER, MARY	BAL	225	12TH WAR
FOWLER, MARY F.	PRI	014	BLADENSB
FOWLER, MATILDA	BAL	210	2ND WARD
FOWLER, MICHA A.	FRE	249	NEW MARK
FOWLER, NACKY	BAL	363	13TH WAR
FOWLER, NANCY	BAL	069	2ND DIST
FOWLER, O. L.	KEN	214	2ND DIST
FOWLER, PERRY	BAL	106	18TH WAR
FOWLER, PERRY	FRE	084	FREDERIC
FOWLER, PETER	BAL	313	12TH WAR
FOWLER, PHIL M.	BAL	274	20TH WAR
FOWLER, PRISCILLA	CAL	057	3RD DIST
FOWLER, REBECCA	CAL	045	3RD DIST
FOWLER, RICHARD	CAR	282	7TH DIST
FOWLER, RICHARD	CAR	282	7TH DIST
FOWLER, RICHARD	ANN	348	3RD DIST
FOWLER, RICHARD W.	BAL	272	12TH WAR
FOWLER, ROBERT	BAL	164	11TH WAR
FOWLER, ROBERT	WAS	287	1ST DIST
FOWLER, RUBEN	BAL	164	11TH WAR
FOWLER, SAMUEL	BAL	336	7TH WARD
FOWLER, SAMUEL	BAL	459	1ST DIST
FOWLER, SAMUEL	PRI	068	NOTTINGH
FOWLER, SAMUEL B.	BAL	074	10TH WAR
FOWLER, SAMUEL P.	CEC	007	ELKTON 3
FOWLER, SARAH	BAL	111	15TH WAR
FOWLER, SUSAN	BAL	097	5TH WARD
FOWLER, SUSAN	CAR	277	7TH DIST
FOWLER, SUSAN	PRI	004	BLADENSB
FOWLER, SUTTON J.	CAL	002	1ST DIST
FOWLER, THOMAS	BAL	041	4TH WARD
FOWLER, THOMAS	BAL	205	17TH WAR
FOWLER, THOMAS	BAL	295	3RD WARD
FOWLER, THOMAS	BAL	393	1ST DIST
FOWLER, WILLIAM	BAL	141	16TH WAR
FOWLER, WILLIAM	BAL	271	12TH WAR
FOWLER, WILLIAM	BAL	070	2ND DIST
FOWLER, WILLIAM	ANN	427	HOWARD D
FOWLER, WILLIAM	CEC	021	ELKTON 3
FOWLER, WILLIAM	BAL	296	17TH WAR
FOWLER, WILLIAM	BAL	134	18TH WAR
FOWLER, WILLIAM	PRI	008	BLADENSB
FOWLER, WILLIAM	PRI	072	MARLBROU
FOWLER, WILLIAM C.	CAL	062	3RD DIST
FOWLER, WILLIAM C.	BAL	355	3RD WARD
FOWLER, WILLIAM H.	BAL	263	2ND WARD
FOWLER, WILLIAM H.	BAL	286	7TH WARD
FOWLER, WILLIAM H.	ST	340	5TH E DI
FOWLER, WILLIAM W.	BAL	444	14TH WAR
FOWLER, GILBERT	CAL	033	2ND DIST
FOWLES, JOHN H.	BAL	287	3RD WARD
FOWLES, MARY R. *	BAL	064	18TH WAR
FOWLING, MARY	BAL	069	2ND DIST
FOWNER, ISAAC	BAL	459	8TH WARD
FOX, A.	BAL	002	15TH WAR
FOX, ALEXANDER	FRE	389	PETERSVI
FOX, ALOSIUS	FRE	167	EMMITTSB
FOX, BALTZER	FRE	293	WOODSBOR
FOX, BALZER	FRE	412	8TH E DI
FOX, BARBARA	CAR	265	WESTMINS
FOX, BARBARA	BAL	434	8TH WARD
FOX, C. F. ADOLPHUS	FRE	059	FREDERIC
FOX, CATHARINE	BAL	437	14TH WAR
FOX, CATHERINE	BAL	386	8TH WARD
FOX, CHALRES J.	BAL	029	18TH WAR
FOX, CHARLES	BAL	076	1ST WARD
FOX, CHARLES F.	FRE	359	CATOCTIN
FOX, CHARLES F. L.	FRE	373	CATOCTIN
FOX, CHARLES F. O.	FRE	061	FREDERIC
FOX, CONRAD	ANN	444	HOWARD D
FOX, CONRAD	BAL	355	1ST DIST
FOX, CONRADT	BAL	254	17TH WAR
FOX, CYRUS	FRE	290	WOODSBOR
FOX, CANIEL	FRE	432	8TH E DI
FOX, CANIEL	BAL	281	1ST DIST
FOX, DEXTER	BAL	251	1ST DIST
FOX, ELIZABETH	ALL	131	8TH E.D.
FOX, ELIZABETH	FRE	083	FREDERIC
FOX, ELIZABETH A.	ANN	413	HOWARD D
FOX, EMIT	FRE	358	CATOCTIN
FOX, FRANCES	BAL	402	14TH WAR
FOX, FRANCIS	HAR	193	3RD DIST
FOX, CEORGE	BAL	232	1ST DIST
FOX, GEORGE	BAL	292	7TH WARD
FOX, GEORGE	WAS	156	HAGERSTO
FOX, GEORGE H.	FRE	151	10TH E D
FOX, GEORGE P.	FRE	151	10TH E D
FOX, HANNAH M.	FRE	152	10TH E D
FOX, HENRY	FRE	258	NEW MARK
FOX, HENRY	FRE	410	8TH E DI
FOX, HENRY	WAS	061	2ND SUBD
FOX, HENRY*	BAL	376	3RD WARD
FOX, HENRY-BLACK	QUE	131	1ST E DI
FOX, HESTER	BAL	228	6TH WARD
FOX, HESTOR	BAL	144	5TH WARD
FOX, HUGH	BAL	197	2ND WARD
FOX, JACOB	FRE	156	10TH E D
FOX, JACOB	FRE	410	8TH E DI
FOX, JACOB	FRE	093	FREDERIC
FOX, JACOB-BLACK	QUE	150	1ST E DI
FOX, JAMES	FRE	259	NEW MARK
FOX, JAMES	BAL	144	1ST WARD
FOX, JAMES	BAL	005	15TH WAR
FOX, JAMES-BLACK	QUE	142	1ST E DI
FOX, JANE	BAL	235	6TH WARD
FOX, JESSE	FRE	282	WOODSBOR
FOX, JOHN	FRE	257	NEW MARK
FOX, JOHN	FRE	187	5TH E DI
FOX, JOHN	FRE	109	CREAGERS
FOX, JOHN	FRE	108	CREAGERS
FOX, JOHN	FRE	083	FREDERIC
FOX, JOHN	FRE	084	FREDERIC
FOX, JOHN	CEC	210	7TH E DI
FOX, JOHN	BAL	233	17TH WAR
FOX, JOHN	BAL	016	9TH WARD
FOX, JOHN	BAL	061	1ST WARD
FOX, JOHN	BAL	114	5TH WARD
FOX, JOHN	BAL	075	2ND DIST
FOX, JOHN	ALL	236	CUMBERLA
FOX, JOHN W.	FRE	085	FREDERIC
FOX, JOSEPHIEN	BAL	316	1ST DIST
FOX, LEWIS	BAL	390	3RD WARD
FOX, LIDDY	BAL	081	4TH WARD
FOX, LUTHER	BAL	042	9TH WARD
FOX, MAGDELANA	FRE	290	WOODSBOR
FOX, MARGARET	BAL	355	8TH WARD
FOX, MARY	BAL	145	2ND DIST
FOX, MARY	BAL	253	12TH WAR
FOX, MARY	BAL	050	15TH WAR
FOX, MARY	WAS	106	2ND DIST
FOX, MARY A.	WAS	156	HAGERSTO
FOX, MARY ANN	BAL	147	5TH WARD
FOX, MARY M.	FRE	453	8TH E DI
FOX, MARYANN	FRE	428	8TH E DI
FOX, MICHAEL	BAL	321	1ST DIST
FOX, NANCY	ANN	468	HOWARD D
FOX, PETER	BAL	244	2ND WARD
FOX, PETER	BAL	273	17TH WAR
FOX, PHILIP	CEC	185	7TH E DI
FOX, REBECCA	BAL	096	5TH WARD
FOX, REBECCA	KEN	296	3RD DIST
FOX, RICHARD	HAR	042	1ST DIST
FOX, SAMUEL	FRE	414	8TH E DI
FOX, SAMUEL	FRE	293	WOODSBOR
FOX, SAMUEL	HAR	194	3RD DIST
FOX, SARAH	SOM	460	HANGARY
FOX, SARAH C.	FRE	420	8TH E DI
FOX, SARAH J.	BAL	068	1ST WARD
FOX, SERECK	HAR	055	1ST DIST
FOX, SOLOMON J.	CAR	389	2ND DIST
FOX, THOMAS	BAL	134	18TH WAR
FOX, THOMAS	BAL	139	16TH WAR
FOX, WILLIAM	HAR	042	1ST DIST
FOX, WILLIAM	FRE	122	CREAGERS
FOX, WILLIAM *	BAL	055	18TH WAR
FOX, WILLIAM H.	BAL	030	18TH WAR
FOXALL, JANE	BAL	022	15TH WAR
FOXALL, MARY	BAL	373	8TH WARD
FOXALL, ZEBEDEE	BAL	018	15TH WAR
FOXBENDER, GILBERT	BAL	177	2ND WARD
FOXCRAFT, ELIZA J.	BAL	020	4TH WARD
FOXCROFT, ELIZA	HAR	114	2ND DIST
FOXCROFT, JAMES	BAL	171	6TH WARD
FOXE, CHARLES *	CAR	340	6TH DIST
FOXENBERGER, ACAM	WAS	268	1ST DIST
FOXENBURGEN, ALFRED	BAL	177	2ND WARD
FOXTER, MAX	PRI	107	PISCATAW
FOXWALL, BENJAMIN L.	BAL	324	3RD WARD
FOXWELE, MARY A.	DOR	444	1ST DIST
FOXWELE, NOAH	DOR	444	1ST DIST
FOXWELL, AHAM*	DOR	411	1ST DIST
FOXWELL, BENJAMIN H.	SOM	433	PRINCESS
FOXWELL, BETSY	DOR	434	1ST DIST
FOXWELL, CATHARINE *	BAL	035	15TH WAR
FOXWELL, CHARELS	BAL	004	1ST WARD
FOXWELL, DOROTHERY	DOR	369	3RD DIVI
FOXWELL, ELZIABETH	ST	306	1ST E DI
FOXWELL, GEORGE	BAL	260	17TH WAR
FOXWELL, JAMES L.	ST	313	1ST E DI
FOXWELL, JANE	DOR	299	1ST DIST
FOXWELL, JOHN*	BAL	388	3RD WARD
FOXWELL, JOSEPH	BAL	093	1ST WARD
FOXWELL, JOSHUA	BAL	026	4TH WARD
FOXWELL, LEVIN	ST	313	1ST E DI
FOXWELL, MARGARETT	BAL	009	4TH WARD
FOXWELL, MARTIN	DOR	338	3RD DIVI
FOXWELL, MARY	ST	267	3RD E DI
FOXWELL, ROBERT	DOR	350	3RD DIVI
FOXWELL, SOLOMON	DOR	349	3RD DIVI
FOXWELL, SUSAN	SOM	463	HANGARY
FOXWELL, SUSAN	SOM	461	HANGARY
FOXWELL, WILLIAM	DOR	355	3RD DIVI
FOXWELL, ZACHARIAH	BAL	032	15TH WAR
FOXWELL, ZIPPORA	BAL	063	15TH WAR
FOY, ALEXANDER	BAL	296	17TH WAR
FOY, ANN	WAS	043	2ND SUBD
FOY, E. A.	BAL	072	10TH WAR
FOY, HENRY*	BAL	376	3RD WARD
FOY, JAMES	BAL	079	15TH WAR
FOY, JOHN H.	BAL	089	5TH WARD
FOY, MARY	BAL	458	1ST DIST
FOY, MARY J.	FRE	066	FREDERIC
FOY, NICHOLAS	WAS	123	HAGERSTO
FOY, PALTUS	HAR	177	3RD DIST
FOY, PETER	BAL	028	1ST WARD
FOY, WILLIAM Z.	BAL	093	15TH WAR
FOYE, JOSEPH	BAL	388	13TH WAR
FOYLE, SOLOMON	BAL	237	12TH WAR
FRACHMER, ISAAC	BAL	065	1ST WARD
FRADRED, NICHOLAS	CEC	084	CHARLEST
FRAE, GEORGE	BAL	010	9TH WARD
FRAGE, WILLIAM	BAL	348	1ST DIST
FRAGER, WESLEY	FRE	060	FREDERIC
FRAGER, WILLIAM	HAR	178	3RD DIST
FRAGUE, SAMUEL *	KEN	218	2ND DIST
FRAGUE, WILLIAM	KEN	210	2ND DIST
FRAHEY, BRIDGETT	BAL	037	4TH WARD
FRAILEY, CHRISTIAN	FRE	002	FREDERIC
FRAILEY, HENRY	FRE	002	FREDERIC
FRAILEY, JOHN	FRE	071	FREDERIC
FRAILEY, JOHN	WAS	153	2ND DIST
FRAILEY, LEONARD	BAL	474	14TH WAR
FRAILEY, MARY A.	FRE	073	FREDERIC
FRAILEY, P. L.	BAL	149	1ST WARD
FRAILEY, PHILLIP	BAL	237	2ND WARD
FRAILEY, THOMAS	FRE	122	CREAGERS
FRAILINGER, MARY	BAL	269	2ND WARD
FRAILLEY, DAVID	FRE	140	CREAGERS
FRAIN, JOHN	ALL	136	4TH E.D.
FRAINER, MARY	ALL	050	10TH E.D
FRAISUR, CHARLES	DOR	363	3RD DIVI
FRAISUR, ELIZA	DOR	364	3RD DIVI
FRAISUR, JOHN	DOR	357	3RD DIVI
FRAISUR, MACE	DOR	357	3RD DIVI
FRAIZER, CHARLES M.	CAL	010	1ST DIST
FRAIZER, ELIZA	BAL	115	5TH WARD
FRAIZER, ELIZA	BAL	092	5TH WARD
FRAIZER, ELIZA	BAL	114	5TH WARD
FRAIZER, SAMUEL	BAL	092	5TH WARD
FRAIZER, SARAH	BAL	266	17TH WAR
FRAIZER, WILLIAM	BAL	265	17TH WAR
FRALEY, FREDERICK	ALL	111	5TH E.D.
FRALEY, JOHN C.	DOR	319	1ST DIST
FRALEY, MAIS	ALL	096	5TH E.D.
FRAME, DAVID	BAL	351	1ST DIST
FRAME, JOSEPH M.	CAR	316	1ST DIST
FRAME, RICHARD	CAR	316	1ST DIST
FRAMES, JAMES P.	BAL	043	15TH WAR
FRAMFREE, DORCAS	MGM	372	BERRYS D
FRAMFREE, SAMUEL	MGM	372	BERRYS D
FRAMIGER, EDWARD H.	BAL	062	1ST WARD
FRAMPROM, EMILY H.	BAL	308	3RD WARD
FRAMPTOM, ALEXANDER	DOR	324	1ST DIST
FRAMPTOM, ASBERRY	DOR	307	1ST DIST
FRAMPTON, CHARLES	TAL	015	EASTON D
FRAMPTON, CHARLES H.	TAL	002	EASTON D
FRAMPTON, EDWARD	TAL	030	EASTON D
FRAMPTON, EELIZABETH	TAL	065	EASTON T
FRAMPTON, ELIZABETH F.	TAL	046	EASTON T
FRAMPTON, ELLEN	TAL	065	EASTON T
FRAMPTON, GEORGE W.	TAL	046	EASTON T
FRAMPTON, JAMES	TAL	038	EASTON D
FRAMPTON, JAMES C.	TAL	062	EASTON D
FRAMPTON, JOHN	TAL	038	EASTON D
FRAMPTON, JOHN H.	TAL	021	EASTON D
FRAMPTON, LEVIN*	TAL	004	EASTON D
FRAMPTON, LUTHER T.	TAL	028	EASTON D
FRAMPTON, MARIAH	TAL	016	EASTON D
FRAMPTON, MARY	TAL	038	EASTON D
FRAMPTON, MARY	TAL	038	EASTON D
FRAMPTON, MARY R.	DOR	317	1ST DIST
FRAMPTON, N.*	TAL	038	EASTON D
FRAMPTON, NANCY	TAL	028	EASTON D
FRAMPTON, RICHARD	TAL	027	EASTON D
FRAMPTON, RICHARD B.	TAL	096	ST MICHA
FRAMPTON, RISDEN	TAL	017	EASTON D
FRAMPTON, SALLY	TAL	038	EASTON D
FRAMPTON, THOMAS	TAL	030	EASTON D
FRAMPTON, THOMAS H.	TAL	027	EASTON D
FRAMPTON, VINCENT	TAL	102	ST MICHA
FRAMPTON, WILLIAM	TAL	038	EASTON D
FRAMY, DANIEL	HAR	174	3RD DIST
FRAMY, JAMES	HAR	174	3RD DIST
FRANASCUS, SALLY	BAL	337	13TH WAR
FRANCAS, ADAM	BAL	253	2ND WARD
FRANCAS, JOHN	BAL	029	1ST WARD
FRANCAS, JOHN-BLACK	BAL	219	2ND WARD
FRANCAS, MARY-BLACK	BAL	223	2ND WARD
FRANCAS, SAMUEL-BLACK	BAL	219	2ND WARD
FRANCAS, THOMAS	BAL	275	2ND WARD
FRANCE, A.	BAL	117	1ST WARD
FRANCE, A.	BAL	333	1ST DIST
FRANCE, ALPHEUS	ALL	036	2ND E.D.
FRANCE, AUGUSTUS	BAL	066	2ND DIST
FRANCE, CARL	BAL	231	2ND WARD
FRANCE, CATHARINE	ALL	037	2ND E.D.
FRANCE, D.	BAL	130	5TH WARD
FRANCE, ELIZABETH	BAL	064	2ND DIST
FRANCE, ELIZABETH	ANN	463	HOWARD D
FRANCE, F.	BAL	233	2ND WARD
FRANCE, FREDERICK	BAL	226	2ND WARD
FRANCE, GEORGE	WAS	300	1ST DIST
FRANCE, HENRY	BAL	338	1ST DIST
FRANCE, JAMES	BAL	079	2ND DIST
FRANCE, JADCB	BAL	239	2ND WARD
FRANCE, JOHN	BAL	266	2ND WARD
FRANCE, JOHN	BAL	218	2ND WARD
FRANCE, JOHN	ALL	027	2ND E.D.
FRANCE, JOHN	ALL	025	2ND E.D.
FRANCE, JOHN	BAL	051	1ST WARD
FRANCE, JOHN JULIUS	BAL	335	13TH WAR
FRANCE, JOHN W.	ANN	471	HOWARD D
FRANCE, JONATHAN	ALL	036	2ND E.D.
FRANCE, JONATHAN	ALL	036	2ND E.D.
FRANCE, JOSEPH	ALL	025	2ND E.D.
FRANCE, JOSEPH	ALL	036	2ND E.D.
FRANCE, JOSEPH	ALL	153	6TH E.D.
FRANCE, JOSEPH	BAL	210	19TH WAR
FRANCE, JOSHUA	ALL	036	2ND E.D.
FRANCE, JULIA A.	BAL	203	19TH WAR
FRANCE, LEVI	ALL	022	2ND E.D.
FRANCE, LEWIS	BAL	178	19TH WAR
FRANCE, LUCY	BAL	275	17TH WAR
FRANCE, R. M. L.	BAL	333	1ST DIST
FRANCE, RACHEL	ANN	434	HOWARD D
FRANCE, RICHARD	HAR	098	2ND DIST
FRANCE, RICHARD	BAL	068	18TH WAR
FRANCE, ROBERT	ALL	021	2ND E.D.
FRANCE, S. L.	BAL	332	1ST DIST
FRANCE, SAMUEL	BAL	338	1ST DIST
FRANCE, THOMAS	ALL	024	3RD E.D.
FRANCE, THOMAS	BAL	138	16TH WAR
FRANCE, THOMAS	BAL	455	14TH WAR
FRANCE, WILLIAM	BAL	104	5TH WARD
FRANCE, WILLIAM	ANN	508	HOWARD D
FRANCE, WILLIAM F.	ALL	163	6TH E.D.
FRANCES, CHARLES	BAL	127	2ND DIST
FRANCES, ELIZA	BAL	080	4TH WARD
FRANCES, J.	BAL	152	1ST WARD
FRANCES, JAMES	BAL	087	2ND DIST
FRANCES, JANE LISTER	BAL	472	14TH WAR
FRANCES, JOHN	BAL	069	4TH WARD
FRANCES, JOHN	BAL	160	1ST WARD
FRANCES, JOHN-BLACK	CAR	169	NO TWP L
FRANCES, JOSHUA	BAL	127	2ND DIST
FRANCES, MARY A.	CEC	090	4TH E DI
FRANCES, PRISCELLER	BAL	091	2ND DIST
FRANCES, ROBERT	BAL	297	7TH WARD
FRANCES, SAMUEL	BAL	090	2ND DIST
FRANCES, THOMAS-	BAL	091	2ND DIST
FRANCHI, CELILIA	BAL	464	14TH WAR
FRANCHI, MARIA	BAL	465	14TH WAR
FRANCHILLI, LOUISA	BAL	008	9TH WARD
FRANCIOLY, FELIX	BAL	042	9TH WARD
FRANCIS L.	BAL	157	1ST WARD
FRANCIS, ABRAHAM	BAL	200	5TH WARD

Name	County	Page	District
FRANCIS. ADITHA	WAS	047	2ND SUBD
FRANCIS. AGNES A.	BAL	219	6TH WARD
FRANCIS. ANN	BAL	101	18TH WAR
FRANCIS. ANN	FRE	396	PETERSVI
FRANCIS, BROTHER	BAL	216	11TH WAR
FRANCIS. BROTHER	BAL	216	11TH WAR
FRANCIS. CHARLES	BAL	151	1ST WARD
FRANCIS, CORBIN	HAR	074	1ST DIST
FRANCIS. CORBIN	HAR	062	1ST DIST
FRANCIS, DANIEL-BLACK	BAL	250	2ND WARD
FRANCIS, DINER	HAR	065	1ST DIST
FRANCIS. ELIAS	BAL	068	10TH WAR
FRANCIS. ELIZA	BAL	118	5TH WARD
FRANCIS. ELLEN	BAL	306	3RD WARD
FRANCIS. ELSEY	BAL	044	15TH WAR
FRANCIS, EMELINE A.	KEN	210	2ND DIST
FRANCIS. F.	BAL	159	1ST WARD
FRANCIS, FLEETWOOD	BAL	335	3RD WARD
FRANCIS. FOUSTINE	BAL	180	11TH WAR
FRANCIS, GEORGE	BAL	290	12TH WAR
FRANCIS. GEORGE	BAL	160	16TH WAR
FRANCIS. GEORGE	BAL	099	10TH WAR
FRANCIS. HARRIET	BAL	248	6TH WARD
FRANCIS. HENRY	CEC	199	7TH E DI
FRANCIS, HESTER A.-BLACK	BAL	220	2ND WARD
FRANCIS. HETTY	BAL	111	5TH WARD
FRANCIS. ISAAC	BAL	127	2ND DIST
FRANCIS, JACOB	HAR	065	1ST DIST
FRANCIS. JAMES-BLACK	FRE	019	FREDERIC
FRANCIS, JANE	BAL	246	20TH WAR
FRANCIS. JANE	KEN	311	3RD DIST
FRANCIS, JEREMIAH	CEC	091	4TH E DI
FRANCIS, JESSEE	BAL	265	7TH WARD
FRANCIS, JOHN	BAL	062	2ND DIST
FRANCIS, JOHN	BAL	334	3RD WARD
FRANCIS, JOHN	BAL	215	2ND WARD
FRANCIS, JOHN	BAL	168	1ST WARD
FRANCIS, JOHN	BAL	456	8TH WARD
FRANCIS. JOHN-MULATTO	BAL	212	2ND WARD
FRANCIS, K.	BAL	115	1ST WARD
FRANCIS. KITTY	WAS	164	HAGERSTO
FRANCIS, LEOPOLD	BAL	194	6TH WARD
FRANCIS, LEVAN	BAL	128	2ND DIST
FRANCIS. MARIA	BAL	127	2ND DIST
FRANCIS, MARY	BAL	443	14TH WAR
FRANCIS, MICHAEL	BAL	320	12TH WAR
FRANCIS. MILLY	KEN	216	2ND DIST
FRANCIS. N. JOHCN	ALL	229	CUMBERLA
FRANCIS. OBBY-BLACK	BAL	245	2ND WARD
FRANCIS. PETER	BAL	168	1ST WARD
FRANCIS, PETER	PRI	005	BLADENSB
FRANCIS. SARAH	BAL	369	8TH WARD
FRANCIS. SARAH	BAL	454	8TH WARD
FRANCIS. THOMAS	BAL	335	7TH WARD
FRANCIS. THOMAS	BAL	262	6TH WARD
FRANCIS. THOMAS	BAL	385	3RD WARD
FRANCIS. THOMAS	BAL	172	1ST WARD
FRANCIS. THOMAS-BLACK	FRE	011	FREDERIC
FRANCIS. WALTER	BAL	026	15TH WAR
FRANCIS. WESLEY	BAL	146	11TH WAR
FRANCIS. WILLIAM	SOM	417	PRINCESS
FRANCIS. WILLIAM	BAL	136	1ST WARD
FRANCIS. WILLIAM	ALL	220	CUMBERLA
FRANCIS, WILLIAM P.	KEN	210	2ND DIST
FRANCIS.EPHRAHAM-BLACK	FRE	033	FREDERIC
FRANCISCO. ELIZA	BAL	302	12TH WAR
FRANCISCO. FRANCIS A.	BAL	299	7TH WARD
FRANCISCO. GEORGE	BAL	302	12TH WAR
FRANCISCO. LUDING	BAL	008	9TH WARD
FRANCISCO. SARAH E.	BAL	312	7TH WARD
FRANCISCUS, FRANCES	BAL	095	2ND DIST
FRANCISS. THEODORE	SOM	426	PRINCESS
FRANCK. MARY	BAL	203	2ND WARD
FRANCKE. AUSTIN F.	BAL	053	15TH WAR
FRANCKE, MICHAEL	BAL	142	16TH WAR
FRANCONIA. FELIX	BAL	020	9TH WARD
FRANEKE. JOHN G.	BAL	014	9TH WARD
FRANES, MARY	BAL	041	1ST WARD
FRANETONE, EDWARD	CAR	136	NO TWP L
FRANEY, PATRICK	ALL	129	4TH E.D.
FRANGEL, ROBERT	CEC	015	ELKTON 3
FRANHOUSER, HENRY	WAS	213	1ST DIST
FRANICS. ANTONIA	BAL	286	2ND WARD
FRANICS, RACHAEL	BAL	306	12TH WAR
FRANIELS. WILLIAM *	BAL	094	2ND DIST
FRANILY. TERESSA	BAL	189	2ND WARD
FRANK. ABRAHAM	BAL	122	1ST WARD
FRANK, ADAM	BAL	306	7TH WARD
FRANK, ANDREW	BAL	187	6TH WARD
FRANK, ANDREW J.	CHA	231	HILLTOP
FRANK, ANN S.	BAL	299	1ST DIST
FRANK, ASCHAR	BAL	386	13TH WAR
FRANK, BENJAMIN	BAL	389	8TH WARD
FRANK, CATHARINE	BAL	200	17TH WAR
FRANK. CHARLES	BAL	161	19TH WAR
FRANK. CLAMME *	ALL	102	5TH E.D.
FRANK. DAVID	BAL	263	2ND WARD
FRANK. CAVID	BAL	213	2ND WARD
FRANK, ELEANORA	BAL	169	6TH WARD
FRANK, ELIZABETH	BAL	317	3RD WARD
FRANK, ELIZABETH	BAL	077	4TH WARD
FRANK. EMMA	ALL	198	CUMBERLA
FRANK, ERNEST	BAL	437	14TH WAR
FRANK. FREDERICK	BAL	001	4TH WARD
FRANK. FREDERICK	BAL	293	7TH WARD
FRANK. FREDERICK W.	BAL	345	3RD WARD
FRANK, GEORGE	BAL	254	2ND WARD
FRANK, GEORGE	BAL	393	14TH WAR
FRANK, GEORGE	BAL	287	17TH WAR
FRANK. GEORGE	CAR	335	6TH DIST
FRANK, GEORGE C.	BAL	284	12TH WAR
FRANK. GEORGE K.	BAL	208	6TH DIST
FRANK. GOTLIPP	BAL	218	17TH WAR
FRANK. HENRY	CAR	375	9TH DIST
FRANK. HENRY	CAR	249	3RD DIST
FRANK. HENRY	CAR	177	8TH DIST
FRANK, HENRY	BAL	338	3RD WARD
FRANK, HENRY	BAL	315	3RD WARD
FRANK, HENRY	BAL	092	10TH WAR
FRANK, J. A.	TAL	014	EASTON D
FRANK. JACOB	BAL	209	17TH WAR
FRANK, JACOB H.	BAL	208	6TH DIST
FRANK. JANE	BAL	208	6TH DIST
FRANK, JOHN	BAL	208	6TH DIST
FRANK. JOHN	BAL	294	7TH WARD
FRANK. JOHN	BAL	066	1ST WARD
FRANK, JOHN	BAL	158	2ND DIST
FRANK. JOHN	ALL	242	CUMBERLA
FRANK, JOHN	BAL	327	7TH WARD
FRANK, JOHN	BAL	252	17TH WAR
FRANK. JOHN	CAR	340	6TH DIST
FRANK. JOHN C.	WOR	259	BERLIN 1
FRANK. JOHN D.	BAL	300	17TH WAR
FRANK. JOHN G.	BAL	291	17TH WAR
FRANK. JOHN P.	BAL	299	1ST DIST
FRANK. JOSEPH	BAL	200	17TH WAR
FRANK, L.	BAL	149	1ST WARD
FRANK. LEESON N.	BAL	222	6TH WARD
FRANK. LEWIS	BAL	300	7TH WARD
FRANK. LEWIS	BAL	387	8TH WARD
FRANK. LEWIS	ALL	103	5TH E.D.
FRANK. MAGDALAM	BAL	066	1ST WARD
FRANK. MARGARET	ALL	208	CUMBERLA
FRANK, MARGARET	BAL	328	7TH WARD
FRANK. MARGARETTA	BAL	196	6TH WARD
FRANK, MOSES	BAL	315	3RD WARD
FRANK, NATHAN	BAL	239	6TH WARD
FRANK. PAULINA	BAL	386	13TH WAR
FRANK. PETER	BAL	427	8TH WARD
FRANK. PETER	BAL	377	8TH WARD
FRANK. PETER	BAL	113	2ND DIST
FRANK. PHILIP	ALL	198	CUMBERLA
FRANK. PHILIP	BAL	299	1ST DIST
FRANK, PHILIP	BAL	198	5TH DIST
FRANK. SAMUEL	BAL	269	7TH WARD
FRANK. SAMUEL	BAL	076	18TH WAR
FRANK. SIMON	BAL	013	9TH WARD
FRANK. WILLIAM	BAL	265	2ND WARD
FRANK. WILLIAM	BAL	267	2ND WARD
FRANK. WILLIAM	BAL	200	2ND WARD
FRANKE. JACOB	BAL	046	9TH WARD
FRANKENBERGER, LEWIS	BAL	107	2ND DIST
FRANKENBERRG. MARGARET	WAS	025	2ND SUBD
FRANKENBERRY. WILLIAM H.	WAS	245	SMITHSBU
FRANKENBUSCH, G.	BAL	150	1ST WARD
FRANKENBUSH. G.	BAL	165	1ST WARD
FRANKFCRTER. DANIEL	CAR	330	MANCHEST
FRANKFORTER. DAVID C.	CAR	330	MANCHEST
FRANKFCRTER, FREDERICK	CAR	356	6TH DIST
FRANKFORTER. JACOB	CAR	328	MANCHEST
FRANKFOTER. JACOB	CAR	174	8TH DIST
FRANKIE. HENRIETTA	BAL	321	1ST DIST
FRANKINFIELD. DANIEL	KEN	248	2ND DIST
FRANKINFIELD. ISAAC	KEN	247	2ND DIST
FRANKLAND. GEORGE W.	BAL	119	1ST WARD
FRANKLE. HANNAH	BAL	029	9TH WARD
FRANKLE. ISAAC	BAL	028	9TH WARD
FRANKLIN. ABRAHAM	ANN	442	HOWARD D
FRANKLIN, ABRAHAM	ANN	344	3RD DIST
FRANKLIN. ALEXANDER	ANN	407	8TH DIST
FRANKLIN. ANDERSON	ANN	284	ANNAPOLI
FRANKLIN. BENJAMIN	ALL	220	CUMBERLA
FRANKLIN. BLANCHE	BAL	097	10TH WAR
FRANKLIN, CHARLES	BAL	088	2ND DIST
FRANKLIN. CHARLES	BAL	114	5TH WARD
FRANKLIN. CHARLES	CAR	373	9TH DIST
FRANKLIN. CHARLES W.	CAR	361	9TH DIST
FRANKLIN. COLUMBUS	WAS	269	1ST DIST
FRANKLIN. DANIEL	PRI	074	MARLBROU
FRANKLIN. DAVID	BAL	229	1ST DIST
FRANKLIN. ELEANA	CHA	237	HILLTOP
FRANKLIN. ELIZA	CAR	364	9TH DIST
FRANKLIN, ELIZA	BAL	294	1ST DIST
FRANKLIN. ELIZA	BAL	226	12TH WAR
FRANKLIN. ELIZA	WOR	257	1ST CENS
FRANKLIN. ELIZABETH	CAR	393	2ND DIST
FRANKLIN. FRANCIS	CAR	283	7TH DIST
FRANKLIN. GEORGE	BAL	407	14TH WAR
FRANKLIN. GEORGE	BAL	113	18TH WAR
FRANKLIN. GEORGE	BAL	088	10TH WAR
FRANKLIN, GEORGE E.	ANN	279	ANNAPOLI
FRANKLIN. GEORGE H.	BAL	456	8TH WARD
FRANKLIN. GEORGE P.	WOR	261	BERLIN 1
FRANKLIN. GRISTY	PRI	051	AQUASCO
FRANKLIN. HANNAH	BAL	313	20TH WAR
FRANKLIN. HENRIETTA	BAL	100	15TH WAR
FRANKLIN. HENRIETTA	BAL	402	3RD WARD
FRANKLIN. HENRY	ANN	345	3RD DIST
FRANKLIN. HENRY D.	CAR	361	9TH DIST
FRANKLIN. HESTER	DOR	364	3RD DIVI
FRANKLIN. HEZEKIAH	CHA	235	HILLTOP
FRANKLIN. HEZEKIAH	CHA	235	HILLTOP
FRANKLIN. IRA	BAL	146	1ST WARD
FRANKLIN. J. B.	CHA	233	HILLTOP
FRANKLIN. J. MISS-	ANN	402	8TH DIST
FRANKLIN, JACK	BAL	223	1ST DIST
FRANKLIN. JACOB	ANN	345	3RD DIST
FRANKLIN. JACOB	BAL	438	1ST DIST
FRANKLIN. JAMES	BAL	044	9TH WARD
FRANKLIN. JAMES	BAL	333	7TH WARD
FRANKLIN. JAMES	CHA	222	ALLENS F
FRANKLIN. JAMES	BAL	170	19TH WAR
FRANKLIN. JARED	BAL	106	2ND DIST
FRANKLIN. JARET	BAL	428	1ST DIST
FRANKLIN, JOHN	FRE	300	WOODSBOR
FRANKLIN. JOHN	BAL	333	13TH WAR
FRANKLIN. JOHN	PRI	034	VANSVILL
FRANKLIN. JOHN	PRI	021	VANSVILL
FRANKLIN. JOHN R.	WOR	299	SNOW HIL
FRANKLIN. JOSEPH	BAL	407	14TH WAR
FRANKLIN. JOSEPH	BAL	185	16TH WAR
FRANKLIN. JOSHUA	CAR	361	9TH DIST
FRANKLIN. JOSHUA D.	BAL	131	16TH WAR
FRANKLIN, JULIA A.	BAL	094	15TH WAR
FRANKLIN. LITTETCN	WOR	260	BERLIN 1
FRANKLIN. M.	BAL	301	20TH WAR
FRANKLIN. MADISON	WOR	299	SNOW HIL
FRANKLIN. MALINDA	CAR	285	7TH DIST
FRANKLIN. MARGARET	BAL	065	15TH WAR
FRANKLIN. MARGARETT	BAL	081	4TH WARD
FRANKLIN. MARIA	ANN	291	ANNAPOLI
FRANKLIN. MARY	CHA	235	HILLTOP
FRANKLIN, MARY	BAL	262	20TH WAR
FRANKLIN. MARY A.	BAL	049	15TH WAR
FRANKLIN. MARY B.	CHA	233	HILLTOP
FRANKLIN. MARY V.	BAL	254	6TH WARD
FRANKLIN. NANCY	WOR	261	BERLIN 1
FRANKLIN. NANCY	PRI	040	VANSVILL
FRANKLIN. NATHAN	CAR	373	9TH DIST
FRANKLIN. NET	WOR	274	BERLIN 1
FRANKLIN. NOEL E.	CHA	264	HILLTOP
FRANKLIN. PETER	BAL	086	15TH WAR
FRANKLIN. PETER	ANN	345	3RD DIST
FRANKLIN, PHILLIP-BLACK	BAL	223	2ND WARD
FRANKLIN, R.	ANN	293	ANNAPOLI
FRANKLIN. REZIN H.	CAR	226	5TH DIST
FRANKLIN. RIZIUR	CAR	362	9TH DIST
FRANKLIN. ROBERT	ANN	410	8TH DIST
FRANKLIN. ROBERT	WOR	259	BERLIN 1
FRANKLIN. RUTH	FRE	435	8TH E DI
FRANKLIN. RYAN	CAR	374	9TH DIST
FRANKLIN, SAMUEL	BAL	052	1ST WARD
FRANKLIN, SEVIN	WOR	262	BERLIN 1
FRANKLIN, SUSAN	CAR	362	9TH DIST
FRANKLIN. T.	BAL	258	12TH WAR
FRANKLIN, THOMAS	ANN	409	8TH DIST
FRANKLIN. THOMAS	ANN	279	ANNAPOLI
FRANKLIN. THOMAS	CAR	358	9TH DIST
FRANKLIN. THOMAS	BAL	108	18TH WAR
FRANKLIN. THOMAS B.	CAR	366	9TH DIST
FRANKLIN. VIRGINIA	BAL	169	6TH WARD
FRANKLIN, WALTER	CHA	288	BOJANTOW
FRANKLIN, WILLIAM	BAL	069	18TH WAR
FRANKLIN. WILLIAM	BAL	066	4TH WARD
FRANKLIN. WILLIAM	BAL	338	13TH WAR
FRANKLIN. WILLIAM	BAL	146	1ST WARD
FRANKLIN. WILLIAM N.	CHA	240	HILLTOP
FRANKLIN,LARKIN	BAL	074	2ND DIST
FRANKLIN.SUSAN	FRE	441	8TH E DI
FRANKLING. JAMES	ANN	416	HOWARD D
FRANLIN. COLUMBUS	FRE	443	8TH E DI
FRANNK. LEON	BAL	013	9TH WARD
FRANT. CAROLINE	FRE	147	10TH E D
FRANT. GODLEY	ALL	197	CUMBERLA
FRANTOM, NATHANIEL	QUE	218	3RD E DI
FRANTON. JOHN W.	QUE	203	3RD E DI
FRANTON, RICHARD S.	CAR	161	NO TWP L
FRANTON. TILGHMAN	CAR	137	NO TWP L
FRANTON, WILLIAM	ANN	350	3RD DIST
FRANTON.SUSAN	QUE	200	3RD E DI
FRANTONE. BAYARD	CAR	137	NO TWP L
FRANTORN, MARY	CAR	157	NO TWP L
FRANTS, PETER	BAL	276	1ST DIST
FRANTUM, ELIZA	KEN	302	3RD DIST
FRANTUM, HARRIET	BAL	273	17TH WAR
FRANTUM, THOMAS	BAL	326	7TH WARD
FRANTURN, HENRY	BAL	311	7TH WARD
FRANTURN. JOHN H.	BAL	293	3RD WARD
FRANTY, HENRY	BAL	244	1ST DIST
FRANTZ, ANN	WAS	121	2ND DIST
FRANTZ. CATHERINE	WAS	105	2ND DIST
FRANTZ. GEORGE	WAS	134	2ND DIST
FRANTZ, GEORGE	ALL	032	2ND E.D.
FRANTZ. HENRY	BAL	268	1ST DIST
FRANTZ, LYDIA	ALL	028	2ND E.D.
FRANTZ, WILLIAM	ALL	024	3RD E.D.
FRANTZ, WILLIAM	BAL	418	1ST DIST
FRANZ. G.	BAL	305	20TH WAR
FRANZ. MINA	BAL	039	4TH WARD
FRASER. JOHN	ST	308	1ST E DI
FRASER. SARAH	BAL	019	15TH WAR
FRASHER. WILLIAM	BAL	130	18TH WAR
FRASHIER, MARY A.	BAL	154	11TH WAR
FRASIER, ANN	BAL	231	6TH WARD
FRASIER. DAVID	BAL	047	15TH WAR
FRASIER. MARY A.	FRE	215	BUCKEYST
FRASIER. MARY E.-BLACK	FRE	230	BUCKEYST
FRASIER, THOMAS	BAL	151	2ND DIST
FRASLER. JOHN	BAL	128	18TH WAR
FRASURE. JOHN	ALL	106	5TH E.D.
FRATTON. BIDDY*	SOM	399	BRINKLEY
FRATZ. LANCHART	ALL	119	5TH E.D.
FRATZ. MNARY	ALL	207	CUMBERLA
FRATZE. JOHN	BAL	476	14TH WAR
FRAUENSHUR. FRANCIS	BAL	089	10TH WAR
FRAUER. ANDREW	BAL	307	1ST DIST
FRAUKINBURY. GEORGE	BAL	234	2ND WARD
FRAXLER. FERDINAND	ALL	244	CUMBERLA
FRAY, GEORGE	BAL	150	2ND DIST
FRAY. JACOB	BAL	125	18TH WAR
FRAY, JOHN H.	BAL	112	15TH WAR
FRAY. MARGARETT*	BAL	039	4TH WARD
FRAY. SAMUEL	BAL	147	2ND DIST
FRAYER. DANIEL	BAL	279	1ST DIST
FRAYER. LUTHER	FRE	019	FREDERIC
FRAZAR. ELIZABETH	BAL	266	1ST DIST
FRAZEE. BARBARA	ALL	026	2ND E.D.
FRAZEE. EDWARD*	TAL	018	EASTON D
FRAZEE. ELISABETH	ALL	026	2ND E.D.
FRAZEE. ELISHA	ALL	026	2ND E.D.
FRAZEE. GEORGE W.	ALL	025	2ND E.D.
FRAZEE, ISAAC	ALL	023	2ND E.D.
FRAZEE. JOHN	ALL	026	2ND E.D.
FRAZEE. JOHN	ALL	026	2ND E.D.
FRAZEE. JONATHAN	ALL	025	2ND E.D.
FRAZEE. MARGARET	ALL	033	2ND E.D.
FRAZEE. MATHIAS	ALL	026	2ND E.D.
FRAZEE. RICHARD	ALL	033	2ND E.D.
FRAZEE. SQUIRE	ALL	027	2ND E.D.
FRAZEE. THURMAN	ALL	027	2ND E.D.
FRAZENBAKER. GEORGE	ALL	003	3RD E.D.
FRAZER. AMRY-MULATTO	FRE	027	FREDERIC
FRAZER. ANN	MGM	333	CRACKLIN
FRAZER. CHARLES-BLACK	FRE	030	FREDERIC
FRAZER, HARRIET	MGM	342	CLARKSBU
FRAZER. HENRY	FRE	027	FREDERIC
FRAZER, HENRY	FRE	052	FREDERIC
FRAZER, J.B.	BAL	236	2ND WARD
FRAZER. JAMES	MGM	342	CLARKSBU
FRAZER, JEREMIAH	FRE	078	FREDERIC
FRAZER. JOHN	BAL	126	16TH WAR
FRAZER, JUDY-BLACK	FRE	044	FREDERIC
FRAZER, LYDIA	BAL	013	15TH WAR
FRAZER, MARIA	FRE	104	FREDERIC
FRAZER. RUTHANN	BAL	306	1ST DIST
FRAZER. SOLOMON	TAL	036	EASTON D
FRAZER. STEPHEN	BAL	306	1ST DIST
FRAZER, SUSAN	BAL	178	16TH WAR
FRAZER. THOMAS	MGM	333	CRACKLIN
FRAZER, WILLIAM	FRE	018	FREDERIC
FRAZER, WILLIAM R.	BAL	063	15TH WAR
FRAZIER, AMELIA	PRI	072	MARLBROU
FRAZIER, ANN	BAL	396	3RD WARD
FRAZIER, ANN	DOR	432	1ST DIST
FRAZIER. ANTHONY	PRI	116	PISCATAW
FRAZIER. ARCHIBALD	HAR	132	2ND DIST
FRAZIER. BASIL	BAL	458	8TH WARD
FRAZIER. BETSY	DOR	317	1ST DIST
FRAZIER. CALEB	QUE	227	4TH E DI
FRAZIER. CHARLES R.	DOR	395	1ST DIST
FRAZIER. CLEMENT	DOR	452	1ST DIST
FRAZIER, CORNELIUS	FRE	013	FREDERIC
FRAZIER, DANIEL	CAR	281	7TH DIST
FRAZIER. DARIAS	KEN	278	1ST DIST
FRAZIER, DAVID	QUE	230	4TH E DI
FRAZIER, DAVID	FRE	017	FREDERIC
FRAZIER, ELIZABETH	TAL	076	EASTON T
FRAZIER, EZEKIEL	DOR	382	1ST DIST
FRAZIER, FRANCES	BAL	118	15TH WAR
FRAZIER, FREDERICK	KEN	258	1ST DIST

Name	County	Page	District
FRAZIER, FRENCH*	BAL	314	3RD WARD
FRAZIER, GEORGE	DOR	308	1ST DIST
FRAZIER, GEORGE	BAL	141	11TH WAR
FRAZIER, HANNAH	BAL	125	16TH WAR
FRAZIER, HARRIET	FRE	260	NEW MARK
FRAZIER, HENRY	ANN	292	ANNAPOLI
FRAZIER, HENRY C.	FRE	379	PETERSVI
FRAZIER, HESTER	ANN	424	HOWARD D
FRAZIER, HINTON	BAL	065	1ST WARD
FRAZIER, JAMES	BAL	027	1ST WARD
FRAZIER, JAMES	BAL	143	1ST WARD
FRAZIER, JAMES	DOR	405	1ST DIST
FRAZIER, JAMES F.	BAL	397	3RD WARD
FRAZIER, JANE	BAL	070	2ND DIST
FRAZIER, JOHN	ANN	427	HOWARD D
FRAZIER, JOHN	BAL	391	3RD WARD
FRAZIER, JOHN	BAL	318	12TH WAR
FRAZIER, JOHN	FRE	395	PETERSVI
FRAZIER, JOHN	BAL	067	4TH WARD
FRAZIER, JOHN	KEN	282	3RD DIST
FRAZIER, JOHN	QUE	228	4TH E DI
FRAZIER, JOHN	PRI	119	PISCATAW
FRAZIER, JOHN A.	PRI	090	MARLBROU
FRAZIER, JOHN F.	DOR	378	1ST DIST
FRAZIER, JOHN JR.	KEN	286	3RD DIST
FRAZIER, JOHN S.	FRE	381	PETERSVI
FRAZIER, JOHN W.	BAL	425	3RD WARD
FRAZIER, JOSEPH	DOR	434	1ST DIST
FRAZIER, JOSEPH	TAL	058	EASTON D
FRAZIER, JOSEPH	BAL	329	1ST DIST
FRAZIER, JOSEPH-BLACK	FRE	196	5TH E DI
FRAZIER, JOSEPHINE	BAL	348	13TH WAR
FRAZIER, JOSIAH	FRE	384	PETERSVI
FRAZIER, LETITIA-BLACK	BAL	203	2ND WARD
FRAZIER, MARIA-BLACK	QUE	185	3RD E DI
FRAZIER, MARY	WAS	227	1ST DIST
FRAZIER, MARY	BAL	305	3RD WARD
FRAZIER, MARY	BAL	318	12TH WAR
FRAZIER, MARY	BAL	416	3RD WARD
FRAZIER, NICHOLAS	BAL	210	19TH WAR
FRAZIER, PALEY	DOR	422	1ST DIST
FRAZIER, PETER-BLACK	FRE	049	FREDERIC
FRAZIER, PHILIP	QUE	227	4TH E DI
FRAZIER, PRISCILLA	BAL	119	2ND DIST
FRAZIER, REASON	PRI	106	PISCATAW
FRAZIER, SAMUEL *	KEN	218	2ND DIST
FRAZIER, SARAH	BAL	420	3RD WARD
FRAZIER, SARAH	PRI	103	SPALDING
FRAZIER, SARAH	BAL	027	1ST WARD
FRAZIER, SARAH S.	DOR	395	1ST DIST
FRAZIER, SUSAN	ANN	292	ANNAPOLI
FRAZIER, THOMAS	QUE	235	4TH E DI
FRAZIER, THOMAS	ANN	274	ANNAPOLI
FRAZIER, THOMAS	DOR	406	1ST DIST
FRAZIER, THOMAS J.	DOR	395	1ST DIST
FRAZIER, W.	DOR	427	1ST DIST
FRAZIER, WALTER	BAL	175	2ND WARD
FRAZIER, WESLEY	ALL	053	10TH E.D
FRAZIER, WILLIAM	ANN	276	ANNAPOLI
FRAZIER, WILLIAM	BAL	242	6TH WARD
FRAZIER, WILLIAM	BAL	411	8TH WARD
FRAZIER, WILLIAM	DOR	395	1ST DIST
FRAZIER, WILLIAM	BAL	334	13TH WAR
FRAZIER, WILLIAM H.-MULAT	QUE	202	3RD E DI
FRAZUR, F.T.	BAL	163	1ST WARD
FRAZURE, ELIZABETH	DOR	322	1ST DIST
FRAZURE, JAMES H.*	DOR	308	1ST DIST
FRAZURE, JOSEPH	DOR	320	1ST DIST
FRAZURE, SOLOMON	DOR	322	1ST DIST
FRAZURE, WILLIAM	DOR	308	1ST DIST
FREAKLE, EZEKIEL*	BAL	336	3RD WARD
FREANER, HENRY	WAS	147	HAGERSTO
FREANER, MARY	WAS	131	HAGERSTO
FREANER, WILLIAM	WAS	153	HAGERSTO
FREATON, CHARLES	BAL	300	17TH WAR
FREAY, CATHARINE	WAS	157	2ND DIST
FREBUR, ANN	BAL	220	19TH WAR
FRECHTEL, CATHARINE *	BAL	375	13TH WAR
FRECKLE, LEWIS	CAR	214	5TH DIST
FREDAWAY, ELLEN	BAL	299	1ST DIST
FREDCALDAG, JOHN	BAL	167	2ND DIST
FREDDEL, CONRAD	BAL	014	9TH WARD
FREDERIC, JACOB	BAL	169	6TH WARD
FREDERICK, ALEXANDER	BAL	324	7TH WARD
FREDERICK, ANGELINE	BAL	130	11TH WAR
FREDERICK, ANN	BAL	065	2ND DIST
FREDERICK, BARBARA	BAL	202	2ND WARD
FREDERICK, CAROLINE	BAL	247	2ND WARD
FREDERICK, CATHARIEN	BAL	166	2ND DIST
FREDERICK, CATHARINE	WAS	177	1ST DIST
FREDERICK, CHARLES F.	BAL	382	8TH WARD
FREDERICK, CHRISTIANA	BAL	438	14TH WAR
FREDERICK, CHRISTOPHER	BAL	208	19TH WAR
FREDERICK, CHRISTOPHER	BAL	229	2ND WARD
FREDERICK, CHRISTOPHER	BAL	109	1ST WARD
FREDERICK, CONRAD	WAS	013	WILLIAMS
FREDERICK, EDWARD	BAL	120	1ST WARD
FREDERICK, ELLEN	BAL	205	6TH WARD
FREDERICK, GEORGE	BAL	247	2ND WARD
FREDERICK, GEROGE	BAL	104	10TH WAR
FREDERICK, H.	BAL	309	12TH WAR
FREDERICK, HANNAH	WAS	211	1ST DIST
FREDERICK, HENRY	BAL	331	13TH WAR
FREDERICK, JACOB	CAR	220	5TH DIST
FREDERICK, JACOB	CEC	034	CHESAPEA
FREDERICK, JACOB	BAL	310	20TH WAR
FREDERICK, JESSE A.	CAR	214	5TH DIST
FREDERICK, JOHN	BAL	219	17TH WAR
FREDERICK, JOHN	FRE	337	MIDDLETO
FREDERICK, JOHN	BAL	097	10TH WAR
FREDERICK, JOHN	BAL	019	9TH WARD
FREDERICK, JOHN	BAL	101	1ST WARD
FREDERICK, JOHN	BAL	021	1ST WARD
FREDERICK, JOHN	BAL	171	2ND DIST
FREDERICK, JOHN	ALL	096	5TH E.D.
FREDERICK, JOHN	WOR	242	1ST CENS
FREDERICK, JOHN W.	BAL	129	11TH WAR
FREDERICK, JOSHUA	BAL	033	2ND DIST
FREDERICK, L.	BAL	310	12TH WAR
FREDERICK, LEWIS	BAL	425	8TH WARD
FREDERICK, LLOYD	CAR	222	5TH DIST
FREDERICK, MARIA	CHA	219	ALLENS F
FREDERICK, MARSH	BAL	435	1ST DIST
FREDERICK, MARY J.	BAL	289	7TH WARD
FREDERICK, MARY J.	FRE	372	CATOCTIN
FREDERICK, MICHAEL A.	BAL	366	13TH WAR
FREDERICK, PETER	BAL	382	8TH WARD
FREDERICK, PETER B.	BAL	038	2ND DIST
FREDERICK, REUBVEN	FRE	318	MIDDLETO
FREDERICK, ROBERT	BAL	044	18TH WAR

Name	County	Page	District
FREDERICK, SHAD LER	BAL	171	2ND DIST
FREDERICK, SUS	BAL	089	18TH WAR
FREDERICK, T	BAL	087	10TH WAR
FREDERICK,	BAL	352	7TH WARD
FREDERI	BAL	324	7TH WARD
FREDER	BAL	238	20TH WAR
FREDER	BAL	242	2ND WARD
FREDER	ANN	463	HOWARD D
FREDEF	BAL	217	6TH WARD
FREDEK	BAL	085	2ND DIST
FREDER	FRE	075	FREDERIC
FREDER	FRE	067	FREDERIC
FREDERI H	BAL	067	1ST WARD
FREDERI ON	FRE	252	NEW MARK
FREDERI MUEL	WAS	212	1ST DIST
FREDERIC ELLIDALE	BAL	235	2ND WARD
FREDHOFF JACOB	ANN	382	4TH DIST
FREDHOFFL, MARY	ANN	382	4TH DIST
FREDHOFRER, GODFREY *	KEN	238	2ND DIST
FREDHOPER, GODFREY *	KEN	238	2ND DIST
FREDINGER, GEORGE	WAS	145	HAGERSTO
FREDLEY, JOHN	ALL	006	3RD E.D.
FREDLOCK, FREDERICK	ALL	045	10TH E.D
FREDLOCK, HENRY	ALL	059	10TH E.D
FREDLOOF, PETER	ALL	230	CUMBERLA
FREDMAN, MARGARET	BAL	122	18TH WAR
FREDRICK, ELIZABETH	BAL	061	18TH WAR
FREDRICK, HENRY	BAL	330	3RD WARD
FREDRICK, JOHN	BAL	207	11TH WAR
FREDRICK, LOUISA	BAL	076	4TH WARD
FREDRICK, MARY	BAL	209	11TH WAR
FREDRICKS, JOHN	BAL	225	2ND WARD
FREDS, JACOB	ALL	184	9TH E.D.
FREDS, REBECCA-MULATTO	FRE	218	BUCKEYST
FREOUND, SPITZNOS	BAL	472	14TH WAR
FREDYARE, JOAB *	ALL	087	5TH E.D.
FREE, ELIZA	PRI	079	QUEEN AN
FREE, HARRIET	BAL	267	20TH WAR
FREE, HENRIETTA	BAL	334	1ST DIST
FREE, JOHN	BAL	439	14TH WAR
FREE, MARGARETT	BAL	131	18TH WAR
FREE, MILTON	BAL	158	16TH WAR
FREE, WALTER	PRI	122	PISCATAW
FREE, WILLIAM	MGM	357	BERRYS D
FREEBERGER, GEORGE	BAL	038	9TH WARD
FREEBERGER, HENRY G.	BAL	116	18TH WAR
FREEBERGER, JAMES M.	BAL	115	18TH WAR
FREEBERGER, JOHN	BAL	031	18TH WAR
FREEBURGER, ELIZA	BAL	017	15TH WAR
FREEBURGER, GEORGE A.	BAL	119	15TH WAR
FREEBURGER, JACOB	BAL	147	16TH WAR
FREEBURGER, RACHELL	BAL	122	5TH WARD
FREEBURY, ELIZABETH	BAL	279	20TH WAR
FREED, ELIZABETH	CAR	343	6TH DIST
FREED, JACOB	CEC	133	6TH E DI
FREEDELL, GEORGE	BAL	218	17TH WAR
FREEDENWALL, HENRY	BAL	380	3RD WARD
FREEDER, HENRY	BAL	279	17TH WAR
FREEDY, MARY	BAL	252	1ST DIST
FREEHEARTY, HUGH	BAL	193	6TH WARD
FREEL, JOSHUA	CEC	061	1ST E DI
FREELAND, AARON	BAL	034	2ND DIST
FREELAND, ALFRED	ANN	300	1ST DIST
FREELAND, CLOE	BAL	186	5TH DIST
FREELAND, CORNELIA	ANN	300	1ST DIST
FREELAND, DANIEL	BAL	252	1ST DIST
FREELAND, DANIEL	BAL	024	2ND DIST
FREELAND, EDWARD B.	BAL	431	1ST DIST
FREELAND, EGBERT	BAL	159	16TH WAR
FREELAND, ELIZA	FRE	106	CREAGERS
FREELAND, ELIZABETH	BAL	208	11TH WAR
FREELAND, ELIZABETH	BAL	305	1ST DIST
FREELAND, ETHELBERT	CAL	037	2ND DIST
FREELAND, FANNY	CAL	022	2ND DIST
FREELAND, FAYETTE	CAL	037	2ND DIST
FREELAND, FRESBY *	BAL	449	8TH WAR
FREELAND, JACOB	BAL	450	8TH WARD
FREELAND, JAMES	BAL	214	6TH DIST
FREELAND, JAMES	CAL	041	3RD DIST
FREELAND, JIM	ANN	300	1ST DIST
FREELAND, JOHN	BAL	433	1ST DIST
FREELAND, JOHN	BAL	305	1ST DIST
FREELAND, JOHN	BAL	034	2ND DIST
FREELAND, JOHN	BAL	045	2ND DIST
FREELAND, JOSEPH	BAL	212	6TH DIST
FREELAND, MAHALA	CAL	020	2ND DIST
FREELAND, MARY	CAL	029	2ND DIST
FREELAND, MARY	FRE	168	EMMITTSB
FREELAND, MARY	BAL	216	6TH DIST
FREELAND, MARY	BAL	128	5TH WARD
FREELAND, NED	ANN	300	1ST DIST
FREELAND, OLIVER H. P.	CAL	020	2ND DIST
FREELAND, RACHEL	CAL	021	2ND DIST
FREELAND, RACHEL	BAL	034	2ND DIST
FREELAND, ROSANNA	BAL	204	6TH DIST
FREELAND, RUTH	BAL	213	6TH DIST
FREELAND, STEPHEN	BAL	213	6TH DIST
FREELAND, STEPHEN	BAL	210	6TH DIST
FREELAND, THOMAS	CAL	021	2ND DIST
FREELAND, THOMAS H.	BAL	475	14TH WAR
FREELAND, WILLIAM	CAL	059	3RD DIST
FREELAND, WILLIAM	BAL	219	5TH DIST
FREELEN, JOHN	FRE	294	WOODSBOR
FREELIN, ELIZA	FRE	294	WOODSBOR
FREELINGER, NICHOLAS	BAL	089	1ST WARD
FREELY, MARY	BAL	024	2ND DIST
FREEM, JACOB	BAL	261	20TH WAR
FREEMA, PHILLIP	ALL	242	CUMBERLA
FREEMAN, ABRAHAM	KEN	270	1ST DIST
FREEMAN, ABRAM-BLACK	QUE	179	2ND E DI
FREEMAN, ALEXANDER	TAL	038	EASTON D
FREEMAN, ALEXANDER	BAL	170	11TH WAR
FREEMAN, ALEXANDER	CAL	003	1ST DIST
FREEMAN, AMELIA	CHA	275	ALLENS F
FREEMAN, ANDREW	BAL	140	1ST WARD
FREEMAN, ANN	BAL	202	11TH WAR
FREEMAN, ANNA	BAL	406	1ST DIST
FREEMAN, BENJAMIN	CAL	034	2ND DIST
FREEMAN, BENJAMIN	CEC	050	1ST E DI
FREEMAN, BENJAMIN	KEN	297	3RD DIST
FREEMAN, BERY	BAL	138	2ND DIST
FREEMAN, C.	BAL	293	12TH WAR
FREEMAN, CATHARINE	TAL	038	EASTON D
FREEMAN, CHARLES	BAL	334	3RD WARD
FREEMAN, CHARLES	BAL	281	2ND WARD
FREEMAN, CHARLES	BAL	149	5TH WARD
FREEMAN, CLARA A.	KEN	229	2ND DIST
FREEMAN, D. MISS-	ANN	301	1ST DIST
FREEMAN, DANIEL	ALL	135	4TH E.D.
FREEMAN, DANIEL W. *	TAL	101	ST MICHA

Name	County	Page	District
FREEMAN, DEBRO		70	11TH WAR
FREEMAN, EDWA		75	ALLENS F
FREEMAN, E		5	ALLENS F
FREEMAN, E		7	7TH E DI
FREEMAN, EL			WESTMINS
FREEMAN, EL			BERRYS D
FREEMAN, EL			1ST WARD
FREEMAN, ELL	AL	128	18TH WAR
FREEMAN, EPH	CAR	348	6TH DIST
FREEMAN, FAN	ANN	499	HOWARD D
FREEMAN, FRAN	BAL	031	9TH WARD
FREEMAN, FRED CK	CAL	033	2ND DIST
FREEMAN, GEORGE	ANN	354	3RD DIST
FREEMAN, GEORGE-BLACK	QUE	191	3RD E DI
FREEMAN, GUSTUVAS	CAL	023	2ND DIST
FREEMAN, HARACE	KEN	211	2ND DIST
FREEMAN, HARRIET	CEC	047	1ST E DI
FREEMAN, HENRIETTA	BAL	030	4TH WARD
FREEMAN, HENRY	MGM	320	CRACKLIN
FREEMAN, HENRY	PRI	010	BLADENSB
FREEMAN, HENRY	BAL	149	5TH WARD
FREEMAN, HENRY H.	CHA	275	ALLENS F
FREEMAN, ISAAC	KEN	247	2ND DIST
FREEMAN, ISAAC	CEC	016	ELKTON 3
FREEMAN, ISAAC	BAL	152	5TH WARD
FREEMAN, ISAAC	WOR	278	BERLIN 1
FREEMAN, J.	BAL	157	1ST WARD
FREEMAN, J.	BAL	157	1ST WARD
FREEMAN, JACOB	QUE	218	3RD E DI
FREEMAN, JACOB	KEN	229	2ND DIST
FREEMAN, JACOB T.	KEN	253	1ST DIST
FREEMAN, JAMES	BAL	107	18TH WAR
FREEMAN, JAMES	BAL	113	18TH WAR
FREEMAN, JOHN	BAL	029	18TH WAR
FREEMAN, JOHN	BAL	114	1ST WARD
FREEMAN, JOHN D.	CHA	232	HILLTOP
FREEMAN, JOHN D.	ST	303	2ND E DI
FREEMAN, JOHN H.	BAL	171	11TH WAR
FREEMAN, JOHN T.	CAL	002	1ST DIST
FREEMAN, JOHN W.	TAL	030	EASTON D
FREEMAN, JONAH D.	BAL	345	7TH WARD
FREEMAN, JOSEPH	CAR	265	WESTMINS
FREEMAN, L.	BAL	318	12TH WAR
FREEMAN, LUCY A.	BAL	057	10TH WAR
FREEMAN, M.	ANN	274	ANNAPOLI
FREEMAN, MARY	BAL	064	10TH WAR
FREEMAN, MARY	CEC	058	1ST E DI
FREEMAN, MARY	CEC	065	1ST E DI
FREEMAN, NANCY-BLACK	QUE	153	1ST E DI
FREEMAN, NATHANIEL	CHA	275	ALLENS F
FREEMAN, NATHANIEL	CHA	230	MIDDLETO
FREEMAN, OWEN	BAL	165	11TH WAR
FREEMAN, PATTY	CEC	014	ELKTON 3
FREEMAN, PERRY	KEN	229	2ND DIST
FREEMAN, REBECCA	KEN	235	2ND DIST
FREEMAN, RICHARD	CEC	175	7TH E DI
FREEMAN, RICHARD	BAL	149	5TH WARD
FREEMAN, RICHARD	BAL	239	6TH WARD
FREEMAN, S.	BAL	168	1ST WARD
FREEMAN, SALLY	TAL	038	EASTON D
FREEMAN, SAMUEL	BAL	050	9TH WARD
FREEMAN, SARAH	BAL	102	15TH WAR
FREEMAN, SARAH	KEN	267	1ST DIST
FREEMAN, SIMON	KEN	241	2ND DIST
FREEMAN, TEMPY	KEN	213	2ND DIST
FREEMAN, THOMAS	BAL	418	3RD WARD
FREEMAN, THOMAS	BAL	401	14TH WAR
FREEMAN, THOMAS	BAL	170	1ST WARD
FREEMAN, THOMAS	BAL	152	1ST WARD
FREEMAN, THOMAS	BAL	286	2ND WARD
FREEMAN, THOMAS L.	ST	307	1ST E DI
FREEMAN, THOMAS-MULATTO	CAR	149	NO TWP L
FREEMAN, TIMOTHY	BAL	300	17TH WAR
FREEMAN, TOM	ANN	336	3RD DIST
FREEMAN, WESLEY	CEC	011	ELKTON 3
FREEMAN, WILLIAM	CEC	033	CHESAPEA
FREEMAN, WILLIAM	BAL	198	19TH WAR
FREEMAN, WILLIAM	KEN	229	2ND DIST
FREEMAN, WILLIAM	BAL	227	6TH WARD
FREEMAN, WILLIAM H.	BAL	104	10TH WAR
FREEMAN, WILLIAM H.	BAL	381	1ST DIST
FREEMAN, WILLIAM H.	CHA	273	ALLENS F
FREEMAN, WILLIAM H.	BAL	069	4TH WARD
FREEMAN,W ILLIAM M.	ST	303	2ND E DI
FREEMFREE, WILLIAM HENRY	MGM	347	BERRYS D
FREEMON, COMFORT	WOR	268	BERLIN 1
FREENEY, JOSHUA	WOR	231	6TH E DI
FREENEY, PETER	SOM	501	SALISBUR
FREENY, BENJAMIN	BAL	013	15TH WAR
FREENY, JOHN	SOM	498	SALISBUR
FREENY, WILLIAM	SOM	487	SALISBUR
FREENY, WILLIAM	WOR	239	6TH E DI
FREER, HORACE	BAL	288	12TH WAR
FREER, JANE	BAL	317	20TH WAR
FREER, MARGARET	BAL	156	11TH WAR
FREER, MICHAEL	BAL	216	19TH WAR
FREER, THOMAS	KEN	251	1ST DIST
FREER, WILLIAM H.	BAL	338	1ST DIST
FREESE, ALEXANDER	BAL	313	20TH WAR
FREESE, JOHN T.	HAR	150	3RD DIST
FREESE, MARY	CAR	405	2ND DIST
FREET, JOHN	CAR	292	7TH DIST
FREETEN, WILLIAM	FRE	294	WOODSBOR
FREETER, JOHN	CEC	059	1ST E DI
FREEZE, ANN E.	FRE	130	CREAGERS
FREEZE, JOSEPH	FRE	129	CREAGERS
FREEZE, MICHAEL	FRE	118	CREAGERS
FREEZE, SUSANNA	FRE	118	CREAGERS
FREGO, ELIZABETH*	DOR	368	3RD DIVI
FREGO, JOHN	BAL	020	2ND DIST
FREIDENHAUS, PAUKELS	BAL	226	2ND WARD
FREIDENRICK, AARON	BAL	367	3RD WARD
FREIDENRICK, FANNY	BAL	367	3RD WARD
FREIDINGER, CHARLES	WAS	145	HAGERSTO
FREIDINGER, GEORGE	WAS	145	HAGERSTO
FREIDINGER, JOHN M.	WAS	145	HAGERSTO
FREIFOYLE, DAVID	BAL	253	12TH WAR
FREILER, JOHN	BAL	003	1ST WARD
FREINSEHT, GEORGE	BAL	165	2ND DIST
FREIS, LOUISA	BAL	297	3RD WARD
FREISBY, CAROLINE	CEC	145	PORT DUP
FREISIG, ERNST	BAL	077	10TH WAR
FREITAG, AUGUST	BAL	072	4TH WARD
FREITZE, PHILIP R.	BAL	154	11TH WAR
FRELA, A.	BAL	203	19TH WAR
FRELAND, SOSKEY	BAL	026	2ND DIST
FRELOCK, EDWARD	ALL	041	2ND E.D.
FREMAN, ALEX-BLACK	CAR	107	NO TWP L
FREMAN, ISAAC	BAL	107	18TH WAR
FREMAN, JOHN-BLACK	CAR	094	NO TWP L

FREMAN, JOHN-BLACK CAR 073 NO TWP L
FREMAN, PHILIP-BLACK CAR 106 NO TWP L
FREMAN, SAMUEL CAR 067 NO TWP L
FREMAN, SARAH-BLACK CAR 070 NO TWP L
FREMAN, WILLIAM BAL 141 1ST WARD
FREMMAN, BENJAMIN CEC 048 1ST E DI
FREMUTH, GEORGE H. BAL 280 1ST DIST
FRENBRAGEN, JAMES C. BAL 290 3RD WARD
FRENCH, ANDREW BAL 079 18TH WAR
FRENCH, ANDREW WAS 143 HAGERSTO
FRENCH, ANN PRI 037 VANSVILL
FRENCH, ANN M.E. WAS 292 1ST DIST
FRENCH, ARTHUR BAL 169 2ND DIST
FRENCH, BENJAMIN PRI 020 VANSVILL
FRENCH, BENJAMIN PRI 037 VANSVILL
FRENCH, CADUALIDER F. J. FRE 070 FREDERIC
FRENCH, CHARELS BAL 001 15TH WAR
FRENCH, CHARLES BAL 227 12TH WAR
FRENCH, CHARLES B. CEC 080 NORTHEAS
FRENCH, CHARLOTT BAL 313 7TH WARD
FRENCH, CHARLOTT* BAL 368 3RD WARD
FRENCH, CORNELIUS BAL 055 4TH WARD
FRENCH, DANIEL WAS 292 1ST DIST
FRENCH, DARIUS BAL 368 3RD WARD
FRENCH, DOMINICK BAL 206 6TH WARD
FRENCH, ELIZA WAS 162 HAGERSTO
FRENCH, ELIZABETH CEC 036 CHESAPEA
FRENCH, ELLEN BAL 367 3RD WARD
FRENCH, GEORGE WAS 132 HAGERSTO
FRENCH, GEORGE WAS 300 1ST DIST
FRENCH, HANNAH BAL 463 14TH WAR
FRENCH, HENRY BAL 343 13TH WAR
FRENCH, J. PRI 115 PISCATAW
FRENCH, JACOB BAL 126 18TH WAR
FRENCH, JAMES E. BAL 025 15TH WAR
FRENCH, JANE WAS 032 2ND SUBD
FRENCH, JASPER BAL 163 2ND DIST
FRENCH, JASPER BAL 418 3RD WARD
FRENCH, JOHN BAL 128 18TH WAR
FRENCH, JOHN BAL 280 2ND WARD
FRENCH, JOHN PRI 115 PISCATAW
FRENCH, JOHN WAS 177 1ST DIST
FRENCH, JOHN C. BAL 032 9TH WARD
FRENCH, JOHN H.W. BAL 189 17TH WAR
FRENCH, JOHN M. BAL 023 1ST WARD
FRENCH, JOSEPH BAL 236 6TH WARD
FRENCH, JOSEPH CAL 059 3RD DIST
FRENCH, MARGARET WAS 102 2ND DIST
FRENCH, MARY A. HAR 190 3RD DIST
FRENCH, MILLIE ANN 317 1ST DIST
FRENCH, NANCY CEC 197 7TH E DI
FRENCH, ORVILL BAL 124 2ND DIST
FRENCH, REBECCA CAL 046 3RD DIST
FRENCH, RICHARD BAL 101 15TH WAR
FRENCH, RICHARD BAL 310 3RD WARD
FRENCH, ROBERT BAL 245 17TH WAR
FRENCH, SAMUEL BAL 219 6TH WARD
FRENCH, THEADORE WAS 177 1ST DIST
FRENCH, THOMAS BAL 040 18TH WAR
FRENCH, WILLIAM KEN 235 2ND DIST
FRENCH, WILLIAM BAL 417 8TH WARD
FRENCHBOX, CAROLINE BAL 155 5TH WARD
FRENCK, HENRY A. FRE 119 CREAGERS
FRENCY, JOHN BAL 071 4TH WARD
FRENCY, SARAH BAL 110 10TH WAR
FRENDERWAY, HENRY H. BAL 213 19TH WAR
FRENINGLE, CONRAD BAL 049 1ST WARD
FRENKER, HENRY BAL 141 1ST WARD
FRENNER, MARY M. WAS 147 HAGERSTO
FRENT, CATHARINE BAL 216 19TH WAR
FRENTINAN, A. A. BAL 321 12TH WAR
FRERALD, JOHN BAL 179 2ND WARD
FRES, FRANCIS BAL 124 5TH WARD
FRESBY, ABRAHAM HAR 145 3RD DIST
FRESBY, DEBBY BAL 320 12TH WAR
FRESH, ALEXANDER ALL 036 2ND E.D.
FRESH, JOHN BAL 409 8TH WARD
FRESH, JOHN BAL 322 1ST DIST
FRESHER, JAMES ALL 056 10TH E.D
FRESHLINE, A. BAL 247 20TH WAR
FRESHOUR, ADAM FRE 063 FREDERIC
FRESHOUR, GREEN FRE 062 FREDERIC
FRESHOUR, HENRY A. * FRE 137 CREAGERS
FRESHOUR, KATHARINE BAL 157 19TH WAR
FRESHOUR, MARY BAL 158 19TH WAR
FRESHOUR, MARY BAL 313 20TH WAR
FRESINHAN, ANDREW * ANN 372 4TH DIST
FRETHORN, WILLIAM BAL 167 1ST WARD
FREW, MARGARET KEN 276 1ST DIST
FREY, CATHARINE BAL 256 2ND WARD
FREY, CHARELS BAL 295 20TH WAR
FREY, CHARLES BAL 082 10TH WAR
FREY, DEBORAH ALL 028 2ND E.D.
FREY, ENOCH WAS 215 1ST DIST
FREY, GAUNTLET BAL 333 3RD WARD
FREY, GEORGE BAL 021 1ST WARD
FREY, GOTLEIB BAL 155 5TH WARD
FREY, HERMAN BAL 083 10TH WAR
FREY, JACOB WAS 157 2ND DIST
FREY, JOHN MGM 350 BERRYS D
FREY, MALVINA BAL 169 6TH WARD
FREY, MARY BAL 092 5TH WARD
FREY, MATHEW ALL 053 10TH E.D
FREY, MICHAEL ALL 047 10TH E.D
FREY, PETER ALL 019 2ND E.D.
FREY, PETER BAL 170 16TH WAR
FREY, SAMUEL BAL 383 13TH WAR
FREY, SARAH ANN ALL 029 2ND E.D.
FREY, SOLOMON ALL 028 2ND E.D.
FREY, SUSAN BAL 204 19TH WAR
FREY, THOMAS ALL 029 2ND E.D.
FREY, WILLIAM ALL 027 2ND E.D.
FREY, WILLIAM ALL 027 2ND E.D.
FREYER, PETER BAL 140 16TH WAR
FREYS, AMANDA BAL 178 19TH WAR
FREYSINGER, HENRY BAL 139 11TH WAR
FREZARE, JOHN ALL 088 5TH E.D.
FRI, CHARLES BAL 209 2ND WARD
FRIAN, JOHN BAL 127 5TH WARD
FRIANT, HENRY BAL 209 17TH WAR
FRIAR, BILL BAL 148 5TH WARD
FRIAR, CHRISTOPHER BAL 027 4TH WARD
FRIAR, PATRICK BAL 066 4TH WARD
FRIAREAUK, CARLINE FRE 033 FREDERIC
FRICK, ABRAHAM WAS 276 RIDGEVIL
FRICK, ABRAHAM WAS 277 LEITERSB
FRICK, ANDREW BAL 129 1ST WARD
FRICK, CHARELS WAS 144 HAGERSTO
FRICK, CHARLES HAR 114 2ND DIST
FRICK, CHRISTIANA WAS 276 RIDGEVIL
FRICK, FLEMING WAS 232 1ST DIST
FRICK, FREDERIC BAL 185 6TH WARD
FRICK, FREDERICK BAL 448 14TH WAR
FRICK, GEORGE BAL 461 14TH WAR
FRICK, HENRY HAR 077 BEL AIR
FRICK, JOHN CAR 203 4TH DIST
FRICK, JOHN WAS 272 RIDGEVIL
FRICK, JOSEPH ALL 249 CUMBERLA
FRICK, MARTHA WAS 147 HAGERSTO
FRICK, RICHARD BAL 444 14TH WAR
FRICK, SAMUEL WAS 231 1ST DIST
FRICK, WILLIAM BAL 444 14TH WAR
FRICK, WILLIAM BAL 319 20TH WAR
FRICK, WILLIAM F. BAL 153 11TH WAR
FRICK, WILLIAM G. BAL 054 1ST WARD
FRICKEL, WILLIAM BAL 267 2ND WARD
FRIDAY, FREDERICK FRE 071 FREDERIC
FRIDAY, HENRY FRE 224 BUCKEYST
FRIDAY, HENRY SR. FRE 408 JEFFERSO
FRIDAY, JAMES B. FRE 204 BUCKEYST
FRIDAY, JOHN FRE 072 FREDERIC
FRIDAY, WILLIAM FRE 095 FREDERIC
FRIDELEY, SOLOMON FRE 120 CREAGERS
FRIDGE, ALEXANDER ANN 287 ANNAPOLI
FRIDINGER, ADAM CAR 349 6TH DIST
FRIDIRGER, CHRISTIAN * WAS 084 2ND SUBD
FRIDMYER, CHRISTIAN * WAS 084 2ND SUBD
FRIDMYER, MARGARET * WAS 078 2ND SUBD
FRIDNIGER, MARGARET * WAS 078 2ND SUBD
FRIED, HENRY* BAL 086 10TH WAR
FRIEDEL, JOHN BAL 039 15TH WAR
FRIEDENWALD, J. BAL 268 2ND WARD
FRIEDMAN, MOSES BAL 347 3RD WARD
FRIEDSHIEMER, CHARLES BAL 405 14TH WAR
FRIELKING, FREDERICK BAL 085 4TH WARD
FRIEN, HENRIETTA BAL 114 11TH WAR
FRIEND, AGNES WAS 142 2ND DIST
FRIEND, ALFRED A. BAL 090 5TH WARD
FRIEND, AMOS ALL 044 10TH E.D
FRIEND, ANDREW ALL 033 2ND E.D.
FRIEND, ANDREW WAS 002 WILLIAMS
FRIEND, ANN BAL 090 5TH WARD
FRIEND, CHRISTOPHER BAL 212 2ND WARD
FRIEND, CORNELIUS ALL 044 10TH E.D
FRIEND, DANIEL ALL 034 2ND E.D.
FRIEND, DORCAS ALL 044 10TH E.D
FRIEND, EDMUND ALL 044 10TH E.D
FRIEND, ELIJAH ALL 043 10TH E.D
FRIEND, ELISABETH ALL 044 10TH E.D
FRIEND, ELISABETH ALL 046 10TH E.D
FRIEND, ELSIABETH ALL 044 10TH E.D
FRIEND, FREEMAN ALL 045 10TH E.D
FRIEND, GABRIEL ALL 033 2ND E.D.
FRIEND, GABRIEL WAS 103 2ND DIST
FRIEND, GABRIEL-BLACK CAR 163 NO TWP L
FRIEND, HARRISON ALL 046 10TH E.D
FRIEND, HENRY ALL 044 10TH E.D
FRIEND, HENRY WAS 203 1ST DIST
FRIEND, HERNY-MULATTO CAR 138 NO TWP L
FRIEND, ISAAC ALL 044 10TH E.D
FRIEND, J.S. ALL 033 2ND E.D.
FRIEND, JACOB ALL 033 2ND E.D.
FRIEND, JAMES ALL 044 10TH E.D
FRIEND, JOAH ALL 032 2ND E.D.
FRIEND, JOHN-BLACK CAR 135 NO TWP L
FRIEND, JONATHAN ALL 032 2ND E.D.
FRIEND, JONATHAN ALL 034 2ND E.D.
FRIEND, JOSEPH ALL 045 10TH E.D
FRIEND, JOSIAH ALL 046 10TH E.D
FRIEND, JSOHUA ALL 032 2ND E.D.
FRIEND, LOUISA ALL 041 2ND E.D.
FRIEND, NANCY ALL 127 4TH E.D.
FRIEND, NATHANIEL ALL 067 10TH E.D
FRIEND, OBED ALL 044 10TH E.D
FRIEND, G.G. ALL 033 2ND E.D.
FRIEND, RACHEL WAS 003 WILLIAMS
FRIEND, REBECCA TAL 076 EASTON T
FRIEND, S.W. ALL 043 10TH E.D
FRIEND, SAMUEL ALL 045 10TH E.D
FRIEND, WILLIAM E. ALL 033 2ND E.D.
FRIEND,MARY B. ALL 046 10TH E.D
FRIER, ANDREW BAL 377 3RD WARD
FRIER, JACOB BAL 417 3RD WARD
FRIER, P. * BAL 316 20TH WAR
FRIERE, JACOB BAL 049 4TH WARD
FRIERMEN, DANIEL BAL 045 1ST WARD
FRIES, JOHN BAL 124 16TH WAR
FRIES, JOHN WAS 124 HAGERSTO
FRIES, OLIVIA BAL 378 3RD WARD
FRIES, PETER WAS 174 FUNKSTOW
FRIES, THORWALD* BAL 078 10TH WAR
FRIES, URICH WAS 124 HAGERSTO
FRIESBACK, RUDOLPH BAL 290 17TH WAR
FRIESE, HENRY BAL 030 15TH WAR
FRIESING, JOSIAH* BAL 304 3RD WARD
FRIESTING, HENRY BAL 031 9TH WARD
FRIEULEY, SUSAN WAS 293 1ST DIST
FRIEZE, GEORGE D. BAL 399 14TH WAR
FRIFOGLE, HENRY BAL 326 1ST DIST
FRIGO, LEVEN DOR 366 3RD DIVI
FRIGO, WILLIAM DOR 367 3RD DIVI
FRIGO, WILLIAM SR.* DOR 367 3RD DIVI
FRIGOE, THOMAS DOR 423 1ST DIST
FRIGOR, ZACHARIA* DOR 403 1ST DIST
FRIGOW, WASHINGTON DOR 387 1ST DIST
FRILAS, ELLEN* TAL 120 ST MICHA
FRIM, PATRICK BAL 043 1ST WARD
FRINCH, ELIZA BAL 270 2ND WARD
FRINCK, HENRY BAL 002 9TH WARD
FRINDSHIP, HENRY BAL 279 2ND WARD
FRINE, HARRY BAL 078 1ST WARD
FRINFRUCK, JOHN WAS 142 HAGERSTO
FRINGER, HENRY L. BAL 237 1ST DIST
FRINGER, JACOB CAR 182 8TH DIST
FRINGER, JAOCB CAR 302 1ST DIST
FRINGER, MARGARET CAR 243 TANEYTOW
FRINGER, MICHAEL CAR 303 1ST DIST
FRINGER, NICHOLAS BAL 218 19TH WAR
FRINGLER, MICHAEL CAR 302 1ST DIST
FRINK, ISAAC BAL 136 5TH WARD
FRINK, L. BAL 151 1ST WARD
FRINYER, WILLIAM BAL 126 1ST WARD
FRISBEY, PERRY-BLACK QUE 127 1ST E DI
FRISBIE, WILLIAM BAL 335 3RD WARD
FRISBY, A. BAL 099 10TH WAR
FRISBY, ALICE-BLACK QUE 201 3RD E DI
FRISBY, ALTHEA HAR 099 2ND DIST
FRISBY, BENJAMIN KEN 215 2ND DIST
FRISBY, BRIGET BAL 289 7TH WARD
FRISBY, CASHER BAL 107 2ND DIST
FRISBY, CHARLES KEN 246 2ND DIST
FRISBY, DAVID CEC 016 ELKTON 3
FRISBY, DEBORAH BAL 260 6TH WARD
FRISBY, DOLLY KEN 313 3RD DIST
FRISBY, E. BAL 072 10TH WAR
FRISBY, ELIZABETH BAL 174 11TH WAR
FRISBY, FRANCIS KEN 210 2ND DIST
FRISBY, GEORGE BAL 287 7TH WARD
FRISBY, HARRIET BAL 279 12TH WAR
FRISBY, HENRIETTA BAL 374 3RD WARD
FRISBY, HENRY KEN 246 2ND DIST
FRISBY, HORACE KEN 257 1ST DIST
FRISBY, J. H. BAL 154 1ST WARD
FRISBY, JAEMS KEN 237 2ND DIST
FRISBY, JAMES KEN 218 2ND DIST
FRISBY, JAMES KEN 224 2ND DIST
FRISBY, JAMES JOHNSON BAL 180 6TH WARD
FRISBY, JANE HAR 097 2ND DIST
FRISBY, JOHN CEC 054 1ST E DI
FRISBY, JOHN BAL 403 14TH WAR
FRISBY, JOSEPH BAL 206 17TH WAR
FRISBY, MARY CEC 037 CHESAPEA
FRISBY, MARY BAL 282 20TH WAR
FRISBY, MARY BAL 176 6TH WARD
FRISBY, MARYANN BAL 411 3RD WARD
FRISBY, MICHAEL KEN 249 2ND DIST
FRISBY, MICHAEL KEN 277 1ST DIST
FRISBY, MILLICENT CEC 011 ELKTON 3
FRISBY, NANCY CEC 145 PORT DUP
FRISBY, NATHANIEL BAL 290 7TH WARD
FRISBY, PERRA KEN 313 3RD DIST
FRISBY, PERRY KEN 260 1ST DIST
FRISBY, PERRY BAL 180 6TH WARD
FRISBY, PERRY BAL 025 15TH WAR
FRISBY, RICAHRD BAL 097 15TH WAR
FRISBY, RICHARD BAL 290 7TH WARD
FRISBY, RICHARD KEN 277 1ST DIST
FRISBY, RICHARD-BLACK QUE 168 2ND E DI
FRISBY, S. BAL 127 5TH WARD
FRISBY, SALLY KEN 219 2ND DIST
FRISBY, SAMUEL BAL 230 19TH WAR
FRISBY, SAMUEL BAL 230 19TH WAR
FRISBY, SAMUEL QUE 217 3RD E DI
FRISBY, SARAH BAL 044 9TH WARD
FRISBY, SPENCER BAL 175 6TH WARD
FRISBY, SUSAN KEN 243 2ND DIST
FRISBY, TEMPERANCE BAL 051 9TH WARD
FRISBY, WILLIAM BAL 043 9TH WARD
FRISBY, WILLIAM KEN 208 2ND DIST
FRISH, CATHERINE BAL 006 1ST WARD
FRISH, CONRAD BAL 104 5TH WARD
FRISH, ELISABETH ALL 035 2ND E.D.
FRISH, ELIZA BAL 207 2ND WARD
FRISH, MARGARET BAL 104 5TH WARD
FRISHMAN, JOHN FRE 124 CREAGERS
FRISKEY, HENRY WAS 153 2ND DIST
FRISOGLE, JOSEPH BAL 266 1ST DIST
FRIST, ANDREW BAL 172 19TH WAR
FRIST, NICHOLAS BAL 088 1ST WARD
FRIST, WILLIAM CEC 156 PORT DUP
FRITCH, CATHARINE WAS 129 HAGERSTO
FRITE, CATHARINE CAR 173 8TH DIST
FRITH, S. BAL 142 1ST WARD
FRITH, SAMUEL BAL 121 1ST WARD
FRITSBY, GIDWAY ALL 212 CUMBERLA
FRITSH, BEN BAL 107 5TH WARD
FRITSLER, JACOB CAR 179 8TH DIST
FRITT, LYDIA FRE 325 MIDDLETO
FRITTER, LOUISA BAL 033 4TH WARD
FRITWELL, GEORGE BAL 321 1ST DIST
FRITZ, ALEXNADER BAL 222 1ST DIST
FRITZ, CHARLES A. BAL 161 19TH WAR
FRITZ, ELIZABETH CAR 393 2ND DIST
FRITZ, ELLENORA CAR 382 2ND DIST
FRITZ, FREDERICK BAL 050 15TH WAR
FRITZ, GEORGE BAL 301 3RD WARD
FRITZ, GOTTEIB BAL 060 2ND DIST
FRITZ, GUNTHEWS CAR 390 2ND DIST
FRITZ, HENRY BAL 298 17TH WAR
FRITZ, HENRY BAL 454 8TH WARD
FRITZ, JAOCB CAR 390 2ND DIST
FRITZ, JOHN CAR 385 2ND DIST
FRITZ, JOHN BAL 235 20TH WAR
FRITZ, JOHN BAL 350 7TH WARD
FRITZ, JOHN BAL 381 3RD WARD
FRITZ, JOHN WAS 187 BOONSBOR
FRITZ, MANUEL BAL 214 2ND WARD
FRITZ, MANZELLA WAS 200 1ST DIST
FRITZ, MARGARET BAL 252 12TH WAR
FRITZ, MATHIAS CAR 382 2ND DIST
FRITZ, MICHAEL BAL 170 2ND DIST
FRITZ, MORDECAI CAR 323 1ST DIST
FRITZ, SARAH CAR 359 9TH DIST
FRITZ, WILLIAM CAR 172 8TH DIST
FRITZ, WILLIAM BAL 328 7TH WARD
FRITZ, WILLIAM WAS 212 1ST DIST
FRITZHES, GEORGE BAL 068 4TH WARD
FRIZBY, JAMES BAL 459 1ST DIST
FRIZE, CHRISTINE BAL 224 19TH WAR
FRIZELFOGAL, MARY BAL 115 11TH WAR
FRIZELL, HENRY HAR 107 2ND DIST
FRIZELL, REBECCA BAL 037 18TH WAR
FRIZER, THOMAS CEC 027 CHESAPEA
FRIZZEL, DAVID CAR 365 9TH DIST
FRIZZEL, JAOCB CAR 365 9TH DIST
FRIZZEL, JESSE CAR 373 9TH DIST
FRIZZEL, JOSHUA CAR 374 9TH DIST
FRIZZEL, ROSANA CAR 373 9TH DIST
FRIZZEL, WASH BAL 291 1ST DIST
FRIZZELL, ISRAEL CAR 214 5TH DIST
FRIZZELL, JESSE CAR 204 4TH DIST
FRIZZELL, JOEL CAR 204 4TH DIST
FRIZZELL, JOHN CAR 201 4TH DIST
FRIZZELL, JOHN CAR 215 5TH DIST
FRIZZELL, JOSHUA CAR 222 5TH DIST
FRIZZELL, MILTON CAR 207 4TH DIST
FRIZZELL, NANCY BAL 114 11TH WAR
FRIZZELL, NIMROD BAL 349 1ST DIST
FRIZZELL, RICHARD CAR 201 4TH DIST
FRIZZELL, WILLIAM CAR 209 5TH DIST
FRIZZELL, WILLIAM BAL 233 1ST DIST
FRIZZELL, WILLIAM D. CAR 215 5TH DIST
FRIZZLE, ANN CAR 405 2ND DIST
FRIZZLE, ISAAC CAR 361 9TH DIST
FRIZZLE, JAMES BAL 292 20TH WAR
FRIZZLE, JAOCB JR. CAR 366 9TH DIST
FRIZZLE, JOHN WAS 169 FUNKSTOW
FRIZZLE, JSOHUA CAR 362 9TH DIST
FRIZZLE, LEONARD CAR 374 9TH DIST
FRIZZLE, M. BAL 239 20TH WAR

Name	County	Page	District
FRIZZLE, MARY A.	CAR	372	9TH DIST
FRIZZLE, RICHARD	CAR	375	9TH DIST
FRIZZLE, WILLIAM	CAR	405	2ND DIST
FRNAKLIN, PATTY	WOR	283	BERLIN 1
FROBASE, HENRY	BAL	356	3RD WARD
FROBORT, HENRY	BAL	057	4TH WARD
FROCK, BENJAMIN	CAR	304	1ST DIST
FROCK, CATHARINE	CAR	316	1ST DIST
FROCK, DANIEL	CAR	316	1ST DIST
FROCK, DANIEL JR.	CAR	321	1ST DIST
FROCK, ELIZABETH	FRE	167	EMMITTSB
FROCK, JACOB	CAR	252	3RD DIST
FROCK, JACOB	CAR	258	3RD DIST
FROCK, JACOB H.	CAR	278	7TH DIST
FROCK, JACOB W.	CAR	261	3RD DIST
FROCK, JOHN	CAR	257	3RD DIST
FROCK, JOHN H.	CAR	347	6TH DIST
FROCK, MARGARET	CAR	292	7TH DIST
FROCK, MARGOALENA	CAR	315	1ST DIST
FROCK, MICHAEL	CAR	277	7TH DIST
FROCK, PETER	CAR	355	6TH DIST
FROCK, PETER	CAR	292	7TH DIST
FROCK, RACHEL	CAR	325	1ST DIST
FROCK, SARAH S.	CAR	325	1ST DIST
FROCK, VALENTINE	CAR	305	1ST DIST
FROCK, WILLIAM	CAR	317	1ST DIST
FROCK, WILLIAM	CAR	261	3RD DIST
FROCK, WILLIAM	BAL	043	2ND DIST
FROG, SAMUEL	BAL	416	1ST DIST
FROMAN, ABRAHAM	HAR	163	3RD DIST
FROMAN, JOHN	HAR	163	3RD DIST
FROMBACK, SUSAN	BAL	464	14TH WAR
FROME, SARAH	BAL	012	9TH WARD
FROMHOLT, JOHN	ALL	149	6TH E.D.
FRONERS, MARY *	BAL	300	1ST DIST
FRONK, GEORGE	FRE	122	CREAGERS
FRONK, HENRY	BAL	283	1ST DIST
FRONK, JOHN	WAS	098	2ND DIST
FRONK, PHILIP	BAL	200	5TH DIST
FRONK, SARAH R.	WAS	098	2ND DIST
FROSBENDER, ELIZA	BAL	100	18TH WAR
FROSESTER, RHODI	ALL	170	6TH E.D.
FROST, ABBISTENE	BAL	325	3RD WARD
FROST, ALICE	PRI	032	VANSVILL
FROST, CATHARINE	ANN	464	HOWARD D
FROST, CHARLOTA	FRE	274	NEW MARK
FROST, ELIAS W.	ANN	432	HOWARD D
FROST, ENOCH	ALL	090	5TH E.D.
FROST, GEORGE	BAL	047	9TH WARD
FROST, HARRIET	ALL	090	5TH E.D.
FROST, HENRY C.	ANN	473	HOWARD D
FROST, JAMES A.	BAL	131	16TH WAR
FROST, JOHN	BAL	088	18TH WAR
FROST, LEONARD	HAR	158	3RD DIST
FROST, MARY	BAL	439	14TH WAR
FROST, MESHECK	ALL	112	5TH E.D.
FROST, RACHEL	ANN	519	HOWARD D
FROST, ROBERT	ANN	426	HOWARD D
FROST, SALLY	SOM	426	PRINCESS
FROST, THOMAS	BAL	300	20TH WAR
FROST, WILHELMINA	BAL	230	6TH WARD
FROST, WILLIAM	ANN	468	HOWARD D
FROST, WILLIAM	BAL	324	3RD WARD
FROST, WILLIAM	ALL	006	3RD E.D.
FROUERS, MARY *	BAL	300	1ST DIST
FROULEY, GEORGE C.	BAL	292	12TH WAR
FROUNTFELDER, SARAH	WAS	216	1ST DIST
FROW, FRANCIS	ALL	257	CUMBERLA
FROWNFELLER, MATILDA	CAR	313	1ST DIST
FROWNFELLER, PETER	CAR	258	3RD DIST
FROWNFELTER, DAVID	CAR	289	7TH DIST
FROWNFELTER, JOHN	CAR	403	2ND DIST
FROWNFELTER, MARY	CAR	259	3RD DIST
FROWNFELTER, MARY	CAR	255	3RD DIST
FROWNFELTER, PETER	CAR	406	2ND DIST
FROWNFELTER, PETER	WAS	274	RIDGEVIL
FROWNFETTER, SUSAN	CAR	349	6TH DIST
FROXEL, FREDERICK W.	FRE	161	EMMITTSB
FRROUNLE, JOHN	FRE	115	CREAGERS
FRUCH, JOHN B.	BAL	129	5TH WARD
FRUCKER, ANDREW	WAS	037	2ND SUBD
FRUD, HENRY*	BAL	086	10TH WAR
FRUMFREE, CALEB	MGM	338	CRACKLIN
FRUMFREE, CHARLES ARTHUR	MGM	348	BERRYS D
FRUNDS, JAMES *	BAL	290	20TH WAR
FRURY, RICHARD	ANN	398	8TH DIST
FRUS, THORWALD*	BAL	078	10TH WAR
FRUSH, CATHARINE	WAS	018	2ND SUBD
FRUSH, GEORGE H.	BAL	170	19TH WAR
FRUSH, GEORGE W.	BAL	395	8TH WARD
FRUSH, JACOB	BAL	343	3RD WARD
FRUSH, JOHN N.	BAL	169	19TH WAR
FRUSH, JULIA A.	BAL	395	8TH WARD
FRUSH, MICHAEL	WAS	018	2ND SUBD
FRUST, JOHN *	BAL	302	20TH WAR
FRUTZ, EMANUEL	WAS	101	2ND DIST
FRY, AARON	WAS	063	2ND SUBD
FRY, ANN C.	WAS	265	1ST DIST
FRY, BENJAMIN	BAL	032	4TH WARD
FRY, CHARLES	CAR	320	1ST DIST
FRY, COLMORE	PRI	014	BLADENSB
FRY, CONRAD	BAL	283	1ST DIST
FRY, DANIEL	WAS	064	2ND SUBD
FRY, DANIEL M.	FRE	135	CREAGERS
FRY, DAVID	WAS	265	1ST DIST
FRY, EDWIN	BAL	429	1ST DIST
FRY, ELIAS	FRE	362	CATOCTIN
FRY, ENOCK	BAL	108	2ND DIST
FRY, EPHRAIM	FRE	360	CATOCTIN
FRY, GEORGE	BAL	171	1ST WARD
FRY, HANNAH	WAS	287	1ST DIST
FRY, HENRY	FRE	360	CATOCTIN
FRY, JAMES	MGM	359	BERRYS D
FRY, JOHN	WAS	228	1ST DIST
FRY, JOHN B.	BAL	393	8TH WARD
FRY, JONATHAN	FRE	360	CATOCTIN
FRY, JONATHAN	MGM	346	CLARKSBU
FRY, L.	BAL	100	10TH WAR
FRY, MARY	FRE	098	FREDERIC
FRY, MATHEW	FRE	024	FREDERIC
FRY, MICHAEL	BAL	211	17TH WAR
FRY, MINERVA	FRE	363	CATOCTIN
FRY, PETER	BAL	192	2ND WARD
FRY, RICHARD	BAL	241	1ST DIST
FRY, SAMUEL	FRE	372	CATOCTIN
FRY, SAMUEL	WAS	265	1ST DIST
FRY, SAMUEL	WAS	252	1ST DIST
FRY, SARAH	WAS	284	1ST DIST
FRY, STEPHEN	BAL	240	1ST DIST
FRYAN, MARY	BAL	067	1ST WARD
FRYE, AARON	WAS	047	2ND SUBD
FRYE, JOSPEH	PRI	103	SPALDING
FRYE, NOAH	PRI	101	SPALDING
FRYE, WILLIAM	PRI	072	MARLBROU
FRYER, ANDREW	BAL	262	1ST DIST
FRYER, BRIDGET	BAL	067	4TH WARD
FRYER, CONRAD	BAL	346	1ST DIST
FRYER, ELIJAH S.	BAL	075	10TH WAR
FRYER, ELIZA J.	BAL	425	8TH WARD
FRYER, ELLEN	BAL	075	10TH WAR
FRYER, HENRY	BAL	259	1ST DIST
FRYER, HENRY	BAL	309	20TH WAR
FRYER, JOSEPH	CEC	167	6TH E DI
FRYER, MARY	BAL	246	6TH WARD
FRYER, THOMAS	BAL	067	4TH WARD
FRYER, WINPED	BAL	254	2ND WARD
FRYHANCE, ELIZABETH	BAL	261	2ND WARD
FRYNE, WILLIAM *	BAL	149	1ST WARD
FSIHER, SANFORD	WAS	245	SMITHSBU
FTIMILIN, WILLIAM	BAL	203	6TH WARD
FUBITZ, SUSAN	BAL	179	19TH WAR
FUCITZ, FREDERICK	SAL	239	2ND WARD
FUCKER, T. H.	BAL	158	1ST WARD
FUCKSBURRY, JOHN	BAL	190	2ND WARD
FUDIT, PETER	BAL	313	12TH WAR
FUEGLE, MARY STANISLAUS S	BAL	316	20TH WAR
FUEK, GEORGE A.	BAL	382	13TH WAR
FUELLY, WILLIAM	BAL	169	1ST WARD
FUEND, ELIZABETH	BAL	013	2ND DIST
FUER, P. *	BAL	316	20TH WAR
FUETON, MARGARET	BAL	288	12TH WAR
FUGATE, MARTIN	BAL	044	2ND DIST
FUGET, ROBERT M.	ALL	216	CUMBERLA
FUGET, THOMAS	BAL	431	1ST DIST
FUGIT, GEORGE	BAL	310	7TH WARD
FUGIT, MARY	BAL	311	7TH WARD
FUGOR, ZACHARIA*	DOR	403	1ST DIST
FUGUSON, WILLIAM	FRE	119	CREAGERS
FUHTHOFF, ANDREW C.*	BAL	411	3RD WARD
FUHTIS, LEWIS R.	MGM	414	MEDLEY 3
FUIST, WILLIAM *	BAL	281	20TH WAR
FUKEENER, FREDERICK	BAL	386	13TH WAR
FUKRMAN, HENRY B.	CAR	172	8TH DIST
FULAN, CATHRINE	BAL	024	18TH WAR
FULDA, BERNARD	BAL	033	1ST WARD
FULDER, AMAN	BAL	382	8TH WARD
FULERTON, PETER	BAL	067	18TH WAR
FULEY, MARY JANE	ALL	201	CUMBERLA
FULFORD, A. M.	BAL	042	4TH WARD
FULFORD, FRANCIS S.	HAR	094	2ND DIST
FULK, CAROLINE	BAL	021	15TH WAR
FULK, GEORGE	ALL	093	5TH E.D.
FULL, ADAM	FRE	071	FREDERIC
FULL, MADORA	FRE	032	FREDERIC
FULL, VILET*	BAL	338	3RD WARD
FULL, WILLIAM	BAL	306	12TH WAR
FULLAADT, GOSTINA	BAL	103	1ST WARD
FULLAN, JOHN	ALL	258	CUMBERLA
FULLAND, MARY	BAL	103	1ST WARD
FULLENKAMP, JOHN H.	BAL	286	17TH WAR
FULLER, A.	BAL	269	20TH WAR
FULLER, A.	BAL	135	1ST WARD
FULLER, ANN	BAL	055	1ST WARD
FULLER, BENJAMIN	BAL	334	1ST DIST
FULLER, CANA	ALL	019	2ND E.D.
FULLER, CHARELS	BAL	110	5TH WARD
FULLER, CHASE	BAL	382	3RD WARD
FULLER, CORNELIA	BAL	023	1ST WARD
FULLER, D.N.	ANN	443	HOWARD D
FULLER, EBENEZER W.	BAL	187	6TH WARD
FULLER, ELEANOR	BAL	197	6TH WARD
FULLER, ELIJAH	ALL	011	3RD E.D.
FULLER, ELISHA	ALL	011	3RD E.D.
FULLER, ELIZA	ANN	466	HOWARD D
FULLER, ELIZABETH	BAL	109	1ST WARD
FULLER, FLORENCE	BAL	412	14TH WAR
FULLER, HENRY	ALL	018	3RD E.D.
FULLER, HESTER A.	BAL	368	3RD WARD
FULLER, ISAAC	BAL	053	18TH WAR
FULLER, ISAIAH	ALL	012	3RD E.D.
FULLER, J.	BAL	228	12TH WAR
FULLER, JAMES	ANN	444	HOWARD D
FULLER, JANE	BAL	235	6TH WARD
FULLER, JOHN	BAL	065	2ND DIST
FULLER, JOHN	BAL	130	1ST WARD
FULLER, JOHN	BAL	254	6TH WARD
FULLER, JOHN L.	BAL	281	2ND WARD
FULLER, JOSEPH	BAL	069	2ND DIST
FULLER, JOSHUA	BAL	175	2ND DIST
FULLER, JOSHUA M.	BAL	235	12TH WAR
FULLER, JOSIAH	BAL	011	1ST WARD
FULLER, JOSIAH M.	BAL	012	1ST WARD
FULLER, LEWIS	BAL	200	17TH WAR
FULLER, MARY F.	BAL	249	1ST DIST
FULLER, MARY J.	BAL	168	16TH WAR
FULLER, MELVILE *	ALL	101	5TH E.D.
FULLER, NANNIE A.	BAL	249	1ST DIST
FULLER, PHILIP	BAL	173	6TH WARD
FULLER, RACHEAL	BAL	179	11TH WAR
FULLER, RICHARD	BAL	412	14TH WAR
FULLER, SAMUEL	BAL	078	2ND DIST
FULLER, SISTER GERALDINE	FRE	197	5TH E DI
FULLER, STEVEN	ALL	101	5TH E.D.
FULLER, THOMAS	BAL	109	1ST WARD
FULLER, THOMAS M.	BAL	285	7TH WARD
FULLER, THOMAS*	DOR	385	1ST DIST
FULLER, WILLIAM	BAL	435	14TH WAR
FULLER, WILLIAM	BAL	092	2ND DIST
FULLER, WILSON	BAL	154	16TH WAR
FULLERTIN, GEORGE	BAL	275	20TH WAR
FULLERTON, ARCHABALD	HAR	071	1ST DIST
FULLERTON, ELIZA	BAL	346	13TH WAR
FULLERTON, PATRICK	BAL	035	4TH WARD
FULLERTON, ROSE	BAL	219	12TH WAR
FULLERTON, SUSANNA	BAL	186	6TH WARD
FULLERTON, THOMAS	BAL	045	4TH WARD
FULLERTON, WILLIAM	BAL	349	7TH WARD
FULLFORD, MARY F.	BAL	196	11TH WAR
FULLINGAINS, BENJAMIN	FRE	217	BUCKEYST
FULLMAN, HARMAN	FRE	075	FREDERIC
FULLMATE, MICHAEL	BAL	242	1ST DIST
FULLMER, LEWIS	FRE	072	FREDERIC
FULLTON, JOHN	BAL	342	13TH WAR
FULMAN, CECELIA	BAL	256	2ND WARD
FULMAN, GABREL	BAL	034	1ST WARD
FULMAN, LEO	BAL	316	3RD WARD
FULMER, ANN R.	FRE	401	JEFFERSO
FULMER, CHARLES	FRE	067	FREDERIC
FULMER, GEORGE	FRE	067	FREDERIC
FULMER, HANNAH	BAL	038	9TH WARD
FULMER, JOHN	BAL	257	1ST DIST
FULMER, JOHN	ALL	222	CUMBERLA
FULMER, JOHN N.	BAL	308	12TH WAR
FULMER, JULIA A.	BAL	082	15TH WAR
FULMER, WILLIAM	FRE	401	JEFFERSC
FULMER, MARY	FRE	401	JEFFERSO
FULP, HENRY	BAL	282	1ST DIST
FULROY, HENRY	FRE	087	FREDERIC
FULSE, JANETA	ALL	109	5TH E.D.
FULSE, JOHN	ALL	108	5TH E.D.
FULSEN, CHARITY	BAL	286	12TH WAR
FULTON, ADONIA	BAL	126	1ST WARD
FULTON, ALBERT K.	BAL	133	5TH WARD
FULTON, ALEXANDER	BAL	250	6TH WARD
FULTON, ALEXANDER	ALL	107	5TH E.D.
FULTON, ALEXANDER	CEC	174	6TH E DI
FULTON, ANN	CEC	087	4TH E DI
FULTON, ANN	CEC	092	4TH E DI
FULTON, ANNA	CEC	101	4TH E DI
FULTON, BARBARA	WAS	263	1ST DIST
FULTON, CAROLINE	CEC	087	4TH E DI
FULTON, CHARLES C.	BAL	133	5TH WARD
FULTON, EDINGTON	BAL	075	4TH WARD
FULTON, ELISA	BAL	046	18TH WAR
FULTON, ELIZABETH	CEC	157	PORT DUP
FULTON, ELIZABETH	FRE	094	FREDERIC
FULTON, ELIZABETH	FRE	138	CREAGERS
FULTON, ELLEN	CEC	119	3RD E DI
FULTON, G. W.	BAL	300	20TH WAR
FULTON, GEORGE	BAL	196	6TH WARD
FULTON, GEORGE A.	CEC	104	4TH E DI
FULTON, GOERGE	WAS	261	1ST DIST
FULTON, HENRY	BAL	406	3RD WARD
FULTON, J.B.H.	BAL	009	EASTERN
FULTON, JACOB	WAS	261	1ST DIST
FULTON, JACOB	CEC	118	4TH E DI
FULTON, JAMES	BAL	244	17TH WAR
FULTON, JAMES	FRE	205	BUCKEYST
FULTON, JAMES	BAL	111	18TH WAR
FULTON, JAMES	BAL	471	14TH WAR
FULTON, JAMES	WAS	261	1ST DIST
FULTON, JAMES	BAL	284	12TH WAR
FULTON, JAMES	BAL	063	10TH WAR
FULTON, JAMES A.	ANN	294	1ST DIST
FULTON, JAMES A.	HAR	075	BEL AIR
FULTON, JANE	CEC	109	4TH E DI
FULTON, JOHN	FRE	303	WOODSBOR
FULTON, JOHN	CEC	210	7TH E DI
FULTON, JOHN	WAS	249	1ST DIST
FULTON, JOHN B.	ANN	295	1ST DIST
FULTON, JOHN C.	HAR	102	2ND DIST
FULTON, JOSEPH	FRE	137	CREAGERS
FULTON, LYMAN	BAL	114	5TH WARD
FULTON, MARY	WAS	263	1ST DIST
FULTON, MOSES	BAL	071	10TH WAR
FULTON, PATRICK	FRE	140	CREAGERS
FULTON, REBECCA	BAL	181	2ND WARD
FULTON, ROBERT	BAL	162	2ND DIST
FULTON, ROBERT DR.	BAL	381	13TH WAR
FULTON, SARAH	HAR	034	1ST DIST
FULTON, SARAH C.	FRE	310	WOODSBOR
FULTON, SOLOMON	FRE	301	WOODSBOR
FULTON, SUSAN	FRE	302	WOODSBOR
FULTON, THOMAS	CEC	089	4TH E DI
FULTON, THOMAS H.	BAL	410	1ST DIST
FULTON, WILLIAM	CEC	092	4TH E DI
FULTON, WILLIAM	WAS	263	1ST DIST
FULTZ, CATHERINE	WAS	107	2ND DIST
FULTZ, ELIZABETH	BAL	299	1ST DIST
FULTZ, GEORGE	WAS	213	1ST DIST
FULTZ, HENRY	WAS	223	1ST DIST
FULTZ, JOHN	WAS	253	1ST DIST
FULTZ, JOHN	ALL	038	2ND E.D.
FULWILER, FERDINAND	WAS	137	HAGERSTO
FUMER, ANN	BAL	018	18TH WAR
FUNALD, D.D.	BAL	163	1ST WARD
FUNCH, WILLIAM	WAS	036	2ND SUBD
FUNCK, HENRY	FRE	126	CREAGERS
FUNCK, MARGARET	FRE	128	CREAGERS
FUNCK, NANCY A.	FRE	119	CREAGERS
FUNCK, WILLIAM	FRE	142	CREAGERS
FUNEY, JAMES	BAL	433	14TH WAR
FUNGER, HENRY	ANN	513	HOWARD D
FUNK, A. REBECCA	WAS	130	HAGERSTO
FUNK, ALEINDA	ALL	215	CUMBERLA
FUNK, ANDREW	WAS	215	1ST DIST
FUNK, ANN M.	WAS	258	1ST DIST
FUNK, DANIEL	WAS	074	2ND SUBD
FUNK, DAVID J.	WAS	220	1ST DIST
FUNK, ELLEN	WAS	129	HAGERSTO
FUNK, GEORGE	WAS	225	1ST DIST
FUNK, GEORGE	BAL	217	6TH WARD
FUNK, GEORGE	BAL	028	2ND DIST
FUNK, HENRY	BAL	108	5TH WARD
FUNK, HENRY	WAS	091	2ND SUBD
FUNK, HENRY	BAL	302	20TH WAR
FUNK, JACOB	BAL	298	17TH WAR
FUNK, JACOB	FRE	230	BUCKEYST
FUNK, JACOB	BAL	311	20TH WAR
FUNK, JACOB	WAS	300	1ST DIST
FUNK, JACOB	WAS	225	1ST DIST
FUNK, JACOB	WAS	185	BOONSBOR
FUNK, JAMES	ALL	180	8TH E.D.
FUNK, JAMES T.	WAS	225	1ST DIST
FUNK, JOHN	WAS	221	1ST DIST
FUNK, JOHN	WAS	252	1ST DIST
FUNK, JOHN	WAS	126	HAGERSTO
FUNK, JOHN	WAS	298	1ST DIST
FUNK, JOHN	BAL	458	1ST DIST
FUNK, JOHN H.	WAS	231	1ST DIST
FUNK, JOSEPH	WAS	131	2ND DIST
FUNK, JULIA	WAS	082	2ND SUBD
FUNK, MARTIN	WAS	231	1ST DIST
FUNK, MARY	WAS	220	1ST DIST
FUNK, MARY	WAS	170	FUNKSTOW
FUNK, MICHAEL	WAS	127	HAGERSTO
FUNK, SAMUEL	WAS	219	1ST DIST
FUNK, WILLIAM	BAL	039	18TH WAR
FUNK, F.H.	BAL	240	2ND WARD
FUNK, MARY ANN	ALL	247	CUMBERLA
FUNKLEY, BENJAMIN	BAL	126	11TH WAR
FUPP, GEORGE	BAL	321	1ST DIST
FURBY, CHARLOTTE A.	BAL	435	8TH WARD
FUREY, WILLIAM	FRE	190	5TH E DI
FURGASON, ANDREW	BAL	097	18TH WAR
FURGASON, ELIZABETH	TAL	007	EASTON D
FURGASON, FRANCES	CEC	102	4TH E DI
FURGASON, J. HENRY	BAL	318	1ST DIST
FURGASON, JAMES	TAL	002	EASTON D
FURGASON, JANE M.	BAL	309	1ST DIST

Name	County	Page	District
FURGASON, MARGARET	FRE	294	WOODSBOR
FURGASCN, ROBERT	ALL	041	2ND E.D.
FURGASON, SAMUEL	CEC	092	4TH E DI
FURGASON, WILIAM	BAL	280	2ND WARD
FURGASON, WILLIAM	BAL	281	1ST DIST
FURGASON, WILLIAM	PRI	006	BLADENSB
FURGASON, WILLIAM	PRI	028	VANSVILL
FURGERSON, B. W.	BAL	040	18TH WAR
FURGERSON, ELIZA	BAL	194	11TH WAR
FURGERSON, GEORGE	CEC	109	3RD E DI
FURGERSON, MARGARET	FRE	142	CREAGERS
FURGERSON, WASHINGTON	ST	318	4TH E DI
FURGESON, ALLEN	CAR	073	NO TWP L
FURGESON, CONSTANTIA	CEC	082	CHARLEST
FURGESON, WILLIAM	BAL	285	17TH WAR
FURGESON,MARY	ALL	213	CUMBERLA
FURGINSON, WILLIAM M.	BAL	410	8TH WARD
FURGISON, CHALRES-BLACK	CAR	070	NO TWP L
FURGISON, ELIZABETH	CAR	074	NO TWP L
FURGURSON, WILLIAM	BAL	438	8TH WARD
FURGUSON, ELISHA	PRI	070	MARLBROU
FURGUSON, HENRY	BAL	401	1ST DIST
FURGUSON, JOHN	HAR	002	1ST DIST
FURGUSON, JOSEPHENE	FRE	285	WOODSBOR
FURGUSON, SAMUEL	WAS	044	2ND SUBD
FURGUSON, SAMUEL L.	BAL	281	17TH WAR
FURGUSON, WILLIAM	BAL	141	5TH WARD
FURGUSON, WILLIAM	BAL	141	5TH WARD
FURGUSSON, WILLIAM T.	BAL	438	8TH WARD
FURHMAN, CONRAD	CAR	343	6TH DIST
FURHMAN, EDWARD	CAR	333	MANCHEST
FURHMAN, HENRY	CAR	343	6TH DIST
FURHMAN, MARTIN	CAR	341	6TH DIST
FURHMAN, SAMUEL B.	CAR	333	MANCHEST
FURHMAN, SOPHIA	CAR	378	2ND DIST
FURLE, SAMUEL	ALL	171	7TH E.D.
FURLEY, WILLIAM	BAL	048	4TH WARD
FURLONG, ANNA	BAL	360	3RD WARD
FURLONG, DENNIS	HAR	055	1ST DIST
FURLONG, ELIZABETH	BAL	011	18TH WAR
FURLONG, ELIZABETH	WAS	097	2ND DIST
FURLONG, HENRY	BAL	046	2ND DIST
FURLONG, JACOB	WAS	025	2ND SUBD
FURLONG, JOANA	BAL	425	1ST DIST
FURLONG, JOHN	WAS	124	2ND DIST
FURLONG, JOHN	BAL	039	4TH WARD
FURLONG, JOSEPHINE	BAL	197	6TH WARD
FURLONG, JUISTIVIRIS *	HAR	011	1ST DIST
FURLONG, MARY	WAS	038	2ND SUBD
FURLONG, NICHOLAS	HAR	009	1ST DIST
FURLONG, ROSE A.	WAS	024	2ND SUBD
FURLONG, SAMUEL	WAS	025	2ND SUBD
FURLONG, SARAH	BAL	078	15TH WAR
FURLONG, THOMAS	BAL	115	18TH WAR
FURLONG, WILLIAM	ALL	220	CUMBERLA
FURLONG, WILLIAM	BAL	354	7TH WARD
FURLONG, WILLLIAM	BAL	424	1ST DIST
FURLONG,ANN	BAL	019	2ND DIST
FURLOUGH, JAMES	ALL	191	9TH E.D.
FURMAN, CATHARINE	TAL	074	EASTON T
FURNACE, ANN	SOM	350	BRINKLEY
FURNACE, ELI	TAL	074	EASTON T
FURNACE, EPHRAIM	SOM	461	HANGARY
FURNACE, HENRIETTA	BAL	387	1ST DIST
FURNACE, LEAH	SOM	350	BRINKLEY
FURNACE, LITTLETON	SOM	465	HANGARY
FURNAN, LUKE	BAL	377	13TH WAR
FURNASE, MATILDA*	TAL	002	EASTON D
FURNEY, DENNIS	BAL	053	18TH WAR
FURNEY, JOHN S.	BAL	079	18TH WAR
FURNEY, REBECCA	BAL	058	18TH WAR
FURNEY, SARAH	BAL	057	18TH WAR
FURNIP, WILLIAM	SOM	400	BRINKLEY
FURR, MARY	BAL	230	2ND WARD
FURR, WILLIAM	BAL	132	11TH WAR
FURREY, ABRAHAM	FRE	450	8TH E DI
FURRY, JOHN *	WAS	168	FUNKSTOW
FURRY, SUSAN	WAS	194	1ST DIST
FURRY, WILLIAM	WAS	171	FUNKSTOW
FURTENEERGER, JESSE	ANN	330	2ND DIST
FURTH, SAMUEL A.	BAL	025	2ND DIST
FURY, JOHN	WAS	025	2ND SUBD
FURY, MICHAEL	ALL	051	10TH E.D
FURZE, EVELINE *	BAL	317	20TH WAR
FUSCH, JONES *	BAL	298	20TH WAR
FUSET, JONES *	BAL	298	20TH WAR
FUSHMAN, JOHN	CAR	347	6TH DIST
FUSLEY, WILLIAM J.	BAL	268	12TH WAR
FUSOF, CAROLINE	BAL	118	5TH WARD
FUSS, ADAM	CAR	401	2ND DIST
FUSS, DAVID	CAR	388	2ND DIST
FUSSELL, B. F.	BAL	076	10TH WAR
FUSSELL, CLARRISSA	BAL	146	5TH WARD
FUSSELL, JOSEPH	BAL	141	5TH WARD
FUSTER, CHRISTOPHER *	BAL	162	2ND DIST
FUSTING, JOSEPH P.	BAL	320	1ST DIST
FUSTNER, LIZEE	BAL	209	11TH WAR
FUTHERER, VERONICA SIS- *	BAL	316	20TH WAR
FUTHORN, WILLIAM	BAL	167	1ST WARD
FUTSELBERGER, PETER	BAL	373	8TH WARD
FUTTERER, LEWIS	WAS	122	HAGERSTO
FUTY, JOHN	BAL	221	2ND WARD
FUTZ, GEORGE H.	BAL	263	2ND WARD
FYAN, ROBERT	FRE	202	5TH E DI
FYFFE, THOMAS H.	MGM	407	MEDLEY 3
FYTER, THOMAS	BAL	161	1ST WARD
GAAS, MARGARET	BAL	217	6TH WARD
GAAVENSTINE, CORA*	BAL	055	4TH WARD
GABBEN, JOHN	BAL	043	18TH WAR
GABBY, JAMES	WAS	274	RIDGEVIL
GABE, CHARLES A.	WAS	182	BOONSBOR
GABELINE, MARY	BAL	376	3RD WARD
GABLE, CATHERINE G.	BAL	389	8TH WARD
GABLE, CHARLES	BAL	101	5TH WARD
GABLE, CHARLES	BAL	006	EASTERN
GABLE, HENRY	BAL	191	6TH WARD
GABLE, HENRY	BAL	166	16TH WAR
GABLE, JOHN	BAL	138	18TH WAR
GABLE, LOUISA	BAL	125	16TH WAR
GABLE, MARY	BAL	398	1ST DIST
GABLE, MICHAEL	BAL	101	5TH WARD
GABLE, MICHAEL	BAL	135	2ND DIST
GABLE, ROBERT	BAL	197	17TH WAR
GABLEN, LEWIS	BAL	167	2ND DIST
GABLEN, LISITTE	BAL	166	2ND DIST
GABLER, CHARLES	BAL	270	7TH WARD
GABLES, MINNA	BAL	003	18TH WAR
GABLIER, BENJAMIN	WAS	170	FUNKSTOW
GABOTH, CHARLES	BAL	386	13TH WAR
GABREATH, JAMES	HAR	005	1ST DIST
GABRIEL, ABRAHAM	WAS	185	BOONSBOR
GABRIEL, CATHARINE	WAS	296	1ST DIST
GABRIELS, MORDEON	BAL	098	1ST WARD
GABRY, DANNEY	WOR	305	2ND E DI
GABVEN, CHARLES *	BAL	021	18TH WAR
GADD, ELIZA	BAL	097	10TH WAR
GADD, JOHN	BAL	131	18TH WAR
GADD, LUTHER C.	BAL	270	7TH WARD
GADD, LYDIA	CAR	090	NO TWP L
GADD, MARY	DOR	364	3RD DIVI
GADD, ROBERT	DOR	365	3RD DIVI
GADDARD, ELIAS	FRE	256	NEW MARK
GADDART, SANCHART	BAL	271	2ND WARD
GADDERS, ALEXANDER	BAL	342	13TH WAR
GADDES, PERREY	BAL	459	8TH WARD
GADDES, REBECCA	BAL	205	11TH WAR
GADDESS, ALEXANDER	BAL	033	9TH WARD
GADDIS, JOHN	KEN	304	3RD DIST
GADDO, MICHAEL	BAL	413	14TH WAR
GADE, JOHN	BAL	101	10TH WAR
GADER, JOHN	ALL	231	CUMBERLA
GADIN, HARRY	WAS	093	2ND SUBD
GADNER, BENJAMIN	BAL	161	1ST WARD
GADSHER, JOHN H.	BAL	368	8TH WARD
GAEHL, MARY	BAL	111	15TH WAR
GAEHLE, LEWIS	BAL	416	14TH WAR
GAEHLE, WILLIAM	BAL	416	14TH WAR
GAES, ADAM	BAL	166	6TH WARD
GAFFANY, TOM	ANN	414	HOWARD D
GAFFARY, CHARLES *	HAR	199	3RD DIST
GAFFNEY, ELLEN	MGM	403	ROCKERLE
GAFFNEY, ELLEN	BAL	441	8TH WARD
GAFFNEY, MARY	BAL	133	5TH WARD
GAFFNEY, PATRICK	BAL	447	8TH WARD
GAFFORD, ANN	BAL	073	15TH WAR
GAFFORD, ANN	BAL	052	18TH WAR
GAFFORD, BENJAMIN	QUE	176	2ND E DI
GAFFORD, JACOB W.	QUE	211	3RD E DI
GAFFORD, JAMES	QUE	170	2ND E DI
GAFFORD, JAMES	WOR	260	BERLIN 1
GAFFORD, JANE	BAL	169	19TH WAR
GAFFORD, JAOCB-BLACK	QUE	175	2ND E DI
GAFFORD, PHILIP	QUE	180	2ND E DI
GAFFORD, SAMUEL	QUE	159	2ND E DI
GAFFORD, SOLOMON	ANN	314	1ST DIST
GAFFREY, ANTHONY	BAL	168	1ST WARD
GAFFY, JOHN	BAL	002	EASTERN
GAGAN, MICHAEL	BAL	271	1ST DIST
GAGAR, CHARLES	BAL	399	1ST DIST
GAGAR, PHILLIP	ANN	270	ANNAPOLI
GAGAWAY, LETHY A.	PRI	093	MARLBROU
GAGAWAY, WILLAIM	PRI	091	MARLBROU
GAGE, CHARLES	HAR	035	1ST DIST
GAGE, ISAAC	HAR	001	1ST DIST
GAGE, ISAAC	HAR	159	3RD DIST
GAGE, MARY E.	HAR	031	1ST DIST
GAGE, WILLIAM L.	SOM	365	BRINKLEY
GAGER, SAMUEL	BAL	050	4TH WARD
GAGES, AUSTIN	CHA	253	MIDDLETO
GAGES, JOSPEH	CHA	254	MIDDLETO
GAGIL, HENRY	WAS	280	LEITERSB
GAHAGAN, THOMAS	BAL	163	11TH WAR
GAHAMAN, ELIZABETH	WAS	271	1ST DIST
GAHLE, HENRY	BAL	463	14TH WAR
GAIENNIE, GEORGE W.	FRE	20	5TH E DI
GAIL, G. W.	BAL	470	14TH WAR
GAILE, JOHN	BAL	129	1ST WARD
GAILHER, MARY L.	PRI	004	BLADENSB
GAILOR, LAVINA	WAS	219	1ST DIST
GAILOR, PETER	WAS	223	1ST DIST
GAILOR, WILLIAM	WAS	219	1ST DIST
GAILY, JANE	BAL	431	1ST DIST
GAILY, MICHAEL	BAL	419	14TH WAR
GAIN, BELITHA *	SOM	410	DUBLIN D
GAIN, ELIZA	WOR	185	7TH E DI
GAIN, JAMES	BAL	051	2ND DIST
GAIN, MARY	BAL	395	1ST DIST
GAIN, MATEA F.	BAL	402	1ST DIST
GAIN, POLLY	BAL	209	6TH DIST
GAIN, RACHAEL	BAL	208	6TH DIST
GAINE, ANTHONY	BAL	138	1ST WARD
GAINER, ELIZABETH	ALL	158	6TH E.D.
GAINER, EPHRAIM	CAR	390	2ND DIST
GAINER, LANEHART	BAL	163	2ND DIST
GAINER, MARTIN	CAR	383	2ND DIST
GAINES, EDMUND P.	BAL	008	EASTERN
GAINES, ELLEN S.	BAL	010	1ST WARD
GAINES, EMILY J.	BAL	036	15TH WAR
GAINES, H.	BAL	287	20TH WAR
GAINES, JOHN	BAL	212	17TH WAR
GAINES, JOHN	BAL	091	15TH WAR
GAINES, JOHN W.	BAL	023	9TH WARD
GAINES, JOSEPH	BAL	192	17TH WAR
GAINES, LEAH	BAL	434	14TH WAR
GAINES, LEVIN	BAL	339	3RD WARD
GAINES, MARTHA	BAL	171	11TH WAR
GAINES, MARTIN	BAL	212	17TH WAR
GAINES, MARY	BAL	078	15TH WAR
GAINES, MARY ANN	BAL	005	4TH WARD
GAINES, MARY V.	BAL	009	EASTERN
GAINES, MOSES	BAL	091	15TH WAR
GAINES, NANTZY	BAL	315	3RD WARD
GAINES, NOAH	BAL	041	15TH WAR
GAINES, PRESCILLA	WAS	154	HAGERSTO
GAINES, RICHARD	BAL	073	18TH WAR
GAINES, WILLIAM	BAL	169	11TH WAR
GAINES, WILLIAM	BAL	315	3RD WARD
GAINES, WILLIAM	BAL	153	1ST WARD
GAINGAN, ANTHONY	ALL	053	10TH E.D
GAINOR,BEDELIA	ALL	219	CUMBERLA
GAINS, ANTHONEY	DOR	326	3RD DIVI
GAINS, CAROLINE	BAL	191	17TH WAR
GAINS, CHARLES	BAL	001	9TH WARD
GAINS, CHARLOTTE	BAL	019	1ST WARD
GAINS, EVANS-BLACK	BAL	178	2ND WARD
GAINS, JAMES	BAL	191	17TH WAR
GAINS, JOHN	BAL	337	3RD WARD
GAINS, MANTZY	BAL	339	3RD WARD
GAINS, MARY M.	BAL	171	16TH WAR
GAINS, MOSES	BAL	096	15TH WAR
GAINS, PHILIP	BAL	259	1ST DIST
GAINS, STEPHEN	DOR	363	3RD DIVI
GAINS, STEWART	BAL	093	15TH WAR
GAINS, WILLIAM	BAL	352	3RD WARD
GAIRUS, CHARLES	BAL	192	17TH WAR
GAITELEY, BRIDGET	BAL	002	15TH WAR
GAITHA, FREDERICA	MGM	335	CRACKLIN
GAITHA, GEORGE	MGM	328	CRACKLIN
GAITHA, SAMUEL R.	MGM	328	CRACKLIN
GAITHA, SAMUEL R.	MGM	333	CRACKLIN
GAITHA, WILLIAM B.	MGM	327	CRACKLIN
GAITHA, WILLIAM L.	MGM	334	CRACKLIN
GAITHER, ALFRED	BAL	475	14TH WAR
GAITHER, BEAL	ANN	385	4TH DIST
GAITHER, BENJAMIN	ANN	439	HOWARD D
GAITHER, CATHARINE	ANN	432	HOWARD D
GAITHER, CATHARINE	BAL	107	18TH WAR
GAITHER, CHARLES	ANN	470	HOWARD D
GAITHER, DENNIS	ANN	368	4TH DIST
GAITHER, EDWIN	WAS	233	1ST DIST
GAITHER, ELI	ANN	373	4TH DIST
GAITHER, ELIJAH	ANN	511	HOWARD D
GAITHER, ELISHA R.	MGM	324	CRACKLIN
GAITHER, ELIZA	BAL	357	3RD WARD
GAITHER, ELIZA A.	BAL	176	16TH WAR
GAITHER, ELIZABETH	PRI	023	VANSVILL
GAITHER, EPHRAIM	MGM	327	CRACKLIN
GAITHER, EVAN	ANN	479	HOWARD D
GAITHER, FLETCHER	BAL	395	8TH WARD
GAITHER, FRANKLIN	ANN	431	HOWARD D
GAITHER, GEORGE R.	ANN	472	HOWARD D
GAITHER, GEORGE W.	BAL	177	16TH WAR
GAITHER, GREENBURY	ANN	495	HOWARD D
GAITHER, HANNAH	ANN	444	HOWARD D
GAITHER, HENRY	MGM	332	CRACKLIN
GAITHER, ISAIAH	ANN	419	HOWARD D
GAITHER, JAMES B.	MGM	318	CRACKLIN
GAITHER, JAMES F.	ANN	414	HOWARD D
GAITHER, JERRY	ANN	444	HOWARD D
GAITHER, JOHN	ANN	324	2ND DIST
GAITHER, JOHN	PRI	087	QUEEN AN
GAITHER, JOHN D.	FRE	442	8TH E DI
GAITHER, JOHN M.	ANN	325	2ND DIST
GAITHER, LUCY	PRI	045	VANSVILL
GAITHER, LUCY-BLACK	FRE	229	BUCKEYST
GAITHER, MARGARET	FRE	023	FREDERIC
GAITHER, MARIA	ANN	384	4TH DIST
GAITHER, MARIA	BAL	136	16TH WAR
GAITHER, MARTHA	ANN	436	HOWARD D
GAITHER, MARY	ANN	496	HOWARD D
GAITHER, MARY	BAL	357	13TH WAR
GAITHER, MATILDA	WAS	136	HAGERSTO
GAITHER, MICHAEL*	BAL	331	3RD WARD
GAITHER, MISS-	ANN	363	4TH DIST
GAITHER, NANCY	PRI	043	VANSVILL
GAITHER, PERRY	ANN	488	HOWARD D
GAITHER, PRUDENCE A.	ANN	436	HOWARD D
GAITHER, RACHEL	ANN	479	HOWARD D
GAITHER, RACHEL A.	ANN	444	HOWARD D
GAITHER, RACHEL A.	ANN	432	HOWARD D
GAITHER, RICAHRD	BAL	405	14TH WAR
GAITHER, RICHARD D.	FRE	442	8TH E DI
GAITHER, SALLY	ANN	388	4TH DIST
GAITHER, SAMUEL	ANN	511	HOWARD D
GAITHER, SINGLETON	ANN	379	4TH DIST
GAITHER, THOMAS D.	MGM	327	CRACKLIN
GAITHER, THOMAS J.	ANN	384	4TH DIST
GAITHER, WASHINGTON	ANN	511	HOWARD D
GAITHER, WASHINGTON	BAL	177	16TH WAR
GAITHER, WILLIAM H.	ANN	431	HOWARD D
GAITLY, PATRICK	BAL	179	2ND WARD
GAITRELL, JOHN	MGM	342	CLARKSBU
GAL, GEORGE	KEN	245	2ND DIST
GALAGAN, MARY	BAL	168	11TH WAR
GALAGER, JOHN	BAL	360	1ST DIST
GALAGHER, FERDINAND H.	BAL	019	18TH WAR
GALAGHER, HUGH	BAL	053	18TH WAR
GALAGHER, MARGARET	BAL	152	11TH WAR
GALAGHER, MARY	BAL	152	11TH WAR
GALAGHER, MARY	WAS	011	WILLIAMS
GALAGHER, MICHEAL	BAL	023	18TH WAR
GALAGHER, PHILIP	BAL	034	18TH WAR
GALAGHER, ROSALA	BAL	212	11TH WAR
GALAHER, JAMES	ALL	081	5TH E.D.
GALALESPIE, NATHAN	BAL	043	2ND DIST
GALAN, THOMAS	BAL	418	14TH WAR
GALAVAN, MORTCMAS	BAL	408	1ST DIST
GALAWAY, ANN	BAL	188	11TH WAR
GALAWAY, ELIZA	BAL	063	18TH WAR
GALAWAY, HILLERY-BLACK	FRE	040	FREDERIC
GALAWAY, ISABEL B.	HAR	031	1ST DIST
GALAWAY, JOHN	BAL	107	18TH WAR
GALAWAY, JOSHUA	CEC	043	CHESAPEA
GALAWAY, VINCENT A.	BAL	097	18TH WAR
GALBERT, LEWIS	BAL	402	14TH WAR
GALBOT, CAROLINE	BAL	303	12TH WAR
GALBREATH, ALEXANDER	HAR	032	1ST DIST
GALBREATH, JOHN F.	HAR	032	1ST DIST
GALBREATH, SARAH	CAR	246	3RD DIST
GALBREATH, THOAMS	HAR	037	1ST DIST
GALBRETH, SAMUEL	BAL	385	3RD WARD
GALBRETH, SAMUEL L.	BAL	386	3RD WARD
GALDEMAN, AUGUST	BAL	289	1ST DIST
GALDHILL, JAMES	FRE	358	CATOCTIN
GALDHILL, JAMES T.	FRE	341	MIDDLETO
GALDING, WILLIAM H.	BAL	134	1ST WARD
GALE, ALEXANDER	CEC	010	ELKTON 3
GALE, ANN	BAL	181	11TH WAR
GALE, ANNE	BAL	246	20TH WAR
GALE, BENJAMIN	CEC	128	5TH E DI
GALE, CHARLES	SOM	554	TYASKIN
GALE, EDWARD	SOM	534	QUANTICO
GALE, ELIZA	KEN	256	1ST DIST
GALE, FRANCIS	KEN	233	2ND DIST
GALE, G. G.	BAL	332	1ST DIST
GALE, GEORGE	BAL	178	11TH WAR
GALE, GEORGE	ANN	307	1ST DIST
GALE, GEORGE	SOM	475	TRAPPE D
GALE, GEORGE	SOM	533	QUANTICO
GALE, GEORGE C.	BAL	346	7TH WARD
GALE, GEORGE L.	SOM	429	PRINCESS
GALE, HENRY	SOM	533	QUANTICO
GALE, HENRY L.	HAR	153	3RD DIST
GALE, HOOPER	SOM	547	TYASKIN
GALE, ISAAC	KEN	264	1ST DIST
GALE, ISAAC	KEN	263	1ST DIST
GALE, J. R.	BAL	157	1ST WARD
GALE, JAMES	BAL	065	1ST WARD
GALE, JAMES	KEN	249	2ND DIST
GALE, JAMES	CEC	168	6TH E DI
GALE, JAMES E.	BAL	082	15TH WAR
GALE, JOHN	BAL	110	5TH WARD
GALE, JOHN	SOM	428	PRINCESS
GALE, JOHN	KEN	260	1ST DIST
GALE, JOHN	SOM	534	QUANTICO
GALE, JOHN E.	KEN	243	2ND DIST
GALE, JOSEPH	CEC	163	6TH E DI
GALE, JOSEPH	CEC	130	6TH E DI
GALE, JOSHUA	SOM	430	PRINCESS
GALE, LEAH	BAL	343	13TH WAR

Name	County	Page	District
GALE, LEVIN	SOM	533	QUANTICO
GALE, LEVINE	BAL	181	11TH WAR
GALE, LYDIA	CEC	185	7TH E DI
GALE, MARGH *	BAL	149	2ND DIST
GALE, MARY	BAL	346	7TH WARD
GALE, MARY	KEN	213	2ND DIST
GALE, RACHAEL	BAL	285	2ND WARD
GALE, REZIN	BAL	069	15TH WAR
GALE, RICHARD	KEN	255	1ST DIST
GALE, ROBERT	BAL	388	3RD WARD
GALE, ROBERT	CEC	177	7TH E DI
GALE, ROBERT W.	ANN	299	1ST DIST
GALE, ROSE	SOM	521	BARREN C
GALE, SAMUEL	HAR	207	3RD DIST
GALE, SARAH	BAL	206	17TH WAR
GALE, SARAH	BAL	160	2ND DIST
GALE, SARAH	BAL	026	9TH WARD
GALE, SARAH J.	CEC	129	6TH E DI
GALE, STEPHEN	BAL	255	1ST DIST
GALE, SUSAN	SOM	530	QUANTICO
GALE, THOMAS	BAL	157	2ND DIST
GALE, THOMAS	BAL	148	2ND DIST
GALE, THOMAS J.*	TAL	067	EASTON T
GALE, THOMAS J.*	TAL	067	EASTON T
GALE, WILLIAM	SOM	388	BRINKLEY
GALE, WILLIAM	SOM	434	PRINCESS
GALEGHEN, JAMES	BAL	124	11TH WAR
GALEN, ANNE	BAL	177	11TH WAR
GALENAR, NICHOLAS	BAL	264	2ND WARD
GALEON, RICHARD	BAL	432	1ST DIST
GALER, JOHN	FRE	325	MIDDLETO
GALER, WILLIAM B.	PRI	004	BLADENSB
GALES, JOSEPH	BAL	177	11TH WAR
GALES, JOSIAH A.	BAL	142	1ST WARD
GALES, RACHAL	KEN	261	1ST DIST
GALES, RACHAL	KEN	254	1ST DIST
GALESBY, HAMILTON	BAL	123	18TH WAR
GALESE, PATRICK	BAL	109	2ND DIST
GALESPIE, MATILDA	BAL	414	8TH WARD
GALESSPIE, DIANA*	BAL	042	4TH WARD
GALET, JOHN	BAL	127	2ND DIST
GALEY, LEWIS	BAL	118	1ST WARD
GALEY, ROBERT	HAR	025	1ST DIST
GALHER, ELIZABETH-MULATTO	FRE	242	NEW MARK
GALIAN, ROBERT	HAR	004	1ST DIST
GALICE, FRANCIS	BAL	362	8TH WARD
GALICE, THOMAS	WAS	158	2ND DIST
GALIGER, JOHN	HAR	185	3RD DIST
GALIGHER, BENJAMIN	WAS	245	SMITHSBU
GALIGHER, JAMES A.	FRE	035	FREDERIC
GALIGHER, PATRICK	FRE	069	FREDERIC
GALIGHER, ELZIABETH	FRE	012	FREDERIC
GALIM, CATHERIN M.	ALL	219	CUMBERLA
GALION, ARON	WAS	107	2ND DIST
GALIONAY, ROBERT M.	BAL	224	12TH WAR
GALL, CATHARINE	BAL	277	1ST DIST
GALL, JOHN	TAL	070	EASTON T
GALL, JOHN	FRE	138	CREAGERS
GALL, JULIA	BAL	440	1ST DIST
GALL, LITTLETON	CEC	144	PORT DUP
GALL, MARGARET	CAL	027	2ND DIST
GALL, WILLIAM	BAL	287	1ST DIST
GALL, WILLIAM	WAS	255	1ST DIST
GALLAGAN, ALLACE	BAL	379	1ST DIST
GALLAGAR, ABERT	BAL	294	1ST DIST
GALLAGAR, CHARLES R.	BAL	287	1ST DIST
GALLAGER, ANN	BAL	120	5TH WARD
GALLAGER, ED	BAL	042	1ST WARD
GALLAGER, EPHRIAM	BAL	366	1ST DIST
GALLAGER, JAMES	BAL	399	1ST DIST
GALLAGER, JANE	BAL	256	17TH WAR
GALLAGER, LYDIA	PRI	027	VANSVILL
GALLAGER, MARY	BAL	186	11TH WAR
GALLAGER, NICHOLAS	BAL	460	1ST DIST
GALLAGER, RICHARD	BAL	278	1ST DIST
GALLAGER, ROSE	BAL	251	1ST DIST
GALLAGER, SUSAN	BAL	205	17TH WAR
GALLAGER, WILLIAM	BAL	127	5TH WARD
GALLAGHER, ADAM	BAL	047	1ST WARD
GALLAGHER, ANN	BAL	161	6TH WARD
GALLAGHER, ANN	BAL	042	15TH WAR
GALLAGHER, CHARLOTTE	BAL	204	6TH WARD
GALLAGHER, FRANCIS	BAL	038	15TH WAR
GALLAGHER, FRANCIS	BAL	159	16TH WAR
GALLAGHER, FRANCIS	BAL	260	20TH WAR
GALLAGHER, HUGH	BAL	441	8TH WARD
GALLAGHER, JAMES	BAL	033	15TH WAR
GALLAGHER, JAMES	BAL	290	3RD WARD
GALLAGHER, JAMES	BAL	193	19TH WAR
GALLAGHER, JOHN	BAL	216	19TH WAR
GALLAGHER, JOHN	BAL	224	19TH WAR
GALLAGHER, JOHN	BAL	242	20TH WAR
GALLAGHER, MARGARET	BAL	035	15TH WAR
GALLAGHER, MARIA	BAL	212	11TH WAR
GALLAGHER, MARTON	BAL	025	9TH WARD
GALLAGHER, MARY	BAL	195	6TH WARD
GALLAGHER, MARY	BAL	091	10TH WAR
GALLAGHER, MARY	BAL	403	3RD WARD
GALLAGHER, MARY	BAL	360	13TH WAR
GALLAGHER, MARY A.	BAL	035	15TH WAR
GALLAGHER, MICHAEL	BAL	345	13TH WAR
GALLAGHER, PATRICK	BAL	288	7TH WARD
GALLAGHER, PATRICK	BAL	139	5TH WARD
GALLAGHER, PATRICK C.	BAL	033	18TH WAR
GALLAGHER, ROBERT	CEC	097	4TH E DI
GALLAGHER, ROBERT	BAL	236	6TH WARD
GALLAGHER, SARAH	BAL	316	20TH WAR
GALLAGHER, STEWART H.	CEC	091	4TH E DI
GALLAGHER, SUSAN	CEC	094	4TH E DI
GALLAGHER, SYLVESTER	WAS	124	HAGERSTO
GALLAGHER, THOMAS	BAL	273	12TH WAR
GALLAGHER, WILLIAM	BAL	021	9TH WARD
GALLAHAN, JANE	PRI	074	MARLBROU
GALLAHAN, JOHN	PRI	078	MARLBROU
GALLAHAN, SAMUEL	PRI	119	PISCATAW
GALLAHAN, THOMAS	PRI	081	QUEEN AN
GALLAHAN, WILLIAM	PRI	119	PISCATAW
GALLAHAR, JOHN	BAL	252	1ST DIST
GALLAHER, ABRAHAM	CEC	162	6TH E DI
GALLAHER, ANN	ALL	196	CUMBERLA
GALLAHER, ELIZABETH	FRE	449	8TH E DI
GALLAHER, ENOCH	CEC	141	6TH E DI
GALLAHER, JOHN	ALL	073	5TH E.D.
GALLAHER, JOHN T.	CEC	108	3RD E DI
GALLAHER, JOSEPH	CEC	152	PORT DUP
GALLAHER, LYDIA A.	CEC	012	ELKTON 3
GALLAHER, MARGARET	ALL	237	CUMBERLA
GALLAHER, MARTHA J.	CEC	006	ELKTON 3
GALLAHER, MARY	CEC	007	ELKTON 3
GALLAHER, MATTEHW	CEC	110	4TH E DI
GALLAHER, MOSES	CEC	011	ELKTON 3
GALLAHER, PATRICK	BAL	345	13TH WAR
GALLAHER, PETER	ALL	239	CUMBERLA
GALLAHER, RICHARD	FRE	449	8TH E DI
GALLAHER, ROBERT	CEC	097	4TH E DI
GALLAHER, ROBINSON	CEC	108	3RD E DI
GALLAHER, SARAH	CEC	116	3RD E DI
GALLAHER, SARAH J.	CEC	127	5TH E DI
GALLAHER, THOMAS	BAL	304	17TH WAR
GALLAKER, EDWIN	CEC	142	6TH E DI
GALLAKER, MARSDINE	PRI	026	VANSVILL
GALLAKER, WILLIAM	ANN	512	HOWARD D
GALLASPIA, ANTHONY	WAS	163	2ND DIST
GALLASPIE, HANNAH	BAL	161	19TH WAR
GALLAWAY, ELISHA	BAL	047	2ND DIST
GALLAWAY, ELIZABETH	BAL	425	14TH WAR
GALLAWAY, ELIZABETH A.	BAL	383	3RD WARD
GALLAWAY, GREENBURG	BAL	294	3RD WARD
GALLAWAY, HANNAH	BAL	005	9TH WARD
GALLAWAY, JOHN	HAR	158	3RD DIST
GALLAWAY, JOHN F. A.	BAL	384	3RD WARD
GALLAWAY, MARGARIT	BAL	312	1ST DIST
GALLAWAY, MARY	BAL	398	1ST DIST
GALLAWAY, MOSES	HAR	157	3RD DIST
GALLAWAY, ROBERT	BAL	356	3RD WARD
GALLAWAY, SAMUEL	BAL	312	1ST DIST
GALLAWAY, THOMAS	BAL	446	1ST DIST
GALLAWAY, WILLIAM	BAL	359	3RD WARD
GALLAWAY, WILLIAM	BAL	125	1ST WARD
GALLAWAY, WILLIAM	BAL	118	18TH WAR
GALLAWAY, MOSES	HAR	160	3RD DIST
GALLBRIDGE, R.C.	BAL	001	18TH WAR
GALLE, PETER	FRE	216	BUCKEYST
GALLE, SARAH A.	FRE	215	BUCKEYST
GALLE, PETER	FRE	232	BUCKEYST
GALLEGER, GRACE	BAL	454	8TH WARD
GALLEGER, PATRICK	BAL	380	8TH WARD
GALLEN, JACOB	BAL	166	2ND DIST
GALLEON, JOHN P.	FRE	098	FREDERIC
GALLER, AUGSUTS	BAL	166	2ND DIST
GALLEY, WILLIAM	BAL	260	20TH WAR
GALLICER, JOHN *	WAS	117	2ND DIST
GALLIER, JOHN *	WAS	117	2ND DIST
GALLIGAN, MICHAEL	PRI	107	PISCATAW
GALLIGAR, FRANCES	BAL	111	15TH WAR
GALLIGHAN, MARY J.	WAS	151	2ND DIST
GALLIGHER, BRIDGET	BAL	093	1ST WARD
GALLIGHER, JAMES	BAL	300	17TH WAR
GALLIGHER, LESLIE	BAL	008	9TH WARD
GALLINGER, PHILIP	FRE	321	MIDDLETO
GALLION, ALEXANDER	HAR	121	2ND DIST
GALLION, AQUILLA L.	HAR	121	2ND DIST
GALLION, BENJAMIN T.	HAR	162	3RD DIST
GALLION, CALEB	HAR	128	2ND DIST
GALLION, HANNAH	HAR	140	2ND DIST
GALLION, JAMES B.	HAR	121	2ND DIST
GALLION, JOSEPH	HAR	125	2ND DIST
GALLION, JOSEPH P.	HAR	131	2ND DIST
GALLION, LOUISA	FRE	399	FREDERIC
GALLION, MARGARET	WAS	301	1ST DIST
GALLION, MARY H.	HAR	185	3RD DIST
GALLION, MARY L.	BAL	450	14TH WAR
GALLION, REBECCA A.	HAR	131	2ND DIST
GALLION, STANSBURY	HAR	137	2ND DIST
GALLION, WILLIAM	WAS	302	1ST DIST
GALLISAMS, JOHN	BAL	469	14TH WAR
GALLIWAY, MARIAN	BAL	288	3RD WARD
GALLIWAY, MARY	BAL	288	3RD WARD
GALLON, CECELIA	BAL	234	12TH WAR
GALLOP, RATCHELL	HAR	177	3RD DIST
GALLOP, SARY	HAR	207	3RD DIST
GALLOWAY, ABSALOM	HAR	106	2ND DIST
GALLOWAY, AUGUSTA	BAL	291	20TH WAR
GALLOWAY, ELLEN	BAL	344	7TH WARD
GALLOWAY, EUGENIA	HAR	106	2ND DIST
GALLOWAY, HESTER	ANN	331	2ND DIST
GALLOWAY, ISAAC	CEC	169	6TH E DI
GALLOWAY, ISAAC M.	CEC	170	6TH E DI
GALLOWAY, ISAAH	BAL	156	1ST WARD
GALLOWAY, JAMES	ANN	378	4TH DIST
GALLOWAY, JAMES	BAL	450	1ST DIST
GALLOWAY, JAMES	CAL	060	3RD DIST
GALLOWAY, JAMES	PRI	004	BLADENSB
GALLOWAY, JANE	ALL	066	10TH E.D
GALLOWAY, JOHN	BAL	238	6TH WARD
GALLOWAY, JOHN	HAR	088	2ND DIST
GALLOWAY, LUCY	BAL	317	7TH WARD
GALLOWAY, LYDIA	CEC	009	ELKTON 3
GALLOWAY, MARGARET	BAL	301	17TH WAR
GALLOWAY, MARGARET	ANN	330	2ND DIST
GALLOWAY, MOSES	BAL	141	2ND DIST
GALLOWAY, ROSANNA	CEC	210	7TH E DI
GALLOWAY, ROSETTA	CAL	059	3RD DIST
GALLOWAY, SAMUEL	HAR	076	BEL AIR
GALLOWAY, SAMUEL	ANN	378	4TH DIST
GALLOWAY, SAMUEL	WAS	158	HAGERSTO
GALLOWAY, SIN *	CAL	027	2ND DIST
GALLOWAY, W. L.	BAL	156	1ST WARD
GALLOWAY, WILLIAM	BAL	140	2ND DIST
GALLOWAY, WILLIAM	BAL	062	2ND DIST
GALLOWAY, WILLIAM	CAL	029	2ND DIST
GALLOWAY, WILLIAM	CAL	024	2ND DIST
GALLOWAY, WILLIAM	HAR	076	BEL AIR
GALLOWERS, LEEDY	BAL	099	2ND DIST
GALLSPIE, JONATHAN	BAL	141	2ND DIST
GALLUP, EDWARD B.	BAL	173	16TH WAR
GALLUP, JOHN F.	BAL	383	3RD WARD
GALLUP, MARYANN	BAL	357	3RD WARD
GALLUP, OLIVER	HAR	181	3RD DIST
GALLWAY, LYDIA	CEC	031	CHESAPEA
GALLY, SUSAN	FRE	136	CREAGERS
GALMITH, PETER	CAR	385	2ND DIST
GALOR, NOAH	ANN	461	HOWARD D
GALOWAY, ANN	BAL	154	2ND DIST
GALOWAY, ISAAC-BLACK	CAR	070	NO TWP L
GALOWAY, MARY	WAS	167	1ST DIST
GALOWAY, RACHAEL-BLACK	FRE	012	FREDERIC
GALOWAY, RAGEOUS	WAS	289	1ST DIST
GALT, ELIZABETH	BAL	312	3RD WARD
GALT, ELWOOD	BAL	346	3RD WARD
GALT, HENRY	BAL	320	3RD WARD
GALT, JANE	BAL	079	10TH WAR
GALT, MATHEW	BAL	084	18TH WAR
GALT, SAMUEL	CAR	310	1ST DIST
GALT, SAMUEL	CAR	310	1ST DIST
GALT, SARAH	CAR	312	1ST DIST
GALT, STERLING	CAR	311	1ST DIST
GALT, THOMAS	BAL	123	1ST WARD
GALUITH, WILLET	FRE	020	FREDERIC
GALUP, ELDRIGE	HAR	150	3RD DIST
GALVEZ, MISS S.	FRE	199	5TH E DI
GALVIN, ROBERT	ALL	077	5TH E.D.
GALVIN, ROGER	CAR	220	5TH DIST
GALWAY, JAMES	BAL	314	20TH WAR
GALWAY, LOYD	ANN	327	2ND DIST
GALWAY, MARGARETT	BAL	092	18TH WAR
GALWAY, MARIA	BAL	314	20TH WAR
GALWAY, MARY	BAL	285	20TH WAR
GALWAY, THOMAS A.	BAL	285	20TH WAR
GALY, MARTIN	ALL	227	CUMBERLA
GALYLAND, HENRY	BAL	451	8TH WARD
GAMAGE, ANTONIA	BAL	167	1ST WARD
GAMAURAN, ELIZABETH	BAL	359	13TH WAR
GAMBB, JOHN	BAL	128	1ST WARD
GAMBELL, ANDREW	CEC	197	7TH E DI
GAMBELL, RACHEL	BAL	168	19TH WAR
GAMBERE, SUSAN J.*	BAL	063	4TH WARD
GAMBIE, CHRISTIANA	ST	307	1ST E DI
GAMBIE, JOHN	BAL	316	3RD WARD
GAMBIEL, MARY J.	ANN	278	ANNAPOLI
GAMBIL, DAVID	BAL	128	18TH WAR
GAMBILL, JOHN	BAL	070	2ND DIST
GAMBILL, MARY	BAL	078	1ST WARD
GAMBLE, ANN	BAL	403	14TH WAR
GAMBLE, CHARLES	CEC	132	6TH E DI
GAMBLE, CHARLES A.	BAL	455	14TH WAR
GAMBLE, DAVID	FRE	197	5TH E DI
GAMBLE, EMMA	KEN	265	1ST DIST
GAMBLE, FRANCIS	BAL	452	14TH WAR
GAMBLE, JAMES	BAL	368	8TH WARD
GAMBLE, JAMES	BAL	236	6TH WARD
GAMBLE, JANE	BAL	060	4TH WARD
GAMBLE, JOHN	CEC	134	6TH E DI
GAMBLE, JOHN	HAR	155	3RD DIST
GAMBLE, JOHN	CEC	094	4TH E DI
GAMBLE, MATILDA	BAL	381	3RD WARD
GAMBLE, RICHARD	BAL	109	18TH WAR
GAMBLE, ROBERT	BAL	394	8TH WARD
GAMBLE, ROBERT A.	KEN	236	2ND DIST
GAMBLE, SARAH A.	BAL	368	8TH WARD
GAMBLE, STANSBURY	KEN	246	2ND DIST
GAMBLE, THOMAS	BAL	459	8TH WARD
GAMBLE, THOMAS	WAS	007	WILLIAMS
GAMBLE, THOMAS B.	BAL	308	3RD WARD
GAMBLE, WILLIAM	MGM	428	CLARKSTR
GAMBRA, MARY *	ANN	337	3RD DIST
GAMBREL, GIDEON	CAR	143	NO TWP L
GAMBREL, JOHN	TAL	002	EASTON D
GAMBRELL, AUGUSTUS	BAL	273	12TH WAR
GAMBRELL, MARY*	TAL	026	EASTON D
GAMBRICE, THOMAS	DOR	430	1ST DIST
GAMBRIEL, JAMES	CAR	151	NO TWP L
GAMBRIEL, JOHN	CAR	151	NO TWP L
GAMBRIEL, MARY	CAR	152	NO TWP L
GAMBRIEL, RICHARDSON	DOR	436	1ST DIST
GAMBRIL, JAMES	BAL	304	3RD WARD
GAMBRILE, RICHARD	ANN	471	HOWARD D
GAMBRILL, ABAGALE	BAL	402	1ST DIST
GAMBRILL, CHARLES	BAL	402	1ST DIST
GAMBRILL, ELIZABETH	BAL	218	19TH WAR
GAMBRILL, GEORGE	ANN	424	HOWARD D
GAMBRILL, GEORGE	ANN	424	HOWARD D
GAMBRILL, H. N.	BAL	298	1ST DIST
GAMBRILL, HANNAH	ANN	419	HOWARD D
GAMBRILL, HENRY	BAL	071	2ND DIST
GAMBRILL, JAMES H.	FRE	272	NEW MARK
GAMBRILL, JOHN W.	BAL	409	1ST DIST
GAMBRILL, JOSHUA	ANN	424	HOWARD D
GAMBRILL, LYDIA	ANN	379	4TH DIST
GAMBRILL, MARGARET	ANN	460	HOWARD D
GAMBRILL, PETER	ANN	387	4TH DIST
GAMBRILL, ROBERT	BAL	233	6TH WARD
GAMBRILL, STEVENS	ANN	378	4TH DIST
GAMBRILL, WILLIAM	ANN	455	HOWARD D
GAMBRILL, WILLIAM	BAL	352	1ST DIST
GAMBRILL, WILLIAM	SOM	449	DAMES QU
GAMBRILL, ELI	BAL	075	2ND DIST
GAMBROL, JAMES	TAL	026	EASTON D
GAMBULL, WILLIAM	BAL	224	19TH WAR
GAME, HENRY	SOM	489	SALISBUR
GAME, JAMES	SOM	508	BARREN C
GAME, JOHN	SOM	554	TYASKIN
GAME, NOAH	SOM	554	TYASKIN
GAME, ROBERT	BAL	151	6TH WARD
GAMEL, WALTER	BAL	377	1ST DIST
GAMER, JAMES	ALL	216	CUMBERLA
GAMER, JOHN	FRE	091	FREDERIC
GAMER, LEVICA	BAL	208	6TH WARD
GAMES, JOHN	BAL	071	2ND DIST
GAMES, NANCY	CAL	023	2ND DIST
GAMGAN, PATRICK	ALL	136	4TH E.D.
GAMHILL, MARY	ANN	311	1ST DIST
GAMIE, GEORGE	BAL	444	8TH WARD
GAMMEL, GEORGE	BAL	291	1ST DIST
GAMMELL, JACOB	CAR	355	6TH DIST
GAMMEN, GEORGE	BAL	161	1ST WARD
GAMMON, GEORGE	BAL	170	1ST WARD
GAMON, PETUES *	BAL	082	2ND DIST
GANAN, MCIHAE	BAL	164	2ND DIST
GANARY, MICHAEL	ALL	244	CUMBERLA
GANBRILL, ELIZA	QUE	123	1ST E DI
GANBY, JACOB	DOR	361	3RD DIVI
GANBY, LEIGHER	DOR	361	3RD DIVI
GANDER, CONA	ALL	258	CUMBERLA
GANDER, MINA	BAL	374	13TH WAR
GANDER, WILLIAM	BAL	023	1ST WARD
GANE, JOHN	BAL	219	19TH WAR
GANE, LIZZY*	BAL	307	3RD WARD
GANELLSON, HENRY	FRE	268	NEW MARK
GANER, FRANCIS	BAL	241	12TH WAR
GANER, PATRICK	BAL	164	2ND DIST
GANER, THOMAS	CEC	068	5TH E DI
GANES, ELIZABETH-MULATTO	BAL	227	2ND WARD
GANES, JANE E.	BAL	229	2ND WARD
GANES, JOHN	DOR	362	3RD DIVI
GANES, JOSEPH	TAL	008	EASTON D
GANET, JAMES*	BAL	392	3RD WARD
GANETT, JOHN *	ANN	423	HOWARD D
GANG, LIZZY*	BAL	307	3RD WARD
GANGWAY, N.	BAL	262	12TH WAR
GANHARD, EDWARD	BAL	142	1ST WARD
GANKLE, JOHN	BAL	244	2ND WARD
GANLACLETT, THEODORE *	CAR	266	WESTMINS
GANLEY, JOHN	BAL	335	1ST DIST
GANLEY, WILLIAM	MGM	381	ROCKERLE
GANNET, PRISCILLA	BAL	260	2ND WARD
GANNETT, JOHN	BAL	261	2ND WARD
GANNON, SALLY	BAL	374	3RD WARD
GANNON, AMELIA	BAL	105	2ND DIST
GANNON, ANN	BAL	287	12TH WAR

Name	County	Page	District
GANNON, CAROLINE	BAL	104	10TH WAR
GANNON, CATHERINE C.	FRE	025	FREDERIC
GANNON, ELIZABETH M.	FRE	025	FREDERIC
GANNON, F.	TAL	004	EASTON D
GANNON, JAMES	TAL	018	EASTON D
GANNON, JAMES	BAL	106	2ND DIST
GANNON, JOHN	BAL	121	16TH WAR
GANNON, MARY	TAL	088	ST MICHA
GANNON, MICHAEL	BAL	003	9TH WARD
GANNON, NATHAN P.	TAL	076	EASTON T
GANNON, NOB	BAL	266	17TH WAR
GANNON, ROBERT H.	TAL	076	EASTON T
GANNON, ROBERT W.	TAL	107	ST MICHA
GANNON, SARAH	FRE	021	FREDERIC
GANNON, SARAH	BAL	329	7TH WARD
GANNON, SARAH	BAL	396	8TH WARD
GANNON, SARAH A.C.	FRE	025	FREDERIC
GANNON, SARAH E.	TAL	076	EASTON T
GANNON, THOMAS	TAL	035	EASTON D
GANNON, WASHINGTON	BAL	133	16TH WAR
GANNON,LEVIN-BLACK	CAR	158	NO TWP L
GANNON,MARY	FRE	203	5TH E DI
GANNOR, JAMES	TAL	027	EASTON D
GANNY, MARY	BAL	046	1ST WARD
GANOGLE, MICHAEL	FRE	106	CREAGERS
GANS, JACOB	WAS	247	SMITHSBU
GANSEY, JOSEPH	BAL	248	6TH WARD
GANT, ALFRED	BAL	261	20TH WAR
GANT, ANN M.	FRE	379	PETERSVI
GANT, ANN M.	BAL	121	16TH WAR
GANT, ANNA-BLACK	FRE	011	FREDERIC
GANT, CATHARINE	BAL	260	20TH WAR
GANT, CHARLES	BAL	181	16TH WAR
GANT, HESTER	FRE	265	NEW MARK
GANT, JOHN	ST	286	2ND E DI
GANT, JOHN C.	FRE	093	FREDERIC
GANT, JOHN M.	BAL	370	13TH WAR
GANT, MARY	BAL	115	15TH WAR
GANT, OTHO T.	BAL	240	20TH WAR
GANT, PERRY	BAL	102	15TH WAR
GANT, REBECCA	BAL	073	15TH WAR
GANT, RICHARD	BAL	239	12TH WAR
GANT, SARAH ANN	ALL	257	CUMBERLA
GANT, STEPHEN-MULATTO	FRE	011	FREDERIC
GANT, THOMAS	BAL	025	15TH WAR
GANT, WILLIAM	FRE	379	PETERSVI
GANT, WILLIAM	BAL	163	19TH WAR
GANT,ANNA-BLACK	FRE	241	NEW MARK
GANTER, SARAH	WAS	164	HAGERSTO
GANTICE, HENRY	BAL	109	1ST WARD
GANTRILL, SINGLETON	FRE	424	8TH E DI
GANTRILL, SOLOMON	FRE	425	8TH E DI
GANTRUM, PETER	BAL	302	1ST DIST
GANTT, ANN M.	CAL	015	1ST DIST
GANTT, BENJAMIN E.	ANN	362	4TH DIST
GANTT, CHARLES	CAL	056	3RD DIST
GANTT, CHARLES F.	CAL	012	1ST DIST
GANTT, CHARLES T.	CAL	058	3RD DIST
GANTT, JOHN	ANN	404	8TH DIST
GANTT, MARY	CAL	050	3RD DIST
GANTT, PATRICK	CAL	025	2ND DIST
GANTT, RICHARD H.	CAL	056	3RD DIST
GANTT, THOMAS J.	CAL	058	3RD DIST
GANTT, THOMAS P. *	ANN	321	2ND DIST
GANTT, VIRGIL	CAL	028	2ND DIST
GANTT, WILLIAM T. DR-	ANN	324	2ND DIST
GANTZ, ANNA	WAS	219	1ST DIST
GANTZ, CATHARINE	WAS	218	1ST DIST
GANTZ, ELIZABETH	WAS	185	BOONSBOR
GANTZ, HENRY	WAS	220	1ST DIST
GANTZ, JOHN	WAS	220	1ST DIST
GANTZ, MARGARET A.	WAS	188	BOONSBOR
GANTZ, MARTIN	WAS	214	1ST DIST
GANTZ, PETER	WAS	218	1ST DIST
GANTZ, SAMUEL	WAS	294	1ST DIST
GANTZ, SARAH	WAS	219	1ST DIST
GANTZILL, A.	BAL	282	2ND WARD
GAPE, PUN	BAL	292	12TH WAR
GARAGAN, BARNEY	BAL	272	1ST DIST
GARAGAR, PATER	BAL	273	1ST DIST
GARAHAM, ELIZABETH	WAS	139	HAGERSTO
GARAMIRE, JACOB	FRE	387	PETERSVI
GARANER, RICHARD J.	QUE	246	5TH E DI
GARBER, ADAM	FRE	422	8TH E DI
GARBER, ANN	FRE	291	WOODSBOR
GARBER, ANN H.	FRE	439	8TH E DI
GARBER, CATHARINE	FRE	413	8TH E DI
GARBER, CHRISTIAN	FRE	444	8TH E DI
GARBER, DAVID	FRE	411	8TH E DI
GARBER, ENOCH	FRE	413	8TH E DI
GARBER, ESTHER	CAR	407	2ND DIST
GARBER, HENRIETTA	FRE	411	8TH E DI
GARBER, HENRY	FRE	422	8TH E DI
GARBER, HENRY	BAL	006	EASTERN
GARBER, JACOB	FRE	437	8TH E DI
GARBER, LYDIA	FRE	289	WOODSBOR
GARBER, MARTIN	CAR	317	1ST DIST
GARBER, MARY J.	FRE	434	8TH E DI
GARBER, SAMUEL	FRE	444	8TH E DI
GARBER, SOLOMON	FRE	444	8TH E DI
GARBER, SOLOMON	FRE	432	8TH E DI
GARBER, WILLIAM	FRE	415	8TH E DI
GARBOUR, DAVID	BAL	167	1ST WARD
GARCETT, JESSE	BAL	114	2ND DIST
GARCY, PETER	ALL	247	CUMBERLA
GARCY, SAMUEL	ALL	146	6TH E.D.
GARCY,MARY	ALL	247	CUMBERLA
GARDAN, ELIZA	BAL	327	13TH WAR
GARDEN, RACHAEL	BAL	304	3RD WARD
GARDEN,LAURA-MULATTO	FRE	039	FREDERIC
GARDENER, ALFRED W.	CHA	284	BOJANTOW
GARDENER, ANN	BAL	200	6TH WARD
GARDENER, BENJAMIN	CHA	291	MIDDLETO
GARDENER, EDWARD	CHA	217	ALLENS F
GARDENER, EDWARD C.	CHA	284	BOJANTOW
GARDENER, EDWARD Z.	CHA	268	BOJANTOW
GARDENER, ELIAS	BAL	291	12TH WAR
GARDENER, ELIZABETH	TAL	033	EASTON D
GARDENER, ELLEN	ANN	289	ANNAPOLI
GARDENER, GEORGE W.	ANN	431	HOWARD D
GARDENER, JAEMS R.	TAL	089	ST MICHA
GARDENER, JAMES	BAL	312	3RD WARD
GARDENER, JOHN	ANN	291	ANNAPOLI
GARDENER, JOHN T.	CHA	252	BOJANTOW
GARDENER, MARIA	BAL	040	18TH WAR
GARDENER, SOPHIA M.	TAL	003	EASTON D
GARDENHOUR, THOMAS B.	WAS	249	1ST DIST
GARDENOUR, GEORGE	WAS	248	SMITHSBU
GARDENOUR, JACOB	WAS	065	2ND SUBD
GARDINE, ANN	CHA	278	BOJANTOW

Name	County	Page	District
GARDINE, WILLIAM	CHA	230	MIDDLETO
GARDINER, ABRAHAM	ANN	374	4TH DIST
GARDINER, ALDERSON	BAL	225	6TH WARD
GARDINER, ANN	BAL	051	18TH WAR
GARDINER, ANNA	MGM	326	CRACKLIN
GARDINER, BENEDICT	PRI	092	MARLBROU
GARDINER, BENJAMIN	BAL	229	6TH WARD
GARDINER, BENNETT	TAL	077	EASTON T
GARDINER, C.	PRI	052	AQUASCO
GARDINER, CHARLES	TAL	088	ST MICHA
GARDINER, CHARLES L.	CHA	276	ALLENS F
GARDINER, DAVID S.*	DOR	448	1ST DIST
GARDINER, EDWARD W.	CHA	276	ALLENS F
GARDINER, ELIZABETH	TAL	081	ST MICHA
GARDINER, ELIZABETH	PRI	014	BLADENSB
GARDINER, ELIZABETH A.	BAL	379	3RD WARD
GARDINER, FRANCIS	BAL	027	9TH WARD
GARDINER, GEORGE	PRI	091	MARLBROU
GARDINER, GEORGE	PRI	070	MARLBROU
GARDINER, GEORGE	CHA	293	BOJANTOW
GARDINER, GEORGE F.	BAL	225	6TH WARD
GARDINER, GEORGE H.	CHA	293	BOJANTOW
GARDINER, GEORGE H.	CHA	260	MIDDLETO
GARDINER, HENRY	CHA	284	BOJANTOW
GARDINER, HENRY	CEC	060	1ST E DI
GARDINER, IGNATIVAS	CHA	293	BOJANTOW
GARDINER, JAMES	TAL	028	EASTON D
GARDINER, JANE R.	CEC	144	PORT DUP
GARDINER, JOHN	CEC	083	CHARLEST
GARDINER, JOHN	TAL	036	EASTON D
GARDINER, JOHN B.	BAL	060	18TH WAR
GARDINER, JOHN H.	ST	295	2ND E DI
GARDINER, JONATHAN	ANN	333	2ND DIST
GARDINER, JOSEPH	MGM	326	CRACKLIN
GARDINER, JOSEPH B.	CHA	276	ALLENS F
GARDINER, M. HELEN	BAL	212	11TH WAR
GARDINER, SARA	CHA	240	HILLTOP
GARDINER, SARAH	ANN	369	4TH DIST
GARDINER, STANTLEY	TAL	092	ST MICHA
GARDINER, SYLVESTER F.	CHA	254	MIDDLETO
GARDINER, TECUMSEH	ANN	319	2ND DIST
GARDINER, THOMAS J.	CHA	278	BOJANTOW
GARDINER, THOMAS S.	CHA	267	MIDDLETO
GARDINER, THOMAS W.	ST	297	2ND E DI
GARDINER, WASHINGTON	PRI	104	PISCATAW
GARDINER, WILLIAM	BAL	225	6TH WARD
GARDINER,RICHARD H.	BAL	296	12TH WAR
GARDINR, DORATHAY	CHA	283	BOJANTOW
GARDMAN, PATRICK	ALL	236	CUMBERLA
GARDNER, ACHSAH	ANN	390	4TH DIST
GARDNER, AGUSTUS M.	BAL	159	11TH WAR
GARDNER, ALEXANDER	CAR	137	NO TWP L
GARDNER, ALIDA A.	ANN	521	HOWARD D
GARDNER, ALLONIUS	CHA	283	BOJANTOW
GARDNER, ANN S.	CAR	095	NO TWP L
GARDNER, ARCHIBALD	ANN	379	4TH DIST
GARDNER, BENJAMIN	BAL	134	1ST WARD
GARDNER, BENJAMIN	BAL	126	1ST WARD
GARDNER, BENJAMIN	BAL	066	4TH WARD
GARDNER, BORIUS	BAL	375	13TH WAR
GARDNER, CHARLES	BAL	284	17TH WAR
GARDNER, CHARLES H.	QUE	234	4TH E DI
GARDNER, CHRISTOPHER	BAL	422	14TH WAR
GARDNER, D.G.F.	BAL	166	1ST WARD
GARDNER, DAVID	QUE	224	4TH E DI
GARDNER, DEBORAH	QUE	231	4TH E DI
GARDNER, ELACE	CHA	278	BOJANTOW
GARDNER, ELI	BAL	043	18TH WAR
GARDNER, ELIZA C.	FRE	034	FREDERIC
GARDNER, ELIZABETH	BAL	128	18TH WAR
GARDNER, ELIZABETH	BAL	383	1ST DIST
GARDNER, ELIZABETH	BAL	458	8TH WARD
GARDNER, ELL. *	ANN	396	8TH DIST
GARDNER, ELLEN	BAL	108	18TH WAR
GARDNER, EMRTINE *	QUE	242	5TH E DI
GARDNER, EPHRAIM	BAL	168	16TH WAR
GARDNER, FLINN.	CAR	271	WESTMINS
GARDNER, FRANCES	BAL	064	10TH WAR
GARDNER, FRANCIS	BAL	019	15TH WAR
GARDNER, FRANCIS	QUE	233	4TH E DI
GARDNER, FRANSES	WAS	080	2ND SUBD
GARDNER, GEORGE	BAL	126	1ST WARD
GARDNER, GEORGE	BAL	136	1ST WARD
GARDNER, GEORGE	BAL	125	1ST WARD
GARDNER, GEORGE B.	BAL	420	3RD WARD
GARDNER, GEORGE E.	BAL	384	8TH WARD
GARDNER, GEORGE W.	BAL	182	19TH WAR
GARDNER, HASKNAL B.	BAL	277	2ND WARD
GARDNER, HENERETTA	SOM	425	PRINCESS
GARDNER, HENRIETTA	FRE	321	MIDDLETO
GARDNER, HENRY	HAR	204	3RD DIST
GARDNER, HENRY	FRE	270	NEW MARK
GARDNER, HENRY	CAR	074	NO TWP L
GARDNER, HENRY	BAL	157	16TH WAR
GARDNER, ISAAC	BAL	291	3RD WARD
GARDNER, ISAAC	BAL	409	1ST DIST
GARDNER, ISABEL	BAL	244	20TH WAR
GARDNER, ISAIAH .	BAL	006	15TH WAR
GARDNER, J.	BAL	153	1ST WARD
GARDNER, JACOB	WAS	246	SMITHSBU
GARDNER, JAMES	ST	319	4TH E DI
GARDNER, JAMES	BAL	065	15TH WAR
GARDNER, JAMES	BAL	375	3RD WARD
GARDNER, JAMES	BAL	034	1ST WARD
GARDNER, JAMES	BAL	303	17TH WAR
GARDNER, JAMES B.	BAL	415	3RD WARD
GARDNER, JAMS	BAL	109	18TH WAR
GARDNER, JOHN	HAR	204	3RD DIST
GARDNER, JOHN	FRE	013	FREDERIC
GARDNER, JOHN	BAL	097	1ST WARD
GARDNER, JOHN	BAL	090	1ST WARD
GARDNER, JOHN	BAL	126	1ST WARD
GARDNER, JOHN	ANN	382	4TH DIST
GARDNER, JOHN	ANN	390	4TH DIST
GARDNER, JOHN	ST	348	5TH E DI
GARDNER, JOHN	MGM	438	CLARKSTR
GARDNER, JOHN	QUE	233	4TH E DI
GARDNER, JOHN	QUE	239	5TH E DI
GARDNER, JOHN M.	BAL	382	8TH WARD
GARDNER, JOHNSEY	BAL	242	1ST DIST
GARDNER, JOSEEPH	BAL	384	8TH WARD
GARDNER, JOSEPH	BAL	367	8TH WARD
GARDNER, JOSEPH	CAR	242	TANEYTOW
GARDNER, JOSEPH	CAR	330	MANCHEST
GARDNER, JOSHUA	TAL	079	ST MICHA
GARDNER, JULIA	ANN	316	1ST DIST
GARDNER, LETITIA	BAL	309	3RD WARD
GARDNER, LEVINA	SOM	414	DUBLIN D
GARDNER, LUCRETIA	BAL	302	17TH WAR
GARDNER, LUTHER	CAR	072	NO TWP L

Name	County	Page	District
GARDNER, MADELIN	BAL	069	1ST WARD
GARDNER, MARGARET	ANN	303	1ST DIST
GARDNER, MARGARET	ANN	397	8TH DIST
GARDNER, MARGARET E.	BAL	162	11TH WAR
GARDNER, MARIA	BAL	252	1ST DIST
GARDNER, MARIA	BAL	248	2ND WARD
GARDNER, MARINDA	BAL	322	3RD WARD
GARDNER, MARTHA E.	BAL	004	1ST WARD
GARDNER, MARY	FRE	126	CREAGERS
GARDNER, MARY	BAL	053	4TH WARD
GARDNER, MARY	BAL	082	4TH WARD
GARDNER, MARY	WAS	039	2ND SUBD
GARDNER, MARY	KEN	271	1ST DIST
GARDNER, MARY E.	BAL	010	1ST WARD
GARDNER, NELSON	QUE	232	4TH E DI
GARDNER, NICHOLAS	BAL	223	1ST DIST
GARDNER, PATIENCE	BAL	034	4TH WARD
GARDNER, PETER	BAL	212	2ND WARD
GARDNER, PHILIP	BAL	234	12TH WAR
GARDNER, RICHARD	ANN	268	ANNAPOLI
GARDNER, RICHARD	QUE	224	4TH E DI
GARDNER, RICHARD F.	FRE	044	FREDERIC
GARDNER, ROBERT	QUE	230	4TH E DI
GARDNER, ROBERT	QUE	253	5TH E DI
GARDNER, ROBERT	WAS	063	2ND SUBD
GARDNER, ROBERT	BAL	366	8TH WARD
GARDNER, RUSSELL	BAL	174	1ST WARD
GARDNER, RUTH	BAL	089	15TH WAR
GARDNER, S.	BAL	164	1ST WARD
GARDNER, SALLY A.	TAL	008	EASTON D
GARDNER, SAM	ANN	397	8TH DIST
GARDNER, SAMUEL	BAL	159	1ST WARD
GARDNER, SAMUEL	BAL	156	1ST WARD
GARDNER, SAMUEL	BAL	144	1ST WARD
GARDNER, SUSAN	BAL	303	7TH WARD
GARDNER, SUSAN V.	BAL	351	7TH WARD
GARDNER, THEADORE	FRE	137	CREAGERS
GARDNER, THOMAS	ANN	273	ANNAPOLI
GARDNER, WILIAM	QUE	231	4TH E DI
GARDNER, WILLIAM	QUE	224	4TH E DI
GARDNER, WILLIAM	SOM	363	BRINKLEY
GARDNER, WILLIAM	WAS	105	2ND DIST
GARDNER, WILLIAM	WAS	102	2ND DIST
GARDNER, WILLIAM	ANN	391	4TH DIST
GARDNER, WILLIAM	ANN	304	1ST DIST
GARDNER, WILLIAM	BAL	283	7TH WARD
GARDNER, WILLIAM	BAL	357	8TH WARD
GARDNER, WILLIAM	BAL	246	2ND WARD
GARDNER, WILLIAM	BAL	331	13TH WAR
GARDNER, WILLIAM	FRE	173	5TH E DI
GARDNER, WILLIAM	FRE	422	8TH E DI
GARDNER, WILLIAM C.	BAL	140	1ST WARD
GARDNER, WILLIAM C.	BAL	165	1ST WARD
GARDNER, WILLIAM F.	BAL	069	18TH WAR
GARDNER, WILLIAM R.	BAL	456	8TH WARD
GARES, ELIZABETH	BAL	229	2ND WARD
GARES, JULIA	BAL	204	11TH WAR
GARET, ADAM	CEC	047	1ST E DI
GARET, CHARLES	BAL	127	1ST WARD
GARET, ELLEN	BAL	057	1ST WARD
GARET, HARRIETT	BAL	332	13TH WAR
GARET, JAMES*	BAL	392	3RD WARD
GARET, JOHN	BAL	233	2ND WARD
GARET, JOHN	BAL	014	1ST WARD
GARET, LEMUEL H.	BAL	433	1ST DIST
GARET, MARY	BAL	014	1ST WARD
GARET, THOMAS	BAL	057	1ST WARD
GARETSON, BENNET	BAL	235	1ST DIST
GARETSON, JAMES A.	HAR	190	3RD DIST
GARETSON, RICHARD F.	HAR	190	3RD DIST
GARETT, JULIANNA	CEC	086	4TH E DI
GARETT, MARY	ANN	458	HOWARD D
GARETT, THOMAS *	ANN	321	2ND DIST
GARETY, MARY A.	BAL	272	2ND WARD
GARETY, PATRICK	ALL	143	6TH E.D.
GARETY, PATRICK	ALL	053	10TH E.D
GAREY, CORNELIUS	ALL	118	5TH E.D.
GAREY, FRANCES	BAL	272	7TH WARD
GAREY, GEORGE	ALL	147	6TH E.D.
GAREY, HESTER	ALL	118	5TH E.D.
GAREY, JOHN	ALL	147	6TH E.D.
GAREY, JOHN W.	BAL	297	7TH WARD
GAREY, MATHEW	CAR	138	NO TWP L
GAREY, SAMUEL	ALL	147	6TH E.D.
GAREY, THOMAS F.	CAR	111	NO TWP L
GAREY, WILLIAM	ALL	099	5TH E.D.
GARHMAN, DARKUS	BAL	009	EASTERN
GARIER, WILLIAM	FRE	096	FREDERIC
GARITY, THOMAS	ALL	143	6TH E.D.
GARKEN, WILLIAM	ALL	057	10TH E.D
GARKENS, SAMUEL L.	BAL	357	13TH WAR
GARKINS, SARAH JANE	BAL	358	13TH WAR
GARLAN, MATILDA	WAS	130	HAGERSTO
GARLAND, ALEXENA	ALL	212	CUMBERLA
GARLAND, CAROLINE	BAL	380	13TH WAR
GARLAND, JAMES D.	BAL	149	1ST WARD
GARLAND, M.	ANN	279	ANNAPOLI
GARLEEK, ANTHONY	ALL	112	5TH E.D.
GARLETZ, BAZAL T.	ALL	013	3RD E.D.
GARLIER, JOHN	BAL	346	1ST DIST
GARLING, JOHN	WAS	162	HAGERSTO
GARLINGER, BENJAMIN A.	WAS	246	SMITHSBU
GARLINGER, HORATIO	WAS	235	1ST DIST
GARLINGER, MARY A.	WAS	106	2ND DIST
GARLINGER, RACHAEL	WAS	247	SMITHSBU
GARLINGER, SAMUEL	WAS	253	1ST DIST
GARLITZ, CHRISTIAN	ALL	004	3RD E.D.
GARLITZ, HART E.	ALL	004	3RD E.D.
GARLITZ, HENRY	ALL	004	3RD E.D.
GARLITZ, HENRY	ALL	014	3RD E.D.
GARLITZ, JACOB	ALL	009	3RD E.D.
GARLITZ, JOHN	ALL	004	3RD E.D.
GARLITZ, JONAS	ALL	011	3RD E.D.
GARLITZ, SARAH	ALL	016	3RD E.D.
GARLITZ, WILLIAM	ALL	005	3RD E.D.
GARMAGE, ED	BAL	159	1ST WARD
GARMAN, GEORGE	BAL	298	17TH WAR
GARMAN, THOMAS	ALL	049	10TH E.D
GARMINGTON, JOHN	BAL	167	11TH WAR
GARNAN, DANIEL	FRE	375	CATOCTIN
GARNAN, DANIEL	FRE	373	CATOCTIN
GARNER, ABRAHAM	CAR	321	1ST DIST
GARNER, ABRAM	CAL	026	2ND DIST
GARNER, ALFRED	CAR	379	2ND DIST
GARNER, ALVA C.	CAR	321	1ST DIST
GARNER, ANN	ANN	403	8TH DIST
GARNER, BENJAMIN	PRI	055	AQUASCO
GARNER, CAROLINE	BAL	046	15TH WAR
GARNER, CAROLINE R.	ST	331	4TH E DI
GARNER, CHARLES	CHA	266	MIDDLETO

GARNER, CHARLES W. BAL 294 3RD WARD
GARNER, CHARLES-BLACK CAR 107 NO TWP L
GARNER, CLEMENTINE CAR 065 NO TWP L
GARNER, DANIEL PRI 054 AQUASCO
GARNER, EDMOND CAR 195 4TH DIST
GARNER, ELIZA PRI 055 AQUASCO
GARNER, EMELINE BAL 116 5TH WARD
GARNER, EVAN H. CAR 196 4TH DIST
GARNER, FRANCIS BAL 338 1ST DIST
GARNER, FREEBORN CAR 211 5TH DIST
GARNER, GEORGE CAR 322 1ST DIST
GARNER, GEORGE WAS 151 2ND DIST
GARNER, HENRY G. ST 333 4TH E DI
GARNER, HENRY-BLACK FRE 029 FREDERIC
GARNER, HETTY PRI 088 SPALDING
GARNER, J. T. BAL 332 1ST DIST
GARNER, JABEZ F. CAR 206 4TH DIST
GARNER, JACOB CAR 378 2ND DIST
GARNER, JANE ANN 521 HOWARD D
GARNER, JESSE CAR 190 4TH DIST
GARNER, JESSE PRI 054 AQUASCO
GARNER, JOEL FRE 361 CATOCTIN
GARNER, JOHN CAR 378 2ND DIST
GARNER, JOHN CAR 380 2ND DIST
GARNER, JOHN PRI 056 AQUASCO
GARNER, JOHN A. ST 344 5TH E DI
GARNER, JOSPEH CAR 302 1ST DIST
GARNER, LEVI QUE 210 3RD E DI
GARNER, LOVELESS CAR 208 5TH DIST
GARNER, LOYD WAS 028 2ND SUBD
GARNER, LUCINDA BAL 046 15TH WAR
GARNER, LUCY ANN 521 HOWARD D
GARNER, LUCY CHA 234 HILLTOP
GARNER, M. PRI 054 AQUASCO
GARNER, MARY PRI 089 SPALDING
GARNER, MARY BAL 161 6TH WARD
GARNER, MARY A. WAS 200 1ST DIST
GARNER, MARY A. WAS 200 1ST DIST
GARNER, MARY E.K. CAL 051 3RD DIST
GARNER, MICHAEL PRI 056 AQUASCO
GARNER, NIMRAD CAR 200 4TH DIST
GARNER, RICHMOND J. CHA 234 HILLTOP
GARNER, ROBERT CEC 074 5TH E DI
GARNER, SAMUEL PRI 056 AQUASCO
GARNER, SAMUEL ST 331 4TH E DI
GARNER, SRAH PRI 056 AQUASCO
GARNER, THOMAS BAL 059 2ND DIST
GARNER, TISSE * CAR 321 1ST DIST
GARNER, WALTER WAS 047 2ND SUBD
GARNER, WILLIAM PRI 058 NOTTINGH
GARNER, WILLIAM PRI 055 AQUASCO
GARNER, WILLIAM PRI 056 AQUASCO
GARNER, WILLIAM BAL 400 1ST DIST
GARNER, WILLIAM H. ST 316 4TH E DI
GARNER, WILLIAM T. PRI 056 AQUASCO
GARNER, WILLIAM T. CHA 261 MIDDLETO
GARNET, C. BAL 130 1ST WARD
GARNET, CHARLES BAL 125 1ST WARD
GARNET, J. BAL 163 1ST WARD
GARNET, MICHAEL CEC 064 1ST E DI
GARNET, REBECA BAL 269 20TH WAR
GARNETT, E. H. BAL 108 10TH WAR
GARNETT, MADISON-BLACK QUE 171 2ND E DI
GARNETT, ROBERT BAL 088 15TH WAR
GARNEY, SISTER ROSE FRE 198 5TH E DI
GARNS, ROBERT WAS 277 RIDGEVIL
GARRAGAN, MICHAEL BAL 274 1ST DIST
GARRAND, E. BAL 096 10TH WAR
GARRATTY, RODGEN BAL 168 2ND DIST
GARRET, ABRAM BAL 098 2ND DIST
GARRET, BASEL BAL 286 1ST DIST
GARRET, DOLLY BAL 148 16TH WAR
GARRET, EDWIN CAR 349 6TH DIST
GARRET, FRANCES ANN 329 2ND DIST
GARRET, GEORGE W. BAL 286 1ST DIST
GARRET, GRACY ANN 275 ANNAPOLI
GARRET, HANSON BAL 286 1ST DIST
GARRET, JACOB BAL 310 12TH WAR
GARRET, JACOB BAL 375 8TH WARD
GARRET, JAMES BAL 077 2ND DIST
GARRET, JOHN BAL 276 1ST DIST
GARRET, JOHN C. BAL 433 1ST DIST
GARRET, LEMUEL H. BAL 434 1ST DIST
GARRET, MARGARET BAL 068 2ND DIST
GARRET, MARTHA BAL 290 12TH WAR
GARRET, MARTIN BAL 131 2ND DIST
GARRET, MARY ANN 279 ANNAPOLI
GARRET, MARY FRE 117 CREAGERS
GARRET, MICHAEL ANN 376 4TH DIST
GARRET, MICHAEL BAL 273 1ST DIST
GARRET, PATRICK BAL 086 2ND DIST
GARRET, PATRICK BAL 400 1ST DIST
GARRET, ROBERT BAL 456 14TH WAR
GARRET, THOAMS BAL 453 14TH WAR
GARRET, WILLIAM MGM 401 ROCKERLE
GARRETSON, ALEXANDER BAL 291 7TH WARD
GARRETSON, ARTHUR BAL 093 5TH WARD
GARRETSON, CORNELIUS BAL 443 8TH WARD
GARRETSON, ELIZABETH J. BAL 215 6TH WARD
GARRETSON, FRELOVE S. DOR 373 1ST DIST
GARRETSON, GEORGE CEC 012 ELKTON 3
GARRETSON, HANAH BAL 384 8TH WARD
GARRETSON, JERAMIAH CEC 065 1ST E DI
GARRETSON, LEVIN SOM 535 QUANTICO
GARRETSON, MARY A. CEC 004 ELKTON 3
GARRETSON, SUSAN BAL 455 8TH WARD
GARRETSON, THOMAS SOM 534 QUANTICO
GARRETSON, WILLIAM BAL 439 8TH WARD
GARRETT, A.B. BAL 141 1ST WARD
GARRETT, AMANDA WAS 091 2ND SUBD
GARRETT, AMOS ANN 329 2ND DIST
GARRETT, ANN CEC 103 4TH E DI
GARRETT, ANN CEC 102 4TH E DI
GARRETT, ANNA-BLACK QUE 178 2ND E DI
GARRETT, BARTON V. FRE 384 PETERSVI
GARRETT, BENJAMIN HAR 019 1ST DIST
GARRETT, BENJAMIN BAL 036 2ND DIST
GARRETT, BIDDY ANN 376 4TH DIST
GARRETT, DANIEL BAL 116 15TH WAR
GARRETT, DANIEL CAR 330 MANCHEST
GARRETT, EDWARD BAL 209 17TH WAR
GARRETT, EDWARD WAS 091 2ND SUBD
GARRETT, ELIZA BAL 101 15TH WAR
GARRETT, ELIZABETH ANN 508 HOWARD D
GARRETT, ELLEN BAL 373 3RD WARD
GARRETT, GRACY ANN 278 ANNAPOLI
GARRETT, HARRIET CEC 111 4TH E DI
GARRETT, HENRY CAR 347 6TH DIST
GARRETT, HENRY QUE 204 3RD E DI
GARRETT, HENRY A. MGM 379 ROCKERLE
GARRETT, HENRY S. HAR 153 3RD DIST
GARRETT, HESTER HAR 147 3RD DIST
GARRETT, ISAAC HAR 019 1ST DIST
GARRETT, JOHN CEC 105 3RD E DI
GARRETT, JOHN BAL 303 17TH WAR
GARRETT, JOHN QUE 245 5TH E DI
GARRETT, JOHN BAL 062 2ND DIST
GARRETT, JOHN BAL 152 2ND DIST
GARRETT, JOHN BAL 188 5TH DIST
GARRETT, JOHN * ANN 423 HOWARD D
GARRETT, JOHN M. BAL 229 19TH WAR
GARRETT, JOSEPH FRE 218 BUCKEYST
GARRETT, LEAH CEC 145 PORT DUP
GARRETT, LEVI BAL 347 7TH WARD
GARRETT, MARGARET BAL 112 15TH WAR
GARRETT, MARGARET HAR 016 1ST DIST
GARRETT, MARGARETT BAL 031 4TH WARD
GARRETT, MARIA BAL 113 15TH WAR
GARRETT, MARTHA BAL 336 3RD WARD
GARRETT, MATILDA BAL 150 11TH WAR
GARRETT, MICHAEL BAL 303 17TH WAR
GARRETT, P. ANN 280 ANNAPOLI
GARRETT, RICHARD BAL 138 2ND DIST
GARRETT, RICHARD BAL 304 17TH WAR
GARRETT, RICHARD HAR 019 1ST DIST
GARRETT, ROBERT M. BAL 222 19TH WAR
GARRETT, SAMUEL HAR 018 1ST DIST
GARRETT, SAMUEL BAL 062 2ND DIST
GARRETT, SOLOMON BAL 124 11TH WAR
GARRETT, SOPHIA BAL 010 4TH WARD
GARRETT, SOPHIA BAL 011 4TH WARD
GARRETT, SUSAN BAL 174 11TH WAR
GARRETT, THOMAS BAL 031 4TH WARD
GARRETT, THOMAS CAR 109 NO TWP L
GARRETT, THOMAS MGM 378 ROCKERLE
GARRETT, THOMAS CEC 096 4TH E DI
GARRETT, THOMAS B. BAL 107 15TH WAR
GARRETT, WILLIAM BAL 349 7TH WARD
GARRETT, WILLIAM ANN 328 2ND DIST
GARRETT, WILSON ANN 270 ANNAPOLI
GARRETT,W ILLIAM BAL 009 EASTERN
GARRETTSON, AGNES KEN 241 2ND DIST
GARRETTSON, FREEBORN BAL 234 20TH WAR
GARRETTSON, FREEBORN BAL 294 20TH WAR
GARRETTSON, GEORGE H. HAR 096 2ND DIST
GARRETTSON, JOEL R. HAR 080 2ND DIST
GARRETTSON, JOHN HAR 092 2ND DIST
GARRETTSON, RACHAEL KEN 241 2ND DIST
GARRETTSON, RICHARD HAR 095 2ND DIST
GARRETTSON, SAMUEL F. BAL 162 19TH WAR
GARRETTSON, SARAH BAL 182 6TH WARD
GARRETTSON, WILEY BAL 232 6TH WARD
GARRETTY, MARGARET ALL 072 5TH E.D.
GARRETTY, PATRICK ALL 072 5TH E.D.
GARRETY, PATRICK ALL 140 6TH E.D.
GARRIETT, HANNAH M. BAL 165 11TH WAR
GARRIGAN, JAMES HAR 102 2ND DIST
GARRIMAN, CATHARINE ALL 031 2ND E.D.
GARRING, REBECCA WAS 132 2ND DIST
GARRINGER, MARGARET WAS 151 HAGERSTO
GARRIOT, FRANCIS V. CHA 236 HILLTOP
GARRISH, JOHN BAL 154 2ND DIST
GARRISH, JOSEPH WAS 005 WILLIAMS
GARRISON, ANN M. SOM 530 QUANTICO
GARRISON, CORNELIUS CEC 028 CHESAPEA
GARRISON, DANIEL BAL 255 1ST DIST
GARRISON, DAVID TAL 004 EASTON D
GARRISON, DAVID H. BAL 029 18TH WAR
GARRISON, EMMA MGM 330 CRACKLIN
GARRISON, FRANCIS BAL 121 16TH WAR
GARRISON, GABRIEL HAR 175 3RD DIST
GARRISON, GEORGE BAL 155 5TH WARD
GARRISON, JAMES ANN 462 HOWARD D
GARRISON, JAMES CAR 166 NO TWP L
GARRISON, JAMES HAR 061 1ST DIST
GARRISON, JOB BAL 141 2ND DIST
GARRISON, JOHN HAR 062 1ST DIST
GARRISON, KATY MGM 335 CRACKLIN
GARRISON, MICHAEL BAL 354 13TH WAR
GARRISON, NICHOLAS MGM 327 CRACKLIN
GARRISON, REBECCA HAR 050 1ST DIST
GARRISON, SARANNAH * BAL 340 13TH WAR
GARRISON, THOMAS BAL 028 1ST WARD
GARRISON,WINGATE BAL 037 1ST WARD
GARRISSON, ELIZA BAL 224 17TH WAR
GARRISSON, HENRY BAL 152 5TH WARD
GARRISSON, JULIAN BAL 254 17TH WAR
GARRIT, RICHARD BAL 062 1ST WARD
GARRITER, WILLIAM BAL 454 8TH WARD
GARRITT, CHARLES PRI 011 BLADENSB
GARRITT, JOHN BAL 029 1ST WARD
GARRITTSON, B. T. BAL 052 9TH WARD
GARRITTY, BARNEY BAL 122 5TH WARD
GARRITY, CATHARINE BAL 244 6TH WARD
GARRITY, PATRICK ALL 227 CUMBERLA
GARRITY, ROGER BAL 006 9TH WARD
GARRITY,PHILIP ALL 173 7TH E.D.
GARRLLIAM, JEHUE FRE 268 NEW MARK
GARRNT, GEORGE BAL 033 9TH WARD
GARROD, L. BAL 148 1ST WARD
GARROT, JACOB BAL 047 1ST WARD
GARROTT, AUGUSTUS BAL 330 13TH WAR
GARROTT, BARTON FRE 383 PETERSVI
GARROTT, DELIA BAL 330 13TH WAR
GARROTT, E. WAS 021 2ND SUBD
GARROTT, JOHN D. FRE 396 PETERSVI
GARROTT, JOHN P. FRE 391 PETERSVI
GARROTT, RICHARD BAL 330 13TH WAR
GARROTT, SARAH BAL 342 13TH WAR
GARROTT, THOMAS BAL 354 13TH WAR
GARROTT, WILLIAM BAL 179 16TH WAR
GARRTH, JULIOUS FRE 044 FREDERIC
GARRTT, CHARLES A. BAL 045 9TH WARD
GARRY, CATHARINE BAL 195 2ND WARD
GARRY, JAMES KEN 222 2ND DIST
GARRY, MICHAL M. WAS 099 2ND DIST
GARSCHE, ELIZABETH FRE 066 FREDERIC
GARSE, FREDERICK BAL 270 17TH WAR
GARSON, JOHN BAL 125 1ST WARD
GARSON, SUSAN ALL 149 6TH E.D.
GARTH, WILLIAM ALL 122 4TH E.D.
GARTHER, BENJAMIN BAL 200 19TH WAR
GARTHER, DENNIS BAL 269 20TH WAR
GARTHER, RICHARD BAL 029 1ST WARD
GARTHER, THOMAS ALL 024 3RD E.D.
GARTHER, VIOLETTA BAL 343 13TH WAR
GARTIELL, RICAHRD FRE 423 8TH E DI
GARTLETZ, REBECCA ALL 001 3RD E.D.
GARTNER, MICHAEL WAS 153 2ND DIST
GARTNER, PETER FRE 352 MIDDLETO
GARTON, CHARLES E. ALL 223 CUMBERLA
GARTON, MARY S. BAL 016 18TH WAR
GARTON, MONROE C. ALL 222 CUMBERLA
GARTON, SARAH ALL 219 CUMBERLA
GARTON, WILLIAM C. BAL 259 17TH WAR
GARTRELL, BENJAMIN MGM 337 CRACKLIN
GARTRELL, BUSHROD MGM 337 CRACKLIN
GARTRELL, NICHOLAS MGM 337 CRACKLIN
GARTRELL, REBECCA MGM 326 CRACKLIN
GARTRELL,W ILLIAM B. FRE 204 BUCKEYST
GARTSIDE, HENRY BAL 362 1ST DIST
GARTSIDE, JAMES BAL 355 1ST DIST
GARTSIDE, JOHN BAL 361 1ST DIST
GARTSIDE, JOHN BAL 304 1ST DIST
GARTSIDE, RUTH BAL 361 1ST DIST
GARTSIDE, SARAH BAL 433 1ST DIST
GARTT, ELIZA CAL 050 3RD DIST
GARTY, JAMES ALL 136 4TH E.D.
GARVE, PATRICK * ALL 069 5TH E.D.
GARVEN, HENRY C. WAS 129 HAGERSTO
GARVER, BENS WAS 277 RIDGEVIL
GARVER, BRIDGET ANN 471 HOWARD D
GARVER, DAVID WAS 277 RIDGEVIL
GARVER, ELIZA A. WAS 245 SMITHSBU
GARVER, FRANCIS BAL 354 13TH WAR
GARVER, JACOB WAS 275 RIDGEVIL
GARVER, JOSEPH WAS 258 1ST DIST
GARVER, JOSEPH WAS 197 1ST DIST
GARVER, SUSAN WAS 269 1ST DIST
GARVER, WILLIAM WAS 197 1ST DIST
GARVEY, JAMES ALL 239 CUMBERLA
GARVEY, JAMES BAL 245 6TH WARD
GARVEY, JAMES BAL 183 11TH WAR
GARVEY, JOHN BAL 096 5TH WARD
GARVEY, MARY BAL 176 11TH WAR
GARVEY, PATRICK BAL 405 8TH WARD
GARVEY, THOMAS BAL 276 1ST DIST
GARVIE, JACOB BAL 322 1ST DIST
GARVIE, LOUISA BAL 322 1ST DIST
GARVIN, CELIA BAL 366 8TH WARD
GARVIN, ELLEN BAL 402 3RD WARD
GARVIN, GEORGE BAL 149 16TH WAR
GARVIN, HENRY BAL 358 8TH WARD
GARVIN, JOHN WAS 301 1ST DIST
GARVIN, PATRICK BAL 366 8TH WARD
GARVIN, PATRICK BAL 280 1ST DIST
GARVIN, ROSAN WAS 300 1ST DIST
GARVIN, TABITHA CEC 172 6TH E DI
GARVIN, THOMAS CEC 172 6TH E DI
GARVIN, THOMAS BAL 444 1ST DIST
GARVING, REBECCA * WAS 132 2ND DIST
GARVIS, J.H. BAL 164 1ST WARD
GARVTHROP, JAMES BAL 204 19TH WAR
GARVY, PATRICK BAL 275 1ST DIST
GARY, CAROLINE ANN 382 4TH DIST
GARY, GASHEL TAL 068 EASTON T
GARY, HARRY SOM 530 QUANTICO
GARY, JOHN BAL 298 3RD WARD
GARY, MILLY-BLACK ST 302 2ND E DI
GARY, REBECCA TAL 074 EASTON T
GARY, ROBERT TAL 077 EASTON T
GARY, STEPHEN WOR 291 9TH E DI
GARY, THOMAS BAL 047 9TH WARD
GARYNG, GEORGE* ALL 035 2ND E.D.
GASAWAY, A. E. CAR 232 5TH DIST
GASAWAY, DANIEL CAR 230 5TH DIST
GASAWAY, EZEKIAL CAL 063 3RD DIST
GASAWAY, GEORGE CAL 064 3RD DIST
GASAWAY, GEORGE H. FRE 303 WOODSBOR
GASAWAY, HARRIET-BLACK FRE 016 FREDERIC
GASAWAY, JANE CAL 037 2ND DIST
GASAWAY, MARIA BAL 096 2ND DIST
GASAWAY, MARTHA WAS 138 HAGERSTO
GASAWAY, NATHAN FRE 084 FREDERIC
GASAWAY, SAMUEL CAR 229 5TH DIST
GASGO, MARY PRI 110 PISCATAW
GASH, ELIZA-BLACK BAL 217 2ND WARD
GASH, ELIZABETH BAL 204 2ND WARD
GASH, FRANK-MULATTO BAL 220 2ND WARD
GASH, SARAH BAL 271 20TH WAR
GASHBEY, JAMES BAL 132 2ND DIST
GASHIER, A. BAL 159 1ST WARD
GASKIN, ROBERT BAL 264 20TH WAR
GASKINS, ANN BAL 023 1ST WARD
GASKINS, ELIZABETH BAL 325 12TH WAR
GASKINS, ELIZABETH BAL 253 2ND WARD
GASKINS, FRANCIS BAL 071 18TH WAR
GASKINS, PRISCILLA BAL 022 1ST WARD
GASKINS, THOMAS BAL 149 16TH WAR
GASLEE, EDWIN SOM 472 TRAPPE D
GASLIN, MARY BAL 145 2ND DIST
GASNELL, AARON FRE 440 8TH E DI
GASNELL, JAMES CAR 362 9TH DIST
GASPER, JOHN WAS 290 1ST DIST
GASPER, MARY WAS 156 HAGERSTO
GASPER, SAMUEL WAS 114 2ND DIST
GASS, BARBARA BAL 153 2ND DIST
GASS, JOHN BAL 269 1ST DIST
GASSAWAY, ANN BAL 226 19TH WAR
GASSAWAY, ANN A. BAL 446 14TH WAR
GASSAWAY, CAROLINE-MULATT FRE 218 BUCKEYST
GASSAWAY, CASSANDRA ANN 505 HOWARD D
GASSAWAY, CATHARINE PRI 035 VANSVILL
GASSAWAY, EDWARD QUE 204 3RD E DI
GASSAWAY, FRANCIS BAL 279 12TH WAR
GASSAWAY, FRANK BAL 016 2ND DIST
GASSAWAY, HANAH BAL 043 2ND DIST
GASSAWAY, HARRIET BAL 458 8TH WARD
GASSAWAY, JAMES ANN 315 1ST DIST
GASSAWAY, JAMES-BLACK FRE 217 BUCKEYST
GASSAWAY, JOHN MGM 425 MEDLEY 3
GASSAWAY, JOHN ANN 503 HOWARD D
GASSAWAY, KITZ ANN 298 ANNAPOLI
GASSAWAY, L. ANN 283 ANNAPOLI
GASSAWAY, LOUISA BAL 168 16TH WAR
GASSAWAY, M. ANN 280 ANNAPOLI
GASSAWAY, MARY ANN 280 ANNAPOLI
GASSAWAY, MARY BAL 098 2ND DIST
GASSAWAY, MISS ANN 280 ANNAPOLI
GASSAWAY, NICHOLAS ANN 517 HOWARD D
GASSAWAY, OHN CAL 020 2ND DIST
GASSAWAY, RACHEL ANN 499 HOWARD D
GASSAWAY, RANDOLPH W. ANN 503 HOWARD D
GASSAWAY, REBECCA ANN 273 ANNAPOLI
GASSAWAY, REBECCA ANN 310 1ST DIST
GASSAWAY, REBECCA E.C. BAL 005 15TH WAR
GASSAWAY, SAM R. ANN 443 HOWARD D
GASSAWAY, SIMON ANN 445 HOWARD D
GASSAWAY, SOPHIA TAL 073 EASTON T
GASSAWAY, TIP ANN 443 HOWARD D

Name	County	Page	District
GASSAWAY, WILLIAM	MGM	426	MEDLEY 3
GASSEE, CATHARINE	BAL	348	13TH WAR
GASSMAN, GEORGE	WAS	147	HAGERSTO
GASSMAN, WILLIAM	WAS	147	HAGERSTO
GASSMAR, MARGARET	ALL	234	CUMBERLA
GASSONY, ELIZABETH	BAL	296	12TH WAR
GASTER, ELLEN	WAS	157	2ND DIST
GASTER, JACOB	WAS	156	2ND DIST
GASTIN, WILLIAM	BAL	275	20TH WAR
GASTING, HENRY	BAL	116	11TH WAR
GASTON, JANE	BAL	075	18TH WAR
GASWAY, HENRY	CEC	045	1ST E DI
GASWAY, ROBERT	BAL	024	18TH WAR
GASY, WILLIAM	FRE	293	WOODSBOR
GATARIN, HARRIET	BAL	251	2ND WARD
GATCH, CONDUCE	BAL	184	16TH WAR
GATCH, EDWARD	BAL	381	3RD WARD
GATCH, ELIZABETH	BAL	180	11TH WAR
GATCH, JANE	BAL	295	1ST DIST
GATCH, NICHOLAS	BAL	070	2ND DIST
GATCH, THOMAS	BAL	107	2ND DIST
GATCHEL, JENY	BAL	272	20TH WAR
GATCHEL, MARY	BAL	410	3RD WARD
GATCHELL, E. J.	BAL	043	4TH WARD
GATCHELL, EMORY	BAL	114	1ST WARD
GATCHELL, JOHN G.	BAL	034	4TH WARD
GATCHELL, JOSHUA	CEC	100	3RD E DI
GATCHELL, WILLIAM	HAR	046	1ST DIST
GATCHELL, WILLIAM H.	BAL	157	11TH WAR
GATCHEY, G.H.	BAL	293	12TH WAR
GATCLIFF, GIDEON	CHA	238	HILLTOP
GATELEY, JOHN	BAL	374	8TH WARD
GATELY, PATRICK	ALL	077	5TH E.D.
GATER, JOSEPH	DOR	369	3RD DIVI
GATER, RICHARD	ANN	344	3RD DIST
GATER, THOAMS	ANN	340	3RD DIST
GATES, ANDREW	CHA	253	MIDDLETO
GATES, ANN	CHA	262	MIDDLETO
GATES, ANN	WAS	200	1ST DIST
GATES, ANN P.	MGM	368	BERRYS D
GATES, CHARLES	WAS	014	2ND SUBD
GATES, ELIAS	CHA	253	MIDDLETO
GATES, ELIZABETH	WAS	009	WILLIAMS
GATES, EMILY	CHA	234	HILLTOP
GATES, EZRA	BAL	328	13TH WAR
GATES, GEORGE	MGM	363	BERRYS D
GATES, HANNAH	BAL	028	15TH WAR
GATES, HARIET*	SOM	546	TYASKIN
GATES, HENRY	BAL	110	10TH WAR
GATES, JAMES	BAL	101	2ND DIST
GATES, JAMES	MGM	365	BERRYS D
GATES, JAMES	HAR	120	2ND DIST
GATES, JAMES	HAR	029	1ST DIST
GATES, JAMES	CAL	029	2ND DIST
GATES, JAMES J.	PRI	112	PISCATAW
GATES, JOHN	WAS	199	1ST DIST
GATES, JOHN	ST	265	3RD E DI
GATES, JOHN	CHA	249	MIDDLETO
GATES, JOHN	CEC	045	1ST E DI
GATES, JOSEPH	DOR	415	1ST DIST
GATES, JOSEPH	WAS	009	WILLIAMS
GATES, MARIAH	WAS	009	WILLIAMS
GATES, MARY	FRE	154	10TH E D
GATES, MARY E.	WAS	199	1ST DIST
GATES, MATILDA	ST	280	3RD E DI
GATES, NANCY	WAS	157	HAGERSTO
GATES, RACHEL	WAS	009	WILLIAMS
GATES, REBECCA	WAS	133	HAGERSTO
GATES, RICHARD	WAS	009	WILLIAMS
GATES, RICHARD T.	MGM	369	BERRYS D
GATES, RYON C.	PRI	112	PISCATAW
GATES, SARAH	PRI	112	PISCATAW
GATES, SARAH	BAL	178	11TH WAR
GATES, SOPHIA	BAL	332	3RD WARD
GATES, SUSAN	BAL	237	12TH WAR
GATES, SUSANNA H.	CHA	254	MIDDLETO
GATES, THOMAS	BAL	060	4TH WARD
GATES, THOMAS	WOR	305	2ND E DI
GATES, WASHINGTON	MGM	355	BERRYS D
GATES, WILLIAM	FRE	155	10TH E D
GATES, WILLIAM	FRE	298	WOODSBOR
GATES, WILLIAM	PRI	054	AQUASCO
GATES, WILLIAM	BAL	183	16TH WAR
GATES, WILLIAM H.	MGM	365	BERRYS D
GATES, WILLIAM M.	BAL	329	13TH WAR
GATEWOOD, ELIZABETH	BAL	408	8TH WARD
GATHENER, JOHN	ALL	107	5TH E.D.
GATHER, WARNER	CAR	231	5TH DIST
GATRIO, FORTY	BAL	134	1ST WARD
GATT, WASHINGTON	BAL	059	4TH WARD
GATTEISON, JOHN	BAL	178	2ND WARD
GATTEN, GEORGE	FRE	074	FREDERIC
GATTIS, JESSE	SOM	540	TYASKIN
GATTON, BARTON	ST	326	4TH E DI
GATTON, BENJAMIN F.	FRE	217	BUCKEYST
GATTON, HENRY	ST	315	4TH E DI
GATTON, JESSE	ST	335	4TH E DI
GATTON, MARY	ST	327	4TH E DI
GATTON, ZACHARIAH	MGM	401	ROCKERLE
GATTREL, FRANCIS	CAR	363	9TH DIST
GATTREL, JOHN B.	CAR	370	9TH DIST
GATY, HUGH	PRI	107	PISCATAW
GAUBETY, ADAM	BAL	247	2ND WARD
GAUCHT, SARAH J.	BAL	320	7TH WARD
GAUER, CHRISTOPHER	BAL	122	16TH WAR
GAUFE, PETER	BAL	315	20TH WAR
GAUFF, JOSEPH	KEN	257	1ST DIST
GAUFFMAN, MARGARET	CAR	364	9TH DIST
GAUGER, JAOCB	CAR	315	1ST DIST
GAUGER, MARY A.	WAS	238	CAVETOWN
GAUGH, ALLICE	BAL	407	8TH WARD
GAUGH, JAMES	BAL	126	1ST WARD
GAUGH, JOHN	FRE	139	CREAGERS
GAUGH, JONATHAN	FRE	141	CREAGERS
GAUGH, PERCIVAL	FRE	174	5TH E DI
GAUGHER, ELIZABETH	CAR	259	3RD DIST
GAUGHER, HANAH	CAR	259	3RD DIST
GAUGHEY, HANNAH	ALL	075	5TH E.D.
GAUGHEY, JANE	BAL	028	9TH WARD
GAUGHKIN, ANTHONY *	ALL	076	5TH E.D.
GAUGHKIN, JAMES	ALL	141	6TH E.D.
GAUGHLIN, ANN	ALL	047	10TH E.D
GAUGHLIN, JAMES	ALL	130	4TH E.D.
GAUGHLIN, PATRICK	ALL	048	10TH E.D
GAUGHLIN, PATRICK	ALL	140	6TH E.D.
GAUGHLIN, PATRICK	ALL	052	10TH E.D
GAUGHLIN, PATRICK	ALL	052	10TH E.D
GAUITY, PATRICK	ALL	051	10TH E.D
GAUL, HENRY	WAS	198	1ST DIST
GAUL, JOHN C.	WAS	126	HAGERSTO
GAULINE, JOHN B.	BAL	289	12TH WAR
GAULINE, JOSEPH C.	BAL	194	6TH WARD
GAULT, ADAM	FRE	037	FREDERIC
GAULT, ARCHIBALD	WOR	218	4TH E DI
GAULT, CYRUS	BAL	102	18TH WAR
GAULT, DAVID	WOR	218	4TH E DI
GAULT, GEORGE C.	BAL	341	3RD WARD
GAULT, JAMES	BAL	099	10TH WAR
GAULT, JAMES	WOR	265	BERLIN 1
GAULT, JESSE	WOR	267	BERLIN 1
GAULT, JOHN	ALL	227	CUMBERLA
GAULT, MARY A.	WOR	283	BERLIN 1
GAULT, OBED	WOR	219	4TH E DI
GAULT, SARAH	BAL	098	10TH WAR
GAULT, THOMAS	BAL	326	7TH WARD
GAULT, WILLIAM	WOR	283	BERLIN 1
GAULT, WILLIAM	WOR	269	BERLIN 1
GAULT, RICHARD T.	BAL	119	1ST WARD
GAULTER, A.	BAL	136	1ST WARD
GAULTING, MICHAEL	BAL	349	7TH WARD
GAUMER, ANNA	CAR	332	MANCHEST
GAUMERS, MATHEW	ALL	226	CUMBERLA
GAUNAN, JOHN	ALL	050	10TH E.D
GAUNT, JOHN	BAL	256	6TH WARD
GAUNT, JOHN SR.	BAL	257	6TH WARD
GAUNT, SAMUEL	BAL	167	6TH WARD
GAUNTLANY, DAVID	KEN	289	3RD DIST
GAUST, MARY E.	BAL	240	2ND WARD
GAUT, HENRIETTA	BAL	191	11TH WAR
GAUT, MOSES	BAL	175	11TH WAR
GAUTT, OVERTON	PRI	058	NOTTINGH
GAUTT, SARAH S.	PRI	007	BLADENSB
GAUTT, WILLIAM -BLACK	CAL	056	3RD DIST
GAVAN, M.	BAL	166	1ST WARD
GAVENDER, EDWORD	HAR	145	3RD DIST
GAVENDER, MARY	HAR	145	3RD DIST
GAVER, BARBARA A.	FRE	397	PETERSVI
GAVER, DANIEL	FRE	395	PETERSVI
GAVER, DANIEL	FRE	393	PETERSVI
GAVER, ELIZABETH	FRE	396	PETERSVI
GAVER, GEORGE	FRE	397	PETERSVI
GAVER, GEORGE W.	FRE	372	CATOCTIN
GAVER, JOH	FRE	325	MIDDLETO
GAVER, JOHN	FRE	368	CATOCTIN
GAVER, JOSEPH	FRE	346	MIDDLETO
GAVER, JOSEPH	FRE	346	MIDDLETO
GAVER, MARY	FRE	368	CATOCTIN
GAVER, PETER	FRE	367	CATOCTIN
GAVER, SAMUEL	FRE	397	PETERSVI
GAVER, SUSAN	FRE	328	MIDDLETO
GAVIN, AMELIA	WAS	150	HAGERSTO
GAVIN, JOHN	BAL	146	2ND DIST
GAVIN, JOHN	BAL	275	1ST DIST
GAVLIN, GEORGE	ALL	230	CUMBERLA
GAW, JAMES	ANN	422	HOWARD D
GAW, JANE	ANN	421	HOWARD D
GAW, JOHN	ANN	422	HOWARD D
GAW, JOHN M.	HAR	188	3RD DIST
GAW, WILLIAM	BAL	277	1ST DIST
GAWKER, JAMES	ALL	102	5TH E.D.
GAWKINS, ANTHONY	ALL	143	6TH E.D.
GAWNE, JOHN	BAL	067	15TH WAR
GAWTHROP, WILLIAM	BAL	186	6TH WARD
GAY, JOHN	ALL	104	5TH E.D.
GAY, JOSEPH	CHA	254	MIDDLETO
GAYE, SISTER M.L.	FRE	197	5TH E DI
GAYLARDE, GEORGE	ANN	430	HOWARD D
GAYLE, BENJAMIN	BAL	226	2ND WARD
GAYLE, EDWARD	BAL	014	1ST WARD
GAYLE, ISAAC	BAL	016	1ST WARD
GAYLE, JOSEPH R.	BAL	061	1ST WARD
GAYLE, ROBERT	BAL	229	2ND WARD
GAYLE, ROBERT	SOM	527	QUANTICO
GAYLE, ROBERT E.	BAL	031	1ST WARD
GAYLE, SARAH F.	BAL	032	1ST WARD
GAYLE, TIMOTHY	BAL	092	1ST WARD
GAYLE, WILLIAM-BLACK	BAL	246	2ND WARD
GAYLOR, CAROLINE	BAL	150	5TH WARD
GAYLOR, SAMUEL	ANN	375	4TH DIST
GAYLOR,GEORGE	FRE	397	PETERSVI
GAYNOR, ELLEN	BAL	384	8TH WARD
GAYOSO, FERNANDO	FRE	20	5TH E DI
GAYTHER, JOHN L.	ST	274	3RD E DI
GAYTON, THOMAS	BAL	089	2ND DIST
GAZELL, MARY	BAL	055	1ST WARD
GEACY, ANN	CHA	246	HILLTOP
GEADOEN, ISAAC	HAR	067	1ST DIST
GEAF, PERY	BAL	020	2ND DIST
GEAGE, MOSES	WOR	321	1ST E DI
GEAHAM, JAEMS	BAL	125	2ND DIST
GEAMES, SEJWICK	HAR	035	1ST DIST
GEAMS, GEORGE	HAR	032	1ST DIST
GEAMS, GEORGE	HAR	015	1ST DIST
GEAMS, JAMES	HAR	033	1ST DIST
GEAMS, JOHN	HAR	030	1ST DIST
GEAMS, LERY	HAR	029	1ST DIST
GEAMS, SAMUEL	HAR	031	1ST DIST
GEAN, WILLIAM	BAL	327	1ST DIST
GEANOR, MARY	BAL	087	4TH WARD
GEANS, RICHRD	PRI	080	QUEEN AN
GEAR, JOHN	BAL	447	1ST DIST
GEARE, WILLIAM N.	BAL	037	18TH WAR
GEAREY, RICHARD	BAL	135	18TH WAR
GEAREY, WILLIAM	BAL	171	11TH WAR
GEARHART, CATHARINE	WAS	173	FUNKSTOW
GEARHART, FOLLEDEN	BAL	225	17TH WAR
GEARHART, ISAAC	WAS	028	2ND SUBD
GEARHART, JACOB	BAL	222	17TH WAR
GEARHEART, ELIZABETH	WAS	223	1ST DIST
GEARHEART, JACOB	WAS	291	1ST DIST
GEARHEART, MARY	WAS	293	1ST DIST
GEARISCH, SISTER WALBERGA	FRE	198	5TH E DI
GEARLOCK, HENRY	ALL	088	5TH E.D.
GEARMAN, ISAAC S.	WOR	215	4TH E DI
GEARS, ELIZA	KEN	242	2ND DIST
GEARS, PEREGRINE	KEN	242	2ND DIST
GEARS, WILLIAM	FRE	234	BUCKEYST
GEARY, ANN	BAL	265	7TH WARD
GEARY, DAVID	WAS	093	2ND SUBD
GEARY, ELLEN	BAL	454	8TH WARD
GEARY, JAMES	BAL	395	1ST DIST
GEARY, MARY	BAL	213	11TH WAR
GEARY, THOMAS	WAS	130	HAGERSTO
GEARY, WILLIAM	WAS	094	2ND SUBD
GEARY, WILLIAM	BAL	230	1ST DIST
GEASCUP, MICHAEL	BAL	237	2ND WARD
GEASEY, JOSEPH	FRE	448	8TH E DI
GEASLER, MARY	FRE	233	BUCKEYST
GEASLER, SARAH A.R.	FRE	234	BUCKEYST
GEASY, JOHN	BAL	434	14TH WAR
GEATTY, ELLEN	CAR	285	7TH DIST
GEATTY, HENRY	CAR	397	2ND DIST
GEATTY, HENRY C.	CAR	392	2ND DIST
GEATTY, MILTON	CAR	393	2ND DIST
GEATY, ELIZA A.	CAR	294	7TH DIST
GEAY, P.	BAL	100	10TH WAR
GEBB, GEORGE	BAL	071	2ND DIST
GEBBINS, ROEBRT	ST	299	2ND E DI
GEBBINS, WILLIAM	WOR	350	1ST E DI
GEBERER, CARL	BAL	025	15TH WAR
GEBHARD, CHARLES	BAL	357	13TH WAR
GEBHART, CHARLES	BAL	015	15TH WAR
GEBHART, ELIZABETH	BAL	221	1ST DIST
GEBHART, GEORGE	CAR	352	6TH DIST
GEBHART, JAMES	CEC	004	ELKTON 3
GEBHART, SOLOMON	FRE	060	FREDERIC
GEBI, ZACH *	BAL	281	20TH WAR
GEBKE, HENRY	BAL	147	11TH WAR
GEBLINE, GEORGE	BAL	221	2ND WARD
GECKE, HENRY	BAL	245	12TH WAR
GEDDES, ADAM	BAL	473	14TH WAR
GEDDES, CHARLES	BAL	383	8TH WARD
GEDDES, GEORGE	BAL	452	14TH WAR
GEDDES, ISEBELLA	BAL	035	18TH WAR
GEDDES, JOHN	BAL	062	18TH WAR
GEDDES, JOHN	BAL	414	14TH WAR
GEDDES, WILLIAM G.	BAL	061	18TH WAR
GEDDINGS, EDWARD	BAL	296	7TH WARD
GEDDINGS, ELIZABETH	PRI	009	BLADENSB
GEDDINGS, ELIZABETH	PRI	009	BLADENSB
GEDDINGS, GEORGE W.	PRI	009	BLADENSB
GEDDINGS, JOHN J.	PRI	036	VANSVILL
GEDDIS, DANIEL	BAL	458	8TH WARD
GEDDIS, HENRY	BAL	458	8TH WARD
GEDDIS, JAMES W.	BAL	438	8TH WARD
GEDDIS, JOHN	BAL	091	2ND DIST
GEDNEN, MARY	BAL	458	1ST DIST
GEE, HENRY	BAL	421	3RD WARD
GEE, NICHOLAS	BAL	155	19TH WAR
GEEK, HENRY	ALL	056	10TH E.D
GEEMAN, BALINDA	CAR	277	7TH DIST
GEEMAN, DAVID	CAR	276	7TH DIST
GEER, ALFRED L.	BAL	055	4TH WARD
GEER, ANN E.	BAL	056	4TH WARD
GEER, HENRY	BAL	143	19TH WAR
GEES, GEORGE	BAL	283	12TH WAR
GEES, RICHARD	BAL	296	20TH WAR
GEES, WESLEY	BAL	296	20TH WAR
GEESE, ANDY	ALL	227	CUMBERLA
GEESEY, ANN R.	FRE	137	CREAGERS
GEESEY, DANIEL	FRE	135	CREAGERS
GEESEY, DAVID	FRE	140	CREAGERS
GEESEY, DELANEY	FRE	115	CREAGERS
GEESEY, ELIZABETH	FRE	142	CREAGERS
GEESEY, GEORGE H.	FRE	301	WOODSBOR
GEESEY, JOHN T.	FRE	137	CREAGERS
GEESEY, MARTHA	FRE	306	WOODSBOR
GEESEY, SOPHIAH	FRE	308	WOODSBOR
GEESEY, THEODORE	FRE	309	WOODSBOR
GEETING, EPHRAIM	WAS	073	2ND SUBD
GEETING, RACHEL	WAS	074	2ND SUBD
GEETING, WILLIAM	WAS	074	2ND SUBD
GEETING, WILLIAM O.	WAS	190	1ST DIST
GEETING, WINFIELD	WAS	075	2ND SUBD
GEETY, JAMES *	BAL	317	12TH WAR
GEFREY, MARY *	BAL	447	14TH WAR
GEGAN, JOSEPH	BAL	156	11TH WAR
GEGAN, PHILLIP	ANN	429	HOWARD D
GEGAN, ROBERT	BAL	199	6TH WARD
GEGAN, WILLIAM	BAL	068	2ND DIST
GEGHLER, WILLIAM	BAL	465	14TH WAR
GEGLIN, MARGARET	BAL	163	19TH WAR
GEGUS, ANN	WAS	053	2ND SUBD
GEHAGAN, MARY	BAL	394	14TH WAR
GEHARDT, JOHN	BAL	010	9TH WARD
GEHING, ELIZABETH	BAL	008	9TH WARD
GEHR, ISAAC	WAS	247	SMITHSBU
GEHR, ISAAC H.	WAS	225	1ST DIST
GEHR, MARY	WAS	271	1ST DIST
GEHR, SAMUEL	WAS	123	2ND DIST
GEHR, ULRICH	WAS	275	RIDGEVIL
GEHR, WILLIAM M.	WAS	123	2ND DIST
GEHRIG, CHARLES	BAL	213	6TH WARD
GEHRING, JAMES	BAL	189	6TH WARD
GEHRING, LAURENCE	BAL	251	2ND WARD
GEHRING, MARY	BAL	117	5TH WARD
GEHRING, WILLIAM	BAL	259	6TH WARD
GEHRMAN, AUGUSTUS	BAL	168	16TH WAR
GEHRMANN, CHARLES	BAL	100	10TH WAR
GEHRUNAN, JULIUS	BAL	080	10TH WAR
GEHUSON, CATHARINE	BAL	195	11TH WAR
GEIDER, BENJAMIN	BAL	087	2ND DIST
GEIGEGUS, MATHIAS	FRE	227	BUCKEYST
GEIGER, ANN	MGM	392	ROCKERLE
GEIGER, CHRISTIAN	BAL	089	1ST WARD
GEIGER, ESTHER	CAR	329	MANCHEST
GEIGER, FREDERICK	BAL	044	15TH WAR
GEIGER, JOHN	BAL	017	4TH WARD
GEIGER, MARY A.	CAR	382	2ND DIST
GEIGER, PETER	CAR	400	2ND DIST
GEIGER, SAMUEL	BAL	059	2ND DIST
GEIGER, WILLIAM	BAL	086	10TH WAR
GEIGLER, JULIA E.	FRE	165	EMMITTSB
GEIGLER, RUDOLPH	MGM	394	ROCKERLE
GEIGNER, DANIEL	BAL	105	2ND DIST
GEIGNER, PAUL	BAL	105	2ND DIST
GEILIS, CORDELEY	HAR	177	3RD DIST
GEIMAN, ABRAHAM	CAR	357	6TH DIST
GEIMAN, DANIEL J.	CAR	294	7TH DIST
GEIMAN, DEBORAH	CAR	294	7TH DIST
GEIMAN, JAOCB	CAR	349	6TH DIST
GEIMAN, JOHN	CAR	346	6TH DIST
GEIMAN, JOSEPH	CAR	296	7TH DIST
GEIR, JOHN	WOR	182	6TH E DI
GEIS, ANDREW	BAL	255	7TH WARD
GEISE, ADAM	FRE	197	5TH E DI
GEISE, JARVIS T.	FRE	166	EMMITTSB
GEISE, JOHN	FRE	166	EMMITTSB
GEISE, OLIVIA	BAL	291	20TH WAR
GEISE, THOMAS	BAL	020	15TH WAR
GEISELMAN, JOHN	CAR	336	6TH DIST
GEISELMAN, LYDIA	CAR	388	2ND DIST
GEISELMAN, MICAHEL	FRE	300	WOODSBOR
GEISENCAFFER, CATHARINE	BAL	252	1ST DIST
GEISHELL, ADAM	BAL	212	17TH WAR
GEISINGELFER, JOHN	BAL	144	19TH WAR
GEISINGER, CATHARINE	WAS	129	HAGERSTO
GEISINGER, GEORGE	FRE	335	MIDDLETO
GEISINGER, HARRIET	FRE	312	MIDDLETO
GEISINGER, JAOCB	FRE	108	CREAGERS

Name	County	Page	District
GEISINGER, ROBERT	FRE	351	MIDDLETO
GEISINGER, SAMUEL L.	FRE	312	MIDDLETO
GEISLAN, DEBORAH A.	CEC	146	PORT DUP
GEISLER, JOHN	BAL	305	17TH WAR
GEISON, ANN	BAL	323	1ST DIST
GEISS, CHRISTOPHER	BAL	462	14TH WAR
GEISS, S.M.	CAL	041	3RD DIST
GEIST, JACOB	BAL	101	5TH WARD
GEITTER, JACOB	BAL	303	20TH WAR
GELBACH, GEORGE	BAL	001	EASTERN
GELDMAKER, CARRY	BAL	288	1ST DIST
GELHART, WILLIAM	BAL	098	2ND DIST
GELIN, MICHAEL	BAL	146	19TH WAR
GELKANUN, MARTIN	BAL	446	1ST DIST
GELKNER, HANNAH	BAL	181	11TH WAR
GELLAN, MARGARETT	BAL	235	17TH WAR
GELLER, CASPER	BAL	251	2ND WARD
GELLERS, URIAH	FRE	075	FREDERIC
GELLEY, ELIZABETH	BAL	015	15TH WAR
GELLINGHAM, R.A.	BAL	236	12TH WAR
GELMARTEN, CATHARINE	ALL	083	5TH E.D.
GELMARTIN, JOHN	ALL	049	10TH E.D
GELON, JAMES*	TAL	010	EASTON D
GELON, WILLIAM	TAL	026	EASTON D
GELOR, JAMES*	TAL	010	EASTON D
GELPIN, THORNTON	ALL	046	10TH E.D
GELSMID, HARD	BAL	054	1ST WARD
GELSON, SAMUEL	SOM	419	PRINCESS
GELSTER, BARBARA	BAL	322	7TH WARD
GELSTON, HUGH	BAL	106	10TH WAR
GELT, PHILIP	BAL	063	2ND DIST
GELTHOCHLER, THOMAS *	WAS	077	2ND SUBD
GELTMAKER, JOHN	WAS	077	2ND SUBD
GELTMOCHAR, THOMAS *	WAS	077	2ND SUBD
GELTNEAKER, HENRY	WAS	080	2ND SUBD
GELTUP, PATRICK H.C.	MGM	422	MEDLEY 3
GELTZINGER, JOHN	FRE	357	CATOCTIN
GELWICKS, C.F.	WAS	123	HAGERSTO
GELWICKS, CHARLES F.	FRE	166	EMMITTSB
GELWICKS, GEORGE	FRE	188	5TH E DI
GELWICKS, GEORGE C.	WAS	144	HAGERSTO
GELWICKS, HENRY	FRE	173	5TH E DI
GELWICKS, JACOB	WAS	144	HAGERSTO
GELWICKS, JACOB S.	FRE	166	EMMITTSB
GELWICKS, JOHN	WAS	181	BOONSBOR
GELWICKS, MARGARET	WAS	181	BOONSBOR
GELWICKS, WILLIAM T.	WAS	146	HAGERSTO
GELYER, DAVID	BAL	176	16TH WAR
GEMELL, GERBOT	BAL	304	12TH WAR
GEMELL, REBECCA	BAL	164	19TH WAR
GEMIELL, W. *	BAL	304	12TH WAR
GEMILL, DOUGLAS E.	BAL	303	12TH WAR
GEMMES, SAMUEL M.	ALL	256	CUMBERLA
GEMMIL, MARGARET	HAR	021	1ST DIST
GEMMILE, JOHN	HAR	060	1ST DIST
GEMMILL, JAMES	HAR	049	1ST DIST
GEMMILL, JAMES M.	HAR	041	1ST DIST
GEMMILL, JOHN	BAL	032	2ND DIST
GENAUEL, ELIZABETH	FRE	129	CREAGERS
GENBER, JONATHAN	FRE	426	8TH E DI
GENDHART, JOHN W.	BAL	274	7TH WARD
GENERIE, PETER	PRI	081	QUEEN AN
GENEROUS, THOMAS	BAL	302	7TH WARD
GENERP, MICHAEL	BAL	086	1ST WARD
GENEVIN, SARAH	BAL	146	19TH WAR
GENG, HENRY	ST	336	4TH E DI
GENGMAZER, JOHN	BAL	179	2ND WARD
GENHARNE, SUSAN	BAL	321	12TH WAR
GENN, A.	BAL	303	12TH WAR
GENNALLA, EPHRAIM	BAL	229	6TH WARD
GENNALLS, JAMES	BAL	229	6TH WARD
GENNELL, WILLIAM	HAR	064	1ST DIST
GENNESS, SAMUEL	CEC	188	7TH E DI
GENNETT, JAMES A.	BAL	048	1ST WARD
GENNETT, JOHN L.	BAL	282	2ND WARD
GENNINGS, JOHN	BAL	183	11TH WAR
GENRY, ELIZA	BAL	241	12TH WAR
GENSNER, PETER	BAL	231	2ND WARD
GENST, GEORGE	BAL	008	1ST WARD
GENT, BRIDGET	BAL	064	1ST WARD
GENT, HENRY	BAL	015	15TH WAR
GENT, JOHN	BAL	136	16TH WAR
GENT, JOHN F.	ANN	465	HOWARD D
GENT, JOSHUA	BAL	416	1ST DIST
GENT, MARY	BAL	192	19TH WAR
GENT, PETER	BAL	254	1ST DIST
GENT, POLLY	BAL	196	19TH WAR
GENT, RICHARD	BAL	268	1ST DIST
GENT, THOMAS	BAL	442	1ST DIST
GENT, WILLAIN	BAL	243	1ST DIST
GENT, WILLIAM	BAL	419	1ST DIST
GENTE, ELIZABETH	BAL	277	12TH WAR
GENTER, HENRY	BAL	169	2ND DIST
GENTER, J.	BAL	262	12TH WAR
GENTER, LUCY	BAL	169	2ND DIST
GENTLE, DELILAH	MGM	365	BERRYS D
GENTRO, JULIA	BAL	246	12TH WAR
GENTRY, EMILY	BAL	026	4TH WARD
GENTY, PATRICK	ALL	056	10TH E.D
GEOGHEGAN, CATHARINE *	BAL	052	15TH WAR
GEOGHEGAN, JAMES	DOR	470	1ST DIST
GEOGHEGAN, WILLIAM*	DOR	470	1ST DIST
GEOGHGAN, EMILA	DOR	357	3RD DIVI
GEOGHGAN, JAMES	DOR	358	3RD DIVI
GEOGHGAN, PHILMON	DOR	364	3RD DIVI
GEOGHGAN, WILLIAM	DOR	357	3RD DIVI
GEOGHHEGAN, MICHAEL	BAL	303	3RD WARD
GEOHEGAN, STEWART	BAL	020	15TH WAR
GEOREE, SAMUEL*	DOR	399	1ST DIST
GEORGE W.	BAL	130	1ST WARD
GEORGE, ACH	BAL	155	11TH WAR
GEORGE, ARAMINTA	CEC	071	5TH E DI
GEORGE, BARBARY E.	WAS	230	1ST DIST
GEORGE, BENJAMIN G.	HAR	047	1ST DIST
GEORGE, DAVID	ALL	236	CUMBERLA
GEORGE, ELIZABETH	BAL	056	4TH WARD
GEORGE, ELIZABETH	BAL	056	4TH WARD
GEORGE, ELIZABETH E.	BAL	016	9TH WARD
GEORGE, ENOCH	QUE	153	1ST E DI
GEORGE, ENOCH-DOCTOR	QUE	130	1ST E DI
GEORGE, HARVEY	BAL	445	14TH WAR
GEORGE, HARVEY	BAL	445	14TH WAR
GEORGE, ISAAC S.	BAL	016	9TH WARD
GEORGE, JACOB	SOM	456	DAMES QU
GEORGE, JAMES	BAL	142	11TH WAR
GEORGE, JAMES	CEC	044	CHESAPEA
GEORGE, JAMES B.	BAL	015	9TH WARD
GEORGE, JOHN	BAL	029	2ND DIST
GEORGE, JOHN	ALL	039	2ND E.D.
GEORGE, JOHN	BAL	313	1ST DIST
GEORGE, JOHN	BAL	183	19TH WAR
GEORGE, JOHN	BAL	407	14TH WAR
GEORGE, JOHN	BAL	260	20TH WAR
GEORGE, JOHN B.	BAL	294	7TH WARD
GEORGE, JOHN H.	WAS	233	1ST DIST
GEORGE, JOHN N.	BAL	271	17TH WAR
GEORGE, JOSEPH	CEC	020	ELKTON 3
GEORGE, JOSEPH.*	BAL	339	3RD WARD
GEORGE, JRABER *	BAL	298	12TH WAR
GEORGE, LEONARD	BAL	194	2ND WARD
GEORGE, MATTHIAS	QUE	130	1ST E DI
GEORGE, PARKER-BLACK	WOR	172	6TH E DI
GEORGE, PETER *	BAL	319	12TH WAR
GEORGE, PHILIP T.	BAL	182	11TH WAR
GEORGE, ROSANNA	CEC	141	6TH E DI
GEORGE, S. R.	BAL	147	11TH WAR
GEORGE, SAMUEL	BAL	299	12TH WAR
GEORGE, SARAH	BAL	233	5TH WARD
GEORGE, SARAH H.	BAL	019	2ND DIST
GEORGE, SARAH J.	BAL	016	9TH WARD
GEORGE, STEPHEN	BAL	260	12TH WAR
GEORGE, STEPHEN JR.	BAL	126	16TH WAR
GEORGE, THOMAS	BAL	356	3RD WARD
GEORGE, WILLIAM	BAL	142	1ST WARD
GEORGE, WILLIAM	QUE	210	3RD E DI
GEORGE, WILLIAM E.	BAL	445	14TH WAR
GEORGE, WILLIAM S.	BAL	359	3RD WARD
GEORGE, ZEAKLE C.	BAL	363	1ST DIST
GEPBART, GEORGE	ALL	183	8TH E.D.
GEPHART, CHARLES	ALL	207	CUMBERLA
GEPHART, FREDERICK	BAL	236	2ND WARD
GEPHART, GEORGE C.	BAL	258	6TH WARD
GEPHART, JOANA S. J. A.	BAL	258	6TH WARD
GEPHART, JOHN	BAL	319	3RD WARD
GEPHART, JOHN	BAL	123	16TH WAR
GEPHART, JOHN	ALL	240	CUMBERLA
GEPHART, JOHN JR.	BAL	141	19TH WAR
GEPHART, MARSHAL	ALL	085	5TH E.D.
GEPHART, MARY	ALL	254	CUMBERLA
GEPHART, WILLIAM	ALL	203	CUMBERLA
GEPHEART, JOHN	BAL	471	14TH WAR
GEPP, MARY	BAL	393	3RD WARD
GEPP, WILLHELMINA	BAL	189	6TH WARD
GEPPO, SIMON	CAR	246	3RD DIST
GEPPY, FREDERICK	FRE	034	FREDERIC
GEPSON, THOMAS	HAR	185	3RD DIST
GEPT, NICHOLAS	BAL	118	1ST WARD
GERAD, MICHAEL	BAL	147	11TH WAR
GERANG, THOMAS E.	KEN	286	3RD DIST
GERANS, JULIANNA	BAL	017	2ND DIST
GERANS, NICHOLAS	BAL	044	2ND DIST
GERARD, ISHAMAEL	BAL	472	14TH WAR
GERARD, SALLY	BAL	471	14TH WAR
GERARD, THOMAS	BAL	156	1ST WARD
GERBER, CHRISTIAN	BAL	097	15TH WAR
GERBERT, FREDERICK	BAL	448	8TH WARD
GERBETS, PHILLIP	BAL	005	1ST WARD
GERBIN, JACOK	BAL	203	6TH DIST
GERBRICK, GEORGE	BAL	114	11TH WAR
GERBRICK, MICHAEL	BAL	114	11TH WAR
GERBUCK, FRANCIS	BAL	279	2ND WARD
GERBY, MARGARET	BAL	323	3RD WARD
GERDEMAN, ANTHONY	ALL	145	6TH E.D.
GERDEN, LUCY	WAS	124	2ND DIST
GERDES, ANNA	ALL	245	CUMBERLA
GERDES, HENRY	BAL	043	9TH WARD
GERDING, HENRY	BAL	177	2ND WARD
GEREGNACHEN, MARY	BAL	199	17TH WAR
GEREST, ANN	BAL	193	2ND WARD
GERGENBACK, JOSEPH	BAL	155	1ST WARD
GERGERICK, TIMOTHY	BAL	277	2ND WARD
GERGIN, ANTHONY	BAL	143	2ND DIST
GERGH, DENTON	CAR	273	WESTMINS
GERHARDT, WILLIAM	BAL	009	9TH WARD
GERHART, JACOB	CAR	347	6TH DIST
GERHOREN, JOHN *	BAL	266	2ND WARD
GERHING, JOSEPH	BAL	297	17TH WAR
GERIEN, ANDREW	BAL	039	15TH WAR
GERIMGER, J. *	BAL	318	20TH WAR
GERING, GEORGE	ANN	417	HOWARD D
GERISHERT, SAMUEL	FRE	113	CREAGERS
GERK, J.P. MA	ALL	237	CUMBERLA
GERLACH, CHARLES	BAL	263	20TH WAR
GERLACH, CONRAD	BAL	017	9TH WARD
GERLACH, DEUCK	BAL	230	2ND WARD
GERLAGH, PETER	BAL	045	15TH WAR
GERLAND, WILLIAM	TAL	030	EASTON D
GERMAN, A.	BAL	139	1ST WARD
GERMAN, ADAM	WAS	156	HAGERSTO
GERMAN, AGNES E.	BAL	016	9TH WARD
GERMAN, BENJAMIN	BAL	330	7TH WARD
GERMAN, BENJAMIN JR.	BAL	331	7TH WARD
GERMAN, CATHARINE	BAL	111	1ST WARD
GERMAN, CATHERINE	BAL	061	4TH WARD
GERMAN, CECELIA A.	BAL	355	13TH WAR
GERMAN, CHARLES B.	BAL	340	3RD WARD
GERMAN, CHRISTIAN	BAL	054	1ST WARD
GERMAN, DAVID	BAL	202	11TH WAR
GERMAN, ELIZABETH	BAL	070	2ND DIST
GERMAN, FRANCIS	BAL	133	11TH WAR
GERMAN, FRANCIS	BAL	049	18TH WAR
GERMAN, GEORGE	BAL	253	2ND WARD
GERMAN, GEORGE	BAL	255	2ND WARD
GERMAN, ISAAC	BAL	061	2ND DIST
GERMAN, JOB	BAL	070	2ND DIST
GERMAN, JOHN	BAL	288	3RD WARD
GERMAN, JOHN	CAR	346	6TH DIST
GERMAN, JOSHUA	BAL	114	11TH WAR
GERMAN, MARGARET	BAL	416	14TH WAR
GERMAN, MARY E.	BAL	016	9TH WARD
GERMAN, NICHOLAS	BAL	188	19TH WAR
GERMAN, PATRICK	BAL	197	19TH WAR
GERMAN, PETER	BAL	050	18TH WAR
GERMAN, THOMAS	BAL	066	2ND DIST
GERMAN, THOMAS	BAL	407	8TH WARD
GERMAN, VOLENTINE	BAL	080	1ST WARD
GERMAN, WILLIAM	BAL	152	2ND DIST
GERMANHANSEN, FRANCIS	BAL	313	7TH WARD
GERMANHOUSEN, LEWIS	BAL	391	14TH WAR
GERMANS, GEORGE F.	BAL	012	9TH WARD
GERMANY, MARY	BAL	443	14TH WAR
GERMCH, WILLIAM G.	BAL	256	12TH WAR
GERMER, BENJAMIN *	ANN	343	3RD DIST
GERMER, HENRY	BAL	071	1ST WARD
GERMEROTZ, CHRISTIAN	BAL	113	15TH WAR
GERMILL, L.W.	BAL	259	12TH WAR
GERMINGHAM, JAMES	HAR	071	1ST DIST
GERMODT, DORTON	ALL	216	CUMBERLA
GERNAN, EDWARD	BAL	235	2ND WARD
GERNANA, ANDREW	FRE	416	8TH E DI
GERNANA, JOSPEH A.	CAR	317	1ST DIST
GERNAND, EMANUEL	CAR	256	WESTMINS
GERNAND, JOSEPH	FRE	129	CREAGERS
GERNANEL, JACOB	FRE	117	CREAGERS
GERNHARDT, HERMAN J.	BAL	323	7TH WARD
GERNICH, WILLIAM	BAL	267	12TH WAR
GERNRAIN, MARY	BAL	205	11TH WAR
GEROGE, JOHN	BAL	096	2ND DIST
GEROGE, JOHN S.	BAL	257	1ST DIST
GERRAGE, JOHN	TAL	057	EASTON D
GERRELL, K. M.	BAL	332	1ST DIST
GERRET, MAHOLA	BAL	332	13TH WAR
GERRIEN, FRANCIS	BAL	242	17TH WAR
GERRY, LYDIA	CEC	156	PORT DUP
GERRY, N.	BAL	129	1ST WARD
GERSENRICK, J.	BAL	224	19TH WAR
GERSINGER, COMODORE D.	BAL	190	11TH WAR
GERSINGER, SARAH	PRI	082	QUEEN AN
GERSTELLER, ARNOLD	ALL	138	6TH E.D.
GERSUCH, THOMAS T.	BAL	017	2ND DIST
GERSUCK, THOMAS	BAL	107	2ND DIST
GERSUCK, WILLIAM	BAL	086	2ND DIST
GERT, HARRIET	BAL	152	11TH WAR
GERTAN, WILLIAM	BAL	111	1ST WARD
GERTEN, WILLIAM	BAL	111	1ST WARD
GERTIN, LLOYD	ST	284	2ND E DI
GERTING, BENJAIN	ST	272	3RD E DI
GERTING, CATHARINE	ST	269	3RD E DI
GERTING, FREDERICK	HAR	101	2ND DIST
GERTING, JAMES	ST	277	3RD E DI
GERTING, JAMES B	ST	278	3RD E DI
GERTING, LLOYD	ST	283	3RD E DI
GERTING, MARY E.	ST	285	2ND E DI
GERTING, SARAH A.	ST	267	3RD E DI
GERTING, THOAMS	ST	265	3RD E DI
GERTING, THOAMS	ST	259	3RD E DI
GERTING, WILFRED	ST	263	3RD E DI
GERTRUDE, EMMA	BAL	475	14TH WAR
GERVAN, TRACY	BAL	133	11TH WAR
GERVER, ISAAC	WAS	276	RIDGEVIL
GERVIER, GEORGE *	BAL	319	12TH WAR
GERVILLE, MARY	BAL	420	14TH WAR
GERVIN, JAMES	CEC	016	ELKTON 3
GERVIN, JAMES	BAL	287	12TH WAR
GESBIER, CHARLES	BAL	232	12TH WAR
GESBURG, PHILIP	BAL	270	12TH WAR
GESELL, DEDEIA	BAL	048	18TH WAR
GESEY, JOHN	BAL	275	12TH WAR
GESFURD, CHARLES	BAL	244	17TH WAR
GESFORD, JAMES	BAL	430	8TH WARD
GESFORD, MARTHA	WAS	113	2ND DIST
GESFORT, MARY	WAS	136	2ND DIST
GESFORT, ROBERT	WAS	136	2ND DIST
GESHARD, SOPHIA	BAL	083	2ND DIST
GESMAN, JAMES *	WAS	117	2ND DIST
GESSART, MARGARET	BAL	254	12TH WAR
GESSFORD, WILLIAM	BAL	431	8TH WARD
GESSLEMAN, GEORGE	WAS	134	HAGERSTO
GESSNCE, REBECCA	ALL	045	10TH E.D
GESSNES, WILLIAM	ALL	259	CUMBERLA
GESSO, HENRY	BAL	111	2ND DIST
GEST, EDIDE	BAL	244	12TH WAR
GEST, JULIA	BAL	393	1ST DIST
GEST, MORDECAI	BAL	194	5TH DIST
GESTING, LOUIS	BAL	295	20TH WAR
GETARCAMMER, SOLOMON G. *	BAL	104	18TH WAR
GETCHE, SOPHIA	BAL	213	11TH WAR
GETCHELL, FRANCIS	KEN	228	2ND DIST
GETCHELL, JERAMIAH	CEC	198	7TH E DI
GETCHELL, MARY *	BAL	291	20TH WAR
GETCHELL, YETHA*	BAL	066	4TH WARD
GETCHZ, GEORGE*	BAL	419	3RD WARD
GETES, WILLIAM	WAS	123	2ND DIST
GETHER, GEORGE	BAL	250	20TH WAR
GETHER, JOHN L.	BAL	210	19TH WAR
GETHER, LOUISA	BAL	215	11TH WAR
GETHUER, WILLIAM	BAL	031	18TH WAR
GETINGER, JOHN	BAL	354	7TH WARD
GETINGS, JAMES	FRE	388	PETERSVI
GETMAN,MARTIN	BAL	067	2ND DIST
GETROST, ADAM	BAL	294	17TH WAR
GETTER, BENJAMIN *	BAL	323	12TH WAR
GETTEY, FRANCIS	BAL	353	7TH WARD
GETTEY, MARY A.	BAL	383	8TH WARD
GETTIER, DANIEL G.	FRE	159	EMMITTSB
GETTIER, ELIZABETH	CAR	332	MANCHEST
GETTIER, GOERGE W.	BAL	304	20TH WAR
GETTIER, H. L.	BAL	274	20TH WAR
GETTIER, HENRY	CAR	351	6TH DIST
GETTIER, JOHN	BAL	210	17TH WAR
GETTIER, JOSEPH	FRE	174	5TH E DI
GETTIER, MICHAEL	CAR	329	MANCHEST
GETTIER, PETER	CAR	346	6TH DIST
GETTIER, REBECCA	BAL	261	1ST DIST
GETTIER, WILLIAM *	BAL	273	20TH WAR
GETTIER, WILLIAM P.	BAL	138	16TH WAR
GETTIN, ELEN	BAL	220	1ST DIST
GETTING, JACOB	CAR	249	3RD DIST
GETTINGER, AVINOA A.E.	WAS	299	1ST DIST
GETTINGER, GEORGE	FRE	098	FREDERIC
GETTINGER, JAMES	FRE	034	FREDERIC
GETTINGER, REBECCA H.	FRE	032	FREDERIC
GETTINGS, ABRAM	BAL	070	2ND DIST
GETTINGS, ANN R.	WAS	154	2ND DIST
GETTINGS, FANNY	BAL	111	2ND DIST
GETTINGS, GEORGE W.	MGM	375	ROCKERLE
GETTINGS, HENRY	BAL	058	2ND DIST
GETTINGS, HENRY C.	FRE	398	JEFFERSO
GETTINGS, JAMES	BAL	096	2ND DIST
GETTINGS, JOHN	BAL	094	2ND DIST
GETTINGS, JOHN S.	BAL	451	1ST DIST
GETTINGS, LAMBERT	BAL	211	11TH WAR
GETTINGS, MARY	BAL	439	8TH WARD
GETTINGS, MARY E.	FRE	379	PETERSVI
GETTINGS, RICHARD	BAL	018	18TH WAR
GETTINGS, RUMSEY	BAL	096	2ND DIST
GETTINGS, SMITH	BAL	193	11TH WAR
GETTINGS, WILLIAM	BAL	105	2ND DIST
GETTINGS, WILLIAM	BAL	009	EASTERN
GETTINGS, WILLIAM	MGM	316	CRACKLIN
GETTINGS, WILLIAM C.	WAS	151	2ND DIST
GETTLE, DANIEL	WAS	034	2ND SUBD
GETTLE, DAVID	WAS	105	2ND DIST
GETTLE, MARTHA	WAS	034	2ND SUBD
GETTLE, MARY	WAS	048	2ND SUBD
GETTS, GEORGE	BAL	404	8TH WARD
GETTUST, SARAH	BAL	263	17TH WAR
GETTY, AUGUSTUS	BAL	124	5TH WARD
GETTY, CHARLES	BAL	166	11TH WAR
GETTY, CHARLES E.	ALL	103	5TH E.D.

GETTY, CRAWFORD CEC 005 ELKTON 3
GETTY, ELEANORA BAL 303 1ST DIST
GETTY, HAMILTON C. BAL 201 6TH WARD
GETTY, JAMES CEC 107 3RD E DI
GETTY, JOHN BAL 251 1ST DIST
GETTY, JOHN A. CEC 003 ELKTON 3
GETTY, MARGARET CEC 004 ELKTON 3
GETTY, MARY ANN BAL 128 5TH WARD
GETTY, ROBERT BAL 303 1ST DIST
GETTY, ROBERT BAL 282 2ND WARD
GETY, EDWARD* BAL 345 3RD WARD
GETZ, CHARLES BAL 400 8TH WARD
GETZ, CHRISTIAN BAL 189 17TH WAR
GETZ, EDWARD* BAL 345 3RD WARD
GETZ, J. BAL 093 15TH WAR
GETZ, JOHN BAL 210 17TH WAR
GETZ, LEWIS BAL 224 6TH WARD
GETZ, LUERZ BAL 276 12TH WAR
GETZ, MARGARET* BAL 382 3RD WARD
GETZ, MICHAEL BAL 434 8TH WARD
GETZ, PAUL BAL 257 6TH WARD
GETZ, WILLIAM BAL 285 2ND WARD
GETZANDANER, ANN M. BAL 415 1ST DIST
GETZENDANER, ABRAHAM FRE 304 WOODSBOR
GETZENDANNEN, CAROLINE * ALL 096 5TH E.D.
GETZENDANNER, CHRISTIAN FRE 021 FREDERIC
GETZENDANNER, CHRISTIAN FRE 061 FREDERIC
GETZENDANNER, JONATHAN * FRE 078 FREDERIC
GETZENDANNER, JOSIAH ALL 095 5TH E.D.
GETZENDANNOR, ANN C. FRE 059 FREDERIC
GETZENDENNER, DANIEL FRE 077 FREDERIC
GETZENDENNER, EDWARD FRE 078 FREDERIC
GETZENDENNER, ELIZABETH FRE 077 FREDERIC
GETZENDENNER, FRANCES FRE 078 FREDERIC
GETZENDENNER, JOHN J. FRE 030 FREDERIC
GETZENDENNER, LEWIS FRE 058 FREDERIC
GETZENDENNER, MARGARET FRE 007 FREDERIC
GETZENDENNER, PHINEAS FRE 028 FREDERIC
GETZENDENNER, SUSAN FRE 007 FREDERIC
GETZENDINNER, CHARLES FRE 014 FREDERIC
GETZENDINNER, SARAH FRE 074 FREDERIC
GETZENHORST, FREDERICK BAL 252 2ND WARD
GETZFORD, CHRISTIAN BAL 018 9TH WARD
GEVALES, JOSEPH TAL 083 ST MICHA
GEVANS, MARY WOR 316 2ND E DI
GEVANS, PETER WOR 261 BERLIN I
GEVIN, ROBERT* TAL 014 EASTON O
GEW, REBECCA MGM 337 CRACKLIN
GEYER, SAMUEL FRE 240 NEW MARK
GEYER, WILLIAM BAL 228 19TH WAR
GEYER,ELIZABETH FRE 044 FREDERIC
GEYESTER, SAMUEL WAS 014 WILLIAMS
GEYLIN, GERTRUDE BAL 163 19TH WAR
GGORDON, CATHERINE ALL 235 CUMBERLA
GHANESICKS, CONRAD BAL 252 2ND WARD
GHEISELIN, WILLIAM ANN 316 1ST DIST
GHEISLIN, ELIZABETH ANN 439 HOWARD D
GHER, SOPHIA WAS 123 2ND DIST
GHERDING, JOHN BAL 220 2ND WARD
GHESLIN, ROBERT PRI 067 NOTTINGH
GHIESLIN, ARCHIBALD ANN 459 HOWARD D
GHILDS, GEORGE BAL 073 2ND DIST
GHRATZ, JOHN BAL 226 2ND WARD
GHREE, MARY WAS 106 2ND DIST
GHUN, BRIDGET BAL 241 12TH WAR
GIAINER, JAOCB * BAL 165 2ND DIST
GIBB, ADAM BAL 289 17TH WAR
GIBB, JACOB BAL 292 7TH WARD
GIBBERT, FRANCIS G. BAL 128 1ST WARD
GIBBERT, L. BAL 139 1ST WARD
GIBBIN, JAMES F. BAL 127 1ST WARD
GIBBINS, ANN ST 306 1ST E DI
GIBBINS, JOHN BAL 028 18TH WAR
GIBBINS, MARY BAL 463 1ST DIST
GIBBONS, ANDREW BAL 411 1ST DIST
GIBBONS, ANN BAL 132 2ND DIST
GIBBONS, ANN ELIZABETH QUE 161 2ND E DI
GIBBONS, ANNA FRE 077 FREDERIC
GIBBONS, ARCADIA BAL 026 9TH WARD
GIBBONS, AUGUSTUS F. BAL 378 1ST DIST
GIBBONS, AUSTIN WAS 064 2ND SUBD
GIBBONS, CHARLES CEC 107 3RD E DI
GIBBONS, DANIEL PRI 046 AQUASCO
GIBBONS, DAVID FRE 076 FREDERIC
GIBBONS, ELIZA PRI 052 AQUASCO
GIBBONS, ELIZA BAL 362 8TH WARD
GIBBONS, FANNY SOM 401 BRINKLEY
GIBBONS, FRANCIS A. BAL 391 8TH WARD
GIBBONS, GEORGE T. PRI 049 AQUASCO
GIBBONS, JAMES QUE 164 2ND E DI
GIBBONS, JAMES BAL 151 1ST WARD
GIBBONS, JAMES BAL 139 2ND DIST
GIBBONS, JAMES SOM 436 PRINCESS
GIBBONS, JAMES H. PRI 052 AQUASCO
GIBBONS, JAMES H.S. PRI 059 NOTTINGH
GIBBONS, JANE BAL 337 1ST DIST
GIBBONS, JEREMIAH PRI 064 NOTTINGH
GIBBONS, JOHN FRE 104 FREDERIC
GIBBONS, JOHN LL M.D. BAL 251 1ST DIST
GIBBONS, JOHN S. CHA 294 BOJANTOW
GIBBONS, JOSEPH PRI 047 AQUASCO
GIBBONS, JOSHUA BAL 349 3RD WARD
GIBBONS, JULIA BAL 337 1ST DIST
GIBBONS, MARIA CHA 232 HILLTOP
GIBBONS, MARTHA BAL 062 15TH WAR
GIBBONS, MARY BAL 200 19TH WAR
GIBBONS, MARY P. FRE 065 FREDERIC
GIBBONS, MICHAEL ANN 472 HOWARD D
GIBBONS, MILES FRE 319 MIDDLETO
GIBBONS, MILES PRI 074 MARLBROU
GIBBONS, OSWELL CHA 294 BOJANTOW
GIBBONS, PATRICK ALL 052 10TH E.D
GIBBONS, PETER W. BAL 342 1ST DIST
GIBBONS, RILEY SOM 404 BRINKLEY
GIBBONS, RILEY SOM 466 HANGARY
GIBBONS, SAMUEL BAL 424 3RD WARD
GIBBONS, THEODORE SOM 401 BRINKLEY
GIBBONS, THOMAS BAL 022 9TH WARD
GIBBONS, THOMAS BAL 097 15TH WAR
GIBBONS, THOMAS B. CAL 049 3RD DIST
GIBBONS, THOMAS E. BAL 120 1ST WARD
GIBBONS, WENNA BAL 205 6TH WARD
GIBBONS, WILLIAM ANN 501 HOWARD D
GIBBONS, WILLIAM CHA 294 BOJANTOW
GIBBONS, WILLIAM M. BAL 158 19TH WAR
GIBBS, ABRAM L. CEC 167 6TH E DI
GIBBS, ABRAM-BLACK QUE 169 2ND E DI
GIBBS, ALEXANDER BAL 130 16TH WAR
GIBBS, ALEXANDER BAL 311 12TH WAR
GIBBS, ANN BAL 167 16TH WAR
GIBBS, ARCHIBALD C. ANN 303 1ST DIST
GIBBS, BENJAMIN BAL 192 17TH WAR
GIBBS, CATHERINE CEC 135 6TH E DI
GIBBS, CHARLES H. BAL 037 4TH WARD
GIBBS, CHARLES S. BAL 300 17TH WAR
GIBBS, CLINTON QUE 249 5TH E DI
GIBBS, CORSEY* TAL 001 EASTON D
GIBBS, DRUSILLA A. BAL 013 15TH WAR
GIBBS, E. BAL 138 5TH WARD
GIBBS, EDMOND W. TAL 068 EASTON T
GIBBS, EDWARD A. BAL 037 4TH WARD
GIBBS, ELIZA SOM 467 TRAPPE D
GIBBS, ELIZABETH WAS 151 2ND DIST
GIBBS, ELIZABETH BAL 454 14TH WAR
GIBBS, EMILY BAL 228 17TH WAR
GIBBS, FRANK TAL 004 EASTON D
GIBBS, GEORGE PRI 069 MARLBROU
GIBBS, HARRIETT BAL 117 11TH WAR
GIBBS, HENRY BAL 248 17TH WAR
GIBBS, HESTER ANN BAL 383 13TH WAR
GIBBS, HETTY WOR 316 2ND E DI
GIBBS, J.B. ALL 234 CUMBERLA
GIBBS, JAMES BAL 156 16TH WAR
GIBBS, JAMES BAL 313 7TH WARD
GIBBS, JAMES ALL 195 CUMBERLA
GIBBS, JAMES-BLACK QUE 197 3RD E DI
GIBBS, JAMES-BLACK CAR 104 NO TWP L
GIBBS, JAMES-BLACK CAR 095 NO TWP L
GIBBS, JESSE WOR 183 6TH E DI
GIBBS, JIM-BLACK QUE 182 3RD E DI
GIBBS, JOHN BAL 433 8TH WARD
GIBBS, JOHN BAL 356 3RD WARD
GIBBS, JOHN BAL 125 1ST WARD
GIBBS, JOHN V. PRI 105 PISCATAW
GIBBS, LEWIS BAL 246 6TH WARD
GIBBS, MAHALA ALL 242 CUMBERLA
GIBBS, MARGARET CEC 011 ELKTON 3
GIBBS, MARIA BAL 424 14TH WAR
GIBBS, MARY BAL 013 15TH WAR
GIBBS, MARY PRI 077 MARLBROU
GIBBS, MARY QUE 193 3RD E DI
GIBBS, MARY WOR 322 1ST E DI
GIBBS, MARY A. CEC 036 CHESAPEA
GIBBS, MARY E. BAL 248 17TH WAR
GIBBS, MATILDA-BLACK QUE 183 3RD E DI
GIBBS, NICHOLAS BAL 210 2ND WARD
GIBBS, PERRY-BLACK CAR 166 NO TWP L
GIBBS, RACHEL BAL 375 13TH WAR
GIBBS, REBECCA BAL 118 15TH WAR
GIBBS, RICHARD QUE 207 3RD E DI
GIBBS, RICHARD QUE 249 5TH E DI
GIBBS, RICHARD QUE 250 5TH E DI
GIBBS, ROBERT BAL 114 15TH WAR
GIBBS, ROSANNA BAL 418 14TH WAR
GIBBS, SAMUEL BAL 253 20TH WAR
GIBBS, SAMUEL TAL 009 EASTON D
GIBBS, SPENCER BAL 409 1ST DIST
GIBBS, SUSAN CEC 147 PORT DUP
GIBBS, WILLIAM J. FRE 441 8TH E DI
GIBENS, CHARLES FRE 272 NEW MARK
GIBERSON, EZEKIEL CEC 126 5TH E DI
GIBERSON, JOHN CEC 040 CHESAPEA
GIBERTON, M. BAL 321 12TH WAR
GIBES, CAROLINE WOR 305 2ND E DI
GIBLIN, PATRICK BAL 184 11TH WAR
GIBNER, GEORGE BAL 166 11TH WAR
GIBNER, SARAH C. WAS 122 2ND DIST
GIBNEY, ELIZABETH CEC 158 PORT DUP
GIBNEY, J. BAL 141 1ST WARD
GIBNEY, RICHARDS BAL 072 10TH WAR
GIBNEY, THOMAS BAL 138 5TH WARD
GIBONS, ALEXANDER PRI 047 AQUASCO
GIBOSN, ABRAM BAL 096 2ND DIST
GIBS, GEORGE WOR 310 2ND E DI
GIBS, HARRIET MGM 387 ROCKERLE
GIBS, JOHN HAR 199 3RD DIST
GIBS, JOHN WOR 309 2ND E DI
GIBS, JOHN WOR 309 2ND E DI
GIBS, JOSEPH CEC 033 CHESAPEA
GIBS, JOSEPH-BLACK CAR 099 NO TWP L
GIBS, SARAH BAL 428 1ST DIST
GIBSON, ADAM CEC 188 7TH E DI
GIBSON, AGNESS BAL 463 1ST DIST
GIBSON, ALEXANDER BAL 213 6TH WARD
GIBSON, ALLY MGM 379 ROCKERLE
GIBSON, ANDREW CEC 111 4TH E DI
GIBSON, ANN CAL 038 2ND DIST
GIBSON, ANN BAL 242 20TH WAR
GIBSON, ANN B. CAL 038 2ND DIST
GIBSON, ANN L. BAL 415 14TH WAR
GIBSON, AUGUSTUS CAL 046 3RD DIST
GIBSON, BENJAMIN CEC 170 6TH E DI
GIBSON, BENJAMIN BAL 302 3RD WARD
GIBSON, BIDDY TAL 067 EASTON T
GIBSON, BILL-BLACK QUE 190 3RD E DI
GIBSON, CATHARINE TAL 026 EASTON D
GIBSON, CHARLES BAL 402 3RD WARD
GIBSON, CHARLES BAL 340 7TH WARD
GIBSON, CHARLES C. BAL 320 20TH WAR
GIBSON, CHARLES T. BAL 281 7TH WARD
GIBSON, CHARLES-MULATTO QUE 161 2ND E DI
GIBSON, DANIEL TAL 049 EASTON T
GIBSON, DANIEL-MULATTO CAR 093 NO TWP L
GIBSON, DAVID BAL 057 10TH WAR
GIBSON, DAVID BAL 113 1ST WARD
GIBSON, DOLLY TAL 106 ST MICHA
GIBSON, DORRINGTON QUE 245 5TH E DI
GIBSON, EDWARD TAL 120 ST MICHA
GIBSON, EDWARD BAL 077 10TH WAR
GIBSON, EDWARD BAL 322 7TH WARD
GIBSON, EDWARD-BLACK CAR 105 NO TWP L
GIBSON, ELIJAH ALL 184 9TH E.D.
GIBSON, ELIJAH SOM 453 DAMES QU
GIBSON, ELIZA BAL 256 6TH WARD
GIBSON, ELIZA BAL 228 6TH WARD
GIBSON, ELIZA HAR 135 2ND DIST
GIBSON, ELIZABETH BAL 211 11TH WAR
GIBSON, ELIZABETH CAL 046 3RD DIST
GIBSON, ELIZABETH BAL 461 14TH WAR
GIBSON, ELIZABETH BAL 146 11TH WAR
GIBSON, ELIZABETH BAL 106 1ST WARD
GIBSON, ELIZABETH SOM 450 DAMES QU
GIBSON, ELIZABETH A. BAL 128 16TH WAR
GIBSON, ELLEN BAL 239 1ST DIST
GIBSON, ELLEN CAR 067 NO TWP L
GIBSON, EMELINE QUE 145 1ST E DI
GIBSON, EMILY SOM 420 PRINCESS
GIBSON, FANNIE H. FRE 045 FREDERIC
GIBSON, FRANCIS A. TAL 095 ST MICHA
GIBSON, GABRIEL BAL 378 3RD WARD
GIBSON, GARRISON TAL 030 EASTON D
GIBSON, GARRISON TAL 073 EASTON T
GIBSON, GEORGE TAL 028 EASTON D
GIBSON, GEORGE BAL 144 1ST WARD
GIBSON, GEORGE BAL 139 1ST WARD
GIBSON, GEORGE BAL 103 5TH WARD
GIBSON, GEORGE BAL 230 19TH WAR
GIBSON, GEORGE CAR 293 7TH DIST
GIBSON, GEORGE L. BAL 144 11TH WAR
GIBSON, GEORGE W. ST 315 4TH E DI
GIBSON, GEROGE BAL 319 20TH WAR
GIBSON, GOLDSBOROUGH BAL 126 16TH WAR
GIBSON, H. D. BAL 332 1ST DIST
GIBSON, H.M. BAL 242 20TH WAR
GIBSON, HARRIOTT TAL 098 ST MICHA
GIBSON, HARRY BAL 105 1ST WARD
GIBSON, HENRIETTA CAR 237 UNION TO
GIBSON, HENRIETTA HAR 204 3RD DIST
GIBSON, HENRY BAL 341 13TH WAR
GIBSON, HENRY BAL 300 3RD WARD
GIBSON, HENRY TAL 039 EASTON D
GIBSON, HENRY SOM 449 DAMES QU
GIBSON, HUGH B. CEC 189 7TH E DI
GIBSON, ISAAC CEC 045 1ST E DI
GIBSON, ISAAC BAL 155 5TH WARD
GIBSON, ISAAC-BLACK CAR 168 NO TWP L
GIBSON, ISAAC-BLACK CAR 070 NO TWP L
GIBSON, ISACK TAL 045 EASTON T
GIBSON, ISAIH B. * TAL 114 ST MICHA
GIBSON, JACOB DOR 452 1ST DIST
GIBSON, JACOB HAR 054 1ST DIST
GIBSON, JACOB BAL 156 16TH WAR
GIBSON, JAMES BAL 309 3RD WARD
GIBSON, JAMES BAL 377 1ST DIST
GIBSON, JAMES BAL 104 1ST WARD
GIBSON, JAMES BAL 022 1ST WARD
GIBSON, JAMES BAL 103 2ND DIST
GIBSON, JAMES ANN 447 HOWARD D
GIBSON, JAMES BAL 161 11TH WAR
GIBSON, JAMES BAL 355 13TH WAR
GIBSON, JAMES CEC 143 7TH E DI
GIBSON, JAMES BAL 224 17TH WAR
GIBSON, JAMES WAS 158 2ND DIST
GIBSON, JAMES A. BAL 314 7TH WARD
GIBSON, JAMES H. TAL 046 EASTON T
GIBSON, JANE BAL 163 16TH WAR
GIBSON, JANE-BLACK QUE 193 3RD E DI
GIBSON, JESSE QUE 152 1ST E DI
GIBSON, JOHN HAR 178 3RD DIST
GIBSON, JOHN BAL 071 4TH WARD
GIBSON, JOHN CAL 056 3RD DIST
GIBSON, JOHN FRE 064 FREDERIC
GIBSON, JOHN MGM 388 ROCKERLE
GIBSON, JOHN BAL 237 20TH WAR
GIBSON, JOHN CEC 197 7TH E DI
GIBSON, JOHN BAL 011 18TH WAR
GIBSON, JOHN QUE 248 5TH E DI
GIBSON, JOHN TAL 112 ST MICHA
GIBSON, JOHN BAL 047 9TH WARD
GIBSON, JOHN ALL 217 CUMBERLA
GIBSON, JOHN BAL 254 1ST DIST
GIBSON, JOHN BAL 178 2ND DIST
GIBSON, JOHN BAL 072 1ST WARD
GIBSON, JOHN BAL 365 1ST DIST
GIBSON, JOHN BAL 103 5TH WARD
GIBSON, JOHN BAL 139 1ST WARD
GIBSON, JOHN CHEW TAL 084 ST MICHA
GIBSON, JOHN L. BAL 188 2ND WARD
GIBSON, JOHN R. BAL 286 7TH WARD
GIBSON, JOHN RJ. TAL 114 ST MICHA
GIBSON, JOHN W. QUE 231 4TH E DI
GIBSON, JOHN W. CAR 096 NO TWP L
GIBSON, JOHN-BLACK ST 335 4TH E DI
GIBSON, JOSEPH QUE 251 5TH E DI
GIBSON, JOSEPH TAL 040 EASTON D
GIBSON, JOSEPH CEC 106 3RD E DI
GIBSON, JOSEPH SOM 420 PRINCESS
GIBSON, JOSEPH BAL 144 1ST WARD
GIBSON, JOSEPH BAL 177 16TH WAR
GIBSON, JOSEPH L. BAL 297 20TH WAR
GIBSON, JOSHUA FRE 045 FREDERIC
GIBSON, JOSIAH BAL 343 3RD WARD
GIBSON, LOUISA BAL 205 17TH WAR
GIBSON, LUCINDA BAL 086 4TH WARD
GIBSON, LUCINDA BAL 121 16TH WAR
GIBSON, LUCUS CAR 273 WESTMINS
GIBSON, MACKALL CAL 043 3RD DIST
GIBSON, MALACHI BAL 040 15TH WAR
GIBSON, MALVINA BAL 413 14TH WAR
GIBSON, MARGARET BAL 196 19TH WAR
GIBSON, MARIA BAL 444 14TH WAR
GIBSON, MARIA BAL 340 3RD WARD
GIBSON, MARTHA BAL 365 1ST DIST
GIBSON, MARTHA BAL 242 6TH WARD
GIBSON, MARY BAL 166 11TH WAR
GIBSON, MARY BAL 247 12TH WAR
GIBSON, MARY BAL 043 1ST WARD
GIBSON, MARY BAL 051 4TH WARD
GIBSON, MARY BAL 253 17TH WAR
GIBSON, MARY BAL 108 18TH WAR
GIBSON, MARY TAL 056 EASTON D
GIBSON, MARY A. BAL 424 14TH WAR
GIBSON, MARY A. CAL 042 3RD DIST
GIBSON, MARY A. CEC 112 4TH E DI
GIBSON, MARY A. HAR 146 3RD DIST
GIBSON, MARY A. BAL 287 7TH WARD
GIBSON, MARY G. BAL 137 11TH WAR
GIBSON, MARY-BLACK QUE 188 3RD E DI
GIBSON, METILDA DOR 325 1ST DIST
GIBSON, NASE TAL 074 EASTON T
GIBSON, NASE TAL 077 EASTON T
GIBSON, NELLY CAL 024 2ND DIST
GIBSON, NICHOLAS TAL 077 EASTON T
GIBSON, PATRICK BAL 155 11TH WAR
GIBSON, PATRICK BAL 155 11TH WAR
GIBSON, PERRY TAL 049 EASTON T
GIBSON, PERRY BAL 011 9TH WARD
GIBSON, PERRY BAL 165 1ST WARD
GIBSON, PETER BAL 114 2ND DIST
GIBSON, PETER CAL 048 3RD DIST
GIBSON, PHILEMON BAL 240 20TH WAR
GIBSON, PHILLIS BAL 025 15TH WAR
GIBSON, PRISCILLA BAL 406 1ST DIST
GIBSON, PRISCILLA CAL 046 3RD DIST
GIBSON, PRISILLA TAL 036 EASTON D
GIBSON, REBECCA CEC 113 4TH E DI
GIBSON, RESIN BAL 370 3RD WARD
GIBSON, RICHARD J. TAL 113 ST MICHA
GIBSON, RICHARD-BLACK CAR 093 NO TWP L
GIBSON, ROBERT BAL 055 18TH WAR

Name	County	Page	District
GIBSON, ROBERT	BAL	275	20TH WAR
GIBSON, ROBERT	BAL	376	13TH WAR
GIBSON, ROBERT	BAL	376	13TH WAR
GIBSON, ROBERT	TAL	115	ST MICHA
GIBSON, ROBERT	TAL	024	EASTON D
GIBSON, ROBERT	PRI	007	BLADENSB
GIBSON, ROBERT	BAL	147	5TH WARD
GIBSON, ROBERT	BAL	183	16TH WAR
GIBSON, ROBERT F.	BAL	292	3RD WARD
GIBSON, ROBERT*	DOR	377	1ST DIST
GIBSON, RODOLPH M.	ST	316	4TH E DI
GIBSON, SALLY-BLACK	CAR	074	NO TWP L
GIBSON, SAMUEL	SOM	419	PRINCESS
GIBSON, SARA	BAL	068	4TH WARD
GIBSON,	CEC	005	ELKTON 3
GIBS	QUE	231	4TH E DI
GIBSO ...K	CAR	071	NO TWP L
GIBSO	BAL	243	12TH WAR
GIBSON	BAL	155	11TH WAR
GIBSON	BAL	155	11TH WAR
GIBSON	CAL	045	3RD DIST
GIBSON	BAL	310	7TH WARD
GIBSON, ...CK	CAR	142	NO TWP L
GIBSON,	FRE	115	CREAGERS
GIBSON,	BAL	102	10TH WAR
GIBSON,	BAL	175	2ND WARD
GIBSON,	BAL	200	6TH WARD
GIBSON, T	BAL	023	2ND DIST
GIBSON, TH ... H.	BAL	145	1ST WARD
GIBSON, TH ... H.	BAL	232	1ST DIST
GIBSON, TH ...S-BLACK	QUE	177	2ND E DI
GIBSON, W.J.	QUE	182	3RD E DI
GIBSON, WALTER	BAL	342	3RD WARD
GIBSON, WILLAIM	BAL	099	2ND DIST
GIBSON, WILLAIM	CAR	333	MANCHEST
GIBSON, WILLIAM	CEC	113	4TH E DI
GIBSON, WILLIAM	BAL	032	4TH WARD
GIBSON, WILLIAM	CEC	026	ELKTON 3
GIBSON, WILLIAM	CEC	176	7TH E DI
GIBSON, WILLIAM	CEC	208	7TH E DI
GIBSON, WILLIAM	DOR	314	1ST DIST
GIBSON, WILLIAM	BAL	140	2ND DIST
GIBSON, WILLIAM	BAL	102	5TH WARD
GIBSON, WILLIAM	BAL	290	7TH WARD
GIBSON, WILLIAM	BAL	024	15TH WAR
GIBSON, WILLIAM	SOM	464	HANGARY
GIBSON, WILLIAM	TAL	017	EASTON D
GIBSON, WILLIAM	TAL	022	EASTON D
GIBSON, WILLIAM A.	CAL	040	3RD DIST
GIBSON, WILLIAM F.	BAL	412	14TH WAR
GIBSON, WILLIAM H.	CAL	042	3RD DIST
GIBSON, WILLIAM H.	TAL	097	ST MICHA
GIBSON, WOLLMAN	QUE	229	4TH E DI
GIBSONS, WILLIAM	BAL	411	1ST DIST
GICKLE, GEORGE	BAL	087	1ST WARD
GICKLE, HENRY	BAL	086	1ST WARD
GICKLER, MARY	BAL	413	3RD WARD
GIDDEOSS, JOHN	MGM	441	CLARKSTR
GIDDES, ALEXANDER	BAL	297	12TH WAR
GIDDES, ANDREW	BAL	092	2ND DIST
GIDDINGS, ALFRED	BAL	040	15TH WAR
GIDDINGS, BENJAMIN	BAL	077	10TH WAR
GIDDINGS, C.G.	WAS	021	2ND SUBD
GIDDINGS, ELIZABETH	MGM	357	BERRYS D
GIDDINGS, FANNY	ANN	521	HOWARD D
GIDDINGS, FRANCIS	BAL	131	1ST WARD
GIDDINGS, GEORGE	PRI	009	BLADENSB
GIDDINGS, J.E.	WAS	021	2ND SUBD
GIDDINGS, JOHN THOMAS	MGM	348	BERRYS D
GIDDINGS, MARIA	MGM	365	BERRYS D
GIDDINGS, MARY E.-BLACK	FRE	419	8TH E DI
GIDDINGS, NANCY	BAL	046	2ND DIST
GIDDINGS, SERENER	FRE	223	BUCKEYST
GIDDINON, WILLIAM	CHA	261	MIDDLETO
GIDENER, JONATHAN	CEC	191	5TH E DI
GIDEON, ANGELIC	BAL	205	11TH WAR
GIDER, JOHN	BAL	203	6TH WARD
GIDINGS, JOHN	HAR	202	3RD DIST
GIDLEY, DAVID	BAL	092	15TH WAR
GIDLEY, MARTHA J.	BAL	092	15TH WAR
GIDLEY, MARY	BAL	028	15TH WAR
GIEBLAND, ROSA	BAL	050	4TH WARD
GIER, JOSEPH A.	BAL	027	9TH WARD
GIES, JOHN	BAL	221	1ST DIST
GIESE, JAMES H.	BAL	279	20TH WAR
GIESE, WILLIAM H.	BAL	313	3RD WARD
GIESLAR, ELIZABETH A.	CEC	146	PORT DUP
GIESZ, HENRY	BAL	196	6TH WARD
GIFFEN, ANDREW	BAL	374	1ST DIST
GIFFEN, PAMELIA	BAL	373	1ST DIST
GIFFEN, WILLIAM	BAL	373	1ST DIST
GIFFEN, WILLIAM	BAL	081	18TH WAR
GIFFIN, ELIZA	DOR	404	1ST DIST
GIFFIN, GEORGE	BAL	147	16TH WAR
GIFFIN, SARAH	BAL	258	17TH WAR
GIFFORD, ALEXANDER	BAL	307	7TH WARD
GIFFORD, HUGH	BAL	310	7TH WARD
GIFFORD, JAMES	BAL	343	7TH WARD
GIFFORD, SAMUEL	BAL	153	19TH WAR
GIFFORD, STEPHEN	CEC	164	6TH E DI
GIFFORD, THOMAS	BAL	307	7TH WARD
GIFFORD, THOMAS	BAL	123	1ST WARD
GIFFORD, WILLIAM	BAL	173	1ST WARD
GIFHORN, WILLIAM	BAL	464	14TH WAR
GIFT, ADAM	ALL	188	9TH E.D.
GIFT, JOHN	WAS	071	2ND SUBD
GIFT, JOHN	WAS	062	2ND SUBD
GIFT, SAMUEL	WAS	061	2ND SUBD
GIFTON, JOHN	PRI	080	QUEEN AN
GIGGERS, JOHN	WAS	201	1ST DIST
GIGGINS, JAMES	BAL	104	1ST WARD
GIGGS, LOUISA J.	KEN	285	3RD DIST
GIGUS, ELIZABETH	WAS	198	1ST DIST
GIHAGAN, BRIDGET	BAL	127	11TH WAR
GIL, GEORGE	BAL	032	1ST WARD
GILAN, THOMAS	BAL	160	11TH WAR
GILASPIE, WILLIAM B.	HAR	170	3RD DIST
GILASPY, CATHARINE	BAL	360	1ST DIST
GILBACK, GEORGE JR.	BAL	030	9TH WARD
GILBAD, GEORGE	BAL	352	3RD WARD
GILBAUGH, BARNEY	BAL	390	3RD WARD
GILBAUGH, SARAH	BAL	321	3RD WARD
GILBEE, CATHRINE	BAL	092	18TH WAR
GILBENT, JOHN W.	FRE	250	NEW MARK
GILBERT, A.	BAL	227	12TH WAR
GILBERT, ABRAHAM A.	HAR	072	1ST DIST
GILBERT, ADAM	CAR	296	7TH DIST
GILBERT, AMELIA	BAL	295	12TH WAR
GILBERT, AMOS	HAR	114	2ND DIST
GILBERT, ANN	CEC	169	6TH E DI
GILBERT, ANN	BAL	408	14TH WAR
GILBERT, BELINDA	BAL	129	2ND DIST
GILBERT, BENETT	HAR	161	3RD DIST
GILBERT, BENJAMIN	FRE	023	FREDERIC
GILBERT, CAROLINE	BAL	138	5TH WARD
GILBERT, CARVIL L.	HAR	162	3RD DIST
GILBERT, CHARLES	HAR	118	2ND DIST
GILBERT, CHRISTIAN	WAS	043	2ND SUBD
GILBERT, COMFOT	HAR	161	3RD DIST
GILBERT, DANIEL	KEN	255	1ST DIST
GILBERT, DAVID	FRE	037	FREDERIC
GILBERT, DAVID	CAR	396	2ND DIST
GILBERT, DAVID	WAS	187	BOONSBOR
GILBERT, EDWARD	BAL	339	13TH WAR
GILBERT, ELI	FRE	286	WOODSBOR
GILBERT, EMELINE	BAL	130	2ND DIST
GILBERT, EMMA	BAL	058	1ST WARD
GILBERT, EPHRAIM	HAR	165	3RD DIST
GILBERT, EVE	WAS	236	CAVETOWN
GILBERT, EZRA	FRE	369	CATOCTIN
GILBERT, GEORGE	HAR	162	3RD DIST
GILBERT, GEORGE	FRE	286	WOODSBOR
GILBERT, GEORGE	HAR	203	3RD DIST
GILBERT, GEORGE	KEN	292	3RD DIST
GILBERT, GEORGE A.	FRE	043	FREDERIC
GILBERT, GEORGE T.	HAR	088	2ND DIST
GILBERT, GEORGE W.	WAS	280	LEITERSB
GILBERT, HENRY	HAR	119	2ND DIST
GILBERT, HENRY	HAR	205	3RD DIST
GILBERT, HEZEKIAH	WAS	093	2ND SUBD
GILBERT, ISAAC	CAR	287	7TH DIST
GILBERT, ISAAC	FRE	340	MIDDLETO
GILBERT, ISAAC	FRE	339	MIDDLETO
GILBERT, ISRAEL	FRE	370	CATOCTIN
GILBERT, JACB	WAS	281	LEITERSB
GILBERT, JACOB	WAS	279	LEITERSB
GILBERT, JACOB	CEC	077	NORTHEAS
GILBERT, JAMES	CAR	395	2ND DIST
GILBERT, JAMES	HAR	207	3RD DIST
GILBERT, JAMES	KEN	273	1ST DIST
GILBERT, JAMES	KEN	269	1ST DIST
GILBERT, JAMES	BAL	125	2ND DIST
GILBERT, JANE	BAL	277	7TH WARD
GILBERT, JANE	HAR	058	1ST DIST
GILBERT, JANE	BAL	428	14TH WAR
GILBERT, JARRETT	HAR	149	3RD DIST
GILBERT, JOEL H.	HAR	192	3RD DIST
GILBERT, JOHN	CEC	169	6TH E DI
GILBERT, JOHN	HAR	020	1ST DIST
GILBERT, JOHN	HAR	003	1ST DIST
GILBERT, JOHN	WAS	232	1ST DIST
GILBERT, JOHN B.	FRE	125	CREAGERS
GILBERT, JOHN L.	WAS	236	CAVETOWN
GILBERT, JOHN N.	HAR	112	2ND DIST
GILBERT, JOSEPH	FRE	415	8TH E DI
GILBERT, LEVIN A.	HAR	128	2ND DIST
GILBERT, LEVINA	BAL	197	11TH WAR
GILBERT, LEWIS	BAL	292	12TH WAR
GILBERT, LEWIS	BAL	464	14TH WAR
GILBERT, LEWIS-BLACK	CAR	087	NO TWP L
GILBERT, LOUISA	HAR	086	2ND DIST
GILBERT, MARTIN	BAL	228	17TH WAR
GILBERT, MARY	HAR	115	2ND DIST
GILBERT, MARY A.	HAR	086	2ND DIST
GILBERT, MARY A.	FRE	339	MIDDLETO
GILBERT, MARY C.	WAS	237	CAVETOWN
GILBERT, MICHAEL	HAR	162	3RD DIST
GILBERT, MICHAEL	FRE	286	WOODSBOR
GILBERT, MRS.	BAL	213	19TH WAR
GILBERT, PACKER	BAL	169	11TH WAR
GILBERT, PARKER	HAR	167	3RD DIST
GILBERT, SAMUEL	CAR	398	2ND DIST
GILBERT, SARAH	HAR	167	3RD DIST
GILBERT, SARAH	BAL	117	2ND DIST
GILBERT, SHADARACK R.	HAR	017	1ST DIST
GILBERT, SOPHIAH	FRE	286	WOODSBOR
GILBERT, STEPHEN	CEC	113	4TH E DI
GILBERT, TAYLOR	HAR	162	3RD DIST
GILBERT, THOMAS	CAR	394	2ND DIST
GILBERT, THOMAS	CAR	230	5TH DIST
GILBERT, THOMAS	FRE	390	PETERSVI
GILBERT, THOMAS	BAL	114	1ST WARD
GILBERT, THOMAS L.	BAL	434	1ST DIST
GILBERT, WILLIAM	BAL	292	12TH WAR
GILBERT, WILLIAM	CAR	380	2ND DIST
GILBERT, WILLIAM	HAR	173	3RD DIST
GILBERT, WILLIAM	FRE	286	WOODSBOR
GILBERT, WILLIAM E.	BAL	131	18TH WAR
GILBERT,HENRY	CAR	398	2ND DIST
GILBERTHORP, CATHERINE	BAL	407	3RD WARD
GILBERTHORPE, MARY A.	BAL	098	10TH WAR
GILBEY, BRIDGETT	BAL	034	4TH WARD
GILBONS, MICHAEL	BAL	097	2ND DIST
GILBORT, CHARLES	HAR	195	3RD DIST
GILBORT, ELIZABETH	HAR	195	3RD DIST
GILBORT, JARVIS	HAR	192	3RD DIST
GILBOY, JOHN	ALL	129	4TH E.D.
GILBRIDE, N.	BAL	163	1ST WARD
GILBSON, GEORGE	BAL	089	2ND DIST
GILDAY, MARY	WAS	029	2ND SUBD
GILDEA, ANN ELIZA	BAL	189	11TH WAR
GILDEA, JOHN	BAL	206	6TH WARD
GILDEN, ANN	BAL	189	11TH WAR
GILDEN, ELIZABETH	BAL	125	2ND DIST
GILDEN, FRANCIS	BAL	288	12TH WAR
GILDEN, JOHN H.	BAL	182	16TH WAR
GILDER, JAMES	BAL	393	14TH WAR
GILDER, P.C.L.	QUE	188	3RD E DI
GILDERSLEVE, GEORGE	BAL	157	11TH WAR
GILDERWAY, JOHN	CHA	243	HILLTOP
GILDESRF, AMIN *	CAR	338	6TH DIST
GILDS, GEORGE	FRE	092	FREDERIC
GILE, ESTER	ANN	483	HOWARD D
GILE, EZEKIEL C.	BAL	397	8TH WARD
GILE, MARY E.	CAR	149	NO TWP L
GILE,JOHN	BAL	236	2ND WARD
GILES, AARON	HAR	125	2ND DIST
GILES, AMOS	HAR	124	2ND DIST
GILES, AQUILLA	BAL	073	2ND DIST
GILES, BILL	HAR	093	2ND DIST
GILES, CAROLINE	BAL	255	17TH WAR
GILES, CHARLES H.	HAR	075	BEL AIR
GILES, DANIEL	WAS	158	HAGERSTO
GILES, DEBORAH	BAL	260	6TH WARD
GILES, EDWARD	BAL	244	20TH WAR
GILES, ELIZA	HAR	051	1ST DIST
GILES, ELIZABETH	BAL	202	19TH WAR
GILES, ELIZABETH	WAS	130	HAGERSTO
GILES, ELSY	BAL	202	19TH WAR
GILES, EMERY	BAL	202	19TH WAR
GILES, GEORGE	CEC	099	3RD E DI
GILES, GEORGE	ANN	292	ANNAPOLI
GILES, GUSTAVUS	BAL	137	16TH WAR
GILES, HANAH	BAL	061	2ND DIST
GILES, HARIETT	DOR	371	3RD DIVI
GILES, HARRIETT	HAR	125	2ND DIST
GILES, HENRIETTA	BAL	041	4TH WARD
GILES, HENRY H.	BAL	344	7TH WARD
GILES, ISAAC H.	SOM	527	QUANTICO
GILES, JACOB	HAR	056	1ST DIST
GILES, JACOB	HAR	091	2ND DIST
GILES, JAMES	BAL	278	2ND WARD
GILES, JOHN	CEC	015	ELKTON 3
GILES, JOHN	HAR	121	2ND DIST
GILES, JOHN	SOM	443	DAMES QU
GILES, JOHN ALLEN-BLACK	QUE	202	3RD E DI
GILES, JOHN P.	SOM	509	BARREN C
GILES, JOHN R.	BAL	069	10TH WAR
GILES, JOHN W.	BAL	030	19TH WAR
GILES, JOSEPH	BAL	030	18TH WAR
GILES, JOSEPH	WAS	158	HAGERSTO
GILES, JOSEPH	WAS	044	2ND SUBD
GILES, JOSIAH	BAL	051	15TH WAR
GILES, LYDNIA A.	BAL	317	7TH WARD
GILES, LYPHLET	SOM	527	QUANTICO
GILES, MAHALEY	BAL	252	20TH WAR
GILES, MARTHA	BAL	234	2ND WARD
GILES, MARY	BAL	130	5TH WARD
GILES, MARY	CEC	012	ELKTON 3
GILES, MARY	BAL	202	19TH WAR
GILES, MARY	HAR	003	1ST DIST
GILES, MARY	BAL	135	11TH WAR
GILES, NATHAN	BAL	134	16TH WAR
GILES, RACHEL	ANN	496	HOWARD D
GILES, REBECCA	BAL	073	2ND DIST
GILES, SAL	HAR	048	1ST DIST
GILES, SAMUEL	HAR	099	2ND DIST
GILES, SCIPIO	HAR	124	2ND DIST
GILES, SIDNEY	BAL	186	6TH WARD
GILES, SUSAN	BAL	008	EASTERN
GILES, SUSAN	HAR	119	2ND DIST
GILES, SYDNEY	SOM	525	QUANTICO
GILES, THOMAS	SOM	514	BARREN C
GILES, THOMAS	HAR	086	2ND DIST
GILES, THOMAS	HAR	106	2ND DIST
GILES, THOMAS	CEC	041	CHESAPEA
GILES, THOMAS	CEC	040	CHESAPEA
GILES, URIAS	BAL	011	1ST WARD
GILES, WALLTER	CEC	001	ELKTON 3
GILES, WALTER	BAL	040	4TH WARD
GILES, WILLIAM	CEC	005	ELKTON 3
GILES, WILLIAM	BAL	202	19TH WAR
GILES, WILLIAM	CEC	142	6TH E DI
GILES, WILLIAM	SOM	526	QUANTICO
GILES, WILLIAM F.	BAL	197	11TH WAR
GILESPIE, DANIEL	BAL	092	1ST WARD
GILESPIE, RACHEL H.	BAL	431	1ST DIST
GILESPIE, ROBERT	BAL	288	12TH WAR
GILFOY, WILLIAM	BAL	041	1ST WARD
GILGHRMAN, CHARLES H.	QUE	242	5TH E DI
GILHAM, MARY	ANN	411	8TH DIST
GILHAM, THOMAS	ANN	411	8TH DIST
GILHINSON, DAVID	BAL	103	2ND DIST
GILIS, MARY	CAR	225	5TH DIST
GILISPIE, CATHERINE	BAL	446	8TH WARD
GILL, ABSALOM	BAL	183	19TH WAR
GILL, ALCY	HAR	038	1ST DIST
GILL, ALEXANDER	BAL	381	13TH WAR
GILL, ALEXANDER	BAL	280	2ND WARD
GILL, AMELIA	BAL	417	1ST DIST
GILL, ANN	BAL	237	1ST DIST
GILL, ANN	BAL	320	20TH WAR
GILL, ANN	BAL	317	20TH WAR
GILL, ANNISLE	BAL	081	18TH WAR
GILL, BENJAMIN	BAL	240	1ST DIST
GILL, BYRSON	BAL	381	13TH WAR
GILL, CHARLES	BAL	099	15TH WAR
GILL, CHRISTIAN M.	BAL	240	1ST DIST
GILL, CONRAD	BAL	267	2ND WARD
GILL, D. D.	BAL	356	3RD WARD
GILL, DIDIMUS	BAL	192	5TH DIST
GILL, EDWARD	BAL	238	1ST DIST
GILL, EDWARD DR-	BAL	417	1ST DIST
GILL, ELISHA H.	BAL	387	3RD WARD
GILL, ELISHA P.	BAL	055	1ST WARD
GILL, ELIZA	BAL	243	1ST DIST
GILL, ELIZABETH	BAL	286	1ST DIST
GILL, ELIZABETH	FRE	348	MIDDLETO
GILL, ELIZABETH	CAR	149	NO TWP L
GILL, ELIZABETH	ST	311	1ST E DI
GILL, EMILY	BAL	124	18TH WAR
GILL, G. M.	BAL	107	10TH WAR
GILL, GEORGE	BAL	092	1ST WARD
GILL, GEORGE	BAL	043	18TH WAR
GILL, GEORGE W.	BAL	417	1ST DIST
GILL, HENRY	BAL	446	1ST DIST
GILL, HENRY	BAL	147	5TH WARD
GILL, J. M.	BAL	142	11TH WAR
GILL, JAMES	CAR	148	NO TWP L
GILL, JAMES L. D.	BAL	046	9TH WARD
GILL, JAMES R.	BAL	059	1ST WARD
GILL, JESTSON L.	CAR	185	8TH DIST
GILL, JOHN	BAL	126	1ST WARD
GILL, JOHN	BAL	196	11TH WAR
GILL, JOHN M.	BAL	123	1ST WARD
GILL, JOHN N.W.	ST	331	4TH E DI
GILL, JOHN T.	BAL	237	1ST DIST
GILL, JOSHUA	BAL	245	1ST DIST
GILL, JOSHUA	BAL	190	5TH DIST
GILL, JOSIAH	BAL	452	1ST DIST
GILL, JULIA A.	BAL	004	EASTERN
GILL, LEWIS	BAL	129	18TH WAR
GILL, LOUISA	BAL	317	20TH WAR
GILL, LUTHER	BAL	422	14TH WAR
GILL, MARGARET	BAL	156	11TH WAR
GILL, MARGARET	BAL	169	16TH WAR
GILL, MARTHA	CEC	119	3RD E DI
GILL, MARTHA E.	BAL	331	1ST DIST
GILL, MARTHA LEUEN	CAR	185	8TH DIST
GILL, MOSES B.	BAL	417	1ST DIST
GILL, MR-	BAL	076	15TH WAR
GILL, NICKOLAS	BAL	188	5TH DIST
GILL, NOAH	BAL	257	6TH WARD
GILL, OLIVER C.	CAR	182	8TH DIST
GILL, OWEN A.	BAL	383	13TH WAR
GILL, PATRICK	ALL	258	CUMBERLA
GILL, PRUDENCE	BAL	022	4TH WARD
GILL, REBECCA	BAL	236	1ST DIST
GILL, RICHARD W.	ANN	266	ANNAPOLI
GILL, ROSINA	BAL	032	1ST WARD

Name	County	Page	District
GILL, SARAH	BAL	355	1ST DIST
GILL, SHADRACK	BAL	293	1ST DIST
GILL, SHADRICK	BAL	362	1ST DIST
GILL, STEPHEN	BAL	209	6TH DIST
GILL, WALTER	FRE	022	FREDERIC
GILL, WASHINGTON	BAL	399	8TH WARD
GILL, WILLIAM	BAL	284	12TH WAR
GILL, WILLIAM	CAR	164	NO TWP L
GILL, WILLIAM L.	BAL	196	11TH WAR
GILL,MOSES	BAL	083	1ST WARD
GILL,WILLIAM F.	BAL	228	12TH WAR
GILLACE, ANN C.	BAL	381	8TH WARD
GILLAN, ELIZABETH	BAL	197	19TH WAR
GILLAN, JAMES	BAL	275	1ST DIST
GILLAN, JAMES	BAL	022	9TH WARD
GILLAN, JOHN	BAL	186	16TH WAR
GILLAN, MICHAEL	BAL	449	14TH WAR
GILLAN, WILLIAM T.	BAL	197	19TH WAR
GILLAND, ARTHUR	FRE	067	FREDERIC
GILLAND, CHARLOTTE	BAL	175	11TH WAR
GILLAND, ELLEN	BAL	215	11TH WAR
GILLARD, ALICE	BAL	175	6TH WARD
GILLASPIE, ALEXANDER	CEC	083	CHARLEST
GILLASPIE, CAROLINE	CEC	207	7TH E DI
GILLASPIE, ELIZA	CEC	208	7TH E DI
GILLASPIE, EMALINE	CEC	203	6TH E DI
GILLASPIE, GEORGE	CEC	210	7TH E DI
GILLASPIE, GEORGE	CEC	156	PORT DUP
GILLASPIE, JAMES	CEC	205	7TH E DI
GILLASPIE, JOHN	CEC	083	CHARLEST
GILLASPIS, LYDIA	CEC	210	7TH E DI
GILLASPIE, MOSES	CEC	203	6TH E DI
GILLASPIE, NANCY	CEC	160	6TH E DI
GILLASPIE, REBECCA	CEC	194	7TH E DI
GILLASPIE, ROBERT	CEC	214	7TH E DI
GILLASPIE, ROBERT	CEC	208	7TH E DI
GILLASPIE, SAMUEL	CEC	208	7TH E DI
GILLASPIE, SAMUEL	CEC	129	6TH E DI
GILLASPIE, SARAH	CEC	194	7TH E DI
GILLASPIE, SARAH J.	CEC	154	PORT DUP
GILLASPIE, SUSANNAH	CEC	189	7TH E DI
GILLASPIE, THOMAS J.	CEC	194	7TH E DI
GILLASPIE, WILLIAM	CEC	210	7TH E DI
GILLASPIE, WILLIAM	CEC	206	7TH E DI
GILLASPY, MATHA	HAR	164	3RD DIST
GILLBOY, MARTIN	ALL	053	10TH E.D
GILLCHREST, JOHN	BAL	266	2ND WARD
GILLCHRIST, JOHN	BAL	160	1ST WARD
GILLCOURSE, DANIEL	ALL	053	10TH E.D
GILLELAND, JOHN	FRE	193	5TH E DI
GILLELAND, WILLIAM	FRE	174	5TH E DI
GILLEN, ANN SIS-	BAL	316	20TH WAR
GILLEN, GEORGE	BAL	005	1ST WARD
GILLEN, PATRICK	WAS	159	2ND DIST
GILLEON, ADAM	ALL	102	5TH E.D.
GILLEOY, JOHN *	ALL	052	10TH E.D
GILLER, MARY	BAL	459	1ST DIST
GILLES, RICHARD	BAL	098	15TH WAR
GILLES, SARRAH A.	SOM	519	BARREN C
GILLESPIE, DAVID D.	CEC	127	5TH E DI
GILLESPIE, FRANCIS	BAL	279	2ND WARD
GILLESPIE, MARY*	BAL	111	10TH WAR
GILLESPIE, MATILDA	BAL	360	13TH WAR
GILLESPIE, STEPHEN	BAL	111	10TH WAR
GILLESPIE, WILLIAM	BAL	394	14TH WAR
GILLET, WILLIAM	BAL	144	1ST WARD
GILLETT, GILBERT	BAL	045	15TH WAR
GILLETT, HENRY-BLACK	WOR	340	1ST E DI
GILLEY, IRAEL-MULATTO	BAL	218	2ND WARD
GILLEY, ISAAC	BAL	309	3RD WARD
GILLEY, JOHN	BAL	197	17TH WAR
GILLEY, ROBERT	BAL	050	9TH WARD
GILLEY, SIMON C.	BAL	158	6TH WARD
GILLIAMS, JAOCB	ST	277	3RD E DI
GILLIAMS, L. L.	ST	254	3RD E DI
GILLIAN, JUDAH	BAL	085	18TH WAR
GILLIARD, ALICE	BAL	208	6TH WARD
GILLIARD, NICHOLAS	BAL	229	6TH WARD
GILLIGAN, ROSALINDA	BAL	386	3RD WARD
GILLIGHER, THOMAS	ALL	051	10TH E.D
GILLILAN, DAVID	HAR	081	2ND DIST
GILLIN, BIDDY	BAL	157	16TH WAR
GILLING, MARGARET	BAL	145	19TH WAR
GILLING, MARY	BAL	043	1ST WARD
GILLING, MARY A.	BAL	043	18TH WAR
GILLINGER, THOMAS	WAS	128	HAGERSTO
GILLINGHAM, ANN R.	BAL	213	11TH WAR
GILLINGHAM, C.T.	BAL	002	18TH WAR
GILLINGHAM, DAVID	BAL	063	2ND DIST
GILLINGHAM, DELILA	BAL	076	2ND DIST
GILLINGHAM, EDWARD	BAL	173	16TH WAR
GILLINGHAM, GEORGE	BAL	111	15TH WAR
GILLINGHAM, GEORGE JR.	BAL	073	4TH WARD
GILLINGHAM, H.W.	ALL	013	3RD E.D.
GILLINGHAM, HARVY	ANN	500	HOWARD D
GILLINGHAM, MARY C.	BAL	315	1ST DIST
GILLINGHAM, THOMAS *	BAL	136	2ND DIST
GILLINGS, DAVID L.	BAL	119	2ND DIST
GILLIOTT, JAMES	BAL	198	6TH WARD
GILLIS, ALEXANDER	CAR	225	5TH DIST
GILLIS, ANN M.	WOR	263	BERLIN 1
GILLIS, BENCHAM	SOM	522	BARREN C
GILLIS, CLEMENT	SOM	530	QUANTICO
GILLIS, CLEMENT	SOM	524	BARREN C
GILLIS, DAVID	ALL	078	5TH E.D.
GILLIS, ELLEN	ALL	079	5TH E.D.
GILLIS, HENRY	SOM	443	DAMES QU
GILLIS, HETTY	WOR	261	BERLIN 1
GILLIS, JAMES	SOM	522	BARREN C
GILLIS, JAMES	BAL	127	1ST WARD
GILLIS, JOHN P. R.	WOR	269	BERLIN 1
GILLIS, JOSEPH	SOM	519	BARREN C
GILLIS, JOSEPH	CAR	371	9TH DIST
GILLIS, LEVI	ANN	455	HOWARD D
GILLIS, NAPOLEON	SOM	529	QUANTICO
GILLIS, PORCIUS T.	CAR	225	5TH DIST
GILLIS, REBECCA S.	PRI	002	BLADENSB
GILLIS, SAMUEL	SOM	519	BARREN C
GILLIS, SUSAN	BAL	111	15TH WAR
GILLIS, THOMAS	CAR	225	5TH DIST
GILLIS, THOMAS H.	CAR	225	5TH DIST
GILLIS, URIAH	BAL	182	16TH WAR
GILLISPIA, ANN	BAL	110	5TH WARD
GILLISPIE, REBECCA	QUE	123	1ST E DI
GILLISS, WILLIAM	WOR	229	6TH E DI
GILLMAN, JAMES C.	BAL	194	11TH WAR
GILLMAN, MARY	BAL	219	2ND WARD
GILLMORE, JOHN	BAL	127	11TH WAR
GILLMORE, MARGARETT	BAL	129	11TH WAR
GILLMYER, GEORGE	WAS	137	HAGERSTO
GILLMYER, GEORGE G.	WAS	139	HAGERSTO
GILLON,ELISABETH	ALL	236	CUMBERLA
GILLS, ANN	BAL	369	13TH WAR
GILLS, JOSEPH	BAL	460	8TH WARD
GILLUT, WILLIAM H.	HAR	160	3RD DIST
GILLY, WILLIAM	SOM	508	BARREN C
GILLYAR, WILLIAM	BAL	475	14TH WAR
GILMAN, ANN E.	BAL	240	2ND WARD
GILMAN, CAROLINE	BAL	277	2ND WARD
GILMAN, DORINCK	BAL	046	1ST WARD
GILMAN, ELLEN	BAL	154	16TH WAR
GILMAN, ELLEN	BAL	154	11TH WAR
GILMAN, GEORGE	BAL	126	1ST WARD
GILMAN, HANNAH	BAL	289	12TH WAR
GILMAN, HENRY	BAL	232	12TH WAR
GILMAN, JAMES	BAL	286	2ND WARD
GILMAN, JOHN	BAL	329	13TH WAR
GILMAN, JOSEPH A.	BAL	154	16TH WAR
GILMAN, JUDSON	BAL	417	14TH WAR
GILMAN, LOUISA	BAL	287	12TH WAR
GILMAN, ROBERT *	BAL	082	2ND DIST
GILMAN, THOMAS	BAL	262	2ND WARD
GILMAN, WASH	BAL	323	12TH WAR
GILMAN, WILLIAM	BAL	276	12TH WAR
GILMANS, WILLIAM	BAL	153	11TH WAR
GILMANTON, MAYR	ALL	215	CUMBERLA
GILMAR, JAMES	BAL	148	2ND DIST
GILMER, CHARLES L.	BAL	150	11TH WAR
GILMET, AUGUST	BAL	220	19TH WAR
GILMON, ANN	BAL	053	9TH WARD
GILMON, JOHN	HAR	154	3RD DIST
GILMON, L. R. L.	BAL	142	11TH WAR
GILMOR, MARIAN	BAL	111	10TH WAR
GILMOR, W. W.	BAL	324	12TH WAR
GILMORE, ANN	BAL	006	1ST WARD
GILMORE, ANN	HAR	160	3RD DIST
GILMORE, ANN	BAL	076	18TH WAR
GILMORE, EMMA	BAL	373	8TH WARD
GILMORE, GEORGE	BAL	173	1ST WARD
GILMORE, HERBERT M.	HAR	122	2ND DIST
GILMORE, JAMES	FRE	040	FREDERIC
GILMORE, JAMES	BAL	161	6TH WARD
GILMORE, JOSEPH	BAL	204	6TH WARD
GILMORE, MARGARET	HAR	155	3RD DIST
GILMORE, RACHEL	BAL	221	12TH WAR
GILMORE, RICHARD	BAL	073	10TH WAR
GILMORE, ROB G.	BAL	189	2ND WARD
GILMORE, ROBERT	BAL	186	16TH WAR
GILMORE, ROBERT	BAL	368	8TH WARD
GILMORE, WILLIAM	CEC	091	4TH E DI
GILMORE,G.	BAL	138	1ST WARD
GILMOUR, ANN E.	CEC	105	3RD E DI
GILMOUR, ANNE	BAL	047	9TH WARD
GILMOUR, ELIZABETH	CEC	146	PORT DUP
GILMOUR, JAMES D.	BAL	119	15TH WAR
GILMOUR, JOHN H.	CEC	151	PORT DUP
GILMOUR, LOUISA	CEC	104	4TH E DI
GILMOUR, ROBERT	CEC	104	4TH E DI
GILMOUR,RICHARD	FRE	20	5TH E DI
GILMOURER, NATHANIEL K.	CEC	149	PORT DUP
GILNER, HAWK*	BAL	278	12TH WAR
GILPATRICK, SIMON G.	BAL	153	1ST WARD
GILPEN, GEORGE	ALL	089	5TH E.D.
GILPHIN, J.	BAL	333	1ST DIST
GILPIN, ALBAN	MGM	319	CRACKLIN
GILPIN, ALFRED T.	KEN	285	3RD DIST
GILPIN, HENRY	CEC	085	5TH E DI
GILPIN, HENRY	CEC	099	3RD E DI
GILPIN, JOSEPH	MGM	347	BERRYS D
GILPIN, JOSHUA C.	MGM	348	BERRYS D
GILPIN, MARGARET	CEC	085	5TH E DI
GILPIN, MARY	CEC	085	5TH E DI
GILPIN, RACHEL	BAL	395	14TH WAR
GILPIN, RACHEL	BAL	180	16TH WAR
GILPIN, WILLIAM H.	MGM	349	BERRYS D
GILPON, THOMAS	BAL	381	1ST DIST
GILS, JAMES H.	WAS	110	2ND DIST
GILSON, JAMES	BAL	103	2ND DIST
GILSON, JOHN	CEC	034	CHESAPEA
GILSON, RICHARD	FRE	176	5TH E DI
GILSON, ROBERT*	DOR	377	1ST DIST
GILSON, THOMAS	FRE	176	5TH E DI
GILSON,LCYD-BLACK	CAR	387	2ND DIST
GILYAN, CHARLES	BAL	257	12TH WAR
GILYARD, EDWARD	BAL	400	8TH WARD
GIMBY, NOAH	SOM	489	SALISBUR
GIMES, ACTIER	BAL	182	2ND WARD
GIMINGER, BENEDICT	WAS	123	HAGERSTO
GIMPEL, ELIZA	BAL	080	10TH WAR
GIMPIAN, JOHN	BAL	105	1ST WARD
GIMPLE, DAVID	WAS	173	FUNKSTOW
GIMPLE, JOHN	WAS	206	1ST DIST
GINAMAN, BRIDGET	CEC	033	CHESAPEA
GINAMAN, PATRICK *	BAL	366	1ST DIST
GINAMON, JANE	BAL	359	1ST DIST
GINAMON, MARY E.	BAL	399	1ST DIST
GINDER, HERMAN	BAL	079	1ST WARD
GINDLE, HENRY	CHA	286	BOJANTOW
GINE, HARRIET-BLACK	WOR	344	1ST E DI
GINEMAN, JOHN *	BAL	363	1ST DIST
GINEMAN, THOMAS	BAL	367	1ST DIST
GINERBACK, JOSEPH	BAL	161	1ST WARD
GINERMAN, GEORGE	BAL	011	18TH WAR
GINEY, WILLIAM	BAL	306	12TH WAR
GING, HENRY	ST	346	5TH E DI
GINGELL, ANDREW-MULATTO	MGM	398	ROCKERLE
GINGELL, ELIZABETH-MULATT	MGM	398	ROCKERLE
GINGELL, JAMES-MULATTO	MGM	398	ROCKERLE
GINGELL, JOSEPH	MGM	357	BERRYS D
GINGENBACK, J.	BAL	164	1ST WARD
GINGER, JACOB	HAR	062	1ST DIST
GINGERBACK, J.	BAL	139	1ST WARD
GINGNER, ANDREW	HAR	068	1ST DIST
GINGTON, AGNES	BAL	326	12TH WAR
GINKINS, ABRAHAM	FRE	290	WOODSBOR
GINKINS, CORNEALCUS	CAR	224	5TH DISY
GINLEY, JAMES	BAL	063	1ST WARD
GINN, HANAH	CAR	326	1ST DIST
GINN, JANE-BLACK	WOR	340	1ST E DI
GINN, JAOCB-BLACK	WOR	348	1ST E DI
GINN, JOHN	CEC	065	1ST E DI
GINN, JOHN	CEC	086	4TH E DI
GINN, LITTLETON-BLACK	WOR	334	1ST E DI
GINN, MAGOR-BLACK	WOR	317	2ND E DI
GINN, MILLY-BLACK	WOR	342	1ST E DI
GINN, MOSES	KEN	299	3RD DIST
GINN, MOSES	CEC	066	1ST E DI
GINN, NATHAN	CAR	075	NO TWP L
GINN, SAMUEL	CEC	066	1ST E DI
GINN, SARAH-BLACK	WOR	341	1ST E DI
GINNA, ELIZABETH	CEC	131	5TH E DI
GINNERMAN, ELIZABETH	BAL	044	9TH WARD
GINNERMAN, GEORGE	BAL	209	11TH WAR
GINNES, PATRICK M.	ALL	076	5TH E.D.
GINNINGS, ALEXANDER	CEC	136	6TH E DI
GINNIS, SARAH J. M.	TAL	090	ST MICHA
GINNS, MARY*	BAL	303	3RD WARD
GINNULS, JANE	BAL	330	13TH WAR
GINNY, DANIEL M.	TAL	077	EASTON T
GINRICH, GOERGE	BAL	245	1ST DIST
GINS, WILLIAM H.	BAL	153	19TH WAR
GINTER, GEORGE	CAR	331	MANCHEST
GINTLING, SUSAN	FRE	194	5TH E DI
GINZELL, HENRY	MGM	393	ROCKERLE
GINZELL, JAMES M.	MGM	393	ROCKERLE
GIPE, GOERGE	BAL	310	7TH WARD
GIPHART, CATHERINE	FRE	046	FREDERIC
GIPSON, CHARLES	HAR	196	3RD DIST
GIPSON, EDWARD	HAR	192	3RD DIST
GIPSON, JAMES	CEC	065	1ST E DI
GIPSON, JAMES	WAS	158	2ND DIST
GIPSON, JAMES F.	HAR	200	3RD DIST
GIPSON, JAMES L.	ST	270	3RD E DI
GIPSON, JOHN	HAR	200	3RD DIST
GIPSON, JOHN	ANN	333	2ND DIST
GIPSON, MRS.*	DOR	377	1ST DIST
GIPSON, WASHINGTON	HAR	135	3RD DIST
GIPSON, WILLIAM	CEC	083	CHARLEST
GIRABALDI, CATHERINE	BAL	027	9TH WARD
GIROEN, SARAH *	BAL	279	20TH WAR
GIRDEY, SARAH	BAL	053	9TH WARD
GIRINNA, NANCY	BAL	205	11TH WAR
GIRLINGHURST, GEORGE	BAL	034	15TH WAR
GIRRAGE, CHRISTOPHER *	ANN	354	3RD DIST
GIRTH, EDWARD	BAL	305	7TH WARD
GIRTH, JOHN	HAR	055	1ST DIST
GIRTING, ALEXANDER	ST	260	3RD E DI
GIRTING, ANN	ST	254	3RD E DI
GIRTING, ELIAS	ST	263	3RD E DI
GIRTING, WILLIAM	ST	260	3RD E DI
GIRVIN, GEORGE	BAL	034	15TH WAR
GIRVIN, ROBERT	BAL	200	19TH WAR
GISBERT, A.H.	FRE	212	BUCKEYST
GISBERT, HESTER A.	FRE	212	BUCKEYST
GISBON, ANN-BLACK	QUE	200	3RD E DI
GISBON, C.	BAL	135	1ST WARD
GISBON, JOHN	BAL	004	EASTERN
GISCART, JOHN	BAL	055	4TH WARD
GISCOE, HENRY	BAL	105	1ST WARD
GISE, ALEXANDER	BAL	368	13TH WAR
GISE, JACOB	BAL	419	1ST DIST
GISE, PETER	BAL	433	8TH WARD
GISEKENT, MARGARET	FRE	048	FREDERIC
GISLON, HUGH A.	FRE	174	5TH E DI
GISSEL, WILLIAM	BAL	045	15TH WAR
GISSENDAFNER, MARY	BAL	006	18TH WAR
GISSENDAFNER, WILLIAM	BAL	006	18TH WAR
GISSMEYER, FREDERICK	BAL	065	1ST WARD
GISSON, MARIA	BAL	051	4TH WARD
GISSUPT, CORNELIA	BAL	002	1ST WARD
GIST, CHARLES	BAL	130	18TH WAR
GIST, ELIZA	DOR	380	1ST DIST
GIST, ELIZABETH H.	BAL	118	15TH WAR
GIST, HENRY	BAL	111	18TH WAR
GIST, JOHN	CAR	192	4TH DIST
GIST, JOHN	BAL	370	8TH WARD
GIST, JOHN	BAL	311	1ST DIST
GIST, JOSHUA C.	CAR	372	9TH DIST
GIST, MARGARET	BAL	334	13TH WAR
GIST, MARGRET	CAR	404	2ND DIST
GIST, MARTHA	BAL	320	7TH WARD
GIST, MORDICAI	CAR	284	7TH DIST
GIST, MOSES	BAL	208	6TH DIST
GIST, STATES	CAR	215	5TH DIST
GIST, THOMAS B.	CAR	267	WESTMINS
GIST, THOMAS W.	BAL	105	18TH WAR
GIST, WILLIAM*	TAL	057	EASTON D
GITCHELL, HENRY E.	CEC	117	4TH E DI
GITCHELL, JOB	CEC	161	6TH E DI
GITCHELL, THOMAS	CEC	167	6TH E DI
GITS, JOSEPH	BAL	280	1ST DIST
GITTING, ANN	BAL	058	2ND DIST
GITTINGER, DANIEL	BAL	236	1ST DIST
GITTINGER, GENTILLA R.	WAS	294	1ST DIST
GITTINGER, GEORGE	WAS	206	1ST DIST
GITTINGER, SAMUEL	WAS	300	1ST DIST
GITTINGER, SARAH	BAL	235	1ST DIST
GITTINGER, WILLIAM	CAR	346	6TH DIST
GITTINGS, ALEXANDER	MGM	354	BERRYS D
GITTINGS, CHRISTIAN	MGM	355	BERRYS D
GITTINGS, DANIEL	BAL	193	5TH DIST
GITTINGS, GEORGE W.	FRE	444	8TH E DI
GITTINGS, HERNIETTA	BAL	181	2ND DIST
GITTINGS, JAMES	BAL	110	2ND DIST
GITTINGS, JOHN C.	BAL	429	1ST DIST
GITTINGS, MARTIN L.	MGM	361	BERRYS D
GITTINGS, RACHELL	BAL	097	5TH WARD
GITTINGS, RICHARD	BAL	181	6TH WARD
GITTINGS, RICHARD	MGM	369	BERRYS D
GITTINGS, SARAH P.	FRE	380	PETERSVI
GITTINGS, TABITHA	MGM	361	BERRYS D
GITTINGS, THOMAS	BAL	093	2ND DIST
GITTINGS, WILLIAM	BAL	142	11TH WAR
GITTINGS, WILLIAM H.	MGM	331	CRACKLIN
GITTINGS, WILLIAMS S.	FRE	396	PETERSVI
GITZENDENNER, JOHN B.	FRE	004	FREDERIC
GIVAN, ISAAC	WOR	221	4TH E DI
GIVAN, JAMES R.	WOR	240	6TH E DI
GIVAN, JOHN S.	WOR	221	4TH E DI
GIVAN, JOSEPH	WOR	180	6TH E DI
GIVAN, THOMAS	WOR	221	4TH E DI
GIVANS, ARNOLD	SOM	362	BRINKLEY
GIVANS, BURTON	SOM	415	DUBLIN D
GIVANS, ELIZABETH	SOM	416	DUBLIN D
GIVANS, EMILY	SOM	417	PRINCESS
GIVANS, EZEKIEL	SOM	421	PRINCESS
GIVANS, GEORGE	SOM	414	DUBLIN D
GIVANS, ISAAC	SOM	417	PRINCESS
GIVANS, ISAAC	SOM	393	BRINKLEY
GIVANS, JAMES	SOM	411	DUBLIN D
GIVANS, JOHN	SOM	411	DUBLIN D
GIVANS, LEVIN	SOM	406	DUBLIN D
GIVANS, MARY	SOM	415	DUBLIN D
GIVANS, MARY	SOM	418	PRINCESS
GIVANS, MILLY	SOM	416	DUBLIN D
GIVANS, NOAH	WOR	254	1ST CENS
GIVANS, REUBEN	SOM	415	DUBLIN D
GIVARNY, WILLIAM H.	KEN	286	3RD DIST
GIVEM, CLORA*	DOR	382	1ST DIST
GIVEN, ELIZA	BAL	146	11TH WAR

Name	County	Page	District
GIVEN, ELIZABETH	BAL	081	18TH WAR
GIVEN, MICHAEL	BAL	160	11TH WAR
GIVEN, PHILIP	MGM	328	CRACKLIN
GIVER, JACOB	BAL	083	2ND DIST
GIVEWELL, THOMAS *	ANN	397	8TH DIST
GIVIN, ELIZABETH	BAL	297	20TH WAR
GIVIN, MORN X	BAL	299	12TH WAR
GIVIN, PRICILLA	BAL	122	5TH WARD
GIVIN, ROBERT*	TAL	014	EASTON D
GIVINS, HENRY	WAS	007	WILLIAMS
GIVINS, WILLIAM	BAL	144	16TH WAR
GLAAB, PETER	BAL	194	6TH WARD
GLABB, GEORGE	BAL	265	7TH WARD
GLABB, JOHN	BAL	265	7TH WARD
GLACEN, EDWARD	CEC	208	7TH E DI
GLADDEN, BENJAMIN J.	SOM	517	BARREN C
GLADDEN, EDWARD	BAL	289	17TH WAR
GLADDEN, GEORGE W.	SOM	450	DAMES QU
GLADDEN, JACOB	HAR	009	1ST DIST
GLADDEN, JAMES	HAR	054	1ST DIST
GLADDEN, JAMES W.	HAR	005	1ST DIST
GLADDEN, MARGARET	WOR	304	SNOW HIL
GLADDEN, MARY	HAR	067	1ST DIST
GLADDEN, PEGGY	TAL	097	ST MICHA
GLADDEN, THOMAS	BAL	356	3RD WARD
GLADDING, EMILY	BAL	013	4TH WARD
GLADDING, MATILDA	QUE	185	3RD E DI
GLADE, JOHN B.	HAR	054	1ST DIST
GLADFELLER, EPHRAIM	BAL	297	12TH WAR
GLADFELTER, JOSEPH	BAL	306	1ST DIST
GLADFETTER, ELIZABETH	BAL	307	1ST DIST
GLADFETTER, JOSEPH *	BAL	306	1ST DIST
GLADHILL, BARBARA	FRE	359	CATOCTIN
GLADHILL, DANIEL	FRE	344	MIDDLETO
GLADHILL, JAMES C.	FRE	358	CATOCTIN
GLADHILL, JOHN	FRE	340	MIDDLETO
GLADMAN, ELIZABETH	CAR	374	9TH DIST
GLADMAN, NANCY	BAL	328	1ST DIST
GLADMAN, THOMAS	BAL	328	1ST DIST
GLADSON, REBECCA	BAL	455	8TH WARD
GLAIZE, JOSEPH	WAS	028	2ND SUBD
GLAMACE, JOHN	BAL	212	2ND WARD
GLAN, JOHN	BAL	178	11TH WAR
GLAN, ROBERT W.	BAL	231	6TH WARD
GLAND, MARY A.	BAL	207	19TH WAR
GLANDEN, HINSON	CEC	057	1ST E DI
GLANDER, EBEN	QUE	131	1ST E DI
GLANDER, SARAH*	BAL	103	10TH WAR
GLANDIN, JAMES	TAL	002	EASTON D
GLANDING, CHARLES W.	QUE	143	1ST E DI
GLANDING, ELIZABETH	QUE	208	3RD E DI
GLANDING, GEORGE H.	QUE	146	1ST E DI
GLANDING, JAMES H.	BAL	165	11TH WAR
GLANDING, JOHN	CAR	079	NO TWP L
GLANDING, MARGRETT JANE	CAR	079	NO TWP L
GLANDING, SARAH T.	CAR	147	NO TWP L
GLANDING, THOMAS	BAL	015	18TH WAR
GLANDING, WILIAM	QUE	208	3RD E DI
GLANDING, WILIAM	QUE	208	3RD E DI
GLANDINGS, CENN*	BAL	321	12TH WAR
GLANDON, MARY	BAL	244	12TH WAR
GLANDVILLE, THOMAS	BAL	022	18TH WAR
GLANEN, CATHARINE	BAL	253	1ST DIST
GLANSFIELD, JOHN	CEC	038	CHESAPEA
GLANSHAN, J.M.	BAL	141	1ST WARD
GLANVILLE, ELIZABETH A.	BAL	027	15TH WAR
GLANVILLE, JAMES	BAL	314	1ST DIST
GLANVILLE, JOHN M.	BAL	083	1ST WARD
GLANVILLE, JOHN W.	BAL	120	16TH WAR
GLANVILLE, MARY	BAL	049	15TH WAR
GLARES, MARGARET	BAL	206	2ND WARD
GLARSLIN, MARGARET	BAL	373	13TH WAR
GLARY, JOHN	BAL	230	2ND WARD
GLASBY, MARY E.	BAL	238	6TH WARD
GLASCOME, SOLOMON	BAL	118	5TH WARD
GLASCOW, ALEXANDER G.	BAL	119	15TH WAR
GLASCOW, HENRY	CHA	225	ALLENS F
GLASE, HENRY	CAR	332	MANCHEST
GLASGAW, GEORGE R.	HAR	092	2ND DIST
GLASGO, JOHN	SOM	430	PRINCESS
GLASGO, JOHN	SOM	440	DAMES QU
GLASGO, JOHN	BAL	462	1ST DIST
GLASGO, MARY J.	SOM	446	DAMES QU
GLASGO, RICHARD	PRI	110	PISCATAW
GLASGOW, CUNNINGHAM	HAR	042	1ST DIST
GLASGOW, HENERETTA	SOM	431	PRINCESS
GLASGOW, JAMES	HAR	144	2ND DIST
GLASGOW, MATTHEW	BAL	403	14TH WAR
GLASHAN, THOMAS	BAL	141	1ST WARD
GLASKEY, JAMES	BAL	097	5TH WARD
GLASON, JAMES	BAL	074	10TH WAR
GLASS, E.	BAL	449	8TH WARD
GLASS, ELIZABETH	PRI	056	AQUASCO
GLASS, GEORGE	ALL	202	CUMBERLA
GLASS, HENRY	BAL	095	1ST WARD
GLASS, ISAAC	BAL	378	3RD WARD
GLASS, JONATHAN	ALL	021	2ND E.D.
GLASS, M.	BAL	449	8TH WARD
GLASS, MARGARET	WAS	043	2ND SUBD
GLASS, MARGARETT	FRE	435	8TH E DI
GLASS, MARY	BAL	087	4TH WARD
GLASS, MISS H.	FRE	199	5TH E DI
GLASS, MOSES	ALL	038	2ND E.D.
GLASS, RICHARD	PRI	093	MARLBROU
GLASS, SARAH	CAR	244	3RD DIST
GLASS, THERISA	BAL	262	2ND WARD
GLASS, THOMAS	BAL	071	1ST WARD
GLASS, VALENTINE	WAS	130	HAGERSTO
GLASS, WILLIAM	FRE	184	5TH E DI
GLASS, WILLIAM	FRE	435	8TH E DI
GLASS, WILLIAM D.	DOR	374	1ST DIST
GLASSCOE, ANN B.	BAL	016	18TH WAR
GLASSCOE, MARY C.	BAL	016	18TH WAR
GLASSCOW, JOHN	BAL	118	5TH WARD
GLASSEN, JOHN	CAR	259	3RD DIST
GLASSGO, STEPHEN	BAL	343	7TH WARD
GLATFELTER, JOSEPH	ANN	424	HOWARD D
GLATZELL, JUILA	BAL	006	15TH WAR
GLATZELL, JULIA	BAL	259	2ND WARD
GLAUBER, JACOB	BAL	089	10TH WAR
GLAUDER, SARAH*	BAL	103	10TH WAR
GLAVIN, WILLIAM *	BAL	153	1ST WARD
GLAZE, DANIEL	FRE	099	FREDERIC
GLAZE, WILLIAM	WAS	254	1ST DIST
GLAZE, WILLIAM G.	FRE	246	NEW MARK
GLAZE, WILLIAM T.	MGM	433	CLARKSTR
GLAZEN, JACOB	BAL	118	5TH WARD
GLCKER, THOMAS	BAL	077	2ND DIST
GLDHILL, JOHN	FRE	358	CATOCTIN
GLE, JAMES H.	KEN	259	1ST DIST
GLEANE, MARY	ALL	182	8TH E.D.
GLEASON, CATHARINE	BAL	333	13TH WAR
GLEASON, DANIEL	BAL	366	8TH WARD
GLEASON, GEORGE	BAL	132	1ST WARD
GLEASON, MARY	BAL	031	9TH WARD
GLEATZ, FREDERICK	BAL	230	2ND WARD
GLEAVER, CHARLES	BAL	455	8TH WARD
GLEAVES, DYER	KEN	213	2ND DIST
GLEAVES, HARRIET	QUE	156	2ND E DI
GLEAVES, MARTHA	KEN	210	2ND DIST
GLEAVES, PERE-BLACK	QUE	176	2ND E DI
GLEAVES, WILLIAM	KEN	246	2ND DIST
GLEAVS, JAMES	KEN	218	2ND DIST
GLEEKMAN, JOHN	BAL	327	3RD WARD
GLEEN, JOHN H.	BAL	131	1ST WARD
GLEEN, MICHAEL	KEN	230	2ND DIST
GLEESON, BRIDGET	BAL	026	18TH WAR
GLEGHORN, JAMES	BAL	012	15TH WAR
GLEGHORN, JOHN	BAL	011	15TH WAR
GLEGON, JOHN	FRE	387	PETERSVI
GLEMENSON, JOSEPH-MULATTO	BAL	214	2ND WARD
GLEN, ELLEN S.	TAL	004	EASTON D
GLEN, PARRICK	BAL	273	1ST DIST
GLEN, PETTERSON	BAL	249	1ST DIST
GLENAPRUM, LEVI	BAL	386	13TH WAR
GLENARD, BIDDY	BAL	140	5TH WARD
GLENDY, ELINOR	BAL	447	14TH WAR
GLENEN, THOMAS	CAR	229	5TH DIST
GLENES, MARY *	KEN	215	2ND DIST
GLENN, ADAM	BAL	244	2ND WARD
GLENN, ANN	BAL	367	8TH WARD
GLENN, ANTHONY	ALL	053	10TH E.D
GLENN, ARTHUR	KEN	220	2ND DIST
GLENN, CATHRINE	BAL	015	18TH WAR
GLENN, CAVID	CEC	194	7TH E DI
GLENN, DAVID	BAL	146	1ST WARD
GLENN, ELIZA	BAL	072	15TH WAR
GLENN, ELIZA B.	BAL	363	3RD WARD
GLENN, ELIZABETH	BAL	012	9TH WARD
GLENN, FRANCIS E.*	BAL	408	3RD WARD
GLENN, HANNAH	BAL	441	14TH WAR
GLENN, HENRY	BAL	169	1ST WARD
GLENN, HUGH	HAR	037	1ST DIST
GLENN, JAMES	KEN	232	2ND DIST
GLENN, JAMISORIA	KEN	215	2ND DIST
GLENN, JANE	HAR	053	1ST DIST
GLENN, JANE	BAL	354	7TH WARD
GLENN, JOHN	ALL	155	6TH E.D.
GLENN, JOHN	BAL	388	13TH WAR
GLENN, JOHN JR.	ANN	368	4TH DIST
GLENN, JOSHUA	HAR	069	1ST DIST
GLENN, JOSHUA	BAL	408	3RD WARD
GLENN, MARY E.	ALL	221	CUMBERLA
GLENN, NATHAN	HAR	025	1ST DIST
GLENN, PETER	ALL	141	6TH E.D.
GLENN, PETER	KEN	269	1ST DIST
GLENN, RACHEL	BAL	329	3RD WARD
GLENN, ROBERT	WAS	263	1ST DIST
GLENN, ROBERT	HAR	026	1ST DIST
GLENN, SAMUEL	BAL	328	7TH WARD
GLENN, SAMUEL T.	BAL	397	3RD WARD
GLENN, SRAH	CAR	368	9TH DIST
GLENN, THOMAS	HAR	053	1ST DIST
GLENN, WILLIAM	HAR	022	1ST DIST
GLENN, WILLIAM	BAL	408	3RD WARD
GLENN, WILLIAM	KEN	236	2ND DIST
GLENN, WILLIAM	BAL	377	13TH WAR
GLENN, WILLIAM	BAL	119	18TH WAR
GLENN, WILLIAM	BAL	022	1ST WARD
GLENN, WILLIAM B.	BAL	362	13TH WAR
GLENNAN, RICHARD	BAL	022	9TH WARD
GLENROY, JOHN	BAL	123	5TH WARD
GLES, ANN	BAL	246	20TH WAR
GLESON, HANYMAN	BAL	240	5TH WARD
GLESPIE, WILLIAM Y.	BAL	170	11TH WAR
GLESSAN, JOHN B.	FRE	444	8TH E DI
GLESSNER, WILLIAM	FRE	063	FREDERIC
GLESSONER, HERNY	CAR	266	WESTMINS
GLETNER, JOSEPH	WAS	123	2ND DIST
GLEVES, JAMES F.	KEN	312	3RD DIST
GLEVES, THOMAS	KEN	313	3RD DIST
GLEWEN, CATHARINE	CEC	031	CHESAPEA
GLICK, MICHAL	BAL	294	7TH WARD
GLICKER, HUBDCRE*	BAL	243	12TH WAR
GLIN, PETER	BAL	288	1ST DIST
GLISS, GEORGE R.	BAL	236	12TH WAR
GLISSEN, JOHN	FRE	449	8TH E DI
GLISSEN, SAMUEL	FRE	422	8TH E DI
GLOCKLIN, MARY A.	BAL	325	7TH WARD
GLOINGER, MARY	BAL	340	13TH WAR
GLOISIN, DAVID A.	BAL	272	20TH WAR
GLOOMER, GEORGE	BAL	041	9TH WARD
GLOPER, JOHN	BAL	163	1ST WARD
GLOS, JOHN	BAL	412	8TH WARD
GLOSNER, GEORGE	BAL	359	1ST DIST
GLOSS, CASPAR	ALL	264	CUMBERLA
GLOSS, DANIEL	WAS	085	2ND SUBD
GLOSS, DANIEL	WAS	052	2ND SUBD
GLOSS, FREDERICK	BAL	368	8TH WARD
GLOSS, JACOB	WAS	085	2ND SUBD
GLOSS, MARY	WAS	082	2ND SUBD
GLOSS, WILLIAM	WAS	042	2ND SUBD
GLOSSBRENER, MARY	WAS	281	1ST DIST
GLOSSBRENNER, SUSAN	WAS	140	HAGERSTO
GLOSSER, DAVID	WAS	198	1ST DIST
GLOSSER, JOEL	WAS	198	1ST DIST
GLOSSER, JOHN	WAS	198	1ST DIST
GLOSSER, SARAH	FRE	190	5TH E DI
GLOSSMER, EARNEST	BAL	280	7TH WARD
GLOUSEN, PETER	BAL	073	1ST WARD
GLOUSENER, HENRY	BAL	190	2ND WARD
GLOUSMAN, HENRY L.	BAL	255	1ST DIST
GLOVE, SAMUEL*	DOR	399	1ST DIST
GLOVER, E.	BAL	150	1ST WARD
GLOVER, GEORGE	CEC	150	PORT DUP
GLOVER, JAMES	BAL	298	17TH WAR
GLOVER, JOHN	BAL	298	17TH WAR
GLOVER, JOHN	CEC	158	PORT DUP
GLOVER, JOHN	BAL	410	8TH WARD
GLOVER, JOHN H.	HAR	187	3RD DIST
GLOVER, JOSIAH	BAL	294	3RD WARD
GLOVER, NANCY	CEC	145	PORT DUP
GLOVER, PRISCILLA	BAL	178	6TH WARD
GLOVER, ROBERT	CEC	148	PORT DUP
GLOVER, SEIZER	HAR	187	3RD DIST
GLOVER, THOMAS	BAL	022	15TH WAR
GLOVER, WILLIAM	ANN	279	ANNAPOLI
GLOVER, WILLIAM	MGM	357	BERRYS D
GLOVER, WILLIAM	WAS	021	2ND SUBD
GLOVER, WILLIAM H.	ANN	352	3RD DIST
GLOYD, EDEN	MGM	429	CLARKSTR
GLOYD, GEORGE	PRI	036	VANSVILL
GLOYD, JOHN C.	ANN	469	HOWARD D
GLOYD, SAMUEL	MGM	317	CRACKLIN
GLUCK, C.	BAL	239	20TH WAR
GLUCK, HENRY C.	BAL	269	7TH WARD
GLUCK, WILLIAM	BAL	171	6TH WARD
GLUE, THOMAS	BAL	214	19TH WAR
GLUKERTUSE, A.	BAL	319	12TH WAR
GLUM, PETER	BAL	250	1ST DIST
GLUTZ, JOHN	BAL	206	19TH WAR
GLYDE, S. N.	BAL	269	20TH WAR
GLYDER, NEWTON	CAR	245	3RD DIST
GLYNN, JOHN	BAL	303	3RD WARD
GLYNN, SOPHIA	BAL	304	3RD WARD
GNAGGY, JOHN	ALL	014	3RD E.D.
GNAT, JACOB	BAL	222	19TH WAR
GOADLEN, WILLIAM	ALL	158	6TH E.D.
GOALDEN, JOHN	ALL	158	6TH E.D.
GOAVTY, MARGRET E.	CAR	125	NO TWP L
GOAY, CATHERINE	MGM	433	CLARKSTR
GOBARE, MARY A.	BAL	178	19TH WAR
GOBBIN, JOHN	BAL	068	4TH WARD
GOBBONS, MINERVA A.	MGM	437	CLARKSTR
GOBBY, B.	BAL	139	1ST WARD
GOBEN, JOHN	MGM	381	ROCKERLE
GOBESER, CONRAD *	BAL	292	20TH WAR
GOBRIGHT, JOHN C.	BAL	277	7TH WARD
GOBRIGHT, JOSEPH	BAL	030	9TH WARD
GOBRIGHT, LOUISA	BAL	079	4TH WARD
GOBRIGHT, WILLIAM	BAL	135	5TH WARD
GOBSON, SARAH	MGM	443	CLARKSTR
GOBY, WILLIAM G.	CHA	248	HILLTOP
GOCX, WILLIAM H.	ST	347	5TH E DI
GOCKLIN, ANTONY	BAL	059	1ST WARD
GODAN, JAMES	BAL	409	3RD WARD
GODARD, ELIZABETH	SOM	516	BARREN C
GODARD, HENERETTA	SOM	513	BARREN C
GODARD, J.L.	PRI	120	PISCATAW
GODARD, JOHN	PRI	118	PISCATAW
GODARD, JOHN H.*	SOM	554	TYASKIN
GODARD, MOSES	SOM	502	SALISBUR
GODARD, RICHARD	WAS	026	2ND SUBD
GODDARD, CHARLES	BAL	469	14TH WAR
GODDARD, ELIZABETH	ST	322	4TH E DI
GODDARD, GEORGE	ST	322	4TH E DI
GODDARD, GEORGE W.	ST	326	4TH E DI
GODDARD, HENRY L.	ST	285	2ND E DI
GODDARD, JAMES E.	PRI	104	PISCATAW
GODDARD, Z.	BAL	147	1ST WARD
GODEY, THOMAS	BAL	384	13TH WAR
GODFIELD, H. *	BAL	311	20TH WAR
GODFREY, CHRISTOPHER	BAL	293	3RD WARD
GODFREY, ELIZABETH	WOR	171	6TH E DI
GODFREY, GEORGE	BAL	246	6TH WARD
GODFREY, HENRY	BAL	197	6TH WARD
GODFREY, HENRY	BAL	311	20TH WAR
GODFREY, J.	BAL	273	12TH WAR
GODFREY, JAMES	BAL	395	3RD WARD
GODFREY, JAMES	WOR	172	6TH E DI
GODFREY, JOEL	WOR	249	1ST CENS
GODFREY, JOHN	WOR	188	7TH E DI
GODFREY, JOHN	WOR	172	6TH E DI
GODFREY, JOHN	BAL	179	6TH WARD
GODFREY, JOHN	BAL	115	1ST WARD
GODFREY, JOSEPH	WOR	172	5TH E DI
GODFREY, JOSPEH	WOR	260	BERLIN 1
GODFREY, LEAH	WOR	304	SNOW HIL
GODFREY, LEAH	BAL	458	8TH WARD
GODFREY, MATTHEW	WOR	171	6TH E DI
GODFREY, MATTHIAS	WOR	253	1ST CENS
GODFREY, NANCY SR.	WOR	213	4TH E DI
GODFREY, NATHAN H.	WOR	252	1ST CENS
GODFREY, NICHOLAS	BAL	324	7TH WARD
GODFREY, REBECA W.	BAL	325	7TH WARD
GODFREY, RHODA	WOR	171	6TH E DI
GODFREY, SAMUEL S.	WOR	175	6TH E DI
GODFREY, SARAH	BAL	207	5TH WARD
GODFREY, SARAH	BAL	102	2ND DIST
GODFREY, STEPHEN	WOR	172	6TH E DI
GODFREY, THOMAS	WOR	171	5TH E DI
GODFRIED, H. *	BAL	311	20TH WAR
GODLEY, PERRY	BAL	180	2ND WARD
GODLINE, A. FRANCES	BAL	212	11TH WAR
GODMAN, BAILEY	BAL	209	19TH WAR
GODMAN, CAROLINE	MGM	370	BERRYS D
GODMAN, ELIJAH	PRI	008	BLADENSB
GODMAN, JOHN	PRI	020	VANSVILL
GODMAN, JOHN D.	BAL	304	20TH WAR
GODMAN, MARGARET A.	PRI	042	VANSVILL
GODMAN, PRUDENCE	BAL	094	10TH WAR
GODMAN, SAMUEL	PRI	020	VANSVILL
GODMAN, THOMAS E.	BAL	223	5TH WARD
GODMAN, THOMAS W.	BAL	073	19TH WAR
GODMAN, WILLIAM	BAL	214	19TH WAR
GODMAN, WILLIAM	BAL	215	19TH WAR
GODMIN, HENRY M.	CAR	165	NO TWP L
GODMIN, ISABELL	CAR	165	NO TWP L
GODON, JOHN H.*	SOM	554	TYASKIN
GODRIN, JEREMIAH *	QUE	236	4TH E DI
GODSON, SARAH J.	BAL	193	19TH WAR
GODWIN, ALEXANDER S.	QUE	185	3RD E DI
GODWIN, ANN	QUE	130	2ND E DI
GODWIN, BENJAMIN	HAR	196	3RD DIST
GODWIN, EDWIN	QUE	173	2ND E DI
GODWIN, ELIZA	QUE	208	3RD E DI
GODWIN, ELIZABETH	QUE	142	1ST E DI
GODWIN, ELIZABETH	BAL	405	8TH WARD
GODWIN, EZEKIEL C.	QUE	159	2ND E DI
GODWIN, GEORGE	QUE	173	2ND E DI
GODWIN, HENRY	QUE	161	2ND E DI
GODWIN, HENRY J.	QUE	172	2ND E DI
GODWIN, JAMES	QUE	161	2ND E DI
GODWIN, JAMES	BAL	308	7TH WARD
GODWIN, JAMES	QUE	157	2ND E DI
GODWIN, JAMES	HAR	205	3RD DIST
GODWIN, JOHN E.	BAL	168	6TH WARD
GODWIN, JOSEPH	KEN	267	1ST DIST
GODWIN, LYTTLETON S.	BAL	181	16TH WAR
GODWIN, MARTHA	BAL	168	6TH WARD
GODWIN, SAMUEL	QUE	197	3RD E DI
GODWIN, SAMUEL P.	QUE	128	1ST E DI
GODWIN, SETH	QUE	208	3RD E DI
GODWIN, WILLIAM	MGM	335	CRACKLIN
GODWIN, WILLIAM JR.	BAL	097	15TH WAR
GODWIN, WILLIAM L.	KEN	235	2ND DIST
GOEHEN, HUGH	WAS	155	HAGERSTO
GOERIS, MARY JANE	BAL	193	17TH WAR
GOET, JOHN *	BAL	313	20TH WAR
GOETZ, FRANCIS	FRE	20	5TH E DI

Name	County	Page	District
GOFF, CAROLINE	FRE	353	MIDDLETO
GOFF, FRED	BAL	234	12TH WAR
GCFF, HENRY	BAL	294	12TH WAR
GOFF, JAMES	BAL	185	16TH WAR
GCFF, JAMES	BAL	135	1ST WARD
GOFF, JOHN	BAL	281	1ST DIST
COFF, JOSEPH	BAL	384	13TH WAR
GCFF, PETER	BAL	441	1ST DIST
GOFF, WESLEY	BAL	424	1ST DIST
GOFORTH, CAROLINE	BAL	105	5TH WARD
GOFOURTH, GEROGE	BAL	285	7TH WARD
GCFRON, MARGARET	BAL	435	14TH WAR
GOFSMAN, MARIA A.*	BAL	303	3RD WARD
GOGAN, EDWARD	FRE	084	FREDERIC
GCGAN, JOHN	HAR	081	2ND DIST
GOGGINS, MARY	BAL	427	14TH WAR
GOGGINS, RICHARD	BAL	427	14TH WAR
GCGLE, CHARLES	BAL	284	7TH WARD
GOH, GUSTAW *	BAL	450	14TH WAR
GOH, JACOB	BAL	450	14TH WAR
GCHOE, JOHN	BAL	065	1ST WARD
GOING, A.	BAL	101	10TH WAR
GOING, NATHANIEL	HAR	205	3RD DIST
GCINGS, ANN-MULATTO	FRE	028	FREDERIC
GOINGS, AREMINTA	FRE	087	FREDERIC
GCINGS, CATHERINE	BAL	148	11TH WAR
GCINGS, CYNTHIA-BLACK	FRE	019	FREDERIC
GCINGS, DELILA-MULATTO	FRE	209	BUCKEYST
GOINGS, ELIZEBETH	HAR	204	3RD DIST
GCINGS, GEORGE	HAR	197	3RD DIST
GOINGS, ISAAC	BAL	084	15TH WAR
GOINGS, JAMES-MULATTO	FRE	220	BUCKEYST
GCINGS, JAOCB-MULATTO	FRE	219	BUCKEYST
GOINGS, JOHN	FRE	305	WOODSBOR
GCINGS, JOHN-BLACK	FRE	221	BUCKEYST
GOINGS, JOSEPH-MULATTO	FRE	383	PETERSVI
CCINGS, JOSHUA	FRE	211	BUCKEYST
GCINGS, LORETTA	FRE	077	FREDERIC
GOINGS, LORSON-BLACK	FRE	222	BUCKEYST
GCINGS, MORRIS	FRE	234	BUCKEYST
GOINGS, MORRIS	FRE	096	FREDERIC
GCINGS, PRINER	HAR	205	3RD DIST
GOINGS, WILLIAM	FRE	080	FREDERIC
GOINGS, WILLIAM	FRE	378	PETERSVI
GOINS, JOHN	WAS	250	1ST DIST
GCINS, MARIA-MULATTC	FRE	399	JEFFERSO
GCINS, MARY-MULATTO	FRE	382	PETERSVI
GCLAHCN, ALLA	TAL	091	ST MICHA
GOLAWAY, BENJAMIN	KEN	302	3RD DIST
GOLAWAY, WILLIAM	KEN	291	3RD DIST
GOLB, RICHARD*	TAL	022	EASTON D
GOLBART, JOSEPH	CEC	157	PORT DUP
GOLD, ABRAHAM	BAL	296	3RD WARD
GOLD, C.W.	BAL	161	1ST WARD
GOLD, C.W.	BAL	167	1ST WARD
GCLD, CHARLES	BAL	056	10TH WAR
GCLD, LONDON	BAL	459	8TH WARD
GOLD, MARY A.	BAL	382	8TH WARD
GOLD, REBECCA	BAL	164	19TH WAR
GOLD, SUSANNAH F.	BAL	022	15TH WAR
GOLD, THOMAS	DOR	459	1ST DIST
GCLDABOROUGH, THOMAS	BAL	003	9TH WARD
GOLDAMITH, JAMES H.	BAL	161	11TH WAR
GOLDBERRY, FRANCIS	ST	283	3RD E DI
GOLDRERY, JAMES E.	CHA	222	ALLENS F
GCLDBOROUGH, RICHARD	ALL	056	10TH E.D
GOLDBOROUGH, WILFORC	ST	289	2ND E DI
GOLDBOROUGH, WILLIAM-BLAC	CAR	137	NO TWP L
GCLDBOWUGH, BRICE J.	DOR	430	1ST DIST
GOLDEN, BARNEY	BAL	016	9TH WARD
GOLDEN, CATHARINE	BAL	273	12TH WAR
GCLDEN, CATHERINE	CHA	249	HILLTOP
GCLDEN, CHARLES	BAL	174	11TH WAR
GCLDEN, CHARLES	BAL	408	8TH WARD
GOLDEN, ELIZABETH-BLACK	QUE	146	1ST E DI
GOLDEN, HANNAH	BAL	150	11TH WAR
GCLDEN, HANNAH	BAL	459	1ST DIST
GCLDEN, JAMES	ANN	471	HOWARD D
GOLDEN, JOHN	WAS	152	2ND DIST
GOLDEN, JOHN	WAS	152	2ND DIST
GCLDEN, JOHN A.	CHA	243	HILLTOP
GCLDEN, JOSEPH	WAS	214	1ST DIST
GCLDEN, JOSHUA	BAL	364	13TH WAR
GOLDEN, MARY A.	BAL	408	8TH WARD
GOLDEN, MARY F.	BAL	408	8TH WARD
GOLDEN, MICHAEL	BAL	161	16TH WAR
GOLDEN, NANCY	WAS	200	1ST DIST
GOLDEN, RICHARD	BAL	142	16TH WAR
GOLDEN, THOMAS	ALL	221	CUMBERLA
GCLDEN, WILLIAM	BAL	286	12TH WAR
GOLDEN, WILLIAM	MGM	328	CRACKLIN
GOLDEN, WILLIAM-BLACK	QUE	146	1ST E DI
GOLDENBERG, LEVI	BAL	182	6TH WARD
GOLDER, ARCHIBALD	BAL	341	13TH WAR
GOLDER, HAMILTON	BAL	004	EASTERN
GCLDER, JAMES C.	BAL	204	11TH WAR
GOLDER, LYDIA	BAL	371	13TH WAR
GOLDHAMMER, SELENA	BAL	287	7TH WARD
GCLDMAN, JANE	BAL	341	7TH WARD
GCLDROUROUGH, THOMAS	BAL	260	2ND WARD
GCLDSBERRY, ELIZA	CHA	221	ALLENS F
GOLDSBERRY, ELIZABETH	WAS	164	HAGERSTO
GOLDSBERRY, FRANCIS	ST	284	2ND E DI
GOLDSBERRY, SALLY	ST	281	3RD E DI
GOLDSBERRY, UZ.	CHA	221	ALLENS F
GCLDSBERRY, WILLIAM W.	ST	273	3RD E DI
GOLDSBORO, S.M.	ANN	282	ANNAPOLI
GCLDSBORO, SCIPIO	BAL	197	19TH WAR
GCLDSBORO, THOMAS	WAS	023	2ND SUBD
GCLDSBOROGH, HOWES	ANN	516	HOWARD D
GCLDSBOROUGH, A. M.	BAL	332	1ST DIST
GOLDSBOROUGH, ALEXANDER	ST	299	2ND E DI
GOLDSBOROUGH, ALEXANDER	ST	292	2ND E DI
GOLDSBOROUGH, ALICE	TAL	001	EASTON D
GOLDSBOROUGH, ALLEN M.	TAL	066	EASTON T
GOLDSBOROUGH, ANN	ST	288	2ND E DI
GCLDSBOROUGH, ANN	ST	293	2ND E DI
GOLDSBOROUGH, ANN E.	ST	289	2ND E DI
GOLDSBOROUGH, CALESTIUS	ST	311	1ST E DI
GCLDSBOROUGH, CARROLINE	TAL	014	EASTON D
GOLDSBOROUGH, CHARLES H.	FRE	309	WOODSBOR
GOLDSBOROUGH, CHARLES F.	DOR	375	1ST DIST
GOLDSBOROUGH, DEELY	TAL	092	ST MICHA
GOLDSBOROUGH, E.*	DOR	462	1ST DIST
GOLDSBOROUGH, EDUARD Y.	FRE	013	FREDERIC
GOLDSBOROUGH, EDWARD-BLAC	QUE	147	1ST E DI
GOLDSBOROUGH, ELISHA	BAL	008	4TH WARD
GOLDSBOROUGH, ELLEN	CAR	273	WESTMINS
GOLDSBOROUGH, ELLEN-BLACK	QUE	201	3RD E DI
GOLDSBOROUGH, GEORGE	BAL	121	16TH WAR
GOLDSBORCUGH, GEORGE	BAL	094	15TH WAR
GOLDSBOROUGH, GEORGE W.	CAR	097	NO TWP L
GOLDSBORCUGH, HANNAH	QUE	240	5TH E DI
GOLDSBOROUGH, HARCULOUS-B	CAR	085	NO TWP L
GOLDSBORCUGH, HENRY	BAL	343	3RD WARD
GOLDSBORCUGH, HENRY H.	TAL	078	EASTON T
GOLDSBORCUGH, HOWS*	TAL	020	EASTON D
GOLDSBORCUGH, ISAAC-BLACK	QUE	175	2ND E DI
GOLDSBOROUGH, JAMES	ST	286	2ND E DI
GOLDSBORCUGH, JAMES K.	TAL	066	EASTON T
GOLDSBOROUGH, JAMES N.	TAL	006	EASTON D
GOLDSBORCUGH, JOHN	TAL	067	EASTON T
GOLDSBORCUGH, JOHN	ST	301	2ND E DI
GOLDSBORCUGH, JOHN	BAL	204	2ND WARD
GOLDSBORCUGH, JOHN A.	PRI	063	NOTTINGH
GOLDSBOROUGH, JOHN H.	ST	297	2ND E DI
GOLDSBORCUGH, JOSEPH	QUE	206	3RD E DI
GOLDSBOROUGH, LAVINLL	ST	310	1ST E DI
GOLDSBORCUGH, LEVIN	TAL	106	ST MICHA
GOLDSBOROUGH, M.*	TAL	001	EASTON D
GOLDSBORCUGH, MARCELLUS	ST	289	2ND E DI
GOLDSBOROUGH, MARGARET	TAL	073	EASTON T
GOLDSBORCUGH, MARIAH	TAL	050	EASTON T
GOLDSBORCUGH, MARTIN	TAL	050	EASTON T
GOLDSBOROUGH, MARY	TAL	043	EASTON D
GOLDSBOROUGH, MARY	QUE	206	3RD E DI
GOLDSBOROUGH, MARY-BLACK	CAR	102	NO TWP L
GOLDSBOROUGH, MATHEW T.	TAL	036	EASTON D
GOLDSBOROUGH, N. W.	BAL	313	20TH WAR
GOLDSBOROUGH, NANCY-BLACK	QUE	183	3RD E DI
GOLDSBOROUGH, NICHOLAS	TAL	043	EASTON D
GOLDSBORCUGH, RICHARD F.	DOR	386	1ST DIST
GOLDSBOROUGH, RICHARD	BAL	343	3RD WARD
GOLDSBOROUGH, ROBERT	QUE	186	3RD E DI
GOLDSBORGUGH, ROBERT L.	CEC	009	ELKTON 3
GOLDSBOROUGH, SARAH	BAL	331	3RD WARD
GOLDSBORGUGH, SARAH Y.	DOR	375	1ST DIST
GOLDSBOROUGH, SCIPIO	BAL	153	11TH WAR
GOLDSBOROUGH, VILENDA-MUL	ST	318	4TH E DI
GOLDSBOROUGH, W. T.	DOR	387	1ST DIST
GOLDSBOROUGH, WESLEY-BLAC	CAR	102	NO TWP L
GOLDSBORCUGH, WILLIAM	TAL	006	EASTON D
GOLDSBOROUGH, WILLIAM	TAL	002	EASTON D
GOLDSBORCUGH, WILLIAM	QUE	226	4TH E DI
GOLDSBOROUGH, WILLIAM J.	BAL	249	6TH WARD
GOLDSBOROUGH,ROBERT	CAR	092	NO TWP L
GOLDSBORUGH, ELIZABETH	BAL	399	14TH WAR
GOLDSBOUGH, ABRAHAM-BLACK	CAR	081	NO TWP L
GOLDSBOUROUGH, ALICE J.	BAL	306	7TH WARD
GOLDSBOUROUGH, CHARLOTT	BAL	141	5TH WARD
GOLDSBOURUGH, ELIZABETH	BAL	461	14TH WAR
GOLDSBURY, GEORGE W.	ST	267	3RD E DI
GOLDSBURY, MARY E.	BAL	331	7TH WARD
GOLDSBURY, PHILIP	ANN	405	8TH DIST
GOLDSMILD, ISAAC	BAL	206	2ND WARD
GOLDSMITH, ANNA M.	ST	320	4TH E DI
GOLDSMITH, BENJAMIN H.	CHA	294	BOJANTOW
GOLDSMITH, ELIZA	BAL	137	11TH WAR
GOLDSMITH, GUSTAV	BAL	457	14TH WAR
GOLDSMITH, H.	ANN	281	ANNAPOLI
GOLDSMITH, HENRIETTA	BAL	261	2ND WARD
GOLDSMITH, IRWIN	WAS	154	2ND DIST
GOLDSMITH, JAMES	CHA	278	BOJANTOW
GOLDSMITH, JOHN	HAR	023	1ST DIST
GOLDSMITH, JOHN	ST	319	4TH E DI
GOLDSMITH, JOHN	QUE	182	3RD E DI
GOLDSMITH, JOHN T.	TAL	113	ST MICHA
GOLDSMITH, LEWIS A.	BAL	278	12TH WAR
GOLDSMITH, LYDIA	CHA	294	BOJANTOW
GOLDSMITH, MARGARET	CHA	284	BOJANTOW
GOLDSMITH, MARTHA V.	CHA	284	BOJANTOW
GOLDSMITH, MARTIN	BAL	056	1ST WARD
GOLDSMITH, MARY ANN	QUE	187	3RD E DI
GOLDSMITH, RUBEN	BAL	232	2ND WARD
GOLDSMITH, SAMUEL	ANN	267	ANNAPOLI
GOLDSMITH, SAMUEL H.	BAL	180	11TH WAR
GOLDSMITH, THCMAS	BAL	297	7TH WARD
GOLDSMITH, WILLIAM	BAL	166	2ND DIST
GOLDSMITH, WILLIAM	CHA	284	BOJANTOW
GOLDSMITH, WILLIAM	CAR	363	9TH DIST
GOLDSMITH, Z.H.	ST	319	4TH E DI
GOLDSMUTH, ELIZA	CHA	227	ALLENS F
GOLDSTON, JACOB	BAL	009	9TH WARD
GOLDSTCNE, B.	BAL	150	5TH WARD
GOLDTHAIT, MARY	BAL	103	10TH WAR
GOLER, BILL	CAL	015	1ST DIST
GOLEY, HARRIET A.	CHA	248	HILLTOP
GOLEY, JOHN	ALL	049	10TH E.D
GOLF, HANNAH	BAL	242	20TH WAR
GOLL, JAMES H.	BAL	460	8TH WARD
GOLLAGER, MICHAEL	WAS	163	2ND DIST
GOLLAHER, MARGARET	CEC	110	4TH E DI
GOLLAN, MICHAEL	BAL	180	2ND WARD
GCLLAR, THOMAS	HAR	148	3RD DIST
GOLLATHURN, EDWARD P.	TAL	112	ST MICHA
GOLLEN, JOHN	BAL	110	2ND DIST
GOLLEY, HENRY*	DOR	329	3RD DIVI
GOLLIBERT, SUMON	BAL	362	8TH WARD
GOLLICHER, EUPHERNIA	WAS	246	SMITHSBU
GOLLICHER, MICHAEL	WAS	111	2ND DIST
GOLLICKER, WILLIAM	BAL	250	2ND WARD
GOLLIGHER, CORNELIUS	ALL	053	10TH E.D
GOLLIGHER, JAMES	ALL	052	10TH E.D
GOLLIGHER, MICHAEL	ALL	052	10TH E.D
GOLLIGHER, PATRICK	ALL	052	10TH E.D
GOLLIGHER, PHELIS	ALL	052	10TH E.D
GOLLIHAN, MARY	HAR	148	3RD DIST
GOLLINGHORST, GEORGE	BAL	036	9TH WARD
GOLLINGHORST, HENRY	BAL	009	9TH WARD
GOLLINHORST, GEORGE	BAL	009	9TH WARD
GOLLINHORST, JOHN	BAL	009	9TH WARD
GOLLOBUT, MARY	BAL	043	4TH WARD
GOLLOGHER, JOHN	ALL	052	10TH E.D
GOLLY, DAVID	CAR	313	1ST DIST
GOLLY, ELIZABETH	CAR	413	2ND DIST
GOLLY, JONATHAN	CAR	407	2ND DIST
GOLOT, JOSHUA	FRE	009	FREDERIC
GOLRIGHT, GEORGE N. *	BAL	378	13TH WAR
GOLSBERRY, MARY	HAR	159	3RD DIST
GOLSCHIND, SOLOMON	BAL	065	1ST WARD
GOLSIN, WILLIAM	DOR	309	1ST DIST
GOLT, HENRY	TAL	032	EASTON D
GOLT, JAMES	QUE	214	3RD E DI
GOLT, RACHEL	QUE	139	1ST E DI
GOLT, SARAH	BAL	298	20TH WAR
GOLT, WILLIAM H.	QUE	214	3RD E DI
GOLZ, CYNAKUS	BAL	007	EASTERN
GOMAGE, A.	BAL	171	1ST WARD
GOMBAT, JOSEPH	BAL	412	8TH WARD
GOMBER, EGAN	FRE	036	FREDERIC
GOMBER, ISAAC	FRE	022	FREDERIC
GOMELL, M.G.	BAL	248	12TH WAR
GOMER,ARTHUR	BAL	123	1ST WARD
GOMEROUS, WOLF	BAL	182	2ND WARD
GOMERY, TONN*	DOR	418	1ST DIST
GOMFF, PETER	BAL	370	13TH WAR
GOMLEY, ELIZABETH	HAR	083	2ND DIST
GOMLY, JOHN	BAL	439	14TH WAR
GOMP, CAROLINE	BAL	345	3RD WARD
GOMRY, JAMES*	DOR	413	1ST DIST
GONCE, JOHN	KEN	284	3RD DIST
GOND, ELIZABETH	CEC	069	5TH E DI
GONDA, STEPHEN *	BAL	292	1ST DIST
GONDER, ANDREW	ALL	209	CUMBERLA
GONDER, CATHARINE	CAR	330	MANCHEST
GONDER, THOMAS	ALL	221	CUMBERLA
GONDER, WILLIAM	CAR	334	6TH DIST
GONDERMAN, JOHN	BAL	105	2ND DIST
GONDING, ABRAM	BAL	011	2ND DIST
GONDON, JOHN F.	CAR	379	2ND DIST
GONER, EMMA	BAL	257	12TH WAR
GONER, GEORGE P.	BAL	226	12TH WAR
GONES, JAMES	WAS	062	2ND SUBD
GONG, JOHN H.	ST	322	4TH E DI
GONGEL, HENRY *	BAL	309	20TH WAR
GONN, JOHN	BAL	254	20TH WAR
GONN, MARY	CEC	112	4TH E DI
GONO, ANN *	WAS	159	2ND DIST
GONSO, CHARLOTTE	BAL	092	10TH WAR
GONSO, ELIZABETH	FRE	081	FREDERIC
GONSO, JACOB	FRE	062	FREDERIC
GONSO, SUSAN	FRE	064	FREDERIC
GONSOCK, MARY	FRE	041	FREDERIC
GONTY, JOHN	CAR	117	NO TWP L
GONTY, MARY	CAR	118	NO TWP L
GONURY, JAMES*	DOR	413	1ST DIST
GOOD, BENJAMIN	CHA	270	ALLENS F
GOOD, DAVID M.	WAS	278	LEITERSB
GOOD, ELIZA G.	WAS	028	2ND SUBD
GOOD, GEORGE W.	CHA	282	BOJANTOW
GOOD, HENRY	CHA	272	ALLENS F
GOOD, ICHABOD	BAL	336	13TH WAR
GOOD, JACOB	WAS	265	1ST DIST
GOOD, JANE M.	ST	322	4TH E DI
GOOD, JOHN G.	CHA	271	ALLENS F
GOOD, MICHAEL	BAL	063	18TH WAR
GOOD, NANCY	WAS	148	2ND DIST
GOOD, PASA	CHA	271	ALLENS F
GOOD, PATRICK	ALL	139	6TH E.D.
GOOD, SARAH	BAL	464	14TH WAR
GOODACRE, DANIEL	BAL	002	4TH WARD
GOODALL, MATHEW	BAL	186	11TH WAR
GOODAN, ANDREW	BAL	053	18TH WAR
GOODAN, JANE	BAL	138	5TH WARD
GOODAN, RICHARD	BAL	052	18TH WAR
GOODAUN, AUGUSTAS	BAL	106	18TH WAR
GOODCHECK, ROSINA	BAL	220	17TH WAR
GOODDING, BENJAMIN	BAL	185	5TH DIST
GOODDING, MARY	BAL	190	5TH DIST
GOODE, JOHN	BAL	087	10TH WAR
GOODE, PATRICK	BAL	305	3RD WARD
GOODEN, BETTSY	FRE	262	NEW MARK
GOODEN, JOHN	FRE	275	NEW MARK
GOODEN, JOHN	BAL	324	1ST DIST
GOODEN, JOHN	BAL	228	1ST DIST
GOODEN, JOSEPH	BAL	379	1ST DIST
GOUDEN, LOUISA	BAL	224	1ST DIST
GOODEN, LOYD	FRE	262	NEW MARK
GOODEN, PATRICK	BAL	342	1ST DIST
GOODEN, REBECCA	FRE	065	FREDERIC
GOODEN, RICHARD	BAL	272	1ST DISY
GOODEN, SAMUEL	FRE	265	NEW MARK
GOODEN, SIMON	CAR	334	6TH DIST
GOOCEN, WILLIAM	BAL	428	1ST DIST
GOODEN, WILLIAM-BLACK	FRE	446	8TH E DI
GOODENOTT, JOHN	BAL	174	19TH WAR
GOODCER, GEORGE A.	FRE	265	NEW MARK
GOODEU, PHELINER	FRE	265	NEW MARK
GOODFELLOW, JOSHUA B.	BAL	066	4TH WARD
GOODFELLOW, REUBEN	BAL	164	11TH WAR
GOODHAM, HENRY	BAL	108	5TH WARD
GOODHAM, JAMES B.	BAL	181	11TH WAR
GOODHAN, PHILIP	BAL	033	18TH WAR
GOODHAND, HIRAM	QUE	151	1ST E DI
GOODHAND, HIRAM	QUE	224	4TH E DI
GOODHAND, JOHN	BAL	047	18TH WAR
GOODHAND, JONES	QUE	252	5TH E DI
GOODHAND, MARGARET	BAL	340	13TH WAR
GOODHAND, SARAH	QUE	250	5TH E DI
GOODHAND, WILLIAM	QUE	237	4TH E DI
GOODHARD, CHRISTCPHER	QUE	123	1ST E DI
GOODHARD, JAMES	QUE	233	4TH E DI
GOODHARD, JAMES	QUE	233	4TH E DI
GOODHARD, WILIAM E.	QUE	235	4TH E DI
GOODHARD, WILLIAM K.	QUE	222	4TH E DI
GOODHELL, FREDERICK	BAL	259	20TH WAR
GOODHOUSE, GEORGE	BAL	008	4TH WARD
GOODHUE, MARY E.	BAL	282	7TH WARD
GOODICK, FRANCIS	CHA	227	ALLENS F
GOODIME, JULIA	FRE	036	FREDERIC
GOODING, AARON L.	BAL	185	6TH WARD
GOODING, BENJAMIN	BAL	207	6TH DIST
GOODING, E.	BAL	139	5TH WARD
GOODING, EDWARD	KEN	261	1ST DIST
GOODING, ELIZABETH-BLACK	FRE	031	FREDERIC
GOODING, ELLEN	BAL	430	14TH WAR
GOODING, JAMES	CAR	073	NO TWP L
GOODING, JOHN	KEN	231	2ND DIST
GOODING, JOHN	ALL	004	3RD E.D.
GOODING, LUCY	BAL	227	1ST DIST
GOODING, WILLIAM	KEN	302	3RD DIST
GOODINGDING, JOHN	WAS	184	BOONSBOR
GOODINGTING, GECRGE	WAS	186	BOONSBOR
GOODLAND, S. H.	BAL	473	14TH WAR
GOODLUM, SARAH	ST	325	4TH E DI
GOODMAN, ANN	BAL	317	12TH WAR
GOODMAN, CALEB	BAL	091	2ND DIST
GOODMAN, CHARLES	BAL	144	1ST WARD
GOODMAN, CHARLES	QUE	202	3RD E DI
GOODMAN, EDWARD C.	BAL	103	5TH WARD
GOODMAN, GEORGE A.	BAL	253	12TH WAR
GOODMAN, H.	BAL	137	1ST WARD
GOODMAN, HENRY	BAL	013	9TH WARD
GOODMAN, HONORUIE SIS- *	BAL	316	20TH WAR
GOCDMAN, ISAAC	BAL	137	5TH WARD
GOODMAN, JACOB	FRE	396	PETERSVI
GOODMAN, JACOB	BAL	101	18TH WAR
GOODMAN, JOEL	BAL	274	12TH WAR
GOODMAN, JOHN	CEC	109	4TH E DI
GOODMAN, JOHN	BAL	121	18TH WAR

Name	Co.	Page	District
GOODMAN, JOHN D.	QUE	233	4TH E DI
GOODMAN, JOHN G.	ALL	246	CUMBERLA
GOODMAN, JOHN-MULATTO	FRE	005	FREDERIC
GOODMAN, JOSEPH	FRE	395	PETERSVI
GOODMAN, JOSEPH	BAL	013	9TH WARD
GOODMAN, JOSEPH	BAL	280	7TH WARD
GOODMAN, LAURA	BAL	101	18TH WAR
GOODMAN, LOUIS	BAL	091	10TH WAR
GOODMAN, MARY	FRE	397	PETERSVI
GOODMAN, MARY	FRE	051	FREDERIC
GOODMAN, REBECCA	ANN	266	ANNAPOLI
GOODMAN, SAMUEL	BAL	280	7TH WARD
GOODMAN, SAMUEL	ANN	439	HOWARD D
GOODMAN, WILLIAM	FRE	081	FREDERIC
GOODMAN, HENRY	BAL	122	1ST WARD
GOODMANSON, JAMES H.	BAL	273	7TH WARD
GOODMANSON, PETER	FRE	034	FREDERIC
GOODMUD, SAMUEL	BAL	370	3RD WARD
GOODRICH, GEORGE	PRI	113	PISCATAW
GOODRICH, LEROY	ALL	200	CUMBERLA
GOODRICH, MARY	BAL	291	3RD WARD
GOODRICH, MARY	ST	339	5TH E DI
GOODRICH, THOMAS	WAS	012	WILLIAMS
GOODRICH, THOMAS	BAL	157	1ST WARD
GOODRICH, THOMAS	BAL	159	1ST WARD
GOODRICH, WASHING	BAL	002	9TH WARD
GOODRICK, ANN	CHA	275	ALLENS F
GOODRICK, CALEB	WAS	012	WILLIAMS
GOODRICK, GEORGE	CHA	275	ALLENS F
GOODRICK, GEORGE	BAL	062	4TH WARD
GOODRICK, HENRY	ST	298	2ND E DI
GOODRICK, JOHN	ST	301	2ND E DI
GOODRICK, JOHN T. N.	CHA	223	ALLENS F
GOODRICK, JOSAPHINE B.	CHA	227	ALLENS F
GOODRICK, JOSEPH	ST	298	2ND E DI
GOODRICK, MARY	ST	269	3RD E DI
GOODRICK, MATTHEW	MGM	380	ROCKERLE
GOODRICK, SUSAN	CHA	247	HILLTOP
GOODRICK, SUSAN	BAL	041	4TH WARD
GOODROON, ELENDER	CAL	015	1ST DIST
GOODUCK, ISABELLA	CHA	224	ALLENS F
GOODWARD, WILLIAM	FRE	328	MIDDLETO
GOODWICH, MARY	BAL	273	7TH WARD
GOODWICK, SARAH	CHA	247	HILLTOP
GOODWIN, ANN	BAL	328	7TH WARD
GOODWIN, ANN	ST	267	3RD E DI
GOODWIN, ANNA	KEN	267	1ST DIST
GOODWIN, ANNA	BAL	431	14TH WAR
GOODWIN, BRADFORD	BAL	312	12TH WAR
GOODWIN, C.	BAL	151	1ST WARD
GOODWIN, CALEB	BAL	020	9TH WARD
GOODWIN, CALEB	BAL	013	4TH WARD
GOODWIN, CALEB H.	BAL	210	6TH WARD
GOODWIN, CHARLES	BAL	440	1ST DIST
GOODWIN, CHARLES	BAL	424	14TH WAR
GOODWIN, E.A.	BAL	204	11TH WAR
GOODWIN, ELISHA	CAR	275	7TH DIST
GOODWIN, EPHRAIM	BAL	292	20TH WAR
GOODWIN, GEORGE	BAL	298	1ST DIST
GOODWIN, GEORGE	WOR	194	8TH E DI
GOODWIN, HANNAH	CAR	202	4TH DIST
GOODWIN, HENRY	CAR	375	9TH DIST
GOODWIN, HENRY B.	CHA	269	ALLENS F
GOODWIN, JAMES	BAL	175	2ND DIST
GOODWIN, JAMES	BAL	300	3RD WARD
GOODWIN, JAMES	BAL	339	1ST DIST
GOODWIN, JAMES	BAL	460	8TH WARD
GOODWIN, JAMES	BAL	308	7TH WARD
GOODWIN, JANET	BAL	402	14TH WAR
GOODWIN, JIM	BAL	310	1ST DIST
GOODWIN, JOHN	BAL	338	1ST DIST
GOODWIN, JOHN	BAL	026	1ST WARD
GOODWIN, JOHN	BAL	445	14TH WAR
GOODWIN, JOHN	BAL	444	14TH WAR
GOODWIN, JOHN	WOR	289	9TH E DI
GOODWIN, LYDE	BAL	220	6TH WARD
GOODWIN, MARGARET	BAL	243	12TH WAR
GOODWIN, MARIA	BAL	244	6TH WARD
GOODWIN, MARY	BAL	041	1ST WARD
GOODWIN, MARY AJANE	ST	265	3RD E DI
GOODWIN, MARY E.	ST	334	4TH E DI
GOODWIN, MATILDA	CAR	283	7TH DIST
GOODWIN, NATHAN	QUE	247	5TH E DI
GOODWIN, OMAN	QUE	185	3RD E DI
GOODWIN, PENELOPE	BAL	085	4TH WARD
GOODWIN, R.R.	ANN	267	ANNAPOLI
GOODWIN, REBECA	CAR	175	8TH DIST
GOODWIN, ROSANNA	BAL	001	EASTERN
GOODWIN, RUTH	BAL	306	20TH WAR
GOODWIN, SOLOMON	ANN	355	3RD DIST
GOODWIN, SUSAN A.	CHA	270	ALLENS F
GOODWIN, THOMAS	BAL	169	11TH WAR
GOODWIN, WILLIAM	BAL	159	1ST WARD
GOODWIN, WILLIAM	BAL	158	1ST WARD
GOODWIN, WILLIAM	BAL	203	2ND WARD
GOODWIN, WILLIAM	BAL	181	6TH WARD
GOODWIN, WILLIAM H.	ST	257	3RD E DI
GOODYEAR, CASPER	ALL	260	CUMBERLA
GOOK, REBECCA	WAS	060	2ND SUBD
GOOL, JANE	CEC	018	ELKTON 3
GOOL, SAMUEL-BLACK	CAR	076	NO TWP L
GOOLD, JOHN	BAL	338	3RD WARD
GOOLE, RICHARD	KEN	282	3RD DIST
GOOMAN, WILLIAM R.	ANN	265	ANNAPOLI
GOOR, MARY	BAL	305	12TH WAR
GOOR, THOMAS	KEN	215	2ND DIST
GOORE, CAPREL*	DOR	372	3RD DIVI
GOORE, EDWARD	DOR	347	3RD DIVI
GOORE, NOAH	DOR	332	3RD DIVI
GOORE, STANDLY*	DOR	361	3RD DIVI
GOOSBURY, CHARLES	ANN	348	3RD DIST
GOOSE, CAPREL*	DOR	372	3RD DIVI
GOOSE, PHILLIP	FRE	045	FREDERIC
GOOSE, STANDLY*	DOR	361	3RD DIVI
GOOSEBERRY, HAGERETTA	BAL	225	6TH WARD
GOOSEBERRY, MARGARET	BAL	215	6TH WARD
GOOSEBERRY, WILLIAM	BAL	226	6TH WARD
GOOSTER, LEVEN	DOR	371	3RD DIVI
GOOTEE, CASANDER	DOR	334	3RD DIVI
GOOTEE, EDWARD	DOR	348	3RD DIVI
GOOTEE, EMILY	DOR	465	1ST DIST
GOOTEE, GEORGE W.	DOR	333	3RD DIVI
GOOTEE, GOODMAN	DOR	356	3RD DIVI
GOOTEE, MARGARET	DOR	435	1ST DIST
GOOTEE, MISS*	DOR	453	1ST DIST
GOOTEE, REBECCA	DOR	451	1ST DIST
GOOTEE, SHADRACK	DOR	334	3RD DIVI
GOOTEN, JOHN	WOR	326	1ST E DI
GOOTY, JOHN W.	CAR	123	NO TWP L
GOOTY, THOMAS	WOR	199	8TH E DI
GOPA, GOTLIEB	BAL	273	2ND WARD
GOPAGE, JAMES H.*	TAL	067	EASTON T
GOPAGE, JAMES*	TAL	037	EASTON D
GOPAGE, RICHARD*	TAL	039	EASTON D
GOPE, NELLEY	BAL	357	8TH WARD
GOPPERT, GEORGE	BAL	040	15TH WAR
GORA, EDWARD	ALL	053	10TH E.D
GORCARAN, MARGARET	BAL	003	EASTERN
GORCIA, S.	BAL	158	1ST WARD
GORDAN, BRIDGET	BAL	174	2ND DIST
GORDAN, HARRIET	BAL	320	1ST DIST
GORDAN, ISAAC	CEC	205	7TH E DI
GORDAN, JOHN	CEC	178	7TH E DI
GORDAN, JOHN	BAL	300	12TH WAR
GORDAN, JOHN	BAL	306	12TH WAR
GORDAN, MARY	BAL	411	1ST DIST
GORDEN, ANDREW-BLACK	CAR	075	NO TWP L
GORDEN, CHARLES	BAL	455	1ST DIST
GORDEN, HENERETTA	FRE	129	CREAGERS
GORDEN, HETTY	KEN	244	2ND DIST
GORDEN, JAMES F.	KEN	210	2ND DIST
GORDEN, JOHN H.	BAL	311	1ST DIST
GORDEN, MARY	HAR	033	1ST DIST
GORDEN, OWEN	BAL	454	1ST DIST
GORDEN, PERRY	KEN	271	1ST DIST
GORDEN, PERRY-BLACK	CAR	081	NO TWP L
GORDEN, ROBERT T.	CAR	072	NO TWP L
GORDEN, RUTH	BAL	036	2ND DIST
GORDEN, SAMUEL	HAR	034	1ST DIST
GORDEN, SAMUEL R.	KEN	273	1ST DIST
GORDEN, THERESA	ANN	288	ANNAPOLI
GORDER, ELLEN	BAL	149	11TH WAR
GORDIN, ANN	BAL	260	20TH WAR
GORDIN, JANE	FRE	095	FREDERIC
GORDNER, JOSEPH	ALL	219	CUMBERLA
GORDNER, SARAH	CAR	192	4TH DIST
GORDON, A.B.	BAL	202	11TH WAR
GORDON, ABRAHAM	HAR	080	2ND DIST
GORDON, ALEXANDER	HAR	090	2ND DIST
GORDON, ALEXANDER	MGM	380	ROCKERLE
GORDON, ALEXANDER	BAL	165	1ST WARD
GORDON, AMOS	CEC	070	5TH E DI
GORDON, ANDREW	HAR	108	2ND DIST
GORDON, ANDREW	CEC	122	4TH E DI
GORDON, ARNDT	BAL	045	15TH WAR
GORDON, B.	BAL	282	2ND WARD
GORDON, B.M.	BAL	122	1ST WARD
GORDON, BASIL MRS.	BAL	156	11TH WAR
GORDON, BENJAMIN	CEC	019	ELKTON 3
GORDON, BENJAMIN T.	BAL	318	7TH WARD
GORDON, CAGER	KEN	235	2ND DIST
GORDON, CATHERINE	BAL	037	4TH WARD
GORDON, CATHERINE	BAL	056	1ST WARD
GORDON, CATHERINE	BAL	421	8TH WARD
GORDON, CHARLES	BAL	310	7TH WARD
GORDON, CHARLES	BAL	199	2ND WARD
GORDON, CHARLES	CEC	007	ELKTON 3
GORDON, CHARLES	SOM	485	TRAPP DI
GORDON, CHARLES W.	CEC	008	ELKTON 3
GORDON, CLARRISSA S.	BAL	057	15TH WAR
GORDON, CLEM-BLACK	ST	322	4TH E DI
GORDON, CORNELIUS	BAL	031	15TH WAR
GORDON, CANIEL	BAL	037	1ST WARD
GORDON, DAVID	BAL	006	4TH WARD
GORDON, DAVID L.	WAS	131	HAGERSTO
GORDON, DENNIS	BAL	328	7TH WARD
GORDON, ELIJAH	BAL	097	2ND DIST
GORDON, ELIZA	BAL	107	10TH WAR
GORDON, ELLEN	SOM	519	BARREN C
GORDON, GEORGE	BAL	422	8TH WARD
GORDON, GEORGE	BAL	147	1ST WARD
GORDON, GEORGE	BAL	147	1SY WARD
GORDON, GEORGE	CEC	127	5TH E DI
GORDON, GEORGE	CHA	227	ALLENS F
GORDON, GEORGE W.	BAL	289	3RD WARD
GORDON, HARRIET	BAL	357	8TH WARD
GORDON, HENRY	BAL	356	3RD WARD
GORDON, HENRY D.	BAL	067	18TH WAR
GORDON, J.	BAL	149	1ST WARD
GORDON, J. W. W.	BAL	301	20TH WAR
GORDON, JAMES	BAL	369	8TH WARD
GORDON, JAMES	BAL	097	2ND DIST
GORDON, JAMES E.	CEC	172	6TH E DI
GORDON, JAUIRE	BAL	030	2ND DIST
GORDON, JOHN	BAL	001	EASTERN
GORDON, JOHN	BAL	279	2ND WARD
GORDON, JOHN	BAL	128	1ST WARD
GORDON, JOHN	CEC	134	6TH E DI
GORDON, JOHN	BAL	070	18TH WAR
GORDON, JOHN	CEC	070	5TH E DI
GORDON, JOHN	FRE	150	10TH E D
GORDON, JOHN	CAL	007	1ST DIST
GORDON, JOHN	BAL	387	13TH WAR
GORDON, JOHN	TAL	011	EASTON D
GORDON, JOHN A.	BAL	136	11TH WAR
GORDON, JOHN H.	BAL	056	15TH WAR
GORDON, JOHN T.	BAL	414	3RD WARD
GORDON, JOSEPH	BAL	243	12TH WAR
GORDON, JOSEPH	BAL	317	7TH WARD
GORDON, JOSEPH N.	BAL	064	10TH WAR
GORDON, JOSIAH H.	ALL	234	CUMBERLA
GORDON, JULIA	BAL	317	12TH WAR
GORDON, LEMUEL S.	BAL	056	10TH WAR
GORDON, LYDIA	BAL	012	2ND DIST
GORDON, MARGARET	CEC	070	5TH E DI
GORDON, MARTHA	HAR	108	2ND DIST
GORDON, MARTHA	BAL	190	11TH WAR
GORDON, MARY	BAL	422	3RD WARD
GORDON, MARY	CEC	159	PORT DUP
GORDON, MARY	BAL	061	4TH WARD
GORDON, MARY F.	BAL	056	10TH WAR
GORDON, PATRICK	BAL	457	8TH WARD
GORDON, PHILIP	CEC	068	5TH E DI
GORDON, PROVIDENCE	BAL	445	8TH WARD
GORDON, RACHEL	CEC	004	ELKTON 3
GORDON, REBECCA	BAL	030	9TH WARD
GORDON, RHODA	SOM	524	BARREN C
GORDON, ROBERT	BAL	280	2ND WARD
GORDON, SAMUEL	BAL	097	2ND DIST
GORDON, SAMUEL	CEC	057	1ST E DI
GORDON, SARAH	BAL	414	14TH WAR
GORDON, SARAH A.-MULATTO	BAL	208	2ND WARD
GORDON, SARHA A.	BAL	014	2ND DIST
GORDON, STEPHEN	BAL	164	1ST WARD
GORDON, THOMAS	DOR	443	1ST DIST
GORDON, WILLAIM	BAL	244	17TH WAR
GORDON, WILLAIM	BAL	260	20TH WAR
GORDON, WILLIAM	BAL	006	4TH WARD
GORDON, WILLIAM	BAL	384	3RD WARD
GORDON, WILLIAM	KEN	306	3RD DIST
GORDON, WILLIAM F.	BAL	172	16TH WAR
GORDON, ANTHONY	BAL	046	1ST WARD
GORDON, MARTIN	BAL	019	1ST WARD
GORDON, W ILLIAM	BAL	119	1ST WARD
GORDSHEL, GOERGE W.	BAL	180	19TH WAR
GORDSON, CHARLES *	BAL	293	20TH WAR
GORDY, BENJAMIN	SOM	505	SALISBUR
GORDY, BENJAMIN B.	WOR	219	4TH E DI
GORDY, BENJAMIN H.	SOM	492	SALISBUR
GORDY, ELIJAH M.	WOR	231	6TH E DI
GORDY, FRANCIS L.	WOR	238	6TH E DI
GORDY, GARRETTSON	WOR	214	4TH E DI
GORDY, HENRY	WOR	232	6TH E DI
GORDY, HENRY W.	WOR	231	6TH E DI
GORDY, JAEMS H.	WOR	236	6TH E DI
GORDY, JOHN	WOR	239	6TH E DI
GORDY, JOHN H.	WOR	236	6TH E DI
GORDY, LAURA A.	WOR	214	4TH E DI
GORDY, LEAH K.	WOR	211	4TH E DI
GORDY, LINN SR. *	WOR	209	4TH E DI
GORDY, LUN JR. *	WOR	211	4TH E DI
GORDY, MARGARET	WOR	206	4TH E DI
GORDY, MARY	WOR	198	3TH E DI
GORDY, MARY	WOR	237	6TH E DI
GORDY, MARY A.	WOR	238	6TH E DI
GORDY, NATHAN	WOR	238	6TH E DI
GORDY, NOAH	WOR	234	6TH E DI
GORDY, NOAH	WOR	238	6TH E DI
GORDY, RUFUS J.	WOR	238	6TH E DI
GORDY, SAMUEL	WOR	228	6TH E DI
GORDY, SAMUEL SR.	WOR	231	6TH E DI
GORDY, SAMUEL T.	WOR	211	4TH E DI
GORDY, SPICER	WOR	232	6TH E DI
GORDY, WILLIAM	SOM	507	BARREN C
GORDY, WILLIAM	SOM	469	TRAPPE D
GORDY, WILLIAM Q.	WOR	239	5TH E DI
GORE, CATHARINE	BAL	472	14TH WAR
GORE, CATHERINE	FRE	137	CREAGERS
GORE, CHARLES	BAL	204	6TH DIST
GORE, CHARLES F.	BAL	345	7TH WARD
GORE, CHRISTIAN	BAL	204	6TH DIST
GORE, CLARISSA	BAL	220	1ST DIST
GORE, DAVIS	DOR	430	1ST DIST
GORE, ELIJAH	BAL	238	1ST DIST
GORE, ELIJAH	BAL	253	1ST DIST
GORE, GEORGE	BAL	250	1ST DIST
GORE, GEORGE	BAL	247	1ST DIST
GORE, JAMES*	TAL	037	EASTON D
GORE, JESSE	BAL	224	1ST DIST
GORE, JOHN	ALL	255	CUMBERLA
GORE, JOHN	DOR	433	1ST DIST
GORE, JOHN	BAL	458	14TH WAR
GORE, JOHN	CAR	236	UNION TO
GORE, JOHN W.	TAL	073	EASTON T
GORE, JOHNSEY	BAL	242	1ST DIST
GORE, MARY	BAL	251	1ST DIST
GORE, NICHOLAS	CAR	233	5TH DIST
GORE, ORSON	TAL	037	EASTON D
GORE, PHILIP	CAR	215	5TH DIST
GORE, PHILIP	BAL	111	1ST WARD
GORE, ROBERT C.*	TAL	066	EASTON T
GORE, SAMUEL	BAL	219	6TH DIST
GORE, SAMUEL	BAL	204	6TH DIST
GORE, SAMUEL	CAR	213	5TH DIST
GORE, STEPHEN	CAR	213	5TH DIST
GORE, SUSAN	FRE	066	FREDERIC
GORE, TEMPERANCE	BAL	219	6TH DIST
GORE, THOMAS*	TAL	067	EASTON T
GORE, WILLIAM	BAL	223	1ST DIST
GORELL, JOHN	CEC	186	7TH E DI
GORES, DANIEL J.	DOR	430	1ST DIST
GORES, STANLEY	BAL	083	1ST WARD
GORETZ, BALTZER	ALL	038	2ND E.D.
GORGAN, HENRY	BAL	061	4TH WARD
GORGAN, NICHOLAS	BAL	220	1ST DIST
GORGER, HENRY	BAL	310	12TH WAR
GORGUE, CARL *	BAL	304	20TH WAR
GORHTEY, JAMES	WAS	159	2ND DIST
GORIRY, MARY	WAS	129	HAGERSTO
GORL, ELLEN*	KEN	287	3RD DIST
GORLEY, MOSES	FRE	116	CREAGERS
GORLOS, MARY	BAL	248	12TH WAR
GORMAN, ANN	BAL	369	3RD WARD
GORMAN, ANNA-MULATTO	BAL	224	2ND WARD
GORMAN, BERNARD	BAL	161	11TH WAR
GORMAN, BRIDGET	BAL	414	3RD WARD
GORMAN, CLARA	BAL	116	5TH WARD
GORMAN, EVE	BAL	405	3RD WARD
GORMAN, HENRY	BAL	135	2ND DIST
GORMAN, HENRY	BAL	151	11TH WAR
GORMAN, HESTER	BAL	394	3RD WARD
GORMAN, JAMES	BAL	280	7TH WARD
GORMAN, JAMES	BAL	134	1ST WARD
GORMAN, JAMES	BAL	018	1ST WARD
GORMAN, JAMES	BAL	454	14TH WAR
GORMAN, JAMES W.	BAL	040	4TH WARD
GORMAN, JANE	BAL	307	1ST DIST
GORMAN, JOHN	BAL	127	1ST WARD
GORMAN, JOHN	BAL	125	1ST WARD
GORMAN, JOHN	BAL	152	1ST WARD
GORMAN, JOHN	CAL	062	3RD DIST
GORMAN, MARY	BAL	178	19TH WAR
GORMAN, MARY	BAL	066	2ND DIST
GORMAN, MARY A.	BAL	280	7TH WARD
GORMAN, MARY G.	BAL	004	1ST WARD
GORMAN, MICHAEL	BAL	156	2ND DIST
GORMAN, MICHAEL	BAL	398	3RD WARD
GORMAN, MISS M.	FRE	199	5TH E DI
GORMAN, PATRICK	BAL	316	20TH WAR
GORMAN, PATRICK	ANN	415	HOWARD D
GORMAN, PATRICK	BAL	028	9TH WARD
GORMAN, PATRICK G.	BAL	120	1ST WARD
GORMAN, PETER	ANN	448	HOWARD D
GORMAN, THOMAS W.	BAL	257	12TH WAR
GORMAN, WILLIAM	BAL	124	1ST WARD
GORMAN, WILLIAM	BAL	049	4TH WARD
GORMECE, ELIZABETH	BAL	288	12TH WAR
GORMICHER, DROW	BAL	112	1ST WARD
GORMLY, HENRY	BAL	461	1ST DIST
GORMLY, THOMAS	BAL	355	13TH WAR
GORNAND, HENRY	CAR	213	5TH DIST
GORNE, MICHAEL	CEC	064	1ST E DI
GORNEER, WILLIAM	BAL	312	12TH WAR
GORNELL, ENOCH	BAL	325	7TH WARD
GORNELL, QUINCY A.	BAL	164	19TH WAR
GORNER, MARGARET	ALL	202	CUMBERLA
GORNEST, GRACE F.	BAL	249	12TH WAR
GORNISH, ELIZA	BAL	021	1ST WARD
GORR, CHARLES	BAL	350	7TH WARD
GORR, GEORGE	ALL	037	2ND E.D.

GORR, PHILLIP ALL 036 2ND E.D.
GORRAGE, WILLIAM A. BAL 388 13TH WAR
GORREL, JAMES HAR 026 1ST DIST
GORRELL, ANDREW HAR 129 2ND DIST
GORRELL, GEORGE HAR 118 2ND DIST
GORRELL, HENRY HAR 119 2ND DIST
GORRELL, HENRY HAR 122 2ND DIST
GORRELL, JACKSON HAR 121 2ND DIST
GORRELL, JACKSON HAR 120 2ND DIST
GORRELL, JAMES CEC 077 NORTHEAS
GORRELL, JAMES D. HAR 178 3RD DIST
GORRELL, JOHN HAR 120 2ND DIST
GORRELL, JOHN CEC 073 5TH E DI
GORRELL, RESIN HAR 125 2ND DIST
GORRELL, ROBERT B. HAR 123 2ND DIST
GORRELL, SKIPWITH, C. HAR 121 2ND DIST
GORRELL, WILLIAM CEC 072 5TH E DI
GORRELL, WILLIAM HAR 118 2ND DIST
GORRELL, WILLIAM G. HAR 164 3RD DIST
GORRETT, THEADORA HAR 094 2ND DIST
GORREY, G. BAL 165 1ST WARD
GORSBEN, LUCY BAL 089 2ND DIST
GORSUCH, ANDREW BAL 380 3RD WARD
GORSUCH, ANGELINE BAL 019 2ND DIST
GORSUCH, ANN BAL 025 2ND DIST
GORSUCH, ANN D. DOR 467 1ST DIST
GORSUCH, BENJAMIN CAR 375 9TH DIST
GORSUCH, BENJAMIN H. BAL 288 7TH WARD
GORSUCH, CATHERINE FRE 011 FREDERIC
GORSUCH, CHARLES HAR 140 2ND DIST
GORSUCH, CHARLES B. BAL 425 1ST DIST
GORSUCH, CHARLES H. BAL 276 7TH WARD
GORSUCH, CHARLOTTE BAL 020 2ND DIST
GORSUCH, EDWARD BAL 429 1ST DIST
GORSUCH, ELIZABETH BAL 314 7TH WARD
GORSUCH, ELLEN BAL 025 2ND DIST
GORSUCH, G. BAL 141 5TH WARD
GORSUCH, J. BAL 140 1ST WARD
GORSUCH, JAMES BAL 400 3RD WARD
GORSUCH, JOHN BAL 124 5TH WARD
GORSUCH, JOHN BAL 165 1ST WARD
GORSUCH, JOHN BAL 250 1ST WARD
GORSUCH, JOSEPH BAL 250 1ST DIST
GORSUCH, JOSHUA BAL 017 2ND DIST
GORSUCH, JOSHUA ANN 419 HOWARD D
GORSUCH, KIPIA* BAL 380 3RD WARD
GORSUCH, LEVI BAL 032 2ND DIST
GORSUCH, LEVIN BAL 030 1ST WARD
GORSUCH, LUTHER M. HAR 017 1ST DIST
GORSUCH, MARY BAL 174 16TH WAR
GORSUCH, MARY J. BAL 330 7TH WARD
GORSUCH, NELSON BAL 022 2ND DIST
GORSUCH, NICHOLAS BAL 032 2ND DIST
GORSUCH, NICHOLAS BAL 032 2ND DIST
GORSUCH, NICHOLAS M. BAL 046 4TH WARD
GORSUCH, NOAH BAL 424 1ST DIST
GORSUCH, PEREGRINE BAL 202 6TH WARD
GORSUCH, PHEOBE BAL 092 5TH WARD
GORSUCH, ROBERT BAL 220 6TH WARD
GORSUCH, RUTH BAL 032 2ND DIST
GORSUCH, SAMUEL BAL 035 1ST WARD
GORSUCH, SARAH BAL 278 12TH WAR
GORSUCH, SARAH BAL 181 19TH WAR
GORSUCH, SARAH DOR 466 1ST DIST
GORSUCH, STEPHEN CAR 373 9TH DIST
GORSUCH, STEPHEN BAL 032 2ND DIST
GORSUCH, STEPHEN BAL 051 2ND DIST
GORSUCH, SUSAN BAL 276 7TH WARD
GORSUCH, SUSANNA BAL 181 6TH WARD
GORSUCH, SUSANNAH BAL 048 1ST WARD
GORSUCH, THOMAS BAL 319 20TH WAR
GORSUCH, THOMAS * CAR 203 4TH DIST
GORSUCH, WASHINGTON BAL 217 6TH WARD
GORSUCH, WILLIAM BAL 331 1ST DIST
GORSUCH, WILLIAM BAL 435 8TH WARD
GORSUCH, WILLIAM P. BAL 086 18TH WAR
GORSUCH,WILLIAM BAL 025 2ND DIST
GORSUCK, ANN CAR 203 4TH DIST
GORSUCK, AQUILLA BAL 180 2ND DIST
GORSUCK, BENJAMIN BAL 188 5TH DIST
GORSUCK, BENJAMIN BAL 086 2ND DIST
GORSUCK, ELISHA CAR 206 4TH DIST
GORSUCK, JAMES M. CAR 274 7TH DIST
GORSUCK, JOHN BAL 142 2ND DIST
GORSUCK, JOHN BAL 033 9TH WARD
GORSUCK, JOSHUA BAL 148 2ND DIST
GORSUCK, JOSHUA * BAL 128 2ND DIST
GORSUCK, JULIAN BAL 364 3RD WARD
GORSUCK, LOVELISS CAR 211 5TH DIST
GORSUCK, NATHAN CAR 203 4TH DIST
GORSUCK, NATHAN CAR 269 WESTMINS
GORSUCK, PEREGRINE BAL 414 14TH WAR
GORSUCK, ROBERT * BAL 325 12TH WAR
GORSUCK, THOMAS BAL 094 2ND DIST
GORSUCK, THOMAS FRE 300 WOODSBOR
GORSUDH, THOMAS BAL 406 3RD WARD
GORTEE, BENJAMIN BAL 049 4TH WARD
GORTER, ONNO GOSSE* BAL 070 10TH WAR
GORTHWAY, ELIZABETH BAL 081 1ST WARD
GORTHWAY, ELIZABETH BAL 080 1ST WARD
GORTIS, GOSSEONUS* BAL 070 10TH WAR
GORTON, FRECERICK BAL 273 2ND WARD
GORTON, PHEOBE BAL 266 7TH WARD
GORTON, WILLIAM BAL 273 2ND WARD
GORTON, WILLIAM A. BAL 157 16TH WAR
GOSBEE, SUSAN SOM 460 HANGARY
GOSBERT, NICHOLAS BAL 126 18TH WAR
GOSBIN, MARY E. DOR 309 1ST DIST
GOSBREL, JACOB BAL 045 2ND DIST
GOSBY, ISAAC BAL 456 1ST DIST
GOSCUP, FREDERIC HAR 139 2ND DIST
GOSDEN, JOHN T. BAL 177 6TH WARD
GOSEMAN, JOHN BAL 023 1ST WARD
GOSH, WILLIAM WAS 117 2ND DIST
GOSHEL, HENRY BAL 052 2ND DIST
GOSHELL, PETER BAL 241 2ND WARD
GOSKINS, SAMUEL BAL 461 1ST DIST
GOSLEE, CLEMENT SOM 515 BARREN C
GOSLEE, JACOB SOM 529 QUANTICO
GOSLEE, JAMES M.* SOM 481 TRAPP DI
GOSLEE, JANE SOM 520 BARREN C
GOSLEE, JOHN SOM 532 QUANTICO
GOSLEE, JOHN SOM 473 TRAPPE D
GOSLEE, JOHN S. SOM 499 SALISBUR
GOSLEE, JOHN T. SOM 487 SALISBUR
GOSLEE, LEVI SOM 508 BARREN C
GOSLEE, LEYA SOM 524 BARREN C
GOSLEE, LUCY SOM 504 SALISBUR
GOSLEE, MARY SOM 527 QUANTICO
GOSLEE, RICHARD SOM 549 TYASKIN
GOSLEE, SABRE SOM 533 QUANTICO
GOSLEE, SARAH SOM 330 QUANTICO
GOSLEE, VALENTINE O. SOM 549 TYASKIN
GOSLER, HANNAH ALL 013 3RD E.D.
GOSLIN, ANN M. FRE 035 FREDERIC
GOSLIN, EDWARD R. CAR 125 NO TWP L
GOSLIN, GEORGE BAL 005 EASTERN
GOSLIN, HARRIET BAL 404 14TH WAR
GOSLIN, LEWIS BAL 409 14TH WAR
GOSLIN, MARY DOR 309 1ST DIST
GOSLIN, PHILIP J. BAL 409 14TH WAR
GOSLIN, RICHARD BAL 031 2ND DIST
GOSLIN, WILLIAM L. DOR 316 1ST DIST
GOSLIN,MARGRET BAL 020 2ND DIST
GOSLING, JACK ANN 420 HOWARD D
GOSLING, JOHN BAL 013 15TH WAR
GOSMAN, JAMES * WAS 117 2ND DIST
GOSMELL, VACHEL CAR 216 5TH DIST
GOSNEL, PETER WAS 091 2ND SUBD
GOSNEL, WILLIAM CAR 369 9TH DIST
GOSNEL, WILLIAM H. ANN 457 HOWARD D
GOSNELE, MARTHA CAR 362 9TH DIST
GOSNELL, AARON CAR 370 9TH DIST
GOSNELL, AMOS FRE 391 PETERSVI
GOSNELL, ANN M. BAL 300 1ST DIST
GOSNELL, BEAL CAR 370 9TH DIST
GOSNELL, CASSANORA BAL 306 1ST DIST
GOSNELL, CHARLES A. CAR 404 2ND DIST
GOSNELL, ELLEN CAR 362 9TH DIST
GOSNELL, ELLEN V. ANN 510 HOWARD D
GOSNELL, ELLEN W. BAL 347 13TH WAR
GOSNELL, FRANKLIN BAL 193 6TH WARD
GOSNELL, GEORGE ANN 517 HOWARD D
GOSNELL, GEORGE BAL 446 8TH WARD
GOSNELL, GEORGE H.CLAY BAL 015 18TH WAR
GOSNELL, GEORGE T. BAL 016 18TH WAR
GOSNELL, HEROD BAL 324 1ST DIST
GOSNELL, JAMES CAR 218 5TH DIST
GOSNELL, JERRY BAL 229 1ST DIST
GOSNELL, JESSE ANN 466 HOWARD D
GOSNELL, JOHN CAR 228 5TH DIST
GOSNELL, JOHN FRE 101 FREDERIC
GOSNELL, JOHN L. BAL 007 18TH WAR
GOSNELL, JOHN R. ANN 507 HOWARD D
GOSNELL, JOSEPH H. CAR 372 9TH DIST
GOSNELL, JSEPER CAR 209 5TH DIST
GOSNELL, LEVANA BAL 228 1ST DIST
GOSNELL, LEVI CAR 214 5TH DIST
GOSNELL, LEWIS CAR 232 5TH DIST
GOSNELL, LUTHER R. FRE 391 PETERSVI
GOSNELL, LYDIA A. CAR 367 9TH DIST
GOSNELL, MARICN BAL 324 1ST DIST
GOSNELL, MARY BAL 299 1ST DIST
GOSNELL, MARY A. CAR 372 9TH DIST
GOSNELL, MICHAEL WAS 199 1ST DIST
GOSNELL, MORDICA BAL 400 1ST DIST
GOSNELL, MOSES G. ANN 456 HOWARD D
GOSNELL, NINROD CAR 372 9TH DIST
GOSNELL, PERIGRINE BAL 324 1ST DIST
GOSNELL, PERRY CAR 220 5TH DIST
GOSNELL, PETER BAL 228 1ST DIST
GOSNELL, PETER BAL 228 1ST DIST
GOSNELL, PHILIP J. CAR 232 5TH DIST
GOSNELL, ROBERT CAR 218 5TH DIST
GOSNELL, ROBERT BAL 326 1ST DIST
GOSNELL, RUTH CAR 193 4TH DIST
GOSNELL, SAMUEL CAR 370 9TH DIST
GOSNELL, SARAH BAL 299 1ST DIST
GOSNELL, SARAH BAL 266 1ST DIST
GOSNELL, THOMAS ANN 454 HOWARD D
GOSNELL, THOMAS BAL 193 6TH WARD
GOSNELL, THOMAS S. CAR 221 5TH DIST
GOSNELL, VACHEL BAL 324 1ST DIST
GOSNELL, WASHINGTON CAR 215 5TH DIST
GOSNELL, WILLIAM BAL 325 1ST DIST
GOSNELL, WILLIAM H. CAR 370 9TH DIST
GOSNEY, MARGARET BAL 195 2ND WARD
GOSPENSTRICK, JOHN BAL 202 2ND WARD
GOSS, GOTHELLE BAL 057 4TH WARD
GOSS, JANE BAL 049 4TH WARD
GOSS, JOHN BAL 374 13TH WAR
GOSSAGE, ELIZA TAL 095 ST MICHA
GOSSAGE, ENNAES TAL 097 ST MICHA
GOSSAGE, JAMES H.* TAL 067 EASTON T
GOSSAGE, JAMES* TAL 037 EASTON D
GOSSAGE, MARY TAL 084 ST MICHA
GOSSAGE, RICHARD* TAL 039 EASTON D
GOSSAGE, THOMAS TAL 080 ST MICHA
GOSSAGE, TRISS * TAL 088 ST MICHA
GOSSE GORTER, ONNO* BAL 070 10TH WAR
GOSSE, CATHARINE BAL 111 2ND DIST
GOSSMAN, MARIA A.* BAL 303 3RD WARD
GOSSOP, MARGARET BAL 410 1ST DIST
GOSSUCH, LOVELIS M. FRE 205 BUCKEYST
GOSSUCK, ELISABETH T. BAL 426 14TH WAR
GOSSUM, ALEXANDER PRI 023 VANSVILL
GOST, FRED BAL 251 12TH WAR
GOST, GEORGE WAS 211 1ST DIST
GOSTER, AARON BAL 281 7TH WARD
GOT, JOHN BAL 232 1ST DIST
GOTE, RICHARD J.R MGM 422 MEDLEY 3
GOTEN, JOHN BAL 051 9TH WARD
GOTHURP, R.Y. BAL 174 19TH WAR
GOTIER, FRANCIS CEC 008 ELKTON 3
GOTLIP, ELIZABETH WAS 042 2ND SUBD
GOTSBERRY, GEORGE BAL 287 3RD WARD
GOTT, BENJAMIN CAL 002 1ST DIST
GOTT, EDWIN E. ANN 394 8TH DIST
GOTT, JACKSON BAL 453 1ST DIST
GOTT, JAMES CAL 009 1ST DIST
GOTT, JAMES HAR 055 1ST DIST
GOTT, JOHN BAL 416 1ST DIST
GOTT, JOHN C. MGM 425 MEDLEY 3
GOTT, JOHN H. KEN 309 3RD DIST
GOTT, JOSEPH CAL 002 1ST DIST
GOTT, RICHARD MGM 409 MEDLEY 3
GOTT, SAMUEL ANN 324 2ND DIST
GOTT, THOMAS CAL 033 2ND DIST
GOTT, THOMAS N. MGM 407 MEDLEY 3
GOTT, WILLIAM BAL 299 20TH WAR
GOTT, WILLIAM * BAL 288 20TH WAR
GOTTENFELT, LEWIS BAL 068 1ST WARD
GOTTENMYER, JOSEPH BAL 276 1ST DIST
GOTTHAMER, PETER BAL 338 1ST DIST
GOTTINGHAMER, PETER BAL 434 8TH WARD
GOTZINGER, PETER BAL 349 13TH WAR
GOUCHER, SAMUEL WAS 227 1ST DIST
GOUDA, STEPHEN * BAL 292 1ST DIST
GOUDEY, JOHN ANN 463 HOWARD D
GOUDEY, JOHNATHAN ANN 463 HOWARD D
GOUED, SARAH * BAL 317 12TH WAR
GOUF, ADAM WAS 078 2ND SUBD
GOUF, CATHARINE WAS 064 2ND SUBD
GOUF, GEORGE WAS 079 2ND SUBD
GOUF, HARRY WAS 082 2ND SUBD
GOUF, ISAUH WAS 064 2ND SUBD
GOUF, JOHN WAS 079 2ND SUBD
GOUF, JOSEPH WAS 064 2ND SUBD
GOUF, LUCINDA WAS 079 2ND SUBD
GOUF, MAHLON WAS 079 2ND SUBD
GOUF, MARY WAS 080 2ND SUBD
GOUF, RUAN WAS 082 2ND SUBD
GOUF, SAMUEL WAS 078 2ND SUBD
GOUGE, FREDERICK BAL 183 19TH WAR
GOUGER, JOHN CAR 306 1ST DIST
GOUGH, ABBOUT HAR 192 3RD DIST
GOUGH, ANDREW BAL 131 1ST WARD
GOUGH, ANN BAL 178 6TH WARD
GOUGH, ANN E. ST 283 3RD E DI
GOUGH, ANN E. ST 284 2ND E DI
GOUGH, ANN M. ST 275 3RD E DI
GOUGH, ANN P. BAL 212 11TH WAR
GOUGH, BENEDICT BAL 112 10TH WAR
GOUGH, BENNET ST 284 2ND E DI
GOUGH, BENNET ST 283 3RD E DI
GOUGH, CAROLINE BAL 183 11TH WAR
GOUGH, CASSANDRA BAL 338 1ST DIST
GOUGH, CATHARINE ANN 431 HOWARD D
GOUGH, CHARLES E. ST 283 3RD E DI
GOUGH, DIXON BAL 113 15TH WAR
GOUGH, FANNY BAL 378 3RD WARD
GOUGH, FRANCIS BAL 179 11TH WAR
GOUGH, GEORGE BAL 054 4TH WARD
GOUGH, HARRY D. HAR 144 2ND DIST
GOUGH, JAMES J. ST 266 3RD E DI
GOUGH, JANE BAL 159 6TH WARD
GOUGH, JOEPH FRE 029 FREDERIC
GOUGH, LLOYD BAL 263 12TH WAR
GOUGH, MARILDA BAL 120 18TH WAR
GOUGH, MARTHA BAL 029 9TH WARD
GOUGH, MARY BAL 174 6TH WARD
GOUGH, MARY BAL 140 5TH WARD
GOUGH, PEGGY ANN 431 HOWARD D
GOUGH, PETER ANN 379 4TH DIST
GOUGH, SARAH C. ST 265 3RD E DI
GOUGH, THOMAS BAL 323 7TH WARD
GOUGH, THOMAS G. ST 283 3RD E DI
GOUGH, THOMAS W. ST 284 2ND E DI
GOUGH, THOMAS W. ST 283 3RD E DI
GOUGH, WILLIAM BAL 127 2ND DIST
GOUGH, WILLIAM H. CHA 272 ALLENS F
GOUGHTY, SALLEY WOR 235 5TH E DI
GOUKER, CATHARINE WAS 245 SMITHSBU
GOUKER, DAVID WAS 271 1ST DIST
GOUKER, ELIAS WAS 270 1ST DIST
GOUKER, GEORGE CAR 292 7TH DIST
GOUKER, JAMES WAS 238 CAVETOWN
GOUKER, JULIAN WAS 238 CAVETOWN
GOUKER, WILLIAM BAL 232 1ST DIST
GOUKER, WILLIAM H. WAS 271 1ST DIST
GOULD, ALEXANDER QUE 178 2ND E DI
GOULD, ALEXANDER BAL 275 17TH WAR
GOULD, ALEXANDER BAL 232 17TH WAR
GOULD, ANN CEC 177 7TH E DI
GOULD, ANN BAL 458 14TH WAR
GOULD, ANNA CEC 006 ELKTON 3
GOULD, ANNA KEN 214 2ND DIST
GOULD, ANNE A. BAL 049 15TH WAR
GOULD, CAROLINE-BLACK QUE 155 2ND E DI
GOULD, CASPAR BAL 158 2ND DIST
GOULD, CATHERINE BAL 459 8TH WARD
GOULD, CHRIST. BAL 295 1ST DIST
GOULD, DANIEL HAR 102 2ND DIST
GOULD, DANIEL D. BAL 379 13TH WAR
GOULD, EDWARD BAL 093 10TH WAR
GOULD, ELIZA-BLACK QUE 180 2ND E DI
GOULD, ELIZABETH BAL 192 11TH WAR
GOULD, ELIZABETH BAL 156 11TH WAR
GOULD, FRANCES BAL 297 12TH WAR
GOULD, FRANCES BAL 223 6TH WARD
GOULD, G. FRANCIS BAL 146 5TH WARD
GOULD, GATLY SOM 538 TYASKIN
GOULD, HENRY SOM 531 QUANTICO
GOULD, HESTER QUE 178 2ND E DI
GOULD, HETTY BAL 166 19TH WAR
GOULD, JACOB SOM 523 BARREN C
GOULD, JAMES SOM 547 TYASKIN
GOULD, JAMES SOM 549 TYASKIN
GOULD, JAMES DOR 459 1ST DIST
GOULD, JAMES BAL 198 11TH WAR
GOULD, JAMES A. BAL 072 18TH WAR
GOULD, JOHN BAL 228 17TH WAR
GOULD, JOHN KEN 235 2ND DIST
GOULD, JOHN BAL 101 15TH WAR
GOULD, JOHN WAS 164 HAGERSTO
GOULD, JOHN G. BAL 076 4TH WARD
GOULD, JOHN H. BAL 122 16TH WAR
GOULD, JOHN W. QUE 197 3RD E DI
GOULD, JOHN-BLACK QUE 157 2ND E DI
GOULD, JOSEPH-BLACK QUE 170 2ND E DI
GOULD, MARGARET KEN 220 2ND DIST
GOULD, MARY CEC 008 ELKTON 3
GOULD, MARY BAL 040 9TH WARD
GOULD, MARY BAL 343 3RD WARD
GOULD, NICHOLAS BAL 205 2ND WARD
GOULD, PAINE BAL 283 12TH WAR
GOULD, RACHEL CEC 009 ELKTON 3
GOULD, REBECCA BAL 015 18TH WAR
GOULD, RICHARD BAL 043 15TH WAR
GOULD, ROSETTA SOM 530 QUANTICO
GOULD, SAMUEL QUE 214 3RD E DI
GOULD, SAMUEL BAL 077 10TH WAR
GOULD, SAMUEL BAL 315 3RD WARD
GOULD, STEPHEN-BLACK QUE 152 1ST E DI
GOULD, THOMAS N. BAL 048 15TH WAR
GOULD, WILLIAM QUE 207 3RD E DI
GOULD, WILLIAM QUE 180 2ND E DI
GOULD, WILLIAM-BLACK QUE 172 2ND E DI
GOULD, WILLIAM-BLACK QUE 151 1ST E DI
GOULD, WILLIAM-BLACK QUE 148 1ST E DI
GOULD, ZACHEUS BAL 170 6TH WARD
GOULD,MARIA-BLACK QUE 183 3RD E DI
GOULDE, WILLIAM SOM 435 PRINCESS
GOULDEN, ANTHONY ALL 048 10TH E.D
GOULDEN, BRIDGET ALL 072 5TH E.D.
GOULDEN, JAMES BAL 137 1ST WARD
GOULDEN, JEFFRY BAL 241 6TH WARD
GOULDEN, JOHN ALL 048 10TH E.D
GOULDEN, LUCINDA BAL 241 6TH WARD
GOULDEN, MARY BAL 216 11TH WAR

Name	County	Page	District
GOULDEN, PATRICK	ALL	141	6TH E.D.
GOULDIN, BRIDGET	BAL	380	3RD WARD
GOULDSBOROUGH, FRANCIS	BAL	114	5TH WARD
GOULDSBOUROUGH, F.	BAL	460	1ST DIST
GOULDSBURY, HENRY	BAL	451	1ST DIST
GOULDSMITH, ELIZABETH W.	BAL	348	7TH WARD
GOULEY, CHARLOTTE	BAL	095	10TH WAR
GOULIART, JOHN	BAL	104	18TH WAR
GOULSTEL, ANN*	BAL	416	3RD WARD
GOULT, ALEXANDER	CAR	091	NO TWP L
GOULT, ALEXANDER	CAR	078	NO TWP L
GOULT, HENRIETTA	CAR	166	NO TWP L
GOULT, LEVI	CAR	080	NO TWP L
GOULT, RICHARD	CAR	099	NO TWP L
GOULT, SAMUEL	CAR	078	NO TWP L
GOULT, WILLIAM	CAR	166	NO TWP L
GOULTON, LOUIS E.	BAL	116	1ST WARD
GOULY, GEORGE	BAL	189	11TH WAR
GOUPH, ALEXINA	BAL	091	5TH WARD
GOURD, LAWRENCE	BAL	282	1ST DIST
GOURDLEY, ELIZA	BAL	358	3RD WARD
GOURLEY, GEORGE	BAL	008	4TH WARD
GOURLEY, JAMES	PRI	057	NOTTINGH
GOURLEY, MOSES	FRE	146	10TH E D
GOURLEY, THOMAS	FRE	145	10TH E D
GOURLY, E.	PRI	065	NOTTINGH
GOURLY, THOMAS	PRI	065	NOTTINGH
GOUSE, THOMAS	BAL	315	7TH WARD
GOUSO, LAURA V.	FRE	061	FREDERIC
GOUTNIM, CHARLES	BAL	193	17TH WAR
GOUTY, REBECCA	CAR	148	NO TWP L
GOUTY, SARAH	DOR	325	1ST DIST
GOUTY, WILLIAM	CAR	144	NO TWP L
GOUVERNER, JAMES	BAL	315	20TH WAR
GOUY, WILLIAM H.	CAR	162	NO TWP L
GOUZELEIG, REUBEN	BAL	128	5TH WARD
GOVAN, RICHARD	CEC	145	PORT DUP
GOVANS, AIRABELLA	BAL	427	1ST DIST
GOVE, JAMES*	TAL	037	EASTON D
GOVE, MARGARET	CEC	043	CHESAPEA
GOVE, MARY E.*	TAL	037	EASTON D
GOVE, ROBERT C.*	TAL	066	EASTON T
GOVE, THOMAS*	TAL	067	EASTON T
GOVENS, CHARITY	BAL	153	5TH WARD
GOVENS, DANIEL	BAL	114	5TH WARD
GOVENS, HENRY	CEC	055	1ST E DI
GOVER, BARBARA	BAL	241	1ST DIST
GOVER, CLARA	BAL	107	5TH WARD
GOVER, FREDERICK G.	CAR	204	4TH DIST
GOVER, GIRARD	BAL	088	4TH WARD
GOVER, JACOB	BAL	267	7TH WARD
GOVER, JAMES A.	HAR	152	3RD DIST
GOVER, PETER	BAL	133	1ST WARD
GOVER, PHIL	HAR	145	3RD DIST
GOVER, RICHARD	ANN	343	3RD DIST
GOVER, ROVERT	HAR	027	1ST DIST
GOVER, SAMUEL	FRE	259	NEW MARK
GOVER, SAMUEL	ANN	403	8TH DIST
GOVER, SAMUEL H.	BAL	137	5TH WARD
GOVER, SARAH	HAR	192	3RD DIST
GOVER, TORRY	HAR	045	1ST DIST
GOVER, WILLIAM	BAL	038	2ND DIST
GOVERDENK, CHRISTIAN	BAL	013	2ND DIST
GOVERMAN, ANTHONY	BAL	014	4TH WARD
GOVERMAN, ANTHONY	BAL	014	4TH WARD
GOVRICH, W.	BAL	138	1ST WARD
GOW, ELIZABETH *	WAS	063	2ND SUBD
GOW, JAMES	QUE	186	3RD E DI
GOW, SOLOMAN	TAL	005	EASTON D
GOW, WILLIAM	QUE	199	3RD E DI
GOWAN, C.	BAL	280	12TH WAR
GOWAN, MRS.	ANN	265	ANNAPOLI
GOWEN, MARY	CAR	237	UNION TO
GOWER, ADAM	ALL	060	10TH E.D
GOWER, GEORGE	WAS	027	2ND SUBD
GOWER, HENRY	WAS	169	FUNKSTOW
GOWER, JACOB	WAS	173	FUNKSTOW
GOWER, JACOB	ALL	059	10TH E.D
GOWER, JACOB	ALL	060	10TH E.D
GOWER, JOHN	ALL	060	10TH E.D
GOWER, MARY	WAS	027	2ND SUBD
GOWER, WILLIAM	ALL	060	10TH E.D
GOWTY, MARY*	DOR	321	1ST DIST
GOY, SAMUEL D. *	BAL	301	20TH WAR
GOYALL, THOMAS	BAL	056	18TH WAR
GOYER, FRED	KEN	263	1ST DIST
GOYER, JOHN	KEN	264	1ST DIST
GOYLE, ELLEN	BAL	043	18TH WAR
GR---, J. L.	ANN	346	3RD DIST
GRAB, PETER	BAL	115	11TH WAR
GRABELL, NANCY	BAL	454	1ST DIST
GRABER, CLARA	BAL	354	13TH WAR
GRABILL, ABRAHAM	FRE	433	8TH E DI
GRABILL, JACOB	FRE	283	WOODSBOR
GRABILL, JOHN	FRE	169	5TH E DI
GRABILL, MOSES	FRE	283	WOODSBOR
GRABILL, PETER	FRE	169	5TH E DI
GRABILL, THOMAS	BAL	454	1ST DIST
GRABLE, ELIZABETH	BAL	399	14TH WAR
GRABNER, MARGARETTA	BAL	072	10TH WAR
GRABUR, PETER	BAL	380	1ST DIST
GRACE, AARON B.	BAL	362	3RD WARD
GRACE, ADAM	BAL	416	3RD WARD
GRACE, ALEX	BAL	006	1ST WARD
GRACE, ALFRED	CAR	277	7TH DIST
GRACE, ANDREW	CAR	350	6TH DIST
GRACE, DANIEL	BAL	017	2ND DIST
GRACE, EVALINE	ANN	343	3RD DIST
GRACE, HENRY	CAR	348	6TH DIST
GRACE, J.A.	BAL	275	12TH WAR
GRACE, JACOB	BAL	283	7TH WARD
GRACE, JAMES	BAL	379	13TH WAR
GRACE, JAMES	TAL	096	ST MICHA
GRACE, JAMES	TAL	109	ST MICHA
GRACE, JAMES H.	KEN	296	3RD DIST
GRACE, JESSE	BAL	175	19TH WAR
GRACE, JESSE	ANN	462	HOWARD D
GRACE, JOHN	BAL	147	2ND DIST
GRACE, JOHN	BAL	307	7TH WARD
GRACE, JOHN	BAL	013	4TH WARD
GRACE, JOHN	BAL	241	17TH WAR
GRACE, LAURA V.	BAL	449	14TH WAR
GRACE, MARY	BAL	275	12TH WAR
GRACE, MICHAEL	CAR	305	1ST DIST
GRACE, PRUCILLA	BAL	289	3RD WARD
GRACE, REBECCA	TAL	109	ST MICHA
GRACE, SAMUEL	DOR	416	1ST DIST
GRACE, SARAH	BAL	467	14TH WAR
GRACE, SKINNER	TAL	106	ST MICHA
GRACE, STANTLY*	TAL	025	EASTON D
GRACE, THOMAS	BAL	417	8TH WARD
GRACE, WILLIAM	CEC	072	5TH E DI
GRACE,ELIZABETH	BAL	074	1ST WARD
GRACEN, JOHN	BAL	149	16TH WAR
GRACER, PHILIP D.	BAL	282	12TH WAR
GRACEY, HENRY SR.	BAL	255	6TH WARD
GRACEY, HUGH	BAL	284	7TH WARD
GRACEY, MARY E.	BAL	176	19TH WAR
GRACEY, WILLIAM	BAL	255	6TH WARD
GRACEY, WILLIAM	BAL	315	7TH WARD
GRACHUN, BERNARD	BAL	109	1ST WARD
GRACIE, AUGUSTUS	BAL	416	14TH WAR
GRACY, CATHERINE E.	CEC	166	6TH E DI
GRACY, KNAPPY	BAL	366	3RD WARD
GRACY, WILLAIM	CEC	088	4TH E DI
GRADEN, CHARLES	BAL	413	1ST DIST
GRADER, CONRADT	BAL	270	7TH WARD
GRADILY, WILLIAM	CEC	074	NORTHEAS
GRADSHAW, SAM	BAL	155	1ST WARD
GRADY, JOHN	BAL	127	5TH WARD
GRADY, JOHN	BAL	178	11TH WAR
GRADY, MARGARET	BAL	049	15TH WAR
GRADY, MARY	BAL	063	10TH WAR
GRADY, MARY	BAL	076	2ND DIST
GRADY, MARY	BAL	043	4TH WARD
GRAEEBEL, CHARLES *	BAL	048	18TH WAR
GRAESER, FREDERICKA	BAL	061	15TH WAR
GRAESS, TOBIAS	BAL	425	1ST DIST
GRAF, JOHN	BAL	269	2ND WARD
GRAF, PETER	BAL	114	5TH WARD
GRAF, PHILIP	ALL	209	CUMBERLA
GRAFF, CAROLINE	BAL	048	9TH WARD
GRAFF, CATHERINE	BAL	107	10TH WAR
GRAFF, ELI B.	BAL	054	4TH WARD
GRAFF, EVAN	FRE	247	NEW MARK
GRAFF, FREDERICK B.	BAL	136	11TH WAR
GRAFF, GEORGE W.	MGM	403	ROCKERLE
GRAFF, HENRIETTA	BAL	404	3RD WARD
GRAFF, JAMES J.	ANN	273	ANNAPOLI
GRAFF, JOHN	ALL	216	CUMBERLA
GRAFF, JOHN	BAL	168	16TH WAR
GRAFF, JOHN D.	BAL	292	3RD WARD
GRAFF, JOHN S.	ANN	287	ANNAPOLI
GRAFF, LEOANRD	BAL	241	1ST DIST
GRAFF, MICHIEL	BAL	224	1ST DIST
GRAFF, SUSAN	BAL	418	14TH WAR
GRAFF, THOMAS	BAL	404	3RD WARD
GRAFF, TRAT	ALL	259	CUMBERLA
GRAFF, WILLIAM	BAL	298	3RD WARD
GRAFF, WILLIAM	FRE	233	BUCKEYST
GRAFF,MARY E.	FRE	031	FREDERIC
GRAFFIN, A.	BAL	154	11TH WAR
GRAFFLIN, JOSEPH	BAL	188	16TH WAR
GRAFFLIN, T. C.	BAL	329	13TH WAR
GRAFLIN, JACOB	BAL	002	18TH WAR
GRAFT, ELISABETH	ALL	239	CUMBERLA
GRAFT, JACOB-BLACK	FRE	006	FREDERIC
GRAFT, THOMAS	BAL	425	8TH WARD
GRAFT, THOMAS	BAL	425	8TH WARD
GRAFTON, ANN	BAL	381	13TH WAR
GRAFTON, B.	BAL	140	1ST WARD
GRAFTON, BASIL	HAR	108	2ND DIST
GRAFTON, BENNET	HAR	108	2ND DIST
GRAFTON, CORBIN	HAR	111	2ND DIST
GRAFTON, CURTIS	HAR	116	2ND DIST
GRAFTON, CURTIS	HAR	103	2ND DIST
GRAFTON, ELKANAH	ALL	127	4TH E.D.
GRAFTON, J.	BAL	117	1ST WARD
GRAFTON, JACOB W.	BAL	186	2ND WARD
GRAFTON, JAMES	HAR	108	2ND DIST
GRAFTON, JESSE	HAR	111	2ND DIST
GRAFTON, JOHN	HAR	108	2ND DIST
GRAFTON, JOHN	BAL	116	2ND DIST
GRAFTON, JOSEPH	HAR	120	2ND DIST
GRAFTON, MARK	BAL	339	13TH WAR
GRAFTON, MARTIN	HAR	107	2ND DIST
GRAFTON, NATHAN	HAR	090	2ND DIST
GRAFTON, SAMUEL H.	BAL	063	15TH WAR
GRAFTON, SARAH A.	HAR	112	2ND DIST
GRAFTON, SOPHIA C.	BAL	032	4TH WARD
GRAG, JOSEPH	BAL	241	17TH WAR
GRAG, THOMAS	BAL	241	17TH WAR
GRAHAM, ABRAHAM-BLACK	CAR	087	NO TWP L
GRAHAM, ALEXANDER	HAR	052	1ST DIST
GRAHAM, ALEXANDER H.	TAL	079	ST MICHA
GRAHAM, ALFRED-BLACK	FRE	025	FREDERIC
GRAHAM, ALLEN C.	BAL	067	18TH WAR
GRAHAM, AMELIA	BAL	432	14TH WAR
GRAHAM, ANDREW	BAL	117	11TH WAR
GRAHAM, ANGUS	HAR	114	2ND DIST
GRAHAM, ANN	SOM	551	TYASKIN
GRAHAM, ANN	BAL	043	15TH WAR
GRAHAM, ANN	BAL	172	6TH WARD
GRAHAM, ANTHONY	FRE	244	NEW MARK
GRAHAM, ANTHONY	FRE	265	NEW MARK
GRAHAM, ARCHABALD	FRE	432	8TH E DI
GRAHAM, ARENNA	TAL	084	ST MICHA
GRAHAM, ARIRS	PRI	007	BLADENSB
GRAHAM, ASA	SOM	518	BARREN C
GRAHAM, BENAJAMIN	BAL	252	12TH WAR
GRAHAM, BRIDGETT	MGM	423	MEDLEY 3
GRAHAM, CAROLINE M.	HAR	114	2ND DIST
GRAHAM, CATHERINE	BAL	109	18TH WAR
GRAHAM, CATHERINE	BAL	079	18TH WAR
GRAHAM, CATHERINE-BLACK	FRE	013	FREDERIC
GRAHAM, CELY	TAL	062	EASTON D
GRAHAM, CHARLES-BLACK	FRE	039	FREDERIC
GRAHAM, CHARLOTTE	CEC	052	1ST E DI
GRAHAM, DANIEL	BAL	459	8TH WARD
GRAHAM, DAVID	WAS	130	2ND DIST
GRAHAM, EDMOND	TAL	054	EASTON D
GRAHAM, EDWARD	WAS	021	2ND SUBD
GRAHAM, ELIAS	ALL	134	4TH E.D.
GRAHAM, ELIZA	SOM	517	BARREN C
GRAHAM, ELIZABETH	BAL	335	3RD WARD
GRAHAM, ELIZABETH	BAL	013	18TH WAR
GRAHAM, ELIZABETH-BLACK	FRE	028	FREDERIC
GRAHAM, ELLEN	TAL	076	EASTON T
GRAHAM, EMELINE	TAL	083	ST MICHA
GRAHAM, EZEKIEL	DOR	306	1ST DIST
GRAHAM, FRANCES A.	CEC	203	6TH E DI
GRAHAM, FREDERICK	BAL	048	9TH WARD
GRAHAM, G.	BAL	153	1ST WARD
GRAHAM, GEORGE	BAL	320	3RD WARD
GRAHAM, GEORGE	FRE	265	NEW MARK
GRAHAM, GEORGE A.	WAS	231	1ST DIST
GRAHAM, GEORGE C.	TAL	067	EASTON T
GRAHAM, GEORGE R.	BAL	020	15TH WAR
GRAHAM, GEORGE W.	KEN	286	3RD DIST
GRAHAM, GEORGE W.	PRI	121	PISCATAW
GRAHAM, GEORGE W.	PRI	079	HARLBROU
GRAHAM, GEORGE-BLACK	FRE	044	FREDERIC
GRAHAM, HARRIET	TAL	052	EASTON D
GRAHAM, HARRIET	ALL	258	CUMBERLA
GRAHAM, HARRIET-BLACK	FRE	013	FREDERIC
GRAHAM, HENERY	DOR	364	3RD DIVI
GRAHAM, HESTER	CAR	097	NO TWP L
GRAHAM, IRA	BAL	254	12TH WAR
GRAHAM, ISABELLA	BAL	158	6TH WARD
GRAHAM, ISRAEL J.	BAL	463	14TH WAR
GRAHAM, J. H.	BAL	471	14TH WAR
GRAHAM, JACOB, B.	BAL	250	6TH WARD
GRAHAM, JAMES	BAL	157	6TH WARD
GRAHAM, JAMES	BAL	471	14TH WAR
GRAHAM, JAMES	BAL	468	14TH WAR
GRAHAM, JAMES	CAR	080	NO TWP L
GRAHAM, JAMES	FRE	310	WOODSBOR
GRAHAM, JAMES	CEC	208	7TH E DI
GRAHAM, JAMES	FRE	377	PETERSVI
GRAHAM, JAMES	SOM	517	BARREN C
GRAHAM, JAMES C. G.	CAR	229	5TH DIST
GRAHAM, JOHN	FRE	379	PETERSVI
GRAHAM, JOHN	CEC	203	6TH E DI
GRAHAM, JOHN	DOR	305	1ST DIST
GRAHAM, JOHN	BAL	062	18TH WAR
GRAHAM, JOHN	TAL	079	ST MICHA
GRAHAM, JOHN	QUE	173	2ND E DI
GRAHAM, JOHN	BAL	184	6TH WARD
GRAHAM, JOHN	BAL	173	1ST WARD
GRAHAM, JOHN	BAL	249	6TH WARD
GRAHAM, JOHN	BAL	135	1ST WARD
GRAHAM, JOHN	BAL	141	1ST WARD
GRAHAM, JOHN	BAL	126	1ST WARD
GRAHAM, JOHN	BAL	455	8TH WARD
GRAHAM, JOHN	BAL	078	2ND DIST
GRAHAM, JOHN	BAL	054	9TH WARD
GRAHAM, JOHN	BAL	081	1ST WARD
GRAHAM, JOHN E.	DOR	349	3RD DIVI
GRAHAM, JOHN H.	CEC	005	ELKTON 3
GRAHAM, JOHN T.	SOM	516	BARREN C
GRAHAM, JOSEPH	SOM	495	SALISBUR
GRAHAM, JOSEPH	TAL	078	EASTON T
GRAHAM, JOSIAH	BAL	032	15TH WAR
GRAHAM, JUIANN	TAL	086	ST MICHA
GRAHAM, JULIA	BAL	059	10TH WAR
GRAHAM, KITTY C.	ANN	443	HOWARD D
GRAHAM, LEVIN	SOM	516	BARREN C
GRAHAM, LLOYD	WAS	204	1ST DIST
GRAHAM, LOYD	WAS	106	2ND DIST
GRAHAM, LYDIA	PRI	026	VANSVILL
GRAHAM, MARGARET	BAL	172	19TH WAR
GRAHAM, MARGARET R.	FRE	056	FREDERIC
GRAHAM, MARIA E.	BAL	404	8TH WARD
GRAHAM, MARTHA	BAL	378	1ST DIST
GRAHAM, MARY	BAL	312	1ST DIST
GRAHAM, MARY	CEC	082	CHARLEST
GRAHAM, MARY	BAL	467	14TH WAR
GRAHAM, MARY A.	BAL	082	18TH WAR
GRAHAM, MARY A.	TAL	088	ST MICHA
GRAHAM, MARY L.	BAL	069	4TH WARD
GRAHAM, MARY MISS	ANN	285	ANNAPOLI
GRAHAM, MATILDA	BAL	291	12TH WAR
GRAHAM, MATILDA	BAL	364	13TH WAR
GRAHAM, MICHAEL	BAL	172	6TH WARD
GRAHAM, N.	BAL	158	1ST WARD
GRAHAM, NORRIS	ALL	158	6TH E.D.
GRAHAM, PETER	BAL	065	1ST WARD
GRAHAM, PHILIP	BAL	313	3RD WARD
GRAHAM, PHILIP G.	BAL	017	15TH WAR
GRAHAM, PRISCILLA-MULATTO	FRE	174	5TH E DI
GRAHAM, RACHAEL A.	BAL	208	2ND WARD
GRAHAM, RACHEL E.	CAR	080	NO TWP L
GRAHAM, REBECCA	ANN	468	HOWARD D
GRAHAM, REZIN	ANN	468	HOWARD D
GRAHAM, ROB	BAL	170	1ST WARD
GRAHAM, ROBERT	BAL	460	1ST DIST
GRAHAM, ROBERT	BAL	173	2ND DIST
GRAHAM, ROBERT	BAL	311	1ST DIST
GRAHAM, ROBERT	BAL	030	4TH WARD
GRAHAM, ROSEANNA	CEC	203	6TH E DI
GRAHAM, SALLY	SOM	553	TYASKIN
GRAHAM, SAMUEL	WOR	229	6TH E DI
GRAHAM, SAMUEL B.	FRE	391	PETERSVI
GRAHAM, SARAH	FRE	256	NEW MARK
GRAHAM, SARAH	SOM	517	BARREN C
GRAHAM, SARAH A.	BAL	164	11TH WAR
GRAHAM, SARAH E.	SOM	529	QUANTICO
GRAHAM, SILAS O.P.	BAL	017	15TH WAR
GRAHAM, THEADORE	CEC	207	7TH E DI
GRAHAM, THOMAS	BAL	093	10TH WAR
GRAHAM, THOMAS	SOM	467	TRAPPE D
GRAHAM, THOMAS-BLACK	FRE	011	FREDERIC
GRAHAM, URIAH T.	SOM	510	BARREN C
GRAHAM, WILLIAM	FRE	377	PETERSVI
GRAHAM, WILLIAM	BAL	408	3RD WARD
GRAHAM, WILLIAM	BAL	154	11TH WAR
GRAHAM, WILLIAM	BAL	033	18TH WAR
GRAHAM, WILLIAM	MGM	353	BERRYS D
GRAHAM, WILLIAM	BAL	119	1ST WARD
GRAHAM, WILLIAM	BAL	132	5TH WARD
GRAHAM, WILLIAM	BAL	018	9TH WARD
GRAHAM, WILLIAM R.	PRI	058	NOTTINGH
GRAHAM, WYE	FRE	261	NEW MARK
GRAHAM, ZACHARY B.	CEC	082	CHARLEST
GRAHAM,F RANCIS	BAL	078	2ND DIST
GRAHAME, THOMAS J.	CAL	062	3RD DIST
GRAHAMS, CAMPBELL	CAL	052	3RD DIST
GRAHAN, BELINDA	BAL	015	2ND DIST
GRAHAN, JAMES	BAL	035	1ST WARD
GRAHAN, RACHAEL	BAL	301	1ST DIST
GRAHE, THEODORE	FRE	046	FREDERIC
GRAICE, P.	BAL	148	1ST WARD
GRAIF, WILLIAM	BAL	166	19TH WAR
GRAIG, WILLIAM *	BAL	097	18TH WAR
GRAIL, JOHN	HAR	200	3RD DIST
GRAIL, THOMAS	HAR	148	3RD DIST
GRAIN, HUGH*	BAL	272	20TH WAR
GRAINER, FELIX	BAL	319	12TH WAR
GRAIS, JACOB	BAL	262	12TH WAR
GRALLER, JOHN	BAL	284	2ND WARD
GRAM, WILLIAM	CEC	015	ELKTON 3
GRAMBURY, ANN	BAL	257	1ST DIST
GRAME, FREDERICK	ALL	056	10TH E.D
GRAME, HESTHER	CAR	316	1ST DIST
GRAMLIN, BARBARA	ALL	227	CUMBERLA
GRAMLIN, MARTIN	ALL	227	CUMBERLA
GRAMLIN, THOMAS	ALL	227	CUMBERLA
GRAMMAR, VALENTINE	BAL	270	2ND WARD
GRAMMER, ANDREW	CAR	287	7TH DIST
GRAMMER, CATHERINE	BAL	188	11TH WAR

Name	County	Page	District
GRAMMER, FREDERICK L.	BAL	332	3RD WARD
GRAMMER, G.J.	ANN	267	ANNAPOLI
GRAMMER, HENRIETTA	BAL	135	11TH WAR
GRAMMER, HENRY D.	CAR	287	7TH DIST
GRAMMER, JOHN	CAR	377	2ND DIST
GRAMMER, MARGARET	BAL	332	3RD WARD
GRAMMER, REBECCA	CAR	399	2ND DIST
GRAMMER, SIMON	CAR	330	MANCHEST
GRAMMERS, FREDERICK	BAL	279	2ND WARD
GRAMMON, PATRICK	ALL	214	CUMBERLA
GRAMS, JOHN N.	FRE	394	PETERSVI
GRAN, DEER	BAL	081	18TH WAR
GRANAN, ANNA	BAL	134	5TH WARD
GRANAR, CATHERINE M.	BAL	078	10TH WAR
GRANAR, CHARLES	ALL	232	CUMBERLA
GRAND, VIRGINIA	BAL	195	11TH WAR
GRANDISON, CHARLES	BAL	241	6TH WARD
GRANDLEMYER, JOHN	BAL	227	19TH WAR
GRANDSON, C.	BAL	142	1ST WARD
GRANE, EDWARD	BAL	143	11TH WAR
GRANE, HERMAN H. *	BAL	100	15TH WAR
GRANE, N.	BAL	252	12TH WAR
GRANEL, ANDREW	BAL	061	1ST WARD
GRANER, JOHN	BAL	433	8TH WARD
GRANEY, JOHN	BAL	017	1ST WARD
GRANEY, MARGARET	BAL	047	9TH WARD
GRANEY, MICHAEL	BAL	017	1ST WARD
GRANEY, NELLY	BAL	017	1ST WARD
GRANGER, ANN	DOR	398	1ST DIST
GRANGER, ANN	KEN	284	3RD DIST
GRANGER, BENJAMIN-BLACK	QUE	157	2ND E DI
GRANGER, BENJAMIN-BLACK	QUE	157	2ND E DI
GRANGER, ELIZABETH A.	BAL	137	16TH WAR
GRANGER, HENRY	BAL	420	14TH WAR
GRANGER, HENRY	WAS	132	2ND DIST
GRANGER, JACOB	CAR	335	6TH DIST
GRANGER, JAMES	ANN	338	3RD DIST
GRANGER, JOHN	BAL	110	15TH WAR
GRANGER, JONATHAN	MGM	396	ROCKERLE
GRANGER, JUDSON	MGM	397	ROCKERLE
GRANGER, LEVIN L.	BAL	251	17TH WAR
GRANGER, LOUISE	BAL	241	12TH WAR
GRANGER, MARGARET	BAL	313	20TH WAR
GRANGER, MARIA	KEN	212	2ND DIST
GRANGER, MARY	BAL	035	2ND DIST
GRANGER, MARY A.	PRI	003	BLADENSB
GRANGER, MATT	BAL	220	12TH WAR
GRANGER, NATHAN	BAL	202	17TH WAR
GRANGER, PERE	QUE	230	4TH E DI
GRANGER, REEECCA	DOR	324	1ST DIST
GRANGER, SARAH	BAL	266	12TH WAR
GRANGER, SOPHIA	BAL	220	12TH WAR
GRANGER, STEPHEN	BAL	462	1ST DIST
GRANGER, SUSAN	BAL	115	5TH WARD
GRANGER, THOMAS	PRI	003	BLADENSB
GRANGER, WILLIAM	BAL	246	12TH WAR
GRANGER, WILLIAM	BAL	136	16TH WAR
GRANGER, WILLIAM	MGM	398	ROCKERLE
GRANHAWK, JACOB	QUE	241	5TH E DI
GRANIN, MICHAEL	WAS	055	2ND SUBD
GRANK, B. L.	BAL	149	1ST WARD
GRANKAITZ, JOHN	BAL	080	1ST WARD
GRANLEAD, WILLIAM	BAL	114	1ST WARD
GRANMER, MARY	CAR	270	WESTMINS
GRANNER, CASPAR	BAL	059	1ST WARD
GRANNER, GOTLIEB	BAL	267	2ND WARD
GRANNETT, MARY A.	BAL	251	2ND WARD
GRANNEY, MARGARET	BAL	001	9TH WARD
GRANNITT, GUSTAVUS	BAL	251	2ND WARD
GRANNON, ANN	BAL	383	8TH WARD
GRANNON, PATRICK	BAL	383	8TH WARD
GRANOR, JOHN	BAL	383	8TH WARD
GRANOR, JOHN	BAL	383	8TH WARD
GRANS, GEORGE	BAL	145	1ST WARD
GRANT, ALICE	BAL	449	14TH WAR
GRANT, ANDREW	CEC	020	ELKTON 3
GRANT, ANNIE	HAR	086	2ND DIST
GRANT, CAROLINE	CEC	082	CHARLEST
GRANT, CAROLINE	BAL	331	13TH WAR
GRANT, CATHERINE	BAL	347	3RD WARD
GRANT, CATHERINE	BAL	148	11TH WAR
GRANT, CHARLES	CEC	074	5TH E DI
GRANT, CHARLES	BAL	231	12TH WAR
GRANT, D.	BAL	117	1ST WARD
GRANT, CAVID	BAL	141	1ST WARD
GRANT, CAVID	BAL	125	1ST WARD
GRANT, DAVID	WAS	032	2ND SUBD
GRANT, EDWARD	BAL	361	3RD WARD
GRANT, ELIZA	CEC	128	5TH E DI
GRANT, GEORGE	CEC	096	4TH E DI
GRANT, GEORGE	BAL	146	5TH WARD
GRANT, GEORGE W.	BAL	182	2ND WARD
GRANT, GEORGE W.	HAR	088	2ND DIST
GRANT, GUS	BAL	137	1ST WARD
GRANT, HARRIET	CEC	080	NORTHEAS
GRANT, HENRY	BAL	462	1ST DIST
GRANT, J.	BAL	154	1ST WARD
GRANT, J. J.	BAL	147	1ST WARD
GRANT, J. M.	BAL	255	6TH WARD
GRANT, JACOB	BAL	144	1ST WARD
GRANT, JAMES	BAL	213	6TH WARD
GRANT, JAMES	ANN	467	HOWARD D
GRANT, JAMES	CEC	076	NORTHEAS
GRANT, JAMES	CEC	120	4TH E DI
GRANT, JOHN	CEC	119	3RD E DI
GRANT, JOHN	CEC	076	NORTHEAS
GRANT, JOHN	HAR	059	1ST DIST
GRANT, JOHN	BAL	007	EASTERN
GRANT, JOHN	BAL	136	16TH WAR
GRANT, JOHN	ALL	176	7TH E.D.
GRANT, JOHN W.	MGM	417	MEDLEY 3
GRANT, JOHN W.	KEN	233	2ND DIST
GRANT, JOSEPH	CEC	073	5TH E DI
GRANT, JOSEPH	BAL	388	13TH WAR
GRANT, LAURENCE	HAR	060	1ST DIST
GRANT, MALVINA	BAL	463	1ST DIST
GRANT, MARGARET	BAL	165	6TH WARD
GRANT, MARGARET	CEC	080	NORTHEAS
GRANT, MARGARET	CEC	002	ELKTON 3
GRANT, MARK	BAL	168	6TH WARD
GRANT, MARY	BAL	378	13TH WAR
GRANT, MARY A.	BAL	051	18TH WAR
GRANT, MARY A.	BAL	344	7TH WARD
GRANT, MICHAEL	FRE	001	FREDERIC
GRANT, NANCY	BAL	091	15TH WAR
GRANT, PATRICK	BAL	050	2ND DIST
GRANT, RICHARD	BAL	048	1ST WARD
GRANT, RICHARD S.	BAL	269	7TH WARD
GRANT, ROBERT	BAL	051	9TH WARD
GRANT, SARAH	CEC	081	CHARLEST
GRANT, SEABORN	CEC	080	NORTHEAS
GRANT, SOPHIA	CEC	081	CHARLEST
GRANT, T.	BAL	117	1ST WARD
GRANT, THOAMS	BAL	282	2ND WARD
GRANT, THOMAS	QUE	240	5TH E DI
GRANT, THOMAS	KEN	292	3RD DIST
GRANT, W.	BAL	158	1ST WARD
GRANT, WALTER	BAL	084	2ND DIST
GRANT, WASHINGTON	CEC	096	4TH E DI
GRANT, WILLAIM	BAL	156	2ND DIST
GRANT, WILLIAM	BAL	131	1ST WARD
GRANT, WILLIAM	BAL	012	15TH WAR
GRANT, WILLIAM	CEC	082	CHARLEST
GRANT, WILLIAM	CEC	082	CHARLEST
GRANT, WILLIAM	BAL	052	18TH WAR
GRANT, WILLIAM J.	CEC	091	4TH E DI
GRANT, WILLIAM M.	HAR	093	2ND DIST
GRANT, WILLIAM T.	CEC	074	NORTHEAS
GRANT, ZENOPHON	BAL	266	12TH WAR
GRANT,RICHARD	BAL	064	1ST WARD
GRANTHAM, MARIA	BAL	058	10TH WAR
GRANVILLE, JULIET	BAL	297	12TH WAR
GRANWELL, ELLEN	CEC	044	CHESAPEA
GRANY, HARRISON	BAL	148	11TH WAR
GRANYER, G. R. *	BAL	333	1ST DIST
GRANZER, G. R. *	BAL	333	1ST DIST
GRAP, ANDREW	HAR	199	3RD DIST
GRAPAW, JULIA	BAL	192	11TH WAR
GRAPE, CATHARINE	BAL	217	17TH WAR
GRAPE, CHARLOTTE	BAL	205	6TH WARD
GRAPE, ELIZABETH	BAL	206	6TH WARD
GRAPE, JOHN	BAL	225	17TH WAR
GRAPE, JOHN*	BAL	296	3RD WARD
GRAPES, BARBARA	BAL	079	10TH WAR
GRAPEVINE, CATHARINE	BAL	014	15TH WAR
GRAPIS, CARK *	BAL	224	12TH WAR
GRARRET, BERNARD	FRE	316	MIDDLETO
GRASAY, ELIZABETH	BAL	359	1ST DIST
GRASE, CHARLES	TAL	066	EASTON T
GRASE, FANNY*	TAL	056	EASTON D
GRASE, JAMES*	TAL	005	EASTON D
GRASE, JOHN T.	TAL	111	ST MICHA
GRASE, SARAH*	TAL	065	EASTON T
GRASE, STANTLY*	TAL	025	EASTON D
GRASELY, CHARLES	BAL	262	1ST DIST
GRASER, JACOB	BAL	170	2ND DIST
GRASH, LEWIS	WAS	172	FUNKSTOW
GRASKOPRF, FREDERICK	BAL	386	13TH WAR
GRASLESS, CHARLES*	TAL	005	EASTON D
GRASON, CATHRINE	BAL	024	18TH WAR
GRASON, CHARLES*	TAL	058	EASTON D
GRASON, ELIZA	BAL	084	15TH WAR
GRASON, GEORGE	BAL	162	1ST WARD
GRASON, GEORGE	ANN	317	1ST DIST
GRASON, JAMES	QUE	250	5TH E DI
GRASON, JANE	BAL	065	10TH WAR
GRASON, JANE	BAL	129	16TH WAR
GRASON, JOHN	ST	319	4TH E DI
GRASON, MARY	BAL	147	11TH WAR
GRASON, MARY R.-BLACK	BAL	176	2ND WARD
GRASON, RICHARD	CEC	003	ELKTON 3
GRASON, SAMUEL	BAL	091	15TH WAR
GRASON, SAMUEL	BAL	024	15TH WAR
GRASON, SARAH	CEC	014	ELKTON 3
GRASON, THOMAS	BAL	136	18TH WAR
GRASON, WILLIAM	BAL	024	18TH WAR
GRASON, WILLIAM	BAL	089	15TH WAR
GRASON, WILLIAM	QUE	246	5TH E DI
GRASS, ELIZABETH	CAR	330	MANCHEST
GRASS, EMORY	BAL	246	17TH WAR
GRASS, GEORGE	BAL	277	2ND WARD
GRASS, HENRY	BAL	238	1ST DIST
GRASS, JOHN	CAR	329	MANCHEST
GRASS, JOHN	BAL	283	1ST DIST
GRASS, MICHAEL	BAL	317	1ST DIST
GRASS, ROCHESTER	PRI	074	MARLBROU
GRASS, ROEKSANEY	CAL	009	1ST DIST
GRASS, STEPHEN	BAL	353	1ST DIST
GRASSBEMDER, JOHN *	BAL	131	18TH WAR
GRASSE, JOHN*	BAL	296	3RD WARD
GRASSMAN, SAMUEL	BAL	033	15TH WAR
GRATE, CHARELS E.	FRE	164	EMMITTSB
GRATH, JOANNA M.	BAL	205	11TH WAR
GRATH, PETER M.	BAL	124	1ST WARD
GRATS, JOHN	BAL	289	1ST DIST
GRATY, HUMEN	ANN	449	HOWARD D
GRATY, PHILIP	BAL	227	19TH WAR
GRATZ, ABRAM	BAL	212	2ND WARD
GRATZ, ALEXANDER	BAL	089	1ST WARD
GRATZ, JOHN	BAL	087	1ST WARD
GRATZ, LOUIS	BAL	230	2ND WARD
GRAU, JAMES	TAL	066	EASTON T
GRAUBY, SUSAN	BAL	148	5TH WARD
GRAUFF, CHRISTOPHER	BAL	271	2ND WARD
GRAUFF, MARGRET	BAL	205	2ND WARD
GRAUPNER, FREDERICK	BAL	370	3RD WARD
GRAUPNER, LOUISA	BAL	370	3RD WARD
GRAUSMAN, PHILLIP	BAL	064	1ST WARD
GRAUTHROP, THOMAS	BAL	063	2ND DIST
GRAVE, FANNY*	TAL	056	EASTON D
GRAVE, HERMAN H. *	BAL	100	15TH WAR
GRAVE, JACOB	BAL	102	5TH WARD
GRAVE, JAMES*	TAL	005	EASTON D
GRAVENER, BURTON	WOR	225	4TH E DI
GRAVENER, ISMA	WOR	223	4TH E DI
GRAVENER, WILLIAM	WOR	235	6TH E DI
GRAVENSTINE, CORA*	BAL	055	4TH WARD
GRAVENSTINE, JAMES H.	BAL	055	4TH WARD
GRAVER, JOHN	CEC	142	6TH E DI
GRAVER, MARY	BAL	313	20TH WAR
GRAVER, MARY A.	CEC	143	7TH E DI
GRAVER, RUTH	BAL	376	13TH WAR
GRAVES, ANN	ST	323	4TH E DI
GRAVES, ANN C.	CHA	282	BOJANTOW
GRAVES, BANNER	WAS	162	2ND DIST
GRAVES, BARNEY	BAL	134	16TH WAR
GRAVES, CAROLINE	BAL	258	12TH WAR
GRAVES, CHLOE A.	ST	270	3RD E DI
GRAVES, DAVID	CEC	057	1ST E DI
GRAVES, DENNIS	WAS	160	2ND DIST
GRAVES, DENTON T.	WAS	163	2ND DIST
GRAVES, DINDIN *	KEN	255	1ST DIST
GRAVES, ELEANOR	ST	257	3RD E DI
GRAVES, ELEANOR E.*	ST	269	3RD E DI
GRAVES, ELIZABETH	KEN	216	2ND DIST
GRAVES, ELIZABETH	BAL	416	3RD WARD
GRAVES, ELIZABETH	BAL	347	7TH WARD
GRAVES, ELIZABETH	BAL	184	16TH WAR
GRAVES, ELIZABETH	BAL	346	3RD WARD
GRAVES, ELIZABETH	BAL	265	7TH WARD
GRAVES, EMORY	KEN	256	1ST DIST
GRAVES, FERDENAND	ST	266	3RD E DI
GRAVES, FJOHNW .	ST	268	3RD E DI
GRAVES, FRANCIS	ST	312	1ST E DI
GRAVES, GEORGE	KEN	261	1ST DIST
GRAVES, GEORGE	BAL	147	2ND DIST
GRAVES, HARRIET-BLACK	QUE	126	1ST E DI
GRAVES, HENRY	KEN	255	1ST DIST
GRAVES, HENRY C.	ST	259	3RD E DI
GRAVES, JACOB-BLACK	QUE	133	1ST E DI
GRAVES, JAMES	KEN	214	2ND DIST
GRAVES, JAMES	BAL	377	13TH WAR
GRAVES, JAMES	KEN	256	1ST DIST
GRAVES, JAMES	BAL	170	1ST WARD
GRAVES, JAMES A.	ST	267	3RD E DI
GRAVES, JAMES R.	ST	268	3RD E DI
GRAVES, JANE	WAS	163	2ND DIST
GRAVES, JANE	BAL	382	3RD WARD
GRAVES, JOHN G.	ST	323	4TH E DI
GRAVES, JOHN G.	BAL	055	4TH WARD
GRAVES, JOHN J.	BAL	225	19TH WAR
GRAVES, JOHN P.	ST	268	3RD E DI
GRAVES, JOHN W.	ST	275	3RD E DI
GRAVES, LEWIS	MGM	357	BERRYS D
GRAVES, LOUISA	KEN	254	1ST DIST
GRAVES, MADERID *	HAR	193	3RD DIST
GRAVES, MARGARET	BAL	035	1ST WARD
GRAVES, MARIA	KEN	253	1ST DIST
GRAVES, MARY	BAL	266	7TH WARD
GRAVES, MARY	BAL	301	12TH WAR
GRAVES, MARY	KEN	256	1ST DIST
GRAVES, RAMOND N.	ST	275	3RD E DI
GRAVES, ROBERT	BAL	156	1ST WARD
GRAVES, ROBERT B.	ST	270	3RD E DI
GRAVES, RUBEN	ST	260	3RD E DI
GRAVES, SAMUEL	ST	260	3RD E DI
GRAVES, SAMUEL	BAL	144	5TH WARD
GRAVES, SARAH	BAL	305	12TH WAR
GRAVES, SARAH	ST	332	4TH E DI
GRAVES, SARAH	ST	321	4TH E DI
GRAVES, SILAS	WAS	160	2ND DIST
GRAVES, STEPHEN	KEN	255	1ST DIST
GRAVES, SUSAN	ST	301	2ND E DI
GRAVES, TERESE	ST	266	3RD E DI
GRAVES, THOMAS M.	CAR	317	1ST DIST
GRAVES, WILLIAM	BAL	418	3RD WARD
GRAVES, WILLIAM	KEN	252	1ST DIST
GRAVES, WILLIAM	ST	321	4TH E DI
GRAVES, WILLIAM	KEN	258	1ST DIST
GRAVES, WILLIAM	KEN	261	1ST DIST
GRAVES, WILLIAM	BAL	302	12TH WAR
GRAVES, WILLIAM A.	ST	303	2ND E DI
GRAVES, WILLIAM T.	BAL	145	1ST WARD
GRAVES, ZEPHANIAH	ST	320	4TH E DI
GRAVES,LOUIS	ST	323	4TH E DI
GRAVES,MARY A.	ST	321	4TH E DI
GRAVEY, WILLIAM	BAL	063	18TH WAR
GRAVIS, BARBARY	ST	275	3RD E DI
GRAVNER, BENJAMIN	SOM	518	BARREN C
GRAVNER, BENJAMIN JR.	SOM	518	BARREN C
GRAVNER, THOMAS	SOM	518	BARREN C
GRAVS, WILLIAM	BAL	034	9TH WARD
GRAVY, SUSAN	BAL	063	18TH WAR
GRAVYER, G. R. *	BAL	333	1ST DIST
GRAW, AARON D.	TAL	056	EASTON D
GRAW, JAMES M.	BAL	070	1ST WARD
GRAWE, WILLIAM *	BAL	306	20TH WAR
GRAY, A. L.	BAL	111	15TH WAR
GRAY, ADAMS	BAL	011	4TH WARD
GRAY, ALBERT W.	BAL	356	3RD WARD
GRAY, ALEXANDER	KEN	230	2ND DIST
GRAY, ALICE	FRE	164	EMMITTSB
GRAY, ALICE	BAL	054	15TH WAR
GRAY, ALICE ANN	BAL	373	13TH WAR
GRAY, AMANDA	BAL	064	18TH WAR
GRAY, AMRY	BAL	447	14TH WAR
GRAY, ANDREW	BAL	012	4TH WARD
GRAY, ANDREW	CEC	212	7TH E DI
GRAY, ANDREW	QUE	246	5TH E DI
GRAY, ANN	PRI	102	SPALDING
GRAY, ANN	ST	337	4TH E DI
GRAY, ANN	CHA	246	HILLTOP
GRAY, ANN	CAL	003	1ST DIST
GRAY, ANN	CAL	012	1ST DIST
GRAY, ANN E.	QUE	177	2ND E DI
GRAY, ANN M.	BAL	040	18TH WAR
GRAY, ARAMIAS	WOR	287	BERLIN 1
GRAY, ARAMINTA	BAL	242	6TH WARD
GRAY, ARCHABALD	DOR	351	3RD DIVI
GRAY, ASBERRY-BLACK	CAR	161	NO TWP L
GRAY, BARBARA J.	CAL	001	1ST DIST
GRAY, BASIL B.	CAL	010	1ST DIST
GRAY, BENJAMIN	CAL	035	2ND DIST
GRAY, BENJAMIN	BAL	413	1ST DIST
GRAY, BERMARD	BAL	168	11TH WAR
GRAY, BLADEN	MGM	327	CRACKLIN
GRAY, C.L.	PRI	049	AQUASCO
GRAY, CAROLINE	BAL	291	3RD WARD
GRAY, CARTER E.	BAL	022	18TH WAR
GRAY, CATHARINE	BAL	284	12TH WAR
GRAY, CATHERINE	CAR	133	NO TWP L
GRAY, CATHERINE	CEC	201	6TH E DI
GRAY, CHARITY	BAL	371	3RD WARD
GRAY, CHARLES	BAL	138	1ST WARD
GRAY, CHARLES	BAL	116	2ND DIST
GRAY, CHARLES E.	ANN	359	3RD DIST
GRAY, CHARLES E.	BAL	146	16TH WAR
GRAY, CHARLES H.	BAL	134	11TH WAR
GRAY, CHESTER	BAL	132	2ND DIST
GRAY, CLOWIE M.	ST	337	4TH E DI
GRAY, D.	BAL	136	1ST WARD
GRAY, DANIEL	BAL	088	2ND DIST
GRAY, DANIEL	WOR	247	1ST CENS
GRAY, CAVID	BAL	026	15TH WAR
GRAY, DAVID	BAL	234	20TH WAR
GRAY, CAVID H.	WOR	286	BERLIN 1
GRAY, DAVID S.	WOR	267	BERLIN 1
GRAY, E. T.	WOR	269	BERLIN 1
GRAY, EDWARD	BAL	122	16TH WAR
GRAY, EDWARD	BAL	346	1ST DIST
GRAY, EEMET G. *	TAL	093	ST MICHA
GRAY, ELISHA	BAL	091	2ND DIST
GRAY, ELIXIOUS	PRI	023	VANSVILL
GRAY, ELIZA	BAL	095	15TH WAR
GRAY, ELIZA	BAL	357	8TH WARD
GRAY, ELIZA	ANN	328	2ND DIST
GRAY, ELIZA J.	CEC	010	ELKTON 3
GRAY, ELIZA W.	BAL	468	14TH WAR
GRAY, ELIZABETH	BAL	156	11TH WAR
GRAY, ELIZABETH	MGM	331	CRACKLIN

Name	County	Page	District
[illegible] H	MGM	336	CRACKLIN
GRAY, [illegible] H	BAL	368	13TH WAR
GRAY, ELIZABE H	ALL	009	3RD E.D.
GRAY, ELIZABETH	BAL	094	10TH WAR
GRAY, ELIZABETH	BAL	183	11TH WAR
GRAY, ELIZABETH	PRI	023	VANSVILL
GRAY, ELIZABETH	WOR	282	BERLIN 1
GRAY, ELLEN	BAL	078	18TH WAR
GRAY, EMELINE	CAL	042	3RD DIST
GRAY, EMMA	FRE	066	FREDERIC
GRAY, EPHRAIM	ANN	354	3RD DIST
GRAY, EZEKIEL	BAL	426	14TH WAR
GRAY, FANNEY	BAL	167	19TH WAR
GRAY, FANNY E.	BAL	442	14TH WAR
GRAY, FRANCES H.	BAL	346	3RD WARD
GRAY, FRANCES W.	BAL	347	3RD WARD
GRAY, FRANCIS	MGM	381	ROCKERLE
GRAY, FRANKLIN	BAL	081	1ST WARD
GRAY, GEORGE	BAL	066	1ST WARD
GRAY, GEORGE	ANN	505	HOWARD D
GRAY, GEORGE	BAL	156	1ST WARD
GRAY, GEORGE	CAL	006	1ST DIST
GRAY, GEORGE	FRE	238	NEW MARK
GRAY, GEORGE	BAL	022	18TH WAR
GRAY, GEORGE	HAR	131	2ND DIST
GRAY, GEORGE	WOR	248	1ST CENS
GRAY, GEORGE	ST	337	4TH E DI
GRAY, GEORGE A.	ANN	351	3RD DIST
GRAY, GEORGE B.	WOR	260	BERLIN 1
GRAY, GEORGE W.	WAS	192	1ST DIST
GRAY, GEORGE W.	TAL	067	EASTON T
GRAY, GEORGE W.	BAL	362	3RD WARD
GRAY, GREEN	ANN	350	3RD DIST
GRAY, GREEN	ANN	354	3RD DIST
GRAY, GREGORY	PRI	095	SPALDING
GRAY, GUSTUS	CAL	008	1ST DIST
GRAY, H.	BAL	156	1ST WARD
GRAY, H. A.	BAL	106	10TH WAR
GRAY, HARRIET	ANN	462	HOWARD D
GRAY, HENRIETTA	BAL	132	11TH WAR
GRAY, HENRY	MGM	397	ROCKERLE
GRAY, HENRY	TAL	044	EASTON T
GRAY, HESTER	WOR	211	4TH E DI
GRAY, HESTER	BAL	292	1ST DIST
GRAY, HETTA	WOR	304	SNOW HIL
GRAY, HEZEKIAH	ANN	432	HOWARD D
GRAY, ISAAC	WOR	264	BERLIN 1
GRAY, ISAAC	WOR	172	6TH E DI
GRAY, ISAAC	CEC	089	4TH E DI
GRAY, ISAAC	BAL	302	20TH WAR
GRAY, ISABELLA	CEC	012	ELKTON 3
GRAY, JACOB	WAS	239	CAVETOWN
GRAY, JAMES	TAL	038	EASTON D
GRAY, JAMES	PRI	088	SPALDING
GRAY, JAMES	BAL	199	19TH WAR
GRAY, JAMES	CEC	207	7TH E DI
GRAY, JAMES	CHA	244	HILLTOP
GRAY, JAMES	CEC	059	1ST E DI
GRAY, JAMES	CAL	001	1ST DIST
GRAY, JAMES	MGM	329	CRACKLIN
GRAY, JAMES	HAR	179	3RD DIST
GRAY, JAMES	BAL	075	4TH WARD
GRAY, JAMES	BAL	222	17TH WAR
GRAY, JAMES	CEC	169	6TH E DI
GRAY, JAMES	CEC	171	6TH E DI
GRAY, JAMES	BAL	098	15TH WAR
GRAY, JAMES	BAL	070	10TH WAR
GRAY, JAMES	ANN	322	2ND DIST
GRAY, JAMES	BAL	146	1ST WARD
GRAY, JAMES	BAL	402	3RD WARD
GRAY, JAMES	BAL	271	7TH WARD
GRAY, JAMES B.	WOR	287	BERLIN 1
GRAY, JAMES J.	ANN	310	1ST DIST
GRAY, JAMES M.	BAL	122	5TH WARD
GRAY, JANE	BAL	292	1ST DIST
GRAY, JANE	WOR	291	9TH E DI
GRAY, JANE	CAL	004	1ST DIST
GRAY, JANE	CAL	047	3RD DIST
GRAY, JANE	CHA	241	HILLTOP
GRAY, JERAMIAH	CEC	018	ELKTON 3
GRAY, JIM	WOR	281	BERLIN 1
GRAY, JOHN	WAS	064	2ND SUBD
GRAY, JOHN	WOR	244	1ST CENS
GRAY, JOHN	WAS	207	1ST DIST
GRAY, JOHN	ST	296	2ND E DI
GRAY, JOHN	CHA	248	HILLTOP
GRAY, JOHN	CEC	206	7TH E DI
GRAY, JOHN	MGM	359	BERRYS D
GRAY, JOHN	BAL	049	1ST WARD
GRAY, JOHN	BAL	170	1ST WARD
GRAY, JOHN	BAL	335	3RD WARD
GRAY, JOHN	BAL	342	1ST DIST
GRAY, JOHN	BAL	460	1ST DIST
GRAY, JOHN	BAL	168	11TH WAR
GRAY, JOHN B.	ST	343	5TH E DI
GRAY, JOHN F.	PRI	092	MARLBROU
GRAY, JOHN R.	KEN	230	2ND DIST
GRAY, JOHN R.	DOR	448	1ST DIST
GRAY, JOHN T.	MGM	397	ROCKERLE
GRAY, JOHN T.	BAL	002	4TH WARD
GRAY, JOHN T.	CAL	015	1ST DIST
GRAY, JOHN W.	PRI	112	PISCATAW
GRAY, JOHN W.	BAL	341	3RD WARD
GRAY, JOHN W.	ANN	363	4TH DIST
GRAY, JOHNSON	WOR	264	BERLIN 1
GRAY, JONATHAN	BAL	096	2ND DIST
GRAY, JOSEPH	ANN	345	3RD DIST
GRAY, JOSEPH	BAL	077	10TH WAR
GRAY, JOSEPH	WOR	244	1ST CENS
GRAY, JOSEPH	WOR	246	1ST CENS
GRAY, JOSEPH	HAR	131	2ND DIST
GRAY, JOSEPH	HAR	137	2ND DIST
GRAY, JOSEPH	CHA	248	HILLTOP
GRAY, JOSEPH	CEC	171	6TH E DI
GRAY, JOSEPH	BAL	417	14TH WAR
GRAY, JOSEPH A.	BAL	114	18TH WAR
GRAY, JOSEPH C.	CHA	235	HILLTOP
GRAY, JOSEPH V.	MGM	424	MEDLEY 3
GRAY, JOSHUA	ANN	346	3RD DIST
GRAY, JULIA A.	WOR	304	SNOW HIL
GRAY, JULIAN	BAL	025	4TH WARD
GRAY, KEZIAH	BAL	103	15TH WAR
GRAY, LAURA	BAL	112	5TH WARD
GRAY, LAVINIA	ANN	454	HOWARD D
GRAY, LEMUEL	WOR	244	1ST CENS
GRAY, LEVIN	TAL	061	EASTON D
GRAY, LEVIN J.	DOR	412	1ST DIST
GRAY, LEWIS	BAL	004	15TH WAR
GRAY, LLOYD	ANN	496	HOWARD D
GRAY, MARGARET	BAL	341	13TH WAR

Name	County	Page	District
GRAY, MARGARET	CAL	052	3RD DIST
GRAY, MARGARET	CEC	067	5TH E DI
GRAY, MARIA	BAL	395	14TH WAR
GRAY, MARTHA A.	BAL	361	3RD WARD
GRAY, MARY	ANN	331	2ND DIST
GRAY, MARY	BAL	372	3RD WARD
GRAY, MARY	DOR	432	1ST DIST
GRAY, MARY	CHA	291	MIDDLETO
GRAY, MARY	WOR	299	SNOW HIL
GRAY, MARY	WAS	029	2ND SUBD
GRAY, MARY	WAS	064	2ND SUBD
GRAY, MARY A.	BAL	118	15TH WAR
GRAY, MARY E.	MGM	401	ROCKERLE
GRAY, MARY J.	CHA	248	HILLTOP
GRAY, MATILDA	BAL	470	14TH WAR
GRAY, MATILDA	ANN	451	HOWARD D
GRAY, MATILDA	PRI	059	NOTTINGH
GRAY, NANCY	WOR	248	1ST CENS
GRAY, NANCY	ANN	422	HOWARD D
GRAY, NATHAN	ANN	351	3RD DIST
GRAY, NATHANIEL	WOR	277	BERLIN 1
GRAY, NATHANIEL J.	CAL	009	1ST DIST
GRAY, NELSON	BAL	337	1ST DIST
GRAY, NICHOLAS	ANN	370	4TH DIST
GRAY, NOAH	WOR	281	BERLIN 1
GRAY, OTHO	CEC	145	PORT DUP
GRAY, OTIS H.	BAL	033	1ST WARD
GRAY, P.	BAL	158	1ST WARD
GRAY, P.	BAL	150	1ST WARD
GRAY, PARTRUK	CAL	006	1ST DIST
GRAY, PATRICK	BAL	341	13TH WAR
GRAY, PATRICK	BAL	168	11TH WAR
GRAY, PETER	ANN	413	HOWARD D
GRAY, PETER	WAS	207	1ST DIST
GRAY, PHEBY	WOR	301	SNOW HIL
GRAY, PHILIP	ANN	347	3RD DIST
GRAY, PHILIS	BAL	116	5TH WARD
GRAY, RAINE	ANN	456	HOWARD D
GRAY, RICHARD	BAL	156	16TH WAR
GRAY, RICHARD	ST	338	4TH E DI
GRAY, RICHARD A.	QUE	195	3RD E DI
GRAY, ROBERT	BAL	110	10TH WAR
GRAY, ROBERT	BAL	067	2ND DIST
GRAY, ROBERT	CAL	035	2ND DIST
GRAY, ROBERT	CHA	242	HILLTOP
GRAY, SALLY	BAL	016	18TH WAR
GRAY, SALLY	WOR	269	BERLIN 1
GRAY, SAMUEL	CEC	209	7TH E DI
GRAY, SAMUEL	BAL	110	10TH WAR
GRAY, SAMUEL	BAL	354	1ST DIST
GRAY, SAMUEL	BAL	231	6TH WARD
GRAY, SAMUEL-BLACK	QUE	130	1ST E DI
GRAY, SARAH	BAL	146	11TH WAR
GRAY, SARAH	CAR	143	NO TWP L
GRAY, SARAH	BAL	393	3RD WARD
GRAY, SARAH	BAL	364	8TH WARD
GRAY, SARAH	WOR	276	BERLIN 1
GRAY, SARAH	WOR	277	BERLIN 1
GRAY, SARAH	ST	302	2ND E DI
GRAY, SARDELIA A.	ST	304	2ND E DI
GRAY, SENA	MGM	436	CLARKSTR
GRAY, SHARLOT	TAL	060	EASTON D
GRAY, SIDNEY-MULATTO	WOR	169	6TH E DI
GRAY, SIDNEY-MULATTO	WOR	168	6TH E DI
GRAY, SILAS	BAL	046	18TH WAR
GRAY, STEPHEN	ANN	358	3RD DIST
GRAY, STEPHEN J.	CEC	169	6TH E DI
GRAY, SUSAN	BAL	461	14TH WAR
GRAY, SUSAN	WAS	198	1ST DIST
GRAY, TEMPERANCE	BAL	154	2ND DIST
GRAY, THCAMS	ST	261	3RD E DI
GRAY, THOAMS S.	WOR	303	SNOW HIL
GRAY, THOMAS	WOR	283	BERLIN 1
GRAY, THCMAS	CEC	183	7TH E DI
GRAY, THCMAS	DOR	351	3RD DIVI
GRAY, THOMAS	DOR	316	1ST DIST
GRAY, THCMAS P.	CHA	248	HILLTOP
GRAY, VINCENT	BAL	101	18TH WAR
GRAY, W.	BAL	246	12TH WAR
GRAY, WALTON	BAL	184	16TH WAR
GRAY, WASHINGTON	BAL	424	1ST DIST
GRAY, WESLEY	BAL	260	2ND WARD
GRAY, WESTLEY	BAL	365	3RD WARD
GRAY, WILHELMINA	BAL	034	9TH WARD
GRAY, WILLAIM	PRI	102	SPALDING
GRAY, WILLIAM	WOR	287	BERLIN 1
GRAY, WILLIAM	BAL	233	6TH WARD
GRAY, WILLIAM	BAL	180	6TH WARD
GRAY, WILLIAM	BAL	032	1ST WARD
GRAY, WILLIAM	BAL	136	1ST WARD
GRAY, WILLIAM	BAL	335	3RD WARD
GRAY, WILLIAM	BAL	368	1ST DIST
GRAY, WILLIAM	BAL	027	18TH WAR
GRAY, WILLIAM	CEC	207	7TH E DI
GRAY, WILLIAM	CEC	175	7TH E DI
GRAY, WILLIAM	BAL	475	14TH WAR
GRAY, WILLIAM	CAL	003	1ST DIST
GRAY, WILLIAM	MGM	329	CRACKLIN
GRAY, WILLIAM	MGM	397	ROCKERLE
GRAY, WILLIAM	BAL	112	18TH WAR
GRAY, WILLIAM	HAR	192	3RD DIST
GRAY, WILLIAM B.	BAL	059	4TH WARD
GRAY, WILLIAM N.	PRI	098	SPALDING
GRAY, WILLIAM T.	ANN	356	3RD DIST
GRAY, ZACH	ANN	361	3RD DIST
GRAY, ZACHARIAH	ANN	359	3RD DIST
GRAY,MARIE	BAL	280	12TH WAR
GRAYHAM, ELLIS	BAL	403	8TH WARD
GRAYHAND, JOHN	BAL	180	2ND WARD
GRAYLESS, RACHEL*	TAL	004	EASTON D
GRAYMILLER, GEORGE	ALL	035	2ND E.D.
GRAYMILLER,MARY	ALL	017	3RD E.D.
GRAYSON, ARTHUR	HAR	101	2ND DIST
GRAYSON, JAMES	BAL	142	2ND DIST
GRAYSON, WILLIAM	ANN	389	4TH DIST
GRAYSON, WILLIAM C.	BAL	175	6TH WARD
GRAZELL, JOSEPH	MGM	393	ROCKERLE
GRDEN, MARGARETT	BAL	129	11TH WAR
GREABLE, HENRY	WAS	260	1ST DIST
GREACEY, JOHN	ANN	309	1ST DIST
GREADY, JOHN	BAL	208	11TH WAR
GREADY, MICHAEL	ALL	155	6TH E.D.
GREAGIN, JERRY	BAL	131	2ND DIST
GREAR, MARY	BAL	180	11TH WAR
GREASLY, JACOB F.	BAL	261	1ST DIST
GREASON, GEORGE	BAL	135	16TH WAR
GREASCN, ROBERT	BAL	077	1ST WARD
GREASOR, SYLVESTER	BAL	454	1ST DIST
GREATE, MICHAEL	BAL	250	1ST DIST
GREATFIELD, ELIZA	BAL	351	13TH WAR

Name	County	Page	District
GREAVES, ADEL M.*	DOR	417	1ST DIST
GREAVES, ANN	BAL	329	3RD WARD
GREAVES, ELLENOR P.	ANN	483	HOWARD D
GREAVES, EMELINE J.	BAL	112	15TH WAR
GREAVES, FRANCIS A.	QUE	243	5TH E DI
GREAVES, HANNAH	BAL	099	15TH WAR
GREAVES, MARIA A.	BAL	127	16TH WAR
GREAVES, MARY	BAL	379	3RD WARD
GREAVES, MATHIAS	QUE	243	5TH E DI
GREAVES, REBECCA	BAL	083	1ST WARD
GREB, JOSEPH	BAL	087	1ST WARD
GREBE, SIMON	ANN	425	HOWARD D
GREBE, VALTEEN	ANN	425	HOWARD D
GREBLE, BENJAMIN	BAL	394	8TH WARD
GREBLE, HARVY A.	BAL	394	8TH WARD
GREBLE, HENRIETTA	BAL	210	5TH WARD
GRECKER, CHARLES	BAL	071	1ST WARD
GREDE, HARMAN	BAL	181	18TH WAR
GREDON, WILLIAM	BAL	185	19TH WAR
GREE, JOHN	BAL	090	2ND DIST
GREEBY, JOHN	HAR	185	3RD DIST
GREEHAM, MARGARET	ANN	436	HOWARD D
GREEIVE, WILLIAM *	BAL	306	20TH WAR
GREELAND, SARY J.	HAR	193	3RD DIST
GREELEY, ELIZABETH	FRE	025	FREDERIC
GREEMVALT, JACOB	WAS	267	1ST DIST
GREEMWOOD, JOSEPH BAILE	CAR	364	9TH DIST
GREEN, ----*	TAL	045	EASTON T
GREEN, A.	BAL	147	1ST WARD
GREEN, AARON	ALL	241	CUMBERLA
GREEN, AARON	HAR	185	3RD DIST
GREEN, ABLE	CEC	200	7TH E DI
GREEN, ADALADE	WOR	277	BERLIN 1
GREEN, ADAM	BAL	059	18TH WAR
GREEN, AILSELY	BAL	023	9TH WARD
GREEN, ALEXANDER	BAL	014	2ND DIST
GREEN, ALEXANDER	BAL	156	2ND DIST
GREEN, ALEXANDER	CAR	067	NO TWP L
GREEN, ALEXANDER	TAL	106	ST MICHA
GREEN, ALEXENA	BAL	338	1ST DIST
GREEN, ALEXIOUS	BAL	187	5TH DIST
GREEN, ALICE	BAL	152	16TH WAR
GREEN, ALLEN	BAL	245	6TH WARD
GREEN, ALLEN	ANN	332	2ND DIST
GREEN, AMANDA	ANN	435	HOWARD D
GREEN, AMRTIN	BAL	274	12TH WAR
GREEN, ANDREW	ALL	217	CUMBERLA
GREEN, ANDREW	BAL	129	5TH WARD
GREEN, ANDREW	BAL	188	6TH WARD
GREEN, ANDREW	BAL	400	1ST DIST
GREEN, ANDREW O.	BAL	377	8TH WARD
GREEN, ANDREW S.	CAR	067	NO TWP L
GREEN, ANKER	BAL	153	5TH WARD
GREEN, ANN	BAL	364	8TH WARD
GREEN, ANN	BAL	156	11TH WAR
GREEN, ANN	BAL	021	18TH WAR
GREEN, ANN	BAL	190	19TH WAR
GREEN, ANN	BAL	052	4TH WARD
GREEN, ANN	SOM	522	BARREN C
GREEN, ANN C.	FRE	362	CATOCTIN
GREEN, ANN MARIA	FRE	196	5TH E DI
GREEN, ANN W.	BAL	230	1ST DIST
GREEN, ANN-MULATTO	BAL	219	2ND WARD
GREEN, ANNA-BLACK	QUE	192	3RD E DI
GREEN, ANTHONY B.	SOM	537	TYASKIN
GREEN, ARAMENTER-BLACK	CAR	075	NO TWP L
GREEN, ARCHABLE	SOM	552	TYASKIN
GREEN, ASA	SOM	437	PRINCESS
GREEN, AUGUSTUS-BLACK	CAR	086	NO TWP L
GREEN, B. K.	SOM	356	BRINKLEY
GREEN, BEAL	ANN	372	4TH DIST
GREEN, BENEDICT	FRE	005	FREDERIC
GREEN, BENJA	TAL	113	ST MICHA
GREEN, BENJAMIN	WAS	008	WILLIAMS
GREEN, BENJAMIN	CEC	041	CHESAPEA
GREEN, BENJAMIN	CEC	044	1ST E DI
GREEN, BENJAMIN	ALL	123	4TH E.D.
GREEN, BENJAMIN	BAL	175	6TH WARD
GREEN, BENJAMIN	BAL	309	7TH WARD
GREEN, BENJAMIN	BAL	330	13TH WAR
GREEN, BENNET	HAR	109	2ND DIST
GREEN, BENNETT	CHA	218	ALLENS F
GREEN, BILLY	BAL	051	4TH WARD
GREEN, BRUNETTA	SOM	512	BARREN C
GREEN, CALEB	BAL	217	6TH WARD
GREEN, CAROLINE	BAL	292	17TH WAR
GREEN, CATHARINE	BAL	383	13TH WAR
GREEN, CATHARINE	BAL	349	1ST DIST
GREEN, CATHARINE	SOM	547	TYASKIN
GREEN, CATHERINE	BAL	412	3RD WARD
GREEN, CATHERINE A.	QUE	124	1ST E DI
GREEN, CATHERINE-BLACK	QUE	149	1ST E DI
GREEN, CEZAR-BLACK	FRE	224	BUCKEYST
GREEN, CHALRES-BLACK	BAL	222	2ND WARD
GREEN, CHARELS	BAL	298	12TH WAR
GREEN, CHARITY	FRE	159	EMMITTSB
GREEN, CHARLES	BAL	126	18TH WAR
GREEN, CHARLES	CAR	093	NO TWP L
GREEN, CHARLES	BAL	087	15TH WAR
GREEN, CHARLES	BAL	165	1ST WARD
GREEN, CHARLES	BAL	132	1ST WARD
GREEN, CHARLES	BAL	132	1ST WARD
GREEN, CHARLES	BAL	037	1ST WARD
GREEN, CHARLES	ANN	449	HOWARD D
GREEN, CHARLES	ANN	442	HOWARD D
GREEN, CHARLES B.	BAL	094	5TH WARD
GREEN, CHARLES C.	SOM	386	BRINKLEY
GREEN, CHRISTIANA	FRE	195	5TH E DI
GREEN, CHRISTOPHER-BLACK	CAR	070	NO TWP L
GREEN, CHRISTOPHER-BLACK	QUE	184	3RD E DI
GREEN, CLARA	BAL	031	9TH WARD
GREEN, CLEMENT	MGM	378	ROCKERLE
GREEN, CORDELIS	ANN	480	HOWARD D
GREEN, CORNELIUS	BAL	264	7TH WARD
GREEN, CURLIGHT	MGM	339	CLARKSBU
GREEN, DANIEL	ANN	513	HOWARD D
GREEN, DANIEL	ANN	300	1ST DIST
GREEN, DANIEL K.	ANN	485	HOWARD D
GREEN, DAVID	BAL	337	3RD WARD
GREEN, DAVID	QUE	131	1ST E DI
GREEN, DAVID	BAL	412	14TH WAR
GREEN, DENNIS	ANN	518	HOWARD D
GREEN, DENNIS-BLACK	FRE	441	8TH E DI
GREEN, DOUGLAS	FRE	136	CREAGERS
GREEN, E.	ALL	122	4TH E.D.
GREEN, E. MRS.	ANN	279	ANNAPOLI
GREEN, EASTER	CAL	023	2ND DIST
GREEN, EDWARD	BAL	117	11TH WAR
GREEN, EDWARD	MGM	330	CRACKLIN
GREEN, EHRNY	KEN	244	2ND DIST

Name	County	Page	District
GREEN, EIRIETTA	BAL	354	1ST DIST
GREEN, ELI	BAL	240	12TH WAR
GREEN, ELIAS	WAS	092	2ND SUBD
GREEN, ELIE	WAS	158	HAGERSTO
GREEN, ELINOR	BAL	455	14TH WAR
GREEN, ELISHA	BAL	449	1ST DIST
GREEN, ELISHA	BAL	085	2ND DIST
GREEN, ELIZA	ALL	160	6TH E.D.
GREEN, ELIZA	BAL	404	3RD WARD
GREEN, ELIZA	BAL	003	1ST WARD
GREEN, ELIZA	BAL	184	16TH WAR
GREEN, ELIZA	CAR	223	5TH DIST
GREEN, ELIZA	PRI	064	NOTTINGH
GREEN, ELIZA J.	BAL	020	15TH WAR
GREEN, ELIZABETH	BAL	327	1ST DIST
GREEN, ELIZABETH	WAS	162	HAGERSTO
GREEN, ELIZABETH	QUE	224	4TH E DI
GREEN, ELIZABETH	QUE	172	2ND E DI
GREEN, ELIZABETH	FRE	154	10TH E D
GREEN, ELIZABETH	HAR	153	3RD DIST
GREEN, ELIZABETH	FRE	365	CATOCTIN
GREEN, ELIZABETH	HAR	191	3RD DIST
GREEN, ELIZABETH	BAL	023	18TH WAR
GREEN, ELIZABETH-BLACK	BAL	216	2ND WARD
GREEN, ELLEN	BAL	246	6TH WARD
GREEN, ELLEN	BAL	108	15TH WAR
GREEN, ELLEN	BAL	101	1ST WARD
GREEN, ELLEN	ALL	156	6TH E.D.
GREEN, ELLEN	BAL	094	2ND DIST
GREEN, EMELINE	QUE	222	4TH E DI
GREEN, EMILS	TAL	107	ST MICHA
GREEN, EMILY	BAL	275	2ND WARD
GREEN, EMMA R.	BAL	153	16TH WAR
GREEN, ENOCH	BAL	156	19TH WAR
GREEN, ENREAL	BAL	046	18TH WAR
GREEN, EVELINE	ANN	515	HOWARD D
GREEN, FANNY	TAL	108	ST MICHA
GREEN, FELIX	BAL	285	17TH WAR
GREEN, FERDINAND	BAL	352	7TH WARD
GREEN, FOSTER	CAR	067	NO TWP L
GREEN, FRANCES	BAL	256	2ND WARD
GREEN, FRANCIS	BAL	352	3RD WARD
GREEN, FRANCIS	FRE	366	CATOCTIN
GREEN, FRANCIS	HAR	173	3RD DIST
GREEN, FRANCIS B.	FRE	20	5TH E DI
GREEN, FRANCIS E.	CHA	261	MIDDLETO
GREEN, FREDERICK	SOM	460	HANGARY
GREEN, FREDERICK S.	BAL	431	14TH WAR
GREEN, GAMSON	BAL	330	13TH WAR
GREEN, GEORGE	BAL	009	1ST WARD
GREEN, GEORGE	BAL	379	1ST DIST
GREEN, GEORGE	BAL	120	2ND DIST
GREEN, GEORGE	ANN	360	3RD DIST
GREEN, GEORGE	BAL	314	1ST DIST
GREEN, GEORGE	FRE	369	CATOCTIN
GREEN, GEORGE	BAL	253	20TH WAR
GREEN, GEORGE	FRE	136	CREAGERS
GREEN, GEORGE	BAL	161	19TH WAR
GREEN, GEORGE	CAR	219	5TH DIST
GREEN, GEORGE	CEC	005	ELKTON 3
GREEN, GEORGE	SOM	384	BRINKLEY
GREEN, GEORGE E.	BAL	128	16TH WAR
GREEN, GEORGE M.	BAL	312	1ST DIST
GREEN, GEORGE W.	BAL	033	9TH WARD
GREEN, GEORGE W.	BAL	033	9TH WARD
GREEN, GEORGE W.	FRE	293	WOODSBOR
GREEN, GEORGE W.	MGM	377	ROCKERLE
GREEN, GILES	CHA	283	BOJANTOW
GREEN, GUST-BLACK	FRE	203	5TH E DI
GREEN, H. P.	BAL	471	14TH WAR
GREEN, HANNA	TAL	093	ST MICHA
GREEN, HANNAH	BAL	192	6TH WARD
GREEN, HARRIET	BAL	023	9TH WARD
GREEN, HARRIET	BAL	113	15TH WAR
GREEN, HARRIET	CAR	218	5TH DIST
GREEN, HARRIET	CEC	100	3RD E DI
GREEN, HARRIETT	QUE	232	4TH E DI
GREEN, HENRIETTA	BAL	054	10TH WAR
GREEN, HENRIETTA-BLACK	BAL	224	2ND WARD
GREEN, HENRY	BAL	179	6TH WARD
GREEN, HENRY	BAL	279	12TH WAR
GREEN, HENRY	ANN	302	1ST DIST
GREEN, HENRY	ALL	121	4TH E.D.
GREEN, HENRY	ANN	349	3RD DIST
GREEN, HENRY	BAL	085	2ND DIST
GREEN, HENRY	BAL	011	1ST WARD
GREEN, HENRY	BAL	044	18TH WAR
GREEN, HENRY	CAR	219	5TH DIST
GREEN, HENRY	BAL	197	19TH WAR
GREEN, HENRY	BAL	148	11TH WAR
GREEN, HENRY	CHA	237	HILLTOP
GREEN, HENRY H.	BAL	401	14TH WAR
GREEN, HENRY V.	CAR	098	NO TWP L
GREEN, HESTER-BLACK	BAL	220	2ND WARD
GREEN, HEZEKIAH	BAL	179	11TH WAR
GREEN, HICKMAN	ANN	359	3RD DIST
GREEN, HOOPER	BAL	330	3RD WARD
GREEN, HUGH	BAL	174	11TH WAR
GREEN, IMMANUEL	CAL	035	2ND DIST
GREEN, ISAAC	CAR	181	8TH DIST
GREEN, ISAAC	WAS	253	1ST DIST
GREEN, ISAAC JR.	CAR	176	8TH DIST
GREEN, ISAAC K.	SOM	392	BRINKLEY
GREEN, ISABELLA	BAL	002	18TH WAR
GREEN, ISRIEL	BAL	455	1ST DIST
GREEN, J.	BAL	154	1ST WARD
GREEN, JACOB	BAL	186	5TH WARD
GREEN, JACOB	BAL	222	12TH WAR
GREEN, JACOB	ALL	121	4TH E.D.
GREEN, JACOB	CEC	196	6TH E DI
GREEN, JACOB	CEC	197	7TH E DI
GREEN, JAEMS G.	QUE	231	4TH E DI
GREEN, JAMES	PRI	061	NOTTINGH
GREEN, JAMES	CAR	189	4TH DIST
GREEN, JAMES	FRE	134	CREAGERS
GREEN, JAMES	BAL	001	9TH WARD
GREEN, JAMES	BAL	176	6TH WARD
GREEN, JAMES	BAL	146	1ST WARD
GREEN, JAMES	ALL	259	CUMBERLA
GREEN, JAMES	BAL	030	1ST WARD
GREEN, JAMES	BAL	105	10TH WAR
GREEN, JAMES	BAL	320	12TH WAR
GREEN, JAMES	BAL	070	10TH WAR
GREEN, JAMES	BAL	360	8TH WARD
GREEN, JAMES	BAL	406	3RD WARD
GREEN, JAMES *	BAL	029	18TH WAR
GREEN, JAMES H.	BAL	021	18TH WAR
GREEN, JAMES-BLACK	QUE	123	1ST E DI
GREEN, JAMES-BLACK	QUE	142	1ST E DI
GREEN, JAMES-BLACK	CAR	083	NO TWP L
GREEN, JAMS	MGM	377	ROCKERLE
GREEN, JANE	HAR	176	3RD DIST
GREEN, JANE	BAL	098	18TH WAR
GREEN, JANE	BAL	366	3RD WARD
GREEN, JANE	BAL	061	10TH WAR
GREEN, JANE	BAL	182	11TH WAR
GREEN, JEMS	BAL	355	8TH WARD
GREEN, JERAMIAH	CEC	034	CHESAPEA
GREEN, JESSE	QUE	230	4TH E DI
GREEN, JIM	TAL	042	EASTON O
GREEN, JM	BAL	149	1ST WARD
GREEN, JOHN	BAL	144	5TH WARD
GREEN, JOHN	BAL	168	1ST WARD
GREEN, JOHN	BAL	242	6TH WARD
GREEN, JOHN	BAL	228	6TH WARD
GREEN, JOHN	BAL	204	2ND WARD
GREEN, JOHN	BAL	192	2ND WARD
GREEN, JOHN	BAL	390	8TH WARD
GREEN, JOHN	BAL	460	8TH WARD
GREEN, JOHN	BAL	239	12TH WAR
GREEN, JOHN	BAL	044	15TH WAR
GREEN, JOHN	BAL	042	15TH WAR
GREEN, JOHN	BAL	154	16TH WAR
GREEN, JOHN	BAL	025	1ST WARD
GREEN, JOHN	BAL	178	2ND DIST
GREEN, JOHN	BAL	223	1ST DIST
GREEN, JOHN	BAL	318	1ST DIST
GREEN, JOHN	BAL	318	3RD WARD
GREEN, JOHN	TAL	098	ST MICHA
GREEN, JOHN	WAS	158	HAGERSTO
GREEN, JOHN	TAL	102	ST MICHA
GREEN, JOHN	KEN	305	3RD DIST
GREEN, JOHN	KEN	309	3RD DIST
GREEN, JOHN	CAR	187	8TH DIST
GREEN, JOHN	MGM	374	ROCKERLE
GREEN, JOHN	HAR	079	2ND DIST
GREEN, JOHN	CAR	067	NO TWP L
GREEN, JOHN	BAL	403	14TH WAR
GREEN, JOHN	BAL	146	11TH WAR
GREEN, JOHN	CAL	021	2ND DIST
GREEN, JOHN	CEC	192	5TH E DI
GREEN, JOHN	BAL	284	20TH WAR
GREEN, JOHN E.	BAL	078	10TH WAR
GREEN, JOHN H.	BAL	238	6TH WARD
GREEN, JOHN J.	BAL	208	11TH WAR
GREEN, JOHN N.	BAL	300	7TH WARD
GREEN, JOHN S.	SOM	542	TYASKIN
GREEN, JOHN T.	FRE	055	FREDERIC
GREEN, JOHN T.	MGM	330	CRACKLIN
GREEN, JOHN W.	BAL	089	5TH WARD
GREEN, JOHN*	DOR	439	1ST DIST
GREEN, JOHN-BLACK	QUE	152	1ST E DI
GREEN, JOHN-BLACK	QUE	164	2ND E DI
GREEN, JOHN-MULATTO	FRE	180	5TH E DI
GREEN, JOSEPH	CAL	016	1ST DIST
GREEN, JOSEPH	CEC	196	6TH E DI
GREEN, JOSEPH	CEC	164	6TH E DI
GREEN, JOSEPH	WAS	158	HAGERSTO
GREEN, JOSEPH	WAS	004	WILLIAMS
GREEN, JOSEPH	BAL	461	1ST DIST
GREEN, JOSEPH	BAL	242	6TH WARD
GREEN, JOSEPH	BAL	298	12TH WAR
GREEN, JOSEPH	BAL	180	2ND DIST
GREEN, JOSEPH	BAL	457	8TH WARD
GREEN, JOSEPH	BAL	058	15TH WAR
GREEN, JOSEPH	BAL	311	1ST DIST
GREEN, JOSHUA	BAL	207	19TH WAR
GREEN, JOSHUA	CEC	100	3RD E DI
GREEN, JOSHUA B.	BAL	187	5TH DIST
GREEN, JOSHUA J.	BAL	311	3RD WARD
GREEN, JULIA	BAL	125	2ND DIST
GREEN, JULIA	BAL	071	18TH WAR
GREEN, JULIA	BAL	212	19TH WAR
GREEN, JULIA	SOM	386	BRINKLEY
GREEN, KISSY	SOM	541	TYASKIN
GREEN, KITTY	BAL	143	5TH WARD
GREEN, LAMBERT	QUE	185	3RD E DI
GREEN, LAWRENCE	FRE	369	CATOCTIN
GREEN, LEAH	BAL	186	6TH WARD
GREEN, LEMUEL	QUE	143	1ST E DI
GREEN, LEONARD	MGM	326	CRACKLIN
GREEN, LEONARD	MGM	387	ROCKERLE
GREEN, LEVI	HAR	187	3RD DIST
GREEN, LEVI	CEC	171	6TH E DI
GREEN, LEWIS	CAR	181	8TH DIST
GREEN, LEWIS	ANN	430	HOWARD D
GREEN, LEWIS	BAL	374	3RD WARD
GREEN, LEWIS	PRI	071	MARLBROU
GREEN, LEWIS	PRI	098	SPALDING
GREEN, LEWIS-BLACK	MGM	423	MEDLEY 3
GREEN, LLOYD	MGM	353	BERRYS D
GREEN, LLOYD	ANN	511	HOWARD D
GREEN, LOUIS	BAL	365	1ST DIST
GREEN, LOUISA	BAL	118	15TH WAR
GREEN, LOUISA	SOM	521	BARREN C
GREEN, LOUISA A.	ANN	482	HOWARD D
GREEN, LUCY A.	BAL	449	14TH WAR
GREEN, LYDIA	ALL	239	CUMBERLA
GREEN, LYDIA	WAS	279	LEITERSB
GREEN, LYDIA*	DOR	444	1ST DIST
GREEN, M.	ANN	272	ANNAPOLI
GREEN, M.M.	ANN	279	ANNAPOLI
GREEN, MARGARET	ALL	228	CUMBERLA
GREEN, MARGARET	WAS	137	HAGERSTO
GREEN, MARIA	BAL	283	12TH WAR
GREEN, MARIA	BAL	141	5TH WARD
GREEN, MARIA	BAL	161	6TH WARD
GREEN, MARIA	BAL	052	15TH WAR
GREEN, MARTHA	BAL	442	14TH WAR
GREEN, MARTHA	BAL	203	11TH WAR
GREEN, MARTHA	BAL	200	19TH WAR
GREEN, MARTHA	BAL	413	14TH WAR
GREEN, MARTHA	BAL	074	18TH WAR
GREEN, MARTHA	CEC	053	1ST E DI
GREEN, MARY	BAL	319	7TH WARD
GREEN, MARY	BAL	308	7TH WARD
GREEN, MARY	BAL	373	8TH WARD
GREEN, MARY	BAL	300	12TH WAR
GREEN, MARY	BAL	304	12TH WAR
GREEN, MARY	BAL	239	12TH WAR
GREEN, MARY	BAL	178	11TH WAR
GREEN, MARY	BAL	348	7TH WARD
GREEN, MARY	BAL	148	2ND DIST
GREEN, MARY	ANN	481	HOWARD D
GREEN, MARY	ANN	471	HOWARD D
GREEN, MARY	BAL	384	1ST DIST
GREEN, MARY	BAL	089	5TH WARD
GREEN, MARY	BAL	065	18TH WAR
GREEN, MARY	BAL	419	14TH WAR
GREEN, MARY	BAL	360	13TH WAR
GREEN, MARY	BAL	399	14TH WAR
GREEN, MARY	CAL	054	3RD DIST
GREEN, MARY	BAL	476	14TH WAR
GREEN, MARY	BAL	119	11TH WAR
GREEN, MARY	FRE	188	5TH E DI
GREEN, MARY	KEN	249	2ND DIST
GREEN, MARY	MGM	389	ROCKERLE
GREEN, MARY	QUE	177	2ND E DI
GREEN, MARY	QUE	168	2ND E DI
GREEN, MARY	ST	318	4TH E DI
GREEN, MARY A.	CHA	283	BOJANTOW
GREEN, MARY A.	QUE	154	1ST E DI
GREEN, MARY A.	BAL	020	18TH WAR
GREEN, MARY ANN	BAL	467	14TH WAR
GREEN, MARY E.	QUE	179	2ND E DI
GREEN, MARY E.	BAL	055	9TH WARD
GREEN, MARYJ.	BAL	180	16TH WAR
GREEN, MATHEW	BAL	280	2ND WARD
GREEN, MATHIAS	WAS	193	1ST DIST
GREEN, MATILDA	WAS	157	HAGERSTO
GREEN, MAY	QUE	156	2ND E DI
GREEN, MELCHISDICK	MGM	376	ROCKERLE
GREEN, MICHAEL	FRE	155	10TH E D
GREEN, MICHAEL	BAL	102	5TH WARD
GREEN, MINY	BAL	306	12TH WAR
GREEN, MISS	ANN	256	ANNAPOLI
GREEN, MOSES	ANN	372	4TH DIST
GREEN, MOSES	HAR	014	1ST DIST
GREEN, MRS. M.	ANN	280	ANNAPOLI
GREEN, MRS-	ANN	305	1ST DIST
GREEN, N.H.	ANN	269	ANNAPOLI
GREEN, NACKEY	ANN	455	HOWARD D
GREEN, NACLEY	ANN	461	HOWARD D
GREEN, NANCY	KEN	215	2ND DIST
GREEN, NANCY	BAL	146	11TH WAR
GREEN, NANCY	DOR	314	1ST DIST
GREEN, NANCY	WOR	176	6TH E DI
GREEN, NATHAN	BAL	457	8TH WARD
GREEN, NATHANIEL	CAL	043	3RD DIST
GREEN, NICHOLAS	BAL	314	1ST DIST
GREEN, NICHOLAS	ANN	499	HOWARD D
GREEN, NICHOLAS	BAL	075	1ST WARD
GREEN, NONROD	CAR	336	6TH DIST
GREEN, OTHO	CAR	223	5TH DIST
GREEN, OWEN	ANN	472	HOWARD D
GREEN, PATIENCE	ANN	459	HOWARD D
GREEN, PERRY	ANN	351	3RD DIST
GREEN, PERRY	FRE	430	8TH E DI
GREEN, PETER	CAL	319	1ST DIST
GREEN, PHILANDER	BAL	333	13TH WAR
GREEN, PHILLIP	PRI	064	NOTTINGH
GREEN, PHOEBE	ANN	461	HOWARD D
GREEN, PLULUNENA	BAL	268	20TH WAR
GREEN, PRUCILLA	SOM	435	PRINCESS
GREEN, R. C.	BAL	332	1ST DIST
GREEN, RACHAEL-MULATTO	BAL	241	2ND WARD
GREEN, RACHEL	BAL	086	15TH WAR
GREEN, RACHEL	CAR	068	NO TWP L
GREEN, RACHEL	BAL	169	19TH WAR
GREEN, REBECCA	BAL	019	15TH WAR
GREEN, REBECCA	QUE	228	4TH E DI
GREEN, REBECCA-BLACK	CAR	141	NO TWP L
GREEN, REZIN	ANN	472	HOWARD D
GREEN, RICHARD	BAL	309	3RD WARD
GREEN, RICHARD	BAL	365	3RD WARD
GREEN, RICHARD	BAL	359	3RD WARD
GREEN, RICHARD	BAL	285	1ST DIST
GREEN, RICHARD	HAR	101	2ND DIST
GREEN, RICHARD	BAL	295	20TH WAR
GREEN, RICHARD	MGM	339	CLARKSBU
GREEN, RICHARD C.	BAL	153	16TH WAR
GREEN, ROANAN	CAL	032	2ND DIST
GREEN, ROBERT	CEC	041	CHESAPEA
GREEN, ROBERT	BAL	063	15TH WAR
GREEN, ROBERT	ALL	121	4TH E.D.
GREEN, ROBERT	QUE	227	4TH E DI
GREEN, ROBERT	QUE	223	4TH E DI
GREEN, ROSAN *	BAL	383	13TH WAR
GREEN, RUTH	BAL	168	2ND DIST
GREEN, SALLY	CHA	267	BOJANTOW
GREEN, SAMUEL	FRE	371	CATOCTIN
GREEN, SAMUEL	BAL	111	5TH WARD
GREEN, SAMUEL	ANN	359	3RD DIST
GREEN, SAMUEL	ANN	351	3RD DIST
GREEN, SAMUEL	BAL	061	2ND DIST
GREEN, SAMUEL	QUE	223	4TH E DI
GREEN, SAMUEL L.	BAL	286	7TH WARD
GREEN, SAMUEL*	DOR	453	1ST DIST
GREEN, SAMUEL-BLACK	QUE	170	2ND E DI
GREEN, SARA	CHA	259	MIDDLETO
GREEN, SARAH	CAL	036	2ND DIST
GREEN, SARAH	QUE	171	2ND E DI
GREEN, SARAH	KEN	285	3RD DIST
GREEN, SARAH	SOM	356	BRINKLEY
GREEN, SARAH	PRI	061	NOTTINGH
GREEN, SARAH	BAL	051	2ND DIST
GREEN, SARAH	BAL	091	5TH WARD
GREEN, SARAH	BAL	314	3RD WARD
GREEN, SARAH	BAL	458	1ST DIST
GREEN, SARAH A.	ANN	515	HOWARD D
GREEN, SERCELIA	BAL	062	18TH WAR
GREEN, SISTER ANN	FRE	198	5TH E DI
GREEN, SISTER M.J.	FRE	198	5TH E DI
GREEN, SOPHIA	BAL	378	3RD WARD
GREEN, STEPHEN	CEC	099	3RD E DI
GREEN, STEPHEN	PRI	038	VANSVILL
GREEN, STEPHEN-MULATTO	FRE	189	5TH E DI
GREEN, SURREN-BLACK	CAR	084	NO TWP L
GREEN, SUSAN	BAL	384	1ST DIST
GREEN, SUSAN	BAL	423	1ST DIST
GREEN, SUSAN	ALL	240	CUMBERLA
GREEN, SUSAN	BAL	102	10TH WAR
GREEN, SUSAN	BAL	139	5TH WARD
GREEN, SYNTHA	HAR	173	3RD DIST
GREEN, THOMAS	HAR	073	1ST DIST
GREEN, THOMAS	BAL	097	10TH WAR
GREEN, THOMAS	BAL	047	9TH WARD
GREEN, THOMAS	ANN	343	3RD DIST
GREEN, THOMAS	BAL	312	3RD WARD
GREEN, THOMAS	BAL	281	2ND WARD
GREEN, THOMAS	BAL	062	1ST WARD
GREEN, THOMAS	BAL	189	5TH DIST
GREEN, THOMAS	BAL	026	1ST WARD
GREEN, THOMAS	BAL	198	11TH WAR
GREEN, THOMAS	QUE	224	4TH E DI
GREEN, THOMAS P.	BAL	103	5TH WARD
GREEN, THOMAS S.	QUE	180	2ND E DI
GREEN, VIRGINIA	BAL	101	5TH WARD
GREEN, VIRGINIA	BAL	158	2ND DIST
GREEN, WESLEY	BAL	057	2ND DIST

Name	County	Page	District
GREEN, WILLAIM	BAL	298	12TH WAR
GREEN, WILLIAM	BAL	110	10TH WAR
GREEN, WILLIAM	BAL	053	2ND DIST
GREEN, WILLIAM	BAL	142	2ND DIST
GREEN, WILLIAM	BAL	111	5TH WARD
GREEN, WILLIAM	BAL	334	1ST DIST
GREEN, WILLIAM	BAL	319	1ST DIST
GREEN, WILLIAM	BAL	265	12TH WAR
GREEN, WILLIAM	BAL	425	8TH WARD
GREEN, WILLIAM	ALL	160	6TH E.D.
GREEN, WILLIAM	PRI	061	NOTTINGH
GREEN, WILLIAM	TAL	108	ST MICHA
GREEN, WILLIAM	CAL	032	2ND DIST
GREEN, WILLIAM	BAL	117	11TH WAR
GREEN, WILLIAM	BAL	279	17TH WAR
GREEN, WILLIAM	CAR	271	WESTMINS
GREEN, WILLIAM	FRE	369	CATOCTIN
GREEN, WILLIAM	BAL	373	13TH WAR
GREEN, WILLIAM	BAL	414	14TH WAR
GREEN, WILLIAM	CEC	032	CHESAPEA
GREEN, WILLIAM F.	BAL	309	7TH WARD
GREEN, WILLIAM H.	BAL	398	3RD WARD
GREEN, WILLIAM H.	QUE	173	2ND E DI
GREEN, WILLIAM P.	ST	308	1ST E DI
GREEN, WILLIAM R.	BAL	089	5TH WARD
GREEN, WILLIAM-BLACK	QUE	169	2ND E DI
GREEN, WILLIAM-BLACK	CAR	134	NO TWP L
GREEN, ZEBEDEE	SOM	522	BARREN C
GREEN, ZEDRICK	ANN	372	4TH DIST
GREEN,ASBURY	BAL	134	1ST WARD
GREEN,W ILLIAM	BAL	291	12TH WAR
GREENAGE, ASBURY	QUE	234	4TH E DI
GREENAGE, BENJAMIN	QUE	234	4TH E DI
GREENAGE, JAMES W.-BLACK	QUE	129	1ST E DI
GREENAGE, JAMES-BLACK	QUE	145	1ST E DI
GREENAGE, JESSE	QUE	233	4TH E DI
GREENAGE, MORDECAI	QUE	230	4TH E DI
GREENAGE, RACHAEL	BAL	197	11TH WAR
GREENAGE, THOMAS	BAL	175	11TH WAR
GREENAWALC, HENRIETTA	BAL	135	16TH WAR
GREENBANK, ROBERT	CEC	151	PORT DUP
GREENBARK, JOHN B.	QUE	226	4TH E DI
GREENBAUGH, GEROGE	BAL	421	14TH WAR
GREENBAUM, MINA	BAL	174	19TH WAR
GREENBAUM, MOSES	BAL	386	8TH WARD
GREENBAUM, MYER	BAL	386	8TH WARD
GREENBAUM, NATHAN	BAL	327	7TH WARD
GREENBAUM, WILLIAM	BAL	174	19TH WAR
GREENBERRY, WILLIAM G.	WAS	021	2ND SUBD
GREENBOLT, WILLIAM	CAR	382	2ND DIST
GREENBOLTZ, JAMES	CAR	242	TANEYTOW
GREENBUD, MARGARET	BAL	044	1ST WARD
GREENBUGH, FREDERICK	BAL	043	1ST WARD
GREENBY, SUSAN	CAR	104	NO TWP L
GREENE, AMELIA	ANN	462	HOWARD D
GREENE, ANN E.	BAL	073	15TH WAR
GREENE, HANNAH	FRE	304	WOODSBOR
GREENE, JAMES	HAR	200	3RD DIST
GREENE, JAMES	BAL	180	2ND DIST
GREENE, LOUISA	BAL	378	13TH WAR
GREENE, LUCINDA	ALL	262	CUMBERLA
GREENE, VIRGINIA	BAL	276	12TH WAR
GREENE, WILLIAM	BAL	136	1ST WARD
GREENEBAUM, JOSHUA	BAL	015	9TH WARD
GREENER, CATHARINE	BAL	255	12TH WAR
GREENER, ELLEN	BAL	191	11TH WAR
GREENFELTER, JOSEPH	BAL	464	14TH WAR
GREENFELTER, SIMON	BAL	292	7TH WARD
GREENFIELD, A.	BAL	264	12TH WAR
GREENFIELD, A.H.	BAL	249	12TH WAR
GREENFIELD, AMELIA	HAR	142	2ND DIST
GREENFIELD, AMOS H.	HAR	080	2ND DIST
GREENFIELD, CALEB	BAL	302	12TH WAR
GREENFIELD, CALEB	BAL	117	2ND DIST
GREENFIELD, ELIZABETH	BAL	197	6TH WARD
GREENFIELD, HENRY A.	HAR	186	3RD DIST
GREENFIELD, HERZ	BAL	060	15TH WAR
GREENFIELD, JAMES	ST	285	2ND E DI
GREENFIELD, JOHN F.	ST	341	5TH E DI
GREENFIELD, JOHN G.	ALL	211	CUMBERLA
GREENFIELD, JOSEPHEAN	BAL	337	1ST DIST
GREENFIELD, MARY E.	HAR	132	2ND DIST
GREENFIELD, SAMUEL	MGM	395	ROCKERLE
GREENFIELD, SAMUEL	BAL	095	2ND DIST
GREENFIELD, THOMAS	BAL	010	4TH WARD
GREENFIELD, WALTER	MGM	396	ROCKERLE
GREENFIELD, WILLIAM	BAL	010	4TH WARD
GREENFIELD, WINFORD	BAL	012	18TH WAR
GREENHAND, REBECCA G.	TAL	073	EASTON T
GREENHAWK, CHARLES	TAL	027	EASTON D
GREENHAWK, ELIZA	TAL	017	EASTON D
GREENHAWK, ELIZABETH	TAL	074	EASTON T
GREENHAWK, F. A.	TAL	068	EASTON T
GREENHAWK, JAMES	TAL	067	EASTON T
GREENHAWK, SAMUEL	TAL	017	EASTON D
GREENHAWK, THOMAS	TAL	023	EASTON D
GREENHOLTZ, RACHAEL	CAR	237	UNION TO
GREENHORNE, M.	ANN	282	ANNAPOLI
GREENHOURSER, JOHN	BAL	264	12TH WAR
GREENLAND, ANN	HAR	133	2ND DIST
GREENLAND, CHARLOTTE	HAR	101	2ND DIST
GREENLAND, ELIZA	HAR	131	2ND DIST
GREENLAND, MARY	HAR	134	2ND DIST
GREENLAND, WILLIAM R.	HAR	168	3RD DIST
GREENLEAF, HANSON	PRI	058	NOTTINGH
GREENLEAF, KITTY	ANN	323	2ND DIST
GREENLEAF, ROBERT	PRI	065	NOTTINGH
GREENLEY, EDMOND	PRI	064	NOTTINGH
GREENLEY, WILLIAM	BAL	245	17TH WAR
GREENLOW, MARY	BAL	238	12TH WAR
GREENLY, CHARLES W.	CAR	105	NO TWP L
GREENLY, JAMES	CAR	090	NO TWP L
GREENSBINE, DANIEL	FRE	077	FREDERIC
GREENSEY, LEWIS W. H.	BAL	117	11TH WAR
GREENSFELDER, BERNARD	BAL	053	4TH WARD
GREENSFELDTER, ABRAM	BAL	048	9TH WARD
GREENSTONE, SIMON	ANN	286	ANNAPOLI
GREENTREE, ANDREW	BAL	203	19TH WAR
GREENTREE, CATHARINE	BAL	202	19TH WAR
GREENTREE, ELLEN	BAL	473	14TH WAR
GREENTREE, ELLEN-MULATTO	FRE	221	BUCKEYST
GREENTREE, EZRA	FRE	048	FREDERIC
GREENTREE, SOLOMON*	TAL	023	EASTON D
GREENVILLE, JOHN H.-BLACK	ST	295	2ND E DI
GREENWADE, MOSES	ALL	138	6TH E.D.
GREENWADE, MOSES T.	ALL	136	4TH E.D.
GREENWALT, CHRISTIAN	FRE	072	FREDERIC
GREENWALT, JAMES	WAS	162	HAGERSTO
GREENWALT, MR.	ANN	284	ANNAPOLI
GREENWALT, SARAH	BAL	359	13TH WAR
GREENWAY, ANN	BAL	294	7TH WARD
GREENWAY, E.M.	BAL	202	11TH WAR
GREENWAY, ELIZABETH	BAL	420	3RD WARD
GREENWAY, JAMES	BAL	130	1ST WARD
GREENWAY, JAMES	BAL	178	2ND WARD
GREENWAY, MARIA	BAL	073	15TH WAR
GREENWELL, ABEL	CAL	050	3RD DIST
GREENWELL, ALEXANDER-BLAC	ST	314	1ST E DI
GREENWELL, AMANDA	BAL	398	3RD WARD
GREENWELL, ANN	ST	257	3RD E DI
GREENWELL, ANN M.	ST	273	3RD E DI
GREENWELL, ANN P.	ST	264	3RD E DI
GREENWELL, BENNETT	ST	272	3RD E DI
GREENWELL, EDWARD	ST	264	3RD E DI
GREENWELL, ELEANOR	ST	266	3RD E DI
GREENWELL, ELIZABETH	ST	258	3RD E DI
GREENWELL, ELIZABETH R.	ST	278	3RD E DI
GREENWELL, ENOCH	ST	288	2ND E DI
GREENWELL, FRANCES	MGM	391	ROCKERLE
GREENWELL, FREDERICK J.	ST	258	3RD E DI
GREENWELL, FRENCH V.	ST	265	3RD E DI
GREENWELL, GUSTAUOIS	ST	285	2ND E DI
GREENWELL, HENRY	ST	273	3RD E DI
GREENWELL, HENRY	ST	272	3RD E DI
GREENWELL, JOHN	ST	274	3RD E DI
GREENWELL, JOHN A.	ST	274	3RD E DI
GREENWELL, JOHN A.	ST	304	2ND E DI
GREENWELL, JOHN D.	ST	290	2ND E DI
GREENWELL, JOHN L.	ST	275	3RD E DI
GREENWELL, JOHN T.	ST	286	2ND E DI
GREENWELL, JOSEPH A.	ST	275	3RD E DI
GREENWELL, JOSEPH H.	ST	257	3RD E DI
GREENWELL, JOSEPH K.	ST	286	2ND E DI
GREENWELL, JOSHUA	BAL	134	18TH WAR
GREENWELL, LEGARD	ST	254	3RD E DI
GREENWELL, LOUIS	ST	283	3RD E DI
GREENWELL, LOUIS W.	ST	274	3RD E DI
GREENWELL, MARGARET-BLACK	ST	312	1ST E DI
GREENWELL, MARY	FRE	154	10TH E D
GREENWELL, MARY E.	ST	308	1ST E DI
GREENWELL, MARY S.B.	ST	317	4TH E DI
GREENWELL, PRISCILLA	ST	307	1ST E DI
GREENWELL, ROSA-BLACK	ST	313	1ST E DI
GREENWELL, SAMUEL-BLACK	ST	311	1ST E DI
GREENWELL, TERESE-BLACK	ST	310	1ST E DI
GREENWELL, THOMAS C.	ST	318	4TH E DI
GREENWELL, THOMAS T.	ST	285	2ND E DI
GREENWELL, TOIA	ST	255	3RD E DI
GREENWELL, WILLIAM	ST	278	3RD E DI
GREENWELL, WILLIAM F.	PRI	093	MARLBROU
GREENWELL, WILLIAM G.	ST	279	3RD E DI
GREENWELL, WILLIAM T.	ST	285	2ND E DI
GREENWICH, GEORGE-BLACK	QUE	179	2ND E DI
GREENWICK, EMILY	BAL	111	18TH WAR
GREENWILL, ANN	ST	265	3RD E DI
GREENWOO, ARIAIMA	KEN	210	2ND DIST
GREENWOLD, MICHAEL	HAR	112	2ND DIST
GREENWOOD, ABRAHAM	FRE	430	8TH E DI
GREENWOOD, ANGELIN	BAL	236	12TH WAR
GREENWOOD, BARBARA	CAR	391	2ND DIST
GREENWOOD, BENJAMIN	KEN	210	2ND DIST
GREENWOOD, BETTY	BAL	077	18TH WAR
GREENWOOD, CATHARINE	FRE	428	8TH E DI
GREENWOOD, ELIZABETH	BAL	359	8TH WARD
GREENWOOD, ELLEN	BAL	099	15TH WAR
GREENWOOD, ELLEN	BAL	396	14TH WAR
GREENWOOD, ELLEN A.	BAL	428	14TH WAR
GREENWOOD, FRANKLIN	KEN	303	3RD DIST
GREENWOOD, GEORGE W.	KEN	247	2ND DIST
GREENWOOD, GERGIANNA	QUE	134	1ST E DI
GREENWOOD, HANNA	KEN	297	3RD DIST
GREENWOOD, HARRIET	BAL	231	12TH WAR
GREENWOOD, HARRIETT	BAL	334	13TH WAR
GREENWOOD, HENRY	BAL	301	12TH WAR
GREENWOOD, HENRY	BAL	176	6TH WARD
GREENWOOD, ISAIAH	FRE	428	8TH E DI
GREENWOOD, J.R.	BAL	171	1ST WARD
GREENWOOD, JACOB	BAL	141	11TH WAR
GREENWOOD, JAMES	BAL	231	17TH WAR
GREENWOOD, JAMES	CEC	048	1ST E DI
GREENWOOD, JAMES	QUE	169	2ND E DI
GREENWOOD, JAMES W.	KEN	228	2ND DIST
GREENWOOD, JANE	BAL	234	20TH WAR
GREENWOOD, JOHN	BAL	227	19TH WAR
GREENWOOD, JOHN	CAR	284	7TH DIST
GREENWOOD, JOHN	KEN	213	2ND DIST
GREENWOOD, JOHN	FRE	426	8TH E DI
GREENWOOD, JOHN	BAL	002	18TH WAR
GREENWOOD, JOHN	KEN	269	1ST DIST
GREENWOOD, JOHN	KEN	281	3RD DIST
GREENWOOD, JOHN	ANN	330	2ND DIST
GREENWOOD, JOHN	ALL	250	CUMBERLA
GREENWOOD, JOSEPH	CAR	402	2ND DIST
GREENWOOD, MARGARET	CAR	391	2ND DIST
GREENWOOD, MARIA	BAL	099	5TH WARD
GREENWOOD, MARY A.	KEN	221	2ND DIST
GREENWOOD, MARY A.	KEN	310	3RD DIST
GREENWOOD, MARY E.	BAL	098	5TH WARD
GREENWOOD, PEREGRINE	BAL	396	14TH WAR
GREENWOOD, RICHARD	BAL	049	15TH WAR
GREENWOOD, SAMUEL	BAL	093	15TH WAR
GREENWOOD, SARAH	KEN	211	2ND DIST
GREENWOOD, SARAH	BAL	002	18TH WAR
GREENWOOD, SARAH A.	KEN	306	3RD DIST
GREENWOOD, SUSAN	BAL	070	18TH WAR
GREENWOOD, SUSAN	BAL	268	20TH WAR
GREENWOOD, SUSAN	BAL	329	7TH WARD
GREENWOOD, SUSAN E.	BAL	144	16TH WAR
GREENWOOD, WILLIAM	BAL	098	5TH WARD
GREENWOOD, WILLIAM	BAL	002	18TH WAR
GREENWOOD, WILLIAM	KEN	244	2ND DIST
GREENWOOD, WILLIAM	KEN	270	1ST DIST
GREER, ALEXANDER	BAL	009	15TH WAR
GREER, FIELDER W.	PRI	046	AQUASCO
GREER, GEORGE	BAL	044	9TH WARD
GREER, JAMES	BAL	401	14TH WAR
GREER, JOHN *	BAL	029	18TH WAR
GREER, JOHN*	DOR	439	1ST DIST
GREER, LYDIA*	DOR	444	1ST DIST
GREER, MARY	BAL	109	15TH WAR
GREER, MARY A.	WAS	097	2ND DIST
GREER, MOSES	SOM	485	TRAPP DI
GREER, SAMUEL*	DOR	453	1ST DIST
GREER, SELBY	WOR	221	4TH E DI
GREER, STOKLEY *	WOR	224	4TH E DI
GREER, WILLIAM	BAL	022	9TH WARD
GREERMAN, ELIZABETH	BAL	296	3RD WARD
GREES, TOBIAS	BAL	424	1ST DIST
GREESOR, JOSEPH	BAL	411	14TH WAR
GREEVES, DANIEL	BAL	033	1ST WARD
GREEVY, HENRY	ANN	461	HOWARD D
GREEWALT, DANIEL	WAS	162	HAGERSTO
GREEWALT, ELIZABETH	WAS	181	BOONSBOR
GREEWOOD, ANN	KEN	208	2ND DIST
GREEWOOD, CHARLES	BAL	125	1ST WARD
GREEWOOD, MARY	BAL	265	17TH WAR
GREF, PATRICK	BAL	082	2ND DIST
GREGER, JOHN *	BAL	313	20TH WAR
GREGG, ANDREW	BAL	148	11TH WAR
GREGG, ANN	BAL	339	13TH WAR
GREGG, ELIZABETH	BAL	149	11TH WAR
GREGG, ELIZABETH	WAS	152	2ND DIST
GREGG, HARRIET	BAL	066	10TH WAR
GREGG, JAMES	CEC	122	4TH E DI
GREGG, JOHN	BAL	151	16TH WAR
GREGG, JOHN H.	ALL	113	5TH E.D.
GREGG, JOHN H.	FRE	384	PETERSVI
GREGG, M. H.	BAL	046	9TH WARD
GREGG, PRAISON *	ALL	055	10TH E.D
GREGG, ROBERT	CEC	110	4TH E DI
GREGG, SAMUEL	FRE	377	PETERSVI
GREGG, THOMAS	CEC	123	3RD E DI
GREGOR, JOHN	ALL	135	4TH E.D.
GREGORY, AMOS	BAL	042	15TH WAR
GREGORY, ELLENORA	BAL	245	17TH WAR
GREGORY, HENRY M.	BAL	395	3RD WARD
GREGORY, JAMES	ALL	200	CUMBERLA
GREGORY, JAMES	BAL	460	1ST DIST
GREGORY, JAMES A.	PRI	106	PISCATAW
GREGORY, JOHN	BAL	034	15TH WAR
GREGORY, JOHN	BAL	313	7TH WARD
GREGORY, JOHUA R.	BAL	179	2ND WARD
GREGORY, JOSEPH	BAL	245	17TH WAR
GREGORY, JOSHUA	BAL	394	3RD WARD
GREGORY, LEVINA	WAS	162	2ND DIST
GREGORY, MARY E.	ALL	200	CUMBERLA
GREGORY, MISS P.	FRE	200	5TH E DI
GREGORY, RICHARD	WAS	162	2ND DIST
GREGORY, SAMUEL F.	FRE	384	PETERSVI
GREGORY, SARHA E.	BAL	418	14TH WAR
GREGORY, TAPLEY	BAL	028	15TH WAR
GREGORY, VIRGINIA	BAL	387	3RD WARD
GREGORY, WILLIAM	BAL	228	2ND WARD
GREGORY, WILLIAM	BAL	028	4TH WARD
GREGSLEY, SARAH	BAL	205	2ND WARD
GREHA, AUGUSTUS	FRE	019	FREDERIC
GREHARTH, ANSON	CEC	025	ELKTON 3
GREIB, FREDERICK	PRI	093	MARLBROU
GREIG, HENRY	WAS	136	2ND DIST
GREIGE, HENRY *	BAL	303	12TH WAR
GREIGG, SISTER A.C.	FRE	198	5TH E DI
GREIOR, MATHEW	ANN	458	HOWARD D
GREIR, ROBERT	BAL	104	5TH WARD
GREIVES, HORATIO G.	DOR	417	1ST DIST
GREIVES, JOHN	BAL	290	17TH WAR
GREMLEY, MARY	CAR	066	NO TWP L
GREMLY, DAVID	CAR	103	NO TWP L
GREMLY, ELIZABETH	CAR	066	NO TWP L
GREMM, EUGENE	ANN	469	HOWARD D
GREMUIRE, E.	BAL	320	12TH WAR
GREN, HENRIETTA	BAL	052	9TH WARD
GREN, MARY A.	BAL	009	1ST WARD
GRENALL, CHARLES	BAL	135	1ST WARD
GRENDER, SAMUEL	FRE	204	BUCKEYST
GRENENGER, JOHN	BAL	386	13TH WAR
GRENER, JOHN	BAL	264	12TH WAR
GRENEWALD, SAMUEL	BAL	120	16TH WAR
GRENEWALD, SIMON	BAL	123	16TH WAR
GRENLAND, JOHN	HAR	193	3RD DIST
GRENMINGHER, JAMES	BAL	253	2ND WARD
GRENNWOOD, DANIEL	CAR	402	2ND DIST
GRENY, EMELINE	PRI	115	PISCATAW
GREOME, SARAH *	KEN	241	2ND DIST
GRESBINE, JOHN	BAL	212	19TH WAR
GRESHA, AVELINA	BAL	453	8TH WARD
GRESHAM, THOMAS P.	KEN	233	2ND DIST
GRESHAM, WASHINGTON	KEN	233	2ND DIST
GRESHION, MARY	BAL	199	11TH WAR
GRESON, EPHRAIM	CEC	078	NORTHEAS
GRESS, JOHN	BAL	136	2ND DIST
GRESSEN, CATHARINE	BAL	194	11TH WAR
GRESSON, JOHN	CEC	132	6TH E DI
GRET, VALENTINE	BAL	087	1ST WARD
GRETGER, HENRY	BAL	230	17TH WAR
GRETZBERG, GEORGE	ALL	097	5TH E.D.
GREUBELL, GEORGE	BAL	077	15TH WAR
GREVES, JAMES	CAL	011	1ST DIST
GREVES, JOHN B.	CAL	017	1ST DIST
GREVES, REBECCA	BAL	093	1ST WARD
GREW, CAROLINE	BAL	229	6TH WARD
GREWE, HANNAH	BAL	234	6TH WARD
GREY, A. M.	ANN	345	3RD DIST
GREY, ANN	WAS	060	2ND SUBD
GREY, ANN	WAS	059	2ND SUBD
GREY, ANN E.	WAS	130	HAGERSTO
GREY, CHARLES	ST	325	4TH E DI
GREY, DANIEL	WAS	059	2ND SUBD
GREY, DAVID	WAS	148	2ND DIST
GREY, ELIZABETH	WAS	065	2ND SUBD
GREY, ELIZABETH	BAL	156	5TH WARD
GREY, ELIZABETH-BLACK	QUE	151	1ST E DI
GREY, EPTER	FRE	008	FREDERIC
GREY, GEORGIANNE	BAL	099	5TH WARD
GREY, ISAAC	WAS	149	HAGERSTO
GREY, JOHN	WAS	161	HAGERSTO
GREY, JOHN	WAS	204	1ST DIST
GREY, JOHN	BAL	094	10TH WAR
GREY, JOHN	ANN	391	4TH DIST
GREY, JOHN F.	WAS	085	2ND SUBD
GREY, JOHN P.	WAS	149	HAGERSTO
GREY, JOHNATHAN	ALL	218	CUMBERLA
GREY, JOSEPH	WAS	104	2ND DIST
GREY, JOSEPH-BLACK	FRE	040	FREDERIC
GREY, LETTY	WAS	102	2ND DIST
GREY, LOUISA	BAL	156	5TH WARD
GREY, MARGARET	BAL	155	11TH WAR
GREY, MARY	ANN	331	2ND DIST
GREY, MARY J.	WAS	155	HAGERSTO
GREY, MARY J.-BLACK	FRE	039	FREDERIC
GREY, MATILDA-BLACK	FRE	043	FREDERIC
GREY, NANCY	PRI	106	PISCATAW
GREY, NANCY	ANN	428	HOWARD D
GREY, OTHO	ANN	310	1ST DIST
GREY, RACHEL A.	FRE	305	WOODSBOR
GREY, ROBERT	FRE	083	FREDERIC
GREY, ROBERT	ST	334	4TH E DI
GREY, SARAH	BAL	208	17TH WAR
GREY, THEADORE	FRE	003	FREDERIC
GREY, THOMAS	FRE	369	CATOCTIN
GREY, THOMAS	WAS	138	2ND DIST

Name	County	Page	District
GREY, THOMAS	WAS	065	2ND SUBD
GREY, URIAH	ST	347	5TH E DI
GREY, VIRGINIA WALLON	WAS	136	HAGERSTO
GREY, WILLIAM	ANN	388	4TH DIST
GREY,MATILDA	BAL	077	1ST WARD
GREY,PATRICK	BAL	114	1ST WARD
GREYHAN, EDWARD	HAR	025	1ST DIST
GRFFIN, JOHN	QUE	247	5TH E DI
GRIAR, THOMAS	HAR	110	2ND DIST
GRIBBIN, MARY	FRE	196	5TH E DI
GRIBBON, ALFRED W.	BAL	385	13TH WAR
GRIBIE, BERNARD	BAL	436	8TH WARD
GRICE, ELIZA	BAL	072	2ND DIST
GRICE, GEORGE	BAL	249	6TH WARD
GRICE, J.A.	BAL	011	2ND DIST
GRICE, MARY	BAL	164	16TH WAR
GRICKLEY, THOMAS J.	PRI	007	BLADENSB
GRIDDY, MARY A.	BAL	448	14TH WAR
GRIDING, LEONARD	BAL	204	19TH WAR
GRIDLEY, JOHN	BAL	092	5TH WARD
GRIEDEL, RUTH	BAL	055	9TH WARD
GRIEN, JOSEPH D.	BAL	277	20TH WAR
GRIER, ANN	BAL	252	20TH WAR
GRIER, CAROLINE	BAL	070	10TH WAR
GRIER, JOHN	BAL	376	8TH WARD
GRIER, JOHN	BAL	436	14TH WAR
GRIER, JOHN	WAS	083	2ND SUBD
GRIER, PETER	ALL	208	CUMBERLA
GRIER, ROBERT S.	FRE	162	EMMITTSB
GRIER, SARAH	BAL	280	7TH WARD
GRIERSON, ANDREW	CAL	030	2ND DIST
GRIERSON, ROBERT	CAL	030	2ND DIST
GRIES, JOHN	BAL	225	17TH WAR
GRIES, JOHN G.	BAL	055	15TH WAR
GRIES, NICHOLAS	BAL	351	7TH WARD
GRIES, SARAH *	BAL	280	7TH WARD
GRIEST, AMOS	CEC	121	4TH E DI
GRIEST, GEORGE C.	BAL	043	15TH WAR
GRIEST, JOHN	CEC	166	6TH E DI
GRIEST, JOHN	CEC	167	6TH E DI
GRIEST, LYDIA	CEC	172	6TH E DI
GRIEST, MOSES	BAL	042	15TH WAR
GRIEVES, DAVID F.	BAL	076	15TH WAR
GRIEVES, HENRY	CEC	051	1ST E DI
GRIEVES, MARY	BAL	326	7TH WARD
GRIEVES, POMPEY	CEC	204	6TH E DI
GRIEVES, SAMUEL	CEC	205	7TH E DI
GRIEVES, THOMAS G.	ANN	511	HOWARD D
GRIEVES, WILLIAM	CEC	068	5TH E DI
GRIEZE, HENRY	BAL	025	4TH WARD
GRIFFE, RICHARD	CEC	208	7TH E DI
GRIFFE, WILLIAM	CEC	207	7TH E DI
GRIFFEE, BENJAMIN	CEC	120	4TH E DI
GRIFFEE, ELISHA	CAR	202	4TH DIST
GRIFFEE, WILLIAM JR.	CAR	194	4TH DIST
GRIFFEL, ABRAHAM	CEC	059	1ST E DI
GRIFFEN, DAVID-MULATTO	FRE	419	8TH E DI
GRIFFEN, ELIAS G.	BAL	276	12TH WAR
GRIFFEN, GEORGE-BLACK	FRE	417	8TH E DI
GRIFFEN, HARRIET-MULATTO	FRE	415	8TH E DI
GRIFFEN, JAMES	ALL	221	CUMBERLA
GRIFFEN, JOHN-MULATTO	FRE	415	8TH E DI
GRIFFETH, ALEXANDER	ALL	012	3RD E.D.
GRIFFETH, AMOS	HAR	030	1ST DIST
GRIFFETH, G. L.	BAL	169	11TH WAR
GRIFFETH, HARTER	ALL	012	3RD E.D.
GRIFFETH, HENRY	ALL	013	3RD E.D.
GRIFFETH, HENRY	ALL	012	3RD E.D.
GRIFFETH, JOHN	ALL	019	2ND E.D.
GRIFFETH, SELATHIEL	SOM	532	QUANTICO
GRIFFETT, SELMA	BAL	323	12TH WAR
GRIFFICTH, ALFRED	BAL	382	13TH WAR
GRIFFIEE, JAMES	CAL	018	1ST DIST
GRIFFIFS, JOHN*	BAL	033	4TH WARD
GRIFFILTH, MARIA C.	BAL	345	13TH WAR
GRIFFIN, ALEXANDER	ANN	392	4TH DIST
GRIFFIN, ALEXANDER-BLACK	QUE	156	2ND E DI
GRIFFIN, ALEXANDER-BLACK	QUE	155	2ND E DI
GRIFFIN, ALSEY	QUE	247	5TH E DI
GRIFFIN, ANN-BLACK	FRE	428	8TH E DI
GRIFFIN, ANNA	QUE	133	1ST E DI
GRIFFIN, ANNA M.-BLACK	QUE	187	3RD E DI
GRIFFIN, ANNE	BAL	029	15TH WAR
GRIFFIN, ANTHONY	BAL	124	18TH WAR
GRIFFIN, ASBURY	TAL	060	EASTON D
GRIFFIN, BELITHA	WOR	254	1ST CENS
GRIFFIN, BENJAMINE	BAL	280	7TH WARD
GRIFFIN, BRIDGET	BAL	179	19TH WAR
GRIFFIN, CALEB	MGM	323	CRACKLIN
GRIFFIN, CALEB	TAL	059	EASTON D
GRIFFIN, CAROLINE	KEN	256	1ST DIST
GRIFFIN, CAROLINE	BAL	230	6TH WARD
GRIFFIN, CATHARINE	BAL	205	11TH WAR
GRIFFIN, CHARLES	BAL	281	12TH WAR
GRIFFIN, CHARLES-BLACK	QUE	159	2ND E DI
GRIFFIN, CHRISTIAN	BAL	060	2ND DIST
GRIFFIN, DANIEL	BAL	096	10TH WAR
GRIFFIN, DANIEL	PRI	112	PISCATAW
GRIFFIN, EDWARD	BAL	162	11TH WAR
GRIFFIN, EDWARD	CEC	151	PORT DUP
GRIFFIN, EDWARD*	DOR	383	1ST DIST
GRIFFIN, ELISHA	CAR	137	NO TWP L
GRIFFIN, ELIZA	BAL	124	18TH WAR
GRIFFIN, ELIZA	BAL	205	19TH WAR
GRIFFIN, ELIZABETH	BAL	042	4TH WARD
GRIFFIN, ELIZABETH	BAL	242	2ND WARD
GRIFFIN, ELLEN	BAL	011	1ST WARD
GRIFFIN, ELLEN W.	BAL	353	7TH WARD
GRIFFIN, GEORGE	BAL	270	12TH WAR
GRIFFIN, GEORGE	BAL	014	15TH WAR
GRIFFIN, GEORGE	KEN	233	2ND DIST
GRIFFIN, GEORGE	QUE	250	5TH E DI
GRIFFIN, GREENBURY	QUE	159	2ND E DI
GRIFFIN, HARNETT	KEN	296	3RD DIST
GRIFFIN, HARRIET	BAL	124	16TH WAR
GRIFFIN, HARRIET	BAL	106	15TH WAR
GRIFFIN, HENRIETTA	BAL	068	15TH WAR
GRIFFIN, HENRY	BAL	324	7TH WARD
GRIFFIN, HENRY	BAL	101	2ND DIST
GRIFFIN, HUGH	BAL	312	12TH WAR
GRIFFIN, HYLAND	CEC	046	1ST E DI
GRIFFIN, ISAAC	DOR	389	1ST DIST
GRIFFIN, ISAAC	QUE	241	5TH E DI
GRIFFIN, ISAAC	WOR	286	BERLIN 1
GRIFFIN, JACOB	BAL	269	20TH WAR
GRIFFIN, JACOB	BAL	257	6TH WARD
GRIFFIN, JAMES	BAL	294	7TH WARD
GRIFFIN, JAMES	BAL	308	7TH WARD
GRIFFIN, JAMES	ANN	354	3RD DIST
GRIFFIN, JAMES	BAL	361	3RD WARD
GRIFFIN, JAMES	BAL	230	6TH WARD
GRIFFIN, JAMES	CHA	253	MIDDLETO
GRIFFIN, JAMES	FRE	178	5TH E DI
GRIFFIN, JAMES	HAR	102	2ND DIST
GRIFFIN, JAMES	CEC	065	1ST E DI
GRIFFIN, JAMES	QUE	232	4TH E DI
GRIFFIN, JAMES H.	PRI	105	PISCATAW
GRIFFIN, JAMES-BLACK	QUE	197	3RD E DI
GRIFFIN, JANE	BAL	046	18TH WAR
GRIFFIN, JANE	BAL	419	14TH WAR
GRIFFIN, JARVIS	BAL	288	7TH WARD
GRIFFIN, JERVIS	QUE	246	5TH E DI
GRIFFIN, JOHN	KEN	276	1ST DIST
GRIFFIN, JOHN	PRI	120	PISCATAW
GRIFFIN, JOHN	BAL	402	3RD WARD
GRIFFIN, JOHN	BAL	059	2ND DIST
GRIFFIN, JOHN	ANN	481	HOWARD D
GRIFFIN, JOHN	BAL	116	15TH WAR
GRIFFIN, JOHN	BAL	325	12TH WAR
GRIFFIN, JOHN	BAL	345	13TH WAR
GRIFFIN, JOHN	SOM	424	PRINCESS
GRIFFIN, JOHN	DOR	333	3RD DIVI
GRIFFIN, JOHN	BAL	198	19TH WAR
GRIFFIN, JOHN	CAL	058	3RD DIST
GRIFFIN, JOHN-BLACK	BAL	220	2ND WARD
GRIFFIN, JOHN-BLACK	QUE	172	2ND E DI
GRIFFIN, JOSEPH	CAL	008	1ST DIST
GRIFFIN, JOSEPH G.	TAL	112	ST MICHA
GRIFFIN, JOSHUA	BAL	019	2ND DIST
GRIFFIN, JULIANA E. E.	QUE	239	5TH E DI
GRIFFIN, KATE	BAL	027	18TH WAR
GRIFFIN, LAMBS	WOR	255	1ST CENS
GRIFFIN, LEMUEL G.	BAL	102	15TH WAR
GRIFFIN, LEVI	KEN	256	1ST DIST
GRIFFIN, LEVI J.	BAL	400	3RD WARD
GRIFFIN, LEVIN	BAL	299	7TH WARD
GRIFFIN, LUKE	BAL	003	9TH WARD
GRIFFIN, LYNCH	BAL	003	9TH WARD
GRIFFIN, MACHALA-BLACK	BAL	217	2ND WARD
GRIFFIN, MARGARET	BAL	024	1ST WARD
GRIFFIN, MARGARET	QUE	244	5TH E DI
GRIFFIN, MARGARET	DOR	464	1ST DIST
GRIFFIN, MARGARET	CEC	152	PORT DUP
GRIFFIN, MARIETTA	QUE	193	3RD E DI
GRIFFIN, MARRY	WAS	065	2ND SUBD
GRIFFIN, MARTHA	QUE	245	5TH E DI
GRIFFIN, MARTHA	BAL	243	17TH WAR
GRIFFIN, MARTHA	HAR	099	2ND DIST
GRIFFIN, MARTHA	BAL	224	6TH WARD
GRIFFIN, MARY	BAL	238	6TH WARD
GRIFFIN, MARY	BAL	237	12TH WAR
GRIFFIN, MARY	BAL	281	12TH WAR
GRIFFIN, MARY	BAL	338	3RD WARD
GRIFFIN, MARY	CAL	047	3RD DIST
GRIFFIN, MARY	WOR	286	BERLIN 1
GRIFFIN, MARY A.	BAL	002	18TH WAR
GRIFFIN, MARY L.	PRI	105	PISCATAW
GRIFFIN, MATILDA	WOR	254	1ST CENS
GRIFFIN, MICHAEL	BAL	126	2ND DIST
GRIFFIN, MILBY	WOR	287	BERLIN 1
GRIFFIN, MISS M.	FRE	200	5TH E DI
GRIFFIN, NANCY	DOR	419	1ST DIST
GRIFFIN, NATHAN	BAL	018	2ND DIST
GRIFFIN, NATHAN	BAL	083	2ND DIST
GRIFFIN, NELSON	BAL	269	20TH WAR
GRIFFIN, NICY*	DOR	382	1ST DIST
GRIFFIN, PATTY	BAL	286	12TH WAR
GRIFFIN, PERRY	BAL	102	15TH WAR
GRIFFIN, PHILIP	BAL	413	8TH WARD
GRIFFIN, PINDEN	DOR	416	1ST DIST
GRIFFIN, R.H.	BAL	162	6TH WARD
GRIFFIN, REBECA	CAR	214	5TH DIST
GRIFFIN, RICHARD*	TAL	001	EASTON D
GRIFFIN, ROBERT	BAL	265	17TH WAR
GRIFFIN, ROBERT	BAL	183	6TH WARD
GRIFFIN, ROBERT B.	BAL	309	12TH WAR
GRIFFIN, SALLY	QUE	248	5TH E DI
GRIFFIN, SAMUEL	BAL	338	3RD WARD
GRIFFIN, SAMUEL	BAL	378	13TH WAR
GRIFFIN, SARAH	QUE	132	1ST E DI
GRIFFIN, SARAH	BAL	444	14TH WAR
GRIFFIN, SARAH M.	BAL	080	4TH WARD
GRIFFIN, SIBERIA	BAL	428	14TH WAR
GRIFFIN, SICKY	BAL	064	1ST WARD
GRIFFIN, STEPHEN	BAL	455	1ST DIST
GRIFFIN, STEPHEN	BAL	279	12TH WAR
GRIFFIN, STEPHEN-BLACK	BAL	217	2ND WARD
GRIFFIN, SUSAN	BAL	143	5TH WARD
GRIFFIN, SUSAN	BAL	329	7TH WARD
GRIFFIN, THERESA	BAL	301	7TH WARD
GRIFFIN, THOMAS	BAL	383	8TH WARD
GRIFFIN, THOMAS	BAL	217	6TH WARD
GRIFFIN, THOMAS	BAL	028	9TH WARD
GRIFFIN, THOMAS	BAL	068	1ST WARD
GRIFFIN, THOMAS	BAL	126	2ND DIST
GRIFFIN, THOMAS	BAL	179	19TH WAR
GRIFFIN, THOMAS	DOR	404	1ST DIST
GRIFFIN, THOMAS	HAR	098	2ND DIST
GRIFFIN, THOMAS	WAS	185	BOONSBOR
GRIFFIN, THOMAS	WAS	072	2ND SUBD
GRIFFIN, THOMAS	PRI	070	MARLBROU
GRIFFIN, THOMAS	KEN	269	1ST DIST
GRIFFIN, TIMOTHY	BAL	140	5TH WARD
GRIFFIN, WASHINGTON	DOR	416	1ST DIST
GRIFFIN, WILLIAM	CEC	176	7TH E DI
GRIFFIN, WILLIAM	CAL	041	3RD DIST
GRIFFIN, WILLIAM	BAL	150	1ST WARD
GRIFFIN, WILLIAM	BAL	021	1ST WARD
GRIFFIN, WILLIAM	BAL	346	7TH WARD
GRIFFIN, WILLIAM	BAL	460	8TH WARD
GRIFFIN, WILLIAM	ANN	392	4TH DIST
GRIFFIN, WILLIAM	ANN	406	8TH DIST
GRIFFIN, WILLIAM	QUE	193	3RD E DI
GRIFFIN, WILLIAM	PRI	100	SPALDING
GRIFFIN, WILLIAM H.	WOR	254	1ST CENS
GRIFFIN, WILLIAM H.	PRI	070	MARLBROU
GRIFFIN, WILLIAM J.B.	BAL	120	1ST WARD
GRIFFIN, WILLIAM W.	BAL	008	15TH WAR
GRIFFIN, WILLIAM-BLACK	TAL	038	EASTON D
GRIFFIN,E DWIN	QUE	179	2ND E DI
GRIFFIN,MICHAEL	ALL	208	CUMBERLA
GRIFFINTH, LEWIS	ALL	258	CUMBERLA
GRIFFISS, JOHN*	CAL	049	3RD DIST
GRIFFISS, SARAH	BAL	033	4TH WARD
GRIFFISS, THOMAS*	BAL	148	5TH WARD
GRIFFITH, A.V.	BAL	033	4TH WARD
GRIFFITH, AARON	ANN	521	HOWARD D
GRIFFITH, ABRAHAM	CAR	133	NO TWP L
GRIFFITH, ABRAHAM	CAR	170	NO TWP L
GRIFFITH, ALBERT G.	WAS	071	2ND SUBD
GRIFFITH, ALEXANDER	BAL	061	18TH WAR
GRIFFITH, ALEXANDER JR.	CAR	131	NO TWP L
GRIFFITH, ALFRED	CAR	154	NO TWP L
GRIFFITH, ALICE	ANN	285	ANNAPOLI
GRIFFITH, ALICE	BAL	225	12TH WAR
GRIFFITH, ALLEN	CEC	136	6TH E DI
GRIFFITH, AMANUEL R.	ANN	388	4TH DIST
GRIFFITH, ANDREW	BAL	104	18TH WAR
GRIFFITH, ANN	HAR	200	3RD DIST
GRIFFITH, ANN	BAL	244	20TH WAR
GRIFFITH, ANN	ANN	277	ANNAPOLI
GRIFFITH, ANN	BAL	333	3RD WARD
GRIFFITH, ANNA	BAL	251	6TH WARD
GRIFFITH, ANNA J.	MGM	327	CRACKLIN
GRIFFITH, BARZILLIA	ANN	368	4TH DIST
GRIFFITH, BENJAMIN	ANN	389	4TH DIST
GRIFFITH, BENJAMIN	ANN	403	8TH DIST
GRIFFITH, CALEP	ALL	209	CUMBERLA
GRIFFITH, CATHARINE	KEN	290	3RD DIST
GRIFFITH, CHARLES	BAL	257	6TH WARD
GRIFFITH, CHARLES	ANN	388	4TH DIST
GRIFFITH, CHARLES	BAL	170	16TH WAR
GRIFFITH, CHARLES A.	BAL	365	13TH WAR
GRIFFITH, CHARLES G.	CAR	170	NO TWP L
GRIFFITH, CHARLES R.	BAL	059	10TH WAR
GRIFFITH, CLARA	ANN	389	4TH DIST
GRIFFITH, DANIEL	BAL	149	5TH WARD
GRIFFITH, DAVID	BAL	361	13TH WAR
GRIFFITH, DENNIS	BAL	119	15TH WAR
GRIFFITH, DENNIS A.	ANN	388	4TH D&ST
GRIFFITH, DOROTHEA	ANN	389	4TH DIST
GRIFFITH, EASTER	BAL	087	15TH WAR
GRIFFITH, EDWARD	DOR	335	3RD DIVI
GRIFFITH, EDWORD	BAL	294	1ST DIST
GRIFFITH, ELIAS	HAR	192	3RD DIST
GRIFFITH, ELISHA	WAS	070	2ND SUBD
GRIFFITH, ELIZ	MGM	334	CRACKLIN
GRIFFITH, ELIZA A.	BAL	234	12TH WAR
GRIFFITH, ELIZABETH	CAR	116	NO TWP L
GRIFFITH, ELIZABETH	BAL	205	11TH WAR
GRIFFITH, ELIZABETH	DOR	359	3RD DIVI
GRIFFITH, ELIZABETH	DOR	318	1ST DIST
GRIFFITH, ELIZABETH	BAL	002	15TH WAR
GRIFFITH, ELIZABETH	BAL	112	15TH WAR
GRIFFITH, ELIZABETH A.	ANN	408	8TH DIST
GRIFFITH, ELIZABETH C.	HAR	186	3RD DIST
GRIFFITH, ELLEN	BAL	051	15TH WAR
GRIFFITH, ELLEN	BAL	191	11TH WAR
GRIFFITH, ELLEN	BAL	127	11TH WAR
GRIFFITH, EVELINA	BAL	082	4TH WARD
GRIFFITH, F.C.	BAL	014	15TH WAR
GRIFFITH, FRANCES	WAS	126	HAGERSTO
GRIFFITH, FRANCIS M.	ALL	022	2ND E.D.
GRIFFITH, GABRIEL	MGM	341	CLARKSBU
GRIFFITH, GAUBABUROUGH	DOR	370	3RD DIVI
GRIFFITH, GEORGE	BAL	262	1ST DIST
GRIFFITH, GRACE	ALL	246	CUMBERLA
GRIFFITH, GRACE	BAL	052	1ST WARD
GRIFFITH, HENERY	BAL	141	11TH WAR
GRIFFITH, HENRY	DOR	333	3RD DIVI
GRIFFITH, HENRY	ALL	011	3RD E.D.
GRIFFITH, HENRY	BAL	073	10TH WAR
GRIFFITH, HENRY C.	WAS	071	2ND SUBD
GRIFFITH, HESTER	BAL	334	13TH WAR
GRIFFITH, HORATIO	HAR	179	3RD DIST
GRIFFITH, HOWARD	MGM	333	CRACKLIN
GRIFFITH, HOWARD	BAL	001	18TH WAR
GRIFFITH, ISAAC	MGM	424	MEDLEY 3
GRIFFITH, ISAAC	HAR	176	3RD DIST
GRIFFITH, ISAAC	HAR	193	3RD DIST
GRIFFITH, ISRAEL	BAL	185	5TH DIST
GRIFFITH, ISRAEL	CEC	113	4TH E DI
GRIFFITH, J.	BAL	382	13TH WAR
GRIFFITH, J. JONES	BAL	332	1ST DIST
GRIFFITH, JACOB	BAL	033	9TH WARD
GRIFFITH, JAMES	WAS	243	CAVETOWN
GRIFFITH, JAMES	BAL	173	2ND DIST
GRIFFITH, JAMES	BAL	115	1ST WARD
GRIFFITH, JAMES	BAL	126	2ND DIST
GRIFFITH, JAMES L.	HAR	135	2ND DIST
GRIFFITH, JAMES M.	BAL	124	11TH WAR
GRIFFITH, JANE	BAL	177	2ND DIST
GRIFFITH, JANE	BAL	229	1ST DIST
GRIFFITH, JEFFERSON	BAL	046	9TH WARD
GRIFFITH, JEFFREY M.	MGM	328	CRACKLIN
GRIFFITH, JOHANNA	BAL	108	10TH WAR
GRIFFITH, JOHN	BAL	010	4TH WARD
GRIFFITH, JOHN	MGM	332	CRACKLIN
GRIFFITH, JOHN	HAR	165	3RD DIST
GRIFFITH, JOHN	DOR	350	3RD DIVI
GRIFFITH, JOHN	BAL	078	15TH WAR
GRIFFITH, JOHN	BAL	190	5TH DIST
GRIFFITH, JOHN	BAL	167	1ST WARD
GRIFFITH, JOHN	BAL	174	1ST WARD
GRIFFITH, JOHN	ALL	072	5TH E.D.
GRIFFITH, JOHN	PRI	086	QUEEN AN
GRIFFITH, JOHN A.	BAL	297	7TH WARD
GRIFFITH, JOHN J.	BAL	212	6TH WARD
GRIFFITH, JOHN L.	ANN	406	8TH DIST
GRIFFITH, JOHN L.	HAR	173	3RD DIST
GRIFFITH, JOHN N.	BAL	254	1ST DIST
GRIFFITH, JOHN R.	ANN	380	4TH DIST
GRIFFITH, JOSEPH	CAR	146	NO TWP L
GRIFFITH, JOSEPH	HAR	199	3RD DIST
GRIFFITH, JOSHAWAY	HAR	179	3RD DIST
GRIFFITH, LEVI P.	BAL	291	7TH WARD
GRIFFITH, LEWIS	HAR	159	3RD DIST
GRIFFITH, LEWIS	CAL	050	3RD DIST
GRIFFITH, LEWIS P.	BAL	212	6TH WARD
GRIFFITH, LOUIS DR-	BAL	420	1ST DIST
GRIFFITH, LOUISA	HAR	178	3RD DIST
GRIFFITH, LUCRETIA O.	BAL	170	16TH WAR
GRIFFITH, LYDE	MGM	342	CLARKSBU
GRIFFITH, MANDA	HAR	163	3RD DIST
GRIFFITH, MARTHA	CAL	047	3RD DIST
GRIFFITH, MARTHA	BAL	187	11TH WAR
GRIFFITH, MARTHA H.	KEN	268	1ST DIST
GRIFFITH, MARTIN	ALL	080	5TH E.D.
GRIFFITH, MARY	BAL	421	1ST DIST
GRIFFITH, MARY	BAL	127	11TH WAR
GRIFFITH, MARY	FRE	243	NEW MARK
GRIFFITH, MARY	BAL	177	19TH WAR
GRIFFITH, MARY	BAL	080	4TH WARD
GRIFFITH, MARY	DOR	302	1ST DIST
GRIFFITH, MARY A.	BAL	314	20TH WAR
GRIFFITH, MARY E.	DOR	376	1ST DIST
GRIFFITH, MATILDA	BAL	140	2ND DIST
GRIFFITH, MICHAEL	BAL	091	10TH WAR
GRIFFITH, NATHAN	CEC	136	6TH E DI
GRIFFITH, NICHOLAS	BAL	467	14TH WAR

GRIFFITH, NOBLE CAR 107 NO TWP L
GRIFFITH, ORLANDO ANN 388 4TH DIST
GRIFFITH, ORLANDO ANN 381 4TH DIST
GRIFFITH, OWEN BAL 134 1ST WARD
GRIFFITH, OWEN BAL 265 1ST DIST
GRIFFITH, PERRY CAR 111 NO TWP L
GRIFFITH, PHILEMON MGM 402 ROCKERLE
GRIFFITH, PHILIP MGM 341 CLARKSBU
GRIFFITH, POLLY BAL 176 2ND DIST
GRIFFITH, PRUDENCE MGM 340 CLARKSBU
GRIFFITH, RACHAEL BAL 228 1ST DIST
GRIFFITH, RACHEL FRE 271 NEW MARK
GRIFFITH, REBECCA G. BAL 062 18TH WAR
GRIFFITH, REUBEN CEC 135 6TH E DI
GRIFFITH, RHODA DOR 335 3RD DIVI
GRIFFITH, RICHARD DOR 350 3RD DIVI
GRIFFITH, RICHARD ANN 431 HOWARD D
GRIFFITH, RICHARD H. MGM 329 CRACKLIN
GRIFFITH, RICHARD L. CAL 059 3RD DIST
GRIFFITH, RICHARD W. BAL 438 8TH WARD
GRIFFITH, ROBERT BAL 134 16TH WAR
GRIFFITH, ROBERT DOR 359 3RD DIVI
GRIFFITH, ROBERT DOR 439 1ST DIST
GRIFFITH, ROBERT A. ANN 430 HOWARD D
GRIFFITH, ROBERT R. BAL 189 6TH WARD
GRIFFITH, ROMULIS R. BAL 173 2ND DIST
GRIFFITH, RUTH FRE 246 NEW MARK
GRIFFITH, RUTH H. MGM 329 CRACKLIN
GRIFFITH, SAMUEL BAL 372 3RD WARD
GRIFFITH, SAMUEL C. BAL 108 10TH WAR
GRIFFITH, SAMUEL E. BAL 144 16TH WAR
GRIFFITH, SARAH BAL 424 14TH WAR
GRIFFITH, SARAH A. CAR 160 NO TWP L
GRIFFITH, SEBBEUS FRE 271 NEW MARK
GRIFFITH, SETH CAR 121 NO TWP L
GRIFFITH, SUSAN FRE 047 FREDERIC
GRIFFITH, SUSAN BAL 078 15TH WAR
GRIFFITH, SUSAN E. BAL 012 4TH WARD
GRIFFITH, SUSAN M. BAL 003 15TH WAR
GRIFFITH, T.H. BAL 162 6TH WARD
GRIFFITH, THOMAS BAL 253 12TH WAR
GRIFFITH, THOMAS CAR 134 NO TWP L
GRIFFITH, THOMAS FRE 244 NEW MARK
GRIFFITH, THOMAS MGM 329 CRACKLIN
GRIFFITH, THOMAS DOR 318 1ST DIST
GRIFFITH, THOMAS PRI 102 SPALDING
GRIFFITH, THOMAS MGM 443 CLARKSTR
GRIFFITH, THOMAS D. ANN 445 HOWARD D
GRIFFITH, THOMAS G. BAL 419 1ST DIST
GRIFFITH, ULYSSES MGM 334 CRACKLIN
GRIFFITH, URIAH H. MGM 325 CRACKLIN
GRIFFITH, WALTER MGM 334 CRACKLIN
GRIFFITH, WESLEY CAR 285 7TH DIST
GRIFFITH, WILLIAM DOR 308 1ST DIST
GRIFFITH, WILLIAM CAR 158 NO TWP L
GRIFFITH, WILLIAM CEC 113 4TH E DI
GRIFFITH, WILLIAM BAL 007 EASTERN
GRIFFITH, WILLIAM BAL 420 8TH WARD
GRIFFITH, WILLIAM BAL 194 17TH WAR
GRIFFITH, WILLIAM BAL 254 6TH WARD
GRIFFITH, WILLIAM BAL 132 1ST WARD
GRIFFITH, WILLIAM ANN 389 4TH DIST
GRIFFITH, WILLIAM ALL 080 5TH E.D.
GRIFFITH, WILLIAM E. HAR 190 3RD DIST
GRIFFITH, WILLIAM FINLEY BAL 014 15TH WAR
GRIFFITH, WILLIAM H. HAR 191 3RD DIST
GRIFFITH, WILLIAM H. BAL 409 14TH WAR
GRIFFITH, WILLIAM J. KEN 282 3RD DIST
GRIFFITH, WILLIAM K. CEC 136 6TH E DI
GRIFFITH, WILLIAM W. HAR 172 3RD DIST
GRIFFITH,FRANCES FRE 224 BUCKEYST
GRIFFITH,JOSEPH W. FRE 224 BUCKEYST
GRIFFITHS, G. BAL 115 1ST WARD
GRIFFON, JANE BAL 128 11TH WAR
GRIFFS, ELIZABETH HAR 167 3RD DIST
GRIFIFN, THOMAS K. QUE 239 5TH E DI
GRIFIFTH, SIDNEY FRE 300 WOODSBOR
GRIFIN, SILAS BAL 476 14TH WAR
GRIFITH, GEORGE P. FRE 407 JEFFERSO
GRIFITH, JOHN CAR 223 5TH DIST
GRIGAN, JOHN BAL 068 2ND DIST
GRIGERY, JOHN* TAL 012 EASTON D
GRIGGS, GEORGE BAL 335 3RD WARD
GRIGGS, HARRIET BAL 381 3RD WARD
GRIGGS, JAMES BAL 019 4TH WARD
GRIGGS, WILLIAM BAL 381 3RD WARD
GRIGHTLY, LEONARD CAL 023 2ND DIST
GRIGONY, DAVID BAL 068 2ND DIST
GRIGOREY, JAMES TAL 024 EASTON D
GRIGOREY, WILLIAM A. TAL 016 EASTON D
GRIGORY, AMANDA TAL 039 EASTON D
GRIGORY, RICHARD BAL 152 2ND DIST
GRILL, CHARLES BAL 129 16TH WAR
GRILL, FRANCIS BAL 355 1ST DIST
GRILLE, ADAM * BAL 273 20TH WAR
GRIM, ABRAHAM WAS 086 2ND SUBD
GRIM, ALEXANDER WAS 087 2ND SUBD
GRIM, ALEXANDER WAS 078 2ND SUBD
GRIM, BENJAMIN WAS 088 2ND SUBD
GRIM, CATHARINE WAS 089 2ND SUBD
GRIM, CATHARINE BAL 011 15TH WAR
GRIM, DANIEL WAS 089 2ND SUBD
GRIM, DANIEL WAS 045 2ND SUBD
GRIM, DANIEL B. WAS 082 2ND SUBD
GRIM, DAVID WAS 074 2ND SUBD
GRIM, DAVID WAS 089 2ND SUBD
GRIM, EDWARD D. BAL 011 18TH WAR
GRIM, ELIZA FRE 419 8TH E DI
GRIM, EMANUEL BAL 191 5TH DIST
GRIM, FREDERICK A. WAS 060 2ND SUBD
GRIM, GEORGE ALL 008 3RD E.D.
GRIM, HENRY WAS 089 2ND SUBD
GRIM, JACOB WAS 088 2ND SUBD
GRIM, JACOB BAL 197 5TH DIST
GRIM, JOHN BAL 066 15TH WAR
GRIM, JOHN WAS 201 1ST DIST
GRIM, JOHN J. WAS 082 2ND SUBD
GRIM, JOSEPH WAS 079 2ND SUBD
GRIM, JOSEPH * WAS 048 2ND SUBD
GRIM, LEWIS BAL 236 2ND WARD
GRIM, LOUISA BAL 043 2ND DIST
GRIM, MALIM WAS 189 1ST DIST
GRIM, MARGARET WAS 022 2ND SUBD
GRIM, NATHANIEL WAS 060 2ND SUBD
GRIM, SINAH-BLACK WOR 343 1ST E DI
GRIM, THOMAS WAS 069 2ND SUBD
GRIM, THOMAS FRE 264 NEW MARK
GRIM, WILLIAM D. BAL 009 18TH WAR
GRIMBETS, HENRY BAL 180 2ND WARD
GRIMCO, GREENBURY BAL 302 1ST DIST
GRIME, MAHLON CAR 370 9TH DIST
GRIMER, HUGH CAR 144 NO TWP L
GRIMES, ADAM ALL 259 CUMBERLA
GRIMES, ALBERT T. FRE 222 BUCKEYST
GRIMES, AMBROSE BAL 035 13TH WAR
GRIMES, AMELIA FRE 286 WOODSBOR
GRIMES, ANN BAL 419 3RD WARD
GRIMES, ANN BAL 025 1ST WARD
GRIMES, ANN PRI 103 SPALDING
GRIMES, BASIL ANN 498 HOWARD D
GRIMES, CATHARINE BAL 436 14TH WAR
GRIMES, CHARELS E. BAL 385 13TH WAR
GRIMES, CHARLES BAL 074 18TH WAR
GRIMES, CHARLES ANN 486 HOWARD D
GRIMES, CHARLES BAL 183 11TH WAR
GRIMES, CHARLES PRI 100 SPALDING
GRIMES, CHARLES QUE 223 4TH E DI
GRIMES, CHARLES E. BAL 385 13TH WAR
GRIMES, CORNELIUS CAR 367 9TH DIST
GRIMES, DANIEL BAL 163 6TH WARD
GRIMES, DELILA BAL 079 2ND DIST
GRIMES, DENIS CAR 193 4TH DIST
GRIMES, E. PRI 087 SPALDING
GRIMES, EDWARD BAL 403 14TH WAR
GRIMES, EDWARD M. ANN 469 HOWARD D
GRIMES, ELIAS CAR 308 1ST DIST
GRIMES, ELIJAH ANN 466 HOWARD D
GRIMES, ELIZA CAR 324 1ST DIST
GRIMES, ELIZABETH BAL 175 2ND WARD
GRIMES, ELIZABETH BAL 266 1ST DIST
GRIMES, ELIZABETH QUE 225 4TH E DI
GRIMES, ELLEN BAL 229 19TH WAR
GRIMES, EPHRAIM FRE 294 WOODSBOR
GRIMES, FRANCIS FRE 058 FREDERIC
GRIMES, GASSAWAY S. CAR 367 9TH DIST
GRIMES, GEORGE MGM 438 CLARKSTR
GRIMES, GEORGE ANN 346 3RD DIST
GRIMES, GEORGE ANN 502 HOWARD D
GRIMES, GERIAS A. ANN 465 HOWARD D
GRIMES, GRAFTON BAL 220 1ST DIST
GRIMES, GREENBURY ANN 502 HOWARD D
GRIMES, HESTER BAL 035 18TH WAR
GRIMES, HUGH BAL 371 8TH WARD
GRIMES, J. BAL 167 1ST WARD
GRIMES, J. BAL 148 1ST WARD
GRIMES, JAMILE CAR 363 9TH DIST
GRIMES, JAMES BAL 366 1ST DIST
GRIMES, JAMES WAS 048 2ND SUBD
GRIMES, JANE R. CAR 211 5TH DIST
GRIMES, JOHN CAR 231 5TH DIST
GRIMES, JOHN MGM 410 MEDLEY 3
GRIMES, JOHN MGM 383 ROCKERLE
GRIMES, JOHN PRI 079 MARLBROU
GRIMES, JOHN PRI 121 PISCATAW
GRIMES, JOHN PRI 058 NOTTINGH
GRIMES, JOHN BAL 171 1ST WARD
GRIMES, JOHN BAL 301 7TH WARD
GRIMES, JOHN BAL 282 2ND WARD
GRIMES, JOHN BAL 271 1ST DIST
GRIMES, JOHN T. BAL 345 13TH WAR
GRIMES, JOSHUA CAR 371 9TH DIST
GRIMES, JOSHUA BAL 319 3RD WARD
GRIMES, JULIA CAR 317 1ST DIST
GRIMES, LARKIN ANN 498 HOWARD D
GRIMES, LEVI FRE 280 WOODSBOR
GRIMES, LOTT FRE 173 5TH E DI
GRIMES, LYDOY BAL 229 2ND WARD
GRIMES, M.E. PRI 057 NOTTINGH
GRIMES, MARANDA BAL 277 1ST DIST
GRIMES, MARIA CAR 325 1ST DIST
GRIMES, MARTIN CAR 324 1ST DIST
GRIMES, MARY FRE 130 CREAGERS
GRIMES, MARY FRE 290 WOODSBOR
GRIMES, MARY PRI 003 BLADENSB
GRIMES, MATILDA MGM 349 BERRYS D
GRIMES, NANCY MGM 421 MEDLEY 3
GRIMES, NANCY PRI 054 AQUASCO
GRIMES, NANCY QUE 225 4TH E DI
GRIMES, NOAH B. ANN 486 HOWARD D
GRIMES, OBADIAH WAS 163 2ND DIST
GRIMES, OLIVER CAR 324 1ST DIST
GRIMES, PHEBE BAL 436 14TH WAR
GRIMES, REBECCA WAS 015 2ND SUBD
GRIMES, REBECCA BAL 173 16TH WAR
GRIMES, RICHARD CAR 211 5TH DIST
GRIMES, ROBERT PRI 015 BLADENSB
GRIMES, SAMUEL ANN 492 HOWARD D
GRIMES, SAMUEL BAL 175 2ND WARD
GRIMES, SAMUEL ANN 306 1ST DIST
GRIMES, STEPHEN BAL 152 2ND DIST
GRIMES, SUSANAH BAL 153 2ND DIST
GRIMES, THOMAS ALL 058 10TH E.D
GRIMES, THOMAS PRI 088 SPALDING
GRIMES, THOMAS PRI 067 NOTTINGH
GRIMES, THOMAS CEC 021 ELKTON 3
GRIMES, VINCENT BAL 143 16TH WAR
GRIMES, VIRGINIA BAL 216 6TH WARD
GRIMES, WARNER T. FRE 111 CREAGERS
GRIMES, WARREN FRE 422 8TH E DI
GRIMES, WARRING PRI 067 NOTTINGH
GRIMES, WELSON L. FRE 282 WOODSBOR
GRIMES, WILLAM F. PRI 091 MARLBROU
GRIMES, WILLIAM WAS 118 2ND DIST
GRIMES, WILLIAM QUE 124 1ST E DI
GRIMES, WILLIAM CAR 211 5TH DIST
GRIMES, WILLIAM ANN 312 1ST DIST
GRIMES, WILLIAM BAL 375 1ST DIST
GRIMES, WILLIAM C. FRE 290 WOODSBOR
GRIMES, WILLIAM H. FRE 290 WOODSBOR
GRIMES, WILLIAM H. FRE 125 CREAGERS
GRIMET, JOSEPH BAL 171 19TH WAR
GRIMEWALD, SOLOMON BAL 080 1ST WARD
GRIMM, ELLEN ALL 062 10TH E.D
GRIMM, FREDERICK BAL 152 16TH WAR
GRIMM, JOHN BAL 090 10TH WAR
GRIMM, JOHN WAS 055 2ND SUBD
GRIMM, JOSEPH WAS 055 2ND SUBD
GRIMS, SARAH BAL 302 7TH WARD
GRINADGE, ELIZA KEN 288 3RD DIST
GRINADGE, WALT BAL 227 17TH WAR
GRINAGE, CHRISTOPHER * ANN 354 3RD DIST
GRINAGE, FRANCES A. HAR 173 3RD DIST
GRINAGE, JESSE ANN 356 3RD DIST
GRINAGE, MARTHA BAL 061 10TH WAR
GRINAGE, MARY BAL 133 5TH WARD
GRINAGE, MATILDA BAL 228 17TH WAR
GRINAGE, SOLOMON CAR 107 NO TWP L
GRINBEINAT, VALENTINE BAL 312 12TH WAR
GRINDAGE, JOHN CEC 042 CHESAPEA
GRINDALL, ANN BAL 086 18TH WAR
GRINDALL, JOHN T. BAL 017 15TH WAR
GRINDALL, JOSEPH J. BAL 086 18TH WAR
GRINDALL, WILLIAM BAL 110 18TH WAR
GRINDELL, JOHN H. BAL 064 18TH WAR
GRINDER, JACOB FRE 301 WOODSBOR
GRINDER, MAGDALINE FRE 112 CREAGERS
GRINDER, MARY BAL 034 15TH WAR
GRINDER, MICHAEL FRE 286 WOODSBOR
GRINDGE, JAMES KEN 258 1ST DIST
GRINDLE, BETSY CHA 286 BOJANTOW
GRINDY, FANY W. BAL 204 11TH WAR
GRINEDGE, FREDERIC W. BAL 175 6TH WARD
GRINEL, ELIZA BAL 461 1ST DIST
GRINEL, JOHN A. * BAL 281 7TH WARD
GRINES, BELINDA FRE 303 WOODSBOR
GRINGER, E. L. BAL 322 12TH WAR
GRINGER, JOHN BAL 163 2ND DIST
GRINNAGE, ELY BAL 128 16TH WAR
GRINNAGE, SARAH BAL 106 15TH WAR
GRINNAGE, WILLIAM BAL 183 16TH WAR
GRINNEL, G.W. BAL 127 5TH WARD
GRINNEL, HORACE BAL 458 9TH WARD
GRINNELL, CHARLES A. BAL 321 12TH WAR
GRINNELL, HENRY BAL 160 1ST WARD
GRINNELL, JAMES M. ST 309 1ST E DI
GRINNELL, LUCY FRE 055 FREDERIC
GRINNING, JOSEPH BAL 290 2ND WARD
GRINNUN, JOHN* DOR 457 1ST DIST
GRINTHAL, LES BAL 227 19TH WAR
GRINWALL, JOSEPH WAS 068 2ND SUBD
GRINWELL, THOMAS * ANN 397 8TH DIST
GRIPE, HENRY BAL 069 4TH WARD
GRIPP, CHARLOTTE BAL 154 11TH WAR
GRIPPEL, JOHN CEC 025 ELKTON 3
GRISCORN, BALA BAL 331 13TH WAR
GRISCUM, CHOCKLEY BAL 455 1ST DIST
GRISCUM, POWELL BAL 449 1ST DIST
GRISE, JOHN WAS 040 2ND SUBD
GRISE, MARY BAL 012 2ND DIST
GRISE, ROBERT BAL 291 1ST DIST
GRISELMAN, GEORGE CAR 391 2ND DIST
GRISEMAN, ADAM * BAL 166 2ND DIST
GRISER, CHARLES BAL 460 14TH WAR
GRISKEN, RACHEL CEC 200 7TH E DI
GRISLER, CHRISTIAN CEC 154 PORT DUP
GRISLINE, JOHN BAL 047 1ST WARD
GRISMAN, CHRISTIAN BAL 012 9TH WARD
GRISS, RICHARD C. BAL 275 20TH WAR
GRISSLER, PHILLIP FRE 119 CREAGERS
GRISSUM, MARY M. TAL 093 ST MICHA
GRISSWALD, CHESTER BAL 315 1ST DIST
GRIST, HENRY BAL 105 2ND DIST
GRISUM, JOHN TAL 093 ST MICHA
GRISWALD, H. BAL 332 1ST DIST
GRISWELL, THOMAS * ANN 397 8TH DIST
GRISWOLD, CHARLES BAL 059 2ND DIST
GRISWOLD, EDWARD BAL 025 9TH WARD
GRISWOLD, MARION QUE 203 3RD E DI
GRISWOLD, MARY BAL 063 2ND DIST
GRISWOLD, SIMOND* TAL 041 EASTON D
GRITS, THOMAS * ALL 155 6TH E.D.
GRIVE, FRANCIS BAL 297 12TH WAR
GRIVEL, BENJAMIN BAL 444 1ST DIST
GRIVEN, PERT BAL 218 12TH WAR
GROBEL, MARGARET BAL 255 20TH WAR
GROBIL, GEORGE BAL 255 20TH WAR
GROCE, AARON-BLACK CAR 089 NO TWP L
GROCE, ALPHECY ALL 151 6TH E.D.
GROCE, BOON CAR 066 NO TWP L
GROCE, CASPAR BAL 239 20TH WAR
GROCE, DANIEL-BLACK CAR 084 NO TWP L
GROCE, DANIEL-BLACK CAR 096 NO TWP L
GROCE, ELIZABETH-BLACK ST 347 5TH E DI
GROCE, ELLEN-BLACK CAR 106 NO TWP L
GROCE, JAMES E.-BLACK CAR 070 NO TWP L
GROCE, JAMES-BLACK CAR 070 NO TWP L
GROCE, JAMES-BLACK CAR 107 NO TWP L
GROCE, JOHN CAR 066 NO TWP L
GROCE, JOHN L.-BLACK CAR 075 NO TWP L
GROCE, JOHN-BLACK CAR 105 NO TWP L
GROCE, JOHN-BLACK CAR 150 NO TWP L
GROCE, MARTHA ST 343 5TH E DI
GROCE, NOAH-BLACK CAR 096 NO TWP L
GROCE, NOAH-BLACK CAR 105 NO TWP L
GROCE, SARAH-BLACK CAR 096 NO TWP L
GROCE, STERIN-BLACK CAR 086 NO TWP L
GROCE, SUSAN ALL 093 5TH E.D.
GROCE, THOMAS-BLACK CAR 077 NO TWP L
GROCE, WILIAM-BLACK CAR 105 NO TWP L
GROCE, WILLIAM-BLACK CAR 109 NO TWP L
GROCTEY, CATHARINE BAL 160 6TH WARD
GRODEN, HENRY BAL 142 2ND DIST
GRODER, HENRY BAL 260 1ST DIST
GRODENCKER, AUGUST BAL 077 10TH WAR
GRODER, MICHAEL ALL 035 2ND E.D.
GROF, JOHN BAL 239 1ST DIST
GROFENICOL, DANIEL FRE 371 CATOCTIN
GROFENICOL, JOHN FRE 370 CATOCTIN
GROFENICOL, PETER * FRE 371 CATOCTIN
GROFF, A.E. BAL 227 1ST DIST
GROFF, ABRAHAM BAL 221 1ST DIST
GROFF, ADAM CAL 031 2ND DIST
GROFF, BENJAMIN FRE 181 5TH E DI
GROFF, CHARLES BAL 226 1ST DIST
GROFF, DORINS CAR 320 1ST DIST
GROFF, ELI FRE 181 5TH E DI
GROFF, ELIZABETH CAR 320 1ST DIST
GROFF, FRANCIS B. BAL 227 1ST DIST
GROFF, REBECCA FRE 115 CREAGERS
GROFF, ROBERT J. MGM 407 MEDLEY 3
GROFF, SARAH M. FRE 176 5TH E DI
GROFLIN, GEORGE W. BAL 430 14TH WAR
GROFT, CHRISTIAN BAL 164 6TH WARD
GROFT, GEORGE BAL 257 1ST DIST
GROFTEN, WILLIAM BAL 405 14TH WAR
GROGAN, ANN R. BAL 153 11TH WAR
GROGAN, BRIDGETT BAL 151 2ND DIST
GROGAN, ELIZABETH BAL 187 6TH WARD
GROGAN, MARY BAL 203 6TH WARD
GROGANS, PETER BAL 139 2ND DIST
GROGDEN, SOLOMON ANN 364 4TH DIST
GROGG, DAVID CAR 275 7TH DIST
GROGHAN, ANNA BAL 188 6TH WARD
GROGHEGAN, CATHARINE * BAL 052 15TH WAR
GROH, CHARLES BAL 085 10TH WAR
GROHAN, MARTHA BAL 266 12TH WAR
GROHE, GEORGE BAL 211 19TH WAR
GROHGER, BRIDGET BAL 091 1ST WARD
GROINN, ELLEN WAS 219 1ST DIST
GROKGANS, GEORGE BAL 370 3RD WARD

Name	County	Page	District
GROKNICOL, PETER *	FRE	371	CATOCTIN
GROMARN, CASPER	BAL	411	14TH WAR
GRONEBERG, E.	BAL	038	4TH WARD
GRONNINGER, AUGUST	BAL	059	15TH WAR
GROOD, JAMES	FRE	122	CREAGERS
GROOLD, JOSEPH	CEC	032	CHESAPEA
GROOM, DARIUS	BAL	176	6TH WARD
GROOM, EDWARD	BAL	057	15TH WAR
GROOM, FREDERICK E.	BAL	349	7TH WARD
GROOM, HENRIETTA	BAL	175	6TH WARD
GROOM, HENRY	KEN	289	3RD DIST
GROOM, JOHN	KEN	280	3RD DIST
GROOM, MARY	BAL	376	3RD WARD
GROOM, PETER	HAR	195	3RD DIST
GROOM, S.	TAL	066	EASTON T
GROOM, WILLIAM	BAL	223	6TH WARD
GROOM, WILLIAM H.	TAL	066	EASTON T
GROOME, CAROLINE	KEN	213	2ND DIST
GROOME, ELIZABETH	KEN	214	2ND DIST
GROOME, ELIZABETH M.	TAL	067	EASTON T
GROOME, HENSON	MGM	316	CRACKLIN
GROOME, JOHN G.	CEC	010	ELKTON 3
GROOME, PERRY	KEN	272	1ST DIST
GROOME, SARAH	KEN	214	2ND DIST
GROOMES, WILLIAM	MGM	327	CRACKLIN
GROOMFIELD, MARY	BAL	008	4TH WARD
GROOMIS, WILLIAM J.	BAL	164	1ST WARD
GROOMS, DAVID	WAS	064	2ND SUBD
GROOMS, DAVID	WAS	046	2ND SUBD
GROOMS, JAMES	WAS	071	2ND SUBD
GROOMS, JOHN	WAS	063	2ND SUBD
GROOMS, MARY A.	BAL	397	8TH WARD
GROOMS, NELSON	BAL	302	7TH WARD
GROOMS, NELSON	BAL	416	8TH WARD
GROOMS, PERRY	BAL	141	5TH WARD
GROOMS, RACHELL	BAL	141	5TH WARD
GROOMS, REBECCA	BAL	061	10TH WAR
GROOMS, ROSETTA	BAL	062	10TH WAR
GROOMS, THOMAS	BAL	329	7TH WARD
GROOMS, W. HENRY	BAL	109	10TH WAR
GROOMS, WILLIAM	BAL	397	8TH WARD
GROOMS, WILLIAM	SOM	480	TRAPP DI
GROOP, GEORGE	SOM	361	BRINKLEY
GROOSE, HARRIET	ALL	229	CUMBERLA
GROOSE, ISABELLE	ALL	256	CUMBERLA
GROOSE, JOHN	TAL	104	ST MICHA
GROOSE, RACHEL	ALL	215	CUMBERLA
GROOSSE, A.	BAL	152	1ST WARD
GROOVE, CATHARINE	ALL	040	2ND E.D.
GROOVE, DENNIS*	TAL	006	EASTON D
GROOVER, GEORGE	ALL	225	CUMBERLA
GROOVES, CHARLES	BAL	063	2ND DIST
GROOVES, WILLIAM G.	BAL	116	1ST WARD
GROPE, JOHN	BAL	253	1ST DIST
GROPES, SAVY	CHA	267	MIDDLETO
GRORE, DANUEL D. *	WAS	107	2ND DIST
GROSBY, LEWIS	BAL	275	7TH WARD
GROSBY, SARAH T.	BAL	127	18TH WAR
GROSCUP, ANN J.	BAL	249	6TH WARD
GROSCUP, FREDERIC	BAL	249	6TH WARD
GROSCUP, JOHN	BAL	267	17TH WAR
GROSCUP, MARGARET G.	BAL	258	17TH WAR
GROSE, DANIEL	WAS	022	2ND SUBD
GROSE, DAVID	WAS	022	2ND SUBD
GROSE, HENRY	WAS	022	2ND SUBD
GROSE, MARY	BAL	197	5TH DIST
GROSE, PATH	TAL	077	EASTON T
GROSE, REBECA	TAL	012	EASTON D
GROSE, SALLY	BAL	438	14TH WAR
GROSE, THAELOT	TAL	098	ST MICHA
GROSE, THOMAS	TAL	016	EASTON D
GROSE, THOMAS	TAL	019	EASTON D
GROSE, THOMAS*	TAL	015	EASTON D
GROSE, WESTLEY	FRE	300	WOODSBOR
GROSECUP, JOHN	ALL	210	CUMBERLA
GROSENICOL, JACOB	FRE	366	CATOCTIN
GROSH, ANDREW	WAS	115	2ND DIST
GROSH, ELIZABETH	BAL	420	3RD WARD
GROSH, FREDERICK	WAS	172	FUNKSTOW
GROSH, GEORGE	WAS	162	2ND DIST
GROSH, GOTLEIB	WAS	171	FUNKSTOW
GROSH, JEROME	WAS	292	1ST DIST
GROSH, JOHN	WAS	115	2ND DIST
GROSH, SARAH	WAS	117	2ND DIST
GROSH, SARAH	WAS	101	2ND DIST
GROSHAR, JOSEPH	BAL	115	1ST WARD
GROSNUCK, JOHN	BAL	010	1ST WARD
GROSS, A.	BAL	072	10TH WAR
GROSS, ABRAHAM	BAL	028	15TH WAR
GROSS, ABRAHAM	BAL	038	15TH WAR
GROSS, ADAM	BAL	191	2ND WARD
GROSS, AMOS	ALL	161	6TH E.D.
GROSS, ANN	BAL	028	15TH WAR
GROSS, ANN	WAS	191	1ST DIST
GROSS, AUGUSTA	BAL	265	7TH WARD
GROSS, BENJAMIN	BAL	071	15TH WAR
GROSS, BENJAMIN	BAL	196	17TH WAR
GROSS, BENJAMIN	CAL	033	2ND DIST
GROSS, BENJAMIN	BAL	207	11TH WAR
GROSS, BENJAMIN-MULATTO	BAL	223	2ND WARD
GROSS, BERRY	BAL	229	12TH WAR
GROSS, BETSY	CAL	032	2ND DIST
GROSS, CAROLINE	BAL	121	16TH WAR
GROSS, CATHARINE	BAL	368	13TH WAR
GROSS, CATHARINE	HAR	068	1ST DIST
GROSS, CHARGO	WAS	188	1ST DIST
GROSS, CHARLES	QUE	207	3RD E DI
GROSS, CHARLES	FRE	338	MIDDLETO
GROSS, CHARLES P.	BAL	416	14TH WAR
GROSS, CHARLOTTE	BAL	049	9TH WARD
GROSS, CHARLOTTE	BAL	219	6TH WARD
GROSS, DANIEL	CAR	275	7TH DIST
GROSS, DAVID	BAL	125	16TH WAR
GROSS, DIANAH	BAL	101	15TH WAR
GROSS, DRUSELIA	ALL	161	6TH E.D.
GROSS, EDWARD	CAL	034	2ND DIST
GROSS, ELIA	CAL	023	2ND DIST
GROSS, ELIZA	CAL	027	2ND DIST
GROSS, ELIZABETH	CAL	018	1ST DIST
GROSS, ELIZABETH	CEC	098	4TH E DI
GROSS, ELIZABETH	FRE	407	JEFFERSO
GROSS, ELIZABETH	BAL	103	15TH WAR
GROSS, ELIZABETH	WAS	191	1ST DIST
GROSS, ELIZABETH	WAS	090	2ND SUBD
GROSS, ELIZABETH	WAS	077	2ND SUBD
GROSS, ELLIN	HAR	062	1ST DIST
GROSS, ELNORA	BAL	199	11TH WAR
GROSS, ELSEY	BAL	262	20TH WAR
GROSS, EMMA	CAL	002	1ST DIST
GROSS, FRANCIS H.	CAR	352	6TH DIST
GROSS, FRISBY	CAL	055	3RD DIST
GROSS, G.H.	BAL	164	1ST WARD
GROSS, GEORGE	BAL	170	16TH WAR
GROSS, GEORGE	BAL	447	1ST DIST
GROSS, GEORGE	HAR	017	1ST DIST
GROSS, GEORGE	CAR	178	8TH DIST
GROSS, GEORGE	CAR	175	8TH DIST
GROSS, GRACE	CAL	034	2ND DIST
GROSS, GRACE	BAL	138	16TH WAR
GROSS, HENOLY	CHA	238	HILLTOP
GROSS, HENRY	BAL	111	10TH WAR
GROSS, HENRY	BAL	217	17TH WAR
GROSS, HENRY	BAL	276	17TH WAR
GROSS, HENRY	FRE	332	MIDDLETO
GROSS, HENRY	BAL	311	12TH WAR
GROSS, HENRY	BAL	386	1ST DIST
GROSS, HENRY	BAL	136	2ND DIST
GROSS, HENRY	BAL	087	2ND DIST
GROSS, HENRY-BLACK	FRE	016	FREDERIC
GROSS, HESTER	BAL	115	15TH WAR
GROSS, HESTER	QUE	207	3RD E DI
GROSS, ISAAC	CAL	027	2ND DIST
GROSS, ISABELLA	BAL	461	14TH WAR
GROSS, JACOB	HAR	068	1ST DIST
GROSS, JACOB	WAS	077	2ND SUBD
GROSS, JACOB	WAS	174	FUNKSTOW
GROSS, JACOB	BAL	123	5TH WARD
GROSS, JAMES	BAL	458	8TH WARD
GROSS, JAMES	WAS	104	2ND DIST
GROSS, JAMES	CAL	046	3RD DIST
GROSS, JAMES-MULATTO	ST	342	5TH E DI
GROSS, JANE	CAL	032	2ND DIST
GROSS, JANE	CHA	281	BOJANTOW
GROSS, JANE	BAL	020	15TH WAR
GROSS, JANE	BAL	251	1ST DIST
GROSS, JEREMIAH	BAL	053	15TH WAR
GROSS, JEREMIAH	BAL	084	15TH WAR
GROSS, JOHN	BAL	089	15TH WAR
GROSS, JOHN	BAL	287	1ST DIST
GROSS, JOHN	BAL	008	EASTERN
GROSS, JOHN	CAL	034	2ND DIST
GROSS, JOHN	CAL	041	3RD DIST
GROSS, JOHN	CAL	020	2ND DIST
GROSS, JOHN	CAL	004	1ST DIST
GROSS, JOHN	BAL	021	18TH WAR
GROSS, JOHN	BAL	295	17TH WAR
GROSS, JOHN	TAL	088	ST MICHA
GROSS, JOHN J.	BAL	211	5TH WARD
GROSS, JOHN P.	CAR	189	4TH DIST
GROSS, JOHN W.	FRE	342	MIDDLETO
GROSS, JOSEPH	CAL	047	3RD DIST
GROSS, JOSEPH H.	BAL	195	17TH WAR
GROSS, JOSEPH J.	ANN	469	HOWARD D
GROSS, JOSHUA	CEC	100	3RD E DI
GROSS, JOSIAH	FRE	330	MIDDLETO
GROSS, JOSIAH	BAL	190	17TH WAR
GROSS, KITTY	BAL	078	4TH WARD
GROSS, LAUNA *	BAL	373	13TH WAR
GROSS, LAURA	BAL	094	5TH WARD
GROSS, LAWSON	WAS	053	2ND SUBD
GROSS, LEVI	BAL	129	11TH WAR
GROSS, LEWIS	BAL	280	7TH WARD
GROSS, LUCRETIA	BAL	167	16TH WAR
GROSS, MAHALA	CAL	062	3RD DIST
GROSS, MAJOR	BAL	094	15TH WAR
GROSS, MANZELLA	FRE	331	MIDDLETO
GROSS, MARGARET	CAL	028	2ND DIST
GROSS, MARGARET	CAL	032	2ND DIST
GROSS, MARIA	CAL	061	3RD DIST
GROSS, MARIA	BAL	363	13TH WAR
GROSS, MARIA	BAL	097	15TH WAR
GROSS, MARTHA-BLACK	FRE	036	FREDERIC
GROSS, MARY	BAL	342	13TH WAR
GROSS, MARY	CAL	063	3RD DIST
GROSS, MARY	CAL	035	2ND DIST
GROSS, MARY	BAL	126	11TH WAR
GROSS, MARY	BAL	089	15TH WAR
GROSS, MARY	BAL	167	11TH WAR
GROSS, MARY-BLACK	FRE	046	FREDERIC
GROSS, MICHAEL	WAS	263	1ST DIST
GROSS, MILLY	CAL	055	3RD DIST
GROSS, MILLY	BAL	168	19TH WAR
GROSS, NANCY	CAL	043	3RD DIST
GROSS, NANCY	BAL	137	11TH WAR
GROSS, PETER	BAL	098	2ND DIST
GROSS, PETER	BAL	236	1ST DIST
GROSS, PRINCE	BAL	195	17TH WAR
GROSS, PRISCELLA	CAL	026	2ND DIST
GROSS, PRISCILLA	CAL	027	2ND DIST
GROSS, RACHAEL	BAL	079	15TH WAR
GROSS, RACHEL	BAL	375	1ST DIST
GROSS, REBECCA	CHA	283	BOJANTOW
GROSS, ROBERT	BAL	125	16TH WAR
GROSS, ROBERT	BAL	238	6TH WARD
GROSS, SALMON	BAL	067	4TH WARD
GROSS, SAMSON	BAL	366	13TH WAR
GROSS, SAMUEL	BAL	082	15TH WAR
GROSS, SAMUEL	ANN	304	1ST DIST
GROSS, SAMUEL	WAS	098	2ND CIST
GROSS, SAMUEL	WAS	030	2ND SUBD
GROSS, SARAH	BAL	053	15TH WAR
GROSS, SOPHIA	CAL	008	1ST DIST
GROSS, SUSAN	BAL	127	11TH WAR
GROSS, SUSAN	BAL	190	11TH WAR
GROSS, THOAMS	BAL	375	1ST DIST
GROSS, THOMAS	BAL	460	8TH WARD
GROSS, THOMAS	CAL	061	3RD DIST
GROSS, THOMAS	WAS	105	2ND DIST
GROSS, URIAS	WAS	196	1ST DIST
GROSS, WASHINGTON	BAL	253	17TH WAR
GROSS, WILLIAM	BAL	207	17TH WAR
GROSS, WILLIAM	CAL	036	2ND DIST
GROSS, WILLIAM	CAL	009	1ST DIST
GROSS, WILLIAM	CAL	021	2ND DIST
GROSS, WILLIAM	BAL	139	11TH WAR
GROSS, WILLIAM	BAL	130	18TH WAR
GROSS, WILLIAM	BAL	127	16TH WAR
GROSS, WILLIAM E.	BAL	113	15TH WAR
GROSS, WILLIAM H.	BAL	084	15TH WAR
GROSS, WILLIAM H.	BAL	378	13TH WAR
GROSS, WILLIAM J.	BAL	352	13TH WAR
GROSS, WILLIAM S.	BAL	101	5TH WARD
GROSSENICOL, PETER	FRE	370	CATOCTIN
GROSSGROVE, ANN J.	BAL	017	18TH WAR
GROSSHANTZ, JOHN	CAR	250	3RD DIST
GROSSMEOL, GEORGE	FRE	343	MIDDLETO
GROSSMEOL, JOHN	FRE	348	MIDDLETO
GROSSMEOL, JONATHAN	FRE	366	CATOCTIN
GROSSMIDT, JOHN A. *	FRE	341	MIDDLETO
GROSSNICKEL, JACOB	WAS	216	1ST DIST
GROSSNICOL, JOHN	FRE	370	CATOCTIN
GROSTA, F.	BAL	066	10TH WAR
GROSUCK, GEORGE W.	CAR	203	4TH DIST
GROSUCK, JOHN	BAL	151	2ND DIST
GROT, CHARLES	FRE	005	FREDERIC
GROT, JOHN	BAL	460	1ST DIST
GROTA, MATILDA	BAL	276	17TH WAR
GROTH, B.F.	WAS	004	WILLIAMS
GROTH, HENRY	WAS	005	WILLIAMS
GROTHAN, CHRISTIAN	BAL	007	9TH WARD
GROTHE, CHRISTIAN	BAL	256	6TH WARD
GROTJOHN, AGNES	BAL	444	14TH WAR
GROTS, JOHN	BAL	453	8TH WARD
GROUDEN, JOHN	ALL	249	CUMBERLA
GROUF, HENRY	ALL	259	CUMBERLA
GROUND, JOSEPH	WAS	253	1ST DIST
GROUND, MARY	WAS	038	2ND SUBD
GROUNDEHAMER, MYER	BAL	387	8TH WARD
GROUNGER, JOSEPH	BAL	458	14TH WAR
GROUNGER, MARGARET	BAL	458	14TH WAR
GROUPY, AMANDA V.	HAR	081	2ND DIST
GROUS, BETTY	BAL	417	14TH WAR
GROUS, JAMES	BAL	417	14TH WAR
GROUSE, ADAM	BAL	302	3RD WARD
GROUSE, GEORGE	BAL	034	1ST WARD
GROUSE, PETER	BAL	084	1ST WARD
GROUSE, SOPHIA	BAL	034	1ST WARD
GROUSEM, GODFREY	BAL	181	2ND WARD
GROUSH, JOHN	BAL	200	2ND WARD
GROUSO, WILLIAM H.	FRE	060	FREDERIC
GROUTHAMP, GOTLIEB	BAL	207	2ND WARD
GROVE, ABRAHAM	WAS	137	2ND DIST
GROVE, ABRAHAM	WAS	154	2ND DIST
GROVE, ANNA	BAL	103	5TH WARD
GROVE, ANNA	BAL	406	1ST DIST
GROVE, AUGUSTUS G.	WOR	202	4TH E DI
GROVE, BARBARA	WAS	107	2ND DIST
GROVE, BENBEN	FRE	207	BUCKEYST
GROVE, CATHARINE	CAR	257	3RD DIST
GROVE, CATHARINE F.	WAS	235	1ST DIST
GROVE, CHARLES	WAS	054	2ND SUBD
GROVE, CONRAD	CAR	342	6TH DIST
GROVE, DANIEL	FRE	392	PETERSVI
GROVE, DANIEL	WAS	269	1ST DIST
GROVE, DANIEL L.	WAS	054	2ND SUBD
GROVE, DANUEL D. *	WAS	107	2ND DIST
GROVE, ELIAS	WAS	055	2ND SUBD
GROVE, ELIAS	FRE	087	FREDERIC
GROVE, ELIAS *	WAS	055	2ND SUBD
GROVE, ELIZABETH	WAS	056	2ND SUBD
GROVE, GEORGE	WAS	125	HAGERSTO
GROVE, GEORGE	CAR	341	6TH DIST
GROVE, GEORGE	FRE	324	MIDDLETO
GROVE, GEORGE W.	WAS	028	2ND SUBD
GROVE, HENRY	FRE	207	BUCKEYST
GROVE, HEZEKIAH	CAR	184	8TH DIST
GROVE, ISAAC	WAS	135	2ND DIST
GROVE, JACOB	WAS	109	2ND DIST
GROVE, JACOB	CAR	283	7TH DIST
GROVE, JACOB	FRE	407	JEFFERSO
GROVE, JACOB H.	WAS	036	2ND SUBD
GROVE, JAEMS	HAR	039	1ST DIST
GROVE, JAMES	FRE	120	CREAGERS
GROVE, JAMES	WAS	222	1ST DIST
GROVE, JOHN	WAS	275	RIDGEVIL
GROVE, JOHN	FRE	102	FREDERIC
GROVE, JOHN	FRE	268	NEW MARK
GROVE, JOSEPH	WAS	263	1ST DIST
GROVE, JOSEPH *	WAS	053	2ND SUBD
GROVE, L. JEWETT	WAS	142	2ND DIST
GROVE, LAURA	WAS	043	2ND SUBD
GROVE, LEOANRD S.	FRE	409	JEFFERSO
GROVE, MARTHA J.	BAL	449	14TH WAR
GROVE, MARTIN	FRE	331	MIDDLETO
GROVE, MARTIN	BAL	451	8TH WARD
GROVE, MARY	BAL	233	6TH WARD
GROVE, MARY	BAL	222	1ST DIST
GROVE, MARY	FRE	098	FREDERIC
GROVE, MARY A.	FRE	063	FREDERIC
GROVE, MARY R.	FRE	407	JEFFERSO
GROVE, MILLIE	FRE	057	FREDERIC
GROVE, PETER	FRE	390	PETERSVI
GROVE, PETER	FRE	378	PETERSVI
GROVE, PETER	CAR	226	5TH DIST
GROVE, PHILIP	FRE	385	PETERSVI
GROVE, SAMUEL	FRE	323	MIDDLETO
GROVE, SAMUEL	WAS	237	CAVETOWN
GROVE, SARAH	WAS	092	2ND SUBD
GROVE, SIMON	WAS	227	1ST DIST
GROVE, STEPHEN	WAS	056	2ND SUBD
GROVE, SUSAN	WAS	128	HAGERSTO
GROVE, SUSAN	FRE	207	BUCKEYST
GROVE, WILLIAM	FRE	324	MIDDLETO
GROVE, WILLIAM	WAS	043	2ND SUBD
GROVEMAN, A.	BAL	333	1ST DIST
GROVEN, ELIZABETH	BAL	089	2ND DIST
GROVEN, ELLEN	BAL	090	2ND DIST
GROVEN, WILLIAM	BAL	117	2ND DIST
GROVER, BENJAMIN A.	BAL	356	3RD WARD
GROVER, CHARLES	BAL	459	1ST DIST
GROVER, DAVID	BAL	086	2ND DIST
GROVER, DELILA	BAL	192	5TH DIST
GROVER, DENNIS*	TAL	006	EASTON D
GROVER, GEORGE	FRE	159	EMMITTSB
GROVER, GRAFTON	BAL	095	2ND DIST
CROVER, GRAFTON	BAL	127	1ST WARD
GROVER, JAMES	BAL	091	2ND DIST
GROVER, JAMES	WAS	240	CAVETOWN
GROVER, JOHN A.	CAL	005	1ST DIST
GROVER, MARY	BAL	333	7TH WARD
GROVER, MATTHIAS	ALL	225	CUMBERLA
GROVER, THOASM R.	CAL	017	1ST DIST
GROVER, THOMAS	ANN	419	HOWARD D
GROVER, THOMAS	BAL	455	8TH WARD
GROVERMAN, HENRIETTA	BAL	318	1ST DIST
GROVERMAN, HENRY	BAL	318	1ST DIST
GROVES, ALBERT	CEC	056	1ST E DI
GROVES, ANN	HAR	149	3RD DIST
GROVES, DANIEL-BLACK	QUE	145	1ST E DI
GROVES, DENNIS	ALL	121	4TH E.D.
GROVES, DENNIS	ALL	123	4TH E.D.
GROVES, EMELINE	CHA	247	HILLTOP
GROVES, G.	BAL	138	1ST WARD
GROVES, GEORGE	FRE	249	NEW MARK
GROVES, GEORGE W.	BAL	018	15TH WAR
GROVES, HENRY E.	CHA	247	HILLTOP
GROVES, HENRY-BLACK	QUE	174	2ND E DI
GROVES, JAMES	CHA	228	ALLENS F
GROVES, JESSE	ALL	120	5TH E.D.
GROVES, JOHN	BAL	192	5TH DIST

GROVES, JOHN	CHA	247	HILLTOP
GROVES, JOSEPH	CEC	180	7TH E DI
GROVES, JOSEPH	ALL	243	CUMBERLA
GROVES, JOSIAH	ANN	460	HOWARD D
GROVES, KITTY A.	ANN	510	HOWARD D
GROVES, MARY	ALL	123	4TH E.D.
GROVES, REBECCA-BLACK	QUE	146	1ST E DI
GROVES, THOMAS	CHA	243	HILLTOP
GROVES, WILLIAM G.	BAL	142	1ST WARD
GROVES, WILLIAM H.	BAL	250	17TH WAR
GROVEY, MISS	BAL	158	19TH WAR
GROVING, PHILIP	BAL	147	11TH WAR
GROW, BARBARA	BAL	429	8TH WARD
GROW, ELIAS *	WAS	055	2ND SUBD
GROW, JOHN C.	WAS	036	2ND SUBD
GROW, JOSEPH	WAS	053	2ND SUBD
GROW, LAVINA	WAS	039	2ND SUBD
GROW, WILLIAM	WAS	029	2ND SUBD
GROWDEN, J.	BAL	282	2ND WARD
GROWER, JACOB	BAL	171	6TH WARD
GROWER, JOHN L.	KEN	217	2ND DIST
GROWEY, NATHANIEL	BAL	234	20TH WAR
GROWNE, SARAH *	KEN	241	2ND DIST
GROXWELL, STEPHEN	ST	278	3RD E DI
GROYRAN, JOHN R. *	BAL	319	20TH WAR
GRUB, SAMUEL	FRE	385	PETERSVI
GRUBB, GEORGE M.	BAL	163	19TH WAR
GRUBB, GEORGE W.	BAL	400	14TH WAR
GRUBB, JOHN	BAL	274	20TH WAR
GRUBB, JOHN	BAL	069	18TH WAR
GRUBB, MARGARET	BAL	405	14TH WAR
GRUBB, MARY ANN	BAL	139	19TH WAR
GRUBB, MARY M.	BAL	.63	19TH WAR
GRUBB, RICHARD	BAL	355	8TH WARD
GRUBB, THOMAS	CEC	173	4TH E DI
GRUBB, THOMAS B.	BAL	064	15TH WAR
GRUBB, WASHINGTON A.	BAL	139	19TH WAR
GRUBB, WILLIAM	BAL	355	8TH WARD
GRUBB, WILLIAM A.A.	BAL	102	5TH WARD
GRUBBY, GEORGE	BAL	300	17TH WAR
GRUBEL, ANTHONY	BAL	036	15TH WAR
GRUBER, ANN B.	WAS	132	HAGERSTO
GRUBER, CHARLES	WAS	045	2ND SUBD
GRUBER, DAVID	WAS	215	1ST DIST
GRUBER, ELIZABETH	WAS	117	2ND DIST
GRUBER, FELIX	BAL	223	19TH WAR
GRUBER, GEORGE	WAS	131	HAGERSTO
GRUBER, ISAAC	WAS	004	WILLIAMS
GRUBER, J.	BAL	245	12TH WAR
GRUBER, JACOB	WAS	109	2ND DIST
GRUBER, JACOB	WAS	152	HAGERSTO
GRUBER, JOHN	WAS	164	HAGERSTO
GRUBER, JOHN	WAS	121	HAGERSTO
GRUBER, JOHN	BAL	236	1ST DIST
GRUBER, JOHN D.	WAS	106	2ND DIST
GRUBER, ROBERT	BAL	458	8TH WARD
GRUBER, SAMUEL	WAS	105	2ND DIST
GRUBER, SARAH	WAS	045	2ND SUBD
GRUBY, CATHARINE	BAL	235	12TH WAR
GRUBY, MARY *	BAL	278	20TH WAR
GRUDE, JAMES M.	ALL	132	4TH E.D.
GRUDER, ELIZA	FRE	126	CREAGERS
GRUITT, LITTLETON R.	WOR	215	4TH E DI
GRUL, CONRAD	ANN	389	4TH DIST
GRULL, CATHARINE	BAL	210	6TH DIST
GRUM, DANIEL	WAS	160	HAGERSTO
GRUM, MAJOR-BLACK	WOR	345	1ST E DI
GRUMBE, JES.*	BAL	322	12TH WAR
GRUMBINE, WILLIAM	CAR	269	WESTMINS
GRUMBINE, WILLIAM S.	CAR	281	7TH DIST
GRUMBLE, DEBORAH	ST	285	2ND E DI
GRUMBLE, DEBORAH	ST	284	2ND E DI
GRUMBS, G. A. *	BAL	321	12TH WAR
GRUMLINE, JOHN	FRE	314	MIDDLETO
GRUMMEY, JOHN	BAL	280	2ND WARD
GRUMMOELL, E.	BAL	320	12TH WAR
GRUN, JOSEPH *	WAS	048	2ND SUBD
GRUN, WASHINGTON	CAR	240	TANEYTOW
GRUNBY, JACOB	CAL	027	2ND DIST
GRUNDY, AUGUSTA	BAL	167	11TH WAR
GRUNDY, BILLOSS	BAL	355	13TH WAR
GRUNEBAUMER, ISAAC	BAL	066	4TH WARD
GRUNECER, ANTONIA	BAL	364	13TH WAR
GRUNLY, CAROLINE	HAR	178	3RD DIST
GRUNNARD, JINNY	BAL	173	16TH WAR
GRUNNER, GABRIEL	ALL	113	5TH E.D.
GRURAND, FRANCIS	BAL	121	11TH WAR
GRURTEN, OTHO	BAL	109	2ND DIST
GRUS, CAROLINE	BAL	229	12TH WAR
GRUSCOP, HENRY	BAL	083	2ND DIST
GRUSE, HENRY-BLACK	WOR	338	1ST E DI
GRUSE, JANE-BLACK	WOR	337	1ST E DI
GRUSE, PEGGA-BLACK	WOR	338	1ST E DI
GRUSHON, ABRAHAM	FRE	064	FREDERIC
GRUSHON, CATHERINE	FRE	140	CREAGERS
GRUSHON, GEORGE *	FRE	127	CREAGERS
GRUSHON, WILLIAM	FRE	113	CREAGERS
GRUSHON,ELIAS A.	FRE	002	FREDERIC
GRUSHOR, ANNL.	FRE	107	CREAGERS
GRUSHORD, GEORGE	FRE	024	FREDERIC
GRUSHOW, ABRAHAM	FRE	130	CREAGERS
GRUSINGER, ADAM	BAL	378	8TH WARD
GRUSMAN, GEORGE	BAL	132	2ND DIST
GRUSSEY, F. H.	BAL	119	2ND DIST
GRUSSEY, JACOB	BAL	119	2ND DIST
GRUTTER, JACOB	BAL	021	15TH WAR
GRUVER, CHESTON	BAL	251	6TH WARD
GRUVER, JACOB	BAL	263	17TH WAR
GRUVER, OTTO	BAL	091	5TH WARD
GRUVES, JAMES	BAL	323	1ST DIST
GRYA, ANN	BAL	255	12TH WAR
GRYWOLD, ELLEN M.	ALL	159	6TH E.D.
GSPALL, ELBRIDGE	BAL	181	2ND DIST
GUAADE, CHARLES	BAL	171	1ST WARD
GUAN, Z.	CHA	275	ALLENS F
GUANT, TOM	CHA	256	MIDDLETO
GUARD, JEREMIAH	ALL	023	2ND E.D.
GUBBNITZ, MARTIN	BAL	119	1ST WARD
GUCKEN, THOMAS	ALL	139	6TH E.D.
GUCKER, PATRICK	ALL	051	10TH E.D
GUDDIS, ALEXANDER	BAL	164	19TH WAR
GUDE, ELIZABETH	BAL	007	9TH WARD
GUDE, FREDERICK	BAL	007	9TH WARD
GUDE, JUSTUS	BAL	113	15TH WAR
GUDEN, SARAH *	BAL	279	20TH WAR
GUDGEON, HARRIET	KEN	271	1ST DIST
GUDGEON, JESSE	BAL	063	4TH WARD
GUDGEON, RICHARD	KEN	271	1ST DIST
GUDGEON, VIRGINIA	BAL	063	4TH WARD
GUDLEP, GEORGE	BAL	172	19TH WAR

GUDSHELL, MARGARET	BAL	180	19TH WAR
GUE, GEORGE	MGM	344	CLARKSBU
GUE, HENRY	MGM	341	CLARKSBU
GUE, HENRY	MGM	332	CRACKLIN
GUE, HEZEKIAH	MGM	435	CLARKSTR
GUE, JOSEPH	MGM	326	CRACKLIN
GUE, MARGARET	MGM	342	CLARKSBU
GUEEGAN, ANN M.	BAL	393	8TH WARD
GUEELY, RIHCARD *	WAS	164	2ND DIST
GUEN, JOHN	BAL	138	1ST WARD
GUENING, ROBERT	BAL	162	1ST WARD
GUENTICE, JOHN D.	BAL	153	19TH WAR
GUER, ELEANOR	BAL	291	12TH WAR
GUERE, FRED	BAL	037	18TH WAR
GUESS, ANN	FRE	258	NEW MARK
GUESSFORD, NATHANIEL-BLAC	QUE	170	2ND E DI
GUEST, ELLEN	BAL	130	16TH WAR
GUEST, GEORGE	BAL	153	11TH WAR
GUEST, JANE S.	BAL	072	18TH WAR
GUEST, MOSES	BAL	033	1ST WARD
GUEST, RICHARD T.	BAL	405	3RD WARD
GUEST, SAMUEL	BAL	109	15TH WAR
GUEST, SARAH C.	BAL	134	16TH WAR
GUEYER, LOUISA	WAS	294	1ST DIST
GUFFEN, RICHARD	BAL	047	18TH WAR
GUFFIN, ELLEN	BAL	173	19TH WAR
GUFMAN, JOHN	BAL	363	13TH WAR
GUGAR, JOSEPHINE	BAL	442	14TH WAR
GUGTON, ALBERT G.	FRE	211	BUCKEYST
GUICHARD, SOPHIA	BAL	080	4TH WARD
GUILDHALL, TEMPERANCE	BAL	341	1ST DIST
GUILDNER, HANNAH	BAL	369	13TH WAR
GUILFORD, WILLIAM	MGM	349	BERRYS D
GUILFOYLE, AMELIA	BAL	071	10TH WAR
GUILLE, JOSEPH F.	BAL	099	10TH WAR
GUILLER, CRESELIA E.	FRE	299	WOODSBOR
GUIN, HENRY	BAL	053	18TH WAR
GUINER, JOHN	ALL	251	CUMBERLA
GUINN, BENJAMIN	CHA	222	ALLENS F
GUINN, CHARLES	BAL	320	1ST DIST
GUINN, ELLEN	ALL	246	CUMBERLA
GUINN, JACOB	CEC	151	PORT DUP
GUINN, JANE	BAL	085	18TH WAR
GUINN, MARY	BAL	362	3RD WARD
GUINN, MARY	ALL	128	4TH E.D.
GUINN, WILLIAM	BAL	119	18TH WAR
GUINNER, ELISABETH	ALL	252	CUMBERLA
GUINS, JOHN	BAL	257	2ND WARD
GUIR, ARTHUR	BAL	279	2ND WARD
GUIRE, MICHAL	WAS	137	2ND DIST
GUIS, JANE	BAL	223	12TH WAR
GUIS, LEWIS	BAL	309	7TH WARD
GUISBERT, ANDREW	FRE	140	CREAGERS
GUISBERT, CHRISTIAN	FRE	091	FREDERIC
GUISBERT, JONATHAN	FRE	140	CREAGERS
GUISHARD, SARAH	BAL	419	3RD WARD
GUIST, RACHAEL	BAL	100	18TH WAR
GUISTA, STEPHEN	BAL	001	9TH WARD
GUITEAU, SHERIDAN	BAL	255	6TH WARD
GUITON, JAMES	BAL	435	8TH WARD
GUITON, WILLIAM A.	BAL	402	8TH WARD
GUITZ, ANN T.	FRE	027	FREDERIC
GUITZ, CHARLES	FRE	026	FREDERIC
GUIVEE, JOSEPHINE *	BAL	110	18TH WAR
GULIER, HANNAH	BAL	423	14TH WAR
GULINE, MARY	BAL	298	7TH WARD
GULL, HENRY	BAL	009	18TH WAR
GULL, JHN	BAL	210	2ND WARD
GULL, WILLIAM	SOM	532	QUANTICO
GULLET, ANN	CAR	067	NO TWP L
GULLET, ANN E.	CAR	073	NO TWP L
GULLET, MORRIS	WOR	230	6TH E DI
GULLET, WILLIAM	CAR	068	NO TWP L
GULLETT, ALBERT G.	CAR	169	NO TWP L
GULLETT, GEORGE	SOM	504	SALISBUR
GULLETT, LOVEY	SOM	503	SALISBUR
GULLETT, WILLIAM	SOM	554	TYASKIN
GULLEY, SARAH	BAL	046	15TH WAR
GULLIN, FRANCIS M.	BAL	127	5TH WARD
GULLIN, WILLIAM M.	BAL	356	3RD WARD
GULLY, STEPHEN-BLACK	FRE	407	JEFFERSO
GUMAN, GEORGE	BAL	278	17TH WAR
GUMAR, SARAH R.	BAL	109	1ST WARD
GUMBEYE, KATE	BAL	177	19TH WAR
GUMBRILL, THOMAS	BAL	326	12TH WAR
GUMBY, ELISH-BLACK	WOR	346	1ST E DI
GUMBY, ISAAC-BLACK	WOR	346	1ST E DI
GUMBY, JOSHUA	WOR	248	1ST CENS
GUMLEY, WILLIAM	ANN	429	HOWARD D
GUMMART, MARY	BAL	224	19TH WAR
GUMMEL, G.	BAL	215	19TH WAR
GUMMEL, GEORGE	CAR	350	6TH DIST
GUMMEL, MAGADALENA	CAR	350	6TH DIST
GUMMELL, MARY	CAR	276	7TH DIST
GUMP, G.W.	ALL	215	CUMBERLA
GUMP, HENRY	ALL	215	CUMBERLA
GUMPERD, PETER	ALL	001	3RD E.D.
GUMPERT, JOHN	WAS	125	HAGERSTO
GUNALL, PERRY	BAL	166	1ST WARD
GUNBACK, AMELIA	BAL	003	1ST WARD
GUNBLY, JOHN	WOR	193	8TH E DI
GUNBY, ABRAM-BLACK	WOR	347	1ST E DI
GUNBY, BELL	WOR	251	1ST CENS
GUNBY, EDWARD	WOR	256	1ST CENS
GUNBY, ELISHA J.	SOM	389	BRINKLEY
GUNBY, ELIZABETH A.	BAL	413	3RD WARD
GUNBY, HOWARD-BLACK	WOR	348	1ST E DI
GUNBY, ISAAC-BLACK	WOR	348	1ST E DI
GUNBY, JAMES-BLACK	WOR	348	1ST E DI
GUNBY, JIM	WOR	290	9TH E DI
GUNBY, JOHN	WOR	309	2ND E DI
GUNBY, LEAH	SOM	429	PRINCESS
GUNBY, LEWIS-BLACK	WOR	348	1ST E DI
GUNBY, MARIA	BAL	073	1ST WARD
GUNBY, MARY	WOR	258	1ST CENS
GUNBY, MARY	SOM	450	DAMES QU
GUNBY, MILKY	SOM	390	BRINKLEY
GUNBY, ROBERT-BLACK	WOR	172	6TH E DI
GUNBY, SAMUEL J.	SOM	390	BRINKLEY
GUNBY, WILLIAM	SOM	469	TRAPPE D
GUNBY, WILLIAM	BAL	014	15TH WAR
GUNBY, WILLIAM-BLACK	WOR	330	1ST E DI
GUNCE, GEORGE	CEC	059	1ST E DI
GUNDECKER,G.	BAL	262	12TH WAR
GUNDEFEFKLS, ELIZA	BAL	022	1ST WARD
GUNDEL, CATHERINE	BAL	086	10TH WAR
GUNDER, EDMUND	CAR	331	MANCHEST
GUNDER, NANCY	WAS	035	2ND SUBD
GUNDREY, JOHN A.	BAL	251	6TH WARD
GUNDT, EMILY	BAL	276	20TH WAR

GUNDT, SARAH A.	BAL	276	20TH WAR
GUNDY, JAEMS D.	BAL	298	12TH WAR
GUNEBY, WILLIAM	BAL	245	17TH WAR
GUNEL, JOHN A. *	BAL	281	7TH WARD
GUNINON, JOHN	BAL	110	1ST WARD
GUNINS, WILLIAM *	WAS	086	2ND SUBD
GUNLOCK, AUGUSTUS	FRE	018	FREDERIC
GUNLOCK, CONROD	FRE	018	FREDERIC
GUNLY, SARAH	WOR	275	BERLIN I
GUNN, ANN M.	BAL	362	13TH WAR
GUNN, ELIZABETH	BAL	203	2ND WARD
GUNN, GEORGE	BAL	258	12TH WAR
GUNN, HUGH	BAL	007	4TH WARD
GUNN, MRS-	BAL	122	18TH WAR
GUNN, PATRICK	BAL	007	4TH WARD
GUNNELLE, U.	BAL	315	12TH WAR
GUNNETT, MARY	BAL	334	13TH WAR
GUNNING, WILLIAM	CEC	032	CHESAPEA
GUNNY, JAMES	ALL	107	5TH E.D.
GUNSALLUS, DANIEL	BAL	052	15TH WAR
GUNSBURG, D. A. REV.	BAL	070	4TH WARD
GUNTER, CONRAD	BAL	250	2ND WARD
GUNTER, ELIZABETH	BAL	058	10TH WAR
GUNTER, HARMAN *	BAL	103	2ND DIST
GUNTER, HENRY	BAL	250	2ND WARD
GUNTER, JOHN H.	BAL	049	1ST WARD
GUNTER, MARTHA	WAS	040	2ND SUBD
GUNTER, MARY	BAL	435	14TH WAR
GUNTHER, CONRAD	BAL	410	3RD WARD
GUNTHER, HENRY	BAL	126	16TH WAR
GUNTHER, JOSEPH	BAL	119	15TH WAR
GUNTON, WILLAIM A.	PRI	094	SPALDING
GUNTS, ADAM	BAL	153	2ND DIST
GUNTY, JAMES K.	WOR	228	6TH E DI
GUNWELL, LEVI	BAL	081	1ST WARD
GUNWELL, THOMAS	BAL	081	1ST WARD
GUNY, WILLIAM *	WAS	062	2ND SUBD
GUPERT, JULIANA	BAL	418	14TH WAR
GUPTON, SAMUEL	BAL	089	2ND DIST
GURDON, ELIZA	CHA	246	HILLTOP
GURDON, FELIX-BLACK	ST	335	4TH E DI
GURLEY, ELIZABETH	WAS	291	1ST DIST
GURLEY, FRANCIS A.*	BAL	396	3RD WARD
GURLEY, JAMES	WAS	290	1ST DIST
GURLEY, MARY	WAS	290	1ST DIST
GURLEY, WILLIAM K.	BAL	061	4TH WARD
GURMILL, MARY	BAL	013	9TH WARD
GURNAYS, EDW.	BAL	314	20TH WAR
GURNER, JOHN	BAL	090	1ST WARD
GURNES, CATHARINE	BAL	245	20TH WAR
GURNETT, MARY	BAL	182	19TH WAR
GURNEY, GRIDLEY	BAL	293	3RD WARD
GURNEY, JAMES	BAL	063	1ST WARD
GURRAH, DINAH	CAL	036	2ND DIST
GURRUR, EDWARD	BAL	189	5TH DIST
GURRY, HARRIET	KEN	210	2ND DIST
GURTY, ANN A.	TAL	004	EASTON D
GURTY, DAVID*	TAL	004	EASTON D
GURVER, LAVINIA	BAL	231	19TH WAR
GURVER, MARGADOCK	BAL	189	5TH DIST
GURWELLING, STEPHEN	WOR	326	1ST E DI
GURY, WILLIAM *	WAS	062	2ND SUBD
GUSECUP, GEORGE	ALL	198	CUMBERLA
GUSHARD, PHOEBE	BAL	265	7TH WARD
GUSHASD, LOUISA*	BAL	313	3RD WARD
GUSLEY, GEORGE	ANN	483	HOWARD D
GUSRING, POWLES*	BAL	315	3RD WARD
GUST, CATHARINE	BAL	321	7TH WARD
GUST, JOHN	BAL	457	14TH WAR
GUST, JOSEPH	BAL	086	1ST WARD
GUST, SEBASTIAN	BAL	086	1ST WARD
GUSTAVUS, WILLIAM	BAL	130	1ST WARD
GUSTE, LEWIS	BAL	369	13TH WAR
GUSTING, GEORGE	BAL	221	19TH WAR
GUSTMAN, MICHAEL	BAL	003	4TH WARD
GUSTUS, ABRAM	BAL	353	3RD WARD
GUSTUS, MARGARET	BAL	329	13TH WAR
GUSTWELLEN, ELIZA	WOR	325	1ST E DI
GUSTY, DANIEL	TAL	070	EASTON T
GUSTY, DAVID*	TAL	004	EASTON D
GUSTY, ESAU*	TAL	004	EASTON D
GUSTY, ESAW*	TAL	005	EASTON D
GUSTY, ESAW*	TAL	009	EASTON D
GUTCHAN,ADOLPH	BAL	247	2ND WARD
GUTCHELL,L.	BAL	115	1ST WARD
GUTHERY, OHN	WOR	292	9TH E DI
GUTHNER, JOSEPH	BAL	133	1ST WARD
GUTHORY, JOHN	WOR	313	2ND E DI
GUTHRA, THOMAS	BAL	042	15TH WAR
GUTHREY,HARRISON	ALL	028	2ND E.D.
GUTHRIE, ADAM	FRE	159	5TH E DI
GUTHRIE, ALEXANDER	BAL	058	2ND DIST
GUTHRO, JOSEPH	BAL	111	1ST WARD
GUTHROW, JULIA	BAL	224	5TH WARD
GUTHRY, WILLIAM	CEC	023	ELKTON 3
GUTHWOSSER, CHARLES	BAL	297	3RD WARD
GUTING, JOHN	ST	257	3RD E DI
GUTING, MARIA	ST	251	3RD E DI
GUTMAN, CAROLINE	BAL	117	15TH WAR
GUTRIDGE, LEVI	PRI	006	BLADENSB
GUTRY, MARGARET A.	WOR	165	6TH E DI
GUTRY, WILLIAM W.	WOR	165	6TH E DI
GUTS, CATHERINE	BAL	066	4TH WARD
GUTWALT, MICHAEL	BAL	201	2ND WARD
GUULY, RICHARD *	WAS	164	2ND DIST
GUVERICK, JOHN	BAL	401	1ST DIST
GUVISCHA, CHARLES	BAL	202	2ND WARD
GUWEE, JOSEPHINE *	BAL	110	18TH WAR
GUY, ADAM	HAR	076	BEL AIR
GUY, AMOS	BAL	040	9TH WARD
GUY, ANN	CHA	272	ALLENS F
GUY, ANN MARIA	BAL	152	5TH WARD
GUY, CHARLES	BAL	294	7TH WARD
GUY, ELEANOR	CHA	282	BOJANTOW
GUY, ELIZABETH	BAL	211	11TH WAR
GUY, ELIZABETH	ANN	302	1ST DIST
GUY, ELLEN	BAL	125	11TH WAR
GUY, EMELINE	ST	274	3RD E DI
GUY, FRANCIS	BAL	452	14TH WAR
GUY, FRANCIS E.	ST	271	3RD E DI
GUY, GEORGE	BAL	167	19TH WAR
GUY, GEORGE J.	ST	271	3RD E DI
GUY, HENRIETTA	BAL	054	9TH WARD
GUY, INATIUS	ST	274	3RD E DI
GUY, ISAAC	BAL	177	11TH WAR
GUY, JAMES	BAL	105	5TH WARD
GUY, JAMES H.	BAL	456	8TH WARD
GUY, JOHN	BAL	365	8TH WARD
GUY, JOHN	ST	271	3RD E DI
GUY, JOHN C.	ST	275	3RD E DI

Name	County	Page	District
GUY, JOHN F.	CHA	258	MIDDLETO
GUY, JOHN W.	CHA	258	MIDDLETO
GUY, JOSEPH	ST	271	3RD E DI
GUY, MARY	HAR	110	2ND DIST
GUY, MATTHEW	CHA	280	BOJANTOW
GUY, NICHOLAS-BLACK	FRE	051	FREDERIC
GUY, RACHAEL A.	ST	335	4TH E DI
GUY, RACHEL	BAL	396	14TH WAR
GUY, RICHARD	ST	266	3RD E DI
GUY, RUTH	BAL	196	17TH WAR
GUY, SAMUEL	HAR	018	1ST DIST
GUY, STEPHEN	BAL	098	2ND DIST
GUY, THOMAS P.	ST	271	3RD E DI
GUY, WILLIAM	BAL	050	9TH WARD
GUY, WILLIAM B.	ST	270	3RD E DI
GUYER, JOHN	BAL	022	18TH WAR
GUYER, JOHN W.	FRE	033	FREDERIC
GUYLE, CHARLES	BAL	334	1ST DIST
GUYN, EMILY	BAL	071	2ND DIST
GUYNARD, JANE	BAL	463	1ST DIST
GUYNN, BERNARD	FRE	20	5TH E DI
GUYON, MARTHA	QUE	244	5TH E DI
GUYSE, CONRAD	ALL	038	2ND E.D.
GUYSOER, HARMON	ALL	148	6TH E.D.
GUYTHER, ELIZA A.	ST	296	2ND E DI
GUYTHER, GEORGE	ST	296	2ND E DI
GUYTHER, HENRY	BAL	059	4TH WARD
GUYTHER, JOHN	BAL	161	6TH WARD
GUYTHER, MARY A.	BAL	059	4TH WARD
GUYTON, BEAL L.	BAL	429	14TH WAR
GUYTON, BENJAMIN A.	HAR	048	1ST DIST
GUYTON, EDWARD	BAL	095	2ND DIST
GUYTON, EDWARD M.	HAR	070	1ST DIST
GUYTON, ELIZABETH	BAL	335	7TH WARD
GUYTON, HENRY	BAL	095	2ND DIST
GUYTON, HENRY	HAR	104	2ND DIST
GUYTON, JAMES	HAR	087	2ND DIST
GUYTON, JAMES	HAR	042	1ST DIST
GUYTON, JESSE *	HAR	006	1ST DIST
GUYTON, JOHN	HAR	042	1ST DIST
GUYTON, JOHN	BAL	113	5TH WARD
GUYTON, JOHN H.	BAL	281	1ST DIST
GUYTON, JOSEPH	HAR	042	1ST DIST
GUYTON, JOSHUA	BAL	455	14TH WAR
GUYTON, JOSIAH	HAR	072	1ST DIST
GUYTON, ORVILLE	BAL	429	14TH WAR
GUYTON, ROBERT	HAR	065	2ND DIST
GUYTON, ROSETTA	BAL	116	2ND DIST
GUYTON, SARAH A.	BAL	359	13TH WAR
GUYTON, UNDERWOOD	BAL	128	2ND DIST
GUYTON, WILLIAM	BAL	099	5TH WARD
GUYTON, WILLIAM	BAL	358	13TH WAR
GUYTON, WILLIAM	HAR	046	1ST DIST
GUYTON, WILLIAM	FRE	325	MIDDLETO
GUYTON, WILLIAM A.	HAR	068	1ST DIST
GUYTON,MARGARET	BAL	039	2ND DIST
GUYTZ, LENA	BAL	015	4TH WARD
GUZLOW, ELLEN	BAL	249	2ND WARD
GWEEDIE, JOHN	BAL	244	12TH WAR
GWEENY, PATRICK	BAL	198	11TH WAR
GWIN, MARIA	BAL	044	15TH WAR
GWIN, WILLIAM H.	PRI	116	PISCATAW
GWINN, BENNET F.	PRI	104	PISCATAW
GWINN, ELIZA	BAL	104	10TH WAR
GWINN, JOHN	CEC	150	PORT DUP
GWINN, JOSHUA	BAL	200	6TH WARD
GWINN, MARTHA	BAL	162	6TH WARD
GWINN, MARY E.	WAS	157	HAGERSTO
GWINN, MARY F.	BAL	227	6TH WARD
GWINN, PATRICK	WAS	183	BOONSBOR
GWINN, THOMAS	WAS	004	WILLIAMS
GWINN, THOMAS B.	PRI	116	PISCATAW
GWINN, WILLIAM R.	CEC	151	PORT DUP
GWINN,MARY	WAS	156	HAGERSTO
GWYIN, PETER *	BAL	145	1ST WARD
GWYN, CAROLINE*	BAL	402	3RD WARD
GWYN, CHARLES R.	BAL	070	15TH WAR
GWYNN, JOHN	ANN	284	ANNAPOLI
GWYNN, JOHN H.	PRI	105	PISCATAW
GWYNN, JOHN P.	BAL	007	9TH WARD
GWYNN, MARY	BAL	007	9TH WARD
GWYNN, MISS V.	FRE	199	5TH E DI
GWYNN, ROBERT	BAL	045	15TH WAR
GWYNN, WILLIAM	BAL	078	10TH WAR
GWYUN, WILLIAM	BAL	076	10TH WAR
GYE, GEORGE	SOM	454	DAMES QU
HAAS, ENOCH	BAL	160	6TH WARD
HAAS, H.	BAL	309	12TH WAR
HAAS, JACOB	CAR	268	WESTMINS
HAAS, MARY A.	CAR	405	2ND DIST
HAAS, SOLOMON	BAL	060	15TH WAR
HABBENOT, JAMES	BAL	060	2ND DIST
HABBERSETT, WILLIAM	BAL	188	6TH WARD
HABBERSITT, JOHN	BAL	052	9TH WARD
HABECKER, SUSAN	WAS	285	1ST DIST
HABEL, LEWIS	BAL	068	4TH WARD
HABER, FRANCIS	BAL	105	5TH WARD
HABERSELL, HENRY	BAL	398	8TH WARD
HABERSETT, JACOB	BAL	323	1ST DIST
HABERSETT, JOHN	BAL	322	1ST DIST
HABERSETT, WILLIAM	BAL	074	18TH WAR
HABICHT, LEONARD	BAL	032	15TH WAR
HABLANT, SAMY *	BAL	031	18TH WAR
HABLE, HARMAN	BAL	307	7TH WARD
HABLE, ROSA	BAL	308	7TH WARD
HABLE, SARAH	BAL	283	7TH WARD
HABSON, RICHARD	BAL	246	20TH WAR
HABURN, ARKLIS	BAL	121	11TH WAR
HABURN, BETSY	ANN	372	4TH DIST
HABY, JOHN	BAL	455	1ST DIST
HABY, MARGARET	BAL	455	1ST DIST
HACE, JACOB	BAL	116	1ST WARD
HACET, ANDREW	CEC	062	1ST E DI
HACHET, MOSES	HAR	049	1ST DIST
HACHTER, DAVID	FRE	105	CREAGERS
HACHTER, GEORGE	FRE	105	CREAGERS
HACHTER, HENRY	FRE	098	FREDERIC
HACHTER, JACOB	FRE	105	CREAGERS
HACHTER, JOSHUA	FRE	097	FREDERIC
HACHTER, MARY	FRE	098	FREDERIC
HACHTER, PHEBE A.	FRE	106	CREAGERS
HACHTER, SAMUEL *	FRE	097	FREDERIC
HACK, AUGUSTA	BAL	459	1ST DIST
HACK, BERNARD	BAL	429	8TH WARD
HACK, CASPAR	BAL	459	1ST DIST
HACK, ELIZABETH	HAR	096	2ND DIST
HACK, F. W.	BAL	169	11TH WAR
HACK, FANNY	BAL	387	13TH WAR
HACK, GEORGE	BAL	393	14TH WAR
HACK, GEORGE	BAL	018	4TH WARD
HACK, GEORGE W.	BAL	421	14TH WAR
HACK, JACOB	ANN	463	HOWARD D
HACK, JAMES A.	BAL	291	12TH WAR
HACK, JOHN	BAL	235	2ND WARD
HACK, JOHN B.	BAL	307	7TH WARD
HACK, JOHN W.	BAL	039	18TH WAR
HACK, MARY	BAL	284	20TH WAR
HACK, PETER	BAL	351	7TH WARD
HACK, SIDNEY	BAL	020	4TH WARD
HACK, THOAMS P.	BAL	048	15TH WAR
HACK, WILLIAM	BAL	464	14TH WAR
HACK,ACHEL	ALL	261	CUMBERLA
HACKART, JACOB	BAL	278	1ST DIST
HACKE, JOHN	BAL	232	2ND WARD
HACKEN, BRIDGET	BAL	366	8TH WARD
HACKER, A.	BAL	238	20TH WAR
HACKER, HANNAH	BAL	388	3RD WARD
HACKER, JAMES	SOM	475	TRAPPE D
HACKER, JOHN A.	BAL	455	14TH WAR
HACKER, JOHN C.	BAL	086	10TH WAR
HACKER, PERRY	SOM	475	TRAPPE D
HACKET, ANN F.	KEN	218	2ND DIST
HACKET, CLENTER *	KEN	216	2ND DIST
HACKET, ELIZABETH	BAL	460	14TH WAR
HACKET, FRANK	DOR	424	1ST DIST
HACKET, GEORGE	ST	327	4TH E DI
HACKET, HARRIET A.	MGM	332	CRACKLIN
HACKET, JACOB	CEC	043	CHESAPEA
HACKET, JAMES	DOR	458	1ST DIST
HACKET, JANE	HAR	009	1ST DIST
HACKET, LOYD	ANN	371	4TH DIST
HACKET, MARY	BAL	117	15TH WAR
HACKET, MARY	BAL	361	1ST DIST
HACKET, PATRICK	BAL	034	15TH WAR
HACKET, PERRY	DOR	306	1ST DIST
HACKET, RICHARD	ALL	201	CUMBERLA
HACKET, ROBERT	DOR	424	1ST DIST
HACKET, ROGER	DOR	363	3RD DIVI
HACKET, SUSAN	DOR	440	1ST DIST
HACKET, THOMAS	BAL	278	1ST DIST
HACKET, WINAFORD	BAL	278	1ST DIST
HACKETT, ABRAHAM	CEC	106	3RD E DI
HACKETT, ADAM-BLACK	CAR	087	NO TWP L
HACKETT, AGNESS	BAL	305	7TH WARD
HACKETT, ANN	QUE	209	3RD E DI
HACKETT, ANNA	CEC	005	ELKTON 3
HACKETT, BENJAMIN	BAL	189	17TH WAR
HACKETT, BENJAMIN JR.	BAL	189	17TH WAR
HACKETT, CAROLINE-BLACK	QUE	188	3RD E DI
HACKETT, CASSY-BLACK	QUE	186	3RD E DI
HACKETT, CATHARINE	BAL	250	6TH WARD
HACKETT, CHARLES	ANN	497	HOWARD D
HACKETT, CHARLES	BAL	223	6TH WARD
HACKETT, CHARLES	MGM	332	CRACKLIN
HACKETT, CHARLES R.	KEN	305	3RD DIST
HACKETT, CHARLOTTE-BLACK	QUE	134	1ST E DI
HACKETT, CLARICA	BAL	450	8TH WARD
HACKETT, DAFINEY-BLACK	FRE	223	BUCKEYST
HACKETT, DANIEL	BAL	290	7TH WARD
HACKETT, DARBY	BAL	152	5TH WARD
HACKETT, DEBORAH-BLACK	QUE	149	1ST E DI
HACKETT, ED.	BAL	036	18TH WAR
HACKETT, EDWARD	CAR	115	NO TWP L
HACKETT, EMORY-BLACK	QUE	148	1ST E DI
HACKETT, FREDERICK	BAL	095	2ND DIST
HACKETT, GEORGE A.	BAL	198	6TH WARD
HACKETT, GEORGE-BLACK	QUE	141	1ST E DI
HACKETT, GEORGE-BLACK	QUE	140	1ST E DI
HACKETT, HENRY	QUE	211	3RD E DI
HACKETT, HENRY	QUE	218	3RD E DI
HACKETT, J.	BAL	172	1ST WARD
HACKETT, JAMES	KEN	291	3RD DIST
HACKETT, JAMES	MGM	322	CRACKLIN
HACKETT, JAMES	CEC	057	1ST E DI
HACKETT, JAMES	CEC	014	ELKTON 3
HACKETT, JOHN	DOR	310	1ST DIST
HACKETT, JOHN	BAL	421	8TH WARD
HACKETT, JOSEPHUS	BAL	149	16TH WAR
HACKETT, LIDDY*	BAL	305	3RD WARD
HACKETT, LOUISA	BAL	154	11TH WAR
HACKETT, LUCINDA	BAL	033	18TH WAR
HACKETT, MARIA	BAL	203	17TH WAR
HACKETT, MARY	KEN	305	3RD DIST
HACKETT, MATILDA	KEN	283	3RD DIST
HACKETT, MAY-MULATTO	QUE	153	1ST E DI
HACKETT, MICHAEL	ANN	517	HOWARD D
HACKETT, MOSES	BAL	095	2ND DIST
HACKETT, NANCY	DOR	298	1ST DIST
HACKETT, NANCY	QUE	217	3RD E DI
HACKETT, NANCY	QUE	211	3RD E DI
HACKETT, PERRY	KEN	282	3RD DIST
HACKETT, PHILIP-BLACK	CAR	087	NO TWP L
HACKETT, ROBNERT	BAL	129	2ND DIST
HACKETT, SAMUEL	BAL	166	6TH WARD
HACKETT, SAMUEL	KEN	300	3RD DIST
HACKETT, SARAH	ANN	517	HOWARD D
HACKETT, SARAH	QUE	131	1ST E DI
HACKETT, SOPHIA	KEN	283	3RD DIST
HACKETT, SUSAN	CAR	071	NO TWP L
HACKETT, THOMAS	CAR	092	NO TWP L
HACKETT, THOMAS	DOR	323	1ST DIST
HACKETT, THOMAS	BAL	425	8TH WARD
HACKETT, THOMAS H.	QUE	208	3RD E DI
HACKETT, TILGHMAN	DOR	298	1ST DIST
HACKETT, TILLY-BLACK	QUE	126	1ST E DI
HACKETT, WALTER	MGM	327	CRACKLIN
HACKETT, WESLEY	MGM	321	CRACKLIN
HACKETT, WILLIAM	DOR	298	1ST DIST
HACKETT, WILLIAM	DOR	299	1ST DIST
HACKETT, WILLIAM	ANN	495	HOWARD D
HACKETT, WILLIAM	BAL	323	7TH WARD
HACKETT, WILLIAM	BAL	155	2ND DIST
HACKETT, WILLIAM-BLACK	CAR	079	NO TWP L
HACKEY, PHILLIP	BAL	253	17TH WAR
HACKING, CHARLOTT	BAL	125	11TH WAR
HACKLEY, ANTHONY	BAL	239	17TH WAR
HACKNEY, ANGELINA	MGM	336	CRACKLIN
HACKNEY, JOHN	MGM	338	CRACKLIN
HACKNEY, MARY E.	BAL	223	6TH WARD
HACKNEY, THOMAS	BAL	279	2ND WARD
HACKNEY, WILLIAM	BAL	223	6TH WARD
HACKTEE, ANNE	BAL	265	12TH WAR
HACKTEE, LEONARD	BAL	264	12TH WAR
HACKTEL, GEORGE	BAL	433	14TH WAR
HACKTER, ANN R.	FRE	098	FREDERIC
HACKTER, ARIUS	FRE	099	FREDERIC
HACKTER, CATHERINE	FRE	099	FREDERIC
HACKTER, SOPHIA	FRE	099	FREDERIC
HACOMER, HENRY	BAL	226	17TH WAR
HADAWAY, ALBERT	BAL	326	3RD WARD
HADAWAY, JAMES H.	BAL	014	15TH WAR
HADAWAY, JOHN	KEN	254	1ST DIST
HADAWAY, MARY	BAL	413	3RD WARD
HADAWAY, ROBERT	KEN	230	2ND DIST
HADAWAY, SARAH	BAL	321	3RD WARD
HADAWAY, WILLIAM	BAL	163	16TH WAR
HADDAWAY, CAROLINE	TAL	102	ST MICHA
HADDAWAY, CHARLES W.	TAL	042	EASTON D
HADDAWAY, CLEMENTUR	TAL	111	ST MICHA
HADDAWAY, DANIEL S.	TAL	111	ST MICHA
HADDAWAY, EDWARD	KEN	263	1ST DIST
HADDAWAY, EDWARD	KEN	257	1ST DIST
HADDAWAY, GEORGE W.	TAL	002	EASTON D
HADDAWAY, HOPKINS	TAL	016	EASTON D
HADDAWAY, HUGH	TAL	114	ST MICHA
HADDAWAY, JAMES	KEN	266	1ST DIST
HADDAWAY, JAMES	QUE	187	3RD E DI
HADDAWAY, JOHN	TAL	108	ST MICHA
HADDAWAY, JOHN H.	BAL	085	1ST WARD
HADDAWAY, JOHN P.	TAL	113	ST MICHA
HADDAWAY, JOHN Q.	TAL	087	ST MICHA
HADDAWAY, LOUISA	TAL	109	ST MICHA
HADDAWAY, MARY E.	TAL	102	ST MICHA
HADDAWAY, RICHARD	TAL	115	ST MICHA
HADDAWAY, ROBERT	QUE	207	3RD E DI
HADDAWAY, ROBERT	KEN	251	1ST DIST
HADDAWAY, RUFUS K.	TAL	110	ST MICHA
HADDAWAY, SALLY	TAL	116	ST MICHA
HADDAWAY, THEADORE F.	TAL	109	ST MICHA
HADDAWAY, THOMAS S.	TAL	045	EASTON T
HADDAWAY, THOMAS W.	TAL	115	ST MICHA
HADDAWAY, W. B.	TAL	111	ST MICHA
HADDAWAY, WILLIAM	TAL	115	ST MICHA
HADDAWAY, WILLIAM	TAL	108	ST MICHA
HADDEN, FRANCIS A.	SOM	521	BARREN C
HADDEN, JOHN	BAL	418	3RD WARD
HADDEN, NANCY	WOR	315	2ND E DI
HADDER, CALEB	QUE	218	3RD E DI
HADDER, MARTHA	BAL	097	5TH WARD
HADDER, MARY	BAL	102	10TH WAR
HADDER, SALLY	QUE	220	3RD E DI
HADDER, SALLY	QUE	201	3RD E DI
HADDER, STEPHEN	WOR	265	BERLIN 1
HADDER, WILLIAM	WOR	248	1ST CENS
HADDINOT, GEORGE	BAL	063	2ND DIST
HADDLE, WILLIAM	FRE	134	CREAGERS
HADDOCK, HENRY	BAL	246	17TH WAR
HADDOCK, THOMAS	BAL	027	9TH WARD
HADDOLK, JAMES	WOR	170	6TH E DI
HADDYWAY, JAMES*	DOR	386	1ST DIST
HADEE, J.N.C.	BAL	297	12TH WAR
HADEL, WILLIAM	BAL	130	11TH WAR
HADEN, ALONZO	CHA	226	ALLENS F
HADEN, BETTY	CHA	245	HILLTOP
HADEN, CATHARINE	WAS	149	HAGERSTO
HADEN, CATHARINE	WAS	152	HAGERSTO
HADEN, CATHERINE	BAL	320	20TH WAR
HADEN, FRANCIS	CHA	274	ALLENS F
HADEN, HENRY V.	CHA	273	ALLENS F
HADEN, JAMES	CHA	226	ALLENS F
HADEN, JAMES S.	CHA	225	ALLENS F
HADEN, JOHN	CHA	288	BOJANTOW
HADEN, JOHN	CEC	084	CHARLEST
HADEN, LYDIA	WAS	217	1ST DIST
HADEN, SUSAN	QUE	203	3RD E DI
HADEN, THOMAS D.	CHA	223	ALLENS F
HADEN, WILLIAM J.	CHA	232	HILLTOP
HADIAN, MARTIN	BAL	045	9TH WARD
HADLEY, DEBORAH	BAL	252	6TH WARD
HADLEY, ELIZA	BAL	169	19TH WAR
HADLEY, JAMES	HAR	057	1ST DIST
HADLEY, JOHN W.	BAL	169	19TH WAR
HADLEY, MARGARET	BAL	129	2ND DIST
HADLEY, VINCENT	QUE	140	1ST E DI
HADLEY, WILLIAM	QUE	130	1ST E DI
HADLIN, JOHN	BAL	147	2ND DIST
HADO, EZRA	FRE	257	NEW MARK
HADOCK, MARY A.	WOR	167	6TH E DI
HADOLK, JAMES H.	WOR	167	6TH E DI
HADSON, GABRIEL	ALL	259	CUMBERLA
HADY, JAMES	BAL	092	18TH WAR
HADY, JOHN D.	BAL	295	12TH WAR
HAEFFER, GEORGE	FRE	070	FREDERIC
HAEZA, PATRICK	ALL	050	10TH E.D
HAFELEIGH, JEREMIAH	FRE	163	EMMITTSB
HAFELY, AMANDA	CAR	405	2ND DIST
HAFELY, DAVID	CAR	405	2ND DIST
HAFELY, ISAAC	CAR	407	2ND DIST
HAFELY, JANE	CAR	411	2ND DIST
HAFELY, JESSE	CAR	315	1ST DIST
HAFELY, JOHN	CAR	409	2ND DIST
HAFELY, JONAS	CAR	298	1ST DIST
HAFELY, LEVI	CAR	405	2ND DIST
HAFELY, PETER	CAR	405	2ND DIST
HAFELY, SIMON	CAR	405	2ND DIST
HAFF, ABRAHAM	FRE	017	FREDERIC
HAFFBAUM, GUSTAVUS	BAL	355	13TH WAR
HAFFLER, HEZEKIAH	FRE	259	NEW MARK
HAFFNER, SAMUEL P.	FRE	204	BUCKEYST
HAFNER, DAVID	FRE	293	WOODSBOR
HAFNER, MARGARET	FRE	290	WOODSBOR
HAFNER, WILLIAM	FRE	283	WOODSBOR
HAFS, MARGARET	BAL	399	14TH WAR
HAFT, CONRAD	ALL	260	CUMBERLA
HAGAN, ANN	BAL	371	3RD WARD
HAGAN, ANN	BAL	470	14TH WAR
HAGAN, BRIDGET	ALL	135	4TH E.D.
HAGAN, CAHRLES	BAL	206	11TH WAR
HAGAN, DANIEL	BAL	387	3RD WARD
HAGAN, EDWARD	BAL	357	8TH WARD
HAGAN, H. D.	ALL	071	5TH E.D.
HAGAN, HESTER	CEC	196	6TH E DI
HAGAN, JACOB	BAL	460	1ST DIST
HAGAN, JAMES	BAL	168	2ND DIST
HAGAN, JAMES	BAL	020	15TH WAR
HAGAN, JERAMIAH	CEC	043	CHESAPEA
HAGAN, JOHN	FRE	389	PETERSVI
HAGAN, JOHN H.	BAL	158	16TH WAR
HAGAN, MARK	BAL	246	2ND WARD
HAGAN, MARY	BAL	204	11TH WAR
HAGAN, MARY	WAS	133	2ND DIST
HAGAN, MARY A. O.	BAL	145	11TH WAR
HAGAN, MICHAEL	FRE	075	FREDERIC
HAGAN, PATRICK	BAL	163	11TH WAR
HAGAN, PETER	BAL	280	7TH WARD
HAGAN, PETER	BAL	133	5TH WARD
HAGAN, RICHARD	CEC	104	4TH E DI
HAGAN, RICHARD	BAL	021	18TH WAR
HAGAN, STEREN	FRE	075	FREDERIC
HAGAN, THOMAS	ALL	071	5TH E.D.

Name	County	Page	District
HAGAN, THOMAS	ALL	221	CUMBERLA
HAGAN, THOMAS	BAL	094	2ND DIST
HAGAN, WILLIAM	BAL	213	19TH WAR
HAGAN,MATILDA	FRE	008	FREDERIC
HAGANE, MICHALE	ALL	050	10TH E.D
HAGANER, SOPHIA	BAL	209	6TH WARD
HAGANS, JOHN	[illegible]	[illegible]	ST DIST
HAGAR, JOHN	[illegible]	[illegible]	ETO
HAGAR, JOHN	[illegible]	[illegible]	RLA
HAGAR, PETE	[illegible]	[illegible]	Y 3
HAGAR, SUS	[illegible]	[illegible]	STO
HAGAR, THO	[illegible]	[illegible]	RLA
HAGARD, H.	[illegible]	[illegible]	D
HAGARD, OV	[illegible]	[illegible]	RD
HAGE, JAM	[illegible]	[illegible]	AR
HAGE, JOH	[illegible]	[illegible]	RD
HAGE, PET	BAL	079	1ST WARD
HAGEE, W[illegible]IAM	BAL	226	1ST DIST
HAGELL, ELIZABETH	ST	270	3RD E DI
HAGELL, MARGARET	ST	271	3RD E DI
HAGEN, ADAM	FRE	227	BUCKEYST
HAGEN, BENJAMIN F.	FRE	228	BUCKEYST
HAGEN, BRIDGET	BAL	145	5TH WARD
HAGEN, C.	BAL	228	19TH WAR
HAGEN, GEORGE	CEC	097	4TH E DI
HAGEN, JOHN W.	FRE	233	BUCKEYST
HAGEN, JOSEPHINE	FRE	206	BUCKEYST
HAGEN, PHILIS	WAS	046	2ND SUBD
HAGEN, REBECCA	BAL	078	10TH WAR
HAGEN, RICHARD	FRE	227	BUCKEYST
HAGEN, SARAH	FRE	226	BUCKEYST
HAGENBERGER, MARGARET	WAS	183	BOONSBOR
HAGER, ANDREW	WAS	125	HAGERSTO
HAGER, AUGUSTINE	FRE	075	FREDERIC
HAGER, AUGUSTUS	FRE	092	FREDERIC
HAGER, CHARLES	BAL	003	1ST WARD
HAGER, GEORGE W.	BAL	205	6TH WARD
HAGER, HENRY	BAL	002	1ST WARD
HAGER, HENRY	BAL	163	11TH WAR
HAGER, IGNATIUS B.	FRE	208	BUCKEYST
HAGER, JACOB	BAL	312	7TH WARD
HAGER, JOHN	BAL	189	5TH DIST
HAGER, JOHN	BAL	077	10TH WAR
HAGER, JOHN	WAS	221	1ST DIST
HAGER, JOHN C.	FRE	370	CATOCTIN
HAGER, JONOTHAN	WAS	221	1ST DIST
HAGER, JOSEPH	ALL	221	CUMBERLA
HAGER, MARGARET	CAR	187	4TH DIST
HAGER, MARTIN	FRE	026	FREDERIC
HAGER, RICHARD	BAL	222	1ST DIST
HAGER, SUSAN	WAS	221	1ST DIST
HAGER, SUSANAH	CAR	182	8TH DIST
HAGER, WILLIAM H.	WAS	243	CAVETOWN
HAGERHOUS, CHARLES	BAL	050	1ST WARD
HAGERMAN, ALBERT	WAS	292	1ST DIST
HAGERMAN, ANDREW	WAS	148	HAGERSTO
HAGERMAN, MART A.	WAS	127	HAGERSTO
HAGERMAN, MARTHA	WAS	148	HAGERSTO
HAGERMAN, MARY C.	WAS	176	1ST DIST
HAGERMAN, THOMAS	WAS	299	1ST DIST
HAGERMAN, WILLIAM	WAS	167	1ST DIST
HAGERTY, ANDREW	BAL	172	6TH WARD
HAGERTY, CHARLES	BAL	031	15TH WAR
HAGERTY, CHARLES	BAL	203	17TH WAR
HAGERTY, CHARLES	HAR	139	2ND DIST
HAGERTY, JAMES	BAL	023	4TH WARD
HAGERTY, JOHN R.	BAL	026	2ND DIST
HAGERTY, LEVI	HAR	135	2ND DIST
HAGERTY, MICHAEL	BAL	021	15TH WAR
HAGERTY, PATRICK	ALL	259	CUMBERLA
HAGERTY, SARAH	BAL	026	2ND DIST
HAGERTY, SUSAN	BAL	108	5TH WARD
HAGERTY, THOMAS	BAL	445	1ST DIST
HAGERTY, WILLIAM	BAL	168	11TH WAR
HAGERTY,MICHEL	BAL	043	2ND DIST
HAGERWIST, JOHN B.	BAL	256	1ST DIST
HAGET, HARMAN	ANN	430	HOWARD D
HAGET, HERMAN	BAL	270	2ND WARD
HAGETTON, CHARLES	QUE	244	5TH E DI
HAGEY, JOHN	BAL	131	18TH WAR
HAGG, RACHE	BAL	233	12TH WAR
HAGGAN, AMRK	HAR	206	3RD DIST
HAGGAN, JOHN	BAL	137	16TH WAR
HAGGARTY, SUSAN	ALL	222	CUMBERLA
HAGGER, JOHN W.	BAL	074	15TH WAR
HAGGERMAN, CONRAD	ANN	426	HOWARD D
HAGGERTY, JOHN	BAL	101	1ST WARD
HAGGERTY, JOHN	BAL	032	9TH WARD
HAGGERTY, MARGARET	BAL	350	13TH WAR
HAGGERTY, MARGARET	WAS	153	HAGERSTO
HAGGERTY, MARY	BAL	079	10TH WAR
HAGGERTY, PETER	ALL	052	10TH E.D
HAGGERTY, WILLIAM	BAL	193	19TH WAR
HAGGINS, CHARLES	BAL	149	1ST WARD
HAGGLE, JOHN L. *	BAL	091	18TH WAR
HAGGY, PETER	BAL	232	1ST DIST
HAGHART, EDWARD	BAL	169	2ND DIST
HAGHERITY, MAURICE	BAL	104	19TH WAR
HAGIN, FRANKLIN	CEC	172	6TH E DI
HAGIN, JOHN	BAL	126	1ST WARD
HAGLEMAN, ELZIABETH	BAL	103	1ST WARD
HAGLETON, MARGARET	QUE	248	5TH E DI
HAGLETON, SAMUEL	QUE	219	3RD E DI
HAGNER, ADAM	BAL	131	18TH WAR
HAGNER, ELIZABETH	BAL	135	18TH WAR
HAGNER, GEORGE	BAL	037	18TH WAR
HAGNER, JOSEPHINE	BAL	070	18TH WAR
HAGNER, MARGARET	BAL	181	16TH WAR
HAGNER, MARTIN	WAS	001	WILLIAMS
HAGNER, RICHARD H.	CAL	030	2ND DIST
HAGNER, SUSAN	BAL	131	18TH WAR
HAGNEY, BRIDGET	BAL	195	2ND WARD
HAGON, WILLIAM	BAL	400	9TH WARD
HAGOR, ALEXANDER	ALL	230	CUMBERLA
HAGTHROP, EDWARD	BAL	115	5TH WARD
HAGUE, AUGUSTINE	BAL	346	7TH WARD
HAGUE, DENNIS	BAL	142	19TH WAR
HAGUE, MARY E.	KEN	286	3RD DIST
HAGUE, MATILDA	BAL	442	14TH WAR
HAGUE, WILLIAM	KEN	266	1ST DIST
HAGUES, GEORGE	BAL	156	11TH WAR
HAGY, CATHARINE	BAL	232	1ST DIST
HAGY, JACOB	BAL	232	1ST DIST
HAHAN, GEORGE	CAR	303	1ST DIST
HAHANEY, STEPHEN	CEC	124	5TH E DI
HAHER, JEW *	BAL	320	12TH WAR
HAHLER, GEORGE	WAS	151	HAGERSTO
HAHN, ABRAHAM	FRE	302	WOODSBOR
HAHN, ABRHAAM E.	CAR	312	1ST DIST
HAHN, ADOLPHUS	BAL	265	7TH WARD
HAHN, AHRHART	WAS	264	1ST DIST
HAHN, BARBARY	WAS	149	HAGERSTO
HAHN, CAROLINE	BAL	257	17TH WAR
HAHN, CATHARINE	FRE	180	5TH E DI
HAHN, CATHARINE	BAL	097	15TH WAR
HAHN, CATHERINE	FRE	108	CREAGERS
HAHN, DANIEL	CAR	298	1ST DIST
HAHN, DANIEL H.	CAR	301	1ST DIST
HAHN, DAVID	ALL	058	10TH E.D
HAHN, EDWARD	BAL	335	7TH WARD
HAHN, ELIZABETH	CAR	386	2ND DIST
HAHN, ELIZABETH	CAR	355	6TH DIST
HAHN, EPHRAIM	CAR	313	1ST DIST
HAHN, FRANCIS D.	FRE	131	CREAGERS
HAHN, GEORGE	BAL	326	7TH WARD
HAHN, GEORGE	WAS	149	HAGERSTO
HAHN, HENRY	BAL	193	17TH WAR
HAHN, HENRY	BAL	348	13TH WAR
HAHN, HENRY	FRE	289	WOODSBOR
HAHN, HENRY	BAL	135	18TH WAR
HAHN, HERMAN	BAL	007	18TH WAR
HAHN, JACOB	CAR	261	3RD DIST
HAHN, JACOB	FRE	133	CREAGERS
HAHN, JACOB	FRE	121	CREAGERS
HAHN, JACOB	CAR	292	7TH DIST
HAHN, JOHN	FRE	126	CREAGERS
HAHN, JOHN	CAR	261	3RD DIST
HAHN, JOHN	CAR	395	2ND DIST
HAHN, JOHN	BAL	304	17TH WAR
HAHN, JOHN	BAL	455	14TH WAR
HAHN, JOHN	BAL	386	1ST DIST
HAHN, JOHN	BAL	014	2ND DIST
HAHN, JOHN	KEN	310	3RD DIST
HAHN, JOHN	WAS	011	WILLIAMS
HAHN, JOSEPH E.	CAR	258	3RD DIST
HAHN, JOSIAH	CAR	262	3RD DIST
HAHN, LEVI	FRE	140	CREAGERS
HAHN, LOUIS	BAL	017	18TH WAR
HAHN, LOUISA	BAL	040	15TH WAR
HAHN, M.	FRE	200	5TH E DI
HAHN, PETER	FRE	121	CREAGERS
HAHN, PROVIDENCE	CAR	315	1ST DIST
HAHN, REBECCA	CAR	258	3RD DIST
HAHN, SAMUEL	CAR	313	1ST DIST
HAHN, TOBIAS	CAR	299	1ST DIST
HAHN, WILLIAM	CAR	310	1ST DIST
HAHN, WILLIAM	FRE	310	WOODSBOR
HAHN, WILLIAM	BAL	336	7TH WARD
HAICHMAN, JACOB	FRE	340	MIDDLETO
HAICK, HERMAN	BAL	235	2ND WARD
HAIDA, JUSTICE	BAL	295	1ST DIST
HAIDIE, EMILY*	BAL	372	3RD WARD
HAIFLY, REBECCA	CAR	379	2ND DIST
HAIG, JAMES M.	BAL	420	14TH WAR
HAIGHT, ELIZABETH	ANN	442	HOWARD D
HAIGHT, JESSE	BAL	178	2ND WARD
HAIGHT, NICHOLAS N.	BAL	265	1ST DIST
HAIL, CHARLES	BAL	088	2ND DIST
HAIL, ELIZABETH	BAL	198	5TH DIST
HAIL, JOHN	BAL	188	5TH DIST
HAIL, JOHN	BAL	087	2ND DIST
HAIL, JOHN	DOR	349	3RD DIVI
HAIL, SUSAN	BAL	088	2ND DIST
HAIL, THOMAS	BAL	186	5TH DIST
HAIL, WILLIAM	BAL	197	5TH DIST
HAILEY, ELIZABETH	BAL	061	1ST WARD
HAILEY, JAMES	BAL	123	1ST WARD
HAILEY, JOHN	CEC	074	5TH E DI
HAILEY, JOSEPH	BAL	062	1ST WARD
HAILS, FRANKLIN	CAL	016	1ST DIST
HAIMAN, AUGUSTUS	MGM	390	ROCKERLE
HAIN, H.N.	WAS	132	HAGERSTO
HAIN, HELEN L.	FRE	366	CATOCTIN
HAIN, HENRY *	FRE	366	CATOCTIN
HAIN, JAMES	CEC	108	3RD E DI
HAIN, THOMAS H.*	BAL	375	3RD WARD
HAIN, WILLIAM J.	FRE	363	CATOCTIN
HAINBERG, PENNEY	BAL	301	12TH WAR
HAINE, HESTER	FRE	248	NEW MARK
HAINE, SUSANN	FRE	440	8TH E DI
HAINER, JOHN H.	BAL	259	2ND WARD
HAINER, SAMUEL	CAR	234	UNION TO
HAINES, A. MARIA	BAL	073	18TH WAR
HAINES, ANN	CAR	362	9TH DIST
HAINES, BENJAMIN P. *	BAL	070	18TH WAR
HAINES, DANIEL	FRE	425	8TH E DI
HAINES, DANIEL	KEN	245	2ND DIST
HAINES, DANIEL	BAL	003	15TH WAR
HAINES, DAVID	CEC	033	CHESAPEA
HAINES, DENNIS	CEC	019	ELKTON 3
HAINES, E. J.	CHA	221	ALLENS F
HAINES, ELIZABETH	FRE	426	8TH E DI
HAINES, ESTHER A.	BAL	003	15TH WAR
HAINES, FRANCIS	FRE	307	WOODSBOR
HAINES, HARRIETT	BAL	228	17TH WAR
HAINES, HENRIETTA	ANN	506	HOWARD D
HAINES, HENRY	WAS	066	2ND SUBD
HAINES, HILDA B.	BAL	003	15TH WAR
HAINES, JACOB A.	BAL	216	6TH WARD
HAINES, JAMES	WAS	067	2ND SUBD
HAINES, JERREMIAH	WAS	069	2ND SUBD
HAINES, JESSE	FRE	255	NEW MARK
HAINES, JOHN	FRE	436	8TH E DI
HAINES, JOHN	FRE	422	8TH E DI
HAINES, JOHN	FRE	422	8TH E DI
HAINES, JOSEPH	CAR	287	7TH DIST
HAINES, JOSEPH	WAS	067	2ND SUBD
HAINES, LEWIS	BAL	042	4TH WARD
HAINES, LYNN	WAS	066	2ND SUBD
HAINES, MARIA	KEN	208	2ND DIST
HAINES, MARY	FRE	300	WOODSBOR
HAINES, MARY	ANN	481	HOWARD D
HAINES, MICHAEL	BAL	102	5TH WARD
HAINES, MORDECAI	ANN	481	HOWARD D
HAINES, NATHAN	FRE	435	8TH E DI
HAINES, PETER	CAR	393	2ND DIST
HAINES, REUBEN	CAR	286	7TH DIST
HAINES, ROBERT R.	MGM	401	ROCKERLE
HAINES, SAMUEL	CAR	286	7TH DIST
HAINES, SARAH	FRE	436	8TH E DI
HAINES, SIDNEY	BAL	224	1ST DIST
HAINES, STEPHEN	FRE	427	8TH E DI
HAINES, TOBIAS	FRE	427	8TH E DI
HAINES, WILLIAM	FRE	439	8TH E DI
HAINES, WILLIAM	BAL	190	19TH WAR
HAINES, WILLIAM	CAR	364	9TH DIST
HAINES, WILLIAM M.	FRE	425	8TH E DI
HAINES,EPHRAIM	FRE	415	8TH E DI
HAINEY, JOHN	ALL	051	10TH E.D
HAINEY, MARLIN	BAL	052	18TH WAR
HAINS, ABRAHAM	CAR	373	9TH DIST
HAINS, AGNES	CEC	208	7TH E DI
HAINS, ANDREW	CAR	365	9TH DIST
HAINS, ANDREW	CAR	379	2ND DIST
HAINS, ANNA	CAR	399	2ND DIST
HAINS, BASIL	CEC	163	6TH E DI
HAINS, CHARLES	BAL	165	19TH WAR
HAINS, DANIEL	CAR	363	9TH DIST
HAINS, DAVID	CAR	392	2ND DIST
HAINS, DAVID	CAR	397	2ND DIST
HAINS, EDWARD A.	BAL	120	2ND DIST
HAINS, EDWIN	CEC	165	6TH E DI
HAINS, ELI	CEC	163	6TH E DI
HAINS, ELI	CAR	394	2ND DIST
HAINS, EVE	CAR	362	9TH DIST
HAINS, FRANCIS	CAR	351	6TH DIST
HAINS, GEORGE	CAR	387	2ND DIST
HAINS, GEORGE	CEC	158	PORT DUP
HAINS, HAZEL	ANN	391	4TH DIST
HAINS, HENRY	CAR	393	2ND DIST
HAINS, ISAAC	CAR	395	2ND DIST
HAINS, ISAAC	CEC	062	1ST E DI
HAINS, JOB	CAR	388	2ND DIST
HAINS, JOB	CEC	163	6TH E DI
HAINS, JOB H.	CEC	164	6TH E DI
HAINS, JOEL	CAR	384	2ND DIST
HAINS, JOEL H.	CEC	150	PORT DUP
HAINS, JOHN	CAR	359	9TH DIST
HAINS, JOHN	CAR	351	6TH DIST
HAINS, JOHN	CEC	046	1ST E DI
HAINS, JOSEPH	BAL	075	18TH WAR
HAINS, JOSEPH	CEC	165	6TH E DI
HAINS, JOSEPH	CEC	129	6TH E DI
HAINS, LEWIS	CAR	378	2ND DIST
HAINS, MARY	CAR	388	2ND DIST
HAINS, MARY	CAR	360	9TH DIST
HAINS, MARY	BAL	425	1ST DIST
HAINS, MOSES	CAR	387	2ND DIST
HAINS, NATHAN	CAR	384	2ND DIST
HAINS, NATHAN	CAR	396	2ND DIST
HAINS, RACHEAL	CAR	399	2ND DIST
HAINS, REBECCA	CAR	386	2ND DIST
HAINS, REUBEN	CAR	394	2ND DIST
HAINS, REUBEN	CAR	386	2ND DIST
HAINS, SAMUEL	CEC	162	6TH E DI
HAINS, SAMUEL	CEC	048	1ST E DI
HAINS, SARAH	CEC	214	7TH E DI
HAINS, SARAH A.	CAR	366	9TH DIST
HAINS, SOPHIA	BAL	425	1ST DIST
HAINS, SUSAN	BAL	050	9TH WARD
HAINS, SUSNA E.	CAR	388	2ND DIST
HAINS, WILLAIM	CEC	009	ELKTON 3
HAINS, WILLIAM	CAR	366	9TH DIST
HAINS, WILLIAM	CAR	413	2ND DIST
HAINS, WILLIAM	ANN	391	4TH DIST
HAINS, WILLIAM	BAL	148	2ND DIST
HAIR, CLARA A. M.	FRE	364	CATOCTIN
HAIR, HENRY	CAR	336	6TH DIST
HAIR, JOHN	BAL	197	5TH DIST
HAIR, W. F.	BAL	197	5TH DIST
HAISLET, WILLIAM	ANN	433	HOWARD D
HAISLIP, WALTER A.	CHA	237	HILLTOP
HAISN, ISREAL	CAR	373	9TH DIST
HAITHEN, HANNAH	BAL	204	2ND WARD
HAITMAN, REGINA	BAL	309	12TH WAR
HAITZ, AARON	BAL	236	2ND WARD
HAITZELL, LEE	BAL	269	12TH WAR
HAIZZA, JOHN *	ALL	055	10TH E.D
HAKE, MARY	BAL	372	8TH WARD
HAKEL, HENRY	CEC	050	1ST E DI
HAKER, CONRAD	BAL	010	9TH WARD
HAKESLEY, JOHN	BAL	448	8TH WARD
HAKESLEY, WILLIAM J.	BAL	223	6TH WARD
HAKKINGS, HENRIETTA	WAS	160	2ND DIST
HALA, FRANCIS	WAS	228	1ST DIST
HALADAY, LYDIA-BLACK	CAR	138	NO TWP L
HALAY, JOHN	HAR	013	1ST DIST
HALBACH, CHARLES	BAL	068	10TH WAR
HALBERT, ELIZABETH	WAS	277	RIDGEVIL
HALBERT, HANNAH	FRE	065	FREDERIC
HALBERT, JEMMIMA E.	BAL	396	3RD WARD
HALBERT, JOHN	BAL	222	6TH WARD
HALBERT, LAURA	FRE	042	FREDERIC
HALBERT, MARYANN*	BAL	396	3RD WARD
HALBERT, SAMUEL	BAL	095	2ND DIST
HALBERT, SAMUEL	BAL	093	2ND DIST
HALBY, MARGARET	ALL	226	CUMBERLA
HALDEMAN, LOUISA	ALL	018	3RD E.D.
HALE, ANN J.	BAL	054	15TH WAR
HALE, BETTY	ANN	398	8TH DIST
HALE, CAROLINE S.	MGM	375	ROCKERLE
HALE, CATHARINE	BAL	282	12TH WAR
HALE, CHARLES W.	BAL	002	15TH WAR
HALE, COLIN F.	BAL	157	16TH WAR
HALE, ELIAS	CEC	055	1ST E DI
HALE, ELIZABETH	CEC	091	4TH E DI
HALE, ELIZABETH	DOR	416	1ST DIST
HALE, ELIZABETH	BAL	406	1ST DIST
HALE, EMELINE	ALL	164	6TH E.D.
HALE, GEORGE	TAL	005	EASTON D
HALE, GEORGE	WAS	122	HAGERSTO
HALE, GEORGE W.	WAS	159	HAGERSTO
HALE, HARRIETT	ALL	158	6TH E.D.
HALE, HENRIETTA	BAL	352	8TH WARD
HALE, JAMES E.	DOR	404	1ST DIST
HALE, JAMES W.	WAS	159	HAGERSTO
HALE, JOHN	BAL	138	11TH WAR
HALE, JOSHUA	ANN	493	HOWARD D
HALE, JOSHUA	BAL	350	3RD WARD
HALE, JOSHUA	BAL	350	3RD WARD
HALE, MARGARET	BAL	304	1ST DIST
HALE, MARGARET	HAR	003	1ST DIST
HALE, MARGARET	DOR	470	1ST DIST
HALE, MARIAH	BAL	312	7TH WARD
HALE, MERCY	CEC	168	6TH E DI
HALE, NICHOLAS	BAL	294	1ST DIST
HALE, PHILIP M.	BAL	167	6TH WARD
HALE, SAMUEL	CEC	053	1ST E DI
HALE, SARAH A.	CEC	121	4TH E DI
HALE, SUSAN	DOR	417	1ST DIST
HALE, WALTER	BAL	090	2ND DIST
HALE, WILLIAM	FRE	213	BUCKEYST
HALE, WILLIAM	FRE	213	BUCKEYST
HALE, WILLIAM	CEC	154	PORT DUP
HALE, WILLIAM	MGM	380	ROCKERLE
HALE, WILLIAM H.	BAL	117	15TH WAR
HALE, WILLIAM H.	BAL	456	8TH WARD
HALED, GEORGE	BAL	129	1ST WARD
HALEN, ADAM	BAL	022	2ND DIST
HALES, ANN	CHA	247	HILLTOP

Name	County	No.	District
HALES, HENRY	BAL	157	1ST WARD
HALES, JACOB	SOM	351	BRINKLEY
HALES, MATHIAS	WOR	170	6TH E DI
HALES, SAMUEL	BAL	178	19TH WAR
HALES, WILLIAM	WOR	308	2ND E DI
HALES, WILLIAM A.	WOR	171	6TH E DI
HALETT, A.	BAL	162	1ST WARD
HALEY, AMRY A.	KEN	216	2ND DIST
HALEY, ANN	BAL	402	8TH WARD
HALEY, ANN	BAL	020	1ST WARD
HALEY, ANN	KEN	308	3RD DIST
HALEY, CATHARINE	BAL	135	16TH WAR
HALEY, ELIZABETH	FRE	111	CREAGERS
HALEY, FRANCAS	BAL	257	2ND WARD
HALEY, FRANCIS	ALL	243	CUMBERLA
HALEY, HENRY	BAL	024	15TH WAR
HALEY, JAMES	ALL	252	CUMBERLA
HALEY, JOHN	BAL	004	9TH WARD
HALEY, JOHN	BAL	370	3RD WARD
HALEY, JOHN	BAL	441	1ST DIST
HALEY, LACKEY	ALL	255	CUMBERLA
HALEY, LEAH	BAL	024	1ST WARD
HALEY, MARY	ALL	261	CUMBERLA
HALEY, MARY	BAL	173	11TH WAR
HALEY, MICHAEL	ALL	210	CUMBERLA
HALEY, NICHOLAS	BAL	234	6TH WARD
HALEY, PENELOP	BAL	062	18TH WAR
HALEY, PETE	BAL	126	2ND DIST
HALEY, R. H.	BAL	167	11TH WAR
HALEY, SANDY	BAL	084	15TH WAR
HALEY, THOMAS	BAL	173	11TH WAR
HALEY, WILLIAM	BAL	068	15TH WAR
HALEY, WILLIAM	ALL	050	10TH E.D
HALEY, WILLIAM C.	KEN	216	2ND DIST
HALFEN, GEORGE	ALL	111	5TH E.D.
HALFPENNY, SAMUEL W.	BAL	210	2ND WARD
HALGAMAN, WILLIAM	BAL	243	17TH WAR
HALIGAN, MARY	BAL	475	14TH WAR
HALIN, GEORGE	BAL	245	2ND WARD
HALIN, WASHINGTON	CAR	399	2ND DIST
HALL, A. F.	BAL	147	1ST WARD
HALL, A. G.	BAL	333	1ST DIST
HALL, A. T.	WOR	302	SNOW HIL
HALL, AARON	BAL	134	1ST WARD
HALL, ABNER	TAL	070	EASTON T
HALL, ABSOLAM A.	ANN	332	2ND DIST
HALL, ALBERT	SOM	398	BRINKLEY
HALL, ALEXANDER	BAL	205	6TH WARD
HALL, ALEXANDER	ANN	479	HOWARD D
HALL, ALFRED	BAL	303	3RD WARD
HALL, ALFRED	HAR	121	2ND DIST
HALL, ALLACE	BAL	299	1ST DIST
HALL, AMELIA	BAL	005	EASTERN
HALL, AMELIA	BAL	271	12TH WAR
HALL, AMELIA	SOM	429	PRINCESS
HALL, AMEY	BAL	448	8TH WARD
HALL, ANASTAHA-BLACK	MGM	403	ROCKERLE
HALL, ANDREW	HAR	176	3RD DIST
HALL, ANDREW	ALL	152	6TH E.D.
HALL, ANN	ALL	050	10TH E.D
HALL, ANN	BAL	191	11TH WAR
HALL, ANN	BAL	181	2ND DIST
HALL, ANN	BAL	141	16TH WAR
HALL, ANN	HAR	045	1ST DIST
HALL, ANN	CAL	008	1ST DIST
HALL, ANN	CEC	098	3RD E DI
HALL, ANN	WOR	340	1ST E DI
HALL, ANN	TAL	099	ST MICHA
HALL, ANN	QUE	167	2ND E DI
HALL, ANN E.	QUE	179	2ND E DI
HALL, ANN M.	TAL	074	EASTON T
HALL, ANN M.	CEC	174	6TH E DI
HALL, ANN MARIA	QUE	175	2ND E DI
HALL, ANNA	BAL	353	1ST DIST
HALL, ANNA M.	ANN	333	2ND DIST
HALL, ANNE	BAL	122	16TH WAR
HALL, ANTWINE	ALL	203	CUMBERLA
HALL, AQUILLA	HAR	138	2ND DIST
HALL, ARAMENTA	BAL	337	13TH WAR
HALL, ARENA	BAL	157	16TH WAR
HALL, ARON	BAL	084	4TH WARD
HALL, ARTHUR	BAL	121	16TH WAR
HALL, ARTHUR	BAL	248	6TH WARD
HALL, ASBERRY	KEN	270	1ST DIST
HALL, ASBURY W.	BAL	177	6TH WARD
HALL, AVEY	BAL	197	11TH WAR
HALL, AYRUS	WOR	290	9TH E DI
HALL, B.	BAL	135	1ST WARD
HALL, BASIL	PRI	086	QUEEN AN
HALL, BASIL	BAL	161	11TH WAR
HALL, BASIL D.	ANN	331	2ND DIST
HALL, BENERATA	CEC	064	1ST E DI
HALL, BENJAMIN	PRI	020	VANSVILL
HALL, BENJAMIN	WOR	251	1ST CENS
HALL, BENJAMIN	WAS	153	HAGERSTO
HALL, BENJAMIN E.	BAL	426	14TH WAR
HALL, BETSEY	WOR	340	1ST E DI
HALL, BETSEY	BAL	085	2ND DIST
HALL, BIDDY	BAL	225	19TH WAR
HALL, BILL	ANN	350	3RD DIST
HALL, BOB	ANN	346	3RD DIST
HALL, BRIDGET	WOR	340	1ST E DI
HALL, CALEB	BAL	437	14TH WAR
HALL, CALIB	BAL	353	1ST DIST
HALL, CAROLINE	BAL	014	2ND DIST
HALL, CAROLINE	BAL	399	8TH WARD
HALL, CAROLINE	BAL	062	10TH WAR
HALL, CARROLL	HAR	161	3RD DIST
HALL, CART	BAL	221	12TH WAR
HALL, CARTER A.	BAL	430	14TH WAR
HALL, CATHAIRNE	BAL	101	2ND DIST
HALL, CATHARINE	BAL	175	2ND DIST
HALL, CATHARINE	HAR	155	3RD DIST
HALL, CATHARINE	WAS	302	1ST DIST
HALL, CATHERINE	CEC	213	7TH E DI
HALL, CATHERINE	BAL	075	10TH WAR
HALL, CATHERINE-BLACK	QUE	173	2ND E DI
HALL, CATHRINE	BAL	171	11TH WAR
HALL, CHALRES	CAR	222	5TH DIST
HALL, CHARELS	BAL	257	1ST DIST
HALL, CHARLES	BAL	120	1ST WARD
HALL, CHARLES	BAL	460	8TH WARD
HALL, CHARLES	BAL	100	10TH WAR
HALL, CHARLES	BAL	015	2ND DIST
HALL, CHARLES	BAL	460	1ST DIST
HALL, CHARLES	CEC	212	7TH E DI
HALL, CHARLES	CEC	065	1ST E DI
HALL, CHARLES F.	SOM	351	BRINKLEY
HALL, CHARLOTTE	BAL	236	20TH WAR
HALL, CHARLOTTE	BAL	170	2ND DIST
HALL, CHRISTOPHER	BAL	014	2ND DIST
HALL, CLARA	BAL	080	4TH WARD
HALL, CLINTON	KEN	283	3RD DIST
HALL, CORDELIA G.	BAL	097	10TH WAR
HALL, CORNELIA	FRE	025	FREDERIC
HALL, DANIEL	SOM	433	PRINCESS
HALL, DANIEL A.-MULATTO	FRE	038	FREDERIC
HALL, DAVID	CAR	403	2ND DIST
HALL, DAVID	TAL	069	EASTON T
HALL, DAVID J.	BAL	125	18TH WAR
HALL, DEBBY	BAL	417	3RD WARD
HALL, DIANA	ANN	454	HOWARD D
HALL, DINAH	FRE	259	NEW MARK
HALL, E. W.	ANN	309	1ST DIST
HALL, E.G.W.	PRI	093	MARLBROU
HALL, EDWARD	WOR	252	1ST CENS
HALL, EDWARD	ANN	401	8TH DIST
HALL, EDWARD	ANN	406	8TH DIST
HALL, EDWARD	BAL	280	7TH WARD
HALL, EDWARD	BAL	207	2ND WARD
HALL, EDWARD	BAL	206	19TH WAR
HALL, EDWARD	BAL	153	11TH WAR
HALL, EDWARD *	BAL	092	2ND DIST
HALL, EDWARD L.	BAL	411	3RD WARD
HALL, ELEANOR G.	SOM	361	BRINKLEY
HALL, ELI	CAR	354	6TH DIST
HALL, ELIAS S.	BAL	282	20TH WAR
HALL, ELIHU B.	CEC	132	6TH E DI
HALL, ELIJAH	BAL	345	7TH WARD
HALL, ELIJAH A.	BAL	046	18TH WAR
HALL, ELIJAH T.	SOM	356	BRINKLEY
HALL, ELISHA J.	MGM	319	CRACKLIN
HALL, ELIZA	BAL	431	14TH WAR
HALL, ELIZA	BAL	045	4TH WARD
HALL, ELIZA	CAL	047	3RD DIST
HALL, ELIZA	SOM	415	DUBLIN D
HALL, ELIZA	PRI	057	AQUASCO
HALL, ELIZA	BAL	167	6TH WARD
HALL, ELIZA	BAL	062	10TH WAR
HALL, ELIZA	BAL	318	1ST DIST
HALL, ELIZA E.-BLACK	ST	321	4TH E DI
HALL, ELIZA J.	BAL	123	5TH WARD
HALL, ELIZA J.-MULATTO	FRE	225	BUCKEYST
HALL, ELIZA S.	BAL	109	10TH WAR
HALL, ELIZABETH	BAL	117	15TH WAR
HALL, ELIZABETH	BAL	079	15TH WAR
HALL, ELIZABETH	BAL	081	15TH WAR
HALL, ELIZABETH	ANN	520	HOWARD D
HALL, ELIZABETH	BAL	072	15TH WAR
HALL, ELIZABETH	BAL	074	15TH WAR
HALL, ELIZABETH	CAL	050	3RD DIST
HALL, ELIZABETH	BAL	392	14TH WAR
HALL, ELIZABETH	BAL	208	19TH WAR
HALL, ELIZABETH	BAL	419	3RD WARD
HALL, ELIZABETH	WAS	122	HAGERSTO
HALL, ELIZABETH	WOR	253	1ST CENS
HALL, ELIZABETH A.	BAL	001	9TH WARD
HALL, ELIZABETH D.	QUE	204	3RD E DI
HALL, ELIZABETH P.	WAS	140	HAGERSTO
HALL, ELLEN	BAL	193	11TH WAR
HALL, ELLEN	BAL	445	14TH WAR
HALL, ELLEN	BAL	374	13TH WAR
HALL, EMILY	BAL	357	13TH WAR
HALL, EMILY	BAL	044	15TH WAR
HALL, EMILY	BAL	313	7TH WARD
HALL, ERASTUS Q.	BAL	026	1ST WARD
HALL, ESTEP	ANN	302	1ST DIST
HALL, F.	BAL	151	1ST WARD
HALL, F.	BAL	170	1ST WARD
HALL, FANNY	BAL	425	14TH WAR
HALL, FANNY	WOR	252	1ST CENS
HALL, FENWICK	BAL	191	11TH WAR
HALL, FRANCES	BAL	183	16TH WAR
HALL, FRANCIS	BAL	220	6TH WARD
HALL, FRANCIS	BAL	124	1ST WARD
HALL, FRANCIS A.	SOM	353	BRINKLEY
HALL, FRANKLIN	BAL	114	2ND DIST
HALL, FREBON	BAL	066	1ST WARD
HALL, FREDERICK	BAL	168	2ND DIST
HALL, FREDERICK-BLACK	QUE	161	2ND E DI
HALL, FREDERICK-BLACK	QUE	172	2ND E DI
HALL, FRISBY	KEN	283	3RD DIST
HALL, G.	PRI	073	MARLBROU
HALL, GEORGE	BAL	168	2ND DIST
HALL, GEORGE	BAL	012	2ND DIST
HALL, GEORGE	BAL	032	9TH WARD
HALL, GEORGE	BAL	427	14TH WAR
HALL, GEORGE	HAR	030	1ST DIST
HALL, GEORGE H.	PRI	023	VANSVILL
HALL, GEORGE M.	ST	316	4TH E DI
HALL, GEORGE W.	MGM	319	CRACKLIN
HALL, GEORGE W.	HAR	151	3RD DIST
HALL, GEORGE W.	BAL	184	6TH WARD
HALL, GEORGE WILLIAM	HAR	193	3RD DIST
HALL, GRACE	BAL	342	3RD WARD
HALL, GRACY	ANN	274	ANNAPOLI
HALL, H. C.	BAL	332	1ST DIST
HALL, H. M.	BAL	054	4TH WARD
HALL, HANNAH	BAL	240	6TH WARD
HALL, HANNAH	WOR	339	1ST E DI
HALL, HARRIET	ANN	357	3RD DIST
HALL, HARRIETT	WAS	133	HAGERSTO
HALL, HENRIETTA	BAL	157	11TH WAR
HALL, HENRY	BAL	125	11TH WAR
HALL, HENRY	MGM	365	BERRYS D
HALL, HENRY	MGM	366	BERRYS D
HALL, HENRY	HAR	069	1ST DIST
HALL, HENRY	HAR	102	2ND DIST
HALL, HENRY	HAR	097	2ND DIST
HALL, HENRY	BAL	001	18TH WAR
HALL, HENRY	ANN	322	2ND DIST
HALL, HENRY	BAL	359	3RD WARD
HALL, HENRY	BAL	460	8TH WARD
HALL, HENRY	BAL	127	1ST WARD
HALL, HENRY A.	ANN	401	8TH DIST
HALL, HENRY W.	BAL	198	11TH WAR
HALL, HESTER	BAL	366	3RD WARD
HALL, HORATIO	WAS	094	2ND SUBD
HALL, HOWARD	BAL	137	18TH WAR
HALL, ISAAC	BAL	136	18TH WAR
HALL, ISAAC	CAR	254	3RD DIST
HALL, ISABELLA	BAL	080	4TH WARD
HALL, ISABELLA	BAL	078	4TH WARD
HALL, ISRAEL	BAL	173	6TH WARD
HALL, ISREAL	BAL	239	17TH WAR
HALL, J.B.	WAS	136	HAGERSTO
HALL, J.M.	ANN	270	ANNAPOLI
HALL, JACOB	ANN	294	1ST DIST
HALL, JACOB	BAL	230	1ST DIST
HALL, JACOB	BAL	133	1ST WARD
HALL, JACOB	BAL	353	1ST DIST
HALL, JACOB	BAL	024	18TH WAR
HALL, JACOB	HAR	074	1ST DIST
HALL, JACOB T.	PRI	033	VANSVILL
HALL, JAKE	ANN	337	3RD DIST
HALL, JAMES	BAL	185	5TH DIST
HALL, JAMES	BAL	259	1ST DIST
HALL, JAMES	BAL	214	6TH WARD
HALL, JAMES	BAL	168	1ST WARD
HALL, JAMES	BAL	015	15TH WAR
HALL, JAMES	ANN	448	HOWARD D
HALL, JAMES	BAL	009	EASTERN
HALL, JAMES	SOM	487	SALISBUR
HALL, JAMES	SOM	354	BRINKLEY
HALL, JAMES	WOR	298	9TH E DI
HALL, JAMES	ST	316	4TH E DI
HALL, JAMES	BAL	254	17TH WAR
HALL, JAMES	CEC	127	5TH E DI
HALL, JAMES	BAL	466	14TH WAR
HALL, JAMES	HAR	139	2ND DIST
HALL, JAMES	QUE	143	1ST E DI
HALL, JAMES DR.	BAL	140	11TH WAR
HALL, JAMES F.	QUE	179	2ND E DI
HALL, JAMES H.	ST	316	4TH E DI
HALL, JAMES H.	BAL	093	10TH WAR
HALL, JAMES M.	BAL	128	1ST WARD
HALL, JAMES P.	BAL	178	11TH WAR
HALL, JAMS	WOR	253	1ST CENS
HALL, JANE	BAL	121	11TH WAR
HALL, JANE	BAL	112	10TH WAR
HALL, JANE	BAL	381	13TH WAR
HALL, JANE	HAR	009	1ST DIST
HALL, JASON	ANN	324	2ND DIST
HALL, JASON	ANN	378	4TH DIST
HALL, JEREMIAH	WOR	192	8TH E DI
HALL, JEREMIAH-BLACK	FRE	390	PETERSVI
HALL, JEREMIAH-MULATTO	WOR	166	6TH E DI
HALL, JESSE	ANN	493	HOWARD D
HALL, JIM	BAL	229	1ST DIST
HALL, JOB	BAL	259	17TH WAR
HALL, JOEL	FRE	255	NEW MARK
HALL, JOHN	BAL	123	18TH WAR
HALL, JOHN	BAL	252	17TH WAR
HALL, JOHN	HAR	010	1ST DIST
HALL, JOHN	KEN	230	2ND DIST
HALL, JOHN	KEN	237	2ND DIST
HALL, JOHN	CEC	065	1ST E DI
HALL, JOHN	BAL	234	20TH WAR
HALL, JOHN	CAR	222	5TH DIST
HALL, JOHN	B-L	175	2ND DIST
HALL, JOHN	BAL	172	2ND DIST
HALL, JOHN	BAL	306	3RD WARD
HALL, JOHN	BAL	377	1ST DIST
HALL, JOHN	ANN	322	2ND DIST
HALL, JOHN	ANN	278	ANNAPOLI
HALL, JOHN	BAL	011	15TH WAR
HALL, JOHN	BAL	068	15TH WAR
HALL, JOHN	BAL	309	7TH WARD
HALL, JOHN	BAL	374	8TH WARD
HALL, JOHN	BAL	102	2ND DIST
HALL, JOHN	BAL	155	1ST WARD
HALL, JOHN	KEN	257	1ST DIST
HALL, JOHN	KEN	283	3RD DIST
HALL, JOHN	WOR	252	1ST CENS
HALL, JOHN	SOM	357	BRINKLEY
HALL, JOHN	SOM	398	BRINKLEY
HALL, JOHN	WOR	332	1ST E DI
HALL, JOHN A.	QUE	178	2ND E DI
HALL, JOHN A.	CEC	162	6TH E DI
HALL, JOHN C. C.	HAR	192	3RD DIST
HALL, JOHN D.	BAL	345	7TH WARD
HALL, JOHN H.	BAL	282	7TH WARD
HALL, JOHN N.	CEC	114	3RD E DI
HALL, JOHN S.	ANN	313	1ST DIST
HALL, JOHN T.	ANN	517	HOWARD D
HALL, JOHN T.	CEC	098	3RD E DI
HALL, JOHN T.	BAL	108	18TH WAR
HALL, JOHN T.	FRE	385	PETERSVI
HALL, JOHN W.	MGM	319	CRACKLIN
HALL, JOHN W.	CAL	028	2ND DIST
HALL, JOHN W.	BAL	307	3RD WARD
HALL, JOHN-BLACK	MGM	423	MEDLEY 3
HALL, JOHNW.	MGM	416	MEDLEY 3
HALL, JOHNW.	MGM	407	MEDLEY 3
HALL, JONATHAN	BAL	071	1ST WARD
HALL, JOSEPH	BAL	264	1ST DIST
HALL, JOSEPH	BAL	316	1ST DIST
HALL, JOSEPH	BAL	090	15TH WAR
HALL, JOSEPH	CAL	026	2ND DIST
HALL, JOSEPH	HAR	122	2ND DIST
HALL, JOSEPH	CEC	115	3RD E DI
HALL, JOSEPH	SOM	385	BRINKLEY
HALL, JOSEPH	WOR	257	1ST CENS
HALL, JOSEPHINE	BAL	406	14TH WAR
HALL, JOSHUA	CAR	100	NO TWP L
HALL, JOSHUA	ANN	330	2ND DIST
HALL, JOSHUA	BAL	377	3RD WARD
HALL, JOSHUA	BAL	061	2ND DIST
HALL, JOSIAH	CEC	052	1ST E DI
HALL, JULIA	CEC	210	7TH E DI
HALL, JULIA	WOR	341	1ST E DI
HALL, JULIA A.	HAR	156	3RD DIST
HALL, JULIUS	CAL	062	3RD DIST
HALL, JULIUS T.	WOR	349	1ST E DI
HALL, KATE	BAL	030	9TH WARD
HALL, KINSEY	BAL	178	6TH WARD
HALL, LAURA A.	PRI	025	VANSVILL
HALL, LAZARUS M.	SOM	445	DAMES QU
HALL, LEAH	BAL	026	9TH WARD
HALL, LEONARA J.	BAL	358	3RD WARD
HALL, LEVI	WAS	091	2ND SUBD
HALL, LEVI	CEC	112	4TH E DI
HALL, LEVI-BLACK	FRE	390	PETERSVI
HALL, LEVY	BAL	323	7TH WARD
HALL, LEWIS	BAL	430	8TH WARD
HALL, LEWIS	ANN	493	HOWARD D
HALL, LEWIS	CAR	385	2ND DIST
HALL, LOUIS	BAL	168	16TH WAR
HALL, LOUISA	BAL	252	6TH WARD
HALL, LUCINDA	ANN	497	HOWARD D
HALL, LUCY	ANN	311	1ST DIST
HALL, LYDIA	BAL	060	10TH WAR
HALL, M.A	ANN	269	ANNAPOLI
HALL, MAJOR T.	WOR	343	1ST E DI
HALL, MANN	BAL	173	19TH WAR
HALL, MARGARET	SOM	351	BRINKLEY
HALL, MARGARET	BAL	160	16TH WAR
HALL, MARIA	BAL	332	3RD WARD
HALL, MARIA	BAL	071	15TH WAR
HALL, MARIA	BAL	167	6TH WARD

Name	County	Page	District
HALL, MARIA	ANN	430	HOWARD D
HALL, MARIA	ANN	453	HOWARD D
HALL, MARIA	BAL	237	20TH WAR
HALL, MARIA W.	BAL	159	16TH WAR
HALL, MARIAH	KEN	312	3RD DIST
HALL, MARK	ANN	269	ANNAPOLI
HALL, MARTH AE.	CAR	215	5TH DIST
HALL, MARTHA	BAL	032	18TH WAR
HALL, MARTHA	MGM	320	CRACKLIN
HALL, MARTHA T.	PRI	093	MARLBROU
HALL, MARY	PRI	081	QUEEN AN
HALL, MARY	PRI	077	MARLBROU
HALL, MARY	SOM	352	BRINKLEY
HALL, MARY	WOR	316	2ND E DI
HALL, MARY	PRI	012	BLADENSB
HALL, MARY	HAR	139	2ND DIST
HALL, MARY	CAL	050	3RD DIST
HALL, MARY	BAL	058	4TH WARD
HALL, MARY	FRE	276	NEW MARK
HALL, MARY	ANN	319	2ND DIST
HALL, MARY	BAL	296	12TH WAR
HALL, MARY	BAL	100	2ND DIST
HALL, MARY	BAL	027	9TH WARD
HALL, MARY	BAL	027	9TH WARD
HALL, MARY A.	ANN	439	HOWARD D
HALL, MARY A.	BAL	317	7TH WARD
HALL, MARY A.	BAL	347	7TH WARD
HALL, MARY A.	BAL	266	7TH WARD
HALL, MARY A.	BAL	407	14TH WAR
HALL, MARY C.	HAR	178	3RD DIST
HALL, MARY J.	BAL	346	3RD WARD
HALL, MARY J.	SOM	399	BRINKLEY
HALL, MARY Q.	HAR	071	1ST DIST
HALL, MATILDA	BAL	392	14TH WAR
HALL, MICHAEL	HAR	175	3RD DIST
HALL, MICHAEL	ALL	164	6TH E.D.
HALL, MILLY	BAL	343	3RD WARD
HALL, MILLY	BAL	050	18TH WAR
HALL, MR-	BAL	058	15TH WAR
HALL, NACE	ANN	353	3RD DIST
HALL, NACE	ANN	477	HOWARD D
HALL, NANCY	BAL	028	15TH WAR
HALL, NANCY	BAL	401	14TH WAR
HALL, NANCY	CAR	223	5TH DIST
HALL, NANCY	SOM	357	BRINKLEY
HALL, NANCY	WOR	284	BERLIN 1
HALL, NATHAN	BAL	337	13TH WAR
HALL, NATHAN	BAL	328	7TH WARD
HALL, NATHAN H.	BAL	411	3RD WARD
HALL, NATHANIEL	BAL	082	15TH WAR
HALL, NELSON	CAR	198	4TH DIST
HALL, NELSON	KEN	238	2ND DIST
HALL, NELSON	WOR	250	1ST CENS
HALL, NICHOLAS	FRE	268	NEW MARK
HALL, NICHOLAS E.	CAR	368	9TH DIST
HALL, NOAH	WOR	282	BERLIN 1
HALL, ORANGE	HAR	189	3RD DIST
HALL, OWEN	BAL	167	2ND DIST
HALL, PERRY	ANN	470	HOWARD D
HALL, PETER	ALL	146	6TH E.D.
HALL, PETER	BAL	069	18TH WAR
HALL, PHILIP	KEN	238	2ND DIST
HALL, PRESCELLA	BAL	337	13TH WAR
HALL, PRESTON	BAL	164	11TH WAR
HALL, R. D.	CEC	212	7TH E DI
HALL, RACHAEL-MULATTO	FRE	038	FREDERIC
HALL, RACHAL	FRE	305	WOODSBOR
HALL, REBECCA	CEC	068	5TH E DI
HALL, REBECCA	CAR	247	3RD DIST
HALL, REBECCA	CAR	247	3RD DIST
HALL, REBECCA	CAL	012	1ST DIST
HALL, RICHARD	BAL	217	6TH WARD
HALL, RICHARD	WOR	253	1ST CENS
HALL, RICHARD	QUE	243	5TH E DI
HALL, RICHARD A.-BLACK	FRE	225	BUCKEYST
HALL, RICHARD G.	PRI	034	VANSVILL
HALL, RICHARD H.	BAL	147	11TH WAR
HALL, RICHARD J.	ANN	357	3RD DIST
HALL, RITTY	BAL	100	15TH WAR
HALL, ROBERT	BAL	297	12TH WAR
HALL, ROBERT	BAL	280	12TH WAR
HALL, ROBERT	ANN	351	3RD DIST
HALL, ROBERT	BAL	124	5TH WARD
HALL, ROBERT	ALL	215	CUMBERLA
HALL, ROBERT	CEC	057	1ST E DI
HALL, ROBERT	HAR	071	1ST DIST
HALL, ROBERT	SOM	354	BRINKLEY
HALL, ROBERT	SOM	385	BRINKLEY
HALL, ROBERT	KEN	283	3RD DIST
HALL, ROBERT-BLACK	FRE	225	BUCKEYST
HALL, RODGER	WOR	252	1ST CENS
HALL, ROSA J.	BAL	178	6TH WARD
HALL, ROSENNA	BAL	067	18TH WAR
HALL, ROSINA	BAL	050	15TH WAR
HALL, RUBEN	BAL	264	2ND WARD
HALL, SALLY	ANN	325	2ND DIST
HALL, SAMPSON	WAS	C09	WILLIAMS
HALL, SAMSON	ANN	307	1ST DIST
HALL, SAMUEL	BAL	308	7TH WARD
HALL, SAMUEL	BAL	365	8TH WARD
HALL, SAMUEL	BAL	016	15TH WAR
HALL, SAMUEL	BAL	437	8TH WARD
HALL, SAMUEL	BAL	136	2ND DIST
HALL, SAMUEL	BAL	281	12TH WAR
HALL, SAMUEL	BAL	160	2ND DIST
HALL, SAMUEL	BAL	331	1ST DIST
HALL, SAMUEL	SOM	361	BRINKLEY
HALL, SAMUEL	SOM	354	BRINKLEY
HALL, SAMUEL	WOR	342	1ST E DI
HALL, SAMUEL	CAR	254	3RD DIST
HALL, SAMUEL	BAL	103	18TH WAR
HALL, SAMUEL	BAL	463	14TH WAR
HALL, SAMUEL	QUE	157	2ND E DI
HALL, SAMUEL	CAR	220	5TH DIST
HALL, SANDY	BAL	142	1ST WARD
HALL, SARAH	BAL	226	1ST DIST
HALL, SARAH	BAL	349	7TH WARD
HALL, SARAH	ANN	308	1ST DIST
HALL, SARAH	ANN	311	1ST DIST
HALL, SARAH	ANN	404	8TH DIST
HALL, SARAH	BAL	026	9TH WARD
HALL, SARAH	BAL	037	18TH WAR
HALL, SARAH	HAR	117	2ND DIST
HALL, SARAH	HAR	055	1ST DIST
HALL, SARAH	BAL	424	14TH WAR
HALL, SARAH	WAS	093	2ND SUBD
HALL, SARAH A.	BAL	173	11TH WAR
HALL, SARAH H.	BAL	167	16TH WAR
HALL, SARAH J.	ST	328	4TH E DI
HALL, SARAH S.	SOM	353	BRINKLEY
HALL, SARAH-BLACK	BAL	214	2ND WARD
HALL, SARAH-BLACK	FRE	041	FREDERIC
HALL, SHADRICH	CAR	086	NO TWP L
HALL, SIDNEY C.	BAL	181	2ND DIST
HALL, SISTER M.E ETIENE	FRE	197	5TH E DI
HALL, SOLOMAN	BAL	046	18TH WAR
HALL, SOPHIA	BAL	341	7TH WARD
HALL, STEPHEN*	DOR	417	1ST DIST
HALL, STEVEN	FRE	070	FREDERIC
HALL, SUCKEY	SOM	354	BRINKLEY
HALL, SUSAN	HAR	038	1ST DIST
HALL, SUSAN	HAR	055	1ST DIST
HALL, SUSAN	BAL	357	3RD WARD
HALL, SUSAN H.	BAL	346	3RD WARD
HALL, SUSAN K.	KEN	215	2ND DIST
HALL, SUSANAH	BAL	108	18TH WAR
HALL, SUSANER	HAR	189	3RD DIST
HALL, SUSANNAH	BAL	124	16TH WAR
HALL, THEODORE	WOR	342	1ST E DI
HALL, THOASM L.	BAL	424	1ST DIST
HALL, THOMAS	BAL	015	15TH WAR
HALL, THOMAS	BAL	181	2ND WARD
HALL, THOMAS	BAL	168	1ST WARD
HALL, THOMAS	ANN	311	1ST DIST
HALL, THOMAS	KEN	288	3RD DIST
HALL, THOMAS	DOR	368	3RD DIVI
HALL, THOMAS	MGM	407	MEDLEY 3
HALL, THOMAS	CAL	049	3RD DIST
HALL, THOMAS	BAL	374	13TH WAR
HALL, THOMAS B.	KEN	286	3RD DIST
HALL, THOMAS J.	BAL	115	15TH WAR
HALL, THOMAS J.	ANN	355	3RD DIST
HALL, THOMAS W.	BAL	152	11TH WAR
HALL, THOMAS W.	HAR	193	3RD DIST
HALL, TRACEY-BLACK	BAL	219	2ND WARD
HALL, TUBMAN	SOM	358	BRINKLEY
HALL, W. R.	BAL	333	1ST DIST
HALL, WALTER	BAL	090	2ND DIST
HALL, WASHINGTON	SOM	392	BRINKLEY
HALL, WASHINGTON JR.	BAL	112	10TH WAR
HALL, WELLS R.	BAL	049	1ST WARD
HALL, WILLAIM	BAL	282	2ND WARD
HALL, WILLIAM	BAL	379	3RD WARD
HALL, WILLIAM	BAL	012	2ND DIST
HALL, WILLIAM	BAL	021	9TH WARD
HALL, WILLIAM	BAL	286	12TH WAR
HALL, WILLIAM	BAL	121	16TH WAR
HALL, WILLIAM	BAL	191	17TH WAR
HALL, WILLIAM	BAL	173	16TH WAR
HALL, WILLIAM	ANN	259	ANNAPOLI
HALL, WILLIAM	BAL	431	8TH WARD
HALL, WILLIAM	BAL	394	14TH WAR
HALL, WILLIAM	BAL	126	18TH WAR
HALL, WILLIAM	FRE	248	NEW MARK
HALL, WILLIAM	BAL	377	13TH WAR
HALL, WILLIAM	CEC	173	6TH E DI
HALL, WILLIAM	CEC	171	6TH E DI
HALL, WILLIAM	CEC	177	7TH E DI
HALL, WILLIAM	HAR	013	1ST DIST
HALL, WILLIAM	KEN	255	1ST DIST
HALL, WILLIAM	WAS	127	HAGERSTO
HALL, WILLIAM	QUE	214	3RD E DI
HALL, WILLIAM	WOR	275	BERLIN 1
HALL, WILLIAM	PRI	035	VANSVILL
HALL, WILLIAM	PRI	047	AQUASCO
HALL, WILLIAM A.	HAR	068	1ST DIST
HALL, WILLIAM A.	BAL	014	4TH WARD
HALL, WILLIAM B.	PRI	066	NOTTINGH
HALL, WILLIAM C.	SOM	354	BRINKLEY
HALL, WILLIAM H.	ANN	307	1ST DIST
HALL, WILLIAM H.	ANN	391	4TH DIST
HALL, WILLIAM J.	ANN	330	2ND DIST
HALL, WILLIAM J.	KEN	286	3RD DIST
HALL, WILLIAM L.	BAL	465	14TH WAR
HALL, WILLIAM M.	ST	310	1ST E DI
HALL, WILLIAM M.	PRI	076	MARLBROU
HALL, WILLIAM P.	PRI	042	VANSVILL
HALL, WILLIAM T.	BAL	326	7TH WARD
HALL, WILLIAM W.	BAL	317	7TH WARD
HALL, WILLIAM-MULATTO	FRE	005	FREDERIC
HALL, ZACHARIAH	BAL	082	15TH WAR
HALL, ZACHARIAH	BAL	062	15TH WAR
HALL, ZADOX	WOR	350	1ST E DI
HALL, ZIPPORAH	WOR	341	1ST E DI
HALL,LETTY	CAL	061	3RD DIST
HALL,NATHAN	BAL	064	2ND DIST
HALL,W ILLIAM	QUE	167	2ND E DI
HALLADAY, DANILE	BAL	471	14TH WAR
HALLADAY, SARAH	DOR	310	1ST DIST
HALLAGAN, MICHAEL	BAL	287	1ST DIST
HALLAM, GEORGE*	SOM	366	BRINKLEY
HALLARAN, JAMES O.	PRI	107	PISCATAW
HALLARAN, RACHAEL	BAL	387	3RD WARD
HALLARD, THOMAS	BAL	200	17TH WAR
HALLAWAY, CAROLLINE	BAL	170	11TH WAR
HALLBENK, JOHN	BAL	056	1ST WARD
HALLEN, GRANVILLE O.	BAL	364	13TH WAR
HALLENSTEIN, JULIAS	BAL	038	18TH WAR
HALLER, ABNER*	BAL	152	19TH WAR
HALLER, ABRAHAM	BAL	327	7TH WARD
HALLER, ANN L.	FRE	022	FREDERIC
HALLER, ANN M.	FRE	006	FREDERIC
HALLER, BENEDICT	BAL	066	15TH WAR
HALLER, CARLENE	FRE	011	FREDERIC
HALLER, CATHERINE	FRE	042	FREDERIC
HALLER, CATHERINE	FRE	050	FREDERIC
HALLER, CHARLES H.	FRE	040	FREDERIC
HALLER, DANIEL	FRE	042	FREDERIC
HALLER, DAVID H.	FRE	016	FREDERIC
HALLER, ELIZABETH	FRE	015	FREDERIC
HALLER, GEORGE	FRE	435	8TH E DI
HALLER, GEORGE W.	FRE	318	MIDDLETO
HALLER, HARMON	FRE	348	MIDDLETO
HALLER, JACOB	BAL	104	18TH WAR
HALLER, JOHN	FRE	050	FREDERIC
HALLER, MARY	FRE	015	FREDERIC
HALLER, MARY M.	FRE	006	FREDERIC
HALLER, MICHAEL H.	FRE	014	FREDERIC
HALLER, NICHOLAS	FRE	024	FREDERIC
HALLER, REUBEN H.	FRE	391	PETERSVI
HALLER, SAMUEL	FRE	003	FREDERIC
HALLER, SAMUEL	FRE	070	FREDERIC
HALLER, SARAH L.	FRE	014	FREDERIC
HALLER, SOPHIA M.	FRE	034	FREDERIC
HALLER, THOMAS	FRE	032	FREDERIC
HALLER, TOBIAS W.	FRE	015	FREDERIC
HALLER,ELIZABETH	FRE	398	JEFFERSO
HALLER,ELIZABETH	FRE	401	JEFFERSO
HALLER,MARY	FRE	003	FREDERIC
HALLES, WILLIAM	ALL	202	CUMBERLA
HALLEY, ALEXANDER-BLACK	BAL	217	2ND WARD
HALLEY, CATHERINE	BAL	001	9TH WARD
HALLEY, ELIZABETH	FRE	002	FREDERIC
HALLEY, LEONARD	FRE	002	FREDERIC
HALLEY, SANDY	BAL	171	1ST WARD
HALLIDAY, MARY JANE	BAL	443	14TH WAR
HALLIDAY, ROBERT	BAL	308	20TH WAR
HALLIGAN, OWEN	BAL	002	9TH WARD
HALLING, DAVID	FRE	014	FREDERIC
HALLING, JAOCB	FRE	013	FREDERIC
HALLING, JOSEPH H.	FRE	022	FREDERIC
HALLING, JOSEPH M.	FRE	022	FREDERIC
HALLMAN, JAMES A.	CEC	137	5TH E DI
HALLOCK, MARY E.*	DOR	455	1ST DIST
HALLON, HENRY	BAL	405	8TH WARD
HALLOWELL, GEORGE	CEC	094	4TH E DI
HALLY, ALEXANDER	CHA	285	BUJANTOW
HALLY, RICHARD	CHA	256	MIDDLETO
HALMAN, JOHN	ALL	172	7TH E.D.
HALMOT, JACOB	BAL	004	9TH WARD
HALOR, JOHN	BAL	411	3TH WARD
HALORAN, ANN	BAL	225	12TH WAR
HALPAN, KATE	BAL	137	19TH WAR
HALPIN, BUORET	MGM	402	ROCKERLE
HALPIN, MARY A.	FRE	385	PETERSVI
HALPIN, MICHAEL	BAL	345	7TH WARD
HALPIN, PATRICK	BAL	345	7TH WARD
HALPIN, THOMAS	BAL	211	2ND WARD
HALPIN,MICHAEL	BAL	022	2ND DIST
HALPINE, THOMAS	BAL	125	1ST WARD
HALSE, WILLIAM P.	BAL	286	7TH WARD
HALSEY, MARGARET	BAL	223	19TH WAR
HALSEY, WILLIAM	BAL	120	1ST WARD
HALSH, PATRICK	ALL	047	10TH E.D
HALSTINE, DAVID	BAL	248	6TH WARD
HALT, PAULUS	ALL	240	CUMBERLA
HALTERN, PRESTON	ALL	095	5TH E.D.
HALTHAUS, HENRY	BAL	229	6TH WARD
HALTON, ANN	BAL	149	11TH WAR
HALTON, CHARLES	BAL	319	7TH WARD
HALTON, MARIA	BAL	408	8TH WARD
HALVEY, JOHN	BAL	291	17TH WAR
HALWALDT, C.	BAL	064	10TH WAR
HALY, JOHN	BAL	449	1ST DIST
HALY, MATILDA	PRI	071	MARLBROU
HALZ, THOMAS	BAL	069	2ND DIST
HAM, DANIEL	BAL	314	20TH WAR
HAM, ELIZABETH*	BAL	377	3RD WARD
HAM, ISABELLA	WAS	141	HAGERSTO
HAM, J.	BAL	158	1ST WARD
HAM, J.	BAL	154	1ST WARD
HAM, JOHN	WAS	197	1ST DIST
HAM, L.O.	WAS	141	HAGERSTO
HAM, MARY A.	CEC	002	ELKTON 3
HAMA, JOHN	HAR	151	3RD DIST
HAMACKER, EPHRAIM	WAS	223	1ST DIST
HAMAKER, ELIZABETH	WAS	250	1ST DIST
HAMAKER, SOLOMON	WAS	250	1ST DIST
HAMAN, JOHN	BAL	172	2ND DIST
HAMAN, MINA	BAL	417	8TH WARD
HAMAN, NANCY	DOR	435	1ST DIST
HAMBACK	BAL	234	12TH WAR
HAMBAUGH, GEORGE	HAR	101	2ND DIST
HAMBAUGH, JOHN	HAR	101	2ND DIST
HAMBAUGH, MICHAEL	HAR	101	2ND DIST
HAMBER, WILLIAM H.	BAL	154	1ST WARD
HAMBERG, H.	BAL	129	1ST WARD
HAMBERGER, A.	BAL	153	5TH WARD
HAMBERGER, HANNAH	ALL	115	5TH E.D.
HAMBERGER, KAUFMAN	BAL	013	9TH WARD
HAMBERRY, JESSE	SOM	534	QUANTICO
HAMBERSON, GEORGE	ALL	024	3RD E.D.
HAMBERTSON, THOAMS	ALL	091	5TH E.D.
HAMBLET, JOHN E.	BAL	272	12TH WAR
HAMBLETON, ADAM-BLACK	QUE	146	1ST E DI
HAMBLETON, ALEXANDER	TAL	073	EASTON T
HAMBLETON, ALEXANDER	TAL	086	ST MICHA
HAMBLETON, ANN	TAL	070	EASTON T
HAMBLETON, EDWARD	QUE	160	2ND E DI
HAMBLETON, EDWARD O.	TAL	075	EASTON T
HAMBLETON, GARRISON-BLACK	CAR	072	NO TWP L
HAMBLETON, GEORGE	CAR	097	NO TWP L
HAMBLETON, GEORGE	QUE	169	2ND E DI
HAMBLETON, JAEMS C.	TAL	088	ST MICHA
HAMBLETON, JAMES	QUE	170	2ND E DI
HAMBLETON, JAMES-BLACK	CAR	086	NO TWP L
HAMBLETON, MARY*	TAL	069	EASTON T
HAMBLETON, MATHEW	TAL	059	EASTON D
HAMBLETON, PERRY	TAL	023	EASTON D
HAMBLETON, PHILIMON	TAL	098	ST MICHA
HAMBLETON, PHILIMON	TAL	099	ST MICHA
HAMBLETON, SAMUEL	TAL	099	ST MICHA
HAMBLETON, SAMUEL	TAL	073	EASTON T
HAMBLETON, SARAH	WOR	227	4TH E DI
HAMBLETON, THOMAS	BAL	427	8TH WARD
HAMBLETON, THOMAS E.	BAL	320	12TH WAR
HAMBLETON, WILLIAM	TAL	101	ST MICHA
HAMBLETON, WILLIAM	HAR	182	3RD DIST
HAMBLETON, WILLIAM-BLACK	CAR	076	NO TWP L
HAMBLIN, ASHER B.	WOR	206	4TH E DI
HAMBLIN, BENJAMIN M.	WOR	203	4TH E DI
HAMBLIN, ELIZA	WOR	266	BERLIN 1
HAMBLIN, ELIZABETH	BAL	145	5TH WARD
HAMBLIN, EMMA	BAL	104	10TH WAR
HAMBLIN, JAMES B.	WOR	213	4TH E DI
HAMBLIN, JAMES N.	WOR	206	4TH E DI
HAMBLIN, JOHN	WOR	253	1ST CENS
HAMBLIN, LOUISA	WOR	233	6TH E DI
HAMBLIN, MARSHALL	WOR	203	4TH E DI
HAMBLIN, NATHANIEL	WOR	207	4TH E DI
HAMBLITON, CHARLOTT	QUE	241	5TH E DI
HAMBURG, ALONZO	BAL	115	5TH WARD
HAMBURG, AMELIA	BAL	115	5TH WARD
HAMBURG, FREDERICK	CAR	234	UNION TO
HAMBURG, JACOB	BAL	421	1ST DIST
HAMBURG, JANE	FRE	055	FREDERIC
HAMBURG, JOHN	CAR	312	1ST DIST
HAMBURG, JOSEPH	CAR	312	1ST DIST
HAMBURG, PETER	CAR	312	1ST DIST
HAMBURG, SIDNEY	FRE	059	FREDERIC
HAMBURG, THOMAS*	SOM	551	TYASKIN
HAMBURG, WILLIAM	BAL	388	3RD WARD
HAMBURGER, ISAAC	BAL	090	10TH WAR
HAMBURGH, ELIZABETH	WAS	257	1ST DIST
HAMBURGH, MARGARET	FRE	148	10TH E D
HAMBURY, BARBARA	FRE	028	FREDERIC
HAMBURY, THOMAS	SOM	546	TYASKIN
HAMBURY, THOMAS*	SOM	551	TYASKIN
HAMBY, ELIZA-MULATTO	BAL	223	2ND WARD
HAMBY, MIRIAN	HAR	136	2ND DIST

Name	County	Page	District
HAMBY, SCOTT	HAR	136	2ND DIST
HAMBY, WILLIAM	HAR	158	3RD DIST
HAME, MARY	ANN	273	ANNAPOLI
HAMEL, ELIZA	BAL	261	1ST DIST
HAMEL, HENRY	BAL	145	1ST WARD
HAMEL, JACOB	BAL	366	8TH WARD
HAMEL, E.	BAL	235	2ND WARD
HAMELIN, EMELINE	BAL	446	8TH WARD
HAMELIN, THOMAS	BAL	146	1ST WARD
HAMELTON, CATHERINE	BAL	392	8TH WARD
HAMELTON, RICHARD	BAL	161	2ND DIST
HAMER, BERTHA	BAL	405	8TH WARD
HAMER, CAROLINE	KEN	241	2ND DIST
HAMER, DANIEL	BAL	271	7TH WARD
HAMER, JOHN	BAL	268	2ND WARD
HAMER, JOHN	BAL	115	1ST WARD
HAMER, JOHN	BAL	165	1ST WARD
HAMER, JOSEPH	BAL	175	6TH WARD
HAMER, LEVI	CEC	034	CHESAPEA
HAMER, MARY	BAL	064	4TH WARD
HAMER, MARY A.	BAL	267	7TH WARD
HAMER, PRISCILLA	FRE	144	10TH E D
HAMER, SAMUEL C.	FRE	144	10TH E D
HAMER, WALTER	CEC	188	7TH E DI
HAMER, WILLIAM H.	BAL	113	15TH WAR
HAMERALTY, ROSA	BAL	011	4TH WARD
HAMERICK, SUSAN	FRE	162	EMMITTSB
HAMERSLAW, ISAAC	WAS	067	2ND SUBD
HAMERSLY, JAMES*	DOR	416	1ST DIST
HAMES, BENJAMIN P. *	BAL	070	18TH WAR
HAMES, JAMES	BAL	427	14TH WAR
HAMES, THOMAS	BAL	058	1ST WARD
HAMESLY, JAMES*	DOR	416	1ST DIST
HAMET, JOHN	BAL	029	9TH WARD
HAMFT, CONRAD	ALL	120	5TH E.D.
HAMFT, LEWIS	ALL	120	5TH E.D.
HAMIGAN, AUGUST	BAL	012	9TH WARD
HAMIL, ALEXANDER	BAL	451	8TH WARD
HAMIL, PHILIP	BAL	338	3RD WARD
HAMILBET, ANN	BAL	144	2ND DIST
HAMILE, ANTONEY	BAL	375	8TH WARD
HAMILL, JACKSON	BAL	218	6TH WARD
HAMILL, JAMES	HAR	078	2ND DIST
HAMILL, JOHN	BAL	376	8TH WARD
HAMILL, JOHN	BAL	136	16TH WAR
HAMILL, PATRICK	BAL	455	1ST DIST
HAMILL, THOMAS	DOR	308	1ST DIST
HAMILL, THOMAS	BAL	206	11TH WAR
HAMILTON, ALEXANDER	CHA	259	MIDDLETO
HAMILTON, ALFRED	BAL	283	7TH WARD
HAMILTON, AMELIA	CHA	251	MIDDLETO
HAMILTON, ANN	HAR	043	1ST DIST
HAMILTON, ANN	BAL	024	4TH WARD
HAMILTON, ANN	BAL	186	6TH WARD
HAMILTON, ANN-BLACK	FRE	200	5TH E DI
HAMILTON, ARCHIBALD	BAL	006	15TH WAR
HAMILTON, BENJAMIN	ANN	427	HOWARD D
HAMILTON, C.	ANN	296	1ST DIST
HAMILTON, CALEB	BAL	044	18TH WAR
HAMILTON, CALIB	BAL	358	1ST DIST
HAMILTON, CATHARINE	WAS	174	FUNKSTOW
HAMILTON, CATHERINE	CEC	198	7TH E DI
HAMILTON, CHARITY	FRE	066	FREDERIC
HAMILTON, CHARLES	BAL	458	1ST DIST
HAMILTON, CHARLES	BAL	146	1ST WARD
HAMILTON, CHARLES	BAL	144	1ST WARD
HAMILTON, D.	BAL	166	1ST WARD
HAMILTON, D.	BAL	164	1ST WARD
HAMILTON, DAVID	BAL	115	1ST WARD
HAMILTON, DAVID	HAR	106	2ND DIST
HAMILTON, DOLLY-BLACK	QUE	201	3RD E DI
HAMILTON, EDWARD	QUE	185	3RD E DI
HAMILTON, EDWARD	HAR	083	2ND DIST
HAMILTON, EDWARDINA	FRE	066	FREDERIC
HAMILTON, ELI	ANN	455	HOWARD D
HAMILTON, ELICK	HAR	040	1ST DIST
HAMILTON, ELIZA ANN	ALL	157	6TH E.D.
HAMILTON, ELIZA ANN	ALL	192	9TH E.D.
HAMILTON, ELIZABETH	ALL	190	9TH E.D.
HAMILTON, ELIZABETH	BAL	308	12TH WAR
HAMILTON, ELIZABETH	HAR	041	1ST DIST
HAMILTON, ELIZABETH	BAL	390	13TH WAR
HAMILTON, ELIZABETH	BAL	418	14TH WAR
HAMILTON, ELIZABETH	WAS	245	SMITHSBU
HAMILTON, ELLEN	BAL	180	19TH WAR
HAMILTON, ELLEN	BAL	264	7TH WARD
HAMILTON, ELVIRA	BAL	467	14TH WAR
HAMILTON, EPHRIAM	BAL	373	1ST DIST
HAMILTON, ESTELLE M.	BAL	101	10TH WAR
HAMILTON, FLORENCE	FRE	053	FREDERIC
HAMILTON, GEORGE	BAL	126	11TH WAR
HAMILTON, GEORGE	HAR	139	2ND DIST
HAMILTON, GEORGE	BAL	171	16TH WAR
HAMILTON, GEORGE	BAL	328	1ST DIST
HAMILTON, GEORGE	ANN	442	HOWARD D
HAMILTON, GEORGE	BAL	171	1ST WARD
HAMILTON, GEORGE W.	BAL	079	15TH WAR
HAMILTON, GIRENY	ANN	276	ANNAPOLI
HAMILTON, GOERGE	ANN	440	HOWARD D
HAMILTON, H.	BAL	161	1ST WARD
HAMILTON, HARRIET	TAL	085	ST MICHA
HAMILTON, HARRIS	CHA	252	BOJANTOW
HAMILTON, HENRY	KEN	271	1ST DIST
HAMILTON, HENRY	BAL	202	6TH WARD
HAMILTON, HENSON	MGM	330	CRACKLIN
HAMILTON, HESTER A.	BAL	417	8TH WARD
HAMILTON, HUGH	BAL	160	1ST WARD
HAMILTON, HUGH	CEC	138	6TH E DI
HAMILTON, JABES	BAL	373	1ST DIST
HAMILTON, JACOB	KEN	306	3RD DIST
HAMILTON, JAMES	WAS	167	1ST DIST
HAMILTON, JAMES	BAL	334	1ST DIST
HAMILTON, JAMES	BAL	296	7TH WARD
HAMILTON, JAMES	ANN	295	1ST DIST
HAMILTON, JAMES	CHA	268	BOJANTOW
HAMILTON, JAMES	BAL	131	11TH WAR
HAMILTON, JAMES	BAL	030	18TH WAR
HAMILTON, JAMES L.	BAL	215	6TH WARD
HAMILTON, JAMES S.	BAL	277	1ST DIST
HAMILTON, JAMES W.-BLACK	MGM	431	CLARKSTR
HAMILTON, JANE	BAL	191	6TH WARD
HAMILTON, JEFFERSON	MGM	389	ROCKERLE
HAMILTON, JERUSHA	BAL	372	1ST DIST
HAMILTON, JOEL	BAL	336	1ST DIST
HAMILTON, JOEL	BAL	423	3RD WARD
HAMILTON, JOHN	BAL	187	19TH WAR
HAMILTON, JOHN	CEC	086	4TH E DI
HAMILTON, JOHN	BAL	347	13TH WAR
HAMILTON, JOHN	CHA	229	MIDDLETO
HAMILTON, JOHN	CEC	205	7TH E DI

Name	County	Page	District
HAMILTON, JOHN	FRE	261	NEW MARK
HAMILTON, JOHN	BAL	121	18TH WAR
HAMILTON, JOHN	BAL	117	1ST WARD
HAMILTON, JOHN	BAL	120	1ST WARD
HAMILTON, JOHN	ALL	187	9TH E.D.
HAMILTON, JOHN	BAL	081	15TH WAR
HAMILTON, JOHN	BAL	197	11TH WAR
HAMILTON, JOHN	KEN	305	3RD DIST
HAMILTON, JOHN	KEN	307	3RD DIST
HAMILTON, JOHN L.	WAS	232	1ST DIST
HAMILTON, JOHN W.	FRE	062	FREDERIC
HAMILTON, JOSEPH	HAR	083	2ND DIST
HAMILTON, JOSEPH	CEC	133	6TH E DI
HAMILTON, JOSEPH	BAL	101	2ND DIST
HAMILTON, LAWTON	BAL	423	3RD WARD
HAMILTON, LEONARD-MULATTO	MGM	431	CLARKSTR
HAMILTON, LEVI	ALL	192	9TH E.D.
HAMILTON, LOUISA	CEC	095	4TH E DI
HAMILTON, LUKEY	BAL	305	12TH WAR
HAMILTON, MAHLON	BAL	198	11TH WAR
HAMILTON, MARGARET	BAL	030	9TH WARD
HAMILTON, MARGARET	BAL	299	20TH WAR
HAMILTON, MARGARET	CEC	198	7TH E DI
HAMILTON, MARIA	PRI	084	QUEEN AN
HAMILTON, MARIA L.	FRE	066	FREDERIC
HAMILTON, MARIAN	BAL	251	1ST DIST
HAMILTON, MARY	BAL	182	6TH WARD
HAMILTON, MARY	BAL	272	12TH WAR
HAMILTON, MARY	BAL	052	9TH WARD
HAMILTON, MARY	BAL	062	10TH WAR
HAMILTON, MARY	ALL	191	9TH E.D.
HAMILTON, MARY	ALL	171	7TH E.D.
HAMILTON, MARY	BAL	364	1ST DIST
HAMILTON, MARY	HAR	078	2ND DIST
HAMILTON, MARY	BAL	181	19TH WAR
HAMILTON, MARY	BAL	136	11TH WAR
HAMILTON, MARY E.	KEN	306	3RD DIST
HAMILTON, MARY H.	FRE	066	FREDERIC
HAMILTON, MAXWELL	BAL	131	18TH WAR
HAMILTON, MAXWELL	ALL	068	5TH E.D.
HAMILTON, MRS.	BAL	002	18TH WAR
HAMILTON, PATRICK	CHA	222	ALLENS F
HAMILTON, PATRICK	BAL	146	16TH WAR
HAMILTON, PHILIP	MGM	338	CRACKLIN
HAMILTON, RACHEL	BAL	055	2ND DIST
HAMILTON, REBECCA	BAL	368	8TH WARD
HAMILTON, RICHARD	BAL	255	2ND WARD
HAMILTON, RICHARD	BAL	146	11TH WAR
HAMILTON, ROBERT	BAL	136	18TH WAR
HAMILTON, ROBERT	BAL	066	15TH WAR
HAMILTON, ROBERT	KEN	309	3RD DIST
HAMILTON, ROSS	BAL	242	6TH WARD
HAMILTON, S. P.	ANN	384	4TH DIST
HAMILTON, SALLY-BLACK	MGM	423	MEDLEY 3
HAMILTON, SAMUEL	KEN	215	2ND DIST
HAMILTON, SAMUEL	ANN	298	1ST DIST
HAMILTON, SAMUEL	BAL	301	12TH WAR
HAMILTON, SAMUEL	PRI	036	VANSVILL
HAMILTON, SAMUEL	WAS	075	2ND SUBD
HAMILTON, SARAH	BAL	126	11TH WAR
HAMILTON, SARAH	CEC	204	6TH E DI
HAMILTON, SARAH	CEC	015	ELKTON 3
HAMILTON, SARAH	BAL	414	14TH WAR
HAMILTON, SARAH J.	BAL	296	7TH WARD
HAMILTON, SUSAN	ALL	212	CUMBERLA
HAMILTON, SUSAN	BAL	188	6TH WARD
HAMILTON, TALBOT	BAL	254	1ST DIST
HAMILTON, THOMAS	BAL	077	1ST WARD
HAMILTON, THOMAS	BAL	447	8TH WARD
HAMILTON, THOMAS	CEC	094	4TH E DI
HAMILTON, THOMAS	KEN	308	3RD DIST
HAMILTON, THOMAS	SOM	381	BRINKLEY
HAMILTON, THOMAS	WAS	126	2ND DIST
HAMILTON, THOMAS B.	BAL	189	2ND WARD
HAMILTON, W.	BAL	063	10TH WAR
HAMILTON, W. S.	BAL	332	1ST DIST
HAMILTON, WASHINGTON	ANN	466	HOWARD D
HAMILTON, WESLEY	BAL	337	1ST DIST
HAMILTON, WILLAIM	BAL	433	1ST DIST
HAMILTON, WILLIAM	BAL	089	2ND DIST
HAMILTON, WILLIAM	BAL	138	11TH WAR
HAMILTON, WILLIAM	BAL	269	1ST DIST
HAMILTON, WILLIAM	BAL	169	2ND DIST
HAMILTON, WILLIAM	ALL	190	9TH E.D.
HAMILTON, WILLIAM	ALL	196	CUMBERLA
HAMILTON, WILLIAM	WAS	067	2ND SUBD
HAMILTON, WILLIAM	CHA	222	ALLENS F
HAMILTON, WILLIAM	CHA	253	MIDDLETO
HAMILTON, WILLIAM	CHA	294	BOJANTOW
HAMILTON, WILLIAM	FRE	044	FREDERIC
HAMILTON, WILLIAM H.	FRE	377	PETERSVI
HAMILTON, WILLIAM H.	KEN	210	2ND DIST
HAMILTON, WILLIAM JR.	BAL	100	10TH WAR
HAMILTON, WILLIAM T.	BAL	061	15TH WAR
HAMILTON, WILLIAM T.	WAS	152	HAGERSTO
HAMILTON, WILLIAM-BLACK	MGM	420	MEDLEY 3
HAMILTON, WOODWARD	BAL	110	18TH WAR
HAMILTON,EMILY	ALL	212	CUMBERLA
HAMILTON.JAMES	BAL	079	2ND DIST
HAMILTON.JOHN	BAL	119	1ST WARD
HAMILTON,WILLIAM J.	BAL	033	1ST WARD
HAMINE, L. F.	BAL	356	13TH WAR
HAMING, THOMAS	BAL	400	14TH WAR
HAMINGTGON, CLAYTON	TAL	115	ST MICHA
HAMKHOUSE, PETER	ALL	215	CUMBERLA
HAMKLIN, JOSHUA	WOR	203	4TH E DI
HAMLER, BARTHOLOMEW	ALL	228	CUMBERLA
HAMLER, ELIZABETH	FRE	174	5TH E DI
HAMLER, JOSEPH	ALL	200	CUMBERLA
HAMLETT, A.	BAL	470	14TH WAR
HAMLEY, MARTHA	HAR	157	3RD DIST
HAMLIN, ALICE	BAL	144	19TH WAR
HAMLIN, GEORGE P.	BAL	001	15TH WAR
HAMLIN, JAMES M.	BAL	001	15TH WAR
HAMLIN, JOHN	BAL	370	8TH WARD
HAMLIN, JOSEPH	ALL	215	CUMBERLA
HAMLIN, JSOEPH	ANN	520	HOWARD D
HAMLIN, REBECCA	BAL	196	17TH WAR
HAMLIN, THOMAS	ALL	204	CUMBERLA
HAMLIN, WILLIAM C.	BAL	144	19TH WAR
HAMM, JOHNR.	QUE	123	1ST E DI
HAMMACK, C. M.	BAL	301	3RD WARD
HAMMAN, ELIZABETH-BLACK	WOR	171	6TH E DI
HAMMAN, JAMES	WOR	177	6TH E DI
HAMMAN, JAMES-BLACK	WOR	171	6TH E DI
HAMMAN, JOSHUA-BLACK	WOR	168	6TH E DI
HAMMAN, JOSHUA-BLAKC	WOR	169	6TH E DI
HAMMAN, LITTLETON	WOR	178	6TH E DI
HAMMAN, MARY	WOR	178	6TH E DI
HAMMAN, PETER-BLACK	WOR	171	6TH E DI

Name	County	Page	District
HAMMAN, SAMUEL	WOR	177	6TH E DI
HAMMAN, WILLIAM	WOR	201	3RD E DI
HAMMAR, LEWIS	BAL	111	15TH WAR
HAMMAR, SARAH	CAR	284	7TH DIST
HAMMEL, ANN-BLACK	CAR	127	NO TWP L
HAMMEL, CASPER	BAL	242	17TH WAR
HAMMEL, CHARLES	ALL	095	5TH E.D.
HAMMEL, HUGH	CEC	051	1ST E DI
HAMMEL, JOHN	BAL	234	2ND WARD
HAMMEL, MR.	BAL	232	17TH WAR
HAMMEL, PHILIP	BAL	382	8TH WARD
HAMMEL, SAMUEL	WAS	297	1ST DIST
HAMMEL, SISTER ROMANNA	FRE	197	5TH E DI
HAMMEL, VALENTINE	BAL	234	6TH WARD
HAMMELL, FRANK	ALL	125	4TH E.D.
HAMMELL, MARY	ALL	125	4TH E.D.
HAMMELL, WILLAIM	CEC	052	1ST E DI
HAMMELTON, MARGARET	WAS	127	2ND DIST
HAMMEN, JOHN	WAS	161	HAGERSTO
HAMMEN, JOHN	FRE	425	8TH E DI
HAMMER, CATHARINE	WAS	131	HAGERSTO
HAMMER, ELIZA	BAL	359	13TH WAR
HAMMER, ELIZABETH	WAS	024	2ND SUBD
HAMMER, GABRIEL	CAR	182	8TH DIST
HAMMER, GERHARD	BAL	359	13TH WAR
HAMMER, JANE A.	BAL	016	18TH WAR
HAMMER, JOHN	BAL	312	3RD WARD
HAMMER, MARCILLA	BAL	157	6TH WARD
HAMMER, MATILDA	BAL	360	13TH WAR
HAMMER, PETER	BAL	295	12TH WAR
HAMMER, SAMUEL	BAL	324	12TH WAR
HAMMER, SUSAN	WAS	131	HAGERSTO
HAMMERPHAN, FREDERICK	BAL	349	13TH WAR
HAMMERSLEY, DAVID L.	BAL	304	7TH WARD
HAMMERSLEY, JAMS	MGM	380	ROCKERLE
HAMMERSMITH, JANE	HAR	116	2ND DIST
HAMMERSTED, ALLEY	WAS	148	HAGERSTO
HAMMERSTOUGH, L.	BAL	321	12TH WAR
HAMMET, DAVID	FRE	129	CREAGERS
HAMMET, JOHN	CHA	286	BOJANTOW
HAMMET, MARY	WAS	142	2ND DIST
HAMMETHWICK, GEORGE	ALL	228	CUMBERLA
HAMMETT, ANN E.	ST	291	2ND E DI
HAMMETT, CHALOTTE	ST	290	2ND E DI
HAMMETT, DAVID	CAR	264	WESTMINS
HAMMETT, E.M.	ST	344	5TH E DI
HAMMETT, EMELINE	ST	307	1ST E DI
HAMMETT, ENOCH	ST	285	2ND E DI
HAMMETT, HENRY	ST	290	2ND E DI
HAMMETT, HENRY	ST	317	4TH E DI
HAMMETT, IGNATIUS	ST	290	2ND E DI
HAMMETT, JAMES L. B.	ST	289	2ND E DI
HAMMETT, JAMES MC HELVA	ST	298	2ND E DI
HAMMETT, JANE M.	ST	344	5TH E DI
HAMMETT, JESSE	BAL	258	1ST DIST
HAMMETT, JOHN B.	ST	283	3RD E DI
HAMMETT, MARY	ST	330	4TH E DI
HAMMETT, MARY L.	ST	320	4TH E DI
HAMMETT, MARY S.	ST	307	1ST E DI
HAMMETT, MC KELVA	ST	299	2ND E DI
HAMMETT, ROBERT	BAL	259	1ST DIST
HAMMETT, ROBERT B.	ST	288	2ND E DI
HAMMETT, S.B.	ST	298	2ND E DI
HAMMETT, WILLIAMT .	ST	318	4TH E DI
HAMMILL, CHARLES	BAL	279	2ND WARD
HAMMILL, HENRY	ALL	066	10TH E.D
HAMMILL, ROBERT	BAL	400	8TH WARD
HAMMILTON, ELIZABETH	BAL	388	3RD WARD
HAMMITT, ABELL	ST	256	3RD E DI
HAMMITT, GEORGE E.	ST	285	2ND E DI
HAMMOCK, EMELINE	CHA	239	HILLTOP
HAMMOCK, JOHN L.	CHA	239	HILLTOP
HAMMON, BARBARA	ALL	234	CUMBERLA
HAMMON, CATHARIEN	CAR	230	5TH DIST
HAMMON, CORA	ALL	257	CUMBERLA
HAMMON, EDWARD	ALL	227	CUMBERLA
HAMMON, GEORGE	BAL	315	3RD WARD
HAMMON, HENERY	HAR	203	3RD DIST
HAMMON, JAMES	ST	296	2ND E DI
HAMMON, JOHN	BAL	048	4TH WARD
HAMMON, JOHN A.	BAL	079	4TH WARD
HAMMON, JOHN W.	BAL	469	14TH WAR
HAMMON, MARY	HAR	062	1ST DIST
HAMMON, NATHANIEL	WOR	271	BERLIN I
HAMMON, ROBERT	ALL	082	5TH E.D.
HAMMON, WILLIAM T.	CAR	184	8TH DIST
HAMMOND, A.	WAS	016	2ND SUBD
HAMMOND, ABSOLAM	ANN	352	3RD DIST
HAMMOND, AGNES	BAL	014	18TH WAR
HAMMOND, ALEXANDER	ANN	474	HOWARD D
HAMMOND, ANDREW	WAS	001	WILLIAMS
HAMMOND, ANN	TAL	038	EASTON O
HAMMOND, ANN	TAL	065	EASTON T
HAMMOND, ANN	ANN	378	4TH DIST
HAMMOND, ANN C.	TAL	073	EASTON T
HAMMOND, BILLY	WOR	330	1ST E DI
HAMMOND, BORDICA	WOR	293	9TH E DI
HAMMOND, BOSS-MULATTO	FRE	436	8TH E DI
HAMMOND, CAROLINE	BAL	375	13TH WAR
HAMMOND, CAROLINE	BAL	259	1ST DIST
HAMMOND, CARROLL	FRE	438	8TH E DI
HAMMOND, CATHARINE	BAL	250	17TH WAR
HAMMOND, CATHARINE	CAR	285	7TH DIST
HAMMOND, CATHERINE	BAL	345	3RD WARD
HAMMOND, CATHERINE	BAL	033	9TH WARD
HAMMOND, CATHERINE	WOR	176	6TH E DI
HAMMOND, CEASER	ANN	351	3RD DIST
HAMMOND, CHARLES	ANN	443	HOWARD D
HAMMOND, CHARLES	ANN	381	4TH DIST
HAMMOND, CHARLES	ANN	337	3RD DIST
HAMMOND, CHARLES	TAL	039	EASTON D
HAMMOND, CHARLES	BAL	014	18TH WAR
HAMMOND, CHARLES E.	BAL	101	15TH WAR
HAMMOND, CHARLES W.	BAL	079	15TH WAR
HAMMOND, CIBBY *	ANN	354	3RD DIST
HAMMOND, CLEVIA	BAL	209	19TH WAR
HAMMOND, DANIEL	BAL	153	19TH WAR
HAMMOND, DANIEL-BLACK	FRE	424	8TH E DI
HAMMOND, DAVID	BAL	104	5TH WARD
HAMMOND, DAVID	WAS	129	HAGERSTO
HAMMOND, DAVID	WAS	196	1ST DIST
HAMMOND, DELILA	WAS	202	1ST DIST
HAMMOND, DENNIS	CAR	363	9TH DIST
HAMMOND, DENTON	FRE	410	8TH E DI
HAMMOND, DENTON	ANN	334	2ND DIST
HAMMOND, DOMINIC	BAL	129	2ND DIST
HAMMOND, EDEN-MULATTO	FRE	429	8TH E DI
HAMMOND, EDWARD	ANN	470	HOWARD D
HAMMOND, EDWARD	BAL	149	2ND DIST
HAMMOND, EDWARD	BAL	154	2ND DIST

HAMMOND, EDWARD TAL 071 EASTON T
HAMMOND, EDWARD-BLACK WOR 323 1ST E DI
HAMMOND, EDWIN WAS 036 2ND SUBD
HAMMOND, EDWIN QUE 155 2ND E DI
HAMMOND, ELIZA BAL 318 3RD WARD
HAMMOND, ELIZA BAL 243 12TH WAR
HAMMOND, ELIZA A. FRE 240 NEW MARK
HAMMOND, ELIZABETH FRE 260 NEW MARK
HAMMOND, ELIZABETH MGM 319 CRACKLIN
HAMMOND, ELIZABETH BAL 156 2ND DIST
HAMMOND, ELIZABETH ANN 432 HOWARD D
HAMMOND, ELIZABETH ANN 423 HOWARD D
HAMMOND, ELIZABETH WOR 263 BERLIN 1
HAMMOND, ELIZABETH WAS 181 BOONSBOR
HAMMOND, ELLEN WAS 020 2ND SUBD
HAMMOND, ELLEN ANN 429 HOWARD D
HAMMOND, ELLEN BAL 166 2ND DIST
HAMMOND, EMILENE-MULATTO BAL 210 2ND WARD
HAMMOND, EMMA FRE 262 NEW MARK
HAMMOND, EVAN D. FRE 260 NEW MARK
HAMMOND, EZKIEL WOR 294 9TH E DI
HAMMOND, GEORG G. BAL 439 14TH WAR
HAMMOND, GEORGE TAL 007 EASTON D
HAMMOND, GEORGE BAL 160 1ST WARD
HAMMOND, GEORGE BAL 176 2ND DIST
HAMMOND, GEORGE BAL 025 15TH WAR
HAMMOND, GEORGE W. BAL 229 12TH WAR
HAMMOND, GEORGE W. ANN 368 4TH DIST
HAMMOND, GOERGE BAL 014 18TH WAR
HAMMOND, GRACEY ANN 354 3RD DIST
HAMMOND, GRAFTIN BAL 158 19TH WAR
HAMMOND, H. BAL 158 1ST WARD
HAMMOND, HANSON WAS 168 FUNKSTOW
HAMMOND, HARRIET BAL 285 1ST DIST
HAMMOND, HARRIET MRS- ANN 333 2ND DIST
HAMMOND, HARRY BAL 159 1ST WARD
HAMMOND, HENRIETTA ANN 381 4TH DIST
HAMMOND, HENRIETTA ANN 277 ANNAPOLI
HAMMOND, HENRY BAL 206 6TH WARD
HAMMOND, HENRY BAL 167 1ST WARD
HAMMOND, HENRY BAL 124 1ST WARD
HAMMOND, HENRY BAL 133 1ST WARD
HAMMOND, HENRY BAL 136 1ST WARD
HAMMOND, HENRY BAL 042 18TH WAR
HAMMOND, HENRY H. QUE 131 1ST E DI
HAMMOND, HENRY-MULATTO BAL 178 2ND WARD
HAMMOND, HESTER BAL 355 3RD WARD
HAMMOND, HESTER ANN 351 3RD DIST
HAMMOND, HETTY WOR 291 9TH E DI
HAMMOND, IRA BAL 243 12TH WAR
HAMMOND, IRA BAL 186 19TH WAR
HAMMOND, ISAAC WOR 279 BERLIN 1
HAMMOND, JACOB BAL 462 1ST DIST
HAMMOND, JAMES BAL 142 2ND DIST
HAMMOND, JAMES BAL 166 1ST WARD
HAMMOND, JAMES TAL 014 EASTON D
HAMMOND, JAMES BAL 208 17TH WAR
HAMMOND, JAMES CEC 164 6TH E DI
HAMMOND, JANE ANN 269 ANNAPOLI
HAMMOND, JANE E. WOR 223 4TH E DI
HAMMOND, JEMIMA FRE 056 FREDERIC
HAMMOND, JENNET ALL 196 CUMBERLA
HAMMOND, JERRY ANN 318 2ND DIST
HAMMOND, JESSE WOR 235 6TH E DI
HAMMOND, JIM WOR 291 9TH E DI
HAMMOND, JOHN WAS 037 2ND SUBD
HAMMOND, JOHN WOR 295 9TH E DI
HAMMOND, JOHN WAS 031 2ND SUBD
HAMMOND, JOHN WAS 183 BOONSBOR
HAMMOND, JOHN WAS 192 1ST DIST
HAMMOND, JOHN WAS 203 1ST DIST
HAMMOND, JOHN QUE 207 3RD E DI
HAMMOND, JOHN ANN 270 ANNAPOLI
HAMMOND, JOHN ANN 343 3RD DIST
HAMMOND, JOHN ANN 480 HOWARD D
HAMMOND, JOHN BAL 071 2ND DIST
HAMMOND, JOHN BAL 247 2ND WARD
HAMMOND, JOHN BAL 292 12TH WAR
HAMMOND, JOHN BAL 241 20TH WAR
HAMMOND, JOHN L. BAL 065 10TH WAR
HAMMOND, JONATHAN PRI 093 MARLBROU
HAMMOND, JOSEPH ANN 342 3RD DIST
HAMMOND, JOSIAH WOR 222 4TH E DI
HAMMOND, JOSIAH WAS 201 1ST DIST
HAMMOND, JULIAN BAL 304 1ST DIST
HAMMOND, JULIANN ANN 362 4TH DIST
HAMMOND, LAZARUS WOR 309 2ND E DI
HAMMOND, LLOYD BAL 470 14TH WAR
HAMMOND, LLOYD-MULATTO FRE 218 BUCKEYST
HAMMOND, LOUISA FRE 445 8TH E DI
HAMMOND, LOUISA WAS 040 2ND SUBD
HAMMOND, LOUISA ANN 421 HOWARD D
HAMMOND, M. BAL 178 19TH WAR
HAMMOND, MARGARET BAL 358 13TH WAR
HAMMOND, MARGARET BAL 094 15TH WAR
HAMMOND, MARGARET WAS 032 2ND SUBD
HAMMOND, MARIA BAL 175 11TH WAR
HAMMOND, MARK WOR 290 9TH E DI
HAMMOND, MARRY WAS 053 2ND SUBD
HAMMOND, MARTHA WOR 283 BERLIN 1
HAMMOND, MARTHA ANN 380 4TH DIST
HAMMOND, MARY ANN 378 4TH DIST
HAMMOND, MARY BAL 153 2ND DIST
HAMMOND, MARY BAL 462 1ST DIST
HAMMOND, MARY WAS 201 1ST DIST
HAMMOND, MARY WAS 136 HAGERSTO
HAMMOND, MARY FRE 258 NEW MARK
HAMMOND, MARY MGM 319 CRACKLIN
HAMMOND, MARY A. BAL 068 18TH WAR
HAMMOND, MARY E. BAL 027 9TH WARD
HAMMOND, MARY E.A.K. FRE 240 NEW MARK
HAMMOND, MARY J. FRE 065 FREDERIC
HAMMOND, MATHIAS ANN 471 HOWARD D
HAMMOND, MATILDA A. ANN 424 HOWARD D
HAMMOND, MAURINE WAS 028 2ND SUBD
HAMMOND, MAYON BAL 159 1ST WARD
HAMMOND, MICHAEL BAL 217 2ND WARD
HAMMOND, MICHAEL WAS 302 1ST DIST
HAMMOND, MINTY BAL 180 16TH WAR
HAMMOND, MIRANDA-BLACK MGM 432 CLARKSTR
HAMMOND, MOSES-MULATTO CAR 364 9TH DIST
HAMMOND, NACE ANN 389 4TH DIST
HAMMOND, NACE ANN 390 4TH DIST
HAMMOND, NANCY BAL 032 9TH WARD
HAMMOND, NANCY CEC 102 4TH E DI
HAMMOND, NANCY WAS 001 WILLIAMS
HAMMOND, NANCY WAS 037 2ND SUBD
HAMMOND, NANCY MGM 443 CLARKSTR
HAMMOND, NATHAN WOR 296 9TH E DI
HAMMOND, NATHAN FRE 260 NEW MARK
HAMMOND, NATHAN C. FRE 258 NEW MARK
HAMMOND, NICHOLAS ANN 282 ANNAPOLI
HAMMOND, OLIVER ANN 362 4TH DIST
HAMMOND, OSMOND TAL 090 ST MICHA
HAMMOND, PAUL-BLACK CAR 127 NO TWP L
HAMMOND, PEER WOR 291 9TH E DI
HAMMOND, PETER WOR 310 2ND E DI
HAMMOND, PETER BAL 131 11TH WAR
HAMMOND, PETER BAL 293 1ST DIST
HAMMOND, PHILIP ALL 217 CUMBERLA
HAMMOND, PHILIP FRE 269 NEW MARK
HAMMOND, PIKE-BLACK FRE 440 8TH E DI
HAMMOND, POWELL WAS 037 2ND SUBD
HAMMOND, PRISCILLA FRE 421 8TH E DI
HAMMOND, PRISCILLA ANN 431 HOWARD D
HAMMOND, PRISCILLA ANN 448 HOWARD D
HAMMOND, RACHAEL BAL 054 4TH WARD
HAMMOND, RACHEL TAL 074 EASTON T
HAMMOND, REZIN ANN 337 3RD DIST
HAMMOND, REZIN ANN 513 HOWARD D
HAMMOND, REZIN ANN 519 HOWARD D
HAMMOND, RICHARD ANN 505 HOWARD D
HAMMOND, RICHARD BAL 317 12TH WAR
HAMMOND, RICHARD T. FRE 295 WOODSBOR
HAMMOND, RICHARD-MULATTO BAL 239 2ND WARD
HAMMOND, ROBERT TAL 075 EASTON T
HAMMOND, SALVAGE BAL 256 12TH WAR
HAMMOND, SARAH BAL 354 7TH WARD
HAMMOND, SARAH BAL 072 15TH WAR
HAMMOND, SARAH TAL 010 EASTON D
HAMMOND, SARAH FRE 313 MIDDLETO
HAMMOND, SARAH C.-BLACK MGM 433 CLARKSTR
HAMMOND, SARHA TAL 082 ST MICHA
HAMMOND, SHADRIC BAL 168 16TH WAR
HAMMOND, SILAS CAR 194 4TH DIST
HAMMOND, SILAS-MULATTO CAR 127 NO TWP L
HAMMOND, SOPHIA BAL 287 7TH WARD
HAMMOND, STEPHEN BAL 160 2ND DIST
HAMMOND, STEPHEN R. WOR 261 BERLIN 1
HAMMOND, SUSANNA R. FRE 438 8TH E DI
HAMMOND, SYBILLA MGM 344 CLARKSBU
HAMMOND, SYLVESTER BAL 122 1ST WARD
HAMMOND, THOMAS BAL 329 7TH WARD
HAMMOND, THOMAS ANN 362 4TH DIST
HAMMOND, THOMAS FRE 445 8TH E DI
HAMMOND, THOMAS FRE 033 FREDERIC
HAMMOND, THOMAS FRE 076 FREDERIC
HAMMOND, THOMAS TAL 037 EASTON D
HAMMOND, THOMAS C. BAL 050 9TH WARD
HAMMOND, THOMAS-BLACK CAR 127 NO TWP L
HAMMOND, TILGHMAN TAL 049 EASTON T
HAMMOND, TILGHMAN TAL 048 EASTON T
HAMMOND, TURNER * WOR 298 9TH E DI
HAMMOND, UPTON J. FRE 438 8TH E DI
HAMMOND, VACHAEL CAR 363 9TH DIST
HAMMOND, WALTER C. FRE 243 NEW MARK
HAMMOND, WASHINGTON FRE 262 NEW MARK
HAMMOND, WILLEYTA FRE 268 NEW MARK
HAMMOND, WILLIAM FRE 278 NEW MARK
HAMMOND, WILLIAM CAL 023 2ND DIST
HAMMOND, WILLIAM BAL 041 4TH WARD
HAMMOND, WILLIAM BAL 434 14TH WAR
HAMMOND, WILLIAM WOR 290 9TH E DI
HAMMOND, WILLIAM MGM 443 CLARKSTR
HAMMOND, WILLIAM WAS 048 2ND SUBD
HAMMOND, WILLIAM WAS 051 2ND SUBD
HAMMOND, WILLIAM WOR 235 6TH E DI
HAMMOND, WILLIAM ANN 349 3RD DIST
HAMMOND, WILLIAM ANN 448 HOWARD D
HAMMOND, WILLIAM BAL 140 2ND DIST
HAMMOND, WILLIAM BAL 154 5TH WARD
HAMMOND, WILLIAM L. FRE 303 WOODSBOR
HAMMOND, WILLIAM M. BAL 187 11TH WAR
HAMMOND, WILLIAM P. FRE 240 NEW MARK
HAMMOND, WILLIAM R. WOR 259 BERLIN 1
HAMMOND, WILLIAM T. QUE 207 3RD E DI
HAMMOND,JOHN CAR 373 9TH DIST
HAMMOND,MARGARET ALL 206 CUMBERLA
HAMMONDS, CATHARINE WAS 012 WILLIAMS
HAMMONDS, JOHN WOR 279 BERLIN 1
HAMMONDS, PATZY BAL 325 3RD WARD
HAMMONDS, SAMPSON WOR 249 1ST CENS
HAMMONOTREE, JOHN PRI 027 VANSVILL
HAMMONS, BILL WOR 249 1ST CENS
HAMMONS, JACOB BAL 458 1ST DIST
HAMMONS, MARGARET WOR 249 1ST CENS
HAMMONS, MARY WOR 302 SNOW HIL
HAMMONS, SARAH BAL 058 15TH WAR
HAMMONSON, JOSEPH WOR 306 2ND E DI
HAMMONTREE, HENRY BAL 042 15TH WAR
HAMMUSHLOUGH, JULIUS BAL 382 13TH WAR
HAMNER, CRISTIAN BAL 061 18TH WAR
HAMNER, ELISABETH ALL 213 CUMBERLA
HAMNER, JOHN G. REV. BAL 380 13TH WAR
HAMON, JOHN C. QUE 152 1ST E DI
HAMOND, JAMES BAL 279 2ND WARD
HAMONDTREE, MARY BAL 084 18TH WAR
HAMONDTREE, WILLIAM W. BAL 084 18TH WAR
HAMPEY, ADOLPH BAL 421 3RD WARD
HAMPEY, ELLEN BAL 281 17TH WAR
HAMPHILL, DANIEL WAS 056 2ND SUBD
HAMPHILL, HENRY WAS 054 2ND SUBD
HAMPIN, FREDERICK BAL 117 5TH WARD
HAMPSEY, MARY BAL 327 7TH WARD
HAMPSHIRE, GEORGE BAL 219 6TH DIST
HAMPSHIRE, JACOB W. BAL 209 6TH DIST
HAMPSHIRE, JOHN BAL 203 6TH DIST
HAMPSHIRE, JOHN BAL 456 1ST DIST
HAMPSHIRE, JOSEPH D. BAL 202 6TH DIST
HAMPSHIRE, NANCY BAL 201 6TH DIST
HAMPSON, A. J. BAL 061 10TH WAR
HAMPSON, CHARLES BAL 424 14TH WAR
HAMPSON, MARY BAL 189 11TH WAR
HAMPTINAN, HENIRETTA BAL 241 12TH WAR
HAMPTMAN, JOHN BAL 198 19TH WAR
HAMPTON, ANNA B. BAL 062 10TH WAR
HAMPTON, JESSE BAL 349 1ST DIST
HAMPTON, JOHN BAL 207 17TH WAR
HAMPTON, JOHN QUE 230 4TH E DI
HAMPTON, JOHN C. BAL 282 20TH WAR
HAMPTON, LEVI BAL 281 20TH WAR
HAMPTON, LYDIA BAL 242 12TH WAR
HAMPTON, ROBERT QUE 231 4TH E DI
HAMPTON, SAMUEL QUE 246 5TH E DI
HAMRICK, GEORGE FRE 293 WOODSBOR
HAMRY, ISAAC CEC 063 1ST E DI
HAMSBURGH, CAROLINE WAS 257 1ST DIST
HAMSEY, J. BAL 151 1ST WARD
HAMSEY, JANE BAL 152 11TH WAR
HAMSLEY, HESTER QUE 217 3RD E DI
HAMSLEY, LEIGHER DOR 366 3RD DIVI
HAMSON, SUSAN TAL 109 ST MICHA
HAMSWORTH, MARSILLA WAS 294 1ST DIST
HANA, PHEBE BAL 334 13TH WAR
HANAGAN, ANN BAL 463 1ST DIST
HANAGAN, CATHERINE FRE 105 CREAGERS
HANAGAN, CHARLES BAL 261 2ND WARD
HANAGAN, JONATHAN CEC 127 5TH E DI
HANAGAN, MARGARET BAL 261 2ND WARD
HANAGAN, MARTIN ALL 185 9TH E.D.
HANAGAN, MATILDA BAL 460 1ST DIST
HANAH, ROBERT BAL 345 7TH WARD
HANAHAN, JAMES ALL 140 6TH E.D.
HANAHAN, PATRICK ALL 056 10TH E.D
HANAHAN, PATRICK ALL 048 10TH E.D
HANAY, JACOB KEN 301 3RD DIST
HANAY, JOHN B. BAL 283 20TH WAR
HANBEL, AUGUST BAL 428 8TH WARD
HANBERT, SUSAN R. L. BAL 362 13TH WAR
HANBURY, THOMAS BAL 091 10TH WAR
HANBY, MARY A. BAL 067 2ND DIST
HANCE, AARON BAL 433 1ST DIST
HANCE, ELIZA BAL 264 17TH WAR
HANCE, ELIZABETH PRI 092 MARLBROU
HANCE, FRANCES CAL 016 1ST DIST
HANCE, JAMES BAL 175 16TH WAR
HANCE, JAMES B. KEN 289 3RD DIST
HANCE, JOHN CAL 016 1ST DIST
HANCE, KINSY CAL 033 2ND DIST
HANCE, LEWISA CAL 015 1ST DIST
HANCE, MARVEL ST 345 5TH E DI
HANCE, PERRY KEN 249 2ND DIST
HANCE, RICHARD CAL 024 2ND DIST
HANCE, SAMUEL BAL 238 17TH WAR
HANCE, SARAH CEC 002 ELKTON 3
HANCE, SETH S. BAL 096 10TH WAR
HANCE, T.C. CAL 034 2ND DIST
HANCE, THOMAS CEC 033 CHESAPEA
HANCE, WILLIAM CEC 081 CHARLEST
HANCE, WILLIAM G. BAL 279 2ND WARD
HANCE, YOUNG D. CAL 034 2ND DIST
HANCHERY, JOSHUA FRE 253 NEW MARK
HANCK, CAROLINE BAL 227 12TH WAR
HANCKS, OLIVER* BAL 326 3RD WARD
HANCOCK, ABSALOM* BAL 417 3RD WARD
HANCOCK, CHARLES A. ANN 352 3RD DIST
HANCOCK, DANIEL WOR 321 1ST E DI
HANCOCK, ISABELLA BAL 006 9TH WARD
HANCOCK, JAMES BAL 073 1ST WARD
HANCOCK, JAMES WOR 320 1ST E DI
HANCOCK, JARRET ANN 359 3RD DIST
HANCOCK, JOHN ANN 348 3RD DIST
HANCOCK, JOHN BAL 005 9TH WARD
HANCOCK, JOHN BAL 133 1ST WARD
HANCOCK, JOHN BAL 153 1ST WARD
HANCOCK, JOHN BAL 160 1ST WARD
HANCOCK, JOHN FRE 124 CREAGERS
HANCOCK, MAJOR WOR 329 1ST E DI
HANCOCK, MARIA BAL 257 17TH WAR
HANCOCK, MARSELENA BAL 350 7TH WARD
HANCOCK, ORLANDO ANN 357 3RD DIST
HANCOCK, RACHEL ANN 345 3RD DIST
HANCOCK, SAMUEL BAL 069 2ND DIST
HANCOCK, SAMUEL-MULATTO BAL 214 2ND WARD
HANCOCK, SARAH E. BAL 257 17TH WAR
HANCOCK, SUSAN BAL 051 4TH WARD
HANCOCK, WELTHY WOR 335 1ST E DI
HANCOCK, WESLEY ANN 348 3RD DIST
HANCOCK, WILLIAM BAL 012 9TH WARD
HANCOCK, WILLIAM WOR 321 1ST E DI
HANCOCK, WILLIAM FRE 119 CREAGERS
HANCOCK, WILLIAM FRE 130 CREAGERS
HANCOCK, WILLIAM BAL 298 17TH WAR
HANCOCKS, JOHN BAL 081 4TH WARD
HANCOKE, SUSAN BAL 288 17TH WAR
HANCY, JOHN BAL 214 17TH WAR
HANCY, LITTLETON D. SOM 362 BRINKLEY
HAND, ALEXANDER BAL 315 12TH WAR
HAND, ANN BAL 285 20TH WAR
HAND, CATHARINE KEN 255 1ST DIST
HAND, CATHARINE BAL 109 5TH WARD
HAND, E. X. J. DR- BAL 368 1ST DIST
HAND, HANNAH CEC 042 CHESAPEA
HAND, HENRY BAL 399 3RD WARD
HAND, JOHN BAL 275 7TH WARD
HAND, JOHN BAL 173 1ST WARD
HAND, JONOTHAN S. KEN 214 2ND DIST
HAND, JOSEPH QUE 193 3RD E DI
HAND, LENA BAL 048 15TH WAR
HAND, LEVI FRE 111 CREAGERS
HAND, LIDIA TAL 042 EASTON D
HAND, MARGARET BAL 283 20TH WAR
HAND, MARGARET A. BAL 399 3RD WARD
HAND, MARY TAL 069 EASTON T
HAND, NICHOLAS BAL 156 16TH WAR
HAND, RACHEL D. TAL 069 EASTON T
HAND, SAMUEL ST 308 1ST E DI
HAND, SAMUEL FRE 107 CREAGERS
HAND, SAMUEL FRE 130 CREAGERS
HAND, THOMAS BAL 143 1ST WARD
HAND, THOMAS J. BAL 338 13TH WAR
HAND, THOMAS R. BAL 207 19TH WAR
HAND, WILLIAM CAR 107 NO TWP L
HAND, WILLIAM ALL 243 CUMBERLA
HAND, WILLIAM QUE 198 3RD E DI
HANDCOCK, ALEXANDER CHA 220 ALLENS F
HANDCOCK, HETTY WOR 264 BERLIN 1
HANDCOCK, JAMES WOR 316 2ND E DI
HANDCOCK, JOHN WOR 306 2ND E DI
HANDCOCK, JOHN C. CHA 268 BOJANTOW
HANDCOCK, JOHN T. WOR 234 6TH E DI
HANDCOCK, JOSIAS CHA 290 BOJANTOW
HANDCOCK, LEVI WOR 325 1ST E DI
HANDCOCK, R. S. CHA 248 HILLTOP
HANDCOCK, S. R. CHA 217 ALLENS F
HANDCOCK, SAY CHA 247 HILLTOP
HANDCOCK, WALTER CHA 279 BOJANTOW
HANDCOCK, WILLIAM WOR 220 4TH E DI
HANDCOCK, WILLIAM BAL 370 1ST DIST
HANDCORK, JOHN* TAL 014 EASTON D
HANDEY, CHARLES FRE 273 NEW MARK
HANDISAM, PURDY* TAL 058 EASTON D
HANDKERFER, GARARD CHA 228 ALLENS F
HANDLE, DENNIS FRE 130 CREAGERS
HANDLE, JOHN WAS 025 2ND SUBD
HANDLELON, CORNELIUS CEC 062 1ST E DI
HANDLY, DEWIT C. DOR 433 1ST DIST
HANDLY, HARIATE DOR 430 1ST DIST
HANDLY, MARY* DOR 453 1ST DIST
HANDLY, JOHN D. KEN 253 1ST DIST

Name	County	Page	District
HANDLY, JOSEPH	DOR	364	3RD DIVI
HANDLY, WILLIAM C.	DOR	432	1ST DIST
HANDRAKING, SARAH	BAL	011	4TH WARD
HANDRATTER, CATHERINE	BAL	034	4TH WARD
HANDS, ALEXANDER	TAL	065	EASTON T
HANDS, AUGUST	BAL	237	17TH WAR
HANDS, DENTON	ANN	379	4TH DIST
HANDS, ELIZABETH	ANN	478	HOWARD D
HANDS, GEORGE	BAL	289	12TH WAR
HANDS, GEORGE THOMAS	BAL	146	5TH WARD
HANDS, JANE	BAL	145	5TH WARD
HANDS, JOHN	BAL	355	8TH WARD
HANDS, LOUISA	MGM	438	CLARKSTR
HANDS, MICHAEL	BAL	302	12TH WAR
HANDS, TABITTA	BAL	063	4TH WARD
HANDSON, HENERETTA	CHA	270	ALLENS F
HANDSON, ISACK	CHA	248	HILLTOP
HANDSON, JONAS	CHA	246	HILLTOP
HANDSON, JOSIAS	CHA	262	MIDDLETO
HANDSON, MARY	CHA	231	HILLTOP
HANDSON, SAMUEL	CHA	245	HILLTOP
HANDSON, SUSAN	CHA	246	HILLTOP
HANDST, EDWARD	BAL	279	7TH WARD
HANDWRIGHT, WESLEY	CEC	150	PORT DUP
HANDY, AILSA	WOR	230	6TH E DI
HANDY, ANN	SOM	386	BRINKLEY
HANDY, ANN	SOM	390	BRINKLEY
HANDY, ANN MARIE	BAL	376	13TH WAR
HANDY, ANNA	BAL	053	9TH WARD
HANDY, CALEB	SOM	393	BRINKLEY
HANDY, CAROLINE	BAL	075	15TH WAR
HANDY, CAROLINE	BAL	260	12TH WAR
HANDY, CAROLINE	BAL	420	3RD WARD
HANDY, CAROLINE C.	SOM	503	SALISBUR
HANDY, CATHERINE	DOR	377	1ST DIST
HANDY, CEZAR-BLACK	CAR	068	NO TWP L
HANDY, CHALRES	BAL	135	18TH WAR
HANDY, CHARITY	WAS	155	HAGERSTO
HANDY, CHARLES	TAL	030	EASTON D
HANDY, EASTER	WAS	158	HAGERSTO
HANDY, EBENEZER	WOR	230	6TH E DI
HANDY, EDWARD	SOM	429	PRINCESS
HANDY, EDWARD	BAL	180	11TH WAR
HANDY, EDWARD H.	BAL	095	18TH WAR
HANDY, ELIZABETH	DOR	304	1ST DIST
HANDY, ELLEN	BAL	062	10TH WAR
HANDY, ELLEN	BAL	149	5TH WARD
HANDY, G. M.	BAL	332	1ST DIST
HANDY, GEORGE	SOM	426	PRINCESS
HANDY, GEORGE	BAL	269	20TH WAR
HANDY, GEORGE	SOM	387	BRINKLEY
HANDY, GEORGE	SOM	385	BRINKLEY
HANDY, GEORGE	SOM	354	BRINKLEY
HANDY, GEORGE	SOM	359	BRINKLEY
HANDY, GEORGE D. S.	KEN	241	2ND DIST
HANDY, GEORGE W.	BAL	081	18TH WAR
HANDY, GERUTHA	BAL	040	1ST WARD
HANDY, HANNAH	SOM	387	BRINKLEY
HANDY, HENERETTA	SOM	363	BRINKLEY
HANDY, HENRY	WOR	181	6TH E DI
HANDY, HENRY	BAL	132	1ST WARD
HANDY, HENRY S.	SOM	387	BRINKLEY
HANDY, HESTER	WOR	304	SNOW HIL
HANDY, ISAAC C.	SOM	388	BRINKLEY
HANDY, ISABELA	BAL	147	11TH WAR
HANDY, J.T.	BAL	199	11TH WAR
HANDY, JACOB	SOM	427	PRINCESS
HANDY, JACOB	SOM	489	SALISBUR
HANDY, JAMES	SOM	396	BRINKLEY
HANDY, JAMES	BAL	023	1ST WARD
HANDY, JESSE T.	BAL	403	14TH WAR
HANDY, JOHN	WOR	178	6TH E DI
HANDY, LEAH-BLACK	WOR	339	1ST E DI
HANDY, LEVIN	SOM	437	DAMES QU
HANDY, LEVIN	BAL	054	9TH WARD
HANDY, LINA*	DOR	305	1ST DIST
HANDY, MARGARET	BAL	001	1ST WARD
HANDY, MARGARET	SOM	355	BRINKLEY
HANDY, MARTHA	SOM	359	BRINKLEY
HANDY, MARTHA	KEN	215	2ND DIST
HANDY, MARY	BAL	091	18TH WAR
HANDY, MARY	WOR	241	1ST CENS
HANDY, MARY	BAL	149	5TH WARD
HANDY, MARY	BAL	214	6TH WARD
HANDY, MINTA	BAL	273	17TH WAR
HANDY, PERE-BLACK	QUE	200	3RD E DI
HANDY, PHOEBE	BAL	269	20TH WAR
HANDY, PRICILLA	BAL	149	19TH WAR
HANDY, PRISCILLA	WAS	299	1ST DIST
HANDY, RACHEL	BAL	168	19TH WAR
HANDY, SAMUEL K. DR-	SOM	428	PRINCESS
HANDY, SAMUEL*	DOR	303	1ST DIST
HANDY, SARAH	BAL	376	13TH WAR
HANDY, STEPHEN-BLACK	QUE	202	3RD E DI
HANDY, THOMAS	SOM	387	BRINKLEY
HANDY, THOMAS H.	DOR	374	1ST DIST
HANDY, WASHINGTON R.	BAL	020	4TH WARD
HANDY, WILLAIM W.	SOM	472	TRAPPE D
HANDY, WILLIAM	SOM	460	HANGARY
HANDY, WILLIAM	BAL	167	1ST WARD
HANDY, WILLIAM	BAL	062	10TH WAR
HANDY, WILLIAM	BAL	140	1ST WARD
HANDY, WILLIAM H.	WAS	125	HAGERSTO
HANDY, WILLIAM J.	SOM	366	BRINKLEY
HANDY, WILLIAM W.	BAL	063	15TH WAR
HANE, CHRISTIANA	BAL	179	16TH WAR
HANE, JACOB D.	FRE	014	FREDERIC
HANE, JOHN	FRE	251	NEW MARK
HANE, JOHN	FRE	035	FREDERIC
HANE, JOHN	BAL	187	5TH DIST
HANEE, JESSE J.	CAL	005	1ST DIST
HANELLIN, GEORGE	BAL	021	18TH WAR
HANELY, ROSE	BAL	206	11TH WAR
HANER, DANIEL J.	FRE	398	JEFFERSO
HANER, JACOB	BAL	107	1ST WARD
HANERWOOD, LAVINA *	BAL	321	12TH WAR
HANES, BENJAMIN	CAR	206	4TH DIST
HANES, CHARLES-MULATTO	CAR	165	NO TWP L
HANES, DAVID	CEC	034	CHESAPEA
HANES, DAVID	HAR	093	2ND DIST
HANES, EDWARD	CAR	192	4TH DIST
HANES, ELIZA	BAL	159	19TH WAR
HANES, EMANUEL	FRE	096	FREDERIC
HANES, FLOYD-BLACK	CAR	118	NO TWP L
HANES, FRANCIS	CAR	225	5TH DIST
HANES, HARRIET-BLACK	CAR	074	NO TWP L
HANES, HENRY-BLACK	CAR	164	NO TWP L
HANES, JACOB	FRE	087	FREDERIC
HANES, JACOB	HAR	127	2ND DIST
HANES, JACOB	BAL	312	7TH WARD
HANES, JOHN-BLACK	CAR	118	NO TWP L
HANES, JOSEPH	CAR	194	4TH DIST
HANES, JOSEPH *	WAS	069	2ND SUBD
HANES, LEWIS-BLACK	CAR	113	NO TWP L
HANES, LUSIA	CAR	195	4TH DIST
HANES, MALINDA	ANN	370	4TH DIST
HANES, MARGARET	FRE	024	FREDERIC
HANES, MARY	WAS	062	2ND SUBD
HANES, MARY E.	BAL	159	19TH WAR
HANES, PHILIP	WAS	160	2ND DIST
HANES, RACHEL	BAL	029	18TH WAR
HANES, RACHEL	BAL	353	1ST DIST
HANES, WASHINGTON-BLACK	CAR	134	NO TWP L
HANES, WILLIAM	CAR	206	4TH DIST
HANES, WILLIAM	CAR	194	4TH DIST
HANESON, GEORGE	BAL	118	1ST WARD
HANESON, H.	ALL	152	6TH E.D.
HANESON, PEURE	CEC	063	1ST E DI
HANEST, WILLIAM	ALL	179	7TH E.D.
HANEWELL, JOHN	BAL	137	5TH WARD
HANEY, ALVERA	BAL	141	11TH WAR
HANEY, BENJAMIN	MGM	399	ROCKERLE
HANEY, CAROLINE	BAL	031	15TH WAR
HANEY, ELIZABETH	BAL	020	15TH WAR
HANEY, FRANCES	BAL	410	3RD WARD
HANEY, FRANCIS	SOM	460	HANGARY
HANEY, ISAAC-BLACK	CAR	081	NO TWP L
HANEY, JACOB	BAL	133	18TH WAR
HANEY, JAMES	FRE	090	FREDERIC
HANEY, JAMES	BAL	458	8TH WARD
HANEY, JAMES	BAL	061	2ND DIST
HANEY, JANE	ALL	217	CUMBERLA
HANEY, JANE	ALL	229	CUMBERLA
HANEY, JOHN	BAL	438	8TH WARD
HANEY, JOHN	BAL	064	4TH WARD
HANEY, JOHN	ST	254	3RD E DI
HANEY, LEWIS H.	FRE	323	MIDDLETO
HANEY, MICHAEL	ALL	053	10TH E.D
HANEY, MR.*	BAL	321	3RD WARD
HANEY, PATRICK	ALL	048	10TH E.D
HANEY, SARAH	BAL	215	11TH WAR
HANEY, WILLIAM	BAL	325	3RD WARD
HANEY, WILLIAM	BAL	140	16TH WAR
HANEY, WILLIAM A.	BAL	006	1ST WARD
HANFTLING, GEORGE	BAL	087	15TH WAR
HANFTLING, MARY	BAL	087	15TH WAR
HANGER, HENRY	BAL	207	2ND WARD
HANGLY, MRS.	PRI	075	MARLBROU
HANGMELL, HENRY	BAL	198	6TH WARD
HANGTREY, BARNEY	HAR	103	2ND DIST
HANIES, ELIJAH P.	FRE	271	NEW MARK
HANIES, ELIZABETH MISS-*	BAL	315	20TH WAR
HANIGANE, PATRICK	BAL	101	18TH WAR
HANIHAROT, MARY *	BAL	133	18TH WAR
HANIKEN, ELIZ	BAL	249	12TH WAR
HANILTON, MARY	BAL	300	20TH WAR
HANINGTON, JAMES E.	BAL	275	2ND WARD
HANK, INDEPENDENT	BAL	304	1ST DIST
HANK, J. NEWMAN	MGM	374	ROCKERLE
HANK, JANE SP.B.	MGM	406	MEDLEY 3
HANK, JAMES	BAL	215	6TH DIST
HANK, JOHN	WOR	301	SNOW HIL
HANK, WILLIAM	FRE	447	8TH E DI
HANKEY, ANN *	BAL	225	6TH WARD
HANKEY, FREDERICK	FRE	109	CREAGERS
HANKEY, GEORGE	FRE	116	CREAGERS
HANKEY, HENRY	BAL	070	4TH WARD
HANKEY, JACOB	FRE	366	CATOCTIN
HANKEY, JUSTIANNA	FRE	214	BUCKEYST
HANKEY, MARY	FRE	142	CREAGERS
HANKEY, PETER	FRE	107	CREAGERS
HANKFELT, ANTHONY	FRE	077	FREDERIC
HANKIN, HARMAN	BAL	063	2ND DIST
HANKINS, WILLAIM	BAL	151	1ST WARD
HANKLEY, ELIZABETH	BAL	023	4TH WARD
HANLAN, BRIDGET	BAL	201	11TH WAR
HANLAND, JAMES	BAL	373	8TH WARD
HANLAUFF, HENRY	BAL	253	2ND WARD
HANLAY, VALENTINE	BAL	283	12TH WAR
HANLEA, WILLIAM	BAL	123	1ST WARD
HANLEN, JOHN	BAL	231	17TH WAR
HANLEY, DANIEL	BAL	318	7TH WARD
HANLEY, ELIZA	BAL	319	7TH WARD
HANLEY, JOHN	BAL	285	1ST DIST
HANLEY, JOHN	BAL	144	1ST WARD
HANLEY, MARY	BAL	322	12TH WAR
HANLEY, MARY MRS-	BAL	315	20TH WAR
HANLEY, PHILLIP	FRE	138	CREAGERS
HANLEY, STEURNT *	BAL	222	12TH WAR
HANLEY, THOMAS	BAL	276	1ST DIST
HANLEY, MAGADLINE	FRE	203	5TH E DI
HANLIN, CHRISTY	BAL	312	1ST DIST
HANLIN, DAVID	BAL	281	20TH WAR
HANLIN, MARTIN	ALL	053	10TH E.D
HANLON, MARY S. D.	BAL	153	11TH WAR
HANLON, PATRICK	BAL	206	11TH WAR
HANLON, THOMAS	BAL	443	14TH WAR
HANLY, DANIEL	BAL	449	1ST DIST
HANLY, EDMUND	BAL	469	14TH WAR
HANLY, WILLIAM	DOR	299	1ST DIST
HANLY, OWEN	BAL	020	2ND DIST
HANMESBY, DANIEL	BAL	280	2ND WARD
HANMIS, WILLIAM	BAL	364	13TH WAR
HANN, ABRAHAM	CAR	408	2ND DIST
HANN, CATHARINE	CAR	409	2ND DIST
HANN, HENRY	FRE	159	EMMITTSB
HANN, HENRY	CAR	378	2ND DIST
HANN, HUGH	CAR	390	2ND DIST
HANN, ISAAC	CAR	325	1ST DIST
HANN, JAMES H.	BAL	168	16TH WAR
HANN, JESSE	CAR	408	2ND DIST
HANN, LOUISA	BAL	271	12TH WAR
HANN, MARTHA	FRE	319	MIDDLETO
HANN, MATHIAS	CAR	378	2ND DIST
HANN, PHILIP	CAR	323	1ST DIST
HANN, PHILIP SR.	CAR	242	TANEYTOW
HANN, WILLIAM H.	CAR	391	2ND DIST
HANNA, ACALINE	WAS	266	1ST DIST
HANNA, ALEXANDER	BAL	039	4TH WARD
HANNA, ALFRED	BAL	297	3RD WARD
HANNA, ANDREW	CEC	077	NORTHEAS
HANNA, BENJAMIN	CEC	166	6TH E DI
HANNA, BETHSHEBA T.	BAL	001	4TH WARD
HANNA, CATHARINE	WAS	228	1ST DIST
HANNA, CHARLES	BAL	077	4TH WARD
HANNA, DRUSILLA	WAS	298	1ST DIST
HANNA, GEORGE L.	FRE	253	NEW MARK
HANNA, GERDGE	BAL	231	6TH WARD
HANNA, HUGH BELL *	BAL	311	1ST DIST
HANNA, ISAAC N.	WAS	170	FUNKSTOW
HANNA, JANE	BAL	095	10TH WAR
HANNA, JENNE	BAL	212	11TH WAR
HANNA, JOANNA	CAR	397	2ND DIST
HANNA, JOHN C.	HAR	094	2ND DIST
HANNA, JOSEPH	CEC	172	6TH E DI
HANNA, MARTHA	FRE	043	FREDERIC
HANNA, MICHAEL	ALL	051	10TH E.D
HANNA, NATHAN	CAR	396	2ND DIST
HANNA, ROBERT	WAS	228	1ST DIST
HANNA, RUAN	WAS	231	1ST DIST
HANNA, SAMUEL	CEC	123	3RD E DI
HANNA, SAMUEL	BAL	034	9TH WARD
HANNA, THOMAS H.	BAL	360	13TH WAR
HANNA, WILLIAM	FRE	253	NEW MARK
HANNA, WILLIAM	BAL	239	20TH WAR
HANNA, WILLIAM	BAL	193	11TH WAR
HANNAGAN, JOHN	ALL	053	10TH E.D
HANNAGAN, PHILIP	BAL	281	1ST DIST
HANNAGAN, THOMAS	BAL	102	18TH WAR
HANNAH, BALSH	HAR	094	2ND DIST
HANNAH, CATHARINE	BAL	409	14TH WAR
HANNAH, JAMES	BAL	008	4TH WARD
HANNAH, JANE	ANN	422	HOWARD D
HANNAH, JOHN	HAR	094	2ND DIST
HANNAH, JOHN	HAR	116	2ND DIST
HANNAH, LAURENCE	BAL	060	15TH WAR
HANNAH, MARGARETT	BAL	459	1ST DIST
HANNAH, MARY	BAL	432	14TH WAR
HANNAH, MARY	WAS	155	2ND DIST
HANNAH, MATTHEW	MGM	315	CRACKLIN
HANNAH, RACHEL	BAL	439	1ST DIST
HANNAH, ROBERT	HAR	116	2ND DIST
HANNAH, ROBERT	HAR	094	2ND DIST
HANNAH, ROBERT	WAS	152	2ND DIST
HANNAH, SAMUEL C.	BAL	368	8TH WARD
HANNAH, SARAH	FRE	423	8TH E DI
HANNAH, THOMAS	BAL	345	1ST DIST
HANNAH, WILLIAM	BAL	224	1ST DIST
HANNAH, WILLIAM	HAR	094	2ND DIST
HANNAH, WILLIAM	HAR	084	2ND DIST
HANNAH, WILLIAM	HAR	141	2ND DIST
HANNAH, WILLIAM F.	HAR	075	BEL AIR
HANNAH, W ILLIAM	ALL	188	9TH E.D.
HANNAHAN, FRANCES	ALL	077	5TH E.D.
HANNAMAN, JESSE	BAL	006	4TH WARD
HANNAN, ANN	BAL	191	11TH WAR
HANNAN, AUGUSTUS	BAL	310	3RD WARD
HANNAN, CHRISTIAN	FRE	132	CREAGERS
HANNAN, FRANCIS	BAL	349	3RD WARD
HANNAN, HENRY-BLACK	WOR	173	6TH E DI
HANNAN, JACOB	WAS	048	2ND SUBD
HANNAN, JOHN H.-BLACK	WOR	175	6TH E DI
HANNAN, JOHN-BLACK	WOR	172	6TH E DI
HANNAN, WILLIAM H. *	BAL	079	18TH WAR
HANNO, IRENE	BAL	002	15TH WAR
HANNEGAN, BARNEY	BAL	263	6TH WARD
HANNEGAN, BIDDY	BAL	274	1ST DIST
HANNEGAN, BRIDGET	BAL	050	9TH WARD
HANNEGAN, CATHARINE	BAL	470	14TH WAR
HANNEGAN, MICHAEL	ALL	110	5TH E.D.
HANNEGAR, CHRISTOPHER	ALL	231	CUMBERLA
HANNER, CHRISTIAN	FRE	155	10TH E D
HANNER, ELIZABETH	FRE	151	10TH E D
HANNER, PETER	FRE	155	10TH E D
HANNER, WILLIAM	BAL	037	1ST WARD
HANNES, GEORGE	BAL	122	1ST WARD
HANNEY, JOHN F.	BAL	025	1ST WARD
HANNEY, MARY A.	BAL	165	16TH WAR
HANNICK, JACOB C.	BAL	006	1ST WARD
HANNIGAN, ANN	BAL	262	6TH WARD
HANNIKER, HARMON	BAL	009	9TH WARD
HANNING, ANN	BAL	104	10TH WAR
HANNNAKAN, BRIDGET	ALL	203	CUMBERLA
HANNOMO, HETTY	BAL	290	12TH WAR
HANNON, ANN	BAL	183	2ND WARD
HANNON, HENRY	CHA	232	HILLTOP
HANNON, HENRY V.	CHA	259	MIDDLETO
HANNON, LYSTAIN	BAL	079	1ST WARD
HANNON, NOEL B.	CHA	257	MIDDLETO
HANNOX, THOMAS	BAL	087	2ND DIST
HANNUEL, WILLIAM	BAL	054	1ST WARD
HANNY, JAMES T.	BAL	003	1ST WARD
HANOD, ELIZA A.	BAL	033	1ST WARD
HANOGAN, CECILIA	BAL	278	1ST DIST
HANOR, HAMILTON	SOM	483	TRAPP DI
HANOT, JOSEPH	BAL	191	19TH WAR
HANOVAN, EDWARD	BAL	376	8TH WARD
HANP, JOSEPH	BAL	031	1ST WARD
HANPITT, D.*	BAL	271	20TH WAR
HANPITT, EVA	BAL	271	20TH WAR
HANPT, JHN	BAL	207	2ND WARD
HANRAY, MARY	BAL	449	1ST DIST
HANRIN, HENRY	BAL	304	17TH WAR
HANRIN, MARY	BAL	304	17TH WAR
HANRITY, PATRICK	BAL	068	4TH WARD
HANS, CASPAR*	BAL	087	10TH WAR
HANS, JOHN	BAL	170	16TH WAR
HANSBERBER, I.	BAL	329	13TH WAR
HANSBERGER, MRS.	BAL	329	13TH WAR
HANSBERRY, RACHEAL	WAS	161	HAGERSTO
HANSCHELDT, JACOB P.	BAL	123	1ST WARD
HANSCHILD, HANRICH	BAL	123	1ST WARD
HANSCK, ROBERT	ALL	188	9TH E.D.
HANSE, ERNEST	ALL	120	5TH E.D.
HANSEL, ADAM W.	CEC	138	6TH E DI
HANSEL, DAVID	CEC	075	NORTHEAS
HANSEL, SOLOMON	ALL	111	5TH E.D.
HANSELL, PHILEMON	BAL	161	19TH WAR
HANSEN, CHRISTIAN	BAL	354	1ST DIST
HANSEN, LOUISA	KEN	211	2ND DIST
HANSERSMITH, JOHN	CEC	196	6TH E DI
HANSHAW, AMOS	CEC	210	7TH E DI
HANSHEN, JOHN	FRE	046	FREDERIC
HANSHEW, HENRY	FRE	011	FREDERIC
HANSLER, CHARLES	BAL	030	9TH WARD
HANSLEY, RICHARD	QUE	219	3RD E DI
HANSLING, PETER *	BAL	329	13TH WAR
HANSDER, RACHEL	BAL	334	13TH WAR
HANSON, ALEXANDER	WAS	161	HAGERSTO
HANSON, ALFRED	WAS	166	HAGERSTO
HANSON, ANDREW	BAL	421	1ST DIST
HANSON, ANDREW	ANN	338	3RD DIST
HANSON, ANN	BAL	156	11TH WAR
HANSON, AQUILLA	BAL	137	2ND DIST
HANSON, BECILLA	FRE	057	FREDERIC
HANSON, BENEDICT H.	HAR	116	2ND DIST
HANSON, BENJAMIN	KEN	278	1ST DIST
HANSON, CHARLES	BAL	166	1ST WARD
HANSON, CHARLES G.	ANN	426	HOWARD D
HANSON, CHARLES W.	BAL	353	7TH WARD

Name	County	Page	District
HANSON, D.	BAL	172	1ST WARD
HANSON, E.J.	WAS	021	2ND SUBD
HANSON, EDWARD L.	BAL	419	1ST DIST
HANSON, ELI	BAL	175	2ND DIST
HANSON, ELIAS	BAL	095	5TH WARD
HANSON, ELIZA	BAL	227	6TH WARD
HANSON, ELIZXA	KEN	254	1ST DIST
HANSON, EMILY	BAL	136	5TH WARD
HANSON, F. R.	CAL	031	2ND DIST
HANSON, FORD B.	HAR	116	2ND DIST
HANSON, GEORGE	QUE	179	2ND E DI
HANSON, GEORGE	WAS	149	HAGERSTO
HANSON, GOERGE H.	BAL	295	7TH WARD
HANSON, HARRIET	BAL	274	2ND WARD
HANSON, HENRY	BAL	171	1ST WARD
HANSON, HENRY	BAL	286	2ND WARD
HANSON, HENRY	KEN	256	1ST DIST
HANSON, HENRY	CEC	015	ELKTON 3
HANSON, JAMES	HAR	188	3RD DIST
HANSON, JAMES	WAS	177	1ST DIST
HANSON, JOHN	WAS	166	HAGERSTO
HANSON, JOHN	CEC	016	ELKTON 3
HANSON, JOHN	BAL	298	3RD WARD
HANSON, JOHN	BAL	364	3RD WARD
HANSON, JOHN	ANN	310	1ST DIST
HANSON, JOHN F.	BAL	235	6TH WARD
HANSON, JOHN M.	BAL	295	7TH WARD
HANSON, JOHN P.	BAL	065	15TH WAR
HANSON, JOSIAS H.	ANN	312	1ST DIST
HANSON, LLOYD	FRE	387	PETERSVI
HANSON, LUCY	HAR	079	2ND DIST
HANSON, MARGARET	ALL	177	7TH E.D.
HANSON, MARIAH	KEN	303	3RD DIST
HANSON, MARTHA	ANN	289	ANNAPOLI
HANSON, MARY	BAL	250	6TH WARD
HANSON, MARY	BAL	110	10TH WAR
HANSON, MARY	WAS	279	LEITERSB
HANSON, MATHIAS	WAS	030	2ND SUBD
HANSON, NATHAN	BAL	020	2ND DIST
HANSON, NATHANIEL	BAL	424	1ST DIST
HANSON, NEILL	BAL	068	1ST WARD
HANSON, PETER	BAL	056	4TH WARD
HANSON, PHEBE	BAL	463	14TH WAR
HANSON, RACHEL	BAL	261	6TH WARD
HANSON, SAMUEL	KEN	256	1ST DIST
HANSON, SARAH	BAL	054	4TH WARD
HANSON, THOMAS	WAS	282	1ST DIST
HANSON, THOMAS	WAS	157	HAGERSTO
HANSON, THOMAS	BAL	006	1ST WARD
HANSON, THOMAS	BAL	234	6TH WARD
HANSON, WASHINGTON R.	BAL	319	7TH WARD
HANSON, WILLIAM	BAL	123	1ST WARD
HANSON, WILLIAM	BAL	296	7TH WARD
HANSON, WILLIAM	WAS	169	FUNKSTOW
HANSON, WILLIAM E.	BAL	065	4TH WARD
HANSON,A.B.	FRE	025	FREDERIC
HANSON,PETER	BAL	173	1ST WARD
HANSTEN, JOSEPH	BAL	121	1ST WARD
HANTER, JOHN	CEC	033	CHESAPEA
HANTINGBAYER, ELIZABETH	BAL	071	4TH WARD
HANTZ, CATHERINE*	BAL	331	3RD WARD
HANUS, WILLIAM	BAL	298	3RD WARD
HANVANDI, MARTIN *	WAS	049	2ND SUBD
HANWAY, DAVID	HAR	057	1ST DIST
HANWAY, JOSEPH	HAR	051	1ST DIST
HANWAY, PETER	BAL	224	12TH WAR
HANWAY, SAMUEL	HAR	091	2ND DIST
HANWAY, THOMAS	HAR	100	2ND DIST
HANWAY, THOMAS	HAR	099	2ND DIST
HANWAY, WASHINGTON	HAR	051	1ST DIST
HAPBERT, EMORY	CEC	075	NORTHEAS
HAPE, JACOB	FRE	290	WOODSBOR
HAPE, WILLIAM	CAR	402	2ND DIST
HAPELD, WILLIAM*	DOR	412	1ST DIST
HAPENNER, JOHN	BAL	445	8TH WARD
HAPER, DAVID	CAR	327	1ST DIST
HAPET, HENRY*	TAL	019	EASTON D
HAPETE, ELIZABETH*	DOR	412	1ST DIST
HAPFELD, HENRY	BAL	354	13TH WAR
HAPLER, SIDNEY A.	FRE	411	8TH E DI
HAPNER, MARGARET	BAL	123	18TH WAR
HAPPE, CHRISTOPHER	HAR	061	1ST DIST
HAPPINKS, S.	BAL	130	1ST WARD
HAPPMAN, NICHOLAS	BAL	336	13TH WAR
HAPPMAN, VALENTINE*	BAL	084	4TH WARD
HAPPOLD, GEORGE	BAL	012	15TH WAR
HAPPOLDT, DANIEL J.	BAL	224	6TH WARD
HAPPRAN, GEORGE V.	BAL	081	4TH WARD
HAPPS, CATNIP	BAL	380	8TH WARD
HAPSMAN, ANDREW	BAL	276	1ST DIST
HAPSTENER, LAWRENCE	BAL	224	2ND WARD
HARA, JOHN D.	BAL	355	8TH WARD
HARADA, CHARLES	CEC	039	CHESAPEA
HARADMAN, NICHOLAS	BAL	133	1ST WARD
HARALL, S.	ANN	342	3RD DIST
HARB, PETER	BAL	332	7TH WARD
HARBACK, F.	BAL	152	1ST WARD
HARBAN, JAMES	ANN	496	HOWARD D
HARBAUGH, ANDREW	WAS	256	1ST DIST
HARBAUGH, ANN	FRE	147	10TH E D
HARBAUGH, ANN ELIZABETH	FRE	147	10TH E D
HARBAUGH, BENJAMIN	FRE	143	10TH E D
HARBAUGH, BENJAMIN	BAL	355	3RD WARD
HARBAUGH, CARTON	FRE	314	MIDDLETO
HARBAUGH, CATHARINE	FRE	192	5TH E DI
HARBAUGH, CHARLES	FRE	157	10TH E D
HARBAUGH, CHARLES	BAL	215	5TH DIST
HARBAUGH, CHRIST	FRE	116	CREAGERS
HARBAUGH, DANIEL	FRE	147	10TH E D
HARBAUGH, DAVID	FRE	150	10TH E D
HARBAUGH, DAVID	FRE	093	FREDERIC
HARBAUGH, ELIAS	FRE	147	10TH E D
HARBAUGH, ELIZABETH	FRE	148	10TH E D
HARBAUGH, ELIZABETH	FRE	110	CREAGERS
HARBAUGH, ELIZABETH	CAR	236	UNION TO
HARBAUGH, HENERITTA	FRE	114	CREAGERS
HARBAUGH, HENRY	FRE	147	10TH E D
HARBAUGH, HENRY	FRE	195	5TH E DI
HARBAUGH, JACOB	FRE	148	10TH E D
HARBAUGH, JAMES	BAL	306	7TH WARD
HARBAUGH, JAMES P.	FRE	141	CREAGERS
HARBAUGH, JEREMIAH	FRE	195	5TH E DI
HARBAUGH, JEREMIAH	WAS	256	1ST DIST
HARBAUGH, JEROME	BAL	066	18TH WAR
HARBAUGH, JOHN	FRE	146	10TH E D
HARBAUGH, JOHN	WAS	283	1ST DIST
HARBAUGH, JOHN C.	FRE	145	10TH E D
HARBAUGH, JOHN C.	FRE	194	5TH E DI
HARBAUGH, JONOTHAN	WAS	257	1ST DIST
HARBAUGH, JOSEPH	FRE	143	10TH E D
HARBAUGH, L. H.	FRE	145	10TH E D
HARBAUGH, LEONARD	FRE	146	10TH E D
HARBAUGH, LEVI	FRE	117	CREAGERS
HARBAUGH, LEWIS M.	WAS	148	HAGERSTO
HARBAUGH, LOUIS A.	FRE	288	WOODSBOR
HARBAUGH, LUCINDA	FRE	143	10TH E D
HARBAUGH, MARGARET	FRE	147	10TH E D
HARBAUGH, MARY E.	ALL	026	2ND E.D.
HARBAUGH, MARY JANE	FRE	175	5TH E DI
HARBAUGH, MATTHEW	FRE	254	NEW MARK
HARBAUGH, MORGAN	FRE	312	MIDDLETO
HARBAUGH, SAMUEL G.	FRE	314	MIDDLETO
HARBAUGH, SARAH	CAR	234	UNION TO
HARBAUGH, SOLOMON	FRE	144	10TH E D
HARBAUGH, THOMAS	BAL	353	7TH WARD
HARBAUGH, THOMAS H.	BAL	355	3RD WARD
HARBAUGH, VALENTINE	FRE	146	10TH E D
HARBAUGH, YOST	FRE	157	10TH E D
HARBECK, W.	BAL	119	5TH WARD
HARBERT, ALBERT	KEN	259	1ST DIST
HARBERT, LEWIS	BAL	023	9TH WARD
HARBESAN, JAMES	BAL	257	1ST DIST
HARBET, ADAM	BAL	096	1ST WARD
HARBIN, BENJAMIN	CHA	292	BOJANTOW
HARBIN, L.	PRI	061	NOTTINGH
HARBIN, RICHARD	CHA	292	BOJANTOW
HARBIN, ROBERT	CHA	218	ALLENS F
HARBIN, WALTER	CHA	279	BOJANTOW
HARBIN, WILLIAM S.	FRE	244	NEW MARK
HARBINE, ELIZABETH	WAS	102	2ND DIST
HARBOCX, LEWIS	WAS	084	2ND SUBD
HARBOUGH, ELI	FRE	147	10TH E D
HARBOUGH, GEORGE S.	CAR	229	5TH DIST
HARBRICK, JOHN	ALL	224	CUMBERLA
HARBSTRITH, SISTER MARY	FRE	198	5TH E DI
HARBURK, LYDIA	BAL	051	9TH WARD
HARBURT, WILLIAM F.	BAL	046	9TH WARD
HARBY, MAHALA	BAL	458	1ST DIST
HARCRAY, ELIZABETH	BAL	117	5TH WARD
HARCUM, C. C.	BAL	279	2ND WARD
HARD, EDWARD D.	ANN	488	HOWARD D
HARD, MARY E.	CAL	045	3RD DIST
HARD, POLLY	ANN	485	HOWARD D
HARDACKER, ELIZABETH	CAL	040	3RD DIST
HARDBAUER, WILLIAM	FRE	007	FREDERIC
HARDCARTH, ROBERT E.	CAR	079	NO TWP L
HARDCASTLE, ABRAHAM-BLACK	QUE	183	3RD E DI
HARDCASTLE, ALEXANDER	CAR	094	NO TWP L
HARDCASTLE, EDWARD	CAR	142	NO TWP L
HARDCASTLE, EDWARD M.	TAL	056	EASTON D
HARDCASTLE, EDWIN	QUE	191	3RD E DI
HARDCASTLE, ELIZA	BAL	045	9TH WARD
HARDCASTLE, HARIATT	DOR	462	1ST DIST
HARDCASTLE, JOHN A.	QUE	198	3RD E DI
HARDCASTLE, MARCUS	BAL	284	7TH WARD
HARDCASTLE, MILMAN	DOR	311	1ST DIST
HARDCASTLE, MILMAN	DOR	320	1ST DIST
HARDCASTLE, MORTIMER	QUE	211	3RD E DI
HARDCASTLE, ROBERT H.	QUE	206	3RD E DI
HARDCASTLE, SARAH C.	QUE	128	1ST E DI
HARDCASTLE, SIMON	DOR	307	1ST DIST
HARDCASTLE, WALTER D.	QUE	191	3RD E DI
HARDCASTLE, WILLIAM	CAR	082	NO TWP L
HARDCASTLE, WILLIAM M.	CAR	082	NO TWP L
HARDE, CONRAD	BAL	217	19TH WAR
HARDE, JEREMIAH	BAL	158	11TH WAR
HARDELL, GEORGE	BAL	168	19TH WAR
HARDEN, BENEDICT	CHA	274	ALLENS F
HARDEN, BRIDGET	BAL	299	7TH WARD
HARDEN, CALEB	BAL	196	19TH WAR
HARDEN, CAROLINE	BAL	457	1ST DIST
HARDEN, CHAMBERS*	TAL	006	EASTON D
HARDEN, CHARELS	ALL	101	5TH E.D.
HARDEN, CHARLES	ANN	472	HOWARD D
HARDEN, DELILA	ANN	471	HOWARD D
HARDEN, ELIZA	BAL	374	13TH WAR
HARDEN, ELIZABETH	ANN	471	HOWARD D
HARDEN, FRANCIS A.	ST	335	4TH E DI
HARDEN, GEORGE	ALL	097	5TH E.D.
HARDEN, HARRIET	BAL	344	3RD WARD
HARDEN, HARRIET	CAR	232	5TH DIST
HARDEN, HENRIETTA	ST	318	4TH E DI
HARDEN, HENRY	KEN	262	1ST DIST
HARDEN, HENRY	CAR	199	4TH DIST
HARDEN, HENRY	BAL	448	14TH WAR
HARDEN, HENRY J.	TAL	026	EASTON D
HARDEN, J.	BAL	109	10TH WAR
HARDEN, JACOB	BAL	319	1ST DIST
HARDEN, JAMES	BAL	311	12TH WAR
HARDEN, JAMES	TAL	068	EASTON T
HARDEN, JAMS	ALL	101	5TH E.D.
HARDEN, JESSE	BAL	041	9TH WARD
HARDEN, JOHN	ALL	097	5TH E.D.
HARDEN, JOHN E.	ST	340	5TH E DI
HARDEN, JOHN L.	BAL	362	13TH WAR
HARDEN, JOHN W.	ST	318	4TH E DI
HARDEN, JOSEPH E.	CAR	215	5TH DIST
HARDEN, JULIA A.	ST	319	4TH E DI
HARDEN, KATE	BAL	228	1ST DIST
HARDEN, LEAH	BAL	389	13TH WAR
HARDEN, MARGARET	BAL	320	3RD WARD
HARDEN, MARGARET	TAL	048	EASTON T
HARDEN, MARY	BAL	462	14TH WAR
HARDEN, NICHOLAS L. F.	CAR	214	5TH DIST
HARDEN, PENELOPE	BAL	196	19TH WAR
HARDEN, PERRY	BAL	179	2ND DIST
HARDEN, PHIL	BAL	226	1ST DIST
HARDEN, PRECILIA	CAR	188	4TH DIST
HARDEN, RACHEL	BAL	449	14TH WAR
HARDEN, RACHEL	BAL	220	1ST DIST
HARDEN, RICHARD	BAL	344	3RD WARD
HARDEN, RICHARD	ANN	461	HOWARD D
HARDEN, ROBERT	ANN	515	HOWARD D
HARDEN, SAMUEL G.	CAR	214	5TH DIST
HARDEN, SARAH	BAL	356	1ST DIST
HARDEN, SARAH	ALL	090	5TH E.D.
HARDEN, SARAH E.	ANN	471	HOWARD D
HARDEN, SNOWDEN	CAR	229	5TH DIST
HARDEN, SOPHIA	BAL	227	1ST DIST
HARDEN, STEPHEN	ANN	474	HOWARD D
HARDEN, THOMAS	ANN	369	4TH DIST
HARDEN, THOMAS	TAL	009	EASTON D
HARDEN, WILLIAM	CAR	214	5TH DIST
HARDEN, WILLIAM	KEN	248	2ND DIST
HARDEN, WILLIAM	CHA	261	MIDDLETO
HARDEN, ZACHARIA	ANN	443	HOWARD D
HARDER, HENNY	BAL	390	1ST DIST
HARDER, HENRY	HAR	175	3RD DIST
HARDER, JERRY	BAL	141	11TH WAR
HARDER, MOSES	BAL	224	1ST DIST
HARDER, NATHAN	BAL	238	1ST DIST
HARDERLY, ELIZA	CAL	040	3RD DIST
HARDERSP, NATHAN*	ALL	185	9TH E.D.
HARDESLY, CHARLES C.	ST	323	4TH E DI
HARDESTA, THOMAS	CAL	001	1ST DIST
HARDESTAY, A.	PRI	080	QUEEN AN
HARDESTER, GRACEY, A.	BAL	288	7TH WARD
HARDESTER, HENRY	BAL	197	6TH WARD
HARDESTER, MARY	BAL	032	15TH WAR
HARDESTIR, DAVID	BAL	375	3RD WARD
HARDESTY, ACHSAH	BAL	283	7TH WARD
HARDESTY, ALBERT	ANN	369	4TH DIST
HARDESTY, ANDREW V.*	TAL	004	EASTON D
HARDESTY, ANN L.	ST	259	3RD E DI
HARDESTY, ANN P.	ST	269	3RD E DI
HARDESTY, BENJAMIN	BAL	052	4TH WARD
HARDESTY, CAROLINE	MGM	331	CRACKLIN
HARDESTY, CHARLES R.	BAL	048	15TH WAR
HARDESTY, D.	PRI	112	PISCATAW
HARDESTY, DANILE	CAL	022	2ND DIST
HARDESTY, EDWARD	ANN	312	1ST DIST
HARDESTY, EDWARD D.*	TAL	003	EASTON D
HARDESTY, ELIZA	ANN	380	4TH DIST
HARDESTY, ELIZABETH	ANN	447	HOWARD D
HARDESTY, ELIZABETH	MGM	371	BERRYS D
HARDESTY, ESSIE	ANN	317	1ST DIST
HARDESTY, FRANCIES	MGM	368	BERRYS D
HARDESTY, GEORGE	PRI	087	QUEEN AN
HARDESTY, GEORGE	ST	324	4TH E DI
HARDESTY, GEORGE W.	CAL	032	2ND DIST
HARDESTY, HENRY	BAL	151	11TH WAR
HARDESTY, HENRY	ANN	400	8TH DIST
HARDESTY, JACOB	MGM	371	BERRYS D
HARDESTY, JAMES H.	ANN	268	ANNAPOLI
HARDESTY, JAMES R.	ST	262	3RD E DI
HARDESTY, JOHN	PRI	044	VANSVILL
HARDESTY, JOHN	ANN	349	3RD DIST
HARDESTY, JOHN	CAR	109	NO TWP L
HARDESTY, JOHN J.	BAL	345	3RD WARD
HARDESTY, JOHN W.	ANN	349	3RD DIST
HARDESTY, JOSEPH	CAL	037	2ND DIST
HARDESTY, JOSEPH	CAL	020	2ND DIST
HARDESTY, JOSEPH J.	CAL	020	2ND DIST
HARDESTY, L. YOUNG	CAL	029	2ND DIST
HARDESTY, MARGARET	CAL	059	3RD DIST
HARDESTY, MARY	CAL	055	3RD DIST
HARDESTY, MARY	BAL	006	18TH WAR
HARDESTY, MATHEW	ANN	394	8TH DIST
HARDESTY, MATILDA	BAL	042	4TH WARD
HARDESTY, NICHOLAS	ANN	368	4TH DIST
HARDESTY, PRISCELLA	CAL	020	2ND DIST
HARDESTY, RICHARD	CAL	054	3RD DIST
HARDESTY, RICHARD	ANN	294	1ST DIST
HARDESTY, RICHARD S.	BAL	425	14TH WAR
HARDESTY, ROBERT	CAL	056	3RD DIST
HARDESTY, SAMUEL	CAL	054	3RD DIST
HARDESTY, SAMUEL	MGM	397	ROCKERLE
HARDESTY, THOMAS	MGM	353	BERRYS D
HARDESTY, THOMAS	BAL	124	1ST WARD
HARDESTY, THOMAS	PRI	037	VANSVILL
HARDESTY, THOMAS	ST	283	3RD E DI
HARDESTY, THOMAS G.	ANN	409	8TH DIST
HARDESTY, WASHINGTON	MGM	331	CRACKLIN
HARDESTY, WESTLEY	BAL	307	3RD WARD
HARDESTY, WILLIAM	ANN	304	1ST DIST
HARDESTY, WILLIAM	ANN	316	1ST DIST
HARDESTY, WILLIAM	CAL	058	3RD DIST
HARDESTY, WILLIAM P.	CAL	057	3RD DIST
HARDESTY, WILLIAM T.	CAL	061	3RD DIST
HARDESTY, WILLIAM T.	TAL	067	EASTON T
HARDEUS, ELLEN	QUE	240	5TH E DI
HARDEY, DAVID	CAL	022	2ND DIST
HARDEY, MARY	ANN	517	HOWARD D
HARDFELLOW, HENRY	ALL	197	CUMBERLA
HARDFORD, WASHINGTON	BAL	208	11TH WAR
HARDICAN, SAMUEL	DOR	349	3RD DIVI
HARDIE, ALICE	BAL	372	3RD WARD
HARDIE, EMILY*	BAL	372	3RD WARD
HARDIN, CATHERINE	BAL	430	8TH WARD
HARDIN, CHARLOTT	BAL	137	5TH WARD
HARDIN, ELIZA	ST	261	3RD E DI
HARDIN, ELIZABETH	DOR	422	1ST DIST
HARDIN, ELIZABETH	DOR	434	1ST DIST
HARDIN, HARVY	DOR	422	1ST DIST
HARDIN, HENRY	BAL	240	20TH WAR
HARDIN, J.	BAL	048	9TH WARD
HARDIN, JAMES	BAL	430	8TH WARD
HARDIN, JAMES	DOR	444	1ST DIST
HARDIN, JOHN	MGM	356	BERRYS D
HARDIN, JOHN	BAL	430	8TH WARD
HARDIN, JOSEPH	MGM	355	BERRYS D
HARDIN, LEAH	BAL	043	2ND DIST
HARDIN, MARIA	BAL	114	2ND DIST
HARDIN, MATTHEW	DOR	427	1ST DIST
HARDIN, RICHARD	KEN	211	2ND DIST
HARDIN, ROBERT	DOR	412	1ST DIST
HARDIN, SALEY	DOR	456	1ST DIST
HARDIN, SANDY	BAL	197	17TH WAR
HARDIN, WILLIAM	ALL	089	5TH E.D.
HARDIN, WILLIAM	DOR	409	1ST DIST
HARDIN, WILLIAM	DOR	446	1ST DIST
HARDIN, WILLIAM	CAR	268	WESTMINS
HARDIN, WILLIAM H.	CEC	124	5TH E DI
HARDIN,MARY	BAL	239	12TH WAR
HARDING, ANN	BAL	283	12TH WAR
HARDING, ANN	BAL	283	12TH WAR
HARDING, ANN	CAR	274	7TH DIST
HARDING, ASBURY	ANN	448	HOWARD D
HARDING, CARLINE P.	FRE	034	FREDERIC
HARDING, CLEMENT	DOR	317	1ST DIST
HARDING, CONRAD	ALL	150	6TH E.D.
HARDING, DUSILLA F.	ANN	421	HOWARD D
HARDING, EDWARD	ANN	520	HOWARD D
HARDING, GEORGE	ALL	084	5TH E.D.
HARDING, HENRIETTA	FRE	242	NEW MARK
HARDING, HENRY	MGM	376	ROCKERLE
HARDING, JAMES M.	FRE	012	FREDERIC
HARDING, JANE	BAL	070	4TH WARD
HARDING, JOHN	FRE	253	NEW MARK
HARDING, JOHN	ANN	457	HOWARD D
HARDING, JOHN	ANN	422	HOWARD D
HARDING, JOHN L.	FRE	019	FREDERIC
HARDING, JOHNSON	MGM	401	ROCKERLE
HARDING, JOSEPH	ANN	420	HOWARD D
HARDING, JOSEPH	ANN	476	HOWARD D
HARDING, JOSEPH	ANN	520	HOWARD D
HARDING, JOSIAH	MGM	359	BERRYS D
HARDING, LOYD F.	MGM	421	MEDLEY 3
HARDING, MATHEW	BAL	248	17TH WAR
HARDING, NICHOLAS	ANN	473	HOWARD D

NAME	CO	PAGE	DISTRICT
HARDING, NORMAN B.	FRE	009	FREDERIC
HARDING, OLIVER	FRE	253	NEW MARK
HARDING, PEYTON	MGM	385	ROCKERLE
HARDING, PHILIP	FRE	252	NEW MARK
HARDING, REBECA A.	BAL	279	7TH WARD
HARDING, RICHARD	BAL	316	7TH WARD
HARDING, RICHARD A.	MGM	422	MEDLEY 3
HARDING, SAMUEL	BAL	273	17TH WAR
HARDING, SAMUEL	ANN	480	HOWARD D
HARDING, SARAH	FRE	230	BUCKEYST
HARDING, STEPHEN	KEN	281	3RD DIST
HARDING, VACHEL	ANN	518	HOWARD D
HARDING, WALTIS	BAL	258	12TH WAR
HARDING, WESLEY	BAL	247	17TH WAR
HARDING, WILLIAM	FRE	253	NEW MARK
HARDING, WILLIAM	ANN	484	HOWARD D
HARDIS, EDWARD	WOR	302	SNOW HIL
HARDIS, RACHEL A.	BAL	365	3RD WARD
HARDISTY, J.H.	PRI	104	PISCATAW
HARDISTY, RICHARD	PRI	086	QUEEN AN
HARDISTY, WILLIAM H.	BAL	095	18TH WAR
HARDMAN, ANDREW	BAL	170	2ND DIST
HARDMAN, CAROLINE	FRE	298	WOODSBOR
HARDMAN, CANIEL	ANN	349	3RD DIST
HARDMAN, GEORGE	FRE	301	WOODSBOR
HARDMAN, MAJOR	CAL	009	1ST DIST
HARDMAN, N.	BAL	165	1ST WARD
HARDMAN, NICHOLAS	BAL	134	1ST WARD
HARDMAN, PHILIP	FRE	161	EMMITTSB
HARDMAN, THOMAS	CAL	027	2ND DIST
HARDMAN, THOMAS	CAL	041	3RD DIST
HARDNACHT, CATHARINE	WAS	243	CAVETOWN
HARDNAGLE, FREDERICK	FRE	032	FREDERIC
HARDNER, LOIUSA	BAL	170	2ND DIST
HARDNOCHT, CONRADT	WAS	251	1ST DIST
HARDNOCHT, JACOB	WAS	254	1ST DIST
HARDO, HARRIET A.	BAL	409	14TH WAR
HARDON, JOHN H.	ST	346	5TH E DI
HARDSOCK, JOHN	ALL	185	9TH E.D.
HARDSOCK, WILLIAM	ALL	194	9TH E.D.
HARDSON, ROBERT	CHA	233	HILLTOP
HARDT, GEORGE	MGM	377	ROCKERLE
HARDTNER, JACOB	BAL	003	15TH WAR
HARDUSTY, JOHN	CAL	030	2ND DIST
HARDWICK, HENRY	BAL	046	9TH WARD
HARDY, ABRAHAM	BAL	222	6TH WARD
HARDY, ALBERT	BAL	234	20TH WAR
HARDY, BEN	PRI	097	SPALDING
HARDY, BENJAMIN	ST	310	1ST E DI
HARDY, BIDDY	BAL	048	4TH WARD
HARDY, CATHERINE	BAL	180	11TH WAR
HARDY, CATHERINE P.	CHA	291	MIDDLETO
HARDY, CATHRINE	BAL	048	18TH WAR
HARDY, CHARLES	CHA	252	BOJANTOW
HARDY, CHARLES	BAL	280	2ND WARD
HARDY, DANIEL	BAL	038	1ST WARD
HARDY, EDITH A.	HAR	197	3RD DIST
HARDY, EDWARD	ALL	215	CUMBERLA
HARDY, EDWARD	ANN	483	HOWARD D
HARDY, ELIAS	TAL	039	EASTON D
HARDY, ELIZA	BAL	463	1ST DIST
HARDY, ELIZABETH	BAL	017	9TH WARD
HARDY, ELLEN	ANN	482	HOWARD D
HARDY, ELY	BAL	149	19TH WAR
HARDY, GEORGE	BAL	259	17TH WAR
HARDY, GEORGE	BAL	168	1ST WARD
HARDY, GEORGE	WAS	067	2ND SUBD
HARDY, GEORGE L.	PRI	097	SPALDING
HARDY, GEORGE-MULATTO	ST	342	5TH E DI
HARDY, HANNA	TAL	045	EASTON T
HARDY, HENRIETTA	BAL	233	6TH WARD
HARDY, HENRY	BAL	286	12TH WAR
HARDY, HENRY	SOM	540	TYASKIN
HARDY, HENRY	BAL	203	11TH WAR
HARDY, HIRAM	WAS	069	2ND SUBD
HARDY, HUGH W.	BAL	079	18TH WAR
HARDY, JACOB	CAR	217	5TH DIST
HARDY, JAMES	BAL	449	1ST DIST
HARDY, JAMES H.	ANN	490	HOWARD D
HARDY, JOHN	BAL	134	1ST WARD
HARDY, JOHN	BAL	045	18TH WAR
HARDY, JOHN	CAL	023	2ND DIST
HARDY, JOHN	BAL	149	19TH WAR
HARDY, JOHN	FRE	306	WOODSBOR
HARDY, JOHN	MGM	363	BERRYS D
HARDY, JOHN	PRI	096	SPALDING
HARDY, JOHN F.	CHA	293	BOJANTOW
HARDY, JOHN JR.	BAL	077	18TH WAR
HARDY, JOHN T.	ANN	481	HOWARD D
HARDY, JOSHUA	WAS	150	2ND DIST
HARDY, JSOEPH	BAL	354	7TH WARD
HARDY, LIDE	ANN	500	HOWARD D
HARDY, LYDIA	ANN	459	HOWARD D
HARDY, M.M.A.	PRI	090	MARLBROU
HARDY, MARIA	CHA	257	MIDDLETO
HARDY, MARY	ANN	515	HOWARD D
HARDY, MARY	BAL	359	1ST DIST
HARDY, MARY	BAL	317	1ST DIST
HARDY, MATILDA	SOM	545	TYASKIN
HARDY, MERCER	ANN	500	HOWARD D
HARDY, RICHARD	PRI	041	VANSVILL
HARDY, SAMUEL	SOM	538	TYASKIN
HARDY, SAMUEL	BAL	077	18TH WAR
HARDY, SAMUEL	BAL	204	17TH WAR
HARDY, SARAH	BAL	440	14TH WAR
HARDY, SUMMERFIELD	BAL	427	14TH WAR
HARDY, SUSAN	PRI	100	SPALDING
HARDY, THOMAS	BAL	436	14TH WAR
HARDY, THOMAS	ANN	495	HOWARD D
HARDY, THOMAS	BAL	462	1ST DIST
HARDY, THOMAS	BAL	460	1ST DIST
HARDY, THOMAS	BAL	166	1ST WARD
HARDY, TUBMAN	SOM	550	TYASKIN
HARDY, W.	BAL	164	6TH WARD
HARDY, WILLIAM	ANN	495	HOWARD D
HARDY, WILLIAM	ANN	482	HOWARD D
HARDY, WILLIAM	BAL	098	15TH WAR
HARDY, WILLIAM	BAL	069	18TH WAR
HARDY, WILLIAM H.	ANN	481	HOWARD D
HARDY, WILLIAM H.	BAL	295	3RD WARD
HARDY, ZACHARIA	ANN	483	HOWARD D
HARDZG, SAPHARA	WAS	136	2ND DIST
HARE, ABRAHAM	BAL	202	6TH DIST
HARE, ABRAHAM	BAL	200	5TH DIST
HARE, ANN	CEC	174	6TH E DI
HARE, CHARLES	BAL	414	1ST DIST
HARE, CHARLES	BAL	276	2ND WARD
HARE, CRISTIAN	HAR	176	3RD DIST
HARE, EDWARD	BAL	236	20TH WAR
HARE, EDWARD	BAL	406	3RD WARD
HARE, ELIZA A.	BAL	210	11TH WAR
HARE, ELIZABETH B.	BAL	053	4TH WARD
HARE, EMANUEL	BAL	239	1ST DIST
HARE, EPHRIAM	BAL	305	1ST DIST
HARE, HENRY	BAL	401	1ST DIST
HARE, HETTA	BAL	239	1ST DIST
HARE, HUGH	TAL	017	EASTON D
HARE, HY	BAL	202	6TH DIST
HARE, JACOB	BAL	203	11TH WAR
HARE, JOHN	CAR	172	8TH DIST
HARE, JOHN	BAL	203	6TH DIST
HARE, JOHN	BAL	187	5TH DIST
HARE, JOHN	BAL	199	5TH DIST
HARE, JULIANN	BAL	197	5TH DIST
HARE, JULIANN	CEC	052	1ST E DI
HARE, MARGARET	CAR	176	8TH DIST
HAPE, MARGARET	BAL	199	5TH DIST
HARE, MARY	BAL	305	1ST DIST
HARE, MARY	BAL	447	1ST DIST
HARE, MARY	BAL	216	6TH WARD
HARE, MICHAEL	BAL	308	20TH WAR
HARE, NATHANIEL	CAL	017	1ST DIST
HARE, PETER	WAS	257	1ST DIST
HARE, RICHARD	BAL	470	14TH WAR
HARE, ROBERT H.	ANN	465	HOWARD D
HARE, RUTH	BAL	226	6TH WARD
HARE, SARAH	BAL	203	6TH DIST
HARE, SUSAN	BAL	198	5TH DIST
HARE, THOMAS	BAL	186	16TH WAR
HARE, WILLIAM	BAL	055	4TH WARD
HAREETT, CATHERINE	FRE	039	FREDERIC
HAREHARD, GILBERT A.	BAL	115	1ST WARD
HARELL, HENRY	BAL	005	4TH WARD
HARELY, GEORGE	ST	296	2ND E DI
HARENHINA, CONRADT	BAL	392	8TH WARD
HARERKEMP, CHARLES H.	BAL	255	2ND WARD
HAREY, DANIEL H.	WAS	105	2ND DIST
HAREY, WILLIAM	MGM	389	ROCKERLE
HARFELL, HENRY	BAL	208	2ND WARD
HARFERTY, THOMAS	ALL	046	10TH E.D
HARFIED, GOERGE	BAL	144	19TH WAR
HARFLICK, PHILLIP	BAL	135	11TH WAR
HARFORD, AUGUSTA	BAL	110	15TH WAR
HARFORD, JOHN	BAL	446	14TH WAR
HARFORD, MARY E.	CAR	184	8TH DIST
HARFORD, MARYANN	BAL	371	3RD WARD
HARGAN, DAVID	BAL	131	5TH WARD
HARGATE, ABRAHAM	FRE	072	FREDERIC
HARGATE, DAVID	FRE	074	FREDERIC
HARGATE, HIRAM	FRE	078	FREDERIC
HARGATE, PETER	FRE	002	FREDERIC
HARGATE, ROBERT	FRE	077	FREDERIC
HARGESS, THOMAS M.	SOM	406	DUBLIN D
HARGEST, THOMAS	BAL	002	EASTERN
HARGET, JACOB	FRE	401	JEFFERSO
HARGETT, ABRAHAM	FRE	212	BUCKEYST
HARGETT, CYRUS D.	FRE	208	BUCKEYST
HARGETT, GEORGE	FRE	400	JEFFERSO
HARGETT, JOHN	FRE	213	BUCKEYST
HARGETT, JOHN H.	FRE	208	BUCKEYST
HARGETT, JOHN W.	FRE	210	BUCKEYST
HARGETT, WILLIAM H.	FRE	215	BUCKEYST
HARGIS, JOHN	WOR	327	1ST E DI
HARGIS, MARY W.	WOR	343	1ST E DI
HARGIS, STEPHEN T.	WOR	342	1ST E DI
HARGIS, THOMAS W.	WOR	327	1ST E DI
HARGIS, WILLIAM	SOM	413	DUBLIN D
HARGRAVES, HOLLAND	CEC	119	3RD E DI
HARGRO, CHARELS	WOR	241	1ST CENS
HARGROVE, HENRY	BAL	414	14TH WAR
HARGROVE, STEWART	BAL	414	14TH WAR
HARGROVE, THOMAS	WOR	272	BERLIN 1
HARGROVE, WILLIAM H.	BAL	399	14TH WAR
HARGUS, WILLIAM	BAL	349	7TH WARD
HARGY, ANNM M. *	FRE	293	WOODSBOR
HARIAN, EDWARD	BAL	350	7TH WARD
HARICH, THOMAS*	DOR	382	1ST DIST
HARICK, THOMAS*	DOR	382	1ST DIST
HARIDN, ELLEN	BAL	427	8TH WARD
HARIDY, ISAAC	BAL	352	7TH WARD
HARIE, SHARLOTTE M.*	TAL	035	EASTON D
HARIG, BERNARD L.	BAL	090	15TH WAR
HARIG, JOHN B.	BAL	090	15TH WAR
HARIIS, MARY	BAL	343	1ST DIST
HARINE, HENRY	WAS	286	1ST DIST
HARINGTON, JOHN E.	DOR	366	3RD DIVI
HARINGTON, JOHN J.	DOR	364	3RD DIVI
HARINGTON, MARY	DOR	363	3RD DIVI
HARINGTON, PETER	DOR	366	3RD DIVI
HARIPE, VOLUMNIA O.	ANN	521	HOWARD D
HARIS, HENRY*	DOR	418	1ST DIST
HARIS, ISAAC J. J.	DOR	373	1ST DIST
HARIS, JOSHUA	DOR	426	1ST DIST
HARIS, LLOYD N.	DOR	421	1ST DIST
HARIS, MARY	DOR	424	1ST DIST
HARIS, NOAH*	DOR	395	1ST DIST
HARIS, WILEY*	DOR	420	1ST DIST
HARISE, SAMUEL	BAL	207	19TH WAR
HARISHORN, WJOHN	BAL	204	2ND WARD
HARISON, ANN	DOR	357	3RD DIVI
HARISON, ANN*	DOR	360	3RD DIVI
HARISON, BARBARA-MULATTO	FRE	452	8TH E DI
HARISON, BENJAMIN	DOR	417	1ST DIST
HARISON, BENJAMIN B.	DOR	365	3RD DIVI
HARISON, W. E.*	DOR	452	1ST DIST
HARITER, JANET	BAL	120	5TH WARD
HARK, FREDERICK	BAL	343	7TH WARD
HARKEN, EDWARD	BAL	459	1ST DIST
HARKEN, PATRICK	MGM	381	ROCKER_E
HARKER, ALFRED	BAL	104	5TH WARD
HARKER, ALICE	BAL	196	6TH WARD
HARKER, ANDREW J.	BAL	070	2ND DIST
HARKER, ANN	BAL	205	11TH WAR
HARKER, ELIZABETH	BAL	454	8TH WARD
HARKER, GEORGE	KEN	276	1ST DIST
HARKER, GEORGE W.	BAL	422	8TH WARD
HARKER, JAMES	BAL	439	8TH WARD
HARKER, JOHN	BAL	418	8TH WARD
HARKER, JOHN C.	BAL	246	20TH WAR
HARKER, JOHN J.	BAL	460	8TH WARD
HARKER, JULIUS	BAL	081	1ST WARD
HARKER, MARY F.	BAL	153	19TH WAR
HARKER, SAMUEL	CEC	070	5TH E DI
HARKER, SAMUEL	BAL	101	5TH WARD
HARKER, WILLIAM	BAL	161	19TH WAR
HARKEY, SIMON H.	FRE	042	FREDERIC
HARKING, LEWIS B.	CHA	220	ALLENS F
HARKING, THOMAS	BAL	318	7TH WARD
HARKINS, ANN	HAR	037	1ST DIST
HARKINS, ENEALS-MULATTO	CAR	158	NO TWP L
HARKINS, HANNAH J.	HAR	090	2ND DIST
HARKINS, HENRY	BAL	005	9TH WARD
HARKINS, JAMES H.	HAR	075	BEL AIR
HARKINS, JOHN	BAL	318	7TH WARD
HARKINS, JOSEPH	HAR	108	2ND DIST
HARKINS, MARY	HAR	005	1ST DIST
HARKINS, NEILE	BAL	149	19TH WAR
HARKINS, ROBERT	BAL	025	4TH WARD
HARKINS, SARAH	HAR	114	2ND DIST
HARKINS, STEPHEN	HAR	112	2ND DIST
HARKINS, STEVENSON	HAR	113	2ND DIST
HARKINS, THOMAS	BAL	172	19TH WAR
HARKINS, WILLIAM	HAR	089	2ND DIST
HARKINS, WILLIAM C.	PRI	024	VANSVILL
HARKINS, WILLIAM J.	HAR	005	1ST DIST
HARKLESS, HENRIETTA	TAL	034	EASTON D
HARKLEY, FADRY	BAL	264	1ST DIST
HARKLEY, GEORGE	BAL	289	1ST DIST
HARKMAN, GEORGE	HAR	199	3RD DIST
HARKNESS, M.	BAL	226	19TH WAR
HARKNESS, THOMAS	BAL	244	20TH WAR
HARKNESS, THOMAS	BAL	166	1ST WARD
HARKROM, GEORGE	BAL	154	1ST WARD
HARKUM, HENRY S.	SOM	478	TRAPP DI
HARLAKER, PETER	BAL	227	1ST DIST
HARLAN, EMMA	ANN	521	HOWARD D
HARLAN, JAMES	HAR	053	1ST DIST
HARLAN, JOHN	BAL	096	2ND DIST
HARLAN, JOSIAH T. J.	BAL	374	13TH WAR
HARLAN, MARY A.	BAL	261	6TH WARD
HARLAND, ELLEN	BAL	178	19TH WAR
HARLAND, GEORGE	ALL	180	8TH E.D.
HARLAND, HANNAH	CEC	105	3RD E DI
HARLAND, HENRY J.	HAR	124	2ND DIST
HARLAND, MARGARET	CEC	126	5TH E DI
HARLAND, REUBEN S.	HAR	123	2ND DIST
HARLAND, RICHARD	CAR	224	5TH DIST
HARLAND, STEPHEN B.	CEC	172	6TH E DI
HARLAND, WILLIAM A.	HAR	078	2ND DIST
HARLANG, DANIEL	BAL	055	2ND DIST
HARLEN, JOHN M.	FRE	286	WOODSBOR
HARLES CHARLES	BAL	375	8TH WARD
HARLEY, DAVID	KEN	218	2ND DIST
HARLEY, ELI	PRI	055	AQUASCO
HARLEY, ELIZABETH	BAL	155	2ND DIST
HARLEY, ELIZABETH R.	MGM	445	CLARKSTR
HARLEY, HENRY T.	FRE	032	FREDERIC
HARLEY, JAEMS	BAL	400	14TH WAR
HARLEY, JOHN	PRI	055	AQUASCO
HARLEY, JOHN	ALL	105	5TH E.D.
HARLEY, MARY	BAL	225	6TH WARD
HARLEY, MARY	WOR	187	7TH E DI
HARLEY, NATHAN T.	MGM	396	ROCKERLE
HARLEY, OTHO F.	FRE	394	PETERSVI
HARLEY, ROBERT	BAL	368	3RD WARD
HARLEY, SAMUEL	ALL	109	5TH E.D.
HARLEY, TRUMAN W.	FRE	020	FREDERIC
HARLEY, VIRGINIA	BAL	161	11TH WAR
HARLEY, WILLIAM	FRE	194	5TH E DI
HARLEY,MARY	ALL	212	CUMBERLA
HARLIN, ELLEN	BAL	185	5TH DIST
HARLIN, JESSE	CHA	292	BOJANTOW
HARLIN, WILLIAM	BAL	114	2ND DIST
HARLING, ANN	KEN	290	3RD DIST
HARLOCK, ABRAHAM	KEN	295	3RD DIST
HARLOCK, ALFRED	KEN	310	3RD DIST
HARLOW, BRADFORD	BAL	093	10TH WAR
HARLOW, BRANCH	BAL	093	10TH WAR
HARLOW, CHESTER	BAL	002	4TH WARD
HARLOW, ISAAC	BAL	170	6TH WARD
HARLTZ, CHARLES	ALL	089	5TH E.D.
HARLY, E.	PRI	055	AQUASCO
HARLY, J.L.	PRI	055	AQUASCO
HARLY, JAMES	PRI	055	AQUASCO
HARLY, JOHN	PRI	088	SPALDING
HARLY, NATHANIEL	CHA	259	MIDDLETO
HARM, CATHARINE *	CAR	313	1ST DIST
HARM, ELIZABETH	FRE	111	CREAGERS
HARM, S.A.	WAS	021	2ND SUBD
HARM, W.B.	WAS	021	2ND SUBD
HARMAN, ANN	ANN	374	4TH DIST
HARMAN, ANN	BAL	103	10TH WAR
HARMAN, ANN L.	CAR	398	2ND DIST
HARMAN, BARBARA	BAL	435	14TH WAR
HARMAN, BENJAMIN	CAR	323	1ST DIST
HARMAN, CAROLINE	BAL	382	1ST DIST
HARMAN, DANIEL	CAR	399	2ND DIST
HARMAN, DANIEL	CAR	309	1ST DIST
HARMAN, EDITH	BAL	440	1ST DIST
HARMAN, ELIZA*	BAL	349	3RD WARD
HARMAN, ELIZABETH	BAL	084	15TH WAR
HARMAN, ELIZABETH	CAR	294	7TH DIST
HARMAN, ELIZABETH	BAL	143	11TH WAR
HARMAN, ELIZALA *	BAL	087	2ND DIST
HARMAN, ELLEN	BAL	102	10TH WAR
HARMAN, ELLEN	BAL	133	5TH WARD
HARMAN, FREDERICK G.	ANN	429	HOWARD D
HARMAN, GEORGE	BAL	296	7TH WARD
HARMAN, GEORGE	CAR	284	7TH DIST
HARMAN, GEORGE	FRE	113	CREAGERS
HARMAN, GEORGE	FRE	051	FREDERIC
HARMAN, GEORGE	WAS	160	HAGERSTO
HARMAN, HANNAH	HAR	122	2ND DIST
HARMAN, HANNAH	BAL	369	13TH WAR
HARMAN, ISABEL	BAL	289	20TH WAR
HARMAN, JACOB	CAR	398	2ND DIST
HARMAN, JACOB	CAR	410	2ND DIST
HARMAN, JACOB	ANN	364	4TH DIST
HARMAN, JACOB	BAL	174	2ND DIST
HARMAN, JACOB	BAL	272	1ST DIST
HARMAN, JAMES	BAL	030	1ST WARD
HARMAN, JAMES	ANN	419	HOWARD D
HARMAN, JAMES	BAL	313	7TH WARD
HARMAN, JAMES	WOR	200	3RD E DI
HARMAN, JAMS	BAL	053	2ND DIST
HARMAN, JOHN	ANN	375	4TH DIST
HARMAN, JOHN	BAL	344	7TH WARD
HARMAN, JOHN	BAL	347	7TH WARD
HARMAN, JOHN	BAL	343	7TH WARD
HARMAN, JOHN	WAS	143	HAGERSTO
HARMAN, JOHN	WAS	058	2ND SUBD
HARMAN, JOHN	BAL	051	4TH WARD
HARMAN, JOHN	BAL	419	14TH WAR
HARMAN, JOHN	HAR	047	1ST DIST
HARMAN, JOHN	CAR	315	1ST DIST
HARMAN, JOHN	CAR	289	7TH DIST
HARMAN, JOHN	CAR	240	TANEYTOW
HARMAN, JOHN	BAL	447	14TH WAR
HARMAN, JOHN *	WOR	201	3RD E DI
HARMAN, JOHN E.	QUE	186	3RD E DI

HARMAN, JOSEPH CAR 274 7TH DIST
HARMAN, JOSEPH BAL 210 6TH DIST
HARMAN, LEAN CAR 159 NO TWP L
HARMAN, LEVIN BAL 030 1ST WARD
HARMAN, LITTLETON BAL 099 15TH WAR
HARMAN, MALINDA BAL 305 7TH WARD
HARMAN, MARGARET FRE 102 FREDERIC
HARMAN, MARY BAL 214 11TH WAR
HARMAN, MARY BAL 002 1ST WARD
HARMAN, MARY WOR 185 6TH E DI
HARMAN, MICHAEL BAL 147 2ND DIST
HARMAN, MICHAEL BAL 435 14TH WAR
HARMAN, MINA C. BAL 412 8TH WARD
HARMAN, PHILIP ANN 375 4TH DIST
HARMAN, R. B. BAL 329 13TH WAR
HARMAN, RICHARD BAL 342 7TH WARD
HARMAN, ROBERT BAL 120 11TH WAR
HARMAN, ROBERT K. BAL 349 3RD WARD
HARMAN, SABINA FRE 024 FREDERIC
HARMAN, SAMPSON WOR 189 7TH E DI
HARMAN, SAMUEL CAR 308 1ST DIST
HARMAN, SAMUEL HAR 047 1ST DIST
HARMAN, SAMUEL BAL 128 16TH WAR
HARMAN, SAMUEL BAL 284 7TH WARD
HARMAN, SAMUEL BAL 383 3RD WARD
HARMAN, SAMUEL R. ANN 420 HOWARD D
HARMAN, SARAH CAR 277 7TH DIST.
HARMAN, SARAH J. WOR 189 7TH E DI
HARMAN, SUSAN R. BAL 090 18TH WAR
HARMAN, THOMAS KEN 260 1ST DIST
HARMAN, URIAH CAR 399 2ND DIST
HARMAN, WILLIAM FRE 095 FREDERIC
HARMAN, WILLIAM BAL 398 14TH WAR
HARMAN, WILLIAM WAS 289 1ST DIST
HARMAN, WILLIAM ANN 444 HOWARD D
HARMAN, WILLIAM H. BAL 258 17TH WAR
HARMAN,MICHEL BAL 059 2ND DIST
HARMANSON, JACOB BAL 415 14TH WAR
HARMAR, WILLIAM H. * BAL 079 18TH WAR
HARMEL, GEORGE ALL 228 CUMBERLA
HARMENSON, HETTY WOR 265 BERLIN 1
HARMENSON, JAMES WOR 258 1ST CENS
HARMER, DANIEL CAR 311 1ST DIST
HARMER, JEREMIAH CAR 290 7TH DIST
HARMER, JOSEPH M. HAR 039 1ST DIST
HARMER, JOSHUA HAR 039 1ST DIST
HARMER, PETER BAL 327 7TH WARD
HARMER, SIMON BAL 146 2ND DIST
HARMES, HERMAN BAL 201 17TH WAR
HARMESSON, SUSAN ALL 154 6TH E.D.
HARMETHON,MATILDA BAL 058 2ND DIST
HARMGER, JOHN P. BAL 303 12TH WAR
HARMIN, MARY E. CEC 011 ELKTON 3
HARMIN, NANCY CEC 021 ELKTON 3
HARMINSON, JOSEPH WAS 114 2ND DIST
HARMINSON, RUTH WAS 108 2ND DIST
HARMM, PETER * FRE 121 CREAGERS
HARMMOND, MATILDA FRE 254 NEW MARK
HARMON, CAROLINE E. ANN 386 4TH DIST
HARMON, CHARITY ANN 417 HOWARD D
HARMON, DUCK A.* TAL 002 EASTON D
HARMON, ELIZABETH ANN 386 4TH DIST
HARMON, GEORGE G. DOR 426 1ST DIST
HARMON, IRVIN WOR 315 2ND E DI
HARMON, ISAAC FRE 279 WOODSBOR
HARMON, JACOB SOM 424 PRINCESS
HARMON, JOHN WOR 315 2ND E DI
HARMON, JOHN ANN 386 4TH DIST
HARMON, LANCE FRE 052 FREDERIC
HARMON, LAYRUS WOR 306 2ND E DI
HARMON, M. ANN 339 3RD DIST
HARMON, MARY A. CAR 387 2ND DIST
HARMON, MICHAEL FRE 052 FREDERIC
HARMON, MOSES-BLACK WOR 348 1ST E DI
HARMON, PHILLIP ANN 426 HOWARD D
HARMON, REBECCA ANN 386 4TH DIST
HARMON, REZIN ANN 388 4TH DIST
HARMON, SARAH C. CAR 322 1ST DIST
HARMON, SUSAN WAS 113 2ND DIST
HARMON, WILLIAM WOR 316 2ND E DI
HARMON, WILLIAM BAL 298 20TH WAR
HARMON, WILLIAM-BLACK CAR 151 NO TWP L
HARMOND, JARVIS BAL 288 7TH WARD
HARMONSON, EDWARD WOR 285 BERLIN 1
HARMSTON, MARY BAL 123 2ND DIST
HARMUS, JACOB FRE 297 WOODSBOR
HARN, EDWIN WAS 257 1ST DIST
HARN, ELIZABETH FRE 367 CATOCTIN
HARN, ELIZABETH* BAL 377 3RD WARD
HARN, EPHRIAM CAR 367 9TH DIST
HARN, JOHN CEC 109 3RD E DI
HARN, JOHN FRE 425 8TH E DI
HARN, LOUIS BAL 269 1ST DIST
HARN, MARIA WAS 273 RIDGEVIL
HARN, OVERTON C. FRE 363 CATOCTIN
HARN, SINGLETON W. FRE 441 8TH E DI
HARN, SUSAN FRE 107 CREAGERS
HARN, WILLIAM H. FRE 253 NEW MARK
HARNAN, LEWIS BAL 081 1ST WARD
HARNAR, SAMUEL CAR 314 1ST DIST
HARNBERER, JOHN P. CAR 245 3RD DIST
HARNEGN,JAMES CAR 142 NO TWP L
HARNER, ABRAHAM CAR 320 1ST DIST
HARNER, ANDREW CAR 300 1ST DIST
HARNER, DANIEL CAR 302 1ST DIST
HARNER, DAVID CAR 302 1ST DIST
HARNER, EMANUEL CAR 313 1ST DIST
HARNER, EPHRAIM CAR 310 1ST DIST
HARNER, FREDERICK CAR 300 1ST DIST
HARNER, HANNAH FRE 096 FREDERIC
HARNER, HENRY CEC 176 7TH E DI
HARNER, JACOB FRE 166 EMMITTSB
HARNER, JAMES CAR 298 1ST DIST
HARNER, JOHN C. CEC 149 PORT DUP
HARNER, MARTIN BAL 146 2ND DIST
HARNER, MICHAEL CAR 256 3RD DIST
HARNER, WILLIAM CAR 302 1ST DIST
HARNER, WILLIAM H. CEC 176 7TH E DI
HARNES, THOMAS CEC 017 ELKTON 3
HARNESOM, CHARLES ALL 126 4TH E.D.
HARNESS, JOHN BAL 041 18TH WAR
HARNESS, JOSEPH BAL 041 18TH WAR
HARNESS, WILLIAM * BAL 176 2ND DIST
HARNET, ELIZA* DOR 428 1ST DIST
HARNETT, DANIEL BAL 361 3RD WARD
HARNEY, ANN FRE 273 NEW MARK
HARNEY, JOHN ALL 119 5TH E.D.
HARNEY, JOHN * BAL 025 18TH WAR
HARNEY, LUKE BAL 385 8TH WARD
HARNEY, MARGARET FRE 276 NEW MARK
HARNEY, MISS A. FRE 199 5TH E DI
HARNEY, SUSAN ALL 126 4TH E.D.
HARNIER, ANNA QUE 242 5TH E DI
HARNIGAN, WASHINGTON CEC 118 4TH E DI
HARNING, MARIA FRE 058 FREDERIC
HARNISH, JACOB CAR 313 1ST DIST
HARNISH, JACOB WAS 289 1ST DIST
HARNISH, JOHN WAS 289 1ST DIST
HARNISH, PETER WAS 289 1ST DIST
HARNISH, SAMUEL WAS 289 1ST DIST
HARNON, JAMES BAL 018 2ND DIST
HARNS, WILLIAM BAL 009 EASTERN
HARP, CATHAIRNE FRE 370 CATOCTIN
HARP, DANIEL FRE 186 5TH E DI
HARP, DEBORAH BAL 388 1ST DIST
HARP, EDWARD BAL 346 7TH WARD
HARP, EDWARD TAL 079 ST MICHA
HARP, ELLEN BAL 346 7TH WARD
HARP, HANNAH FRE 348 MIDDLETO
HARP, JACOB WAS 252 1ST DIST
HARP, JAMES CAR 373 9TH DIST
HARP, JOHN FRE 341 MIDDLETO
HARP, JOHN BAL 329 3RD WARD
HARP, JOSHUA WAS 215 1ST DIST
HARP, MARY CEC 078 NORTHEAS
HARP, MARY A. ANN 508 HOWARD D
HARP,GEORGE BAL 161 1ST WARD
HARPE, JOHN FRANCIS BAL 433 14TH WAR
HARPEN, ANN BAL 216 6TH WARD
HARPER, AJMES BAL 308 20TH WAR
HARPER, ALGERNON S.* TAL 057 EASTON D
HARPER, ALLEN CAR 128 NO TWP L
HARPER, ANN R. WAS 168 FUNKSTOW
HARPER, CATHARINE BAL 023 2ND DIST
HARPER, CATHERINE BAL 180 11TH WAR
HARPER, CHARITY WAS 136 HAGERSTO
HARPER, CHARLES WAS 220 1ST DIST
HARPER, CHARLES BAL 180 2ND WARD
HARPER, CHRISTOPHER C. QUE 189 3RD E DI
HARPER, DANIEL BAL 009 15TH WAR
HARPER, DANIEL DOR 298 1ST DIST
HARPER, ELISHA DOR 313 1ST DIST
HARPER, ELIZA FRE 119 CREAGERS
HARPER, ELIZA DOR 386 1ST DIST
HARPER, ELIZABETH FRE 062 FREDERIC
HARPER, ELIZABETH BAL 211 19TH WAR
HARPER, ELLEN V. BAL 177 16TH WAR
HARPER, EMMA BAL 034 9TH WARD
HARPER, EMORY WAS 208 1ST DIST
HARPER, FANNY A. ALL 256 CUMBERLA
HARPER, FRANCES C. QUE 223 4TH E DI
HARPER, FRANCIS T. FRE 013 FREDERIC
HARPER, GEORGE W. DOR 354 3RD DIVI
HARPER, HENRY MGM 439 CLARKSTR
HARPER, ISAIH S. TAL 092 ST MICHA
HARPER, JACOB WAS 050 2ND SUBD
HARPER, JAMES WAS 048 2ND SUBD
HARPER, JAMES DOR 458 1ST DIST
HARPER, JAMES PRI 074 MARLBROU
HARPER, JAMES CAR 096 NO TWP L
HARPER, JAMES BAL 082 18TH WAR
HARPER, JAMES BAL 198 11TH WAR
HARPER, JAMES BAL 232 1ST DIST
HARPER, JAMES K. QUE 189 3RD E DI
HARPER, JAMES L. BAL 341 3RD WARD
HARPER, JHNW . ST 260 3RD E DI
HARPER, JOHN TAL 088 ST MICHA
HARPER, JOHN MGM 380 ROCKERLE
HARPER, JOHN E.-MULATTO BAL 179 2ND WARD
HARPER, JOHN F. DOR 455 1ST DIST
HARPER, JOHN R. BAL 049 9TH WARD
HARPER, JOSEPH BAL 188 5TH DIST
HARPER, JOSEPH A. KEN 249 2ND DIST
HARPER, JULIANN QUE 187 3RD E DI
HARPER, LLOYD BAL 052 9TH WARD
HARPER, MARGARET BAL 314 20TH WAR
HARPER, MARGARETT BAL 053 4TH WARD
HARPER, MARTHA BAL 232 1ST DIST
HARPER, MARTHA J. TAL 058 EASTON D
HARPER, MARY DOR 461 1ST DIST
HARPER, MARY WAS 090 2ND SUBD
HARPER, MARY BAL 306 1ST DIST
HARPER, MARY BAL 371 13TH WAR
HARPER, MARY FRE 389 PETERSVI
HARPER, MARY E. FRE 327 MIDDLETO
HARPER, MARY G. HAR 045 1ST DIST
HARPER, MILAN BAL 061 4TH WARD
HARPER, MILLY BAL 022 1ST WARD
HARPER, NANCY DOR 308 1ST DIST
HARPER, PRESBURY BAL 314 7TH WARD
HARPER, R. ANN 470 HOWARD D
HARPER, REBECCA PRI 050 AQUASCO
HARPER, REBECCA W. QUE 223 4TH E DI
HARPER, RICHARD MGM 382 ROCKERLE
HARPER, RICHARD FRE 094 FREDERIC
HARPER, ROBERT DOR 353 3RD DIVI
HARPER, SABIN* DOR 297 1ST DIST
HARPER, SAMPSON FRE 119 CREAGERS
HARPER, SAMUEL HAR 002 1ST DIST
HARPER, SAMUEL QUE 223 4TH E DI
HARPER, SAMUEL BAL 177 6TH WARD
HARPER, SAMUEL A. HAR 002 1ST DIST
HARPER, SARAH CAR 305 1ST DIST
HARPER, SHADRICH CAR 096 NO TWP L
HARPER, SIDNEY A. BAL 085 18TH WAR
HARPER, THOMAS CAR 139 NO TWP L
HARPER, THOMAS DOR 383 1ST DIST
HARPER, THOMAS BAL 131 1ST WARD
HARPER, THOMAS-MULATTO ST 323 4TH E DI
HARPER, WILLAIM WAS 168 FUNKSTOW
HARPER, WILLIAM PRI 049 AQUASCO
HARPER, WILLIAM WOR 243 1ST CENS
HARPER, WILLIAM BAL 159 1ST WARD
HARPER, WILLIAM BAL 315 12TH WAR
HARPER, WILLIAM BAL 315 12TH WAR
HARPER, WILLIAM BAL 155 19TH WAR
HARPER, WILLIAM CAR 316 1ST DIST
HARPER, WILLIAM MGM 354 BERRYS D
HARPER, WILLIAM H BAL 055 15TH WAR
HARPER, WILLIAM W. HAR 001 1ST DIST
HARPER,WILLIA BAL 067 1ST WARD
HARPISH, MARGARET BAL 453 8TH WARD
HARPS, BENJAMIN-BLACK FRE 442 8TH E DI
HARPS, CHARLOTT CAR 224 5TH DIST
HARPS, CHRISTIAN FRE 034 FREDERIC
HARPS, FRNACIS R. CAR 228 5TH DIST
HARPS, PERRY G. CAR 224 5TH DIST
HARPST, GEORGE FRE 173 5TH E DI
HARPWOOD, JOHN CAL 010 1ST DIST
HARR, CHARLES W. ANN 437 HOWARD D
HARR, ENERARD FRE 148 10TH E D
HARR, ISAAC ANN 316 1ST DIST
HARR, MARY M. FRE 149 10TH E D
HARR, PETER BAL 309 7TH WARD
HARR, WILLIAM E. ANN 436 HOWARD D
HARRAGAN, MARK BAL 445 1ST DIST
HARRARD, SARAH ANN 291 ANNAPOLI
HARRED, CLEM CAL 014 1ST DIST
HARRELL, MARY BAL 184 11TH WAR
HARREN, SAMUEL BAL 184 11TH WAR
HARRESS, PRISCILLA ALL 191 9TH E.D.
HARRET, CHARLES CEC 040 CHESAPEA
HARRET, JOHN A. FRE 058 FREDERIC
HARRETY, STEPHEN BAL 060 1ST WARD
HARREYMAN, THOMAS BAL 323 7TH WARD
HARRGAN, CHRISTOPHER CEC 097 4TH E DI
HARRICK, EDWARD BAL 282 7TH WARD
HARRIE, WILLIAM QUE 253 5TH E DI
HARRIES, ELIZABETH MISS- BAL 315 20TH WAR
HARRIET, LOUISA BAL 214 19TH WAR
HARRIET, SUSAN PRI 097 SPALDING
HARRIETT, HENRY WAS 141 2ND DIST
HARRIGAN, B. BAL 300 12TH WAR
HARRIGAN, BARTLY CEC 123 3RD E DI
HARRIGAN, CATHARINE BAL 061 15TH WAR
HARRIGAN, CORNELIUS BAL 352 7TH WARD
HARRIGAN, ELISHU CEC 131 6TH E DI
HARRIGAN, JOHN CEC 123 3RD E DI
HARRIGAN, JOHN G. BAL 410 8TH WARD
HARRIGAN, JOHN R. FRE 159 EMMITTSB
HARRIGAN, LYDIA WAS 060 2ND SUBD
HARRIGAN, PETER BAL 362 8TH WARD
HARRIGAN, REBECCA CEC 123 3RD E DI
HARRING, JACOB ALL 261 CUMBERLA
HARRINGTON, ALFRED SOM 546 TYASKIN
HARRINGTON, AMES BAL 305 17TH WAR
HARRINGTON, ANDREW BAL 185 6TH WARD
HARRINGTON, CINTHY A. ANN 417 HOWARD D
HARRINGTON, ELEIZA TAL 073 EASTON T
HARRINGTON, ELISHA BAL 182 6TH WARD
HARRINGTON, ELIZABETH TAL 086 ST MICHA
HARRINGTON, ELIZABETH BAL 024 4TH WARD
HARRINGTON, ELLEN BAL 095 10TH WAR
HARRINGTON, EMILY BAL 111 1ST WARD
HARRINGTON, EMILY CEC 056 1ST E DI
HARRINGTON, GEORGE BAL 110 1ST WARD
HARRINGTON, GEORGE W. CAR 098 NO TWP L
HARRINGTON, H.S. BAL 290 12TH WAR
HARRINGTON, HENRY QUE 217 3RD E DI
HARRINGTON, JAMES SOM 551 TYASKIN
HARRINGTON, JAMES CAR 098 NO TWP L
HARRINGTON, JAMES BAL 243 17TH WAR
HARRINGTON, JAMES W. QUE 179 2ND E DI
HARRINGTON, JOHN SOM 462 HANGARY
HARRINGTON, JOHN TAL 088 ST MICHA
HARRINGTON, JOHN WAS 006 WILLIAMS
HARRINGTON, JOHN SOM 541 TYASKIN
HARRINGTON, JOHN BAL 329 13TH WAR
HARRINGTON, JOSEPH B. TAL 112 ST MICHA
HARRINGTON, JULIAN FRE 008 FREDERIC
HARRINGTON, LEVIN BAL 199 17TH WAR
HARRINGTON, LOUISA BAL 382 13TH WAR
HARRINGTON, LUKE BAL 031 4TH WARD
HARRINGTON, MARTHA CEC 193 5TH E DI
HARRINGTON, MARY TAL 079 ST MICHA
HARRINGTON, MATILDA BAL 218 6TH WARD
HARRINGTON, NATHAN TAL 079 ST MICHA
HARRINGTON, RICHARD TAL 080 ST MICHA
HARRINGTON, RICHARD BAL 155 1ST WARD
HARRINGTON, RICHARD BAL 398 3RD WARD
HARRINGTON, ROBERT BAL 038 1ST WARD
HARRINGTON, SAMUEL BAL 296 1ST DIST
HARRINGTON, SAMUEL BAL 259 17TH WAR
HARRINGTON, SAMUEL CAR 102 NO TWP L
HARRINGTON, SARAH E. SOM 490 SALISBUR
HARRINGTON, STEPHEN C. TAL 066 EASTON T
HARRINGTON, SUSAN QUE 186 3RD E DI
HARRINGTON, SUSAN BAL 334 1ST DIST
HARRINGTON, THOMAS ANN 415 HOWARD D
HARRINGTON, THOMAS F. QUE 179 2ND E DI
HARRINGTON, THOMAS W. BAL 098 10TH WAR
HARRINGTON, WILLIAM ALL 204 CUMBERLA
HARRINGTON, WILLIAM QUE 201 3RD E DI
HARRINGTON, WILLIAM DOR 457 1ST DIST
HARRINGTON,JESSE BAL 133 1ST WARD
HARRINGTON,MARY BAL 296 12TH WAR
HARRINGTON,MARY CAR 084 NO TWP L
HARRINGTON,W ILLIAM CAR 073 NO TWP L
HARRINITGTON, HANNAH CEC 198 7TH E DI
HARRIOSN, JAMES P. QUE 236 4TH E DI
HARRIOSN, JULIA TAL 094 ST MICHA
HARRIOSN, KEZIAH BAL 124 2ND DIST
HARRIOSN, W. H. BAL 147 1ST WARD
HARRIOSN, WILLIAM TAL 081 ST MICHA
HARRIS, A. E. MRS- BAL 096 18TH WAR
HARRIS, A. H. BAL 052 9TH WARD
HARRIS, AARON BAL 175 6TH WARD
HARRIS, ABRAM CEC 153 PORT DUP
HARRIS, ABRAM TAL 062 EASTON D
HARRIS, ABRAM TAL 034 EASTON D
HARRIS, ALBERT SOM 391 BRINKLEY
HARRIS, ALBERT CEC 163 6TH E DI
HARRIS, ALEVIA SOM 449 DAMES QU
HARRIS, ALEX BAL 145 1ST WARD
HARRIS, ALEXANDER BAL 076 10TH WAR
HARRIS, ALEXANDER BAL 302 3RD WARD
HARRIS, ALEXANDER WAS 064 2ND SUBD
HARRIS, ALEXANDER CEC 158 PORT DUP
HARRIS, ALEXANDER BAL 048 4TH WARD
HARRIS, ALEXANDER CAR 112 NO TWP L
HARRIS, ALEXANDER KEN 233 2ND DIST
HARRIS, ALEXIA BAL 097 18TH WAR
HARRIS, ALEXIUS CAR 178 8TH DIST
HARRIS, ALFRED C. BAL 020 15TH WAR
HARRIS, ALICE HAR 115 2ND DIST
HARRIS, AMANDA E. CEC 122 4TH E DI
HARRIS, AMELIA BAL 235 20TH WAR
HARRIS, AMELIA BAL 398 3RD WARD
HARRIS, AMELILA BAL 169 11TH WAR
HARRIS, AMOS CAR 179 8TH DIST
HARRIS, ANDREW BAL 177 6TH WARD
HARRIS, ANGEL A. WOR 177 6TH E DI
HARRIS, ANN ST 342 5TH E DI
HARRIS, ANN BAL 150 5TH WARD
HARRIS, ANN BAL 272 12TH WAR
HARRIS, ANN BAL 305 1ST DIST
HARRIS, ANN A.-MULATTO FRE 429 8TH E DI
HARRIS, ANN M. TAL 033 EASTON D
HARRIS, ANNA CEC 038 CHESAPEA
HARRIS, ANNA BAL 453 14TH WAR

Name	County	Page	District
HARRIS, ANNA	BAL	453	1ST DIST
HARRIS, ANTHONEY	ST	254	3RD E DI
HARRIS, ANTHONY	BAL	260	6TH WARD
HARRIS, ANTHONY	ANN	341	3RD DIST
HARRIS, ARTHUR	CAL	037	2ND DIST
HARRIS, B. G.	BAL	045	9TH WARD
HARRIS, B.W.	CEC	036	CHESAPEA
HARRIS, BASIL H.	PRI	108	PISCATAW
HARRIS, BENJAMIN	WAS	122	HAGERSTO
HARRIS, BENJAMIN	BAL	123	11TH WAR
HARRIS, BENJAMIN	BAL	395	8TH WARD
HARRIS, BENJAMIN	BAL	265	12TH WAR
HARRIS, BENJAMIN G.	ST	274	3RD E DI
HARRIS, BETSEY	BAL	178	11TH WAR
HARRIS, BETSEY	BAL	243	20TH WAR
HARRIS, BETSY	BAL	374	13TH WAR
HARRIS, BILL	TAL	097	ST MICHA
HARRIS, CAROLINE	KEN	284	3RD DIST
HARRIS, CAROLINE	CHA	256	MIDDLETO
HARRIS, CAROLINE	HAR	152	3RD DIST
HARRIS, CATHARINE C.	CAL	029	2ND DIST
HARRIS, CATHRINE	BAL	191	11TH WAR
HARRIS, CESULT F.	TAL	080	ST MICHA
HARRIS, CHAPIN A.	BAL	106	10TH WAR
HARRIS, CHARBBTAE	ANN	275	ANNAPOLI
HARRIS, CHARELS	BAL	173	16TH WAR
HARRIS, CHARLES	BAL	025	15TH WAR
HARRIS, CHARLES	BAL	242	2ND WARD
HARRIS, CHARLES	BAL	196	5TH DIST
HARRIS, CHARLES	KEN	260	1ST DIST
HARRIS, CHARLES	CEC	163	6TH E DI
HARRIS, CHARLES	CEC	168	6TH E DI
HARRIS, CHARLES	BAL	064	4TH WARD
HARRIS, CHARLES	BAL	339	13TH WAR
HARRIS, CHARLES F.	BAL	306	3RD WARD
HARRIS, CHARLES W.	BAL	366	3RD WARD
HARRIS, CHARLES-BLACK	CAR	090	NO TWP L
HARRIS, CHARLOTT	BAL	320	7TH WARD
HARRIS, CHARLOTTE	BAL	149	19TH WAR
HARRIS, CHAROLETT	BAL	135	18TH WAR
HARRIS, CORNELIA	BAL	063	18TH WAR
HARRIS, CRISTOPHER	ANN	421	HOWARD D
HARRIS, CUELIA	CAL	014	1ST DIST
HARRIS, D. G.	BAL	149	1ST WARD
HARRIS, DANIEL	BAL	457	1ST DIST
HARRIS, DANIEL	TAL	063	EASTON D
HARRIS, CANIEL JR.	BAL	382	3RD WARD
HARRIS, CANIEL-MULATTC	BAL	239	2ND WARD
HARRIS, DARKEY*	TAL	043	EASTON D
HARRIS, CAVE	HAR	009	1ST DIST
HARRIS, CAVID	BAL	301	17TH WAR
HARRIS, CAVID C.	BAL	014	18TH WAR
HARRIS, DEALY	TAL	074	EASTON T
HARRIS, DINAH	BAL	030	9TH WARD
HARRIS, CORATTEY	BAL	015	2ND DIST
HARRIS, E. J W.	BAL	470	14TH WAR
HARRIS, EASTER	CAL	049	3RD DIST
HARRIS, ECWARD	HAR	032	1ST DIST
HARRIS, EDWARD	FRE	098	FREDERIC
HARRIS, ECWARD	QUE	137	1ST E DI
HARRIS, ECWARD	BAL	347	7TH WARD
HARRIS, EDWARD	BAL	354	7TH WARD
HARRIS, ECWARD	TAL	045	EASTON T
HARRIS, EDWARD	TAL	115	ST MICHA
HARRIS, EDWARD B.	BAL	183	6TH WARD
HARRIS, ELI	BAL	207	19TH WAR
HARRIS, ELI-BLACK	CAR	135	NO TWP L
HARRIS, ELIAS	CEC	005	ELKTON 3
HARRIS, ELISA	BAL	177	2ND DIST
HARRIS, ELISHA	CEC	158	PORT DUP
HARRIS, ELIZA	CEC	122	4TH E DI
HARRIS, ELIZA	BAL	414	14TH WAR
HARRIS, ELIZA	BAL	464	14TH WAR
HARRIS, ELIZA	HAR	166	3RD DIST
HARRIS, ELIZA	FRE	165	EMMITTSB
HARRIS, ELIZA	CEC	193	5TH E DI
HARRIS, ELIZA	BAL	177	2ND DIST
HARRIS, ELIZA	BAL	254	1ST DIST
HARRIS, ELIZA	BAL	401	3RD WARD
HARRIS, ELIZA	BAL	099	15TH WAR
HARRIS, ELIZA MISS-	BAL	315	20TH WAR
HARRIS, ELIZABETH	BAL	289	20TH WAR
HARRIS, ELIZABETH	CAR	142	NO TWP L
HARRIS, ELIZABETH	CEC	151	PORT DUP
HARRIS, ELIZABETH	CAR	326	1ST DIST
HARRIS, ELIZABETH	FRE	298	WOODSBOR
HARRIS, ELIZABETH	BAL	102	10TH WAR
HARRIS, ELIZABETH	BAL	403	3RD WARD
HARRIS, ELIZABETH	BAL	265	7TH WARD
HARRIS, ELIZABETH	BAL	034	9TH WARD
HARRIS, ELIZABETH	BAL	091	2ND DIST
HARRIS, ELIZABETH	BAL	337	3RD WARD
HARRIS, ELIZABETH	ANN	493	HOWARD D
HARRIS, ELIZABETH	BAL	203	6TH DIST
HARRIS, ELIZABETH	TAL	022	EASTON D
HARRIS, ELIZABETH A.	BAL	287	7TH WARD
HARRIS, ELIZABETH E.	CAR	156	NO TWP L
HARRIS, ELIZABETH-BLACK	CAR	093	NO TWP L
HARRIS, ELIZABETH-BLACK	BAL	182	2ND WARD
HARRIS, ELLEN	BAL	033	9TH WARD
HARRIS, ELLEN	BAL	339	13TH WAR
HARRIS, ELLEN	CEC	207	7TH E DI
HARRIS, ELLEN	CEC	016	ELKTON 3
HARRIS, ELLEN	PRI	075	MARLBROU
HARRIS, ELVINA	BAL	111	18TH WAR
HARRIS, ELY	BAL	148	19TH WAR
HARRIS, EMAS-BLACK	CAR	138	NO TWP L
HARRIS, EMELINE	QUE	211	3RD E DI
HARRIS, EMIALS-BLACK	CAR	162	NO TWP L
HARRIS, EMORY	BAL	193	17TH WAR
HARRIS, ENOCH	CEC	198	7TH E DI
HARRIS, EPHRAIM	BAL	452	1ST DIST
HARRIS, ESTER	CAR	286	7TH DIST
HARRIS, FANNY	BAL	101	10TH WAR
HARRIS, FRANCES	QUE	252	5TH E DI
HARRIS, FRANCIS	ANN	492	HOWARD D
HARRIS, FREDERIC	BAL	257	6TH WARD
HARRIS, GEORGE	BAL	285	7TH WARD
HARRIS, GEORGE	BAL	131	1ST WARD
HARRIS, GEORGE	BAL	368	1ST DIST
HARRIS, GECRGE	BAL	346	7TH WARD
HARRIS, GEORGE	SOM	358	BRINKLEY
HARRIS, GEORGE	ST	343	5TH E DI
HARRIS, GEORGE	CEC	008	ELKTON 3
HARRIS, GEORGE	CAR	234	UNION TO
HARRIS, GEORGE	FRE	306	WOODSBOR
HARRIS, GEORGE	BAL	098	18TH WAR
HARRIS, GEORGE	BAL	295	17TH WAR
HARRIS, GEORGE	BAL	062	18TH WAR
HARRIS, GEORGE	CAR	393	2ND DIST
HARRIS, GEORGE	HAR	163	3RD DIST
HARRIS, GEORGE F.	CHA	255	MIDDLETO
HARRIS, GEORGE M.	BAL	197	19TH WAR
HARRIS, GEORGE*	BAL	382	3RD WARD
HARRIS, GIDEON	CAR	091	NO TWP L
HARRIS, GOAN H.	BAL	182	16TH WAR
HARRIS, GRANT	ST	343	5TH E DI
HARRIS, H.	BAL	151	1ST WARD
HARRIS, HANNAH	BAL	142	11TH WAR
HARRIS, HANNER	HAR	153	3RD DIST
HARRIS, HARRIET	KEN	212	2ND DIST
HARRIS, HARRIET	BAL	177	16TH WAR
HARRIS, HARRIET A.	TAL	019	EASTON D
HARRIS, HARRIETT	CAR	066	NO TWP L
HARRIS, HARRY	CAR	141	NO TWP L
HARRIS, HAZZARD	HAR	034	1ST DIST
HARRIS, HENRY	HAR	115	2ND DIST
HARRIS, HENRY	CAR	135	NO TWP L
HARRIS, HENRY	KEN	216	2ND DIST
HARRIS, HENRY	MGM	321	CRACKLIN
HARRIS, HENRY	TAL	014	EASTON D
HARRIS, HENRY	QUE	249	5TH E DI
HARRIS, HENRY	BAL	091	10TH WAR
HARRIS, HENRY	BAL	273	12TH WAR
HARRIS, HENRY	BAL	028	2ND DIST
HARRIS, HENRY	BAL	015	1ST WARD
HARRIS, HENRY R.	CHA	222	ALLENS F
HARRIS, HENRY R.	FRE	309	WOODSBOR
HARRIS, HERRMAN	CEC	155	PORT DUP
HARRIS, HICKS	BAL	321	12TH WAR
HARRIS, HULIA	BAL	192	2ND WARD
HARRIS, INHITTE *	KEN	273	1ST DIST
HARRIS, ISAAC	KEN	271	1ST DIST
HARRIS, ISAAC	KEN	309	3RD DIST
HARRIS, ISAAC	WOR	327	1ST E DI
HARRIS, ISAAC	BAL	015	2ND DIST
HARRIS, ISAAC	BAL	018	2ND DIST
HARRIS, ISAAC	HAR	203	3RD DIST
HARRIS, ISABELLA	BAL	134	16TH WAR
HARRIS, ISABELLA-BLACK	QUE	168	2ND E DI
HARRIS, ISABILA	HAR	190	3RD DIST
HARRIS, ISASH	TAL	093	ST MICHA
HARRIS, J.	BAL	117	1ST WARD
HARRIS, J. MORRISON	BAL	109	10TH WAR
HARRIS, JACOB	BAL	086	15TH WAR
HARRIS, JACOB	BAL	091	15TH WAR
HARRIS, JACOB	BAL	254	12TH WAR
HARRIS, JACOB	TAL	093	ST MICHA
HARRIS, JACOB	QUE	251	5TH E DI
HARRIS, JACOB	CAR	275	7TH DIST
HARRIS, JAMES	DOR	371	3RD DIVI
HARRIS, JAMES	CHA	255	MIDDLETO
HARRIS, JAMES	CHA	259	MIDDLETO
HARRIS, JAMES	BAL	153	11TH WAR
HARRIS, JAMES	CAR	104	NO TWP L
HARRIS, JAMES	CAR	160	NO TWP L
HARRIS, JAMES	BAL	234	20TH WAR
HARRIS, JAMES	BAL	018	4TH WARD
HARRIS, JAMES	SOM	367	BRINKLEY
HARRIS, JAMES	SOM	398	BRINKLEY
HARRIS, JAMES	QUE	194	3RD E DI
HARRIS, JAMES	PRI	078	MARLBROU
HARRIS, JAMES	SOM	483	TRAPP DI
HARRIS, JAMES	BAL	302	12TH WAR
HARRIS, JAMES	BAL	132	16TH WAR
HARRIS, JAMES	BAL	162	1ST WARD
HARRIS, JAMES	BAL	040	9TH WARD
HARRIS, JAMES	BAL	362	8TH WARD
HARRIS, JAMES	BAL	120	5TH WARD
HARRIS, JAMES	ANN	278	ANNAPOLI
HARRIS, JAMES	ALL	174	7TH E.D.
HARRIS, JAMES B.	BAL	416	3RD WARD
HARRIS, JAMES T.	BAL	409	3RD WARD
HARRIS, JAMES T.	BAL	338	3RD WARD
HARRIS, JANE	BAL	104	10TH WAR
HARRIS, JANE	BAL	300	1ST DIST
HARRIS, JANE	CAL	051	3RD DIST
HARRIS, JAOCB	ALL	229	CUMBERLA
HARRIS, JEREMIAH	BAL	174	1ST WARD
HARRIS, JESSE	BAL	322	1ST DIST
HARRIS, JESSEE	BAL	287	7TH WARD
HARRIS, JOHN	BAL	143	1ST WARD
HARRIS, JOHN	BAL	149	5TH WARD
HARRIS, JOHN	BAL	016	1ST WARD
HARRIS, JOHN	ANN	275	ANNAPOLI
HARRIS, JOHN	BAL	266	12TH WAR
HARRIS, JOHN	BAL	459	8TH WARD
HARRIS, JOHN	CAR	128	NO TWP L
HARRIS, JOHN	CAR	067	NO TWP L
HARRIS, JOHN	CAR	286	7TH DIST
HARRIS, JOHN	BAL	009	4TH WARD
HARRIS, JOHN	CAR	179	8TH DIST
HARRIS, JOHN	CEC	208	7TH E DI
HARRIS, JOHN	FRE	451	8TH E DI
HARRIS, JOHN	KEN	225	2ND DIST
HARRIS, JOHN	MGM	335	CRACKLIN
HARRIS, JOHN	HAR	186	3RD DIST
HARRIS, JOHN	PRI	112	PISCATAW
HARRIS, JOHN	SOM	442	DAMES QU
HARRIS, JOHN	QUE	249	5TH E DI
HARRIS, JOHN	TAL	101	ST MICHA
HARRIS, JOHN B.	ST	342	5TH E DI
HARRIS, JOHN E.	SOM	526	QUANTICO
HARRIS, JOHN H.	ST	343	5TH E DI
HARRIS, JOHN H.	TAL	043	EASTON D
HARRIS, JOHN M.	BAL	352	7TH WARD
HARRIS, JOHN T.	ST	280	3RD E DI
HARRIS, JOHN W.	MGM	321	CRACKLIN
HARRIS, JOICE-BLACK	FRE	018	FREDERIC
HARRIS, JOSEPH	FRE	128	CREAGERS
HARRIS, JOSEPH	KEN	252	1ST DIST
HARRIS, JOSEPH	KEN	234	2ND DIST
HARRIS, JOSEPH	HAR	169	3RD DIST
HARRIS, JOSEPH	BAL	448	14TH WAR
HARRIS, JOSEPH	CAL	050	3RD DIST
HARRIS, JOSEPH	QUE	239	5TH E DI
HARRIS, JOSEPH	SOM	350	BRINKLEY
HARRIS, JOSEPH	TAL	082	ST MICHA
HARRIS, JOSEPH	KEN	273	1ST DIST
HARRIS, JOSEPH	PRI	093	MARLBROU
HARRIS, JOSEPH	PRI	027	VANSVILL
HARRIS, JOSEPH	BAL	220	12TH WAR
HARRIS, JOSEPH *	BAL	154	1ST WARD
HARRIS, JOSEPH *	WAS	069	2ND SUBD
HARRIS, JOSEPH H.	ST	339	5TH E DI
HARRIS, JOSEPH P.	TAL	045	EASTON T
HARRIS, JOSEPH P.	BAL	047	18TH WAR
HARRIS, JOSEPHINE	BAL	266	2ND WARD
HARRIS, JSOEPH	BAL	074	15TH WAR
HARRIS, JULIA	TAL	093	ST MICHA
HARRIS, JULIA A.	FRE	309	WOODSBOR
HARRIS, JULIAN	DOR	399	1ST DIST
HARRIS, LAPLISHUM	BAL	129	11TH WAR
HARRIS, LAURA	KEN	227	2ND DIST
HARRIS, LEEDS	BAL	166	5TH WARD
HARRIS, LETHIA A.	BAL	305	3RD WARD
HARRIS, LEVIN	SOM	362	BRINKLEY
HARRIS, LEVIN-BLACK	CAR	136	NO TWP L
HARRIS, LEVINA M.	BAL	049	2ND DIST
HARRIS, LIDDY A.	BAL	128	11TH WAR
HARRIS, LIDIA	TAL	090	ST MICHA
HARRIS, LITTLETON	SOM	403	BRINKLEY
HARRIS, LITTLETON	SOM	442	DAMES QU
HARRIS, LITTLETON	SOM	461	HANGARY
HARRIS, LITTLETON T.	WOR	327	1ST E DI
HARRIS, LLOYD	SOM	442	DAMES QU
HARRIS, LLOYD	DOR	411	1ST DIST
HARRIS, LOUISA	BAL	111	5TH WARD
HARRIS, LOUISA	BAL	187	11TH WAR
HARRIS, LOUISA	BAL	022	1ST WARD
HARRIS, LOYD	BAL	047	2ND DIST
HARRIS, LOYD	BAL	015	2ND DIST
HARRIS, LYDIA	DOR	395	1ST DIST
HARRIS, MACKALL	CAL	022	2ND DIST
HARRIS, MADISCN F.	MGM	397	ROCKERLE
HARRIS, MAHITABLE	BAL	259	17TH WAR
HARRIS, MANE	BAL	245	12TH WAR
HARRIS, MARGARET	BAL	281	20TH WAR
HARRIS, MARGARET-BLACK	BAL	225	2ND WARD
HARRIS, MARIA	BAL	029	15TH WAR
HARRIS, MARIA	BAL	201	17TH WAR
HARRIS, MARIA	HAR	100	2ND DIST
HARRIS, MARIA	HAR	131	2ND DIST
HARRIS, MARIA	BAL	409	3RD WARD
HARRIS, MARIA L.	FRE	100	FREDERIC
HARRIS, MARRIS	BAL	251	20TH WAR
HARRIS, MARTHA	BAL	338	13TH WAR
HARRIS, MARTHA E.	BAL	042	15TH WAR
HARRIS, MARY	BAL	044	15TH WAR
HARRIS, MARY	BAL	193	11TH WAR
HARRIS, MARY	BAL	066	15TH WAR
HARRIS, MARY	BAL	055	15TH WAR
HARRIS, MARY	BAL	309	7TH WARD
HARRIS, MARY	HAR	002	1ST DIST
HARRIS, MARY	SOM	408	DUBLIN D
HARRIS, MARY	SOM	442	DAMES QU
HARRIS, MARY	KEN	283	3RD DIST
HARRIS, MARY	QUE	242	5TH E DI
HARRIS, MARY	TAL	099	ST MICHA
HARRIS, MARY	TAL	007	EASTON D
HARRIS, MARY	PRI	042	VANSVILL
HARRIS, MARY A.	FRE	078	FREDERIC
HARRIS, MARY A.	BAL	366	13TH WAR
HARRIS, MARY A.	BAL	395	14TH WAR
HARRIS, MARY A.	BAL	053	15TH WAR
HARRIS, MARY E.	CEC	122	4TH E DI
HARRIS, MARY E.-MULATTO	ST	330	4TH E DI
HARRIS, MARY J.	BAL	330	3RD WARD
HARRIS, MARY L.	MGM	377	ROCKERLE
HARRIS, MARY R.	SOM	461	HANGARY
HARRIS, MARY-BLACK	ST	338	4TH E DI
HARRIS, MELCHOR	CAR	178	8TH DIST
HARRIS, MICHAEL	BAL	246	1ST DIST
HARRIS, MILKEY	BAL	180	16TH WAR
HARRIS, MINERVA	HAR	092	2ND DIST
HARRIS, MISS E.	FRE	199	5TH E DI
HARRIS, MOSE	HAR	003	1ST DIST
HARRIS, MOSE	HAR	031	1ST DIST
HARRIS, MOSES	BAL	343	3RD WARD
HARRIS, MOSES-BLACK	CAR	146	NO TWP L
HARRIS, N.	BAL	158	1ST WARD
HARRIS, NANCY	BAL	452	1ST DIST
HARRIS, NANCY	DOR	469	1ST DIST
HARRIS, NATHANIEL	BAL	084	18TH WAR
HARRIS, NATHANIEL-BLACK	QUE	168	2ND E DI
HARRIS, NICHOLAS	BAL	202	6TH WARD
HARRIS, NICHOLAS	BAL	172	16TH WAR
HARRIS, NROVAL	BAL	396	14TH WAR
HARRIS, O.C.	PRI	092	MARLBROU
HARRIS, OTHO	FRE	296	WOODSBOR
HARRIS, PATRICK	BAL	099	2ND DIST
HARRIS, PERRY	SOM	462	HANGARY
HARRIS, PETER	ANN	418	HOWARD D
HARRIS, PETER	CAR	131	NO TWP L
HARRIS, PETER	CAR	160	NO TWP L
HARRIS, PETER	CAL	049	3RD DIST
HARRIS, PHILIP	BAL	091	15TH WAR
HARRIS, PHOEBE	BAL	223	12TH WAR
HARRIS, PRISCILLA	BAL	474	14TH WAR
HARRIS, R.J.	CEC	008	ELKTON 3
HARRIS, RACHEL	BAL	243	20TH WAR
HARRIS, RACHEL	BAL	420	1ST DIST
HARRIS, REBECCA	BAL	104	15TH WAR
HARRIS, REBECCA	BAL	187	6TH WARD
HARRIS, REBECCA	CEC	038	CHESAPEA
HARRIS, REBECCA	CEC	168	6TH E DI
HARRIS, RICHARD	CAR	173	8TH DIST
HARRIS, RICHARD	BAL	080	18TH WAR
HARRIS, RICHARD	MGM	389	ROCKERLE
HARRIS, RICHARD	BAL	110	15TH WAR
HARRIS, RICHARD H.	KEN	248	2ND DIST
HARRIS, ROBERT	KEN	228	2ND DIST
HARRIS, ROBERT	HAR	159	3RD DIST
HARRIS, ROBERT	CEC	207	7TH E DI
HARRIS, ROBERT	CAR	130	NO TWP L
HARRIS, ROBERT	BAL	096	15TH WAR
HARRIS, ROBERT	BAL	036	15TH WAR
HARRIS, ROBERT	QUE	250	5TH E DI
HARRIS, ROBERT	SOM	391	BRINKLEY
HARRIS, ROBERT W.	BAL	470	13TH WAR
HARRIS, ROBERT-BLACK	CAR	135	NO TWP L
HARRIS, ROBERT-BLACK	CAR	132	NO TWP L
HARRIS, ROVE-BLACK	CAR	134	NO TWP L
HARRIS, SAMUEL	FRE	418	8TH E DI
HARRIS, SAMUEL	CEC	047	1ST E DI
HARRIS, SAMUEL	BAL	020	4TH WARD
HARRIS, SAMUEL	CEC	164	6TH E DI
HARRIS, SAMUEL	BAL	340	13TH WAR
HARRIS, SAMUEL	DOR	369	3RD DIVI
HARRIS, SAMUEL	KEN	294	3RD DIST
HARRIS, SAMUEL	BAL	102	15TH WAR
HARRIS, SAMUEL	BAL	113	2ND DIST
HARRIS, SAMUEL	BAL	141	1ST WARD
HARRIS, SAMUEL JR.	BAL	111	10TH WAR
HARRIS, SAMUEL-BLACK	QUE	168	2ND E DI
HARRIS, SARAH	KEN	306	3RD DIST
HARRIS, SARAH	SOM	481	TRAPP DI
HARRIS, SARAH	TAL	031	EASTON D
HARRIS, SARAH	BAL	074	15TH WAR
HARRIS, SARAH	BAL	197	5TH DIST

HARRIS, SARAH BAL 196 5TH DIST
HARRIS, SARAH BAL 056 18TH WAR
HARRIS, SARAH A. BAL 091 10TH WAR
HARRIS, SARAH A. ST 260 3RD E DI
HARRIS, SARAH C. TAL 041 EASTON D
HARRIS, SARAH E. FRE 418 8TH E DI
HARRIS, SARRAH A. SOM 541 TYASKIN
HARRIS, SHACE KEN 257 1ST DIST
HARRIS, SHACY KEN 208 2ND DIST
HARRIS, SHARLOTT HAR 164 3RD DIST
HARRIS, SHARLOTT TAL 031 EASTON D
HARRIS, SHARLOTTE CAR 068 NO TWP L
HARRIS, SILVER BAL 067 4TH WARD
HARRIS, SOLOMON SOM 462 HANGARY
HARRIS, SOLOMON BAL 023 9TH WARD
HARRIS, STEPHEN BAL 299 3RD WARD
HARRIS, SUAN BAL 178 16TH WAR
HARRIS, SUSAN BAL 017 15TH WAR
HARRIS, SUSAN BAL 360 8TH WARD
HARRIS, SUSAN ANN 275 ANNAPOLI
HARRIS, SUSAN TAL 012 EASTON D
HARRIS, SUSAN SOM 393 BRINKLEY
HARRIS, SUSAN BAL 411 14TH WAR
HARRIS, SUSAN BAL 425 14TH WAR
HARRIS, SUSAN KEN 251 2ND DIST
HARRIS, SUSANA CAR 384 2ND DIST
HARRIS, THEADORE BAL 273 7TH WARD
HARRIS, THEOPHILUS S. TAL 043 EASTON D
HARRIS, THOMAS SOM 465 HANGARY
HARRIS, THOMAS QUE 195 3RD E DI
HARRIS, THOMAS BAL 294 7TH WARD
HARRIS, THOMAS ANN 290 ANNAPOLI
HARRIS, THOMAS BAL 177 2ND DIST
HARRIS, THOMAS CAR 145 NO TWP L
HARRIS, THOMAS FRE 418 8TH E DI
HARRIS, THOMAS A. BAL 170 1ST WARD
HARRIS, THOMAS G. MGM 377 ROCKERLE
HARRIS, THOMAS H. BAL 168 11TH WAR
HARRIS, THOMAS J. BAL 382 3RD WARD
HARRIS, THOMAS J. BAL 152 16TH WAR
HARRIS, THOMAS-BLACK CAR 089 NO TWP L
HARRIS, THOMAS-BLACK CAR 104 NO TWP L
HARRIS, THOMAS-MULATTO ST 331 4TH E DI
HARRIS, VINCENT QUE 128 1ST E DI
HARRIS, VIOLA PRI 074 MARLBROU
HARRIS, W. G. BAL 153 1ST WARD
HARRIS, W.T. BAL 230 1ST DIST
HARRIS, WESTLY TAL 018 EASTON D
HARRIS, WILLIAM WAS 046 2ND SUBD
HARRIS, WILLIAM SOM 549 TYASKIN
HARRIS, WILLIAM WAS 154 HAGERSTO
HARRIS, WILLIAM BAL 164 1ST WARD
HARRIS, WILLIAM BAL 166 1ST WARD
HARRIS, WILLIAM BAL 034 9TH WARD
HARRIS, WILLIAM BAL 198 2ND WARD
HARRIS, WILLIAM BAL 174 16TH WAR
HARRIS, WILLIAM BAL 380 3RD WARD
HARRIS, WILLIAM BAL 126 1ST WARD
HARRIS, WILLIAM BAL 399 1ST DIST
HARRIS, WILLIAM BAL 452 1ST DIST
HARRIS, WILLIAM BAL 114 5TH WARD
HARRIS, WILLIAM BAL 203 6TH DIST
HARRIS, WILLIAM BAL 205 6TH DIST
HARRIS, WILLIAM ANN 419 HOWARD D
HARRIS, WILLIAM BAL 016 2ND DIST
HARRIS, WILLIAM BAL 031 2ND DIST
HARRIS, WILLIAM ANN 470 HOWARD D
HARRIS, WILLIAM KEN 253 1ST DIST
HARRIS, WILLIAM CAR 113 NO TWP L
HARRIS, WILLIAM CAR 150 NO TWP L
HARRIS, WILLIAM MGM 397 ROCKERLE
HARRIS, WILLIAM MGM 396 ROCKERLE
HARRIS, WILLIAM HAR 051 1ST DIST
HARRIS, WILLIAM FRE 417 8TH E DI
HARRIS, WILLIAM BAL 277 20TH WAR
HARRIS, WILLIAM BAL 272 20TH WAR
HARRIS, WILLIAM DOR 398 1ST DIST
HARRIS, WILLIAM A. BAL 174 16TH WAR
HARRIS, WILLIAM H. SOM 466 HANGARY
HARRIS, WILLIAM J. TAL 102 ST MICHA
HARRIS, WILLIAM J. N. FRE 078 FREDERIC
HARRIS, WILLIAM N. MGM 421 MEDLEY 3
HARRIS, WILLIAM S. BAL 142 1ST WARD
HARRIS, WILLIAM S. BAL 182 2ND WARD
HARRIS, WILLIAM T. BAL 231 1ST DIST
HARRIS, WILLIAM-BLACK CAR 091 NO TWP L
HARRIS, WILLIAM-MULATTO BAL 239 2ND WARD
HARRIS, ZACHARIAH G. MGM 421 MEDLEY 3
HARRIS.T HOAMS FRE 450 8TH E DI
HARRISON, ALEXANDER BAL 475 14TH WAR
HARRISON, ALFRED TAL 085 ST MICHA
HARRISON, ANDREW WAS 223 1ST DIST
HARRISON, ANN BAL 212 11TH WAR
HARRISON, ANN HAR 190 3RD DIST
HARRISON, ANN E. KEN 218 2ND DIST
HARRISON, ANNA BAL 010 9TH WARD
HARRISON, ANNE BAL 109 10TH WAR
HARRISON, ANTHONY ANN 289 ANNAPOLI
HARRISON, ARTHUR S. ST 347 5TH E DI
HARRISON, ASA BAL 405 1ST DIST
HARRISON, AUGUSTA-MULATTO FRE 234 BUCKEYST
HARRISON, BARBARA A. MGM 397 ROCKERLE
HARRISON, BASIL BAL 058 15TH WAR
HARRISON, BENJAMIN ANN 412 HOWARD D
HARRISON, BENJAMIN BAL 249 2ND WARD
HARRISON, BENJAMIN CAL 040 3RD DIST
HARRISON, BENJAMIN BAL 013 18TH WAR
HARRISON, BENJAMIN BAL 358 13TH WAR
HARRISON, BENJAMIN TAL 102 ST MICHA
HARRISON, BENJAMIN F. BAL 336 13TH WAR
HARRISON, BENJAMIN-BLACK QUE 149 1ST E DI
HARRISON, BENN-BLACK QUE 124 1ST E DI
HARRISON, BENONI FRE 404 JEFFERSO
HARRISON, CALVERT ANN 322 2ND DIST
HARRISON, CAROLINE BAL 078 15TH WAR
HARRISON, CAROLINE TAL 115 ST MICHA
HARRISON, CATHARINE FRE 408 JEFFERSO
HARRISON, CATHARINE BAL 337 13TH WAR
HARRISON, CHARLES TAL 082 ST MICHA
HARRISON, CHARLES BAL 370 1ST DIST
HARRISON, CHARLES BAL 370 1ST DIST
HARRISON, CHARLES D. BAL 384 3RD WARD
HARRISON, CHARLES R. CAL 042 3RD DIST
HARRISON, CHARLOTTE BAL 108 15TH WAR
HARRISON, CRARACY CHA 245 HILLTOP
HARRISON, CRISTOPHER TAL 025 EASTON D
HARRISON, DANIEL BAL 308 12TH WAR
HARRISON, DANIEL E. BAL 304 3RD WARD
HARRISON, DAVID S. BAL 208 19TH WAR
HARRISON, DENNIS WAS 091 2ND SUBD
HARRISON, E. M. ALL 062 10TH E.D
HARRISON, EDWARD WOR 282 BERLIN 1
HARRISON, EDWARD TAL 079 ST MICHA
HARRISON, EDWARD TAL 061 EASTON D
HARRISON, EDWARD S.* TAL 038 EASTON D
HARRISON, ELEANOR WOR 272 BERLIN 1
HARRISON, ELISABETH ALL 062 10TH E.D
HARRISON, ELIZA BAL 048 15TH WAR
HARRISON, ELIZA CAR 080 NO TWP L
HARRISON, ELIZABETH CAL 029 2ND DIST
HARRISON, ELIZABETH BAL 088 15TH WAR
HARRISON, ELIZABETH BAL 105 10TH WAR
HARRISON, ELIZABETH WOR 270 BERLIN 1
HARRISON, ELIZABETH TAL 089 ST MICHA
HARRISON, ELIZABETH W. BAL 078 15TH WAR
HARRISON, ELLEN BAL 062 1ST WARD
HARRISON, ENOCH T. BAL 202 19TH WAR
HARRISON, ESHLINDA* BAL 101 10TH WAR
HARRISON, EUDALIA WAS 157 HAGERSTO
HARRISON, FANNY MGM 327 CRACKLIN
HARRISON, FARNEY WOR 303 SNOW HIL
HARRISON, FRANCIS J. BAL 178 11TH WAR
HARRISON, FREDERICK FRE 034 FREDERIC
HARRISON, FREDERICK JR. BAL 414 1ST DIST
HARRISON, FREEBURN TAL 007 EASTON D
HARRISON, GEORGE WAS 112 2ND DIST
HARRISON, GEORGE BAL 194 11TH WAR
HARRISON, GEORGE ALL 207 CUMBERLA
HARRISON, GEORGE CEC 162 6TH E DI
HARRISON, GEORGE B. PRI 020 VANSVILL
HARRISON, GEORGE H. BAL 103 15TH WAR
HARRISON, GEORGE M. ANN 446 HOWARD D
HARRISON, GEORGE W. BAL 279 2ND WARD
HARRISON, GEORGE W. CAL 025 2ND DIST
HARRISON, GIDEON O. ST 344 5TH E DI
HARRISON, H.L. CAL 042 3RD DIST
HARRISON, HALL WAS 021 2ND SUBD
HARRISON, HENRY BAL 224 17TH WAR
HARRISON, HENRY BAL 175 19TH WAR
HARRISON, HENRY BAL 377 3RD WARD
HARRISON, HORACE PRI 021 VANSVILL
HARRISON, HOWARD PRI 021 VANSVILL
HARRISON, HUGH T. REV. ANN 466 HOWARD D
HARRISON, ISAAC BAL 405 1ST DIST
HARRISON, J. BAL 117 1ST WARD
HARRISON, J.P. BAL 351 7TH WARD
HARRISON, JACOB PRI 090 MARLBROU
HARRISON, JACOB CAL 057 3RD DIST
HARRISON, JACOB BAL 002 18TH WAR
HARRISON, JACOB F. WAS 033 2ND SUBD
HARRISON, JACOB-MULATTO FRE 039 FREDERIC
HARRISON, JAEMS CAL 026 2ND DIST
HARRISON, JAMES CAL 041 3RD DIST
HARRISON, JAMES TAL 105 ST MICHA
HARRISON, JAMES TAL 115 ST MICHA
HARRISON, JAMES BAL 008 1ST WARD
HARRISON, JAMES BAL 356 3RD WARD
HARRISON, JAMES BAL 410 1ST DIST
HARRISON, JAMES BAL 136 1ST WARD
HARRISON, JAMES BAL 309 1ST DIST
HARRISON, JAMES BAL 150 1ST WARD
HARRISON, JAMES J. TAL 108 ST MICHA
HARRISON, JAMES JR. TAL 079 ST MICHA
HARRISON, JAMES W. BAL 352 7TH WARD
HARRISON, JAMS ALL 236 CUMBERLA
HARRISON, JANE BAL 065 15TH WAR
HARRISON, JANE BAL 307 12TH WAR
HARRISON, JANE WOR 263 BERLIN 1
HARRISON, JANE CAL 020 2ND DIST
HARRISON, JEF BAL 115 2ND DIST
HARRISON, JEREMIAH TAL 120 ST MICHA
HARRISON, JESSE BAL 378 13TH WAR
HARRISON, JOHN BAL 358 13TH WAR
HARRISON, JOHN BAL 425 3RD WARD
HARRISON, JOHN TAL 104 ST MICHA
HARRISON, JOHN TAL 103 ST MICHA
HARRISON, JOHN PRI 023 VANSVILL
HARRISON, JOHN TAL 090 ST MICHA
HARRISON, JOHN ST 345 5TH E DI
HARRISON, JOHN QUE 178 2ND E DI
HARRISON, JOHN BAL 096 2ND DIST
HARRISON, JOHN BAL 211 6TH WARD
HARRISON, JOHN BAL 280 2ND WARD
HARRISON, JOHN BAL 133 1ST WARD
HARRISON, JOHN BAL 016 1ST WARD
HARRISON, JOHN B. ST 348 5TH E DI
HARRISON, JOHN K. PRI 021 VANSVILL
HARRISON, JOHN T. MGM 389 ROCKERLE
HARRISON, JOHN W. ST 267 3RD E DI
HARRISON, JOHN W. ANN 492 HOWARD D
HARRISON, JOHN-BLACK BAL 219 2ND WARD
HARRISON, JONATAN TAL 102 ST MICHA
HARRISON, JOSEPH WAS 144 2ND DIST
HARRISON, JOSEPH BAL 306 1ST DIST
HARRISON, JOSEPH CAR 157 NO TWP L
HARRISON, JOSEPH H. TAL 092 ST MICHA
HARRISON, JOSEPH J. TAL 116 ST MICHA
HARRISON, JOSEPH N. CHA 276 ALLENS F
HARRISON, JOSEPHC FRE 405 JEFFERSO
HARRISON, JOSEPHINE KEN 238 2ND DIST
HARRISON, JOSHUA TAL 120 ST MICHA
HARRISON, JOSHUA D. MGM 389 ROCKERLE
HARRISON, JOSHUA O.* BAL 384 3RD WARD
HARRISON, KATE BAL 097 10TH WAR
HARRISON, KENSEY QUE 186 3RD E DI
HARRISON, KITTY BAL 151 19TH WAR
HARRISON, LEFCOT BAL 304 7TH WARD
HARRISON, LEMUEL BAL 177 16TH WAR
HARRISON, LEVI TAL 116 ST MICHA
HARRISON, LEVIN CAL 021 2ND DIST
HARRISON, LEWIS BAL 386 13TH WAR
HARRISON, LEWIS CAL 040 3RD DIST
HARRISON, LIDIA R. TAL 105 ST MICHA
HARRISON, LOUISA BAL 001 15TH WAR
HARRISON, LOUISA ANN 405 8TH DIST
HARRISON, LUCRETIA BAL 013 1ST WARD
HARRISON, LYDIA WAS 158 HAGERSTO
HARRISON, MALVINA BAL 248 1ST DIST
HARRISON, MANUEL ANN 434 HOWARD D
HARRISON, MANUEL-BLACK QUE 189 3RD E DI
HARRISON, MARGARET BAL 396 8TH WARD
HARRISON, MARGRET ANN 271 ANNAPOLI
HARRISON, MARIA BAL 167 11TH WAR
HARRISON, MARIA TAL 104 ST MICHA
HARRISON, MARTHA J. TAL 093 ST MICHA
HARRISON, MARY TAL 091 ST MICHA
HARRISON, MARY TAL 010 EASTON D
HARRISON, MARY WAS 136 HAGERSTO
HARRISON, MARY BAL 261 2ND WARD
HARRISON, MARY BAL 126 5TH WARD
HARRISON, MARY CAL 059 3RD DIST
HARRISON, MARY W. WOR 264 BERLIN 1
HARRISON, MARY A. BAL 292 20TH WAR
HARRISON, MARY E. WOR 259 BERLIN 1
HARRISON, MARY J. TAL 116 ST MICHA
HARRISON, MARY L. CAL 021 2ND DIST
HARRISON, MATILDA BAL 378 13TH WAR
HARRISON, MATILDA WOR 278 BERLIN 1
HARRISON, MATILDA ANN 400 8TH DIST
HARRISON, MICHAEL ALL 075 5TH E.D.
HARRISON, N.S. BAL 249 12TH WAR
HARRISON, NACY WOR 264 BERLIN 1
HARRISON, NICOLAS C. TAL 062 EASTON D
HARRISON, NIMORD T. FRE 092 FREDERIC
HARRISON, NINROD CAR 367 9TH DIST
HARRISON, OLIVER TAL 083 ST MICHA
HARRISON, ORD FRE 230 BUCKEYST
HARRISON, PETER BAL 205 2ND WARD
HARRISON, QUIINTIA * TAL 106 ST MICHA
HARRISON, REBECCA CAL 048 3RD DIST
HARRISON, REUBEN H. FRE 247 NEW MARK
HARRISON, RICHARD BAL 033 18TH WAR
HARRISON, RICHARD WAS 128 2ND DIST
HARRISON, RICHARD TAL 038 EASTON D
HARRISON, RICHARD M. QUE 198 3RD E DI
HARRISON, ROBERT WOR 272 BERLIN 1
HARRISON, ROBERT TAL 084 ST MICHA
HARRISON, ROBERT CAL 041 3RD DIST
HARRISON, ROBERT CAL 025 2ND DIST
HARRISON, ROBERT * CAL 020 2ND DIST
HARRISON, ROBERT JR. TAL 084 ST MICHA
HARRISON, SALLY WOR 250 1ST CENS
HARRISON, SALLY ANN QUE 214 3RD E DI
HARRISON, SAMUEL WAS 204 1ST DIST
HARRISON, SAMUEL KEN 304 3RD DIST
HARRISON, SAMUEL TAL 114 ST MICHA
HARRISON, SAMUEL CAL 029 2ND DIST
HARRISON, SAMUEL BAL 169 19TH WAR
HARRISON, SAMUEL S. TAL 082 ST MICHA
HARRISON, SAMUEL T. QUE 170 2ND E DI
HARRISON, SAMUEL T. TAL 085 ST MICHA
HARRISON, SARAH BAL 212 5TH WARD
HARRISON, SARAH BAL 220 6TH WARD
HARRISON, SOPHIA BAL 022 18TH WAR
HARRISON, SUSAN BAL 078 18TH WAR
HARRISON, SUSANAH BAL 044 18TH WAR
HARRISON, SUSANNA BAL 397 8TH WARD
HARRISON, THEOPHILUS CHA 286 BOJANTOW
HARRISON, THOASM HAR 029 1ST DIST
HARRISON, THOMAS HAR 039 1ST DIST
HARRISON, THOMAS KEN 238 2ND DIST
HARRISON, THOMAS BAL 145 11TH WAR
HARRISON, THOMAS BAL 012 15TH WAR
HARRISON, THOMAS ANN 445 HOWARD D
HARRISON, THOMAS BAL 069 1ST WARD
HARRISON, THOMAS BAL 029 1ST WARD
HARRISON, THOMAS BAL 463 1ST DIST
HARRISON, THOMAS TAL 099 ST MICHA
HARRISON, THOMAS TAL 116 ST MICHA
HARRISON, THOMAS A. WOR 241 1ST CENS
HARRISON, VACHEL BAL 273 1ST DIST
HARRISON, WILLIAM ANN 369 4TH DIST
HARRISON, WILLIAM BAL 251 12TH WAR
HARRISON, WILLIAM BAL 333 7TH WARD
HARRISON, WILLIAM BAL 266 2ND WARD
HARRISON, WILLIAM BAL 371 3RD WARD
HARRISON, WILLIAM BAL 393 3RD WARD
HARRISON, WILLIAM BAL 407 8TH WARD
HARRISON, WILLIAM BAL 234 6TH WARD
HARRISON, WILLIAM BAL 088 15TH WAR
HARRISON, WILLIAM TAL 110 ST MICHA
HARRISON, WILLIAM DOR 452 1ST DIST
HARRISON, WILLIAM WAS 115 2ND DIST
HARRISON, WILLIAM BAL 153 11TH WAR
HARRISON, WILLIAM CAL 042 3RD DIST
HARRISON, WILLIAM BAL 131 11TH WAR
HARRISON, WILLIAM BAL 129 11TH WAR
HARRISON, WILLIAM BAL 043 18TH WAR
HARRISON, WILLIAM BAL 204 19TH WAR
HARRISON, WILLIAM E. TAL 109 ST MICHA
HARRISON, WILLIAM E. BAL 279 2ND WARD
HARRISON, WILLIAM G. BAL 390 13TH WAR
HARRISON, WILLIAM H. BAL 125 1ST WARD
HARRISON, WILLIAM H. TAL 094 ST MICHA
HARRISON, WILLIAM H.-BLAC FRE 049 FREDERIC
HARRISON, WILLIAM HENRY CAL 061 3RD DIST
HARRISON, WILLIAM I. CAL 042 3RD DIST
HARRISON, WILLIAM N. BAL 212 6TH WARD
HARRISON, WILLIAM S. BAL 256 6TH WARD
HARRISON, WILLIAM T. CAL 047 3RD DIST
HARRISON, WILLIAM W. TAL 019 EASTON D
HARRISON, WILLIAMC CAL 063 3RD DIST
HARRISON, WSHINGTON QUE 167 2ND E DI
HARRISON, ZEPHANIAH FRE 025 FREDERIC
HARRISON,JOSIAH FRE 025 FREDERIC
HARRISON,ZACHARIAH CAL 052 3RD DIST
HARRISS, ANDREW BAL 100 5TH WARD
HARRISS, ANN BAL 206 17TH WAR
HARRISS, BETSY BAL 134 5TH WARD
HARRISS, CLARA BAL 008 9TH WARD
HARRISS, DANIEL BAL 223 17TH WAR
HARRISS, G. BAL 318 12TH WAR
HARRISS, JACOB BAL 279 17TH WAR
HARRISS, JAMES BAL 098 5TH WARD
HARRISS, JARVIS BAL 193 17TH WAR
HARRISS, JOHN BAL 216 17TH WAR
HARRISS, JOSEPH BAL 216 17TH WAR
HARRISS, JOSHUA BAL 207 2ND WARD
HARRISS, LOUISA BAL 248 1ST DIST
HARRISS, PHILLIS DOR 301 1ST DIST
HARRISS, SAMUEL BAL 276 17TH WAR
HARRISS, SANDY BAL 216 17TH WAR
HARRISS, THOMAS BAL 245 1ST DIST
HARRISS, THOMAS ANN 462 HOWARD D
HARRISS, WILLIAM BAL 207 17TH WAR
HARRISS, WILLIAM H. DOR 319 1ST DIST
HARRISSON, ANN BAL 249 17TH WAR
HARRISSON, CHAMPION BAL 248 17TH WAR
HARRISSON, EMILY BAL 215 17TH WAR
HARRISSON, NATHAN BAL 016 18TH WAR
HARRISSON, THOMAS J. BAL 223 17TH WAR
HARRISSON, WILLIAM BAL 254 17TH WAR
HARRISSON, ZEDEKIAH G. BAL 284 17TH WAR
HARRLS, JOHN BAL 143 2ND DIST
HARROD, CHARELS I. HAR 103 2ND DIST
HARROD, CHARLES HAR 084 2ND DIST
HARROD, CHRISTIANA CAL 032 2ND DIST
HARROD, DERINDA CAL 032 2ND DIST
HARROD, HENNEY BAL 081 15TH WAR
HARROD, JAMES BAL 124 1ST WARD

Name	County	Page	District
HARROD, JAMES	QUE	239	5TH E DI
HARROD, JOHN T.	HAR	103	2ND DIST
HARROD, JOSEPH A.	BAL	132	1ST WARD
HARROD, MAJOR	BAL	456	8TH WARD
HARROD, MARY	BAL	250	6TH WARD
HARROD, MARY G.	BAL	389	3RD WARD
HARROD, OSA	ANN	269	ANNAPOLI
HARROD, SAMUEL	HAR	048	1ST DIST
HARROD, SAMUEL	CAL	054	3RD DIST
HARROD, SARAH	BAL	390	3RD WARD
HARROD, THOMAS	CAL	036	2ND DIST
HARROD, WILLIAM	HAR	084	2ND DIST
HARROD, WILLIAM	HAR	051	1ST DIST
HARROD, WILLIAM	BAL	100	2ND DIST
HARROLD, CATHERINE	BAL	401	3RD WARD
HARROLD, JOHN	BAL	410	3RD WARD
HARROLD, JOHN J.	BAL	044	9TH WARD
HARROLD, LOUISA	BAL	411	3RD WARD
HARROLL, EMILY	BAL	460	8TH WARD
HARRUN, HENRY	PRI	098	SPALDING
HARROSS, HOSEA	ALL	191	9TH E.D.
HARRS, LEWIS	BAL	031	1ST WARD
HARRVEY, ELIZABETH	BAL	142	11TH WAR
HARRY, CAROLINE	FRE	197	5TH E DI
HARRY, DAVID	HAR	011	1ST DIST
HARRY, ELIZABETH	WAS	137	HAGERSTO
HARRY, H. J.	BAL	157	1ST WARD
HARRY, ISABELLA	WAS	131	HAGERSTO
HARRY, J.K.	WAS	122	HAGERSTO
HARRY, JOEL *	HAR	044	1ST DIST
HARRY, JOHN	BAL	075	2ND DIST
HARRY, NICHOLAS	CAR	191	4TH DIST
HARRY, PARMENIA *	FRE	114	CREAGERS
HARRY, SUSAN	WAS	136	HAGERSTO
HARRYMAN, AQUILLA	BAL	098	2ND DIST
HARRYMAN, GEORGE	BAL	030	2ND DIST
HARRYMAN, HEZEKIAH	HAR	098	2ND DIST
HARRYMAN, JOHN SR.	BAL	027	2ND DIST
HARRYMAN, JOSIAH	BAL	185	6TH WARD
HARRYMAN, LABERT	BAL	143	2ND DIST
HARRYMAN, SAMUEL	BAL	220	1ST DIST
HARRYMAN, SARAH	HAR	144	2ND DIST
HARRYMAN, WALTER	BAL	342	3RD WARD
HARRYMAN, WILLIAM	HAR	075	BEL AIR
HARRYMAN, WILLIAM D.	BAL	134	5TH WARD
HARS, MARY	BAL	371	13TH WAR
HARSAID, JANE	BAL	357	13TH WAR
HARSANK, ACAM	BAL	105	1ST WARD
HARSBERGER, MARY	BAL	006	18TH WAR
HARSEL, ELIZABETH	WAS	257	1ST DIST
HARSEN, JEREMIAH	BAL	119	1ST WARD
HARSEY, GEORGE	BAL	025	9TH WARD
HARSEY, LEONARD	BAL	136	2ND DIST
HARSEY, MARY M.	FRE	025	FREDERIC
HARSH, ADAM	CAR	176	8TH DIST
HARSH, CANIEL *	WAS	142	2ND DIST
HARSH, ELIZA	BAL	407	14TH WAR
HARSH, GEORGE	WAS	106	2ND DIST
HARSHAM, CHRISTIAN	FRE	370	CATOCTIN
HARSHAMAN, GEORGE	FRE	371	CATOCTIN
HARSHAMN, CHRISTIAN	FRE	373	CATOCTIN
HARSHAW, NEALIE	ANN	348	3RD DIST
HARSHBAUGH, ABRAHAM	ALL	039	2ND E.D.
HARSHBERGER, CAROLINE	WAS	295	1ST DIST
HARSHBERGER, DANIEL	WAS	295	1ST DIST
HARSHBERGER, JACOB	WAS	295	1ST DIST
HARSHBERGER, JOHN	WAS	296	1ST DIST
HARSHBERGER, TEMPERENCE	BAL	006	18TH WAR
HARSHMAN, CHARLOTTE	FRE	343	MIDDLETO
HARSHMAN, CHRISTIAN	FRE	367	CATOCTIN
HARSHMAN, ELINYART *	FRE	340	MIDDLETO
HARSHMAN, JOHN	FRE	343	MIDDLETO
HARSHMAN, JOHN	FRE	367	CATOCTIN
HARSHMAN, MARY A.	FRE	368	CATOCTIN
HARSHMIER, SAMUEL	FRE	337	MIDDLETO
HARSLOVE, JOHN	BAL	145	1ST WARD
HARSON, CHARLES	BAL	159	19TH WAR
HARSSELL, JEREMIAH	CAR	330	MANCHEST
HARST, JOHN	BAL	365	13TH WAR
HART, ABRAHAM	ANN	314	1ST DIST
HART, ABRAM	CEC	009	ELKTON 3
HART, AMANUEL	DOR	436	1ST DIST
HART, AMI E.	CEC	009	ELKTON 3
HART, ANN	BAL	244	12TH WAR
HART, ANNE J.	ANN	281	ANNAPOLI
HART, ARCHIBALD	BAL	439	14TH WAR
HART, ASA	BAL	210	6TH WARD
HART, BENJAMIN	DOR	348	3RD DIVI
HART, C.	BAL	157	1ST WARD
HART, CATHARINE	BAL	198	19TH WAR
HART, CATHARINE	BAL	299	17TH WAR
HART, CHARLES C.	BAL	026	18TH WAR
HART, CHRISTIAN	BAL	328	7TH WARD
HART, DANIEL	ANN	281	ANNAPOLI
HART, DAVIC	FRE	322	MIDDLETO
HART, EDWARC	DOR	337	3RD DIVI
HART, EDWARD	BAL	364	8TH WARD
HART, EDWARD	WAS	119	2ND DIST
HART, ELIAS	FRE	055	FREDERIC
HART, ELIZA	HAR	147	3RD DIST
HART, ELIZA	BAL	007	EASTERN
HART, ELIZABETH	BAL	155	2ND DIST
HART, EMILA	BAL	463	1ST DIST
HART, FAYETT	WAS	103	2ND DIST
HART, FERDINAND	BAL	358	3RD WARD
HART, FRANCE	HAR	196	3RD DIST
HART, FRANCIS	BAL	132	11TH WAR
HART, FRANCISE B.	BAL	345	13TH WAR
HART, G. C.	BAL	333	1ST DIST
HART, GARRETT	KEN	272	1ST DIST
HART, GEORGE	BAL	094	5TH WARD
HART, GEORGE	ALL	201	CUMBERLA
HART, HENRY	BAL	253	1ST DIST
HART, HENRY	WAS	026	2ND SUBD
HART, HENRY	BAL	312	20TH WAR
HART, JACOB	FRE	002	FREDERIC
HART, JAMES	BAL	194	19TH WAR
HART, JAMES	KEN	271	1ST DIST
HART, JAMES	BAL	020	1ST WARD
HART, JAMES	BAL	020	1ST WARD
HART, JAMES	BAL	174	1ST WARD
HART, JOHN	BAL	109	2ND DIST
HART, JOHN	BAL	134	1ST WARD
HART, JOHN	QUE	195	3RD E DI
HART, JOHN	WAS	044	2ND SUBD
HART, JOHN	BAL	419	3RD WARD
HART, JOHN	CEC	038	CHESAPEA
HART, JOHN	CHA	238	HILLTOP
HART, JOHN	BAL	312	20TH WAR
HART, JOHN	BAL	268	17TH WAR
HART, JOHN D.	WAS	154	2ND DIST
HART, JOSEPH	BAL	299	17TH WAR
HART, JOSEPH	BAL	134	1ST WARD
HART, JOSEPH	BAL	154	2ND DIST
HART, LAWRENCE	CEC	039	CHESAPEA
HART, MARIA	BAL	318	20TH WAR
HART, MARY	CEC	013	ELKTON 3
HART, MARY	BAL	156	11TH WAR
HART, MARY L.	BAL	344	13TH WAR
HART, MICHAEL	BAL	228	2ND WARD
HART, MICHEL	BAL	240	20TH WAR
HART, OLIVIA AMARIDA	BAL	267	17TH WAR
HART, PATRICK	BAL	300	17TH WAR
HART, PHILIP	BAL	130	11TH WAR
HART, RACHAEL	BAL	151	19TH WAR
HART, RICHARD	ANN	364	4TH DIST
HART, RICHARD W.	CHA	235	HILLTOP
HART, ROBERT	CEC	069	5TH E DI
HART, SAMUEL	BAL	070	10TH WAR
HART, SHADE	CEC	016	ELKTON 3
HART, STEPHEN F.	BAL	346	3RD WARD
HART, SUSAN	FRE	123	CREAGERS
HART, SUSAN	WAS	119	2ND DIST
HART, TALBERT	BAL	406	1ST DIST
HART, THCAMS	BAL	358	13TH WAR
HART, THOMAS	BAL	006	EASTERN
HART, WASHINGTON*	DOR	361	3RD DIVI
HART, WILLIAM	BAL	386	13TH WAR
HART, WILLIAM	BAL	148	1ST WARD
HART, WILLIAM	BAL	232	12TH WAR
HART, WILLIAM A.	ALL	181	8TH E.D.
HART, WILLIAM J.	BAL	299	20TH WAR
HART, D.	BAL	118	1ST WARD
HARTADT, LEWIS	BAL	328	13TH WAR
HARTBAUER, CHARLOTT	FRE	007	FREDERIC
HARTE, CATHARINE	DOR	349	3RD DIVI
HARTE, GEORGE	DOR	343	3RD DIVI
HARTEBURG, ISAAC	BAL	037	4TH WARD
HARTELLS, BERDINA	BAL	215	2ND WARD
HARTEN, MARGARET	ALL	005	3RD E.D.
HARTEN, PETER	ALL	006	3RD E.D.
HARTENSTINE, JACCR	CAR	336	6TH DIST
HARTER, PETER	WAS	266	1ST DIST
HARTERY, SARAH	ALL	175	7TH E.D.
HARTESTY, JOHN	FRE	444	8TH E DI
HARTFIELD, WILLIAM	FRE	403	JEFFERSO
HARTGEE, JOHN	ANN	411	8TH DIST
HARTGLER, DANIEL	BAL	091	2ND DIST
HARTGRAUGH, CONRAD	BAL	283	2ND WARD
HARTHORN, ANN M.	WAS	291	1ST DIST
HARTHORN, ESTER	WAS	290	1ST DIST
HARTHORN, JOHN	WAS	290	1ST DIST
HARTHORN, JOSHUA	BAL	468	14TH WAR
HARTHORN, WILLIAM	WAS	155	HAGERSTO
HARTIGAN, CATHARINE	BAL	158	16TH WAR
HARTIGAN, JOHN	BAL	018	9TH WARD
HARTIGAN, THOMAS	BAL	057	15TH WAR
HARTIGAN, WILLIAM	BAL	128	1ST WARD
HARTIGING, JAMES	FRE	384	PETERSVI
HARTIKIN, THOMAS	BAL	304	17TH WAR
HARTINAN, GEORGE	BAL	275	20TH WAR
HARTINAN, MARGARET	BAL	276	20TH WAR
HARTINAN, MICHAEL	BAL	177	2ND WARD
HARTINELL, ELLEN *	BAL	394	1ST DIST
HARTING, PHELTY	WOR	226	4TH E DI
HARTING, WARREN J.	WOR	230	6TH E DI
HARTING, WILLIAM	WOR	239	6TH E DI
HARTINGTON, MARY	BAL	082	1ST WARD
HARTKINS, SAMUEL H.	BAL	372	8TH WARD
HARTLE, EPHRAIM	WAS	235	1ST DIST
HARTLE, JACOB	WAS	228	1ST DIST
HARTLE, JACOB	WAS	242	CAVETOWN
HARTLE, JOHN	WAS	242	CAVETOWN
HARTLEY, ARCHER	BAL	181	11TH WAR
HARTLEY, CATHARINE L.	KEN	223	2ND DIST
HARTLEY, CHARLES	ANN	463	HOWARD D
HARTLEY, EDWARD	KEN	223	2ND DIST
HARTLEY, ELIJAH	ALL	172	7TH E.D.
HARTLEY, ELIZABETH	ALL	183	8TH E.D.
HARTLEY, FRANCIS	BAL	448	8TH WARD
HARTLEY, GEORGE W.	CAR	361	9TH DIST
HARTLEY, HENRY	HAR	108	2ND DIST
HARTLEY, JOHN	ALL	176	7TH E.D.
HARTLEY, JOHN T.	PRI	042	VANSVILL
HARTLEY, JONATHAN	FRE	279	WOODSBOR
HARTLEY, MARIAN	BAL	372	1ST DIST
HARTLEY, MARK	PRI	008	BLADENSB
HARTLEY, NOAMI	BAL	396	8TH WARD
HARTLEY, SAMUEL	MGM	335	CRACKLIN
HARTLEY, WILLIAM	BAL	372	1ST DIST
HARTLINE, BARBARY	BAL	233	17TH WAR
HARTLINE, MICHAEL	BAL	231	17TH WAR
HARTLOCK, KATE	BAL	141	19TH WAR
HARTLOVE, CHARLES H.	BAL	137	16TH WAR
HARTLOVE, RUTH	BAL	229	17TH WAR
HARTLOVE, SARAH	BAL	134	18TH WAR
HARTLOVE, WESLEY	BAL	238	17TH WAR
HARTLOVE, WILLIAM	BAL	234	17TH WAR
HARTLOVER, ENOCK	BAL	134	18TH WAR
HARTLY, CHARLES	ALL	206	CUMBERLA
HARTLY, JOHN	BAL	074	2ND DIST
HARTLY, THOMAS	BAL	371	1ST DIST
HARTMAL, FREDERICK	BAL	402	14TH WAR
HARTMAN, ANDREW	BAL	277	17TH WAR
HARTMAN, ANDREW	BAL	257	6TH WARD
HARTMAN, ANDREW	WAS	142	2ND DIST
HARTMAN, ANDREW J.	WAS	269	1ST DIST
HARTMAN, ANN	PRI	097	SPALDING
HARTMAN, ANNA	BAL	066	1ST WARD
HARTMAN, AQUILA	WAS	118	2ND DIST
HARTMAN, AUGUSTUS	BAL	108	5TH WARD
HARTMAN, BARBARY	BAL	037	18TH WAR
HARTMAN, BENS	WAS	237	CAVETOWN
HARTMAN, CAROLINE	BAL	050	9TH WARD
HARTMAN, CASPER	BAL	280	1ST DIST
HARTMAN, CASPER	BAL	133	11TH WAR
HARTMAN, CATHARINE	BAL	281	1ST DIST
HARTMAN, CHRISTIAN	FRE	069	FREDERIC
HARTMAN, CHRISTOPHER	HAR	203	3RD DIST
HARTMAN, DANIEL	ALL	237	CUMBERLA
HARTMAN, FERDINAND	BAL	079	1ST WARD
HARTMAN, FRANCES	ALL	089	5TH E.D.
HARTMAN, FREDERICK	BAL	109	18TH WAR
HARTMAN, FREDERICK	BAL	063	18TH WAR
HARTMAN, FREDNEY	BAL	066	1ST WARD
HARTMAN, GEORGE	BAL	456	8TH WARD
HARTMAN, GEORGE	BAL	135	11TH WAR
HARTMAN, GEORGE	WAS	265	1ST DIST
HARTMAN, GEORGE	PRI	096	SPALDING
HARTMAN, GERDRANT	BAL	196	6TH WARD
HARTMAN, HENRY	FRE	074	FREDERIC
HARTMAN, HENRY	BAL	174	19TH WAR
HARTMAN, HENRY-BLACK	FRE	215	BUCKEYST
HARTMAN, ISAAC	BAL	026	9TH WARD
HARTMAN, J. P.	BAL	030	4TH WARD
HARTMAN, JACOB	WAS	248	1ST DIST
HARTMAN, JAMES	ALL	096	5TH E.D.
HARTMAN, JOHN	ALL	034	2ND E.D.
HARTMAN, JOHN	BAL	177	2ND WARD
HARTMAN, JOHN	ALL	232	CUMBERLA
HARTMAN, JOHN	BAL	046	2ND DIST
HARTMAN, JOHN	TAL	091	ST MICHA
HARTMAN, JOHN	BAL	055	18TH WAR
HARTMAN, JOHN	BAL	040	18TH WAR
HARTMAN, JOSEPH	BAL	302	17TH WAR
HARTMAN, JOSEPH	BAL	375	8TH WARD
HARTMAN, L.	BAL	314	12TH WAR
HARTMAN, LAZARUS	HAR	123	2ND DIST
HARTMAN, LEWIS	WAS	265	1ST DIST
HARTMAN, LOUIS	BAL	123	16TH WAR
HARTMAN, LOUIS JR.	BAL	123	16TH WAR
HARTMAN, MARGARETT	BAL	075	18TH WAR
HARTMAN, MARGRETT	BAL	072	18TH WAR
HARTMAN, MARTIN	BAL	209	11TH WAR
HARTMAN, MARY	BAL	050	18TH WAR
HARTMAN, MARY	BAL	200	17TH WAR
HARTMAN, MICHAEL	BAL	284	17TH WAR
HARTMAN, NICHOLAS	FRE	273	NEW MARK
HARTMAN, PHILLIPP	BAL	063	18TH WAR
HARTMAN, SAMUEL	BAL	184	16TH WAR
HARTMAN, SIMON	FRE	029	FREDERIC
HARTMAN, SOBENA	BAL	275	7TH WARD
HARTMAN, VALENTINE	FRE	069	FREDERIC
HARTMAN, WILTON	BAL	003	EASTERN
HARTMAN, EZRA	FRE	397	PETERSVI
HARTMAUN, CONRAD	BAL	140	15TH WAR
HARTMYER, HENRY	CAR	328	MANCHEST
HARTMYER, RICHARD	BAL	307	20TH WAR
HARTNACHT, ELIZABETH	WAS	166	1ST DIST
HARTNAN, ELIZABETH *	ALL	102	5TH E.D.
HARTNEN, WILLIAM	BAL	114	11TH WAR
HARTNER, JAMES	BAL	114	11TH WAR
HARTNES, M.	FRE	200	5TH E DI
HARTOG, HARTOGENSIS	BAL	009	9TH WARD
HARTON, B.	BAL	235	20TH WAR
HARTON, THOMAS	FRE	441	8TH E DI
HARTONG, ELIZABETH *	WAS	178	BOONSBOR
HARTSHORN, ALBERT	CEC	171	5TH E DI
HARTSHORN, CHARLES	CEC	147	PORT DEP
HARTSHORN, CHARLES	CEC	214	7TH E DI
HARTSHORN, EDWARD B.	CEC	090	4TH E DI
HARTSHORN, MOSES	CEC	204	6TH E DI
HARTSHORN, MOSES	CEC	213	7TH E DI
HARTSHORN, MOSES	CEC	215	7TH E DI
HARTSHORN, PHILLIS	BAL	023	4TH WARD
HARTSHORN, SAMUEL	BAL	348	3RD WARD
HARTSHORN, WILLIAM	HAR	192	3RD DIST
HARTSHORNE, ISAAC	MGM	331	CRACKLIN
HARTSICK, MARY	BAL	421	8TH WARD
HARTSOCK, CATHARINE	FRE	443	8TH E DI
HARTSOCK, HENRY	FRE	422	8TH E DI
HARTSOCK, HOWARD D.	FRE	410	8TH E DI
HARTSOCK, JACOB	ALL	174	7TH E.D.
HARTSOCK, JOHN A.	FRE	453	8TH E DI
HARTSOCK, JOSEPH	FRE	443	8TH E DI
HARTSOCK, LOTT	FRE	410	8TH E DI
HARTSOKE, JOHN	FRE	282	WOODSBOR
HARTT, GEORGE	KEN	294	3RD DIST
HARTT, JAMES H.	KEN	313	3RD DIST
HARTT, JOHN	KEN	292	3RD DIST
HARTT, JOHN T.	KEN	287	3RD DIST
HARTT, THOMAS	KEN	289	3RD DIST
HARTT, THOMAS D.	KEN	294	3RD DIST
HARTWELL, ELLEN	BAL	394	1ST DIST
HARTWELL, WILLIAM	HAR	085	2ND DIST
HARTY, JAMES	ALL	135	4TH E.D.
HARTYLEY, CORNALIUS	BAL	268	20TH WAR
HARTYMAN, DAVID	WAS	129	HAGERSTO
HARTYMAN, JOHN	WAS	129	HAGERSTO
HARTYMAN, MARGARET	WAS	123	HAGERSTO
HARTZ, SAMPSON	BAL	116	5TH WARD
HARTZARG, ELISETTA	BAL	457	14TH WAR
HARTZEL, ELIZABETH	BAL	236	2ND WARD
HARTZEL, GEORGE	BAL	238	20TH WAR
HARTZELL, DAVID	BAL	426	14TH WAR
HARTZELL, GEORGE	BAL	290	12TH WAR
HARTZELL, JOHN	BAL	255	1ST DIST
HARTZELL, WILLIAM	FRE	178	5TH E DI
HARTZMAN, DANIEL	WAS	167	1ST DIST
HARTZOCK, ANN E.	FRE	133	CREAGERS
HARTZOCK, ANNIE C.	FRF	087	FREDERIC
HARTZOCK, ELIZABETH	FRE	069	FREDERIC
HARTZOCK, JOHN H.	FRE	121	CREAGERS
HARTZOCK, NATHANIEL	FRE	123	CREAGERS
HARTZOCK, THOMAS	FRE	119	CREAGERS
HARTZOCK, WILLIAM	FRE	086	FREDERIC
HARTZOG, ELI	CAR	383	2ND DIST
HARTZOG, EVI	BAL	047	1ST WARD
HARTZOG, GEORGE	BAL	126	16TH WAR
HARTZOG, JOHN P.	BAL	127	16TH WAR
HARTZOG, LAVINA	CAR	391	2ND DIST
HARTZOG, NICHOLAS	CAR	377	2ND DIST
HARTZOY, MARY	BAL	116	11TH WAR
HARTZWELL, WILLIAM H.	PRI	107	PISCATAW
HARVARTY, JOHN	BAL	046	9TH WARD
HARVEN, SUSAN	BAL	123	2ND DIST
HARVER, ELIZABETH	BAL	007	EASTERN
HARVERY, GEORGE	BAL	227	12TH WAR
HARVERY, JOHN K.	BAL	329	1ST DIST
HARVES, HENRY	BAL	018	9TH WARD
HARVEY, ALEXANDER	BAL	057	18TH WAR
HARVEY, ANDREW	BAL	437	14TH WAR
HARVEY, ANN	BAL	127	11TH WAR
HARVEY, ANN	MGM	336	CRACKLIN
HARVEY, ANN	BAL	395	8TH WARD
HARVEY, ANNETTE	ANN	521	HOWARD D
HARVEY, ARCHIBALD	BAL	084	4TH WARD
HARVEY, CATHARINE	BAL	356	1ST DIST
HARVEY, CHARELS	ANN	495	HOWARD D
HARVEY, CHARLES	BAL	304	12TH WAR
HARVEY, CHARLES	BAL	109	15TH WAR
HARVEY, CHARLES	BAL	234	17TH WAR
HARVEY, CHARLES W.	BAL	099	18TH WAR
HARVEY, CHARLOTTE	BAL	175	11TH WAR
HARVEY, CHRISTIAN	MGM	405	ROCKERLE
HARVEY, D.	BAL	157	1ST WARD
HARVEY, DAVID	BAL	171	19TH WAR
HARVEY, DICK	BAL	238	1ST DIST
HARVEY, EDWARD	BAL	148	16TH WAR
HARVEY, EDWARD	ANN	295	1ST DIST

Name	County	Page	District
HARVEY, ELISHA	ALL	065	10TH E.D
HARVEY, ELLEN	BAL	380	1ST DIST
HARVEY, ELLICK	ALL	065	10TH E.D
HARVEY, EMELINE	BAL	083	10TH WAR
HARVEY, EPHRAIM	ALL	063	10TH E.D
HARVEY, GEORGE	ALL	118	5TH E.D.
HARVEY, GEORGE	BAL	043	4TH WARD
HARVEY, GEORGE	WAS	149	2ND DIST
HARVEY, H. H.	WAS	164	HAGERSTO
HARVEY, HANNAH	BAL	110	15TH WAR
HARVEY, HARRIETT	BAL	246	17TH WAR
HARVEY, HENRY D.	BAL	102	10TH WAR
HARVEY, HEZEKIAH	ALL	063	10TH E.D
HARVEY, HYLER	BAL	228	12TH WAR
HARVEY, JAMES	BAL	122	1ST WARD
HARVEY, JAMES	BAL	348	3RD WARD
HARVEY, JAMES	BAL	385	8TH WARD
HARVEY, JAMES	BAL	418	14TH WAR
HARVEY, JAMES	HAR	077	BEL AIR
HARVEY, JAMES	SOM	455	DAMES QU
HARVEY, JAMES A.	PRI	016	BLADENSB
HARVEY, JANE	BAL	109	10TH WAR
HARVEY, JOHN	PRI	013	BLADENSB
HARVEY, JOHN	HAR	084	2ND DIST
HARVEY, JOHN	HAR	004	1ST DIST
HARVEY, JOHN	BAL	246	17TH WAR
HARVEY, JOHN *	BAL	025	18TH WAR
HARVEY, JOHN N.	BAL	410	3RD WARD
HARVEY, JONATHAN	ALL	063	10TH E.D
HARVEY, JOSEPH	BAL	334	7TH WARD
HARVEY, JOSEPH	BAL	220	19TH WAR
HARVEY, JOSEPH A.	WAS	140	HAGERSTO
HARVEY, JOSEPH SR.	BAL	019	18TH WAR
HARVEY, JOSHUA	BAL	092	18TH WAR
HARVEY, JOSHUA	BAL	429	14TH WAR
HARVEY, JOSHUA	BAL	167	2ND DIST
HARVEY, JOSHUA-BLACK	QUE	127	1ST E DI
HARVEY, LEVI	ANN	441	HOWARD D
HARVEY, LEVY	BAL	071	18TH WAR
HARVEY, M.*	BAL	114	11TH WAR
HARVEY, MARGARET	PRI	039	VANSVILL
HARVEY, MARGARET	KEN	259	1ST DIST
HARVEY, MARY	FRE	338	MIDDLETO
HARVEY, MARY	BAL	176	11TH WAR
HARVEY, MOSES	HAR	201	3RD DIST
HARVEY, NATHANIEL B.	ALL	065	10TH E.D
HARVEY, NELLY	PRI	068	NOTTINGH
HARVEY, NOAH	ALL	063	10TH E.D
HARVEY, PATIENCE	BAL	106	15TH WAR
HARVEY, PHEBE	CAL	051	3RD DIST
HARVEY, RICHARD	ANN	384	4TH DIST
HARVEY, RICHARD	PRI	017	BLADENSB
HARVEY, SAMUEL	KEN	259	1ST DIST
HARVEY, SAMUEL	ALL	067	10TH E.D
HARVEY, SAMUEL	BAL	171	2ND DIST
HARVEY, SARAH	BAL	090	5TH WARD
HARVEY, SARAH	FRE	338	MIDDLETO
HARVEY, SOLOMON	ALL	057	10TH E.D
HARVEY, SOLOMON B.	ALL	066	10TH E.D
HARVEY, SOPHIA	CEC	080	NORTHEAS
HARVEY, SOPHIA	HAR	124	2ND DIST
HARVEY, THOMAS	BAL	448	14TH WAR
HARVEY, THOMAS	BAL	171	2ND DIST
HARVEY, THOMAS	BAL	044	15TH WAR
HARVEY, THOMAS	PRI	005	BLADENSB
HARVEY, THOMAS JR.	PRI	014	BLADENSB
HARVEY, THOMAS P.	BAL	408	14TH WAR
HARVEY, UPTON	BAL	420	14TH WAR
HARVEY, WILLIAM	BAL	066	18TH WAR
HARVEY, WILLIAM	PRI	042	VANSVILL
HARVEY, WILLIAM	TAL	116	ST MICHA
HARVEY, WILLIAM	PRI	064	NOTTINGH
HARVEY, WILLIAM	ALL	063	10TH E.D
HARVEY, ZACHARY	ANN	339	3RD DIST
HARVEY.RODES	BAL	007	EASTERN
HARVIN, JOSIAS B.	CHA	275	ALLENS F
HARVIN, MARHATCHERSON, AN	ST	270	3RD E DI
HARVY, ANDREW	CEC	108	3RD E DI
HARVY, ANN	CHA	248	HILLTOP
HARVY, BRIDGET	BAL	442	1ST DIST
HARVY, FRANCIS	DOR	443	1ST DIST
HARVY, FRANKLIN	CEC	155	PORT DUP
HARVY, JAMES H.	ANN	469	HOWARD D
HARVY, JESSE	CEC	092	4TH E DI
HARVY, JOHN	CEC	108	3RD E DI
HARVY, JOHN	CAR	109	NO TWP L
HARVY, JOHN	ALL	198	CUMBERLA
HARVY, MARIA	BAL	463	14TH WAR
HARVY, MARY E.*	DOR	308	1ST DIST
HARVY, PATRICK	BAL	441	1ST DIST
HARVY, PHILLIP	DOR	447	1ST DIST
HARVY, WILLIAM	CAR	227	5TH DIST
HARVY, WILLIAM	HAR	041	1ST DIST
HARWELL, EATON	BAL	003	9TH WARD
HARWICK, HENRY	BAL	191	17TH WAR
HARWIG, CASPAR	BAL	304	20TH WAR
HARWIG, EVA	BAL	305	20TH WAR
HARWOOD, ALEXANDER	ANN	404	8TH DIST
HARWOOD, ALICE E.	TAL	018	EASTON D
HARWOOD, ANN R.	BAL	134	11TH WAR
HARWOOD, BENJAMIN	ANN	295	1ST DIST
HARWOOD, ELIZABETH	PRI	065	NOTTINGH
HARWOOD, ELLEN	ANN	289	ANNAPOLI
HARWOOD, EMILY	BAL	078	10TH WAR
HARWOOD, HENRIETTA M.	MGM	422	MEDLEY 3
HARWOOD, HENRY D.	TAL	008	EASTON D
HARWOOD, ISAAC	ANN	350	3RD DIST
HARWOOD, JAMES	ANN	292	ANNAPOLI
HARWOOD, JAMES H.	ANN	327	2ND DIST
HARWOOD, JANE	BAL	125	11TH WAR
HARWOOD, JOHN	ANN	323	2ND DIST
HARWOOD, JOHN H.	MGM	435	CLARKSTR
HARWOOD, MARGARET	BAL	029	18TH WAR
HARWOOD, MARY	BAL	115	11TH WAR
HARWOOD, MARY D.	ANN	316	1ST DIST
HARWOOD, MARY E.	QUE	189	3RD E DI
HARWOOD, MISS	ANN	279	ANNAPOLI
HARWOOD, NANCY	PRI	076	MARLBROU
HARWOOD, R.	PRI	067	NOTTINGH
HARWOOD, RICHARD	ANN	295	1ST DIST
HARWOOD, RICHARD A.	PRI	080	QUEEN AN
HARWOOD, S.	BAL	059	10TH WAR
HARWOOD, SAMUEL	HAR	128	2ND DIST
HARWOOD, SPRIGG	ANN	298	1ST DIST
HARWOOD, THOMA SN.	FRE	211	BUCKEYST
HARWOOD, THOMAS	TAL	018	EASTON D
HARWOOD, VALENTINE	BAL	288	7TH WARD
HARWOOD, W. COL-	ANN	294	1ST DIST
HARWOOD, WILLIAM	PRI	080	QUEEN AN
HARY, CASPAR	BAL	216	19TH WAR
HARZARD, WILLIAM	BAL	306	12TH WAR
HARZPANY, JACOB	BAL	015	9TH WARD
HASBAND, LAREY G.	HAR	166	3RD DIST
HASBAUGH, CAROLINE	BAL	039	18TH WAR
HASBROKE, HANNON	ALL	215	CUMBERLA
HASBURN, WILLIAM	FRE	026	FREDERIC
HASE, MAHALA	DOR	371	3RD DIVI
HASE, MARGARETT	BAL	109	5TH WARD
HASED, JOHN	HAR	194	3RD DIST
HASEL, THOMAS P.	CEC	042	CHESAPEA
HASELETT, ROBERT	BAL	129	5TH WARD
HASELIP, GEORGE	BAL	395	1ST DIST
HASELTON, ROBERT	BAL	149	11TH WAR
HASEMAN, MALANA	BAL	418	8TH WARD
HASEMAN, MARY	BAL	418	8TH WARD
HASEMAN, VERGINIA	BAL	418	8TH WARD
HASFIELDT, ADAM	BAL	249	6TH WARD
HASH, CHRISTINE	BAL	260	12TH WAR
HASH, HENRY	BAL	117	11TH WAR
HASHEL, NICKOLAS	BAL	215	6TH DIST
HASHERMOST, CATHARINE	WAS	068	2ND SUBD
HASHETT, ADAM*	BAL	004	4TH WARD
HASHLEP, JOHN*	TAL	036	EASTON D
HASIMAN, ANDREW	BAL	275	1ST DIST
HASING, RICHARD	WOR	264	BERLIN I
HASINGTON, ROBERT	BAL	227	17TH WAR
HASKELL, ALEXANDER	BAL	209	2ND WARD
HASKELL, JOHN	BAL	130	1ST WARD
HASKELL, JOHN	BAL	467	14TH WAR
HASKELL, JOHNH.	BAL	467	14TH WAR
HASKELL, THEODORE J.	BAL	173	16TH WAR
HASKEN, SUSAN	BAL	285	20TH WAR
HASKET, SARAH	BAL	357	13TH WAR
HASKET, THOMAS	ALL	220	CUMBERLA
HASKILL, JOHN	BAL	126	1ST WARD
HASKINE, J.	BAL	148	1ST WARD
HASKINS, ANTHONY	BAL	110	10TH WAR
HASKINS, BARKLEY	TAL	056	EASTON D
HASKINS, CHARLES	TAL	094	ST MICHA
HASKINS, DAFFEY	BAL	174	11TH WAR
HASKINS, GEORGE	BAL	083	18TH WAR
HASKINS, J.	BAL	140	1ST WARD
HASKINS, JAMES	BAL	138	5TH WARD
HASKINS, JAMES	HAR	009	1ST DIST
HASKINS, JANE	BAL	085	18TH WAR
HASKINS, L.	BAL	160	1ST WARD
HASKINS, LUCRETIA	BAL	075	15TH WAR
HASKINS, MARY A.*	DOR	376	1ST DIST
HASKINS, MARY M.	TAL	071	EASTON T
HASLAM, FREDERICK	BAL	109	5TH WARD
HASLAM, THOMAS	BAL	379	13TH WAR
HASLAN, SAMUEL *	BAL	207	6TH WARD
HASLEP, CATHARINE *	BAL	393	1ST DIST
HASLER, CATHARINE *	BAL	393	1ST DIST
HASLET, JOHN	ALL	214	CUMBERLA
HASLETON, SOLOMON	BAL	302	3RD WARD
HASLETT, CAROLINE-BLACK	BAL	219	2ND WARD
HASLETT, GEORGE	BAL	183	19TH WAR
HASLETT, SARAH	BAL	376	13TH WAR
HASLEY, CATHARINE. *	BAL	393	1ST DIST
HASLIN, PATRICK	ANN	413	HOWARD D
HASLINGER, ANREAS	BAL	162	16TH WAR
HASLIP, ELSY	BAL	257	20TH WAR
HASLIP, MARY A.	ANN	439	HOWARD D
HASLIP, REBECCA	PRI	020	VANSVILL
HASLIPP, ANN	BAL	035	13TH WAR
HASLITT, ROBERT	BAL	061	2ND DIST
HASLITT, THOMAS	BAL	061	2ND DIST
HASLUP, ANDREW	ANN	441	HOWARD D
HASLUP, CHARLES G.	ANN	439	HOWARD D
HASLUP, HENRY	BAL	235	6TH WARD
HASLUP, HORACE	ANN	431	HOWARD D
HASLUP, JOHN	ANN	440	HOWARD D
HASLUP, JOHN*	BAL	100	10TH WAR
HASLUP, OLIVER W.	BAL	087	15TH WAR
HASLUP, REZIN	BAL	102	10TH WAR
HASLUP, RUTH A.	BAL	100	10TH WAR
HASLUP, SARAH A.	MGM	323	CRACKLIN
HASLUP, WILLIAM L.	ANN	431	HOWARD D
HASMAN, HENRY	BAL	044	18TH WAR
HASNER, JOSHUA	BAL	150	2ND DIST
HASON, JAMES	CEC	043	CHESAPEA
HASPELMORN, MARY	FRE	129	CREAGERS
HASPER, SARAH-BLACK	FRE	008	FREDERIC
HASS, ANTHONY	BAL	112	10TH WAR
HASS, AUGUSTUS	BAL	468	14TH WAR
HASSAM, ANDREW	BAL	290	7TH WARD
HASSAN, JOSEPH	ALL	253	CUMBERLA
HASSAN, LEWIS	ALL	118	5TH E.D.
HASSBACH, CHRISTIAN	BAL	215	17TH WAR
HASSELD, WILLIAM*	DOR	412	1ST DIST
HASSELL, CASPAR	BAL	058	18TH WAR
HASSEN, ELLEN D.	ALL	238	CUMBERLA
HASSER, SISTER MARY	FRE	198	5TH E DI
HASSET, ABSALOM	CEC	199	7TH E DI
HASSET, JOHN	WAS	154	2ND DIST
HASSETT, JAMES	QUE	222	4TH E DI
HASSETT, JOHN	BAL	246	17TH WAR
HASSETT, SAMUEL	QUE	215	3RD E DI
HASSETT, THOANS	WAS	113	2ND DIST
HASSEY, ANNEE*	BAL	109	10TH WAR
HASSHOOF, DANIEL	BAL	124	1ST WARD
HASSIAN, MALCOLM	BAL	035	1ST WARD
HASSIAN, MARY	BAL	196	2ND WARD
HASSLBECK, W.	BAL	449	8TH WARD
HASSLEBERGER, WILLIAM	BAL	021	2ND DIST
HASSLETT, WILLIAM	BAL	111	5TH WARD
HASSON, GEORGE	CEC	203	6TH E DI
HASSON, GERTRUDE	ALL	119	5TH E.D.
HASSON, HENRIETTA	CEC	188	7TH E DI
HASSON, JAMES	CEC	083	CHARLEST
HASSON, JAMES	BAL	279	7TH WARD
HASSON, JOHN	BAL	087	4TH WARD
HASSON, MACY	CEC	202	6TH E DI
HASSON, MICHAEL	ANN	340	3RD DIST
HASSON, SAMUEL	CEC	188	7TH E DI
HASSON, WASHINGTON	CEC	182	7TH E DI
HASSPER, J. *	BAL	295	1ST DIST
HASSY, WILLIAM	ANN	376	5TH DIST
HASSYER, J. *	BAL	295	1ST DIST
HAST, HERMAN	BAL	040	18TH WAR
HASTELL, BENJAMIN	BAL	340	13TH WAR
HASTEY, DAVID	WAS	140	2ND DIST
HASTING, AGNES	SOM	498	SALISBUR
HASTING, ALEXANDER	SOM	471	TRAPPE D
HASTING, ELISHA	WOR	226	4TH E DI
HASTING, FRANCES	SOM	498	SALISBUR
HASTING, JAMES	SOM	496	SALISBUR
HASTING, JOSHUA	SOM	502	SALISBUR
HASTING, LEMUEL M.	WOR	239	6TH E DI
HASTING, MAJOR	WOR	263	BERLIN I
HASTING, MICHAEL J.	WOR	226	4TH E DI
HASTING, NANCY	WOR	234	6TH E DI
HASTING, RENATTUS	SOM	494	SALISBUR
HASTING, RICHARD	WOR	264	BERLIN I
HASTING, RICHARD JR.	WOR	270	BERLIN I
HASTING, SARAH E.	SOM	499	SALISBUR
HASTING, STEPHEN	SOM	488	SALISBUR
HASTING, WILLIAM	SOM	498	SALISBUR
HASTING, WINDER	SOM	494	SALISBUR
HASTING, WINDER	WOR	239	6TH E DI
HASTINGS, EDWARD	WOR	249	1ST CENS
HASTINGS, HENRY	WOR	265	BERLIN I
HASTINGS, JAMES	BAL	306	12TH WAR
HASTINGS, JANE	BAL	191	11TH WAR
HASTINGS, JANE	CEC	115	3RD E DI
HASTINGS, JOHN	DOR	426	1ST DIST
HASTINGS, JOHN	HAR	108	2ND DIST
HASTINGS, JOHN	BAL	280	7TH WARD
HASTINGS, JOHN	WOR	257	BERLIN I
HASTINGS, JOSHUA	WOR	271	BERLIN I
HASTINGS, LAURENCE	WOR	269	BERLIN I
HASTINGS, SAMUEL	WOR	275	BERLIN I
HASTINGS, SAMUEL	HAR	108	2ND DIST
HASTINGS, THOMAS	SOM	469	TRAPPE D
HASTINGS, WASHINGTON	CAR	125	NO TWP L
HASTINGS, WESTLEY	WOR	279	BERLIN I
HASTINGS, WILLIAM	WOR	287	BERLIN I
HASTON, THOMAS	BAL	106	2ND DIST
HASTRAM, CHARLOTTE	BAL	110	1ST WARD
HASTRAM, FREDERICK	BAL	110	1ST WARD
HASTUP, JOHN*	BAL	100	10TH WAR
HASTY.HESTER	CAR	104	NO TWP L
HASWELL, J.	BAL	210	19TH WAR
HASWELL, J.	BAL	172	1ST WARD
HASWELL, JOHN	BAL	140	16TH WAR
HATCH, JANE	BAL	174	11TH WAR
HATCH, JESSE	BAL	140	1ST WARD
HATCH, JOHN L.	BAL	311	12TH WAR
HATCH, MADELINE	BAL	457	14TH WAR
HATCH, NATHAN T.	BAL	282	12TH WAR
HATCH, SAMUEL T.	BAL	276	20TH WAR
HATCHER, EDWARD	CHA	219	ALLENS F
HATCHER, JOHN	CHA	235	HILLTOP
HATCHER, ROBERT	CHA	230	MIDDLETO
HATCHERSON, BARTUS	KEN	235	2ND DIST
HATCHERSON, CAROLINE	KEN	209	2ND DIST
HATCHERSON, MARY	KEN	266	1ST DIST
HATCHESON, MARTHA E.	BAL	060	15TH WAR
HATCHISON, WELTHEY *	TAL	096	ST MICHA
HATCHNER, JOHN	BAL	056	18TH WAR
HATCHNER, MARY	BAL	056	18TH WAR
HATE, GEROGE A.	BAL	220	12TH WAR
HATESTEAD, CHIS	BAL	208	19TH WAR
HATFAU, WILLIAM H.	BAL	257	2ND WARD
HATFEILD, WILLIAM H.	CAR	370	9TH DIST
HATFIELD, BENJAMIN	ANN	510	HOWARD D
HATFIELD, DANIEL	CAR	370	9TH DIST
HATFIELD, JOHN	CAR	226	5TH DIST
HATFIELD, JOSIAH	CAR	225	5TH DIST
HATFIELD, MARGARET R.	CAR	370	9TH DIST
HATFIELD, MARY R.	BAL	086	18TH WAR
HATFIELD, ROBERT	WAS	155	HAGERSTO
HATFIELD, THOMAS	ANN	515	HOWARD D
HATHAWAY, EDMOND	BAL	157	1ST WARD
HATHAWAY, LUCINDA	WAS	184	BOONSBOR
HATHAWAY, WILLIAM	WOR	325	1ST E DI
HATHELL, CHRISTIAN	BAL	421	14TH WAR
HATHERLEY, JOAB	FRE	088	FREDERIC
HATHERLY, ELIZABETH	FRE	342	MIDDLETO
HATHERS, ANDREW	CEC	041	CHESAPEA
HATHERS, ANNA	CEC	042	CHESAPEA
HATHEWAY, MARY A.	BAL	467	14TH WAR
HATKA, EDWARD	ANN	413	HOWARD D
HATLEY, SARAH E.	ALL	167	6TH E.D.
HATLINE, JOHN	BAL	283	1ST DIST
HATRHISON, CEASER	TAL	077	EASTON T
HATSEN, ELIZABTH	BAL	082	1ST WARD
HATSOFF, MICHEL	BAL	322	7TH WARD
HATSON, EDWARD	DOR	423	1ST DIST
HATSON, GRACE	ALL	255	CUMBERLA
HATSON, LYDY-MULATTO	FRE	015	FREDERIC
HATSON, SAMUEL	ALL	215	CUMBERLA
HATSON, SARAH C.-MULATTO	FRE	017	FREDERIC
HATT, ELIZA	FRE	016	FREDERIC
HATTAN, JOSIAH	WAS	104	2ND DIST
HATTEN, DAVID	WAS	122	2ND DIST
HATTEN, EBERELLA	BAL	429	14TH WAR
HATTER, FREDRICKER	CAR	204	4TH DIST
HATTER, MARTIN	BAL	112	5TH WARD
HATTKINS, H.	BAL	170	1ST WARD
HATTON, A.	PRI	120	PISCATAW
HATTON, ANN	PRI	111	PISCATAW
HATTON, ANN M.	BAL	254	7TH WARD
HATTON, CAROLINE M.	BAL	056	10TH WAR
HATTON, DORINDA	PRI	058	NOTTINGH
HATTON, E.	PRI	108	PISCATAW
HATTON, ELEANOR	PRI	111	PISCATAW
HATTON, ELLEN	BAL	341	7TH WARD
HATTON, GEORGE	BAL	329	7TH WARD
HATTON, GEORGE W.	BAL	414	8TH WARD
HATTON, GEORGE W.	BAL	209	5TH WARD
HATTON, HENRY	BAL	328	7TH WARD
HATTON, HENRY	PRI	098	SPALDING
HATTON, HENRY D.	PRI	108	PISCATAW
HATTON, JONATHAN	ANN	270	ANNAPOLI
HATTON, JOSEPH C.	PRI	106	PISCATAW
HATTON, LOUISA	BAL	158	6TH WARD
HATTON, M.E.	PRI	118	PISCATAW
HATTON, SUSAN	BAL	158	6TH WARD
HATTON, THOMAS	ANN	464	HOWARD D
HATTON, THOMAS	PRI	118	PISCATAW
HATTON, WILLIAM H.	PRI	105	PISCATAW
HATTON, ZACHARIAH	BAL	130	2ND DIST
HATTS, GEORGE	ALL	004	3RD E.D.
HATZ, SAMUEL	BAL	299	3RD WARD
HATZEL, HENRY	BAL	405	14TH WAR
HATZEL, SAMUEL	WAS	030	2ND SUBD
HATZELL, JACOB	BAL	118	18TH WAR
HATZELL, LENONARD	BAL	118	18TH WAR
HATZELL,MATILDA	ALL	238	CUMBERLA
HAUBECKER, CHRISTIAN	WAS	121	2ND DIST
HAUBERT, DANIEL	BAL	164	11TH WAR
HAUBERT, HENRY C.S.	CAL	052	3RD DIST
HAUBT, T.	BAL	018	9TH WARD
HAUCK, CHRISTOF	BAL	414	8TH WARD
HAUCKMAN, SARAH	CAR	277	7TH DIST
HAUD, THOMAS B.	BAL	298	3RD WARD
HAUEISEN, MARY	BAL	189	6TH WARD
HAUER, CATHERINE	FRE	018	FREDERIC

Name	County	Page	District
HAUER, DANUEL	WAS	105	2ND DIST
HAUER, GEORGE	WAS	105	2ND DIST
HAUER, JACOB *	BAL	101	18TH WAR
HAUER, WILLIAM	FRE	025	FREDERIC
HAUER,NICHOLS D.	FRE	028	FREDERIC
HAUFAN, ZACHARIAH	FRE	256	NEW MARK
HAUFMAN, FALCENER	BAL	111	2ND DIST
HAUGH, ANDREW	CAR	299	1ST DIST
HAUGH, CATHARINE	CAR	313	1ST DIST
HAUGH, DAVID	FRE	279	WOODSBOR
HAUGH, ELIZA	FRE	280	WOODSBOR
HAUGH, ELIZA	FRE	281	WOODSBOR
HAUGH, GEORGE	CAR	312	1ST DIST
HAUGH, HENRY	FRE	279	WOODSBOR
HAUGH, JACOB	FRE	281	WOODSBOR
HAUGH, JOHN	FRE	234	BUCKEYST
HAUGH, JOHN	CAR	326	1ST DIST
HAUGH, JOHN W.	CAR	241	TANEYTOW
HAUGH, JOSEPH	CAR	300	1ST DIST
HAUGH, JOSIAH	CAR	301	1ST DIST
HAUGH, JOSIAH L.	FRE	280	WOODSBOR
HAUGH, MARY J.	BAL	066	15TH WAR
HAUGH, PETER	CAR	313	1ST DIST
HAUGH, PHILIP W.	WAS	208	1ST DIST
HAUGH, QULEAN	FRE	279	WOODSBOR
HAUGH, SUSANNA	FRE	413	8TH E DI
HAUGH, WILLIAM	CAR	241	TANEYTOW
HAUGH, WILLIAM	FRE	108	CREAGERS
HAUGHEY, BENJAMIN M.	BAL	278	1ST DIST
HAUGHEY, FRANCIS	BAL	253	1ST DIST
HAUGHEY, GEORGE	BAL	199	2ND WARD
HAUGHEY, HUGH	HAR	104	2ND DIST
HAUGHEY, JAMES	BAL	008	EASTERN
HAUGHEY, MARY A.	BAL	424	3RD WARD
HAUGHEY, SUSN	HAR	104	2ND DIST
HAUGHEY, VIXTECIA	BAL	383	1ST DIST
HAUGHREY, CATHARINE	BAL	406	1ST DIST
HAUGHT, RICHARD	BAL	445	14TH WAR
HAUGHTER, ELIZA	BAL	340	13TH WAR
HAUGHTER, JOHN	BAL	052	1ST WARD
HAUGHY, THOMAS	BAL	234	1ST DIST
HAUK, JOHN	WAS	139	HAGERSTO
HAUK, MARY	BAL	305	1ST DIST
HAUK, MARY A.	WAS	139	HAGERSTO
HAUKEY, ANN *	BAL	225	6TH WARD
HAUKINS, GEORGE	CEC	159	PORT DUP
HAUKINS, REBECCA	FRE	076	FREDERIC
HAUKINS, REBECCA	FRE	101	FREDERIC
HAUKINS, ROSETTA	BAL	157	11TH WAR
HAUKNER, VIOLET	BAL	186	2ND WARD
HAUL, ADELINE B.	HAR	178	3RD DIST
HAUL, JAMESB.	BAL	044	1ST WARD
HAULER, NATHAN	CAR	072	NO TWP L
HAULEY, HANNAH	CEC	129	6TH E DI
HAULY, BIDDY	BAL	020	2ND DIST
HAUN, CATHARIEN	CAR	199	4TH DIST
HAUN, ELIZABETH	FRE	164	EMMITTSB
HAUN, JACOB	FRE	134	CREAGERS
HAUN, JOSEPH	FRE	134	CREAGERS
HAUN, MARGARET	FRE	183	5TH E DI
HAUPS, WILLIAM	BAL	257	2ND WARD
HAUPT, CASPAR	BAL	166	16TH WAR
HAUPT, DAVID	BAL	118	15TH WAR
HAUPT, EDWARD	BAL	166	16TH WAR
HAUPT, ELIZABETH A.	BAL	324	7TH WARD
HAUPT, JOHN	BAL	205	17TH WAR
HAUPT, LOUISA	BAL	204	17TH WAR
HAUPT, MARGARET	BAL	027	9TH WARD
HAUPT, ROSELLA	BAL	118	15TH WAR
HAUR, HENRY	WAS	164	HAGERSTO
HAURER, SUSAN	FRE	128	CREAGERS
HAUS, CASPAR*	BAL	087	10TH WAR
HAUS, JOHN	WAS	164	HAGERSTO
HAUS, MARIA	WAS	160	HAGERSTO
HAUS, MARY	WAS	160	HAGERSTO
HAUS, SAMUEL	WAS	234	1ST DIST
HAUSCH, GEORGE	BAL	335	7TH WARD
HAUSE, A.	BAL	137	1ST WARD
HAUSE, BENJAMIN	WAS	148	2ND DIST
HAUSE, CATHARINE	WAS	241	CAVETOWN
HAUSE, EZRA	ALL	061	10TH E.D
HAUSE, GEORGE	BAL	287	17TH WAR
HAUSE, JACOB	WAS	143	2ND DIST
HAUSE, JOHN	WAS	148	2ND DIST
HAUSE, JOHN	PRI	091	MARLBROU
HAUSE, PATRICK	BAL	459	1ST DIST
HAUSE, PETER	BAL	323	1ST DIST
HAUSE, WILLIAM	BAL	012	2ND DIST
HAUSE, WILLIAM F.	ANN	303	1ST DIST
HAUSEMAN, WILSON	BAL	212	6TH DIST
HAUSER, WILLIAM P.	FRE	242	NEW MARK
HAUSIN, PETER	BAL	075	1ST WARD
HAUSS, WILLIAM	FRE	178	5TH E DI
HAUTH, JOHN	BAL	251	2ND WARD
HAUVER, MARTIN	FRE	365	CATOCTIN
HAUY, SAMUEL	MGM	333	CRACKLIN
HAVE, HENRY	BAL	011	18TH WAR
HAVELIN, ASAHEN	HAR	091	2ND DIST
HAVELIN, BARTELTT	HAR	091	2ND DIST
HAVELIN, CHRISTONA	BAL	429	8TH WARD
HAVELIN, JOHN	HAR	120	2ND DIST
HAVELINO, PATRICK	HAR	120	2ND DIST
HAVELL, ROSS	BAL	454	8TH WARD
HAVELOW, JAMES	CEC	048	1ST E DI
HAVENER, A.P.	PRI	067	NOTTINGH
HAVENER, ANTHONY	BAL	262	12TH WAR
HAVENER, BENEDICT	PRI	095	SPALDING
HAVENER, DANIEL	PRI	066	NOTTINGH
HAVENER, JOHN	BAL	464	14TH WAR
HAVENER, OVERTON	PRI	090	MARLBROU
HAVENER, SAMUEL S.	BAL	038	18TH WAR
HAVERCOSS, HENRY	BAL	442	8TH WARD
HAVERHARD, G.	BAL	156	1ST WARD
HAVERICH, FRANCIS	BAL	327	3RD WARD
HAVERLOW, JAMES	CEC	048	1ST E DI
HAVERLY, JOHN	ALL	201	CUMBERLA
HAVERSE, NICHOLAS	DOR	451	1ST DIST
HAVERSTEAD, ELI	CAR	313	1ST DIST
HAVESTEY, JOHN	BAL	365	8TH WARD
HAVEY, ANDREW	BAL	001	EASTERN
HAVEY, J.	BAL	173	1ST WARD
HAVILAND, G.	BAL	140	1ST WARD
HAVILINO, AGNESS	HAR	120	2ND DIST
HAVINDER, THOMAS*	DOR	314	1ST DIST
HAVINGTON, AMANCA	BAL	419	8TH WARD
HAVNER, B.	BAL	161	1ST WARD
HAVNEW, ANDREW	ALL	136	4TH E.D.
HAVVECUTTE, FREDERICK	ANN	440	HOWARD D
HAW, ANN	BAL	314	12TH WAR
HAW, JOHN	BAL	285	2ND WARD
HAW, JOHN	BAL	348	1ST DIST
HAW, PATRICK	ALL	057	10TH E.D
HAWAMET, LAURA V.	WAS	215	1ST DIST
HAWARD, BENJAMIN	DOR	339	3RD DIVI
HAWARD, JOHN H.	HAR	201	3RD DIST
HAWARD, JOHN W.*	DOR	328	3RD DIVI
HAWARD, JOHN*	DOR	338	3RD DIVI
HAWARD, LEE	HAR	201	3RD DIST
HAWARD, SILAS	DOR	339	3RD DIVI
HAWARD, WILLIAM J.	WAS	153	2ND DIST
HAWELL, SAMUEL	BAL	003	9TH WARD
HAWES, ALFRED	BAL	050	9TH WARD
HAWK, ANDREWS	ALL	035	2ND E.D.
HAWK, AUGUSTUS	BAL	273	1ST DIST
HAWK, DAVID	BAL	133	5TH WARD
HAWK, ISAAC	ALL	163	6TH E.D.
HAWK, JACOB	WAS	194	1ST DIST
HAWK, JESSEE	BAL	318	7TH WARD
HAWK, JOHN S.	WAS	109	2ND DIST
HAWK, JOSEPH	ANN	414	HOWARD D
HAWK, LEONARD	BAL	352	1ST DIST
HAWK, MARGARET	BAL	115	5TH WARD
HAWK, MARGARET	ALL	034	2ND E.D.
HAWK, MARIA	BAL	332	7TH WARD
HAWK, MARY J.	FRE	183	5TH E DI
HAWK, MICHAEL	ALL	031	2ND E.D.
HAWK, PHEBE	ALL	195	CUMBERLA
HAWK, RACHEL	ALL	032	2ND E.D.
HAWK, REBECCA	BAL	190	2ND WARD
HAWK, SARAH	ALL	178	7TH E.D.
HAWK, THOMAS	BAL	271	1ST DIST
HAWKEN, WILLIAM H.	WAS	240	CAVETOWN
HAWKER, ANN	WAS	237	CAVETOWN
HAWKES, JOSEPH A.	FRE	214	BUCKEYST
HAWKES, PHILIP	FRE	214	BUCKEYST
HAWKIN, L. W. B.	CHA	230	BOJANTOW
HAWKIN, MARGARET	WAS	155	HAGERSTO
HAWKIN, SAMUEL	WAS	115	2ND DIST
HAWKIN, WILLIAM	WAS	155	HAGERSTO
HAWKING, HENRIETTA	BAL	034	9TH WARD
HAWKINGS, JACOB	WAS	148	2ND DIST
HAWKINS, AARON	ANN	342	3RD DIST
HAWKINS, ADALINE	BAL	286	1ST DIST
HAWKINS, ALEXANDER	KEN	211	2ND DIST
HAWKINS, ALEXNADER	BAL	190	17TH WAR
HAWKINS, ALLICE	BAL	046	18TH WAR
HAWKINS, ANDREW	KEN	308	3RD DIST
HAWKINS, ANN	PRI	115	PISCATAW
HAWKINS, ANN	BAL	133	18TH WAR
HAWKINS, ANN	HAR	001	1ST DIST
HAWKINS, ANN G.	BAL	317	3RD WARD
HAWKINS, ANNA	KEN	229	2ND DIST
HAWKINS, ANNE	BAL	096	15TH WAR
HAWKINS, AQUILLA	BAL	329	7TH WARD
HAWKINS, ARCHIBALD	BAL	002	EASTERN
HAWKINS, BENJAMIN	MGM	420	MEDLEY 3
HAWKINS, BETTY	PRI	059	NOTTINGH
HAWKINS, CALEB-BLACK	QUE	146	1ST E DI
HAWKINS, CAROLINE	CHA	229	MIDDLETO
HAWKINS, CAROLINE	ANN	436	HOWARD D
HAWKINS, CHARITY	ANN	367	4TH DIST
HAWKINS, CHARLES	BAL	142	2ND DIST
HAWKINS, CHARLES	BAL	076	2ND DIST
HAWKINS, CHARLES	BAL	142	5TH WARD
HAWKINS, CHARLES	BAL	281	20TH WAR
HAWKINS, CHARLES	BAL	204	19TH WAR
HAWKINS, CHARLES	CAL	061	3RD DIST
HAWKINS, CHARLES	BAL	204	17TH WAR
HAWKINS, CHARLES R.	BAL	052	9TH WARD
HAWKINS, DANIEL	BAL	255	12TH WAR
HAWKINS, DEBORAH	BAL	011	2ND DIST
HAWKINS, E.	BAL	059	10TH WAR
HAWKINS, EDWARD	BAL	196	17TH WAR
HAWKINS, EDWARD	BAL	262	20TH WAR
HAWKINS, EDWARD	CEC	042	CHESAPEA
HAWKINS, EDWARD	TAL	071	EASTON T
HAWKINS, ELEANOR	MGM	395	ROCKERLE
HAWKINS, ELIZA	BAL	256	20TH WAR
HAWKINS, ELIZA	BAL	183	11TH WAR
HAWKINS, ELIZABETH	BAL	110	10TH WAR
HAWKINS, ELIZABETH	BAL	256	1ST DIST
HAWKINS, ELLEN	CEC	008	ELKTON 3
HAWKINS, ELY-BLACK	FRE	232	BUCKEYST
HAWKINS, EMANUEL	BAL	374	13TH WAR
HAWKINS, EMANUEL	BAL	286	1ST DIST
HAWKINS, EMELINE	BAL	238	6TH WARD
HAWKINS, EMILY	BAL	094	10TH WAR
HAWKINS, EMILY	ANN	417	HOWARD D
HAWKINS, EMILY	WAS	157	HAGERSTO
HAWKINS, ENOCH	BAL	426	8TH WARD
HAWKINS, FLORA	BAL	254	1ST DIST
HAWKINS, FRANCIS	CHA	285	BOJANTOW
HAWKINS, FREDERICK	BAL	093	18TH WAR
HAWKINS, GEORGE	CEC	183	7TH E DI
HAWKINS, GEORGE	BAL	137	5TH WARD
HAWKINS, GEORGE T.	WAS	002	WILLIAMS
HAWKINS, GEORGE W.	BAL	320	1ST DIST
HAWKINS, HARRIET	BAL	126	5TH WARD
HAWKINS, HARRIET	BAL	026	15TH WAR
HAWKINS, HENRY	BAL	203	17TH WAR
HAWKINS, HENRY	CAL	027	2ND DIST
HAWKINS, HESTER	CEC	175	7TH E DI
HAWKINS, HESTER	BAL	107	18TH WAR
HAWKINS, HILLEARY	CAL	024	2ND DIST
HAWKINS, HOARCE	BAL	167	2ND DIST
HAWKINS, HUS.	BAL	230	12TH WAR
HAWKINS, IRA JAMES	MGM	381	ROCKERLE
HAWKINS, ISAAC	FRE	314	MIDDLETO
HAWKINS, ISAAC	ANN	331	2ND DIST
HAWKINS, ISAIH	BAL	309	3RD WARD
HAWKINS, JACOB	BAL	352	1ST DIST
HAWKINS, JAMES	BAL	435	8TH WARD
HAWKINS, JAMES	ANN	337	3RD DIST
HAWKINS, JAMES	BAL	137	2ND DIST
HAWKINS, JAMES	BAL	129	16TH WAR
HAWKINS, JAMES	BAL	474	14TH WAR
HAWKINS, JAMES	CEC	043	CHESAPEA
HAWKINS, JAMES	WAS	002	WILLIAMS
HAWKINS, JAMES JR.	MGM	380	ROCKERLE
HAWKINS, JANE	MGM	442	CLARKSTR
HAWKINS, JANE-BLACK	QUE	149	1ST E DI
HAWKINS, JEREMIAH	WAS	149	2ND DIST
HAWKINS, JOHN	WAS	114	2ND DIST
HAWKINS, JOHN	KEN	220	2ND DIST
HAWKINS, JOHN	HAR	120	2ND DIST
HAWKINS, JOHN	HAR	068	1ST DIST
HAWKINS, JOHN	BAL	425	3RD WARD
HAWKINS, JOHN	CAL	056	3RD DIST
HAWKINS, JOHN	DOR	375	1ST DIST
HAWKINS, JOHN	ANN	363	4TH DIST
HAWKINS, JOHN	BAL	148	2ND DIST
HAWKINS, JOHN	BAL	096	2ND DIST
HAWKINS, JOHN	BAL	286	1ST DIST
HAWKINS, JOHN G.	ANN	388	4TH DIST
HAWKINS, JOHN S.	HAR	131	2ND DIST
HAWKINS, JOHN W.	CHA	228	ALLENS F
HAWKINS, JOHN W.	BAL	171	16TH WAR
HAWKINS, JONATHAN S.	ANN	302	1ST DIST
HAWKINS, JOSEPH	ANN	342	3RD DIST
HAWKINS, JOSEPH	ANN	425	HOWARD D
HAWKINS, JOSEPH-BLACK	QUE	159	2ND E DI
HAWKINS, JOSEPHINE	ANN	439	HOWARD D
HAWKINS, JOSIAH	KEN	212	2ND DIST
HAWKINS, JOSIAS	CHA	229	MIDDLETO
HAWKINS, KEZIAH	BAL	388	13TH WAR
HAWKINS, KITTY	ANN	417	HOWARD D
HAWKINS, L.	BAL	152	1ST WARD
HAWKINS, LIDIA	HAR	124	2ND DIST
HAWKINS, LOUIS	ANN	387	4TH DIST
HAWKINS, LUCY	ANN	451	HOWARD D
HAWKINS, LUTHER	BAL	196	19TH WAR
HAWKINS, M.	ANN	272	ANNAPOLI
HAWKINS, MARGARET	ANN	419	HOWARD D
HAWKINS, MARGARET	ANN	490	HOWARD D
HAWKINS, MARGARET	ANN	505	HOWARD D
HAWKINS, MARIA	BAL	019	18TH WAR
HAWKINS, MARINDA	HAR	038	1ST DIST
HAWKINS, MARTHA	BAL	110	15TH WAR
HAWKINS, MARTHA	BAL	253	6TH WARD
HAWKINS, MARY	ANN	342	3RD DIST
HAWKINS, MARY	ANN	375	4TH DIST
HAWKINS, MARY	BAL	041	1ST WARD
HAWKINS, MARY	BAL	430	8TH WARD
HAWKINS, MARY	BAL	007	9TH WARD
HAWKINS, MARY	CAR	088	NO TWP L
HAWKINS, MARY	BAL	380	13TH WAR
HAWKINS, MARY	BAL	431	14TH WAR
HAWKINS, MARY	BAL	420	14TH WAR
HAWKINS, MARY E.	BAL	216	17TH WAR
HAWKINS, MARY E.	HAR	026	1ST DIST
HAWKINS, MARY E.	ANN	340	3RD DIST
HAWKINS, MARY H.	CHA	223	ALLENS F
HAWKINS, MARY-BLACK	FRE	030	FREDERIC
HAWKINS, MATILDA	ALL	256	CUMBERLA
HAWKINS, NACE	ANN	354	3RD DIST
HAWKINS, PAT	BAL	224	1ST DIST
HAWKINS, PATIENCE	PRI	062	NOTTINGH
HAWKINS, PATRICK	BAL	042	1ST WARD
HAWKINS, PEGGY	ANN	416	HOWARD D
HAWKINS, PETER	FRE	102	FREDERIC
HAWKINS, PHEBE	MGM	442	CLARKSTR
HAWKINS, PHILIP G.	HAR	177	3RD DIST
HAWKINS, RACHAEL	CHA	285	BOJANTOW
HAWKINS, RACHEL	BAL	474	14TH WAR
HAWKINS, RASHILL	BAL	195	17TH WAR
HAWKINS, RICHARD	BAL	403	1ST DIST
HAWKINS, RICHARD	FRE	252	NEW MARK
HAWKINS, RICHARD	PRI	013	BLADENSB
HAWKINS, ROBERT S.	ANN	339	3RD DIST
HAWKINS, ROSETTA	BAL	334	1ST DIST
HAWKINS, SAMUEL	ANN	445	HOWARD D
HAWKINS, SAMUEL	HAR	129	2ND DIST
HAWKINS, SAMUEL	BAL	238	17TH WAR
HAWKINS, SARAH	BAL	305	17TH WAR
HAWKINS, SOLOMON	ANN	356	3RD DIST
HAWKINS, SOPHIA	BAL	399	8TH WARD
HAWKINS, STEPHEN	BAL	128	2ND DIST
HAWKINS, SUSAN	BAL	356	13TH WAR
HAWKINS, TAMAR	BAL	474	14TH WAR
HAWKINS, THEODORE	ANN	384	4TH DIST
HAWKINS, THOMAS	DOR	307	1ST DIST
HAWKINS, THOMAS	MGM	394	ROCKERLE
HAWKINS, THOMAS W.	BAL	310	3RD WARD
HAWKINS, W.H.	WAS	005	WILLIAMS
HAWKINS, WALLACE W.	BAL	163	16TH WAR
HAWKINS, WALTER	SOM	466	HANGARY
HAWKINS, WILLIAM	PRI	049	AQUASCO
HAWKINS, WILLIAM	BAL	137	2ND DIST
HAWKINS, WILLIAM	BAL	286	1ST DIST
HAWKINS, WILLIAM	HAR	042	1ST DIST
HAWKINS, WILLIAM	BAL	345	13TH WAR
HAWKINS, WILLIAM	CAL	027	2ND DIST
HAWKINS, WILLIAM	HAR	131	2ND DIST
HAWKINS, WILLIAM	HAR	163	3RD DIST
HAWKINS, WILLIAM H.	BAL	404	1ST DIST
HAWKINS, WLE.	WAS	001	WILLIAMS
HAWKISN, MARGARET-BLACK	ST	329	4TH E DI
HAWKISN, MILLE	BAL	188	5TH DIST
HAWKS, JACOB	BAL	194	11TH WAR
HAWL, ABRAM	HAR	146	3RD DIST
HAWL, HENRY	HAR	177	3RD DIST
HAWL, JOHN S.	HAR	176	3RD DIST
HAWL, MARY F.	HAR	153	3RD DIST
HAWL, SAMUEL	HAR	199	3RD DIST
HAWL, SUSANER	HAR	152	3RD DIST
HAWLAND, PATRICK	BAL	429	1ST DIST
HAWLEY, ANDREW	BAL	079	1ST WARD
HAWLEY, JOHN	CAR	167	NO TWP L
HAWLY, MICHAEL	BAL	275	1ST DIST
HAWMAN, FREDERICK	FRE	023	FREDERIC
HAWMAN, JOHN J.	FRE	349	MIDDLETO
HAWMAN, PHILIP J.	FRE	021	FREDERIC
HAWN, BARBARA	BAL	284	1ST DIST
HAWNER, JACOB	FRE	152	10TH E D
HAWS, ELIZA	WAS	252	1ST DIST
HAWS, JOHN	WAS	290	1ST DIST
HAWS, SAUSAN	WAS	229	1ST DIST
HAWS, WASHINGTON	SOM	504	SALISBUR
HAWSAMNEUL, MICHAEL *	ALL	169	6TH E.D.
HAWSER, NICHOLAS	BAL	307	1ST DIST
HAWSKINS, JOHN	HAR	029	1ST DIST
HAWSON, HENRY	BAL	131	1ST WARD
HAWTHORN, DAVID	WAS	289	1ST DIST
HAWTHORN, JAMES	BAL	376	3RD WARD
HAWTHORN, JOHN	BAL	281	1ST DIST
HAWTHORNE, GEORGE	BAL	215	11TH WAR
HAWTHORNE, MARGARET	BAL	148	19TH WAR
HAWZE, FREDERICK JR.	BAL	022	15TH WAR
HAX, CHRISTIAN	BAL	307	7TH WARD
HAX, JOHN A.	BAL	288	3RD WARD
HAX, JOHN P.	BAL	089	18TH WAR
HAXEL, WILLIAM	BAL	112	10TH WAR
HAY, AMANDA T.	BAL	002	4TH WARD
HAY, ANN F.	BAL	009	4TH WARD
HAY, CONRAD	BAL	006	15TH WAR
HAY, ELIZABETH D.	BAL	004	EASTERN
HAY, GEORGE	BAL	108	5TH WARD
HAY, GEORGE	BAL	065	18TH WAR
HAY, GEORGE	BAL	435	14TH WAR
HAY, JANE	BAL	002	4TH WARD

Name	County	Page	District
HAY, JESSE	BAL	074	18TH WAR
HAY, JOHN	BAL	242	12TH WAR
HAY, JOHN	BAL	110	15TH WAR
HAY, JOHN-BLACK	FRE	439	8TH E DI
HAY, MARGRETT	BAL	048	18TH WAR
HAY, MENSLY	BAL	350	7TH WARD
HAY, RACHAEL	FRE	423	8TH E DI
HAY, REBECCA	BAL	459	1ST DIST
HAY, STEPHEN	BAL	326	1ST DIST
HAY, THADIAUS	FRE	438	8TH E DI
HAY,RACHAEL	FRE	438	8TH E DI
HAYALL, EDWARD	ANN	315	1ST DIST
HAYARD, J.	BAL	117	1ST WARD
HAYARD, LUCY	CEC	160	6TH E DI
HAYBURN, FRANCIS	BAL	160	11TH WAR
HAYCOCK, HENRY	HAR	182	3RD DIST
HAYCOCK, JEMIMA	BAL	370	1ST DIST
HAYDEN, A. REBECCA	ST	273	3RD E DI
HAYDEN, AMBROSE	CAR	279	7TH DIST
HAYDEN, BASIL	CAR	270	WESTMINS
HAYDEN, BERNARD	BAL	103	18TH WAR
HAYDEN, CECELIA	ST	333	4TH E DI
HAYDEN, CHARLE	ST	331	4TH E DI
HAYDEN, CHARLOTTE	BAL	197	19TH WAR
HAYDEN, EDWARD	BAL	218	2ND WARD
HAYDEN, ELIZA	BAL	019	1ST WARD
HAYDEN, ELIZA E.	ST	319	4TH E DI
HAYDEN, ELIZABETH	ST	333	4TH E DI
HAYDEN, ELIZABETH	ST	275	3RD E DI
HAYDEN, ELIZABETH	BAL	116	5TH WARD
HAYDEN, ELIZABETH	QUE	135	1ST E DI
HAYDEN, ELIZABETH H.	ANN	458	HOWARD D
HAYDEN, GEORGE	ANN	349	3RD DIST
HAYDEN, GEORGE	ST	274	3RD E DI
HAYDEN, H. E.	BAL	333	1ST DIST
HAYDEN, H. M.	BAL	141	11TH WAR
HAYDEN, H.G.	ST	333	4TH E DI
HAYDEN, IGNATIUS	ST	272	3RD E DI
HAYDEN, ISAAC	QUE	188	3RD E DI
HAYDEN, ISAAC	BAL	170	2ND DIST
HAYDEN, ISAAC	BAL	241	6TH WARD
HAYDEN, JAMES L.	ST	260	3RD E DI
HAYDEN, JANE	ST	277	3RD E DI
HAYDEN, JANE MISS	PRI	046	AQUASCO
HAYDEN, JOANNA	ST	271	3RD E DI
HAYDEN, JOHN B.	ST	285	2ND E DI
HAYDEN, JOHN R.	ALL	210	CUMBERLA
HAYDEN, JONATHAN SR.	ST	332	4TH E DI
HAYDEN, JOSEPH	ST	335	4TH E DI
HAYDEN, JOSEPH J.	ST	279	3RD E DI
HAYDEN, JULIANN	ST	338	4TH E DI
HAYDEN, L. S.	BAL	332	1ST DIST
HAYDEN, LEONARD	ST	260	3RD E DI
HAYDEN, MARGARET	QUE	135	1ST E DI
HAYDEN, MARIA	BAL	141	11TH WAR
HAYDEN, MARY	FRE	066	FREDERIC
HAYDEN, RICHARD	ST	270	3RD E DI
HAYDEN, ROBERT	BAL	295	3RD WARD
HAYDEN, SARAH	BAL	170	2ND DIST
HAYDEN, STEPHEN	ST	257	3RD E DI
HAYDEN, THOMAS F.	ST	332	4TH E DI
HAYDEN, WILLIAM	ST	267	3RD E DI
HAYDEN, WILLIAM	ST	256	3RD E DI
HAYDEN, WILLIAM	ST	265	3RD E DI
HAYDEN, WILLIAM	BAL	170	1ST WARD
HAYDEN, WILLIAM G.	ST	336	4TH E DI
HAYDEN, WILLIAM H.	ST	279	3RD E DI
HAYDEN,ANNA	QUE	135	1ST E DI
HAYDER, ELIZABETH A.C.	ST	334	4TH E DI
HAYDER, ZACHARIAH	ST	334	4TH E DI
HAYDON, ALICIA	FRE	040	FREDERIC
HAYDON, CHARLOTTE *	ANN	290	ANNAPOLI
HAYER, JACOB	CEC	056	1ST E DI
HAYES, ANN	BAL	326	3RD WARD
HAYES, CHARLES	BAL	282	2ND WARD
HAYES, DANIEL	BAL	120	1ST WARD
HAYES, DAVID	BAL	115	18TH WAR
HAYES, ELIZABETH	BAL	122	16TH WAR
HAYES, EMILY	BAL	326	3RD WARD
HAYES, HENRY	BAL	377	13TH WAR
HAYES, JAMES	BAL	059	18TH WAR
HAYES, JANE	BAL	049	9TH WARD
HAYES, JOHN	BAL	159	1ST WARD
HAYES, JOHN	FRE	384	PETERSVI
HAYES, JOHN B.	BAL	030	2ND DIST
HAYES, JULIA A.	BAL	097	10TH WAR
HAYES, MARY	BAL	102	10TH WAR
HAYES, PETER	BAL	322	3RD WARD
HAYES, ROBERT J.	HAR	004	1ST DIST
HAYES, THOMAS	BAL	027	9TH WARD
HAYES, WALTER*	BAL	064	4TH WARD
HAYETER, HARRIET	BAL	430	14TH WAR
HAYETT, PETER L. *	WAS	171	FUNKSTOW
HAYGHE, JOSEPH*	BAL	399	3RD WARD
HAYGKE, JOSEPH*	BAL	399	3RD WARD
HAYGLE, HENRY CLAY	BAL	092	18TH WAR
HAYGLE, JOHN L. *	BAL	091	18TH WAR
HAYKEMP, HARMON	BAL	423	14TH WAR
HAYKOCK, SOLOMON	HAR	187	3RD DIST
HAYLAND, ELIZA	BAL	475	14TH WAR
HAYLE, JOSIAH	BAL	014	2ND DIST
HAYLE, PHEBY	PRI	061	NOTTINGH
HAYLER, W.	BAL	149	1ST WARD
HAYLETT, JOSHUA M.	BAL	300	3RD WARD
HAYLEY, JOHN	BAL	172	2ND DIST
HAYLOR, MARGARET*	BAL	071	10TH WAR
HAYLY, JAMES	SOM	544	TYASKIN
HAYLY, ROBERT	SOM	489	SALISBUR
HAYMAN, ANN B.	BAL	059	18TH WAR
HAYMAN, CORNELUS	SOM	469	TRAPPE D
HAYMAN, DAVID J.	WOR	198	8TH E DI
HAYMAN, GEORGE	SOM	465	HANGARY
HAYMAN, GILLIS W.	SOM	482	TRAPP DI
HAYMAN, HAMILTON	SOM	469	TRAPPE D
HAYMAN, HANDY	WOR	198	8TH E DI
HAYMAN, HENRY	WOR	194	8TH E DI
HAYMAN, HENRY	SOM	534	QUANTICO
HAYMAN, HENRY	SOM	424	PRINCESS
HAYMAN, HESTER	SOM	470	TRAPPE D
HAYMAN, ISAAC	WOR	187	7TH E DI
HAYMAN, JAMES	SOM	437	PRINCESS
HAYMAN, JAMES D.	WOR	187	7TH E DI
HAYMAN, JAMES W.	WOR	233	6TH E DI
HAYMAN, JACOB H.	WOR	212	4TH E DI
HAYMAN, JEPTHA	SOM	400	BRINKLEY
HAYMAN, JOHN	WOR	180	6TH E DI
HAYMAN, JOHN	SOM	471	TRAPPE D
HAYMAN, JOHN	SOM	423	PRINCESS
HAYMAN, JOHN K.*	SOM	482	TRAPP DI
HAYMAN, LATITIA	SOM	482	TRAPP DI
HAYMAN, LEVIN P.	SOM	422	PRINCESS
HAYMAN, LITTLETON	SOM	476	TRAPPE D
HAYMAN, LIZA	SOM	460	HANGARY
HAYMAN, MARGARET	SOM	424	PRINCESS
HAYMAN, NANCY	SOM	437	PRINCESS
HAYMAN, REBECCA	SOM	424	PRINCESS
HAYMAN, REBECCA A.	SOM	423	PRINCESS
HAYMAN, ROBERT H.	WOR	206	4TH E DI
HAYMAN, SARAH J.	FRE	069	FREDERIC
HAYMAN, THEODORE	SOM	467	HANGARY
HAYMAN, URIAH	SOM	422	PRINCESS
HAYMAN, WILLIAM	SOM	431	PRINCESS
HAYNE, C.	FRE	200	5TH E DI
HAYNE, CHRISTOPHER	BAL	081	1ST WARD
HAYNE, JOHNG.	BAL	109	1ST WARD
HAYNE, MARY A.	BAL	284	7TH WARD
HAYNE, THOMAS	KEN	273	1ST DIST
HAYNE, WESLEY	BAL	410	14TH WAR
HAYNE, WILLIAM	KEN	249	2ND DIST
HAYNEAN, JOHN H.	BAL	015	1ST WARD
HAYNEL, ADOLPHUS F. DR.	BAL	343	13TH WAR
HAYNER, FRANCIS	BAL	015	1ST WARD
HAYNER, MARTIN	BAL	239	12TH WAR
HAYNES, ANNA	BAL	373	8TH WARD
HAYNES, CHARLES	BAL	284	20TH WAR
HAYNES, CHARLES	BAL	283	20TH WAR
HAYNES, HENRY	BAL	069	10TH WAR
HAYNES, HESTER	BAL	067	15TH WAR
HAYNES, IBO. T.	BAL	104	15TH WAR
HAYNES, JAMES	BAL	279	2ND WARD
HAYNES, JESSE	ANN	450	HOWARD D
HAYNES, JOHN	BAL	155	1ST WARD
HAYNES, JOHN	FRE	364	CATOCTIN
HAYNES, JOHN	WAS	081	2ND SUBD
HAYNES, JOHN C.	WAS	066	2ND SUBD
HAYNES, JOHN T.	ANN	504	HOWARD D
HAYNES, RACHEL	ANN	481	HOWARD D
HAYNES, ROBERT	BAL	238	2ND WARD
HAYNES, SARAH	BAL	373	8TH WARD
HAYNES, STEVEN	WAS	081	2ND SUBD
HAYNES, THOMAS	WAS	078	2ND SUBD
HAYNES, THOMAS	BAL	295	3RD WARD
HAYNES, URIAH	ANN	438	HOWARD D
HAYNES, WILLIAM	ANN	412	HOWARD D
HAYNES, WILLIAM	WAS	081	2ND SUBD
HAYNES, WILLIAM	BAL	445	14TH WAR
HAYNES, WILLIAM	BAL	145	19TH WAR
HAYNIA, W.J.	BAL	171	1ST WARD
HAYRE, HENRY	ALL	010	3RD E.D.
HAYS, A.*	DOR	410	1ST DIST
HAYS, ABNER	WAS	278	LEITERSB
HAYS, ABRAHAM	CAR	308	1ST DIST
HAYS, ALEX	BAL	181	2ND DIST
HAYS, ANN	BAL	053	9TH WARD
HAYS, ANN M.	FRE	039	FREDERIC
HAYS, ARTHUR	FRE	202	5TH E DI
HAYS, BENJAMIN	ANN	319	2ND DIST
HAYS, BETSY	DOR	410	1ST DIST
HAYS, BRIDGET	BAL	254	20TH WAR
HAYS, CATHARINE	FRE	377	PETERSVI
HAYS, CATHARINE	BAL	030	2ND DIST
HAYS, CATHARINE	BAL	201	11TH WAR
HAYS, CATHARINE	WAS	187	BOONSBOR
HAYS, CHALMANEY	SOM	356	BRINKLEY
HAYS, CHARLES	FRE	118	CREAGERS
HAYS, CHRISTIANA	WAS	055	2ND SUBD
HAYS, DAVID	PRI	055	AQUASCO
HAYS, DAVID	BAL	167	11TH WAR
HAYS, DAVID E.	WAS	129	2ND DIST
HAYS, DEBORAH	CAR	307	1ST DIST
HAYS, DOROTHY A.*	DOR	422	1ST DIST
HAYS, EDWARD	WAS	055	2ND SUBD
HAYS, EDWARD L.	MGM	382	ROCKERLE
HAYS, ELIZABETH	CEC	016	ELKTON 3
HAYS, ELIZABETH	FRE	167	EMMITTSB
HAYS, ELIZABETH	BAL	085	18TH WAR
HAYS, EMILY A.	BAL	136	18TH WAR
HAYS, GABRIEL	HAR	074	1ST DIST
HAYS, GABRIEL	BAL	057	2ND DIST
HAYS, GEORGE	HAR	035	1ST DIST
HAYS, GEORGE	BAL	036	18TH WAR
HAYS, GEORGE	BAL	033	18TH WAR
HAYS, GEORGE	BAL	207	17TH WAR
HAYS, GEORGE W.	FRE	015	FREDERIC
HAYS, GEORGE W.	WAS	156	2ND DIST
HAYS, GOODLOUR	FRE	364	CATOCTIN
HAYS, HARRIET-BLACK	FRE	433	8TH E DI
HAYS, HARRIETT B.	HAR	140	2ND DIST
HAYS, HENRY	CEC	071	5TH E DI
HAYS, HENRY	WAS	200	1ST DIST
HAYS, J.C.	WAS	042	2ND SUBD
HAYS, J.T.	BAL	292	12TH WAR
HAYS, JACOB	BAL	418	1ST DIST
HAYS, JAMES	BAL	117	2ND DIST
HAYS, JAMES	BAL	091	1ST WARD
HAYS, JAMES	BAL	282	2ND WARD
HAYS, JAMES	FRE	128	CREAGERS
HAYS, JAMES A.	BAL	152	1ST WARD
HAYS, JAMES H.	BAL	183	6TH WARD
HAYS, JAMES-BLACK	FRE	442	8TH E DI
HAYS, JANE	CEC	016	ELKTON 3
HAYS, JEMIMA	BAL	260	12TH WAR
HAYS, JOHN	BAL	270	12TH WAR
HAYS, JOHN	BAL	185	2ND WARD
HAYS, JOHN	BAL	355	8TH WARD
HAYS, JOHN	BAL	401	3RD WARD
HAYS, JOHN	BAL	073	1ST WARD
HAYS, JOHN	BAL	270	1ST DIST
HAYS, JOHN	BAL	018	1ST WARD
HAYS, JOHN	BAL	168	2ND DIST
HAYS, JOHN	BAL	111	2ND DIST
HAYS, JOHN	ALL	240	CUMBERLA
HAYS, JOHN	ANN	320	2ND DIST
HAYS, JOHN	CAR	316	1ST DIST
HAYS, JOHN	FRE	022	FREDERIC
HAYS, JOHN	CEC	088	4TH E DI
HAYS, JOHN	BAL	079	18TH WAR
HAYS, JOHN	CEC	065	1ST E DI
HAYS, JOHN	HAR	199	3RD DIST
HAYS, JOHN	BAL	398	14TH WAR
HAYS, JOHN B.	CEC	061	1ST E DI
HAYS, JOHN E.	HAR	206	3RD DIST
HAYS, JOSEPH	BAL	193	19TH WAR
HAYS, JOSEPH	FRE	110	CREAGERS
HAYS, JOSEPH	HAR	134	2ND DIST
HAYS, JOSEPH	WAS	181	BOONSBOR
HAYS, JOSIAH	CAR	359	9TH DIST
HAYS, JOSIAH	FRE	368	CATOCTIN
HAYS, KETURAH	FRE	015	FREDERIC
HAYS, LEOANRD	MGM	423	MEDLEY 3
HAYS, LEVIN	FRE	152	10TH E D
HAYS, MARGARET	SOM	476	TRAPPE D
HAYS, MARTHA	BAL	309	12TH WAR
HAYS, MARY A.	BAL	088	15TH WAR
HAYS, MARY D.	BAL	167	11TH WAR
HAYS, MARY E.	BAL	159	16TH WAR
HAYS, MARY J.	CAR	316	1ST DIST
HAYS, MARY M.	FRE	341	MIDDLETO
HAYS, MICHAEL	ALL	072	5TH E.D.
HAYS, MICHAEL S.	BAL	160	19TH WAR
HAYS, MOSES-BLACK	FRE	428	8TH E DI
HAYS, NANCY	SOM	462	HANGARY
HAYS, NATHANIEL W.S.	HAR	084	2ND DIST
HAYS, PATRICK	BAL	208	11TH WAR
HAYS, PETER D.	BAL	406	3RD WARD
HAYS, PHILEMON	BAL	232	1ST DIST
HAYS, POLLY	BAL	146	11TH WAR
HAYS, POLLY	SOM	475	TRAPPE D
HAYS, PRISILLA	BAL	205	11TH WAR
HAYS, REBECCA	ANN	463	HOWARD D
HAYS, RICHARD	DOR	409	1ST DIST
HAYS, ROBERT	BAL	400	14TH WAR
HAYS, ROBERT	CEC	049	1ST E DI
HAYS, ROBERT	BAL	081	18TH WAR
HAYS, ROBERT	CEC	088	4TH E DI
HAYS, ROBERT	BAL	182	6TH WARD
HAYS, SAMUEL	CEC	053	1ST E DI
HAYS, SAMUEL	BAL	228	17TH WAR
HAYS, SAMUEL J.	BAL	136	18TH WAR
HAYS, SAMUEL S.	MGM	424	MEDLEY 3
HAYS, SAMUEL S. JR.	MGM	410	MEDLEY 3
HAYS, SARAH	BAL	145	16TH WAR
HAYS, SARAH	WAS	201	1ST DIST
HAYS, SARAH A.	FRE	279	WOODSBOR
HAYS, SHARLOT A.	ST	258	3RD E DI
HAYS, SILVEY	ST	258	3RD E DI
HAYS, SISTER M.R.	FRE	198	5TH E DI
HAYS, SPALDING	PRI	061	NOTTINGH
HAYS, STEPHEN	CEC	008	ELKTON 3
HAYS, SUSAN	CEC	048	1ST E DI
HAYS, SUSAN G.	BAL	355	8TH WARD
HAYS, SUSAN R.	FRE	362	CATOCTIN
HAYS, TERESE	ST	261	3RD E DI
HAYS, THOMAS	FRE	111	CREAGERS
HAYS, THOMAS	BAL	061	10TH WAR
HAYS, THOMAS A.	HAR	075	BEL AIR
HAYS, THOMAS A. JR.	HAR	092	2ND DIST
HAYS, THOMAS J.	HAR	092	2ND DIST
HAYS, THOMAS M.	CEC	093	4TH E DI
HAYS, WASHINGTON	QUE	127	1ST E DI
HAYS, WILLIAM	BAL	301	17TH WAR
HAYS, WILLIAM	FRE	363	CATOCTIN
HAYS, WILLIAM	CEC	049	1ST E DI
HAYS, WILLIAM	BAL	256	17TH WAR
HAYS, WILLIAM	BAL	458	14TH WAR
HAYS, WILLIAM	BAL	356	8TH WARD
HAYS, WILLIAM	ALL	062	10TH E.D
HAYS, WILLIAM	ANN	383	4TH DIST
HAYS, WILLIAM	BAL	269	12TH WAR
HAYS, WILLIAM S.	FRE	229	BUCKEYST
HAYS,DENNIS	BAL	020	2ND DIST
HAYS,EDWARD	ALL	247	CUMBERLA
HAYSE, CHARLES H.	PRI	010	BLADENSB
HAYSE, FIELDER	PRI	011	BLADENSB
HAYSE, FIELDER	PRI	010	BLADENSB
HAYSE, GEORGE	BAL	011	2ND DIST
HAYSE, SAMUEL	PRI	012	BLADENSB
HAYSE, WILLIAM	PRI	012	BLADENSB
HAYTON, JAMES	BAL	200	19TH WAR
HAYWANE, E. E.	TAL	069	EASTON T
HAYWARD, ANN	TAL	037	EASTON D
HAYWARD, ARTHUR	WOR	176	6TH E DI
HAYWARD, CHARLES	BAL	047	15TH WAR
HAYWARD, DINER	SOM	408	DUBLIN D
HAYWARD, E. H.	TAL	074	EASTON T
HAYWARD, ELIZA E.	TAL	069	EASTON T
HAYWARD, ELIZABETH	PRI	001	BLADENSB
HAYWARD, GUSTAVUS*	TAL	005	EASTON D
HAYWARD, HARRIET	TAL	062	EASTON D
HAYWARD, HARRIET	TAL	070	EASTON T
HAYWARD, HARRIET	BAL	183	6TH WARD
HAYWARD, HENRICA	BAL	037	18TH WAR
HAYWARD, JOHN	DOR	440	1ST DIST
HAYWARD, JOHN E. SR.	WOR	200	3RD E DI
HAYWARD, JOSHUA-BLACK	WOR	173	5TH E DI
HAYWARD, LEAH-BLACK	WOR	172	6TH E DI
HAYWARD, NEHEMIAH P.	BAL	075	15TH WAR
HAYWARD, REBECCA	BAL	268	17TH WAR
HAYWARD, SARAH	SOM	426	PRINCESS
HAYWARD, SHADRICK	SOM	409	DUBLIN D
HAYWARD, THOMAS	TAL	036	EASTON D
HAYWARD, THOMAS H.	BAL	300	17TH WAR
HAYWARD, WILLIAM	TAL	003	EASTON D
HAYWOOD, EDWARD	BAL	230	12TH WAR
HAYWOOD, EDWARD G.	WAS	021	2ND SUBD
HAYWOOD, J. H.	BAL	147	11TH WAR
HAYWOOD, JACOB	BAL	404	14TH WAR
HAYWOOD, JOHN	BAL	331	7TH WARD
HAYWOOD, JOHN	BAL	053	9TH WARD
HAYWOOD, JOHN	BAL	458	1ST DIST
HAYWOOD, JOHN A.	ST	305	1ST E DI
HAYWOOD, JOSEPH	ST	308	1ST E DI
HAYWOOD, MARIA	BAL	104	10TH WAR
HAYWOOD, PHILIP H.	ANN	266	ANNAPOLI
HAYWOOD, RISE	BAL	231	12TH WAR
HAYWOOD, WILLIAM H.	BAL	192	19TH WAR
HAYWORTH, GEORGE R.	ANN	452	HOWARD D
HAYWORTH, MARGARET	BAL	356	1ST DIST
HAYZARD, SARAH	CAR	140	NO TWP L
HAZAL, JETSON	ST	330	4TH E DI
HAZARD, CORNELIA	CAL	052	3RD DIST
HAZARD, JAMES	BAL	310	3RD WARD
HAZARD, JOHN F.	ANN	327	2ND DIST
HAZARD, JONATHAN	CEC	044	CHESAPEA
HAZARD, LEWIS A.	ANN	325	2ND DIST
HAZEL, ANN M.	TAL	044	EASTON D
HAZEL, EDWARD J.	TAL	026	EASTON D
HAZEL, JOHN H.	ALL	121	4TH E.D.
HAZEL, MANLOVE	BAL	059	10TH WAR
HAZEL, PHILLIP	ALL	236	CUMBERLA
HAZEL, RICHARD A.	BAL	454	8TH WARD
HAZEL, WILLIAM H.	ST	329	4TH E DI
HAZELGROVE, WILLIAM*	BAL	094	10TH WAR
HAZELHURST, EMMA	BAL	229	19TH WAR
HAZELL, BENJAMIN	KEN	306	3RD DIST
HAZELL, JAMES	KEN	308	3RD DIST
HAZELL, JOHNATHAN	KEN	309	3RD DIST
HAZELTON, DAVID	QUE	242	3TH E DI
HAZELTOP, BETSY	ANN	313	2ND DIST
HAZELWAFF, CHRISTIAN	BAL	033	1ST WARD

HAZEN, WILLIAM	BAL	452	14TH WAR
HAZILTON, THOMAS	BAL	127	1ST WARD
HAZLE, JAMES L.	QUE	150	1ST E DI
HAZLE, JAMES W.	QUE	131	1ST E DI
HAZLEGROVE, GEORGE	BAL	042	9TH WARD
HAZLEHURST, HENRY R.	BAL	098	10TH WAR
HAZLEHURST, R.P.	ALL	216	CUMBERLA
HAZLEHURST, SAMUEL	BAL	228	19TH WAR
HAZLET, JAMES	HAR	056	1ST DIST
HAZLETON, ALEXANDER	QUE	234	4TH E DI
HAZLETON, CHARLES	QUE	227	4TH E DI
HAZLETON, ELIZABETH-BLACK	QUE	183	3RD E DI
HAZLETON, FRANCES	QUE	227	4TH E DI
HAZLETON, IRENE	QUE	212	3RD E DI
HAZLETON, JAMES	BAL	301	3RD WARD
HAZLETON, JERE	QUE	235	4TH E DI
HAZLETON, JOHN	QUE	228	4TH E DI
HAZLETON, JULIA-BLACK	QUE	187	3RD E DI
HAZLETON, ROBERT	BAL	188	19TH WAR
HAZLIP, DAVID	BAL	307	3RD WARD
HAZY, HARRIET	BAL	452	14TH WAR
HAZY, MARY E.	BAL	452	14TH WAR
HAZZARD, CHORLOT	WOR	273	BERLIN I
HAZZARD, E.	BAL	070	10TH WAR
HAZZARD, JACOB H.	TAL	065	EASTON T
HAZZARD, JOHN	TAL	085	ST MICHA
HAZZARD, JOSEPHINE E.	BAL	070	10TH WAR
HAZZARD, POLLARD	TAL	072	EASTON T
HAZZARD, SUSAN	WOR	262	BERLIN I
HBRUNT, JANE	BAL	362	13TH WAR
HEUSSARD, HENRY	CAR	369	9TH DIST
HEACK, PETE	BAL	053	1ST WARD
HEACK, WILLIAM	ALL	241	CUMBERLA
HEAD, CECILIUS	FRE	056	FREDERIC
HEAD, ELEY H.	BAL	180	16TH WAR
HEAD, JOHN S.	BAL	045	1ST WARD
HEAD, WASHINGTON	BAL	049	18TH WAR
HEAD, WILLAIM T.	ALL	066	10TH E.D
HEAD, WILLIAM Y.	FRE	272	NEW MARK
HEADEN, HESTER	CEC	083	CHARLEST
HEADGES, SARAH	BAL	226	12TH WAR
HEADINGTON, WILLIAM	BAL	358	1ST DIST
HEADLAND, JOHN	ANN	386	4TH DIST
HEADLEN, GEORGE	BAL	060	1ST WARD
HEADLEY, MILES	BAL	151	1ST WARD
HEADLINE, JOHN	BAL	046	1ST WARD
HEADLOW, WILLIAM	BAL	146	1ST WARD
HEADLY, JONATHAN	CEC	162	6TH E DI
HEADLY, THOMAS	DOR	429	1ST DIST
HEADNER, ANDREW	BAL	282	1ST DIST
HEADRICH, MARY	WAS	294	1ST DIST
HEADWARDLY, MARY	BAL	278	17TH WAR
HEADY, MARY A.	WAS	156	2ND DIST
HEAEN, GEORGE A. H.	WOR	216	4TH E DI
HEAFERAN, PETER	BAL	022	2ND DIST
HEAFLEICH, ELIZABETH	BAL	187	6TH WARD
HEAFLEICH, JACOB D.	BAL	308	3RD WARD
HEAGUE, HENRY	BAL	372	8TH WARD
HEAGY, CATHARINE	CAR	243	TANEYTOW
HEAHS, ELIZABETH	BAL	110	10TH WAR
HEAKER, JESSE	ALL	160	6TH E.D.
HEAKEY, JACOB	WAS	016	2ND SUBD
HEALAND, EDWARD	BAL	136	1ST WARD
HEALD, JAMES H.	HAR	088	2ND DIST
HEALD, JOHN H.H.	BAL	204	11TH WAR
HEALD, WILLAM	BAL	446	14TH WAR
HEALD, WILLIAM H.	BAL	235	6TH WARD
HEALEY, JOSEPH	BAL	286	2ND WARD
HEALEY, PATRICK	ALL	049	10TH E.D
HEALEY, WILLIAM	BAL	229	19TH WAR
HEALTON, RICHARD H.	BAL	035	9TH WARD
HEALY, AGNES E. A.	BAL	063	4TH WARD
HEALY, ANGELINE	BAL	059	15TH WAR
HEALY, CATHERINE	ALL	213	CUMBERLA
HEALY, CATHERINE	BAL	083	10TH WAR
HEALY, ELIZABETH	HAR	013	1ST DIST
HEALY, FRANCIS	BAL	132	11TH WAR
HEALY, FRANCIS	CHA	224	ALLENS F
HEALY, JAMES E.	BAL	355	3RD WARD
HEALY, JOHN	ALL	211	CUMBERLA
HEALY, JOHN	BAL	018	4TH WARD
HEALY, MARY	BAL	357	13TH WAR
HEALY, MARY	BAL	359	3RD WARD
HEALY, MICHAEL	ALL	228	CUMBERLA
HEALY, PATRICK	HAR	154	3RD DIST
HEALY, THOMAS A.	ALL	238	CUMBERLA
HEALY, THOMAS M.	ALL	238	CUMBERLA
HEAM, BENJAMIN	WOR	237	6TH E DI
HEAM, HARRIET	WOR	217	4TH E DI
HEAM, ISAAC	WOR	198	8TH E DI
HEAM, JONATHAN	WOR	233	6TH E DI
HEAM, JOSEPH *	WOR	236	6TH E DI
HEAM, PETER	WOR	200	8TH E DI
HEAM, ROBERT	WOR	216	4TH E DI
HEAM, Y.	WOR	218	4TH E DI
HEAMER, PATRICK	BAL	148	1ST WARD
HEANE, EBENEZER	BAL	064	1ST WARD
HEANY, JAMES	WOR	342	1ST E DI
HEAPS, ARCHABALD	BAL	403	14TH WAR
HEAPS, ARCHY	HAR	042	1ST DIST
HEAPS, BENJAMIN	HAR	011	1ST DIST
HEAPS, BENJAMIN B.	BAL	175	2ND WARD
HEAPS, CATHARINE	HAR	024	1ST DIST
HEAPS, J. B.	BAL	115	11TH WAR
HEAPS, JAMES	BAL	151	1ST WARD
HEAPS, JOHN	BAL	227	1ST DIST
HEAPS, JOHN	HAR	011	1ST DIST
HEAPS, JOHN B.	HAR	054	1ST DIST
HEAPS, MARGARETT	BAL	222	2ND WARD
HEAPS, MARY	BAL	227	1ST DIST
HEAPS, ROBERT S.	BAL	227	1ST DIST
HEAPS, WILLIAM	HAR	011	1ST DIST
HEARALD, ANTONY J.	HAR	037	1ST DIST
HEARD, BENEDICT J.	BAL	433	9TH WARD
HEARD, CHARLOTTE	ST	321	4TH E DI
HEARD, EDMOND	ST	311	1ST E DI
HEARD, FRANKLIN A.	ST	279	3RD E DI
HEARD, HARRIET E.	WAS	126	HAGERSTO
HEARD, IGNATIUS	ST	258	3RD E DI
HEARD, JAEMS W.	ST	258	3RD E DI
HEARD, JAMES E.	ST	278	3RD E DI
HEARD, JAMES H.	ST	279	3RD E DI
HEARD, JAMES M.	ST	295	2ND E DI
HEARD, JANE	ST	263	3RD E DI
HEARD, M.L.V.L.	ST	260	3RD E DI
HEARD, REBECCA L.	WAS	021	2ND SUBD
HEARD, WILLIAM J.	ST	259	3RD E DI
HEARD, WILLIAM J.	WAS	140	HAGERSTO
HEARN, A.J.	ST	312	1ST E DI
HEARN, ALFRED C.	BAL	247	12TH WAR
HEARN, AMANDA	ANN	501	HOWARD D
HEARN, ARTEMAS	SOM	513	BARREN C
HEARN, BENJAMIN	ANN	498	HOWARD D
HEARN, BENJAMIN	SOM	503	SALISBUR
HEARN, BENJAMIN G.*	SOM	501	SALISBUR
HEARN, CHARLES	DOR	447	1ST DIST
HEARN, CHARLES R.	SOM	501	SALISBUR
HEARN, ELIZA J.	WOR	204	4TH E DI
HEARN, ELIZABETH	SOM	500	SALISBUR
HEARN, HANDY	ANN	471	HOWARD D
HEARN, HARIET	WOR	242	1ST CENS
HEARN, HESTER	SOM	503	SALISBUR
HEARN, HYRAM	SOM	470	TRAPPE D
HEARN, ICHABOD	SOM	501	SALISBUR
HEARN, ISAAC SR.	SOM	553	TYASKIN
HEARN, JACOB	ANN	502	HOWARD D
HEARN, JOHN	SOM	505	SALISBUR
HEARN, JOHN	WOR	238	6TH E DI
HEARN, JOHN S.	ANN	502	HOWARD D
HEARN, JOHN W.	WOR	342	1ST E DI
HEARN, JULIA	SOM	500	SALISBUR
HEARN, MARIA	SOM	501	SALISBUR
HEARN, MARTHA	ANN	479	HOWARD D
HEARN, MARY E.	SOM	491	SALISBUR
HEARN, MERILL	SOM	499	SALISBUR
HEARN, MORRIS	SOM	490	SALISBUR
HEARN, MOSES	SOM	504	SALISBUR
HEARN, NOAH	SOM	505	SALISBUR
HEARN, POLLY	SOM	502	SALISBUR
HEARN, RICHARD	SOM	383	BRINKLEY
HEARN, RIDSON	ANN	501	HOWARD D
HEARN, SARAH	WOR	237	6TH E DI
HEARN, SARAH A.	SOM	503	SALISBUR
HEARN, SEVA	SOM	502	SALISBUR
HEARN, THOMAS	WOR	239	6TH E DI
HEARN, WILLIAM	SOM	498	SALISBUR
HEARN, WILLIAM L.	SOM	490	SALISBUR
HEARN, WILLIAM L.	BAL	129	1ST WARD
HEARN, WILLIAM W.*	DOR	386	1ST DIST
HEARNE, CAROLINE	DOR	447	1ST DIST
HEARNS, BENJAMIN	BAL	210	11TH WAR
HEARNS, JANE-BLACK	ANN	502	HOWARD D
HEARPNER, NICHOLAS	WOR	339	1ST E DI
HEARSEY, HESTER	BAL	278	2ND WARD
HEART, ALEXANDER	BAL	012	18TH WAR
HEART, ELIZABETH	BAL	408	14TH WAR
HEART, FRANCIS B.	PRI	008	BLADENSB
HEART, GEORGE W.	BAL	457	14TH WAR
HEART, MARGARET	BAL	385	1ST DIST
HEART, MARY	BAL	457	14TH WAR
HEART, SUSAN	BAL	446	14TH WAR
HEARTER, NICHOLAS	FRE	063	FREDERIC
HEARTER, WILLIAM	BAL	220	1ST DIST
HEARTLEY, JAMES	BAL	221	1ST DIST
HEARTLEY, JAMES	BAL	456	1ST DIST
HEARTLEY, JOHN	BAL	194	19TH WAR
HEARTLEY, STGEPHEN	BAL	187	19TH WAR
HEARTLOVE, ASBURY	BAL	444	14TH WAR
HEARTLY, PRISCILLA	BAL	111	1ST WARD
HEARY, HENRY	ALL	245	CUMBERLA
HEASEN, FREDERICK*	WAS	017	2ND SUBD
HEASS, WATT *	BAL	341	3RD WARD
HEASTON, JOHN	BAL	299	12TH WAR
HEASTON, MILLY*	BAL	142	1ST WARD
HEATER, WILLIAM *	SOM	489	SALISBUR
HEATH, ANN	BAL	166	2ND DIST
HEATH, BENJAMIN T.	BAL	338	13TH WAR
HEATH, CAROLINE	CEC	148	PORT DUP
HEATH, D.P.	CEC	125	5TH E DI
HEATH, DANIEL D.	BAL	169	1ST WARD
HEATH, DURDEN *	ANN	445	HOWARD D
HEATH, ELISHA S.	QUE	251	5TH E DI
HEATH, ELIZABETH	BAL	049	15TH WAR
HEATH, ESHMEL	BAL	032	4TH WARD
HEATH, FRANCIS W.	SOM	418	PRINCESS
HEATH, FREDERICK	BAL	137	18TH WAR
HEATH, GEORGE	BAL	143	19TH WAR
HEATH, HARLOW W.	SOM	403	BRINKLEY
HEATH, HENRY	BAL	065	10TH WAR
HEATH, HENRY	BAL	460	1ST DIST
HEATH, HORACE W.	SOM	403	BRINKLEY
HEATH, ISABELLA	PRI	024	VANSVILL
HEATH, JAMES	CEC	083	CHARLEST
HEATH, JAMES P.	SOM	484	TRAPP DI
HEATH, JOHN	BAL	297	12TH WAR
HEATH, JOHN	BAL	170	6TH WARD
HEATH, JOHN T.	CEC	140	5TH E DI
HEATH, JULIA A.	CEC	125	5TH E DI
HEATH, LAURA	CAR	193	4TH DIST
HEATH, LEAH	ANN	357	3RD DIST
HEATH, MARY	SOM	403	BRINKLEY
HEATH, MARY	BAL	348	7TH WARD
HEATH, MARY E.	BAL	354	7TH WARD
HEATH, MARY O.	PRI	023	VANSVILL
HEATH, MISS A.	BAL	272	12TH WAR
HEATH, MISS L.	FRE	199	5TH E DI
HEATH, RICHARD	FRE	198	5TH E DI
HEATH, ROBERT	PRI	026	VANSVILL
HEATH, ROSETTA	ANN	348	3RD DIST
HEATH, SARAH	TAL	077	EASTON T
HEATH, SARAH	QUE	252	5TH E DI
HEATH, SARAH	CEC	084	CHARLEST
HEATH, STEPHEN P.	CEC	190	5TH E DI
HEATH, THOMAS	PRI	023	VANSVILL
HEATH, THOMAS	CEC	079	NORTHEAS
HEATH, UPTON S.	SOM	441	DAMES QU
HEATH, WILBUR W.	BAL	197	11TH WAR
HEATH, WILLIAM	PRI	024	VANSVILL
HEATH, WILLIAM	SOM	546	TYASKIN
HEATH, WILLIAM	SOM	544	TYASKIN
HEATH, WILLIAM	QUE	251	5TH E DI
HEATH, WILLIAM	QUE	224	4TH E DI
HEATH, WILLIAM	BAL	137	1ST WARD
HEATHCOCT, JOHN	CEC	140	5TH E DI
HEATLY, JOSEPH	HAR	202	3RD DIST
HEATON, ANDREW	BAL	172	1ST WARD
HEATON, JACOB	HAR	018	1ST DIST
HEATON, JOHN	WAS	147	HAGERSTO
HEATON, SARAH	HAR	025	1ST DIST
HEATOR, VINCENT	CEC	118	4TH E DI
HEATSHANO, PAUL A.	BAL	166	2ND DIST
HEATTY, J.	BAL	163	1ST WARD
HEATTY, MARY	BAL	166	1ST WARD
HEATYMAN, M.	CEC	149	PORT DUP
HEAUGHNAGEL, PHILIP	BAL	219	19TH WAR
HEAVES, JAMES	BAL	234	1ST DIST
HEAVNER, AGUSTUS	BAL	152	1ST WARD
HEBB, EDWARD T.	BAL	218	2ND WARD
HEBB, ELIZABETH	FRE	209	BUCKEYST
HEBB, H.F.	WAS	039	2ND SUBD
HEBB, HENRY	ST	319	4TH E DI
HEBB, JOHN	ALL	255	CUMBERLA
HEBB, PRISCILLA	ANN	426	HOWARD D
HEBB, REBECCA	ST	300	1ST E DI
HEBB, RICHARD H.	ST	298	2ND E DI
HEBB, SUSAN	PRI	114	PISCATAW
HEBB, SUSAN	ALL	239	CUMBERLA
HEBB, THOMAS	ST	293	2ND E DI
HEBB, VLAN L.	ST	348	5TH E DI
HEBB, WILLIAM	ST	298	2ND E DI
HEBBARD, JOHN M.	MGM	319	CRACKLIN
HEBE, HOPEWELL	FRE	20	5TH E DI
HEBER, J.H.	BAL	149	19TH WAR
HEBERER, CAROLINE	BAL	260	17TH WAR
HEBERMEAHL, MARGARET	BAL	25[illegible]	17TH WAR
HEBERT, SAMUEL	ANN	373	4TH DIST
HEBLER, FREDERICK	BAL	354	13TH WAR
HEBNER, CHARLES	BAL	256	17TH WAR
HEBNER, DANIEL	HAR	063	1ST DIST
HEBREW, EDWARD	BAL	247	20TH WAR
HEBREW, JOHN *	KEN	220	2ND DIST
HEBRON, JOHN *	KEN	220	2ND DIST
HEBRON, RICHARD	ANN	445	HOWARD D
HEBROW, JOHN *	KEN	220	2ND DIST
HEBROW, JOSEPH J.	HAR	134	2ND DIST
HEBURN, DAVID	BAL	039	1ST WARD
HEBURN, PETER	ANN	370	4TH DIST
HECHT, ASHER	BAL	073	4TH WARD
HECHT, ELIAS	BAL	112	10TH WAR
HECHT, JAMES B.	BAL	227	12TH WAR
HECHT, SAMUEL	BAL	296	7TH WARD
HECK, ADAM	BAL	019	15TH WAR
HECK, ANDREW	BAL	010	15TH WAR
HECK, CHARLES L.	HAR	114	2ND DIST
HECK, ELIZABETH	WAS	181	BOONSBOR
HECK, GEORGE	BAL	030	1ST WARD
HECK, GEROME	ALL	110	5TH E.D.
HECK, HENRY	WAS	208	1ST DIST
HECK, JACOB	WAS	048	2ND SUBD
HECK, JAMES	CAR	313	1ST DIST
HECK, JOHN	WAS	181	BOONSBOR
HECK, JOHN	WAS	183	BOONSBOR
HECK, JOHN	BAL	224	6TH WARD
HECK, LANEHAM	WAS	188	1ST DIST
HECK, LEWIS	WAS	200	1ST DIST
HECK, MARY	CEC	039	CHESAPEA
HECK, MEDESSA *	FRE	350	MIDDLETO
HECK, NICHOLAS	CAR	312	1ST DIST
HECK, PETER	CAR	314	1ST DIST
HECK, PETER	WAS	197	1ST DIST
HECK, PETER	WAS	181	BOONSBOR
HECK, SARAH	WAS	093	2ND SUBD
HECK, WILLIAM	BAL	147	5TH WARD
HECKART, DAVID	CEC	154	PORT DUP
HECKART, JOHN J.	CEC	146	PORT DUP
HECKATHORN, CHRISTIAN	FRE	044	FREDERIC
HECKATHORN, WILLIAM	BAL	088	18TH WAR
HECKENDORN, JACOB	CEC	006	ELKTON 3
HECKER, CHARLES	KEN	228	2ND DIST
HECKET, JACKSON	CEC	053	1ST E DI
HECKLEYER, HENRY	WAS	165	HAGERSTO
HECKLINE, CATHARINE	WAS	278	LEITERSB
HECKMAN, CATHARINE	WAS	155	HAGERSTO
HECKMAN, CHRISTIAN	WAS	155	HAGERSTO
HECKMAN, HARRIET	FRE	056	FREDERIC
HECKMAN, LAWRANCE	BAL	379	8TH WARD
HECKMAN, MARY	BAL	203	6TH DIST
HECKMAN, SOLOMON	BAL	211	6TH DIST
HECKMAN, THEODORE	BAL	370	1ST DIST
HECKROOTE, WILLIAM H	WAS	102	2ND DIST
HECKROTTE, CHARLES	BAL	105	15TH WAR
HECKROTTE, ISABEL	ALL	025	2ND E.D.
HECKROTTE, JOHN S.	MGM	335	CRACKLIN
HECKROTTE, WILLIAM *	BAL	056	15TH WAR
HECKS, ALASON	CHA	251	MIDDLETO
HECKS, GILES	CAR	166	NO TWP L
HECKS, SAMUEL	FRE	075	FREDERIC
HECKSEL, CHRISTIAN	CAR	353	6TH DIST
HECKT, REUBEN	BAL	297	3RD WARD
HECOM, JAMES	BAL	009	EASTERN
HECTER, ELBERT	FRE	204	BUCKEYST
HECTOR, ANNA	BAL	247	6TH WARD
HECTRICK, THOMAS	BAL	160	19TH WAR
HECTROPE, HENRIETTA	ANN	508	HOWARD D
HECTROPE, MARGARET	ANN	508	HOWARD D
HEDDEMAN, HENRY*	BAL	346	3RD WARD
HEDDIN, MARY	BAL	390	8TH WARD
HEDDINGER, MICHAEL H.	BAL	305	3RD WARD
HEDDINOT, CHARLES	BAL	064	2ND DIST
HEDDLE, GEORGE	FRE	108	CREAGERS
HEDDLE, JAMES	FRE	122	CREAGERS
HEDDRICKSON, CATHAINE	ALL	037	2ND E.D.
HEDELLE, MARINA A.	FRE	118	CREAGERS
HEDERBACHT, ABRAM	BAL	252	12TH WAR
HEDERICK, ANTON	BAL	402	14TH WAR
HEDGE, GEORGE	BAL	208	11TH WAR
HEDGE, MARY	FRE	336	MIDDLETO
HEDGES, DANIEL	FRE	091	FREDERIC
HEDGES, JOHN A.	FRE	097	FREDERIC
HEDGES, WILLIAM	BAL	167	19TH WAR
HEDGES, WILLIAM	BAL	354	13TH WAR
HEDGET, MICHEL	DOR	363	3RD DIVI
HEDGTES, ENOS	FRE	091	FREDERIC
HEDINGER, CATHARINE	BAL	224	6TH WARD
HEDINGER, DANIEL	BAL	155	2ND DIST
HEDINGER, JAMES	BAL	349	3RD WARD
HEDINGER, JOHN	ALL	221	CUMBERLA
HEDLAND, HANNAH	BAL	359	1ST DIST
HEDLEY, CHARLES	BAL	002	15TH WAR
HEDLEY, HENRY	KEN	226	2ND DIST
HEDLEY, SARAH	KEN	225	2ND DIST
HEDON, ANN	WAS	073	2ND SUBD
HEDRAER, MARGARET	BAL	320	12TH WAR
HEDRICH, CATHARINE	BAL	025	2ND DIST
HEDRICH, ELIZABETH	BAL	026	2ND DIST
HEDRICH, JOHN	BAL	025	2ND DIST
HEDRICH, SARAH	WAS	040	2ND SUBD
HEDRICK, ALICE	BAL	052	2ND DIST
HEDRICK, CHRISTIAN	FRE	016	FREDERIC
HEDRICK, DANIEL	BAL	023	2ND DIST
HEDRICK, ELIZABETH	BAL	402	14TH WAR
HEDRICK, JOHN	BAL	230	2ND WARD
HEDRICK, JOHN	WAS	301	1ST DIST
HEDRICK, JOHN *	FRE	355	MIDDLETO
HEDRICK, JOSEPH T.	BAL	299	7TH WARD
HEDRICK, LID	BAL	207	11TH WAR
HEDRICK, MARY	BAL	163	2ND DIST
HEDRICK, MARY	BAL	299	1ST DIST
HEDRICK, MARY	WAS	039	2ND SUBD
HEDRICK, MARY A.	BAL	299	7TH WARD

Name	County	Page	District
HEDRICK, RICHARD	BAL	308	7TH WARD
HEDRICK, ROBERT	BAL	026	2ND DIST
HEDRICK, VICY	CEC	116	3RD E DI
HEDRICK, WILLIAM	BAL	163	2ND DIST
HEDRICK, WILLIAM	BAL	393	1ST DIST
HEDRICKS, ANDREW	BAL	353	3RD WARD
HEDRICKS, GEORGE	BAL	051	2ND DIST
HEDRICKS, GOERGE	BAL	336	7TH WARD
HEDWICK, MARGRETT	BAL	204	11TH WAR
HEEDY, JACOB	WAS	075	2ND SUBD
HEELAN, AGNES	FRE	336	MIDDLETO
HEEMAN, ANN	WOR	305	SNOW HIL
HEER, GEORGE	WAS	138	2ND DIST
HEER, JOHN H.	WAS	128	2ND DIST
HEERMAN, ELIZA	BAL	005	15TH WAR
HEERWAGEN, AUGUST	BAL	166	16TH WAR
HEESLER, JOHN	BAL	065	4TH WARD
HEFER, DANIEL	WAS	083	2ND SUBD
HEFF, MARY	WAS	041	2ND SUBD
HEFFERN, HUGH	BAL	176	11TH WAR
HEFFIELD, HENRY	BAL	001	18TH WAR
HEFFINGTON, WILLIAM	BAL	213	19TH WAR
HEFFLAN, PATRICK	BAL	099	1ST WARD
HEFFLEFINGER, J.A.	ALL	215	CUMBERLA
HEFFLER, HORACE	FRE	239	NEW MARK
HEFFNER, AGNES	BAL	121	11TH WAR
HEFFNER, DAVID	WAS	125	HAGERSTO
HEFFNER, EDWARD	BAL	013	15TH WAR
HEFFNER, GEORGE	FRE	214	BUCKEYST
HEFFNER, JOHN	FRE	093	FREDERIC
HEFFNER, MARY	BAL	027	9TH WARD
HEFFNER, MICHAEL	FRE	130	CREAGERS
HEFFNER, SAMUEL	FRE	099	FREDERIC
HEFFNER, SAMUEL	FRE	064	FREDERIC
HEFFNER, T.	BAL	276	20TH WAR
HEFLER, JERDENAN	BAL	433	8TH WARD
HEFNER, DANIEL	MGM	407	MEDLEY 3
HEFNER, JOHN	MGM	415	MEDLEY 3
HEFNER, MARY A.	FRE	284	WOODSBOR
HEFNER, MICHAEL	BAL	421	14TH WAR
HEFRON, CATHERINE	BAL	406	3RD WARD
HEFSONG, MARGARET	FRE	336	MIDDLETO
HEGAN, JSOEPH	FRE	067	FREDERIC
HEGDON, HENRY	BAL	324	7TH WARD
HEGENBOTHANE, MARY	BAL	148	2ND DIST
HEGGS, WILLIAM H.	CHA	289	BOJANTOW
HEGHAM, CATHARINE	BAL	266	12TH WAR
HEGINBOTHAM, CHARLES	BAL	147	2ND DIST
HEGLE, JOSEPH	BAL	011	2ND DIST
HEGMETT, JAMES	CAR	092	NO TWP L
HEHON, JAMES	CEC	150	PORT DUP
HEICHMAN, GEORGE	BAL	244	2ND WARD
HEICKLER, JOHN	BAL	018	9TH WARD
HEICKS, HANNAH	BAL	303	1ST DIST
HEIDER, CHRISTIAN	BAL	044	9TH WARD
HEIDMAN, AUGUST H.	BAL	121	5TH WARD
HEIF, EDWARD	BAL	151	5TH WARD
HEIGER, WILLIAM	BAL	105	1ST WARD
HEIGH, SAMUEL	BAL	180	19TH WAR
HEIGHT, ANN M.	BAL	366	3RD WARD
HEIGHT, GROVE	BAL	276	7TH WARD
HEIGHT, ISABEL	CAL	033	2ND DIST
HEIGHT, JACOB	BAL	274	12TH WAR
HEIGHT, SARAH J.	BAL	357	3RD WARD
HEIGHT, WILLIAM	BAL	373	3RD WARD
HEIGHT, WILLIAM HENRY	CAL	034	2ND DIST
HEIGHTHS, CATHARINE	BAL	230	2ND WARD
HEIGHTMAN, MARYANN	BAL	379	3RD WARD
HEIGISHAMA, CHRISTOPHA	BAL	262	2ND WARD
HEIGLE, SAMUEL *	BAL	090	2ND DIST
HEIKNER, LEWIS	BAL	312	12TH WAR
HEILAN, GEORGE	CAR	275	7TH DIST
HEILAND, LEWIS	BAL	102	1ST WARD
HEILBOW, GEORGE	BAL	315	3RD WARD
HEILBURN, MICHAEL	BAL	382	13TH WAR
HEILDMAN, ABRAHAM	ALL	022	2ND E.D.
HEILDMAN, HESTER	ALL	022	2ND E.D.
HEILMAN, REGINA	ALL	007	3RD E.D.
HEIM, ALBERT	BAL	159	6TH WARD
HEIM, ANDREW	FRE	011	FREDERIC
HEIM, DAVID	BAL	184	6TH WARD
HEIM, JOHN	BAL	030	15TH WAR
HEIMAN, BERNARD	BAL	332	3RD WARD
HEIMAN, CHRISTIAN	BAL	052	1ST WARD
HEIMAN, JAMES	BAL	008	4TH WARD
HEIMAN, JOHN	BAL	243	2ND WARD
HEIMER, EMANUEL	BAL	052	1ST WARD
HEIMERIER, WILLIAM	BAL	063	1ST WARD
HEIMILLER, HENRY	BAL	199	6TH WARD
HEIMS, ELLEN	FRE	406	JEFFERSO
HEIMS, JOHN	FRE	377	PETERSVI
HEIMS, SUSAN M.	FRE	400	JEFFERSO
HEIN, CHRISTOPHER	BAL	204	19TH WAR
HEIN, HENRY	BAL	220	17TH WAR
HEIN, MICHAEL	BAL	219	19TH WAR
HEIN, STEPHEN	BAL	259	2ND WARD
HEINDLE, GEORGE	CAR	338	6TH DIST
HEINDLE, JOSHUA	CAR	339	6TH DIST
HEINE, SEBASTIAN	BAL	057	4TH WARD
HEINEP, C.	BAL	153	1ST WARD
HEINER, CHARLOTTE	BAL	052	4TH WARD
HEINER, CHRISTIAN	BAL	024	1ST WARD
HEINER, ELIAS	BAL	051	9TH WARD
HEINER, FRANCIS	BAL	330	3RD WARD
HEINER, FRANK	BAL	031	1ST WARD
HEINER, FREDERICK	BAL	260	2ND WARD
HEINER, GEORGE	BAL	244	6TH WARD
HEINER, GEORGE	BAL	146	19TH WAR
HEINER, HENRY *	FRE	110	CREAGERS
HEINER, ISABEL	BAL	228	19TH WAR
HEINER, JACOB	BAL	031	1ST WARD
HEINER, LEVI	FRE	101	FREDERIC
HEINER, RACHEL	BAL	166	16TH WAR
HEINER, REBECCA	BAL	175	6TH WARD
HEINER, SAMUEL	CAR	388	2ND DIST
HEINER, WILLIAM	CAR	323	1ST DIST
HEINER, WILLIAM	FRE	114	CREAGERS
HEINES, THEADORE	BAL	023	1ST WARD
HEINGER, FREDERICK	BAL	285	17TH WAR
HEINICK, EARNEST	BAL	064	1ST WARD
HEINIG, WILLIAM	BAL	092	10TH WAR
HEINKER, AUGUSTUS	BAL	244	2ND WARD
HEINLEIN, MICHAEL	BAL	024	15TH WAR
HEINOR, HENRY	HAR	129	2ND DIST
HEINSERLING, DANIEL	BAL	275	17TH WAR
HEINSMAN, CATHARINE	WAS	158	HAGERSTO
HEIPLE, JOHN	BAL	276	2ND WARD
HEIR, JOHN	HAR	200	3RD DIST
HEIRAGHTY, PATRICK	ALL	048	10TH E.D
HEIRD, RICHARD H.	BAL	045	9TH WARD
HEIRMON, LEVIN	WOR	307	2ND E DI
HEIRONERMUS, H. M.	BAL	474	14TH WAR
HEIRONIMUS, GEORGE	BAL	049	9TH WARD
HEIRS, JAMS	BAL	252	12TH WAR
HEIS, CHARLES	BAL	242	17TH WAR
HEISE, MARY	CAR	391	2ND DIST
HEISER, CONRAD	BAL	104	1ST WARD
HEISER, DAVID	CAR	348	6TH DIST
HEISER, GEORGE	BAL	303	17TH WAR
HEISER, HENRY	BAL	461	14TH WAR
HEISER, HUGH	BAL	059	1ST WARD
HEISKEL, A.	PRI	117	PISCATAW
HEISLER, ELIZABETH	BAL	267	12TH WAR
HEISLER, JOHN F.	BAL	043	4TH WARD
HEISLING, WILLIAM	BAL	291	17TH WAR
HEISS, J. H.	BAL	333	1ST DIST
HEISS, NATHAN	BAL	256	2ND WARD
HEIST, JACOB	WAS	270	1ST DIST
HEIST, THOMAS W.	CAR	311	1ST DIST
HEISTER, MATILDA	WAS	178	BOONSBOR
HEISTER, THOMAS MCK. *	WAS	162	HAGERSTO
HEITTHNER, WILLIAM	BAL	031	9TH WARD
HEIZE, GEORGE	BAL	245	2ND WARD
HELARD, ELLEN	BAL	218	2ND WARD
HELAWAY, MID-BLACK	FRE	446	8TH E DI
HELCH, GARY	CAR	133	NO TWP L
HELD, LOUISA	BAL	062	15TH WAR
HELDBERGER, WILLIAM	BAL	068	18TH WAR
HELDEBRAND, BENOVALL	CAR	185	8TH DIST
HELDEBRAND, ELIZABETH	CAR	178	8TH DIST
HELDEBRAND, GEORGE	CAR	186	8TH DIST
HELDEBRAND, JACOB	CAR	178	8TH DIST
HELDEBRAND, JOHN	CAR	184	8TH DIST
HELDEBRAND, LEAH	CAR	183	8TH DIST
HELDEBRAND, NOAH	CAR	177	8TH DIST
HELDEBRAND, THOMAS	CAR	178	8TH DIST
HELDHART, JOHN	BAL	253	2ND WARD
HELDIFER, JOHN	ALL	257	CUMBERLA
HELDMAN, HENRY	BAL	381	8TH WARD
HELDRICH, MARY E.	BAL	213	17TH WAR
HELDRICH, WILLAM	BAL	213	17TH WAR
HELEM, WILLIAM	BAL	184	6TH WARD
HELEMAN, HIRAM	ALL	171	7TH E.D.
HELEMAN, JOHN	ALL	172	7TH E.D.
HELEMAN, WILLIAM	ALL	004	3RD E.D.
HELENE, GEORGE	WAS	142	HAGERSTO
HELENNS, LEWIS H.	BAL	098	1ST WARD
HELER, ANDREW	BAL	255	20TH WAR
HELFICK, CATHARINE E.	CAR	292	7TH DIST
HELFICK, LEWIS	CAR	292	7TH DIST
HELFICK, WILLIAM	CAR	295	7TH DIST
HELFINBINE, HENRY	BAL	458	14TH WAR
HELFRISH, GEORGE	BAL	004	18TH WAR
HELFRY, CATHERINE	ALL	224	CUMBERLA
HELFRY, RANDOLPH	ALL	224	CUMBERLA
HELFRY, VALENTINE	ALL	224	CUMBERLA
HELGE, ALEXSNDER	BAL	468	14TH WAR
HELGERT, GEORGE	WAS	161	2ND DIST
HELINE, JOHN M.	CAR	363	9TH DIST
HELING, CATHARINE	CEC	066	1ST E DI
HELING, JOHANNAH	BAL	200	11TH WAR
HELINKIN, MARGARET	BAL	196	11TH WAR
HELIP, SUSAN	BAL	259	1ST DIST
HELIRCH, COORNROD *	BAL	110	2ND DIST
HELKER, HENRY	ALL	035	2ND E.D.
HELKER, HENRY	ALL	037	2ND E.D.
HELL, CATHERINE*	BAL	382	3RD WARD
HELL, RACHEL-BLACK	FRE	242	NEW MARK
HELLEARY, LEVI	ALL	085	5TH E.D.
HELLEAY, JAMES	FRE	267	NEW MARK
HELLEBREDLE, URIAH	CAR	314	1ST DIST
HELLEBREST, PETER	CAR	303	1ST DIST
HELLEMSTATTOR, TERESSA *	ALL	169	6TH E.D.
HELLEN, CHARLOTTE	FRE	403	JEFFERSO
HELLEN, CLIFTON	MGM	319	CRACKLIN
HELLEN, JAMES	CAL	017	1ST DIST
HELLEN, JOSEPH J.	CAL	007	1ST DIST
HELLEN, REBECCA	BAL	079	4TH WARD
HELLEN, SOLOMON	BAL	062	2ND DIST
HELLEN, SOPHIA	DOR	317	1ST DIST
HELLEN, THOMAS	BAL	398	3RD WARD
HELLENA, JONATHAN	WAS	256	1ST DIST
HELLENCOME, MARY	BAL	212	2ND WARD
HELLENS, ELIZABETH	BAL	042	1ST WARD
HELLENSTRUFF, JOSEPH	KEN	289	3RD DIST
HELLER, AUGUSTUS	BAL	191	2ND WARD
HELLER, DANIEL	WAS	099	2ND DIST
HELLER, DANIEL	WAS	100	2ND DIST
HELLER, DAVID	WAS	136	2ND DIST
HELLER, ELI	WAS	109	2ND DIST
HELLER, GEORGE	WAS	108	2ND DIST
HELLER, JACOB JR.	FRE	403	JEFFERSO
HELLER, JACOB SR.	FRE	403	JEFFERSO
HELLER, JOHN	BAL	454	8TH WARD
HELLER, SIDEL	BAL	217	17TH WAR
HELLER, SIMON	BAL	063	15TH WAR
HELLER, WILLIAM	BAL	386	13TH WAR
HELLER, ANN M.	FRE	403	JEFFERSO
HELLEY, WILLIAM G.	CAR	202	4TH DIST
HELLFINCH, JOHN	BAL	149	19TH WAR
HELLGOST, LEON	BAL	406	1ST DIST
HELLIARD, HENRY	BAL	418	3RD WARD
HELLINS, JOSEPH	BAL	044	1ST WARD
HELLMAM, SAMUEL	WAS	282	1ST DIST
HELLMAN, BERTHA V.	WAS	283	1ST DIST
HELLMAN, HENRY	BAL	267	2ND WARD
HELLMAN, HENRY	BAL	099	2ND DIST
HELLMAN, JOSEPH	ANN	415	HOWARD D
HELLMAN, JOSEPH	BAL	115	5TH WARD
HELLMAN, MARY	WAS	283	1ST DIST
HELLMAN, WASHINGTON	WAS	031	2ND SUBD
HELLMER, LEWIS	HAR	153	3RD DIST
HELLSTEIN, PHILIP	BAL	258	5TH WARD
HELLTRUM, AUGUST	BAL	209	17TH WAR
HELLUMSTRAP, WILLIAM	KEN	290	3RD DIST
HELLWIG, AUGUSTUS	BAL	230	19TH WAR
HELM, ISABELLA	BAL	209	6TH WARD
HELM, JOHN	BAL	219	6TH WARD
HELM, JOHN H.	BAL	209	6TH WARD
HELM, MARY	ST	274	3RD E DI
HELMA, PAUL	BAL	102	15TH WAR
HELMAN, JACOB	BAL	209	11TH WAR
HELMAN, MICHAEL	FRE	164	EMMITTSB
HELMER, GODFREY	ALL	121	4TH E.D.
HELMER, RATCHELL	HAR	179	3RD DIST
HELMET, SARAH	BAL	229	19TH WAR
HELMIKE, H.	BAL	136	1ST WARD
HELMING, GEORGE R.	BAL	130	18TH WAR
HELMING, WILLIAM	BAL	130	18TH WAR
HELMIRE, CAROLINE	BAL	304	3RD WARD
HELMKEN, HENRY	BAL	089	10TH WAR
HELMLEY, GILES	BAL	291	16TH WAR
HELMLING, EMMA	BAL	152	16TH WAR
HELMLING, HENRY	BAL	151	16TH WAR
HELMLING, SAMUEL	BAL	414	1ST DIST
HELMS, B.	BAL	207	19TH WAR
HELMS, BEAL	ANN	422	HOWARD D
HELMS, DANIEL	BAL	235	1ST DIST
HELMS, HENRY	BAL	233	1ST DIST
HELMS, MARY	BAL	236	1ST DIST
HELMS, MARY	BAL	193	5TH DIST
HELMS, OLIVER	ANN	422	HOWARD D
HELMS, WILLIAM	WAS	167	1ST DIST
HELMSLEY, ELLEN A.	BAL	058	10TH WAR
HELMSLEY, HENRY	BAL	185	6TH WARD
HELMSLEY, HORACE	BAL	050	9TH WARD
HELMSLEY, WILLIAM	BAL	379	3RD WARD
HELMSMALLER, T. B.	BAL	045	9TH WARD
HELMSTALLER, ANTHONY	ALL	169	6TH E.D.
HELMSTOFFER, C.	BAL	213	19TH WAR
HELMUTH, H.	BAL	332	1ST DIST
HELMUTH, O.	BAL	333	1ST DIST
HELMUTH, W. T.	BAL	332	1ST DIST
HELNER, HENRY	BAL	205	2ND WARD
HELPIN, ANDREW	ALL	237	CUMBERLA
HELPLESS, CHARLES	BAL	258	12TH WAR
HELPMAN, HENRY	BAL	202	11TH WAR
HELPS, ELIJAH *	HAR	010	1ST DIST
HELSBA, THOMAS	DOR	319	1ST DIST
HELSBEY, SOLOMON	ANN	255	ANNAPOLI
HELSBY, JOHN W.	TAL	044	EASTON D
HELSBY, NANCY*	TAL	044	EASTON T
HELSBY, PAMELIA	BAL	425	8TH WARD
HELSBY, SAMUEL	BAL	225	6TH WARD
HELSBY, SARAH E.	DOR	427	1ST DIST
HELSBY, THOMAS	TAL	057	EASTON D
HELSER, ELIZABETH	WAS	139	2ND DIST
HELSER, SOLOMAN	WAS	139	2ND DIST
HELSEY, FERDINAND	WAS	161	HAGERSTO
HELSHER, FREDERIC	BAL	194	5TH WARD
HELSM, ZADEE	BAL	072	1ST WARD
HELSSMAN, HAL	BAL	316	12TH WAR
HELT, JOHN	FRE	073	FREDERIC
HELTEBRECKT, JACOB	CAR	304	1ST DIST
HELTEBRIDLE, MARY E.	CAR	314	1ST DIST
HELTON, JOHN *	ANN	354	3RD DIST
HELTY, JOHN *	FRE	115	CREAGERS
HELTZ, WILLIAM	BAL	140	1ST WARD
HELWICH, CONRAD	BAL	355	1ST DIST
HELWICK, ANDREW	ALL	250	CUMBERLA
HELWIG, AUGUST	BAL	066	15TH WAR
HELWIG, GEORGE	BAL	132	5TH WARD
HELWING, GUSTAVE	BAL	025	1ST WARD
HELZER, JACOB	BAL	062	15TH WAR
HELZOZ, JOHN	BAL	120	11TH WAR
HEMAKE, LOUIS	BAL	193	2ND WARD
HEMAN, CHARLOTTE	BAL	201	11TH WAR
HEMAN, MARGARET	BAL	273	12TH WAR
HEMBER, ANN	BAL	212	11TH WAR
HEMBER, MICHAEL	BAL	250	2ND WARD
HEMBLEY, MARGARET	WAS	158	HAGERSTO
HEMBLY, JOHN	CHA	227	ALLENS F
HEMEN, ELIZABETH	HAR	147	3RD DIST
HEMEN, FRANCE	BAL	013	2ND DIST
HEMENNY, JOHN	BAL	282	12TH WAR
HEMER, GATTY*	WOR	301	SNOW HIL
HEMER, JOHN	BAL	398	3RD WARD
HEMER, MATILDA	HAR	151	3RD DIST
HEMER, WILLIAM	CEC	044	CHESAPEA
HEMERSLAE, MARTHA	WAS	149	HAGERSTO
HEMETINE, SARAH	ALL	122	4TH E.D.
HEMILTON, CATHARINE	FRE	268	NEW MARK
HEMING, JOHN	BAL	216	2ND WARD
HEMING, MARTIN	BAL	012	9TH WARD
HEMINGWAY, C. E.	WOR	255	BERLIN 1
HEMINGWAY, JAMES	WOR	261	BERLIN 1
HEMINGWAY, JESSE	WOR	266	BERLIN 1
HEMLER, JOHN	BAL	215	17TH WAR
HEMLER, PETER	FRE	195	5TH E DI
HEMLING, ANTHONY	BAL	242	17TH WAR
HEMLING, ANTHONY	BAL	035	15TH WAR
HEMLING, FREDERICK	CAR	192	4TH DIST
HEMLING, HARRY A.	BAL	241	17TH WAR
HEMLING, JOHN	BAL	273	20TH WAR
HEMLY, AUGUSTUS	BAL	072	2ND DIST
HEMLY, JOHN	ST	296	2ND E DI
HEMMAN, JACOB	BAL	166	2ND DIST
HEMMELBAUGH, LEANHART	BAL	210	17TH WAR
HEMMELL, CATHERINE	FRE	002	FREDERIC
HEMMERICK, B.	BAL	320	12TH WAR
HEMMICK, ELIZABETH	BAL	205	17TH WAR
HEMMICK, GEORGE A.	ANN	422	HOWARD D
HEMMICK, JACOB	BAL	347	13TH WAR
HEMMON, ASA	DOR	300	1ST DIST
HEMMON, J. RATLEFF*	DOR	300	1ST DIST
HEMMOND, MARY	WOR	314	2ND E DI
HEMMRICK, JACOB	BAL	235	17TH WAR
HEMMTINGER, J.	BAL	259	12TH WAR
HEMONS, JOHN	SOM	541	TYASKIN
HEMONS, SARAH	SOM	541	TYASKIN
HEMORE, SAMUEL	HAR	158	3RD DIST
HEMP, ABRAHAM	FRE	399	JEFFERSO
HEMP, JOHN	FRE	406	JEFFERSO
HEMP, JULIANN	FRE	399	JEFFERSO
HEMPHILL, AMELIA	WAS	113	2ND DIST
HEMPHILL, EVANS	CEC	012	ELKTON 3
HEMPHILL, JAMES	CEC	022	ELKTON 3
HEMPHILL, WILLIAM	WAS	065	2ND SUBD
HEMPLER, CONSTANTINE	WAS	122	HAGERSTO
HEMPNASS, ELIABETH	BAL	072	1ST WARD
HEMPSTON, ZADOCK	MGM	422	MEDLEY 3
HEMPSTONE, DORCAS A.	ANN	521	HOWARD D
HEMPT, EDWARD	BAL	340	3RD WARD
HEMRICHOUSER, WILLIAM H.	WAS	155	HAGERSTO
HEMSLEY, J.	ANN	273	ANNAPOLI
HEMSLEY, JACK	WAS	158	HAGERSTO
HEMSLEY, JOHN C.	QUE	210	3RD E DI
HEMSLEY, LLOYD J.	QUE	190	3RD E DI
HEMSLEY, MARIA	BAL	357	8TH WARD
HEMSLEY, P.	ANN	258	ANNAPOLI
HEMSLEY, P. F.	TAL	011	EASTON D
HEMSLEY, R. F.	TAL	066	EASTON T
HEMSLEY, RICHARD-BLACK	QUE	191	3RD E DI
HEMSLEY, SAMUEL	QUE	210	3RD E DI
HEMSLEY, SARH	WAS	133	HAGERSTO
HEMSLEY, WILLIAM DR.	TAL	074	EASTON T
HEMSLY, ANN	BAL	449	14TH WAR
HEMSLY, JOSHUA	BAL	436	14TH WAR
HEMSLY, MARY J.	CHA	293	BOJANTOW
HEMSLY, SHARLOT	TAL	029	EASTON D

Name	County	Page	District
HEMSTON, ARMSTEAD T.	FRE	409	JEFFERSO
HEMSWORTH, ELIZABETH	WAS	219	1ST DIST
HENALTY, PATRICK *	BAL	175	2ND DIST
HENBEICK, DANIEL	BAL	179	2ND WARD
HENBERRY, ELIZA	BAL	215	11TH WAR
HENCH, LEWIS	BAL	168	2ND DIST
HENCHE, ANN	BAL	210	19TH WAR
HENCKE, CATHARINE	BAL	335	13TH WAR
HENCOCK, GOERGE	BAL	200	11TH WAR
HENDEN, SALLY	BAL	246	12TH WAR
HENDERGAN, PATRICK	BAL	017	1ST WARD
HENDERICKS, MARTIN	HAR	078	2ND DIST
HENDERONS, JOHN	BAL	443	14TH WAR
HENDEROSN, EZEKIEL	WOR	283	BERLIN 1
HENDEROSN, GEORGE	CAR	212	5TH DIST
HENDERCSN, HENRY	BAL	319	12TH WAR
HENDEROSN, JONATHAN	ALL	163	6TH E.D.
HENDEROSN, MARY	WOR	279	BERLIN 1
HENDEROSN, WILLIAM	WOR	283	BERLIN 1
HENDERSON, ANDREW	FRE	036	FREDERIC
HENDERSON, ANN	SOM	397	BRINKLEY
HENDERSON, ANTHONY	BAL	200	2ND WARD
HENDERSON, ARCHABALD	HAR	016	1ST DIST
HENDERSON, BENJAMIN	CEC	094	4TH E DI
HENDERSON, BENJAMIN	BAL	382	8TH WARD
HENDERSON, BENJAMIN	BAL	109	5TH WARD
HENDERSON, BENJAMIN	WOR	283	BERLIN 1
HENDERSON, BENJAMIN	SOM	499	SALISBUR
HENDERSON, CARLINE	FRE	051	FREDERIC
HENDERSON, CASSANDER	CEC	011	ELKTON 3
HENDERSON, CHARELS	BAL	472	14TH WAR
HENDERSON, CHARLES	BAL	024	18TH WAR
HENDERSON, CHARLES	WAS	162	2ND DIST
HENDERSON, CHARLOTTE	BAL	212	19TH WAR
HENDERSON, CAVID	SOM	379	BRINKLEY
HENDERSON, CAVID	BAL	300	1ST DIST
HENDERSON, DENARD	WOR	289	9TH E DI
HENDERSON, DINAH	CEC	120	4TH E DI
HENDERSON, E.	BAL	063	10TH WAR
HENDERSON, ELEANOR	WOR	229	6TH E DI
HENDERSON, ELIZA	BAL	269	20TH WAR
HENDERSON, ELIZABETH	BAL	043	4TH WARD
HENDERSON, ELIZABETH	BAL	298	12TH WAR
HENDERSON, ELLEN	BAL	395	8TH WARD
HENDERSON, ELLEN	WAS	156	HAGERSTO
HENDERSON, EMMA	BAL	278	1ST DIST
HENDERSON, FRANCES	WOR	229	6TH E DI
HENDERSON, FRANCES	SOM	490	SALISBUR
HENDERSON, FRANCIS	HAR	016	1ST DIST
HENDERSON, GEORGE	BAL	460	8TH WARD
HENDERSON, GUSTAVUS	BAL	087	4TH WARD
HENDERSON, GUSTAVUS	BAL	424	3RD WARD
HENDERSON, HANNAH	WOR	282	BERLIN 1
HENDERSON, HARMAN	CEC	153	PORT DUP
HENDERSON, HARRIET	BAL	243	20TH WAR
HENDERSON, HENRY	WOR	329	1ST E DI
HENDERSON, HENRY	SOM	402	BRINKLEY
HENDERSON, HENRY	BAL	296	1ST DIST
HENDERSON, HENRY B.	WOR	329	1ST E DI
HENDERSON, HESTER	CEC	110	4TH E DI
HENDERSON, HETTEY	BAL	331	7TH WARD
HENDERSON, ISRAEL	CEC	091	4TH E DI
HENDERSON, J.	BAL	155	1ST WARD
HENDERSON, J.F.	WOR	342	1ST E DI
HENDERSON, JAMES	WOR	333	1ST E DI
HENDERSON, JAMES	WOR	329	1ST E DI
HENDERSON, JAMES	WOR	276	BERLIN 1
HENDERSON, JAMES	BAL	332	13TH WAR
HENDERSON, JAMES	BAL	087	18TH WAR
HENDERSON, JAMES	BAL	018	4TH WARD
HENDERSON, JAMES A.	BAL	026	9TH WARD
HENDERSON, JAMES A. JR.	BAL	026	9TH WARD
HENDERSON, JAMES H.	BAL	337	7TH WARD
HENDERSON, JAMES N.	HAR	017	1ST DIST
HENDERSON, JAMES S.	WOR	350	1ST E DI
HENDERSON, JAMES T.	ANN	502	HOWARD D
HENDERSON, JAMES-BLACK	BAL	212	2ND WARD
HENDERSON, JANE	BAL	414	1ST DIST
HENDERSON, JANE	WOR	178	6TH E DI
HENDERSON, JOHN	SOM	483	TRAPP DI
HENDERSON, JOHN	WOR	334	1ST E DI
HENDERSON, JOHN	BAL	148	1ST WARD
HENDERSON, JOHN	BAL	108	10TH WAR
HENDERSON, JOHN	BAL	384	8TH WARD
HENDERSON, JOHN	BAL	395	8TH WARD
HENDERSON, JOHN	BAL	424	3RD WARD
HENDERSON, JOHN	CEC	093	4TH E DI
HENDERSON, JOHN B.	HAR	072	1ST DIST
HENDERSON, JOHN H.	CAR	374	9TH DIST
HENDERSON, JOHN J.	MGM	338	CRACKLIN
HENDERSON, JOHN S.	CEC	025	ELKTON 3
HENDERSON, JOSPEH	CEC	109	4TH E DI
HENDERSON, KITTINA	BAL	264	12TH WAR
HENDERSON, LAMBERT	WOR	260	BERLIN 1
HENDERSON, LEVIN	WOR	333	1ST E DI
HENDERSON, LEVIN	WOR	332	1ST E DI
HENDERSON, LYDIA	CAR	373	9TH DIST
HENDERSON, M.	BAL	099	10TH WAR
HENDERSON, MARANCA	BAL	319	1ST DIST
HENDERSON, MARIA	BAL	335	3RD WARD
HENDERSON, MARY	BAL	109	5TH WARD
HENDERSON, MARY	BAL	350	3RD WARD
HENDERSON, MARY	BAL	189	19TH WAR
HENDERSON, MARY	HAR	032	1ST DIST
HENDERSON, MARY	BAL	458	14TH WAR
HENDERSON, MARY	WOR	342	1ST E DI
HENDERSON, MARY A.	BAL	233	2ND WARD
HENDERSON, MARY J.	BAL	064	4TH WARD
HENDERSON, MATILDA	SOM	426	PRINCESS
HENDERSON, NOAH	WOR	333	1ST E DI
HENDERSON, O. P.	ALL	163	6TH E.D.
HENDERSON, POLLY	WOR	333	1ST E DI
HENDERSON, POLLY	WOR	341	1ST E DI
HENDERSON, REBECCA	WOR	331	1ST E DI
HENDERSON, RICHARD	ALL	162	6TH E.D.
HENDERSON, ROBERT	BAL	291	3RD WARD
HENDERSON, ROBERT	BAL	036	4TH WARD
HENDERSON, ROBERT T.	HAR	072	1ST DIST
HENDERSON, ROUSE	SOM	405	DUBLIN D
HENDERSON, SALLY	WOR	280	BERLIN 1
HENDERSON, SAMUEL	WOR	329	1ST E DI
HENDERSON, SAMUEL	BAL	287	12TH WAR
HENDERSON, SARAH	WOR	329	1ST E DI
HENDERSON, SARAH	HAR	097	2ND DIST
HENDERSON, SARAH	HAR	016	1ST DIST
HENDERSON, SARAH	HAR	173	3RD DIST
HENDERSON, SARAH	FRE	030	FREDERIC
HENDERSON, SARAH-BLACK	BAL	208	2ND WARD
HENDERSON, SUSAN	BAL	062	10TH WAR
HENDERSON, SUSAN	WAS	162	HAGERSTO
HENDERSON, T.	BAL	140	1ST WARD
HENDERSON, THOMAS	BAL	357	3RD WARD
HENDERSON, THOMAS	WOR	339	1ST E DI
HENDERSON, THOMAS	SOM	460	HANGARY
HENDERSON, THOMAS	HAR	071	1ST DIST
HENDERSON, WILLIAM	BAL	012	4TH WARD
HENDERSON, WILLIAM	BAL	385	13TH WAR
HENDERSON, WILLIAM	BAL	074	18TH WAR
HENDERSON, WILLIAM	BAL	262	6TH WARD
HENDERSON, WILLIAM	ALL	160	6TH E.D.
HENDERSON, WILLIAM M.	BAL	232	2ND WARD
HENDERSON, WILLIAM W.	MGM	380	ROCKERLE
HENDERSON,JANE	BAL	276	12TH WAR
HENDERSON,MANN	BAL	280	12TH WAR
HENDERSON,W ILLIAM	BAL	170	1ST WARD
HENDESON, JAMES	BAL	083	2ND DIST
HENDICE, GEORGE	BAL	031	1ST WARD
HENDICK, MARTIN	BAL	115	2ND DIST
HENDISON, JOHN	CEC	060	1ST E DI
HENDLE, ELISABETH	ALL	260	CUMBERLA
HENDLE, ELIZABETH	ALL	264	CUMBERLA
HENDLE, HENRY	ALL	260	CUMBERLA
HENDLE, MARY	CHA	290	BOJANTOW
HENDLEY, JOHN	BAL	026	4TH WARD
HENDLEY, JOSEPH	BAL	213	19TH WAR
HENDLEY, JOSEPH	BAL	155	19TH WAR
HENDON, BENJAMIN	HAR	106	2ND DIST
HENDON, JAMES	HAR	087	2ND DIST
HENDON, JOSIAS	HAR	049	1ST DIST
HENDOW, THOMAS	HAR	092	2ND DIST
HENDRIC, MARGARET	BAL	122	2ND DIST
HENDRIC, MICHAEL	BAL	122	2ND DIST
HENDRICK, ELIZA	BAL	281	12TH WAR
HENDRICK, MOSES	BAL	073	2ND DIST
HENDRICKS, ANNE	BAL	373	3RD WARD
HENDRICKS, CATHARINE	CAR	388	2ND DIST
HENDRICKS, CHARLES	BAL	373	3RD WARD
HENDRICKS, JAMES	CHA	257	MIDDLETO
HENDRICKS, JOHN	BAL	031	2ND DIST
HENDRICKS, JSOHUA	BAL	034	2ND DIST
HENDRICKS, WILLIAM	BAL	190	6TH WARD
HENDRICKSON, ANN	CEC	094	4TH E DI
HENDRICKSON, ANN E.	BAL	033	4TH WARD
HENDRICKSON, HENRY	BAL	033	4TH WARD
HENDRICKSON, LETITIA	ALL	251	CUMBERLA
HENDRICKSON, MARGARET F.	BAL	047	15TH WAR
HENDRICKSON,MATILDA	ALL	225	CUMBERLA
HENDRIKSON, JOHN	FRE	416	8TH E DI
HENDRIX, HENRY	QUE	168	2ND E DI
HENDRIX, JOHN	QUE	167	2ND E DI
HENDRIX, LODI	QUE	172	2ND E DI
HENDRIX, MARTHA A.	QUE	167	2ND E DI
HENDRIX, SUSAN	QUE	169	2ND E DI
HENDRIX, THOMAS H.	QUE	165	2ND E DI
HENDRIX, WILLIAM	QUE	168	2ND E DI
HENDRIX, WILLIAM	KEN	275	1ST DIST
HENDRIX, WILLIAM H.	QUE	167	2ND E DI
HENDUDAL, MAJOR	WOR	324	1ST E DI
HENDY, MARGRET	ANN	275	ANNAPOLI
HENEKIN, JOHN	BAL	247	17TH WAR
HENENTON, JOHN	CEC	065	1ST E DI
HENER, LOUISA	BAL	252	12TH WAR
HENER, MARY	BAL	241	12TH WAR
HENERN, WILLIAM	CEC	061	1ST E DI
HENERSON, CHARLES	ST	345	5TH E DI
HENERSON, THOMAS G.	ST	345	5TH E DI
HENERSON,T HOMAS E.	ST	345	5TH E DI
HENERY, CATHARINE	BAL	071	1ST WARD
HENERY, PETER	BAL	072	1ST WARD
HENERY, ROBERT	HAR	190	3RD DIST
HENERY, WILLIAM -BLACK	CAR	073	NO TWP L
HENESEE, SAMUEL	TAL	046	EASTON T
HENESEY, EDWARD	TAL	050	EASTON T
HENESEY, ELIZABETH	TAL	044	EASTON D
HENESLEY, SHARLOTT	TAL	024	EASTON D
HENESSY, PETER	WAS	198	1ST DIST
HENESSY, THOMAS	WAS	198	1ST DIST
HENESTOPHEL, JACOB	CAR	180	8TH DIST
HENEWAY, THOMAS	SOM	415	DUBLIN D
HENEY, MICHAEL	BAL	257	6TH WARD
HENGEL, JOHN	BAL	244	2ND WARD
HENGER, MARGARET	BAL	245	2ND WARD
HENGST, SOLOMON	CAR	337	6TH DIST
HENHER, CUFF	FRE	247	NEW MARK
HENICK, REBECCA	BAL	391	1ST DIST
HENICKLEW, MARTIN	CAR	338	6TH DIST
HENICKS, CHRISTOPHER	BAL	390	1ST DIST
HENICKS, GEORGE C.	BAL	406	1ST DIST
HENICKS, ROBERT W.	BAL	406	1ST DIST
HENING, ELMA	BAL	218	2ND WARD
HENING, JAMES	ALL	028	2ND E.D.
HENING, LEWIS	BAL	308	12TH WAR
HENING, WILLIAM	BAL	353	3RD WARD
HENINGTON, H.	BAL	282	2ND WARD
HENISH, CASPARD	BAL	327	3RD WARD
HENISH, JESSE	BAL	171	1ST WARD
HENISLER, CLEMMON	BAL	108	1ST WARD
HENKEL, AUGUST	BAL	201	6TH WARD
HENKEL, BARBARA	BAL	373	3RD WARD
HENKEL, FREDERICK	ALL	056	10TH E.D
HENKEL, HENRY	BAL	068	15TH WAR
HENKEL, PETER	BAL	104	15TH WAR
HENKEL, PHILIP	BAL	373	3RD WARD
HENKEL, THEODORE	BAL	373	3RD WARD
HENKERKAMP, WILLIAM	BAL	406	14TH WAR
HENKING, HENRY	BAL	037	9TH WARD
HENKLE, CHRISTIAN	BAL	284	2ND WARD
HENKLE, DAVID	ALL	161	6TH E.D.
HENKLE, JACOB	BAL	211	2ND WARD
HENKLE, WILLIAM	ALL	157	6TH E.D.
HENKLEMAN, CHRISTIAN	BAL	251	2ND WARD
HENKLEMAN, JOHN	BAL	218	2ND WARD
HENKLEMAN, M.	BAL	209	2ND WARD
HENLEBEK, JOSEPH	BAL	089	1ST WARD
HENLEIN, MORET	BAL	065	4TH WARD
HENLEY, CHARLES	BAL	141	2ND DIST
HENLEY, ELIZABETH	MGM	384	ROCKERLE
HENLEY, HENRY	BAL	159	2ND DIST
HENLEY, JOHN	BAL	173	1ST WARD
HENLEY, JOHN P.	MGM	322	CRACKLIN
HENLEY, LUCRETIA*	BAL	314	3RD WARD
HENLEY, MARGARET	MGM	318	CRACKLIN
HENLEY, MARY E.	MGM	322	CRACKLIN
HENLEY, MATTHEW	BAL	145	1ST WARD
HENLEY, PATRICK	MGM	324	CRACKLIN
HENLEY, ROBERT	BAL	118	1ST WARD
HENLEY, WILLIAM	MGM	383	ROCKERLE
HENLINE, DANIEL	ALL	062	10TH E.D
HENLINE, JOHN	WAS	153	2ND DIST
HENLTON, WILLIAM	BAL	124	1ST WARD
HENLUE, MARGRET	BAL	192	2ND WARD
HENLY, DAVID	BAL	057	4TH WARD
HENLY, ICHABOD*	DOR	440	1ST DIST
HENLY, MARY*	DOR	382	1ST DIST
HENMAN, SARAH	BAL	036	15TH WAR
HENMAN, WALTER L.	BAL	120	2ND DIST
HENN, ELISHA P.	BAL	056	2ND DIST
HENNAMAN, JOHN G.	BAL	266	12TH WAR
HENNAN, F.	BAL	252	12TH WAR
HENNEBERGER, G.W.	WAS	126	HAGERSTO
HENNEBERGER, HIRAM	BAL	329	13TH WAR
HENNEBERGER, J.J.	WAS	126	HAGERSTO
HENNEBERGER, JOHN	WAS	125	HAGERSTO
HENNEBERRY, ELIZABETH	BAL	233	6TH WARD
HENNELEY, GEORGE	BAL	251	20TH WAR
HENNEMAN, WILLIAM H.	BAL	033	15TH WAR
HENNERMAN, JOHN	BAL	001	EASTERN
HENNESEY, TIMOTHY	PRI	028	VANSVILL
HENNESSEY, HUGH	BAL	031	4TH WARD
HENNESSY, MISS M.	FRE	200	5TH E DI
HENNESSY, MR-	BAL	061	15TH WAR
HENNEY, JANE	KEN	274	1ST DIST
HENNICK, JESSE	BAL	174	1ST WARD
HENNICK, JOHN C.	BAL	139	16TH WAR
HENNICK, JOSIAS G.	BAL	139	16TH WAR
HENNICK, POLLY	BAL	257	1ST DIST
HENNIMAN, GABRIEL	CAR	283	7TH DIST
HENNING, ADAM	BAL	255	2ND WARD
HENNING, ALEXANDER	ST	298	2ND E DI
HENNING, ALFRED	BAL	185	2ND WARD
HENNING, CATHARINE	BAL	185	2ND WARD
HENNING, ELIZABETH	BAL	273	2ND WARD
HENNING, ELIZABETH	BAL	121	11TH WAR
HENNING, GEROGE	BAL	075	18TH WAR
HENNING, JAMES G.	MGM	443	CLARKSTR
HENNING, JEREMIAH	BAL	153	16TH WAR
HENNING, JOHN	BAL	235	2ND WARD
HENNING, JULIUS	BAL	351	3RD WARD
HENNING, LIONI	BAL	114	5TH WARD
HENNING, MARY L.	BAL	172	19TH WAR
HENNING, ROBERT M.	ST	304	2ND E DI
HENNING, TIMOTHY	PRI	027	VANSVILL
HENNING, WILLIAM	BAL	293	20TH WAR
HENNING, WILLIAM	BAL	040	15TH WAR
HENNINGS, EMERT A.	BAL	384	13TH WAR
HENNINGS, VIRGINIA	BAL	394	8TH WARD
HENNIS, JANE	BAL	060	15TH WAR
HENNIS, PETER	BAL	281	2ND WARD
HENNISS, JOHN	BAL	018	4TH WARD
HENNIX, EDWARD	BAL	422	8TH WARD
HENNIX, EDWARD G.	BAL	296	7TH WARD
HENNIX, MARY	BAL	445	8TH WARD
HENNSLEY, ANN	TAL	073	EASTON T
HENNX, AMANDA	BAL	445	8TH WARD
HENNY, JOHN	BAL	294	12TH WAR
HENNYBERGER, WILLIAM	BAL	049	4TH WARD
HENNYMAN, JOSHUA	BAL	050	4TH WARD
HENPMAN, JUSTUS	BAL	077	1ST WARD
HENR, ANN	BAL	067	2ND DIST
HENRICK, MARY	BAL	363	3RD WARD
HENRICKEL, ELLEN	BAL	253	5TH WARD
HENRICKEL, GEORGE W.	BAL	252	6TH WARD
HENRICKS, CATHARINE	BAL	462	1ST DIST
HENRIX, ----*	TAL	025	EASTON D
HENRIX, MARY	BAL	316	12TH WAR
HENRIX, THOMAS J.	BAL	250	6TH WARD
HENRY, A. S.	BAL	475	14TH WAR
HENRY, AARON	MGM	366	BERRYS D
HENRY, ABENI A.	BAL	119	11TH WAR
HENRY, ABRAHAM	BAL	204	5TH DIST
HENRY, ABRAHAM	BAL	225	1ST DIST
HENRY, ABSENT	BAL	174	11TH WAR
HENRY, ALEXANDER	BAL	055	4TH WARD
HENRY, ANDREW-BLACK	CAR	105	NO TWP L
HENRY, ANN	HAR	040	1ST DIST
HENRY, ANN	BAL	052	9TH WARD
HENRY, ANN	DOR	461	1ST DIST
HENRY, ANN	WAS	121	HAGERSTO
HENRY, ANN-BLACK	CAR	072	NO TWP L
HENRY, ANN-BLACK	CAR	071	NO TWP L
HENRY, ARTHUR	BAL	163	11TH WAR
HENRY, BEN	PRI	086	QUEEN AN
HENRY, BEN	PRI	084	QUEEN AN
HENRY, BENJAMIN	BAL	129	2ND DIST
HENRY, BIDDY	BAL	148	11TH WAR
HENRY, BILL	WOR	316	2ND E DI
HENRY, BINA	DOR	389	1ST DIST
HENRY, BRIDGET	BAL	110	10TH WAR
HENRY, BRIDGET	BAL	014	1ST WARD
HENRY, CAROLINE	CAR	275	7TH DIST
HENRY, CATHERINE	BAL	075	4TH WARD
HENRY, CATHINE *	BAL	095	18TH WAR
HENRY, CHARELS	QUE	219	3RD E DI
HENRY, CHARELS	QUE	208	3RD E DI
HENRY, CHARLES	KEN	297	3RD DIST
HENRY, CHARLES	DOR	446	1ST DIST
HENRY, CHARLES	BAL	447	1ST DIST
HENRY, CHARLES	BAL	280	7TH WARD
HENRY, CHARLES	BAL	134	1ST WARD
HENRY, CHARLES	BAL	242	6TH WARD
HENRY, CHLOE	ALL	224	CUMBERLA
HENRY, CYRUS	DOR	309	1ST DIST
HENRY, DALLAN *	BAL	140	19TH WAR
HENRY, DANIEL	BAL	136	2ND DIST
HENRY, DANIEL	BAL	220	5TH WARD
HENRY, DANIEL M.	DOR	377	1ST DIST
HENRY, DANIEL-BLACK	CAR	076	NO TWP L
HENRY, DANIL	DOR	464	1ST DIST
HENRY, DECKHARD	BAL	271	2ND WARD
HENRY, DICK	DOR	433	1ST DIST
HENRY, DOLEY	DOR	385	1ST DIST
HENRY, DUTCH	BAL	075	18TH WAR
HENRY, EDWARD J.	WOR	274	BERLIN 1
HENRY, ELI	CAR	378	2ND DIST
HENRY, ELIZA	BAL	158	16TH WAR
HENRY, ELIZABETH	ANN	515	HOWARD D
HENRY, ELIZABETH	BAL	268	12TH WAR
HENRY, ELIZABETH	BAL	062	4TH WARD
HENRY, FENNERS	BAL	252	2ND WARD
HENRY, FRANCIS J.	DOR	376	1ST DIST
HENRY, FRANK	BAL	126	16TH WAR
HENRY, FREDERICK	BAL	041	1ST WARD
HENRY, FREDERICK	DOR	409	1ST DIST
HENRY, GEORGE	DOR	432	1ST DIST
HENRY, GEORGE	CAR	275	7TH DIST
HENRY, GEORGE	BAL	302	20TH WAR
HENRY, GEORGE	HAR	114	2ND DIST
HENRY, GEORGE	BAL	326	7TH WARD
HENRY, GEORGE	BAL	203	6TH DIST
HENRY, GEORGE	BAL	161	1ST WARD

Name	County	Page	District
HENRY, GEORGE	WAS	121	HAGERSTO
HENRY, GEORGE K.	BAL	013	9TH WARD
HENRY, GEORGE W.	BAL	282	20TH WAR
HENRY, GEROGE	BAL	291	20TH WAR
HENRY, HARRIET-BLACK	CAR	073	NO TWP L
HENRY, HARRIET-BLACK	CAR	074	NO TWP L
HENRY, HARRIETT	KEN	297	3RD DIST
HENRY, HENRIETTA	BAL	423	14TH WAR
HENRY, HENRIETTA	BAL	131	16TH WAR
HENRY, HENRY	ALL	197	CUMBERLA
HENRY, HENRY	ALL	197	CUMBERLA
HENRY, HERMAN	BAL	005	9TH WARD
HENRY, HERMAN	BAL	024	18TH WAR
HENRY, HESTER	SOM	405	DUBLIN D
HENRY, HORACE	ALL	105	5TH E.D.
HENRY, HOSEY	SOM	500	SALISBUR
HENRY, ISAAC	DOR	308	1ST DIST
HENRY, ISAAC	CAR	119	NO TWP L
HENRY, ISAAC JR.	BAL	044	18TH WAR
HENRY, ISACK*	TAL	061	EASTON D
HENRY, J.S.	BAL	163	6TH WARD
HENRY, JACOB	CAR	275	7TH DIST
HENRY, JACOB	DOR	406	1ST DIST
HENRY, JACOB C.	BAL	169	6TH WARD
HENRY, JAMES	BAL	157	1ST WARD
HENRY, JAMES	BAL	240	6TH WARD
HENRY, JAMES	BAL	003	9TH WARD
HENRY, JAMES	BAL	426	8TH WARD
HENRY, JAMES	BAL	105	10TH WAR
HENRY, JAMES	BAL	127	2ND DIST
HENRY, JAMES	DOR	389	1ST DIST
HENRY, JAMES	BAL	208	17TH WAR
HENRY, JAMES	QUE	229	4TH E DI
HENRY, JAMES	WOR	201	3RD E DI
HENRY, JAMES	QUE	206	3RD E DI
HENRY, JAMES	TAL	032	EASTON D
HENRY, JAMES E.	BAL	216	17TH WAR
HENRY, JAMES W.	DOR	446	1ST DIST
HENRY, JANE	BAL	344	13TH WAR
HENRY, JOHN	DOR	408	1ST DIST
HENRY, JOHN	DOR	418	1ST DIST
HENRY, JOHN	DOR	406	1ST DIST
HENRY, JOHN	DOR	370	3RD DIVI
HENRY, JOHN	BAL	471	14TH WAR
HENRY, JOHN	BAL	023	4TH WARD
HENRY, JOHN	BAL	216	19TH WAR
HENRY, JOHN	CAR	285	7TH DIST
HENRY, JOHN	KEN	246	2ND DIST
HENRY, JOHN	QUE	193	3RD E DI
HENRY, JOHN	WAS	125	HAGERSTO
HENRY, JOHN	WAS	200	1ST DIST
HENRY, JOHN	WOR	201	3RD E DI
HENRY, JOHN	QUE	248	5TH E DI
HENRY, JOHN	DOR	464	1ST DIST
HENRY, JOHN	WAS	133	HAGERSTO
HENRY, JOHN	BAL	295	12TH WAR
HENRY, JOHN	BAL	446	8TH WARD
HENRY, JOHN	BAL	154	1ST WARD
HENRY, JOHN	ALL	105	5TH E.D.
HENRY, JOHN	BAL	304	3RD WARD
HENRY, JOHN	BAL	318	3RD WARD
HENRY, JOHN	BAL	279	2ND WARD
HENRY, JOHN C.	DOR	385	1ST DIST
HENRY, JOHN G.	BAL	213	17TH WAR
HENRY, JOHN P. M.	WOR	255	1ST CENS
HENRY, JOHN-BLACK	WOR	335	1ST E DI
HENRY, JOHN-BLACK	CAR	076	NO TWP L
HENRY, JOSEPH	BAL	277	7TH WARD
HENRY, JOSEPH	ALL	155	6TH E.D.
HENRY, JSOHUA-BLACK	CAR	108	NO TWP L
HENRY, JULIA A.	WOR	263	BERLIN 1
HENRY, LELTY	ALL	225	CUMBERLA
HENRY, LEVIN	WOR	343	1ST E DI
HENRY, LEVIN	TAL	063	EASTON D
HENRY, LEVIN	DOR	311	1ST DIST
HENRY, LEWIS	BAL	210	17TH WAR
HENRY, LOUISA	BAL	067	4TH WARD
HENRY, MAJOR	BAL	243	6TH WARD
HENRY, MAREAN	ALL	105	5TH E.D.
HENRY, MARGARET	BAL	158	16TH WAR
HENRY, MARY	BAL	462	1ST DIST
HENRY, MARY	BAL	054	1ST WARD
HENRY, MARY	DOR	386	1ST DIST
HENRY, MARY	BAL	026	18TH WAR
HENRY, MARY D.	CEC	010	ELKTON 3
HENRY, MARY C.	BAL	318	1ST DIST
HENRY, MARY E.	BAL	004	1ST WARD
HENRY, MARY J.	BAL	083	4TH WARD
HENRY, MATHEW	ALL	248	CUMBERLA
HENRY, MATILDA	BAL	219	6TH WARD
HENRY, MICAHEL	BAL	315	12TH WAR
HENRY, MICHAEL	BAL	220	2ND WARD
HENRY, MICHAEL	BAL	400	3RD WARD
HENRY, MICHAEL	CAR	275	7TH DIST
HENRY, MORDICA	PRI	085	QUEEN AN
HENRY, NANCY	HAR	006	1ST DIST
HENRY, NEGRO	BAL	459	8TH WARD
HENRY, PATRICK	CEC	059	1ST E DI
HENRY, PETER	CAR	336	6TH DIST
HENRY, PETER	BAL	281	2ND WARD
HENRY, PETER SR.	CAR	336	6TH DIST
HENRY, PHILEMON	BAL	217	19TH WAR
HENRY, RACHEL	CEC	202	6TH E DI
HENRY, REUBEN	CAR	370	9TH DIST
HENRY, RHODY	FRE	400	JEFFERSO
HENRY, RICHARD	QUE	225	4TH E DI
HENRY, RICHARD-BLACK	QUE	199	3RD E DI
HENRY, ROBERT	BAL	029	18TH WAR
HENRY, ROBERT J.	WOR	281	BERLIN 1
HENRY, SAMUEL	CEC	099	3RD E DI
HENRY, SAMUEL	BAL	287	20TH WAR
HENRY, SAMUEL	BAL	208	19TH WAR
HENRY, SAMUEL H.	ANN	413	HOWARD D
HENRY, SAMUEL T.	BAL	096	18TH WAR
HENRY, SAMUEL-BLACK	QUE	136	1ST E DI
HENRY, SAMUEL-BLACK	QUE	189	3RD E DI
HENRY, SAMUEL-BLACK	QUE	202	3RD E DI
HENRY, SARAH	DOR	309	1ST DIST
HENRY, SARAH	BAL	240	12TH WAR
HENRY, SARAH G.	BAL	267	1ST DIST
HENRY, SARAH-BLACK	CAR	070	NO TWP L
HENRY, SUSAN	BAL	020	1ST WARD
HENRY, SUSAN	BAL	252	12TH WAR
HENRY, SUSAN	BAL	077	15TH WAR
HENRY, THACIUS	BAL	344	7TH WARD
HENRY, THOMAS	BAL	310	7TH WARD
HENRY, THOMAS	BAL	303	3RD WARD
HENRY, THOMAS	BAL	012	4TH WARD
HENRY, THOMAS	DOR	409	1ST DIST
HENRY, THOMAS	QUE	216	3RD E DI
HENRY, THOMAS	TAL	017	EASTON D
HENRY, THOMAS	WAS	157	HAGERSTO
HENRY, THOMAS	WAS	157	HAGERSTO
HENRY, THOMAS	PRI	084	QUEEN AN
HENRY, VALENT	BAL	239	12TH WAR
HENRY, WILIAM	QUE	235	4TH E DI
HENRY, WILLIAM	QUE	236	4TH E DI
HENRY, WILLIAM	QUE	241	5TH E DI
HENRY, WILLIAM	QUE	240	5TH E DI
HENRY, WILLIAM	WAS	141	HAGERSTO
HENRY, WILLIAM	SOM	500	SALISBUR
HENRY, WILLIAM	WOR	273	BERLIN 1
HENRY, WILLIAM	QUE	211	3RD E DI
HENRY, WILLIAM	QUE	217	3RD E DI
HENRY, WILLIAM	BAL	020	15TH WAR
HENRY, WILLIAM	BAL	450	1ST DIST
HENRY, WILLIAM	BAL	260	2ND WARD
HENRY, WILLIAM	BAL	033	1ST WARD
HENRY, WILLIAM	BAL	021	9TH WARD
HENRY, WILLIAM	DOR	420	1ST DIST
HENRY, WILLIAM	CAR	400	2ND DIST
HENRY, WILLIAM	FRE	351	MIDDLETO
HENRY, WILLIAM	CEC	034	CHESAPEA
HENRY, WILLIAM	DOR	311	1ST DIST
HENRY, WILLIAM	QUE	137	1ST E DI
HENRY, WILLIAM	CEC	065	1ST E DI
HENRY, WILLIAM	CAR	275	7TH DIST
HENRY, WILLIAM	BAL	048	18TH WAR
HENRY, WILLIAM	SOM	435	PRINCESS
HENRY, WILLIAM J.	BAL	242	6TH WARD
HENRY, WILLIAM L.	BAL	088	18TH WAR
HENRY, WILLIAM M.	BAL	457	8TH WARD
HENRY, WILLIAM*	DOR	461	1ST DIST
HENRY, WILLIAM-BLACK	QUE	185	3RD E DI
HENRY, WILLIAM-BLACK	QUE	183	3RD E DI
HENRY, WILLIAM-BLACK	QUE	183	3RD E DI
HENRY, WILLIAM-BLACK	QUE	189	3RD E DI
HENRY, WILLIAM-BLACK	QUE	203	3RD E DI
HENRY, WILLIAM-BLACK	QUE	127	1ST E DI
HENRY, WILLIAMP	QUE	200	3RD E DI
HENRY, ZADOK P.	WOR	262	BERLIN 1
HENRY,MARIA	FRE	032	FREDERIC
HENRY,ROBERT-BLACK	QUE	129	1ST E DI
HENRYKET, LUTHER	BAL	456	8TH WARD
HENSEL, HENRY	BAL	121	18TH WAR
HENSEL, WILLIAM *	HAR	032	1ST DIST
HENSEY, HENRY	BAL	374	3RD WARD
HENSEY, THOMAS	MGM	391	ROCKERLE
HENSHAW, ANN	BAL	282	20TH WAR
HENSHAW, ANN	ANN	272	ANNAPOLI
HENSHAW, CHAELS	ALL	091	5TH E.D.
HENSHAW, JAMES G.	BAL	427	14TH WAR
HENSICKS, CAROLINE	FRE	131	CREAGERS
HENSIE, WILLIAM *	HAR	032	1ST DIST
HENSLER, SARAH	FRE	182	5TH E DI
HENSLEY, HESTER	ANN	279	ANNAPOLI
HENSLEY, JAMES	QUE	210	3RD E DI
HENSLEY, JOHN	QUE	129	1ST E DI
HENSLEY, JOHN	BAL	120	11TH WAR
HENSLEY, SAMUEL	QUE	211	3RD E DI
HENSMAN, HENRY	BAL	330	13TH WAR
HENSON, ALFRED	BAL	177	16TH WAR
HENSON, ANN	BAL	237	20TH WAR
HENSON, ANN M.	CAL	050	3RD DIST
HENSON, ANN R.	BAL	026	15TH WAR
HENSON, CHARLES	ANN	348	3RD DIST
HENSON, CHARLES	FRE	400	JEFFERSO
HENSON, CHARLOTTE *	ANN	290	ANNAPOLI
HENSON, DAVID	BAL	216	17TH WAR
HENSON, DEANA	BAL	272	1ST DIST
HENSON, ELIZA	BAL	263	12TH WAR
HENSON, ELIZA	BAL	131	16TH WAR
HENSON, ELLEN	BAL	247	6TH WARD
HENSON, ELLEN	PRI	075	MARLBROU
HENSON, FREDERICK	BAL	100	15TH WAR
HENSON, GEORGE	BAL	121	16TH WAR
HENSON, HENRIETTA	BAL	002	9TH WARD
HENSON, HENRIETTA	BAL	126	11TH WAR
HENSON, HENRY	BAL	154	5TH WARD
HENSON, HENRY	BAL	125	5TH WARD
HENSON, HENRY	ANN	401	8TH DIST
HENSON, ISAAC	CAL	050	3RD DIST
HENSON, JACOB	BAL	301	12TH WAR
HENSON, JACOB-BLACK	BAL	217	2ND WARD
HENSON, JAMES	BAL	078	10TH WAR
HENSON, JAMES	BAL	003	15TH WAR
HENSON, JAMES	BAL	024	1ST WARD
HENSON, JAMES	BAL	361	13TH WAR
HENSON, JAMES E.	BAL	129	16TH WAR
HENSON, JAMES H.	BAL	026	15TH WAR
HENSON, JOHN	PRI	074	MARLBROU
HENSON, JOSHUA	ANN	362	4TH DIST
HENSON, JOSHUA	ANN	363	4TH DIST
HENSON, JULIA A.	BAL	122	16TH WAR
HENSON, KITTY	BAL	179	2ND DIST
HENSON, L.	ANN	272	ANNAPOLI
HENSON, LAURA	BAL	118	11TH WAR
HENSON, LOUIS	BAL	141	16TH WAR
HENSON, LOUISA	BAL	005	15TH WAR
HENSON, LUCY	BAL	389	13TH WAR
HENSON, LUCY A.	BAL	102	15TH WAR
HENSON, LUSINODA	HAR	196	3RD DIST
HENSON, MARY	BAL	257	20TH WAR
HENSON, MARY	ANN	290	ANNAPOLI
HENSON, PATTY	BAL	122	16TH WAR
HENSON, PETER	BAL	096	15TH WAR
HENSON, PHILLIS	ANN	278	ANNAPOLI
HENSON, REBECCA	BAL	154	5TH WARD
HENSON, SAMUEL	ANN	309	1ST DIST
HENSON, SAMUEL	BAL	091	15TH WAR
HENSON, SAMUEL	BAL	096	15TH WAR
HENSON, SARAH	BAL	119	11TH WAR
HENSON, SUSAN	BAL	075	4TH WARD
HENSON, TERESA	FRE	064	FREDERIC
HENSON, THOMAS	ANN	309	1ST DIST
HENSON, WESLEY	BAL	089	15TH WAR
HENSON, WILLIAM	BAL	239	6TH WARD
HENSON, WILLIAM	BAL	317	3RD WARD
HENSON, WILLIAM	BAL	252	17TH WAR
HENSTON, BENJAMIN F. *	KEN	214	2ND DIST
HENSTON, EDWARD *	KEN	255	1ST DIST
HENSTON, SARAH	WOR	237	6TH E DI
HENT, MOSES	WOR	179	6TH E DI
HENTEN, PETER	BAL	159	1ST WARD
HENTEN, ROBERT	BAL	115	1ST WARD
HENTHORN, THOMAS	BAL	135	16TH WAR
HENTINAN, ELTEY	BAL	309	12TH WAR
HENTMAN, DANIEL	BAL	259	2ND WARD
HENTON, ELIZABETH	BAL	121	2ND DIST
HENTON, JOSEPH J.	MGM	401	ROCKERLE
HENTON, LEWES	HAR	205	3RD DIST
HENTOR, WILLAIM	BAL	115	2ND DIST
HENTRACK, JOSEPH H.	FRE	422	8TH E DI
HENTRESS, FRANCIS	BAL	121	1ST WARD
HENTZ, CHARLES	BAL	169	16TH WAR
HENTZ, JOHN	BAL	304	1ST DIST
HENUREXON, ELLEN	ALL	202	CUMBERLA
HENUREXON, SAMUEL	ALL	202	CUMBERLA
HENWICK, MARY C.	BAL	399	8TH WARD
HENWOOD, EDWARD	BAL	350	3RD WARD
HENYAN, ELIZABETH	BAL	248	20TH WAR
HENZLLENG, ELIZA	BAL	382	13TH WAR
HEODS, NANCY	CAR	253	3RD DIST
HEPBERN, SARAH J.	BAL	227	6TH WARD
HEPBRON, GREORGE	KEN	248	2ND DIST
HEPBRON, JOHN T.	KEN	248	2ND DIST
HEPBRON, THOMAS	KEN	246	2ND DIST
HEPBURN, CATHERINE A.	PRI	027	VANSVILL
HEPBURN, ELIZA J.	PRI	027	VANSVILL
HEPBURN, GEORGE	PRI	021	VANSVILL
HEPBURN, GEORGE L.	BAL	410	3RD WARD
HEPBURN, HENRY	MGM	404	ROCKERLE
HEPBURN, HENRY	BAL	052	2ND DIST
HEPBURN, JERRY	BAL	135	18TH WAR
HEPBURN, JOSEPH	CAL	048	3RD DIST
HEPBURN, LOUISA	BAL	122	11TH WAR
HEPBURN, PRISSILLA	PRI	038	VANSVILL
HEPEY, BENJAMIN	KEN	281	3RD DIST
HEPHEARD, MARGRET	CAR	102	NO TWP L
HEPIREIN, SAMUEL	MGM	388	ROCKERLE
HEPLINGER, GEORGE	BAL	460	14TH WAR
HEPMAN, JOHN	BAL	111	2ND DIST
HEPP, ADAM	BAL	093	1ST WARD
HEPPER, MARY	FRE	113	CREAGERS
HEPPERCK, GEORG	BAL	103	1ST WARD
HEPPINS, RICHARD	CAL	028	2ND DIST
HEPPLE, CASPER	ALL	104	5TH E.D.
HEPRONE, FRANCIS	BAL	106	1ST WARD
HEPSLEY, JOSEPH F.	ANN	494	HOWARD D
HEPSLY, CALEP	WAS	064	2ND SUBD
HEPTON, ELIZA	BAL	121	2ND DIST
HER, SUSAN	FRE	432	8TH E DI
HERALD, JOHN	BAL	352	1ST DIST
HERALD, MARGARET	BAL	425	8TH WARD
HERBARD, NICHOLAS	ALL	119	5TH E.D.
HERBAUGH, HENRY H.	CAR	236	UNION TO
HERBERSON, WILLIAM	HAR	125	2ND DIST
HERBERT, A.C.	HAR	168	3RD DIST
HERBERT, ALEXANDER-BLACK	ST	336	4TH E DI
HERBERT, ANN E.	ST	273	3RD E DI
HERBERT, AUGUSTUS	ST	315	4TH E DI
HERBERT, B.J.	WAS	281	1ST DIST
HERBERT, BENEDICT-BLACK	ST	335	4TH E DI
HERBERT, BETSEY	CHA	219	ALLENS F
HERBERT, CATHARINE	HAR	155	3RD DIST
HERBERT, CHARLES	BAL	243	6TH WARD
HERBERT, CHARLES W.	HAR	151	3RD DIST
HERBERT, CHARLOTTE	CHA	218	ALLENS F
HERBERT, CHRISTIAN	ALL	227	CUMBERLA
HERBERT, CLARACY	CHA	227	ALLENS F
HERBERT, DAVID	WAS	187	BOONSBOR
HERBERT, DELILIA	WAS	186	BOONSBOR
HERBERT, ECWARD	ANN	314	1ST DIST
HERBERT, ELIZABETH	BAL	144	2ND DIST
HERBERT, ELIZABETH	ST	327	4TH E DI
HERBERT, ELIZABETH	ST	314	1ST E DI
HERBERT, EVE	BAL	400	8TH WARD
HERBERT, F.D.	WAS	139	HAGERSTO
HERBERT, FRANCIS	BAL	316	1ST DIST
HERBERT, GEORGE	BAL	400	8TH WARD
HERBERT, GEORGE	ST	293	2ND E DI
HERBERT, GIDEON	BAL	321	1ST DIST
HERBERT, GUSTAV	BAL	005	9TH WARD
HERBERT, HUSBAND	BAL	166	19TH WAR
HERBERT, IRAH	HAR	171	3RD DIST
HERBERT, JAMES H.	BAL	409	3RD WARD
HERBERT, JAMES H.	BAL	141	1ST WARD
HERBERT, JANE	HAR	141	2ND DIST
HERBERT, JEREMIAH	CHA	269	ALLENS F
HERBERT, JESSE	FRE	314	MIDDLETO
HERBERT, JOHN	CHA	221	ALLENS F
HERBERT, JOHN	BAL	142	5TH WARD
HERBERT, JOHN	ST	327	4TH E DI
HERBERT, JOHN	WAS	157	HAGERSTO
HERBERT, JOHN C.	ST	273	3RD E DI
HERBERT, JOHN E.	ST	327	4TH E DI
HERBERT, JOHN F.	BAL	413	8TH WARD
HERBERT, JOHN W.	FRE	314	MIDDLETO
HERBERT, JOSEPH	CHA	226	ALLENS F
HERBERT, JOSEPH	BAL	432	8TH WARD
HERBERT, JOSEPH	BAL	320	1ST DIST
HERBERT, JOSEPH	ST	332	4TH E DI
HERBERT, JOSEPH C.	HAR	168	3RD DIST
HERBERT, JOSEPH W.	ST	265	3RD E DI
HERBERT, JULIA	BAL	277	20TH WAR
HERBERT, KATE	BAL	385	3RD WARD
HERBERT, LOUIS-BLACK	ST	335	4TH E DI
HERBERT, MARTHY A.	HAR	146	3RD DIST
HERBERT, MARY	ST	327	4TH E DI
HERBERT, MARY	PRI	045	VANSVILL
HERBERT, MARY	BAL	443	8TH WARD
HERBERT, MATTHIAS H.	MGM	378	ROCKERLE
HERBERT, NICHOLAS	BAL	390	1ST WARD
HERBERT, PERRY	WAS	210	1ST DIST
HERBERT, PHILIP	ST	332	4TH E DI
HERBERT, PHILIP	WAS	178	BOONSBOR
HERBERT, PRISCILLA	BAL	015	9TH WARD
HERBERT, RICHARD	BAL	317	1ST DIST
HERBERT, ROSEAN	BAL	457	8TH WARD
HERBERT, SAMUEL	WAS	139	HAGERSTO
HERBERT, SAMUEL	BAL	152	11TH WAR
HERBERT, SAMUEL J.	FRE	392	PETERSVI
HERBERT, SARAH	BAL	035	15TH WAR
HERBERT, STEWART	WAS	148	HAGERSTO
HERBERT, TERRY W.	ALL	170	6TH E.D.
HERBERT, THOMAS	BAL	030	1ST WARD
HERBERT, THOMAS L.	ANN	517	HOWARD D
HERBERT, WALTER	ST	289	2ND E DI
HERBERT, WILLIAM	ST	332	4TH E DI
HERBERT, WILLIAM	BAL	470	14TH WAR
HERBERT, WILLIAM T.	ST	298	2ND E DI
HERBET, JOSEPH	BAL	087	2ND DIST
HERBICH, SIMON	BAL	084	10TH WAR
HERBLE, ANDREW	CAR	377	2ND DIST
HERBST, JOHN	CAR	345	5TH DIST
HERBURTSON, WILLIAM	HAR	130	2ND DIST
HERBY, JAMES E.	ST	298	2ND E DI
HERCE, EPHRAIM-MULATTO	FRE	434	8TH E DI
HERCH, JACOB	CAR	347	5TH DIST
HERCHENHEIN, HENRY	BAL	166	6TH WARD

Name	County	Page	District
HERD, BETSY	BAL	412	14TH WAR
HERD, EZRA	FRE	129	CREAGERS
HERD, JOHN	BAL	334	7TH WARD
HERD, JOSHUA	FRE	264	NEW MARK
HERD, MARCUS-MULATTO	FRE	014	FREDERIC
HERD, MARGARET	BAL	350	3RD WARD
HERD, MARY	BAL	350	3RD WARD
HERD, MICHAEL M.	BAL	353	7TH WARD
HERD, SARAH J.-BLACK	FRE	437	8TH E DI
HERD, WILLIAM	BAL	421	3RD WARD
HERDMAN, WILLIAM	SOM	484	TRAPP DI
HERDY, AUGSUT	BAL	379	13TH WAR
HEREFORD, J.B.	PRI	070	MARLBROU
HEREN, THOMAS	ALL	104	5TH E.D.
HERETAGE, JOSEPH	KEN	245	2ND DIST
HERFORD, MIER S.	BAL	294	3RD WARD
HERGAN, HUGH	BAL	180	11TH WAR
HERGENS, G.	BAL	142	1ST WARD
HERGERHIMER, VIRGINIA	FRE	205	BUCKEYST
HERGERSHIMER, PETER	FRE	006	FREDERIC
HERGERT, THOMAS	WAS	130	2ND DIST
HERGESHEIMER, SOPHIA	FRE	061	FREDERIC
HERGET, EDWARD C.	BAL	126	16TH WAR
HERGET, JOHN B.	BAL	126	16TH WAR
HERGINHINE, JOHN	BAL	303	7TH WARD
HERGOT, ECKHERT	CAR	273	WESTMINS
HERHENROTEN, MICHAEL	BAL	133	11TH WAR
HERHOLD, MARIA	BAL	002	18TH WAR
HERIEMAN, G.C.	BAL	293	12TH WAR
HERIMAN, JOSEPH	CEC	215	7TH E DI
HERIN, HESTER	BAL	274	2ND WARD
HERING, JOSHUA W.	FRE	410	8TH E DI
HERING, MARRY	FRE	425	8TH E DI
HERITAGE, WILLIAM	WAS	011	WILLIAMS
HERLEY, JAMES	BAL	234	1ST DIST
HERLEY, ORGAN	FRE	397	PETERSVI
HERLICK, CHARLES H.	BAL	014	9TH WARD
HERLING, CATHARINE	BAL	014	15TH WAR
HERLING, GOERGE	BAL	136	16TH WAR
HERLING, LEWIS	WAS	185	BOONSBOR
HERLOCK, BENJAMIN	BAL	129	16TH WAR
HERLSOCK, FREDERICK	ALL	185	9TH E.D.
HERLST, ELVIS	HAR	150	3RD DIST
HERLY, HENRY	BAL	162	19TH WAR
HERMAN, AARON	BAL	103	5TH WARD
HERMAN, AARON	WAS	278	LEITERSB
HERMAN, ABRHAM	BAL	261	2ND WARD
HERMAN, ANN	BAL	167	11TH WAR
HERMAN, C.	BAL	104	10TH WAR
HERMAN, CASPER	BAL	259	2ND WARD
HERMAN, CLEMENS	BAL	323	3RD WARD
HERMAN, CONRAD	BAL	227	17TH WAR
HERMAN, DERRIAS	HAR	174	3RD DIST
HERMAN, DERRIAS	HAR	174	3RD DIST
HERMAN, ELIZABETH	BAL	261	6TH WARD
HERMAN, ELIZABETH	BAL	092	10TH WAR
HERMAN, FRANCIS	BAL	421	8TH WARD
HERMAN, H.	BAL	137	5TH WARD
HERMAN, IRA	BAL	220	19TH WAR
HERMAN, J.	BAL	261	12TH WAR
HERMAN, JACOB	BAL	348	3RD WARD
HERMAN, JOSHUA	BAL	367	3RD WARD
HERMAN, MARTIN	BAL	202	17TH WAR
HERMAN, MARY	BAL	108	5TH WARD
HERMAN, PHILIP	BAL	013	9TH WARD
HERMAN, WILLIAM	BAL	459	8TH WARD
HERMANGE, ELLEN	FRE	161	EMMITTSB
HERMANN, JACOB	BAL	164	6TH WARD
HERMANTT, EUGENE	BAL	013	2ND DIST
HERMER, AMOS	BAL	222	1ST DIST
HERMER, HENRY	BAL	052	1ST WARD
HERMER, SOPHIA *	BAL	308	12TH WAR
HERMER, WILLIAM J.	BAL	223	1ST DIST
HERMISON, THOMAS	BAL	295	12TH WAR
HERMIUS, FREDERICK	BAL	237	2ND WARD
HERMNA, NICKOLAS	BAL	207	17TH WAR
HERMON, JACOB	HAR	155	3RD DIST
HERMON, MICHAEL	BAL	335	13TH WAR
HERMON, QUGANDA	BAL	336	13TH WAR
HERNER, HENRY	BAL	144	1ST WARD
HERNER, WILLIAM	BAL	269	20TH WAR
HERNET, GEORGE	BAL	206	19TH WAR
HERNEY, MARY ANN*	BAL	333	3RD WARD
HERNEY, MRS. M.	BAL	152	19TH WAR
HERNICK, FRANK	BAL	218	19TH WAR
HERNICK, JOSEPH	BAL	219	19TH WAR
HERNSWING, AUGUST	BAL	275	17TH WAR
HERNY, JACOB JR.	CAR	275	7TH DIST
HERNY, JULIUS	BAL	181	19TH WAR
HEROLD, ELIZABETH	BAL	029	1ST WARD
HEROLD, FREDERICK	BAL	087	15TH WAR
HEROLT, PETER	BAL	227	2ND WARD
HERON, ALEXANDER	BAL	074	10TH WAR
HERON, JAMES W.	BAL	033	4TH WARD
HERONAME, MARY	HAR	203	3RD DIST
HERPREY, CHARLES H.	BAL	166	1ST WARD
HERR, CHRSITIANA	BAL	380	13TH WAR
HERR, ELIZABETH A.	WAS	131	HAGERSTO
HERR, EMANUL	WAS	179	BOONSBOR
HERR, ISAAC	BAL	315	12TH WAR
HERR, JOHN	BAL	048	9TH WARD
HERR, JOHN	WAS	013	WILLIAMS
HERR, RODOLPH	WAS	110	2ND DIST
HERRAND, JOHN T.	CHA	231	HILLTOP
HERRARA, MISS M.	FRE	199	5TH E DI
HERRCIES, THOMAS	CAR	115	NO TWP L
HERREMAN, ANTONY *	BAL	146	2ND DIST
HERREN, PHILIP	HAR	183	3RD DIST
HERREN, WILLIAM	ALL	221	CUMBERLA
HERRERA, GENERAL	BAL	392	14TH WAR
HERRICK, ELLEN	KEN	291	3RD DIST
HERRING, BENJAMIN W.	BAL	319	3RD WARD
HERRING, CARLINE	FRE	054	FREDERIC
HERRING, CHRISTIAN	FRE	313	MIDDLETO
HERRING, DANIEL	CAR	324	1ST DIST
HERRING, DANIEL C.	FRE	315	MIDDLETO
HERRING, DAVID	BAL	322	3RD WARD
HERRING, EDWAD	FRE	035	FREDERIC
HERRING, GEORGE	ALL	226	CUMBERLA
HERRING, GEORGE W.	BAL	015	4TH WARD
HERRING, GODFREY	BAL	215	2ND WARD
HERRING, H.W.	BAL	137	1ST WARD
HERRING, HENRY	BAL	378	3RD WARD
HERRING, HENRY	BAL	027	4TH WARD
HERRING, HERNY	FRE	312	MIDDLETO
HERRING, JACOB	ALL	033	2ND E.D.
HERRING, JEREMIAH	BAL	029	4TH WARD
HERRING, JOHN	FRE	315	MIDDLETO
HERRING, JOHN	BAL	336	7TH WARD
HERRING, JOHN Q. A.	BAL	081	4TH WARD
HERRING, JOSEPH	ALL	226	CUMBERLA
HERRING, JOSHUA	WAS	240	CAVETOWN
HERRING, LLOYD H.	FRE	313	MIDDLETO
HERRING, LOUIS	BAL	298	1ST DIST
HERRING, MARGARET	BAL	172	19TH WAR
HERRING, MARY	FRE	212	BUCKEYST
HERRING, ORIGONAL	BAL	098	10TH WAR
HERRING, SARAH	KEN	215	2ND DIST
HERRING, SARAH	FRE	392	PETERSVI
HERRING, SOPHIA	BAL	278	1ST DIST
HERRING, SYLVESTER	ALL	243	CUMBERLA
HERRING, WILLIAM	CAR	324	1ST DIST
HERRINGTON, GEORGEAN	BAL	346	1ST DIST
HERRINGTON, JOHN	BAL	229	19TH WAR
HERRINGTON, JOHN	BAL	219	17TH WAR
HERRINGTON, JOHN	SOM	463	HANGARY
HERRINGTON, WILLIAM	SOM	463	HANGARY
HERRIS, EDWARD L.	FRE	315	MIDDLETO
HERRIS, THOMAS G.	WAS	042	2ND SUBD
HERRIT, ANDREW	BAL	219	17TH WAR
HERRITT, THOMAS	BAL	231	19TH WAR
HERROD, WALTER	HAR	188	3RD DIST
HERRON, FREDERICK	BAL	146	2ND DIST
HERRON, JAMES	HAR	076	BEL AIR
HERRY, DORRITY	ANN	286	ANNAPOLI
HERRY, WILLIAM	HAR	152	3RD DIST
HERRYON,, SALCONI	BAL	294	12TH WAR
HERSBAUM, JOHANNA	BAL	008	4TH WARD
HERSCHAL, THOMAS	BAL	107	1ST WARD
HERSCHBOUGH, HENRY	BAL	213	2ND WARD
HERSEN, SUSAN	HAR	203	3RD DIST
HERSEY, ELIZA D.	FRE	387	PETERSVI
HERSEY, JOHN	QUE	175	2ND E DI
HERSEY, THOMAS H.	KEN	311	3RD DIST
HERSH, JOHN	CAR	289	7TH DIST
HERSH, JOHN	FRE	170	5TH E DI
HERSH, JOHN R.	FRE	171	5TH E DI
HERSH, MARY E.	BAL	430	14TH WAR
HERSHAW, JAMES	BAL	112	5TH WARD
HERSHBERGER, JAMES W.	FRE	099	FREDERIC
HERSHBERGER, MALINDA	WAS	179	BOONSBOR
HERSHBOUGH, ISAAC	BAL	221	2ND WARD
HERSHEY, CHRISTIANA	WAS	024	2ND SUBD
HERSHEY, DAVID	MGM	419	MEDLEY 3
HERSHEY, ELIZABETH	WAS	159	HAGERSTO
HERSHEY, ISAAC	WAS	141	HAGERSTO
HERSHEY, JACOB	WAS	024	2ND SUBD
HERSHEY, JOHN	WAS	301	1ST DIST
HERSHEY, JOHN	WAS	158	HAGERSTO
HERSHEY, LYDIA	WAS	302	1ST DIST
HERSHIDE, FANNY	FRE	196	5TH E DI
HERSHIDE, JOSEPH	FRE	188	5TH E DI
HERSHLY, GEORGE	BAL	473	14TH WAR
HERSHY, JOSEPH	WAS	125	HAGERSTO
HERSING, JOHN L.	BAL	295	3RD WARD
HERST, SARAH E.	HAR	058	1ST DIST
HERSY, WILLIAM	CEC	048	1ST E DI
HERSYE, A.M.	MGM	424	MEDLEY 3
HERT, JACOB	BAL	015	9TH WARD
HERT, TOBIAS	BAL	014	9TH WARD
HERTEL, RUDOLPH	BAL	304	7TH WARD
HERTIGE, ELIZABETH	CAR	095	NO TWP L
HERTMAN, BENJAMIN	WAS	279	LEITERSB
HERTMAN, DAVID	WAS	123	2ND DIST
HERTMAN, FREDERICK	WAS	271	1ST DIST
HERTMAN, JOHN	WAS	158	2ND DIST
HERTMAN, ROSANNA	WAS	279	LEITERSB
HERTZ, FANNY	BAL	318	20TH WAR
HERTZBAG,MYER	BAL	050	1ST WARD
HERVERY, ELIZA	BAL	269	20TH WAR
HERVEY, CATHERINE	BAL	127	11TH WAR
HERVEY, CHARLES	ALL	181	8TH E.D.
HERVY, FREDERICK	CEC	084	CHARLEST
HERWICK, AUGUSTUS	FRE	027	FREDERIC
HERWIG, LEWIS	BAL	276	17TH WAR
HERWIG, MARIA	BAL	369	13TH WAR
HERYKE, JOHN	BAL	161	19TH WAR
HERZBERG, LAZARUS	BAL	063	15TH WAR
HERZBERG, PHILIP	BAL	013	9TH WARD
HERZBERG, SALIGSMAN	BAL	016	9TH WARD
HERZINGER, JACOB	BAL	240	2ND WARD
HESBURGH, LEWIS	BAL	033	1ST WARD
HESCHER, ARTHUR-BLACK	FRE	241	NEW MARK
HESEY, JOHN	CEC	053	1ST E DI
HESH, CHARLES	BAL	276	7TH WARD
HESIMAN, HENRIETTA	BAL	260	2ND WARD
HESKET, THOMAS	WAS	093	2ND SUBD
HESKIT, ALCINDA	WAS	093	2ND SUBD
HESLEN, RICHARD M.	BAL	048	15TH WAR
HESLER, CATHERINE	BAL	020	9TH WARD
HESLER, JOHN	BAL	215	2ND WARD
HESLER, MARY	BAL	216	2ND WARD
HESLETINE, C.C.	WAS	002	WILLIAMS
HESLINGER, JOHN	BAL	159	16TH WAR
HESMER, MARY	BAL	181	11TH WAR
HESOR, MARY	BAL	381	3RD WARD
HESPIS, FRANCIS	BAL	193	19TH WAR
HESS, ABRAHAM	CAR	304	1ST DIST
HESS, ANN M.	WAS	215	1ST DIST
HESS, CATHARINE	WAS	227	1ST DIST
HESS, CHARLES	BAL	264	20TH WAR
HESS, CONRAD	BAL	255	2ND WARD
HESS, CONSTANT	BAL	011	18TH WAR
HESS, DANIEL	CAR	387	2ND DIST
HESS, DANIEL	CAR	300	1ST DIST
HESS, ELIAS	HAR	157	3RD DIST
HESS, ELIZABETH	FRE	213	BUCKEYST
HESS, EMILY	BAL	071	10TH WAR
HESS, FRANK A.	BAL	090	1ST WARD
HESS, FREDERICK	BAL	071	10TH WAR
HESS, FREDERICK	BAL	438	8TH WARD
HESS, GEORGE	CAR	377	2ND DIST
HESS, GEORGE	HAR	067	1ST DIST
HESS, HENRIETTA	BAL	269	7TH WARD
HESS, HENRY	HAR	061	1ST DIST
HESS, HENRY	CAR	301	1ST DIST
HESS, HENRY	WAS	152	HAGERSTO
HESS, JACOB	CAR	251	3RD DIST
HESS, JACOB	CAR	411	2ND DIST
HESS, JACOB*	BAL	082	4TH WARD
HESS, JANE	CAR	388	2ND DIST
HESS, JOHN	CAR	386	2ND DIST
HESS, JOHN	CAR	301	1ST DIST
HESS, JOHN JR.	CAR	387	2ND DIST
HESS, JOSEPH	CAR	207	4TH DIST
HESS, JOSEPH	BAL	432	14TH WAR
HESS, JOSHUA	BAL	312	1ST DIST
HESS, LOUISA	BAL	088	1ST WARD
HESS, MARGARET	BAL	429	8TH WARD
HESS, SAMUEL	BAL	314	12TH WAR
HESS, SAMUEL	CAR	303	1ST DIST
HESS, SAMUEL R.	CAR	299	1ST DIST
HESS, WILLIAM	HAR	116	2ND DIST
HESS, WILLIAM	BAL	123	15TH WAR
HESS, WILLIAM	ANN	384	4TH DIST
HESSA, FREDERICK	HAR	101	2ND DIST
HESSER, ABRAHAM	FRE	295	WOODSBOR
HESSER, ELIZAVBETH	FRE	305	WOODSBOR
HESSER, GEORGE	FRE	115	CREAGERS
HESSER, LIZZIE A.	ANN	452	HOWARD D
HESSER, MATILDA	FRE	304	WOODSBOR
HESSER, REBECCA	CAR	327	1ST DIST
HESSEY, HEATHERTON	KEN	295	3RD DIST
HESSEY, JAMES	BAL	297	20TH WAR
HESSEY, RHEUBEN	BAL	387	1ST DIST
HESSIAN, WILLIAM	ALL	127	4TH E.D.
HESSILING, WILLIAM A.	BAL	300	17TH WAR
HESSIN, CHARLES	BAL	054	2ND DIST
HESSLER, GEORGE	BAL	193	2ND WARD
HESSNER, CONRAD	BAL	247	2ND WARD
HESSNER, JOHN	BAL	276	2ND WARD
HESSON, ABRAHAM	CAR	247	3RD DIST
HESSON, ABRAHAM	CAR	247	3RD DIST
HESSON, ABRAHAM	CAR	409	2ND DIST
HESSON, ABRAHAM	CAR	411	2ND DIST
HESSON, BALTZER	CAR	260	3RD DIST
HESSON, BENJAMIN	CAR	256	3RD DIST
HESSON, CATHARINE	CAR	255	3RD DIST
HESSON, ELLEN	CAR	395	2ND DIST
HESSON, JAMES	CAR	405	2ND DIST
HESSON, JAOCB	CAR	255	3RD DIST
HESSON, JEROME	CAR	405	2ND DIST
HESSON, JOHN	CAR	406	2ND DIST
HESSON, JOHN	CAR	197	4TH DIST
HESSON, JOSEPH	CAR	250	3RD DIST
HESSON, MARGARET	CAR	255	3RD DIST
HESSON, MARY	CAR	403	2ND DIST
HESSON, PETER	CAR	407	2ND DIST
HESSON, PETER	CAR	258	3RD DIST
HESSON, SAMUEL	CAR	260	3RD DIST
HESSON, SAVILLA	CAR	259	3RD DIST
HESSON, WILLIAM	FRE	182	5TH E DI
HESSON, WILLIAM H.	CAR	262	3RD DIST
HESSON,JESSE	CAR	406	2ND DIST
HESSON,MARGARET	CAR	405	2ND DIST
HESSONG, ERAZA	FRE	340	MIDDLETO
HESSONG, JOHN	FRE	368	CATOCTIN
HESTER, DAVID	WAS	254	1ST DIST
HESTER, FRANCES	BAL	225	12TH WAR
HESTER, JOHN	BAL	228	12TH WAR
HESTER, MARY	QUE	130	1ST E DI
HESTER, MARY F.	BAL	243	12TH WAR
HESTER, MICHAEL	BAL	239	2ND WARD
HESTLER, CATHERINE	BAL	008	9TH WARD
HESTNER, J.	BAL	258	12TH WAR
HESTON, HAMEL E.	BAL	380	13TH WAR
HESTON, WILLIAM T.	BAL	422	1ST DIST
HETDANS, WILLIAM	BAL	257	2ND WARD
HETESHEW, GEORGE	FRE	110	CREAGERS
HETHER, WILLIAM	CAR	086	NO TWP L
HETHERS, HENRIETTA*	TAL	008	EASTON D
HETHORNE, BENJAMIN	ST	344	5TH E DI
HETINGHOUSER, FREDERICK	WAS	188	1ST DIST
HETLER, SARAH	FRE	137	CREAGERS
HETNEN, CHARLES *	BAL	107	18TH WAR
HETRICK, GEORGE W.	BAL	217	6TH DIST
HETRICK, JOHN	ALL	036	2ND E.D.
HETRICKS, CHARLES	ALL	037	2ND E.D.
HETSEL, WILLIAM	FRE	095	FREDERIC
HETT, HENRY	BAL	331	13TH WAR
HETT, JOSHUA*	BAL	351	3RD WARD
HETTEN, GEORGE	BAL	116	11TH WAR
HETTENKOUSE, LUCINDA	FRE	354	MIDDLETO
HETTER, JOHN	PRI	109	PISCATAW
HETTERLEY, ELIZABETH	FRE	163	EMMITTSB
HETTERLEY, EYRIE	FRE	187	5TH E DI
HETTERLEY, HANNAH R.	FRE	187	5TH E DI
HETTERLEY, LOUISA	FRE	166	EMMITTSB
HETTERLY, CAROLINE	FRE	160	EMMITTSB
HETTESLEY, HARRIET	FRE	129	CREAGERS
HETTON, ELIZA A.	ST	296	2ND E DI
HETTON, JAMES	BAL	027	2ND DIST
HETTS, ISAAC	HAR	163	3RD DIST
HETZ, GEORGE	ALL	006	3RD E.D.
HETZEL, JOHN	BAL	359	13TH WAR
HETZELL, JOHN	BAL	056	1ST WARD
HETZER, CHARLES	ALL	218	CUMBERLA
HETZER, ELIZABETH	WAS	012	WILLIAMS
HETZER, JOHN	WAS	005	WILLIAMS
HETZER, LEONARD	BAL	029	15TH WAR
HETZLER, FRANCIS	BAL	337	7TH WARD
HETZLER, JULIA A.	BAL	327	7TH WARD
HEUBEHMAN, GEORGE	BAL	065	4TH WARD
HEUBNER, ADAM	BAL	336	13TH WAR
HEUEL, SACHARAH	BAL	302	1ST DIST
HEUETT, WILLIAM	FRE	140	CREAGERS
HEUGST, BENJAMIN	BAL	187	6TH WARD
HEUISLER, GEORGE A.	BAL	317	20TH WAR
HEULEY, LUCRETIA*	BAL	314	3RD WARD
HEURING, JACOB	BAL	303	1ST DIST
HEURSLEY, RICHARD	BAL	067	1ST WARD
HEUSEHEN, CHRISTOPHER	BAL	047	4TH WARD
HEUSH, ABRAHAM	BAL	289	1ST DIST
HEUSON, CHARLOTTE *	ANN	290	ANNAPOLI
HEUSTON, ANNA	BAL	372	3RD WARD
HEUSTON, ANNIE	BAL	365	3RD WARD
HEUSTON, EMILY	SOM	492	SALISBUR
HEUSTON, MILLY*	SOM	489	SALISBUR
HEUSTON, SAMUEL P.	SOM	517	BARREN C
HEUSTOR, JACOB	BAL	058	4TH WARD
HEUT BOKELLEN, A. R. MRS-	BAL	333	1ST DIST
HEUT BOKELLEN, BRITHA MIS	BAL	333	1ST DIST
HEUT, BOKKELEN, MARY MISS	BAL	333	1ST DIST
HEVEN, CATHERINE	BAL	156	11TH WAR
HEVEREN, ANDREW	ALL	078	5TH E.D.
HEVERLY, ELIZABETH	BAL	421	14TH WAR
HEVERN, WILLIAM	BAL	159	2ND DIST
HEVERS, HENRY	BAL	228	6TH WARD
HEVERTIN, JOHN	BAL	078	1ST WARD
HEVERTY, MAGDALENE	BAL	165	2ND DIST
HEVNER, BENJAMIN *	BAL	144	1ST WARD
HEVONER, CATHERINE	BAL	359	8TH WARD
HEVREN, ANDREW	ALL	078	5TH E.D.
HEWALT, JOHN B.	BAL	041	1ST WARD
HEWELL, FRANCIS W.	BAL	354	7TH WARD
HEWELL, JAMES	SOM	359	BRINKLEY
HEWELL, LEWIS	BAL	097	5TH WARD
HEWES, ANN	BAL	405	1ST DIST
HEWES, ANNA	BAL	215	11TH WAR
HEWES, DAVID	BAL	405	1ST DIST

Name	County	Page	District
HEWES, ELBRIDGET	HAR	083	2ND DIST
HEWES, JAMES E.	BAL	076	15TH WAR
HEWES, JOHN G.	BAL	431	14TH WAR
HEWET, AMANDA	BAL	370	3RD WARD
HEWET, ELI	CAR	229	5TH DIST
HEWET, SOPHIA	HAR	002	1ST DIST
HEWETT, ANDREW K.	BAL	051	4TH WARD
HEWETT, ANN	CEC	149	PORT DUP
HEWETT, ANN E.	BAL	407	14TH WAR
HEWETT, CHARLES	FRE	087	FREDERIC
HEWETT, HENRY	CEC	003	ELKTON 3
HEWETT, HENRY	BAL	167	1ST WARD
HEWETT, J.	BAL	147	1ST WARD
HEWETT, JACOB	WAS	064	2ND SUBD
HEWETT, JOHN	BAL	059	15TH WAR
HEWETT, MARY	WAS	106	2ND DIST
HEWETT, MARY E.	BAL	052	4TH WARD
HEWETT, MARY J.	FRE	137	CREAGERS
HEWETT, MILISSA	FRE	343	MIDDLETO
HEWETT, NATHAN	BAL	147	11TH WAR
HEWETT, RACHEL	BAL	376	13TH WAR
HEWETT, REBECCA	DOR	345	3RD DIVI
HEWETT, THOMAS	HAR	091	2ND DIST
HEWIT, ELIZABETH	BAL	287	12TH WAR
HEWIT, PRUDENCE	HAR	051	1ST DIST
HEWIT, R. E.	BAL	069	10TH WAR
HEWIT, VIRGINIA	BAL	186	2ND WARD
HEWIT, WESTLY	HAR	051	1ST DIST
HEWITT, ANN E.	QUE	148	1ST E DI
HEWITT, BENJAMIN	ST	288	2ND E DI
HEWITT, ELIZA	HAR	092	2ND DIST
HEWITT, ELMER	BAL	007	9TH WARD
HEWITT, FRANKLIN W.	BAL	041	4TH WARD
HEWITT, GEORGE	HAR	091	2ND DIST
HEWITT, HENRIETTA	QUE	225	4TH E DI
HEWITT, HENRY	QUE	204	3RD E DI
HEWITT, HENRY	QUE	139	1ST E DI
HEWITT, JESSE T.	QUE	150	1ST E DI
HEWITT, JOHN	BAL	276	20TH WAR
HEWITT, JOHN H.	BAL	099	5TH WARD
HEWITT, MARTHA G.	QUE	150	1ST E DI
HEWITT, MARY D.	BAL	347	13TH WAR
HEWITT, MARY E.	BAL	311	7TH WARD
HEWITT, MARY J	HAR	083	2ND DIST
HEWITT, REZIN D.	ANN	516	HOWARD D
HEWITT, ROBERT M.	MGM	319	CRACKLIN
HEWITT, THOMAS	QUE	149	1ST E DI
HEWITT, THOMAS	HAR	087	2ND DIST
HEWITT, UDIAH	BAL	020	9TH WARD
HEWITT, WILLIAM	QUE	173	2ND E DI
HEWLET, CAROLINE	BAL	265	17TH WAR
HEWLETT, ANN M.	BAL	038	4TH WARD
HEWLETT, J. W.	BAL	332	1ST DIST
HEWLETT, MARY	BAL	264	7TH WARD
HEWLEY, PATRICK	BAL	109	18TH WAR
HEWS, ELIZA	CEC	020	ELKTON 3
HEWS, GEORGE	CEC	047	1ST E DI
HEWS, JACOB	CEC	155	PORT DUP
HEWS, JASON	DOR	346	3RD DIVI
HEWS, JOHN	BAL	220	19TH WAR
HEWS, JOHN T.	BAL	461	14TH WAR
HEWS, MARGARET	CEC	112	4TH E DI
HEWS, MARTHA	CEC	113	4TH E DI
HEWS, THOMAS	CEC	137	6TH E DI
HEWSTON, JOHN	BAL	327	3RD WARD
HEWSY, JOHN	CEC	062	1ST E DI
HEX, VALENTINE	BAL	247	2ND WARD
HEX, WILLIAM	ALL	243	CUMBERLA
HEXTER, DAVID	ST	256	3RD E DI
HEY, FREDERICK	BAL	105	1ST WARD
HEYBAIN, COLLINS	BAL	199	19TH WAR
HEYCHEW, BERNARD	WAS	247	SMITHSBU
HEYDAW, FREDERICK W.	BAL	391	1ST DIST
HEYDEN, MARY	BAL	164	2ND DIST
HEYDER, MARY	CAR	314	1ST DIST
HEYLAND, LAZARUS	BAL	302	3RD WARD
HEYLER, CHARLES	BAL	084	1ST WARD
HEYLET, JOHN *	ALL	166	6TH E.D.
HEYMES, JOHN	PRI	107	PISCATAW
HEYMIRE, ANDREW	WAS	032	2ND SUBD
HEYN, JOHN	BAL	034	18TH WAR
HEYNER, F.	BAL	152	1ST WARD
HEYSER, CHRISTIAN	FRE	012	FREDERIC
HEYSER, LEWIS	FRE	052	FREDERIC
HEZE, SERENA-MULATTO	BAL	176	2ND WARD
HGNAM, WILLIAM	BAL	441	8TH WARD
HHINDY, JONAS	BAL	321	20TH WAR
HIAMEN, LOUISA	ALL	169	6TH E.D.
HIATT, JAMES	ALL	216	CUMBERLA
HIBB, CATHARINE	BAL	272	12TH WAR
HIBB, GEORGE H.	ST	272	3RD E DI
HIBBARD, JOB	CAR	398	2ND DIST
HIBBARD, JOSIAH	CAR	398	2ND DIST
HIBBARD, SILAS	CAR	398	2ND DIST
HIBBARD, THEODORE	CAR	402	2ND DIST
HIBBERT, ISRAEL	BAL	083	4TH WARD
HIBBERT, THOMAS	BAL	123	1ST WARD
HIBECK, ELIZABETH	BAL	368	13TH WAR
HIBECK, VALENTINE	BAL	368	13TH WAR
HIBERAN, CODNRAD *	BAL	114	2ND DIST
HIBERIA, WILLIAM	BAL	381	1ST DIST
HIBET, JOHN	CEC	177	7TH E DI
HIBLITZELL, THOMS T.	ALL	225	CUMBERLA
HIBNER, ALEXANDER	BAL	236	6TH WARD
HIBNER, BARBARA	BAL	170	6TH WARD
HIBNER, JOHN N.	BAL	067	2ND DIST
HIBSELBARGER, MARGARET	BAL	081	10TH WAR
HICHCOCK, ABRAHAM D.	HAR	049	1ST DIST
HICHCOCK, CHARLES B.	HAR	049	1ST DIST
HICHCOCK, SARAH	HAR	023	1ST DIST
HICHCOCK, SARAH	BAL	331	7TH WARD
HICHCOCK, WILLIAM	HAR	049	1ST DIST
HICHEW, EPHRAIM	WAS	272	RIDGEVIL
HICHEW, SAMUEL	BAL	325	3RD WARD
HICHEW, WILLIAM	WAS	272	RIDGEVIL
HICHINS, WILLIAM	BAL	331	3RD WARD
HICHISON, MARGARET	BAL	032	1ST WARD
HICK, HENRY	BAL	142	1ST WARD
HICK, HENRY	BAL	129	1ST WARD
HICK, JOSEPH	BAL	448	14TH WAR
HICK, MARGARET	BAL	322	7TH WARD
HICK, SARAH	BAL	312	12TH WAR
HICKER, CATHARINE	BAL	086	1ST WARD
HICKEY, EDWARD	BAL	353	13TH WAR
HICKEY, J.	BAL	158	1ST WARD
HICKEY, JAMES	BAL	075	2ND DIST
HICKEY, JAMES	BAL	352	13TH WAR
HICKEY, JAMES	QUE	191	3RD E DI
HICKEY, JAMES D.	FRE	184	5TH E DI
HICKEY, JOHN	BAL	316	20TH WAR
HICKEY, JOHN	BAL	156	19TH WAR
HICKEY, JOHN	BAL	149	2ND DIST
HICKEY, JOHN F.	BAL	119	5TH WARD
HICKEY, MARGARET	BAL	321	20TH WAR
HICKEY, MARGARETT	BAL	042	4TH WARD
HICKEY, MARTIN	BAL	359	8TH WARD
HICKEY, MARY	BAL	067	15TH WAR
HICKEY, MARY EUSTACHIA SI	BAL	316	20TH WAR
HICKEY, MICHAEL J.	BAL	366	13TH WAR
HICKEY, PATRICK	HAR	044	1ST DIST
HICKEY, PATRICK	BAL	279	20TH WAR
HICKEY, THOMAS	HAR	045	1ST DIST
HICKEY, WILLIAM	CEC	062	1ST E DI
HICKHAM, JOHN	FRE	108	CREAGERS
HICKINER, JOHN	ALL	039	2ND E.D.
HICKING, JOHN	ALL	104	5TH E.D.
HICKINS, GARNER	ST	275	3RD E DI
HICKLE, AUGUSTUS	BAL	065	2ND DIST
HICKLESS, MARGARET	FRE	071	FREDERIC
HICKLEY, CATHARINE R.	BAL	212	11TH WAR
HICKLEY, CATHERINE	BAL	045	4TH WARD
HICKLEY, R. J.	BAL	220	12TH WAR
HICKLEY, THOMAS	BAL	251	12TH WAR
HICKLY, ELENOR	BAL	320	12TH WAR
HICKMAN, ADAM P.	BAL	012	9TH WARD
HICKMAN, ALICE	BAL	004	EASTERN
HICKMAN, AMANDA	BAL	045	15TH WAR
HICKMAN, ANN	BAL	001	1ST WARD
HICKMAN, ANN	WOR	242	1ST CENS
HICKMAN, ANN S.	FRE	026	FREDERIC
HICKMAN, ANTHONY	BAL	316	1ST DIST
HICKMAN, CHARLES	CAR	093	NO TWP L
HICKMAN, CHARLES	TAL	031	EASTON D
HICKMAN, CHARLES T.	BAL	018	18TH WAR
HICKMAN, CYRUS	WAS	190	1ST DIST
HICKMAN, EDWARD	BAL	097	10TH WAR
HICKMAN, ELIZABETH	SOM	382	BRINKLEY
HICKMAN, EMERSON	BAL	018	18TH WAR
HICKMAN, FREDERICK	BAL	078	1ST WARD
HICKMAN, GEORGE	BAL	091	10TH WAR
HICKMAN, GEORGE H.	BAL	101	10TH WAR
HICKMAN, GEORGE L.	SOM	420	PRINCESS
HICKMAN, GEORGE T.	MGM	381	ROCKERLE
HICKMAN, ISAAC	SOM	381	BRINKLEY
HICKMAN, ISRIAH	WAS	149	2ND DIST
HICKMAN, JAMES	BAL	334	7TH WARD
HICKMAN, JANE	BAL	104	2ND DIST
HICKMAN, JESSE	WOR	257	BERLIN 1
HICKMAN, JOHN	WOR	291	9TH E DI
HICKMAN, JOHN	BAL	383	8TH WARD
HICKMAN, JOSHUA	WOR	291	9TH E DI
HICKMAN, LEMUEL	WOR	266	BERLIN 1
HICKMAN, MARGARET	BAL	453	8TH WARD
HICKMAN, MARGARET	BAL	069	10TH WAR
HICKMAN, MARY	BAL	078	1ST WARD
HICKMAN, MARY	WOR	242	1ST CENS
HICKMAN, MARY A.	WOR	313	2ND E DI
HICKMAN, N.	BAL	033	4TH WARD
HICKMAN, SAMUEL	BAL	416	3RD WARD
HICKMAN, THEODORE	SOM	420	PRINCESS
HICKMAN, THOMAS	WAS	074	2ND SUBD
HICKMAN, THOMAS	SOM	387	BRINKLEY
HICKMAN, THOMASV.	FRE	034	FREDERIC
HICKMAN, WILLIAM H.	BAL	218	6TH WARD
HICKMAN, WILLIAM T.	MGM	426	MEDLEY 3
HICKMON, BALEY	WOR	260	BERLIN 1
HICKMON, CHARLES	CAR	116	NO TWP L
HICKMON, EMALINE	WOR	293	9TH E DI
HICKOCK, T.	BAL	283	20TH WAR
HICKOX, ELIZABETH	BAL	261	12TH WAR
HICKOX, MARY	BAL	262	12TH WAR
HICKRON, ANN	WAS	149	2ND DIST
HICKS, ALBERTY E. A.	DOR	448	1ST DIST
HICKS, AMELIA	BAL	240	20TH WAR
HICKS, ANN	BAL	044	4TH WARD
HICKS, ANNIE	BAL	336	3RD WARD
HICKS, ASEL	BAL	433	1ST DIST
HICKS, BEN	BAL	441	8TH WARD
HICKS, BEN	BAL	070	4TH WARD
HICKS, CHARLES	CAL	064	3RD DIST
HICKS, CHARLES	BAL	197	19TH WAR
HICKS, COLUMBUS	DOR	444	1ST DIST
HICKS, EASTER-BLACK	CAR	090	NO TWP L
HICKS, EDWARD	BAL	122	1ST WARD
HICKS, ELIZA	DOR	455	1ST DIST
HICKS, ELIZA J.	BAL	337	3RD WARD
HICKS, ENNEAS	QUE	214	3RD E DI
HICKS, ERASMUS-MULATTO	FRE	040	FREDERIC
HICKS, EVELINE	WAS	297	1ST DIST
HICKS, GEORGE	WAS	297	1ST DIST
HICKS, GEORGE	BAL	251	12TH WAR
HICKS, GEORGE W.	DOR	321	1ST DIST
HICKS, H.G.	BAL	159	1ST WARD
HICKS, HARRIET	BAL	029	9TH WARD
HICKS, HARRIET	CAL	045	3RD DIST
HICKS, HENRY	PRI	095	SPALDING
HICKS, HENRY-BLACK	ST	336	4TH E DI
HICKS, HESTER	BAL	346	7TH WARD
HICKS, HETTY	QUE	197	3RD E DI
HICKS, HOOPER C.*	DOR	448	1ST DIST
HICKS, HORACE	BAL	150	16TH WAR
HICKS, HUSELIA*	DOR	444	1ST DIST
HICKS, ISAAC	BAL	027	2ND DIST
HICKS, ISAAC	BAL	087	2ND DIST
HICKS, JAMES B.	CAR	166	NO TWP L
HICKS, JANE	BAL	251	12TH WAR
HICKS, JANE	ST	273	3RD E DI
HICKS, JERRY	BAL	301	12TH WAR
HICKS, JOHN	BAL	087	2ND DIST
HICKS, JOHN-BLACK	QUE	191	3RD E DI
HICKS, JOHN-BLACK	CAR	090	NO TWP L
HICKS, JOSHUA	HAR	061	1ST DIST
HICKS, JOSHUA	BAL	018	2ND DIST
HICKS, LAZARUS	WAS	296	1ST DIST
HICKS, LEBANYA	BAL	441	8TH WARD
HICKS, LEVIN	QUE	175	2ND E DI
HICKS, MARGARET	PRI	049	AQUASCO
HICKS, MARIA	ST	276	3RD E DI
HICKS, MARTIN	QUE	218	3RD E DI
HICKS, MARY	BAL	262	6TH WARD
HICKS, MARY	BAL	293	7TH WARD
HICKS, MARY	BAL	088	4TH WARD
HICKS, MARY .E	WAS	297	1ST DIST
HICKS, MARY A.-BLACK	ST	307	1ST E DI
HICKS, MATILDA-BLACK	CAR	079	NO TWP L
HICKS, PRISCILLA	BAL	135	16TH WAR
HICKS, REUBEN	BAL	411	14TH WAR
HICKS, RICHARD D.	CAR	093	NO TWP L
HICKS, ROBERT	BAL	469	14TH WAR
HICKS, SALLY	CAR	149	NO TWP L
HICKS, SARAH	BAL	056	2ND DIST
HICKS, SYLVIA	BAL	167	19TH WAR
HICKS, THOMAS	DOR	450	1ST DIST
HICKS, THOMAS E.	BAL	066	15TH WAR
HICKS, THOMAS H.	DOR	469	1ST DIST
HICKS, THOMAS J.	DOR	450	1ST DIST
HICKS, WILLIAM	BAL	052	15TH WAR
HICKS,LAWRENCE	BAL	109	1ST WARD
HICKS,MARY-BLACK	QUE	189	3RD E DI
HICKSON, FRANCES	BAL	297	7TH WARD
HICKSON, SORCAS	BAL	361	13TH WAR
HICKSON, W.	BAL	293	12TH WAR
HICKSON,ELIZA	CAR	396	2ND DIST
HICKSON,JOHN	CAR	396	2ND DIST
HICKY, SIMEON	BAL	070	1ST WARD
HICKY, THOMAS	BAL	070	1ST WARD
HICUS, COSANDER	CAR	183	8TH DIST
HIDE, ANN	CAR	398	2ND DIST
HIDE, JOHN J.	BAL	116	18TH WAR
HIDE, SARAH	BAL	083	18TH WAR
HIDELAND, JOHN	BAL	320	1ST DIST
HIDENHOUSE, LEWIS	WAS	055	2ND SUBD
HIDER, JOHN	FRE	432	8TH E DI
HIDER, LEDIS	BAL	417	14TH WAR
HIDLE, CHARLES	BAL	200	17TH WAR
HIDLEBOUGH, JOHN	BAL	459	1ST DIST
HIONECK, MARGARET	WAS	039	2ND SUBD
HIEGLY, WILLIAM	WAS	125	HAGERSTO
HIEHAEL, JAMES	BAL	404	8TH WARD
HIEL, JANE	CHA	278	BOJANTOW
HIELBRAN, ROSE	BAL	014	9TH WARD
HIELHOLTZ, ALFRED	FRE	147	10TH E D
HIELLEN, ELIZABETH	ST	290	2ND E DI
HIELMAN, FREDRICKA	BAL	007	9TH WARD
HIELRICK, CHRISTIAN	FRE	090	FREDERIC
HIEMILLER, WILLIAM	BAL	033	9TH WARD
HIER, HANNAH	ALL	200	CUMBERLA
HIER, HERMON	BAL	047	1ST WARD
HIER, JOSHUA F.	ALL	199	CUMBERLA
HIES, ROSE	BAL	317	12TH WAR
HIES, WILLIAM	BAL	283	2ND WARD
HIET, ELIE	WAS	060	2ND SUBD
HIET, GEORGE	HAR	190	3RD DIST
HIET, WILLIAM	BAL	306	1ST DIST
HIETHER, ELIZABETH	BAL	018	9TH WARD
HIETT, LEVIN	SOM	473	TRAPPE D
HIFER, EMANUEL	FRE	396	PETERSVI
HIGAN, FREDERICK	BAL	127	5TH WARD
HIGANBOTHAN, MARGARET	BAL	036	1ST WARD
HIGBY, MERRY	BAL	257	20TH WAR
HIGBY, SAMUEL	BAL	096	1ST WARD
HIGCHCOCK, JOSEPH	BAL	003	1ST WARD
HIGDEN, JOHN	CHA	270	ALLENS F
HIGDEN, JOHN F. S.	CHA	270	ALLENS F
HIGDEN, LEONARD	ST	349	5TH E DI
HIGDEN, STANALAWS	CHA	232	HILLTOP
HIGDEON, JOHN	MGM	415	MEDLEY 3
HIGDON, BAPTIST	BAL	197	17TH WAR
HIGDON, CATHERINE	CHA	246	HILLTOP
HIGDON, FRANCY	CHA	280	BOJANTOW
HIGDON, HENRY	BAL	198	17TH WAR
HIGDON, JAMES W.	MGM	414	MEDLEY 3
HIGDON, JOSEPH	ST	323	4TH E DI
HIGDON, LEAH M.	BAL	332	7TH WARD
HIGDON, LORA C.	CHA	288	BOJANTOW
HIGDON, MARGARET	BAL	112	5TH WARD
HIGDON, RALPH	BAL	197	17TH WAR
HIGDON, SYLVESTER	BAL	423	8TH WARD
HIGDON, THOMAS	BAL	331	7TH WARD
HIGDON, WILLIAM J.	BAL	445	8TH WARD
HIGENBOTTOM, THOMAS	BAL	280	7TH WARD
HIGERSHIMER, JAMES	FRE	040	FREDERIC
HIGGANS, MICHAEL	BAL	042	1ST WARD
HIGGANS, WILLIAM	BAL	275	2ND WARD
HIGGENS, JOHN	SOM	516	BARREN C
HIGGERSON, JOHN	HAR	198	3RD DIST
HIGGINBOTHAM, L.	BAL	080	4TH WARD
HIGGINBOTHAM, WILLIAM	BAL	233	6TH WARD
HIGGINS, AMANDA	BAL	138	5TH WARD
HIGGINS, ANNA M.	BAL	077	10TH WAR
HIGGINS, ANTHONY	BAL	001	4TH WARD
HIGGINS, ARGALUS	QUE	204	3RD E DI
HIGGINS, ASA	BAL	088	4TH WARD
HIGGINS, CHARLES	CAL	049	3RD DIST
HIGGINS, CHARLES	WAS	101	2ND DIST
HIGGINS, CHARLOTTE	BAL	200	11TH WAR
HIGGINS, CHARLTTE	BAL	220	12TH WAR
HIGGINS, DANIEL	TAL	109	ST MICHA
HIGGINS, DARCUS	QUE	253	5TH E DI
HIGGINS, EDWARD	BAL	001	15TH WAR
HIGGINS, ELIZABETH	BAL	442	14TH WAR
HIGGINS, ELLEN	BAL	054	9TH WARD
HIGGINS, EMILY	BAL	004	1ST WARD
HIGGINS, ERI	MGM	405	ROCKERLE
HIGGINS, HANNAH	WAS	260	1ST DIST
HIGGINS, HENRIETTA	WOR	193	8TH E DI
HIGGINS, HILLORY	MGM	355	BERRYS D
HIGGINS, JACOB	BAL	004	1ST WARD
HIGGINS, JAME SH.	MGM	405	ROCKERLE
HIGGINS, JAMES	DOR	431	1ST DIST
HIGGINS, JAMES	FRE	382	PETERSVI
HIGGINS, JAMES	BAL	297	12TH WAR
HIGGINS, JAMES W.	ALL	180	8TH E.D.
HIGGINS, JAMES*	MGM	400	ROCKERLE
HIGGINS, JEFFERSON	BAL	314	3RD WARD
HIGGINS, JESSE T.	ANN	482	HOWARD D
HIGGINS, JOHN	MGM	407	MEDLEY 3
HIGGINS, JOHN	BAL	031	9TH WARD
HIGGINS, JOHN	BAL	190	2ND WARD
HIGGINS, JOHN	PRI	019	VANSVILL
HIGGINS, JOHN	WAS	301	1ST DIST
HIGGINS, JOHN H.	TAL	029	EASTON D
HIGGINS, JOHN H.	MGM	377	ROCKERLE
HIGGINS, JOSEPH	BAL	287	20TH WAR
HIGGINS, JOSHUA	CAR	220	5TH DIST
HIGGINS, JOSIAH	ANN	333	2ND DIST
HIGGINS, JOSIAH	WAS	098	2ND DIST
HIGGINS, JOSIAH	TAL	048	EASTON T
HIGGINS, LEDONA	WAS	127	2ND DIST
HIGGINS, MARGARET	BAL	315	3RD WARD
HIGGINS, MARGARETT	TAL	106	ST MICHA
HIGGINS, MARGRETT	BAL	085	4TH WARD
HIGGINS, MARIA	CAR	067	NO TWP L
HIGGINS, MARIA	BAL	122	5TH WARD
HIGGINS, MARTIN J.	BAL	168	6TH WARD
HIGGINS, MARY	MGM	338	CRACKLIN
HIGGINS, MARY	BAL	357	13TH WAR
HIGGINS, MARY A.	MGM	387	ROCKERLE
HIGGINS, MARY A.	PRI	020	VANSVILL
	QUE	251	5TH E DI

HIGGINS, MARY J. BAL 138 5TH WARD
HIGGINS, MICHAEL BAL 043 1ST WARD
HIGGINS, OLIVIA MGM 372 BERRYS D
HIGGINS, RANSOM ALL 184 9TH E.D.
HIGGINS, RICHARD ANN 333 2ND DIST
HIGGINS, RICHARD WAS 302 1ST DIST
HIGGINS, ROBERT TAL 086 ST MICHA
HIGGINS, SAMUEL DOR 463 1ST DIST
HIGGINS, SAMUEL MGM 404 ROCKERLE
HIGGINS, SUSANAH BAL 086 4TH WARD
HIGGINS, T. G. BAL 152 1ST WARD
HIGGINS, THOMAS BAL 026 4TH WARD
HIGGINS, THOMAS WAS 136 2ND DIST
HIGGINS, THOMAS L. F. MGM 367 BERRYS D
HIGGINS, THOMAS T. BAL 049 9TH WARD
HIGGINS, WILLIAM BAL 395 3RD WARD
HIGGINS, WILLIAM BAL 006 4TH WARD
HIGGINS, WILLIAM FRE 003 FREDERIC
HIGGINS, WILLIAM FRE 033 FREDERIC
HIGGINS, WILLIAM WAS 121 2ND DIST
HIGGINS, WILLIAM QUE 204 3RD E DI
HIGGINS, WILLIAM DOR 452 1ST DIST
HIGGONS, JAMES BAL 356 8TH WARD
HIGGS, ALETHE A. ST 347 5TH E DI
HIGGS, ALEXANDER ST 271 3RD E DI
HIGGS, ALEXANDER ST 262 3RD E DI
HIGGS, AMELIA WAS 201 1ST DIST
HIGGS, BETTS CHA 272 ALLENS F
HIGGS, GEORGE H. ST 333 4TH E DI
HIGGS, HENRY WAS 162 2ND DIST
HIGGS, JAMES WAS 053 2ND SUBD
HIGGS, JAMES R. ST 335 4TH E DI
HIGGS, JOHN WAS 140 2ND DIST
HIGGS, JOHN CHA 287 BOJANTOW
HIGGS, JOHN C. ST 323 4TH E DI
HIGGS, JULIANNA KEN 293 3RD DIST
HIGGS, MARY E. ANN 408 8TH DIST
HIGGS, SAMUEL ST 338 4TH E DI
HIGGS, SAMUEL CHA 272 ALLENS F
HIGGS, SISTER J.P. FRE 197 5TH E DI
HIGGS, WILLIAM F. ST 339 5TH E DI
HIGH, B. M. BAL 138 11TH WAR
HIGH, BENJAMIN F. BAL 044 18TH WAR
HIGH, CAROLINE BAL 272 12TH WAR
HIGH, CATHARINE S. BAL 090 5TH WARD
HIGH, CHARLES BAL 185 16TH WAR
HIGH, CHARLES SOM 382 BRINKLEY
HIGH, DAVID BAL 245 20TH WAR
HIGH, ELIZABETH BAL 012 15TH WAR
HIGH, ISABELLA BAL 196 5TH DIST
HIGH, ISABELLA BAL 197 5TH DIST
HIGH, JAMES BAL 322 7TH WARD
HIGH, JAMES BAL 202 19TH WAR
HIGH, JAMES BAL 202 19TH WAR
HIGH, JAMES KEN 287 3RD DIST
HIGH, JOHN SOM 388 BRINKLEY
HIGH, JOHN BAL 120 16TH WAR
HIGH, JOHN T. BAL 468 14TH WAR
HIGH, JOHN W. BAL 162 16TH WAR
HIGH, JOSEPH BAL 184 16TH WAR
HIGH, JULIA BAL 014 4TH WARD
HIGH, MARTIN BAL 038 4TH WARD
HIGH, MARY SOM 389 BRINKLEY
HIGH, SARAH BAL 202 19TH WAR
HIGH, SARAH BAL 041 18TH WAR
HIGH, SARAH BAL 213 2ND WARD
HIGH, WILLIAM BAL 202 19TH WAR
HIGH, WILLIM BAL 163 16TH WAR
HIGHAN, JOHN BAL 190 2ND WARD
HIGHBAND, ASBERRY HAR 206 3RD DIST
HIGHBEE, NICHOLAS BAL 397 14TH WAR
HIGHBERGER, ADAM WAS 045 2ND SUBD
HIGHBERGER, CATHARINE WAS 042 2ND SUBD
HIGHBERGER, DANIEL WAS 016 2ND SUBD
HIGHBERGER, GEORGE WAS 033 2ND SUBD
HIGHBERGER, JACOB WAS 047 2ND SUBD
HIGHBERGER, JACOB WAS 038 2ND SUBD
HIGHBERGER, JOSEPH WAS 064 2ND SUBD
HIGHBERGER, MARY WAS 046 2ND SUBD
HIGHBERGER, MARY WAS 038 2ND SUBD
HIGHBERGER, NATHAN WAS 038 2ND SUBD
HIGHBERGER, SARAH WAS 060 2ND SUBD
HIGHEY, ELANTHAN FRE 161 EMMITTSB
HIGHFIELD, THOMAS CHA 248 HILLTOP
HIGHGOHASER, CHARLES BAL 109 1ST WARD
HIGHLAND, CATHARINE BAL 018 2ND DIST
HIGHLAND, JAMES DOR 377 1ST DIST
HIGHMILLER, HARMAN BAL 268 1ST DIST
HIGHMILLER, JOHN BAL 268 1ST DIST
HIGHS, JOSIAH DOR 409 1ST DIST
HIGHT, AMELIA BAL 417 14TH WAR
HIGHT, NINTY* DOR 388 1ST DIST
HIGHT, SENICA* DOR 387 1ST DIST
HIGHT, WILLIAM BAL 138 1ST WARD
HIGHTMAN, JACOB FRE 395 PETERSVI
HIGHTMAN, JOHN FRE 395 PETERSVI
HIGHWAFF, CAROL BAL 017 4TH WARD
HIGINBOTHAM, EDWARD BAL 033 4TH WARD
HIGINBOTHAM, JOHN BAL 032 4TH WARD
HIGINBOTHAM, MARY BAL 093 1ST WARD
HIGISTON, MARGARET BAL 320 20TH WAR
HIGLAND, JACOB BAL 291 12TH WAR
HIGLE, ELIZA BAL 456 1ST DIST
HIGLEY, JOHN BAL 257 20TH WAR
HIGLEY, TALE BAL 060 15TH WAR
HIGMUTT, ROBERT CAR 143 NO TWP L
HIGNAT, CAROLINE BAL 251 6TH WARD
HIGNATT, JOHN J. BAL 233 17TH WAR
HIGNELL, JANE QUE 209 3RD E DI
HIGNET, CATHARINE BAL 463 1ST DIST
HIGNETT, SOPHIA QUE 216 3RD E DI
HIGNULL, JAMES CAR 116 NO TWP L
HIGNUTT, ANN-BLACK CAR 149 NO TWP L
HIGNUTT, EMANUEL CAR 119 NO TWP L
HIGNUTT, JOHN CAR 150 NO TWP L
HIGNUTT, SARAH A. CAR 107 NO TWP L
HIGROT, FREDERICK BAL 305 17TH WAR
HIGS, ANN WAS 036 2ND SUBD
HIGSON, GEORGE BAL 190 11TH WAR
HIILL, MATILDA WOR 312 2ND E DI
HIL, MARY N. CHA 279 BOJANTOW
HILA, ADAM * HAR 017 1ST DIST
HILA, JACOB * HAR 074 1ST DIST
HILA, WILLIAM * HAR 074 1ST DIST
HILAND, BENJAMIN BAL 289 1ST DIST
HILAND, JAMES BAL 429 1ST DIST
HILAND, THOMAS BAL 429 1ST DIST
HILBBERT, MARY J. BAL 435 14TH WAR
HILBERG, FRANCIS L. BAL 043 9TH WARD
HILBERG, FREDERICK BAL 083 10TH WAR

HILBERT, ADAM BAL 388 3RD WARD
HILBERT, FREDERICK BAL 388 3RD WARD
HILBERT, HENRY BAL 435 14TH WAR
HILBERT, HENRY FRE 354 MIDDLETO
HILBERT, JOHN BAL 239 20TH WAR
HILBERT, JOHN BAL 019 18TH WAR
HILBERT, L. BAL 320 12TH WAR
HILBERT, LENARD CAR 197 4TH DIST
HILBERT, PHILIP BAL 254 20TH WAR
HILBERY, WILLIAM BAL 315 20TH WAR
HILBUIGH, ADAM BAL 177 2ND WARD
HILBURG, FRANCIS L. BAL 441 14TH WAR
HILBURN, LYDIA BAL 444 14TH WAR
HILBURN, SAMUEL BAL 443 14TH WAR
HILCARD, DANIEL BAL 206 5TH DIST
HILCARD, HY BAL 205 6TH DIST
HILD, AMAM * HAR 017 1ST DIST
HILD, HENRY HAR 083 2ND DIST
HILD, JACOB HAR 062 1ST DIST
HILD, JOHN HAR 061 1ST DIST
HILD, JOSEPH BAL 209 6TH WARD
HILD, MARY BAL 208 6TH WARD
HILDABRAND, JOHN FRE 225 BUCKEYST
HILDALGC, NICHOLAS FRE 20 5TH E DI
HILDDERBERGE, SMAUEL ALL 252 CUMBERLA
HILDE, PUNY BAL 254 12TH WAR
HILDEBRAND, ADAM C. WAS 246 SMITHSBU
HILDEBRAND, AUGUST BAL 099 2ND DIST
HILDEBRAND, CONRAD WAS 207 1ST DIST
HILDEBRAND, GEORGE ALL 224 CUMBERLA
HILDEBRAND, GEORGE BAL 448 14TH WAR
HILDEBRAND, H.W. BAL 193 19TH WAR
HILDEBRAND, JACOB BAL 256 1ST DIST
HILDEBRAND, PETER BAL 386 13TH WAR
HILDEBRAND, RACHAEL BAL 430 14TH WAR
HILDEBRAND, SAMUEL BAL 370 13TH WAR
HILDEBRAND, STEPHEN ANN 456 HOWARD D
HILDEBRAND, WILLIAM BAL 466 14TH WAR
HILDEBRANDT, AMANDA FRE 083 FREDERIC
HILDEBRANDT, EZRA FRE 082 FREDERIC
HILDEBRANDT, JOHN FRE 081 FREDERIC
HILDEBRANDT, JOSHUA FRE 091 FREDERIC
HILDEBRANDT, JULIAN FRE 091 FREDERIC
HILDEBRANDT, LEWIS M. FRE 091 FREDERIC
HILDEBRANDT, MARGARETT BAL 022 18TH WAR
HILDEBRANDT, WILLIAM FRE 097 FREDERIC
HILDEBRANT, ANN BAL 459 1ST DIST
HILDEBRIDEL, JACOB BAL 010 15TH WAR
HILDEBRIDLE, FRANCIS A. WAS 252 1ST DIST
HILDEBRIDLE, MARY WAS 215 1ST DIST
HILDEHANDT, CATHARINE C. FRE 086 FREDERIC
HILDEIDE, JAMES FRE 114 CREAGERS
HILDERBRAND, GEORGE BAL 128 11TH WAR
HILDERBRAND, HENRY BAL 128 18TH WAR
HILDERBRANDT, CHARLES BAL 007 9TH WARD
HILDERBRANT, CONRAD BAL 027 1ST WARD
HILDING, ELIZABETH QUE 176 2ND E DI
HILDITCH, JOHN BAL 183 6TH WARD
HILDITCH, RUELMA * BAL 184 6TH WARD
HILDMAN, ANN BAL 301 1ST DIST
HILDRETH, JAMES H. BAL 109 5TH WARD
HILDRETH, JEREMIAH ALL 238 CUMBERLA
HILDRETH, MARTHA ALL 239 CUMBERLA
HILE, ANN CEC 119 3RD E DI
HILE, CATHARINE HAR 084 2ND DIST
HILE, DANIEL WAS 041 2ND SUBD
HILE, ELIZABETH* DOR 407 1ST DIST
HILE, HENRIETTA WAS 040 2ND SUBD
HILE, JOHN WAS 041 2ND SUBD
HILE, JONATHAN WAS 041 2ND SUBD
HILE, LEVI Y. MGM 369 BERRYS D
HILE, WILLIAM WAS 039 2ND SUBD
HILES, ISAIH BAL 019 2ND DIST
HILES, JACOB FRE 114 CREAGERS
HILESHEW, ISRAEL CAR 240 TANEYTOW
HILETT, NICHOLAS FRE 246 NEW MARK
HILFRICH, CONRAD ALL 227 CUMBERLA
HILGARDURE, CATHARINE BAL 285 2ND WARD
HILGARDURE, GEORGE BAL 285 2ND WARD
HILGE, JOHN BAL 127 18TH WAR
HILGER, SARAH BAL 438 8TH WARD
HILGERFORTH, MARGARET BAL 447 14TH WAR
HILHECT, FREDERICK * FRE 155 10TH E D
HILIGER, GEORGE BAL 072 2ND DIST
HILKINS, CHARLES WAS 143 HAGERSTO
HILKIRD, WILLIAM BAL 131 1ST WARD
HILL MARY A. BAL 306 7TH WARD
HILL, A. BAL 117 1ST WARD
HILL, A.P. PRI 117 PISCATAW
HILL, ADDISON SOM 544 TYASKIN
HILL, AINY FRE 257 NEW MARK
HILL, ALEX BAL 011 9TH WARD
HILL, ALEXANDER CEC 102 4TH E DI
HILL, ALEXANDER CEC 102 4TH E DI
HILL, ALFRED ALL 152 6TH E.D.
HILL, AMELIA ANN 468 HOWARD D
HILL, ANDREW BAL 124 1ST WARD
HILL, ANIY * FRE 257 NEW MARK
HILL, ANN MGM 320 CRACKLIN
HILL, ANN BAL 391 14TH WAR
HILL, ANN BAL 090 2ND DIST
HILL, ANN BAL 199 11TH WAR
HILL, ANN BAL 405 1ST DIST
HILL, ANN SOM 505 SALISBUR
HILL, ANN E. ST 262 3RD E DI
HILL, ANN L. FRE 005 FREDERIC
HILL, ANTHONY BAL 122 18TH WAR
HILL, ANTHONY FRE 294 WOODSBOR
HILL, ANTHONY BAL 332 13TH WAR
HILL, AUGUSTUS BAL 228 12TH WAR
HILL, BARBARA FRE 114 CREAGERS
HILL, BENEDICK R. HAR 206 3RD DIST
HILL, CAPT, R.M. BAL 003 18TH WAR
HILL, CAROLINE BAL 172 6TH WARD
HILL, CARRILL KEN 265 1ST DIST
HILL, CASSY MGM 347 BERRYS D
HILL, CATHARINE C. ST 322 4TH E DI
HILL, CATHERINE PRI 011 BLADENSB
HILL, CATHERINE BAL 059 10TH WAR
HILL, CATHERINE* BAL 382 3RD WARD
HILL, CHALROTTE BAL 418 14TH WAR
HILL, CHARLES BAL 286 7TH WARD
HILL, CHARLES BAL 179 11TH WAR
HILL, CHARLES BAL 117 5TH WARD
HILL, CHARLES BAL 318 1ST DIST
HILL, CHARLES BAL 312 1ST DIST
HILL, CHARLES WOR 302 SNOW HIL
HILL, CHARLES SOM 448 DAMES QU
HILL, CHARLES PRI 076 MARLBROU
HILL, CHARLES WOR 245 1ST CENS

HILL, CHARLES C. PRI 083 QUEEN AN
HILL, CHLOE BAL 056 10TH WAR
HILL, CLEM ANN 300 1ST DIST
HILL, CLEMENT C. PRI 078 MARLBROU
HILL, CORNELIUS WAS 209 1ST DIST
HILL, DANIEL BAL 017 15TH WAR
HILL, DAVID BAL 123 1ST WARD
HILL, DAVID WOR 201 3RD E DI
HILL, DAVID FRE 297 WOODSBOR
HILL, E. W. BAL 280 20TH WAR
HILL, EBENEZER BAL 315 3RD WARD
HILL, ELANOR WOR 245 1ST CENS
HILL, ELIAS BAL 192 2ND WARD
HILL, ELIAS MGM 319 CRACKLIN
HILL, ELIJAH CEC 159 PORT DUP
HILL, ELIJAH CEC 101 4TH E DI
HILL, ELIJAH CEC 102 4TH E DI
HILL, ELIZA BAL 363 13TH WAR
HILL, ELIZA DOR 315 1ST DIST
HILL, ELIZA BAL 459 1ST DIST
HILL, ELIZABETH BAL 303 3RD WARD
HILL, ELIZABETH BAL 402 3RD WARD
HILL, ELIZABETH CEC 173 6TH E DI
HILL, ELIZABETH BAL 205 17TH WAR
HILL, ELIZABETH CEC 102 4TH E DI
HILL, ELIZABETH CAR 321 1ST DIST
HILL, ELIZABETH HAR 185 3RD DIST
HILL, ELIZABETH ST 322 4TH E DI
HILL, ELIZABETH WAS 066 2ND SUBD
HILL, ELIZABETH* DOR 407 1ST DIST
HILL, ELIZABETH-BLACK FRE 413 8TH E DI
HILL, ELLEN HAR 154 3RD DIST
HILL, ELLEN CEC 148 PORT DUP
HILL, ELLEN BAL 084 15TH WAR
HILL, ELZA DOR 315 1ST DIST
HILL, EMUND ALL 151 6TH E.D.
HILL, EVE C. FRE 140 CREAGERS
HILL, EWMUA MGM 340 BERRYS D
HILL, F.H. BAL 135 1ST WARD
HILL, FANNY BAL 139 11TH WAR
HILL, FREDERICK BAL 143 2ND DIST
HILL, G. H. BAL 333 1ST DIST
HILL, GARRISON-BLACK CAR 165 NO TWP L
HILL, GEORGE HAR 027 1ST DIST
HILL, GEORGE BAL 314 7TH WARD
HILL, GEORGE BAL 253 1ST DIST
HILL, GEORGE WOR 258 1ST CENS
HILL, GEORGE WAS 223 1ST DIST
HILL, GEORGE WOR 337 1ST E DI
HILL, GEORGE WOR 336 1ST E DI
HILL, GEORGE A. CEC 156 PORT DUP
HILL, GEORGE V. HAR 054 1ST DIST
HILL, GEORGE W. MGM 388 ROCKERLE
HILL, GEORGE-MULATTO FRE 431 8TH E DI
HILL, GIDEON FRE 289 WOODSBOR
HILL, HARIOTT DOR 409 1ST DIST
HILL, HARMER HAR 169 3RD DIST
HILL, HARRIET BAL 050 9TH WARD
HILL, HARRIET ALL 196 CUMBERLA
HILL, HAZEL MGM 371 BERRYS D
HILL, HENRIETTA FRE 410 8TH E DI
HILL, HENRIETTA-BLACK FRE 050 FREDERIC
HILL, HENRY FRE 300 WOODSBOR
HILL, HENRY CAR 274 7TH DIST
HILL, HENRY ST 341 5TH E DI
HILL, HENSON MGM 338 CRACKLIN
HILL, HESTER FRE 264 NEW MARK
HILL, HESTER BAL 194 11TH WAR
HILL, HIRAM BAL 123 1ST WARD
HILL, HUMPHREY C. ANN 454 HOWARD D
HILL, ISAAC CEC 172 6TH E DI
HILL, ISAAC BAL 005 4TH WARD
HILL, ISAAC CAR 108 NO TWP L
HILL, ISAAC-BLACK QUE 183 3RD E DI
HILL, ISAIAH BAL 109 10TH WAR
HILL, J. BAL 152 1ST WARD
HILL, JACOB-BLACK FRE 029 FREDERIC
HILL, JAEMS WOR 315 2ND E DI
HILL, JAMES WOR 281 BERLIN I
HILL, JAMES BAL 204 11TH WAR
HILL, JAMES CAL 061 3RD DIST
HILL, JAMES CEC 156 PORT DUP
HILL, JAMES HAR 172 3RD DIST
HILL, JAMES HAR 155 3RD DIST
HILL, JAMES CHA 278 BOJANTOW
HILL, JAMES MGM 371 BERRYS D
HILL, JAMES BAL 079 10TH WAR
HILL, JAMES ANN 417 HOWARD D
HILL, JAMES BAL 164 2ND DIST
HILL, JAMES BAL 144 1ST WARD
HILL, JAMES H. ST 262 3RD E DI
HILL, JAMES W. MGM 338 CRACKLIN
HILL, JAN CEC 212 7TH E DI
HILL, JANE HAR 182 3RD DIST
HILL, JANE BAL 417 3RD WARD
HILL, JANE BAL 211 6TH WARD
HILL, JANE E. CEC 133 6TH E DI
HILL, JARETT HAR 165 3RD DIST
HILL, JASON QUE 136 1ST E DI
HILL, JEREMIAH DOR 300 1ST DIST
HILL, JOHN BAL 379 13TH WAR
HILL, JOHN HAR 187 3RD DIST
HILL, JOHN CHA 283 BOJANTOW
HILL, JOHN BAL 183 19TH WAR
HILL, JOHN MGM 380 ROCKERLE
HILL, JOHN MGM 380 ROCKERLE
HILL, JOHN MGM 389 ROCKERLE
HILL, JOHN SOM 441 DAMES QU
HILL, JOHN FRE 294 WOODSBOR
HILL, JOHN CAR 277 7TH DIST
HILL, JOHN CEC 102 4TH E DI
HILL, JOHN BAL 169 6TH WARD
HILL, JOHN BAL 136 5TH WARD
HILL, JOHN BAL 236 5TH WARD
HILL, JOHN BAL 135 1ST WARD
HILL, JOHN BAL 169 2ND DIST
HILL, JOHN BAL 072 10TH WAR
HILL, JOHN BAL 309 1ST DIST
HILL, JOHN ANN 397 8TH DIST
HILL, JOHN BAL 095 5TH WARD
HILL, JOHN BAL 403 1ST DIST
HILL, JOHN WAS 046 2ND SUBD
HILL, JOHN PRI 094 SPALDING
HILL, JOHN E. BAL 219 6TH WARD
HILL, JOHN E. MGM 338 CRACKLIN
HILL, JOHN F. HAR 186 3RD DIST
HILL, JOHN H. BAL 071 10TH WAR
HILL, JOHN J. WOR 201 3RD E DI
HILL, JOHN R. WOR 262 BERLIN I
HILL, JOHN T. CAR 206 4TH DIST

HILL, JOHN W. MGM 372 BERRYS D
HILL, JOSEPH BAL 414 14TH WAR
HILL, JOSEPH WAS 063 2ND SUBD
HILL, JOSEPH BAL 239 6TH WARD
HILL, JOSEPH BAL 156 1ST WARD
HILL, JOSEPH BAL 153 1ST WARD
HILL, JOSEPH BAL 170 1ST WARD
HILL, JOSEPH BAL 120 1ST WARD
HILL, JOSEPH BAL 119 1ST WARD
HILL, JOSEPH B. PRI 117 PISCATAW
HILL, JOSEPH S. BAL 332 13TH WAR
HILL, JOSEPH S. ANN 396 8TH DIST
HILL, JOSEPH T. QUE 135 1ST E DI
HILL, JOSEPHINE FRE 159 EMMITTSB
HILL, JOSH * BAL 142 2ND DIST
HILL, JOSHUA BAL 244 6TH WARD
HILL, JULIA BAL 291 7TH WARD
HILL, JULIA ST 340 5TH E DI
HILL, LEMUEL WOR 245 1ST CENS
HILL, LEVI CEC 111 4TH E DI
HILL, LEWIS CAR 305 1ST DIST
HILL, LEWIS H. BAL 090 15TH WAR
HILL, LONDON BAL 095 15TH WAR
HILL, LORNEZA BAL 100 2ND DIST
HILL, M.A. BAL 262 20TH WAR
HILL, MAJOR WOR 279 BERLIN 1
HILL, MAJOR WOR 326 1ST E DI
HILL, MANCY BAL 094 1ST WARD
HILL, MARGARET BAL 162 16TH WAR
HILL, MARGARET BAL 094 10TH WAR
HILL, MARGARET WOR 201 3RD E DI
HILL, MARGARET CEC 172 6TH E DI
HILL, MARGARET BAL 111 10TH WAR
HILL, MARIA BAL 012 18TH WAR
HILL, MARK BAL 133 11TH WAR
HILL, MARRIA HAR 203 3RD DIST
HILL, MARTHA BAL 099 10TH WAR
HILL, MARTHA BAL 079 15TH WAR
HILL, MARTHA BAL 164 6TH WARD
HILL, MARTHA-MULATTO FRE 184 5TH E DI
HILL, MARY HAR 146 3RD DIST
HILL, MARY HAR 174 3RD DIST
HILL, MARY HAR 174 3RD DIST
HILL, MARY BAL 443 14TH WAR
HILL, MARY BAL 085 4TH WARD
HILL, MARY BAL 067 4TH WARD
HILL, MARY HAR 082 2ND DIST
HILL, MARY BAL 118 15TH WAR
HILL, MARY BAL 167 16TH WAR
HILL, MARY WOR 178 6TH E DI
HILL, MARY PRI 095 SPALDING
HILL, MARY SOM 484 TRAPP DI
HILL, MARY WOR 314 2ND E DI
HILL, MARY ST 340 5TH E DI
HILL, MARY A. BAL 379 13TH WAR
HILL, MARY O. FRE 066 FREDERIC
HILL, MARY J. BAL 081 18TH WAR
HILL, MAY ANN 396 8TH DIST
HILL, MICHAEL ST 254 3RD E DI
HILL, MISS L. FRE 199 5TH E DI
HILL, NANCY BAL 157 11TH WAR
HILL, NANCY WOR 313 2ND E DI
HILL, NARCISSA BAL 205 17TH WAR
HILL, NATHAN HAR 158 3RD DIST
HILL, NATHANIEL CEC 084 CHARLEST
HILL, NICHOLAS HAR 062 1ST DIST
HILL, PERRY CEC 153 PORT DUP
HILL, PHILIP PRI 011 BLADENSB
HILL, PHILIP ST 340 5TH E DI
HILL, PIPPIN BAL 078 10TH WAR
HILL, RATE R. BAL 333 13TH WAR
HILL, REBECCA CAR 385 2ND DIST
HILL, RICHARD CEC 098 3RD E DI
HILL, RICHARD BAL 379 13TH WAR
HILL, RICHARD CAR 290 7TH DIST
HILL, RICHARD CAR 303 1ST DIST
HILL, RICHARD ANN 410 8TH DIST
HILL, RICHARD BAL 154 2ND DIST
HILL, RICHARD WAS 019 2ND SUBD
HILL, RICHARD PRI 068 NOTTINGH
HILL, RICHARD D. ANN 397 8TH DIST
HILL, RICHARD L. PRI 077 MARLBROU
HILL, RICHARD T. PRI 004 BLADENSB
HILL, ROBERT WAS 064 2ND SUBD
HILL, ROBERT BAL 135 2ND DIST
HILL, ROBERT BAL 139 11TH WAR
HILL, ROSE BAL 320 1ST DIST
HILL, ROSIN BAL 243 2ND WARD
HILL, RUFUS BAL 117 1ST WARD
HILL, RUPLE HAR 168 3RD DIST
HILL, SALLY WOR 284 BERLIN 1
HILL, SALLY WOR 269 BERLIN 1
HILL, SALLY WOR 321 1ST E DI
HILL, SAMEUL BAL 405 1ST DIST
HILL, SAMUEL BAL 377 3RD WARD
HILL, SAMUEL ANN 472 HOWARD D
HILL, SAMUEL BAL 195 17TH WAR
HILL, SAMUEL BAL 059 10TH WAR
HILL, SAMUEL BAL 025 4TH WARD
HILL, SARAH BAL 129 11TH WAR
HILL, SARAH CAL 050 3RD DIST
HILL, SARAH CEC 195 6TH E DI
HILL, SARAH BAL 169 16TH WAR
HILL, SARAH BAL 346 7TH WARD
HILL, SARAH BAL 349 7TH WARD
HILL, SARAH ANN ALL 166 6TH E.D.
HILL, SARAH ANN BAL 235 17TH WAR
HILL, SARAH-BLACK FRE 043 FREDERIC
HILL, SARAH-MULATTO FRE 243 NEW MARK
HILL, SEVERN WOR 201 3RD E DI
HILL, SOPHIA WOR 201 3RD E DI
HILL, SOPHIA BAL 383 8TH WARD
HILL, STEPHEN BAL 327 3RD WARD
HILL, STEPHEN FRE 297 WOODSBOR
HILL, STEPHEN P. BAL 429 14TH WAR
HILL, SUSAN BAL 134 16TH WAR
HILL, SUSAN ST 262 3RD E DI
HILL, SUSAN J. HAR 082 2ND DIST
HILL, SYLVIA BAL 290 20TH WAR
HILL, THOMAS ST 260 3RD E DI
HILL, THOMAS BAL 135 16TH WAR
HILL, THOMAS BAL 357 8TH WARD
HILL, THOMAS BAL 125 2ND DIST
HILL, THOMAS BAL 302 1ST DIST
HILL, THOMAS BAL 215 6TH WARD
HILL, THOMAS B. BAL 460 1ST DIST
HILL, THOMAS J. ST 262 3RD E DI
HILL, W. DOR 384 1ST DIST
HILL, WASHINGTON HAR 039 1ST DIST
HILL, WILLAIM CEC 016 ELKTON 3
HILL, WILLAIM BAL 084 2ND DIST
HILL, WILLIAM BAL 058 2ND DIST
HILL, WILLIAM BAL 107 5TH WARD
HILL, WILLIAM BAL 008 1ST WARD
HILL, WILLIAM BAL 127 16TH WAR
HILL, WILLIAM ALL 158 6TH E.D.
HILL, WILLIAM BAL 459 8TH WARD
HILL, WILLIAM MGM 388 ROCKERLE
HILL, WILLIAM FRE 298 WOODSBOR
HILL, WILLIAM BAL 283 20TH WAR
HILL, WILLIAM BAL 272 17TH WAR
HILL, WILLIAM BAL 458 14TH WAR
HILL, WILLIAM FRE 166 EMMITTSB
HILL, WILLIAM FRE 106 CREAGERS
HILL, WILLIAM CEC 119 3RD E DI
HILL, WILLIAM CAR 241 TANEYTOW
HILL, WILLIAM SOM 502 SALISBUR
HILL, WILLIAM WAS 260 1ST DIST
HILL, WILLIAM B. PRI 075 MARLBROU
HILL, WILLIAM C. HAR 199 3RD DIST
HILL, WILLIAM D. ST 340 5TH E DI
HILL, WILLIAM H. BAL 121 18TH WAR
HILL, WILLIAM H. BAL 251 17TH WAR
HILL, WILLIAM T. KEN 249 2ND DIST
HILL, WILLIAM W. PRI 011 BLADENSB
HILL, WILLIAM-MULATTO FRE 184 5TH E DI
HILL, WORTHY C. CEC 173 6TH E DI
HILL, ZACHARIAH ST 262 3RD E DI
HILL, ZENI CEC 216 7TH E DI
HILL,G EROGE WAS 261 1ST DIST
HILL,LUCY-BLACK FRE 010 FREDERIC
HILLAN, JERRY BAL 229 12TH WAR
HILLAN, SAMUEL MGM 424 MEDLEY 3
HILLAN, THOMAS BAL 285 12TH WAR
HILLARD, JAMES MGM 427 MEDLEY 3
HILLARY, CHARLES-BLACK FRE 230 BUCKEYST
HILLARY, GEORGE W. PRI 078 MARLBROU
HILLARY, HENRY PRI 079 MARLBROU
HILLARY, MARGARET BAL 225 6TH WARD
HILLDEBRANDT, HENRY BAL 078 18TH WAR
HILLDITCH, THOMAS J. BAL 106 18TH WAR
HILLEAEY, JEREMIAH FRE 249 NEW MARK
HILLEANY, JAMES ALL 226 CUMBERLA
HILLEARLY, CLEMENT T. PRI 015 BLADENSB
HILLEARY, ANN C. FRE 395 PETERSVI
HILLEARY, DAVID E. FRE 394 PETERSVI
HILLEARY, HIGHMAN FRE 381 PETERSVI
HILLEARY, JANE FRE 396 PETERSVI
HILLEARY, JOHN MGM 319 CRACKLIN
HILLEARY, JOHN H. FRE 391 PETERSVI
HILLEARY, JOHN Q. FRE 383 PETERSVI
HILLEARY, JOHN W. FRE 382 PETERSVI
HILLEARY, LEVI R. ALL 235 CUMBERLA
HILLEARY, REBECCA FRE 382 PETERSVI
HILLEARY, SARAH FRE 382 PETERSVI
HILLEARY, SARAH MGM 426 MEDLEY 3
HILLEARY, SARAH Q. PRI 016 BLADENSB
HILLEARY, THEODORE PRI 017 BLADENSB
HILLEARY, THOMAS FRE 380 PETERSVI
HILLEARY, TILGHMAN MGM 319 CRACKLIN
HILLEARY, WALTER H. PRI 016 BLADENSB
HILLEARY, WALTER S. PRI 015 BLADENSB
HILLEARY, WILLIAM J.G. ALL 213 CUMBERLA
HILLEAY, WILLIAM H. FRE 381 PETERSVI
HILLEBRAND, ANN BAL 025 2ND DIST
HILLEBRAND, LOUISA FRE 072 FREDERIC
HILLEBRECT, JOHN * CAR 310 1ST DIST
HILLEBRIDEL, DAVID CAR 391 2ND DIST
HILLEN, CHRISTOPHER BAL 106 2ND DIST
HILLEN, FRANCIS A. BAL 134 11TH WAR
HILLEN, LEWIS BAL 101 2ND DIST
HILLEN, ROBINA BAL 062 2ND DIST
HILLER, ELIZABETH BAL 041 2ND DIST
HILLER, FIDE BAL 288 1ST DIST
HILLER, FREDERIC BAL 256 6TH WARD
HILLER, MARGARET ALL 006 3RD E.D.
HILLERAY, MARY T. PRI 015 BLADENSB
HILLERBIDLE, JOHN CAR 292 7TH DIST
HILLERY, CHARLES-BLACK FRE 046 FREDERIC
HILLERY, HENRY FRE 327 MIDDLETO
HILLERY, HOWARD CAR 369 9TH DIST
HILLERY, WILLIAM H. BAL 129 18TH WAR
HILLERY, WILLIAM-BLACK CAR 398 2ND DIST
HILLET, ARNST BAL 169 2ND DIST
HILLEY, LUDWIG BAL 181 16TH WAR
HILLHIDE, DANIEL FRE 133 CREAGERS
HILLHIDE, DANIEL FRE 132 CREAGERS
HILLHIDE, FREDERICK FRE 117 CREAGERS
HILLHIDE, JOSEPH FRE 113 CREAGERS
HILLIARD, BENJAMIN BAL 247 17TH WAR
HILLIARD, CHRISTIAN WAS 146 HAGERSTO
HILLIARD, HEZEKIAH BAL 241 20TH WAR
HILLIARD, JANE WAS 151 HAGERSTO
HILLIARD, MARIA J. BAL 420 3RD WARD
HILLIARY, JOHN M. PRI 041 VANSVILL
HILLIDAY, AGNESS FRE 067 FREDERIC
HILLIDAY, DAVID BAL 164 2ND DIST
HILLIDAY, WILLIAM BAL 421 8TH WARD
HILLMAN, AUGUSTUS BAL 194 6TH WARD
HILLMAN, GEORGE-MULATTO FRE 434 8TH E DI
HILLMAN, JOHN BAL 390 13TH WAR
HILLMAN, JOHN BAL 400 8TH WARD
HILLMAN, MOSES BAL 110 10TH WAR
HILLMAN, NANCY WOR 228 6TH E DI
HILLMAN, NANCY-BLACK FRE 004 FREDERIC
HILLMAN, PHILIP BAL 353 13TH WAR
HILLOCK, STEPHEN BAL 116 11TH WAR
HILLOWAY, THOMAS WOR 249 1ST CENS
HILLS, C.B. PRI 057 NOTTINGH
HILLS, EDWARD BAL 013 18TH WAR
HILLS, SAMUEL BAL 210 19TH WAR
HILLS, WESLEY BAL 136 2ND DIST
HILLSCOME, HENRY CAR 273 WESTMINS
HILLTERNER, THOMAS FRE 134 CREAGERS
HILLTLEBRIDLE, ELI CAR 238 UNION TO
HILMAN, CASA FRE 101 FREDERIC
HILMAN, CHRISTIAN BAL 248 2ND WARD
HILMAN, H. BAL 310 20TH WAR
HILMAN, JAMES W. SOM 476 TRAPPE D
HILMANN, HESTER BAL 030 9TH WARD
HILMER, ANN BAL 273 7TH WARD
HILSON, JOHN BAL 157 1ST WARD
HILSTON, SAMUEL WOR 313 2ND E DI
HILT, FREDERICK HAR 145 3RD DIST
HILT, GEORGE BAL 129 11TH WAR
HILT, MARY BAL 132 5TH WARD
HILT, NICHOLAS CAR 369 9TH DIST
HILTABIDEL, JACOB CAR 210 5TH DIST
HILTABIDLE, JOSEPH FRE 366 CATOCTIN
HILTABIDLE, SERENA FRE 367 CATOCTIN
HILTEBRIDLE, PLOMEY S. * CAR 310 1ST DIST
HILTELBUDLE, JOHN CAR 387 2ND DIST
HILTERBIDLE, DAVID CAR 268 WESTMINS
HILTERBIDLE, ERREL CAR 292 7TH DIST
HILTERBIDLE, LYDIA CAR 265 WESTMINS
HILTERBRAN, JOHN CAR 349 6TH DIST
HILTLEBRIDLE, MARY CAR 395 2ND DIST
HILTON, EDWARD BAL 266 7TH WARD
HILTON, ELIJAH Y. FRE 238 NEW MARK
HILTON, ELIZABETH FRE 210 BUCKEYST
HILTON, ELIZABETH BAL 200 17TH WAR
HILTON, ELIZABETH ST 313 1ST E DI
HILTON, GEORGE BAL 291 1ST DIST
HILTON, GEORGE W. MGM 329 CRACKLIN
HILTON, HARMA HAR 188 3RD DIST
HILTON, HENRY MGM 345 CLARKSBU
HILTON, HENRY ST 273 3RD E DI
HILTON, HENRY K. FRE 029 FREDERIC
HILTON, ISAAC HAR 125 2ND DIST
HILTON, JAMES CEC 087 4TH E DI
HILTON, JAMES BAL 143 1ST WARD
HILTON, JOHN MGM 424 MEDLEY 3
HILTON, JOHN MGM 416 MEDLEY 3
HILTON, JOHN * ANN 354 3RD DIST
HILTON, JOSHUA BAL 340 1ST DIST
HILTON, KITTY BAL 043 2ND DIST
HILTON, LLOYD MGM 329 CRACKLIN
HILTON, LORA BAL 340 1ST DIST
HILTON, LYDIA BAL 153 5TH WARD
HILTON, MARY FRE 022 FREDERIC
HILTON, ORUX BAL 101 5TH WARD
HILTON, ROBERT BAL 355 8TH WARD
HILTON, SAMUEL T. MGM 344 CLARKSBU
HILTON, THOMAS MGM 344 CLARKSBU
HILTON, THOMAS MGM 338 CRACKLIN
HILTON, WALTER MGM 432 CLARKSTR
HILTON, WILLIAM BAL 266 7TH WARD
HILTON, WILLIAM BAL 391 1ST DIST
HILTON, WILLIAM BAL 040 9TH WARD
HILTON, WILLIAM BAL 329 7TH WARD
HILTON, WILLIAM H. FRE 023 FREDERIC
HILTON, WILLIAM L. ST 306 1ST E DI
HILTON, WILSON MGM 333 CRACKLIN
HILTON,WILLIAM MGM 424 MEDLEY 3
HILTZ, CHARLES BAL 125 5TH WARD
HILTZ, JAMES BAL 168 1ST WARD
HILTZ, WILLIAM BAL 126 5TH WARD
HILYER, ELIZABETH BAL 230 19TH WAR
HIMAN, WILLIAM ALL 128 4TH E.D.
HIMEL, AUGUSTINE WAS 056 2ND SUBD
HIMELMAN, JACOB BAL 331 1ST DIST
HIMES, CHARLOTTE ALL 187 9TH E.D.
HIMES, ELIZABETH WAS 088 2ND SUBD
HIMES, ELIZABETH A. FRE 208 BUCKEYST
HIMES, FRANCIS FRE 077 FREDERIC
HIMES, GEORGE WAS 055 2ND SUBD
HIMES, GEORGE WAS 240 CAVETOWN
HIMES, GEORGE WAS 240 CAVETOWN
HIMES, HARRIET FRE 405 JEFFERSO
HIMES, JACOB WAS 045 2ND SUBD
HIMES, JOHN FRE 149 10TH E D
HIMES, JOHN ALL 187 9TH E.D.
HIMES, JOSEPH WAS 088 2ND SUBD
HIMES, MARY E. WAS 249 1ST DIST
HIMES, SAMUEL WAS 088 2ND SUBD
HIMES, SAMUEL WAS 089 2ND SUBD
HIMES, SAMUEL L. FRE 378 PETERSVI
HIMES, THOMAS-BLACK FRE 038 FREDERIC
HIMES, WILLIAM FRE 151 10TH E D
HIMES, WILLIAM M. CAR 232 5TH DIST
HIMEY, MARY J. BAL 019 1ST WARD
HIMMEL, JACOB BAL 184 6TH WARD
HIMMEL, LEOPOLD BAL 090 10TH WAR
HIMMELL, DAVID FRE 131 CREAGERS
HIMMELL, JACOB FRE 023 FREDERIC
HIMMELL, JOHN D. FRE 059 FREDERIC
HIMMELL, MICHAEL FRE 129 CREAGERS
HIMPLE, JOHN CEC 155 PORT DUP
HINAKER, JUSTINA BAL 459 1ST DIST
HINAMAN, AVY* TAL 045 EASTON T
HINAN, JOHN G. BAL 208 2ND WARD
HINAY, LAURENCE ALL 258 CUMBERLA
HINBURRY, ISACHER FRE 021 FREDERIC
HINCHLIFF, URETH BAL 255 1ST DIST
HINCHMAN, ELIZA BAL 136 18TH WAR
HINCKLEY, GEORGE KEN 269 1ST DIST
HINDAMYER, JOHN BAL 284 1ST DIST
HINDEMAN, ROBERT CEC 201 6TH E DI
HINDEMAN, SAMUEL CEC 201 6TH E DI
HINDER, FREDERICK BAL 102 10TH WAR
HINDES, ELIZABETH HAR 072 1ST DIST
HINDES, GEORGE BAL 008 18TH WAR
HINDES, ISABELLA HAR 073 1ST DIST
HINDES, JAMES BAL 025 18TH WAR
HINDES, MARIA BAL 136 5TH WARD
HINDES, MOSES BAL 108 10TH WAR
HINDES, MOSES G. BAL 111 15TH WAR
HINDIN, ELIZABETH * BAL 313 1ST DIST
HINDLE, ELIZABETH WAS 095 2ND SUBD
HINDLE, JOHN WAS 250 1ST DIST
HINDLE, JOHN BAL 145 1ST WARD
HINDLE, MATILDA BAL 298 1ST DIST
HINDLE, WILLIAM CHA 290 BOJANTOW
HINDLE,THOMS BAL 120 1ST WARD
HINDLEY, ANN TAL 008 EASTON D
HINDLIN, PATRICK HAR 156 3RD DIST
HINDLINE, JOHN BAL 161 19TH WAR
HINDMAN, ABRAM CEC 012 ELKTON 3
HINDMAN, ANDREW BAL 448 14TH WAR
HINDMAN, AUGUST BAL 288 7TH WARD
HINDMAN, DANIEL ANN 355 3RD DIST
HINDMAN, JACOB ANN 319 2ND DIST
HINDMAN, RACHEL ANN 353 3RD DIST
HINDMAN, SARAH BAL 125 16TH WAR
HINDS, AUTHER BAL 317 7TH WARD
HINDS, AUTHER BAL 279 7TH WARD
HINDS, CONRAD BAL 099 18TH WAR
HINDS, DELBERTT BAL 093 2ND DIST
HINDS, HENRY BAL 407 8TH WARD
HINDS, HENRY BAL 099 18TH WAR
HINDS, J. BAL 163 1ST WARD
HINDS, JOSHUA BAL 093 2ND DIST
HINDS, MARIA BAL 304 7TH WARD
HINDS, MARY BAL 175 2ND WARD
HINDS, SARAH BAL 316 7TH WARD
HINDS, WILLIAM BAL 115 5TH WARD
HINDS, WILLIAM BAL 457 8TH WARD
HINE, BOLUS ALL 198 CUMBERLA
HINE, CASPER ALL 198 CUMBERLA
HINE, CHRISTIAN BAL 271 17TH WAR

Name	County	Page	District
HINE, GEORGE	BAL	319	7TH WARD
HINE, GEORGE	WAS	078	2ND SUBD
HINE, GEORGE	WAS	062	2ND SUBD
HINE, JOHN	WAS	046	2ND SUBD
HINE, JOHN	WAS	047	2ND SUBD
HINE, JOHN	WAS	078	2ND SUBD
HINE, JOHN	ALL	047	10TH E.D
HINE, JOHN	BAL	384	1ST DIST
HINE, JOSEPH	WAS	079	2ND SUBD
HINE, MARRY	WAS	080	2ND SUBD
HINE, MICHAEL	ALL	049	10TH E.D
HINE, PETER	ALL	229	CUMBERLA
HINE,S ANN	BAL	256	12TH WAR
HINE,S GEORGE-BLACK	QUE	194	3RD E DI
HINEBAUGH, DANIEL	ALL	038	2ND E.D.
HINELIN, ELIZABETH *	BAL	313	1ST DIST
HINELINE, GEORGE	BAL	315	1ST DIST
HINEMAN, GEORGE M.	BAL	271	7TH WARD
HINER, C.	BAL	139	1ST WARD
HINER, HENRY	BAL	303	3RD WARD
HINER, HENRY	WAS	010	WILLIAMS
HINER, JOHN	CAR	193	4TH DIST
HINER, SAMUEL	BAL	305	7TH WARD
HINERY, RACHEL*	DOR	367	3RD DIVI
HINES, A. W.	DOR	454	1ST DIST
HINES, ALSEY-BLACK	CAR	075	NO TWP L
HINES, ANN	WAS	087	2ND SUBD
HINES, ANN	WAS	090	2ND SUBD
HINES, ANN E.	BAL	293	3RD WARD
HINES, ANTHONY	CAR	331	MANCHEST
HINES, AUTHOR	CAR	066	NO TWP L
HINES, CARGLET	BAL	110	1ST WARD
HINES, CAROLINE	BAL	424	14TH WAR
HINES, CATHARINE	CAR	326	1ST DIST
HINES, CHRISTIAN	BAL	021	15TH WAR
HINES, DANILE	BAL	179	2ND DIST
HINES, DAVID	CAR	233	5TH DIST
HINES, DAVID	WAS	087	2ND SUBD
HINES, DENNIS	HAR	139	2ND DIST
HINES, E.M.	BAL	135	1ST WARD
HINES, EDWARD	ANN	359	3RD DIST
HINES, ELIAS	FRE	213	BUCKEYST
HINES, ELIZABETH	CAR	216	5TH DIST
HINES, ELIZABETH	TAL	070	EASTON T
HINES, ENOCH	WAS	038	2ND SUBD
HINES, EVE-BLACK	CAR	084	NO TWP L
HINES, FRANCIS	BAL	125	18TH WAR
HINES, GEORGE	CAR	329	MANCHEST
HINES, GEORGE	BAL	165	1ST WARD
HINES, GEORGE N.	KEN	245	2ND DIST
HINES, GEORGE-BLACK	CAR	069	NO TWP L
HINES, GOERGE	BAL	006	1ST WARD
HINES, HENRY	BAL	270	2ND WARD
HINES, HENRY	QUE	239	5TH E DI
HINES, HUGH	TAL	015	EASTON D
HINES, JAMES	TAL	076	EASTON T
HINES, JAMES	QUE	222	4TH E DI
HINES, JAMES	BAL	249	1ST DIST
HINES, JAMES	CAR	065	NO TWP L
HINES, JAMES H.	BAL	096	18TH WAR
HINES, JAMES-BLACK	CAR	069	NO TWP L
HINES, JOHANNA	BAL	236	17TH WAR
HINES, JOHN	CEC	068	5TH E DI
HINES, JOHN	CEC	047	1ST E DI
HINES, JOHN	CEC	051	1ST E DI
HINES, JOHN	FRE	073	FREDERIC
HINES, JOHN	BAL	270	12TH WAR
HINES, JOHN	BAL	352	1ST DIST
HINES, JOHN	KEN	258	1ST DIST
HINES, JOHN	WAS	037	2ND SUBD
HINES, JOHN	TAL	111	ST MICHA
HINES, JOHN A.	BAL	266	1ST DIST
HINES, JOHN C.	BAL	098	10TH WAR
HINES, JOHN J.	BAL	299	12TH WAR
HINES, JOSEPH	CEC	148	PORT DEP
HINES, JOSHUA-BLACK	CAR	070	NO TWP L
HINES, LEWIS	FRE	214	BUCKEYST
HINES, LORA	BAL	266	1ST DIST
HINES, MARGARET	BAL	209	6TH WARD
HINES, MARY	BAL	423	3RD WARD
HINES, MARY	CAR	254	3RD DIST
HINES, MARY	WAS	037	2ND SUBD
HINES, MARY A.	BAL	423	14TH WAR
HINES, MICAHEL	WAS	036	2ND SUBD
HINES, NELLY	BAL	228	12TH WAR
HINES, PATRICK	BAL	022	2ND DIST
HINES, PETE	BAL	034	1ST WARD
HINES, PHILIP	CEC	047	1ST E DI
HINES, PHILLIP	FRE	307	WOODSBOR
HINES, RACHEL	QUE	209	3RD E DI
HINES, SAMUEL	CEC	184	7TH E DI
HINES, SMAUEL	CAR	066	NO TWP L
HINES, SOPHIA	BAL	229	19TH WAR
HINES, SUSAN	CEC	066	1ST E DI
HINES, SUSAN	BAL	250	1ST DIST
HINES, THOMAS	BAL	103	2ND DIST
HINES, THOMAS	ALL	051	10TH E.D
HINES, THOMAS	CEC	048	1ST E DI
HINES, THOMAS	CEC	190	5TH E DI
HINES, URIAS	WAS	190	BOONSBOR
HINES, WILLIAM	CEC	012	ELKTON 3
HINES, WILLIAM-BLACK	QUE	142	1ST E DI
HINGH, JOHN	KEN	212	2ND DIST
HINGINS, JOHN	BAL	460	1ST DIST
HINGLE, EMILY	BAL	242	12TH WAR
HINGLE, JOHN	BAL	072	1ST WARD
HINGLE, JOHN	BAL	211	17TH WAR
HINGSTON, E.	BAL	282	2ND WARD
HINKEL, ELIZABETH	BAL	040	9TH WARD
HINKELMAN, FREDERICK	BAL	083	10TH WAR
HINKELMAN, GEORGE	BAL	020	9TH WARD
HINKELMAN, PETER	BAL	020	9TH WARD
HINKET, DAVID	CEC	018	ELKTON 3
HINKHOUSE, FREDERICK	CAR	311	1ST DIST
HINKINS, RICHARD	BAL	309	1ST DIST
HINKLE, ALPHECY B.	ALL	161	6TH E.D.
HINKLE, BATHAUSER	BAL	322	7TH WARD
HINKLE, CONRAD	BAL	303	20TH WAR
HINKLE, ELI REV.	BAL	234	1ST DIST
HINKLE, ELIZABETH	BAL	459	1ST DIST
HINKLE, GEORGE	ALL	161	6TH E.D.
HINKLE, GEORGE	FRE	345	MIDDLETO
HINKLE, GEORGE	CAR	352	6TH DIST
HINKLE, GEORGE P.	ALL	157	6TH E.D.
HINKLE, JOHN	ALL	161	6TH E.D.
HINKLE, JOHN	BAL	333	7TH WARD
HINKLE, JOHN	CAR	352	6TH DIST
HINKLE, JOHN	WAS	150	2ND DIST
HINKLE, JOHN T.	ALL	161	6TH E.D.
HINKLE, JOHN W.	BAL	068	18TH WAR
HINKLE, JOSEPH	BAL	100	18TH WAR
HINKLE, MARGARET	BAL	175	2ND WARD
HINKLE, MARTIN	BAL	298	7TH WARD
HINKLE, PETER	BAL	322	7TH WARD
HINKLE, SAMUEL	WAS	133	2ND DIST
HINKLE, WILLIAM	BAL	309	7TH WARD
HINKLE,MARGARET	BAL	175	2ND WARD
HINKLEMAN, ANDREW	BAL	120	11TH WAR
HINKLEMAN, JOHN	BAL	351	13TH WAR
HINKLEMANN, HENRY	BAL	164	16TH WAR
HINKLEY, EDWARD	BAL	261	12TH WAR
HINKS, CHARLES D.	BAL	431	14TH WAR
HINKS, JOSEPH H.	BAL	145	1ST WARD
HINKS, MARY	BAL	425	14TH WAR
HINKS, SAMUEL	BAL	406	14TH WAR
HINKS, SAMUEL	BAL	092	2ND DIST
HINKSON, ANN	BAL	304	7TH WARD
HINLEY, JOHN	WAS	142	HAGERSTO
HINLEY, JOHN J.	BAL	279	20TH WAR
HINLINE, JOHN	BAL	381	8TH WARD
HINLY, W. J.	DOR	434	1ST DIST
HINMAN, ISRAEL	BAL	477	14TH WAR
HINMAN, TRUMAN	BAL	336	3RD WARD
HINMILLER, JACOB	BAL	242	20TH WAR
HINN, JANE	WAS	195	1ST DIST
HINNAMON, SAMUEL	CAR	070	NO TWP L
HINNED, JACOB *	BAL	076	18TH WAR
HINNING, HENRY	ALL	225	CUMBERLA
HINSELING, JOHN	BAL	269	17TH WAR
HINSET, AUGUSTUS	BAL	402	1ST DIST
HINSEY, H.	BAL	071	18TH WAR
HINSLEY, JOHN	BAL	380	8TH WARD
HINSON, AREMNTA	CAR	068	NO TWP L
HINSON, BENJAMIN	BAL	141	5TH WARD
HINSON, BENJAMIN T.	BAL	398	14TH WAR
HINSON, CAROLINE	BAL	357	8TH WARD
HINSON, CATHERINE-BLACK	CAR	133	NO TWP L
HINSON, CHARLES	CAR	082	NO TWP L
HINSON, CHRISTIAN	WAS	068	2ND SUBD
HINSON, DAVID	BAL	192	11TH WAR
HINSON, EDWARD	CEC	049	1ST E DI
HINSON, ELIZABETH	CAR	086	NO TWP L
HINSON, ELIZABETH-BLACK	CAR	147	NO TWP L
HINSON, EMORY-BLACK	QUE	144	1ST E DI
HINSON, HENRY	CEC	047	1ST E DI
HINSON, HENRY	BAL	412	3RD WARD
HINSON, HENRY	HAR	204	3RD DIST
HINSON, J. ALEX	BAL	166	11TH WAR
HINSON, JACOB	BAL	092	15TH WAR
HINSON, JAMES	CEC	079	NORTHEAS
HINSON, JAMES	QUE	210	3RD E DI
HINSON, JAMES*	BAL	337	3RD WARD
HINSON, JANE-BLACK	CAR	099	NO TWP L
HINSON, JOSEPH	DOR	469	1ST DIST
HINSON, JOSHUA	CEC	018	ELKTON 3
HINSON, JOSHUA	BAL	267	7TH WARD
HINSON, LOUIZA	BAL	119	5TH WARD
HINSON, MILLER	BAL	357	8TH WARD
HINSON, NAT*	TAL	019	EASTON D
HINSON, OLIVER	BAL	201	11TH WAR
HINSON, PERRY	CEC	064	1ST E DI
HINSON, PHILIP	BAL	346	7TH WARD
HINSON, RACHAEL	BAL	388	8TH WARD
HINSON, RICHARD	HAR	204	3RD DIST
HINSON, SOLOMON*	DOR	392	1ST DIST
HINSON, THOMAS	BAL	005	4TH WARD
HINSON, WILLIAM	CAR	081	NO TWP L
HINSOR, SOLOMON*	DOR	392	1ST DIST
HINSTON, LOUISA *	KEN	253	1ST DIST
HINT, WILLIAM REV.	BAL	336	13TH WAR
HINTEMYER, LEWIS	FRE	080	FREDERIC
HINTON, B.	ANN	299	1ST DIST
HINTON, BENJAMIN	BAL	439	1ST DIST
HINTON, CHARITY	QUE	204	3RD E DI
HINTON, DANIEL	BAL	165	11TH WAR
HINTON, DANIEL	BAL	141	11TH WAR
HINTON, EDWARD	ANN	305	1ST DIST
HINTON, ELIZABETH	BAL	306	1ST DIST
HINTON, ELLEN	BAL	300	1ST DIST
HINTON, J. H.	BAL	084	10TH WAR
HINTON, JAMES	BAL	349	1ST DIST
HINTON, JOHN	BAL	023	18TH WAR
HINTON, JOSEPH	CAL	001	1ST DIST
HINTON, JULIA	WAS	031	2ND SUBD
HINTON, MARRY	WAS	086	2ND SUBD
HINTON, PLATER	CEC	215	7TH E DI
HINTON, PRISCILLA	CAL	006	1ST DIST
HINTON, PRISSILLA	BAL	349	1ST DIST
HINTON, RICHARD	BAL	141	11TH WAR
HINTON, RUTH	PRI	002	BLADENSB
HINTON, THEADORE	BAL	344	1ST DIST
HINTON, THOMAS	BAL	006	15TH WAR
HINTON, THOMAS	BAL	143	1ST WARD
HINTON, THOMAS	FRE	300	WOODSBOR
HINTON, WILIAM	CAL	010	1ST DIST
HINTON, WILLIAM	MGM	371	BERRYS D
HINTON, WILLIAM	BAL	418	8TH WARD
HINTON, WILLIAM	BAL	419	1ST DIST
HINTON, WILLIAM H.	MGM	427	MEDLEY 3
HINTON, WILLIAM W.	BAL	001	1ST WARD
HINTON, WILSON S.	BAL	143	1ST WARD
HINTON, ZACKARIAH	BAL	121	2ND DIST
HINTSON, DANIEL	TAL	070	EASTON T
HINTSON, DANIEL	TAL	070	EASTON T
HINTSON, THEODORE	TAL	096	ST MICHA
HINTZ, JOHN	BAL	462	1ST DIST
HINTZ, MARY A.	BAL	135	16TH WAR
HINTZ, RICHARD	BAL	304	1ST DIST
HINTZE, T. E. B.	BAL	026	9TH WARD
HINVAR, JOHN	BAL	208	2ND WARD
HINVERS, NICHOLAS	BAL	018	4TH WARD
HINZE, LYDIA	BAL	061	15TH WAR
HIORN, JOHN *	BAL	272	1ST DIST
HIP, MARY E.	BAL	190	2ND WARD
HIPKINS, CALEB	BAL	277	17TH WAR
HIPKINS, E. W. MR.	FRE	076	FREDERIC
HIPKINS, WILLIAM *	BAL	422	1ST DIST
HIPKINS,WILHELMINA	BAL	078	2ND DIST
HIPLEY, SARAH	BAL	402	14TH WAR
HIPP, FREDERICK	BAL	004	15TH WAR
HIPPENSTEAL, JOHN	FRE	124	CREAGERS
HIPSEY, ARCHIBALD	BAL	371	1ST DIST
HIPSEY, BRIDGET	BAL	171	11TH WAR
HIPSLEY, BENJAMIN F.	CAR	372	9TH DIST
HIPSLEY, CATHARINE	BAL	353	7TH WARD
HIPSLEY, CHARLES	BAL	356	1ST DIST
HIPSLEY, CHARLES	ANN	512	HOWARD D
HIPSLEY, CHARLES	BAL	105	18TH WAR
HIPSLEY, EVAN	BAL	346	1ST DIST
HIPSLEY, FREEBORN	ANN	467	HOWARD D
HIPSLEY, HENRY	ANN	511	HOWARD D
HIPSLEY, JOHN T.H.	ANN	486	HOWARD D
HIPSLEY, JOSHUA	BAL	443	14TH WAR
HIPSLEY, JOSHUA	CAR	223	5TH DIST
HIPSLEY, MALVINA	BAL	078	2ND DIST
HIPSLEY, PERMENUS	BAL	345	1ST DIST
HIPSLEY, REBECCA	ANN	459	HOWARD D
HIPSLEY, REZIN H.	ANN	519	HOWARD D
HIPSLEY, SOLOMON	ANN	468	HOWARD D
HIPWELL, SUSAN	BAL	333	13TH WAR
HIR, HENRY	BAL	236	2ND WARD
HIRKLE, JOHN	WAS	302	1ST DIST
HIRL, ADAM	BAL	247	2ND WARD
HIRLT, CHARLES	BAL	155	2ND DIST
HIRODE, ELIZABETH	BAL	319	20TH WAR
HIRSCH, CHRISTIAN	BAL	085	10TH WAR
HIRSCH, CONRAD	ANN	414	HOWARD D
HIRSCH, FREDERICK	ANN	414	HOWARD D
HIRSH, JACOB	BAL	012	15TH WAR
HIRSH, JOHN A.	BAL	287	17TH WAR
HIRSH, MARTIN	BAL	287	17TH WAR
HIRSH, PETER	BAL	247	17TH WAR
HIRSK, JOSEPH	BAL	448	14TH WAR
HIRST, LOUIS	BAL	106	2ND DIST
HIRST, SARAH E.	BAL	374	3RD WARD
HIRT, ELIE	WAS	043	2ND SUBD
HIRTZ, CHARLES *	BAL	318	20TH WAR
HISE, WILLIAM	BAL	253	17TH WAR
HISEMAN, ABRAHAM	BAL	261	2ND WARD
HISER, ALEANORA	BAL	242	1ST DIST
HISER, CATHAIRNE	CAR	348	6TH DIST
HISER, CATHARINE	BAL	461	1ST DIST
HISER, ELIZABETH	BAL	393	1ST DIST
HISER, ENOCH	BAL	242	1ST DIST
HISER, FREDERICK	BAL	440	1ST DIST
HISER, HENRY	BAL	174	19TH WAR
HISER, JACOB	CAR	348	6TH DIST
HISER, JAMES	BAL	262	1ST DIST
HISER, JOHN	BAL	303	3RD WARD
HISER, LEWIS	CAR	304	1ST DIST
HISER, MARY	BAL	241	12TH WAR
HISER, MARY	BAL	199	17TH WAR
HISER, MRS-	BAL	305	1ST DIST
HISER, SAMUEL L.	BAL	248	20TH WAR
HISER, SARAH	BAL	213	6TH DIST
HISER, WILLIAM	BAL	442	1ST DIST
HISER, WILLIAM	BAL	305	1ST DIST
HISER, WILLIAM R.	BAL	227	1ST DIST
HISEY, HENRY	BAL	083	18TH WAR
HISH, CATHERINE	BAL	276	7TH WARD
HISHER, CONRAD	BAL	188	19TH WAR
HISHER, RACHEL	BAL	197	19TH WAR
HISINGER, PETER	ALL	225	CUMBERLA
HISK, RUFUS	CEC	161	6TH E DI
HISKET, THOMAS	WAS	093	2ND SUBD
HISKEY, VIRGINIA	BAL	109	18TH WAR
HISLEY, ELY *	BAL	054	18TH WAR
HISS, AUGUSTA	BAL	105	15TH WAR
HISS, BENJAMIN	BAL	277	17TH WAR
HISS, ELIZABETH G.	BAL	012	4TH WARD
HISS, FREDERICK	BAL	460	8TH WARD
HISS, GEORGE M.	BAL	012	2ND DIST
HISS, HEINEMAN *	BAL	146	1ST WARD
HISS, JACOB*	BAL	082	4TH WARD
HISS, JESSE S.	BAL	189	2ND WARD
HISS, JOHN	BAL	132	2ND DIST
HISS, PHILIP	BAL	418	3RD WARD
HISS, PHILIP	BAL	320	20TH WAR
HISS, WILLIAM	BAL	079	4TH WARD
HISS, WILLIAM	BAL	069	2ND DIST
HISSENGER, WILLIAM	ANN	325	2ND DIST
HISSEY, ARIANA	BAL	145	16TH WAR
HISSEY, ARICHABLD	BAL	077	18TH WAR
HISSEY, ELI	BAL	231	19TH WAR
HISSEY, ELI	BAL	457	8TH WARD
HISSEY, ELY *	BAL	054	18TH WAR
HISSEY, MARY A.	BAL	083	18TH WAR
HISSEY, SOPHIA	BAL	385	1ST DIST
HISSEY, WILLIAM	BAL	145	16TH WAR
HISSEY, WILLIAM	BAL	328	13TH WAR
HISSEY, WILLIAM	BAL	022	18TH WAR
HISSKINS, WILLIAM *	BAL	422	1ST DIST
HIST, WILLIAM	BAL	126	2ND DIST
HISTER, WESLEY	BAL	391	14TH WAR
HISTERMAN, WILLAIM	BAL	303	7TH WARD
HISTON, MARY A.	BAL	403	1ST DIST
HITCH, ASBURY	SOM	485	TRAPP DI
HITCH, DR.	BAL	228	19TH WAR
HITCH, ELIZABETH	CAR	123	NO TWP L
HITCH, ELIZABETH	SOM	504	SALISBUR
HITCH, ELIZABETH	BAL	339	3RD WARD
HITCH, EZEKIEL	SOM	505	SALISBUR
HITCH, GEORGE	BAL	287	12TH WAR
HITCH, GEORGE W.	SOM	500	SALISBUR
HITCH, GEORGE W.	SOM	532	QUANTICO
HITCH, JANE	SOM	554	TYASKIN
HITCH, MARY	SOM	472	TRAPPE D
HITCH, MARY E.	BAL	214	17TH WAR
HITCH, MATTHEW	BAL	038	1ST WARD
HITCH, MOLLY	SOM	422	PRINCESS
HITCH, NELLY	SOM	500	SALISBUR
HITCH, NELLY	SOM	502	SALISBUR
HITCH, ROBERT	SOM	525	QUANTICO
HITCH, SAMUEL	WOR	193	8TH E DI
HITCH, SARAH	SOM	505	SALISBUR
HITCH, SARAH J.	SOM	462	HANGARY
HITCH, THOMAS	SOM	504	SALISBUR
HITCH, THOMAS	WOR	191	8TH E DI
HITCH, WASHINGTON H.	WOR	194	8TH E DI
HITCH, WILLIAM	SOM	485	TRAPP DI
HITCHCOCK, ABRAHAM	HAR	021	1ST DIST
HITCHCOCK, ALBERT	ALL	047	10TH E.D
HITCHCOCK, BENNET	HAR	059	1ST DIST
HITCHCOCK, CATHARINE	BAL	359	1ST DIST
HITCHCOCK, CHARLES F.	HAR	152	3RD DIST
HITCHCOCK, DENNIS	HAR	020	1ST DIST
HITCHCOCK, ELISHA	CEC	072	5TH E DI
HITCHCOCK, ELISHA	BAL	132	2ND DIST
HITCHCOCK, ELIZABETH	BAL	385	3RD WARD
HITCHCOCK, ELIZABETH	BAL	407	8TH WARD
HITCHCOCK, GABRIEL	BAL	330	1ST DIST
HITCHCOCK, ISABELLA	BAL	165	16TH WAR
HITCHCOCK, JAMES	BAL	330	1ST DIST
HITCHCOCK, JOHN	HAR	016	1ST DIST
HITCHCOCK, JOSEPH K.	BAL	165	11TH WAR
HITCHCOCK, JOSHUA K.	BAL	165	11TH WAR
HITCHCOCK, LESTER	ALL	046	10TH E.D
HITCHCOCK, LEVI	ANN	306	1ST DIST
HITCHCOCK, LEWIS L.	BAL	087	18TH WAR
HITCHCOCK, LUTHER M.	HAR	024	1ST DIST

Name	County	Page	District
HITCHCOCK, MARIA	CEC	169	6TH E DI
HITCHCOCK, SAMUEL	CEC	179	7TH E DI
HITCHCOCK, SARAH	CEC	136	6TH E DI
HITCHCOCK, SARAH J.	BAL	390	8TH WARD
HITCHCOCK, WILLIAM T.	BAL	165	11TH WAR
HITCHENS, EDWARD J.	WOR	204	4TH E DI
HITCHENS, JOSEPH	WOR	206	4TH E DI
HITCHENS, WILLIAM	SOM	464	HANGARY
HITCHEW, BARNARD	BAL	325	1ST DIST
HITCHINGS, GEORGE	BAL	340	7TH WARD
HITCHINGS, JAMES	BAL	031	1ST WARD
HITCHINGS, JANE	BAL	434	8TH WARD
HITCHINGS, JOHN	BAL	340	7TH WARD
HITCHINGS, SAMUEL	BAL	302	7TH WARD
HITCHINS, EDWARD	BAL	330	3RD WARD
HITCKCOCK, GEORGE	BAL	109	18TH WAR
HITEMAN, JACOB	FRE	326	MIDDLETO
HITER, HANNAH	CAR	379	2ND DIST
HITESHEN, SAMUEL	BAL	267	12TH WAR
HITESHEW, ABRAHAM	CAR	327	1ST DIST
HITESHEW, CHARLES	CAR	320	1ST DIST
HITESHEW, DANIEL	FRE	313	MIDDLETO
HITESHEW, DAVID	FRE	165	EMMITTSB
HITESHEW, EPHRAIM	CAR	378	2ND DIST
HITESHEW, GIDEON	CAR	302	1ST DIST
HITESHEW, HANNAH	CAR	237	UNION TO
HITESHEW, JEREMIAH	FRE	072	FREDERIC
HITESHEW, MARY C.	CAR	377	2ND DIST
HITESHEW, PHILLIP	FRE	094	FREDERIC
HITESHEW, WILLIAM	CAR	237	UNION TO
HITESHEW, WILLIAM	FRE	182	5TH E DI
HITESHIRE, ISRAEL	FRE	307	WOODSBOR
HITESKEW, CHARLES	CAR	237	UNION TO
HITMAN, JULIUS	HAR	086	2ND DIST
HITMER, HENRY	FRE	108	CREAGERS
HITRELBERGER, ELIZABETH*	BAL	059	4TH WARD
HITSELBERGER, JOHN A.	BAL	137	16TH WAR
HITSELBERGER, JOSEPH	BAL	395	8TH WARD
HITSLER, CHARLES	BAL	453	8TH WARD
HITTABIDER, GEORGE	FRE	367	CATOCTIN
HITTCH, JOSHUA	BAL	141	2ND DIST
HITTERBRIDLE, EMANUEL	CAR	407	2ND DIST
HITTIE, MORTON	BAL	239	12TH WAR
HITTLEBRIDL, DANIEL	CAR	408	2ND DIST
HITTMEYER, ADOLPH	BAL	062	15TH WAR
HITTON, FREDERICK	BAL	202	2ND WARD
HITTZ, PHILLIP	BAL	260	2ND WARD
HITZCE, REGINA	BAL	244	12TH WAR
HITZEL, GOTLEIB	WAS	061	2ND SUBD
HITZELBERGER, ELIZABETH	BAL	260	6TH WARD
HITZELBERGER, ELIZABETH*	BAL	059	4TH WARD
HITZELBERGER, HANNAH	BAL	287	17TH WAR
HITZELBERGER, JOHN	BAL	155	11TH WAR
HITZELBERGER, MARY E.	BAL	214	11TH WAR
HITZELBERGER, STEPHEN	BAL	099	18TH WAR
HITZELBERGER, STEPHEN	BAL	100	18TH WAR
HITZELBERGER, WILLIAM	BAL	133	11TH WAR
HITZELBERGER, WILLIAM	BAL	259	6TH WARD
HITZELLBERGER, ADAM	ANN	417	HOWARD D
HITZIE, HENRY P.	BAL	243	12TH WAR
HIVELY, MARY	CAR	331	MANCHEST
HIVER, CHARLES	BAL	024	4TH WARD
HIVES, JOSHUA	BAL	386	1ST DIST
HIXEN, JOHN	HAR	018	1ST DIST
HIXENBOUGH, CATHERINE	ALL	115	5TH E.D.
HIXER, FRANCES	HAR	058	1ST DIST
HIXON, MARY ANN	BAL	325	3RD WARD
HIXON, SUSAN	BAL	225	19TH WAR
HIXSLY, LEVI	BAL	077	2ND DIST
HJOLVENSON, H.	BAL	137	1ST WARD
HLLAND, JOHN R.	FRE	227	BUCKEYST
HLLEY, JANE	BAL	041	1ST WARD
HMACKALL, ELIZABETH W.	BAL	033	9TH WARD
HMPHIA, JOSEPH	CEC	012	ELKTON 3
HNSON, WILLIAM	QUE	131	1ST E DI
HOACK, JOHN	BAL	200	11TH WAR
HOAGES, CATHERINE	BAL	022	9TH WARD
HOAM, DAVID	ALL	135	4TH E.D.
HOARNE, ROSE	BAL	431	14TH WAR
HOATS, ELIZA J.	CAL	023	2ND DIST
HOBAN, MARY	BAL	104	18TH WAR
HOBAN, VINELEN*	DOR	406	1ST DIST
HOBART, HASS	BAL	203	2ND WARD
HOBB, ANDREW A.	BAL	221	19TH WAR
HOBB, CATHARINE	BAL	267	20TH WAR
HOBB, LUCRETIA	QUE	216	3RD E DI
HOBB, MARY	BAL	276	12TH WAR
HOBB, ROSE	BAL	278	12TH WAR
HOBB, SAMUEL	BAL	220	12TH WAR
HOBBITZELL, GEORGE	ALL	226	CUMBERLA
HOBBLZELL, JOHN F.	ALL	212	CUMBERLA
HOBBRENER, SUSAN	WAS	284	1ST DIST
HOBBS, ALEXANDER	BAL	187	19TH WAR
HOBBS, ALEXANDER H.	BAL	059	10TH WAR
HOBBS, ALMIRA V.	ANN	504	HOWARD D
HOBBS, BERNARD	BAL	023	9TH WARD
HOBBS, BRICE	ANN	414	HOWARD D
HOBBS, BRICE H.	BAL	081	18TH WAR
HOBBS, CALEB	BAL	050	18TH WAR
HOBBS, CALEB	ANN	514	HOWARD D
HOBBS, CATHARINE	ANN	494	HOWARD D
HOBBS, CATHARINE	BAL	050	15TH WAR
HOBBS, CATHARINE	FRE	184	5TH E DI
HOBBS, CHARLES	ANN	305	1ST DIST
HOBBS, CHARLES A.	ANN	503	HOWARD D
HOBBS, CORNELIUS	ANN	470	HOWARD D
HOBBS, DANIEL	TAL	038	EASTON D
HOBBS, DANIEL D. L.	BAL	235	6TH WARD
HOBBS, EDWAD	CAR	092	NO TWP L
HOBBS, ELIZA	TAL	038	EASTON D
HOBBS, ELIZABETH	BAL	074	18TH WAR
HOBBS, ELLEN	SOM	541	TYASKIN
HOBBS, ELLEN	BAL	117	5TH WARD
HOBBS, ELTON	BAL	284	12TH WAR
HOBBS, EPHRAIM	ANN	506	HOWARD D
HOBBS, GAERIEL	BAL	015	1ST WARD
HOBBS, GEORGE	ANN	418	HOWARD D
HOBBS, GEORGE	BAL	404	14TH WAR
HOBBS, GERARD	ANN	511	HOWARD D
HOBBS, GOERGE W.	ANN	502	HOWARD D
HOBBS, HAZEL	MGM	349	BERRYS D
HOBBS, JAMES	SOM	525	BARREN C
HOBBS, JAMES H.	ANN	502	HOWARD D
HOBBS, JANE	BAL	127	11TH WAR
HOBBS, JESSE	FRE	250	NEW MARK
HOBBS, JOHANNA	BAL	031	9TH WARD
HOBBS, JOHN	BAL	236	6TH WARD
HOBBS, JOHN	BAL	421	8TH WARD
HOBBS, JOHN	FRE	178	5TH E DI
HOBBS, JOSEPH	BAL	348	1ST DIST
HOBBS, JOSEPH R.	ANN	504	HOWARD D
HOBBS, JOSHUA	FRE	164	EMMITTSB
HOBBS, LANCELOT	ANN	488	HOWARD D
HOBBS, LAURA	BAL	031	9TH WARD
HOBBS, LAURA V.	BAL	051	18TH WAR
HOBBS, LEONARD	FRE	255	NEW MARK
HOBBS, LEVIN	ST	296	2ND E DI
HOBBS, LEVIN W. C.	MGM	443	CLARKSTR
HOBBS, LEWIS	BAL	090	1ST WARD
HOBBS, LITTLETON	BAL	037	1ST WARD
HOBBS, LOWEL	ANN	514	HOWARD D
HOBBS, MARGARET E.	SOM	523	BARREN C
HOBBS, MARTHA M.	FRE	204	BUCKEYST
HOBBS, MARY	BAL	003	18TH WAR
HOBBS, MARY	FRE	007	FREDERIC
HOBBS, MARY	BAL	081	4TH WARD
HOBBS, MARY	BAL	022	1ST WARD
HOBBS, MARY	BAL	278	12TH WAR
HOBBS, MARY E.	TAL	052	EASTON D
HOBBS, MILTON	ANN	506	HOWARD D
HOBBS, NATHAN	MGM	337	CRACKLIN
HOBBS, NATHAN	CAR	109	NO TWP L
HOBBS, NATHAN C.	ANN	504	HOWARD D
HOBBS, PEREGRINE	ANN	504	HOWARD D
HOBBS, REZIN	MGM	340	CLARKSBU
HOBBS, RHODA	MGM	444	CLARKSTR
HOBBS, RIGEN	FRE	043	FREDERIC
HOBBS, ROBERT	TAL	038	EASTON D
HOBBS, SAMUEL	MGM	438	CLARKSTR
HOBBS, SAMUEL	BAL	337	7TH WARD
HOBBS, SAMUEL T.	BAL	029	9TH WARD
HOBBS, SARAH	BAL	301	3RD WARD
HOBBS, SARAH	BAL	406	14TH WAR
HOBBS, SETH	WOR	227	4TH E DI
HOBBS, THOMAS	TAL	037	EASTON D
HOBBS, THOMAS B.	ANN	504	HOWARD D
HOBBS, THOMAS J.	MGM	327	CRACKLIN
HOBBS, THOMAS R.	ANN	475	HOWARD D
HOBBS, VIRGINIA	TAL	038	EASTON D
HOBBS, WARNER	CAR	396	2ND DIST
HOBBS, WASHINGTON	BAL	053	4TH WARD
HOBBS, WILLIAM	FRE	308	WOODSBOR
HOBBS, WILLIAM	BAL	163	19TH WAR
HOBBS, WILLIAM	MGM	439	CLARKSTR
HOBBS, WILLIAM	BAL	003	9TH WARD
HOBBS, WILLIAM A. G.	QUE	248	5TH E DI
HOBBS, WILLIAM P. T.	BAL	084	4TH WARD
HOBBS, WILSON L.	ANN	519	HOWARD D
HOBBS, YELBURTON	BAL	288	3RD WARD
HOBBS,CLARA	FRE	045	FREDERIC
HOBER, LAURENCE	HAR	045	1ST DIST
HOBERCAMP, CATHARINE	ALL	133	4TH E.D.
HOBERCAMP, JOHN	ALL	132	4TH E.D.
HOBERG, ELIZABETH	BAL	186	6TH WARD
HOBERT, THOMAS	BAL	073	2ND DIST
HOBHORST, CASPER	BAL	066	10TH WAR
HOBING, FRITZ	BAL	436	14TH WAR
HOBISON, MARK	ANN	514	HOWARD D
HOBLETZELL, JACOB	ALL	094	5TH E.D.
HOBLETZELL, JAMES	ALL	094	5TH E.D.
HOBLETZELL, MISSOURI	BAL	430	14TH WAR
HOBLEZELL, ANN E.	ALL	157	6TH E.D.
HOBLITZELL, GEORGE	ALL	253	CUMBERLA
HOBLITZELL, JOHN	ALL	231	CUMBERLA
HOBLITZELL, WILLIAM	ALL	242	CUMBERLA
HOBS, CALIB	BAL	336	1ST DIST
HOBS, GUSTAVAS	CAR	221	5TH DIST
HOBS, HENRY	CAR	101	NO TWP L
HOBS, HESTER	BAL	342	1ST DIST
HOBS, JOHN	BAL	458	1ST DIST
HOBS, RACHELL	HAR	154	3RD DIST
HOBS, THOMAS	BAL	337	1ST DIST
HOBS, TITUS J.	CAR	102	NO TWP L
HOBSINGER, FRANCIS	BAL	422	14TH WAR
HOBSON, BENJAMIN	BAL	183	6TH WARD
HOBSON, JOHN	BAL	054	9TH WARD
HOBSON, JOHN	BAL	332	13TH WAR
HOBSON, JOHN	BAL	471	14TH WAR
HOBSON, WILLIAM L.	BAL	211	11TH WAR
HOBURN, JOHN	BAL	285	17TH WAR
HOCH, JACOB	BAL	081	10TH WAR
HOCHAN, J. GEORGE	BAL	043	18TH WAR
HOCHEMER, HENRY	BAL	065	4TH WARD
HOCK, ADAM	PRI	107	PISCATAW
HOCK, CHARLOTT	WOR	313	2ND E DI
HOCK, THOMAS	CEC	025	ELKTON 3
HOCKCOTT, ANDREW	BAL	166	2ND DIST
HOCKDALE, THOMAS	BAL	328	13TH WAR
HOCKENNY, DOLLY	CEC	181	7TH E DI
HOCKENSMITH, H.J.	FRE	172	5TH E DI
HOCKENSMITH, JOHN	FRE	172	5TH E DI
HOCKENSMITH, JOHN	FRE	171	5TH E DI
HOCKENSMITH, JULIA A.	FRE	166	EMMITTSB
HOCKENSMITH, WILLIAM	FRE	173	5TH E DI
HOCKER, CHARLES	CEC	186	7TH E DI
HOCKERSMAN, JOSHUA *	CAR	315	1ST DIST
HOCKEY, GEORGE	CAR	298	1ST DIST
HOCKING, NANCY	ALL	105	5TH E.D.
HOCKING, WILLIAM	ALL	104	5TH E.D.
HOCKINS, JARRET	BAL	347	3RD WARD
HOCKSPRINGER, ISAAC	BAL	214	2ND WARD
HOCKSTER, MEYER	BAL	193	2ND WARD
HOD, BENJAMIN	ANN	513	HOWARD D
HODDEMAN, HENRY*	BAL	346	3RD WARD
HODDEN, JOHN G.	BAL	279	2ND WARD
HODDENOT, MARIA	BAL	063	2ND DIST
HODDIGIN, LIDIA	TAL	054	EASTON D
HODDINOT, ELIZABETH	BAL	064	2ND DIST
HODDLER, GEORGE	FRE	116	CREAGERS
HODDMAN, S. OWINGS	BAL	217	11TH WAR
HODDS, THOMAS	CEC	056	1ST E DI
HODGE, ALFRED	BAL	365	1ST DIST
HODGE, CHARLES	CAL	055	3RD DIST
HODGE, EDWARD	BAL	459	8TH WARD
HODGE, EDWRD	BAL	474	14TH WAR
HODGE, FRANCES	BAL	322	12TH WAR
HODGE, JAMES	BAL	236	17TH WAR
HODGE, JAOCB	ALL	180	8TH E.D.
HODGE, JOHN	BAL	366	1ST DIST
HODGE, JOHN	BAL	155	1ST WARD
HODGE, JOHN	BAL	114	1ST WARD
HODGE, JOHN	CAL	044	3RD DIST
HODGE, JOHN-BLACK	MGM	403	ROCKERLE
HODGE, JOSEPH	PRI	091	MARLBROU
HODGE, JULIA	WOR	264	BERLIN 1
HODGE, MARGARET	WOR	263	BERLIN 1
HODGE, MARGARET	MGM	378	ROCKERLE
HODGE, SAMUEL	ANN	379	4TH DIST
HODGE, SUSAN	MGM	348	BERRYS D
HODGE, THOMAS	BAL	157	1ST WARD
HODGE, WALTER	MGM	379	ROCKERLE
HODGE, WASHINGTON	MGM	315	CRACKLIN
HODGE, WILLIAM H.	MGM	338	CRACKLIN
HODGER, J.	BAL	113	1ST WARD
HODGERS, JAMES	BAL	137	18TH WAR
HODGERS, MARGARET J.	CHA	231	HILLTOP
HODGERS, THOMAS	ST	315	4TH E DI
HODGERS, THOMAS	ST	348	5TH E DI
HODGES, ABRAHAM	BAL	153	16TH WAR
HODGES, ANN	BAL	035	9TH WARD
HODGES, ARCHIBALD	ANN	344	3RD DIST
HODGES, B.B.	PRI	074	MARLBROU
HODGES, BENJAIN M. JR.	BAL	217	11TH WAR
HODGES, BENJAMIN	PRI	077	MARLBROU
HODGES, BENJAMIN	BAL	080	10TH WAR
HODGES, BENJAMIN M.	BAL	108	10TH WAR
HODGES, CHARLES	ANN	344	3RD DIST
HODGES, CHARLES	ANN	326	2ND DIST
HODGES, CHRISTINA	BAL	297	3RD WARD
HODGES, CLINTON-BLACK	CAR	087	NO TWP L
HODGES, EDMUND	BAL	115	18TH WAR
HODGES, ELIZABETH	CHA	261	MIDDLETO
HODGES, GEORGE	BAL	424	8TH WARD
HODGES, GEORGE	WAS	150	2ND DIST
HODGES, HENRIETTA	BAL	153	16TH WAR
HODGES, HENRY	BAL	299	7TH WARD
HODGES, JAMES	BAL	038	9TH WARD
HODGES, JAMES	BAL	134	11TH WAR
HODGES, JAMES W.	HAR	085	2ND DIST
HODGES, JANE	BAL	118	15TH WAR
HODGES, JILEMER	PRI	091	MARLBROU
HODGES, JOHN	PRI	077	MARLBROU
HODGES, JOHN	ANN	499	HOWARD D
HODGES, JOHN	BAL	288	17TH WAR
HODGES, JOHN T.	ANN	327	2ND DIST
HODGES, JOSEPH	PRI	100	SPALDING
HODGES, JOSEPH	WAS	150	2ND DIST
HODGES, MARGARET	BAL	299	3RD WARD
HODGES, MARGARET	ANN	367	4TH DIST
HODGES, MARY	MGM	420	MEDLEY 3
HODGES, MARY	BAL	053	4TH WARD
HODGES, MATILDA A.	MGM	420	MEDLEY 3
HODGES, RICHARD	KEN	235	2ND DIST
HODGES, ROBERT	BAL	074	10TH WAR
HODGES, S.	ANN	346	3RD DIST
HODGES, SALLIE	ANN	294	1ST DIST
HODGES, SALLY	BAL	025	9TH WARD
HODGES, SAMUEL	BAL	181	2ND DIST
HODGES, SAMUEL	WAS	150	2ND DIST
HODGES, SAMUEL	KEN	269	1ST DIST
HODGES, SARAH	BAL	102	10TH WAR
HODGES, SARAH A.	BAL	067	15TH WAR
HODGES, SARAH E.	MGM	358	BERRYS D
HODGES, SOLOMON	BAL	401	1ST DIST
HODGES, THOMAS	MGM	420	MEDLEY 3
HODGES, THOMAS	BAL	007	4TH WARD
HODGES, THOMAS H.	BAL	203	11TH WAR
HODGES, THOMAS H.	ANN	327	2ND DIST
HODGES, WESLEY	BAL	236	12TH WAR
HODGES, WILLIAM	BAL	014	1ST WARD
HODGESKIN, MEDORAH	PRI	056	AQUASCO
HODGESKIN, THOMAS	PRI	075	MARLBROU
HODGIN, JOSEPH	BAL	187	19TH WAR
HODGKIN, THEODORE	CAL	051	3RD DIST
HODGKINSON, JOHN	BAL	054	4TH WARD
HODGKINSON, JOHN	BAL	004	EASTERN
HODGKISS, ANN	BAL	075	10TH WAR
HODGSON, JAMES B.	BAL	420	8TH WARD
HODGY, J.S.	BAL	173	1ST WARD
HODINS, GEORGE	BAL	260	12TH WAR
HODKINS, CHRIS	BAL	227	12TH WAR
HODLE, MARY	ALL	231	CUMBERLA
HODNEY, JAMES R.	BAL	161	19TH WAR
HODSON, JOHN H.	DOR	455	1ST DIST
HODSON, LEVIN	DOR	466	1ST DIST
HODSON, MARGARET	BAL	058	10TH WAR
HODSON, NANCY*	DOR	383	1ST DIST
HODSON, SARAH	BAL	076	10TH WAR
HODSON, THOMAS	PRI	009	BLADENSB
HODSON, THOMAS S.	DOR	451	1ST DIST
HOE, ANNA	BAL	402	1ST DIST
HOE, JACOB	BAL	370	1ST DIST
HOE, LUCY	BAL	181	2ND DIST
HOEG, MARY A.	BAL	146	11TH WAR
HOEKENSMITH, TOBIAS	FRE	161	EMMITTSB
HOELAND, WILLIAM	BAL	227	12TH WAR
HOEN, AUGUSTAS	BAL	209	11TH WAR
HOEN, HENRY	BAL	293	7TH WARD
HOEN, WILLIAM	BAL	022	2ND DIST
HOENGE, GEORGE	BAL	188	19TH WAR
HOENIG, JOHN	BAL	075	10TH WAR
HOET, CHARLES	BAL	275	20TH WAR
HOEY, JOHN	BAL	451	8TH WARD
HOFEE, JAMES T.	TAL	080	ST MICHA
HOFERBERT, ADAM	ALL	197	CUMBERLA
HOFF, ABRAHAM	ALL	022	2ND E.D.
HOFF, ANDREW	CAR	319	1ST DIST
HOFF, ANDREW	BAL	349	13TH WAR
HOFF, ELISHA	ALL	171	7TH E.D.
HOFF, ELIZABETH	FRE	001	FREDERIC
HOFF, GEORGE	BAL	100	2ND DIST
HOFF, GEORGE	BAL	356	8TH WARD
HOFF, HENRY	FRE	414	8TH E DI
HOFF, JACOB	BAL	260	1ST DIST
HOFF, JAMES	BAL	158	2ND DIST
HOFF, JOHN	CAR	189	4TH DIST
HOFF, JOHN	WAS	017	2ND SUBD
HOFF, JOHN H.	FRE	003	FREDERIC
HOFF, JOHN L.	BAL	218	19TH WAR
HOFF, LEWIS	BAL	221	19TH WAR
HOFF, MARGARET	BAL	087	4TH WARD
HOFF, MARGARET	WAS	012	WILLIAMS
HOFF, MARGARET L.	BAL	221	19TH WAR
HOFF, RACHEL	BAL	144	2ND DIST
HOFF, SAMUEL	ALL	022	2ND E.D.
HOFF, URSELA	BAL	122	18TH WAR
HOFF, VIRGINIA	FRE	205	BUCKEYST
HOFF, WILLIAM L.	CAR	245	3RD DIST
HOFFACKER, FREDERICK	CAR	352	5TH DIST
HOFFACKER, HENRY M.	CAR	335	5TH DIST
HOFFACKER, JACOB	CAR	338	6TH DIST
HOFFACKER, JOHN	CAR	338	6TH DIST
HOFFECKER, ABRAM B.	QUE	163	2ND E DI
HOFFER, BARBARA	WAS	209	1ST DIST
HOFFER, CATHARINE	WAS	292	1ST DIST
HOFFER, ELIZABETH	WAS	301	1ST DIST
HOFFER, HENRY	WAS	301	1ST DIST
HOFFER, JACOB C.	WAS	209	1ST DIST
HOFFER, JOHN	WAS	200	1ST DIST
HOFFER, MICHAEL	WAS	297	1ST DIST

Name	County	Page	District
HOFFER, SOPHIA	WAS	085	2ND SUBD
HOFFER, SUSAN	WAS	219	1ST DIST
HOFFEY, JOSEPH	BAL	111	18TH WAR
HOFFIE, MARY	BAL	068	2ND DIST
HOFFIN, MICHAEL	BAL	105	2ND DIST
HOFFINGTON, JAMES	SOM	516	BARREN C
HOFFKEY, ADLADE	BAL	037	18TH WAR
HOFFLEIN, MARTHA	BAL	422	3RD WARD
HOFFMAN, AARON	BAL	306	20TH WAR
HOFFMAN, ABRAHAM	BAL	092	18TH WAR
HOFFMAN, ANDERSON	BAL	193	19TH WAR
HOFFMAN, ANN	BAL	237	12TH WAR
HOFFMAN, ANNA	ALL	206	CUMBERLA
HOFFMAN, AUGUSTSU	BAL	327	13TH WAR
HOFFMAN, C.	BAL	238	20TH WAR
HOFFMAN, C.	BAL	238	20TH WAR
HOFFMAN, CAROLINE	BAL	233	2ND WARD
HOFFMAN, CAROLINE	BAL	405	8TH WARD
HOFFMAN, CASPAR	FRE	079	FREDERIC
HOFFMAN, CASPER	CAR	338	6TH DIST
HOFFMAN, CATHARINE	FRE	214	BUCKEYST
HOFFMAN, CATHARINE	FRE	357	CATOCTIN
HOFFMAN, CATHARINE	WAS	257	1ST DIST
HOFFMAN, CHARLES	FRE	399	JEFFERSO
HOFFMAN, CHARLES	BAL	004	18TH WAR
HOFFMAN, CHARLES	BAL	217	17TH WAR
HOFFMAN, CHARLES	BAL	439	14TH WAR
HOFFMAN, CHARLES	BAL	427	14TH WAR
HOFFMAN, CHARLES	FRE	20	5TH E DI
HOFFMAN, CHARLES	BAL	226	12TH WAR
HOFFMAN, CHARLES	BAL	004	EASTERN
HOFFMAN, CHARLES	BAL	245	1ST DIST
HOFFMAN, CHARLES F.	BAL	315	20TH WAR
HOFFMAN, CHRISTIAN	BAL	230	2ND WARD
HOFFMAN, CHRISTIAN	WAS	273	RIDGEVIL
HOFFMAN, CHRISTOPHER	BAL	407	8TH WARD
HOFFMAN, CONRAD	BAL	008	15TH WAR
HOFFMAN, DANIEL P.	BAL	435	14TH WAR
HOFFMAN, DAVID	ALL	025	2ND E.D.
HOFFMAN, DAVID W.	BAL	160	16TH WAR
HOFFMAN, DEETS	BAL	416	8TH WARD
HOFFMAN, ED.	BAL	307	20TH WAR
HOFFMAN, ELENOR	FRE	398	JEFFERSO
HOFFMAN, ELISABETH	ALL	024	3RD E.D.
HOFFMAN, ELIZA	BAL	265	7TH WARD
HOFFMAN, ELIZA L.	BAL	160	16TH WAR
HOFFMAN, ELIZABETH	BAL	412	1ST DIST
HOFFMAN, ELIZABETH	BAL	204	6TH DIST
HOFFMAN, ELIZABETH	BAL	155	5TH WARD
HOFFMAN, ELIZABETH	FRE	018	FREDERIC
HOFFMAN, ELIZABETH	BAL	088	18TH WAR
HOFFMAN, ELIZABETH	FRE	321	MIDDLETO
HOFFMAN, ELIZABETH	WAS	030	2ND SUBD
HOFFMAN, ELIZABETH A.	BAL	088	18TH WAR
HOFFMAN, EMANUEL	BAL	445	8TH WARD
HOFFMAN, EMELINE	CAR	347	6TH DIST
HOFFMAN, EMILY	BAL	282	12TH WAR
HOFFMAN, EPHRAIM	BAL	306	20TH WAR
HOFFMAN, EZRA	FRE	009	FREDERIC
HOFFMAN, F.	BAL	211	2ND WARD
HOFFMAN, FRANCIS	CAR	180	8TH DIST
HOFFMAN, FREDERICK	BAL	214	19TH WAR
HOFFMAN, FREDERICK B.	BAL	122	11TH WAR
HOFFMAN, GEORGE	BAL	455	14TH WAR
HOFFMAN, GEORGE	BAL	383	13TH WAR
HOFFMAN, GEORGE	FRE	110	CREAGERS
HOFFMAN, GEORGE	BAL	161	1ST WARD
HOFFMAN, GEORGE	BAL	010	15TH WAR
HOFFMAN, GEORGE	ALL	049	10TH E.D
HOFFMAN, GEORGE	WAS	043	2ND SUBD
HOFFMAN, GEORGE	WAS	220	1ST DIST
HOFFMAN, GEORGE F.	FRE	385	PETERSVI
HOFFMAN, GEORGE L.	BAL	176	16TH WAR
HOFFMAN, GEORGE M.	BAL	214	19TH WAR
HOFFMAN, GOERGE B.	BAL	216	11TH WAR
HOFFMAN, GOTTEIB	BAL	233	2ND WARD
HOFFMAN, HENRIETTA	BAL	155	11TH WAR
HOFFMAN, HENRY	BAL	040	4TH WARD
HOFFMAN, HENRY	BAL	211	19TH WAR
HOFFMAN, HENRY	FRE	375	CATOCTIN
HOFFMAN, HENRY	BAL	217	17TH WAR
HOFFMAN, HENRY	CAR	283	7TH DIST
HOFFMAN, HENRY	CAR	382	2ND DIST
HOFFMAN, HENRY	ALL	235	CUMBERLA
HOFFMAN, HENRY	WAS	261	1ST DIST
HOFFMAN, HY B.	BAL	204	6TH DIST
HOFFMAN, HY H.	BAL	208	6TH DIST
HOFFMAN, IGNATUS	BAL	146	11TH WAR
HOFFMAN, J.	BAL	216	19TH WAR
HOFFMAN, J. LATIMER	BAL	111	10TH WAR
HOFFMAN, JACOB	FRE	074	FREDERIC
HOFFMAN, JACOB	WAS	260	1ST DIST
HOFFMAN, JACOB	WAS	271	1ST DIST
HOFFMAN, JAMES	BAL	255	2ND WARD
HOFFMAN, JAMES A.	FRE	398	JEFFERSO
HOFFMAN, JAOCB	FRE	025	FREDERIC
HOFFMAN, JAOCB	FRE	042	FREDERIC
HOFFMAN, JOHANNA	BAL	109	1ST WARD
HOFFMAN, JOHN	BAL	058	1ST WARD
HOFFMAN, JOHN	BAL	252	2ND WARD
HOFFMAN, JOHN	BAL	379	8TH WARD
HOFFMAN, JOHN	BAL	135	2ND DIST
HOFFMAN, JOHN	ALL	096	5TH E.D.
HOFFMAN, JOHN	BAL	426	8TH WARD
HOFFMAN, JOHN	BAL	050	15TH WAR
HOFFMAN, JOHN	BAL	029	15TH WAR
HOFFMAN, JOHN	BAL	181	6TH WARD
HOFFMAN, JOHN	FRE	079	FREDERIC
HOFFMAN, JOHN	BAL	025	4TH WARD
HOFFMAN, JOHN	BAL	012	4TH WARD
HOFFMAN, JOHN	BAL	415	3RD WARD
HOFFMAN, JOHN	CAR	362	9TH DIST
HOFFMAN, JOHN	BAL	073	18TH WAR
HOFFMAN, JOHN	BAL	253	17TH WAR
HOFFMAN, JOHN	KEN	245	2ND DIST
HOFFMAN, JOHN	BAL	154	19TH WAR
HOFFMAN, JOHN	WAS	273	RIDGEVIL
HOFFMAN, JOHN	WAS	074	2ND SUBD
HOFFMAN, JOHN	WAS	190	1ST DIST
HOFFMAN, JOHN B.	BAL	332	13TH WAR
HOFFMAN, JOHN E.	WAS	130	HAGERSTO
HOFFMAN, JOHN F.	BAL	150	16TH WAR
HOFFMAN, JOHN H.	FRE	110	CREAGERS
HOFFMAN, JOHN M.	BAL	176	16TH WAR
HOFFMAN, JOHN S.	ALL	235	CUMBERLA
HOFFMAN, JOHN W.	FRE	349	MIDDLETO
HOFFMAN, JOSEPH	FRE	357	CATOCTIN
HOFFMAN, JOSEPH H.	BAL	444	14TH WAR
HOFFMAN, JULIAN	BAL	057	4TH WARD
HOFFMAN, JY	FRE	077	FREDERIC
HOFFMAN, LANHART	BAL	444	14TH WAR
HOFFMAN, LEWIS	BAL	208	19TH WAR
HOFFMAN, M.C.	WAS	010	WILLIAMS
HOFFMAN, MARGARET	BAL	425	14TH WAR
HOFFMAN, MARTIN	FRE	358	CATOCTIN
HOFFMAN, MARY	FRE	078	FREDERIC
HOFFMAN, MARY	BAL	174	16TH WAR
HOFFMAN, MARY	BAL	138	5TH WARD
HOFFMAN, MARY A.	BAL	442	8TH WARD
HOFFMAN, MARY D.	BAL	153	11TH WAR
HOFFMAN, MARY E.	BAL	435	14TH WAR
HOFFMAN, MATHIAS	WAS	299	1ST DIST
HOFFMAN, MATHIAS	WAS	273	RIDGEVIL
HOFFMAN, MICHAEL	WAS	292	1ST DIST
HOFFMAN, MICHAEL	WAS	209	1ST DIST
HOFFMAN, MICHAEL	FRE	347	MIDDLETO
HOFFMAN, MICHAEL	CAR	328	MANCHEST
HOFFMAN, MICHAEL	BAL	285	2ND WARD
HOFFMAN, MICHAEL	BAL	153	16TH WAR
HOFFMAN, MICHEAL	BAL	137	18TH WAR
HOFFMAN, MILLA	BAL	166	11TH WAR
HOFFMAN, OLLIVER H.	FRE	214	BUCKEYST
HOFFMAN, P.B.	WAS	154	HAGERSTO
HOFFMAN, PETER	WAS	238	CAVETOWN
HOFFMAN, PETER	BAL	126	11TH WAR
HOFFMAN, PETER B.	BAL	216	6TH DIST
HOFFMAN, PRUDENCE	FRE	324	MIDDLETO
HOFFMAN, RANDOLPH	WAS	220	1ST DIST
HOFFMAN, ROBERT	FRE	393	PETERSVI
HOFFMAN, ROSETTA	BAL	154	16TH WAR
HOFFMAN, SAMUEL	BAL	248	2ND WARD
HOFFMAN, SAMUEL	FRE	374	CATOCTIN
HOFFMAN, SAMUEL	CAR	398	2ND DIST
HOFFMAN, SAMUEL	FRE	292	WOODSBOR
HOFFMAN, SAMUEL	BAL	153	11TH WAR
HOFFMAN, SARAH R.	BAL	301	7TH WARD
HOFFMAN, SEVILLA	WAS	272	RIDGEVIL
HOFFMAN, SOPHIA	BAL	273	12TH WAR
HOFFMAN, SUSAN	WAS	074	2ND SUBD
HOFFMAN, T.	BAL	163	1ST WARD
HOFFMAN, THOMAS	BAL	074	15TH WAR
HOFFMAN, THOMAS C.	BAL	075	15TH WAR
HOFFMAN, TILGHMAN	BAL	028	18TH WAR
HOFFMAN, VALENTINE	BAL	231	17TH WAR
HOFFMAN, VALENTINE	BAL	081	10TH WAR
HOFFMAN, WELBERS*	BAL	327	3RD WARD
HOFFMAN, WILLAIM	BAL	378	13TH WAR
HOFFMAN, WILLAIM D.	BAL	208	6TH DIST
HOFFMAN, WILLIAM	BAL	321	7TH WARD
HOFFMAN, WILLIAM	BAL	054	15TH WAR
HOFFMAN, WILLIAM	CAR	323	MANCHEST
HOFFMAN, WILLIAM	BAL	140	19TH WAR
HOFFMAN, WILLIAM	FRE	071	FREDERIC
HOFFMAN, WILLIAM G.	FRE	267	NEW MARK
HOFFMAN, WILLIAM H.	BAL	204	6TH DIST
HOFFMAN, WILLIAM J.	BAL	204	6TH DIST
HOFFMAN, WILLIAM P.	BAL	345	13TH WAR
HOFFMAN, WINDER	BAL	028	18TH WAR
HOFFMAN, D.L.	ALL	238	CUMBERLA
HOFFMAN, JOHN	ALL	235	CUMBERLA
HOFFMER, LEONARD	ALL	205	CUMBERLA
HOFFNAGLE, SEBASTIAN	BAL	267	2ND WARD
HOFFNAGLE, WILLIAM	BAL	090	18TH WAR
HOFFNER, JAMES SMITH	ALL	207	CUMBERLA
HOFFNER, JOHN	FRE	112	CREAGERS
HOFFNER, JOSEPH	ALL	207	CUMBERLA
HOFFOR, JACOB	WAS	191	1ST DIST
HOFFUTE, WILLIAM *	MGM	385	ROCKERLE
HOFMAN, GEORGE	BAL	096	10TH WAR
HOFMAN, JACOB	BAL	276	2ND WARD
HOFMAN, JOHNJ.	ALL	219	CUMBERLA
HOFMAN, WILLIAM F.	CEC	137	6TH E DI
HOFMASTER, ELIZA	WAS	088	2ND SUBD
HOFMASTER, GEORGE	WAS	070	2ND SUBD
HOFMASTER, JOHN	WAS	070	2ND SUBD
HOFMASTER, JOHN	WAS	088	2ND SUBD
HOFMEISTER, AUGUST	BAL	229	6TH WARD
HOFMEISTER, GEORGE	BAL	199	6TH WARD
HOFMEISTER, HENRY	BAL	236	6TH WARD
HOFMER, VALENTINE	BAL	070	18TH WAR
HOFNER, ADAM	BAL	321	7TH WARD
HOFOCKER, HY	BAL	202	6TH DIST
HOFOCKER, JOHN	BAL	203	6TH DIST
HOFOCKER, SAMUEL	BAL	204	6TH DIST
HOFSNIDER, GEORGE	BAL	010	9TH WARD
HOFSTATER, JOSEPH	BAL	069	2ND DIST
HOFUS, JOHN	CAR	307	1ST DIST
HOGAN, DANIEL	BAL	316	20TH WAR
HOGAN, EDWARD	BAL	144	5TH WARD
HOGAN, ELIZABETYH	BAL	472	14TH WAR
HOGAN, ELLEN R.	ALL	102	5TH E.D.
HOGAN, FRANCIS	BAL	191	2ND WARD
HOGAN, JAMES	BAL	177	2ND WARD
HOGAN, JAMES	BAL	244	20TH WAR
HOGAN, JOHN	BAL	316	20TH WAR
HOGAN, JOHN	BAL	113	2ND DIST
HOGAN, JOHN	BAL	006	EASTERN
HOGAN, JOSEPH	BAL	214	11TH WAR
HOGAN, MARGARET	BAL	382	8TH WARD
HOGAN, MARY	BAL	022	9TH WARD
HOGAN, MARY	BAL	418	3RD WARD
HOGAN, MARY	BAL	474	14TH WAR
HOGAN, MATTHEW	BAL	239	6TH WARD
HOGAN, MICHAEL	BAL	128	2ND DIST
HOGAN, MICHAEL	ALL	152	6TH E.D.
HOGAN, MICHAEL	FRE	067	FREDERIC
HOGAN, PATRICK	ALL	056	10TH E.D
HOGAN, PATRICK	ALL	084	5TH E.D.
HOGAN, PATRICK	BAL	173	2ND DIST
HOGAN, SILVEY	BAL	418	3RD WARD
HOGAN, STEPHEN	BAL	357	1ST DIST
HOGAN, THOMAS	ALL	101	5TH E.D.
HOGAN, THOMAS	BAL	390	3RD WARD
HOGAN, WILLIAM	BAL	240	1ST DIST
HOGAN, MICHAEL	BAL	131	1ST WARD
HOGANDY, ADAM	MGM	405	ROCKERLE
HOGANS, MARY A.	BAL	156	11TH WAR
HOGART, JAMES	PRI	008	BLADENSB
HOGCH, JAMES	BAL	391	14TH WAR
HOGE, JOHN H.	BAL	370	1ST DIST
HOGE, LEVY	BAL	106	18TH WAR
HOGE, ROSE	ALL	078	5TH E.D.
HOGENDORF, ELIAS	BAL	070	15TH WAR
HOGENS, MARY	CEC	041	CHESAPEA
HOGEWELL, ELIZABETH	BAL	195	11TH WAR
HOGG, CASPAR	BAL	170	2ND DIST
HOGG, CHARLES	BAL	071	10TH WAR
HOGG, HORACE	BAL	124	1ST WARD
HOGG, JAMES	BAL	087	4TH WARD
HOGG, JAMES H.	BAL	395	14TH WAR
HOGG, JAMES H.	BAL	257	12TH WAR
HOGG, JOHN	BAL	245	12TH WAR
HOGG, JOHN	BAL	123	5TH WARD
HOGG, JOHN	BAL	294	20TH WAR
HOGG, JOHN R.	CEC	009	ELKTON 3
HOGG, JOHN R.	CEC	009	ELKTON 3
HOGG, JOHN W.	BAL	098	10TH WAR
HOGG, LEWIS	CEC	171	6TH E DI
HOGG, M.	BAL	253	20TH WAR
HOGG, MARTHA	BAL	124	11TH WAR
HOGG, MARY	CEC	004	ELKTON 3
HOGG, RACHEL	BAL	365	13TH WAR
HOGG, ROBERT E.	BAL	318	20TH WAR
HOGG, SAMUEL	CEC	197	7TH E DI
HOGG, SAMUEL R.	FRE	036	FREDERIC
HOGG, THOMAS R.	ANN	508	HOWARD D
HOGG, W.	BAL	139	5TH WARD
HOGG, WILLIAM	BAL	218	6TH DIST
HOGG, WILLIAM H.	BAL	096	18TH WAR
HOGGINS, MARY-MULATTO	FRE	011	FREDERIC
HOGLE, NICHOLAS	ALL	230	CUMBERLA
HOGMAN, SARAH M.	SOM	400	BRINKLEY
HOGMIRE, RICHARD	BAL	303	20TH WAR
HOGROOK, ADAM	ALL	168	6TH E.D.
HOHEAN, TIMOTHY	BAL	216	11TH WAR
HOHMAN, JOHN	BAL	288	20TH WAR
HOHN, BERNARD	BAL	019	4TH WARD
HOHN, JOHN	BAL	154	19TH WAR
HOHN, LEVI	BAL	370	3RD WARD
HOHN, MARGARET	BAL	153	16TH WAR
HOHN, MEANE	BAL	156	19TH WAR
HOHNE, JACOB	BAL	234	17TH WAR
HOIL, JOHN	HAR	074	1ST DIST
HOISEE, SARAH	BAL	251	17TH WAR
HOKAMP, JOSEPH	BAL	052	18TH WAR
HOKE, GEORGE	BAL	319	12TH WAR
HOKE, JACOB	FRE	174	5TH E DI
HOKE, JACOB	HAR	160	3RD DIST
HOKE, MICHAEL	FRE	174	5TH E DI
HOLADY, ENOCH-BLACK	CAR	092	NO TWP L
HOLADY, JAMES-BLACK	CAR	078	NO TWP L
HOLAIN, JOHN	ALL	056	10TH E.D
HOLAND, CAROLINE	MGM	349	BERRYS D
HOLAND, NATHAN	MGM	420	MEDLEY 3
HOLAWAY, CHARLES C.	HAR	184	3RD DIST
HOLAWAY, WILLIAM	HAR	182	3RD DIST
HOLBEIM, MARTIN	BAL	011	9TH WARD
HOLBERGER, CHARLES	BAL	130	11TH WAR
HOLBERGER, JACOB	WAS	279	LEITERSB
HOLBERT, CATHARINE	WAS	138	HAGERSTO
HOLBERT, DANIEL	WAS	139	2ND DIST
HOLBERT, JAMES	WAS	121	2ND DIST
HOLBERT, JOHN	WAS	137	2ND DIST
HOLBERT, MICHAL	WAS	139	2ND DIST
HOLBERT, ROBERT	BAL	451	14TH WAR
HOLBINE, ADAM	BAL	022	4TH WARD
HOLBORN, CAROLINE	BAL	422	3RD WARD
HOLBOURN, J.W.	BAL	173	1ST WARD
HOLBRANER, THOMAS M. *	FRE	285	WOODSBOR
HOLBRENER, LYDIA	WAS	236	CAVETOWN
HOLBRENNER, REBECCA	WAS	274	RIDGEVIL
HOLBROOK, ANN J.	SOM	441	DAMES QU
HOLBROOK, JACOB	BAL	294	20TH WAR
HOLBROOK, JAMES	BAL	339	13TH WAR
HOLBROOK, JANE L.	BAL	312	3RD WARD
HOLBROOK, JOSHUA	BAL	075	4TH WARD
HOLBROOK, MARGARETT E.	BAL	369	8TH WARD
HOLBROOK, MARY J.	BAL	395	8TH WARD
HOLBROOK, MATILDA	SOM	446	DAMES QU
HOLBROOK, SAMUEL G.	SOM	440	DAMES QU
HOLBROOK, SETH	BAL	330	1ST DIST
HOLBROOK, THOMAS	BAL	045	15TH WAR
HOLBROOK, WILLIAM	CAR	107	NO TWP L
HOLBROOK, CATHERINE H.	FRE	238	NEW MARK
HOLBROOKE, MARGARET	BAL	464	14TH WAR
HOLBROOKS, ANN L.	BAL	381	3RD WARD
HOLBROOKS, ELIZA	BAL	083	4TH WARD
HOLBROOKS, FRANCES	BAL	362	3RD WARD
HOLBROOKS, MARY	BAL	055	4TH WARD
HOLBROT, WILLIAM	BAL	090	2ND DIST
HOLBRUME, JOHN H.	FRE	304	WOODSBOR
HOLBRUMER, GEORGE	FRE	294	WOODSBOR
HOLBRUNNER, ADAM	FRE	285	WOODSBOR
HOLBRUNNER, HENRY	FRE	286	WOODSBOR
HOLBRUNNER, JOHN	FRE	302	WOODSBOR
HOLBS, BRICE H.	BAL	081	18TH WAR
HOLBS, ELIZABETH	ANN	495	HOWARD D
HOLD, JOSEPH	BAL	023	1ST WARD
HOLDAVER, JOHN	BAL	202	2ND WARD
HOLDEFER, HENRY	BAL	199	2ND WARD
HOLDEN, ANN	BAL	360	1ST DIST
HOLDEN, ENOCH P.	BAL	030	4TH WARD
HOLDEN, J.	BAL	135	1ST WARD
HOLDEN, J. F.	BAL	332	1ST DIST
HOLDEN, J. S.	BAL	286	2ND WARD
HOLDEN, JACOB	CEC	118	4TH E DI
HOLDEN, JAMES	BAL	121	1ST WARD
HOLDEN, JAMES	BAL	075	10TH WAR
HOLDEN, JOSEPH	CAR	093	NO TWP L
HOLDEN, JOSEPH K.	BAL	216	19TH WAR
HOLDEN, MARY	BAL	265	2ND WARD
HOLDEN, PATRICK	BAL	222	6TH WARD
HOLDEN, PHILLIS	BAL	115	15TH WAR
HOLDER, ELIZABETH	SOM	524	BARREN C
HOLDER, HIRAM	BAL	217	17TH WAR
HOLDER, WILLIAM	SOM	508	BARREN C
HOLDER, WILLIAM	WOR	203	4TH E DI
HOLDER, ZEBIDEE	WOR	234	6TH E DI
HOLDERG, MAJOR-BLACK	WOR	335	1ST E DI
HOLDERMAN, PETER	ALL	216	CUMBERLA
HOLDERS, ANNA	BAL	015	18TH WAR
HOLDET, JOHN M.	BAL	159	19TH WAR
HOLDIN, JAMES M.	BAL	187	19TH WAR
HOLDING, ELIZABETH	QUE	149	1ST E DI
HOLDING, ELIZABETH	QUE	173	2ND E DI
HOLDING, JAMES	QUE	163	2ND E DI
HOLDING, JOHN	QUE	162	2ND E DI
HOLDING, JOHN F.	QUE	162	2ND E DI
HOLDING, RICHARD T.	QUE	133	1ST E DI
HOLDING, WILLIAM	BAL	160	1ST WARD
HOLDTERSA, WILLIAM *	BAL	141	2ND DIST
HOLEAN, CHARLOTTE M.	DOR	433	1ST DIST
HOLEAN, HARRY	DOR	432	1ST DIST
HOLEAN, MARGARET	BAL	332	13TH WAR
HOLEAN, SAMUEL*	DOR	444	1ST DIST
HOLEAN, WILLIAM*	DOR	453	1ST DIST
HOLEBERGER, SAMUEL	WAS	013	WILLIAMS
HOLEBROOKS, JACOB	BAL	284	7TH WARD
HOLEBROOKS, PATRICK M.	BAL	370	8TH WARD
HOLEIS, DELIA*	DOR	433	1ST DIST

Name	County	Page	District
HOLENBAUGH, JOHN	CAR	179	8TH DIST
HOLENBERGER, REBECCA	CAR	407	2ND DIST
HOLENSHADE, JOHN	HAR	019	1ST DIST
HOLENSWORTH, JESSE	CAR	219	5TH DIST
HOLER, CHARLES	BAL	303	12TH WAR
HOLER, CONRAD	BAL	105	2ND DIST
HOLER, DAVID	CAR	303	1ST DIST
HOLETER, GEORGE B.	FRE	402	JEFFERSO
HOLEY, THOMAS M.	FRE	110	CREAGERS
HOLEY, WILLIAM	ALL	171	7TH E.D.
HOLF, SALLY	BAL	206	6TH DIST
HOLFIELD, JOSEPH	BAL	272	12TH WAR
HOLIDAY, EDWARD	BAL	423	3RD WARD
HOLIDAY, ELISHA	DOR	455	1ST DIST
HOLIDAY, GEORGE	WAS	055	2ND SUBD
HOLIDAY, H.	WAS	021	2ND SUBD
HOLIDAY, MARY	DOR	384	1ST DIST
HOLIDAY, R.T.	WAS	025	2ND SUBD
HOLIDAY, SUSAN MARTHA	BAL	406	14TH WAR
HOLIDAY, VICTORIA	BAL	184	19TH WAR
HOLIDEN, MICHAEL	BAL	032	18TH WAR
HOLINGSWORTH, MARY	CAR	188	4TH DIST
HOLIS, AMOS	HAR	194	3RD DIST
HOLIWICK, WILLIAM	BAL	314	12TH WAR
HOLL, CATHARIN	CAR	368	9TH DIST
HOLL, MARGARET	ST	348	5TH E DI
HOLLABERGER, JOHN	WAS	228	1ST DIST
HOLLACAY, ELIZABETH	BAL	009	EASTERN
HOLLADAY, JESSE	BAL	097	5TH WARD
HOLLACAY, JOHN	HAR	177	3RD DIST
HOLLADAY, RICHARD	CEC	045	1ST E DI
HOLLADAY, RICHARD	TAL	022	EASTON D
HOLLADAY, THOMAS R.	TAL	003	EASTON D
HOLLADY, RICHARD	CEC	003	ELKTON 3
HOLLAHOCK, JOHN	BAL	321	1ST DIST
HOLLAM, SOLOMON	BAL	121	1ST WARD
HOLLAN, JESE*	DOR	427	1ST DIST
HOLLAN, THOMAS*	DOR	431	1ST DIST
HOLLAND, ALBERT	BAL	273	12TH WAR
HOLLAND, ALECK	ANN	302	1ST DIST
HOLLAND, ALEX	ALL	261	CUMBERLA
HOLLAND, ALLICE	WOR	274	BERLIN 1
HOLLAND, ANN	BAL	097	2ND DIST
HOLLAND, ANN	ANN	453	HOWARD D
HOLLAND, ANN	ANN	268	ANNAPOLI
HOLLAND, ANN	BAL	424	8TH WARD
HOLLAND, ANNA	ANN	496	HOWARD D
HOLLAND, ARAMINTA	CEC	017	ELKTON 3
HOLLAND, BENJAMIN	HAR	085	2ND DIST
HOLLAND, BENJAMIN	WOR	273	BERLIN 1
HOLLAND, BERNARD	BAL	044	9TH WARD
HOLLAND, CAROLINE	ANN	511	HOWARD D
HOLLAND, CAROLINE	FRE	065	FREDERIC
HOLLAND, CASANDRA	FRE	414	8TH E DI
HOLLAND, CATHARINE	HAR	039	1ST DIST
HOLLAND, CATHERINE	BAL	349	3RD WARD
HOLLAND, CECELIA	BAL	205	11TH WAR
HOLLAND, CHARLES	MGM	332	CRACKLIN
HOLLAND, CHARLES	BAL	355	1ST DIST
HOLLAND, CHARLES	BAL	078	2ND DIST
HOLLAND, CLARRISSA	ANN	455	HOWARD D
HOLLAND, DANIEL	PRI	092	MARLBROU
HOLLAND, DARKY-BLACK	FRE	434	8TH E DI
HOLLAND, DAVY	CAL	025	2ND DIST
HOLLAND, DENIS	BAL	350	1ST DIST
HOLLAND, DENNIS	BAL	062	2ND DIST
HOLLAND, DNAIEL	ANN	417	HOWARD D
HOLLAND, EDWARD	CEC	080	NORTHEAS
HOLLAND, EDWARD	WOR	257	1ST CENS
HOLLAND, EDWARD	MGM	441	CLARKSTR
HOLLAND, EDWIN S.	ANN	344	3RD DIST
HOLLAND, ELIAS	MGM	334	CRACKLIN
HOLLAND, ELIZA	BAL	348	13TH WAR
HOLLAND, ELIZABETH	BAL	084	1ST WARD
HOLLAND, ELIZABETH	ANN	291	ANNAPOLI
HOLLAND, ELIZABETH	WOR	265	BERLIN 1
HOLLAND, ELLEN	BAL	075	10TH WAR
HOLLAND, ELNORA	BAL	031	18TH WAR
HOLLAND, EMMA	MGM	374	ROCKERLE
HOLLAND, ENOCH	MGM	430	CLARKSTR
HOLLAND, EPHEN	HAR	194	3RD DIST
HOLLAND, ESTHER	WOR	183	6TH E DI
HOLLAND, ESWIN	CAR	198	4TH DIST
HOLLAND, FANNY	TAL	109	ST MICHA
HOLLAND, FRANCIS	BAL	218	17TH WAR
HOLLAND, FREDERICK	CEC	073	5TH E DI
HOLLAND, GEORGE	CAL	055	3RD DIST
HOLLAND, GEORGE	SOM	394	BRINKLEY
HOLLAND, GEORGE	BAL	439	8TH WARD
HOLLAND, GEORGE A.	BAL	301	7TH WARD
HOLLAND, GEORGE E.	SOM	366	BRINKLEY
HOLLAND, GEORGE-BLACK	CAR	169	NO TWP L
HOLLAND, GEORGIANA	ANN	457	HOWARD D
HOLLAND, GRAFTON	MGM	332	CRACKLIN
HOLLAND, H.L.	ANN	266	ANNAPOLI
HOLLAND, HANNA *	WOR	305	2ND E DI
HOLLAND, HARRIET	CAL	059	3RD DIST
HOLLAND, HARRIET J.	ANN	460	HOWARD D
HOLLAND, HENRIETTA	BAL	384	3RD WARD
HOLLAND, HENRY	BAL	216	17TH WAR
HOLLAND, HESTER	BAL	163	16TH WAR
HOLLAND, HESTER A.	SOM	358	BRINKLEY
HOLLAND, HILLEARY	CAL	029	2ND DIST
HOLLAND, ISAAC	MGM	366	BERRYS D
HOLLAND, ISAAC	SOM	435	PRINCESS
HOLLAND, ISAAC	WOR	294	9TH E DI
HOLLAND, ISAAC	BAL	097	2ND DIST
HOLLAND, ISAAC	ANN	474	HOWARD D
HOLLAND, ISAAC	BAL	127	2ND DIST
HOLLAND, ISAAC-BLACK	WOR	323	1ST E DI
HOLLAND, ISAIAH	BAL	452	14TH WAR
HOLLAND, JACOB	CEC	089	4TH E DI
HOLLAND, JAMES	HAR	109	2ND DIST
HOLLAND, JAMES	HAR	086	2ND DIST
HOLLAND, JAMES	CEC	019	ELKTON 3
HOLLAND, JAMES	CEC	026	ELKTON 3
HOLLAND, JAMES	WOR	310	2ND E DI
HOLLAND, JAMES	WOR	316	2ND E DI
HOLLAND, JAMES	WOR	257	1ST CENS
HOLLAND, JAMES	TAL	106	ST MICHA
HOLLAND, JAMES	BAL	127	2ND DIST
HOLLAND, JAMES	BAL	038	9TH WARD
HOLLAND, JAMES D.	CEC	153	PORT DEP
HOLLAND, JAMES H.	WOR	320	1ST E DI
HOLLAND, JAMES W.	WOR	286	BERLIN 1
HOLLAND, JAMES #.	ANN	268	ANNAPOLI
HOLLAND, JANE	WOR	257	1ST CENS
HOLLAND, JESSE	WOR	256	1ST CENS
HOLLAND, JESSE	WOR	287	BERLIN 1
HOLLAND, JESSE	BAL	245	17TH WAR
HOLLAND, JOHANAH	BAL	439	8TH WARD
HOLLAND, JOHN	BAL	173	6TH WARD
HOLLAND, JOHN	BAL	117	2ND DIST
HOLLAND, JOHN	ANN	485	HOWARD D
HOLLAND, JOHN	ANN	458	HOWARD D
HOLLAND, JOHN	BAL	271	1ST DIST
HOLLAND, JOHN	CEC	125	5TH E DI
HOLLAND, JOHN	CAR	164	NO TWP L
HOLLAND, JOHN	CAL	045	3RD DIST
HOLLAND, JOHN	WOR	292	9TH E DI
HOLLAND, JOHN	WOR	310	2ND E DI
HOLLAND, JOHN	WOR	323	1ST E DI
HOLLAND, JOHN	WOR	324	1ST E DI
HOLLAND, JOHN A.	HAR	091	2ND DIST
HOLLAND, JOHN C.	BAL	071	10TH WAR
HOLLAND, JOHN G.	ANN	434	HOWARD D
HOLLAND, JOHN G.	BAL	219	6TH WARD
HOLLAND, JOHN H.	SOM	367	BRINKLEY
HOLLAND, JOHN R.	BAL	191	11TH WAR
HOLLAND, JOHN S.	FRE	227	BUCKEYST
HOLLAND, JOHN W.	BAL	119	2ND DIST
HOLLAND, JOHN-BLACK	CAR	105	NO TWP L
HOLLAND, JOHN-BLACK	CAR	128	NO TWP L
HOLLAND, JOSEPH	BAL	123	1ST WARD
HOLLAND, JOSHUA	BAL	044	18TH WAR
HOLLAND, JOSHUA	WOR	308	2ND E DI
HOLLAND, JOSHUA	WOR	308	2ND E DI
HOLLAND, JOSHUA E.	WOR	186	7TH E DI
HOLLAND, L. O.	BAL	157	1ST WARD
HOLLAND, LEAH-BLACK	WOR	325	1ST E DI
HOLLAND, LEVIN	WOR	296	9TH E DI
HOLLAND, LEVIN-BLACK	WOR	323	1ST E DI
HOLLAND, LOUISA	HAR	090	2ND DIST
HOLLAND, LYDIA	BAL	093	10TH WAR
HOLLAND, MARGARET	WOR	324	1ST E DI
HOLLAND, MARGARET A.	BAL	352	7TH WARD
HOLLAND, MARIA	BAL	055	15TH WAR
HOLLAND, MARINDA	BAL	328	7TH WARD
HOLLAND, MARTHA	BAL	116	2ND DIST
HOLLAND, MARTHA	MGM	368	BERRYS D
HOLLAND, MARTHA	BAL	317	20TH WAR
HOLLAND, MARY	BAL	317	20TH WAR
HOLLAND, MARY	FRE	247	NEW MARK
HOLLAND, MARY	ALL	234	CUMBERLA
HOLLAND, MARY	BAL	353	7TH WARD
HOLLAND, MARY	SOM	366	BRINKLEY
HOLLAND, MARY	WAS	154	HAGERSTO
HOLLAND, MARY A.	SOM	365	BRINKLEY
HOLLAND, MARY E.	HAR	086	2ND DIST
HOLLAND, MARY M.	WOR	281	BERLIN 1
HOLLAND, MATHEW	BAL	280	1ST DIST
HOLLAND, MATILDA	MGM	376	ROCKERLE
HOLLAND, MEDFIELD	BAL	368	3RD WARD
HOLLAND, MOSES	CAR	184	8TH DIST
HOLLAND, MOSES-BLACK	WOR	334	1ST E DI
HOLLAND, NANCY	SOM	366	BRINKLEY
HOLLAND, NANCY	HAR	086	2ND DIST
HOLLAND, NATHAN	MGM	384	ROCKERLE
HOLLAND, NELLY	QUE	205	3RD E DI
HOLLAND, OLIVER	WOR	179	6TH E DI
HOLLAND, P.	ANN	344	3RD DIST
HOLLAND, PATRICK	ALL	057	10TH E.D
HOLLAND, PERRY	TAL	108	ST MICHA
HOLLAND, POLLY	QUE	193	3RD E DI
HOLLAND, RACHAEL	SOM	366	BRINKLEY
HOLLAND, REBECCA	QUE	193	3RD E DI
HOLLAND, REBECCA	BAL	115	2ND DIST
HOLLAND, RICHARD	WOR	345	1ST E DI
HOLLAND, RICHARD W.	FRE	228	BUCKEYST
HOLLAND, RICHARD-BLACK	WOR	324	1ST E DI
HOLLAND, ROBERT	ANN	347	3RD DIST
HOLLAND, ROBERT	BAL	009	EASTERN
HOLLAND, ROBERT	BAL	440	8TH WARD
HOLLAND, ROBERT W.	HAR	144	2ND DIST
HOLLAND, S.	BAL	116	1ST WARD
HOLLAND, S.	BAL	136	1ST WARD
HOLLAND, S.C.	BAL	166	1ST WARD
HOLLAND, SAMUEL	BAL	285	1ST DIST
HOLLAND, SAMUEL	CEC	089	4TH E DI
HOLLAND, SAMUEL	CEC	137	6TH E DI
HOLLAND, SAMUEL-MULATTO	FRE	225	BUCKEYST
HOLLAND, SARAH	MGM	330	CRACKLIN
HOLLAND, SARAH	BAL	197	6TH WARD
HOLLAND, SARAH	ANN	485	HOWARD D
HOLLAND, SARAH	WOR	270	BERLIN 1
HOLLAND, SARAH E.	MGM	335	CRACKLIN
HOLLAND, SINGLETON	ANN	517	HOWARD D
HOLLAND, SMITH	SOM	386	BRINKLEY
HOLLAND, SOLOMON	BAL	242	6TH WARD
HOLLAND, SOLOMON	BAL	063	4TH WARD
HOLLAND, STOCKLEY	SOM	435	PRINCESS
HOLLAND, SUSAN	WOR	184	6TH E DI
HOLLAND, THOMAS	WOR	185	6TH E DI
HOLLAND, THOMAS	WOR	182	6TH E DI
HOLLAND, THOMAS	SOM	385	BRINKLEY
HOLLAND, THOMAS	CEC	044	CHESAPEA
HOLLAND, THOMAS	CAL	020	2ND DIST
HOLLAND, THOMAS	BAL	135	5TH WARD
HOLLAND, THOMAS	ALL	056	10TH E.D
HOLLAND, THOMAS J.	SOM	425	PRINCESS
HOLLAND, WASHINGTON	BAL	119	2ND DIST
HOLLAND, WESLEY	CAL	021	2ND DIST
HOLLAND, WILLIAM	HAR	194	3RD DIST
HOLLAND, WILLIAM	CEC	074	5TH E DI
HOLLAND, WILLIAM	CEC	101	4TH E DI
HOLLAND, WILLIAM	BAL	348	3RD WARD
HOLLAND, WILLIAM	BAL	052	9TH WARD
HOLLAND, WILLIAM	BAL	143	16TH WAR
HOLLAND, WILLIAM	BAL	313	7TH WARD
HOLLAND, WILLIAM	WOR	325	1ST E DI
HOLLAND, WILLIAM	SOM	360	BRINKLEY
HOLLAND, WILLIAM	SOM	371	BRINKLEY
HOLLAND, WILLIAM	WOR	271	BERLIN 1
HOLLAND, WILLIAM	TAL	036	EASTON D
HOLLAND, WILLIAM	QUE	139	2ND E DI
HOLLAND, WILLIAM H.	WOR	303	SNOW HIL
HOLLAND, WILLIAM H.	BAL	245	17TH WAR
HOLLAND, WILLIAM J.	SOM	366	BRINKLEY
HOLLAND, WILLIAM J.	WOR	185	7TH E DI
HOLLAND, WILLIAM R.	BAL	077	1ST WARD
HOLLAND, WILLIAM V.	DOR	315	1ST DIST
HOLLANDER, ALEXANDER	BAL	253	20TH WAR
HOLLANDER, CHARLES	BAL	017	4TH WARD
HOLLANDER, DEVESKE	BAL	131	2ND DIST
HOLLANDS, JOSEPH	BAL	405	1ST DIST
HOLLARD, WILLAIM	QUE	213	3RD E DI
HOLLARS, WILLIAMS	FRE	120	CREAGERS
HOLLASH, ELEANOR	WOR	309	2ND E DI
HOLLAWAY, EPHRAIM	SOM	495	SALISBUR
HOLLAWAY, JOHN	SOM	495	SALISBUR
HOLLAWAY, LIDDY	BAL	077	4TH WARD
HOLLBROOK, HENRY	CAR	189	4TH DIST
HOLLEBAUGH, JOEL V.	FRE	003	FREDERIC
HOLLEIMEYER, GEORGE	BAL	020	9TH WARD
HOLLEN, JAMES	BAL	214	11TH WAR
HOLLEN, MINEA	BAL	308	12TH WAR
HOLLENBAUGH, JESSE	BAL	197	5TH DIST
HOLLENBAUGH, JOHN	BAL	202	6TH DIST
HOLLENBAUGH, SUSAN	BAL	442	1ST DIST
HOLLENBERGER, ELIAS	CAR	304	1ST DIST
HOLLENBERGER, ELIZA	FRE	107	CREAGERS
HOLLENBERGER, JACOB M.	CAR	409	2ND DIST
HOLLENBERGER, JOHN	CAR	408	2ND DIST
HOLLENBERGER, PETER	CAR	385	2ND DIST
HOLLENBERGER, WILLIAM F.	CAR	407	2ND DIST
HOLLENBERGER, WILLIAM	CAR	304	1ST DIST
HOLLENVAUGH, JESSE	BAL	196	5TH DIST
HOLLER, RANDOLPH	FRE	294	WOODSBOR
HOLLETT, JAMES	BAL	194	19TH WAR
HOLLEY, ANN	BAL	370	8TH WARD
HOLLEY, DELIA	BAL	088	4TH WARD
HOLLEY, DORCAS	BAL	024	9TH WARD
HOLLEY, FRANCIS	BAL	118	18TH WAR
HOLLEY, JAMES	BAL	233	20TH WAR
HOLLEY, LOUIS-MULATTO	ST	342	5TH E DI
HOLLEY, S.	BAL	320	12TH WAR
HOLLEY, THOMAS	HAR	175	3RD DIST
HOLLEY, WILLIAM-BLACK	ST	347	5TH E DI
HOLLEY, EMILY-BLACK	ST	345	5TH E DI
HOLLHONS, HERMON	BAL	379	13TH WAR
HOLLIDA, CHINA	SOM	553	TYASKIN
HOLLIDA, PETER	HAR	059	1ST DIST
HOLLIDA, WILLIAM*	SOM	536	TYASKIN
HOLLIDAY, AGNES A.	BAL	084	4TH WARD
HOLLIDAY, ANN	BAL	347	13TH WAR
HOLLIDAY, CHARLES	QUE	211	3RD E DI
HOLLIDAY, CHARLOTT	BAL	134	11TH WAR
HOLLIDAY, DAVID	BAL	373	13TH WAR
HOLLIDAY, DAVID *	BAL	306	12TH WAR
HOLLIDAY, ELSEY	FRE	066	FREDERIC
HOLLIDAY, GEORGE S.	KEN	213	2ND DIST
HOLLIDAY, HENRY	BAL	165	6TH WARD
HOLLIDAY, HERCILLA	BAL	176	6TH WARD
HOLLIDAY, ISAAC-BLACK	QUE	140	1ST E DI
HOLLIDAY, JAMES	BAL	225	6TH WARD
HOLLIDAY, JAMES	BAL	180	15TH WAR
HOLLIDAY, JAMES	ALL	127	4TH E.D.
HOLLIDAY, JAMES	BAL	341	7TH WARD
HOLLIDAY, JAMES T.	BAL	402	8TH WARD
HOLLIDAY, JESSE T.	BAL	218	5TH WARD
HOLLIDAY, JOHN	BAL	103	2ND DIST
HOLLIDAY, JOHN	DOR	464	1ST DIST
HOLLIDAY, JOHN-BLACK	QUE	152	1ST E DI
HOLLIDAY, JOSEPH	DOR	464	1ST DIST
HOLLIDAY, JOSHUA	ALL	035	2ND E.D.
HOLLIDAY, MARGARET	FRE	189	5TH E DI
HOLLIDAY, MARIA	BAL	134	11TH WAR
HOLLIDAY, MARTHA-BLACK	QUE	181	2ND E DI
HOLLIDAY, MARY	BAL	216	11TH WAR
HOLLIDAY, MARY A. L.	BAL	207	6TH WARD
HOLLIDAY, PRICILLA	BAL	129	11TH WAR
HOLLIDAY, RAECHAEL	BAL	170	11TH WAR
HOLLIDAY, SARAH A.	BAL	009	4TH WARD
HOLLIDAY, SUSAN	BAL	091	15TH WAR
HOLLIDAY, THOMAS	BAL	077	10TH WAR
HOLLIDAY, THOMAS	ANN	314	1ST DIST
HOLLIDAY, URBAN	PRI	065	NOTTINGH
HOLLIDAY, WILLIAM	KEN	211	2ND DIST
HOLLIDAY, WILLIAM H.	DOR	464	1ST DIST
HOLLIDAY, WILLIAM H.	ALL	215	CUMBERLA
HOLLIDAY, WILLIAM S.	ANN	320	2ND DIST
HOLLIDAY, WILLIAM T.	ANN	304	1ST DIST
HOLLIDAY, WILLIAM*	SOM	536	TYASKIN
HOLLIFIELD, WILLIAM	ANN	467	HOWARD D
HOLLIGAN, SAMUEL	BAL	280	2ND WARD
HOLLIN, GEORGE	BAL	348	3RD WARD
HOLLIN, LUCY	BAL	288	12TH WAR
HOLLINBERGER, DAVID	WAS	189	1ST DIST
HOLLINBERGER, MOSES	CAR	385	2ND DIST
HOLLING, ELIZABETH	CEC	006	ELKTON 3
HOLLING, GEORGE	BAL	041	15TH WAR
HOLLINGBERGER, JOSEPH	BAL	015	2ND DIST
HOLLINGBERGER, LOUIS H.	BAL	015	2ND DIST
HOLLINGS, ARCHIBALD	BAL	073	2ND DIST
HOLLINGSHAD, DAVID	BAL	037	2ND DIST
HOLLINGSHEAD, CAROLINE R.	BAL	079	15TH WAR
HOLLINGSHEAD, D. A.	BAL	070	18TH WAR
HOLLINGSHEAD, FRANCIS	BAL	075	15TH WAR
HOLLINGSHEAD, JOHN	BAL	090	15TH WAR
HOLLINGSHEAD, MARY	BAL	138	16TH WAR
HOLLINGSHEAD, SAMUEL	BAL	138	16TH WAR
HOLLINGSOWRTH, ELEXANDER	HAR	179	3RD DIST
HOLLINGSOWRTH, THOMAS	WAS	279	LEITERSB
HOLLINGSWORTH, ALEXANDER	BAL	140	16TH WAR
HOLLINGSWORTH, AMOS	HAR	085	2ND DIST
HOLLINGSWORTH, ANN D.	BAL	361	13TH WAR
HOLLINGSWORTH, BARTON	BAL	020	2ND DIST
HOLLINGSWORTH, COL J.	WAS	135	HAGERSTO
HOLLINGSWORTH, CYRUS	BAL	471	14TH WAR
HOLLINGSWORTH, ELEN	HAR	174	3RD DIST
HOLLINGSWORTH, ELIZA K.	BAL	086	4TH WARD
HOLLINGSWORTH, ELLEN	CEC	007	ELKTON 3
HOLLINGSWORTH, ELY	HAR	098	2ND DIST
HOLLINGSWORTH, GEORGE	QUE	192	3RD E DI
HOLLINGSWORTH, HARRIET	HAR	157	3RD DIST
HOLLINGSWORTH, HENRY	HAR	097	2ND DIST
HOLLINGSWORTH, JAMES	BAL	347	3RD WARD
HOLLINGSWORTH, JESSE	HAR	097	2ND DIST
HOLLINGSWORTH, JOHN	HAR	098	2ND DIST
HOLLINGSWORTH, JOHN	WAS	246	SMITHSBU
HOLLINGSWORTH, KEZIAH	BAL	311	7TH WARD
HOLLINGSWORTH, MARTHA J.	WAS	245	SMITHSBU
HOLLINGSWORTH, MARY	BAL	013	18TH WAR
HOLLINGSWORTH, MARY E.	CEC	013	ELKTON 3
HOLLINGSWORTH, NATHANIEL	HAR	098	2ND DIST
HOLLINGSWORTH, NOBLE	CAR	077	NO TWP L
HOLLINGSWORTH, PRICILLA	BAL	358	8TH WARD
HOLLINGSWORTH, RACHEL	CEC	128	5TH E DI
HOLLINGSWORTH, ROBERT	CEC	127	5TH E DI
HOLLINGSWORTH, ROBERT	HAR	098	2ND DIST
HOLLINGSWORTH, RUTH	BAL	292	3RD WARD
HOLLINGSWORTH, SAMUEL	CEC	006	ELKTON 3
HOLLINGSWORTH, SARAH A.	CAR	077	NO TWP L
HOLLINGSWORTH, SOPHIA	BAL	199	11TH WAR
HOLLINGSWORTH, WILLAIM	BAL	011	15TH WAR
HOLLINGSWORTH, WILLIAM B.	BAL	229	19TH WAR
HOLLINGWORTH, ABRAM	BAL	098	2ND DIST
HOLLINGWORTH, ELIJAH	BAL	133	2ND DIST
HOLLINGWORTH, ELIZABETH	CEC	005	ELKTON 3
HOLLINGWORTH, FRANCIS	BAL	013	18TH WAR

Name	County	Page	District
HOLLINGWORTH, HARRIET	CEC	177	7TH E DI
HOLLINGWORTH, J.	BAL	254	12TH WAR
HOLLINGWORTH, LYDIA	BAL	144	11TH WAR
HOLLINGWORTH, MC HENRY	BAL	248	1ST DIST
HOLLINGWORTH, SAMUEL	CEC	034	CHESAPEA
HOLLINGWORTH, SUSAN	CAR	075	NO TWP L
HOLLINOT, SIMON	BAL	079	2ND DIST
HOLLINS, C. H.	BAL	148	11TH WAR
HOLLINS, DANIEL F.	BAL	131	11TH WAR
HOLLINS, EDWARD	BAL	425	8TH WARD
HOLLINS, FRANCIS	BAL	117	11TH WAR
HOLLINS, GEORGE H.-BLACK	FRE	008	FREDERIC
HOLLINS, HANNAH	BAL	196	11TH WAR
HOLLINS, J. SMITH	BAL	039	9TH WARD
HOLLINS, JOHN	BAL	295	3RD WARD
HOLLINS, JOHNAS	BAL	130	11TH WAR
HOLLINS, JOSEPH C.	BAL	039	9TH WARD
HOLLINS, LUCY	BAL	152	11TH WAR
HOLLINS, MRS.	BAL	080	4TH WARD
HOLLINS, NANCY	BAL	133	5TH WARD
HOLLINS, ROBERT L.	BAL	151	11TH WAR
HOLLINS, SANDS	BAL	081	2ND DIST
HOLLINS, TORBIT	BAL	081	2ND DIST
HOLLINS, WILLIAM	BAL	313	12TH WAR
HOLLINSHADE, ANGELINE	BAL	048	2ND DIST
HOLLINSHADE, PRISCILLA	BAL	024	2ND DIST
HOLLINSWORTH, HENRIETTA	WAS	245	SMITHSBU
HOLLIS, ANN	BAL	242	12TH WAR
HOLLIS, ARAMINTA	CEC	072	5TH E DI
HOLLIS, BENJAMIN D.	HAR	182	3RD DIST
HOLLIS, CATHARINE	HAR	125	2ND DIST
HOLLIS, CLINTON	KEN	286	3RD DIST
HOLLIS, DELIA*	DOR	433	1ST DIST
HOLLIS, DENNIS	ANN	498	HOWARD D
HOLLIS, EMLY	HAR	202	3RD DIST
HOLLIS, FRANCIS	HAR	151	3RD DIST
HOLLIS, FRANCIS	BAL	381	13TH WAR
HOLLIS, GEORGE C.	KEN	294	3RD DIST
HOLLIS, GEORGIANA	ANN	499	HOWARD D
HOLLIS, HANNAH	HAR	173	3RD DIST
HOLLIS, HARRIET	ANN	499	HOWARD D
HOLLIS, HENRY	HAR	179	3RD DIST
HOLLIS, HENRY	KEN	311	3RD DIST
HOLLIS, ISAAC	CEC	101	4TH E DI
HOLLIS, JAMES	HAR	124	2ND DIST
HOLLIS, JAMES	CHA	226	ALLENS F
HOLLIS, JAMES-BLACK	QUE	142	1ST E DI
HOLLIS, JARRETT	HAR	113	2ND DIST
HOLLIS, JO-BLACK	QUE	193	3RD E DI
HOLLIS, JOHN	CEC	192	5TH E DI
HOLLIS, JOHN	BAL	122	5TH WARD
HOLLIS, JOSEPH-BLACK	QUE	194	3RD E DI
HOLLIS, LOUISA	DOR	463	1ST DIST
HOLLIS, MARY	DOR	449	1ST DIST
HOLLIS, MARY E.	DOR	463	1ST DIST
HOLLIS, MILEY*	DOR	411	1ST DIST
HOLLIS, NEVETT	SOM	514	BARREN C
HOLLIS, PARKER	HAR	095	2ND DIST
HOLLIS, SAMUEL	SOM	508	BARREN C
HOLLIS, SARAH A.	BAL	170	11TH WAR
HOLLIS, SILAS	CAR	164	NO TWP L
HOLLIS, SYLVESTER	SOM	513	BARREN C
HOLLIS, THOMAS*	BAL	242	12TH WAR
HOLLIS, WESLEY	BAL	169	1ST WARD
HOLLIS, WILLIAM	DOR	451	1ST DIST
HOLLMAN, BENJAMIN F.	WAS	150	2ND DIST
HOLLMAN, CATHARINE	WAS	012	WILLIAMS
HOLLOCK, JESSE	CAR	127	NO TWP L
HOLLOCK, JOHN	WOR	298	9TH E DI
HOLLOCK, MARY E.*	DOR	455	1ST DIST
HOLLOCK, SUSAN	CAR	116	NO TWP L
HOLLOR, SYBYL	HAR	193	3RD DIST
HOLLOWAY, AERAM	WOR	246	1ST CENS
HOLLOWAY, ANAMAS	WOR	243	1ST CENS
HOLLOWAY, ANANIAS	WOR	275	BERLIN 1
HOLLOWAY, ANANCY	WOR	245	1ST CENS
HOLLOWAY, CHARLES	BAL	001	18TH WAR
HOLLOWAY, DANIEL	WOR	235	6TH E DI
HOLLOWAY, EDWIN	CEC	001	ELKTON 3
HOLLOWAY, ELIJAH	WOR	234	6TH E DI
HOLLOWAY, ELISHA	WOR	234	6TH E DI
HOLLOWAY, ELIZABETH	HAR	119	2ND DIST
HOLLOWAY, FANNY	WOR	241	1ST CENS
HOLLOWAY, GEORGE	WOR	258	1ST CENS
HOLLOWAY, GEORGE	BAL	001	18TH WAR
HOLLOWAY, HENRY	WOR	214	4TH E DI
HOLLOWAY, HUGH S.	HAR	033	1ST DIST
HOLLOWAY, ISAAC	WOR	241	1ST CENS
HOLLOWAY, JAMES	WOR	244	1ST CENS
HOLLOWAY, JOHN	BAL	114	5TH WARD
HOLLOWAY, JOSHUA J.	WOR	167	6TH E DI
HOLLOWAY, JOSHUA JR.	WOR	220	4TH E DI
HOLLOWAY, JOSHUA SR.	WOR	232	6TH E DI
HOLLOWAY, MARY J.	BAL	109	5TH WARD
HOLLOWAY, MC KINNA	WOR	276	BERLIN 1
HOLLOWAY, MRS.	WOR	260	BERLIN 1
HOLLOWAY, REBECCA	HAR	122	2ND DIST
HOLLOWAY, RICHARD	HAR	084	2ND DIST
HOLLOWAY, ROBERT	BAL	110	5TH WARD
HOLLOWAY, SAMUEL	WOR	282	BERLIN 1
HOLLOWAY, SAMUEL	WOR	246	1ST CENS
HOLLOWAY, WILLIAM R.	HAR	123	2ND DIST
HOLLY, ABRAHAM-BLACK	ST	297	2ND E DI
HOLLY, ALBERT	ALL	200	CUMBERLA
HOLLY, ANN-BLACK	ST	346	5TH E DI
HOLLY, CHARLES	ST	254	3RD E DI
HOLLY, CHARLES H.-BLACK	ST	301	2ND E DI
HOLLY, DAVID	PRI	021	VANSVILL
HOLLY, DAVID	PRI	021	VANSVILL
HOLLY, GEORGE	BAL	234	20TH WAR
HOLLY, GEORGE	CEC	157	PORT DUP
HOLLY, GEORGE-MULATTO	ST	347	5TH E DI
HOLLY, GOERGE	BAL	150	16TH WAR
HOLLY, HARRIET-BLACK	ST	341	5TH E DI
HOLLY, HENRY-BLACK	ST	294	2ND E DI
HOLLY, JACKSON	ST	280	3RD E DI
HOLLY, JACOB	ST	283	3RD E DI
HOLLY, JAMES	KEN	249	2ND DIST
HOLLY, JOHN	KEN	252	1ST DIST
HOLLY, JOHN	HAR	159	3RD DIST
HOLLY, JOHN-BLACK	ST	300	2ND E DI
HOLLY, JOHN-MULATTO	ST	303	2ND E DI
HOLLY, JUTIEL *	ST	283	3RD E DI
HOLLY, JUTIEL *	ST	284	2ND E DI
HOLLY, LOUIS	KEN	226	2ND DIST
HOLLY, MARY ANN	BAL	388	13TH WAR
HOLLY, SARAH-BLACK	ST	294	2ND E DI
HOLLY, STEPHEN	ST	261	3RD E DI
HOLLY, SUSANER	HAR	150	3RD DIST
HOLLY, TACETUS N.	WAS	104	2ND DIST
HOLLY, TACTIS	WAS	104	2ND DIST
HOLLY, THOMAS	ST	270	3RD E DI
HOLLY, THOMAS	ST	263	3RD E DI
HOLLY, THOMAS-BLACK	ST	305	2ND E DI
HOLLY, THOMAS-MULATTO	ST	302	2ND E DI
HOLLY, WILLAIM	BAL	244	1ST DIST
HOLLY, WILLIAM	ST	329	4TH E DI
HOLLYDAY, DAVID	MGM	374	ROCKERLE
HOLLYDAY, E.H.	PRI	065	NOTTINGH
HOLLYDAY, FRANCES-BLACK	QUE	202	3RD E DI
HOLLYDAY, GEORGE-BLACK	QUE	201	3RD E DI
HOLLYDAY, HENRY	QUE	196	3RD E DI
HOLLYDAY, HENRY-BLACK	QUE	201	3RD E DI
HOLLYDAY, JAMES E.L.	PRI	061	NOTTINGH
HOLLYDAY, JANE	BAL	255	1ST DIST
HOLLYDAY, MARY	BAL	255	1ST DIST
HOLLYDAY, SARAH	BAL	253	17TH WAR
HOLLYDAY, WILLIAM	QUE	215	3RD E DI
HOLLYDEYCKE, EDWARD	ANN	276	ANNAPOLI
HOLLYDEYCKER, ELLEN	ANN	275	ANNAPOLI
HOLLZMAN, SAMUEL	ALL	093	5TH E.D.
HOLMAD, JOHN B.	BAL	045	9TH WARD
HOLMAN, DAVID	BAL	160	19TH WAR
HOLMAN, JOHN H.	BAL	009	9TH WARD
HOLMANS, SAMUEL	BAL	099	18TH WAR
HOLMBS, ELIZABETH	BAL	363	1ST DIST
HOLMEAD, JOHN	CHA	270	ALLENS F
HOLMEN, CHARLES	BAL	119	1ST WARD
HOLMES, A.	BAL	046	9TH WARD
HOLMES, AARON	CEC	017	ELKTON 3
HOLMES, ALLEN	BAL	020	15TH WAR
HOLMES, ARCHIBALD	WAS	086	2ND SUBD
HOLMES, CATHARINE	BAL	373	13TH WAR
HOLMES, DAVID	BAL	172	19TH WAR
HOLMES, DAVID	BAL	103	18TH WAR
HOLMES, DAVID	BAL	313	1ST DIST
HOLMES, ELI	BAL	310	20TH WAR
HOLMES, ELIAS	CAR	293	7TH DIST
HOLMES, ELIZA	ANN	390	4TH DIST
HOLMES, ELIZABETH	BAL	317	7TH WARD
HOLMES, ELIZABETH	BAL	301	17TH WAR
HOLMES, EMEALS-BLACK	CAR	140	NO TWP L
HOLMES, EMIALS-BLACK	CAR	162	NO TWP L
HOLMES, GEORGE	BAL	282	17TH WAR
HOLMES, GEORGE	BAL	145	1ST WARD
HOLMES, HARRIET	BAL	069	15TH WAR
HOLMES, HARRIET	FRE	036	FREDERIC
HOLMES, HENRY	BAL	274	17TH WAR
HOLMES, HEZEKIAH	FRE	396	PETERSVI
HOLMES, IGNATIUS-BLACK	MGM	421	MEDLEY 3
HOLMES, J. M.	BAL	106	18TH WAR
HOLMES, JAMES	BAL	330	13TH WAR
HOLMES, JAMES	BAL	246	6TH WARD
HOLMES, JAMES	BAL	163	6TH WARD
HOLMES, JAMESH.	CAR	142	NO TWP L
HOLMES, JANE	BAL	226	19TH WAR
HOLMES, JEROME	BAL	168	19TH WAR
HOLMES, JOHN	BAL	209	11TH WAR
HOLMES, JOHN	FRE	049	FREDERIC
HOLMES, JOHN	BAL	269	20TH WAR
HOLMES, JOHN	CAR	284	7TH DIST
HOLMES, JOHN	BAL	019	9TH WARD
HOLMES, JOHN	BAL	185	11TH WAR
HOLMES, JOHN	ALL	176	7TH E.D.
HOLMES, JOHN	BAL	254	1ST DIST
HOLMES, JOHN B.	BAL	048	2ND DIST
HOLMES, JOHN E.	BAL	076	4TH WARD
HOLMES, JOHN H.	BAL	114	11TH WAR
HOLMES, JOHN W.	ALL	213	CUMBERLA
HOLMES, JOSEPH	BAL	298	17TH WAR
HOLMES, JULIA	WAS	059	2ND SUBD
HOLMES, LOUISA	BAL	201	6TH WARD
HOLMES, LUCRETIA	BAL	073	15TH WAR
HOLMES, MAHLON T.	BAL	103	18TH WAR
HOLMES, MARTIN	WAS	070	2ND SUBD
HOLMES, MARY	QUE	217	3RD E DI
HOLMES, MARY	BAL	088	4TH WARD
HOLMES, MARY	DOR	375	1ST DIST
HOLMES, MARY	BAL	128	5TH WARD
HOLMES, MOSES	BAL	062	10TH WAR
HOLMES, PHILETUS	BAL	397	3RD WARD
HOLMES, POLLARD-BLACK	CAR	157	NO TWP L
HOLMES, RICHARD	BAL	303	20TH WAR
HOLMES, ROBERT	FRE	193	5TH E DI
HOLMES, ROBERT S.	BAL	310	7TH WARD
HOLMES, SALLY ANN	QUE	187	3RD E DI
HOLMES, SAMUEL	BAL	259	1ST DIST
HOLMES, SAMUEL	BAL	331	1ST DIST
HOLMES, SAMUEL	BAL	301	17TH WAR
HOLMES, SARAH	BAL	373	3RD WARD
HOLMES, SARAH J.	BAL	225	17TH WAR
HOLMES, SOLOMON	DOR	313	1ST DIST
HOLMES, SOLOMON	CAR	158	NO TWP L
HOLMES, SOMERVILLE	BAL	004	EASTERN
HOLMES, THOMAS	BAL	243	2ND WARD
HOLMES, THOMAS	BAL	300	17TH WAR
HOLMES, THOMAS	HAR	148	3RD DIST
HOLMES, VICTOR	BAL	050	2ND DIST
HOLMES, W. H.	BAL	332	1ST DIST
HOLMES, WILLIAM	BAL	396	3RD WARD
HOLMES, WILLIAM	BAL	135	1ST WARD
HOLMES, WILLIAM	BAL	165	2ND DIST
HOLMES, C.	BAL	137	1ST WARD
HOLMON, PETER	ALL	104	5TH E.D.
HOLMS, GEORGE	BAL	332	7TH WARD
HOLMS, JANE	BAL	226	17TH WAR
HOLMS, JOHN	DOR	339	3RD DIVI
HOLMS, MARY	CEC	016	ELKTON 3
HOLMS, SERENIA	BAL	096	18TH WAR
HOLOWAY, FRANCIS	CEC	093	4TH E DI
HOLSEHART, AMCS	BAL	068	15TH WAR
HOLSER, ANTHONY	ALL	223	CUMBERLA
HOLSEY, RICHARD	MGM	434	CLARKSTR
HOLSON, JOHN	BAL	129	2ND DIST
HOLSON, JOHN	BAL	027	18TH WAR
HOLSTEIN, HAMILTON	BAL	030	4TH WARD
HOLSTEIN, MARTHA	KEN	247	2ND DIST
HOLSTEIN, PETER	BAL	055	9TH WARD
HOLSTEIN, RACHEL	BAL	125	16TH WAR
HOLSTEIN, WILLIAM H.	BAL	132	16TH WAR
HOLSTEN, LEVIN	WOR	169	6TH E DI
HOLSTER, RODOLPH	ALL	245	CUMBERLA
HOLSTON, ADALYA R.	WOR	291	9TH E DI
HOLSTON, BENJAIN	WOR	306	2ND E DI
HOLSTON, JAMES	WOR	290	9TH E DI
HOLSTON, JAMES	WOR	321	1ST E DI
HOLSTON, JOHN	WOR	293	9TH E DI
HOLSTON, ZADOK	WOR	293	9TH E DI
HOLSWORTH, COLIN F.	QUE	172	2ND E DI
HOLSWORTH, GEORGE	QUE	173	2ND E DI
HOLSWORTH, JOHN G.	QUE	165	2ND E DI
HOLT, ALLEY-BLACK	ST	325	4TH E DI
HOLT, CHARLES W.	QUE	190	3RD E DI
HOLT, DANIEL	BAL	184	2ND WARD
HOLT, ELIZABETH	CEC	116	3RD E DI
HOLT, ELIZABETH-MULATTO	ST	325	4TH E DI
HOLT, ENOCH	BAL	279	7TH WARD
HOLT, GEORGE H.	BAL	187	16TH WAR
HOLT, GEORGE W.	MGM	392	ROCKERLE
HOLT, GREENSBURY	SOM	522	BARREN C
HOLT, ISAAC	CEC	115	3RD E DI
HOLT, JAMES	FRE	384	PETERSVI
HOLT, JOHN	FRE	119	CREAGERS
HOLT, JOHN	CHA	287	BOJANTOW
HOLT, JOHN	CAR	091	NO TWP L
HOLT, JOHN G.	BAL	028	9TH WARD
HOLT, JOHN W.	CEC	116	3RD E DI
HOLT, JOHN-MULATTO	ST	333	4TH E DI
HOLT, JOSHUA	BAL	412	3RD WARD
HOLT, LEONARD-MULATTO	ST	322	4TH E DI
HOLT, MARY D.	MGM	400	ROCKERLE
HOLT, MARY E.-MULATTO	ST	325	4TH E DI
HOLT, PETER-MULATTO	ST	322	4TH E DI
HOLT, RUTH	ALL	138	6TH E.D.
HOLT, SARAH A.	BAL	387	3RD WARD
HOLT, STEPHEN*	DOR	417	1ST DIST
HOLT, SUSAN	PRI	105	PISCATAW
HOLT, THOMAS	MGM	381	ROCKERLE
HOLT, WASHINGTON	CEC	067	5TH E DI
HOLT, WILLAIM	BAL	177	19TH WAR
HOLTEN, GEORGE-BLACK	CAR	398	2ND DIST
HOLTEN, HENRY	CAR	327	1ST DIST
HOLTEN, MARY H.	BAL	187	11TH WAR
HOLTEN, WILLIAM	KEN	229	2ND DIST
HOLTENBERGER, PETER	CAR	388	2ND DIST
HOLTER, MARY	BAL	063	2ND DIST
HOLTER, SAMUEL	FRE	402	JEFFERSO
HOLTER, WILLIAM	FRE	073	FREDERIC
HOLTER, WILLIAM	FRE	073	FREDERIC
HOLTHAUS, F. D.	BAL	095	10TH WAR
HOLTHOUS, MARGARET	WAS	135	2ND DIST
HOLTIDY, JAMES	ANN	276	ANNAPOLI
HOLTIZMAN, URIAH *	BAL	303	12TH WAR
HOLTMAN, HENRY	BAL	196	6TH WARD
HOLTON, ANN E.	ST	303	2ND E DI
HOLTON, BARNEY	BAL	367	8TH WARD
HOLTON, BETSEY	WOR	296	9TH E DI
HOLTON, DAVID	BAL	315	7TH WARD
HOLTON, ELLEN	BAL	153	11TH WAR
HOLTON, FRANK	BAL	092	1ST WARD
HOLTON, GEORGE	BAL	443	8TH WARD
HOLTON, JOHN	BAL	099	18TH WAR
HOLTON, JOHN	BAL	059	18TH WAR
HOLTON, MARGARET	BAL	069	10TH WAR
HOLTON, MARGARETT	BAL	191	11TH WAR
HOLTON, WILLIAM	WOR	295	9TH E DI
HOLTS, ANN	BAL	415	3RD WARD
HOLTS, F.	BAL	007	4TH WARD
HOLTS, FREDERICK R.	BAL	458	8TH WARD
HOLTS, LOUISA	BAL	370	8TH WARD
HOLTT, MAHALA	CAL	040	3RD DIST
HOLTT, PHILIP	CAL	051	3RD DIST
HOLTT, THOMAS J.	CAL	021	2ND DIST
HOLTZ, ALBERT B.	FRE	092	FREDERIC
HOLTZ, BENEDICT	FRE	100	FREDERIC
HOLTZ, CATHARINE	FRE	307	WOODSBOR
HOLTZ, CATHARINE	BAL	219	6TH WARD
HOLTZ, ELIZABETH	FRE	119	CREAGERS
HOLTZ, EMANUEL	BAL	310	12TH WAR
HOLTZ, F.H.	BAL	159	1ST WARD
HOLTZ, FREDERICK	BAL	222	17TH WAR
HOLTZ, GEORGE	FRE	048	FREDERIC
HOLTZ, HARRIET	FRE	049	FREDERIC
HOLTZ, HESTER	BAL	184	2ND WARD
HOLTZ, JACOB	FRE	092	FREDERIC
HOLTZ, JACOB	WAS	213	1ST DIST
HOLTZ, JACOB O.	BAL	303	12TH WAR
HOLTZ, JESSE	FRE	121	CREAGERS
HOLTZ, JOHN	FRE	091	FREDERIC
HOLTZ, SAMUEL	WAS	213	1ST DIST
HOLTZ, SUSAN	BAL	304	12TH WAR
HOLTZAPPLE, FREDERICK	FRE	105	CREAGERS
HOLTZE, ADELINE	BAL	400	14TH WAR
HOLTZE, PETER CASPAR	BAL	429	14TH WAR
HOLTZMAN, AMERICA B.	PRI	020	YANSVILL
HOLTZMAN, ANDREW J.	ALL	156	6TH E.D.
HOLTZMAN, C. C.	BAL	074	10TH WAR
HOLTZMAN, CHARLES	ALL	146	6TH E.D.
HOLTZMAN, CHRISTIAN	FRE	357	CATOCTIN
HOLTZMAN, ELIZABETH	FRE	419	8TH E DI
HOLTZMAN, GEORGE	BAL	303	12TH WAR
HOLTZMAN, JACOB	FRE	357	CATOCTIN
HOLTZMAN, JOHN	ALL	219	CUMBERLA
HOLTZMAN, JOHN H.	ALL	208	CUMBERLA
HOLTZMAN, JOHN T.	PRI	020	VANSVILL
HOLTZMAN, MARYH	FRE	357	CATOCTIN
HOLTZMAN, THOMAS	BAL	242	12TH WAR
HOLTZMAN, WILLIAM	ALL	095	5TH E.D.
HOLTZMAN, WILLIAM	BAL	084	10TH WAR
HOLTZMAN, WILLIAM	FRE	374	CATOCTIN
HOLTZMAR, GEORGE	BAL	227	2ND WARD
HOLWICK, JOHN	BAL	352	13TH WAR
HOLWICK, PAUL	BAL	352	13TH WAR
HOLY, GEORGE C.	BAL	239	20TH WAR
HOLYHASE, JOHN	BAL	085	1ST WARD
HOMAN, AMELIA-MULATTO	FRE	242	NEW MARK
HOMAN, ANN	BAL	251	12TH WAR
HOMAN, ROSE	BAL	421	14TH WAR
HOMARHAUSER, WILLIAM	BAL	227	2ND WARD
HOMAS, CHARLES*	TAL	005	EASTON D
HOMAS, WILLIAM	CAR	066	NO TWP L
HOME, WESLEY	ANN	274	ANNAPOLI
HOMEL, JOHN	BAL	359	1ST DIST
HOMEL, JOSHUA	BAL	351	3RD WARD
HOMER, ANN*	TAL	050	EASTON T
HOMER, BRIGET	BAL	458	1ST DIST
HOMER, CECELIA	BAL	257	2ND WARD
HOMER, CHRISTIAN	BAL	341	3RD WARD
HOMER, CURTIS	BAL	423	8TH WARD
HOMER, DANIEL	TAL	051	EASTON D
HOMER, EMILY C.	TAL	051	EASTON D
HOMER, HARRIET	TAL	051	EASTON D
HOMER, HENRY	TAL	051	EASTON D
HOMER, SOPHIA	BAL	402	8TH WARD
HOMER, WESLEY	BAL	060	10TH WAR
HOMERBECKER, MARTIN	BAL	197	17TH WAR
HOMERICK, ANDREW	FRE	157	10TH E D
HOMERICK, LYDIA ANN	FRE	157	10TH E D
HOMES, ANN	CHA	221	ALLENS F
HOMES, BARTLEY *	WAS	051	2ND SUBD

HOMES, CATHARINE HAR 148 3RD DIST
HOMES, DANIEL BAL 150 2ND DIST
HOMES, DAVID WAS 084 2ND SUBD
HOMES, ELEANOR CHA 221 ALLENS F
HOMES, ELIAS WAS 088 2ND SUBD
HOMES, HENRY TAL 001 EASTON D
HOMES, HORATIO WAS 085 2ND SUBD
HOMES, JACOB WAS 121 2ND DIST
HOMES, JERMIAH WAS 084 2ND SUBD
HOMES, JOHN WAS 121 2ND DIST
HOMES, JOHN ST 314 1ST E DI
HOMES, JOHN M. ALL 211 CUMBERLA
HOMES, JOSIAH TAL 025 EASTON D
HOMES, MARY HAR 153 3RD DIST
HOMES, SAMUEL WAS 085 2ND SUBD
HOMES, SIMON WAS 087 2ND SUBD
HOMES, SUSAN WAS 121 2ND DIST
HOMES, VICTOR HAR 063 1ST DIST
HOMES, VICTOR HAR 045 1ST DIST
HOMES, WILLIAM CHA 220 ALLENS F
HOMMAN, GABRIEL ALL 236 CUMBERLA
HOMMOND, GRAFTON FRE 260 NEW MARK
HOMMOND, WILLIAM-BLACK CAR 127 NO TWP L
HOMON, MATHIAS BAL 355 1ST DIST
HOMONS, JACOB HAR 061 1ST DIST
HOMPHREY, EANAS BAL 391 1ST DIST
HOMPHREY, ENOS BAL 391 1ST DIST
HOMRICK, JOHN FRE 109 CREAGERS
HON, DANIEL CAR 189 4TH DIST
HON, JOSEPH CAR 192 4TH DIST
HONAMON, LUDWICK BAL 287 1ST DIST
HONCK, SAMUEL BAL 303 20TH WAR
HONO, NICY DOR 430 1ST DIST
HONDEN, ROBERT BAL 269 20TH WAR
HONDY, WILLIAM* DOR 303 1ST DIST
HONE, CHARLES FRE 20 5TH E DI
HONE, CHARLES ALL 024 3RD E.D.
HONE, ELIZABETH FRE 353 MIDDLETO
HONE, ELLEN BAL 470 14TH WAR
HONE, JOHN ALL 057 10TH E.D
HONE, PATRICK ALL 240 CUMBERLA
HONES, JESSEE KEN 225 2ND DIST
HONES, MARY BAL 136 11TH WAR
HONEY, CATHERINE KEN 284 3RD DIST
HONEY, FREDERICK QUE 235 4TH E DI
HONEY, JANE QUE 225 4TH E DI
HONEY, NICHOLAS T. CEC 125 5TH E DI
HONEY, PERE QUE 225 4TH E DI
HONEY, THOMAS QUE 225 4TH E DI
HONEYWELL, CAHRLES BAL 162 19TH WAR
HONEYWELL, JANE BAL 103 10TH WAR
HONGMEYER, JOHN BAL 060 1ST WARD
HONIES, CATHARINE BAL 476 14TH WAR
HONIKER, PETER FRE 162 EMMITTSB
HONING, GEORGE BAL 333 7TH WARD
HONRES, GOERG-EBLACK CAR 076 NO TWP L
HONSAR, WESLEY MGM 389 ROCKERLE
HONSAR, WILLIAM MGM 380 ROCKERLE
HONSBERRY, HENRY WAS 196 1ST DIST
HONSHEW, GEORGE B. FRE 082 FREDERIC
HONSTEIN, ADAM WAS 256 1ST DIST
HONTER, ANN ALL 252 CUMBERLA
HONTON, REEECCA HAR 160 3RD DIST
HONTZ, JOHN FRE 127 CREAGERS
HONTZE, OLIVER BAL 471 14TH WAR
HONY, FREDERICK BAL 369 1ST DIST
HOOBER, GUTTIP HAR 016 1ST DIST
HOOBS, THOMAS BAL 064 18TH WAR
HOOD, ALBERT ANN 454 HOWARD D
HOOD, ALEXANDER W. FRE 224 BUCKEYST
HOOD, BASIL FRE 424 8TH E DI
HOOD, BASIL FRE 425 8TH E DI
HOOD, BENJAMIN FRE 386 PETERSVI
HOOD, CATHARINE FRE 387 PETERSVI
HOOD, CATHARINE E. FRE 424 8TH E DI
HOOD, CHARLES W. CAR 230 5TH DIST
HOOD, CHARLES W. CAR 230 5TH DIST
HOOD, ELISABETH ANN 383 4TH DIST
HOOD, ELIZA BAL 044 18TH WAR
HOOD, ELIZABETH ANN 423 HOWARD D
HOOD, ELIZABETH PRI 026 VANSVILL
HOOD, GEORGE FRE 424 8TH E DI
HOOD, GEORGE A. FRE 407 JEFFERSO
HOOD, GEORGE W. FRE 424 8TH E DI
HOOD, HENRY FRE 424 8TH E DI
HOOD, HENRY W. ANN 471 HOWARD D
HOOD, ISAIAH ANN 493 HOWARD D
HOOD, J. W. BAL 337 13TH WAR
HOOD, JAMES CAR 363 9TH DIST
HOOD, JAMES ANN 493 HOWARD D
HOOD, JAMES BAL 396 1ST DIST
HOOD, JAMES H. FRE 023 FREDERIC
HOOD, JANE CEC 148 PORT DUP
HOOD, JOHN ANN 512 HOWARD D
HOOD, JOHN ANN 383 4TH DIST
HOOD, JOHN BAL 054 9TH WARD
HOOD, JOHN PRI 026 VANSVILL
HOOD, JOHN PRI 039 VANSVILL
HOOD, JOSHUA ANN 513 HOWARD D
HOOD, LEVIN ANN 493 HOWARD D
HOOD, LEWIS ANN 389 4TH DIST
HOOD, MARY BAL 316 7TH WARD
HOOD, RACHEL CAR 227 5TH DIST
HOOD, RACHEL FRE 249 NEW MARK
HOOD, SAMUEL CAR 368 9TH DIST
HOOD, THOMAS CAR 361 9TH DIST
HOOD, THOMAS CEC 054 1ST E DI
HOOD, THOMAS H. ANN 503 HOWARD D
HOOD, WILLIAM ANN 423 HOWARD D
HOOD, WILLIAM G. CAR 227 5TH DIST
HOOE, CIRANISON BAL 187 11TH WAR
HOOER, RACHEL HAR 094 2ND DIST
HOOF, JOHN S. BAL 053 18TH WAR
HOOF, PETER BAL 293 17TH WAR
HOOF, WILLIAM WOR 241 1ST CENS
HOOFAVER, FRED BAL 145 2ND DIST
HOOFF, EDWARD BAL 465 14TH WAR
HOOFINE, JACOB WAS 236 CAVETOWN
HOOFMAN, AMELIA BAL 007 9TH WARD
HOOFMAN, EDWARD P. ALL 157 6TH E.D.
HOOFMAN, GEORGE BAL 367 1ST DIST
HOOFMAN, GEORGE BAL 048 1ST WARD
HOOFMAN, JOHN BAL 128 18TH WAR
HOOFMAN, LEVI BAL 379 1ST DIST
HOOFMAN, MARY E. HAR 130 2ND DIST
HOOFMAN, PETER BAL 296 20TH WAR
HOOFMAN, RICHARD BAL 269 20TH WAR
HOOFMAN, WILLIAM ANN 429 HOWARD D
HOOFMASTER, HENRY BAL 016 4TH WARD
HOOFMIESTER, MARY BAL 012 9TH WARD
HOOFNAGLE, BARTHOLOMEW BAL 285 2ND WARD
HOOFNAGLE, CONRAD BAL 205 2ND WARD
HOOFNAGLE, ELLENORA BAL 092 18TH WAR
HOOFNAGLE, JOHN BAL 015 15TH WAR
HOOFNAGLE, JOHN BAL 253 2ND WARD
HOOFNAGLE, LYDIA BAL 012 15TH WAR
HOOFNAGLE, MARTIN BAL 258 2ND WARD
HOOFNAGLE, RICHARD ANN 430 HOWARD D
HOOFNAGLE, RICHARD H. BAL 031 15TH WAR
HOOFNER, JOHN BAL 427 8TH WARD
HOOFNOCK, ATHONY BAL 428 8TH WARD
HOOFPAUGH, JOHN BAL 068 18TH WAR
HOOK, ALBERT BAL 179 2ND DIST
HOOK, ANN BAL 068 2ND DIST
HOOK, CATHARINE BAL 417 1ST DIST
HOOK, CATHARINE CAR 235 UNION TO
HOOK, CATHARINE A. BAL 406 1ST DIST
HOOK, CHARLES F. BAL 206 6TH WARD
HOOK, CONRAD CAR 187 4TH DIST
HOOK, CONRAD JR. BAL 415 1ST DIST
HOOK, EMMA BAL 287 17TH WAR
HOOK, ENOCH BAL 205 19TH WAR
HOOK, FREDERICK BAL 355 13TH WAR
HOOK, FREDERICK BAL 326 3RD WARD
HOOK, GEORGE C. BAL 374 8TH WARD
HOOK, GOERGE BAL 222 17TH WAR
HOOK, GRANBURG BAL 099 1ST WARD
HOOK, GREENBURY ALL 231 CUMBERLA
HOOK, GUSTAVUS BAL 401 1ST DIST
HOOK, HENRY F. BAL 440 14TH WAR
HOOK, ISAAC BAL 412 1ST DIST
HOOK, JACOB BAL 132 5TH WARD
HOOK, JACOB BAL 114 11TH WAR
HOOK, JAMES CAR 199 4TH DIST
HOOK, JAMES ALL 175 7TH E.D.
HOOK, JAMES WAS 162 2ND DIST
HOOK, JOHN BAL 395 1ST DIST
HOOK, JOHN BAL 294 12TH WAR
HOOK, JOHN BAL 233 17TH WAR
HOOK, JOHN H. BAL 276 12TH WAR
HOOK, JOHN L. ALL 032 2ND E.D.
HOOK, JONATHON BAL 277 1ST DIST
HOOK, JOSEPH BAL 296 1ST DIST
HOOK, JOSEPH BAL 375 1ST DIST
HOOK, JOSIAS BAL 395 1ST DIST
HOOK, JULIA A. BAL 375 8TH WARD
HOOK, JULIA A.* DOR 429 1ST DIST
HOOK, M. ANN 309 1ST DIST
HOOK, MARCUS R. BAL 355 3RD WARD
HOOK, MARIA BAL 158 6TH WARD
HOOK, MARY BAL 289 3RD WARD
HOOK, MARY A. CAR 200 4TH DIST
HOOK, MARY ANN BAL 139 5TH WARD
HOOK, NELSON BAL 173 2ND DIST
HOOK, NICHOLAS BAL 294 17TH WAR
HOOK, RADOLPH BAL 408 1ST DIST
HOOK, REASON ALL 251 CUMBERLA
HOOK, RICHARD BAL 401 1ST DIST
HOOK, RICHARD PRI 063 NOTTINGH
HOOK, ROBERT ANN 508 HOWARD D
HOOK, SAMUEL BAL 408 1ST DIST
HOOK, SAMUEL D. CAL 012 1ST DIST
HOOK, SAMUEL K. ALL 032 2ND E.D.
HOOK, SARAH ALL 206 CUMBERLA
HOOK, SOPHIA BAL 347 1ST DIST
HOOK, THOMAS CAR 326 1ST DIST
HOOK, THOMAS B. BAL 406 1ST DIST
HOOK, WILLAIM BAL 133 5TH WARD
HOOK, WILLIAM BAL 402 1ST DIST
HOOK, WILLIAM BAL 173 2ND DIST
HOOKE, KEZIAH ALL 213 CUMBERLA
HOOKER, E. R. DOR 374 1ST DIST
HOOKER, GEORGE BAL 148 2ND DIST
HOOKER, HENRY* DOR 459 1ST DIST
HOOKER, JACOB BAL 412 1ST DIST
HOOKER, JAMES CAR 386 2ND DIST
HOOKER, JESSE CAR 222 5TH DIST
HOOKER, JOSEPH* DOR 377 1ST DIST
HOOKER, JOSHUA HAR 106 2ND DIST
HOOKER, LLOYD HAR 074 1ST DIST
HOOKER, MALINDA BAL 338 7TH WARD
HOOKER, MARTHA CEC 181 7TH E DI
HOOKER, MARY DOR 329 3RD DIVI
HOOKER, MARY BAL 359 1ST DIST
HOOKER, NEWTON* DOR 455 1ST DIST
HOOKER, REBECCA BAL 424 1ST DIST
HOOKER, SAMUEL BAL 454 1ST DIST
HOOKER, SAMUEL BAL 236 1ST DIST
HOOKER, TOBIAS BAL 180 6TH WARD
HOOKER, V. P.* DOR 453 1ST DIST
HOOKER, WILLIAM BAL 136 1ST WARD
HOOKER, WILLIAM B. BAL 354 1ST DIST
HOOKER, WILLIAM* DOR 454 1ST DIST
HOOLBROCK, HENRY SOM 436 PRINCESS
HOON, JOHN ALL 163 6TH E.D.
HOONER, HENRIETTA WAS 008 WILLIAMS
HOONER, STEPHEN FRE 159 EMMITTSB
HOONEY, AMELINE* TAL 026 EASTON D
HOONEY, ANN* TAL 002 EASTON D
HOONEY, THOMAS* TAL 025 EASTON D
HOOOVER, CATHERINE FRE 059 FREDERIC
HOOP, CONRAD ALL 120 5TH E.D.
HOOPE, P. R. F. DOR 378 1ST DIST
HOOPER, A. MRS- BAL 315 20TH WAR
HOOPER, AARON DOR 333 3RD DIVI
HOOPER, ABRAHAM CAL 013 1ST DIST
HOOPER, AMANDA M. BAL 137 16TH WAR
HOOPER, AMASSA BAL 212 6TH WARD
HOOPER, ANN L. ST 286 2ND E DI
HOOPER, ANNA DOR 378 1ST DIST
HOOPER, BENJAMIN A. BAL 046 15TH WAR
HOOPER, BETSEY BAL 102 2ND DIST
HOOPER, CATHARINE DOR 333 3RD DIVI
HOOPER, CHARLES DOR 359 3RD DIVI
HOOPER, CHARLES FRE 368 CATOCTIN
HOOPER, CHARLES BAL 188 2ND WARD
HOOPER, CHARLES V. DOR 347 3RD DIVI
HOOPER, CHARLOTTE BAL 039 18TH WAR
HOOPER, D. M. BAL 323 12TH WAR
HOOPER, DAVID BAL 153 2ND DIST
HOOPER, DAVID CAR 361 9TH DIST
HOOPER, EDWARD BAL 055 4TH WARD
HOOPER, ELEY BAL 221 12TH WAR
HOOPER, ELIZA DOR 379 1ST DIST
HOOPER, ELIZA J. BAL 009 1ST WARD
HOOPER, ELIZABETH BAL 089 10TH WAR
HOOPER, ELIZABETH BAL 305 3RD WARD
HOOPER, ELIZABETH BAL 312 7TH WARD
HOOPER, ELIZABETH DOR 357 3RD DIVI
HOOPER, EZEKIEL ANN 337 3RD DIST
HOOPER, FLORENCE T. BAL 021 4TH WARD
HOOPER, GEORGE CAL 035 2ND DIST
HOOPER, GEORGE BAL 189 17TH WAR
HOOPER, HARRIET BAL 111 15TH WAR
HOOPER, HENERY DOR 359 3RD DIVI
HOOPER, HENERY DOR 331 3RD DIVI
HOOPER, HENRIETTA BAL 347 7TH WARD
HOOPER, HENRY BAL 142 1ST WARD
HOOPER, HENRY BAL 121 1ST WARD
HOOPER, HENRY BAL 148 1ST WARD
HOOPER, HENRY BAL 161 1ST WARD
HOOPER, HENRY BAL 273 17TH WAR
HOOPER, HENRY SOM 525 QUANTICO
HOOPER, HENRY* DOR 459 1ST DIST
HOOPER, HERCULES MGM 325 CRACKLIN
HOOPER, ISRAEL BAL 077 15TH WAR
HOOPER, J. B. BAL 332 1ST DIST
HOOPER, J. P. BAL 333 1ST DIST
HOOPER, JACOB BAL 084 15TH WAR
HOOPER, JACOB DOR 357 3RD DIVI
HOOPER, JAMES BAL 258 17TH WAR
HOOPER, JAMES BAL 236 17TH WAR
HOOPER, JAMES CAL 029 2ND DIST
HOOPER, JAMES BAL 301 3RD WARD
HOOPER, JAMES BAL 307 3RD WARD
HOOPER, JAMES BAL 216 6TH WARD
HOOPER, JAMES BAL 048 15TH WAR
HOOPER, JAMES WOR 228 6TH E DI
HOOPER, JAMES WAS 127 2ND DIST
HOOPER, JAMES A. BAL 082 4TH WARD
HOOPER, JAMES B. BAL 049 18TH WAR
HOOPER, JAMES J. BAL 039 18TH WAR
HOOPER, JAMES JR. BAL 072 15TH WAR
HOOPER, JAMES T. ST 285 2ND E DI
HOOPER, JANE BAL 011 4TH WARD
HOOPER, JOHN BAL 275 17TH WAR
HOOPER, JOHN DOR 359 3RD DIVI
HOOPER, JOHN FRE 021 FREDERIC
HOOPER, JOHN BAL 009 EASTERN
HOOPER, JOHN BAL 088 2ND DIST
HOOPER, JOHN E. DOR 453 1ST DIST
HOOPER, JOHN J. BAL 210 6TH WARD
HOOPER, JOHN P. BAL 048 15TH WAR
HOOPER, JOHN T. SOM 487 SALISBUR
HOOPER, JOSEPH DOR 330 3RD DIVI
HOOPER, JOSEPH M. BAL 223 6TH WARD
HOOPER, JOSEPH T.H. CAR 360 9TH DIST
HOOPER, JOSEPH* DOR 377 1ST DIST
HOOPER, JOSIAH DOR 428 1ST DIST
HOOPER, JULIA A. CAR 360 9TH DIST
HOOPER, LEVENTA BAL 130 11TH WAR
HOOPER, LEVIN BAL 278 20TH WAR
HOOPER, LOUISA BAL 077 15TH WAR
HOOPER, LUCY A. BAL 209 19TH WAR
HOOPER, MARGARET BAL 053 15TH WAR
HOOPER, MARGRETT CAR 140 NO TWP L
HOOPER, MARIA D. DOR 374 1ST DIST
HOOPER, MARY BAL 447 14TH WAR
HOOPER, MARY DOR 331 3RD DIVI
HOOPER, MARY ST 287 2ND E DI
HOOPER, MARY A. BAL 007 4TH WARD
HOOPER, MARY E. BAL 117 11TH WAR
HOOPER, MARY J. BAL 088 4TH WARD
HOOPER, MARY J. BAL 305 3RD WARD
HOOPER, MARY M. BAL 075 15TH WAR
HOOPER, MARY M. KEN 259 1ST DIST
HOOPER, MARY MISS- BAL 315 20TH WAR
HOOPER, MARY S. CAL 011 1ST DIST
HOOPER, MARY S. DOR 331 3RD DIVI
HOOPER, MARY S. DOR 331 3RD DIVI
HOOPER, MICHAEL BAL 016 18TH WAR
HOOPER, NATHANIEL BAL 284 7TH WARD
HOOPER, NEWTON* DOR 455 1ST DIST
HOOPER, OCTAVIUS T. CAL 018 1ST DIST
HOOPER, OLIVIA BAL 476 14TH WAR
HOOPER, PAMELIA BAL 302 7TH WARD
HOOPER, PRICELLA* DOR 332 3RD DIVI
HOOPER, PRISCILLA BAL 335 13TH WAR
HOOPER, PRUDENCE BAL 192 11TH WAR
HOOPER, RACHEL DOR 414 1ST DIST
HOOPER, RACHEL A. BAL 098 10TH WAR
HOOPER, ROBERT BAL 052 15TH WAR
HOOPER, ROBERT DOR 333 3RD DIVI
HOOPER, ROSEANN DOR 330 3RD DIVI
HOOPER, SAMUEL DOR 332 3RD DIVI
HOOPER, SAMUEL BAL 261 17TH WAR
HOOPER, SAMUEL BAL 391 3RD WARD
HOOPER, SAMUEL BAL 167 1ST WARD
HOOPER, SARAH BAL 221 12TH WAR
HOOPER, SARAH BAL 088 2ND DIST
HOOPER, STEPHEN HAR 093 2ND DIST
HOOPER, STEPHEN H. BAL 167 6TH WARD
HOOPER, SYE* DOR 414 1ST DIST
HOOPER, THOMAS FRE 021 FREDERIC
HOOPER, THOMAS FRE 442 8TH E DI
HOOPER, THOMAS BAL 078 15TH WAR
HOOPER, THOMAS BAL 092 10TH WAR
HOOPER, THOMAS BAL 115 1ST WARD
HOOPER, THOMAS D. BAL 243 17TH WAR
HOOPER, THOMAS J. BAL 353 7TH WARD
HOOPER, THOMAS W. BAL 053 15TH WAR
HOOPER, THOMAS-BLACK BAL 216 2ND WARD
HOOPER, V. P.* DOR 453 1ST DIST
HOOPER, WASHINGTON BAL 171 16TH WAR
HOOPER, WILIAM CAL 031 2ND DIST
HOOPER, WILLIAM BAL 020 4TH WARD
HOOPER, WILLIAM BAL 323 12TH WAR
HOOPER, WILLIAM BAL 139 16TH WAR
HOOPER, WILLIAM BAL 109 1ST WARD
HOOPER, WILLIAM BAL 022 1ST WARD
HOOPER, WILLIAM BAL 075 1ST WARD
HOOPER, WILLIAM ANN 346 3RD DIST
HOOPER, WILLIAM BAL 269 7TH WARD
HOOPER, WILLIAM A. FRE 001 FREDERIC
HOOPER, WILLIAM E. BAL 011 4TH WARD
HOOPER, WILLIAM H. FRE 264 NEW MARK
HOOPER, WILLIAM H. BAL 332 3RD WARD
HOOPER, WILLIAM W.* DOR 446 1ST DIST
HOOPER, WILLIAM* DOR 454 1ST DIST
HOOPKINS, RUTH A. FRE 277 NEW MARK
HOOPMAN, FRANCIS BAL 031 1ST WARD
HOOPMAN, JACOB HAR 164 3RD DIST
HOOPMAN, JOHN HAR 207 3RD DIST
HOOPMAN, JOHN W. HAR 164 3RD DIST
HOOPMAN, MARY A. BAL 026 1ST WARD
HOOPPER, J. ANN 282 ANNAPOLI
HOOPRA, SARAH C. HAR 164 3RD DIST
HOOPS, AMOS BAL 015 1ST WARD
HOOPS, CALEB BAL 258 1ST DIST
HOOPS, CLARA CEC 205 7TH E DI

Name	County	Page	Locality
HOOPS, DARLINGTON	HAR	112	2ND DIST
HOOPS, FRANKLIN B.	BAL	030	1ST WARD
HOOPS, GEORGE W.	BAL	030	1ST WARD
HOOPS, JANE	BAL	076	4TH WARD
HOOPS, PHOEEE	HAR	112	2ND DIST
HOOPS, SARAH	WAS	068	2ND SUBD
HOOPS, SILUS	HAR	082	2ND DIST
HOORICH, FRANCIS	CAR	365	9TH DIST
HOOS, JOHN	BAL	086	10TH WAR
HOOSLEY, JOHN	BAL	039	2ND DIST
HOOSLEY, MATILDA	BAL	039	2ND DIST
HOOSLEY, MATILDA	BAL	039	2ND DIST
HOOSTER, CECILIA *	BAL	282	1ST DIST
HOOTE, HENRY	BAL	435	8TH WARD
HOOTON, J.	BAL	150	1ST WARD
HOOTZEL, AUSTIN	ALL	004	3RD E.D.
HOOVE, JOHN	BAL	382	3RD WARD
HOOVER, ADAM	BAL	043	18TH WAR
HOOVER, ADAM L.	CAR	184	8TH DIST
HOOVER, ANDREW	WAS	178	BOONSBOR
HOOVER, ANN M.	ALL	212	CUMBERLA
HOOVER, BENJAMIN	WAS	266	1ST DIST
HOOVER, CHARLES	BAL	019	1ST WARD
HOOVER, CHRISTIAN	WAS	199	1ST DIST
HOOVER, CURLITE	WAS	253	1ST DIST
HOOVER, DANIEL	CAR	184	8TH DIST
HOOVER, DANIEL	FRE	366	CATOCTIN
HOOVER, DANIEL	FRE	181	5TH E DI
HOOVER, DAVID	WAS	250	1ST DIST
HOOVER, DAVID	WAS	269	1ST DIST
HOOVER, DAVID	WAS	012	WILLIAMS
HOOVER, ELIE	WAS	269	1ST DIST
HOOVER, ELIZABETH	WAS	257	1ST DIST
HOOVER, ELIZABETH	WAS	273	RIDGEVIL
HOOVER, ELIZABETH	BAL	213	11TH WAR
HOOVER, ELIZABETH	ALL	010	3RD E.D.
HOOVER, ELIZABETH	BAL	086	10TH WAR
HOOVER, ELIZABETH	BAL	182	16TH WAR
HOOVER, EZRA	WAS	232	1ST DIST
HOOVER, FRANCES	BAL	122	18TH WAR
HOOVER, FRANCIS J.	FRE	168	EMMITTSB
HOOVER, FREDERICK	BAL	313	7TH WARD
HOOVER, GEORGE	BAL	090	1ST WARD
HOOVER, GEORGE	BAL	460	1ST DIST
HOOVER, GIDEON	FRE	362	CATOCTIN
HOOVER, HARIET	WAS	012	WILLIAMS
HOOVER, HENRY	BAL	049	18TH WAR
HOOVER, HENRY	BAL	015	18TH WAR
HOOVER, HESTER	WAS	273	RIDGEVIL
HOOVER, HY	BAL	192	5TH DIST
HOOVER, ISABELLA	WAS	240	CAVETOWN
HOOVER, JACOB	WAS	229	1ST DIST
HOOVER, JACOB	WAS	273	RIDGEVIL
HOOVER, JACCB	ALL	015	3RD E.D.
HOOVER, JACOB	ALL	047	10TH E.D
HOOVER, JACOB	BAL	031	18TH WAR
HOOVER, JACOB	FRE	375	CATOCTIN
HOOVER, JAOCB	FRE	185	5TH E DI
HOOVER, JAOCB	BAL	450	14TH WAR
HOOVER, JESSE	FRE	174	5TH E DI
HOOVER, JOHN	FRE	159	EMMITTSB
HOOVER, JOHN	FRE	185	5TH E DI
HOOVER, JOHN	FRE	362	CATOCTIN
HOOVER, JOHN	BAL	213	19TH WAR
HOOVER, JOHN	FRE	349	MIDDLETO
HOOVER, JOHN	BAL	193	5TH DIST
HOOVER, JOHN	BAL	313	7TH WARD
HOOVER, JOHN	BAL	086	10TH WAR
HOOVER, JOHN	BAL	292	12TH WAR
HOOVER, JOHN	WAS	090	2ND SUBD
HOOVER, JOHN L.	CAR	184	8TH DIST
HOOVER, JOHN W.	BAL	289	20TH WAR
HOOVER, JOSEPH	CAR	352	6TH DIST
HOOVER, JOSEPH	BAL	315	20TH WAR
HOOVER, LAURA C.	BAL	147	19TH WAR
HOOVER, LYDIA	ALL	251	CUMBERLA
HOOVER, MARTIN	WAS	250	1ST DIST
HOOVER, MARY	BAL	311	3RD WARD
HOOVER, MARY A. V.	FRE	168	EMMITTSB
HOOVER, MICHAEL	ALL	176	7TH E.D.
HOOVER, NANCY	WAS	273	RIDGEVIL
HOOVER, PETER	BAL	192	5TH DIST
HOOVER, REEECCA	BAL	122	18TH WAR
HOOVER, SAMUEL	FRE	363	CATOCTIN
HOOVER, SAMUEL	WAS	252	1ST DIST
HOOVER, SARAH	ALL	251	CUMBERLA
HOOVER, SIMEON	FRE	362	CATOCTIN
HOOVER, SOLOMON	WAS	243	CAVETOWN
HOOVER, SUSAN	WAS	251	1ST DIST
HOOVER, WILLIAM	WAS	248	1ST DIST
HOOVER, WILLIAM	BAL	380	8TH WARD
HOOVER,CARLISLE	ALL	015	3RD E.D.
HOOVER,MARY C.	FRE	184	5TH E DI
HOOVER,MILLIA	CAR	354	6TH DIST
HOOVES, JACOB	ALL	199	CUMBERLA
HOOVRUS, WILLIAM	FRE	106	CREAGERS
HOOWE, SAMUEL	BAL	296	3RD WARD
HOPBACH, ADAM*	BAL	089	10TH WAR
HOPE, ANDREW	HAR	023	1ST DIST
HOPE, ANN	BAL	407	14TH WAR
HOPE, DANIEL	BAL	327	13TH WAR
HOPE, DANIEL JR.	TAL	083	ST MICHA
HOPE, DAVID	BAL	022	15TH WAR
HOPE, ELIZABETH	HAR	062	1ST DIST
HOPE, GEORGE	BAL	335	1ST DIST
HOPE, GEORGE W.	CAR	325	1ST DIST
HOPE, HANNAH	FRE	396	PETERSVI
HOPE, JAMES	HAR	070	1ST DIST
HOPE, JOHN	ALL	103	5TH E.D.
HOPE, JOHN	TAL	065	EASTON T
HOPE, JULIA	BAL	429	1ST DIST
HOPE, JULIA	BAL	429	1ST DIST
HOPE, SARAH J.	FRE	132	CREAGERS
HOPE, THOMAS	HAR	059	1ST DIST
HOPE, WILLIAM	HAR	070	1ST DIST
HOPE, WILLIAM	FRE	107	CREAGERS
HOPE, WILLIAM	BAL	054	9TH WARD
HOPE, WILLIAM	BAL	188	2ND WARD
HOPE, WILLIAM	SOM	459	HANGARY
HOPE, WILLIAM H.	BAL	054	9TH WARD
HOPERGROVES, WILLIAM	CEC	026	ELKTON 3
HOPEWELL, BENJAMIN-BLACK	FRE	242	NEW MARK
HOPEWELL, DAVID	WAS	161	HAGERSTO
HOPEWELL, GEORGE-BLACK	ST	292	2ND E DI
HOPEWELL, JACOB-MULATTO	FRE	238	NEW MARK
HOPEWELL, JAMES	WAS	032	2ND SUBD
HOPEWELL, JAMES R.	ST	292	2ND E DI
HOPEWELL, KITTY	BAL	073	10TH WAR
HOPEWELL, LUCRETIA-BLACK	ST	298	2ND E DI
HOPEWELL, PETER	WAS	090	2ND SUBD
HOPEWELL, RACHEAL	WAS	163	HAGERSTO
HOPEWELL, THOMAS	QUE	211	3RD E DI
HOPEY, CHARLES*	TAL	019	EASTON D
HOPKINS, ----*	BAL	037	4TH WARD
HOPKINS, ABEL	BAL	175	2ND DIST
HOPKINS, ALFRED H.	TAL	044	EASTON T
HOPKINS, ALICE	HAR	127	2ND DIST
HOPKINS, AMANDA	HAR	122	2ND DIST
HOPKINS, ANN	MGM	334	CRACKLIN
HOPKINS, ANN	CEC	210	7TH E DI
HOPKINS, ANN	BAL	186	5TH DIST
HOPKINS, ANN	BAL	026	1ST WARD
HOPKINS, ANN	BAL	325	12TH WAR
HOPKINS, ANN E.	BAL	294	3RD WARD
HOPKINS, ANN M.	BAL	011	15TH WAR
HOPKINS, ANN W.	BAL	159	19TH WAR
HOPKINS, ANNA M.	ANN	459	HOWARD D
HOPKINS, BEN*	DOR	464	1ST DIST
HOPKINS, BENJAMIN	TAL	044	EASTON D
HOPKINS, BENJAMIN	TAL	045	EASTON T
HOPKINS, BETSEY	QUE	212	3RD E DI
HOPKINS, C.	BAL	152	1ST WARD
HOPKINS, CHALKLEY	BAL	382	13TH WAR
HOPKINS, CHARLES	BAL	126	11TH WAR
HOPKINS, CHARLES	BAL	440	8TH WARD
HOPKINS, CHARLES E.	TAL	010	EASTON D
HOPKINS, CHARLES W.	DOR	373	1ST DIST
HOPKINS, CHARLES W.	HAR	003	1ST DIST
HOPKINS, CHARLOTTE	BAL	258	6TH WARD
HOPKINS, CORNELIUS	BAL	232	1ST DIST
HOPKINS, DANIEL	ANN	421	HOWARD D
HOPKINS, DANIEL	ANN	457	HOWARD D
HOPKINS, DANIEL	BAL	126	11TH WAR
HOPKINS, DAVID	ALL	120	5TH E.D.
HOPKINS, DAVID	WOR	304	SNOW HIL
HOPKINS, DAVID E.	ANN	505	HOWARD D
HOPKINS, DEBORAH	BAL	383	13TH WAR
HOPKINS, DOROTHEA	BAL	001	15TH WAR
HOPKINS, EDWARD	ANN	267	ANNAPOLI
HOPKINS, EDWARD	DOR	365	3RD DIVI
HOPKINS, EDWARD	QUE	222	4TH E DI
HOPKINS, EDWARD	QUE	235	4TH E DI
HOPKINS, EDWORD A.	HAR	192	3RD DIST
HOPKINS, ELIJAH	SOM	439	DAMES QU
HOPKINS, ELIZA	TAL	068	EASTON T
HOPKINS, ELIZA R.	BAL	384	13TH WAR
HOPKINS, ELIZABETH	BAL	297	20TH WAR
HOPKINS, ELIZABETH	ST	313	1ST E DI
HOPKINS, ELIZABETH	TAL	087	ST MICHA
HOPKINS, ELIZABETH	SOM	529	QUANTICO
HOPKINS, ELIZABETH	BAL	166	11TH WAR
HOPKINS, ELIZABETH-BLACK	CAR	069	NO TWP L
HOPKINS, ELLA	BAL	378	1ST DIST
HOPKINS, ELLEN	BAL	080	4TH WARD
HOPKINS, ELLEN	MGM	352	BERRYS D
HOPKINS, ELLEN E.	HAR	150	3RD DIST
HOPKINS, EPHRAIM	HAR	002	1ST DIST
HOPKINS, EPHRAIM	HAR	003	1ST DIST
HOPKINS, FANNY	BAL	001	EASTERN
HOPKINS, FRANKLIN	BAL	225	2ND WARD
HOPKINS, GEORGE	BAL	226	12TH WAR
HOPKINS, GEORGE	SOM	439	DAMES QU
HOPKINS, GEORGE	SOM	535	QUANTICO
HOPKINS, GEORGE H.	TAL	079	ST MICHA
HOPKINS, GEORGE W.	SOM	439	DAMES QU
HOPKINS, GEORGE W.	HAR	125	2ND DIST
HOPKINS, GEORGE-BLACK	FRE	220	BUCKEYST
HOPKINS, GEORGE-MULATTO	CAR	069	NO TWP L
HOPKINS, GERARD	ANN	321	2ND DIST
HOPKINS, GERRARD T.	BAL	001	15TH WAR
HOPKINS, GIDEON P.	BAL	134	16TH WAR
HOPKINS, GRACEY A.	BAL	053	15TH WAR
HOPKINS, GREENBURY*	BAL	308	3RD WARD
HOPKINS, H.	BAL	072	10TH WAR
HOPKINS, HANNAH	BAL	173	11TH WAR
HOPKINS, HARRISON	TAL	050	EASTON T
HOPKINS, HENNERETTA	BAL	205	11TH WAR
HOPKINS, HENNRIETTA	BAL	163	11TH WAR
HOPKINS, HENRY	CEC	147	PORT DUP
HOPKINS, HENRY	TAL	035	EASTON D
HOPKINS, HENRY F.	SOM	528	QUANTICO
HOPKINS, HENRY P.	TAL	010	EASTON D
HOPKINS, HENRY W.	HAR	001	1ST DIST
HOPKINS, HENRY-BLACK	FRE	220	BUCKEYST
HOPKINS, HESTER	ANN	331	2ND DIST
HOPKINS, HOWARD	BAL	278	20TH WAR
HOPKINS, ISAAC	SOM	552	TYASKIN
HOPKINS, ISAAC	KEN	292	3RD DIST
HOPKINS, ISAAC G.	ANN	318	2ND DIST
HOPKINS, ISAAC H.	ANN	324	2ND DIST
HOPKINS, JACOB	TAL	009	EASTON D
HOPKINS, JAMES	TAL	026	EASTON D
HOPKINS, JAMES	SOM	551	TYASKIN
HOPKINS, JAMES	TAL	050	EASTON T
HOPKINS, JAMES	TAL	076	EASTON T
HOPKINS, JAMES	ANN	297	1ST DIST
HOPKINS, JAMES	BAL	185	11TH WAR
HOPKINS, JAMES	BAL	448	8TH WARD
HOPKINS, JAMES	HAR	030	1ST DIST
HOPKINS, JAMES	HAR	118	2ND DIST
HOPKINS, JAMES	BAL	422	14TH WAR
HOPKINS, JAMES	CAR	097	NO TWP L
HOPKINS, JAMES	BAL	415	3RD WARD
HOPKINS, JAMES	BAL	003	18TH WAR
HOPKINS, JAMES A.	SOM	544	TYASKIN
HOPKINS, JAMES C.	BAL	003	18TH WAR
HOPKINS, JAMES H.	TAL	076	EASTON T
HOPKINS, JAMES L.	ANN	332	2ND DIST
HOPKINS, JAMES M.	TAL	103	ST MICHA
HOPKINS, JAMES SR.	QUE	236	4TH E DI
HOPKINS, JAMES T.	BAL	416	3RD WARD
HOPKINS, JANE	BAL	276	7TH WARD
HOPKINS, JANNEL	MGM	320	CRACKLIN
HOPKINS, JARNETT	HAR	117	2ND DIST
HOPKINS, JARRET-BLACK	MGM	432	CLARKSTR
HOPKINS, JESS	TAL	095	ST MICHA
HOPKINS, JESSE K.	WOR	341	1ST E DI
HOPKINS, JOEL	ANN	413	HOWARD D
HOPKINS, JOHN	ANN	313	1ST DIST
HOPKINS, JOHN	BAL	128	2ND DIST
HOPKINS, JOHN	BAL	149	2ND DIST
HOPKINS, JOHN	BAL	061	2ND DIST
HOPKINS, JOHN	TAL	072	EASTON T
HOPKINS, JOHN	WOR	349	1ST E DI
HOPKINS, JOHN	MGM	356	BERRYS D
HOPKINS, JOHN	HAR	045	1ST DIST
HOPKINS, JOHN	HAR	027	1ST DIST
HOPKINS, JOHN	HAR	153	3RD DIST
HOPKINS, JOHN	BAL	451	14TH WAR
HOPKINS, JOHN	BAL	469	14TH WAR
HOPKINS, JOHN *	BAL	312	12TH WAR
HOPKINS, JOHN A.	HAR	002	1ST DIST
HOPKINS, JOHN B.	BAL	013	18TH WAR
HOPKINS, JOHN H.	ANN	303	1ST DIST
HOPKINS, JOHN H.	SOM	551	TYASKIN
HOPKINS, JOHN M.	HAR	141	2ND DIST
HOPKINS, JOHN N.	BAL	062	18TH WAR
HOPKINS, JOHN R.	TAL	025	EASTON D
HOPKINS, JOHN SR.	SOM	526	QUANTICO
HOPKINS, JOHN W.	BAL	013	18TH WAR
HOPKINS, JOHN W.	HAR	030	1ST DIST
HOPKINS, JOHN Y.	BAL	168	11TH WAR
HOPKINS, JOHNZZY	PRI	016	BLADENSB
HOPKINS, JOKE *	HAR	026	1ST DIST
HOPKINS, JONATHAN E.	ANN	505	HOWARD D
HOPKINS, JOSEPH	BAL	290	1ST DIST
HOPKINS, JOSEPH	HAR	033	1ST DIST
HOPKINS, JOSEPH	BAL	447	14TH WAR
HOPKINS, JOSEPH	BAL	335	13TH WAR
HOPKINS, JOSEPH	CEC	131	6TH E DI
HOPKINS, JOSEPH	SOM	552	TYASKIN
HOPKINS, JOSEPH	SOM	358	BRINKLEY
HOPKINS, JOSEPH E.	BAL	353	7TH WARD
HOPKINS, JOSHUA	HAR	027	1ST DIST
HOPKINS, JOSIAH	DOR	382	1ST DIST
HOPKINS, JULIA	BAL	120	2ND DIST
HOPKINS, L. N.	BAL	322	12TH WAR
HOPKINS, LEVEN M.	DOR	332	3RD DIVI
HOPKINS, LEVI	MGM	331	CRACKLIN
HOPKINS, LEVI	BAL	019	2ND DIST
HOPKINS, LEWIS	HAR	034	1ST DIST
HOPKINS, LOUISA	CEC	146	PORT DUP
HOPKINS, LUCY	MGM	338	CRACKLIN
HOPKINS, LYDIA	MGM	348	BERRYS D
HOPKINS, MANUEL	SOM	515	BARREN C
HOPKINS, MARGARET	SOM	547	TYASKIN
HOPKINS, MARGARET	ST	310	1ST E DI
HOPKINS, MARGARET	HAR	027	1ST DIST
HOPKINS, MARGARFT*	TAL	056	EASTON D
HOPKINS, MARIA	BAL	076	10TH WAR
HOPKINS, MARIAH	WOR	331	1ST E DI
HOPKINS, MARSH	BAL	302	20TH WAR
HOPKINS, MARTHA	BAL	158	11TH WAR
HOPKINS, MARTHA	CEC	103	4TH E DI
HOPKINS, MARY	CEC	213	7TH E DI
HOPKINS, MARY	HAR	125	2ND DIST
HOPKINS, MARY	BAL	058	10TH WAR
HOPKINS, MARY	BAL	274	1ST DIST
HOPKINS, MARY	BAL	230	1ST DIST
HOPKINS, MARY	ALL	214	CUMBERLA
HOPKINS, MARY	BAL	259	5TH WARD
HOPKINS, MARY	BAL	187	6TH WARD
HOPKINS, MARY	BAL	035	9TH WARD
HOPKINS, MARY A.	HAR	133	2ND DIST
HOPKINS, MARY A.	BAL	079	4TH WARD
HOPKINS, MARY A.	FRE	243	NEW MARK
HOPKINS, MARY B.	BAL	163	16TH WAR
HOPKINS, MARY C.	ANN	362	4TH DIST
HOPKINS, MARY M.	BAL	215	11TH WAR
HOPKINS, MARY M.	TAL	073	EASTON T
HOPKINS, MATTHEW	DOR	319	1ST DIST
HOPKINS, MELISSA	QUE	237	4TH E DI
HOPKINS, MITCHELL	SOM	526	QUANTICO
HOPKINS, NANCY	SOM	526	QUANTICO
HOPKINS, NANCY	ANN	362	4TH DIST
HOPKINS, NATHAN	TAL	025	EASTON D
HOPKINS, NATHANIEL	KEN	282	3RD DIST
HOPKINS, NICOLAS	CAR	159	NO TWP L
HOPKINS, P.-BLACK	FRE	033	FREDERIC
HOPKINS, PETER	MGM	333	CRACKLIN
HOPKINS, PETER	BAL	231	12TH WAR
HOPKINS, PHILIP	MGM	351	BERRYS D
HOPKINS, PHILIP	CEC	151	PORT DUP
HOPKINS, PHILIP	PRI	043	VANSVILL
HOPKINS, PHILIP G.	BAL	226	5TH WARD
HOPKINS, POLLY A.	DOR	465	1ST DIST
HOPKINS, PRISCILLA	BAL	068	10TH WAR
HOPKINS, PRISCILLA	BAL	344	13TH WAR
HOPKINS, PRUSILLA	SOM	554	TYASKIN
HOPKINS, R.	BAL	162	1ST WARD
HOPKINS, RACHEL A.	MGM	367	BERRYS D
HOPKINS, REBECCA	BAL	234	6TH WARD
HOPKINS, REBECCA-MULATTO	BAL	214	2ND WARD
HOPKINS, REUBEN	MGM	366	BERRYS D
HOPKINS, REUBEN-BLACK	FRE	246	NEW MARK
HOPKINS, RICHARD	MGM	350	BERRYS D
HOPKINS, RICHARD	HAR	130	2ND DIST
HOPKINS, RICHARD	HAR	129	2ND DIST
HOPKINS, RICHARD	BAL	171	1ST WARD
HOPKINS, RICHARD	ANN	325	2ND DIST
HOPKINS, RICHARD	ANN	332	2ND DIST
HOPKINS, RICHARD	BAL	124	1ST WARD
HOPKINS, RICHARD	BAL	336	3RD WARD
HOPKINS, RICHARD	SOM	528	QUANTICO
HOPKINS, RICHARD S.	ANN	368	4TH DIST
HOPKINS, RICHARD S.	HAR	014	1ST DIST
HOPKINS, RICHARD-BLACK	BAL	136	1ST WARD
HOPKINS, ROBERT M.	BAL	224	6TH WARD
HOPKINS, ROSS	FRE	277	NEW MARK
HOPKINS, SALLY	BAL	058	10TH WAR
HOPKINS, SALLY	SOM	515	BARREN C
HOPKINS, SALLY	SOM	553	TYASKIN
HOPKINS, SAM	BAL	197	11TH WAR
HOPKINS, SAMEUL	ANN	364	4TH DIST
HOPKINS, SAMUEL	ALL	055	10TH E.D
HOPKINS, SAMUEL	SOM	507	BARREN C
HOPKINS, SAMUEL	SOM	515	BARREN C
HOPKINS, SAMUEL	PRI	039	VANSVILL
HOPKINS, SAMUEL	HAR	030	1ST DIST
HOPKINS, SAMUEL	HAR	129	2ND DIST
HOPKINS, SAMUEL	HAR	178	3RD DIST
HOPKINS, SAMUEL B.	TAL	072	EASTON T
HOPKINS, SAMUEL G.	BAL	294	3RD WARD
HOPKINS, SAMUEL P.	HAR	154	3RD DIST
HOPKINS, SARAH	HAR	027	1ST DIST
HOPKINS, SARAH	BAL	129	18TH WAR
HOPKINS, SARAH	BAL	100	5TH WARD
HOPKINS, SARAH A.	HAR	125	2ND DIST
HOPKINS, SARAH M.	HAR	171	3RD DIST
HOPKINS, SEPTIMUS	ANN	430	HOWARD D
HOPKINS, SEXTUS	ANN	385	4TH DIST
HOPKINS, SOLOMAN J.*	TAL	007	EASTON D
HOPKINS, SOLOMON	TAL	040	EASTON D
HOPKINS, SOPHIA	BAL	282	7TH WARD
HOPKINS, STEPHEN	SOM	461	HANGARY
HOPKINS, STEPHEN R.	SOM	535	QUANTICO
HOPKINS, SUSAN	TAL	066	EASTON T
HOPKINS, SUSAN	BAL	003	15TH WAR
HOPKINS, TAMY	CHA	257	MIDDLETO
HOPKINS, THOAMS	HAR	029	1ST DIST

Name	Co.	Page	Locality
HOPKINS, THOAS	BAL	114	1ST WARD
HOPKINS, THOMAS	BAL	025	1ST WARD
HOPKINS, THOMAS	BAL	282	2ND WARD
HOPKINS, THOMAS	ANN	428	HOWARD D
HOPKINS, THOMAS	BAL	166	1ST WARD
HOPKINS, THOMAS	FRE	383	PETERSVI
HOPKINS, THOMAS	FRE	20	5TH E DI
HOPKINS, THOMAS	DOR	367	3RD DIVI
HOPKINS, THOMAS	PRI	044	VANSVILL
HOPKINS, THOMAS	TAL	015	EASTON D
HOPKINS, THOMAS C.	HAR	150	3RD DIST
HOPKINS, THOMAS C.	BAL	359	3RD WARD
HOPKINS, THOMAS E.	BAL	396	8TH WARD
HOPKINS, THOMAS F.	TAL	024	EASTON D
HOPKINS, THOMAS S.	PRI	040	VANSVILL
HOPKINS, VILOT	TAL	065	EASTON T
HOPKINS, VIOLET	HAR	033	1ST DIST
HOPKINS, WAKEMAN B.	HAR	123	2ND DIST
HOPKINS, WILLIAM	HAR	172	3RD DIST
HOPKINS, WILLIAM	KEN	252	1ST DIST
HOPKINS, WILLIAM	HAR	119	2ND DIST
HOPKINS, WILLIAM	SOM	438	DAMES QU
HOPKINS, WILLIAM	DOR	393	1ST DIST
HOPKINS, WILLIAM	BAL	028	4TH WARD
HOPKINS, WILLIAM	BAL	017	4TH WARD
HOPKINS, WILLIAM	BAL	418	3RD WARD
HOPKINS, WILLIAM	BAL	068	18TH WAR
HOPKINS, WILLIAM	QUE	236	4TH E DI
HOPKINS, WILLIAM	BAL	025	9TH WARD
HOPKINS, WILLIAM	BAL	026	9TH WARD
HOPKINS, WILLIAM	BAL	164	6TH WARD
HOPKINS, WILLIAM	BAL	128	2ND DIST
HOPKINS, WILLIAM	ANN	395	8TH DIST
HOPKINS, WILLIAM	BAL	134	16TH WAR
HOPKINS, WILLIAM A.	PRI	035	VANSVILL
HOPKINS, WILLIAM C.	ANN	399	8TH DIST
HOPKINS, WILLIAM E.	ALL	209	CUMBERLA
HOPKINS, WILLIAM E.	HAR	147	3RD DIST
HOPKINS, WILLIAM F.	BAL	110	15TH WAR
HOPKINS, WILLIAM H.	BAL	187	2ND WARD
HOPKINS, WILLIAM M.	BAL	019	18TH WAR
HOPKINS, WILLIAM S.	BAL	109	15TH WAR
HOPKINS, WILLIAM*	DOR	460	1ST DIST
HOPKINS, PHILIP	CAR	156	NO TWP L
HOPKINSON, FRANCIS	BAL	063	18TH WAR
HOPKINSON, M. A. DR.	BAL	340	13TH WAR
HOPKISN, J. L.	BAL	475	14TH WAR
HOPLINS, THOMAS R.	BAL	169	1ST WARD
HOPP, RUTH	BAL	152	11TH WAR
HOPP, WILLIAM	FRE	444	8TH E DI
HOPP, WILLIAM	BAL	405	8TH WARD
HOPPE, A.E.	BAL	241	12TH WAR
HOPPE, ASHTON	CAR	354	6TH DIST
HOPPE, DAVID	CAR	294	7TH DIST
HOPPE, HERMAN	BAL	115	15TH WAR
HOPPE, JOH NH.	CAR	294	7TH DIST
HOPPE, LEAH	CAR	246	3RD DIST
HOPPELL, GEORGE	BAL	289	7TH WARD
HOPPELL, LAWRANCE	BAL	126	18TH WAR
HOPPENSTADLER, ELIZA	BAL	403	14TH WAR
HOPPER, ASAHEL	BAL	087	2ND DIST
HOPPER, CATHARINE	BAL	112	15TH WAR
HOPPER, DANIEL C.	QUE	200	3RD E DI
HOPPER, ELLEN	BAL	403	8TH WARD
HOPPER, GEORGE	MGM	323	CRACKLIN
HOPPER, JAMES	HAR	145	3RD DIST
HOPPER, JOHN A.	HAR	145	3RD DIST
HOPPER, P.B.	QUE	182	3RD E DI
HOPPER, SAMUEL	ANN	476	HOWARD D
HOPPER, SAMUEL W. T.	BAL	364	13TH WAR
HOPPER, THOMAS W.	BAL	475	14TH WAR
HOPPER, WASHINGTON	BAL	402	8TH WARD
HOPPER, WILLIAM J.	QUE	184	3RD E DI
HOPPER, WILLIAM	QUE	182	3RD E DI
HOPPS, MARY A.	BAL	183	11TH WAR
HOPS, FANNY	BAL	058	10TH WAR
HOPS, FANNY	BAL	323	12TH WAR
HOPS, WASHINGTON	HAR	203	3RD DIST
HOPSON, ELLEN	BAL	053	9TH WARD
HOPWELL, ALFRED	FRE	241	NEW MARK
HOPWELL, ANGELICA	ST	307	1ST E DI
HOPWOOD, JAMES	FRE	008	FREDERIC
HOPWOOD, JOSEPH	MGM	344	CLARKSBU
HOPWOOD, JOSHUA	FRE	084	FREDERIC
HOPWOOD, JOSHUA	ALL	243	CUMBERLA
HORACE, ANNA	BAL	268	12TH WAR
HORACE, ISABELLA	BAL	293	3RD WARD
HORADA, HENRY	CEC	039	CHESAPEA
HORALL, HENRIETTA	ANN	379	4TH DIST
HORAN, ANDREW	FRE	069	FREDERIC
HORAN, ELLEN	WAS	020	2ND SUBD
HORAN, MICHAEL	WAS	019	2ND SUBD
HORAN, PATRICK	ALL	048	10TH E.D
HORBER, HAVEN *	BAL	378	13TH WAR
HORBEY, JAMES F.	BAL	281	20TH WAR
HORBICT, ARVILLA	BAL	167	11TH WAR
HORDERSON, FRANCIS *	BAL	316	12TH WAR
HORDLEY, CHARLES	BAL	129	1ST WARD
HORELIES, THOMAS	ALL	102	5TH E.D.
HOREW, WILLIAM	BAL	208	6TH WARD
HORETER, WILLIAM H.	QUE	225	4TH E DI
HOREY, BUDGET	BAL	287	12TH WAR
HORFFETT, BENJAMIN	FRE	408	JEFFERSO
HORFMAN, HENRY F.	BAL	007	9TH WARD
HORFREY, LETITIA	BAL	022	9TH WARD
HORGAN, OLIVER J.	QUE	242	5TH E DI
HORICK, EDWARD	BAL	250	2ND WARD
HORICK, MONTELL	BAL	173	19TH WAR
HORIDAY, MICHAEL	HAR	205	3RD DIST
HORINE, ANN	FRE	351	MIDDLETO
HORINE, CATHERINE ANN	ALL	211	CUMBERLA
HORINE, CONRAD	WAS	226	1ST DIST
HORINE, JOEL	FRE	403	JEFFERSO
HORINE, JOHN	FRE	350	MIDDLETO
HORINE, JOHN	WAS	178	BOONSBOR
HORINE, LUTHER	FRE	394	PETERSVI
HORINE, SAMUEL T.	FRE	394	PETERSVI
HORINE, SMAUEL	WAS	229	1ST DIST
HORINE, TOBIAS	FRE	394	PETERSVI
HORIS, RUTH ANN	CAR	282	7TH DIST
HORIS, SAMUEL*	DOR	418	1ST DIST
HORLEY, WILLIAM	BAL	131	1ST WARD
HORMAH, FREDERICK	BAL	132	11TH WAR
HORMAN, ADAM	BAL	302	3RD WARD
HORMAN, ANDREW O.	FRE	100	FREDERIC
HORMAN, AUGUSTUS	MGM	438	CLARKSTR
HORMAN, GEORGE	BAL	085	2ND DIST
HORMAN, HENRY	BAL	367	13TH WAR
HORMAN, JOHN	BAL	370	3RD WARD
HORMAN, JOHN R.	FRE	046	FREDERIC
HORMAN, LOUDY	SOM	452	DAMES QU
HORMAN, PETER	BAL	287	1ST DIST
HORN, ADAM	HAR	074	1ST DIST
HORN, ALEXANDER	BAL	307	20TH WAR
HORN, BENJAMIN	BAL	312	20TH WAR
HORN, BRIDGETT	BAL	052	4TH WARD
HORN, CATHARINE	BAL	398	1ST DIST
HORN, CATHARINE	ALL	156	6TH E.D.
HORN, CHRISTIANA	WAS	162	HAGERSTO
HORN, CORBINA *	BAL	039	18TH WAR
HORN, DANIEL	BAL	111	18TH WAR
HORN, DAVID R.	BAL	016	2ND DIST
HORN, ELIZABETH	BAL	334	3RD WARD
HORN, ELLEN	BAL	308	12TH WAR
HORN, ELLIS P.	BAL	043	2ND DIST
HORN, FRANCIS	BAL	225	6TH WARD
HORN, FREDERICK	BAL	367	1ST DIST
HORN, FREDERICK	BAL	307	1ST DIST
HORN, GEORGE	BAL	328	3RD WARD
HORN, GEORGE	BAL	388	8TH WARD
HORN, HANNAH	BAL	408	14TH WAR
HORN, HENRY	BAL	028	18TH WAR
HORN, HENRY	BAL	412	1ST DIST
HORN, HENRY J.	HAR	068	1ST DIST
HORN, HERNY	BAL	408	14TH WAR
HORN, JACOB	BAL	323	12TH WAR
HORN, JAMES	BAL	002	9TH WARD
HORN, JOHN	BAL	300	1ST DIST
HORN, JOHN	BAL	062	18TH WAR
HORN, JOHN D.	HAR	009	1ST DIST
HORN, JOHN V.	BAL	383	1ST DIST
HORN, JOSEPH	BAL	275	12TH WAR
HORN, LIDY	BAL	205	2ND WARD
HORN, LOUIS	BAL	122	2ND DIST
HORN, MARTIN	ALL	156	6TH E.D.
HORN, MARY	BAL	307	1ST DIST
HORN, MARY	BAL	160	16TH WAR
HORN, MARY	BAL	269	1ST DIST
HORN, MARY A.	BAL	412	1ST DIST
HORN, NATHANIEL	BAL	110	2ND DIST
HORN, PETER	WAS	143	HAGERSTO
HORN, PETER OF H.	WAS	290	1ST DIST
HORN, SAMUEL	BAL	059	18TH WAR
HORN, THOMAS	BAL	072	1ST WARD
HORN, WILLIAM	HAR	061	1ST DIST
HORN, WILLIAM S.	ALL	165	6TH E.D.
HORNBEN, H.	BAL	261	12TH WAR
HORNBLOWER, THOMAS	ANN	492	HOWARD D
HORNBROOCK, SARAH	BAL	223	19TH WAR
HORNE, CHRISTIAN	BAL	170	2ND DIST
HORNE, GEORGE	WAS	084	2ND SUBD
HORNE, JOHN	BAL	354	7TH WARD
HORNE, MICHAEL	WAS	027	2ND SUBD
HORNE, RUTH	WAS	084	2ND SUBD
HORNE, THOMAS	BAL	253	6TH WARD
HORNEGOSE, JOSEPH	BAL	415	14TH WAR
HORNER, ABEL	BAL	242	17TH WAR
HORNER, ABRAHAM	BAL	101	1ST WARD
HORNER, ABRAHAM	BAL	100	1ST WARD
HORNER, ALEBERT	BAL	268	20TH WAR
HORNER, ANN E.	TAL	002	EASTON D
HORNER, CATHARINE	ANN	417	HOWARD D
HORNER, DAVID	SOM	451	DAMES QU
HORNER, DAVID	CAR	285	7TH DIST
HORNER, ELIZABETH	SOM	547	TYASKIN
HORNER, FRANCIS F.	CAR	192	4TH DIST
HORNER, FREDRICK	BAL	022	18TH WAR
HORNER, GEORGE	CEC	215	7TH E DI
HORNER, GEORGE	SOM	464	HANGARY
HORNER, GEORGE W.	FRE	294	WOODSBOR
HORNER, JAMES	SOM	448	DAMES QU
HORNER, JAMES	SOM	464	HANGARY
HORNER, JOHN	SOM	452	DAMES QU
HORNER, JOHN	SOM	464	HANGARY
HORNER, JOHN W.	SOM	542	TYASKIN
HORNER, JOSEPH	TAL	102	ST MICHA
HORNER, JOSEPH	BAL	258	17TH WAR
HORNER, KITTY	SOM	465	HANGARY
HORNER, LANIA	BAL	268	20TH WAR
HORNER, LOUDY *	SOM	452	DAMES QU
HORNER, LUCINDA	SOM	542	TYASKIN
HORNER, MARIAH	SOM	544	TYASKIN
HORNER, SAMUEL	TAL	012	EASTON D
HORNER, SARAH	SOM	452	DAMES QU
HORNER, SARAH E.	SOM	542	TYASKIN
HORNER, SARAH E.	CEC	025	ELKTON 3
HORNER, SPENCER	DOR	313	1ST DIST
HORNER, THOMAS*	TAL	025	EASTON D
HORNER, TRAVERS	SOM	452	DAMES QU
HORNER, WILLIAM	SOM	464	HANGARY
HORNER, WILLIAM	SOM	542	TYASKIN
HORNER, WILLIAM	DOR	309	1ST DIST
HORNES, A. B.	ST	254	3RD E DI
HORNES, BARTLEY *	WAS	051	2ND SUBD
HORNES, CATHARINE	CAR	199	4TH DIST
HORNES, JACOB	CAR	203	4TH DIST
HORNESS, EMIL	BAL	386	13TH WAR
HORNET, W.	BAL	151	1ST WARD
HORNEY, AMELINE*	TAL	026	EASTON D
HORNEY, BENJAMIN	TAL	002	EASTON D
HORNEY, CAROLINE	QUE	159	2ND E DI
HORNEY, CURTIS-MULATTO	CAR	138	NO TWP L
HORNEY, EBEN-BLACK	CAR	122	NO TWP L
HORNEY, EDWARD	BAL	079	1ST WARD
HORNEY, ELIZABETH-MULATTO	CAR	138	NO TWP L
HORNEY, JAMES P.	TAL	032	EASTON D
HORNEY, JOHN	QUE	248	5TH E DI
HORNEY, JOHN	CAR	134	NO TWP L
HORNEY, MARIA V.	BAL	059	1ST WARD
HORNEY, MARY	BAL	330	7TH WARD
HORNEY, MARY	BAL	115	15TH WAR
HORNEY, SAMUEL	BAL	020	1ST WARD
HORNEY, THOMAS	BAL	058	1ST WARD
HORNEY, THOMAS	BAL	266	17TH WAR
HORNEY, THOMAS	QUE	249	5TH E DI
HORNEY, THOMAS	QUE	249	5TH E DI
HORNEY, THOMAS*	TAL	025	EASTON D
HORNEY, WILLIAM	TAL	026	EASTON D
HORNEY, WILLIAM	BAL	013	15TH WAR
HORNEY, WILLIAM	BAL	255	2ND WARD
HORNING, REUBEN	CAR	370	9TH DIST
HORNNER, LARY ANN	HAR	154	3RD DIST
HORNS, HENRY	ALL	225	CUMBERLA
HORNSBY, ADDA	BAL	072	10TH WAR
HORNYCAMP, JOHN	ALL	118	5TH E.D.
HORPER, JOHN N.	BAL	433	14TH WAR
HORRESIFER, JACOB	CAR	244	3RD DIST
HORREY, HANNAH *	BAL	369	13TH WAR
HORRIGAN, ANN	TAL	053	EASTON D
HORRISON, HARRIETT	BAL	043	18TH WAR
HORROW, MARY	BAL	148	11TH WAR
HORS, SILAS	CAR	321	1ST DIST
HORSE, FOULTANE	BAL	269	17TH WAR
HORSE, FRANCES T. *	BAL	275	20TH WAR
HORSE, MICHAEL	FRE	085	FREDERIC
HORSEMAN, ARNOLD	DOR	442	1ST DIST
HORSEMAN, ARNOLD*	DOR	439	1ST DIST
HORSEMAN, ENNALES*	DOR	442	1ST DIST
HORSEMAN, GEORGE	DOR	442	1ST DIST
HORSEMAN, JAMES D.	CHA	285	BOJANTOW
HORSEMAN, JASON	CHA	285	BOJANTOW
HORSEMAN, JOB	DOR	442	1ST DIST
HORSEMAN, JOHN	ALL	145	6TH E.D.
HORSEMAN, JOSIAH	DOR	411	1ST DIST
HORSEMAN, MARY H.	DOR	439	1ST DIST
HORSENEN, ERNEST	ALL	147	6TH E.D.
HORSEY, ADAM	SOM	484	TRAPP DI
HORSEY, ALBERT	SOM	382	BRINKLEY
HORSEY, ALBERT	SOM	374	BRINKLEY
HORSEY, ANGELINE	SOM	409	DUBLIN D
HORSEY, CATHARINE	BAL	242	20TH WAR
HORSEY, CHARLES	SOM	525	QUANTICO
HORSEY, CHARLES	QUE	210	3RD E DI
HORSEY, COSMER	SOM	484	TRAPP DI
HORSEY, EDWAN K.	SOM	388	BRINKLEY
HORSEY, EDWARD	SOM	441	DAMES QU
HORSEY, EDWARD C.	SOM	526	QUANTICO
HORSEY, ELBERT	DOR	438	1ST DIST
HORSEY, ELIJAH*	DOR	438	1ST DIST
HORSEY, ELIZABETH	WOR	340	1ST E DI
HORSEY, EMILY J.	BAL	265	17TH WAR
HORSEY, EPHRAIM	SOM	394	BRINKLEY
HORSEY, EPHRAIM	SOM	394	BRINKLEY
HORSEY, EPHRAIM	SOM	362	BRINKLEY
HORSEY, GEORGE	WOR	193	8TH E DI
HORSEY, GEORGE	BAL	026	9TH WARD
HORSEY, HENRY	SOM	502	SALISBUR
HORSEY, HENRY	SOM	404	BRINKLEY
HORSEY, HESTER	BAL	089	10TH WAR
HORSEY, ISAAC	SOM	365	BRINKLEY
HORSEY, ISAAC	SOM	387	BRINKLEY
HORSEY, JOHN	SOM	409	DUBLIN D
HORSEY, JOHN C.	SOM	365	BRINKLEY
HORSEY, JOHN H.	CAR	132	NO TWP L
HORSEY, JOSEPH	SOM	387	BRINKLEY
HORSEY, JOSHUA P.	SOM	388	BRINKLEY
HORSEY, JOSIAH	SOM	394	BRINKLEY
HORSEY, LEAR	BAL	054	4TH WARD
HORSEY, MAJOR*	DOR	438	1ST DIST
HORSEY, MARIAH	SOM	404	BRINKLEY
HORSEY, MARY	SOM	409	DUBLIN D
HORSEY, MARY J.	BAL	061	4TH WARD
HORSEY, NANCY	SOM	467	HANGARY
HORSEY, OUTERBRIDGE	BAL	111	10TH WAR
HORSEY, PETER J.	BAL	144	1ST WARD
HORSEY, ROBB-BLACK	WOR	346	1ST E DI
HORSEY, ROBERT	SOM	417	PRINCESS
HORSEY, ROBERT	SOM	429	PRINCESS
HORSEY, SALLY	SOM	433	PRINCESS
HORSEY, SALLY	SOM	404	BRINKLEY
HORSEY, SALLY	SOM	386	BRINKLEY
HORSEY, SAMUEL	SOM	404	BRINKLEY
HORSEY, SARAH	SOM	384	BRINKLEY
HORSEY, SARAH	SOM	525	QUANTICO
HORSEY, SEVENIA	BAL	406	8TH WARD
HORSEY, STEPHEN	SOM	389	BRINKLEY
HORSEY, SUSAN	SOM	394	BRINKLEY
HORSEY, SUSAN	SOM	488	SALISBUR
HORSEY, SUSAN	SOM	526	QUANTICO
HORSEY, THOMAS	SOM	402	BRINKLEY
HORSEY, THOMAS	SOM	391	BRINKLEY
HORSEY, WILLIAM	SOM	470	TRAPPE D
HORSEY, WILLIAM	BAL	310	1ST DIST
HORSEY, WILLIAM	CAR	170	NO TWP L
HORSKEY, PATRICK	CEC	129	6TH E DI
HORSMACK, GEORGE	BAL	140	5TH WARD
HORSMAN, ALEXANDER	SOM	541	TYASKIN
HORSMAN, ARNOLD	DOR	352	3RD DIVI
HORSMAN, JACKSON	SOM	547	TYASKIN
HORSMAN, JESSEY	SOM	448	DAMES QU
HORSMAN, JOHN	DOR	342	3RD DIVI
HORSMAN, JULIA A.	SOM	544	TYASKIN
HORSMAN, MARGRET	DOR	346	3RD DIVI
HORSMAN, MARGRETT	DOR	345	3RD DIVI
HORSMAN, MOSELEY	SOM	523	BARREN C
HORSMAN, PERRY	SOM	543	TYASKIN
HORSMAN, ROBERT	SOM	540	TYASKIN
HORSMAN, SALLY	SOM	485	TRAPP DI
HORSMAN, SARAH	BAL	296	17TH WAR
HORSMAN, SEVERN	SOM	542	TYASKIN
HORSMAN, SUSAN	SOM	547	TYASKIN
HORSMAN, SUSAN	SOM	546	TYASKIN
HORSMAN, THOMAS	DOR	352	3RD DIVI
HORSMAN, WILLIAM	SOM	448	DAMES QU
HORSNER, WILLIAM	BAL	021	1ST WARD
HORSRISH, CATHARINE *	WAS	162	HAGERSTO
HORST, ABRAHAM	WAS	284	1ST DIST
HORST, CATHARINE	WAS	292	1ST DIST
HORST, CHRISTIAN	WAS	283	1ST DIST
HORST, CONRAD	BAL	210	2ND WARD
HORST, GEORGE	BAL	445	8TH WARD
HORST, JOHN	WAS	291	1ST DIST
HORST, MARTIN	BAL	109	5TH WARD
HORST, MICAHEL	WAS	291	1ST DIST
HORSTER, CECILIA *	BAL	282	1ST DIST
HORSTHEIMER, EARNEST	BAL	063	1ST WARD
HORSTMAN, CHARLES	BAL	404	3RD WARD
HORSTMAN, ELIZABETH	BAL	176	6TH WARD
HORSTMAN, J.E.	BAL	129	1ST WARD
HORSTMAN, LEO	BAL	138	18TH WAR
HORSTMEYER, WILLIAM	BAL	086	1ST WARD
HORT, JOSEPH	FRE	079	FREDERIC
HORTA, ANTHONY	BAL	051	4TH WARD
HORTENBAKER, WILLIAM	FRE	401	JEFFERSO
HORTER, JAMES	QUE	203	3RD E DI
HORTER, RICHARD	QUE	229	4TH E DI
HORTLEY, GEORGE	BAL	121	1ST WARD
HORTMAN, CATHERINE	BAL	399	8TH WARD
HORTON, AMOS D.	FRE	388	PETERSVI
HORTON, CATHERINE P.	BAL	368	8TH WARD
HORTON, ELLENDER	CAR	366	9TH DIST
HORTON, HECTOR	FRE	306	WOODSBOR
HORTON, JAMES M.	BAL	368	8TH WARD
HORTON, LAURA	BAL	065	15TH WAR
HORTON, MALCOLM	FRE	388	PETERSVI
HORTON, ROSETTA	QUE	223	4TH E DI
HORTON, WILLIAM	BAL	030	18TH WAR
HORTON, WILLIAM L.	HAR	177	3RD DIST
HORTON, RICHARD	MGM	410	MEDLEY 3
HORTZEL, ADAM *	WAS	053	2ND SUBD

Name	County	Page	District
HORVAN, J.	BAL	261	12TH WAR
HORVELL, EDWARD C.	BAL	112	5TH WARD
HORVILL, MARY	HAR	203	3RD DIST
HORWING, ANDREW	BAL	211	6TH DIST
HORWITZ, ALBERT	BAL	050	9TH WARD
HORWITZ, JONAS	BAL	325	12TH WAR
HORY, WILLIAM	BAL	060	4TH WARD
HORYE, MARY	ALL	257	CUMBERLA
HOS, MARTHA	CAR	221	5TH DIST
HOSBURN, WILLIAM	CEC	084	CHARLEST
HOSE, DAVID	WAS	106	2ND DIST
HOSE, GEORGE	WAS	225	1ST DIST
HOSE, HARTMAN	WAS	161	2ND DIST
HOSE, HENRY	WAS	253	1ST DIST
HOSE, ISABELLA	WAS	177	1ST DIST
HOSE, JACOB	WAS	133	2ND DIST
HOSE, JACOB	WAS	238	CAVETOWN
HOSE, JOHN	WAS	160	HAGERSTO
HOSE, JOHN	ALL	224	CUMBERLA
HOSE, MARY	WAS	149	HAGERSTO
HOSE, PETER	WAS	253	1ST DIST
HOSE, SOLOMON	WAS	266	1ST DIST
HOSEL, HENRY	BAL	004	15TH WAR
HOSEMAN, E. P.	BAL	165	11TH WAR
HOSENGE, JOSEPH	ALL	228	CUMBERLA
HOSET, ADAM	BAL	012	9TH WARD
HOSEY, MEEDA	SOM	522	BARREN C
HOSFORD, ANN	BAL	303	1ST DIST
HOSFORD, ELIZABETH	BAL	235	6TH WARD
HOSFORD, ELIZABETH	BAL	302	20TH WAR
HOSHAL, SHADRACK	BAL	042	15TH WAR
HOSHEL, CALEB	BAL	201	6TH DIST
HOSHEL, EPHRAIM	BAL	212	6TH DIST
HOSHEL, ISAAC	BAL	201	6TH DIST
HOSHEL, JESSE	BAL	201	6TH DIST
HOSHEL, MELCHOR	BAL	201	6TH DIST
HOSHEL, NICKOLAS	BAL	201	6TH DIST
HOSHEL, REBECCA	BAL	201	6TH DIST
HOSHELL, JOHN	BAL	444	1ST DIST
HOSICK, ROBERT	BAL	129	1ST WARD
HOSIER, JULIA	WOR	278	BERLIN 1
HOSIER, MATILDA	WOR	206	4TH E DI
HOSIMER, AMOS H.	BAL	064	18TH WAR
HOSIMER, HORACE B.	BAL	064	18TH WAR
HOSKEY, BERNARD	BAL	173	6TH WARD
HOSKINS, CHEYNEY	HAR	093	2ND DIST
HOSKINS, EDITH	HAR	087	2ND DIST
HOSKINS, ELIZABETH	HAR	140	2ND DIST
HOSKINS, GEORGE	FRE	046	FREDERIC
HOSKINS, HIRAM	HAR	078	2ND DIST
HOSKINS, JESSE	HAR	095	2ND DIST
HOSKINS, JOSEPH	HAR	096	2ND DIST
HOSKINS, JOSEPH T.	HAR	079	2ND DIST
HOSKINS, MARGARET	ALL	007	3RD E.D.
HOSKINS, MARY A.*	DOR	376	1ST DIST
HOSKINS, PHILEMON	HAR	096	2ND DIST
HOSKINS, VIOLETTU	FRE	380	PETERSVI
HOSKINSON, ANDREW J.	MGM	415	MEDLEY 3
HOSKINSON, HILEAN JR.	MGM	406	MEDLEY 3
HOSKINSON, HILEARY	MGM	406	MEDLEY 3
HOSKINSON, REBECCA	MGM	355	BERRYS D
HOSKIRS, WILLIAM	CEC	145	PORT DUP
HOSLER, ELI	BAL	260	6TH WARD
HOSLINGER, ANNA	BAL	199	6TH WARD
HOSLINGER, LEWIS	BAL	227	19TH WAR
HOSMER, CHARLES	BAL	051	9TH WARD
HOSMER, MARGRET	BAL	067	18TH WAR
HOSNEIDER, HENRY	BAL	053	1ST WARD
HOSNER, SARAH C.*	TAL	048	EASTON T
HOSPELHONE, RACHAEL	FRE	191	5TH E DI
HOSPELHORN, JOSEPH	FRE	187	5TH E DI
HOSPELHORNS, JAMES	FRE	187	5TH E DI
HOSS, GEORGE	ALL	199	CUMBERLA
HOSS, JOHN	BAL	018	4TH WARD
HOSS, JOHN F.	BAL	026	4TH WARD
HOSSBACH, ADAM*	BAL	089	10TH WAR
HOSSBAUCH, PHILLIP	BAL	214	17TH WAR
HOSSBAUGH, GEORGE	BAL	232	17TH WAR
HOSSE, CHARLES	CAR	215	5TH DIST
HOSSE, MARY	CAR	214	5TH DIST
HOSSELBERGER, GEORGE	BAL	235	17TH WAR
HOSSELBOCK, GEORGE	FRE	206	BUCKEYST
HOSSEY, LEVIN-BLACK	WOR	338	1ST E DI
HOSSMAN, ANDREW	BAL	005	15TH WAR
HOSSMAN, CATHARINE	BAL	006	15TH WAR
HOSSOFRASS, SARAH	BAL	001	9TH WARD
HOST, JOHN	BAL	350	7TH WARD
HOST, WILLIAM	BAL	020	1ST WARD
HOSTEHOPE, JOHN	WAS	128	2ND DIST
HOSTELTER, DAVID	CAR	245	3RD DIST
HOSTER, NICHOLAS	BAL	309	1ST DIST
HOSTUTLER, JACOB	ALL	070	5TH E.D.
HOSTZEL, ADAM	WAS	053	2ND SUBD
HOSUER, HENRY	ALL	216	CUMBERLA
HOSUTTER, BARBARA	CAR	303	1ST DIST
HOTCHKISS, S.	BAL	277	20TH WAR
HOTEN, JAMES A.	KEN	255	1ST DIST
HOTEN, JAMES A. *	KEN	255	1ST DIST
HOTHERLY, JOSEPH	FRE	365	CATOCTIN
HOTHOUS, JACOB	WAS	135	2ND DIST
HOTING, MARTIN	BAL	167	1ST WARD
HOTON, LOUIS	ALL	055	10TH E.D
HOTON, REVIL	WOR	330	1ST E DI
HOTSTELTER, JOHN	WAS	146	HAGERSTO
HOTT, AARON	BAL	266	1ST DIST
HOTT, LETITIA*	DOR	391	1ST DIST
HOTTENBERGER, WILLIAM	BAL	419	8TH WARD
HOTZ, MARTIN	FRE	050	FREDERIC
HOTZE, JOHN R. A.	BAL	040	15TH WAR
HOTZEL, LEWIS	WAS	076	2ND SUBD
HOTZEL, SAMUEL	WAS	076	2ND SUBD
HOUARD, HENRY-BLACK	FRE	005	FREDERIC
HOUCH, FRANCIS	BAL	427	8TH WARD
HOUCH, MICHAEL	BAL	025	4TH WARD
HOUCK, A.V.	BAL	246	12TH WAR
HOUCK, APPALONIA	CAR	331	MANCHEST
HOUCK, CARLINE	FRE	112	CREAGERS
HOUCK, CHARLES	BAL	104	18TH WAR
HOUCK, CLARA A.	BAL	224	17TH WAR
HOUCK, DANIEL	FRE	135	CREAGERS
HOUCK, DANIEL	FRE	081	FREDERIC
HOUCK, DAVID	FRE	047	FREDERIC
HOUCK, DAVID	CAR	332	MANCHEST
HOUCK, DAVID W.	CAR	178	8TH DIST
HOUCK, EDWARD	FRE	238	NEW MARK
HOUCK, ELISHA	CAR	382	2ND DIST
HOUCK, ELIZABETH	CAR	383	2ND DIST
HOUCK, ELIZABETH	CAR	347	6TH DIST
HOUCK, ELIZABETH	BAL	127	16TH WAR
HOUCK, EZRA	FRE	058	FREDERIC
HOUCK, FREDERIC	BAL	324	12TH WAR
HOUCK, GEORGE	BAL	128	1ST WARD
HOUCK, GEORGE	FRE	054	FREDERIC
HOUCK, GEORGE	CAR	328	MANCHEST
HOUCK, GEORGE	CAR	181	8TH DIST
HOUCK, GEORGE H.	BAL	026	18TH WAR
HOUCK, GOTFRIED	BAL	027	4TH WARD
HOUCK, HANSON	CAR	316	1ST DIST
HOUCK, HENRY	BAL	103	18TH WAR
HOUCK, HENRY	CAR	348	6TH DIST
HOUCK, HENRY	FRE	103	FREDERIC
HOUCK, HENRY	BAL	262	12TH WAR
HOUCK, JACB	FRE	434	8TH E DI
HOUCK, JACOB	CAR	213	5TH DIST
HOUCK, JACOB	BAL	128	1ST WARD
HOUCK, JACOB	BAL	279	2ND WARD
HOUCK, JACOB	WAS	097	2ND DIST
HOUCK, JAOCB	CAR	332	MANCHEST
HOUCK, JAOCB W.	CAR	174	8TH DIST
HOUCK, JOHN	CAR	175	8TH DIST
HOUCK, JOHN	CAR	178	8TH DIST
HOUCK, JOHN	FRE	060	FREDERIC
HOUCK, JOHN	FRE	250	NEW MARK
HOUCK, JOHN	BAL	137	1ST WARD
HOUCK, JOHN J.	FRE	010	FREDERIC
HOUCK, JOSHUA	FRE	130	CREAGERS
HOUCK, LEREMY	BAL	263	20TH WAR
HOUCK, LUCINDA	CAR	182	8TH DIST
HOUCK, MARY	CAR	182	8TH DIST
HOUCK, MATTHIAS	BAL	266	12TH WAR
HOUCK, MICHAEL	FRE	090	FREDERIC
HOUCK, PETER	FRE	089	FREDERIC
HOUCK, PETER	FRE	089	FREDERIC
HOUCK, PETER	CAR	328	MANCHEST
HOUCK, RUTH A.	CAR	178	8TH DIST
HOUCK, SAMUEL	WAS	111	2ND DIST
HOUCK, WILLIAM	CAR	344	6TH DIST
HOUCK, WILLIAM JR.	CAR	179	8TH DIST
HOUCKS, HENRY	FRE	196	5TH E DI
HOUCY, GEORGE	CEC	209	7TH E DI
HOUD, HENRY	BAL	008	1ST WARD
HOUGH, BENJAMIN	BAL	030	18TH WAR
HOUGH, CHARLES A.	BAL	109	15TH WAR
HOUGH, CRISANDA	BAL	079	18TH WAR
HOUGH, IWLLIAM	BAL	259	6TH WARD
HOUGH, JOHN	ST	330	4TH E DI
HOUGH, JOHN M.	BAL	348	13TH WAR
HOUGH, MANETTA S.	BAL	410	14TH WAR
HOUGH, MARY	BAL	082	18TH WAR
HOUGH, ROBERT	BAL	196	11TH WAR
HOUGH, SAMUEL H.	BAL	157	11TH WAR
HOUGH,PHILIP	ST	315	4TH E DI
HOUGHT, ADAM	BAL	010	EASTERN
HOUGHTON, MARY H.	BAL	338	13TH WAR
HOUHOF, JOHN	ALL	200	CUMBERLA
HOUK, JOHN	BAL	235	1ST DIST
HOULAHAN, CHRISTOPHER	BAL	388	3RD WARD
HOULSON, WILLIAM	BAL	018	9TH WARD
HOULTON, RUTH	BAL	412	3RD WARD
HOULTON, WILLIAM	BAL	009	4TH WARD
HOUN, MARTIN	BAL	194	6TH WARD
HOUP, LEWIS	WAS	198	1ST DIST
HOUPMAN, PHILLIP	FRE	028	FREDERIC
HOUPT, ANTHONY	FRE	047	FREDERIC
HOUPT, DAVID	WAS	199	1ST DIST
HOUPT, ELIZABETH	FRE	334	MIDDLETO
HOUPT, EZRA	WAS	210	1ST DIST
HOUPT, HENRY	FRE	353	MIDDLETO
HOUPT, JACOB	FRE	352	MIDDLETO
HOUPT, JACOB	WAS	185	BOONSBOR
HOUPT, JOHN	FRE	357	CATOCTIN
HOUPT, JONATHAN	FRE	334	MIDDLETO
HOUPT, LAURA	BAL	210	6TH DIST
HOUPT, NICHOLAS	FRE	350	MIDDLETO
HOUPT, OLIVER	FRE	182	5TH E DI
HOUPT, SOLOMON	FRE	350	MIDDLETO
HOUPT, WILLIAM	FRE	353	MIDDLETO
HOUR, JOHN	CAR	187	8TH DIST
HOURECH, DANIEL *	BAL	289	1ST DIST
HOUSAN, LEWIS	BAL	284	2ND WARD
HOUSE, AAMON	ALL	192	9TH E.D.
HOUSE, ANDREW	FRE	404	JEFFERSO
HOUSE, BENJAMIN-MULATTO	FRE	405	JEFFERSO
HOUSE, CHARLES	BAL	298	3RD WARD
HOUSE, CHESTIANNA	ALL	059	10TH E.D
HOUSE, CORNELIUS	FRE	079	FREDERIC
HOUSE, DAVID	ALL	194	9TH E.D.
HOUSE, DORCAS	ALL	193	9TH E.D.
HOUSE, EDWARD	ANN	396	8TH DIST
HOUSE, EDWARD	BAL	341	3RD WARD
HOUSE, ELI P.	FRE	392	PETERSVI
HOUSE, ELIE	WAS	151	HAGERSTO
HOUSE, FREDERICK	BAL	137	16TH WAR
HOUSE, GEORGE	WOR	313	2ND E DI
HOUSE, GEORGE E.	FRE	227	BUCKEYST
HOUSE, GEORGE J.	WAS	129	HAGERSTO
HOUSE, GREENBURG J.R.	FRE	392	PETERSVI
HOUSE, HENRY	WAS	131	2ND DIST
HOUSE, HENRY L.	FRE	247	NEW MARK
HOUSE, ISAAC	BAL	259	20TH WAR
HOUSE, JOHN	FRE	392	PETERSVI
HOUSE, JOHN	WAS	131	2ND DIST
HOUSE, JOHN	BAL	356	8TH WARD
HOUSE, JOSEPH	WAS	178	BOONSBOR
HOUSE, JOSEPH	WAS	189	1ST DIST
HOUSE, LEVI	FRE	325	MIDDLETO
HOUSE, LUTHER-MULATTO	FRE	405	JEFFERSO
HOUSE, MARGARET	BAL	086	2ND DIST
HOUSE, MARTIN W.E.	FRE	396	PETERSVI
HOUSE, MARY	CEC	153	PORT DUP
HOUSE, MARY M.	FRE	024	FREDERIC
HOUSE, MC CENEY	ANN	303	1ST DIST
HOUSE, MICHAEL	BAL	304	20TH WAR
HOUSE, POLLY	WAS	126	HAGERSTO
HOUSE, REBECCA	FRE	024	FREDERIC
HOUSE, SAMUEL	CAL	059	3RD DIST
HOUSE, SAMUEL	WAS	233	1ST DIST
HOUSE, SAUSON	FRE	378	PETERSVI
HOUSE, WILLIAM	FRE	324	MIDDLETO
HOUSE, WILLIAM	FRE	324	MIDDLETO
HOUSE, WILLIAM	BAL	252	6TH WARD
HOUSE, WILLIAM	BAL	134	1ST WARD
HOUSE, WILLIAM	BAL	123	1ST WARD
HOUSE, WILLIAM A.	BAL	059	15TH WAR
HOUSE, WILLIAM R.	FRE	405	JEFFERSO
HOUSE, ZACHARIAH	CAL	050	3RD DIST
HOUSE .SOLOMON	BAL	058	1ST WARD
HOUSEHOLDER, CATHARINE	WAS	294	1ST DIST
HOUSEHOLDER, ELIZABETH	WAS	004	WILLIAMS
HOUSEHOLDER, MARY	WAS	004	WILLIAMS
HOUSEHOLDER, PHILIP	WAS	123	HAGERSTO
HOUSEHOLDER, WILLIAM	WAS	144	HAGERSTO
HOUSEMAN, A. C.	BAL	112	18TH WAR
HOUSEMAN, WILLIAM	BAL	204	6TH DIST
HOUSEN, HENRY	BAL	072	4TH WARD
HOUSEN, LOUIS	BAL	247	17TH WAR
HOUSEN, MAHALA	WAS	178	BOONSBOR
HOUSENVALT, JOHN	BAL	251	12TH WAR
HOUSER, ABRAHAM	WAS	067	2ND SUBD
HOUSER, ABRAHAM	FRE	385	PETERSVI
HOUSER, ANDREW	WAS	237	CAVETOWN
HOUSER, BARNETT	WAS	281	LEITERSB
HOUSER, BARNEY	WAS	038	2ND SUBD
HOUSER, DENNIS	FRE	242	NEW MARK
HOUSER, ISRAEL	FRE	250	NEW MARK
HOUSER, JACOB	WAS	043	2ND SUBD
HOUSER, JACOB	WAS	053	2ND SUBD
HOUSER, JACOB	WAS	088	2ND SUBD
HOUSER, JOHN	WAS	089	2ND SUBD
HOUSER, JOHN	WAS	237	CAVETOWN
HOUSER, MARRY	WAS	068	2ND SUBD
HOUSER, PETER	WAS	069	2ND SUBD
HOUSER, SAMUEL	WAS	069	2ND SUBD
HOUSER, SAMUEL	WAS	246	SMITHSBU
HOUSER, SAMUEL H.	FRE	216	BUCKEYST
HOUSER, THEODORE	FRE	242	NEW MARK
HOUSEROLDER, SAMUEL	ALL	169	6TH E.D.
HOUSIER, ELIZABETH	WOR	170	6TH E DI
HOUSIER, MARY	WOR	199	8TH E DI
HOUST, D.	BAL	238	20TH WAR
HOUSTIE, ELIZA	BAL	406	14TH WAR
HOUSTON, AARON-BLACK	FRE	234	BUCKEYST
HOUSTON, ABRAHAM *	KEN	214	2ND DIST
HOUSTON, AGNESS	FRE	055	FREDERIC
HOUSTON, AMEY	KEN	239	2ND DIST
HOUSTON, ANN	CAR	151	NO TWP L
HOUSTON, ANN	KEN	252	1ST DIST
HOUSTON, ANN	BAL	118	5TH WARD
HOUSTON, ANN	BAL	067	10TH WAR
HOUSTON, BENJAMIN F. *	KEN	214	2ND DIST
HOUSTON, BILL	WOR	270	BERLIN 1
HOUSTON, CAMPLAND	BAL	012	1ST WARD
HOUSTON, EDEWARD-BLACK	WOR	331	1ST E DI
HOUSTON, EDWARD	KEN	255	1ST DIST
HOUSTON, EMILY	WOR	230	6TH E DI
HOUSTON, FLETCHER	CEC	194	7TH E DI
HOUSTON, GEORGE	WAS	164	HAGERSTO
HOUSTON, HARRIET	KEN	263	1ST DIST
HOUSTON, HARRIET A.	BAL	132	16TH WAR
HOUSTON, HENRY	KEN	275	1ST DIST
HOUSTON, HENRY *.	DOR	454	1ST DIST
HOUSTON, HENRY-BLACK	WOR	332	1ST E DI
HOUSTON, ISAAC-BLACK	WOR	350	1ST E DI
HOUSTON, J.	BAL	151	1ST WARD
HOUSTON, JAMES	CEC	133	6TH E DI
HOUSTON, JOHN	HAR	021	1ST DIST
HOUSTON, JOHN M.	WOR	350	1ST E DI
HOUSTON, JOHN T.	DOR	319	1ST DIST
HOUSTON, JUDIA-BLACK	WOR	350	1ST E DI
HOUSTON, LEVIN	WOR	228	6TH E DI
HOUSTON, LEVIN	BAL	273	17TH WAR
HOUSTON, LOUISA *	KEN	253	1ST DIST
HOUSTON, LUCY	BAL	258	12TH WAR
HOUSTON, MARY	BAL	317	20TH WAR
HOUSTON, MARY	WOR	271	BERLIN 1
HOUSTON, ROBERT-BLACK	WOR	170	6TH E DI
HOUSTON, RODNEY	ALL	216	CUMBERLA
HOUSTON, SAMUEL	WOR	229	6TH E DI
HOUSTON, SAMUEL	KEN	254	1ST DIST
HOUSTON, SARAH	KEN	263	1ST DIST
HOUSTON, SARAH-BLACK	WOR	334	1ST E DI
HOUSTON, WILLIAM	BAL	148	16TH WAR
HOUSTON, YORK	WOR	327	1ST E DI
HOUTAHN, LUTHER *	FRE	342	MIDDLETO
HOUX, WILLIAM J.	FRE	110	CREAGERS
HOUZE, ELISHA	CAL	051	3RD DIST
HOVEN, MICHAEL	BAL	298	20TH WAR
HOVER, DANIEL	WAS	248	1ST DIST
HOVER, FREDERICK	BAL	409	1ST DIST
HOVER, HENRY	WAS	161	HAGERSTO
HOVER, JOHN	WAS	161	HAGERSTO
HOVER, JOSEPH	BAL	432	8TH WARD
HOVER, PETER	BAL	398	1ST DIST
HOVEST, LEVILLA	WAS	275	RIDGEVIL
HOVEY, E. D.	BAL	147	1ST WARD
HOVID, LUCINDA	ANN	512	HOWARD D
HOVIS, ADAM	FRE	189	5TH E DI
HOVNEY, ANN*	TAL	002	EASTON D
HOVNEY, JOHNSON	TAL	117	ST MICHA
HOVVER, SUSAN	FRE	362	CATOCTIN
HOVY, NANCY	BAL	247	12TH WAR
HOW, ALICE	HAR	203	3RD DIST
HOW, CHARLOTTE	BAL	018	2ND DIST
HOW, CYRUS	HAR	202	3RD DIST
HOW, HENNERY	HAR	202	3RD DIST
HOW, JAMES	HAR	193	3RD DIST
HOW, JOHN	HAR	198	3RD DIST
HOW, JOSIA	HAR	202	3RD DIST
HOW, REBECCA R.	ST	307	1ST E DI
HOW, SUSANNA R.	ST	285	2ND E DI
HOW, THOMAS	BAL	352	7TH WARD
HOW, WILLIAM	HAR	194	3RD DIST
HOWANCE, JOHN *	BAL	073	18TH WAR
HOWARD, A.	PRI	076	MARLBROU
HOWARD, A. C.	WOR	303	SNOW HIL
HOWARD, ADAM	FRE	018	FREDERIC
HOWARD, ALEXANDER	FRE	129	CREAGERS
HOWARD, ALEXANDER	ST	269	3RD E DI
HOWARD, ALEXANDER	ANN	290	ANNAPOLI
HOWARD, ALFRED	WAS	206	1ST DIST
HOWARD, ALFRED	MGM	369	BERRYS D
HOWARD, ALLEN B.	ANN	326	2ND DIST
HOWARD, AMANDA	HAR	060	1ST DIST
HOWARD, AMELIA	MGM	328	CRACKLIN
HOWARD, AMELIA	BAL	025	9TH WARD
HOWARD, AMELIA	PRI	002	BLADENSB
HOWARD, AMERICA	WAS	240	CAVETOWN
HOWARD, ANGELINA	MGM	331	CRACKLIN
HOWARD, ANN	BAL	204	11TH WAR
HOWARD, ANN	BAL	414	3RD WARD
HOWARD, ANN	TAL	033	EASTON D
HOWARD, ANN	ST	266	3RD E DI
HOWARD, ANN	PRI	088	SPALDING
HOWARD, ANN	BAL	183	2ND WARD
HOWARD, ANN	ANN	453	HOWARD D
HOWARD, ANN	BAL	378	1ST DIST
HOWARD, ANN M.	CAL	047	3RD DIST
HOWARD, ANNA	CEC	183	7TH E DI
HOWARD, ANNA M.	FRE	274	NEW MARK
HOWARD, ARAMINTA-BLACK	QUE	194	3RD E DI

Name	County	Page	District
HOWARD, ARNOLD	SOM	408	DUBLIN D
HOWARD, ASBURY	KEN	214	2ND DIST
HOWARD, AUGUSTUS	BAL	394	8TH WARD
HOWARD, BEACHAM*	SOM	507	BARREN C
HOWARD, BEAN	CHA	261	MIDDLETO
HOWARD, BEN	CAL	063	3RD DIST
HOWARD, BENCHAM*	SOM	507	BARREN C
HOWARD, BENEDICT J.	ST	276	3RD E DI
HOWARD, BENJAMIN	FRE	423	8TH E DI
HOWARD, BENJAMIN	KEN	242	2ND DIST
HOWARD, BENJAMIN	KEN	222	2ND DIST
HOWARD, BENJAMIN	BAL	031	18TH WAR
HOWARD, BENJAMIN	BAL	247	1ST DIST
HOWARD, BENJAMIN C. *	BAL	278	1ST DIST
HOWARD, BETSY	WAS	148	HAGERSTO
HOWARD, BEVY C. *	BAL	278	1ST DIST
HOWARD, BILL	BAL	455	1ST DIST
HOWARD, BOYD	CEC	185	7TH E DI
HOWARD, C.*	DOR	426	1ST DIST
HOWARD, CATHAIRNE	BAL	395	14TH WAR
HOWARD, CATHARINE	BAL	254	12TH WAR
HOWARD, CATHARINE	PRI	085	QUEEN AN
HOWARD, CATHARINE	ST	317	4TH E DI
HOWARD, CATHERINE	BAL	164	11TH WAR
HOWARD, CATHERINE	FRE	019	FREDERIC
HOWARD, CATHERINE	CHA	222	ALLENS F
HOWARD, CECELIA	BAL	458	1ST DIST
HOWARD, CHARLES	BAL	080	2ND DIST
HOWARD, CHARLES	BAL	125	2ND DIST
HOWARD, CHARLES	BAL	026	9TH WARD
HOWARD, CHARLES	BAL	042	9TH WARD
HOWARD, CHARLES	BAL	165	6TH WARD
HOWARD, CHARLES	BAL	105	10TH WAR
HOWARD, CHARLES	BAL	211	11TH WAR
HOWARD, CHARLES	BAL	321	20TH WAR
HOWARD, CHARLES	HAR	033	1ST DIST
HOWARD, CHARLES	BAL	235	20TH WAR
HOWARD, CHARLES H.	BAL	075	4TH WARD
HOWARD, CHARLES J.	BAL	113	15TH WAR
HOWARD, CHARLES R.	ANN	520	HOWARD D
HOWARD, CORNELIA	BAL	116	15TH WAR
HOWARD, CORNELIUS	BAL	335	3RD WARD
HOWARD, CORNELIUS H.	BAL	335	3RD WARD
HOWARD, DAVID	BAL	277	1ST DIST
HOWARD, DENNIS	BAL	126	18TH WAR
HOWARD, DENNIS D.	FRE	438	8TH E DI
HOWARD, DENNISS	FRE	255	NEW MARK
HOWARD, EASTER	BAL	336	3RD WARD
HOWARD, EASTER	SOM	495	SALISBUR
HOWARD, EBEN	SOM	409	DUBLIN D
HOWARD, EDWARD	FRE	070	FREDERIC
HOWARD, EDWARD	SOM	386	BRINKLEY
HOWARD, EDWARD	BAL	121	2ND DIST
HOWARD, ELEN	CAR	206	4TH DIST
HOWARD, ELI	BAL	034	2ND DIST
HOWARD, ELI B.	ANN	292	ANNAPOLI
HOWARD, ELI D.	BAL	346	3RD WARD
HOWARD, ELISHA	FRE	229	BUCKEYST
HOWARD, ELIZA	CEC	199	7TH E DI
HOWARD, ELIZA	BAL	426	1ST DIST
HOWARD, ELIZA	BAL	323	1ST DIST
HOWARD, ELIZA	BAL	348	3RD WARD
HOWARD, ELIZA J.	BAL	113	5TH WARD
HOWARD, ELIZABETH	BAL	043	2ND DIST
HOWARD, ELIZABETH	BAL	300	12TH WAR
HOWARD, ELIZABETH R.	FRE	230	BUCKEYST
HOWARD, ELIZABETH R.	MGM	375	ROCKERLE
HOWARD, ELLEN	BAL	278	1ST DIST
HOWARD, ELLEN H.	BAL	181	2ND DIST
HOWARD, EZEKIEL	WOR	324	1ST E DI
HOWARD, FRANCES	BAL	213	11TH WAR
HOWARD, FRANCIS	BAL	071	1ST WARD
HOWARD, FRANCIS	BAL	113	1ST WARD
HOWARD, FRANCS E.	ALL	192	9TH E.D.
HOWARD, GEORGE	ANN	391	4TH DIST
HOWARD, GEORGE	BAL	024	1ST WARD
HOWARD, GEORGE	ALL	221	CUMBERLA
HOWARD, GEORGE	BAL	153	5TH WARD
HOWARD, GEORGE	BAL	065	4TH WARD
HOWARD, GEORGE	SOM	402	BRINKLEY
HOWARD, GEORGE A.J.	ANN	496	HOWARD D
HOWARD, GEORGE R.	CEC	010	ELKTON 3
HOWARD, GEORGE W.	BAL	430	14TH WAR
HOWARD, GEORGE W.	BAL	082	1ST WARD
HOWARD, GEORGE W.	ST	274	3RD E DI
HOWARD, GILLIS	SOM	443	DAMES QU
HOWARD, GREENBURY	MGM	316	CRACKLIN
HOWARD, HAMILTON P.	PRI	023	VANSVILL
HOWARD, HANAH-BLACK	CAR	164	NO TWP L
HOWARD, HANNAH	CEC	091	4TH E DI
HOWARD, HANNAH	BAL	148	5TH WARD
HOWARD, HARRIET	ANN	518	HOWARD D
HOWARD, HARRIET	BAL	403	8TH WARD
HOWARD, HARRIET	MGM	321	CRACKLIN
HOWARD, HARRIET	BAL	417	14TH WAR
HOWARD, HARRIET A.	MGM	321	CRACKLIN
HOWARD, HENRIETTA	BAL	135	2ND DIST
HOWARD, HENRIETTA	BAL	068	2ND DIST
HOWARD, HENRIETTA	BAL	199	11TH WAR
HOWARD, HENRY	BAL	058	2ND DIST
HOWARD, HENRY	BAL	096	5TH WARD
HOWARD, HENRY	BAL	296	12TH WAR
HOWARD, HENRY	HAR	179	3RD DIST
HOWARD, HENRY	CHA	259	MIDDLETO
HOWARD, HENRY	WOR	242	1ST CENS
HOWARD, HESTER	SOM	399	BRINKLEY
HOWARD, HESTER	WOR	333	1ST E DI
HOWARD, HESTER	SOM	409	DUBLIN D
HOWARD, HESTER	ANN	285	ANNAPOLI
HOWARD, HEZEKIAH	ANN	304	1ST DIST
HOWARD, HEZEKIAH	ANN	305	1ST DIST
HOWARD, HOCK	BAL	314	3RD WARD
HOWARD, ISAAC	BAL	095	5TH WARD
HOWARD, ISAAC	FRE	070	FREDERIC
HOWARD, ISAIAH	BAL	286	20TH WAR
HOWARD, J.	BAL	148	1ST WARD
HOWARD, JACKSON	CHA	225	ALLENS F
HOWARD, JACOB	MGM	381	ROCKERLE
HOWARD, JACOB	FRE	266	NEW MARK
HOWARD, JACOB	BAL	232	6TH WARD
HOWARD, JACOB	BAL	424	1ST DIST
HOWARD, JACOB	BAL	020	2ND DIST
HOWARD, JACOB C.	CEC	008	ELKTON 3
HOWARD, JAMES	CAR	203	4TH DIST
HOWARD, JAMES	BAL	301	17TH WAR
HOWARD, JAMES	BAL	137	2ND DIST
HOWARD, JAMES	BAL	415	1ST DIST
HOWARD, JAMES	BAL	418	1ST DIST
HOWARD, JAMES	BAL	135	5TH WARD
HOWARD, JAMES	BAL	165	11TH WAR
HOWARD, JAMES	BAL	349	7TH WARD
HOWARD, JAMES	WOR	332	1ST E DI
HOWARD, JAMES	ST	269	3RD E DI
HOWARD, JAMES	SOM	478	TRAPP DI
HOWARD, JAMES	TAL	034	EASTON D
HOWARD, JAMES E.	KEN	226	2ND DIST
HOWARD, JAMES W.	MGM	382	ROCKERLE
HOWARD, JANE	BAL	073	18TH WAR
HOWARD, JANE	BAL	398	14TH WAR
HOWARD, JANE-MULATTO	FRE	010	FREDERIC
HOWARD, JANET	BAL	407	14TH WAR
HOWARD, JEMIMA	CAR	360	9TH DIST
HOWARD, JEREMIAH	BAL	004	EASTERN
HOWARD, JOCAM*	DOR	376	1ST DIST
HOWARD, JOHN	FRE	275	NEW MARK
HOWARD, JOHN	KEN	212	2ND DIST
HOWARD, JOHN	CAL	056	3RD DIST
HOWARD, JOHN	BAL	136	11TH WAR
HOWARD, JOHN	FRE	010	FREDERIC
HOWARD, JOHN	CHA	256	MIDDLETO
HOWARD, JOHN	HAR	059	1ST DIST
HOWARD, JOHN	MGM	332	CRACKLIN
HOWARD, JOHN	FRE	133	CREAGERS
HOWARD, JOHN	BAL	210	19TH WAR
HOWARD, JOHN	BAL	428	14TH WAR
HOWARD, JOHN	BAL	417	14TH WAR
HOWARD, JOHN	BAL	219	17TH WAR
HOWARD, JOHN	BAL	130	2ND DIST
HOWARD, JOHN	BAL	026	2ND DIST
HOWARD, JOHN	BAL	174	11TH WAR
HOWARD, JOHN	ALL	011	3RD E.D.
HOWARD, JOHN	BAL	146	1ST WARD
HOWARD, JOHN	BAL	403	3RD WARD
HOWARD, JOHN	BAL	242	1ST DIST
HOWARD, JOHN *	WOR	332	1ST E DI
HOWARD, JOHN C.	BAL	073	18TH WAR
HOWARD, JOHN E.	BAL	469	14TH WAR
HOWARD, JOHN MRS.	BAL	278	1ST DIST
HOWARD, JOHN S.	BAL	152	11TH WAR
HOWARD, JOHN W.*	CHA	295	HILLTOP
HOWARD, JOHN*	DOR	328	3RD DIVI
HOWARD, JOHNSTON	DOR	338	3RD DIVI
HOWARD, JOSEPH	BAL	090	18TH WAR
HOWARD, JOSEPH	BAL	244	20TH WAR
HOWARD, JOSEPH	KEN	248	2ND DIST
HOWARD, JOSEPH	BAL	418	14TH WAR
HOWARD, JOSEPH	BAL	033	1ST WARD
HOWARD, JOSEPH	BAL	172	2ND DIST
HOWARD, JOSEPH	ANN	297	1ST DIST
HOWARD, JOSEPH	BAL	462	1ST DIST
HOWARD, JOSEPH	PRI	079	QUEEN AN
HOWARD, JOSEPH A.	ST	276	3RD E DI
HOWARD, JOSEPH-BLACK	CAR	169	NO TWP L
HOWARD, JOSEPHRE	FRE	242	NEW MARK
HOWARD, JOSHUA	BAL	434	14TH WAR
HOWARD, JOSHUA	BAL	051	4TH WARD
HOWARD, JOSHUA	BAL	243	1ST DIST
HOWARD, KISSIAH	SOM	447	DAMES QU
HOWARD, L.	BAL	165	1ST WARD
HOWARD, LEAH	DOR	454	1ST DIST
HOWARD, LEE	HAR	197	3RD DIST
HOWARD, LENARD-MULATTO	FRE	401	JEFFERSO
HOWARD, LEONARD	FRE	204	BUCKEYST
HOWARD, LEONARD	ST	278	3RD E DI
HOWARD, LEVI	BAL	179	2ND DIST
HOWARD, LEWIS	BAL	080	2ND DIST
HOWARD, LLOYD	BAL	363	13TH WAR
HOWARD, LOUISA	BAL	161	6TH WARD
HOWARD, LOUISA	BAL	145	16TH WAR
HOWARD, LOUISA M.	BAL	296	7TH WARD
HOWARD, LUCY	BAL	015	4TH WARD
HOWARD, LYDIA	BAL	033	9TH WARD
HOWARD, MAJOR	CEC	153	PORT DUP
HOWARD, MALINDA	BAL	447	1ST DIST
HOWARD, MARGARET	BAL	093	5TH WARD
HOWARD, MARGARET	ANN	465	HOWARD D
HOWARD, MARGARET	ANN	292	ANNAPOLI
HOWARD, MARGARET	BAL	194	11TH WAR
HOWARD, MARGARET	WAS	123	HAGERSTO
HOWARD, MARIA	BAL	220	6TH WARD
HOWARD, MARIA	BAL	083	18TH WAR
HOWARD, MARTHA	HAR	079	2ND DIST
HOWARD, MARTHA	ANN	265	ANNAPOLI
HOWARD, MARTHA	WAS	123	HAGERSTO
HOWARD, MARTHA A.	BAL	215	11TH WAR
HOWARD, MARY	CEC	106	3RD E DI
HOWARD, MARY	DOR	336	3RD DIVI
HOWARD, MARY	KEN	215	2ND DIST
HOWARD, MARY	BAL	212	11TH WAR
HOWARD, MARY	KEN	261	1ST DIST
HOWARD, MARY	BAL	125	2ND DIST
HOWARD, MARY	BAL	119	5TH WARD
HOWARD, MARY A.	ANN	418	HOWARD D
HOWARD, MARY A.	ANN	292	ANNAPOLI
HOWARD, MARY A.	BAL	244	6TH WARD
HOWARD, MARY A.	SOM	395	BRINKLEY
HOWARD, MARY C.	BAL	369	13TH WAR
HOWARD, MARY D.	BAL	098	15TH WAR
HOWARD, MARY E.	BAL	175	16TH WAR
HOWARD, MARY E.	ANN	521	HOWARD D
HOWARD, MARY G.	CEC	139	6TH E DI
HOWARD, MARY M.	BAL	073	4TH WARD
HOWARD, MARY-BLACK	CAR	115	NO TWP L
HOWARD, MARY-MULATTO	FRE	033	FREDERIC
HOWARD, MATILDA	BAL	002	18TH WAR
HOWARD, MATTA	WAS	048	2ND SUBD
HOWARD, MAYANTHIA	BAL	178	11TH WAR
HOWARD, MINERVIA	FRE	443	8TH E DI
HOWARD, MOSES	HAR	110	2ND DIST
HOWARD, NANY	BAL	378	1ST DIST
HOWARD, NATHAN	HAR	201	3RD DIST
HOWARD, NATHANIEL	BAL	206	11TH WAR
HOWARD, NICHOLAS	ALL	001	3RD E.D.
HOWARD, NICKOLAS	BAL	153	5TH WARD
HOWARD, NOAH H.	SOM	515	BARREN C
HOWARD, OLIVIA	SOM	425	PRINCESS
HOWARD, PHEBE	HAR	087	2ND DIST
HOWARD, PHOEBE E.	HAR	088	2ND DIST
HOWARD, PRICELLA	SOM	385	BRINKLEY
HOWARD, PRISCILLA	KEN	210	2ND DIST
HOWARD, PRISSILLY*	DOR	449	1ST DIST
HOWARD, PURDENCE	CAR	232	5TH DIST
HOWARD, RACHAEL	SOM	494	SALISBUR
HOWARD, REBECCA	SOM	400	BRINKLEY
HOWARD, REBECCA	BAL	031	18TH WAR
HOWARD, REBECCA	DOR	302	1ST DIST
HOWARD, RICHARD	FRE	423	8TH E DI
HOWARD, RICHARD	BAL	032	9TH WARD
HOWARD, RICHARD T.	CEC	139	6TH E DI
HOWARD, ROBERT	CEC	144	PORT DUP
HOWARD, ROBERT	CAL	057	3RD DIST
HOWARD, ROBERT	HAR	174	3RD DIST
HOWARD, ROBERT	BAL	181	2ND DIST
HOWARD, ROBERT R.	ANN	503	HOWARD D
HOWARD, ROSETTA	CEC	153	PORT DUP
HOWARD, SALLY	BAL	430	14TH WAR
HOWARD, SAMUEL	FRE	222	BUCKEYST
HOWARD, SAMUEL	BAL	093	5TH WARD
HOWARD, SAMUEL	BAL	166	1ST WARD
HOWARD, SAMUEL	ALL	196	CUMBERLA
HOWARD, SAMUEL	BAL	019	2ND DIST
HOWARD, SARAH	BAL	462	1ST DIST
HOWARD, SARAH	BAL	189	11TH WAR
HOWARD, SARAH	BAL	179	16TH WAR
HOWARD, SARAH	BAL	150	16TH WAR
HOWARD, SARAH	BAL	251	2ND WARD
HOWARD, SARAH	CEC	139	6TH E DI
HOWARD, SARAH	WAS	028	2ND SUBD
HOWARD, SARAH J.	BAL	339	7TH WARD
HOWARD, SARAH J.	BAL	014	1ST WARD
HOWARD, SARAH W.	FRE	020	FREDERIC
HOWARD, SARHA	BAL	467	14TH WAR
HOWARD, SARRAH	DOR	356	3RD DIVI
HOWARD, SILAS	CAR	271	WESTMINS
HOWARD, SOLOMAN	BAL	158	1ST WARD
HOWARD, SOPHIA	BAL	188	11TH WAR
HOWARD, STACY	BAL	142	11TH WAR
HOWARD, STEPHEN	BAL	191	5TH DIST
HOWARD, SUSAN	BAL	165	11TH WAR
HOWARD, SUSAN	BAL	260	6TH WARD
HOWARD, SUSAN	BAL	122	16TH WAR
HOWARD, SUSAN	BAL	345	1ST DIST
HOWARD, SUSANNA	SOM	354	BRINKLEY
HOWARD, T. C. B.	ST	270	3RD E DI
HOWARD, THOMAS	ANN	326	2ND DIST
HOWARD, THOMAS	BAL	336	1ST DIST
HOWARD, THOMAS	BAL	132	1ST WARD
HOWARD, THOMAS	ALL	218	CUMBERLA
HOWARD, THOMAS	SOM	377	BRINKLEY
HOWARD, THOMAS	SOM	394	BRINKLEY
HOWARD, THOMAS	SOM	506	BARREN C
HOWARD, THOMAS	BAL	077	18TH WAR
HOWARD, THOMAS	CEC	001	ELKTON 3
HOWARD, THOMAS G.	BAL	095	5TH WARD
HOWARD, THOMAS H.	FRE	046	FREDERIC
HOWARD, THOMAS J.	BAL	466	14TH WAR
HOWARD, VACHEL	BAL	024	18TH WAR
HOWARD, W.	ANN	344	3RD DIST
HOWARD, WASHINGTON	CHA	258	MIDDLETO
HOWARD, WESLEY	BAL	175	2ND WARD
HOWARD, WILLIAM	BAL	034	9TH WARD
HOWARD, WILLIAM	BAL	243	5TH WARD
HOWARD, WILLIAM	BAL	148	5TH WARD
HOWARD, WILLIAM	BAL	209	2ND WARD
HOWARD, WILLIAM	ANN	355	3RD DIST
HOWARD, WILLIAM	BAL	009	EASTERN
HOWARD, WILLIAM	ANN	485	HOWARD D
HOWARD, WILLIAM	BAL	127	1ST WARD
HOWARD, WILLIAM	BAL	277	7TH WARD
HOWARD, WILLIAM	BAL	384	3RD WARD
HOWARD, WILLIAM	BAL	399	8TH WARD
HOWARD, WILLIAM	BAL	457	8TH WARD
HOWARD, WILLIAM	BAL	004	9TH WARD
HOWARD, WILLIAM	BAL	191	5TH DIST
HOWARD, WILLIAM	CHA	247	HILLTOP
HOWARD, WILLIAM	FRE	002	FREDERIC
HOWARD, WILLIAM	BAL	031	18TH WAR
HOWARD, WILLIAM	CEC	058	1ST E DI
HOWARD, WILLIAM	CEC	061	1ST E DI
HOWARD, WILLIAM	CAL	033	2ND DIST
HOWARD, WILLIAM	CEC	010	ELKTON 3
HOWARD, WILLIAM	BAL	417	14TH WAR
HOWARD, WILLIAM	BAL	363	13TH WAR
HOWARD, WILLIAM	FRE	273	NEW MARK
HOWARD, WILLIAM	CHA	275	ALLENS F
HOWARD, WILLIAM	SOM	506	BARREN C
HOWARD, WILLIAM	PRI	088	SPALDING
HOWARD, WILLIAM	PRI	107	PISCATAW
HOWARD, WILLIAM	SOM	386	BRINKLEY
HOWARD, WILLIAM B.	MGM	417	MEDLEY 3
HOWARD, WILLIAM G.	FRE	020	FREDERIC
HOWARD, WILLIAM H.	CEC	157	PORT DUP
HOWARD, WILLIAM K.	BAL	030	2ND DIST
HOWARD, WILLIAM M.	BAL	004	9TH WARD
HOWARD, WILLIAM T.	CEC	109	4TH E DI
HOWARD, PRISCILLA-BLACK	BAL	219	2ND WARD
HOWBLE, ELIZABETH A.	BAL	303	3RD WARD
HOWCK, GEORGE	CAR	181	8TH DIST
HOWCK, WILLIAM	CAR	181	8TH DIST
HOWDEN, JOSEPH	BAL	057	1ST WARD
HOWDEN, LUCY	BAL	037	9TH WARD
HOWE, ALEXANDER L.	BAL	068	4TH WARD
HOWE, ALICE	BAL	162	6TH WARD
HOWE, ANN	HAR	079	2ND DIST
HOWE, CHARLES	ALL	259	CUMBERLA
HOWE, DANIEL	BAL	134	18TH WAR
HOWE, GEORGE	BAL	158	2ND DIST
HOWE, GEORGE	BAL	146	1ST WARD
HOWE, GEORGE L. C.	BAL	055	4TH WARD
HOWE, GEORGE W.	FRE	395	PETERSVI
HOWE, HENRY	HAR	053	1ST DIST
HOWE, HENRY	BAL	145	1ST WARD
HOWE, JAMES	ALL	221	CUMBERLA
HOWE, JAMES	HAR	030	1ST DIST
HOWE, JOHN	BAL	132	1ST WARD
HOWE, MARY F.	BAL	024	18TH WAR
HOWE, MATTHEW L.	BAL	430	14TH WAR
HOWE, PATRICK	ALL	049	10TH E.D
HOWE, PERY	FRE	230	BUCKEYST
HOWE, REBECCA	BAL	014	18TH WAR
HOWE, ROBERT	BAL	135	2ND DIST
HOWE, SARAH	PRI	113	PISCATAW
HOWE, THOMAS	BAL	169	11TH WAR
HOWE, THOMAS L.	HAR	010	1ST DIST
HOWE, WESLEY	BAL	014	18TH WAR
HOWE, WILLIAM	BAL	023	18TH WAR
HOWEL, MARY	FRE	257	NEW MARK
HOWEL, SUSAN	CHA	252	BOJANTOW
HOWELL, ABIGALE	BAL	063	13TH WAR
HOWELL, ANNA	BAL	002	9TH WARD
HOWELL, ANNE J.	CEC	002	ELKTON 3
HOWELL, DARIUS C.	BAL	134	16TH WAR
HOWELL, EILY	BAL	231	12TH WAR
HOWELL, EMILY JANE	BAL	340	13TH WAR
HOWELL, FANNY	BAL	156	11TH WAR
HOWELL, GEORGEANNE	BAL	269	7TH WARD
HOWELL, HORATIO	CEC	002	ELKTON 3
HOWELL, JAMES	KEN	284	3RD DIST
HOWELL, JAMES P.	CEC	026	ELKTON 3
HOWELL, JOHN B.	BAL	149	11TH WAR

HOWELL, JOSEPH CHA 279 BOJANTOW
HOWELL, L. BAL 154 11TH WAR
HOWELL, LOUISA BAL 257 20TH WAR
HOWELL, MARY CAL 057 3RD DIST
HOWELL, ROBERT BAL 097 5TH WARD
HOWELL, SAMUEL CEC 055 1ST E DI
HOWELL, T. H. BAL 284 20TH WAR
HOWELL, WILLIAM CEC 202 6TH E DI
HOWELL, WILLIAM BAL 309 3RD WARD
HOWELL, WILLIAM BAL 276 2ND WARD
HOWELL, WILLIAM BAL 188 11TH WAR
HOWELL, WILLIAM KEN 304 3RD DIST
HOWELL, WILLIAM F. PRI 081 QUEEN AN
HOWELL, WILLIAM T. BAL 002 9TH WARD
HOWER, JOHNATHAN WAS 099 2ND DIST
HOWERSON, MR. ANN 284 ANNAPOLI
HOWES, EDWARD MGM 317 CRACKLIN
HOWES, JAMES G. MGM 318 CRACKLIN
HOWES, LEVIN MGM 318 CRACKLIN
HOWES, SARAH A. BAL 160 16TH WAR
HOWES, WILLIAM MGM 339 CLARKSBU
HOWETH, JAMES F. DOR 450 1ST DIST
HOWETH, JOHN SOM 364 BRINKLEY
HOWETH, LEVIN SOM 367 BRINKLEY
HOWETH, WILLIAM SOM 356 BRINKLEY
HOWETT, MARY BAL 231 19TH WAR
HOWINGS, NANCY* BAL 103 10TH WAR
HOWINSON, SARAH BAL 383 8TH WARD
HOWISH, PETER BAL 258 2ND WARD
HOWISON, ANN BAL 186 6TH WARD
HOWITH, WILLIAM DOR 458 1ST DIST
HOWITT, ELIZABETH HAR 118 2ND DIST
HOWITT, JOHN HAR 118 2ND DIST
HOWITZ, BENJAMIN F. BAL 362 13TH WAR
HOWK, FREDERICK ALL 197 CUMBERLA
HOWLAND, ANDREW BAL 144 1ST WARD
HOWLAND, JOHN BAL 116 1ST WARD
HOWLAND, JOHN KEN 294 3RD DIST
HOWLAND, MARGARET BAL 355 3RD WARD
HOWLAND, MARK PRI 021 VANSVILL
HOWLAND, REBECCA M. BAL 388 13TH WAR
HOWLANE, MARY A. PRI 005 BLADENSB
HOWLEN, JAMES PRI 017 BLADENSB
HOWLETT, ANDREW J. HAR 042 1ST DIST
HOWLETT, JOHN ALL 071 5TH E.D.
HOWLETT, MATHEY HAR 147 3RD DIST
HOWLETT, WILLIAM HAR 147 3RD DIST
HOWLEY, CATHERINE BAL 055 4TH WARD
HOWLEY, CHARELY HAR 198 3RD DIST
HOWLEY, MAY A. BAL 212 11TH WAR
HOWLY, WILLIAM* DOR 414 1ST DIST
HOWMAN, WILLIAM BAL 078 1ST WARD
HOWN, MARTIN * BAL 194 6TH WARD
HOWRY, JANE ANN 437 HOWARD D
HOWSE, WILLIAM BAL 089 10TH WAR
HOWSE, WILLIAM CAL 058 3RD DIST
HOWSER, CECELIA BAL 208 6TH WARD
HOWSER, GEORGE BAL 105 2ND DIST
HOWSER, GEORGE BAL 285 7TH WARD
HOWSER, H.S. BAL 135 5TH WARD
HOWSER, JACOB BAL 135 5TH WARD
HOWSER, JACOB BAL 281 17TH WAR
HOWSER, JAMES BAL 281 17TH WAR
HOWSER, LEWIS A. BAL 136 5TH WARD
HOWSER, MARTHA CAR 369 9TH DIST
HOWSER, PHILIP CAR 368 9TH DIST
HOWSIE, THOMAS * WOR 199 8TH E DI
HOWSIER, EDWARD WOR 180 6TH E DI
HOWSIER, ELANOR WOR 171 6TH E DI
HOWSIER, JOSHUA WOR 171 6TH E DI
HOWTEN, SUAN BAL 140 16TH WAR
HOWYER, AMOS BAL 383 8TH WARD
HOX, HENRY BAL 254 12TH WAR
HOXLEY, SPENCER WAS 138 HAGERSTO
HOXON, MARTHA BAL 431 14TH WAR
HOXTER, ANDREW TAL 005 EASTON D
HOXTER, EELIZABETH* TAL 005 EASTON D
HOXTER, JAOCB QUE 231 4TH E DI
HOXTER, MARY A.* TAL 005 EASTON D
HOXTER, NOAH* TAL 004 EASTON D
HOXTON, JOHN T. PRI 098 SPALDING
HOY, ACSHA A. FRE 423 8TH E DI
HOY, ALEXANDER BAL 094 18TH WAR
HOY, ANN BAL 094 2ND DIST
HOY, ELVIRA BAL 327 7TH WARD
HOY, JOHN ALL 257 CUMBERLA
HOY, MARIAM WAS 244 SMITHSBU
HOY, MARY HAR 078 2ND DIST
HOY, RACHEL BAL 129 2ND DIST
HOY, SUSAN FRE 292 WOODSBOR
HOYD, GEORGE WAS 006 WILLIAMS
HOYD, LAURENCE WAS 006 WILLIAMS
HOYE, BRIDGET WAS 007 WILLIAMS
HOYE, DANIEL ALL 055 10TH E.D
HOYE, EDWAD ALL 042 10TH E.D
HOYE, ELISABETH ALL 043 10TH E.D
HOYE, ELISABETH ALL 055 10TH E.D
HOYE, JOHN ALL 062 10TH E.D
HOYE, JOHN G. PRI 046 AQUASCO
HOYES, WALTER* BAL 064 4TH WARD
HOYL, CHARLES * HAR 018 1ST DIST
HOYLE, ELIZABETH MGM 418 MEDLEY 3
HOYLE, GEORGE BAL 008 9TH WARD
HOYLE, GOERGE MGM 418 MEDLEY 3
HOYLE, JOHN SR. MGM 418 MEDLEY 3
HOYLE, WILLIAM L. PRI 051 AQUASCO
HOYT, ANDREW D. BAL 051 9TH WARD
HOYT, CHARLES HAR 084 2ND DIST
HOYT, CHARLES * HAR 018 1ST DIST
HOYT, E. K. DOR 448 1ST DIST
HOYTT, ADAM BAL 343 3RD WARD
HOZZARD, ROBERT DOR 387 1ST DIST
HREALER, CASPER BAL 250 2ND WARD
HRIFFITH, HENRY MGM 333 CRACKLIN
HRINED, JACOB * BAL 076 18TH WAR
HRLENT, CHARLES BAL 227 2ND WARD
HRLENT, GEORGE BAL 227 2ND WARD
HRORNEY, SARAH TAL 111 ST MICHA
HSHAW, PETER BAL 041 1ST WARD
HSOMERVILLE, JAMES H.-BLA ST 307 1ST E DI
HUBALL, MARY BAL 353 7TH WARD
HUBARD, JOHN DOR 360 3RD DIVI
HUBART, ADAM BAL 443 8TH WARD
HUBBARD, ALEXANDER* BAL 042 4TH WARD
HUBBARD, ANDREW DOR 364 3RD DIVI
HUBBARD, ANDREW BAL 167 1ST WARD
HUBBARD, BETSEY BAL 339 1ST DIST
HUBBARD, CALEP DOR 361 3RD DIVI
HUBBARD, CAROLINE BAL 099 5TH WARD
HUBBARD, DANIEL BAL 417 8TH WARD
HUBBARD, DANIEL DOR 309 1ST DIST
HUBBARD, DANIEL DOR 377 1ST DIST
HUBBARD, DAVID WAS 235 1ST DIST
HUBBARD, EDWARD TAL 081 ST MICHA
HUBBARD, ELIJAH CAL 048 3RD DIST
HUBBARD, ELIZABETH BAL 407 3RD WARD
HUBBARD, ELIZABETH BAL 270 17TH WAR
HUBBARD, FOSTER DOR 317 1ST DIST
HUBBARD, FOSTER DOR 323 1ST DIST
HUBBARD, FRANCES DOR 313 1ST DIST
HUBBARD, FRANCIS BAL 091 18TH WAR
HUBBARD, GEORGE W. BAL 243 6TH WARD
HUBBARD, GEORGE W. BAL 042 1ST WARD
HUBBARD, HENRY BAL 336 3RD WARD
HUBBARD, HENRY BAL 270 17TH WAR
HUBBARD, HENRY A. BAL 100 5TH WARD
HUBBARD, HOOPER DOR 322 1ST DIST
HUBBARD, ISAAC DOR 298 1ST DIST
HUBBARD, JAME BAL 039 1ST WARD
HUBBARD, JAMES BAL 325 7TH WARD
HUBBARD, JAMES ANN 276 ANNAPOLI
HUBBARD, JAMES DOR 314 1ST DIST
HUBBARD, JAMES G. BAL 372 8TH WARD
HUBBARD, JERE DOR 429 1ST DIST
HUBBARD, JEREMIAH BAL 069 18TH WAR
HUBBARD, JOHN DOR 399 1ST DIST
HUBBARD, JOHN BAL 260 17TH WAR
HUBBARD, JOHN BAL 114 11TH WAR
HUBBARD, JOHN BAL 314 7TH WARD
HUBBARD, JOHN BAL 184 6TH WARD
HUBBARD, JOHN BAL 331 7TH WARD
HUBBARD, JULIA DOR 379 1ST DIST
HUBBARD, L. BAL 150 1ST WARD
HUBBARD, L. BAL 152 1ST WARD
HUBBARD, LAURA BAL 378 1ST DIST
HUBBARD, MARGARET WAS 283 1ST DIST
HUBBARD, MARGARETT BAL 070 18TH WAR
HUBBARD, MARY BAL 159 11TH WAR
HUBBARD, MARY E. BAL 372 8TH WARD
HUBBARD, NANCY BAL 016 15TH WAR
HUBBARD, PERRY DOR 297 1ST DIST
HUBBARD, PETER DOR 322 1ST DIST
HUBBARD, RACHEAL CAR 396 2ND DIST
HUBBARD, RACHEL BAL 214 17TH WAR
HUBBARD, RACHEL BAL 258 12TH WAR
HUBBARD, SAMUEL* BAL 413 3RD WARD
HUBBARD, SARAH A. BAL 324 3RD WARD
HUBBARD, SILAS TAL 018 EASTON D
HUBBARD, SKINNER DOR 394 1ST DIST
HUBBARD, SOCRATES FRE 400 JEFFERSO
HUBBARD, SOLOMON BAL 325 7TH WARD
HUBBARD, SUSAN BAL 037 4TH WARD
HUBBARD, THOMAS CAR 105 NO TWP L
HUBBARD, THOMAS BAL 360 1ST DIST
HUBBARD, THOMAS TAL 086 ST MICHA
HUBBARD, THOMAS S. BAL 163 6TH WARD
HUBBARD, THOMASL DOR 318 1ST DIST
HUBBARD, WILLIAM DOR 321 1ST DIST
HUBBARD, WILLIAM BAL 099 5TH WARD
HUBBARD, WILLIAM BAL 320 3RD WARD
HUBBARD, WILLIAM BAL 324 3RD WARD
HUBBARD, WILLIAM BAL 032 15TH WAR
HUBBARD, WILLIAM ANN 276 ANNAPOLI
HUBBARD, WILLIAM BAL 059 1ST WARD
HUBBART, SAMUEL* BAL 413 3RD WARD
HUBBEARD, CHARLES CAR 115 NO TWP L
HUBBEARD, ELIZA-BLACK CAR 113 NO TWP L
HUBBEARD, SARAH CAR 095 NO TWP L
HUBBED, MARY E. BAL 397 14TH WAR
HUBBEL, BENEDICT BAL 375 8TH WARD
HUBBEL, PETER BAL 054 18TH WAR
HUBBELL, EDWARD WOR 289 9TH E DI
HUBBELL, PAMELIA BAL 378 13TH WAR
HUBBELL, SARAH BAL 241 12TH WAR
HUBBETS, O. BAL 115 1ST WARD
HUBBOAD, JESSE CAR 165 NO TWP L
HUBBOARD, BARBERY-BLACK CAR 155 NO TWP L
HUBBOARD, BARROTT-BLACK CAR 124 NO TWP L
HUBBOARD, BEACHAMP-BLACK CAR 158 NO TWP L
HUBBOARD, CHARLES CAR 159 NO TWP L
HUBBOARD, CLEMENT DOR 470 1ST DIST
HUBBOARD, CLEMENT DOR 452 1ST DIST
HUBBOARD, DANIEL-BLACK CAR 155 NO TWP L
HUBBOARD, ELIAS CAR 162 NO TWP L
HUBBOARD, ELIZABETH DOR 399 1ST DIST
HUBBOARD, ENNALS CAR 165 NO TWP L
HUBBOARD, GREENTREE-BLACK CAR 123 NO TWP L
HUBBOARD, HENRY CAR 163 NO TWP L
HUBBOARD, HENRY DOR 403 1ST DIST
HUBBOARD, HENRY DOR 400 1ST DIST
HUBBOARD, HENRY DOR 399 1ST DIST
HUBBOARD, HENRY* DOR 405 1ST DIST
HUBBOARD, JAMES CAR 146 NO TWP L
HUBBOARD, JESSE CAR 157 NO TWP L
HUBBOARD, JESSE CAR 161 NO TWP L
HUBBOARD, JOHN DOR 403 1ST DIST
HUBBOARD, JOHN K. CAR 145 NO TWP L
HUBBOARD, JOSEPH DOR 454 1ST DIST
HUBBOARD, LEMUEL CAR 144 NO TWP L
HUBBOARD, LEVIN CAR 158 NO TWP L
HUBBOARD, MARGARET DOR 399 1ST DIST
HUBBOARD, MARY DOR 402 1ST DIST
HUBBOARD, MARY-BLACK CAR 127 NO TWP L
HUBBOARD, MICHAL CAR 126 NO TWP L
HUBBOARD, MILLY ANN DOR 399 1ST DIST
HUBBOARD, MITCHEL CAR 150 NO TWP L
HUBBOARD, PETER CAR 117 NO TWP L
HUBBOARD, POULSON-BLACK CAR 138 NO TWP L
HUBBOARD, ROBERT DOR 402 1ST DIST
HUBBOARD, SARAH DOR 399 1ST DIST
HUBBOARD, THOMAS DOR 403 1ST DIST
HUBBOARD, THOMAS DOR 399 1ST DIST
HUBBOARD, TIGHMAN CAR 125 NO TWP L
HUBBOARD, TILGHINAR CAR 137 NO TWP L
HUBBOARD, TILGHMAN CAR 129 NO TWP L
HUBBOARD, WILLIAM DOR 401 1ST DIST
HUBBOARD, WRIGHT CAR 128 NO TWP L
HUBBOARD,PETER-BLACK CAR 155 NO TWP L
HUBBORD, L. BAL 147 1ST WARD
HUBBOURD, ANDREW S. DOR 379 1ST DIST
HUBBROWN, NANCY PRI 013 BLADENSB
HUBBS, CHARLES CAR 395 2ND DIST
HUBBURT, WILLIAM BAL 059 2ND DIST
HUBEL, ROSINA BAL 366 8TH WARD
HUBER, EDWARD BAL 163 11TH WAR
HUBER, JOHN BAL 049 18TH WAR
HUBER, MARY BAL 446 14TH WAR
HUBER, PHILIP FRE 20 5TH E DI
HUBERT, GEROGE BAL 449 8TH WARD
HUBRICH, FERDINAND BAL 127 16TH WAR
HUCHENS, JANE HAR 152 3RD DIST
HUCHING, MARY F. BAL 129 18TH WAR
HUCHINGS, PETER A. BAL 129 18TH WAR
HUCHINS, MANN BAL 300 12TH WAR
HUCHT, HENRY BAL 372 13TH WAR
HUCK, JAMES ALL 241 CUMBERLA
HUCK, JOHN ALL 209 CUMBERLA
HUCK, JOHN J. WAS 264 1ST DIST
HUCK, JULIANN ALL 210 CUMBERLA
HUCKETT, JAMES BAL 191 11TH WAR
HUCKLE, GEORGE W. BAL 260 2ND WARD
HUCOM, JOHN BAL 092 5TH WARD
HUDDELSTON, WILLIAM MGM 394 ROCKERLE
HUDDERS, JAMES W. CEC 112 4TH E DI
HUDDESTON, JOHN BAL 019 1ST WARD
HUDDLESTON, GEORGE MGM 393 ROCKERLE
HUDDLESTON, JOHN PRI 037 VANSVILL
HUDDLESTON, MARY A. PRI 024 VANSVILL
HUDE, JOHN T. E. ANN 353 3RD DIST
HUDE, SOPHIA BAL 150 11TH WAR
HUDGING, WILLIAM H. BAL 120 1ST WARD
HUDGINS, JESSE L. BAL 048 1ST WARD
HUDGINS, JOEL BAL 007 4TH WARD
HUDGINS, JOHN BAL 007 4TH WARD
HUDGINS, JOHN BAL 012 15TH WAR
HUDGINS, JOHN W. BAL 060 15TH WAR
HUDGINS, MARGARET FRANCIS BAL 216 6TH WARD
HUDGINS, WILLIAM BAL 216 6TH WARD
HUDGINS, WILLIAM B. BAL 049 4TH WARD
HUDIS, AGUSTUS BAL 256 2ND WARD
HUDLMIEN, CHARLES L. MGM 390 ROCKERLE
HUDOSN,HOOPER, D. CAR 103 NO TWP L
HUDSON, AARON WOR 313 2ND E DI
HUDSON, ANDREW BAL 230 12TH WAR
HUDSON, ANN ANN 461 HOWARD D
HUDSON, ANNA BAL 276 2ND WARD
HUDSON, ARENIA WOR 246 1ST CENS
HUDSON, BELETHA WOR 247 1ST CENS
HUDSON, BENJAMIN WOR 298 9TH E DI
HUDSON, BENJAMIN SOM 364 BRINKLEY
HUDSON, CAROLINE BAL 269 20TH WAR
HUDSON, CHARLOTT BAL 030 18TH WAR
HUDSON, COMFORT WOR 263 BERLIN I
HUDSON, DANIEL WOR 290 9TH E DI
HUDSON, DAVID D. WOR 179 6TH E DI
HUDSON, DAVID W. BAL 311 3RD WARD
HUDSON, DRUCILLA WOR 316 2ND E DI
HUDSON, ELIZA BAL 461 1ST DIST
HUDSON, ELIZA BAL 256 17TH WAR
HUDSON, ELIZABETH SOM 397 BRINKLEY
HUDSON, EMELINE BAL 338 3RD WARD
HUDSON, EPHRAIM WOR 241 1ST CENS
HUDSON, GEORGE WOR 315 2ND E DI
HUDSON, GEORGE WOR 264 BERLIN I
HUDSON, GEORGE BAL 093 18TH WAR
HUDSON, GEROGE BAL 080 18TH WAR
HUDSON, HANDY WOR 314 2ND E DI
HUDSON, HARRIET BAL 230 12TH WAR
HUDSON, HENRY WOR 183 6TH E DI
HUDSON, HENRY CAR 210 5TH DIST
HUDSON, HENRY BAL 135 18TH WAR
HUDSON, HESTER WOR 319 1ST E DI
HUDSON, ISAAC WOR 250 1ST CENS
HUDSON, ISAAC WOR 250 1ST CENS
HUDSON, ISAAC WOR 248 1ST CENS
HUDSON, ISAAC BAL 104 5TH WARD
HUDSON, JAMES WOR 245 1ST CENS
HUDSON, JAMES WOR 338 1ST E DI
HUDSON, JAMES CEC 035 CHESAPEA
HUDSON, JAMES BAL 341 13TH WAR
HUDSON, JAMES BAL 287 20TH WAR
HUDSON, JAMES C. WOR 208 4TH E DI
HUDSON, JANE-BLACK CAR 146 NO TWP L
HUDSON, JEHU WOR 280 BERLIN I
HUDSON, JEHU E. WOR 245 1ST CENS
HUDSON, JOHN WOR 241 1ST CENS
HUDSON, JOHN WOR 282 BERLIN I
HUDSON, JOHN WOR 290 9TH E DI
HUDSON, JOHN FRE 174 5TH E DI
HUDSON, JOHN BAL 142 1ST WARD
HUDSON, JOHN A. FRE 048 FREDERIC
HUDSON, JOHN B. CAR 103 NO TWP L
HUDSON, JOHN L. WOR 323 1ST E DI
HUDSON, JOHN M. KEN 241 2ND DIST
HUDSON, JOHS. BAL 031 18TH WAR
HUDSON, JOSEPH CAR 102 NO TWP L
HUDSON, JOSEPH BAL 127 1ST WARD
HUDSON, JOSIAH WOR 279 BERLIN I
HUDSON, JULIA A. WOR 179 6TH E DI
HUDSON, L. J. BAL 111 10TH WAR
HUDSON, LABEN WOR 336 1ST E DI
HUDSON, LEMUEL KEN 285 3RD DIST
HUDSON, LEVEINA WOR 336 1ST E DI
HUDSON, LEVI BAL 347 7TH WARD
HUDSON, LITTLETON SOM 396 BRINKLEY
HUDSON, LOUISA WOR 308 2ND E DI
HUDSON, LUCRETIA G. FRE 007 FREDERIC
HUDSON, MARGARET WOR 270 BERLIN I
HUDSON, MARGARET WOR 324 1ST E DI
HUDSON, MARIA WOR 263 BERLIN I
HUDSON, MARIAH WOR 279 BERLIN I
HUDSON, MARY SOM 390 BRINKLEY
HUDSON, MARY CAR 104 NO TWP L
HUDSON, MARY CEC 037 CHESAPEA
HUDSON, MARY CEC 037 CHESAPEA
HUDSON, MARY ALL 217 CUMBERLA
HUDSON, MARY E. WOR 278 BERLIN I
HUDSON, MARY ML WOR 242 1ST CENS
HUDSON, MATTHEW BAL 003 15TH WAR
HUDSON, MICHAEL BAL 390 1ST DIST
HUDSON, MILBY WOR 312 2ND E DI
HUDSON, MOSES WOR 335 1ST E DI
HUDSON, NANCY WOR 244 1ST CENS
HUDSON, PHILLIP WOR 278 BERLIN I
HUDSON, RACHAEL BAL 066 1ST WARD
HUDSON, RICHARD WOR 256 1ST CENS
HUDSON, RICHARD C. BAL 043 18TH WAR
HUDSON, ROBERT BAL 369 3RD WARD
HUDSON, SABIN WOR 306 2ND E DI
HUDSON, SARAH WOR 246 1ST CENS
HUDSON, SARAH SOM 392 BRINKLEY
HUDSON, SARAH BAL 341 13TH WAR
HUDSON, SARAH W. MISS- ANN 372 4TH DIST
HUDSON, SELBY WOR 305 2ND E DI
HUDSON, SNANIAS WOR 284 BERLIN I
HUDSON, SUSAN WOR 244 1ST CENS
HUDSON, THOMAS WOR 287 BERLIN I
HUDSON, THOMAS WAS 179 BOONSBOR
HUDSON, THOMAS QUE 163 2ND E DI
HUDSON, THOMAS BAL 019 1ST WARD

Name	County	Page	District
HUDSON, THOMAS	BAL	365	1ST DIST
HUDSON, UGENIA	BAL	327	1ST DIST
HUOSON, WALTER	WOR	243	1ST CENS
HUDSON, WILLIAM	WOR	165	6TH E DI
HUDSON, WILLIAM	WOR	268	BERLIN 1
HUDSON, WILLIAM	BAL	364	1ST DIST
HUDSON, WILLIAM	BAL	066	1ST WARD
HUDSON, WILLIAM	BAL	050	1ST WARD
HUDSON, WILLIAM	BAL	276	2ND WARD
HUDSON, WILLIAM	BAL	318	12TH WAR
HUDSON, WILLIAM	CEC	029	CHESAPEA
HUDSON, WILLIAM B.	BAL	452	14TH WAR
HUDSON, WILLIAM D.	WOR	258	1ST CENS
HUDSON, WILLIAM L.	WOR	256	1ST CENS
HUEBRENNER, DANIEL	ALL	201	CUMBERLA
HUEING, JOHN	BAL	184	2ND WARD
HUENBERGER, WILLIAM H.	WAS	102	2ND DIST
HUEPNER, ADAM	BAL	021	18TH WAR
HUEPNER, MARTIN	BAL	005	18TH WAR
HUERT, JOHN*	DOR	392	1ST DIST
HUES, HENERETTA	SOM	465	HANGARY
HUES, JOHN	WOR	274	BERLIN 1
HUES, PATRICK	BAL	400	1ST DIST
HUESTEW, MARGARET	CAR	307	1ST DIST
HUET, AUGUSTIN	BAL	025	9TH WARD
HUET, NANCY	BAL	229	1ST DIST
HUETT, THOMAS	BAL	140	1ST WARD
HUEY, JAMES	BAL	186	6TH WARD
HUEY, JANE	BAL	167	2ND DIST
HUEZELMEIER, WILLIAM	BAL	077	10TH WAR
HUF, RACHIEL	HAR	007	1ST DIST
HUFE, HENRY *	BAL	279	1ST DIST
HUFF, ABRAHAM	HAR	007	1ST DIST
HUFF, ANDRWE	BAL	166	2ND DIST
HUFF, GEORGE	ALL	004	3RD E.D.
HUFF, GEORGE	HAR	031	1ST DIST
HUFF, JASPER	ALL	157	6TH E.D.
HUFF, JESSE	HAR	007	1ST DIST
HUFF, JOHN	HAR	007	1ST DIST
HUFF, JOHN	ALL	157	6TH E.D.
HUFF, JOHN	BAL	226	2ND WARD
HUFF, JOHN L.	BAL	471	14TH WAR
HUFF, JOSEPH B.	HAR	122	2ND DIST
HUFF, SUSAN B.	FRE	205	BUCKEYST
HUFF, THOMAS R.	HAR	031	1ST DIST
HUFF, TOBIAS	ALL	029	2ND E.D.
HUFF, WALTER	CAR	104	NO TWP L
HUFF, ZEBULON	ALL	030	2ND E.D.
HUFF,NARCISSA	ALL	225	CUMBERLA
HUFFER, JOSEPH L.	FRE	323	MIDDLETO
HUFFER, MARIA	FRE	349	MIDDLETO
HUFFERY, WILLIAM	BAL	197	2ND WARD
HUFFEY, MICHAEL	BAL	197	2ND WARD
HUFFIELD, ABIGAL	BAL	001	18TH WAR
HUFFINGTON, JAMES	SOM	476	TRAPPE D
HUFFINGTON, JOHN	BAL	428	14TH WAR
HUFFINGTON, JONATHAN	SOM	476	TRAPPE D
HUFFINGTON, MARGARET	DOR	456	1ST DIST
HUFFINGTON, MARY E.	DOR	390	1ST DIST
HUFFINGTON, REBECCA	DOR	456	1ST DIST
HUFFINGTON, WILLIAM	SOM	549	TYASKIN
HUFFINGTON, WILLIAM	DOR	390	1ST DIST
HUFFINGTON, WILLIAM	ANN	460	HOWARD D
HUFFINGTON, WILLIAM W.	BAL	289	3RD WARD
HUFFMAN, ELIZABETH	WAS	225	1ST DIST
HUFFMAN, FREDRICK	BAL	008	4TH WARD
HUFFMAN, GEORG	BAL	232	2ND WARD
HUFFMAN, GEORGE	BAL	383	13TH WAR
HUFFMAN, HENRY	BAL	231	2ND WARD
HUFFMAN, ISAAC	CAR	178	8TH DIST
HUFFMAN, JACOB	HAR	083	2ND DIST
HUFFMAN, JAOCB SR.	FRE	414	8TH E DI
HUFFMAN, LEFMAN*	BAL	399	3RD WARD
HUFFMAN, THOMAS	FRE	414	8TH E DI
HUFFORD, NANCY	ALL	013	3RD E.D.
HUFFSTATE, JOSEPH	BAL	103	2ND DIST
HUFFSTIDLER, REBECCA	BAL	400	8TH WARD
HUFLER, CHARLES	BAL	146	1ST WARD
HUFLIN, CHARLES	BAL	279	2ND WARD
HUFNENCH, NEWMAN	BAL	147	11TH WAR
HUFTY, O.P.	BAL	139	1ST WARD
HUGANES, JOHN	CEC	048	1ST E DI
HUGARY, EDWARD	CEC	035	CHESAPEA
HUGEN, CATHARINE	BAL	401	1ST DIST
HUGENEIR, MELISSAS*	DOR	380	1ST DIST
HUGENS, THOMAS	CEC	037	CHESAPEA
HUGER, HENRY	FRE	217	BUCKEYST
HUGERSHIMER, SAMUEL	FRE	003	FREDERIC
HUGES, GEORGE	BAL	442	1ST DIST
HUGES, JANE	BAL	426	1ST DIST
HUGES, SARAH	BAL	426	1ST DIST
HUGESHIMER, DAVID	FRE	217	BUCKEYST
HUGETT, GEORGE	WAS	274	RIDGEVIL
HUGETT, JACOB L.	WAS	274	RIDGEVIL
HUGG, ELIZABETH A.	BAL	223	6TH WARD
HUGG, GEORGE	CEC	176	7TH E DI
HUGG, HENRIETTA	BAL	335	3RD WARD
HUGG, JACOB W.	BAL	411	3RD WARD
HUGG, MARGARET	BAL	089	1ST WARD
HUGG, MARY	BAL	213	6TH WARD
HUGG, RICHARD	BAL	308	12TH WAR
HUGGAN, JOHN	ALL	069	5TH E.D.
HUGGENS, HAMILTON	BAL	387	1ST DIST
HUGGINS, BETS	CEC	098	3RD E DI
HUGGINS, CATHARINE	HAR	153	3RD DIST
HUGGINS, ELIZABETH	BAL	225	1ST DIST
HUGGINS, JAMES	HAR	017	1ST DIST
HUGGINS, MARY	CEC	103	4TH E DI
HUGGINS, WILLAM	BAL	182	19TH WAR
HUGGON, JOHN	ALL	069	5TH E.D.
HUGH, EDWARD	ALL	181	8TH E.D.
HUGH, EMELINE	BAL	266	12TH WAR
HUGH, JOHN	CEC	057	1ST E DI
HUGH, THOMGHUNDER *	BAL	155	2ND DIST
HUGHE, RICHARD	BAL	155	19TH WAR
HUGHE, WILLIAM	BAL	181	19TH WAR
HUGHEEY, ISEBELLA	BAL	117	18TH WAR
HUGHENS, JOHN T.	HAR	147	3RD DIST
HUGHES T. L.	BAL	095	10TH WAR
HUGHES, A.D.	BAL	267	12TH WAR
HUGHES, ABRAM	CEC	159	PORT DUP
HUGHES, ABRAM	TAL	020	EASTON D
HUGHES, ALICE	BAL	170	16TH WAR
HUGHES, AMOS	HAR	130	2ND DIST
HUGHES, ANN	BAL	045	18TH WAR
HUGHES, ANN	BAL	475	14TH WAR
HUGHES, ANN	BAL	042	2ND DIST
HUGHES, ANNA T.	BAL	096	5TH WARD
HUGHES, ANTHONY	ALL	129	4TH E.D.
HUGHES, AQUILLA	BAL	262	12TH WAR
HUGHES, ARTHUR	BAL	077	15TH WAR
HUGHES, BENJAMIN	MGM	339	CLARKSBU
HUGHES, BIDDY	BAL	064	15TH WAR
HUGHES, BRIDGET	BAL	454	8TH WARD
HUGHES, BRIDGET	BAL	070	10TH WAR
HUGHES, BRIDGET	BAL	394	3RD WARD
HUGHES, BRIDGET	BAL	372	3RD WARD
HUGHES, BRIDGET	BAL	205	11TH WAR
HUGHES, CALEB	SOM	537	TYASKIN
HUGHES, CATHARINE	WAS	136	HAGERSTO
HUGHES, CATHERINE	BAL	126	11TH WAR
HUGHES, CATHERINE	BAL	317	20TH WAR
HUGHES, CATHERINE	BAL	377	3RD WARD
HUGHES, CATHERINE	BAL	188	11TH WAR
HUGHES, CHARLOTTE	BAL	014	2ND DIST
HUGHES, CHARLOTTE	SOM	537	TYASKIN
HUGHES, CHRIS	BAL	231	19TH WAR
HUGHES, CHRISTOPHER	BAL	242	20TH WAR
HUGHES, DANIEL	FRE	055	FREDERIC
HUGHES, DANIEL B.	FRE	095	FREDERIC
HUGHES, DAVID	WAS	260	1ST DIST
HUGHES, DAVID	ALL	070	5TH E.D.
HUGHES, EDITH	BAL	119	2ND DIST
HUGHES, EDWARD	BAL	457	8TH WARD
HUGHES, EDWARD	BAL	405	3RD WARD
HUGHES, EDWARD	BAL	306	3RD WARD
HUGHES, EDWARD	BAL	171	1ST WARD
HUGHES, EDWARD	WAS	009	WILLIAMS
HUGHES, EDWARD	HAR	046	1ST DIST
HUGHES, EDWARD	BAL	264	20TH WAR
HUGHES, EDWARD	BAL	379	13TH WAR
HUGHES, ELANDA	BAL	275	2ND WARD
HUGHES, ELIJAH	BAL	228	12TH WAR
HUGHES, ELIZA	BAL	249	12TH WAR
HUGHES, ELIZA	BAL	335	7TH WARD
HUGHES, ELIZA	BAL	312	12TH WAR
HUGHES, ELIZA	HAR	018	1ST DIST
HUGHES, ELIZA	CAR	232	5TH DIST
HUGHES, ELIZABETH	BAL	200	19TH WAR
HUGHES, ELIZABETH	QUE	243	5TH E DI
HUGHES, ELLEN	PRI	096	SPALDING
HUGHES, ELLEN	BAL	103	10TH WAR
HUGHES, ELLEN	BAL	445	8TH WARD
HUGHES, ELLEN	BAL	192	11TH WAR
HUGHES, ELLEN	BAL	179	11TH WAR
HUGHES, ELLEN	BAL	271	7TH WARD
HUGHES, ELY	BAL	020	2ND DIST
HUGHES, EUPHRIA	BAL	212	11TH WAR
HUGHES, EVAN	ANN	412	HOWARD D
HUGHES, EVERETT G.	HAR	172	3RD DIST
HUGHES, FANNEY	CAR	217	5TH DIST
HUGHES, FELIX	BAL	188	11TH WAR
HUGHES, FRANCIS H.	HAR	078	2ND DIST
HUGHES, GEORGE	FRE	239	NEW MARK
HUGHES, GEORGE	BAL	383	3RD WARD
HUGHES, GEORGE	BAL	309	12TH WAR
HUGHES, GEORGE A.	BAL	150	11TH WAR
HUGHES, GEORGE H.	BAL	070	15TH WAR
HUGHES, GEORGE W.	ANN	308	1ST DIST
HUGHES, HANDY	HAR	175	3RD DIST
HUGHES, HARRIET	WAS	281	LEITERSB
HUGHES, HENRY	WAS	164	2ND DIST
HUGHES, HENRY	QUE	146	1ST E DI
HUGHES, HENRY	ALL	135	4TH E.D.
HUGHES, HENRY	BAL	152	2ND DIST
HUGHES, HESTER	BAL	264	12TH WAR
HUGHES, HESTER A.	TAL	048	EASTON T
HUGHES, HESTOR	BAL	250	17TH WAR
HUGHES, HUGH	BAL	392	8TH WARD
HUGHES, HUGH R.	WAS	171	FUNKSTOW
HUGHES, HUGHY	FRE	214	BUCKEYST
HUGHES, ISAAC	WOR	339	1ST E DI
HUGHES, ISABELLA	WAS	164	HAGERSTO
HUGHES, ISAIAH	WAS	156	HAGERSTO
HUGHES, ISRAEL	BAL	400	8TH WARD
HUGHES, JAEMS	BAL	070	18TH WAR
HUGHES, JAME	BAL	102	2ND DIST
HUGHES, JAMES	ALL	232	CUMBERLA
HUGHES, JAMES	BAL	385	8TH WARD
HUGHES, JAMES	BAL	140	1ST WARD
HUGHES, JAMES	BAL	192	11TH WAR
HUGHES, JAMES	BAL	460	8TH WARD
HUGHES, JAMES	BAL	457	8TH WARD
HUGHES, JAMES	BAL	001	15TH WAR
HUGHES, JAMES	BAL	346	7TH WARD
HUGHES, JAMES	BAL	112	1ST WARD
HUGHES, JAMES	ALL	142	6TH E.D.
HUGHES, JAMES	ALL	149	6TH E.D.
HUGHES, JAMES	BAL	300	17TH WAR
HUGHES, JAMES	BAL	128	18TH WAR
HUGHES, JAMES	CAR	192	4TH DIST
HUGHES, JAMES	BAL	420	3RD WARD
HUGHES, JAMES	BAL	253	20TH WAR
HUGHES, JAMES	FRE	034	FREDERIC
HUGHES, JAMES	WAS	142	2ND DIST
HUGHES, JAMES C.	ALL	162	6TH E.D.
HUGHES, JANE	BAL	347	7TH WARD
HUGHES, JANE	BAL	083	15TH WAR
HUGHES, JANE	BAL	158	19TH WAR
HUGHES, JESSE	TAL	067	EASTON T
HUGHES, JOANNA	BAL	236	6TH WARD
HUGHES, JOHN	BAL	291	12TH WAR
HUGHES, JOHN	BAL	344	7TH WARD
HUGHES, JOHN	BAL	184	11TH WAR
HUGHES, JOHN	BAL	184	11TH WAR
HUGHES, JOHN	BAL	064	15TH WAR
HUGHES, JOHN	BAL	112	1ST WARD
HUGHES, JOHN	BAL	101	1ST WARD
HUGHES, JOHN	BAL	264	7TH WARD
HUGHES, JOHN	ALL	231	CUMBERLA
HUGHES, JOHN	TAL	048	EASTON T
HUGHES, JOHN	WAS	004	WILLIAMS
HUGHES, JOHN	SOM	447	DAMES QU
HUGHES, JOHN	BAL	015	4TH WARD
HUGHES, JOHN	BAL	040	18TH WAR
HUGHES, JOHN	HAR	130	2ND DIST
HUGHES, JOHN	BAL	158	11TH WAR
HUGHES, JOHN H.	MGM	408	MEDLEY 3
HUGHES, JON	BAL	010	9TH WARD
HUGHES, JOSEPH	BAL	101	2ND DIST
HUGHES, JOSEPH	ALL	247	CUMBERLA
HUGHES, JOSEPH	CAR	284	7TH DIST
HUGHES, JOSEPH M.	WAS	144	HAGERSTO
HUGHES, JOSHUA	HAR	017	1ST DIST
HUGHES, JOSIAH	BAL	279	17TH WAR
HUGHES, JOSIAH	BAL	375	13TH WAR
HUGHES, LAURA	WAS	136	HAGERSTO
HUGHES, LEASHEA	BAL	054	18TH WAR
HUGHES, LUCRETIA	BAL	410	3RD WARD
HUGHES, LYDIA A.	BAL	349	7TH WARD
HUGHES, MARGARET	BAL	346	7TH WARD
HUGHES, MARGARET	BAL	029	18TH WAR
HUGHES, MARGARET	BAL	254	17TH WAR
HUGHES, MARGARET S.	BAL	103	10TH WAR
HUGHES, MARIA	BAL	213	2ND WARD
HUGHES, MARTHA	BAL	271	2ND WARD
HUGHES, MARTHA	BAL	153	2ND DIST
HUGHES, MARTIN	BAL	109	1ST WARD
HUGHES, MARTIN	ALL	053	10TH E.D
HUGHES, MARTIN	ALL	048	10TH E.D
HUGHES, MARY	BAL	279	7TH WARD
HUGHES, MARY	BAL	213	6TH WARD
HUGHES, MARY	BAL	236	12TH WAR
HUGHES, MARY	BAL	042	2ND DIST
HUGHES, MARY	BAL	347	13TH WAR
HUGHES, MARY	BAL	230	19TH WAR
HUGHES, MARY	MGM	374	ROCKERLE
HUGHES, MARY	BAL	160	11TH WAR
HUGHES, MARY	FRE	001	FREDERIC
HUGHES, MARY A.	BAL	289	3RD WARD
HUGHES, MARYANN	BAL	368	3RD WARD
HUGHES, MICHAEL	ANN	423	HOWARD D
HUGHES, MICHAEL	ALL	052	10TH E.D
HUGHES, MICHAEL	ALL	057	10TH E.D
HUGHES, MICHAEL	BAL	159	16TH WAR
HUGHES, MICHEAL	BAL	071	18TH WAR
HUGHES, MORRIS	BAL	014	1ST WARD
HUGHES, NANCY	HAR	194	3RD DIST
HUGHES, NAPOLSON*	BAL	080	4TH WARD
HUGHES, PATRICK	BAL	316	20TH WAR
HUGHES, PATRICK	BAL	036	4TH WARD
HUGHES, PATRICK	BAL	091	5TH WARD
HUGHES, PATRICK	BAL	002	9TH WARD
HUGHES, PATRICK	BAL	019	9TH WARD
HUGHES, PATRICK	BAL	381	8TH WARD
HUGHES, PETER	BAL	420	14TH WAR
HUGHES, PHILIP	BAL	158	16TH WAR
HUGHES, RACHEL	BAL	133	2ND DIST
HUGHES, RACHEL	BAL	133	2ND DIST
HUGHES, RICHARD	ALL	053	10TH E.D
HUGHES, RICHARD	HAR	046	1ST DIST
HUGHES, ROBERT	BAL	287	20TH WAR
HUGHES, ROBERT	BAL	023	2ND DIST
HUGHES, ROSA	BAL	170	16TH WAR
HUGHES, ROSA	BAL	054	4TH WARD
HUGHES, ROSE H.	BAL	017	9TH WARD
HUGHES, SAMUEL	CAR	202	4TH DIST
HUGHES, SARAH	BAL	068	4TH WARD
HUGHES, SARAH	BAL	086	18TH WAR
HUGHES, SARAH	BAL	235	6TH WARD
HUGHES, SARAH	BAL	315	7TH WARD
HUGHES, SCOTT	BAL	335	3RD WARD
HUGHES, SCOTT	HAR	130	2ND DIST
HUGHES, SINGLEOTN	CAR	228	5TH DIST
HUGHES, SOPHIA	FRE	051	FREDERIC
HUGHES, SOPHIA	ALL	247	CUMBERLA
HUGHES, SUSAN	BAL	133	5TH WARD
HUGHES, SUSAN	BAL	019	4TH WARD
HUGHES, SUSAN	WAS	098	2ND DIST
HUGHES, SUSAN W.	BAL	038	4TH WARD
HUGHES, SUSANA	HAR	171	3RD DIST
HUGHES, THERESA	BAL	264	7TH WARD
HUGHES, THOMAS	BAL	170	1ST WARD
HUGHES, THOMAS	ALL	082	5TH E.D.
HUGHES, THOMAS	BAL	458	8TH WARD
HUGHES, THOMAS	BAL	007	15TH WAR
HUGHES, THOMAS	BAL	100	1ST WARD
HUGHES, THOMAS	BAL	175	19TH WAR
HUGHES, THOMAS	BAL	175	19TH WAR
HUGHES, WILLAIM	ANN	465	HOWARD D
HUGHES, WILLAM	HAR	070	1ST DIST
HUGHES, WILLIAM	HAR	081	2ND DIST
HUGHES, WILLIAM	CAR	202	4TH DIST
HUGHES, WILLIAM	BAL	092	18TH WAR
HUGHES, WILLIAM	BAL	127	18TH WAR
HUGHES, WILLIAM	FRE	239	NEW MARK
HUGHES, WILLIAM	BAL	362	3RD WARD
HUGHES, WILLIAM	BAL	346	7TH WARD
HUGHES, WILLIAM	BAL	340	7TH WARD
HUGHES, ZLERIS	HAR	074	1ST DIST
HUGHES,CHARLES	BAL	269	12TH WAR
HUGHES,EDWARD	FRE	391	PETERSVI
HUGHES,MARGARET	ALL	262	CUMBERLA
HUGHES,MARIN	BAL	249	12TH WAR
HUGHES,NASAN	BAL	041	2ND DIST
HUGHES,WILLIAM	CAR	384	2ND DIST
HUGHEY, JOHN	BAL	243	2ND WARD
HUGHEY, MARY	DOR	321	1ST DIST
HUGHEY, ROBERT	TAL	005	EASTON D
HUGHEY, SARAH	CAR	158	NO TWP L
HUGHEY, THOMAS	QUE	186	3RD E DI
HUGHL, MARY	BAL	090	2ND DIST
HUGHLETT, JOHN	DOR	308	1ST DIST
HUGHLETT, MARGARET	TAL	075	EASTON T
HUGHLETT, MRY	TAL	078	EASTON T
HUGHLETT, THOMAS	DOR	325	1ST DIST
HUGHLETT, WILLIAM R.	TAL	052	EASTON D
HUGHS, A. W.	TAL	038	EASTON D
HUGHS, AARON	DOR	447	1ST DIST
HUGHS, ANTHONY	TAL	077	EASTON T
HUGHS, ARTHUR	DOR	439	1ST DIST
HUGHS, BETTY H.	CHA	257	MIDDLETO
HUGHS, CHARLES	DOR	453	1ST DIST
HUGHS, DERNWOOD*	DOR	425	1ST DIST
HUGHS, EDWARD	BAL	160	11TH WAR
HUGHS, GEORGE	ALL	205	CUMBERLA
HUGHS, GEORGE-BLACK	BAL	218	2ND WARD
HUGHS, ISAAC	ALL	203	CUMBERLA
HUGHS, JAMES	ALL	203	CUMBERLA
HUGHS, JAMES	BAL	349	1ST DIST
HUGHS, JAMES	DOR	389	1ST DIST
HUGHS, JAMIMA	BAL	151	5TH WARD
HUGHS, JOHN	BAL	225	2ND WARD
HUGHS, JOHN	BAL	039	1ST WARD
HUGHS, JOHN	DOR	420	1ST DIST
HUGHS, JOHN	DOR	442	1ST DIST
HUGHS, JOHN	FRE	159	EMMITTSB
HUGHS, JOHN	FRE	145	10TH E D
HUGHS, JOHN	CHA	218	ALLENS F
HUGHS, LEAH	DOR	438	1ST DIST
HUGHS, LEVIN T.	SOM	536	TYASKIN
HUGHS, LITTLETON	DOR	420	1ST DIST
HUGHS, MARGARET	BAL	268	2ND WARD
HUGHS, MARY	FRE	168	EMMITTSB
HUGHS, PATRICK	BAL	250	2ND WARD
HUGHS, ROBERT	DOR	422	1ST DIST
HUGHS, ROBERT	CAR	227	5TH DIST
HUGHS, SARAH	BAL	029	1ST WARD
HUGHS, SISTER M.S.	FRE	198	5TH E DI
HUGHS, THOMAS	BAL	017	1ST WARD

HUGHS, THOMAS BAL 266 2ND WARD
HUGHS, THOMAS SOM 536 TYASKIN
HUGHS, WILLIAM DOR 422 1ST DIST
HUGHS, WILLIAM DOR 422 1ST DIST
HUGHS, WILLIAM DOR 409 1ST DIST
HUGHS, WILLIAM DOR 421 1ST DIST
HUGHY, MARY BAL 393 3RD WARD
HUGINS, A.L. ALL 215 CUMBERLA
HUGO, DORAS FRE 031 FREDERIC
HUGO, HENRY BAL 027 9TH WARD
HUGS, MICHAEL BAL 449 14TH WAR
HUGS, THOMAS L. FRE 234 BUCKEYST
HUGWET, LOUISA A. BAL 014 18TH WAR
HUHN, JACOB FRE 358 CATOCTIN
HUHN, JOHN BAL 011 9TH WARD
HUHR, ELIZABETH BAL 102 10TH WAR
HUIKLE, WILLIAM* BAL 421 3RD WARD
HUIST, MARY BAL 001 1ST WARD
HUITZE, LOUISA BAL 323 12TH WAR
HUKLE, CHRISITAN BAL 260 2ND WARD
HULBERT, JOSEPH P. BAL 376 13TH WAR
HULBINE, JOHN BAL 253 1ST DIST
HULBURGH, MATTHIAS BAL 066 1ST WARD
HULD, EDWARD H. TAL 076 EASTON T
HULDING, CLIA BAL 180 2ND WARD
HULE, WILLIAM ALL 161 6TH E.D.
HULEN, MARY L. WAS 057 2ND SUBD
HULER, PHILIP BAL 345 13TH WAR
HULET, THOMAS BAL 168 1ST WARD
HULETT, JAMES BAL 142 1ST WARD
HULETT, THOMAS BAL 117 1ST WARD
HULETT, THOMSA BAL 118 1ST WARD
HULFINCH, JACOB BAL 149 19TH WAR
HULINE, JOSEPH BAL 279 2ND WARD
HULL, AARON BAL 140 1ST WARD
HULL, AARON BAL 135 1ST WARD
HULL, ABEL A. HAR 091 2ND DIST
HULL, ABRAHAM WAS 147 2ND DIST
HULL, AVON BAL 173 11TH WAR
HULL, BEACHAM G. SOM 527 QUANTICO
HULL, BENJAMIN FRE 103 FREDERIC
HULL, DAVID FRE 107 CREAGERS
HULL, ELIAS BAL 233 20TH WAR
HULL, ELIZABETH FRE 032 FREDERIC
HULL, ELIZABETH TAL 075 EASTON T
HULL, ELIZABETH BAL 207 6TH WARD
HULL, ELIZABETH * BAL 304 12TH WAR
HULL, ELIZABETH * TAL 075 EASTON T
HULL, EUGENE C. FRE 099 FREDERIC
HULL, GEORGE W. FRE 446 8TH E DI
HULL, GOERGE BAL 333 7TH WARD
HULL, ISAAC CAR 254 3RD DIST
HULL, JACOB FRE 431 8TH E DI
HULL, JACOB WAS 147 2ND DIST
HULL, JAMES CAL 059 3RD DIST
HULL, JOEL FRE 026 FREDERIC
HULL, JOHN WAS 146 2ND DIST
HULL, JOHN WAS 146 2ND DIST
HULL, JOHN ALL 061 10TH E.D
HULL, JOHN BAL 402 1ST DIST
HULL, JOHN T. ALL 160 6TH E.D.
HULL, JUBIUS FRE 295 WOODSBOR
HULL, MARIAH SOM 391 BRINKLEY
HULL, MARY BAL 139 5TH WARD
HULL, MILCAH A. BAL 070 10TH WAR
HULL, NAPOLEON B. WAS 102 2ND DIST
HULL, PETER WAS 145 2ND DIST
HULL, REBECCA FRE 103 FREDERIC
HULL, RICHARD BAL 015 4TH WARD
HULL, ROBERT BAL 109 10TH WAR
HULL, SALEY D. DOR 431 1ST DIST
HULL, SAMUEL CAR 254 3RD DIST
HULL, SAMUEL CAR 365 9TH DIST
HULL, SAMUEL* TAL 001 EASTON D
HULL, SARAH J. ALL 061 10TH E.D
HULL, SUSAN TAL 076 EASTON T
HULL, TEDEMAN FRE 099 FREDERIC
HULL, THOMAS J. BAL 110 5TH WARD
HULL, WILLIAM BAL 226 12TH WAR
HULL, WILLIAM FRE 107 CREAGERS
HULL, WILLIAM SOM 521 BARREN C
HULL, WILLIAM H. CAR 254 3RD DIST
HULLEY, F. BAL 170 1ST WARD
HULLEY, JOHN BAL 217 17TH WAR
HULLING, PHILIP WAS 122 2ND DIST
HULLINGER, LEWIS ALL 070 5TH E.D.
HULLS, C. G. BAL 150 1ST WARD
HULLS, JOHN BAL 092 5TH WARD
HULLY, MITILDA BAL 201 11TH WAR
HULOW, CATHARINE CAR 242 TANEYTOW
HULREMAN, HENRY BAL 210 17TH WAR
HULSE, ISAAC JR. BAL 057 15TH WAR
HULSE, JAMES BAL 346 13TH WAR
HULSE, JOHN BAL 071 10TH WAR
HULSE, JOHN WAS 204 1ST DIST
HULSE, MAREY BAL 251 12TH WAR
HULSE, MICHAEL WAS 135 HAGERSTO
HULSE, WILLIAM BAL 329 3RD WARD
HULSE, WILLIAM FRE 315 MIDDLETO
HULSE, WILLIAM D. BAL 330 3RD WARD
HULSELMAN, LOUIS BAL 117 15TH WAR
HULST, HENRY CEC 205 7TH E DI
HULTMAN, ELIZA BAL 368 8TH WARD
HULTZ, ROBERT BAL 120 11TH WAR
HULTZHIMER, CHRISTOPHER FRE 084 FREDERIC
HULTZHIMER, MARGARET FRE 085 FREDERIC
HUM, LEWIS FRE 116 CREAGERS
HUMAKER, HENRY BAL 333 13TH WAR
HUMAN, JOHN TAL 031 EASTON D
HUMAN, MARGARET DOR 424 1ST DIST
HUMAS, EDMUND CAL 047 3RD DIST
HUMBAUGH, CLARA L. WAS 150 HAGERSTO
HUMBERSON, JACOB ALL 121 4TH E.D.
HUMBERSON, JOHN S. ALL 112 5TH E.D.
HUMBERSON, SALEM ALL 113 5TH E.D.
HUMBERSON, WILLIAM ALL 112 5TH E.D.
HUMBERSON, WILLIAM ALL 114 5TH E.D.
HUMBERT, ADAM CAR 260 3RD DIST
HUMBERT, CHRISTIAN CAR 408 2ND DIST
HUMBERT, GEORGE CAR 247 3RD DIST
HUMBERT, JOHN CAR 406 2ND DIST
HUMBERT, JOHN CAR 407 2ND DIST
HUMBERT, JOHN BAL 260 20TH WAR
HUMBERT, NICHOLAS BAL 259 20TH WAR
HUMBIRD, JACOB ALL 211 CUMBERLA
HUMBLEBROOK, SARAH ANN 435 HOWARD D
HUMBRIGHT, , EMANUEL ALL 220 CUMBERLA
HUMBUG, ELIZABETH-BLACK FRE 048 FREDERIC
HUMBURD, JOHN ALL 211 CUMBERLA
HUME, ISABELLA BAL 427 14TH WAR
HUME, JANE BAL 145 19TH WAR
HUME, WILLIAM BAL 426 14TH WAR
HUMERICK, HENRY FRE 145 10TH E D
HUMERT, CASPAR BAL 206 19TH WAR
HUMES, FELIX F. BAL 311 1ST DIST
HUMES, MARY BAL 095 5TH WARD
HUMES, MARY BAL 152 19TH WAR
HUMES, SAMUEL BAL 074 2ND DIST
HUMES, THOMAS JR. BAL 095 5TH WARD
HUMES, VIVALDI BAL 160 19TH WAR
HUMGERFORD, ANNM. CAL 027 2ND DIST
HUMICUMB, DINA* BAL 345 3RD WARD
HUMILLER, J. BAL 245 12TH WAR
HUMM, EDWARD FRE 121 CREAGERS
HUMM, PETER FRE 112 CREAGERS
HUMM, PETER * FRE 121 CREAGERS
HUMMA, M. BAL 259 12TH WAR
HUMMAN, JOHN BAL 304 12TH WAR
HUMMEL, AUGUST BAL 259 12TH WAR
HUMMELL, PATRICK ALL 126 4TH E.D.
HUMMER, ADAM FRE 293 WOODSBOR
HUMMER, DAVID ALL 109 5TH E.D.
HUMMER, HENRY FRE 293 WOODSBOR
HUMPH, JACOB BAL 216 19TH WAR
HUMPH, LOUISA BAL 216 19TH WAR
HUMPHAYES, NANTZY* BAL 400 3RD WARD
HUMPHEYS, HECTOR ANN 293 ANNAPOLI
HUMPHEYS, JOHN C. KEN 259 1ST DIST
HUMPHISS, WILLIAM* SOM 531 QUANTICO
HUMPHREIS, THOMAS BAL 004 1ST WARD
HUMPHREY, ANN BAL 154 11TH WAR
HUMPHREY, DAVID BAL 166 1ST WARD
HUMPHREY, ELIZA ANN 380 4TH DIST
HUMPHREY, HONARY ANN 503 HOWARD D
HUMPHREY, SALLY H. WOR 237 6TH E DI
HUMPHREY, VERUS * WOR 240 6TH E DI
HUMPHREYS, ANDREW BAL 003 9TH WARD
HUMPHREYS, ASARIAH SOM 426 PRINCESS
HUMPHREYS, CATHEL SOM 495 SALISBUR
HUMPHREYS, DAVID ANN 442 HOWARD D
HUMPHREYS, GEORGE W. SOM 495 SALISBUR
HUMPHREYS, HENRY BAL 157 16TH WAR
HUMPHREYS, HRMPHREY SOM 493 SALISBUR
HUMPHREYS, JAMES CAL 004 1ST DIST
HUMPHREYS, JAMES M. SOM 426 PRINCESS
HUMPHREYS, JOHN BAL 214 17TH WAR
HUMPHREYS, LOUISA BAL 146 16TH WAR
HUMPHREYS, MARTHA ANN 293 ANNAPOLI
HUMPHREYS, MARY A. BAL 019 15TH WAR
HUMPHREYS, MISS A. FRE 199 5TH E DI
HUMPHREYS, OWEN T. BAL 168 16TH WAR
HUMPHREYS, ROBERT ANN 380 4TH DIST
HUMPHREYS, THOMAS BAL 083 1ST WARD
HUMPHRIES, AVENDER BAL 442 8TH WARD
HUMPHRIES, CHARLES H. BAL 456 8TH WARD
HUMPHRIES, EDWARD CEC 098 3RD E DI
HUMPHRIES, ELIZABETH BAL 341 7TH WARD
HUMPHRIES, FRANCIS BAL 247 1ST DIST
HUMPHRIES, J. R. WAS 183 BOONSBOR
HUMPHRIES, J.B. WAS 021 2ND SUBD
HUMPHRIES, JOHN PRI 089 SPALDING
HUMPHRIES, JOSEPH BAL 128 1ST WARD
HUMPHRIES, RICHARD BAL 413 8TH WARD
HUMPHRIES, WILLIAM BAL 401 3RD WARD
HUMPHRIES, WILLIAM BAL 111 2ND DIST
HUMPHRISS, CLOA SOM 535 QUANTICO
HUMPHRISS, EMORY F. SOM 488 SALISBUR
HUMPHRISS, FOUNTAIN B. SOM 487 SALISBUR
HUMPHRISS, FRANCES SOM 491 SALISBUR
HUMPHRISS, JOSEPH SOM 526 QUANTICO
HUMPHRISS, JOSEPHUS SOM 531 QUANTICO
HUMPHRISS, MARGARET SOM 531 QUANTICO
HUMPHRISS, MARGARET W. SOM 530 QUANTICO
HUMPHRY, CINDERELLA BAL 205 11TH WAR
HUMPHRYES, NANTZY* BAL 400 3RD WARD
HUMPLING, ANN BAL 269 20TH WAR
HUMPREYS, PETER A. TAL 103 ST MICHA
HUMRISS, CHARLES W. SOM 532 QUANTICO
HUMRICHOUSE, CHARLES W. BAL 333 3RD WARD
HUMRICHOUSER, FREDERICK WAS 129 HAGERSTO
HUMRICHOUSER, MALVINA WAS 153 HAGERSTO
HUMRICHOUSER, MARY C. WAS 153 HAGERSTO
HUMRICHOUSER, WILLIAM * WAS 172 FUNKSTOW
HUMRICK, FREDERICK FRE 342 MIDDLETO
HUMRICK, ZACHARIAH FRE 107 CREAGERS
HUNA, ELIZA FRE 292 WOODSBOR
HUNDDINGTON, PACE CHA 283 BOJANTOW
HUNDERLOCKER, JOHN BAL 326 3RD WARD
HUNDERMARK, CONRAD BAL 238 1ST DIST
HUNDINGTON, JEREMIAH CHA 271 ALLENS F
HUNDLEY, MARY SOM 454 DAMES QU
HUNDLEY, WILLIAM SOM 454 DAMES QU
HUNGER, HENRY BAL 104 2ND DIST
HUNGERFORD, BASIL BAL 472 14TH WAR
HUNGERFORD, BENJAMIN CAL 013 1ST DIST
HUNGERFORD, ELIZABETH CAL 013 1ST DIST
HUNGERFORD, JAMES BAL 220 1ST DIST
HUNGERFORD, JESSE CAL 007 1ST DIST
HUNGERFORD, THOMAS BAL 464 14TH WAR
HUNGERFORD, WILLIAM BAL 227 19TH WAR
HUNGERFORD, WILLIAM S. CAL 041 3RD DIST
HUNGERFORD, ZACHARIAH CAL 013 1ST DIST
HUNICHENN, GERHARD BAL 051 15TH WAR
HUNICK, JOHN BAL 264 20TH WAR
HUNIERICK, MICHAEL FRE 118 CREAGERS
HUNITZ, FRED BAL 273 20TH WAR
HUNK, HENRY WAS 024 2ND SUBD
HUNKMYER, SOLOMON BAL 133 11TH WAR
HUNLEIN, MARTIN BAL 161 16TH WAR
HUNN, HENRY * BAL 311 20TH WAR
HUNNA, J.H.* BAL 228 12TH WAR
HUNNEGAR, FRANCIS ALL 221 CUMBERLA
HUNOLD, GEORGE * BAL 386 1ST DIST
HUNSBERGER, ENOS BAL 048 15TH WAR
HUNSCHE, JOHN G. BAL 247 12TH WAR
HUNSEPER, HENRY* ALL 181 8TH E.D.
HUNSICKER, ALBERT BAL 333 3RD WARD
HUNSON, FRISBY BAL 033 9TH WARD
HUNSON, LUCY KEN 295 3RD DIST
HUNSTON, JESSE BAL 244 12TH WAR
HUNT, A.W. BAL 222 2ND WARD
HUNT, ALVERDA M. BAL 218 6TH WARD
HUNT, ANN ANN 421 HOWARD D
HUNT, ANN N. BAL 145 5TH WARD
HUNT, ANN R. BAL 025 1ST WARD
HUNT, ASBURY H. FRE 045 FREDERIC
HUNT, B. BAL 188 2ND WARD
HUNT, BETSEY TAL 106 ST MICHA
HUNT, CALEB BAL 045 2ND DIST
HUNT, CALEB CHA 262 MIDDLETO
HUNT, CLOE A. BAL 008 4TH WARD
HUNT, DANIEL BAL 457 8TH WARD
HUNT, DAVID WAS 115 2ND DIST
HUNT, ELENOR CHA 262 MIDDLETO
HUNT, ELI CHA 250 MIDDLETO
HUNT, ELIZABETH BAL 069 18TH WAR
HUNT, ELIZABETH TAL 107 ST MICHA
HUNT, ELIZABETH BAL 146 5TH WARD
HUNT, ELIZABETH BAL 357 1ST DIST
HUNT, EMMA L. BAL 424 1ST DIST
HUNT, F. G. BAL 012 18TH WAR
HUNT, GEORGE BAL 167 1ST WARD
HUNT, GEORGE BAL 380 8TH WARD
HUNT, GEORGE A. CHA 282 BOJANTOW
HUNT, GERMAN BAL 210 19TH WAR
HUNT, HENRY BAL 188 2ND WARD
HUNT, ISAAC J. SOM 491 SALISBUR
HUNT, JAMES BAL 004 EASTERN
HUNT, JAMES BAL 051 9TH WARD
HUNT, JAMES R. TAL 113 ST MICHA
HUNT, JESSE BAL 457 1ST DIST
HUNT, JESSE BAL 472 14TH WAR
HUNT, JESSE J. FRE 043 FREDERIC
HUNT, JOHN ANN 355 3RD DIST
HUNT, JOHN BAL 441 8TH WARD
HUNT, JOHN ANN 408 8TH DIST
HUNT, JOHN H. BAL 145 5TH WARD
HUNT, JOHN W. BAL 145 5TH WARD
HUNT, JOHN W. CHA 262 MIDDLETO
HUNT, JOSEPH BAL 302 12TH WAR
HUNT, JOSEPH R. CHA 291 MIDDLETO
HUNT, JUDA BAL 001 18TH WAR
HUNT, JUDSON CHA 280 BOJANTOW
HUNT, LEWIS C. ANN 522 HOWARD D
HUNT, LUONEY BAL 186 2ND WARD
HUNT, MARGARET BAL 061 10TH WAR
HUNT, MARSHAL CEC 165 6TH E DI
HUNT, MARY A. SOM 491 SALISBUR
HUNT, MARY J. TAL 104 ST MICHA
HUNT, MARY J. BAL 145 5TH WARD
HUNT, MATHEW BAL 437 1ST DIST
HUNT, MICHAEL BAL 432 14TH WAR
HUNT, MITCHELL SOM 491 SALISBUR
HUNT, OLIVER BAL 056 2ND DIST
HUNT, PATRICK BAL 420 14TH WAR
HUNT, PETER L. TAL 107 ST MICHA
HUNT, PHILIP S. ALL 154 6TH E.D.
HUNT, PRUDENCE BAL 188 16TH WAR
HUNT, RACHEL BAL 038 2ND DIST
HUNT, ROBERT K. BAL 367 3RD WARD
HUNT, SAMUEL BAL 322 12TH WAR
HUNT, SAMUEL TAL 107 ST MICHA
HUNT, SAMUEL BAL 427 14TH WAR
HUNT, SAMUEL BAL 428 14TH WAR
HUNT, SAMUEL C. BAL 457 1ST DIST
HUNT, SEVIN TAL 112 ST MICHA
HUNT, STEPHEN BAL 143 19TH WAR
HUNT, SUTTON D. * TAL 109 ST MICHA
HUNT, THOMAS BAL 438 1ST DIST
HUNT, THOMAS BAL 281 2ND WARD
HUNT, THOMAS H. BAL 236 12TH WAR
HUNT, WASHINGTON KEN 277 1ST DIST
HUNT, WILLIAM PRI 105 PISCATAW
HUNT, WILLIAM BAL 399 8TH WARD
HUNT, WILLIAM BAL 192 2ND WARD
HUNT, WILLIAM A. BAL 098 18TH WAR
HUNT, WILLIE BAL 031 2ND DIST
HUNTEMULLER, HERMAN F. BAL 119 15TH WAR
HUNTER, AGNES BAL 317 20TH WAR
HUNTER, ANDREW BAL 285 7TH WARD
HUNTER, ANN BAL 057 4TH WARD
HUNTER, ANN QUE 182 3RD E DI
HUNTER, ANNA M. MGM 358 BERRYS D
HUNTER, AUGUSTA CEC 023 ELKTON 3
HUNTER, CHARLES MGM 388 ROCKERLE
HUNTER, CHARLES H. HAR 192 3RD DIST
HUNTER, DANIEL HAR 059 1ST DIST
HUNTER, DANIEL CAR 280 7TH DIST
HUNTER, DENTON WAS 155 2ND DIST
HUNTER, ELENORA BAL 066 18TH WAR
HUNTER, ELIZABETH MGM 417 MEDLEY 3
HUNTER, ELIZABETH BAL 077 4TH WARD
HUNTER, ELIZABETH HAR 175 3RD DIST
HUNTER, ELIZABETH BAL 318 12TH WAR
HUNTER, ELLEN BAL 417 3RD WARD
HUNTER, ESTHER CEC 100 3RD E DI
HUNTER, FRANCAS BAL 232 2ND WARD
HUNTER, GEORGE W. HAR 200 3RD DIST
HUNTER, GOERGE H. PRI 111 PISCATAW
HUNTER, HUGH BAL 190 19TH WAR
HUNTER, JAMES BAL 170 16TH WAR
HUNTER, JAMES H. ANN 279 ANNAPOLI
HUNTER, JAMES H.M. WAS 135 HAGERSTO
HUNTER, JANE ALL 249 CUMBERLA
HUNTER, JEROME BAL 155 19TH WAR
HUNTER, JOANNA CEC 031 CHESAPEA
HUNTER, JOHN CAR 284 7TH DIST
HUNTER, JOHN BAL 252 20TH WAR
HUNTER, JOHN BAL 255 6TH WARD
HUNTER, JOHN BAL 209 6TH DIST
HUNTER, JOHN WAS 028 2ND SUBD
HUNTER, JOHN H. FRE 040 FREDERIC
HUNTER, JOHN M. BAL 186 6TH WARD
HUNTER, JOHN R. BAL 364 8TH WARD
HUNTER, JOSEPH BAL 113 1ST WARD
HUNTER, JOSEPH BAL 022 4TH WARD
HUNTER, M. A. ALL 111 5TH E.D.
HUNTER, MARTHA FRE 066 FREDERIC
HUNTER, MARTHA BAL 265 20TH WAR
HUNTER, MARY BAL 242 20TH WAR
HUNTER, MARY BAL 111 10TH WAR
HUNTER, MARY ALL 087 5TH E.D.
HUNTER, MARY A. BAL 419 8TH WARD
HUNTER, MARY L. FRE 065 FREDERIC
HUNTER, MARY T. BAL 003 4TH WARD
HUNTER, MILBOURN MGM 357 BERRYS D
HUNTER, N. B. BAL 152 1ST WARD
HUNTER, NANCY BAL 190 11TH WAR
HUNTER, NANCY H. ANN 521 HOWARD D
HUNTER, PETER BAL 039 2ND DIST
HUNTER, PLEASANT BAL 435 1ST DIST
HUNTER, RANNY W. WAS 206 1ST DIST
HUNTER, REBECCA WAS 286 1ST DIST
HUNTER, REBECCA CEC 020 ELKTON 3
HUNTER, ROBERT CAR 282 7TH DIST
HUNTER, ROBERT BAL 155 19TH WAR
HUNTER, ROBERT W. PRI 109 PISCATAW
HUNTER, SAMUEL BAL 160 11TH WAR
HUNTER, SARAH HAR 114 2ND DIST
HUNTER, SUSAN BAL 360 8TH WARD

Name	County	Page	District
HUNTER, THOMAS	BAL	040	2ND DIST
HUNTER, THOMAS	MGM	402	ROCKERLE
HUNTER, THOMAS	BAL	003	4TH WARD
HUNTER, THOMAS Q.	CAL	021	2ND DIST
HUNTER, THOMAS T.	PRI	043	VANSVILL
HUNTER, WILLIAM	CAR	072	NO TWP L
HUNTER, WILLIAM	CEC	020	ELKTON 3
HUNTER, WILLIAM	CEC	019	ELKTON 3
HUNTER, WILLIAM	ANN	515	HOWARD D
HUNTER, CASSAY-BLACK	FRE	218	BUCKEYST
HUNTERLAUGH, JOHN	BAL	230	2ND WARD
HUNTINGDON, ANN	CHA	271	ALLENS F
HUNTINGDON, CYRUS	HAR	151	3RD DIST
HUNTINGTON, ANDREW B.	BAL	438	8TH WARD
HUNTINGTON, ANN M.	ST	338	4TH E DI
HUNTINGTON, BENEDICT	ST	339	5TH E DI
HUNTINGTON, IGNATIUS	ST	335	4TH E DI
HUNTINGTON, JOHN	SOM	499	SALISBUR
HUNTINGTON, JOHN B.P	ST	333	4TH E DI
HUNTLEMAN, AUGUST	BAL	024	4TH WARD
HUNTLEY, E. K.	ALL	092	5TH E.D.
HUNTMAN, JOHN S.	BAL	088	1ST WARD
HUNTRESS, F.F.	BAL	129	1ST WARD
HUNTRESS, FRANCIS	BAL	133	1ST WARD
HUNTS, JAOCB	FRE	052	FREDERIC
HUNTS, JOHN	BAL	044	9TH WARD
HUNTSBERRY, CATHARINE	WAS	193	1ST DIST
HUNTSBERRY, JOSEPH	WAS	058	2ND SUBD
HUNTSMAN, CHRISTIANA	BAL	422	14TH WAR
HUNTT, ELIZABETH	CAL	063	3RD DIST
HUNTT, GILBERT	CAL	054	3RD DIST
HUNTT, RICHARD	CAL	059	3RD DIST
HUNTTER, PHILEMON G.	HAR	178	3RD DIST
HUNTZELLMAN, JOHN A.	BAL	215	2ND WARD
HUNWOOD, H. M. *	BAL	149	1ST WARD
HUPER, ELIZA*	TAL	068	EASTON T
HUPP, PETER	BAL	306	7TH WARD
HUPSMER, GEORGE	BAL	077	1ST WARD
HUPTFELT, CHRISTOPHER	BAL	454	14TH WAR
HURBERT, ANNA	ALL	200	CUMBERLA
HURBERT, CHARLES	ALL	200	CUMBERLA
HURBERT, SAMUEL	ALL	200	CUMBERLA
HURBEY, GEORGE	ALL	107	5TH E.D.
HURBIN, ANN	CAR	396	2ND DIST
HURD, JOHN	ALL	218	CUMBERLA
HURD, SMITH	ALL	218	CUMBERLA
HURD, WILLIAM	BAL	412	14TH WAR
HURD, JOSEPH	CAR	104	NO TWP L
HURD, RACHEL	CAR	105	NO TWP L
HURDLE, ELIZA	BAL	213	11TH WAR
HURDLE, MARANDA	PRI	016	BLADENSB
HURDLE, NOAH	FRE	389	PETERSVI
HURDLE, ROBERT	BAL	348	13TH WAR
HURDY, WILLIAM	CEC	038	CHESAPEA
HUREST, LOUIS	BAL	192	2ND WARD
HURFORD, ELI	CEC	142	6TH E DI
HURGELL, HOVEN	BAL	175	2ND WARD
HURIN, HENRY *	BAL	311	20TH WAR
HURKLE, WILLIAM*	BAL	421	3RD WARD
HURLAND, SUSAN	CEC	191	5TH E DI
HURLEY, ADAM	CAR	329	MANCHEST
HURLEY, ARTHUR	BAL	303	1ST DIST
HURLEY, CALEB	DOR	407	1ST DIST
HURLEY, CHARLES A.	BAL	169	19TH WAR
HURLEY, CLINTON	DOR	351	3RD DIVI
HURLEY, DENNIS	BAL	112	18TH WAR
HURLEY, EDWARD	BAL	071	10TH WAR
HURLEY, ELIZA	WAS	143	HAGERSTO
HURLEY, ELIZABETH	FRE	364	CATOCTIN
HURLEY, HEZEKIAH	WAS	151	HAGERSTO
HURLEY, JAMES	WAS	230	1ST DIST
HURLEY, JAMES J.	WAS	152	HAGERSTO
HURLEY, JOHN	FRE	364	CATOCTIN
HURLEY, JOHN	BAL	184	6TH WARD
HURLEY, JOHN	BAL	204	6TH WARD
HURLEY, LANTE*	DOR	345	3RD DIVI
HURLEY, LEVIN	FRE	364	CATOCTIN
HURLEY, LEVY L.	DOR	341	3RD DIVI
HURLEY, MARTHA	CHA	286	BOJANTOW
HURLEY, MARY	TAL	090	ST MICHA
HURLEY, MICHAEL	BAL	164	2ND DIST
HURLEY, OBED	MGM	444	CLARKSTR
HURLEY, P.M.	ALL	218	CUMBERLA
HURLEY, SALEM	PRI	005	BLADENSB
HURLEY, WESTLEY	DOR	351	3RD DIVI
HURLEY, WILLIAM	BAL	128	1ST WARD
HURLEY, WILLIAM L.	MGM	442	CLARKSTR
HURLEY, ZACHARIAH	SOM	374	BRINKLEY
HURLOCK, ABRAHAM	KEN	306	3RD DIST
HURLOCK, CAVID	QUE	178	2ND E DI
HURLOCK, GEORGE T.	QUE	180	2ND E DI
HURLOCK, HENIETTA	KEN	227	2ND DIST
HURLOCK, JAMES	DOR	316	1ST DIST
HURLOCK, JAMES	DOR	308	1ST DIST
HURLOCK, JEFFERSON	DOR	307	1ST DIST
HURLOCK, JOHN	DOR	306	1ST DIST
HURLOCK, JOHN	DOR	309	1ST DIST
HURLOCK, JOHN	KEN	227	2ND DIST
HURLOCK, SAMUEL	KEN	306	3RD DIST
HURLOCK, SARAH	DOR	315	1ST DIST
HURLOCK, WASHINGTON	DOR	309	1ST DIST
HURLOCK, WILLIAM	DOR	322	1ST DIST
HURLOCK, WILLIS	DOR	312	1ST DIST
HURLY, A.*	DOR	442	1ST DIST
HURLY, A.*	DOR	443	1ST DIST
HURLY, ALEXANDER	DOR	412	1ST DIST
HURLY, ALFRED	DOR	442	1ST DIST
HURLY, ALGERNON*	DOR	441	1ST DIST
HURLY, ASA	DOR	443	1ST DIST
HURLY, BRANNOCK B.*	DOR	442	1ST DIST
HURLY, C.*	DOR	442	1ST DIST
HURLY, CAIN*	DOR	441	1ST DIST
HURLY, CHARLES A.	DOR	412	1ST DIST
HURLY, CLINTON*	DOR	442	1ST DIST
HURLY, CONSTANT	DOR	439	1ST DIST
HURLY, CURTIS	DOR	445	1ST DIST
HURLY, DENNIS	DOR	442	1ST DIST
HURLY, DOROTHY	DOR	408	1ST DIST
HURLY, ELIJAH	DOR	445	1ST DIST
HURLY, ELIJAH R.	DOR	440	1ST DIST
HURLY, EVEN	CHA	286	BOJANTOW
HURLY, FANNY*	DOR	441	1ST DIST
HURLY, GEORGE	DOR	443	1ST DIST
HURLY, GRIFFIN	DOR	441	1ST DIST
HURLY, HENRY	DOR	434	1ST DIST
HURLY, HUTSON	DOR	441	1ST DIST
HURLY, ICHABOD*	DOR	440	1ST DIST
HURLY, JACKSON	DOR	435	1ST DIST
HURLY, JAMES	DOR	422	1ST DIST
HURLY, JENKINS	DOR	439	1ST DIST
HURLY, JOB	DOR	441	1ST DIST
HURLY, JOHANNA	WAS	026	2ND SUBD
HURLY, JOHN J.	DOR	442	1ST DIST
HURLY, JOSEPH	DOR	442	1ST DIST
HURLY, JOSEPH	DOR	442	1ST DIST
HURLY, LACY*	DOR	443	1ST DIST
HURLY, LAFAYETTE	DOR	439	1ST DIST
HURLY, M. D.*	DOR	443	1ST DIST
HURLY, MARGARET	DOR	443	1ST DIST
HURLY, MARIA*	DOR	434	1ST DIST
HURLY, MARY	DOR	438	1ST DIST
HURLY, MARY*	DOR	382	1ST DIST
HURLY, MATILDY	DOR	412	1ST DIST
HURLY, MICAH*	DOR	444	1ST DIST
HURLY, MISTER	DOR	443	1ST DIST
HURLY, NOAH	DOR	443	1ST DIST
HURLY, P. MINNY*	DOR	442	1ST DIST
HURLY, RICHARD	DOR	443	1ST DIST
HURLY, S. E.	DOR	442	1ST DIST
HURLY, SALEY	DOR	441	1ST DIST
HURLY, SAMUEL	DOR	444	1ST DIST
HURLY, STEPHEN	DOR	422	1ST DIST
HURLY, THOMPSON*	DOR	441	1ST DIST
HURLY, TILGHMAN	DOR	435	1ST DIST
HURLY, W. W.*	DOR	442	1ST DIST
HURLY, WILLIAM	DOR	440	1ST DIST
HURLY, WILLIAM	CAR	343	6TH DIST
HURN, MARIA	BAL	035	18TH WAR
HURN, SARAH	FRE	299	WOODSBOR
HUROLL, SUSAN	MGM	391	ROCKERLE
HUROT, SAMUEL J.	WOR	190	8TH E DI
HURRGIES, JOHN H. *	BAL	070	15TH WAR
HURRICKS, CHRISTOPHER	BAL	469	14TH WAR
HURRING, JACOB	BAL	172	19TH WAR
HURROLD, GEORGE *	BAL	386	1ST DIST
HURRY, JOHN C.	ST	274	3RD E DI
HURST, BENNET	BAL	461	1ST DIST
HURST, CATHERINE	BAL	279	20TH WAR
HURST, CHARLES	BAL	417	14TH WAR
HURST, CONRAD	BAL	110	10TH WAR
HURST, E.	ANN	282	ANNAPOLI
HURST, ELIZABETH	BAL	432	14TH WAR
HURST, ELLIOD*	DOR	458	1ST DIST
HURST, GEORGE W.	BAL	299	7TH WARD
HURST, JACOB	BAL	286	20TH WAR
HURST, JOHN	SOM	375	BRINKLEY
HURST, JOHN F.	DOR	378	1ST DIST
HURST, JOHN*	DOR	392	1ST DIST
HURST, JOSEPH	PRI	025	VANSVILL
HURST, LOUISA	BAL	281	20TH WAR
HURST, MARY D.	FRE	065	FREDERIC
HURST, NATHAN	BAL	391	3RD WARD
HURST, SAMUEL J.	DOR	381	1ST DIST
HURST, SARAH	DOR	381	1ST DIST
HURST, SARAH	BAL	058	10TH WAR
HURST, SARAH A.	DOR	459	1ST DIST
HURST, SARAH A.	DOR	459	1ST DIST
HURST, SOPHIA	DOR	392	1ST DIST
HURST, WILLIAM	DOR	456	1ST DIST
HURST, WILLIAM	SOM	550	TYASKIN
HURT, EBENEZER	SOM	511	BARREN C
HURT, EDWARD	PRI	106	PISCATAW
HURT, MARY S.	BAL	233	6TH WARD
HURT, THOMAS W.	BAL	298	7TH WARD
HURT, WALTER	BAL	081	4TH WARD
HURTER, MATHIAS	FRE	095	FREDERIC
HURTLE, GEORGE	WAS	265	1ST DIST
HURTLE, GEORGE	WAS	265	1ST DIST
HURTMAN, CATHARINE	WAS	223	1ST DIST
HURTT, CHRISTOPHER	BAL	286	17TH WAR
HURTT, EDGAR	BAL	029	9TH WARD
HURTT, HENRY N.	BAL	327	13TH WAR
HURTT, JAMES	KEN	295	3RD DIST
HURTT, JAMES A.	BAL	376	8TH WARD
HURTT, JAMES C.	KEN	284	3RD DIST
HURTT, MARGARET	BAL	189	6TH WARD
HURTT, MILIA M.	KEN	284	3RD DIST
HURTT, WILLIAM	KEN	301	3RD DIST
HURZY, ELIZA-BLACK	BAL	217	2ND WARD
HUSAMANN, ERNEST	BAL	184	5TH DIST
HUSBAIN, MICHAEL	CAR	234	UNION TO
HUSBAND, JAMES E.	BAL	094	10TH WAR
HUSBAND, JOSEPH	BAL	063	15TH WAR
HUSBAND, JOSHUA	HAR	014	1ST DIST
HUSBAND, RUTH W.	HAR	014	1ST DIST
HUSBAND, WILLIAM	BAL	270	12TH WAR
HUSBANDS, ELIAS	FRE	054	FREDERIC
HUSBANDS, HESEKIAH	BAL	154	5TH WARD
HUSDENWALDON, CATHARINE M	BAL	031	15TH WAR
HUSE, F.A.	BAL	231	1ST DIST
HUSE, GABREL	DOR	369	3RD DIVI
HUSE, HENRY *	BAL	279	1ST DIST
HUSE, JAMES	DOR	298	1ST DIST
HUSE, JAMES	DOR	349	3RD DIVI
HUSE, JAMES	WOR	315	2ND E DI
HUSE, JOHN	DOR	324	1ST DIST
HUSE, JOHN	DOR	349	3RD DIVI
HUSE, WILLIS E.	DOR	298	1ST DIST
HUSEL, JOHN	CEC	059	1ST E DI
HUSELBAUGH, JOHN	CAR	216	5TH DIST
HUSELBOUGH, FREDERICK	BAL	278	2ND WARD
HUSEN, FRANCES	BAL	441	1ST DIST
HUSER, ELI	BAL	455	14TH WAR
HUSEY, E.	BAL	073	1ST WARD
HUSEY, GEORGE	CEC	059	1ST E DI
HUSH, ELIZABETH	BAL	331	7TH WARD
HUSH, JAMES	BAL	414	3RD WARD
HUSH, JOSEPH	WAS	163	2ND DIST
HUSH, SAMUEL C.	BAL	398	1ST DIST
HUSHBACK, AUGASTAS	BAL	052	18TH WAR
HUSHBECK, CHARLES	BAL	052	18TH WAR
HUSHETT, ADAM*	BAL	004	4TH WARD
HUSICK, THOMAS*	DOR	382	1ST DIST
HUSK, JOSEPH	CEC	161	6TH E DI
HUSKEY, MARY	BAL	103	5TH WARD
HUSLET, JOHN	BAL	247	12TH WAR
HUSON, CHARELS	CAL	014	1ST DIST
HUSPERGER, HENRY	FRE	324	MIDDLETO
HUSPERGER, WILLIAMS J.	FRE	392	PETERSVI
HUSS, JAMES	CEC	173	6TH E DI
HUSSELL, JOHN	BAL	105	1ST WARD
HUSSELL, WILLIAM	BAL	169	1ST WARD
HUSSEY, ANNEE*	BAL	109	10TH WAR
HUSSEY, CATHARINE	BAL	001	15TH WAR
HUSSEY, ELIZA J.	BAL	225	6TH WARD
HUSSEY, FRANCES A.*	BAL	109	10TH WAR
HUSSEY, JACOB Z.	BAL	050	15TH WAR
HUSSEY, JAMES	BAL	111	5TH WARD
HUSSEY, JAMES	BAL	040	18TH WAR
HUSSEY, JOSEPH	BAL	280	2ND WARD
HUSSEY, MARTIN	BAL	017	4TH WARD
HUSSEY, OBIT	BAL	038	4TH WARD
HUSSEY, SUSAN	BAL	283	2ND WARD
HUST, ANN*	DOR	381	1ST DIST
HUST, F.	BAL	172	1ST WARD
HUST, NATHANIEL	HAR	057	1ST DIST
HUSTED, HENRY A.	WOR	329	1ST E DI
HUSTER, ANDREW	BAL	122	18TH WAR
HUSTER, GEORGE	BAL	240	1ST DIST
HUSTER, GOTLIEP	BAL	240	1ST DIST
HUSTEW, JOHN P.	CAR	302	1ST DIST
HUSTIN, WILLIAM GEORGE	BAL	183	19TH WAR
HUSTON, JAMES	BAL	364	8TH WARD
HUSTON, JAMES	BAL	299	7TH WARD
HUSTON, JOHN	BAL	460	8TH WARD
HUSTON, MARGARET	BAL	252	20TH WAR
HUSTON, MARGARET J.	BAL	365	8TH WARD
HUSTON, MARY	BAL	315	12TH WAR
HUSTON, WILLIAM	BAL	231	12TH WAR
HUSTON, MARY L.	CAR	398	2ND DIST
HUSTY, HAGEN	BAL	155	2ND DIST
HUT, AMELIA	WOR	312	2ND E DI
HUT, ELIZABETH	WOR	183	6TH E DI
HUT, FREDERICK	WOR	313	2ND E DI
HUT, HENRY H.	WOR	201	3RD E DI
HUT, LEVIN	WOR	178	6TH E DI
HUT, MAJOR	WOR	185	6TH E DI
HUT, MOSES	WOR	184	6TH E DI
HUT, MOSES	WOR	178	6TH E DI
HUT, SARAH	WOR	310	2ND E DI
HUT, WILLIAM	WOR	301	SNOW HIL
HUT, WILLIAM	WOR	181	6TH E DI
HUTCH, H.	BAL	287	12TH WAR
HUTCHEN, JAMES	BAL	356	3RD WARD
HUTCHEN, SAMUEL	CHA	282	BOJANTOW
HUTCHENS, ALEXANDER	QUE	244	5TH E DI
HUTCHENS, ALEXANDER	QUE	242	5TH E DI
HUTCHENS, ANN	HAR	050	1ST DIST
HUTCHENS, BARNET	QUE	244	5TH E DI
HUTCHENS, HENRIETTA	QUE	248	5TH E DI
HUTCHENS, JAMES	BAL	047	2ND DIST
HUTCHENS, JERVIS	QUE	250	5TH E DI
HUTCHENS, JOHN	HAR	070	1ST DIST
HUTCHENS, JOSEPH	QUE	248	5TH E DI
HUTCHENS, MARY D.	BAL	047	2ND DIST
HUTCHENS, NICHOLAS	BAL	050	2ND DIST
HUTCHENS, NICHOLAS	HAR	069	1ST DIST
HUTCHENS, PHIL	QUE	252	5TH E DI
HUTCHENS, RICHARD	BAL	047	2ND DIST
HUTCHENS, RICHARD	BAL	381	1ST DIST
HUTCHENS, SUSAN	BAL	462	1ST DIST
HUTCHENS, WILLIAM R.	HAR	062	1ST DIST
HUTCHENS, RICHARD	BAL	047	2ND DIST
HUTCHENSON, ROBERT	ALL	110	5TH E.D.
HUTCHERSON, JOHN	DOR	359	3RD DIVI
HUTCHERSON, SARAH A.	PRI	003	BLADENSB
HUTCHERSON, THOMAS N.	PRI	004	BLADENSB
HUTCHESON, JOHN J.	WOR	303	SNOW HIL
HUTCHESON, MARY A.	BAL	054	4TH WARD
HUTCHESON, THOMAS	MGM	394	ROCKERLE
HUTCHINGS, ALONZO	BAL	388	8TH WARD
HUTCHINGS, MARGARET	BAL	407	8TH WARD
HUTCHINGS, SARAH	BAL	282	7TH WARD
HUTCHINS, ALEXANDER	BAL	151	5TH WARD
HUTCHINS, ALEXANDER-BLACK	CAR	132	NO TWP L
HUTCHINS, ANN	BAL	138	2ND DIST
HUTCHINS, ASBURY	BAL	046	15TH WAR
HUTCHINS, BENJAMIN	BAL	112	5TH WARD
HUTCHINS, BENJAMIN	ST	305	1ST E DI
HUTCHINS, CAROLINE	ST	340	5TH E DI
HUTCHINS, CHARLES-BLACK	QUE	158	2ND E DI
HUTCHINS, DANIEL	BAL	199	6TH WARD
HUTCHINS, DAVID	CAL	022	2ND DIST
HUTCHINS, ELI	CAL	032	2ND DIST
HUTCHINS, ELIZABETH	BAL	317	20TH WAR
HUTCHINS, ELIZABETH	BAL	363	13TH WAR
HUTCHINS, ELIZABETH	BAL	137	2ND DIST
HUTCHINS, ELIZABETH E.	CAL	025	2ND DIST
HUTCHINS, EMILY-BLACK	QUE	184	3RD E DI
HUTCHINS, FRANCES	BAL	248	5TH WARD
HUTCHINS, FRANCIS	CAR	100	NO TWP L
HUTCHINS, FRANK	BAL	191	19TH WAR
HUTCHINS, GEORGE	BAL	277	17TH WAR
HUTCHINS, HARRIET	BAL	130	2ND DIST
HUTCHINS, HARRIET-BLACK	CAR	148	NO TWP L
HUTCHINS, HENRY	CAL	034	2ND DIST
HUTCHINS, JAMES	BAL	112	5TH WARD
HUTCHINS, JAMES L.	ST	349	5TH E DI
HUTCHINS, JAMES-BLACK	ST	333	4TH E DI
HUTCHINS, JANE	BAL	076	15TH WAR
HUTCHINS, JOHN	BAL	120	1ST WARD
HUTCHINS, JOHN	CAL	025	2ND DIST
HUTCHINS, JOHN JR.	CAL	034	2ND DIST
HUTCHINS, JOHN M.	BAL	144	1ST WARD
HUTCHINS, JOHN-BLACK	CAR	083	NO TWP L
HUTCHINS, JOSHUA	BAL	047	2ND DIST
HUTCHINS, LAURA	BAL	149	5TH WARD
HUTCHINS, LUKE	ST	336	4TH E DI
HUTCHINS, MARIA	BAL	061	4TH WARD
HUTCHINS, MERAH	BAL	053	1ST WARD
HUTCHINS, MIRANDA	BAL	058	2ND DIST
HUTCHINS, NANCY	CAL	018	1ST DIST
HUTCHINS, NATHAN	CAR	100	NO TWP L
HUTCHINS, NICHOLAS	BAL	292	7TH WARD
HUTCHINS, NICKOLAS	BAL	111	5TH WARD
HUTCHINS, OWEN	KEN	260	1ST DIST
HUTCHINS, PERRY	TAL	012	EASTON D
HUTCHINS, PHILIP-BLACK	QUE	169	2ND E DI
HUTCHINS, POMPEY-BLACK	QUE	144	1ST E DI
HUTCHINS, REBECCA	CAL	028	2ND DIST
HUTCHINS, RICHARD-BLACK	ST	329	4TH E DI
HUTCHINS, ROBERT	BAL	172	6TH WARD
HUTCHINS, S. S.	BAL	321	1ST DIST
HUTCHINS, SAMUEL	BAL	257	6TH WARD
HUTCHINS, SAMUEL	BAL	255	12TH WAR
HUTCHINS, SOLOMON	CAR	065	NO TWP L
HUTCHINS, SUSAN	BAL	097	5TH WARD
HUTCHINS, THEADORE	TAL	008	EASTON D
HUTCHINS, THOMAS J.	CAL	030	2ND DIST
HUTCHINS, WILLIAM	CAL	037	2ND DIST
HUTCHINSON, ANN	QUE	125	1ST E DI
HUTCHINSON, ARTHUR	BAL	101	15TH WAR
HUTCHINSON, BENJAMIN O.	BAL	231	2ND WARD
HUTCHINSON, C.	ANN	277	ANNAPOLI
HUTCHINSON, EBENEZER	WOR	180	6TH E DI
HUTCHINSON, FRANK	BAL	092	5TH WARD
HUTCHINSON, GEORGE	BAL	090	10TH WAR
HUTCHINSON, H. M.	TAL	092	ST MICHA
HUTCHINSON, HENRY	ALL	135	4TH E.D.
HUTCHINSON, JAMES	BAL	101	15TH WAR

HUTCHINSON, JAMES BAL 097 5TH WARD
HUTCHINSON, JAMES ANN 344 3RD DIST
HUTCHINSON, JAMES A. DOR 461 1ST DIST
HUTCHINSON, JOHN F. FRE 404 JEFFERSO
HUTCHINSON, JOHN H. HAR 146 3RD DIST
HUTCHINSON, JOHN* TAL 012 EASTON D
HUTCHINSON, JOHN-BLACK CAR 083 NO TWP L
HUTCHINSON, JOSEPH M. BAL 106 5TH WARD
HUTCHINSON, MARY ANN 285 ANNAPOLI
HUTCHINSON, MARY BAL 425 3RD WARD
HUTCHINSON, MARY QUE 208 3RD E DI
HUTCHINSON, MARY A. BAL 041 4TH WARD
HUTCHINSON, MARY ANN BAL 347 3RD WARD
HUTCHINSON, MARY J. BAL 078 15TH WAR
HUTCHINSON, NANCY DOR 433 1ST DIST
HUTCHINSON, RICHARD CEC 002 ELKTON 3
HUTCHINSON, ROBERT BAL 261 17TH WAR
HUTCHINSON, ROBERT A. MGM 372 BERRYS D
HUTCHINSON, SAMUEL QUE 125 1ST E DI
HUTCHINSON, SARAH BAL 108 5TH WARD
HUTCHINSON, SOPHIA DOR 452 1ST DIST
HUTCHINSON, TIMOTHY BAL 097 5TH WARD
HUTCHINSON, WILLIAM HAR 036 1ST DIST
HUTCHISON, ANDREW CEC 043 CHESAPEA
HUTCHISON, ANN CEC 043 CHESAPEA
HUTCHISON, DAVID CEC 013 ELKTON 3
HUTCHISON, FRANCES CEC 011 ELKTON 3
HUTCHISON, JAMES BAL 457 8TH WARD
HUTCHISON, JOHN CAR 137 NO TWP L
HUTCHISON, LUCRETIA PRI 003 BLADENSB
HUTCHISON, MARGARET TAL 027 EASTON D
HUTCHISON, MARY CEC 037 CHESAPEA
HUTCHISON, NEALY TAL 096 ST MICHA
HUTCHISON, ROBERT HAR 035 1ST DIST
HUTCHISON, SUSAN CAR 152 NO TWP L
HUTCHISON, THOMAS BAL 072 4TH WARD
HUTCHISON,BARBARA CAR 382 2ND DIST
HUTE, CONRADT BAL 433 8TH WARD
HUTER, JOHN MGM 384 ROCKERLE
HUTERMAN, JOHN BAL 055 2ND DIST
HUTESON, LITTLETON WOR 301 SNOW HIL
HUTH, JOHN BAL 126 1ST WARD
HUTH, MARTIN BAL 107 1ST WARD
HUTHCENS, WILLIAM QUE 244 5TH E DI
HUTHCINSON, SARAH BAL 178 2ND DIST
HUTHES, BRIDGET BAL 472 14TH WAR
HUTHES, CLEMENTINE BAL 134 2ND DIST
HUTHES, JOHN BAL 134 2ND DIST
HUTMAN, MICHAEL BAL 089 1ST WARD
HUTN, HENRY BAL 229 2ND WARD
HUTNER, MARY CAR 075 NO TWP L
HUTNINGTON, WILLIAM ST 345 5TH E DI
HUTSBERRY, HILERY WAS 191 1ST DIST
HUTSBURGER, JOHN BAL 283 1ST DIST
HUTSEL, SARAH WAS 210 1ST DIST
HUTSELL, JACOB WAS 191 1ST DIST
HUTSELL, JOHN WAS 188 1ST DIST
HUTSELL, JOHN WAS 213 1ST DIST
HUTSON, DANIEL ALL 151 6TH E.D.
HUTSON, EDWARD BAL 321 3RD WARD
HUTSON, ELIZA BAL 023 15TH WAR
HUTSON, GEORGE ALL 156 6TH E.D.
HUTSON, HENRY ALL 138 6TH E.D.
HUTSON, HENRY BAL 286 2ND WARD
HUTSON, JACOB ALL 151 6TH E.D.
HUTSON, LITTLETON* DOR 434 1ST DIST
HUTSON, MARGARETT DOR 317 1ST DIST
HUTSON, MARIAH TAL 117 ST MICHA
HUTSON, ROBERT CAR 210 5TH DIST
HUTSON, WILLIAM HAR 020 1ST DIST
HUTSON, WILLIAM W. CEC 189 7TH E DI
HUTT, AGUSTUS-MULATTO BAL 223 2ND WARD
HUTT, ELIJ WOR 302 SNOW HIL
HUTT, MARY BAL 072 15TH WAR
HUTT, NANCY BAL 076 15TH WAR
HUTT, SALLY BAL 143 5TH WARD
HUTT, WILLIAM SOM 534 QUANTICO
HUTTON, ADRIANNA HAR 179 3RD DIST
HUTTON, ANN BAL 339 13TH WAR
HUTTON, BETSEY BAL 159 16TH WAR
HUTTON, BURN BAL 367 3RD WARD
HUTTON, CATHARINE BAL 282 12TH WAR
HUTTON, CATHARINE BAL 129 5TH WARD
HUTTON, CATHARINE FRE 166 EMMITTSB
HUTTON, ELISHA BAL 358 8TH WARD
HUTTON, ELIZABETH BAL 205 2ND WARD
HUTTON, ELIZABETH BAL 203 2ND WARD
HUTTON, ENOCH MGM 322 CRACKLIN
HUTTON, FORGUS CEC 016 ELKTON 3
HUTTON, FRANCES A. CAL 041 3RD DIST
HUTTON, GARON M.* BAL 108 10TH WAR
HUTTON, JAMES ANN 320 2ND DIST
HUTTON, JANE BAL 100 10TH WAR
HUTTON, JOB BAL 050 18TH WAR
HUTTON, JOHN BAL 358 8TH WARD
HUTTON, JOHN ANN 475 HOWARD D
HUTTON, JOSEPH CHA 219 ALLENS F
HUTTON, JOSEPH G. BAL 276 7TH WARD
HUTTON, LAVINIA C. MGM 322 CRACKLIN
HUTTON, LOUISA BAL 352 7TH WARD
HUTTON, MARY ANN 274 ANNAPOLI
HUTTON, MARY BAL 212 6TH WARD
HUTTON, MARY CEC 006 ELKTON 3
HUTTON, MARY BAL 380 13TH WAR
HUTTON, NACE ANN 354 3RD DIST
HUTTON, ORLANDO MGM 319 CRACKLIN
HUTTON, PERREY BAL 459 8TH WARD
HUTTON, PLEASANTS BAL 064 10TH WAR
HUTTON, RACHAEL CHA 219 ALLENS F
HUTTON, ROBERT BAL 452 1ST DIST
HUTTON, THOMAS BAL 300 17TH WAR
HUTTON, WILLAIM BAL 239 20TH WAR
HUTTON, WILLFORD BAL 247 17TH WAR
HUTTON, WILLIAM BAL 197 2ND WARD
HUTTON, WILLIAM BAL 152 5TH WARD
HUTTON, WILLIAM D. CEC 006 ELKTON 3
HUTTS, CHARLOTT BAL 152 5TH WARD
HUTTUM, JESSEY M. HAR 179 3RD DIST
HUTZEL, JACOB FRE 333 MIDDLETO
HUTZEL, SUSAN FRE 335 MIDDLETO
HUTZLER, JOHN BAL 177 2ND WARD
HUTZLER, MOSES BAL 268 7TH WARD
HUXLEY, JOHN BAL 188 11TH WAR
HUYETT, DANIEL WAS 229 1ST DIST
HUYETT, DANIEL OF J. WAS 231 1ST DIST
HUYETT, ELIZABETH WAS 229 1ST DIST
HUYETT, ELLEN M. WAS 219 1ST DIST
HUYETT, HENRY WAS 235 1ST DIST
HUYETT, JOHN H. WAS 126 2ND DIST
HUYETT, MARY C. WAS 256 1ST DIST
HUYETT, PETER L. * WAS 171 FUNKSTOW
HUYETT, SAMUEL C. WAS 228 1ST DIST
HUYETT, SUSANNA WAS 231 1ST DIST
HUYETT, WILLIAM WAS 229 1ST DIST
HUYETTE, JEREMIAH WAS 227 1ST DIST
HUYNSOR, EZEKIEL QUE 246 5TH E DI
HUYOCK, CHRIS BAL 228 12TH WAR
HUZZA, COLUMBUS BAL 187 6TH WARD
HUZZA, JOHN BAL 203 6TH WARD
HWEGMAN, JOHN ALL 013 3RD E.D.
HWINTER, H. BAL 160 1ST WARD
HY, ANN BAL 272 7TH WARD
HYAE, MARGARETT FRE 443 8TH E DI
HYALL, HENRY FRE 253 NEW MARK
HYAT, ELLEN BAL 472 14TH WAR
HYATT, ALPHEUS BAL 178 19TH WAR
HYATT, ALPHEUS BAL 004 EASTERN
HYATT, CHARLES BAL 126 16TH WAR
HYATT, CHRISTOPHER C. PRI 004 BLADENSB
HYATT, CHRISTOPHER C. PRI 004 BLADENSB
HYATT, ELI H. FRE 344 MIDDLETO
HYATT, ELIJAH BAL 339 1ST DIST
HYATT, ELLA MGM 437 CLARKSTR
HYATT, GEORGE W. MGM 344 CLARKSBU
HYATT, JAMES D. FRE 344 MIDDLETO
HYATT, JESSE MGM 411 MEDLEY 3
HYATT, JOHN MGM 435 CLARKSTR
HYATT, JOHN BAL 365 8TH WARD
HYATT, LEVI T. MGM 437 CLARKSTR
HYATT, LLOYD H. FRE 322 MIDDLETO
HYATT, MARGARET FRE 344 MIDDLETO
HYATT, MARY A. MGM 438 CLARKSTR
HYATT, MARY E. MGM 418 MEDLEY 3
HYATT, MESHART MGM 442 CLARKSTR
HYATT, MIRANDA FRE 244 NEW MARK
HYATT, PHILIP FRE 322 MIDDLETO
HYATT, RICHARD PRI 043 VANSVILL
HYATT, RICHARD H. BAL 080 15TH WAR
HYATT, SARAH R. MGM 437 CLARKSTR
HYATT, SOPHIA BAL 049 4TH WARD
HYATT, SUSANNA PRI 036 VANSVILL
HYATT, THOMAS FRE 244 NEW MARK
HYATT, WESLEY PRI 043 VANSVILL
HYATT,MARY BAL 080 1ST WARD
HYBECK, FREDERICK BAL 081 10TH WAR
HYBERGER, JOSEPH WAS 179 BOONSBOR
HYDA, JOSEPH HAR 203 3RD DIST
HYDE, ADAM BAL 127 1ST WARD
HYDE, AMASA BAL 325 12TH WAR
HYDE, ANN BAL 173 19TH WAR
HYDE, ANNA BAL 269 20TH WAR
HYDE, BARBARA PRI 058 NOTTINGH
HYDE, CHARLES ANN 270 ANNAPOLI
HYDE, CLEMENCE S. BAL 057 10TH WAR
HYDE, DANIEL ANN 475 HOWARD D
HYDE, DANIEL F. ANN 271 ANNAPOLI
HYDE, DANIEL L. ANN 270 ANNAPOLI
HYDE, ELISHA C. FRE 209 BUCKEYST
HYDE, F.C. ANN 267 ANNAPOLI
HYDE, FRANCIS BAL 057 10TH WAR
HYDE, FRANCIS BAL 182 11TH WAR
HYDE, HENRY BAL 006 9TH WARD
HYDE, HENRY K. BAL 382 13TH WAR
HYDE, JAMES ANN 274 ANNAPOLI
HYDE, JOHN BAL 019 15TH WAR
HYDE, LAURA ANN 268 ANNAPOLI
HYDE, M. BAL 332 13TH WAR
HYDE, MARGARET BAL 131 5TH WARD
HYDE, MOSES BAL 390 8TH WARD
HYDE, OLIVER BAL 107 5TH WARD
HYDE, RACHAEL FRE 443 8TH E DI
HYDE, RACHAEL FRE 435 8TH E DI
HYDE, RICHARD H. BAL 073 10TH WAR
HYDE, SAMUEL G. BAL 057 10TH WAR
HYDE, THOMAS FRE 443 8TH E DI
HYDE, THOMAS T. PRI 056 AQUASCO
HYDE, THOMAS W. MGM 420 MEDLEY 3
HYDE, WILLIAM J. BAL 126 5TH WARD
HYDE,WILLIAMS BAL 138 1ST WARD
HYDECKER, HILEMINER FRE 031 FREDERIC
HYDER, CATHARIEN CAR 236 UNION TO
HYDER, ENGLED BAL 273 12TH WAR
HYDER, HENRY BAL 219 17TH WAR
HYDER, ISAAC CAR 308 1ST DIST
HYDER, ISAAC CAR 402 2ND DIST
HYDER, JACOB FRE 291 WOODSBOR
HYDER, JOHN BAL 233 2ND WARD
HYDER, JOHN W. FRE 432 8TH E DI
HYDER, MARY C. FRE 303 WOODSBOR
HYDER, RICHARD QUE 179 2ND E DI
HYE, HENRY BAL 219 17TH WAR
HYEHARIS, ANTONE BAL 251 2ND WARD
HYER, AGNES BAL 135 11TH WAR
HYER, F.C. BAL 169 1ST WARD
HYER, FREDERICK H. WAS 137 HAGERSTO
HYER, JOHN BAL 380 8TH WARD
HYERN, CHRISTOPHER BAL 075 1ST WARD
HYERS, J. BAL 150 1ST WARD
HYETH, JAMES H. BAL 173 6TH WARD
HYETT, ELIZABETH WAS 172 FUNKSTOW
HYGINS, MARY E. MGM 400 ROCKERLE
HYGIS, GOTLIEB WAS 134 HAGERSTO
HYGIS, HENRY WAS 153 HAGERSTO
HYKES, JACOB WAS 283 1ST DIST
HYLAMA, HESTER BAL 276 7TH WARD
HYLAND, ALLEN SOM 499 SALISBUR
HYLAND, ANDREW BAL 005 9TH WARD
HYLAND, BETSEY SOM 503 SALISBUR
HYLAND, EDWARD BAL 005 9TH WARD
HYLAND, EDWARD CEC 022 ELKTON 3
HYLAND, ELISHA SOM 491 SALISBUR
HYLAND, GEORGE SOM 468 TRAPPE D
HYLAND, GEORGE CEC 080 NORTHEAS
HYLAND, GEORGE R. BAL 070 15TH WAR
HYLAND, HENRY BAL 096 5TH WARD
HYLAND, HENRY OR- SOM 438 DAMES QU
HYLAND, HESTER CEC 184 7TH E DI
HYLAND, JACOB CEC 075 NORTHEAS
HYLAND, JOHN CEC 071 5TH E DI
HYLAND, JOSHUA CEC 091 4TH E DI
HYLAND, LAMBERT CEC 079 NORTHEAS
HYLAND, LAMBERT W. BAL 333 13TH WAR
HYLAND, LEMUEL SOM 459 HANGARY
HYLAND, MARIAH SOM 515 BARREN C
HYLAND, MARY CEC 079 NORTHEAS
HYLAND, RACHEL CEC 071 5TH E DI
HYLAND, RICHARD KEN 285 3RD DIST
HYLAND, ROBERT H. BAL 097 5TH WARD
HYLAND, RUTH CEC 076 NORTHEAS
HYLAND, SOLOMON SOM 533 QUANTICO
HYLAND, STEPHEN CEC 075 NORTHEAS
HYLAND, STEPHEN CEC 071 5TH E DI
HYLAND, STEPHEN BAL 178 19TH WAR
HYLAND, WASHINGTON CEC 069 5TH E DI
HYLAND, WILLIAM R. CEC 072 5TH E DI
HYLANDT, JAMES C. BAL 064 10TH WAR
HYLE, ALBERT WAS 104 2ND DIST
HYLE, ANDREW PRI 032 VANSVILL
HYLE, JOSEPH BAL 011 2ND DIST
HYLE, JOSEPH CAR 244 3RD DIST
HYLER, JOHN BAL 125 1ST WARD
HYLER, JOHN BAL 281 2ND WARD
HYLER, LEWIS BAL 225 17TH WAR
HYLEY, TIMOTHY ALL 071 5TH E.D.
HYLSE, JAMES WAS 189 1ST DIST
HYMAN, ANTHONY * KEN 224 2ND DIST
HYMAN, CHRISTOPHER C. BAL 187 6TH WARD
HYMAN, JOHN BAL 179 16TH WAR
HYMAN, JOHN K. SOM 482 TRAPP DI
HYMAN, LEONARD ALL 021 2ND E.D.
HYMENS, GEORGE ALL 105 5TH E.D.
HYMER, JOHN KEN 264 1ST DIST
HYMES, HENRY BAL 140 2ND DIST
HYMES, ROSEANNA BAL 106 15TH WAR
HYMES, WILLIAM BAL 153 1ST WARD
HYMITTER, HARMAN BAL 208 2ND WARD
HYMN, JOHN W. BAL 457 8TH WARD
HYND, J. BAL 139 1ST WARD
HYNO, JOSEPH BAL 129 1ST WARD
HYNER, GEORGE W. KEN 265 1ST DIST
HYNES, BENAJAH ANN 462 HOWARD D
HYNES, BENJAMIN BAL 105 18TH WAR
HYNES, JAMES BAL 172 2ND DIST
HYNES, JOHN ANN 462 HOWARD D
HYNES, JOSIAH BAL 087 18TH WAR
HYNES, PATRICK BAL 102 2ND DIST
HYNES, SARAH BAL 245 6TH WARD
HYNIE, WILLIAM BAL 430 8TH WARD
HYNSON, ANN-BLACK QUE 178 2ND E DI
HYNSON, ANTHONY * KEN 224 2ND DIST
HYNSON, BENJAMIN KEN 237 2ND DIST
HYNSON, CHARLOTTE KEN 293 3RD DIST
HYNSON, ELIZA BAL 235 6TH WARD
HYNSON, FANNY BAL 363 3RD WARD
HYNSON, GEORGE BAL 245 6TH WARD
HYNSON, GEORGE KEN 221 2ND DIST
HYNSON, HANNAH A. KEN 241 2ND DIST
HYNSON, HENRY KEN 217 2ND DIST
HYNSON, J. * QUE 241 5TH E DI
HYNSON, JAMES KEN 224 2ND DIST
HYNSON, JOHN C. KEN 265 1ST DIST
HYNSON, JOHN R. BAL 209 19TH WAR
HYNSON, JOHN W. QUE 190 3RD E DI
HYNSON, JOSEPH KEN 216 2ND DIST
HYNSON, JOSEPH BAL 431 14TH WAR
HYNSON, LAURA S. KEN 268 1ST DIST
HYNSON, LUCY KEN 251 2ND DIST
HYNSON, MARY KEN 244 2ND DIST
HYNSON, MARY BAL 377 13TH WAR
HYNSON, MARY E. KEN 222 2ND DIST
HYNSON, NATHANIEL T. KEN 246 2ND DIST
HYNSON, NELLY KEN 251 2ND DIST
HYNSON, PETER QUE 242 5TH E DI
HYNSON, RICHARD * KEN 214 2ND DIST
HYNSON, THOMAS BAL 164 1ST WARD
HYNSON, THOMAS W. KEN 245 2ND DIST
HYNSON, VIRGINIA KEN 245 2ND DIST
HYOT, WILMER CEC 033 CHESAPEA
HYRE, WASHINGTON * KEN 216 2ND DIST
HYRENS, JOHN R. KEN 213 2ND DIST
HYRICH, ADOLF BAL 266 1ST DIST
HYRONS, JAMES S. KEN 284 3RD DIST
HYSER, AARON DON WAS 130 HAGERSTO
HYSER, ELEANOR MGM 408 MEDLEY 3
HYSER, GEORGE F. WAS 204 1ST DIST
HYSER, JOHN WAS 204 1ST DIST
HYSER, MARGARET BAL 053 15TH WAR
HYSINGER, CHRISTIAN WAS 102 2ND DIST
HYSON, * BAL 192 5TH DIST
HYSON, ELIZABETH BAL 247 17TH WAR
HYSON, GEORGE BAL 269 17TH WAR
HYSON, JAMES FRE 009 FREDERIC
HYSON, JAMES H. BAL 091 5TH WARD
HYSON, MARY BAL 360 13TH WAR
HYSON, ROBERT BAL 247 17TH WAR
HYSON, SOLOMON BAL 247 17TH WAR
HYSON, THOMAS BAL 172 1ST WARD
HYSON, WILLIAM BAL 031 15TH WAR
HYSSONG, ADAM WAS 133 2ND DIST
HYST, ADAM CAR 323 1ST DIST
HYST, MATILDA CAR 323 1ST DIST
HYTMAN, A. BAL 167 1ST WARD
HYUSON, MARIA ANN 465 HOWARD D
IACBZAS, H. G. BAL 312 12TH WAR
IAGO, PATRICK ALL 053 10TH E.D
IAMS, JANE R. ANA 366 4TH DIST
IANA, ELSEY CAL 014 1ST DIST
IANEY, RICHARD M. BAL 102 2ND DIST
IBLING, ELIZABETH BAL 171 19TH WAR
IBLING, HANNAH BAL 171 19TH WAR
ICAMRON, MALTY HAR 154 3RD DIST
ICEFEATOLE, FERDINAND ALL 055 10TH E.D
ICEFELT, LAZARUS BAL 314 3RD WARD
ICEFELT, ROZENA BAL 314 3RD WARD
ICHERER, JOHN BAL 312 20TH WAR
ICHLER, CHARLES BAL 295 20TH WAR
ICHNAR, JOHN BAL 253 12TH WAR
ICHNER, FREDERICK HAR 153 3RD DIST
ICKENICK, JACOB BAL 269 2ND WARD
ICKES, ANDERW CAR 309 1ST DIST
ICKES, FRANCILLA FRE 173 5TH E DI
ICKES, JAMES FRE 175 5TH E DI
ICKEY, HENRY BAL 302 20TH WAR
ICSSELL, ANN ST 287 2ND E DI
IDDINGS, CALEB P. BAL 318 1ST DIST
IDDINGS, WILLIAM P. BAL 001 18TH WAR
IDEMILLER, R. BAL 215 6TH DIST
IDSNEY, RICHARD ANN 373 4TH DIST
IDZINFRETZ, DANIEL BAL 233 2ND WARD
IERLAND, PERRY BAL 075 4TH WARD
IFERD, MARY WAS 266 1ST DIST
IFLIND, CUOLIP HAR 200 3RD DIST
IFORD, CHRISTIAN FRE 316 MIDDLETO
IFORD, DANIEL FRE 332 MIDDLETO
IFORD, HENRY FRE 331 MIDDLETO
IFORD, REBECCA FRE 313 MIDDLETO
IFORD, WILLIAM FRE 331 MIDDLETO
IGANS, JOHN BAL 069 18TH WAR
IGENBRODE, SUSAN FRE 129 CREAGERS
IGHRAIN, JOHN BAL 171 11TH WAR

Name	County	Page	District
IGHRON, MARGARET	BAL	430	8TH WARD
IGLEHARD, THOMAS J.	BAL	114	15TH WAR
IGLEHART, ALPHEUS	MGM	352	BERRYS D
IGLEHART, ANN MRS-	BAL	315	20TH WAR
IGLEHART, DENTON	ANN	474	HOWARD D
IGLEHART, EDMOND	ANN	511	HOWARD D
IGLEHART, EDW.	BAL	315	20TH WAR
IGLEHART, GARRISON	ANN	449	HOWARD D
IGLEHART, HARRIET	ANN	474	HOWARD D
IGLEHART, JAMES A.	ANN	312	1ST DIST
IGLEHART, JAMES H.	ANN	266	ANNAPOLI
IGLEHART, JAMES SR.	ANN	266	ANNAPOLI
IGLEHART, JESSE	ANN	372	4TH DIST
IGLEHART, JOEL	ANN	471	HOWARD D
IGLEHART, JOHN	ANN	296	1ST DIST
IGLEHART, JOHN	FRE	20	5TH E DI
IGLEHART, JULIA A.	ANN	324	2ND DIST
IGLEHART, LARKIN	ANN	484	HOWARD D
IGLEHART, MARGARET	ANN	483	HOWARD D
IGLEHART, MARY	ANN	484	HOWARD D
IGLEHART, MARY	MGM	335	CRACKLIN
IGLEHART, WILLIAM	ANN	479	HOWARD D
IGLEHART, WILLIAM H.	BAL	002	15TH WAR
IGLEHEART, ANN W.	ANN	463	HOWARD D
IGLEHEART, GEORGE W.	PRI	021	VANSVILL
IGLEHEART, ISAAC	PRI	043	VANSVILL
IGLEHEART, JOHN W.	ANN	295	1ST DIST
IGLEHEART, MARTHA A.	PRI	021	VANSVILL
IGLEHEART, MARY	ANN	481	HOWARD D
IGLEHEART, RICHARD SR.	ANN	450	HOWARD D
IGLEHEART, ROSALIE	PRI	056	AQUASCO
IGLEHEART, TIGHMAN	ANN	502	HOWARD D
IGLER, CHARLES	BAL	460	14TH WAR
IGMAN, MARGRETT E.	BAL	104	18TH WAR
IGO, MICHEAL	BAL	023	18TH WAR
IGON, GEORGE	BAL	301	7TH WARD
IHLEA, JACOB	BAL	056	4TH WARD
IHLEA, RACHEL	BAL	020	2ND DIST
IHOPFF, MARGARET *	BAL	156	2ND DIST
IJAMS, ISAAC P.	ANN	412	HOWARD D
IJAMS, JOHN	BAL	260	6TH WARD
IJAMS, JOHN W.	ANN	366	4TH DIST
IJAMS, OLIVER	BAL	070	10TH WAR
IJAMS, RICHARD *	FRE	269	NEW MARK
IJAMS, WILLIAM	BAL	053	4TH WARD
IJAMS, WILLIAM	BAL	050	9TH WARD
IJULOES, WILLIAM	BAL	287	12TH WAR
IKER, JOHN	ALL	008	3RD E.D.
IKER, SAMUEL	ALL	007	3RD E.D.
ILAN, DAVID	BAL	236	2ND WARD
ILAND, HENRY	BAL	277	12TH WAR
ILAR, FANNY	BAL	427	1ST DIST
ILEE, PETER JR.	FRE	289	WOODSBOR
ILEE, TEREPLA A.	FRE	280	WOODSBOR
ILER, ANN M.	FRE	288	WOODSBOR
ILER, CATHARINE A.	FRE	290	WOODSBOR
ILER, HORATIO	FRE	310	WOODSBOR
ILER, JACOB	FRE	290	WOODSBOR
ILER, JACOB	FRE	105	CREAGERS
ILER, JOHN	FRE	113	CREAGERS
ILER, JOHN W.	FRE	414	8TH E DI
ILER, JOSHUA	FRE	093	FREDERIC
ILER, JULIA A.	CAR	379	2ND DIST
ILER, MARGARET	FRE	296	WOODSBOR
ILER, MARGARET A.	FRE	279	WOODSBOR
ILER, MATILCA	FRE	288	WOODSBOR
ILER, NATHANIEL	FRE	130	CREAGERS
ILER, PETER	FRE	297	WOODSBOR
ILER, PETGER	FRE	290	WOODSBOR
ILER, SARAH	FRE	443	8TH E DI
ILER, SOLOMON	FRE	128	CREAGERS
ILER, WILLIAM	FRE	290	WOODSBOR
ILER, WILLIAM	FRE	291	WOODSBOR
ILER, ZUBAN	FRE	279	WOODSBOR
ILER, MARY	FRE	427	8TH E DI
ILES, JOHN	ANN	470	HOWARD D
ILET, HENRIETTA	BAL	040	4TH WARD
ILEY, JACOB	HAR	004	1ST DIST
ILEY, JAMES W.	HAR	005	1ST DIST
ILGEN, SAMUEL	CAR	411	2ND DIST
ILGENFRITZ, MARGARET	BAL	372	8TH WARD
ILGIN, PENFIELD	HAR	054	1ST DIST
ILIFER, MARTIN	WAS	035	2ND SUBD
ILLIAMBERRY, DAVID	BAL	008	9TH WARD
ILON, PERRY*	BAL	077	10TH WAR
IMANHAUSEN, JOHN	BAL	221	6TH WARD
IMES, CLARENCE	BAL	269	20TH WAR
IMES, JOHN W.	BAL	268	20TH WAR
IMESS, WILLAIM J.	BAL	273	7TH WARD
IMHOFF, ELIZABETH	BAL	120	16TH WAR
IMHOFF, GEORGE	BAL	120	16TH WAR
IMMER, SUSANNA	WAS	274	RIDGEVIL
IMMLER, CHARLES A.	BAL	104	15TH WAR
IMMOHE, JOHN E.	BAL	385	3RD WARD
IMPEY, JOHN	BAL	267	7TH WARD
IMPEY, SARAH	ANN	336	3RD DIST
INDERMAN, JEREMIAH	BAL	365	13TH WAR
INDERRICDEN, JOSEPH*	BAL	098	10TH WAR
INDERRIEDEN, JOSEPH*	BAL	098	10TH WAR
INE, CHARLES	BAL	442	14TH WAR
INEMER, ELIZABETH	BAL	038	4TH WARD
INEZ, THOMAS	ALL	195	CUMBERLA
INFELT, GEORGE	ALL	007	3RD E.D.
INFELT, MARY J.	ALL	011	3RD E.D.
ING, EDWARD*	BAL	312	3RD WARD
ING, JOHN H.	BAL	064	10TH WAR
INGALLS, DIMOND	BAL	114	18TH WAR
INGALS, LOUISA	BAL	357	1ST DIST
INGE, ROSA	WOR	180	6TH E DI
INGEIALL, CHARLES J.	BAL	312	12TH WAR
INGELKING, FREDERIC	BAL	231	6TH WARD
INGEMAN, JOSHUA	FRE	063	FREDERIC
INGER, MARY	ALL	177	7TH E.D.
INGERSON, ALEXANDER	SOM	474	TRAPPE D
INGERSON, WILLIAM	SOM	473	TRAPPE D
INGHAM, JOHN	BAL	422	1ST DIST
INGHAM, JOHN	BAL	145	1ST WARD
INGHAM, THOMAS	BAL	427	1ST DIST
INGHAM, WILLIAM	BAL	043	15TH WAR
INGHONE, WILLIAM H.	BAL	117	1ST WARD
INGLASS, ANN M.	WAS	133	HAGERSTO
INGLE, GEORGE	BAL	263	12TH WAR
INGLE, JOHN	BAL	353	3RD WARD
INGLE, JUDITH	BAL	406	3RD WARD
INGLE, REUBEN	MGM	435	CLARKSTR
INGLE, SPRINGER	BAL	078	2ND DIST
INGLE, WILLAIM	ANN	508	HOWARD D
INGLE, WILLIAM	HAR	060	1ST DIST
INGLEBECK, ELIZABETH	BAL	080	1ST WARD
INGLEHARD, STEPHEN	BAL	108	2ND DIST
INGLEHART, JOHN	BAL	108	2ND DIST
INGLEHART, MICHAEL	HAR	040	1ST DIST
INGLEHEART, ABRAHAM	BAL	379	3RD WARD
INGLEMAN, JOSEPH	BAL	404	8TH WARD
INGLES, ELLEN	BAL	212	19TH WAR
INGLES, GEORGE	BAL	365	13TH WAR
INGLES, JAMES	BAL	313	20TH WAR
INGLESBY, MARY	BAL	032	4TH WARD
INGLESON, ROBERT	BAL	350	7TH WARD
INGLING, D. J.	BAL	408	14TH WAR
INGLIS, HARRIET	BAL	454	14TH WAR
INGLISH, SARAH A.	ANN	509	HOWARD D
INGMAN, AMBROSE	WAS	126	HAGERSTO
INGMAN, RACHEL	BAL	346	1ST DIST
INGMAN, SARAH	FRE	095	FREDERIC
INGNEST, FREDERICK	BAL	124	1ST WARD
INGRAHAM, JAMES	HAR	090	2ND DIST
INGRAHAM, JOHN	BAL	201	6TH DIST
INGRAHAM, ANDREW	BAL	136	1ST WARD
INGRAM, CHARLES	WAS	161	2ND DIST
INGRAM, ELIZA	BAL	333	3RD WARD
INGRAM, ELIZABETH	WAS	071	2ND SUBD
INGRAM, EVEN	WAS	146	2ND DIST
INGRAM, GEOREG	FRE	313	MIDDLETO
INGRAM, JOHN	MGM	350	BERRYS D
INGRAM, LYTHA	WAS	067	2ND SUBD
INGRAM, MARY	SOM	521	BARREN C
INGRAM, MARY	FRE	316	MIDDLETO
INGRAM, ROBERT-BLACK	ST	327	4TH E DI
INGRAM, WILLIAM	BAL	162	1ST WARD
INGRIAM, EDWARD	WAS	229	1ST DIST
INGRIAM, ELIZABETH	WAS	187	BOONSBOR
INGRIAM, JOHN	WAS	219	1ST DIST
INGRIM, FRANKLIN	WAS	067	2ND SUBD
INGRIM, JOSEPH	WAS	068	2ND SUBD
INGRUM, ELIZABETH	HAR	037	1ST DIST
INGUIN, J.W.	BAL	139	1ST WARD
INGUM, CASPER	BAL	025	4TH WARD
INHOF, GEORGE	BAL	196	6TH WARD
INKLEMYER, WOLFGONG	BAL	381	8TH WARD
INKS, GEORGE	ALL	002	3RD E.D.
INLAND, PETER	BAL	073	1ST WARD
INLING, HENRY	BAL	087	1ST WARD
INLOES, ABRA	BAL	460	1ST DIST
INLOES, DANIEL	BAL	120	1ST WARD
INLOES, ELIZABETH	BAL	405	3RD WARD
INLOES, ENOCH	BAL	089	15TH WAR
INLOES, FRANK H.	BAL	145	11TH WAR
INLOES, INSAN	BAL	110	15TH WAR
INLOES, J.S.	BAL	246	2ND WARD
INLOES, JAMES	BAL	123	1ST WARD
INLOES, MARTHA	BAL	066	18TH WAR
INLOES, MARY A.	BAL	166	16TH WAR
INLOES, MAY J.	BAL	167	11TH WAR
INLOES, REBECCA	BAL	112	15TH WAR
INLOES, WILLIAM*	BAL	416	3RD WARD
INLOSE, LAURA	BAL	294	3RD WARD
INMAN, W. P.	BAL	470	14TH WAR
INNES, ALLEN L.	BAL	095	10TH WAR
INNES, ELIZABETH*	TAL	022	EASTON D
INNES, THOAMS	ALL	087	5TH E.D.
INNIS, ELIZABETH*	TAL	022	EASTON D
INNIS, JOSHUA	BAL	091	15TH WAR
INNOCENCE, M. SIS-	BAL	062	18TH WAR
INOLOES, WILLIAM*	BAL	416	3RD WARD
INSCO, JAMES H.	BAL	230	17TH WAR
INSKEEP, DAVID	ALL	117	5TH E.D.
INSKEEP, JAMES	ALL	123	4TH E.D.
INSKEEP, WILLIAM B.	ALL	134	4TH E.D.
INSKIP, WILLIAM	ALL	052	10TH E.D
INSLEY, ANDREW	DOR	348	3RD DIVI
INSLEY, ANDREW J.	DOR	353	3RD DIVI
INSLEY, ANN	SOM	543	TYASKIN
INSLEY, CATHARINE	DOR	347	3RD DIVI
INSLEY, DECATUR	BAL	038	4TH WARD
INSLEY, DENARD	SOM	543	TYASKIN
INSLEY, EASAW*	DOR	353	3RD DIVI
INSLEY, ELIZABETH	DOR	351	3RD DIVI
INSLEY, GEORGE	DOR	331	3RD DIVI
INSLEY, HARRIET	BAL	416	3RD WARD
INSLEY, HENERY	DOR	350	3RD DIVI
INSLEY, JACOB	DOR	458	1ST DIST
INSLEY, JOHN	SOM	543	TYASKIN
INSLEY, JOHN	DOR	300	1ST DIST
INSLEY, JOSEPH	DOR	350	3RD DIVI
INSLEY, LOUISA	SOM	446	DAMES QU
INSLEY, MARCILLUS	DOR	410	1ST DIST
INSLEY, MARGARET	SOM	445	DAMES QU
INSLEY, MARY A.	DOR	345	3RD DIVI
INSLEY, SARRAH A.	DOR	351	3RD DIVI
INSLEY, SUSAN*	DOR	377	1ST DIST
INSLEY, SWAN	DOR	347	3RD DIVI
INSLEY, THOMAS	DOR	306	1ST DIST
INSLEY, VALENTINE	SOM	548	TYASKIN
INSLEY, VALENTINE	SOM	511	BARREN C
INSLEY, WILLIAM	SOM	543	TYASKIN
INSLEY, WILLIAM	BAL	040	15TH WAR
INSLEY, ZEBEDEE	DOR	354	3RD DIVI
INSLOW, JAMES	BAL	125	1ST WARD
INSLOW, WILLIAM	BAL	125	1ST WARD
INSLY, JACOB	DOR	448	1ST DIST
INSLY, WILLIAM*	DOR	447	1ST DIST
INSTY, MARY J.	BAL	274	2ND WARD
INTRE, MARY	BAL	422	14TH WAR
INTREPELL, THOMAS	BAL	395	1ST DIST
INWRIGHT, JOHN	BAL	461	14TH WAR
IORR, CHARLES *	BAL	153	1ST WARD
IPRY, ELIZABETH	DOR	309	1ST DIST
IRAGUIN, A.	BAL	162	1ST WARD
IRAGUR, CHARLES	BAL	144	1ST WARD
IRBIN, LUCRETIA	BAL	273	17TH WAR
IREBY, PRUDENT	BAL	215	11TH WAR
IREDALE, THOMAS	BAL	222	6TH WARD
IREEP, HENRY*	BAL	065	4TH WARD
IREES, WILLIAM M.	BAL	072	4TH WARD
IRELAN, JOHN	BAL	185	6TH WARD
IRELAND, ANN	BAL	064	10TH WAR
IRELAND, BENJAMIN	CAL	051	3RD DIST
IRELAND, BENJAMIN	CAL	043	3RD DIST
IRELAND, BENJAMIN H.	CAL	005	1ST DIST
IRELAND, CATHARINE	BAL	203	2ND WARD
IRELAND, CHARLES T.	KEN	220	2ND DIST
IRELAND, DAVID	BAL	231	12TH WAR
IRELAND, DRUSILLA	CAL	011	1ST DIST
IRELAND, EDWARD	CAR	215	5TH DIST
IRELAND, ELIZABETH A.	BAL	014	15TH WAR
IRELAND, GEORGE	CAR	216	5TH DIST
IRELAND, GEORGE	CAL	011	1ST DIST
IRELAND, GEORRGE	CAL	010	1ST DIST
IRELAND, HANNAH	KEN	286	3RD DIST
IRELAND, HANNAH W.	KEN	292	3RD DIST
IRELAND, HARRIETT	BAL	133	11TH WAR
IRELAND, ISAAC A.	CAR	166	NO TWP L
IRELAND, JAMES	CAL	043	3RD DIST
IRELAND, JANE	HAR	078	2ND DIST
IRELAND, JANE	BAL	461	1ST DIST
IRELAND, JOHN	BAL	301	17TH WAR
IRELAND, JOHN F.	CAL	010	1ST DIST
IRELAND, JOHN M.	CEC	129	6TH E DI
IRELAND, LYDA ANN	CAL	037	2ND DIST
IRELAND, LYDIA	CAR	274	7TH DIST
IRELAND, MARGARET	CAL	025	2ND DIST
IRELAND, MARGRETT	CAR	070	NO TWP L
IRELAND, MARY	BAL	047	15TH WAR
IRELAND, MARY E.	BAL	214	11TH WAR
IRELAND, MARY H.	CAL	010	1ST DIST
IRELAND, MARY J.	BAL	279	7TH WARD
IRELAND, MILLY	BAL	075	4TH WARD
IRELAND, NATHAN	CEC	102	4TH E DI
IRELAND, RACHEL	ANN	353	3RD DIST
IRELAND, REBECCA	CAL	024	2ND DIST
IRELAND, RICHARD	CAR	075	NO TWP L
IRELAND, RICHARD	CAL	051	3RD DIST
IRELAND, RICHARD	BAL	310	3RD WARD
IRELAND, SALLY	BAL	203	11TH WAR
IRELAND, SAMUEL	BAL	289	7TH WARD
IRELAND, SARAH	ANN	277	ANNAPOLI
IRELAND, SARAH	CAL	045	3RD DIST
IRELAND, SARAH	CAR	074	NO TWP L
IRELAND, THOMAS	CAL	049	3RD DIST
IRELAND, THOMAS	ANN	271	ANNAPOLI
IRELAND, WILLIAM	BAL	049	2ND DIST
IRELAND, WILLIAM	CAL	057	3RD DIST
IRELY, GEORGE	WAS	097	2ND DIST
IREMAN, CATHARIN	CAR	358	9TH DIST
IREMAN, JOHN	CAR	363	9TH DIST
IREMAN, WILLIAM	BAL	129	16TH WAR
IRENBERGER, HENRY	WAS	300	1ST DIST
IRENTROUT, BARBARA	BAL	345	7TH WARD
IRENWITH, GEERGE	FRE	447	8TH E DI
IRESTON, CLEMENTINE*	BAL	105	10TH WAR
IRICK, HENRY	WAS	202	1ST DIST
IRIE, C.	BAL	129	1ST WARD
IRIEL, MRS-	BAL	341	1ST DIST
IRISH, LOVINA	ALL	215	CUMBERLA
IRISH, MARY	ALL	217	CUMBERLA
IRISH, PATRICK	BAL	232	1ST DIST
IRLAN, MARGARET	BAL	295	20TH WAR
IRLAND, ANN E.*	TAL	003	EASTON D
IRLAND, ROADY *	TAL	076	EASTON T
IRNEY, MRS.	BAL	151	5TH WARD
IROMIS, C.	BAL	130	1ST WARD
IRON, BIDDY	BAL	296	20TH WAR
IRON, GEORGIANA	BAL	325	12TH WAR
IRONBRIN, REBECCA	BAL	032	15TH WAR
IRONMONGER, EDWARD L.	BAL	111	10TH WAR
IRONMONGER, MARY	BAL	299	7TH WARD
IRONS, DIANNA	BAL	139	5TH WARD
IRONS, EMANUEL	BAL	066	4TH WARD
IRONS, JOHN	BAL	226	2ND WARD
IRONS, JOHN	ALL	064	10TH E.D
IRONS, JOSEPH	ALL	063	10TH E.D
IRONS, M. KENNY	BAL	280	2ND WARD
IRONS, MARY	ALL	061	10TH E.D
IRONS, MARY	BAL	218	2ND WARD
IRONS, MARY	QUE	244	5TH E DI
IRONS, MICHAEL	FRE	188	5TH E DI
IRONS, ROBERT	BAL	083	4TH WARD
IRONS, SARAH	BAL	339	7TH WARD
IRONS, SOPHIA	FRE	182	5TH E DI
IRONS, TETIS H.	CAR	082	NO TWP L
IRONS, THOMAS	BAL	307	7TH WARD
IRONS, VANBUREN	ALL	143	6TH E.D.
IROOTENDICK, DENOA *	BAL	091	18TH WAR
IRRINGTON, WASHBURN	PRI	030	VANSVILL
IRUN, GEORGE	BAL	121	1ST WARD
IRVAN, JAMES	BAL	115	2ND DIST
IRVAN, MARTHA	BAL	148	5TH WARD
IRVAN, MICHAEL	HAR	147	3RD DIST
IRVEEN, JOHN	PRI	049	AQUASCO
IRVIN, ANN	BAL	289	12TH WAR
IRVIN, DAVID	BAL	401	8TH WARD
IRVIN, E.	BAL	061	10TH WAR
IRVIN, EDWARD	WOR	228	6TH E DI
IRVIN, EMILINE	BAL	197	11TH WAR
IRVIN, FRANCIS	BAL	474	14TH WAR
IRVIN, HENRY	BAL	025	18TH WAR
IRVIN, HENRY	BAL	372	13TH WAR
IRVIN, J.G.	BAL	168	1ST WARD
IRVIN, JACOB	BAL	261	17TH WAR
IRVIN, JOHN	BAL	148	19TH WAR
IRVIN, JOHN	ALL	031	2ND E.D.
IRVIN, JOSEPH	BAL	124	16TH WAR
IRVIN, JOSEPH W.	BAL	201	17TH WAR
IRVIN, JOSEPHINE	BAL	215	11TH WAR
IRVIN, MARGARET	ANN	451	HOWARD D
IRVIN, MARY	ALL	047	10TH E.D
IRVIN, MARY A.	BAL	053	9TH WARD
IRVIN, MATT	BAL	282	12TH WAR
IRVIN, ROBERT	BAL	232	2ND WARD
IRVIN, ROBERT	BAL	399	1ST DIST
IRVIN, SAMUEL	WAS	147	HAGERSTO
IRVIN, SAUL	WOR	228	6TH E DI
IRVIN, THOAMS	BAL	128	18TH WAR
IRVIN, WILLIAM	CEC	093	4TH E DI
IRVIN, WILLIAM	BAL	457	8TH WARD
IRVIN, WILLIAM I.	BAL	286	7TH WARD
IRVINE, AMBROSE	BAL	103	10TH WAR
IRVINE, CHARLOTT	BAL	111	5TH WARD
IRVINE, ELIZABETH	BAL	285	20TH WAR
IRVINE, SARAH	BAL	049	4TH WARD
IRVINE, WILLIAM	PRI	107	PISCATAW
IRVING, CAROLINE	BAL	025	15TH WAR
IRVING, CATHARINE	ANN	465	HOWARD D
IRVING, GEORGE G.	SOM	505	SALISBUR
IRVING, GEORGIANA	BAL	341	7TH WARD
IRVING, HENRY	BAL	021	9TH WARD
IRVING, JAMES	BAL	277	20TH WAR
IRVING, JAMES-BLACK	BAL	224	2ND WARD
IRVING, LEVIN	BAL	098	15TH WAR
IRVING, MARGARET	BAL	066	2ND DIST
IRVING, PEGGY	SOM	492	SALISBUR
IRVING, ROBERT	BAL	065	2ND DIST
IRVING, SANDY	SOM	502	SALISBUR
IRVING, THOMAS J.	BAL	262	6TH WARD
IRVING, WILLIAM	BAL	341	7TH WARD
IRWIN, ABNER	CEC	133	6TH E DI
IRWIN, ANN	BAL	195	11TH WAR
IRWIN, DANIEL	WAS	127	2ND DIST
IRWIN, DAVID	WAS	124	2ND DIST

Name	County	Page	District
IRWIN, ELIZA	CEC	131	6TH E DI
IRWIN, GEORGE	BAL	419	14TH WAR
IRWIN, GEORGE	BAL	287	20TH WAR
IRWIN, GEORGE	BAL	142	1ST WARD
IRWIN, GEORGE W.	BAL	372	13TH WAR
IRWIN, HENRY J.	BAL	452	14TH WAR
IRWIN, ISAAC	BAL	148	2ND DIST
IRWIN, JACOB	WAS	041	2ND SUBD
IRWIN, JAMES	WAS	218	1ST DIST
IRWIN, JAMES	FRE	159	EMMITTSB
IRWIN, JESSE	CEC	118	4TH E DI
IRWIN, JOHN J.	CEC	137	6TH E DI
IRWIN, JOHN W.	CEC	137	6TH E DI
IRWIN, MARIAH	WAS	010	WILLIAMS
IRWIN, MARY	WAS	155	HAGERSTO
IRWIN, MATILDA	WAS	110	2ND DIST
IRWIN, SARAH	WAS	217	1ST DIST
IRWIN, THOMAS	BAL	166	2ND DIST
IRWIN, VICTORIA	CEC	145	PORT DUP
IRWIN, WILLIAM	CEC	144	PORT DUP
IRWIN, WILLIAM	CEC	155	PORT DUP
ISAAC R.	CAL	023	2ND DIST
ISAAC, BENJAMIN	ANN	315	1ST DIST
ISAAC, CHARLES	ALL	208	CUMBERLA
ISAAC, GODFREY	BAL	123	5TH WARD
ISAAC, GRAFTON J.	PRI	057	AQUASCO
ISAAC, HENRY C.	ALL	208	CUMBERLA
ISAAC, JANE	BAL	117	11TH WAR
ISAAC, JONATHAN	BAL	349	1ST DIST
ISAAC, JOSEPH	PRI	057	AQUASCO
ISAAC, JOSEPH	PRI	122	PISCATAW
ISAAC, JOSEPHUS	ANN	494	HOWARD D
ISAAC, LEANNA	BAL	019	18TH WAR
ISAAC, MARTHA	BAL	180	16TH WAR
ISAAC, MINTY	CAL	054	3RD DIST
ISAAC, REBECCA C.	BAL	013	18TH WAR
ISAAC, RICHAR	CAL	023	2ND DIST
ISAAC, RICHARD	BAL	179	16TH WAR
ISAAC, RICHARD OF JOSEPH	PRI	121	PISCATAW
ISAAC, RICHARD W.	PRI	086	QUEEN AN
ISAAC, WILLIAM C.	BAL	280	2ND WARD
ISAACE, EDWARD	CAL	061	3RD DIST
ISAACKS, JARRETT	BAL	346	7TH WARD
ISAACS, GEORGE W.	ANN	452	HOWARD D
ISAACS, HENRY	BAL	150	2ND DIST
ISAACS, JOHN	ANN	459	HOWARD D
ISAACS, JOHN	BAL	231	19TH WAR
ISAACS, JOSEPH	BAL	102	2ND DIST
ISAACS, JULIA	ANN	390	4TH DIST
ISAACS, LEWIS	CEC	130	6TH E DI
ISAACS, LOUISA	BAL	338	7TH WARD
ISAACS, MARIA	BAL	073	10TH WAR
ISAACS, MATILDA	BAL	395	14TH WAR
ISAACS, RICHARD	ANN	444	HOWARD D
ISAACS, RUTH A.	BAL	179	6TH WARD
ISAACS, SAMUEL L.	ANN	497	HOWARD D
ISAACS, THOMAS	ANN	459	HOWARD D
ISAACS, WILLIAM	DOR	458	1ST DIST
ISAACS, ZEDEKIAH M.	ANN	459	HOWARD D
ISACKS, HARRIET	BAL	379	3RD WARD
ISACKS, JAMES	CEC	130	6TH E DI
ISACS, WILLIAM A.J.	ANN	459	HOWARD D
ISADORA, IDA	CAR	291	7TH DIST
ISAFETTER, ISAAC	BAL	227	2ND WARD
ISAMS, FRANKLIN	BAL	003	18TH WAR
ISAMS, W.	BAL	004	18TH WAR
ISATT, ELIZABETH	BAL	023	18TH WAR
ISBORN, SARAH	WAS	173	FUNKSTOW
ISCHUDY, BARBAR	QUE	123	1ST E DI
ISEBROUGHT, BATBAY	BAL	135	11TH WAR
ISELY, JACOB	BAL	307	20TH WAR
ISEMAN, GEORGE	BAL	242	20TH WAR
ISEMINGER, GEORGE	WAS	168	FUNKSTOW
ISEMINGER, MICHAEL	WAS	168	FUNKSTOW
ISEMINGER, MICHAEL	WAS	172	FUNKSTOW
ISEMINGER, SARAH	WAS	172	FUNKSTOW
ISENBERGER, PETER	FRE	427	8TH E DI
ISENBRUEST, JOHN	BAL	253	20TH WAR
ISENDORF, JOSEPHENE	BAL	327	3RD WARD
ISENHART, JACOB	ALL	091	5TH E.D.
ISENHART, SUSAN	ALL	091	5TH E.D.
ISENHOWER, WILLIAM	CAR	346	6TH DIST
ISENWACKER, ADOLPH	BAL	090	1ST WARD
ISER, BARBARA	FRE	436	8TH E DI
ISER, GEORGE	FRE	442	8TH E DI
ISER, JOHN	BAL	297	17TH WAR
ISER, MARGARET	BAL	358	1ST DIST
ISEREAL, RICHARD	PRI	028	VANSVILL
ISET, WILLIAM	BAL	284	1ST DIST
ISHAM, WILLIAM	BAL	161	1ST WARD
ISHUM, ELIJAH	WOR	249	1ST CENS
ISHUM, ELISHA	WOR	248	1ST CENS
ISHUM, JAOCB	WOR	241	1ST CENS
ISHUM, JOHN	WOR	249	1ST CENS
ISHUM, JOHN	WOR	248	1ST CENS
ISHUM, WILLIAM	BAL	171	1ST WARD
ISIMINGER, HENRY	WAS	169	FUNKSTOW
ISINER, HENRY	HAR	060	1ST DIST
ISINER, HENRY	HAR	060	1ST DIST
ISING, JOHN	HAR	107	2ND DIST
ISINGER, LEAME*	BAL	354	3RD WARD
ISINGER, LIME*	BAL	077	4TH WARD
ISINGER, SIME*	BAL	077	4TH WARD
ISLAND, JAMES	BAL	316	3RD WARD
ISLE, BRIDGET	BAL	419	1ST DIST
ISLE, BRIDGET	ALL	076	5TH E.D.
ISLEINFELT, CASPER	BAL	313	1ST DIST
ISLES,ELIZABETH	BAL	028	2ND DIST
ISLEY, ISAAC	CEC	017	ELKTON 3
ISLEY, MARY	CEC	017	ELKTON 3
ISLEY, PETER	BAL	299	3RD WARD
ISLIER, MARGARET	BAL	237	2ND WARD
ISLRICH, ACAM	HAR	107	2ND DIST
ISMCOT, ANDREW	CHA	273	ALLENS F
ISRAEL, ELIZABETH	BAL	241	2ND WARD
ISRAEL, ELIZABETH	BAL	248	12TH WAR
ISRAEL, GEORGE W.	MGM	442	CLARKSTR
ISRAEL, SARAH	BAL	275	12TH WAR
ISRAEL, THOMAS B.	BAL	260	12TH WAR
ISREAL, JACOB	BAL	036	18TH WAR
ISREAL, MARKS	WAS	130	HAGERSTO
ISREAL, NELSON	CAR	396	2ND DIST
ISREAL, WILLIAM	BAL	079	18TH WAR
ISRIEL, NANCY	BAL	226	1ST DIST
ISRIEL, OWEN	BAL	432	1ST DIST
ISRREAL, JOHN	CAR	395	2ND DIST
ITE, JOSEPH	BAL	436	8TH WARD
ITEN,ALBERT	BAL	168	1ST WARD
ITENEYER, SUSAN	WAS	211	1ST DIST
ITINGER, CATHARINE	BAL	322	12TH WAR
ITLGHMAN, LOUISA	TAL	094	ST MICHA
ITNIER, SAMUEL	FRE	323	MIDDLETO
ITSON, F.	BAL	135	1ST WARD
ITSON,HENRY	BAL	134	1ST WARD
ITTS, TERESA	BAL	384	3RD WARD
IUISBERT, JONATHAN	FRE	092	FREDERIC
IVERS, JAMES	CHA	256	MIDDLETO
IVES, ELMIRA M.	CEC	131	6TH E DI
IVES, JOHN	BAL	062	2ND DIST
IVES, MARY J.	BAL	146	5TH WARD
IVES, THOMAS J.	HAR	146	3RD DIST
IVEY, JOHN	KEN	227	2ND DIST
IVIN, PHILLIP	ALL	049	10TH E.D
IVLAND, ANN E.*	TAL	003	EASTON D
IVUMRON, TINT*	ALL	207	CUMBERLA
IVY, DOROTHY	ST	263	3RD E DI
IVY, ELIZA	KEN	273	1ST DIST
IVY, HENRY F.	ST	320	4TH E DI
IVY, MARY E.	KEN	258	1ST DIST
IVY, MARY MISS-	BAL	315	20TH WAR
IWINS, WILLIAM	HAR	167	3RD DIST
IYBRAND, HENRY	BAL	202	2ND WARD
IZAR, JOSHUA	BAL	459	8TH WARD
IZELL, JACOB	BAL	260	1ST DIST
IZER, GEORGE	BAL	212	6TH WARD
IZERDENTZ, JOHN*	BAL	380	3RD WARD
J//U, GABRIEL	SOM	451	DAMES QU
JACHIN, BARBARA	BAL	403	1ST DIST
JACK, ALLY	CAL	025	2ND DIST
JACK, ANDREW	WAS	161	2ND DIST
JACK, CHARLES	WAS	134	HAGERSTO
JACK, HARRIET	CEC	207	7TH E DI
JACK, JAMES	ALL	106	5TH E.D.
JACK, JOHN	BAL	222	12TH WAR
JACKE, JOHN	BAL	116	11TH WAR
JACKELL, NCIHOLAS	ANN	469	HOWARD D
JACKERSON, S.	BAL	085	10TH WAR
JACKOSN, CATHARINE E.	BAL	274	2ND WARD
JACKS, ISAAC	CAL	024	2ND DIST
JACKS, KATER	CAL	024	2ND DIST
JACKSON,	PRI	069	MARLBROU
JACKSON, -----*	BAL	084	10TH WAR
JACKSON, A.	BAL	236	20TH WAR
JACKSON, AARON	BAL	176	19TH WAR
JACKSON, AARON	CAR	083	NO TWP L
JACKSON, ABRAHAM	BAL	369	3RD WARD
JACKSON, ABRAHAM	ANN	353	3RD DIST
JACKSON, ABRAM	ANN	351	3RD DIST
JACKSON, ADDISON	BAL	093	15TH WAR
JACKSON, ADELINE	BAL	398	8TH WARD
JACKSON, AGNES	BAL	128	16TH WAR
JACKSON, ALBERT	BAL	040	1ST WARD
JACKSON, ALEXANDER	CEC	189	7TH E DI
JACKSON, ALEXANDER	CEC	199	7TH E DI
JACKSON, ALEXANDER	CEC	212	7TH E DI
JACKSON, ALEXANDER C.	MGM	372	BERRYS D
JACKSON, ALEXANDR J. W.	BAL	467	14TH WAR
JACKSON, ALICE	ANN	418	HOWARD D
JACKSON, ALICE	BAL	175	11TH WAR
JACKSON, ALONZO	CEC	179	7TH E DI
JACKSON, AMANDA	BAL	083	4TH WARD
JACKSON, AMANDA	HAR	050	1ST DIST
JACKSON, AMANUEL	DOR	384	1ST DIST
JACKSON, AMELIA A.	BAL	096	5TH WARD
JACKSON, AMELINE	TAL	032	EASTON D
JACKSON, AMOS	CEC	179	7TH E DI
JACKSON, ANDREW	CEC	081	CHARLEST
JACKSON, ANDREW	PRI	084	QUEEN AN
JACKSON, ANDREW	SOM	514	BARREN C
JACKSON, ANDREW	BAL	144	1ST WARD
JACKSON, ANDREW	BAL	128	5TH WARD
JACKSON, ANDREW	BAL	167	1ST WARD
JACKSON, ANDREW-BLACK	FRE	234	BUCKEYST
JACKSON, ANDREW-MULATTO	BAL	216	2ND WARD
JACKSON, ANN	BAL	302	7TH WARD
JACKSON, ANN	BAL	382	13TH WAR
JACKSON, ANN	BAL	276	17TH WAR
JACKSON, ANN	BAL	339	13TH WAR
JACKSON, ANN	TAL	118	ST MICHA
JACKSON, ANN J.	BAL	247	17TH WAR
JACKSON, ANN M.	DOR	380	1ST DIST
JACKSON, ANN M.	DOR	440	1ST DIST
JACKSON, ANN M.	BAL	007	1ST WARD
JACKSON, ANN MARIA	BAL	146	5TH WARD
JACKSON, ANN MARIA	BAL	193	17TH WAR
JACKSON, ANN R.	FRE	043	FREDERIC
JACKSON, ANN-BLACK	CAR	126	NO TWP L
JACKSON, ANNA	BAL	339	13TH WAR
JACKSON, ANNA M.	BAL	069	2ND DIST
JACKSON, ANTHONY-MULATTO	CAR	359	9TH DIST
JACKSON, ANTHCNY-MULATTO	FRE	428	8TH E DI
JACKSON, AREAN	BAL	191	2ND WARD
JACKSON, ARTHUR	BAL	090	15TH WAR
JACKSON, ARTHUR	BAL	074	15TH WAR
JACKSON, AUGUSTUS-MULATTO	FRE	451	8TH E DI
JACKSON, AUTHER	BAL	456	8TH WARD
JACKSON, BAKER	MGM	442	CLARKSTR
JACKSON, BARBARA	BAL	125	16TH WAR
JACKSON, BARRETT	CEC	101	4TH E DI
JACKSON, BEN*	DOR	425	1ST DIST
JACKSON, BENJAMIN	DOR	385	1ST DIST
JACKSON, BENJAMIN	BAL	085	2ND DIST
JACKSON, BENJAMIN	BAL	375	1ST DIST
JACKSON, BETHIAH	BAL	162	16TH WAR
JACKSON, BETSEY	KEN	282	3RD DIST
JACKSON, BETSY	BAL	033	9TH WARD
JACKSON, BOYD	BAL	154	5TH WARD
JACKSON, BRIDGET	BAL	180	2ND WARD
JACKSON, C.	ANN	274	ANNAPOLI
JACKSON, CAIN	BAL	002	15TH WAR
JACKSON, CALEB	BAL	363	3RD WARD
JACKSON, CALEB	CEC	209	7TH E DI
JACKSON, CANFAT	BAL	276	12TH WAR
JACKSON, CAROLINE	BAL	385	1ST DIST
JACKSON, CAROLINE	BAL	114	5TH WARD
JACKSON, CAROLINE	BAL	305	3RD WARD
JACKSON, CAROLINE	ANN	443	HOWARD D
JACKSON, CAROLINE-BLACK	QUE	142	1ST E DI
JACKSON, CATHARINE	BAL	265	12TH WAR
JACKSON, CATHARINE	BAL	283	2ND WARD
JACKSON, CATHARINE	TAL	090	ST MICHA
JACKSON, CATHARINE	WAS	041	2ND SUBD
JACKSON, CATHERIN	CAR	095	NO TWP L
JACKSON, CATHERINE	CAR	148	NO TWP L
JACKSON, CHARITY	DOR	449	1ST DIST
JACKSON, CHARLES	SOM	475	TRAPPE D
JACKSON, CHARLES	KEN	260	1ST DIST
JACKSON, CHARLES	SOM	485	TRAPP DI
JACKSON, CHARLES	DOR	464	1ST DIST
JACKSON, CHARLES	DOR	383	1ST DIST
JACKSON, CHARLES	CEC	184	7TH E DI
JACKSON, CHARLES	BAL	144	1ST WARD
JACKSON, CHARLES	BAL	132	1ST WARD
JACKSON, CHARLES H.	BAL	425	8TH WARD
JACKSON, CHARLES H.	QUE	161	2ND E DI
JACKSON, CHARLES M.	BAL	109	15TH WAR
JACKSON, CHARLES-BLACK	FRE	229	BUCKEYST
JACKSON, CHARLOTTE	DOR	424	1ST DIST
JACKSON, CHARLOTTE	BAL	456	14TH WAR
JACKSON, CHARLOTTE	BAL	032	4TH WARD
JACKSON, CHRISTINA	BAL	289	7TH WARD
JACKSON, COLUMBUS	PRI	063	NOTTINGH
JACKSON, CRISTY A.-BLACK	FRE	231	BUCKEYST
JACKSON, CUTY	DOR	311	1ST DIST
JACKSON, DANIEL	DOR	319	1ST DIST
JACKSON, DANIEL	DOR	431	1ST DIST
JACKSON, DANIEL	SOM	489	SALISBUR
JACKSON, DANIL	DOR	465	1ST DIST
JACKSON, DARKUS	BAL	122	5TH WARD
JACKSON, DAVID	BAL	159	1ST WARD
JACKSON, DAVID	BAL	130	16TH WAR
JACKSON, DEANA	BAL	314	3RD WARD
JACKSON, DELIA	BAL	473	14TH WAR
JACKSON, E.	BAL	099	10TH WAR
JACKSON, EDWARD	FRE	301	WOODSBOR
JACKSON, EDWARD	CEC	184	7TH E DI
JACKSON, EDWARD	CEC	185	7TH E DI
JACKSON, EDWARD	CEC	186	7TH E DI
JACKSON, EDWARD	CEC	083	CHARLEST
JACKSON, EDWARD	CEC	083	CHARLEST
JACKSON, EDWARD	SOM	400	BRINKLEY
JACKSON, EDWARD	PRI	069	MARLBROU
JACKSON, ELEN	CHA	293	BOJANTOW
JACKSON, ELI	ANN	432	HOWARD D
JACKSON, ELIHU	WOR	236	6TH E DI
JACKSON, ELISHA	BAL	085	2ND DIST
JACKSON, ELISHA	BAL	189	5TH DIST
JACKSON, ELISHA	CAR	186	8TH DIST
JACKSON, ELIZA	BAL	319	12TH WAR
JACKSON, ELIZA	BAL	330	1ST DIST
JACKSON, ELIZA	BAL	022	9TH WARD
JACKSON, ELIZA A.	DOR	425	1ST DIST
JACKSON, ELIZA J.	BAL	142	16TH WAR
JACKSON, ELIZABETH	BAL	121	16TH WAR
JACKSON, ELIZABETH	BAL	292	3RD WARD
JACKSON, ELIZABETH	ALL	109	5TH E.D.
JACKSON, ELIZABETH	QUE	140	1ST E DI
JACKSON, ELIZABETH	HAR	003	1ST DIST
JACKSON, ELIZABETH	QUE	214	3RD E DI
JACKSON, ELIZABETH	WAS	043	2ND SUBD
JACKSON, ELLEN	ANN	472	HOWARD D
JACKSON, ELLEN-BLACK	CAR	161	NO TWP L
JACKSON, EMELINE	DOR	441	1ST DIST
JACKSON, EMILY	DOR	424	1ST DIST
JACKSON, EMILY	BAL	205	11TH WAR
JACKSON, EMILY	BAL	241	1ST DIST
JACKSON, EMILY	BAL	078	1ST WARD
JACKSON, EMILY	BAL	286	7TH WARD
JACKSON, EMILY C.	DOR	379	1ST DIST
JACKSON, EMILY*	TAL	032	EASTON D
JACKSON, EMILY-BLACK	BAL	183	2ND WARD
JACKSON, FANNY	BAL	188	2ND WARD
JACKSON, FANNY-MULATTO	BAL	214	2ND WARD
JACKSON, FLETCHER	CAR	083	NO TWP L
JACKSON, FLY	BAL	295	20TH WAR
JACKSON, FRANCES	WAS	055	2ND SUBD
JACKSON, FRANCIS	BAL	189	19TH WAR
JACKSON, FRANCIS	CEC	180	7TH E DI
JACKSON, G.	BAL	173	1ST WARD
JACKSON, GARRIT	MGM	340	CLARKSBU
JACKSON, GASTAVUS	ST	260	3RD E DI
JACKSON, GEORGE	TAL	020	EASTON D
JACKSON, GEORGE	WOR	293	9TH E DI
JACKSON, GEORGE	MGM	436	CLARKSTR
JACKSON, GEORGE	DOR	452	1ST DIST
JACKSON, GEORGE	SOM	523	BARREN C
JACKSON, GEORGE	PRI	120	PISCATAW
JACKSON, GEORGE	PRI	119	PISCATAW
JACKSON, GEORGE	CEC	186	7TH E DI
JACKSON, GEORGE	BAL	341	13TH WAR
JACKSON, GEORGE	HAR	085	2ND DIST
JACKSON, GEORGE	CAR	359	9TH DIST
JACKSON, GEORGE	BAL	189	2ND WARD
JACKSON, GEORGE	BAL	246	6TH WARD
JACKSON, GEORGE	BAL	171	2ND DIST
JACKSON, GEORGE	BAL	105	1ST WARD
JACKSON, GEORGE	BAL	050	9TH WARD
JACKSON, GEORGE D.	SOM	541	TYASKIN
JACKSON, GEORGE S.W.	BAL	331	7TH WARD
JACKSON, GEORGEANNA	BAL	040	1ST WARD
JACKSON, GERARD-BLACK	ST	337	4TH E DI
JACKSON, GREGORY	BAL	169	1ST WARD
JACKSON, GREOGYR	BAL	123	1ST WARD
JACKSON, H.	BAL	229	19TH WAR
JACKSON, HAGAR	BAL	237	20TH WAR
JACKSON, HANEY	HAR	050	1ST DIST
JACKSON, HANNAH	BAL	099	10TH WAR
JACKSON, HARRIET	PRI	101	SPALDING
JACKSON, HARRISON	BAL	143	1ST WARD
JACKSON, HECTOR	BAL	379	3RD WARD
JACKSON, HENERITTA	DOR	311	1ST DIST
JACKSON, HENRIETTA	BAL	261	20TH WAR
JACKSON, HENRIETTA-BLACK	CAR	069	NO TWP L
JACKSON, HENRY	BAL	433	14TH WAR
JACKSON, HENRY	BAL	108	10TH WAR
JACKSON, HENRY	BAL	102	1ST WARD
JACKSON, HENRY	BAL	167	6TH WARD
JACKSON, HENRY	ANN	462	HOWARD D
JACKSON, HENRY	ANN	466	HOWARD D
JACKSON, HENRY	ANN	275	ANNAPOLI
JACKSON, HENRY	ANN	414	HOWARD D
JACKSON, HENRY	BAL	375	1ST DIST
JACKSON, HENRY	PRI	094	SPALDING
JACKSON, HENRY	WOR	293	9TH E DI
JACKSON, HENRY	TAL	024	EASTON D
JACKSON, HENRY	WAS	046	2ND SUBD
JACKSON, HENRY	DOR	469	1ST DIST
JACKSON, HENRY F.	BAL	469	14TH WAR
JACKSON, HENRY-BLACK	MGM	420	MEDLEY 3
JACKSON, HENRY-BLACK	ST	346	5TH E DI
JACKSON, HETTY	WOR	290	9TH E DI
JACKSON, HORACE	DOR	371	3RD DIVI
JACKSON, HOWARD	BAL	160	2ND DIST
JACKSON, HUGH	SOM	498	SALISBUR
JACKSON, IGNATIOUS	BAL	340	7TH WARD
JACKSON, ISAAAC	BAL	106	10TH WAR
JACKSON, ISAAC	SOM	498	SALISBUR
JACKSON, ISAAC	PRI	029	VANSVILL
JACKSON, ISAAC	BAL	363	13TH WAR
JACKSON, ISAAC	CEC	209	7TH E DI

Name	County	Page	District
JACKSON, ISAAC	BAL	284	17TH WAR
JACKSON, ISAAC-MULATTO	CAR	384	2ND DIST
JACKSON, ISABEL	BAL	467	14TH WAR
JACKSON, ISABEL	BAL	462	1ST DIST
JACKSON, ISRAEL M.	PRI	035	VANSVILL
JACKSON, J.	BAL	163	1ST WARD
JACKSON, J.	BAL	153	1ST WARD
JACKSON, J.	BAL	152	1ST WARD
JACKSON, J.J.	PRI	101	SPALDING
JACKSON, JACOB	BAL	031	1ST WARD
JACKSON, JACOB	BAL	097	2ND DIST
JACKSON, JACOB	DOR	364	3RD DIVI
JACKSON, JAMES	CHA	257	MIDDLETO
JACKSON, JAMES	CHA	234	HILLTOP
JACKSON, JAMES	CHA	247	HILLTOP
JACKSON, JAMES	CAR	327	1ST DIST
JACKSON, JAMES	BAL	033	18TH WAR
JACKSON, JAMES	BAL	350	13TH WAR
JACKSON, JAMES	CEC	168	6TH E DI
JACKSON, JAMES	BAL	216	11TH WAR
JACKSON, JAMES	BAL	024	2ND DIST
JACKSON, JAMES	BAL	008	1ST WARD
JACKSON, JAMES	BAL	233	6TH WARD
JACKSON, JAMES	BAL	094	5TH WARD
JACKSON, JAMES	BAL	046	9TH WARD
JACKSON, JAMES	BAL	106	15TH WAR
JACKSON, JAMES	BAL	101	15TH WAR
JACKSON, JAMES	BAL	077	10TH WAR
JACKSON, JAMES	ANN	274	ANNAPOLI
JACKSON, JAMES	TAL	118	ST MICHA
JACKSON, JAMES	TAL	110	ST MICHA
JACKSON, JAMES	WOR	312	2ND E DI
JACKSON, JAMES H.	TAL	050	EASTON T
JACKSON, JAMES M.	BAL	307	3RD WARD
JACKSON, JAMES R.	ANN	402	8TH DIST
JACKSON, JAMES R.	BAL	160	16TH WAR
JACKSON, JAMES-BLACK	BAL	208	2ND WARD
JACKSON, JAMES-BLACK	BAL	228	2ND WARD
JACKSON, JAMES-MULATTO	BAL	222	2ND WARD
JACKSON, JANE	BAL	429	14TH WAR
JACKSON, JANE	BAL	462	14TH WAR
JACKSON, JANE	CAL	009	1ST DIST
JACKSON, JANE	HAR	085	2ND DIST
JACKSON, JANE-BLACK	FRE	227	BUCKEYST
JACKSON, JASPER M.	PRI	009	BLADENSB
JACKSON, JASPER M.	PRI	036	VANSVILL
JACKSON, JEFFREY	TAL	028	EASTON D
JACKSON, JEREMIAH	BAL	141	16TH WAR
JACKSON, JOHN	BAL	387	3RD WARD
JACKSON, JOHN	BAL	143	1ST WARD
JACKSON, JOHN	ANN	388	4TH DIST
JACKSON, JOHN	ANN	270	ANNAPOLI
JACKSON, JOHN	BAL	188	5TH DIST
JACKSON, JOHN	BAL	170	2ND DIST
JACKSON, JOHN	BAL	122	1ST WARD
JACKSON, JOHN	BAL	073	1ST WARD
JACKSON, JOHN	BAL	244	1ST DIST
JACKSON, JOHN	BAL	259	1ST DIST
JACKSON, JOHN	BAL	432	8TH WARD
JACKSON, JOHN	WAS	064	2ND SUBD
JACKSON, JOHN	KEN	309	3RD DIST
JACKSON, JOHN	DOR	385	1ST DIST
JACKSON, JOHN	DOR	422	1ST DIST
JACKSON, JOHN	FRE	301	WOODSBOR
JACKSON, JOHN	CEC	148	PORT DUP
JACKSON, JOHN	CEC	083	CHARLEST
JACKSON, JOHN	BAL	284	20TH WAR
JACKSON, JOHN	HAR	121	2ND DIST
JACKSON, JOHN	CHA	267	BOJANTOW
JACKSON, JOHN	FRE	189	5TH E DI
JACKSON, JOHN A.	BAL	298	7TH WARD
JACKSON, JOHN C.	CEC	168	6TH E DI
JACKSON, JOHN C.	FRE	302	WOODSBOR
JACKSON, JOHN H.	BAL	204	17TH WAR
JACKSON, JOHN H.	BAL	040	18TH WAR
JACKSON, JOHN R.	HAR	019	1ST DIST
JACKSON, JOHN T.	BAL	237	20TH WAR
JACKSON, JOHN T.	CAR	302	1ST DIST
JACKSON, JOHN W.	CEC	184	7TH E DI
JACKSON, JOHN W.	CEC	190	5TH E DI
JACKSON, JOHN W.-BLACK	BAL	222	2ND WARD
JACKSON, JOHN W.-BLACK	BAL	223	2ND WARD
JACKSON, JOHN-BLACK	BAL	222	2ND WARD
JACKSON, JOHN-BLACK	BAL	222	2ND WARD
JACKSON, JOHN-MULATTO	FRE	434	8TH E DI
JACKSON, JOHN-MULATTO	FRE	231	BUCKEYST
JACKSON, JONATHAN	BAL	362	3RD WARD
JACKSON, JONATHAN	BAL	117	1ST WARD
JACKSON, JONATHAN H.	SOM	541	TYASKIN
JACKSON, JOSEPH	TAL	110	ST MICHA
JACKSON, JOSEPH	BAL	166	1ST WARD
JACKSON, JOSEPH	BAL	142	1ST WARD
JACKSON, JOSEPH	BAL	456	8TH WARD
JACKSON, JOSEPH	BAL	218	19TH WAR
JACKSON, JOSEPH	FRE	107	CREAGERS
JACKSON, JOSEPH	CAR	142	NO TWP L
JACKSON, JOSEPH A.	CAL	055	3RD DIST
JACKSON, JOSEPH H.	ALL	077	5TH E.D.
JACKSON, JOSEPH L.	BAL	014	1ST WARD
JACKSON, JOSHUA	BAL	236	2ND WARD
JACKSON, JOSHUA	BAL	085	2ND DIST
JACKSON, JOSHUA	CEC	099	3RD E DI
JACKSON, JOSHUA	SOM	544	TYASKIN
JACKSON, L. MRS.	BAL	329	13TH WAR
JACKSON, L.J.	PRI	082	QUEEN AN
JACKSON, LARINDA	BAL	248	17TH WAR
JACKSON, LEAH	WOR	296	9TH E DI
JACKSON, LEONARD	MGM	340	CLARKSBU
JACKSON, LEVI	CEC	118	4TH E DI
JACKSON, LEVI	TAL	028	EASTON D
JACKSON, LEVIN	QUE	214	3RD E DI
JACKSON, LEWIS	HAR	048	1ST DIST
JACKSON, LEWIS-BLACK	FRE	434	8TH E DI
JACKSON, LIBBY	BAL	134	5TH WARD
JACKSON, LIDIA	BAL	380	1ST DIST
JACKSON, LITTLETON	SOM	532	QUANTICO
JACKSON, LIZZA	BAL	328	1ST DIST
JACKSON, LOFIRE W.	HAR	162	3RD DIST
JACKSON, LOUISA	BAL	344	7TH WARD
JACKSON, LOUISANNA *	BAL	143	2ND DIST
JACKSON, LUCINDA	BAL	457	8TH WARD
JACKSON, LUCY	BAL	347	13TH WAR
JACKSON, LUCY	BAL	039	4TH WARD
JACKSON, LYDIA	MGM	366	BERRYS D
JACKSON, MANLSBY	BAL	016	1ST WARD
JACKSON, MANLSLY	BAL	016	1ST WARD
JACKSON, MANUEL	ANN	275	ANNAPOLI
JACKSON, MARGARET	ANN	323	2ND DIST
JACKSON, MARGARET	BAL	346	7TH WARD
JACKSON, MARGARET	BAL	397	3RD WARD
JACKSON, MARGARET	WAS	162	HAGERSTO
JACKSON, MARGRET	ANN	275	ANNAPOLI
JACKSON, MARIA	BAL	177	11TH WAR
JACKSON, MARIA	QUE	205	3RD E DI
JACKSON, MARIA	BAL	146	11TH WAR
JACKSON, MARIA	BAL	166	19TH WAR
JACKSON, MARTHA	TAL	035	EASTON D
JACKSON, MARTHA	BAL	162	11TH WAR
JACKSON, MARTHA	BAL	077	1ST WARD
JACKSON, MARTHA	BAL	247	6TH WARD
JACKSON, MARTHA	BAL	056	10TH WAR
JACKSON, MARTHA-BLACK	FRE	028	FREDERIC
JACKSON, MARTIN	HAR	048	1ST DIST
JACKSON, MARY	FRE	043	FREDERIC
JACKSON, MARY	CHA	257	MIDDLETO
JACKSON, MARY	CHA	243	HILLTOP
JACKSON, MARY	DOR	433	1ST DIST
JACKSON, MARY	DOR	422	1ST DIST
JACKSON, MARY	BAL	121	18TH WAR
JACKSON, MARY	BAL	155	11TH WAR
JACKSON, MARY	BAL	155	11TH WAR
JACKSON, MARY	BAL	470	14TH WAR
JACKSON, MARY	CAR	094	NO TWP L
JACKSON, MARY	BAL	128	11TH WAR
JACKSON, MARY	BAL	268	17TH WAR
JACKSON, MARY	BAL	207	17TH WAR
JACKSON, MARY	BAL	045	4TH WARD
JACKSON, MARY	BAL	068	4TH WARD
JACKSON, MARY	CEC	147	PORT DUP
JACKSON, MARY	MGM	315	CRACKLIN
JACKSON, MARY	BAL	177	16TH WAR
JACKSON, MARY	BAL	059	1ST WARD
JACKSON, MARY	BAL	457	8TH WARD
JACKSON, MARY	BAL	298	7TH WARD
JACKSON, MARY	BAL	370	1ST DIST
JACKSON, MARY	ST	291	2ND E DI
JACKSON, MARY	TAL	115	ST MICHA
JACKSON, MARY T.	BAL	008	1ST WARD
JACKSON, MARY T.	FRE	301	WOODSBOR
JACKSON, MARY-BLACK	CAR	133	NO TWP L
JACKSON, MATILDA	BAL	086	15TH WAR
JACKSON, MATILDA	ANN	454	HOWARD D
JACKSON, MILKY	DOR	390	1ST DIST
JACKSON, MOLLY	BAL	104	10TH WAR
JACKSON, NACE	ANN	276	ANNAPOLI
JACKSON, NANCY	BAL	255	12TH WAR
JACKSON, NANCY	TAL	117	ST MICHA
JACKSON, NAOMI	BAL	210	6TH WARD
JACKSON, NATHAN	PRI	103	SPALDING
JACKSON, NATHAN	CEC	201	6TH E DI
JACKSON, NICHOLAS	DOR	441	1ST DIST
JACKSON, NICHOLAS	ANN	416	HOWARD D
JACKSON, NOAH	SOM	541	TYASKIN
JACKSON, OCTAVO	BAL	290	1ST DIST
JACKSON, OWEN	TAL	033	EASTON D
JACKSON, PARIS	BAL	108	10TH WAR
JACKSON, PATIENCE	PRI	103	SPALDING
JACKSON, PERRY	KEN	262	1ST DIST
JACKSON, PERRY-BLACK	MGM	425	MEDLEY 3
JACKSON, PETER	BAL	388	8TH WARD
JACKSON, PETER-BLACK	FRE	386	PETERSVI
JACKSON, PETR	ANN	466	HOWARD D
JACKSON, PHEBY	BAL	182	11TH WAR
JACKSON, PHILIP	CEC	147	PORT DUP
JACKSON, PHILIP	CEC	083	CHARLEST
JACKSON, PHILIP	QUE	179	2ND E DI
JACKSON, PHILLUS-BLACK	FRE	017	FREDERIC
JACKSON, POLLY	SOM	523	BARREN C
JACKSON, PRISCILLA	BAL	418	14TH WAR
JACKSON, PRISCILLA	BAL	390	13TH WAR
JACKSON, PROSPER	BAL	286	12TH WAR
JACKSON, PURNAL	WOR	330	1ST E DI
JACKSON, RACHAEL	ANN	289	ANNAPOLI
JACKSON, RACHEL	BAL	227	6TH WARD
JACKSON, RACHEL	CEC	184	7TH E DI
JACKSON, RACHEL	CAR	333	MANCHEST
JACKSON, RACHEL A.	WAS	196	1ST DIST
JACKSON, RALPH	BAL	393	1ST DIST
JACKSON, RANDAL	BAL	344	3RD WARD
JACKSON, REBECCA	BAL	162	11TH WAR
JACKSON, REBECCA	BAL	368	3RD WARD
JACKSON, REBECCA	FRE	189	5TH E DI
JACKSON, REBECCA	BAL	020	4TH WARD
JACKSON, RESETTA	BAL	060	15TH WAR
JACKSON, RICHARD	BAL	377	1ST DIST
JACKSON, RICHARD	QUE	144	1ST E DI
JACKSON, RICHARD	CAL	028	2ND DIST
JACKSON, RICHARD J.	HAR	122	2ND DIST
JACKSON, ROBERT	FRE	452	8TH E DI
JACKSON, ROBERT	CEC	194	7TH E DI
JACKSON, ROBERT	BAL	449	8TH WARD
JACKSON, ROBERT	BAL	291	7TH WARD
JACKSON, ROBERT-MULATTO	FRE	411	8TH E DI
JACKSON, ROSE	BAL	141	11TH WAR
JACKSON, ROSE-BLACK	FRE	221	BUCKEYST
JACKSON, RUTH	BAL	172	2ND DIST
JACKSON, RUTHA *	QUE	251	5TH E DI
JACKSON, S. T.	BAL	097	10TH WAR
JACKSON, S.H.	BAL	165	1ST WARD
JACKSON, SALLY	WOR	330	1ST E DI
JACKSON, SALLY M.	WOR	282	BERLIN 1
JACKSON, SAM	DOR	436	1ST DIST
JACKSON, SAMUEL	HAR	196	3RD DIST
JACKSON, SAMUEL	BAL	122	11TH WAR
JACKSON, SAMUEL	BAL	136	11TH WAR
JACKSON, SAMUEL	CEC	189	7TH E DI
JACKSON, SAMUEL	BAL	285	17TH WAR
JACKSON, SAMUEL	CEC	179	7TH E DI
JACKSON, SAMUEL	CEC	144	PORT DUP
JACKSON, SAMUEL	BAL	373	13TH WAR
JACKSON, SAMUEL	BAL	205	17TH WAR
JACKSON, SAMUEL	BAL	353	13TH WAR
JACKSON, SAMUEL	QUE	176	2ND E DI
JACKSON, SAMUEL	SOM	520	BARREN C
JACKSON, SAMUEL	BAL	220	5TH WARD
JACKSON, SAMUEL	BAL	193	17TH WAR
JACKSON, SAMUEL	BAL	195	17TH WAR
JACKSON, SAMUEL	BAL	152	16TH WAR
JACKSON, SAMUEL	BAL	293	1ST DIST
JACKSON, SAMUEL	ANN	432	HOWARD D
JACKSON, SAMUEL	ANN	418	HOWARD D
JACKSON, SAMUEL A.	BAL	184	15TH WAR
JACKSON, SAMUEL J.	KEN	227	2ND DIST
JACKSON, SAMUEL R.	WOR	184	6TH E DI
JACKSON, SAMUEL T.	SOM	544	TYASKIN
JACKSON, SARAH	WOR	314	2ND E DI
JACKSON, SARAH	CEC	098	3RD E DI
JACKSON, SARAH A.	BAL	146	11TH WAR
JACKSON, SARAH J.	CAR	359	9TH DIST
JACKSON, SOLOMON	DOR	388	1ST DIST
JACKSON, SOPHIA	TAL	032	EASTON D
JACKSON, STEPHEN	DOR	409	1ST DIST
JACKSON, STEPHEN	DOR	430	1ST DIST
JACKSON, STEPHEN	HAR	032	1ST DIST
JACKSON, STEPHEN	ANN	462	HOWARD D
JACKSON, STEPHEN-BLACK	WOR	333	1ST E DI
JACKSON, STEVEN	ALL	073	5TH E.D.
JACKSON, SUSAN	ANN	278	ANNAPOLI
JACKSON, SUSAN	BAL	044	9TH WARD
JACKSON, SUSAN	BAL	382	8TH WARD
JACKSON, SUSAN	SOM	544	TYASKIN
JACKSON, SUSAN T.	BAL	434	14TH WAR
JACKSON, T.	BAL	177	19TH WAR
JACKSON, THOMAS	DOR	424	1ST DIST
JACKSON, THOMAS	DOR	407	1ST DIST
JACKSON, THOMAS	CEC	085	5TH E DI
JACKSON, THOMAS	MGM	350	BERRYS D
JACKSON, THOMAS	FRE	102	FREDERIC
JACKSON, THOMAS	CHA	221	ALLENS F
JACKSON, THOMAS	BAL	241	20TH WAR
JACKSON, THOMAS	CHA	258	MIDDLETO
JACKSON, THOMAS	WOR	312	2ND E DI
JACKSON, THOMAS	WAS	046	2ND SUBD
JACKSON, THOMAS	WAS	066	2ND SUBD
JACKSON, THOMAS	BAL	262	2ND WARD
JACKSON, THOMAS	BAL	143	1ST WARD
JACKSON, THOMAS	BAL	142	2ND DIST
JACKSON, THOMAS	BAL	114	1ST WARD
JACKSON, THOMAS	BAL	162	1ST WARD
JACKSON, THOMAS	BAL	388	1ST DIST
JACKSON, THOMAS A.	CHA	222	ALLENS F
JACKSON, THOMAS B.	BAL	146	1ST WARD
JACKSON, THOMAS H.	CAR	186	8TH DIST
JACKSON, THOMAS L.	KEN	240	2ND DIST
JACKSON, THOMAS-BLACK	CAR	142	NO TWP L
JACKSON, VICTOR	CEC	143	7TH E DI
JACKSON, VICTOR	HAR	086	2ND DIST
JACKSON, VINCENT	BAL	344	1ST DIST
JACKSON, VINCENT R.	BAL	157	16TH WAR
JACKSON, VINSON	PRI	115	PISCATAW
JACKSON, VIRGINIA	MGM	379	ROCKERLE
JACKSON, WARNER	BAL	120	1ST WARD
JACKSON, WASHINGTON	PRI	090	MARLBROU
JACKSON, WASHINGTON	QUE	205	3RD E DI
JACKSON, WASHINGTON-BLACK	FRE	223	BUCKEYST
JACKSON, WHITTINGTON	BAL	374	3RD WARD
JACKSON, WILLAIM	BAL	260	20TH WAR
JACKSON, WILLAIM	PRI	102	SPALDING
JACKSON, WILLAIM	WOR	228	6TH E DI
JACKSON, WILLIAM	SOM	543	TYASKIN
JACKSON, WILLIAM	TAL	105	ST MICHA
JACKSON, WILLIAM	QUE	205	3RD E DI
JACKSON, WILLIAM	TAL	091	ST MICHA
JACKSON, WILLIAM	CEC	189	7TH E DI
JACKSON, WILLIAM	DOR	385	1ST DIST
JACKSON, WILLIAM	FRE	302	WOODSBOR
JACKSON, WILLIAM	HAR	035	1ST DIST
JACKSON, WILLIAM	CEC	125	5TH E DI
JACKSON, WILLIAM	CEC	165	6TH E DI
JACKSON, WILLIAM	CAR	083	NO TWP L
JACKSON, WILLIAM	CAR	071	NO TWP L
JACKSON, WILLIAM	FRE	106	CREAGERS
JACKSON, WILLIAM	CEC	089	4TH E DI
JACKSON, WILLIAM	BAL	238	2ND WARD
JACKSON, WILLIAM	BAL	123	1ST WARD
JACKSON, WILLIAM	BAL	121	1ST WARD
JACKSON, WILLIAM	BAL	175	2ND DIST
JACKSON, WILLIAM	BAL	305	12TH WAR
JACKSON, WILLIAM	BAL	463	1ST DIST
JACKSON, WILLIAM	BAL	153	1ST WARD
JACKSON, WILLIAM	BAL	159	1ST WARD
JACKSON, WILLIAM	BAL	161	1ST WARD
JACKSON, WILLIAM	ALL	057	10TH E.D
JACKSON, WILLIAM	ALL	172	7TH E.D.
JACKSON, WILLIAM	BAL	162	11TH WAR
JACKSON, WILLIAM	BAL	004	15TH WAR
JACKSON, WILLIAM D.-BLACK	FRE	224	BUCKEYST
JACKSON, WILLIAM H.	BAL	208	6TH WARD
JACKSON, WILLIAM H.	BAL	156	16TH WAR
JACKSON, WILLIAM I.	BAL	164	1ST WARD
JACKSON, WILLIAM S.	DOR	447	1ST DIST
JACKSON, WILLIAM*	DOR	465	1ST DIST
JACKSON, WILLIAM-BLACK	ST	313	4TH E DI
JACKSON, WILLIAM-BLACK	FRE	018	FREDERIC
JACKSON, WILLIAM-BLACK	CAR	169	NO TWP L
JACKSON, WILLIAM-BLACK	CAR	169	NO TWP L
JACKSON, WILLIS	BAL	199	11TH WAR
JACKSON,BENJAMIN M.	BAL	027	2ND DIST
JACKSON,ELIZA-BLACK	CAR	106	NO TWP L
JACKSON,JACOB	BAL	124	1ST WARD
JACKSON,JAMES	BAL	063	1ST WARD
JACKSON,JOHN	BAL	137	1ST WARD
JACKSON,SUSAN	BAL	203	2ND WARD
JACO, SAMUEL	ALL	032	2ND E.D.
JACOB, ADAM	BAL	236	20TH WAR
JACOB, ANDREW	BAL	253	20TH WAR
JACOB, ANN	BAL	253	12TH WAR
JACOB, ANNA	ANN	294	1ST DIST
JACOB, ASENET	BAL	232	17TH WAR
JACOB, CATHERINE	BAL	370	3RD WARD
JACOB, DANIEL	BAL	240	1ST DIST
JACOB, EDWARD	ANN	404	8TH DIST
JACOB, EDWIN	CAR	277	7TH DIST
JACOB, ELIZABETH	ANN	267	ANNAPOLI
JACOB, EVA	BAL	245	20TH WAR
JACOB, HOWARD	ANN	348	3RD DIST
JACOB, JACOB	BAL	295	1ST DIST
JACOB, JAMES	BAL	274	12TH WAR
JACOB, JOHN	BAL	248	20TH WAR
JACOB, MEYER	BAL	015	9TH WARD
JACOB, MICHAEL	BAL	009	1ST WARD
JACOB, RICHARD J.	ANN	391	4TH DIST
JACOB, WILLIAM H.	CAR	295	7TH DIST
JACOBI, GEORGE	BAL	397	14TH WAR
JACOBI, MARY	HAR	076	BEL AIR
JACOBI, THOMAS J.	HAR	076	BEL AIR
JACOBS, ABRAHAM	BAL	274	1ST DIST
JACOBS, ADAM	CAR	400	2ND DIST
JACOBS, AMANDA	DOR	447	1ST DIST
JACOBS, ANGELINA	ALL	133	4TH E.D.
JACOBS, ANN	BAL	066	1ST WARD
JACOBS, ANN	BAL	128	11TH WAR
JACOBS, ARRAMINTA	KEN	297	3RD DIST
JACOBS, ASA	ALL	133	4TH E.D.
JACOBS, BARBARA	FRE	277	NEW MARK
JACOBS, BETSY	ANN	363	4TH DIST
JACOBS, C. W.	WOR	263	BERLIN 1
JACOBS, CATHARINE	BAL	217	2ND WARD
JACOBS, CHARLES	ANN	275	ANNAPOLI
JACOBS, DANIEL	WAS	283	1ST DIST

Name	County	Page	District
JACOBS, DANIEL	FRE	263	NEW MARK
JACOBS, DAVID	FRE	259	NEW MARK
JACOBS, DAVID	WAS	065	2ND SUBD
JACOBS, DAVID	ALL	133	4TH E.D.
JACOBS, DAVID	BAL	302	7TH WARD
JACOBS, DENNIS	BAL	280	1ST DIST
JACOBS, DORSEY	ANN	358	3RD DIST
JACOBS, EDWARD	KEN	253	1ST DIST
JACOBS, EDWARD C.	WAS	021	2ND SUBD
JACOBS, ELIZA	BAL	391	14TH WAR
JACOBS, ELIZA	BAL	056	10TH WAR
JACOBS, ELIZABETH	ALL	123	4TH E.D.
JACOBS, EMANUEL	WAS	194	1ST DIST
JACOBS, FRANK	DOR	299	1ST DIST
JACOBS, FREDERICK	BAL	100	18TH WAR
JACOBS, FREDERICK	BAL	004	9TH WARD
JACOBS, GEORGE	BAL	199	6TH WARD
JACOBS, GEORGE	BAL	456	1ST DIST
JACOBS, GEORGE	CAR	206	4TH DIST
JACOBS, GEORGE W.	FRE	234	BUCKEYST
JACOBS, HENRY	MGM	348	BERRYS D
JACOBS, HENRY	FRE	074	FREDERIC
JACOBS, HENRY	ALL	122	4TH E.D.
JACOBS, HENRY	KEN	259	1ST DIST
JACOBS, HENRY *	KEN	277	1ST DIST
JACOBS, HETTY S.	HAR	128	2ND DIST
JACOBS, HINCAMEY	ALL	133	4TH E.D.
JACOBS, IGNATUS	FRE	359	CATOCTIN
JACOBS, J.H.	BAL	107	1ST WARD
JACOBS, JACOB	ALL	133	4TH E.D.
JACOBS, JAMES	ANN	370	4TH DIST
JACOBS, JAMES M.	BAL	328	3RD WARD
JACOBS, JAMES M.	HAR	094	2ND DIST
JACOBS, JANE	FRE	262	NEW MARK
JACOBS, JOHN	FRE	372	CATOCTIN
JACOBS, JOHN	BAL	417	3RD WARD
JACOBS, JOHN	ANN	338	3RD DIST
JACOBS, JOHN	ANN	330	2ND DIST
JACOBS, JOHN	BAL	199	6TH WARD
JACOBS, JOHN	BAL	391	3RD WARD
JACOBS, JOHN A.	CAR	388	2ND DIST
JACOBS, JOHN C.	BAL	097	18TH WAR
JACOBS, JOHN F.	BAL	236	17TH WAR
JACOBS, JOHN-BLACK	WOR	332	1ST E DI
JACOBS, JOHN-MULATTO	FRE	208	BUCKEYST
JACOBS, JOSEPH	WAS	048	2ND SUBD
JACOBS, JOSEPH M.	FRE	448	8TH E DI
JACOBS, JULIAN	BAL	099	1ST WARD
JACOBS, JULIA	ANN	268	ANNAPOLI
JACOBS, JULIA	BAL	227	17TH WAR
JACOBS, KENDLE M.	DOR	321	1ST DIST
JACOBS, LEVENY	BAL	254	20TH WAR
JACOBS, LEVI	ALL	133	4TH E.D.
JACOBS, LOUIS	BAL	165	16TH WAR
JACOBS, MARGARET	ALL	122	4TH E.D.
JACOBS, MARGARETT	BAL	045	4TH WARD
JACOBS, MARIA	BAL	304	7TH WARD
JACOBS, MARK	BAL	285	7TH WARD
JACOBS, MARTHA E.	BAL	274	17TH WAR
JACOBS, MARY	FRE	243	NEW MARK
JACOBS, MARY	DOR	447	1ST DIST
JACOBS, MARY	BAL	378	1ST DIST
JACOBS, MARY A.	BAL	115	11TH WAR
JACOBS, MATTHEW	ALL	121	4TH E.D.
JACOBS, MICHAEL	FRE	108	CREAGERS
JACOBS, NORMAN	ALL	124	4TH E.D.
JACOBS, OLIVER	WAS	092	2ND SUBD
JACOBS, PERRY	KEN	274	1ST DIST
JACOBS, PETER	BAL	462	1ST DIST
JACOBS, PRICILLA	BAL	286	7TH WARD
JACOBS, RACHAEL	KEN	253	1ST DIST
JACOBS, SAMUEL	BAL	013	9TH WARD
JACOBS, SAMUEL	BAL	071	15TH WAR
JACOBS, SARAH	BAL	069	10TH WAR
JACOBS, SARAH	HAR	080	2ND DIST
JACOBS, SARAH P.	BAL	149	16TH WAR
JACOBS, THEODORE	FRE	427	8TH E DI
JACOBS, THOMAS	BAL	306	12TH WAR
JACOBS, THOMAS A.	KEN	282	3RD DIST
JACOBS, THOMAS-BLACK	WOR	322	1ST E DI
JACOBS, WILHELMINA	ANN	382	4TH DIST
JACOBS, WILLIAM	ALL	117	5TH E.D.
JACOBS, WILLIAM	KEN	278	1ST DIST
JACOBS, WILLIAM	FRE	106	CREAGERS
JACOBS, WILLIAM	FRE	108	CREAGERS
JACOBS, WILLIAM	BAL	080	18TH WAR
JACOBS, WILLIAM HENRY	MGM	348	BERRYS D
JACOBS, ZACHARIAH	BAL	149	16TH WAR
JACOBSEN, HENRY G.	BAL	080	15TH WAR
JACOBSON, H.	BAL	117	1ST WARD
JACOBSON, H.	BAL	166	1ST WARD
JACOBSON, H.	BAL	171	1ST WARD
JACQUES, MARY	WAS	102	2ND DIST
JAEBOT, JANE	BAL	289	12TH WAR
JAEKINS, JOSEPH *	BAL	413	1ST DIST
JAG, PEGGY	BAL	030	2ND DIST
JAGER, ANTHONY	BAL	386	13TH WAR
JAGER, JOHN	BAL	220	2ND WARD
JAHATS, S.	ANN	284	ANNAPOLI
JAHUM, ELIZABETH	BAL	351	7TH WARD
JAIHN, SOLOMON	BAL	265	2ND WARD
JAINER, JOHN	BAL	119	1ST WARD
JAKCSON, JOSHUA	CAR	334	6TH DIST
JAKEES, HENRY	BAL	186	11TH WAR
JAKES, CHARLOTTE	BAL	369	13TH WAR
JAKES, FREDERICK	BAL	132	11TH WAR
JAKES, GEORGE	BAL	171	1ST WARD
JAKES, RALPH	BAL	132	11TH WAR
JAMAR, ELIZABETH	CAR	148	NO TWP L
JAMAR, JAMES H.	CEC	005	ELKTON 3
JAMAR, RUBEN	CEC	006	ELKTON 3
JAMAR, SUSAN	BAL	442	14TH WAR
JAMART, MICHAEL	BAL	029	9TH WARD
JAMASON, WILLIAM	BAL	134	1ST WARD
JAME, REBECCA	SOM	489	SALISBUR
JAMEISON, JOHN J.	FRE	273	NEW MARK
JAMERSON, WALTER	CHA	267	BOJANTOW
JAMES, ABEL	HAR	038	1ST DIST
JAMES, ABEL	BAL	174	2ND DIST
JAMES, ABLE D.	BAL	227	1ST DIST
JAMES, ACHSHAH	BAL	355	13TH WAR
JAMES, ALEXANDER	CAR	144	NO TWP L
JAMES, ALLEN	TAL	077	EASTON T
JAMES, AMOS	WAS	033	2ND SUBD
JAMES, AMOS	ALL	162	6TH E.D.
JAMES, AN	HAR	139	2ND DIST
JAMES, ANN	HAR	135	2ND DIST
JAMES, ANN	BAL	203	17TH WAR
JAMES, ANN	BAL	298	12TH WAR
JAMES, ANN M.	BAL	378	3RD WARD

Name	County	Page	District
JAMES, ANNA A.	TAL	104	ST MICHA
JAMES, B.	BAL	072	10TH WAR
JAMES, BAKER	FRE	094	FREDERIC
JAMES, BANE	BAL	257	12TH WAR
JAMES, BENJAMIN-BLACK	FRE	049	FREDERIC
JAMES, BENNETT	WAS	030	2ND SUBD
JAMES, BETSY	DOR	399	1ST DIST
JAMES, CAROLINE	HAR	096	2ND DIST
JAMES, CAROLINE	BAL	221	17TH WAR
JAMES, CASSIAH	CEC	130	6TH E DI
JAMES, CATHERINE	BAL	317	20TH WAR
JAMES, CHALRES	MGM	423	MEDLEY 3
JAMES, CHARLES	BAL	161	11TH WAR
JAMES, CHARLES	BAL	165	2ND DIST
JAMES, CHARLES *	BAL	292	1ST DIST
JAMES, CHARLES E.	MGM	401	ROCKERLE
JAMES, CHARLOTTE	ANN	356	3RD DIST
JAMES, CHRISTIAN	BAL	154	19TH WAR
JAMES, CYRUS-BLACK	FRE	048	FREDERIC
JAMES, DANIEL	BAL	270	17TH WAR
JAMES, DANIEL N.	CAR	147	NO TWP L
JAMES, DAVID	BAL	453	14TH WAR
JAMES, DAVID	CEC	206	7TH E DI
JAMES, E.	BAL	153	1ST WARD
JAMES, EDWARD	BAL	190	6TH WARD
JAMES, EDWARD	BAL	401	14TH WAR
JAMES, EDWARD	BAL	231	17TH WAR
JAMES, EDWARD T.	TAL	053	EASTON D
JAMES, ELIAS	FRE	211	BUCKEYST
JAMES, ELIZA	BAL	213	11TH WAR
JAMES, ELIZA A.	DOR	300	1ST DIST
JAMES, ELIZABETH	BAL	348	13TH WAR
JAMES, ELIZABETH	HAR	013	1ST DIST
JAMES, ELIZABETH	HAR	040	1ST DIST
JAMES, ELIZABETH	BAL	088	18TH WAR
JAMES, ELIZABETH	BAL	083	18TH WAR
JAMES, ELIZABETH A.	TAL	102	ST MICHA
JAMES, ELLEN	BAL	084	15TH WAR
JAMES, FANNY	HAR	093	2ND DIST
JAMES, FIELDING	HAR	141	2ND DIST
JAMES, FLORA	BAL	168	19TH WAR
JAMES, GEORGE	BAL	418	14TH WAR
JAMES, GEORGE	HAR	131	2ND DIST
JAMES, GEORGE	BAL	146	5TH WARD
JAMES, GEORGE	ANN	416	HOWARD D
JAMES, GEORGE	BAL	110	1ST WARD
JAMES, GEORGE	BAL	054	1ST WARD
JAMES, GEORGE	BAL	255	6TH WARD
JAMES, GEORGE	BAL	459	1ST DIST
JAMES, GEORGE	WOR	229	6TH E DI
JAMES, GEORGE J.	WOR	310	2ND E DI
JAMES, GEORGIANA	BAL	189	5TH DIST
JAMES, GRANDISON	BAL	213	6TH WARD
JAMES, H.	BAL	376	8TH WARD
JAMES, HANAH*	BAL	118	1ST WARD
JAMES, HARRIET	DOR	434	1ST DIST
JAMES, HARRIET	WAS	100	2ND DIST
JAMES, HENRY	TAL	034	EASTON D
JAMES, HENRY	TAL	069	EASTON T
JAMES, HENRY	WAS	200	1ST DIST
JAMES, HENRY	BAL	243	17TH WAR
JAMES, HENRY	FRE	063	FREDERIC
JAMES, HENRY	BAL	099	1ST WARD
JAMES, HENRY	BAL	057	10TH WAR
JAMES, HIRAM	BAL	144	5TH WARD
JAMES, HJENRY	BAL	178	2ND DIST
JAMES, HORATIO	MGM	400	ROCKERLE
JAMES, ISAAC	DOR	306	1ST DIST
JAMES, ISAAC	BAL	077	4TH WARD
JAMES, ISAAC*	DOR	435	1ST DIST
JAMES, JACOB	HAR	132	2ND DIST
JAMES, JACOB-BLACK	CAR	130	NO TWP L
JAMES, JAMES	DOR	397	1ST DIST
JAMES, JAMES M. C.	WOR	229	6TH E DI
JAMES, JANE	TAL	034	EASTON D
JAMES, JOHN	TAL	040	EASTON D
JAMES, JOHN	TAL	034	EASTON D
JAMES, JOHN	WAS	049	2ND SUBD
JAMES, JOHN	TAL	061	EASTON D
JAMES, JOHN	WAS	161	2ND DIST
JAMES, JOHN	DOR	399	1ST DIST
JAMES, JOHN	BAL	399	14TH WAR
JAMES, JOHN	HAR	103	2ND DIST
JAMES, JOHN	FRE	434	8TH E DI
JAMES, JOHN	BAL	114	1ST WARD
JAMES, JOHN	BAL	158	2ND DIST
JAMES, JOHN	BAL	251	1ST DIST
JAMES, JOHN	BAL	213	6TH WARD
JAMES, JOHN	BAL	125	1ST WARD
JAMES, JOHN	BAL	309	3RD WARD
JAMES, JOHN	ALL	170	6TH E.D.
JAMES, JOHN	ALL	135	4TH E.D.
JAMES, JOHN	ALL	080	5TH E.D.
JAMES, JOHN C.	TAL	052	EASTON D
JAMES, JOHN D.	ALL	080	5TH E.D.
JAMES, JOHN H.	BAL	206	17TH WAR
JAMES, JOHN J.	MGM	378	ROCKERLE
JAMES, JOHN L.	BAL	050	1ST WARD
JAMES, JOSEPH	HAR	027	1ST DIST
JAMES, JOSEPH	BAL	084	4TH WARD
JAMES, JOSEPH	FRE	306	WOODSBOR
JAMES, JOSEPH	QUE	147	1ST E DI
JAMES, JOSEPH	TAL	104	ST MICHA
JAMES, JOSEPH H.	TAL	041	EASTON D
JAMES, JOSEPH-BLACK	QUE	147	1ST E DI
JAMES, JOSHUA	HAR	132	2ND DIST
JAMES, JULIAN	BAL	375	1ST DIST
JAMES, KENNEY	BAL	067	10TH WAR
JAMES, LANT	HAR	141	2ND DIST
JAMES, LAURENA	SOM	513	BARREN C
JAMES, LEVI	BAL	012	1ST WARD
JAMES, LOUIZA	CAR	154	NO TWP L
JAMES, LYDIA	BAL	307	12TH WAR
JAMES, M.	BAL	148	1ST WARD
JAMES, MALINDA-BLACK	FRE	051	FREDERIC
JAMES, MARIA	BAL	279	12TH WAR
JAMES, MARIAH	TAL	035	EASTON D
JAMES, MARIE	BAL	286	20TH WAR
JAMES, MARIE*	DOR	383	1ST DIST
JAMES, MARY	FRE	094	FREDERIC
JAMES, MARY	BAL	346	13TH WAR
JAMES, MARY	BAL	063	10TH WAR
JAMES, MARY	BAL	163	16TH WAR
JAMES, MARY	BAL	178	16TH WAR
JAMES, MARY	BAL	037	9TH WARD
JAMES, MARY J.	TAL	052	EASTON D
JAMES, MATHEW	TAL	026	EASTON D
JAMES, MILLY	BAL	302	12TH WAR
JAMES, N.	BAL	161	1ST WARD
JAMES, NACHAN	BAL	269	20TH WAR

Name	County	Page	District
JAMES, NANCY	BAL	139	2ND DIST
JAMES, NATHAN	BAL	248	1ST DIST
JAMES, PEGGY	BAL	108	5TH WARD
JAMES, PERRY-BLACK	CAR	131	NO TWP L
JAMES, PETER	ANN	486	HOWARD D
JAMES, PETER-BLACK	CAR	156	NO TWP L
JAMES, PHILLIP	ANN	320	2ND DIST
JAMES, RACHAL	ALL	143	6TH E.D.
JAMES, REBECCA	BAL	251	1ST DIST
JAMES, REBECCA	HAR	048	1ST DIST
JAMES, RELUE	BAL	249	12TH WAR
JAMES, RESIN	WAS	032	2ND SUBD
JAMES, RHESA	WAS	019	2ND SUBD
JAMES, ROBERT	HAR	057	1ST DIST
JAMES, ROBERT-BLACK	QUE	185	3RD E DI
JAMES, ROSA	BAL	077	10TH WAR
JAMES, ROSETTA	BAL	067	10TH WAR
JAMES, S.	BAL	269	20TH WAR
JAMES, SAMUEL	HAR	036	1ST DIST
JAMES, SAMUEL	HAR	039	1ST DIST
JAMES, SAMUEL	HAR	087	2ND DIST
JAMES, SAMUEL	BAL	238	17TH WAR
JAMES, SAMUEL	BAL	286	12TH WAR
JAMES, SAMUEL	BAL	430	8TH WARD
JAMES, SARAH	BAL	023	4TH WARD
JAMES, SARAH C.	TAL	056	EASTON D
JAMES, SENSEY	TAL	075	EASTON T
JAMES, SOLOMON	WAS	138	HAGERSTO
JAMES, SOLOMON	WAS	138	HAGERSTO
JAMES, SUSAN	BAL	075	10TH WAR
JAMES, SUSANAH	BAL	013	4TH WARD
JAMES, SUSANNAH	BAL	203	11TH WAR
JAMES, THOMAS	BAL	101	10TH WAR
JAMES, THOMAS	BAL	003	1ST WARD
JAMES, THOMAS	BAL	156	2ND DIST
JAMES, THOMAS	BAL	384	3RD WARD
JAMES, THOMAS C.	BAL	263	2ND WARD
JAMES, THOMAS M.	HAR	104	2ND DIST
JAMES, UPTON	HAR	055	1ST DIST
JAMES, URIAS	CAR	405	2ND DIST
JAMES, VILETTA	BAL	181	2ND DIST
JAMES, VIOLETTA	BAL	293	20TH WAR
JAMES, WALTER	WAS	028	2ND SUBD
JAMES, WALTER	WAS	052	2ND SUBD
JAMES, WASHINGTON	FRE	015	FREDERIC
JAMES, WILLIAM	HAR	084	2ND DIST
JAMES, WILLIAM	HAR	142	2ND DIST
JAMES, WILLIAM	TAL	033	EASTON D
JAMES, WILLIAM	TAL	037	EASTON D
JAMES, WILLIAM	WAS	111	2ND DIST
JAMES, WILLIAM	TAL	003	EASTON D
JAMES, WILLIAM	TAL	102	ST MICHA
JAMES, WILLIAM	QUE	239	5TH E DI
JAMES, WILLIAM	QUE	210	3RD E DI
JAMES, WILLIAM	QUE	201	3RD E DI
JAMES, WILLIAM	SOM	493	SALISBUR
JAMES, WILLIAM	BAL	115	2ND DIST
JAMES, WILLIAM	BAL	140	2ND DIST
JAMES, WILLIAM C.	HAR	141	2ND DIST
JAMES, WILLIAM S.	DOR	373	1ST DIST
JAMES, WILLIAM-BLACK	CAR	135	NO TWP L
JAMES, WILLIAM-BLACK	CAR	071	NO TWP L
JAMES, WILLIAM-BLACK	QUE	201	3RD E DI
JAMES, WILLIAM-BLACK	QUE	199	3RD E DI
JAMES.DANIEL	BAL	125	1ST WARD
JAMES.MARY	BAL	033	1ST WARD
JAMES.RICHARD	BAL	128	1ST WARD
JAMES.WILLIAM	QUE	198	3RD E DI
JAMES.WILLIAM	QUE	201	3RD E DI
JAMESON, ANDREW	BAL	132	1ST WARD
JAMESON, ANDREW	BAL	305	1ST DIST
JAMESON, BENJAMIN	CHA	245	HILLTOP
JAMESON, BENJAMIN H.	CHA	269	ALLENS F
JAMESON, ELIZA	CHA	258	BOJANTOW
JAMESON, ELIZA	CHA	257	MIDDLETO
JAMESON, F.A.	ALL	192	9TH E.D.
JAMESON, HORATIO G. DR.	BAL	346	13TH WAR
JAMESON, HY A.	ALL	192	9TH E.D.
JAMESON, JANE	BAL	297	3RD WARD
JAMESON, JOHNSTON	CAR	307	1ST DIST
JAMESON, L.M.	ALL	174	7TH E.D.
JAMESON, MARY J.	CHA	293	BOJANTOW
JAMESON, REBECCA	BAL	013	4TH WARD
JAMESON, SAMUEL	CAR	293	7TH DIST
JAMESON, SAMUEL	CHA	276	ALLENS F
JAMESON, THOMAS A.	CHA	258	MIDDLETO
JAMESON, WILLAIM	BAL	352	7TH WARD
JAMESON, WILLIAM	ALL	107	5TH E.D.
JAMESON,IGNATIUS	MGM	421	MEDLEY 3
JAMIESON, ANDREW	BAL	079	10TH WAR
JAMIESON, ANDREW	BAL	079	10TH WAR
JAMIESON, CATHARINE	BAL	250	6TH WARD
JAMIESON, MARIAH	WAS	084	2ND SUBD
JAMIESON, SARAH	BAL	461	14TH WAR
JAMILSON, JAMES M.	BAL	213	5TH DIST
JAMISON, ALEXANDER	FRE	228	BUCKEYST
JAMISON, ALEXIUS	FRE	067	FREDERIC
JAMISON, ANN	BAL	149	11TH WAR
JAMISON, ARCHIBALD	BAL	173	19TH WAR
JAMISON, C. C.	BAL	061	10TH WAR
JAMISON, CAHTARINE	FRE	227	BUCKEYST
JAMISON, CAROLINE	CEC	100	3RD E DI
JAMISON, CECELIA	ALL	192	9TH E.D.
JAMISON, DAVID	BAL	100	2ND DIST
JAMISON, GEORGE	CEC	100	3RD E DI
JAMISON, HANNAH	CEC	089	4TH E DI
JAMISON, HORATIO G.	QUE	180	2ND E DI
JAMISON, JAMES	WAS	062	2ND SUBD
JAMISON, JAMES L.	CEC	112	4TH E DI
JAMISON, JOHN	CEC	100	3RD E DI
JAMISON, JOHN	WAS	061	2ND SUBD
JAMISON, JOHN	BAL	089	5TH WARD
JAMISON, LOUISA	BAL	061	10TH WAR
JAMISON, MALRY	BAL	052	9TH WARD
JAMISON, MARY	BAL	314	20TH WAR
JAMISON, PHILIP	WAS	061	2ND SUBD
JAMISON, RICHARD B.	ALL	032	2ND E.D.
JAMISON, ROBERT JR.	BAL	084	15TH WAR
JAMISON, SARAH	CEC	200	7TH E DI
JAMISON, THOMAS	WOR	264	BERLIN 1
JAMISON, THOMAS W.	BAL	052	9TH WARD
JAMISON, WILLIAM	BAL	387	8TH WARD
JAMISON, WILLIAM	BAL	020	15TH WAR
JAMISON, WILLIAM	BAL	121	1ST WARD
JAMISON, WILLIAM	BAL	320	20TH WAR
JAMISON, WILLIAM	CEC	123	3RD E DI
JAMISON, WILLIAM D.	BAL	149	11TH WAR
JAMISON, WILLIAM D.	BAL	149	11TH WAR
JAMISON, WILLIAM J.	BAL	173	19TH WAR
JAMMESON, JOHN	BAL	171	6TH WARD

JAMMISON, MARY BAL 112 5TH WARD
JAMP, JOSIAH DOR 380 1ST DIST
JAMS, HANNAH* DOR 434 1ST DIST
JAMS, HARRIETT J. FRE 424 8TH E DI
JAMS, JOHN D. BAL 269 12TH WAR
JAMS, MARIE* DOR 383 1ST DIST
JAMSON, AMELIA CHA 293 BOJANTOW
JANAGAN, DAVID BAL 001 1ST WARD
JANE, ELIZA BAL 141 19TH WAR
JANE, WILLIAM BAL 017 1ST WARD
JANEHARPIER, JOHN BAL 226 2ND WARD
JANES, CHARLES * BAL 292 1ST DIST
JANES, CLARISSA BAL 452 1ST DIST
JANES, EDWARD BAL 393 1ST DIST
JANES, GEORGE BAL 461 1ST DIST
JANES, JAMES BAL 462 1ST DIST
JANES, JOHN BAL 257 2ND WARD
JANES, MARY BAL 459 1ST DIST
JANES, THOMAS R. BAL 355 1ST DIST
JANEST, JESSE BAL 254 12TH WAR
JANETT, B. BAL 118 1ST WARD
JANETT, CHARLES BAL 120 1ST WARD
JANETTE, JOHUTA * ALL 107 5TH E.D.
JANEY, RICHARD M. BAL 102 2ND DIST
JANEY, TABITHA BAL 229 12TH WAR
JANISON, ROBERT M. BAL 001 1ST WARD
JANK, JOHN BAL 107 1ST WARD
JANKINS, JAMES H. BAL 298 7TH WARD
JANNER, GEORGE CEC 125 5TH E DI
JANNESS, JAMES HAR 099 2ND DIST
JANNETT, THOMAS BAL 241 12TH WAR
JANNEY, ELI CEC 139 6TH E DI
JANNEY, HANNAH H. BAL 383 13TH WAR
JANNEY, JOHN CEC 139 6TH E DI
JANNEY, JOHN T. MGM 319 CRACKLIN
JANNEY, THOMAS CEC 139 6TH E DI
JANNY, MARGARET BAL 263 2ND WARD
JANPEN, J. BAL 167 1ST WARD
JANSBURY, ANNA BAL 359 13TH WAR
JANSEN, J. BAL 162 1ST WARD
JANSEN, JOHN G. BAL 161 1ST WARD
JANSON, HENRY BAL 159 1ST WARD
JANSON, J. BAL 166 1ST WARD
JANSON, J. BAL 136 1ST WARD
JANSON, JAME SH. BAL 017 2ND DIST
JANUARY, DANIEL BAL 291 20TH WAR
JANUAY, JANE BAL 061 2ND DIST
JAOCB, BANE BAL 255 12TH WAR
JAONE, CASANDER F. HAR 191 3RD DIST
JAOSN, EPHRAIM CAR 393 2ND DIST
JAQUES, DENTON WAS 114 2ND DIST
JAQUES, GEORGE L. WAS 115 2ND DIST
JAQUES, GIDEON CEC 140 6TH E DI
JAQUES, LANCELOTT WAS 123 2ND DIST
JAR, SARAH WOR 298 9TH E DI
JARBEC, JOANNA ST 305 2ND E DI
JARBOE, ELIZABETH ST 261 3RD E DI
JARBOE, ELLEN PRI 101 SPALDING
JARBOE, ELLEN CAL 035 2ND DIST
JARBOE, FRANCIS M. ST 280 3RD E DI
JARBOE, GEORGE W. ST 322 4TH E DI
JARBOE, JAMES T. ST 337 4TH E DI
JAREOE, JAMES T. ST 285 2ND E DI
JARBOE, JOHN B. ST 255 3RD E DI
JARBOE, JOHN B. ST 321 4TH E DI
JARBOE, JOHN R. BAL 087 4TH WARD
JARBOE, JOHN W. BAL 262 12TH WAR
JARBOE, MARGARET FRE 403 JEFFERSO
JARBOE, MATTHEW ST 277 3RD E DI
JARBOE, RAPHAEL FRE 166 EMMITTSB
JARBOE, SAMUEL FRE 222 BUCKEYST
JARBOE, THOMAS ST 278 3RD E DI
JARBOE, WILLIAM A. PRI 101 SPALDING
JARBOE, WILLIAM H. ALL 215 CUMBERLA
JARBOE, WILLIAM J. ST 308 1ST E DI
JARBOR, J. A. ST 280 3RD E DI
JARBOR, SARAH ST 276 3RD E DI
JARBOUR, DAVID BAL 157 1ST WARD
JARBSON, WILLIAM TAL 115 ST MICHA
JARERS, JARREIT MGM 407 MEDLEY 3
JARET, JACOB ALL 092 5TH E.D.
JARET, MARY ALL 092 5TH E.D.
JARGER, HARMAN ANN 471 HOWARD D
JARIETT, MARGRET DOR 361 3RD DIVI
JARKSON, PETER TAL 074 EASTON T
JARMAN, GEORGE WOR 254 1ST CENS
JARMAN, HANNAH CAR 099 NO TWP L
JARMAN, JOHN-BLACK CAR 068 NO TWP L
JARMAN, LOUIZA CAR 097 NO TWP L
JARMAN, NATHAN CAR 076 NO TWP L
JARMAN, ROBERT CAR 075 NO TWP L
JARMAN, SAMUEL KEN 301 3RD DIST
JARMAN, SAMUEL J. QUE 137 1ST E DI
JARMAN, WESLEY QUE 219 3RD E DI
JARMON, ANANIAS WOR 282 BERLIN 1
JARMON, ANANIAS WOR 266 BERLIN 1
JARMON, JESSE WOR 255 1ST CENS
JARMON, JOHN WOR 281 BERLIN 1
JARMON, JOHN WOR 285 BERLIN 1
JARMON, KENDAL T. WOR 294 9TH E DI
JARMON, LITTLETON WOR 251 1ST CENS
JARMON, LOTTY WOR 267 BERLIN 1
JARMON, MARGARET WOR 255 1ST CENS
JARMON, MC KINNA WOR 257 1ST CENS
JARMOT, J.E. BAL 135 1ST WARD
JARN, JOHN * CAR 331 MANCHEST
JARNHART, CATHERINE FRE 058 FREDERIC
JARR, WESLEY B.* BAL 085 10TH WAR
JARRALL, JOHN BAL 280 2ND WARD
JARREL, ANN E. QUE 141 1ST E DI
JARREL, CHARLES E. CAR 166 NO TWP L
JARREL, RICHARD QUE 146 1ST E DI
JARREL, ROBERT QUE 140 1ST E DI
JARREL, WILLIAM H. QUE 146 1ST E DI
JARRELL, RICHARD-BLACK CAR 076 NO TWP L
JARRELL, SAMUEL-BLACK QUE 128 1ST E DI
JARRELL, THOMAS CAR 076 NO TWP L
JARRETT, ABRAHAM SOM 544 TYASKIN
JARRETT, ABRAHAM L. HAR 077 BEL AIR
JARRETT, ASBURY BAL 040 4TH WARD
JARRETT, CAROLINE BAL 249 17TH WAR
JARRETT, DEVERAUX HAR 059 1ST DIST
JARRETT, EDWARD HAR 059 1ST DIST
JARRETT, ELIZABETH L. HAR 140 2ND DIST
JARRETT, FRANCES BAL 284 7TH WARD
JARRETT, HAYARD SOM 543 TYASKIN
JARRETT, HENRY C. BAL 044 4TH WARD
JARRETT, J. BAL 151 1ST WARD
JARRETT, JACOB HAR 105 2ND DIST
JARRETT, JACOB HAR 088 2ND DIST
JARRETT, JESSE BAL 088 2ND DIST
JARRETT, JOHN BAL 123 16TH WAR
JARRETT, JOHN BAL 282 17TH WAR
JARRETT, LAFEVER BAL 140 5TH WARD
JARRETT, LUTHER M. HAR 070 1ST DIST
JARRETT, MANN BAL 300 12TH WAR
JARRETT, MITCHELL SOM 541 TYASKIN
JARRIE, JOHN* SOM 392 BRINKLEY
JARVES, ROBERT CEC 125 5TH E DI
JARVIS, AMELIA BAL 085 15TH WAR
JARVIS, AMOS BAL 087 15TH WAR
JARVIS, ANNA BAL 188 6TH WARD
JARVIS, CORNELIA F.* BAL 109 15TH WAR
JARVIS, EDGAR WOR 262 BERLIN 1
JARVIS, EDWARD WOR 279 BERLIN 1
JARVIS, ELIZABETH WOR 270 BERLIN 1
JARVIS, ELIZABETH WOR 201 3RD E DI
JARVIS, ELIZABETH BAL 023 9TH WARD
JARVIS, ELIZABETH MGM 407 MEDLEY 3
JARVIS, ELIZABETH BAL 077 18TH WAR
JARVIS, EMILY CEC 197 7TH E DI
JARVIS, FRANCIS CEC 118 4TH E DI
JARVIS, GEORGE WOR 300 SNOW HIL
JARVIS, HENDAL WOR 262 BERLIN 1
JARVIS, HENNETTA * BAL 344 13TH WAR
JARVIS, HENRY W. WOR 261 BERLIN 1
JARVIS, ISAIH* DOR 438 1ST DIST
JARVIS, J.H. BAL 162 1ST WARD
JARVIS, JAMES CEC 128 5TH E DI
JARVIS, JAMES SOM 428 PRINCESS
JARVIS, JAMES W. BAL 283 20TH WAR
JARVIS, JOHN BAL 376 3RD WARD
JARVIS, JOHN BAL 371 1ST DIST
JARVIS, LEONARD BAL 105 10TH WAR
JARVIS, MARY BAL 302 7TH WARD
JARVIS, NANCY SOM 465 HANGARY
JARVIS, SARAH BAL 186 6TH WARD
JARVIS, SARAH SOM 425 PRINCESS
JARVIS, SARAH CEC 128 5TH E DI
JARVIS, SEVERN WOR 264 BERLIN 1
JARVIS, SOPHIA BAL 048 4TH WARD
JARVIS, WILLIAM DOR 381 1ST DIST
JARVIS, WILLIAM H. BAL 310 7TH WARD
JASLINE, WILLIAM W. BAL 123 1ST WARD
JASON, AARON ANN 511 HOWARD D
JASON, ELIZA-BLACK MGM 420 MEDLEY 3
JASON, ELLEN-BLACK MGM 425 MEDLEY 3
JASON, JOHN BAL 084 1ST WARD
JASON, REBECCA ANN 487 HOWARD D
JASON, RICHARD-BLACK MGM 422 MEDLEY 3
JASON, WILLIAM J. BAL 317 3RD WARD
JASPER, ELIZABETH BAL 049 1ST WARD
JASPER, JOSEPH TAL 054 EASTON D
JASPER, WILLIAM DOR 299 1ST DIST
JATJE, HENY BAL 186 2ND WARD
JATTERSON, JAMES BAL 177 19TH WAR
JAUFMAN, BENJAMIN FRE 103 FREDERIC
JAWES, CHARLES * BAL 292 1ST DIST
JAWS, ISAAC* SOM 370 BRINKLEY
JAY, JOHN HAR 164 3RD DIST
JAY, JOSEPH W. BAL 084 15TH WAR
JAY, JOSH HAR 029 1ST DIST
JAY, SAMUEL HAR 105 2ND DIST
JAY, SARAH BAL 311 3RD WARD
JAY, THOMAS W. BAL 076 15TH WAR
JAYCE, NICKOLAS BAL 184 5TH DIST
JOUFFIDLD, ZIPPORAH A. WOR 299 SNOW HIL
JEAN, GEORGE HENRY BAL 466 14TH WAR
JEAN, J. BAL 241 12TH WAR
JEAN, MARCELLA BAL 193 19TH WAR
JEANERET, CHARLES BAL 038 9TH WARD
JEANES, MARY BAL 299 1ST DIST
JEANES, NANCY PRI 085 QUEEN AN
JEANS, ANN BAL 050 18TH WAR
JEANS, EDWARD H. CEC 131 6TH E DI
JEANS, FRANCES A. ANN 477 HOWARD D
JEANS, GEORGE ANN 438 HOWARD D
JEANS, JOSEPH ANN 444 HOWARD D
JEANS, MARY E. ANN 438 HOWARD D
JEANS, RICHARD BAL 210 11TH WAR
JEANS, TIBATHA ANN 436 HOWARD D
JEANS, WILLIAM CEC 090 4TH E DI
JEBI, JOHN * BAL 281 20TH WAR
JECKES, CAROLINE BAL 214 19TH WAR
JECOMPT, JAMES R.* DOR 307 1ST DIST
JEDRICKS, DANIEL * FRE 088 FREDERIC
JEELEY, JOHN WAS 238 CAVETOWN
JEENS, JANE HAR 001 1ST DIST
JEFERSON, BENJAMIN-BLACK CAR 385 2ND DIST
JEFFERIES, JOHN BAL 218 17TH WAR
JEFFERIS, LYDIA BAL 110 15TH WAR
JEFFEROSN, JOHN TAL 085 ST MICHA
JEFFERS, ANN E. BAL 056 18TH WAR
JEFFERS, BENJAMIN HAR 205 3RD DIST
JEFFERS, BENJAMIN ANN 496 HOWARD D
JEFFERS, CHARLOTTE BAL 046 9TH WARD
JEFFERS, ELIZABETH QUE 232 4TH E DI
JEFFERS, JAMES BAL 173 2ND DIST
JEFFERS, JANE BAL 395 14TH WAR
JEFFERS, JOHN ANN 474 HOWARD D
JEFFERS, JOHN R. QUE 232 4TH E DI
JEFFERS, JOHN-BLACK QUE 131 1ST E DI
JEFFERS, JOSEPH-BLACK QUE 131 1ST E DI
JEFFERS, JOSEPHINE QUE 201 3RD E DI
JEFFERS, MARY-BLACK QUE 125 1ST E DI
JEFFERS, MOSES QUE 230 4TH E DI
JEFFERS, RICHARD QUE 226 4TH E DI
JEFFERS, SAMUEL HAR 016 1ST DIST
JEFFERS, SAMUEL ANN 416 HOWARD D
JEFFERS, TIMOTHY ANN 417 HOWARD D
JEFFERSON, ANN BAL 408 8TH WARD
JEFFERSON, CHARLOTTE DOR 452 1ST DIST
JEFFERSON, DELIA DOR 415 1ST DIST
JEFFERSON, EDWARD J. TAL 091 ST MICHA
JEFFERSON, ELIZA MGM 368 BERRYS D
JEFFERSON, ELIZA BAL 175 11TH WAR
JEFFERSON, ELIZABETH BAL 179 11TH WAR
JEFFERSON, ELLEN BAL 344 7TH WARD
JEFFERSON, ELLEN BAL 120 11TH WAR
JEFFERSON, FRANCIS TAL 086 ST MICHA
JEFFERSON, FRANCIS A. BAL 315 3RD WARD
JEFFERSON, G. PRI 107 PISCATAW
JEFFERSON, GEORGE W. DOR 369 3RD DIVI
JEFFERSON, GEORGIANA BAL 057 10TH WAR
JEFFERSON, GUSTAVUS TAL 086 ST MICHA
JEFFERSON, HENRY BAL 302 7TH WARD
JEFFERSON, ISABELLA BAL 131 11TH WAR
JEFFERSON, JAMES BAL 131 11TH WAR
JEFFERSON, JAMES BAL 439 14TH WAR
JEFFERSON, JAMES TAL 086 ST MICHA
JEFFERSON, JAMES TAL 084 ST MICHA
JEFFERSON, JERREY DOR 357 3RD DIVI
JEFFERSON, JOHN B. BAL 083 1ST WARD
JEFFERSON, JOSEPH CAR 107 NO TWP L
JEFFERSON, MARY BAL 325 3RD WARD
JEFFERSON, MATILDA L. BAL 408 8TH WARD
JEFFERSON, NOAH TAL 091 ST MICHA
JEFFERSON, OTHO CAL 047 3RD DIST
JEFFERSON, RICAHRD BAL 391 14TH WAR
JEFFERSON, STEPHEN BAL 113 15TH WAR
JEFFERSON, THOMAS BAL 416 3RD WARD
JEFFERSON, THOMAS PRI 106 PISCATAW
JEFFERSON, THOMAS J. TAL 086 ST MICHA
JEFFERSON, WILLIAM TAL 016 EASTON D
JEFFERSON, WILLIAM CAL 023 2ND DIST
JEFFERSON,S ARAH BAL 036 1ST WARD
JEFFESON, ANN-BLACK BAL 219 2ND WARD
JEFFEYS, MARY BAL 422 1ST DIST
JEFFREES, MARGARET ALL 150 6TH E.D.
JEFFREIS, SAMUEL BAL 143 5TH WARD
JEFFRERS, BARWIN CEC 019 ELKTON 3
JEFFREY, BENJAMIN BAL 054 18TH WAR
JEFFREY, ELISABETH ANN 387 4TH DIST
JEFFREY, ELIZA BAL 204 6TH WARD
JEFFREY, JAMES HAR 207 3RD DIST
JEFFREY, JAMES H. ANN 503 HOWARD D
JEFFREY, JOHN T. BAL 182 6TH WARD
JEFFREY, JOHN W. HAR 078 2ND DIST
JEFFREY, LINA BAL 249 20TH WAR
JEFFREY, PETER PRI 006 BLADENSB
JEFFREY, RICHARD ANN 387 4TH DIST
JEFFREY, THOMAS HAR 120 2ND DIST
JEFFREYS, CHARLES HAR 105 2ND DIST
JEFFREYS, JOSEPH BAL 148 16TH WAR
JEFFRIES, ALEXANDER BAL 158 16TH WAR
JEFFRIES, ALICE ANN 416 HOWARD D
JEFFRIES, BEN BAL 106 5TH WARD
JEFFRIES, CHARLOTTE BAL 068 15TH WARD
JEFFRIES, ELIZABETH BAL 332 3RD WARD
JEFFRIES, EMILY BAL 272 20TH WAR
JEFFRIES, GRANVILLE L. CEC 134 6TH E DI
JEFFRIES, JANE BAL 061 10TH WAR
JEFFRIES, JOSEPH ALL 159 6TH E.D.
JEFFRIES, M. BAL 294 20TH WAR
JEFFRIES, MADISON J. BAL 272 20TH WAR
JEFFRIES, MARGARET BAL 013 1ST WARD
JEFFRIES, MARY BAL 298 1ST DIST
JEFFRIES, MARY BAL 017 15TH WAR
JEFFRIES, MARY E. BAL 089 10TH WAR
JEFFRIES, SARAH BAL 211 5TH WARD
JEFFRIES, THOMAS BAL 399 1ST DIST
JEFFRIES, THOMAS R. BAL 271 7TH WARD
JEFFRIES, THORNTON ALL 151 6TH E.D.
JEFFRIES, WILLIAM CEC 019 ELKTON 3
JEFFRIES, WILLIAM J. BAL 280 2ND WARD
JEFFRY, TIMOTHY BAL 132 18TH WAR
JEFFY, JOHN BAL 167 11TH WAR
JEFRIES, SARAH L. BAL 261 1ST DIST
JEKENHOWER, CATHARINE BAL 284 17TH WAR
JEKINS, ANN BAL 215 6TH WARD
JELDAN, MARGARET BAL 268 12TH WAR
JELLISON, MARGARET BAL 231 12TH WAR
JELVA, A. BAL 159 1ST WARD
JEMERSON, JOHN KEN 283 3RD DIST
JEMES, STEPHEN HAR 001 1ST DIST
JEMESON, JACOB S. ALL 240 CUMBERLA
JEMISSON, PERRY KEN 267 1ST DIST
JEMKER, HENRY BAL 124 1ST WARD
JEMMEN, OTTER BAL 251 2ND WARD
JEMMERSON, CHARLES BAL 115 18TH WAR
JEMMINGS, CHARLES BAL 155 1ST WARD
JEMS, ADDA ALL 119 5TH E.D.
JENDERS, B.E. ALL 242 CUMBERLA
JENET, JOSEPH BAL 321 7TH WARD
JENETT, NICHOLAS BAL 159 2ND DIST
JENGINS, JOHN C. BAL 261 12TH WAR
JENGLESEKER ALL 009 3RD E.D.
JENIFER, ANN CHA 289 MIDDLETO
JENIFER, BEN DOR 384 1ST DIST
JENIFER, ELIZA PRI 047 AQUASCO
JENIFER, JAMES C. CHA 219 ALLENS F
JENIFER, RACHAEL-BLACK FRE 042 FREDERIC
JENINGS, MARY ANN 425 HOWARD D
JENK, JOHN BAL 124 1ST WARD
JENKEN, MORRIS CAR 236 UNION TO
JENKENS, JOSEPH S. CHA 222 ALLENS F
JENKIN, JOHN BAL 037 9TH WARD
JENKINS, A. PRI 071 MARLBROU
JENKINS, ADALINE DOR 368 3RD DIVI
JENKINS, ADAM P. FRE 202 5TH E DI
JENKINS, ALEXANDER SOM 535 QUANTICO
JENKINS, ALEXANDER BAL 179 11TH WAR
JENKINS, ALFRED BAL 345 3RD WARD
JENKINS, AMELIA BAL 325 3RD WARD
JENKINS, ANDREW-MULATTO MGM 399 ROCKERLE
JENKINS, ANN BAL 150 11TH WAR
JENKINS, ANN BAL 118 5TH WARD
JENKINS, ANN ANN 481 HOWARD D
JENKINS, ANN H. BAL 014 2ND DIST
JENKINS, ANN M. WOR 303 SNOW HIL
JENKINS, ANTHONY H. BAL 054 15TH WAR
JENKINS, ASA CHA 221 ALLENS F
JENKINS, AUGUSTUS ANN 324 2ND DIST
JENKINS, BEN* DOR 463 1ST DIST
JENKINS, BENJAMIN WAS 160 2ND DIST
JENKINS, C. D. BAL 075 10TH WAR
JENKINS, CAROLINE S. BAL 327 3RD WARD
JENKINS, CATHARINE ALL 125 4TH E.D.
JENKINS, CHARLES WAS 160 2ND DIST
JENKINS, CHARLES CHA 262 MIDDLETO
JENKINS, CHARLES CHA 257 MIDDLETO
JENKINS, CHARLES FRE 029 FREDERIC
JENKINS, CHARLES CAL 046 3RD DIST
JENKINS, CHARLOTTE BAL 246 20TH WAR
JENKINS, CHARLOTTE BAL 268 12TH WAR
JENKINS, CLARA TAL 075 EASTON T
JENKINS, CROMWELL WOR 345 1ST E DI
JENKINS, CYRUS BAL 196 19TH WAR
JENKINS, DAVID WAS 011 WILLIAMS
JENKINS, DAVID* SOM 488 SALISBUR
JENKINS, EDWARD TAL 067 EASTON T
JENKINS, EDWARD CHA 226 ALLENS F
JENKINS, EDWARD BAL 139 11TH WAR
JENKINS, EDWARD BAL 181 11TH WAR
JENKINS, EDWARD Y. BAL 150 11TH WAR
JENKINS, ELEY BAL 139 19TH WAR
JENKINS, ELISHA ALL 144 6TH E.D.
JENKINS, ELIZA CEC 151 PORT DUP
JENKINS, ELIZABETH ALL 010 3RD E.D.
JENKINS, ELIZABETH BAL 178 11TH WAR

Name	County	Page	Locality
JENKINS, ELIZABETH	BAL	096	2ND DIST
JENKINS, ELIZABETH	WAS	158	2ND DIST
JENKINS, ELIZABETH	PRI	072	MARLBROU
JENKINS, ELIZABETH	WOR	198	8TH E DI
JENKINS, ELIZABETH	SOM	481	TRAPP DI
JENKINS, ELIZABETH A.	BAL	096	2ND DIST
JENKINS, ELLEN	WAS	157	HAGERSTO
JENKINS, ELLEN	BAL	148	11TH WAR
JENKINS, ELLEN	BAL	260	20TH WAR
JENKINS, ELSEY*	SOM	358	BRINKLEY
JENKINS, EMILY	CHA	274	ALLENS F
JENKINS, EMILY E.	PRI	016	BLADENSB
JENKINS, EMILY J.	BAL	326	3RD WARD
JENKINS, ENOCH	BAL	286	2ND WARD
JENKINS, ERA	ALL	144	6TH E.D.
JENKINS, F. K.	BAL	037	9TH WARD
JENKINS, FELIX	BAL	472	14TH WAR
JENKINS, FRANCES	FRE	221	BUCKEYST
JENKINS, FRANCIS	CHA	281	BOJANTOW
JENKINS, FRANCIS	BAL	300	12TH WAR
JENKINS, FRANK	DOR	392	1ST DIST
JENKINS, FREDERICK	ALL	056	10TH E.D
JENKINS, FREDERICK	BAL	273	1ST DIST
JENKINS, FRISBY	BAL	025	15TH WAR
JENKINS, FRISBY	BAL	161	11TH WAR
JENKINS, G. F.	BAL	332	1ST DIST
JENKINS, GEORGE	BAL	413	1ST DIST
JENKINS, GEORGE	BAL	193	11TH WAR
JENKINS, GEORGE	BAL	155	5TH WARD
JENKINS, GEORGE	BAL	424	8TH WARD
JENKINS, GEORGE	CAL	022	2ND DIST
JENKINS, GEORGE	TAL	097	ST MICHA
JENKINS, GEORGE	PRI	080	QUEEN AN
JENKINS, GEORGE	WAS	197	1ST DIST
JENKINS, GEORGE C.	FRE	202	5TH E DI
JENKINS, GEORGE P.	CHA	294	BOJANTOW
JENKINS, GEORGE W.	BAL	094	18TH WAR
JENKINS, GEORGE W.	TAL	048	EASTON T
JENKINS, GEORGE*	SOM	481	TRAPP DI
JENKINS, GEORGEANNA	CHA	241	HILLTOP
JENKINS, GRAFTON	FRE	209	BUCKEYST
JENKINS, H.	BAL	172	1ST WARD
JENKINS, H.	BAL	063	10TH WAR
JENKINS, HARRIET	BAL	152	5TH WARD
JENKINS, HARRIET	BAL	190	19TH WAR
JENKINS, HENRY	BAL	054	15TH WAR
JENKINS, HENRY	BAL	365	3RD WARD
JENKINS, HENRY	BAL	176	2ND DIST
JENKINS, HENRY	WOR	266	BERLIN 1
JENKINS, HENRY W.	BAL	047	9TH WARD
JENKINS, HORATIO	DOR	463	1ST DIST
JENKINS, HUGH	BAL	103	10TH WAR
JENKINS, HUGH	BAL	150	2ND DIST
JENKINS, IDA	FRE	379	PETERSVI
JENKINS, IGNATIUS	BAL	083	2ND DIST
JENKINS, ISABELLA	BAL	176	16TH WAR
JENKINS, J.	BAL	295	12TH WAR
JENKINS, JACOB	BAL	129	11TH WAR
JENKINS, JAMES	BAL	215	17TH WAR
JENKINS, JAMES	BAL	215	17TH WAR
JENKINS, JAMES	BAL	045	4TH WARD
JENKINS, JAMES	ANN	482	HOWARD D
JENKINS, JAMES	BAL	067	1ST WARD
JENKINS, JAMES	BAL	249	2ND WARD
JENKINS, JAMES	WOR	197	8TH E DI
JENKINS, JAMES B.	TAL	020	EASTON D
JENKINS, JANE	WOR	198	8TH E DI
JENKINS, JANE	CAR	114	NO TWP L
JENKINS, JANE E.	CEC	166	6TH E DI
JENKINS, JANE-BLACK	CAL	056	3RD DIST
JENKINS, JAVIS	WOR	190	8TH E DI
JENKINS, JOAB	BAL	273	1ST DIST
JENKINS, JOE*	DOR	460	1ST DIST
JENKINS, JOHN	PRI	059	NOTTINGH
JENKINS, JOHN	TAL	001	EASTON D
JENKINS, JOHN	WAS	062	2ND SUBD
JENKINS, JOHN	BAL	273	1ST DIST
JENKINS, JOHN	BAL	090	10TH WAR
JENKINS, JOHN	BAL	173	1ST WARD
JENKINS, JOHN	ANN	377	4TH DIST
JENKINS, JOHN	ALL	054	10TH E.D
JENKINS, JOHN	BAL	250	17TH WAR
JENKINS, JOHN	BAL	243	20TH WAR
JENKINS, JOHN C.	FRE	202	5TH E DI
JENKINS, JOHN H.	CHA	288	BOJANTOW
JENKINS, JOHN H.	BAL	079	4TH WARD
JENKINS, JOHN H.	TAL	033	EASTON D
JENKINS, JOHN J.	PRI	072	MARLBROU
JENKINS, JOHN J.	CHA	229	MIDDLETO
JENKINS, JOHN L.	CEC	151	PORT DUP
JENKINS, JOHN W.	BAL	250	17TH WAR
JENKINS, JOHN W.	CHA	263	MIDDLETO
JENKINS, JOHN*	SOM	503	SALISBUR
JENKINS, JOSEPH	DOR	463	1ST DIST
JENKINS, JOSEPH	CHA	279	BOJANTOW
JENKINS, JOSEPH	FRE	390	PETERSVI
JENKINS, JOSEPH	BAL	212	11TH WAR
JENKINS, JOSEPH	BAL	425	3RD WARD
JENKINS, JOSEPH	BAL	273	1ST DIST
JENKINS, JOSEPH	ANN	341	3RD DIST
JENKINS, JOSEPH F.	BAL	275	12TH WAR
JENKINS, JOSHUA	BAL	402	3RD WARD
JENKINS, JOSHUA-MULATTO	BAL	250	2ND WARD
JENKINS, JULIA	BAL	275	12TH WAR
JENKINS, L.	PRI	120	PISCATAW
JENKINS, LANATIOUS	CHA	245	HILLTOP
JENKINS, LEAH	BAL	118	15TH WAR
JENKINS, LEVI	ALL	021	2ND E.D.
JENKINS, LEVIN	DOR	463	1ST DIST
JENKINS, LILLY A.	BAL	036	4TH WARD
JENKINS, LOUISA	BAL	133	16TH WAR
JENKINS, LUCINDA	CHA	279	BOJANTOW
JENKINS, LUCY	DOR	463	1ST DIST
JENKINS, LUKE	BAL	138	1ST WARD
JENKINS, LYDIA H.	BAL	366	13TH WAR
JENKINS, M. C.	BAL	193	11TH WAR
JENKINS, MARGARET	CAL	044	3RD DIST
JENKINS, MARGARET	TAL	112	ST MICHA
JENKINS, MARGARET	WAS	033	2ND SUBD
JENKINS, MARGRETT	CAR	115	NO TWP L
JENKINS, MARIA	DOR	434	1ST DIST
JENKINS, MARIA	PRI	080	QUEEN AN
JENKINS, MARK W.	BAL	002	EASTERN
JENKINS, MARTHA J.	WOR	198	8TH E DI
JENKINS, MARY	TAL	100	ST MICHA
JENKINS, MARY	ST	289	2ND E DI
JENKINS, MARY	ALL	235	CUMBERLA
JENKINS, MARY	DOR	431	1ST DIST
JENKINS, MARY	CHA	281	BOJANTOW
JENKINS, MARY A.	BAL	357	1ST DIST
JENKINS, MARY G.	CHA	241	HILLTOP
JENKINS, MARY H. K.*	TAL	043	EASTON D
JENKINS, MARY*	SOM	505	SALISBUR
JENKINS, MICHAEL-BLACK	ST	293	2ND E DI
JENKINS, MICHELLA	BAL	212	11TH WAR
JENKINS, MOSES	DOR	446	1ST DIST
JENKINS, MRS.	BAL	092	5TH WARD
JENKINS, NANCE	BAL	422	1ST DIST
JENKINS, NATHANIEL	BAL	175	16TH WAR
JENKINS, NATHANIEL P.	TAL	104	ST MICHA
JENKINS, OLIVER L.	BAL	312	12TH WAR
JENKINS, PERPETIE	BAL	212	11TH WAR
JENKINS, PERRY	BAL	249	12TH WAR
JENKINS, PETER K.	DOR	316	1ST DIST
JENKINS, PHILIP	CHA	273	ALLENS F
JENKINS, PRECILLA	BAL	402	3RD WARD
JENKINS, RACHAEL	BAL	194	11TH WAR
JENKINS, RACHAEL	BAL	170	11TH WAR
JENKINS, RACHAEL J.	BAL	062	4TH WARD
JENKINS, REBECCA	BAL	213	11TH WAR
JENKINS, REID	ALL	153	6TH E.D.
JENKINS, RICHARD	ANN	382	4TH DIST
JENKINS, RICHARD	DOR	391	1ST DIST
JENKINS, RICHARD L.	PRI	109	PISCATAW
JENKINS, RIRIA A.	PRI	016	BLADENSB
JENKINS, ROBERT	MGM	417	MEDLEY 3
JENKINS, ROBERT	BAL	025	15TH WAR
JENKINS, ROBERT	BAL	029	2ND DIST
JENKINS, ROSINA	BAL	214	11TH WAR
JENKINS, ROSINA	BAL	214	11TH WAR
JENKINS, SAMUEL	BAL	271	2ND WARD
JENKINS, SAMUEL	BAL	100	10TH WAR
JENKINS, SAMUEL	BAL	061	10TH WAR
JENKINS, SAMUEL-BLACK	BAL	214	2ND WARD
JENKINS, SARA A.	CHA	242	HILLTOP
JENKINS, SARA A.	CHA	241	HILLTOP
JENKINS, SARAH	BAL	214	11TH WAR
JENKINS, SARAH	BAL	087	2ND DIST
JENKINS, SARAH A. H.	PRI	016	BLADENSB
JENKINS, SARAH-BLACK	QUE	171	2ND E DI
JENKINS, SARAHANN*	BAL	351	3RD WARD
JENKINS, SIDNEY	BAL	453	14TH WAR
JENKINS, SIMEON	ALL	144	6TH E.D.
JENKINS, SOPHIA	BAL	413	3RD WARD
JENKINS, STEPHEN-BLACK	WOR	329	1ST E DI
JENKINS, STEPHEN-BLACK	WOR	322	1ST E DI
JENKINS, SUSAN	TAL	036	EASTON D
JENKINS, SUSAN	WOR	192	8TH E DI
JENKINS, SUSAN	CEC	007	ELKTON 3
JENKINS, SUSAN	CHA	262	MIDDLETO
JENKINS, SUSANAH	PRI	106	PISCATAW
JENKINS, THEODORE	PRI	035	VANSVILL
JENKINS, THOMAS	WOR	196	8TH E DI
JENKINS, THOMAS	TAL	052	EASTON D
JENKINS, THOMAS	ANN	324	2ND DIST
JENKINS, THOMAS	BAL	251	1ST DIST
JENKINS, THOMAS	BAL	021	1ST WARD
JENKINS, THOMAS	ANN	422	HOWARD D
JENKINS, THOMAS	BAL	099	5TH WARD
JENKINS, THOMAS C.	BAL	183	11TH WAR
JENKINS, THOMAS P.	BAL	147	5TH WARD
JENKINS, THOMAS R.	BAL	079	4TH WARD
JENKINS, UPTON	BAL	469	14TH WAR
JENKINS, VIRGINIA	CHA	273	ALLENS F
JENKINS, WILFORD	CHA	218	ALLENS F
JENKINS, WILLIAM	CHA	274	ALLENS F
JENKINS, WILLIAM	CEC	165	6TH E DI
JENKINS, WILLIAM	CEC	036	CHESAPEA
JENKINS, WILLIAM	DOR	392	1ST DIST
JENKINS, WILLIAM	BAL	107	18TH WAR
JENKINS, WILLIAM	BAL	303	17TH WAR
JENKINS, WILLIAM	BAL	169	1ST WARD
JENKINS, WILLIAM	BAL	458	8TH WARD
JENKINS, WILLIAM	BAL	271	1ST DIST
JENKINS, WILLIAM	ANN	382	4TH DIST
JENKINS, WILLIAM	BAL	178	16TH WAR
JENKINS, WILLIAM	PRI	059	NOTTINGH
JENKINS, WILLIAM	PRI	069	MARLBROU
JENKINS, WILLIAM	TAL	049	EASTON T
JENKINS, WILLIAM	DOR	455	1ST DIST
JENKINS, WILLIAM H.	BAL	408	8TH WARD
JENKINS, WILLIAM O.	BAL	298	7TH WARD
JENKINS, WILLIAM W.	WAS	159	2ND DIST
JENKINS, WILLIMA	WAS	092	2ND SUBD
JENKINS, ZACHARIAH	FRE	095	FREDERIC
JENKINS,ALFRED	BAL	260	12TH WAR
JENKINS,KITTY	CAL	061	3RD DIST
JENKINS,LAMBERT	ST	348	5TH E DI
JENKINS,NANCY J.	ALL	033	2ND E.D.
JENKINS,WILLIAM	PRI	115	PISCATAW
JENKISN, H.	BAL	172	1ST WARD
JENKISN, H.	BAL	152	1ST WARD
JENKS, ELIZABETH	BAL	137	5TH WARD
JENKS, FRANS H.	BAL	098	10TH WAR
JENKS, WILLAM D.	FRE	033	FREDERIC
JENNES, MARY	CEC	080	NORTHEAS
JENNESS, ANNA	BAL	169	6TH WARD
JENNESS, JOHN A.	HAR	188	3RD DIST
JENNESS, LEVY L.	HAR	179	3RD DIST
JENNET, CANIEL	BAL	436	1ST DIST
JENNET, JOHN A.	BAL	227	1ST DIST
JENNEY, MARGARET	BAL	228	12TH WAR
JENNEY, MARGARET	CEC	110	4TH E DI
JENNIFER, DANIEL JR.	BAL	076	2ND DIST
JENNIFER, JOHN*	DOR	388	1ST DIST
JENNIFER, MARGARET	DOR	388	1ST DIST
JENNING, SAMUEL	WAS	088	2ND SUBD
JENNING, WILLIAM	BAL	257	20TH WAR
JENNING, WILLIAM	BAL	110	5TH WARD
JENNINGS, ABRAHAM	BAL	110	18TH WAR
JENNINGS, ANNA	BAL	181	6TH WARD
JENNINGS, AUSTIN	ANN	346	3RD DIST
JENNINGS, CATHERINE	BAL	358	8TH WARD
JENNINGS, CHARELS	BAL	153	5TH WARD
JENNINGS, CHARLES	BAL	123	1ST WARD
JENNINGS, CONRAD	BAL	306	12TH WAR
JENNINGS, ELIZABETH	QUE	139	1ST E DI
JENNINGS, F.	FRE	200	5TH E DI
JENNINGS, FRANCIS	BAL	158	19TH WAR
JENNINGS, HENRY	BAL	279	12TH WAR
JENNINGS, HENRY	ANN	325	2ND DIST
JENNINGS, HENRY	ANN	326	2ND DIST
JENNINGS, JACOB F.	CEC	147	PORT DUP
JENNINGS, JOHN	ANN	351	3RD DIST
JENNINGS, JOHN	BAL	038	2ND DIST
JENNINGS, JOHN L.	BAL	107	1ST WARD
JENNINGS, MARIA	ANN	308	1ST DIST
JENNINGS, MARY	BAL	110	10TH WAR
JENNINGS, MARY A.	BAL	311	3RD WARD
JENNINGS, MICHAEL	BAL	166	6TH WARD
JENNINGS, MICHEAL	BAL	103	18TH WAR
JENNINGS, NATHAN	BAL	224	17TH WAR
JENNINGS, PATRICK	BAL	165	6TH WARD
JENNINGS, PATRICK	ALL	106	5TH E.D.
JENNINGS, RICHARD	ANN	311	1ST DIST
JENNINGS, ROBERT	BAL	364	3RD WARD
JENNINGS, ROBERT	HAR	018	1ST DIST
JENNINGS, SAMUEL	BAL	224	17TH WAR
JENNINGS, SAMUEL	BAL	040	4TH WARD
JENNINGS, SAMUEL	BAL	346	7TH WARD
JENNINGS, SAMUEL	BAL	346	7TH WARD
JENNINGS, SARAH	BAL	195	2ND WARD
JENNINGS, SARAH	BAL	107	10TH WAR
JENNINGS, THOMAS	BAL	343	7TH WARD
JENNINGS, THOMAS	ANN	322	2ND DIST
JENNINGS, THOMAS	ALL	056	10TH E.D
JENNINGS, THOMAS	BAL	234	20TH WAR
JENNINGS, THOMAS	BAL	224	17TH WAR
JENNINGS, THOMAS	BAL	067	4TH WARD
JENNINGS, VINA	ANN	330	2ND DIST
JENNINGS, WILLIAM	ANN	310	1ST DIST
JENNINGS, WILLIAM	BAL	169	1ST WARD
JENNISS, DAVID	CEC	194	7TH E DI
JENNY, H.	BAL	281	12TH WAR
JENNY, JANE	BAL	209	19TH WAR
JENNY, MARY	BAL	282	12TH WAR
JENRALS, WILLIAM	ANN	330	2ND DIST
JENSFIELD, A.A.	BAL	140	1ST WARD
JENSFIELD, MARY	BAL	297	3RD WARD
JENSON, ISABEL	BAL	239	12TH WAR
JENSON, JACKSON *	KEN	253	1ST DIST
JENSON, MARY	BAL	227	12TH WAR
JENSS, JOHN *	CAR	308	1ST DIST
JENSS, SAMUEL *	CAR	309	1ST DIST
JENT, HANNAH	BAL	116	5TH WARD
JERDONE, MARIA C.	ANN	521	HOWARD D
JEREWAY, JAMES	BAL	131	1ST WARD
JERGAN, WILLIAM	ALL	234	CUMBERLA
JERKEN, SARAH	BAL	290	20TH WAR
JERKER, W.*	BAL	293	12TH WAR
JERKIER, JOHN	BAL	293	12TH WAR
JERKLE, HARMON	BAL	105	1ST WARD
JERMAN, JOSEPH	BAL	070	2ND DIST
JEROME, BROTHER	BAL	216	11TH WAR
JEROME, BROTHER	BAL	216	11TH WAR
JEROME, HAGAR	BAL	084	15TH WAR
JEROME, JESSE	KEN	258	1ST DIST
JEROME, JOHN H.T.	BAL	248	12TH WAR
JEROME, MARY	BAL	441	8TH WARD
JEROME, SARAH	KEN	250	2ND DIST
JEROS, JOHN	DOR	408	1ST DIST
JERRETT, JULIA	BAL	089	2ND DIST
JERRY, LUCIUS A.	CEC	146	PORT DUP
JERRY, NANCY	BAL	171	2ND DIST
JERVIS, CORNELIA F.*	BAL	109	15TH WAR
JERVIS, ISAIH*	DOR	438	1ST DIST
JERVIS, JOHN	KEN	290	3RD DIST
JERVIS, SOPHIA	KEN	290	3RD DIST
JERVIS, W.H.	BAL	127	1ST WARD
JERVIS, WALTER	HAR	171	3RD DIST
JESLAND, OLIVER C.*	BAL	292	12TH WAR
JESLER, ELIJAH	CAR	127	NO TWP L
JESLER, JOHN	CAR	130	NO TWP L
JESLER, WILLIAM	CAR	111	NO TWP L
JESS, EDWARD	ANN	432	HOWARD D
JESS, WILLAIM	BAL	413	14TH WAR
JESSOP, AMANDA C.	BAL	035	9TH WARD
JESSOP, CHARLES	BAL	086	2ND DIST
JESSOP, CHARLES	BAL	425	1ST DIST
JESSOP, GEORGE	BAL	022	2ND DIST
JESSOP, JAMES O.	FRE	450	8TH E DI
JESSOP, JOSHUA	BAL	087	2ND DIST
JESSOP, JOSHUA	BAL	032	9TH WARD
JESSOP, PRISCILLA	BAL	230	5TH WARD
JESSOP, RICHARD O.	CAL	042	3RD DIST
JESSOP, WILLIAM	BAL	022	2ND DIST
JESSOP, WILLIAM W.	BAL	455	14TH WAR
JESSUP, ANN	BAL	181	19TH WAR
JESSUP, CHARLES	KEN	263	1ST DIST
JESSUP, D.B.	BAL	223	1ST DIST
JESSUP, DELINA	BAL	375	1ST DIST
JESSUP, JOHN	CAR	068	NO TWP L
JESSUP, SAMUEL	BAL	181	19TH WAR
JESSUP, SUSAN	WAS	010	WILLIAMS
JESTER, ANNA A.	KEN	311	3RD DIST
JESTER, BENJAMIN E.	KEN	310	3RD DIST
JESTER, BENNETT	CAR	143	NO TWP L
JESTER, JAMES	CAR	161	NO TWP L
JESTER, JAMES B.	TAL	029	EASTON D
JESTER, JOHN	KEN	301	3RD DIST
JESTER, JOHN H.	CAR	073	NO TWP L
JESTER, JOHN-BLACK	CAR	069	NO TWP L
JESTER, JOHN-MULATTO	WOR	338	1ST E DI
JESTER, MARSHALL	CEC	029	CHESAPEA
JESTER, MITCHELL	WOR	298	9TH E DI
JESTER, PETER	CAR	145	NO TWP L
JESTER, PHILIP R.	CEC	058	1ST E DI
JESTER, RHODA-BLACK	QUE	171	2ND E DI
JESTER, RICHARD	TAL	005	EASTON D
JESTER, RICHARD	CAR	108	NO TWP L
JESTER, SAMUEL	CAR	125	NO TWP L
JESTER, SARAH	CAR	144	NO TWP L
JESTER, WILLIAM	DOR	308	1ST DIST
JESTER, WILLIAM	TAL	005	EASTON D
JESTUS, WILLIAM	WOR	278	BERLIN 1
JESURAN, ANNA M.	BAL	429	14TH WAR
JESURE, GEORGE	BAL	250	20TH WAR
JESURE, JACOB	BAL	250	20TH WAR
JETT, CHARLES W.	BAL	037	9TH WARD
JETT, EDWARD	BAL	044	9TH WARD
JETT, ELLEN L.	ANN	521	HOWARD D
JETT, ELVIRA	ANN	521	HOWARD D
JETT, LLOVEL C.	BAL	106	18TH WAR
JETTER, JAMES LANGEN	BAL	103	5TH WARD
JEVENS, JOHN W.	BAL	059	10TH WAR
JEWDEN, ELIJA	BAL	134	1ST WARD
JEWELL, CHARLES	KEN	222	2ND DIST
JEWELL, CHARLES H. *	KEN	234	2ND DIST
JEWELL, DANIEL	KEN	295	3RD DIST
JEWELL, ELIZABETH	QUE	251	5TH E DI
JEWELL, ELIZABETH	BAL	136	5TH WARD
JEWELL, GUSTAVUS	MGM	430	CLARKSTR
JEWELL, JAMES	KEN	273	1ST DIST
JEWELL, JOSEPH	ANN	279	ANNAPOLI
JEWELL, LUTHER	CAR	115	NO TWP L
JEWELL, MAJOR	CAR	109	NO TWP L
JEWELL, REBECCA	BAL	274	12TH WAR
JEWELL, RICHARD	BAL	274	12TH WAR
JEWELL, SAMUEL	CAR	065	NO TWP L
JEWELL, THOMAS	CAR	114	NO TWP L

Name	County	Page	District
JEWELL, WILLIAM	KEN	231	2ND DIST
JEWELL, WILLIAM	ANN	279	ANNAPOLI
JEWETT, GRACE	SOM	376	BRINKLEY
JEWETT, ISAAC	SOM	383	BRINKLEY
JEWETT, ISAAC	SOM	367	BRINKLEY
JEWETT, ISAAC W.	BAL	030	9TH WARD
JEWETT, NANCY	SOM	383	BRINKLEY
JEWETT, NELLY	SOM	376	BRINKLEY
JEWETT, SAMUEL	SOM	367	BRINKLEY
JEWETT, WHITTINGTON	SOM	375	BRINKLEY
JEWETT, WILLAIM	BAL	154	1ST WARD
JEWETT, WILLIAM	BAL	158	1ST WARD
JEWETT, WILLIAM	KEN	280	3RD DIST
JEWIT, JOHN	HAR	014	1ST DIST
JEWITT, JOHN	HAR	001	1ST DIST
JEWITT, MILTHY-BLACK	BAL	214	2ND WARD
JEWS, ABRAM	DOR	422	1ST DIST
JEWS, ADAM	DOR	426	1ST DIST
JEWS, HOOPER	DOR	423	1ST DIST
JEWS, JOHN	DOR	412	1ST DIST
JEWS, NED*	DOR	408	1ST DIST
JEYES, ELIZABETH	BAL	083	15TH WAR
JHACKSON, ELIZBAETH-BLACK	WOR	340	1ST E DI
JICE, CATHARINE	BAL	234	17TH WAR
JICE, FLORENY	BAL	221	19TH WAR
JICE, THOMAS	HAR	195	3RD DIST
JIFFRIES, MARGARET J.	BAL	011	1ST WARD
JIGINFETTER, JANE	BAL	060	4TH WARD
JILES, HESTER	DOR	418	1ST DIST
JILES, JERE	CAL	062	3RD DIST
JILES, JOHN	ANN	342	3RD DIST
JILES, NANCY	WAS	060	2ND SUBD
JILES, WILLIAM	HAR	207	3RD DIST
JILGHMAN, FLOYD-BLACK	CAR	087	NO TWP L
JILLIARD, JOHN	BAL	424	3RD WARD
JILVESTHOM, JOHN	WOR	302	SNOW HIL
JIM, VIRGINIA *	BAL	281	20TH WAR
JIMASON, ANN	FRE	044	FREDERIC
JIMASON, TERESA	FRE	044	FREDERIC
JIMESON, LUCINDA	FRE	040	FREDERIC
JIN, LEWIS-BLACK	WOR	332	1ST E DI
JINERELS, MASEY *	ANN	353	3RD DIST
JINES, CHARLES	KEN	251	2ND DIST
JINES, CLEMENTS F. *	KEN	250	2ND DIST
JINES, SAMUEL	QUE	189	3RD E DI
JINGLING, HENRY	BAL	108	5TH WARD
JINGOE, JERRY	TAL	098	ST MICHA
JINKEN, AUSTIN	BAL	136	11TH WAR
JINKENS, WILLIAM-BLACK	FRE	420	8TH E DI
JINKINS, A. BRADFORD	BAL	191	11TH WAR
JINKINS, ANN*	DOR	301	1ST DIST
JINKINS, DAVID*	SOM	488	SALISBUR
JINKINS, ELISHA	SOM	410	DUBLIN D
JINKINS, ELIZA	BAL	050	18TH WAR
JINKINS, ELIZABETH	SOM	481	TRAPP DI
JINKINS, ELSEY*	SOM	358	BRINKLEY
JINKINS, GEORGE*	SOM	481	TRAPP DI
JINKINS, HANNAH	BAL	137	11TH WAR
JINKINS, HANNAH-MULATTO	FRE	450	8TH E DI
JINKINS, HENRY *	CHA	241	HILLTOP
JINKINS, JOHN*	SOM	503	SALISBUR
JINKINS, JOHN-BLACK	FRE	452	8TH E DI
JINKINS, JOSHUA	BAL	422	1ST DIST
JINKINS, L. A.	BAL	191	11TH WAR
JINKINS, LITTLETON	SOM	468	TRAPPE D
JINKINS, MARY H. K.*	TAL	043	EASTON D
JINKINS, MARY*	SOM	505	SALISBUR
JINKINS, PHOEBY	BAL	068	18TH WAR
JINKINS, RICHARD E.	SOM	472	TRAPPE D
JINKINS, SAMUEL	WAS	118	2ND DIST
JINKINS, THOMAS	BAL	103	18TH WAR
JINKINS, WESLEY	SOM	489	SALISBUR
JINKINS, WILLIAM A.	BAL	016	18TH WAR
JINN, NELSON	ALL	045	10TH E.D
JINNESS, MILTON	CEC	111	4TH E DI
JINNEY, JESSE	CEC	139	6TH E DI
JINNEY, JOHN T.	CEC	160	6TH E DI
JINNEY, PHILLIP	CEC	182	7TH E DI
JINNEY, ROBERT	CEC	163	6TH E DI
JINNEY, THOMAS	CEC	140	5TH E DI
JINNINGS, JOSEPH	BAL	072	18TH WAR
JINNINGS, THOMAS	BAL	458	1ST DIST
JINNRAL, AUSTIN *	ANN	352	3RD DIST
JIRGA, CHARLES	BAL	008	9TH WARD
JOANS, GEORGE	BAL	209	11TH WAR
JOB, REBECCA	BAL	237	6TH WARD
JOB, WILLIAM	ANN	290	ANNAPOLI
JOBES, CHARLES U.	BAL	402	8TH WARD
JOBES, ELLEN	CAR	291	7TH DIST
JOBES, GEORGE	BAL	402	8TH WARD
JOBES, MARY	CAR	296	7TH DIST
JOBES, NICHOLAS	CAR	285	7TH DIST
JOBS, CHARLES-MULATTO	FRE	415	8TH E DI
JOBS, SARAH	FRE	450	8TH E DI
JOBS, WILLIAM-MULATTC	FRE	425	8TH E DI
JOBS, MARY-MULATTO	FRE	440	8TH E DI
JOCHINHURST, WILLIAM	BAL	192	2ND WARD
JOE, ELIZABETH	FRE	300	WOODSBOR
JOEL, GUSTAOUS	BAL	356	13TH WAR
JOELBOTT, JAMES	BAL	288	12TH WAR
JOELING, REBECCA	BAL	254	12TH WAR
JOENS, ABRAHAM	FRE	073	FREDERIC
JOENS, CATHARINE	BAL	121	2ND DIST
JOENS, CHARLES H.	BAL	281	2ND WARD
JOENS, DAVID	CAR	201	4TH DIST
JOENS, E.	BAL	155	1ST WARD
JOENS, ELISHA	BAL	166	2ND DIST
JOENS, ELIZABETH	CAR	305	1ST DIST
JOENS, EZEKIEL	BAL	430	8TH WARD
JOENS, GEORGE	BAL	118	18TH WAR
JOENS, GEORGE	WOR	273	BERLIN 1
JOENS, HESTER	WOR	303	SNOW HIL
JOENS, HEZE	CAL	021	2ND DIST
JOENS, ISAAC	WOR	260	BERLIN 1
JOENS, J. B.	BAL	147	1ST WARD
JOENS, JACKSCN	QUE	225	4TH E DI
JOENS, JAMES	WOR	193	8TH E DI
JOENS, JOHN	BAL	376	13TH WAR
JOENS, LETITIA	CAR	296	7TH DIST
JOENS, MARGARET	QUE	240	5TH E DI
JOENS, MARTHA ANN	QUE	224	4TH E DI
JOENS, MARY	CAL	026	2ND DIST
JOENS, MITTY	WOR	254	1ST CENS
JOENS, OBIDA W.	WOR	255	1ST CENS
JOENS, PETER	CAR	207	4TH DIST
JOENS, SAMUEL	BAL	362	13TH WAR
JOENS, SIDNEY	WOR	298	9TH E DI
JOENS, SRAH	BAL	422	14TH WAR
JOENS, STEPHEN	BAL	178	2ND DIST
JOENS, SUSAN	BAL	353	13TH WAR
JOENS, WILLIAM	BAL	339	13TH WAR
JOENS, WILLIAM	BAL	150	1ST WARD
JOENS, WILLIAM	WOR	193	8TH E DI
JOENS, WILLIAM	QUE	206	3RD E DI
JOENS, WILLIMA	WOR	270	BERLIN 1
JOGG, ABNER *	BAL	158	1ST WARD
JOHANAMAN, MARY	ALL	120	5TH E.D.
JOHANAS, MARTIN	BAL	289	1ST DIST
JOHANNES, CHARLES	BAL	120	1ST WARD
JOHANNES, EDWARD	BAL	120	1ST WARD
JOHANNES, MARTIN	BAL	131	1ST WARD
JOHHSTON, JOHN	BAL	270	7TH WARD
JOHN, AUG.	BAL	321	12TH WAR
JOHN, CATHARINE	BAL	339	13TH WAR
JOHN, CHARLES	BAL	080	10TH WAR
JOHN, DANIEL-BLACK	QUE	190	3RD E DI
JOHN, DAVID	HAR	131	2ND DIST
JOHN, ELSY	BAL	248	20TH WAR
JOHN, ENOS	CEC	002	ELKTON 3
JOHN, GEORGE .	BAL	328	3RD WARD
JOHN, HENRY	BAL	148	11TH WAR
JOHN, JAMES	FRE	168	EMMITTSB
JOHN, MARGARET	BAL	104	2ND DIST
JOHN, MISS K.	FRE	198	5TH E DI
JOHN, PERE	HAR	075	BEL AIR
JOHN, WESLEY	BAL	315	1ST DIST
JOHNES, HARRIET	BAL	230	12TH WAR
JOHNES, HENRY	BAL	159	1ST WARD
JOHNES, JOHN	BAL	116	1ST WARD
JOHNEZ, ZIELDER G.*	DOR	326	3RD DIVI
JOHNOM, GEORGE	ALL	011	3RD E.D.
JOHNOSN, ANN	WOR	230	6TH E DI
JOHNOSN, ANNA	BAL	468	14TH WAR
JOHNOSN, ANTOLINER	CAL	009	1ST DIST
JOHNOSN, ARALANTA	WOR	291	9TH E DI
JOHNOSN, BENJAMIN	BAL	467	14TH WAR
JOHNOSN, CHARELS	BAL	157	1ST WARD
JOHNOSN, CHARLES	BAL	172	16TH WAR
JOHNOSN, CHARLOTTE	BAL	337	13TH WAR
JOHNOSN, DENNIS	BAL	179	2ND DIST
JOHNOSN, EBIN	WOR	308	2ND E DI
JOHNOSN, ELIZABETH	BAL	381	13TH WAR
JOHNOSN, HENRY	WOR	315	2ND E DI
JOHNOSN, ISAAC	KEN	297	3RD DIST
JOHNOSN, ISAIAH T.	WOR	201	3RD E DI
JOHNOSN, JAMES	BAL	187	19TH WAR
JOHNOSN, JAMES J.	CAL	001	1ST DIST
JOHNOSN, JANETT B.	BAL	309	12TH WAR
JOHNOSN, JOHN H.	WOR	201	3RD E DI
JOHNOSN, JOSEPH	WOR	231	6TH E DI
JOHNOSN, MARY	TAL	089	ST MICHA
JOHNOSN, MARY ADELINE	BAL	389	13TH WAR
JOHNOSN, NED	WOR	293	9TH E DI
JOHNOSN, PURNELL	WOR	315	2ND E DI
JOHNOSN, RACHEL	BAL	439	14TH WAR
JOHNOSN, SAMUEL	BAL	224	12TH WAR
JOHNOSN, STEPHEN	WOR	309	2ND E DI
JOHNOSN, THOMAS	WOR	247	1ST CENS
JOHNOSN, THOMAS	QUE	240	5TH E DI
JOHNOSN, THOMAS	CAR	187	4TH DIST
JOHNOSN, THOMAS D.	BAL	474	14TH WAR
JOHNS, ALEXANDER	BAL	409	14TH WAR
JOHNS, ANN	BAL	348	13TH WAR
JOHNS, ASBERRY-BLACK	CAR	157	NO TWP L
JOHNS, CATHARINE	CEC	085	5TH E DI
JOHNS, CATHERINE	BAL	458	8TH WARD
JOHNS, CATHERINE-BLACK	CAR	162	NO TWP L
JOHNS, CHARLES	QUE	252	5TH E DI
JOHNS, CHARLES G.	BAL	234	2ND WARD
JOHNS, CHARLOTTE-BLACK	QUE	126	1ST E DI
JOHNS, DEBY	DOR	324	1ST DIST
JOHNS, EDWORD F.	HAR	189	3RD DIST
JOHNS, EEAVE*	TAL	002	EASTON D
JOHNS, ELIAS	BAL	242	2ND WARD
JOHNS, ELIZ	BAL	229	12TH WAR
JOHNS, ELIZA	BAL	307	7TH WARD
JOHNS, ELIZA	BAL	213	2ND WARD
JOHNS, ELIZA-BLACK	CAR	140	NO TWP L
JOHNS, ELLEN	BAL	203	19TH WAR
JOHNS, FRANCES A.	ST	264	3RD E DI
JOHNS, FRANCIS	BAL	452	14TH WAR
JOHNS, FRISBY	BAL	459	8TH WARD
JOHNS, H. V. D.	BAL	314	20TH WAR
JOHNS, HARRIETT-BLACK	CAR	146	NO TWP L
JOHNS, HENRY	BAL	454	14TH WAR
JOHNS, HENRY	BAL	254	2ND WARD
JOHNS, HENRY	BAL	271	7TH WARD
JOHNS, HENRY	BAL	077	15TH WAR
JOHNS, HENRY	BAL	315	3RD WARD
JOHNS, HENRY	WAS	024	2ND SUBD
JOHNS, HESTER-BLACK	QUE	126	1ST E DI
JOHNS, ISAAC	BAL	150	16TH WAR
JOHNS, JACOB*	DOR	314	1ST DIST
JOHNS, JANE E.	CHA	275	ALLENS F
JOHNS, JEFFERSON	BAL	114	15TH WAR
JOHNS, JOHN	BAL	244	1ST DIST
JOHNS, JOHN T.	BAL	422	1ST DIST
JOHNS, JOSEPH	BAL	295	3RD WARD
JOHNS, JOSEPH	BAL	126	16TH WAR
JOHNS, JOSHUA	DOR	314	1ST DIST
JOHNS, LEAN-BLACK	CAR	141	NO TWP L
JOHNS, LEONARD H.	ALL	208	CUMBERLA
JOHNS, LIDNER*	BAL	051	4TH WARD
JOHNS, LORA V.	BAL	366	1ST DIST
JOHNS, LOUISA	BAL	058	4TH WARD
JOHNS, LUCINDA	CHA	246	HILLTOP
JOHNS, MAHLIN	BAL	272	20TH WAR
JOHNS, MARGARETT A.	DOR	299	1ST DIST
JOHNS, MARRGARET	ALL	255	CUMBERLA
JOHNS, MARY	BAL	441	8TH WARD
JOHNS, MATHEN-BLACK	CAR	137	NO TWP L
JOHNS, MICHAEL	BAL	243	2ND WARD
JOHNS, MILLY	BAL	076	15TH WAR
JOHNS, NICHOLAS	ANN	420	HOWARD D
JOHNS, OTHELLO	BAL	457	8TH WARD
JOHNS, RANDOLPH	BAL	277	7TH WARD
JOHNS, RHUBEN	BAL	317	1ST DIST
JOHNS, RICHARD	BAL	255	12TH WAR
JOHNS, RICHARD	BAL	243	1ST DIST
JOHNS, ROBERT-BLACK	QUE	178	2ND E DI
JOHNS, SARAH	BAL	389	8TH WARD
JOHNS, SARAH	HAR	189	3RD DIST
JOHNS, SARAH-BLACK	CAR	084	NO TWP L
JOHNS, SIONER*	BAL	051	4TH WARD
JOHNS, STEPHEN S.	HAR	001	1ST DIST
JOHNS, THOMAS	ALL	103	5TH E.D.
JOHNS, THOMAS	ANN	303	1ST DIST
JOHNS, WASHINGTON-BLACK	BAL	250	2ND WARD
JOHNS, WILLARD-BLACK	CAR	141	NO TWP L
JOHNS, WILLIAM	DOR	413	1ST DIST
JOHNS, WILLIAM	ANN	303	1ST DIST
JOHNS, WILLIAM	BAL	007	1ST WARD
JOHNS, WILLIAM	ALL	255	CUMBERLA
JOHNS, WILLIAM	BAL	021	9TH WARD
JOHNS, WILLIAM H.	HAR	023	1ST DIST
JOHNS, WILLIAM L.	BAL	292	7TH WARD
JOHNSJON, ELIZABETH E.	DOR	320	1ST DIST
JOHNSON, SUSAN	BAL	214	5TH WARD
JOHNSON, A.	BAL	168	1ST WARD
JOHNSON, A.	BAL	117	1ST WARD
JOHNSON, A.	ANN	271	ANNAPOLI
JOHNSON, A.	BAL	255	12TH WAR
JOHNSON, A.	BAL	251	20TH WAR
JOHNSON, A.	PRI	080	QUEEN AN
JOHNSON, A. C.	BAL	317	3RD WARD
JOHNSON, AARON	BAL	077	15TH WAR
JOHNSON, AARON	SOM	383	BRINKLEY
JOHNSON, AARON	CAR	093	NO TWP L
JOHNSON, ABIGAIL	QUE	242	5TH E DI
JOHNSON, ABRAHAM	PRI	038	VANSVILL
JOHNSON, ABRAHAM	FRE	240	NEW MARK
JOHNSON, ABRAHAM	BAL	152	16TH WAR
JOHNSON, ABRAHAM	BAL	130	1ST WARD
JOHNSON, ABRAM	BAL	171	1ST WARD
JOHNSON, ADAM	SOM	385	BRINKLEY
JOHNSON, ADAM	SOM	365	BRINKLEY
JOHNSON, ADDISON	ANN	347	3RD DIST
JOHNSON, ADELINE	BAL	199	2ND WARD
JOHNSON, ADELINE	BAL	103	15TH WAR
JOHNSON, ADELINE	BAL	205	11TH WAR
JOHNSON, ADLINE	BAL	111	18TH WAR
JOHNSON, ADOLPH	BAL	079	1ST WARD
JOHNSON, AGNES	BAL	124	16TH WAR
JOHNSON, AIRY	ANN	474	HOWARD D
JOHNSON, ALBERT	BAL	203	17TH WAR
JOHNSON, ALESON	ALL	110	5TH E.D.
JOHNSON, ALEXANDER	BAL	084	15TH WAR
JOHNSON, ALEXANDER	BAL	066	10TH WAR
JOHNSON, ALEXANDER	BAL	276	17TH WAR
JOHNSON, ALEXANDER	BAL	408	14TH WAR
JOHNSON, ALEXANDER	CHA	261	MIDDLETO
JOHNSON, ALEXANDER	DOR	344	3RD DIVI
JOHNSON, ALEXANDER	BAL	228	19TH WAR
JOHNSON, ALEXANDER	BAL	225	19TH WAR
JOHNSON, ALEXANDER	BAL	290	17TH WAR
JOHNSON, ALEXANDER	BAL	286	17TH WAR
JOHNSON, ALEXANDER-BLACK	QUE	197	3RD E DI
JOHNSON, ALEXANDER-MULATT	BAL	208	2ND WARD
JOHNSON, ALFORD	BAL	121	1ST WARD
JOHNSON, ALFRED	BAL	156	1ST WARD
JOHNSON, ALFRED	BAL	159	1ST WARD
JOHNSON, ALFRED	BAL	101	15TH WAR
JOHNSON, ALFRED	ANN	351	3RD DIST
JOHNSON, ALFRED	CEC	042	CHESAPEA
JOHNSON, ALFRED	KEN	232	2ND DIST
JOHNSON, ALFRED D.	WOR	199	8TH E DI
JOHNSON, ALGE	SOM	518	BARREN C
JOHNSON, ALICE	CEC	201	5TH E DI
JOHNSON, ALICE	BAL	258	17TH WAR
JOHNSON, ALLE	CAL	008	1ST DIST
JOHNSON, ALPHEUS	ANN	430	HOWARD D
JOHNSON, ALSOLUM	FRE	086	FREDERIC
JOHNSON, ALVERTA	BAL	128	18TH WAR
JOHNSON, ALWARD	DOR	336	3RD DIVI
JOHNSON, AMANDA	HAR	067	1ST DIST
JOHNSON, AMANDA	HAR	153	3RD DIST
JOHNSON, AMANDA	BAL	230	12TH WAR
JOHNSON, AMELIA	BAL	103	15TH WAR
JOHNSON, AMELIA	MGM	362	BERRYS D
JOHNSON, AMELIA	BAL	111	10TH WAR
JOHNSON, AMELIA-BLACK	FRE	242	NEW MARK
JOHNSON, AMERICAN	BAL	046	2ND DIST
JOHNSON, AMRY	HAR	201	3RD DIST
JOHNSON, AMY	BAL	339	13TH WAR
JOHNSON, ANDREW	ANN	301	1ST DIST
JOHNSON, ANDREW	TAL	090	ST MICHA
JOHNSON, ANDREW	TAL	089	ST MICHA
JOHNSON, ANN	QUE	174	2ND E DI
JOHNSON, ANN	BAL	075	2ND DIST
JOHNSON, ANN	ANN	457	HOWARD D
JOHNSON, ANN	ANN	362	4TH DIST
JOHNSON, ANN	BAL	097	2ND DIST
JOHNSON, ANN	BAL	105	10TH WAR
JOHNSON, ANN	BAL	133	5TH WARD
JOHNSON, ANN	BAL	002	1ST WARD
JOHNSON, ANN	BAL	257	17TH WAR
JOHNSON, ANN	BAL	087	4TH WARD
JOHNSON, ANN	BAL	066	4TH WARD
JOHNSON, ANN	BAL	395	14TH WAR
JOHNSON, ANN	CAL	002	1ST DIST
JOHNSON, ANN	FRE	062	FREDERIC
JOHNSON, ANN	BAL	225	19TH WAR
JOHNSON, ANN	BAL	414	3RD WARD
JOHNSON, ANN	BAL	413	3RD WARD
JOHNSON, ANN B.	CAR	257	3RD DIST
JOHNSON, ANN E.	BAL	317	3RD WARD
JOHNSON, ANN E.	WAS	029	2ND SUBD
JOHNSON, ANN M.	QUE	251	5TH E DI
JOHNSON, ANN M.	BAL	368	3RD WARD
JOHNSON, ANN M.	BAL	005	15TH WAR
JOHNSON, ANN M.-BLACK	BAL	176	2ND WARD
JOHNSON, ANN R. B.	MGM	413	MEDLEY 3
JOHNSON, ANN S.	BAL	007	9TH WARD
JOHNSON, ANNA	BAL	109	5TH WARD
JOHNSON, ANNA	BAL	328	1ST DIST
JOHNSON, ANNA	BAL	181	16TH WAR
JOHNSON, ANNA	CEC	008	ELKTON 3
JOHNSON, ANNA	CEC	145	PORT DUP
JOHNSON, ANNA-BLACK	QUE	202	3RD E DI
JOHNSON, ANTHONY M.	ANN	430	HOWARD D
JOHNSON, AQUILLA	BAL	171	16TH WAR
JOHNSON, AQUILLA	BAL	182	2ND WARD
JOHNSON, ARA	ANN	357	3RD DIST
JOHNSON, ARCHIBALD	ANN	340	3RD DIST
JOHNSON, ARCHIBALD	BAL	446	14TH WAR
JOHNSON, ARLEDIA	BAL	174	11TH WAR
JOHNSON, ARON	WAS	124	2ND DIST
JOHNSON, ARTEMAS	ANN	475	HOWARD D
JOHNSON, ARTHUR	ALL	095	5TH E.D.
JOHNSON, ARTHUR L.	BAL	251	12TH WAR
JOHNSON, ASBURY	BAL	189	6TH WARD
JOHNSON, ASBURY-BLACK	QUE	162	2ND E DI
JOHNSON, AUGUSTUS	ANN	412	HOWARD D
JOHNSON, AUGUSTUS	BAL	344	13TH WAR
JOHNSON, AUGUSTUS	FRE	386	PETERSVI
JOHNSON, AUGUSTUS J.	WOR	185	6TH E DI
JOHNSON, AZEL	ALL	177	7TH E.D.
JOHNSON, BAKER	ANN	324	2ND DIST
JOHNSON, BARBARA	BAL	053	15TH WAR
JOHNSON, BARRETT	HAR	108	2ND DIST

Name	County	Page	District
JOHNSON, BASIL	ANN	484	HOWARD D
JOHNSON, BASIL	ANN	356	3RD DIST
JOHNSON, BASIL	BAL	091	15TH WAR
JOHNSON, BECKY	BAL	227	1ST DIST
JOHNSON, BEN	BAL	059	2ND DIST
JOHNSON, BEN	MGM	360	BERRYS D
JOHNSON, BEN A.	PRI	106	PISCATAW
JOHNSON, BENEDICT	ANN	459	HOWARD D
JOHNSON, BENJAIN	BAL	170	2ND DIST
JOHNSON, BENJAMIN	BAL	230	1ST DIST
JOHNSON, BENJAMIN	BAL	055	2ND DIST
JOHNSON, BENJAMIN	BAL	017	2ND DIST
JOHNSON, BENJAMIN	WOR	235	6TH E DI
JOHNSON, BENJAMIN	MGM	420	MEDLEY 3
JOHNSON, BENJAMIN	CEC	134	6TH E DI
JOHNSON, BENJAMINB.	WOR	168	6TH E DI
JOHNSON, BENJANIN	DOR	355	3RD DIVI
JOHNSON, BESTEY	TAL	088	ST MICHA
JOHNSON, BETSEY	WOR	276	BERLIN 1
JOHNSON, BETSEY	TAL	112	ST MICHA
JOHNSON, BETSY	CAL	025	2ND DIST
JOHNSON, BETSY	BAL	126	5TH WARD
JOHNSON, BIDDY	SOM	522	BARREN C
JOHNSON, BILL	ANN	394	8TH DIST
JOHNSON, BLINDA-BLACK	BAL	220	2ND WARD
JOHNSON, BRITANIA	ST	282	3RD E DI
JOHNSON, C.A.	BAL	174	1ST WARD
JOHNSON, C.J.	BAL	141	1ST WARD
JOHNSON, CALEB	ANN	317	1ST DIST
JOHNSON, CALEB	BAL	321	1ST DIST
JOHNSON, CALEB	BAL	222	17TH WAR
JOHNSON, CAMILLA	CEC	072	5TH E DI
JOHNSON, CARLOS	BAL	117	15TH WAR
JOHNSON, CAROLIN	BAL	085	15TH WAR
JOHNSON, CAROLINE	BAL	160	16TH WAR
JOHNSON, CAROLINE	BAL	089	5TH WARD
JOHNSON, CAROLINE	HAR	071	1ST DIST
JOHNSON, CAROLINE	HAR	052	1ST DIST
JOHNSON, CAROLINE	MGM	330	CRACKLIN
JOHNSON, CAROLINE	MGM	330	CRACKLIN
JOHNSON, CAROLINE	PRI	105	PISCATAW
JOHNSON, CAROLINE	WOR	270	BERLIN 1
JOHNSON, CASSANDRA	BAL	260	6TH WARD
JOHNSON, CASSANDRA	BAL	049	15TH WAR
JOHNSON, CATHARINE	BAL	243	12TH WAR
JOHNSON, CATHARINE	BAL	424	1ST DIST
JOHNSON, CATHARINE	BAL	080	15TH WAR
JOHNSON, CATHARINE	BAL	130	16TH WAR
JOHNSON, CATHARINE	CEC	077	NORTHEAS
JOHNSON, CATHARINE	FRE	215	BUCKEYST
JOHNSON, CATHERINE	FRE	245	NEW MARK
JOHNSON, CATHERINE	BAL	279	20TH WAR
JOHNSON, CATHERINE	BAL	032	4TH WARD
JOHNSON, CATHERINE	BAL	068	10TH WAR
JOHNSON, CATHERINE	ALL	218	CUMBERLA
JOHNSON, CAVY	ANN	433	HOWARD D
JOHNSON, CEPTON	FRE	093	FREDERIC
JOHNSON, CHARITY	HAR	187	3RD DIST
JOHNSON, CHARITY	ANN	415	HOWARD D
JOHNSON, CHARITY	ANN	349	3RD DIST
JOHNSON, CHARITY	BAL	169	6TH WARD
JOHNSON, CHARITY	BAL	255	1ST DIST
JOHNSON, CHARITY	SOM	510	BARREN C
JOHNSON, CHARLES	SOM	394	BRINKLEY
JOHNSON, CHARLES	QUE	211	3RD E DI
JOHNSON, CHARLES	BAL	009	1ST WARD
JOHNSON, CHARLES	BAL	081	1ST WARD
JOHNSON, CHARLES	BAL	285	1ST DIST
JOHNSON, CHARLES	BAL	215	6TH WARD
JOHNSON, CHARLES	BAL	192	6TH WARD
JOHNSON, CHARLES	BAL	144	5TH WARD
JOHNSON, CHARLES	BAL	163	1ST WARD
JOHNSON, CHARLES	BAL	036	9TH WARD
JOHNSON, CHARLES	ANN	350	3RD DIST
JOHNSON, CHARLES	ANN	460	HOWARD D
JOHNSON, CHARLES	BAL	115	2ND DIST
JOHNSON, CHARLES	BAL	077	15TH WAR
JOHNSON, CHARLES	ANN	498	HOWARD D
JOHNSON, CHARLES	BAL	012	9TH WARD
JOHNSON, CHARLES	BAL	136	1ST WARD
JOHNSON, CHARLES	BAL	142	1ST WARD
JOHNSON, CHARLES	BAL	137	1ST WARD
JOHNSON, CHARLES	ANN	292	ANNAPOLI
JOHNSON, CHARLES	ALL	069	5TH E.D.
JOHNSON, CHARLES	BAL	037	4TH WARD
JOHNSON, CHARLES	FRE	231	BUCKEYST
JOHNSON, CHARLES	DOR	438	1ST DIST
JOHNSON, CHARLES	CEC	064	1ST E DI
JOHNSON, CHARLES	CAL	025	2ND DIST
JOHNSON, CHARLES P.	CHA	272	ALLENS F
JOHNSON, CHARLES H.	CAL	050	3RD DIST
JOHNSON, CHARLES H.	BAL	372	3RD WARD
JOHNSON, CHARLES-BLACK	BAL	136	1ST WARD
JOHNSON, CHARLES-BLACX	FRE	451	8TH E DI
JOHNSON, CHARLES-BLACK	QUE	197	3RD E DI
JOHNSON, CHARLOTT	WOR	313	2ND E DI
JOHNSON, CHARLOTTE	SOM	531	QUANTICO
JOHNSON, CHARLOTTE	BAL	086	18TH WAR
JOHNSON, CHARLOTTE	MGM	420	MEDLEY 3
JOHNSON, CHARLOTTE	ANN	290	ANNAPOLI
JOHNSON, CHARLOTTE	ANN	331	2ND DIST
JOHNSON, CHARLOTTE	BAL	223	12TH WAR
JOHNSON, CHARLOTTE	BAL	070	15TH WAR
JOHNSON, CHARLOTTE	ANN	516	HOWARD D
JOHNSON, CHARLOTTE	BAL	121	16TH WAR
JOHNSON, CHARLOTTE	BAL	189	6TH WARD
JOHNSON, CHAUNCEY	BAL	079	15TH WAR
JOHNSON, CHESTON	ALL	070	5TH E.D.
JOHNSON, CHRISTOPHER	MGM	433	CLARKSTR
JOHNSON, CHRISTOPHER	HAR	196	3RD DIST
JOHNSON, CLARISSA	BAL	015	2ND DIST
JOHNSON, CLEM	BAL	166	19TH WAR
JOHNSON, CONSTANT	BAL	057	4TH WARD
JOHNSON, CORDELIA	BAL	351	3RD WARD
JOHNSON, CORNELIUS	ALL	042	10TH E.D
JOHNSON, CORNELIUS	BAL	379	3RD WARD
JOHNSON, CRISSY	ANN	353	3RD DIST
JOHNSON, CROMWELL	BAL	044	2ND DIST
JOHNSON, CUPID	CEC	200	7TH E DI
JOHNSON, CYRUS	BAL	115	1ST WARD
JOHNSON, CYRUS	BAL	114	1ST WARD
JOHNSON, CYRUS	ANN	496	HOWARD D
JOHNSON, CYRUS	SOM	387	BRINKLEY
JOHNSON, DAFNEY	ANN	291	ANNAPOLI
JOHNSON, DANIEL	ANN	370	4TH DIST
JOHNSON, DANIEL	WOR	186	7TH E DI
JOHNSON, DANIEL	DOR	462	1ST DIST
JOHNSON, DANIEL	DOR	339	3RD DIVI
JOHNSON, DANIEL	CEC	129	6TH E DI
JOHNSON, DANIEL	BAL	126	11TH WAR
JOHNSON, DANIL	DOR	466	1ST DIST
JOHNSON, DARIUS	BAL	180	6TH WARD
JOHNSON, DAVID	BAL	022	2ND DIST
JOHNSON, DAVID	BAL	022	2ND DIST
JOHNSON, DAVID	SOM	385	BRINKLEY
JOHNSON, DAVID	SOM	393	BRINKLEY
JOHNSON, DAVID	ST	257	3RD E DI
JOHNSON, DAVID	ST	257	3RD E DI
JOHNSON, DAVID	TAL	002	EASTON D
JOHNSON, DAVID	CAL	040	3RD DIST
JOHNSON, DAVID	BAL	214	17TH WAR
JOHNSON, DAVID	FRE	416	8TH E DI
JOHNSON, DAVID	CEC	070	5TH E DI
JOHNSON, DAVID	CAR	388	2ND DIST
JOHNSON, DAVID	HAR	146	3RD DIST
JOHNSON, DAVID S.	SOM	393	BRINKLEY
JOHNSON, DAVID-MULATTO	FRE	038	FREDERIC
JOHNSON, DELIA	PRI	025	VANSVILL
JOHNSON, DELIAH	WAS	118	2ND DIST
JOHNSON, DELINA	FRE	383	PETERSVI
JOHNSON, DELOIS	BAL	115	5TH WARD
JOHNSON, DEWEY	BAL	166	19TH WAR
JOHNSON, DENARD	SOM	390	BRINKLEY
JOHNSON, DENWOOD	DOR	339	3RD DIVI
JOHNSON, DENWOOD-BLACK	CAR	096	NO TWP L
JOHNSON, DERON	BAL	235	12TH WAR
JOHNSON, DEWY	BAL	029	2ND DIST
JOHNSON, DINAH	BAL	010	EASTERN
JOHNSON, DINAH	BAL	115	11TH WAR
JOHNSON, DINAH	BAL	066	18TH WAR
JOHNSON, DORCAS	FRE	056	FREDERIC
JOHNSON, DORCAS	BAL	176	6TH WARD
JOHNSON, E.	BAL	150	1ST WARD
JOHNSON, E.	BAL	149	1ST WARD
JOHNSON, E.	BAL	072	10TH WAR
JOHNSON, EDWARD	BAL	127	16TH WAR
JOHNSON, EDWARD	BAL	103	10TH WAR
JOHNSON, EDWARD	BAL	228	6TH WARD
JOHNSON, EDWARD	ALL	230	CUMBERLA
JOHNSON, EDWARD	BAL	087	2ND DIST
JOHNSON, EDWARD	BAL	231	12TH WAR
JOHNSON, EDWARD	ANN	289	ANNAPOLI
JOHNSON, EDWARD	ALL	001	3RD E.D.
JOHNSON, EDWARD	BAL	107	1ST WARD
JOHNSON, EDWARD	BAL	055	1ST WARD
JOHNSON, EDWARD	HAR	083	2ND DIST
JOHNSON, EDWARD	BAL	062	18TH WAR
JOHNSON, EDWARD	CEC	081	CHARLEST
JOHNSON, EDWARD	DOR	336	3RD DIVI
JOHNSON, EDWARD	CEC	153	PORT DUP
JOHNSON, EDWARD	CAR	229	5TH DIST
JOHNSON, EDWARD	ST	286	2ND E DI
JOHNSON, EDWARD	WOR	324	1ST E DI
JOHNSON, EDWARD H.	ST	332	4TH E DI
JOHNSON, EDWARD*	DOR	453	1ST DIST
JOHNSON, EDWARD-BLACK	BAL	223	2ND WARD
JOHNSON, EDWIN	BAL	211	19TH WAR
JOHNSON, ELEANOR	CHA	239	HILLTOP
JOHNSON, ELENOR	FRE	382	PETERSVI
JOHNSON, ELENOR C.	FRE	406	JEFFERSO
JOHNSON, ELI	BAL	243	20TH WAR
JOHNSON, ELIJAH	BAL	115	15TH WAR
JOHNSON, ELIJAH	SOM	394	BRINKLEY
JOHNSON, ELIJAH	SOM	384	BRINKLEY
JOHNSON, ELISABETH	ALL	042	10TH E.D
JOHNSON, ELISABETH	ALL	257	CUMBERLA
JOHNSON, ELISHA	BAL	059	2ND DIST
JOHNSON, ELISHA	BAL	244	1ST DIST
JOHNSON, ELISHA	HAR	026	1ST DIST
JOHNSON, ELIZA	HAR	017	1ST DIST
JOHNSON, ELIZA	BAL	032	4TH WARD
JOHNSON, ELIZA	BAL	031	4TH WARD
JOHNSON, ELIZA	BAL	417	14TH WAR
JOHNSON, ELIZA	CEC	075	NORTHEAS
JOHNSON, ELIZA	BAL	121	11TH WAR
JOHNSON, ELIZA	KEN	219	2ND DIST
JOHNSON, ELIZA	BAL	292	1ST DIST
JOHNSON, ELIZA	BAL	227	1ST DIST
JOHNSON, ELIZA	ANN	379	4TH DIST
JOHNSON, ELIZA	ALL	085	5TH E.D.
JOHNSON, ELIZA	BAL	110	10TH WAR
JOHNSON, ELIZA	BAL	043	9TH WARD
JOHNSON, ELIZA	BAL	241	12TH WAR
JOHNSON, ELIZA	BAL	068	15TH WAR
JOHNSON, ELIZA	BAL	114	5TH WARD
JOHNSON, ELIZA	ANN	497	HOWARD D
JOHNSON, ELIZA	BAL	432	1ST DIST
JOHNSON, ELIZA	BAL	372	3RD WARD
JOHNSON, ELIZA	KEN	288	3RD DIST
JOHNSON, ELIZA	TAL	096	ST MICHA
JOHNSON, ELIZA A.	BAL	073	15TH WAR
JOHNSON, ELIZA A.	BAL	174	11TH WAR
JOHNSON, ELIZA J.	BAL	003	15TH WAR
JOHNSON, ELIZA J.	BAL	191	17TH WAR
JOHNSON, ELIZA J.	BAL	417	3RD WARD
JOHNSON, ELIZABETH	CEC	002	ELKTON 3
JOHNSON, ELIZABETH	BAL	208	19TH WAR
JOHNSON, ELIZABETH	BAL	012	4TH WARD
JOHNSON, ELIZABETH	BAL	114	11TH WAR
JOHNSON, ELIZABETH	CAL	043	3RD DIST
JOHNSON, ELIZABETH	BAL	412	14TH WAR
JOHNSON, ELIZABETH	CEC	137	6TH E DI
JOHNSON, ELIZABETH	BAL	344	13TH WAR
JOHNSON, ELIZABETH	BAL	061	4TH WARD
JOHNSON, ELIZABETH	BAL	249	17TH WAR
JOHNSON, ELIZABETH	MGM	422	MEDLEY 3
JOHNSON, ELIZABETH	HAR	062	1ST DIST
JOHNSON, ELIZABETH	HAR	058	1ST DIST
JOHNSON, ELIZABETH	SOM	408	DUBLIN D
JOHNSON, ELIZABETH	DOR	340	3RD DIVI
JOHNSON, ELIZABETH	DOR	361	3RD DIVI
JOHNSON, ELIZABETH	CEC	192	5TH E DI
JOHNSON, ELIZABETH	FRE	337	MIDDLETO
JOHNSON, ELIZABETH	BAL	091	15TH WAR
JOHNSON, ELIZABETH	BAL	077	10TH WAR
JOHNSON, ELIZABETH	BAL	007	9TH WARD
JOHNSON, ELIZABETH	BAL	379	3RD WARD
JOHNSON, ELIZABETH	BAL	446	1ST DIST
JOHNSON, ELIZABETH	BAL	306	3RD WARD
JOHNSON, ELIZABETH	BAL	200	6TH WARD
JOHNSON, ELIZABETH	BAL	124	5TH WARD
JOHNSON, ELIZABETH	TAL	036	EASTON D
JOHNSON, ELIZABETH	PRI	027	VANSVILL
JOHNSON, ELIZABETH-BLACK	BAL	185	2ND WARD
JOHNSON, ELLEN	BAL	458	1ST DIST
JOHNSON, ELLEN	BAL	113	5TH WARD
JOHNSON, ELLEN	BAL	100	5TH WARD
JOHNSON, ELLEN	BAL	378	1ST DIST
JOHNSON, ELLEN	BAL	052	9TH WARD
JOHNSON, ELLEN	BAL	328	13TH WAR
JOHNSON, ELLEN	SOM	491	SALISBUR
JOHNSON, ELLEN	SOM	493	SALISBUR
JOHNSON, ELLEN	BAL	042	4TH WARD
JOHNSON, ELLEN J.	BAL	433	14TH WAR
JOHNSON, ELMIRA	WOR	289	9TH E DI
JOHNSON, EMALINE	WOR	275	BERLIN 1
JOHNSON, EMALINE	CEC	066	1ST E DI
JOHNSON, EMELINE	SOM	384	BRINKLEY
JOHNSON, EMILINE	BAL	152	11TH WAR
JOHNSON, EMILINE	BAL	110	5TH WARD
JOHNSON, EMILY	BAL	317	3RD WARD
JOHNSON, EMILY	BAL	122	5TH WARD
JOHNSON, EMILY	BAL	180	6TH WARD
JOHNSON, EMILY	BAL	250	6TH WARD
JOHNSON, EMMA	TAL	087	ST MICHA
JOHNSON, EMORY	BAL	240	6TH WARD
JOHNSON, ENNALS	CAR	121	NO TWP L
JOHNSON, ENOCH	CEC	133	6TH E DI
JOHNSON, EPHRAIM	MGM	340	CLARKSBU
JOHNSON, ESTER	SOM	405	DUBLIN D
JOHNSON, EUGENIA	ANN	371	4TH DIST
JOHNSON, EZEKIEL	BAL	115	1ST WARD
JOHNSON, EZEKIEL	DOR	344	3RD DIVI
JOHNSON, EZEKIEL	TAL	087	ST MICHA
JOHNSON, EZEKIEL C.	BAL	336	3RD WARD
JOHNSON, F.	BAL	172	1ST WARD
JOHNSON, FANNY	BAL	133	5TH WARD
JOHNSON, FANNY	BAL	110	5TH WARD
JOHNSON, FANNY	TAL	084	ST MICHA
JOHNSON, FANNY	BAL	264	17TH WAR
JOHNSON, FERGUS	BAL	186	19TH WAR
JOHNSON, FLORIAL	PRI	014	BLADENSB
JOHNSON, FRANCES	QUE	235	4TH E DI
JOHNSON, FRANCES	BAL	179	19TH WAR
JOHNSON, FRANCES	BAL	241	6TH WARD
JOHNSON, FRANCES A.	HAR	029	1ST DIST
JOHNSON, FRANCES J.	BAL	099	15TH WAR
JOHNSON, FRANCINER	CAR	214	5TH DIST
JOHNSON, FRANCIS	BAL	160	19TH WAR
JOHNSON, FRANCIS	BAL	105	1ST WARD
JOHNSON, FRANCIS	BAL	243	1ST DIST
JOHNSON, FRANCIS	QUE	246	5TH E DI
JOHNSON, FRANCIS A.	BAL	446	1ST DIST
JOHNSON, FRANCIS H.	CHA	218	ALLENS F
JOHNSON, FRANCIS V.	BAL	060	10TH WAR
JOHNSON, FRANK	BAL	080	2ND DIST
JOHNSON, FRANK	BAL	081	2ND DIST
JOHNSON, FREDERICK	ALL	262	CUMBERLA
JOHNSON, FREDERICK	BAL	106	1ST WARD
JOHNSON, FREDERICK	BAL	159	11TH WAR
JOHNSON, FREDERICK	ST	280	3RD E DI
JOHNSON, FREDERICK	TAL	118	ST MICHA
JOHNSON, FREDERICK	KEN	278	1ST DIST
JOHNSON, FREDERICK *	BAL	301	12TH WAR
JOHNSON, G. M.	BAL	332	1ST DIST
JOHNSON, G.P.	BAL	165	1ST WARD
JOHNSON, GEORGE	BAL	168	1ST WARD
JOHNSON, GEORGE	BAL	227	6TH WARD
JOHNSON, GEORGE	BAL	207	6TH WARD
JOHNSON, GEORGE	BAL	463	1ST DIST
JOHNSON, GEORGE	BAL	279	12TH WAR
JOHNSON, GEORGE	BAL	152	16TH WAR
JOHNSON, GEORGE	ANN	346	3RD DIST
JOHNSON, GEORGE	BAL	041	2ND DIST
JOHNSON, GEORGE	ANN	290	ANNAPOLI
JOHNSON, GEORGE	DOR	453	1ST DIST
JOHNSON, GEORGE	PRI	039	VANSVILL
JOHNSON, GEORGE	QUE	235	4TH E DI
JOHNSON, GEORGE	WOR	344	1ST E DI
JOHNSON, GEORGE	SOM	371	BRINKLEY
JOHNSON, GEORGE	SOM	369	BRINKLEY
JOHNSON, GEORGE	SOM	359	BRINKLEY
JOHNSON, GEORGE	WOR	275	BERLIN 1
JOHNSON, GEORGE	WOR	309	2ND E DI
JOHNSON, GEORGE	DOR	314	1ST DIST
JOHNSON, GEORGE	BAL	199	19TH WAR
JOHNSON, GEORGE	HAR	097	2ND DIST
JOHNSON, GEORGE	BAL	253	17TH WAR
JOHNSON, GEORGE	BAL	253	17TH WAR
JOHNSON, GEORGE	BAL	250	17TH WAR
JOHNSON, GEORGE	BAL	382	13TH WAR
JOHNSON, GEORGE	FRE	129	CREAGERS
JOHNSON, GEORGE	BAL	453	14TH WAR
JOHNSON, GEORGE	BAL	459	14TH WAR
JOHNSON, GEORGE	CEC	095	4TH E DI
JOHNSON, GEORGE .*	ANN	453	HOWARD D
JOHNSON, GEORGE A.	HAR	153	3RD DIST
JOHNSON, GEORGE A. H. M.	BAL	043	15TH WAR
JOHNSON, GEORGE JR.	CEC	095	4TH E DI
JOHNSON, GEORGE P.	BAL	315	20TH WAR
JOHNSON, GEORGE P.	BAL	308	3RD WARD
JOHNSON, GEORGE W.	BAL	010	1ST WARD
JOHNSON, GEORGE W.	HAR	203	3RD DIST
JOHNSON, GEORGE W.	HAR	196	3RD DIST
JOHNSON, GEORGE-BLACK	QUE	200	3RD E DI
JOHNSON, GEORGIANA	BAL	216	6TH WARD
JOHNSON, GEORGIANA	BAL	031	9TH WARD
JOHNSON, GERARD	ANN	310	1ST DIST
JOHNSON, GEROGE	HAR	006	1ST DIST
JOHNSON, GINTUS	CEC	020	ELKTON 3
JOHNSON, GOERGE	BAL	134	16TH WAR
JOHNSON, GOERGE J.	HAR	186	3RD DIST
JOHNSON, GRACE	BAL	038	9TH WARD
JOHNSON, GRACE	BAL	168	2ND DIST
JOHNSON, GRAFTON	BAL	117	5TH WARD
JOHNSON, GREENBURY	ANN	485	HOWARD D
JOHNSON, H.	BAL	165	1ST WARD
JOHNSON, H.	BAL	153	11TH WAR
JOHNSON, H. F.	BAL	333	1ST DIST
JOHNSON, H.*	TAL	035	EASTON D
JOHNSON, HAGAN	BAL	044	9TH WARD
JOHNSON, HAGAR	BAL	105	10TH WAR
JOHNSON, HAGAR	CAL	044	3RD DIST
JOHNSON, HAMBELTON	DOR	336	3RD DIVI
JOHNSON, HAMILTON	BAL	107	18TH WAR
JOHNSON, HAMILTON	ANN	474	HOWARD D
JOHNSON, HANNA	CAL	014	1ST DIST
JOHNSON, HANNAH	BAL	399	14TH WAR
JOHNSON, HANNAH	HAR	204	3RD DIST
JOHNSON, HANNAH	HAR	085	2ND DIST
JOHNSON, HANNAH	ANN	425	HOWARD D
JOHNSON, HANNAH	BAL	057	10TH WAR
JOHNSON, HANNAH	BAL	462	1ST DIST
JOHNSON, HANNAH	BAL	260	1ST DIST
JOHNSON, HANNAH	BAL	066	15TH WAR
JOHNSON, HANNAH	SOM	501	SALISBUR
JOHNSON, HANNAH-BLACK	QUE	153	1ST E DI
JOHNSON, HARRIET	BAL	429	14TH WAR
JOHNSON, HARRIET	WOR	299	SNOW HIL
JOHNSON, HARRIET	WOR	268	BERLIN 1

JOHNSON, HARRIET WOR 276 BERLIN I
JOHNSON, HARRIET BAL 236 12TH WAR
JOHNSON, HARRIET BAL 331 1ST DIST
JOHNSON, HARRIET BAL 057 10TH WAR
JOHNSON, HARRIET ANN 479 HOWARD D
JOHNSON, HARRIET BAL 239 6TH WARD
JOHNSON, HARRIET ANN 336 3RD DIST
JOHNSON, HARRIET A. BAL 167 19TH WAR
JOHNSON, HARRIET-MULATTO FRE 233 BUCKEYST
JOHNSON, HARRIOTT BAL 338 3RD WARD
JOHNSON, HARRIS QUE 233 4TH E DI
JOHNSON, HARRY BAL 151 1ST WARD
JOHNSON, HARVEY ALL 171 7TH E.D.
JOHNSON, HARVEY F. SR. SOM 383 BRINKLEY
JOHNSON, HARY DOR 463 1ST DIST
JOHNSON, HARY DOR 461 1ST DIST
JOHNSON, HELEN BAL 174 19TH WAR
JOHNSON, HENREITTA BAL 074 1ST WARD
JOHNSON, HENRIETTA BAL 132 16TH WAR
JOHNSON, HENRIETTA BAL 416 3RD WARD
JOHNSON, HENRIETTA KEN 210 2ND DIST
JOHNSON, HENRIETTA BAL 466 14TH WAR
JOHNSON, HENRIETTA CAR 079 NO TWP L
JOHNSON, HENRIETTA-MULATT ST 299 2ND E DI
JOHNSON, HENRIETTE-BLACK CAR 090 NO TWP L
JOHNSON, HENRY BAL 161 11TH WAR
JOHNSON, HENRY BAL 166 19TH WAR
JOHNSON, HENRY DOR 420 1ST DIST
JOHNSON, HENRY BAL 408 3RD WARD
JOHNSON, HENRY CAR 188 4TH DIST
JOHNSON, HENRY BAL 045 4TH WARD
JOHNSON, HENRY BAL 376 13TH WAR
JOHNSON, HENRY BAL 353 13TH WAR
JOHNSON, HENRY HAR 097 2ND DIST
JOHNSON, HENRY BAL 314 20TH WAR
JOHNSON, HENRY HAR 041 1ST DIST
JOHNSON, HENRY SOM 412 DUBLIN D
JOHNSON, HENRY FRE 391 PETERSVI
JOHNSON, HENRY KEN 281 3RD DIST
JOHNSON, HENRY SOM 382 BRINKLEY
JOHNSON, HENRY QUE 244 5TH E DI
JOHNSON, HENRY QUE 226 4TH E DI
JOHNSON, HENRY ST 264 3RD E DI
JOHNSON, HENRY SOM 391 BRINKLEY
JOHNSON, HENRY SOM 393 BRINKLEY
JOHNSON, HENRY WAS 065 2ND SUBD
JOHNSON, HENRY SOM 521 BARREN C
JOHNSON, HENRY PRI 038 VANSVILL
JOHNSON, HENRY SOM 530 QUANTICO
JOHNSON, HENRY BAL 128 16TH WAR
JOHNSON, HENRY BAL 130 16TH WAR
JOHNSON, HENRY BAL 050 9TH WARD
JOHNSON, HENRY BAL 055 9TH WARD
JOHNSON, HENRY BAL 082 1ST WARD
JOHNSON, HENRY BAL 105 1ST WARD
JOHNSON, HENRY ANN 384 4TH DIST
JOHNSON, HENRY BAL 151 1ST WARD
JOHNSON, HENRY BAL 152 1ST WARD
JOHNSON, HENRY BAL 463 1ST DIST
JOHNSON, HENRY BAL 378 1ST DIST
JOHNSON, HENRY ANN 519 HOWARD D
JOHNSON, HENRY BAL 029 2ND DIST
JOHNSON, HENRY ANN 345 3RD DIST
JOHNSON, HENRY BAL 005 EASTERN
JOHNSON, HENRY ALL 257 CUMBERLA
JOHNSON, HENRY BAL 010 EASTERN
JOHNSON, HENRY BAL 075 2ND DIST
JOHNSON, HENRY BAL 129 1ST WARD
JOHNSON, HENRY BAL 280 2ND WARD
JOHNSON, HENRY C. CEC 143 7TH E DI
JOHNSON, HENRY J. SOM 392 BRINKLEY
JOHNSON, HENRY JR. BAL 005 9TH WARD
JOHNSON, HENRY T. BAL 157 16TH WAR
JOHNSON, HENRY-BLACK QUE 203 3RD E DI
JOHNSON, HENRY-BLACK QUE 178 2ND E DI
JOHNSON, HENRY-MULATTO BAL 222 2ND WARD
JOHNSON, HESTER BAL 130 16TH WAR
JOHNSON, HESTER BAL 093 15TH WAR
JOHNSON, HESTER BAL 043 15TH WAR
JOHNSON, HESTER ANN 463 HOWARD D
JOHNSON, HESTER SOM 491 SALISBUR
JOHNSON, HESTER CAR 222 5TH DIST
JOHNSON, HESTER A. TAL 010 EASTON D
JOHNSON, HESTER A. BAL 126 16TH WAR
JOHNSON, HESTER A. BAL 378 3RD WARD
JOHNSON, HESTER A.-BLACK BAL 208 2ND WARD
JOHNSON, HESTER-BLACK CAR 161 NO TWP L
JOHNSON, HESTOR ANN BAL 203 17TH WAR
JOHNSON, HETIA WOR 304 SNOW HIL
JOHNSON, HETTY A. CEC 132 6TH E DI
JOHNSON, HEWIT BAL 148 5TH WARD
JOHNSON, HIRAM BAL 057 10TH WAR
JOHNSON, HIRAM BAL 106 5TH WARD
JOHNSON, HORACE DOR 337 3RD DIVI
JOHNSON, HORACE BAL 243 20TH WAR
JOHNSON, HORATIO ANN 485 HOWARD D
JOHNSON, HOSEA CEC 213 7TH E DI
JOHNSON, HOWARD BAL 076 18TH WAR
JOHNSON, HY BAL 186 5TH DIST
JOHNSON, IBBY TAL 099 ST MICHA
JOHNSON, IGNATIUS CHA 241 HILLTOP
JOHNSON, ISAAC BAL 231 17TH WAR
JOHNSON, ISAAC CEC 181 7TH E DI
JOHNSON, ISAAC BAL 039 4TH WARD
JOHNSON, ISAAC HAR 014 1ST DIST
JOHNSON, ISAAC WOR 281 BERLIN 1
JOHNSON, ISAAC KEN 296 3RD DIST
JOHNSON, ISAAC SOM 383 BRINKLEY
JOHNSON, ISAAC SOM 371 BRINKLEY
JOHNSON, ISAAC SOM 372 BRINKLEY
JOHNSON, ISAAC ANN 447 HOWARD D
JOHNSON, ISAAC BAL 069 2ND DIST
JOHNSON, ISAAC BAL 052 9TH WARD
JOHNSON, ISAAC BAL 077 15TH WAR
JOHNSON, ISAAC BAL 301 12TH WAR
JOHNSON, ISAAC BAL 301 12TH WAR
JOHNSON, ISAAC ALL 092 5TH E.D.
JOHNSON, ISAAC ALL 186 9TH E.D.
JOHNSON, ISAAC H. BAL 037 15TH WAR
JOHNSON, ISAAC-BLACK WOR 334 1ST E DI
JOHNSON, ISAAC-BLACK QUE 143 1ST E DI
JOHNSON, ISABEL BAL 300 20TH WAR
JOHNSON, ISABELLA BAL 167 19TH WAR
JOHNSON, ISAIAH BAL 121 16TH WAR
JOHNSON, ISRAEL BAL 213 6TH DIST
JOHNSON, J. BAL 332 1ST DIST
JOHNSON, J. ANN 345 3RD DIST
JOHNSON, J. BAL 115 1ST WARD
JOHNSON, J. BAL 151 1ST WARD
JOHNSON, J. BAL 157 1ST WARD
JOHNSON, J. BAL 148 1ST WARD
JOHNSON, J. BAL 129 1ST WARD
JOHNSON, J. BAL 129 1ST WARD
JOHNSON, J. C. BAL 332 1ST DIST
JOHNSON, J. G. BAL 048 18TH WAR
JOHNSON, J. H. BAL 148 1ST WARD
JOHNSON, J. H. BAL 156 1ST WARD
JOHNSON, J. M. BAL 156 1ST WARD
JOHNSON, J.H. BAL 174 1ST WARD
JOHNSON, J.H.T. BAL 158 1ST WARD
JOHNSON, J.P. BAL 170 1ST WARD
JOHNSON, JACKSON ALL 042 10TH E.D
JOHNSON, JACOB ANN 314 1ST DIST
JOHNSON, JACOB BAL 271 2ND WARD
JOHNSON, JACOB ANN 347 3RD DIST
JOHNSON, JACOE BAL 046 2ND DIST
JOHNSON, JACOB BAL 049 15TH WAR
JOHNSON, JACOB FRE 368 CATOCTIN
JOHNSON, JACOB HAR 160 3RD DIST
JOHNSON, JACOB HAR 112 2ND DIST
JOHNSON, JACOB CEC 180 7TH E DI
JOHNSON, JACOB DOR 307 1ST DIST
JOHNSON, JACOB WOR 315 2ND E DI
JOHNSON, JACOB C. CEC 003 ELKTON 3
JOHNSON, JACOB-BLACK FRE 437 8TH E DI
JOHNSON, JAMES DOR 320 1ST DIST
JOHNSON, JAMES CEC 135 6TH E DI
JOHNSON, JAMES CEC 133 6TH E DI
JOHNSON, JAMES CEC 138 6TH E DI
JOHNSON, JAMES CEC 187 7TH E DI
JOHNSON, JAMES CEC 167 6TH E DI
JOHNSON, JAMES BAL 213 17TH WAR
JOHNSON, JAMES BAL 216 17TH WAR
JOHNSON, JAMES HAR 115 2ND DIST
JOHNSON, JAMES HAR 020 1ST DIST
JOHNSON, JAMES SOM 411 DUBLIN D
JOHNSON, JAMES HAR 063 1ST DIST
JOHNSON, JAMES MGM 359 BERRYS D
JOHNSON, JAMES HAR 135 2ND DIST
JOHNSON, JAMES CAL 022 2ND DIST
JOHNSON, JAMES CAL 001 1ST DIST
JOHNSON, JAMES CAL 052 3RD DIST
JOHNSON, JAMES CAR 065 NO TWP L
JOHNSON, JAMES WOR 295 9TH E DI
JOHNSON, JAMES SOM 384 BRINKLEY
JOHNSON, JAMES SOM 383 BRINKLEY
JOHNSON, JAMES KEN 304 3RD DIST
JOHNSON, JAMES ST 341 5TH E DI
JOHNSON, JAMES TAL 118 ST MICHA
JOHNSON, JAMES WOR 176 6TH E DI
JOHNSON, JAMES BAL 047 2ND DIST
JOHNSON, JAMES BAL 096 2ND DIST
JOHNSON, JAMES BAL 089 2ND DIST
JOHNSON, JAMES BAL 094 2ND DIST
JOHNSON, JAMES BAL 035 2ND DIST
JOHNSON, JAMES BAL 282 2ND WARD
JOHNSON, JAMES ANN 324 2ND DIST
JOHNSON, JAMES ALL 090 5TH E.D.
JOHNSON, JAMES ALL 090 5TH E.D.
JOHNSON, JAMES ANN 275 ANNAPOLI
JOHNSON, JAMES BAL 207 2ND WARD
JOHNSON, JAMES BAL 198 2ND WARD
JOHNSON, JAMES BAL 186 2ND WARD
JOHNSON, JAMES BAL 028 9TH WARD
JOHNSON, JAMES BAL 110 5TH WARD
JOHNSON, JAMES BAL 120 1ST WARD
JOHNSON, JAMES BAL 121 1ST WARD
JOHNSON, JAMES BAL 157 2ND DIST
JOHNSON, JAMES BAL 108 15TH WAR
JOHNSON, JAMES BAL 108 15TH WAR
JOHNSON, JAMES BAL 106 15TH WAR
JOHNSON, JAMES BAL 289 12TH WAR
JOHNSON, JAMES BAL 183 16TH WAR
JOHNSON, JAMES BAL 195 17TH WAR
JOHNSON, JAMES A. HAR 161 3RD DIST
JOHNSON, JAMES A. BAL 243 20TH WAR
JOHNSON, JAMES E.* DOR 356 3RD DIVI
JOHNSON, JAMES H. BAL 169 1ST WARD
JOHNSON, JAMES H. WOR 231 6TH E DI
JOHNSON, JAMES HENRY DOR 297 1ST DIST
JOHNSON, JAMES JR. MGM 359 BERRYS D
JOHNSON, JAMES N. CHA 286 BOJANTOW
JOHNSON, JAMES N. BAL 339 1ST DIST
JOHNSON, JAMES W. BAL 094 10TH WAR
JOHNSON, JAMES-BLACK FRE 396 PETERSVI
JOHNSON, JAMES-MULATTO BAL 246 2ND WARD
JOHNSON, JANE BAL 093 10TH WAR
JOHNSON, JANE BAL 106 10TH WAR
JOHNSON, JANE BAL 093 5TH WARD
JOHNSON, JANE BAL 097 5TH WARD
JOHNSON, JANE BAL 135 5TH WARD
JOHNSON, JANE BAL 185 6TH WARD
JOHNSON, JANE BAL 231 1ST DIST
JOHNSON, JANE CHA 245 HILLTOP
JOHNSON, JANE KEN 218 2ND DIST
JOHNSON, JANE HAR 066 1ST DIST
JOHNSON, JANE BAL 423 14TH WAR
JOHNSON, JANE BAL 264 17TH WAR
JOHNSON, JANE BAL 295 17TH WAR
JOHNSON, JANE WAS 044 2ND SUBD
JOHNSON, JANE PRI 001 BLADENSB
JOHNSON, JANE BARNES ANN 419 HOWARD D
JOHNSON, JANES ANN 473 HOWARD D
JOHNSON, JARAD BAL 089 2ND DIST
JOHNSON, JARRED HAR 177 3RD DIST
JOHNSON, JARRET BAL 099 5TH WARD
JOHNSON, JARRET BAL 173 16TH WAR
JOHNSON, JEFFERSON ANN 482 HOWARD D
JOHNSON, JEFFERY-BLACK QUE 136 1ST E DI
JOHNSON, JEFFREY ANN 367 4TH DIST
JOHNSON, JEMIMA-BLACK FRE 220 BUCKEYST
JOHNSON, JEREMIAH BAL 137 16TH WAR
JOHNSON, JERRY KEN 238 2ND DIST
JOHNSON, JESSE BAL 160 1ST WARD
JOHNSON, JESSY HAR 179 3RD DIST
JOHNSON, JETHRO CEC 139 6TH E DI
JOHNSON, JIM WOR 304 SNOW HIL
JOHNSON, JIM WOR 275 BERLIN 1
JOHNSON, JIM WOR 274 BERLIN 1
JOHNSON, JOEL BAL 220 12TH WAR
JOHNSON, JOHN BAL 185 6TH WARD
JOHNSON, JOHN BAL 205 2ND WARD
JOHNSON, JOHN BAL 197 2ND WARD
JOHNSON, JOHN BAL 177 6TH WARD
JOHNSON, JOHN BAL 240 6TH WARD
JOHNSON, JOHN BAL 183 16TH WAR
JOHNSON, JOHN BAL 078 10TH WAR
JOHNSON, JOHN BAL 121 16TH WAR
JOHNSON, JOHN BAL 121 16TH WAR
JOHNSON, JOHN ANN 358 3RD DIST
JOHNSON, JOHN ANN 341 3RD DIST
JOHNSON, JOHN BAL 090 2ND DIST
JOHNSON, JOHN BAL 096 2ND DIST
JOHNSON, JOHN BAL 075 2ND DIST
JOHNSON, JOHN BAL 027 2ND DIST
JOHNSON, JOHN BAL 142 2ND DIST
JOHNSON, JOHN BAL 149 2ND DIST
JOHNSON, JOHN BAL 136 2ND DIST
JOHNSON, JOHN BAL 129 2ND DIST
JOHNSON, JOHN BAL 103 2ND DIST
JOHNSON, JOHN BAL 130 2ND DIST
JOHNSON, JOHN ANN 516 HOWARD D
JOHNSON, JOHN ANN 505 HOWARD D
JOHNSON, JOHN BAL 334 3RD WARD
JOHNSON, JOHN BAL 308 3RD WARD
JOHNSON, JOHN BAL 153 2ND DIST
JOHNSON, JOHN BAL 105 1ST WARD
JOHNSON, JOHN BAL 121 1ST WARD
JOHNSON, JOHN BAL 103 1ST WARD
JOHNSON, JOHN BAL 005 1ST WARD
JOHNSON, JOHN BAL 082 1ST WARD
JOHNSON, JOHN BAL 125 1ST WARD
JOHNSON, JOHN BAL 125 1ST WARD
JOHNSON, JOHN BAL 132 1ST WARD
JOHNSON, JOHN BAL 127 1ST WARD
JOHNSON, JOHN BAL 131 1ST WARD
JOHNSON, JOHN BAL 388 3RD WARD
JOHNSON, JOHN BAL 146 1ST WARD
JOHNSON, JOHN BAL 138 1ST WARD
JOHNSON, JOHN BAL 139 1ST WARD
JOHNSON, JOHN ANN 282 ANNAPOLI
JOHNSON, JOHN ANN 316 1ST DIST
JOHNSON, JOHN ANN 325 2ND DIST
JOHNSON, JOHN ALL 109 5TH E.D.
JOHNSON, JOHN WOR 275 BERLIN 1
JOHNSON, JOHN WOR 276 BERLIN 1
JOHNSON, JOHN WOR 272 BERLIN 1
JOHNSON, JOHN WOR 273 BERLIN 1
JOHNSON, JOHN WOR 304 SNOW HIL
JOHNSON, JOHN WAS 066 2ND SUBD
JOHNSON, JOHN TAL 019 EASTON D
JOHNSON, JOHN PRI 080 QUEEN AN
JOHNSON, JOHN KEN 297 3RD DIST
JOHNSON, JOHN KEN 295 3RD DIST
JOHNSON, JOHN KEN 291 3RD DIST
JOHNSON, JOHN ST 319 4TH E DI
JOHNSON, JOHN SOM 383 BRINKLEY
JOHNSON, JOHN SOM 395 BRINKLEY
JOHNSON, JOHN ST 265 3RD E DI
JOHNSON, JOHN BAL 253 17TH WAR
JOHNSON, JOHN CEC 165 6TH E DI
JOHNSON, JOHN HAR 183 3RD DIST
JOHNSON, JOHN BAL 163 19TH WAR
JOHNSON, JOHN BAL 168 19TH WAR
JOHNSON, JOHN CEC 078 NORTHEAS
JOHNSON, JOHN CEC 066 1ST E DI
JOHNSON, JOHN CEC 066 1ST E DI
JOHNSON, JOHN HAR 061 1ST DIST
JOHNSON, JOHN MGM 369 BERRYS D
JOHNSON, JOHN HAR 095 2ND DIST
JOHNSON, JOHN HAR 086 2ND DIST
JOHNSON, JOHN MGM 413 MEDLEY 3
JOHNSON, JOHN CEC 051 1ST E DI
JOHNSON, JOHN CEC 051 1ST E DI
JOHNSON, JOHN CEC 035 CHESAPEA
JOHNSON, JOHN BAL 201 19TH WAR
JOHNSON, JOHN A BAL 005 15TH WAR
JOHNSON, JOHN A. CEC 001 ELKTON 3
JOHNSON, JOHN A. FRE 305 WOODSBOR
JOHNSON, JOHN A. PRI 014 BLADENSB
JOHNSON, JOHN C. BAL 433 14TH WAR
JOHNSON, JOHN C. CAL 001 1ST DIST
JOHNSON, JOHN H. BAL 284 17TH WAR
JOHNSON, JOHN H. BAL 240 6TH WARD
JOHNSON, JOHN J. BAL 046 15TH WAR
JOHNSON, JOHN JAMES BAL 279 17TH WAR
JOHNSON, JOHN K. FRE 336 MIDDLETO
JOHNSON, JOHN K. FRE 338 MIDDLETO
JOHNSON, JOHN L. HAR 115 2ND DIST
JOHNSON, JOHN L. CHA 293 BOJANTOW
JOHNSON, JOHN M. BAL 293 20TH WAR
JOHNSON, JOHN M. BAL 024 9TH WARD
JOHNSON, JOHN N. DOR 320 1ST DIST
JOHNSON, JOHN S. WOR 314 2ND E DI
JOHNSON, JOHN T. CHA 241 HILLTOP
JOHNSON, JOHN T. BAL 096 18TH WAR
JOHNSON, JOHN T. BAL 061 4TH WARD
JOHNSON, JOHN T. BAL 199 19TH WAR
JOHNSON, JOHN T. ANN 276 ANNAPOLI
JOHNSON, JOHN T. BAL 027 2ND DIST
JOHNSON, JOHN T. ANN 427 HOWARD D
JOHNSON, JOHN W. BAL 128 1ST WARD
JOHNSON, JOHN W. BAL 008 1ST WARD
JOHNSON, JOHN W. QUE 148 1ST E DI
JOHNSON, JOHN W. BAL 128 11TH WAR
JOHNSON, JOHN-BLACK CAR 097 NO TWP L
JOHNSON, JOHN-BLACK CAR 072 NO TWP L
JOHNSON, JOHN-BLACK FRE 011 FREDERIC
JOHNSON, JOHN-BLACK WOR 169 6TH E DI
JOHNSON, JOHN-BLACK WOR 168 6TH E DI
JOHNSON, JOHN-BLACK QUE 159 2ND E DI
JOHNSON, JOHN-MULATTO BAL 214 2ND WARD
JOHNSON, JOHNATHAN ALL 229 CUMBERLA
JOHNSON, JOHSUA ALL 001 3RD E.D.
JOHNSON, JONATHAN ALL 097 5TH E.D.
JOHNSON, JOSEPH BAL 140 2ND DIST
JOHNSON, JOSEPH ANN 340 3RD DIST
JOHNSON, JOSEPH BAL 356 3RD WARD
JOHNSON, JOSEPH BAL 239 1ST DIST
JOHNSON, JOSEPH BAL 133 1ST WARD
JOHNSON, JOSEPH BAL 142 1ST WARD
JOHNSON, JOSEPH BAL 143 1ST WARD
JOHNSON, JOSEPH BAL 107 15TH WAR
JOHNSON, JOSEPH BAL 111 15TH WAR
JOHNSON, JOSEPH BAL 092 15TH WAR
JOHNSON, JOSEPH ST 261 3RD E DI
JOHNSON, JOSEPH TAL 087 ST MICHA
JOHNSON, JOSEPH FRE 129 CREAGERS
JOHNSON, JOSEPH BAL 247 17TH WAR
JOHNSON, JOSEPH CAR 284 7TH DIST
JOHNSON, JOSEPH MGM 419 MEDLEY 3
JOHNSON, JOSEPH FRE 336 MIDDLETO
JOHNSON, JOSEPH BAL 115 18TH WAR
JOHNSON, JOSEPH-BLACK CAR 103 NO TWP L
JOHNSON, JOSHUA BAL 083 4TH WARD
JOHNSON, JOSHUA KEN 239 2ND DIST
JOHNSON, JOSHUA BAL 293 20TH WAR
JOHNSON, JOSHUA CEC 042 CHESAPEA
JOHNSON, JOSHUA WOR 199 8TH E DI
JOHNSON, JOSHUA SOM 521 BARREN C

Name	County	Page	District
JOHNSON, JOSHUA	PRI	038	VANSVILL
JOHNSON, JOSHUA	BAL	366	3RD WARD
JOHNSON, JOSHUA	BAL	041	1ST WARD
JOHNSON, JOSHUA	BAL	044	2ND DIST
JOHNSON, JOSHUA	ANN	473	HOWARD D
JOHNSON, JOSHUA	BAL	010	EASTERN
JOHNSON, JOSHUA C.	WOR	184	6TH E DI
JOHNSON, JOSIAH	WOR	199	8TH E DI
JOHNSON, JOSIAH	SOM	505	SALISBUR
JOHNSON, JSOHUA-BLACK	CAR	155	NO TWP L
JOHNSON, JULIA	DOR	453	1ST DIST
JOHNSON, JULIA	WOR	303	SNOW HIL
JOHNSON, JULIA	ANN	472	HOWARD D
JOHNSON, JULIA	ALL	213	CUMBERLA
JOHNSON, JULIA	BAL	378	1ST DIST
JOHNSON, JULIA A.	BAL	096	15TH WAR
JOHNSON, JULIA A.	BAL	122	16TH WAR
JOHNSON, JULIA A.	BAL	042	9TH WARD
JOHNSON, JULIANA	ALL	263	CUMBERLA
JOHNSON, JULIANN	KEN	296	3RD DIST
JOHNSON, JULIANN A.	ALL	001	3RD E.D.
JOHNSON, JULIANNE	BAL	193	17TH WAR
JOHNSON, JUSTUS A.*	TAL	067	EASTON T
JOHNSON, KEZIAH	BAL	081	15TH WAR
JOHNSON, KEZIAH	BAL	046	2ND DIST
JOHNSON, L.	BAL	144	5TH WARD
JOHNSON, L.	BAL	240	20TH WAR
JOHNSON, L. O.	BAL	410	14TH WAR
JOHNSON, L. J.	BAL	286	2ND WARD
JOHNSON, L.A.	ANN	275	ANNAPOLI
JOHNSON, L.E.	WAS	021	2ND SUBD
JOHNSON, LAMBERT R.	CAL	001	1ST DIST
JOHNSON, LANTY	WOR	296	9TH E DI
JOHNSON, LARINA	KEN	241	2ND DIST
JOHNSON, LARKIN	ANN	449	HOWARD D
JOHNSON, LAURA	BAL	092	5TH WARD
JOHNSON, LAURA	BAL	421	14TH WAR
JOHNSON, LAURA	CAR	207	4TH DIST
JOHNSON, LAURA C.	HAR	031	1ST DIST
JOHNSON, LAUSON	CHA	240	HILLTOP
JOHNSON, LAVINIA	BAL	381	13TH WAR
JOHNSON, LAVINIA	BAL	193	17TH WAR
JOHNSON, LAVINIA	KEN	277	1ST DIST
JOHNSON, LEAH	WOR	201	3RD E DI
JOHNSON, LEAH	WOR	201	3RD E DI
JOHNSON, LEAH	SOM	433	PRINCESS
JOHNSON, LEAMOD	HAR	038	1ST DIST
JOHNSON, LEIGHER	DOR	371	3RD DIVI
JOHNSON, LEONARD	ANN	373	4TH DIST
JOHNSON, LETTA	BAL	011	2ND DIST
JOHNSON, LEVI	ANN	471	HOWARD D
JOHNSON, LEVI	CEC	151	PORT DUP
JOHNSON, LEVI	WOR	189	7TH E DI
JOHNSON, LEVI	SOM	532	QUANTICO
JOHNSON, LEVI	PRI	119	PISCATAW
JOHNSON, LEVI	PRI	119	PISCATAW
JOHNSON, LEVI	WAS	094	2ND SUBD
JOHNSON, LEVIN	WOR	316	2ND E DI
JOHNSON, LEVIN-BLACK	CAR	141	NO TWP L
JOHNSON, LEWIS	FRE	319	MIDDLETO
JOHNSON, LEWIS	BAL	024	2ND DIST
JOHNSON, LEWIS	BAL	242	6TH WARD
JOHNSON, LEWIS	BAL	145	1ST WARD
JOHNSON, LIDIA	BAL	289	1ST DIST
JOHNSON, LITTLETON	CAL	012	1ST DIST
JOHNSON, LITTLETON	WOR	289	9TH E DI
JOHNSON, LITTLETON	SOM	382	BRINKLEY
JOHNSON, LLOYD	BAL	043	9TH WARD
JOHNSON, LLOYD J.	PRI	066	NOTTINGH
JOHNSON, LORENZO	ANN	483	HOWARD D
JOHNSON, LORING	WOR	261	BERLIN 1
JOHNSON, LOT	MGM	370	BERRYS D
JOHNSON, LOTT	ANN	485	HOWARD D
JOHNSON, LOUISA	BAL	355	3RD WARD
JOHNSON, LOUISA	BAL	382	3RD WARD
JOHNSON, LOUISA	BAL	323	12TH WAR
JOHNSON, LOUISA	BAL	311	12TH WAR
JOHNSON, LOUISA	CAL	037	2ND DIST
JOHNSON, LOUISA	FRE	316	MIDDLETO
JOHNSON, LOVERM	DOR	337	3RD DIVI
JOHNSON, LOYD	ANN	344	3RD DIST
JOHNSON, LOYD	ANN	358	3RD DIST
JOHNSON, LUCRETIA	BAL	016	4TH WARD
JOHNSON, LUCY	CEC	201	6TH E DI
JOHNSON, LUCY	BAL	264	17TH WAR
JOHNSON, LUCY	ANN	343	3RD DIST
JOHNSON, LUCY	BAL	425	1ST DIST
JOHNSON, LUCY J.	CEC	006	ELKTON 3
JOHNSON, LUCY-BLACK	FRE	449	8TH E DI
JOHNSON, LUNDY	HAR	115	2ND DIST
JOHNSON, LUTHER	BAL	131	5TH WARD
JOHNSON, LYDIA	BAL	078	2ND DIST
JOHNSON, LYDIA	CEC	209	7TH E DI
JOHNSON, LYDIA	CEC	055	1ST E DI
JOHNSON, M.*	DOR	410	1ST DIST
JOHNSON, M.*	DOR	425	1ST DIST
JOHNSON, M.N.	BAL	259	12TH WAR
JOHNSON, MACISON	BAL	155	19TH WAR
JOHNSON, MANUEL	ANN	349	3RD DIST
JOHNSON, MARCELLUS	BAL	106	15TH WAR
JOHNSON, MARCELLUS	WOR	239	6TH E DI
JOHNSON, MARGARET	TAL	109	ST MICHA
JOHNSON, MARGARET	PRI	014	BLADENSB
JOHNSON, MARGARET	WOR	324	1ST E DI
JOHNSON, MARGARET	BAL	126	16TH WAR
JOHNSON, MARGARET	BAL	027	15TH WAR
JOHNSON, MARGARET	BAL	215	6TH WARD
JOHNSON, MARGARET	ANN	291	ANNAPOLI
JOHNSON, MARGARET	BAL	166	19TH WAR
JOHNSON, MARGARET	BAL	257	20TH WAR
JOHNSON, MARGARET	MGM	409	MEDLEY 3
JOHNSON, MARGARET	CHA	285	BOJANTOW
JOHNSON, MARGARET W.	SOM	426	PRINCESS
JOHNSON, MARGRETT-BLACK	CAR	086	NO TWP L
JOHNSON, MARIA	BAL	404	14TH WAR
JOHNSON, MARIA	BAL	321	20TH WAR
JOHNSON, MARIA	FRE	322	MIDDLETO
JOHNSON, MARIA	BAL	068	18TH WAR
JOHNSON, MARIA	BAL	053	18TH WAR
JOHNSON, MARIA	CEC	168	6TH E DI
JOHNSON, MARIA	CEC	138	6TH E DI
JOHNSON, MARIA	BAL	206	17TH WAR
JOHNSON, MARIA	BAL	363	13TH WAR
JOHNSON, MARIA	BAL	260	12TH WAR
JOHNSON, MARIA	BAL	071	15TH WAR
JOHNSON, MARIA	BAL	077	15TH WAR
JOHNSON, MARIA	ANN	422	HOWARD D
JOHNSON, MARIA	BAL	115	5TH WARD
JOHNSON, MARIA	BAL	356	3RD WARD
JOHNSON, MARIA	BAL	353	3RD WARD
JOHNSON, MARIA-BLACK	QUE	152	1ST E DI
JOHNSON, MARIAH	WOR	279	BERLIN 1
JOHNSON, MARIAH F.	TAL	039	EASTON D
JOHNSON, MARIAH-BLACK	CAR	073	NO TWP L
JOHNSON, MARRISS	BAL	225	17TH WAR
JOHNSON, MARTHA	BAL	435	14TH WAR
JOHNSON, MARTHA	BAL	388	13TH WAR
JOHNSON, MARTHA	FRE	365	CATOCTIN
JOHNSON, MARTHA	WOR	260	BERLIN 1
JOHNSON, MARTHA	BAL	174	2ND DIST
JOHNSON, MARTHA	BAL	100	15TH WAR
JOHNSON, MARTHA	BAL	299	12TH WAR
JOHNSON, MARTHA	ALL	072	5TH E.D.
JOHNSON, MARTHA	BAL	223	6TH WARD
JOHNSON, MARTHA E.	BAL	028	2ND DIST
JOHNSON, MARTHA J.	WAS	148	2ND DIST
JOHNSON, MARY	ST	270	3RD E DI
JOHNSON, MARY	QUE	239	5TH E DI
JOHNSON, MARY	WOR	282	BERLIN 1
JOHNSON, MARY	WOR	300	SNOW HIL
JOHNSON, MARY	WOR	307	2ND E DI
JOHNSON, MARY	WOR	309	2ND E DI
JOHNSON, MARY	TAL	096	ST MICHA
JOHNSON, MARY	WOR	230	6TH E DI
JOHNSON, MARY	SOM	497	SALISBUR
JOHNSON, MARY	KEN	264	1ST DIST
JOHNSON, MARY	ANN	357	3RD DIST
JOHNSON, MARY	ANN	341	3RD DIST
JOHNSON, MARY	ANN	472	HOWARD D
JOHNSON, MARY	BAL	086	2ND DIST
JOHNSON, MARY	ANN	448	HOWARD D
JOHNSON, MARY	ANN	466	HOWARD D
JOHNSON, MARY	ANN	431	HOWARD D
JOHNSON, MARY	ANN	430	HOWARD D
JOHNSON, MARY	BAL	144	5TH WARD
JOHNSON, MARY	BAL	129	5TH WARD
JOHNSON, MARY	BAL	124	5TH WARD
JOHNSON, MARY	ANN	282	ANNAPOLI
JOHNSON, MARY	BAL	096	15TH WAR
JOHNSON, MARY	BAL	060	10TH WAR
JOHNSON, MARY	BAL	058	10TH WAR
JOHNSON, MARY	BAL	181	16TH WAR
JOHNSON, MARY	BAL	263	1ST DIST
JOHNSON, MARY	BAL	121	5TH WARD
JOHNSON, MARY	BAL	339	3RD WARD
JOHNSON, MARY	BAL	072	15TH WAR
JOHNSON, MARY	BAL	265	12TH WAR
JOHNSON, MARY	BAL	220	12TH WAR
JOHNSON, MARY	BAL	222	12TH WAR
JOHNSON, MARY	BAL	226	12TH WAR
JOHNSON, MARY	BAL	174	11TH WAR
JOHNSON, MARY	BAL	252	20TH WAR
JOHNSON, MARY	CEC	195	6TH E DI
JOHNSON, MARY	DOR	339	3RD DIVI
JOHNSON, MARY	DOR	348	3RD DIVI
JOHNSON, MARY	DOR	355	3RD DIVI
JOHNSON, MARY	BAL	269	20TH WAR
JOHNSON, MARY	BAL	393	14TH WAR
JOHNSON, MARY	CAR	084	NO TWP L
JOHNSON, MARY	BAL	462	14TH WAR
JOHNSON, MARY	BAL	418	14TH WAR
JOHNSON, MARY	BAL	370	13TH WAR
JOHNSON, MARY	BAL	045	4TH WARD
JOHNSON, MARY	KEN	218	2ND DIST
JOHNSON, MARY	HAR	125	2ND DIST
JOHNSON, MARY	BAL	065	18TH WAR
JOHNSON, MARY	BAL	282	17TH WAR
JOHNSON, MARY	CEC	098	3RD E DI
JOHNSON, MARY	DOR	410	1ST DIST
JOHNSON, MARY	FRE	233	BUCKEYST
JOHNSON, MARY	SOM	433	PRINCESS
JOHNSON, MARY	HAR	098	2ND DIST
JOHNSON, MARY	BAL	011	4TH WARD
JOHNSON, MARY	CEC	020	ELKTON 3
JOHNSON, MARY	BAL	229	19TH WAR
JOHNSON, MARY	BAL	229	19TH WAR
JOHNSON, MARY	BAL	234	20TH WAR
JOHNSON, MARY A.	BAL	175	19TH WAR
JOHNSON, MARY A.	BAL	441	14TH WAR
JOHNSON, MARY A.	BAL	049	15TH WAR
JOHNSON, MARY A.	BAL	186	16TH WAR
JOHNSON, MARY A.	BAL	080	15TH WAR
JOHNSON, MARY A.	BAL	116	15TH WAR
JOHNSON, MARY A.	BAL	036	9TH WARD
JOHNSON, MARY A.	ANN	341	3RD DIST
JOHNSON, MARY A.	BAL	119	2ND DIST
JOHNSON, MARY A.	WOR	283	BERLIN 1
JOHNSON, MARY ANN	BAL	001	15TH WAR
JOHNSON, MARY E.	BAL	235	6TH WARD
JOHNSON, MARY E.	PRI	008	BLADENSB
JOHNSON, MARY F.	CEC	091	4TH E DI
JOHNSON, MARY J.	ST	278	3RD E DI
JOHNSON, MARY J.	BAL	106	15TH WAR
JOHNSON, MARY L.*	BAL	365	3RD WARD
JOHNSON, MARY P.	BAL	295	12TH WAR
JOHNSON, MARY S.	BAL	005	9TH WARD
JOHNSON, MARY T.	BAL	206	19TH WAR
JOHNSON, MARY V.	CHA	239	HILLTOP
JOHNSON, MARY-BLACK	FRE	453	8TH E DI
JOHNSON, MATHEW	BAL	206	17TH WAR
JOHNSON, MATHIAS	BAL	041	4TH WARD
JOHNSON, MATHIAS	DOR	434	1ST DIST
JOHNSON, MATILDA	BAL	249	12TH WAR
JOHNSON, MATILCA	PRI	024	VANSVILL
JOHNSON, MATILDA C.	BAL	071	15TH WAR
JOHNSON, MICHAEL	CEC	048	1ST E DI
JOHNSON, MICHAL	HAR	206	3RD DIST
JOHNSON, MILBY	WOR	315	2ND E DI
JOHNSON, MILKY	BAL	105	5TH WARD
JOHNSON, MILLY	BAL	327	3RD WARD
JOHNSON, MINGO	CEC	194	7TH E DI
JOHNSON, MINTY*	DOR	296	1ST DIST
JOHNSON, MONROE	BAL	268	17TH WAR
JOHNSON, MOSES	BAL	186	19TH WAR
JOHNSON, MOSES	BAL	125	11TH WAR
JOHNSON, MOSES	ANN	287	ANNAPOLI
JOHNSON, MRS.	BAL	150	5TH WARD
JOHNSON, N.	BAL	155	1ST WARD
JOHNSON, NANCY	BAL	145	5TH WARD
JOHNSON, NANCY	ANN	302	1ST DIST
JOHNSON, NANCY	BAL	115	15TH WAR
JOHNSON, NANCY	BAL	134	16TH WAR
JOHNSON, NANCY	BAL	155	11TH WAR
JOHNSON, NANCY	BAL	155	11TH WAR
JOHNSON, NANCY	CEC	041	CHESAPEA
JOHNSON, NANCY	CEC	181	7TH E DI
JOHNSON, NANCY	BAL	031	18TH WAR
JOHNSON, NANCY	WOR	187	7TH E DI
JOHNSON, NANCY	QUE	248	5TH E DI
JOHNSON, NASE	MGM	328	CRACKLIN
JOHNSON, NATHANIEL	CEC	060	1ST E DI
JOHNSON, NATHANIEL	HAR	100	2ND DIST
JOHNSON, NEBO	WOR	234	6TH E DI
JOHNSON, NED	BAL	258	1ST DIST
JOHNSON, NELSON	ALL	085	5TH E.D.
JOHNSON, NELSON	BAL	429	1ST DIST
JOHNSON, NEVILINA	BAL	135	5TH WARD
JOHNSON, NEVILLE	BAL	135	5TH WARD
JOHNSON, NICHOLAS	ANN	359	3RD DIST
JOHNSON, NICHOLAS	CEC	020	ELKTON 3
JOHNSON, NICK	ANN	326	2ND DIST
JOHNSON, NOAH	KEN	307	3RD DIST
JOHNSON, OLIVER	CAR	214	5TH DIST
JOHNSON, OLIVER	HAR	109	2ND DIST
JOHNSON, OLIVIA	BAL	071	15TH WAR
JOHNSON, P.	BAL	166	1ST WARD
JOHNSON, P.	BAL	165	1ST WARD
JOHNSON, P.	BAL	161	1ST WARD
JOHNSON, P.	BAL	158	1ST WARD
JOHNSON, P.	BAL	116	1ST WARD
JOHNSON, P.	BAL	137	1ST WARD
JOHNSON, P.	BAL	239	20TH WAR
JOHNSON, P. R.	BAL	329	13TH WAR
JOHNSON, P.H.	BAL	166	1ST WARD
JOHNSON, PATIENCE	BAL	175	6TH WARD
JOHNSON, PATIENCE	DOR	453	1ST DIST
JOHNSON, PATTY	BAL	028	2ND DIST
JOHNSON, PERE	QUE	208	3RD E DI
JOHNSON, PERRY	SOM	530	QUANTICO
JOHNSON, PERRY	KEN	239	2ND DIST
JOHNSON, PETER	FRE	416	8TH E DI
JOHNSON, PETER	CAL	052	3RD DIST
JOHNSON, PETER	WOR	311	2ND E DI
JOHNSON, PETER	WOR	277	BERLIN 1
JOHNSON, PETER	BAL	171	1ST WARD
JOHNSON, PETER	BAL	162	1ST WARD
JOHNSON, PETER	BAL	138	1ST WARD
JOHNSON, PETER	BAL	142	1ST WARD
JOHNSON, PETER	BAL	133	1ST WARD
JOHNSON, PETER	BAL	281	2ND WARD
JOHNSON, PETER	BAL	124	1ST WARD
JOHNSON, PETER	BAL	168	2ND DIST
JOHNSON, PETER	BAL	024	1ST WARD
JOHNSON, PETER	BAL	175	11TH WAR
JOHNSON, PETER	BAL	316	1ST DIST
JOHNSON, PETER	ANN	274	ANNAPOLI
JOHNSON, PETER	ANN	297	1ST DIST
JOHNSON, PHEBE	ANN	367	4TH DIST
JOHNSON, PHIL	QUE	238	5TH E DI
JOHNSON, PHILIP	ANN	377	4TH DIST
JOHNSON, PHILIP	BAL	068	2ND DIST
JOHNSON, PHILIP	BAL	190	5TH DIST
JOHNSON, PHILIP	BAL	095	15TH WAR
JOHNSON, PHILIP	BAL	346	3RD WARD
JOHNSON, PHILIP	BAL	346	3RD WARD
JOHNSON, PHILIP	BAL	387	1ST DIST
JOHNSON, PHILIS	BAL	153	16TH WAR
JOHNSON, PHILLIP	BAL	245	6TH WARD
JOHNSON, PHILLIS	CEC	012	ELKTON 3
JOHNSON, PLEASANT	ALL	095	5TH E.D.
JOHNSON, PLEASANT	WOR	296	9TH E DI
JOHNSON, PLEASANT-BLACK	WOR	341	1ST E DI
JOHNSON, POLLARD	CEC	070	5TH E DI
JOHNSON, PRELATE J.	ANN	444	HOWARD D
JOHNSON, PRESZ	BAL	198	6TH WARD
JOHNSON, PRISCILLA	ANN	418	HOWARD D
JOHNSON, PRISCILLA	ANN	298	1ST DIST
JOHNSON, PRISSY	ANN	416	HOWARD D
JOHNSON, PURNELL	SOM	505	SALISBUR
JOHNSON, PURNELL JR.	WOR	198	8TH E DI
JOHNSON, PURNELL SR.	WOR	190	8TH E DI
JOHNSON, PURSY	BAL	168	19TH WAR
JOHNSON, QUESA	ALL	172	7TH E.D.
JOHNSON, R.	ANN	345	3RD DIST
JOHNSON, RACHAEL	BAL	005	1ST WARD
JOHNSON, RACHAEL	SOM	517	BARREN C
JOHNSON, RACHALE	BAL	283	2ND WARD
JOHNSON, RACHEAL	BAL	146	11TH WAR
JOHNSON, RACHEAL	BAL	276	20TH WAR
JOHNSON, RACHEL	BAL	251	20TH WAR
JOHNSON, RACHEL	BAL	168	19TH WAR
JOHNSON, RACHEL	CEC	064	1ST E DI
JOHNSON, RACHEL	BAL	062	1ST WARD
JOHNSON, RACHEL	BAL	054	2ND DIST
JOHNSON, RACHEL	BAL	054	2ND DIST
JOHNSON, RACHEL	ANN	474	HOWARD D
JOHNSON, RACHEL	BAL	165	6TH WARD
JOHNSON, RACHEL	BAL	337	3RD WARD
JOHNSON, RACHEL	BAL	403	1ST DIST
JOHNSON, RACHEL	BAL	360	1ST DIST
JOHNSON, RACHEL	TAL	065	EASTON T
JOHNSON, RACHEL	TAL	014	EASTON D
JOHNSON, RACHEL	TAL	001	EASTON D
JOHNSON, RACHEL A.	BAL	391	3RD WARD
JOHNSON, RACHEL A.	BAL	462	14TH WAR
JOHNSON, RACHEL-BLACK	QUE	176	2ND E DI
JOHNSON, RACHELL	BAL	109	5TH WARD
JOHNSON, RACHIEL-BLACK	CAR	071	NO TWP L
JOHNSON, RANDOLPH	ANN	420	HOWARD D
JOHNSON, REBECCA	BAL	385	3RD WARD
JOHNSON, REBECCA	ALL	030	2ND E.D.
JOHNSON, REBECCA	BAL	151	16TH WAR
JOHNSON, REBECCA	BAL	178	16TH WAR
JOHNSON, REBECCA	BAL	007	15TH WAR
JOHNSON, REBECCA	CAR	080	NO TWP L
JOHNSON, REBECCA	CEC	075	NORTHEAS
JOHNSON, REBECCA	KEN	297	3RD DIST
JOHNSON, REBECCA-BLACK	CAR	138	NO TWP L
JOHNSON, REBECCA-BLACK	QUE	143	1ST E DI
JOHNSON, REUBEN	BAL	119	5TH WARD
JOHNSON, REUBEN A.	ANN	486	HOWARD D
JOHNSON, REVERDY	BAL	100	10TH WAR
JOHNSON, RHODA	WOR	274	BERLIN 1
JOHNSON, RICAHRD W.	CAL	017	1ST DIST
JOHNSON, RICHARD	CAL	015	1ST DIST
JOHNSON, RICHARD	HAR	149	3RD DIST
JOHNSON, RICHARD	DOR	428	1ST DIST
JOHNSON, RICHARD	CHA	239	HILLTOP
JOHNSON, RICHARD	FRE	382	PETERSVI
JOHNSON, RICHARD	BAL	344	13TH WAR
JOHNSON, RICHARD	WAS	067	2ND SUBD
JOHNSON, RICHARD	KEN	277	1ST DIST
JOHNSON, RICHARD	KEN	305	3RD DIST
JOHNSON, RICHARD	WAS	129	2ND DIST
JOHNSON, RICHARD	BAL	127	16TH WAR
JOHNSON, RICHARD	BAL	126	16TH WAR
JOHNSON, RICHARD	ANN	476	HOWARD D
JOHNSON, RICHARD	BAL	238	12TH WAR
JOHNSON, RICHARD	BAL	241	6TH WARD
JOHNSON, RICHARD	BAL	040	9TH WARD

JOHNSON, RICHARD C. ALL 262 CUMBERLA
JOHNSON, RICHARD L. BAL 016 4TH WARD
JOHNSON, RITTY MGM 359 BERRYS D
JOHNSON, ROBERT BAL 175 19TH WAR
JOHNSON, ROBERT CEC 177 7TH E DI
JOHNSON, ROBERT FRE 032 FREDERIC
JOHNSON, ROBERT HAR 156 3RD DIST
JOHNSON, ROBERT BAL 399 14TH WAR
JOHNSON, ROBERT BAL 409 14TH WAR
JOHNSON, ROBERT ANN 345 3RD DIST
JOHNSON, ROBERT BAL 160 1ST WARD
JOHNSON, ROBERT BAL 311 3RD WARD
JOHNSON, ROBERT BAL 128 1ST WARD
JOHNSON, ROBERT WAS 117 2ND DIST
JOHNSON, ROBERT SOM 359 BRINKLEY
JOHNSON, ROBERT TAL 118 ST MICHA
JOHNSON, ROBERT D. BAL 230 6TH WARD
JOHNSON, ROBERT-BLACK BAL 216 2ND WARD
JOHNSON, ROBERT-MULATTO BAL 208 2ND WARD
JOHNSON, RODOLPH B. ANN 338 3RD DIST
JOHNSON, ROGER DOR 319 1ST DIST
JOHNSON, ROSAN BAL 044 2ND DIST
JOHNSON, ROSE BAL 267 17TH WAR
JOHNSON, ROSETTA BAL 358 13TH WAR
JOHNSON, ROSETTA ANN 278 ANNAPOLI
JOHNSON, SALLY BAL 119 5TH WARD
JOHNSON, SALLY BAL 257 17TH WAR
JOHNSON, SALLY HAR 205 3RD DIST
JOHNSON, SALLY WOR 335 1ST E DI
JOHNSON, SALLY WOR 307 2ND E DI
JOHNSON, SALLY WOR 316 2ND E DI
JOHNSON, SALLY A. TAL 038 EASTON D
JOHNSON, SAMEUL BAL 237 20TH WAR
JOHNSON, SAMEUL ANN 399 8TH DIST
JOHNSON, SAMUEL ALL 001 3RD E.D.
JOHNSON, SAMUEL ANN 395 8TH DIST
JOHNSON, SAMUEL ANN 298 1ST DIST
JOHNSON, SAMUEL ANN 360 3RD DIST
JOHNSON, SAMUEL BAL 098 2ND DIST
JOHNSON, SAMUEL ALL 236 CUMBERLA
JOHNSON, SAMUEL BAL 257 6TH WARD
JOHNSON, SAMUEL BAL 053 15TH WAR
JOHNSON, SAMUEL BAL 024 15TH WAR
JOHNSON, SAMUEL BAL 041 15TH WAR
JOHNSON, SAMUEL BAL 128 16TH WAR
JOHNSON, SAMUEL BAL 190 17TH WAR
JOHNSON, SAMUEL BAL 093 15TH WAR
JOHNSON, SAMUEL BAL 103 15TH WAR
JOHNSON, SAMUEL BAL 053 9TH WARD
JOHNSON, SAMUEL BAL 077 10TH WAR
JOHNSON, SAMUEL BAL 053 1ST WARD
JOHNSON, SAMUEL BAL 184 5TH DIST
JOHNSON, SAMUEL BAL 365 3RD WARD
JOHNSON, SAMUEL BAL 121 1ST WARD
JOHNSON, SAMUEL BAL 278 1ST DIST
JOHNSON, SAMUEL CAR 220 5TH DIST
JOHNSON, SAMUEL CAR 217 5TH DIST
JOHNSON, SAMUEL CEC 040 CHESAPEA
JOHNSON, SAMUEL CEC 036 CHESAPEA
JOHNSON, SAMUEL FRE 260 NEW MARK
JOHNSON, SAMUEL BAL 251 17TH WAR
JOHNSON, SAMUEL BAL 378 13TH WAR
JOHNSON, SAMUEL BAL 378 13TH WAR
JOHNSON, SAMUEL CEC 135 6TH E DI
JOHNSON, SAMUEL DOR 320 1ST DIST
JOHNSON, SAMUEL CEC 198 7TH E DI
JOHNSON, SAMUEL DOR 344 3RD DIVI
JOHNSON, SAMUEL DOR 361 3RD DIVI
JOHNSON, SAMUEL MGM 431 CLARKSTR
JOHNSON, SAMUEL CEC 098 3RD E DI
JOHNSON, SAMUEL WOR 308 2ND E DI
JOHNSON, SAMUEL SOM 371 BRINKLEY
JOHNSON, SAMUEL SOM 521 BARREN C
JOHNSON, SAMUEL WOR 199 8TH E DI
JOHNSON, SAMUEL QUE 222 4TH E DI
JOHNSON, SAMUEL H. HAR 160 3RD DIST
JOHNSON, SAMUEL S. HAR 033 1ST DIST
JOHNSON, SAMUEL T. WOR 308 2ND E DI
JOHNSON, SAMUEL T. WOR 277 BERLIN 1
JOHNSON, SAMUEL* TAL 066 EASTON T
JOHNSON, SAMUEL-BLACK CAR 166 NO TWP L
JOHNSON, SANDY PRI 076 MARLBROU
JOHNSON, SANDY ANN 341 3RD DIST
JOHNSON, SARAH BAL 075 2ND DIST
JOHNSON, SARAH BAL 368 3RD WARD
JOHNSON, SARAH BAL 085 15TH WAR
JOHNSON, SARAH BAL 017 15TH WAR
JOHNSON, SARAH BAL 180 11TH WAR
JOHNSON, SARAH BAL 001 15TH WAR
JOHNSON, SARAH BAL 372 3RD WARD
JOHNSON, SARAH BAL 261 2ND WARD
JOHNSON, SARAH ALL 055 10TH E.D
JOHNSON, SARAH ALL 213 CUMBERLA
JOHNSON, SARAH BAL 099 5TH WARD
JOHNSON, SARAH BAL 345 3RD WARD
JOHNSON, SARAH BAL 228 6TH WARD
JOHNSON, SARAH SOM 395 BRINKLEY
JOHNSON, SARAH SOM 392 BRINKLEY
JOHNSON, SARAH WOR 275 BERLIN 1
JOHNSON, SARAH WOR 257 1ST CENS
JOHNSON, SARAH CEC 066 1ST E DI
JOHNSON, SARAH CEC 190 5TH E DI
JOHNSON, SARAH BAL 240 20TH WAR
JOHNSON, SARAH BAL 375 13TH WAR
JOHNSON, SARAH CEC 158 PORT DUP
JOHNSON, SARAH CEC 167 6TH E DI
JOHNSON, SARAH CEC 186 7TH E DI
JOHNSON, SARAH BAL 153 19TH WAR
JOHNSON, SARAH BAL 455 14TH WAR
JOHNSON, SARAH A. HAR 045 1ST DIST
JOHNSON, SARAH A. ST 274 3RD E DI
JOHNSON, SARAH A. B. FRE 338 MIDDLETO
JOHNSON, SARAH A.-BLACK CAR 145 NO TWP L
JOHNSON, SARAH J. BAL 153 16TH WAR
JOHNSON, SARAH-BLACK CAR 161 NO TWP L
JOHNSON, SARAH-BLACK FRE 383 PETERSVI
JOHNSON, SARAH-BLACK WOR 349 1ST E DI
JOHNSON, SARHA ANN BAL 361 13TH WAR
JOHNSON, SELBY WOR 311 2ND E DI
JOHNSON, SELENA BAL 119 11TH WAR
JOHNSON, SERENE BAL 244 6TH WARD
JOHNSON, SEVERN BAL 128 16TH WAR
JOHNSON, SHADE HAR 100 2ND DIST
JOHNSON, SHADE HAR 100 2ND DIST
JOHNSON, SIDNEY DOR 297 1ST DIST
JOHNSON, SILAS BAL 118 11TH WAR
JOHNSON, SILAS ANN 399 8TH DIST
JOHNSON, SILAS ANN 398 8TH DIST
JOHNSON, SOLOMON HAR 070 1ST DIST
JOHNSON, SOPHIA CEC 050 1ST E DI
JOHNSON, SOPHIA BAL 093 10TH WAR
JOHNSON, SOPHIA BAL 421 1ST DIST
JOHNSON, STANLEY BAL 364 13TH WAR
JOHNSON, STEPHEN CEC 040 CHESAPEA
JOHNSON, STEPHEN CEC 073 5TH E DI
JOHNSON, STEPHEN HAR 126 2ND DIST
JOHNSON, STEPHEN BAL 116 5TH WARD
JOHNSON, STEPHEN ANN 319 2ND DIST
JOHNSON, STEPHEN ANN 484 HOWARD D
JOHNSON, STEPHEN WOR 197 8TH E DI
JOHNSON, STEPHEN-BLACK WOR 338 1ST E DI
JOHNSON, SUSAN SOM 526 QUANTICO
JOHNSON, SUSAN WOR 279 BERLIN 1
JOHNSON, SUSAN TAL 006 EASTON D
JOHNSON, SUSAN BAL 104 5TH WARD
JOHNSON, SUSAN BAL 044 9TH WARD
JOHNSON, SUSAN BAL 312 12TH WAR
JOHNSON, SUSAN BAL 179 6TH WARD
JOHNSON, SUSAN BAL 153 5TH WARD
JOHNSON, SUSAN BAL 036 15TH WAR
JOHNSON, SUSAN BAL 436 14TH WAR
JOHNSON, SUSAN MGM 354 BERRYS D
JOHNSON, SUSAN BAL 139 11TH WAR
JOHNSON, SUSAN BAL 205 11TH WAR
JOHNSON, SUSAN BAL 280 20TH WAR
JOHNSON, SUSAN DOR 396 1ST DIST
JOHNSON, SUSAN F. MGM 354 BERRYS D
JOHNSON, SUSANNA BAL 446 14TH WAR
JOHNSON, SUSANNAH CEC 167 6TH E DI
JOHNSON, T. BAL 117 1ST WARD
JOHNSON, TABITHA WOR 324 1ST E DI
JOHNSON, THEADORE TAL 071 EASTON T
JOHNSON, THEADORE BAL 025 1ST WARD
JOHNSON, THEODORE-BLACK BAL 179 2ND WARD
JOHNSON, THERESA BAL 266 2ND WARD
JOHNSON, THOMAS BAL 239 2ND WARD
JOHNSON, THOMAS BAL 255 2ND WARD
JOHNSON, THOMAS BAL 128 1ST WARD
JOHNSON, THOMAS BAL 145 1ST WARD
JOHNSON, THOMAS BAL 172 1ST WARD
JOHNSON, THOMAS BAL 154 1ST WARD
JOHNSON, THOMAS BAL 158 1ST WARD
JOHNSON, THOMAS BAL 163 1ST WARD
JOHNSON, THOMAS BAL 101 1ST WARD
JOHNSON, THOMAS BAL 100 1ST WARD
JOHNSON, THOMAS BAL 002 9TH WARD
JOHNSON, THOMAS BAL 063 10TH WAR
JOHNSON, THOMAS BAL 167 16TH WAR
JOHNSON, THOMAS BAL 405 1ST DIST
JOHNSON, THOMAS BAL 344 3RD WARD
JOHNSON, THOMAS BAL 071 2ND DIST
JOHNSON, THOMAS ANN 416 HOWARD D
JOHNSON, THOMAS ANN 344 3RD DIST
JOHNSON, THOMAS ALL 001 3RD E.D.
JOHNSON, THOMAS ALL 019 2ND E.D.
JOHNSON, THOMAS ANN 303 1ST DIST
JOHNSON, THOMAS ALL 159 6TH E.D.
JOHNSON, THOMAS WOR 296 9TH E DI
JOHNSON, THOMAS WOR 295 9TH E DI
JOHNSON, THOMAS SOM 500 SALISBUR
JOHNSON, THOMAS SOM 504 SALISBUR
JOHNSON, THOMAS BAL 070 4TH WARD
JOHNSON, THOMAS BAL 059 4TH WARD
JOHNSON, THOMAS BAL 399 14TH WAR
JOHNSON, THOMAS BAL 397 14TH WAR
JOHNSON, THOMAS BAL 476 14TH WAR
JOHNSON, THOMAS MGM 376 ROCKERLE
JOHNSON, THOMAS HAR 104 2ND DIST
JOHNSON, THOMAS HAR 112 2ND DIST
JOHNSON, THOMAS HAR 088 2ND DIST
JOHNSON, THOMAS HAR 051 1ST DIST
JOHNSON, THOMAS FRE 405 JEFFERSO
JOHNSON, THOMAS DOR 362 3RD DIVI
JOHNSON, THOMAS DOR 319 1ST DIST
JOHNSON, THOMAS CHA 235 HILLTOP
JOHNSON, THOMAS HAR 139 2ND DIST
JOHNSON, THOMAS KEN 217 2ND DIST
JOHNSON, THOMAS CHA 286 BOJANTOW
JOHNSON, THOMAS CHA 288 BOJANTOW
JOHNSON, THOMAS BAL 097 18TH WAR
JOHNSON, THOMAS BAL 036 4TH WARD
JOHNSON, THOMAS E. PRI 114 PISCATAW
JOHNSON, THOMAS L. CEC 135 6TH E DI
JOHNSON, THOMAS M. BAL 417 1ST DIST
JOHNSON, THOMAS P. BAL 434 14TH WAR
JOHNSON, TIMOTHY ANN 517 HOWARD D
JOHNSON, TOBIAS HAR 085 2ND DIST
JOHNSON, TOBIAS WAS 136 2ND DIST
JOHNSON, TOBY BAL 097 2ND DIST
JOHNSON, TRACY-BLACK BAL 219 2ND WARD
JOHNSON, URIAH BAL 167 6TH WARD
JOHNSON, URIAH ST 263 3RD E DI
JOHNSON, URIAH CAL 049 3RD DIST
JOHNSON, VAGES BAL 334 1ST DIST
JOHNSON, VANCE DOR 313 1ST DIST
JOHNSON, VIRGINIA BAL 199 6TH WARD
JOHNSON, W. WAS 002 WILLIAMS
JOHNSON, W.C. ANN 286 ANNAPOLI
JOHNSON, W.H. ANN 285 ANNAPOLI
JOHNSON, WALTER MGM 354 BERRYS D
JOHNSON, WASHINGTON DOR 425 1ST DIST
JOHNSON, WESLEY BAL 100 2ND DIST
JOHNSON, WHITELY CAR 146 NO TWP L
JOHNSON, WHITTINGTON SOM 384 BRINKLEY
JOHNSON, WILIAM QUE 244 5TH E DI
JOHNSON, WILILAM S. BAL 286 2ND WARD
JOHNSON, WILLAIM BAL 001 15TH WAR
JOHNSON, WILLAIM ANN 460 HOWARD D
JOHNSON, WILLAIM BAL 116 5TH WARD
JOHNSON, WILLAIM BAL 231 17TH WAR
JOHNSON, WILLAIM F. BAL 414 1ST DIST
JOHNSON, WILLIAM BAL 431 1ST DIST
JOHNSON, WILLIAM BAL 432 1ST DIST
JOHNSON, WILLIAM BAL 430 1ST DIST
JOHNSON, WILLIAM BAL 406 1ST DIST
JOHNSON, WILLIAM BAL 348 3RD WARD
JOHNSON, WILLIAM BAL 443 1ST DIST
JOHNSON, WILLIAM BAL 091 5TH WARD
JOHNSON, WILLIAM BAL 092 2ND DIST
JOHNSON, WILLIAM ANN 369 4TH DIST
JOHNSON, WILLIAM BAL 040 2ND DIST
JOHNSON, WILLIAM BAL 007 EASTERN
JOHNSON, WILLIAM BAL 286 2ND WARD
JOHNSON, WILLIAM BAL 044 15TH WAR
JOHNSON, WILLIAM BAL 259 12TH WAR
JOHNSON, WILLIAM ANN 292 ANNAPOLI
JOHNSON, WILLIAM ANN 277 ANNAPOLI
JOHNSON, WILLIAM BAL 315 1ST DIST
JOHNSON, WILLIAM BAL 190 6TH WARD
JOHNSON, WILLIAM BAL 202 6TH WARD
JOHNSON, WILLIAM BAL 173 6TH WARD
JOHNSON, WILLIAM BAL 152 1ST WARD
JOHNSON, WILLIAM BAL 166 1ST WARD
JOHNSON, WILLIAM BAL 164 1ST WARD
JOHNSON, WILLIAM BAL 232 6TH WARD
JOHNSON, WILLIAM BAL 085 15TH WAR
JOHNSON, WILLIAM BAL 122 16TH WAR
JOHNSON, WILLIAM BAL 152 16TH WAR
JOHNSON, WILLIAM BAL 138 16TH WAR
JOHNSON, WILLIAM BAL 108 15TH WAR
JOHNSON, WILLIAM BAL 116 1ST WARD
JOHNSON, WILLIAM BAL 115 1ST WARD
JOHNSON, WILLIAM BAL 284 1ST DIST
JOHNSON, WILLIAM BAL 021 1ST WARD
JOHNSON, WILLIAM BAL 024 1ST WARD
JOHNSON, WILLIAM BAL 250 1ST DIST
JOHNSON, WILLIAM BAL 142 1ST WARD
JOHNSON, WILLIAM BAL 145 1ST WARD
JOHNSON, WILLIAM BAL 131 1ST WARD
JOHNSON, WILLIAM BAL 134 1ST WARD
JOHNSON, WILLIAM BAL 133 1ST WARD
JOHNSON, WILLIAM BAL 243 2ND WARD
JOHNSON, WILLIAM BAL 264 2ND WARD
JOHNSON, WILLIAM BAL 251 6TH WARD
JOHNSON, WILLIAM BAL 282 2ND WARD
JOHNSON, WILLIAM DOR 305 1ST DIST
JOHNSON, WILLIAM CEC 134 5TH E DI
JOHNSON, WILLIAM BAL 064 4TH WARD
JOHNSON, WILLIAM BAL 339 13TH WAR
JOHNSON, WILLIAM CAR 129 NO TWP L
JOHNSON, WILLIAM CAL 055 3RD DIST
JOHNSON, WILLIAM BAL 468 14TH WAR
JOHNSON, WILLIAM BAL 457 14TH WAR
JOHNSON, WILLIAM HAR 205 3RD DIST
JOHNSON, WILLIAM FRE 273 NEW MARK
JOHNSON, WILLIAM MGM 347 BERRYS D
JOHNSON, WILLIAM MGM 332 CRACKLIN
JOHNSON, WILLIAM KEN 239 2ND DIST
JOHNSON, WILLIAM FRE 118 CREAGERS
JOHNSON, WILLIAM FRE 416 8TH E DI
JOHNSON, WILLIAM BAL 279 20TH WAR
JOHNSON, WILLIAM HAR 024 1ST DIST
JOHNSON, WILLIAM MGM 356 BERRYS D
JOHNSON, WILLIAM MGM 379 ROCKERLE
JOHNSON, WILLIAM MGM 359 BERRYS D
JOHNSON, WILLIAM FRE 088 FREDERIC
JOHNSON, WILLIAM BAL 236 20TH WAR
JOHNSON, WILLIAM BAL 411 3RD WARD
JOHNSON, WILLIAM BAL 096 18TH WAR
JOHNSON, WILLIAM CAR 390 2ND DIST
JOHNSON, WILLIAM BAL 068 18TH WAR
JOHNSON, WILLIAM QUE 242 5TH E DI
JOHNSON, WILLIAM ST 281 3RD E DI
JOHNSON, WILLIAM WAS 126 2ND DIST
JOHNSON, WILLIAM WOR 305 SNOW HIL
JOHNSON, WILLIAM TAL 015 EASTON D
JOHNSON, WILLIAM WAS 061 2ND SUBD
JOHNSON, WILLIAM SOM 498 SALISBUR
JOHNSON, WILLIAM SOM 493 SALISBUR
JOHNSON, WILLIAM PRI 075 MARLBROU
JOHNSON, WILLIAM KEN 307 3RD DIST
JOHNSON, WILLIAM KEN 281 3RD DIST
JOHNSON, WILLIAM CORT FRE 409 JEFFERSO
JOHNSON, WILLIAM F. FRE 044 FREDERIC
JOHNSON, WILLIAM H. HAR 052 1ST DIST
JOHNSON, WILLIAM H. FRE 382 PETERSVI
JOHNSON, WILLIAM H. MGM 319 CRACKLIN
JOHNSON, WILLIAM H. BAL 083 4TH WARD
JOHNSON, WILLIAM H. ST 265 3RD E DI
JOHNSON, WILLIAM H. BAL 241 1ST DIST
JOHNSON, WILLIAM H. BAL 090 5TH WARD
JOHNSON, WILLIAM J. SOM 391 BRINKLEY
JOHNSON, WILLIAM J. SOM 390 BRINKLEY
JOHNSON, WILLIAM J. TAL 005 EASTON D
JOHNSON, WILLIAM J. MGM 425 MEDLEY 3
JOHNSON, WILLIAM M. CAL 029 2ND DIST
JOHNSON, WILLIAM M. BAL 260 2ND WARD
JOHNSON, WILLIAM P. WOR 308 2ND E DI
JOHNSON, WILLIAM R. CAL 024 2ND DIST
JOHNSON, WILLIAM T. SOM 426 PRINCESS
JOHNSON, WILLIAM T. BAL 137 16TH WAR
JOHNSON, WILLIAM U. CHA 239 HILLTOP
JOHNSON, WILLIAM W. SOM 427 PRINCESS
JOHNSON, WILLIAM W. BAL 261 17TH WAR
JOHNSON, WILLIAM-BLACK MGM 401 ROCKERLE
JOHNSON, WILLIAM-BLACK MGM 398 ROCKERLE
JOHNSON, WILLIAM-BLACK MGM 412 MEDLEY 3
JOHNSON, WILLIAM-BLACK CAR 071 NO TWP L
JOHNSON, WILLIAM-BLACK CAR 128 NO TWP L
JOHNSON, WILLIAM-BLACK CAR 131 NO TWP L
JOHNSON, WILLIAM-BLACK QUE 136 1ST E DI
JOHNSON, WILLIAM-MULATTO BAL 223 2ND WARD
JOHNSON, WILLIAMA BAL 044 4TH WARD
JOHNSON, WILLMOT BAL 136 11TH WAR
JOHNSON, WILSON BAL 292 1ST DIST
JOHNSON, WORTHINGTON FRE 070 FREDERIC
JOHNSON, ZACH ANN 356 3RD DIST
JOHNSON, ZACH ANN 359 3RD DIST
JOHNSON, ZACHARIAH FRE 317 MIDDLETO
JOHNSON, ZACHARIAH F. MGM 375 ROCKERLE
JOHNSON, ZEKIEL DOR 341 3RD DIVI
JOHNSON,BARNEY BAL 001 EASTERN
JOHNSON,E.J. BAL 173 1ST WARD
JOHNSON,EZEKIAL C. BAL 163 1ST WARD
JOHNSON,HARRIET A. ALL 001 3RD E.D.
JOHNSON,HENRY BAL 138 1ST WARD
JOHNSON,J. BAL 165 1ST WARD
JOHNSON,JAMES B. BAL 116 1ST WARD
JOHNSON,JAMES M BAL 237 12TH WAR
JOHNSON,JAMES T. FRE 234 BUCKEYST
JOHNSON,JOHN BAL 126 1ST WARD
JOHNSON,JOSEPH BAL 125 1ST WARD
JOHNSON,MARY FRE 234 BUCKEYST
JOHNSON,MARY B. FRE 406 JEFFERSO
JOHNSON,P. BAL 160 1ST WARD
JOHNSON,PETER BAL 125 1ST WARD
JOHNSON,PETER BAL 064 1ST WARD
JOHNSON,PRISCILLA BAL 053 2ND DIST
JOHNSON,RICHARD FRE 048 FREDERIC
JOHNSON,WILLIAM BAL 123 1ST WARD
JOHNSON,WILLIAM BAL 167 1ST WARD
JOHNSON,WILLIAM BAL 142 1ST WARD
JOHNSON,WILLIAM BAL 140 1ST WARD
JOHNSONSON, WASHINGTON * KEN 277 1ST DIST
JOHNSTON, ADAM BAL 173 11TH WAR
JOHNSTON, ALFRED BAL 294 7TH WARD
JOHNSTON, ANN BAL 460 1ST DIST
JOHNSTON, ANN BAL 115 11TH WAR
JOHNSTON, ANN BAL 134 11TH WAR
JOHNSTON, ANN BAL 155 11TH WAR

Name	County	Page	Location
JOHNSTON, ARCHIBALD	BAL	397	8TH WARD
JOHNSTON, ARIANA	BAL	360	8TH WARD
JOHNSTON, BENJAMIN	BAL	184	11TH WAR
JOHNSTON, CALEB	BAL	119	11TH WAR
JOHNSTON, CAROLINE	BAL	138	11TH WAR
JOHNSTON, CAROLINE	BAL	446	8TH WARD
JOHNSTON, CATHARINE	WAS	164	HAGERSTO
JOHNSTON, CHARLES	BAL	129	11TH WAR
JOHNSTON, CHARLES	BAL	135	18TH WAR
JOHNSTON, CHARLES H.	BAL	302	7TH WARD
JOHNSTON, CHARLOTT	BAL	271	7TH WARD
JOHNSTON, CHARLOTTE	BAL	149	11TH WAR
JOHNSTON, CHRISTOPHER	BAL	402	8TH WARD
JOHNSTON, CORDIALIA	WAS	141	HAGERSTO
JOHNSTON, DAVID	WAS	159	HAGERSTO
JOHNSTON, CAVID	WAS	293	1ST DIST
JOHNSTON, DEBORAH	BAL	386	8TH WARD
JOHNSTON, DELIAH	BAL	408	8TH WARD
JOHNSTON, EDGAR	BAL	083	18TH WAR
JOHNSTON, EDWARD	WAS	125	HAGERSTO
JOHNSTON, ELIJA	BAL	136	11TH WAR
JOHNSTON, ELISA	BAL	012	18TH WAR
JOHNSTON, ELIZA	BAL	127	11TH WAR
JOHNSTON, ELIZA	BAL	269	20TH WAR
JOHNSTON, ELIZA	BAL	355	8TH WARD
JOHNSTON, ELIZABET	HAR	091	2ND DIST
JOHNSTON, ELIZABETH	HAR	076	BEL AIR
JOHNSTON, ELIZABETH	CAR	354	6TH DIST
JOHNSTON, ELIZABETH	BAL	279	7TH WARD
JOHNSTON, ELLEN	BAL	154	11TH WAR
JOHNSTON, EMILY J.	BAL	083	18TH WAR
JOHNSTON, EMMA	WAS	206	1ST DIST
JOHNSTON, EMORY	BAL	184	11TH WAR
JOHNSTON, FRANCIS	CAR	409	2ND DIST
JOHNSTON, FREDERICK	BAL	320	7TH WARD
JOHNSTON, GEORGE	BAL	318	7TH WARD
JOHNSTON, GEORGE	BAL	458	8TH WARD
JOHNSTON, GEORGE	BAL	136	18TH WAR
JOHNSTON, GEORGE	BAL	128	10TH WAR
JOHNSTON, GEORGE	WAS	278	LEITERSB
JOHNSTON, GEORGE W.	BAL	264	7TH WARD
JOHNSTON, HANAH	BAL	457	8TH WARD
JOHNSTON, HANNAH	BAL	024	18TH WAR
JOHNSTON, HANNAH	BAL	142	11TH WAR
JOHNSTON, HANNAH	BAL	138	11TH WAR
JOHNSTON, HARRIET	CEC	036	CHESAPEA
JOHNSTON, HARRIETT	BAL	144	11TH WAR
JOHNSTON, HENRIETTA	BAL	456	8TH WARD
JOHNSTON, HENRY	BAL	265	7TH WARD
JOHNSTON, HENRY	BAL	366	8TH WARD
JOHNSTON, HENRY	BAL	460	1ST DIST
JOHNSTON, HENRY	BAL	024	18TH WAR
JOHNSTON, HERNY	BAL	452	8TH WARD
JOHNSTON, HETTY	CAR	235	UNION TO
JOHNSTON, HIRAM	BAL	166	11TH WAR
JOHNSTON, HOWARD	BAL	405	8TH WARD
JOHNSTON, ISAAC	BAL	155	11TH WAR
JOHNSTON, ISAAK	BAL	456	8TH WARD
JOHNSTON, J.S.	BAL	254	12TH WAR
JOHNSTON, JACOB	BAL	002	18TH WAR
JOHNSTON, JAMES	BAL	019	18TH WAR
JOHNSTON, JAMES	BAL	011	18TH WAR
JOHNSTON, JAMES	BAL	136	18TH WAR
JOHNSTON, JAMES	BAL	201	11TH WAR
JOHNSTON, JAMES	BAL	397	8TH WARD
JOHNSTON, JAMES	BAL	277	7TH WARD
JOHNSTON, JAMES	BAL	250	6TH WARD
JOHNSTON, JAMES	BAL	316	7TH WARD
JOHNSTON, JAMES	WAS	246	SMITHSBU
JOHNSTON, JAMES W.	BAL	360	8TH WARD
JOHNSTON, JANE	BAL	073	10TH WAR
JOHNSTON, JANE	BAL	171	11TH WAR
JOHNSTON, JANE	BAL	135	18TH WAR
JOHNSTON, JANE	BAL	388	13TH WAR
JOHNSTON, JANE	BAL	424	3RD WARD
JOHNSTON, JOHN	BAL	128	11TH WAR
JOHNSTON, JOHN	BAL	139	11TH WAR
JOHNSTON, JOHN	BAL	371	8TH WARD
JOHNSTON, JOHN	BAL	304	7TH WARD
JOHNSTON, JOHN	BAL	184	6TH WARD
JOHNSTON, JOHN P.	BAL	398	8TH WARD
JOHNSTON, JONAS	BAL	364	8TH WARD
JOHNSTON, JOSEPH	BAL	357	8TH WARD
JOHNSTON, JOSEPH	BAL	388	8TH WARD
JOHNSTON, JOSEPH	BAL	335	7TH WARD
JOHNSTON, JOSEPH	ST	318	4TH E DI
JOHNSTON, JOSHUA T.	BAL	344	7TH WARD
JOHNSTON, JULIA	BAL	283	7TH WARD
JOHNSTON, JULIA	BAL	412	8TH WARD
JOHNSTON, KILTEY	BAL	438	8TH WARD
JOHNSTON, LEE	BAL	255	20TH WAR
JOHNSTON, LEVI	BAL	353	1ST DIST
JOHNSTON, LEWIS	WAS	178	BOONSBOR
JOHNSTON, LOUIS	BAL	220	1ST DIST
JOHNSTON, LOUISA	BAL	121	11TH WAR
JOHNSTON, LUCY	BAL	318	12TH WAR
JOHNSTON, MAHALA	BAL	216	11TH WAR
JOHNSTON, MALVINA	BAL	140	11TH WAR
JOHNSTON, MARGARET	BAL	015	18TH WAR
JOHNSTON, MARGARET	BAL	287	7TH WARD
JOHNSTON, MARGARET	WAS	265	1ST DIST
JOHNSTON, MARIA	BAL	350	7TH WARD
JOHNSTON, MARIA P.	BAL	340	7TH WARD
JOHNSTON, MARTHA	BAL	192	11TH WAR
JOHNSTON, MARTHA	BAL	021	18TH WAR
JOHNSTON, MARTHA	BAL	014	18TH WAR
JOHNSTON, MARTHA A.	BAL	326	7TH WARD
JOHNSTON, MARY	BAL	166	11TH WAR
JOHNSTON, MARY	BAL	276	7TH WARD
JOHNSTON, MARY	BAL	275	7TH WARD
JOHNSTON, MARY	BAL	406	8TH WARD
JOHNSTON, MARY	BAL	405	8TH WARD
JOHNSTON, MARY	BAL	369	8TH WARD
JOHNSTON, MARY	BAL	283	1ST DIST
JOHNSTON, MARY	BAL	131	11TH WAR
JOHNSTON, HARY	BAL	127	11TH WAR
JOHNSTON, HARY	BAL	129	18TH WAR
JOHNSTON, MARY A.	BAL	341	7TH WARD
JOHNSTON, MARY A.	BAL	443	8TH WARD
JOHNSTON, MICHAEL	BAL	414	8TH WARD
JOHNSTON, MITILDA	BAL	211	11TH WAR
JOHNSTON, MOSES	BAL	354	7TH WARD
JOHNSTON, MRS. E.	BAL	148	11TH WAR
JOHNSTON, OSCAR	BAL	304	7TH WARD
JOHNSTON, P. B.	BAL	146	11TH WAR
JOHNSTON, REBECCA	BAL	342	7TH WARD
JOHNSTON, RICHARD	BAL	340	7TH WARD
JOHNSTON, RICHARD	BAL	354	7TH WARD
JOHNSTON, RICHARD	BAL	172	11TH WAR
JOHNSTON, RICHARD	BAL	112	18TH WAR
JOHNSTON, ROBERT	HAR	005	1ST DIST
JOHNSTON, ROBERT	BAL	257	12TH WAR
JOHNSTON, ROSS	BAL	279	2ND WARD
JOHNSTON, SAMUEL	WAS	159	HAGERSTO
JOHNSTON, SARAH	BAL	403	8TH WARD
JOHNSTON, SARAH	BAL	197	11TH WAR
JOHNSTON, SARAH	BAL	024	18TH WAR
JOHNSTON, SARAH	BAL	013	18TH WAR
JOHNSTON, SARAH	BAL	216	11TH WAR
JOHNSTON, SARAH J.	BAL	341	7TH WARD
JOHNSTON, SIMON	BAL	135	18TH WAR
JOHNSTON, STEPHEN	BAL	206	11TH WAR
JOHNSTON, STEPHEN	BAL	276	7TH WARD
JOHNSTON, SUSAN	WAS	152	HAGERSTO
JOHNSTON, SUSANA	CAR	369	9TH DIST
JOHNSTON, THERESA	BAL	275	7TH WARD
JOHNSTON, THOMAS	BAL	291	7TH WARD
JOHNSTON, THOMAS	BAL	016	4TH WARD
JOHNSTON, THOMAS JR.	BAL	364	13TH WAR
JOHNSTON, TRUMAN	WAS	195	1ST DIST
JOHNSTON, WALTER	WAS	293	1ST DIST
JOHNSTON, WILLIAM	WAS	205	1ST DIST
JOHNSTON, WILLIAM	BAL	043	4TH WARD
JOHNSTON, WILLIAM	CAR	333	MANCHEST
JOHNSTON, WILLIAM	BAL	131	11TH WAR
JOHNSTON, WILLIAM	BAL	136	18TH WAR
JOHNSTON, WILLIAM	BAL	308	7TH WARD
JOHNSTON, WILLIAM	BAL	300	7TH WARD
JOHNSTON, WILLIAM	BAL	353	7TH WARD
JOHNSTON, WILLIAM	BAL	456	8TH WARD
JOHNSTON, WILLIAM	BAL	456	8TH WARD
JOHNSTON, WILLIAM	BAL	458	8TH WARD
JOHNSTON, WILLIAM H.	BAL	460	8TH WARD
JOHNSTON, WILLIAM H.	FRE	151	10TH E D
JOHNSTON, WILLIAM HENRY	CAR	372	9TH DIST
JOHNSTON, WILLIAM O.	BAL	300	7TH WARD
JOHNSTON, WILLIAM T.	CAR	379	2ND DIST
JOHNSTON,ROBERT-BLACK	CAR	384	2ND DIST
JOHNTON, J.	WAS	020	2ND SUBD
JOHNTSON, JOSEPH	BAL	272	1ST DIST
JOHNWITH, RICHARD	QUE	126	1ST E DI
JOHONAHAS, JOHN G.	BAL	020	18TH WAR
JOHOSN, MARY	CAL	002	1ST DIST
JOHSNON, ELIZABETH	BAL	270	12TH WAR
JOHSNON, H.	BAL	118	1ST WARD
JOHSNON, JEMIMA	BAL	046	2ND DIST
JOHSNON, JOHN	BAL	105	1ST WARD
JOHSNON, JOHN	BAL	122	1ST WARD
JOHSNON, JOHN	ALL	152	6TH E.D.
JOHSNON, JOSEPH	ALL	245	CUMBERLA
JOHSNON, JULIANNA	ALL	044	10TH E.D
JOHSNON, MARY-BLACK	CAR	085	NO TWP L
JOHSNON, SAMUEL-BLACK	CAR	090	NO TWP L
JOHSNON, WILLIAM	BAL	286	12TH WAR
JOHSNON, WILLIAM	BAL	172	1ST WARD
JOHSON, ABIGAIL	BAL	224	12TH WAR
JOHSON, J. P.	BAL	152	1ST WARD
JOHSON, WILIAM	BAL	156	1ST WARD
JOICE, BILL	BAL	456	1ST DIST
JOICE, CHARLES	WAS	092	2ND SUBD
JOICE, DANIEL	BAL	377	13TH WAR
JOICE, ELIZABETH	BAL	378	13TH WAR
JOICE, ELIZABETH	BAL	100	10TH WAR
JOICE, GEORGE	BAL	175	2ND DIST
JOICE, GEORGE	BAL	174	2ND DIST
JOICE, GEORGE	BAL	395	8TH WARD
JOICE, GEORGE H.	BAL	245	17TH WAR
JOICE, HARRIET	ANN	271	ANNAPOLI
JOICE, JOHN	BAL	426	1ST DIST
JOICE, JOHN	FRE	096	FREDERIC
JOICE, JOSEPH	BAL	461	1ST DIST
JOICE, JOSHUA	BAL	160	6TH WARD
JOICE, LAWRENCE	ALL	047	10TH E.D
JOICE, MARY	BAL	454	8TH WARD
JOICE, MARY	BAL	419	3RD WARD
JOICE, MARY E.	BAL	371	3RD WARD
JOICE, NACE	BAL	068	2ND DIST
JOICE, NOAH	CEC	023	ELKTON 3
JOICE, OLIVER	BAL	378	13TH WAR
JOICE, RICHARD	HAR	195	3RD DIST
JOICE, RICHARD	BAL	215	6TH WARD
JOICE, SUSAN	BAL	455	1ST DIST
JOICE, THOMAS	BAL	237	6TH WARD
JOICE, WILLIAM	ANN	346	3RD DIST
JOICE, WILLIAM	BAL	249	6TH WARD
JOINOON, WILLIAM	BAL	108	2ND DIST
JOINER, ALICE	QUE	236	4TH E DI
JOINER, CHARLES	KEN	228	2ND DIST
JOINER, CHARLOTTE A.*	BAL	064	4TH WARD
JOINER, DAVID	KEN	228	2ND DIST
JOINER, EDITHA	KEN	228	2ND DIST
JOINER, GEROGE	KEN	258	1ST DIST
JOINER, JOHN EDWARD	BAL	263	17TH WAR
JOINER, JOSHUA	BAL	356	3RD WARD
JOINER, LOUISA	QUE	233	4TH E DI
JOINER, MARY	BAL	275	2ND WARD
JOINER, ROBERT	CAR	111	NO TWP L
JOINER, THOMAS	QUE	229	4TH E DI
JOINER, WILLIAM	KEN	267	1ST DIST
JOINER, WILLIAM	KEN	273	1ST DIST
JOINER, WILLIAM	CAR	111	NO TWP L
JOINER, WILLIAM	BAL	263	17TH WAR
JOINES, JOHN	BAL	191	6TH WARD
JOINS, ELIZABETH	WOR	329	1ST E DI
JOKELY, MARGRETT-MULATTO	CAR	069	NO TWP L
JOLANS, JACOB*	DOR	314	1ST DIST
JOLEFIL, GEORGE W.B.	QUE	148	1ST E DI
JOLEY, DICK	DOR	418	1ST DIST
JOLEY, EASEN*	DOR	406	1ST DIST
JOLEY, HENRY	DOR	425	1ST DIST
JOLEY, HOOPER*	DOR	448	1ST DIST
JOLEY, JOHN	DOR	409	1ST DIST
JOLEY, JOHN	DOR	383	1ST DIST
JOLEY, LEVIN*	DOR	377	1ST DIST
JOLEY, LEVINIA	DOR	417	1ST DIST
JOLEY, LIBY*	DOR	469	1ST DIST
JOLEY, MILKY	DOR	387	1ST DIST
JOLEY, SIMON	DOR	445	1ST DIST
JOLEY, SOPHIA	DOR	419	1ST DIST
JOLEY, WILLIAM	DOR	441	1ST DIST
JOLIE, PHILIP	BAL	230	19TH WAR
JOLLEY, ELIZA	HAR	014	1ST DIST
JOLLEY, ELIZABETH	BAL	142	11TH WAR
JOLLEY, GEORGE	BAL	387	3RD WARD
JOLLEY, GEORGE	BAL	056	1ST WARD
JOLLEY, ISAAC	BAL	330	7TH WARD
JOLLEY, PATRICK	BAL	024	9TH WARD
JOLLEY, RICHARD G.	BAL	345	7TH WARD
JOLLEY, THOMA	BAL	119	1ST WARD
JOLLIVERT, JOSEPH	BAL	006	1ST WARD
JOLLY, HENRY	QUE	250	5TH E DI
JOLLY, JACOB	ALL	187	9TH E.D.
JOLLY, JOHN A.	BAL	452	1ST DIST
JOLLY, LEIN	QUE	217	3RD E DI
JOLLY, LEVIN-BLACK	QUE	160	2ND E DI
JOLLY, MARY	BAL	101	18TH WAR
JOLLY, MARY	BAL	053	18TH WAR
JOLLY, SARAH	QUE	251	5TH E DI
JOLLY, WILLIAM H.	BAL	030	2ND DIST
JOLSON,J.P.	BAL	169	1ST WARD
JOMES, ISAAC*	DOR	435	1ST DIST
JOMES, SAMUEL	ANN	280	ANNAPOLI
JOMIS, T. J.	BAL	149	1ST WARD
JOMLINSON, FREDERICK*	BAL	311	3RD WARD
JOMRY, ELIJAH	DOR	414	1ST DIST
JONAS, JACOB	BAL	387	1ST DIST
JONAS, MARY F.	BAL	386	8TH WARD
JONBES, LOUIZA	CAR	155	NO TWP L
JONOS, MARGARET	SOM	461	HANGARY
JONE, EDWARD	BAL	293	7TH WARD
JONE, ISAAC	BAL	124	2ND DIST
JONE, JAMES	WOR	335	1ST E DI
JONE, MARGARET	BAL	346	7TH WARD
JONE, VALENTINE-MULATTO	FRE	409	JEFFERSO
JONE,S HENRY	CAL	038	2ND DIST
JONE,S JAMES	BAL	068	10TH WAR
JONEES, CLEMENT F.	BAL	064	10TH WAR
JONES, A.	BAL	173	1ST WARD
JONES, A. D. REV-	BAL	332	1ST DIST
JONES, AARON	BAL	112	10TH WAR
JONES, ABRAHAM	FRE	447	8TH E DI
JONES, ABRAHAM	CAR	411	2ND DIST
JONES, ABRAHAM	BAL	358	1ST DIST
JONES, ABRAHAM	BAL	173	1ST WARD
JONES, ABRAHAM	ANN	465	HOWARD D
JONES, ACCARY	BAL	010	18TH WAR
JONES, ACSHA	BAL	085	15TH WAR
JONES, ADAM	SOM	465	HANGARY
JONES, ADAM	SOM	459	HANGARY
JONES, ADISON	WAS	095	2ND SUBD
JONES, ADOLPHUS-MULATTO	FRE	242	NEW MARK
JONES, AGNES	ANN	461	HOWARD D
JONES, AGNES	BAL	188	11TH WAR
JONES, AGNESS B.	CHA	224	ALLENS F
JONES, ALABAMA	BAL	411	3RD WARD
JONES, ALEXANDER	BAL	152	19TH WAR
JONES, ALEXANDER	SOM	428	PRINCESS
JONES, ALEXANDER	BAL	329	13TH WAR
JONES, ALEXANDER	BAL	394	3RD WARD
JONES, ALEXINE	BAL	412	3RD WARD
JONES, ALFRED	BAL	123	18TH WAR
JONES, ALFRED	FRE	161	EMMITTSB
JONES, ALFRED	BAL	393	3RD WARD
JONES, ALFRED	BAL	313	12TH WAR
JONES, ALFRED	BAL	013	1ST WARD
JONES, ALFRED H.	SOM	427	PRINCESS
JONES, ALLY	TAL	116	ST MICHA
JONES, ALONZE	BAL	160	1ST WARD
JONES, ALSEY	SOM	453	DAMES QU
JONES, AMAN	BAL	414	1ST DIST
JONES, AMANDA	BAL	019	15TH WAR
JONES, AMAS	DOR	342	3RD DIVI
JONES, AMELIA	BAL	255	17TH WAR
JONES, AMELIA	WOR	200	3RD E DI
JONES, AMELIA	WOR	208	4TH E DI
JONES, AMELIA	WOR	350	1ST E DI
JONES, AMELIA-BLACK	WOR	170	6TH E DI
JONES, AMERICAN	BAL	371	1ST DIST
JONES, AMEY	BAL	448	8TH WARD
JONES, AMOS	BAL	342	1ST DIST
JONES, AMOS	KEN	225	2ND DIST
JONES, AMOS	BAL	167	19TH WAR
JONES, ANDREW	FRE	102	FREDERIC
JONES, ANDREW	BAL	452	1ST DIST
JONES, ANDREW	BAL	245	6TH WARD
JONES, ANDREW J.	ANN	466	HOWARD D
JONES, ANDREW*	DOR	302	1ST DIST
JONES, ANGELINE	BAL	105	5TH WARD
JONES, ANN	ALL	234	CUMBERLA
JONES, ANN	BAL	230	12TH WAR
JONES, ANN	BAL	054	15TH WAR
JONES, ANN	BAL	363	3RD WARD
JONES, ANN	BAL	159	2ND DIST
JONES, ANN	BAL	096	10TH WAR
JONES, ANN	BAL	314	7TH WARD
JONES, ANN	BAL	113	15TH WAR
JONES, ANN	BAL	303	7TH WARD
JONES, ANN	BAL	357	8TH WARD
JONES, ANN	ANN	388	4TH DIST
JONES, ANN	ALL	075	5TH E.D.
JONES, ANN	MGM	322	CRACKLIN
JONES, ANN	DOR	352	3RD DIVI
JONES, ANN	BAL	019	4TH WARD
JONES, ANN	BAL	030	4TH WARD
JONES, ANN	BAL	033	18TH WAR
JONES, ANN	BAL	134	11TH WAR
JONES, ANN	BAL	146	11TH WAR
JONES, ANN	SOM	450	DAMES QU
JONES, ANN	KEN	288	3RD DIST
JONES, ANN	WAS	038	2ND SUBD
JONES, ANN E.	BAL	089	15TH WAR
JONES, ANN E.	BAL	086	15TH WAR
JONES, ANN M.	ALL	245	CUMBERLA
JONES, ANN M.	BAL	227	6TH WARD
JONES, ANN M.	CEC	089	4TH E DI
JONES, ANN M.	FRE	446	8TH E DI
JONES, ANN M.	BAL	136	18TH WAR
JONES, ANN W.	SOM	431	PRINCESS
JONES, ANNA	CAR	302	1ST DIST
JONES, ANNA	MGM	325	CRACKLIN
JONES, ANNA M.	MGM	371	BERRYS D
JONES, AQUILLA	HAR	040	1ST DIST
JONES, AQUILLA	BAL	439	1ST DIST
JONES, ARNOLD	WAS	130	2ND DIST
JONES, ARON	MGM	435	CLARKSTP
JONES, ARTHUR	BAL	356	1ST DIST
JONES, ARTHUR	CEC	057	1ST E DI
JONES, ASBERY	BAL	163	11TH WAR
JONES, ASBURY	BAL	444	14TH WAR
JONES, AUBRY	BAL	463	14TH WAR
JONES, AUDRY	BAL	107	18TH WAR
JONES, AUMITTA	BAL	078	4TH WARD
JONES, AUTHER	BAL	317	7TH WARD
JONES, BARGILLA	ST	299	2ND E DI
JONES, BASIL	CAL	009	1ST DIST
JONES, BELL	BAL	067	4TH WARD
JONES, BELL	WOR	300	SNOW HIL
JONES, BEN	CAL	048	3RD DIST
JONES, BENJAMIN	CAL	048	3RD DIST
JONES, BENJAMIN	BAL	154	19TH WAR

JONES, BENJAMIN	QUE	127	1ST E DI
JONES, BENJAMIN	QUE	123	1ST E DI
JONES, BENJAMIN	DOR	346	3RD DIVI
JONES, BENJAMIN	BAL	185	6TH WARD
JONES, BENJAMIN	ANN	360	3RD DIST
JONES, BENJAMIN	ANN	469	HOWARD D
JONES, BENJAMIN	ANN	398	8TH DIST
JONES, BENJAMIN J.	SOM	548	TYASKIN
JONES, BENJAMIN T.	BAL	438	8TH WARD
JONES, BENJAMIN W.	BAL	347	3RD WARD
JONES, BENJAMIN-BLACK	FRE	242	NEW MARK
JONES, BENNETT	BAL	001	4TH WARD
JONES, BENSON	BAL	250	20TH WAR
JONES, BETSEY	BAL	087	4TH WARD
JONES, BETSEY	BAL	168	11TH WAR
JONES, BETSEY	ANN	450	HOWARD D
JONES, BETSEY	SOM	459	HANGARY
JONES, BETSEY	SOM	400	BRINKLEY
JONES, BETSY	WOR	325	1ST E DI
JONES, BETSY	BAL	138	5TH WARD
JONES, BETTY	BAL	319	20TH WAR
JONES, BOYSTON	BAL	063	4TH WARD
JONES, BRISTER	BAL	011	2ND DIST
JONES, BROOK	MGM	426	MEDLEY 3
JONES, C.	BAL	305	20TH WAR
JONES, CADWALDER	HAR	041	1ST DIST
JONES, CALEB	SOM	447	DAMES QU
JONES, CALEB M.	ST	309	1ST E DI
JONES, CALEP	DOR	346	3RD DIVI
JONES, CALVIN	CEC	036	CHESAPEA
JONES, CAROLINE	CAL	046	3RD DIST
JONES, CAROLINE	BAL	200	6TH WARD
JONES, CAROLINE	BAL	021	15TH WAR
JONES, CAROLINE	BAL	411	1ST DIST
JONES, CAROLINE	BAL	045	9TH WARD
JONES, CAROLINE	BAL	055	9TH WARD
JONES, CATHARINE	ANN	505	HOWARD D
JONES, CATHARINE	BAL	197	11TH WAR
JONES, CATHARINE	BAL	252	6TH WARD
JONES, CATHARINE	BAL	175	19TH WAR
JONES, CATHARINE	BAL	202	19TH WAR
JONES, CATHARINE	DOR	381	1ST DIST
JONES, CATHARINE	KEN	229	2ND DIST
JONES, CATHARINE	WAS	282	1ST DIST
JONES, CATHARINE	WOR	290	9TH E DI
JONES, CATHARINE A.	BAL	134	16TH WAR
JONES, CATHARINE M.-BLACK	FRE	208	BUCKEYST
JONES, CATHARINE S.	BAL	032	18TH WAR
JONES, CATHARINE-MULATTO	FRE	408	JEFFERSO
JONES, CATHERINE	BAL	045	4TH WARD
JONES, CATHERINE	BAL	068	10TH WAR
JONES, CATHERINE	BAL	027	1ST WARD
JONES, CATHERINE	WAS	122	2ND DIST
JONES, CATO	ANN	307	1ST DIST
JONES, CECELIA	BAL	214	17TH WAR
JONES, CELELIA	CAL	030	2ND DIST
JONES, CELEY	SOM	448	DAMES QU
JONES, CHARELS	TAL	098	ST MICHA
JONES, CHARELS	BAL	301	12TH WAR
JONES, CHARLES	ALL	072	5TH E.D.
JONES, CHARLES	BAL	234	1ST DIST
JONES, CHARLES	BAL	080	1ST WARD
JONES, CHARLES	BAL	128	1ST WARD
JONES, CHARLES	BAL	146	1ST WARD
JONES, CHARLES	BAL	030	15TH WAR
JONES, CHARLES	BAL	248	12TH WAR
JONES, CHARLES	BAL	449	1ST DIST
JONES, CHARLES	BAL	149	5TH WARD
JONES, CHARLES	BAL	244	6TH WARD
JONES, CHARLES	WOR	289	9TH E DI
JONES, CHARLES	SOM	447	DAMES QU
JONES, CHARLES	PRI	078	MARLBROU
JONES, CHARLES	SOM	484	TRAPP DI
JONES, CHARLES	FRE	404	JEFFERSO
JONES, CHARLES	BAL	188	19TH WAR
JONES, CHARLES	BAL	321	20TH WAR
JONES, CHARLES	MGM	360	BERRYS D
JONES, CHARLES	SOM	443	DAMES QU
JONES, CHARLES B.	MGM	402	ROCKERLE
JONES, CHARLES H.	BAL	333	13TH WAR
JONES, CHARLES W.	BAL	235	1ST DIST
JONES, CHARLES-MULATTO	BAL	219	2ND WARD
JONES, CHARLOTTE	BAL	302	12TH WAR
JONES, CHARLOTTE	BAL	331	3RD WARD
JONES, CHARLOTTE	BAL	247	12TH WAR
JONES, CHARLOTTE	SOM	414	DUBLIN D
JONES, CHARLOTTE	CAR	397	2ND DIST
JONES, CHARLOTTE A.	MGM	421	MEDLEY 3
JONES, CHRISTOPHER	CEC	054	1ST E DI
JONES, CHRISTOPHER	CEC	062	1ST E DI
JONES, CIRENDA	SOM	447	DAMES QU
JONES, CLEMENT	ST	312	1ST E DI
JONES, CLEMENT	ANN	379	4TH DIST
JONES, CLEMENTINE	BAL	208	6TH WARD
JONES, CLINTON L.	KEN	226	2ND DIST
JONES, COLLINS	BAL	001	9TH WARD
JONES, COMFORT	FRE	316	MIDDLETO
JONES, CORNELIUS	BAL	207	6TH DIST
JONES, CRISTIAN	BAL	018	18TH WAR
JONES, CROWNEN	ANN	302	1ST DIST
JONES, CYRUS	SOM	470	TRAPPE D
JONES, D. DR-	SOM	443	DAMES QU
JONES, DANIEL	HAR	114	2ND DIST
JONES, DANIEL	KEN	249	2ND DIST
JONES, DANIEL	KEN	222	2ND DIST
JONES, DANIEL	DOR	347	3RD DIVI
JONES, DANIEL	WOR	293	9TH E DI
JONES, DANIEL	ALL	070	5TH E.D.
JONES, DANIEL	ANN	472	HOWARD D
JONES, DANIEL T.	FRE	223	BUCKEYST
JONES, DAVID	BAL	303	17TH WAR
JONES, DAVID	BAL	241	17TH WAR
JONES, DAVID	ALL	123	4TH E.D.
JONES, DAVID	BAL	433	1ST DIST
JONES, DAVID	BAL	450	1ST DIST
JONES, DAVID	BAL	101	5TH WARD
JONES, DAVID	BAL	327	13TH WAR
JONES, DAVID	BAL	081	15TH WAR
JONES, DAVID	BAL	152	2ND DIST
JONES, DAVID	BAL	277	1ST DIST
JONES, DAVID	BAL	278	2ND WARD
JONES, DAVID	KEN	263	1ST DIST
JONES, DAVID	QUE	234	4TH E DI
JONES, DAVID A.	BAL	134	16TH WAR
JONES, DAVID B.	CAR	251	3RD DIST
JONES, DAVID F.	FRE	213	BUCKEYST
JONES, DAVID P.	BAL	032	18TH WAR
JONES, DAVID-BLACK	FRE	025	FREDERIC
JONES, DEEBY	ANN	421	HOWARD D
JONES, DEBORAH-BLACK	QUE	179	2ND E DI
JONES, DELPHINE	BAL	284	20TH WAR
JONES, DENIAS S. *	TAL	086	ST MICHA
JONES, DENNARD	BAL	045	15TH WAR
JONES, DIANA	BAL	043	9TH WARD
JONES, DICK	ANN	314	1ST DIST
JONES, DINWOOD	BAL	051	9TH WARD
JONES, DOROTHY A.	DOR	376	1ST DIST
JONES, DORSEY	BAL	191	19TH WAR
JONES, E.	BAL	238	17TH WAR
JONES, E.	BAL	150	5TH WARD
JONES, E.	BAL	281	2ND WARD
JONES, EBEY	DOR	306	1ST DIST
JONES, EBLING	BAL	161	1ST WARD
JONES, EDUARD	BAL	244	12TH WAR
JONES, EDWARD	BAL	184	11TH WAR
JONES, EDWARD	BAL	170	11TH WAR
JONES, EDWARD	BAL	126	1ST WARD
JONES, EDWARD	ANN	299	1ST DIST
JONES, EDWARD	BAL	005	EASTERN
JONES, EDWARD	BAL	112	5TH WARD
JONES, EDWARD	DOR	304	1ST DIST
JONES, EDWARD	BAL	214	17TH WAR
JONES, EDWARD	CHA	255	MIDDLETO
JONES, EDWARD	CEC	058	1ST E DI
JONES, EDWARD	TAL	085	ST MICHA
JONES, EDWARD	WOR	327	1ST E DI
JONES, EDWARD	WOR	294	9TH E DI
JONES, EDWARD J.	WOR	319	1ST E DI
JONES, EDWIN	BAL	237	12TH WAR
JONES, ELBE	WOR	316	2ND E DI
JONES, ELEANOR	SOM	469	TRAPPE D
JONES, ELEANOR	SOM	466	HANGARY
JONES, ELENORA	QUE	185	3RD E DI
JONES, ELI	SOM	391	BRINKLEY
JONES, ELI	ANN	464	HOWARD D
JONES, ELI	BAL	165	2ND DIST
JONES, ELI	BAL	365	3RD WARD
JONES, ELIAS	BAL	177	19TH WAR
JONES, ELIAS N.	HAR	036	1ST DIST
JONES, ELIJAH	HAR	012	1ST DIST
JONES, ELIJAH	BAL	086	1ST WARD
JONES, ELIJAH	BAL	030	2ND DIST
JONES, ELISA	BAL	120	2ND DIST
JONES, ELISA H.	ANN	288	ANNAPOLI
JONES, ELISHA	BAL	063	15TH WAR
JONES, ELISHA	BAL	436	1ST DIST
JONES, ELISHA	BAL	345	1ST DIST
JONES, ELISHA	BAL	289	17TH WAR
JONES, ELISHA	BAL	305	17TH WAR
JONES, ELISHA	CHA	231	HILLTOP
JONES, ELISHA	WOR	349	1ST E DI
JONES, ELISHA	MGM	442	CLARKSTR
JONES, ELIZA	BAL	250	20TH WAR
JONES, ELIZA	SOM	441	DAMES QU
JONES, ELIZA	BAL	336	13TH WAR
JONES, ELIZA	DOR	401	1ST DIST
JONES, ELIZA	KEN	212	2ND DIST
JONES, ELIZA	BAL	349	1ST DIST
JONES, ELIZA	BAL	303	3RD WARD
JONES, ELIZA	BAL	305	1ST DIST
JONES, ELIZA	BAL	296	12TH WAR
JONES, ELIZA	BAL	113	15TH WAR
JONES, ELIZA J.	BAL	317	7TH WARD
JONES, ELIZA-BLACK	QUE	134	1ST E DI
JONES, ELIZA-BLACK	WOR	350	1ST E DI
JONES, ELIZABETH	WOR	341	1ST E DI
JONES, ELIZABETH	WOR	336	1ST E DI
JONES, ELIZABETH	SOM	460	HANGARY
JONES, ELIZABETH	SOM	465	HANGARY
JONES, ELIZABETH	WOR	165	6TH E DI
JONES, ELIZABETH	WAS	211	1ST DIST
JONES, ELIZABETH	WOR	247	1ST CENS
JONES, ELIZABETH	SOM	496	SALISBUR
JONES, ELIZABETH	FRE	210	BUCKEYST
JONES, ELIZABETH	BAL	263	17TH WAR
JONES, ELIZABETH	DOR	302	1ST DIST
JONES, ELIZABETH	SOM	414	DUBLIN D
JONES, ELIZABETH	MGM	396	ROCKERLE
JONES, ELIZABETH	FRE	032	FREDERIC
JONES, ELIZABETH	DOR	345	3RD DIVI
JONES, ELIZABETH	DOR	344	3RD DIVI
JONES, ELIZABETH	BAL	072	18TH WAR
JONES, ELIZABETH	CAR	189	4TH DIST
JONES, ELIZABETH	BAL	114	15TH WAR
JONES, ELIZABETH	BAL	074	1ST WARD
JONES, ELIZABETH	BAL	164	2ND DIST
JONES, ELIZABETH	BAL	451	1ST DIST
JONES, ELIZABETH	BAL	337	3RD WARD
JONES, ELIZABETH	BAL	053	15TH WAR
JONES, ELIZABETH	BAL	054	15TH WAR
JONES, ELIZABETH	BAL	250	12TH WAR
JONES, ELIZABETH	BAL	124	2ND DIST
JONES, ELIZABETH	ANN	465	HOWARD D
JONES, ELIZABETH	BAL	394	3RD WARD
JONES, ELIZABETH	BAL	258	2ND WARD
JONES, ELIZABETH	BAL	257	2ND WARD
JONES, ELIZABETH A.	BAL	103	15TH WAR
JONES, ELIZABETH A.	BAL	158	19TH WAR
JONES, ELIZABETH-BLACK	ST	319	4TH E DI
JONES, ELIZABETHJ	KEN	258	1ST DIST
JONES, ELLEN	KEN	265	1ST DIST
JONES, ELLEN	PRI	095	SPALDING
JONES, ELLEN	PRI	095	SPALDING
JONES, ELLEN	TAL	112	ST MICHA
JONES, ELLEN	HAR	042	1ST DIST
JONES, ELLEN	BAL	047	4TH WARD
JONES, ELLEN	BAL	112	15TH WAR
JONES, ELLEN	BAL	028	15TH WAR
JONES, ELLENOR	DOR	467	1ST DIST
JONES, ELLIS	CEC	003	ELKTON 3
JONES, ELSEY	DOR	351	3RD DIVI
JONES, ELTRENA	DOR	322	1ST DIST
JONES, EMALINE	SOM	452	DAMES QU
JONES, EMELINE	BAL	449	8TH WARD
JONES, EMELINE	BAL	391	3RD WARD
JONES, EMELINE	BAL	180	2ND WARD
JONES, EMILY	BAL	301	20TH WAR
JONES, EMILY	BAL	236	17TH WAR
JONES, EMILY	BAL	361	13TH WAR
JONES, EMILY	BAL	013	18TH WAR
JONES, EMILY	BAL	082	18TH WAR
JONES, EMILY	BAL	126	11TH WAR
JONES, EMILY R.	BAL	163	16TH WAR
JONES, EMMA	WOR	298	9TH E DI
JONES, EMMANUEL	BAL	049	15TH WAR
JONES, EMORY	BAL	240	5TH WARD
JONES, ENNIS	SOM	539	TYASKIN
JONES, ENNIS	SOM	431	PRINCESS
JONES, ENOCH	WAS	020	2ND SUBD
JONES, EPHRAIM	CAR	303	1ST DIST
JONES, EPHRAIM W.	WOR	294	9TH E DI
JONES, ETHAN A.	PRI	044	VANSVILL
JONES, EVAN	MGM	399	ROCKERLE
JONES, EVAN	MGM	322	CRACKLIN
JONES, EVAN	MGM	322	CRACKLIN
JONES, EVANS-BLACK	BAL	219	2ND WARD
JONES, EWARD	FRE	446	8TH E DI
JONES, EYNCH	BAL	187	2ND WARD
JONES, EZEKEL	DOR	347	3RD DIVI
JONES, EZEKIEL	HAR	040	1ST DIST
JONES, EZEKIEL	HAR	054	1ST DIST
JONES, EZEKIEL	BAL	350	3RD WARD
JONES, EZRA	WAS	184	BOONSBOR
JONES, FANNY	BAL	122	5TH WARD
JONES, FANY	BAL	170	11TH WAR
JONES, FELIZ	KEN	263	1ST DIST
JONES, FRANCES	BAL	365	13TH WAR
JONES, FRANCIS	FRE	300	WOODSBOR
JONES, FRANCIS	SOM	329	QUANTICO
JONES, FRANCIS	PRI	095	SPALDING
JONES, FRANCIS	WOR	294	9TH E DI
JONES, FRANCIS	BAL	031	15TH WAR
JONES, FRANCIS A.	ST	303	2ND E DI
JONES, FRANCIS A.*	BAL	406	3RD WARD
JONES, FRANCIS S.	FRE	447	8TH E DI
JONES, FRANKLIN	BAL	130	1ST WARD
JONES, FREDERICK	BAL	080	4TH WARD
JONES, FREDERICK	TAL	028	EASTON D
JONES, FURBIT	BAL	304	3RD WARD
JONES, G.	BAL	147	1ST WARD
JONES, G.	BAL	148	1ST WARD
JONES, G. S.	BAL	158	1ST WARD
JONES, G. W.	TAL	093	ST MICHA
JONES, G.S.	BAL	170	1ST WARD
JONES, GABRIEL	DOR	344	3RD DIVI
JONES, GARRETT	CAR	099	NC T&P L
JONES, GATTY	SOM	432	PRINCESS
JONES, GEORGE	SOM	443	DAMES QU
JONES, GEORGE	HAR	091	2ND DIST
JONES, GEORGE	FRE	069	FREDERIC
JONES, GEORGE	CAL	061	3RD DIST
JONES, GEORGE	CAL	063	3RD DIST
JONES, GEORGE	DOR	366	3RD DIVI
JONES, GEORGE	DOR	327	3RD DIVI
JONES, GEORGE	DOR	347	3RD DIVI
JONES, GEORGE	CEC	203	6TH E DI
JONES, GEORGE	FRE	335	MIDDLETO
JONES, GEORGE	KEN	232	2ND DIST
JONES, GEORGE	CEC	005	ELKTON 3
JONES, GEORGE	BAL	130	5TH WARD
JONES, GEORGE	BAL	144	5TH WARD
JONES, GEORGE	BAL	374	3RD WARD
JONES, GEORGE	BAL	326	3RD WARD
JONES, GEORGE	BAL	347	1ST DIST
JONES, GEORGE	BAL	458	8TH WARD
JONES, GEORGE	BAL	157	2ND DIST
JONES, GEORGE	ANN	343	3RD DIST
JONES, GEORGE	TAL	031	EASTON D
JONES, GEORGE	SOM	457	DAMES QU
JONES, GEORGE	SOM	461	HANGARY
JONES, GEORGE ANNA*	SOM	482	TRAPP DI
JONES, GEORGE H.	SOM	460	HANGARY
JONES, GEORGE L.	BAL	020	1ST WARD
JONES, GEORGE P.	HAR	019	1ST DIST
JONES, GEORGE R.	ANN	401	8TH DIST
JONES, GEORGE W.	BAL	162	6TH WARD
JONES, GEORGE W.	BAL	413	3RD WARD
JONES, GEORGE W.	DOR	370	3RD DIVI
JONES, GEORGE W.*	BAL	310	3RD WARD
JONES, GEORGE W.-BLACK	FRE	225	BUCKEYST
JONES, GEORGE-BLACK	FRE	231	BUCKEYST
JONES, GEORGEANNA*	SOM	482	TRAPP DI
JONES, GEORGIANA	BAL	106	10TH WAR
JONES, GEORGIANNA	BAL	200	11TH WAR
JONES, GEORGINANA	BAL	366	13TH WAR
JONES, GERALDINE	BAL	014	4TH WARD
JONES, GILBERT	BAL	226	19TH WAR
JONES, GILES	WOR	325	1ST E DI
JONES, GOERGE	BAL	024	15TH WAR
JONES, GOFFRO	BAL	475	14TH WAR
JONES, GRACE	CAL	021	2ND DIST
JONES, GRACE	SOM	447	DAMES QU
JONES, GRISONTON	BAL	164	2ND DIST
JONES, GUSTAVAS	MGM	319	CRACKLIN
JONES, H.	BAL	134	5TH WARD
JONES, H.	BAL	130	1ST WARD
JONES, HAMILTON	SOM	419	PRINCESS
JONES, HANAH*	DOR	434	1ST DIST
JONES, HANNAH	BAL	397	14TH WAR
JONES, HANNAH	BAL	417	3RD WARD
JONES, HANNAH	BAL	074	18TH WAR
JONES, HANNAH	BAL	049	1ST WARD
JONES, HANNAH	BAL	274	12TH WAR
JONES, HANNAH	BAL	454	1ST DIST
JONES, HANNAH	WAS	187	BOONSBOR
JONES, HANNAH A.	BAL	312	3RD WARD
JONES, HANNAH P.	BAL	473	14TH WAR
JONES, HANSON	WAS	004	WILLIAMS
JONES, HARIET	SOM	364	BRINKLEY
JONES, HARMON	CEC	022	ELKTON 3
JONES, HARRIET	CEC	043	CHESAPEA
JONES, HARRIET	BAL	474	14TH WAR
JONES, HARRIET	BAL	406	14TH WAR
JONES, HARRIET	BAL	158	11TH WAR
JONES, HARRIET	BAL	316	20TH WAR
JONES, HARRIET	BAL	057	15TH WAR
JONES, HARRIET	ANN	312	1ST DIST
JONES, HARRIETT	BAL	216	11TH WAR
JONES, HARRIS	SOM	448	DAMES QU
JONES, HARY	DOR	435	1ST DIST
JONES, HAZAR	FRE	240	NEW MARK
JONES, HELEN M.	BAL	443	14TH WAR
JONES, HEMBRY	BAL	202	11TH WAR
JONES, HENRIETTA	BAL	133	16TH WAR
JONES, HENRIETTA	BAL	108	15TH WAR
JONES, HENRIETTA	BAL	293	7TH WARD
JONES, HENRIETTA	BAL	212	6TH WARD
JONES, HENRIETTA	BAL	213	6TH WARD
JONES, HENRIETTA	BAL	197	19TH WAR
JONES, HENRIETTA	TAL	111	ST MICHA
JONES, HENRIETTA-BLACK	FRE	304	PETERSVI
JONES, HENRY	BAL	407	14TH WAR
JONES, HENRY	FRE	332	MIDDLETO
JONES, HENRY	SOM	418	PRINCESS
JONES, HENRY	FRE	076	FREDERIC
JONES, HENRY	HAR	110	2ND DIST
JONES, HENRY	MGM	358	BERRYS D
JONES, HENRY	KEN	236	2ND DIST
JONES, HENRY	KEN	235	2ND DIST
JONES, HENRY	HAR	141	2ND DIST

Name	County	Page	District
JONES, HENRY	BAL	216	17TH WAR
JONES, HENRY	CEC	144	PORT DUP
JONES, HENRY	PRI	087	SPALDING
JONES, HENRY	SOM	545	TYASKIN
JONES, HENRY	PRI	079	QUEEN AN
JONES, HENRY	SOM	485	TRAPP DI
JONES, HENRY	SOM	448	DAMES QU
JONES, HENRY	KEN	267	1ST DIST
JONES, HENRY	KEN	267	1ST DIST
JONES, HENRY	WAS	173	FUNKSTOW
JONES, HENRY	WOR	316	2ND E DI
JONES, HENRY	WOR	320	1ST E DI
JONES, HENRY	ST	260	3RD E DI
JONES, HENRY	WAS	148	2ND DIST
JONES, HENRY	WOR	295	9TH E DI
JONES, HENRY	WAS	071	2ND SUBD
JONES, HENRY	BAL	093	15TH WAR
JONES, HENRY	BAL	144	16TH WAR
JONES, HENRY	BAL	053	9TH WARD
JONES, HENRY	BAL	170	16TH WAR
JONES, HENRY	BAL	455	8TH WARD
JONES, HENRY	BAL	262	12TH WAR
JONES, HENRY	BAL	346	7TH WARD
JONES, HENRY	BAL	325	3RD WARD
JONES, HENRY	BAL	058	1ST WARD
JONES, HENRY	BAL	123	1ST WARD
JONES, HENRY	ANN	343	3RD DIST
JONES, HENRY	BAL	149	2ND DIST
JONES, HENRY B.	SOM	446	DAMES QU
JONES, HENRY P.	BAL	031	9TH WARD
JONES, HENRY S.	ST	280	3RD E DI
JONES, HERSHEY *	WAS	174	FUNKSTOW
JONES, HESTER	BAL	248	12TH WAR
JONES, HESTER	BAL	158	19TH WAR
JONES, HESTER A.	BAL	406	8TH WARD
JONES, HESTER A.	WOR	169	6TH E DI
JONES, HESTOR A.	BAL	100	5TH WARD
JONES, HESTOR ANN	BAL	303	17TH WAR
JONES, HETTY	SOM	437	PRINCESS
JONES, HETTY	CAL	021	2ND DIST
JONES, HINTSON	TAL	116	ST MICHA
JONES, HIRAM	KEN	265	1ST DIST
JONES, HIRAM	HAR	036	1ST DIST
JONES, HIRAM	ALL	161	6TH E.D.
JONES, HONOR	FRE	450	8TH E DI
JONES, HORATIO	DOR	468	1ST DIST
JONES, HOWARD	BAL	027	4TH WARD
JONES, HTOMAS	ANN	346	3RD DIST
JONES, HUGH	BAL	126	5TH WARD
JONES, HUGH	BAL	189	17TH WAR
JONES, HUGH	HAR	035	1ST DIST
JONES, IDO BLANCH	BAL	162	6TH WARD
JONES, IGNATIUS-BLACK	ST	325	4TH E DI
JONES, ISAAC	SOM	473	TRAPPE D
JONES, ISAAC	KEN	312	3RD DIST
JONES, ISAAC	WOR	322	1ST E DI
JONES, ISAAC	WAS	067	2ND SUBD
JONES, ISAAC	WOR	254	1ST CENS
JONES, ISAAC	BAL	202	6TH WARD
JONES, ISAAC	BAL	329	13TH WAR
JONES, ISAAC	ANN	297	1ST DIST
JONES, ISAAC	BAL	280	2ND WARD
JONES, ISAAC	BAL	162	11TH WAR
JONES, ISAAC	BAL	178	19TH WAR
JONES, ISAAC	CAR	188	4TH DIST
JONES, ISAAC	BAL	275	20TH WAR
JONES, ISAAC	CAR	280	7TH DIST
JONES, ISAAC	BAL	117	18TH WAR
JONES, ISAAC D.	SOM	446	DAMES QU
JONES, ISAAC D.	SOM	450	DAMES QU
JONES, ISAAC R.	WOR	348	1ST E DI
JONES, ISAAC-BLACK	QUE	125	1ST E DI
JONES, ISABELLA	BAL	193	19TH WAR
JONES, ISABELLA	BAL	049	4TH WARD
JONES, ISABELLA	BAL	086	15TH WAR
JONES, ISAIAH	BAL	197	11TH WAR
JONES, ISARH	TAL	097	ST MICHA
JONES, ISMA	WOR	172	6TH E DI
JONES, ISRAEL	BAL	244	6TH WARD
JONES, ISRAEL	BAL	291	3RD WARD
JONES, J.	BAL	147	1ST WARD
JONES, J.	BAL	264	20TH WAR
JONES, J.R.	WAS	121	HAGERSTO
JONES, JAE*	BAL	424	3RD WARD
JONES, JACKSON	CAL	055	3RD DIST
JONES, JACKSON-BLACK	FRE	191	5TH E DI
JONES, JACOB	FRE	341	MIDDLETO
JONES, JACOB	DOR	340	3RD DIVI
JONES, JACOB	CEC	162	6TH E DI
JONES, JACOB	BAL	032	18TH WAR
JONES, JACOB	SOM	461	HANGARY
JONES, JACOB	WAS	019	2ND SUBD
JONES, JACOB	ANN	317	1ST DIST
JONES, JACOB	BAL	155	2ND DIST
JONES, JACOB L.	MGM	387	ROCKERLE
JONES, JACOB P.	BAL	032	18TH WAR
JONES, JAMES	BAL	076	18TH WAR
JONES, JAMES	CEC	053	1ST E DI
JONES, JAMES	SOM	413	DUBLIN D
JONES, JAMES	SOM	440	DAMES QU
JONES, JAMES	HAR	098	2ND DIST
JONES, JAMES	HAR	015	1ST DIST
JONES, JAMES	BAL	057	4TH WARD
JONES, JAMES	DOR	340	3RD DIVI
JONES, JAMES	BAL	293	20TH WAR
JONES, JAMES	BAL	282	20TH WAR
JONES, JAMES	BAL	226	19TH WAR
JONES, JAMES	BAL	236	20TH WAR
JONES, JAMES	QUE	141	1ST E DI
JONES, JAMES	HAR	179	3RD DIST
JONES, JAMES	CAL	036	2ND DIST
JONES, JAMES	CAL	036	2ND DIST
JONES, JAMES	CAL	057	3RD DIST
JONES, JAMES	CAR	081	NO TWP L
JONES, JAMES	BAL	131	11TH WAR
JONES, JAMES	CAR	158	NO TWP L
JONES, JAMES	FRE	294	WOODSBOR
JONES, JAMES	KEN	213	2ND DIST
JONES, JAMES	BAL	172	2ND DIST
JONES, JAMES	BAL	036	1ST WARD
JONES, JAMES	BAL	028	1ST WARD
JONES, JAMES	BAL	115	1ST WARD
JONES, JAMES	ANN	268	ANNAPOLI
JONES, JAMES	ALL	046	10TH E.D
JONES, JAMES	BAL	144	1ST WARD
JONES, JAMES	BAL	145	1ST WARD
JONES, JAMES	BAL	284	7TH WARD
JONES, JAMES	BAL	308	7TH WARD
JONES, JAMES	BAL	129	1ST WARD
JONES, JAMES	BAL	260	6TH WARD
JONES, JAMES	BAL	463	1ST DIST
JONES, JAMES	BAL	334	3RD WARD
JONES, JAMES	BAL	337	3RD WARD
JONES, JAMES	BAL	167	6TH WARD
JONES, JAMES	BAL	043	9TH WARD
JONES, JAMES	BAL	030	9TH WARD
JONES, JAMES	BAL	168	1ST WARD
JONES, JAMES	BAL	196	11TH WAR
JONES, JAMES	BAL	061	15TH WAR
JONES, JAMES	BAL	054	9TH WARD
JONES, JAMES	BAL	098	15TH WAR
JONES, JAMES	BAL	040	2ND DIST
JONES, JAMES	WOR	285	BERLIN 1
JONES, JAMES	WOR	303	SNOW HIL
JONES, JAMES	SOM	476	TRAPPE D
JONES, JAMES	KEN	303	3RD DIST
JONES, JAMES	DOR	459	1ST DIST
JONES, JAMES	KEN	256	1ST DIST
JONES, JAMES	KEN	263	1ST DIST
JONES, JAMES	KEN	288	3RD DIST
JONES, JAMES	KEN	289	3RD DIST
JONES, JAMES	WOR	320	1ST E DI
JONES, JAMES	WOR	319	1ST E DI
JONES, JAMES	DOR	469	1ST DIST
JONES, JAMES	WAS	188	BOONSBOR
JONES, JAMES	PRI	077	MARLBROU
JONES, JAMES A.	KEN	278	1ST DIST
JONES, JAMES A.	BAL	180	2ND WARD
JONES, JAMES A.	BAL	014	4TH WARD
JONES, JAMES C.	BAL	032	9TH WARD
JONES, JAMES E	BAL	393	14TH WAR
JONES, JAMES H.	BAL	411	3RD WARD
JONES, JAMES M.	CAR	159	NO TWP L
JONES, JAMES M.	SOM	533	QUANTICO
JONES, JAMES G.	TAL	083	ST MICHA
JONES, JAMES W.	ALL	263	CUMBERLA
JONES, JAMS	TAL	115	ST MICHA
JONES, JANE	WAS	156	HAGERSTO
JONES, JANE	SOM	466	HANGARY
JONES, JANE	BAL	157	11TH WAR
JONES, JANE	BAL	155	11TH WAR
JONES, JANE	CHA	274	ALLENS F
JONES, JANE	BAL	335	13TH WAR
JONES, JANE	SOM	420	PRINCESS
JONES, JANE	HAR	038	1ST DIST
JONES, JANE	HAR	041	1ST DIST
JONES, JANE R.	ANN	309	1ST DIST
JONES, JARRELD-BLACK	FRE	383	PETERSVI
JONES, JARUS*	DOR	435	1ST DIST
JONES, JEFF	BAL	236	20TH WAR
JONES, JEMIMA	CEC	003	ELKTON 3
JONES, JEMIMA	BAL	057	4TH WARD
JONES, JEMIMA	BAL	363	1ST DIST
JONES, JEMIMA	BAL	238	2ND WARD
JONES, JENETTA	WOR	255	1ST CENS
JONES, JENKINS H.	BAL	077	15TH WAR
JONES, JEREMIAH	BAL	371	1ST DIST
JONES, JEREMIAH	ANN	365	4TH DIST
JONES, JERRY	ANN	451	HOWARD D
JONES, JERRY	DOR	346	3RD DIVI
JONES, JESSE	WOR	289	9TH E DI
JONES, JESSE	WOR	298	9TH E DI
JONES, JESSE	SOM	541	TYASKIN
JONES, JIM	CAL	031	2ND DIST
JONES, JOHN	CAR	151	NO TWP L
JONES, JOHN	BAL	403	14TH WAR
JONES, JOHN	BAL	399	14TH WAR
JONES, JOHN	BAL	453	14TH WAR
JONES, JOHN	CAR	078	NO TWP L
JONES, JOHN	BAL	471	14TH WAR
JONES, JOHN	BAL	275	17TH WAR
JONES, JOHN	BAL	272	17TH WAR
JONES, JOHN	CEC	183	7TH E DI
JONES, JOHN	BAL	216	17TH WAR
JONES, JOHN	BAL	243	17TH WAR
JONES, JOHN	BAL	364	13TH WAR
JONES, JOHN	CAR	291	7TH DIST
JONES, JOHN	CAR	301	1ST DIST
JONES, JOHN	BAL	026	4TH WARD
JONES, JOHN	DOR	435	1ST DIST
JONES, JOHN	FRE	205	BUCKEYST
JONES, JOHN	SOM	413	DUBLIN D
JONES, JOHN	HAR	014	1ST DIST
JONES, JOHN	HAR	011	1ST DIST
JONES, JOHN	HAR	004	1ST DIST
JONES, JOHN	HAR	004	1ST DIST
JONES, JOHN	MGM	367	BERRYS D
JONES, JOHN	MGM	398	ROCKERLE
JONES, JOHN	MGM	415	MEDLEY 3
JONES, JOHN	QUE	141	1ST E DI
JONES, JOHN	QUE	153	1ST E DI
JONES, JOHN	HAR	128	2ND DIST
JONES, JOHN	FRE	113	CREAGERS
JONES, JOHN	CEC	052	1ST E DI
JONES, JOHN	CAR	251	3RD DIST
JONES, JOHN	PRI	089	SPALDING
JONES, JOHN	PRI	101	SPALDING
JONES, JOHN	PRI	096	SPALDING
JONES, JOHN	SOM	479	TRAPP DI
JONES, JOHN	WOR	276	BERLIN 1
JONES, JOHN	WOR	289	9TH E DI
JONES, JOHN	WAS	008	WILLIAMS
JONES, JOHN	WAS	029	2ND SUBD
JONES, JOHN	SOM	454	DAMES QU
JONES, JOHN	SOM	461	HANGARY
JONES, JOHN	SOM	447	DAMES QU
JONES, JOHN	SOM	463	HANGARY
JONES, JOHN	KEN	271	1ST DIST
JONES, JOHN	DOR	455	1ST DIST
JONES, JOHN	DOR	455	1ST DIST
JONES, JOHN	WAS	172	FUNKSTOW
JONES, JOHN	WAS	185	BOONSBOR
JONES, JOHN	TAL	070	EASTON T
JONES, JOHN	WOR	344	1ST E DI
JONES, JOHN	WOR	326	1ST E DI
JONES, JOHN	WOR	319	1ST E DI
JONES, JOHN	WOR	321	1ST E DI
JONES, JOHN	WAS	132	2ND DIST
JONES, JOHN	QUE	245	5TH E DI
JONES, JOHN	ANN	445	HOWARD D
JONES, JOHN	ANN	360	3RD DIST
JONES, JOHN	ALL	257	CUMBERLA
JONES, JOHN	BAL	149	2ND DIST
JONES, JOHN	BAL	110	2ND DIST
JONES, JOHN	BAL	123	2ND DIST
JONES, JOHN	BAL	070	2ND DIST
JONES, JOHN	BAL	069	2ND DIST
JONES, JOHN	BAL	330	3RD WARD
JONES, JOHN	BAL	330	3RD WARD
JONES, JOHN	BAL	101	5TH WARD
JONES, JOHN	BAL	321	3RD WARD
JONES, JOHN	BAL	302	3RD WARD
JONES, JOHN	BAL	291	3RD WARD
JONES, JOHN	BAL	436	1ST DIST
JONES, JOHN	BAL	053	9TH WARD
JONES, JOHN	BAL	101	15TH WAR
JONES, JOHN	BAL	154	16TH WAR
JONES, JOHN	BAL	279	12TH WAR
JONES, JOHN	BAL	134	1ST WARD
JONES, JOHN	BAL	310	7TH WARD
JONES, JOHN	BAL	279	2ND WARD
JONES, JOHN	BAL	365	8TH WARD
JONES, JOHN	BAL	310	1ST DIST
JONES, JOHN	ANN	399	8TH DIST
JONES, JOHN	ALL	111	5TH E.D.
JONES, JOHN	ALL	089	5TH E.D.
JONES, JOHN	ALL	080	5TH E.D.
JONES, JOHN	BAL	020	9TH WARD
JONES, JOHN	BAL	168	1ST WARD
JONES, JOHN	BAL	167	6TH WARD
JONES, JOHN	BAL	147	5TH WARD
JONES, JOHN	BAL	157	1ST WARD
JONES, JOHN	BAL	178	11TH WAR
JONES, JOHN	BAL	028	13TH WAR
JONES, JOHN	BAL	119	1ST WARD
JONES, JOHN	BAL	160	2ND DIST
JONES, JOHN	BAL	161	2ND DIST
JONES, JOHN	BAL	172	2ND DIST
JONES, JOHN	BAL	122	1ST WARD
JONES, JOHN	BAL	005	1ST WARD
JONES, JOHN	BAL	272	1ST DIST
JONES, JOHN *	ALL	162	6TH E.D.
JONES, JOHN A.	MGM	416	MEDLEY 3
JONES, JOHN A.	BAL	057	4TH WARD
JONES, JOHN A.	BAL	044	4TH WARD
JONES, JOHN B.	BAL	124	1ST WARD
JONES, JOHN C.	MGM	392	ROCKERLE
JONES, JOHN D.	BAL	071	4TH WARD
JONES, JOHN E.	CAL	022	2ND DIST
JONES, JOHN F.	PRI	070	MARLBROU
JONES, JOHN F.	WOR	217	4TH E DI
JONES, JOHN H.	SOM	447	DAMES QU
JONES, JOHN H.	ANN	325	2ND DIST
JONES, JOHN J.	ST	255	3RD E DI
JONES, JOHN L.	CEC	154	PORT DUP
JONES, JOHN L.T.	MGM	427	MEDLEY 3
JONES, JOHN M.	BAL	241	6TH WARD
JONES, JOHN M.	ALL	227	CUMBERLA
JONES, JOHN M. JR.	SOM	461	HANGARY
JONES, JOHN OF CHARLES	BAL	234	1ST DIST
JONES, JOHN P.	HAR	015	1ST DIST
JONES, JOHN P.	BAL	158	11TH WAR
JONES, JOHN Q.	BAL	026	18TH WAR
JONES, JOHN R.	CAR	111	NO TWP L
JONES, JOHN R.	DOR	301	1ST DIST
JONES, JOHN R.	BAL	058	15TH WAR
JONES, JOHN S.	BAL	104	18TH WAR
JONES, JOHN T.	QUE	239	5TH E DI
JONES, JOHN W.	SOM	446	DAMES QU
JONES, JOHN W.	TAL	101	ST MICHA
JONES, JOHN W.	BAL	050	4TH WARD
JONES, JOHN W.	HAR	178	3RD DIST
JONES, JOHN W.	KEN	234	2ND DIST
JONES, JOHN W.	DOR	442	1ST DIST
JONES, JOHN W.	DOR	352	3RD DIVI
JONES, JOHN W.	BAL	030	15TH WAR
JONES, JOHN W.	BAL	241	6TH WARD
JONES, JOHN Z. A.	SOM	446	DAMES QU
JONES, JOHN-BLACK	ST	338	4TH E DI
JONES, JOHN-BLACK	FRE	225	BUCKEYST
JONES, JOHNATHAN	KEN	302	3RD DIST
JONES, JOHNES	BAL	039	2ND DIST
JONES, JOHNSEY	BAL	357	1ST DIST
JONES, JONAS	ANN	461	HOWARD D
JONES, JONOTHAN	WAS	292	1ST DIST
JONES, JONS. P. B.	BAL	042	18TH WAR
JONES, JOSEPH	DOR	351	3RD DIVI
JONES, JOSEPH	QUE	146	1ST E DI
JONES, JOSEPH	CAR	149	NO TWP L
JONES, JOSEPH	BAL	135	11TH WAR
JONES, JOSEPH	HAR	015	1ST DIST
JONES, JOSEPH	BAL	319	20TH WAR
JONES, JOSEPH	BAL	196	19TH WAR
JONES, JOSEPH	PRI	004	BLADENSB
JONES, JOSEPH	SOM	469	TRAPPE D
JONES, JOSEPH	SOM	451	DAMES QU
JONES, JOSEPH	KEN	295	3RD DIST
JONES, JOSEPH	PRI	071	MARLBROU
JONES, JOSEPH	SOM	544	TYASKIN
JONES, JOSEPH	ANN	365	4TH DIST
JONES, JOSEPH	BAL	093	5TH WARD
JONES, JOSEPH	BAL	203	6TH WARD
JONES, JOSEPH A.	BAL	127	16TH WAR
JONES, JOSEPH C.	FRE	385	PETERSVI
JONES, JOSEPH F.	BAL	300	3RD WARD
JONES, JOSEPH H.	FRE	027	FREDERIC
JONES, JOSEPH H.	ST	344	5TH E DI
JONES, JOSEPH H.	TAL	098	ST MICHA
JONES, JOSEPH J.	PRI	020	VANSVILL
JONES, JOSEPH T.	BAL	081	18TH WAR
JONES, JOSEPH*	BAL	380	3RD WARD
JONES, JOSEPHINE	BAL	100	5TH WARD
JONES, JOSEPHINE	BAL	184	2ND WARD
JONES, JOSEPHINE	BAL	429	14TH WAR
JONES, JOSHUA	HAR	003	1ST DIST
JONES, JOSHUA	SOM	444	DAMES QU
JONES, JOSHUA	BAL	211	11TH WAR
JONES, JOSHUA	FRE	331	MIDDLETO
JONES, JOSHUA	BAL	450	1ST DIST
JONES, JOSHUA	BAL	419	1ST DIST
JONES, JOSHUA	BAL	375	3RD WARD
JONES, JOSHUA	BAL	025	1ST WARD
JONES, JOSHUA	WAS	103	2ND DIST
JONES, JOSHUA	PRI	028	VANSVILL
JONES, JOSHUA	ST	259	3RD E DI
JONES, JOSHUA W.	HAR	013	1ST DIST
JONES, JOSIAH	FRE	300	WOODSBOR
JONES, JOSIAH-BLACK	FRE	232	BUCKEYST
JONES, JOSPHE A.	MGM	393	ROCKERLE
JONES, JUDA-BLACK	FRE	245	NEW MARK
JONES, JUDY	PRI	095	SPALDING
JONES, JULIA	BAL	030	18TH WAR
JONES, JULIA	BAL	066	18TH WAR
JONES, JULIA	CHA	271	ALLENS F
JONES, JULIA	BAL	275	12TH WAR
JONES, JULIA A.	BAL	116	15TH WAR
JONES, JULIA A.	CAR	330	MANCHEST
JONES, JULIAN	BAL	418	3RD WARD
JONES, JULIET	CAL	027	2ND DIST
JONES, KATE	BAL	053	9TH WARD

Name	County	Page	Locality
JONES, KETTY	BAL	261	12TH WAR
JONES, KINSEY	BAL	289	17TH WAR
JONES, KINZY	CAL	058	3RD DIST
JONES, KITTURA	DOR	364	3RD DIVI
JONES, L.A.	PRI	105	PISCATAW
JONES, LAKE	BAL	018	15TH WAR
JONES, LAURA	BAL	246	20TH WAR
JONES, LEA	BAL	207	6TH DIST
JONES, LEAH	SOM	443	DAMES QU
JONES, LEAH	SOM	447	DAMES QU
JONES, LEAR	BAL	086	4TH WARD
JONES, LEEANA	BAL	361	1ST DIST
JONES, LEMUEL	ANN	472	HOWARD D
JONES, LEMUEL	BAL	057	4TH WARD
JONES, LEONARD	CAL	055	3RD DIST
JONES, LEONARD	WAS	083	2ND SUBD
JONES, LETTY	BAL	080	4TH WARD
JONES, LEVEN	DOR	365	3RD DIVI
JONES, LEVI	CAR	296	7TH DIST
JONES, LEVIN	DOR	326	3RD DIVI
JONES, LEVIN	CAR	138	NO TWP L
JONES, LEVIN	SOM	434	PRINCESS
JONES, LEVIN	DOR	392	1ST DIST
JONES, LEVIN	SOM	450	DAMES QU
JONES, LEVIN	SOM	487	SALISBUR
JONES, LEVIN	SOM	486	TRAPP DI
JONES, LEVIN	BAL	046	15TH WAR
JONES, LEVIN	BAL	342	7TH WARD
JONES, LEVIN	BAL	033	1ST WARD
JONES, LEVIN H.	BAL	333	7TH WARD
JONES, LEVIN J.	WOR	256	1ST CENS
JONES, LEVIN J.	WOR	327	1ST E DI
JONES, LEVISA	HAR	030	1ST DIST
JONES, LEVZ	FRE	206	BUCKEYST
JONES, LEWIS	BAL	120	18TH WAR
JONES, LEWIS	HAR	008	1ST DIST
JONES, LEWIS	FRE	357	CATOCTIN
JONES, LEWIS	BAL	360	13TH WAR
JONES, LEWIS	QUE	126	1ST E DI
JONES, LEWIS	WOR	341	1ST E DI
JONES, LEWIS	BAL	033	9TH WARD
JONES, LEWIS T.	QUE	236	4TH E DI
JONES, LIDDY	BAL	118	18TH WAR
JONES, LIDIA	TAL	021	EASTON D
JONES, LIDIA	TAL	015	EASTON D
JONES, LINDY	HAR	070	1ST DIST
JONES, LITTLETON-BLACK	WOR	170	6TH E DI
JONES, LLOYD	FRE	025	FREDERIC
JONES, LLOYD-BLACK	FRE	234	BUCKEYST
JONES, LONORA	BAL	321	3RD WARD
JONES, LOUIS	BAL	209	19TH WAR
JONES, LOUISA	BAL	226	19TH WAR
JONES, LOUISA	CAR	283	7TH DIST
JONES, LOUISA	BAL	248	12TH WAR
JONES, LOUISA	BAL	281	1ST DIST
JONES, LOUISA	SOM	452	DAMES QU
JONES, LOUISA	WOR	229	6TH E DI
JONES, LOUZA	CAR	106	NO TWP L
JONES, LOYD	FRE	242	NEW MARK
JONES, LOYD	ANN	499	HOWARD D
JONES, LOYD S.	MGM	420	MEDLEY 3
JONES, LUCRICIA	BAL	125	11TH WAR
JONES, LUCY	BAL	300	20TH WAR
JONES, LUCY	BAL	039	9TH WARD
JONES, LUCY	ANN	313	1ST DIST
JONES, LUCY	WAS	022	2ND SUBD
JONES, LUCY ANN	ALL	263	CUMBERLA
JONES, LUTHER M.	TAL	005	EASTON D
JONES, LYNCH	WAS	034	2ND SUBD
JONES, M.	ANN	281	ANNAPOLI
JONES, M. A.	BAL	072	10TH WAR
JONES, M.C.	ST	312	1ST E DI
JONES, M.J.	WAS	007	WILLIAMS
JONES, MAGDALINE	WAS	047	2ND SUBD
JONES, MAHALA	SOM	550	TYASKIN
JONES, MAHALA A.	BAL	020	15TH WAR
JONES, MAHALAH	BAL	248	6TH WARD
JONES, MAJOR	DOR	435	1ST DIST
JONES, MAJOR W.	WOR	337	1ST E DI
JONES, MALINDA	BAL	055	4TH WARD
JONES, MALVINA	PRI	049	AQUASCO
JONES, MARANDA	BAL	422	3RD WARD
JONES, MARCELLUS	SOM	461	HANGARY
JONES, MARCSES	ALL	101	5TH E.D.
JONES, MARGARET	BAL	273	2ND WARD
JONES, MARGARET	BAL	304	7TH WARD
JONES, MARGARET	BAL	396	8TH WARD
JONES, MARGARET	BAL	225	12TH WAR
JONES, MARGARET	BAL	430	8TH WARD
JONES, MARGARET	BAL	198	17TH WAR
JONES, MARGARET	BAL	021	9TH WARD
JONES, MARGARET	BAL	207	2ND WARD
JONES, MARGARET	BAL	313	3RD WARD
JONES, MARGARET	BAL	364	3RD WARD
JONES, MARGARET	SOM	475	TRAPPE D
JONES, MARGARET	PRI	025	VANSVILL
JONES, MARGARET	PRI	074	MARLBROU
JONES, MARGARET	FRE	345	MIDDLETO
JONES, MARGARET	BAL	144	19TH WAR
JONES, MARGARET	BAL	252	20TH WAR
JONES, MARGARET	BAL	149	11TH WAR
JONES, MARGARETT	BAL	208	11TH WAR
JONES, MARGARETT	BAL	037	18TH WAR
JONES, MARGARETT A.	BAL	050	4TH WARD
JONES, MARGARETTA	BAL	171	16TH WAR
JONES, MARGRETT	DOR	345	3RD DIVI
JONES, MARI	BAL	280	20TH WAR
JONES, MARIA	BAL	281	20TH WAR
JONES, MARIA	CAR	089	NO TWP L
JONES, MARIA	BAL	144	19TH WAR
JONES, MARIA	KEN	210	2ND DIST
JONES, MARIA	BAL	205	19TH WAR
JONES, MARIA	CEC	019	ELKTON 3
JONES, MARIA	BAL	094	15TH WAR
JONES, MARIA	BAL	259	5TH WARD
JONES, MARIA	WOR	196	8TH E DI
JONES, MARIA	WOR	197	8TH E DI
JONES, MARIA G.	BAL	086	4TH WARD
JONES, MARIA-BLACK	ST	325	4TH E DI
JONES, MARIAH	SOM	430	PRINCESS
JONES, MARIETTA	BAL	187	6TH WARD
JONES, MARION P.	ANN	457	HOWARD D
JONES, MARSHALL	BAL	311	20TH WAR
JONES, MARSHALL	WAS	156	HAGERSTO
JONES, MARTHA	WOR	278	BERLIN 1
JONES, MARTHA	BAL	419	14TH WAR
JONES, MARTHA	KEN	238	2ND DIST
JONES, MARTHA	BAL	119	15TH WAR
JONES, MARTHA	BAL	206	6TH DIST
JONES, MARTHA A.	WOR	269	BERLIN 1
JONES, MARTHA E.	ST	259	3RD E DI
JONES, MARTIN	MGM	444	CLARKSTR
JONES, MARTIN	BAL	275	1ST DIST
JONES, MARY	BAL	048	1ST WARD
JONES, MARY	BAL	172	2ND DIST
JONES, MARY	BAL	010	1ST WARD
JONES, MARY	BAL	311	3RD WARD
JONES, MARY	BAL	091	5TH WARD
JONES, MARY	BAL	451	1ST DIST
JONES, MARY	BAL	463	1ST DIST
JONES, MARY	BAL	094	5TH WARD
JONES, MARY	BAL	116	5TH WARD
JONES, MARY	BAL	089	15TH WAR
JONES, MARY	BAL	120	16TH WAR
JONES, MARY	BAL	167	16TH WAR
JONES, MARY	BAL	053	9TH WARD
JONES, MARY	BAL	291	12TH WAR
JONES, MARY	BAL	330	13TH WAR
JONES, MARY	BAL	295	12TH WAR
JONES, MARY	ANN	461	HOWARD D
JONES, MARY	BAL	003	EASTERN
JONES, MARY	BAL	082	2ND DIST
JONES, MARY	BAL	138	2ND DIST
JONES, MARY	BAL	205	2ND WARD
JONES, MARY	BAL	204	2ND WARD
JONES, MARY	BAL	151	5TH WARD
JONES, MARY	BAL	132	5TH WARD
JONES, MARY	BAL	298	7TH WARD
JONES, MARY	BAL	410	8TH WARD
JONES, MARY	BAL	239	12TH WAR
JONES, MARY	BAL	024	15TH WAR
JONES, MARY	BAL	168	11TH WAR
JONES, MARY	BAL	256	12TH WAR
JONES, MARY	BAL	072	15TH WAR
JONES, MARY	BAL	316	1ST DIST
JONES, MARY	BAL	311	1ST DIST
JONES, MARY	PRI	016	BLADENSB
JONES, MARY	WAS	088	2ND SUBD
JONES, MARY	WAS	017	2ND SUBD
JONES, MARY	WOR	295	9TH E DI
JONES, MARY	WAS	122	2ND DIST
JONES, MARY	SOM	462	HANGARY
JONES, MARY	DOR	459	1ST DIST
JONES, MARY	KEN	303	3RD DIST
JONES, MARY	SOM	536	TYASKIN
JONES, MARY	PRI	100	SPALDING
JONES, MARY	QUE	134	1ST E DI
JONES, MARY	HAR	137	2ND DIST
JONES, MARY	CHA	286	BOJANTOW
JONES, MARY	BAL	433	14TH WAR
JONES, MARY	BAL	065	4TH WARD
JONES, MARY	BAL	063	4TH WARD
JONES, MARY	BAL	385	13TH WAR
JONES, MARY	BAL	362	13TH WAR
JONES, MARY	HAR	030	1ST DIST
JONES, MARY	CEC	020	ELKTON 3
JONES, MARY	BAL	182	19TH WAR
JONES, MARY	BAL	421	3RD WARD
JONES, MARY	DOR	448	1ST DIST
JONES, MARY	CAL	028	2ND DIST
JONES, MARY	CAR	124	NO TWP L
JONES, MARY	BAL	392	14TH WAR
JONES, MARY	BAL	281	20TH WAR
JONES, MARY	BAL	298	20TH WAR
JONES, MARY	DOR	346	3RD DIVI
JONES, MARY	DOR	345	3RD DIVI
JONES, MARY	FRE	399	JEFFERSO
JONES, MARY	FRE	008	FREDERIC
JONES, MARY A.	FRE	278	NEW MARK
JONES, MARY A.	TAL	116	ST MICHA
JONES, MARY A.	WAS	293	1ST DIST
JONES, MARY ANN	FRE	171	5TH E DI
JONES, MARY B.	BAL	201	6TH WARD
JONES, MARY C.	BAL	444	14TH WAR
JONES, MARY C.A.-BLACK	BAL	208	2ND WARD
JONES, MARY E.	BAL	086	15TH WAR
JONES, MARY E.	BAL	234	1ST DIST
JONES, MARY E.	MGM	409	MEDLEY 3
JONES, MARY E.	BAL	047	18TH WAR
JONES, MARY J.	MGM	430	CLARKSTR
JONES, MARY J.	BAL	222	17TH WAR
JONES, MARY J.	BAL	209	6TH WARD
JONES, MARY L.*	BAL	365	3RD WARD
JONES, MARY S.	BAL	025	15TH WAR
JONES, MARY W.	ANN	437	HOWARD D
JONES, MATILDA	BAL	110	10TH WAR
JONES, MATILDA	ANN	288	ANNAPOLI
JONES, MATILDA	CAR	207	4TH DIST
JONES, MATILDA	SOM	461	HANGARY
JONES, MATILDA	SOM	446	DAMES QU
JONES, MATILDA T.	BAL	333	13TH WAR
JONES, MATILDY	DOR	468	1ST DIST
JONES, MATTHEW	CAL	024	2ND DIST
JONES, MATTHEW	CAL	023	2ND DIST
JONES, MAURICE	BAL	326	12TH WAR
JONES, MEMOREY	TAL	046	EASTON T
JONES, MERITY	BAL	210	17TH WAR
JONES, MESABELL	KEN	298	3RD DIST
JONES, MICHAEL	KEN	277	1ST DIST
JONES, MICHAEL-BLACK	FRE	409	JEFFERSO
JONES, MICHAL	WAS	109	2ND DIST
JONES, MILCHEL	DOR	344	3RD DIVI
JONES, MILES	CEC	026	ELKTON 3
JONES, MILES	ST	264	3RD E DI
JONES, MILLY	WOR	335	1ST E DI
JONES, MILLY	SOM	469	TRAPPE D
JONES, MILLY	SOM	511	BARREN C
JONES, MILLY	SOM	438	DAMES QU
JONES, MISS M.	FRE	199	5TH E DI
JONES, MITCHELL	SOM	550	TYASKIN
JONES, MITCHELL	BAL	095	15TH WAR
JONES, MOSES	BAL	192	11TH WAR
JONES, MOSES	QUE	194	3RD E DI
JONES, MOSES	QUE	152	1ST E DI
JONES, MOSES W.	WOR	344	1ST E DI
JONES, MOSES*	DOR	435	1ST DIST
JONES, MOSES-BLACK	FRE	415	8TH E DI
JONES, MRS. HARRIETT	BAL	015	13TH WAR
JONES, NACY	HAR	071	1ST DIST
JONES, NANCY	SOM	426	PRINCESS
JONES, NANCY	DOR	322	1ST DIST
JONES, NANCY	BAL	144	19TH WAR
JONES, NANCY	CAR	224	5TH DIST
JONES, NANCY	BAL	200	17TH WAR
JONES, NANCY	QUE	250	5TH E DI
JONES, NANCY	SOM	450	DAMES QU
JONES, NANCY	SOM	462	HANGARY
JONES, NANCY	SOM	466	HANGARY
JONES, NANCY	SOM	459	HANGARY
JONES, NANCY	WOR	299	SNOW HIL
JONES, NANCY	WAS	046	2ND SUBD
JONES, NANCY	BAL	167	16TH WAR
JONES, NANCY	BAL	147	5TH WARD
JONES, NANCY	BAL	020	9TH WARD
JONES, NANCY	BAL	345	1ST DIST
JONES, NATH	WOR	260	BERLIN 1
JONES, NATHAN	ANN	365	4TH DIST
JONES, NATHAN	FRE	247	NEW MARK
JONES, NATHAN	MGM	386	ROCKERLE
JONES, NATHAN C.	TAL	072	EASTON T
JONES, NEAL	BAL	116	1ST WARD
JONES, NEAMIAH	SOM	461	HANGARY
JONES, NELSON	PRI	074	MARLBROU
JONES, NICHOLAS	SOM	461	HANGARY
JONES, NICHOLAS	BAL	126	11TH WAR
JONES, NICHOLAS H.	SOM	448	DAMES QU
JONES, NICK S.	BAL	110	5TH WARD
JONES, NOAH	BAL	227	17TH WAR
JONES, OBED	WOR	317	2ND E DI
JONES, OLIVER	HAR	137	2ND DIST
JONES, OLIVER P.	KEN	261	1ST DIST
JONES, OWEN C.	CAR	169	NO TWP L
JONES, OWEN D.	BAL	353	1ST DIST
JONES, PARMELIA	BAL	029	15TH WAR
JONES, PATIENCE	BAL	294	20TH WAR
JONES, PERCILLA	BAL	402	3RD WARD
JONES, PERY	KEN	209	2ND DIST
JONES, PETER	SOM	412	DUBLIN D
JONES, PETER	BAL	173	11TH WAR
JONES, PETER	BAL	124	1ST WARD
JONES, PETER	BAL	144	5TH WARD
JONES, PETER	BAL	154	5TH WARD
JONES, PHENEAS	KEN	211	2ND DIST
JONES, PHEOBE	BAL	135	5TH WARD
JONES, PHILEMON	ANN	432	HOWARD D
JONES, PHILIP	BAL	448	8TH WARD
JONES, PHILIP	CAL	044	3RD DIST
JONES, PLAIMER*	BAL	420	3RD WARD
JONES, PRICELLA	SOM	437	PRINCESS
JONES, PRISCILLA	CAL	063	3RD DIST
JONES, PRISCILLA	BAL	103	10TH WAR
JONES, PURNELL J.	WOR	240	6TH E DI
JONES, QUNCE *	BAL	307	12TH WAR
JONES, R.	BAL	172	1ST WARD
JONES, RACHAEL	SOM	447	DAMES QU
JONES, RACHEAL	WAS	138	HAGERSTO
JONES, RACHEL	WOR	295	9TH E DI
JONES, RACHEL	BAL	363	8TH WARD
JONES, RACHEL A.	BAL	356	13TH WAR
JONES, RACHELL	BAL	246	17TH WAR
JONES, RALPH S.	ALL	240	CUMBERLA
JONES, RAPHAEL	FRE	307	WOODSBOR
JONES, RBEECCA	BAL	043	1ST WARD
JONES, REBECA	BAL	290	7TH WARD
JONES, REBECA	BAL	446	8TH WARD
JONES, REBECCA	BAL	013	18TH WAR
JONES, REBECCA	BAL	061	18TH WAR
JONES, REBECCA	BAL	454	14TH WAR
JONES, REBECCA	BAL	409	14TH WAR
JONES, REBECCA	BAL	048	15TH WAR
JONES, REBECCA	BAL	053	15TH WAR
JONES, REBECCA	BAL	073	15TH WAR
JONES, REBECCA	ANN	422	HOWARD D
JONES, REBECCA	BAL	180	6TH WARD
JONES, REBECCA	BAL	342	1ST DIST
JONES, REBECCA	TAL	079	ST MICHA
JONES, REBECCA	SOM	452	DAMES QU
JONES, REBECCA	QUE	163	2ND E DI
JONES, REBECCA C.	HAR	114	2ND DIST
JONES, REBECCA W.	KEN	266	1ST DIST
JONES, REDDON	CEC	031	CHESAPEA
JONES, REUBEN E.	BAL	211	5TH DIST
JONES, REZIN	ANN	512	HOWARD D
JONES, REZIN	ANN	465	HOWARD D
JONES, RHODA	CAL	041	3RD DIST
JONES, RICAHRD V.	ST	259	3RD E DI
JONES, RICHARD	ST	276	3RD E DI
JONES, RICHARD	WAS	021	2ND SUBD
JONES, RICHARD	PRI	049	AQUASCO
JONES, RICHARD	CAR	081	NO TWP L
JONES, RICHARD	MGM	416	MEDLEY 3
JONES, RICHARD	CEC	113	4TH E DI
JONES, RICHARD	BAL	377	13TH WAR
JONES, RICHARD	BAL	280	20TH WAR
JONES, RICHARD	KEN	238	2ND DIST
JONES, RICHARD	ANN	442	HOWARD D
JONES, RICHARD	ANN	374	4TH DIST
JONES, RICHARD	BAL	396	8TH WARD
JONES, RICHARD	BAL	238	2ND WARD
JONES, RICHARD	BAL	024	1ST WARD
JONES, RICHARD	ANN	297	1ST DIST
JONES, RICHARD	ANN	298	1ST DIST
JONES, RICHARD B.	CEC	102	4TH E DI
JONES, RICHARD E.	ANN	275	ANNAPOLI
JONES, RICHARD J. C.	QUE	229	4TH E DI
JONES, RICHARD W.	KEN	263	1ST DIST
JONES, RICHARD W.	BAL	046	1ST WARD
JONES, RICHARD W.	ANN	446	HOWARD D
JONES, RILEY	WOR	167	6TH E DI
JONES, RITEY	DOR	470	1ST DIST
JONES, ROBECCA	BAL	131	11TH WAR
JONES, ROBERT	CAR	146	NO TWP L
JONES, ROBERT	CAR	092	NO TWP L
JONES, ROBERT	CEC	105	3RD E DI
JONES, ROBERT	KEN	233	2ND DIST
JONES, ROBERT	DOR	344	3RD DIVI
JONES, ROBERT	DOR	349	3RD DIVI
JONES, ROBERT	BAL	258	17TH WAR
JONES, ROBERT	BAL	241	17TH WAR
JONES, ROBERT	SOM	427	PRINCESS
JONES, ROBERT	WOR	174	6TH E DI
JONES, ROBERT	SOM	462	HANGARY
JONES, ROBERT	TAL	116	ST MICHA
JONES, ROBERT	TAL	105	ST MICHA
JONES, ROBERT	WAS	010	WILLIAMS
JONES, ROBERT	TAL	098	ST MICHA
JONES, ROBERT	BAL	052	1ST WARD
JONES, ROBERT	BAL	053	1ST WARD
JONES, ROBERT	BAL	170	2ND DIST
JONES, ROBERT	BAL	234	5TH WARD
JONES, ROBERT	BAL	159	1ST WARD
JONES, ROBERT	BAL	101	15TH WAR
JONES, ROBERT	BAL	142	16TH WAR
JONES, ROBERT C.	TAL	020	EASTON D
JONES, ROBERT C.	MGM	395	ROCKERLE
JONES, ROBERT H.	SOM	359	BRINKLEY
JONES, ROBERT S.	HAR	038	1ST DIST
JONES, ROBERT S.	ANN	402	8TH DIST
JONES, ROBERT V.	SOM	484	TRAPP DI
JONES, ROBINSON	CEC	179	7TH E DI

Name	County	Page	District
JONES, RODY*	DOR	448	1ST DIST
JONES, ROGER	DOR	366	3RD DIVI
JONES, ROGERS	BAL	010	9TH WARD
JONES, ROMAN	CEC	031	CHESAPEA
JONES, ROSA L.	BAL	382	3RD WARD
JONES, ROSANNA	CAL	048	3RD DIST
JONES, ROSE	BAL	138	11TH WAR
JONES, ROSE A.	DOR	366	3RD DIVI
JONES, ROSE A.	BAL	035	15TH WAR
JONES, ROSE E.	BAL	417	14TH WAR
JONES, ROSEANNA	BAL	221	17TH WAR
JONES, ROSETTA	SOM	457	DAMES QU
JONES, RUBEN F.	TAL	102	ST MICHA
JONES, RUTH	BAL	171	11TH WAR
JONES, RUTH	ALL	097	5TH E.D.
JONES, S. C.	BAL	470	14TH WAR
JONES, SALLY	SOM	426	PRINCESS
JONES, SALLY	BAL	242	12TH WAR
JONES, SALLY	SOM	463	HANGARY
JONES, SALLY	SOM	366	BRINKLEY
JONES, SALLY	WAS	158	HAGERSTO
JONES, SALLY	WOR	294	9TH E DI
JONES, SALLY A.	WOR	292	9TH E DI
JONES, SALLY A.	SOM	458	DAMES QU
JONES, SALLY A.	DOR	374	1ST DIST
JONES, SALLY ANN	SOM	423	PRINCESS
JONES, SALLY M.	WOR	256	1ST CENS
JONES, SAMUEL	WOR	287	BERLIN 1
JONES, SAMUEL	WOR	274	BERLIN 1
JONES, SAMUEL	SOM	449	DAMES QU
JONES, SAMUEL	WAS	173	FUNKSTOW
JONES, SAMUEL	WOR	350	1ST E DI
JONES, SAMUEL	MGM	370	BERRYS D
JONES, SAMUEL	CEC	150	PORT DUP
JONES, SAMUEL	BAL	251	17TH WAR
JONES, SAMUEL	DOR	345	3RD DIVI
JONES, SAMUEL	BAL	298	20TH WAR
JONES, SAMUEL	BAL	246	20TH WAR
JONES, SAMUEL	FRE	408	JEFFERSO
JONES, SAMUEL	CAR	204	4TH DIST
JONES, SAMUEL	FRE	346	MIDDLETO
JONES, SAMUEL	BAL	279	17TH WAR
JONES, SAMUEL	BAL	056	18TH WAR
JONES, SAMUEL	BAL	035	15TH WAR
JONES, SAMUEL	ANN	396	8TH DIST
JONES, SAMUEL	ALL	001	3RD E.D.
JONES, SAMUEL	ANN	384	4TH DIST
JONES, SAMUEL	ANN	287	ANNAPOLI
JONES, SAMUEL	BAL	194	17TH WAR
JONES, SAMUEL	BAL	150	5TH WARD
JONES, SAMUEL	BAL	120	1ST WARD
JONES, SAMUEL	ANN	373	4TH DIST
JONES, SAMUEL B. D.	SOM	535	QUANTICO
JONES, SAMUEL R.	HAR	175	3RD DIST
JONES, SAMUEL T.	CEC	032	CHESAPEA
JONES, SAMUEL W.	SOM	424	PRINCESS
JONES, SAMUEL-BLACK	QUE	155	2ND E DI
JONES, SAMUEL-BLACK	WOR	169	6TH E DI
JONES, SARAH	SOM	446	DAMES QU
JONES, SARAH	SOM	461	HANGARY
JONES, SARAH	KEN	309	3RD DIST
JONES, SARAH	PRI	084	QUEEN AN
JONES, SARAH	WAS	033	2ND SUBD
JONES, SARAH	WAS	072	2ND SUBD
JONES, SARAH	SOM	415	DUBLIN D
JONES, SARAH	SOM	436	PRINCESS
JONES, SARAH	SOM	443	DAMES QU
JONES, SARAH	HAR	045	1ST DIST
JONES, SARAH	MGM	411	MEDLEY 3
JONES, SARAH	CEC	031	CHESAPEA
JONES, SARAH	BAL	414	3RD WARD
JONES, SARAH	CEC	094	4TH E DI
JONES, SARAH	BAL	236	17TH WAR
JONES, SARAH	BAL	412	14TH WAR
JONES, SARAH	BAL	086	4TH WARD
JONES, SARAH	FRE	278	NEW MARK
JONES, SARAH	CAL	042	3RD DIST
JONES, SARAH	CAL	053	3RD DIST
JONES, SARAH	CAL	020	2ND DIST
JONES, SARAH	BAL	146	11TH WAR
JONES, SARAH	BAL	144	11TH WAR
JONES, SARAH	BAL	178	2ND DIST
JONES, SARAH	BAL	133	16TH WAR
JONES, SARAH	BAL	320	7TH WARD
JONES, SARAH	BAL	127	16TH WAR
JONES, SARAH	ANN	323	2ND DIST
JONES, SARAH	ALL	074	5TH E.D.
JONES, SARAH	ALL	055	10TH E.D
JONES, SARAH	BAL	233	12TH WAR
JONES, SARAH	BAL	246	12TH WAR
JONES, SARAH	BAL	273	12TH WAR
JONES, SARAH	BAL	254	6TH WARD
JONES, SARAH	BAL	346	1ST DIST
JONES, SARAH	BAL	310	3RD WARD
JONES, SARAH	BAL	437	1ST DIST
JONES, SARAH A.	BAL	094	15TH WAR
JONES, SARAH A.	BAL	174	6TH WARD
JONES, SARAH C.	HAR	077	BEL AIR
JONES, SARAH D.	ANN	422	HOWARD D
JONES, SARAH E.	BAL	313	7TH WARD
JONES, SARAH J.	BAL	262	6TH WARD
JONES, SARAH J.	BAL	287	7TH WARD
JONES, SARAH J.	BAL	040	18TH WAR
JONES, SARAH T.	WOR	319	1ST E DI
JONES, SARRAH	DOR	366	3RD DIVI
JONES, SEWELL	SOM	460	HANGARY
JONES, SHERRY-BLACK	QUE	197	3RD E DI
JONES, SHOCKLEY	CEC	103	4TH E DI
JONES, SIBA	WOR	307	2ND E DI
JONES, SIDNEY	BAL	411	1ST DIST
JONES, SIDONIA	CEC	010	ELKTON 3
JONES, SILAS	QUE	163	2ND E DI
JONES, SISTER ELIZA	FRE	198	5TH E DI
JONES, SMAUEL	BAL	254	12TH WAR
JONES, SNANCY	WOR	169	6TH E DI
JONES, SOLLERS D.	BAL	360	3RD WARD
JONES, SOLOMON	BAL	015	2ND DIST
JONES, SOLOMON	DOR	315	1ST DIST
JONES, SOMERSET	MGM	323	CRACKLIN
JONES, SOPHIA	QUE	141	1ST E DI
JONES, SOPHIA	BAL	207	17TH WAR
JONES, SOPHIA	BAL	083	2ND DIST
JONES, SOPHIA-	BAL	087	2ND DIST
JONES, SOPHIA	BAL	251	2ND WARD
JONES, SOPHIA	BAL	078	15TH WAR
JONES, SOPHIA	BAL	227	2ND WARD
JONES, SOPHIA-BLACK	FRE	017	FREDERIC
JONES, SPENCER	CEC	180	7TH E DI
JONES, SPENCER	SOM	450	DAMES QU
JONES, STEPHEN	BAL	423	3RD WARD
JONES, STEPHEN	HAR	077	BEL AIR
JONES, STEPHEN	DOR	435	1ST DIST
JONES, STEPHEN	BAL	315	12TH WAR
JONES, STEPHEN	BAL	449	8TH WARD
JONES, STEPHEN	BAL	320	3RD WARD
JONES, SUSAN	BAL	097	15TH WAR
JONES, SUSAN	BAL	089	15TH WAR
JONES, SUSAN	BAL	190	17TH WAR
JONES, SUSAN	BAL	287	7TH WARD
JONES, SUSAN	BAL	405	3RD WARD
JONES, SUSAN	BAL	045	1ST WARD
JONES, SUSAN	HAR	086	2ND DIST
JONES, SUSAN	BAL	235	20TH WAR
JONES, SUSAN	CAR	092	NO TWP L
JONES, SUSAN	SOM	448	DAMES QU
JONES, SUSAN H.	BAL	043	4TH WARD
JONES, SUSAN-BLACK	FRE	220	BUCKEYST
JONES, SUSANAH	BAL	114	18TH WAR
JONES, SUSANNAH	BAL	436	1ST DIST
JONES, SYLVESTER	BAL	207	17TH WAR
JONES, SYLVESTER	HAR	032	1ST DIST
JONES, SYLVESTER	PRI	088	SPALDING
JONES, TABITHA	CAR	182	8TH DIST
JONES, TABITHA	BAL	258	6TH WARD
JONES, TEMPRENCE	BAL	397	3RD WARD
JONES, THEOPHILLAS	CEC	204	6TH E DI
JONES, THEOPILLUS	CEC	206	7TH E DI
JONES, THOMAS	BAL	279	20TH WAR
JONES, THOMAS	BAL	037	4TH WARD
JONES, THOMAS	CAR	296	7TH DIST
JONES, THOMAS	CAR	305	1ST DIST
JONES, THOMAS	HAR	041	1ST DIST
JONES, THOMAS	SOM	445	DAMES QU
JONES, THOMAS	BAL	201	17TH WAR
JONES, THOMAS	KEN	209	2ND DIST
JONES, THOMAS	KEN	211	2ND DIST
JONES, THOMAS	CAL	022	2ND DIST
JONES, THOMAS	CAL	049	3RD DIST
JONES, THOMAS	CAL	041	3RD DIST
JONES, THOMAS	CAR	088	NO TWP L
JONES, THOMAS	KEN	216	2ND DIST
JONES, THOMAS	CEC	052	1ST E DI
JONES, THOMAS	BAL	374	3RD WARD
JONES, THOMAS	BAL	281	2ND WARD
JONES, THOMAS	BAL	110	5TH WARD
JONES, THOMAS	BAL	365	3RD WARD
JONES, THOMAS	BAL	152	2ND DIST
JONES, THOMAS	BAL	171	16TH WAR
JONES, THOMAS	BAL	167	16TH WAR
JONES, THOMAS	BAL	006	9TH WARD
JONES, THOMAS	BAL	265	12TH WAR
JONES, THOMAS	BAL	154	1ST WARD
JONES, THOMAS	BAL	245	6TH WARD
JONES, THOMAS	BAL	188	2ND WARD
JONES, THOMAS	ANN	450	HOWARD D
JONES, THOMAS	BAL	149	2ND DIST
JONES, THOMAS	BAL	138	2ND DIST
JONES, THOMAS	PRI	069	MARLBROU
JONES, THOMAS	SOM	487	SALISBUR
JONES, THOMAS	KEN	282	3RD DIST
JONES, THOMAS	WOR	277	BERLIN 1
JONES, THOMAS	WOR	327	1ST E DI
JONES, THOMAS	WOR	349	1ST E DI
JONES, THOMAS	WAS	156	HAGERSTO
JONES, THOMAS	WAS	154	HAGERSTO
JONES, THOMAS	ST	264	3RD E DI
JONES, THOMAS B.	WOR	299	SNOW HIL
JONES, THOMAS C.	CAR	078	NO TWP L
JONES, THOMAS H.	CAL	045	3RD DIST
JONES, THOMAS H.	SOM	485	TRAPP DI
JONES, THOMAS J.	DOR	467	1ST DIST
JONES, THOMAS J.	SOM	446	DAMES QU
JONES, THOMAS L.	MGM	411	MEDLEY 3
JONES, THOMAS L.	BAL	360	3RD WARD
JONES, THOMAS N.	CHA	274	ALLENS F
JONES, THOMAS O.	BAL	441	14TH WAR
JONES, THOMAS R.	QUE	135	1ST E DI
JONES, THOMAS W.	FRE	033	FREDERIC
JONES, THOMAS W.	BAL	342	3RD WARD
JONES, THOMAS W.	WAS	137	HAGERSTO
JONES, THOMAS*	DOR	468	1ST DIST
JONES, THOMAS-BLACK	ST	310	1ST E DI
JONES, THOMAS-MULATTO	FRE	415	8TH E DI
JONES, THOMPSON	BAL	349	3RD WARD
JONES, THOMSA	BAL	119	1ST WARD
JONES, UNAS	BAL	051	1ST WARD
JONES, URIAH	BAL	259	12TH WAR
JONES, VALENTINE-MULATTO	FRE	407	JEFFERSO
JONES, VERLINDA	PRI	008	BLADENSB
JONES, VIOLET	BAL	178	19TH WAR
JONES, W.	BAL	100	10TH WAR
JONES, WAHSINGTON	CAR	188	4TH DIST
JONES, WALLACE	CAR	165	NO TWP L
JONES, WALTER	BAL	198	6TH WARD
JONES, WALTER R.	BAL	463	14TH WAR
JONES, WALTY	WOR	166	6TH E DI
JONES, WASHINGTON	CAL	014	1ST DIST
JONES, WASHINGTON	CEC	029	CHESAPEA
JONES, WASHINGTON	DOR	315	1ST DIST
JONES, WELTHY H.	CAR	296	7TH DIST
JONES, WESLEY	CEC	043	CHESAPEA
JONES, WESLEY	ANN	387	4TH DIST
JONES, WHITINGTON	WOR	290	9TH E DI
JONES, WILIAM	WOR	198	8TH E DI
JONES, WILLAIM	BAL	228	17TH WAR
JONES, WILLAM	BAL	209	17TH WAR
JONES, WILLAMENOR*	DOR	337	3RD DIVI
JONES, WILLIAM	DOR	325	1ST DIST
JONES, WILLIAM	DOR	351	3RD DIVI
JONES, WILLIAM	FRE	034	FREDERIC
JONES, WILLIAM	BAL	245	20TH WAR
JONES, WILLIAM	CEC	190	5TH E DI
JONES, WILLIAM	CEC	202	6TH E DI
JONES, WILLIAM	FRE	446	8TH E DI
JONES, WILLIAM	BAL	227	17TH WAR
JONES, WILLIAM	BAL	204	17TH WAR
JONES, WILLIAM	CEC	017	ELKTON 3
JONES, WILLIAM	BAL	409	3RD WARD
JONES, WILLIAM	CAR	182	8TH DIST
JONES, WILLIAM	CEC	004	ELKTON 3
JONES, WILLIAM	BAL	025	4TH WARD
JONES, WILLIAM	BAL	398	14TH WAR
JONES, WILLIAM	BAL	468	14TH WAR
JONES, WILLIAM	CAR	088	NO TWP L
JONES, WILLIAM	CAR	081	NO TWP L
JONES, WILLIAM	BAL	444	14TH WAR
JONES, WILLIAM	CAR	106	NO TWP L
JONES, WILLIAM	CAR	154	NO TWP L
JONES, WILLIAM	QUE	144	1ST E DI
JONES, WILLIAM	KEN	222	2ND DIST
JONES, WILLIAM	MGM	425	MEDLEY 3
JONES, WILLIAM	SOM	432	PRINCESS
JONES, WILLIAM	SOM	437	PRINCESS
JONES, WILLIAM	HAR	087	2ND DIST
JONES, WILLIAM	MGM	357	BERRYS D
JONES, WILLIAM	CEC	079	NORTHEAS
JONES, WILLIAM	BAL	305	17TH WAR
JONES, WILLIAM	HAR	198	3RD DIST
JONES, WILLIAM	FRE	220	BUCKEYST
JONES, WILLIAM	FRE	332	MIDDLETO
JONES, WILLIAM	TAL	108	ST MICHA
JONES, WILLIAM	WAS	085	2ND SUBD
JONES, WILLIAM	WAS	009	WILLIAMS
JONES, WILLIAM	WAS	030	2ND SUBD
JONES, WILLIAM	WAS	282	1ST DIST
JONES, WILLIAM	ST	311	1ST E DI
JONES, WILLIAM	SOM	465	HANGARY
JONES, WILLIAM	SOM	463	HANGARY
JONES, WILLIAM	SOM	467	HANGARY
JONES, WILLIAM	SOM	476	TRAPPE D
JONES, WILLIAM	SOM	473	TRAPPE D
JONES, WILLIAM	QUE	179	2ND E DI
JONES, WILLIAM	QUE	198	3RD E DI
JONES, WILLIAM	QUE	205	3RD E DI
JONES, WILLIAM	KEN	309	3RD DIST
JONES, WILLIAM	KEN	302	3RD DIST
JONES, WILLIAM	WAS	125	HAGERSTO
JONES, WILLIAM	WAS	237	CAVETOWN
JONES, WILLIAM	WOR	336	1ST E DI
JONES, WILLIAM	TAL	079	ST MICHA
JONES, WILLIAM	WOR	319	1ST E DI
JONES, WILLIAM	QUE	243	5TH E DI
JONES, WILLIAM	ALL	087	5TH E.D.
JONES, WILLIAM	ANN	321	2ND DIST
JONES, WILLIAM	ANN	280	ANNAPOLI
JONES, WILLIAM	ALL	120	5TH E.D.
JONES, WILLIAM	BAL	154	1ST WARD
JONES, WILLIAM	BAL	171	1ST WARD
JONES, WILLIAM	BAL	044	9TH WARD
JONES, WILLIAM	BAL	034	9TH WARD
JONES, WILLIAM	BAL	100	10TH WAR
JONES, WILLIAM	BAL	102	10TH WAR
JONES, WILLIAM	BAL	190	17TH WAR
JONES, WILLIAM	BAL	311	12TH WAR
JONES, WILLIAM	BAL	081	15TH WAR
JONES, WILLIAM	BAL	171	11TH WAR
JONES, WILLIAM	BAL	338	7TH WARD
JONES, WILLIAM	BAL	044	1ST WARD
JONES, WILLIAM	BAL	342	3RD WARD
JONES, WILLIAM	BAL	094	5TH WARD
JONES, WILLIAM	BAL	413	1ST DIST
JONES, WILLIAM	BAL	314	3RD WARD
JONES, WILLIAM	BAL	358	1ST DIST
JONES, WILLIAM	BAL	358	1ST DIST
JONES, WILLIAM	BAL	462	1ST DIST
JONES, WILLIAM	BAL	459	1ST DIST
JONES, WILLIAM	BAL	123	2ND DIST
JONES, WILLIAM	ANN	450	HOWARD D
JONES, WILLIAM	ANN	430	HOWARD D
JONES, WILLIAM	BAL	062	2ND DIST
JONES, WILLIAM	ANN	362	4TH DIST
JONES, WILLIAM	BAL	232	2ND WARD
JONES, WILLIAM	BAL	377	8TH WARD
JONES, WILLIAM B.	BAL	384	3RD WARD
JONES, WILLIAM B.	BAL	003	1ST WARD
JONES, WILLIAM B.	BAL	054	9TH WARD
JONES, WILLIAM B.	WOR	209	4TH E DI
JONES, WILLIAM B. SR.	SOM	439	DAMES QU
JONES, WILLIAM C.	SOM	430	PRINCESS
JONES, WILLIAM CRAIG	BAL	219	17TH WAR
JONES, WILLIAM F.	DOR	392	1ST DIST
JONES, WILLIAM F.	DOR	337	3RD DIVI
JONES, WILLIAM G.	DOR	352	3RD DIVI
JONES, WILLIAM H.	SOM	433	PRINCESS
JONES, WILLIAM H.	BAL	046	18TH WAR
JONES, WILLIAM H.	QUE	139	1ST E DI
JONES, WILLIAM H.	CAR	093	NO TWP L
JONES, WILLIAM H.	BAL	149	11TH WAR
JONES, WILLIAM H.	WOR	190	8TH E DI
JONES, WILLIAM H.	WOR	327	1ST E DI
JONES, WILLIAM H.	WAS	021	2ND SUBD
JONES, WILLIAM H.	WOR	278	BERLIN 1
JONES, WILLIAM H.	WOR	299	9TH E DI
JONES, WILLIAM H.	TAL	015	EASTON D
JONES, WILLIAM H.	BAL	273	2ND WARD
JONES, WILLIAM H.	BAL	030	15TH WAR
JONES, WILLIAM H.	BAL	199	11TH WAR
JONES, WILLIAM H.	BAL	175	11TH WAR
JONES, WILLIAM H.	BAL	182	2ND WARD
JONES, WILLIAM J.	CEC	005	ELKTON 3
JONES, WILLIAM L.	BAL	075	4TH WARD
JONES, WILLIAM M.	DOR	302	1ST DIST
JONES, WILLIAM P.	CEC	129	6TH E DI
JONES, WILLIAM R.	QUE	141	1ST E DI
JONES, WILLIAM R.	SOM	427	PRINCESS
JONES, WILLIAM R.	BAL	261	5TH WARD
JONES, WILLIAM R.	TAL	112	ST MICHA
JONES, WILLIAM T.	BAL	135	1ST WARD
JONES, WILLIAM T.	BAL	125	1ST WARD
JONES, WILLIAM T.	ANN	394	8TH DIST
JONES, WILLIAM T. DR-	BAL	352	1ST DIST
JONES, WILLIAM W.	WAS	145	HAGERSTO
JONES, WILLIAM W.	DOR	371	3RD DIVI
JONES, WILLIAM W.-MULATTO	ST	318	4TH E DI
JONES, WILLIAM-BLACK	QUE	179	2ND E DI
JONES, WILLIAM-BLACK	QUE	161	2ND E DI
JONES, WILLIAM-BLACK	MGM	398	ROCKERLE
JONES, WRIGHTSON	TAL	079	ST MICHA
JONES, ZACHARIAH	MGM	436	CLARKSTR
JONES, ZACHARY-BLACK	CAR	386	2ND DIST
JONES, ZACHRIAH	BAL	003	9TH WARD
JONES, ZEBEDEE	DOR	347	3RD DIVI
JONES,AMIE	FRE	030	FREDERIC
JONES,MARTIN	CAR	148	NO TWP L
JONES,MARY	CAR	107	NO TWP L
JONES,TLABOT	BAL	120	1ST WARD
JONEY, BENJAMIN	BAL	314	20TH WAR
JONEY, MARY	BAL	295	17TH WAR
JONEZS, SUSAN	BAL	383	13TH WAR
JONH, JOSEPH	BAL	010	EASTERN
JONHOFF, JOHN	BAL	069	10TH WAR
JONKHARR, MARY	WOR	307	2ND E DI
JONON, ISABELLA	BAL	226	12TH WAR
JONS, HARRIET	BAL	366	13TH WAR
JONS, SAMUEL	WOR	328	1ST E DI
JONSON, ANN	BAL	314	12TH WAR
JONSON, ANN	BAL	274	1ST DIST
JONSON, CATHARINE	BAL	261	12TH WAR
JONSON, CHARLOTTE	BAL	306	12TH WAR
JONSON, EDWARD	KEN	255	1ST DIST

Name	Co.	No.	District
JONSCN. EDWARD	KEN	255	1ST DIST
JONSON. EDWIN	KEN	255	1ST DIST
JONSON. EDWIN	KEN	254	1ST DIST
JONSCN. EMILY	KEN	270	1ST DIST
JONSON. G.	BAL	299	20TH WAR
JONSCN. HARRIET	BAL	309	12TH WAR
JONSUN. HARRIETT	BAL	314	20TH WAR
JCNSON. HENRIETTA	KEN	266	1ST DIST
JONSCN. HENRY	KEN	263	1ST DIST
JONSCN. HESTER	KEN	261	1ST DIST
JONSCN. JACKSON *	KEN	253	1ST DIST
JONSCN. JAMES	HAR	146	3RD DIST
JCNSCN. JAMES	KEN	270	1ST DIST
JONSCN. JAMES	KEN	268	1ST DIST
JONSON. JOHN	KEN	263	1ST DIST
JONSCN. JOHN	KEN	258	1ST DIST
JONSCN. LEVI	KEN	256	1ST DIST
JONSON. MARY	BAL	298	12TH WAR
JONSON. MARY	BAL	273	12TH WAR
JONSCN. ROBERT	BAL	279	12TH WAR
JONSON. THCMAS	KEN	255	1ST DIST
JONSON. WILLIAM	KEN	244	2ND DIST
JONSCN. WILLIAM	KEN	256	1ST DIST
JONSON. WILLIAM	KEN	261	1ST DIST
JONSCN.REBECCA	BAL	265	12TH WAR
JCNSTON. BARBARA F.	WAS	124	2ND DIST
JONTH. C.	BAL	158	1ST WARD
JCNTY. GEORGE B.	BAL	233	1ST DIST
JOOKS. JOHN	WOR	269	BERLIN 1
JOPPA. AMANDA	MGM	372	BERRYS D
JOPPA. ELIAS	BAL	315	1ST DIST
JOPPA. HARRY	MGM	371	BERRYS D
JOPPA. JOHN	MGM	331	CRACKLIN
JOPPA. LOUISA	MGM	349	BERRYS D
JCPPA. MARTHA	MGM	371	BERRYS D
JORDAN. ANN	BAL	062	4TH WARD
JORDAN. ANNIE M. L.	WOR	229	6TH E DI
JORDAN. BRIDGET	BAL	100	1ST WARD
JORDAN. CHARLES	BAL	015	9TH WARD
JCRDAN. CHARLES	BAL	315	20TH WAR
JORDAN. CHRISTOPHER	BAL	303	20TH WAR
JCRDAN. CONRAD R.	WOR	228	6TH E DI
JORDAN. DANIEL	BAL	204	2ND WARD
JORDAN. ELIAS	CAR	206	4TH DIST
JORDAN. EPHRAIM	CEC	109	4TH E DI
JORDAN. FANNY T.	BAL	073	15TH WAR
JORCAN. FERDINAND	BAL	083	4TH WARD
JORDAN. HANSCN P.	WOR	229	6TH E DI
JORCAN. HENRY	BAL	124	1ST WARD
JURDAN. HEZEKIAH	CAR	354	6TH DIST
JORDAN. JAMES	BAL	281	12TH WAR
JORDAN. JAMES	ANN	450	HOWARD D
JORDAN. JOHN	BAL	015	1ST WARD
JCRDAN. JOHN	BAL	194	2ND WARD
JORDAN. JOHN .B	BAL	168	16TH WAR
JORDAN. JOHN E.	CAR	203	4TH DIST
JORDAN. JOHN L.	WAS	066	2ND SUBD
JORDAN. JOHN M.	BAL	396	1ST DIST
JORDAN. JULIA	BAL	033	9TH WARD
JCRDAN. LOUISA	BAL	080	4TH WARD
JORDAN. LUCINDA	BAL	152	16TH WAR
JORDAN. LUTHER	BAL	162	19TH WAR
JORDAN. MARTHA	BAL	162	19TH WAR
JORDAN. MARY	CEC	109	4TH E DI
JCRCAN. NELSON	BAL	343	3RD WARD
JORDAN. PATRICK	FRE	067	FREDERIC
JORDAN. SAMUEL	SOM	399	BRINKLEY
JORDAN. SOLOMON	BAL	194	6TH WARD
JORDAN. THOMAS	BAL	142	1ST WARD
JORDAN. WILLIAM	BAL	359	8TH WARD
JORDAN. WILLIAM	BAL	152	2ND DIST
JCRDAN. WILLIAM	CEC	120	3RD E DI
JORCAN. WILLIAM	CAR	221	5TH DIST
JORDAN. WILLIAM	CAR	200	4TH DIST
JORCAN. WILLIAM H.	DOR	381	1ST DIST
JORDAN.FREDERICK	BAL	068	1ST WARD
JORDAN.JOHN	WAS	009	WILLIAMS
JORDEN. ANN	BAL	239	12TH WAR
JORDEN. CASANDER	HAR	056	1ST DIST
JORDEN. JOSEPH	CEC	110	4TH E DI
JORDEN. THOMAS-MULATTO	ST	293	2ND E DI
JORDEN. WILLIAM	CAR	111	NO TWP L
JCRDEN.ROBERT	BAL	019	1ST WARD
JORDEN.W ILLIAM	CAR	164	NO TWP L
JORDCN. ANN	BAL	125	5TH WARD
JCRDCN. ANN JANE	BAL	371	13TH WAR
JCRDCN. BETSY	BAL	138	5TH WARD
JORDON. CATHERINE	BAL	085	18TH WAR
JORDCN. ELIAS	CAR	206	4TH DIST
JORDON. ESTHER	CAR	402	2ND DIST
JORDCN. GEORGE-BLACK	FRE	231	BUCKEYST
JORDCN. HARRIET	BAL	389	13TH WAR
JORDCN. HERMAN	BAL	048	15TH WAR
JORDON. HIRAM	CAR	365	9TH DIST
JORDCN. ISABELLA	BAL	215	11TH WAR
JORDON. ISABELLA	BAL	215	11TH WAR
JORDON. ISOM	BAL	041	15TH WAR
JORDCN. J.	BAL	143	5TH WARD
JORDCN. JAMES B.	BAL	093	18TH WAR
JORDON. JOHN	BAL	165	6TH WARD
JORDCN. JCHN	BAL	118	5TH WARD
JCRDON. JOSEPH R.	ALL	255	CUMBERLA
JORDCN. OWEN	BAL	185	11TH WAR
JCRDON. REBECCA	BAL	076	18TH WAR
JORDCN. SAMUEL	CAR	230	5TH DIST
JCRDCN. SAMUEL B.	BAL	054	18TH WAR
JORDON. ZACHARIAH L.	CAR	202	4TH DIST
JORDCN.WILLIAM	BAL	054	1ST WARD
JORK. JOHN	BAL	133	1ST WARD
JORS. ALICE	BAL	239	20TH WAR
JORSEY. ELLEN	BAL	298	12TH WAR
JOSBOWD. CORDIELA	HAR	183	3RD DIST
JOSE. A.	BAL	159	1ST WARD
JOSE. FRANCES	BAL	066	4TH WARD
JOSEHANCE. CHARLES	BAL	111	18TH WAR
JOSELINE. BARNEY	ALL	105	5TH E.D.
JOSEPH JAMES	BAL	019	9TH WARD
JOSEPH. ALOYSUES	ST	285	2ND E DI
JCSEPH. FRANK	BAL	125	1ST WARD
JCSEPH. FRANKLIN	BAL	280	2ND WARD
JOSEPH. GEORGE	BAL	374	8TH WARD
JOSEPH. J.	BAL	153	1ST WARD
JOSEPH. JOHN	BAL	166	1ST WARD
JOSEPH. JOHN	BAL	294	12TH WAR
JCSEPH. LESTER ANN *	BAL	312	12TH WAR
JOSEPH. MARGARET	BAL	194	11TH WAR
JOSEPH. MARTHA	BAL	001	15TH WAR
JOSEPH. REBECCA	ST	271	3RD E DI
JOSEPH. REHRBAUGH	CAR	247	3RD DIST
JOSEPH. WILLIAM	BAL	161	11TH WAR
JOSEPH. WILLIAM	BAL	430	8TH WARD
JOSEPH. WILLIAM H.	BAL	337	13TH WAR
JOSEPHS. JOHN	BAL	018	4TH WARD
JOSEPHS. JOHN	BAL	138	1ST WARD
JOSEPHS. MICHAEL	BAL	320	3RD WARD
JOSEPHS. WILLIAM	BAL	006	4TH WARD
JCSHANA. ELIZABETH	BAL	225	2ND WARD
JCSHBOT. CHARLES	BAL	074	2ND DIST
JOSHEPHS. ISABELLA	BAL	006	4TH WARD
JOSHUA. BROTHER	BAL	216	11TH WAR
JOSHUA. MARIA	BAL	344	3RD WARD
JCSLIN.SHEPHERD	QUE	135	1ST E DI
JOTTERALL. S. B.	BAL	333	1ST DIST
JOUET. ANN M.	BAL	249	17TH WAR
JOUKS. RUTH A. *	BAL	025	9TH WARD
JOUNGST. AUGUST	BAL	322	1ST DIST
JOUNTAIN. JOHN	BAL	372	13TH WAR
JOURDAN. CHARLES M.	HAR	124	2ND DIST
JOURDAN. ELIZABETH	BAL	386	8TH WARD
JOURDAN. FREDERICKA	BAL	390	8TH WARD
JOURDAN. JANE	ALL	158	6TH E.D.
JOURDAN. JANE	HAR	113	2ND DIST
JOURDAN. JOHN F.	HAR	105	2ND DIST
JOURDAN. JOHN W.	HAR	124	2ND DIST
JOURDAN. MARY	HAR	113	2ND DIST
JOURDAN. WILLIAM	HAR	076	BEL AIR
JOURDAN. WILLIAM	BAL	462	1ST DIST
JCURDON. JOHN	BAL	156	1ST WARD
JOURNAY. EDWARD	BAL	128	18TH WAR
JOURNEY. CAROLINE	BAL	350	13TH WAR
JOURNEY. ELIZABETH	ANN	321	2ND DIST
JOURNEY. RICHARD	ANN	435	HOWARD D
JOURNEY. SUSAN	BAL	066	15TH WAR
JOURNEY. WILLIAM	ANN	311	1ST DIST
JOURS. GEORGE	BAL	372	8TH WARD
JOUTZEY. WILLIAM	FRE	144	10TH E D
JOWLS. JAMES	BAL	015	9TH WARD
JOWS. ARINA	TAL	026	EASTON D
JOY. ANN	BAL	083	18TH WAR
JOY. ANN E.	ST	303	2ND E DI
JOY. B.	BAL	150	1ST WARD
JOY. DOROTHY	ST	299	2ND E DI
JOY. EDMCND B.	ST	264	3RD E DI
JCY. EDWARD	ST	330	4TH E DI
JOY. EDWARD	BAL	294	7TH WARD
JCY. ENOUD	BAL	073	2ND DIST
JOY. ENOCH	WAS	185	BOONSBOR
JOY. GEORGE W.	FRE	399	JEFFERSO
JOY. HENRIETTA	ST	264	3RD E DI
JOY. J.B.	BAL	138	1ST WARD
JOY. JAMES	ST	255	3RD E DI
JOY. JAMES	FRE	336	MIDDLETO
JOY. JAMES E.	ST	292	2ND E DI
JOY. JANE M. R.	ST	265	3RD E DI
JOY. JOHN	PRI	012	BLADENSB
JOY. MARY L.	ST	285	2ND E DI
JOY. MARY L.	ST	284	2ND E DI
JOY. SAMUEL J.	BAL	311	3RD WARD
JOY. STEVEN	FRE	336	MIDDLETO
JOY. WILLIAM	PRI	105	PISCATAW
JOY. WILLIAM M.	ST	255	3RD E DI
JOYCE. ANN	BAL	053	2ND DIST
JOYCE. CHARLES	ANN	456	HOWARD D
JOYCE. FRANCES	BAL	086	10TH WAR
JOYCE. GEORGE H.	CEC	004	ELKTON 3
JOYCE. HENRIETTA	BAL	047	2ND DIST
JOYCE. HENRY	BAL	078	2ND DIST
JOYCE. HENRY	ALL	129	4TH E.D.
JOYCE. JAMES	BAL	143	1ST WARD
JOYCE. JAMES	BAL	362	3RD WARD
JOYCE. MARK	BAL	030	2ND DIST
JOYCE. MARY	BAL	056	2ND DIST
JOYCE. MARY	BAL	156	16TH WAR
JOYCE. MICHAEL	BAL	154	16TH WAR
JOYCE. OWEN A.	BAL	362	3RD WARD
JCYCE. PATRICK	ALL	127	4TH E.D.
JOYCE. REBECCA	BAL	312	7TH WARD
JOYCE. RICHARD	MGM	389	ROCKERLE
JOYCE. SISTER ELLEN	FRE	198	5TH E DI
JOYCE. STEPHEN J.	BAL	119	11TH WAR
JOYCE. THERESA	BAL	112	5TH WARD
JOYCE. THCMAS	BAL	132	2ND DIST
JOYCE. TCBIAS	ALL	139	6TH E.D.
JOYCE. WILLIAM	BAL	146	1ST WARD
JOYCE. WILLIAM H.	BAL	312	7TH WARD
JOYCE. WILLIAM N.	BAL	035	9TH WARD
JOYES. EDWARD	BAL	118	5TH WARD
JOYES. MARY ANN	BAL	117	5TH WARD
JOYHNSON. MARY A.	ST	338	4TH E DI
JOYNES. DANIEL	BAL	184	6TH WARD
JOYNES. EDMUND G.	BAL	235	6TH WARD
JCYNES. PHEBE	BAL	030	2ND DIST
JOYNES. THOASM	BAL	146	1ST WARD
JCYSER. JESSE	BAL	117	5TH WARD
JREEP. HENRY*	BAL	065	4TH WARD
JRUSTY. AARON	BAL	376	13TH WAR
JTOMKINS. J. R.	CHA	223	ALLENS F
JUBB. E. J.	ANN	348	3RD DIST
JUBB. EMILY	BAL	101	1ST WARD
JUBB. HENRY	ANN	356	3RD DIST
JUBB. JOHN	ANN	358	3RD DIST
JUBB. REUBEN	BAL	100	1ST WARD
JUBB. REUBEN	BAL	101	1ST WARD
JUBB. RICHARD	BAL	093	1ST WARD
JUBB. WILLIAM	ANN	352	3RD DIST
JUBILE. FRANK	SOM	358	BRINKLEY
JUBILEE. JANE	BAL	086	15TH WAR
JUDAH. DAIVD	BAL	155	11TH WAR
JUDAH. ELIZABETH	ALL	010	3RD E.D.
JUDAH. RINAT	BAL	240	20TH WAR
JUDD. HENRY R.	HAR	105	2ND DIST
JUDD. JOHN	HAR	114	2ND DIST
JUDD. SARAH	HAR	114	2ND DIST
JUDD. WILLIAM	HAR	106	2ND DIST
JUDEFIND. CHARLES	BAL	037	15TH WAR
JUDEFIND. JOHN	BAL	094	15TH WAR
JUDGE. HENRY	BAL	343	13TH WAR
JUDGE. JOHN	BAL	075	10TH WAR
JUDGE. PATRICK	ALL	136	4TH E.D.
JUDGE. PATRICK	WAS	164	2ND DIST
JUDGE. THOMAS	ALL	051	10TH E.D
JUDGEE. MARY *	BAL	030	18TH WAR
JUDICK. JOSEPH	BAL	290	12TH WAR
JUDKIN. L.M.	BAL	134	1ST WARD
JUDKINS. L. M.	BAL	147	1ST WARD
JUDKINS. RICHARD	BAL	275	2ND WARD
JUDKINS. ROSELLE	ALL	235	CUMBERLA
JUDKNS. L.M.	BAL	135	1ST WARD
JUDLIN. ELIZABETH	BAL	205	6TH WARD
JUDLIN. HENRY J.	BAL	032	9TH WARD
JUDSON. EPHRAIM	ANN	511	HOWARD D
JUDSON. WILLIAM	BAL	420	8TH WARD
JUDY. HENRY W.	FRE	207	BUCKEYST
JUDY. MARTHA	MGM	442	CLARKSTR
JUDY. THOMAS L.	FRE	218	BUCKEYST
JUDY. WILLIAM A.	FRE	206	BUCKEYST
JUG. EDWARD*	BAL	312	3RD WARD
JUGNETTI. JOSHUA	BAL	008	9TH WARD
JULERS. MARY-BLACK	CAR	101	NO TWP L
JULIA. FRANCIS	ALL	215	CUMBERLA
JULIA. MISS	BAL	137	11TH WAR
JULIUS. CATHARINE	WAS	123	HAGERSTO
JULIUS. GEORGE	WAS	204	1ST DIST
JULIUS. JOHN	WAS	128	HAGERSTO
JULDES. GILLS	BAL	180	2ND WARD
JULDES. J. L.	BAL	142	11TH WAR
JULY. BETSY-BLACK	FRE	451	8TH E DI
JULY. MICHAEL	BAL	069	2ND DIST
JUMB. THOMAS	CEC	056	1ST E DI
JUMBO. MARY	BAL	146	19TH WAR
JUMIF. CATHARINE*	WAS	044	2ND SUBD
JUMILLEN. BARBARY	BAL	090	2ND DIST
JUMIS. JAMES E.	CAR	265	WESTMINS
JUMIS. MARGARET A. E.	CAR	265	WESTMINS
JUMP. ABRAHAM	CAR	071	NO TWP L
JUMP. ALBERT	QUE	170	2ND E DI
JUMP. ALEXANDER C.	TAL	110	ST MICHA
JUMP. ALMIRA	CAR	137	NO TWP L
JUMP. ANDREW	QUE	251	5TH E DI
JUMP. CHARLES	TAL	021	EASTON D
JUMP. CLARINDA	QUE	213	3RD E DI
JUMP. DANIEL	CAR	106	NO TWP L
JUMP. EDWIN P.	QUE	247	5TH E DI
JUMP. ELIZABETH-BLACK	QUE	201	3RD E DI
JUMP. ELLEN W.	CEC	075	NORTHEAS
JUMP. HENRY	QUE	213	3RD E DI
JUMP. HENRY T.	KEN	247	2ND DIST
JUMP. HENRYP	BAL	377	3RD WARD
JUMP. INDIANA	QUE	186	3RD E DI
JUMP. ISACK	TAL	047	EASTON T
JUMP. JAMES	QUE	214	3RD E DI
JUMP. JOHN	QUE	200	3RD E DI
JUMP. JOHN	CAR	147	NO TWP L
JUMP. JOHN W.	TAL	068	EASTON T
JUMP. JOSEPHENE	TAL	014	EASTON D
JUMP. LYDIA	KEN	300	3RD DIST
JUMP. MARGARET A.	TAL	068	EASTON T
JUMP. ROBERT	TAL	070	EASTON T
JUMP. ROBERT	CAR	169	NO TWP L
JUMP. ROBERT H.	TAL	017	EASTON D
JUMP. SALATHIEL P.	QUE	213	3RD E DI
JUMP. SAMUEL	QUE	185	3RD E DI
JUMP. SARAH E.	DOR	455	1ST DIST
JUMP. SOPHIA	TAL	059	EASTON D
JUMP. THOMAS	TAL	010	EASTON D
JUMP. WILLIAM	TAL	052	EASTON D
JUMP. WILLIAM	DOR	455	1ST DIST
JUMPER. ADAM	DOR	326	3RD DIVI
JUMPER. SALLY	WAS	149	HAGERSTO
JUNEMER. LEWIS	BAL	363	8TH WARD
JUNES. XAVIERA	BAL	212	11TH WAR
JUNIPER. JOSHUA	CAR	265	WESTMINS
JUNKE. HANSON	ALL	021	2ND E.D.
JUNKER. PHILIP	BAL	008	15TH WAR
JUNKS. ELIZABETH	BAL	080	4TH WARD
JUNN. MARSHA	BAL	290	12TH WAR
JUNP. SALLY	QUE	190	3RD E DI
JUNP. WILLIAM L.	QUE	188	3RD E DI
JUNSE. JACOB	FRE	271	NEW MARK
JURDEN. SAMUEL	BAL	002	1ST WARD
JURIN. JACOB	FRE	271	NEW MARK
JURIN. LOYD	FRE	277	NEW MARK
JURIN. MANAH	FRE	278	NEW MARK
JURIN. THOMAS-MULATTO	FRE	243	NEW MARK
JURNEY. BASIL	KEN	208	2ND DIST
JURNEY. JAMES E.	KEN	208	2ND DIST
JURNEY. JANE	BAL	345	13TH WAR
JUROR. NANTZY*	BAL	403	3RD WARD
JURRY. JOHN	BAL	265	17TH WAR
JURSINS. MARY*	BAL	088	10TH WAR
JURVIS. MARIA	CEC	090	4TH E DI
JURY. GEORGE	BAL	260	17TH WAR
JURY. WILLIAM	BAL	235	17TH WAR
JUSLEY. SUSAN*	DOR	377	1ST DIST
JUSTER. ELWOOD	ALL	127	4TH E.D.
JUSTICE. ADAM	BAL	326	3RD WARD
JUSTICE. ANN M.	BAL	312	3RD WARD
JUSTICE. ANTHONY	ALL	118	5TH E.D.
JUSTICE. CLODIUS	WAS	254	1ST DIST
JUSTICE. DAVID	FRE	443	8TH E DI
JUSTICE. EMILY	BAL	466	14TH WAR
JUSTICE. HENRY	BAL	377	1ST DIST
JUSTICE. ISRAEL	HAR	049	1ST DIST
JUSTICE. JACOB	WAS	269	1ST DIST
JUSTICE. JAMES	SOM	419	PRINCESS
JUSTICE. JANE	BAL	063	15TH WAR
JUSTICE. JOHN	BAL	170	19TH WAR
JUSTICE. LEWIS	KEN	224	2ND DIST
JUSTICE. MALON	BAL	397	1ST DIST
JUSTICE. MATILDA	WAS	251	1ST DIST
JUSTICE. REBECCA	BAL	388	1ST DIST
JUSTICE. TABITHA	SOM	420	PRINCESS
JUSTICE. WILLIAM	FRE	422	8TH E DI
JUSTIE. WILLIAM *	BAL	149	1ST WARD
JUSTLY. EDWARD	CAR	098	NO TWP L
JUSTON. CLEMENTINE	BAL	105	10TH WAR
JUSTUS. JOHN	BAL	441	1ST DIST
JUSTUS. MARY	BAL	055	18TH WAR
JUSTUS. SARAH	BAL	113	15TH WAR
JUSTUS. WILLIAM L.	BAL	036	4TH WARD
JUXTER. FRANK	BAL	099	2ND DIST
JYMANCK. FRANK	BAL	261	2ND WARD
K	CAR	132	NO TWP L
K	QUE	194	3RD E DI
K	ST	307	1ST E DI
K	WOR	331	1ST E DI
KABENNOYHEE. JOHN*	BAL	238	12TH WAR
KABERNAGH. JOHNH.	BAL	459	14TH WAR
KABLER. JOHN	BAL	351	13TH WAR
KABLETON. ANN	BAL	050	9TH WARD
KABLUD. CHARLES	BAL	072	2ND DIST
KACHRAM. JOSEPH	BAL	280	2ND WARD
KACK. GEORGE	BAL	300	17TH WAR
KADDAY. MARTIN	ANN	413	HOWARD D
KADLE. ABRAHAM	WAS	211	1ST DIST
KADLE. MATILDA	FRE	349	MIDDLETO
KADY. GEORGE	ALL	202	CUMBERLA
KADY. JAMES R.	ALL	209	CUMBERLA
KADY. MARK	ANN	426	HOWARD D
KAESER. GEORGE D.	BAL	179	6TH WARD

NAME	CO	PAGE	DISTRICT
KAESTING, AUGUST	BAL	456	8TH WARD
KAFFENBERGER, GEORGE	ANN	462	HOWARD D
KAGEL, CATHERINE	BAL	281	7TH WARD
KAGG, JANE *	BAL	289	20TH WAR
KAGLE, JOHN	ALL	257	CUMBERLA
KAHEARTY, JOHN	FRE	109	CREAGERS
KAHEL, JOHN	ALL	257	CUMBERLA
KAHL, JOHN	BAL	220	2ND WARD
KAHLART, CHARLES	BAL	295	3RD WARD
KAHLART, HENRY	BAL	294	3RD WARD
KAHLER, ADAM	BAL	437	14TH WAR
KAHLER, CHRISTIAN	FRE	030	FREDERIC
KAHLOF, HENRY	BAL	133	1ST WARD
KAHN, DOREICE	BAL	070	4TH WARD
KAHN, JOSEPH*	BAL	314	3RD WARD
KAHN, JOSHUA*	BAL	314	3RD WARD
KAHN, MARY	BAL	321	3RD WARD
KAHNS, JOHN*	BAL	070	4TH WARD
KAILER, CATHARINE	WAS	172	FUNKSTO*
KAILER, JOSEPH	BAL	166	2ND DIST
KAILOR, DAVID	FRE	338	MIDDLETO
KAILOR, JAMES	FRE	338	MIDDLETO
KAIN, BERNHARD*	BAL	091	10TH WAR
KAIN, CATHARINE	CEC	018	ELKTON 3
KAIN, DAVID	CEC	004	ELKTON 3
KAIN, ELIZA	BAL	026	2ND DIST
KAIN, ESTHER	CEC	153	PORT DUP
KAIN, FRANCIS	CEC	082	CHARLEST
KAIN, HANNAH	BAL	122	5TH WARD
KAIN, JOHN	CEC	046	1ST E DI
KAIN, JOSEPH	BAL	316	20TH WAR
KAIN, PATRICK	CEC	083	CHARLEST
KAIN, ROSE	CEC	050	1ST E DI
KAIN, SARAH	CEC	038	CHESAPEA
KAIN, WILLIAM	CEC	038	CHESAPEA
KAIN, WILLIAM	CEC	167	6TH E DI
KAIN,CONRAD	BAL	060	1ST WARD
KAINE, JOHN	BAL	200	17TH WAR
KAINE, MICHAEL	BAL	200	17TH WAR
KAINE, PATRICK	BAL	300	17TH WAR
KAINE,ROBERT	BAL	122	1ST WARD
KAINER, JAMES	BAL	163	2ND DIST
KAINEY, PETER	ALL	055	10TH E.D
KAINS, THOMAS	BAL	234	2ND WARD
KAIS, JOHN	BAL	210	17TH WAR
KAISER, ELIZABETH	BAL	007	9TH WARD
KAITH, FREDERICK	BAL	254	20TH WAR
KAIZER, CHARLES	BAL	108	5TH WARD
KAKEL, WILLIAM SR.	CAR	336	6TH DIST
KALBAUGH, MICHAEL	ALL	126	4TH E.D.
KALBFUS, LEWIS	BAL	431	14TH WAR
KALBFUS, LEWIS SR.	BAL	392	14TH WAR
KALBFUS, THEODORE	BAL	197	6TH WARD
KALBFUS, WILLIAM	BAL	333	7TH WARD
KALCHART, JOHN	BAL	142	5TH WARD
KALDENBACK, MATHIAS	PRI	065	NOTTINGH
KALDENBACK, MATHIAS J.	PRI	065	NOTTINGH
KALDENDBACK, ANDREW	PRI	116	PISCATAW
KALEON, GEORGE	BAL	072	2ND DIST
KALER, HENRY	BAL	076	2ND DIST
KALER, ISAAC	BAL	233	12TH WAR
KALER, JACOB	BAL	076	2ND DIST
KALER, WILLIAM	BAL	103	2ND DIST
KALFFUS, DANIEL	BAL	217	19TH WAR
KALFMAN, HENRY	BAL	123	18TH WAR
KALKENBACH, J. WILLIAM	BAL	018	15TH WAR
KALXENBACH, LOUISA	BAL	018	15TH WAR
KALKENBACH, WILLIAM	BAL	018	15TH WAR
KALKMAN CHARLES	BAL	317	1ST DIST
KALKMAN, ALEXANDER E.	ANN	462	HOWARD D
KALKMAN, CAROLINE	BAL	317	1ST DIST
KALKMAN, V. H.	BAL	101	10TH WAR
KALL, JOHN	BAL	204	2ND WARD
KALLARY, CATHERINE	BAL	003	9TH WARD
KALLFOUS, FREDERICK	BAL	319	7TH WARD
KALMAN, MARY	ALL	086	5TH E.D.
KALN, JACOB	BAL	072	2ND DIST
KALP, JOHN	BAL	384	1ST DIST
KALT, FLORENTINA	BAL	060	4TH WARD
KALTERBACK, CHRISTIAN	BAL	015	15TH WAR
KALVELAGE, JOHN	BAL	244	17TH WAR
KALVELEDGE, HENRY	BAL	286	17TH WAR
KAME, JOHN *	BAL	099	2ND DIST
KAMERAUGH, MATHEW	BAL	231	17TH WAR
KAMES, D.H.	WAS	006	WILLIAMS
KAMM, GERARD	BAL	095	10TH WAR
KAMM, JULIUS*	BAL	087	10TH WAR
KAMMARD, GEORGE	BAL	008	15TH WAR
KAMP, CATHARINE	ALL	021	2ND E.D.
KAMP, JOHN	ALL	020	2ND E.D.
KAMP, JOHN	ALL	020	2ND E.D.
KAMP, JONATHAN	ALL	012	3RD E.D.
KAMP, SOLOMON	WAS	221	1ST DIST
KAMPER, MARGARET	BAL	283	2ND WARD
KAMPHER, ANDREW	BAL	294	17TH WAR
KAN, DAVID*	TAL	056	EASTON D
KANADY, JAMES C.	HAR	130	2ND DIST
KANADY, THOMAS	BAL	313	1ST DIST
KANAGA, DAVID	FRE	061	FREDERIC
KANAN, JAMES	ALL	181	8TH E.D.
KANAN, JOHN	BAL	062	10TH WAR
KANAF, LOUIS	BAL	432	1ST DIST
KANAPRAS, ELIZABETH	BAL	335	13TH WAR
KANO, PATRICK	BAL	092	1ST WARD
KANO, REBECA	BAL	222	19TH WAR
KANDALL, WILLIAM	BAL	133	1ST WARD
KANDER, ELIZABETH	BAL	261	12TH WAR
KANDY, JACOB	BAL	071	2ND DIST
KANE, AMANDA	BAL	214	11TH WAR
KANE, AMELIA S.	BAL	069	15TH WAR
KANE, ANN	BAL	326	7TH WARD
KANE, ANNA	BAL	043	9TH WARD
KANE, ANNE	BAL	051	15TH WAR
KANE, BENJAMIN	FRE	177	5TH E DI
KANE, BENJAMIN-BLACK	CAR	079	NO TWP L
KANE, BRIDGET	BAL	368	8TH WARD
KANE, CHARLES	BAL	037	18TH WAR
KANE, CHARLOTTE	BAL	348	3RD WARD
KANE, CORNELIUS	BAL	069	2ND DIST
KANE, DAVID	BAL	132	1ST WARD
KANE, DAVID	BAL	356	3RD WARD
KANE, EMILY	BAL	215	11TH WAR
KANE, FRANCES	BAL	327	3RD WARD
KANE, GODLOVE K.	BAL	296	3RD WARD
KANE, GOERGE P.	BAL	207	11TH WAR
KANE, ISABELLA	BAL	185	2ND WARD
KANE, JAMES	BAL	246	2ND WARD
KANE, JAMES	BAL	380	8TH WARD
KANE, JAMES	BAL	176	11TH WAR
KANE, JAMES	BAL	076	10TH WAR
KANE, JAMES	HAR	113	2ND DIST
KANE, JOANNA	BAL	166	16TH WAR
KANE, JOHN	BAL	040	9TH WARD
KANE, JOHN	BAL	159	1ST WARD
KANE, JOHN	BAL	091	5TH WARD
KANE, JOHN	BAL	097	1ST WARD
KANE, JOHN	BAL	046	1ST WARD
KANE, JOHN	HAR	089	2ND DIST
KANE, JOHN	HAR	107	2ND DIST
KANE, JOHN	BAL	304	17TH WAR
KANE, JOHN	FRE	246	NEW MARK
KANE, LAURA	BAL	352	1ST DIST
KANE, LEWIS	BAL	308	20TH WAR
KANE, M.	FRE	200	5TH E DI
KANE, MARCELLES-BLACK	CAR	084	NO TWP L
KANE, MARGARET	BAL	024	9TH WARD
KANE, MARTHA	HAR	128	2ND DIST
KANE, MARY	BAL	170	11TH WAR
KANE, MARY	BAL	001	9TH WARD
KANE, MARY	BAL	377	8TH WARD
KANE, MARY	BAL	288	7TH WARD
KANE, MARY	BAL	405	3RD WARD
KANE, MARY A.	WAS	122	HAGERSTO
KANE, MARY-MULATTO	BAL	212	2ND WARD
KANE, MATHIAS	BAL	420	8TH WARD
KANE, MICHAEL	ALL	142	6TH E.D.
KANE, NANCY	BAL	462	14TH WAR
KANE, NELEY	BAL	367	8TH WARD
KANE, PATRICK	BAL	208	11TH WAR
KANE, PRINA	HAR	128	2ND DIST
KANE, R. D.	BAL	147	1ST WARD
KANE, RACHEL	BAL	313	20TH WAR
KANE, RICHARD	BAL	169	19TH WAR
KANE, RICHARD	BAL	085	15TH WAR
KANE, RICHARD	BAL	072	2ND DIST
KANE, ROSA	BAL	046	9TH WARD
KANE, SARAH	HAR	078	2ND DIST
KANE, SARAH C.	HAR	089	2ND DIST
KANE, THOMAS	MGM	381	ROCKERLE
KANE, THOMAS	BAL	073	18TH WAR
KANE, THOMAS	BAL	119	15TH WAR
KANE, THOMAS	ANN	461	HOWARD D
KANE, VIRGINIA	BAL	421	1ST DIST
KANE, W.	BAL	170	1ST WARD
KANE, WILLIAM	BAL	327	1ST DIST
KANE, WILLIAM	BAL	113	5TH WARD
KANE, WILLIAM	BAL	022	18TH WAR
KANE, WILLIAM	FRE	169	5TH E DI
KANE, WILLIAM H.	HAR	124	2ND DIST
KANE, WILLIAM H.	BAL	379	3RD WARD
KANFMAN, HENRY	BAL	158	2ND DIST
KANHAM, SIMON	BAL	259	2ND WARD
KANN, BERNHARD*	BAL	091	10TH WAR
KANN, JULIUS*	BAL	087	10TH WAR
KANN, LAKEY	BAL	217	2ND WARD
KANNADA, BENJAMIN	CEC	066	1ST E DI
KANNADA, JAMES	CEC	066	1ST E DI
KANNEKE, CHARLES	PRI	107	PISCATAW
KANNER, JOHN	BAL	055	1ST WARD
KANODE, DAVID	FRE	226	BUCKEYST
KANODE, JACOB	FRE	225	BUCKEYST
KANODE, JEREMIAH J.R.	FRE	230	BUCKEYST
KANODE, MARTIN R.	FRE	225	BUCKEYST
KANOUF, GEORGE	WAS	242	CAVETOWN
KANOUFF, GEORGE H.	FRE	224	BUCKEYST
KANOUFF, JOHN W.	FRE	219	BUCKEYST
KANOUFF, MARY A.	FRE	223	BUCKEYST
KANOUFF, MARY M.	FRE	224	BUCKEYST
KANSO, JOHN	BAL	113	1ST WARD
KANTNER, GEORGE	FRE	048	FREDERIC
KANTNER, JOHN	FRE	050	FREDERIC
KANTZ, MANTILLA	CAR	333	MANCHEST
KAOUFFE, MARY *	FRE	166	EMMITTSB
KAPERT, HENRY	BAL	192	19TH WAR
KAPLISE, HENRY	BAL	288	17TH WAR
KARBINE, THOMAS	WAS	132	HAGERSTO
KARE, DAVID*	TAL	056	EASTON D
KARE, ELIZA E.	TAL	077	EASTON T
KARGATE, SAMUEL	FRE	072	FREDERIC
KARIN, JOHN	BAL	281	2ND WARD
KARKLEY, JOHN W.	BAL	003	18TH WAR
KARLBORE, HENRY	BAL	030	1ST WARD
KARLES, CHRISTINA	BAL	454	8TH WARD
KARN, CHARLES	BAL	350	13TH WAR
KARN, EZRA L.	FRE	395	PETERSVI
KARN, GEORGE	FRE	397	PETERSVI
KARN, JOHN	BAL	087	15TH WAR
KARN, PATRICK	BAL	343	1ST DIST
KARN, PHILIP	FRE	393	PETERSVI
KARN, SARAH A.	FRE	394	PETERSVI
KARN, THOMAS P.	FRE	393	PETERSVI
KARNES, THOMAS	BAL	018	4TH WARD
KARNEY, JAMES	BAL	035	2ND DIST
KARNEY, JOHN	BAL	448	1ST DIST
KARNEY, JOHN	BAL	387	3RD WARD
KARNEY, MARY	BAL	411	1ST DIST
KARNEY, THOMAS	ANN	265	ANNAPOLI
KARNICA, MICHAEL	BAL	225	2ND WARD
KARNS, JOHN	BAL	183	16TH WAR
KARNS, MARGARETT	WAS	215	1ST DIST
KARNS, PATRICK	BAL	443	1ST DIST
KARNS, SOPHIA	WAS	206	1ST DIST
KARP, ANDREW	BAL	351	13TH WAR
KARPER, BARNEY	FRE	075	FREDERIC
KARR, ANNY	HAR	086	2ND DIST
KARRER, GEORGE	BAL	231	6TH WARD
KARRICHER, GEORGE	CAR	356	6TH DIST
KARRICK, MARY A.	BAL	410	1ST DIST
KARSER, JOSEPH	BAL	265	7TH WARD
KARSNER, DAVID F.	CEC	028	CHESAPEA
KARUS, CHARELS A.	BAL	378	13TH WAR
KARVER, BERNARD	BAL	258	20TH WAR
KASE, GEORGE L.	ANN	479	HOWARD D
KASE, JOHN	ANN	479	HOWARD D
KASHIEL, JOHN	BAL	390	3RD WARD
KASSINDIGHT, LEWIS	BAL	213	17TH WAR
KASSMAUL, GEORGE F.	FRE	083	FREDERIC
KASSOCK, JAMES M.	BAL	163	1ST WARD
KASTER, SARAH *.*	BAL	115	15TH WAR
KATARCH, FREDERICK	BAL	272	2ND WARD
KATCH, JAMES E.	CHA	275	ALLENS F
KATE, DANIEL	BAL	120	2ND DIST
KATELSTINE, PHILLIP	BAL	235	2ND WARD
KATENKAMF, DETRICK	BAL	182	19TH WAR
KATENKAMF, JULIA	BAL	182	19TH WAR
KATHE, GEORGE	BAL	185	19TH WAR
KATHMANN, JOHN	BAL	175	6TH WARD
KATIN, JOHN	BAL	222	19TH WAR
KATING, CAROLINE	BAL	254	2ND WARD
KATINGER, JACOB	WAS	122	2ND DIST
KATS, ADELINE	BAL	296	7TH WARD
KATTSHILL, JEMIMAH	WAS	128	2ND DIST
KATZ, EMMA	BAL	371	13TH WAR
KATZ, JOHN	BAL	371	13TH WAR
KATZBERGER, GEORGE	FRE	083	FREDERIC
KATZMILLER, ZEBULUM *	FRE	130	CREAGERS
KAUB, CHARLES	BAL	416	1ST DIST
KAUFFETT, JAMES B.	BAL	359	3RD WARD
KAUFFMAN, CHRISTOPHER	BAL	133	18TH WAR
KAUFFMAN, DANE	BAL	271	12TH WAR
KAUFFMAN, JACOB	BAL	068	2ND DIST
KAUFFMAN, JAMES W.	FRE	332	MIDDLETO
KAUFFMAN, JOHN C.	BAL	118	15TH WAR
KAUFFMAN, JOHN T.	HAR	062	1ST DIST
KAUFFMAN, LEWIS	BAL	139	16TH WAR
KAUFFMAN, MARGARET	BAL	118	15TH WAR
KAUFFMAN, MARTHA	WAS	190	1ST DIST
KAUFFMAN, NICHOLAS	BAL	378	8TH WARD
KAUFFMAN, THOMAS	BAL	034	2ND DIST
KAUFFMAN, WILLIAM	BAL	437	1ST DIST
KAUFMAN, ELIZABETH	FRE	082	FREDERIC
KAUFMAN, ELIZABETH	HAR	084	2ND DIST
KAUFMAN, FRED	BAL	437	1ST DIST
KAUFMAN, FREDERIC	BAL	254	6TH WARD
KAUFMAN, FREDERICKA	BAL	235	17TH WAR
KAUFMAN, HENRY	FRE	025	FREDERIC
KAUFMAN, HIRAM	BAL	214	19TH WAR
KAUFMAN, J.H.	BAL	229	19TH WAR
KAUFMAN, J.H.	BAL	229	19TH WAR
KAUFMAN, JESSE	BAL	214	19TH WAR
KAUFMAN, JOHN	FRE	063	FREDERIC
KAUFMAN, JOSEPH	BAL	226	17TH WAR
KAUFMAN, LAUREN *	FRE	064	FREDERIC
KAUFMAN, MARTIN L.	FRE	091	FREDERIC
KAUFMAN, MARY	BAL	407	14TH WAR
KAUFMAN, SOPHIA	BAL	250	2ND WARD
KAUFMAN, WARNER	FRE	014	FREDERIC
KAUFMAN, WILLIAM	FRE	063	FREDERIC
KAUGH, PETER	BAL	344	7TH WARD
KAULBUS, FREDERICK	BAL	052	1ST WARD
KAUM, S. J.	BAL	090	10TH WAR
KAUSLER, CATHARINE	WAS	135	HAGERSTO
KAVENAUGH, MARGARET	BAL	392	14TH WAR
KAY, GEORGE	HAR	057	1ST DIST
KAY, GEORGE	BAL	115	1ST WARD
KAY, J. M.	BAL	150	1ST WARD
KAY, J.M.	BAL	136	1ST WARD
KAY, JAMES	BAL	046	2ND DIST
KAY, JAMES	BAL	027	18TH WAR
KAY, JAMES	CEC	088	4TH E DI
KAY, MARTIN	BAL	461	1ST DIST
KAY, RACHAEL V.	FRE	396	PETERSVI
KAYLER, MARY	BAL	156	19TH WAR
KAYLINE, SUSANA	CAR	256	3RD DIST
KAYLOR, ELENA	BAL	014	18TH WAR
KAYLOR, GEORGE	BAL	017	9TH WARD
KAYLOR, GEORGE	BAL	447	8TH WARD
KAYLOR, HENRY	BAL	038	4TH WARD
KAYLOR, JOHN	BAL	011	18TH WAR
KAYLOR, JOHN	SOM	492	SALISBUR
KAYLOR, THOMAS	BAL	017	9TH WARD
KAYLOR, THOMAS	BAL	017	9TH WARD
KAYS, A.*	DOR	410	1ST DIST
KAYS, DOROTHY A.*	DOR	422	1ST DIST
KAYS, WILLIAM	BAL	138	1ST WARD
KAYTON, JOHN	BAL	018	1ST WARD
KAYTON, REBECCA	BAL	433	14TH WAR
KAYWOOD, ELLENORAH	FRE	331	MIDDLETO
KAYWOOD, GOERGE T.	ANN	286	ANNAPOLI
KAYWOOD,ELLENCR	ST	338	4TH E DI
KEACH, AARON	HAR	053	1ST DIST
KEACH, CATHARINE	BAL	051	2ND DIST
KEACH, CYRIL	BAL	041	9TH WARD
KEACH, ELISABETH	ALL	253	CUMBERLA
KEACH, HENRY	CEC	172	5TH E DI
KEACH, LAWSON P.	BAL	091	5TH WARD
KEACH, SAMUEL	ST	343	5TH E DI
KEACH, SUSANNA	ST	340	5TH E DI
KEAFAEVER, JACOB	FRE	322	MIDDLETO
KEAFAUVER, DANIEL *	FRE	319	MIDDLETO
KEAFAUVER, JOHN	BAL	425	14TH WAR
KEAFER, NICHOLAS	BAL	343	1ST DIST
KEAFEUWN, GEORGE *	FRE	322	MIDDLETO
KEAFRUWER, JOHN	FRE	316	MIDDLETO
KEAGEY, ABRAHAM	BAL	221	1ST DIST
KEAGLE, GEORGE	BAL	215	6TH WARD
KEAKIN, FRANCIS	BAL	310	20TH WAR
KEAKLE, FREDERICK	CAR	297	7TH DIST
KEALER, HEANTHA	BAL	241	1ST DIST
KEALHEFER, CATHARINE	WAS	125	HAGERSTO
KEALHOFER, GEORGE	WAS	132	HAGERSTO
KEALHOFER, JOHN	WAS	141	HAGERSTO
KEALPOFER, HENRY	WAS	132	HAGERSTO
KEAMER, JOHN	BAL	012	9TH WARD
KEAMER, JOHN D.	WAS	136	HAGERSTO
KEAN, ALEXANDER	BAL	170	1ST WARD
KEAN, ANN	BAL	141	19TH WAR
KEAN, ELIZABETH	FRE	066	FREDERIC
KEAN, GEORGE	BAL	080	2ND DIST
KEAN, JOHN	CAR	190	4TH DIST
KEAN, MICHAEL	ALL	051	10TH E.D
KEAN, WILLIAM	FRE	20	5TH E DI
KEAN,MICHAEL	BAL	097	1ST WARD
KEANE, HUGH	BAL	157	6TH WARD
KEANE, JOHN	BAL	038	9TH WARD
KEANNER, MARY	BAL	039	9TH WARD
KEANNY, CATHERINE	BAL	155	11TH WAR
KEANNY, DARBY	ALL	129	4TH E.D.
KEARIRN, ANN M.	BAL	243	2ND WARD
KEARL, CAHRLES F.	WAS	010	WILLIAMS
KEARMEY, ANN	BAL	316	20TH WAR
KEARN, ANN	CAR	105	NO TWP L
KEARNED, JOHN	BAL	021	2ND DIST
KEARNEY, ANDREW	HAR	083	2ND DIST
KEARNEY, BRIDGET	HAR	085	2ND DIST
KEARNEY, ELLEN	ALL	234	CUMBERLA
KEARNEY, FRANCIS	HAR	085	2ND DIST
KEARNEY, JOHN	HAR	086	2ND DIST
KEARNEY, JOHN	BAL	159	19TH WAR
KEARNEY, JOHN	ALL	223	CUMBERLA
KEARNEY, JOHN	ALL	246	CUMBERLA
KEARNEY, JOHN	WAS	162	HAGERSTO
KEARNEY, MATILDA	WAS	155	HAGERSTO
KEARNEY, MATTHEW	ALL	088	5TH E.D.
KEARNEY, MICHAEL	ALL	078	5TH E.D.
KEARNEY, PATRICK	BAL	120	16TH WAR
KEARNEY, PATRICK	HAR	085	2ND DIST
KEARNEY, ROSAN	WAS	291	1ST DIST
KEARNS, CATHERINE	BAL	406	3RD WARD
KEARNY, ISAAC	BAL	257	2ND WARD

Name	County	Page	District
KEARNY, JONATHAN	BAL	075	1ST WARD
KEARSHNER, ANDREW	WAS	298	1ST DIST
KEARSHNER, CANIEL	WAS	294	1ST DIST
KEARSHNER, CAVID	WAS	160	HAGERSTO
KEARSHNER, IRA	WAS	302	1ST DIST
KEARSHNER, ISIAH	WAS	302	1ST DIST
KEARSHNER, JONOTHAN	WAS	299	1ST DIST
KEARSHNER, SUSAN	WAS	267	1ST DIST
KEAS, ANDY	HAR	034	1ST DIST
KEAS, JOHN	HAR	034	1ST DIST
KEASLECKER, JACOB	WAS	290	1ST DIST
KEASLY, CHARLES A.	KEN	286	3RD DIST
KEATES, WILLIAM	BAL	160	1ST WARD
KEATES, WILLIAM	BAL	161	1ST WARD
KEATH, JANE A.C.	BAL	354	7TH WARD
KEATH, JOHN A.	HAR	036	1ST DIST
KEATH, SARAH	BAL	458	1ST DIST
KEATH, ZACHARIAH	BAL	216	6TH DIST
KEATH, ZACHARIAH	BAL	216	6TH DIST
KEATING, ELIZABETH	QUE	188	3RD E DI
KEATING, JAMES S.	BAL	126	1ST WARD
KEATING, MARY J.	FRE	065	FREDERIC
KEATINGE, JOHN	HAR	118	2ND DIST
KEATLY, WILLIAM	CEC	171	6TH E DI
KEATTEY, EDWARD T.	HAR	134	2ND DIST
KEATTING, TEMPERANCE	KEN	284	3RD DIST
KEATTING, WILLIAM	KEN	231	2ND DIST
KEATTING, WILLIAM	KEN	237	2ND DIST
KEATTY, JOHN	HAR	134	2ND DIST
KEAVE, WILLIAM	BAL	129	18TH WAR
KEAVER, CHRISTIAN	BAL	314	20TH WAR
KEAWER, URSULA M.	BAL	257	1ST DIST
KEAWORTH, CHARLES B.	BAL	405	1ST DIST
KEBBS, EDWARD*	TAL	051	EASTON D
KECK, ERNEST	BAL	281	12TH WAR
KECK, GEORGE	BAL	297	1ST DIST
KECK, JAMES*	TAL	065	EASTON T
KECK, SAMUEL *	BAL	292	1ST DIST
KECK, SAMUEL G.	BAL	292	1ST DIST
KECKLER, ELIZABETH	WAS	278	LEITERSB
KEDDEN, JAMES	BAL	163	1ST WARD
KEDDLE, SAMUEL	FRE	117	CREAGERS
KEE, ANN	WAS	150	HAGERSTO
KEE, LOUISA	CEC	163	6TH E DI
KEE, OSCAR	FRE	129	CREAGERS
KEE, WILLIM	TAL	071	EASTON T
KEEBER, DANE	BAL	225	12TH WAR
KEEBS, HARRIET	TAL	071	EASTON T
KEEBY, ELIZABETH	FRE	260	NEW MARK
KEECH, CATHARINE	PRI	056	AQUASCO
KEECH, JOHN	CHA	220	ALLENS F
KEECH, JOHN R.	HAR	079	2ND DIST
KEECH, WILLIAM S.	CHA	280	BOJANTOW
KEECK, JOHN E.	ST	345	5TH E DI
KEEDER, CHARLES	WAS	146	HAGERSTO
KEEDING, JOSEPH	WAS	190	1ST DIST
KEEDY, ALFRED	WAS	190	1ST DIST
KEEDY, D. H.	WAS	182	BOONSBOR
KEEDY, DANIEL	WAS	081	2ND SUBD
KEEDY, H.J.	WAS	038	2ND SUBD
KEEDY, HENRY	WAS	082	2ND SUBD
KEEDY, J. J.	WAS	190	1ST DIST
KEEDY, JACOB	WAS	197	1ST DIST
KEEDY, JELIS C.	WAS	182	BOONSBOR
KEEDY, JONAS	WAS	074	2ND SUBD
KEEDY, RACHEAL A.	WAS	190	1ST DIST
KEEDY, SAMUEL	WAS	190	1ST DIST
KEEEFER, MARY	WAS	142	HAGERSTO
KEEF, MICHAEL	FRE	065	FREDERIC
KEEF, WILLIAM	WAS	134	2ND DIST
KEEFE, CATHARINE	BAL	319	12TH WAR
KEEFE, CATHERINE	FRE	066	FREDERIC
KEEFE, NICHOALS	WAS	100	2ND DIST
KEEFE, NICKOLAS	WAS	024	2ND SUBD
KEEFE, WILLIAM	BAL	083	2ND DIST
KEEFER, ABRAM	ALL	188	9TH E.D.
KEEFER, ANN M.	FRE	053	FREDERIC
KEEFER, CATHARINE A.	CAR	242	TANEYTOW
KEEFER, CHARLES F.	FRE	032	FREDERIC
KEEFER, CHARLOTT	FRE	021	FREDERIC
KEEFER, CHRISTINA	FRE	064	FREDERIC
KEEFER, CHRISTOPHER	WAS	301	1ST DIST
KEEFER, DAVID	CAR	269	WESTMINS
KEEFER, DAVID	FRE	186	5TH E DI
KEEFER, CAVID	FRE	135	5TH E DI
KEEFER, DENNIS P.	FRE	064	FREDERIC
KEEFER, ELIZABETH	FRE	049	FREDERIC
KEEFER, FREDERICX	FRE	042	FREDERIC
KEEFER, FREDERICK	BAL	147	2ND DIST
KEEFER, GEORGE	CAR	408	2ND DIST
KEEFER, GEORGE	FRE	268	NEW MARK
KEEFER, GEORGE	WAS	100	2ND DIST
KEEFER, HIRAM	FRE	036	FREDERIC
KEEFER, ISAAC	CAR	408	2ND DIST
KEEFER, JACOB	FRE	207	BUCKEYST
KEEFER, JACOB	FRE	064	FREDERIC
KEEFER, JAMES	CAR	268	WESTMINS
KEEFER, JANE	CAR	386	2ND DIST
KEEFER, JOHN	FRE	041	FREDERIC
KEEFER, JOHN	FRE	280	WOODSBOR
KEEFER, JOHN	WAS	072	2ND SUBD
KEEFER, JOSEPH	FRE	433	8TH E DI
KEEFER, JOSEPH A.	FRE	164	EMMITTSB
KEEFER, LEWIS	FRE	108	CREAGERS
KEEFER, MARGARET	FRE	042	FREDERIC
KEEFER, MICHAEL	FRE	033	FREDERIC
KEEFER, MICHAL	WAS	139	2ND DIST
KEEFER, MOSES	WAS	150	HAGERSTO
KEEFER, NICHOLAS	FRE	032	FREDERIC
KEEFER, PETER	FRE	020	FREDERIC
KEEFER, ROSANNA	WAS	160	HAGERSTO
KEEFER, SAMUEL	FRE	140	CREAGERS
KEEFER, SAMUEL	FRE	280	WOODSBOR
KEEFER, THEADORE P.	FRE	064	FREDERIC
KEEFER, THEOBALD	WAS	160	HAGERSTO
KEEFER, THOMAS	CAR	307	1ST DIST
KEEFER, WILLIAM	FRE	128	CREAGERS
KEEFER, WILLIAM	CAR	382	2ND DIST
KEEFER, WILLIAM	BAL	102	18TH WAR
KEEFER,EPHRAIM	CAR	408	2ND DIST
KEEFHOVER, GEORGE W. *	WAS	185	BOONSBOR
KEEGAN, JOHN	BAL	166	16TH WAR
KEEHAN, MICHEAL	BAL	104	18TH WAR
KEEHUE, AUGUSTUS	BAL	045	1ST WARD
KEELAN, M. SIS- *	BAL	062	18TH WAR
KEELAND, CATHERINE	BAL	395	8TH WARD
KEELCUFF, GEORGE	QUE	124	1ST E DI
KEELEN, PATRICK	BAL	033	4TH WARD
KEELER, ELIZABETH	BAL	133	16TH WAR
KEELER, FREDERICK	ALL	263	CUMBERLA
KEELER, JOHN H.	ALL	239	CUMBERLA
KEELER, WILLIAM	CAR	340	6TH DIST
KEELEY, MARY	BAL	193	11TH WAR
KEELEY, STEPHEN	BAL	021	9TH WARD
KEELHOLTZ, WILLIAM	BAL	297	12TH WAR
KEELING, FREDERICK *	BAL	284	1ST DIST
KEELOR, MARY	BAL	058	10TH WAR
KEELTY, RICHARD	BAL	100	18TH WAR
KEELY, MATILDA*	TAL	041	EASTON D
KEELY, PATRICK H.	BAL	267	20TH WAR
KEELY, SARAH	PRI	096	SPALDING
KEELY, WILLMOT*	TAL	045	EASTON T
KEEM, STEWART	DOR	372	3RD DIVI
KEEMER, HARRIET	BAL	078	15TH WAR
KEEMER, JESSEE	KEN	257	1ST DIST
KEEN, A.D.	HAR	177	3RD DIST
KEEN, ADAM	BAL	429	8TH WARD
KEEN, AQUILLA	HAR	163	3RD DIST
KEEN, B.H.	HAR	163	3RD DIST
KEEN, BENJAMIN G.	DOR	334	3RD DIVI
KEEN, CHARLES	DOR	371	3RD DIVI
KEEN, CHARLES T.-BLACK	QUE	143	1ST E DI
KEEN, DANIEL	DOR	367	3RD DIVI
KEEN, DECLAN	HAR	186	3RD DIST
KEEN, DRAPER	DOR	368	3RD DIVI
KEEN, DRAPER	DOR	372	3RD DIVI
KEEN, DRAPER	DOR	367	3RD DIVI
KEEN, DUKE	DOR	366	3RD DIVI
KEEN, EDWARD	BAL	262	1ST DIST
KEEN, EMILA	DOR	372	3RD DIVI
KEEN, FREDERICK	BAL	080	1ST WARD
KEEN, GANDLAMP	BAL	216	2ND WARD
KEEN, GEORGE	BAL	164	2ND DIST
KEEN, GEORGE N.	BAL	023	4TH WARD
KEEN, GEORGE W.	DOR	372	3RD DIVI
KEEN, JACOB-BLACK	QUE	142	1ST E DI
KEEN, JAMES	DOR	370	3RD DIVI
KEEN, JAMES	QUE	160	2ND E DI
KEEN, JAMES S.	QUE	151	1ST E DI
KEEN, JOHN	DOR	365	3RD DIVI
KEEN, JOHN R.	DOR	326	3RD DIVI
KEEN, JOHN-BLACK	QUE	155	2ND E DI
KEEN, JOHN-BLACK	QUE	176	2ND E DI
KEEN, JOSEPH	BAL	250	2ND WARD
KEEN, JOSIAH	DOR	365	3RD DIVI
KEEN, JULIA A.	QUE	134	1ST E DI
KEEN, L.L.	HAR	163	3RD DIST
KEEN, LEVEN	DOR	356	3RD DIVI
KEEN, LEVEN L.	DOR	334	3RD DIVI
KEEN, MARCELUS D.	DOR	326	3RD DIVI
KEEN, MARGRET	DOR	369	3RD DIVI
KEEN, MARY	DOR	332	3RD DIVI
KEEN, MARY	DOR	361	3RD DIVI
KEEN, MARY S.	BAL	157	16TH WAR
KEEN, MARY-BLACK	QUE	179	2ND E DI
KEEN, MOSES	ANN	320	2ND DIST
KEEN, MOSES L.	DOR	372	3RD DIVI
KEEN, MURREY	DOR	368	3RD DIVI
KEEN, NATHANIEL B.	HAR	163	3RD DIST
KEEN, NED	ANN	320	2ND DIST
KEEN, PATRICK	HAR	175	3RD DIST
KEEN, ROBERT	DOR	360	3RD DIVI
KEEN, SARRAH	DOR	362	3RD DIVI
KEEN, STEPHEN	DOR	334	3RD DIVI
KEEN, SUSAN	DOR	333	3RD DIVI
KEEN, THOMAS	CEC	060	1ST E DI
KEEN, VACHEL	DOR	356	3RD DIVI
KEEN, WILLIAM	DOR	360	3RD DIVI
KEEN, WILLIAM	BAL	459	1ST DIST
KEEN, WILLIAM-BLACK	QUE	148	1ST E DI
KEEN, WILLIAM-BLACK	QUE	148	1ST E DI
KEENAN, AN R.	BAL	006	18TH WAR
KEENAN, ANN	BAL	234	20TH WAR
KEENAN, ANN	BAL	257	12TH WAR
KEENAN, BRIDGET	BAL	356	13TH WAR
KEENAN, BRIDGETT	BAL	036	4TH WARD
KEENAN, DANIEL	BAL	027	18TH WAR
KEENAN, DANIEL	BAL	050	15TH WAR
KEENAN, EDWARD	BAL	127	11TH WAR
KEENAN, ELIZABETH	BAL	102	10TH WAR
KEENAN, FREDRICX	BAL	050	18TH WAR
KEENAN, HENRY	PRI	107	PISCATAW
KEENAN, JAMES*	BAL	070	10TH WAR
KEENAN, JOHN	FRE	203	5TH E DI
KEENAN, JOSEPH A.	BAL	231	19TH WAR
KEENAN, MARGARET	BAL	194	19TH WAR
KEENAN, MARGARET	BAL	050	15TH WAR
KEENAN, MARGARETT*	BAL	036	4TH WARD
KEENAN, MARY ANN	BAL	433	14TH WAR
KEENAN, MICHAEL	BAL	199	2ND WARD
KEENAN, PATRICK	ALL	055	10TH E.D
KEENAN, SIMON	BAL	068	4TH WARD
KEENAN, WILLIAM	BAL	138	11TH WAR
KEENAN,MARY	FRE	203	5TH E DI
KEENE, BENJAMIN	DOR	423	1ST DIST
KEENE, CHARELS	BAL	146	1ST WARD
KEENE, CHARLES*	DOR	356	3RD DIVI
KEENE, EMILY J.	BAL	078	15TH WAR
KEENE, EUGENE L.	DOR	413	1ST DIST
KEENE, HENRY	DOR	413	1ST DIST
KEENE, JAMES	BAL	032	9TH WARD
KEENE, JOHN	BAL	182	16TH WAR
KEENE, JOHN	DOR	394	1ST DIST
KEENE, JCHN	BAL	054	4TH WARD
KEENE, JOHN H.	BAL	177	2ND DIST
KEENE, JOHN R.	DOR	412	1ST DIST
KEENE, JOHNY.	CAR	134	NO TWP L
KEENE, LENOX R.	BAL	075	15TH WAR
KEENE, LETTIE*	DOR	470	1ST DIST
KEENE, LEVANNA	DOR	469	1ST DIST
KEENE, MARY	HAR	137	2ND DIST
KEENE, MARY A.	DOR	413	1ST DIST
KEENE, PETE	DOR	413	1ST DIST
KEENE, PETER	DOR	421	1ST DIST
KEENE, RICHARD A.	DOR	427	1ST DIST
KEENE, SAMUEL	DOR	359	3RD DIVI
KEENE, SIMEON-BLACK	QUE	126	1ST E DI
KEENE, THOMAS	DOR	356	3RD DIVI
KEENE, WESTLEY	DOR	361	3RD DIVI
KEENEN, JOSEPH	BAL	087	10TH WAR
KEENER, ANTHONY	BAL	006	4TH WARD
KEENER, BRIDGET	BAL	453	14TH WAR
KEENER, C.H.	BAL	137	1ST WARD
KEENER, CHRISTIAN	BAL	071	15TH WAR
KEENER, DAVID	BAL	262	1ST DIST
KEENER, DAVID	BAL	387	13TH WAR
KEENER, FREDERICK	BAL	277	7TH WARD
KEENER, JOHN	BAL	033	9TH WARD
KEENER, LEWIS	BAL	392	14TH WAR
KEENER, MARY	HAR	099	2ND DIST
KEENER, SOPHIA	BAL	071	15TH WAR
KEENER, WILLIAM C.	BAL	450	8TH WARD
KEENNGH, JAMES *	BAL	069	18TH WAR
KEENRIGHT, NICHOLAS	BAL	070	18TH WAR
KEEPEE, HENRY	TAL	105	ST MICHA
KEEPER, ADELINE	CEC	151	PORT DUP
KEEPER, DORATHY	CEC	147	PORT DUP
KEEPER, SOPHIA	FRE	097	FREDERIC
KEEPER.S JOSEPH	FRE	186	5TH E DI
KEEPERS, CECELIA	FRE	161	EMMITTSB
KEEPERS, JOHN B.	FRE	185	5TH E DI
KEEPERS, MARY A.	BAL	316	20TH WAR
KEEPHOVER, GEORGE W.	WAS	185	BOONSBOR
KEER, CHARLES	WAS	149	2ND DIST
KEER, JAMES	BAL	009	18TH WAR
KEER, JAMES	HAR	198	3RD DIST
KEER, JOHN	BAL	085	18TH WAR
KEER, SAMUEL	WAS	143	2ND DIST
KEERFOOT, BARBARY	WAS	174	FUNKSTOW
KEERITH, JAMES	BAL	037	18TH WAR
KEERL, JOHN C.	BAL	467	14TH WAR
KEERL, MARTHA	BAL	467	14TH WAR
KEERLE, MARY A.-MULATTO	BAL	208	2ND WARD
KEERLE, WILLIAM	BAL	007	18TH WAR
KEERO, WILLIAM	HAR	183	3RD DIST
KEERTA, WILLIAM	BAL	230	2ND WARD
KEES, ANN	BAL	157	6TH WARD
KEES, ANTHONY	TAL	077	EASTON T
KEES, JAMES	CEC	168	6TH E DI
KEES, JAMES	CEC	170	6TH E DI
KEES, MARGARET	CEC	166	6TH E DI
KEES, MARGARET	CEC	023	ELKTON 3
KEES, RICHARD	BAL	136	5TH WARD
KEES, SALLY	CAR	267	WESTMINS
KEESE, DAVID L.	CAR	245	3RD DIST
KEESE, JACOB J.	CAR	245	3RD DIST
KEESFOOT, BARBARY *	WAS	174	FUNKSTOW
KEESMACH, EMILY	BAL	218	17TH WAR
KEESSER, JOHN	BAL	302	3RD WARD
KEETH, JACOB	FRE	449	8TH E DI
KEETHLEY, JOHN	TAL	081	ST MICHA
KEETING, GEORGE	HAR	150	3RD DIST
KEETS, JOHN	QUE	240	5TH E DI
KEETS, MARY	CAR	068	NO TWP L
KEETS, PERDUE	CAR	084	NO TWP L
KEETZ, JAMES H.	TAL	082	ST MICHA
KEEVE, JOHN N.	PRI	065	NOTTINGH
KEEVEL, CLANCY	BAL	382	8TH WARD
KEEVER, JOHN	BAL	064	18TH WAR
KEEVER, MARY A.	BAL	252	20TH WAR
KEEVER, SAMUEL	BAL	460	1ST DIST
KEFAUER, GEORGE	WAS	082	2ND SUBD
KEFAURER, HENRY	WAS	085	2ND SUBD
KEFAURER, JOHN SR.	WAS	079	2ND SUBD
KEFAURER, SUSAN	WAS	080	2ND SUBD
KEFAURER, THEODORE	WAS	085	2ND SUBD
KEFEEBRING, JOHN *	FRE	370	CATOCTIN
KEFEEBRING, SAMUEL	FRE	370	CATOCTIN
KEFFER, JOHN	BAL	011	15TH WAR
KEFFER, SINAH	BAL	011	15TH WAR
KEFLER, PAWLES	BAL	277	1ST DIST
KEFOVER, MARY	ALL	034	2ND E.D.
KEGG, ELIZA A.	BAL	061	18TH WAR
KEGHT, EMANUEL	ALL	118	5TH E.D.
KEGLOW, JACOB	CAR	299	1ST DIST
KEGLOW, JACOB	CAR	299	1ST DIST
KEGRIER, MICHAEL	BAL	074	2ND DIST
KEHIN, ALEXANDER	BAL	221	12TH WAR
KEHLER, GEORGE	BAL	282	1ST DIST
KEHLER, MARY	ALL	258	CUMBERLA
KEHLY, PHILIP	BAL	257	1ST DIST
KEHN, EDWARD	FRE	432	8TH E DI
KEHN, JOHN	CAR	240	TANEYTOW
KEHNER, JOHN	BAL	176	2ND WARD
KEHO, MARY	BAL	109	1ST WARD
KEHOE, ELIZA	BAL	055	9TH WARD
KEHOE, JAMES	BAL	028	9TH WARD
KEHOE, JOHN	BAL	194	19TH WAR
KEHOE, PATRICK	ANN	412	HOWARD D
KEHOE, THOMAS	BAL	012	2ND DIST
KEHOE,TIMOTHY	BAL	064	1ST WARD
KEHOU, MARY E.	BAL	215	11TH WAR
KEHRBAUGH, MARY	CAR	247	3RD DIST
KEIBY, JOHN *	KEN	213	2ND DIST
KEICH, JAMES	ST	345	5TH E DI
KEICH, JAMES F.	ST	343	5TH E DI
KEICH, JOHN H.	CHA	217	ALLENS F
KEICHNE, ELIZABETH	FRE	024	FREDERIC
KEIDIGER, HENRY	BAL	255	2ND WARD
KEIFER, DANIEL	WAS	147	2ND DIST
KEIFER, GEORGE	WAS	147	2ND DIST
KEIFER, GEORGE	ALL	188	9TH E.D.
KEIFER, GEORGE	ALL	190	9TH E.D.
KEIFER, HENRY	ALL	188	9TH E.D.
KEIFER, HENRY	BAL	131	5TH WARD
KEIFER, JACOB	ALL	188	9TH E.D.
KEIFER, JACOB	CAR	307	1ST DIST
KEIFER, LEWIS	CAR	359	9TH DIST
KEIFER, MARTHA	CAR	307	1ST DIST
KEIFER, MARY J.	WAS	257	1ST DIST
KEIFER, PAUL	ANN	427	HOWARD D
KEIFF, MICHAEL O.	BAL	108	5TH WARD
KEIGHLER, JOHN	BAL	311	7TH WARD
KEIGHLER, JOHN	BAL	440	8TH WARD
KEIGHNER, JOHN	BAL	391	3RD WARD
KEIGHTEN, MARY	BAL	146	11TH WAR
KEIGHTER, MARY	BAL	146	11TH WAR
KEIHOLTZ, CHARLES	BAL	134	18TH WAR
KEIK, GEORGE	BAL	224	2ND WARD
KEIL, CATHARINE	BAL	023	15TH WAR
KEIL, JOHN	BAL	023	15TH WAR
KEIL, JOSEPH	ALL	036	10TH E.D
KEILER, JACOB	WAS	207	1ST DIST
KEILER, LILIA	WAS	216	1ST DIST
KEILER, THOMAS	WAS	207	1ST DIST
KEILEY, M.	BAL	137	1ST WARD
KEILHOLTY, WILLIAM	BAL	050	18TH WAR
KEILHOLTZ, JACOB	BAL	180	16TH WAR
KEILING, FREDERICK *	BAL	284	1ST DIST
KEILMAN, DAVID	ALL	086	5TH E.D.
KEILMAN, JACOB *	ALL	086	5TH E.D.
KEILMUTTZ, JACOB	BAL	339	3RD WARD
KEILY, EDWARD	BAL	123	18TH WAR
KEIM, BARBARA	CAR	395	2ND DIST
KEIMON, DANIEL	BAL	098	18TH WAR
KEIN, GEORGE	HAR	188	3RD DIST
KEIN, JAMES W.	HAR	164	3RD DIST
KEINAN, MARGARETT*	BAL	036	4TH WARD
KEINS, JOSEPH	FRE	299	WOODSBOR
KEINSTER, WILLIAM	BAL	268	2ND WARD

KEIPER, CHRISTIAN WAS 160 HAGERSTO
KEIPER, GEORGE WAS 147 HAGERSTO
KEIR, JOHN W. DOR 447 1ST DIST
KEIR, JOSIAH* DOR 447 1ST DIST
KEIRLE, GEORGE H. BAL 446 14TH WAR
KEIRLE, HENRY * BAL 298 20TH WAR
KEIRLE, JOHN W.* BAL 312 3RD WARD
KEIRLE, MATHEW BAL 124 11TH WAR
KEIRLE, ROBERT BAL 127 1ST WARD
KEIRLE, THOMAS BAL 160 11TH WAR
KEIS, BRUTUS BAL 120 5TH WARD
KEISEL, JOHN BAL 335 7TH WARD
KEISER, DANIEL CAR 252 3RD DIST
KEISER, HENRY BAL 289 17TH WAR
KEISER, JOHN BAL 050 15TH WAR
KEISER, JOHN ALL 197 CUMBERLA
KEISER, JOSEHP BAL 082 15TH WAR
KEISER, LUDWIG WAS 124 HAGERSTO
KEISER, NICHOLAS BAL 050 15TH WAR
KEISER, PHEBE CAR 302 1ST DIST
KEISLER, FANDREW FRE 209 BUCKEYST
KEISLER, HENRY BAL 222 17TH WAR
KEISLER, HERMINANS BAL 070 1ST WARD
KEISLER, MICHAEL BAL 280 1ST DIST
KEISLIN, ANDREW BAL 259 2ND WARD
KEISMOBEL, FREDERICK BAL 373 13TH WAR
KEISNER, MICHAEL BAL 081 1ST WARD
KEISON, T. BAL 281 2ND WARD
KEISTER, ANN BAL 229 6TH WARD
KEISTER, EDWARD T.H. BAL 091 5TH WARD
KEISTER, MARY BAL 080 1ST WARD
KEITCH, GEORGE PRI 021 VANSVILL
KEITEL, A.C. BAL 213 19TH WAR
KEITH, CANIEL BAL 024 1ST WARD
KEITH, EMIL BAL 296 3RD WARD
KEITH, GEORGE MGM 338 CRACKLIN
KEITH, HORATIO MGM 372 BERRYS D
KEITH, HUGH BAL 186 19TH WAR
KEITH, JOHN BAL 245 6TH WARD
KEITH, JOHN H. PRI 027 VANSVILL
KEITH, JOHN-MULATTO BAL 222 2ND WARD
KEITH, JOSEPH BAL 244 6TH WARD
KEITH, MARTIN JR. BAL 150 11TH WAR
KEITH, MARY FRE 066 FREDERIC
KEITH, SARAH BAL 187 19TH WAR
KEITH, TIMOTHY ANN 468 HOWARD D
KEITH, WILLIAM ANN 446 HOWARD D
KEITMILLER, HENRY BAL 239 17TH WAR
KEITTRLY, JANE BAL 225 2ND WARD
KEITZ, HENRY L. BAL 090 5TH WARD
KEIZER, GEORGE HAR 143 2ND DIST
KELAN, MICHAEL BAL 233 2ND WARD
KELAND, JOHN BAL 460 1ST DIST
KELBAUGH, ADAM CAR 191 4TH DIST
KELBAUGH, CHRISTIAN BAL 186 5TH DIST
KELBAUGH, ELIZABETH BAL 196 5TH DIST
KELBAUGH, HENRY CAR 181 8TH DIST
KELBAUGH, JOHN CAR 171 8TH DIST
KELBAUGH, JOHN BAL 191 19TH WAR
KELBAUGH, JOHN BAL 028 2ND DIST
KELBAUGH, SAMUE CAR 201 4TH DIST
KELBAUGH, WILLIAM BAL 195 5TH DIST
KELBERGER, DAVID BAL 253 12TH WAR
KELDOW, GEORGE W. ALL 124 4TH E.D.
KELEN, RUDOLPH FRE 267 NEW MARK
KELENBECK, JOHN ALL 070 5TH E.D.
KELEON, TERRENCE ALL 136 4TH E.D.
KELER, JOHN BAL 406 8TH WARD
KELES, SUSAN ALL 037 2ND E.D.
KELEY, MICHAEL ALL 155 6TH E.D.
KELGALLON, JOHN ALL 139 6TH E.D.
KELGAM, ELIZABETH MGM 398 ROCKERLE
KELHIOUSE, FREDERICK ALL 200 CUMBERLA
KELIGENBERG, ALEXANDER BAL 356 13TH WAR
KELIGIAR, MARTHA M. ST 344 5TH E DI
KELISON, ROBERT CHA 246 HILLTOP
KELKERRER, SARAH ALL 101 5TH E.D.
KELL, DARKESS BAL 119 18TH WAR
KELL, FRANCIS HAR 130 2ND DIST
KELL, GEORGE HAR 130 2ND DIST
KELL, GEORGE HAR 082 2ND DIST
KELL, MARIA HAR 092 2ND DIST
KELL, MARTHA HAR 051 1ST DIST
KELL, MARY HAR 052 1ST DIST
KELL, MARY BAL 100 2ND DIST
KELL, POWELL BAL 275 2ND WARD
KELL, SARAH HAR 082 2ND DIST
KELL, SUSAN BAL 111 5TH WARD
KELL, THOMAS HAR 131 2ND DIST
KELL, VINCENT HAR 174 3RD DIST
KELL, VINCENT HAR 174 3RD DIST
KELL, WILLIAM HAR 175 3RD DIST
KELLAND, JAMES PRI 108 PISCATAW
KELLAR, CONRAD BAL 074 1ST WARD
KELLAR, JACOB BAL 402 14TH WAR
KELLAR, JACOB B. FRE 243 NEW MARK
KELLAR, MARY FRE 259 NEW MARK
KELLAR, NATHAN WAS 077 2ND SUBD
KELLAR, THOMAS WAS 024 2ND SUBD
KELLARD, THOMAS ALL 109 5TH E.D.
KELLAY, MICHAEL* BAL 031 4TH WARD
KELLEN, WILLIAM BAL 057 2ND DIST
KELLENBERGER, JOHN H. MGM 395 ROCKERLE
KELLER, ABRAHAM BAL 215 6TH DIST
KELLER, ADAM FRE 315 MIDDLETO
KELLER, ANN FRE 044 FREDERIC
KELLER, ANN M. FRE 400 JEFFERSO
KELLER, BARBARA FRE 030 FREDERIC
KELLER, BENJAMIN ALL 038 2ND E.D.
KELLER, BENJAMIN WAS 043 2ND SUBD
KELLER, C.W. BAL 139 1ST WARD
KELLER, CATHERINE FRE 025 FREDERIC
KELLER, CATHERINE BAL 109 18TH WAR
KELLER, CHARLES FRE 025 FREDERIC
KELLER, CHARLES BAL 044 4TH WARD
KELLER, CHARLES BAL 080 10TH WAR
KELLER, CLARENCE FRE 051 FREDERIC
KELLER, CLARISSA BAL 296 1ST DIST
KELLER, CROLINE FRE 322 MIDDLETO
KELLER, DAVID FRE 311 MIDDLETO
KELLER, CAVID FRE 398 JEFFERSO
KELLER, CAVID FRE 391 PETERSVI
KELLER, CAVID BAL 204 6TH WARD
KELLER, ELIAS FRE 116 CREAGERS
KELLER, ELIZA BAL 088 10TH WAR
KELLER, ELIZABETH FRE 402 JEFFERSO
KELLER, ELIZABETH FRE 318 MIDDLETO
KELLER, ELIZABETH BAL 044 4TH WARD
KELLER, FRANCES BAL 166 2ND DIST
KELLER, FRANCES M. ALL 197 CUMBERLA
KELLER, FREDERICK FRE 445 8TH E DI
KELLER, FREDERICK H. FRE 023 FREDERIC
KELLER, GEORGE BAL 354 13TH WAR
KELLER, GEORGE FRE 315 MIDDLETO
KELLER, GEORGE ALL 038 2ND E.D.
KELLER, GEORGE BAL 252 2ND WARD
KELLER, GEORGE W. BAL 269 7TH WARD
KELLER, HARRIET BAL 189 5TH DIST
KELLER, HENRY BAL 098 1ST WARD
KELLER, HENRY FRE 049 FREDERIC
KELLER, HENRY FRE 347 MIDDLETO
KELLER, HENRY CAR 357 6TH DIST
KELLER, HENRY H. CAR 186 8TH DIST
KELLER, JACOB BAL 083 10TH WAR
KELLER, JACOB WAS 130 HAGERSTO
KELLER, JAMES BAL 053 9TH WARD
KELLER, JAMES BAL 180 6TH WARD
KELLER, JAOCB FRE 041 FREDERIC
KELLER, JOEL FRE 320 MIDDLETO
KELLER, JOHN BAL 296 1ST DIST
KELLER, JOHN ALL 196 CUMBERLA
KELLER, JOHN BAL 457 8TH WARD
KELLER, JOHN WAS 206 1ST DIST
KELLER, JOHN F. BAL 294 7TH WARD
KELLER, JOHN H. BAL 016 9TH WARD
KELLER, JOHN H. FRE 398 JEFFERSO
KELLER, JOHN P. FRE 307 WOODSBOR
KELLER, JONATHAN FRE 230 BUCKEYST
KELLER, JONATHAN FRE 347 MIDDLETO
KELLER, JOSEPH BAL 354 13TH WAR
KELLER, JOSEPH BAL 295 7TH WARD
KELLER, JOSEPH ALL 149 6TH E.D.
KELLER, JOSEPH BAL 215 6TH DIST
KELLER, JOSEPH BAL 430 1ST DIST
KELLER, JOSEPH C. FRE 206 BUCKEYST
KELLER, JOSHUA BAL 415 1ST DIST
KELLER, JOSIAH BAL 202 19TH WAR
KELLER, LUCINDA ALL 027 2ND E.D.
KELLER, MALINDA FRE 352 MIDDLETO
KELLER, MALINDA FRE 208 BUCKEYST
KELLER, MARGARET BAL 218 19TH WAR
KELLER, MARGARET BAL 099 2ND DIST
KELLER, MARY A. BAL 103 18TH WAR
KELLER, MARY E. WAS 130 HAGERSTO
KELLER, MILTON ALL 219 CUMBERLA
KELLER, N. J. BAL 276 20TH WAR
KELLER, OTHA S. BAL 285 7TH WARD
KELLER, PETER ALL 176 7TH E.D.
KELLER, PHILIP BAL 307 7TH WARD
KELLER, PHILIP BAL 201 5TH DIST
KELLER, PHILIP CAR 354 6TH DIST
KELLER, PHILIP WAS 130 HAGERSTO
KELLER, REBECCA WAS 127 HAGERSTO
KELLER, ROSANNA FRE 317 MIDDLETO
KELLER, SAMUEL ALL 036 2ND E.D.
KELLER, SARAH BAL 215 6TH DIST
KELLER, SARAH WAS 140 HAGERSTO
KELLER, SARAH A. BAL 381 8TH WARD
KELLER, SARAH C. ALL 057 10TH E.D
KELLER, SARAH J. BAL 403 1ST DIST
KELLER, SOLOMON WAS 286 1ST DIST
KELLER, THOMAS A. ALL 057 10TH E.D
KELLER, WILLIAM ALL 165 6TH E.D.
KELLER, WILLIAM ALL 196 CUMBERLA
KELLER, WILLIAM BAL 133 5TH WARD
KELLER, WILLIAM BAL 227 1ST DIST
KELLER, WILLIAM FRE 347 MIDDLETO
KELLER, WILLIAM H. FRE 016 FREDERIC
KELLER, WILLIAM H. WAS 133 2ND DIST
KELLER, WILLIAM J. BAL 319 20TH WAR
KELLER,A. BAL 285 12TH WAR
KELLER,LOUISA FRE 016 FREDERIC
KELLER,MARY FRE 425 8TH E DI
KELLEY, ANDREW J. PRI 033 VANSVILL
KELLEY, ANN SOM 443 DAMES QU
KELLEY, ANN BAL 026 4TH WARD
KELLEY, ANN CEC 105 3RD E DI
KELLEY, ANN B. FRE 063 FREDERIC
KELLEY, B.B. BAL 137 5TH WARD
KELLEY, BARNEY BAL 374 1ST DIST
KELLEY, BENJAMIN BAL 397 8TH WARD
KELLEY, BESSEY BAL 438 8TH WARD
KELLEY, BRIDGET BAL 409 8TH WARD
KELLEY, CATHARINE BAL 252 1ST DIST
KELLEY, CATHERINE BAL 390 8TH WARD
KELLEY, CATHERINE BAL 356 8TH WARD
KELLEY, CATHERINE E. FRE 051 FREDERIC
KELLEY, CORNELIUS A. BAL 013 2ND DIST
KELLEY, DANIE ALL 050 10TH E.D
KELLEY, EDMUND ALL 044 10TH E.D
KELLEY, EDWARD BAL 022 2ND DIST
KELLEY, EDWARD HAR 035 1ST DIST
KELLEY, EDWARD WOR 311 2ND E DI
KELLEY, ELIZA BAL 109 5TH WARD
KELLEY, ELIZABETH-BLACK QUE 132 1ST E DI
KELLEY, ELLEN BAL 307 3RD WARD
KELLEY, ELLEN BAL 366 3RD WARD
KELLEY, ELLEN PRI 030 VANSVILL
KELLEY, FREDERICK FRE 053 FREDERIC
KELLEY, G. B. BAL 152 1ST WARD
KELLEY, GEORGE BAL 060 1ST WARD
KELLEY, GEORGE BAL 132 1ST WARD
KELLEY, HENRY FRE 051 FREDERIC
KELLEY, HENRY BAL 288 17TH WAR
KELLEY, HUGH BAL 408 8TH WARD
KELLEY, JACOB HAR 010 1ST DIST
KELLEY, JAMES FRE 054 FREDERIC
KELLEY, JAMES FRE 076 FREDERIC
KELLEY, JAMES BAL 416 8TH WARD
KELLEY, JAMES BAL 146 1ST WARD
KELLEY, JAMES BAL 141 1ST WARD
KELLEY, JAMES BAL 158 1ST WARD
KELLEY, JAMES BAL 118 5TH WARD
KELLEY, JAMES ALL 240 CUMBERLA
KELLEY, JAMES ALL 052 10TH E.D
KELLEY, JAMES BAL 349 7TH WARD
KELLEY, JOHN BAL 446 8TH WARD
KELLEY, JOHN BAL 460 8TH WARD
KELLEY, JOHN ALL 053 10TH E.D
KELLEY, JOHN ALL 053 10TH E.D
KELLEY, JOHN BAL 114 2ND DIST
KELLEY, JOHN BAL 405 8TH WARD
KELLEY, JOHN BAL 408 8TH WARD
KELLEY, JOHN CAR 188 4TH DIST
KELLEY, JOHN KEN 299 3RD DIST
KELLEY, JOHN C. BAL 114 11TH WAR
KELLEY, JOHN J. BAL 279 2ND WARD
KELLEY, JOHN T. BAL 363 1ST DIST
KELLEY, JONAH DOR 313 1ST DIST
KELLEY, JOSEPH BAL 155 1ST WARD
KELLEY, JOSHUA KEN 312 3RD DIST
KELLEY, LARILLA FRE 103 FREDERIC
KELLEY, LEVI CAR 203 4TH DIST
KELLEY, LOFTUS BAL 139 5TH WARD
KELLEY, LYDIA FRE 063 FREDERIC
KELLEY, MARCUS BAL 127 1ST WARD
KELLEY, MARGARET BAL 389 8TH WARD
KELLEY, MARTIN BAL 454 8TH WARD
KELLEY, MARY BAL 424 8TH WARD
KELLEY, MARY BAL 286 7TH WARD
KELLEY, MARY BAL 375 3RD WARD
KELLEY, MARY A. BAL 363 8TH WARD
KELLEY, MARY J. BAL 150 5TH WARD
KELLEY, MICHAEL BAL 367 8TH WARD
KELLEY, MICHAEL* BAL 031 4TH WARD
KELLEY, NICHOLAS CAR 188 4TH DIST
KELLEY, OLEVIA BAL 404 8TH WARD
KELLEY, PATERICK CAR 185 8TH DIST
KELLEY, PATRICK BAL 301 17TH WAR
KELLEY, PATRICK ALL 052 10TH E.D
KELLEY, PATRICK ALL 195 CUMBERLA
KELLEY, PENDLETON BAL 159 1ST WARD
KELLEY, PETER BAL 104 18TH WAR
KELLEY, PONDEXTER BAL 123 1ST WARD
KELLEY, PRICE BAL 052 2ND DIST
KELLEY, RACHEL BAL 435 8TH WARD
KELLEY, RICHARD BAL 356 8TH WARD
KELLEY, ROBET BAL 132 1ST WARD
KELLEY, SAMUEL ALL 016 3RD E.D.
KELLEY, SARAH HAR 157 3RD DIST
KELLEY, SARAH P. QUE 207 3RD E DI
KELLEY, SARRAH BAL 389 8TH WARD
KELLEY, SOLOMON BAL 114 1ST WARD
KELLEY, STEWART BAL 051 2ND DIST
KELLEY, SUSAN BAL 366 1ST DIST
KELLEY, THOMAS BAL 405 8TH WARD
KELLEY, THOMAS BAL 360 8TH WARD
KELLEY, THOMAS ALL 053 10TH E.D
KELLEY, TIMOTHY HAR 157 3RD DIST
KELLEY, WARNER-BLACK QUE 150 1ST E DI
KELLEY, WILLIAM HAR 124 2ND DIST
KELLEY, WILLIAM BAL 118 18TH WAR
KELLEY, WILLIAM BAL 251 17TH WAR
KELLEY, WILLIAM BAL 280 2ND WARD
KELLEY, WILLIAM BAL 145 2ND DIST
KELLEY, WILLIAM BAL 156 1ST WARD
KELLEY, WILLIAM KEN 265 1ST DIST
KELLEY, WILLIAM B. ALL 057 10TH E.D
KELLEY, WILLIAM G. CAR 202 4TH DIST
KELLEY, WILLIAM J. BAL 367 1ST DIST
KELLEY,MATTHEW BAL 097 1ST WARD
KELLINGER, JACOB BAL 194 2ND WARD
KELLINSTINE, EVE BAL 436 8TH WARD
KELLMAN, CHARLES BAL 321 7TH WARD
KELLMIRE, MAX BAL 352 13TH WAR
KELLOG, ANNA M. CEC 080 NORTHEAS
KELLOG, EBINASER HAR 056 1ST DIST
KELLOG, ELIZABETH BAL 098 5TH WARD
KELLOGG, JOHN BAL 470 14TH WAR
KELLOGG, ORSON BAL 108 10TH WAR
KELLUM, BRIDGET WOR 201 3RD E DI
KELLUM, ELIZABETH BAL 172 6TH WARD
KELLUM, JOHN SOM 392 BRINKLEY
KELLUM, LEVEN WOR 310 2ND E DI
KELLUM, LEWIS BAL 360 3RD WARD
KELLUM, SALLEY BAL 454 8TH WARD
KELLUM, WILLIAM SOM 500 SALISBUR
KELLY, A. D. BAL 045 18TH WAR
KELLY, AGUSTAS BAL 140 11TH WAR
KELLY, AMANDA ALL 153 6TH E.D.
KELLY, ANN BAL 186 11TH WAR
KELLY, ANN BAL 162 2ND DIST
KELLY, ANN BAL 177 2ND DIST
KELLY, ANN BAL 134 16TH WAR
KELLY, ANN BAL 385 13TH WAR
KELLY, ANN BAL 213 11TH WAR
KELLY, ANN BAL 300 20TH WAR
KELLY, BASIL BAL 186 5TH DIST
KELLY, BRIDGET BAL 330 13TH WAR
KELLY, BRIDGET ALL 218 CUMBERLA
KELLY, BRIDGET BAL 193 19TH WAR
KELLY, BRIDGET BAL 337 13TH WAR
KELLY, BRIDGET BAL 123 18TH WAR
KELLY, BRIGET BAL 274 1ST DIST
KELLY, BRIGET BAL 462 1ST DIST
KELLY, CALEB BAL 186 16TH WAR
KELLY, CAROLINE CAR 399 2ND DIST
KELLY, CAROLINE BAL 062 18TH WAR
KELLY, CATHARINE BAL 368 13TH WAR
KELLY, CATHARINE BAL 460 1ST DIST
KELLY, CATHARINE BAL 446 1ST DIST
KELLY, CATHARINE BAL 054 2ND DIST
KELLY, CATHARINE BAL 223 6TH WARD
KELLY, CATHARINE BAL 228 2ND WARD
KELLY, CATHERINE BAL 314 3RD WARD
KELLY, CATHERINE BAL 097 10TH WAR
KELLY, CATHERINE BAL 101 10TH WAR
KELLY, CHARLES ALL 153 6TH E.D.
KELLY, CHARLES FRE 067 FREDERIC
KELLY, CHARLES WOR 321 1ST E DI
KELLY, CHARLES A. BAL 091 18TH WAR
KELLY, CHARLOTTE BAL 178 11TH WAR
KELLY, DANIEL BAL 179 11TH WAR
KELLY, DANIEL WOR 233 5TH E DI
KELLY, DANIEL QUE 219 3RD E DI
KELLY, DAVID ALL 031 2ND E.D.
KELLY, DAVID ANN 473 HOWARD D
KELLY, DAVID H. CAR 399 2ND DIST
KELLY, DAVIS WOR 199 8TH E DI
KELLY, DENNIS CAR 138 NO TWP L
KELLY, DENNIS BAL 112 1ST WARD
KELLY, DENNIS BAL 302 1ST DIST
KELLY, EDWARD BAL 302 1ST DIST
KELLY, EDWARD BAL 161 2ND DIST
KELLY, EDWARD BAL 436 1ST DIST
KELLY, EDWARD BAL 265 2ND WARD
KELLY, EDWARD CAR 389 2ND DIST
KELLY, EILZABETH WOR 299 SNOW HIL
KELLY, ELEANOR A. SOM 445 DAMES QU
KELLY, ELI V. BAL 354 7TH WARD
KELLY, ELIJAH WOR 276 BERLIN I
KELLY, ELIJAH WOR 224 4TH E DI
KELLY, ELIJAH W. WOR 157 5TH E DI
KELLY, ELIZA BAL 219 12TH WAR
KELLY, ELIZA BAL 168 11TH WAR
KELLY, ELIZA ALL 077 5TH E.D.
KELLY, ELIZABETH BAL 025 2ND DIST
KELLY, ELIZABETH BAL 105 15TH WAR
KELLY, ELIZABETH WOR 275 BERLIN I
KELLY, ELLEN BAL 330 13TH WAR

Name	County	Page	District
KELLY, ELLEN	ALL	140	6TH E.D.
KELLY, ELLEN	BAL	169	11TH WAR
KELLY, ELLEN	BAL	451	1ST DIST
KELLY, ELLEN	BAL	406	14TH WAR
KELLY, ELLEN	BAL	087	4TH WARD
KELLY, ELLEN	BAL	175	19TH WAR
KELLY, EMANUEL	BAL	239	17TH WAR
KELLY, FANNY	BAL	214	11TH WAR
KELLY, FANNY	ANN	351	3RD DIST
KELLY, FRANCIS	BAL	272	12TH WAR
KELLY, FRANCIS	BAL	320	1ST DIST
KELLY, FRANCIS	BAL	199	6TH WARD
KELLY, FRANCIS	TAL	015	EASTON D
KELLY, FRANKLIN	WOR	168	6TH E DI
KELLY, G. J.	BAL	309	12TH WAR
KELLY, GEORGE	BAL	385	1ST DIST
KELLY, GEORGE	BAL	390	1ST DIST
KELLY, GEORGE	WOR	289	9TH E DI
KELLY, GEORGE	WOR	200	8TH E DI
KELLY, GEORGE	SOM	527	QUANTICO
KELLY, GEORGE	BAL	395	14TH WAR
KELLY, GEORGE	CAR	390	2ND DIST
KELLY, GEORGE	HAR	150	3RD DIST
KELLY, HANNAH	BAL	296	12TH WAR
KELLY, HANNAH	BAL	101	2ND DIST
KELLY, HANNAH M.	CEC	102	4TH E DI
KELLY, HENRY	CEC	177	7TH E DI
KELLY, HENRY	FRE	053	FREDERIC
KELLY, HENRY	BAL	385	1ST DIST
KELLY, HENRY	BAL	286	2ND WARD
KELLY, HENRY	BAL	246	2ND WARD
KELLY, HENRY	WOR	168	6TH E DI
KELLY, HENRY	WOR	169	6TH E DI
KELLY, HENRY P.	WOR	211	4TH E DI
KELLY, HEZKIAH	WOR	224	4TH E DI
KELLY, HEZRON N.	ANN	385	4TH DIST
KELLY, HUGH	BAL	461	1ST DIST
KELLY, HUGH	PRI	107	PISCATAW
KELLY, HUGH	BAL	121	18TH WAR
KELLY, ISAAC	BAL	069	18TH WAR
KELLY, ISABELLA	BAL	431	14TH WAR
KELLY, ISABELLA	BAL	011	1ST WARD
KELLY, JACKSON	ALL	030	2ND E.D.
KELLY, JACOB	FRE	062	FREDERIC
KELLY, JAMES	SOM	443	DAMES QU
KELLY, JAMES	BAL	419	14TH WAR
KELLY, JAMES	CAR	331	MANCHEST
KELLY, JAMES	KEN	252	1ST DIST
KELLY, JAMES	BAL	208	11TH WAR
KELLY, JAMES	FRE	383	PETERSVI
KELLY, JAMES	ALL	048	10TH E.D
KELLY, JAMES	ALL	171	7TH E.D.
KELLY, JAMES	ALL	142	6TH E.D.
KELLY, JAMES	BAL	284	1ST DIST
KELLY, JAMES	BAL	253	1ST DIST
KELLY, JAMES	BAL	437	1ST DIST
KELLY, JAMES	BAL	184	16TH WAR
KELLY, JAMES	BAL	203	6TH WARD
KELLY, JAMES	BAL	220	2ND WARD
KELLY, JAMES	BAL	237	6TH WARD
KELLY, JAMES	BAL	033	9TH WARD
KELLY, JAMES	BAL	028	9TH WARD
KELLY, JAMES	PRI	031	VANSVILL
KELLY, JAMES	WOR	168	6TH E DI
KELLY, JAMES	WOR	169	6TH E DI
KELLY, JAMES	KEN	265	1ST DIST
KELLY, JAMES	WAS	195	1ST DIST
KELLY, JAMES	WAS	203	1ST DIST
KELLY, JAMES	WAS	161	2ND DIST
KELLY, JAMES C.	WOR	169	6TH E DI
KELLY, JAMES C.	WOR	168	6TH E DI
KELLY, JAMES F.	SOM	445	DAMES QU
KELLY, JAMS	CAR	248	3RD DIST
KELLY, JANE	BAL	192	6TH WARD
KELLY, JANE	BAL	291	12TH WAR
KELLY, JEPTHA	SOM	471	TRAPPE D
KELLY, JEREMIAH	BAL	076	10TH WAR
KELLY, JOHN	BAL	110	10TH WAR
KELLY, JOHN	BAL	175	2ND WARD
KELLY, JOHN	BAL	180	2ND WARD
KELLY, JOHN	BAL	439	1ST DIST
KELLY, JOHN	BAL	387	1ST DIST
KELLY, JOHN	ALL	155	6TH E.D.
KELLY, JOHN	ALL	055	10TH E.D
KELLY, JOHN	ALL	031	2ND E.D.
KELLY, JOHN	ANN	322	2ND DIST
KELLY, JOHN	ALL	084	5TH E.D.
KELLY, JOHN	ALL	181	8TH E.D.
KELLY, JOHN	ALL	204	CUMBERLA
KELLY, JOHN	BAL	268	2ND WARD
KELLY, JOHN	BAL	163	11TH WAR
KELLY, JOHN	BAL	039	15TH WAR
KELLY, JOHN	SOM	471	TRAPPE D
KELLY, JOHN	WOR	201	3RD E DI
KELLY, JOHN	BAL	023	18TH WAR
KELLY, JOHN	BAL	026	18TH WAR
KELLY, JOHN	SOM	421	PRINCESS
KELLY, JOHN	BAL	281	20TH WAR
KELLY, JOHN	CEC	192	5TH E DI
KELLY, JOHN	BAL	151	11TH WAR
KELLY, JOHN	KEN	248	2ND DIST
KELLY, JOHN	KEN	251	2ND DIST
KELLY, JOHN	BAL	385	13TH WAR
KELLY, JOHN	BAL	131	18TH WAR
KELLY, JOHN	BAL	112	18TH WAR
KELLY, JOHN	BAL	156	19TH WAR
KELLY, JOHN	BAL	191	19TH WAR
KELLY, JOHN	BAL	003	4TH WARD
KELLY, JOHN	BAL	003	4TH WARD
KELLY, JOHN A.	CAR	271	WESTMINS
KELLY, JOHN C.	BAL	229	12TH WAR
KELLY, JOHN J.	BAL	316	20TH WAR
KELLY, JOSEPH	CAR	399	2ND DIST
KELLY, JOSEPH	MGM	351	BERRYS D
KELLY, JOSEPH	FRE	185	5TH E DI
KELLY, JOSEPH	BAL	114	11TH WAR
KELLY, JOSEPH	BAL	325	1ST DIST
KELLY, JOSEPH	BAL	273	1ST DIST
KELLY, JOSEPH	BAL	024	2ND DIST
KELLY, JOSHUA	WOR	198	8TH E DI
KELLY, JOSHUA J.	WOR	233	6TH E DI
KELLY, JULIA	BAL	307	1ST DIST
KELLY, KAINS	BAL	400	1ST DIST
KELLY, LAWRENCE	BAL	398	14TH WAR
KELLY, LEAH	ANN	367	4TH DIST
KELLY, LEONARD	WOR	223	4TH E DI
KELLY, LETITIA	BAL	028	9TH WARD
KELLY, LEWIS	FRE	182	5TH E DI
KELLY, LOUISA	BAL	076	18TH WAR
KELLY, LUCINDA	BAL	077	15TH WAR
KELLY, LUKE	ALL	258	CUMBERLA
KELLY, LUKE	BAL	176	11TH WAR
KELLY, LUKE	CEC	102	4TH E DI
KELLY, LUKS	BAL	017	18TH WAR
KELLY, MARGARET	BAL	407	3RD WARD
KELLY, MARGARET	ALL	238	CUMBERLA
KELLY, MARGARET	BAL	333	13TH WAR
KELLY, MARGARET	BAL	126	5TH WARD
KELLY, MARGARET A.	BAL	163	16TH WAR
KELLY, MARGRET	BAL	180	2ND WARD
KELLY, MARIA	BAL	089	5TH WARD
KELLY, MARTHA	BAL	254	12TH WAR
KELLY, MARTIN	BAL	302	1ST DIST
KELLY, MARTIN	BAL	226	19TH WAR
KELLY, MARY	BAL	023	4TH WARD
KELLY, MARY	BAL	007	18TH WAR
KELLY, MARY	BAL	469	14TH WAR
KELLY, MARY	CAR	401	2ND DIST
KELLY, MARY	FRE	397	PETERSVI
KELLY, MARY	BAL	013	15TH WAR
KELLY, MARY	BAL	390	1ST DIST
KELLY, MARY	BAL	334	1ST DIST
KELLY, MARY	BAL	332	13TH WAR
KELLY, MARY	BAL	077	10TH WAR
KELLY, MARY	ALL	260	CUMBERLA
KELLY, MARY	ALL	108	5TH E.D.
KELLY, MARY	SOM	447	DAMES QU
KELLY, MARY	WOR	299	SNOW HIL
KELLY, MARY A.	WOR	201	3RD E DI
KELLY, MARY A.	BAL	017	2ND DIST
KELLY, MARY A.	BAL	115	15TH WAR
KELLY, MARY E.	KEN	248	2ND DIST
KELLY, MARY J.	BAL	362	13TH WAR
KELLY, MARY J.	WOR	231	6TH E DI
KELLY, MARY-BLACK	CAR	394	2ND DIST
KELLY, MATILDA	BAL	213	11TH WAR
KELLY, MATILDA	WAS	217	1ST DIST
KELLY, MERNIA	BAL	121	11TH WAR
KELLY, MICHAEL	BAL	421	14TH WAR
KELLY, MICHAEL	FRE	393	PETERSVI
KELLY, MICHAEL	BAL	128	18TH WAR
KELLY, MICHAEL	HAR	086	2ND DIST
KELLY, MICHAEL	WAS	299	1ST DIST
KELLY, MICHAEL	BAL	077	10TH WAR
KELLY, MICHAEL	BAL	004	EASTERN
KELLY, MICHAEL	ALL	258	CUMBERLA
KELLY, MICHAEL	ALL	180	8TH E.D.
KELLY, MICHAEL	BAL	448	1ST DIST
KELLY, MICHAEL	BAL	412	1ST DIST
KELLY, MICHAEL	BAL	414	1ST DIST
KELLY, MICHAEL	BAL	166	11TH WAR
KELLY, MICHAEL	BAL	227	2ND WARD
KELLY, MILES	PRI	045	VANSVILL
KELLY, MILLY	ANN	476	HOWARD D
KELLY, MISS M.	FRE	199	5TH E DI
KELLY, MORDECAI	BAL	147	16TH WAR
KELLY, NALAM	BAL	209	11TH WAR
KELLY, NANCY	BAL	411	1ST DIST
KELLY, NOAH	SOM	448	DAMES QU
KELLY, PATRICK	WAS	159	HAGERSTO
KELLY, PATRICK	BAL	408	1ST DIST
KELLY, PATRICK	BAL	445	1ST DIST
KELLY, PATRICK	BAL	154	16TH WAR
KELLY, PATRICK	BAL	111	15TH WAR
KELLY, PATRICK	BAL	281	12TH WAR
KELLY, PATRICK	BAL	312	12TH WAR
KELLY, PATRICK	ALL	258	CUMBERLA
KELLY, PATRICK	ALL	240	CUMBERLA
KELLY, PATRICK	ALL	141	6TH E.D.
KELLY, PATRICK	ALL	195	CUMBERLA
KELLY, PATRICK	ALL	056	10TH E.D
KELLY, PATRICK	BAL	019	1ST WARD
KELLY, PATRICK	BAL	028	9TH WARD
KELLY, PATRICK	FRE	163	EMMITTSB
KELLY, PATRICK	BAL	411	14TH WAR
KELLY, PETER	BAL	159	11TH WAR
KELLY, PETER	BAL	274	1ST DIST
KELLY, PETER	ALL	127	4TH E.D.
KELLY, PETER	BAL	118	2ND DIST
KELLY, PETER	BAL	129	16TH WAR
KELLY, PHILIP	BAL	274	1ST DIST
KELLY, R.	BAL	166	1ST WARD
KELLY, RACHEAL	CAR	390	2ND DIST
KELLY, REBECCA	BAL	005	EASTERN
KELLY, RICHARD	ALL	129	4TH E.D.
KELLY, ROBERT	BAL	135	16TH WAR
KELLY, ROBERT	BAL	257	2ND WARD
KELLY, ROBERT	BAL	143	1ST WARD
KELLY, ROSA	BAL	094	10TH WAR
KELLY, ROSANNA	BAL	038	15TH WAR
KELLY, ROSANNA	BAL	469	14TH WAR
KELLY, RUFUS	CAR	108	NO TWP L
KELLY, SALLY	BAL	065	15TH WAR
KELLY, SAMUEL	ANN	480	HOWARD D
KELLY, SAMUEL	BAL	220	2ND WARD
KELLY, SAMUEL	TAL	071	EASTON T
KELLY, SAMUEL	WAS	194	1ST DIST
KELLY, SAMUEL	WAS	220	1ST DIST
KELLY, SAMUEL	WOR	220	4TH E DI
KELLY, SAMUEL	SOM	490	SALISBUR
KELLY, SAMUEL	WOR	306	2ND E DI
KELLY, SARAH	BAL	203	11TH WAR
KELLY, SARAH	BAL	110	10TH WAR
KELLY, SARAH	BAL	444	1ST DIST
KELLY, SARAH	BAL	389	13TH WAR
KELLY, SARAH	CAR	142	NO TWP L
KELLY, SARAH	BAL	347	13TH WAR
KELLY, SARAH	BAL	047	4TH WARD
KELLY, SARAH A.	ANN	519	HOWARD D
KELLY, SARAH A.	BAL	393	3RD WARD
KELLY, SARAH E.	CAR	141	NO TWP L
KELLY, SISTER M.P.	FRE	198	5TH E DI
KELLY, SOPHIA	BAL	211	11TH WAR
KELLY, SOPHIA	BAL	123	11TH WAR
KELLY, SUSAN	SOM	425	PRINCESS
KELLY, TERENCE	BAL	205	19TH WAR
KELLY, TERENCE	BAL	285	12TH WAR
KELLY, THOAMS	SOM	449	DAMES QU
KELLY, THOMAS	WOR	313	2ND E DI
KELLY, THOMAS	WAS	144	HAGERSTO
KELLY, THOMAS	BAL	448	1ST DIST
KELLY, THOMAS	BAL	445	1ST DIST
KELLY, THOMAS	BAL	448	1ST DIST
KELLY, THOMAS	BAL	452	1ST DIST
KELLY, THOMAS	BAL	038	15TH WAR
KELLY, THOMAS	BAL	164	11TH WAR
KELLY, THOMAS	BAL	144	2ND DIST
KELLY, THOMAS	ALL	077	5TH E.D.
KELLY, THOMAS	BAL	273	1ST DIST
KELLY, THOMAS	BAL	129	11TH WAR
KELLY, THOMAS	KEN	233	2ND DIST
KELLY, THOMAS	BAL	342	13TH WAR
KELLY, THOMAS	BAL	368	13TH WAR
KELLY, THOMAS	CEC	143	PORT DUP
KELLY, THOMAS	BAL	032	18TH WAR
KELLY, THOMAS G.	CAR	365	9TH DIST
KELLY, TIMOTHY	BAL	374	13TH WAR
KELLY, TIMOTHY	BAL	005	4TH WARD
KELLY, WASHINGTON	TAL	097	ST MICHA
KELLY, WASHINGTON-BLACK	FRE	385	PETERSVI
KELLY, WILLIAM	FRE	385	PETERSVI
KELLY, WILLIAM	BAL	022	18TH WAR
KELLY, WILLIAM	BAL	080	18TH WAR
KELLY, WILLIAM	KEN	224	2ND DIST
KELLY, WILLIAM	CAR	111	NO TWP L
KELLY, WILLIAM	CAR	142	NO TWP L
KELLY, WILLIAM	WAS	017	2ND SUBD
KELLY, WILLIAM	BAL	169	2ND DIST
KELLY, WILLIAM	BAL	116	1ST WARD
KELLY, WILLIAM	BAL	051	2ND DIST
KELLY, WILLIAM	BAL	051	2ND DIST
KELLY, WILLIAM	BAL	448	1ST DIST
KELLY, WILLIAM	BAL	120	5TH WARD
KELLY, WILLIAM	BAL	024	9TH WARD
KELLY, WILLIAM	BAL	154	1ST WARD
KELLY, WILLIAM H.	BAL	114	5TH WARD
KELLY, WILLIAM S.	WOR	169	6TH E DI
KELLY, WILLIAM T.	BAL	184	16TH WAR
KELLY, ZACHARIAH	WOR	170	6TH E DI
KELLY,F RANKLIN	WOR	169	6TH E DI
KELLY,LAWSON	MGM	406	MEDLEY 3
KELLY,MARY	BAL	293	12TH WAR
KELLY,ZIPPORAH	WOR	169	6TH E DI
KELMAN, SARAH	BAL	322	7TH WARD
KELMARTIN, THOMAS	BAL	449	1ST DIST
KELMSER, GEORGE	BAL	251	2ND WARD
KELP, FERDINAN	BAL	370	8TH WARD
KELPIEN, HANDY	WOR	303	SNOW HIL
KELSEY, BENJAMIN	BAL	012	4TH WARD
KELSEY, ELI	BAL	084	4TH WARD
KELSEY, HENRY	BAL	012	4TH WARD
KELSH, PATRICK *	BAL	378	13TH WAR
KELSLER, JACOB	ALL	025	2ND E.D.
KELSO, BECCA	BAL	194	17TH WAR
KELSO, GEORGE G.	BAL	032	4TH WARD
KELSO, JANE	BAL	057	10TH WAR
KELSO, JOHN	ALL	225	CUMBERLA
KELSO, JOHN	BAL	085	4TH WARD
KELSO, JOHN	SOM	355	BRINKLEY
KELSO, JOHN R.	BAL	381	13TH WAR
KELSO, LOUISA	BAL	159	16TH WAR
KELSO, LUCRETIA	BAL	453	14TH WAR
KELSO, M.	BAL	099	10TH WAR
KELSO, MARIA	BAL	248	1ST DIST
KELSO, MARTHA	BAL	046	4TH WARD
KELSO, SARAH	BAL	345	1ST DIST
KELSO, THOMAS	BAL	085	4TH WARD
KELSO, WILLIAM	CEC	195	6TH E DI
KELSO, WILLIAM	BAL	394	3RD WARD
KELSO, WILLIAM A.	SOM	355	BRINKLEY
KELSON, ALLEN*	TAL	045	EASTON T
KELSON, ELIZABETH	CEC	164	6TH E DI
KELSON, GIDEON-BLACK	QUE	196	3RD E DI
KELSON, JAMES*	TAL	048	EASTON T
KELSON, JOHN B.	WOR	324	1ST E DI
KELSON, NATHAN-BLACK	CAR	101	NO TWP L
KELSON, RACHEL	BAL	057	10TH WAR
KELSON, SAMUEL-BLACK	CAR	101	NO TWP L
KELSOR, JOHN	KEN	213	2ND DIST
KELSY, DAVID	WAS	039	2ND SUBD
KELSY, FRANKLIN	WAS	040	2ND SUBD
KELTER, CONRAD	ALL	198	CUMBERLA
KELTNER, F. G.	BAL	018	4TH WARD
KELTNER, MARY	BAL	018	4TH WARD
KELTON, COULTON	BAL	278	12TH WAR
KELTON, THEODORE	BAL	277	12TH WAR
KELTTLER, WILLIAM	BAL	043	9TH WARD
KELTY, HARRIETT	BAL	101	5TH WARD
KELTY, JOHN W.	BAL	149	16TH WAR
KELVINGTON, SAMUEL	CEC	088	4TH E DI
KEMAN, ELLEN	BAL	099	5TH WARD
KEMAN, JOHN	BAL	099	5TH WARD
KEMAN, JOHN	BAL	444	8TH WARD
KEMAN, MICHAEL	BAL	444	8TH WARD
KEMBERLY, ELIZA	ALL	092	5TH E.D.
KEMBERLY, MARIA	ALL	099	5TH E.D.
KEMBLA, WILLIAM *	BAL	219	12TH WAR
KEMBLE, THOMAS D.	BAL	100	10TH WAR
KEMBLE, WILLIAM	BAL	383	1ST DIST
KEMBLES, NELSON	QUE	159	2ND E DI
KEMERIDGE, BRIDGET	BAL	360	8TH WARD
KEMKLE, MARY C.	BAL	345	13TH WAR
KEMLIN, MARGARET A.	BAL	329	3RD WARD
KEMMEL, CAROLINE	BAL	052	4TH WARD
KEMMEL, PETER	ALL	038	2ND E.D.
KEMMELMAN, ANDREW*	BAL	339	3RD WARD
KEMMER, HENRY	BAL	010	9TH WARD
KEMMET, CASPER	BAL	321	1ST DIST
KEMMET, EVE	BAL	322	1ST DIST
KEMMIER, SAMLIN *	BAL	308	12TH WAR
KEMMON, PETER S.	BAL	369	8TH WARD
KEMOUGH, GEORGE	BAL	229	2ND WARD
KEMP, ABRAHAM	FRE	045	FREDERIC
KEMP, ADALINE	BAL	219	6TH DIST
KEMP, ALIRE	TAL	084	ST MICHA
KEMP, ALISON	BAL	003	18TH WAR
KEMP, ANN	BAL	017	4TH WARD
KEMP, ANN	TAL	103	ST MICHA
KEMP, ANN	BAL	260	2ND WARD
KEMP, ANN M.	BAL	371	3RD WARD
KEMP, ANNA S.*	TAL	048	EASTON T
KEMP, BARBARA	FRE	426	8TH E DI
KEMP, BERNARD	FRE	381	PETERSVI
KEMP, CATHARINE	FRE	046	FREDERIC
KEMP, CATHARINE	BAL	250	17TH WAR
KEMP, CATHARINE	FRE	281	WOODSBOR
KEMP, CHARLES	BAL	461	14TH WAR
KEMP, COLLUMBUS	FRE	289	WOODSBOR
KEMP, DANIEL L.	FRE	305	WOODSBOR
KEMP, DANIEL M.	FRE	303	WOODSBOR
KEMP, DAVID	FRE	097	FREDERIC
KEMP, DAVID	FRE	407	JEFFERSO
KEMP, DAVID	WAS	173	FUNKSTOW
KEMP, E..EN*	TAL	001	EASTON D
KEMP, EDWARD	FRE	103	FREDERIC
KEMP, EDWARD D.	BAL	145	11TH WAR
KEMP, ELIZABETH	FRE	090	FREDERIC
KEMP, ELIZABETH	TAL	017	EASTON D
KEMP, ELIZABETH	SOM	525	QUANTICO
KEMP, EMILY A.	BAL	454	14TH WAR

KEMP, GEORGE FRE 084 FREDERIC
KEMP, GEORGE BAL 439 14TH WAR
KEMP, GEORGE WAS 221 1ST DIST
KEMP, GOERGE BAL 188 19TH WAR
KEMP, H. BAL 144 5TH WARD
KEMP, HARRIETT ALL 104 5TH E.D.
KEMP, HENRETTA BAL 204 19TH WAR
KEMP, HENRIETTA BAL 300 3RD WARD
KEMP, HENRY BAL 192 11TH WAR
KEMP, HENRY BAL 188 19TH WAR
KEMP, HENRY BAL 203 19TH WAR
KEMP, HERMAN BAL 204 19TH WAR
KEMP, HERNIETTA FRE 065 FREDERIC
KEMP, HOSEA BAL 183 5TH DIST
KEMP, JACOB MGM 364 BERRYS D
KEMP, JACOB JR. MGM 365 BERRYS D
KEMP, JAMES QUE 138 1ST E DI
KEMP, JAMES D. BAL 010 1ST WARD
KEMP, JAMES L. BAL 194 2ND WARD
KEMP, JAMES T. BAL 101 15TH WAR
KEMP, JOHN BAL 110 10TH WAR
KEMP, JOHN BAL 239 1ST DIST
KEMP, JOHN ALL 060 10TH E.D
KEMP, JOHN BAL 146 11TH WAR
KEMP, JOHN FRE 295 WOODSBOR
KEMP, JOHN DOR 433 1ST DIST
KEMP, JOHN TAL 111 ST MICHA
KEMP, JOHN W. TAL 110 ST MICHA
KEMP, JOSEPH FRE 245 NEW MARK
KEMP, JOSEPH BAL 228 17TH WAR
KEMP, JOSEPH BAL 240 20TH WAR
KEMP, JOSEPH F. BAL 126 16TH WAR
KEMP, JOSHUA BAL 183 5TH DIST
KEMP, JOSHUA FRE 309 WOODSBOR
KEMP, JOSHUA JR. BAL 183 5TH DIST
KEMP, LEMUEL SOM 485 TRAPP DI
KEMP, LEWIS FRE 099 FREDERIC
KEMP, LEWIS BAL 204 19TH WAR
KEMP, LOUISA TAL 067 EASTON T
KEMP, MARIE L. BAL 158 19TH WAR
KEMP, MARY BAL 105 18TH WAR
KEMP, MARY FRE 213 BUCKEYST
KEMP, MARY BAL 462 14TH WAR
KEMP, MARY CAR 327 1ST DIST
KEMP, MARY A. QUE 239 5TH E DI
KEMP, MARY A. TAL 031 EASTON D
KEMP, MARY A. BAL 168 11TH WAR
KEMP, MARY* BAL 323 3RD WARD
KEMP, MATILDA BAL 407 14TH WAR
KEMP, PETER BAL 001 18TH WAR
KEMP, PETER FRE 308 WOODSBOR
KEMP, PETER FRE 281 WOODSBOR
KEMP, RICHARD BAL 047 4TH WARD
KEMP, RICHARD BAL 131 5TH WARD
KEMP, ROBERT TAL 067 EASTON T
KEMP, ROBERT REV- SOM 426 PRINCESS
KEMP, RUTH BAL 157 19TH WAR
KEMP, SAMUEL BAL 055 18TH WAR
KEMP, SAMUEL TAL 036 EASTON D
KEMP, SAMUEL BAL 183 5TH DIST
KEMP, SAMUEL T. TAL 048 EASTON T
KEMP, SARAH TAL 003 EASTON D
KEMP, SARAH BAL 344 13TH WAR
KEMP, SHADE BAL 196 5TH DIST
KEMP, SHADRACK BAL 183 5TH DIST
KEMP, SIMON BAL 011 4TH WARD
KEMP, SOLOMON FRE 245 NEW MARK
KEMP, STEVER FRE 096 FREDERIC
KEMP, THOMAS TAL 054 EASTON D
KEMP, THOMAS H. QUE 223 4TH E DI
KEMP, VIRGINIA QUE 247 5TH E DI
KEMP, WARREN P. BAL 124 16TH WAR
KEMP, WILLAIM PRI 102 SPALDING
KEMP, WILLIAM DOR 451 1ST DIST
KEMP, WILLIAM TAL 020 EASTON D
KEMP, WILLIAM BAL 405 3RD WARD
KEMP, WILLIAM BAL 388 8TH WARD
KEMP, WILLIAM FRE 072 FREDERIC
KEMP, WILLIAM BAL 127 18TH WAR
KEMP, WILLIAM BAL 155 11TH WAR
KEMP, WILLIAM A. KEN 247 2ND DIST
KEMP, WILLIAM C. FRE 382 PETERSVI
KEMP, WILLIAM D. TAL 082 ST MICHA
KEMP, WILLIAM E. BAL 240 1ST DIST
KEMP, WILLIAM H. BAL 427 1ST DIST
KEMP, WILLIAM H. TAL 102 ST MICHA
KEMP, WILLIAM M. BAL 456 14TH WAR
KEMP, WILLIAM P. TAL 100 ST MICHA
KEMP, WILLIAM T. TAL 030 EASTON D
KEMP,COLUMBUS FRE 204 BUCKEYST
KEMP,LYDIA ALL 014 3RD E.D.
KEMP,MARTIN BAL 069 1ST WARD
KEMP,OBADIAH BAL 004 EASTERN
KEMP,WATTERS BAL 181 2ND WARD
KEMPER, JOHN BAL 130 16TH WAR
KEMPER, JOHN BAL 088 10TH WAR
KEMPER, JOHN G. BAL 129 16TH WAR
KEMPER, JUILIA BAL 457 14TH WAR
KEMPER, MARY FRE 197 5TH E DI
KEMPER, SAMUEL BAL 006 18TH WAR
KEMPERS, FRANZ H. BAL 008 4TH WARD
KEMPHER, JACOB CAR 333 MANCHEST
KEMPHER, MOSES BAL 203 17TH WAR
KEMPHER,MICHEAL CAR 406 2ND DIST
KEMPHERP, MOSES BAL 203 17TH WAR
KEMPIS, THOMAS BAL 168 2ND DIST
KEMPLE, ELISHA BAL 471 14TH WAR
KEMPS, HENNAN BAL 018 9TH WARD
KEMPT, RACHAELL BAL 131 5TH WARD
KEN, CASANARY* DOR 384 1ST DIST
KEN, WILLIM BAL 168 2ND DIST
KENADA, JOHN SOM 394 BRINKLEY
KENADY, HENRY BAL 461 1ST DIST
KENADY, JOHN BAL 408 1ST DIST
KENADY, JOHN BAL 346 1ST DIST
KENADY, MARCIA BAL 402 1ST DIST
KENADY, MARY BAL 390 1ST DIST
KENADY, MARY A. BAL 317 1ST DIST
KENADY, MICHAEL BAL 406 1ST DIST
KENADY, R.A. WAS 040 2ND SUBD
KENADY, SARAH BAL 378 1ST DIST
KENADY, WILLIAM BAL 404 1ST DIST
KENAHAN, THOMAS BAL 035 15TH WAR
KENAMON, HENRY CAR 159 NO TWP L
KENAN, EDWARD ALL 150 6TH E.D.
KENAN, JOSEPH BAL 003 9TH WARD
KENAN, JOSEPH WAS 162 HAGERSTO
KENAN, PETER ALL 150 6TH E.D.
KENANABT, AUGUST BAL 051 1ST WARD
KENARD, CELENA BAL 359 8TH WARD
KENARD, ELIZABETH KEN 290 3RD DIST
KENARD, GEORGE HAR 164 3RD DIST
KENARD, HANDY HAR 178 3RD DIST
KENARD, WILCAT HAR 185 3RD DIST
KENARD, STEPHEN KEN 295 3RD DIST
KENARD, THOMAS HAR 160 3RD DIST
KENARD, WILLIAM B. KEN 284 3RD DIST
KENBLER, MATTHEW BAL 013 15TH WAR
KENBLES, MARGARET QUE 158 2ND E DI
KENBLES, ROBERT QUE 158 2ND E DI
KENBLES, STEPHEN W. QUE 157 2ND E DI
KENBOTTOM, ANNA FRE 437 8TH E DI
KENBY, ALLEN BAL 049 1ST WARD
KENDALL, BARBARY ANN 418 HOWARD D
KENDALL, DAVID B. KEN 289 3RD DIST
KENDALL, ELI BAL 347 1ST DIST
KENDALL, HARACE KEN 264 1ST DIST
KENDALL, HARACE KEN 232 2ND DIST
KENDALL, HENRY M. BAL 009 18TH WAR
KENDALL, JAMES KEN 264 1ST DIST
KENDALL, JESSEE KEN 264 1ST DIST
KENDALL, MARY R. KEN 268 1ST DIST
KENDALL, MRS. MARY BAL 020 18TH WAR
KENDALL, PRUDENCE H. ALL 254 CUMBERLA
KENDALL, STEPHEN KEN 267 1ST DIST
KENDALL, STEPHEN KEN 266 1ST DIST
KENDALL, THOMAS KEN 267 1ST DIST
KENDALL, THOMAS KEN 283 3RD DIST
KENDALL, THOMAS J. KEN 285 3RD DIST
KENDALL, WILLIAM BAL 131 1ST WARD
KENDERSON, MARY CEC 085 5TH E DI
KENDICK, JOHN CHA 243 HILLTOP
KENDIRCK, GEORGE PRI 106 PISCATAW
KENDLE, AUGUSTA BAL 193 5TH DIST
KENDLE, BARBARA BAL 348 1ST DIST
KENDLE, CAROLINE BAL 242 12TH WAR
KENDLE, GEORGE WAS 239 CAVETOWN
KENDLE, JOHN H. ALL 181 8TH E.D.
KENDLEY, GEORGE F. FRE 274 NEW MARK
KENDRICK, GEORGE PRI 114 PISCATAW
KENDRICK, HENRY BAL 218 19TH WAR
KENDRICK, JANE PRI 113 PISCATAW
KENDRICK, MARY BAL 414 3RD WARD
KENDRICK, S. BAL 141 1ST WARD
KENDRICK, WILLIAM CHA 264 MIDDLETO
KENEDY, EZEKIEL ALL 172 7TH E.D.
KENEDY, FRANCIS WAS 213 1ST DIST
KENEDY, JANE BAL 046 2ND DIST
KENEDY, JOHN ANN 460 HOWARD D
KENEDY, MARY BAL 310 1ST DIST
KENEDY, NICHOLAS R. BAL 388 8TH WARD
KENEDY, SARAH BAL 093 5TH WARD
KENEDY, WILLIAM BAL 286 1ST DIST
KENEDY, WILLIAM H. BAL 017 18TH WAR
KENEDY, WILLIAM W. BAL 260 17TH WAR
KENEDY,THOMAS BAL 008 EASTERN
KENEL, JOHN BAL 092 2ND DIST
KENEMAN, JOHN A. CHA 269 ALLENS F
KENER, GEORGE J. BAL 271 7TH WARD
KENERD, HARKLESS HAR 205 3RD DIST
KENERICKS, BASIL FRE 088 FREDERIC
KENEY, ELI FRE 302 WOODSBOR
KENFELDER, ANN S. BAL 269 20TH WAR
KENFMAN, WILLIAM FRE 267 NEW MARK
KENIAN, JOHN BAL 033 1ST WARD
KENIKUVETZ, H.P. BAL 127 5TH WARD
KENIVEDA, JAMES ALL 155 6TH E.D.
KENK, JACOB BAL 120 11TH WAR
KENKAUGH, HENRY BAL 095 1ST WARD
KENLEIN, MATHIAS BAL 280 1ST DIST
KENLER, JOHN BAL 273 20TH WAR
KENLEVILLE, DAVID * BAL 218 12TH WAR
KENLEY, ANN BAL 323 12TH WAR
KENLEY, LUCY HAR 003 1ST DIST
KENLEY, MARGARET HAR 036 1ST DIST
KENLEY, THOMAS BAL 072 18TH WAR
KENLEY, WILLIAM * HAR 030 1ST DIST
KENLINO, JOHN BAL 176 2ND WARD
KENLY, EDWARD BAL 406 14TH WAR
KENLY, JOHN BAL 455 14TH WAR
KENLY, PRISCILLA BAL 456 14TH WAR
KENLY, SUSAN BAL 437 14TH WAR
KENLY, WILLAM HAR 174 3RD DIST
KENN, THOMAS ALL 128 4TH E.D.
KENNA, JAMES W. BAL 395 8TH WARD
KENNA, MARGARET BAL 305 20TH WAR
KENNADA, ELIZA DOR 320 1ST DIST
KENNADA, GEORGE DOR 321 1ST DIST
KENNADY, JAMES CEC 205 7TH E DI
KENNADY, JAMES N. KEN 222 2ND DIST
KENNALLY, MARY* BAL 400 3RD WARD
KENNAN, ELLEN BAL 260 12TH WAR
KENNAN, JAMES BAL 159 11TH WAR
KENNAN, MARY BAL 455 1ST DIST
KENNAN, OWEN BAL 158 11TH WAR
KENNAR, EDWARD FRE 259 NEW MARK
KENNARD, ALEXANDER BAL 154 11TH WAR
KENNARD, ALEXANDER A. BAL 159 19TH WAR
KENNARD, AMELIA BAL 382 13TH WAR
KENNARD, BOLRAS BAL 129 18TH WAR
KENNARD, CATHERINE BAL 375 3RD WARD
KENNARD, ELIZABETH TAL 071 EASTON T
KENNARD, EMELINE KEN 252 1ST DIST
KENNARD, GEORGE J. BAL 222 6TH WARD
KENNARD, HARRIET BAL 147 11TH WAR
KENNARD, HENRY BAL 190 17TH WAR
KENNARD, HENRY BAL 120 2ND DIST
KENNARD, HOARCE TAL 077 EASTON T
KENNARD, HORRACE TAL 016 EASTON D
KENNARD, ISABEL HAR 132 2ND DIST
KENNARD, ISABEL HAR 121 2ND DIST
KENNARD, JAMES KEN 230 2ND DIST
KENNARD, JAMES KEN 225 2ND DIST
KENNARD, JAMES BAL 310 12TH WAR
KENNARD, JOHN A. KEN 230 2ND DIST
KENNARD, JOHN H. BAL 120 2ND DIST
KENNARD, JOSEPH BAL 014 15TH WAR
KENNARD, JOSEPH KEN 213 2ND DIST
KENNARD, JOSEPH KEN 272 1ST DIST
KENNARD, JOSHUA QUE 157 2ND E DI
KENNARD, KITTY BAL 206 17TH WAR
KENNARD, LEVI CEC 065 1ST E DI
KENNARD, LEVI BAL 425 8TH WARD
KENNARD, MARIA E. BAL 123 5TH WARD
KENNARD, MARY BAL 311 12TH WAR
KENNARD, MARY BAL 046 18TH WAR
KENNARD, MARY BAL 252 17TH WAR
KENNARD, MOSES KEN 244 2ND DIST
KENNARD, NICHOLAS TAL 399 ST MICHA
KENNARD, P. A. MRS- BAL 065 18TH WAR
KENNARD, PIERRY CEC 059 1ST E DI
KENNARD, SAMUEL KEN 232 2ND DIST
KENNARD, SARAH E. KEN 244 2ND DIST
KENNARD, SARAH T. KEN 242 2ND DIST
KENNARD, THOMAS H. KEN 223 2ND DIST
KENNARD, THOMAS H. KEN 249 2ND DIST
KENNARD, THOMAS J. BAL 002 18TH WAR
KENNARD, THOMAS W. BAL 121 1ST WARD
KENNARD, WILLIAM BAL 317 3RD WARD
KENNARD, WILLIAM KEN 294 3RD DIST
KENNARD, WILLIAM H. BAL 018 18TH WAR
KENNARD, WILLIAM H. BAL 381 13TH WAR
KENNARD,B.T. BAL 138 1ST WARD
KENNARD,JAMES J. BAL 141 1ST WARD
KENNARY, MICHAEL BAL 267 20TH WAR
KENNEDA, WILLIAM ALL 251 CUMBERLA
KENNEDAY, CATHERINE ALL 235 CUMBERLA
KENNEDAY, HUGH BAL 002 9TH WARD
KENNEDAY, MARY J. CEC 110 4TH E DI
KENNEDAY, MATILDA-BLACK QUE 201 3RD E DI
KENNEDER, DAVID * ALL 099 5TH E.D.
KENNEDY, ADALINE BAL 397 3RD WARD
KENNEDY, ALEXANDER BAL 161 6TH WARD
KENNEDY, AMRY A. BAL 294 20TH WAR
KENNEDY, ANDREW BAL 170 6TH WARD
KENNEDY, ANDREW E. BAL 106 10TH WAR
KENNEDY, ANN BAL 098 10TH WAR
KENNEDY, ANN BAL 355 13TH WAR
KENNEDY, ANN BAL 029 4TH WARD
KENNEDY, ANNA BAL 417 14TH WAR
KENNEDY, ANNE BAL 067 10TH WAR
KENNEDY, ANTHONY BAL 108 10TH WAR
KENNEDY, BENJAMIN BAL 122 1ST WARD
KENNEDY, BRIDGET BAL 355 3RD WARD
KENNEDY, BRIDGET BAL 003 9TH WARD
KENNEDY, BRIDGET BAL 145 11TH WAR
KENNEDY, CATHARINE BAL 107 5TH WARD
KENNEDY, CATHERINE BAL 356 3RD WARD
KENNEDY, CATHERINE BAL 052 4TH WARD
KENNEDY, CATHERINE BAL 029 4TH WARD
KENNEDY, CATHRINE BAL 023 18TH WAR
KENNEDY, CHARLES BAL 145 11TH WAR
KENNEDY, CHARLES BAL 279 12TH WAR
KENNEDY, DAVID FRE 039 FREDERIC
KENNEDY, DENNIS BAL 433 8TH WARD
KENNEDY, DENNIS BAL 425 8TH WARD
KENNEDY, DRISILLA WAS 198 1ST DIST
KENNEDY, ELIZABETH BAL 006 18TH WAR
KENNEDY, ELIZABETH BAL 215 11TH WAR
KENNEDY, ELLEN BAL 397 3RD WARD
KENNEDY, ELLEN J. BAL 137 5TH WARD
KENNEDY, ESIKEL BAL 028 18TH WAR
KENNEDY, FELIX BAL 023 18TH WAR
KENNEDY, FRANCIS BAL 017 18TH WAR
KENNEDY, GEORGE FRE 023 FREDERIC
KENNEDY, GEORGE A. BAL 020 15TH WAR
KENNEDY, GEORGE G. WAS 197 1ST DIST
KENNEDY, GEORGE K. BAL 121 1ST WARD
KENNEDY, GOERGE L. WAS 198 1ST DIST
KENNEDY, H. BAL 100 10TH WAR
KENNEDY, HENRY BAL 025 18TH WAR
KENNEDY, HOWARD ALL 159 6TH E.D.
KENNEDY, JACOB B. CEC 201 6TH E DI
KENNEDY, JAMES HAR 059 1ST DIST
KENNEDY, JAMES BAL 352 7TH WARD
KENNEDY, JAMES BAL 131 5TH WARD
KENNEDY, JAMES M. BAL 063 18TH WAR
KENNEDY, JAMES P. BAL 207 19TH WAR
KENNEDY, JANE BAL 099 10TH WAR
KENNEDY, JANE BAL 310 7TH WARD
KENNEDY, JOANNA BAL 156 16TH WAR
KENNEDY, JOHANER BAL 184 2ND WARD
KENNEDY, JOHN BAL 033 9TH WARD
KENNEDY, JOHN BAL 156 1ST WARD
KENNEDY, JOHN BAL 271 7TH WARD
KENNEDY, JOHN BAL 279 2ND WARD
KENNEDY, JOHN BAL 031 15TH WAR
KENNEDY, JOHN BAL 270 12TH WAR
KENNEDY, JOHN BAL 286 2ND WARD
KENNEDY, JOHN BAL 010 18TH WAR
KENNEDY, JOHN CEC 108 3RD E DI
KENNEDY, JOHN HAR 050 1ST DIST
KENNEDY, JOHN BAL 445 14TH WAR
KENNEDY, JOHN B. BAL 111 10TH WAR
KENNEDY, JOHN W. WAS 157 1ST DIST
KENNEDY, KATE BAL 141 19TH WAR
KENNEDY, LAURENCE BAL 122 11TH WAR
KENNEDY, LAWRENCE BAL 365 13TH WAR
KENNEDY, LYDIA WAS 136 HAGERSTO
KENNEDY, MARGARET BAL 352 7TH WAR
KENNEDY, MARGARETT BAL 001 18TH WAR
KENNEDY, MARGRETT BAL 073 18TH WAR
KENNEDY, MARTIN BAL 356 8TH WARD
KENNEDY, MARY BAL 221 5TH WARD
KENNEDY, MARY BAL 073 18TH WAR
KENNEDY, MARY E. BAL 226 12TH WAR
KENNEDY, MORDIAI BAL 170 11TH WAR
KENNEDY, PATRICK ALL 071 5TH E.D.
KENNEDY, PATRICK BAL 103 18TH WAR
KENNEDY, PATRICK HAR 059 1ST DIST
KENNEDY, PETER BAL 030 9TH WARD
KENNEDY, PHILIP G. HAR 050 1ST DIST
KENNEDY, PHILLIP BAL 005 9TH WARD
KENNEDY, RACHEL BAL 289 20TH WAR
KENNEDY, SARAH BAL 093 10TH WAR
KENNEDY, SARAH BAL 314 12TH WAR
KENNEDY, SUSAN BAL 200 19TH WAR
KENNEDY, THOMAS HAR 059 1ST DIST
KENNEDY, THOMAS BAL 426 8TH WARD
KENNEDY, THOMAS BAL 314 3RD WARD
KENNEDY, TIMOTHY BAL 280 2ND WARD
KENNEDY, WILLIAM BAL 142 1ST WARD
KENNEDY, WILLIAM BAL 048 1ST WARD
KENNEDY, WILLIAM BAL 058 1ST WARD
KENNEDY, WILLIAM ALL 251 CUMBERLA
KENNEDY, WILLIAM BAL 002 EASTERN
KENNEDY, WILLIAM T. HAR 116 2ND DIST
KENNEDY, WILLIAM W. BAL 084 15TH WAR
KENNEDY,PATRICK BAL 091 1ST WARD
KENNELLY, MISS BAL 139 5TH WARD
KENNEMAN, CHARLES* TAL 002 EASTON D
KENNEMANN, KUNIGUNDE * BAL 102 15TH WAR
KENNEMON, JOHN TAL 111 ST MICHA
KENNEN, JOHN BAL 079 2ND DIST
KENNER, ABRAHAM FRE 414 8TH E DI
KENNER, ALEXANDER WAS 160 2ND DIST
KENNER, ELIZA WAS 139 HAGERSTO
KENNER, ISAAC WAS 270 1ST DIST
KENNER, MARGARET FRE 414 8TH E DI
KENNER, MARY BAL 301 7TH WARD

Name	County	Page	District
KENNER, SOPHIA	BAL	100	2ND DIST
KENNER, WILLIAM	WAS	258	1ST DIST
KENNERD, FREDERICK	BAL	064	4TH WARD
KENNERLY, COLUMBUS	SOM	534	QUANTICO
KENNERLY, ELIZABETH	SOM	518	BARREN C
KENNERLY, HENRY	SOM	529	QUANTICO
KENNERLY, IRVING	SOM	533	QUANTICO
KENNERLY, ISAAC	SOM	514	BARREN C
KENNERLY, JANE	SOM	425	PRINCESS
KENNERLY, JULIA A.	SOM	527	QUANTICO
KENNERLY, LUTHER	SOM	516	BARREN C
KENNERLY, WHITTINGTON	SOM	517	BARREN C
KENNERLY, WILLIAM A.	SOM	533	QUANTICO
KENNERMAN, JAMES	TAL	035	EASTON D
KENNET, JOHN	BAL	024	2ND DIST
KENNEY, ANDREW	BAL	144	2ND DIST
KENNEY, AUGUSTINE	BAL	341	7TH WARD
KENNEY, AUGUSTUS	BAL	362	8TH WARD
KENNEY, BENJAMIN	BAL	188	2ND WARD
KENNEY, CATHARINE	ALL	073	5TH E.D.
KENNEY, EDWARD	ALL	051	10TH E.D
KENNEY, FRANCIS	BAL	295	20TH WAR
KENNEY, JAMES	BAL	269	17TH WAR
KENNEY, JAMES	BAL	043	1ST WARD
KENNEY, JOHN	BAL	159	19TH WAR
KENNEY, MARGARET	ALL	103	5TH E.D.
KENNEY, MARTIN	ALL	053	10TH E.D
KENNEY, MARY	BAL	385	3RD WARD
KENNEY, MARY	BAL	102	5TH WARD
KENNEY, MARY F.	BAL	335	7TH WARD
KENNEY, MICHAEL	ALL	068	5TH E.D.
KENNEY, MICHAEL	BAL	035	1ST WARD
KENNEY, MICHAEL	BAL	027	4TH WARD
KENNEY, OWEN M.	BAL	355	8TH WARD
KENNEY, PATRICK	ALL	235	CUMBERLA
KENNEY, THOMAS	ALL	098	5TH E.D.
KENNEY, THOMAS	BAL	371	1ST DIST
KENNEY, THOMAS	BAL	283	17TH WAR
KENNEY, WILLIAM	BAL	286	17TH WAR
KENNEY,LEVIN	CAR	121	NO TWP L
KENNGER, J. W. *	ALL	090	5TH E.D.
KENNING, DAVID	BAL	037	1ST WARD
KENNOUS, ADELINE	BAL	337	7TH WARD
KENNOW, MARY	FRE	072	FREDERIC
KENNRICK, JOHN	BAL	173	19TH WAR
KENNS, HENRY M.	ALL	210	CUMBERLA
KENNUMAN, WILLIAM A.	TAL	095	ST MICHA
KENNY, ANN	BAL	244	12TH WAR
KENNY, ANNE	BAL	074	15TH WAR
KENNY, CATHERINE	BAL	083	10TH WAR
KENNY, CONRAD	BAL	046	1ST WARD
KENNY, DAVID	BAL	419	1ST DIST
KENNY, ELIZABETH	BAL	079	4TH WARD
KENNY, FRANCIS	BAL	387	1ST DIST
KENNY, JAMES	ALL	254	CUMBERLA
KENNY, JAMES	BAL	036	9TH WARD
KENNY, JOHN	BAL	218	6TH WARD
KENNY, JOSEPH L.	CAR	126	NO TWP L
KENNY, MARGARET	BAL	316	20TH WAR
KENNY, NANCY	WOR	228	6TH E DI
KENNY, P.T.	CAL	062	3RD DIST
KENNY, PATRICK	BAL	203	6TH WARD
KENNY, PATRICK	BAL	442	1ST DIST
KENNY, PATRICK	ALL	129	4TH E.D.
KENNY, PETER	BAL	046	1ST WARD
KENNY, RICHARD	BAL	044	9TH WARD
KENNY, SISTER MARY	FRE	198	5TH E DI
KENNY, THOMAS	BAL	215	6TH WARD
KENNY, THOMAS	BAL	450	1ST DIST
KENNY, THOMAS	BAL	010	9TH WARD
KENNY, TIMOTHY	BAL	028	15TH WAR
KENNY, WILLIAM	BAL	044	1ST WARD
KENNYDY, JOSEPH	BAL	462	1ST DIST
KENP, ANN *	BAL	103	18TH WAR
KENP, MARY*	BAL	323	3RD WARD
KENSELER, SARAH*	BAL	335	3RD WARD
KENSENDORFF, AMELIA	BAL	190	11TH WAR
KENSER, CATHERINE	BAL	428	8TH WARD
KENSER, MARY	BAL	238	17TH WAR
KENSEY, JOHN	ALL	106	5TH E.D.
KENSHALER, MICHAEL	BAL	154	2ND DIST
KENSINGER, JOSEPH	ALL	005	3RD E.D.
KENSLOE, PATRICK	WAS	163	2ND DIST
KENSON, HENRIETTA	BAL	030	9TH WARD
KENT, ALICE L.	BAL	375	13TH WAR
KENT, C.H.	BAL	163	1ST WARD
KENT, DANIEL	ANN	327	2ND DIST
KENT, DANIEL	ANN	287	ANNAPOLI
KENT, DANIEL	CAL	048	3RD DIST
KENT, DAVID	ALL	025	2ND E.D.
KENT, DAVID	BAL	155	1ST WARD
KENT, DINAH	CAL	041	3RD DIST
KENT, ELIZABETH A.	BAL	311	7TH WARD
KENT, EVELINE W.	TAL	044	EASTON D
KENT, FANNY	BAL	013	2ND DIST
KENT, HARRY-BLACK	QUE	198	3RD E DI
KENT, HENRY	CAL	048	3RD DIST
KENT, J.Y.	CAL	062	3RD DIST
KENT, JAMES	BAL	137	1ST WARD
KENT, JAMES	ANN	398	8TH DIST
KENT, JAMES W.	CAL	062	3RD DIST
KENT, JOHN	CEC	030	CHESAPEA
KENT, JOHN	BAL	040	15TH WAR
KENT, JOHN-BLACK	CAR	071	NO TWP L
KENT, JOSEPH	BAL	074	2ND DIST
KENT, JOSEPH	ANN	349	3RD DIST
KENT, JOSHAWAY	HAR	206	3RD DIST
KENT, JULIA	ANN	350	3RD DIST
KENT, MARY	PRI	069	MARLBROU
KENT, PATRICK	BAL	134	2ND DIST
KENT, PHILIP	BAL	197	19TH WAR
KENT, RALPH	PRI	109	PISCATAW
KENT, SARAH	CAL	042	3RD DIST
KENT, SARAH	BAL	013	2ND DIST
KENT, THOMAS H.	CAL	055	3RD DIST
KENT, THOMAS R.	ANN	312	1ST DIST
KENT, WILLIAM	BAL	094	5TH WARD
KENT, WILLIAM	BAL	147	11TH WAR
KENT, WILLIAM	BAL	223	17TH WAR
KENT, WILLIAM	HAR	054	1ST DIST
KENTCH, PETER	BAL	082	1ST WARD
KENTEINS, PETER	WOR	316	2ND E DI
KENTENBENE, JACOBINA	BAL	061	4TH WARD
KENTINBINE, MARY	BAL	062	4TH WARD
KENTLINE, MICHAEL	CAR	353	6TH DIST
KENTON, SOLOMON	CAR	129	NO TWP L
KENTON,RACHEL	QUE	196	3RD E DI
KENTS, POWEL	BAL	356	8TH WARD
KENTZ, HENRY	BAL	446	8TH WARD
KENTZ, JACOB S.	BAL	242	12TH WAR
KENTZ, WILLIAM	BAL	276	2ND WARD
KENUN, ELKANA	HAR	154	3RD DIST
KENYON, PETER J.*	BAL	418	3RD WARD
KEOCH, ALEXANDER	PRI	044	VANSVILL
KEOFT, JOHN	BAL	104	2ND DIST
KEOGH, A.	FRE	200	5TH E DI
KEOHLER, ELIZABETH	BAL	456	1ST DIST
KEOHLER, WILLIAM F.	BAL	220	1ST DIST
KEONCE, WASHINGTON *	ANN	351	3RD DIST
KEPHART, ANN	BAL	453	8TH WARD
KEPHART, DAVID	CAR	303	1ST DIST
KEPHART, EUGENIA B.	FRE	065	FREDERIC
KEPHART, GEORGE	CAR	379	2ND DIST
KEPHART, HARMAN	FRE	073	FREDERIC
KEPHART, MATHEW	CAR	332	MANCHEST
KEPHART, PETER	FRE	020	FREDERIC
KEPHART, PETER J.	FRE	319	MIDDLETO
KEPHART, PHILIP	BAL	048	9TH WARD
KEPHAS, JOSEPH	BAL	458	8TH WARD
KEPLE, THOMAS *	BAL	145	2ND DIST
KEPLER, ABSALOM	FRE	401	JEFFERSO
KEPLER, ANDREW JR.	FRE	405	JEFFERSO
KEPLER, ANDREW SR.	FRE	408	JEFFERSO
KEPLER, CONSTANCE	BAL	394	14TH WAR
KEPLER, EMILY	BAL	124	18TH WAR
KEPLER, GEORGE W.	BAL	212	6TH WARD
KEPLER, HENRY	ALL	255	CUMBERLA
KEPLER, HENRY	BAL	321	20TH WAR
KEPLER, ISRAEL	FRE	407	JEFFERSO
KEPLER, JOHN	FRE	329	MIDDLETO
KEPLER, LLOYD A.	FRE	399	JEFFERSO
KEPLER, MARY E.	BAL	077	4TH WARD
KEPLER, RACHAEL	FRE	399	JEFFERSO
KEPLER, SARAH	FRE	408	JEFFERSO
KEPLER, WILLIAM	BAL	216	6TH WARD
KEPLING, JOHN	FRE	381	PETERSVI
KEPLINGER, DAVID	WAS	204	1ST DIST
KEPLINGER, EDWIN	WAS	221	1ST DIST
KEPLINGER, ELIZABETH	BAL	256	12TH WAR
KEPLINGER, GEORGE L.	BAL	400	8TH WARD
KEPLINGER, HANNAH	BAL	268	20TH WAR
KEPLINGER, JOHN	BAL	202	6TH WARD
KEPLINGER, JONOTHAN	WAS	221	1ST DIST
KEPLINGER, MARY	BAL	023	18TH WAR
KEPLINGER, MICHAEL	WAS	220	1ST DIST
KEPLINGER, NICHOLAS	WAS	196	1ST DIST
KEPLINGER, WILLIMA	CAR	184	8TH DIST
KEPLINGLER, ROSINA	BAL	399	8TH WARD
KEPP, MORGANN	FRE	413	8TH E DI
KEPP,WESLEY	FRE	453	8TH E DI
KEPPEL, JOHN	BAL	311	20TH WAR
KEPPLER, MARGARET	BAL	233	6TH WARD
KEPTNER, ENOS	FRE	162	EMMITTSB
KER, JOHN	ALL	140	6TH E.D.
KER, LAMBERT	SOM	427	PRINCESS
KER, SAMUEL	SOM	427	PRINCESS
KER, SAMUEL J. S.	SOM	528	QUANTICO
KER, WILLIAM*	SOM	477	TRAPP DI
KERBES, SAMUEL	TAL	095	ST MICHA
KERBEY, MARY E.	QUE	249	5TH E DI
KERBIG, THOMAS R.	BAL	272	12TH WAR
KERBY, BENJAMIN	ALL	093	5TH E.D.
KERBY, BENJAMIN	TAL	091	ST MICHA
KERBY, BENJAMIN	KEN	313	3RD DIST
KERBY, CHARLES	BAL	051	9TH WARD
KERBY, CLOWDESBUS *	TAL	099	ST MICHA
KERBY, CORNELIUS	ST	291	2ND E DI
KERBY, CORNLEIUS F.	ST	287	2ND E DI
KERBY, DEBER	TAL	101	ST MICHA
KERBY, EDWARD	BAL	447	14TH WAR
KERBY, EDWARD*	TAL	019	EASTON D
KERBY, ELIZA C.	TAL	096	ST MICHA
KERBY, ELLEN	KEN	313	3RD DIST
KERBY, ELSHA	TAL	083	ST MICHA
KERBY, FANNY	TAL	100	ST MICHA
KERBY, GEORGE W.	PRI	002	BLADENSB
KERBY, HORIM *	TAL	101	ST MICHA
KERBY, ISACK*	TAL	035	EASTON D
KERBY, ISAK	TAL	036	EASTON D
KERBY, JAMES*	TAL	065	EASTON T
KERBY, JOHN	KEN	290	3RD DIST
KERBY, JOHN	KEN	213	2ND DIST
KERBY, JOSHUA	BAL	308	3RD WARD
KERBY, LAMBERT	TAL	056	EASTON D
KERBY, LUIS	TAL	081	ST MICHA
KERBY, MARY	TAL	088	ST MICHA
KERBY, MARY	TAL	081	ST MICHA
KERBY, RACHEL-BLACK	CAR	113	NO TWP L
KERBY, SAMUEL R.	BAL	434	8TH WARD
KERBY, SILAS*	TAL	025	EASTON D
KERBY, SOLOMON	PRI	024	VANSVILL
KERBY, SUSAN	BAL	320	3RD WARD
KERBY, THOMAS	FRE	417	8TH E DI
KERBY, THOMAS H.	TAL	080	ST MICHA
KERBY, WESTLEY	TAL	029	EASTON D
KERBY, WILLIAM	PRI	106	PISCATAW
KERBY, WILLIAM	ALL	093	5TH E.D.
KERBY, WILLIAM	BAL	129	1ST WARD
KERBY, WILLIAM A.	TAL	051	EASTON D
KERBY, WILLIAM H.	TAL	087	ST MICHA
KERBY, WILLIAM*	TAL	020	EASTON D
KERBY, WILLIAM*	TAL	017	EASTON D
KERBY, ZEBLON H.	HAR	180	3RD DIST
KERBY,JACOB	CAR	091	NO TWP L
KERBY,MATILDA	ST	313	1ST E DI
KERCHENBOUGH, JOHN	BAL	256	2ND WARD
KERCHER, ANTHONY	BAL	293	17TH WAR
KERCHER, FREDERICK	BAL	119	18TH WAR
KERCHEVAL, JOHN	WAS	095	2ND SUBD
KERCHNER, FRANCIS	BAL	114	5TH WARD
KERCHNER, JOHN	WAS	107	2ND DIST
KERCHNER, KILLIAN	BAL	255	2ND WARD
KERCHNER, MARY	BAL	113	15TH WAR
KERCHNER, SUSAN	WAS	106	2ND DIST
KERCHNER, WILLIAM	BAL	113	5TH WARD
KEREBY, GODFREY	BAL	006	18TH WAR
KERER, JAMES	BAL	263	20TH WAR
KERFER, JOHN	BAL	216	17TH WAR
KERFOD, WILLIAM	WAS	220	1ST DIST
KERFOOT, A.A.	WAS	019	2ND SUBD
KERFOOT, ANDREW	WAS	102	2ND DIST
KERFOOT, GEORGE W.	WAS	102	2ND DIST
KERFOOT, JAMES	WAS	101	2ND DIST
KERFOOT, JOHN B.	WAS	018	2ND SUBD
KERFOOT, ROBERT	BAL	334	13TH WAR
KERICH, LAZARUS	BAL	301	3RD WARD
KERK, MATILDA*	TAL	002	EASTON D
KERKET, JACOB	WAS	100	2ND DIST
KERKNER, RICHARD	ANN	314	1ST DIST
KERLEW, FRANKLIN	CAR	234	UNION TO
KERLEY, EDWARD	BAL	364	3RD WARD
KERLINGER, ELIZA	BAL	326	7TH WARD
KERLINGER, ELIZABETH	CAR	333	MANCHEST
KERLINGER, GEORGE	BAL	394	14TH WAR
KERLINGER, JACOB	CAR	328	MANCHEST
KERLINGS, HENRY M.	BAL	234	2ND WARD
KERMAN, JACOB	BAL	314	1ST DIST
KERMAN, JOHN	BAL	394	1ST DIST
KERMAN, JOHN A.	BAL	134	1ST WARD
KERMAN, MARY	BAL	016	9TH WARD
KERMAN, MICHAEL	BAL	125	11TH WAR
KERMAN, THOMAS	BAL	406	8TH WARD
KERMER, AMELIA	BAL	017	9TH WARD
KERMICHALY, HUGH	WAS	164	2ND DIST
KERN, ARTHUR	ALL	246	CUMBERLA
KERN, JOHN	ALL	246	CUMBERLA
KERN, JOHN	ALL	233	CUMBERLA
KERN, JOHN	BAL	127	1ST WARD
KERN, RUTH	ALL	177	7TH E.D.
KERNAN, ANN	ALL	255	CUMBERLA
KERNAN, BERNARD	BAL	070	4TH WARD
KERNAN, CAROLINE	BAL	415	14TH WAR
KERNAN, EDWARD	BAL	071	10TH WAR
KERNAN, ELLEN	BAL	182	6TH WARD
KERNAN, HUGH	PRI	036	VANSVILL
KERNAN, JAMES	PRI	036	VANSVILL
KERNAN, JAMES	BAL	072	10TH WAR
KERNAN, JAMES H.	BAL	026	4TH WARD
KERNAN, JAMES W.	BAL	010	15TH WAR
KERNAN, JOHN	BAL	030	2ND DIST
KERNAN, JOHN	BAL	418	8TH WARD
KERNAN, LAWRENCE	FRE	202	5TH E DI
KERNAN, MARY	BAL	424	8TH WARD
KERNAN, MARY*	BAL	418	3RD WARD
KERNAN, PETER	BAL	072	15TH WAR
KERNAN, ROBERT	BAL	432	8TH WARD
KERNAN, SAMUEL	BAL	258	5TH WARD
KERNAN, THERESE	BAL	181	6TH WARD
KERNAN, THOMS	ALL	181	8TH E.D.
KERNAN, WILLIAM	BAL	280	2ND WARD
KERNARD, MARY	BAL	183	2ND WARD
KERNEILLEY, GEORGE	BAL	149	1ST WARD
KERNER, AMELIA	BAL	017	9TH WARD
KERNER, CAROLINE	BAL	038	4TH WARD
KERNER, CHRISTIAN D.	BAL	454	14TH WAR
KERNER, ELLEN	BAL	057	15TH WAR
KERNER, JOHN F.	BAL	038	4TH WARD
KERNER, MARGARET	BAL	018	9TH WARD
KERNER, MARGARET	BAL	017	9TH WARD
KERNER, SIMON	BAL	081	1ST WARD
KERNEY, BRIDGET	BAL	353	7TH WARD
KERNEY, JAMES	ALL	237	CUMBERLA
KERNEY, JAMES	BAL	115	18TH WAR
KERNEY, JOHN	ALL	079	5TH E.D.
KERNEY, MARGARET	ALL	216	CUMBERLA
KERNEY, MARGARET	BAL	119	15TH WAR
KERNEY, MARY ANN*	BAL	333	3RD WARD
KERNEY, MATHIAS J.	BAL	120	5TH WARD
KERNEY, MICHAEL	ALL	237	CUMBERLA
KERNEY, PATRICK	ALL	239	CUMBERLA
KERNEY, PHILIP	BAL	336	3RD WARD
KERNEY, SAMUEL	BAL	179	6TH WARD
KERNEY, THOMAS	BAL	007	15TH WAR
KERNEY, WESLEY	CAR	309	1ST DIST
KERNS, ELIZABETH	CAR	309	1ST DIST
KERNS, LAURENCE	BAL	017	9TH WARD
KERNS, MARGARET	ALL	216	CUMBERLA
KERNS, MARY T.	BAL	380	3RD WARD
KERNS, ROBERT	ALL	231	CUMBERLA
KERNVEN, P.	BAL	140	1ST WARD
KERR, ANN W.	BAL	435	1ST DIST
KERR, BENJAMIN	SOM	478	TRAPP DI
KERR, CHARLOTTE	SOM	477	TRAPP DI
KERR, EDWARD	BAL	009	15TH WAR
KERR, EDWARD	BAL	010	15TH WAR
KERR, FRANCIS	BAL	039	15TH WAR
KERR, ISABELLA	BAL	153	16TH WAR
KERR, JACOB R.	BAL	059	15TH WAR
KERR, JAMES	BAL	105	5TH WARD
KERR, JAMES	WAS	098	2ND DIST
KERR, JOHN	BAL	231	5TH WARD
KERR, JOHN B.	BAL	169	2ND DIST
KERR, JOHN BOZMAN	TAL	078	EASTON T
KERR, JOSEPH B.	BAL	050	9TH WARD
KERR, JOSIAH*	DOR	447	1ST DIST
KERR, LEAH	SOM	477	TRAPP DI
KERR, LURY H.	TAL	078	EASTON T
KERR, M.	DOR	434	1ST DIST
KERR, MARY E.	FRE	065	FREDERIC
KERR, MARY J.	CAR	270	WESTMINS
KERR, ROBERT	BAL	105	5TH WARD
KERR, SAMUEL	KEN	226	2ND DIST
KERR, SAMUEL C.	MGM	378	ROCKERLE
KERR, SARAH	BAL	339	13TH WAR
KERR, SARAH	BAL	348	1ST DIST
KERR, SARAH	BAL	241	5TH WARD
KERR, WILLIAM	CEC	128	5TH E DI
KERR, WILLIAM	BAL	058	18TH WAR
KERRGER, SOPHIA *	BAL	070	18TH WAR
KERRICK, EDWARD	KEN	291	3RD DIST
KERRIGAN, EDWARD	BAL	262	6TH WARD
KERRIGN, JAMES	FRE	165	EMMITTSB
KERRLE, NATHANIEL	BAL	274	12TH WAR
KERRS, JOHN W.	MGM	378	ROCKERLE
KERRS, WILLIAM	ALL	177	7TH E.D.
KERRY, W.	BAL	153	1ST WARD
KERSEY, ANN	BAL	096	5TH WARD
KERSEY, DEBBY	TAL	109	ST MICHA
KERSEY, ELIZA	CAR	102	NO TWP L
KERSEY, MARGARET	QUE	235	4TH E DI
KERSEY, WILLIAM	BAL	423	8TH WARD
KERSEY, WILLIAM*	TAL	055	EASTON D
KERSHAW, EDWARD	BAL	244	20TH WAR
KERSHAW, JAMES L.	CAL	003	1ST DIST
KERSHAW, JANE	CEC	087	4TH E DI
KERSHAW, JOHN	BAL	244	20TH WAR
KERSHAW, JOHN W.	CAL	005	1ST DIST
KERSHAW, WILLIAM	CEC	088	4TH E DI
KERSHERER, MARY	FRE	006	FREDERIC
KERSHNER, BENJAMIN F.	BAL	330	13TH WAR
KERSHNER, DAVID	ALL	214	CUMBERLA
KERSHNER, GEORGE	WAS	118	2ND DIST
KERSHNER, GUSTAVUS	WAS	134	2ND DIST
KERSHNER, JAMES	WAS	162	HAGERSTO
KERSLER, JOHN	BAL	217	19TH WAR
KERSTER, EMILY	BAL	125	16TH WAR
KERSTZER, THEODORE	BAL	466	14TH WAR
KERT, HENRIETTA*	TAL	018	EASTON D
KERT, MATILDA*	TAL	002	EASTON D
KERTH, HARRIET	ALL	245	CUMBERLA

Name	County	Page	District
KERTHLEY, THOMAS	HAR	161	3RD DIST
KERTHLEY, THOMAS *	TAL	082	ST MICHA
KERTIS, MARY ANN	BAL	086	4TH WARD
KERTLEY, JAMES	BAL	166	6TH WARD
KERTZ, SABASTIN	HAR	145	3RD DIST
KERVICK, KEERN	ALL	253	CUMBERLA
KERVIN, J. K.	BAL	049	4TH WARD
KERVIN, JOHN	BAL	050	4TH WARD
KERWAN, JAMES*	DOR	334	3RD DIVI
KERWAN, JOHN	DOR	336	3RD DIVI
KERWAN, SAMUEL	DOR	335	3RD DIVI
KERWAN, SOLOMON F.*	DOR	360	3RD DIVI
KERWAN, THOMAS*	DOR	339	3RD DIVI
KERWIN, ROBERT*	BAL	353	3RD WARD
KESAELING, GEORGE	FRE	311	MIDDLETO
KESKETT, L. C.	WAS	049	2ND SUBD
KESLER, CASPER	BAL	192	2ND WARD
KESLER, EPTER	WAS	279	LEITERSB
KESLER, IRA S.	BAL	260	12TH WAR
KESLER, JACOB	FRE	230	BUCKEYST
KESLER, JOHN	HAR	177	3RD DIST
KESLEY, GEORGE	BAL	125	16TH WAR
KESMAN, NICHOLAS	BAL	143	2ND DIST
KESMODIE, F.	BAL	315	12TH WAR
KESNODER, MARTIN*	BAL	097	10TH WAR
KESSEBRING, DAWALT	CAR	271	WESTMINS
KESSELRING, FRANCIS	CAR	273	WESTMINS
KESSELRING, JAMES	CAR	260	3RD DIST
KESSELRING, JOHN	CAR	314	1ST DIST
KESSELRING, MICHAEL	CAR	312	1ST DIST
KESSEN, JOHN	BAL	013	2ND DIST
KESSER, MICHAEL	FRE	230	BUCKEYST
KESSLER, ARAMENTA	FRE	027	FREDERIC
KESSLER, CATHARINE	CAR	331	MANCHEST
KESSLER, CATHERINE	BAL	019	9TH WARD
KESSLER, CHRISTIAN	BAL	256	1ST DIST
KESSLER, CONRADT	BAL	434	8TH WARD
KESSLER, ELIZABETH	FRE	453	8TH E DI
KESSLER, FREDERICK	BAL	007	15TH WAR
KESSLER, J. G.	BAL	081	10TH WAR
KESSLER, JACOB	CAR	330	MANCHEST
KESSLER, JOHN	BAL	003	15TH WAR
KESSLER, MARGARET	BAL	011	15TH WAR
KESSLER, MARY H.	WAS	115	2ND DIST
KESSLER, MATTHEW	BAL	249	20TH WAR
KESSLER, MICHAEL	BAL	198	19TH WAR
KESSLER, NELSON	WAS	135	2ND DIST
KESSLER, THOMAS	FRE	213	BUCKEYST
KESSLERING, GEORGE	CAR	313	1ST DIST
KESSLIN, C.	BAL	271	12TH WAR
KESSNER, HENRY	BAL	193	2ND WARD
KESTE, MARGARET*	DOR	406	1ST DIST
KESTER, ELIZABETH	CAR	332	MANCHEST
KESTER, MARGARET*	DOR	406	1ST DIST
KESTLER, ANDREW	BAL	048	18TH WAR
KESTLER, CHRISTIANA	BAL	200	11TH WAR
KESTON, FREDERICK	BAL	366	3RD WARD
KESTUS, WILTON	HAR	182	3RD DIST
KETAL, JOHN	BAL	137	1ST WARD
KETCHAM, WILLIAM	BAL	076	1ST WARD
KETCHUM, STEPHEN	WOR	316	2ND E DI
KETHORN, JOHN	BAL	084	1ST WARD
KETLAND, WILLAIM	PRI	108	PISCATAW
KETLER, FRANCES	BAL	025	4TH WARD
KETLING, MARGARET	BAL	213	19TH WAR
KETROUSE, HENRY	FRE	094	FREDERIC
KETROWS, CATHARINE	FRE	095	FREDERIC
KETS, SARAH *	WAS	062	2ND SUBD
KETSOW, JOHN	FRE	090	FREDERIC
KETTENBARG, SIMON*	BAL	067	4TH WARD
KETTING, JERO	BAL	212	19TH WAR
KETTLE, MARY	BAL	365	13TH WAR
KETTLER, CATHERINE	BAL	002	9TH WARD
KETTLER, FREDERICK	BAL	380	3RD WARD
KETTLER, GEORGE	FRE	001	FREDERIC
KETTLEWELL, JOHN	BAL	188	16TH WAR
KETTNER, FRANEL*	BAL	018	4TH WARD
KETTONE, ISAAC	FRE	053	FREDERIC
KETTY, WILLAIM	BAL	204	17TH WAR
KEUBETS, JOHN	FRE	075	FREDERIC
KEULEY, WILLIAM	HAR	030	1ST DIST
KEUP, ANN *	BAL	103	18TH WAR
KEUTZER, CHARLES T.	BAL	062	10TH WAR
KEVINGTON, PAT S.	BAL	153	19TH WAR
KEVITZ, CHRISTIAN*	BAL	340	3RD WARD
KEW, JOHN M.	BAL	446	8TH WARD
KEWIN, ROBERT*	BAL	353	3RD WARD
KEWSLEY, ELIZABETH	BAL	236	17TH WAR
KEWSLEY, WENSEL	BAL	236	17TH WAR
KEXEL, A.	BAL	220	2ND WARD
KEY, ABNER	BAL	056	18TH WAR
KEY, ABRAM	CAL	021	2ND DIST
KEY, ANGELINA	FRE	265	NEW MARK
KEY, ANN	FRE	203	5TH E DI
KEY, ASBURY-BLACK	CAR	388	2ND DIST
KEY, CALEB	MGM	443	CLARKSTR
KEY, D. M.	BAL	333	1ST DIST
KEY, E.R.	BAL	137	1ST WARD
KEY, EDMOND	PRI	062	NOTTINGH
KEY, ELIAS-BLACK	FRE	437	8TH E DI
KEY, ELLEN	BAL	279	7TH WARD
KEY, GEORGE-MULATTO	FRE	452	8TH E DI
KEY, GLLEN	FRE	247	NEW MARK
KEY, H. G. L.	ST	266	3RD E DI
KEY, HENRY-BLACK	FRE	439	8TH E DI
KEY, HIRAM-MULATTO	FRE	011	FREDERIC
KEY, HIRAM-MULATTO	FRE	420	8TH E DI
KEY, JAMES	FRE	123	CREAGERS
KEY, JAMES-BLACK	FRE	437	8TH E DI
KEY, JEREMIAH-BLACK	CAR	385	2ND DIST
KEY, JOHN H.	ST	336	4TH E DI
KEY, JOHN K.	CAR	329	MANCHEST
KEY, JONAS-MULATTO	FRE	425	8TH E DI
KEY, JOSEPH	BAL	150	1ST WARD
KEY, JOSEPH H.	HAR	079	2ND DIST
KEY, JULIA	BAL	042	15TH WAR
KEY, LYDIA	CAR	377	2ND DIST
KEY, MALINDA E.	FRE	265	NEW MARK
KEY, MARGARET	FRE	088	FREDERIC
KEY, MARY	BAL	210	11TH WAR
KEY, MARY	CAL	042	3RD DIST
KEY, MARY E.	CHA	233	HILLTOP
KEY, MARY J.	BAL	078	10TH WAR
KEY, MATILDA-BLACK	FRE	422	8TH E DI
KEY, MRS. F.S.	BAL	205	11TH WAR
KEY, OWEN	WAS	164	2ND DIST
KEY, RICHARD	HAR	079	2ND DIST
KEY, SAMUEL	FRE	100	FREDERIC
KEY, SAMUEL-BLACK	FRE	433	8TH E DI
KEY, SARAH	ST	267	3RD E DI
KEY, SENAH-BLACK	FRE	421	8TH E DI
KEY, STEPHEN-BLACK	FRE	431	8TH E DI
KEY, SUSAN	WAS	151	HAGERSTO
KEY, UPTON S.	CAL	060	3RD DIST
KEY, WASHINGTON	ANN	456	HOWARD D
KEY, WILLIAM-MULATTO	FRE	023	FREDERIC
KEY, ZACHARAH	FRE	123	CREAGERS
KEYE, ELIE	WAS	012	WILLIAMS
KEYE, FRANKLIN	WAS	010	WILLIAMS
KEYER, JAMES	BAL	121	11TH WAR
KEYES, JOHN	BAL	165	1ST WARD
KEYHEART, ANDREW	PRI	028	VANSVILL
KEYHEART, ANDREW	PRI	028	VANSVILL
KEYHEART, CATHERINE	PRI	029	VANSVILL
KEYHOLES, GEORGE*	DOR	381	1ST DIST
KEYHOTES, GEORGE*	DOR	381	1ST DIST
KEYL, WILLIAM	BAL	356	13TH WAR
KEYLER, JOHN G.	BAL	392	14TH WAR
KEYLOR, JOHN	ALL	234	CUMBERLA
KEYS, ALEX*	DOR	434	1ST DIST
KEYS, ALEXANDER	ANN	445	HOWARD D
KEYS, ALEXANDER	BAL	217	6TH DIST
KEYS, ANN	BAL	387	8TH WARD
KEYS, ANN O.*	DOR	447	1ST DIST
KEYS, ANNE	BAL	101	15TH WAR
KEYS, ARAMINTA	BAL	227	6TH WARD
KEYS, BAYLEY	BAL	149	11TH WAR
KEYS, CABLE	BAL	114	18TH WAR
KEYS, CHANDLER	MGM	378	ROCKERLE
KEYS, CHARLES	HAR	085	2ND DIST
KEYS, CHARLES	BAL	027	2ND DIST
KEYS, DAVID	CAR	293	7TH DIST
KEYS, ELEANBOR T.	ST	307	1ST E DI
KEYS, ELIZABETH	TAL	053	EASTON D
KEYS, ELIZABETH	BAL	328	3RD WARD
KEYS, ELLEN	BAL	068	15TH WAR
KEYS, ELLEN	BAL	241	17TH WAR
KEYS, FIELDING	ANN	446	HOWARD D
KEYS, FRANCIS S.	BAL	315	1ST DIST
KEYS, FREDERICK	BAL	144	19TH WAR
KEYS, GEORGE	BAL	027	2ND DIST
KEYS, GEORGE	WAS	282	1ST DIST
KEYS, HARRIETT	BAL	070	18TH WAR
KEYS, HARRIETT E.	DOR	312	1ST DIST
KEYS, HENRIETTA	BAL	045	4TH WARD
KEYS, HENRY	BAL	312	1ST DIST
KEYS, HORATIO	BAL	345	1ST DIST
KEYS, HUGH	BAL	362	8TH WARD
KEYS, HUGH	BAL	125	11TH WAR
KEYS, J.	BAL	139	1ST WARD
KEYS, JAMES	ANN	479	HOWARD D
KEYS, JAMES	BAL	180	6TH WARD
KEYS, JAMES	BAL	102	1ST WARD
KEYS, JAMES N.	BAL	009	4TH WARD
KEYS, JAMS	BAL	020	1ST WARD
KEYS, JEREMIAH	BAL	290	1ST DIST
KEYS, JERRY	BAL	025	18TH WAR
KEYS, JOHN	HAR	041	1ST DIST
KEYS, JOHN	HAR	173	3RD DIST
KEYS, JOHN	BAL	123	1ST WARD
KEYS, JOHN	BAL	196	5TH DIST
KEYS, JOHN	BAL	294	7TH WARD
KEYS, JOHN	BAL	294	7TH WARD
KEYS, JOHN	TAL	028	EASTON D
KEYS, JOHN H.	BAL	026	18TH WAR
KEYS, JOSEPH T.	BAL	345	13TH WAR
KEYS, JUDSON	WAS	201	1ST DIST
KEYS, LAREY	BAL	308	7TH WARD
KEYS, LIZZA L.	BAL	316	1ST DIST
KEYS, LOTTY*	DOR	315	1ST DIST
KEYS, MARGARET	BAL	386	8TH WARD
KEYS, MARGARETT	DOR	320	1ST DIST
KEYS, MARSHALL	BAL	056	18TH WAR
KEYS, MARY E.	DOR	314	1ST DIST
KEYS, MARY E.	BAL	028	4TH WARD
KEYS, MATILDA	BAL	217	6TH DIST
KEYS, PETER	BAL	117	5TH WARD
KEYS, PETER	ANN	445	HOWARD D
KEYS, PHILIP	ALL	255	CUMBERLA
KEYS, REACHEL	BAL	205	11TH WAR
KEYS, RHODY	BAL	071	4TH WARD
KEYS, SAMUEL	BAL	279	7TH WARD
KEYS, SAMUEL*	DOR	447	1ST DIST
KEYS, SARAH A.	BAL	295	7TH WARD
KEYS, SOPHIA	TAL	082	ST MICHA
KEYS, STEPHEN	CAR	294	7TH DIST
KEYS, STEPHEN	CAR	285	7TH DIST
KEYS, THOMAS	BAL	048	9TH WARD
KEYS, WILLIAM	BAL	424	1ST DIST
KEYS, WILLIAM	BAL	350	3RD WARD
KEYS, WILLIAM	BAL	178	6TH WARD
KEYS, WILLIAM H.	BAL	071	4TH WARD
KEYS, WILLIS	CAR	154	NO TWP L
KEYSE, S.	BAL	332	1ST DIST
KEYSEN, JOHN	BAL	111	2ND DIST
KEYSER, ADAM	ALL	242	CUMBERLA
KEYSER, ANDREW	BAL	460	1ST DIST
KEYSER, ANNA	BAL	100	15TH WAR
KEYSER, ANTHONY	BAL	211	17TH WAR
KEYSER, BARBARA	BAL	324	1ST DIST
KEYSER, BENJAMIN	FRE	099	FREDERIC
KEYSER, CASPAR	BAL	238	20TH WAR
KEYSER, CATHARINE	FRE	091	FREDERIC
KEYSER, CATHARINE	BAL	195	11TH WAR
KEYSER, CHARLES H.	BAL	352	7TH WARD
KEYSER, CHARLES M.	BAL	268	12TH WAR
KEYSER, CHRISTOPHER	BAL	277	2ND WARD
KEYSER, D. W.	BAL	061	18TH WAR
KEYSER, DANIEL	WAS	263	1ST DIST
KEYSER, FRANCIS	HAR	107	2ND DIST
KEYSER, GEORGE	BAL	121	18TH WAR
KEYSER, GODFREY	CAR	330	MANCHEST
KEYSER, HENRY	WAS	184	BOONSBOR
KEYSER, HENRY	BAL	323	1ST DIST
KEYSER, HENRY	BAL	169	6TH WARD
KEYSER, HENRY	ALL	168	6TH E.D.
KEYSER, HESTER	BAL	456	14TH WAR
KEYSER, HETTY	BAL	460	14TH WAR
KEYSER, JACOB	FRE	057	FREDERIC
KEYSER, JOHN	FRE	094	FREDERIC
KEYSER, JOHN	BAL	131	2ND DIST
KEYSER, JOHN	BAL	064	1ST WARD
KEYSER, JOHN	WAS	252	1ST DIST
KEYSER, JOHN	WAS	215	1ST DIST
KEYSER, JOHN	WAS	286	1ST DIST
KEYSER, JOHN W.	BAL	083	1ST WARD
KEYSER, KNOX	ALL	001	3RD E.D.
KEYSER, LAVINIA	WAS	223	1ST DIST
KEYSER, MARGARET	WAS	184	BOONSBOR
KEYSER, MARGARET	BAL	096	1ST WARD
KEYSER, MARIA	WAS	182	BOONSBOR
KEYSER, MARY	BAL	056	1ST WARD
KEYSER, MARY	BAL	002	15TH WAR
KEYSER, MARY E.	ANN	521	HOWARD D
KEYSER, MICHAEL F.	BAL	439	14TH WAR
KEYSER, MOSES	BAL	064	15TH WAR
KEYSER, NICHOLAS	BAL	287	12TH WAR
KEYSER, PHILLIP	FRE	099	FREDERIC
KEYSER, SAMUEL	FRE	091	FREDERIC
KEYSER, SAMUEL J.	BAL	157	11TH WAR
KEYSER, SOPHIA	BAL	288	12TH WAR
KEYSER, WILLIAM	BAL	325	1ST DIST
KEYSER, WILLIAM	BAL	332	1ST DIST
KEYSES, LIVINA	WAS	186	BOONSBOR
KEYSEVGER, ELLEN	ALL	090	5TH E.D.
KEYSNEE, JOHN	ALL	054	10TH E.D
KEYSNEE, SAMUEL	ALL	054	10TH E.D
KEYSNER, JAMES	ALL	053	10TH E.D
KEYSOR, HENRY	BAL	056	4TH WARD
KEYSOR, SOLOMON	BAL	018	4TH WARD
KEYTH, NANCY	BAL	345	1ST DIST
KEYWORTH, JOHN	BAL	132	5TH WARD
KEYWORTH, THOMAS	BAL	223	19TH WAR
KEZSIE, HENRY	ALL	055	10TH E.D
KHIETH, SARAH	BAL	095	5TH WARD
KHILERT, HENRY	BAL	047	9TH WARD
KHILERT, HENRY S.	BAL	047	9TH WARD
KHROAN, JACOB	BAL	105	1ST WARD
KIAB, STEPHEN*	DOR	384	1ST DIST
KIAH, EDWARD	BAL	294	17TH WAR
KIAH, ROBERT	DOR	368	3RD DIVI
KIAR, PRISCILLA	BAL	093	10TH WAR
KIBBER, CATHARIEN	BAL	419	14TH WAR
KIBBER, JOHN	BAL	446	8TH WARD
KIBBIN, J. G. M.*	BAL	115	11TH WAR
KIBBLE, ANN	SOM	479	TRAPP DI
KIBBLE, MARY	SOM	487	SALISBUR
KIBBS, EDWARD*	TAL	051	EASTON D
KIBBY, WILLIAM	BAL	297	17TH WAR
KIBLER, CATHERINE	BAL	389	8TH WARD
KIBLER, HENRY	CEC	040	CHESAPEA
KIBLER, MARY	CEC	040	CHESAPEA
KICK, JACOB J.	CEC	131	6TH E DI
KICK, SAMUEL *	BAL	292	1ST DIST
KICKLEY, FRANCIS	BAL	164	2ND DIST
KICKY, MARY	CHA	283	BOJANTOW
KID, ANN	BAL	102	5TH WARD
KID, CHARLES	BAL	427	14TH WAR
KID, CHARLES H.	BAL	427	14TH WAR
KID, JOHN	BAL	427	14TH WAR
KID, JOHN H.	BAL	025	2ND DIST
KID, JOSHUA	BAL	025	2ND DIST
KID, JULIAN	BAL	435	1ST DIST
KID, MOSES	BAL	025	2ND DIST
KID, RACHEL	BAL	304	1ST DIST
KIDD, AMANDA	BAL	313	7TH WARD
KIDD, ANDREW	CEC	147	PORT DUP
KIDD, BALINDA	HAR	077	BEL AIR
KIDD, BENJAMIN	BAL	111	10TH WAR
KIDD, DAVID	BAL	214	6TH DIST
KIDD, ELIAS	BAL	215	6TH DIST
KIDD, ELIZABETH	BAL	206	6TH DIST
KIDD, ELIZABETH	BAL	445	8TH WARD
KIDD, GEORGE	CEC	156	PORT DUP
KIDD, GEORGE W.	FRE	422	8TH E DI
KIDD, JACOB	CEC	120	4TH E DI
KIDD, JAMES	CEC	180	7TH E DI
KIDD, JAMES	BAL	397	8TH WARD
KIDD, JAMES	BAL	357	8TH WARD
KIDD, JOHN	BAL	033	2ND DIST
KIDD, JOHN B.	BAL	039	2ND DIST
KIDD, JOSHUA	BAL	064	2ND DIST
KIDD, JOSHUA	BAL	285	7TH WARD
KIDD, JULIA	BAL	301	1ST DIST
KIDD, LEONIDAS	CEC	157	PORT DUP
KIDD, LEWIS	BAL	442	8TH WARD
KIDD, LYDIA	BAL	096	10TH WAR
KIDD, MILTON Y.	CEC	156	PORT DUP
KIDD, REBECCA	CEC	149	PORT DUP
KIDD, ROBERT	BAL	050	2ND DIST
KIDD, WILLIAM G.	FRE	410	8TH E DI
KIDD,JOSEPH	FRE	450	8TH E DI
KIDDER, CAMILLUS	BAL	062	10TH WAR
KIDDER, ELIZABETH L.	BAL	462	14TH WAR
KIDDIES, JAMES	BAL	348	3RD WARD
KIDGLEY, RICHARD-MULATTO	FRE	411	8TH E DI
KIDLER, GEORGE	FRE	390	PETERSVI
KIDROY, THOMAS	ALL	241	CUMBERLA
KIDWELL, ANN	PRI	055	AQUASCO
KIDWELL, B.J.	PRI	060	NOTTINGH
KIDWELL, CHARLES	MGM	318	CRACKLIN
KIDWELL, DANIEL	BAL	259	1ST DIST
KIDWELL, DILILAH	PRI	061	NOTTINGH
KIDWELL, ELIZABETH	PRI	042	VANSVILL
KIDWELL, FRANCIS	MGM	374	ROCKERLE
KIDWELL, FRANCIS L.	BAL	361	13TH WAR
KIDWELL, HARRIOTT	WAS	103	2ND DIST
KIDWELL, HENRIETTA	FRE	222	BUCKEYST
KIDWELL, J.	PRI	062	NOTTINGH
KIDWELL, J. HARRISON	WAS	110	2ND DIST
KIDWELL, JAMES	PRI	059	NOTTINGH
KIDWELL, JAMES	PRI	060	NOTTINGH
KIDWELL, JOHN	PRI	071	MARLBROU
KIDWELL, JOHN	ANN	359	3RD DIST
KIDWELL, JOHN W.	PRI	094	SPALDING
KIDWELL, L.	PRI	065	NOTTINGH
KIDWELL, MARY	PRI	059	NOTTINGH
KIDWELL, MARY A.	ST	342	5TH E DI
KIDWELL, ROBERT	BAL	077	18TH WAR
KIDWELL, SARAH	PRI	053	AQUASCO
KIDWELL, WILLIAM	PRI	061	NOTTINGH
KIEBARD, BEAL	ST	337	4TH E DI
KIEHL, GEORGE	WAS	293	1ST DIST
KIEL, JOHN H.	BAL	038	4TH WARD
KIELEY, DAVID *	BAL	288	1ST DIST
KIELHOLTZ, ANN	FRE	191	5TH E DI
KIELHOLTZ, BENJAMIN	FRE	191	5TH E DI
KIELHOLTZ, DAVID	FRE	190	5TH E DI
KIEM, JAMES	DOR	368	3RD DIVI
KIEM, JOHN	DOR	368	3RD DIVI
KIER, CHARLES	HAR	100	2ND DIST
KIER, MILLY	BAL	316	3RD WARD
KIER, THOMAS	BAL	115	1ST WARD
KIERNAN, JAMES	BAL	140	1ST WARD
KIERNS, SAPHEN	BAL	254	12TH WAR
KIERSING, PHILIP	BAL	205	19TH WAR
KIES, BENJAMIN C.	BAL	083	18TH WAR
KIESTER, MADALINE	BAL	275	2ND WARD
KIETZER, ELIZA	WAS	174	FUNKSTOW
KIFEL, GEORGE	BAL	410	14TH WAR

Name	County	Page	District
KIFEL, HENRY N.	BAL	411	14TH WAR
KIFER, CASPER	BAL	039	15TH WAR
KIFFLE, ANN C.	BAL	466	14TH WAR
KIGGINS, JAMES*	BAL	314	3RD WARD
KIGGIS, VIRGIL	BAL	128	1ST WARD
KIGHT, COMS	ALL	127	4TH E.D.
KIGHT, CORNELIUS	ALL	067	10TH E.D
KIGHT, ENOCH	ALL	125	4TH E.D.
KIGHT, HENRY	ALL	127	4TH E.D.
KIGHT, HENRY	ALL	130	4TH E.D.
KIGHT, JOHN	ALL	127	4TH E.D.
KIGHT, JOHN	ALL	127	4TH E.D.
KIGHT, JOSHUA	ALL	126	4TH E.D.
KIGHT, JOSIAH	ALL	129	4TH E.D.
KIGHT, MARYANN	ALL	125	4TH E.D.
KIGHT, WILLIAM	ALL	124	4TH E.D.
KIGHT, WILLIAM	ALL	127	4TH E.D.
KIGN, MICHAL	BAL	327	1ST DIST
KIHR, FLONARY	BAL	231	19TH WAR
KIKIRK, GEORGE	FRE	345	MIDDLETO
KILBAUGH, CONRAD	BAL	187	5TH DIST
KILBAUGH, JOHN	BAL	004	18TH WAR
KILBERTH, JOHN	CEC	069	5TH E DI
KILBOCKIN, MARGARET	BAL	352	7TH WARD
KILBORN, CECILIA	MGM	319	CRACKLIN
KILBOUN, E. G.	BAL	046	18TH WAR
KILBOURN, ANDREW	BAL	172	19TH WAR.
KILBOURN, L.	BAL	238	20TH WAR
KILBOURN, M.	BAL	258	12TH WAR
KILBOURNE, A.	BAL	152	1ST WARD
KILBRAITH, THOMAS	BAL	407	14TH WAR
KILBURN, DIANA T.	BAL	063	4TH WARD
KILCHENSTEIN, ELIZA	BAL	089	10TH WAR
KILDEER, JOHN	BAL	113	1ST WARD
KILDENBECK, JOHN	BAL	009	18TH WAR
KILE, GEORGE	BAL	189	19TH WAR
KILEE, LEWIS	BAL	119	18TH WAR
KILEHOLTS, GEORGE	BAL	392	8TH WARD
KILER, CHARLES	CAL	020	2ND DIST
KILER, ISAAC	FRE	440	8TH E DI
KILER, MELLY	CAL	042	3RD DIST
KILER, NATHANIEL	CAL	020	2ND DIST
KILER, NELSON	CAL	052	3RD DIST
KILES, REUBEN	ALL	154	6TH E.D.
KILGAN, J.	BAL	196	2ND WARD
KILGOM, ALEXANDER	MGM	379	ROCKERLE
KILGONE, CHARLES J.	MGM	379	ROCKERLE
KILGOUR, JAMES E.	ST	341	5TH E DI
KILGOUR, JOHN A.T.	MGM	399	ROCKERLE
KILKELLY, ELLEN	BAL	405	14TH WAR
KILKELLY, ELLEN	BAL	383	1ST DIST
KILL, JOHN	ALL	056	10TH E.D
KILL, JOHN	CAR	185	8TH DIST
KILLARD, FRANCIS	BAL	083	10TH WAR
KILLARD, MARY	BAL	059	10TH WAR
KILLBRIDGE, THOMAS	ANN	468	HOWARD D
KILLDOLPH, PATRICK	BAL	170	11TH WAR
KILLDORE, ARTHUR*	BAL	076	10TH WAR
KILLDORE, MICHAEL *	ALL	078	5TH E.D.
KILLDOVE, ARTHUR*	BAL	076	10TH WAR
KILLOUFF, PATRICK	ALL	048	10TH E.D
KILLELA, THOMAS	BAL	231	19TH WAR
KILLEN, BARBARA	BAL	060	1ST WARD
KILLEN, JUDITH	BAL	245	20TH WAR
KILLEN, MARGARET	BAL	392	14TH WAR
KILLEN, MATHEW	BAL	010	EASTERN
KILLEN, MICHAEL	BAL	281	17TH WAR
KILLEN, PATRICK	BAL	082	2ND DIST
KILLENSTINE, ADAM	BAL	433	8TH WARD
KILLER, BARNEY	BAL	011	2ND DIST
KILLER, DAVID	CAR	365	9TH DIST
KILLER, WILLIAM	BAL	080	1ST WARD
KILLERD, ELIZA	BAL	076	15TH WAR
KILLERMAN, JACOB	BAL	021	2ND DIST
KILLETS, HERMAN	FRE	020	FREDERIC
KILLFOIL, JOHN	ALL	048	10TH E.D
KILLIN, JANE	BAL	017	2ND DIST
KILLIN, R.S.	BAL	287	12TH WAR
KILLINGS, WILLIAMS	BAL	181	6TH WARD
KILLINGSWORTH, MANLOVE	CEC	010	ELKTON 3
KILLINGSWORTH, OLIVER	CEC	206	7TH E DI
KILLION, MARGARET E.	FRE	021	FREDERIC
KILLION, PHILLIP	FRE	070	FREDERIC
KILLION, THOMAS	ALL	049	10TH E.D
KILLKANNON, THOMAS	BAL	208	11TH WAR
KILLKENY, SAMUEL *	BAL	041	18TH WAR
KILLKERRY, SAMUEL *	BAL	041	18TH WAR
KILLMAN, ADELINE	CEC	152	PORT DUP
KILLMAN, CHARLES	CHA	254	MIDDLETO
KILLMAN, JOHN E.	CEC	152	PORT DUP
KILLMAN, MARY	BAL	142	16TH WAR
KILLMAN, NICHOLAS	ANN	274	ANNAPOLI
KILLMAN, RICHARD	HAR	162	3RD DIST
KILLMAN, TRYNA	CHA	254	MIDDLETO
KILLMAN, WASHINGTON	BAL	013	1ST WARD
KILLMAN, WILLAIM	QUE	243	5TH E DI
KILLMAN, WILLIAM	TAL	090	ST MICHA
KILLMARTIN, MICHEL	ALL	052	10TH E.D
KILLME, R JOHN	BAL	064	1ST WARD
KILLSON, ALLIN	TAL	052	EASTON D
KILLSON, SAMUEL-BLACK	CAR	079	NO TWP L
KILLSON, WILLIAM	TAL	052	EASTON D
KILLSVY, PATRICK	ALL	048	10TH E.D
KILMAN, N.	ANN	283	ANNAPOLI
KILMAN, THOMAS	BAL	352	3RD WARD
KILMAN, THOMAS	BAL	353	3RD WARD
KILMER, WILLIAM	BAL	061	18TH WAR
KILMOND, WILLIAM	BAL	020	18TH WAR
KILPATRICK, HUGH	BAL	405	1ST DIST
KILPATRICK, JAMES	BAL	242	1ST DIST
KILPATRICK, M.	BAL	219	19TH WAR
KILPATRICK, MARY	BAL	356	3RD WARD
KILPATRICK, THOMAS	BAL	218	19TH WAR
KILPATRICK, WILLIAM	BAL	219	19TH WAR
KILPSTINE, L. F.	ALL	067	10TH E.D
KILSON, BENJAMIN	TAL	048	EASTON T
KILSON, HENRY	TAL	055	EASTON D
KILSON, HERNY	CAR	101	NO TWP L
KILSON, JAMES*	TAL	048	EASTON T
KILSON, JOSHUA-BLACK	CAR	080	NO TWP L
KILSON, MARY-BLACK	CAR	073	NO TWP L
KILSON, PERRY-BLACK	CAR	102	NO TWP L
KILSON, RACHAEL	BAL	050	15TH WAR
KILSON, RACHEL	TAL	048	EASTON T
KILSON, SAMUEL-BLACK	CAR	101	NO TWP L
KILSTON, HENRY	BAL	280	2ND WARD
KILTENSTEIN, STEPHEN*	BAL	091	10TH WAR
KILTY, CATHERINE	BAL	140	11TH WAR
KILWELL, AUGUST	BAL	284	7TH WARD
KILYNER, JOHN	BAL	254	20TH WAR
KIMBAL, RACHEL	BAL	010	1ST WARD
KIMBALEY, HARREY	BAL	383	8TH WARD
KIMBALL, HORRIST	BAL	057	18TH WAR
KIMBERLEY, EDWARD	BAL	405	8TH WARD
KIMBERLEY, ELIZABETH	BAL	451	8TH WARD
KIMBERLEY, JEREMIAH M.	BAL	399	8TH WARD
KIMBERLEY, SAMUEL	BAL	454	8TH WARD
KIMBERLY, ANN	BAL	133	5TH WARD
KIMBERLY, CATHARINE	ALL	098	5TH E.D.
KIMBERLY, CORNELIA	BAL	126	5TH WARD
KIMBERLY, ELIJAH B.	BAL	454	8TH WARD
KIMBERLY, JOHN	ALL	102	5TH E.D.
KIMBERLY, JOHN	ALL	098	5TH E.D.
KIMBERLY, MARY	BAL	236	17TH WAR
KIMBERLY, NATHAN	BAL	246	2ND WARD
KIMBERMAN, FREDERICK	BAL	087	1ST WARD
KIMBERTES, WILLIAM H.	BAL	405	8TH WARD
KIMBLE, ALFRED W.	HAR	186	3RD DIST
KIMBLE, ANDREW	ALL	040	2ND E.D.
KIMBLE, CHANEY	ALL	017	3RD E.D.
KIMBLE, ELIZABETH	CEC	101	4TH E DI
KIMBLE, FRANCIS	BAL	292	7TH WARD
KIMBLE, HENRY	CEC	093	4TH E DI
KIMBLE, HENRY	HAR	181	3RD DIST
KIMBLE, HERMAN	BAL	320	7TH WARD
KIMBLE, JACOB	ALL	039	2ND E.D.
KIMBLE, JOHN F.	BAL	393	8TH WARD
KIMBLE, LEREW	BAL	101	2ND DIST
KIMBLE, LOUISA	HAR	186	3RD DIST
KIMBLE, MARY	CEC	085	5TH E DI
KIMBLE, MARY	BAL	061	4TH WARD
KIMBLE, SALMON*	BAL	061	4TH WARD
KIMBLE, SAMUEL	ALL	040	2ND E.D.
KIMBLE, SARAH	CEC	112	4TH E DI
KIMBLE, STEPHEN	BAL	167	6TH WARD
KIMBLE, ZACHRIA	HAR	194	3RD DIST
KIMBLE, ZACHRIA JR.	HAR	194	3RD DIST
KIMBY, EZEKIL	HAR	197	3RD DIST
KIMBY, RUEBEN S.	BAL	200	17TH WAR
KIME, FREDERICK	BAL	045	18TH WAR
KIMLER, JACOB F.	WAS	245	SMITHSBU
KIMLY, CHRISTIAN	BAL	219	17TH WAR
KIMMAR, ELIZABETH	BAL	441	14TH WAR
KIMMEL, ANTHONY	FRE	422	8TH E DI
KIMMEL, FREDERICK	CAR	402	2ND DIST
KIMMEL, JACOB	ALL	038	2ND E.D.
KIMMEL, JACOB	BAL	050	2ND DIST
KIMMEL, JOHN	FRE	200	5TH E DI
KIMMEL, LEWIS	ALL	038	2ND E.D.
KIMMEL,CHRISTIAN	ALL	045	10TH E.D
KIMMEL,WILLIAM	BAL	067	2ND DIST
KIMMELL, JOHN	BAL	055	15TH WAR
KIMMELL, JOSEPH	CAR	291	7TH DIST
KIMMELL, ROBERT	WAS	195	1ST DIST
KIMMELL, THERESA	CAR	291	7TH DIST
KIMMET, PHILIP	BAL	018	9TH WARD
KIMMEY, HARRIETT	DOR	321	1ST DIST
KIMMY, ELSY*	DOR	451	1ST DIST
KIMMY, SAMUEL	DOR	296	1ST DIST
KIMONS, THOMAS	BAL	152	1ST WARD
KIMP, THOMAS	BAL	039	1ST WARD
KIMPE, JACOB	BAL	184	11TH WAR
KIMPH, PHILLIP	BAL	265	2ND WARD
KINAKIN, JOHN	SOM	508	BARREN C
KINARD, HOWARD	HAR	189	3RD DIST
KINAS, SMAUEL D.	BAL	232	2ND WARD
KINCADE, LOUIS	BAL	131	18TH WAR
KINCAID, MARGARET	BAL	195	6TH WARD
KINCHCOMB, BEAL C.	BAL	023	2ND DIST
KIND, BENJAMIN	HAR	112	2ND DIST
KINDALL, WILLAIM	BAL	001	1ST WARD
KINDAY, MARY	BAL	225	12TH WAR
KINDEL, JOSEPH	CEC	057	1ST E DI
KINDER, CATHERINE	MGM	414	MEDLEY 3
KINDER, DILILA	MGM	439	CLARKSTR
KINDER, JOSEPH	WAS	035	2ND SUBD
KINDER, JULIUS	BAL	103	5TH WARD
KINDER, ROBERT	MGM	430	CLARKSTR
KINDER, SARAH A.	MGM	425	MEDLEY 3
KINDER, WILLIAM	MGM	444	CLARKSTR
KINDIG, FRANCIS	BAL	239	1ST DIST
KINDIG, SAMUEL	CAR	237	UNION TO
KINDLE, SUSAN	WAS	048	2ND SUBD
KINDLE, WILLIAM	WAS	239	CAVETOWN
KINDLEY, MARTHA	SOM	399	BRINKLEY
KINDRICK, ADLINE	CHA	264	HILLTOP
KINDRICK, HELY	CHA	264	HILLTOP
KINDY, PHILIP	BAL	447	1ST DIST
KINE, A. *	ALL	076	5TH E.D.
KINE, CHARLES *	FRE	251	NEW MARK
KINE, EDWARD	ALL	076	5TH E.D.
KINE, PATRICK	ALL	088	5TH E.D.
KINE, PATRICK	ANN	414	HOWARD D
KINE, PETER	ANN	427	HOWARD D
KINE, SUSAN	BAL	350	7TH WARD
KINE, SUSAN	BAL	382	8TH WARD
KINEAR, J. C.	BAL	332	1ST DIST
KINECAIN, JULIA A.	WOR	266	BERLIN 1
KINECAN, ISAAC	WOR	266	BERLIN 1
KINEDOLLAR, JOHN	CAR	243	TANEYTOW
KINEL, WILLIAM	HAR	178	3RD DIST
KINEMAN, WILLIAM	CAR	185	8TH DIST
KINEMON, CHARLES	CHA	261	MIDDLETO
KINES, CUOLIP	BAL	263	17TH WAR
KINES, DANIEL	ALL	075	5TH E.D.
KINES, FRANCIS	BAL	250	17TH WAR
KINESMAN, MARY	BAL	278	20TH WAR
KINEY, ANNA	BAL	171	2ND DIST
KINEY, HENRY	FRE	288	WOODSBOR
KING, ADALINE	SOM	429	PRINCESS
KING, ALEXANDER	ALL	147	6TH E.D.
KING, ALEXANDER	BAL	152	15TH WAR
KING, ALEXANDER W.	CEC	080	NORTHEAS
KING, ALFRED C.	BAL	392	1ST DIST
KING, AMANDA	BAL	419	14TH WAR
KING, AMANDA E.	MGM	441	CLARKSTR
KING, AMERICA-BLACK	FRE	221	BUCKEYST
KING, AMOS	BAL	108	1ST WARD
KING, ANDREW	WAS	211	1ST DIST
KING, ANN	PRI	001	BLADENSB
KING, ANN	BAL	060	1ST WARD
KING, ANN	BAL	058	1ST WARD
KING, ANN	ALL	087	5TH E.D.
KING, ANN	BAL	351	13TH WAR
KING, ANN	BAL	048	18TH WAR
KING, ANN	CAR	358	9TH DIST
KING, ANN	SOM	430	PRINCESS
KING, ANN	MGM	330	CRACKLIN
KING, ANN M.	FRE	069	FREDERIC
KING, ANN-BLACK	MGM	432	CLARKSTR
KING, AUGUST	BAL	024	1ST WARD
KING, BARTLY	BAL	060	1ST WARD
KING, BENJAMIN	ANN	402	8TH DIST
KING, BENJAMIN	CAR	194	4TH DIST
KING, BERNARD	BAL	248	6TH WARD
KING, BIDDY	BAL	059	4TH WARD
KING, BRIDGET	BAL	441	8TH WARD
KING, BRIGET	BAL	460	1ST DIST
KING, CAORLINE	CAR	283	7TH DIST
KING, CAROLINE	BAL	405	3RD WARD
KING, CASSA	CAL	033	2ND DIST
KING, CATH	BAL	321	12TH WAR
KING, CATHARINE	BAL	296	17TH WAR
KING, CATHARINE	BAL	175	19TH WAR
KING, CATHERINE	BAL	275	20TH WAR
KING, CATHERINE	BAL	033	9TH WARD
KING, CHARES	BAL	186	16TH WAR
KING, CHARLES	BAL	324	12TH WAR
KING, CHARLES	BAL	353	7TH WARD
KING, CHARLES	ANN	414	HOWARD D
KING, CHARLES	BAL	020	2ND DIST
KING, CHARLES	BAL	073	2ND DIST
KING, CHARLES	BAL	436	14TH WAR
KING, CHARLES F.	BAL	364	3RD WARD
KING, CHARLES T.	BAL	356	3RD WARD
KING, CHARLES W.	ST	292	2ND E DI
KING, CHARLOTT	BAL	024	9TH WARD
KING, CHARLOTTE	PRI	056	AQUASCO
KING, CHRISTIAN	WAS	020	2ND SUBD
KING, CHRISTIAN	BAL	023	1ST WARD
KING, CHRISTOPHER C.	ST	255	3RD E DI
KING, COLUMBUS	ALL	136	4TH E.D.
KING, CONRAD	FRE	006	FREDERIC
KING, DANIEL	WAS	156	HAGERSTO
KING, DANIEL	PRI	120	PISCATAW
KING, DANIEL	PRI	120	PISCATAW
KING, DANIEL-BLACK	CAR	084	NO TWP L
KING, DAVID	MGM	351	BERRYS D
KING, DAVID	BAL	120	2ND DIST
KING, DAVID	BAL	102	5TH WARD
KING, DINARD	HAR	190	3RD DIST
KING, EDMUND	PRI	004	BLADENSB
KING, EDWARD	MGM	443	CLARKSTR
KING, EDWARD-BLACK	FRE	047	FREDERIC
KING, ELIZA	CEC	082	CHARLEST
KING, ELIZA	PRI	102	SPALDING
KING, ELIZA	BAL	121	2ND DIST
KING, ELIZA	BAL	088	15TH WAR
KING, ELIZA W. A.	SOM	430	PRINCESS
KING, ELIZABETH	CEC	163	6TH E DI
KING, ELIZABETH	CAR	301	1ST DIST
KING, ELIZABETH	BAL	225	19TH WAR
KING, ELIZABETH	BAL	302	1ST DIST
KING, ELIZABETH	BAL	170	6TH WARD
KING, ELIZABETH	PRI	102	SPALDING
KING, ELIZABETH	PRI	017	BLADENSB
KING, ELLEN J.	WAS	023	2ND SUBD
KING, EMELINE	PRI	001	BLADENSB
KING, EMILY P.	BAL	046	4TH WARD
KING, EMUND	CAR	322	1ST DIST
KING, ERNST	BAL	300	17TH WAR
KING, F. X.	BAL	080	10TH WAR
KING, FANNY-MULATTO	BAL	094	18TH WAR
KING, FRANCES	MGM	432	CLARKSTR
KING, FRANCIS	BAL	353	7TH WARD
KING, FREDERICK	CEC	058	1ST E DI
KING, FREDERICK	FRE	079	FREDERIC
KING, G.	BAL	209	2ND WARD
KING, G.L.	BAL	150	1ST WARD
KING, G.W.	WAS	139	HAGERSTO
KING, GARARD	ANN	271	ANNAPOLI
KING, GEORG EW.	ST	299	2ND E DI
KING, GEORGE	CAL	048	3RD DIST
KING, GEORGE	SOM	441	DAMES QU
KING, GEORGE	CAR	255	3RD DIST
KING, GEORGE	CEC	044	CHESAPEA
KING, GEORGE	MGM	329	CRACKLIN
KING, GEORGE	BAL	001	1ST WARD
KING, GEORGE	BAL	066	1ST WARD
KING, GEORGE	BAL	130	2ND DIST
KING, GEORGE	BAL	253	2ND WARD
KING, GEORGE H.	BAL	288	12TH WAR
KING, GEORGE L.	ST	266	3RD E DI
KING, GEORGE R.	WAS	124	2ND DIST
KING, GEORGE R.	BAL	066	15TH WAR
KING, GEORGE R.	BAL	057	18TH WAR
KING, GEORGE T.	MGM	422	MEDLEY 3
KING, GEORGE W.	BAL	441	14TH WAR
KING, GEORGE W.	BAL	458	1ST DIST
KING, HAMILTON-BLACK	FRE	409	JEFFERSO
KING, HARRIETT	QUE	226	4TH E DI
KING, HARRY-BLACK	CAR	138	NO TWP L
KING, HELO	BAL	355	8TH WARD
KING, HENRIETTA	BAL	162	16TH WAR
KING, HENRIETTA	CAR	273	WESTMINS
KING, HENRIETTA	BAL	016	18TH WAR
KING, HENRY	FRE	010	FREDERIC
KING, HENRY	SOM	420	PRINCESS
KING, HENRY	HAR	190	3RD DIST
KING, HENRY	FRE	248	NEW MARK
KING, HENRY	BAL	460	1ST DIST
KING, HENRY	BAL	220	6TH WARD
KING, HENRY	WAS	189	1ST DIST
KING, HENRY	PRI	110	PISCATAW
KING, HENRY	SOM	502	SALISBUR
KING, HENRY S.	BAL	012	18TH WAR
KING, HESTER	BAL	094	15TH WAR
KING, HESTER	BAL	306	12TH WAR
KING, HIRAM	CEC	127	5TH E DI
KING, ISAAC	BAL	059	2ND DIST
KING, ISABELLA	FRE	167	EMMITTSB
KING, ISRAEL L.	ALL	064	10TH E.D
KING, J. T.	BAL	021	18TH WAR
KING, JACOB	BAL	035	18TH WAR
KING, JACOB	BAL	213	19TH WAR
KING, JACOB	WAS	276	RIDGEVIL
KING, JAEMS J.	SOM	417	PRINCESS
KING, JAMES	MGM	415	MEDLEY 3
KING, JAMES	BAL	239	17TH WAR
KING, JAMES	CAL	050	3RD DIST
KING, JAMES	CAL	031	2ND DIST
KING, JAMES	PRI	010	BLADENSB
KING, JAMES	PRI	011	BLADENSB
KING, JAMES	PRI	095	SPALDING
KING, JAMES	PRI	035	VANSVILL
KING, JAMES	WOR	230	6TH E DI
KING, JAMES	ANN	374	4TH DIST
KING, JAMES	BAL	186	16TH WAR
KING, JAMES	BAL	200	2ND WARD
KING, JAMES	BAL	307	3RD WARD

Name	County	Page	District
KING, JAMES A.	ST	303	2ND E DI
KING, JAMES E.	ST	258	3RD E DI
KING, JAMES JR.	PRI	010	BLADENSB
KING, JAMES O.	CHA	220	ALLENS F
KING, JAMES P.	CAL	063	3RD DIST
KING, JAMES R.	TAL	083	ST MICHA
KING, JAMES T.	BAL	332	13TH WAR
KING, JANE	BAL	007	9TH WARD
KING, JANE	BAL	010	1ST WARD
KING, JANE	PRI	095	SPALDING
KING, JANE	SOM	420	PRINCESS
KING, JANE	HAR	044	1ST DIST
KING, JANE	FRE	275	NEW MARK
KING, JEMIMA	CAR	254	3RD DIST
KING, JESSE	FRE	071	FREDERIC
KING, JESSE	ALL	063	10TH E.D
KING, JESSE	ALL	012	3RD E.D.
KING, JOHN	ALL	173	7TH E.D.
KING, JOHN	ALL	183	8TH E.D.
KING, JOHN	BAL	076	1ST WARD
KING, JOHN	BAL	357	3RD WARD
KING, JOHN	BAL	121	1ST WARD
KING, JOHN	BAL	002	9TH WARD
KING, JOHN	BAL	171	11TH WAR
KING, JOHN	BAL	463	1ST DIST
KING, JOHN	BAL	414	1ST DIST
KING, JOHN	BAL	163	1ST WARD
KING, JOHN	BAL	385	8TH WARD
KING, JOHN	BAL	231	2ND WARD
KING, JOHN	BAL	127	1ST WARD
KING, JOHN	FRE	087	FREDERIC
KING, JOHN	BAL	282	17TH WAR
KING, JOHN	BAL	108	18TH WAR
KING, JOHN	CAL	050	3RD DIST
KING, JOHN	BAL	476	14TH WAR
KING, JOHN	CEC	206	7TH E DI
KING, JOHN	BAL	287	20TH WAR
KING, JOHN	BAL	298	20TH WAR
KING, JOHN	BAL	423	14TH WAR
KING, JOHN	BAL	047	4TH WARD
KING, JOHN	FRE	131	CREAGERS
KING, JOHN	PRI	120	PISCATAW
KING, JOHN	PRI	106	PISCATAW
KING, JOHN	WAS	177	1ST DIST
KING, JOHN	PRI	009	BLADENSB
KING, JOHN	WOR	268	BERLIN 1
KING, JOHN	ST	304	2ND E DI
KING, JOHN	WAS	241	CAVETOWN
KING, JOHN	WAS	204	1ST DIST
KING, JOHN A.	MGM	441	CLARKSTR
KING, JOHN A.	PRI	007	BLADENSB
KING, JOHN C.	BAL	163	16TH WAR
KING, JOHN D.	MGM	441	CLARKSTR
KING, JOHN H.	SOM	427	PRINCESS
KING, JOHN H.-BLACK	MGM	418	MEDLEY 3
KING, JOHN L.	ST	257	3RD E DI
KING, JOHN R.	WAS	139	HAGERSTO
KING, JOHN R.	WAS	292	1ST DIST
KING, JOHN T.	MGM	352	BERRYS D
KING, JOHN T.	CAL	050	3RD DIST
KING, JOHN T.	CAL	027	2ND DIST
KING, JOHN W.	BAL	014	4TH WARD
KING, JOHN W.	BAL	273	2ND WARD
KING, JOSEPH	BAL	132	1ST WARD
KING, JOSEPH	BAL	136	1ST WARD
KING, JOSEPH	BAL	149	16TH WAR
KING, JOSEPH	ANN	403	8TH DIST
KING, JOSEPH	FRE	137	CREAGERS
KING, JOSEPH	HAR	119	2ND DIST
KING, JOSEPH	BAL	412	14TH WAR
KING, JOSEPH	BAL	081	18TH WAR
KING, JOSEPH	ST	272	3RD E DI
KING, JOSEPH JR.	BAL	105	10TH WAR
KING, JOSEPH S.	FRE	354	MIDDLETO
KING, JOSHUA	ST	303	2ND E DI
KING, JULIA A.	BAL	316	7TH WARD
KING, JULIAN	ST	292	2ND E DI
KING, JULIANA	BAL	438	14TH WAR
KING, KITTY	CAL	052	3RD DIST
KING, LEAH	BAL	456	14TH WAR
KING, LEVI	PRI	012	BLADENSB
KING, LEWIS	CEC	163	6TH E DI
KING, LEWIS	HAR	016	1ST DIST
KING, LEWIS	FRE	004	FREDERIC
KING, LEWIS	BAL	267	12TH WAR
KING, LIDIA	BAL	453	1ST DIST
KING, LIVINGSTON	BAL	144	19TH WAR
KING, LOUIS	BAL	458	1ST DIST
KING, LOYD	MGM	410	MEDLEY 3
KING, LUCY	BAL	136	18TH WAR
KING, LUTHER G.	MGM	441	CLARKSTR
KING, LYTTLETON	BAL	133	2ND DIST
KING, MARGARET	BAL	100	5TH WARD
KING, MARGARET	DOR	303	1ST DIST
KING, MARGARET	BAL	003	18TH WAR
KING, MARGARETT	BAL	111	5TH WARD
KING, MARIA	BAL	157	11TH WAR
KING, MARIA	MGM	342	CLARKSBU
KING, MARK	BAL	241	2ND WARD
KING, MARTHA	ANN	449	HOWARD D
KING, MARTHA	CEC	028	CHESAPEA
KING, MARTHA	WOR	245	1ST CENS
KING, MARTIN	WAS	144	HAGERSTO
KING, MARY	PRI	117	PISCATAW
KING, MARY	PRI	056	AQUASCO
KING, MARY	CAR	185	8TH DIST
KING, MARY	FRE	160	EMMITTSB
KING, MARY	CAL	020	2ND DIST
KING, MARY	BAL	059	18TH WAR
KING, MARY	BAL	341	13TH WAR
KING, MARY	BAL	141	19TH WAR
KING, MARY	BAL	167	19TH WAR
KING, MARY	BAL	105	2ND DIST
KING, MARY	BAL	090	5TH WARD
KING, MARY	BAL	257	12TH WAR
KING, MARY	ANN	403	8TH DIST
KING, MARY	ALL	183	8TH E.D.
KING, MARY	BAL	203	2ND WARD
KING, MARY	BAL	058	1ST WARD
KING, MARY A.	BAL	455	8TH WARD
KING, MARY A.	BAL	070	10TH WAR
KING, MARY A.	BAL	084	4TH WARD
KING, MARY A.	CAR	248	3RD DIST
KING, MARY A.J.	FRE	234	BUCKEYST
KING, MARY C.	CAL	041	3RD DIST
KING, MARY E.	FRE	191	5TH E DI
KING, MARY H.	CHA	273	ALLENS F
KING, MARY J.	DOR	304	1ST DIST
KING, MARY L.	BAL	014	4TH WARD
KING, MARY L.	ST	278	3RD E DI
KING, MARY S.	ST	338	4TH E DI
KING, MATHEW	ALL	102	5TH E.D.
KING, MATILDA	BAL	356	1ST DIST
KING, MATILDA	BAL	248	6TH WARD
KING, MATILDA	CAL	034	2ND DIST
KING, MICHAEL	ANN	500	HOWARD D
KING, MICHAEL	BAL	293	1ST DIST
KING, MIDDLETON	MGM	436	CLARKSTR
KING, MOSES	BAL	016	9TH WARD
KING, MR.	ANN	470	HOWARD D
KING, MRS.	BAL	238	17TH WAR
KING, NANCY	BAL	078	18TH WAR
KING, NANCY	SOM	429	PRINCESS
KING, NANCY	MGM	437	CLARKSTR
KING, NICEY	SOM	433	PRINCESS
KING, NICHOLAS	BAL	454	14TH WAR
KING, OWEN	BAL	075	10TH WAR
KING, PATIENCE G.	BAL	067	15TH WAR
KING, PATRICK	BAL	079	10TH WAR
KING, PATRICK	BAL	314	3RD WARD
KING, PATRICK	ALL	053	10TH E.D
KING, PETER	WAS	294	1ST DIST
KING, PETER	WAS	262	1ST DIST
KING, PETER-BLACK	CAR	161	NO TWP L
KING, PHILIP	ANN	464	HOWARD D
KING, PHILLIP	PRI	104	PISCATAW
KING, QUINTON	BAL	352	7TH WARD
KING, R. J. H.	SOM	418	PRINCESS
KING, RACHEL	HAR	099	2ND DIST
KING, REBECCA	MGM	367	BERRYS D
KING, REBECCA	CEC	164	6TH E DI
KING, REBECCA	CEC	048	1ST E DI
KING, RICHARD	BAL	046	9TH WARD
KING, RICHARD	BAL	024	9TH WARD
KING, RICHARD	PRI	082	QUEEN AN
KING, RICHARD B.	ST	288	2ND E DI
KING, ROBERT	ST	304	2ND E DI
KING, ROBERT	SOM	414	DUBLIN D
KING, ROBERT	BAL	085	18TH WAR
KING, ROBERT G.	BAL	045	9TH WARD
KING, ROSE	BAL	062	10TH WAR
KING, ROSETTA	ANN	338	3RD DIST
KING, RUFUS	MGM	441	CLARKSTR
KING, RUTH	ALL	028	2ND E.D.
KING, SALLIE E.	ANN	521	HOWARD D
KING, SALLY	BAL	108	15TH WAR
KING, SALLY	SOM	418	PRINCESS
KING, SAMUEL	CAR	383	2ND DIST
KING, SAMUEL	BAL	234	20TH WAR
KING, SAMUEL	BAL	201	17TH WAR
KING, SAMUEL	BAL	124	18TH WAR
KING, SAMUEL	ANN	454	HOWARD D
KING, SAMUEL	SOM	350	BRINKLEY
KING, SAMUEL	WOR	238	6TH E DI
KING, SAMUEL H.	BAL	274	2ND WARD
KING, SAMUEL M.	CAL	017	1ST DIST
KING, SARAH	DOR	417	1ST DIST
KING, SARAH	CEC	127	5TH E DI
KING, SARAH	BAL	079	15TH WAR
KING, SARAH	ALL	070	5TH E.D.
KING, SARAH	BAL	002	9TH WARD
KING, SARAH	BAL	245	12TH WAR
KING, SARAH	PRI	010	BLADENSB
KING, SARAH A.	FRE	399	JEFFERSO
KING, SARAH E.	BAL	130	18TH WAR
KING, SARAH E.	FRE	087	FREDERIC
KING, SARAH H.	WAS	122	2ND DIST
KING, SARAH J.	ALL	147	6TH E.D.
KING, SARAH J.	BAL	060	10TH WAR
KING, SARAH M.	BAL	204	2ND WARD
KING, SIMEON W.	CEC	165	6TH E DI
KING, SOLOMAN	BAL	399	8TH WARD
KING, SUSAN	CAL	034	2ND DIST
KING, SUSAN	CAL	031	2ND DIST
KING, SUSAN	CAL	029	2ND DIST
KING, SUSAN	BAL	226	19TH WAR
KING, SUSAN	CAR	380	2ND DIST
KING, SUSAN J.	BAL	027	9TH WARD
KING, SUSANA	ALL	003	3RD E.D.
KING, SYLVSTER	PRI	088	SPALDING
KING, THOMAS	PRI	103	SPALDING
KING, THOMAS	ANN	315	1ST DIST
KING, THOMAS	BAL	396	8TH WARD
KING, THOMAS	BAL	094	15TH WAR
KING, THOMAS	BAL	243	12TH WAR
KING, THOMAS	BAL	002	9TH WARD
KING, THOMAS	BAL	352	7TH WARD
KING, THOMAS	ANN	373	4TH DIST
KING, THOMAS	BAL	050	2ND DIST
KING, THOMAS	ANN	488	HOWARD D
KING, THOMAS	BAL	119	1ST WARD
KING, THOMAS	CAR	391	2ND DIST
KING, THOMAS	BAL	299	17TH WAR
KING, THOMAS	CAR	193	4TH DIST
KING, THOMAS	MGM	374	ROCKERLE
KING, THOMAS F.	ALL	041	2ND E.D.
KING, THOMAS W.	CAL	062	3RD DIST
KING, VINCENT	HAR	014	1ST DIST
KING, VINCENT	PRI	010	BLADENSB
KING, VIRGINIA	WAS	292	1ST DIST
KING, WALTER A.	PRI	013	BLADENSB
KING, WALTER A.	PRI	013	BLADENSB
KING, WALTER J.	FRE	233	BUCKEYST
KING, WALTER S.	CAL	040	3RD DIST
KING, WARREN	MGM	422	MEDLEY 3
KING, WILLAIM	CAR	265	WESTMINS
KING, WILLAIM	BAL	093	2ND DIST
KING, WILLIAM	ANN	336	3RD DIST
KING, WILLIAM	BAL	108	1ST WARD
KING, WILLIAM	BAL	173	11TH WAR
KING, WILLIAM	BAL	156	1ST WARD
KING, WILLIAM	BAL	296	17TH WAR
KING, WILLIAM	BAL	029	18TH WAR
KING, WILLIAM	FRE	086	FREDERIC
KING, WILLIAM	SOM	420	PRINCESS
KING, WILLIAM	CAL	005	1ST DIST
KING, WILLIAM	CEC	206	7TH E DI
KING, WILLIAM F.	ANN	440	HOWARD D
KING, WILLIAM G.	BAL	189	19TH WAR
KING, WILLIAM H.	BAL	214	19TH WAR
KING, WILLIAM H.	BAL	270	7TH WARD
KING, WILLIAM J.	BAL	140	5TH WARD
KING, WILLIAM J. C.	BAL	102	18TH WAR
KING, WILLIAM JR.	CAR	269	WESTMINS
KING, WILLIAM T.	CEC	163	5TH E DI
KING, ZACHARIAH	FRE	224	BUCKEYST
KING, CARLENE	FRE	027	FREDERIC
KING, LANCHART	BAL	231	2ND WARD
KING, MARY	BAL	059	2ND DIST
KING, PERRY-BLACK	FRE	224	BUCKEYST
KING, SINGLETON	FRE	227	BUCKEYST
KING, STEPHEN R.	BAL	134	2ND WARD
KINGCADE, BARBARY	BAL	093	18TH WAR
KINGCADE, CATHARINE	BAL	123	5TH WARD
KINGDON, MARY	BAL	237	12TH WAR
KINGHAM, ELEANOR	BAL	136	2ND DIST
KINGHAM, WILLIAN	BAL	135	2ND DIST
KINGHOM, ELIZABETH T.	BAL	073	4TH WARD
KINGHT, EDWARD A.	BAL	312	12TH WAR
KINGLAND, ZENIA	FRE	450	8TH E DI
KINGLE, JOHN	BAL	105	2ND DIST
KINGLE, JOHN	BAL	265	2ND WARD
KINGLY, MICHAEL	BAL	159	11TH WAR
KINGMIRE, E.	BAL	279	12TH WAR
KINGOLD, JOHN	CAR	221	5TH DIST
KINGROSE, ROBERT	BAL	092	1ST WARD
KINGS, WILLIAM	FRE	086	FREDERIC
KINGSBERRY, JOHN	BAL	271	17TH WAR
KINGSBERRY, MARY	FRE	234	BUCKEYST
KINGSBURY, JOHN W.	PRI	072	MARLBROU
KINGSBURY, NANCY	PRI	067	NOTTINGH
KINGSBURY, SARAH	PRI	072	MARLBROU
KINGSBURY, WILLIAM O..	MGM	426	MEDLEY 3
KINGSHOW, ELIZA *	BAL	261	6TH WARD
KINGSLY, THOMAS	CHA	283	BOJANTOW
KINGSMIRE, GEORGE	BAL	286	20TH WAR
KINGSMORE, MARY	BAL	104	2ND DIST
KINGSTON, J.	BAL	147	1ST WARD
KINGSWORTH, WILLIAM	BAL	241	17TH WAR
KININGMONGER, LEWIS	BAL	137	1ST WARD
KINKE, MICHAEL	PRI	039	VANSVILL
KINKEAD, JAMES	CEC	027	CHESAPEA
KINKEAD, JERAMIAH	CEC	027	CHESAPEA
KINKEAD, JOHN	CEC	099	3RD E DI
KINKEAD, JOHN	CEC	085	5TH E DI
KINKED, JOEL	CEC	033	CHESAPEA
KINKER, JAMES *	BAL	200	5TH DIST
KINKER, JOHN	BAL	316	1ST DIST
KINKHOUSE, HENRY	BAL	109	16TH WAR
KINKLE, ADAM	WAS	133	HAGERSTO
KINKLE, CHARLES	WAS	132	HAGERSTO
KINKLE, JAMES C. OR-	BAL	062	18TH WAR
KINKLE, JAOCB M.	FRE	031	FREDERIC
KINLEY, JAMES B.	HAR	121	2ND DIST
KINLEY, JOHN	BAL	040	2ND DIST
KINLEY, MARY	BAL	117	15TH WAR
KINLY, DANIEL	HAR	155	3RD DIST
KINLY, GEORGE W.	HAR	200	3RD DIST
KINLY, LYDIA A.	BAL	032	1ST WARD
KINNA, JAMES	FRE	344	MIDDLETO
KINNA, JOHN	FRE	344	MIDDLETO
KINNA, MARY A.	FRE	323	MIDDLETO
KINNA, MARY A.	FRE	382	PETERSVI
KINNA, SAMSON	FRE	322	MIDDLETO
KINNA, SAMUEL	FRE	344	MIDDLETO
KINNAKIN, JAMES	SOM	508	BARREN C
KINNAMAN, GOLDSBOROUGH	QUE	219	3RD E DI
KINNAMON, JORDEN	CAR	083	NO TWP L
KINNAMON, PETER	TAL	024	EASTON D
KINNAMON, WILLIAM	DOR	308	1ST DIST
KINNAMOR, MARGARET	DOR	435	1ST DIST
KINNAMOR, REBECCA L.*	DOR	434	1ST DIST
KINNANOE, CLINTON*	DOR	434	1ST DIST
KINNARD, ADAM	MGM	374	ROCKERLE
KINNARD, NICHOLAS	BAL	075	4TH WARD
KINNARD, VIRGINIA S.	BAL	062	1ST WARD
KINNEAR, JOHN	BAL	131	1ST WARD
KINNEDY, CLEMENT	PRI	005	BLADENSB
KINNELY, CATHERINE	BAL	421	3RD WARD
KINNEMAN, FRANCIS	BAL	063	2ND DIST
KINNEMAN, PERRY S.*	BAL	052	4TH WARD
KINNEMON, BETSEY	BAL	001	15TH WAR
KINNEY, ELSY	DOR	427	1ST DIST
KINNEY, GEORGE	WAS	228	1ST DIST
KINNEY, JACOB	FRE	416	8TH E DI
KINNEY, JAEMS	BAL	169	2ND DIST
KINNEY, JOHN	FRE	432	8TH E DI
KINNEY, JOHN SR.	FRE	415	8TH E DI
KINNEY, JONATHAN*	DOR	426	1ST DIST
KINNEY, MARGARET	BAL	052	15TH WAR
KINNEY, MARGARETT	FRE	416	8TH E DI
KINNEY, PETER	BAL	148	5TH WARD
KINNEY, ROBERT M.*	SOM	358	BRINKLEY
KINNEY, THOMAS	BAL	391	3RD WARD
KINNEY, THOMAS J.G.	BAL	141	16TH WAR
KINNEY, WILLIAM	BAL	144	16TH WAR
KINNEY, WILLIAM	FRE	209	BUCKEYST
KINNEY, WILLIAM	SOM	425	PRINCESS
KINNEY, WILLIAM JR.	FRE	417	8TH E DI
KINNEY.WILLIAM	MGM	420	MEDLEY 3
KINNIER, ALEXANDER	BAL	186	6TH WARD
KINNIER, GEORGE	BAL	301	7TH WARD
KINNINGHAM, SARAH	BAL	261	1ST DIST
KINNWOOD, WILLIAM L.	MGM	370	BERRYS D
KINNY, MARIAH	FRE	422	8TH E DI
KINNY, MARY	BAL	418	3RD WARD
KINNY, PRUDY	DOR	451	1ST DIST
KINOM, PETER	BAL	259	12TH WAR
KINOR, GEORGE	FRE	266	NEW MARK
KINSEL, EMMA	BAL	030	9TH WARD
KINSEL, HENRY	BAL	102	2ND DIST
KINSEL, MARGARET	WAS	015	2ND SUBD
KINSEL, MARY	WAS	163	2ND DIST
KINSELL, JOSEPH	WAS	124	2ND DIST
KINSELO, ANDREW	CEC	026	ELKTON 3
KINSELO, NATHAN	CEC	026	ELKTON 3
KINSELO, ROBERT	CEC	017	ELKTON 3
KINSELO, SAMUEL	CEC	107	3RD E DI
KINSELO, SAMUEL	CEC	119	3RD E DI
KINSELT, MARY	WAS	123	2ND DIST
KINSENDORF, CHARLES H.	BAL	386	8TH WARD
KINSENDORF, JANE	ANN	417	HOWARD D
KINSER, CHARLES	BAL	320	7TH WARD
KINSEY, BENJAMIN	BAL	298	1ST DIST
KINSEY, BENJAMIN	MGM	327	CRACKLIN
KINSEY, CHARK	HAR	044	1ST DIST
KINSEY, GEORGE F.	MGM	335	CRACKLIN
KINSEY, HANNAH A.	BAL	068	18TH WAR
KINSEY, LEVI	MGM	335	CRACKLIN
KINSEY, PETER	BAL	429	8TH WARD
KINSEY, REBECCA	MGM	327	CRACKLIN
KINSEY, SAMUEL	ANN	460	HOWARD D
KINSEY, SETH	HAR	044	1ST DIST
KINSEY, SLACY	BAL	067	18TH WAR
KINSEY, THOMAS	BAL	081	4TH WARD
KINSEYER, CHRISTIAN	FRE	411	8TH E DI
KINSIG, GEORGE	BAL	074	1ST WARD
KINSLER, FERDINAND	BAL	049	9TH WARD
KINSLER, JACOB	BAL	350	7TH WARD
KINSLEY, BARNEY	BAL	035	15TH WAR

Name	County	Page	District
KINSLEY, MICHAEL	BAL	093	1ST WARD
KINSLEY, SARAH	BAL	198	2ND WARD
KINSLEY, THOAMS	ALL	070	5TH E.D.
KINSLEY, WILLIAM	BAL	197	2ND WARD
KINSON, JOHN	CEC	212	7TH E DI
KINSOR, SOLOMON*	DOR	392	1ST DIST
KINTED, HENRY *	BAL	367	1ST DIST
KINTEMYER, LEWIS	FRE	080	FREDERIC
KINTETS, BARBARA	FRE	103	FREDERIC
KINTIG, JACOB	WAS	277	RIDGEVIL
KINTON, HENRY	KEN	209	2ND DIST
KINTY, SAMUEL	BAL	030	18TH WAR
KINTZ, CHARLES *	BAL	273	20TH WAR
KINTZ, FREDERICK	FRE	082	FREDERIC
KINTZ, JACOB	FRE	082	FREDERIC
KINTZER, JACOB	BAL	326	7TH WARD
KINTZMAN, ELIZABETH	BAL	345	7TH WARD
KINYON, PETER J.*	BAL	418	3RD WARD
KINZER, GEORGE	BAL	377	1ST DIST
KINZER, JASPER	FRE	414	8TH E DI
KINZER, JOHN	FRE	410	8TH E DI
KINZER, NICHOLAS	BAL	196	6TH WARD
KINZEY, CHRISTIAN SR.	FRE	432	8TH E DI
KIOH, G.S.	BAL	225	2ND WARD
KIOLL, JOHN	TAL	107	ST MICHA
KIPE, JOHN	FRE	192	5TH E DI
KIPE, JOHN	FRE	160	EMMITTSB
KIPENT, MARY	BAL	371	8TH WARD
KIPLER, JUNE	BAL	215	19TH WAR
KIPLINGER, JOHN	BAL	211	6TH DIST
KIPP, JOHN	FRE	098	FREDERIC
KIPP, JOHN W.	BAL	118	15TH WAR
KIPPS, ELIZA	BAL	401	8TH WARD
KIRBEY, PERE-BLACK	QUE	160	2ND E DI
KIRBY, ANN	BAL	068	1ST WARD
KIRBY, ANN	ANN	373	4TH DIST
KIRBY, ANN R.	BAL	098	1ST WARD
KIRBY, ANN R.	BAL	404	8TH WARD
KIRBY, BASIL	BAL	356	1ST DIST
KIRBY, BASIL	BAL	328	1ST DIST
KIRBY, C.	BAL	129	1ST WARD
KIRBY, CAROLINE	BAL	298	20TH WAR
KIRBY, CATHARINE	BAL	343	1ST DIST
KIRBY, CHRISTIANA	BAL	339	7TH WARD
KIRBY, DANE	BAL	267	12TH WAR
KIRBY, DENIS	BAL	408	1ST DIST
KIRBY, E.	BAL	150	1ST WARD
KIRBY, EDUARD	BAL	072	1ST WARD
KIRBY, EDWARD*	TAL	019	EASTON D
KIRBY, ELIZA	ANN	354	3RD DIST
KIRBY, ELIZABETH	BAL	211	6TH WARD
KIRBY, ELIZABETH	DOR	298	1ST DIST
KIRBY, ELIZZBETH	WOR	256	1ST CENS
KIRBY, ELLEN	BAL	129	11TH WAR
KIRBY, FRANCIS	TAL	021	EASTON D
KIRBY, FRANCIS	PRI	087	SPALDING
KIRBY, FRANCIS	BAL	205	6TH WARD
KIRBY, FREDERICK	BAL	437	8TH WARD
KIRBY, GEORGE M.	HAR	137	2ND DIST
KIRBY, HANNA	TAL	021	EASTON D
KIRBY, HENRIETTA*	DOR	415	1ST DIST
KIRBY, HENRY	BAL	128	1ST WARD
KIRBY, HINSOR*	DOR	403	1ST DIST
KIRBY, ISAAC	QUE	205	3RD E DI
KIRBY, ISACK*	TAL	035	EASTON D
KIRBY, J.B.	PRI	118	PISCATAW
KIRBY, JAME SH.	BAL	101	1ST WARD
KIRBY, JAMES	BAL	035	15TH WAR
KIRBY, JAMES	BAL	059	15TH WAR
KIRBY, JAMES	BAL	185	6TH WARD
KIRBY, JAMES	ANN	354	3RD DIST
KIRBY, JAMES	BAL	191	19TH WAR
KIRBY, JAMES H.	QUE	154	1ST E DI
KIRBY, JANE	QUE	154	1ST E DI
KIRBY, JANE	BAL	066	1ST WARD
KIRBY, JOHN	ALL	108	5TH E.D.
KIRBY, JOHN	BAL	226	19TH WAR
KIRBY, JOHN	DOR	392	1ST DIST
KIRBY, JOHN	BAL	209	17TH WAR
KIRBY, JOHN T.	BAL	356	1ST DIST
KIRBY, JOHN W.	BAL	105	15TH WAR
KIRBY, JOSEPH	BAL	371	8TH WARD
KIRBY, JOSEPH	QUE	154	1ST E DI
KIRBY, JOSEPH	BAL	278	17TH WAR
KIRBY, JOSEPH W.	PRI	052	AQUASCO
KIRBY, JOSIAH	TAL	016	EASTON D
KIRBY, JULIA	BAL	191	19TH WAR
KIRBY, MARGARET	BAL	370	3RD WARD
KIRBY, MARGRETT-BLACK	CAR	115	NO TWP L
KIRBY, MARIA	BAL	278	17TH WAR
KIRBY, MARIAH	TAL	020	EASTON D
KIRBY, MARY	BAL	370	3RD WARD
KIRBY, MARY	ALL	108	5TH E.D.
KIRBY, MARY	ANN	355	3RD DIST
KIRBY, MARY A.	BAL	039	9TH WARD
KIRBY, MARY A.	BAL	010	4TH WARD
KIRBY, MATILDA*	TAL	041	EASTON D
KIRBY, MORCECAI	QUE	169	2ND E DI
KIRBY, MORDECAI T.	QUE	212	3RD E DI
KIRBY, PHILIP	ALL	093	5TH E.D.
KIRBY, RICHARD W.	BAL	059	1ST WARD
KIRBY, ROBERT	BAL	330	7TH WARD
KIRBY, ROBERT	CAR	273	WESTMINS
KIRBY, SAMUEL-BLACK	QUE	149	1ST E DI
KIRBY, SARAH	BAL	039	9TH WARD
KIRBY, SILAS*	TAL	025	EASTON D
KIRBY, THOMAS	BAL	097	1ST WARD
KIRBY, THOMAS	BAL	132	1ST WARD
KIRBY, WILLIAM	BAL	283	2ND WARD
KIRBY, WILLIAM	BAL	139	1ST WARD
KIRBY, WILLIAM	TAL	046	EASTON T
KIRBY, WILLIAM	QUE	213	3RD E DI
KIRBY, WILLIAM	BAL	004	18TH WAR
KIRBY, WILLIAM	BAL	122	11TH WAR
KIRBY, WILLIAM	BAL	232	17TH WAR
KIRBY, WILLIAM	DOR	381	1ST DIST
KIRBY, WILLIAM	FRE	260	NEW MARK
KIRBY, WILLIAM H.	TAL	026	EASTON D
KIRBY, WILLMOT*	TAL	045	EASTON T
KIRBY, ZACHARIAH	BAL	337	1ST DIST
KIRBY,CALVIN	BAL	059	1ST WARD
KIRBY,MERIL	ST	307	1ST E DI
KIRCHBAUM, ADAM	BAL	008	15TH WAR
KIRCHENBAN, REBECCA W.*	BAL	119	15TH WAR
KIRCHENBANER, GEORGE MART	BAL	018	15TH WAR
KIRCHENBAU, REBECCA W.*	BAL	119	15TH WAR
KIRCHENBAUER, CHARLES	BAL	029	15TH WAR
KIRCHNER, FERDINAND	BAL	370	13TH WAR
KIRK, ABNER	CEC	129	6TH E DI
KIRK, ALLEN	CEC	164	6TH E DI
KIRK, ALPHONA C.	CEC	162	6TH E DI
KIRK, ANN	CEC	131	6TH E DI
KIRK, ANNIE	BAL	377	13TH WAR
KIRK, BARTON	ST	310	1ST E DI
KIRK, BENJAMIN F.	CEC	133	6TH E DI
KIRK, C.	BAL	304	20TH WAR
KIRK, CALEB	CEC	121	4TH E DI
KIRK, CALEB G.	HAR	099	2ND DIST
KIRK, CAROLINE L.	CEC	132	6TH E DI
KIRK, CHARLES	BAL	334	13TH WAR
KIRK, CORNELIA	CEC	128	5TH E DI
KIRK, DAVID	BAL	165	11TH WAR
KIRK, ELIM	CEC	163	6TH E DI
KIRK, ELISHA	CEC	195	6TH E DI
KIRK, ELISHA E.	CEC	128	5TH E DI
KIRK, ELIZA	BAL	307	3RD WARD
KIRK, ELLIS	CEC	113	4TH E DI
KIRK, EMILY J.	CEC	133	6TH E DI
KIRK, GEORGE	HAR	086	2ND DIST
KIRK, GEORGE W.	BAL	415	14TH WAR
KIRK, HENRIETTA*	TAL	018	EASTON D
KIRK, HENRY C.	BAL	417	14TH WAR
KIRK, HENRY N.	ST	300	2ND E DI
KIRK, HOWELL	CEC	163	6TH E DI
KIRK, ISAAC	BAL	008	EASTERN
KIRK, JACOB	HAR	052	1ST DIST
KIRK, JACOB W.	CEC	163	6TH E DI
KIRK, JAMES	CEC	199	7TH E DI
KIRK, JAMES	BAL	165	11TH WAR
KIRK, JESSE A.	CEC	162	6TH E DI
KIRK, JOHN	BAL	391	1ST DIST
KIRK, JOHN A.	BAL	084	4TH WARD
KIRK, JOHN R	HAR	076	BEL AIR
KIRK, JOSEPH	CEC	132	6TH E DI
KIRK, JOSIAH F.	CEC	118	4TH E DI
KIRK, LOUIS	CEC	067	5TH E DI
KIRK, LUCY F.	CEC	165	6TH E DI
KIRK, MAHLON	MGM	367	BERRYS D
KIRK, MARGARET	CEC	168	6TH E DI
KIRK, MARY	BAL	083	4TH WARD
KIRK, MARY A.	BAL	396	1ST DIST
KIRK, MARY H.	CEC	161	6TH E DI
KIRK, RACHEL	MGM	331	CRACKLIN
KIRK, REUBEN	CEC	132	6TH E DI
KIRK, REUBEN H.	CEC	142	6TH E DI
KIRK, RICHARD L.	MGM	361	BERRYS D
KIRK, ROBERT	BAL	106	2ND DIST
KIRK, ROBERT	BAL	123	1ST WARD
KIRK, SAMUEL	BAL	061	10TH WAR
KIRK, SAMUEL	BAL	207	6TH WARD
KIRK, SAMUEL	HAR	118	2ND DIST
KIRK, THOMAS	CAR	102	NO TWP L
KIRK, THOMAS C.	ST	303	2ND E DI
KIRK, TIMOTHY	MGM	338	CRACKLIN
KIRK, W. ALEXANDER	ST	312	1ST E DI
KIRK, WASHINGTON	BAL	398	14TH WAR
KIRK, WILLIAM	CEC	132	6TH E DI
KIRK, WILLIAM	CEC	132	6TH E DI
KIRK, WILLIAM	CEC	076	NORTHEAS
KIRK, WILLIAM	BAL	449	1ST DIST
KIRK, WILLIAM J.	BAL	209	19TH WAR
KIRK, WILSON A.	CEC	132	6TH E DI
KIRKHAM, LYDIA A.	CEC	077	NORTHEAS
KIRKHART, WILLIAM	WAS	089	2ND SUBD
KIRKLAND, ALEXANDER	BAL	456	14TH WAR
KIRKLAND, EDWARD	BAL	187	11TH WAR
KIRKLAND, HENRY C.	BAL	115	5TH WARD
KIRKLAND, J. W.	BAL	332	1ST DIST
KIRKLAND, JOHN	BAL	156	1ST WARD
KIRKLEY, THOMAS	BAL	226	19TH WAR
KIRKMAN, JOHN W.	BAL	157	16TH WAR
KIRKMAN, MARY	CAR	147	NO TWP L
KIRKNER, H.	BAL	238	12TH WAR
KIRKNER, HENRY	BAL	238	12TH WAR
KIRKOFF, HENRY	BAL	394	1ST DIST
KIRKPATRICK, D.	BAL	267	20TH WAR
KIRKPATRICK, ELIZA	BAL	178	19TH WAR
KIRKPATRICK, JOHN	BAL	265	12TH WAR
KIRKPATRICK, JOHN	WAS	143	2ND DIST
KIRKPATRICK, WILLIAM	BAL	457	1ST DIST
KIRKPATRICK, WILLIAM	BAL	318	20TH WAR
KIRKWOOD, AGNES	HAR	023	1ST DIST
KIRKWOOD, ARCHABALD	HAR	073	1ST DIST
KIRKWOOD, CHARLES P.	BAL	341	1ST DIST
KIRKWOOD, HOPE	HAR	073	1ST DIST
KIRKWOOD, JAMES	HAR	073	1ST DIST
KIRKWOOD, JOHN	BAL	287	17TH WAR
KIRKWOOD, JOHN	BAL	287	17TH WAR
KIRKWOOD, JOHN B.	HAR	018	1ST DIST
KIRKWOOD, JOHN H.	HAR	023	1ST DIST
KIRKWOOD, PHILLIP	BAL	287	17TH WAR
KIRKWOOD, RICHARD	HAR	023	1ST DIST
KIRKWOOD, ROBERT	HAR	018	1ST DIST
KIRKWOOD, SARAH	BAL	015	18TH WAR
KIRKWOOD, WALLACE	PRI	005	BLADENSB
KIRKWOOD, WILLIAM	CEC	096	4TH E DI
KIRKWOOD, WILLIAM	BAL	235	17TH WAR
KIRKWOOD, WILLIAM	BAL	038	2ND DIST
KIRLMAN, J. F.	BAL	149	1ST WARD
KIRLY, WILLIAM	BAL	249	2ND WARD
KIRRIGNER, JOSHUA	BAL	025	4TH WARD
KIRSH, FREDERIC	BAL	191	6TH WARD
KIRSHAW, CHARLES C.	CAL	001	1ST DIST
KIRSHAW, JOHN	CAL	001	1ST DIST
KIRSSELOR, THOMAS	CEC	026	ELKTON 3
KIRT, CASPER	BAL	248	2ND WARD
KIRTHLEY, JAMES	TAL	082	ST MICHA
KIRTIS, THOMAS *	WAS	073	2ND SUBD
KIRTY, AUGUSTAS *	BAL	113	18TH WAR
KIRTZ, ANGUSTAS *	BAL	113	18TH WAR
KIRTZ, MARTIN	HAR	068	1ST DIST
KIRVIN, MARY	SOM	463	HANGARY
KIRWAN, GEORGE	BAL	288	17TH WAR
KIRWAN, JOHN	BAL	019	15TH WAR
KIRWAN, JOHN H.	BAL	090	15TH WAR
KIRWAN, LOVEY	DOR	347	3RD DIVI
KIRWAN, PETER	DOR	355	3RD DIVI
KIRWAN, SOLOMON F.*	DOR	360	3RD DIVI
KIRWAN, THOMAS*	DOR	339	3RD DIVI
KIRWAN, WILLIAM T.	BAL	174	16TH WAR
KIRWIN, ZEBADE	BAL	264	17TH WAR
KIRY, MARY	BAL	412	14TH WAR
KISENDAFFER, FRED	BAL	138	2ND DIST
KISER, ANDREW	FRE	397	PETERSVI
KISER, HELENA	BAL	365	8TH WARD
KISER, HENRY	BAL	102	2ND DIST
KISEWETTER, CHARLES	BAL	349	3RD WARD
KISH, JACOB	MGM	399	ROCKERLE
KISNER, CHRIATOPHER	MGM	363	BERRYS D
KISNER, DANIEL	BAL	336	13TH WAR
KISNER, JACOB	FRE	279	WOODSBOR
KISNER, WILLIAM	MGM	394	ROCKERLE
KISONG, GEORGE R.	FRE	026	FREDERIC
KISS, JOHN	WAS	266	1ST DIST
KISS, WILLIAM	BAL	279	2ND WARD
KISSECKER, CHRISTIAN	BAL	021	15TH WAR
KISSEL, EMANUEL	WAS	278	LEITERSB
KISSEL, JACOB	WAS	278	LEITERSB
KISSEL, JOHN	WAS	262	1ST DIST
KISSELL, MARGARET	BAL	081	15TH WAR
KISSELL, SARAH A.	BAL	300	7TH WARD
KISSERT, P.	BAL	259	20TH WAR
KISSICK, HENRY	BAL	144	16TH WAR
KISSINGER, ANN	WAS	162	HAGERSTO
KISSINGER, CATHARINE	WAS	280	LEITERSB
KISSINGER, ELIZABETH	WAS	280	LEITERSB
KISSINGER, GEORGE	WAS	275	RIDGEVIL
KISSINGER, GEORGE	WAS	262	1ST DIST
KISSINGER, WILLIAM	WAS	023	2ND SUBD
KISSMAN, JOHN	BAL	099	2ND DIST
KIST, AMELIA	HAR	102	2ND DIST
KIST, FREDERICK	BAL	216	19TH WAR
KISTER, MARY	BAL	425	14TH WAR
KISTER, RICHARD	BAL	138	18TH WAR
KISTNER, CONRAD	BAL	233	6TH WARD
KITCHEN, GEORGE	MGM	378	ROCKERLE
KITCHEN, SARAH-BLACK	WOR	333	1ST E DI
KITCHENS, CATHARINE	BAL	026	15TH WAR
KITCHENS, ELIZA-BLACK	WOR	333	1ST E DI
KITCHIE, AUGUSTINE	BAL	212	11TH WAR
KITCHINGER, FREDERICK	BAL	148	19TH WAR
KITE, JES	BAL	021	2ND DIST
KITE, JOSEPH	BAL	300	7TH WARD
KITE, JOSEPH B.	BAL	300	7TH WARD
KITELY, CLARISSA	BAL	131	16TH WAR
KITENBERGER, GEORGE	BAL	033	15TH WAR
KITHLY, HESTER A.	HAR	191	3RD DIST
KITLER, FREDERICK	BAL	434	8TH WARD
KITLER, JOHN A.	BAL	145	16TH WAR
KITLING, OLEVIA	BAL	356	1ST DIST
KITNER, GODFREY	BAL	191	2ND WARD
KITSMILLER, WILLIAM	WAS	118	2ND DIST
KITT, JOSHUA	HAR	142	2ND DIST
KITTEANING, FREDERICKX	FRE	144	10TH E D
KITTENSTEIN, STEPHEN*	BAL	091	10TH WAR
KITTER, JOHN	BAL	128	1ST WARD
KITTERING, CHARLES	BAL	415	8TH WARD
KITTERING, PETER	BAL	414	8TH WARD
KITTLE, ALWIRE	BAL	351	13TH WAR
KITTLE, JOSEPH	BAL	219	2ND WARD
KITTLER, AUGUST	BAL	261	2ND WARD
KITTLER, FREDERIC	BAL	197	6TH WARD
KITTLEWELL, SAMUEL	TAL	015	EASTON D
KITTS, BARNEY	ANN	311	1ST DIST
KITTS, DAVID	BAL	157	19TH WAR
KITTS, JOHN	BAL	171	11TH WAR
KITZELLER, BASS JR.	BAL	212	11TH WAR
KITZMILLER, COLUMBUS	ALL	066	10TH E.D
KITZMILLER, DAVID	WAS	301	1ST DIST
KITZMILLER, HIRAM	FRE	415	8TH E DI
KITZMILLER, JACOB	WAS	214	1ST DIST
KITZMILLER, JACOB	WAS	212	1ST DIST
KITZMILLER, JOHN	WAS	190	1ST DIST
KITZMILLER, SAMUEL	CAR	371	9TH DIST
KITZMILLER, SUSAN	WAS	024	2ND SUBD
KITZMILLER, WASHINGTON	WAS	181	BOONSBOR
KITZMILLER, WILLIAM	WAS	299	1ST DIST
KIU, JOHN *	BAL	150	1ST WARD
KIZANDREFER, LAUREN	BAL	087	1ST WARD
KIZNER, JOHN	BAL	131	5TH WARD
KKIDWELL, THOMAS	MGM	354	BERRYS D
KLAENLA, FREDERICK	BAL	166	6TH WARD
KLANNER, JACOB	BAL	282	12TH WAR
KLAR, G.*	BAL	272	20TH WAR
KLARE, CHRISTIAN	BAL	146	16TH WAR
KLARE, JOHN B.	BAL	145	16TH WAR
KLASKE, MIECZYSTAN	BAL	357	13TH WAR
KLASSEN, ANDREW	BAL	282	12TH WAR
KLAUMBURG, AUGUSTUS	BAL	039	4TH WARD
KLAUSSEN, CHARLES F.	BAL	282	12TH WAR
KLAY, CORNELIUS	FRE	256	NEW MARK
KLAY, ZAHULON	FRE	256	NEW MARK
KLEAS, GEORGE	FRE	405	JEFFERSO
KLEEN, HENRY	BAL	254	20TH WAR
KLEES, HENRY	BAL	077	10TH WAR
KLEG, ELLEN	BAL	222	1ST DIST
KLEG, JOSEPH	BAL	225	1ST DIST
KLEIBER, ELIZABETH	BAL	087	15TH WAR
KLEIBLINE, GOTLIEB	CAR	340	6TH DIST
KLEIBUCKER, BERNARD	BAL	022	9TH WARD
KLEIN, ELIZABETH	BAL	042	9TH WARD
KLEIN, FREDERICK	BAL	259	2ND WARD
KLEIN, JOHN	BAL	031	1ST WARD
KLEIN, PETER S.	BAL	254	12TH WAR
KLEIN, WILLIAM	BAL	203	6TH WARD
KLEINSDENST, ANTHONY	BAL	210	2ND WARD
KLEINSMITH, ADAM	BAL	110	15TH WAR
KLEM, CAROLINE	BAL	265	20TH WAR
KLEPPITCH, ANN R.	BAL	155	19TH WAR
KLEPPITCH, CHARLES F.	BAL	288	12TH WAR
KLEPR, HENRY	BAL	060	1ST WARD
KLEPSTINE, AMELIA *	ALL	124	4TH E.D.
KLEPSTINE, DORCAS E.	ALL	123	4TH E.D.
KLEPSTINE, WILLIAM	ALL	145	6TH E.D.
KLESE, SOLOMON	FRE	098	FREDERIC
KLESNI, ANNE	BAL	215	11TH WAR
KLESSEL, FRANCIS	BAL	038	15TH WAR
KLESSEL, JOHN	BAL	008	15TH WAR
KLESSEL, STEPHEN	BAL	037	15TH WAR
KLESSNER, WILLAIM	BAL	454	14TH WAR
KLIE, JACOB *	BAL	379	13TH WAR
KLIEN, GEORGE	BAL	018	9TH WARD
KLIENFELLER, JESSE	BAL	438	8TH WARD
KLIGHLE, LEWIS	FRE	021	FREDERIC
KLIMHEN, GEORGE	BAL	181	16TH WAR
KLINE, ANTHONY	WAS	226	1ST DIST
KLINE, CAROLINE	BAL	458	14TH WAR
KLINE, CHRISTIMA	WAS	239	CAVETOWN
KLINE, DANIEL	WAS	224	1ST DIST
KLINE, DANIEL	FRE	351	MIDDLETO
KLINE, DANIEL	FRE	360	CATOCTIN
KLINE, DAVID	FRE	360	CATOCTIN
KLINE, ELIZABETH	WAS	160	HAGERSTO
KLINE, ELIZABETH	BAL	277	2ND WARD
KLINE, FREDERICK	BAL	167	2ND DIST
KLINE, FREDERICK	FRE	082	FREDERIC
KLINE, GEORGE	BAL	098	2ND DIST
KLINE, GEORGE	WAS	133	2ND DIST
KLINE, GEORGE	WAS	149	HAGERSTO
KLINE, GEORGE	WAS	208	1ST DIST

Name	County	Page	Location
KLINE, GEORGE A.	FRE	368	CATOCTIN
KLINE, GEORGE W.	WAS	133	2ND DIST
KLINE, GODFREY	BAL	097	15TH WAR
KLINE, HANNAH	WAS	241	CAVETOWN
KLINE, HARRY	FRE	004	FREDERIC
KLINE, HENRY	WAS	224	1ST DIST
KLINE, HENRY	BAL	265	2ND WARD
KLINE, HIRAM	FRE	363	CATOCTIN
KLINE, ISAAC	WAS	220	1ST DIST
KLINE, JACOB	FRE	361	CATOCTIN
KLINE, JACOB	FRE	360	CATOCTIN
KLINE, JANE	WAS	125	HAGERSTO
KLINE, JOHN	FRE	371	CATOCTIN
KLINE, JOHN	BAL	277	2ND WARD
KLINE, JOHN	BAL	123	16TH WAR
KLINE, JOHN	BAL	076	1ST WARD
KLINE, JOHN	BAL	082	1ST WARD
KLINE, JOSEPH	BAL	387	8TH WARD
KLINE, JOSEPHINE	BAL	379	13TH WAR
KLINE, LENHART	BAL	350	13TH WAR
KLINE, LEWIS	FRE	341	MIDDLETO
KLINE, MARY E.	BAL	214	11TH WAR
KLINE, MARY H.	WAS	133	2ND DIST
KLINE, MICHAEL	FRE	361	CATOCTIN
KLINE, PAUL	FRE	361	CATOCTIN
KLINE, PETER	FRE	080	FREDERIC
KLINE, PETER	FRE	101	FREDERIC
KLINE, PHILIP	FRE	368	CATOCTIN
KLINE, PHILIP	FRE	368	CATOCTIN
KLINE, SAMUEL	FRE	372	CATOCTIN
KLINE, SAMUEL	WAS	243	CAVETOWN
KLINE, SAMUEL	BAL	438	1ST DIST
KLINE, SARAH	FRE	348	MIDDLETO
KLINE, STEREN	FRE	004	FREDERIC
KLINE, SUSAN	WAS	117	2ND DIST
KLINE, TELPHY	BAL	240	17TH WAR
KLINE, WILLIAM	BAL	351	13TH WAR
KLINE, WILLIAM	FRE	353	MIDDLETO
KLINE, WILLIAM	WAS	123	2ND DIST
KLINE, WILLIAM	WAS	140	HAGERSTO
KLINE, WILLIAM	BAL	023	15TH WAR
KLINE, WILLIAM L.	WAS	116	2ND DIST
KLINEDINST, ANDREW	BAL	442	1ST DIST
KLINEFELT, SAMUEL	BAL	271	17TH WAR
KLINEFELTER, AUGUSTUS	BAL	072	2ND DIST
KLINEFELTER, HENRY	BAL	329	3RD WARD
KLINEWELL, JOHN F.	FRE	007	FREDERIC
KLING, DAVID	FRE	420	8TH E DI
KLING, ELIZABETH	BAL	096	10TH WAR
KLING, JOHN	BAL	129	16TH WAR
KLINGAMAN, LEWIS	BAL	263	2ND WARD
KLINGENHEFFER, CATHARINE	BAL	168	16TH WAR
KLINIBECK, L.	BAL	090	5TH WARD
KLINTINE, JOHN	BAL	340	3RD WARD
KLIPSTINE, LEWIS F.	ALL	067	10TH E.D
KLIPSTONE, CATHARINE	ALL	067	10TH E.D
KLIRLEIN, BARBARA	BAL	061	4TH WARD
KLOCKGETHER, DEDERICK	BAL	117	15TH WAR
KLOMAN, FELIX	BAL	405	14TH WAR
KLOMM, FREDRICA	BAL	086	10TH WAR
KLOPPENSTEIN, JACOB	BAL	135	16TH WAR
KLORE, ADAM	BAL	266	1ST DIST
KLORE, CATHARINE	BAL	267	1ST DIST
KLORMAN, SEBASTIAN	BAL	196	6TH WARD
KLOTZ, ADAM F.	BAL	039	9TH WARD
KLOUCHESCHICK, FRANCIS	BAL	002	18TH WAR
KLUCK, ELIZABETH	BAL	157	19TH WAR
KLUCK, LOUIS	BAL	157	19TH WAR
KLUGE, JACOB	BAL	162	16TH WAR
KLUMP, JACOB	BAL	246	6TH WARD
KLUMP, MATHIAS	BAL	192	17TH WAR
KLUMP, MICHEAL	BAL	273	20TH WAR
KLUMPER, FERDINAND W.	BAL	213	6TH WARD
KLUN, WILLIAM	BAL	239	12TH WAR
KLUNEMAN, FREDERICK	BAL	467	14TH WAR
KLUNGER, JOHN	BAL	084	1ST WARD
KLUNK, CAROLINE	BAL	274	7TH WARD
KLUNZ, JOHN	BAL	268	7TH WARD
KLUTZBACH, HENRY	BAL	118	15TH WAR
KNABB, JOHN	BAL	301	3RD WARD
KNABE, WILLIAM	BAL	283	12TH WAR
KNABE, ZACHARIAH	CAR	268	WESTMINS
KNACKSTADT, THOMAS	BAL	105	5TH WARD
KNADY, TIMOTHY	HAR	156	3RD DIST
KNAGG, EMAN	ALL	013	3RD E.D.
KNAGG, ERNAN	ALL	013	3RD E.D.
KNAKLE, GEORGE	BAL	247	2ND WARD
KNAKLE, JOHN	BAL	247	2ND WARD
KNAN, MARGARET	BAL	404	8TH WARD
KNAP, CONRAD	BAL	178	16TH WAR
KNAP, THOMAS	BAL	336	3RD WARD
KNAPP, AMRY	BAL	096	18TH WAR
KNAPP, BARNHARDT	BAL	006	15TH WAR
KNAPP, CHARLES	BAL	116	1ST WARD
KNAPP, HENRY	BAL	326	3RD WARD
KNAPP, J.	BAL	157	1ST WARD
KNAPP, JOHN	BAL	233	20TH WAR
KNAPP, JOSPEH M.	BAL	343	13TH WAR
KNAPP, LYDIA	BAL	281	12TH WAR
KNAPP, WILLIAM	BAL	043	9TH WARD
KNAPP, WILLIAM	BAL	012	9TH WARD
KNAPP, WILLIAM	BAL	096	18TH WAR
KNAPT, JOHN	BAL	176	2ND DIST
KNARK, MARY	BAL	016	9TH WARD
KNAUF, HOWER	BAL	259	12TH WAR
KNAUF, JESSE	BAL	302	20TH WAR
KNAUF, MICHAEL	BAL	120	18TH WAR
KNAUF, WILLIAM	BAL	336	13TH WAR
KNAUFF, JACOB	FRE	114	CREAGERS
KNAUFF, JACOB	FRE	047	FREDERIC
KNAUFMAN, JOHN	BAL	017	9TH WARD
KNAWELER, AGUST	BAL	240	2ND WARD
KNAW, MARY E.	BAL	073	4TH WARD
KNEARIN, HENRY	BAL	243	2ND WARD
KNEASY, ADOLPHUS	WAS	125	HAGERSTO
KNEBAL, JOHN H.	BAL	084	1ST WARD
KNECHT, FLORENCE	ALL	020	2ND E.D.
KNECHT, FRANCIS J.	BAL	041	15TH WAR
KNECHT, MICHAEL	ALL	020	2ND E.D.
KNEELAN, HANNAH	BAL	207	6TH WARD
KNEELAND, ELISHA	BAL	456	8TH WARD
KNEELAND, ELISHA	BAL	285	7TH WARD
KNEEN, THOMAS	BAL	185	16TH WAR
KNELL, ANDREW	BAL	182	16TH WAR
KNELL, G.A.	BAL	246	20TH WAR
KNELL, HENRY	BAL	306	20TH WAR
KNELL, JOSEPH	BAL	253	20TH WAR
KNELL, RICHARD	BAL	051	1ST WARD
KNELL, SOPHIA	BAL	409	14TH WAR
KNELL,MARY E.	BAL	051	1ST WARD
KNELLER, FREDERICK	CAR	341	6TH DIST
KNELLER, GODFREY	CAR	355	6TH DIST
KNELLER, JOHN	BAL	362	13TH WAR
KNELLER, NATHAN	CAR	274	7TH DIST
KNEP, ANN	BAL	318	1ST DIST
KNEP, MARGARET	BAL	309	1ST DIST
KNEPPER, WILLIAM	WAS	103	2ND DIST
KNETTLE, ROBERT H.	BAL	143	1ST WARD
KNEWLLR, CATHARINE	BAL	362	13TH WAR
KNGIHT, LUCINDA	FRE	415	8TH E DI
KNICKMAN, JOHN	BAL	135	16TH WAR
KNIFE, EDWARD	BAL	293	12TH WAR
KNIGHT, A.	BAL	101	10TH WAR
KNIGHT, ALEXANDER	HAR	095	2ND DIST
KNIGHT, ANN	CAR	386	2ND DIST
KNIGHT, ANN E.	BAL	033	18TH WAR
KNIGHT, ANN E.	CEC	024	ELKTON 3
KNIGHT, ANTHONY	BAL	218	17TH WAR
KNIGHT, CASANDER	HAR	149	3RD DIST
KNIGHT, CATHARINE	KEN	289	3RD DIST
KNIGHT, CECILIA	BAL	409	1ST DIST
KNIGHT, CORA	CEC	187	7TH E DI
KNIGHT, DORATHY	BAL	360	1ST DIST
KNIGHT, ELIZA	BAL	164	2ND DIST
KNIGHT, ELIZABETH	BAL	360	1ST DIST
KNIGHT, ELIZABETH	BAL	330	1ST DIST
KNIGHT, ELIZABETH	BAL	072	10TH WAR
KNIGHT, ELIZABETH	CEC	186	7TH E DI
KNIGHT, ELIZABETH	HAR	173	3RD DIST
KNIGHT, EZIKEL	BAL	033	18TH WAR
KNIGHT, GEORGE	HAR	181	3RD DIST
KNIGHT, GEORGE	BAL	128	18TH WAR
KNIGHT, GEORGE	ANN	520	HOWARD D
KNIGHT, GEORGE	BAL	023	15TH WAR
KNIGHT, H.	BAL	138	1ST WARD
KNIGHT, H.	BAL	159	1ST WARD
KNIGHT, HANNAH	ALL	161	6TH E.D.
KNIGHT, HARRISON	FRE	063	FREDERIC
KNIGHT, HENRIETTA	ST	325	4TH E DI
KNIGHT, HENRY	BAL	279	2ND WARD
KNIGHT, HENRY	BAL	286	2ND WARD
KNIGHT, HENRY	BAL	359	1ST DIST
KNIGHT, HENRY	BAL	198	17TH WAR
KNIGHT, HORACE	BAL	173	2ND DIST
KNIGHT, HUMPHREY	BAL	134	1ST WARD
KNIGHT, IGNATIOUS	BAL	329	1ST DIST
KNIGHT, ISAAC	BAL	259	12TH WAR
KNIGHT, ISAAC	ALL	157	6TH E.D.
KNIGHT, JACOB	BAL	440	8TH WARD
KNIGHT, JACOB	CAR	195	4TH DIST
KNIGHT, JAMES	CEC	061	1ST E DI
KNIGHT, JAMES	BAL	453	1ST DIST
KNIGHT, JAMES	BAL	100	10TH WAR
KNIGHT, JAMES T.	HAR	032	1ST DIST
KNIGHT, JANE	BAL	053	1ST WARD
KNIGHT, JOHN	BAL	320	1ST DIST
KNIGHT, JOHN	ALL	211	CUMBERLA
KNIGHT, JOHN	HAR	094	2ND DIST
KNIGHT, JOHN	CEC	024	ELKTON 3
KNIGHT, JOHN	BAL	133	18TH WAR
KNIGHT, JOHN	BAL	156	19TH WAR
KNIGHT, JOHN	BAL	144	19TH WAR
KNIGHT, JOHN	FRE	202	5TH E DI
KNIGHT, JOHN	CEC	154	PORT DUP
KNIGHT, JOHN	BAL	082	4TH WARD
KNIGHT, JOHN	BAL	082	4TH WARD
KNIGHT, JOHN	FRE	447	8TH E DI
KNIGHT, JOHN B.	HAR	205	3RD DIST
KNIGHT, JOHN H.	BAL	231	19TH WAR
KNIGHT, JONATHAN	BAL	171	6TH WARD
KNIGHT, JOSHAWAY W.	HAR	195	3RD DIST
KNIGHT, LOUISA	BAL	299	17TH WAR
KNIGHT, MARGARET	BAL	088	2ND DIST
KNIGHT, MARGARET	ALL	231	CUMBERLA
KNIGHT, MARY	BAL	173	2ND DIST
KNIGHT, MARY	BAL	411	8TH WARD
KNIGHT, MARY	BAL	282	17TH WAR
KNIGHT, MARY	BAL	013	18TH WAR
KNIGHT, MARY C.	BAL	204	19TH WAR
KNIGHT, MATILDA	BAL	123	2ND DIST
KNIGHT, MICHAEL	BAL	032	18TH WAR
KNIGHT, MICHAEL	BAL	063	18TH WAR
KNIGHT, NANCY	BAL	023	18TH WAR
KNIGHT, NATH.	BAL	300	20TH WAR
KNIGHT, PERRY	BAL	094	18TH WAR
KNIGHT, PETER	CAR	280	7TH DIST
KNIGHT, PETER	BAL	015	1ST WARD
KNIGHT, PETER	BAL	315	12TH WAR
KNIGHT, ROBERT	BAL	003	9TH WARD
KNIGHT, ROBERT	HAR	002	1ST DIST
KNIGHT, SAMUEL	HAR	195	3RD DIST
KNIGHT, SAMUEL	BAL	139	2ND DIST
KNIGHT, SARAH	BAL	099	1ST WARD
KNIGHT, SARAH	PRI	032	VANSVILL
KNIGHT, SARAH A.	HAR	171	3RD DIST
KNIGHT, SARAH J.	HAR	173	3RD DIST
KNIGHT, SARAH J.	HAR	181	3RD DIST
KNIGHT, SISTER M.E.	FRE	197	5TH E DI
KNIGHT, THEADORE	CEC	186	7TH E DI
KNIGHT, THOMAS	BAL	115	11TH WAR
KNIGHT, THOMAS	BAL	131	2ND DIST
KNIGHT, THOMAS C.	BAL	152	1ST WARD
KNIGHT, W. M.	BAL	333	1ST DIST
KNIGHT, WESTLY	HAR	067	1ST DIST
KNIGHT, WILLIAM	HAR	171	3RD DIST
KNIGHT, WILLIAM	BAL	011	18TH WAR
KNIGHT, WILLIAM	CEC	047	1ST E DI
KNIGHT, WILLIAM	BAL	127	2ND DIST
KNIGHT, WILLIAM	BAL	221	12TH WAR
KNIGHT, WILLIAM F.	BAL	344	13TH WAR
KNIGHT, WILLIAM H.	BAL	020	15TH WAR
KNIGHT, ZEIXEL	BAL	100	18TH WAR
KNIGHT,LEVINIA	FRE	415	8TH E DI
KNIGHT,WILLIAM	BAL	254	2ND WARD
KNIGHTART, ADAM	BAL	371	1ST DIST
KNIGHTON, CATHARINE	ANN	404	8TH DIST
KNIGHTON, ELLEN	ANN	311	1ST DIST
KNIGHTON, HANNAH	ANN	269	ANNAPOLI
KNIGHTON, RICHARD	ANN	288	ANNAPOLI
KNIGHTON, THOMAS	BAL	307	3RD WARD
KNIGHTON, THOMAS H.	ANN	312	1ST DIST
KNILL, WILLIAM	FRE	074	FREDERIC
KNIPE, WILLIAM H.	BAL	088	18TH WAR
KNIPLY, JOHN	PRI	107	PISCATAW
KNIPP, JACOB	BAL	199	17TH WAR
KNIPPLE, BARBARA	CAR	348	6TH DIST
KNIPPLE, DAVID	CAR	296	7TH DIST
KNIPPLE, EDWARD H.	CAR	324	1ST DIST
KNIPPLE, ELLEN	CAR	296	7TH DIST
KNIPPLE, HENRY	CAR	258	3RD DIST
KNIPPLE, JACOB	CAR	267	WESTMINS
KNIPPLE, JACOB	CAR	324	1ST DIST
KNIPPLE, JOHN	CAR	348	6TH DIST
KNIPPLE, MARY	CAR	349	6TH DIST
KNIRER, JOHN *	FRE	313	MIDDLETO
KNISS, WILLIAM	BAL	082	10TH WAR
KNITED, HENRY *	BAL	367	1ST DIST
KNIVE, SARAH	BAL	315	1ST DIST
KNOBB, CAROLINE	BAL	356	3RD WARD
KNOBBS, LUCY*	BAL	408	3RD WARD
KNOBLOCK, CHARLOTT	BAL	453	8TH WARD
KNOBLOCK, JOHN C.	BAL	453	8TH WARD
KNOCH, GEORGE	BAL	039	15TH WAR
KNOCHE, CATHARINE	BAL	374	13TH WAR
KNOCK, EZEKEL	CAR	228	5TH DIST
KNOCK, HENRY	BAL	018	18TH WAR
KNOCK, JAMES	KEN	250	2ND DIST
KNOCK, JESSEY	KEN	305	3RD DIST
KNOCK, JOHN	KEN	243	2ND DIST
KNOCK, MARY	CAR	228	5TH DIST
KNOCK, NELLY	BAL	135	11TH WAR
KNOCK, THOMAS	ANN	513	HOWARD D
KNOCKER, PATRICK	ALL	056	10TH E.D
KNOCKTON, MARY	BAL	188	6TH WARD
KNODDY, LUDEWICK	BAL	390	3RD WARD
KNODE, CATHARINE	WAS	038	2ND SUBD
KNODE, CORNELIUS	WAS	087	2ND SUBD
KNODE, DANIEL	WAS	172	FUNKSTOW
KNODE, FRISBY	WAS	030	2ND SUBD
KNODE, GEORGE	WAS	087	2ND SUBD
KNODE, HENRY	WAS	056	2ND SUBD
KNODE, HEZEKIAH	WAS	069	2ND SUBD
KNODE, ISREAL	WAS	128	HAGERSTO
KNODE, JACOB	WAS	213	1ST DIST
KNODE, JACOB H.	WAS	155	HAGERSTO
KNODE, JOHN E.	WAS	221	1ST DIST
KNODE, LEWIS A.	WAS	222	1ST DIST
KNODE, MARY	WAS	172	FUNKSTOW
KNODE, MARY	WAS	094	2ND SUBD
KNODE, OLIVER	WAS	187	BOONSBOR
KNODE, REBECCA	WAS	302	1ST DIST
KNODE, SIMON	WAS	172	FUNKSTOW
KNODE, URIAH	WAS	056	2ND SUBD
KNODE, WILLIAM	WAS	170	FUNKSTOW
KNODE, WILLIAM	WAS	258	1ST DIST
KNODER, DANIEL	WAS	215	1ST DIST
KNODER, JOHN G.	WAS	132	HAGERSTO
KNODER, WILLAIM	WAS	148	HAGERSTO
KNODLE, BARBARA	WAS	203	1ST DIST
KNODLE, ELIAS	WAS	033	2ND SUBD
KNODLE, GEORGE	WAS	121	HAGERSTO
KNODLE, JACOB	WAS	192	1ST DIST
KNODLE, JOHN	WAS	185	BOONSBOR
KNODLE, JOHN	WAS	121	HAGERSTO
KNODLE, JONATHAN	WAS	035	2ND SUBD
KNODLE, JONOTHAN S.	WAS	192	1ST DIST
KNODLE, JOSIAH	WAS	182	BOONSBOR
KNODLE, KNODLE	WAS	202	1ST DIST
KNODLE, LYDIA	WAS	162	HAGERSTO
KNODLE, SAMUEL	WAS	203	1ST DIST
KNODLE, SAMUEL	WAS	033	2ND SUBD
KNODLE, WILLIAM	WAS	128	HAGERSTO
KNOFF, JACOB	WAS	256	1ST DIST
KNOGHT, LANE Y.	BAL	224	12TH WAR
KNOLE, JOSEPH R.	CAR	231	5TH DIST
KNOLL, DINAH	BAL	368	13TH WAR
KNOLLS, DAVID	CAR	067	NO TWP L
KNOLT, JAMES L.	BAL	445	8TH WARD
KNOLTS, GEORGE P.*	BAL	389	3RD WARD
KNOMAN, FRANK	BAL	066	4TH WARD
KNOMMAR, JAMES	BAL	413	14TH WAR
KNONEBERG, FRANCIS	BAL	410	14TH WAR
KNONIG, JACOB	BAL	142	5TH WARD
KNOOKS, BENJAMIN	BAL	151	11TH WAR
KNOOOKS, WILLIAM	FRE	384	PETERSVI
KNOOR, ANN M.	BAL	369	3RD WARD
KNOOTZ, ALICE L.	CAR	317	1ST DIST
KNOP, LUDWIG	BAL	379	13TH WAR
KNOPP, GEORGE	HAR	053	1ST DIST
KNOPP, S.	BAL	309	20TH WAR
KNOPS, MARGARET	BAL	143	2ND DIST
KNOR, WILLIAM	BAL	350	7TH WARD
KNORLIENS, HENRY	BAL	290	17TH WAR
KNORR, JOHN	BAL	329	13TH WAR
KNOST, WILLIAM	ALL	229	CUMBERLA
KNOTE, WILLIAM	CAR	336	6TH DIST
KNOTT, ALEXANDER B.	MGM	430	CLARKSTR
KNOTT, BENEDICT	FRE	188	5TH E DI
KNOTT, CHARLES	BAL	336	13TH WAR
KNOTT, CHRISTIAN	BAL	343	7TH WARD
KNOTT, CLEMEN	PRI	114	PISCATAW
KNOTT, DAVIES	ALL	217	CUMBERLA
KNOTT, EDWARD	ST	309	1ST E DI
KNOTT, EDWARD	MGM	417	MEDLEY 3
KNOTT, ELIZABETH	FRE	188	5TH E DI
KNOTT, FRANCIS A.	FRE	379	PETERSVI
KNOTT, HENRY	ST	321	4TH E DI
KNOTT, JAMES A.	CAL	040	3RD DIST
KNOTT, JAMES H.	ST	315	4TH E DI
KNOTT, JAMES H.	ST	330	4TH E DI
KNOTT, JAMES M.	BAL	009	18TH WAR
KNOTT, JANE	ST	285	2ND E DI
KNOTT, JOHN B.	ST	259	3RD E DI
KNOTT, JOHN B.	MGM	430	CLARKSTR
KNOTT, JOHN H.	ST	336	4TH E DI
KNOTT, JOHN H.	PRI	116	PISCATAW
KNOTT, JOHNT.	MGM	431	CLARKSTR
KNOTT, JOSEPH	FRE	175	5TH E DI
KNOTT, JOSEPH	BAL	110	18TH WAR
KNOTT, MARY A.	ST	262	3RD E DI
KNOTT, MARY J.	ST	260	3RD E DI
KNOTT, RICHARD	PRI	106	PISCATAW
KNOTT, RICHARD	ST	337	4TH E DI
KNOTT, ROSA	ST	278	3RD E DI
KNOTT, SARAH E.	BAL	445	8TH WARD
KNOTT, SOHPIA	BAL	207	19TH WAR
KNOTT, STANISLAUS	MGM	425	MEDLEY 3
KNOTT, STEPHEN	BAL	064	18TH WAR
KNOTT, THOMAS	ST	300	2ND E DI
KNOTT, THOMAS	PRI	058	NOTTINGH
KNOTT, WILLIAM	KEN	260	1ST DIST
KNOTT, WILLIAM	ST	261	3RD E DI
KNOTT, WILLIAM H.	ST	260	3RD E DI
KNOTTS, ALEXANDER	QUE	210	3RD E DI
KNOTTS, BASIL	BAL	080	2ND DIST
KNOTTS, GEORGE E.	KEN	241	2ND DIST
KNOTTS, GEORGE P.*	BAL	389	3RD WARD
KNOTTS, GREENBERRY	QUE	208	3RD E DI
KNOTTS, GREENBERRY JR.	QUE	208	3RD E DI
KNOTTS, ISAAC	QUE	209	3RD E DI

Name	County	Page	District
KNOTTS, JACOB	KEN	261	1ST DIST
KNOTTS, JAMES	KEN	254	1ST DIST
KNOTTS, JOHN	KEN	216	2ND DIST
KNOTTS, JOSHUA-BLACK	QUE	193	3RD E DI
KNOTTS, MANFEE	QUE	155	2ND E DI
KNOTTS, MARTHA	QUE	167	2ND E DI
KNOTTS, MARY	QUE	165	2ND E DI
KNOTTS, MARY	QUE	208	3RD E DI
KNOTTS, MARY E.	BAL	389	3RD WARD
KNOTTS, REUBEN	QUE	192	3RD E DI
KNOTTS, SARAH E.	KEN	216	2ND DIST
KNOTTS, THOMAS	QUE	168	2ND E DI
KNOTTS, WILLIAM	QUE	200	3RD E DI
KNOTTS, WILLIAM	CEC	004	ELKTON 3
KNOTTS, WILLIAM-BLACK	QUE	147	1ST E DI
KNOTTS, WILLIAM-BLACK	QUE	147	1ST E DI
KNOUF, WILLIAM	BAL	228	1ST DIST
KNOUFF, JACOB	WAS	266	1ST DIST
KNOUFFE, ANNIE	FRE	167	EMMITTSB
KNOUFFE, JAMES	FRE	165	EMMITTSB
KNOUFFE, JOHN	FRE	180	5TH E DI
KNOUGH, JAMES	BAL	129	16TH WAR
KNOUGH, JOHN F.	BAL	043	18TH WAR
KNOUS, LEWIS*	BAL	027	4TH WARD
KNOW, JOSEPH	BAL	162	11TH WAR
KNOWDLE, L.	BAL	135	5TH WARD
KNOWEL, ANN	BAL	392	3RD WARD
KNOWEL, JAMES	ALL	200	CUMBERLA
KNOWEL, TERESA*	BAL	387	3RD WARD
KNOWL, TERESA*	BAL	387	3RD WARD
KNOWLAN, MARY	BAL	013	4TH WARD
KNOWLEN, PETER	BAL	036	9TH WARD
KNOWLES, EDWARD	BAL	353	7TH WARD
KNOWLES, FRANCES	ALL	109	5TH E.D.
KNOWLES, GEORGE	MGM	360	BERRYS D
KNOWLES, HENRY	BAL	127	5TH WARD
KNOWLES, JAMES	BAL	026	9TH WARD
KNOWLES, JAMES	BAL	093	1ST WARD
KNOWLES, JOHN	BAL	356	3RD WARD
KNOWLES, JOHN	BAL	275	2ND WARD
KNOWLES, LEWIS	BAL	137	1ST WARD
KNOWLES, LEWIS	BAL	172	1ST WARD
KNOWLES, RHODA	SOM	510	BARREN C
KNOWLES, S.	BAL	141	1ST WARD
KNOWLES, SAMUEL	BAL	130	1ST WARD
KNOWLES, THOMAS I.	BAL	020	1ST WARD
KNOWLES, WILLIAM G.	BAL	084	15TH WAR
KNOWLEY, BENJAMIN	QUE	170	2ND E DI
KNOWLS, EPRIM W.	BAL	312	7TH WARD
KNOWT, ROBERT	BAL	140	5TH WARD
KNOX, ADAM	BAL	151	16TH WAR
KNOX, ALBERT	WOR	303	SNOW HIL
KNOX, ALFRED	BAL	043	15TH WAR
KNOX, ANN L.	BAL	174	11TH WAR
KNOX, BARBARA	CAR	310	1ST DIST
KNOX, CATHARINE	BAL	176	19TH WAR
KNOX, DAVID	BAL	173	19TH WAR
KNOX, DAVIS W.	FRE	353	MIDDLETO
KNOX, EDWARD	BAL	002	4TH WARD
KNOX, EDWARD	WOR	299	SNOW HIL
KNOX, ELIJAH J.	WOR	297	9TH E DI
KNOX, HENRY	ANN	506	HOWARD D
KNOX, ISAAC	WOR	257	1ST CENS
KNOX, JAEMS	WOR	274	BERLIN 1
KNOX, JAMES	WOR	260	BERLIN 1
KNOX, JAMES	WOR	299	SNOW HIL
KNOX, JAMES	WOR	300	SNOW HIL
KNOX, JAMES C.R.	ANN	515	HOWARD D
KNOX, JOHN	BAL	100	10TH WAR
KNOX, JOHN	ANN	480	HOWARD D
KNOX, JOHN	WOR	304	SNOW HIL
KNOX, JOHN	WOR	307	2ND E DI
KNOX, JOHN	WOR	336	1ST E DI
KNOX, JOSEPH	ALL	046	10TH E.D
KNOX, JOSEPH	BAL	274	17TH WAR
KNOX, JOSHUA	ANN	498	HOWARD D
KNOX, JULIUS	BAL	421	3RD WARD
KNOX, MARY	FRE	162	EMMITTSB
KNOX, MARY A.	CAR	123	NO TWP L
KNOX, MIDDLETON	BAL	070	4TH WARD
KNOX, PETER	BAL	421	3RD WARD
KNOX, SAMUEL	CEC	125	5TH E DI
KNOX, SARAH	ANN	503	HOWARD D
KNOX, SIMEON	ALL	041	2ND E.D.
KNOX, WILLAIM	ANN	480	HOWARD D
KNOX, WILLIAM	ANN	427	HOWARD D
KNOX, WILLIAM	WOR	335	1ST E DI
KNOX, WILLIAM	WOR	308	2ND E DI
KNOX, WILLIAM	WOR	294	9TH E DI
KNOX, WILLIAM	WOR	284	BERLIN 1
KNOX, WILLIAM	QUE	214	3RD E DI
KNOYRE, HANNAH	ALL	008	3RD E.D.
KNUP, MARGARET	BAL	128	16TH WAR
KNUTTSEN, AUGUSTUS	BAL	311	20TH WAR
KNUTTSEN, WILLIAM	BAL	311	20TH WAR
KOANS, FRANCIS	BAL	456	1ST DIST
KOBB, CATHERINE	FRE	024	FREDERIC
KOBB, WILLIAM	FRE	058	FREDERIC
KOBOLD, HENRY	BAL	409	1ST DIST
KOCH, AMELIA	WAS	161	HAGERSTO
KOCH, BERNARD	BAL	112	10TH WAR
KOCH, CATHRINE	BAL	140	19TH WAR
KOCH, FREDERICK	BAL	352	13TH WAR
KOCH, JACOB	BAL	321	20TH WAR
KOCH, JOHN	FRE	20	5TH E DI
KOCH, LOUISA	BAL	095	10TH WAR
KOCH, LOUISA	BAL	188	16TH WAR
KOCHLER, ERNEST	BAL	109	1ST WARD
KOCHLER, DOROTHA	FRE	032	FREDERIC
KOCK, EARNEST	BAL	143	2ND DIST
KOCK, GEORGE	WAS	138	HAGERSTO
KOCKLER, THOMAS	BAL	109	1ST WARD
KOEBER, CHARLES	BAL	066	1ST WARD
KOECHLING, ANTONIA	BAL	389	3RD WARD
KOECHLING, LUCY	BAL	388	3RD WARD
KOEHLER, JOHN	BAL	029	15TH WAR
KOEHLER, MARY	BAL	030	15TH WAR
KOEHLER, NICHOLAS	BAL	119	15TH WAR
KOENIG, WILLIAM	ALL	034	10TH E.D
KOERNER, JACOB	BAL	256	12TH WAR
KOESTER, HENRY	FRE	001	FREDERIC
KOESTNER, THOMAS	BAL	238	6TH WARD
KOETHE, EMANUEL	BAL	091	10TH WAR
KOETHE, WILLIAM	BAL	090	10TH WAR
KOFF, VALENTINE	BAL	017	9TH WARD
KOFFER, WILLEMINA	CEC	041	CHESAPEA
KOFFMAN, ADAM	FRE	150	10TH E D
KOFFMAN, DAVID	FRE	192	5TH E DI
KOFFMAN, GEORGE	FRE	191	5TH E DI
KOHBURY, HARRY W.	ANN	290	ANNAPOLI

Name	County	Page	District
KOHLENBURG, ADAM*	FRE	230	BUCKEYST
KOHLENBURG, ADAM	FRE	209	BUCKEYST
KOHLENBURG, CHARLES A.	FRE	234	BUCKEYST
KOHLENBURG, DANIEL H.	FRE	206	BUCKEYST
KOHLER, ANNA	BAL	302	12TH WAR
KOHLER, GEORGE	WAS	273	RIDGEVIL
KOHLER, HENRY	BAL	240	12TH WAR
KOHLER, JACOB	BAL	135	11TH WAR
KOHLER, MARGARET J.	BAL	063	15TH WAR
KOHLHOSS, GEORGE W.	FRE	210	BUCKEYST
KOHLHOSS, REBECCA-MULATTO	FRE	208	BUCKEYST
KOHLKOSS, CHRISTIAN	FRE	231	BUCKEYST
KOHLSCHIRT, WILLIAM*	BAL	112	10TH WAR
KOHN, CHARLES	BAL	044	1ST WARD
KOHN, LENA	BAL	391	3RD WARD
KOHN, LEWIS	BAL	125	5TH WARD
KOHN, NATHAN	WAS	130	HAGERSTO
KOHN, NATHAN	WAS	130	HAGERSTO
KOINSMAN, GEORGE	BAL	253	2ND WARD
KOKLHOSS, BENJAMIN	FRE	229	BUCKEYST
KOKLHOSS, FREDERICK	FRE	230	BUCKEYST
KOKLHOSS, WILLIAM	FRE	229	BUCKEYST
KOLB, CHARLOTTE	FRE	049	FREDERIC
KOLB, DANIEL	FRE	059	FREDERIC
KOLB, DANIEL	FRE	017	FREDERIC
KOLB, DAVID	FRE	286	WOODSBOR
KOLB, DAVID	FRE	109	CREAGERS
KOLB, ELIZABETH	FRE	051	FREDERIC
KOLB, FREDERICK	FRE	049	FREDERIC
KOLB, GEORGE	BAL	304	17TH WAR
KOLB, HENRY	BAL	125	16TH WAR
KOLB, J. GEORGE	BAL	040	18TH WAR
KOLB, JOHN W.	FRE	109	CREAGERS
KOLB, JOSIAH	FRE	108	CREAGERS
KOLB, MICHEAL C.	BAL	039	18TH WAR
KOLB, MUHL	FRE	058	FREDERIC
KOLB, RAMER	FRE	050	FREDERIC
KOLB, WILSON W.	FRE	102	FREDERIC
KOLB.LUTHER	FRE	051	FREDERIC
KOLFFAGER, FREDERICK	ALL	231	CUMBERLA
KOLFFAGER, GERTRUDE	ALL	232	CUMBERLA
KOLLEN, DANIEL	BAL	057	2ND DIST
KOLLER, HENRY	BAL	094	18TH WAR
KOLLER, WILLIAM	BAL	031	2ND DIST
KOLLOCK, GEORGE-BLACK	WOR	335	1ST E DI
KOLLOCK, JANE-BLACK	WOR	335	1ST E DI
KOLLOCK, LEWIS-BLACK	WOR	335	1ST E DI
KOLLOCK, MARY-BLACK	WOR	336	1ST E DI
KOLLYLEE, ROGER	BAL	346	13TH WAR
KOLM, DAVID J.	BAL	139	1ST WARD
KOLP, ANN	BAL	120	11TH WAR
KOLP, JOHN	BAL	082	10TH WAR
KOLP, MICHAEL	BAL	352	3RD WARD
KOLT, FREDERICK	FRE	005	FREDERIC
KOLT, JACOB	FRE	040	FREDERIC
KOLTENBERGER, CHRISTOPHER	BAL	091	10TH WAR
KOMERAT, HENRIETTA	BAL	107	10TH WAR
KOMPSON, CHARLES	FRE	244	NEW MARK
KONBERGER, CHARLES	BAL	310	12TH WAR
KONE, ANDREW	BAL	166	19TH WAR
KONE, ANDREW J.	BAL	080	4TH WARD
KONE, DANIEL	BAL	088	15TH WAR
KONE, FLORENCE	BAL	166	19TH WAR
KONE, JESSE	HAR	011	1ST DIST
KONE, MARY J.	BAL	088	15TH WAR
KONE, THOMAS	BAL	070	2ND DIST
KONERIDER, HENRY	HAR	123	2ND DIST
KONES, ALMIRA	BAL	129	11TH WAR
KONET, GEORGE	BAL	040	9TH WARD
KONIG, ANN	BAL	116	15TH WAR
KONIG, FREDERICK	BAL	265	12TH WAR
KONIG, GEORGE	BAL	432	14TH WAR
KONIG, JACOB	BAL	458	8TH WARD
KONIG, M.	BAL	142	5TH WARD
KONING, ADAM	BAL	107	1ST WARD
KONING, GEORGE	BAL	205	2ND WARD
KONK, ELIZABETH	BAL	412	3RD WARD
KONK, ELIZABETH	CAR	291	7TH DIST
KONKLIN, ANN	BAL	318	1ST DIST
KONKLIN, JOHN	BAL	298	3RD WARD
KONLIN, LUKE	HAR	006	1ST DIST
KONTZE, LEWIS	BAL	410	14TH WAR
KONZE, LOUIS	BAL	125	16TH WAR
KOOCH, ADELINE	BAL	182	16TH WAR
KOOCH, ELIZABETH	BAL	054	15TH WAR
KOOCH, ELIZABETH	WAS	153	HAGERSTO
KOOCHEGY, ELIZABETH	BAL	401	14TH WAR
KOOGLE, ADAM	FRE	341	MIDDLETO
KOOGLE, ADAM	FRE	354	MIDDLETO
KOOGLE, CHRISTIAN	FRE	347	MIDDLETO
KOOGLE, DANIEL	FRE	353	MIDDLETO
KOOGLE, DANIEL	FRE	334	MIDDLETO
KOOGLE, DAVID	FRE	334	MIDDLETO
KOOGLE, ISAAC	FRE	311	MIDDLETO
KOOGLE, JACOB	FRE	331	MIDDLETO
KOOGLE, JOHN	FRE	345	MIDDLETO
KOOGLE, JOSHUA D.	FRE	333	MIDDLETO
KOOGLE, MALINDA	FRE	347	MIDDLETO
KOOK, JOHN T.	QUE	172	2ND E DI
KOOK, JOSEPH*	DOR	429	1ST DIST
KOOLMAN, RICHARD	BAL	085	10TH WAR
KOOLS, SOPHIA	BAL	248	12TH WAR
KOOM, ANDREW	CAR	243	TANEYTOW
KOON, CATHARINE	BAL	417	14TH WAR
KOON, DANIEL	WAS	228	1ST DIST
KOON, FORENTZ	BAL	218	19TH WAR
KOON, LEONARD	WAS	029	2ND SUBD
KOON, MICHAEL J.	BAL	321	1ST DIST
KOON, MR-	BAL	051	15TH WAR
KOONE, HENRY	CAR	378	2ND DIST
KOONE, MARY	BAL	116	11TH WAR
KOONES, JAMES	BAL	165	11TH WAR
KOONS, ABRAHAM	CAR	257	3RD DIST
KOONS, BENJAMIN	CAR	307	1ST DIST
KOONS, CHARELS H.	BAL	362	13TH WAR
KOONS, CONRAD	CAR	306	1ST DIST
KOONS, ELI	BAL	391	1ST DIST
KOONS, ELIZABETH	CAR	279	7TH DIST
KOONS, ELIZABETH	BAL	408	14TH WAR
KOONS, EMANIEL	CAR	290	7TH DIST
KOONS, ESTHER	CAR	257	3RD DIST
KOONS, FREDERIC	CAR	289	7TH DIST
KOONS, GEORGE	CAR	254	3RD DIST
KOONS, HENRY	CAR	260	3RD DIST
KOONS, JACOB	BAL	376	1ST DIST
KOONS, JAOCB	CAR	379	2ND DIST
KOONS, JOHN	CAR	379	2ND DIST
KOONS, JOHN	CAR	253	3RD DIST
KOONS, JOHN	CAR	242	TANEYTOW
KOONS, JUDWELL A.	ANN	446	HOWARD D

Name	County	Page	District
KOONS, MARY	BAL	122	2ND DIST
KOONS, MARY E.	CAR	385	2ND DIST
KOONS, N. C.	BAL	471	14TH WAR
KOONS, PHILIP	WAS	227	1ST DIST
KOONS, SARAH	CAR	261	3RD DIST
KOONS, WILLIAM	CAR	327	1ST DIST
KOONS, WILLIAM W.	FRE	287	WOODSBOR
KOONS,ELIZABETH	CAR	384	2ND DIST
KOONSMAN, WILLIAM H.	BAL	031	15TH WAR
KOONTY, DANIEL	ALL	059	10TH E.D
KOONTZ, ABRAHAM	CAR	327	1ST DIST
KOONTZ, ABRAHAM	CAR	311	1ST DIST
KOONTZ, ABRAHAM	FRE	099	FREDERIC
KOONTZ, ABRAHAM	WAS	204	1ST DIST
KOONTZ, ANDREW	FRE	172	5TH E DI
KOONTZ, ANDREW	CAR	301	1ST DIST
KOONTZ, ANN R.	CAR	388	2ND DIST
KOONTZ, CATHARINE	FRE	165	EMMITTSB
KOONTZ, CATHARINE	ALL	126	4TH E.D.
KOONTZ, CATHERINE	FRE	129	CREAGERS
KOONTZ, COLUMBIA	FRE	037	FREDERIC
KOONTZ, DANIEL	ALL	172	7TH E.D.
KOONTZ, DANIEL	ALL	178	7TH E.D.
KOONTZ, DANIEL	WAS	154	HAGERSTO
KOONTZ, DAVID	FRE	107	CREAGERS
KOONTZ, DAVID	CAR	292	7TH DIST
KOONTZ, DENNIS	ALL	221	CUMBERLA
KOONTZ, ELIAS	CAR	333	MANCHEST
KOONTZ, ELIZABETH	FRE	162	EMMITTSB
KOONTZ, ELIZABETH	FRE	233	BUCKEYST
KOONTZ, ELIZABETH	ALL	173	7TH E.D.
KOONTZ, ELIZABETH J.	CAR	384	2ND DIST
KOONTZ, EMILY J.	FRE	116	CREAGERS
KOONTZ, EPHRAIM	CAR	327	1ST DIST
KOONTZ, EPHRAIM	WAS	196	1ST DIST
KOONTZ, GEORGE	FRE	146	10TH E D
KOONTZ, GEORGE	FRE	032	FREDERIC
KOONTZ, GEORGE	FRE	394	PETERSVI
KOONTZ, GODFREY	FRE	031	FREDERIC
KOONTZ, HENRY	WAS	214	1ST DIST
KOONTZ, HENRY	WAS	177	1ST DIST
KOONTZ, HENRY	ALL	121	4TH E.D.
KOONTZ, HENRY	ALL	122	4TH E.D.
KOONTZ, HENRY COLUM	WAS	232	1ST DIST
KOONTZ, ISAAC	CAR	386	2ND DIST
KOONTZ, JACOB	ALL	114	5TH E.D.
KOONTZ, JAOCB	ALL	114	5TH E.D.
KOONTZ, JCOB	FRE	132	CREAGERS
KOONTZ, JOHN	FRE	026	FREDERIC
KOONTZ, JOHN	FRE	394	PETERSVI
KOONTZ, JOHN	FRE	331	MIDDLETO
KOONTZ, JOHN	CAR	237	UNION TO
KOONTZ, JOHN	ALL	114	5TH E.D.
KOONTZ, JOHN	ALL	179	7TH E.D.
KOONTZ, JOHN	BAL	100	2ND DIST
KOONTZ, JOHN	WAS	260	1ST DIST
KOONTZ, JOHN D.	FRE	394	PETERSVI
KOONTZ, JOSIAH	CAR	382	2ND DIST
KOONTZ, JULIAN	WAS	176	1ST DIST
KOONTZ, LEWIS	WAS	176	1ST DIST
KOONTZ, MAHALAH	CAR	317	1ST DIST
KOONTZ, MARIA	WAS	140	HAGERSTO
KOONTZ, NICHOLAS	ALL	172	7TH E.D.
KOONTZ, PAUL	FRE	180	5TH E DI
KOONTZ, PETER	CAR	317	1ST DIST
KOONTZ, REBECCA	CAR	325	1ST DIST
KOONTZ, REBECCA	FRE	054	FREDERIC
KOONTZ, SAMUEL	CAR	317	1ST DIST
KOONTZ, SAMUEL	ALL	114	5TH E.D.
KOONTZ, SARAH	ALL	113	5TH E.D.
KOONTZ, THOMAS	CAR	400	2ND DIST
KOONTZ, UPTON	FRE	159	EMMITTSB
KOONTZ, WILLIAM	CAR	267	WESTMINS
KOONTZ, WILLIAM	WAS	203	1ST DIST
KOONTZ, WILLIAM	WAS	289	1ST DIST
KOOSEL, MOSES	BAL	257	7TH WARD
KOOSKE, HENRIETTA	BAL	074	4TH WARD
KOOTER, GEORGE	WAS	007	WILLIAMS
KOOZER, ELIZABETH	FRE	315	MIDDLETO
KOPHART, JOSHUA	FRE	321	MIDDLETO
KOPLEPH, JOHN	BAL	320	12TH WAR
KOPP, FERDINAND	BAL	015	15TH WAR
KOPP, JOHN	BAL	015	15TH WAR
KOPP, JOSEPH	CAR	333	MANCHEST
KOPP, MARGARET	CAR	328	MANCHEST
KOPP, MARGARET	CAR	353	6TH DIST
KOPP, SARAH	CAR	332	MANCHEST
KOPP, SOPHIA	BAL	015	15TH WAR
KOPPLEMAN, JOHN	BAL	104	2ND DIST
KOPPLER, ANDREW	BAL	164	6TH WARD
KORDSON, HENRY	BAL	281	2ND WARD
KORNER, CONRAD	BAL	122	16TH WAR
KORNER, FREDERICKER	BAL	123	16TH WAR
KORNER, JOHN	BAL	180	6TH WARD
KORNER, PAULINE	BAL	123	16TH WAR
KORNIG, JOHN	BAL	009	9TH WARD
KORNMAN, HENRY	BAL	162	16TH WAR
KORNMAN, PETER *	BAL	374	13TH WAR
KORNMANN, HENRY	BAL	072	4TH WARD
KORNS, ANN M.	ALL	225	CUMBERLA
KORRCH, LOUIS	BAL	089	10TH WAR
KORUG, PHILEGG	BAL	080	1ST WARD
KOSENTHAL, CHARLES	MGM	388	ROCKERLE
KOSER, ELLEN	BAL	428	14TH WAR
KOSMAN, FREDERIC	BAL	165	6TH WARD
KOSS, JAMES E.	BAL	133	1ST WARD
KOSTAR, JOHN G.	BAL	255	12TH WAR
KOSTER, ALBERT	BAL	217	17TH WAR
KOSTER, MARY A.	BAL	076	15TH WAR
KOSTER, MARY C.	BAL	272	2ND WARD
KOSTERBERRY, ELIZABETH	BAL	217	17TH WAR
KOSURE, JESSE	BAL	410	14TH WAR
KOTE, FANNEY	BAL	329	7TH WARD
KOTHE, FREDERICK	BAL	185	19TH WAR
KOTT, LETITIA*	DOR	391	1ST DIST
KOUGOTTEN, JACOB	BAL	131	3TH WARD
KOZH, ELIZA	BAL	314	7TH WARD
KOZIER, CHARLES H.	BAL	132	1ST WARD
KRABOR, FREDERICK	BAL	072	4TH WARD
KRACHT, C. F.	BAL	382	1ST DIST
KRADE, FREDERICK	BAL	439	8TH WARD
KRAFF, GEORGE	BAL	279	1ST DIST
KRAFFT, ELIZA	BAL	105	10TH WAR
KRAFT, ADAM	BAL	249	20TH WAR
KRAFT, FREDERICK	BAL	103	15TH WAR
KRAFT, GEORGE	BAL	148	19TH WAR
KRAFT, GEORGE	BAL	227	19TH WAR
KRAFT, JACOB	BAL	221	19TH WAR
KRAFT, JACOB	BAL	058	15TH WAR
KRAFT, JACOB	BAL	200	11TH WAR

Name	County	Page	District
KRAFT, JOHN	BAL	253	12TH WAR
KRAFT, JOHN	BAL	253	12TH WAR
KRAFT, JOHN	BAL	236	20TH WAR
KRAFT, JOHN J.	BAL	397	8TH WARD
KRAFT, JULIA	BAL	249	20TH WAR
KRAFT, LAME	BAL	221	19TH WAR
KRAFT, MARGARET	BAL	120	5TH WARD
KRAFT, MICHAEL	BAL	191	19TH WAR
KRAFT, PETER	BAL	090	18TH WAR
KRAFT, PHILLIP	BAL	120	5TH WARD
KRAFT, SUSAN	BAL	228	19TH WAR
KRAFT, SUSAN	BAL	412	3RD WARD
KRAGER, GEORGE	BAL	436	8TH WARD
KRAGER, HENRY	BAL	436	8TH WARD
KRAGER, LAURA J.	BAL	055	18TH WAR
KRAGER, PETER	BAL	056	18TH WAR
KRAGGS, ROBERT	BAL	413	3RD WARD
KRAIGER, ELIZA J. B.	BAL	103	18TH WAR
KRAINE, ANN	BAL	189	11TH WAR
KRAISER, CATHERINE	BAL	019	9TH WARD
KRAITSIR, GEORGE	BAL	082	10TH WAR
KRAME, WILLIAM	BAL	252	2ND WARD
KRAMEL, CHRISTIAN	BAL	224	2ND WARD
KRAMEL, JULIUS	BAL	225	2ND WARD
KRAMER, BERNHARDT	BAL	111	10TH WAR
KRAMER, CATHARINE	BAL	087	15TH WAR
KRAMER, FRANCS	BAL	216	2ND WARD
KRAMER, FREDERICK W.	FRE	226	BUCKEYST
KRAMER, HENRY	BAL	356	8TH WARD
KRAMER, HENRY	BAL	270	7TH WARD
KRAMER, JACOB	BAL	009	1ST WARD
KRAMER, JAMES	BAL	016	15TH WAR
KRAMER, JO W.	BAL	294	20TH WAR
KRAMER, JOHN	BAL	392	8TH WARD
KRAMER, JOHN	BAL	381	8TH WARD
KRAMER, JOHN C.	BAL	087	15TH WAR
KRAMER, LEWIS	WAS	125	HAGERSTO
KRAMER, MARGARET	BAL	336	13TH WAR
KRAMER, P.	BAL	139	1ST WARD
KRAMER, SAMUEL	BAL	056	15TH WAR
KRAMMEL, HENRY	BAL	211	2ND WARD
KRANDERMAN, CHARLES	BAL	294	17TH WAR
KRANE, PHILIP	BAL	049	9TH WARD
KRANEWALD, ABRAHAM	BAL	308	7TH WARD
KRANEY, MICHAEL	BAL	273	2ND WARD
KRANLING, CONRAD	BAL	094	1ST WARD
KRANLING, GEORGE	BAL	094	1ST WARD
KRANF, JACOB	BAL	048	1ST WARD
KRANTY, JOHN *	ANN	415	HOWARD D
KRANTZ, FREDERICK	FRE	305	WOODSBOR
KRANTZ, HERNY	CAR	331	MANCHEST
KRANTZ, JOHN	CAR	328	MANCHEST
KRANTZ, JOHN	ANN	415	HOWARD D
KRANTZ, WILLIAM	CAR	353	6TH DIST
KRANTZ, WILLIAM	FRE	062	FREDERIC
KRANZER, JOHN	BAL	353	13TH WAR
KRAPH, DANIEL	ANN	424	HOWARD D
KRAPH, JACOB	ANN	419	HOWARD D
KRAQMER, CATHARINE	BAL	350	13TH WAR
KRASGMESTER, JOSEPH *	ALL	098	5TH E.D.
KRASISE, ERRERT *	BAL	037	18TH WAR
KRASTEL, JOSEPH	BAL	108	2ND DIST
KRATCH, MARY	BAL	268	2ND WARD
KRATH, WILLIAM	BAL	158	1ST WARD
KRATS, HENRY	BAL	352	3RD WARD
KRATZ, CHARLES	BAL	165	6TH WARD
KRATZ, HENRY	BAL	004	15TH WAR
KRATZ, JOHN	BAL	133	16TH WAR
KRATZINSTINE, MARY	BAL	399	14TH WAR
KRAUFF, JACOB	BAL	049	1ST WARD
KRAUFF, JACOB	BAL	047	1ST WARD
KRAUGHN, GEORGE	BAL	259	2ND WARD
KRAUGHN, MARGRET	BAL	259	2ND WARD
KRAUS, ABRAHAM	BAL	092	10TH WAR
KRAUS, ADOLPHUS	BAL	228	19TH WAR
KRAUSE, JOHN	BAL	277	17TH WAR
KRAUSE, JOHN	BAL	010	15TH WAR
KRAUSS, -----*	BAL	084	10TH WAR
KRAUSS, ALBERT	CEC	167	6TH E DI
KRAUSS, ANTHONY	CEC	142	6TH E DI
KRAUSS, BARNARD	CEC	005	ELKTON 3
KRAUSS, BARNARD	CEC	194	7TH E DI
KRAUSS, HENRY	CEC	160	6TH E DI
KRAUSS, JACOB	CEC	199	7TH E DI
KRAUSS, JOHN H.	CEC	171	6TH E DI
KRAUSS, JOSEPH	CEC	167	6TH E DI
KRAUSS, LEONARD	CEC	199	7TH E DI
KRAUSS, LEONARD	CEC	199	7TH E DI
KRAUSS, MARY	CEC	200	7TH E DI
KRAUSS, THOMAS	CEC	167	6TH E DI
KRAUSS, THOMAS M.	CEC	199	7TH E DI
KRAUTH, LOUISA	FRE	008	FREDERIC
KRAUTH, SUSAN	FRE	007	FREDERIC
KRAUVER, FREDERICK	BAL	253	2ND WARD
KRAWLE, LEWIS	BAL	109	1ST WARD
KREAGE, HANNAH	BAL	383	1ST DIST
KREAGER, GEORGE	BAL	284	12TH WAR
KREAKLE, GEORGE	BAL	052	1ST WARD
KREAMER, CATHARINE	BAL	271	12TH WAR
KREAMER, JACOB	BAL	272	20TH WAR
KREAR, JACOB	BAL	308	7TH WARD
KREBS, CATHARINE	BAL	311	7TH WARD
KREBS, DAVID	BAL	111	1ST WARD
KREBS, EDWARD	BAL	382	13TH WAR
KREBS, ELIZA C.	TAL	096	ST MICHA
KREBS, ELIZABETH	BAL	140	19TH WAR
KREBS, ELIZABETH	BAL	195	6TH WARD
KREBS, GEORGE	BAL	140	19TH WAR
KREBS, GEORGE C.	BAL	426	14TH WAR
KREBS, GEORGE W.	BAL	175	16TH WAR
KREBS, HENRY	BAL	429	8TH WARD
KREBS, HENRY	WAS	090	2ND SUBD
KREBS, JACOB	BAL	330	7TH WARD
KREBS, JOHN	WAS	091	2ND SUBD
KREBS, JOHN	WAS	108	2ND DIST
KREBS, JOHN W.	BAL	393	14TH WAR
KREBS, MARGARET	BAL	167	16TH WAR
KREBS, MARY C.	BAL	425	14TH WAR
KREBS, WILLIAM	BAL	311	7TH WARD
KREBS, WILLIMA H.W.	BAL	175	16TH WAR
KREBY, F.	BAL	150	1ST WARD
KREEMER, CRISTOPHER	BAL	206	11TH WAR
KREEPER, HENRY	ALL	013	3RD E.D.
KREFFING, CATHERINE G.*	BAL	075	10TH WAR
KREGBAUM, HENRY	ALL	113	5TH E.D.
KREGBAUM, PETER	ALL	146	6TH E.D.
KREGEL, ANN	BAL	162	6TH WARD
KREGEL, OTTO W.	BAL	162	6TH WARD
KREGER, FREDERICK	BAL	125	16TH WAR
KREGER, GEORGE	BAL	008	15TH WAR
KREGER, LEWIS	BAL	459	14TH WAR
KREGER, WILLIAM	BAL	007	15TH WAR
KREGLOW, CATHARINE	CAR	301	1ST DIST
KREGLOW, JOHN	CAR	301	1ST DIST
KREGLOW, JONAS	CAR	299	1ST DIST
KREIDER, CATHARINE	WAS	133	HAGERSTO
KREIDER, REBECCA	BAL	335	3RD WARD
KREIDLER, JAMES	WAS	121	HAGERSTO
KREIDLER, SUSAN	WAS	121	HAGERSTO
KREIG, ANN E.	BAL	034	4TH WARD
KREIGER, DANIEL	BAL	091	10TH WAR
KREIGH, ADAM	WAS	136	2ND DIST
KREIGH, EDWIN P.	WAS	144	HAGERSTO
KREIGH, ELIE	WAS	144	HAGERSTO
KREIGH, JACOB	WAS	130	2ND DIST
KREIGH, JOHN	WAS	164	2ND DIST
KREIGH, JOHN A.	WAS	149	2ND DIST
KREIGH, LEOURIA	WAS	144	2ND DIST
KREIGH, LUDERICK	CAR	201	4TH DIST
KREIGH, MARY A.	WAS	134	2ND DIST
KREIGH, NANCEY	WAS	126	2ND DIST
KREIGH, WILLIAM	WAS	133	2ND DIST
KREIGHEN, ARMINA	BAL	129	11TH WAR
KREIN, JOHN	BAL	086	10TH WAR
KREIN, LEWIS	BAL	279	20TH WAR
KREIS, HENRY	ANN	467	HOWARD D
KREIS, LOUISA	WAS	285	1ST DIST
KREIS, PETER	BAL	293	12TH WAR
KREISE, PETER	BAL	278	2ND WARD
KREITT, WILMINER *	BAL	037	18TH WAR
KREITZER, SEBASTIAN	BAL	221	6TH WARD
KREMAN, W. H. E.	BAL	096	18TH WAR
KREMER, ANN A.	BAL	302	3RD WARD
KREMER, BARBARA	BAL	395	3RD WARD
KREMER, CHARLES	BAL	302	3RD WARD
KREMER, ELIZA	BAL	016	4TH WARD
KREMER, JAMES C.	BAL	020	18TH WAR
KREMER, JOSEPH	BAL	088	15TH WAR
KREMS, JAMES	BAL	225	12TH WAR
KREPPS, CATHARINE	WAS	209	1ST DIST
KREPPS, JOSEPH A.	WAS	286	1ST DIST
KREPPS, WILLIAM	WAS	286	1ST DIST
KREPS, ELIZABETH	WAS	286	1ST DIST
KREPS, JACOB	WAS	110	2ND DIST
KREPS, JOHN	WAS	007	WILLIAMS
KREPS, JOHN M.	WAS	027	2ND SUBD
KREPS, JOHN R.	WAS	282	1ST DIST
KREPS, MICHAEL	WAS	012	WILLIAMS
KREPS, SUSAN	WAS	109	2ND DIST
KRERTGER, THEODORE	BAL	017	9TH WARD
KRESNER, JOSEPH	BAL	022	18TH WAR
KRESS, PETER	BAL	014	9TH WARD
KRESSENNADOER, A.	BAL	044	9TH WARD
KRESSINAN, GEHART	BAL	263	2ND WARD
KRESZ, CONRAD	BAL	256	6TH WARD
KRETCHER, HENRY	KEN	243	2ND DIST
KRETS, COLUMBUS	ANN	348	3RD DIST
KRETZER, ANNA	WAS	162	HAGERSTO
KRETZER, DANIEL	WAS	024	2ND SUBD
KRETZER, DAVID	WAS	058	2ND SUBD
KRETZER, HIRAM	WAS	047	2ND SUBD
KRETZER, JAMES	WAS	062	2ND SUBD
KRETZER, MARY	WAS	039	2ND SUBD
KRETZINGER, DAVID	WAS	176	1ST DIST
KRETZINGER, JACOB	WAS	301	1ST DIST
KRETZINGER, MARY C.	WAS	232	1ST DIST
KRICK, LINAH*	WOR	308	2ND E DI
KRICK, WELEY	WAS	126	HAGERSTO
KRIDELER, JACOB F.	BAL	244	20TH WAR
KRIDELER, SARAH	BAL	245	20TH WAR
KRIEBA, CAROLINE	BAL	029	9TH WARD
KRIEBLE, ANDREW	BAL	030	1ST WARD
KRIEDLER, GEORGE	WAS	208	1ST DIST
KRIEG, CHRISTIAN	BAL	456	1ST DIST
KRIEGH, GEORGE W.	WAS	122	2ND DIST
KRIEL, CHRISTIANA	BAL	402	14TH WAR
KRIEL, ELEANORA	BAL	068	15TH WAR
KRIELY, THOMAS	BAL	032	1ST WARD
KRIESS, CHARLES	BAL	081	1ST WARD
KRIETZER, CHRISTOPH	BAL	019	9TH WARD
KRIGBAUM, WILLIAM	ALL	113	5TH E.D.
KRIGLE, FREDERICK L.	ANN	486	HOWARD D
KRIH, MARTIN	CAR	331	MANCHEST
KRIKWOOD, ABEL	HAR	074	1ST DIST
KRIPER, GEORGE	BAL	320	12TH WAR
KRIPHINE, ELISABETH	BAL	298	3RD WARD
KRIPHINE, GEORGE	BAL	299	3RD WARD
KRISE, CONRAD	BAL	105	2ND DIST
KRISE, DANIEL	FRE	156	10TH E D
KRISE, ELIAS	FRE	109	CREAGERS
KRISE, JOHN	BAL	367	13TH WAR
KRISE, JOHN	BAL	109	2ND DIST
KRISE, JOHN F.	BAL	367	13TH WAR
KRISE, SOLOMON	FRE	176	5TH E DI
KRISE, WILLIAM	FRE	168	EMMITTSB
KRISKS, SAMUEL	BAL	252	20TH WAR
KRITCHMAN, LEWIS	BAL	011	4TH WARD
KRITEMAN, PHILIP	BAL	002	EASTERN
KRITEMAN, SARAH	BAL	003	EASTERN
KRITZER, HANAH	WAS	040	2ND SUBD
KRITZER, HENRIETTA	WAS	040	2ND SUBD
KRITZER, JOHN	WAS	040	2ND SUBD
KRITZER, JOHN	BAL	381	8TH WARD
KRNOTZ, CATHARINE	WAS	151	HAGERSTO
KROCH, CASPAR	BAL	060	2ND DIST
KROCK, CHRISTIAN	BAL	156	19TH WAR
KROCKER, ANNE	BAL	044	15TH WAR
KRODER, JOHN	BAL	259	2ND WARD
KROENING, G. B.	BAL	122	18TH WAR
KROFT, DORATHA	FRE	094	FREDERIC
KROFT, HENRY	BAL	010	9TH WARD
KROFT, MICHAEL	BAL	009	15TH WAR
KROFT, SOPHIA	BAL	419	14TH WAR
KROGER, CLAMENS	BAL	214	17TH WAR
KROGER, J. J. R. DR-	BAL	050	18TH WAR
KROH, PHILIP	BAL	035	2ND DIST
KROH, THEODORE	BAL	378	13TH WAR
KROK, DANIEL	HAR	077	BEL AIR
KROK, JOHN	CAR	344	6TH DIST
KROK, PHILIP	HAR	077	BEL AIR
KROKER, JAMES	BAL	134	1ST WARD
KROLL, JOHN	CAR	288	7TH DIST
KROMBIHLER, ZAVIER	BAL	416	14TH WAR
KROMEN, CHRISTIAN	BAL	081	10TH WAR
KROMET, FREDERICK	FRE	275	NEW MARK
KROMET, GEORGE	FRE	247	NEW MARK
KROMM, LOUIS	BAL	081	10TH WAR
KRONAN, JOHN	BAL	160	6TH WARD
KRONGE, MICHAEL*	BAL	332	3RD WARD
KRONMILLER, GEORGE	BAL	109	5TH WARD
KRONTY, ALBINA *	WAS	164	HAGERSTO
KRONTZ, CATHARINE	WAS	151	HAGERSTO
KRONTZ, CATHARINE	FRE	210	BUCKEYST
KROOPH, FREDERICK	BAL	049	1ST WARD
KROSEL, EIRSHLIN *	BAL	068	18TH WAR
KROTZER, JOSEPH	WAS	225	1ST DIST
KROTZER, SARAH	WAS	221	1ST DIST
KROUCH, WILLIAM W.	BAL	373	1ST DIST
KROUSE, CAROLINE	BAL	401	14TH WAR
KROUSE, DAVID	BAL	301	17TH WAR
KROUSE, PETER	WAS	236	CAVETOWN
KROUSE, SOLOMON	WAS	237	CAVETOWN
KROUSS, WILLIAM	BAL	258	17TH WAR
KROUT, BENJAMIN	BAL	438	1ST DIST
KROUT, ELIZABETH	BAL	438	1ST DIST
KROUT, MICHAEL	CAR	317	1ST DIST
KROUT, SARAH A.	BAL	373	1ST DIST
KROWN, STEPHEN	BAL	366	3RD WARD
KROZER, J. J. R. DR- *	BAL	050	18TH WAR
KROZIER, ISREAL	BAL	240	17TH WAR
KRUGER, JOHN P.	BAL	017	9TH WARD
KRUM, CATHARINE	BAL	259	12TH WAR
KRUMMAR, JOHN	BAL	476	14TH WAR
KRUMNIE, JOHN H.	BAL	092	5TH WARD
KRUSE, RUDOLPH	BAL	134	1ST WARD
KRUTZ, CHRISTIAN	BAL	329	3RD WARD
KRUTZ, S.	BAL	318	12TH WAR
KUBER, JOHN	BAL	324	7TH WARD
KUBS, WILLIAM*	TAL	020	EASTON D
KUBY, FRISBY	TAL	076	EASTON T
KUBY, WILLIAM*	TAL	017	EASTON D
KUCIX, JOHN	BAL	299	3RD WARD
KUEFOY, HENRY	BAL	071	10TH WAR
KUERN, GEORGE	BAL	259	12TH WAR
KUFIER, JOHN	BAL	173	19TH WAR
KUGER, FRANCIS H. *	BAL	070	18TH WAR
KUGG, JANE *	BAL	289	20TH WAR
KUGLER, GEORGE	BAL	063	2ND DIST
KUGLER, SAMUEL	BAL	168	16TH WAR
KUGLER, THOMAS	BAL	083	10TH WAR
KUHIRT, PAULINA	BAL	070	4TH WARD
KUHL, CHARLES	BAL	158	16TH WAR
KUHL, JACOB	BAL	154	19TH WAR
KUHL, PHILIP	BAL	120	16TH WAR
KUHL, WILLIAM	BAL	158	16TH WAR
KUHLMAN, HERMAN	BAL	009	9TH WARD
KUHLMAN, JOHN	BAL	038	18TH WAR
KUHN, ALFRED	BAL	277	12TH WAR
KUHN, AUET	BAL	251	12TH WAR
KUHN, AUGUSTUS C.	BAL	240	5TH WARD
KUHN, CATHERINE	BAL	328	3RD WARD
KUHN, CYRUS C.	CAR	388	2ND DIST
KUHN, ELIZABETH	FRE	024	FREDERIC
KUHN, ELIZABETH A. C.	FRE	377	PETERSVI
KUHN, GEORGE	FRE	379	PETERSVI
KUHN, GEORGE	BAL	213	17TH WAR
KUHN, GEORGE	FRE	160	EMMITTSB
KUHN, GEORGE W.	BAL	195	19TH WAR
KUHN, HENRY	FRE	364	CATOCTIN
KUHN, JACOB	FRE	311	MIDDLETO
KUHN, JACOB	BAL	328	3RD WARD
KUHN, JACOB	WAS	117	2ND DIST
KUHN, JOHN	WAS	065	2ND SUBD
KUHN, JOHN	BAL	292	12TH WAR
KUHN, JOHN	FRE	358	CATOCTIN
KUHN, JOHN	BAL	002	18TH WAR
KUHN, JOHN	CAR	328	MANCHEST
KUHN, JOHN	CAR	270	WESTMINS
KUHN, JOHN J.	BAL	114	5TH WARD
KUHN, JOSEPH	BAL	205	19TH WAR
KUHN, JOSHUA	BAL	303	12TH WAR
KUHN, MARY	FRE	361	CATOCTIN
KUHN, MARY A.	FRE	311	MIDDLETO
KUHN, PETER	WAS	066	2ND SUBD
KUHN, PETER	WAS	065	2ND SUBD
KUHN, PHILIP	FRE	359	CATOCTIN
KUHN, WILLIAM	FRE	377	PETERSVI
KUIN, HENRY	ALL	167	6TH E.D.
KULESE, MARY	FRE	244	NEW MARK
KULEY, ELIZABETH O.	BAL	200	11TH WAR
KULIN, DAVID	CAR	269	WESTMINS
KULIN, JOHN	BAL	312	20TH WAR
KULLE, CATHARINE *	BAL	300	20TH WAR
KULLENS, THOMAS	BAL	194	2ND WARD
KULLMAN, ELIZABETH	BAL	060	15TH WAR
KULMAN, ADOLPH	BAL	269	2ND WARD
KULP, SOPHIA	BAL	230	6TH WARD
KULUTY, RANDOLPH	BAL	067	18TH WAR
KUMANON, JOHN-BLACK	CAR	162	NO TWP L
KUMERT, MICHAEL	BAL	017	9TH WARD
KUMMELL, JOSIAH	CAR	330	MANCHEST
KUMMER, EREHARST	BAL	239	2ND WARD
KUMP, DANIEL DEIHL	CAR	247	3RD DIST
KUMP, DAVID	CAR	247	3RD DIST
KUMP, ELIZABETH	CAR	347	3RD DIST
KUMP, HENRY	FRE	280	WOODSBOR
KUMP, JACOB	CAR	247	3RD DIST
KUMP, JACOB H.	CAR	247	3RD DIST
KUMP, JOHN	FRE	170	5TH E DI
KUMP, LYDIA A.	CAR	252	3RD DIST
KUMP, PETER	CAR	252	3RD DIST
KUNAER, GEORGE	CAR	274	7TH DIST
KUNAN, JAMES*	BAL	070	10TH WAR
KUNAN, THOMAS *	BAL	143	1ST WARD
KUNCLE, HENRY	HAR	039	1ST DIST
KUNE, CHARLOTTE	HAR	094	2ND DIST
KUNE, JOHN H.	BAL	069	2ND DIST
KUNECT, JACOB	BAL	269	2ND WARD
KUNIAMON, JOHN	CAR	098	NO TWP L
KUNITZ, HENRY	BAL	065	2ND DIST
KUNKEL, JOHN B.	FRE	034	FREDERIC
KUNKEL, SIDNEY	FRE	034	FREDERIC
KUNKLE, HENRY	HAR	049	1ST DIST
KUNKLE, JOHN	FRE	025	FREDERIC
KUNNS, EMANUEL	CAR	265	WESTMINS
KUNRIGHT, WASHINGTON	BAL	265	1ST DIST
KUNSMAN, WILLIAM H.	BAL	047	18TH WAR
KUNTZ, ELLEN C.	CAR	329	MANCHEST
KUNTZ, MARY	BAL	088	4TH WARD
KUPER, FRANCIS	BAL	237	5TH WARD
KUPP, GEORGE	BAL	053	18TH WAR
KUR, ADELINE	BAL	015	4TH WARD
KURITY, CHRISTINA*	BAL	389	3RD WARD
KURITZ, CHRISTINA*	BAL	389	3RD WARD
KURNER, CATHARINE	FRE	377	PETERSVI
KURNNOT, EVA	BAL	171	19TH WAR
KURNNOT, JOHN	BAL	170	19TH WAR
KURSEY, ISIAH	PRI	025	VANSVILL
KURTS, MARY	BAL	291	7TH WARD
KURTZ, ANN	BAL	053	4TH WARD

Name	County	Page	District
KURTZ, CHARLES *	BAL	273	20TH WAR
KURTZ, DANIEL	BAL	141	19TH WAR
KURTZ, FREDERICK	BAL	385	8TH WARD
KURTZ, JOHN	CAR	404	2ND DIST
KURTZ, JOHN H.	BAL	444	8TH WARD
KURTZ, JOSEPH	BAL	154	5TH WARD
KURTZ, JSOHUA	CAR	352	6TH DIST
KURTZ, LOUISA	BAL	369	1ST DIST
KURTZ, MARY	BAL	282	12TH WAR
KURTZE, LEWIS	BAL	467	14TH WAR
KURTZER, JOHN	HAR	137	2ND DIST
KUSER, DANIEL	FRE	205	BUCKEYST
KUSER, JACOB	FRE	206	BUCKEYST
KUSEY, JOHN	TAL	066	EASTON T
KUSH, STEPHEN	BAL	232	2ND WARD
KUSHAF, HENRY	BAL	122	2ND DIST
KUSHMIRE, MARY	BAL	368	13TH WAR
KUSHNER, MARGARET	FRE	005	FREDERIC
KUSMAUL, LAURENCE	BAL	230	6TH WARD
KUSNER, HENRY	BAL	079	1ST WARD
KUST, HENRY	BAL	115	15TH WAR
KUSTER, A.	BAL	237	12TH WAR
KUSTER, SARAH W.*	BAL	115	15TH WAR
KUSTLER, MARY *	BAL	110	2ND DIST
KUTES, THOMAS *	WAS	073	2ND SUBD
KUTHLEY, JOHN	TAL	036	EASTON D
KUTTER, MARY E.	BAL	090	15TH WAR
KUTY, HINTSON*	TAL	010	EASTON D
KUTZING, LUDWIG	WAS	047	2ND SUBD
KYAR, GEORGE	BAL	275	17TH WAR
KYARD, CHARLES	BAL	040	1ST WARD
KYARD, LEWIS	BAL	276	2ND WARD
KYDER, MARY A.	CAR	244	3RD DIST
KYER, JOHN	BAL	243	6TH WARD
KYLE, ADAM B.	BAL	072	15TH WAR
KYLE, CATHRIEN	BAL	171	11TH WAR
KYLE, CATHRINE	BAL	171	11TH WAR
KYLE, CHRISTGPHER	BAL	226	17TH WAR
KYLE, HUGH T.	HAR	040	1ST DIST
KYLE, JOHN	BAL	390	3RD WARD
KYLE, SAMUEL	HAR	039	1ST DIST
KYLE, SAMUEL	BAL	375	13TH WAR
KYLE, THOMAS	BAL	414	3RD WARD
KYLE, WILLIAM	HAR	040	1ST DIST
KYLE, WILLIAM	BAL	126	11TH WAR
KYNE, PATRICK	ANN	428	HOWARD D
KYNOCK, JOHN	BAL	392	14TH WAR
KYPER, LYDIA	WAS	209	1ST DIST
KYSER, WILLIAM	WAS	140	HAGERSTO
KZSER, DAVID	ALL	037	2ND E.D.
L	ALL	020	2ND E.D.
L//U, HENRY	SOM	452	DAMES QU
LA BATTE, EUGENIA	BAL	205	11TH WAR
LA BRUNT, MARY	BAL	148	5TH WARD
LA MARTRE, CHRISTIANA	BAL	233	2ND WARD
LAACKE, WILLAIM	BAL	202	17TH WAR
LAACKMAN, ELIZABETH	BAL	338	1ST DIST
LABARK, ELIZABETH	BAL	369	8TH WARD
LABARKE, ELI	BAL	364	13TH WAR
LABARKE, MORRISON	BAL	364	13TH WAR
LABEL, JOHN*	BAL	393	3RD WARD
LABERERE, NICHOLAS	BAL	059	15TH WAR
LABEY, THOMAS	BAL	145	19TH WAR
LABMAN, EDWARD	ST	256	3RD E DI
LABOISSIERE, MATILDA	BAL	074	10TH WAR
LABREAR, FRANCIS	BAL	288	17TH WAR
LABREAR, NICHOLAS	BAL	292	17TH WAR
LABROQUERE, BENARD T.	BAL	189	6TH WARD
LABROQUERE, CATHARINE	BAL	190	6TH WARD
LACATES, CHARLES W.	SOM	483	TRAPP DI
LACE, GEORGE W.	BAL	308	7TH WARD
LACE, REBECCA	BAL	367	1ST DIST
LACENANER, JOHN	BAL	066	1ST WARD
LACEPT, JOHN	BAL	116	1ST WARD
LACET, PAT	BAL	156	2ND DIST
LACEY,ALEXANDER	BAL	252	2ND WARD
LACHKNER, HENRY	BAL	181	2ND WARD
LACHKNER, JACOB	BAL	181	2ND WARD
LACK, CHARLES B.	BAL	295	3RD WARD
LACK, TABITHA	BAL	295	3RD WARD
LACKARD, JOHN	CAR	201	4TH DIST
LACKEM, BARNEY	BAL	348	13TH WAR
LACKERMAN, LEWIS	BAL	034	1ST WARD
LACKET, NACE	WAS	062	2ND SUBD
LACKEY, ELIZABETH	BAL	332	7TH WARD
LACKEY, ISABELA	BAL	388	8TH WARD
LACKEY, MARTHA	HAR	071	1ST DIST
LACKEY, WILLIAM	BAL	130	1ST WARD
LACKEY, WILLIAM P.	BAL	353	7TH WARD
LACKILL, WILLIAM J.*	DOR	458	1ST DIST
LACKLAND, MARY	CEC	190	5TH E DI
LACKLAND, NATHAN	CEC	191	5TH E DI
LACKLAND, THOMAS	CEC	141	6TH E DI
LACKLAND, WILLIAM	CEC	163	6TH E DI
LACKMAN, ANDREW	SOM	363	BRINKLEY
LACKMAN, BERTA	BAL	320	1ST DIST
LACKMAN, FANNY	BAL	396	14TH WAR
LACKMAN, COERGE	BAL	266	1ST DIST
LACKMAN, HENRY	BAL	126	16TH WAR
LACKMAN, NATHAN	BAL	396	14TH WAR
LACKNER, ANDREW	BAL	192	2ND WARD
LACOMBER, J.	BAL	210	19TH WAR
LACOMPT, JAMES	BAL	407	14TH WAR
LACOMPT, MARY	BAL	306	1ST DIST
LACOMPT,LOUIZA	CAR	147	NO TWP L
LACOMPTE, ELIZABETH	BAL	146	11TH WAR
LACOMPTE, JAMES	SOM	511	BARREN C
LACOMPTE, JOHN H.	SOM	510	BARREN C
LACONICK, LAZARO	BAL	331	3RD WARD
LACOTER, ELLEN	BAL	158	19TH WAR
LACOTES, ELIJAH	SOM	472	TRAPPE D
LACOTES, JULIA A.	SOM	427	PRINCESS
LACOTES, WILLIAM	SOM	426	PRINCESS
LACOUR, W. L.	BAL	169	19TH WAR
LACROSS, FRANCIS A.	BAL	231	17TH WAR
LACY, DORCAS	ST	328	4TH E DI
LACY, DOROTHY	DOR	416	1ST DIST
LACY, ELLEN	BAL	030	4TH WARD
LACY, ELLEN	BAL	312	12TH WAR
LACY, GEORGE	CEC	150	PORT DUP
LACY, JAMES	BAL	313	12TH WAR
LACY, JOHN	BAL	313	12TH WAR
LACY, JOSEPH	CHA	231	HILLTOP
LACY, MARTHA	ST	339	4TH E DI
LACY, RICHARD	BAL	380	3RD WARD
LACY, WILLIAM	CEC	062	1ST E DI
LADD, ANN	BAL	093	18TH WAR
LADDY, MOSES	BAL	125	18TH WAR
LADEKE, FREDERICK	MGM	390	ROCKERLE
LADERMAN, JOHN	BAL	434	8TH WARD
LADLER, JOHN	FRE	250	NEW MARK
LADMON, LAWRENCE	BAL	434	8TH WARD
LADON, SAMUEL	CEC	205	7TH E DI
LADSON, ANN	BAL	142	11TH WAR
LADUE, SUSAN	BAL	296	12TH WAR
LAESAR, CHRISTIANA	BAL	370	8TH WARD
LAFABIL, FRANCIS G.	BAL	327	7TH WARD
LAFAILLE, JOHN	BAL	388	13TH WAR
LAFAIT, JOHN	BAL	114	1ST WARD
LAFAVRE, MARY F.	BAL	295	3RD WARD
LAFERITY, JAMES	BAL	189	11TH WAR
LAFERTY, EDWARD	BAL	153	2ND DIST
LAFERVER, LEWIS	BAL	045	9TH WARD
LAFETRA, SOPHIA P.	BAL	110	5TH WARD
LAFEVER, DAVID	BAL	100	5TH WARD
LAFFELL, CHARLES	MGM	317	CRACKLIN
LAFFELL, MAHLON	ANN	500	HOWARD D
LAFFER, ANDREW	BAL	018	1ST WARD
LAFFER, HENRY	BAL	312	3RD WARD
LAFFER, SARAH	BAL	338	13TH WAR
LAFFERTY, CATHARINE	BAL	318	7TH WARD
LAFFERTY, ELIZA	BAL	415	8TH WARD
LAFFERTY, ELIZA	BAL	377	8TH WARD
LAFFERTY, HUGH	BAL	279	2ND WARD
LAFFERTY, JANE	BAL	411	8TH WARD
LAFFERTY, JOHN	BAL	415	8TH WARD
LAFFERTY, MARY	BAL	298	7TH WARD
LAFFERTY, MARY	BAL	282	12TH WAR
LAFFERTY, MICHAEL	BAL	356	8TH WARD
LAFFERTY, MISS E.	FRE	200	5TH E DI
LAFFERTY, PAT	BAL	165	19TH WAR
LAFFERTY, ROBERT	BAL	418	8TH WARD
LAFFIELD, JAMES	BAL	153	1ST WARD
LAFFIN, THOMAS*	TAL	023	EASTON D
LAFFINGTON, FRANCIS	BAL	079	10TH WAR
LAFFRAN, CHARLES*	BAL	028	4TH WARD
LAFITTE, H.B.	BAL	296	12TH WAR
LAFITY, DIANAH	CAR	175	8TH DIST
LAFLEUR, A.J.	BAL	259	20TH WAR
LAFLEUR, ELIZABETH	BAL	287	20TH WAR
LAFONT, MARY	BAL	031	4TH WARD
LAFORD, MARY	BAL	294	17TH WAR
LAGAN, MARY	FRE	449	8TH E DI
LAGAR, JOHN	ALL	163	6TH E.D.
LAGUE, WILLAIM	CAR	201	4TH DIST
LAGUR, PATIENCE	ALL	174	7TH E.D.
LAHAM, MICHAEL	BAL	150	2ND DIST
LAHAN, PAT	BAL	150	2ND DIST
LAHEY, CATHARINE	BAL	073	1ST WARD
LAHEY, MARGARET	BAL	145	19TH WAR
LAHM, ELIZABETH	WAS	280	LEITERSB
LAHM, G.W.L.	WAS	280	LEITERSB
LAHUT, JOHN S.	BAL	081	15TH WAR
LAIK, ROSEANA	WAS	056	2ND SUBD
LAIN, EDWARD C.	HAR	046	1ST DIST
LAIN, HARMAN	WAS	061	2ND SUBD
LAIN, MARY	BAL	058	1ST WARD
LAINE, JOHN A.	KEN	294	3RD DIST
LAINE, JOHN T.	BAL	064	18TH WAR
LAINE, LOUIZA	BAL	128	5TH WARD
LAINE, PATRICK	BAL	291	17TH WAR
LAINE, REBECCA	FRE	399	JEFFERSO
LAINE, WILLIAM	BAL	192	17TH WAR
LAINER, MARTHA	BAL	060	18TH WAR
LAING, RODALPH	BAL	259	12TH WAR
LAING, SYLVESTER	BAL	193	6TH WARD
LAING, WILLIAM	BAL	092	10TH WAR
LAINGAN, MICHAEL	ALL	048	10TH E.D
LAINHARDT, BALTHAZAR	BAL	191	6TH WARD
LAINHARDT, WILLIAM	BAL	015	9TH WARD
LAIRD, ABRAHAM	ALL	087	5TH E.D.
LAIRD, ANN	BAL	023	2ND DIST
LAIRD, ANNA	SOM	371	BRINKLEY
LAIRD, ROBERT	ALL	086	5TH E.D.
LAIRD, THOMAS	BAL	402	1ST DIST
LAIRMORE, JONATHAN	TAL	103	ST MICHA
LAISKEN, WILLIAM	BAL	304	20TH WAR
LAISSY, FREDERICK	ALL	242	CUMBERLA
LAITHAM, LOUISA	FRE	160	EMMITTSB
LAITHEISER, JOHN R.	BAL	386	13TH WAR
LAITZ, C.	BAL	243	12TH WAR
LAKE, ANN M.	DOR	381	1ST DIST
LAKE, CORDELIA	BAL	097	10TH WAR
LAKE, CORDILIA	DOR	355	3RD DIVI
LAKE, GABREL P.	DOR	338	3RD DIVI
LAKE, JACK	DOR	334	3RD DIVI
LAKE, JAMES N.*	DOR	377	1ST DIST
LAKE, JAMES*	DOR	308	1ST DIST
LAKE, JERREY	DOR	338	3RD DIVI
LAKE, JOHN	DOR	335	3RD DIVI
LAKE, JOHN	BAL	386	3RD WARD
LAKE, JOHN A. J.	BAL	387	3RD WARD
LAKE, JOHN*	DOR	315	1ST DIST
LAKE, LEVINA	DOR	312	1ST DIST
LAKE, M.A.	ANN	271	ANNAPOLI
LAKE, MARY A.	BAL	205	11TH WAR
LAKE, MOSES	ANN	271	ANNAPOLI
LAKE, OBEDIAH	DOR	335	3RD DIVI
LAKE, RUBEN	CEC	068	5TH E DI
LAKE, SAMUEL	DOR	338	3RD DIVI
LAKE, SAMUEL	WAS	137	2ND DIST
LAKE, THOMAS	WAS	006	WILLIAMS
LAKE, THOMAS	WAS	014	WILLIAMS
LAKE, THOMAS	CEC	067	5TH E DI
LAKELEDER, THOMAS	FRE	306	WOODSBOR
LAKELIDER, JOHN	FRE	310	WOODSBOR
LAKEMAM, MARTHA A.*	BAL	323	3RD WARD
LAKENAN, MARTHA A.	BAL	319	3RD WARD
LAKER, JOHN	ALL	149	6TH E.D.
LAKER, JOHN	BAL	166	1ST WARD
LAKER, JOHN W.*	BAL	421	3RD WARD
LAKER, MICHAEL J.	BAL	420	3RD WARD
LAKER, SAMUEL	BAL	365	1ST DIST
LAKERS, ANDREW J.	ANN	479	HOWARD D
LAKERS, CATHARINE	ANN	453	HOWARD D
LAKERS, ELIZABETH	ANN	437	HOWARD D
LAKERS, WILLIAM	ANN	440	HOWARD D
LAKEY, MICHAEL	BAL	180	11TH WAR
LAKEY, MOSES	BAL	153	2ND DIST
LAKFORD, JOHN	WOR	342	1ST E DI
LAKIN, JOHN H.	WAS	178	BOONSBOR
LAKIN, MARGARET	ALL	150	6TH E.D.
LAKIN, WILLIAM H.	FRE	408	JEFFERSO
LAKIN.ABRAHAM	FRE	408	JEFFERSO
LAKINS, JACOB	FRE	395	PETERSVI
LAKMAN, BERNHARD	BAL	370	3RD WARD
LAKY, RICHARD	ANN	475	HOWARD D
LALEY, WILLIAM H.	FRE	059	FREDERIC
LALLEY, JOHN	ALL	049	10TH E.D
LALMON, WADNEL L.*	BAL	423	3RD WARD
LALOM, FRANCES*	BAL	031	4TH WARD
LALON, RICHARD *	WAS	094	2ND SUBD
LALOR, SISTER M.C.	FRE	197	5TH E DI
LAMAN, ELIZABETH V.	CHA	281	BOJANTOW
LAMAN, FOREMAN	CEC	030	CHESAPEA
LAMAN, HENRY	FRE	226	BUCKEYST
LAMAN, MOSES	BAL	014	9TH WARD
LAMAR, ANNA M.	FRE	219	BUCKEYST
LAMAR, BENONI S.	FRE	218	BUCKEYST
LAMAR, BETTY	MGM	322	CRACKLIN
LAMAR, CHRISTINA	BAL	072	15TH WAR
LAMAR, MARVIN	PRI	083	QUEEN AN
LAMAR, MARY	CHA	281	BOJANTOW
LAMAR, MARY	BAL	121	11TH WAR
LAMAR, RICHARD	CHA	281	BOJANTOW
LAMAR, RICHARD J.	FRE	056	FREDERIC
LAMAR, THOMA	FRE	406	JEFFERSO
LAMAR, THOMAS	CEC	189	7TH E DI
LAMAR, WILLIAM B.	FRE	396	PETERSVI
LAMARD, WILLIAM L.	ALL	169	6TH E.D.
LAMATER, C.	BAL	130	1ST WARD
LAMATON, EPHRAIM	BAL	117	1ST WARD
LAMAX, DAVID*	BAL	315	3RD WARD
LAMAY, JOHN	CEC	103	4TH E DI
LAMB, ALEXANDER	BAL	290	20TH WAR
LAMB, AMELIA	CAR	094	NO TWP L
LAMB, CHARLES	BAL	020	2ND DIST
LAMB, CANIEL	KEN	263	1ST DIST
LAMB, DAVID	BAL	238	12TH WAR
LAMB, FRANCIS B.	FRE	090	FREDERIC
LAMB, GOERGE M.	BAL	160	16TH WAR
LAMB, HENRY	BAL	102	18TH WAR
LAMB, HEZEKIAH	FRE	334	MIDDLETO
LAMB, JAMES	KEN	253	1ST DIST
LAMB, JOHN	BAL	049	1ST WARD
LAMB, JOHN	WAS	238	CAVETOWN
LAMB, JOHN E.	BAL	020	2ND DIST
LAMB, JOHN SR.	ANN	288	ANNAPOLI
LAMB, JOHN T.	QUE	183	3RD E DI
LAMB, JOHN W.	ST	312	1ST E DI
LAMB, JONATHAN D.	BAL	345	13TH WAR
LAMB, JOSEPH	BAL	290	20TH WAR
LAMB, MARY	ANN	287	ANNAPOLI
LAMB, MARY E.	ST	312	1ST E DI
LAMB, MICHAEL	BAL	091	1ST WARD
LAMB, MICHAEL	BAL	175	16TH WAR
LAMB, MICHAEL *	BAL	125	18TH WAR
LAMB, PETER	KEN	280	3RD DIST
LAMB, RACHEL	KEN	310	3RD DIST
LAMB, ROBERT	BAL	290	20TH WAR
LAMB, ROBERT	ANN	322	2ND DIST
LAMB, SARAH	BAL	204	2ND WARD
LAMB, SARAH	BAL	205	2ND WARD
LAMB, THOMAS	BAL	325	7TH WARD
LAMB, WILLIAM	KEN	253	1ST DIST
LAMB, WILLIAM B.	FRE	096	FREDERIC
LAMBDEN, ANDREW G.	BAL	038	1ST WARD
LAMBDEN, CAROLINE	BAL	212	11TH WAR
LAMBDEN, CHARLOTTE	BAL	418	14TH WAR
LAMBDEN, DANIEL	BAL	038	1ST WARD
LAMBDEN, EDWARD	WOR	331	1ST E DI
LAMBDEN, J. W.	KEN	223	2ND DIST
LAMBDEN, JOHN W.	WOR	331	1ST E DI
LAMBDEN, LEAH	WOR	328	1ST E DI
LAMBDEN, PRISSILLA-BLACK	WOR	332	1ST E DI
LAMBDEN, ROBERT	WOR	332	1ST E DI
LAMBDEN, ROBERT-BLACK	WOR	332	1ST E'DI
LAMBDEN, SAMUEL	WOR	331	1ST E DI
LAMBDEN, STEPHEN-BLACK	WOR	340	1ST E DI
LAMBDEN, THOMAS	WOR	331	1ST E DI
LAMBDEN, THOMAS	BAL	071	1ST WARD
LAMBDEN, THOMAS K.	BAL	053	1ST WARD
LAMBDEN,RICHARD	BAL	030	1ST WARD
LAMBDIN, CHARLES W.	BAL	073	15TH WAR
LAMBDIN, ELIZABETH P.	BAL	090	10TH WAR
LAMBDIN, J. M.	BAL	073	10TH WAR
LAMBDIN, JOHN	BAL	418	14TH WAR
LAMBDIN, MARY A.	BAL	060	10TH WAR
LAMBDIN, W. K.	BAL	060	10TH WAR
LAMBDIN, WILLAM	BAL	219	17TH WAR
LAMBDING, ISAAC	WOR	339	1ST E DI
LAMBERS, ANN R.	BAL	090	15TH WAR
LAMBERS, BARNEY	PRI	039	VANSVILL
LAMBERSON, ISAAC	WOR	346	1ST E DI
LAMBERSON, JOHN	WOR	326	1ST E DI
LAMBERSON, JOSEPH	FRE	218	BUCKEYST
LAMBERSON, LEVIN	WOR	350	1ST E DI
LAMBERT, ABRAM	BAL	189	19TH WAR
LAMBERT, AGUST	BAL	263	2ND WARD
LAMBERT, ALLISON	BAL	264	2ND WARD
LAMBERT, CALVIN	WAS	255	1ST DIST
LAMBERT, CATHARINE	PRI	111	PISCATAW
LAMBERT, CATHARINE	WAS	280	LEITERSB
LAMBERT, CATHERINE	FRE	108	CREAGERS
LAMBERT, CATHERINE	FRE	074	FREDERIC
LAMBERT, CHRISTIAN	BAL	249	2ND WARD
LAMBERT, CONRAD	BAL	188	6TH WARD
LAMBERT, DANIEL	FRE	221	BUCKEYST
LAMBERT, DAVID	FRE	445	8TH E DI
LAMBERT, DAVID M.	FRE	015	FREDERIC
LAMBERT, EDWARD	KEN	221	2ND DIST
LAMBERT, ELIAS	WAS	215	1ST DIST
LAMBERT, ELIJAH	DOR	304	1ST DIST
LAMBERT, ELIZABETH	WAS	075	2ND SUBD
LAMBERT, ELIZABETH*	DOR	301	1ST DIST
LAMBERT, FRANCIS H.	CAR	399	2ND DIST
LAMBERT, FREDERICK	FRE	004	FREDERIC
LAMBERT, GEORGE	CAR	304	1ST DIST
LAMBERT, GEORGE	CAR	272	WESTMINS
LAMBERT, GEORGE	WAS	265	1ST DIST
LAMBERT, GOERGE	CAR	178	8TH DIST
LAMBERT, HARRIET	FRE	006	FREDERIC
LAMBERT, HENRY	KEN	220	2ND DIST
LAMBERT, HENRY	BAL	121	5TH WARD
LAMBERT, JACKSON	CAR	178	8TH DIST
LAMBERT, JACOB	CAR	241	TANEYTOW
LAMBERT, JACOB	WAS	245	SMITHSBU
LAMBERT, JAMES	KEN	254	1ST DIST
LAMBERT, JAMES	BAL	173	1ST WARD
LAMBERT, JESSE	CAR	397	2ND DIST
LAMBERT, JOHN	CAR	404	2ND DIST
LAMBERT, JOHN	CAR	401	2ND DIST
LAMBERT, JOHN	BAL	278	2ND WARD
LAMBERT, JOHN	WAS	265	1ST DIST
LAMBERT, JOHN	WAS	075	2ND SUBD
LAMBERT, JOHN	WAS	190	1ST DIST
LAMBERT, JOHN J.	PRI	110	PISCATAW
LAMBERT, JOSEPH	WAS	078	2ND SUBD
LAMBERT, JOSEPH	BAL	262	17TH WAR
LAMBERT, JOSEPH	FRE	073	FREDERIC

Name	County	Page	District
LAMBERT, MARY	BAL	245	12TH WAR
LAMBERT, MARY J.	CEC	159	PORT DUP
LAMBERT, PHILIP	BAL	233	6TH WARD
LAMBERT, ROBERT H.	BAL	006	1ST WARD
LAMBERT, ROSINA	BAL	366	8TH WARD
LAMBERT, SARAH E.	DOR	304	1ST DIST
LAMBERT, SARAH N.	BAL	025	9TH WARD
LAMBERT, SUSAN	FRE	330	MIDDLETO
LAMBERT, SUSAN	WAS	074	2ND SUBD
LAMBERT, URIAH	CAR	315	1ST DIST
LAMBERT, WILLIAM	FRE	078	FREDERIC
LAMBERT, WILLIAM T.	CEC	159	PORT DUP
LAMBERTON, CHRISTIAN	BAL	253	1ST DIST
LAMBERTSON, DANIEL	WOR	270	BERLIN I
LAMBERTSON, JOHN	WOR	297	9TH E DI
LAMBERTSON, POLLY	WOR	329	1ST E DI
LAMBERTSON, ROSA	WOR	344	1ST E DI
LAMBERTT, THOMAS	KEN	238	2ND DIST
LAMBET, WILLIAM	WAS	191	1ST DIST
LAMBETH, RICHARD	CAL	047	3RD DIST
LAMBETH, WILLIAM	CAL	047	3RD DIST
LAMBIE, MARY	BAL	300	7TH WARD
LAMBLIN, JOHN R.	BAL	108	15TH WAR
LAMBORN, LEWIS DR.	CAR	270	WESTMINS
LAMBOURNE, WILLIAM	ANN	424	HOWARD D
LAMBPERT, ELIZABETH	CAR	326	1ST DIST
LAMBPERT, SUSAN	CAR	285	7TH DIST
LAMBRAN, CAROLINE	BAL	221	12TH WAR
LAMBRIGHT, CHRISTOPHER	BAL	437	8TH WARD
LAMBRIGHT, GEORGE	FRE	092	FREDERIC
LAMBRIGHT, HENRIETTA	BAL	437	8TH WARD
LAMBRIGHT, HENRY	BAL	064	2ND DIST
LAMBRIGHT, HENRY	FRE	308	WOODSBOR
LAMBRIGHT, JACOB	FRE	063	FREDERIC
LAMBRIGHT, JOHN	FRE	064	FREDERIC
LAMBRIGHT, MICHAEL	FRE	054	FREDERIC
LAMBRIGHT, WILLIAM	ALL	181	8TH E.D.
LAMDEN, ARTHUR	SOM	372	BRINKLEY
LAMDEN, DANIEL	CAR	097	NO TWP L
LAMDEN, EDWARD	BAL	289	3RD WARD
LAMDEN, HARRIET	WOR	182	6TH E DI
LAMCEN, JAMES	BAL	462	1ST DIST
LAMDEN, LANCEY	SOM	356	BRINKLEY
LAMDEN, RICHARD	SOM	355	BRINKLEY
LAMDEN, SAMUEL J.	SOM	354	BRINKLEY
LAMDEN, THOMAS	BAL	046	15TH WAR
LAMDEN, THOMAS*	SOM	354	BRINKLEY
LAMDIN, ANN	BAL	331	3RD WARD
LAMDIN, CAROLINE	TAL	117	ST MICHA
LAMDIN, KITTY*	TAL	053	EASTON D
LAMDIN, ROBERT P.*	BAL	413	3RD WARD
LAMDIN, ROBERT*	TAL	117	ST MICHA
LAMDIN, THOMAS J.	BAL	419	3RD WARD
LAMDIN, WILLIAM W. JUN.	TAL	117	ST MICHA
LAMDIN, WILLIAM W.*	TAL	117	ST MICHA
LAMER, GEORGE W.	ALL	067	10TH E.D
LAMER, GRACE	HAR	146	3RD DIST
LAMMOTT, ABRAHAM	CAR	207	4TH DIST
LAMMOTT, CHARLOTTE	BAL	210	6TH DIST
LAMMOTT, HARRISON	CAR	183	8TH DIST
LAMMOTT, JACOB	CAR	184	8TH DIST
LAMMOTT, JACOB	CAR	341	6TH DIST
LAMMOTT, JOHN	CAR	183	8TH DIST
LAMMOTT, LEVI	BAL	209	6TH DIST
LAMMOTT, MARGARET	CAR	183	8TH DIST
LAMNOTT, DAVID F.	CAR	380	2ND DIST
LAMO, MARY ELIZABETH	QUE	183	3RD E DI
LAMON, A.	BAL	116	1ST WARD
LAMP, JOHN	BAL	313	7TH WARD
LAMPECHT, HENRY	BAL	080	10TH WAR
LAMPERT, ABRAHAM	CAR	401	2ND DIST
LAMPERT, DANIEL	CAR	398	2ND DIST
LAMPERT, DAVID	CAR	303	1ST DIST
LAMPERT, JERAMIAH	CAR	241	TANEYTOW
LAMPERT, WILLIAM	CAR	281	7TH DIST
LAMPHER, ASAHEL	HAR	096	2ND DIST
LAMPHER, C.	BAL	136	5TH WARD
LAMPHER, JOHN	BAL	063	1ST WARD
LAMPHER, JOHN	HAR	096	2ND DIST
LAMPHER, WILLIAM	BAL	152	1ST WARD
LAMPHER, WILLIAM L.	HAR	096	2ND DIST
LAMPING, WILLIAM	BAL	162	2ND DIST
LAMPKIN, CHARLES	BAL	426	14TH WAR
LAMPLEY, HESTOR	BAL	072	4TH WARD
LAMPLEY, OLIVER E.*	BAL	071	4TH WARD
LAMPCONER, ALBERT	BAL	367	3RD WARD
LAMPRICH, WILLIAM	BAL	060	2ND DIST
LAMPSON, COLONEL	BAL	307	3RD WARD
LAMPSON, MARTHA*	BAL	075	4TH WARD
LAMPSON, WASHINGTON	BAL	067	4TH WARD
LAMPTON, MISS E.	FRE	200	5TH E DI
LAMUTH, HENRY	BAL	279	1ST DIST
LAMY, JOHN H.	PRI	048	AQUASCO
LANAHAN, ANN	BAL	091	10TH WAR
LANAHAN, DARBY	ALL	136	4TH E.D.
LANAHAN, JOHN	ALL	142	6TH E.D.
LANAHAN, M.	ANN	296	1ST DIST
LANAHAN, MICHAEL	BAL	445	14TH WAR
LANAHAN, SAMUEL J.	BAL	163	16TH WAR
LANAHAN, THOMAS M.	BAL	051	4TH WARD
LANAHAN, WILLIAM	BAL	163	16TH WAR
LANAN, PATRICK	BAL	449	1ST DIST
LANAN, PATRICK	BAL	382	1ST DIST
LANARLAND, HNERY *	BAL	371	13TH WAR
LANAY, WESLEY *	ANN	359	3RD DIST
LANBDEN, CHESTER-BLACK	QUE	154	1ST E DI
LANBDEN, WILLIAM S.	BAL	037	1ST WARD
LANBERT, BERNARD	BAL	068	1ST WARD
LANBOUGH, VALENTINE	BAL	251	2ND WARD
LANBRACH, CHRISTOPHER	BAL	206	6TH WARD
LANBRACH, CHRISTOPHER	BAL	206	6TH WARD
LANBRIGHT, PHILIP D.	BAL	097	18TH WAR
LANBY, JOHN	MGM	389	ROCKERLE
LANBY, JOHN	MGM	389	ROCKERLE
LANCASTER, ALECTIOUS	CHA	273	ALLENS F
LANCASTER, ANDREW	ALL	122	4TH E.D.
LANCASTER, ANN	BAL	120	5TH WARD
LANCASTER, ANN	BAL	476	14TH WAR
LANCASTER, B.F.	WAS	219	1ST DIST
LANCASTER, BARBARA	MGM	355	BERRYS D
LANCASTER, BENJAMIN	CHA	226	ALLENS F
LANCASTER, BENJAMIN	WAS	019	2ND SUBD
LANCASTER, BENJAMIN	WAS	031	2ND SUBD
LANCASTER, BENJAMIN	BAL	191	11TH WAR
LANCASTER, CHARITY	MGM	352	BERRYS D
LANCASTER, CHARLES	CHA	226	ALLENS F
LANCASTER, CHRISTIANA	WAS	157	HAGERSTO
LANCASTER, COLLUMBUS	CHA	227	ALLENS F
LANCASTER, COLONUS	CHA	272	ALLENS F
LANCASTER, EDWARD	MGM	351	BERRYS D
LANCASTER, ELIZA	BAL	308	12TH WAR
LANCASTER, GEORGE	BAL	105	18TH WAR
LANCASTER, HANNAH	BAL	055	4TH WARD
LANCASTER, HARIET	WAS	031	2ND SUBD
LANCASTER, HENRIETTA	CHA	225	ALLENS F
LANCASTER, HENRY	ALL	022	2ND E.D.
LANCASTER, HESTER	ALL	083	5TH E.D.
LANCASTER, IRA	BAL	206	19TH WAR
LANCASTER, ISAIAH	BAL	459	8TH WARD
LANCASTER, ISAIAH	BAL	349	3RD WARD
LANCASTER, JESSIE	BAL	349	3RD WARD
LANCASTER, JOHN	ALL	115	5TH E.D.
LANCASTER, JOHN	CHA	227	ALLENS F
LANCASTER, JOHN	MGM	351	BERRYS D
LANCASTER, JOHN	HAR	082	2ND DIST
LANCASTER, JOHN	HAR	087	2ND DIST
LANCASTER, JOHN	BAL	316	20TH WAR
LANCASTER, JOHN D.	BAL	120	5TH WARD
LANCASTER, LUCINDA	MGM	353	BERRYS D
LANCASTER, MARY	BAL	217	17TH WAR
LANCASTER, REBECCA	WAS	031	2ND SUBD
LANCASTER, SINCLAIR	WAS	031	2ND SUBD
LANCASTER, SUSAN	HAR	080	2ND DIST
LANCASTER, THEOPHILUS	PRI	013	BLADENSB
LANCASTER, THOMAS	MGM	354	BERRYS D
LANCASTER, THOMAS	ALL	119	5TH E.D.
LANCASTER, THOMAS	BAL	137	16TH WAR
LANCASTER, THOMAS	BAL	376	3RD WARD
LANCASTER, WASHINGTON	CHA	226	ALLENS F
LANCASTER, WILLIAM	BAL	184	19TH WAR
LANCE, CHRIST.	BAL	299	1ST DIST
LANCE, HENRY	BAL	460	1ST DIST
LANCE, JOHN	BAL	463	14TH WAR
LANCE, OLIVER	BAL	393	14TH WAR
LANCE, SARAH *	BAL	403	1ST DIST
LANCET, CASPAR	BAL	401	3RD WARD
LANCEY, ISAAC	BAL	159	1ST WARD
LANCHAN, JOHN	BAL	169	2ND DIST
LANCHART, MARY	BAL	264	2ND WARD
LANCHESTER, ANN	BAL	122	18TH WAR
LANCK, JOHN	BAL	064	15TH WAR
LANCKEY, HENRY	BAL	096	15TH WAR
LANCO, SARAH	BAL	173	2ND DIST
LANCO, SARAH	BAL	408	1ST DIST
LANCO, SARAH *	BAL	403	1ST DIST
LAND, ANN	BAL	019	4TH WARD
LANDALE, THOMAS *	BAL	062	18TH WAR
LANDEN, ANN	ANN	281	ANNAPOLI
LANDEN, EZEKIEL	SOM	372	BRINKLEY
LANDEN, JAMES	BAL	023	15TH WAR
LANDEN, RICHARD*	SOM	354	BRINKLEY
LANDEN, SARAH	SOM	355	BRINKLEY
LANDEN, WILLIAM J.*	SOM	397	BRINKLEY
LANDENSLAGER, JOHN	BAL	237	1ST DIST
LANDENSLAGER, JOHN	BAL	236	1ST DIST
LANDENSLAYER, C.	BAL	272	20TH WAR
LANDENSLAYER, WILLIAM	BAL	273	20TH WAR
LANDER, ALFRED	CAR	235	UNION TO
LANDER, CATHARINE	BAL	062	2ND DIST
LANDER, CONRACT	BAL	428	8TH WARD
LANDER, WILLIAM	BAL	100	10TH WAR
LANDERBOCH, GEROGE	BAL	307	20TH WAR
LANDERMAN, F.	BAL	157	1ST WARD
LANDERMAN, HENRY R.*	BAL	422	3RD WARD
LANDERMAN, MARY	FRE	426	8TH E DI
LANDERS, CELENIA*	BAL	067	4TH WARD
LANDERS, EDWARD J.*	BAL	043	4TH WARD
LANDERS, EMILY*	BAL	336	3RD WARD
LANDERS, GEORGE W.	BAL	409	14TH WAR
LANDERS, GEORGE*	BAL	023	4TH WARD
LANDERS, JACOB	CAR	391	2ND DIST
LANDERS, JAMES*	BAL	421	3RD WARD
LANDERS, JOHN	FRE	186	5TH E DI
LANDERS, JOHN	BAL	315	1ST DIST
LANDERS, JOHN*	BAL	039	4TH WARD
LANDERS, LAURA*	BAL	044	4TH WARD
LANDERS, PERRY D.	BAL	173	1ST WARD
LANDETH, ROBERT	BAL	135	1ST WARD
LANDETT, JAMES	BAL	126	1ST WARD
LANDFORD, EDWARD	BAL	393	9TH WARD
LANDHART, AUGUST	BAL	276	2ND WARD
LANDIE, THOMAS	BAL	310	7TH WARD
LANDIN, ELIZABETH	SOM	443	DAMES QU
LANDING, ATTA	SOM	399	BRINKLEY
LANDING, GEORGE W.	WOR	342	1ST E DI
LANDING, HENRY	WOR	329	1ST E DI
LANDING, SALLY	WOR	349	1ST E DI
LANDING, SAMUEL T.	WOR	341	1ST E DI
LANDING, SUSAN	WOR	340	1ST E DI
LANDING, WILLIAM	SOM	397	BRINKLEY
LANDIS, ABRAHAM	CAR	391	2ND DIST
LANDIS, CATHARINE	WAS	277	LEITERSB
LANDIS, CHARLES	DOR	413	1ST DIST
LANDIS, D. C.*	BAL	052	4TH WARD
LANDIS, EDMOND*	BAL	383	3RD WARD
LANDIS, HENRY	WAS	222	1ST DIST
LANDIS, JESSE	FRE	041	FREDERIC
LANDIS, MARY	WAS	222	1ST DIST
LANDIS, SAMUEL	BAL	419	1ST DIST
LANDLEY, MARY A.	BAL	122	11TH WAR
LANDMAN, HENRY	BAL	398	14TH WAR
LANDMAN, HENRY	BAL	422	14TH WAR
LANDMAN, JAMES	QUE	228	4TH E DI
LANDMAN, PERE-BLACK	QUE	125	1ST E DI
LANDMAN, SUSAN	QUE	236	4TH E DI
LANDMAN, SUSAN	QUE	222	4TH E DI
LANDMAN, THOMAS	QUE	228	4TH E DI
LANDNER, THOMAS	BAL	366	13TH WAR
LANDON, ANDREW	PRI	100	SPALDING
LANDON, JOHN	SOM	353	BRINKLEY
LANDON, JOSHUA*	BAL	340	3RD WARD
LANDON, SARAH	SOM	553	TYASKIN
LANDORGAN, JOHN	BAL	148	16TH WAR
LANDOVER, JAMES	FRE	028	FREDERIC
LANDRE, SAMUEL	FRE	20	5TH E DI
LANDRICK, NANCY	MGM	360	BERRYS D
LANDRIS, MICHAEL	BAL	449	14TH WAR
LANDRY, JOHN	FRE	20	5TH E DI
LANDS, ANN*	BAL	061	4TH WARD
LANDS, BETSEY*	BAL	085	4TH WARD
LANDS, JANE*	BAL	053	4TH WARD
LANDS, SALMON*	BAL	078	4TH WARD
LANDS, WILLIAM	BAL	150	1ST WARD
LANDSDALE, THOMAS	BAL	356	1ST DIST
LANDSLAGER, CONRAD	BAL	015	18TH WAR
LANDSLY, OCTAVIA *	BAL	375	13TH WAR
LANDSTREET, L.	BAL	429	14TH WAR
LANDUM, SUSAN	ANN	286	ANNAPOLI
LANDUS, WILLIAM C.	FRE	141	CREAGERS
LANDWAY, HENRY	ALL	197	CUMBERLA
LANDY, THOMAS	BAL	152	5TH WARD
LANE, ABHRAIM	BAL	060	18TH WAR
LANE, ABRHAN	BAL	139	11TH WAR
LANE, ANDREW	ALL	107	5TH E.D.
LANE, ANN	BAL	329	13TH WAR
LANE, ANN	BAL	353	7TH WARD
LANE, ANN	BAL	075	4TH WARD
LANE, BETSEY	BAL	043	9TH WARD
LANE, BRIDGET	BAL	061	15TH WAR
LANE, BRIDGET	BAL	003	9TH WARD
LANE, CAIN	DOR	308	1ST DIST
LANE, CALEB	CAR	290	7TH DIST
LANE, CAROLINE	BAL	025	1ST WARD
LANE, CATHARINE	FRE	165	EMMITTSB
LANE, CHARLES	CAR	077	NO TWP L
LANE, CHARLES	BAL	430	1ST DIST
LANE, CHARLES G.	WAS	129	HAGERSTO
LANE, CHRISTOPHER	BAL	338	13TH WAR
LANE, E. E.	BAL	332	1ST DIST
LANE, EDWARD	BAL	407	8TH WARD
LANE, EDWARD	KEN	285	3RD DIST
LANE, ELIZA	BAL	082	15TH WAR
LANE, ELIZA C.	DOR	298	1ST DIST
LANE, ELIZABETH	BAL	450	14TH WAR
LANE, ELIZABETH	CAR	072	NO TWP L
LANE, ELIZABETH	CAR	148	NO TWP L
LANE, ELIZABETH	BAL	417	1ST DIST
LANE, ELIZABETH	BAL	256	12TH WAR
LANE, ELIZABETH	WOR	184	6TH E DI
LANE, ELIZABETH-BLACK	CAR	078	NO TWP L
LANE, EMILY	BAL	290	20TH WAR
LANE, FRANCIS	WOR	258	1ST CENS
LANE, GEORGE	BAL	417	1ST DIST
LANE, HEMSLEY	QUE	125	1ST E DI
LANE, HENRY	BAL	367	3RD WARD
LANE, HENRY	ANN	314	1ST DIST
LANE, HENRY	ANN	326	2ND DIST
LANE, HEZEKIAH	SOM	409	DUBLIN D
LANE, JACOB	FRE	085	FREDCRIC
LANE, JAMES	CEC	033	CHESAPEA
LANE, JAMES	TAL	032	EASTON D
LANE, JAMES B.	BAL	382	8TH WARD
LANE, JAMES H.	TAL	028	EASTON D
LANE, JOHN	WOR	183	6TH E DI
LANE, JOHN	ANN	325	2ND DIST
LANE, JOHN	BAL	272	1ST DIST
LANE, JOHN	QUE	133	1ST E DI
LANE, JOHN	CAR	388	2ND DIST
LANE, JOHN *	SOM	466	HANGARY
LANE, JOHN C.	WAS	129	HAGERSTO
LANE, JOHN C.	FRE	338	MIDDLETO
LANE, JOHN L.	ANN	501	HOWARD D
LANE, JOHN V.	KEN	290	3RD DIST
LANE, JOSEPH	ANN	320	2ND DIST
LANE, JOSEPH M.	BAL	392	3RD WARD
LANE, JOSHUA	BAL	415	1ST DIST
LANE, JOSHUA	FRE	156	10TH E D
LANE, LEVINA	BAL	294	3RD WARD
LANE, LLOYD	BAL	170	16TH WAR
LANE, LOUISA	WAS	147	HAGERSTO
LANE, MARY	BAL	273	1ST DIST
LANE, MARY	HAR	184	3RD DIST
LANE, MARY	BAL	290	20TH WAR
LANE, MARY M.	QUE	137	1ST E DI
LANE, MATILDA	QUE	127	1ST E DI
LANE, MICHAEL	BAL	276	1ST DIST
LANE, N.	BAL	154	1ST WARD
LANE, NANCY	BAL	233	12TH WAR
LANE, NELLY	ANN	301	1ST DIST
LANE, PADDY	BAL	272	1ST DIST
LANE, RACHAEL	BAL	147	11TH WAR
LANE, REBECCA	HAR	154	3RD DIST
LANE, RICHARD	CAL	036	2ND DIST
LANE, RICHARD	ANN	289	ANNAPOLI
LANE, RICHARD A.	TAL	070	EASTON T
LANE, RICHARD C.	TAL	082	ST MICHA
LANE, SAMUEL	QUE	127	1ST E DI
LANE, SAMUEL H.	ANN	458	HOWARD D
LANE, SARAH	BAL	099	10TH WAR
LANE, SARAH	BAL	089	5TH WARD
LANE, SARAH	BAL	381	3RD WARD
LANE, SARAH	SOM	415	DUBLIN D
LANE, SHADRICK-BLACK	WOR	334	1ST E DI
LANE, STEPHEN	BAL	164	1ST WARD
LANE, TERRY	DOR	366	3RD DIVI
LANE, THOAMS G.	WOR	256	1ST CENS
LANE, THOMAS	TAL	044	EASTON D
LANE, THOMAS	KEN	284	3RD DIST
LANE, THOMAS	CAL	057	3RD DIST
LANE, THOMAS	CAL	056	3RD DIST
LANE, THOMAS	CAR	078	NO TWP L
LANE, THOMAS	CEC	034	CHESAPEA
LANE, THOMAS	BAL	281	2ND WARD
LANE, THOMAS	BAL	458	1ST DIST
LANE, THOMAS A.	BAL	081	4TH WARD
LANE, TOM	ANN	296	1ST DIST
LANE, VALENTINE	BAL	378	8TH WARD
LANE, WILLIAM	BAL	340	3RD WARD
LANE, WILLIAM	BAL	042	9TH WARD
LANE, WILLIAM	CEC	038	CHESAPEA
LANE, WILLIAM	DOR	321	1ST DIST
LANE, WILLIAM	FRE	088	FREDERIC
LANE, WILLIAM	TAL	018	EASTON D
LANE, WILLIAM H.	QUE	170	2ND E DI
LANE, WILLIAM M.	WOR	195	8TH E DI
LANEEN, PETER	ALL	129	4TH E.D.
LANEFIELD, PATRICK	CEC	031	CHESAPEA
LANEHAN, ELIZA	BAL	044	4TH WARD
LANEHARDT, GEORGE	BAL	047	1ST WARD
LANEHARLT, PETER	BAL	254	2ND WARD
LANEHART, GEORGE	BAL	102	2ND DIST
LANEHART, JOHN	BAL	457	8TH WARD
LANEHART, JONATHAN	BAL	136	16TH WAR
LANEHEART, WILLIAM	ALL	251	CUMBERLA
LANEKIN, BRIDGET	BAL	422	8TH WARD
LANER, ANDREW	BAL	239	20TH WAR
LANER, GEORGE	BAL	348	13TH WAR
LANER, JOHN	BAL	180	19TH WAR
LANER, PETER	CAR	178	8TH DIST
LANERBECK, JOHN	BAL	242	20TH WAR
LANERS, HEZEKIAH	BAL	113	1ST WARD
LANES, JOHN	FRE	075	FREDERIC
LANESTREET, JOHN	BAL	141	19TH WAR
LANEY, NANCY	WAS	007	WILLIAMS
LANEY, ROBERT V.	ALL	237	CUMBERLA
LANEY, SAMUEL	WAS	120	2ND DIST
LANFARE, WILLIAM*	BAL	342	3RD WARD
LANFEAT, JOHN	BAL	144	1ST WARD
LANFLICK, PATRICK	BAL	209	11TH WAR
LANFULL, JAMES	BAL	167	1ST WARD

Name	County	Page	District
LANG, ANN	BAL	082	15TH WAR
LANG, CORNELIUS B.	BAL	368	3RD WARD
LANG, COULBORN	SOM	496	SALISBUR
LANG, EMILY	MGM	356	BERRYS D
LANG, GEORGE	BAL	339	3RD WARD
LANG, HENRY	BAL	262	2ND WARD
LANG, HENRY	FRE	280	WOODSBOR
LANG, JOHN	BAL	127	1ST WARD
LANG, JOHN	ALL	052	10TH E.D
LANG, JOHN	QUE	161	2ND E DI
LANG, LUDERICK	CAR	199	4TH DIST
LANG, MARGARET	BAL	367	13TH WAR
LANG, MARY	QUE	195	3RD E DI
LANG, PETER	FRE	440	8TH E DI
LANG, ROBERT	BAL	262	2ND WARD
LANG, WILLIAM	CAR	199	4TH DIST
LANG, WILLIAM P.*	BAL	325	3RD WARD
LANGAN, JAMES	BAL	127	1ST WARD
LANGDEN, SUSAN	FRE	039	FREDERIC
LANGDIN, FRANKLIN	CEC	162	6TH E DI
LANGDIN, SARAH	CEC	154	PORT DUP
LANGDON, BARCLAY	ALL	127	4TH E.D.
LANGDON, GILES S.	CEC	162	6TH E DI
LANGDON, HEZEKIAH	ANN	357	3RD DIST
LANGDON, JOHN J.	BAL	050	9TH WARD
LANGE, AUGUSTUS	BAL	252	12TH WAR
LANGE, JACOB	BAL	253	12TH WAR
LANGE, JOHN G.	BAL	091	18TH WAR
LANGE, MATILDA	BAL	259	12TH WAR
LANGER, DAVID	BAL	146	1ST WARD
LANGFILT, WILLIAM	TAL	039	EASTON D
LANGFORD, AMELIA	SOM	422	PRINCESS
LANGFORD, ANN	SOM	409	DUBLIN D
LANGFORD, AUGUSTA	SOM	407	DUBLIN D
LANGFORD, BENJAMIN	SOM	416	PRINCESS
LANGFORD, ELIJAH S.	SOM	392	BRINKLEY
LANGFORD, ELIZA	CAR	153	NO TWP L
LANGFORD, GATTY	SOM	409	DUBLIN D
LANGFORD, HENRY	SOM	397	BRINKLEY
LANGFORD, HENRY J.	SOM	404	BRINKLEY
LANGFORD, HIRAM	SOM	425	PRINCESS
LANGFORD, HURDEMAN	CAR	151	NO TWP L
LANGFORD, ISAAC L.*	SOM	393	BRINKLEY
LANGFORD, JOHN	SOM	447	DAMES QU
LANGFORD, JOHN H.	SOM	421	PRINCESS
LANGFORD, JOHN L.	SOM	429	PRINCESS
LANGFORD, JOSEPH B. J.	SOM	385	BRINKLEY
LANGFORD, JOSEPH P.	DOR	458	1ST DIST
LANGFORD, JOSHUA	SOM	422	PRINCESS
LANGFORD, LAZARUS	SOM	396	BRINKLEY
LANGFORD, LEVIN	SOM	385	BRINKLEY
LANGFORD, LEVIN	DOR	445	1ST DIST
LANGFORD, LITTLETON	SOM	429	PRINCESS
LANGFORD, MARY	DOR	450	1ST DIST
LANGFORD, NANCY S.	SOM	395	BRINKLEY
LANGFORD, NATHAN J.	SOM	392	BRINKLEY
LANGFORD, NICHOLAS	DOR	437	1ST DIST
LANGFORD, PATSEY	SOM	397	BRINKLEY
LANGFORD, SARAH	SOM	390	BRINKLEY
LANGFORD, THOMAS	SOM	394	BRINKLEY
LANGFORD, THOMAS	SOM	417	PRINCESS
LANGFORD, TUBMAN	SOM	398	BRINKLEY
LANGFORD, WASHINGTON	SOM	390	BRINKLEY
LANGFORD, WILLIAM	CAR	143	NO TWP L
LANGFORD, WILLIAM	BAL	025	1ST WARD
LANGFORD, WILLIAM	BAL	078	1ST WARD
LANGFORD, WILLIAM D.	SOM	394	BRINKLEY
LANGFORD, WILLIAM H.	SOM	485	TRAPP DI
LANGFORD, ZACHARIAH	DOR	437	1ST DIST
LANGGOOD, MOSES	BAL	048	1ST WARD
LANGKORN, JOHN	BAL	179	6TH WARD
LANGLES, JOHN H.	CHA	281	BOJANTOW
LANGLEY, AMRY E.	ST	310	1ST E DI
LANGLEY, ANN E.	ST	309	1ST E DI
LANGLEY, BETSEY	BAL	283	17TH WAR
LANGLEY, CATHARINE	BAL	251	6TH WARD
LANGLEY, CHARLOTTE	CHA	285	BOJANTOW
LANGLEY, DANIEL W.	ST	313	1ST E DI
LANGLEY, EDWARD	BAL	283	7TH WARD
LANGLEY, EDWARD	BAL	339	3RD WARD
LANGLEY, GEORGE	BAL	396	1ST DIST
LANGLEY, GEORGE	BAL	385	1ST DIST
LANGLEY, GEORGE	HAR	004	1ST DIST
LANGLEY, GEORGE H.	CHA	281	BOJANTOW
LANGLEY, GUSTAVAS	CHA	279	BOJANTOW
LANGLEY, HENRY M.	ST	312	1ST E DI
LANGLEY, IGNATIUS J.	ST	313	1ST E DI
LANGLEY, IGNATIUS V.	ST	305	2ND E DI
LANGLEY, JAMES	BAL	118	18TH WAR
LANGLEY, JAMES L.	ST	309	1ST E DI
LANGLEY, JAMES L.	ST	310	1ST E DI
LANGLEY, JOHN	CHA	282	BOJANTOW
LANGLEY, JOHN	BAL	299	17TH WAR
LANGLEY, JOSEPH	PRI	058	NOTTINGH
LANGLEY, L.	PRI	066	NOTTINGH
LANGLEY, MARY A.	BAL	287	7TH WARD
LANGLEY, MARY E.	ST	273	3RD E DI
LANGLEY, MRS.	PRI	089	SPALDING
LANGLEY, PHILIP G.	ST	313	1ST E DI
LANGLEY, RICHARD H.	ST	277	3RD E DI
LANGLEY, ROMIA	BAL	233	20TH WAR
LANGLEY, SYLVESTER	ST	348	5TH E DI
LANGLEY, T.A.	ST	310	1ST E DI
LANGLEY, WILLIAM	ST	284	2ND E DI
LANGLEY, WILLIAM	ST	285	2ND E DI
LANGLEY, WILLIAM B.	ST	312	1ST E DI
LANGLEY, WILLIAM R.	ST	310	1ST E DI
LANGLEY, WILLIAM W.	PRI	053	AQUASCO
LANGLY, CHARLES	BAL	112	2ND DIST
LANGLY, ELLEN	BAL	299	17TH WAR
LANGLY, HENRY	CHA	292	BOJANTOW
LANGLY, JOHN	CHA	279	BOJANTOW
LANGLY, JOHN B.	CHA	279	BOJANTOW
LANGLY, MARY	ALL	217	CUMBERLA
LANGLY, RUTH	BAL	111	2ND DIST
LANGLY, SOLOMON	PRI	072	MARLBROU
LANGLY, WILLIAM	PRI	098	SPALDING
LANGLY, WILLIAM B.	PRI	053	AQUASCO
LANGLY, Z.	CHA	267	BOJANTOW
LANGON, ELLEN	ALL	073	5TH E.D.
LANGON, MICHAEL	ALL	073	5TH E.D.
LANGON, PATRICK	ALL	142	6TH E.D.
LANGOOD, NICHOLAS	BAL	031	1ST WARD
LANGOR, FANNEY	BAL	299	7TH WARD
LANGOR, HERMAN	BAL	206	6TH WARD
LANGOR, PHILLIS	CEC	053	1ST E DI
LANGREL, ALEXANDER	DOR	340	3RD DIVI
LANGREL, ANN	DOR	351	3RD DIVI
LANGREL, HENERY	DOR	351	3RD DIVI
LANGREL, JOBE T.	DOR	351	3RD DIVI
LANGREL, JOBE*	DOR	351	3RD DIVI
LANGREL, JOHN*	DOR	345	3RD DIVI
LANGREL, WILLIAM	DOR	351	3RD DIVI
LANGSDAB, HUGH	DOR	377	1ST DIST
LANGSDALE, CYRUS	SOM	485	TRAPP DI
LANGSDALE, JAMES R.	SOM	549	TYASKIN
LANGSDALE, MARY	WOR	237	6TH E DI
LANGSDALE, MARY	SOM	538	TYASKIN
LANGSDALE, MARY	SOM	544	TYASKIN
LANGSDALE, NICY	SOM	514	BARREN C
LANGSDALE, ROBERT	SOM	522	BARREN C
LANGSDALE, SARAH A.	SOM	526	QUANTICO
LANGSTEAD, HERMAN	BAL	253	2ND WARD
LANGSTON, ANN H.	BAL	356	13TH WAR
LANGSTON, ELIZABETH A.	CAL	005	1ST DIST
LANGSTON, GEORGE E.	BAL	375	13TH WAR
LANGSTON, LAWRENC *	BAL	070	15TH WAR
LANGSTON, WILLAIM	BAL	125	5TH WARD
LANGSWELL, ANN E.	BAL	310	1ST DIST
LANGTRA, JAMES	BAL	116	1ST WARD
LANGUAY, ELLEN	BAL	213	11TH WAR
LANGUM, WILLIAM	BAL	151	1ST WARD
LANGWELL, SARAH	BAL	150	2ND DIST
LANGWINTINE, PETER *	BAL	125	2ND DIST
LANHAM, ANN	PRI	008	BLADENSB
LANHAM, JANE	PRI	030	VANSVILL
LANHAM, NANCY	MGM	376	ROCKERLE
LANHAM, TRUMAN	PRI	015	BLADENSB
LANHAM, WILLIAM	MGM	388	ROCKERLE
LANHAY, THOMAS	BAL	127	1ST WARD
LANI, HARMAN *	WAS	061	2ND SUBD
LANIER, LEWIS	BAL	047	9TH WARD
LANIMORE, ANN M.*	TAL	067	EASTON T
LANIMORE, NICHOLAS P.*	TAL	067	EASTON T
LANIMORE, THOMAS	TAL	027	EASTON D
LANIMORE, WILLIAM*	TAL	030	EASTON D
LANIN, PATRICK	BAL	286	1ST DIST
LANING, FRANCES	BAL	039	1ST WARD
LANING, JOHN	BAL	039	1ST WARD
LANING, WILLIAM	WAS	162	HAGERSTO
LANK, JOHN M.	BAL	146	19TH WAR
LANK, JOSEPH H.	BAL	390	8TH WARD
LANKENBY, MARGARET *	BAL	111	2ND DIST
LANKFACE, ISAAC	BAL	160	2ND DIST
LANKFORD, ADAM	SOM	385	BRINKLEY
LANKFORD, AMANCA W.	BAL	192	2ND WARD
LANKFORD, ANN *	BAL	160	2ND DIST
LANKFORD, BENJAMIN	SOM	389	BRINKLEY
LANKFORD, EDWARD	SOM	362	BRINKLEY
LANKFORD, EDWARD	BAL	458	14TH WAR
LANKFORD, FREEBORN	SOM	530	QUANTICO
LANKFORD, GEORGE	SOM	534	QUANTICO
LANKFORD, GEORGE	SOM	371	BRINKLEY
LANKFORD, GEORGE*	DOR	323	1ST DIST
LANKFORD, HENRY S.	BAL	061	15TH WAR
LANKFORD, HESTER	BAL	038	1ST WARD
LANKFORD, HETTY	SOM	354	BRINKLEY
LANKFORD, ISABELLA	SOM	366	BRINKLEY
LANKFORD, JAMES	SOM	374	BRINKLEY
LANKFORD, JOHA H.	WOR	185	6TH E DI
LANKFORD, JOSEPH	SOM	386	BRINKLEY
LANKFORD, JOSIAH-BLACK	WOR	342	1ST E DI
LANKFORD, LILLY A.	DOR	307	1ST DIST
LANKFORD, LOVEY*	DOR	306	1ST DIST
LANKFORD, NANCY C.*	SOM	309	BARREN C
LANKFORD, ROBERT	SOM	386	BRINKLEY
LANKFORD, SARAH A.	SOM	366	BRINKLEY
LANKFORD, SARAH*	SOM	521	BARREN C
LANKFORD, SMITH	SOM	365	BRINKLEY
LANKFORD, SUSAN	SOM	389	BRINKLEY
LANKFORD, TURPIN*	DOR	305	1ST DIST
LANKFORD, WILEY	BAL	061	15TH WAR
LANKFORD, WILLIAM	DOR	307	1ST DIST
LANKFORD, WILLIAM H.*	SOM	377	BRINKLEY
LANKFORD, WILLIAM L.	SOM	365	BRINKLEY
LANKHOUSE, CHRISTIAN	BAL	145	2ND DIST
LANKIN, JOSHUA	BAL	133	1ST WARD
LANLER, PATRICK	QUE	224	4TH E DI
LANLINE, JANE *	BAL	299	20TH WAR
LANMAN, WESLEY	ANN	448	HOWARD D
LANMAN, WILLIAM	BAL	084	15TH WAR
LANMOR, WILLIAM*	DOR	404	1ST DIST
LANN, JESSE F.	CEC	075	NORTHEAS
LANNAN, MARY	BAL	371	3RD WARD
LANNAN, PETER	ALL	129	4TH E.D.
LANNAN, WILLIAM	ALL	129	4TH E.D.
LANNDS, JOHN *	BAL	351	13TH WAR
LANNER, ANN	ST	288	2ND E DI
LANNER, JAMES H.*	BAL	305	3RD WARD
LANNER, NICHOLAS	BAL	221	2ND WARD
LANNER, VINCENT	FRE	334	MIDDLETO
LANNING, GEORGE	BAL	466	14TH WAR
LANNING, HENRY M.	BAL	160	16TH WAR
LANOGAN, JOHN	BAL	070	1ST WARD
LANON, MARY M.	BAL	274	2ND WARD
LANON, PETER	BAL	274	2ND WARD
LANRMAN, FRANKLIN	QUE	245	5TH E DI
LANRON, ANN	BAL	237	20TH WAR
LANSBACK, HENRY	BAL	058	1ST WARD
LANSDALE, CHRISTCPHER W.	MGM	394	ROCKERLE
LANSDALE, ELIZA C.	PRI	042	VANSVILL
LANSDALE, ELIZABETH-BLACK	FRE	245	NEW MARK
LANSDALE, ISAAC W.	BAL	358	13TH WAR
LANSDALE, LAURA V.	PRI	036	VANSVILL
LANSDALE, MARY	MGM	375	ROCKERLE
LANSDALE, MARY E.	BAL	118	15TH WAR
LANSDALE, WILLIAM	ANN	510	HOWARD D
LANSDALE, WILLIAM-BLACK	FRE	245	NEW MARK
LANSDALE, ISAAC-BLACK	FRE	239	NEW MARK
LANSDIE, WILLIAM *	ANN	326	2ND DIST
LANSDOWN, EDWARD L.	BAL	056	4TH WARD
LANSEY, HARRIET A.	BAL	095	15TH WAR
LANSEY, HENRY	BAL	020	15TH WAR
LANSFIELD, STEPHEN	BAL	132	11TH WAR
LANSINGER, JACOB	FRE	148	10TH E D
LANSINGER, WILLIAM	FRE	145	10TH E D
LANSON, ELIZ	BAL	187	5TH DIST
LANSON, MARGARET	BAL	144	19TH WAR
LANSON, HENRY S.	BAL	062	1ST WARD
LANSSING, HERMAN	BAL	302	3RD WARD
LANSTETH, SAMUEL	BAL	039	9TH WARD
LANT, MICHAEL *	BAL	125	18TH WAR
LANTANE, ABRAHAM	BAL	238	2ND WARD
LANTHOOVER, JOHN	BAL	042	18TH WAR
LANTIER, LOUIS E.	BAL	130	5TH WARD
LANTMAN, CONRAD	BAL	249	2ND WARD
LANTS, JOHN P.	BAL	168	6TH WARD
LANTY, HENRY	WAS	189	1ST DIST
LANTY, JACOB	WAS	074	2ND SUBD
LANTZ, CHRISTIAN	WAS	008	WILLIAMS
LANTZ, CHRISTIAN	WAS	281	LEITERSB
LANTZ, CHRISTIAN	WAS	242	CAVETOWN
LANTZ, CHRISTIAN	FRE	194	5TH E DI
LANTZ, DAVID	WAS	241	CAVETOWN
LANTZ, ELIZABETH	WAS	280	LEITERSB
LANTZ, GEORGE	WAS	281	LEITERSB
LANTZ, GEORGE	CAR	399	2ND DIST
LANTZ, JACOB	WAS	111	2ND DIST
LANTZ, JACOB	BAL	133	16TH WAR
LANTZ, JOHN	CAR	401	2ND DIST
LANTZ, JOHN	FRE	150	10TH E D
LANTZ, JOHN G.	BAL	133	16TH WAR
LANUM, BEN	PRI	084	QUEEN AN
LANUM, JOHN *	WAS	060	2ND SUBD
LANUM, L.	PRI	117	PISCATAW
LANUN, ANN	PRI	101	SPALDING
LANUN, RICHARD	PRI	120	PISCATAW
LANYON, BRIDGET	ALL	135	4TH E.D.
LAONE, JOSEPH	HAR	191	3RD DIST
LAOR, SISTER M. DAMION	FRE	197	5TH E DI
LAP, CATHARINE	ALL	072	5TH E.D.
LAPAN, JOHN	BAL	348	7TH WARD
LAPAN, MARY	BAL	348	7TH WARD
LAPEAN, VICTOR	CEC	080	NORTHEAS
LAPELL, WILLIAM S.	KEN	210	2ND DIST
LAPETY, PHIL	BAL	235	20TH WAR
LAPIER, AUSLEEN	BAL	156	2ND DIST
LAPORT, ARNOLD	BAL	047	18TH WAR
LAPORT, CHARLES	BAL	115	1ST WARD
LAPORT, CHARLES	BAL	113	1ST WARD
LAPORVILLE, ALFRED P. *	BAL	259	6TH WARD
LAPOTT, CHARLES	BAL	168	1ST WARD
LAPP, DANIEL*	BAL	371	3RD WARD
LAPP, DAVID	BAL	408	8TH WARD
LAPP, DENNIS	BAL	459	8TH WARD
LAPP, JACOB*	BAL	077	4TH WARD
LAPP, JOHN	BAL	278	12TH WAR
LAPP, JOSHUA F.*	BAL	367	3RD WARD
LAPP, LYDIA	BAL	106	2ND DIST
LAPP, SOPHIA	BAL	358	13TH WAR
LAPP, WILLIAM	BAL	361	3RD WARD
LAPPIN, PATRICK	BAL	447	1ST DIST
LAPRADE, JOHN B.	BAL	363	13TH WAR
LARABEE, ANNE	BAL	115	15TH WAR
LARACY, JACOB F.	BAL	389	8TH WARD
LARACY, JOHN	BAL	388	8TH WARD
LARACY, MATHEW	BAL	328	7TH WARD
LARAMER, ELIZABETH	BAL	041	15TH WAR
LARAMER, JAMES	WAS	153	HAGERSTO
LARB, ELTONE	BAL	051	9TH WARD
LARBOKEN, JOHN	BAL	428	8TH WARD
LARCH, EMMA	ANN	520	HOWARD D
LARCH, EMMA	ANN	520	HOWARD D
LARCH, HENRY	FRE	015	FREDERIC
LARCH, MARY J.	BAL	248	6TH WARD
LARCH, RICHARD	BAL	247	6TH WARD
LARCO, J.	BAL	166	1ST WARD
LARD, BETSEY	SOM	369	BRINKLEY
LARD, JAMES W.	DOR	375	1ST DIST
LARD, JOHN S.*	SOM	368	BRINKLEY
LARD, LEAH	SOM	391	BRINKLEY
LARD, THOMAS	SOM	466	HANGARY
LARD, WILLIAM	SOM	466	HANGARY
LARD, WILLIAMINA*	DOR	375	1ST DIST
LARDO, NATHANIEL	BAL	082	4TH WARD
LARDY, THOMAS	HAR	186	3RD DIST
LARE, MARY	FRE	272	NEW MARK
LARE, THOMAS	BAL	261	12TH WAR
LARE, WILLIAM	BAL	235	20TH WAR
LAREA, A.	BAL	166	1ST WARD
LAREMAR, LOUIZA	CAR	148	NO TWP L
LAREW, CHARLES J.	BAL	427	14TH WAR
LARF, GOLFRIED *	BAL	444	8TH WARD
LARGAN, GERRARD	BAL	385	8TH WARD
LARGE, CHRISTPHER	BAL	112	18TH WAR
LARGE, CLARISSA E.	BAL	313	12TH WAR
LARGE, JONATHAN	BAL	348	3RD WARD
LARGE, MOSES*	BAL	374	3RD WARD
LARGE, ORATHER M.	BAL	112	18TH WAR
LARGIN, JOHN	BAL	143	1ST WARD
LARGNOUSE, MARY ANN	BAL	356	13TH WAR
LARGUE, CHARLES	BAL	202	2ND WARD
LARIDERSKY, WILLIAM	BAL	288	20TH WAR
LARIDGE, HENRY	BAL	036	9TH WARD
LARIGAN, MARGARET	BAL	001	9TH WARD
LARIMORE, EDWARD G.	TAL	103	ST MICHA
LARIMORE, JSOHUA N.	TAL	071	EASTON T
LARK, AMANDA	ALL	246	CUMBERLA
LARK, JAMES	ANN	348	3RD DIST
LARK, LAWRANCE	BAL	005	EASTERN
LARK, STEPHEN	ANN	348	3RD DIST
LARK, THOMAS	BAL	017	1ST WARD
LARKEY, JAMES	BAL	059	15TH WAR
LARKIN, ALFRED F.	BAL	325	1ST DIST
LARKIN, ANDREW	BAL	114	1ST WARD
LARKIN, BERNARD	BAL	315	20TH WAR
LARKIN, CATHARINE	BAL	013	15TH WAR
LARKIN, ELIZA	BAL	001	9TH WARD
LARKIN, JACOB	BAL	204	6TH WARD
LARKIN, JAMES	ANN	324	2ND DIST
LARKIN, JOHN	ALL	056	10TH E.D
LARKIN, LAWRENCE	ALL	049	10TH E.D
LARKIN, M.	ANN	279	ANNAPOLI
LARKIN, MARKET	BAL	460	14TH WAR
LARKIN, MARY	ANN	285	ANNAPOLI
LARKIN, MARY	ANN	286	ANNAPOLI
LARKIN, MARY	ALL	072	5TH E.D.
LARKIN, MICHAL	BAL	281	7TH WARD
LARKIN, PATRICK	BAL	449	1ST DIST
LARKIN, PRISCILLA	BAL	078	10TH WAR
LARKIN, THOMAS	ALL	143	6TH E.D.
LARKIN, THOMAS	CAR	220	5TH DIST
LARKIN, TIMOTHY	BAL	283	17TH WAR
LARKIN, WILLAIM	ANN	272	ANNAPOLI
LARKIN, WILLIAM	BAL	033	4TH WARD
LARKINAS, WILLIAM	BAL	060	1ST WARD
LARKING, JOHN	BAL	171	1ST WARD
LARKINS WILLIAM H.	BAL	083	4TH WARD
LARKINS, CARVENILA M.	FRE	220	BUCKEYST
LARKINS, DENNIS	BAL	338	7TH WARD
LARKINS, ELIZA	BAL	463	14TH WAR
LARKINS, ELLEN	BAL	355	8TH WARD
LARKINS, HERLY	BAL	248	20TH WAR
LARKINS, JAMES	WAS	094	2ND SUBD
LARKINS, JANE	FRE	222	BUCKEYST
LARKINS, JANE	ANN	291	ANNAPOLI
LARKINS, JOHN	FRE	073	FREDERIC
LARKINS, JOHN	FRE	123	CREAGERS
LARKINS, JOSEPH	WOR	321	1ST E DI
LARKINS, JOSHUA	BAL	330	7TH WARD

Name	County	Page	District
LARKINS, JULIA	ANN	289	ANNAPOLI
LARKINS, MARY	BAL	010	4TH WARD
LARKINS, MARY E.	BAL	333	7TH WARD
LARKINS, R.	ANN	280	ANNAPOLI
LARKINS, RACHAEL	FRE	022	FREDERIC
LARKINS, STEPHEN	BAL	356	8TH WARD
LARKINS, WILLIAM	ANN	290	ANNAPOLI
LARKINS, WILLIAM	BAL	437	8TH WARD
LARMARE, EBENEZER*	SOM	544	TYASKIN
LARMORE, ALFRED	SOM	540	TYASKIN
LARMORE, EBENEZER	SOM	543	TYASKIN
LARMORE, EBENEZER*	SOM	544	TYASKIN
LARMORE, ELIZABETH	SOM	539	TYASKIN
LARMORE, ELLEN	SOM	539	TYASKIN
LARMORE, GEORGE	SOM	538	TYASKIN
LARMORE, GEORGE	SOM	547	TYASKIN
LARMORE, GEORGE	SOM	552	TYASKIN
LARMORE, GEORGE H.	SOM	542	TYASKIN
LARMORE, JAMES	SOM	492	SALISBUR
LARMORE, JAMES A.	SOM	531	QUANTICO
LARMORE, JAMES M.	SOM	545	TYASKIN
LARMORE, JOHN	SOM	540	TYASKIN
LARMORE, JOHN D.	SOM	541	TYASKIN
LARMORE, MARCELLUS	SOM	547	TYASKIN
LARMORE, MARGARET	SOM	540	TYASKIN
LARMORE, MARY	SOM	547	TYASKIN
LARMORE, MARY F.	SOM	493	SALISBUR
LARMORE, PRUSILLA	SOM	544	TYASKIN
LARMORE, REUBEN D.	SOM	539	TYASKIN
LARMORE, RICHARD	SOM	542	TYASKIN
LARMOUR, WILLIAM B.	BAL	047	18TH WAR
LARNAX, DAVID*	BAL	315	3RD WARD
LARNO, WILLIAM *	SOM	439	DAMES QU
LARNER, HENRY	BAL	382	8TH WARD
LAROGUE, ALEX B.	BAL	322	12TH WAR
LAROGUE, EDWARD	BAL	064	10TH WAR
LAROGUE, J. M.	BAL	074	10TH WAR
LAROLEIS, RICHARD	BAL	231	12TH WAR
LAROUNG, KITTY	ANN	314	1ST DIST
LAROUNG, MARTHA	ANN	313	1ST DIST
LAROUNG, SARAH	ANN	313	1ST DIST
LAROY, BENJAMIN	FRE	248	NEW MARK
LAROZE, CHAPPAN	BAL	144	1ST WARD
LARP, AUGUST	BAL	405	14TH WAR
LARP, CHRISTOPHER	BAL	405	14TH WAR
LARQUAY, ANN M.	BAL	213	11TH WAR
LARRABEE, EDWARD W.	BAL	052	9TH WARD
LARRABEE, EPHRAIM	BAL	055	9TH WARD
LARRABEE, WILLIAM F.	MGM	347	BERRYS D
LARRAGY, DENNIS	BAL	354	13TH WAR
LARRAGY, WILLIAM	BAL	354	13TH WAR
LARRAMORE, BRIDGET	DOR	433	1ST DIST
LARRIMORE, ANN	TAL	108	ST MICHA
LARRIMORE, ANN M.*	TAL	067	EASTON T
LARRIMORE, JAMES S.	TAL	094	ST MICHA
LARRIMORE, JOHN H.	QUE	253	5TH E DI
LARRIMORE, LUCRETIA	TAL	055	EASTON D
LARRIMORE, MARY	TAL	109	ST MICHA
LARRIMORE, MARY	ANN	310	1ST DIST
LARRIMORE, REBECCA	TAL	111	ST MICHA
LARRIMORE, ROBERT	TAL	091	ST MICHA
LARRIMORE, ROBERT T.*	TAL	067	EASTON T
LARRIMORE, SARAH	TAL	108	ST MICHA
LARRIMORE, THEODORE	QUE	252	5TH E DI
LARRIMORE, WILLIAM	TAL	105	ST MICHA
LARSEN, C.	BAL	172	1ST WARD
LARSH, CATHARINE	BAL	352	13TH WAR
LARSH, JAMES C. DR-	BAL	373	1ST DIST
LARSH, JOHN	WOR	192	8TH E DI
LARSH, SILAS M.D.	BAL	223	1ST DIST
LARSON, D.	BAL	152	1ST WARD
LARSON,P.L.	BAL	137	1ST WARD
LARTZ, RHEIM	BAL	251	12TH WAR
LARUCK, HENRY	BAL	415	14TH WAR
LARUE, ISAAC	ALL	009	3RD E.D.
LARUE, SHADRACH	ALL	009	3RD E.D.
LARVEE, ELIZA	BAL	269	20TH WAR
LARWOOD, ALBERT	QUE	176	2ND E DI
LARWOOD, ALFRED	QUE	167	2ND E DI
LARY, SAMUEL	QUE	195	3RD E DI
LASCELL, JOSEPH	BAL	220	19TH WAR
LASCELL, WILLIAM	BAL	220	19TH WAR
LASCER, FREDERICK	PRI	092	MARLBROU
LASCER, ZEDOCH	PRI	090	MARLBROU
LASE, PHILIP	CAR	386	2ND DIST
LASE, WILLIAM	FRE	261	NEW MARK
LASEER, DORINDA	PRI	091	MARLBROU
LASH, ANN	BAL	232	2ND WARD
LASH, MARIA	BAL	076	15TH WAR
LASH, WILLIAM	ALL	052	10TH E.D
LASHLEY, GEORGE	ALL	187	9TH E.D.
LASHLEY, JACOB	ALL	187	9TH E.D.
LASHLEY, ROBERT	ALL	187	9TH E.D.
LASKER, ANN	HAR	154	3RD DIST
LASKER, ELIZA	ANN	438	HOWARD D
LASKEY, WILLER	BAL	220	17TH WAR
LASLEY, GEORGE	CEC	001	ELKTON 3
LASPAW, JAMES	BAL	035	18TH WAR
LASSAN, JAMES	CEC	057	1ST E DI
LASSCER, J.T.	PRI	052	AQUASCO
LASSELL, MARY A.	KEN	221	2ND DIST
LASSER, JOHN W.	PRI	059	NOTTINGH
LASSEY, J. H.	BAL	139	19TH WAR
LASSIA, LOUIS	BAL	180	2ND WARD
LASSITER, CHARLES	BAL	199	19TH WAR
LASSUM, EDWARD	BAL	200	5TH DIST
LAST, RICHARD	ALL	073	5TH E.D.
LASTER, NACKEY	BAL	086	18TH WAR
LATAMCN, ROBERT	BAL	117	1ST WARD
LATCH, CATHARINE	BAL	320	1ST DIST
LATCHEL, MARY C.*	TAL	048	EASTON T
LATCHENO, SETH	WOR	279	BERLIN 1
LATCHERSON, ELEANOR	BAL	032	15TH WAR
LATCHFORD, FRANCIS	ANN	440	HOWARD D
LATCHFORD, GEORGE	BAL	313	1ST DIST
LATCHFORD, GEORGE	ANN	391	4TH DIST
LATCHFORD, JOHN	ANN	430	HOWARD D
LATCHFORD, JOHN	BAL	445	1ST DIST
LATCHFORD, JOHN	PRI	038	VANSVILL
LATCHFORD, JOHN C.	PRI	038	VANSVILL
LATCHFORD, MARGARET A.	ANN	431	HOWARD D
LATCHFORD, PAT	ANN	431	HOWARD D
LATCHUM, JOSEPH	WOR	242	1ST CENS
LATCHUM, MARY K.	SOM	414	DUBLIN D
LATE, CATHERINE	FRE	113	CREAGERS
LATE, GEORGE	FRE	113	CREAGERS
LATE, JOHN D.	FRE	222	BUCKEYST
LATE, JONATHAN	WAS	164	HAGERSTO
LATE, MARIA	FRE	042	FREDERIC
LATELL, WILLIAM	BAL	468	14TH WAR
LATEN, ERE	BAL	196	2ND WARD
LATER, JAMES*	BAL	079	4TH WARD
LATHAM, ANN	CAR	369	9TH DIST
LATHAM, EDWARD	BAL	415	3RD WARD
LATHAM, ROBERT	FRE	022	FREDERIC
LATHAM, ROSANA	BAL	084	4TH WARD
LATHAM, SARAH R.	BAL	415	3RD WARD
LATHBERRY, WILLIAM	WOR	242	1ST CENS
LATHCUM, MATILDAY	WOR	249	1ST CENS
LATHE, ELY	BAL	231	17TH WAR
LATHNAN, MARY	ALL	225	CUMBERLA
LATHUM, GEORE W.	ST	259	3RD E DI
LATHUM, GEORGE W.	ST	263	3RD E DI
LATHUM, HENRY E.	ST	259	3RD E DI
LATHUM, JAMES	ST	263	3RD E DI
LATHUM, MATTHEW	ST	259	3RD E DI
LATHUM, THOMAS W.	ST	259	3RD E DI
LATHUM, ZACHARIAH	ST	263	3RD E DI
LATIMER, BENJAMIN C.	BAL	291	7TH WARD
LATIMER, C. W.	BAL	157	1ST WARD
LATIMER, ELIZABETH	BAL	103	10TH WAR
LATIMER, JAMES B.	BAL	057	10TH WAR
LATIMER, JOHN M. S.	CHA	273	ALLENS F
LATIMER, R. B.	BAL	470	14TH WAR
LATIMER, R. W.	BAL	470	14TH WAR
LATIMER, WILLIAM	BAL	377	13TH WAR
LATIMORE, JANE H.	PRI	115	PISCATAW
LATIMORE, JOSEPH T.	PRI	104	PISCATAW
LATIMORE, R.B.	PRI	114	PISCATAW
LATIN, PLUMMER	ANN	446	HOWARD D
LATINER, MARY	BAL	127	18TH WAR
LATLEBERRY, ARTHUR	WOR	313	2ND E DI
LATON, SAMUEL	BAL	289	20TH WAR
LATOR, ALBERT	BAL	432	14TH WAR
LATOURNER, PETER G.	BAL	133	1ST WARD
LATRIE, PLUMER	ANN	397	8TH DIST
LATROBE, BENJAMIN H.	BAL	157	11TH WAR
LATROBE, J. H. B.	ANN	424	HOWARD D
LATROBE, JOHN H. B.	BAL	099	10TH WAR
LATSHIL, JOHN*	TAL	038	EASTON D
LATTER, EMORY	BAL	120	2ND DIST
LATTER, REBECCA	BAL	302	3RD WARD
LATTERFIELD, MARY	BAL	344	13TH WAR
LATTIER, WILLIAM	BAL	134	5TH WARD
LATTIN, WILLAIM	ANN	445	HOWARD D
LATTIRS, JACOB	BAL	150	19TH WAR
LATTOURRETTA, JOHN	CEC	101	4TH E DI
LATTY, JOHN J.	BAL	043	4TH WARD
LATTY, JOSEPH*	BAL	006	4TH WARD
LATTY, MARGARET	BAL	253	6TH WARD
LATUR, JOSEPH	BAL	068	4TH WARD
LATURER, WESLEY	BAL	128	5TH WARD
LATURNAN, JOHN B.	BAL	012	1ST WARD
LAUB, CATHERINE	MGM	392	ROCKERLE
LAUB, HENRY C.	FRE	400	JEFFERSO
LAUBLEBAUGH, MARTHA B. *	BAL	062	18TH WAR
LAUDALE, THOMAS *	BAL	062	18TH WAR
LAUDAMON, GEORGE	CAR	260	3RD DIST
LAUDANSLEIGR, ADAM	BAL	231	6TH WARD
LAUDASLAGER, GEORGE	BAL	460	1ST DIST
LAUDDER, SAMUEL	HAR	165	3RD DIST
LAUDE, JOSEPH	ALL	056	10TH E.D
LAUDENSLAGER, ANN	BAL	352	1ST DIST
LAUDENSLAGER, PEGGY	BAL	236	1ST DIST
LAUDER, CHARLES	BAL	278	7TH WARD
LAUDER, FLORENCENE *	BAL	223	6TH WARD
LAUDER, JAMES	BAL	462	1ST DIST
LAUDIMAN, JAMES	BAL	289	3RD WARD
LAUDIMER, ROBERT	BAL	382	3RD WARD
LAUDNER, JOHN	BAL	201	2ND WARD
LAUER, HENRY	BAL	063	15TH WAR
LAUER, IGNATIUS	BAL	063	15TH WAR
LAUERS, BARBARA	BAL	328	1ST DIST
LAUFLIN, DANIEL	HAR	120	2ND DIST
LAUFTUN, CATHARINE	BAL	215	11TH WAR
LAUGHER, JOHN S.	HAR	102	2ND DIST
LAUGHLAN, CHARLES	BAL	367	8TH WARD
LAUGHLAN, JAMES	BAL	361	8TH WARD
LAUGHLAN, JOHN	BAL	430	8TH WARD
LAUGHLAN, JOHN O.	BAL	364	8TH WARD
LAUGHLIN, ANNA	ANN	303	1ST DIST
LAUGHLIN, DAVID	BAL	200	19TH WAR
LAUGHLIN, EDWARD M.	BAL	367	8TH WARD
LAUGHLIN, EDWARD O.	BAL	173	11TH WAR
LAUGHLIN, ELIZABETH	BAL	200	19TH WAR
LAUGHLIN, IFRIS	BAL	200	19TH WAR
LAUGHLIN, JAMES	HAR	120	2ND DIST
LAUGHLIN, JOHN	HAR	133	2ND DIST
LAUGHLIN, JOHN	BAL	444	1ST DIST
LAUGHLIN, LOUISA	ANN	315	1ST DIST
LAUGHLIN, MARGARET J.	BAL	177	16TH WAR
LAUGHLIN, MARY	ANN	325	2ND DIST
LAUGHLIN, MARY E.	BAL	201	19TH WAR
LAUGHLIN, MR. O.	BAL	139	5TH WARD
LAUGHLIN, R.	ANN	269	ANNAPOLI
LAUGHLIN, RICHARD	HAR	133	2ND DIST
LAUGHLIN, ROBERT B.	BAL	160	11TH WAR
LAUGHLIN, SABINA	BAL	218	12TH WAR
LAUGHLIN, WILLIAM	HAR	127	2ND DIST
LAUGHLIN, WILLIAM	BAL	200	19TH WAR
LAUGHLIN, WILLIAM L.	HAR	143	2ND DIST
LAUGHMAN, FREDERICK	BAL	378	1ST DIST
LAUGHNA, PATRICK	BAL	407	1ST DIST
LAUGHRAN, PATRICK	ANN	460	HOWARD D
LAUGHRIDGE, WILLIAM	WAS	090	2ND SUBD
LAUGHTON, RACHEL	BAL	093	10TH WAR
LAUHFORD, ARTHUR	WOR	193	8TH E DI
LAUK, GEORGE	WOR	223	4TH E DI
LAUKFORD, WILLIAM	BAL	237	2ND WARD
LAUMER, JAMES	DOR	369	3RD DIVI
LAUMING, ANN	BAL	150	16TH WAR
LAUMOR, WILLIAM*	DOR	404	1ST DIST
LAUNAES, CATHARINE *	BAL	352	13TH WAR
LAUNDANER, GEORGE	BAL	171	19TH WAR
LAUNDERBAUGH, FREDERICK	BAL	398	14TH WAR
LAUNEY, HANNAH J.	BAL	407	14TH WAR
LAUNEY, IGNATIUS	ST	258	3RD E DI
LAUNEY, JOHN F.	ST	258	3RD E DI
LAUNEY, MARY E.	ST	259	3RD E DI
LAUNS, WILLIAM	BAL	011	1ST WARD
LAUR, LOUISA	BAL	256	12TH WAR
LAUREL, ANMARIA	ANN	287	ANNAPOLI
LAUREL, WILLIAM	CEC	078	NORTHEAS
LAUREMAN, PETER G. *	BAL	316	12TH WAR
LAURENCE, ANN L.	BAL	050	4TH WARD
LAURENCE, ANN-BLACK	ST	305	2ND E DI
LAURENCE, ANN-MULATTO	ST	306	1ST E DI
LAURENCE, CATHERINE	BAL	301	3RD WARD
LAURENCE, ELIZABETH	ST	318	4TH E DI
LAURENCE, FRANCES	ANN	436	HOWARD D
LAURENCE, GILBERT	ALL	203	CUMBERLA
LAURENCE, HEALON-MULATTO	ST	306	1ST E DI
LAURENCE, HENRY	CAR	283	7TH DIST
LAURENCE, ISAIAH	CEC	154	PORT DUP
LAURENCE, JAMES-MULATTO	ST	307	1ST E DI
LAURENCE, JOHN	ST	319	4TH E DI
LAURENCE, JOHN	CHA	257	MIDDLETO
LAURENCE, JOHN F.	ST	317	4TH E DI
LAURENCE, JOHN SR.	ST	319	4TH E DI
LAURENCE, MARYAN	BAL	360	3RD WARD
LAURENCE, REBECCA-BLACK	ST	294	2ND E DI
LAURENCE, UPTON	ALL	173	7TH E.D.
LAURENCE, WILLIAM	BAL	153	11TH WAR
LAURENSON, FRANCIS B.	BAL	413	1ST DIST
LAURENSON, JAMES P.	BAL	064	10TH WAR
LAURENSON, SOPHIA	BAL	010	4TH WARD
LAURISON, WILILAM W.	BAL	455	14TH WAR
LAUS, LUKE	WOR	244	1ST CENS
LAUSBACKER, CRISTIAN	BAL	132	18TH WAR
LAUSDALE, HARRY A.	PRI	036	VANSVILL
LAUSDALE, KITTY A.	ANN	510	HOWARD D
LAUSDALE, NANCY	ANN	510	HOWARD D
LAUSH, CONRAD	CAR	404	2ND DIST
LAUSON, JOHN B.	CHA	234	HILLTOP
LAUSON, LAURT *	BAL	317	12TH WAR
LAUSTER, JOHN D.	BAL	308	7TH WARD
LAUVER, MARY	WAS	002	WILLIAMS
LAUVER, SAMUEL A.	CAR	190	4TH DIST
LAUVILL, MARGARET	BAL	218	17TH WAR
LAUVRE, ELLIOTT J.	WAS	252	1ST DIST
LAVAY, JOSEPHINE	BAL	121	16TH WAR
LAVEILLE, JAMES	CAL	011	1ST DIST
LAVELL, ELLEN	BAL	130	5TH WARD
LAVELL, JOHN	BAL	164	19TH WAR
LAVELLE, ANTHONY	ALL	047	10TH E.D
LAVELLE, ELLEN	BAL	073	2ND DIST
LAVELLE, PATRICK	ALL	047	10TH E.D
LAVELY, WILLIAM P.	WAS	151	HAGERSTO
LAVEN, JAMES	CEC	065	1ST E DI
LAVENDER, BENJAMIN A.	BAL	341	13TH WAR
LAVENDER, GEORGE	BAL	099	18TH WAR
LAVENTINE, MANUEL	BAL	007	1ST WARD
LAVIELLE, URIAH	CAL	003	1ST DIST
LAVILLE, LEON	BAL	044	4TH WARD
LAVILLE, MARY	BAL	072	15TH WAR
LAVILLE, WILLIAM	BAL	465	14TH WAR
LAVIN, ANNA	BAL	312	12TH WAR
LAVINER, MARY E.	BAL	061	1ST WARD
LAVINES, MARGARET	BAL	114	11TH WAR
LAVIRE, BIDDY	BAL	042	4TH WARD
LAVIS, LOUISA*	DOR	444	1ST DIST
LAVIT, SARAH *	ANN	411	8TH DIST
LAVORY, THOMAS V.	BAL	396	14TH WAR
LAVRA, ANN	BAL	388	1ST DIST
LAW, ANN W. *	ANN	417	HOWARD D
LAW, BARRON DE. *	BAL	074	18TH WAR
LAW, JAMES	ANN	280	ANNAPOLI
LAW, JAMES	BAL	337	7TH WARD
LAW, JOHN*	TAL	026	EASTON D
LAW, ROBERT BROWN *	BAL	406	1ST DIST
LAW, RUTH	BAL	227	1ST DIST
LAW, SARAH F.	BAL	068	18TH WAR
LAWCO, JOHN	BAL	012	2ND DIST
LAWDENSLAGER, EVE	CAR	178	8TH DIST
LAWDENSLAGER, PHILIP	CAR	182	8TH DIST
LAWDER, ELIZABETH	BAL	102	1ST WARD
LAWDER, ELIZABETH A.	BAL	191	6TH WARD
LAWDER, JOHN	BAL	102	1ST WARD
LAWEING, WILLIAM *	BAL	267	1ST DIST
LAWEMON, EDWARD *	QUE	238	5TH E DI
LAWENSON, MARGARITT	BAL	216	11TH WAR
LAWERSON, KESIAH	CEC	130	6TH E DI
LAWES, JESSE	BAL	267	1ST DIST
LAWES, JOHN F.*	BAL	311	3RD WARD
LAWEY, THOMAS*	BAL	110	10TH WAR
LAWFEY, LEWIS	BAL	441	8TH WARD
LAWFULL, JAMES	BAL	172	1ST WARD
LAWIHARDT, MARY *	BAL	133	18TH WAR
LAWKINS, MARY	BAL	353	7TH WARD
LAWLER, JAMES	BAL	165	1ST WARD
LAWLER, JAMES	BAL	134	18TH WAR
LAWLER, JOHN	BAL	023	18TH WAR
LAWLER, LAWRENCE*	BAL	387	3RD WARD
LAWLESS, JOHN	CEC	011	ELKTON 3
LAWMAN, CHARLES	MGM	423	MEDLEY 3
LAWMAN, SARH	CAR	226	5TH DIST
LAWN, CHRISTOPHER	BAL	090	10TH WAR
LAWN, JAMES J.	BAL	319	20TH WAR
LAWN, WILLIAM	WAS	066	2ND SUBD
LAWOSN, JAMES D.	FRE	277	NEW MARK
LAWOTN, ELIZABETH	ANN	359	3RD DIST
LAWPON, ANTHONY	WAS	028	2ND SUBD
LAWRANCE, CATHARINE	BAL	349	7TH WARD
LAWRANCE, ISA	BAL	024	18TH WAR
LAWRANCE, PATRICK	BAL	025	18TH WAR
LAWRANCE, RICHARD	BAL	352	7TH WARD
LAWRASON, HANNAH	BAL	090	15TH WAR
LAWRENCE, ANN	BAL	250	6TH WARD
LAWRENCE, ANN M.	TAL	095	ST MICHA
LAWRENCE, CATHARINE M.	WAS	136	HAGERSTO
LAWRENCE, CORNELIUS	CEC	176	7TH E DI
LAWRENCE, DAVID H.	BAL	283	2ND WARD
LAWRENCE, ELISABETH	ANN	343	3RD DIST
LAWRENCE, ELIZABETH	WAS	137	HAGERSTO
LAWRENCE, ELIZABETH	WAS	136	HAGERSTO
LAWRENCE, ELLEN	BAL	061	15TH WAR
LAWRENCE, EMILY A.	KEN	213	2ND DIST
LAWRENCE, ESTHER	SOM	435	PRINCESS
LAWRENCE, F.	BAL	164	1ST WARD
LAWRENCE, FLORENCE	HAR	174	3RD DIST
LAWRENCE, FRANCIS L.	BAL	250	12TH WAR
LAWRENCE, GEORGE	FRE	167	EMMITTSB
LAWRENCE, GEORGE W.	CAL	049	3RD DIST
LAWRENCE, HARKLES	BAL	020	1ST WARD
LAWRENCE, HELLEN F.	BAL	284	2ND WARD
LAWRENCE, HENRY	BAL	169	6TH WARD
LAWRENCE, HENRY	FRE	047	FREDERIC
LAWRENCE, IRA	BAL	172	19TH WAR
LAWRENCE, JACOB	FRE	169	5TH E DI
LAWRENCE, JACOB	WAS	250	1ST DIST
LAWRENCE, JAMES	MGM	418	MEDLEY 3
LAWRENCE, JEFFERSON	KEN	228	2ND DIST
LAWRENCE, JESSE	BAL	024	18TH WAR
LAWRENCE, JOHN	HAR	034	1ST DIST
LAWRENCE, JOHN	BAL	397	14TH WAR
LAWRENCE, JOHN	KEN	213	2ND DIST
LAWRENCE, JOHN	BAL	172	1ST WARD
LAWRENCE, JOHN	BAL	300	3RD WARD
LAWRENCE, JOHN H.	TAL	108	ST MICHA
LAWRENCE, JOHN M.	BAL	329	3RD WARD

LAWRENCE, JOHN M. BAL 119 1ST WARD
LAWRENCE, JOSEPH BAL 177 2ND DIST
LAWRENCE, LEONARD PRI 103 SPALDING
LAWRENCE, LOUISA BAL 251 12TH WAR
LAWRENCE, MARY C. BAL 209 19TH WAR
LAWRENCE, MARY J. FRE 065 FREDERIC
LAWRENCE, MARY L. BAL 341 13TH WAR
LAWRENCE, MATHEW TAL 104 ST MICHA
LAWRENCE, PURNELL SOM 526 QUANTICO
LAWRENCE, RICHARD TAL 112 ST MICHA
LAWRENCE, RICHARD BAL 041 1ST WARD
LAWRENCE, RICHARD BAL 240 6TH WARD
LAWRENCE, RICHARD ALL 236 CUMBERLA
LAWRENCE, RICHARC T. PRI 005 BLADENSB
LAWRENCE, SAMUEL BAL 117 1ST WARD
LAWRENCE, SARAH WAS 122 HAGERSTO
LAWRENCE, SARAH M. FRE 439 8TH E DI
LAWRENCE, STEPHENS FRE 439 8TH E DI
LAWRENCE, THOMAS J. ANN 400 8TH DIST
LAWRENCE, VALENTINE BAL 205 17TH WAR
LAWRENCE, WILLAIM BAL 158 1ST WARD
LAWRENCE, WILLIAM ANN 435 HOWARD D
LAWRENCE, WILLIAM BAL 108 18TH WAR
LAWRENCE, WILLIAM KEN 300 3RD DIST
LAWRENCE, WILLIAM GEORGE BAL 258 17TH WAR
LAWRENCE, WILLIAM M. BAL 064 4TH WARD
LAWRENCESON, WILLIAM L. BAL 145 1ST WARD
LAWRENE, FRANCIS BAL 251 12TH WAR
LAWRENSON, ELIZA BAL 017 15TH WAR
LAWRENSON, J. BAL 151 1ST WARD
LAWRY, JOHN ANN 350 3RD DIST
LAWS, ALEXANDER CEC 062 1ST E DI
LAWS, AMOS WOR 244 1ST CENS
LAWS, ELIJAH WOR 167 6TH E DI
LAWS, ELIZABETH A. WOR 168 6TH E DI
LAWS, EVANS DOR 388 1ST DIST
LAWS, GEORGE SOM 470 TRAPPE D
LAWS, GILBERT WOR 334 1ST E DI
LAWS, HANNAH-BLACK WOR 329 1ST E DI
LAWS, JAMES CAR 107 NO TWP L
LAWS, JOHN SOM 485 TRAPP DI
LAWS, PRICELLA SOM 485 TRAPP DI
LAWS, WILLIAM DOR 467 1ST DIST
LAWS, WILLIAM WOR 168 6TH E DI
LAWS, WIULLIAM WOR 169 6TH E DI
LAWSEN, LEVIN BAL 163 1ST WARD
LAWSON, ANN BAL 460 14TH WAR
LAWSON, BEN PRI 067 NOTTINGH
LAWSON, BENNET R. BAL 388 3RD WARD
LAWSON, CATHARINE CAR 361 9TH DIST
LAWSON, CATHARINE-BLACK FRE 438 8TH E DI
LAWSON, DAVID BAL 157 11TH WAR
LAWSON, EDWARD BAL 200 5TH DIST
LAWSON, ELIZA-MULATTO FRE 438 8TH E DI
LAWSON, ELIZABETH CHA 234 HILLTOP
LAWSON, FRANK SOM 383 BRINKLEY
LAWSON, GABRIEL L. C. MGM 436 CLARKSTR
LAWSON, GABRIEL T. FRE 277 NEW MARK
LAWSON, HANNAH* SOM 381 BRINKLEY
LAWSON, HARIET SOM 376 BRINKLEY
LAWSON, ISAAC SOM 376 BRINKLEY
LAWSON, ISAAC SOM 377 BRINKLEY
LAWSON, ISAAC SOM 381 BRINKLEY
LAWSON, JACOB BAL 204 11TH WAR
LAWSON, JAMES BAL 169 1ST WARD
LAWSON, JAMES PRI 064 NOTTINGH
LAWSON, JAMES BAL 260 20TH WAR
LAWSON, JAMES BAL 303 20TH WAR
LAWSON, JAMES JR. SOM 377 BRINKLEY
LAWSON, JAMES JR. SOM 378 BRINKLEY
LAWSON, JAMES U. MGM 435 CLARKSTR
LAWSON, JESSE FRE 289 WOODSBOR
LAWSON, JHN S. FRE 256 NEW MARK
LAWSON, JOHN SOM 380 BRINKLEY
LAWSON, JOHN SOM 383 BRINKLEY
LAWSON, JOHN T. SOM 380 BRINKLEY
LAWSON, LAWRASON D.* SOM 381 BRINKLEY
LAWSON, LEVE ANN FRE 276 NEW MARK
LAWSON, MARIAH SOM 377 BRINKLEY
LAWSON, MARY MGM 440 CLARKSTR
LAWSON, MATILDA HAR 132 2ND DIST
LAWSON, NANCY SOM 378 BRINKLEY
LAWSON, NANCY SOM 375 BRINKLEY
LAWSON, OLIVER BAL 404 3RD WARD
LAWSON, PRISCILLA BAL 455 1ST DIST
LAWSON, RICHARD CAR 156 NO TWP L
LAWSON, ROBERT BAL 134 11TH WAR
LAWSON, ROBERT BAL 283 12TH WAR
LAWSON, SAMUEL DOR 438 1ST DIST
LAWSON, SANDY BAL 455 1ST DIST
LAWSON, STEPHEN BAL 070 10TH WAR
LAWSON, THOMAS BAL 444 8TH WARD
LAWSON, THOMAS BAL 023 2ND DIST
LAWSON, THOMAS CAR 340 6TH DIST
LAWSON, TRAVES SOM 377 BRINKLEY
LAWSON, WILLAIM BAL 108 5TH WARD
LAWSON, WILLIAM SOM 376 BRINKLEY
LAWSON, WILLIAM SOM 375 BRINKLEY
LAWSON, WILLIAM SOM 381 BRINKLEY
LAWSON, WILLIAM-BLACK FRE 231 BUCKEYST
LAWSON,ABRAHAM FRE 205 BUCKEYST
LAWSON,LYDIA-BLACK FRE 451 8TH E DI
LAWTER, WILHELMINA BAL 215 6TH WARD
LAWTON, CAROLINE BAL 087 15TH WAR
LAWTON, JOHN BAL 341 1ST DIST
LAWTON, JOHN BAL 158 19TH WAR
LAWTON, JOHN W. BAL 090 15TH WAR
LAWTON, REBECCA ANN 359 3RD DIST
LAWTON, RICHARD BAL 244 17TH WAR
LAWTON, SARAH A. ANN 359 3RD DIST
LAWTON, WILLIAM BAL 394 1ST DIST
LAWUM, JOHN * WAS 060 2ND SUBD
LAWYER, GEORGE BAL 017 18TH WAR
LAWYER, IRA B. CAR 350 6TH DIST
LAWYER, MARY E. BAL 085 4TH WARD
LAX, ADY* BAL 069 4TH WARD
LAX, CHARLES BAL 381 8TH WARD
LAX, JOSEPH BAL 069 4TH WARD
LAX, THEODORE* BAL 069 4TH WARD
LAXSELL, MARTHA * FRE 276 NEW MARK
LAY, ANN M. BAL 212 11TH WAR
LAY, JOHN BAL 416 14TH WAR
LAYDEN, JAEMS BAL 263 2ND WARD
LAYER, CATHARINE BAL 015 1ST WARD
LAYER, CHRISTIAN BAL 219 17TH WAR
LAYER, DAVID BAL 249 17TH WAR
LAYFIELD, ABAGIAL K. WOR 211 4TH E DI
LAYFIELD, AMANDA SOM 482 TRAPP DI
LAYFIELD, CHARLOTTE WOR 196 8TH E DI
LAYFIELD, EDWARD SOM 468 TRAPPE D

LAYFIELD, ELIZABETH SOM 538 TYASKIN
LAYFIELD, EPHRAIM W. WOR 225 4TH E DI
LAYFIELD, GEORGE SOM 548 TYASKIN
LAYFIELD, GEORGE BAL 043 1ST WARD
LAYFIELD, GEORGE B. WOR 226 4TH E DI
LAYFIELD, GEORGE W. SOM 417 PRINCESS
LAYFIELD, ISAAC WOR 215 4TH E DI
LAYFIELD, ISAAC BAL 269 7TH WARD
LAYFIELD, JAMES WOR 196 8TH E DI
LAYFIELD, JAMES SOM 467 HANGARY
LAYFIELD, JOHN SOM 468 TRAPPE D
LAYFIELD, JOHN SOM 411 DUBLIN D
LAYFIELD, JOHN* SOM 361 BRINKLEY
LAYFIELD, LEVIN SOM 421 PRINCESS
LAYFIELD, NANCY* SOM 360 BRINKLEY
LAYFIELD, PO.LY SOM 417 PRINCESS
LAYFIELD, POLLY SOM 467 HANGARY
LAYFIELD, RICHARD SOM 490 SALISBUR
LAYFIELD, ROBERT WOR 236 6TH E DI
LAYFIELD, SALLY SOM 403 BRINKLEY
LAYFIELD, SOLOMON SOM 460 HANGARY
LAYFIELD, THOMAS SOM 492 SALISBUR
LAYFIELD, WILLIAM HAR 180 3RD DIST
LAYFIELD, WILLIAM W. WOR 232 6TH E DI
LAYFIELD, WILLIAM W. TAL 080 ST MICHA
LAYHAN, LYDIA CAR 387 2ND DIST
LAYHAY, ELIZABETH BAL 112 1ST WARD
LAYHUNT, PATRICK BAL 173 11TH WAR
LAYMAN, EDWARD BAL 102 1ST WARD
LAYMAN, GEORGE FRE 105 CREAGERS
LAYMAN, JACOB FRE 206 BUCKEYST
LAYMAN, JACOB FRE 189 5TH E DI
LAYMAN, JOSEPH BAL 320 20TH WAR
LAYMAN, LACE ANN 320 2ND DIST
LAYMAN, ROBERT BAL 210 17TH WAR
LAYMAN, SUSAN BAL 143 11TH WAR
LAYMAN, THOAMS BAL 288 20TH WAR
LAYMAN, TOON ALL 086 5TH E.D.
LAYMARE, THOMAS N. KEN 287 3RD DIST
LAYMON, BEN PRI 084 QUEEN AN
LAYMON, HENRY PRI 098 SPALDING
LAYPOLE, JOHN H. FRE 378 PETERSVI
LAYSON, ELIJAH HAR 052 1ST DIST
LAYTERBACK, CHARLES BAL 337 13TH WAR
LAYTON, ELIZABETH WOR 248 1ST CENS
LAYTON, JAMES DOR 449 1ST DIST
LAYTON, JOHN MGM 441 CLARKSTR
LAYTON, JOHN MGM 323 CRACKLIN
LAYTON, JOHN R. MGM 439 CLARKSTR
LAYTON, JOSIAH* DOR 441 1ST DIST
LAYTON, LAURA S. TAL 066 EASTON T
LAYTON, MARY TAL 082 ST MICHA
LAYTON, MARY A. MGM 323 CRACKLIN
LAYTON, NICHOLAS HAR 111 2ND DIST
LAYTON, TUABALEN CAR 114 NO TWP L
LAYTON, WILLIAM DOR 441 1ST DIST
LAYTON, WILLIAM WOR 219 4TH E DI
LAYTON, WILLIAM BAL 119 1ST WARD
LAYTON, WILLIAM BAL 170 1ST WARD
LAYTON, WILLIAM BAL 172 1ST WARD
LAZENBY, JAMES T. MGM 365 BERRYS D
LAZENBY, JOHN BAL 029 9TH WARD
LAZENBY, MARY MGM 365 BERRYS D
LAZIER, AZA ALL 164 6TH E.D.
LAZIER, JOHN ALL 173 7TH E.D.
LAZIER, WILLIAM ALL 164 6TH E.D.
LAZTON, SAMUEL WOR 250 1ST CENS
LBOWDAN, E. BAL 157 1ST WARD
LCASER, GEORGE FRE 096 FREDERIC
LCATHERMAN, JACOB FRE 367 CATOCTIN
LCHELS, A. BAL 449 8TH WARD
LE BAUGH, CHARLES A. BAL 310 3RD WARD
LE BOHN, CHARLES BAL 141 19TH WAR
LE BON, CHARLES* BAL 083 10TH WAR
LE BOU, CHARLES* BAL 083 10TH WAR
LE BROU, JOSHUA* BAL 368 3RD WARD
LE COMPT, DAVID BAL 344 3RD WARD
LE COMPTE, ADELINE M. DOR 433 1ST DIST
LE COMPTE, ALFRED DOR 374 1ST DIST
LE COMPTE, ANTHONY* DOR 426 1ST DIST
LE COMPTE, CHARLES DOR 431 1ST DIST
LE COMPTE, CHARLES DOR 446 1ST DIST
LE COMPTE, DELILA BAL 017 4TH WARD
LE COMPTE, EDWARD W. DOR 375 1ST DIST
LE COMPTE, EMILY DOR 375 1ST DIST
LE COMPTE, EUGENE D. DOR 375 1ST DIST
LE COMPTE, FLORENCE E. DOR 459 1ST DIST
LE COMPTE, GEORGE DOR 441 1ST DIST
LE COMPTE, HARISCN DOR 419 1ST DIST
LE COMPTE, HENRY M. T. DOR 375 1ST DIST
LE COMPTE, J.* DOR 412 1ST DIST
LE COMPTE, JAMES DOR 434 1ST DIST
LE COMPTE, JAMES DOR 383 1ST DIST
LE COMPTE, JOAB DOR 402 1ST DIST
LE COMPTE, JOHN W. DOR 431 1ST DIST
LE COMPTE, JOSEPH DOR 428 1ST DIST
LE COMPTE, LEAH DOR 422 1ST DIST
LE COMPTE, MARGARET E. DOR 375 1ST DIST
LE COMPTE, MARY DOR 451 1ST DIST
LE COMPTE, MARY A. DOR 450 1ST DIST
LE COMPTE, MARY J. BAL 313 3RD WARD
LE COMPTE, NEHEMIAH DOR 391 1ST DIST
LE COMPTE, PETER G. DOR 408 1ST DIST
LE COMPTE, REBECCA DOR 448 1ST DIST
LE COMPTE, SAMEL DOR 394 1ST DIST
LE COMPTE, SAMUEL W. DOR 379 1ST DIST
LE COMPTE, SARAH DOR 438 1ST DIST
LE COMPTE, SOLOMON DOR 395 1ST DIST
LE COMPTE, THOMAS DOR 386 1ST DIST
LE COMPTE, THOMAS DOR 386 1ST DIST
LE COMPTE, THOMAS DOR 432 1ST DIST
LE COMPTE, WILLIAM G. DOR 386 1ST DIST
LE COMPTE, WILLIAM W. DOR 381 1ST DIST
LE COMPTEE, SAMUEL D. DOR 374 1ST DIST
LE DUANE, CATHERINE PRI 028 VANSVILL
LE MERCHANT, JOSEPH * ANN 417 HOWARD D
LEA, ANN E. ST 314 1ST E DI
LEA, CALEB BAL 316 12TH WAR
LEA, EDWARD MGM 348 BERRYS D
LEA, ELIZABETH E. MGM 331 CRACKLIN
LEA, THOMAS MGM 338 CRACKLIN
LEABREESE, RICHARD* BAL 403 3RD WARD
LEABRY, LEVIA* BAL 349 3RD WARD
LEACH, BENJAMIN BAL 253 6TH WARD
LEACH, C. BAL 152 1ST WARD
LEACH, C. L. BAL 059 18TH WAR
LEACH, DAVID WAS 126 2ND DIST
LEACH, EDWARD BAL 282 2ND WARD
LEACH, ELEANOR ST 284 2ND E DI
LEACH, ELIAS WAS 131 2ND DIST

LEACH, GEORGE SOM 359 BRINKLEY
LEACH, GEORGE * TAL 091 ST MICHA
LEACH, GEORGE P. ST 288 2ND E DI
LEACH, GEORGE W. ST 288 2ND E DI
LEACH, HANAH BAL 276 7TH WARD
LEACH, HARRIET BAL 011 1ST WARD
LEACH, JACOB WAS 127 2ND DIST
LEACH, JAMES BAL 213 6TH DIST
LEACH, JAMES BAL 442 8TH WARD
LEACH, JAMES BAL 393 14TH WAR
LEACH, JAMES H. BAL 394 14TH WAR
LEACH, JANE BAL 026 2ND DIST
LEACH, JOHN BAL 039 9TH WARD
LEACH, JOHN ST 259 3RD E DI
LEACH, JOHN E. ST 274 3RD E DI
LEACH, JOSEPH BAL 159 1ST WARD
LEACH, JOSEPH BAL 063 1ST WARD
LEACH, MARY-BLACK ST 337 4TH E DI
LEACH, NANCY SOM 354 BRINKLEY
LEACH, RACHEL ANN 503 HOWARD D
LEACH, RACHEL W. ANN 498 HOWARD D
LEACH, REBECCA ST 277 3RD E DI
LEACH, SAMUEL WAS 155 2ND DIST
LEACH, SARAH ST 309 1ST E DI
LEACH, SARAH HAR 192 3RD DIST
LEACH, SOPHIA BAL 421 3RD WARD
LEACH, THOMAS ANN 412 HOWARD D
LEACH, WILLIAM BAL 045 9TH WARD
LEACH, WILLIAM BAL 441 8TH WARD
LEACH, WILLIAM T. ST 275 3RD E DI
LEACHE, JESSE BAL 374 13TH WAR
LEADDY, ELIZABETH BAL 114 18TH WAR
LEADINGHAM, CHRISTINA MGM 363 BERRYS D
LEADMAN, GEORGE-BLACK CAR 133 NO TWP L
LEADMAN, GEORGE-BLACK CAR 134 NO TWP L
LEADMAN, IGNATICLS CAR 106 NO TWP L
LEAENHAM, SHADEIST * TAL 112 ST MICHA
LEAF, HENRY BAL 243 1ST DIST
LEAF, JOHN BAL 418 1ST DIST
LEAF, JOHN H. BAL 419 1ST DIST
LEAF, JOSEPH BAL 421 1ST DIST
LEAF, MATILDA BAL 241 1ST DIST
LEAF, SAMUEL H. BAL 127 18TH WAR
LEAGER, BENEDICK HAR 206 3RD DIST
LEAGER, CHARLES H. HAR 159 3RD DIST
LEAGER, JAMES HAR 193 3RD DIST
LEAGER, MARGARET HAR 206 3RD DIST
LEAGER, SILLITIAN HAR 204 3RD DIST
LEAGHTY, WILLIAM ALL 022 2ND E.D.
LEAGUE, ABRAHAM BAL 414 3RD WARD
LEAGUE, CAROLINE BAL 074 18TH WAR
LEAGUE, CHARLES BAL 414 3RD WARD
LEAGUE, COLUMBUS W. BAL 388 8TH WARD
LEAGUE, COLUMBUS BAL 256 17TH WAR
LEAGUE, ELIZABETH BAL 058 4TH WARD
LEAGUE, EMILY L. BAL 035 4TH WARD
LEAGUE, JAMES BAL 163 6TH WARD
LEAGUE, JOSEPH BAL 197 6TH WARD
LEAGUE, JOSIAH BAL 151 2ND DIST
LEAGUE, LUKE BAL 139 5TH WARD
LEAGUE, LUKE BAL 335 7TH WARD
LEAGUE, MARSELIUS BAL 126 11TH WAR
LEAGUE, NATHANIEL* BAL 309 3RD WARD
LEAGUE, THOMAS C. BAL 367 3RD WARD
LEAGUE, THOMAS M. BAL 368 3RD WARD
LEAGUE, WILLIAM BAL 151 2ND DIST
LEAGUE, WILLIAM H. BAL 172 1ST WARD
LEAH, CATHARINE BAL 245 2ND WARD
LEAH, CORAD BAL 245 2ND WARD
LEAH, JACOB FRE 003 FREDERIC
LEAHAST, ELIZABETH BAL 457 14TH WAR
LEAHINKINKLE, CHARLES BAL 443 14TH WAR
LEAHMAN, FREDERICK BAL 228 2ND WARD
LEAHMAN, GEORGE BAL 390 3RD WARD
LEAHMAN, NICHOLAS BAL 289 1ST DIST
LEAHY, TERESA BAL 415 3RD WARD
LEAK, ANN ANN 514 HOWARD D
LEAK, LOUISA HAR 068 1ST DIST
LEAKE, HENRY MGM 332 CRACKLIN
LEAKE, SARAH E.R. MGM 405 ROCKERLE
LEAKE, THOMAS CEC 089 4TH E DI
LEAKENS, FANNY WAS 148 HAGERSTO
LEAKIN, ALICE B. B. FRE 065 FREDERIC
LEAKIN, CATHARINE ANN 493 HOWARD D
LEAKIN, G.C. BAL 193 11TH WAR
LEAKIN, JOHN W. ALL 208 CUMBERLA
LEAKIN, SHEPHERD A. BAL 471 14TH WAR
LEAKINS, DENNIS FRE 296 WOODSBOR
LEAKINS, JOHN BAL 233 20TH WAR
LEAKINS, JOHN F. FRE 412 8TH E DI
LEAKINS, MARY FRE 415 8TH E DI
LEAKINS, MOSES ALL 193 9TH E.D.
LEAKINS, SARAH FRE 416 8TH E DI
LEAKINS, THOMAS FRE 421 8TH E DI
LEAKITT, ANN M. BAL 143 11TH WAR
LEAKY, JOHN BAL 206 5TH DIST
LEAMAN, GEORGE BAL 210 6TH DIST
LEAMAN, JACOB BAL 090 18TH WAR
LEAMAN, JOSEPH MGM 428 MEDLEY 3
LEAMAN, LOUIS BAL 288 1ST DIST
LEAMAN, LOUISA BAL 289 1ST DIST
LEAMAN, MARY MGM 333 CRACKLIN
LEAMAN, PETER BAL 319 12TH WAR
LEAMAN, SOLOMON MGM 430 CLARKSTR
LEAMAN, THEODORE BAL 345 13TH WAR
LEAMAN, WILLIAM H. BAL 127 18TH WAR
LEAMAR, FREDERICK BAL 314 1ST DIST
LEAMOT, A. BAL 140 1ST WARD
LEAN, ADAM BAL 271 17TH WAR
LEAN, SOPHIA BAL 357 13TH WAR
LEANAHAM, THOMAS TAL 105 ST MICHA
LEANARD, H. BAL 153 5TH WARD
LEANER, SARAH BAL 303 12TH WAR
LEANEY, HENRY* TAL 019 EASTON D
LEANING, JOHN BAL 279 1ST DIST
LEANING., GEORGE BAL 302 3RD WARD
LEANON, NANCEY WAS 117 2ND DIST
LEANS, JOHN K. BAL 330 13TH WAR
LEANTON, ANN BAL 099 18TH WAR
LEANTON, JOSEPH BAL 099 18TH WAR
LEANY, GEORGE ALL 231 CUMBERLA
LEAONRD, JOSEPH WOR 235 6TH E DI
LEAONRD, WILLIAM J. WOR 230 6TH E DI
LEAONRD, WILLIAM V. TAL 095 ST MICHA
LEAPLEY, GEORGE N. FRE 215 BUCKEYST
LEAPLEY, PETER N. FRE 223 BUCKEYST
LEAPOLD, ANDREW WAS 124 HAGERSTO
LEAPOLD, LOUISA WAS 287 1ST DIST
LEAPOLD, PHILIP WAS 201 1ST DIST
LEAPOLD, SUSAN WAS 229 1ST DIST

LEAPOLO, WILLIAM	WAS	191	1ST DIST
LEAPOLE, HENRY	BAL	282	1ST DIST
LEAR, EDWARD	BAL	113	18TH WAR
LEAR, FREDERICK	ALL	250	CUMBERLA
LEAR, GEORGE H.	FRE	215	BUCKEYST
LEAR, MARY	BAL	125	18TH WAR
LEAR, MARY	BAL	383	3RD WARD
LEAR, MICHAEL	ALL	043	10TH E.D
LEAR, MOSES	FRE	378	PETERSVI
LEAR, RICHARD	BAL	118	1ST WARD
LEAR, SOPHIA	ALL	250	CUMBERLA
LEARBOROUGH, ELLEN	BAL	053	1ST WARD
LEARIGHT, H.H.	ALL	240	CUMBERLA
LEARKIN, HARRIET A.	BAL	160	11TH WAR
LEARN, JOHN	CEC	121	4TH E DI
LEARNING, SARAH	FRE	098	FREDERIC
LEARNY, JAMES	BAL	273	1ST DIST
LEARS, MARTHA A.*	BAL	084	4TH WARD
LEARY, ANN	BAL	229	2ND WARD
LEARY, CATHERINE	BAL	025	1ST WARD
LEARY, CORNELIUS L. L.*	BAL	393	3RD WARD
LEARY, DANIEL	ALL	135	4TH E.D.
LEARY, DENNIS	BAL	155	1ST WARD
LEARY, EDWARD	ALL	134	4TH E.D.
LEARY, EDWARD	WAS	016	2ND SUBD
LEARY, ELIZABETH	BAL	040	9TH WARD
LEARY, GEORGE	KEN	232	2ND DIST
LEARY, J. E.	BAL	332	1ST DIST
LEARY, JAMES S.	KEN	247	2ND DIST
LEARY, LAWRENCE	BAL	420	14TH WAR
LEARY, MARGARET	BAL	470	14TH WAR
LEARY, MARGARET	BAL	372	3RD WARD
LEARY, MARTHA A.	BAL	008	18TH WAR
LEARY, MARY	BAL	399	8TH WARD
LEARY, MICHAEL	BAL	169	11TH WAR
LEARY, PRIMUS-BLACK	QUE	130	1ST E DI
LEARY, SARAH-BLACK	QUE	131	1ST E DI
LEARY, STEPHEN	ANN	522	HOWARD D
LEARY, THOMAS H. H.	BAL	004	1ST WARD
LEARY, WILLIAM	BAL	006	1ST WARD
LEARY, WILLIAM S.	BAL	005	15TH WAR
LEARY, WILLIAM S.	BAL	016	15TH WAR
LEAS, CHARLES A.	BAL	042	15TH WAR
LEAS, GEORGE	KEN	233	2ND DIST
LEAS, JANE R.	BAL	403	14TH WAR
LEAS, MICHAEL	WAS	243	CAVETOWN
LEAS, POTTY	WAS	124	HAGERSTO
LEASE, ANDREW J.	FRE	419	8TH E DI
LEASE, CATHARINE	FRE	257	NEW MARK
LEASE, CHARLES	FRE	258	NEW MARK
LEASE, CHARLES	ALL	019	2ND E.D.
LEASE, DAVID	CAR	346	6TH DIST
LEASE, EDWARD	FRE	022	FREDERIC
LEASE, ELIZABETH	FRE	258	NEW MARK
LEASE, EZRA	FRE	095	FREDERIC
LEASE, GEORGE	FRE	052	FREDERIC
LEASE, GEORGE	FRE	052	FREDERIC
LEASE, GEORGE	CAR	343	6TH DIST
LEASE, GEORGE	CAR	248	3RD DIST
LEASE, GEORGE H.	FRE	013	FREDERIC
LEASE, GIDEON	FRE	257	NEW MARK
LEASE, HENRY	CAR	343	6TH DIST
LEASE, JACOB	WAS	143	HAGERSTO
LEASE, JOHN	CAR	347	6TH DIST
LEASE, JOHN	FRE	257	NEW MARK
LEASE, MARY	FRE	257	NEW MARK
LEASE, MIJACH *	FRE	257	NEW MARK
LEASE, UPTON	FRE	421	8TH E DI
LEASE, WILLIAM	CAR	349	6TH DIST
LEASE, WILLIAM	FRE	052	FREDERIC
LEASER, DANIEL	FRE	330	MIDDLETO
LEASER, JOHN	FRE	143	10TH E D
LEASER, SOLOMON	FRE	364	CATOCTIN
LEASON, PATRICK	BAL	346	1ST DIST
LEASURE, ANTHONY	WAS	160	2ND DIST
LEASURE, ISAAC	WAS	117	2ND DIST
LEASURE, JONAS	WAS	235	1ST DIST
LEATCH, JAMES	PRI	035	VANSVILL
LEATHE, DANIEL	BAL	106	18TH WAR
LEATHER, HENRY	FRE	014	FREDERIC
LEATHER, JOHN	FRE	231	BUCKEYST
LEATHER, JOHN	BAL	212	17TH WAR
LEATHER, LEWIS M.L.	WAS	273	RIDGEVIL
LEATHER, MICHAEL	FRE	233	BUCKEYST
LEATHERBERRY, JOHN	BAL	417	14TH WAR
LEATHERBERRY, JOHN	BAL	471	14TH WAR
LEATHERBERRY, LEVIN	BAL	208	17TH WAR
LEATHERBERRY, LEVIN T.	SOM	537	TYASKIN
LEATHERBERRY, MARY	QUE	174	2ND E DI
LEATHERBERRY, PERRY	QUE	252	5TH E DI
LEATHERBERRY, VIRGINIA	BAL	013	9TH WARD
LEATHERBURY, ANN	SOM	458	DAMES QU
LEATHERBURY, EDWARD	SOM	462	HANGARY
LEATHERBURY, HENRY	SOM	460	HANGARY
LEATHERBURY, HENRY	SOM	532	QUANTICO
LEATHERBURY, JAMES	SOM	532	QUANTICO
LEATHERBURY, MARY	SOM	483	TRAPP DI
LEATHERBURY, ROBERT	SOM	461	HANGARY
LEATHERBURY, SAMUEL	KEN	211	2ND DIST
LEATHERBURY, SARAH E.	SOM	482	TRAPP DI
LEATHERBURY,ELIZA	QUE	139	1ST E DI
LEATHERMAN, DANIEL	FRE	370	CATOCTIN
LEATHERMAN, ELIAS	FRE	367	CATOCTIN
LEATHERMAN, GEORGE	FRE	387	PETERSVI
LEATHERMAN, GODFREY	FRE	371	CATOCTIN
LEATHERMAN, JACOB	FRE	368	CATOCTIN
LEATHERMAN, JACOB	WAS	252	1ST DIST
LEATHERMAN, JACOB W.	FRE	340	MIDDLETO
LEATHERMAN, JOHN	FRE	362	CATOCTIN
LEATHERWOOD, DEBORA	ALL	251	CUMBERLA
LEATHERWOOD, HAMSON	CAR	225	5TH DIST
LEATHERWOOD, JESSE	CAR	225	5TH DIST
LEATHERWOOD, JOHN	CAR	225	5TH DIST
LEATHERWOOD, JOHN H.	BAL	058	15TH WAR
LEATHERWOOD, PRISCILLA	BAL	031	15TH WAR
LEATHEUNS, HENRY	KEN	308	3RD DIST
LEATON, WILLIAM	BAL	222	1ST DIST
LEAUNER, GEORGE	BAL	114	18TH WAR
LEAUS, CHARLES	BAL	136	2ND DIST
LEAVANCY, CHARLES *	BAL	145	1ST WARD
LEAVENDALL, LEAP	BAL	226	2ND WARD
LEAVER, JOSEPH	BAL	320	7TH WARD
LEAVERTON, JAMES	KEN	272	1ST DIST
LEAVERTON, JESSE	KEN	272	1ST DIST
LEAVERTON, WILLIAM	KEN	272	1ST DIST
LEAVIS, SARAH	TAL	118	ST MICHA
LEAVY, ALBINA	BAL	145	5TH WARD
LEAVY, ANN	BAL	137	11TH WAR
LEAVY, PATRICK	BAL	413	8TH WARD
LEBARCH, AUGUSTUS	BAL	185	6TH WARD
LEBAUGH, MARYAN L.	BAL	310	3RD WARD
LEBBE, WILIAM	BAL	148	1ST WARD
LEBENHESCN, CLEINEUVI *	BAL	043	18TH WAR
LEBODE, FELIX	BAL	097	10TH WAR
LEBOW, JACOB	CEC	040	CHESAPEA
LEBRAND, GEORGE W.	KEN	287	3RD DIST
LEBRICK, CONROD	WAS	142	2ND DIST
LECARY, SAMUEL	CEC	140	6TH E DI
LECH, HENRY	BAL	431	8TH WARD
LECHE, DAVID	BAL	092	2ND DIST
LECHIE, ROBERT	BAL	160	2ND DIST
LECHLEITER, ALEXANDER	FRE	014	FREDERIC
LECHTENBERGER, MICHAEL	BAL	127	16TH WAR
LECHTLITTER, CATHARINE	FRE	419	8TH E DI
LECK, MAHLAH	ANN	498	HOWARD D
LECKEY, CUNNINGHAM	BAL	146	5TH WARD
LECKIE, JOHN B.*	DOR	454	1ST DIST
LECKIE, JOHN C.*	DOR	454	1ST DIST
LECKIE, SARAH *	BAL	217	6TH WARD
LECKLER, SARAH	BAL	268	20TH WAR
LECKRONE, JACOB	WAS	212	1ST DIST
LECKTITTER, JOSEPH	BAL	350	1ST DIST
LECOMPT, ELIZA	WOR	304	SNOW HIL
LECOMPT, JAMES	BAL	298	7TH WARD
LECOMPT, JAMES R.*	DOR	307	1ST DIST
LECOMPT, JOHN	BAL	177	6TH WARD
LECOMPT, MARIA	BAL	311	7TH WARD
LECOMPT, MARY	BAL	114	5TH WARD
LECOMPT, SOPHIA*	DOR	313	1ST DIST
LECOMPT, WILLIAM K.	DOR	320	1ST DIST
LECOMPTE, BOIS	BAL	003	15TH WAR
LECOMPTE, LLOYD	BAL	040	15TH WAR
LECOMPTE, MARGARET	BAL	435	14TH WAR
LECOMPTER, GRANVILLE N.	DOR	374	1ST DIST
LECOMPTON, WILLIAM N.	DOR	373	1ST DIST
LECOUMPT, JANE	BAL	380	8TH WARD
LECOUNT, CALOB	HAR	043	1ST DIST
LECOUNT, PRUDENCE	HAR	043	1ST DIST
LECTOR, MARY	BAL	229	6TH WARD
LECURE, FARYTINE	BAL	221	12TH WAR
LECUSTAND, DENICE A. *	BAL	042	18TH WAR
LECVINTER, JOHN	BAL	268	20TH WAR
LEDABERRY, WILLIAM Y.	BAL	144	19TH WAR
LEDDAN, PATRICK	BAL	409	14TH WAR
LEDDAWEARE, CECELIA	BAL	048	2ND DIST
LEDDEN, GEORGE	BAL	345	7TH WARD
LEDDEN, RICHARD	BAL	442	14TH WAR
LEDDENHAM, SHADERICK *	TAL	106	ST MICHA
LEDDEY, MARY C.	BAL	406	8TH WARD
LEDDIN, BENJAMIN	BAL	336	7TH WARD
LEDDIN, CATHARINE	BAL	337	7TH WARD
LEDDINUM, WILLIAM H.	TAL	066	EASTON T
LEDDY, OWEN	ALL	057	10TH E.D
LEDECUN, ELIZABETH *	BAL	274	1ST DIST
LEDEMAN, WILLIAM	BAL	161	1ST WARD
LEDENHAM, JESSE A.*	TAL	010	EASTON D
LEDENHAM, NANCY*	TAL	060	EASTON D
LEDENHAN, MARY J.	TAL	038	EASTON D
LEDENHANMER, MARY	BAL	030	18TH WAR
LEDERER, FRANK	BAL	092	10TH WAR
LEDERER, JOHN T.	FRE	209	BUCKEYST
LEDERER, PETER	BAL	087	10TH WAR
LEDGER, BRIDGET L.	BAL	017	18TH WAR
LEDGEWOOD, OWEN	FRE	286	WOODSBOR
LEDGEWOOD, WASHINGTON	FRE	307	WOODSBOR
LEDGWOOD,MALINDA	FRE	033	FREDERIC
LEDLER, JOHN	BAL	094	1ST WARD
LEDLEY, AJCOB	BAL	127	18TH WAR
LEDLEY, DANIEL	BAL	158	16TH WAR
LEDLEY, ELIZABETH	BAL	168	16TH WAR
LEDLEY, NANCY	BAL	403	1ST DIST
LEDLEY, SARAH	BAL	129	18TH WAR
LEDLEY, SUSAN	BAL	274	20TH WAR
LEDLOW, ISAAC	BAL	128	2ND DIST
LEDMAN, ANN E.	BAL	301	3RD WARD
LEDMAN, JOHN	BAL	283	17TH WAR
LEDMAN, WILLIAM	BAL	301	3RD WARD
LEDMORROW, CATHARINE	BAL	352	7TH WARD
LEDNEHAM, ELIZABETH S.	TAL	094	ST MICHA
LEDNEME, ELIZABETH A.*	BAL	290	3RD WARD
LEDNUM, ELIZABETH	BAL	333	7TH WARD
LEDNUM, RACHEL A.	BAL	333	7TH WARD
LEDSINGER, RICHARD	BAL	419	8TH WARD
LEDUNN, SARAH	PRI	025	VANSVILL
LEDY, DAVID	WAS	283	1ST DIST
LEE, A.H.	CAL	048	3RD DIST
LEE, ABRAHAM	ALL	063	10TH E.D
LEE, ABRAHAM-MULATTO	FRE	187	5TH E DI
LEE, ABRAM	TAL	105	ST MICHA
LEE, ALBERT	BAL	076	4TH WARD
LEE, ALBERT	BAL	404	1ST DIST
LEE, ALICE	BAL	372	13TH WAR
LEE, AMELIA	PRI	012	BLADENSB
LEE, AMIEL	HAR	193	3RD DIST
LEE, ANDREW	BAL	155	1ST WARD
LEE, ANDREW	BAL	172	6TH WARD
LEE, ANN	BAL	461	1ST DIST
LEE, ANN	ALL	063	10TH E.D
LEE, ANN	BAL	475	14TH WAR
LEE, ANN	HAR	112	2ND DIST
LEE, ANN	HAR	092	2ND DIST
LEE, ANN	WAS	011	WILLIAMS
LEE, ANN E.	ANN	276	ANNAPOLI
LEE, ANN*	BAL	416	3RD WARD
LEE, ANNIE	BAL	375	13TH WAR
LEE, AQUILLA	QUE	236	4TH E DI
LEE, ARCHIBALD	BAL	371	8TH WARD
LEE, BARBARA	BAL	075	4TH WARD
LEE, BEAL	BAL	410	1ST DIST
LEE, BENJAMIN	BAL	422	1ST DIST
LEE, BENJAMIN	BAL	017	2ND DIST
LEE, BENJAMIN	CAR	183	8TH DIST
LEE, BENJAMIN	WAS	031	2ND SUBD
LEE, BENJAMIN	PRI	083	QUEEN AN
LEE, BETSY	DOR	468	1ST DIST
LEE, CAROLINE	CEC	113	4TH E DI
LEE, CATHARINE	BAL	337	7TH WARD
LEE, CATHERINE	ALL	225	CUMBERLA
LEE, CELIA	MGM	380	ROCKERLE
LEE, CELVA	BAL	316	20TH WAR
LEE, CHARLES	HAR	092	2ND DIST
LEE, CHARLES	HAR	026	1ST DIST
LEE, CHARLES	BAL	058	4TH WARD
LEE, CHARLES	BAL	440	14TH WAR
LEE, CHARLES	CEC	130	6TH E DI
LEE, CHARLES	BAL	100	10TH WAR
LEE, CHARLES L.	BAL	174	6TH WARD
LEE, CHARLES R.	BAL	174	6TH WARD
LEE, CHARLOTTE	BAL	075	15TH WAR
LEE, CHARLOTTE	BAL	047	18TH WAR
LEE, CHRISTOPHER	HAR	147	3RD DIST
LEE, CRISTIAN A.	BAL	073	18TH WAR
LEE, DANIEL	HAR	020	1ST DIST
LEE, DANIEL	BAL	178	2ND DIST
LEE, DANIEL P.	BAL	143	16TH WAR
LEE, DAVID	HAR	088	2ND DIST
LEE, DAVID	BAL	371	13TH WAR
LEE, DAVID-BLACK	FRE	021	FREDERIC
LEE, DAVIED	HAR	202	3RD DIST
LEE, DEBORAH	BAL	109	2ND DIST
LEE, DENHARD	BAL	240	6TH WARD
LEE, DIANA	CEC	124	5TH E DI
LEE, DORCAS	WAS	090	2ND SUBD
LEE, DUDLEY	ALL	065	10TH E.D
LEE, E. GEORGE	BAL	295	7TH WARD
LEE, EDWARD	BAL	267	7TH WARD
LEE, EDWARD	ANN	310	1ST DIST
LEE, EDWARD	BAL	164	16TH WAR
LEE, EDWARD	KEN	215	2ND DIST
LEE, EDWARD	HAR	017	1ST DIST
LEE, EDWARD	CEC	059	1ST E DI
LEE, EDWARD*	TAL	059	EASTON D
LEE, ELEN	DOR	360	3RD DIVI
LEE, ELI	BAL	148	2ND DIST
LEE, ELIAS	BAL	053	18TH WAR
LEE, ELISABETH	ALL	021	2ND E.D.
LEE, ELISHA	BAL	085	10TH WAR
LEE, ELIZA	BAL	452	1ST DIST
LEE, ELIZA A.	BAL	352	7TH WARD
LEE, ELIZA A.-BLACK	BAL	217	2ND WARD
LEE, ELIZABETH	BAL	023	15TH WAR
LEE, ELIZABETH	BAL	057	10TH WAR
LEE, ELIZABETH	BAL	099	2ND DIST
LEE, ELIZABETH	HAR	114	2ND DIST
LEE, ELIZABETH	MGM	358	BERRYS D
LEE, ELIZABETH	BAL	349	13TH WAR
LEE, ELIZABETH C.	BAL	331	7TH WARD
LEE, ELIZABETH-MULATTO	MGM	430	CLARKSTR
LEE, ELIZAH	BAL	083	2ND DIST
LEE, ELLEN	BAL	020	15TH WAR
LEE, ELLEN A.	MGM	424	MEDLEY 3
LEE, EMILY A.	BAL	029	18TH WAR
LEE, EMLY-BLACK	FRE	029	FREDERIC
LEE, ENDOSIA	ANN	385	4TH DIST
LEE, EVE	ALL	061	10TH E.D
LEE, F.	BAL	332	1ST DIST
LEE, FREDERICK	ALL	064	10TH E.D
LEE, GEORG	BAL	118	1ST WARD
LEE, GEORGE	ALL	064	10TH E.D
LEE, GEORGE	BAL	332	13TH WAR
LEE, GEORGE	BAL	191	17TH WAR
LEE, GEORGE	BAL	302	12TH WAR
LEE, GEORGE	HAR	009	1ST DIST
LEE, GEORGE	CEC	015	ELKTON 3
LEE, GOERGE W.	BAL	253	12TH WAR
LEE, HAMILTON	BAL	428	1ST DIST
LEE, HANNAH	CEC	040	CHESAPEA
LEE, HANNAH	HAR	106	2ND DIST
LEE, HANNAH	HAR	030	1ST DIST
LEE, HARRY	BAL	314	12TH WAR
LEE, HENRY	BAL	143	1ST WARD
LEE, HENRY	CEC	040	CHESAPEA
LEE, HENRY	CAR	358	9TH DIST
LEE, HENRY	DOR	384	1ST DIST
LEE, HENRY	WAS	128	2ND DIST
LEE, HESTER A.*	DOR	436	1ST DIST
LEE, HOOPER	DOR	463	1ST DIST
LEE, HOOPER	DOR	464	1ST DIST
LEE, HUGH	HAR	040	1ST DIST
LEE, ISAAC	HAR	138	2ND DIST
LEE, ISAAC	KEN	283	3RD DIST
LEE, ISABEL S.	HAR	013	1ST DIST
LEE, ISABELLA	CEC	183	7TH E DI
LEE, ISABELLA	BAL	430	1ST DIST
LEE, ISABELLA	BAL	353	7TH WARD
LEE, J. HENRY	BAL	057	10TH WAR
LEE, JACKSON T.	QUE	135	1ST E DI
LEE, JACOB	CEC	098	4TH E DI
LEE, JACOB	BAL	202	6TH WARD
LEE, JACOB A.	BAL	077	15TH WAR
LEE, JAMES	BAL	130	5TH WARD
LEE, JAMES	BAL	025	9TH WARD
LEE, JAMES	BAL	306	3RD WARD
LEE, JAMES	BAL	377	1ST DIST
LEE, JAMES	ANN	411	8TH DIST
LEE, JAMES	ANN	311	1ST DIST
LEE, JAMES	ALL	130	4TH E.D.
LEE, JAMES	BAL	173	2ND DIST
LEE, JAMES	BAL	123	1ST WARD
LEE, JAMES	BAL	141	2ND DIST
LEE, JAMES	CEC	180	7TH E DI
LEE, JAMES	CEC	152	PORT DUP
LEE, JAMES	BAL	344	13TH WAR
LEE, JAMES	BAL	435	14TH WAR
LEE, JAMES	MGM	364	BERRYS D
LEE, JAMES	CHA	249	HILLTOP
LEE, JAMES	KEN	301	3RD DIST
LEE, JAMES C.	HAR	092	2ND DIST
LEE, JAMES E.	CHA	231	HILLTOP
LEE, JAMES H.	BAL	036	4TH WARD
LEE, JAMES H.	BAL	410	14TH WAR
LEE, JAMES H.	ANN	355	3RD DIST
LEE, JANE	BAL	028	2ND DIST
LEE, JANE	BAL	003	15TH WAR
LEE, JANE	TAL	024	EASTON D
LEE, JESSE	BAL	190	17TH WAR
LEE, JESSE	CAR	210	5TH DIST
LEE, JESSE	CAR	402	2ND DIST
LEE, JESSE W.	BAL	183	6TH WARD
LEE, JESSIAH	BAL	311	7TH WARD
LEE, JO	BAL	172	1ST WARD
LEE, JOE	DOR	453	1ST DIST
LEE, JOHN	KEN	310	3RD DIST
LEE, JOHN	WAS	077	2ND SUBD
LEE, JOHN	WAS	046	2ND SUBD
LEE, JOHN	QUE	251	5TH E DI
LEE, JOHN	BAL	126	5TH WARD
LEE, JOHN	BAL	204	6TH WARD
LEE, JOHN	BAL	204	2ND WARD
LEE, JOHN	BAL	288	7TH WARD
LEE, JOHN	BAL	020	15TH WAR
LEE, JOHN	BAL	014	15TH WAR
LEE, JOHN	BAL	007	9TH WARD
LEE, JOHN	BAL	180	11TH WAR
LEE, JOHN	BAL	181	11TH WAR
LEE, JOHN	BAL	176	2ND DIST
LEE, JOHN	ANN	311	1ST DIST
LEE, JOHN	ALL	065	10TH E.D
LEE, JOHN	ALL	095	5TH E.D.
LEE, JOHN	ANN	317	1ST DIST

Name	County	Page	District
LEE, JOHN	ALL	152	6TH E.D.
LEE, JOHN	BAL	423	1ST DIST
LEE, JOHN	DOR	384	1ST DIST
LEE, JOHN	BAL	136	18TH WAR
LEE, JOHN	FRE	257	NEW MARK
LEE, JOHN	BAL	153	19TH WAR
LEE, JOHN	CEC	015	ELKTON 3
LEE, JOHN	BAL	016	4TH WARD
LEE, JOHN	FRE	386	PETERSVI
LEE, JOHN	HAR	007	1ST DIST
LEE, JOHN	HAR	140	2ND DIST
LEE, JOHN A.	BAL	028	18TH WAR
LEE, JOHN B.	BAL	383	13TH WAR
LEE, JOHN H.-MULATTO	FRE	010	FREDERIC
LEE, JOHN R.	SOM	537	TYASKIN
LEE, JOHN W.	QUE	142	1ST E DI
LEE, JOHN W.	CAR	076	NO TWP L
LEE, JOHN W.	BAL	305	12TH WAR
LEE, JOHN W.	BAL	014	2ND DIST
LEE, JOHN*	TAL	007	EASTON D
LEE, JOHN-BLACK	CAR	163	NO TWP L
LEE, JOSEPH	DOR	368	3RD DIVI
LEE, JOSEPH	ANN	344	3RD DIST
LEE, JOSEPH	ANN	311	1ST DIST
LEE, JOSEPH	BAL	342	7TH WARD
LEE, JOSEPH	BAL	240	6TH WARD
LEE, JOSHAH	BAL	032	2ND DIST
LEE, JOSHUA	BAL	179	6TH WARD
LEE, JOSIAH	BAL	107	10TH WAR
LEE, JUDITH	BAL	076	15TH WAR
LEE, JULIA	BAL	130	11TH WAR
LEE, JULIA	QUE	236	4TH E DI
LEE, KATE-BLACK	FRE	200	5TH E DI
LEE, LATTICE	MGM	380	ROCKERLE
LEE, LAURA	BAL	273	12TH WAR
LEE, LEVI	WAS	046	2ND SUBD
LEE, LEVIN	DOR	461	1ST DIST
LEE, LEVIN	BAL	177	6TH WARD
LEE, LEVY	BAL	071	18TH WAR
LEE, LICKE	BAL	180	11TH WAR
LEE, LONDON	HAR	127	2ND DIST
LEE, M. A.	BAL	134	11TH WAR
LEE, MARGARET	BAL	274	7TH WARD
LEE, MARGARET A.	BAL	430	14TH WAR
LEE, MARGARET ANN	BAL	203	17TH WAR
LEE, MARGARETT	BAL	020	4TH WARD
LEE, MARIA	BAL	357	13TH WAR
LEE, MARTHA	BAL	352	1ST DIST
LEE, MARTHA-BLACK	FRE	182	5TH E DI
LEE, MARTHA-MULATTO	FRE	218	BUCKEYST
LEE, MARY	CEC	168	6TH E DI
LEE, MARY	BAL	068	4TH WARD
LEE, MARY	BAL	334	13TH WAR
LEE, MARY	HAR	027	1ST DIST
LEE, MARY	FRE	066	FREDERIC
LEE, MARY	BAL	458	1ST DIST
LEE, MARY	BAL	069	15TH WAR
LEE, MARY	BAL	042	15TH WAR
LEE, MARY	ANN	327	2ND DIST
LEE, MARY	BAL	254	1ST DIST
LEE, MARY A.	BAL	225	6TH WARD
LEE, MARY D.	FRE	387	PETERSVI
LEE, MARY D.	FRE	387	PETERSVI
LEE, MARY E.	BAL	088	15TH WAR
LEE, MARY E.	BAL	144	16TH WAR
LEE, MARY JANE	ALL	208	CUMBERLA
LEE, MICHAEL	BAL	117	2ND DIST
LEE, MISS M.	FRE	199	5TH E DI
LEE, MISS-	ANN	303	1ST DIST
LEE, MOSES	BAL	142	2ND DIST
LEE, MOSES	BAL	067	1ST WARD
LEE, MOUNTZ	BAL	132	11TH WAR
LEE, MRS.	BAL	225	17TH WAR
LEE, NACE	WAS	130	2ND DIST
LEE, NANCY	HAR	107	2ND DIST
LEE, NANCY	BAL	090	18TH WAR
LEE, NANCY	BAL	109	2ND DIST
LEE, NATHANIEL	BAL	238	6TH WARD
LEE, NATHANIEL	BAL	411	3RD WARD
LEE, PAINER	HAR	200	3RD DIST
LEE, PARKER H.	HAR	093	2ND DIST
LEE, PERE	QUE	242	5TH E DI
LEE, PERE	QUE	242	5TH E DI
LEE, PERRY	QUE	252	5TH E DI
LEE, PETER-MULATTO	FRE	189	5TH E DI
LEE, PHILIP	CAR	179	8TH DIST
LEE, PHILIP	BAL	437	14TH WAR
LEE, PRISCILLA	PRI	004	BLADENSB
LEE, PRISCILLA	BAL	030	9TH WARD
LEE, R.	BAL	149	1ST WARD
LEE, R. C.	BAL	150	1ST WARD
LEE, R. E.	BAL	283	20TH WAR
LEE, RACHEL	BAL	453	14TH WAR
LEE, RACHEL	BAL	042	9TH WARD
LEE, RACHEL	BAL	275	12TH WAR
LEE, RACHEL	BAL	358	1ST DIST
LEE, RACHEL	WAS	046	2ND SUBD
LEE, RALPH	BAL	175	16TH WAR
LEE, RALPH	HAR	159	3RD DIST
LEE, RALPH S.	HAR	202	3RD DIST
LEE, RHODA	BAL	405	14TH WAR
LEE, RICHARD	CAL	033	2ND DIST
LEE, RICHARD	CAR	163	NO TWP L
LEE, RICHARD	BAL	075	18TH WAR
LEE, RICHARD	DOR	466	1ST DIST
LEE, RICHARD B.	BAL	292	3RD WARD
LEE, RITCHILL *	HAR	191	3RD DIST
LEE, ROBERT	HAR	030	1ST DIST
LEE, ROBERT	MGM	429	CLARKSTR
LEE, ROBERT	BAL	306	3RD WARD
LEE, ROBERT	ALL	215	CUMBERLA
LEE, ROBERT	WAS	104	2ND DIST
LEE, ROBERT	DOR	461	1ST DIST
LEE, ROBERT FISH	TAL	014	EASTON D
LEE, ROBERT K.	BAL	125	1ST WARD
LEE, ROBERT K.	BAL	128	1ST WARD
LEE, RODNEY	BAL	292	17TH WAR
LEE, ROSA	BAL	076	15TH WAR
LEE, SAMUEL	BAL	180	16TH WAR
LEE, SAMUEL	BAL	070	18TH WAR
LEE, SAMUEL	BAL	196	19TH WAR
LEE, SAMUEL	BAL	250	20TH WAR
LEE, SAMUEL	CEC	205	7TH E DI
LEE, SAMUEL	CEC	204	6TH E DI
LEE, SAMUEL	BAL	071	4TH WARD
LEE, SAMUL	BAL	191	5TH DIST
LEE, SAMULE W.	HAR	029	1ST DIST
LEE, SARAH	HAR	041	1ST DIST
LEE, SARAH	HAR	019	1ST DIST
LEE, SARAH	BAL	203	17TH WAR
LEE, SARAH	BAL	083	15TH WAR
LEE, SARAH A.	ANN	355	3RD DIST
LEE, SARAH L.	BAL	187	11TH WAR
LEE, SAVILLA	CEC	130	6TH E DI
LEE, SOPHIA	CEC	049	1ST E DI
LEE, SOPHIA	BAL	300	3RD WARD
LEE, STEPHEN	ANN	303	1ST DIST
LEE, STEPHEN L.	ANN	316	1ST DIST
LEE, STEPHEN S.	BAL	186	11TH WAR
LEE, SUSAN	BAL	028	15TH WAR
LEE, SUSAN	BAL	075	18TH WAR
LEE, SUSAN	CAL	016	1ST DIST
LEE, SUSAN	BAL	456	14TH WAR
LEE, SUSAN	WAS	071	2ND SUBD
LEE, SUSANAH	BAL	081	18TH WAR
LEE, SUSANNAH	BAL	143	16TH WAR
LEE, THOMAS	ANN	292	ANNAPOLI
LEE, THOMAS	ANN	311	1ST DIST
LEE, THOMAS	BAL	036	2ND DIST
LEE, THOMAS	BAL	124	1ST WARD
LEE, THOMAS	BAL	274	1ST DIST
LEE, THOMAS	CAR	221	5TH DIST
LEE, THOMAS	CAR	216	5TH DIST
LEE, THOMAS	BAL	284	20TH WAR
LEE, THOMAS	DOR	325	1ST DIST
LEE, THOMAS	DOR	437	1ST DIST
LEE, THOMAS	DOR	459	1ST DIST
LEE, THOMAS S.	FRE	387	PETERSVI
LEE, VINCENT	QUE	143	1ST E DI
LEE, W.	BAL	126	18TH WAR
LEE, WALTER	BAL	353	7TH WARD
LEE, WASHINGTON	HAR	152	3RD DIST
LEE, WESLEY	ALL	064	10TH E.D
LEE, WILLAIM	BAL	178	2ND DIST
LEE, WILLIAM	BAL	254	1ST DIST
LEE, WILLIAM	ALL	130	4TH E.D.
LEE, WILLIAM	BAL	331	7TH WARD
LEE, WILLIAM	BAL	029	2ND DIST
LEE, WILLIAM	BAL	098	2ND DIST
LEE, WILLIAM	BAL	100	10TH WAR
LEE, WILLIAM	BAL	384	1ST DIST
LEE, WILLIAM	QUE	140	1ST E DI
LEE, WILLIAM	MGM	335	CRACKLIN
LEE, WILLIAM	BAL	153	19TH WAR
LEE, WILLIAM	BAL	204	19TH WAR
LEE, WILLIAM	BAL	315	20TH WAR
LEE, WILLIAM	HAR	029	1ST DIST
LEE, WILLIAM	HAR	119	2ND DIST
LEE, WILLIAM	DOR	452	1ST DIST
LEE, WILLIAM PRICE	HAR	197	3RD DIST
LEE, WILLIAM T.*	TAL	021	EASTON D
LEE, WILLIAM W.	ALL	063	10TH E.D
LEE, WILLIAM W.	BAL	304	7TH WARD
LEE, WILLIAM*	DOR	424	1ST DIST
LEE, WILLIAM-MULATTO	FRE	224	BUCKEYST
LEE, Y.	BAL	200	19TH WAR
LEE, Z. COLLINS	BAL	135	11TH WAR
LEE,CHARLES	BAL	256	12TH WAR
LEE,JOHN-BLACK	MGM	422	MEDLEY 3
LEE,MARY-BLACK	FRE	189	5TH E DI
LEE,WESLEY	BAL	055	2ND DIST
LEEARY, FRANCIS X. *	BAL	313	12TH WAR
LEEBOED, FRANCIS	FRE	128	CREAGERS
LEEBROOKS, MARIA C.	FRE	110	CREAGERS
LEECE, SILAS	ALL	137	4TH E.D.
LEECH, AMOS	CEC	109	3RD E DI
LEECH, ELIZA	CEC	004	ELKTON 3
LEECH, FRISBY T.	CEC	128	5TH E DI
LEECH, JOHN P.	CEC	127	5TH E DI
LEECH, MAIANN	ALL	072	5TH E.D.
LEECH, MARTHA	BAL	154	5TH WARD
LEECH, MARTHA	CEC	104	4TH E DI
LEECH, MOSES	ALL	068	5TH E.D.
LEECH, ROBERTH	CEC	077	NORTHEAS
LEECH, SARAH	CEC	088	4TH E DI
LEECH, WILLIAM	BAL	355	3RD WARD
LEECHER, JOSEPH	CEC	164	6TH E DI
LEEDENMAN, CHRISTOPHER	BAL	203	19TH WAR
LEEDS, MARY	BAL	221	12TH WAR
LEEDY, JACOB	BAL	190	19TH WAR
LEEDY, JOSEPH	FRE	380	PETERSVI
LEEE, MARIA-MULATTO	MGM	398	ROCKERLE
LEEFE, PETER	FRE	20	5TH E DI
LEEGAR, BENJAMI	QUE	126	1ST E DI
LEEGER, GOTLEIB	WAS	160	HAGERSTO
LEEGHTY, URIAS	ALL	038	2ND E.D.
LEEKE, BENJAMIN	ANN	474	HOWARD D
LEEKE, DAVIDGE.	MGM	332	CRACKLIN
LEEKE, JAMES	BAL	033	18TH WAR
LEEKE, MARY	MGM	332	CRACKLIN
LEEKE, THOMAS	ANN	519	HOWARD D
LEEKE, WESLEY	BAL	184	2ND WARD
LEEKIE, SARAH *	BAL	217	6TH WARD
LEEL, JOHN	BAL	451	14TH WAR
LEEMAN, LEWIS	FRE	103	FREDERIC
LEEMON, JOHN	BAL	002	15TH WAR
LEEMY, JAMES	CEC	008	ELKTON 3
LEENY, JOHN	BAL	235	20TH WAR
LEES, JAMES	BAL	365	1ST DIST
LEES, JEREMIAH	WAS	233	1ST DIST
LEES, JOSEPH	BAL	077	2ND DIST
LEES, NANCY	WAS	162	HAGERSTO
LEES, WILLIAM	BAL	005	18TH WAR
LEESE, WILLIAM L.	BAL	367	13TH WAR
LEESER, LOUIS A.	BAL	061	15TH WAR
LEESON, JAMES	BAL	302	20TH WAR
LEESON, PATRICK	ANN	425	HOWARD D
LEESON,WILLIAM C.	BAL	174	1ST WARD
LEET, FERDINAND	BAL	261	1ST DIST
LEETES, JOSHUA	CAR	105	NO TWP L
LEETS, HENRY	BAL	221	12TH WAR
LEETZ, CHARLES	BAL	306	12TH WAR
LEETZ, VALENTINE	BAL	458	1ST DIST
LEEVERS, A. Y.	BAL	142	11TH WAR
LEFARINGER, CLARA	BAL	229	2ND WARD
LEFENER, SAMUEL	WAS	007	WILLIAMS
LEFEVER, A.E.	WAS	017	2ND SUBD
LEFEVER, DAMIEL	WAS	017	2ND SUBD
LEFEVER, HENRY	WAS	007	WILLIAMS
LEFEVER, HENRY OF GEORGE	WAS	020	2ND SUBD
LEFEVER, JOHN	FRE	189	5TH E DI
LEFEVOR, SARAH	ALL	092	5TH E.D.
LEFEVRE, ABRAHAM	BAL	296	3RD WARD
LEFEVRE, CHARLES	BAL	055	15TH WAR
LEFEVRE, HAMILTON	HAR	062	1ST DIST
LEFFER, HENRY	HAR	070	1ST DIST
LEFFERMAN, WILLIAM	BAL	356	8TH WARD
LEFFLER, ANN	BAL	261	12TH WAR
LEFFLER, ANN	BAL	276	17TH WAR
LEFFLER, CHARLES	BAL	135	16TH WAR
LEFFLER, GEORGE	BAL	451	1ST DIST
LEFFLER, GEORGE R.	BAL	185	16TH WAR
LEFFLER, HENRY	BAL	339	7TH WARD
LEFFLER, MARY	HAR	034	1ST DIST
LEFFLER, MARY A.	BAL	080	1ST WARD
LEFFLER, PHILIP	BAL	155	6TH WARD
LEFLER, ANDREW	BAL	034	18TH WAR
LEFLER, DANIEL	BAL	259	17TH WAR
LEFLER, ISIDORE	CAR	345	6TH DIST
LEFLER, JOHN	MGM	398	ROCKERLE
LEFLIN, RICHARD	HAR	162	3RD DIST
LEFRIED, FREDERICK*	BAL	024	4TH WARD
LEFTER, PHILLIP	BAL	181	11TH WAR
LEFTON, JEREMIAH	FRE	362	CATOCTIN
LEGAAR, THOMAS	PRI	050	AQUASCO
LEGAE, JOSEPH	BAL	410	8TH WARD
LEGAN, JAMES	BAL	141	1ST WARD
LEGAN, JAMES	ANN	444	HOWARD D
LEGAR, JOSEPH	CAR	092	NO TWP L
LEGAR, MARY E.	CAR	089	NO TWP L
LEGAR, SUSAN	CAR	070	NO TWP L
LEGAR,ROBERT	CAR	101	NO TWP L
LEGART, SARHA	BAL	410	14TH WAR
LEGER, JONATHAN	BAL	382	1ST DIST
LEGER, NATHANIEL	HAR	196	3RD DIST
LEGER, WILLIAM	KEN	260	1ST DIST
LEGETT, ROBERT	WAS	071	2ND SUBD
LEGG, AGUILLA	QUE	235	4TH E DI
LEGG, BENJAMIN	KEN	266	1ST DIST
LEGG, CLARISSA	QUE	243	5TH E DI
LEGG, ELIZA	BAL	060	15TH WAR
LEGG, ELIZABETH-BLACK	QUE	128	1ST E DI
LEGG, GEORGE	QUE	208	3RD E DI
LEGG, HARRIET	BAL	087	15TH WAR
LEGG, HARRIS	QUE	228	4TH E DI
LEGG, HENRY	QUE	232	4TH E DI
LEGG, HENRY	BAL	257	6TH WARD
LEGG, HOLTER	QUE	232	4TH E DI
LEGG, JACOB C.	QUE	228	4TH E DI
LEGG, JAMES	ANN	271	ANNAPOLI
LEGG, JAMES H.	KEN	231	2ND DIST
LEGG, JAOC3 W.	QUE	226	4TH E DI
LEGG, JOHN	BAL	325	7TH WARD
LEGG, JOHN C.	QUE	228	4TH E DI
LEGG, JOHN V.	QUE	181	2ND E DI
LEGG, JOHN W.	QUE	230	4TH E DI
LEGG, JOHN W.	QUE	150	1ST E DI
LEGG, MARGARET	QUE	234	4TH E DI
LEGG, MARY	QUE	231	4TH E DI
LEGG, MARY	BAL	327	13TH WAR
LEGG, MATILDA	BAL	198	17TH WAR
LEGG, MOSES	QUE	232	4TH E DI
LEGG, MOSES	KEN	252	1ST DIST
LEGG, REUBEN	QUE	235	4TH E DI
LEGG, RICHARD	CAR	089	NO TWP L
LEGG, THOMAS	KEN	228	2ND DIST
LEGG, WILLIAM	QUE	231	4TH E DI
LEGG, WILLIAM	KEN	264	1ST DIST
LEGG, WILLIAM B.	QUE	211	3RD E DI
LEGG, WILLIAM H.	QUE	234	4TH E DI
LEGGET, CHARLES	BAL	475	14TH WAR
LEGGETT, JAMES	WAS	222	1ST DIST
LEGGETT, JAMES	WAS	280	LEITERSB
LEGGETT, MARGARET E.	WAS	222	1ST DIST
LEGGETT, MARY	WAS	184	BOONSBOR
LEGGETT, WALTER	HAR	048	1ST DIST
LEGHLER, FRANCES A.	FRE	264	NEW MARK
LEGLER, JAMES	ALL	141	6TH E.D.
LEGLER, MARTHA	ALL	134	4TH E.D.
LEGO, RACHEL	BAL	122	16TH WAR
LEGORE, EZRA	CAR	261	3RD DIST
LEGORE, JACOB	CAR	408	2ND DIST
LEGORE, SUSAN	CAR	261	3RD DIST
LEGRAND, JOHN C.	BAL	098	10TH WAR
LEGRAND, SARAH	ST	292	2ND E DI
LEGROVE, ELIZABETH	BAL	054	18TH WAR
LEGS, DANIEL	HAR	144	2ND DIST
LEHAY, MICHAEL	BAL	089	5TH WARD
LEHIGH, INASTASIA	BAL	292	20TH WAR
LEHIGH, WILLIAM	BAL	291	20TH WAR
LEHL, CONRAD	BAL	288	12TH WAR
LEHLAGER, F.	BAL	037	4TH WARD
LEHMAN, CHARLES	BAL	089	10TH WAR
LEHMAN, GEORGE	BAL	166	6TH WARD
LEHMAN, GEORGE S.	ALL	006	3RD E.D.
LEHMAN, GEORGE W.	ALL	005	3RD E.D.
LEHMAN, JACOB	BAL	089	18TH WAR
LEHMAN, JACOB	WAS	268	1ST DIST
LEHMAN, JOHN A.	BAL	165	5TH WARD
LEHMANN, J. C.	BAL	072	4TH WARD
LEHN, WILSON	CAR	242	TANEYTOW
LEHNAR, JOSEPH	BAL	124	16TH WAR
LEHNHOFF, WILHELMINA	BAL	165	6TH WARD
LEHNHOFF, WILLIAM	BAL	164	5TH WARD
LEHOULIER, CHARLES	BAL	127	5TH WARD
LEHR, ROBERT	BAL	105	10TH WAR
LEHRS, NICK	BAL	140	5TH WARD
LEIAPOLD, FREDERICK	WAS	150	HAGERSTO
LEIB, JACOB	BAL	132	5TH WARD
LEIB, JOHN	PRI	040	VANSVILL
LEIB, THOMAS	BAL	002	15TH WAR
LEIBEN, ANDREW	BAL	048	18TH WAR
LEIBENSTINE, PHILIP	BAL	460	1ST DIST
LEIBERT, REGINA	BAL	075	4TH WARD
LEICE, WILLAIM	ALL	089	5TH E.D.
LEICH, RUTH	BAL	006	9TH WARD
LEICHTY, BARBARA	WAS	226	1ST DIST
LEICHTY, HENRY	WAS	226	1ST DIST
LEIDER, FREDERICK*	BAL	031	4TH WARD
LEIDY, JACOB	FRE	132	CREAGERS
LEIF, HENRY	BAL	030	4TH WARD
LEIF, MARY A.	BAL	194	2ND WARD
LEIFERT, COONROD	BAL	109	2ND DIST
LEIFLER, JOSEPH	HAR	123	2ND DIST
LEIGH, A. K.*	TAL	056	EASTON D
LEIGH, HENRIETTA M.	FRE	034	FREDERIC
LEIGH, JAMES A.	ST	297	2ND E DI
LEIGH, LOUIS H.	ST	275	3RD E DI
LEIGH, MARIA	ST	279	3RD E DI
LEIGH, MARIA	BAL	316	20TH WAR
LEIGH, MARY A.	ST	314	1ST E DI
LEIGH, SARAH	BAL	039	9TH WARD
LEIGH, SHARLOTTE	TAL	039	EASTON D
LEIGH, SUSAN	ST	313	1ST E DI
LEIGHER, ELIZBETH	BAL	269	2ND WARD
LEIGHIN, NICHOLAS	ALL	019	2ND E.D.
LEIGHT, CORNELIUS	WAS	162	HAGERSTO
LEIGHT, DANIEL	WAS	286	1ST DIST
LEIGHT, JOHN	BAL	433	1ST DIST
LEIGHT, JOSIAH	BAL	433	1ST DIST

Name	Co.	No.	District
LEIGHTY, SAMUEL	ALL	088	5TH E.D.
LEIGMAN, GOTLIEB	FRE	128	CREAGERS
LEIHBOUGH, LOUIS *	ALL	083	5TH E.D.
LEILARD, THOMAS	BAL	147	2ND DIST
LEILICK, MICHAEL	FRE	090	FREDERIC
LEIM, ELIZABETH *	FRE	054	FREDERIC
LEIN, JOHN	ALL	152	6TH E.D.
LEINER, ABHRIAM	BAL	060	18TH WAR
LEINHARD, GEORGE	BAL	108	5TH WARD
LEINLINE, JANE *	BAL	299	20TH WAR
LEINSZ, FREDERICK	BAL	291	20TH WAR
LEINZ, DANIEL	BAL	194	6TH WARD
LEIP, VALENTINE	BAL	307	7TH WARD
LEIPP, GEORGE	BAL	220	17TH WAR
LEIS, LEMUEL	WOR	214	4TH E DI
LEISEURE, JONATHAN	FRE	271	NEW MARK
LEISHEAR, RICHARD	BAL	367	1ST DIST
LEISHER, ELIJAH	BAL	351	1ST DIST
LEISHER, JAMES	BAL	446	1ST DIST
LEISHER, THOMAS	BAL	351	1ST DIST
LEISON, PATRICK	BAL	463	1ST DIST
LEISOURE, JOHN T.	MGM	442	CLARKSTR
LEISS, ANN MARIA	FRE	114	CREAGERS
LEISS, CAROLINE	FRE	157	10TH E D
LEISS, ELIJAH	FRE	157	10TH E D
LEISS, SAMUEL	FRE	118	CREAGERS
LEISTER, CONRAD	BAL	117	5TH WARD
LEISTER, DANIEL	CAR	247	3RD DIST
LEISTER, DAVID	CAR	251	3RD DIST
LEISTER, EDWARD	CAR	251	3RD DIST
LEISTER, HENRY	CAR	354	6TH DIST
LEISTER, ISAREL	CAR	191	4TH DIST
LEISTER, ISRIEL	BAL	224	1ST DIST
LEISTER, JACOB	CAR	251	3RD DIST
LEISTER, JAMES	CAR	248	3RD DIST
LEISTER, JOHN	CAR	304	1ST DIST
LEISTER, JOSEPH	CAR	247	3RD DIST
LEISTER, JOSEPH	CAR	247	3RD DIST
LEISTER, LEVI	WAS	245	SMITHSBU
LEISTER, LYDIA	CAR	268	WESTMINS
LEISTER, MAGDALENA	CAR	247	3RD DIST
LEISTER, MARY	CAR	404	2ND DIST
LEISTER, NICHOLAS	WAS	249	1ST DIST
LEISTER, THOMAS	BAL	013	18TH WAR
LEISURE, JAMES A.	WAS	161	2ND DIST
LEISY, MARGARET	WAS	143	HAGERSTO
LEIT, ROSINA	BAL	261	2ND WARD
LEITCH, BENJAMIN	ANN	408	8TH DIST
LEITCH, EDWARD	BAL	124	5TH WARD
LEITCH, HENRY M.	ANN	402	8TH DIST
LEITCH, JAMES	CAL	040	3RD DIST
LEITCH, JOHN F.	BAL	297	7TH WARD
LEITCH, LEONARD C.	CAL	064	3RD DIST
LEITCH, ROBERT	PRI	030	VANSVILL
LEITCH, SARAH	ANN	405	8TH DIST
LEITCH, THOMAS	ANN	408	8TH DIST
LEITCH, THOMAS	ANN	402	8TH DIST
LEITCH, WILLIAM F.	ANN	402	8TH DIST
LEITCH, WILLIAM J.	CAL	064	3RD DIST
LEITCHTON, JAMES C.	HAR	176	3RD DIST
LEITCHTON, JOHN W.	HAR	169	3RD DIST
LEITER, ABRAHAM	WAS	014	2ND SUBD
LEITER, ANDREW	WAS	239	CAVETOWN
LEITER, BARBARA	WAS	281	LEITERSB
LEITER, ISAAC	WAS	278	LEITERSB
LEITER, JACOB	WAS	298	1ST DIST
LEITER, JACOB	WAS	055	2ND SUBD
LEITER, JAMES M.	WAS	278	LEITERSB
LEITER, JOHN	WAS	287	1ST DIST
LEITER, MARY	WAS	278	LEITERSB
LEITER, SAMUEL	WAS	278	LEITERSB
LEITER, SAMUEL	WAS	026	2ND SUBD
LEITER, THOMAS	WAS	278	LEITERSB
LEITH, CAROLINE	BAL	149	19TH WAR
LEITH, CHARLES	BAL	123	1ST WARD
LEITHBERCHER, MARY	BAL	372	13TH WAR
LEITZ, A.	BAL	238	20TH WAR
LEITZ, ADAM	BAL	131	5TH WARD
LEITZ, BRIDGET	BAL	104	2ND DIST
LEITZ, CHARLES	BAL	370	13TH WAR
LEITZ, DANIEL	BAL	086	10TH WAR
LEITZ, DORNTHY	BAL	369	13TH WAR
LEITZ, JOHN	BAL	237	2ND WARD
LEITZ, JOHN W.	BAL	060	1ST WARD
LEIWS, DELPHENA	FRE	102	FREDERIC
LEIWS, HANDY	WOR	234	BERLIN 1
LEIXSEY, JUSTUS	BAL	016	9TH WARD
LEKERLTS, ELIZA	WOR	346	1ST E DI
LEKEY, THOMAS	FRE	009	FREDERIC
LEKINS, WILLIAM	FRE	213	BUCKEYST
LELAND, AUGUSTUS	BAL	073	2ND DIST
LELAND, C.	BAL	129	1ST WARD
LELAND, JOHN	CHA	243	HILLTOP
LELAND, LEVEN	CHA	234	HILLTOP
LELAND, LORENZO	CHA	244	HILLTOP
LELAND, LUTHER T.	CHA	244	HILLTOP
LELIS, PERGRAMIS	BAL	124	11TH WAR
LELL, CHARLES	BAL	128	2ND DIST
LELLY, JOHN T.*	BAL	071	4TH WARD
LELRON, HENRY	BAL	155	2ND DIST
LELSBY, MARY	BAL	412	8TH WARD
LELTZ, DANIEL	FRE	354	MIDDLETO
LEMANS, NANCY	PRI	118	PISCATAW
LEMBZ, GEORGE	BAL	105	2ND DIST
LEMERING, PHILIP*	BAL	029	4TH WARD
LEMEPLACK, PRUDENCE	BAL	143	19TH WAR
LEMKUHL, JOHN	BAL	460	1ST DIST
LEMKUHL, SOPHIA	BAL	032	15TH WAR
LEMLY, JOHN G.	BAL	074	2ND DIST
LEMLY, SUSANNAH	BAL	074	2ND DIST
LEMMA, ANDREW *	BAL	422	8TH WARD
LEMMAN, ROBERT*	BAL	406	3RD WARD
LEMMES, BENEDICT J.	PRI	115	PISCATAW
LEMMES, DAVID	PRI	059	NOTTINGH
LEMMES, GABRIEL	BAL	212	11TH WAR
LEMMES, MARY	PRI	048	AQUASCO
LEMMES, SAMUEL	PRI	088	SPALDING
LEMMES, WILLIAM	PRI	083	NOTTINGH
LEMMIN, ELIZABETH	BAL	310	12TH WAR
LEMMON, A. L.	BAL	146	11TH WAR
LEMMON, CATHARINE	CAR	267	WESTMINS
LEMMON, CECELIA	BAL	031	9TH WARD
LEMMON, DAVID	ANN	304	HOWARD D
LEMMON, ELIZA	BAL	107	10TH WAR
LEMMON, ELIZA	BAL	287	1ST DIST
LEMMON, ELLEN	BAL	422	1ST DIST
LEMMON, JACOB	BAL	205	19TH WAR
LEMMON, JOHN	BAL	306	3RD WARD
LEMMON, JOHN L.	BAL	280	1ST DIST
LEMMON, JOHNATHAN H.	HAR	004	1ST DIST
LEMMON, JOSHUA F.	BAL	286	12TH WAR
LEMMON, RACHEL	BAL	394	3RD WARD
LEMMON, REBECCA	CAR	282	7TH DIST
LEMMON, RICHARD	MGM	429	CLARKSTR
LEMMON, RICHARD	BAL	280	1ST DIST
LEMMON, ROBERT C.	BAL	245	20TH WAR
LEMMON, ROBERT JR.	ANN	368	4TH DIST
LEMMON, ROBERT*	BAL	406	3RD WARD
LEMMON, S. A.	BAL	146	11TH WAR
LEMMON, WILLIAM	BAL	118	18TH WAR
LEMMON, WILLIAM J.	WOR	233	6TH E DI
LEMMONS, HENRIETTA	BAL	152	11TH WAR
LEMMONS, RICHARD	BAL	142	16TH WAR
LEMMONS, VICTORIA	BAL	268	17TH WAR
LEMMONS, WILLIAM	MGM	382	ROCKERLE
LEMMONS, WILLIAM	BAL	302	7TH WARD
LEMMORE, MR.	BAL	233	17TH WAR
LEMMY, JAMES E. *	TAL	102	ST MICHA
LEMNON, WILLIAM MRS.	BAL	139	11TH WAR
LEMON, CATHERINE	BAL	008	4TH WARD
LEMON, G.	BAL	150	1ST WARD
LEMON, GEORGE	HAR	016	1ST DIST
LEMON, GEORGE	CAR	412	2ND DIST
LEMON, GEORGE	CEC	106	3RD E DI
LEMON, ISAAC A.	HAR	154	3RD DIST
LEMON, JAMES	BAL	051	4TH WARD
LEMON, JANE	BAL	458	1ST DIST
LEMON, JOHN	ANN	377	4TH DIST
LEMON, JOHN	ALL	049	10TH E.D
LEMON, JOSEPH	BAL	369	13TH WAR
LEMON, LOUIZA	DOR	343	3RD DIVI
LEMON, RICHARD	BAL	274	1ST DIST
LEMON, RICHARD	SOM	489	SALISBUR
LEMON, ROBERT	BAL	276	1ST DIST
LEMON, SAMUE	BAL	073	1ST WARD
LEMON, SAMUEL	BAL	119	1ST WARD
LEMON, SCMEFIELD	BAL	116	11TH WAR
LEMON, THOMAS	BAL	140	2ND DIST
LEMON,JESSE	CAR	402	2ND DIST
LEMONS, LINDA	BAL	457	1ST DIST
LEMONS, WILLIAM*	DOR	328	3RD DIVI
LEMPTE, ELIZABETH	BAL	296	12TH WAR
LEN	BAL	128	1ST WARD
LENAHAM, MATHEW	BAL	448	8TH WARD
LENARD, JACOB	WAS	143	HAGERSTO
LENARD, MARTHA*	TAL	054	EASTON D
LENARD, PATRICK	BAL	294	1ST DIST
LENARD, ROBERT *	TAL	076	EASTON T
LENARD, SUSAN A.	TAL	101	ST MICHA
LENBIN, MARGARET	BAL	201	2ND WARD
LENCYCUM, HARMAN *	BAL	293	1ST DIST
LENDENFELTER, JOHN	BAL	281	12TH WAR
LENDKINS, JAMES	BAL	311	12TH WAR
LENER, MARY *	BAL	359	13TH WAR
LENEY, MOSES	BAL	154	1ST WARD
LENFT, PHILLIP *	FRE	115	CREAGERS
LENHART, HENRY F.	FRE	230	BUCKEYST
LENIG, ADAM	HAR	107	2ND DIST
LENING, PRISCILLA *	BAL	302	20TH WAR
LENLINE, NATHAN*	BAL	073	4TH WARD
LENNE, PAUL	BAL	250	20TH WAR
LENNECK, HENRY	CAR	357	6TH DIST
LENNEN, JOHN	BAL	021	18TH WAR
LENNON, DANIEL	BAL	404	3RD WARD
LENNON, JOHN	ALL	055	10TH E.D
LENNOX, ANN	BAL	003	18TH WAR
LENNOX, EDWARD	CEC	028	CHESAPEA
LENNY, PRISCILLA *	BAL	302	20TH WAR
LENONI, ANTHONY	BAL	081	10TH WAR
LENOR, GEORGE*	BAL	269	20TH WAR
LENOT, ADE	BAL	272	12TH WAR
LENOX, THOMAS	BAL	215	17TH WAR
LENRISE, MICHAEL	ALL	246	CUMBERLA
LENRWOND, JOHN H. *	BAL	043	18TH WAR
LENRY, ELIZABETH	BAL	415	14TH WAR
LENSE, CATHARINE	HAR	095	2ND DIST
LENSHOW, CHARLES	BAL	134	11TH WAR
LENSMER, GEORGE	ALL	227	CUMBERLA
LENT, CONRAD	BAL	249	2ND WARD
LENT, HARRIET	BAL	280	12TH WAR
LENTBECKER, GEORGE	BAL	235	2ND WARD
LENTE, JOSHUA*	BAL	026	4TH WARD
LENTHECUM, ELEANOR	FRE	275	NEW MARK
LENTHIAUM, ELIZABETH	FRE	275	NEW MARK
LENTHICUM, MARY	BAL	066	10TH WAR
LENTHIEUM, SLINGSBURY	ANN	472	HOWARD D
LENTMAN, JOHN	CEC	095	4TH E DI
LENTMAN, JOHNATHAN	CEC	104	4TH E DI
LENTMAN, LAWRENCE	CEC	102	4TH E DI
LENTMAN, LAWRENCE	CEC	104	4TH E DI
LENTMAN, MARY	CEC	101	4TH E DI
LENTMAN, SUSAN*	CEC	102	4TH E DI
LENTNER, FRANCIS	BAL	220	17TH WAR
LENTROUGH, FREDUCA	BAL	216	2ND WARD
LENTROUGH, H.	BAL	215	2ND WARD
LENTS, CHARELS	CAR	264	WESTMINS
LENTZ, CAROLINE	BAL	087	10TH WAR
LENTZ, CHARLES	BAL	102	5TH WARD
LENTZ, CHARLES	BAL	143	19TH WAR
LENTZ, CHARLES W.	BAL	429	14TH WAR
LENTZ, CONRAD	BAL	044	9TH WARD
LENTZ, CONRAD	BAL	037	15TH WAR
LENTZ, DAVID	BAL	253	12TH WAR
LENTZ, ELIZABETH	BAL	001	18TH WAR
LENTZ, ELIZABETH	FRE	040	FREDERIC
LENTZ, HANNAH	FRE	151	10TH E D
LENTZ, HENRY	BAL	299	3RD WARD
LENTZ, JACOB	BAL	298	7TH WARD
LENTZ, JAMES	BAL	125	1ST WARD
LENTZ, JOHN	BAL	299	3RD WARD
LENTZ, JOHN	BAL	131	2ND WARD
LENTZ, JOSEPH	ALL	232	CUMBERLA
LENTZ, LEWIS H.	BAL	267	12TH WAR
LENTZ, PETER	BAL	061	1ST WARD
LENVENER, M. ABEL	BAL	329	13TH WAR
LENY, J.	BAL	129	1ST WARD
LENY, THOMAS	BAL	123	1ST WARD
LENZ, AUGUST	BAL	276	12TH WAR
LENZ, REGINA	BAL	276	12TH WAR
LEOD, JOHN M.	BAL	135	1ST WARD
LEOD, PATRICK H.	MGM	416	MEDLEY 3
LEON, JACOB	BAL	239	6TH WARD
LEON, SAMUEL	BAL	096	10TH WAR
LEONANE, MARY	TAL	120	ST MICHA
LEONARD, A.	BAL	118	1ST WARD
LEONARD, ABRAHAM	WOR	230	6TH E DI
LEONARD, AMANCY	BAL	050	18TH WAR
LEONARD, AMASA	BAL	289	20TH WAR
LEONARD, ANN	DOR	404	1ST DIST
LEONARD, ANN	BAL	157	6TH WARD
LEONARD, ANNIS	FRE	155	10TH E D
LEONARD, ARAMINTA	WOR	229	6TH E DI
LEONARD, CATHARINE	ANN	521	HOWARD D
LEONARD, DANIEL	BAL	045	1ST WARD
LEONARD, DANIEL	TAL	090	ST MICHA
LEONARD, EDWARD	TAL	051	EASTON D
LEONARD, ELEANOR	SOM	495	SALISBUR
LEONARD, ELIZABETH	SOM	496	SALISBUR
LEONARD, ELIZABETH	BAL	160	6TH WARD
LEONARD, ELIZABETH	BAL	308	12TH WAR
LEONARD, ELIZABETH	BAL	003	15TH WAR
LEONARD, FRANCIS O. P.	MGM	377	ROCKERLE
LEONARD, FREDERICK	ALL	136	4TH E.D.
LEONARD, G. W. C.	TAL	004	EASTON D
LEONARD, G.C.	BAL	141	1ST WARD
LEONARD, GEORGE	BAL	133	1ST WARD
LEONARD, GEORGE	BAL	299	20TH WAR
LEONARD, GEORGE E.	ALL	069	5TH E.D.
LEONARD, GEORGE HEAM, LEW	WOR	230	6TH E DI
LEONARD, GREENBURY	SOM	497	SALISBUR
LEONARD, HANNAH	CEC	130	6TH E DI
LEONARD, HENRY	SOM	498	SALISBUR
LEONARD, HENRY	SOM	525	QUANTICO
LEONARD, ISAAC	SOM	497	SALISBUR
LEONARD, JAMES	TAL	051	EASTON D
LEONARD, JEREMIAH	TAL	089	ST MICHA
LEONARD, JEREMIAH	PRI	006	BLADENSB
LEONARD, JOHN	TAL	037	EASTON D
LEONARD, JOHN	SOM	530	QUANTICO
LEONARD, JOHN	BAL	018	4TH WARD
LEONARD, JOHN	BAL	004	9TH WARD
LEONARD, JOHN	BAL	446	1ST DIST
LEONARD, JOHN A.B.	MGM	411	MEDLEY 3
LEONARD, JOHN G.	BAL	021	1ST WARD
LEONARD, JOHN H.	TAL	090	ST MICHA
LEONARD, JOHN J.	WOR	216	4TH E DI
LEONARD, JOHN S.	TAL	096	ST MICHA
LEONARD, JOHN T.	PRI	113	PISCATAW
LEONARD, JONATHAN	TAL	054	EASTON D
LEONARD, JOSEPH	BAL	165	1ST WARD
LEONARD, JOSHUA	SOM	497	SALISBUR
LEONARD, JOSHUA	WOR	219	4TH E DI
LEONARD, JOSHUA	TAL	092	ST MICHA
LEONARD, LEVY	DOR	361	3RD DIVI
LEONARD, LEWIS	DOR	325	1ST DIST
LEONARD, LYDIA	BAL	189	17TH WAR
LEONARD, MARTHA	WOR	229	6TH E DI
LEONARD, MARY	SOM	493	SALISBUR
LEONARD, MARY	TAL	024	EASTON D
LEONARD, MARY	TAL	090	ST MICHA
LEONARD, MARY	BAL	317	20TH WAR
LEONARD, MARY A.	PRI	068	NOTTINGH
LEONARD, MARY A.	WAS	123	HAGERSTO
LEONARD, MOSES	WOR	229	6TH E DI
LEONARD, NATHAN	TAL	054	EASTON D
LEONARD, NOAH	WOR	230	6TH E DI
LEONARD, NOAH	CAR	071	NO TWP L
LEONARD, PATRICK	BAL	079	15TH WAR
LEONARD, PATRICK	BAL	440	1ST DIST
LEONARD, PERRY	SOM	500	SALISBUR
LEONARD, RIDGEAWAY	TAL	091	ST MICHA
LEONARD, ROBERT	BAL	086	15TH WAR
LEONARD, ROBSON CAPT.	TAL	098	ST MICHA
LEONARD, ROSE	SOM	497	SALISBUR
LEONARD, ROSEANNA	TAL	096	ST MICHA
LEONARD, SAMUEL	SOM	495	SALISBUR
LEONARD, SAMUEL	WAS	143	HAGERSTO
LEONARD, SAMUEL K.	TAL	050	EASTON T
LEONARD, SARAH A.	WOR	166	6TH E DI
LEONARD, STEVEN	ALL	217	CUMBERLA
LEONARD, THEODOCIA	SOM	493	SALISBUR
LEONARD, THOMAS	TAL	097	ST MICHA
LEONARD, THOMAS	BAL	172	1ST WARD
LEONARD, THOMAS	ALL	057	10TH E.D
LEONARD, THOMAS	BAL	370	8TH WARD
LEONARD, THOMAS	BAL	292	17TH WAR
LEONARD, THOMAS B.	TAL	104	ST MICHA
LEONARD, THOMAS H.	TAL	044	EASTON D
LEONARD, WILLAIM	WOR	234	6TH E DI
LEONARD, WILLIAM	SOM	489	SALISBUR
LEONARD, WILLIAM	TAL	050	EASTON T
LEONARD, WILLIAM	CAR	117	NO TWP L
LEONARD, WILLIAM	BAL	396	14TH WAR
LEONARD, WILLIAM	BAL	361	8TH WARD
LEONARD, WILLIAM	BAL	053	9TH WARD
LEONARD, WILLIAM K.	TAL	055	EASTON D
LEONARD, WILLIAM L.	BAL	105	18TH WAR
LEONARD, WILLIAM T.	BAL	393	8TH WARD
LEONARD,EDWARD	BAL	247	12TH WAR
LEONRAD, THOMAS	TAL	090	ST MICHA
LEONRAD, WILLIAM	WOR	229	6TH E DI
LEOPOLD, CHARLES	ALL	251	CUMBERLA
LEORY, ANN	BAL	020	4TH WARD
LEOTTI, LEWIS F.*	BAL	031	4TH WARD
LEPALEY, JOHN	MGM	425	MEDLEY 3
LEPART, GEORGE	BAL	230	17TH WAR
LEPER, GEORGE A.	BAL	219	12TH WAR
LEPER, JOHN	HAR	101	2ND DIST
LEPERST, WILLIAM *	ALL	120	5TH E.D.
LEPERTER, LOWIS	BAL	028	18TH WAR
LEPEY, JOHN	FRE	300	WOODSBOR
LEPP, GEORGE	BAL	311	20TH WAR
LEPP, GEORGE	BAL	277	12TH WAR
LEPP,LEWIS	BAL	277	12TH WAR
LEPPARD, JACOB	WAS	149	2ND DIST
LEPPE, PETER	FRE	200	5TH E DI
LEPPEL, WILLIAM	BAL	114	11TH WAR
LEPPER, FREDERICK	BAL	161	16TH WAR
LEPPER, WILLIAM	CAL	057	3RD DIST
LEPPERT, MARGARET	BAL	043	9TH WARD
LEPPISH, NICHOLAS	BAL	207	5TH WARD
LEPPO, JACOB	CAR	397	2ND DIST
LEPPO, DAVID	CAR	249	3RD DIST
LEPSON, DANIEL	BAL	054	18TH WAR
LEPSON, DORIELY	BAL	050	18TH WAR
LEPSON, GEORGE A.	BAL	056	18TH WAR
LERAND, GEORGE	BAL	055	1ST WARD
LERCH, AUGUSTUS	ANN	334	1ST DIST
LERCH, CONRAD	FRE	022	FREDERIC
LERCH, MORETZ	BAL	063	15TH WAR
LERCHTY, WILLIAM	ALL	039	3RD E.D.
LEREDAY, WILLIAM*	TAL	003	EASTON D
LEREW, CHARLES J.	BAL	470	14TH WAR
LEREW, JAMES	BAL	060	18TH WAR
LEREW, JAMES	BAL	115	5TH WARD
LEREW, ROBERT	ANN	414	HOWARD D
LEREW, SARAH	BAL	159	6TH WARD
LEREW, SUSAN	BAL	116	5TH WARD
LERICE, GEORGE *	BAL	091	2ND DIST
LERMAN, THOMAS*	DOR	341	3RD DIVI

Name	County	Page	District
LERMMES, MIDDLETON	ALL	257	CUMBERLA
LERMON, ANDREW H.	HAR	184	3RD DIST
LEROAKE, ANN	BAL	134	18TH WAR
LERONDES, ELOISE	BAL	097	10TH WAR
LEROY, JOSEPH	BAL	142	2ND DIST
LERSBAUGH, GEORGE	WAS	159	HAGERSTO
LERSEY, JOHN G.	BAL	214	19TH WAR
LERSH, JOHN	BAL	002	1ST WARD
LERSTER, A.B.	ALL	180	8TH E.D.
LERTES, JOHN *	BAL	417	1ST DIST
LERVEY, HARRIET	HAR	151	3RD DIST
LERVOURUM, LEWIS	BAL	423	14TH WAR
LERY, SARAH R.	FRE	007	FREDERIC
LESAGE, JAMES	KEN	300	3RD DIST
LESBY, MARY	HAR	181	3RD DIST
LESER, MINA	BAL	309	12TH WAR
LESEWARD, JOSEPH	BAL	026	2ND DIST
LESFAURIES, ALEXANDER	BAL	044	15TH WAR
LESH, CAROLINE	BAL	073	18TH WAR
LESH, FRANCIS	BAL	071	18TH WAR
LESHBAUGH, MARY	ALL	093	5TH E.D.
LESHEY, ELIZABETH	BAL	245	20TH WAR
LESHOEN, EZRA	FRE	097	FREDERIC
LESKAL, SAMUEL	ALL	020	2ND E.D.
LESKILET, MARY A.*	DOR	306	1ST DIST
LESKILET, SISSEY*	DOR	307	1ST DIST
LESKLIT, MARY A.*	DOR	306	1ST DIST
LESLEY, JOHN	PRI	096	SPALDING
LESLEY, L.	ANN	283	ANNAPOLI
LESLIE, ELIZABETH	WAS	073	2ND SUBD
LESLIE, JOHN	BAL	459	14TH WAR
LESLIE, JOHN	BAL	458	14TH WAR
LESLIE, MARY	BAL	029	1ST WARD
LESLIE, OWEN	CEC	136	6TH E DI
LESLIE, RACHEL	WAS	086	2ND SUBD
LESLIE, ROBERT	BAL	281	20TH WAR
LESNE, JOHN	BAL	142	19TH WAR
LESNER, ELIZABETH	BAL	142	19TH WAR
LESOUND, JOHN	BAL	035	2ND DIST
LESSEE, THOMAS	BAL	035	18TH WAR
LESSING, JAMES	BAL	252	12TH WAR
LESSING, JOHN	BAL	207	11TH WAR
LESSNER, JOHN B.	BAL	197	17TH WAR
LESSON, WILLAIM O.	BAL	150	1ST WARD
LESSURE, AUGUSTUS L.	WAS	260	1ST DIST
LESSURE, DAVID	WAS	194	1ST DIST
LESSURE, FREDERICK	WAS	260	1ST DIST
LESTER, CHARLES M.	WAS	237	CAVETOWN
LESTER, DANIEL	BAL	152	19TH WAR
LESTER, JAMES	BAL	304	12TH WAR
LESTER, JAMES	BAL	061	2ND DIST
LESTER, JOSHUA	CAR	166	NO TWP L
LESTER, MARCELLUS	CAR	104	NO TWP L
LESTER, SHIPLEY	BAL	146	16TH WAR
LESTER, THOMAS	CAR	166	NO TWP L
LESTER, WILLIAM H.	BAL	144	16TH WAR
LESTMAN, PHILLIP	BAL	237	2ND WARD
LESTUER, MARY	BAL	128	16TH WAR
LESURE, SUSAN	WAS	266	1ST DIST
LET, NANCY	WAS	073	2ND SUBD
LETCHTHALER, JOHN	BAL	063	1ST WARD
LETH, ELIZABETH*	BAL	059	4TH WARD
LETH, THOMAS B.*	BAL	082	4TH WARD
LETHELIN, ALECANDER L.	CAL	016	1ST DIST
LETHERBRIDGE, ANN	BAL	058	10TH WAR
LETHERBURY, LIDIA	KEN	262	1ST DIST
LETHERBURY, SAMUEL	KEN	212	2ND DIST
LETHERWOOD,RANDOLPH	FRE	439	8TH E DI
LETHLIEG, EUSTAS	BAL	318	7TH WARD
LETHOUSE, CHRISTOPHER	BAL	278	7TH WARD
LETMATE, CHARLES A.	BAL	207	6TH WARD
LETRUM, AMBROSE	BAL	131	2ND DIST
LETSINGER, ANN	BAL	102	2ND DIST
LETSINGER, HARRIET	BAL	023	2ND DIST
LETSINGER, JOSEPH	BAL	028	2ND DIST
LETSINGER, MAYBURY	BAL	102	2ND DIST
LETT, EVERETT G.	ANN	496	HOWARD D
LETT, JOHN C.	ANN	495	HOWARD D
LETT, WASHINGTON V.	ANN	495	HOWARD D
LETTEN, JAMES*	BAL	084	4TH WARD
LETTERHURST, HENRY	BAL	045	15TH WAR
LETTIN, SOPHIA	BAL	204	2ND WARD
LETTON, BUEL	MGM	400	ROCKERLE
LETTON, MICHAEL G.	MGM	375	ROCKERLE
LETTY, BERNARD	CAR	149	NO TWP L
LEUM, ISAAC	CEC	038	CHESAPEA
LEURWOND, JOHN H. *	BAL	043	18TH WAR
LEUTBAKER, CHRISTIAN	BAL	350	3RD WARD
LEUTHER, JOSEPH	FRE	069	FREDERIC
LEUTHOER, CHRISTIAN	BAL	199	19TH WAR
LEUTMYER, NANCY	WAS	056	2ND SUBD
LEVALL, PATRICK	ALL	140	6TH E.D.
LEVALLIN, JOHN	BAL	049	4TH WARD
LEVAN, ISAAC	BAL	458	8TH WARD
LEVANCEY, ETHAN*	BAL	036	4TH WARD
LEVANCY, GEORGE	BAL	374	8TH WARD
LEVANDER, MYER	BAL	087	1ST WARD
LEVANTON, JOHN	ALL	244	CUMBERLA
LEVATOR, HENRY S.*	TAL	005	EASTON D
LEVATT, WASHINGTON	BAL	246	6TH WARD
LEVEAGE, MARCUS	BAL	120	11TH WAR
LEVEE, HENRIETTA	BAL	457	14TH WAR
LEVEL, MARY	ALL	241	CUMBERLA
LEVELL, PATRICK	ALL	142	6TH E.D.
LEVELLY, HARRY	ANN	265	ANNAPOLI
LEVENETON, HANNAH	CAR	155	NO TWP L
LEVENITE, FREDERICK	WAS	285	1ST DIST
LEVENTON, AUTHOR	CAR	155	NO TWP L
LEVEOCERE, F. P. E.	BAL	322	12TH WAR
LEVER, WILLIAM	CEC	167	5TH E DI
LEVERING, AARON R.	BAL	468	14TH WAR
LEVERING, ANDREW J.	BAL	073	15TH WAR
LEVERING, ARON	BAL	290	3RD WARD
LEVERING, COCATER	CAR	323	1ST DIST
LEVERING, EDWARD	BAL	310	1ST DIST
LEVERING, ELIZA	BAL	236	6TH WARD
LEVERING, ELLEN	BAL	142	19TH WAR
LEVERING, EUGENE	BAL	111	15TH WAR
LEVERING, FREDERICK A.	BAL	112	15TH WAR
LEVERING, HANNAH	BAL	090	15TH WAR
LEVERING, LAWRENCE	BAL	007	EASTERN
LEVERING, SARAH R.	HAR	082	2ND DIST
LEVERING, SUSAN	BAL	269	20TH WAR
LEVERING, SUSANA	BAL	443	8TH WARD
LEVERING, THOMAS W.	BAL	071	15TH WAR
LEVERING, WILLIAM L.	BAL	225	12TH WAR
LEVERNTON, LEMUEL	CAR	125	NO TWP L
LEVERTON, ANN M.*	TAL	062	EASTON D
LEVERTOM, EDWARD	QUE	180	2ND E DI
LEVERTON, GARY	KEN	264	1ST DIST
LEVERTON, HENRY B.*	TAL	032	EASTON D
LEVERTON, JESSE J.	TAL	033	EASTON D
LEVERTON, MARY L.	QUE	180	2ND E DI
LEVERTON, RICHARD	KEN	272	1ST DIST
LEVET, WILLIAM	CAR	219	5TH DIST
LEVEY, EMILY	BAL	046	18TH WAR
LEVI, ABRAHAM	WAS	124	HAGERSTO
LEVI, EDWIN	BAL	164	1ST WARD
LEVI, GEORGE	CAL	050	3RD DIST
LEVI, GERSON	WAS	132	HAGERSTO
LEVI, JAMES	BAL	236	20TH WAR
LEVI, JOSEPH	BAL	004	15TH WAR
LEVI, MATILDA	BAL	399	8TH WARD
LEVI, MILLY	CAL	061	3RD DIST
LEVI, NANCY	BAL	300	7TH WARD
LEVI, NELLY	CAL	050	3RD DIST
LEVI, SOLOMAN L.	WAS	100	2ND DIST
LEVIC, JAMES	QUE	138	1ST E DI
LEVILLEN, JAMES L.	BAL	111	1ST WARD
LEVIN, ANN	BAL	256	12TH WAR
LEVIN, DANIEL	BAL	152	19TH WAR
LEVIN, DORA	BAL	213	2ND WARD
LEVIN, PATRICK	ALL	076	5TH E.D.
LEVINBY, HENRY *	BAL	144	1ST WARD
LEVING, VALENTINE	BAL	427	8TH WARD
LEVINGSTON, BENJAMIN	WOR	190	8TH E DI
LEVINGTON, WILLIAM	BAL	302	7TH WARD
LEVIS, ANN	FRE	180	5TH E DI
LEVIS, ANTHONY	FRE	117	CREAGERS
LEVIS, ANTHONY	FRE	117	CREAGERS
LEVIS, JOSEPH	FRE	180	5TH E DI
LEVIS, NATHANIEL	FRE	119	CREAGERS
LEVIS, NORRIS	CEC	105	3RD E DI
LEVISON, SAMUEL	BAL	386	13TH WAR
LEVITTE, E. G.	BAL	153	1ST WARD
LEVIZER, JULIA	BAL	270	2ND WARD
LEVLEM, A.	BAL	282	2ND WARD
LEVNE, RICHARD	BAL	232	12TH WAR
LEVRAGE, NATHANIEL	QUE	132	1ST E DI
LEVRAGE, WILLIAM	QUE	164	2ND E DI
LEVUS, W.W.	HAR	153	3RD DIST
LEVUTON, HENRY B.*	TAL	032	EASTON D
LEVUTON, JESSE*	TAL	061	EASTON D
LEVUTON, MARGARET*	TAL	016	EASTON D
LEVUTON, MARY*	TAL	006	EASTON D
LEVUTOR, JAMES*	TAL	006	EASTON D
LEVUTOR, MARY A.*	TAL	007	EASTON D
LEVUTOR, WILLIAM P.*	TAL	004	EASTON D
LEVY, ANN	BAL	202	11TH WAR
LEVY, ANN E.	FRE	312	MIDDLETO
LEVY, EDWARD M.	ANN	413	HOWARD D
LEVY, ELEANOR	BAL	169	16TH WAR
LEVY, HERMAN	BAL	248	6TH WARD
LEVY, JOHN	HAR	168	3RD DIST
LEVY, JOSEPH M.	BAL	333	3RD WARD
LEVY, MARIA	BAL	001	EASTERN
LEVY, PERRY J.	FRE	312	MIDDLETO
LEVY, SAMUEL	BAL	301	20TH WAR
LEVY, THOMAS P.	BAL	071	4TH WARD
LEVY, WILLIAM D.	BAL	055	4TH WARD
LEW, HENRY	BAL	460	8TH WARD
LEW, JEFFERSON	BAL	047	1ST WARD
LEWDER, ADAM	BAL	428	8TH WARD
LEWEL, HENRY	ANN	465	HOWARD D
LEWELL, ANN	ANN	437	HOWARD D
LEWELL, AUGUSTUS	ANN	288	ANNAPOLI
LEWELL, DANIEL G	ANN	433	HOWARD D
LEWELL, ELIZA	ANN	288	ANNAPOLI
LEWELL, JANE	BAL	138	11TH WAR
LEWELL, JOHN T.	ANN	437	HOWARD D
LEWELL, MARY R.	BAL	312	3RD WARD
LEWELL, SEPTERMS D.	HAR	191	3RD DIST
LEWELL, THOMAS	ANN	288	ANNAPOLI
LEWELL, TRUSTUM F.*	BAL	371	3RD WARD
LEWELLAN, LYDIA	BAL	092	1ST WARD
LEWELLAN, THOMAS	BAL	091	1ST WARD
LEWELLEN, M.	BAL	038	1ST WARD
LEWELLEN, THOMAS	BAL	303	17TH WAR
LEWELLYM, SARAH	ALL	116	5TH E.D.
LEWEN, BARNARD	BAL	168	11TH WAR
LEWEN, HENRY	BAL	255	1ST DIST
LEWEN, JOHN	BAL	258	1ST DIST
LEWEN, LEROY	BAL	074	15TH WAR
LEWEN, THOMAS	BAL	294	1ST DIST
LEWEN, WILLIAM	BAL	254	1ST DIST
LEWER, ABERT	BAL	426	8TH WARD
LEWES, CHARLOTT	BAL	459	1ST DIST
LEWEY, ANDREW	HAR	197	3RD DIST
LEWIE, JOHN	BAL	374	3RD WARD
LEWIN, ISAAC	BAL	299	7TH WARD
LEWIN, JOHN	HAR	008	1ST DIST
LEWIN, JOHN	HAR	031	1ST DIST
LEWIN, JOHN H.	BAL	258	1ST DIST
LEWIN, JOSEPH	BAL	299	7TH WARD
LEWIN, MEUGEN	CHA	276	ALLENS F
LEWIN, WILLIAM	BAL	253	1ST DIST
LEWIS, ISAIH*	DOR	438	1ST DIST
LEWIS, A.	BAL	148	1ST WARD
LEWIS, AARON	CAR	130	NO TWP L
LEWIS, ABNER	BAL	053	18TH WAR
LEWIS, ABRAHAM	BAL	219	6TH WARD
LEWIS, ALEXANDER	PRI	109	PISCATAW
LEWIS, ALFRED G.	QUE	196	3RD E DI
LEWIS, ALFRED M.	DOR	443	1ST DIST
LEWIS, ALLEN T.	BAL	160	16TH WAR
LEWIS, AMANDA	QUE	249	5TH E DI
LEWIS, ANDREW	BAL	230	12TH WAR
LEWIS, ANDREW	BAL	410	3RD WARD
LEWIS, ANN	BAL	252	2ND WARD
LEWIS, ANN E.	BAL	242	2ND WARD
LEWIS, ANN E.	BAL	098	5TH WARD
LEWIS, ANN-MULATTO	FRE	437	8TH E DI
LEWIS, ANNA	ANN	521	HOWARD D
LEWIS, ANNA R.	BAL	114	5TH WARD
LEWIS, ANNA-BLACK	QUE	174	2ND E DI
LEWIS, ANTHONY	BAL	462	1ST DIST
LEWIS, ANTONY	BAL	041	2ND DIST
LEWIS, ARNOLD T.	MGM	439	CLARKSTR
LEWIS, ASE M.	FRE	063	FREDERIC
LEWIS, B.	BAL	152	1ST WARD
LEWIS, BAINBRIDGE	BAL	124	1ST WARD
LEWIS, BAINBRIDGE	BAL	122	1ST WARD
LEWIS, BEHO *	WOR	308	2ND E DI
LEWIS, BENJAMIN	CAR	208	5TH DIST
LEWIS, BERNARD	FRE	154	10TH E D
LEWIS, BETSA	WOR	301	SNOW HIL
LEWIS, BETSEY	WOR	263	BERLIN 1
LEWIS, CALEB	MGM	344	CLARKSBU
LEWIS, CANE	DOR	331	3RD DIVI
LEWIS, CAROLINE	BAL	274	20TH WAR
LEWIS, CAROLINE	BAL	021	4TH WARD
LEWIS, CAROLINE	FRE	055	FREDERIC
LEWIS, CAROLINE	BAL	439	14TH WAR
LEWIS, CAROLINE	BAL	259	7TH WARD
LEWIS, CASH	BAL	272	20TH WAR
LEWIS, CASPAR	BAL	250	20TH WAR
LEWIS, CATHARINE	CEC	081	CHARLEST
LEWIS, CATHARINE	CEC	082	CHARLEST
LEWIS, CATHARINE	QUE	232	4TH E DI
LEWIS, CHARLES	BAL	219	17TH WAR
LEWIS, CHARLES	BAL	158	1ST WARD
LEWIS, CHARLES	ANN	367	4TH DIST
LEWIS, CHARLES	BAL	094	5TH WARD
LEWIS, CHARLES E.	BAL	146	1ST WARD
LEWIS, CHARLES E.	CEC	006	ELKTON 3
LEWIS, CHARLOT	BAL	450	1ST DIST
LEWIS, CHARLOTT	WOR	247	1ST CENS
LEWIS, CHRISTIAN*	BAL	368	3RD WARD
LEWIS, CORDEALIA	HAR	152	3RD DIST
LEWIS, DANIEL	CEC	117	4TH E DI
LEWIS, DANIEL	FRE	363	CATOCTIN
LEWIS, DANIEL	ALL	045	10TH E.D
LEWIS, DAVID	FRE	220	BUCKEYST
LEWIS, DAVID	WAS	117	2ND DIST
LEWIS, DAVID J.	HAR	086	2ND DIST
LEWIS, E.	PRI	105	PISCATAW
LEWIS, EASTER	DOR	296	1ST DIST
LEWIS, EBENEZAR L.	CEC	140	5TH E DI
LEWIS, EDED	ALL	120	5TH E.D.
LEWIS, EDMOND H.	BAL	390	1ST DIST
LEWIS, EDWARD	BAL	171	16TH WAR
LEWIS, EDWARD	BAL	171	16TH WAR
LEWIS, EDWARD	CEC	128	5TH E DI
LEWIS, EDWARD	MGM	439	CLARKSTR
LEWIS, EDWARD B.	CEC	005	ELKTON 3
LEWIS, ELISHA	DOR	420	1ST DIST
LEWIS, ELISHA	HAR	159	3RD DIST
LEWIS, ELIZ J.	QUE	192	3RD E DI
LEWIS, ELIZA	KEN	265	1ST DIST
LEWIS, ELIZA	BAL	316	20TH WAR
LEWIS, ELIZA	BAL	125	11TH WAR
LEWIS, ELIZA	BAL	395	14TH WAR
LEWIS, ELIZABETH	FRE	328	MIDDLETO
LEWIS, ELIZABETH	BAL	078	4TH WARD
LEWIS, ELIZABETH	BAL	051	18TH WAR
LEWIS, ELIZABETH	SOM	362	BRINKLEY
LEWIS, ELIZABETH	BAL	100	15TH WAR
LEWIS, ELIZABETH	BAL	316	3RD WARD
LEWIS, ELIZABETH	BAL	040	9TH WARD
LEWIS, ELIZABETH	BAL	072	15TH WAR
LEWIS, ELIZABETH	BAL	330	7TH WARD
LEWIS, ELLEN	WOR	342	1ST E DI
LEWIS, ELLEN	PRI	039	VANSVILL
LEWIS, EMILEY	DOR	327	3RD DIVI
LEWIS, EMILY	BAL	241	12TH WAR
LEWIS, EMILY	BAL	186	11TH WAR
LEWIS, EMILY	BAL	197	11TH WAR
LEWIS, EMILY	BAL	245	1ST DIST
LEWIS, EUGENE R.	BAL	178	6TH WARD
LEWIS, F.	BAL	228	19TH WAR
LEWIS, FRANCES A.	BAL	388	8TH WARD
LEWIS, FRANCIS	BAL	027	15TH WAR
LEWIS, FRANCIS	BAL	417	14TH WAR
LEWIS, FRANCIS	BAL	122	11TH WAR
LEWIS, FRANCIS	BAL	134	11TH WAR
LEWIS, FRANKLIN	BAL	459	8TH WARD
LEWIS, FREDUS E.	CEC	108	3RD E DI
LEWIS, GARRISON-BLACK	CAR	119	NO TWP L
LEWIS, GEORG EW.	BAL	222	19TH WAR
LEWIS, GEORGE	BAL	406	14TH WAR
LEWIS, GEORGE	BAL	029	1ST WARD
LEWIS, GEORGE	QUE	232	4TH E DI
LEWIS, GEORGE	QUE	244	5TH E DI
LEWIS, GEORGE M.	CHA	220	ALLENS F
LEWIS, GEORGE W.	BAL	119	11TH WAR
LEWIS, GEORGE W.	BAL	293	1ST DIST
LEWIS, GEORGEANNA	BAL	232	2ND WARD
LEWIS, GOERGE	BAL	020	15TH WAR
LEWIS, H. J.	BAL	155	1ST WARD
LEWIS, HANCY	BAL	389	8TH WARD
LEWIS, HARRIET	BAL	207	2ND WARD
LEWIS, HARRIOTT	BAL	076	4TH WARD
LEWIS, HENERY	DOR	338	3RD DIVI
LEWIS, HENRY	BAL	103	18TH WAR
LEWIS, HENRY	BAL	141	1ST WARD
LEWIS, HENRY	ALL	045	10TH E.D
LEWIS, HENRY	ALL	070	5TH E.D.
LEWIS, HENRY	ANN	429	HOWARD D
LEWIS, HENRY	QUE	227	4TH E DI
LEWIS, HENRY	SOM	487	SALISBUR
LEWIS, HENRY	WOR	308	2ND E DI
LEWIS, HORNER	BAL	471	14TH WAR
LEWIS, ISAAC	WOR	216	4TH E DI
LEWIS, ISAAC	BAL	207	6TH DIST
LEWIS, ISAAC A.	WOR	165	6TH E DI
LEWIS, ISAAC W.	WOR	221	4TH E DI
LEWIS, ISAAC-MULATTO	CAR	093	NO TWP L
LEWIS, JACOB	CAR	088	NO TWP L
LEWIS, JACOB	FRE	234	BUCKEYST
LEWIS, JACOB	QUE	224	4TH E DI
LEWIS, JACOB-BLACK	CAR	075	NO TWP L
LEWIS, JAEMS	BAL	438	14TH WAR
LEWIS, JAMEA	KEN	286	3RD DIST
LEWIS, JAMES	KEN	273	1ST DIST
LEWIS, JAMES	QUE	188	3RD E DI
LEWIS, JAMES	WOR	214	4TH E DI
LEWIS, JAMES	SOM	543	TYASKIN
LEWIS, JAMES	PRI	023	VANSVILL
LEWIS, JAMES	WOR	256	1ST CENS
LEWIS, JAMES	KEN	234	2ND DIST
LEWIS, JAMES	BAL	274	7TH WARD
LEWIS, JAMES	BAL	040	1ST WARD
LEWIS, JAMES M.	BAL	178	6TH WARD
LEWIS, JAMES M.	SOM	524	BARREN C
LEWIS, JAMES R.	DOR	446	1ST DIST
LEWIS, JEREMIAH	FRE	245	NEW MARK
LEWIS, JEREMIAH	CAR	127	NO TWP L
LEWIS, JEREMIAH	MGM	436	CLARKSTR
LEWIS, JESSE	CAR	093	NO TWP L
LEWIS, JESSE	BAL	098	15TH WAR
LEWIS, JESSEE	DOR	321	1ST DIST
LEWIS, JOHN	DOR	331	3RD DIVI
LEWIS, JOHN	FRE	363	CATOCTIN
LEWIS, JOHN	FRE	382	PETERSVI
LEWIS, JOHN	BAL	271	20TH WAR
LEWIS, JOHN	BAL	146	11TH WAR
LEWIS, JOHN	MGM	332	CRACKLIN
LEWIS, JOHN	BAL	235	17TH WAR
LEWIS, JOHN	BAL	058	4TH WARD
LEWIS, JOHN	BAL	256	17TH WAR

Name	County	Page	District
LEWIS, JOHN	BAL	310	20TH WAR
LEWIS, JOHN	FRE	059	FREDERIC
LEWIS, JOHN	MGM	332	ROCKERLE
LEWIS, JOHN	BAL	128	16TH WAR
LEWIS, JOHN	BAL	276	12TH WAR
LEWIS, JOHN	BAL	035	1ST WARD
LEWIS, JOHN	BAL	358	3RD WARD
LEWIS, JOHN	BAL	373	3RD WARD
LEWIS, JOHN	BAL	132	1ST WARD
LEWIS, JOHN	BAL	371	1ST DIST
LEWIS, JOHN	BAL	387	1ST DIST
LEWIS, JOHN	BAL	458	1ST DIST
LEWIS, JOHN	BAL	095	5TH WARD
LEWIS, JOHN	BAL	114	5TH WARD
LEWIS, JOHN	BAL	105	5TH WARD
LEWIS, JOHN	BAL	106	5TH WARD
LEWIS, JOHN	BAL	331	3RD WARD
LEWIS, JOHN	ANN	473	HOWARD D
LEWIS, JOHN	ANN	478	HOWARD D
LEWIS, JOHN	ALL	073	5TH E.D.
LEWIS, JOHN	ALL	074	5TH E.D.
LEWIS, JOHN	ALL	044	10TH E.D
LEWIS, JOHN	BAL	311	1ST DIST
LEWIS, JOHN	BAL	457	8TH WARD
LEWIS, JOHN	BAL	348	7TH WARD
LEWIS, JOHN	BAL	170	11TH WAR
LEWIS, JOHN	PRI	021	VANSVILL
LEWIS, JOHN	SOM	544	TYASKIN
LEWIS, JOHN	WOR	216	4TH E DI
LEWIS, JOHN	QUE	210	3RD E DI
LEWIS, JOHN	QUE	224	4TH E DI
LEWIS, JOHN	WAS	124	2ND DIST
LEWIS, JOHN D.	QUE	219	3RD E DI
LEWIS, JOHN F.	BAL	036	1ST WARD
LEWIS, JOHN JR.	BAL	262	6TH WARD
LEWIS, JOHN L.	FRE	154	10TH E D
LEWIS, JOHN M.	BAL	255	1ST DIST
LEWIS, JOHN R.	MGM	436	CLARKSTR
LEWIS, JOHN T.*	BAL	380	3RD WARD
LEWIS, JOHN W.	PRI	040	VANSVILL
LEWIS, JOHNY.	FRE	245	NEW MARK
LEWIS, JONATHAN	MGM	342	CLARKSBU
LEWIS, JOSEPH	QUE	137	1ST E DI
LEWIS, JOSEPH	BAL	299	20TH WAR
LEWIS, JOSEPH	WAS	064	2ND SUBD
LEWIS, JOSEPH	BAL	061	1ST WARD
LEWIS, JOSEPH	BAL	124	1ST WARD
LEWIS, JOSEPH	BAL	122	1ST WARD
LEWIS, JOSEPH	ALL	044	10TH E.D
LEWIS, JOSEPH	ALL	045	10TH E.D
LEWIS, JOSEPH	BAL	408	1ST DIST
LEWIS, JOSEPH H.	WAS	117	2ND DIST
LEWIS, JOSEPH H.	HAR	080	2ND DIST
LEWIS, JOSEPH N.	BAL	338	13TH WAR
LEWIS, JOSEPH-BLACK	CAR	100	NO TWP L
LEWIS, JOSEPHINE	QUE	233	4TH E DI
LEWIS, JOSEPHINE	BAL	457	8TH WARD
LEWIS, JOSHUA	HAR	071	1ST DIST
LEWIS, JOSHUA H.	WOR	165	6TH E DI
LEWIS, JOSHUA H. JR.	WOR	167	6TH E DI
LEWIS, JOSHUA L.	BAL	041	4TH WARD
LEWIS, JULIA	WOR	215	4TH E DI
LEWIS, KENDAL M.	SOM	523	BARREN C
LEWIS, KENDALL P.	WOR	216	4TH E DI
LEWIS, KENDE*	DOR	434	1ST DIST
LEWIS, L.	PRI	109	PISCATAW
LEWIS, LEVIN	DOR	439	1ST DIST
LEWIS, LEVIN	DOR	413	1ST DIST
LEWIS, LEWIS D.	ANN	306	1ST DIST
LEWIS, LOUIS	ANN	522	HOWARD D
LEWIS, LOUIS	BAL	295	12TH WAR
LEWIS, LOUISA	DOR	382	1ST DIST
LEWIS, LOUISA*	DOR	444	1ST DIST
LEWIS, MANNING*	DOR	438	1ST DIST
LEWIS, MANNY-MULATTO	BAL	223	2ND WARD
LEWIS, MARANDA	DOR	321	1ST DIST
LEWIS, MARGARET	FRE	056	FREDERIC
LEWIS, MARGARET	BAL	318	1ST DIST
LEWIS, MARGARET	BAL	262	6TH WARD
LEWIS, MARGARET	WAS	127	HAGERSTO
LEWIS, MARGARETT ANN	BAL	215	17TH WAR
LEWIS, MARIA	BAL	242	6TH WARD
LEWIS, MARIA	BAL	053	9TH WARD
LEWIS, MARIA	BAL	229	1ST DIST
LEWIS, MARIAH	FRE	217	BUCKEYST
LEWIS, MARIETTA	QUE	219	3RD E DI
LEWIS, MARTHA	CEC	051	1ST E DI
LEWIS, MARTHA	BAL	464	14TH WAR
LEWIS, MARTHA	BAL	395	1ST DIST
LEWIS, MARTIN	BAL	280	20TH WAR
LEWIS, MARY	BAL	211	11TH WAR
LEWIS, MARY	CAR	128	NO TWP L
LEWIS, MARY	BAL	196	19TH WAR
LEWIS, MARY	BAL	065	18TH WAR
LEWIS, MARY	BAL	459	8TH WARD
LEWIS, MARY	BAL	019	15TH WAR
LEWIS, MARY	BAL	240	12TH WAR
LEWIS, MARY	SOM	503	SALISBUR
LEWIS, MARY	SOM	361	BRINKLEY
LEWIS, MARY A.	CEC	068	5TH E DI
LEWIS, MARY A.	BAL	167	19TH WAR
LEWIS, MARY E.	BAL	348	13TH WAR
LEWIS, MARY E.	MGM	433	CLARKSTR
LEWIS, MARY E.	BAL	044	15TH WAR
LEWIS, MARY E.	BAL	170	11TH WAR
LEWIS, MARY L.	BAL	214	11TH WAR
LEWIS, MARY-BLACK	QUE	173	2ND E DI
LEWIS, MARY-MULATTO	FRE	405	JEFFERSO
LEWIS, MARY-MULATTO	FRE	412	8TH E DI
LEWIS, MARY-MULATTO	FRE	451	8TH E DI
LEWIS, MATILDA	BAL	245	1ST DIST
LEWIS, MICHAEL	CAR	408	2ND DIST
LEWIS, MICHAEL	WAS	216	1ST DIST
LEWIS, MILO	BAL	025	18TH WAR
LEWIS, MINOS H.	DOR	313	1ST DIST
LEWIS, MINUS	SOM	429	PRINCESS
LEWIS, MITILDA	BAL	128	11TH WAR
LEWIS, N.W.	WAS	288	1ST DIST
LEWIS, NANCY	DOR	420	1ST DIST
LEWIS, NANCY	MGM	336	CRACKLIN
LEWIS, NATHAN	CAR	231	5TH DIST
LEWIS, NEILD	DOR	345	3RD DIVI
LEWIS, NELLEY	BAL	389	8TH WARD
LEWIS, NICHOLAS	BAL	450	1ST DIST
LEWIS, NOAH W.	SOM	523	BARREN C
LEWIS, PATIENCE	CAR	211	5TH DIST
LEWIS, PATTY	WAS	046	2ND SUBD
LEWIS, PERRY	ANN	497	HOWARD D
LEWIS, PETER	BAL	016	1ST WARD
LEWIS, PETER	WOR	217	4TH E DI
LEWIS, PHILIP	BAL	446	1ST DIST
LEWIS, PHILLIP	ALL	044	10TH E.D
LEWIS, PRISCILLA	BAL	254	1ST DIST
LEWIS, R.	BAL	118	1ST WARD
LEWIS, R.	BAL	139	1ST WARD
LEWIS, R.	BAL	098	10TH WAR
LEWIS, R.	BAL	170	1ST WARD
LEWIS, RACHEL	WOR	204	4TH E DI
LEWIS, RACHEL	DOR	411	1ST DIST
LEWIS, REBECCA	DOR	409	1ST DIST
LEWIS, REBECCA	QUE	172	2ND E DI
LEWIS, REBECCA	QUE	234	4TH E DI
LEWIS, REBECCA	BAL	380	3RD WARD
LEWIS, REBECCA	BAL	282	1ST DIST
LEWIS, REUBEN	CAR	285	7TH DIST
LEWIS, RICHARD	BAL	379	1ST DIST
LEWIS, RICHARD	BAL	456	8TH WARD
LEWIS, RILEY	WOR	214	4TH E DI
LEWIS, RISPAH A. M.	MGM	439	CLARKSTR
LEWIS, ROBERT	WAS	032	2ND SUBD
LEWIS, ROBERT	WOR	167	6TH E DI
LEWIS, ROBERT	BAL	321	1ST DIST
LEWIS, ROBERT	DOR	328	3RD DIVI
LEWIS, ROBERT J.	MGM	395	ROCKERLE
LEWIS, SALLY	WOR	216	4TH E DI
LEWIS, SALLY	WAS	188	BOONSBOR
LEWIS, SAMUEL	WAS	220	1ST DIST
LEWIS, SAMUEL	CEC	195	6TH E DI
LEWIS, SAMUEL	BAL	301	1ST DIST
LEWIS, SARAH	BAL	048	2ND DIST
LEWIS, SARAH	BAL	304	20TH WAR
LEWIS, SARAH	BAL	171	19TH WAR
LEWIS, SARAH	MGM	338	CRACKLIN
LEWIS, SARAH	FRE	153	10TH E D
LEWIS, SARAH A.	DOR	411	1ST DIST
LEWIS, SARAH A.	BAL	003	4TH WARD
LEWIS, SARAH E.	CAR	209	5TH DIST
LEWIS, SARAH L.	CEC	114	3RD E DI
LEWIS, SARAH R.	BAL	052	18TH WAR
LEWIS, SARRAH	DOR	362	3RD DIVI
LEWIS, SIBLY-BLACK	FRE	219	BUCKEYST
LEWIS, STEPHEN	BAL	095	5TH WARD
LEWIS, STEPHEN	MGM	442	CLARKSTR
LEWIS, TENNEY	QUE	214	3RD E DI
LEWIS, THOAMS	BAL	108	13TH WAR
LEWIS, THOMA SH.	FRE	228	BUCKEYST
LEWIS, THOMAS	FRE	255	NEW MARK
LEWIS, THOMAS	FRE	259	NEW MARK
LEWIS, THOMAS	DOR	331	3RD DIVI
LEWIS, THOMAS	CEC	117	4TH E DI
LEWIS, THOMAS	BAL	331	3RD WARD
LEWIS, THOMAS	ALL	070	5TH E.D.
LEWIS, THOMAS	BAL	258	6TH WARD
LEWIS, W.	BAL	282	2ND WARD
LEWIS, WASHINGTON	MGM	376	ROCKERLE
LEWIS, WESLEY	WAS	147	HAGERSTO
LEWIS, WILLIAM	WAS	190	1ST DIST
LEWIS, WILLIAM	QUE	233	4TH E DI
LEWIS, WILLIAM	WOR	343	1ST E DI
LEWIS, WILLIAM	WOR	328	1ST E DI
LEWIS, WILLIAM	QUE	169	2ND E DI
LEWIS, WILLIAM	SOM	453	DAMES QU
LEWIS, WILLIAM	TAL	008	EASTON D
LEWIS, WILLIAM	FRE	056	FREDERIC
LEWIS, WILLIAM	CEC	118	4TH E DI
LEWIS, WILLIAM	BAL	300	17TH WAR
LEWIS, WILLIAM	CAR	277	7TH DIST
LEWIS, WILLIAM	BAL	297	20TH WAR
LEWIS, WILLIAM	BAL	150	19TH WAR
LEWIS, WILLIAM	FRE	260	NEW MARK
LEWIS, WILLIAM	FRE	220	BUCKEYST
LEWIS, WILLIAM	DOR	410	1ST DIST
LEWIS, WILLIAM	BAL	387	1ST DIST
LEWIS, WILLIAM	BAL	427	1ST DIST
LEWIS, WILLIAM	BAL	103	2ND DIST
LEWIS, WILLIAM	BAL	457	8TH WARD
LEWIS, WILLIAM	BAL	175	11TH WAR
LEWIS, WILLIAM	BAL	004	15TH WAR
LEWIS, WILLIAM	BAL	431	8TH WARD
LEWIS, WILLIAM	BAL	170	1ST WARD
LEWIS, WILLIAM	BAL	172	1ST WARD
LEWIS, WILLIAM	BAL	168	1ST WARD
LEWIS, WILLIAM	BAL	129	5TH WARD
LEWIS, WILLIAM A.-MULATTO	FRE	436	8TH E DI
LEWIS, WILLIAM C.	BAL	007	1ST WARD
LEWIS, WILLIAM D.	FRE	003	FREDERIC
LEWIS, WILLIAM S.	WOR	165	6TH E DI
LEWIS, WILLIAM T.	MGM	382	ROCKERLE
LEWIS, WILLIAM-MULATTO	FRE	436	8TH E DI
LEWIS, WILSON	DOR	332	3RD DIVI
LEWIS, WILSON	BAL	282	1ST DIST
LEWIS, ZADOCK S.	WOR	218	4TH E DI
LEWIS, ZEKEAH	ALL	119	5TH E.D.
LEWIS, ZEKIEL	CAR	111	NO TWP L
LEWIS, ZIPPA	WOR	278	BERLIN 1
LEWIS,ANNA M.	QUE	184	3RD E DI
LEWIS,MARTHA B.	BAL	073	2ND DIST
LEWISON,ANTONE	BAL	105	1ST WARD
LEWISSON, CHARLES	BAL	157	16TH WAR
LEWIT, SARAH *	ANN	411	8TH DIST
LEWITT, JOHN-MULATTO	BAL	223	2ND WARD
LEWYGOUS, ELIZA	BAL	197	19TH WAR
LEWYT, CAROLINE	BAL	120	5TH WARD
LEWYT, SOLOMON H.	BAL	120	5TH WARD
LEYDEN, WILLIAM A.A.*	CAR	132	NO TWP L
LEYH, SARAH*	TAL	061	EASTON D
LEYHOLD, HANNAH	BAL	084	10TH WAR
LEYHOLD, LOUIS	BAL	087	10TH WAR
LEYPOLD, ELIZABETH	WAS	193	1ST DIST
LEYPOLD, ELIZABETH*	BAL	080	10TH WAR
LEYPOLE, JOHN	WAS	188	1ST DIST
LEYTON, SOPHIA C.	BAL	069	4TH WARD
LIALS, JOHN*	BAL	369	3RD WARD
LIALS, SARAH A.	BAL	369	3RD WARD
LIAR, MATILDA	BAL	265	1ST DIST
LIAS, GEORGE	KEN	253	1ST DIST
LIB, STEPHEN	BAL	281	17TH WAR
LIBBEY, EDWIN	BAL	198	19TH WAR
LIBBEY, HARRY	BAL	198	19TH WAR
LIBBEY, JOANNA	BAL	203	19TH WAR
LIBBY, EMALINE	SOM	511	BARREN C
LIBBY, HENRY	ANN	347	3RD DIST
LIBBY, JOHN	ANN	347	3RD DIST
LIBBY, SARAH	SOM	514	BARREN C
LIBBY, WINDER	SOM	508	BARREN C
LIBE, MARY	BAL	150	11TH WAR
LIBEL, JOHN*	BAL	027	4TH WARD
LIBELHOLT, JOHN	BAL	050	18TH WAR
LIBEN, HENRY	BAL	132	2ND DIST
LIBER, JOHN	BAL	381	8TH WARD
LIBERT, CHARLES	WAS	212	1ST DIST
LIBERTS, GERARD*	BAL	349	3RD WARD
LIBERTY, ANN	BAL	170	19TH WAR
LIBERTY, SARAH	BAL	341	7TH WARD
LIBLA, MARY	BAL	448	8TH WARD
LIBLE, JOHN	BAL	322	7TH WARD
LIBURN, SAMUEL	BAL	026	18TH WAR
LICHTY, DANIEL	FRE	137	5TH E DI
LICKE, THOMAS N.	BAL	155	11TH WAR
LICKEL, FRANCIS	FRE	254	NEW MARK
LICKETT, JAMES H.	BAL	176	11TH WAR
LICKLIDER, JOHN	FRE	093	FREDERIC
LICKMAN, WILLIAM	BAL	375	8TH WARD
LICOUNT, MACEY	CAL	036	2ND DIST
LICUTAND, DENICE *	BAL	042	18TH WAR
LIDART, LEVI	BAL	387	1ST DIST
LIDAY, GEORGE W.	WAS	284	1ST DIST
LIDAY, SOLOMON	WAS	284	1ST DIST
LIDAY, WILSON	WAS	284	1ST DIST
LIDDA, JAMES	CEC	062	1ST E DI
LIDDLE, JOSEPH	BAL	007	4TH WARD
LIDDLE, ROBERT	BAL	264	7TH WARD
LIDDLE, THOMAS	BAL	443	1ST DIST
LIDDLE, WILLIAM	BAL	122	1ST WARD
LIDEN, JOHN	BAL	399	1ST DIST
LIDENHAM, DANIEL	TAL	112	ST MICHA
LIDER, JOHN	BAL	377	8TH WARD
LIDES, MARGARETT*	BAL	030	4TH WARD
LIDES, WILLIAM*	BAL	029	4TH WARD
LIDEY, HENRY	WAS	244	SMITHSBU
LIDID, WILLIAM	BAL	369	1ST DIST
LIDINGS, LOYD	HAR	189	3RD DIST
LIDINS, LOUISA	HAR	190	3RD DIST
LIDLEY, EDWARD C.	HAR	004	1ST DIST
LIDMAN,WILHELMINA	BAL	075	1ST WARD
LIDWELL, JOSEPH	CEC	142	6TH E DI
LIE, KATE	BAL	153	19TH WAR
LIEB, JACOB	BAL	112	10TH WAR
LIEBAGOD, MARGARET	BAL	276	1ST DIST
LIEBBERT, CHRISTIAN	BAL	251	2ND WARD
LIEBE, GODFRIED	BAL	207	19TH WAR
LIEBEN, JOHN F.	BAL	001	EASTERN
LIEBLER, H.	BAL	449	8TH WARD
LIEBLINE, GEORGE	BAL	234	1ST DIST
LIECHTENBERG, FREDERICK	BAL	300	17TH WAR
LIENS, CHARLES	KEN	264	1ST DIST
LIEPLINE, DAVID	BAL	236	1ST DIST
LIERNY, MICHAEL	BAL	174	2ND DIST
LIERS, MARY	BAL	390	13TH WAR
LIES, JANE	BAL	339	1ST DIST
LIESHBAUGH, JACOB	ALL	098	5TH E.D.
LIESON, JAMES G.	BAL	440	1ST DIST
LIESS, ELIAS	FRE	115	CREAGERS
LIESTER, ABRAHAM	CAR	191	4TH DIST
LIESTER, ABRAHAM	CAR	191	4TH DIST
LIESTER, DAVID	CAR	276	7TH DIST
LIETENZHAL, HENRY	BAL	353	13TH WAR
LIETZ, JACOB	BAL	273	20TH WAR
LIFE, ROBERT	FRE	016	FREDERIC
LIFEVORE, ELI P.	FRE	159	EMMITTSB
LIFFER, CHARLES	BAL	024	4TH WARD
LIFRIED, ELIZA	BAL	025	4TH WARD
LIFRIED, FREDERICK*	BAL	024	4TH WARD
LIFTON, WILLIAM	FRE	128	CREAGERS
LIGENFELDER, VIRGINIA	BAL	297	3RD WARD
LIGGET, JOHN H.	CAR	327	1ST DIST
LIGGETT, ELIZABETH	BAL	035	4TH WARD
LIGGETT, JOHN	WAS	224	1ST DIST
LIGGETT, JOHN	WAS	223	1ST DIST
LIGHAMS, CINTHEA	BAL	232	6TH WARD
LIGHOER, ELIZABETH	FRE	334	MIDDLETO
LIGHOER, HENRY	FRE	317	MIDDLETO
LIGHOER, PETGER	FRE	334	MIDDLETO
LIGHT, ELIAS	BAL	239	1ST DIST
LIGHT, JACOB	BAL	368	1ST DIST
LIGHT, JACOB	BAL	118	18TH WAR
LIGHT, JACOB	BAL	106	18TH WAR
LIGHT, JOHN	BAL	044	2ND DIST
LIGHT, LAURENCE	BAL	166	2ND DIST
LIGHT, LEAH	DOR	415	1ST DIST
LIGHT, MARY	BAL	277	20TH WAR
LIGHTBACK, LOUISIA	BAL	239	2ND WARD
LIGHTBURN, JAMES	CEC	008	ELKTON 3
LIGHTER, JOHN	FRE	073	FREDERIC
LIGHTER, LAUSON	FRE	073	FREDERIC
LIGHTFOOT, MARY	BAL	075	10TH WAR
LIGHTNER, AARON	BAL	132	2ND DIST
LIGHTNER, AGNES M.	BAL	105	5TH WARD
LIGHTNER, AMOS	CAR	409	2ND DIST
LIGHTNER, BENJAMIN	FRE	090	FREDERIC
LIGHTNER, CHRISTOPHER	BAL	389	8TH WARD
LIGHTNER, DAVIS	CAR	264	WESTMINS
LIGHTNER, DEORAH	CAR	378	2ND DIST
LIGHTNER, FREDERICK	FRE	123	CREAGERS
LIGHTNER, HENRY	BAL	237	17TH WAR
LIGHTNER, HENRY	BAL	106	5TH WARD
LIGHTNER, HENRY	WAS	097	2ND DIST
LIGHTNER, HENRY L.	WAS	101	2ND DIST
LIGHTNER, JAMES	FRE	135	CREAGERS
LIGHTNER, JOSEPH	FRE	139	CREAGERS
LIGHTNER, JOSEPH	BAL	262	17TH WAR
LIGHTNER, JOSHUA	FRE	139	CREAGERS
LIGHTNER, MARGARET	BAL	263	17TH WAR
LIGHTNER, MATILDA	BAL	398	8TH WARD
LIGHTNER, NATHANIEL	BAL	398	8TH WARD
LIGHTNER, PETER	CAR	348	6TH DIST
LIGHTNER, PRESLEY T.	FRE	107	CREAGERS
LIGHTNER, RACHAEL	FRE	136	CREAGERS
LIGHTNER, RACHAEL	FRE	137	CREAGERS
LIGHTNER, ROBERT-BLACK	CAR	393	2ND DIST
LIGHTNER, WILLIAM	FRE	139	CREAGERS
LIGHTNER, WILLIAM P.	BAL	199	6TH WARD
LIGHTREAD, GEORGE	BAL	073	2ND DIST
LIGHTS, JOHN	BAL	211	17TH WAR
LIGHTS, RICHARD	BAL	023	9TH WARD
LIGHTSINGER, ANDREW	QUE	154	1ST E DI
LIGON, MARY T.	ANN	465	HOWARD D
LIGON, THOMAS W.	ANN	465	HOWARD D
LIGTZBEY, HENRY W.	BAL	167	11TH WAR
LIJAH, MARIA	BAL	348	1ST DIST
LIKE, CHRISTINA	BAL	170	2ND DIST
LIKENS, OTHO	WAS	046	2ND SUBD
LIKEY, LEWIS*	BAL	013	4TH WARD
LIKINS, ANDREW	WAS	162	HAGERSTO
LILBURN, ROBERT F.	ST	308	1ST E DI
LILES, HARRIET	FRE	023	FREDERIC
LILES, HARRIET-BLACK	FRE	042	FREDERIC
LILES, JACOB	ST	254	3RD E DI
LILES, JAMES-BLACK	FRE	048	FREDERIC
LILES, JOSEPH-BLACK	FRE	017	FREDERIC

Name	County	Page	District
LILES, MARY-BLACK	QUE	157	2ND E DI
LILES, THOMAS J.-BLACK	FRE	010	FREDERIC
LILET, MARGARET	ALL	259	CUMBERLA
LILIENTHOL, FREDERICK%	BAL	157	19TH WAR
LILLAHY, ROBERT	TAL	072	EASTON T
LILLARD, ESTEP E. *	ANN	408	8TH DIST
LILLARD, JEROME	MGM	440	CLARKSTR
LILLELL, BETSEY *	BAL	068	18TH WAR
LILLER, FRECERICK	BAL	296	3RD WARD
LILLET, ELIZABETH	BAL	233	20TH WAR
LILLEY, CAROLINE	BAL	043	4TH WARD
LILLEY, ELIAS	FRE	182	5TH E DI
LILLEY, ELIZA J.	SOM	407	DUBLIN D
LILLEY, G. A.	ANN	337	3RD DIST
LILLEY, WILLIAM	CEC	109	4TH E DI
LILLIBRIDGE, GEORGE	ANN	439	HOWARD D
LILLIN, MICHAEL	KEN	292	3RD DIST
LILLIS, HARRY	BAL	156	19TH WAR
LILLRED, WILLIAM	BAL	149	19TH WAR
LILLY, ABRAHAM	BAL	121	16TH WAR
LILLY, ADAM	BAL	346	1ST DIST
LILLY, AIRY	FRE	087	FREDERIC
LILLY, ALONZO	BAL	319	20TH WAR
LILLY, ANN	BAL	078	15TH WAR
LILLY, ANNE	BAL	047	15TH WAR
LILLY, CATHARINE	BAL	378	1ST DIST
LILLY, CHARLOTTE J.	BAL	214	11TH WAR
LILLY, DANIEL	CEC	190	5TH E DI
LILLY, ELERY	BAL	256	20TH WAR
LILLY, ELIZA	BAL	337	1ST DIST
LILLY, G. W.	BAL	298	20TH WAR
LILLY, GEORGE	BAL	258	1ST DIST
LILLY, GEORGE W.	BAL	113	1ST WARD
LILLY, J.R.	BAL	173	1ST WARD
LILLY, JACKSON	BAL	053	4TH WARD
LILLY, JAMES	BAL	345	1ST DIST
LILLY, JOHN	BAL	349	1ST DIST
LILLY, JOHN	BAL	364	1ST DIST
LILLY, JOHN	HAR	088	2ND DIST
LILLY, JOHN	CEC	105	3RD E DI
LILLY, JOSHUA	ALL	084	5TH E.D.
LILLY, LUCINDA R.	BAL	225	6TH WARD
LILLY, MARGARET	BAL	363	1ST DIST
LILLY, MARY C.	FRE	065	FREDERIC
LILLY, MARY A.	BAL	311	1ST DIST
LILLY, ONORA	BAL	366	1ST DIST
LILLY, PETER	BAL	131	16TH WAR
LILLY, PETER	BAL	071	4TH WARD
LILLY, RICHARD	BAL	043	4TH WARD
LILLY, RICHARD	CEC	044	1ST E DI
LILLY, RICHARD	CEC	044	CHESAPEA
LILLY, RICHARD	BAL	347	1ST DIST
LILLY, ROBERT	ANN	451	HOWARD D
LILLY, ROBERT B.	BAL	214	11TH WAR
LILLY, SAMUEL	CAR	346	6TH DIST
LILLY, SAMUEL	BAL	372	1ST DIST
LILLY, SAMUEL	ANN	516	HOWARD D
LILLY, SARAH	BAL	125	5TH WARD
LILLY, SARAH	FRE	062	FREDERIC
LILLY, THOMAS	HAR	116	2ND DIST
LILLY, THOMAS	ST	308	1ST E DI
LILLY, WILLIAM	BAL	364	1ST DIST
LILLY, WILLIAM	ANN	468	HOWARD D
LILLY, ZACHARIAH	BAL	364	1ST DIST
LILPIN, CHARLES	FRE	132	CREAGERS
LILSOR, CHARLES H.*	DOR	341	3RD DIVI
LILTIG, THOMAS	HAR	139	2ND DIST
LILY, CHARLES	CEC	190	5TH E DI
LILY, MARGARET	BAL	101	5TH WARD
LILY, WASHINGTON	ANN	367	4TH DIST
LIMAN, CATHARIEN	HAR	034	1ST DIST
LIMAN, CHARLES*	BAL	396	3RD WARD
LIMBERRY, DAVID	BAL	017	4TH WARD
LIMBERRY, JOHN	BAL	377	13TH WAR
LIMBERRY, ROBERT*	BAL	391	3RD WARD
LIMBERRY, WASHINGTON	BAL	377	13TH WAR
LIMBORRY, ROBERT*	BAL	391	3RD WARD
LIMBRECK, ELIZABETH	BAL	450	8TH WARD
LIMBRICKS, TEMPEY	BAL	328	3RD WARD
LIMBY, JOHN	BAL	072	2ND DIST
LIMEKILLER, MATTHEW	BAL	131	16TH WAR
LIMERICK, MARY	BAL	229	2ND WARD
LIMERS, ROBERT	BAL	168	1ST WARD
LIMES, ADAM	WAS	124	2ND DIST
LIMES, HANAH	BAL	455	8TH WARD
LIMGREN, JOHN	CEC	108	3RD E DI
LIMIENBERGER, CATHERINE	BAL	081	18TH WAR
LIMMY, ROBERT	BAL	205	19TH WAR
LIMOR, SOPHIAH	DOR	370	3RD DIVI
LIMRATH, WILLIAM	BAL	068	10TH WAR
LIMROAD, CONRAD*	BAL	326	3RD WARD
LIMUS, HENRY*	SOM	497	SALISBUR
LINAN, JOHN	BAL	335	1ST DIST
LINAN, WILLIAM	BAL	273	2ND WARD
LINARD, BIDDY	BAL	294	1ST DIST
LINAT, SAMUEL L.	BAL	253	12TH WAR
LINBER, DAVID	CEC	060	1ST E DI
LINBERGER, KITTY	BAL	437	14TH WAR
LINBURN, D. VAN*	BAL	271	20TH WAR
LINBURY, S.	BAL	156	1ST WARD
LINCE, A. L.	BAL	152	1ST WARD
LINCH, ABRAHAM	BAL	076	18TH WAR
LINCH, BELSORA*	TAL	065	EASTON T
LINCH, BENJAMIN	BAL	451	8TH WARD
LINCH, ELIZABETH	HAR	059	1ST DIST
LINCH, GEORGE	WAS	117	2ND DIST
LINCH, ISAAC	WOR	275	BERLIN 1
LINCH, JAMES	WOR	208	4TH E DI
LINCH, JAMES M.*	DOR	319	1ST DIST
LINCH, JOHN	PRI	050	AQUASCO
LINCH, LEAH	WOR	279	BERLIN 1
LINCH, LOTTY	WOR	275	BERLIN 1
LINCH, MARGARET	WOR	278	BERLIN 1
LINCH, MARY	BAL	260	2ND WARD
LINCH, MARY A.	BAL	103	18TH WAR
LINCH, NORIA	BAL	198	11TH WAR
LINCH, RICHARD	FRE	230	BUCKEYST
LINCH, SUSAN	BAL	299	12TH WAR
LINCH, WILLAIM	HAR	071	1ST DIST
LINCH, WILLIAM*	TAL	065	EASTON T
LINCHENCUM, RUTH	BAL	040	18TH WAR
LINCHENCUN, HENRY W.	BAL	079	18TH WAR
LINCK, CATHARIEN	CAR	200	4TH DIST
LINCK, HENRY	BAL	186	19TH WAR
LINCK, WILLIAM*	BAL	027	4TH WARD
LINCKAMPER, HENRY	BAL	108	5TH WARD
LINCKER, ELIZA	BAL	080	10TH WAR
LINCOLN, CORNELIA F.	CEC	166	6TH E DI
LINCOLN, E.	BAL	139	19TH WAR
LINCOLN, ISRAEL	BAL	134	1ST WARD
LINCOLN, J.	BAL	136	1ST WARD
LINCOLN, JACOB	ALL	101	5TH E.D.
LINCOLN, JOHN	CEC	165	6TH E DI
LINCOLN, JOSEPH	BAL	207	19TH WAR
LINCOLN, JOSIAH L.	BAL	309	12TH WAR
LINCOLN, NATHAN	BAL	145	11TH WAR
LINCUM, MARY	FRE	318	MIDDLETO
LINCUTANO, DENICE	BAL	042	18TH WAR
LINCY, JAMES	WAS	124	2ND DIST
LIND, AUGUST	BAL	459	8TH WARD
LIND, GEORGE	BAL	103	15TH WAR
LIND, ROBERT *	KEN	235	2ND DIST
LIND, T. H.	BAL	157	1ST WARD
LINDA, JOHN	QUE	169	2ND E DI
LINDAL, ELIZABETH	BAL	367	3RD WARD
LINDAL, JOHN	BAL	109	2ND DIST
LINDAL, PETER	WOR	281	BERLIN 1
LINDALL, RACHEL	BAL	026	9TH WARD
LINDAMAN, CATHARINE	CAR	348	6TH DIST
LINDAMAN, ELIZABETH	CAR	347	6TH DIST
LINDAMON, EVE	BAL	454	1ST DIST
LINDAMORE, HARRIET	BAL	451	1ST DIST
LINDAMORE, WILLIAM	HAR	202	3RD DIST
LINDAMORE, WILLIAM	HAR	201	3RD DIST
LINDBURY, A. F.	BAL	146	1ST WARD
LINDEMAN, CONRAD	BAL	076	15TH WAR
LINDEMAN, CONRAD JR.	BAL	076	15TH WAR
LINDEMAN, EDWARD	BAL	464	14TH WAR
LINDEMAN, FREDERICK	BAL	040	15TH WAR
LINDEMAN, MARGARET	BAL	131	16TH WAR
LINDEMAN, WILLIAM	BAL	080	10TH WAR
LINDEMANN, HARMAN N.	BAL	166	16TH WAR
LINDEN, JAMES	ALL	249	CUMBERLA
LINDEN, JAMES	CEC	135	6TH E DI
LINDENBAUM, HENRY	BAL	366	13TH WAR
LINDENBERGER, DANIEL C.	BAL	028	15TH WAR
LINDENBERGER, GEORGE-MULA	FRE	042	FREDERIC
LINDENBERGER, HANNA	BAL	040	4TH WARD
LINDENBERGER, JOHN H.	BAL	121	16TH WAR
LINDENBORN, DAVID	BAL	197	6TH WARD
LINDENER, ELLEN	BAL	062	1ST WARD
LINDENHALL, MARTHA	CEC	141	6TH E DI
LINDENMANN, ANN M.	BAL	125	16TH WAR
LINDENMORE, SARAH	BAL	009	EASTERN
LINDER, ALFRED	BAL	210	19TH WAR
LINDER, ANTHONY	BAL	210	6TH DIST
LINDER, LENEA	BAL	110	5TH WARD
LINDERMAN, HENRY	BAL	459	8TH WARD
LINDERMAN, JOHN	BAL	168	6TH WARD
LINDERMAN, LOUIS	BAL	005	EASTERN
LINDERMAN, NICHOLAS	BAL	352	13TH WAR
LINDHARDT, GEORGE	BAL	126	11TH WAR
LINDLE, JODE	BAL	396	1ST DIST
LINDLE, WILLIAM M.	BAL	301	1ST DIST
LINDLEIN, ERHARDT	BAL	022	15TH WAR
LINDLEY, ELIZABETH	FRE	419	8TH E DI
LINDLY, JAMES	BAL	460	1ST DIST
LINDOLPH, JOSEPH	BAL	156	19TH WAR
LINDORD, JOSEPH	BAL	384	13TH WAR
LINDSAY, AMOS	BAL	212	11TH WAR
LINDSAY, ELIZABETH	BAL	281	12TH WAR
LINDSAY, EPHRAIM	CAR	375	9TH DIST
LINDSAY, GEORGE W.	BAL	288	12TH WAR
LINDSAY, ISABEL	BAL	212	11TH WAR
LINDSAY, LEWIS	CAR	362	9TH DIST
LINDSAY, LEWIS	CAR	382	2ND DIST
LINDSAY, MARY	BAL	211	6TH DIST
LINDSAY, MUASTASIA *	BAL	418	14TH WAR
LINDSAY, RACHEL	BAL	097	1ST WARD
LINDSAY, SARAH	CAR	272	WESTMINS
LINDSEY, ANDREW B.	HAR	031	1ST DIST
LINDSEY, BENJAMIN	FRE	440	8TH E DI
LINDSEY, CHARLOTTE	BAL	149	11TH WAR
LINDSEY, CHARLOTTE W.-BLA	QUE	194	3RD E DI
LINDSEY, E.	PRI	108	PISCATAW
LINDSEY, ELIZABETH	BAL	148	11TH WAR
LINDSEY, ELIZABETH	BAL	207	6TH WARD
LINDSEY, FRANCIS	BAL	034	9TH WARD
LINDSEY, HANNAH	CAR	215	5TH DIST
LINDSEY, HARRIET	BAL	015	1ST WARD
LINDSEY, HENRIETTA	BAL	160	16TH WAR
LINDSEY, HUGH	BAL	019	2ND DIST
LINDSEY, JAMES W.	BAL	018	9TH WARD
LINDSEY, JOHN	BAL	087	18TH WAR
LINDSEY, JOHN D.	FRE	440	8TH E DI
LINDSEY, JOHN D.	BAL	182	16TH WAR
LINDSEY, JOHN H.	BAL	388	8TH WARD
LINDSEY, JOHN H.	CAR	208	5TH DIST
LINDSEY, MARY	BAL	012	9TH WARD
LINDSEY, MARY E.	BAL	329	7TH WARD
LINDSEY, MATTHIAS	WOR	329	1ST E DI
LINDSEY, NANCY	HAR	013	1ST DIST
LINDSEY, SAMUEL	CAR	224	5TH DIST
LINDSEY, SARAH	FRE	435	8TH E DI
LINDSEY, WILLIAM	BAL	145	11TH WAR
LINDSEY, WILLIAM	QUE	170	2ND E DI
LINDSLEY, BENJAMIN	BAL	184	19TH WAR
LINDSLEY, BENJAMIN	BAL	060	15TH WAR
LINDSLEY, MRS.	BAL	184	19TH WAR
LINDVILLE, MARY C.	BAL	226	6TH WARD
LINDWALL, J. *	BAL	281	2ND WARD
LINE, ARTHUR	ALL	103	5TH E.D.
LINE, S. W.	BAL	316	12TH WAR
LINEBACK, MARTHEW L.	BAL	324	7TH WARD
LINEBAUGH, BENJAMIN	FRE	344	MIDDLETO
LINEBAUGH, BENJAMIN	WAS	291	1ST DIST
LINEBAUGH, CHRISTIANA	BAL	359	1ST DIST
LINEBAUGH, DANIEL	FRE	351	MIDDLETO
LINEBAUGH, HENRY	BAL	358	1ST DIST
LINEBAUGH, JOHN	FRE	341	MIDDLETO
LINEBAUGH, JOHN	FRE	351	MIDDLETO
LINEBERG, JOHN	BAL	263	12TH WAR
LINEBERGER, CATHERINE	BAL	264	7TH WARD
LINEBERGER, CHARLOTTE A.	ANN	424	HOWARD D
LINEBERGER, KITTEY	BAL	338	7TH WARD
LINEBERGER, MATILDA	BAL	351	1ST DIST
LINEBERGH, RUDOLPH	BAL	133	11TH WAR
LINEGANBER, HENRY	BAL	370	8TH WARD
LINEHART, HENRY	BAL	256	1ST DIST
LINEHOFF, PETER	BAL	159	2ND DIST
LINEKEMPLER, ANN	BAL	408	8TH WARD
LINENBERGER, MARY	BAL	170	11TH WAR
LINENBOW, ELIZABETH	BAL	180	6TH WARD
LINENER, GEORGE*	BAL	410	3RD WARD
LINER, ALEXANDER	BAL	290	1ST DIST
LINER, CASPER	BAL	215	19TH WAR
LINER, JOHN	BAL	229	19TH WAR
LINER, LOUIS F.	BAL	289	1ST DIST
LINERE, ARNOLD	FRE	149	10TH E D
LINEROEVER, GEORGE	BAL	274	20TH WAR
LINERWOOD, JIM	BAL	232	12TH WAR
LINES, DANIEL *	WAS	186	BOONSBOR
LINES, HENRY	ALL	044	10TH E.D
LINES, JANE	ALL	234	CUMBERLA
LINEWEVER, NOAH	CAR	353	6TH DIST
LING, GEORGE	BAL	090	1ST WARD
LING, HENRY	BAL	380	8TH WARD
LING, SUSAN	BAL	002	4TH WARD
LINGAFFETTY, WILLIAM	FRE	332	MIDDLETO
LINGENBOCK, FRED	BAL	295	12TH WAR
LINGENFELTER, CATHARINE	BAL	198	19TH WAR
LINGERMAN, RUDOLPH	BAL	197	11TH WAR
LINGERVALD, ANDREW	BAL	186	19TH WAR
LINGEWALD, MARGARET	BAL	186	19TH WAR
LINGFILTER, JACOB*	TAL	068	EASTON T
LINGHAM, EDWARD	HAR	005	1ST DIST
LINGHAMS, LOUISA	BAL	058	2ND DIST
LINGHAN, EDWARD	HAR	104	2ND DIST
LINGHAN, MARY	HAR	144	2ND DIST
LINGIN, SARAH	WAS	226	1ST DIST
LINGINGFELTER, PETER	CAR	192	4TH DIST
LINGLEWALD, F.H.	BAL	248	2ND WARD
LINGO, DANIEL	KEN	296	3RD DIST
LINGO, JOHN	ALL	219	CUMBERLA
LINGO, WILLIAM M.	KEN	246	2ND DIST
LINGSELL, REBECCA E.	DOR	303	1ST DIST
LINGUM, ROBERT	HAR	191	3RD DIST
LINGUN,FANNY	BAL	050	2ND DIST
LINGWIN, ROBERT	HAR	204	3RD DIST
LINHARD, ANDREW	BAL	095	10TH WAR
LINHARD, THOMAS	BAL	208	5TH WARD
LINICOMB, FRANCIS	BAL	116	15TH WAR
LINIEUMAR, JOHN	BAL	075	18TH WAR
LININGER, JACOB	FRE	169	5TH E DI
LINIS, BEN	ANN	285	ANNAPOLI
LINK, ADAM	BAL	279	1ST DIST
LINK, ADAM	FRE	303	WOODSBOR
LINK, CATHARINE	BAL	081	15TH WAR
LINK, CHRISTOPHER	BAL	290	17TH WAR
LINK, DANIEL	FRE	303	WOODSBOR
LINK, ELIZABETH	WAS	228	1ST DIST
LINK, FREDERICK	WAS	235	1ST DIST
LINK, JACOB	FRE	096	FREDERIC
LINK, JOHN	BAL	279	1ST DIST
LINK, JOHN	ALL	226	CUMBERLA
LINK, LEWIS	FRE	419	8TH E DI
LINK, LOUISA	BAL	372	3RD WARD
LINK, PHILIP	BAL	326	12TH WAR
LINK, SIMON	BAL	431	8TH WARD
LINK, THOMAS	BAL	298	17TH WAR
LINKARDS, GEORGE	BAL	284	2ND WARD
LINKENFELTER, GEORGE	BAL	380	8TH WARD
LINKER, C.	BAL	215	19TH WAR
LINKER, CATHERINE	FRE	247	NEW MARK
LINKIN, LAURENCE	WAS	132	HAGERSTO
LINKIN, SUSANA*	BAL	318	3RD WARD
LINKINS, JOSEPH	CHA	242	HILLTOP
LINKINS, PETER	CHA	240	HILLTOP
LINKINS, THOMAS	CHA	242	HILLTOP
LINKLER, ELIZABETH	BAL	342	7TH WARD
LINKTINE, SAMUEL	WAS	286	1ST DIST
LINKUM, EMMA	MGM	326	CRACKLIN
LINKUM, PERRY	MGM	335	CRACKLIN
LINKUM, RACHEL	MGM	326	CRACKLIN
LINLOPE, CHRISTIN	HAR	203	3RD DIST
LINLY, ROSE	BAL	151	11TH WAR
LINMAN, CHARLOTTE	WAS	257	1ST DIST
LINMAN, WILLIAM	BAL	094	18TH WAR
LINN, ABRAHAM	CAR	326	1ST DIST
LINN, ANN	BAL	231	6TH WARD
LINN, CATHARINE	BAL	452	14TH WAR
LINN, CATHARINE	FRE	177	5TH E DI
LINN, CATHARINE A.	CAR	391	2ND DIST
LINN, D.	BAL	281	2ND WARD
LINN, DANIEL	FRE	091	FREDERIC
LINN, DAVID O.	BAL	469	14TH WAR
LINN, ELIJAH	WAS	118	2ND DIST
LINN, GEORGE*	BAL	269	20TH WAR
LINN, HANAH	CAR	326	1ST DIST
LINN, JACOB	FRE	061	FREDERIC
LINN, JAMES	ANN	481	HOWARD D
LINN, JOHN	ANN	485	HOWARD D
LINN, MARY	BAL	414	8TH WARD
LINN, MOSES	MGM	338	CRACKLIN
LINN, PARMELIA	FRE	061	FREDERIC
LINN, PATRICK	BAL	272	1ST DIST
LINN, PERRY	ANN	462	HOWARD D
LINN, RACHEL	ANN	517	HOWARD D
LINN, REUBEN	MGM	337	CRACKLIN
LINN, SARAH	CAR	302	1ST DIST
LINN, WILLIAM	BAL	127	1ST WARD
LINNANVAN, ANN TERESA SIS	BAL	316	20TH WAR
LINNDWEAVER, HENRY L.	BAL	122	11TH WAR
LINNEFERLDEN, JOHN	BAL	136	11TH WAR
LINNEHAN, DENNIS	ANN	475	HOWARD D
LINNENBEAVER, PETER	BAL	123	11TH WAR
LINNENBERY, DANIEL	BAL	076	18TH WAR
LINNER, CONRAD	ANN	425	HOWARD D
LINNET, JAMES	ALL	141	6TH E.D.
LINNGAR, CAROLINE	BAL	444	14TH WAR
LINNING, SOPHRONIA	BAL	257	20TH WAR
LINNUS, MARIA	BAL	138	11TH WAR
LINPT, RACHEL	BAL	212	19TH WAR
LINS, ANN M.*	TAL	034	EASTON D
LINS, BENJAMIN*	TAL	029	EASTON D
LINS, GEORGE	BAL	026	15TH WAR
LINS, RACHEL*	TAL	031	EASTON D
LINSEY, ALICE	BAL	121	2ND DIST
LINSEY, ANTHONY	BAL	444	1ST DIST
LINSEY, ARCHIBALD*	BAL	376	3RD WARD
LINSEY, CATHERINE	BAL	010	4TH WARD
LINSEY, CHARLOTTE	BAL	378	3RD WARD
LINSEY, CHARLOTTE	BAL	259	6TH WARD
LINSEY, ELIZA	BAL	353	7TH WARD
LINSEY, ELLEN	BAL	370	3RD WARD
LINSEY, JANE	WAS	124	2ND DIST
LINSEY, JOHN	PRI	118	PISCATAW
LINSEY, JOHN	FRE	440	8TH E DI
LINSEY, MARY	BAL	121	2ND DIST
LINSEY, SAMUEL	BAL	259	6TH WARD
LINSEY, SAMUEL	BAL	249	2ND WARD
LINSEY, THOMAS	PRI	114	PISCATAW
LINSEY, WILLIAM	PRI	108	PISCATAW
LINSHEAME, JOSEPH	FRE	239	NEW MARK
LINSINHEM, ABRAHAM	BAL	019	9TH WARD
LINSLY, HENRY *	BAL	273	7TH WARD
LINSON, ABAGAL	HAR	181	3RD DIST
LINSON, PETER	HAR	181	3RD DIST
LINSTED, HAMUETEL E. *	ANN	352	3RD DIST
LINSTED, MARY	ANN	351	3RD DIST

LINSTED, SANDY ANN 352 3RD DIST
LINSY, CHARLOTTE DOR 450 1ST DIST
LINSY, NICHOLAS BAL 011 15TH WAR
LINSY, SAMUEL CEC 209 7TH E DI
LINSY, WILLIAM CEC 028 CHESAPEA
LINT, FREDRICK BAL 007 4TH WARD
LINT, JOSEPH BAL 211 19TH WAR
LINT, SEBASTIN BAL 248 2ND WARD
LINTCH, MARIA PRI 001 BLADENSB
LINTCH, MICHAEL PRI 039 VANSVILL
LINTCH, PATRICK PRI 033 VANSVILL
LINTEHCUM, HESIKIAH BAL 296 17TH WAR
LINTER, MARY A. BAL 264 2ND WARD
LINTERMAN, HERNY FRE 095 FREDERIC
LINTHECUM, EDWARD FRE 381 PETERSVI
LINTHECUM, FREDERICK BAL 261 17TH WAR
LINTHECUM, SAMUEL BAL 288 17TH WAR
LINTHECUM, WILLIAM H. FRE 383 PETERSVI
LINTHENCUM, CHARLES BAL 118 18TH WAR
LINTHENCUM, WILLIAM O. BAL 040 18TH WAR
LINTHGAUM, MATHIAS BAL 274 1ST DIST
LINTHIAN, GASSAWAYH W. MGM 430 CLARKSTR
LINTHICAM, OTHO W. FRE 230 BUCKEYST
LINTHICAW, JOHN H.L. FRE 230 BUCKEYST
LINTHICUM, AMELIA ANN 332 2ND DIST
LINTHICUM, ANN C. MGM 418 MEDLEY 3
LINTHICUM, BEN ANN 270 ANNAPOLI
LINTHICUM, ELIZABETH A. B BAL 080 15TH WAR
LINTHICUM, GOERGE ANN 346 3RD DIST
LINTHICUM, HARRIET BAL 289 20TH WAR
LINTHICUM, HEZEKIAH ANN 473 HOWARD D
LINTHICUM, HEZEKIAH ANN 338 3RD DIST
LINTHICUM, JAMES S. S. ANN 338 3RD DIST
LINTHICUM, JOHN ANN 331 2ND DIST
LINTHICUM, JOHN N. ANN 313 1ST DIST
LINTHICUM, JOHN W. ANN 472 HOWARD D
LINTHICUM, JOSHUA ANN 332 2ND DIST
LINTHICUM, LLOYD M. ANN 496 HOWARD D
LINTHICUM, OTHO DOR 468 1ST DIST
LINTHICUM, RICHARD* DOR 466 1ST DIST
LINTHICUM, STEPHEN ANN 304 1ST DIST
LINTHICUM, SWEETZER ANN 338 3RD DIST
LINTHICUM, THALES BAL 159 16TH WAR
LINTHICUM, THEODORE ANN 333 2ND DIST
LINTHICUM, THOMAS ANN 332 2ND DIST
LINTHICUM, WESLEY ANN 463 HOWARD D
LINTHICUM, WILLIAM ANN 338 3RD DIST
LINTHICUM, WILLIAM A. ANN 338 3RD DIST
LINTHICUM, ZACHARIA DOR 466 1ST DIST
LINTHIDEN, JOHN M. * FRE 314 MIDDLETO
LINTICHUM, DAVID DOR 367 3RD DIVI
LINTICHUM, FRANCES DOR 365 3RD DIVI
LINTICHUM, SARRAH DOR 370 3RD DIVI
LINTICHUM, ZACARIAH DOR 369 3RD DIVI
LINTON, DANIEL FRE 335 MIDDLETO
LINTON, DANIEL FRE 084 FREDERIC
LINTON, HANNAH SOM 431 PRINCESS
LINTON, HERMAN BAL 062 15TH WAR
LINTON, ISAAC BAL 097 2ND DIST
LINTON, JACOB SOM 359 BRINKLEY
LINTON, JAMES ALL 136 4TH E.D.
LINTON, JOHN BAL 329 1ST DIST
LINTON, JOHN BAL 420 1ST DIST
LINTON, JOHN BAL 279 2ND WARD
LINTON, JOHN FRE 085 FREDERIC
LINTON, JOHN * BAL 022 18TH WAR
LINTON, JOSEPH BAL 185 5TH DIST
LINTON, JOSEPHENE CEC 149 PORT DUP
LINTON, MAJOR SOM 461 HANGARY
LINTON, MARGARET CEC 184 7TH E DI
LINTON, MARY CEC 079 NORTHEAS
LINTON, SAMUEL CEC 193 5TH E DI
LINTON, THOMAS FRE 086 FREDERIC
LINTON, WILLIAM BAL 139 19TH WAR
LINTON, WILLIAM ESQ. BAL 238 17TH WAR
LINTZ, JOHN BAL 318 7TH WARD
LINTZ, WILLIAM BAL 286 7TH WARD
LINTZMER, G. BAL 308 20TH WAR
LINZ, JOHN BAL 229 6TH WARD
LINZERS, ELIZ WOR 337 1ST E DI
LION, MARY A. BAL 026 9TH WARD
LIONS, ELIZA CAR 105 NO TWP L
LIONS, ELLEN BAL 288 7TH WARD
LIPE, FREDERICK BAL 440 14TH WAR
LIPES, JOSHUA BAL 261 1ST DIST
LIPKER, WILLIAM BAL 142 16TH WAR
LIPP, ADAM BAL 142 5TH WARD
LIPP, FREDERICK BAL 350 13TH WAR
LIPP, MARGARET BAL 021 15TH WAR
LIPPARD, HENRY BAL 213 2ND WARD
LIPPENCOTT, JOSEPH HAR 076 BEL AIR
LIPPENCOTT, JOSEPH M HAR 076 BEL AIR
LIPPERD, MARGARET BAL 017 9TH WARD
LIPPERGD, GEORGE BAL 264 12TH WAR
LIPPETT, GEORGE ST 266 3RD E DI
LIPPEY, JESSE L. BAL 149 16TH WAR
LIPPEY, LEWIS BAL 198 19TH WAR
LIPPINCOTT, JAMES B. BAL 105 5TH WARD
LIPPITT, IRA BAL 183 19TH WAR
LIPPLE, GEORGE BAL 239 2ND WARD
LIPPLE, SAMUEL BAL 213 19TH WAR
LIPPO, ANN CAR 176 8TH DIST
LIPPO, JABEZ CAR 191 4TH DIST
LIPPO, JAOCB CAR 182 8TH DIST
LIPPOLD, LEWIS ALL 264 CUMBERLA
LIPPS, JOHN FRE 012 FREDERIC
LIPPY, BENJAMIN CAR 351 6TH DIST
LIPPY, GEORGE CAR 398 2ND DIST
LIPPY, JACOB CAR 350 6TH DIST
LIPPY, JOHN CAR 248 3RD DIST
LIPPY, JOSEPH CAR 175 8TH DIST
LIPPY, JUILA CAR 245 3RD DIST
LIPSCOMB, SUSAN B. FRE 065 FREDERIC
LIPTES, JOHN CEC 054 1ST E DI
LIPTON, JOSHUA BAL 451 1ST DIST
LIPTON, REBECCA-BLACK FRE 034 FREDERIC
LIPTON, WILLIAM B. HAR 067 1ST DIST
LIRATA, VICTOR BAL 173 2ND DIST
LIRTLE, ELIZABETH J. BAL 150 19TH WAR
LIRTY, REBECCA ST 290 2ND E DI
LIRUS, NACE FRE 064 FREDERIC
LISBY, DAVID * BAL 131 2ND DIST
LISBY, HARRY HAR 186 3RD DIST
LISBY, HORATIO PRI 119 PISCATAW
LISBY, JOHN N. PRI 096 SPALDING
LISBY, JOSEPH HAR 193 3RD DIST
LISBY, MARY PRI 081 QUEEN AN
LISBY, SARAH HAR 167 3RD DIST
LISBY, WILLIAM HAR 175 3RD DIST
LISCOMB, ELIZABETH BAL 228 6TH WARD
LISE, SMITH WAS 038 2ND SUBD
LISELL, PHILIP BAL 182 11TH WAR
LISER, ANDREW ANN 443 HOWARD D
LISER, DANIEL FRE 365 CATOCTIN
LISETTER, AMALMY BAL 142 19TH WAR
LISHA, MARY BAL 069 15TH WAR
LISHEAR, ELIJAH ANN 511 HOWARD D
LISHPAW, JOHN BAL 179 2ND DIST
LISK, MARIA CEC 054 1ST E DI
LISK, WILLIAM* DOR 312 1ST DIST
LISLES, BETTY-MULATTO FRE 392 PETERSVI
LISLES, DANIEL * WAS 186 BOONSBOR
LISLES, ELIZABETH WAS 291 1ST DIST
LISLES, HENRY WAS 196 1ST DIST
LISLES, RACHAEL WAS 196 1ST DIST
LISLEY, JOSEPH CEC 033 CHESAPEA
LISON, JOHN CEC 046 1ST E DI
LISRO, HENRY ANN 413 HOWARD D
LISSER, CHARLES WAS 130 HAGERSTO
LIST, CHRISTIAN BAL 334 3RD WARD
LIST, ELIZABETH BAL 241 20TH WAR
LIST, FREDERIC BAL 014 9TH WARD
LIST, FREDERICK BAL 004 18TH WAR
LIST, J.J. BAL 259 12TH WAR
LIST, JACOB BAL 214 19TH WAR
LIST, JOHN BAL 205 6TH DIST
LIST, JOHN A. BAL 181 16TH WAR
LISTER, ARTHUR BAL 025 15TH WAR
LISTER, ESTHER WOR 177 6TH E DI
LISTER, JOHN BAL 096 15TH WAR
LISTER, JOHN F. BAL 111 18TH WAR
LISTER, JOSEPH WAS 075 2ND SUBD
LISTER, NATHANIEL CAR 175 8TH DIST
LISTNER, NICHOLAS BAL 242 20TH WAR
LISTON, EDWARD BAL 408 1ST DIST
LISUS, EASTER-BLACK FRE 023 FREDERIC
LITCHFEILD, SAMUEL A. BAL 057 18TH WAR
LITCHFIELD, CHRISTIANA BAL 336 1ST DIST
LITCHFIELD, ELIZABETH BAL 066 18TH WAR
LITCHFIELD, LYZIE A. ANN 435 HOWARD D
LITCHFIELD, WILLIAM ANN 420 HOWARD D
LITCHTHER, JUSTUS BAL 285 2ND WARD
LITE, GEORGE HAR 153 3RD DIST
LITHGONE, ANNA M. BAL 031 9TH WARD
LITINGER, JAEMS HAR 199 3RD DIST
LITLE, DAVID-BLACK QUE 133 1ST E DI
LITLE, HARRIET BAL 359 13TH WAR
LITMAN, HENRY BAL 075 18TH WAR
LITSINGER, JAMES BAL 166 2ND DIST
LITSINGER, JOHN BAL 006 EASTERN
LITSINGER, MATILDA BAL 023 2ND DIST
LITTELL, PHILIP D. ST 277 3RD E DI
LITTELL, WILLIAM BAL 100 10TH WAR
LITTEN, LEVI WAS 138 2ND DIST
LITTER, MORRIS BAL 329 13TH WAR
LITTEWAY, ELIZABETH CEC 032 CHESAPEA
LITTEWAY, LOUIS CEC 031 CHESAPEA
LITTIG, AUGUSTUS* BAL 057 4TH WARD
LITTIG, CALEB B. BAL 313 3RD WARD
LITTIG, LUTHER BAL 195 11TH WAR
LITTIG, PHILIP* BAL 321 3RD WARD
LITTIG, REZIAH BAL 340 13TH WAR
LITTLE, AARON QUE 247 5TH E DI
LITTLE, ADAM CEC 084 CHARLEST
LITTLE, ALEXANDER CEC 103 4TH E DI
LITTLE, AMOS CAR 286 7TH DIST
LITTLE, AMOS CAR 354 6TH DIST
LITTLE, ANN BAL 010 18TH WAR
LITTLE, ANN ALL 241 CUMBERLA
LITTLE, ANN M. BAL 298 3RD WARD
LITTLE, ANN M. BAL 457 8TH WARD
LITTLE, APPELONG CEC 147 PORT DUP
LITTLE, CATHARINE BAL 242 12TH WAR
LITTLE, CHARLES ALL 171 7TH E.D.
LITTLE, CHARLES A. BAL 441 8TH WARD
LITTLE, CHRISTOPHER CEC 081 CHARLEST
LITTLE, D.F. WAS 152 HAGERSTO
LITTLE, DANIEL WAS 191 1ST DIST
LITTLE, DANIEL CAR 397 2ND DIST
LITTLE, DAVID CAR 255 3RD DIST
LITTLE, ENOCH FRE 266 NEW MARK
LITTLE, FANNY BAL 047 15TH WAR
LITTLE, GEORGE BAL 043 9TH WARD
LITTLE, GEORGE CAR 365 9TH DIST
LITTLE, GEORGE CAR 247 3RD DIST
LITTLE, GEORGE L. CAR 246 3RD DIST
LITTLE, HANNAH CAR 382 2ND DIST
LITTLE, HENRY FRE 110 CREAGERS
LITTLE, HENRY FRE 192 5TH E DI
LITTLE, HENRY G. BAL 281 2ND WARD
LITTLE, JACOB B. CAR 332 MANCHEST
LITTLE, JAMES CEC 083 CHARLEST
LITTLE, JAMES CEC 084 CHARLEST
LITTLE, JAMES CEC 144 PORT DUP
LITTLE, JAMES BAL 362 13TH WAR
LITTLE, JAMES BAL 227 19TH WAR
LITTLE, JAMES BAL 312 7TH WARD
LITTLE, JAMES BAL 169 1ST WARD
LITTLE, JAMES BAL 439 1ST DIST
LITTLE, JAMES T. BAL 052 9TH WARD
LITTLE, JANE BAL 035 4TH WARD
LITTLE, JANE CEC 072 5TH E DI
LITTLE, JAOCB CAR 402 2ND DIST
LITTLE, JAUB FRE 015 FREDERIC
LITTLE, JEREMIAH BAL 178 2ND DIST
LITTLE, JOHN BAL 312 7TH WARD
LITTLE, JOHN BAL 255 2ND WARD
LITTLE, JOHN BAL 255 6TH WARD
LITTLE, JOHN CAR 288 7TH DIST
LITTLE, JOHN CAR 281 7TH DIST
LITTLE, JOHN BAL 200 19TH WAR
LITTLE, JOHN CAR 213 5TH DIST
LITTLE, JOHN CEC 144 PORT DUP
LITTLE, JOHN CEC 132 6TH E DI
LITTLE, JOHN CEC 186 7TH E DI
LITTLE, JOHN A. BAL 104 15TH WAR
LITTLE, JOHN H. WAS 182 BOONSBOR
LITTLE, JOHNATHAN WAS 097 2ND DIST
LITTLE, JOSEPH WAS 147 HAGERSTO
LITTLE, JOSEPH ALL 023 2ND E.D.
LITTLE, JOSEPH BAL 118 18TH WAR
LITTLE, JOSEPH MGM 394 ROCKERLE
LITTLE, JOSEPH H. CAR 331 MANCHEST
LITTLE, JOSHUA KEN 306 3RD DIST
LITTLE, LAZARUS QUE 248 5TH E DI
LITTLE, LOTT-BLACK FRE 242 NEW MARK
LITTLE, LOUISA BAL 018 2ND DIST
LITTLE, LUCY BAL 099 5TH WARD
LITTLE, MARIA C. CAR 296 7TH DIST
LITTLE, MARY WAS 033 2ND SUBD
LITTLE, MARY E. CEC 026 ELKTON 3
LITTLE, MARY EMANUEL SIS- BAL 316 20TH WAR
LITTLE, MATILDA TAL 038 EASTON D
LITTLE, NANCY ALL 156 6TH E.D.
LITTLE, NORTH BAL 220 1ST DIST
LITTLE, PATRICK BAL 162 16TH WAR
LITTLE, PATRICK WAS 149 2ND DIST
LITTLE, PETER CAR 296 7TH DIST
LITTLE, PHILLIP BAL 225 17TH WAR
LITTLE, PRISSY* DOR 414 1ST DIST
LITTLE, RICHARD BAL 343 3RD WARD
LITTLE, ROBERT BAL 027 15TH WAR
LITTLE, ROBERT CEC 148 PORT DUP
LITTLE, ROBERT BAL 034 4TH WARD
LITTLE, SAMUEL HAR 112 2ND DIST
LITTLE, SAMUEL WAS 098 2ND DIST
LITTLE, SAMUEL H. WAS 126 HAGERSTO
LITTLE, SAMUEL-BLACK QUE 133 1ST E DI
LITTLE, THOMAS CEC 088 4TH E DI
LITTLE, THOMAS FRE 018 FREDERIC
LITTLE, THOMAS BAL 324 3RD WARD
LITTLE, THOMAS BAL 102 1ST WARD
LITTLE, THOMAS G. BAL 178 16TH WAR
LITTLE, TRUMAN W. FRE 390 PETERSVI
LITTLE, W. W. BAL 471 14TH WAR
LITTLE, WALTER BAL 222 1ST DIST
LITTLE, WASHINGTON BAL 249 1ST DIST
LITTLE, WILLIAM BAL 261 2ND WARD
LITTLE, WILLIAM CEC 197 7TH E DI
LITTLE, WILLIAM CEC 070 5TH E DI
LITTLE, WILLIAM CAR 245 3RD DIST
LITTLE, WILLIAM H. CEC 144 PORT DUP
LITTLE,ELIZABETH CAR 393 2ND DIST
LITTLE,JESSE T. FRE 400 JEFFERSO
LITTLE,JOHN L. FRE 025 FREDERIC
LITTLEFIELD, HERNY FRE 129 CREAGERS
LITTLEFIELD, RUFUS BAL 362 13TH WAR
LITTLEFIELD, SOPHIA BAL 246 6TH WARD
LITTLEFORD, ADDISON PRI 072 MARLBROU
LITTLEFORD, JOHN PRI 065 NOTTINGH
LITTLEFORD, THOMAS PRI 061 NOTTINGH
LITTLES, JANE FRE 065 FREDERIC
LITTLES, WILLIAM FRE 125 CREAGERS
LITTLETON, ALBINA E. DOR 375 1ST DIST
LITTLETON, AMELIA WOR 216 4TH E DI
LITTLETON, ARA L. WOR 216 4TH E DI
LITTLETON, DANIEL J. WOR 214 4TH E DI
LITTLETON, EDMUN DL. WOR 218 4TH E DI
LITTLETON, ELIZA J. WOR 219 4TH E DI
LITTLETON, HESTER A. WOR 222 4TH E DI
LITTLETON, HIRAM WOR 206 4TH E DI
LITTLETON, IRVIN S. WOR 218 4TH E DI
LITTLETON, ISAAC WOR 204 4TH E DI
LITTLETON, JAMES WOR 218 4TH E DI
LITTLETON, JAMES C. WOR 219 4TH E DI
LITTLETON, JAMES M. WOR 217 4TH E DI
LITTLETON, JOHN WOR 219 4TH E DI
LITTLETON, JOHN WOR 218 4TH E DI
LITTLETON, JOHN W. WOR 255 1ST CENS
LITTLETON, LEMUEL WOR 218 4TH E DI
LITTLETON, MARION DOR 374 1ST DIST
LITTLETON, MATILDA . WOR 215 4TH E DI
LITTLETON, MINOR C. WOR 218 4TH E DI
LITTLETON, POLLY WOR 215 4TH E DI
LITTLETON, THOMAS WOR 219 4TH E DI
LITTLETON, THOMAS W. WOR 218 4TH E DI
LITTLETON, WILLIAM WOR 218 4TH E DI
LITTLETON, WILLIAM B. WOR 215 4TH E DI
LITTLETON, WILLIAM C.* DOR 375 1ST DIST
LITTLETON, WILLIAM J. DOR 320 1ST DIST
LITTMAN, HERMAN BAL 104 2ND DIST
LITTON, CALEB WAS 119 2ND DIST
LITTON, THOMAS BAL 357 3RD WARD
LITTS, LEWIS BAL 282 2ND WARD
LITZ, FRANCIS BAL 353 13TH WAR
LITZ, GEORGE BAL 021 2ND DIST
LITZ, GEORGE BAL 223 12TH WAR
LITZ, JOSEPH BAL 032 2ND DIST
LITZINGER, HENRY BAL 447 1ST DIST
LITZINGER, JOHN W. BAL 283 20TH WAR
LITZLER, BENNETT BAL 190 19TH WAR
LIUTHIEUM, SUSAN O.* BAL 013 4TH WARD
LIVEENEY, CATHERINE BAL 355 8TH WARD
LIVELY, ELLEN * BAL 289 20TH WAR
LIVELY, ISAIAH KEN 256 1ST DIST
LIVELY, JAMES BAL 063 10TH WAR
LIVELY, SAMUEL KEN 243 2ND DIST
LIVENGSTON, E. BAL 151 1ST WARD
LIVERGOOD, JESSE ALL 040 2ND E.D.
LIVERGOOD, PRISCILLA ALL 018 3RD E.D.
LIVERING, ALEXANDER T. HAR 082 2ND DIST
LIVERMORE, ORIGEN R. BAL 058 15TH WAR
LIVERS, ELIZABETH BAL 396 1ST DIST
LIVERS,SOPHIER FRE 214 BUCKEYST
LIVERTY, JAMES BAL 158 1ST WARD
LIVES, JOSEPH FRE 180 5TH E DI
LIVES, WILLIAM BAL 155 1ST WARD
LIVEY, ALFRED BAL 474 14TH WAR
LIVEZEY, JACOB HAR 102 2ND DIST
LIVEZEY, PRISCILLA HAR 103 2ND DIST
LIVEZEY, THOMAS HAR 103 2ND DIST
LIVINGSTON, BENA BAL 006 15TH WAR
LIVINGSTON, CAROLINE BAL 135 5TH WARD
LIVINGSTON, ELIZABETH BAL 244 6TH WARD
LIVINGSTON, EMANUEL BAL 161 1ST WARD
LIVINGSTON, EMILY BAL 035 15TH WAR
LIVINGSTON, FRANCIS BAL 231 17TH WAR
LIVINGSTON, GEORGE M. WOR 198 8TH E DI
LIVINGSTON, JANE SOM 475 TRAPPE D
LIVINGSTON, JOHN SOM 474 TRAPPE D
LIVINGSTON, JOHN WOR 196 8TH E DI
LIVINGSTON, JOHN CEC 123 3RD E DI
LIVINGSTON, JOHN BAL 422 14TH WAR
LIVINGSTON, JOHN BAL 145 1ST WARD
LIVINGSTON, LEAH SOM 474 TRAPPE D
LIVINGSTON, LORENZO BAL 165 6TH WARD
LIVINGSTON, MARCUS BAL 128 1ST WARD
LIVINGSTON, PETER WOR 191 8TH E DI
LIVINGSTON, PETER BAL 334 13TH WAR
LIVINGSTON, SAMUEL WOR 197 8TH E DI
LIVINGSTON, SAMUEL L. BAL 423 14TH WAR
LIVINGSTON, SANDY WOR 197 8TH E DI
LIVINGSTON, SARAH CEC 135 6TH E DI
LIVINGSTON, SARAH A. BAL 248 6TH WARD
LIVINGSTON, SARAH E. BAL 013 15TH WAR
LIVINGSTON, SETH F. BAL 012 15TH WAR
LIVINGSTON, STEPHEN SOM 474 TRAPPE D
LIVINGSTON, WILLIAM SOM 492 SALISBUR
LIVINGSTON, WILLIAM DOR 381 1ST DIST
LIVINGSTONE, JOHN CEC 216 7TH E DI

Name	County	Page	District
LIVINTHAL, LEVI	BAL	391	3RD WARD
LIVIS, ARNOLD	FRE	184	5TH E DI
LIVIS, MARGARET	FRE	186	5TH E DI
LIVIS, THOMAS	FRE	184	5TH E DI
LIVUS, SYLVESTER-BLACK	FRE	041	FREDERIC
LIVZEY, GEORGE	HAR	103	2ND DIST
LIYLE, ELIZABETH	BAL	368	13TH WAR
LIZAR, WESLEY	WAS	283	1ST DIST
LIZEAR, ANN	MGM	333	CRACKLIN
LIZEAR, CORNELIAS	MGM	371	BERRYS D
LIZEAR, ELIAS	MGM	371	BERRYS D
LIZEAR, ELIAS JR.	MGM	349	BERRYS D
LIZEAR, JOHN	MGM	366	BERRYS D
LIZEAR, JOSEPH H.	ANN	509	HOWARD D
LIZEAR, LEVI	MGM	315	CRACKLIN
LIZEAR, PERRY	MGM	371	BERRYS D
LIZEAR, SAMUEL	MGM	356	BERRYS D
LIZEAR, THOMAS G.	MGM	337	CRACKLIN
LIZER, GEORGE	WAS	188	1ST DIST
LIZER, HENRY	WAS	226	1ST DIST
LIZER, HENRY	WAS	220	1ST DIST
LIZER, JOHN	WAS	229	1ST DIST
LIZER, JOHN	WAS	233	1ST DIST
LIZER, JOHN	WAS	252	1ST DIST
LIZER, MARY	WAS	222	1ST DIST
LIZER, WILLIAM	WAS	233	1ST DIST
LIZZARD, HETTA	BAL	311	1ST DIST
LLOYD, AND	BAL	280	12TH WAR
LLOYD, B. RUSH	BAL	101	10TH WAR
LLOYD, BENJAMIN	ALL	075	5TH E.D.
LLOYD, BENS	WAS	299	1ST DIST
LLOYD, EDMOND	FRE	407	JEFFERSO
LLOYD, EDWARD	QUE	236	4TH E DI
LLOYD, ELIZA	BAL	242	2ND WARD
LLOYD, ELIZABETH	BAL	227	6TH WARD
LLOYD, ELIZABETH	DOR	305	1ST DIST
LLOYD, FANY-MULATTO	BAL	246	2ND WARD
LLOYD, FRISBY	BAL	055	4TH WARD
LLOYD, GEORGE	SOM	425	PRINCESS
LLOYD, GEORGE	BAL	186	11TH WAR
LLOYD, HENRIETTA	DOR	373	1ST DIST
LLOYD, JACOB	BAL	195	17TH WAR
LLOYD, JAMES	QUE	232	4TH E DI
LLOYD, JAMES	QUE	236	4TH E DI
LLOYD, JAMES W.	BAL	419	3RD WARD
LLOYD, JANE	BAL	120	2ND DIST
LLOYD, JEMIMA	BAL	417	1ST DIST
LLOYD, JOHN	ALL	124	4TH E.D.
LLOYD, JOHN	DOR	303	1ST DIST
LLOYD, JOHN A.	BAL	403	1ST DIST
LLOYD, JULIANN-BLACK	QUE	185	3RD E DI
LLOYD, MARGARET	BAL	222	17TH WAR
LLOYD, MARIA	BAL	353	13TH WAR
LLOYD, MARY	KEN	260	1ST DIST
LLOYD, MARY	BAL	339	1ST DIST
LLOYD, MARY P.	BAL	158	16TH WAR
LLOYD, MITCHELL	CAR	137	NO TWP L
LLOYD, PATY	KEN	214	2ND DIST
LLOYD, PERRY	BAL	240	6TH WARD
LLOYD, PHILEMON	BAL	350	3RD WARD
LLOYD, PHILIP	BAL	254	20TH WAR
LLOYD, RICHARD	BAL	227	6TH WARD
LLOYD, RICHARD B.	BAL	111	15TH WAR
LLOYD, SAMUEL	BAL	022	1ST WARD
LLOYD, SETH	ALL	080	5TH E.D.
LLOYD, STEPHEN	BAL	417	1ST DIST
LLOYD, THOMAS	BAL	065	15TH WAR
LLOYD, THOMAS	BAL	243	2ND WARD
LLOYD, THOMAS	BAL	305	17TH WAR
LLOYD, THOMAS	KEN	259	1ST DIST
LLOYD, THOMAS J.	BAL	022	1ST WARD
LLOYD, WILLIAM	BAL	033	9TH WARD
LLOYD, WILLIAM	QUE	165	2ND E DI
LLOYD, WILLIAM	BAL	057	18TH WAR
LLOYD, WILLIAM R.	FRE	218	BUCKEYST
LLOYD, WILSON L.	BAL	025	18TH WAR
LLOYDE, C. C.	TAL	067	EASTON T
LLOYDE, DANIEL	TAL	011	EASTON D
LLOYDE, DIANNA	TAL	016	EASTON D
LLOYDE, DIANNA	TAL	019	EASTON D
LLOYDE, DIBBY*	TAL	045	EASTON T
LLOYDE, EDWARD	TAL	025	EASTON D
LLOYDE, ELLEN	TAL	070	EASTON T
LLOYDE, GEORGE M.	TAL	080	ST MICHA
LLOYDE, ISACK*	TAL	033	EASTON D
LLOYDE, JAMES P.	TAL	053	EASTON D
LLOYDE, MONTGOMERY	TAL	047	EASTON T
LLOYDE, NELLY	TAL	059	EASTON D
LLOYDE, ROBERT N.	TAL	047	EASTON T
LLOYDE, THOMAS	TAL	035	EASTON D
LLOYDE, THOMAS C.	TAL	045	EASTON T
LLOYDE, UGENIA*	TAL	043	EASTON D
LLOYDS, MARY	BAL	329	3RD WARD
LLUDLEN, MARGARETT	BAL	132	18TH WAR
LOAD, ELIZABETH M.	MGM	382	ROCKERLE
LOAD, MARY	MGM	336	CRACKLIN
LOAE, GEORGE	ALL	058	10TH E.D
LOAE, HENRY	ALL	057	10TH E.D
LOAE, JOHN C.	ALL	057	10TH E.D
LOAE, WINNIFRED	ALL	058	10TH E.D
LOAN, ELIZABETH	BAL	422	3RD WARD
LOAN, JOSEPH	BAL	422	3RD WARD
LOAN, MARTHA L.	BAL	005	4TH WARD
LOAN, REBECCA	BAL	188	2ND WARD
LOANE, EDWARD	BAL	129	16TH WAR
LOANE, EDWARD*	BAL	026	4TH WARD
LOANE, GEORGE	BAL	046	4TH WARD
LOANE, GEORGE*	BAL	035	4TH WARD
LOANE, JABEZ	BAL	047	4TH WARD
LOANE, JOHN *	BAL	297	20TH WAR
LOANE, MARY	BAL	047	4TH WARD
LOANE, SARAH	BAL	327	13TH WAR
LOANE, SARAH	BAL	238	6TH WARD
LOANEY, WILLIAM	BAL	183	11TH WAR
LOAPER, BASIL	MGM	440	CLARKSTR
LOAR, ELISABETH	ALL	018	3RD E.D.
LOAR, ELIZA	ALL	016	3RD E.D.
LOAR, HENRY P.	ALL	132	4TH E.D.
LOAR, JOHN	ALL	015	3RD E.D.
LOAR, PETER	ALL	016	3RD E.D.
LOARE, JOHN *	BAL	297	20TH WAR
LOATS, JOHN	FRE	023	FREDERIC
LOBB, DANIEL	FRE	345	MIDDLETO
LOBBEY, LEWIS	BAL	288	7TH WARD
LOBE, GEORGE	BAL	114	2ND DIST
LOBECK, JAMES	BAL	066	2ND DIST
LOBER, GEORGE*	BAL	113	15TH WAR
LOBIN, FRANCIS *	BAL	116	2ND DIST
LOBSTINE, JOHN E.	CAR	097	NO TWP L
LOBUS, PHILLIP	BAL	201	2ND WARD
LOCCKI, ELIZABETH	BAL	356	13TH WAR
LOCHBAUM, FREDERICK	BAL	126	16TH WAR
LOCHER, BRIDGET A.*	BAL	384	3RD WARD
LOCHER, ELIZABETH	WAS	172	FUNKSTOW
LOCHMAN, THOMAS	BAL	377	3RD WARD
LOCHMAN, THOMAS J.	BAL	377	3RD WARD
LOCHMYER, LOUIS	BAL	303	20TH WAR
LOCHNER, JOHN	BAL	284	1ST DIST
LOCHTE, ANDREW	MGM	394	ROCKERLE
LOCK, AMELIA	BAL	300	12TH WAR
LOCK, FRED	BAL	041	18TH WAR
LOCK, FREDERICK	FRE	291	WOODSBOR
LOCK, HENRY N.	BAL	172	16TH WAR
LOCK, ISAAC	CEC	021	ELKTON 3
LOCK, MARK W.	BAL	168	1ST WARD
LOCK, MARY	FRE	291	WOODSBOR
LOCK, MARY	BAL	364	13TH WAR
LOCK, MATHIAS	FRE	090	FREDERIC
LOCK, SARAH	BAL	376	13TH WAR
LOCK, MARK	BAL	135	1ST WARD
LOCKARD, DAVID	CEC	138	6TH E DI
LOCKARD, HENRY	BAL	230	1ST DIST
LOCKARD, JAMES	CAR	201	4TH DIST
LOCKARD, JOHN	CAR	199	4TH DIST
LOCKARD, MARY	CEC	196	6TH E DI
LOCKARD, MARY W.	BAL	230	1ST DIST
LOCKARD, WILLIAM	CAR	199	4TH DIST
LOCKARD, WILLIAM	CAR	197	4TH DIST
LOCKE, CAROLINE M.	BAL	198	6TH WARD
LOCKE, CHRISTOPHER	BAL	146	19TH WAR
LOCKE, DAVID	BAL	387	13TH WAR
LOCKE, JAMES D. W. C.	WAS	100	2ND DIST
LOCKE, JOHN	ALL	119	5TH E.D.
LOCKE, SAMUEL-BLACK	BAL	224	2ND WARD
LOCKEMAN, ELIZA	KEN	285	3RD DIST
LOCKEMAN, RHODA	CAR	148	NO TWP L
LOCKEMAN, STEPHEN	CAR	072	NO TWP L
LOCKENTON, JOSEPH	BAL	061	18TH WAR
LOCKER, ANN-BLACK	FRE	406	JEFFERSO
LOCKER, BRIDGET A.*	BAL	384	3RD WARD
LOCKER, HENRY	WAS	196	1ST DIST
LOCKER, JAMES	PRI	099	SPALDING
LOCKER, JAMES	PRI	117	PISCATAW
LOCKER, MATTHEW	BAL	030	15TH WAR
LOCKER, RACHEL	PRI	119	PISCATAW
LOCKER, RICHARD H.	PRI	077	MARLBROU
LOCKER, SAMUEL	FRE	177	5TH E DI
LOCKER, VIRGINIA	PRI	078	MARLBROU
LOCKERD, JOHN	BAL	131	16TH WAR
LOCKERMAN, ALLEN-BLACK	CAR	068	NO TWP L
LOCKERMAN, ALLEN-BLACK	CAR	132	NO TWP L
LOCKERMAN, ARNOLD	WAS	122	2ND DIST
LOCKERMAN, BENJAMIN	KEN	291	3RD DIST
LOCKERMAN, ELIZA	BAL	384	13TH WAR
LOCKERMAN, FRANCIS P.	ANN	285	ANNAPOLI
LOCKERMAN, HARRIET	BAL	104	15TH WAR
LOCKERMAN, HARRIET	KEN	244	2ND DIST
LOCKERMAN, HENRY-BLACK	CAR	094	NO TWP L
LOCKERMAN, JAMES	CAR	065	NO TWP L
LOCKERMAN, JAMES	WOR	345	1ST E DI
LOCKERMAN, JAMES	WOR	301	SNOW HIL
LOCKERMAN, JOHN	WOR	335	1ST E DI
LOCKERMAN, JOHN-BLACK	CAR	105	NO TWP L
LOCKERMAN, JOSHUA	DOR	387	1ST DIST
LOCKERMAN, JOSHUA	WOR	335	1ST E DI
LOCKERMAN, LOUIZA-BLACK	CAR	168	NO TWP L
LOCKERMAN, MARKE	DOR	358	3RD DIVI
LOCKERMAN, MOSES	QUE	213	3RD E DI
LOCKERMAN, NANCY	WOR	303	SNOW HIL
LOCKERMAN, RICHARD	CAR	130	NO TWP L
LOCKERMAN, SAMUEL	BAL	260	6TH WARD
LOCKERMAN, SARAH	QUE	179	2ND E DI
LOCKERMAN, SUSAN	BAL	240	6TH WARD
LOCKERMAN, THOMAS	CAR	130	NO TWP L
LOCKERMAN, TOWNLY	ANN	285	ANNAPOLI
LOCKERMAN, W. E.	BAL	325	12TH WAR
LOCKERMAN, WILLIAM	CAR	150	NO TWP L
LOCKERMAN, WILLIAM	KEN	291	3RD DIST
LOCKERT, JOSHUA	CAR	280	7TH DIST
LOCKERT, THOMAS	BAL	097	5TH WARD
LOCKERY, GEORGE	HAR	092	2ND DIST
LOCKERY, JOHN	HAR	142	2ND DIST
LOCKERY, MICHAEL	HAR	142	2ND DIST
LOCKES, ALEXANDER	BAL	125	11TH WAR
LOCKET, WILLIAM	BAL	320	7TH WARD
LOCKETT, WILLIAM	BAL	351	7TH WARD
LOCKEY, BENJAMIN	SOM	404	BRINKLEY
LOCKEY, LENERETTA	SOM	433	PRINCESS
LOCKIE, ANN	BAL	411	8TH WARD
LOCKINGLAND, BALDES	BAL	257	1ST DIST
LOCKLAND, ANDREW	WAS	129	HAGERSTO
LOCKLAND, BRIDGET	BAL	105	18TH WAR
LOCKLAND, F.	BAL	155	1ST WARD
LOCKLAND, J.	BAL	141	1ST WARD
LOCKLAND, JOHN	BAL	263	20TH WAR
LOCKLAND, SARAH	BAL	264	20TH WAR
LOCKLAND, SARAH	WAS	132	HAGERSTO
LOCKLAND, T.	BAL	136	1ST WARD
LOCKMAN, CATHARINE	BAL	206	6TH DIST
LOCKMAN, JOHN	BAL	133	1ST WARD
LOCKMAN, LEVIN	BAL	071	4TH WARD
LOCKMAN, MARGARET	BAL	307	20TH WAR
LOCKMAN, WILLIAM	ANN	370	4TH DIST
LOCKMEYER, JOSEPH	BAL	448	14TH WAR
LOCKNER, JOHN	ALL	258	CUMBERLA
LOCKRIDGE, GEORGE	WAS	211	1ST DIST
LOCKS, BENJAMIN	CAL	008	1ST DIST
LOCKS, DINAH	BAL	229	2ND WARD
LOCKS, ELLEN	BAL	381	3RD WARD
LOCKS, GEORGE	WAS	289	1ST DIST
LOCKS, HARRIET-BLACK	FRE	016	FREDERIC
LOCKS, JIM	CAL	027	2ND DIST
LOCKS, JOHN	WAS	290	1ST DIST
LOCKS, JOHN	BAL	162	2ND DIST
LOCKS, JOHN-BLACK	BAL	224	2ND WARD
LOCKS, MARIA	FRE	312	MIDDLETO
LOCKS, MARY	CAL	033	2ND DIST
LOCKS, MATILDA	FRE	095	FREDERIC
LOCKS, PERRY	BAL	316	3RD WARD
LOCKS, RACHEL	CAL	027	2ND DIST
LOCKS, RICHARD	BAL	382	3RD WARD
LOCKS, SOLOMON	FRE	085	FREDERIC
LOCKSTRAMP, JACOB*	BAL	354	3RD WARD
LOCKWOOD, CHARLES	BAL	084	10TH WAR
LOCKWOOD, DANIEL	BAL	209	19TH WAR
LOCKWOOD, EDUARD	BAL	180	2ND WARD
LOCKWOOD, EDWARD	CEC	063	1ST E DI
LOCKWOOD, JOHN	BAL	139	19TH WAR
LOCKWOOD, JOHN	BAL	033	9TH WARD
LOCKWOOD, JOHN	BAL	105	1ST WARD
LOCKWOOD, MR.	ANN	283	ANNAPOLI
LOCKWOOD, R. M.	BAL	191	11TH WAR
LOCKWOOD, WILLIAM	ALL	237	CUMBERLA
LOCLWOOD, ELISON	BAL	400	14TH WAR
LOCO, JOSEPH	HAR	063	1ST DIST
LODER, ALEXANDER	BAL	168	16TH WAR
LODER, MARY J.	BAL	372	1ST DIST
LODERM, ELLEN	BAL	026	1ST WARD
LODGE, HARRIET	ALL	229	CUMBERLA
LODGE, LAURENCE	MGM	390	ROCKERLE
LODGE, MARTHA	MGM	390	ROCKERLE
LODGE, MARY A.	PRI	027	VANSVILL
LODI, MARGARET	BAL	217	19TH WAR
LODI, PETER	BAL	217	19TH WAR
LODIER, JOHN	BAL	281	12TH WAR
LODINE, ANN	CEC	164	6TH E DI
LODINE, D.	BAL	157	1ST WARD
LODIR, ANN	BAL	168	16TH WAR
LODOR, ELIZABETH	BAL	178	16TH WAR
LOEFFLER, CHARLES	BAL	168	6TH WARD
LOEFFLER, WILLIAM	BAL	352	13TH WAR
LOEFLAND, ELIZABETH	BAL	136	2ND DIST
LOENS, EDWARD	BAL	061	1ST WARD
LOEW, JOHN	CAR	214	5TH DIST
LOFER, CHRISTIAN	BAL	091	2ND DIST
LOFF, SAMUEL B.	BAL	331	13TH WAR
LOFFLER, RICHARD	BAL	191	6TH WARD
LOFFTUS, RICHARD	BAL	098	18TH WAR
LOFTEN, DANIEL	TAL	027	EASTON D
LOFTIS, FRANCIS	BAL	095	2ND DIST
LOFTON, REBECCA	TAL	032	EASTON D
LOFTUS, EDWARD *	BAL	081	18TH WAR
LOFTUS, FRANCES	BAL	116	2ND DIST
LOFTUS, HYLAND	BAL	257	17TH WAR
LOFTUS, JAMES	BAL	103	2ND DIST
LOFTUS, JOHN	ALL	072	5TH E.D.
LOFTUS, MARY	BAL	102	2ND DIST
LOFTUS, MICHAEL	BAL	150	2ND DIST
LOFTUS, NATH.	BAL	318	20TH WAR
LOFTUS, NATHANIEL	BAL	401	1ST DIST
LOFTUS, OWEN	ALL	072	5TH E.D.
LOFTUS, THOMAS	ALL	052	10TH E.D
LOGA, NOAH	BAL	227	17TH WAR
LOGAN, ALEXANDER	BAL	217	6TH WARD
LOGAN, ANN	PRI	009	BLADENSB
LOGAN, BERNARD	BAL	132	16TH WAR
LOGAN, BRIDGET	BAL	006	EASTERN
LOGAN, CATHARINE	BAL	352	7TH WARD
LOGAN, CATHERINE	BAL	097	10TH WAR
LOGAN, CHARLES	BAL	046	15TH WAR
LOGAN, DANIEL	ALL	179	7TH E.D.
LOGAN, GEORGE	WAS	053	2ND SUBD
LOGAN, GEORGE	WAS	201	1ST DIST
LOGAN, GEORGE W.	BAL	153	16TH WAR
LOGAN, GEORGE-BLACK	WOR	342	1ST E DI
LOGAN, H. M.	BAL	293	20TH WAR
LOGAN, HUGH	WAS	272	RIDGEVIL
LOGAN, J. M	BAL	169	19TH WAR
LOGAN, JAMES	BAL	264	17TH WAR
LOGAN, JAMES	BAL	175	19TH WAR
LOGAN, JAMES	BAL	186	19TH WAR
LOGAN, JAMES	BAL	331	3RD WARD
LOGAN, JOHN	CEC	033	CHESAPEA
LOGAN, JOHN	CEC	140	5TH E DI
LOGAN, JOSEPH T.	BAL	434	14TH WAR
LOGAN, LOUISA	BAL	162	19TH WAR
LOGAN, MARGARET	CEC	211	7TH E DI
LOGAN, MARGARET	CEC	216	7TH E DI
LOGAN, MARGARET	BAL	340	7TH WARD
LOGAN, MARGARET A.	CEC	138	6TH E DI
LOGAN, MARY	CEC	187	7TH E DI
LOGAN, MARY	BAL	316	20TH WAR
LOGAN, MARY	BAL	157	11TH WAR
LOGAN, MARY	BAL	165	11TH WAR
LOGAN, MARY	BAL	121	5TH WARD
LOGAN, MARY MISS-	BAL	315	20TH WAR
LOGAN, MICHAEL	BAL	191	2ND WARD
LOGAN, NANCY	BAL	355	8TH WARD
LOGAN, NELSON	SOM	428	PRINCESS
LOGAN, O.	BAL	173	1ST WARD
LOGAN, RACHEAL	WAS	155	HAGERSTO
LOGAN, ROBERT	BAL	132	1ST WARD
LOGAN, ROBERT	CEC	134	6TH E DI
LOGAN, ROBERT	BAL	294	20TH WAR
LOGAN, ROSANA	FRE	020	FREDERIC
LOGAN, SAMUEL	CEC	212	7TH E DI
LOGAN, SAMUEL	CEC	020	ELKTON 3
LOGAN, SAMUEL	CEC	081	CHARLEST
LOGAN, SAMUEL	BAL	181	2ND WARD
LOGAN, SAMUEL	ALL	200	CUMBERLA
LOGAN, SARAH	BAL	104	5TH WARD
LOGAN, SARAH	BAL	106	10TH WAR
LOGAN, THOAMS J.	WAS	162	2ND DIST
LOGAN, THOMAS	BAL	115	1ST WARD
LOGAN, THOMAS	CEC	080	NORTHEAS
LOGAN, THOMAS	CEC	084	CHARLEST
LOGAN, THOMAS	CEC	079	NORTHEAS
LOGAN, THOMAS	FRE	067	FREDERIC
LOGAN, THOMAS	FRE	035	FREDERIC
LOGAN, WILLIAM	CEC	066	1ST E DI
LOGAN, WILLIAM	CEC	211	7TH E DI
LOGAN, WILLIAM	CEC	186	7TH E DI
LOGAN, WILLIAM	CEC	189	7TH E DI
LOGAN, WILLIAM	WAS	155	HAGERSTO
LOGAN, WILLIAM	WAS	155	HAGERSTO
LOGAN, WILLIAM	WAS	288	1ST DIST
LOGANS, THOMAS	BAL	152	5TH WARD
LOGE, WILLIAM	BAL	092	15TH WAR
LOGE, WILLIAM	CEC	040	CHESAPEA
LOGEMAN, DAVID	BAL	240	17TH WAR
LOGEMAN, HENRY	BAL	041	9TH WARD
LOGEN, JAMES *	KEN	226	2ND DIST
LOGEN, JOHN	BAL	016	9TH WARD
LOGERTY, CATHARINE	BAL	172	2ND DIST
LOGG, HARRIOTT	BAL	070	4TH WARD
LOGG, JOSIAH	SOM	435	PRINCESS
LOGG, NELSON	SOM	462	HANGARY
LOGGE, FREDERICK	FRE	065	FREDERIC
LOGGEMAN, MARY *	BAL	238	6TH WARD
LOGGERNAN, MARY *	BAL	238	6TH WARD
LOGGINS, HARY	BAL	321	1ST DIST
LOGGINS, JOHN	BAL	222	1ST DIST
LOGGINS, PETER	BAL	238	1ST DIST
LOGGINS, SAMUEL	BAL	242	1ST DIST
LOGHRAN, JANE	BAL	035	1ST WARD
LOGIE, ELEANOR	BAL	025	15TH WAR
LOGIE, SALLY A.	BAL	025	15TH WAR
LOGINS, C.	PRI	108	PISCATAW
LOGN, JAMES	WOR	267	BERLIN 1
LOGN, MARY	BAL	465	14TH WAR

Name	County	Page	District
LOGRDEN, WILLIAM	ALL	083	5TH E.D.
LOGRDON, JOSEPH	ALL	083	5TH E.D.
LOGRDON, RACHEL	ALL	083	5TH E.D.
LOGRDON, WILLIAM	ALL	153	6TH E.D.
LOGSDEN, JOHN	BAL	250	1ST DIST
LOGSDEN, MARY E.	BAL	204	11TH WAR
LOGSDEN, WILLIAM	BAL	285	1ST DIST
LOGSDON, JOSEPH	ALL	023	2ND E.D.
LOGSDON, LEONARD	ALL	084	5TH E.D.
LOGSDON, MARY	BAL	306	7TH WARD
LOGSDON, MARY J.	ALL	024	3RD E.D.
LOGSDON, SISTER ISABELLA	FRE	197	5TH E DI
LOGSDON, WILLIAM	ALL	070	5TH E.D.
LOGSDON, WILLIAM	ALL	135	4TH E.D.
LOGSDON,SIMEON	ALL	035	2ND E.D.
LOGSTON, MARY	ALL	260	CUMBERLA
LOGUE, ALICE	BAL	110	10TH WAR
LOGUE, ANDREW	BAL	128	2ND DIST
LOGUE, ANDREW J.	CAR	196	4TH DIST
LOGUE, ELIZABETH	BAL	366	8TH WARD
LOGUE, ELLEN	ALL	145	6TH E.D.
LOGUE, FRANCIS	CAR	288	7TH DIST
LOGUE, GEORGE*	BAL	033	4TH WARD
LOGUE, JAMES	BAL	013	9TH WARD
LOGUE, JEFFERSON	CAR	197	4TH DIST
LOGUE, JESSE	CAR	281	7TH DIST
LOGUE, JOHN	BAL	259	17TH WAR
LOGUE, JOSEPH	BAL	124	11TH WAR
LOGUE, JOSHUA	CAR	288	7TH DIST
LOGUE, JOSHUA	CAR	293	7TH DIST
LOGUE, MARY	CAR	281	7TH DIST
LOGUE, MARY	ALL	147	6TH E.D.
LOGUE, MARY A.	BAL	406	8TH WARD
LOGUE, MICHAEL	BAL	406	8TH WARD
LOGUE, MICHAEL	BAL	008	EASTERN
LOGUE, PETER	BAL	277	12TH WAR
LOGUE, REUBEN	CAR	280	7TH DIST
LOGUE, WILLIAM	BAL	336	7TH WARD
LOGY, JOSIAH	SOM	435	PRINCESS
LOGY, NELSON	SOM	462	HANGARY
LOGY, SALLY	SOM	435	PRINCESS
LOGY, SALLY *	SOM	435	PRINCESS
LOHER, PETER	ALL	016	3RD E.D.
LOHL, ADAM	BAL	352	13TH WAR
LOHMAN, AUGUSTINE	BAL	356	3RD WARD
LOHMAN, CAROLINE	WAS	280	LEITERSB
LOHMAN, CHRISTIAN	BAL	354	13TH WAR
LOHMAN, DANIEL	WAS	279	LEITERSB
LOHMAN, DANIEL	WAS	279	LEITERSB
LOHMAN, ELIZABETH	WAS	280	LEITERSB
LOHMAN, GEORGE	WAS	243	CAVETOWN
LOHMAN, HENRY	BAL	271	2ND WARD
LOHMAN, JACOB	WAS	278	LEITERSB
LOHMAN, JACOB	WAS	285	1ST DIST
LOHMAN, JOHN	WAS	280	LEITERSB
LOHMAN, JOHN	WAS	278	LEITERSB
LOHMAN, MARY	WAS	203	1ST DIST
LOHMULLER, FREDERICK	BAL	065	4TH WARD
LOHR, ABRAHAM	FRE	114	CREAGERS
LOHR, ANDREW	CAR	248	3RD DIST
LOHR, JACOB	FRE	153	10TH E D
LOHR, JOHN	FRE	183	5TH E DI
LOHRMAN, JOHN H.	BAL	240	17TH WAR
LOINES, JOANNA	BAL	219	19TH WAR
LOISBOUGH, MARTIN L.*	BAL	081	4TH WARD
LOISTER, JANE	ALL	244	CUMBERLA
LOIUS, CAROLINE	FRE	057	FREDERIC
LOKER, JOHN W.*	BAL	421	3RD WARD
LOKER, REBECCA	ST	307	1ST E DI
LOKER, ROBERT	ST	310	1ST E DI
LOKER, THOMAS	ST	293	2ND E DI
LOKER, WILLIAM A.	ST	278	3RD E DI
LOKER, WILLIAM H.	ST	312	1ST E DI
LOKEY, HARRIET W.	WOR	189	7TH E DI
LOKEY, JOSEPH	BAL	071	10TH WAR
LOKEY, THOMAS	SOM	461	HANGARY
LOKMAN, HENRY	WAS	241	CAVETOWN
LOLLERS, JAMES*	BAL	308	3RD WARD
LOLLY, ABRAHAM	KEN	308	3RD DIST
LOMAN, ANN	TAL	090	ST MICHA
LOMAN, CAMILLUS-BLACK	QUE	143	1ST E DI
LOMAN, EMMA	BAL	075	4TH WARD
LOMAN, ISAAC	BAL	118	5TH WARD
LOMAN, JOHN	QUE	175	2ND E DI
LOMAN, LAURANCE	BAL	074	4TH WARD
LOMAN, MARY	QUE	151	1ST E DI
LOMAN, WILLIAM	QUE	139	1ST E DI
LOMAN, WILLIAM *	BAL	133	18TH WAR
LOMANS, MARY	QUE	136	1ST E DI
LOMAS, BETTY	CHA	249	MIDDLETO
LOMAS, FREDERICK	BAL	263	2ND WARD
LOMAS, JAMES-MULATTO	BAL	225	2ND WARD
LOMAS, MARY C.	MGM	317	CRACKLIN
LOMAX, BETTY	CHA	241	HILLTOP
LOMAX, ELIZA	ANN	405	8TH DIST
LOMAX, GEORGE-BLACK	BAL	221	2ND WARD
LOMAX, JAMES	CHA	271	ALLENS F
LOMAX, JAMES	TAL	116	ST MICHA
LOMAX, JOHN	CHA	260	MIDDLETO
LOMAX, JOHN W.	CHA	223	ALLENS F
LOMAX, RACHEL*	BAL	050	4TH WARD
LOMAX, RICHARD B.	ST	282	3RD E DI
LOMAX, WILLIAM	ANN	405	8TH DIST
LOMAY, CAROLINE	BAL	357	3RD WARD
LOMAY, RACHEL*	BAL	050	4TH WARD
LOMIS, CHARLES F.	BAL	209	17TH WAR
LOMMER, F.	BAL	156	1ST WARD
LOMS, SAMUEL	FRE	341	MIDDLETO
LOMYERSE, CATHARINE	FRE	322	MIDDLETO
LON, HARRIET-MULATTO	FRE	242	NEW MARK
LONC, EDWARD	CAR	154	NO TWP L
LOND, JOHN	CAR	157	NO TWP L
LONDANER, SAMUEL	BAL	030	15TH WAR
LONDENBERRY, MICHAEL	BAL	226	17TH WAR
LONDENSTAGER, SOLOMON *	BAL	111	18TH WAR
LONDON, DANIEL	ALL	169	6TH E.D.
LONDON, JULIANN	ALL	001	3RD E.D.
LONE, DANIEL	BAL	392	8TH WARD
LONE, JOHN	BAL	269	7TH WARD
LONE, JOHN	QUE	154	1ST E DI
LONE, MARTHA	BAL	319	7TH WARD
LONEHLER, WILLIAM	FRE	009	FREDERIC
LONEMAN, ANN	BAL	087	18TH WAR
LONEMAN, OTMARN	BAL	416	14TH WAR
LONERSTAEDTER, JACOB	BAL	060	15TH WAR
LONEY, BENJAMIN	BAL	134	1ST WARD
LONEY, GEORGE *	WAS	115	2ND DIST
LONEY, H. E.	BAL	319	20TH WAR
LONEY, HANNAH	CEC	063	1ST E DI
LONEY, JOHN	BAL	280	20TH WAR
LONEY, MARGARET	BAL	275	7TH WARD
LONEY, MARTHA	BAL	266	7TH WARD
LONEY, WILLIAM A.	BAL	280	20TH WAR
LONG, ABRAHAM	FRE	430	8TH E DI
LONG, ADAM	BAL	291	17TH WAR
LONG, ANN	BAL	463	1ST DIST
LONG, ANN M.	BAL	154	16TH WAR
LONG, ANN M.	CEC	161	6TH E DI
LONG, ANNA	WAS	234	1ST DIST
LONG, AQUEDA	ALL	172	7TH E.D.
LONG, ARTHUR	BAL	292	1ST DIST
LONG, BARBARA	FRE	134	CREAGERS
LONG, BARBARA	FRE	332	MIDDLETO
LONG, BENJAMIN	HAR	077	BEL AIR
LONG, BENJAMIN	WAS	035	2ND SUBD
LONG, CATHARINE	WOR	327	1ST E DI
LONG, CATHARINE	FRE	331	MIDDLETO
LONG, CATHERINE	FRE	108	CREAGERS
LONG, CHARLES	BAL	337	13TH WAR
LONG, CHARLES	ST	346	5TH E DI
LONG, CHARLES	ALL	152	6TH E.D.
LONG, CHRISTIAN	CAR	217	5TH DIST
LONG, CHRISTOPHER	FRE	401	JEFFERSO
LONG, CONRAD	ALL	152	6TH E.D.
LONG, CONRAD	BAL	216	6TH WARD
LONG, DANIEL	FRE	440	8TH E DI
LONG, DANIEL	FRE	423	8TH E DI
LONG, DAVID	SOM	414	DUBLIN D
LONG, DAVID	BAL	222	6TH WARD
LONG, DAVID	BAL	081	15TH WAR
LONG, DAVID	BAL	107	2ND DIST
LONG, DAVID	WAS	025	2ND SUBD
LONG, DAVID	WAS	032	2ND SUBD
LONG, DAVID W.	BAL	137	18TH WAR
LONG, DENWOOD	CAR	066	NO TWP L
LONG, EDWARD	BAL	210	19TH WAR
LONG, EDWARD	SOM	466	HANGARY
LONG, EDWARD P.	CHA	222	ALLENS F
LONG, EDWIN M.	SOM	402	BRINKLEY
LONG, ELIAS	ALL	014	3RD E.D.
LONG, ELIZA	CEC	013	ELKTON 3
LONG, ELIZA	CEC	040	CHESAPEA
LONG, ELIZABETH	FRE	007	FREDERIC
LONG, ELIZABETH	BAL	438	14TH WAR
LONG, ELIZABETH	ST	329	4TH E DI
LONG, ELIZABETH	WAS	017	2ND SUBD
LONG, ELLENOR	ANN	452	HOWARD D
LONG, EMALINE S.	CAR	218	5TH DIST
LONG, EMILY	ST	274	3RD E DI
LONG, EPHRAIM	FRE	326	MIDDLETO
LONG, EUGINE T.	CHA	230	MIDDLETO
LONG, EVELINE	BAL	230	19TH WAR
LONG, GEORGE	BAL	240	17TH WAR
LONG, GEORGE	BAL	103	18TH WAR
LONG, GEORGE	WAS	245	SMITHSBU
LONG, GEORGE S.	ST	340	5TH E DI
LONG, GERTRUDE	BAL	378	1ST DIST
LONG, GOERGE	BAL	116	5TH WARD
LONG, H. R.	BAL	066	10TH WAR
LONG, HANNAH	BAL	152	19TH WAR
LONG, HENRY	BAL	294	17TH WAR
LONG, HENRY	BAL	258	20TH WAR
LONG, HENRY	HAR	074	1ST DIST
LONG, HENRY	BAL	458	1ST DIST
LONG, HENRY	BAL	245	1ST DIST
LONG, HENRY	BAL	262	2ND WARD
LONG, HENRY	ST	326	4TH E DI
LONG, HENRY	QUE	173	2ND E DI
LONG, HENRY	WAS	167	1ST DIST
LONG, HERNY	WOR	342	1ST E DI
LONG, ISAAC	WAS	017	2ND SUBD
LONG, ISAIAH	BAL	340	7TH WARD
LONG, J.	BAL	141	1ST WARD
LONG, J. L.	BAL	150	1ST WARD
LONG, J. R.	BAL	332	1ST DIST
LONG, J.H.	ALL	240	CUMBERLA
LONG, JACOB	WAS	148	2ND DIST
LONG, JACOB	WAS	197	1ST DIST
LONG, JACOB	FRE	191	5TH E DI
LONG, JACOB *	WAS	077	2ND SUBD
LONG, JAMES	ST	328	4TH E DI
LONG, JAMES	WOR	186	7TH E DI
LONG, JAMES	BAL	454	14TH WAR
LONG, JAMES	BAL	143	1ST WARD
LONG, JAMES	BAL	293	12TH WAR
LONG, JAMES E.N.	ST	303	2ND E DI
LONG, JAMES T.	ST	346	5TH E DI
LONG, JAMES W.	WAS	004	WILLIAMS
LONG, JANE	FRE	331	MIDDLETO
LONG, JESSE	WAS	002	WILLIAMS
LONG, JOHN	WAS	005	WILLIAMS
LONG, JOHN	WAS	004	WILLIAMS
LONG, JOHN	ST	339	4TH E DI
LONG, JOHN	ST	305	1ST E DI
LONG, JOHN	WAS	255	1ST DIST
LONG, JOHN	WAS	255	1ST DIST
LONG, JOHN	BAL	458	14TH WAR
LONG, JOHN	BAL	458	14TH WAR
LONG, JOHN	FRE	187	5TH E DI
LONG, JOHN	FRE	184	5TH E DI
LONG, JOHN	HAR	155	3RD DIST
LONG, JOHN	SOM	416	DUBLIN D
LONG, JOHN	BAL	318	20TH WAR
LONG, JOHN	CHA	230	MIDDLETO
LONG, JOHN	FRE	402	JEFFERSO
LONG, JOHN	BAL	050	18TH WAR
LONG, JOHN	ANN	425	HOWARD D
LONG, JOHN	BAL	343	7TH WARD
LONG, JOHN B.	BAL	245	1ST DIST
LONG, JOHN C.	ST	318	4TH E DI
LONG, JOHN D.	BAL	023	19TH WAR
LONG, JOHN J.	BAL	004	1ST WARD
LONG, JOHN P.	FRE	123	CREAGERS
LONG, JOHN S.	FRE	440	8TH E DI
LONG, JOHN T.	CHA	230	MIDDLETO
LONG, JOHN W.	ST	346	5TH E DI
LONG, JOSEPH	BAL	470	14TH WAR
LONG, JOSEPH	BAL	207	17TH WAR
LONG, JOSEPH	FRE	354	MIDDLETO
LONG, JOSEPH	WAS	033	2ND SUBD
LONG, JOSEPH	ST	261	3RD E DI
LONG, JOSEPH	ST	261	3RD E DI
LONG, JOSEPHINE	BAL	214	11TH WAR
LONG, JOSIAH	SOM	415	DUBLIN D
LONG, JOSIAH	SOM	409	DUBLIN D
LONG, JULIA	BAL	111	15TH WAR
LONG, L.N.B.	BAL	186	2ND WARD
LONG, LEAH-BLACK	WOR	333	1ST E DI
LONG, LEROY	BAL	180	11TH WAR
LONG, LEVI	BAL	013	15TH WAR
LONG, LEWIS	BAL	135	1ST WARD
LONG, LIDIA-BLACK	WOR	343	1ST E DI
LONG, LINUS	ST	330	4TH E DI
LONG, LITTLETON	SOM	428	PRINCESS
LONG, LOUIS	BAL	092	10TH WAR
LONG, LOUIS	BAL	463	1ST DIST
LONG, LYDIANN	FRE	426	8TH E DI
LONG, MALINDA	CEC	121	4TH E DI
LONG, MARGARET	BAL	093	2ND DIST
LONG, MARIA	WAS	177	1ST DIST
LONG, MARIAH	SOM	362	BRINKLEY
LONG, MARTHA	BAL	102	18TH WAR
LONG, MARTHA E.	CHA	231	HILLTOP
LONG, MARTIN	FRE	139	CREAGERS
LONG, MARY	CEC	121	4TH E DI
LONG, MARY	SOM	416	DUBLIN D
LONG, MARY	BAL	214	19TH WAR
LONG, MARY	SOM	396	BRINKLEY
LONG, MARY	BAL	115	5TH WARD
LONG, MARY	BAL	128	5TH WARD
LONG, MARY	BAL	360	3RD WARD
LONG, MARY A.	SOM	490	SALISBUR
LONG, MARY B.D.	ALL	186	9TH E.D.
LONG, MARY E.	BAL	001	15TH WAR
LONG, MARY E.	FRE	441	8TH E DI
LONG, MARY*	SOM	550	TYASKIN
LONG, MICHAEL	BAL	207	19TH WAR
LONG, MICHAEL	BAL	234	17TH WAR
LONG, MICHAEL	BAL	028	9TH WARD
LONG, NATHANIEL	WAS	017	2ND SUBD
LONG, NORMAND	ALL	010	3RD E.D.
LONG, PETER	CAR	250	3RD DIST
LONG, PHILLIS-BLACK	WOR	340	1ST E DI
LONG, RACHEL	WOR	266	BERLIN 1
LONG, RICHARD	ST	346	5TH E DI
LONG, RICHARD	SOM	458	DAMES QU
LONG, RICHARD D.	BAL	312	1ST DIST
LONG, ROBERT	BAL	300	12TH WAR
LONG, ROBERT H.	BAL	119	1ST WARD
LONG, ROBERT H.	SOM	359	BRINKLEY
LONG, ROSANNA	BAL	181	11TH WAR
LONG, SAMUEL	BAL	032	9TH WARD
LONG, SAMUEL	BAL	399	1ST DIST
LONG, SAMUEL	BAL	396	3RD WARD
LONG, SAMUEL K.	BAL	299	1ST DIST
LONG, SARAH	ALL	228	CUMBERLA
LONG, SARAH	SOM	358	BRINKLEY
LONG, SARAH	SOM	414	DUBLIN D
LONG, SARAH	FRE	178	5TH E DI
LONG, SARAH	BAL	152	11TH WAR
LONG, SARAH	BAL	404	14TH WAR
LONG, SARAH S.	ANN	403	8TH DIST
LONG, SIMON	WAS	017	2ND SUBD
LONG, SOPHIA	BAL	360	3RD WARD
LONG, STEPHEN	FRE	168	EMMITTSB
LONG, SUSAN	WAS	198	1ST DIST
LONG, SUSANNA	ST	289	2ND E DI
LONG, SYDNEY C.	SOM	426	PRINCESS
LONG, THOMAS	SOM	425	PRINCESS
LONG, THOMAS	CEC	040	CHESAPEA
LONG, THOMAS O.	ST	348	5TH E DI
LONG, UPTON	ALL	152	6TH E.D.
LONG, WILIAM	BAL	410	14TH WAR
LONG, WILLIAM	CAR	199	4TH DIST
LONG, WILLIAM	SOM	417	PRINCESS
LONG, WILLIAM	FRE	134	CREAGERS
LONG, WILLIAM	CHA	232	HILLTOP
LONG, WILLIAM	BAL	233	1ST DIST
LONG, WILLIAM	BAL	261	2ND WARD
LONG, WILLIAM	DOR	469	1ST DIST
LONG, WILLIAM A.	CEC	121	4TH E DI
LONG, WILLIAM H.	FRE	436	8TH E DI
LONG, WILLIAM H. C.	SOM	401	BRINKLEY
LONG, WILLIAM J.	WOR	343	1ST E DI
LONG, WILLIAM P.*	BAL	325	3RD WARD
LONG,MOCKY	ST	347	5TH E DI
LONGA, GEORGE	BAL	135	2ND DIST
LONGALEASE, NICHOLAS	CEC	019	ELKTON 3
LONGANECKER, ABRAHAM	WAS	241	CAVETOWN
LONGANECKER, REBECCA	WAS	251	1ST DIST
LONGBAUGH, JOHN	ALL	230	CUMBERLA
LONGCOPE, WILLIAM	BAL	145	5TH WARD
LONGE, PRISCILLA	BAL	462	14TH WAR
LONGENFIETER, JAMES	BAL	254	12TH WAR
LONGER, CASPER	BAL	290	17TH WAR
LONGER, MRS.	BAL	233	17TH WAR
LONGFELLOW, ANN J.	CEC	004	ELKTON 3
LONGFELLOW, DAVID R.	QUE	153	1ST E DI
LONGFELLOW, EMILY	KEN	292	3RD DIST
LONGFELLOW, EMILY A.	BAL	433	8TH WARD
LONGFELLOW, MARY W.	KEN	228	2ND DIST
LONGFELLOW, WILLIAM	KEN	213	2ND DIST
LONGGATH, ADOLPH	BAL	437	14TH WAR
LONGHANEY, FRANCES	BAL	265	2ND WARD
LONGHRAN, HENRY J.	BAL	096	10TH WAR
LONGHRAN, MARY	BAL	019	9TH WARD
LONGHREN, BRIDGET	BAL	399	14TH WAR
LONGLEY, REBECCA	BAL	159	19TH WAR
LONGLEY, SAMUEL	BAL	158	19TH WAR
LONGLY, JOHN	CAR	300	1ST DIST
LONGLY, THOMAS	CAR	310	1ST DIST
LONGLY, WILLIAM	BAL	225	1ST DIST
LONGMAN, CATHARINE	FRE	346	MIDDLETO
LONGMAN, GEORGE	FRE	351	MIDDLETO
LONGMAN, HUGH	ST	284	2ND E DI
LONGMAN, JACOB	FRE	342	MIDDLETO
LONGMAN, JACOB	FRE	351	MIDDLETO
LONGMAN, JOSEPH	FRE	373	CATOCTIN
LONGMER, LEAH	WAS	198	1ST DIST
LONGMIRE, JOHN	PRI	080	QUEEN AN
LONGMORE, HUGH	ST	283	3RD E DI
LONGMORE, SAMUEL	BAL	181	2ND DIST
LONGNECKER, DAVID	BAL	086	2ND DIST
LONGNECKER, DAVID	BAL	086	2ND DIST
LONGNECKER, JOHN	BAL	440	1ST DIST
LONGNOSE, WILLIAM	BAL	045	9TH WARD
LONGS, ISAAC	FRE	331	MIDDLETO
LONGS, LYDIA	WAS	033	2ND SUBD
LONGS, MATILDA	BAL	299	12TH WAR
LONGSDORFF, ADAM J.	WAS	103	2ND DIST
LONGWELL, BETTY	BAL	125	11TH WAR
LONGWELL, CATHARINE	BAL	076	18TH WAR
LONGWELL, DAVID	BAL	009	18TH WAR
LONGWELL, JANE	CAR	273	WESTMINS
LONGWELL, JANE	BAL	121	11TH WAR
LONGWELL, JOHN K.	CAR	273	WESTMINS
LONGWORTH, HESTER	BAL	334	1ST DIST
LONICE, MARY*	BAL	422	3RD WARD
LONNY, PASGIL	BAL	153	5TH WARD
LONWORTH, SARAH	BAL	347	13TH WAR

Name	County	Page	District
LOO, JOHN	BAL	021	15TH WAR
LOOBY, THOMAS	BAL	311	20TH WAR
LOOCKERMAN, CHARLES-BLACK	CAR	083	NO TWP L
LOOCKERMAN, JULIANNA	QUE	243	5TH E DI
LOOCKERMAN, THOMAS G.	BAL	109	10TH WAR
LOODE, MICHAEL	ALL	143	6TH E.D.
LOOHY, ANN*	BAL	027	4TH WARD
LOOKAMAR, THEADORE*	TAL	056	EASTON D
LOOKENSLAND, CATHERINE	FRE	129	CREAGERS
LOOKERMAN, BENJAMIN	TAL	071	EASTON T
LOOKERMAN, GEORGE W.	DOR	450	1ST DIST
LOOKERMAR, THEADORE R.*	TAL	056	EASTON D
LOOKINBELL, JOHN	CAR	254	3RD DIST
LOOKINGBEAL, AUGUST	CAR	267	WESTMINS
LOOKINGBEAL, JACOB	CAR	291	7TH DIST
LOOKINGBEAL, PETER	CAR	291	7TH DIST
LOOKINGBELL, PETER	CAR	254	3RD DIST
LOOKINGBILL, JOHN	CAR	244	3RD DIST
LOOKINGBILL, PETER	FRE	428	8TH E DI
LOOKINGBILL, SAMUEL	CAR	244	3RD DIST
LOOKINGLAND, JOHN A.	BAL	263	1ST DIST
LOOKINLAND, MARGARET L.	BAL	264	1ST DIST
LOOKINLAND, MARY	WAS	196	1ST DIST
LOOKINSLAND, GEORGE	WAS	149	HAGERSTO
LOOKUMAN, EDWARD*	TAL	011	EASTON D
LOOKY, JOHN	BAL	142	1ST WARD
LOOMAN, F.	BAL	149	1ST WARD
LOOMAN, MARY	ANN	376	4TH DIST
LOOMEY, SUSAN	BAL	118	2ND DIST
LOONEY, AGNESS	BAL	147	11TH WAR
LOONEY, CHALRES	BAL	132	18TH WAR
LOONEYE, THOMAS	ALL	048	10TH E.D
LOOPER, JOHN T.	MGM	439	CLARKSTR
LOOSE, JOHNATHAN	WAS	099	2ND DIST
LOOSE, JOSEPH B.	WAS	267	1ST DIST
LOOSE, MARY C.	WAS	099	2ND DIST
LOOSEY, HARRIET	BAL	368	3RD WARD
LOP, ELIZABETH	WAS	056	2ND SUBD
LOP, JACOB	WAS	056	2ND SUBD
LOPER, A.	BAL	159	1ST WARD
LOPER, AMOS	BAL	162	1ST WARD
LOPER, CATHERINE	MGM	352	BERRYS D
LOPER, IGNATIUS	MGM	437	CLARKSTR
LOPER, JAMES P.	MGM	351	BERRYS D
LOPER, JOHN A.	PRI	001	BLADENSB
LOPER, JOSPEH	MGM	352	BERRYS D
LOPER, MARY	MGM	352	BERRYS D
LOPER, N.	BAL	154	1ST WARD
LOPER, WILSON L.	MGM	437	CLARKSTR
LOPIER, JOHN	CEC	115	3RD E DI
LOPOLD, MICAHEL	BAL	103	2ND DIST
LOPP, DAVID	WAS	232	1ST DIST
LOPP, GEROGE	WAS	185	BOONSBOR
LOPP, JOHN	WAS	192	1ST DIST
LOPP, JOHN	WAS	212	1ST DIST
LOPP, JOHN	BAL	366	13TH WAR
LOPP, SAMUEL	WAS	183	BOONSBOR
LOPPY, CAROLINE*	BAL	008	4TH WARD
LOPTEN, STEPHEN	CEC	065	1ST E DI
LOPTKAUP, WILLIAM	BAL	237	2ND WARD
LOPTON, LOUIS	CEC	053	1ST E DI
LORAH, WILLIAM	ALL	059	10TH E.D
LORAN, CHARLES	BAL	455	8TH WARD
LORAN, MARY	BAL	357	3RD WARD
LORD, ABEL	DOR	461	1ST DIST
LORD, ABRAHAM	CAR	120	NO TWP L
LORD, ALEXANDRE	BAL	150	1ST WARD
LORD, AMELIA	DOR	458	1ST DIST
LORD, BENJAMIN	SOM	368	BRINKLEY
LORD, BENJAMIN	BAL	137	2ND DIST
LORD, BETSEY	BAL	459	8TH WARD
LORD, CHARLES	BAL	387	13TH WAR
LORD, CYRUS	DOR	455	1ST DIST
LORD, DANIEL	CEC	088	4TH E DI
LORD, EDWARD	CAR	121	NO TWP L
LORD, ELIZA W.	TAL	098	ST MICHA
LORD, ELSY	DOR	461	1ST DIST
LORD, HENRY*	DOR	458	1ST DIST
LORD, JAMES	DOR	457	1ST DIST
LORD, JAMES	PRI	048	AQUASCO
LORD, JEREMIAH	SOM	368	BRINKLEY
LORD, JOHN	SOM	384	BRINKLEY
LORD, JOHN	CAR	129	NO TWP L
LORD, LEVI	SOM	369	BRINKLEY
LORD, MARY E.	CAR	126	NO TWP L
LORD, MORSE	DOR	460	1ST DIST
LORD, SEVERN	SOM	371	BRINKLEY
LORD, THOMAS	SOM	368	BRINKLEY
LORD, THOMAS*	SOM	369	BRINKLEY
LORE, GEORGE	BAL	099	2ND DIST
LORE, MARY A. Y.	BAL	159	11TH WAR
LORE, MARY C.	PRI	109	PISCATAW
LORENTZ, AMELIA	BAL	181	6TH WARD
LORENTZ, ELIZABETH	FRE	313	MIDDLETO
LORENTZ, GEORGE	FRE	273	NEW MARK
LORENTZ, HENRY	BAL	338	1ST DIST
LORENTZ, HENRY	BAL	338	1ST DIST
LORENTZ, JACOB	FRE	313	MIDDLETO
LORENTZ, MARTIN	BAL	011	15TH WAR
LORENTZ, WILLIAM	FRE	314	MIDDLETO
LORENZO, JOSEPH	BAL	280	2ND WARD
LORER, CATHARINE	BAL	230	1ST DIST
LOREY, GEORGE *	WAS	115	2ND DIST
LORFING, JOHN	BAL	016	9TH WARD
LORG, WILLIAM	BAL	333	13TH WAR
LORI, JOHN	BAL	249	1ST DIST
LORICK, MAGDALENA	BAL	440	14TH WAR
LORING, JAMES	BAL	163	1ST WARD
LORITZ, JACOB	BAL	367	8TH WARD
LORMAN, JOHN	BAL	322	3RD WARD
LORONDIS, EMMA	BAL	314	20TH WAR
LORSBEY, WILLIAM	BAL	006	4TH WARD
LORSBOUGH, MARTIN L.*	BAL	081	4TH WARD
LORSHBAUGH, PHILIP	WAS	294	1ST DIST
LORT, FRANKLIN W.	CEC	068	5TH E DI
LORTON, CHARLES	BAL	252	17TH WAR
LORVE, THOMAS M.	BAL	203	19TH WAR
LORVENEHUL, SARAH *	BAL	322	12TH WAR
LORY, JACOB *	WAS	077	2ND SUBD
LORYMAN, ELIAS	WAS	034	2ND SUBD
LORYMAN, JOHN	WAS	060	2ND SUBD
LOSCIRNE, HENRY	BAL	231	2ND WARD
LOSE, ANN-BLACK	FRE	244	NEW MARK
LOSEY, ABRAHAM R.	WAS	101	2ND DIST
LOSEY, JOHN	WAS	098	2ND DIST
LOSH, JOSEPH	ALL	046	10TH E.D
LOSKCANE, JANE *	BAL	258	2ND WARD
LOSOM, DAVID	CEC	069	5TH E DI
LOSS, CAROLINE	BAL	381	3RD WARD
LOSSOM, JOHN	CEC	069	5TH E DI
LOTCHFORD, JOSEPH	BAL	197	19TH WAR
LOTH, BERNARD	BAL	141	1ST WARD
LOTMAN, CHARLOTTE	CEC	020	ELKTON 3
LOTMAN, NICHOLAS	CEC	020	ELKTON 3
LOTON, WILLIAM	HAR	019	1ST DIST
LOTT, CHRISTIAN	BAL	312	20TH WAR
LOTT, CORNLIUS	FRE	118	CREAGERS
LOTTON, MORTIMER	ALL	012	3RD E.D.
LOTTY, JOSEPH*	BAL	006	4TH WARD
LOTZ, GEORGE F.	BAL	132	16TH WAR
LOTZ, JOHN	BAL	132	16TH WAR
LOTZ, JOHN M.	BAL	119	1ST WARD
LOUALL, JEREMIAH *	BAL	184	6TH WARD
LOUCE, HENRY	BAL	114	11TH WAR
LOUCK, HY	BAL	191	5TH DIST
LOUCK, IMLIAM *	BAL	195	5TH DIST
LOUCK, JACOB	BAL	204	6TH DIST
LOUCK, JOHN	BAL	187	5TH DIST
LOUCK, JOHN C.	BAL	194	5TH DIST
LOUCK, MAGDALINE	BAL	195	5TH DIST
LOUD, ADAM	DOR	320	1ST DIST
LOUD, CHARLOTTE	BAL	014	18TH WAR
LOUD, JOHN W.	KEN	234	2ND DIST
LOUD, P. H. *	BAL	154	1ST WARD
LOUDASLAGER, NANCY	WAS	035	2ND SUBD
LOUDE, JOSEPH E.	BAL	167	11TH WAR
LOUDE, THEDORE	BAL	102	18TH WAR
LOUDEN, WINNE	ALL	227	CUMBERLA
LOUDENBAUGH, JOEPH	BAL	416	14TH WAR
LOUDENSLAGER, EVERHARD	WAS	137	HAGERSTO
LOUDENSLAGER, LYDIA	WAS	176	1ST DIST
LOUDENSLAGER, MARY	WAS	142	HAGERSTO
LOUDENSLAGER, SYLVIANN	BAL	456	8TH WARD
LOUDENSLAGER, THEODORE	BAL	161	16TH WAR
LOUDENSLEGER, EVERHARD	WAS	151	HAGERSTO
LOUDENSLEGER, PHILIP	CAR	256	3RD DIST
LOUDENSLEGER, SARAH	WAS	162	HAGERSTO
LOUDENSLEGER, SOLOMON	WAS	207	1ST DIST
LOUDENSTAGER, SOLOMON *	BAL	111	18TH WAR
LOUDENSTAYER, THEODORE	BAL	423	14TH WAR
LOUDER, JOSHUA	CAR	324	1ST DIST
LOUDER, PHILIP	CEC	148	PORT DUP
LOUDER, VERLINDA	ANN	478	HOWARD D
LOUDERMAN, JOHN	BAL	423	3RD WARD
LOUDERMELL, ELIZA	ALL	228	CUMBERLA
LOUDERS, AUTHER	WAS	275	RIDGEVIL
LOUDERS, JACOB	FRE	124	CREAGERS
LOUDESLAGER, HENRY	WAS	176	1ST DIST
LOUDESLEGER, AUGUSTUS	WAS	299	1ST DIST
LOUDESLEGER, JOHN	WAS	207	1ST DIST
LOUDINKLAGER, SILVANUS	BAL	074	4TH WARD
LOUDT, PETER	WAS	257	1ST DIST
LOUDY, MARY	SOM	433	PRINCESS
LOUERHOFF, JOHN*	BAL	342	3RD WARD
LOUFT, JOHN M.	BAL	143	11TH WAR
LOUGE, DAVID	BAL	221	1ST DIST
LOUGE, ELIJAH	BAL	228	1ST DIST
LOUGE, ELZIA	CAR	413	2ND DIST
LOUGE, HENRY	BAL	274	1ST DIST
LOUGE, JOHN	BAL	282	1ST DIST
LOUGE, JOHN	BAL	276	1ST DIST
LOUGE, LEWIS	FRE	064	FREDERIC
LOUGH, ARTHUR	BAL	093	10TH WAR
LOUGH, JOSEPH	BAL	063	10TH WAR
LOUGH, MARTHA	BAL	059	2ND DIST
LOUGH, SISTER FERDINAND	FRE	197	5TH E DI
LOUGHLIN, ELLEN O.	BAL	054	4TH WARD
LOUGHLIN, MARIA O.	BAL	098	5TH WARD
LOUGHLIN, SISTER M.P.	FRE	198	5TH E DI
LOUGHLING, ANN	CEC	173	6TH E DI
LOUGHNER, GEORGE	FRE	062	FREDERIC
LOUGHRAN, MICHAEL	BAL	033	9TH WARD
LOUGHRAN, PATRICK	BAL	165	6TH WARD
LOUGHRY, PATRICK	CAR	369	9TH DIST
LOUGHTON, MADGE	BAL	231	12TH WAR
LOUICE, MARY*	BAL	422	3RD WARD
LOUIS, JOHN	BAL	256	12TH WAR
LOUIS, JULIA	BAL	057	10TH WAR
LOUIS, LOUIS	BAL	005	15TH WAR
LOUIS, MARY	BAL	384	13TH WAR
LOUIS, SOPHIA	KEN	238	2ND DIST
LOUIS, WILLIAM	HAR	179	3RD DIST
LOUIS, WILLIAM	MGM	381	ROCKERLE
LOUISA, MARY-BLACK	QUE	185	3RD E DI
LOUISIN, WILLIAM	BAL	199	2ND WARD
LOUMAN, EMORY	BAL	146	2ND DIST
LOUMOINE, LOUISA*	BAL	330	3RD WARD
LOUPHINDEN, MOSES	BAL	256	2ND WARD
LOUR, PETER	BAL	460	14TH WAR
LOUREY, E.	BAL	139	1ST WARD
LOUREY, FRANCIS	BAL	153	2ND DIST
LOUREY, JULIANA	QUE	230	4TH E DI
LOUREY, MISS M.	FRE	199	5TH E DI
LOURSBAUGH, WILLIAM	WAS	133	HAGERSTO
LOURY, HANSON	BAL	030	9TH WARD
LOURY, ROBERT H.	BAL	383	3RD WARD
LOUSE, JOHN	BAL	235	20TH WAR
LOUT, GEORGE	WAS	147	HAGERSTO
LOUTS, LEWIS	CAR	345	6TH DIST
LOUTZ, DAVID	BAL	423	1ST DIST
LOUVESTRE, SUSAN	BAL	205	11TH WAR
LOVALL, JOHN	ALL	140	6TH E.D.
LOVALL, PATRICK	ALL	141	6TH E.D.
LOVAY, HANAH	BAL	385	8TH WARD
LOVE, AGNES A.	CEC	156	PORT DUP
LOVE, ANN	CAR	147	NO TWP L
LOVE, ANN	WAS	143	HAGERSTO
LOVE, AUGUSTA	BAL	252	17TH WAR
LOVE, BENNET	HAR	042	1ST DIST
LOVE, BENNETT	CEC	174	6TH E DI
LOVE, BETSEY	BAL	128	11TH WAR
LOVE, ELLEN	BAL	001	18TH WAR
LOVE, FANNY	BAL	020	2ND DIST
LOVE, GEORGE	HAR	076	BEL AIR
LOVE, HARRIOT	BAL	276	20TH WAR
LOVE, HENRY	BAL	129	18TH WAR
LOVE, JACOB	HAR	048	1ST DIST
LOVE, JAMES	HAR	076	BEL AIR
LOVE, JAMES	BAL	022	18TH WAR
LOVE, JAMES	CEC	174	6TH E DI
LOVE, JAMES B.*	TAL	018	EASTON D
LOVE, JOHN	MGM	399	ROCKERLE
LOVE, JOSEPH K.	BAL	120	16TH WAR
LOVE, JOSSE M.	BAL	249	12TH WAR
LOVE, JULIA C.	FRE	039	FREDERIC
LOVE, KEZIA	BAL	061	10TH WAR
LOVE, MARTHA A.	CEC	096	4TH E DI
LOVE, MARY	CEC	172	6TH E DI
LOVE, MARY	BAL	274	20TH WAR
LOVE, MARY	KEN	312	3RD DIST
LOVE, PERRY S.	TAL	018	EASTON D
LOVE, PHILIP	BAL	121	2ND DIST
LOVE, PHILIP G.	ST	333	4TH E DI
LOVE, PRESILLA	BAL	139	11TH WAR
LOVE, ROBERT	HAR	031	1ST DIST
LOVE, ROBERT	QUE	128	1ST E DI
LOVE, SAMUEL	HAR	031	1ST DIST
LOVE, SAMUEL T.	TAL	021	EASTON D
LOVE, SCHOCKLY	CEC	174	6TH E DI
LOVE, SOLLOMON	TAL	073	EASTON T
LOVE, THOMAS	CAR	139	NO TWP L
LOVE, THOMAS	BAL	019	2ND DIST
LOVE, WILLIAM	BAL	128	11TH WAR
LOVE, WILLIAM	BAL	345	13TH WAR
LOVE, WILLIAM	BAL	098	18TH WAR
LOVE, WILLIAM	ST	270	3RD E DI
LOVE, WILLIAM C.	ST	270	3RD E DI
LOVE, WILLIAM DR-	BAL	096	18TH WAR
LOVE, ZEBALON	WAS	144	HAGERSTO
LOVEALL, DAVID	BAL	188	2ND WARD
LOVEALL, ELIAS	CAR	288	7TH DIST
LOVEALL, ELISHA	BAL	186	5TH DIST
LOVEALL, GREENBURY	CAR	182	8TH DIST
LOVEALL, JANE	CAR	392	2ND DIST
LOVEALL, JOHN	CAR	393	2ND DIST
LOVEALL, JOHN	CAR	175	8TH DIST
LOVEALL, LUCINDA	CAR	175	8TH DIST
LOVEALL, MARGARET	BAL	340	1ST DIST
LOVEALL, MARY	CAR	189	4TH DIST
LOVEALL, THOMAS	CAR	391	2ND DIST
LOVEALL, WILLIAM	BAL	340	1ST DIST
LOVEDAY, CHARLES	BAL	291	7TH WARD
LOVEDAY, PERRY	BAL	130	16TH WAR
LOVEDAY, THOAMS	KEN	208	2ND DIST
LOVEDERS, A. J.	TAL	074	EASTON T
LOVEGROVE, FOLGER P.	BAL	046	9TH WARD
LOVEGROVE, JAMES	BAL	129	5TH WARD
LOVEGROVE, THOMAS J.	BAL	186	6TH WARD
LOVEING, SYLVESTER	BAL	144	1ST WARD
LOVEJET, EMON	BAL	171	19TH WAR
LOVEJOY, GEORGE W.	MGM	345	CLARKSBU
LOVEJOY, JOHN J.	PRI	004	BLADENSB
LOVEJOY, LUCY	BAL	022	4TH WARD
LOVEJOY, MARGARET	BAL	213	11TH WAR
LOVEJOY, P. R.	BAL	101	10TH WAR
LOVEJOY, PERRY G.	ANN	491	HOWARD D
LOVEJOY, SAMUEL	BAL	460	14TH WAR
LOVEJOY, SAMUEL	FRE	009	FREDERIC
LOVEJOY, WILLIAM	BAL	064	2ND DIST
LOVEJOY, WILLIAM H.	BAL	195	11TH WAR
LOVELACE, CHARLOTTE	MGM	359	BERRYS D
LOVELACE, TERSA	CHA	251	MIDDLETO
LOVELAND, HANFORD	BAL	015	4TH WARD
LOVELESS, ANN	BAL	155	2ND DIST
LOVELESS, ELISHA	PRI	083	QUEEN AN
LOVELESS, JAMES	PRI	092	MARLBROU
LOVELESS, JAMES	PRI	062	NOTTINGH
LOVELESS, JOHN	PRI	081	QUEEN AN
LOVELESS, THOMAS	PRI	075	MARLBROU
LOVELEY, AMANUEL	FRE	019	FREDERIC
LOVELIS, MARY A.	ANN	296	1ST DIST
LOVELL, ADALINE	BAL	058	2ND DIST
LOVELL, ANN E.	BAL	378	8TH WARD
LOVELL, CYNTHA	CAR	175	8TH DIST
LOVELL, EDWARD	ALL	143	6TH E.D.
LOVELL, ELLEN	BAL	213	19TH WAR
LOVELL, HENRY	ALL	141	6TH E.D.
LOVELL, HONOR	ALL	241	CUMBERLA
LOVELL, MARY	BAL	012	18TH WAR
LOVELL, PETGER	ALL	142	6TH E.D.
LOVELL, SOLOMAN	BAL	188	2ND WARD
LOVELLA, OWEN	BAL	472	14TH WAR
LOVELY, ELLEN *	BAL	289	20TH WAR
LOVELY, EMANUEL	FRE	079	FREDERIC
LOVELY, HENRY	BAL	150	5TH WARD
LOVELY, MALINDA	BAL	087	18TH WAR
LOVEN, JOHN	BAL	122	11TH WAR
LOVER, MARY E.	BAL	122	11TH WAR
LOVERING, GEORGE A.	BAL	341	7TH WARD
LOVERING, GEORGE A.	BAL	341	7TH WARD
LOVERT, ARAMINTA	CEC	075	NORTHEAS
LOVESS, GEORGE	ST	326	4TH E DI
LOVESS, JOSEPH M.	ST	326	4TH E DI
LOVET, ARAMINTA	CEC	068	5TH E DI
LOVET, MARGARET	BAL	301	1ST DIST
LOVET, WILLIAM	BAL	255	1ST DIST
LOVETT, CONNOR	BAL	004	9TH WARD
LOVETT, JOHN	ALL	116	5TH E.D.
LOVETT, JOSHUA P.	HAR	174	3RD DIST
LOVETT, JOSHUA P.	HAR	174	3RD DIST
LOVITT, H.	BAL	117	1ST WARD
LOW, ANDREW	BAL	161	2ND DIST
LOW, ELIZABETH	HAR	202	3RD DIST
LOW, EMMA J.	BAL	288	17TH WAR
LOW, FRANKLIN	QUE	228	4TH E DI
LOW, FREDERICK	BAL	103	15TH WAR
LOW, JAMES P.	BAL	127	1ST WARD
LOW, JEREMIAH	HAR	019	1ST DIST
LOW, JEREMIAH	HAR	024	1ST DIST
LOW, JOHN	BAL	108	15TH WAR
LOW, JOHN	BAL	229	1ST DIST
LOW, JOHN	WAS	142	2ND DIST
LOW, JOSEPH	ANN	451	HOWARD D
LOW, JOSEPH B.	TAL	117	ST MICHA
LOW, JOSHUA	HAR	047	1ST DIST
LOW, MARY	WAS	099	2ND DIST
LOW, MARY	BAL	282	7TH WARD
LOW, MARY	BAL	256	6TH WARD
LOW, PRUDENCE	ANN	495	HOWARD D
LOW, REBECCA	BAL	033	2ND DIST
LOW.REASON	HAR	024	1ST DIST
LOWAGE, WILIAM	BAL	157	1ST WARD
LOWALT, FANNEY	CAR	184	8TH DIST
LOWBAR, ARINENTTA	BAL	177	11TH WAR
LOWBAR, CHARLES H.	BAL	177	11TH WAR
LOWDE, MARGARET	BAL	084	18TH WAR
LOWDEN, FRANSIS	WAS	055	2ND SUBD
LOWDEN, LEVI	BAL	022	1ST WARD
LOWDEN, MARGARET	BAL	130	5TH WARD
LOWDEN, WILLIAM	BAL	295	17TH WAR
LOWDER, ELIZA	BAL	397	14TH WAR
LOWDER, GODFREED	BAL	260	1ST DIST
LOWDER, JOHN P.	BAL	194	19TH WAR
LOWDERMELK, HANSON	ALL	096	5TH E.D.
LOWDERMILK, JOHN V.	ALL	024	3RD E.D.
LOWE, ADELAID	FRE	044	FREDERIC
LOWE, ALEXANDER	ALL	139	6TH E.D.
LOWE, ALFRED	BAL	231	1ST DIST
LOWE, ANDREW	CEC	170	6TH E DI
LOWE, ANDREW	PRI	004	BLADENSB

LOWE, ASA BAL 211 6TH DIST
LOWE, B.L.A. PRI 119 PISCATAW
LOWE, CALEB HAR 097 2ND DIST
LOWE, CAROLINE PRI 005 BLADENSB
LOWE, CLEMMTAN * TAL 103 ST MICHA
LOWE, CORNELIUS* BAL 022 4TH WARD
LOWE, DANIEL BAL 173 6TH WARD
LOWE, CANIEL U. BAL 021 2ND DIST
LOWE, CAVID BAL 183 16TH WAR
LOWE, DAVID CAR 199 4TH DIST
LOWE, EDWARD BAL 230 1ST DIST
LOWE, EDWARD TAL 115 ST MICHA
LOWE, ELIZA BAL 032 18TH WAR
LOWE, ELIZABETH CAR 218 5TH DIST
LOWE, ELIZABETH MGM 322 CRACKLIN
LOWE, ELIZABETH BAL 424 1ST DIST
LOWE, EPHRAIM CEC 074 5TH E DI
LOWE, ESMA CAR 104 NO TWP L
LOWE, FRANCES DOR 304 1ST DIST
LOWE, FRANCIS BAL 126 16TH WAR
LOWE, GEORGE FRE 063 FREDERIC
LOWE, GEORGE SOM 501 SALISBUR
LOWE, HENRY QUE 253 5TH E DI
LOWE, HENRY FRE 008 FREDERIC
LOWE, JAMES FRE 193 5TH E DI
LOWE, JAMES FRE 193 5TH E DI
LOWE, JAMES FRE 239 NEW MARK
LOWE, JAMES PRI 049 AQUASCO
LOWE, JAMES BAL 060 15TH WAR
LOWE, JAMES W. TAL 109 ST MICHA
LOWE, JAMES W. PRI 066 NOTTINGH
LOWE, JOHN SOM 504 SALISBUR
LOWE, JOHN SOM 500 SALISBUR
LOWE, JOHN ALL 220 CUMBERLA
LOWE, JOHN BAL 259 6TH WARD
LOWE, JOHN FRE 253 NEW MARK
LOWE, JOHN FRE 038 FREDERIC
LOWE, JOHN CAR 238 UNION TO
LOWE, JOHN D. HAR 010 1ST DIST
LOWE, JOHN H. MGM 411 MEDLEY 3
LOWE, JOHN H. BAL 060 10TH WAR
LOWE, JOHN H. PRI 119 PISCATAW
LOWE, JOSE MGM 441 CLARKSTR
LOWE, JOSEPH BAL 366 1ST DIST
LOWE, JOSHUA BAL 033 2ND DIST
LOWE, JOSHUA MGM 440 CLARKSTR
LOWE, JULIANN BAL 216 6TH DIST
LOWE, KITTMA TAL 111 ST MICHA
LOWE, LEVI B. BAL 405 3RD WARD
LOWE, LEVIN SOM 526 QUANTICO
LOWE, LLOYD ALL 184 9TH E.D.
LOWE, MARGARETT DOR 313 1ST DIST
LOWE, MARGRETT A. E. BAL 106 18TH WAR
LOWE, MARY BAL 335 13TH WAR
LOWE, MARY BAL 073 15TH WAR
LOWE, MARY QUE 240 5TH E DI
LOWE, NATHAN PRI 001 BLADENSB
LOWE, NATHANIEL MGM 403 ROCKERLE
LOWE, NICHOLAS CAR 176 8TH DIST
LOWE, NICHOLAS BAL 286 2ND WARD
LOWE, NINIAN MGM 411 MEDLEY 3
LOWE, PHILLIP FRE 042 FREDERIC
LOWE, RACHEL BAL 405 1ST DIST
LOWE, RALPH SOM 523 BARREN C
LOWE, ROBERT BAL 287 3RD WARD
LOWE, ROSIANNA CEC 197 7TH E DI
LOWE, RUTH CEC 170 6TH E DI
LOWE, SALLY DOR 313 1ST DIST
LOWE, SAMUEL O. BAL 027 4TH WARD
LOWE, SARAH BAL 454 14TH WAR
LOWE, SHADA SOM 498 SALISBUR
LOWE, SUSANAH BAL 285 1ST DIST
LOWE, THOMAS PRI 101 SPALDING
LOWE, THOMAS PRI 101 SPALDING
LOWE, THOMAS SOM 534 QUANTICO
LOWE, THOMAS G. BAL 131 1ST WARD
LOWE, THOMAS J. TAL 102 ST MICHA
LOWE, URITH FRE 021 FREDERIC
LOWE, WARING PRI 010 BLADENSB
LOWE, WESLEY DOR 313 1ST DIST
LOWE, WILLIAM DOR 313 1ST DIST
LOWE, WILLIAM CHA 219 ALLENS F
LOWE, WILLIAM CAR 104 NO TWP L
LOWE, WILLIAM FRE 193 5TH E DI
LOWE, WILLIAM WAS 114 2ND DIST
LOWE, WILLIAM BAL 393 3RD WARD
LOWE, WILLIAM BAL 161 2ND DIST
LOWE, WILLIAM S. TAL 115 ST MICHA
LOWE, WILLIAM W. TAL 102 ST MICHA
LOWE, WILLIAM W. CAR 159 NO TWP L
LOWE, WILLIAM* BAL 387 3RD WARD
LOWE, ZACHARIAH MGM 428 CLARKSTR
LOWELL, B. BAL 163 1ST WARD
LOWELL, CHARLES B. FRE 021 FREDERIC
LOWELL, RUBEN BAL 330 3RD WARD
LOWELL, WILLIAM FRE 021 FREDERIC
LOWER, CATHARINE BAL 343 7TH WARD
LOWER, CONRADT BAL 343 7TH WARD
LOWER, MARY BAL 408 3RD WARD
LOWER, MICHAEL ALL 057 10TH E.D
LOWERING, CHRISTIAN BAL 070 1ST WARD
LOWERS, EDWARD ALL 062 10TH E.D
LOWERS, ELIE FRE 265 NEW MARK
LOWERS, ELIZABETH CAR 290 7TH DIST
LOWERS, J. M. BAL 470 14TH WAR
LOWERY, BARBARA A. BAL 351 7TH WARD
LOWERY, BRUSE CEC 083 CHARLEST
LOWERY, EDWARD BAL 302 17TH WAR
LOWERY, EDWARD CEC 038 CHESAPEA
LOWERY, ELIZA BAL 156 11TH WAR
LOWERY, ELIZABETH BAL 141 11TH WAR
LOWERY, GEORGE N. BAL 067 18TH WAR
LOWERY, HENRY ALL 059 10TH E.D
LOWERY, HUGH BAL 288 7TH WARD
LOWERY, JAMES W. BAL 184 2ND WARD
LOWERY, JANE BAL 116 5TH WARD
LOWERY, JOHN ALL 059 10TH E.D
LOWERY, JOHN BAL 305 17TH WAR
LOWERY, JOHN CEC 120 4TH E DI
LOWERY, JOHN CEC 092 4TH E DI
LOWERY, JOHN BAL 099 18TH WAR
LOWERY, JOHN D. BAL 002 1ST WARD
LOWERY, LOUIS-BLACK FRE 012 FREDERIC
LOWERY, LUCY BAL 136 11TH WAR
LOWERY, MARGARET A. BAL 419 8TH WARD
LOWERY, MARIA BAL 149 11TH WAR
LOWERY, MARY CEC 111 4TH E DI
LOWERY, MARY CEC 119 3RD E DI
LOWERY, MARY BAL 136 5TH WARD
LOWERY, PHEBE BAL 116 5TH WARD

LOWERY, SOLLOMON FRE 209 BUCKEYST
LOWERY, STEPHEN TAL 058 EASTON D
LOWERY, THOMAS BAL 456 8TH WARD
LOWERY, VINTON BAL 099 18TH WAR
LOWERY, WILLIAM WAS 137 HAGERSTO
LOWERY, WILLIAM SOM 533 QUANTICO
LOWERY, WILLIAM L. TAL 120 ST MICHA
LOWERY,C. BAL 114 1ST WARD
LOWEY, MARY A.* BAL 303 3RD WARD
LOWIS, MARY KEN 219 2ND DIST
LOWKAMP, J. H. BAL 133 11TH WAR
LOWKAUP, CHARLES BAL 133 11TH WAR
LOWMAN, A. BAL 227 19TH WAR
LOWMAN, CHARITY ANN 388 4TH DIST
LOWMAN, DENTON ANN 381 4TH DIST
LOWMAN, ELIZABETH FRE 245 NEW MARK
LOWMAN, GUSTAVUS ANN 495 HOWARD D
LOWMAN, JACOB MGM 423 MEDLEY 3
LOWMAN, JOHN ANN 381 4TH DIST
LOWMAN, JOHN H. BAL 279 2ND WARD
LOWMAN, MARY A. ANN 381 4TH DIST
LOWMAN, MATTHIAS ANN 390 4TH DIST
LOWMAN, PERRY G. CAR 366 9TH DIST
LOWMAN, WILLIAM CAR 363 9TH DIST
LOWMEGER, WILLIAM BAL 157 2ND DIST
LOWNDES, BENJAMIN O. PRI 005 BLADENSB
LOWNDS, CHARLES* TAL 027 EASTON D
LOWNDS, JAMES BAL 125 5TH WARD
LOWNELS, LOUISA ALL 195 CUMBERLA
LOWNES, ELENORA ANN 462 HOWARD D
LOWRE, CHRISTIAN WAS 253 1ST DIST
LOWREY, AMANDA BAL 392 3RD WARD
LOWREY, ANN AM. QUE 207 3RD E DI
LOWREY, BARBARA BAL 112 1ST WARD
LOWREY, J. BAL 288 20TH WAR
LOWREY, JAMES QUE 241 5TH E DI
LOWREY, JOHN BAL 019 4TH WARD
LOWREY, JOHN BAL 260 2ND WARD
LOWREY, POLLY QUE 241 5TH E DI
LOWREY, WILLIAM QUE 222 4TH E DI
LOWREY, WILLIAM WAS 291 1ST DIST
LOWRIE, JOHN MGM 381 ROCKERLE
LOWRY, AMON ANN 444 HOWARD D
LOWRY, B. BAL 137 1ST WARD
LOWRY, BARBARA BAL 250 6TH WARD
LOWRY, ELIZABETH BAL 049 4TH WARD
LOWRY, GEORGE ALL 143 6TH E.D.
LOWRY, GEORGE WAS 223 1ST DIST
LOWRY, GEORGE M WAS 222 1ST DIST
LOWRY, HANSON BAL 046 9TH WARD
LOWRY, HENRY BAL 134 2ND DIST
LOWRY, HENRY WAS 235 1ST DIST
LOWRY, HENRY WAS 264 1ST DIST
LOWRY, HENRY WAS 287 1ST DIST
LOWRY, JAMES WAS 229 1ST DIST
LOWRY, JAMES D. BAL 288 3RD WARD
LOWRY, JANE ANN 285 ANNAPOLI
LOWRY, JOHN ALL 105 5TH E.D.
LOWRY, JOHN BAL 163 16TH WAR
LOWRY, JOHN BAL 387 3RD WARD
LOWRY, JULIA A. FRE 340 MIDDLETO
LOWRY, MARY BAL 374 13TH WAR
LOWRY, MARY BAL 055 4TH WARD
LOWRY, MARY A.* BAL 303 3RD WARD
LOWRY, RICHARD ALL 214 CUMBERLA
LOWRY, ROBERT H. BAL 114 15TH WAR
LOWRY, SARAH FRE 355 MIDDLETO
LOWRY, WILLIAM BAL 077 1ST WARD
LOWRY, WILLIAM WAS 228 1ST DIST
LOWRY, WILLIAM H. WAS 177 1ST DIST
LOWS, ROBERT BAL 281 2ND WARD
LOWSON, WILLIAM WAS 020 2ND SUBD
LOWTHER, JAMES BAL 072 18TH WAR
LOWTHER, WILLIAM BAL 146 19TH WAR
LOWTHIA, RUTH BAL 071 18TH WAR
LOX, ADY* BAL 069 4TH WARD
LOX, THEODORE* BAL 069 4TH WARD
LOY, DANIEL L. FRE 115 CREAGERS
LOY,LOUISA FRE 043 FREDERIC
LOYD, ANDREW E. CHA 223 ALLENS F
LOYD, ANDRW BAL 185 5TH DIST
LOYD, ANN CEC 035 CHESAPEA
LOYD, ARENA ANN 446 HOWARD D
LOYD, EDWARD BAL 128 2ND DIST
LOYD, EDWARD CEC 008 ELKTON 3
LOYD, EDWARD B. SOM 425 PRINCESS
LOYD, ELIZA CHA 223 ALLENS F
LOYD, ELIZABETH CHA 223 ALLENS F
LOYD, ELLIZABETH BAL 366 8TH WARD
LOYD, FRANCIS CHA 223 ALLENS F
LOYD, GEORGE W. CEC 166 6TH E DI
LOYD, HENRIETTA BAL 366 8TH WARD
LOYD, ISACK* TAL 004 EASTON D
LOYD, JAMES SOM 520 BARREN C
LOYD, JOHN SOM 521 BARREN C
LOYD, JOHN BAL 244 1ST DIST
LOYD, JOHN CEC 034 CHESAPEA
LOYD, JOHN L. CAR 192 4TH DIST
LOYD, JOSEPH CHA 224 ALLENS F
LOYD, LORONE CEC 062 1ST E DI
LOYD, MARY CEC 061 1ST E DI
LOYD, MARY BAL 194 11TH WAR
LOYD, MARY SOM 520 BARREN C
LOYD, MICHAEL BAL 113 1ST WARD
LOYD, MITCHEL SOM 499 SALISBUR
LOYD, NICHOLAS T. CEC 061 1ST E DI
LOYD, PETER SOM 522 BARREN C
LOYD, RICHARD CAR 284 7TH DIST
LOYD, SAMUEL CEC 182 7TH E DI
LOYD, SAMUEL WOR 342 1ST E DI
LOYD, SAMUEL BAL 431 1ST DIST
LOYD, STEPHEN BAL 230 1ST DIST
LOYD, THOMAS CHA 223 ALLENS F
LOYD, THOMAS CHA 233 HILLTOP
LOYD, U. CHA 220 ALLENS F
LOYD, WILLIAM SOM 520 BARREN C
LOYD, WILLIAM B. BAL 026 1ST WARD
LOYD, Y. CHA 220 ALLENS F
LOYDA, WILLIAM-BLACK BAL 222 2ND WARD
LOYDBECKER, JOHN BAL 111 2ND DIST
LOYDE, NIMROD BAL 243 1ST DIST
LOYLE, GEORGE S. WAS 104 2ND DIST
LOZE, M. BAL 286 2ND WARD
LOZMAN, JOHN FRE 396 PETERSVI
LRYON, JOHN BAL 133 1ST WARD
LRYUM, JOHN BAL 047 1ST WARD
LSIMS, MARGARET BAL 294 3RD WARD
LTOOKS, AMI E. V. DOR 375 1ST DIST
LUBE, GEORGE FRE 114 CREAGERS
LUBEN, ISAAC BAL 252 12TH WAR

LUBER, JOHN BAL 436 8TH WARD
LUBERY, ISAAC BAL 067 4TH WARD
LUBEY, HENRY FRE 303 WOODSBOR
LUBHARM, WOLFGANG FRE 052 FREDERIC
LUBIN,MICHAEL ALL 228 CUMBERLA
LUBLE.ELIZABETH BAL 035 1ST WARD
LUBLINE, FREDERICK BAL 238 1ST DIST
LUBMAN, MARY BAL 187 2ND WARD
LUBOLD, JACOB BAL 021 15TH WAR
LUBRICH, S. BAL 102 10TH WAR
LUBS, ANDREW BAL 156 1ST WARD
LUCABAUGH, ADAM CAR 336 6TH DIST
LUCABAUGH, HENRY CAR 336 6TH DIST
LUCABAUGH, PETER CAR 339 6TH DIST
LUCABAUGH, PETER M. CAR 344 6TH DIST
LUCADERE, SARAH BAL 076 10TH WAR
LUCAN, GEORGE BAL 074 2ND DIST
LUCAS, ANN BAL 151 19TH WAR
LUCAS, BASIL BAL 130 2ND DIST
LUCAS, CHARLES ANN 348 3RD DIST
LUCAS, CHRISTIAN * BAL 139 2ND DIST
LUCAS, CHRISTIANA FRE 257 NEW MARK
LUCAS, EDWARD BAL 321 7TH WARD
LUCAS, EDWARD QUE 180 2ND E DI
LUCAS, ELISABETH ALL 229 CUMBERLA
LUCAS, ELIZABETH QUE 178 2ND E DI
LUCAS, ELIZABETH BAL 015 4TH WARD
LUCAS, ELIZABETH BAL 407 14TH WAR
LUCAS, EMILY-MULATTO CAR 149 NO TWP L
LUCAS, FIELDING JR. BAL 057 10TH WAR
LUCAS, FRANCIS BAL 218 19TH WAR
LUCAS, GEORGE BAL 375 13TH WAR
LUCAS, GEORGE H. CHA 228 BOJANTOW
LUCAS, HANNAH BAL 105 10TH WAR
LUCAS, HENRY BAL 046 18TH WAR
LUCAS, ISAAC BAL 277 17TH WAR
LUCAS, JAMES BAL 358 13TH WAR
LUCAS, JAMES ANN 337 3RD DIST
LUCAS, JAMES BAL 132 5TH WARD
LUCAS, JAMES ALL 172 7TH E.D.
LUCAS, JAMES QUE 188 3RD E DI
LUCAS, JAMES B. BAL 044 1ST WARD
LUCAS, JOHN BAL 124 1ST WARD
LUCAS, JOHN ST 284 2ND E DI
LUCAS, JOHN ST 285 2ND E DI
LUCAS, JOHN CHA 257 MIDDLETO
LUCAS, JOHN B. PRI 024 VANSVILL
LUCAS, JOHN F. CHA 270 ALLENS F
LUCAS, JOHN F. CHA 270 ALLENS F
LUCAS, JOHN H. QUE 209 3RD E DI
LUCAS, JOHN L. BAL 446 8TH WARD
LUCAS, JOSHUA SR. BAL 193 17TH WAR
LUCAS, LENA CEC 183 7TH E DI
LUCAS, LEVERINA BAL 295 3RD WARD
LUCAS, LUCY ALL 224 CUMBERLA
LUCAS, LUTHER QUE 216 3RD E DI
LUCAS, MARY BAL 046 18TH WAR
LUCAS, MARY A. BAL 212 17TH WAR
LUCAS, MARY B. BAL 053 15TH WAR
LUCAS, MARY C. CAR 203 4TH DIST
LUCAS, MARY-BLACK CAR 144 NO TWP L
LUCAS, MATILDA BAL 068 15TH WAR
LUCAS, MRS. F.A. BAL 015 18TH WAR
LUCAS, O. BAL 153 1ST WARD
LUCAS, O. BAL 139 1ST WARD
LUCAS, OBEDIAH BAL 129 1ST WARD
LUCAS, OSBORNE ANN 423 HOWARD D
LUCAS, PETER BAL 253 2ND WARD
LUCAS, PETER B. BAL 225 2ND WARD
LUCAS, RACHEL BAL 339 13TH WAR
LUCAS, RACHEL-BLACK QUE 187 3RD E DI
LUCAS, ROBERT BAL 062 2ND DIST
LUCAS, SAMUEL BAL 020 2ND DIST
LUCAS, SAMUEL BAL 053 15TH WAR
LUCAS, SARAH KEN 291 3RD DIST
LUCAS, SARAH E. QUE 127 1ST E DI
LUCAS, THOMAS BAL 244 1ST DIST
LUCAS, THOMAS O. BAL 209 6TH WARD
LUCAS, THOMAS W. BAL 109 18TH WAR
LUCAS, WASHINGTON BAL 143 1ST WARD
LUCAS, WASHINGTON WAS 159 HAGERSTO
LUCAS, WILLIAM QUE 207 3RD E DI
LUCAS, WILLIAM QUE 217 3RD E DI
LUCAS, WILLIAM BAL 038 9TH WARD
LUCAS, WILLIAM A. CAR 149 NO TWP L
LUCAS, WILLIAM B. BAL 254 6TH WARD
LUCAS, WILLIAM H. WAS 138 2ND DIST
LUCBER, FRANCIS FRE 028 FREDERIC
LUCHTON, SAMPSON HAR 191 3RD DIST
LUCKAS, CHRISTIAN CEC 061 1ST E DI
LUCKES, JOHN CEC 038 CHESAPEA
LUCKET, CLARISSA H. FRE 403 JEFFERSO
LUCKET, CLEM-BLACK FRE 243 NEW MARK
LUCKET, JACOB WAS 121 HAGERSTO
LUCKET, JAMES FRE 122 CREAGERS
LUCKET, JOHN FRE 124 CREAGERS
LUCKET, REBECCA FRE 162 EMMITTSB
LUCKETT, BETSY M FRE 398 JEFFERSO
LUCKETT, HENRIETTA L. FRE 407 JEFFERSO
LUCKETT, JOHN R. BAL 214 6TH WARD
LUCKETT, JOSIAH C. FRE 377 PETERSVI
LUCKETT, MARIA HALL BAL 214 6TH WARD
LUCKETT, NACE WAS 070 2ND SUBD
LUCKETT, RALPH FRE 046 FREDERIC
LUCKETT, ROGER C. BAL 073 15TH WAR
LUCKETT, WILLIAM* BAL 045 4TH WARD
LUCKEY, MARY L. BAL 340 3RD WARD
LUCKINGTON, WILLIAM BAL 439 14TH WAR
LUCKMAN, JOHN ALL 007 3RD E.D.
LUCMAN, FREDERICK BAL 050 1ST WARD
LUCOS, ANNA M. QUE 204 3RD E DI
LUCRETIA, MARY CAR 287 7TH DIST
LUCUS, ANDREW WAS 140 2ND DIST
LUCUS, BAZZELL CAR 210 5TH DIST
LUCUS, CLEM-MULATTO FRE 005 FREDERIC
LUCUS, ELEN J. CAR 208 5TH DIST
LUCUS, JAMES WAS 145 2ND DIST
LUCUS, JAMES-MULATTO FRE 407 JEFFERSO
LUCUS, MARGARET WAS 145 2ND DIST
LUCUS, MARY E. FRE 226 BUCKEYST
LUCY, THOMAS JR.* ANN 506 HOWARD D
LUCY, TIMOTHY ALL 172 7TH E.D.
LUCYS, EDMUND ALL 243 CUMBERLA
LUDDEN, LEMUEL BAL 374 13TH WAR
LUDEN, JOHN BAL 397 14TH WAR
LUDEN, JOHN ALL 155 6TH E.D.
LUDEN, MARGARET BAL 231 12TH WAR
LUDENDAY, HENRY ALL 258 CUMBERLA
LUDENKIN, JOHN P. BAL 405 14TH WAR
LUDFORD, THOMAS BAL 134 1ST WARD

LUDLEY, MARY BAL 422 14TH WAR
LUDLOFF, JACOB BAL 200 2ND WARD
LUDLOW, JANE ANN 372 4TH DIST
LUDLOW, SOPHIA BAL 329 3RD WARD
LUDROW, ESTER* BAL 053 4TH WARD
LUDVIGH, SAMUEL BAL 041 4TH WARD
LUDWELL, SAMUEL E. HAR 150 3RD DIST
LUDWICK, ADAM BAL 443 14TH WAR
LUDWICK, CATHARINE BAL 080 1ST WARD
LUDWICK, JACOB FRE 329 MIDDLETO
LUDWICK, JOHN BAL 017 4TH WARD
LUDWICK, LYDIA FRE 331 MIDDLETO
LUDWIG, A. BAL 143 19TH WAR
LUDWIG, JOHN BAL 406 14TH WAR
LUDWIG, LOUIS BAL 208 19TH WAR
LUDY, JACOB FRE 362 CATOCTIN
LUDY, NICHOLAS FRE 351 MIDDLETO
LUDY, NICHOLAS JR. FRE 349 MIDDLETO
LUE, BRIDGET BAL 017 15TH WAR
LUE, SARAH * ANN 338 3RD DIST
LUEMAL, JOHN BAL 145 1ST WARD
LUEMAN, HANNAH BAL 246 20TH WAR
LUFFBORD, HARRIET M. MGM 391 ROCKERLE
LUFRIE, JOHN BAL 162 2ND WARD
LUFT, JOHN BAL 274 7TH WARD
LUGARS, FREDERICK BAL 339 1ST DIST
LUGENBED, JOHN H. FRE 441 8TH E DI
LUGENBEEL, CATHERINE FRE 054 FREDERIC
LUGENBEEL, MARGARETT FRE 442 8TH E DI
LUGENBEEL, MOSES FRE 003 FREDERIC
LUGGANS, MARGARET * BAL 336 1ST DIST
LUGH, GEORGE ST 258 3RD E DI
LUGH, GEORGE ST 316 4TH E DI
LUGH, MARY ST 285 2ND E DI
LUGH, WILLIAM G. ST 312 1ST E DI
LUHER, MICHAEL BAL 320 20TH WAR
LUIRE, MARIA* BAL 041 4TH WARD
LUIS, NICHOLAS TAL 081 ST MICHA
LUISHER, ASHUAH BAL 035 18TH WAR
LUISLEY, ABRAHAM L. HAR 046 1ST DIST
LUITON, JOHN * BAL 022 18TH WAR
LUITZ, ADAM BAL 106 1ST WARD
LUKE, FRANCIS BAL 288 7TH WARD
LUKE, J.A. BAL 259 12TH WAR
LUKE, JOSEPH BAL 362 13TH WAR
LUKE, LUKE BAL 045 9TH WARD
LUKE, VIRGINIA BAL 213 11TH WAR
LUKE, WILIAM BAL 157 1ST WARD
LUKE, BMARY WAS 016 2ND SUBD
LUKEHART, LAWRENCE BAL 337 13TH WAR
LUKENS, MARY J. FRE 065 FREDERIC
LUKINBIEL, PETER FRE 436 8TH E DI
LUKINGLAND, SUSANNAH BAL 355 13TH WAR
LUKINS, JULIA BAL 124 2ND DIST
LUKNEF, ANDREW BAL 226 17TH WAR
LUKNER, CHRISTOPHER BAL 225 17TH WAR
LUKNER, FREDERICK BAL 225 17TH WAR
LULEY, JAMES-BLACK FRE 446 8TH E DI
LULTREN, THOMAS D.* BAL 084 4TH WARD
LULTZ, CHRISTE ANN FRE 077 FREDERIC
LUM, CHARLES CEC 012 ELKTON 3
LUM, CHARLES BAL 007 1ST WARD
LUM, GEORGE WAS 227 1ST DIST
LUM, HESTER A. CAR 091 NO TWP L
LUM, JAMES W. BAL 351 3RD WARD
LUM, MARTHA CEC 075 NORTHEAS
LUMAN, CATHARINE BAL 192 2ND WARD
LUMAN, ELIZABETH FRE 008 FREDERIC
LUMAN, HENRY BAL 112 2ND DIST
LUMAN, SAMUEL WAS 210 1ST DIST
LUMAN, SAMUEL S. ALL 238 CUMBERLA
LUMB, CATHARINE WAS 266 1ST DIST
LUMB, ROBERT WAS 235 1ST DIST
LUMBAR, WILLIAM CEC 060 1ST E DI
LUMBARD, ALBERT BAL 369 3RD WARD
LUMBERG, HENRIETTA BAL 013 9TH WARD
LUMBERSON, EMELINE BAL 012 15TH WAR
LUMBERSON, JOHN BAL 145 2ND DIST
LUMKINS, HENRY ST 341 5TH E DI
LUMM, LUKE BAL 284 17TH WAR
LUMMA, LOUISA FRE 268 NEW MARK
LUMMES, ANGELINE BAL 331 1ST DIST
LUMPKIN, JOHN S. ST 292 2ND E DI
LUMPTFORD, JOHN PRI 107 PISCATAW
LUMPTON, THOMAS BAL 298 7TH WARD
LUMSDEN, WILLIAM D. BAL 028 15TH WAR
LUMWALT, ALEXANDER BAL 096 18TH WAR
LUNAN, ANTHONY ALL 242 CUMBERLA
LUNAN, GEORGE BAL 397 1ST DIST
LUNBURY, JOHANNA BAL 407 14TH WAR
LUNBY, CAROLINE BAL 338 7TH WARD
LUND, OLIVER W. CEC 179 7TH E DI
LUNDERGILL, JOSHUA CAR 281 7TH DIST
LUNDERLAND, BASIL* BAL 371 3RD WARD
LUNDERLUN, JOHN W. BAL 297 7TH WARD
LUNDT, MARY BAL 174 16TH WAR
LUNDT, SARAH BAL 174 16TH WAR
LUNDUN, GEORGE ANNA BAL 186 11TH WAR
LUNENBERGER, GEORGE BAL 002 18TH WAR
LUNENSTINE, LEWIS BAL 392 14TH WAR
LUNES, B.S. BAL 171 1ST WARD
LUNGDEN, SAMUEL G. WAS 140 HAGERSTO
LUNIS, MARY ANN 288 ANNAPOLI
LUNN, JOHN BAL 323 3RD WARD
LUNNAR, SYLVESTER* BAL 411 3RD WARD
LUNSON, CHARITY* BAL 306 3RD WARD
LUNT, ELLEN BAL 292 1ST DIST
LUNTZ, ADAM BAL 161 2ND DIST
LUPPY, GEORGE BAL 201 19TH WAR
LUPTON, ELIJAH F.* BAL 077 4TH WARD
LUPTON, ELISHA F. BAL 355 3RD WARD
LUPTON, ELISHA J. BAL 026 9TH WARD
LUPTON, MARTHA BAL 436 14TH WAR
LUPTON, REBECCA V. BAL 217 11TH WAR
LURAM, HENRY BAL 278 1ST DIST
LURAS, VIN* TAL 034 EASTON D
LURDUR, ISAAC* BAL 315 3RD WARD
LURENBERGER, SAMUEL ANN 472 HOWARD D
LURIGETON, SALLY * WOR 240 6TH E DI
LURKETT, MOUNTJOY B. FRE 045 FREDERIC
LURLULET, CECILIA BAL 248 12TH WAR
LURMAN, GUSTAVUS BAL 334 1ST DIST
LURREVASTY, MARGARET BAL 307 3RD WARD
LURT, BRIDGETT* BAL 062 4TH WARD
LURT, JOHN BAL 097 1ST WARD
LURTY, EMELINE BAL 239 6TH WARD
LURTY, SARAH BAL 473 14TH WAR
LUSBY, AMELIA BAL 419 3RD WARD
LUSBY, ANN CEC 051 1ST E DI
LUSBY, ANN M. BAL 071 15TH WAR
LUSBY, ARAMINTA KEN 303 3RD DIST
LUSBY, BEAL ANN 322 2ND DIST
LUSBY, BENJAMIN W. ANN 321 2ND DIST
LUSBY, CALEB F. BAL 308 3RD WARD
LUSBY, CHARLES KEN 259 1ST DIST
LUSBY, CHARLES W. BAL 160 16TH WAR
LUSBY, EDWARD BAL 054 15TH WAR
LUSBY, ELI ANN 321 2ND DIST
LUSBY, ELIZABETH CEC 070 5TH E DI
LUSBY, ELLEN BAL 380 8TH WARD
LUSBY, HENRY BAL 129 1ST WARD
LUSBY, HENRY BAL 424 8TH WARD
LUSBY, HENRY BAL 134 1ST WARD
LUSBY, HENRY BAL 061 10TH WAR
LUSBY, HENRY E. ANN 346 3RD DIST
LUSBY, HENRY H. BAL 028 15TH WAR
LUSBY, JAMES B. KEN 221 2ND DIST
LUSBY, JOHN KEN 259 1ST DIST
LUSBY, JOHN H. CEC 064 1ST E DI
LUSBY, JOHN R. KEN 257 1ST DIST
LUSBY, JOSIAH KEN 227 2ND DIST
LUSBY, NICHOLAS BAL 326 1ST DIST
LUSBY, PASOLOW CAL 012 1ST DIST
LUSBY, PATRICK BAL 092 1ST WARD
LUSBY, ROBERT KEN 297 3RD DIST
LUSBY, THOMAS KEN 227 2ND DIST
LUSBY, THOMAS KEN 209 2ND DIST
LUSBY, WILLIAM CEC 056 1ST E DI
LUSBY, WILLIAM QUE 188 3RD E DI
LUSBY, WILLIAM BAL 124 1ST WARD
LUSBY, WILLIAM BAL 053 9TH WARD
LUSCLELECT, JOHN CAR 390 2ND DIST
LUSCLELECT, MARY CAR 393 2ND DIST
LUSCLELECT, SARAH J. CAR 387 2ND DIST
LUSCLELECT, WILLIAM H. CAR 361 9TH DIST
LUSCOLETT, WILLIAM FRE 429 8TH E DI
LUSK, JOHN BAL 292 3RD WARD
LUSKIN, JOHN BAL 339 3RD WARD
LUSLER, JOSEPH HAR 072 1ST DIST
LUSLEY, JAMES B. * KEN 221 2ND DIST
LUSLEY, JOHN CAL 013 1ST DIST
LUSLEY, THOMAS KEN 227 2ND DIST
LUSLIN, ANN BAL 131 2ND DIST
LUSLY, WILLIAM A. CAL 014 1ST DIST
LUSSELL, MAGARET ALL 196 CUMBERLA
LUST, MARY BAL 186 11TH WAR
LUSTAT, JOSEPH BAL 108 2ND DIST
LUSTER, HANNAH BAL 156 2ND DIST
LUSTER, NORRIS HAR 178 3RD DIST
LUSTER, WILLIAM HAR 183 3RD DIST
LUSTERLATE, DAVID BAL 117 18TH WAR
LUSTNAUER, CHARLES BAL 291 20TH WAR
LUTCHTON, ELIZABETH HAR 191 3RD DIST
LUTEMAN, GARRETT ALL 154 6TH E.D.
LUTER, CHARLES BAL 014 4TH WARD
LUTER, ELIZABETH BAL 231 19TH WAR
LUTER, JAMES* BAL 079 4TH WARD
LUTES, JOHN * BAL 417 1ST DIST
LUTHE, CATHARINE BAL 225 12TH WAR
LUTHER, CHRIST. BAL 292 1ST DIST
LUTHER, EMMA L. ANN 521 HOWARD D
LUTHER, GEORGE BAL 454 14TH WAR
LUTHER, MARTIN CAR 404 2ND DIST
LUTHER, NANCY WAS 144 HAGERSTO
LUTHERLAND, WILLIAM BAL 204 2ND WARD
LUTHERLOR, SARAH QUE 208 3RD E DI
LUTHERN, JOHN BAL 259 1ST DIST
LUTHERN, JOHN BAL 252 1ST DIST
LUTHNER, LANHART BAL 082 1ST WARD
LUTIS, JOHN BAL 081 2ND DIST
LUTLA, RICHARD BAL 178 19TH WAR
LUTLER, JAMES BAL 178 19TH WAR
LUTLER, MARTHA O. BAL 393 14TH WAR
LUTLZER, JOHN FRE 073 FREDERIC
LUTMAN, ALBERT BAL 447 8TH WARD
LUTMAN, WILLIAM BAL 133 1ST WARD
LUTRO, BERNHARD* BAL 403 3RD WARD
LUTT, MARY BAL 202 19TH WAR
LUTTER, CATHARINE FRE 311 MIDDLETO
LUTTON, JAMES BAL 120 2ND DIST
LUTTON, WILLAM BAL 081 2ND DIST
LUTTRAND, JOHN ALL 252 CUMBERLA
LUTTS, ELIZABETH A. BAL 379 13TH WAR
LUTTZ, JOHN A. J. BAL 021 9TH WARD
LUTTZ, NICKOLAS BAL 096 5TH WARD
LUTTZER, JOHN FRE 213 BUCKEYST
LUTY, C. F. BAL 168 19TH WAR
LUTY, VALENTINE BAL 155 19TH WAR
LUTZ, A.J. WAS 019 2ND SUBD
LUTZ, ANDREW BAL 442 1ST DIST
LUTZ, ANN BAL 326 12TH WAR
LUTZ, BENJAMIN WAS 108 2ND DIST
LUTZ, CHARLES BAL 231 2ND WARD
LUTZ, CONRAD BAL 086 10TH WAR
LUTZ, ELIZABETH BAL 442 1ST DIST
LUTZ, GEORGE FRE 082 FREDERIC
LUTZ, GEORGIANNA KEN 219 2ND DIST
LUTZ, HENRY WAS 110 2ND DIST
LUTZ, ISAAC FRE 284 WOODSBOR
LUTZ, JAMES BAL 166 2ND WARD
LUTZ, JOHN BAL 188 6TH WARD
LUTZ, JOHN BAL 137 1ST WARD
LUTZ, JOHN BAL 004 9TH WARD
LUTZ, JOHN BAL 069 1ST WARD
LUTZ, JOHN HAR 017 1ST DIST
LUTZ, JOHN Q. BAL 021 9TH WARD
LUTZ, JOSEPH BAL 312 7TH WARD
LUTZ, LEWIS FRE 346 MIDDLETO
LUTZ, MARIA FRE 348 MIDDLETO
LUTZ, MICHAEL FRE 027 FREDERIC
LUTZ, PETER BAL 224 2ND WARD
LUTZ, PETER BAL 324 12TH WAR
LUTZ, SAMUEL WAS 015 2ND SUBD
LUTZ, TOBIAS BAL 104 2ND DIST
LUTZ, VALENTINE BAL 104 2ND DIST
LUTZE, MARY BAL 096 10TH WAR
LUVE, MATILDA BAL 220 19TH WAR
LUVOY, DANIEL * BAL 310 1ST DIST
LUVOY, SUSAN BAL 310 1ST DIST
LUX, CHARLES BAL 143 2ND DIST
LWW, WLLWN BAL 180 11TH WAR
LYATT, HENRY BAL 116 1ST WARD
LYATT, MICHAELL BAL 312 12TH WAR
LYBARGER, JOHN ALL 164 6TH E.D.
LYBURN, JOHN BAL 282 17TH WAR
LYBURN, JULIANN BAL 254 17TH WAR
LYCERT, E. BAL 237 12TH WAR
LYCETT, EDWARD L. BAL 019 18TH WAR
LYCETT, WILLIAM BAL 013 4TH WARD
LYCHFIELD, JOHN BAL 337 1ST DIST
LYCOT, JAMES-BLACK BAL 212 2ND WARD
LYDAN, JOHN ANN 475 HOWARD D
LYDAY, HENRY W. WAS 230 1ST DIST
LYDAY, SAMUEL WAS 280 LEITERSB
LYDDAM, MARY MGM 356 BERRYS D
LYDDANE, ANN MGM 395 ROCKERLE
LYDDANE, JAMES E. MGM 395 ROCKERLE
LYDDANE, LAWRENCE MGM 374 ROCKERLE
LYDDANE, MARGARET MGM 353 BERRYS D
LYDDANE, MARY MGM 405 ROCKERLE
LYDDANE, MICHAEL MGM 363 BERRYS D
LYDDANE, PATRICK MGM 363 BERRYS D
LYDDANE, SARAH H. MGM 376 ROCKERLE
LYDDANE, THOMAS MGM 395 ROCKERLE
LYDEN, ANDERTON CAR 119 NO TWP L
LYDEN, EDWARD W. CAR 165 NO TWP L
LYDEN, MICHAEL BAL 472 14TH WAR
LYDEN, PATRICK ANN 424 HOWARD D
LYDEN, SHADRICK CAR 119 NO TWP L
LYDY, HENRY FRE 247 NEW MARK
LYDY, JOHN FRE 018 FREDERIC
LYDY, JOSEPH FRE 142 CREAGERS
LYDY, MARY FRE 052 FREDERIC
LYDY, MARY A. FRE 028 FREDERIC
LYDY, WILLIAM FRE 128 CREAGERS
LYDYANL, MOSES BAL 159 2ND DIST
LYEIBERT, HENRY BAL 126 1ST WARD
LYERS, MAGDALENE WAS 052 2ND SUBD
LYESTER, JOHN WAS 007 WILLIAMS
LYETH, JOHN MC FARREN * BAL 138 18TH WAR
LYETH, SAMUEL BAL 241 17TH WAR
LYETT, SAMUEL* BAL 241 17TH WAR
LYFER, JOSEPH BAL 428 8TH WARD
LYFORD, MARGARET M. BAL 335 13TH WAR
LYFORD, W. G. BAL 060 10TH WAR
LYFTHLE, MARY * BAL 103 2ND DIST
LYGAD, JOHN * BAL 143 1ST WARD
LYGRDON, THOMAS ALL 153 6TH E.D.
LYLES, BARBARY MRS- ANN 406 8TH DIST
LYLES, BARNEY MGM 404 ROCKERLE
LYLES, DAVID WAS 062 2ND SUBD
LYLES, GEORGE D. ANN 402 8TH DIST
LYLES, GEORGE H. CAL 046 3RD DIST
LYLES, HENRY* BAL 025 4TH WARD
LYLES, JEREMIAH BAL 245 6TH WARD
LYLES, JERRY-BLACK FRE 209 BUCKEYST
LYLES, JESSE ANN 502 HOWARD D
LYLES, JOHN WAS 046 2ND SUBD
LYLES, JULIA BAL 001 9TH WARD
LYLES, MARIA E. BAL 212 11TH WAR
LYLES, MARIAH ANN 408 8TH DIST
LYLES, MARTHA A. BAL 025 4TH WARD
LYLES, OCTAVIUS M. ANN 405 8TH DIST
LYLES, R. PRI 110 PISCATAW
LYLES, ROSE WAS 136 2ND DIST
LYLES, SAMUEL CAL 045 3RD DIST
LYLES, THOMAS FRE 234 BUCKEYST
LYLES, THOMAS PRI 106 PISCATAW
LYLES, VACHEL MGM 435 CLARKSTR
LYLES, WILHELMINA CAL 045 3RD DIST
LYLES, WILLIAM ANN 400 8TH DIST
LYLES, WILLIAM H. PRI 114 PISCATAW
LYLES, WILLIAM L. PRI 114 PISCATAW
LYLES, WILSON CAL 061 3RD DIST
LYLLA, LERA BAL 010 EASTERN
LYLLE, JOHN BAL 018 15TH WAR
LYMAN, HENRY BAL 465 14TH WAR
LYMAN, JAMES ALL 231 CUMBERLA
LYMAN, JOHN BAL 175 2ND DIST
LYMAR, CHARLES BAL 282 17TH WAR
LYMEN, JOHN J. WAS 266 1ST DIST
LYNCH, ALFRED KEN 250 2ND DIST
LYNCH, ANDREW CEC 056 1ST E DI
LYNCH, ANDREW A. DR- BAL 368 1ST DIST
LYNCH, ANN BAL 462 1ST DIST
LYNCH, ANN BAL 067 2ND DIST
LYNCH, ANN ALL 159 6TH E.D.
LYNCH, ANN BAL 153 11TH WAR
LYNCH, ANNA BAL 083 10TH WAR
LYNCH, ANNA M. QUE 226 4TH E DI
LYNCH, BLACKSTON WAS 288 1ST DIST
LYNCH, CATHARINE BAL 319 12TH WAR
LYNCH, CATHARINE BAL 099 1ST WARD
LYNCH, CATHERINE ALL 217 CUMBERLA
LYNCH, CATHERINE CEC 137 6TH E DI
LYNCH, CHARLES ALL 249 CUMBERLA
LYNCH, CHARLES BAL 282 2ND WARD
LYNCH, CHARLES PRI 056 AQUASCO
LYNCH, CHARLES E. BAL 191 11TH WAR
LYNCH, CHARLOTTE QUE 209 3RD E DI
LYNCH, CHRISTIAN CAR 280 7TH DIST
LYNCH, DANIEL BAL 120 2ND DIST
LYNCH, DANIEL BAL 088 10TH WAR
LYNCH, DANIEL BAL 293 12TH WAR
LYNCH, DANIEL BAL 314 3RD WARD
LYNCH, DAVID D. CHA 281 BOJANTOW
LYNCH, DENNIS BAL 020 2ND DIST
LYNCH, EDWARD BAL 067 2ND DIST
LYNCH, EDWARD ANN 472 HOWARD D
LYNCH, EDWARD BAL 132 16TH WAR
LYNCH, EDWARD BAL 358 8TH WARD
LYNCH, EDWARD PRI 060 NOTTINGH
LYNCH, ELISHU CEC 134 6TH E DI
LYNCH, ELIZA BAL 004 EASTERN
LYNCH, ELIZA A. BAL 450 8TH WARD
LYNCH, ELIZABETH QUE 235 4TH E DI
LYNCH, ELIZABETH WAS 171 FUNKSTOW
LYNCH, ELLEN ALL 103 5TH E.D.
LYNCH, ELLEN FRE 387 PETERSVI
LYNCH, FRANK BAL 472 14TH WAR
LYNCH, GEORGE CEC 184 7TH E DI
LYNCH, GEORGE BAL 140 2ND DIST
LYNCH, GEORGE BAL 296 1ST DIST
LYNCH, GEORGE W. BAL 401 1ST DIST
LYNCH, GRACE BAL 140 2ND DIST
LYNCH, HAMILTON KEN 223 2ND DIST
LYNCH, HARIET WAS 022 2ND SUBD
LYNCH, HARMAN ANN 324 2ND DIST
LYNCH, HASSON CEC 192 5TH E DI
LYNCH, HENNIS BAL 120 2ND DIST
LYNCH, HENRY BAL 131 2ND DIST
LYNCH, HENRY BAL 044 1ST WARD
LYNCH, HENRY D. PRI 047 AQUASCO
LYNCH, HESTER BAL 055 1ST WARD
LYNCH, HUGH ALL 128 4TH E.D.
LYNCH, HUGH BAL 059 15TH WAR
LYNCH, IVE * BAL 317 20TH WAR
LYNCH, J. S. BAL 095 10TH WAR
LYNCH, JAMES ALL 142 6TH E.D.
LYNCH, JAMES ALL 200 CUMBERLA

Name	County	Page	District
LYNCH, JAMES	BAL	282	2ND WARD
LYNCH, JAMES	BAL	397	8TH WARD
LYNCH, JAMES	FRE	034	FREDERIC
LYNCH, JAMES	CEC	179	7TH E DI
LYNCH, JAMES	QUE	173	2ND E DI
LYNCH, JANE	CEC	134	6TH E DI
LYNCH, JEREMIAH	BAL	400	3RD WARD
LYNCH, JEREMIAH	BAL	400	1ST DIST
LYNCH, JETHRO	BAL	185	5TH DIST
LYNCH, JOHN	BAL	160	2ND DIST
LYNCH, JOHN	BAL	168	2ND DIST
LYNCH, JOHN	BAL	447	1ST DIST
LYNCH, JOHN	BAL	427	1ST DIST
LYNCH, JOHN	ALL	049	10TH E.D
LYNCH, JOHN	CEC	123	3RD E DI
LYNCH, JOHN	KEN	231	2ND DIST
LYNCH, JOHN	CEC	066	1ST E DI
LYNCH, JOHN	BAL	292	17TH WAR
LYNCH, JOHN	CEC	111	4TH E DI
LYNCH, JOHN	QUE	188	3RD E DI
LYNCH, JOHN	WAS	288	1ST DIST
LYNCH, JOHN C.	BAL	105	1ST WARD
LYNCH, JOHN H.	BAL	183	6TH WARD
LYNCH, JOHN W.	BAL	206	17TH WAR
LYNCH, JOHN W.	MGM	380	ROCKERLE
LYNCH, JOSEPH	BAL	317	7TH WARD
LYNCH, JOSEPH	BAL	198	11TH WAR
LYNCH, JOSEPH E.	SOM	502	SALISBUR
LYNCH, JOSHUA	BAL	148	2ND DIST
LYNCH, JOSHUA	SOM	426	PRINCESS
LYNCH, JULIA	BAL	058	4TH WARD
LYNCH, LAWRENCE	FRE	067	FREDERIC
LYNCH, LIDIA	BAL	302	7TH WARD
LYNCH, LOUIS	BAL	167	19TH WAR
LYNCH, LUKE	BAL	181	11TH WAR
LYNCH, MARGARET	BAL	020	9TH WARD
LYNCH, MARGARET	FRE	385	PETERSVI
LYNCH, MARGARET	CEC	009	ELKTON 3
LYNCH, MARTIN	BAL	259	2ND WARD
LYNCH, MARY	BAL	197	2ND WARD
LYNCH, MARY	ALL	223	CUMBERLA
LYNCH, MARY	ALL	255	CUMBERLA
LYNCH, MARY	BAL	097	2ND DIST
LYNCH, MARY	BAL	178	16TH WAR
LYNCH, MARY	BAL	011	4TH WARD
LYNCH, MARY	BAL	373	13TH WAR
LYNCH, MARY	KEN	250	2ND DIST
LYNCH, MARY	HAR	156	3RD DIST
LYNCH, MARY	PRI	049	AQUASCO
LYNCH, MARY	WAS	154	2ND DIST
LYNCH, MARY *	BAL	277	1ST DIST
LYNCH, MARY J.	CEC	123	3RD E DI
LYNCH, MATTHEW	ALL	078	5TH E.D.
LYNCH, MICHAEL	ALL	079	5TH E.D.
LYNCH, MICHAEL	BAL	424	1ST DIST
LYNCH, MICHAEL	CAR	278	7TH DIST
LYNCH, MICHAEL	CAR	279	7TH DIST
LYNCH, NICHOLAS	BAL	392	3RD WARD
LYNCH, PATRICK	ALL	119	5TH E.D.
LYNCH, PATRICK	BAL	283	1ST DIST
LYNCH, PATRICK	BAL	157	2ND DIST
LYNCH, PATRICK	BAL	192	6TH WARD
LYNCH, PATRICK	BAL	127	5TH WARD
LYNCH, PATRICK	CAR	244	3RD DIST
LYNCH, PERRY	KEN	250	2ND DIST
LYNCH, ROBERT	BAL	239	1ST DIST
LYNCH, ROSSE	WAS	162	HAGERSTO
LYNCH, RUTH C.	BAL	254	6TH WARD
LYNCH, SAMUEL	CEC	178	7TH E DI
LYNCH, SAMUEL N.	SOM	510	BARREN C
LYNCH, SARAH E.	QUE	175	2ND E DI
LYNCH, SIMON P.	WAS	182	BOONSBOR
LYNCH, STEPHEN	BAL	399	3RD WARD
LYNCH, T. A.	ANN	358	3RD DIST
LYNCH, THEODORE	BAL	007	4TH WARD
LYNCH, THOMAS	CAR	297	7TH DIST
LYNCH, THOMAS	CEC	178	7TH E DI
LYNCH, THOMAS	QUE	155	2ND E DI
LYNCH, THOMAS	CAR	254	3RD DIST
LYNCH, THOMAS	MGM	418	MEDLEY 3
LYNCH, THOMAS	BAL	168	2ND DIST
LYNCH, THOMAS	BAL	283	1ST DIST
LYNCH, THOMAS	BAL	048	1ST WARD
LYNCH, THOMAS	BAL	034	1ST WARD
LYNCH, THOMAS	BAL	462	1ST DIST
LYNCH, THOMAS	WAS	184	BOONSBOR
LYNCH, THOMAS	ST	300	2ND E DI
LYNCH, THOMAS	WAS	049	2ND SUBD
LYNCH, THOMAS A.	ST	334	4TH E DI
LYNCH, WALTER	CAL	031	2ND DIST
LYNCH, WILLIAM	MGM	396	ROCKERLE
LYNCH, WILLIAM	CEC	074	NORTHEAS
LYNCH, WILLIAM	CEC	140	5TH E DI
LYNCH, WILLIAM	FRE	409	JEFFERSO
LYNCH, WILLIAM	WAS	029	2ND SUBD
LYNCH, WILLIAM	BAL	390	1ST DIST
LYNCH, WILLIAM	BAL	399	1ST DIST
LYNCH, WILLIAM	BAL	157	2ND DIST
LYNCH, WILLIAM	BAL	003	EASTERN
LYNCH, WILLIAM	BAL	078	2ND DIST
LYNCH, WILLIAM N.	KEN	247	2ND DIST
LYNCH, WILLIAM T.	CEC	079	NORTHEAS
LYNCH, WILLIAM T.	QUE	211	3RD E DI
LYNCH, WILSON	CEC	134	6TH E DI
LYNCH, WOOLMAN E.	QUE	234	4TH E DI
LYNDSAY, ANN	BAL	419	3RD WARD
LYNDSY, SANDY	WAS	032	2ND SUBD
LYNEB, JOHN	ALL	103	5TH E.D.
LYNER, JOHN	ALL	119	5TH E.D.
LYNES, BARBARA D.	BAL	383	13TH WAR
LYNIH, MARY *	BAL	277	1ST DIST
LYNINE, MINERVA	BAL	146	19TH WAR
LYNN, ALICE	PRI	084	QUEEN AN
LYNN, EVE	FRE	283	WOODSBOR
LYNN, GALLOWAY	ALL	260	CUMBERLA
LYNN, GEORGE	ALL	090	5TH E.D.
LYNN, ISAAC	FRE	170	5TH E DI
LYNN, J.	BAL	138	1ST WARD
LYNN, JACOB	FRE	115	CREAGERS
LYNN, JAMES C.	ALL	257	CUMBERLA
LYNN, JOHN	FRE	173	5TH E DI
LYNN, JOHN	WAS	080	2ND SUBD
LYNN, JOSEPH	FRE	126	CREAGERS
LYNN, MARGARET	ALL	181	8TH E.D.
LYNN, SAMUEL	FRE	172	5TH E DI
LYNN, SARAH	PRI	084	QUEEN AN
LYNN, SARAH C.	CHA	282	BOJANTOW
LYNN, WILLIAM	FRE	171	5TH E DI
LYNN, WILLIAM	ALL	264	CUMBERLA
LYNN, WILLIAM	ALL	241	CUMBERLA

Name	County	Page	District
LYNN, WILLIAM H.	BAL	159	16TH WAR
LYNNE, THOMAS	BAL	220	19TH WAR
LYNTHECUM, THOMAS F.	BAL	362	1ST DIST
LYNTHRAM, MARY	BAL	168	2ND DIST
LYOD, ELLEN G.	BAL	197	11TH WAR
LYON, ALEXANDER	CHA	264	HILLTOP
LYON, AMELIA	CHA	266	MIDDLETO
LYON, ANDREW	CEC	159	PORT DUP
LYON, ANN	ST	348	5TH E DI
LYON, BETTY	CHA	266	MIDDLETO
LYON, BETTY	CHA	276	ALLENS F
LYON, CHARLES G.	BAL	250	1ST DIST
LYON, DANIEL	BAL	168	2ND DIST
LYON, ELLEN	BAL	301	3RD WARD
LYON, F.Y.	BAL	138	1ST WARD
LYON, GEORGE F.	HAR	130	3RD DIST
LYON, GEORGIANNA	CHA	282	BOJANTOW
LYON, HENRIETTA	BAL	250	12TH WAR
LYON, HENRY M.	CHA	283	BOJANTOW
LYON, JOB	BAL	119	1ST WARD
LYON, JOHN	CEC	153	PORT DUP
LYON, JOHN	PRI	112	PISCATAW
LYON, JOHN B.	ST	327	4TH E DI
LYON, JOHN B.	CHA	272	ALLENS F
LYON, JOHN C.	BAL	052	9TH WARD
LYON, LAWRENCE	BAL	262	1ST DIST
LYON, MARGARET	CEC	108	3RD E DI
LYON, MARGARET	BAL	456	14TH WAR
LYON, MARY	BAL	162	19TH WAR
LYON, MARY	CHA	221	ALLENS F
LYON, RAGER	BAL	187	19TH WAR
LYON, ROBERT	BAL	364	8TH WARD
LYON, SAMUEL	BAL	248	1ST DIST
LYON, SARAH	MGM	325	CRACKLIN
LYON, SOPHIA	BAL	410	1ST DIST
LYON, SUSAN	CHA	263	MIDDLETO
LYON, THOMAS	BAL	348	1ST DIST
LYON, WILLIAM	ST	340	5TH E DI
LYON, WILLIAM A.	CHA	270	ALLENS F
LYON, WILLIAM M.	CHA	262	MIDDLETO
LYON, JOHN	BAL	066	1ST WARD
LYONS, ABBY	BAL	171	16TH WAR
LYONS, ANDREW	BAL	374	13TH WAR
LYONS, ANN	BAL	407	14TH WAR
LYONS, ANN	BAL	440	1ST DIST
LYONS, ANN	BAL	064	15TH WAR
LYONS, ANN	BAL	046	9TH WARD
LYONS, CALEB	BAL	155	1ST WARD
LYONS, CATHARINE	BAL	344	7TH WARD
LYONS, CHARLES	BAL	078	15TH WAR
LYONS, CHARLES	DOR	453	1ST DIST
LYONS, CHARLOTTE	BAL	055	15TH WAR
LYONS, CORNELIUS	BAL	360	8TH WARD
LYONS, CORNELIUS	BAL	350	13TH WAR
LYONS, EDWARD C.	ANN	421	HOWARD D
LYONS, ELIZA	BAL	008	1ST WARD
LYONS, ELLENORA	WAS	209	1ST DIST
LYONS, ELLENORA A.	BAL	033	18TH WAR
LYONS, JACOB	WAS	188	1ST DIST
LYONS, JAMES	CAL	040	3RD DIST
LYONS, JANE	BAL	308	20TH WAR
LYONS, JERE	QUE	222	4TH E DI
LYONS, JEREMIAH	BAL	134	2ND DIST
LYONS, JESSE	FRE	111	CREAGERS
LYONS, JOHN	CAL	052	3RD DIST
LYONS, JOHN	BAL	421	8TH WARD
LYONS, JOHN	BAL	153	16TH WAR
LYONS, JOHN	ALL	047	10TH E.D
LYONS, JOHN	WAS	198	1ST DIST
LYONS, M.C.	BAL	229	19TH WAR
LYONS, MARGARET	ALL	081	5TH E.D.
LYONS, MARTIN	WAS	201	1ST DIST
LYONS, MARY	ALL	098	5TH E.D.
LYONS, MARY	BAL	459	1ST DIST
LYONS, MARY	BAL	028	4TH WARD
LYONS, MARY	BAL	150	11TH WAR
LYONS, MARY J.	BAL	375	13TH WAR
LYONS, MATTHEW	BAL	041	9TH WARD
LYONS, MICHAEL	ALL	143	6TH E.D.
LYONS, MICHAEL	ALL	108	5TH E.D.
LYONS, MICHAEL	ALL	136	4TH E.D.
LYONS, MOSES	BAL	116	1ST WARD
LYONS, MOSES	BAL	116	1ST WARD
LYONS, NANCY	BAL	094	1ST WARD
LYONS, OWEN	ALL	047	10TH E.D
LYONS, PATRICK	ALL	048	10TH E.D
LYONS, PATRICK	ALL	053	10TH E.D
LYONS, PATRICK	ALL	081	5TH E.D.
LYONS, PATRICK	ALL	209	CUMBERLA
LYONS, PATRICK	BAL	071	10TH WAR
LYONS, PATRICK	ALL	241	CUMBERLA
LYONS, PATRICK	BAL	028	4TH WARD
LYONS, PETER	ALL	184	9TH E.D.
LYONS, R. K.	BAL	316	12TH WAR
LYONS, RACHEL	BAL	100	5TH WARD
LYONS, RICHARD H.	BAL	075	18TH WAR
LYONS, ROBERT	BAL	106	18TH WAR
LYONS, SALLY	FRE	388	PETERSVI
LYONS, SAMUEL H.	BAL	153	11TH WAR
LYONS, WILLIAM	CAL	053	3RD DIST
LYONS, WILLIAM	FRE	281	WOODSBOR
LYONS, WILLIAM	FRE	112	CREAGERS
LYONS, WILLIAM	BAL	169	1ST WARD
LYONS, JAMES	BAL	065	1ST WARD
LYONS, MOSES	BAL	167	1ST WARD
LYSER, CATHERINE	PRI	026	VANSVILL
LYSER, MARGARET	PRI	039	VANSVILL
LYSHEAR, JAMES	ANN	502	HOWARD D
LYSHEAR, MARTHA J.	ANN	435	HOWARD D
LYSHEAR, ROBERT	ANN	441	HOWARD D
LYSHEAR, WILLIAM	ANN	435	HOWARD D
LYSHEARS, WILLIAM L.	BAL	408	14TH WAR
LYSINGER, SARAH	KEN	301	3RD DIST
LYSINNER, GEORGE	BAL	054	15TH WAR
LYSLY, JOHN	HAR	178	3RD DIST
LYSON, JOHN C.	BAL	476	14TH WAR
LYSON, SARAH	BAL	104	10TH WAR
LYTCHFIELD, WILLIAM	BAL	337	1ST DIST
LYTH, ROBERT A.	BAL	026	9TH WARD
LYTLE, GEORGE W.	HAR	072	1ST DIST
LYTLE, HANNAH	BAL	107	10TH WAR
LYTLE, JAMES	HAR	117	2ND DIST
LYTLE, JAMES	HAR	017	1ST DIST
LYTLE, JAMES	WAS	284	1ST DIST
LYTLE, JOHN	HAR	011	1ST DIST
LYTLE, JOHN	HAR	176	3RD DIST
LYTLE, JOHN H. E.	BAL	109	10TH WAR
LYTLE, MARGARETT S.	HAR	131	2ND DIST
LYTLE, RACHEL	HAR	130	2ND DIST
LYTLE, ROBERT A.	HAR	018	1ST DIST

Name	County	Page	District
LYTLE, THOMAS	HAR	105	2ND DIST
LYTLE, WILLAIM	HAR	068	1ST DIST
LYTTLE, ANN F.	BAL	266	2ND WARD
LYTTLE, CHARITY	BAL	041	2ND DIST
LYTTLE, DANIEL	BAL	422	14TH WAR
LYTTLE, FREELAND	BAL	122	5TH WARD
LYTTLE, GEORGE	BAL	033	2ND DIST
LYTTLE, JOHN	BAL	155	2ND DIST
LYTTLE, ROBERT	ALL	155	6TH E.D.
LYTTLE, THOMAS	BAL	041	2ND DIST
LYTTLE, WILLIAM B.	BAL	378	13TH WAR
LYTTON, SAMUEL	MGM	358	BERRYS D
M COLBY, ALEXANDER	BAL	115	1ST WARD
M COY, ELLEN	BAL	430	14TH WAR
M DOUGAL, JOHN	BAL	132	1ST WARD
M GRAW, GOERGE W.	BAL	119	1ST WARD
M O DONOHOE, FLORENCE	FRE	20	5TH E DI
MA CORMAC, JAMES	CHA	219	ALLENS F
MA GEE, RUTH	CAR	287	7TH DIST
MA GERK, J.P.	ALL	237	CUMBERLA
MAAIOTT, AUGUSTUS	FRE	274	NEW MARK
MAAS, JOHN	BAL	086	10TH WAR
MAAS, JOHN N.	MGM	354	BERRYS D
MABEE, THADIUS	BAL	295	7TH WARD
MABEL, D.	BAL	215	19TH WAR
MABEN, ANDREW	BAL	334	7TH WARD
MABER, JOHN	BAL	206	19TH WAR
MABERRY, P.	BAL	282	2ND WARD
MABERSEY, JAMES	MGM	388	ROCKERLE
MABERY, JOHN	BAL	122	18TH WAR
MABERY, JOSEPHINE E.	BAL	123	18TH WAR
MABERY, MARK	BAL	124	18TH WAR
MABERY, MARY E.	BAL	121	18TH WAR
MABEY, MARY	BAL	173	19TH WAR
MABONE, JAMES	ALL	145	6TH E.D.
MABURRY, P.	BAL	172	1ST WARD
MAC CLAY, JOHN REV.	BAL	256	1ST DIST
MAC DONALD, JAMES	BAL	223	6TH WARD
MAC INTYRE, ROSE	BAL	447	14TH WAR
MAC KENNEY, BENJAMIN	CAL	009	1ST DIST
MAC KILROY, JAMES	BAL	400	1ST DIST
MAC PHERSON, SAMUEL	BAL	132	16TH WAR
MACABE, DAVID	BAL	218	6TH DIST
MACABE, THOMAS	BAL	218	6TH DIST
MACAFEE, JOHN	FRE	156	10TH E D
MACAFEE, MARY	FRE	145	10TH E D
MACAFFEE, IGNATIUS JR.	FRE	156	10TH E D
MACALESE, ARCHIBALD	BAL	419	8TH WARD
MACALLY, SARAH	BAL	164	19TH WAR
MACARRIER, MARY	BAL	211	6TH WARD
MACASSE, EDWARD	BAL	101	1ST WARD
MACATEE, CLEMENT	HAR	045	1ST DIST
MACATEE, GEORGE J.	HAR	012	1ST DIST
MACATEE, HENRY	HAR	012	1ST DIST
MACATEE, IGNATIUS G.	HAR	037	1ST DIST
MACATEE, MARY F. G.	HAR	013	1ST DIST
MACATEE, SAMUEL	HAR	005	1ST DIST
MACATEE, SYLVESTER	HAR	012	1ST DIST
MACAULAY, ELIJAH *	BAL	207	6TH WARD
MACAULAY, WILLIAM E.	BAL	215	6TH WARD
MACAULEY, CHARLES F.	FRE	316	MIDDLETO
MACAULEY, ELIZABETH	BAL	438	14TH WAR
MACAULEY, MRS.	BAL	095	5TH WARD
MACAVAY, LURENNA	BAL	152	16TH WAR
MACAY, ELIJAH *	BAL	207	6TH WARD
MACCABLISTER, NICKOLAS	BAL	105	5TH WARD
MACCAULEY, WILLIAM	BAL	150	11TH WAR
MACCUBBIN, HENRY W.	BAL	170	16TH WAR
MACCUBBIN, JULIA A.	BAL	215	6TH WARD
MACCUBLEIN, JOHN K.L. DR.	PRI	065	NOTTINGH
MACDANIEL, WILLIAM	CAL	025	2ND DIST
MACE, ALFRED	BAL	114	5TH WARD
MACE, ANN	BAL	006	9TH WARD
MACE, C.*	BAL	007	4TH WARD
MACE, CASSY	DOR	392	1ST DIST
MACE, CATHARINE	WAS	216	1ST DIST
MACE, CHARLES*	DOR	409	1ST DIST
MACE, EVEY	DOR	316	1ST DIST
MACE, FRANKLIN	CEC	052	1ST E DI
MACE, GEORGE	DOR	392	1ST DIST
MACE, GEORGE	WAS	216	1ST DIST
MACE, HARY*	DOR	410	1ST DIST
MACE, JACOB	WAS	231	1ST DIST
MACE, JOHN	DOR	419	1ST DIST
MACE, JOHN	ANN	411	8TH DIST
MACE, JOHN	ANN	285	ANNAPOLI
MACE, JOHN	ANN	286	ANNAPOLI
MACE, JOHN H.	BAL	198	11TH WAR
MACE, JOHN H.	BAL	026	4TH WARD
MACE, JOSEPH	BAL	297	17TH WAR
MACE, OLIVER	BAL	122	5TH WARD
MACE, SAMUEL B.	CEC	052	1ST E DI
MACE, SARAH	SOM	450	DAMES QU
MACE, SARH	HAR	188	3RD DIST
MACE, SOPHIA V.	MGM	374	ROCKERLE
MACE, STEPHEN	BAL	122	5TH WARD
MACE, THOMAS	BAL	065	15TH WAR
MACE, THOMAS	DOR	419	1ST DIST
MACE, THOMAS	PRI	109	PISCATAW
MACE, WILLIAM	BAL	017	15TH WAR
MACE, WILLIAM H.	DOR	423	1ST DIST
MACEDE, AUTHER M. *	BAL	065	18TH WAR
MACEEN, HENRY	CEC	056	1ST E DI
MACELESE, ANN E.	BAL	420	8TH WARD
MACELWEE, WILLIAM	BAL	291	7TH WARD
MACENTIRE, SAMUEL	BAL	275	17TH WAR
MACENTREE, ELLEN	BAL	132	18TH WAR
MACER, CHARLES	DOR	368	3RD DIVI
MACER, JAMES	DOR	364	3RD DIVI
MACESTER, ISRAEL	BAL	018	1ST WARD
MACFARLAN, MALCOM REV.	BAL	370	13TH WAR
MACFARLAND, HARRIET	BAL	403	3RD WARD
MACGAUDER, A.J.	WAS	286	1ST DIST
MACGILL, CHARLES	WAS	154	HAGERSTO
MACGILL, DAVAGE	WAS	154	HAGERSTO
MACGILL, MARIA	BAL	173	16TH WAR
MACGINNIS, FRANCES E.	BAL	138	16TH WAR
MACGINNIS, PHILIP	BAL	137	16TH WAR
MACGOWEN, MARY	BAL	398	1ST DIST
MACGRUDER, SARAH	FRE	364	CATOCTIN
MACGRUNA, SUSANNA	FRE	312	MIDDLETO
MACGUDER, JONAS	FRE	353	MIDDLETO
MACH, WASHINGTON	BAL	263	12TH WAR
MACHADI, JOHN	BAL	312	12TH WAR
MACHALE, MARTIN	BAL	409	3RD WARD
MACHALE, MARY	BAL	410	3RD WARD
MACHALL, JOHN	CAL	048	3RD DIST
MACHARD, MARY	BAL	254	1ST DIST
MACHAST, LORENZO	BAL	122	1ST WARD
MACHEN, GEORGEAN	BAL	375	1ST DIST

Name	County	Page	District
MACHEN, JOSHUA	BAL	375	1ST DIST
MACHEN, MARY E.	BAL	135	18TH WAR
MACHEN, NANCY	BAL	385	1ST DIST
MACHEN, WILLIA	BAL	441	1ST DIST
MACHER, BENJAMIN	BAL	400	14TH WAR
MACHER, JOHN	BAL	130	1ST WARD
MACHER, JOHN S.	BAL	129	16TH WAR
MACHER, THOMAS	BAL	409	14TH WAR
MACHER, WILLIAM O.	BAL	146	16TH WAR
MACHINHAMMERS, JANE*	BAL	342	3RD WARD
MACHIONET, SEBASTIAN	BAL	007	9TH WARD
MACHIONETT, MARIA	BAL	008	9TH WARD
MACHLIN, JOHN	ALL	169	6TH E.D.
MACHREY, JAMES*	TAL	048	EASTON T
MACHTER, DANIEL	FRE	090	FREDERIC
MACI, C.*	BAL	007	4TH WARD
MACINSON, WILLAIM Q. M. *	TAL	112	ST MICHA
MACINTYRE, WILLIAM W.	BAL	344	3RD WARD
MACK, ELIZA	BAL	415	3RD WARD
MACK, HARRY	BAL	233	1ST DIST
MACK, HENRY	BAL	390	1ST DIST
MACK, JOHN-BLACK	ST	328	4TH E DI
MACK, LUKE	HAR	140	2ND DIST
MACK, MARY A.	BAL	079	4TH WARD
MACK, MARYAN	BAL	333	3RD WARD
MACK, PATRICK	BAL	149	2ND DIST
MACK, THOMAS	BAL	202	17TH WAR.
MACKALA, WILLIAM	KEN	299	3RD DIST
MACKALE, ANN	MGM	381	ROCKERLE
MACKALE, HENRY C.	CEC	003	ELKTON 3
MACKALL, C.	PRI	074	MARLBROU
MACKALL, ELIZABETH	CAL	059	3RD DIST
MACKALL, FANNY	CAL	054	3RD DIST
MACKALL, FANNY	CAL	025	2ND DIST
MACKALL, JAMES	PRI	062	NOTTINGH
MACKALL, JAMES J.	CAL	005	1ST DIST
MACKALL, LEONARD	BAL	358	13TH WAR
MACKALL, LOUIS	PRI	061	NOTTINGH
MACKALL, MARGARET	MGM	383	ROCKERLE
MACKALL, MARY	CAL	061	3RD DIST
MACKALL, MARY	BAL	444	14TH WAR
MACKALL, RACHEL	CAL	062	3RD DIST
MACKALL, RICHARD	CAL	052	3RD DIST
MACKALL, RICHARD G.	CAL	046	3RD DIST
MACKALL, SAMUEL	CAL	048	3RD DIST
MACKALL, SARAH	CAL	021	2ND DIST
MACKALL, SUSAN P.	CAL	027	2ND DIST
MACKALL, WILLIAM	CAL	049	3RD DIST
MACKALL, WILLIAM G.	ANN	312	1ST DIST
MACKALL,W ILLIAM	CAL	061	3RD DIST
MACKEE, J.	BAL	130	1ST WARD
MACKELROY, JOHN	BAL	214	11TH WAR
MACKELWARRY, RICHARC	BAL	263	17TH WAR
MACKEMULE, ANDERSON*	BAL	354	3RD WARD
MACKEN, ELIZABETH	BAL	359	1ST DIST
MACKEN, THOMAS	BAL	135	18TH WAR
MACKENHAMMER, JOHN	BAL	076	15TH WAR
MACKENHEIMER, FREDERICK *	BAL	365	13TH WAR
MACKENNY, DENNIS	BAL	026	9TH WARD
MACKENSIE, GEORGE N.	BAL	319	20TH WAR
MACKENY, RUFUS	BAL	130	1ST WARD
MACKENZIE, JOHN C.	BAL	107	10TH WAR
MACKENZIE, JOHN P.	BAL	107	10TH WAR
MACKENZIE, JULIA A.	BAL	038	15TH WAR
MACKENZIE, JULIA A.	BAL	383	13TH WAR
MACKENZIE, SARAH	BAL	070	10TH WAR
MACKER, J.	BAL	139	1ST WARD
MACKER, PETER	FRE	373	CATOCTIN
MACKEROEN, SARAH	BAL	334	1ST DIST
MACKERSON, JOHN	HAR	013	1ST DIST
MACKEY, AARON	BAL	395	14TH WAR
MACKEY, ALEXANDER H.	TAL	004	EASTON D
MACKEY, ALEXANDER L.	ANN	443	HOWARD D
MACKEY, ANDREW	BAL	150	1ST WARD
MACKEY, ANN	TAL	104	ST MICHA
MACKEY, BOIL	CEC	211	7TH E DI
MACKEY, CATHARINE	BAL	475	14TH WAR
MACKEY, CATHARINE	BAL	185	6TH WARD
MACKEY, DAVID	CEC	110	4TH E DI
MACKEY, ELIZABETH*	TAL	030	EASTON D
MACKEY, H.	BAL	116	1ST WARD
MACKEY, H. C.	TAL	069	EASTON T
MACKEY, HENRY	BAL	161	1ST WARD
MACKEY, HENRY	BAL	162	1ST WARD
MACKEY, HENRY	BAL	136	1ST WARD
MACKEY, JAMES	BAL	147	5TH WARD
MACKEY, JAMES	CEC	095	4TH E DI
MACKEY, JAMES	CEC	110	4TH E DI
MACKEY, JIM	TAL	042	EASTON D
MACKEY, JOHN	TAL	049	EASTON T
MACKEY, JOHN	CEC	111	4TH E DI
MACKEY, JOSEPH	TAL	037	EASTON D
MACKEY, MARGARET	BAL	317	20TH WAR
MACKEY, MARGARET	BAL	321	3RD WARD
MACKEY, MARIA	DOR	385	1ST DIST
MACKEY, MICHAEL	BAL	202	17TH WAR
MACKEY, MILEY*	DOR	385	1ST DIST
MACKEY, RACHEL	CEC	140	5TH E DI
MACKEY, RALPH*	TAL	061	EASTON D
MACKEY, ROBERT	WAS	176	1ST DIST
MACKEY, SAMUEL*	TAL	045	EASTON T
MACKEY, WILLIAM	CEC	005	ELKTON 3
MACKILROY, ELIZABETH	BAL	224	6TH WARD
MACKIN, CATHARINE	BAL	126	5TH WARD
MACKIN, JOSEPH	BAL	316	20TH WAR
MACKIN, MARY	BAL	030	9TH WARD
MACKIN, MARY	BAL	309	7TH WARD
MACKIN, SAMUEL	FRE	361	CATOCTIN
MACKIN, THOMAS	BAL	140	1ST WARD
MACKIN, WILLIAM	FRE	238	NEW MARK
MACKINGTYRE, JOSHUA G.	BAL	155	16TH WAR
MACKISON, CHARLES	ANN	460	HOWARD D
MACKISON, DANIEL	BAL	339	1ST DIST
MACKLIN, JAMES	HAR	075	BEL AIR
MACKLIN, MARY	BAL	376	8TH WARD
MACKLY, DAVID	CAR	327	1ST DIST
MACKLY, JACOB	CAR	327	1ST DIST
MACKLY, JAMES	CAR	326	1ST DIST
MACKLY, MICHAEL	CAR	326	1ST DIST
MACKMER, TIMOTHY	BAL	265	17TH WAR
MACKMER, WILLIAM	BAL	265	17TH WAR
MACKRILL, JAMES	BAL	140	1ST WARD
MACKTER, PHILLIP	FRE	089	FREDERIC
MACKUBIN, GEORGE	ANN	266	ANNAPOLI
MACKY, J.	BAL	063	10TH WAR
MACKY, JOHN	BAL	011	1ST WARD
MACKY, MARY	BAL	446	14TH WAR
MACKY, SARAH L.	DOR	454	1ST DIST
MACKY, WILLIAM T.	DOR	453	1ST DIST
MACLEA, ELIZABETH	BAL	083	10TH WAR
MACLIN, ASBURY	ANN	388	4TH DIST
MACLIN, ELISABETH	ANN	388	4TH DIST
MACLIN, LITTLETON	ANN	478	HOWARD D
MACLIN, SARAH A.	ANN	431	HOWARD D
MACNAMEE, GEORGE	WAS	174	FUNKSTOW
MACNAMEE, MARGARET	WAS	166	1ST DIST
MACOMB, GIDEON	BAL	091	18TH WAR
MACON, SAMUELL	ANN	281	ANNAPOLI
MACOREW, ELIZA B.	ANN	487	HOWARD D
MACORMICK, PATRICK	BAL	275	1ST DIST
MACOTTER, JOSEPH	BAL	037	15TH WAR
MACOUNT, PRISSILLA	CAL	002	1ST DIST
MACRADA, JAMES	CAL	013	1ST DIST
MACSENDA, HENRY	BAL	105	1ST WARD
MACTER, MARY	BAL	111	2ND DIST
MACTIEN, SAMUEL	BAL	127	11TH WAR
MACTIER, JANE	BAL	338	13TH WAR
MACTIER, SARAH	BAL	074	15TH WAR
MACTIN, JOHN	BAL	353	3RD WARD
MACTINER, MARGARET	BAL	223	12TH WAR
MACTUMER, TIMCTHY	BAL	266	17TH WAR
MACUBBIN, ALFRED	BAL	125	2ND DIST
MACUBBIN, CHARLES S.	BAL	234	6TH WARD
MACUBBIN, GEORGE	BAL	125	2ND DIST
MACUBBIN, NELSON	BAL	234	6TH WARD
MACUBBIN, NICHOLAS	BAL	125	2ND DIST
MACUBBIN, RICHARE	BAL	292	20TH WAR
MACUBBINE, SUSAN	BAL	029	9TH WARD
MACULBIN, ROBET W.	BAL	379	13TH WAR
MACUTCHING, MARGARET	CAR	353	6TH DIST
MADAR, SARAH	BAL	173	2ND DIST
MADARG, HENRY C.	FRE	226	BUCKEYST
MADARY, CHLOE	FRE	230	BUCKEYST
MADARY, JOHN A.	FRE	232	BUCKEYST
MADARY, TRECY	FRE	232	BUCKEYST
MADDEL, JOHN	BAL	282	1ST DIST
MADDEN, AMANDA	BAL	128	2ND DIST
MADDEN, ANN	BAL	044	9TH WARD
MADDEN, ANTHONY	ALL	143	6TH E.D.
MADDEN, BRIDGET	BAL	261	2ND WARD
MADDEN, DAVID	BAL	283	20TH WAR
MADDEN, DOLLY	TAL	096	ST MICHA
MADDEN, ELIZABETH	WAS	296	1ST DIST
MADDEN, ELIZABETH	BAL	084	15TH WAR
MADDEN, ELLEN	ANN	428	HOWARD D
MADDEN, FERDINAND	BAL	127	1ST WARD
MADDEN, GEORGE	TAL	001	EASTON D
MADDEN, GEORGEAN	BAL	335	1ST DIST
MADDEN, HENRY	HAR	153	3RD DIST
MADDEN, ISACK	TAL	069	EASTON T
MADDEN, ISAIH	TAL	073	EASTON T
MADDEN, JACOB	TAL	029	EASTON D
MADDEN, JACOB	ANN	456	HOWARD D
MADDEN, JAMES	BAL	337	1ST DIST
MADDEN, JAMES	ANN	413	HOWARD D
MADDEN, JAMES	TAL	018	EASTON D
MADDEN, JESSE	BAL	240	1ST DIST
MADDEN, JOAB	BAL	242	1ST DIST
MADDEN, JOE	TAL	066	EASTON T
MADDEN, JOHN	ALL	142	6TH E.D.
MADDEN, JOHN	ALL	214	CUMBERLA
MADDEN, JOHN	BAL	414	1ST DIST
MADDEN, JOHN	ANN	428	HOWARD D
MADDEN, JOHN	BAL	047	9TH WARD
MADDEN, JOHN	BAL	247	20TH WAR
MADDEN, JOHN C.	CEC	028	CHESAPEA
MADDEN, JOHN F.	BAL	099	15TH WAR
MADDEN, JOSHUA	BAL	165	2ND DIST
MADDEN, JULIA A.	BAL	239	6TH WARD
MADDEN, LAWRENCE	ALL	053	10TH E.D
MADDEN, LYDIA	BAL	396	14TH WAR
MADDEN, MARGARET	BAL	253	17TH WAR
MADDEN, MARY	BAL	408	14TH WAR
MADDEN, MARY	ALL	214	CUMBERLA
MADDEN, MARY	BAL	118	5TH WARD
MADDEN, MARY C.	BAL	169	16TH WAR
MADDEN, MICHAEL	ALL	085	5TH E.D.
MADDEN, PETER	BAL	396	14TH WAR
MADDEN, RUTH	ANN	449	HOWARD D
MADDEN, SAMUEL	BAL	275	12TH WAR
MADDEN, SAMUEL	BAL	238	1ST DIST
MADDEN, SARAH	BAL	223	1ST DIST
MADDEN, SOPHIA	ANN	419	HOWARD D
MADDEN, THOMAS	BAL	169	16TH WAR
MADDEN, THOMAS	BAL	044	4TH WARD
MADDEN, WILLIAM	BAL	164	19TH WAR
MADDEN, WILLIAM*	TAL	028	EASTON D
MADDER, MORECAI	BAL	040	2ND DIST
MADDER, WILLIAM*	TAL	028	EASTON D
MADDEY, ALEXANDER	BAL	332	7TH WARD
MADDIN, JAMES	HAR	017	1ST DIST
MADDIN, JOHN	TAL	038	EASTON D
MADDIN, MARY	BAL	375	3RD WARD
MADDIN, PHILASE*	TAL	038	EASTON D
MADDISON, ANN	BAL	104	18TH WAR
MADDISON, J.	BAL	141	1ST WARD
MADDOCK, JOHN	CEC	010	ELKTON 3
MADDOCKS, MARY	BAL	298	1ST DIST
MADDON, EVAN E.	HAR	084	2ND DIST
MADDON, JOSEPH	HAR	084	2ND DIST
MADDON, MARTIN	BAL	382	8TH WARD
MADDON, THOMAS B.	BAL	158	1ST WARD
MADDOX, AMANDA	CHA	263	MIDDLETO
MADDOX, ANN	BAL	055	15TH WAR
MADDOX, CAROLINE	BAL	207	17TH WAR
MADDOX, CATHARINE	BAL	230	17TH WAR
MADDOX, CATHARINE	BAL	016	18TH WAR
MADDOX, CHARLES	BAL	195	17TH WAR
MADDOX, CHARLES J.	ST	264	3RD E DI
MADDOX, CHARLES T.	BAL	058	10TH WAR
MADDOX, CULBERT	BAL	075	4TH WARD
MADDOX, DIXON	WOR	334	1ST E DI
MADDOX, EDWARD	KEN	216	2ND DIST
MADDOX, ELDEN	BAL	174	19TH WAR
MADDOX, ELIJAH	WOR	277	BERLIN 1
MADDOX, ELIZABETH	CHA	218	ALLENS F
MADDOX, ELIZABETH H.	WOR	182	6TH E DI
MADDOX, ELKANC	BAL	209	17TH WAR
MADDOX, FREDERICK	CHA	261	MIDDLETO
MADDOX, GEORGE	CHA	277	BOJANTOW
MADDOX, GEORGE	BAL	229	12TH WAR
MADDOX, GEORGE	BAL	457	8TH WARD
MADDOX, GEORGE A.	BAL	103	16TH WAR
MADDOX, GEORGE H.	BAL	160	6TH WARD
MADDOX, GEORGE W.	BAL	273	17TH WAR
MADDOX, HENRY	SOM	408	DUBLIN D
MADDOX, HENRY	BAL	161	6TH WARD
MADDOX, HENRY	BAL	159	6TH WARD
MADDOX, HENRY	BAL	265	12TH WAR
MADDOX, JAMES	BAL	068	15TH WAR
MADDOX, JAMES F.	CHA	257	MIDDLETO
MADDOX, JANE	CHA	236	HILLTOP
MADDOX, JANE	BAL	077	4TH WARD
MADDOX, JOHN	BAL	094	18TH WAR
MADDOX, JOHN	WAS	021	2ND SUBD
MADDOX, JOHN B.	CHA	217	ALLENS F
MADDOX, JOHN O.	CHA	217	ALLENS F
MADDOX, JOHN S.	CHA	224	ALLENS F
MADDOX, JOSEPH	CHA	263	MIDDLETO
MADDOX, JULIA	BAL	265	12TH WAR
MADDOX, LEWIS	CHA	239	HILLTOP
MADDOX, MARGARET	BAL	070	15TH WAR
MADDOX, MARIA	BAL	119	15TH WAR
MADDOX, MARRION	CHA	289	MIDDLETO
MADDOX, MARY	BAL	253	17TH WAR
MADDOX, MARY	BAL	069	2ND DIST
MADDOX, NANCY	BAL	240	6TH WARD
MADDOX, NANCY	BAL	326	1ST DIST
MADDOX, PETER	BAL	131	2ND DIST
MADDOX, PRISCILLA	PRI	095	SPALDING
MADDOX, ROSA	ST	274	3RD E DI
MADDOX, SAMUEL	SOM	350	BRINKLEY
MADDOX, SARAH	BAL	131	2ND DIST
MADDOX, SPENCER	BAL	044	15TH WAR
MADDOX, THOMAS	WAS	203	1ST DIST
MADDOX, THOMAS	BAL	073	18TH WAR
MADDOX, THOMAS H.	ST	278	3RD E DI
MADDOX, WILLIAM	BAL	153	16TH WAR
MADDOX, WILLIAM	BAL	094	1ST WARD
MADDOX, WILLIAM A.	CHA	223	ALLENS F
MADDOX, WILLIAM H.	WOR	278	BERLIN 1
MADDOX, WILLIAM L.	ST	277	3RD E DI
MADDOX, WILLLIAM	PRI	016	BLADENSB
MADDOX, ZOSA A.	BAL	249	1ST DIST
MADDRIS, ELIJAH L.	WOR	183	6TH E DI
MADDUR, JOHN	WOR	180	6TH E DI
MADDUX, ABIGAIL	SOM	431	PRINCESS
MADDUX, ARDETTA*	SOM	489	SALISBUR
MADDUX, BENJAMIN	WOR	231	6TH E DI
MADDUX, BENJAMIN	SOM	392	BRINKLEY
MADDUX, CALEB	SOM	357	BRINKLEY
MADDUX, CALEB	SOM	358	BRINKLEY
MADDUX, DANIEL	SOM	352	BRINKLEY
MADDUX, DAVID	SOM	360	BRINKLEY
MADDUX, EDWARD	SOM	434	PRINCESS
MADDUX, ELIJAH	WOR	188	7TH E DI
MADDUX, ELIZABETH	SOM	501	SALISBUR
MADDUX, ELIZABETH	SOM	414	DUBLIN D
MADDUX, EMALINE	SOM	360	BRINKLEY
MADDUX, FANNY	SOM	431	PRINCESS
MADDUX, GEORGE	SOM	361	BRINKLEY
MADDUX, HENRY	SOM	413	DUBLIN D
MADDUX, HENRY S.	SOM	352	BRINKLEY
MADDUX, HESTER	WOR	228	6TH E DI
MADDUX, HETTY	SOM	481	TRAPP DI
MADDUX, HEZAKIAH	WOR	237	6TH E DI
MADDUX, ISAAC	SOM	354	BRINKLEY
MADDUX, ISAAC	SOM	445	DAMES QU
MADDUX, JAMES	SOM	418	PRINCESS
MADDUX, JANE	SOM	353	BRINKLEY
MADDUX, JANE	SOM	490	SALISBUR
MADDUX, JESSE	SOM	359	BRINKLEY
MADDUX, JOHN	SOM	358	BRINKLEY
MADDUX, JOHN	SOM	471	TRAPPE D
MADDUX, JOHN	SOM	421	PRINCESS
MADDUX, JOHN T.	BAL	371	3RD WARD
MADDUX, LAURA	SOM	352	BRINKLEY
MADDUX, LAZARUS	WOR	183	6TH E DI
MADDUX, LEVIN	SOM	493	SALISBUR
MADDUX, LEVIN	SOM	421	PRINCESS
MADDUX, LITTLETON	SOM	438	DAMES QU
MADDUX, LITTLETON	SOM	415	DUBLIN D
MADDUX, LITTLETON	SOM	353	BRINKLEY
MADDUX, MARTIN L.	SOM	489	SALISBUR
MADDUX, MARY	SOM	431	PRINCESS
MADDUX, MILLY	SOM	361	BRINKLEY
MADDUX, REBECCA	SOM	392	BRINKLEY
MADDUX, ROBERT	SOM	392	BRINKLEY
MADDUX, ROBERT	SOM	359	BRINKLEY
MADDUX, SARAH	SOM	353	BRINKLEY
MADDUX, SARAH R.	SOM	352	BRINKLEY
MADDUX, SPENCER	SOM	364	BRINKLEY
MADDUX, THOMAS	SOM	353	BRINKLEY
MADDUX, THOMAS	WOR	183	6TH E DI
MADDUX, THOMAS	SOM	408	DUBLIN D
MADDUX, WILLIAM	SOM	419	PRINCESS
MADDUX, WILLIAM H.	SOM	362	BRINKLEY
MADDUX, WILSOW	WOR	237	6TH E DI
MADDUX, ZADOCK	SOM	438	DAMES QU
MADEN, JAMES	WAS	068	2ND SUBD
MADEN, JOHN	CAR	388	2ND DIST
MADER, JOHN	ALL	097	5TH E.D.
MADER, LEWIS	ALL	098	5TH E.D.
MADES, PHILIP	WAS	189	1ST DIST
MADEWELL, JOHN	BAL	283	7TH WARD
MADIGAN, THOMAS	BAL	208	11TH WAR
MADIN, ELLEN	ANN	376	4TH DIST
MADISON, BOSS-BLACK	CAR	108	NO TWP L
MADISON, ELIZABETH	BAL	205	11TH WAR
MADISON, LLOYD ALBERTA	BAL	026	15TH WAR
MADISON, SAMUEL	ANN	460	HOWARD D
MADKINS, WILLIAM	DOR	368	3RD DIVI
MADNERS, R.	BAL	135	1ST WARD
MADORE, FRANCIS	ALL	221	CUMBERLA
MADOX, JOB	BAL	224	17TH WAR
MADOX, SARAH	BAL	224	17TH WAR
MADSEN, J.	BAL	150	1ST WARD
MADUEN, HARRIET-BLACK	BAL	219	2ND WARD
MAE, JULIA A.L.-BLACK	ST	320	4TH E DI
MAEGRANER, JOHN *	FRE	362	CATOCTIN
MAEKALL, JANE	MGM	379	ROCKERLE
MAEPRESS, J.	BAL	168	1ST WARD
MAESS, CONRADV	BAL	390	3RD WARD
MAEVER, JACOB J. *	CAR	236	UNION TO
MAFFEE, ANGELO	BAL	051	9TH WARD
MAFFEE, ANGELO	BAL	050	9TH WARD
MAFFEE, MARY E.	BAL	051	9TH WARD
MAFFIT, CORNELIA	BAL	111	10TH WAR
MAFFIT, JOHN L.	CEC	120	3RD E DI
MAFFIT, SAMUEL L.	CEC	005	ELKTON 3
MAFFIT, STANSBURY	QUE	186	3RD E DI
MAFFITT, CHARLES	CEC	082	CHARLEST
MAGAN, MICHAEL	ALL	150	6TH E.D.
MAGANRAN, JAMES L.	BAL	131	1ST WARD
MAGATHA, MARY	BAL	381	1ST DIST
MAGAUGHEY, ROSE	BAL	020	9TH WARD
MAGAULIN, ELEANOR A.	BAL	226	6TH WARD
MAGAW, SAMUEL	HAR	076	BEL AIR
MAGDALINE	BAL	281	1ST DIST
MAGDALINE, MARY	QUE	245	5TH E DI

MAGE, AMELIA BAL 402 8TH WARD
MAGEE, ABSOLOM CAR 199 4TH DIST
MAGEE, AGNIS CHA 261 MIDDLETO
MAGEE, AQUILER CAR 198 4TH DIST
MAGEE, AUGUSTAS CAR 176 8TH DIST
MAGEE, JESSE ALL 158 6TH E.D.
MAGEE, JOHN CAR 190 4TH DIST
MAGEE, JOHN CAR 383 2ND DIST
MAGEE, JOHN BAL 073 4TH WARD
MAGEE, MARGARET BAL 293 7TH WARD
MAGEE, MARTHA A. BAL 442 8TH WARD
MAGEE, MARY BAL 260 1ST DIST
MAGEE, MARY JUSTINE SIS- BAL 316 20TH WAR
MAGEE, MARY* BAL 401 3RD WARD
MAGEE, PETER SOM 417 PRINCESS
MAGEE, ROSANNA ALL 107 5TH E.D.
MAGEE, SUSAN CAR 384 2ND DIST
MAGEE, THOMAS C. PRI 013 BLADENSB
MAGELL, CHARLES PRI 021 VANSVILL
MAGELLE, SARAH ALL 157 6TH E.D.
MAGENDER, ARCHIBALD S. PRI 003 BLADENSB
MAGENDER, JONATHAN W. ALL 264 CUMBERLA
MAGER, CHARLES H. ST 323 4TH E DI
MAGER, JOHN BAL 029 1ST WARD
MAGER, MARTIN BAL 099 18TH WAR
MAGER,EDWIN BAL 029 1ST WARD
MAGERS, ELIAS BAL 011 4TH WARD
MAGERS, ELIZABETH BAL 332 7TH WARD
MAGERS, GEORGE W. BAL 303 12TH WAR
MAGERS, NICKOLAS BAL 056 2ND DIST
MAGERS, SAMUEL BAL 302 7TH WARD
MAGERS, WILLIAM BAL 092 10TH WAR
MAGGANES, CHARLOTTE BAL 205 11TH WAR
MAGGIN, A. BAL 157 1ST WARD
MAGHAM, THOMAS MGM 390 ROCKERLE
MAGHAN, CATHERINE MGM 390 ROCKERLE
MAGHAN, RACHEL MGM 390 ROCKERLE
MAGHER, ELIZA BAL 017 4TH WARD
MAGIBORNY, BRIDGET * HAR 034 1ST DIST
MAGIE, MARY* BAL 401 3RD WARD
MAGIER, DANIEL O. B. BAL 179 11TH WAR
MAGILL, BENEDICT ST 302 2ND E DI
MAGILL, ELIZABETH ST 255 3RD E DI
MAGILL, FREDERICK ST 255 3RD E DI
MAGILL, JHON F. ST 272 3RD E DI
MAGILL, JOHN BAL 221 6TH WARD
MAGILL, JOHN B. BAL 222 6TH WARD
MAGILL, JOHN W. ST 285 2ND E DI
MAGILL, JOSEPH A. ST 255 3RD E DI
MAGILL, LLOYD BAL 120 16TH WAR
MAGILL, MATTHEW ST 256 3RD E DI
MAGILL, MICHAEL BAL 256 17TH WAR
MAGILL, WILLIAM BAL 105 5TH WARD
MAGIN, NANCY BAL 259 20TH WAR
MAGINITY, HENRY BAL 191 6TH WARD
MAGINLY, MIKE ANN 336 3RD DIST
MAGINNIS, HERNIETTER FRE 205 BUCKEYST
MAGINNIS, JOSEPH PRI 036 VANSVILL
MAGINNIS, RICHARD MGM 354 BERRYS D
MAGINNIS, THOMAS BAL 017 9TH WARD
MAGINNISS, JOHN BAL 183 6TH WARD
MAGINNITY, JOHN BAL 192 6TH WARD
MAGIURE, JOSEPH BAL 168 2ND DIST
MAGNE, R. H. BAL 021 18TH WAR
MAGNEDER, MARKER R. MGM 397 ROCKERLE
MAGNEDER, ZADOCK-BLACK FRE 028 FREDERIC
MAGNER, ELIZABETH BAL 060 18TH WAR
MAGNES, ROSE BAL 178 11TH WAR
MAGNESS, APRKER HAR 093 2ND DIST
MAGNESS, BENJAMIN BAL 251 6TH WARD
MAGNESS, CHARLES H. HAR 093 2ND DIST
MAGNESS, ELIJAH HAR 139 2ND DIST
MAGNESS, ISABELA BAL 388 8TH WARD
MAGNESS, JAMES BAL 377 8TH WARD
MAGNESS, JAMES HAR 141 2ND DIST
MAGNESS, JOHN HAR 095 2ND DIST
MAGNESS, JOHN R. HAR 083 2ND DIST
MAGNESS, LEE HAR 095 2ND DIST
MAGNESS, NATHANIEL HAR 104 2ND DIST
MAGNESS, PARKER HAR 075 BEL AIR
MAGNESS, SAMUEL A. ANN 426 HOWARD D
MAGNESS, THOMAS BAL 122 5TH WARD
MAGNESS, ZACHARIAH BAL 138 16TH WAR
MAGNEW, EDWIN BAL 094 18TH WAR
MAGNUS, CHARLES BAL 370 3RD WARD
MAGORY, JOHN BAL 131 1ST WARD
MAGOWAN, JOHN BAL 175 6TH WARD
MAGQUESS, BARBARA J. CAL 022 2ND DIST
MAGRADER, GREENBY ALL 094 5TH E.D.
MAGRAM, R. N. BAL 155 11TH WAR
MAGRAN, JAMES ALL 088 5TH E.D.
MAGRAN, JOHN ALL 082 5TH E.D.
MAGRANE, MICHAEL * ALL 143 6TH E.D.
MAGRATH, JOHN BAL 038 15TH WAR
MAGRAUDER, JAMES MGM 340 CLARKSBU
MAGRAW, ARTHUR SOM 479 TRAPP DI
MAGRAW, ASBURY SOM 446 DAMES QU
MAGRAW, AUSTIN CEC 121 4TH E DI
MAGRAW, CATHARINE BAL 255 6TH WARD
MAGRAW, ELIZABETH SOM 479 TRAPP DI
MAGRAW, JAMES ALL 129 4TH E.D.
MAGRAW, JAMES BAL 199 6TH WARD
MAGRAW, JAMES BAL 264 17TH WAR
MAGRAW, JOHN BAL 201 6TH WARD
MAGRAW, JOHN SOM 480 TRAPP DI
MAGRAW, JOSEPH DOR 356 3RD DIVI
MAGRAW, LEONARD CEC 183 7TH E DI
MAGRAW, MARGARET SOM 439 DAMES QU
MAGRAW, REBECCA CEC 122 4TH E DI
MAGRAW, SALLY SOM 481 TRAPP DI
MAGRAW, SAMUEL HAR 088 2ND DIST
MAGRAW, SARAH BAL 338 13TH WAR
MAGRAW, SCPTEMUS CEC 126 5TH E DI
MAGRAW, WILLIAM SOM 420 PRINCESS
MAGRE, JOHN MGM 399 ROCKERLE
MAGRE, MARY E. CAR 236 UNION TO
MAGRUDA, CAROLINE MGM 317 CRACKLIN
MAGRUDA, HENRY MGM 328 CRACKLIN
MAGRUCA, MARRION CHA 277 BOJANTOW
MAGRUDA, MARTHA CHA 285 BOJANTOW
MAGRUCA, ZACHARIAH L. MGM 334 CRACKLIN
MAGRUDER, A. PRI 051 AQUASCO
MAGRUDER, ADAM BAL 194 17TH WAR
MAGRUDER, ALEXANDER PRI 071 MARLBROU
MAGRUDER, ALICE BAL 338 13TH WAR
MAGRUDER, ANDREW PRI 051 AQUASCO
MAGRUDER, ANN PRI 078 MARLBROU
MAGRUDER, EDWIE MGM 321 CRACKLIN
MAGRUDER, C. PRI 051 AQUASCO
MAGRUDER, C.C. PRI 075 MARLBROU
MAGRUDER, C.W. PRI 084 QUEEN AN
MAGRUDER, CAROLINE M. MGM 316 CRACKLIN
MAGRUDER, CATHERINE B. MGM 381 ROCKERLE
MAGRUDER, E. PRI 106 PISCATAW
MAGRUDER, EDWARD PRI 012 BLADENSB
MAGRUDER, EDWIN-BLACK MGM 400 ROCKERLE
MAGRUDER, ELISABETH M. ANN 327 2ND DIST
MAGRUDER, ELLEANOR MGM 324 CRACKLIN
MAGRUDER, EMILY C. PRI 108 PISCATAW
MAGRUDER, FIELDER PRI 011 BLADENSB
MAGRUDER, FRANCIS BAL 395 8TH WARD
MAGRUDER, GEORGE ANN 276 ANNAPOLI
MAGRUDER, GREENBERRY MGM 388 ROCKERLE
MAGRUDER, H. C. BAL 148 11TH WAR
MAGRUDER, HENSON PRI 118 PISCATAW
MAGRUDER, JAMES A. WAS 005 WILLIAMS
MAGRUDER, JANE MGM 339 CLARKSBU
MAGRUDER, JANE P. PRI 004 BLADENSB
MAGRUDER, JEFFERY P. T. MGM 329 CRACKLIN
MAGRUDER, JESSE BAL 460 14TH WAR
MAGRUDER, JOHN A. CAL 002 1ST DIST
MAGRUDER, JOHN B. PRI 016 BLADENSB
MAGRUDER, JOHN R. BAL 090 15TH WAR
MAGRUDER, JULIAN MGM 378 ROCKERLE
MAGRUDER, L. PRI 109 PISCATAW
MAGRUDER, LEWIS MGM 390 ROCKERLE
MAGRUDER, MABEY N. PRI 015 BLADENSB
MAGRUDER, MARY PRI 015 BLADENSB
MAGRUDER, MILLEY BAL 126 5TH WARD
MAGRUDER, NACE MGM 434 CLARKSTR
MAGRUDER, OLIVER B. PRI 019 VANSVILL
MAGRUDER, OTHO MGM 317 CRACKLIN
MAGRUDER, PETER PRI 118 PISCATAW
MAGRUDER, POLLY PRI 041 VANSVILL
MAGRUDER, REBECCA MGM 379 ROCKERLE
MAGRUDER, RICAHRD R. BAL 383 13TH WAR
MAGRUDER, RICHARD MGM 395 ROCKERLE
MAGRUDER, RUFUS K. MGM 442 CLARKSTR
MAGRUDER, SAMUEL T. MGM 381 ROCKERLE
MAGRUDER, SAMUEL W. MGM 395 ROCKERLE
MAGRUDER, THOMAS BAL 376 13TH WAR
MAGRUDER, W. PRI 106 PISCATAW
MAGRUDER, WALTER MGM 325 CRACKLIN
MAGRUDER, WESLEY L. MGM 401 ROCKERLE
MAGRUDER, WILLIAM B. MGM 321 CRACKLIN
MAGRUDER, WILLIAM W. MGM 399 ROCKERLE
MAGRUNDER, JOHN R. BAL 383 13TH WAR
MAGS, JERRY BAL 019 2ND DIST
MAGSCLEVE, JOHN BAL 105 1ST WARD
MAGUGHRAN, CATHERINE BAL 373 8TH WARD
MAGUIRE, B. BAL 166 1ST WARD
MAGUIRE, CATHARINE BAL 314 12TH WAR
MAGUIRE, CATHARINE ALL 069 5TH E.D.
MAGUIRE, CHRIS BAL 231 12TH WAR
MAGUIRE, ELLEN BAL 003 9TH WARD
MAGUIRE, JAMES W.* BAL 389 3RD WARD
MAGUIRE, JOHN BAL 254 6TH WARD
MAGUIRE, JOHN BAL 188 11TH WAR
MAGUIRE, JOHN BAL 290 12TH WAR
MAGUIRE, JOHN BAL 160 11TH WAR
MAGUIRE, JOHN BAL 114 11TH WAR
MAGUIRE, JOHN BAL 153 19TH WAR
MAGUIRE, JOHN* DOR 359 3RD DIVI
MAGUIRE, JOSEPH W.* BAL 389 3RD WARD
MAGUIRE, M. BAL 135 1ST WARD
MAGUIRE, MARY BAL 390 3RD WARD
MAGUIRE, MARY BAL 045 15TH WAR
MAGUIRE, PHILLIP KEN 278 1ST DIST
MAGUIRE, SISTER B. FRE 198 5TH E DI
MAGUIRE, THOMAS BAL 254 20TH WAR
MAGUIRE, THOMAS BAL 139 19TH WAR
MAGUIRE, THOMAS BAL 264 12TH WAR
MAGUIRE, W.T. BAL 158 6TH WARD
MAGUNE, MATHEW ALL 150 6TH E.D.
MAGUNESS, ELIZABETH ALL 183 8TH E.D.
MAGURDER, MARIA BAL 364 13TH WAR
MAGURDER, SARAH BAL 449 8TH WARD
MAGURIE, JULIA A. BAL 181 6TH WARD
MAHA, JOHN BAL 005 EASTERN
MAHADY, ANN FRE 066 FREDERIC
MAHAL,ELMIRA BAL 083 1ST WARD
MAHALEY, SAMON BAL 118 5TH WARD
MAHALEY, SUSAN ANN 265 ANNAPOLI
MAHAM, WILLIAM BAL 248 1ST DIST
MAHAMMETT, JERRY * FRE 076 FREDERIC
MAHAMMETT, MARGARET FRE 076 FREDERIC
MAHAN, ANN CEC 097 4TH E DI
MAHAN, ANN E. HAR 151 3RD DIST
MAHAN, CATHARIEN BAL 150 2ND DIST
MAHAN, EDWARD BAL 109 2ND DIST
MAHAN, GOERGE CEC 002 ELKTON 3
MAHAN, JAMES HAR 156 3RD DIST
MAHAN, JAMES B. CEC 090 4TH E DI
MAHAN, JOHN ANN 281 ANNAPOLI
MAHAN, JOSEPH CEC 002 ELKTON 3
MAHAN, JOSEPH L. CEC 002 ELKTON 3
MAHAN, LUCY BAL 422 3RD WARD
MAHAN, LUCY CEC 140 6TH E DI
MAHAN, MARY A. CEC 098 4TH E DI
MAHAN, NANCY BAL 085 15TH WAR
MAHAN, ROBERT M.* TAL 052 EASTON D
MAHAN, SARAH J. CEC 103 4TH E DI
MAHAN, WILLIAM BAL 114 2ND DIST
MAHANA, BASIL BAL 065 15TH WAR
MAHANA, WILLIAM J. CAR 236 UNION TO
MAHANEY, ABIGAIL CEC 125 5TH E DI
MAHANEY, DAVID FRE 224 BUCKEYST
MAHANEY, JAMES BAL 161 6TH WARD
MAHANEY, JEREMIAH CEC 125 5TH E DI
MAHANEY, JEREMIAH CEC 123 3RD E DI
MAHANEY, JOHN CEC 124 5TH E DI
MAHANEY, JOHN CEC 020 ELKTON 3
MAHANEY, MARY C. BAL 185 16TH WAR
MAHANNA, GEORGE CAR 265 WESTMINS
MAHANNY, ELISHA CEC 079 NORTHEAS
MAHANY, BRIDET BAL 448 1ST DIST
MAHANY, DAVID ALL 008 3RD E.D.
MAHANY, ELIZA BAL 011 2ND DIST
MAHANY, FLORANCE HAR 146 3RD DIST
MAHANY, GEORGE ALL 008 3RD E.D.
MAHANY, JOHN CEC 109 3RD E DI
MAHANY, JOHN BAL 430 14TH WAR
MAHANY,ALCINDA ALL 008 3RD E.D.
MAHARAIN, LOUISA BAL 476 14TH WAR
MAHARD, SAMUEL BAL 271 17TH WAR
MAHAY, BRIDGET BAL 105 5TH WARD
MAHENY, RACHEL BAL 275 12TH WAR
MAHER, CATHERINE BAL 319 20TH WAR
MAHER, JOHN BAL 111 2ND DIST
MAHER, JOHN BAL 127 5TH WARD
MAHER, THOAMS H. BAL 301 1ST DIST
MAHEW, ELLEN BAL 181 11TH WAR
MAHEY, JAMES BAL 020 9TH WARD
MAHI, PETER BAL 248 2ND WARD
MAHLERS, HERMAN BAL 029 15TH WAR
MAHLEY, MARGRETT BAL 059 18TH WAR
MAHLON, JOHN BAL 220 6TH WARD
MAHN, EZELINE FRE 078 FREDERIC
MAHN, JOHN FRE 079 FREDERIC
MAHNA, SOLOMA FRE 079 FREDERIC
MAHNAY, MARY ALL 194 9TH E.D.
MAHNE, DANIEL FRE 083 FREDERIC
MAHNE, JESSE FRE 080 FREDERIC
MAHNE, JOHN J. FRE 083 FREDERIC
MAHNE, JOSHUA FRE 082 FREDERIC
MAHOLLAND, MARY BAL 104 10TH WAR
MAHOMET, JOSIAH WAS 148 HAGERSTO
MAHOMMET, JERRY WAS 199 1ST DIST
MAHON, ANN ALL 226 CUMBERLA
MAHON, ELIZABETH D. BAL 074 4TH WARD
MAHON, JAMES BAL 358 3RD WARD
MAHON, JOHN BAL 091 1ST WARD
MAHON, JOHN ALL 262 CUMBERLA
MAHON, JOHN BAL 136 1ST WARD
MAHON, MARY ALL 217 CUMBERLA
MAHON, ROSE BAL 110 10TH WAR
MAHONE, ENIS WAS 164 2ND DIST
MAHONE, MATHIAS BAL 285 7TH WARD
MAHONE, WILLIAM WAS 164 2ND DIST
MAHONEY, DAVID L. FRE 213 BUCKEYST
MAHONEY, DAVID L. FRE 213 BUCKEYST
MAHONEY, ELISHA BAL 271 17TH WAR
MAHONEY, F.G. BAL 137 1ST WARD
MAHONEY, FRANCIS BAL 125 1ST WARD
MAHONEY, JAMES BAL 413 8TH WARD
MAHONEY, MARGARET FRE 208 BUCKEYST
MAHONEY, MARGARET BAL 266 20TH WAR
MAHONEY, MARY J. CHA 240 HILLTOP
MAHONEY, MARY M. FRE 065 FREDERIC
MAHONEY, RICHARD PRI 107 PISCATAW
MAHONEY, SAMUEL FRE 224 BUCKEYST
MAHONEY, SISTER M.D. FRE 198 5TH E DI
MAHONEY, SOPHINE BAL 222 12TH WAR
MAHONEY, SUSAN BAL 461 14TH WAR
MAHONEY, T. BAL 072 10TH WAR
MAHONEY, THERESA BAL 213 11TH WAR
MAHONEY, WILLIAM J. FRE 213 BUCKEYST
MAHONY, DOMONICK DOR 453 1ST DIST
MAHONY, FERDINAND BAL 461 14TH WAR
MAHONY, FRANK BAL 137 1ST WARD
MAHONY, HARRISON CEC 192 5TH E DI
MAHONY, JOSEPH CEC 211 7TH E DI
MAHONY, THOMAS ALL 220 CUMBERLA
MAHONY, WILLIAM ALL 182 8TH E.D.
MAHONY, WILLIAM CEC 190 5TH E DI
MAHONY, WILLIAM FRE 399 JEFFERSO
MAHOOL, JAMES BAL 120 2ND DIST
MAHOOL, SARAH BAL 120 2ND DIST
MAHORE, DAVID FRE 079 FREDERIC
MAHORE, WILLIAM ALL 226 CUMBERLA
MAHR, JOHN N. BAL 215 19TH WAR
MAHUN, CATHERINE MISS- BAL 315 20TH WAR
MAIDEN, M. G. BAL 152 1ST WARD
MAIDLOW, CHARLES BAL 173 2ND DIST
MAIE, ANN BAL 020 4TH WARD
MAIKEN, G. BAL 137 1ST WARD
MAIL, JOHN ALL 054 10TH E.D
MAIL, LUKE ALL 056 10TH E.D
MAIN, DANIEL FRE 342 MIDDLETO
MAIN, FREDERICK FRE 346 MIDDLETO
MAIN, GEORGE FRE 333 MIDDLETO
MAIN, GEORGE FRE 336 MIDDLETO
MAIN, GEORGE A. FRE 336 MIDDLETO
MAIN, JOHN J. FRE 344 MIDDLETO
MAIN, JOSHUA H. FRE 346 MIDDLETO
MAIN, LEWIS FRE 344 MIDDLETO
MAIN, LYDIA FRE 351 MIDDLETO
MAIN, MARY A. FRE 319 MIDDLETO
MAIN, REBECCA FRE 314 MIDDLETO
MAIN, SUSANNA R. FRE 346 MIDDLETO
MAIN, WILLIAM FRE 346 MIDDLETO
MAINAY, THOMAS * ALL 050 10TH E.D
MAINE, ANN BAL 286 17TH WAR
MAINE, DANIEL FRE 006 FREDERIC
MAINE, EDWARD FRE 095 FREDERIC
MAINE, HENRY M. FRE 138 CREAGERS
MAINE, JOHN FRE 095 FREDERIC
MAINE, JOHN BAL 135 1ST WARD
MAINE, JOHN BAL 124 1ST WARD
MAINE, JOHN BAL 170 1ST WARD
MAINE, SUSAN S. FRE 402 JEFFERSO
MAINER, JOHN H. WOR 179 6TH E DI
MAINER, PETER BAL 169 11TH WAR
MAING, NANCY CAR 200 4TH DIST
MAINHART, DANIEL FRE 097 FREDERIC
MAINHART, ELIZABETH FRE 095 FREDERIC
MAINHART, HERNY FRE 321 MIDDLETO
MAINLEY, THOMAS BAL 268 7TH WARD
MAINTZA, MARY E. FRE 320 MIDDLETO
MAINTZER, JOHN FRE 334 MIDDLETO
MAINTZER, SAMUEL FRE 328 MIDDLETO
MAIRS, JOHN BAL 420 1ST DIST
MAIRS, SARAH BAL 418 1ST DIST
MAISEL, FREDERICK BAL 368 1ST DIST
MAITLAND, BENJAMIN BAL 475 14TH WAR
MAITLAND, WILLIAM C. BAL 156 1ST WARD
MAITLAND, WILLIAM L. BAL 476 14TH WAR
MAJOR, JAMES J. BAL 065 4TH WARD
MAJOR, MABEL FRE 066 FREDERIC
MAJOR, WILLIAM QUE 186 3RD E DI
MAJOR, WILLIAM R. PRI 009 BLADENSB
MAJORN, MARY * ALL 083 5TH E.D.
MAJORS, AHDEN FRE 177 5TH E DI
MAJORS, EBE SOM 522 BARREN C
MAJORS, J.W. BAL 003 EASTERN
MAJORS, JAOCB MGM 425 MEDLEY 3
MAJORS, JOHN S. MGM 425 MEDLEY 3
MAJORS, KINDAL SOM 521 BARREN C
MAJORS, LEVIN SOM 521 BARREN C
MAJORS, WILLIAM FRE 320 MIDDLETO
MAJORS, WILLIAM G. SOM 522 BARREN C
MAKAY, LUCINDA ANN 464 HOWARD D
MAKE, MARY BAL 185 2ND WARD
MAKEL, SAMUEL WAS 131 2ND DIST
MAKELL, JOHN D. WAS 130 2ND DIST
MAKEN, PATRICK CEC 044 CHESAPEA
MAKEN, THOMAS ALL 103 5TH E.D.
MAKEPEACE, ROYAL BAL 056 10TH WAR
MAKER, ELLEN R. MGM 402 ROCKERLE
MAKER, HENRY BAL 004 4TH WARD

Name	County	Page	District
MAKER, MARY	BAL	001	18TH WAR
MAKER, MARY A.	WAS	194	1ST DIST
MAKEUSKER, JOHN	ALL	080	5TH E.D.
MAKIN, MARY	BAL	184	11TH WAR
MAKIN, R. G. *	BAL	303	12TH WAR
MAKLE, MARIA	WAS	299	1ST DIST
MAKLET, MARGARET	BAL	264	12TH WAR
MAKLEY, JOHN	BAL	053	18TH WAR
MALACAN, ELIZABETH	MGM	429	CLARKSTR
MALAGAN, MINTY	BAL	450	14TH WAR
MALAGER, G. HENRY	BAL	228	19TH WAR
MALALLY, MARY	BAL	073	2ND DIST
MALAMBRE, EMELINE	BAL	030	2ND DIST
MALAMBRE, JOHN	CAR	397	2ND DIST
MALARY, JOHN	BAL	146	2ND DIST
MALBACK, THOAMS	WAS	111	2ND DIST
MALBON, JAMES	BAL	067	15TH WAR
MALCAHAN, ANN	ALL	209	CUMBERLA
MALCHOUSEN, SOLOMON	BAL	303	7TH WARD
MALCO, JOHN	BAL	222	17TH WAR
MALCOLM, JAMES	BAL	088	4TH WARD
MALCOM, JANET B.	BAL	066	10TH WAR
MALCOM, JOHN	CAR	066	NO TWP L
MALCOM, OTHMAN	HAR	183	3RD DIST
MALCOMB, MARY	SOM	483	TRAPP DI
MALCOMB, SALLY	SOM	433	PRINCESS
MALCOMB, WILLIAM	SOM	463	HANGARY
MALOLA, THOMAS	CEC	071	5TH E DI
MALE, PRISCILA	ALL	013	3RD E.D.
MALEHORN, ANN	CAR	197	4TH DIST
MALEHORN, ELIZABETH	CAR	275	7TH DIST
MALEHORN, JOHN	CAR	282	7TH DIST
MALFIELD, FREDERICK	BAL	277	2ND WARD
MALGROEY, JOHN	ALL	139	6TH E.D.
MALHAN, THOMAS	BAL	238	2ND WARD
MALHOOR, GEORGE	BAL	215	11TH WAR
MALHORN, JAMES	BAL	244	1ST DIST
MALICK, BARBARA	BAL	259	20TH WAR
MALIDAY, MALAKIA	BAL	044	18TH WAR
MALIG, CHARLES W.	BAL	155	1ST WARD
MALIN, SAMUEL	KEN	308	3RD DIST
MALINA, BRICE	ANN	366	4TH DIST
MALINCE, LEONARD	ANN	373	4TH DIST
MALINGER, MARGARET	ALL	248	CUMBERLA
MALINE, FRANCIS A.	BAL	046	9TH WARD
MALINE, JAMES	SOM	476	TRAPPE D
MALING, ANDREW	BAL	284	1ST DIST
MALL, FREDERICK	BAL	220	19TH WAR
MALL, UPTON R.	HAR	071	1ST DIST
MALLABY, THOMAS	BAL	417	8TH WARD
MALLACKIN, BENJAMIN	FRE	209	BUCKEYST
MALLACKS, JOHN	FRE	260	NEW MARK
MALLALIEW, JOHN	BAL	246	1ST DIST
MALLAN, HENRY	BAL	351	1ST DIST
MALLARD, JOHN	BAL	258	2ND WARD
MALLARD, PERRY	KEN	271	1ST DIST
MALLARNEY, MARY	BAL	460	1ST DIST
MALLAS, MARY	BAL	370	13TH WAR
MALLEN, BARNEY	ALL	239	CUMBERLA
MALLEN, CATHARINE	FRE	386	PETERSVI
MALLEN, FRANCIS	BAL	363	1ST DIST
MALLEN, JOHN	ALL	225	CUMBERLA
MALLEN, MAICHE	ALL	105	5TH E.D.
MALLENIN, JOHN	FRE	246	NEW MARK
MALLER, JONATHAN	BAL	150	11TH WAR
MALLER, JOSEPH	BAL	257	6TH WARD
MALLER, WILLIAM	WAS	065	2ND SUBD
MALLET, JOHN	WOR	310	2ND E DI
MALLET, JOHN	WOR	318	2ND E DI
MALLET, ROBERT	HAR	022	1ST DIST
MALLET, SAMUEL	WOR	310	2ND E DI
MALLETT, JAMES	WOR	311	2ND E DI
MALLETT, JAMES	WOR	317	2ND E DI
MALLETT, WILLIAM	WOR	317	2ND E DI
MALLEY, FENTON	BAL	152	11TH WAR
MALLEY, MARY A.	BAL	178	19TH WAR
MALLICAN, JAMES	MGM	402	ROCKERLE
MALLICAN, REUBEN	MGM	364	BERRYS D
MALLIKEN, NATHAN B.	MGM	353	BERRYS D
MALLILEN, JOHN *	ANN	342	3RD DIST
MALLIN, FRANCIS	ALL	242	CUMBERLA
MALLINCKRODT, WILLIAM H.	BAL	064	15TH WAR
MALLINER, NATHANIEL	BAL	247	20TH WAR
MALLING, BENJAMIN	ALL	073	5TH E.D.
MALLINGLEY, G.L.	HAR	147	3RD DIST
MALLINGLY, ELIZA	BAL	362	13TH WAR
MALLINGLY, ELLEN	ALL	097	5TH E.D.
MALLIS, ANN	BAL	226	19TH WAR
MALLMAN, RUDOLPH	ANN	413	HOWARD D
MALLON, CATHARINE	BAL	195	6TH WARD
MALLON, ELIZABETH	BAL	382	8TH WARD
MALLON, JAMES	BAL	363	8TH WARD
MALLON, JOHN	BAL	070	15TH WAR
MALLON, JULIA	BAL	340	7TH WARD
MALLON, THOMAS	BAL	340	7TH WARD
MALLONCE, GEORGE L.	BAL	176	16TH WAR
MALLONCE, JOHN *	BAL	062	18TH WAR
MALLONE, ELIZABETH	BAL	183	5TH DIST
MALLONE, JOHONNAH	BAL	041	18TH WAR
MALLONE, WILLIAM	BAL	038	15TH WAR
MALLONEE, MARY	BAL	282	7TH WARD
MALLONEE, PATRICK	BAL	383	8TH WARD
MALLONEY, JOHN	BAL	271	12TH WAR
MALLONEY, JOHN	BAL	083	18TH WAR
MALLONY, THOMAS	ALL	139	6TH E.D.
MALLORY, EARTHOLOMEW	ALL	152	6TH E.D.
MALLORY, BRIDGET	ALL	263	CUMBERLA
MALLORY, DANIEL	BAL	025	9TH WARD
MALLORY, H.	BAL	234	20TH WAR
MALLORY, ROSE	BAL	152	11TH WAR
MALLORY, THOMAS	ALL	053	10TH E.D
MALLOTT, SARAH	WAS	141	HAGERSTC
MALLOY, CHARLES P.	BAL	421	3RD WARD
MALLOY, MARY*	BAL	346	3RD WARD
MALLY, JAMES S.	ALL	021	2ND E.D.
MALOOY, PATRICK	BAL	285	1ST DIST
MALOLEIN, RICHARD	CAR	193	4TH DIST
MALON, ANGELA	BAL	212	11TH WAR
MALONCE, HYANTHA	BAL	244	1ST DIST
MALONE, ALEXANDER	WOR	194	8TH E DI
MALONE, ANN	BAL	038	15TH WAR
MALONE, BENJAMIN	FRE	318	MIDDLETO
MALONE, BRIDGET	BAL	094	10TH WAR
MALONE, CATHARINE	SOM	477	TRAPP DI
MALONE, CHARLES	WAS	145	HAGERSTO
MALONE, CHARLES	FRE	095	FREDERIC
MALONE, DENNIS	BAL	055	9TH WARD
MALONE, DOMINICK	ANN	413	HOWARD D
MALONE, ELIZABETH	SOM	494	SALISBUR
MALONE, ELIZABETH	SOM	459	HANGARY
MALONE, FREDERICK	BAL	155	2ND DIST
MALONE, GEORGE	FRE	327	MIDDLETO
MALONE, HENRY	SOM	482	TRAPP DI
MALONE, INCREASE	ALL	170	7TH E.D.
MALONE, JAMES S.*	BAL	404	3RD WARD
MALONE, JANE	BAL	023	1ST WARD
MALONE, JANE	BAL	100	5TH WARD
MALONE, JASPER	ALL	171	7TH E.D.
MALONE, JOHN	BAL	098	5TH WARD
MALONE, JOHN	BAL	045	1ST WARD
MALONE, JOHN	BAL	403	3RD WARD
MALONE, JOHN	BAL	263	2ND WARD
MALONE, JOHN	ANN	423	HOWARD D
MALONE, JOHN	BAL	055	2ND DIST
MALONE, JOHN	SOM	477	TRAPP DI
MALONE, JOHN	CAL	002	1ST DIST
MALONE, JOSIAH	BAL	439	1ST DIST
MALONE, JOSIAH	BAL	441	1ST DIST
MALONE, LEMON	SOM	472	TRAPPE D
MALONE, LEVIN	SOM	476	TRAPPE D
MALONE, M.	FRE	200	5TH E DI
MALONE, MARY	BAL	472	14TH WAR
MALONE, MARY	BAL	021	18TH WAR
MALONE, MARY	WOR	197	8TH E DI
MALONE, MARY	ALL	211	CUMBERLA
MALONE, MARY P.	FRE	065	FREDERIC
MALONE, MICHAEL	HAR	048	1ST DIST
MALONE, PATRICK	ANN	412	HOWARD D
MALONE, POLLY	SOM	476	TRAPPE D
MALONE, PRUCILLA	SOM	478	TRAPP DI
MALONE, SALLY	SOM	482	TRAPP DI
MALONE, SAMUEL	BAL	195	17TH WAR
MALONE, SANDY	SOM	478	TRAPP DI
MALONE, SARAH	BAL	439	1ST DIST
MALONE, SARAH	BAL	049	2ND DIST
MALONE, THOMAS	SOM	473	TRAPPE D
MALONE, WESLEY	SOM	503	SALISBUR
MALONE, WILLIAM	SOM	481	TRAPP DI
MALONE,RACHAEL	BAL	026	1ST WARD
MALONEE, HEZAKIAH	BAL	417	1ST DIST
MALONEE, MARICN	ST	307	1ST E DI
MALONEY, DEBORAH	QUE	242	5TH E DI
MALONEY, DENNIS	ALL	069	5TH E.D.
MALONEY, FRANCIS	BAL	168	1ST WARD
MALONEY, GILBERT	BAL	431	14TH WAR
MALONEY, HENRY	TAL	034	EASTON D
MALONEY, HUGH	BAL	356	3RD WARD
MALONEY, JOHN	BAL	063	1ST WARD
MALONEY, PATRICK	ALL	050	10TH E.D
MALONEY, PATRICK	ANN	315	1ST DIST
MALONEY, PETER	ALL	052	10TH E.D
MALONEY, WESTLEY	TAL	024	EASTON D
MALONEY,GEORGE	BAL	170	1ST WARD
MALONY, BRIDGET	BAL	255	1ST DIST
MALONY, JOHN	ALL	128	4TH E.D.
MALONY, MARIA	BAL	006	1ST WARD
MALOON, MARY	BAL	367	8TH WARD
MALORE, ARCHE *	BAL	261	2ND WARD
MALOT, ANN	WAS	016	2ND SUBD
MALOT, BENJAMIN	WAS	029	2ND SUBD
MALOT, ISAAC	WAS	035	2ND SUBD
MALOT, JOHN S.	WAS	030	2ND SUBD
MALOT, JOSEPH*	WAS	035	2ND SUBD
MALOT, SARAH	WAS	029	2ND SUBD
MALOUN, MARY	WAS	004	WILLIAMS
MALOWE, MARGARET	BAL	106	1ST WARD
MALOWNEY, JOHN	MGM	393	ROCKERLE
MALOWREY, JOHN	WAS	055	2ND SUBD
MALOY, GEORGE	ALL	074	5TH E.D.
MALOY, JOHN	ALL	070	5TH E.D.
MALOY, JOHN	WAS	064	2ND SUBD
MALOY, LAURENCE	ANN	469	HOWARD D
MALOY, WILLIAM	QUE	202	3RD E DI
MALREADY, WILLIAM	ALL	098	5TH E.D.
MALRINE, THOMAS	FRE	20	5TH E DI
MALSBERGER, JOSEPH	KEN	288	3RD DIST
MALTA, LAURA	BAL	356	13TH WAR
MALTINGLEY, JOHN	CAL	017	1ST DIST
MALTOCKS, ARTHAN *	FRE	264	NEW MARK
MALVEN, JAEMS	ALL	146	6TH E.D.
MALVINA, BRIDGET	BAL	272	1ST DIST
MALVINA, PETER *	BAL	271	1ST DIST
MALVINA, SUSAN	QUE	127	1ST E DI
MALYPETH, L.	BAL	282	2ND WARD
MAM, JACOB *	BAL	063	18TH WAR
MAN, AQUILLA	BAL	404	1ST DIST
MAN, CONRAD	CAR	192	4TH DIST
MAN, PATRICK	ALL	248	CUMBERLA
MAN, SARAH *	BAL	334	1ST DIST
MANACA, JOHN L.	ANN	484	HOWARD D
MANACA, JOSEPH R.	BAL	247	12TH WAR
MANACA, REUBEN	ANN	513	HOWARD D
MANAGAN, PHILIP	BAL	264	1ST DIST
MANAHAN, DAVID	WAS	123	2ND DIST
MANAHAN, FRANCINA	CAR	395	2ND DIST
MANAHAN, PATRICK	BAL	131	1ST WARD
MANAHAN, THOMAS S.	HAR	194	3RD DIST
MANAN, TENUCE	BAL	193	2ND WARD
MANANEY, HENRY W.	CEC	139	6TH E DI
MANBEL, CHARLES	BAL	062	4TH WARD
MANCARTER, HARRIET	MGM	398	ROCKERLE
MANCOCK, SARAH C. *	ANN	402	8TH DIST
MANCOM, NANCY	QUE	140	1ST E DI
MAND, HY.	BAL	288	1ST DIST
MANDEL, MERA	BAL	010	EASTERN
MANDEN, ELIAS *	BAL	276	20TH WAR
MANDER, JAMES	KEN	304	3RD DIST
MANDER, JOSEPH	KEN	304	3RD DIST
MANDER, SAMUEL	KEN	311	3RD DIST
MANDER, SAMUEL	KEN	305	3RD DIST
MANDER, THOMAS	KEN	306	3RD DIST
MANDER, THOMAS	KEN	285	3RD DIST
MANDERS, ELIZABETH A.	SOM	552	TYASKIN
MANDERS, JOSEPH	SOM	551	TYASKIN
MANDERS, MARY E. F.	SOM	552	TYASKIN
MANDEVILLE, KATE	ANN	308	1ST DIST
MANDFIELD, THOMAS	TAL	085	ST MICHA
MANDFORT, ELIZABETH	CEC	027	CHESAPEA
MANDINGHOLE, CALEB	CEC	200	7TH E DI
MANDLLHAUSE, HENRY *	BAL	309	12TH WAR
MANDRACHA, AUGUSTINE	FRE	202	5TH E DI
MANDRACHA, MISS C.	FRE	198	5TH E DI
MANDRACHA, MISS H.	FRE	199	5TH E DI
MANDRACHA, MISS J.	FRE	199	5TH E DI
MANDUAL, SARAH E.	CAR	122	NO TWP L
MANDUAL, WILLIAM	CAR	121	NO TWP L
MANE, TERRANCE	BAL	399	8TH WARD
MANEANS, ELIZABETH	BAL	334	1ST DIST
MANEILLAS, J.	BAL	159	1ST WARD
MANELIN, FRANCIS	CAR	396	2ND DIST
MANENTY, A.	FRE	200	5TH E DI
MANERD, JOHN	ANN	269	ANNAPOLI
MANERY, MOSES *	KEN	256	1ST DIST
MANES, JOHN	ALL	102	5TH E.D.
MANES, MARY	BAL	050	9TH WARD
MANES, SUSAN.	HAR	086	2ND DIST
MANETT, WILLIAM	CAL	008	1ST DIST
MANEUR, GEORGE	BAL	266	1ST DIST
MANEY, JOHN	BAL	273	20TH WAR
MANEY, SARAH	FRE	028	FREDERIC
MANFIELD, B. C.	BAL	155	1ST WARD
MANGAN, TIMOTHY	BAL	448	1ST DIST
MANGEEN, MARTHA	ANN	402	8TH DIST
MANGEN, JAMES	BAL	062	2ND DIST
MANGER, ADAM	CAR	294	7TH DIST
MANGER, JOHN	CAR	294	7TH DIST
MANGHAN, LEVI	CAR	375	9TH DIST
MANGHLIN, BRIDGET	ALL	072	5TH E.D.
MANGINE, CATHARINE	FRE	375	CATOCTIN
MANGLE, GEORGE	BAL	045	1ST WARD
MANGLE, JOHN	BAL	405	14TH WAR
MANGNUM, WILLIAM	PRI	014	BLADENSB
MANGUM, BILLY	ANN	395	8TH DIST
MANGUM, GEORGE	PRI	075	MARLBROU
MANGUM, HENRY	PRI	061	NOTTINGH
MANGUM, JAMES	PRI	019	VANSVILL
MANGUM, JAMES H.	PRI	001	BLADENSB
MANGUM, JOHN	ANN	307	1ST DIST
MANGUM, ZACHARIAH	PRI	016	BLADENSB
MANGUME, ZACHARIAH	PRI	012	BLADENSB
MANHALL, JACOB	BAL	029	2ND DIST
MANIEL, MARY	BAL	449	1ST DIST
MANIER, PANE	BAL	163	19TH WAR
MANIERS, JOHN	WAS	149	HAGERSTO
MANIES, SAMUEL	ALL	217	CUMBERLA
MANIFIELD, SALLY A.	ANN	422	HOWARD D
MANIFOLD, ELIZABETH	BAL	279	7TH WARD
MANIFOLD, JANE	HAR	020	1ST DIST
MANIFOLD, WILLIAM	BAL	279	7TH WARD
MANIGAN, ANN	BAL	210	2ND WARD
MANIHAN, DENNIS	FRE	149	10TH E D
MANIHAN, ELIZABETH *	FRE	149	10TH E D
MANIHAN, HENRY	FRE	151	10TH E D
MANIHAN, JAMES	FRE	150	10TH E D
MANIHAN, JONAS	FRE	149	10TH E D
MANIHAN, MARY	ALL	218	CUMBERLA
MANIHAN, SAMUEL	FRE	149	10TH E D
MANING, EDWARD	BAL	160	1ST WARD
MANIS, AMELIA	BAL	269	2ND WARD
MANIS, MARIA	BAL	139	19TH WAR
MANIS, MARY *	BAL	300	20TH WAR
MANK, PHILIP	BAL	274	12TH WAR
MANK, WILLIAM B.	FRE	079	FREDERIC
MANKEALL, ELIZABETH	WOR	314	2ND E DI
MANKEY, DAVID	FRE	314	MIDDLETO
MANKIN, HENRY	BAL	164	2ND DIST
MANKIN, ISAIAH	BAL	098	10TH WAR
MANKIN, J.H.	BAL	159	1ST WARD
MANKIN, JAMES	BAL	155	16TH WAR
MANKIN, MARY T.	CHA	248	HILLTOP
MANKIN, THEODOSIA	ST	307	1ST E DI
MANKINS, DOLLY	CHA	246	HILLTOP
MANLEFF, JOHN	CEC	047	1ST E DI
MANLEY, BRIDGET	ALL	069	5TH E.D.
MANLEY, JAMES	ALL	069	5TH E.D.
MANLEY, JAMES	BAL	278	7TH WARD
MANLEY, JOHN	ALL	056	10TH E.D
MANLEY, JULIA	BAL	053	15TH WAR
MANLEY, MARY	CEC	004	ELKTON 3
MANLEY, RODNEY	BAL	228	2ND WARD
MANLIFF, MARK	CEC	056	1ST E DI
MANLIFF, SARAH	CEC	045	1ST E DI
MANLOVE, JOHN	CAR	094	NO TWP L
MANLOVE, JOSEPH M.	KEN	295	3RD DIST
MANLOVE, SOPHIA	KEN	286	3RD DIST
MANLOVE, WILLIAM	CEC	100	3RD E DI
MANLOW, ALFRED	MGM	351	BERRYS D
MANLOW, BENJAMIN H.	MGM	352	BERRYS D
MANLOW, JULIUS	MGM	352	BERRYS D
MANLOW, OLIVER V.	MGM	352	BERRYS D
MANLY, BETSEY	BAL	458	1ST DIST
MANLY, CLAYTON	CEC	016	ELKTON 3
MANLY, ELIZABETH	BAL	413	3RD WARD
MANLY, JOHN	BAL	460	14TH WAR
MANLY, JOHN	BAL	400	1ST DIST
MANLY, JOHN	BAL	176	16TH WAR
MANLY, MARY A.	BAL	275	2ND WARD
MANLY, NICHOLAS	CEC	119	3RD E DI
MANLY, SAMUEL	BAL	127	5TH WARD
MANLY, STEPHEN	BAL	232	17TH WAR
MANLY, WILLIAM	CEC	072	5TH E DI
MANLY, WILLIAM	BAL	111	1ST WARD
MANN, ANN	BAL	353	7TH WARD
MANN, ANNA	KEN	301	3RD DIST
MANN, AQUILLA	BAL	254	1ST DIST
MANN, CECELIA	BAL	274	7TH WARD
MANN, CHARLES	BAL	095	5TH WARD
MANN, EARNEST	BAL	060	4TH WARD
MANN, ELIZABETH	BAL	341	7TH WARD
MANN, ELIZABETH	WAS	152	2ND DIST
MANN, GEORGE	BAL	338	7TH WARD
MANN, GEORGE	BAL	295	3RD WARD
MANN, GRACE	KEN	310	3RD DIST
MANN, HENRIETTA	BAL	413	1ST DIST
MANN, HENRY	KEN	312	3RD DIST
MANN, JACOB *	BAL	063	18TH WAR
MANN, JAMES	BAL	121	18TH WAR
MANN, JAMES	WAS	152	2ND DIST
MANN, JOHN	BAL	283	12TH WAR
MANN, JOHN	BAL	283	12TH WAR
MANN, JOHN J.	BAL	422	3RD WARD
MANN, JOSEPH	KEN	309	3RD DIST
MANN, JOSEPH	WAS	097	2ND DIST
MANN, JOSEPH C.	KEN	298	3RD DIST
MANN, JOSEPH R.	BAL	041	9TH WARD
MANN, JOSHUA L. P.	BAL	078	4TH WARD
MANN, LOUISA L.	HAR	071	1ST DIST
MANN, MARGARET	BAL	082	1ST WARD
MANN, MARY	BAL	310	7TH WARD
MANN, MARY L.	BAL	079	4TH WARD
MANN, MICHAEL	BAL	091	1ST WARD
MANN, NANCY	BAL	203	11TH WAR
MANN, RACHEL	KEN	313	3RD DIST
MANN, SARAH AN	BAL	256	1ST DIST
MANN, THOMAS J.	KEN	302	3RD DIST
MANN, THOMAS M.	BAL	111	15TH WAR
MANN, WILLIAM	BAL	125	16TH WAR
MANN, WILLIAM	BAL	020	4TH WARD
MANN, WILLIAM	BAL	019	18TH WAR
MANN, WILLIAM	BAL	115	11TH WAR

Name	County	Page	District
MANNA, JOHN	ALL	156	6TH E.D.
MANNAGER, NICHOLAS	BAL	456	8TH WARD
MANNAHAN, CATHARINE	FRE	430	8TH E DI
MANNAHAN, DENNIS	ALL	242	CUMBERLA
MANNAHAN, MARY	ALL	261	CUMBERLA
MANNAHAN, MARY	ALL	210	CUMBERLA
MANNAHAN, DAREY	ALL	236	CUMBERLA
MANNAKEE, ELIZABETH A.	MGM	372	BERRYS D
MANNAKEE, REUBEN	MGM	327	CRACKLIN
MANNAKER, WILLIAM	MGM	320	CRACKLIN
MANNAN, PATRICK	BAL	449	1ST DIST
MANNER, CHARLES A.	BAL	201	2ND WARD
MANNER, JAMES B.	BAL	297	7TH WARD
MANNER, LORENTZ	BAL	175	6TH WARD
MANNER, PERNEELEN	CEC	029	CHESAPEA
MANNER, SUSAN	KEN	270	1ST DIST
MANNERING, MARY	BAL	020	2ND DIST
MANNERS, JOSEAS H.	CEC	144	PORT DUP
MANNIKHUYSEN, FANNY	BAL	097	10TH WAR
MANNING, ANN	DOR	453	1ST DIST
MANNING, ANTHONY	DOR	453	1ST DIST
MANNING, CATHARINE	BAL	029	15TH WAR
MANNING, ELIZABETH	BAL	067	15TH WAR
MANNING, ELLEN	BAL	035	9TH WARD
MANNING, EUGENA	DOR	454	1ST DIST
MANNING, HENRIETTA	ST	283	3RD E DI
MANNING, HENRIETTA	ST	284	2ND E DI
MANNING, HENRY S.	BAL	067	15TH WAR
MANNING, JAMES	BAL	305	12TH WAR
MANNING, JAMES	ALL	031	2ND E.D.
MANNING, JAMES	FRE	029	FREDERIC
MANNING, JAMES C.	BAL	325	12TH WAR
MANNING, JAMES H.	BAL	208	2ND WARD
MANNING, JOHN	CAR	079	NO TWP L
MANNING, JOHN	PRI	112	PISCATAW
MANNING, JOSEPH	PRI	112	PISCATAW
MANNING, JULIA	CAR	272	WESTMINS
MANNING, MARTHA	BAL	456	14TH WAR
MANNING, MARTHA A.	ANN	339	3RD DIST
MANNING, MARY	ALL	152	6TH E.D.
MANNING, MICHAEL	ALL	243	CUMBERLA
MANNING, PATRICK	ALL	236	CUMBERLA
MANNING, PATRICK	ALL	167	6TH E.D.
MANNING, PATRICK	BAL	446	1ST DIST
MANNING, PATRICK	BAL	266	1ST DIST
MANNING, R.	BAL	149	1ST WARD
MANNING, REUBEN	ALL	074	5TH E.D.
MANNING, RICHARD	ALL	031	2ND E.D.
MANNING, RICHARD	CAR	271	WESTMINS
MANNING, SAMUEL	BAL	082	18TH WAR
MANNING, WALTER J.	BAL	031	9TH WARD
MANNING, WILLIAM	ANN	339	3RD DIST
MANNING, WILLIAM	BAL	130	1ST WARD
MANNING, WILLIAM F.	DOR	441	1ST DIST
MANNIS, MARY *	BAL	300	20TH WAR
MANNS, JAMES *	BAL	245	6TH WARD
MANNS, JOHN A.	BAL	339	7TH WARD
MANNS, ROSINA	BAL	359	8TH WARD
MANNY, LEVI	CEC	035	CHESAPEA
MANNY, MARGARET	BAL	069	1ST WARD
MANOCA, MASHAE	DOR	368	3RD DIVI
MANOCA, RACHEL	DOR	368	3RD DIVI
MANOCH, PATRICK	ALL	139	6TH E.D.
MANOHAN, GEORG	CAR	391	2ND DIST
MANOKE, EMILY	BAL	350	3RD WARD
MANOKEY, CHARLES	BAL	023	9TH WARD
MANON, ISAAC	BAL	185	19TH WAR
MANON, LENARD	WAS	145	2ND DIST
MANON, PETER	WAS	147	2ND DIST
MANOR, JAMES	KEN	270	1ST DIST
MANRO, CHARLES	BAL	276	20TH WAR
MANRO, HENRIETTA	BAL	277	20TH WAR
MANS, ISAAC R.	MGM	355	BERRYS D
MANS, MARGARET	BAL	025	15TH WAR
MANSARET, MARY	BAL	352	1ST DIST
MANSDOONG, CHRISTINE	BAL	250	20TH WAR
MANSELL, REBECCA	BAL	230	17TH WAR
MANSERICHER, L.	BAL	449	8TH WARD
MANSFIELD, ADELAIDE	BAL	141	19TH WAR
MANSFIELD, ALICE	BAL	198	19TH WAR
MANSFIELD, B.	BAL	129	1ST WARD
MANSFIELD, CHARLES	BAL	161	1ST WARD
MANSFIELD, CHARLES	BAL	007	1ST WARD
MANSFIELD, CHARLES H.	TAL	079	ST MICHA
MANSFIELD, DAVID	BAL	409	14TH WAR
MANSFIELD, EDWARD	KEN	209	2ND DIST
MANSFIELD, EDWARD	TAL	007	EASTON D
MANSFIELD, ELIZABETH	BAL	321	3RD WARD
MANSFIELD, ELLEN A.	BAL	208	2ND WARD
MANSFIELD, JAMES	KEN	234	2ND DIST
MANSFIELD, JAMES D.	TAL	083	ST MICHA
MANSFIELD, JEMIMIA	BAL	373	1ST DIST
MANSFIELD, JOHN	BAL	327	1ST DIST
MANSFIELD, JOHN	KEN	258	1ST DIST
MANSFIELD, LEVI	BAL	271	12TH WAR
MANSFIELD, MARGARITTA E.	BAL	277	1ST DIST
MANSFIELD, MATILDA	BAL	332	3RD WARD
MANSFIELD, MATTHEW	QUE	245	5TH E DI
MANSFIELD, NATHAN	KEN	300	3RD DIST
MANSFIELD, REBECCA	BAL	167	16TH WAR
MANSFIELD, RICHARD L.	TAL	085	ST MICHA
MANSFIELD, THOMAS	BAL	171	1ST WARD
MANSFIELD, WILLIAM	BAL	134	2ND DIST
MANSFIELD, WILLIAM A.	BAL	329	1ST DIST
MANSFIELDER, DANIEL	BAL	476	14TH WAR
MANSHIP, CHARLE	CAR	105	NO TWP L
MANSHIP, CHARLES	CAR	106	NO TWP L
MANSHIP, ELIJAH	CAR	116	NO TWP L
MANSHIP, ELLEN	BAL	204	6TH WARD
MANSHIP, HENRY	ANN	352	3RD DIST
MANSHIP, ISART	TAL	080	ST MICHA
MANSHIP, LUTHER	BAL	063	10TH WAR
MANSHIP, NATHAN	CAR	149	NO TWP L
MANSHIP, RACHIEL	CAR	147	NO TWP L
MANSHIP, RICHARD B.	TAL	043	EASTON D
MANSHIP, SAMUEL	BAL	179	16TH WAR
MANSHOUR, JOHN	FRE	172	5TH E DI
MANSON, CHARLES	BAL	073	10TH WAR
MANSON, ELIJAH	MGM	366	BERRYS D
MANSON, MARGARET	BAL	008	9TH WARD
MANSON, RUFUS*	DOR	432	1ST DIST
MANSON, SARAH	BAL	026	1ST WARD
MANSON, WILLIAM	QUE	142	1ST E DI
MANSTEAD, CATHARINE T.	FRE	002	FREDERIC
MANTELL, LEWIS	BAL	276	2ND WARD
MANTICE, HENRY	BAL	136	2ND DIST
MANTLE, CATHARINE	BAL	336	7TH WARD
MANTLE, ELIAS	ANN	507	HOWARD D
MANTLY, JOEL	BAL	336	1ST DIST
MANTY, E.	BAL	228	19TH WAR

Name	County	Page	District
MANTZ, ALEXANDER K.	BAL	027	9TH WARD
MANTZ, ANN C.	FRE	055	FREDERIC
MANTZ, CASPAR	FRE	040	FREDERIC
MANTZ, CATHERINE	FRE	013	FREDERIC
MANTZ, CHARLES	FRE	011	FREDERIC
MANTZ, CYRUS	FRE	043	FREDERIC
MANTZ, EDWARD	FRE	033	FREDERIC
MANTZ, ELIZA	FRE	034	FREDERIC
MANTZ, FRANCIS	FRE	057	FREDERIC
MANTZ, HARRIET	FRE	012	FREDERIC
MANTZ, JOHN A	WAS	038	2ND SUBD
MANTZ, MILLE	FRE	028	FREDERIC
MANTZ, PETER	FRE	011	FREDERIC
MANTZ, WILLIAM	FRE	030	FREDERIC
MANTZE, SOPHIA	BAL	404	14TH WAR
MANUEL, ELIZABETH	BAL	168	11TH WAR
MANUEL, GEORGE	BAL	115	1ST WARD
MANUEL, GEORGE-BLACK	WOR	320	1ST E DI
MANUEL, HARRIET-BLACK	WOR	322	1ST E DI
MANUEL, JAMES-BLACK	WOR	322	1ST E DI
MANUEL, JAMES-BLACK	WOR	347	1ST E DI
MANUEL, JAMES-BLACK	WOR	347	1ST E DI
MANUEL, JOHN-BLACK	WOR	347	1ST E DI
MANUEL, LUCY	ALL	227	CUMBERLA
MANUEL, MARGARET-BLACK	WOR	322	1ST E DI
MANUEL, MARY-BLACK	WOR	348	1ST E DI
MANUEL, POLLY-BLACK	WOR	348	1ST E DI
MANUEL, TIMOTHY	ALL	239	CUMBERLA
MANUNLY, MICHAEL	ALL	051	10TH E.D
MANWAN, JOHN	BAL	268	1ST DIST
MANWELL, CHARLES	ST	274	3RD E DI
MANWELL, JOHN	FRE	247	NEW MARK
MANWELL, THOMAS*	TAL	008	EASTON D
MANY, AUNTZ-BLACK	BAL	208	2ND WARD
MANY, DANIEL *	BAL	281	20TH WAR
MANY, PENNEL D.	CEC	037	CHESAPEA
MANYARD, BENJAMIN	FRE	255	NEW MARK
MANYARD, NATHAN	FRE	254	NEW MARK
MANYDIER, ELIZABETH	HAR	106	2ND DIST
MAPEY, RICHARD	KEN	288	3RD DIST
MAPEY, THOMAS	KEN	292	3RD DIST
MAPIS, PETER M.	BAL	199	19TH WAR
MAPLY, JAMES D.	FRE	267	NEW MARK
MAPP, RICHARD	BAL	332	13TH WAR
MAQUIN, JOHN	BAL	252	20TH WAR
MAR, DANIEL	BAL	169	2ND DIST
MAR, EMMELINE	BAL	422	14TH WAR
MARA, J.D.O.	BAL	269	12TH WAR
MARA, PATRICK	BAL	350	13TH WAR
MARADA, DANIEL	SOM	354	BRINKLEY
MARAN, ANDREW	MGM	364	BERRYS D
MARAN, ELLEN	MGM	364	BERRYS D
MARAN, GABRIEL	BAL	247	1ST DIST
MARAN, LEND	BAL	246	1ST DIST
MARAN, LEONARD	BAL	417	1ST DIST
MARAN, MICHAEL	BAL	272	1ST DIST
MARAN, RUTH	BAL	414	1ST DIST
MARANE, SUSAN	ANN	288	ANNAPOLI
MARARD, JOHN SR.	ANN	322	2ND DIST
MARARNTY, MICHAEL	ALL	141	6TH E.D.
MARATES, MARGARET	WAS	130	2ND DIST
MARBARY, JOSEPH	CHA	236	HILLTOP
MARBARY, LEONARD	CHA	257	MIDDLETO
MARBERRY, WILLIAM	WAS	132	HAGERSTO
MARBERY, WILLIAM	BAL	207	11TH WAR
MARBEY, LUKE	BAL	341	13TH WAR
MARBIN, HANNAH H.	WAS	128	HAGERSTO
MARBLE, ELIZABETH	DOR	312	1ST DIST
MARBLE, GEORGE	DOR	314	1ST DIST
MARBLE, GEORGE W.	DOR	296	1ST DIST
MARBURER, CHRISTIAN	BAL	113	15TH WAR
MARBURG, WILLIAM A.	BAL	043	9TH WARD
MARBURY, B. F.	BAL	332	1ST DIST
MARBURY, ELISABETH	BAL	424	14TH WAR
MARBURY, ELIZABETH M.	PRI	005	BLADENSB
MARBURY, JOHN W.	PRI	116	PISCATAW
MARBURY, SUSAN F.	PRI	116	PISCATAW
MARCERON, DANIEL S.	BAL	407	1ST DIST
MARCH, CAROLINE	BAL	064	15TH WAR
MARCH, HANNAH	BAL	402	14TH WAR
MARCH, MICHAEL	BAL	249	20TH WAR
MARCH, PHILLIP	BAL	243	17TH WAR
MARCH, RICHARD	BAL	384	3RD WARD
MARCHAND, LEWIS L.	BAL	118	1ST WARD
MARCHANT, MARGARET E.	BAL	155	16TH WAR
MARCHANT, ROBERT A.	BAL	154	16TH WAR
MARCHANT, THOMAS	WAS	134	HAGERSTO
MARCHBANK, ISABELLA	CEC	135	6TH E DI
MARCHBANK, ROBERT	BAL	222	6TH WARD
MARCHELLAS, ELIZABETH	BAL	345	13TH WAR
MARCHEW, AUGUSTUS	BAL	243	20TH WAR
MARCOLFF, MARY	BAL	043	9TH WARD
MARCUS, HYLAND	CEC	015	ELKTON 3
MARCUS, JOHN	BAL	144	1ST WARD
MARCY, EMMA	PRI	006	BLADENSB
MARDEN, CHARLES	BAL	429	1ST DIST
MARDEN, NATHAN	PRI	098	SPALDING
MARDEN, SAVERS	BAL	103	1ST WARD
MARDUE, WALTER	CHA	237	HILLTOP
MARE, THOMAS P.	BAL	386	13TH WAR
MAREAU, CHARLES	ANN	452	HOWARD D
MAREIN, FLETCHER*	DOR	447	1ST DIST
MARES, EMANUEL-BLACK	FRE	048	FREDERIC
MARES, LEONARD	FRE	076	FREDERIC
MAREUSE, JOHN	BAL	041	4TH WARD
MARFELT, FREDERICK	BAL	463	14TH WAR
MARFIELD, PENELOPE	BAL	078	15TH WAR
MARFIELD, SAMUEL*	BAL	371	3RD WARD
MARFIELD, WILLIAM-BLACK	CAR	397	2ND DIST
MARG, FREDERICK A.	BAL	120	1ST WARD
MARGAN, CATHARINE	BAL	250	1ST DIST
MARGAN, MORDICA	BAL	440	1ST DIST
MARGAR, THOMAS J.	BAL	401	1ST DIST
MARGAREAT, HENRY *	BAL	452	8TH WARD
MARGARET, BALTZER	ALL	167	6TH E.D.
MARGE, ELLEN	BAL	273	12TH WAR
MARGE, WILLIAM	BAL	262	1ST DIST
MARGILLE, MARY	BAL	458	1ST DIST
MARGOY, PATRICK	WAS	149	2ND DIST
MARGRUDER, REZIN	FRE	315	MIDDLETO
MARHES, JANE	TAL	083	ST MICHA
MARHES, REBECCA	TAL	074	EASTON T
MARHEY, AARON	TAL	104	ST MICHA
MARHEY, HAZIE	TAL	095	ST MICHA
MARHEY, WILLIAM	TAL	104	ST MICHA
MARHIESER, JOHN	BAL	027	9TH WARD
MARHSAL, HUGH	TAL	083	ST MICHA
MARHSALL, CONRAD	BAL	197	5TH DIST
MARHSALL, ROSENA	WOR	259	BERLIN 1
MARHTER, PHILLIP	FRE	089	FREDERIC

Name	County	Page	District
MARIA, ANNA	QUE	227	4TH E DI
MARIA, ANNA-BLACK	QUE	194	3RD E DI
MARIAM, JANE	ST	341	5TH E DI
MARIAN, CHAELS	BAL	388	13TH WAR
MARIE, JOHN *	WAS	164	HAGERSTO
MARILDR, SARAH A.	WAS	144	2ND DIST
MARIN, LARABABLE*	DOR	449	1ST DIST
MARIN, RICHARD	BAL	347	7TH WARD
MARINE, CHARLES	DOR	301	1ST DIST
MARINE, DAVID	SOM	512	BARREN C
MARINE, ELIZABETH	DOR	367	3RD DIVI
MARINE, ISAIK*	DOR	467	1ST DIST
MARINE, JAMES	DOR	302	1ST DIST
MARINE, JERIPH	DOR	369	3RD DIVI
MARINE, JERREY	DOR	369	3RD DIVI
MARINE, JERREY	DOR	367	3RD DIVI
MARINE, JOHN	DOR	301	1ST DIST
MARINE, MARY	DOR	301	1ST DIST
MARINE, MATTHEW	SOM	511	BARREN C
MARINE, RHODA	SOM	509	BARREN C
MARINE, SARAH	DOR	421	1ST DIST
MARINE, SHARLOTT	DOR	366	3RD DIVI
MARINE, WILLIAM J.	SOM	511	BARREN C
MARINER, AMELIA	BAL	012	9TH WARD
MARINER, THOMAS	BAL	012	9TH WARD
MARINER, W. W.	BAL	063	10TH WAR
MARINES, GEORGE *	CAR	317	1ST DIST
MARING, DANIEL	CAR	310	1ST DIST
MARING, DANIEL E.	CAR	311	1ST DIST
MARING, DAVID	CAR	311	1ST DIST
MARING, GEORGE	CAR	317	1ST DIST
MARING, JACOB	CAR	315	1ST DIST
MARING, JACOB	CAR	290	7TH DIST
MARINK, ELY	BAL	156	19TH WAR
MARINS, WILLIAM	CAR	308	1ST DIST
MARIO, JOHN *	WAS	164	HAGERSTO
MARION, ANN	BAL	428	14TH WAR
MARION, F.	WAS	211	1ST DIST
MARION, FRANCIS	ALL	239	CUMBERLA
MARION, JOHN	BAL	447	1ST DIST
MARION, MARY L.	BAL	051	9TH WARD
MARION, RACHAEL	BAL	150	11TH WAR
MARION, THOMAS	BAL	444	1ST DIST
MARIOTT, BRECILLA	BAL	410	14TH WAR
MARIOTT, ELIZABETH A.	ANN	487	HOWARD D
MARIOTT, THOMAS	MGM	331	CRACKLIN
MARIS, ANTOINA	BAL	129	1ST WARD
MARIS, FREDERICK	BAL	204	19TH WAR
MARIS, JACOB*	CAL	031	4TH WARD
MARIS, JOHN	PRI	031	VANSVILL
MARIS, LEWIS R.	BAL	155	15TH WAR
MARIS, MAHALIKE	BAL	169	11TH WAR
MARIS, MARGERY	PRI	031	VANSVILL
MARIS, SUSAN	BAL	184	19TH WAR
MARISCHER, HENRY	BAL	095	10TH WAR
MARISDORFER, J.	BAL	206	19TH WAR
MARITN, A.	BAL	150	1ST WARD
MARITN, ABNER	WOR	280	BERLIN 1
MARITN, CAHRLES	BAL	147	1ST WARD
MARITN, CHARLES	BAL	148	1ST WARD
MARITN, HARRIET	BAL	173	2ND DIST
MARITN, J.	BAL	154	1ST WARD
MARITN, LUTHER A.	BAL	194	5TH DIST
MARITN, MARTHA	BAL	124	2ND DIST
MARITN, MARY	BAL	368	13TH WAR
MARITN, MORDICAI	BAL	194	5TH DIST
MARITN, SAMUEL	BAL	463	14TH WAR
MARITT, SARAH	FRE	206	BUCKEYST
MARITT, WILLIAM	FRE	206	BUCKEYST
MARIX, RICHARD	BAL	382	1ST DIST
MARK, AMELIA	MGM	352	BERRYS D
MARK, ANNA	CAR	304	1ST DIST
MARK, BARTHLY	FRE	095	FREDERIC
MARK, GEORGE	BAL	287	1ST DIST
MARK, HAMILTON J.	ANN	451	HOWARD D
MARK, HENRIETTA	MGM	351	BERRYS D
MARK, JOHN	BAL	058	18TH WAR
MARK, KITTY	MGM	352	BERRYS D
MARK, PATRICK	BAL	118	2ND DIST
MARK, PETER	CAR	304	1ST DIST
MARK, SUSANNA	ANN	451	HOWARD D
MARK, WILLIAM	FRE	239	NEW MARK
MARK, WILLIAM	CEC	191	5TH E DI
MARKADING, CAROLINE	BAL	035	9TH WARD
MARKALL, ELIZABETH G.	CAL	007	1ST DIST
MARKBERGER, PETER*	BAL	001	4TH WARD
MARKEE, JACOB	CEC	092	4TH E DI
MARKEE, JOHN	CEC	095	4TH E DI
MARKEL, ANN E.	BAL	046	1ST WARD
MARKEL, HENRY	FRE	118	CREAGERS
MARKEL, SARAH	BAL	058	10TH WAR
MARKELL, CHARLES	BAL	475	14TH WAR
MARKELL, FRANCES	BAL	366	13TH WAR
MARKELL, GOERGE	FRE	032	FREDERIC
MARKELL, HENRY	BAL	117	5TH WARD
MARKELL, HENRY	BAL	117	5TH WARD
MARKELL, JOHN	FRE	012	FREDERIC
MARKELL, LEWIS	FRE	014	FREDERIC
MARKELL, AMELIA	FRE	015	FREDERIC
MARKENHEIMER, GEORGE L.	PRI	082	QUEEN AN
MARKER, AMANDA	FRE	375	CATOCTIN
MARKER, CHARLES	CHA	230	BOJANTOW
MARKER, DAVID	CAR	395	2ND DIST
MARKER, EDES	BAL	158	19TH WAR
MARKER, EZRA	FRE	341	MIDDLETO
MARKER, HENRY	FRE	363	CATOCTIN
MARKER, JACOB	CAR	297	7TH DIST
MARKER, JACOB	WAS	037	2ND SUBD
MARKER, JAMES	WAS	036	2ND SUBD
MARKER, JOHN	FRE	361	CATOCTIN
MARKER, JOHN	CAR	408	2ND DIST
MARKER, JOHN	FRE	308	WOODSBOR
MARKER, JOHN	BAL	226	12TH WAR
MARKER, JOHN L.	WAS	284	1ST DIST
MARKER, MARY J.	TAL	087	ST MICHA
MARKER, MICHAEL	FRE	374	CATOCTIN
MARKER, REBERA*	TAL	069	EASTON T
MARKER, SAMUEL	WAS	204	1ST DIST
MARKER, TABITHA	BAL	226	12TH WAR
MARKES, JOHN	BAL	226	19TH WAR
MARKET, GEORGE H.	ST	343	5TH E DI
MARKET, STEPHEN	BAL	046	1ST WARD
MARKEY, CHRISTOPHER	BAL	189	5TH DIST
MARKEY, DAVID J.	FRE	046	FREDERIC
MARKEY, ELIZABETH	BAL	204	6TH DIST
MARKEY, ELIZABETH*	TAL	030	EASTON D
MARKEY, GEORGE	BAL	202	6TH DIST
MARKEY, JACOB	BAL	201	6TH DIST
MARKEY, JOHN D.	FRE	047	FREDERIC
MARKEY, LUCY E.R.	FRE	046	FREDERIC

MARKEY, PATRICK BAL 019 9TH WARD
MARKEY, SIMEON BAL 211 6TH DIST
MARKEY, THOAMS BAL 150 1ST WARD
MARKHY, THOMAS S. BAL 006 1ST WARD
MARKIN, ANN BAL 025 9TH WARD
MARKING, PETER BAL 231 17TH WAR
MARKLAN, ALISAN HAR 002 1ST DIST
MARKLAN, JAMES W. BAL 218 12TH WAR
MARKLAND, ANN J. BAL 181 19TH WAR
MARKLAND, EELIZABETH TAL 040 EASTON D
MARKLAND, F. C. BAL 068 10TH WAR
MARKLAND, F. C. BAL 068 10TH WAR
MARKLAND, J.F. BAL 232 17TH WAR
MARKLAND, JAMES F. BAL 234 17TH WAR
MARKLAND, RICHARC TAL 040 EASTON D
MARKLAND, WILLIAM T. BAL 189 5TH DIST
MARKLE, ADAM CAR 343 6TH DIST
MARKLE, CATHARINE CAR 352 6TH DIST
MARKLE, JACOB CAR 275 7TH DIST
MARKLE, JACOB ALL 044 10TH E.D
MARKLE, JOHN CAR 345 6TH DIST
MARKLE, MARY CAR 258 3RD DIST
MARKLE, SAMUEL BAL 335 1ST DIST
MARKLE, WILLIAM CAR 277 7TH DIST
MARKLEY, DAVID BAL 122 2ND DIST
MARKLIN, CHARLES E. HAR 031 1ST DIST
MARKLING, JOHN T. BAL 113 18TH WAR.
MARKMOL, FREDERICK BAL 215 19TH WAR
MARKNEY, MARGARET WAS 158 HAGERSTO
MARKOLF, MARY BAL 374 13TH WAR
MARKS, AGNES BAL 178 16TH WAR
MARKS, CATHARINE ANN 441 HOWARD D
MARKS, CATHERINE ALL 213 CUMBERLA
MARKS, CHARLOTTE PRI 002 BLADENSB
MARKS, CORNELIUS BAL 146 1ST WARD
MARKS, DANIEL BAL 428 1ST DIST
MARKS, ELIZABETH ALL 196 CUMBERLA
MARKS, ELIZABETH ST 291 2ND E DI
MARKS, ELIZABETH PRI 059 NOTTINGH
MARKS, FREDERICK CAR 309 1ST DIST
MARKS, HENRY CHA 230 BOJANTOW
MARKS, JOHN BAL 317 12TH WAR
MARKS, JOHN BAL 055 1ST WARD
MARKS, LEMUEL ANN 441 HOWARD D
MARKS, MARY J. BAL 239 1ST DIST
MARKS, NICHOLAS WAS 128 2ND DIST
MARKS, NIMROD ANN 439 HOWARD D
MARKS, OSCAR M. ST 291 2ND E DI
MARKS, R. H. BAL 063 10TH WAR
MARKS, THOMAS WAS 292 1ST DIST
MARKT, AUGUSTUS ALL 127 4TH E.D.
MARKUS, JAMES CEC 017 ELKTON 3
MARKWARD, WILLIAM PRI 009 BLADENSB
MARKWOOD, GEORGE FRE 094 FREDERIC
MARL, JAMES ALL 054 10TH E.D
MARLBROUGH, ELIZA BAL 167 16TH WAR
MARLEY, BENJAMIN BAL 090 18TH WAR
MARLEY, CATHARINE BAL 234 17TH WAR
MARLEY, JAMES BAL 098 18TH WAR
MARLEY, JAMES R. BAL 077 18TH WAR
MARLEY, JOHN BAL 112 18TH WAR
MARLEY, JOHN * BAL 090 18TH WAR
MARLIN, JOHN H. BAL 009 1ST WARD
MARLL, JOSEPH W. MGM 378 ROCKERLE
MARLON, TABITHA PRI 036 VANSVILL
MARLOR, ELLEN WAS 144 2ND DIST
MARLOU, MARY C. CHA 251 MIDDLETO
MARLOW, A. W. CHA 252 BOJANTOW
MARLOW, ALFRED H. CHA 251 MIDDLETO
MARLOW, ANN M. MGM 325 CRACKLIN
MARLOW, HANSON FRE 386 PETERSVI
MARLOW, JAMES ANN 480 HOWARD D
MARLOW, LAUSON CHA 251 MIDDLETO
MARLOW, LEVI MGM 332 CRACKLIN
MARLOW, PARMENIE * FRE 380 PETERSVI
MARLOW, RICHARD MGM 356 BERRYS D
MARLOW, SOPHIA ANN 458 HOWARD D
MARLOW, THOMAS MGM 331 CRACKLIN
MARLOW, WILLIAM CHA 253 MIDDLETO
MARLOWE, CHRISTY PRI 058 NOTTINGH
MARLOWE, HENRY PRI 087 SPALDING
MARLOWE, LUISCOE * FRE 106 CREAGERS
MARMADUKE, JAMES WAS 026 2ND SUBD
MARMADUKE, JAMES WAS 025 2ND SUBD
MARMADUKE, LEWIS WAS 055 2ND SUBD
MARMELSTEEL, LOUISA BAL 376 3RD WARD
MARNES, JACOB CEC 212 7TH E DI
MARNOTT, RICHARD W. BAL 380 13TH WAR
MARNWICK, HENRY BAL 437 14TH WAR
MAROBECK, SEBASTIAN BAL 270 12TH WAR
MAROKY, JULIA DOR 419 1ST DIST
MARON, R. BAL 126 1ST WARD
MAROY, JOHN BAL 251 17TH WAR
MARPLE, BENJAMIN BAL 158 16TH WAR
MARPUGH, HARMAN BAL 166 16TH WAR
MARQUART, FREDERICK CAR 409 2ND DIST
MARQUESS, HENRY W. CAL 053 3RD DIST
MARQUESS, JOHN CAL 046 3RD DIST
MARQUESS, WILLIAM CAL 057 3RD DIST
MARR, ANDREW WAS 149 HAGERSTO
MARR, EVILLA C. WAS 149 HAGERSTO
MARR, GEORGE BAL 009 15TH WAR
MARR, JAMES PRI 006 BLADENSB
MARR, JAMES BAL 003 18TH WAR
MARR, JAMES D. BAL 059 18TH WAR
MARR, JOHN BAL 240 2ND WARD
MARR, LENOX BAL 047 18TH WAR
MARR, ROSANNA WAS 146 HAGERSTO
MARR, SARAH * BAL 334 1ST DIST
MARR, SARAH D. BAL 193 11TH WAR
MARR, SOPHIA BAL 184 2ND WARD
MARR, THOMAS S. ST 333 4TH E DI
MARR, WALTER CHA 260 MIDDLETO
MARR, WILLIAM BAL 317 1ST DIST
MARRARD, SAMUEL ANN 272 ANNAPOLI
MARRATT, JULIAN BAL 358 1ST DIST
MARRCOTT, WILLIAM H. ANN 517 HOWARD D
MARRE, BARBARA WAS 065 2ND SUBD
MARRET, HENRY WOR 330 1ST E DI
MARRIA, ANN * BAL 093 18TH WAR
MARRIATT, CHARLOTT BAL 356 1ST DIST
MARRIET, JAMES BAL 369 8TH WARD
MARRIET, JOSEPH BAL 267 1ST DIST
MARRIET, WILLIAM H. BAL 351 1ST DIST
MARRIETT, THOMAS D. BAL 462 14TH WAR
MARRINE, JAMES B. TAL 060 EASTON D
MARRION, JOHN BAL 079 10TH WAR
MARRIOT, JOHNATHAN ANN 446 HOWARD D
MARRIOT, THOMAS BAL 357 1ST DIST
MARRIOT, WASH. BAL 267 1ST DIST
MARRIOTT, ALLEN ANN 311 1ST DIST
MARRIOTT, ALPHEUS W. FRE 045 FREDERIC
MARRIOTT, ANN BAL 364 1ST DIST
MARRIOTT, ANN BAL 371 1ST DIST
MARRIOTT, ANN M. * BAL 067 18TH WAR
MARRIOTT, B. W. ANN 306 1ST DIST
MARRIOTT, CALEP BAL 171 11TH WAR
MARRIOTT, CHARLES MGM 388 ROCKERLE
MARRIOTT, CHARLOTTE BAL 366 1ST DIST
MARRIOTT, ELISHA ANN 316 1ST DIST
MARRIOTT, ELIZABETH ANN 366 4TH DIST
MARRIOTT, GEORGE BAL 097 5TH WARD
MARRIOTT, GEORGE W. PRI 067 AQUASCO
MARRIOTT, HARRIET ANN 338 3RD DIST
MARRIOTT, J. MC KINN BAL 204 11TH WAR
MARRIOTT, JAMES C. BAL 463 14TH WAR
MARRIOTT, JOHN BAL 418 14TH WAR
MARRIOTT, JOHN BAL 261 6TH WARD
MARRIOTT, JOHN H. BAL 260 6TH WARD
MARRIOTT, JOSHUA BAL 366 1ST DIST
MARRIOTT, N. ANN 338 3RD DIST
MARRIOTT, R. ANN 338 3RD DIST
MARRIOTT, RACHEL ANN 376 4TH DIST
MARRIOTT, RICHARD ANN 294 1ST DIST
MARRIOTT, SARAH BAL 050 2ND DIST
MARRIOTT, SARAH BAL 129 11TH WAR
MARRIOTT, SUSANAH BAL 371 1ST DIST
MARRIOTT, WILLIAM BAL 357 1ST DIST
MARRIOTT, WILLIAM BAL 048 9TH WARD
MARRIOTT, WILLIAM H. BAL 389 13TH WAR
MARRIS, HANNAH A. BAL 434 1ST DIST
MARRISS, BETSEY A. SOM 536 TYASKIN
MARRLEY, RICHARD BAL 246 12TH WAR
MARROKY, KESTE* DOR 388 1ST DIST
MARROKY, W.* DOR 388 1ST DIST
MARROTT, RICHARD W. BAL 153 19TH WAR
MARROW, DANIEL BAL 005 EASTERN
MARROW, FRANCES BAL 226 1ST DIST
MARROW, PETER WAS 040 2ND SUBD
MARROWBACK, MARY BAL 117 11TH WAR
MARRS, JOHN CAR 313 1ST DIST
MARRS, LYDIA BAL 468 14TH WAR
MARRY, DANIEL * BAL 281 20TH WAR
MARRY, ELIZABETH BAL 104 2ND DIST
MARRY, JOHN ALL 190 9TH E.D.
MARRY, JORDAN CAL 026 2ND DIST
MARRY, JSOIAH BAL 141 1ST WARD
MARS, BENJAMIN FRE 346 MIDDLETO
MARS, JAMES ANN 428 HOWARD D
MARS, JERRY ANN 324 2ND DIST
MARS, JOSEPH B. BAL 431 1ST DIST
MARS, M. BAL 163 1ST WARD
MARS, MARIA FRE 058 FREDERIC
MARS, POLLY ANN 428 HOWARD D
MARS, SARAH BAL 229 12TH WAR
MARSCH, JOHN BAL 371 13TH WAR
MARSDEAN, ELLEN BAL 282 20TH WAR
MARSDEN, ELIAS * BAL 276 20TH WAR
MARSDEN, H. BAL 234 12TH WAR
MARSDEN, JAMES BAL 388 1ST DIST
MARSDEN, JAMES BAL 287 20TH WAR
MARSDEN, JOHN ANN 514 HOWARD D
MARSEILLIS, MARY BAL 205 2ND WARD
MARSELL, JAMES ALL 227 CUMBERLA
MARSELL, MARY J. BAL 223 17TH WAR
MARSELLA, ADENE BAL 077 15TH WAR
MARSEY, WILLIAM R. BAL 347 13TH WAR
MARSFELDER, CHARLES BAL 138 16TH WAR
MARSFELDER, LEWIS BAL 204 17TH WAR
MARSH, ALEXANDER BAL 241 1ST DIST
MARSH, ANDREW G. BAL 196 5TH DIST
MARSH, AQUILLA BAL 461 1ST DIST
MARSH, CALEB BAL 435 1ST DIST
MARSH, CASPER BAL 289 1ST DIST
MARSH, CATHARINE BAL 087 15TH WAR
MARSH, CATHERINE BAL 371 8TH WARD
MARSH, CATHERINE FRE 065 FREDERIC
MARSH, CHARLES BAL 184 5TH DIST
MARSH, CHARLES SOM 463 HANGARY
MARSH, CHARLOTE WOR 311 2ND E DI
MARSH, CHESTER BAL 455 8TH WARD
MARSH, DAVID BAL 287 1ST DIST
MARSH, ELIJAH BAL 097 2ND DIST
MARSH, ELIZABETH BAL 043 2ND DIST
MARSH, ELIZABETH BAL 431 1ST DIST
MARSH, ELIZABETH BAL 214 6TH DIST
MARSH, ELIZABETH FRE 059 FREDERIC
MARSH, ELIZABETH QUE 134 1ST E DI
MARSH, EMILY BAL 320 3RD WARD
MARSH, GEORGE BAL 420 1ST DIST
MARSH, GEORGE BAL 142 2ND DIST
MARSH, GEORGE BAL 185 5TH DIST
MARSH, HANNAH BAL 340 13TH WAR
MARSH, HENRY KEN 293 3RD DIST
MARSH, HENRY C. BAL 226 12TH WAR
MARSH, JACOB BAL 213 6TH DIST
MARSH, JAMES BAL 444 1ST DIST
MARSH, JAMES BAL 188 5TH DIST
MARSH, JAMES BAL 128 1ST WARD
MARSH, JAMES BAL 212 6TH WARD
MARSH, JOHN BAL 455 1ST DIST
MARSH, JOHN CAR 396 2ND DIST
MARSH, JOHN CAR 253 3RD DIST
MARSH, JOHN E. KEN 290 3RD DIST
MARSH, JOHN K. BAL 305 7TH WARD
MARSH, JOSEPH WAS 224 1ST DIST
MARSH, JOSHUA BAL 351 3RD WARD
MARSH, JOSHUA BAL 086 2ND DIST
MARSH, JOSIAH BAL 178 2ND DIST
MARSH, LEWIS BAL 371 8TH WARD
MARSH, MARIA BAL 038 2ND DIST
MARSH, MARY BAL 042 9TH WARD
MARSH, MASON R. FRE 027 FREDERIC
MARSH, NICKOLAS BAL 055 2ND DIST
MARSH, OTTIS W. WAS 126 HAGERSTO
MARSH, PATIENCE BAL 111 10TH WAR
MARSH, PHEBE CAR 260 3RD DIST
MARSH, PHILLIP WOR 291 9TH E DI
MARSH, RICHARD BAL 184 5TH DIST
MARSH, SALOME BAL 303 7TH WARD
MARSH, SARAH M. BAL 256 6TH WARD
MARSH, THEODORE WOR 274 BERLIN 1
MARSH, THEODORE WOR 301 SNOW HIL
MARSH, THOMAS WOR 307 2ND E DI
MARSH, THOMAS BAL 184 5TH DIST
MARSH, THOMAS BAL 202 2ND WARD
MARSH, THOMAS CAR 219 5TH DIST
MARSH, THOMAS CAR 219 5TH DIST
MARSH, WALTER H. SOM 463 HANGARY
MARSH, WILLIAM BAL 056 2ND DIST
MARSHA, THOMAS BAL 021 2ND DIST
MARSHAL, BENNETT TAL 104 ST MICHA
MARSHAL, EDWARD C. BAL 313 3RD WARD
MARSHAL, ELIJAH TAL 098 ST MICHA
MARSHAL, ELIZA CEC 030 CHESAPEA
MARSHAL, ELLEN TAL 097 ST MICHA
MARSHAL, GREENBURY TAL 082 ST MICHA
MARSHAL, HENRIETTA BAL 340 3RD WARD
MARSHAL, JAMES TAL 113 ST MICHA
MARSHAL, JAMES CAR 121 NO TWP L
MARSHAL, JAMES H. TAL 019 EASTON D
MARSHAL, JEREMIAH TAL 089 ST MICHA
MARSHAL, JOHN TAL 084 ST MICHA
MARSHAL, JOHN TAL 118 ST MICHA
MARSHAL, JOHN CEC 131 6TH E DI
MARSHAL, JOSEPH CEC 029 CHESAPEA
MARSHAL, JOSEPH TAL 089 ST MICHA
MARSHAL, MARIANNA CEC 030 CHESAPEA
MARSHAL, MARY TAL 116 ST MICHA
MARSHAL, MARY A. TAL 075 EASTON T
MARSHAL, NOAH TAL 092 ST MICHA
MARSHAL, PHILIP L. BAL 384 3RD WARD
MARSHAL, SAMUEL TAL 058 EASTON D
MARSHAL, SAMUEL CEC 130 6TH E DI
MARSHAL, STEPHEN BAL 399 3RD WARD
MARSHAL, WILLIAM TAL 041 EASTON D
MARSHAL, WILLIAM G. BAL 005 EASTERN
MARSHALE, EANAN A.* DOR 373 1ST DIST
MARSHALE, JOHN B. DOR 405 1ST DIST
MARSHALE, LURANY DOR 374 1ST DIST
MARSHALE, REBECCA CEC 151 PORT DUP
MARSHALE, SARAH* DOR 408 1ST DIST
MARSHALE, THOMAS DOR 404 1ST DIST
MARSHALL, ALEXANDER BAL 274 17TH WAR
MARSHALL, ALEXANDER TAL 041 EASTON D
MARSHALL, ALFRED J. CAR 334 MANCHEST
MARSHALL, ANN BAL 039 18TH WAR
MARSHALL, ANN BAL 055 1ST WARD
MARSHALL, ANN BAL 311 12TH WAR
MARSHALL, ANN G. CHA 256 MIDDLETO
MARSHALL, ANTOINE BAL 397 14TH WAR
MARSHALL, BOND P. DOR 465 1ST DIST
MARSHALL, C. BAL 300 12TH WAR
MARSHALL, CAROLINE DOR 378 1ST DIST
MARSHALL, CATHARINE BAL 124 5TH WARD
MARSHALL, CHARLES BAL 140 1ST WARD
MARSHALL, CHARLES BAL 339 3RD WARD
MARSHALL, CHARLES WAS 014 2ND SUBD
MARSHALL, CHARLES SOM 394 BRINKLEY
MARSHALL, CHARLES SOM 402 BRINKLEY
MARSHALL, CHRISTIAN BAL 003 4TH WARD
MARSHALL, CHRISTINA WAS 073 2ND SUBD
MARSHALL, CONRAD BAL 196 5TH DIST
MARSHALL, DANIEL BAL 234 2ND WARD
MARSHALL, DAVID E. BAL 131 1ST WARD
MARSHALL, DENTON BAL 249 2ND WARD
MARSHALL, E.C. PRI 111 PISCATAW
MARSHALL, EANAN A.* DOR 373 1ST DIST
MARSHALL, EDWARD BAL 134 11TH WAR
MARSHALL, EDWARD BAL 362 13TH WAR
MARSHALL, EDWARD WAS 072 2ND SUBD
MARSHALL, EDWARD SOM 391 BRINKLEY
MARSHALL, EDWARD BAL 311 12TH WAR
MARSHALL, ELEANOR A.H. PRI 112 PISCATAW
MARSHALL, ELIJA DOR 429 1ST DIST
MARSHALL, ELIJAH DOR 398 1ST DIST
MARSHALL, ELIJAH DOR 399 1ST DIST
MARSHALL, ELIJAH DOR 400 1ST DIST
MARSHALL, ELIZA WOR 348 1ST E DI
MARSHALL, ELIZABETH SOM 392 BRINKLEY
MARSHALL, ELIZABETH WAS 009 WILLIAMS
MARSHALL, ELIZABETH WOR 314 2ND E DI
MARSHALL, ELIZABETH DOR 429 1ST DIST
MARSHALL, ELIZABETH BAL 417 14TH WAR
MARSHALL, ELIZABETH QUE 146 1ST E DI
MARSHALL, ELIZABETH BAL 373 3RD WARD
MARSHALL, ELLEN BAL 117 5TH WARD
MARSHALL, ELLEN BAL 117 5TH WARD
MARSHALL, EMANUEL BAL 133 11TH WAR
MARSHALL, ENNALS BAL 159 6TH WARD
MARSHALL, EPHRAIM SOM 395 BRINKLEY
MARSHALL, EUNALL F. BAL 173 1ST WARD
MARSHALL, FRANCIS BAL 378 13TH WAR
MARSHALL, FRANCIS BAL 223 19TH WAR
MARSHALL, GEORGE BAL 124 11TH WAR
MARSHALL, GEORGE WOR 262 BERLIN 1
MARSHALL, GEORGE WOR 265 BERLIN 1
MARSHALL, GEORGE-BLACK PRI 024 VANSVILL
MARSHALL, HARIATT J. WOR 334 1ST E DI
MARSHALL, HARRIET DOR 400 1ST DIST
MARSHALL, HENRY TAL 099 ST MICHA
MARSHALL, HENRY BAL 197 19TH WAR
MARSHALL, HENRY CAR 276 7TH DIST
MARSHALL, HENSON BAL 035 9TH WARD
MARSHALL, HETTY ANN 325 2ND DIST
MARSHALL, ISAAC SOM 473 TRAPPE D
MARSHALL, ISAIAH BAL 260 6TH WARD
MARSHALL, J.H.M. SOM 397 BRINKLEY
MARSHALL, JAEMS BAL 115 1ST WARD
MARSHALL, JAMES BAL 413 14TH WAR
MARSHALL, JAMES CAR 185 8TH DIST
MARSHALL, JAMES DOR 386 1ST DIST
MARSHALL, JAMES BAL 405 14TH WAR
MARSHALL, JAMES SOM 428 PRINCESS
MARSHALL, JAMES BAL 321 3RD WARD
MARSHALL, JAMES WAS 201 1ST DIST
MARSHALL, JAMES WAS 030 2ND SUBD
MARSHALL, JAMES WAS 072 2ND SUBD
MARSHALL, JAMES E. QUE 193 3RD E DI
MARSHALL, JAMES W. BAL 162 1ST WARD
MARSHALL, JANE BAL 304 20TH WAR
MARSHALL, JENNY BAL 151 19TH WAR
MARSHALL, JESE DOR 468 1ST DIST
MARSHALL, JESSE BAL 148 1ST WARD
MARSHALL, JIM WOR 275 BERLIN 1
MARSHALL, JOHN SOM 398 BRINKLEY
MARSHALL, JOHN SOM 454 DAMES QU
MARSHALL, JOHN PRI 078 MARLBROU
MARSHALL, JOHN BAL 034 9TH WARD
MARSHALL, JOHN BAL 172 1ST WARD
MARSHALL, JOHN BAL 191 2ND WARD
MARSHALL, JOHN BAL 291 3RD WARD
MARSHALL, JOHN BAL 089 10TH WAR
MARSHALL, JOHN BAL 056 15TH WAR
MARSHALL, JOHN DOR 398 1ST DIST
MARSHALL, JOHN DOR 402 1ST DIST
MARSHALL, JOHN DOR 429 1ST DIST
MARSHALL, JOHN FRE 071 FREDERIC
MARSHALL, JOHN BAL 474 14TH WAR
MARSHALL, JOHN BAL 442 14TH WAR

Name	County	Page	District
MARSHALL, JOHN	BAL	209	17TH WAR
MARSHALL, JOHN	CHA	269	ALLENS F
MARSHALL, JOHN D.	WOR	301	SNOW HIL
MARSHALL, JOHN E.	BAL	158	6TH WARD
MARSHALL, JOHN E. H.	WOR	299	SNOW HIL
MARSHALL, JOHN E. H.	WOR	262	BERLIN 1
MARSHALL, JOHN P.	WOR	265	BERLIN 1
MARSHALL, JOHN T.	BAL	324	3RD WARD
MARSHALL, JOHN W.	BAL	103	15TH WAR
MARSHALL, JOHNW.	BAL	388	13TH WAR
MARSHALL, JOSIAH	WOR	259	BERLIN 1
MARSHALL, JULIA	BAL	369	13TH WAR
MARSHALL, K.	BAL	142	1ST WARD
MARSHALL, LEVIN	BAL	378	3RD WARD
MARSHALL, LEVIN	DOR	426	1ST DIST
MARSHALL, LEWIS	DOR	396	1ST DIST
MARSHALL, LEWIS	ALL	212	CUMBERLA
MARSHALL, MARGARET	BAL	055	15TH WAR
MARSHALL, MARGARET	DOR	402	1ST DIST
MARSHALL, MARGARET	DOR	428	1ST DIST
MARSHALL, MARGARET	WOR	290	9TH E DI
MARSHALL, MARGARETT	DOR	451	1ST DIST
MARSHALL, MARGARETT	BAL	114	11TH WAR
MARSHALL, MARIA	BAL	232	12TH WAR
MARSHALL, MARIA	BAL	025	15TH WAR
MARSHALL, MARK	DOR	451	1ST DIST
MARSHALL, MARY	WOR	181	6TH E DI
MARSHALL, MARY	ALL	202	CUMBERLA
MARSHALL, MARY	BAL	434	14TH WAR
MARSHALL, MARY	CHA	288	BOJANTOW
MARSHALL, MARY A.	DOR	400	1ST DIST
MARSHALL, MARY A.	BAL	419	3RD WARD
MARSHALL, MARY A.	ANN	419	HOWARD D
MARSHALL, MARY J.	BAL	077	18TH WAR
MARSHALL, NANCY	SOM	476	TRAPPE D
MARSHALL, NANCY DARLY	PRI	025	VANSVILL
MARSHALL, NICHOLAS	TAL	089	ST MICHA
MARSHALL, NICHOLAS	BAL	046	15TH WAR
MARSHALL, PHILIP	CHA	287	BOJANTOW
MARSHALL, R.	BAL	141	1ST WARD
MARSHALL, R.	BAL	136	1ST WARD
MARSHALL, R.	BAL	136	1ST WARD
MARSHALL, RACHAEL	BAL	158	11TH WAR
MARSHALL, RACHEL	WAS	075	2ND SUBD
MARSHALL, REBECCA	BAL	259	1ST DIST
MARSHALL, RICHARD	BAL	140	1ST WARD
MARSHALL, RICHARD	BAL	171	1ST WARD
MARSHALL, RICHARD	BAL	164	1ST WARD
MARSHALL, RICHARD	PRI	021	VANSVILL
MARSHALL, RICHARD	TAL	091	ST MICHA
MARSHALL, RICHARD H.	PRI	069	MARLBROU
MARSHALL, RICHARD H.	FRE	033	FREDERIC
MARSHALL, ROBERT	DOR	392	1ST DIST
MARSHALL, ROBERT	PRI	100	SPALDING
MARSHALL, ROBERT	BAL	127	5TH WARD
MARSHALL, ROBERT	BAL	027	15TH WAR
MARSHALL, ROBERT H.	SOM	394	BRINKLEY
MARSHALL, RUBEN J.	TAL	117	ST MICHA
MARSHALL, RUTH	CEC	157	PORT DUP
MARSHALL, SALLY	WOR	213	4TH E DI
MARSHALL, SAMUEL	BAL	249	1ST DIST
MARSHALL, SARAH	BAL	300	1ST DIST
MARSHALL, SARAH	BAL	051	9TH WARD
MARSHALL, SARAH	PRI	112	PISCATAW
MARSHALL, SARAH	WAS	075	2ND SUBD
MARSHALL, SARAH	BAL	248	17TH WAR
MARSHALL, SARAH*	DOR	408	1ST DIST
MARSHALL, SIDNEY	BAL	078	10TH WAR
MARSHALL, SOLOMON	BAL	012	1ST WARD
MARSHALL, SOLOMON	BAL	212	17TH WAR
MARSHALL, SUSAN	BAL	107	5TH WARD
MARSHALL, THOMAS	BAL	116	1ST WARD
MARSHALL, THOMAS	BAL	022	15TH WAR
MARSHALL, THOMAS	BAL	073	18TH WAR
MARSHALL, THOMAS	BAL	091	18TH WAR
MARSHALL, THOMAS	WAS	070	2ND SUBD
MARSHALL, THOMAS	SOM	363	BRINKLEY
MARSHALL, THOMAS H.	DOR	393	1ST DIST
MARSHALL, THOMAS J.	PRI	111	PISCATAW
MARSHALL, W. E.	BAL	470	14TH WAR
MARSHALL, WILLIAM	BAL	157	11TH WAR
MARSHALL, WILLIAM	DOR	400	1ST DIST
MARSHALL, WILLIAM	DOR	394	1ST DIST
MARSHALL, WILLIAM	HAR	204	3RD DIST
MARSHALL, WILLIAM	BAL	212	17TH WAR
MARSHALL, WILLIAM	SOM	356	BRINKLEY
MARSHALL, WILLIAM	WAS	131	2ND DIST
MARSHALL, WILLIAM	WOR	283	BERLIN 1
MARSHALL, WILLIAM	WOR	282	BERLIN 1
MARSHALL, WILLIAM	BAL	026	15TH WAR
MARSHALL, WILLIAM	BAL	040	1ST WARD
MARSHALL, WILLIAM	BAL	123	5TH WARD
MARSHALL, WILLIAM	BAL	309	1ST DIST
MARSHALL, WILLIAM B.	CHA	287	BOJANTOW
MARSHALL, WILLIAM H.	WOR	319	1ST E DI
MARSHALL, WILLIAM H.	PRI	070	MARLBROU
MARSHALL, WILLIAM M.	WAS	141	HAGERSTO
MARSHALL, WILLIAM T.	SOM	399	BRINKLEY
MARSHALL, WILSON	CEC	142	6TH E DI
MARSHALL, ZADOK	WOR	259	BERLIN 1
MARSHALL,ROBERT	BAL	114	1ST WARD
MARSHALS, JAMES	BAL	458	8TH WARD
MARSHBANK, ANN	CEC	151	PORT DUP
MARSHBANK, JOHN D.	CEC	150	PORT DUP
MARSHBANK, ROBERT	CEC	005	ELKTON 3
MARSHBANK, THEODORE L.	CEC	157	PORT DUP
MARSHEL, WILLIAM	CAR	121	NO TWP L
MARSHELL, MARGARETT	BAL	058	18TH WAR
MARSHEN, GERRAND *	BAL	429	8TH WARD
MARSHEY, MARY *	TAL	101	ST MICHA
MARSHEY, THEADORE	TAL	091	ST MICHA
MARSHIP, GEORGE	CAR	066	NO TWP L
MARSHLAND, RICHARD JR.*	TAL	068	EASTON T
MARSHOALL, ISAAC T.	SOM	399	BRINKLEY
MARSLLER, HARRY	BAL	232	17TH WAR
MARSTERS, JOSEPH D.	BAL	317	12TH WAR
MARSTERS, WILLIAM	BAL	120	1ST WARD
MARSTON, EUSTINA	BAL	061	15TH WAR
MARSTON, JOSEPH H.	BAL	461	14TH WAR
MARSTON, L. W.	BAL	318	12TH WAR
MARSTON, MOSES T.	BAL	422	14TH WAR
MARSTON, SARAH	BAL	321	12TH WAR
MARSTOW, JOSEPH R.	BAL	461	14TH WAR
MART, WILLIAM	WAS	277	RIDGEVIL
MARTAIN, JOHN *	WAS	135	2ND DIST
MARTAIN, MARY	CEC	102	4TH E DI
MARTAIN, SARAH	CEC	092	4TH E DI
MARTEL, PETER	BAL	049	1ST WARD
MARTEL, PETER	BAL	049	1ST WARD
MARTENBIAH, JOHN	FRE	360	CATOCTIN
MARTENE, MARY	WAS	044	2ND SUBD
MARTENEY, GEORGE	WAS	145	HAGERSTO
MARTENGE, JOHN	WAS	153	HAGERSTO
MARTENYE, JACOB	WAS	200	1ST DIST
MARTER, ELIZA	BAL	093	18TH WAR
MARTHA, JAMES	QUE	243	5TH E DI
MARTHA, JAMES	BAL	048	9TH WARD
MARTHA, STACKER A.	CHA	289	MIDDLETO
MARTHENA, WILLIAM	FRE	161	EMMITTSB
MARTHER,EDWARD	BAL	136	1ST WARD
MARTHLAND, MARY K.	BAL	424	1ST DIST
MARTHLER, JOHN *	FRE	089	FREDERIC
MARTIN, A.	BAL	153	1ST WARD
MARTIN, A.C.	WAS	004	WILLIAMS
MARTIN, ADALINE	BAL	079	4TH WARD
MARTIN, ADAM	WAS	279	LEITERSB
MARTIN, ALECE	BAL	046	4TH WARD
MARTIN, ALEXANDER	BAL	221	17TH WAR
MARTIN, ALLEN	BAL	164	11TH WAR
MARTIN, AMELIA	WOR	176	6TH E DI
MARTIN, ANDREW	BAL	218	12TH WAR
MARTIN, ANN	BAL	463	1ST DIST
MARTIN, ANN	BAL	070	2ND DIST
MARTIN, ANN	TAL	069	EASTON T
MARTIN, ANN	ST	274	3RD E DI
MARTIN, ANN	BAL	274	17TH WAR
MARTIN, ANN	HAR	117	2ND DIST
MARTIN, ANN M.	TAL	028	EASTON D
MARTIN, ANTHONY L.	MGM	368	BERRYS D
MARTIN, ANTOINE	BAL	129	1ST WARD
MARTIN, ANTONE	BAL	124	1ST WARD
MARTIN, ANTONIA	BAL	122	1ST WARD
MARTIN, ARCHIBALD	BAL	122	5TH WARD
MARTIN, ASHTON A.	BAL	375	3RD WARD
MARTIN, AUTONEA	BAL	278	2ND WARD
MARTIN, BARBARA	WAS	279	LEITERSB
MARTIN, BARBARA A.	WAS	272	RIDGEVIL
MARTIN, BENJAMIN	MGM	392	ROCKERLE
MARTIN, BETSEY	BAL	167	11TH WAR
MARTIN, BEZELEEL	HAR	052	1ST DIST
MARTIN, C.	BAL	162	1ST WARD
MARTIN, C.H.	HAR	062	1ST DIST
MARTIN, CAROLINE	BAL	010	4TH WARD
MARTIN, CAROLINE	KEN	285	3RD DIST
MARTIN, CASPER	ALL	019	2ND E.D.
MARTIN, CATHERINE	BAL	011	4TH WARD
MARTIN, CATHERINE*	BAL	340	3RD WARD
MARTIN, CHARELS	BAL	122	5TH WARD
MARTIN, CHARELS H.	ANN	519	HOWARD D
MARTIN, CHARLES	BAL	429	1ST DIST
MARTIN, CHARLES	BAL	335	1ST DIST
MARTIN, CHARLES	ST	257	3RD E DI
MARTIN, CHARLES A.	WAS	145	HAGERSTO
MARTIN, CHARLOTT	KEN	288	3RD DIST
MARTIN, CHRISTIANNA	BAL	181	2ND DIST
MARTIN, COMFORT	BAL	085	18TH WAR
MARTIN, CULBERTSON	BAL	257	12TH WAR
MARTIN, CURTIS	CAR	180	8TH DIST
MARTIN, C.C.	WAS	131	HAGERSTO
MARTIN, DANIEL	TAL	059	EASTON D
MARTIN, DAVID	CAR	327	1ST DIST
MARTIN, DAVID	CAR	327	1ST DIST
MARTIN, DAVID	BAL	020	18TH WAR
MARTIN, DAVID	CAR	247	3RD DIST
MARTIN, DAVID	BAL	432	14TH WAR
MARTIN, DAVID	BAL	471	14TH WAR
MARTIN, DAVID	BAL	393	14TH WAR
MARTIN, DAVID	ALL	059	10TH E.D
MARTIN, DAVID	BAL	045	2ND DIST
MARTIN, E. D.	WOR	299	SNOW HIL
MARTIN, EASTER	WAS	024	2ND SUBD
MARTIN, EDWARD	BAL	035	9TH WARD
MARTIN, EDWARD	DOR	301	1ST DIST
MARTIN, EDWARD	FRE	173	5TH E DI
MARTIN, EDWARD	FRE	133	CREAGERS
MARTIN, EDWARD E.	BAL	340	1ST DIST
MARTIN, EDWARD J.	BAL	252	12TH WAR
MARTIN, ELEANOR	BAL	086	4TH WARD
MARTIN, ELIAZA V.	CHA	257	MIDDLETO
MARTIN, ELISABETH	ALL	222	CUMBER_A
MARTIN, ELIZA	BAL	121	2ND DIST
MARTIN, ELIZA	BAL	114	15TH WAR
MARTIN, ELIZA	BAL	248	17TH WAR
MARTIN, ELIZA	CAL	056	3RD DIST
MARTIN, ELIZA	BAL	149	11TH WAR
MARTIN, ELIZA	BAL	451	14TH WAR
MARTIN, ELIZA	HAR	108	2ND DIST
MARTIN, ELIZABETH	BAL	248	17TH WAR
MARTIN, ELIZABETH	BAL	274	20TH WAR
MARTIN, ELIZABETH	BAL	403	8TH WARD
MARTIN, ELLEN	BAL	353	7TH WARD
MARTIN, ELLWOOD	CEC	159	PORT DUP
MARTIN, EMANUEL	WAS	262	1ST DIST
MARTIN, EMILY	BAL	244	6TH WARD
MARTIN, ENNALS	TAL	075	EASTON T
MARTIN, ERASTMUS	FRE	122	CREAGERS
MARTIN, ESTER	HAR	006	1ST DIST
MARTIN, ESTHER-BLACK	QUE	164	2ND E DI
MARTIN, ESTMAN	BAL	100	18TH WAR
MARTIN, FRANCES	BAL	049	9TH WARD
MARTIN, FRANCIS	ALL	059	10TH E.D
MARTIN, FREDERICK	BAL	254	2ND WARD
MARTIN, FREDERICK	ALL	241	CUMBERLA
MARTIN, GAHAN	BAL	300	17TH WAR
MARTIN, GARRET	ALL	201	CUMBERLA
MARTIN, GEORGE	ALL	071	5TH E.D.
MARTIN, GEORGE	BAL	074	2ND DIST
MARTIN, GEORGE	BAL	132	1ST WARD
MARTIN, GEORGE	BAL	276	7TH WARD
MARTIN, GEORGE	BAL	343	7TH WARD
MARTIN, GEORGE	BAL	030	15TH WAR
MARTIN, GEORGE	BAL	335	3RD WARD
MARTIN, GEORGE	BAL	122	1ST WARD
MARTIN, GEORGE	BAL	300	17TH WAR
MARTIN, GEORGE	BAL	068	18TH WAR
MARTIN, GEORGE	CHA	269	ALLENS F
MARTIN, GEORGE	KEN	243	2ND DIST
MARTIN, GEORGE	FRE	003	FREDERIC
MARTIN, GEORGE	CAR	180	8TH DIST
MARTIN, GEORGE	FRE	286	WOODSBOR
MARTIN, GEORGE L. *	KEN	265	1ST DIST
MARTIN, GEORGE T.	BAL	431	14TH WAR
MARTIN, GEORGE W.	BAL	470	14TH WAR
MARTIN, GEORGIANNA	KEN	266	1ST DIST
MARTIN, GEROGE	KEN	251	2ND DIST
MARTIN, GREENBURY	BAL	010	1ST WARD
MARTIN, GREENBURY	BAL	175	6TH WARD
MARTIN, GUSTAVUS	FRE	172	5TH E DI
MARTIN, H.	BAL	118	1ST WARD
MARTIN, H.	BAL	139	1ST WARD
MARTIN, H.	BAL	140	1ST WARD
MARTIN, H.A.	CAR	369	9TH DIST
MARTIN, H.B.	BAL	233	1ST DIST
MARTIN, HANSON	MGM	376	ROCKERLE
MARTIN, HARRIET	TAL	044	EASTON D
MARTIN, HELEN A.	DOR	376	1ST DIST
MARTIN, HENRY	KEN	248	2ND DIST
MARTIN, HENRY	HAR	182	3RD DIST
MARTIN, HENRY	BAL	391	14TH WAR
MARTIN, HENRY	BAL	071	4TH WARD
MARTIN, HENRY	WAS	276	RIDGEVIL
MARTIN, HENRY	WAS	219	1ST DIST
MARTIN, HENRY	BAL	254	2ND WARD
MARTIN, HENRY	BAL	117	5TH WARD
MARTIN, HENRY	BAL	062	15TH WAR
MARTIN, HENRY	ALL	228	CUMBERLA
MARTIN, HENRY	BAL	135	2ND DIST
MARTIN, HENRY	BAL	146	16TH WAR
MARTIN, HENRY H.	BAL	071	15TH WAR
MARTIN, HESTER	BAL	151	11TH WAR
MARTIN, HOLLY	ALL	082	5TH E.D.
MARTIN, IRA	BAL	173	19TH WAR
MARTIN, IRVIN	BAL	196	19TH WAR
MARTIN, ISAAC	CAR	187	4TH DIST
MARTIN, ISAAC	BAL	305	7TH WARD
MARTIN, ISAAC	BAL	098	1ST WARD
MARTIN, ISAAC J.	ANN	455	HOWARD D
MARTIN, J.	BAL	282	2ND WARD
MARTIN, J. *	BAL	154	1ST WARD
MARTIN, J. H.	ANN	422	HOWARD D
MARTIN, J.S.	BAL	242	2ND WARD
MARTIN, JACOB	ALL	082	5TH E.D.
MARTIN, JACOB	ALL	182	8TH E.D.
MARTIN, JACOB	BAL	172	16TH WAR
MARTIN, JACOB	FRE	173	5TH E DI
MARTIN, JACOB	WAS	215	1ST DIST
MARTIN, JACOB	KEN	263	1ST DIST
MARTIN, JACOB	WAS	298	1ST DIST
MARTIN, JACOB *	KEN	272	1ST DIST
MARTIN, JACOB S.	CAR	411	2ND DIST
MARTIN, JAEMS H.	TAL	074	EASTON T
MARTIN, JAMES	FRE	216	BUCKEYST
MARTIN, JAMES	BAL	153	19TH WAR
MARTIN, JAMES	BAL	083	18TH WAR
MARTIN, JAMES	BAL	088	18TH WAR
MARTIN, JAMES	BAL	269	7TH WARD
MARTIN, JAMES	BAL	389	8TH WARD
MARTIN, JAMES	BAL	375	3RD WARD
MARTIN, JAMES	ANN	344	3RD DIST
MARTIN, JAMES	BAL	125	5TH WARD
MARTIN, JAMES	BAL	124	1ST WARD
MARTIN, JAMES	BAL	069	15TH WAR
MARTIN, JAMES	BAL	334	1ST DIST
MARTIN, JAMES-BLACK	WOR	172	6TH E DI
MARTIN, JEREMIAH	FRE	114	CREAGERS
MARTIN, JESSE	FRE	131	CREAGERS
MARTIN, JOHN	FRE	178	5TH E DI
MARTIN, JOHN	HAR	181	3RD DIST
MARTIN, JOHN	MGM	330	CRACKLIN
MARTIN, JOHN	BAL	013	4TH WARD
MARTIN, JOHN	BAL	216	11TH WAR
MARTIN, JOHN	BAL	402	14TH WAR
MARTIN, JOHN	CEC	154	PORT DUP
MARTIN, JOHN	HAR	014	1ST DIST
MARTIN, JOHN	HAR	011	1ST DIST
MARTIN, JOHN	FRE	095	FREDERIC
MARTIN, JOHN	HAR	031	1ST DIST
MARTIN, JOHN	FRE	019	FREDERIC
MARTIN, JOHN	BAL	289	20TH WAR
MARTIN, JOHN	FRE	377	PETERSVI
MARTIN, JOHN	TAL	056	EASTON D
MARTIN, JOHN	WAS	123	2ND DIST
MARTIN, JOHN	TAL	050	EASTON T
MARTIN, JOHN	BAL	391	1ST DIST
MARTIN, JOHN	BAL	165	11TH WAR
MARTIN, JOHN	BAL	008	9TH WARD
MARTIN, JOHN	BAL	200	11TH WAR
MARTIN, JOHN	BAL	367	3RD WARD
MARTIN, JOHN	BAL	169	2ND DIST
MARTIN, JOHN	BAL	190	5TH DIST
MARTIN, JOHN	BAL	164	6TH WARD
MARTIN, JOHN	BAL	056	2ND DIST
MARTIN, JOHN	BAL	026	2ND DIST
MARTIN, JOHN	BAL	030	2ND DIST
MARTIN, JOHN	BAL	120	16TH WAR
MARTIN, JOHN	ALL	047	10TH E.D
MARTIN, JOHN	ALL	019	2ND E.D.
MARTIN, JOHN	ALL	135	4TH E.D.
MARTIN, JOHN A.	KEN	262	1ST DIST
MARTIN, JOHN A.	FRE	174	5TH E DI
MARTIN, JOHN F.	BAL	274	12TH WAR
MARTIN, JOHN H.	BAL	108	10TH WAR
MARTIN, JOHN H. T.	BAL	034	15TH WAR
MARTIN, JOHN H.B.	ST	299	2ND E DI
MARTIN, JOHN J.	KEN	262	1ST DIST
MARTIN, JOHN L.	ANN	519	HOWARD D
MARTIN, JOHN R.	DOR	423	1ST DIST
MARTIN, JOHN S.	TAL	044	EASTON D
MARTIN, JOHN W.	TAL	044	EASTON D
MARTIN, JOHN W.	BAL	160	1ST WARD
MARTIN, JOSEPH	BAL	172	1ST WARD
MARTIN, JOSEPH	BAL	219	2ND WARD
MARTIN, JOSEPH	KEN	287	3RD DIST
MARTIN, JOSEPH	KEN	263	1ST DIST
MARTIN, JOSEPH	KEN	257	1ST DIST
MARTIN, JOSEPH	FRE	171	5TH E DI
MARTIN, JOSEPH	FRE	181	5TH E DI
MARTIN, JOSEPH	BAL	350	13TH WAR
MARTIN, JOSEPH	BAL	089	18TH WAR
MARTIN, JOSEPH T.	CEC	199	7TH E DI
MARTIN, JOSHUA	QUE	242	5TH E DI
MARTIN, JOSHUA	BAL	190	5TH DIST
MARTIN, JOSHUA	BAL	302	1ST DIST
MARTIN, JULIA	BAL	067	10TH WAR
MARTIN, JULIA	BAL	201	17TH WAR
MARTIN, JULIA W.R.	FRE	174	5TH E DI
MARTIN, LEAH	MGM	405	ROCKERLE
MARTIN, LENNOX J.	ANN	519	HOWARD D
MARTIN, LENOX	ALL	175	7TH E.D.
MARTIN, LEVI	CAR	185	8TH DIST
MARTIN, LEVI	CAR	199	4TH DIST
MARTIN, LEVIN	WOR	181	6TH E DI
MARTIN, LEVISA	CAR	150	NO TWP L
MARTIN, LEWIS	HAR	191	3RD DIST
MARTIN, LITTLETON-BLACK	WOR	173	6TH E DI
MARTIN, LLOYD	HAR	052	1ST DIST
MARTIN, LLOYD	HAR	108	2ND DIST
MARTIN, LORNA	MGM	378	ROCKERLE
MARTIN, LOUIS	ALL	019	2ND E.D.
MARTIN, LOUISA	FRE	418	8TH E DI

Name	County	Page	District
MARTIN, LUSAN	BAL	355	3RD WARD
MARTIN, LUTHER	BAL	193	5TH DIST
MARTIN, LUTHER	BAL	103	15TH WAR
MARTIN, LUTHER	HAR	043	1ST DIST
MARTIN, LYDIA	BAL	231	12TH WAR
MARTIN, M.E.	BAL	160	19TH WAR
MARTIN, MARGARET	BAL	153	16TH WAR
MARTIN, MARGARET	BAL	135	16TH WAR
MARTIN, MARGARET	BAL	200	5TH DIST
MARTIN, MARGARET	ALL	220	CUMBERLA
MARTIN, MARGARETT	HAR	111	2ND DIST
MARTIN, MARGARETT	BAL	016	18TH WAR
MARTIN, MARIA	BAL	213	6TH WARD
MARTIN, MARIA	BAL	405	8TH WARD
MARTIN, MARIAH-BLACK	WOR	317	2ND E DI
MARTIN, MARRIOTT	BAL	070	15TH WAR
MARTIN, MARTHA	BAL	302	3RD WARD
MARTIN, MARTHA A.	BAL	345	3RD WARD
MARTIN, MARY	BAL	426	1ST DIST
MARTIN, MARY	BAL	309	7TH WARD
MARTIN, MARY	BAL	164	6TH WARD
MARTIN, MARY	WAS	138	HAGERSTO
MARTIN, MARY	BAL	120	11TH WAR
MARTIN, MARY	BAL	199	19TH WAR
MARTIN, MARY	CAR	312	1ST DIST
MARTIN, MARY	FRE	165	EMMITTSB
MARTIN, MARY	CHA	292	BOJANTOW
MARTIN, MARY .	WAS	215	1ST DIST
MARTIN, MARY A.	BAL	122	18TH WAR
MARTIN, MARY D.	WAS	016	2ND SUBD
MARTIN, MARY E.	BAL	161	19TH WAR
MARTIN, MARY E.	HAR	108	2ND DIST
MARTIN, MARY J.	TAL	078	EASTON T
MARTIN, MASSEY	MGM	387	ROCKERLE
MARTIN, MATHIAS	CAR	412	2ND DIST
MARTIN, MATTHIAS	FRE	170	5TH E DI
MARTIN, MICAJAH	CAR	218	5TH DIST
MARTIN, MICHAEL	CHA	289	BOJANTOW
MARTIN, MICHAEL	BAL	343	7TH WARD
MARTIN, MICHAEL	BAL	274	1ST DIST
MARTIN, MICHAEL	BAL	273	1ST DIST
MARTIN, MINA	BAL	369	8TH WARD
MARTIN, NANCY	BAL	215	6TH DIST
MARTIN, NANCY	CAR	218	5TH DIST
MARTIN, NANTZY	BAL	312	3RD WARD
MARTIN, NATHAIEL	WOR	200	3RD E DI
MARTIN, NATHAN	MGM	378	ROCKERLE
MARTIN, NATHANIEL	WAS	153	HAGERSTO
MARTIN, NATHANIEL	WAS	153	HAGERSTO
MARTIN, NICHOLAS	TAL	042	EASTON D
MARTIN, NICHOLAS	WAS	293	1ST DIST
MARTIN, NICHOLAS	CAR	197	4TH DIST
MARTIN, NICHOLAS JR.	TAL	044	EASTON D
MARTIN, NORRIS	BAL	334	1ST DIST
MARTIN, OXFORD	KEN	270	1ST DIST
MARTIN, PATRICK	BAL	037	1ST WARD
MARTIN, PATRICK	BAL	457	8TH WARD
MARTIN, PATRICK	ALL	143	6TH E.D.
MARTIN, PAUL	BAL	200	17TH WAR
MARTIN, PAUL	BAL	348	13TH WAR
MARTIN, PETER	CAR	217	5TH DIST
MARTIN, PETER	ALL	059	10TH E.D
MARTIN, PHILANEA	BAL	215	11TH WAR
MARTIN, PHILIP	HAR	096	2ND DIST
MARTIN, PHILIP	HAR	095	2ND DIST
MARTIN, PHILIP	TAL	010	EASTON D
MARTIN, POLLY	BAL	147	11TH WAR
MARTIN, RACHEL	ALL	184	9TH E.D.
MARTIN, RACHEL	BAL	076	10TH WAR
MARTIN, RACHEL	BAL	102	10TH WAR
MARTIN, REBECCA	BAL	411	1ST DIST
MARTIN, RICHARD	BAL	385	13TH WAR
MARTIN, RICHARD	WOR	303	SNOW HIL
MARTIN, ROBERT	WAS	016	2ND SUBD
MARTIN, ROBERT	BAL	185	19TH WAR
MARTIN, ROBERT	DOR	317	1ST DIST
MARTIN, ROBERT	BAL	088	2ND DIST
MARTIN, ROSANA	BAL	014	1ST WARD
MARTIN, ROSE	BAL	128	5TH WARD
MARTIN, ROSETIA	BAL	344	13TH WAR
MARTIN, ROSETTA	BAL	141	16TH WAR
MARTIN, RUCOLPH	CAR	312	1ST DIST
MARTIN, SALLY	BAL	199	17TH WAR
MARTIN, SAMUEL	MGM	378	ROCKERLE
MARTIN, SAMUEL	SOM	410	DUBLIN D
MARTIN, SAMUEL	HAR	138	2ND DIST
MARTIN, SAMUEL	BAL	034	18TH WAR
MARTIN, SAMUEL	BAL	087	18TH WAR
MARTIN, SAMUEL	WAS	282	1ST DIST
MARTIN, SAMUEL	WAS	265	1ST DIST
MARTIN, SAMUEL B.	BAL	317	3RD WARD
MARTIN, SAMUEL J.	BAL	122	1ST WARD
MARTIN, SAMUEL T.	BAL	110	15TH WAR
MARTIN, SARAH	BAL	001	1ST WARD
MARTIN, SARAH	BAL	027	2ND DIST
MARTIN, SARAH	ANN	434	HOWARD D
MARTIN, SARAH	BAL	304	7TH WARD
MARTIN, SARAH C.	BAL	098	1ST WARD
MARTIN, SARAH R.	BAL	312	3RD WARD
MARTIN, SAYLOR	CAR	394	2ND DIST
MARTIN, SIMON	BAL	087	15TH WAR
MARTIN, SISTER ELIZABETH	FRE	198	5TH E DI
MARTIN, SMITH	PRI	053	AQUASCO
MARTIN, SOLOMON	BAL	434	14TH WAR
MARTIN, SOPHIA	FRE	041	FREDERIC
MARTIN, STEPHEN G.	WAS	280	LEITERSB
MARTIN, SUSAN	ST	342	5TH E DI
MARTIN, SUSAN	WAS	208	1ST DIST
MARTIN, SUSAN	BAL	432	14TH WAR
MARTIN, SUSANA	BAL	008	EASTERN
MARTIN, THOAMS	SOM	433	PRINCESS
MARTIN, THOMAS	HAR	101	2ND DIST
MARTIN, THOMAS	HAR	108	2ND DIST
MARTIN, THOMAS	HAR	065	1ST DIST
MARTIN, THOMAS	BAL	267	17TH WAR
MARTIN, THOMAS	BAL	457	14TH WAR
MARTIN, THOMAS	BAL	121	2ND DIST
MARTIN, THOMAS	BAL	107	2ND DIST
MARTIN, THOMAS	BAL	150	2ND DIST
MARTIN, THOMAS	BAL	166	1ST WARD
MARTIN, THOMAS	BAL	229	6TH WARD
MARTIN, THOMAS	ALL	143	6TH E.D.
MARTIN, THOMAS	BAL	023	15TH WAR
MARTIN, THOMAS	WAS	215	1ST DIST
MARTIN, THOMAS	PRI	047	AQUASCO
MARTIN, THOMAS C.	TAL	016	EASTON D
MARTIN, THOMAS E.	HAR	076	BEL AIR
MARTIN, THOMAS M.	BAL	011	4TH WARD
MARTIN, THOMAS S.	CHA	255	MIDDLETO
MARTIN, THOMAS W.*	TAL	044	EASTON D

Name	County	Page	District
MARTIN, V.	BAL	137	1ST WARD
MARTIN, W. N.	DOR	389	1ST DIST
MARTIN, WAKEMAN	HAR	102	2ND DIST
MARTIN, WALTER	BAL	089	2ND DIST
MARTIN, WALTER	BAL	064	2ND DIST
MARTIN, WASHINGTON	BAL	236	1ST DIST
MARTIN, WASHINGTON	BAL	193	5TH DIST
MARTIN, WASHINGTON	FRE	166	EMMITTSB
MARTIN, WESLEY	CEC	208	7TH E DI
MARTIN, WILLIAM	BAL	244	20TH WAR
MARTIN, WILLIAM	FRE	194	5TH E DI
MARTIN, WILLIAM	HAR	124	2ND DIST
MARTIN, WILLIAM	FRE	124	CREAGERS
MARTIN, WILLIAM	FRE	095	FREDERIC
MARTIN, WILLIAM	BAL	365	13TH WAR
MARTIN, WILLIAM	BAL	353	13TH WAR
MARTIN, WILLIAM	CAR	385	2ND DIST
MARTIN, WILLIAM	BAL	123	1ST WARD
MARTIN, WILLIAM	BAL	306	1ST DIST
MARTIN, WILLIAM	ANN	424	HOWARD D
MARTIN, WILLIAM	BAL	140	2ND DIST
MARTIN, WILLIAM	BAL	190	2ND WARD
MARTIN, WILLIAM	BAL	302	3RD WARD
MARTIN, WILLIAM	BAL	418	1ST DIST
MARTIN, WILLIAM	BAL	207	6TH DIST
MARTIN, WILLIAM	SOM	468	TRAPPE D
MARTIN, WILLIAM	SOM	365	BRINKLEY
MARTIN, WILLIAM A.	ALL	073	5TH E.D.
MARTIN, WILLIAM C.	FRE	059	FREDERIC
MARTIN, WILLIAM E.	CAL	056	3RD DIST
MARTIN, WILLIAM G.	HAR	181	3RD DIST
MARTIN, WILLIAM H.	BAL	325	3RD WARD
MARTIN, WILLIAM H.	BAL	383	8TH WARD
MARTIN, WILLIAM J.	KEN	262	1ST DIST
MARTIN, WILLIAM S.	ST	342	5TH E DI
MARTIN, WILLIAM W.	FRE	159	EMMITTSB
MARTIN,A HIA	FRE	181	5TH E DI
MARTIN,CALEB	BAL	021	2ND DIST
MARTIN,MARTHA-BLACK	FRE	418	8TH E DI
MARTINE, JOSEPH	BAL	110	18TH WAR
MARTINET, WILLIAM C.	BAL	398	8TH WARD
MARTINETT, CHARLES F.	BAL	269	17TH WAR
MARTINGRUE, WILLIAM	BAL	209	11TH WAR
MARTINS, JOHN	DOR	456	1ST DIST
MARTINS, MARY	BAL	442	14TH WAR
MARTON, DANIEL	HAR	176	3RD DIST
MARTON, HETTA	HAR	170	3RD DIST
MARTON, JAMES	HAR	198	3RD DIST
MARTON, JOHN	WAS	089	2ND SUBD
MARTON, JOSEPH	HAR	197	3RD DIST
MARTON, LEWIS	HAR	170	3RD DIST
MARTON, MOSES	HAR	146	3RD DIST
MARTY, JACOB *	WAS	061	2ND SUBD
MARTY, MARGARET	WAS	075	2ND SUBD
MARTZ, CARLINE	FRE	097	FREDERIC
MARTZ, DANIEL	WAS	214	1ST DIST
MARTZ, DANIEL L.	FRE	100	FREDERIC
MARTZ, DAVID	WAS	191	1ST DIST
MARTZ, GEORGE	FRE	100	FREDERIC
MARTZ, JACOB	FRE	332	MIDDLETO
MARTZ, JACOB *	WAS	061	2ND SUBD
MARTZ, JOHN	FRE	330	MIDDLETO
MARVAL, PRETTEMAN*	TAL	057	EASTON D
MARVAL, PRITTEMAN JR.	TAL	057	EASTON D
MARVELL, JOHN	SOM	495	SALISBUR
MARVELL, MARY	SOM	495	SALISBUR
MARVELL, THOMAS	SOM	512	BARREN C
MARVIN, TARABABLE*	DOR	449	1ST DIST
MARVIN, WILLIAM	MGM	409	MEDLEY 3
MARWINE, CATHARINE	BAL	098	5TH WARD
MARY, ANN	CHA	249	MIDDLETO
MARY, ANNAH	ALL	211	CUMBERLA
MARY, BRIDGET	BAL	007	9TH WARD
MARY, HOLLIS	HAR	095	2ND DIST
MARY, JOHN	CEC	072	5TH E DI
MARYARD, RUTH	FRE	255	NEW MARK
MARYFILLE, MARIE	BAL	236	12TH WAR
MARYMAN, CAROLINE	ST	262	3RD E DI
MARYMAN, JAMES A.	ST	275	3RD E DI
MARYMAN, MORGAN	ST	254	3RD E DI
MARYNE, DRUCILLA	BAL	278	7TH WARD
MARZ, MARGARET	BAL	238	6TH WARD
MARZ, PHILIP	BAL	237	6TH WARD
MASAL, JOHN	WAS	153	HAGERSTO
MASCLINE, ELIZABETH	BAL	299	17TH WAR
MASDIN, HESAKIAH	KEN	300	3RD DIST
MASE, CHARLES	BAL	068	2ND DIST
MASE, GOERGE	BAL	119	1ST WARD
MASE, JOHN	ALL	004	3RD E.D.
MASELINE, MATHERA H.	BAL	300	17TH WAR
MASEMER, THOMAS	BAL	436	1ST DIST
MASEMINGER, JOHN	BAL	314	1ST DIST
MASEMORE, SUSAN	BAL	216	6TH DIST
MASEMORE,ZEDEKIAH	BAL	050	2ND DIST
MASEN, BILLY	CAL	034	2ND DIST
MASEN, ROBERT	BAL	160	1ST WARD
MASEWILL, JOHN	BAL	120	1ST WARD
MASH, GEORGE	BAL	313	1ST DIST
MASH, JACKSON	CEC	075	NORTHEAS
MASH, THOMAS	BAL	168	1ST WARD
MASH, WILLIAM	BAL	117	15TH WAR
MASHALL, CHARLES	BAL	175	2ND DIST
MASHCOT, AUGUSTA*	BAL	102	10TH WAR
MASHELEY, JANE H.	ANN	281	ANNAPOLI
MASHER, SAMUEL *	TAL	071	EASTON T
MASHEY, JOSEPH	BAL	218	19TH WAR
MASHEY, SAMUEL*	TAL	045	EASTON T
MASHREY, JAMES*	TAL	048	EASTON T
MASIMER, LENARD	CAR	172	8TH DIST
MASIN, JOHN G.	BAL	248	2ND WARD
MASIN, WILLIAM *	ANN	365	4TH DIST
MASINER, SAMUEL	HAR	025	1ST DIST
MASINER, SUSAN	BAL	206	6TH DIST
MASINER, WILLIAM	BAL	206	6TH DIST
MASINO, PAUL	BAL	031	4TH WARD
MASK, GEORGE	BAL	062	15TH WAR
MASK, ISAAC G.	BAL	009	18TH WAR
MASK, JOHN	BAL	145	1ST WARD
MASK, MARY	ANN	438	HOWARD D
MASKELL,JACOB	FRE	042	FREDERIC
MASKER, REBERA*	TAL	069	EASTON T
MASKEY, RALPH*	TAL	061	EASTON D
MASLIN, GEORGE	KEN	306	3RD DIST
MASLIN, GEORGE L.	KEN	265	1ST DIST
MASLIN, JACOB *	KEN	263	1ST DIST
MASLIN, JACOB *	KEN	272	1ST DIST
MASLIN, JAMES	CEC	056	1ST E DI
MASLIN, JOSEPH	ANN	388	4TH DIST
MASLIN, JOSEPH *	KEN	263	1ST DIST
MASN, ELIZA	CAL	006	1ST DIST

Name	County	Page	District
MASNER, MARGARET	ALL	220	CUMBERLA
MASOMER, LYDIA	BAL	206	5TH DIST
MASON, ABRAHAM	BAL	266	7TH WARD
MASON, ALEXANDER-BLACK	ST	308	1ST E DI
MASON, ANDREW	QUE	213	3RD E DI
MASON, ANN	ST	319	4TH E DI
MASON, ANN	BAL	463	1ST DIST
MASON, ANN	BAL	170	16TH WAR
MASON, ANN E.-MULATTO	ST	307	1ST E DI
MASON, ANN L.-BLACK	QUE	125	1ST E DI
MASON, ANNE	BAL	146	16TH WAR
MASON, BABEL A.	WOR	324	1ST E DI
MASON, BEN	BAL	171	2ND DIST
MASON, BENJAMIN	BAL	013	2ND DIST
MASON, BENJAMIN	HAR	067	1ST DIST
MASON, BENJAMIN	FRE	269	NEW MARK
MASON, BENNETT S.	SOM	422	PRINCESS
MASON, BETSEY	CHA	237	HILLTOP
MASON, BRIDGET	BAL	403	8TH WARD
MASON, CATHARINE	BAL	167	16TH WAR
MASON, CHARLES	BAL	173	1ST WARD
MASON, CHARLES	BAL	226	6TH WARD
MASON, CHARLES	QUE	246	5TH E DI
MASON, DANIEL	WOR	348	1ST E DI
MASON, DANILLA	BAL	195	2ND WARD
MASON, EDWARD	BAL	192	6TH WARD
MASON, EDWARD	SOM	432	PRINCESS
MASON, EDWARD	MGM	377	ROCKERLE
MASON, EDWARD-BLACK	CAR	170	NO TWP L
MASON, ELIZA	BAL	424	14TH WAR
MASON, ELIZABETH	BAL	157	11TH WAR
MASON, ELIZABETH	BAL	291	12TH WAR
MASON, ELIZABETH	BAL	254	12TH WAR
MASON, ELIZABETH H.	TAL	068	EASTON T
MASON, ELLEN J.	BAL	137	5TH WARD
MASON, EMORY-BLACK	CAR	093	NO TWP L
MASON, FANNY	BAL	460	1ST DIST
MASON, FREDERICK	BAL	193	2ND WARD
MASON, G.	BAL	154	1ST WARD
MASON, GEORG	BAL	100	2ND DIST
MASON, GEORGE	CEC	153	PORT DUP
MASON, GEORGE C.	CHA	248	HILLTOP
MASON, GEORGE E.-MULATTO	ST	305	2ND E DI
MASON, GEORGE W.	BAL	410	14TH WAR
MASON, GEORGE W.	QUE	157	2ND E DI
MASON, GEORGE-MULATTO	ST	302	2ND E DI
MASON, H.M.	WAS	021	2ND SUBD
MASON, HARRIET	BAL	170	16TH WAR
MASON, HARRIET-BLACK	QUE	157	2ND E DI
MASON, HENRY	ST	289	2ND E DI
MASON, HENRY M. REV.	TAL	074	EASTON T
MASON, HENRY-BLACK	ST	291	2ND E DI
MASON, HENRY-BLACK	ST	293	2ND E DI
MASON, HENRY-BLACK	QUE	157	2ND E DI
MASON, HUBBARD	BAL	420	8TH WARD
MASON, INDIANA	QUE	171	2ND E DI
MASON, ISAAC	QUE	218	3RD E DI
MASON, ISAAC	KEN	311	3RD DIST
MASON, ISAAC-BLACK	CAR	150	NO TWP L
MASON, ISABEL	BAL	425	8TH WARD
MASON, ISACK	TAL	059	EASTON D
MASON, J.Y.	BAL	204	11TH WAR
MASON, JACOB	BAL	406	1ST DIST
MASON, JACOB	TAL	009	EASTON D
MASON, JAME SJR.	WOR	335	1ST E DI
MASON, JAMES	TAL	072	EASTON T
MASON, JAMES	WAS	095	2ND SUBD
MASON, JAMES	BAL	165	6TH WARD
MASON, JAMES	BAL	126	11TH WAR
MASON, JAMES	CEC	045	1ST E DI
MASON, JAMES A.	BAL	091	18TH WAR
MASON, JAMES D.	BAL	020	4TH WARD
MASON, JAMES H.-BLACK	QUE	152	1ST E DI
MASON, JAMES K.	SOM	376	BRINKLEY
MASON, JANE	BAL	134	11TH WAR
MASON, JERRE	ST	275	3RD E DI
MASON, JOHN	SOM	355	BRINKLEY
MASON, JOHN	TAL	067	EASTON T
MASON, JOHN	WOR	335	1ST E DI
MASON, JOHN	WOR	320	1ST E DI
MASON, JOHN	QUE	181	2ND E DI
MASON, JOHN	TAL	120	ST MICHA
MASON, JOHN	TAL	120	ST MICHA
MASON, JOHN	CHA	294	BOJANTOW
MASON, JOHN	CEC	046	1ST E DI
MASON, JOHN	CEC	092	4TH E DI
MASON, JOHN	BAL	432	14TH WAR
MASON, JOHN	BAL	108	18TH WAR
MASON, JOHN	DOR	435	1ST DIST
MASON, JOHN	BAL	195	2ND WARD
MASON, JOHN	BAL	028	15TH WAR
MASON, JOHN	BAL	052	9TH WARD
MASON, JOHN	BAL	300	12TH WAR
MASON, JOHN E.-MULATTO	ST	294	2ND E DI
MASON, JOHN F.	WAS	159	HAGERSTO
MASON, JOHN-BLACK	ST	303	2ND E DI
MASON, JOHN-BLACK	CAR	093	NO TWP L
MASON, JOHN-MULATTO	ST	296	2ND E DI
MASON, JOSEPH	CAL	009	1ST DIST
MASON, JOSEPH	BAL	183	16TH WAR
MASON, JOSEPH-MULATTO	ST	298	2ND E DI
MASON, JOSEPHINE	BAL	195	2ND WARD
MASON, JOSIAH	SOM	379	BRINKLEY
MASON, JULIA	BAL	063	2ND DIST
MASON, JULIA	BAL	131	11TH WAR
MASON, JULIAN	BAL	347	3RD WARD
MASON, LEWIS	WOR	335	1ST E DI
MASON, LLOYD	WAS	204	1ST DIST
MASON, LOUIS-MULATTO	ST	302	2ND E DI
MASON, LOUISA	BAL	410	14TH WAR
MASON, LOUISA D.	HAR	202	3RD DIST
MASON, LUCINDA	MGM	435	CLARKSTR
MASON, LUTHER H.	FRE	048	FREDERIC
MASON, MARIA	BAL	325	1ST DIST
MASON, MARSELLAR*	SOM	378	BRINKLEY
MASON, MARTHA	BAL	460	14TH WAR
MASON, MARTHA	QUE	144	1ST E DI
MASON, MARTHA J.	CAR	209	5TH DIST
MASON, MARTHA T.	CHA	238	HILLTOP
MASON, MARY	FRE	274	NEW MARK
MASON, MARY	BAL	015	18TH WAR
MASON, MARY	WAS	141	HAGERSTO
MASON, MARY	QUE	190	3RD E DI
MASON, MARY	BAL	063	2ND DIST
MASON, MARY	BAL	239	6TH WARD
MASON, MARY	BAL	141	16TH WAR
MASON, MARY	BAL	356	3RD WARD
MASON, MARY	BAL	088	1ST WARD
MASON, MARY A.	FRE	269	NEW MARK
MASON, MARY A.	CHA	289	MIDDLETO

Name	County	Page	District
MASON, MARY K.	BAL	165	11TH WAR
MASON, MARY K.	WAS	136	2ND DIST
MASON, MARY V.	BAL	121	16TH WAR
MASON, MAY	FRE	274	NEW MARK
MASON, MAY E.	FRE	241	NEW MARK
MASON, MC CLURE	ALL	058	10TH E.D
MASON, MIKEL M.	WOR	320	1ST E DI
MASON, MINGO	QUE	218	3RD E DI
MASON, NOAH	CAR	188	4TH DIST
MASON, NOBLE	BAL	289	12TH WAR
MASON, PETER	WOR	329	1ST E DI
MASON, PETER	WOR	330	1ST E DI
MASON, POMPEY-BLACK	QUE	199	3RD E DI
MASON, R.	BAL	163	1ST WARD
MASON, R.B.	BAL	194	19TH WAR
MASON, RACHAEL	BAL	131	11TH WAR
MASON, RACHEL	TAL	054	EASTON D
MASON, REBECA J.	CAR	209	5TH DIST
MASON, REBECCA	WAS	128	2ND DIST
MASON, RICHARD	BAL	423	3RD WARD
MASON, RICHARD	BAL	424	3RD WARD
MASON, RICHARD	BAL	037	4TH WARD
MASON, RICHARD	BAL	158	1ST WARD
MASON, RICHARD	BAL	154	1ST WARD
MASON, RICHARD	BAL	195	2ND WARD
MASON, RICHARD C.	BAL	394	3RD WARD
MASON, RICHARD C.	BAL	088	4TH WARD
MASON, RICHARD-BLACK	ST	294	2ND E DI
MASON, ROBERT	BAL	459	8TH WARD
MASON, SALLY A.	TAL	103	ST MICHA
MASON, SAMUEL	KEN	310	3RD DIST
MASON, SAMUEL	WAS	143	2ND DIST
MASON, SAMUEL	BAL	331	3RD WARD
MASON, SAMUEL I.	BAL	136	1ST WARD
MASON, SARAH	WAS	102	2ND DIST
MASON, SARAH J.	QUE	218	3RD E DI
MASON, SMAUEL F.	BAL	126	1ST WARD
MASON, SOLOMON	BAL	138	5TH WARD
MASON, STEPHEN	WOR	330	1ST E DI
MASON, STEPHEN	SOM	445	DAMES QU
MASON, SUSAN	DOR	298	1ST DIST
MASON, SYLVESTER	BAL	338	3RD WARD
MASON, THOMAS	WOR	330	1ST E DI
MASON, THOMAS	WAS	138	2ND DIST
MASON, THOMAS	KEN	306	3RD DIST
MASON, THOMAS M.	TAL	120	ST MICHA
MASON, THOMAS-BLACK	CAR	093	NO TWP L
MASON, THOMSPON	BAL	291	12TH WAR
MASON, VIRGINIA	WAS	159	HAGERSTC
MASON, WESLEY	BAL	244	17TH WAR
MASON, WILLIAM	BAL	046	4TH WARD
MASON, WILLIAM	BAL	045	4TH WARD
MASON, WILLIAM	BAL	126	11TH WAR
MASON, WILLIAM	SOM	393	BRINKLEY
MASON, WILLIAM	ST	278	3RD E DI
MASON, WILLIAM	ST	283	3RD E DI
MASON, WILLIAM	TAL	074	EASTON T
MASON, WILLIAM	WOR	344	1ST E DI
MASON, WILLIAM	QUE	247	5TH E DI
MASON, WILLIAM	QUE	179	2ND E DI
MASON, WILLIAM	BAL	309	12TH WAR
MASON, WILLIAM	BAL	397	3RD WARD
MASON, WILLIAM	BAL	282	2ND WARD
MASON, WILLIAM	BAL	261	12TH WAR
MASON, WILLIAM	BAL	038	15TH WAR
MASON, WILLIAM	BAL	095	2ND DIST
MASON, WILLIAM	ANN	365	4TH DIST
MASON, WILLIAM C.	BAL	322	3RD WARD
MASON, WILLIAM H.	SOM	376	BRINKLEY
MASON, WILLIAM L.	BAL	438	1ST DIST
MASON, WILLIAM T.	ST	267	3RD E DI
MASON, ZACHARIAH	BAL	048	9TH WARD
MASON,HENRY-BLACK	QUE	178	2ND E DI
MASON,MARY	BAL	204	2ND WARD
MASONHAMER, ADAM	CAR	406	2ND DIST
MASONHAMMER, PETER	CAR	250	3RD DIST
MASONHEIMER, HENRY	CAR	411	2ND DIST
MASONHEIMER, HERNY	CAR	330	MANCHEST
MASONHEIMER, JACOB	CAR	409	2ND DIST
MASOR, ANN	DOR	370	3RD DIVI
MASPHY, JOHN	BAL	102	1ST WARD
MASS, CAROLINE	BAL	125	11TH WAR
MASS, CATHARINE	BAL	184	5TH DIST
MASS, SAMUEL	BAL	272	12TH WAR
MASS, SAUL	BAL	125	11TH WAR
MASSANER, ANN	WAS	146	HAGERSTO
MASSAW, ELIAS	WAS	242	CAVETOWN
MASSAW, JACOB	WAS	142	HAGERSTO
MASSEY, ANN	WOR	274	BERLIN 1
MASSEY, AQUILLA	HAR	031	1ST DIST
MASSEY, BECFORD	KEN	293	3RD DIST
MASSEY, BEN	WOR	274	BERLIN 1
MASSEY, BEN	WOR	274	BERLIN 1
MASSEY, BENJAMIN H.	KEN	293	3RD DIST
MASSEY, CHARLES	ALL	256	CUMBERLA
MASSEY, CLARA	KEN	309	3RD DIST
MASSEY, DAVID	WOR	275	BERLIN 1
MASSEY, EBEN L.	KEN	293	3RD DIST
MASSEY, ELIJAH E.	QUE	124	1ST E DI
MASSEY, ELIZABETH	BAL	393	3RD WARD
MASSEY, ELIZABETH	BAL	264	2ND WARD
MASSEY, EMILY A.	QUE	124	1ST E DI
MASSEY, GEORGE	KEN	304	3RD DIST
MASSEY, HENRY C.	KEN	293	3RD DIST
MASSEY, ISAAC	HAR	031	1ST DIST
MASSEY, JAMES	BAL	292	17TH WAR
MASSEY, JAMES	KEN	309	3RD DIST
MASSEY, JAMES	WOR	275	BERLIN 1
MASSEY, JAMES A.	TAL	073	EASTON T
MASSEY, JOHN A.	WOR	249	1ST CENS
MASSEY, JOHN K.	WOR	276	BERLIN 1
MASSEY, JOHN W.	HAR	003	1ST DIST
MASSEY, JOSIAH	KEN	302	3RD DIST
MASSEY, KENDAL	WOR	275	BERLIN 1
MASSEY, KENDAL	WOR	293	9TH E DI
MASSEY, LEVIN	KEN	297	3RD DIST
MASSEY, MARTHA	WOR	272	BERLIN 1
MASSEY, MARTHA	BAL	129	11TH WAR
MASSEY, MARY	BAL	098	18TH WAR
MASSEY, MARY	KEN	304	3RD DIST
MASSEY, MARY	BAL	246	12TH WAR
MASSEY, MARY A.	BAL	077	18TH WAR
MASSEY, MARY E.	BAL	129	11TH WAR
MASSEY, PHEBE-BLACK	QUE	137	1ST E DI
MASSEY, PURNELL	WOR	280	BERLIN 1
MASSEY, RACHEL	WOR	274	BERLIN 1
MASSEY, RILEY	WOR	280	BERLIN 1
MASSEY, ROBERT	BAL	143	1ST WARD
MASSEY, RUFUS	WOR	256	1ST CENS
MASSEY, SAMUEL	WOR	263	BERLIN 1
MASSEY, SARAH	BAL	058	15TH WAR
MASSEY, SHELLY	WOR	280	BERLIN 1
MASSEY, STEPHEN	QUE	224	4TH E DI
MASSEY, THOMAS	KEN	293	3RD DIST
MASSEY, WARREN P.	SOM	514	BARREN C
MASSEY, WILLIAM	SOM	506	BARREN C
MASSEY, WILLIAM	QUE	174	2ND E DI
MASSEY, WILLIAM	WOR	330	1ST E DI
MASSEY, WILLIAM T.	SOM	350	BRINKLEY
MASSICOT, AUGUSTUS	BAL	315	20TH WAR
MASSICOT, EDWARD	BAL	400	3RD WARD
MASSICOT, WILLIAM A.	BAL	399	3RD WARD
MASSICOTT, CATHERINE	BAL	024	4TH WARD
MASSIE, PAUL	BAL	315	20TH WAR
MASSON, CHARLES	BAL	208	17TH WAR
MASSON, CHARLES A.	BAL	376	3RD WARD
MASSON, JAMES	BAL	335	7TH WARD
MASSON, THOMAS	BAL	308	7TH WARD
MASSXON, NICHOLAS	BAL	073	1ST WARD
MASSY, FRANCIS	CHA	292	BOJANTOW
MASSY, JAMES	CEC	062	1ST E DI
MASSY, JOHN R.	MGM	319	CRACK_IN
MASSY, JULIA	WOR	260	BERLIN 1
MASSY, LUKE	WOR	260	BERLIN 1
MASSY, MARY	CEC	002	ELKTON 3
MASSY, MILLY	KEN	305	3RD DIST
MASSY, MILLY	SOM	530	QUANTICO
MASSY, RACHAEL	ALL	056	10TH E.D
MASSY, SAMUEL	CEC	041	CHESAPEA
MASSY, THOMAS	CEC	041	CHESAPEA
MASSY, WALTER	CAR	111	NO TWP L
MASSY, WILLIAM B.	CAR	095	NO TWP L
MAST, DANIEL	BAL	093	2ND DIST
MAST, JOHN *	BAL	093	2ND DIST
MASTAIN, ELIZABETH	CHA	222	ALLENS F
MASTAYER, CHARLES	BAL	271	20TH WAR
MASTELL, EMILY	BAL	411	8TH WARD
MASTER, AMADA	WAS	099	2ND DIST
MASTER, CONRAD	WAS	254	1ST DIST
MASTER, ELIZABETH	WAS	116	2ND DIST
MASTER, ELIZABETH	BAL	178	19TH WAR
MASTER, GEORGE	ALL	225	CUMBERLA
MASTER, HENRY	CAR	245	3RD DIST
MASTER, MARGARET	CAR	299	1ST DIST
MASTERMAN, CHARLES A.	BAL	366	8TH WARD
MASTERMANN, JAMES	BAL	376	3RD WARD
MASTERS, CATHARINE	PRI	095	SPALDING
MASTERS, CHARLES	BAL	347	3RD WARD
MASTERS, HENRY	WAS	128	2ND DIST
MASTERS, JACOB B.	WAS	099	2ND DIST
MASTERS, JOHN	WAS	099	2ND DIST
MASTERS, MARY	BAL	252	20TH WAR
MASTERS, MARYANN	BAL	354	3RD WARD
MASTERS, RICHARD	ALL	264	CUMBERLA
MASTERS, SAMUEL	WAS	101	2ND DIST
MASTERS, THOMAS B.C.	ALL	169	6TH E.D.
MASTERS, WILLIAM C.	SOM	519	BARREN C
MASTERSON, JOHN	BAL	284	7TH WARD
MASTERTON, JAMES	BAL	221	12TH WAR
MASTIERTON, CHARLES	BAL	218	12TH WAR
MASTINDALE, SAMUEL	CEC	041	CHESAPEA
MASTLAND, THOMAS	BAL	117	1ST WARD
MASTON, JAMES	CEC	181	7TH E DI
MASTON, PERRY	CEC	181	7TH E DI
MASWELL, ELIZABETH	CEC	164	6TH E DI
MASWELL, WILLIAM	BAL	133	1ST WARD
MASY, GEORGE	CAL	034	2ND DIST
MATCENY, CAROLINE	FRE	347	MIDDLETO
MATCHELL, JAMES	BAL	060	18TH WAR
MATCHEN, JONN	BAL	082	18TH WAR
MATCHETE, THOMAS	DOR	412	1ST DIST
MATCHETT, JAMES	BAL	234	17TH WAR
MATEENY, MARGARET	FRE	313	MIDDLETO
MATENA, HENRY	FRE	382	PETERSVI
MATER, JOHN W.	BAL	126	1ST WARD
MATER, WILLIAM	BAL	212	2ND WARD
MATH, CENRAD	BAL	080	1ST WARD
MATH, JOHN	BAL	078	1ST WARD
MATHANY, DANIEL*	BAL	421	3RD WARD
MATHANY, ELEANOR	ST	304	2ND E DI
MATHANY, LOUISA	BAL	421	3RD WARD
MATHARY, MARY C.	CHA	286	BOJANTOW
MATHAS, JOHN W.	BAL	126	1ST WARD
MATHCOT, AUGUSTA*	BAL	102	10TH WAR
MATHENY, JOHN	FRE	119	CREAGERS
MATHER, FRANCES	BAL	076	10TH WAR
MATHER, THOMAS	HAR	191	3RD DIST
MATHERS, CATHARINE	BAL	211	6TH DIST
MATHERS, EDWRAD	BAL	211	6TH DIST
MATHERS, JERAMIAH-BLACK	CAR	381	2ND DIST
MATHERS, JESSE	BAL	192	5TH DIST
MATHERS, ROSANNA	BAL	209	6TH DIST
MATHERS, WILLIAM	BAL	211	6TH DIST
MATHERW, ELIZABETH Z.	CHA	280	BOJANTOW
MATHES, BELINDA	BAL	417	8TH WARD
MATHES, THOMAS	CAR	192	4TH DIST
MATHEUS, JOHN	BAL	278	2ND WARD
MATHEW, CATHERINE	BAL	030	9TH WARD
MATHEW, DENNIS	BAL	097	2ND DIST
MATHEW, ELIZABETH-BLACK	CAR	082	NO TWP L
MATHEW, FRANCIS	CHA	225	ALLENS F
MATHEW, ISAAC	BAL	015	18TH WAR
MATHEW, JOHN-BLACK	CAR	082	NO TWP L
MATHEW, NATHAN B.	MGM	345	CLARKSBU
MATHEW, NICKOLAS	WAS	089	2ND SUBD
MATHEW, PRICOLLE-BLACK	CAR	085	NO TWP L
MATHEW, RACHEL-BLACK	CAR	082	NO TWP L
MATHEW, WILLIAM	BAL	402	1ST DIST
MATHEW, WILLIAM E.	BAL	143	11TH WAR
MATHEWS, ABE	ANN	343	3RD DIST
MATHEWS, ABRAHAM	ANN	342	3RD DIST
MATHEWS, ADALINE	ANN	369	4TH DIST
MATHEWS, AGNES	BAL	216	6TH DIST
MATHEWS, ALEXANDER	CAR	170	NO TWP L
MATHEWS, ALFRED	BAL	020	2ND DIST
MATHEWS, ALZA	BAL	286	1ST DIST
MATHEWS, AMERISA	TAL	018	EASTON D
MATHEWS, AMOS	ANN	336	3RD DIST
MATHEWS, ANDREW	ANN	461	HOWARD D
MATHEWS, ANDREW	BAL	459	8TH WARD
MATHEWS, ANN P.	ANN	447	HOWARD D
MATHEWS, ARCHIBALD	ANN	372	4TH DIST
MATHEWS, BARNEY	BAL	161	11TH WAR
MATHEWS, BENJAMIN	BAL	019	2ND DIST
MATHEWS, BETTY	BAL	145	11TH WAR
MATHEWS, BRIDGET	BAL	456	14TH WAR
MATHEWS, CAROLINE	BAL	149	11TH WAR
MATHEWS, CAROLINE	HAR	143	2ND DIST
MATHEWS, CASSA	ANN	385	4TH DIST
MATHEWS, CHARLES	ANN	441	HOWARD D
MATHEWS, CHARLES	BAL	283	2ND WARD
MATHEWS, CHARLES	TAL	022	EASTON D
MATHEWS, CHARLES-BLACK	FRE	434	8TH E DI
MATHEWS, CHARLOTTE	BAL	047	4TH WARD
MATHEWS, CHARLOTTE	BAL	415	8TH WARD
MATHEWS, CHARLOTTE	ANN	432	HOWARD D
MATHEWS, CHRISTIAN	BAL	463	1ST DIST
MATHEWS, DANIEL	BAL	148	11TH WAR
MATHEWS, DENNIS	BAL	138	11TH WAR
MATHEWS, DNAIEL	BAL	018	2ND DIST
MATHEWS, E.	ANN	271	ANNAPOLI
MATHEWS, EDWARD	BAL	216	6TH DIST
MATHEWS, EDWARD A.	TAL	032	EASTON D
MATHEWS, EDWIN	BAL	198	11TH WAR
MATHEWS, EELIZABETH*	TAL	020	EASTON D
MATHEWS, EHNRY	CAR	290	7TH DIST
MATHEWS, ELI	BAL	426	1ST DIST
MATHEWS, ELIZA	BAL	138	5TH WARD
MATHEWS, ELIZA	BAL	144	11TH WAR
MATHEWS, ELIZA	CHA	222	ALLENS F
MATHEWS, ELLEN	BAL	106	5TH WARD
MATHEWS, ELLEN A.	WOR	310	2ND E DI
MATHEWS, ESTHER	ANN	372	4TH DIST
MATHEWS, F.F.	BAL	161	1ST WARD
MATHEWS, FANNY	BAL	209	11TH WAR
MATHEWS, FRANCIS	WAS	193	1ST DIST
MATHEWS, GARRISCN	TAL	062	EASTON D
MATHEWS, GEORGE	BAL	011	18TH WAR
MATHEWS, GEORGE	ANN	371	4TH DIST
MATHEWS, GEORGE	BAL	205	11TH WAR
MATHEWS, GEORGE	ALL	024	3RD E.D.
MATHEWS, GEORGE K.	WOR	329	1ST E DI
MATHEWS, GEORGE N.	CHA	240	HILLTOP
MATHEWS, GEORGE W.	CAR	191	4TH DIST
MATHEWS, GUSTAVUS	ANN	424	HOWARD D
MATHEWS, HANAH	WAS	063	2ND SUBD
MATHEWS, HARRIET	ANN	367	4TH DIST
MATHEWS, HARRIET	ANN	307	1ST DIST
MATHEWS, HARRIET A.	PRI	025	VANSVILL
MATHEWS, HARRIET-BLACK	CAR	085	NO TWP L
MATHEWS, HARRIETT	BAL	116	11TH WAR
MATHEWS, HARRY	ANN	268	ANNAPOLI
MATHEWS, HENRY	CAR	271	WESTMINS
MATHEWS, HENRY CLAY	BAL	126	5TH WARD
MATHEWS, HENRY-BLACK	CAR	386	2ND DIST
MATHEWS, HESTER	BAL	334	1ST DIST
MATHEWS, HITTY	BAL	266	20TH WAR
MATHEWS, ISAAC	BAL	333	1ST DIST
MATHEWS, ISAAC	BAL	368	1ST DIST
MATHEWS, ISAAC	WOR	336	1ST E DI
MATHEWS, ISRAEL-BLACK	FRE	450	8TH E DI
MATHEWS, JACOB *	BAL	320	1ST DIST
MATHEWS, JAMES	BAL	143	5TH WARD
MATHEWS, JAMES	ALL	238	CUMBERLA
MATHEWS, JAMES	BAL	192	17TH WAR
MATHEWS, JAMES	CAR	241	TANEYTOW
MATHEWS, JAMES	BAL	203	17TH WAR
MATHEWS, JAMES	BAL	203	17TH WAR
MATHEWS, JAMES	FRE	310	WOODSBOR
MATHEWS, JAMES B.	ANN	498	HOWARD D
MATHEWS, JAMES T.	TAL	058	EASTON D
MATHEWS, JAMES-BLACK	CAR	071	NO TWP L
MATHEWS, JANE	BAL	216	6TH DIST
MATHEWS, JANE-MULATTO	FRE	023	FREDERIC
MATHEWS, JOEL	BAL	019	2ND DIST
MATHEWS, JOHN	ALL	242	CUMBERLA
MATHEWS, JOHN	ANN	516	HOWARD D
MATHEWS, JOHN	BAL	339	1ST DIST
MATHEWS, JOHN	BAL	339	1ST DIST
MATHEWS, JOHN	BAL	349	1ST DIST
MATHEWS, JOHN	BAL	427	1ST DIST
MATHEWS, JOHN	BAL	311	1ST DIST
MATHEWS, JOHN	BAL	185	11TH WAR
MATHEWS, JOHN	BAL	303	1ST DIST
MATHEWS, JOHN	BAL	449	14TH WAR
MATHEWS, JOHN	BAL	439	14TH WAR
MATHEWS, JOHN	FRE	139	CREAGERS
MATHEWS, JOHN	KEN	306	3RD DIST
MATHEWS, JOHN D.	BAL	421	1ST DIST
MATHEWS, JOHN H.	BAL	172	6TH WARD
MATHEWS, JOHN H.	TAL	034	EASTON D
MATHEWS, JOHN M.	BAL	397	8TH WARD
MATHEWS, JOHN T.	WAS	097	2ND DIST
MATHEWS, JOHN W.	TAL	017	EASTON D
MATHEWS, JONAS	CEC	096	4TH E DI
MATHEWS, JOSEPH	ANN	501	HOWARD D
MATHEWS, JOSEPH	BAL	168	11TH WAR
MATHEWS, JOSEPH S.	TAL	066	EASTON T
MATHEWS, JOSEPH-BLACK	CAR	083	NO TWP L
MATHEWS, JOSEPH-BLACK	CAR	098	NO TWP L
MATHEWS, JOSHIA	BAL	050	18TH WAR
MATHEWS, JOSHUA	BAL	145	5TH WARD
MATHEWS, JULIA	BAL	145	5TH WARD
MATHEWS, JULIA	ANN	459	HOWARD D
MATHEWS, JULIANA	ANN	516	HOWARD D
MATHEWS, JULIANA	BAL	212	11TH WAR
MATHEWS, KITTY	BAL	453	14TH WAR
MATHEWS, LAVINIA	ANN	453	HOWARD D
MATHEWS, LEWIS H.	CAR	249	3RD DIST
MATHEWS, LEWISA	BAL	039	18TH WAR
MATHEWS, LIZZA	BAL	357	1ST DIST
MATHEWS, LUCY	BAL	211	11TH WAR
MATHEWS, LYDIA-BLACK	CAR	398	2ND DIST
MATHEWS, MARGARET	ANN	371	4TH DIST
MATHEWS, MARGARET A.	BAL	083	18TH WAR
MATHEWS, MARIA	WAS	132	HAGERSTO
MATHEWS, MARSHALL	BAL	316	1ST DIST
MATHEWS, MART A.	CAL	014	1ST DIST
MATHEWS, MARY	BAL	413	14TH WAR
MATHEWS, MARY	FRE	029	FREDERIC
MATHEWS, MARY	ANN	454	HOWARD D
MATHEWS, MARY	BAL	176	11TH WAR
MATHEWS, MEALY-BLACK	FRE	435	8TH E DI
MATHEWS, MILLIA	BAL	074	18TH WAR
MATHEWS, MORDICA H.	BAL	423	1ST DIST
MATHEWS, MOSES	HAR	142	2ND DIST
MATHEWS, NANCY	ANN	450	HOWARD D
MATHEWS, NICHOLAS	ANN	371	4TH DIST
MATHEWS, NICHOLAS	BAL	260	1ST DIST
MATHEWS, NICK	ANN	444	HOWARD D
MATHEWS, NICKOLAS	BAL	202	17TH WAR
MATHEWS, OWEN	BAL	176	11TH WAR
MATHEWS, OWENS	BAL	068	4TH WARD
MATHEWS, PATHY*	BAL	077	4TH WARD
MATHEWS, PATRICK	ALL	242	CUMBERLA
MATHEWS, PERRY	BAL	006	18TH WAR
MATHEWS, PERRY	KEN	274	1ST DIST
MATHEWS, PETER	ALL	250	CUMBERLA
MATHEWS, PRESILLA	BAL	138	11TH WAR
MATHEWS, PRISCILLA	BAL	426	1ST DIST

Name	Co.	Page	District
MATHEWS, PRISCILLA	ANN	382	4TH DIST
MATHEWS, RACHEL	BAL	322	1ST DIST
MATHEWS, RACHEL	BAL	036	2ND DIST
MATHEWS, RACHEL	CAR	223	5TH DIST
MATHEWS, REBECCA	BAL	425	1ST DIST
MATHEWS, RICHARD	BAL	402	1ST DIST
MATHEWS, RICHARD	BAL	408	8TH WARD
MATHEWS, ROBERT	FRE	134	CREAGERS
MATHEWS, ROBERT	WOR	332	1ST E DI
MATHEWS, ROSILLA	FRE	132	CREAGERS
MATHEWS, SAMUEL	DOR	357	3RD DIVI
MATHEWS, SAMUEL	ANN	372	4TH DIST
MATHEWS, SAMUEL	BAL	248	1ST DIST
MATHEWS, SAMUEL G.	ANN	508	HOWARD D
MATHEWS, SAMUEL H.	BAL	421	1ST DIST
MATHEWS, SARAH	BAL	342	1ST DIST
MATHEWS, SARAH	BAL	152	16TH WAR
MATHEWS, SARAH	BAL	410	14TH WAR
MATHEWS, SARRAH	DOR	358	3RD DIVI
MATHEWS, SARRAH	DOR	359	3RD DIVI
MATHEWS, SHEARD	ALL	025	2ND E.D.
MATHEWS, SOLOMON	ANN	311	1ST DIST
MATHEWS, SUSAN	BAL	114	15TH WAR
MATHEWS, TAHTHA	BAL	018	2ND DIST
MATHEWS, THERESA	BAL	101	5TH WARD
MATHEWS, THOMAS	BAL	425	1ST DIST
MATHEWS, THOMAS	BAL	017	2ND DIST
MATHEWS, THOMAS	ANN	482	HOWARD D
MATHEWS, THOMAS	BAL	345	7TH WARD
MATHEWS, THOMAS	DOR	345	3RD DIVI
MATHEWS, THOMAS	HAR	138	2ND DIST
MATHEWS, THOMAS	TAL	055	EASTON D
MATHEWS, THOMAS	WOR	332	1ST E DI
MATHEWS, THOMAS	ST	317	4TH E DI
MATHEWS, THOMAS B.	BAL	421	1ST DIST
MATHEWS, THOMAS B.-BLACK	CAR	083	NO TWP L
MATHEWS, THOMAS J.	BAL	047	4TH WARD
MATHEWS, THOMAS R.	BAL	298	1ST DIST
MATHEWS, TOM	ANN	337	3RD DIST
MATHEWS, W.H.	CAR	403	2ND DIST
MATHEWS, WASHINGTON	CAL	016	1ST DIST
MATHEWS, WILLIAM	FRE	276	NEW MARK
MATHEWS, WILLIAM	BAL	047	4TH WARD
MATHEWS, WILLIAM	FRE	105	CREAGERS
MATHEWS, WILLIAM	BAL	319	1ST DIST
MATHEWS, WILLIAM	BAL	273	1ST DIST
MATHEWS, WILLIAM	BAL	386	1ST DIST
MATHEWS, WILLIAM	BAL	216	6TH DIST
MATHEWS, WILLIAM	BAL	217	6TH DIST
MATHEWS, WILLIAM	BAL	353	7TH WARD
MATHEWS, WILLIAM	BAL	017	2ND DIST
MATHEWS, WILLIAM	ANN	378	4TH DIST
MATHEWS, WILLIAM	ANN	456	HOWARD D
MATHEWS, WILLIAM	BAL	054	2ND DIST
MATHEWS, WILLIAM	TAL	053	EASTON D
MATHEWS, WILLIAM	WOR	349	1ST E DI
MATHEWS, WILLIAM	TAL	018	EASTON D
MATHEWS, WILLIAM H.	ANN	421	HOWARD D
MATHEWS, BASIL-BLACK	FRE	417	8TH E DI
MATHEWS, MARY-MULATTO	CAR	089	NO TWP L
MATHIAS, BENJAMIN	CAR	245	3RD DIST
MATHIAS, BENJAMIN	CAR	250	3RD DIST
MATHIAS, CORNELIAS	CAR	251	3RD DIST
MATHIAS, DANIEL	CAR	250	3RD DIST
MATHIAS, DANIEL	FRE	136	CREAGERS
MATHIAS, DAVID	CAR	347	6TH DIST
MATHIAS, ELIZA	ANN	509	HOWARD D
MATHIAS, FRANCIS	CAR	404	2ND DIST
MATHIAS, GRIFFITH	FRE	113	CREAGERS
MATHIAS, J.	BAL	173	1ST WARD
MATHIAS, JACOB	CAR	354	6TH DIST
MATHIAS, JACOB	CAR	273	WESTMINS
MATHIAS, JOHN	CAR	273	WESTMINS
MATHIAS, JOHN	CAR	387	2ND DIST
MATHIAS, JOHN A.	BAL	258	12TH WAR
MATHIAS, JOSEPH	CAR	266	WESTMINS
MATHIAS, MARGARET	FRE	078	FREDERIC
MATHIAS, NICHOLAS	FRE	303	WOODSBOR
MATHIAS, O. H. P.	CAR	266	WESTMINS
MATHIAS, PERRY	CAR	350	6TH DIST
MATHIAS, PHILLIP	FRE	110	CREAGERS
MATHIAS, RACHAEL	CAR	350	6TH DIST
MATHIAS, REUBEN	CAR	259	3RD DIST
MATHIAS, SAMUEL	CAR	350	6TH DIST
MATHIAS, WILLIAM A. DR.	CAR	273	WESTMINS
MATHIAS, WILLIAM G.	CAR	268	WESTMINS
MATHIAS, WILLIAM L.	HAR	183	3RD DIST
MATHIESON, JOHN	BAL	103	18TH WAR
MATHIEW, JOHN	BAL	010	15TH WAR
MATHINS, ELIAS	BAL	426	1ST DIST
MATHIOTT, ELIZABETH	BAL	013	4TH WARD
MATHIOTT, JOHN B.	BAL	224	6TH WARD
MATHIS, JACOB	HAR	183	3RD DIST
MATHIS, JULIUS	HAR	183	3RD DIST
MATHON, MARTIN	HAR	092	2ND DIST
MATHONA, MARGARET	FRE	103	FREDERIC
MATHRESS, ELIZABETH	CAR	235	UNION TO
MATHUCE, THOMAS	BAL	124	5TH WARD
MATHUNS, JACOB *	BAL	320	1ST DIST
MATINGLEY, SARAH	HAR	147	3RD DIST
MATKIN, LEVIN	BAL	027	15TH WAR
MATKINS, JOSEPHUS-BLACK	CAR	406	2ND DIST
MATKINS, ZEBEDER	BAL	127	1ST WARD
MATKINSON, WILLIAM	CEC	157	PORT DUP
MATLER, SUSAN	BAL	356	13TH WAR
MATLETT, JULIUT	BAL	026	9TH WARD
MATLOCK, EDWARD W.	BAL	162	1ST WARD
MATLOCK, WILLIAM	BAL	162	1ST WARD
MATLOCK, WILLIAM	BAL	163	1ST WARD
MATMILLER, VICTOR	BAL	215	19TH WAR
MATNEY, JOSEPH	DOR	328	3RD DIVI
MATNEY, MARY*	DOR	335	3RD DIVI
MATNEY, RICHARD	BAL	168	1ST WARD
MATONE, BRIDGET	ALL	147	6TH E.D.
MATOX, JAMES	WAS	089	2ND SUBD
MATSEL, CHARLES	CAR	380	2ND DIST
MATSEN, JOHN	FRE	145	10TH E D
MATSEN, MARY-BLACK	FRE	182	5TH E DI
MATSEN, PRISCILLA-BLACK	FRE	182	5TH E DI
MATSEN, WILLIAM-BLACK	FRE	188	5TH E DI
MATSER, JOSEPH	FRE	145	10TH E D
MATSON, CHARLES	BAL	225	19TH WAR
MATSON, ELIZABETH	CEC	173	6TH E DI
MATSON, GEORGE A.	FRE	211	BUCKEYST
MATSON, HARRIET	BAL	383	13TH WAR
MATSON, JAMES	CEC	173	6TH E DI
MATSON, JOSEPH	CHA	271	ALLENS F
MATSON, JOSEPH	BAL	316	7TH WARD
MATSON, RODERICK G.	CHA	232	HILLTOP
MATSON, SAMUEL D.	CHA	232	HILLTOP
MATSON, SARA	CHA	271	ALLENS F
MATSON, SARAH	CEC	169	6TH E DI
MATTAGE, SUSAN L.	BAL	277	2ND WARD
MATTE, SARAH-BLACK	BAL	217	2ND WARD
MATTE, THOMAS-BLACK	BAL	217	2ND WARD
MATTEE, ISAAC-BLACK	CAR	069	NO TWP L
MATTELL, ANN F.	BAL	187	11TH WAR
MATTEN, REUBEN-BLACK	FRE	223	BUCKEYST
MATTENA, MARY C.	WAS	012	WILLIAMS
MATTER, MARY-BLACK	CAR	076	NO TWP L
MATTER, POMEY-BLACK	CAR	088	NO TWP L
MATTER, ROBERT	QUE	214	3RD E DI
MATTERGLY, JOHN	ALL	084	5TH E.D.
MATTESON, SAMUEL J.	BAL	290	3RD WARD
MATTEWS, EMILY	BAL	237	12TH WAR
MATTHARS, MARIA	BAL	419	14TH WAR
MATTHEW, CAROLINE	BAL	259	6TH WARD
MATTHEW, ELIZABETH	CHA	227	ALLENS F
MATTHEW, GRACE	BAL	280	12TH WAR
MATTHEW, H.	BAL	280	12TH WAR
MATTHEW, ISAAC	BAL	224	19TH WAR
MATTHEW, JOHN	CHA	289	MIDDLETO
MATTHEW, LEMUEL	BAL	253	20TH WAR
MATTHEW, MARY	BAL	246	12TH WAR
MATTHEW, PETER	WAS	151	2ND DIST
MATTHEW, REZEN	CHA	295	HILLTOP
MATTHEW, RICHARD	BAL	168	19TH WAR
MATTHEW, SUSAN	BAL	282	12TH WAR
MATTHEW, WILLIAM	CHA	290	BOJANTOW
MATTHEW, WILLIMA	BAL	168	19TH WAR
MATTHEWS, ADAM	DOR	448	1ST DIST
MATTHEWS, AMELIA JANE-BLA	FRE	197	5TH E DI
MATTHEWS, AMOS	BAL	121	16TH WAR
MATTHEWS, AMOS	BAL	178	2ND DIST
MATTHEWS, ANN	BAL	133	16TH WAR
MATTHEWS, ANN	BAL	066	10TH WAR
MATTHEWS, ANN	BAL	380	13TH WAR
MATTHEWS, BASIL	MGM	331	CRACKLIN
MATTHEWS, BENJAMIN	BAL	429	1ST DIST
MATTHEWS, BETSEY	BAL	314	20TH WAR
MATTHEWS, BETSY	BAL	424	14TH WAR
MATTHEWS, CATHARINE	BAL	256	20TH WAR
MATTHEWS, CATHARINE	BAL	297	12TH WAR
MATTHEWS, CHARLES	BAL	240	12TH WAR
MATTHEWS, CHARLES	BAL	269	20TH WAR
MATTHEWS, CHARLES	CEC	139	6TH E DI
MATTHEWS, CHARLES	SOM	396	BRINKLEY
MATTHEWS, CHLOE	BAL	238	12TH WAR
MATTHEWS, CLARA	BAL	106	10TH WAR
MATTHEWS, CORNELIA	MGM	397	ROCKERLE
MATTHEWS, CYRUS	BAL	074	2ND DIST
MATTHEWS, DANIEL	WOR	199	8TH E DI
MATTHEWS, DAVID	DOR	454	1ST DIST
MATTHEWS, DINER	DOR	309	1ST DIST
MATTHEWS, EDWARD	HAR	077	BEL AIR
MATTHEWS, EDWARD	SOM	485	TRAPP DI
MATTHEWS, ELI	BAL	052	9TH WARD
MATTHEWS, ELIZA	BAL	337	13TH WAR
MATTHEWS, ELIZABETH	BAL	338	13TH WAR
MATTHEWS, ELIZABETH	BAL	212	6TH WARD
MATTHEWS, ELLEN	BAL	252	12TH WAR
MATTHEWS, EMELINE	BAL	251	12TH WAR
MATTHEWS, EMMERSON	BAL	359	13TH WAR
MATTHEWS, ESTHER	SOM	396	BRINKLEY
MATTHEWS, FANNY	BAL	073	15TH WAR
MATTHEWS, FOONEY	BAL	431	14TH WAR
MATTHEWS, FRANCIS	CHA	226	ALLENS F
MATTHEWS, FREDERICK	BAL	273	2ND WARD
MATTHEWS, GEORGE	BAL	239	12TH WAR
MATTHEWS, GEORGE	BAL	252	20TH WAR
MATTHEWS, GEORGE	BAL	269	20TH WAR
MATTHEWS, GEORGE	HAR	053	1ST DIST
MATTHEWS, GEORGE	SOM	395	BRINKLEY
MATTHEWS, GEORGE	SOM	538	TYASKIN
MATTHEWS, GEORGE P.	BAL	114	15TH WAR
MATTHEWS, HANNAH	BAL	160	16TH WAR
MATTHEWS, HARRIET A.	BAL	158	6TH WARD
MATTHEWS, HENRIETTA-BLACK	FRE	452	8TH E DI
MATTHEWS, HENRY	SOM	410	DUBLIN D
MATTHEWS, HENRY	BAL	166	19TH WAR
MATTHEWS, HENRY	BAL	312	12TH WAR
MATTHEWS, HENRY W.	SOM	397	BRINKLEY
MATTHEWS, HESTER	BAL	011	15TH WAR
MATTHEWS, ISAAC	BAL	204	19TH WAR
MATTHEWS, ISABEL	HAR	044	1ST DIST
MATTHEWS, JACOB	FRE	258	NEW MARK
MATTHEWS, JACOB F.	HAR	025	1ST DIST
MATTHEWS, JAMES	SOM	436	PRINCESS
MATTHEWS, JAMES	CEC	007	ELKTON 3
MATTHEWS, JAMES	BAL	248	12TH WAR
MATTHEWS, JAMES	BAL	075	15TH WAR
MATTHEWS, JAMES	BAL	153	1ST WARD
MATTHEWS, JAMES	BAL	046	9TH WARD
MATTHEWS, JAMES	BAL	172	6TH WARD
MATTHEWS, JAMES	BAL	118	1ST WARD
MATTHEWS, JAMES	ALL	176	7TH E.D.
MATTHEWS, JAMES	WOR	188	7TH E DI
MATTHEWS, JAMES	WOR	199	8TH E DI
MATTHEWS, JAMES-MULATTO	MGM	431	CLARKSTR
MATTHEWS, JESSEE W.	CEC	121	4TH E DI
MATTHEWS, JOHN	CEC	139	6TH E DI
MATTHEWS, JOHN	MGM	367	BERRYS D
MATTHEWS, JOHN	BAL	274	20TH WAR
MATTHEWS, JOHN	ALL	173	7TH E.D.
MATTHEWS, JOHN	ALL	181	8TH E.D.
MATTHEWS, JOHN	ANN	411	8TH DIST
MATTHEWS, JOHN	ALL	104	5TH E.D.
MATTHEWS, JOHN	ALL	116	5TH E.D.
MATTHEWS, JOHN	BAL	033	1ST WARD
MATTHEWS, JOHN	BAL	221	6TH WARD
MATTHEWS, JOHN	BAL	020	9TH WARD
MATTHEWS, JOHN	BAL	230	12TH WAR
MATTHEWS, JOHN E.	BAL	191	6TH WARD
MATTHEWS, JOHN W.	QUE	230	4TH E DI
MATTHEWS, JONAS	FRE	174	5TH E DI
MATTHEWS, JOSEPH	BAL	140	19TH WAR
MATTHEWS, L.	BAL	117	1ST WARD
MATTHEWS, LEVIN	SOM	429	PRINCESS
MATTHEWS, LEWIS	FRE	186	5TH E DI
MATTHEWS, LIDDLE	BAL	379	13TH WAR
MATTHEWS, LOUIS	BAL	218	19TH WAR
MATTHEWS, MARGARET	BAL	372	13TH WAR
MATTHEWS, MARGARET	BAL	339	13TH WAR
MATTHEWS, MARGARET	BAL	166	19TH WAR
MATTHEWS, MARGARET	CEC	190	5TH E DI
MATTHEWS, MARGARET	BAL	018	9TH WARD
MATTHEWS, MARY	BAL	106	10TH WAR
MATTHEWS, MARY	BAL	255	20TH WAR
MATTHEWS, MARY	FRE	265	NEW MARK
MATTHEWS, MARY	DOR	376	1ST DIST
MATTHEWS, MARY	BAL	374	13TH WAR
MATTHEWS, MARY	SOM	407	DUBLIN D
MATTHEWS, MARY	BAL	444	14TH WAR
MATTHEWS, MARY J.	BAL	105	10TH WAR
MATTHEWS, MRS.	QUE	243	5TH E DI
MATTHEWS, NANCY	DOR	464	1ST DIST
MATTHEWS, O.	BAL	313	12TH WAR
MATTHEWS, PETER	BAL	116	1ST WARD
MATTHEWS, PETER	BAL	123	1ST WARD
MATTHEWS, PIERSON	CEC	139	6TH E DI
MATTHEWS, RACHEL	BAL	375	13TH WAR
MATTHEWS, RACHEL	BAL	314	20TH WAR
MATTHEWS, RACHEL	CEC	095	4TH E DI
MATTHEWS, REBECCA	CEC	075	NORTHEAS
MATTHEWS, REBECCA	WAS	150	HAGERSTO
MATTHEWS, REBECCA	WAS	133	HAGERSTO
MATTHEWS, RICHARD	BAL	246	12TH WAR
MATTHEWS, SALEY*	DOR	376	1ST DIST
MATTHEWS, SAMUEL	BAL	230	12TH WAR
MATTHEWS, SAMUEL	BAL	302	12TH WAR
MATTHEWS, SAMUEL	SOM	396	BRINKLEY
MATTHEWS, SARAH H.	WOR	179	6TH E DI
MATTHEWS, SARAH S.	BAL	073	15TH WAR
MATTHEWS, SOPHIA	BAL	057	10TH WAR
MATTHEWS, STEPHEN	CHA	290	BOJANTOW
MATTHEWS, SUSAN	BAL	233	12TH WAR
MATTHEWS, T.	BAL	117	1ST WARD
MATTHEWS, THOMAS	BAL	073	10TH WAR
MATTHEWS, THOMAS	BAL	201	6TH WARD
MATTHEWS, THOMAS	BAL	262	6TH WARD
MATTHEWS, THOMAS	MGM	320	CRACKLIN
MATTHEWS, THOMAS	SOM	439	DAMES QU
MATTHEWS, THOMAS	SOM	436	PRINCESS
MATTHEWS, THOMAS D.	BAL	171	6TH WARD
MATTHEWS, VICTORIA	BAL	158	6TH WARD
MATTHEWS, WHITTINGTON	SOM	410	DUBLIN D
MATTHEWS, WILLAIM	BAL	421	14TH WAR
MATTHEWS, WILLIAM	MGM	409	MEDLEY 3
MATTHEWS, WILLIAM	SOM	410	DUBLIN D
MATTHEWS, WILLIAM	SOM	425	PRINCESS
MATTHEWS, WILLIAM	CHA	275	ALLENS F
MATTHEWS, WILLIAM	CEC	191	5TH E DI
MATTHEWS, WILLIAM	BAL	161	1ST WARD
MATTHEWS, WILLIAM	BAL	229	12TH WAR
MATTHEWS, WILSON	MGM	351	BERRYS D
MATTHIAS, GEORGE	BAL	473	14TH WAR
MATTHIAS, MATTHEW	BAL	110	10TH WAR
MATTHIAS, MOSES	BAL	279	12TH WAR
MATTHIAS, REBECCA	CEC	095	4TH E DI
MATTIE, JAMES	BAL	382	13TH WAR
MATTILOY, MARY	DOR	392	1ST DIST
MATTIN, CATHERINE*	BAL	340	3RD WARD
MATTING, ELIZA	BAL	282	17TH WAR
MATTINGLEY, FRANCIS	ALL	084	5TH E.D.
MATTINGLEY, GEORGE	ST	269	3RD E DI
MATTINGLEY, JAMES F.	ST	269	3RD E DI
MATTINGLEY, JOSEPH H.	ST	284	2ND E DI
MATTINGLEY, MARY F.	BAL	062	4TH WARD
MATTINGLEY, SYLVESTER	ST	269	3RD E DI
MATTINGLEY, WILLIAM	ST	318	4TH E DI
MATTINGLEY, WILLIAM	BAL	041	4TH WARD
MATTINGLEY, ZACHARIAH	ST	267	3RD E DI
MATTINGLY, ALEXANDER	ST	334	4TH E DI
MATTINGLY, AMANDA	MGM	336	CRACKLIN
MATTINGLY, ANN	ST	320	4TH E DI
MATTINGLY, ANN M.	MGM	336	CRACKLIN
MATTINGLY, BAPTIST	ALL	245	CUMBERLA
MATTINGLY, CLEMENT	ST	276	3RD E DI
MATTINGLY, DOMINICK	ALL	044	10TH E.D
MATTINGLY, EDWARD M.	ST	321	4TH E DI
MATTINGLY, ELIZABETH-MULA	ST	334	4TH E DI
MATTINGLY, ELZIABETH	ST	320	4TH E DI
MATTINGLY, FRANCIS	ST	326	4TH E DI
MATTINGLY, FRANCIS L.	ST	327	4TH E DI
MATTINGLY, GEORGE	ST	340	5TH E DI
MATTINGLY, GEORGE	ALL	232	CUMBERLA
MATTINGLY, GEORGE S.	ST	326	4TH E DI
MATTINGLY, HANSON	ALL	072	5TH E.D.
MATTINGLY, HENRY	ST	346	5TH E DI
MATTINGLY, HENRY	CHA	270	ALLENS F
MATTINGLY, JOHN	BAL	249	17TH WAR
MATTINGLY, JOHN	BAL	077	18TH WAR
MATTINGLY, JOHN	ST	341	5TH E DI
MATTINGLY, JOHN	ST	318	4TH E DI
MATTINGLY, JOHN A.	ST	335	4TH E DI
MATTINGLY, JOHN E.	ST	338	4TH E DI
MATTINGLY, JOHN E.	ALL	222	CUMBERLA
MATTINGLY, JOHN G.	CHA	264	HILLTOP
MATTINGLY, JOSEPH H.	CHA	263	MIDDLETO
MATTINGLY, JOSEPH H.	ST	285	2ND E DI
MATTINGLY, JULIA	CHA	274	ALLENS F
MATTINGLY, JULIAN	CHA	268	BOJANTOW
MATTINGLY, LEVINIA	ST	346	5TH E DI
MATTINGLY, MARY	ST	335	4TH E DI
MATTINGLY, MARY	ANN	486	HOWARD D
MATTINGLY, MARY J.	ST	315	4TH E DI
MATTINGLY, MONICA	CHA	217	ALLENS F
MATTINGLY, PETER J.N.	ST	326	4TH E DI
MATTINGLY, SARAH	ANN	446	HOWARD D
MATTINGLY, SARAH A.	ST	325	4TH E DI
MATTINGLY, SUSAN	ALL	113	5TH E.D.
MATTINGLY, SUSANNA	ST	322	4TH E DI
MATTINGLY, SYLVESTER	ALL	084	5TH E.D.
MATTINGLY, THOMAS	PRI	065	NOTTINGH
MATTINGLY, WILLIAM	ST	278	3RD E DI
MATTINGLY, BARBAR	ALL	221	CUMBERLA
MATTINGSLY, DORETY	BAL	127	18TH WAR
MATTINGSLY, JOHN A.	BAL	128	18TH WAR
MATTIOS, GEORGE-MULATTO	ST	330	4TH E DI
MATTISON, GEORGE	BAL	170	16TH WAR
MATTISON, JOHN I.	BAL	290	3RD WARD
MATTOCK, R. C.	BAL	062	10TH WAR
MATTOCKS, HARRIET	BAL	381	13TH WAR
MATTON, J.W.	BAL	174	1ST WARD
MATTON, JAMES	BAL	141	2ND DIST
MATTON, SUSAN	HAR	096	2ND DIST
MATTOX, E. DEMINIA	ST	332	4TH E DI
MATTOX, EDMUND S.T.	ST	331	4TH E DI
MATTOX, FRANK	BAL	429	14TH WAR
MATTOX, GEORGE F.	ST	332	4TH E DI
MATTOX, HANNAH	BAL	434	14TH WAR
MATTOX, JOHN	FRE	097	FREDERIC
MATTOX, MARIA	BAL	413	14TH WAR
MATTS, LEONIZA	BAL	294	12TH WAR
MATUM, EDWARD	BAL	113	1ST WARD
MAUAN, SILSA	BAL	388	13TH WAR
MAUB, ROBERT	BAL	168	1ST WARD
MAUCOCK, SARAH C. *	ANN	402	8TH DIST
MAUER, GEORGE H.	BAL	120	11TH WAR
MAUGENS, DAVID	FRE	374	CATOCTIN

Name	County	Page	District
MAUGH, PATRICK	HAR	083	2ND DIST
MAUGHER, MARY J.	BAL	252	6TH WARD
MAUGHLIN, PHILLIP	ALL	071	5TH E.D.
MAUGHLIN, WILLIAM W.	BAL	251	6TH WARD
MAUGHT, A.C.H.	FRE	391	PETERSVI
MAUGHT, CONRAD W.	FRE	397	PETERSVI
MAUGHT, HENRY	FRE	386	PETERSVI
MAUGHT, MARY	FRE	391	PETERSVI
MAUGHT, SAMUEL	FRE	386	PETERSVI
MAUGHT, THOMAS J.	FRE	391	PETERSVI
MAUGHT, WILLIAM	FRE	386	PETERSVI
MAUL, ELLEN	BAL	300	3RD WARD
MAUL, JOHN	BAL	001	9TH WARD
MAUL, MARY	BAL	211	17TH WAR
MAUL, PRISCILLA	HAR	096	2ND DIST
MAUL, REBECCA	HAR	079	2ND DIST
MAULBERRY, JANE	BAL	347	1ST DIST
MAULDEN, BENJAMIN	CEC	068	5TH E DI
MAULDEN, EVAN	CEC	152	PORT DUP
MAULDEN, JAMES	CEC	076	NORTHEAS
MAULDEN, JOHN	CEC	068	5TH E DI
MAULDEN, MILLICENT	CEC	075	NORTHEAS
MAULDEN, ZEBULON	CEC	077	NORTHEAS
MAULDER, JOHN	CEC	076	NORTHEAS
MAULDIN, JOHN	CEC	068	5TH E DI
MAULDING, ENOCH	CAL	004	1ST DIST
MAULEY, JAMES	BAL	205	2ND WARD
MAULSBY, DAVID L.	BAL	113	5TH WARD
MAULSBY, GEORGE	BAL	096	2ND DIST
MAULSBY, JANE	HAR	088	2ND DIST
MAULSBY, MORRIS	HAR	082	2ND DIST
MAULSBY, SARAH	FRE	029	FREDERIC
MAULSBY, SUSAN	BAL	086	4TH WARD
MAULSBY, WILLIAM J.	BAL	105	10TH WAR
MAULSUD, SAMUEL	BAL	160	11TH WAR
MAULWY, ROBERT	BAL	003	4TH WARD
MAULY, JOHN	BAL	151	1ST WARD
MAULY, MARY	BAL	240	2ND WARD
MAUN, JOSEPH	BAL	390	13TH WAR
MAUNEY, ELIZABETH	BAL	085	2ND DIST
MAUNS, JAMES *	BAL	245	6TH WARD
MAUPH, JOHN *	BAL	082	2ND DIST
MAUPIN, J. C.	BAL	475	14TH WAR
MAURACE, ELIZABETH	BAL	343	1ST DIST
MAURE, HENRY	BAL	120	11TH WAR
MAURER, HENRY	BAL	231	6TH WARD
MAURICE, JAMES	ST	317	4TH E DI
MAURICE, JOHN	BAL	421	3RD WARD
MAURICE, MARY	BAL	357	1ST DIST
MAURY, JAMES C.	BAL	441	14TH WAR
MAURY, MARTHA A.	BAL	441	14TH WAR
MAUS, JACOB	CAR	313	1ST DIST
MAUS, LEVI C.	CAR	313	1ST DIST
MAUSER, ADOLPH	BAL	263	12TH WAR
MAUSER, JOHN	BAL	038	18TH WAR
MAUSSER, JOHN	BAL	105	5TH WARD
MAUSTEAD, CECELIA	BAL	283	20TH WAR
MAVEL, ANTONIA	CEC	023	ELKTCN 3
MAWBERRY, ELLEN	BAL	269	1ST DIST
MAWBLER, AMANDA	BAL	111	18TH WAR
MAWBRAY, MARY	BAL	033	1ST WARD
MAWEY, THOMAS	BAL	047	9TH WARD
MAWLDON, JOHN	BAL	093	1ST WARD
MAWRICE, JOHN B.	CHA	266	MIDDLETO
MAX, JOHN	BAL	219	19TH WAR
MAX, JOHN	CHA	229	MIDDLETO
MAXCEY, EDWARD	BAL	134	1ST WARD
MAXEL, ABRAHAM	FRE	138	CREAGERS
MAXEL, SAMUEL	FRE	175	5TH E DI
MAXEY, ED	BAL	142	1ST WARD
MAXEY, ECWARD	BAL	368	3RD WARD
MAXFIELD, ANN	HAR	163	3RD DIST
MAXFIELD, CATHARINE	BAL	415	14TH WAR
MAXFIELD, DORCAS	BAL	076	10TH WAR
MAXFIELD, ISAAC	BAL	134	5TH WARD
MAXFIELD, JAMES	HAR	184	3RD DIST
MAXFIELD, JANE	HAR	053	1ST DIST
MAXFIELD, JOHN	BAL	422	8TH WARD
MAXFIELD, MOSES	BAL	145	1ST WARD
MAXFIELD, SAMUEL*	BAL	371	3RD WARD
MAXFIELD, SARAH	BAL	302	1ST DIST
MAXWELL, ALEXANDER	BAL	072	2ND DIST
MAXWELL, ALEXANDER	CEC	009	ELKTON 3
MAXWELL, ALLEN	CEC	003	ELKTON 3
MAXWELL, AMANDA	BAL	276	12TH WAR
MAXWELL, AMOS	HAR	184	3RD DIST
MAXWELL, ANN	BAL	408	3RD WARD
MAXWELL, ANNA	BAL	014	18TH WAR
MAXWELL, BRIDGET	ALL	237	CUMBERLA
MAXWELL, CHARLES	CEC	006	ELKTON 3
MAXWELL, CHARLES	BAL	001	4TH WARD
MAXWELL, CHARLES G.	BAL	140	1ST WARD
MAXWELL, DAVID	CEC	164	6TH E DI
MAXWELL, DAVID	BAL	278	20TH WAR
MAXWELL, EDWARD	ALL	218	CUMBERLA
MAXWELL, ELIZA	BAL	044	1ST WARD
MAXWELL, FRANCES E.	BAL	308	7TH WARD
MAXWELL, GECRGE	BAL	038	1ST WARD
MAXWELL, GEORGE	BAL	109	18TH WAR
MAXWELL, JAMES	BAL	105	1ST WARD
MAXWELL, JAMES L.	CEC	152	PORT DUP
MAXWELL, JAMES W.	CEC	153	PORT DUP
MAXWELL, JOHN	BAL	363	13TH WAR
MAXWELL, JOHN	HAR	092	2ND DIST
MAXWELL, JOHN	BAL	112	1ST WARD
MAXWELL, JCHN	BAL	286	7TH WARD
MAXWELL, JOHN	BAL	041	9TH WARD
MAXWELL, JOHN V.	BAL	182	11TH WAR
MAXWELL, JOSEPH	BAL	166	11TH WAR
MAXWELL, MARY	BAL	261	1ST DIST
MAXWELL, MARY E.	CEC	164	6TH E DI
MAXWELL, PERRY	KEN	296	3RD DIST
MAXWELL, PHEBE	HAR	125	2ND DIST
MAXWELL, REBECCA	BAL	199	11TH WAR
MAXWELL, ROBERT	BAL	036	1ST WARD
MAXWELL, SAMUEL	BAL	044	1ST WARD
MAXWELL, SAMUEL	BAL	302	20TH WAR
MAXWELL, SAMUEL	CEC	090	4TH E DI
MAXWELL, SARAH	BAL	240	6TH WARD
MAXWELL, THOMAS	ALL	243	CUMBERLA
MAXWELL, THOMAS	CEC	164	6TH E DI
MAXWELL, WILLIA MG.	HAR	174	3RD DIST
MAXWELL, WILLIAM	HAR	184	3RD DIST
MAXWELL, WILLIAM	KEN	246	2ND DIST
MAXWELL, WILLIAM	BAL	024	9TH WARD
MAXWELL, WILLIAM	BAL	226	2ND WARD
MAXWELL, WILLIAM	BAL	140	1ST WARD
MAXWELL, WILLIAM	BAL	133	1ST WARD
MAXWELL, WILLIAM	KEN	296	3RD DIST
MAXWELL, WILLIAM B.	BAL	125	1ST WARD
MAXWOOD, BENEDICT	HAR	126	2ND DIST
MAXWOOD, HENRY	HAR	127	2ND DIST
MAY, AUGUSTUS	CAR	411	2ND DIST
MAY, BENJAMIN F.	CEC	004	ELKTON 3
MAY, BRIDGET O.	BAL	411	3RD WARD
MAY, CAROLINE	WAS	129	HAGERSTO
MAY, CHARLES	BAL	229	2ND WARD
MAY, DORCAS	BAL	272	20TH WAR
MAY, EDWARD	BAL	254	12TH WAR
MAY, ELIZABETH	CAR	102	NO TWP L
MAY, FRANCES	BAL	255	6TH WARD
MAY, FRANCIS	BAL	101	18TH WAR
MAY, FREDERICK	BAL	400	14TH WAR
MAY, FREDERICK	BAL	142	19TH WAR
MAY, GECRGE	BAL	055	18TH WAR
MAY, GECRGE	BAL	382	3RD WARD
MAY, GEORGE F.	WAS	145	HAGERSTO
MAY, GEORGE L.	CEC	124	5TH E DI
MAY, HENRY	CEC	058	1ST E DI
MAY, 'HENRY	BAL	387	13TH WAR
MAY, JAMES	KEN	291	3RD DIST
MAY, JAMES	BAL	370	8TH WARD
MAY, JAMES A.	BAL	338	13TH WAR
MAY, JANE	BAL	370	8TH WARD
MAY, JANE	BAL	323	1ST DIST
MAY, JOHN	BAL	378	8TH WARD
MAY, JOHN	BAL	035	15TH WAR
MAY, JOHN	BAL	065	1ST WARD
MAY, JOHN	BAL	195	5TH DIST
MAY, JOHN	BAL	364	13TH WAR
MAY, JOHN	BAL	303	20TH WAR
MAY, JOSHUA	QUE	123	1ST E DI
MAY, LOUISA	WAS	130	HAGERSTO
MAY, MARGARET	BAL	378	8TH WARD
MAY, MARY	WAS	159	HAGERSTO
MAY, MARY	BAL	088	4TH WARD
MAY, MARY	BAL	460	14TH WAR
MAY, MAY	WAS	173	FUNKSTOW
MAY, MERCY K.	WAS	164	HAGERSTO
MAY, HOBERT	BAL	365	8TH WARD
MAY, ROSALIE	BAL	388	13TH WAR
MAY, SARAH	QUE	159	2ND E DI
MAY, SISTER LUCIA	FRE	197	5TH E DI
MAY, SOLOMON	BAL	254	6TH WARD
MAY, SOPHIA	BAL	344	13TH WAR
MAY, STEPHEN	BAL	420	8TH WARD
MAY, THCMAS	BAL	135	1ST WARD
MAY, THCMAS	BAL	154	1ST WARD
MAY, THOMAS	CAR	103	NO TWP L
MAY, W. L. MISS-	ANN	368	4TH DIST
MAY, W.C.T.	BAL	142	19TH WAR
MAY, WILLIAM	BAL	401	14TH WAR
MAY, WILLIAM	BAL	399	14TH WAR
MAY, WILLIAM	BAL	145	1ST WARD
MAY, WILLIAM H.	BAL	040	9TH WARD
MAY, WILLIAM H.	CEC	004	ELKTON 3
MAY,EDWARD	BAL	121	1ST WARD
MAYBEE, JONATHAN	FRE	087	FREDERIC
MAYBERRY, ALBERT G.	FRE	009	FREDERIC
MAYBERRY, ELIZABETH	WAS	036	2ND SUBD
MAYBERRY, JACCB-BLACK	FRE	420	8TH E DI
MAYBERRY, JESTINIAN	FRE	004	FREDERIC
MAYBERRY, MARY	FRE	002	FREDERIC
MAYBERRY, PHEBE	CEC	087	4TH E DI
MAYBURY, GRACE	BAL	053	2ND DIST
MAYBURY, MARK	BAL	148	16TH WAR
MAYBURY, THOMAS	BAL	448	14TH WAR
MAYDALENA, MARY	BAL	233	12TH WAR
MAYDWELL, JOHN	BAL	172	6TH WARD
MAYDWELL, WILLIAM B.	BAL	304	3RD WARD
MAYDWELL, WILLIAM H.	BAL	304	3RD WARD
MAYEL, JAMES	BAL	130	1ST WARD
MAYER, ARY	BAL	244	1ST DIST
MAYER, BRANZ	BAL	320	20TH WAR
MAYER, CHARLES F.	BAL	249	12TH WAR
MAYER, CHARLES F.	BAL	196	11TH WAR
MAYER, ERNESTINE	MGM	394	ROCKERLE
MAYER, FREDERICK	BAL	125	16TH WAR
MAYER, HENRY	CAR	266	WESTMINS
MAYER, PATRICK	ANN	514	HOWARD D
MAYERS, SMAUEL	BAL	033	2ND DIST
MAYERS, SWAN	BAL	185	5TH DIST
MAYES, ELIY	BAL	223	12TH WAR
MAYES, GEORGE W.	BAL	363	8TH WARD
MAYES, HENRY	BAL	337	3RD WARD
MAYFIELD, JOHN J.	ANN	459	HOWARD D
MAYFORD, THOMAS	BAL	281	2ND WARD
MAYGANGLE, HENRIETTA	FRE	020	FREDERIC
MAYGER, PAMILIA	BAL	087	4TH WARD
MAYGER, RICHARD	BAL	087	4TH WARD
MAYHEW, J.	BAL	147	1ST WARD
MAYHEW, JAMES	WAS	243	CAVETOWN
MAYHEW, JOHN	WAS	279	LEITERSB
MAYHEW, JOHN	WAS	287	1ST DIST
MAYHEW, JOHN	BAL	262	20TH WAR
MAYHEW, JOHN	FRE	120	CREAGERS
MAYHEW, JOSEPH P.	WAS	279	LEITERSB
MAYHEW, MARY H.	WAS	266	1ST DIST
MAYHEW, WASHINGTON	WAS	264	1ST DIST
MAYHEW, WILLIAM E.	BAL	146	11TH WAR
MAYHUGH, JOHN W.	PRI	090	MARLBROU
MAYHUGH, PHILLIP	PRI	090	MARLBROU
MAYHUGH, SARAH	PRI	090	MARLBROU
MAYHUGH, WILLIAM	PRI	073	MARLBROU
MAYICE, DANIEL	BAL	207	19TH WAR
MAYLAND, F.	BAL	163	1ST WARD
MAYLOR, SAMUEL	WAS	144	2ND DIST
MAYLOT, ELLEN	WAS	097	2ND DIST
MAYNADEN, ELIZA	BAL	086	2ND DIST
MAYNADIER, CATHARINE L.	HAR	087	2ND DIST
MAYNADIER, WILLIAM M.	HAR	087	2ND DIST
MAYNAN, GEORGE	BAL	292	12TH WAR
MAYNARD, CHARELS	HAR	177	3RD DIST
MAYNARD, DENNIS H.	FRE	434	8TH E DI
MAYNARD, DOLLY	CAL	057	3RD DIST
MAYNARD, ELENORE	FRE	433	8TH E DI
MAYNARD, EPHRAIM	FRE	427	8TH E DI
MAYNARD, JAMES A.	BAL	396	8TH WARD
MAYNARD, JAMES H.	FRE	427	8TH E DI
MAYNARD, JOHN	BAL	256	12TH WAR
MAYNARD, JOHN H.	ANN	269	ANNAPOLI
MAYNARD, JULIANN	TAL	095	ST MICHA
MAYNARD, M.	ANN	283	ANNAPOLI
MAYNARD, PHIEBE	BAL	321	12TH WAR
MAYNARD, ROBERT F.	BAL	065	15TH WAR
MAYNARD, STEPHEN	CAL	034	2ND DIST
MAYNARD, THOMAS	FRE	447	8TH E DI
MAYNARD, THOMAS G.	FRE	446	8TH E DI
MAYNARD, THOMAS H.	TAL	065	EASTON T
MAYNARD, WILLIAM	BAL	052	15TH WAR
MAYNE, JAMES L.	BAL	204	19TH WAR
MAYNE, NANCY	BAL	273	7TH WARD
MAYNER, ANN	BAL	277	20TH WAR
MAYNES, J.	BAL	165	1ST WARD
MAYNIRE, ELLEN	BAL	228	19TH WAR
MAYNIRE, JOHN	BAL	264	20TH WAR
MAYNS, MARIA	BAL	184	5TH DIST
MAYO, A.	BAL	136	1ST WARD
MAYO, CATHERINE	BAL	294	20TH WAR
MAYO, ELIZA	BAL	280	20TH WAR
MAYO, ISAAC	ANN	315	1ST DIST
MAYO, J.	BAL	149	1ST WARD
MAYO, JOHN	BAL	151	16TH WAR
MAYO, SAMUEL	BAL	385	13TH WAR
MAYOY, PATRICK *	WAS	149	2ND DIST
MAYOY, THOMAS	WAS	150	2ND DIST
MAYPOLE, JOHN J.	BAL	210	17TH WAR
MAYPOLE, TOBIAS	BAL	210	17TH WAR
MAYPOLE, TOBIAS	BAL	274	17TH WAR
MAYRILLA, JACOB	WAS	215	1ST DIST
MAYS, ABRAHAM	BAL	188	5TH DIST
MAYS, ELIZABETH	HAR	116	2ND DIST
MAYS, ELIZABETH	FRE	254	NEW MARK
MAYS, EMILY	BAL	256	12TH WAR
MAYS, JACOB	FRE	266	NEW MARK
MAYS, JAMES	BAL	030	2ND DIST
MAYS, JAMES F.	BAL	305	1ST DIST
MAYS, JEREMIAH	BAL	454	1ST DIST
MAYS, JOHN	BAL	056	2ND DIST
MAYS, JOHN C.	BAL	433	1ST DIST
MAYS, JOHN P. JR.	BAL	433	1ST DIST
MAYS, LEWIS	BAL	018	2ND DIST
MAYS, NANCY	BAL	385	1ST DIST
MAYS, RACHEL	BAL	055	2ND DIST
MAYS, ROBERT	BAL	219	6TH DIST
MAYS, ROBERT	BAL	272	20TH WAR
MAYS, SARAH	BAL	152	11TH WAR
MAYSE, ROWAN	BAL	045	2ND DIST
MAYSILLA, HENRY	WAS	214	1ST DIST
MAYSILLA, JOHN *	WAS	171	FUNKSTOW
MAYSILLER, HENRY	WAS	214	1ST DIST
MAYSON, EDWARD	WOR	338	1ST E DI
MAYSON, WILLSON	WOR	317	2ND E DI
MAYVILLA, JOHN *	WAS	171	FUNKSTOW
MAYWARD, SUSAN A.	BAL	081	1ST WARD
MAZEL, PHILIP	BAL	075	10TH WAR
MAZICKS, ELIZABETH	CAR	126	NO TWP L
MC CANDY, PATRICK	ALL	140	6TH E.D.
MC ABEE, ANN	BAL	318	7TH WARD
MC ABEE, CHARLES W.	FRE	223	BUCKEYST
MC ABEE, JOHN W.	BAL	124	18TH WAR
MC ABEE, WILLIAM B.	WAS	140	HAGERSTO
MC ADAM, MISS M.	FRE	199	5TH E DI
MC ADAM, SAMUEL	CHA	244	HILLTOP
MC ADOW, SUSAN	BAL	109	5TH WARD
MC AFEE, ARCHIBALD	FRE	152	10TH E D
MC AFEE, JAMES	BAL	256	20TH WAR
MC AFEE, JOHN	BAL	272	20TH WAR
MC AFEE, WILLIAM	BAL	253	20TH WAR
MC AHALIE, ELIZABETH	ALL	217	CUMBERLA
MC ALBER, HUGH J.	FRE	024	FREDERIC
MC ALDERWINE, ALFRED	ALL	253	CUMBERLA
MC ALEE, ROSANNA	FRE	019	FREDERIC
MC ALEER, ANN	BAL	454	14TH WAR
MC ALEESE, PATRICK	BAL	275	2ND WARD
MC ALEESE, PHEBE	BAL	053	4TH WARD
MC ALESTER, RICHARD	BAL	446	8TH WARD
MC ALIER, CHARLES	ALL	215	CUMBERLA
MC ALISE, THOMAS	BAL	020	9TH WARD
MC ALISTER, ARCHIBALD E.	BAL	365	8TH WARD
MC ALISTER, CHARLOTTE	WOR	206	4TH E DI
MC ALISTER, DANIEL	BAL	364	8TH WARD
MC ALISTER, DANIEL	BAL	173	1ST WARD
MC ALISTER, DAVID	CEC	031	CHESAPEA
MC ALISTER, GEORGE W.	WAS	163	2ND DIST
MC ALISTER, HIRAM	BAL	166	11TH WAR
MC ALISTER, HIRAM	BAL	058	10TH WAR
MC ALISTER, JAMDS	BAL	285	7TH WARD
MC ALISTER, JAMES	BAL	128	1ST WARD
MC ALISTER, MARY	BAL	188	6TH WARD
MC ALISTER, MARY A.	BAL	274	7TH WARD
MC ALISTER, SARAH	BAL	293	7TH WARD
MC ALISTER, THOMAS	BAL	459	1ST DIST
MC ALISTER, WILLIAM	BAL	266	7TH WARD
MC ALISTER, WILLIAM	BAL	285	1ST DIST
MC ALISTER, WILLIAM JR.	BAL	454	8TH WARD
MC ALL, MARY	CHA	278	BOJANTOW
MC ALLEN, GEORGE W.	WOR	186	7TH E DI
MC ALLEN, LEWIN	WOR	305	SNOW HIL
MC ALLEN, LUCRETEN	WOR	183	6TH E DI
MC ALLEN, WILLIAM A.	WOR	201	3RD E DI
MC ALLER, ANNE	BAL	191	11TH WAR
MC ALLESE, EDWARD	BAL	280	2ND WARD
MC ALLESTER, MARY	BAL	219	12TH WAR
MC ALLIN, THOMAS W.	BAL	280	2ND WARD
MC ALLISTER, ADAM	SOM	462	HANGARY
MC ALLISTER, ALEXANDER	BAL	220	6TH WARD
MC ALLISTER, ALEXANDER	CAR	307	1ST DIST
MC ALLISTER, ARCHIBALD	BAL	003	4TH WARD
MC ALLISTER, CHARLES	QUE	157	2ND E DI
MC ALLISTER, DANIEL	BAL	110	18TH WAR
MC ALLISTER, ELIZA	BAL	447	14TH WAR
MC ALLISTER, ELIZA	BAL	092	1ST WARD
MC ALLISTER, ELIZABETH	SOM	495	SALISBUR
MC ALLISTER, JAMES	SOM	496	SALISBUR
MC ALLISTER, JAMES	CAR	301	1ST DIST
MC ALLISTER, JANE	BAL	166	11TH WAR
MC ALLISTER, JANE	BAL	057	10TH WAR
MC ALLISTER, JESSE	SOM	495	SALISBUR
MC ALLISTER, JOHN	BAL	285	1ST DIST
MC ALLISTER, JOHN	BAL	115	1ST WARD
MC ALLISTER, JOHN	BAL	106	5TH WARD
MC ALLISTER, JOSEPH	BAL	253	1ST DIST
MC ALLISTER, MARGARET	BAL	250	6TH WARD
MC ALLISTER, MARTHA	WAS	137	2ND DIST
MC ALLISTER, MARY	BAL	250	6TH WARD
MC ALLISTER, MARY	BAL	058	10TH WAR
MC ALLISTER, MARY	BAL	319	20TH WAR
MC ALLISTER, MARY A.	BAL	254	1ST DIST
MC ALLISTER, NATHAN	BAL	009	4TH WARD
MC ALLISTER, R.	BAL	318	20TH WAR
MC ALLISTER, RICHARD	BAL	053	4TH WARD
MC ALLISTER, ROBERT	BAL	381	3RD WARD
MC ALLISTER, SPENCER E.	SOM	522	BARREN C
MC ALLISTER, WILLIAM H.	BAL	185	16TH WAR
MC ALLY, ARCHIBALD	BAL	133	1ST WARD
MC ALOY, MARY	WAS	149	2ND DIST
MC ALROY, WILLIAM	WAS	048	2ND SUBD
MC ALUR, HUGH	FRE	024	FREDERIC
MC ALWIE, WILLIAM	BAL	368	13TH WAR

MC ANALLY, MARGARET ALL 052 10TH E.D
MC ANALLY, WILLIAM ALL 056 10TH E.D
MC ANANLY, THOMAS * ALL 051 10TH E.D
MC ANARY, FRANK ALL 181 8TH E.D.
MC ANCARNY, MICHAEL ALL 049 10TH E.D
MC ANDEY, THOMAS ALL 143 6TH E.D.
MC ANDREW, FRANCIS ALL 209 CUMBERLA
MC ANDREW, JOHN BAL 274 1ST DIST
MC ANDREW, MARGARET BAL 394 14TH WAR
MC ANDRY, JAMES ALL 143 6TH E.D.
MC ANOVEY, PATRICK ALL 143 6TH E.D.
MC ARDEL, RACHAEL BAL 066 15TH WAR
MC ARDLE, THOMAS BAL 289 7TH WARD
MC ARDLE, THOMAS BAL 176 19TH WAR
MC ARTHER, SAMUEL FRE 140 CREAGERS
MC ARTHUR, COLIN BAL 060 15TH WAR
MC ASIER, GEORGE ALL 231 CUMBERLA
MC ASLESTER, ELIZABETH BAL 432 1ST DIST
MC ATEE, FRANCIS FRE 065 FREDERIC
MC ATEE, JAMES W. MGM 418 MEDLEY 3
MC ATEE, JOHN ALL 176 7TH E.D.
MC ATEE, JOHN S. MGM 428 CLARKSTR
MC ATEE, LUCY HAR 114 2ND DIST
MC ATEE, MICHAEL ALL 150 6TH E.D.
MC ATEE, NATHANIEL ALL 175 7TH E.D.
MC ATEE, SUSAN WAS 246 SMITHSBU
MC ATEE, THOMAS K. WAS 103 2ND DIST
MC ATEE, WILLIAM MGM 432 CLARKSTR
MC ATEE, WILLIAM B. WAS 302 1ST DIST
MC ATEER, MAARGARET FRE 182 5TH E DI
MC ATER, CHARITY MGM 418 MEDLEY 3
MC ATHANY, JAMES* BAL 416 3RD WARD
MC AULEY, ZACHARIA ANN 449 HOWARD D
MC AUTHER, MARGARETT BAL 114 11TH WAR
MC AVOY, CATHARINE ANN 501 HOWARD D
MC AVOY, DENNIS BAL 216 11TH WAR
MC AVOY, ELLEN BAL 285 17TH WAR
MC AVOY, FELEX BAL 285 17TH WAR
MC AVOY, FRANCIS BAL 044 18TH WAR
MC AVOY, FRANCIS ANN 500 HOWARD D
MC AVOY, HUGH BAL 128 5TH WARD
MC AVOY, JAMES BAL 127 5TH WARD
MC AVOY, JOHN F. ANN 422 HOWARD D
MC AVOY, JOSEPH ANN 469 HOWARD D
MC AVOY, MARY BAL 172 11TH WAR
MC AVOY, MARY BAL 140 11TH WAR
MC AVOY, MICHAEL BAL 172 11TH WAR
MC AVOY, PATRICK WAS 025 2ND SUBD
MC BAIN, ARSHILLIA * CHA 247 HILLTOP
MC BEE, THOMAS BAL 302 1ST DIST
MC BERDEL, MARY BAL 268 2ND WARD
MC BETNEY, A. BAL 170 1ST WARD
MC BIRNEY, WILLIAM BAL 006 9TH WARD
MC BLAIR, CHARLES H. BAL 379 1ST DIST
MC BLAIR, MARGARET BAL 379 1ST DIST
MC BLAIR, WILLIAM ANN 318 2ND DIST
MC BOBIE, ELISABETH ALL 045 10TH E.D
MC BRATY, JOHN BAL 027 9TH WARD
MC BRIAN, ADAM BAL 021 1ST WARD
MC BRIDE, ABRAHAM FRE 329 MIDDLETO
MC BRIDE, ANDREW BAL 421 1ST DIST
MC BRIDE, ANNA BAL 298 1ST DIST
MC BRIDE, ANTHONY FRE 160 EMMITTSB
MC BRIDE, ARTHUR BAL 149 2ND DIST
MC BRIDE, CATHARINE FRE 331 MIDDLETO
MC BRIDE, CATHERINE BAL 416 8TH WARD
MC BRIDE, DENNIS BAL 252 20TH WAR
MC BRIDE, EDWARD FRE 184 5TH E DI
MC BRIDE, EDWARD BAL 247 12TH WAR
MC BRIDE, ELLEN BAL 015 18TH WAR
MC BRIDE, FRANCIS WAS 268 1ST DIST
MC BRIDE, GARRET DOR 450 1ST DIST
MC BRIDE, GEORGE WAS 193 1ST DIST
MC BRIDE, HENRY FRE 330 MIDDLETO
MC BRIDE, HENRY C. FRE 331 MIDDLETO
MC BRIDE, JAMES BAL 056 18TH WAR
MC BRIDE, JAMES BAL 056 2ND DIST
MC BRIDE, JAMES BAL 211 6TH DIST
MC BRIDE, JOHN CEC 103 4TH E DI
MC BRIDE, JOHN FRE 203 5TH E DI
MC BRIDE, MARK BAL 155 2ND DIST
MC BRIDE, MARY BAL 283 12TH WAR
MC BRIDE, MATHEW ALL 150 6TH E.D.
MC BRIDE, MRS. BAL 153 19TH WAR
MC BRIDE, NICHOLAS BAL 300 1ST DIST
MC BRIDE, PETER FRE 329 MIDDLETO
MC BRIDE, SAMUEL DOR 432 1ST DIST
MC BRIDE, SAMUEL ALL 192 9TH E.D.
MC BRIDE, SARAH BAL 127 11TH WAR
MC BRIDE, SARAH A. CEC 092 4TH E DI
MC BRIDE, WILLIAM FRE 330 MIDDLETO
MC BRIDE, WILLIAM FRE 328 MIDDLETO
MC BRIDE, WILLIAM WAS 080 2ND SUBD
MC BRIDE, WILLIAM* DOR 381 1ST DIST
MC BRIETY, JOSHUA SOM 490 SALISBUR
MC BRIETY, WILLIAM BAL 038 4TH WARD
MC BUNNEY, CLELLAND * BAL 100 2ND DIST
MC CAAN, ANDREW-BLACK FRE 175 5TH E DI
MC CABE, ANN BAL 106 18TH WAR
MC CABE, ANN BAL 350 13TH WAR
MC CABE, ANN BAL 356 8TH WARD
MC CABE, AUGUSTUS QUE 182 3RD E DI
MC CABE, B.* BAL 110 10TH WAR
MC CABE, BRIDGET BAL 249 12TH WAR
MC CABE, BRIDGET BAL 132 11TH WAR
MC CABE, CATHERINE BAL 405 8TH WARD
MC CABE, ELISABETH ALL 025 2ND E.D.
MC CABE, FRANCES QUE 183 3RD E DI
MC CABE, GEORGE E. BAL 164 19TH WAR
MC CABE, HENRY BAL 065 4TH WARD
MC CABE, HY ALL 043 10TH E.D
MC CABE, JAMES CEC 008 ELKTON 3
MC CABE, JAMES CEC 099 3RD E DI
MC CABE, JAMES PRI 036 VANSVILL
MC CABE, JEFFERSON BAL 125 11TH WAR
MC CABE, JOHN BAL 407 8TH WARD
MC CABE, JOHN BAL 007 15TH WAR
MC CABE, JOHN BAL 092 10TH WAR
MC CABE, JOHN BAL 019 9TH WARD
MC CABE, MARGARET QUE 182 3RD E DI
MC CABE, MARY BAL 380 8TH WARD
MC CABE, MARY CEC 013 ELKTON 3
MC CABE, MICHAEL BAL 178 11TH WAR
MC CABE, PATRICK ALL 042 10TH E.D
MC CABE, PATRICK BAL 226 19TH WAR
MC CABE, RICHARD BAL 316 20TH WAR
MC CABE, ROSANNA BAL 179 11TH WAR
MC CABE, ROSE M. HAR 146 3RD DIST
MC CABE, SOLOMON BAL 187 11TH WAR
MC CABE, SOLOMON BAL 187 11TH WAR
MC CABE, TERESSA BAL 171 16TH WAR
MC CABE, THEODORE ANN 340 3RD DIST
MC CABE, VIOLET CEC 109 3RD E DI
MC CABE, WILLIAM BAL 302 17TH WAR
MC CABE, WILLIAM ALL 025 2ND E.D.
MC CABEN, ALEXANDER BAL 178 11TH WAR
MC CABLE, MICHAEL BAL 163 11TH WAR
MC CADDAR, GILBERT ALL 087 5TH E.D.
MC CADDEN, MARGARET BAL 235 6TH WARD
MC CADDEN, PETER BAL 361 8TH WARD
MC CADDEY, BARNEY BAL 363 8TH WARD
MC CADDIN, DANIEL BAL 089 5TH WARD
MC CADDIN, MARGARET BAL 375 8TH WARD
MC CADDIN, OWEN BAL 361 8TH WARD
MC CADDON, J. BAL 169 1ST WARD
MC CADE, VIOLET CEC 109 3RD E DI
MC CAEN, JAMES ALL 241 CUMBERLA
MC CAFALIN, ANN BAL 260 1ST DIST
MC CAFFEN, MICHAEL BAL 014 2ND DIST
MC CAFFERRY, JAMES BAL 283 17TH WAR
MC CAFFERTY, ANN BAL 156 11TH WAR
MC CAFFERTY, ANN BAL 047 15TH WAR
MC CAFFERTY, CATHARINE BAL 165 6TH WARD
MC CAFFERTY, HENRY BAL 182 6TH WARD
MC CAFFERTY, JOHN BAL 253 6TH WARD
MC CAFFERTY, MARY BAL 457 8TH WARD
MC CAFFERTY, MARY BAL 071 15TH WAR
MC CAFFERTY, MICHAEL HAR 102 2ND DIST
MC CAFFERTY, THOMAS CEC 041 CHESAPEA
MC CAFFERTY, WILLIAM H. BAL 078 4TH WARD
MC CAFFERY, JOHN CEC 058 1ST E DI
MC CAFFEY, PATRICK BAL 422 14TH WAR
MC CAFFEY, THEODORE FRE 398 JEFFERSO
MC CAFFNEY, SISTER ANNE FRE 198 5TH E DI
MC CAFFNEY, THOMAS A. FRE 20 5TH E DI
MC CAFFREE, MARGARET ALL 203 CUMBERLA
MC CAFFREY, GEORGE FRE 202 5TH E DI
MC CAFFREY, GEORGE BAL 353 13TH WAR
MC CAFFREY, ICHA * BAL 343 13TH WAR
MC CAFFREY, JANE MRS- BAL 315 20TH WAR
MC CAFFREY, JOHN FRE 20 5TH E DI
MC CAFFREY, MARY BAL 316 12TH WAR
MC CAFFREY, MICHAEL FRE 028 FREDERIC
MC CAFFREY, PATRICK BAL 351 13TH WAR
MC CAFFREY, PATRICK WAS 026 2ND SUBD
MC CAFFREY, SUSAN BAL 061 10TH WAR
MC CAFFREY, T.J. ALL 049 10TH E.D
MC CAFFREY, THOMAS WAS 026 2ND SUBD
MC CAFFREY, THOMAS CAR 227 5TH DIST
MC CAFFRY, THOMAS BAL 422 14TH WAR
MC CAFFRY, THOMAS BAL 197 2ND WARD
MC CAFNEY, BYAN CEC 024 ELKTON 3
MC CAGAN, JOHN BAL 447 8TH WARD
MC CAGAN, MICHAEL BAL 447 8TH WARD
MC CAGE, HUGH BAL 400 1ST DIST
MC CAHAN, CATHERINE FRE 031 FREDERIC
MC CAHAN, DANIEL BAL 360 3RD WARD
MC CAHAN, EUPHEMIA BAL 360 3RD WARD
MC CAHAN, GEORGE BAL 106 18TH WAR
MC CAHAN, HANNA FRE 044 FREDERIC
MC CAHEY, CATHERINE BAL 033 9TH WARD
MC CAHEY, JAMES BAL 281 7TH WARD
MC CAHILL, PATRICK FRE 20 5TH E DI
MC CAIB, JOHN WOR 249 1ST CENS
MC CAIN, ANN BAL 088 18TH WAR
MC CAIN, BRIDGE BAL 411 14TH WAR
MC CAIN, CHARLES FRE 444 8TH E DI
MC CAIN, ELIZABETH WAS 152 HAGERSTO
MC CAIN, JAMES WAS 144 HAGERSTO
MC CAIN, JOHN ALL 213 CUMBERLA
MC CAIN, MARY BAL 388 1ST DIST
MC CAIN, THOMAS WAS 150 HAGERSTO
MC CAIN, THOMAS WAS 150 HAGERSTO
MC CAINE, ELIZABETH BAL 281 20TH WAR
MC CAINE, JAMES BAL 277 2ND WARD
MC CAKE, CATHARINE BAL 016 18TH WAR
MC CALCOT, CHARLES ALL 181 8TH E.D.
MC CALDWELL, SAMUEL BAL 422 14TH WAR
MC CALEB, ANN ANN 401 8TH DIST
MC CALISTER, JAMES CEC 026 ELKTON 3
MC CALISTER, JOHN W. CAR 326 1ST DIST
MC CALISTER, MARY WOR 262 BERLIN 1
MC CALISTER, WILLIAM HAR 145 3RD DIST
MC CALL, ANN BAL 137 11TH WAR
MC CALL, CATHARINE BAL 442 14TH WAR
MC CALL, DANIEL WAS 160 HAGERSTO
MC CALL, DAVID WAS 160 HAGERSTO
MC CALL, HUGH BAL 020 9TH WARD
MC CALL, HUGH BAL 010 15TH WAR
MC CALL, J. BAL 147 1ST WARD
MC CALL, JAMES BAL 136 16TH WAR
MC CALL, JAMES CEC 067 5TH E DI
MC CALL, JOHN CEC 082 CHARLEST
MC CALL, JOHN BAL 177 16TH WAR
MC CALL, JOHN BAL 010 15TH WAR
MC CALL, JOHN BAL 150 1ST WARD
MC CALL, JOSEPH BAL 136 16TH WAR
MC CALL, MARY ANN 451 HOWARD D
MC CALL, MARY BAL 294 17TH WAR
MC CALL, MICHAEL BAL 285 17TH WAR
MC CALL, MICHAEL BAL 292 17TH WAR
MC CALL, PATRICK BAL 280 17TH WAR
MC CALL, PATRICK BAL 257 6TH WARD
MC CALL, R. BAL 147 1ST WARD
MC CALL, R. BAL 163 1ST WARD
MC CALL, R. BAL 148 1ST WARD
MC CALLAHER, HENRY BAL 353 13TH WAR
MC CALLAN, JAMES BAL 156 11TH WAR
MC CALLEN, JAMES D. WOR 299 SNOW HIL
MC CALLION, CATHARINE FRE 196 5TH E DI
MC CALLION,MARY JANE FRE 193 5TH E DI
MC CALLISTER, MARY A.* DOR 454 1ST DIST
MC CALLISTER, R.H. BAL 069 1ST WARD
MC CALLISTER, SAMUEL* DOR 412 1ST DIST
MC CALLISTER, THOMAS DOR 411 1ST DIST
MC CALLISTER, TOROBABLE* DOR 443 1ST DIST
MC CALLOP, WILLIAM ALL 106 5TH E.D.
MC CALLOUGH, ROBERT ALL 096 5TH E.D.
MC CALLOUGH, WILLIAM CEC 145 PORT DUP
MC CALLY, JOHN BAL 155 1ST WARD
MC CALLY, JOHN TAL 106 ST MICHA
MC CALLY, WILLIAM ALL 218 CUMBERLA
MC CALRAN, PATRICK ALL 205 CUMBERLA
MC CALSKEY, JOHN BAL 438 1ST DIST
MC CAMARON, MARTHA WAS 252 1ST DIST
MC CAMAS, J.M. BAL 039 2ND DIST
MC CAMBRIDGE, DANIEL BAL 091 5TH WARD
MC CAMBRIDGE, HUGH BAL 127 16TH WAR
MC CAMBRIDGE, JOHN BAL 091 5TH WARD
MC CAMERON, THOMAS WAS 228 1ST DIST
MC CAMMERN, ALEXANDER WAS 127 2ND DIST
MC CAMPBENLY, MARGARET BAL 119 5TH WARD
MC CAN, ANN BAL 023 4TH WARD
MC CAN, ANNA BAL 411 14TH WAR
MC CAN, CHARLES * HAR 015 1ST DIST
MC CAN, CHARLEY HAR 146 3RD DIST
MC CAN, ELLEN ALL 084 5TH E.D.
MC CAN, L. BAL 153 1ST WARD
MC CAN, MARY * BAL 048 18TH WAR
MC CAN, PHILIP BAL 335 13TH WAR
MC CAN, ROSAN * WAS 049 2ND SUBD
MC CAN, SARAH HAR 015 1ST DIST
MC CANCE, SAMUEL BAL 472 14TH WAR
MC CANCHAN, CATHARINE ALL 128 4TH E.D.
MC CANCHRAE, THOMAS BAL 092 1ST WARD
MC CANDLER, WILLIAM WAS 075 2ND SUBD
MC CANDLESS, GEORGE S. BAL 077 10TH WAR
MC CANDLESS, RICHARD L. HAR 131 2ND DIST
MC CANDLIS, CHRISTIAN BAL 179 19TH WAR
MC CANDLISS, MARKS ALL 050 10TH E.D
MC CANDRIN, CATHARINE BAL 407 14TH WAR
MC CANDY, EDWARD ALL 140 6TH E.D.
MC CANDY, SARAH ALL 140 6TH E.D.
MC CANE, CATHARINE BAL 195 11TH WAR
MC CANE, JOHN BAL 118 1ST WARD
MC CANELY, CHARLES BAL 019 9TH WARD
MC CANLAR, JOHN ALL 142 6TH E.D.
MC CANLEY, JOSEPH BAL 164 19TH WAR
MC CANLEY, MARY A. * ANN 309 1ST DIST
MC CANLEY, WILLAIM BAL 137 2ND DIST
MC CANLIS, THOMAS ALL 225 CUMBERLA
MC CANN, ALEXANDER BAL 069 15TH WAR
MC CANN, ANOS BAL 143 11TH WAR
MC CANN, BIDDY BAL 319 20TH WAR
MC CANN, BRIDDY BAL 213 2ND WARD
MC CANN, CATHERINE BAL 037 4TH WARD
MC CANN, EDWARD BAL 161 19TH WAR
MC CANN, EDWARD BAL 102 5TH WARD
MC CANN, ELIZABETH BAL 192 19TH WAR
MC CANN, ELLEN BAL 195 2ND WARD
MC CANN, FRANK BAL 181 11TH WAR
MC CANN, HENRIETTA BAL 466 14TH WAR
MC CANN, HENRY BAL 161 16TH WAR
MC CANN, HENRY G. BAL 094 10TH WAR
MC CANN, J. BAL 135 1ST WARD
MC CANN, JAMES BAL 108 5TH WARD
MC CANN, JAMES BAL 285 1ST DIST
MC CANN, JANE TAL 170 11TH WAR
MC CANN, JOHN BAL 131 5TH WARD
MC CANN, JOHN WAS 155 2ND DIST
MC CANN, LORD BAL 295 17TH WAR
MC CANN, MARGARET BAL 161 16TH WAR
MC CANN, MARY BAL 053 9TH WARD
MC CANN, MARY BAL 215 11TH WAR
MC CANN, MARY BAL 005 4TH WARD
MC CANN, MICHAEL BAL 187 16TH WAR
MC CANN, MICHAEL BAL 211 6TH WARD
MC CANN, ROSE BAL 183 11TH WAR
MC CANN, SUMMERS ALL 059 10TH E.D
MC CANN, THOMAS BAL 022 9TH WARD
MC CANN, WILLIAM BAL 131 5TH WARD
MC CANNA, MARGARETT BAL 068 4TH WARD
MC CANNA, MISHAL M.* TAL 006 EASTON D
MC CANNEY, FRANCIS BAL 216 11TH WAR
MC CANNON, E. G. FRE 309 WOODSBOR
MC CANNON, JAMES BAL 155 2ND DIST
MC CANNON, JANE BAL 054 18TH WAR
MC CANNORE, CHARLES FRE 034 FREDERIC
MC CANORY, MARY BAL 315 12TH WAR
MC CANTER, DANIEL ALL 139 6TH E.D.
MC CAP, PEBE WOR 188 7TH E DI
MC CARAPHIN, JOHN BAL 047 15TH WAR
MC CARCERAN, THOMAS BAL 044 2ND DIST
MC CARCLE, WILLIAM WAS 150 HAGERSTO
MC CARDELL, A.C. WAS 016 2ND SUBD
MC CARDELL, JOHN BAL 130 11TH WAR
MC CARDELL, RICHARD P. WAS 010 WILLIAMS
MC CARDELL, W.C. WAS 011 WILLIAMS
MC CARDELL, W.D. WAS 016 2ND SUBD
MC CARDLE, ANN BAL 157 11TH WAR
MC CARDLE, JAMES CEC 201 6TH E DI
MC CARDLE, JAMES CEC 134 6TH E DI
MC CARDLE, JANE CEC 209 7TH E DI
MC CARDLE, LUCY CEC 201 6TH E DI
MC CARDLE, M. BAL 012 9TH WARD
MC CARDLE, MARY A. CEC 165 6TH E DI
MC CARDLE, RACHEL CEC 158 PORT DUP
MC CARDLE, ROSE BAL 125 5TH WARD
MC CARDLE, WILLOUGHBY WAS 264 1ST DIST
MC CARDLES, JONATHAN CEC 168 6TH E DI
MC CARDY, JOHN FRE 182 5TH E DI
MC CARDY, MARY J. BAL 358 13TH WAR
MC CARHEY, MARY BAL 011 18TH WAR
MC CARIN, MICHAEL PRI 039 VANSVILL
MC CARLAND, HENRIETTA* TAL 042 EASTON D
MC CARLTON, JOHN ALL 213 CUMBERLA
MC CARM, HUGH ALL 135 4TH E.D.
MC CARMICK, PATRICK FRE 393 PETERSVI
MC CARN, CHARLES BAL 469 14TH WAR
MC CARN, HUGH ANN 520 HOWARD D
MC CARN, JULIA FRE 079 FREDERIC
MC CARN, MARGARET WAS 013 WILLIAMS
MC CARNT, MICHAEL BAL 292 12TH WAR
MC CAROT, JOHN * BAL 281 1ST DIST
MC CARR, CAROLINE ANN 265 ANNAPOLI
MC CARR, CHARLES * HAR 015 1ST DIST
MC CARR, EPHRAIM HAR 064 1ST DIST
MC CARR, JOHN MGM 410 MEDLEY 3
MC CARR, MARY * BAL 048 18TH WAR
MC CARR, ROSAN * WAS 049 2ND SUBD
MC CARR, THOMAS HAR 067 1ST DIST
MC CARROLL, JACOB CEC 126 5TH E DI
MC CARROLL, JANE BAL 322 12TH WAR
MC CARRON, PATRICK BAL 049 9TH WARD
MC CARSON, JOSEPH* TAL 015 EASTON D
MC CART, GEORGE BAL 006 9TH WARD
MC CART, NANCY BAL 406 8TH WARD
MC CARTA, LANENDER CEC 084 CHARLEST
MC CARTER, CHARLES BAL 383 8TH WARD
MC CARTER, CHARLES BAL 133 1ST WARD
MC CARTER, MARGARET BAL 081 10TH WAR
MC CARTER, SPENCER DOR 367 3RD DIVI
MC CARTER, WILLIAM BAL 318 20TH WAR
MC CARTEY, EDWARD BAL 321 7TH WARD
MC CARTEY, ELLEN BAL 119 5TH WARD
MC CARTEY, JOSEPH BAL 143 1ST WARD
MC CARTEY, WILLIAM BAL 150 5TH WARD
MC CARTHY, ANN BAL 314 20TH WAR
MC CARTHY, CHARLES BAL 171 6TH WARD
MC CARTHY, D. BAL 157 1ST WARD

Name	County	Page	District
MC CARTHY. DENNIS	FRE	067	FREDERIC
MC CARTHY. DENNIS	BAL	418	3RD WARD
MC CARTHY. JANE	BAL	097	5TH WARD
MC CARTHY. JOHN	BAL	418	3RD WARD
MC CARTHY. JOHN	PRI	107	PISCATAW
MC CARTHY. MISS M.	FRE	199	5TH E DI
MC CARTHY. MISS R.	FRE	199	5TH E DI
MC CARTHY. SARAH	BAL	094	10TH WAR
MC CARTHY. TIMOTHY	BAL	418	3RD WARD
MC CARTLEY. JOHN	BAL	124	1ST WARD
MC CARTNEY. AMRY	BAL	327	13TH WAR
MC CARTNEY. BETSEY	CEC	098	3RD E DI
MC CARTNEY. ELIZABETH	CEC	149	PORT DUP
MC CARTNEY. FRANCIS	BAL	258	17TH WAR
MC CARTNEY. JAMES	CEC	122	4TH E DI
MC CARTNEY. JAMES	BAL	089	5TH WARD
MC CARTNEY. JANE	BAL	172	16TH WAR
MC CARTNEY. JOHN	CEC	213	7TH E DI
MC CARTNEY. MICHAEL	FRE	069	FREDERIC
MC CARTNEY. MICHAEL	FRE	335	MIDDLETO
MC CARTNEY. PETER	BAL	278	1ST DIST
MC CARTNEY. ROBERT	BAL	106	2ND DIST
MC CARTNEY. SARAH	CEC	098	3RD E DI
MC CARTNEY. SERJEREK	BAL	253	1ST DIST
MC CARTNY. MARGARET	FRE	066	FREDERIC
MC CARTNY. PETER	HAR	061	1ST DIST
MC CARTY C.	BAL	142	1ST WARD
MC CARTY. A.	ALL	004	3RD E.D.
MC CARTY. ADAM	WAS	144	2ND DIST
MC CARTY. ANN	BAL	006	9TH WARD
MC CARTY. AQUILLA	ALL	056	10TH E.D
MC CARTY. AUSTIN	BAL	048	9TH WARD
MC CARTY. CALLAHAN	ALL	249	CUMBERLA
MC CARTY. CATHARINE M.	WAS	140	2ND DIST
MC CARTY. CHARLES L.	WAS	274	RIDGEVIL
MC CARTY. DENNIS	BAL	035	18TH WAR
MC CARTY. EDWARD	ALL	056	10TH E.D
MC CARTY. ELLEN	QUE	186	3RD E DI
MC CARTY. EUGENE	BAL	086	10TH WAR
MC CARTY. F.	BAL	137	1ST WARD
MC CARTY. ISAAC	ALL	056	10TH E.D
MC CARTY. J.	BAL	163	1ST WARD
MC CARTY. JAMES	ALL	090	5TH E.D.
MC CARTY. JAMES	BAL	097	18TH WAR
MC CARTY. JEREMIAH	WAS	164	2ND DIST
MC CARTY. JERREY	BAL	186	19TH WAR
MC CARTY. JOHN	HAR	070	1ST DIST
MC CARTY. JOHN	MGM	331	CRACKLIN
MC CARTY. JOHN	ALL	112	5TH E.D.
MC CARTY. JOHN	ANN	306	1ST DIST
MC CARTY. M.	BAL	319	20TH WAR
MC CARTY. MARGARET A.	TAL	067	EASTON T
MC CARTY. MARY	BAL	038	9TH WARD
MC CARTY. MARY	BAL	262	12TH WAR
MC CARTY. MICHAEL	ALL	253	CUMBERLA
MC CARTY. NANCY	BAL	042	4TH WARD
MC CARTY. PETER E.	BAL	150	16TH WAR
MC CARTY. ROBERT	BAL	188	2ND WARD
MC CARTY. ROBERT	WAS	164	2ND DIST
MC CARTY. S.	FRE	200	5TH E DI
MC CARTY. SAMUEL	FRE	119	CREAGERS
MC CARTY. SARAH	ALL	006	3RD E.D.
MC CARTY. SUSAN	BAL	139	11TH WAR
MC CARTY. THOMAS	CAR	077	NO TWP L
MC CARTY. WILLIAM	FRE	095	FREDERIC
MC CARTY. WILLIAM	ANN	311	1ST DIST
MC CARY. MARY	ALL	261	CUMBERLA
MC CASCEW. HUGH	WAS	001	WILLIAMS
MC CASKEN.ROSE	ALL	209	CUMBERLA
MC CASKEY. ELLIS	HAR	156	3RD DIST
MC CASKEY. JOHN	BAL	221	1ST DIST
MC CASLIN. ANDREW	BAL	323	3RD WARD
MC CASLIN. CATHARINE	BAL	054	2ND DIST
MC CASLIN. CATHERINE	BAL	025	2ND DIST
MC CASLIN. JOHN	BAL	039	2ND DIST
MC CASLIN. MARIA	BAL	309	1ST DIST
MC CASLIN. WILLIAM J.	BAL	154	1ST WARD
MC CASSEN. THOMAS	ALL	049	10TH E.D
MC CATBIN. THOMAS L.	MGM	393	ROCKERLE
MC CATCHAY. WILLIAM J.*	BAL	330	3RD WARD
MC CATCHY. MARYANN	BAL	330	3RD WARD
MC CATHIDAY. ANNA	BAL	072	10TH WAR
MC CAUGHY. ALEXANDER	BAL	350	7TH WARD
MC CAUL. JOHN	BAL	289	7TH WARD
MC CAUL. OWEN	BAL	176	11TH WAR
MC CAULAY. MARTHA	BAL	222	6TH WARD
MC CAULEY. ABRAHAM	BAL	173	1ST WARD
MC CAULEY. ABSOLEM	CEC	115	3RD E DI
MC CAULEY. ANN	CEC	114	3RD E DI
MC CAULEY. ANN	FRE	043	FREDERIC
MC CAULEY. ANN	PRI	025	VANSVILL
MC CAULEY. CLARK	ANN	344	3RD DIST
MC CAULEY. DAVID H.	BAL	373	8TH WARD
MC CAULEY. ELIZABETH	BAL	140	2ND DIST
MC CAULEY. GEORGE	ANN	323	2ND DIST
MC CAULEY. HENRY	CEC	114	3RD E DI
MC CAULEY. ISAAC	ANN	444	HOWARD D
MC CAULEY. JAMES	CEC	114	3RD E DI
MC CAULEY. JETHRO	CEC	115	3RD E DI
MC CAULEY. JOHN	CEC	117	4TH E DI
MC CAULEY. JOHN	MGM	319	CRACKLIN
MC CAULEY. JOHN	CEC	005	ELKTON 3
MC CAULEY. JOHN	ANN	362	4TH DIST
MC CAULEY. JOHN	BAL	122	5TH WARD
MC CAULEY. JOHN	BAL	137	16TH WAR
MC CAULEY. JOHN	BAL	137	16TH WAR
MC CAULEY. JOSEPH	BAL	365	13TH WAR
MC CAULEY. JOSHUA	ANN	417	HOWARD D
MC CAULEY. LAWRENCE	ANN	469	HOWARD D
MC CAULEY. MARGARET	ANN	310	1ST DIST
MC CAULEY. MARGARET	CEC	090	4TH E DI
MC CAULEY. MARSHALL	ANN	418	HOWARD D
MC CAULEY. MARTHA J.	CEC	120	3RD E DI
MC CAULEY. MARY	CEC	114	3RD E DI
MC CAULEY. MARY A.	PRI	029	VANSVILL
MC CAULEY. MARY A. *	ANN	309	1ST DIST
MC CAULEY. MICHAEL	ALL	129	4TH E.D.
MC CAULEY. RACHEL	CEC	119	3RD E DI
MC CAULEY. RICHARD	BAL	021	15TH WAR
MC CAULEY. SAMUEL	CEC	117	4TH E DI
MC CAULEY. SAMUEL	WAS	233	1ST DIST
MC CAULEY. SOLOMON	ANN	353	3RD DIST
MC CAULEY. THOMAS	ANN	444	HOWARD D
MC CAULEY. THOMAS	ANN	414	HOWARD D
MC CAULEY. WILLIAM	ANN	327	2ND DIST
MC CAULEY. ZACH	ANN	349	3RD DIST
MC CAULIFF. HENNOREY	BAL	125	5TH WARD
MC CAULY. DANIEL J.	CEC	119	3RD E DI
MC CAULY. HANNAH V.	FRE	065	FREDERIC
MC CAULY. JOHN	CEC	107	3RD E DI
MC CAULY. JOHN	ALL	241	CUMBERLA
MC CAULY. NICHOLAS	ANN	439	HOWARD D
MC CAULY. WILLIAM	BAL	367	3RD WARD
MC CAUN. D.	BAL	248	12TH WAR
MC CAUN. MARY	BAL	028	4TH WARD
MC CAUNNAE. M.	BAL	449	8TH WARD
MC CAUSLAND. ELIZABETH	HAR	004	1ST DIST
MC CAUSLAND. ISABELLA	BAL	236	6TH WARD
MC CAUSLAND. JAMES	BAL	153	19TH WAR
MC CAUSLIN. ANN	HAR	004	1ST DIST
MC CAUT. JOHN	BAL	184	2ND WARD
MC CAVERTY. PATRICK	CEC	066	1ST E DI
MC CAWT. JOHN *	BAL	281	1ST DIST
MC CAY. JOSHUA	BAL	329	13TH WAR
MC CEMAS. JAMES	BAL	227	12TH WAR
MC CEMAS. SARAH	BAL	158	19TH WAR
MC CENEY. ANNA	BAL	301	20TH WAR
MC CENEY. CAROLINE	BAL	065	10TH WAR
MC CENEY. EDWARD	ANN	297	1ST DIST
MC CENEY. JACOB M.	ANN	300	1ST DIST
MC CENNY. SUSAN	BAL	429	14TH WAR
MC CENY. BIDDY*	BAL	422	3RD WARD
MC CERRY. BIDDY*	BAL	422	3RD WARD
MC CEVER. PATRICK	BAL	277	1ST DIST
MC CHEM. PETER	HAR	101	2ND DIST
MC CHENEY. JESSE	ALL	005	3RD E.D.
MC CHERRY. JOHN	BAL	254	1ST DIST
MC CHESNHY. JOSEPH	FRE	274	NEW MARK
MC CHICKNER. HANNAH *	BAL	099	2ND DIST
MC CHILLEY. WILLIAM *	BAL	365	13TH WAR
MC CHRISTY. MARGARET	BAL	081	10TH WAR
MC CINLEY. NELSON	WAS	150	2ND DIST
MC CLAIN. A.	WAS	016	2ND SUBD
MC CLAIN. ELIZABETH	WAS	004	WILLIAMS
MC CLAIN. ELIZABETH	WOR	276	BERLIN 1
MC CLAIN. ELIZABETH-BLACK	ST	295	2ND E DI
MC CLAIN. JAMES	SOM	361	BRINKLEY
MC CLAIN. JAMES E.	WAS	108	2ND DIST
MC CLAIN. JOHN	WAS	036	2ND SUBD
MC CLAIN. JOHN	WAS	094	2ND SUBD
MC CLAIN. JOHN	FRE	144	10TH E D
MC CLAIN. JOHN D.	WAS	132	2ND DIST
MC CLAIN. JOSEPH	FRE	143	10TH E D
MC CLAIN. LYDIA-BLACK	ST	295	2ND E DI
MC CLAIN. MARGARETTE	HAR	102	2ND DIST
MC CLAIN. MARTHA	WAS	112	2ND DIST
MC CLAIN. MATILDA	WOR	284	BERLIN 1
MC CLAIN. MATILDA	WOR	255	1ST CENS
MC CLAIN. OWEN	WAS	103	2ND DIST
MC CLAIN. PETER	FRE	143	10TH E D
MC CLAIN. SAMUEL	BAL	369	8TH WARD
MC CLAINE. GEORGE W.	PRI	020	VANSVILL
MC CLAINE. MARY	WAS	099	2ND DIST
MC CLAIR. AMANDA	BAL	323	12TH WAR
MC CLAIR. MARY	HAR	018	1ST DIST
MC CLANAHAN. ELLEN	BAL	051	15TH WAR
MC CLANAHAN. JAMES	BAL	050	15TH WAR
MC CLANAHAN. JAMES	BAL	418	8TH WARD
MC CLANAHAN. JAMES	BAL	311	1ST DIST
MC CLANAHAN. JAMES	WAS	009	WILLIAMS
MC CLANE. JAMES	DOR	360	3RD DIVI
MC CLANE. JOSEPH	HAR	099	2ND DIST
MC CLANEHAN. REUBEN	BAL	095	5TH WARD
MC CLANNAHAN. ELIZA	WAS	101	2ND DIST
MC CLANNAHAN. JANE	BAL	019	1ST WARD
MC CLANNAHAN. MATTHEW	ALL	212	CUMBERLA
MC CLANNON. JOHN	BAL	245	20TH WAR
MC CLARA. JOHNY	WAS	086	2ND SUBD
MC CLARE. SAMUEL	BAL	164	1ST WARD
MC CLAREN. JANE	BAL	388	1ST DIST
MC CLARY. BENJAMIN	BAL	215	6TH DIST
MC CLARY. CHARLOTTE	BAL	216	6TH DIST
MC CLARY. CHARLOTTE	BAL	216	6TH DIST
MC CLARY. JOHN	ALL	214	CUMBERLA
MC CLARY. JOHN	BAL	002	15TH WAR
MC CLARY. MARY	BAL	038	9TH WARD
MC CLASKEY. AIRA	BAL	392	1ST DIST
MC CLASKEY. ALFRED	BAL	230	6TH WARD
MC CLASKEY. ELIZABETH	BAL	034	15TH WAR
MC CLASKEY. JOHN	BAL	226	6TH WARD
MC CLASKEY. LOUISA	BAL	255	6TH WARD
MC CLASKEY. MARY	BAL	116	2ND DIST
MC CLASKEY. MICHAEL	BAL	118	2ND DIST
MC CLASKEY. MICHAEL	BAL	116	2ND DIST
MC CLASKEY. SAMUEL	BAL	333	7TH WARD
MC CLASKEY. WILLAIM	BAL	149	5TH WARD
MC CLASKEY. WILLIAM	BAL	149	5TH WARD
MC CLASKY. ANN	BAL	286	20TH WAR
MC CLASKY. JAMES	CEC	036	CHESAPEA
MC CLASTER. THOMS	BAL	286	2ND WARD
MC CLATCHAY. WILLIAM J.	BAL	330	3RD WARD
MC CLATCHIE. MARGARET	BAL	269	7TH WARD
MC CLAY. DAVID	ALL	214	CUMBERLA
MC CLAY. MARGARET	BAL	193	19TH WAR
MC CLAY. WILLIAM	CEC	008	ELKTON 3
MC CLAYLAND. THOMAS*	TAL	058	EASTON D
MC CLAYRY. ARAMINTY	KEN	299	3RD DIST
MC CLAYTON. ROSINA	BAL	401	8TH WARD
MC CLEAN. JOHN	BAL	365	3RD WARD
MC CLEAREY. JOHN	BAL	420	8TH WARD
MC CLEARY. ANDREW	FRE	405	JEFFERSO
MC CLEARY. ANN	CEC	116	3RD E DI
MC CLEARY. ANNA	CEC	031	CHESAPEA
MC CLEARY. CATHERINE	ALL	238	CUMBERLA
MC CLEARY. JAMES	BAL	012	15TH WAR
MC CLEARY. JOHN	CEC	116	3RD E DI
MC CLEARY. JOHN	QUE	207	3RD E DI
MC CLEARY. JOHN T.	CEC	125	5TH E DI
MC CLEARY. JULIA A.	BAL	012	15TH WAR
MC CLEARY. PETER	ALL	023	2ND E.D.
MC CLEARY. ROBERT	BAL	463	14TH WAR
MC CLEERY. JOHN	BAL	182	19TH WAR
MC CLEERY. ROBERT	BAL	023	4TH WARD
MC CLEESTER. ROBERT	BAL	286	20TH WAR
MC CLEESTER. SARAH A.	BAL	299	7TH WARD
MC CLEIST. A.	BAL	151	1ST WARD
MC CLELAN. JAMES	BAL	200	19TH WAR
MC CLELAN. JAMES A.	FRE	303	WOODSBOR
MC CLELAND. HESTER A.	BAL	124	11TH WAR
MC CLELAND. MILES	DOR	448	1ST DIST
MC CLELAND. ROBERT	BAL	445	1ST DIST
MC CLELLAN. ANDREW	BAL	160	16TH WAR
MC CLELLAN. BENJAMIN F.	BAL	174	16TH WAR
MC CLELLAN. EDWARD	BAL	262	20TH WAR
MC CLELLAN. JANE	BAL	144	19TH WAR
MC CLELLAN. JANE	BAL	374	13TH WAR
MC CLELLAN. JOHN	BAL	264	1ST DIST
MC CLELLAN. MARY E.*	BAL	417	3RD WARD
MC CLELLAN. THOMAS	BAL	222	1ST DIST
MC CLELLAN. THOMAS	BAL	374	3RD WARD
MC CLELLAN. WILLIAM	BAL	275	20TH WAR
MC CLELLAND. ALEXANDER	ALL	069	5TH E.D.
MC CLELLAND. ALFRED	CEC	066	1ST E DI
MC CLELLAND. GEORGE	BAL	006	9TH WARD
MC CLELLAND. ISABELLA	BAL	387	8TH WARD
MC CLELLAND. JAMES	CEC	066	1ST E DI
MC CLELLAND. JOHN	CAR	270	WESTMINS
MC CLELLAND. JOSEPH	ALL	200	CUMBERLA
MC CLELLAND. MARGARET	BAL	203	19TH WAR
MC CLELLAND. SUSAN M.	ST	297	2ND E DI
MC CLELLAND. THOMAS	ALL	235	CUMBERLA
MC CLELLAND. WILLIAM	ALL	223	CUMBERLA
MC CLELLAND. WILLIAM	BAL	203	19TH WAR
MC CLELLAR. MARY E.*	BAL	417	3RD WARD
MC CLELLIN. SUSAN	BAL	144	19TH WAR
MC CLENA. GEORGE	SOM	441	DAMES QU
MC CLENAHAN. WILLIAM*	BAL	424	3RD WARD
MC CLENAN. JOHN	BAL	367	13TH WAR
MC CLENAN. MARY	SOM	460	HANGARY
MC CLENAN. SAMUEL	CAR	380	2ND DIST
MC CLENATHAN. EBANEZER	CEC	183	7TH E DI
MC CLENATHAN. JOSIAH	CEC	153	PORT DUP
MC CLENHAM. WILLIAM B.	BAL	296	3RD WARD
MC CLENLAND. CARY	BAL	050	18TH WAR
MC CLENNAN. ANN B.	BAL	121	11TH WAR
MC CLENNAN. GEORGE	BAL	283	12TH WAR
MC CLENNAN. GEORGIANA	BAL	192	11TH WAR
MC CLENNAN. JAMES	BAL	002	4TH WARD
MC CLENNAN. JOHN	BAL	399	3RD WARD
MC CLENNATHER. SARAH	CEC	090	4TH E DI
MC CLENNON. JOHN D. *	FRE	097	FREDERIC
MC CLENTICK. JAMES	CEC	198	7TH E DI
MC CLENTOCK. JOHN M.	BAL	346	13TH WAR
MC CLEREY. ANDREW	BAL	430	8TH WARD
MC CLERRY. ARTHUR	BAL	262	2ND WARD
MC CLERY. REBECCA	FRE	043	FREDERIC
MC CLETERY. JANE *	BAL	069	18TH WAR
MC CLEWEL. SARAH	CEC	200	7TH E DI
MC CLEYMOUT. WILLIAM	BAL	186	2ND WARD
MC CLIAN. WILLIAM B.	WAS	108	2ND DIST
MC CLINEHAN. REUBEN	BAL	239	17TH WAR
MC CLING. RACHIL	HAR	074	1ST DIST
MC CLINOCK. JAMES	CEC	184	7TH E DI
MC CLINTOCK. ALEXANDER	BAL	185	16TH WAR
MC CLINTOCK. MATHEW	BAL	310	7TH WARD
MC CLORAY. HUGH	BAL	302	17TH WAR
MC CLOSKEY. DANIEL	BAL	115	2ND DIST
MC CLOSKEY. MARY	ALL	008	3RD E.D.
MC CLOSKEY. SISTER M.G.	FRE	198	5TH E DI
MC CLOSKEY. WILLIAM	FRE	20	5TH E DI
MC CLOSKY. ELIZA	ALL	008	3RD E.D.
MC CLOSMKEY. JOHN	FRE	20	5TH E DI
MC CLOUD. J.	BAL	168	1ST WARD
MC CLOUSEY. MARGARET	BAL	232	2ND WARD
MC CLOY. CATHARINE	BAL	249	12TH WAR
MC CLOY. PETER	BAL	241	20TH WAR
MC CLUEN. PATRICK	ALL	049	10TH E.D
MC CLUNE. JOHN	BAL	179	11TH WAR
MC CLUNEY. MARGARET	BAL	340	7TH WARD
MC CLUNEY. MARY	BAL	340	7TH WARD
MC CLUNEY. THOMAS	BAL	340	7TH WARD
MC CLUNG. ANNA R.	ANN	521	HOWARD D
MC CLUNG. DANIEL	BAL	048	2ND DIST
MC CLUNG. ELIZA	WAS	015	2ND SUBD
MC CLUNG. ELIZABETH	HAR	062	1ST DIST
MC CLUNG. MARY	BAL	387	3RD WARD
MC CLUNG. ROBERT	HAR	016	1ST DIST
MC CLUNG. ROBERT	HAR	020	1ST DIST
MC CLUNG. ROBERT R.	HAR	074	1ST DIST
MC CLUR. JAMES	ALL	068	5TH E.D.
MC CLURE. CHRISTOPHER C.	CEC	149	PORT DUP
MC CLURE. ELIZABETH	HAR	181	3RD DIST
MC CLURE. ELIZABETH	BAL	193	6TH WARD
MC CLURE. ELIZABETH	BAL	372	3RD WARD
MC CLURE. J.	BAL	224	12TH WAR
MC CLURE. JOHN	BAL	220	6TH WARD
MC CLURE. MARTHA	HAR	052	1ST DIST
MC CLURMAN. ANDREW	PRI	026	VANSVILL
MC CLUSKEY. BRIDGET	BAL	448	14TH WAR
MC CLUSKEY. CHARLES	ALL	056	10TH E.D
MC CLUSKEY. DANIEL	BAL	041	1ST WARD
MC CLUSKEY. THOMAS	BAL	406	8TH WARD
MC CLUSKY. JAMES	BAL	202	6TH WARD
MC CLUSKY. MARGARET	BAL	313	20TH WAR
MC CLUSKY. PATRICK	ALL	155	6TH E.D.
MC CLUSKY. SARAH	BAL	462	14TH WAR
MC CLUSTY. JOHN	HAR	198	3RD DIST
MC CLY. JANE*	BAL	371	3RD WARD
MC COBB. THOMAS F.	BAL	330	13TH WAR
MC COBB. WILLIAM	BAL	383	8TH WARD
MC COFFIE. THOMAS	CAR	206	4TH DIST
MC COHAN. D.	BAL	117	1ST WARD
MC COLE. MARTIN	ALL	129	4TH E.D.
MC COLGAN. BERNARD	BAL	015	9TH WARD
MC COLGAN. DENNIS	BAL	079	10TH WAR
MC COLGAN. EASTER	BAL	149	16TH WAR
MC COLGAN. JANE	BAL	392	14TH WAR
MC COLGAN. JOHN	BAL	079	10TH WAR
MC COLGAN. MARY	BAL	213	11TH WAR
MC COLGAN. MICHAEL	BAL	257	6TH WARD
MC COLGAN. PATRICK	BAL	062	18TH WAR
MC COLIGAN. CHARLES	BAL	183	11TH WAR
MC COLISTER. WILLIAM	WAS	223	1ST DIST
MC COLL. MARY	BAL	118	15TH WAR
MC COLLESTER. N.	BAL	282	2ND WARD
MC COLLEY. CHARLES	ALL	180	8TH E.D.
MC COLLIGAN. ELLEN	BAL	115	5TH WARD
MC COLLIN. CORNELIUS	BAL	116	11TH WAR
MC COLLINS. SARAH	BAL	200	19TH WAR
MC COLLISTER. ALFRED E.	WOR	210	4TH E DI
MC COLLISTER. J.	BAL	173	1ST WARD
MC COLLISTER. MARY A.*	DOR	454	1ST DIST
MC COLLISTER. ROBERT*	DOR	457	1ST DIST
MC COLLISTER. WILLIAM	HAR	054	1ST DIST
MC COLLISTON. EMILY	DOR	454	1ST DIST
MC COLLOCK. ELIZABETH	FRE	011	FREDERIC
MC COLLOUGH. DENNIS	BAL	195	2ND WARD
MC COLLOUGH. JOHN	BAL	395	1ST DIST
MC COLLUM. DANIEL	BAL	200	19TH WAR
MC COLLUM. ELIZA	BAL	257	12TH WAR
MC COLLUM. ELIZABETH	BAL	164	19TH WAR
MC COLLUM. HUGH	BAL	033	18TH WAR
MC COLLUM. JAMES	BAL	164	1ST WARD
MC COLLUM. JOHN	CAR	265	WESTMINS
MC COLLUM. SOPHIA	BAL	138	18TH WAR
MC COLLUM. WILLIAM	BAL	292	12TH WAR
MC COLM. MATHEW	BAL	032	9TH WARD
MC COLOGAN. JOHN	BAL	127	5TH WARD
MC COLOGAN. REV-	BAL	062	18TH WAR
MC COLOUGH. MARY A.	BAL	187	11TH WAR

Name	County	Page	District
MC COLUTIS, BENJAMIN-BLAC	CAR	088	NO TWP L
MC COMACK, BRIDGET	WAS	145	2ND DIST
MC COMACK, CHARITY	BAL	114	2ND DIST
MC COMAS, ABBUT G.	HAR	199	3RD DIST
MC COMAS, ALEXANDER	HAR	064	1ST DIST
MC COMAS, ALEXANDER	BAL	304	7TH WARD
MC COMAS, AMOS	BAL	072	18TH WAR
MC COMAS, ANN	BAL	042	9TH WARD
MC COMAS, AQUILA	BAL	093	18TH WAR
MC COMAS, BARNET	HAR	138	2ND DIST
MC COMAS, CASANDRE	HAR	190	3RD DIST
MC COMAS, CHARITY	HAR	098	2ND DIST
MC COMAS, CHARLES	HAR	203	3RD DIST
MC COMAS, DAVID	BAL	007	4TH WARD
MC COMAS, ELIZA	BAL	070	2ND DIST
MC COMAS, ELIZABETH	BAL	259	6TH WARD
MC COMAS, ELIZABETH	HAR	203	3RD DIST
MC COMAS, ELIZABETH	HAR	067	1ST DIST
MC COMAS, ELIZABETH B.	BAL	311	7TH WARD
MC COMAS, EMELINE	KEN	234	2ND DIST
MC COMAS, EZEKIEL	HAR	026	1ST DIST
MC COMAS, F.C.	WAS	018	2ND SUBD
MC COMAS, FRANCIS	BAL	145	11TH WAR
MC COMAS, GABRIEL	HAR	058	1ST DIST
MC COMAS, GEORGE A.	BAL	360	8TH WARD
MC COMAS, GEORGE W.	BAL	061	18TH WAR
MC COMAS, GILBERT	BAL	122	5TH WARD
MC COMAS, HARRIETT	HAR	183	3RD DIST
MC COMAS, HENRY D.	BAL	061	18TH WAR
MC COMAS, ISAAC	BAL	433	1ST DIST
MC COMAS, ISABEL	BAL	089	18TH WAR
MC COMAS, JACOB	BAL	070	2ND DIST
MC COMAS, JAMES	BAL	033	18TH WAR
MC COMAS, JAMES	KEN	233	2ND DIST
MC COMAS, JAMES	HAR	022	1ST DIST
MC COMAS, JAMES	HAR	018	1ST DIST
MC COMAS, JAMES	HAR	197	3RD DIST
MC COMAS, JAMES	BAL	029	4TH WARD
MC COMAS, JOHN	HAR	097	2ND DIST
MC COMAS, JOHN C.	HAR	188	3RD DIST
MC COMAS, JOHN E.	HAR	195	3RD DIST
MC COMAS, JOHN R.	HAR	097	2ND DIST
MC COMAS, JOSHUA	HAR	017	1ST DIST
MC COMAS, LEE	BAL	115	18TH WAR
MC COMAS, MARGARET A.	BAL	320	7TH WARD
MC COMAS, MARY	BAL	048	15TH WAR
MC COMAS, NICHOLAS D.	HAR	076	BEL AIR
MC COMAS, OLIVER J. M.	BAL	361	8TH WARD
MC COMAS, ROBERT	BAL	089	18TH WAR
MC COMAS, RUTH	HAR	199	3RD DIST
MC COMAS, SARAH	HAR	051	1ST DIST
MC COMAS, SARAH	HAR	187	3RD DIST
MC COMAS, SARAH	BAL	218	6TH DIST
MC COMAS, SARAH*	BAL	095	10TH WAR
MC COMAS, SIDNEY A.	BAL	184	6TH WARD
MC COMAS, SOLOMON	HAR	138	2ND DIST
MC COMAS, STEPHEN	BAL	004	18TH WAR
MC COMAS, THOMAS	BAL	140	5TH WARD
MC COMAS, WILLAIM	BAL	122	5TH WARD
MC COMAS, WILLIAM	BAL	179	6TH WARD
MC COMAS, WILLIAM	HAR	120	2ND DIST
MC COMAS, WILLIAM	HAR	054	1ST DIST
MC COMAS, WILLIAM	HAR	201	3RD DIST
MC COMAS, WILLIAM	BAL	403	14TH WAR
MC COMAS, WILLIAM R.	BAL	428	14TH WAR
MC COMAS, ZACHARIAH	WAS	131	HAGERSTO
MC COMAY, WILLIAM	BAL	148	19TH WAR
MC COMB, ALEXANDER	BAL	421	8TH WARD
MC COMBS, ANN	CAR	149	NO TWP L
MC COMBS, GEORGE	HAR	055	1ST DIST
MC COMMONS, SARY A.	HAR	164	3RD DIST
MC COMONS, BENJIMAN D.	HAR	165	3RD DIST
MC COMONS, JOHN	HAR	165	3RD DIST
MC COMUCK, JOHN P.	BAL	178	2ND DIST
MC CONCKI, LUCY H.	CHA	231	HILLTOP
MC CONCKY, MARY	BAL	065	1ST WARD
MC CONDEN, THOMAS	ALL	090	5TH E.D.
MC CONE, JOHN	ALL	160	6TH E.D.
MC CONE, JOHN	BAL	165	11TH WAR
MC CONIKER, ANN	QUE	208	3RD E DI
MC CONKEY, BRIDGET	BAL	474	14TH WAR
MC CONKEY, GEORGE	BAL	176	2ND DIST
MC CONKEY, JAMES	BAL	145	11TH WAR
MC CONKEY, JAMES	BAL	032	4TH WAR
MC CONKEY, M.	BAL	248	12TH WAR
MC CONKEY, MARY	BAL	053	4TH WARD
MC CONKEY, WILLIAM	BAL	145	11TH WAR
MC CONKLIN, SARAH	BAL	156	16TH WAR
MC CONLAY, JOHN	BAL	425	1ST DIST
MC CONLY, SAMUEL	BAL	218	6TH DIST
MC CONN, C.	BAL	055	9TH WARD
MC CONN, MARGARET	BAL	258	12TH WAR
MC CONN, RICHARD	BAL	291	12TH WAR
MC CONN, SARAH	BAL	262	20TH WAR
MC CONN, WILLIAM	BAL	024	9TH WARD
MC CONNAS, ISAAC	BAL	171	11TH WAR
MC CONNEER, TERESA	BAL	280	20TH WAR
MC CONNEL, JAMES	BAL	095	5TH WARD
MC CONNEL, THOMAS	BAL	014	4TH WARD
MC CONNELL, EDWARD	BAL	161	11TH WAR
MC CONNELL, FRANCES	CEC	086	4TH E DI
MC CONNELL, GOERGE	BAL	199	19TH WAR
MC CONNELL, HUGH	BAL	161	11TH WAR
MC CONNELL, JACOB D.	CEC	112	4TH E DI
MC CONNELL, JAMES	CEC	120	4TH E DI
MC CONNELL, JAMES	HAR	090	2ND DIST
MC CONNELL, JAMES	BAL	462	1ST DIST
MC CONNELL, JOHN	BAL	163	11TH WAR
MC CONNELL, JOHN	BAL	146	5TH WARD
MC CONNELL, JOHN	ALL	115	5TH E.D.
MC CONNELL, JOHN	BAL	277	20TH WAR
MC CONNELL, JOHN C.	BAL	058	15TH WAR
MC CONNELL, MARY	BAL	163	11TH WAR
MC CONNELL, MARY	BAL	213	2ND WARD
MC CONNELL, NANCY	CEC	120	4TH E DI
MC CONNELL, P.	BAL	125	1ST WARD
MC CONNELL, RACHEL	BAL	395	1ST DIST
MC CONNELL, ROBERT	BAL	015	4TH WARD
MC CONNELL, ROBERT	WAS	117	2ND DIST
MC CONNELL, SARAH	BAL	273	12TH WAR
MC CONNELL, THOMAS	BAL	056	1ST WARD
MC CONNELL, THOMAS	CEC	135	6TH E DI
MC CONNELL, WILLIAM	BAL	218	12TH WAR
MC CONNER, ARTHUR	BAL	173	11TH WAR
MC CONNER, CLEMET*	TAL	011	EASTON D
MC CONNER, DAVID	BAL	148	19TH WAR
MC CONNER, JAMES	BAL	173	11TH WAR
MC CONNER, MARY	BAL	319	20TH WAR
MC CONNOLLY, DUNCAN	BAL	033	18TH WAR
MC CONOKIN, JOHN	QUE	247	5TH E DI
MC CONOMY, AUGUSTINE	FRE	20	5TH E DI
MC CONVILL, JAMES	BAL	271	17TH WAR
MC CONVILLE, EDWARD	BAL	281	7TH WARD
MC COO, ANN	CHA	241	HILLTOP
MC COOL, MICHAEL	BAL	042	9TH WARD
MC CORDON, J.	BAL	135	1ST WARD
MC CORE, ROBERT*	TAL	038	EASTON D
MC CORKEY, NATHAN	BAL	163	16TH WAR
MC CORKLE, ELIZABETH	CEC	202	6TH E DI
MC CORKLE, JAMES A.	CAR	194	4TH DIST
MC CORKLE, JOHN	CEC	039	CHESAPEA
MC CORLICK, STEPHEN	CEC	171	6TH E DI
MC CORMACK, BRIAN	BAL	302	17TH WAR
MC CORMACK, J.	BAL	090	5TH WARD
MC CORMACK, JAMES	BAL	109	5TH WARD
MC CORMACK, JAMES	BAL	395	3RD WARD
MC CORMACK, JAMES	BAL	135	5TH WARD
MC CORMACK, JAMES	BAL	047	1ST WARD
MC CORMACK, MARGARET	BAL	077	1ST WARD
MC CORMACK, MARY A.	FRE	308	WOODSBOR
MC CORMACK, SARAH	BAL	111	5TH WARD
MC CORMACK, THOMAS	FRE	385	PETERSVI
MC CORMACK, WILLIAM	BAL	294	17TH WAR
MC CORMACK, WILLIAM	BAL	148	5TH WARD
MC CORMACK, WILLIAM	WAS	127	2ND DIST
MC CORMIC, ALICE	BAL	414	8TH WARD
MC CORMIC, BIDDEY	BAL	360	8TH WARD
MC CORMIC, JOHN	BAL	360	8TH WARD
MC CORMICH, MICHAEL	BAL	179	11TH WAR
MC CORMICK, A.	BAL	228	19TH WAR
MC CORMICK, ALEXANDER	BAL	002	15TH WAR
MC CORMICK, ANN	BAL	205	6TH WARD
MC CORMICK, ANN	BAL	284	12TH WAR
MC CORMICK, ARCHIBALD	BAL	047	9TH WARD
MC CORMICK, ASA	BAL	268	12TH WAR
MC CORMICK, BRIDGET	BAL	330	13TH WAR
MC CORMICK, CATHARINE	ALL	077	5TH E.D.
MC CORMICK, CATHARINE	ALL	072	5TH E.D.
MC CORMICK, CHARLES	BAL	183	6TH WARD
MC CORMICK, EDWARD	ALL	105	5TH E.D.
MC CORMICK, EDWARD	ALL	050	10TH E.D
MC CORMICK, EDWARD	HAR	114	2ND DIST
MC CORMICK, ELIZABETH	BAL	451	1ST DIST
MC CORMICK, FRANCIS	ALL	071	5TH E.D.
MC CORMICK, FRANCIS	BAL	101	1ST WARD
MC CORMICK, FRANK	ALL	061	10TH E.D
MC CORMICK, FRANK	ALL	050	10TH E.D
MC CORMICK, GEORGE	FRE	092	FREDERIC
MC CORMICK, JAMES	CEC	199	7TH E DI
MC CORMICK, JAMES	ALL	019	2ND E.D.
MC CORMICK, JAMES	BAL	046	9TH WARD
MC CORMICK, JAMES	BAL	103	10TH WAR
MC CORMICK, JAMES M.	HAR	106	2ND DIST
MC CORMICK, JOHN	BAL	238	20TH WAR
MC CORMICK, JOHN	ALL	005	3RD E.D.
MC CORMICK, JOHN	BAL	113	1ST WARD
MC CORMICK, JOHN	WAS	164	2ND DIST
MC CORMICK, MARY	WAS	126	HAGERSTO
MC CORMICK, MARY ANN	BAL	090	5TH WARD
MC CORMICK, MICHAEL	BAL	448	1ST DIST
MC CORMICK, MICHAEL	BAL	088	10TH WAR
MC CORMICK, NEVIN W.	CEC	199	7TH E DI
MC CORMICK, PATRICK	BAL	112	10TH WAR
MC CORMICK, PATRICK	BAL	441	1ST DIST
MC CORMICK, PATRICK	ALL	105	5TH E.D.
MC CORMICK, PATRICK	BAL	199	2ND WARD
MC CORMICK, PETER	BAL	276	1ST DIST
MC CORMICK, PETER	BAL	022	2ND DIST
MC CORMICK, REBECA	CAR	217	5TH DIST
MC CORMICK, ROBERT	WAS	124	2ND DIST
MC CORMICK, ROGER	ALL	050	10TH E.D
MC CORMICK, TABITHA	BAL	181	19TH WAR
MC CORMICK, THOMAS	ALL	071	5TH E.D.
MC CORMICK, THOMAS	BAL	183	6TH WARD
MC CORMICK, WILLIAM	BAL	175	2ND DIST
MC CORMICK, WILLIAM	BAL	253	12TH WAR
MC CORMICK, WILLIAM	BAL	183	19TH WAR
MC CORMICK, WILLIAM	WAS	145	2ND DIST
MC CORMICK, WILLIAM H.	BAL	333	3RD WARD
MC CORMICK, WILLIAM L.	BAL	320	20TH WAR
MC CORMICK, WILLIAM T.	BAL	008	18TH WAR
MC CORNACK, SAMUEL	BAL	388	3RD WARD
MC CORNAS, JOSEPH	BAL	279	12TH WAR
MC CORSE, CHARLES	CEC	026	ELKTON 3
MC CORTER, P.	BAL	130	1ST WARD
MC CORTY, ANN	BAL	273	2ND WARD
MC CORY, JOHN	BAL	310	1ST DIST
MC COSH, SAMUEL C.	BAL	385	13TH WAR
MC COSHINY, MARGARETTE	BAL	133	11TH WAR
MC COSKER, PHILIP	BAL	200	6TH WARD
MC COSKERY, JOSEPH	FRE	284	WOODSBOR
MC COSKEY, CATHEIRNE	ALL	253	CUMBERLA
MC COSKEY, MARGARET	BAL	179	11TH WAR
MC COTEE, WILLIAM	DOR	389	1ST DIST
MC COTTEE, JOSEPH*	DOR	389	1ST DIST
MC COTTEN, JOSEPH*	DOR	389	1ST DIST
MC COTTHER, PETER	CEC	130	6TH E DI
MC COTTISON, TOROBABLE*	DOR	443	1ST DIST
MC COUBRAY, THOMAS	BAL	340	3RD WARD
MC COULL, ROBERT	BAL	241	6TH WARD
MC COULL, ROBERT	BAL	240	6TH WARD
MC COULY, -----	BAL	333	1ST DIST
MC COUNT, AUTHER	BAL	455	8TH WARD
MC COUNT, RYSON	BAL	338	3RD WARD
MC COURT, ANN	BAL	194	2ND WARD
MC COURT, HENRIETTA	BAL	004	9TH WARD
MC COURT, JAMES	BAL	163	6TH WARD
MC COURT, JAMES	BAL	062	4TH WARD
MC COURT, JOHN	BAL	401	3RD WARD
MC COURT, MARY	BAL	114	5TH WARD
MC COURT, MICHAEL	BAL	192	11TH WAR
MC COURT, SARAH	BAL	125	5TH WARD
MC COURT, THOMAS A.	BAL	163	6TH WARD
MC COURTLAND, PATRICK	BAL	037	1ST WARD
MC COURTNEY, SAMUEL	HAR	006	1ST DIST
MC COURTNYE, JAMES	BAL	168	2ND DIST
MC COVAL, ISAAC	CEC	050	1ST E DI
MC COWAN, HUGH	HAR	140	2ND DIST
MC COWAN, MILLICENT	CEC	081	CHARLEST
MC COWAN, SAMUEL	CEC	081	CHARLEST
MC COWAN, SAMUEL	CEC	151	PORT DUP
MC COWAN, SOPHIA	CEC	190	5TH E DI
MC COWLEF, MARY	BAL	387	13TH WAR
MC COY, ABAGAIL	BAL	012	4TH WARD
MC COY, AGNES	BAL	057	10TH WAR
MC COY, ALEXANDER	ALL	155	6TH E.D.
MC COY, ALEXANDER	BAL	362	13TH WAR
MC COY, ALEXANDER	CEC	117	4TH E DI
MC COY, ALEXANDER	FRE	084	FREDERIC
MC COY, ANDREW	BAL	139	5TH WARD
MC COY, ANDREW	WAS	168	FUNKSTOW
MC COY, ANDREW	WAS	052	2ND SUBD
MC COY, ANN A.	BAL	448	14TH WAR
MC COY, ARCHABALD	WAS	170	FUNKSTOW
MC COY, ARCHABALD	WAS	194	1ST DIST
MC COY, ARCHABALD	WAS	221	1ST DIST
MC COY, B.	BAL	149	11TH WAR
MC COY, CAROLINE	BAL	261	17TH WAR
MC COY, CHALES	BAL	387	13TH WAR
MC COY, DANIEL	BAL	336	13TH WAR
MC COY, DANIEL	BAL	297	12TH WAR
MC COY, DAVID	HAR	032	1ST DIST
MC COY, DAVID G.	HAR	032	1ST DIST
MC COY, DAVID H.	CAL	049	3RD DIST
MC COY, EDMOND	BAL	371	13TH WAR
MC COY, EDWARD	BAL	015	4TH WARD
MC COY, ELIZABETH	CEC	091	4TH E DI
MC COY, ELIZABETH	BAL	394	8TH WARD
MC COY, ELIZABETH J.	BAL	261	17TH WAR
MC COY, ELIZABETH T.	BAL	024	9TH WARD
MC COY, ELLEN	WAS	050	2ND SUBD
MC COY, EMANUL	WAS	175	FUNKSTOW
MC COY, GEORGEANA	BAL	266	2ND WARD
MC COY, HANNAH	CEC	137	6TH E DI
MC COY, HENRY	BAL	232	12TH WAR
MC COY, HENRY CLAY	BAL	146	1ST WARD
MC COY, HUGH	BAL	179	11TH WAR
MC COY, JAMES	ALL	077	5TH E.D.
MC COY, JAMES	BAL	045	18TH WAR
MC COY, JAMES	CEC	198	7TH E DI
MC COY, JAMES	BAL	136	18TH WAR
MC COY, JAMES	WAS	221	1ST DIST
MC COY, JAMES G.	BAL	050	9TH WARD
MC COY, JANE	BAL	266	2ND WARD
MC COY, JANE	BAL	145	5TH WARD
MC COY, JEREMIAH	WAS	221	1ST DIST
MC COY, JOHN	BAL	213	6TH WARD
MC COY, JOHN	BAL	280	7TH WARD
MC COY, JOHN	BAL	338	3RD WARD
MC COY, JOHN	CEC	191	5TH E DI
MC COY, JOHN	BAL	012	4TH WARD
MC COY, JOHN H.	WAS	030	2ND SUBD
MC COY, JOHNM-MULATTO	BAL	176	2ND WARD
MC COY, JOSEPH	HAR	047	1ST DIST
MC COY, JULIA	HAR	043	1ST DIST
MC COY, L. H. F.	BAL	333	1ST DIST
MC COY, M.S.	BAL	227	12TH WAR
MC COY, MARGARET	BAL	106	5TH WARD
MC COY, MARGARET	BAL	111	5TH WARD
MC COY, MARTHA	ALL	214	CUMBERLA
MC COY, MARY	BAL	365	3RD WARD
MC COY, MARY	BAL	228	19TH WAR
MC COY, MARY	BAL	081	4TH WARD
MC COY, MARY	WAS	044	2ND SUBD
MC COY, MARY	WAS	118	2ND DIST
MC COY, MOSES	WAS	156	2ND DIST
MC COY, OSCAR	BAL	280	20TH WAR
MC COY, RACHEL	BAL	189	6TH WARD
MC COY, RICHARD B.	HAR	039	1ST DIST
MC COY, SAMUEL	BAL	232	12TH WAR
MC COY, SISTER A.S.	FRE	198	5TH E DI
MC COY, STEPHEN	BAL	299	3RD WARD
MC COY, SUSAN	WAS	116	2ND DIST
MC COY, WASHINGTON	WAS	082	2ND SUBD
MC COY, WILLIAM	WAS	170	FUNKSTOW
MC COY, WILLIAM	BAL	353	7TH WARD
MC COY, WILLIAM	BAL	119	1ST WARD
MC COY, WILLIAM	BAL	122	1ST WARD
MC COY, WILLIAM	HAR	041	1ST DIST
MC COY, WILLIAM	BAL	223	19TH WAR
MC CRABGER, RICHARD	ALL	155	6TH E.D.
MC CRACKAN, JAMES	BAL	201	17TH WAR
MC CRACKAN, JOHN	BAL	202	17TH WAR
MC CRACKEN, JAMES	BAL	171	6TH WARD
MC CRACKEN, JOHN	MGM	380	ROCKERLE
MC CRACKEN, JOHN	CEC	075	NORTHEAS
MC CRACKEN, MARTHA	HAR	141	2ND DIST
MC CRACKEN, THOMAS	BAL	028	15TH WAR
MC CRACKIN, DAVID	HAR	179	3RD DIST
MC CRACKIN, JOHN A.	QUE	171	2ND E DI
MC CRACKIN, MARY	HAR	128	2ND DIST
MC CRACLIN, G.	BAL	137	1ST WARD
MC CRADY, BENJAMIN	SOM	396	BRINKLEY
MC CRADY, BENJAMIN	SOM	387	BRINKLEY
MC CRADY, CLEMENT	SOM	400	BRINKLEY
MC CRADY, ELIZABETH	SOM	387	BRINKLEY
MC CRADY, ISAAC	SOM	398	BRINKLEY
MC CRADY, JAMES*	DOR	351	3RD DIVI
MC CRADY, RILEY	SOM	397	BRINKLEY
MC CRADY, THOMAS	SOM	382	BRINKLEY
MC CRADY, THOMAS A.	SOM	387	BRINKLEY
MC CRAFT, NATHAN	WAS	055	2ND SUBD
MC CRAFT, VALENTINE	WAS	045	2ND SUBD
MC CRAIGHT, DAVID	BAL	041	15TH WAR
MC CRAN, MICHAEL	BAL	449	14TH WAR
MC CRARY, CAROLINE	FRE	382	PETERSVI
MC CRARY, ELIZABETH	ALL	172	7TH E.D.
MC CRARY, THEADORE	ALL	195	CUMBERLA
MC CRAW, ROSEANNA	BAL	384	13TH WAR
MC CRAY, JAMES	CEC	010	ELKTON 3
MC CREA,	BAL	207	2ND WARD
MC CREA, ADAM	WAS	138	2ND DIST
MC CREA, EDWARD	CEC	095	4TH E DI
MC CREA, ELLEN	BAL	098	5TH WARD
MC CREA, JAMES	BAL	135	18TH WAR
MC CREA, JAMES H.	CEC	110	4TH E DI
MC CREA, JOSEPH	CEC	111	4TH E DI
MC CREA, JOSEPH	BAL	342	7TH WARD
MC CREA, MARY	BAL	210	19TH WAR
MC CREA, MARY	CEC	127	5TH E DI
MC CREA, RODERICK	BAL	089	5TH WARD
MC CREA, SAMUEL	CEC	110	4TH E DI
MC CREA, SARAH	BAL	424	14TH WAR
MC CREA, SARAH	BAL	442	14TH WAR
MC CREA, SOPHIA	BAL	064	10TH WAR
MC CREA, THOMAS	ANN	451	HOWARD D
MC CREA, THOMSA	BAL	132	1ST WARD
MC CREA, WILLIAM D.	CEC	101	4TH E DI
MC CREADDY, MICHAEL	BAL	040	9TH WARD
MC CREADY, CONNER	DOR	439	1ST DIST
MC CREADY, GEORGE	DOR	432	1ST DIST
MC CREADY, HARVEY J.	BAL	033	15TH WAR
MC CREADY, JOHN	DOR	432	1ST DIST
MC CREADY, JONATHAN	DOR	444	1ST DIST
MC CREADY, MARGARET A.	BAL	295	7TH WARD
MC CREADY, MESHACK	DOR	434	1ST DIST
MC CREAN, SAMUEL	BAL	310	3RD WARD
MC CREARY, -----*	BAL	107	10TH WAR
MC CREARY, GEORGE	CEC	113	4TH E DI
MC CREARY, JANE	CEC	111	4TH E DI

MC CREARY, JOHN CEC 105 3RD E DI
MC CREARY, LOUIS CEC 197 7TH E DI
MC CREARY, THOMAS CEC 011 ELKTON 3
MC CREARY, THOMAS BAL 144 1ST WARD
MC CREARY, WASHINGTON CEC 005 ELKTON 3
MC CREARY, WILLIAM CEC 118 4TH E DI
MC CREASY, ANN CEC 191 5TH E DI
MC CRECY, MARY C. ALL 210 CUMBERLA
MC CRERY, JOHN BAL 101 2ND DIST
MC CREW, THOMAS BAL 245 17TH WAR
MC CREY, CHARLES CEC 012 ELKTON 3
MC CREY, MARGARET CEC 012 ELKTON 3
MC CREY, SAMUEL CAR 307 1ST DIST
MC CRIBBIN, JAMES BAL 181 19TH WAR
MC CRISTAL, ELLEN* BAL 387 3RD WARD
MC CRISTAL, JOHN BAL 261 2ND WARD
MC CROCKER, JAMES BAL 216 6TH DIST
MC CRODEN, JAMES BAL 291 7TH WARD
MC CROFF, NATHAN WAS 044 2ND SUBD
MC CRONE, JOHN BAL 338 1ST DIST
MC CROWN, ROSANNA BAL 151 11TH WAR
MC CROY, ELEANORA BAL 345 13TH WAR
MC CROY, SARAH JANE BAL 255 17TH WAR
MC CROY, THOMAS BAL 255 17TH WAR
MC CRUBERY, ANN FRE 044 FREDERIC
MC CUBBEN, JEREMIAH BAL 379 1ST DIST
MC CUBBEN, JOHN BAL 437 1ST DIST
MC CUBBIN, AARON H. BAL 192 6TH WARD
MC CUBBIN, CHARLES ANN 358 3RD DIST
MC CUBBIN, CLARA BAL 066 10TH WAR
MC CUBBIN, DAVID BAL 362 8TH WARD
MC CUBBIN, GEORGE BAL 096 5TH WARD
MC CUBBIN, GEORGE QUE 248 5TH E DI
MC CUBBIN, JOHN D. BAL 334 7TH WARD
MC CUBBIN, JOSHUA BAL 387 8TH WARD
MC CUBBIN, LLOYD BAL 126 2ND DIST
MC CUBBIN, LLOYD BAL 128 2ND DIST
MC CUBBIN, LOVINIA BAL 339 3RD WARD
MC CUBBIN, MARY A. BAL 387 8TH WARD
MC CUBBIN, MISS ANN 282 ANNAPOLI
MC CUBBIN, NICHOLAS BAL 298 7TH WARD
MC CUBBIN, RICHARD BAL 034 9TH WARD
MC CUBBIN, RICHARD C. ANN 320 2ND DIST
MC CUBBIN, SALLY QUE 248 5TH E DI
MC CUBBIN, SAMUEL BAL 112 5TH WARD
MC CUBBIN, SAMUEL BAL 114 5TH WARD
MC CUBBIN, THOMAS BAL 126 2ND DIST
MC CUBBIN, THOMAS S. ALL 247 CUMBERLA
MC CUBBINS, JOHN * BAL 126 2ND DIST
MC CUBBINS, MARGARET E. BAL 443 8TH WARD
MC CUBBINS, THOMAS BAL 450 8TH WARD
MC CUBRAY, ELEN BAL 122 5TH WARD
MC CUBRAY, LOUIZA BAL 122 5TH WARD
MC CUE, JOHN BAL 442 1ST DIST
MC CUE, PATRICK ALL 129 4TH E.D.
MC CUE, PATRICK WAS 150 2ND DIST
MC CUEN, HUGHEY BAL 281 1ST DIST
MC CUEN, JAMES BAL 131 1ST WARD
MC CUEN, JOHN ALL 135 4TH E.D.
MC CUEN, PATRICK BAL 453 1ST DIST
MC CUFFRY, ANN ST 308 1ST E DI
MC CUIE, HUGH BAL 144 1ST WARD
MC CULLA, DUCITA HAR 147 3RD DIST
MC CULLA, ROBERT BAL 397 1ST DIST
MC CULLAH, WILLIAM BAL 463 1ST DIST
MC CULLER, CATHARINE BAL 213 11TH WAR
MC CULLER, GEORGE S. HAR 153 3RD DIST
MC CULLER, JAMES BAL 171 11TH WAR
MC CULLER, WILLIAM HAR 071 1ST DIST
MC CULLERS, DENNIS BAL 105 18TH WAR
MC CULLEY, MARGARET BAL 213 11TH WAR
MC CULLEY, WILLIAM BAL 264 17TH WAR
MC CULLIN, HUGH BAL 377 3RD WARD
MC CULLOB, GEORGE COLL. * ALL 090 5TH E.D.
MC CULLOCK, J. BAL 140 5TH WARD
MC CULLOCK, ROSE-BLACK BAL 208 2ND WARD
MC CULLOH, CHARLES M. ALL 255 CUMBERLA
MC CULLOH, DAVIS ALL 199 CUMBERLA
MC CULLOH, ELIZA ALL 255 CUMBERLA
MC CULLOH, JOSEPH ALL 235 CUMBERLA
MC CULLOH, SAMUEL BAL 073 15TH WAR
MC CULLOK, ARCHABALD BAL 233 1ST DIST
MC CULLOP, ROBERT ALL 106 5TH E.D.
MC CULLOT, ELIZ BAL 245 12TH WAR
MC CULLOUGH, ALEXANDER CEC 173 6TH E DI
MC CULLOUGH, AMBROSE BAL 214 6TH DIST
MC CULLOUGH, ANN BAL 169 11TH WAR
MC CULLOUGH, CATHARINE CEC 008 ELKTON 3
MC CULLOUGH, DEBORAH CEC 126 5TH E DI
MC CULLOUGH, DELIA CEC 008 ELKTON 3
MC CULLOUGH, DUNCAN BAL 330 3RD WARD
MC CULLOUGH, GEORGE CEC 003 ELKTON 3
MC CULLOUGH, GEORGE BAL 425 3RD WARD
MC CULLOUGH, HENRY BAL 007 EASTERN
MC CULLOUGH, HIRAM CEC 004 ELKTON 3
MC CULLOUGH, JAMES CEC 129 6TH E DI
MC CULLOUGH, JAMES CEC 193 5TH E DI
MC CULLOUGH, JAMES CEC 197 7TH E DI
MC CULLOUGH, JAMES BAL 218 6TH DIST
MC CULLOUGH, JAMES BAL 205 6TH DIST
MC CULLOUGH, JAMES H. DR. BAL 338 13TH WAR
MC CULLOUGH, JAMES N. CEC 151 PORT DUP
MC CULLOUGH, JANE BAL 273 7TH WARD
MC CULLOUGH, JETHRO CEC 077 NORTHEAS
MC CULLOUGH, JOHN CEC 151 PORT DUP
MC CULLOUGH, JOHN CEC 151 PORT DUP
MC CULLOUGH, JOHN CEC 173 6TH E DI
MC CULLOUGH, JOHN CEC 195 6TH E DI
MC CULLOUGH, JOHN FRE 194 5TH E DI
MC CULLOUGH, JOHN BAL 001 EASTERN
MC CULLOUGH, JOHN BAL 187 11TH WAR
MC CULLOUGH, JOHN ALL 096 5TH E.D.
MC CULLOUGH, JOHN A. FRE 168 EMMITTSB
MC CULLOUGH, JOHN M. ANN 342 3RD DIST
MC CULLOUGH, JOHN W. CEC 145 PORT DUP
MC CULLOUGH, JONAS FRE 174 5TH E DI
MC CULLOUGH, JONATHAN CEC 197 7TH E DI
MC CULLOUGH, JOSEPH FRE 169 5TH E DI
MC CULLOUGH, JOSEPH CEC 120 4TH E DI
MC CULLOUGH, LUCY CEC 196 6TH E DI
MC CULLOUGH, MARTHA CEC 203 6TH E DI
MC CULLOUGH, MARY CEC 208 7TH E DI
MC CULLOUGH, MARY FRE 145 10TH E D
MC CULLOUGH, MARY CEC 149 PORT DUP
MC CULLOUGH, NANCY CEC 173 6TH E DI
MC CULLOUGH, NATHANIEL BAL 420 14TH WAR
MC CULLOUGH, OLIVAR CEC 077 NORTHEAS
MC CULLOUGH, PASMO ANN 270 ANNAPOLI
MC CULLOUGH, RICHARD BAL 064 10TH WAR
MC CULLOUGH, SAMUEL BAL 379 8TH WARD

MC CULLOUGH, SARAH A. BAL 093 10TH WAR
MC CULLOUGH, SOPHIA CEC 003 ELKTON 3
MC CULLOUGH, WILLIAM CEC 180 6TH E DI
MC CULLOUGH, WILLIAM CEC 195 6TH E DI
MC CULLOUGH, WILLIAM BAL 391 8TH WARD
MC CULLOUGH, WILLIAM ALL 179 7TH E.D.
MC CULLOUGH, WILLIAM BAL 209 6TH DIST
MC CULLOUGHT, JOHN BAL 045 9TH WARD
MC CULLUM, EDWARD BAL 212 6TH DIST
MC CULLUM, JAMES BAL 142 1ST WARD
MC CULLUM, PHILIP BAL 029 15TH WAR
MC CULOH, GEORGE W. ALL 090 5TH E.D.
MC CULOT, WILLIAM R. ALL 206 CUMBERLA
MC CULTBAN, JAMES BAL 265 2ND WARD
MC CUMMINS, AMOS CEC 166 6TH E DI
MC CUMMINS, CASANDRA HAR 130 2ND DIST
MC CUMMINS, JOSEPH CEC 161 6TH E DI
MC CUMMINS, MARGARET CEC 158 PORT DUP
MC CUMMINS, ZEBULON HAR 122 2ND DIST
MC CUMMONS, EDWARD HAR 132 2ND DIST
MC CURD, SARAH J. CEC 155 PORT DUP
MC CURDY, DENNIS BAL 293 3RD WARD
MC CURDY, MARY J. BAL 181 2ND DIST
MC CURDY, SAMUEL BAL 238 6TH WARD
MC CURDY, SAMUEL ALL 217 CUMBERLA
MC CURLEY, FELIX BAL 049 18TH WAR
MC CURLEY, JAMES BAL 373 13TH WAR
MC CURLY, ELIZABETH BAL 041 18TH WAR
MC CURLY, JOHN BAL 041 18TH WAR
MC CURRY, JOHN BAL 232 6TH WARD
MC CURTH, MATTHEW FRE 246 NEW MARK
MC CURYO, ALEXANDER FRE 216 BUCKEYST
MC CUSKEE, ANN V. ALL 235 CUMBERLA
MC CUSKER, HUGH WAS 156 2ND DIST
MC CUSKEY, THOMAS BAL 010 18TH WAR
MC CUSKY, MARGARET ALL 213 CUMBERLA
MC CUTCHAN, GEORGE BAL 089 15TH WAR
MC CUTCHEN, EMMA BAL 409 14TH WAR
MC CUTCHION, JAMES BAL 259 17TH WAR
MC CUTHEN, JAMES CAR 181 8TH DIST
MC CVEY, MARY BAL 151 11TH WAR
MC DADE, ALEXANDER FRE 396 PETERSVI
MC DADE, CHARLES WAS 024 2ND SUBD
MC DADE, DAVID BAL 104 18TH WAR
MC DADE, DAVID FRE 081 FREDERIC
MC DADE, ELLEN FRE 327 MIDDLETO
MC DADE, HENRY ANN 440 HOWARD D
MC DADE, SAMUEL WAS 293 1ST DIST
MC DADE, SAMUEL A. BAL 104 18TH WAR
MC DADE, WALTER WAS 012 WILLIAMS
MC DADE, WALTER WAS 034 2ND SUBD
MC DALE, DAVID BAL 203 2ND WARD
MC DALL, DAVID BAL 195 19TH WAR
MC DALLE, SAMUEL FRE 001 FREDERIC
MC DANIEL, ALEN CHA 253 MIDDLETO
MC DANIEL, ANN ANN 424 HOWARD D
MC DANIEL, BENJAMIN R. TAL 103 ST MICHA
MC DANIEL, BETSEY TAL 020 EASTON D
MC DANIEL, BETTY CHA 242 HILLTOP
MC DANIEL, CATHERINE TAL 020 EASTON D
MC DANIEL, CHARLES W. TAL 109 ST MICHA
MC DANIEL, DANIEL FRE 265 NEW MARK
MC DANIEL, DAVID SOM 357 BRINKLEY
MC DANIEL, DAVID SOM 355 BRINKLEY
MC DANIEL, ELIZABETH WOR 306 2ND E DI
MC DANIEL, ELIZABETH QUE 208 3RD E DI
MC DANIEL, ELIZABETH CHA 234 HILLTOP
MC DANIEL, ELIZABETH BAL 017 15TH WAR
MC DANIEL, ENOS FRE 190 5TH E DI
MC DANIEL, FREDERICK BAL 320 12TH WAR
MC DANIEL, HARRIET FRE 040 FREDERIC
MC DANIEL, HARRIET WAS 156 HAGERSTO
MC DANIEL, JAMES SOM 356 BRINKLEY
MC DANIEL, JAMES SOM 437 DAMES QU
MC DANIEL, JAMES BAL 378 13TH WAR
MC DANIEL, JOE* TAL 059 EASTON D
MC DANIEL, JOHN WOR 189 7TH E DI
MC DANIEL, JOHN SOM 503 SALISBUR
MC DANIEL, JOHN FRE 001 FREDERIC
MC DANIEL, JOHN KEN 209 2ND DIST
MC DANIEL, JOHN BAL 112 18TH WAR
MC DANIEL, JOHN ALL 172 7TH E.D.
MC DANIEL, JOHN ALL 139 6TH E.D.
MC DANIEL, JOHN W. TAL 100 ST MICHA
MC DANIEL, JUDSON CHA 250 MIDDLETO
MC DANIEL, JULIANNA ANN 416 HOWARD D
MC DANIEL, LEMUEL CHA 291 MIDDLETO
MC DANIEL, MARGARET SOM 440 DAMES QU
MC DANIEL, MARTIN BAL 123 18TH WAR
MC DANIEL, MARY BAL 388 13TH WAR
MC DANIEL, MARY A. TAL 057 EASTON D
MC DANIEL, MICHAEL ALL 072 5TH E.D.
MC DANIEL, PRICILLA CHA 292 BOJANTOW
MC DANIEL, SAMUEL DOR 320 1ST DIST
MC DANIEL, SAMUEL WAS 229 1ST DIST
MC DANIEL, SARA CHA 228 BOJANTOW
MC DANIEL, SARAH SOM 445 DAMES QU
MC DANIEL, SARAH BAL 294 12TH WAR
MC DANIEL, STEPHEN WOR 310 2ND E DI
MC DANIEL, SUSAN A.-BLACK QUE 163 2ND E DI
MC DANIEL, THOMAS WOR 313 2ND E DI
MC DANIEL, THOMAS CHA 274 ALLENS F
MC DANIEL, THOMAS-BLACK QUE 197 3RD E DI
MC DANIEL, THOMAS-BLACK QUE 198 3RD E DI
MC DANIEL, WILLIAM BAL 119 1ST WARD
MC DANIEL, WILLIAM M. SOM 355 BRINKLEY
MC DANIEL, WILLIAM P. WAS 012 WILLIAMS
MC DANIELS, BRIDGET ALL 196 CUMBERLA
MC DANIELS, JAMES BAL 330 1ST DIST
MC DANILLL, MARTHA CHA 279 BOJANTOW
MC DANNA, PATRICK ANN 424 HOWARD D
MC DANNELL, WILLIAM CEC 018 ELKTON 3
MC DANOUGH, MARY BAL 278 2ND WARD
MC DAVID, CLEMENT ALL 013 3RD E.D.
MC DAVID, JOHN ALL 012 3RD E.D.
MC DAVID, JOHN ALL 145 6TH E.D.
MC DAVIT, FRANCIS BAL 443 1ST DIST
MC DEAITT, JAMES ANN 469 HOWARD D
MC DEMITY, LUKE ALL 055 10TH E.D
MC DEMROTT, MARY BAL 247 12TH WAR
MC DENGALL, ELIZABETH BAL 205 2ND WARD
MC DENNALS, R. BAL 161 1ST WARD
MC DENNIT, EDWARD ALL 196 CUMBERLA
MC DERIAT, THOMAS BAL 241 2ND WARD
MC DERITT, CHARLES FRE 084 FREDERIC
MC DERITT, JOHN FRE 087 FREDERIC
MC DERITT, REBECCA FRE 078 FREDERIC
MC DERITT, SAMUEL FRE 072 FREDERIC
MC DERMAT, MRS- BAL 285 1ST DIST
MC DERMIT, BARNARD BAL 455 1ST DIST

MC DERMIT, ELLEN BAL 378 1ST DIST
MC DERMIT, LUKE BAL 449 1ST DIST
MC DERMIT, MARY WAS 011 WILLIAMS
MC DERMIT, OWEN BAL 400 1ST DIST
MC DERMITT, ROSEANA BAL 356 1ST DIST
MC DERMOT, ALICE BAL 359 8TH WARD
MC DERMOT, BARNES BAL 359 8TH WARD
MC DERMOT, DANIEL ALL 069 5TH E.D.
MC DERMOT, DANIEL . HAR 103 2ND DIST
MC DERMOT, FRANCIS BAL 469 14TH WAR
MC DERMOT, FRANCIS WAS 118 2ND DIST
MC DERMOT, JAMES BAL 016 9TH WARD
MC DERMOT, JOHN ALL 226 CUMBERLA
MC DERMOT, JOHN CAR 237 UNION TO
MC DERMOT, MICHAEL BAL 100 2ND DIST
MC DERMOT, PATRICK BAL 097 2ND DIST
MC DERMOT, PATRICK ALL 046 10TH E.D
MC DERMOT, SUSAN BAL 275 2ND WARD
MC DERMOT, TERRENCE BAL 184 16TH WAR
MC DERMOT, THOMAS BAL 021 15TH WAR
MC DERMOT, THOMAS BAL 376 13TH WAR
MC DERMOT,RICHARD FRE 193 5TH E DI
MC DERMOTE, ANGATINE ALL 069 5TH E.D.
MC DERMOTT, CHARLES BAL 015 4TH WARD
MC DERMOTT, EDWARD HAR 085 2ND DIST
MC DERMOTT, J. BAL 148 1ST WARD
MC DERMOTT, JAMES BAL 380 8TH WARD
MC DERMOTT, JANE BAL 303 3RD WARD
MC DERMOTT, JANE BAL 341 3RD WARD
MC DERMOTT, MARGRETT BAL 064 18TH WAR
MC DERMOTT, MARTIN ALL 141 6TH E.D.
MC DERMOTT, MARY A. BAL 123 11TH WAR
MC DERMOTT, MARY ALBERT S BAL 316 20TH WAR
MC DERMOTT, PETER FRE 067 FREDERIC
MC DERMOTT, PETER ALL 135 4TH E.D.
MC DERMOTT, THOAMS ALL 143 6TH E.D.
MC DERMOTT, THOMAS ALL 152 6TH E.D.
MC DERMOTT, TIMOTHY BAL 177 11TH WAR
MC DERMOTT, WILLIAM T. BAL 033 9TH WARD
MC DERMUTT, JOHN FRE 045 FREDERIC
MC DERNOT, JOHN FRE 20 5TH E DI
MC DERNOT, MARY BAL 183 2ND WARD
MC DEVIET, JOHN BAL 367 8TH WARD
MC DEVIT, CORNELIUS BAL 367 8TH WARD
MC DEVIT, JAMES BAL 367 8TH WARD
MC DEVIT, JOHN BAL 367 8TH WARD
MC DEVITT, AGNUS BAL 379 13TH WAR
MC DEVITT, DAVID BAL 264 20TH WAR
MC DEVITT, EDWARD BAL 041 9TH WARD
MC DEVITT, JAMES PRI 107 PISCATAW
MC DEVITT, NEAL BAL 379 13TH WAR
MC DEVITT, SARAH BAL 085 15TH WAR
MC DEVITT, THOMAS ANN 282 ANNAPOLI
MC DIVET, MARY BAL 439 14TH WAR
MC DIVITT, JOHN BAL 157 6TH WARD
MC DOLE, SAMUEL CEC 122 4TH E DI
MC DOLE, SOPHIA CEC 147 PORT DUP
MC DONAGH, JAMES* BAL 395 3RD WARD
MC DONAL, ELEXANDER HAR 154 3RD DIST
MC DONAL, MATHEW CAR 192 4TH DIST
MC DONALD, ABRAM BAL 031 2ND DIST
MC DONALD, ALEXANDER ALL 069 5TH E.D.
MC DONALD, ALEXANDER BAL 295 12TH WAR
MC DONALD, ANDREW BAL 192 11TH WAR
MC DONALD, ANGUS BAL 002 15TH WAR
MC DONALD, ANN BAL 191 11TH WAR
MC DONALD, ANTHONY ALL 140 6TH E.D.
MC DONALD, CATHARINE BAL 443 1ST DIST
MC DONALD, CATHARINE BAL 384 13TH WAR
MC DONALD, CATHERINA BAL 155 11TH WAR
MC DONALD, CATHERINE BAL 023 4TH WARD
MC DONALD, CHARLES BAL 261 12TH WAR
MC DONALD, CHARLES BAL 422 8TH WARD
MC DONALD, CHARLES BAL 070 2ND DIST
MC DONALD, CHARLES BAL 285 1ST DIST
MC DONALD, CHARLES L. BAL 313 12TH WAR
MC DONALD, CHARLES S. BAL 065 10TH WAR
MC DONALD, DANIEL ALL 136 4TH E.D.
MC DONALD, DANIEL BAL 158 11TH WAR
MC DONALD, DAVID BAL 264 2ND WARD
MC DONALD, DEBORAH BAL 071 2ND DIST
MC DONALD, DOMINICK ALL 143 6TH E.D.
MC DONALD, ELIZABETH BAL 187 11TH WAR
MC DONALD, ELIZABETH BAL 385 1ST DIST
MC DONALD, ELLEN BAL 092 5TH WARD
MC DONALD, ELLEN BAL 057 15TH WAR
MC DONALD, ELLEN ALL 062 10TH E.D
MC DONALD, ELLEN BAL 050 9TH WARD
MC DONALD, ELLEN BAL 019 9TH WARD
MC DONALD, ENOS ALL 105 5TH E.D.
MC DONALD, GEORGE BAL 206 11TH WAR
MC DONALD, GRACE BAL 191 11TH WAR
MC DONALD, HARRIET E. BAL 073 15TH WAR
MC DONALD, HENRY SOM 414 DUBLIN D
MC DONALD, ISAAC BAL 141 1ST WARD
MC DONALD, ISABELLA BAL 165 11TH WAR
MC DONALD, J. BAL 286 2ND WARD
MC DONALD, J. BAL 149 1ST WARD
MC DONALD, J. BAL 149 1ST WARD
MC DONALD, J. BAL 066 10TH WAR
MC DONALD, J. BAL 118 1ST WARD
MC DONALD, J. M. BAL 322 12TH WAR
MC DONALD, JAMES BAL 319 7TH WARD
MC DONALD, JAMES BAL 122 1ST WARD
MC DONALD, JAMES BAL 124 1ST WARD
MC DONALD, JAMES BAL 152 1ST WARD
MC DONALD, JAMES BAL 170 1ST WARD
MC DONALD, JAMES BAL 006 9TH WARD
MC DONALD, JAMES BAL 132 1ST WARD
MC DONALD, JAMES BAL 071 2ND DIST
MC DONALD, JAMES PRI 030 VANSVILL
MC DONALD, JOANNA BAL 206 6TH WARD
MC DONALD, JOHN BAL 172 1ST WARD
MC DONALD, JOHN BAL 127 5TH WARD
MC DONALD, JOHN BAL 032 2ND DIST
MC DONALD, JOHN BAL 134 1ST WARD
MC DONALD, JOHN BAL 133 1ST WARD
MC DONALD, JOHN BAL 280 2ND WARD
MC DONALD, JOHN BAL 269 7TH WARD
MC DONALD, JOHN BAL 460 8TH WARD
MC DONALD, JOHN BAL 188 11TH WAR
MC DONALD, JOHN BAL 446 8TH WARD
MC DONALD, JOHN BAL 125 1ST WARD
MC DONALD, JOHN BAL 116 1ST WARD
MC DONALD, JOHN BAL 275 1ST DIST
MC DONALD, JOHN ALL 079 5TH E.D.
MC DONALD, JOHN BAL 091 5TH WARD
MC DONALD, JOHN BAL 092 18TH WAR
MC DONALD, JOHN CEC 088 4TH E DI
MC DONALD, JOHN F. BAL 369 13TH WAR

Name	County	Page	District
MC DONALD, JOSEPH	BAL	004	1ST WARD
MC DONALD, JOSEPH	BAL	134	1ST WARD
MC DONALD, JULIA A.	BAL	181	6TH WARD
MC DONALD, LAWRENCE	BAL	424	14TH WAR
MC DONALD, LILLY	BAL	087	1ST WARD
MC DONALD, MALCOM	BAL	143	1ST WARD
MC DONALD, MARGARET	BAL	288	17TH WAR
MC DONALD, MARGARET	BAL	470	14TH WAR
MC DONALD, MARGARET	WAS	009	WILLIAMS
MC DONALD, MARIA	BAL	096	1ST WARD
MC DONALD, MARSHAL	SOM	421	PRINCESS
MC DONALD, MARY	SOM	440	DAMES QU
MC DONALD, MARY	CEC	088	4TH E DI
MC DONALD, MARY	BAL	380	13TH WAR
MC DONALD, MARY	BAL	029	4TH WARD
MC DONALD, MARY	BAL	266	20TH WAR
MC DONALD, MARY	ALL	096	5TH E.D.
MC DONALD, MARY	BAL	174	11TH WAR
MC DONALD, MARY	BAL	053	2ND DIST
MC DONALD, MARY A.	BAL	070	2ND DIST
MC DONALD, MARY J.	BAL	213	11TH WAR
MC DONALD, MICHAEL	BAL	091	1ST WARD
MC DONALD, MICHAEL	BAL	172	2ND DIST
MC DONALD, MICHAEL	WAS	126	HAGERSTO
MC DONALD, OWEN	BAL	305	7TH WARD
MC DONALD, PATIENCE	SOM	434	PRINCESS
MC DONALD, PATRICK	BAL	177	2ND DIST
MC DONALD, PATRICK	BAL	017	1ST WARD
MC DONALD, PATRICK	BAL	275	1ST DIST
MC DONALD, PATRICK	BAL	014	2ND DIST
MC DONALD, PATRICK	BAL	005	EASTERN
MC DONALD, PATRICK	ALL	073	5TH E.D.
MC DONALD, PATRICK	ALL	052	10TH E.D
MC DONALD, PETER	ALL	053	10TH E.D
MC DONALD, PETER	BAL	329	13TH WAR
MC DONALD, PETER	SOM	409	DUBLIN D
MC DONALD, RANDELL	ALL	142	6TH E.D.
MC DONALD, RICHARD	BAL	181	6TH WARD
MC DONALD, RICHARD	BAL	213	2ND WARD
MC DONALD, RICHARD	HAR	073	1ST DIST
MC DONALD, ROANNON	ALL	053	10TH E.D
MC DONALD, ROBERT	BAL	257	6TH WARD
MC DONALD, ROSE	BAL	179	11TH WAR
MC DONALD, SABINA	BAL	427	1ST DIST
MC DONALD, SALLY	BAL	047	4TH WARD
MC DONALD, SAMUEL B.	CEC	112	4TH E DI
MC DONALD, SARAH	BAL	412	3RD WARD
MC DONALD, SARAH	BAL	319	7TH WARD
MC DONALD, SARAH	BAL	275	1ST DIST
MC DONALD, SARAH ANN	ALL	096	5TH E.D.
MC DONALD, STEPHEN	BAL	363	8TH WARD
MC DONALD, THOMAS	BAL	443	1ST DIST
MC DONALD, THOMAS	BAL	092	5TH WARD
MC DONALD, THOMAS	PRI	107	PISCATAW
MC DONALD, WILLIAM	BAL	327	1ST DIST
MC DONALD, WILLIAM	BAL	147	1ST WARD
MC DONALD, WILLIAM	CEC	126	5TH E DI
MC DONALD, WILLIAM H.	SOM	409	DUBLIN D
MC DONALD, WILLIAM H.	SOM	414	DUBLIN D
MC DONALD, WILLIAM J.	MGM	356	BERRYS D
MC DONALLY, JAMES	BAL	355	8TH WARD
MC DONAUGH, SISTER PAULIN	FRE	203	5TH E DI
MC DONEL, JAMES	ALL	142	6TH E.D.
MC DONELL, JOHN	BAL	165	19TH WAR
MC DONELL, LUCY	CEC	087	4TH E DI
MC DONGAL, AGNES	ALL	263	CUMBERLA
MC DONLAD, NICHOLAS	BAL	449	14TH WAR
MC DONNEL, BENJAMIN	BAL	286	20TH WAR
MC DONNEL, EDWARD	BAL	422	3RD WARD
MC DONNEL, JACOB	FRE	108	CREAGERS
MC DONNEL, JOHN	BAL	356	3RD WARD
MC DONNELL, ARTHUR	BAL	056	4TH WARD
MC DONNELL, BARNEY	ANN	520	HOWARD D
MC DONNELL, BIDDY	BAL	193	19TH WAR
MC DONNELL, BRIDGET	ALL	212	CUMBERLA
MC DONNELL, CHARLES	BAL	175	19TH WAR
MC DONNELL, ELIZABETH	FRE	126	CREAGERS
MC DONNELL, ELLEN	BAL	215	11TH WAR
MC DONNELL, JAMES	BAL	039	15TH WAR
MC DONNELL, JOHN W.	CEC	087	4TH E DI
MC DONNELL, MICHAEL	BAL	072	4TH WARD
MC DONNELL, PETER	ALL	208	CUMBERLA
MC DONNELL, SAMUEL	CEC	087	4TH E DI
MC DONNELL, SARAH	BAL	027	4TH WARD
MC DONNELL, SARAH	BAL	300	20TH WAR
MC DONNELL, SOLOMON*	BAL	017	4TH WARD
MC DONNELL, SUSAN	BAL	312	3RD WARD
MC DONNELL, WILLIAM	CEC	087	4TH E DI
MC DONNELL, WILLIAM	CEC	096	4TH E DI
MC DONNELL, WILLIAM	CEC	085	5TH E DI
MC DONNIER, AMBROSE	BAL	313	12TH WAR
MC DONOEYU, ANTHONY *	ALL	140	6TH E.D.
MC DONOLD, ALEXANDER	BAL	125	5TH WARD
MC DONOLD, DENNIS	HAR	101	2ND DIST
MC DONOUGH, BARNY	BAL	017	1ST WARD
MC DONOUGH, JAMES	MGM	372	BERRYS D
MC DONOUGH, JOHN	FRE	390	PETERSVI
MC DONOUGH, JOHN	WAS	256	1ST DIST
MC DONOUGH, JOSEPH	MGM	381	ROCKERLE
MC DONOUGH, JOSHUA	MGM	408	MEDLEY 3
MC DONOUGH, MARGARET	BAL	110	5TH WARD
MC DONOUGH, MARY	BAL	292	17TH WAR
MC DONOUGH, MILES	BAL	375	8TH WARD
MC DONOUGH, THOMAS	FRE	389	PETERSVI
MC DONOUGH, WILLIAM	BAL	021	2ND DIST
MC DORMAN, GEORGE	SOM	442	DAMES QU
MC DORMAN, POLLY	SOM	446	DAMES QU
MC DORMAN, WILLIAM	SOM	444	DAMES QU
MC DORMIT, CORNELIUS	HAR	038	1ST DIST
MC DOUELL, JAMES	BAL	033	9TH WARD
MC DOUGAL, JANE	BAL	153	11TH WAR
MC DOUGAL, MARGARET	BAL	362	13TH WAR
MC DOUGAL, MISS D.	FRE	199	5TH E DI
MC DOUGAL, MISS G.	FRE	198	5TH E DI
MC DOUGALL, HUGH	BAL	146	1ST WARD
MC DOUGAN, SAMUEL	ALL	102	5TH E.D.
MC DOUNEY, MARY	BAL	438	14TH WAR
MC DOUOUGH, JOHN *	BAL	111	2ND DIST
MC DOVET, JOHN	ALL	073	5TH E.D.
MC DOW, ANN R.	HAR	097	2ND DIST
MC DOW, SARAH J.	HAR	097	2ND DIST
MC DOWELL, ALEXANDER	CEC	212	7TH E DI
MC DOWELL, ANDREW	BAL	117	18TH WAR
MC DOWELL, CHARLES	CEC	198	7TH E DI
MC DOWELL, ELIZABETH	BAL	296	20TH WAR
MC DOWELL, ELIZABETH	BAL	024	4TH WARD
MC DOWELL, ELLEN	BAL	257	17TH WAR
MC DOWELL, ELLEN	BAL	091	5TH WARD
MC DOWELL, FRANCIS	BAL	136	18TH WAR
MC DOWELL, FREDERICK	ANN	343	3RD DIST
MC DOWELL, GEORGE H.	BAL	056	15TH WAR
MC DOWELL, HAMILTON	BAL	181	6TH WARD
MC DOWELL, JAMES	BAL	097	5TH WARD
MC DOWELL, JAMES	BAL	052	9TH WARD
MC DOWELL, JANE	BAL	182	6TH WARD
MC DOWELL, JOHN	BAL	161	6TH WARD
MC DOWELL, JOHN	ANN	343	3RD DIST
MC DOWELL, M.	BAL	063	10TH WAR
MC DOWELL, M. CATHERINE	BAL	317	20TH WAR
MC DOWELL, MARGARET	BAL	349	13TH WAR
MC DOWELL, NATHAN	WAS	274	RIDGEVIL
MC DOWELL, NELSON	CEC	203	6TH E DI
MC DOWELL, PERRY	BAL	443	14TH WAR
MC DOWELL, R.	BAL	094	10TH WAR
MC DOWELL, REESE	CEC	202	6TH E DI
MC DOWELL, SAMUEL	WAS	280	LEITERSB
MC DOWELL, THOMAS	BAL	097	5TH WARD
MC DOWNEY, ANN	BAL	468	14TH WAR
MC DRUMELL, HENRY S.	BAL	289	3RD WARD
MC DUELL, HENRY	FRE	393	PETERSVI
MC DUELL, ROBERT	FRE	382	PETERSVI
MC DUGAL, ELIZA	BAL	306	7TH WARD
MC DUKEHEART, SAMUEL*	BAL	051	4TH WARD
MC DURMIT, OWEN	BAL	356	8TH WARD
MC EINTIRE, JAMES	ALL	195	CUMBERLA
MC ELDER, EDWARD	BAL	150	19TH WAR
MC ELDEREY, HUGH	BAL	058	10TH WAR
MC ELDERRY, HENRY	BAL	259	6TH WARD
MC ELDERY, HUGH	BAL	265	17TH WAR
MC ELDOWNEY, JOHN	BAL	247	12TH WAR
MC ELDOWNEY, ROBERT	BAL	073	15TH WAR
MC ELDRA, SOPHIA	CEC	153	PORT DUP
MC ELDRY, ELLEN	BAL	371	3RD WARD
MC ELDRY, WILLIAM	BAL	291	1ST DIST
MC ELEER, FRANCES	BAL	448	1ST DIST
MC ELEER, FRANCES	BAL	448	1ST DIST
MC ELEER, FRANCIS	BAL	363	8TH WARD
MC ELEER, MARGARET	BAL	448	1ST DIST
MC ELFEISH, THOMAS	ALL	165	9TH E.D.
MC ELFISH, DAVID	ALL	193	9TH E.D.
MC ELFISH, ELSEY	ALL	174	7TH E.D.
MC ELFISH, EMELINE	ALL	191	9TH E.D.
MC ELFISH, HANNAH	ALL	193	9TH E.D.
MC ELFISH, JAMES	ALL	193	9TH E.D.
MC ELFISH, OWEN	ALL	193	9TH E.D.
MC ELFISH, OWEN	ALL	193	9TH E.D.
MC ELFISH, THOMAS	ALL	189	9TH E.D.
MC ELFRESH, CATHARINE M.	BAL	220	1ST DIST
MC ELFRESH, CHARLES T.	FRE	227	BUCKEYST
MC ELFRESH, DAVIS	BAL	232	1ST DIST
MC ELFRESH, ELLENOR	FRE	228	BUCKEYST
MC ELFRESH, HENRY	FRE	033	FREDERIC
MC ELFRESH, JOHN	FRE	245	NEW MARK
MC ELFRESH, JOHN J.	BAL	359	13TH WAR
MC ELFRESH, SARAH	MGM	433	CLARKSTR
MC ELHANEYK JOHN	BAL	393	14TH WAR
MC ELHANY, BRIDGET	BAL	285	17TH WAR
MC ELHENY, ROBERT	BAL	275	1ST DIST
MC ELHINNY, ELISABETH	ANN	376	4TH DIST
MC ELLROY, JAMES	BAL	127	5TH WARD
MC ELNELLY, JAMES L.	BAL	149	19TH WAR
MC ELNELLY, THOMAS	BAL	149	19TH WAR
MC ELOY, ROBERT	BAL	101	1ST WARD
MC ELPHESH, RACHEL G.	FRE	243	NEW MARK
MC ELRAY, ISABELLA	BAL	443	14TH WAR
MC ELROY, ANN	BAL	263	20TH WAR
MC ELROY, ANN	BAL	210	6TH WARD
MC ELROY, ANN	BAL	090	5TH WARD
MC ELROY, CATHARINE	BAL	005	EASTERN
MC ELROY, CATHERINE	FRE	066	FREDERIC
MC ELROY, DANIEL	HAR	084	2ND DIST
MC ELROY, DANIEL	BAL	064	15TH WAR
MC ELROY, ELIZABETH	BAL	461	14TH WAR
MC ELROY, GEORGE	BAL	089	5TH WARD
MC ELROY, GRACE	BAL	188	19TH WAR
MC ELROY, JAMES	BAL	187	19TH WAR
MC ELROY, JAMES	FRE	202	5TH E DI
MC ELROY, JAMES	BAL	110	10TH WAR
MC ELROY, JANE	BAL	213	11TH WAR
MC ELROY, JANE	BAL	154	19TH WAR
MC ELROY, JOHN	BAL	148	19TH WAR
MC ELROY, JOHN	BAL	263	20TH WAR
MC ELROY, JOHN	BAL	277	20TH WAR
MC ELROY, JOHN	BAL	418	8TH WARD
MC ELROY, MARGARET	BAL	215	11TH WAR
MC ELROY, MARY	BAL	134	5TH WARD
MC ELROY, PATRICK	BAL	089	5TH WARD
MC ELROY, ROBERT	BAL	100	5TH WARD
MC ELROY, S.	BAL	154	19TH WAR
MC ELROY, SARAH	BAL	400	1ST DIST
MC ELROY, THOMAS	BAL	082	10TH WAR
MC ELROY, THOMAS	BAL	057	15TH WAR
MC ELRVAIN, JOHN *	BAL	282	1ST DIST
MC ELVENNY, JOHN	BAL	280	1ST DIST
MC ELVERY, ANN	BAL	186	19TH WAR
MC ELVIN, MARGARET	BAL	281	20TH WAR
MC ELWAIN, JOHN *	BAL	282	1ST DIST
MC ELWEL, WILLIAM	BAL	237	6TH WARD
MC ENALLY, ELLEN	ALL	078	5TH E.D.
MC ENALLY, MICHAEL	ALL	078	5TH E.D.
MC ENALLY, PATRICK	ALL	076	5TH E.D.
MC ENALLY, PATRICK	ALL	084	5TH E.D.
MC ENALLY, PATRICK	ALL	143	6TH E.D.
MC ENANCH, JOHN	BAL	399	1ST DIST
MC ENDALL, THOMAS	BAL	169	1ST WARD
MC ENICH, ARCHIBALD	BAL	399	1ST DIST
MC ENNIS, DOROTHY	BAL	316	20TH WAR
MC ENNOTT, JOHN	BAL	264	2ND WARD
MC ENTIRE, JAMES	ALL	123	4TH E.D.
MC ENTIRE, JANE	BAL	295	1ST DIST
MC ENTIRER, JOHN	BAL	295	1ST DIST
MC ENTRE, JAMES	ALL	195	CUMBERLA
MC EVERS, JULIET E. *	BAL	389	13TH WAR
MC EVOY, DAVID	WAS	161	2ND DIST
MC EVOY, MARY	BAL	255	12TH WAR
MC EWEN, MARY	BAL	052	9TH WARD
MC EWEN, SINCLAIR	BAL	144	19TH WAR
MC EWIN, ELIZABETH	CEC	092	4TH E DI
MC EWING, HENRY	PRI	026	VANSVILL
MC EWING, ROBERT	PRI	027	VANSVILL
MC FADDEN, ANN M.	BAL	138	18TH WAR
MC FADDEN, CATHARINE	WAS	161	2ND DIST
MC FADDEN, CORNELIUS	BAL	410	8TH WARD
MC FADDEN, DENNIS	BAL	138	18TH WAR
MC FADDEN, JOHN	BAL	471	14TH WAR
MC FADDEN, JOSEPH A.	FRE	399	JEFFERSO
MC FADDEN, LOUISA	BAL	051	1ST WARD
MC FADDEN, MARY	BAL	165	11TH WAR
MC FADDEN, MARY	BAL	161	11TH WAR
MC FADDEN, P.	BAL	254	20TH WAR
MC FADDEN, SARAH	TAL	114	ST MICHA
MC FADDIN, CHARLES G.	HAR	129	2ND DIST
MC FADDIN, DENNIS	FRE	161	EMMITTSB
MC FADDIN, JANE	HAR	124	2ND DIST
MC FADDIN, JOHN	HAR	036	1ST DIST
MC FADDIN, P.	BAL	315	20TH WAR
MC FADDIN, SAMUEL	HAR	132	2ND DIST
MC FADDIN, THOMAS	HAR	111	2ND DIST
MC FADDON, ANN	HAR	032	1ST DIST
MC FADDON, ELIZA	BAL	248	6TH WARD
MC FADDON, JOHN	HAR	094	2ND DIST
MC FADDON, MARGARET A.	BAL	333	7TH WARD
MC FADDON, ROBERT	HAR	043	1ST DIST
MC FADDON, SAMEUL	ANN	439	HOWARD D
MC FADEN, JOHN	BAL	289	3RD WARD
MC FADIEN, JOHN	CEC	167	6TH E DI
MC FADIEN, JOSEPH	CEC	100	3RD E DI
MC FADIN, ALEXANDER	CEC	100	3RD E DI
MC FADON, HUGH	BAL	367	13TH WAR
MC FADON, MARGARETT	BAL	023	4TH WARD
MC FADON, P.	BAL	103	10TH WAR
MC FADON, SASANNAH	BAL	367	13TH WAR
MC FALL, MARGARET	BAL	121	5TH WARD
MC FALL, MARY	BAL	063	10TH WAR
MC FALL, SAMUEL	BAL	132	1ST WARD
MC FALLEN, JOHN	BAL	203	19TH WAR
MC FALLON, CAROLINE	BAL	002	9TH WARD
MC FALLOW, JOHN	ALL	141	6TH E.D.
MC FARLAN, DANIEL	BAL	359	8TH WARD
MC FARLAND, ARCH	BAL	124	1ST WARD
MC FARLAND, CATHERINE	BAL	042	9TH WARD
MC FARLAND, EDWARD	BAL	403	3RD WARD
MC FARLAND, ELIAS	CAR	395	2ND DIST
MC FARLAND, GEORGE	CEC	037	CHESAPEA
MC FARLAND, HOLDEANN	CEC	152	PORT DUP
MC FARLAND, JAMES	BAL	185	11TH WAR
MC FARLAND, JOHN	BAL	281	2ND WARD
MC FARLAND, JOHN	BAL	125	1ST WARD
MC FARLAND, JOHN	BAL	156	1ST WARD
MC FARLAND, JOHN	BAL	007	1ST WARD
MC FARLAND, JOHN	ALL	106	5TH E.D.
MC FARLAND, JOHN	BAL	155	16TH WAR
MC FARLAND, JOHN	CEC	152	PORT DUP
MC FARLAND, JOHN	TAL	070	EASTON T
MC FARLAND, JOHN HJR.	TAL	071	EASTON T
MC FARLAND, MARGARET	BAL	185	11TH WAR
MC FARLAND, MARIA J.	BAL	259	1ST DIST
MC FARLAND, MARY	BAL	393	1ST DIST
MC FARLAND, PETER	BAL	023	9TH WARD
MC FARLAND, PETER	BAL	359	8TH WARD
MC FARLAND, REBECCA	CEC	021	ELKTON 3
MC FARLAND, SAMUEL	ALL	113	5TH E.D.
MC FARLAND, SARAH	CEC	037	CHESAPEA
MC FARLAND, THOMAS	BAL	382	1ST DIST
MC FARLAND, THOMAS	BAL	039	2ND DIST
MC FARLAND, VIRGINIA	BAL	282	1ST DIST
MC FARLANE, WILLIAM	BAL	042	2ND DIST
MC FARLIN, PATRICK	HAR	101	2ND DIST
MC FARLINE, MARGARET	BAL	007	1ST WARD
MC FARREN LYETH, JOHN *	BAL	138	18TH WAR
MC FARREN, J.	BAL	166	1ST WARD
MC FARREN, JAMES	WAS	258	1ST DIST
MC FARRES, JOHN	ALL	202	CUMBERLA
MC FAUL, BRIGET	BAL	460	1ST DIST
MC FAUL, CATHERINE	BAL	161	11TH WAR
MC FAUL, CHARLES	BAL	161	11TH WAR
MC FAUL, ENEAS *	BAL	313	20TH WAR
MC FAUL, JAMES	BAL	181	11TH WAR
MC FAUL, JOHN	BAL	161	11TH WAR
MC FAUL, JOHN *	BAL	294	20TH WAR
MC FAWBLE, JOSEPH *	BAL	418	1ST DIST
MC FAY, JAMES	BAL	128	2ND DIST
MC FAY, SAMUEL	BAL	445	8TH WARD
MC FEARNAM, ANN	BAL	442	8TH WARD
MC FEBEY, BARNETT	HAR	152	3RD DIST
MC FEE, JAMES	BAL	320	3RD WARD
MC FEE, JAMES	BAL	174	1ST WARD
MC FEE, JOHN	BAL	378	1ST DIST
MC FEELY, EDWARD	BAL	186	19TH WAR
MC FEELY, JOHN F.	QUE	245	5TH E DI
MC FEELY, RACHEL B.	QUE	184	3RD E DI
MC FERSON, FANNY	BAL	379	1ST DIST
MC FIRE, D.	BAL	115	1ST WARD
MC FOGGY, DANIEL	ALL	218	CUMBERLA
MC FOLAND, LAWRENCE	BAL	447	8TH WARD
MC FREDERICK, JAMES	ANN	442	HOWARD D
MC GAHAN, JOHN	BAL	364	8TH WARD
MC GAHAN, MARY A.	BAL	188	16TH WAR
MC GAHAN, ROSINE	BAL	358	8TH WARD
MC GAHAN, WILLIAM	BAL	316	7TH WARD
MC GAHN, MARY	WAS	013	WILLIAMS
MC GAHUN, JOHN	FRE	022	FREDERIC
MC GAIN, MARGARETT	BAL	098	18TH WAR
MC GAIN, SARAH	BAL	250	2ND WARD
MC GAINEY, JOHN	BAL	001	9TH WARD
MC GAIRTY, MARY J.	BAL	360	8TH WARD
MC GALAUGHLIN, MARY	ALL	244	CUMBERLA
MC GALL, KAMBLE	BAL	187	19TH WAR
MC GALLIGEN, JOHN	ALL	040	2ND E.D.
MC GAN, JOSEPH	ALL	049	10TH E.D
MC GAN, MICHAEL *	BAL	146	2ND DIST
MC GANN, ELLEN	BAL	331	13TH WAR
MC GAR, PATRICK	ALL	229	CUMBERLA
MC GAREY, DAVID	BAL	456	8TH WARD
MC GARITY, J.	BAL	296	20TH WAR
MC GARITY, PATRICK	BAL	355	8TH WARD
MC GARN, CHARLES	BAL	464	14TH WAR
MC GARRA, JOHN	BAL	322	1ST DIST
MC GARREL, BARNEY	BAL	333	3RD WARD
MC GARRIGILL, JOHN	BAL	333	7TH WARD
MC GARRITY, JOHN	BAL	268	17TH WAR
MC GARRITY, WILLIAM	BAL	134	5TH WARD
MC GARTH, JAMES	BAL	200	19TH WAR
MC GARTLAND, ELLEN	BAL	344	13TH WAR
MC GARTLAND, MARY	BAL	344	13TH WAR
MC GARVEY, ELLEN	BAL	150	19TH WAR
MC GARVIN, ANN	BAL	158	2ND DIST
MC GARY, BRIDGET	ALL	254	CUMBERLA
MC GARY, JAMES	FRE	308	WOODSBOR
MC GARY, JOHN	FRE	204	BUCKEYST
MC GARY, JOHN	BAL	131	1ST WARD
MC GATH, ANN	BAL	292	17TH WAR
MC GAUGH, JOHN	BAL	240	6TH WARD
MC GAUGHLAN, THOMAS	BAL	055	1ST WARD
MC GAUGHRAN, PHILIP	FRE	216	BUCKEYST
MC GAUVERN, BARTHOLOMEW	BAL	240	6TH WARD
MC GAVERN, JOHN	BAL	173	11TH WAR
MC GAVIN, BRIDGET	BAL	432	14TH WAR
MC GAW, ANN	BAL	019	4TH WARD
MC GAW, AQUILA	HAR	187	3RD DIST

Name	County	Page	District
MC GAW, JOHN	HAR	161	3RD DIST
MC GAW, JOHN C.*	BAL	050	4TH WARD
MC GAW, MICHAEL	BAL	022	1ST WARD
MC GAW, ROBERT	HAR	188	3RD DIST
MC GAW, SALLY ANN	BAL	047	2ND DIST
MC GAWIN, THOMAS	BAL	274	7TH WARD
MC GAY, MARGARET	BAL	201	11TH WAR
MC GAYDEN, JAMES	BAL	126	1ST WARD
MC GEAN, MANAS E.	BAL	269	20TH WAR
MC GEAN, SAMUEL	BAL	058	1ST WARD
MC GEARY, M.	BAL	032	9TH WARD
MC GEATH, LAWRENCE	BAL	169	2ND DIST
MC GEDDY, JOHN	BAL	329	13TH WAR
MC GEE, ALEXANDER	BAL	136	2ND DIST
MC GEE, ANN	WOR	245	1ST CENS
MC GEE, BENJAMIN	BAL	389	3RD WARD
MC GEE, BETSEY	SOM	424	PRINCESS
MC GEE, BRIDGET	BAL	112	18TH WAR
MC GEE, CATHERINE	BAL	100	10TH WAR
MC GEE, DANIEL	BAL	134	2ND DIST
MC GEE, DAVID	HAR	102	2ND DIST
MC GEE, ELIZA	BAL	054	9TH WARD
MC GEE, ELIZABETH	FRE	339	MIDDLETO
MC GEE, ELLEN	BAL	261	17TH WAR
MC GEE, FINTON	FRE	343	MIDDLETO
MC GEE, FRANCIS	BAL	026	18TH WAR
MC GEE, GEORGE T.	CEC	065	1ST E DI
MC GEE, HANNAH	ALL	213	CUMBERLA
MC GEE, HUGH	BAL	047	9TH WARD
MC GEE, HUGH	WAS	179	BOONSBOR
MC GEE, JAMES	WAS	132	HAGERSTO
MC GEE, JAMES	BAL	051	9TH WARD
MC GEE, JAMES	BAL	021	2ND DIST
MC GEE, JAMES	BAL	412	1ST DIST
MC GEE, JAMES	CEC	053	1ST E DI
MC GEE, JAMES	CEC	121	4TH E DI
MC GEE, JAMES	HAR	098	2ND DIST
MC GEE, JAMES	HAR	057	1ST DIST
MC GEE, JAMES	HAR	160	3RD DIST
MC GEE, JAMES W.	BAL	084	18TH WAR
MC GEE, JAMES W.	FRE	311	MIDDLETO
MC GEE, JESSA	WOR	245	1ST CENS
MC GEE, JOHN	WOR	245	1ST CENS
MC GEE, JOHN	BAL	422	14TH WAR
MC GEE, JOHN	BAL	231	19TH WAR
MC GEE, JOHN	BAL	178	19TH WAR
MC GEE, JOHN	BAL	163	2ND DIST
MC GEE, JOHN	BAL	237	12TH WAR
MC GEE, JOHN	BAL	235	12TH WAR
MC GEE, JOSEPH	DOR	380	1ST DIST
MC GEE, LEWIS	FRE	092	FREDERIC
MC GEE, LION	BAL	332	7TH WARD
MC GEE, MARIAH	WOR	280	BERLIN 1
MC GEE, MARY	DOR	386	1ST DIST
MC GEE, MARY	BAL	026	18TH WAR
MC GEE, MICHAEL	BAL	213	17TH WAR
MC GEE, NANCY	WOR	247	1ST CENS
MC GEE, PAT	BAL	141	5TH WARD
MC GEE, PATRICK	BAL	008	EASTERN
MC GEE, PATTERSON	BAL	420	14TH WAR
MC GEE, PETER	FRE	234	BUCKEYST
MC GEE, ROBERT	BAL	412	1ST DIST
MC GEE, ROSE	BAL	118	5TH WARD
MC GEE, SALLY	BAL	283	12TH WAR
MC GEE, SARAH	WOR	247	1ST CENS
MC GEE, SIMON	BAL	077	4TH WARD
MC GEE, SUSANNA	BAL	212	11TH WAR
MC GEE, THOMAS	PRI	103	SPALDING
MC GEE, THOMAS	ALL	262	CUMBERLA
MC GEE, THOMAS	BAL	013	1ST WARD
MC GEE, WILLIAM	QUE	188	3RD E DI
MC GEE, WILLIAM	BAL	258	17TH WAR
MC GEE, WILLIAM	CEC	154	PORT DUP
MC GEE, WILLIAM	CEC	010	ELKTON 3
MC GEEHAN, MILES	BAL	033	15TH WAR
MC GEERY, JAMES	BAL	039	15TH WAR
MC GEESTER, ALICE	BAL	090	1ST WARD
MC GEHE, ABRAHAM	BAL	276	2ND WARD
MC GEIGAN, ELIZABETH	BAL	051	1ST WARD
MC GEN, THOMAS	BAL	213	17TH WAR
MC GENIRE, ANN	BAL	241	2ND WARD
MC GENITY, MARGARET	BAL	193	11TH WAR
MC GENN, ROSANNA	BAL	379	13TH WAR
MC GENNIS, ROSANNA	BAL	077	4TH WARD
MC GENUS, MARY	BAL	103	2ND DIST
MC GEOCH, MARY*	BAL	084	4TH WARD
MC GEOGH, JOHN	BAL	366	3RD WARD
MC GERNITY, ROSANNA	BAL	136	11TH WAR
MC GETTINGEN, ELIZA	ALL	020	2ND E.D.
MC GEW, JAMES	BAL	083	1ST WAR
MC GHEE, EDWARD	BAL	035	15TH WAR
MC GHEE, JANE	BAL	028	4TH WARD
MC GHEEHAN, EDWARD	CAR	281	7TH DIST
MC GHOFFER, HENRY	BAL	159	19TH WAR
MC GIBBENS, GEORGE	ALL	150	6TH E.D.
MC GIBBIN, ELIZA J.	BAL	068	18TH WAR
MC GIBBON, JAMES	ALL	086	5TH E.D.
MC GIDDEGON, CATHERINE	ALL	237	CUMBERLA
MC GIFF, PATRICK	BAL	002	9TH WARD
MC GIFFEN, JOHN	BAL	083	18TH WAR
MC GIFFERN, CLAUDIUS	BAL	098	10TH WAR
MC GIFFIN, ANN	BAL	229	19TH WAR
MC GILL, ARABELLA W.	FRE	398	JEFFERSO
MC GILL, EDWAD	FRE	220	BUCKEYST
MC GILL, GEORGE	BAL	293	1ST DIST
MC GILL, J.	BAL	162	1ST WARD
MC GILL, JOHN	WAS	158	2ND DIST
MC GILL, LUCY ANN	BAL	386	13TH WAR
MC GILL, NANCY	BAL	066	15TH WAR
MC GILL, OLOVER P.	BAL	413	1ST DIST
MC GILL, PATRICK	BAL	401	14TH WAR
MC GILL, PATRICK	FRE	409	JEFFERSO
MC GILL, RICHARD	BAL	057	15TH WAR
MC GILL, ROBERT	FRE	033	FREDERIC
MC GILL, ROSE	BAL	213	11TH WAR
MC GILL, SARAH	BAL	183	16TH WAR
MC GILL, THOMAS	BAL	385	13TH WAR
MC GILL, THOMAS J.	FRE	398	JEFFERSO
MC GILL, WILLIAM	BAL	081	1ST WARD
MC GILLEY, PATRICK	BAL	040	9TH WARD
MC GIM, ANN	ALL	254	CUMBERLA
MC GIMNA, JOHN*	TAL	007	EASTON D
MC GIN, H.	BAL	230	19TH WAR
MC GINAGILL, JAMES	CEC	187	7TH E DI
MC GINESS, JOHN	BAL	262	1ST DIST
MC GINIVE, THOMAS	BAL	241	2ND WARD
MC GINLEY, CATHARINE	BAL	455	1ST DIST
MC GINLEY, JAMES	BAL	074	15TH WAR
MC GINN, JAMES	BAL	201	11TH WAR
MC GINN, JAMES R.	BAL	199	11TH WAR
MC GINNES, GEORGE	CEC	177	7TH E DI
MC GINNES, PETER	ALL	081	5TH E.D.
MC GINNES, ROBERT	FRE	281	WOODSBOR
MC GINNESS, BENJAMIN R. *	KEN	281	3RD DIST
MC GINNESS, JOHN	BAL	260	1ST DIST
MC GINNESS, JOHN	BAL	068	1ST WARD
MC GINNESS, JOHN P.	ALL	082	5TH E.D.
MC GINNESS, MARY	BAL	068	4TH WARD
MC GINNESS, MARY *	KEN	281	3RD DIST
MC GINNESS, NATHANIEL	KEN	284	3RD DIST
MC GINNESS, TARBETT C.	KEN	284	3RD DIST
MC GINNEY, JAMES	BAL	177	11TH WAR
MC GINNEY, PATRICK	BAL	177	11TH WAR
MC GINNEY, PATRICK	BAL	014	4TH WARD
MC GINNIS, A.	BAL	148	1ST WARD
MC GINNIS, ARTHEN	BAL	102	1ST WARD
MC GINNIS, ARTHUR	BAL	051	1ST WARD
MC GINNIS, ARTHUR	BAL	401	3RD WARD
MC GINNIS, ARTHUR	FRE	167	EMMITTSB
MC GINNIS, CECELIA	BAL	316	20TH WAR
MC GINNIS, ELIZABETH	BAL	143	2ND DIST
MC GINNIS, FRANCIS J.	BAL	355	3RD WARD
MC GINNIS, HARRIET	BAL	353	13TH WAR
MC GINNIS, HESTER*	TAL	014	EASTON D
MC GINNIS, JACOB J.	TAL	090	ST MICHA
MC GINNIS, JAMES	BAL	127	1ST WARD
MC GINNIS, JAMES	BAL	048	9TH WARD
MC GINNIS, JOHN	BAL	007	EASTERN
MC GINNIS, JOHN	BAL	185	2ND WARD
MC GINNIS, JOHN	ALL	155	6TH E.D.
MC GINNIS, JOHN	BAL	309	20TH WAR
MC GINNIS, JOHN	BAL	020	4TH WARD
MC GINNIS, JOHN	BAL	303	17TH WAR
MC GINNIS, MANES	ANN	496	HOWARD D
MC GINNIS, MARY	BAL	341	7TH WARD
MC GINNIS, MICHEAL	BAL	055	18TH WAR
MC GINNIS, PATRICK	BAL	341	7TH WARD
MC GINNIS, PATRICK	BAL	309	7TH WARD
MC GINNIS, R.	BAL	139	19TH WAR
MC GINNIS, ROSA	BAL	215	11TH WAR
MC GINNIS, SUSAN	BAL	215	11TH WAR
MC GINNIS, THOMAS	BAL	154	1ST WARD
MC GINNIS, VAN	ALL	059	10TH E.D
MC GINNISS, WILLIAM	KEN	284	3RD DIST
MC GINNITY, MARGARET	BAL	099	10TH WAR
MC GINNY, JOHN	TAL	067	EASTON T
MC GINNY, JOHN	TAL	006	EASTON D
MC GINNY, SAMUEL H.	TAL	012	EASTON D
MC GIRCK, HENRY	BAL	017	18TH WAR
MC GIRCK, JAMES	BAL	017	18TH WAR
MC GIRE, BIRDGET	BAL	314	20TH WAR
MC GIRGIN, JAMES *	FRE	126	CREAGERS
MC GIRK, JOSEPH	BAL	401	14TH WAR
MC GIRK, PETER	BAL	225	19TH WAR
MC GIRLEY, JOHN	BAL	047	9TH WARD
MC GITTIGAN, WILLAIM	ANN	500	HOWARD D
MC GITTIGEN, JAMES	ALL	020	2ND E.D.
MC GIVENEY, JAMES	BAL	027	4TH WARD
MC GIVENEY, JAMES	BAL	016	4TH WARD
MC GIVINS, WILLIAM	BAL	070	4TH WARD
MC GIVNEY, EDWARD	ALL	081	5TH E.D.
MC GIVNEY, JOHN	BAL	403	3RD WARD
MC GLANAN, KITTY	BAL	355	13TH WAR
MC GLANGHLIN, JOHN	ALL	210	CUMBERLA
MC GLANGHLIN, LEWIS	ALL	210	CUMBERLA
MC GLANNAN, THOMAS	BAL	444	14TH WAR
MC GLASER, JOSEPH	BAL	171	1ST WARD
MC GLASHAM, J.	BAL	157	1ST WARD
MC GLATTEN, DICK	DOR	423	1ST DIST
MC GLAUGHLIN, HENRY	ALL	210	CUMBERLA
MC GLAUGHLIN, MARY A.	FRE	019	FREDERIC
MC GLAUGHLIN, PETER	ALL	245	CUMBERLA
MC GLAUGHLIN, THOMAS	ALL	254	CUMBERLA
MC GLEANY, ELLEN	TAL	066	EASTON T
MC GLEN, ELLEN	BAL	304	1ST DIST
MC GLENAN, PATRICK	BAL	459	1ST DIST
MC GLENN, JOHN	QUE	250	5TH E DI
MC GLENN, MICHAEL	ALL	156	6TH E.D.
MC GLENNAN, D. MR.	BAL	133	11TH WAR
MC GLENNAN, HENRY	BAL	291	20TH WAR
MC GLINER, JOHN	BAL	163	2ND DIST
MC GLINN, MICHAEL	BAL	390	3RD WARD
MC GLOCKLAN, ANN	BAL	366	8TH WARD
MC GLOEKLIN, GEORGE	QUE	196	3RD E DI
MC GLONE, EDWARD	BAL	144	1ST WARD
MC GLONE, GEORGE	BAL	137	11TH WAR
MC GLONE, JANE	BAL	157	11TH WAR
MC GLONE, JOHN	BAL	179	11TH WAR
MC GLONE, MARY	BAL	137	11TH WAR
MC GLOSLIN, ANTONY	HAR	158	3RD DIST
MC GLOSLIN, THOMAS	HAR	146	3RD DIST
MC GLOSSHAN, CHARLES *	BAL	280	2ND WARD
MC GLOTEN, W.*	DOR	456	1ST DIST
MC GLOTHER, JOSEPH	WOR	266	BERLIN 1
MC GLOTHLIN, JOSEPH	CEC	136	6TH E DI
MC GLOTTEN, DANIEL	DOR	420	1ST DIST
MC GLOTTEN, DAVID	DOR	421	1ST DIST
MC GLOTTEN, ELIZABETH*	DOR	457	1ST DIST
MC GLOTTEN, HUGH	DOR	458	1ST DIST
MC GLOUGHLING, ELLEN	BAL	187	16TH WAR
MC GLOUNE, BARBARY	BAL	188	11TH WAR
MC GLUE, THOMAS	BAL	155	1ST WARD
MC GOBRIN, M.	BAL	143	5TH WARD
MC GODDIN, JOHN	BAL	409	3RD WARD
MC GOMMON, MARY	BAL	394	14TH WAR
MC GONEGAL, DANIEL	HAR	141	2ND DIST
MC GONEGAL, ROBERT	CAR	095	NO TWP L
MC GONEGILE, JOSHUA	CAR	097	NO TWP L
MC GONIGAL, JAMES	WAS	137	HAGERSTO
MC GONIGAL, JOHN	WAS	137	HAGERSTO
MC GONIGAL, JOHN	WAS	134	HAGERSTO
MC GOOD, RICHMOND MRS.	BAL	192	11TH WAR
MC GOODWIN, P. *	BAL	315	20TH WAR
MC GOOKIN, JOHN	BAL	311	1ST DIST
MC GORDON, JOSEPH	BAL	432	14TH WAR
MC GORE, JAMES	WAS	026	2ND SUBD
MC GORE, PATRICK	WAS	026	2ND SUBD
MC GORGAN, MALLY	BAL	179	19TH WAR
MC GORVAN, HUGH	BAL	200	19TH WAR
MC GOUCE, GEORGE C.	BAL	310	12TH WAR
MC GOUFFIN, JAMES	BAL	161	11TH WAR
MC GOUKIN, CATHARINE *	BAL	165	2ND DIST
MC GOURT, AURTHUR	BAL	271	17TH WAR
MC GOVAN, WILLIAM	BAL	190	19TH WAR
MC GOVERN, DANIEL	BAL	302	17TH WAR
MC GOVERN, JOHN	BAL	201	19TH WAR
MC GOVERN, M.	BAL	099	10TH WAR
MC GOVERN, MARIA	BAL	054	9TH WARD
MC GOVERN, WILLIAM	WAS	263	1ST DIST
MC GOWAN, ANN	BAL	134	5TH WARD
MC GOWAN, BERNARD	BAL	152	16TH WAR
MC GOWAN, BRIDGET	BAL	188	2ND WARD
MC GOWAN, BRIDGET	BAL	383	8TH WARD
MC GOWAN, DANIEL	BAL	298	12TH WAR
MC GOWAN, ELLEN	BAL	130	5TH WARD
MC GOWAN, FRANCES	ALL	156	6TH E.D.
MC GOWAN, GRACE	BAL	463	1ST DIST
MC GOWAN, GRIDGET	BAL	312	20TH WAR
MC GOWAN, HENRY	BAL	193	11TH WAR
MC GOWAN, HENRY	ANN	455	HOWARD D
MC GOWAN, HUGH	BAL	464	14TH WAR
MC GOWAN, JAMES	BAL	460	1ST DIST
MC GOWAN, JAMES	BAL	291	7TH WARD
MC GOWAN, JOHN	ALL	075	5TH E.D.
MC GOWAN, JOHN	BAL	455	14TH WAR
MC GOWAN, NANCY	BAL	243	12TH WAR
MC GOWAN, PATRICK	BAL	173	11TH WAR
MC GOWAN, PETER	BAL	345	7TH WARD
MC GOWAN, PETER	BAL	028	4TH WARD
MC GOWAN, QANN	ALL	078	5TH E.D.
MC GOWEN, MARGARET	BAL	384	8TH WARD
MC GOWEN, N.	BAL	173	1ST WARD
MC GOWEN, PATRICK	BAL	305	3RD WARD
MC GOWER, ANTHONY	ALL	069	5TH E.D.
MC GOWER, FRANCIS	BAL	464	14TH WAR
MC GOWN, CHARLES	ALL	215	CUMBERLA
MC GOWN, JOSEPH	BAL	012	2ND DIST
MC GOWN, SARAH	ALL	247	CUMBERLA
MC GRADGAN, JOHN	BAL	193	11TH WAR
MC GRAFF, JOHN	FRE	221	BUCKEYST
MC GRAFF, OWEN	BAL	444	1ST DIST
MC GRAGOR, MARGARETT	BAL	463	1ST DIST
MC GRAIN, LEREANCE	BAL	170	11TH WAR
MC GRANLAGHAN, ELIZA	ANN	414	HOWARD D
MC GRATH, BRIDGETT	BAL	170	2ND DIST
MC GRATH, DOLLY	SOM	542	TYASKIN
MC GRATH, EDWARD	BAL	257	12TH WAR
MC GRATH, EDWARD	BAL	023	9TH WARD
MC GRATH, EDWARD	BAL	050	9TH WARD
MC GRATH, EMILY	SOM	488	SALISBUR
MC GRATH, HUGH	BAL	082	2ND DIST
MC GRATH, JAMES	BAL	168	2ND DIST
MC GRATH, JAMES	WAS	047	2ND SUBD
MC GRATH, JOHN	BAL	062	2ND DIST
MC GRATH, JOHN	BAL	077	15TH WAR
MC GRATH, JOHN	BAL	187	16TH WAR
MC GRATH, JOHN	BAL	296	12TH WAR
MC GRATH, KATE	BAL	101	5TH WARD
MC GRATH, LEWIS	SOM	432	PRINCESS
MC GRATH, MARGARET	ALL	245	CUMBERLA
MC GRATH, MARY ANN	BAL	097	10TH WAR
MC GRATH, MARY E.	BAL	076	10TH WAR
MC GRATH, STEPHEN	BAL	469	14TH WAR
MC GRATH, THOMAS	WOR	196	8TH E DI
MC GRATH, THOMAS H.	BAL	059	15TH WAR
MC GRATH, WILLIAM	BAL	300	17TH WAR
MC GRATH, WILLIAM JR.	WOR	197	8TH E DI
MC GRATH, WILLIAM SR.	WOR	194	8TH E DI
MC GRATT, SUSAN	BAL	213	11TH WAR
MC GRAW, ALICE	BAL	280	7TH WARD
MC GRAW, ANN	BAL	308	3RD WARD
MC GRAW, ANN	BAL	304	3RD WARD
MC GRAW, ANN	CAR	148	NO TWP L
MC GRAW, BETSEY	BAL	063	1ST WARD
MC GRAW, BETSEY	SOM	353	BRINKLEY
MC GRAW, BRIDGET	BAL	339	3RD WARD
MC GRAW, CAROLINE	HAR	193	3RD DIST
MC GRAW, CATHERINE	BAL	036	4TH WARD
MC GRAW, D.	BAL	118	1ST WARD
MC GRAW, DANIEL	WAS	037	2ND SUBD
MC GRAW, ELIZABETH	SOM	488	SALISBUR
MC GRAW, ELIZABETH	BAL	304	3RD WARD
MC GRAW, ELIZABETH	BAL	164	6TH WARD
MC GRAW, FRANCES	FRE	168	EMMITTSB
MC GRAW, HANNAH	BAL	050	1ST WARD
MC GRAW, JAMES	BAL	032	1ST WARD
MC GRAW, JAMES	BAL	340	3RD WARD
MC GRAW, JAMES	BAL	340	3RD WARD
MC GRAW, JAMES C.	ALL	254	CUMBERLA
MC GRAW, JESSE	SOM	354	BRINKLEY
MC GRAW, JOHN	BAL	164	6TH WARD
MC GRAW, JOHN	BAL	279	7TH WARD
MC GRAW, JOHN	ALL	071	5TH E.D.
MC GRAW, JOHN	HAR	194	3RD DIST
MC GRAW, MARGART	HAR	157	3RD DIST
MC GRAW, MARIAH	SOM	479	TRAPP DI
MC GRAW, MARY	BAL	346	3RD WARD
MC GRAW, OWEN	BAL	210	2ND WARD
MC GRAW, REDMON	ALL	129	4TH E.D.
MC GRAW, ROBERT F.	HAR	175	3RD DIST
MC GRAW, SARAH	BAL	357	1ST DIST
MC GRAW, SARAH	SOM	355	BRINKLEY
MC GRAWS, JOHN	QUE	126	1ST E DI
MC GRAY, CATHARINE	BAL	290	12TH WAR
MC GREAN, ANDY	BAL	114	5TH WARD
MC GREAR, PATRICK	BAL	304	17TH WAR
MC GREAVY HANAH	BAL	444	8TH WARD
MC GREAVY, MARGARET	BAL	445	8TH WARD
MC GREEDY, MARY	CEC	149	PORT DUP
MC GREEN, RODGER	CAR	082	NO TWP L
MC GREEVY, W.	BAL	289	12TH WAR
MC GREGOR, ABRICK	PRI	017	BLADENSB
MC GREGOR, ELEN	BAL	150	11TH WAR
MC GREGOR, GEORGE	BAL	259	6TH WAR
MC GREGOR, JAMES	BAL	006	9TH WARD
MC GREGOR, JAMES	WOR	263	BERLIN 1
MC GREGOR, JANE	CEC	089	4TH E DI
MC GREGOR, JOHN	CEC	089	4TH E DI
MC GREGOR, WILIAM	WAS	034	2ND SUBD
MC GREROY, JOHN	BAL	287	12TH WAR
MC GREROY, REBECCA	BAL	289	12TH WAR
MC GREWY, ARTHUR	BAL	246	12TH WAR
MC GRICE, CLARA	BAL	252	12TH WAR
MC GRIFFIN, JAMES	ALL	015	3RD E.D.
MC GRIFFIN, JAMES	BAL	044	18TH WAR
MC GRIM, THOMAS	ALL	230	CUMBERLA
MC GROCH, MARY*	BAL	084	4TH WARD
MC GROGAN, CHARLES	ALL	081	5TH E.D.
MC GROGAN, ELLEN	ALL	081	5TH E.D.
MC GROTH, R.	BAL	135	1ST WARD
MC GROW, MARGARET	QUE	208	3RD E DI
MC GROW, PATRICK	BAL	447	1ST DIST
MC GRUDE, JAMES	ALL	132	4TH E.D.
MC GRUDER, ANNA	FRE	120	CREAGERS
MC GRUDER, BURGES	ALL	244	CUMBERLA
MC GRUDER, HANNAH	FRE	114	CREAGERS
MC GRUDER, MISS A.	FRE	199	5TH E DI
MC GRUDER, SUSAN	ALL	249	CUMBERLA
MC GTOBER, JACOB	DOR	383	1ST DIST
MC GTOLLER, LEAH	DOR	429	1ST DIST

Name	County	Page	District
MC GUE, GEORGE	MGM	441	CLARKSTR
MC GUEN, HENRY	ALL	218	CUMBERLA
MC GUFFAN, ANTHONY	BAL	172	11TH WAR
MC GUFFIN, WILLIAM	BAL	465	14TH WAR
MC GUGAN, J.	BAL	117	1ST WARD
MC GUGIN, ANN	BAL	124	5TH WARD
MC GUIGAN, ELIZABETH	BAL	401	3RD WARD
MC GUIGAN, IGNIS	HAR	011	1ST DIST
MC GUIGAN, JOHN	BAL	121	11TH WAR
MC GUIGAN, JOHN A.	FRE	065	FREDERIC
MC GUIGAN, MARY	BAL	125	5TH WARD
MC GUIGAN, MISS A.	FRE	199	5TH E DI
MC GUIGAN, THOMAS	BAL	360	8TH WARD
MC GUIGEN, BARNEY	BAL	286	17TH WAR
MC GUIGGIN, AUTHER J.	TAL	067	EASTON T
MC GUILIN, MICHAEL	BAL	457	8TH WARD
MC GUIN, BRIDGET	BAL	141	11TH WAR
MC GUIN, WILLIAM	ALL	150	6TH E.D.
MC GUINCY, OLIVER*	BAL	005	4TH WARD
MC GUINN, WILLIAM	BAL	385	13TH WAR
MC GUINNESS, ROBERT	CEC	212	7TH E DI
MC GUIRE, ANDREW	BAL	282	2ND WARD
MC GUIRE, ANDREW	BAL	197	2ND WARD
MC GUIRE, ANN E.	QUE	245	5TH E DI
MC GUIRE, ARTHUR	BAL	122	1ST WARD
MC GUIRE, BERNARD	BAL	242	17TH WAR
MC GUIRE, BRIDGET C.	WAS	279	LEITERSB
MC GUIRE, CHANY	CAR	096	NO TWP L
MC GUIRE, CHARLES B.	WAS	247	SMITHSBU
MC GUIRE, ELISABETH	ALL	074	5TH E.D.
MC GUIRE, ELIZA	BAL	277	2ND WARD
MC GUIRE, ELLEN	ANN	413	HOWARD D
MC GUIRE, GEORGE	BAL	097	5TH WARD
MC GUIRE, GEORGE	BAL	264	17TH WAR
MC GUIRE, HUGH	ALL	105	5TH E.D.
MC GUIRE, HUGH	ALL	139	6TH E.D.
MC GUIRE, HUGH	DOR	468	1ST DIST
MC GUIRE, JAMES	ALL	102	5TH E.D.
MC GUIRE, JAMES	BAL	366	8TH WARD
MC GUIRE, JAMES	BAL	405	8TH WARD
MC GUIRE, JAMES	BAL	247	1ST DIST
MC GUIRE, JAMES	BAL	165	1ST WARD
MC GUIRE, JAMES	BAL	099	18TH WAR
MC GUIRE, JAMES	FRE	20	5TH E DI
MC GUIRE, JANE	WAS	137	2ND DIST
MC GUIRE, JOHN	CAR	079	NO TWP L
MC GUIRE, JOHN	BAL	127	5TH WARD
MC GUIRE, JOHN	BAL	121	5TH WARD
MC GUIRE, JOHN	BAL	006	9TH WARD
MC GUIRE, MARGARET	BAL	174	2ND DIST
MC GUIRE, MARTHA	BAL	098	2ND DIST
MC GUIRE, MARTIN	ALL	102	5TH E.D.
MC GUIRE, MARY	BAL	056	2ND DIST
MC GUIRE, MATILDA	ALL	206	CUMBERLA
MC GUIRE, MICHAEL	ALL	070	5TH E.D.
MC GUIRE, NANCY	BAL	410	14TH WAR
MC GUIRE, OWEN	BAL	426	8TH WARD
MC GUIRE, OWEN	WAS	124	2ND DIST
MC GUIRE, PAT	BAL	460	1ST DIST
MC GUIRE, PATERICK	CAR	231	5TH DIST
MC GUIRE, PATRICK	BAL	134	5TH WARD
MC GUIRE, PATRICK	BAL	144	1ST WARD
MC GUIRE, ROGER	BAL	031	15TH WAR
MC GUIRE, SAMUEL	ALL	206	CUMBERLA
MC GUIRE, SAMUEL R.	CEC	147	PORT DUP
MC GUIRE, THOMAS	CAR	092	NO TWP L
MC GUIRE, THOMAS	BAL	104	18TH WAR
MC GUIRE, THOMAS	FRE	065	FREDERIC
MC GUIRE, THOMAS	ALL	150	6TH E.D.
MC GUIRE, THOMAS	BAL	161	1ST WARD
MC GUIRE, URIAH	BAL	286	17TH WAR
MC GUIRE, WILLIAM	BAL	124	5TH WARD
MC GUIRE, WILLIAM	KEN	293	3RD DIST
MC GUIRE,MICHAEL	QUE	163	2ND E DI
MC GUIRKAN, JOSEPH	BAL	102	5TH WARD
MC GUITY, MARY	BAL	183	11TH WAR
MC GUMERY, JAMES	DOR	351	3RD DIVI
MC GUMEY, A.	BAL	252	20TH WAR
MC GUNIGAN, CAHRELS	BAL	167	19TH WAR
MC GUNN, JAMES	BAL	233	12TH WAR
MC GURGAN, JOHN L.	CEC	173	6TH E DI
MC GURIE, ELLEN	BAL	317	20TH WAR
MC GURIN, BRIDGET	ANN	483	HOWARD D
MC GURK, CATHARINE	BAL	123	5TH WARD
MC GURK, MARGARET	BAL	235	20TH WAR
MC GURK, THERESA	BAL	096	10TH WAR
MC GURK, THOMAS	BAL	235	20TH WAR
MC GURKINS, JAMES	CEC	213	7TH E DI
MC GURKINS, JOHN	CEC	213	7TH E DI
MC GURNIS, MARY	ALL	242	CUMBERLA
MC GURON, JAMES	BAL	159	11TH WAR
MC GUTCHEON, EMMA	BAL	476	14TH WAR
MC GUTHY, FELIX	BAL	296	20TH WAR
MC HALE,MCHEL	BAL	076	2ND DIST
MC HALL, ELOCK	ALL	085	5TH E.D.
MC HANEN, EMILY	BAL	009	EASTERN
MC HANEY, JOHN	BAL	010	9TH WARD
MC HANNEY, JOHN	BAL	002	9TH WARD
MC HAPPY, ROBERT	CEC	021	ELKTON 3
MC HARG, BRIDGET	BAL	008	15TH WAR
MC HARG, SAMUEL	BAL	008	15TH WAR
MC HARTHEY, MARY	BAL	342	13TH WAR
MC HAVE, MARGARETT	BAL	172	11TH WAR
MC HEALD, ELIZABETH	BAL	023	18TH WAR
MC HEDRY, JANE	BAL	190	11TH WAR
MC HENDEREN, JOHN	BAL	017	1ST WARD
MC HENRY, BRIDGET	BAL	241	2ND WARD
MC HENRY, EDWARD	BAL	053	4TH WARD
MC HENRY, GEORGE	HAR	048	1ST DIST
MC HENRY, HENRY	FRE	113	CREAGERS
MC HENRY, HUGH	BAL	101	10TH WAR
MC HENRY, JAMES	ALL	208	CUMBERLA
MC HENRY, JAMES	BAL	288	20TH WAR
MC HENRY, JAMES	BAL	141	11TH WAR
MC HENRY, JOHN	BAL	297	20TH WAR
MC HENRY, JOHN	ALL	042	10TH E.D
MC HENRY, JOHN	WOR	345	1ST E DI
MC HENRY, JOHN H.	FRE	123	CREAGERS
MC HENRY, JOSEPH	BAL	145	19TH WAR
MC HENRY, MILCAH	BAL	196	11TH WAR
MC HENRY, N.	BAL	316	20TH WAR
MC HENRY, RAMSEY	HAR	107	2ND DIST
MC HENRY, SALLY	BAL	459	14TH WAR
MC HENRY, WILLIAM	BAL	146	19TH WAR
MC HENRY, WILLIAM	CEC	142	6TH E DI
MC HENRY, WILLIAM	BAL	266	7TH WARD
MC HERD, ELIZABETH	KEN	287	3RD DIST
MC HERSON, SAMUEL	BAL	088	1ST WARD
MC HOWARD, LENARD	HAR	182	3RD DIST
MC HUMPHREYS, JAMES	SOM	426	PRINCESS
MC IEGUE, THOMAS *	ALL	127	4TH E.D.
MC ILDEN, THOMAS	CEC	089	4TH E DI
MC ILHANEY, ROBERT	BAL	052	2ND DIST
MC ILHANEY, MARSHALL	FRE	20	5TH E DI
MC ILHEARNE, FRANCIS	FRE	20	5TH E DI
MC ILHENEY, NANCY	WAS	123	HAGERSTO
MC ILHENNY, ANN M.	WAS	124	HAGERSTO
MC ILHENNY, CHARLES	WAS	152	HAGERSTO
MC ILHENNY, ELIZABETH	WAS	126	HAGERSTO
MC ILHENNY, JOHN	WAS	129	HAGERSTO
MC ILHENNY, JOHN H.	BAL	108	10TH WAR
MC ILHENNY, LUTITIA	WAS	152	HAGERSTO
MC ILHENNY, MARY J.	BAL	159	16TH WAR
MC ILHENNY, MICHAEL	WAS	152	HAGERSTO
MC ILLURD, JAMES	BAL	233	1ST DIST
MC ILLVANE, JEREMIAH	HAR	118	2ND DIST
MC ILOWINE, MARIA *	BAL	274	20TH WAR
MC ILRANEY, BERNARD	BAL	228	2ND WARD
MC ILROY, JAMES	BAL	253	6TH WARD
MC ILROY, JOHN	BAL	070	4TH WARD
MC ILROY, MARY	BAL	107	10TH WAR
MC ILVAIN, DONALD	BAL	099	10TH WAR
MC ILVAIN, JOHN	BAL	053	9TH WARD
MC ILVAIN, JOHN	WAS	268	1ST DIST
MC ILVAIN, MARGARET	MGM	339	CLARKSBU
MC ILVAIN, WILLAIM	BAL	401	14TH WAR
MC ILVAINE, DAVID	BAL	173	19TH WAR
MC ILVAINE, ELZEY	BAL	173	19TH WAR
MC ILVENY, ELLEN	BAL	179	19TH WAR
MC INCID, CATHERINE	ALL	208	CUMBERLA
MC INETREY, JANE	BAL	307	3RD WARD
MC INGHAM, WILLIAM M.	BAL	165	19TH WAR
MC INGZRE, PATRICK	BAL	411	14TH WAR
MC INTEE, MARY	BAL	121	11TH WAR
MC INTIRE, ALICE	BAL	193	11TH WAR
MC INTIRE, ANDREW	BAL	047	9TH WARD
MC INTIRE, ANDREW	CEC	015	ELKTON 3
MC INTIRE, ANDREW	CEC	004	ELKTON 3
MC INTIRE, CHARLES	WAS	286	1ST DIST
MC INTIRE, DANIEL	BAL	130	1ST WARD
MC INTIRE, G.W.	WAS	141	HAGERSTO
MC INTIRE, J.	BAL	161	1ST WARD
MC INTIRE, JAMES	CEC	016	ELKTON 3
MC INTIRE, JMES	BAL	294	12TH WAR
MC INTIRE, JOHN	BAL	160	1ST WARD
MC INTIRE, JOHN	KEN	290	3RD DIST
MC INTIRE, JOHN J.	CEC	122	4TH E DI
MC INTIRE, JOSEPH	BAL	292	12TH WAR
MC INTIRE, MARGARET	BAL	018	15TH WAR
MC INTIRE, MARGARET	ALL	123	4TH E.D.
MC INTIRE, MARY	BAL	215	11TH WAR
MC INTIRE, MARY	CEC	015	ELKTON 3
MC INTIRE, MARY	CEC	016	ELKTON 3
MC INTIRE, PATRICK	BAL	164	2ND DIST
MC INTIRE, PHILIP	BAL	192	11TH WAR
MC INTIRE, REBECCA	WAS	156	HAGERSTO
MC INTIRE, ROBERT J.	CEC	175	7TH E DI
MC INTIRE, SUSAN	WAS	151	HAGERSTO
MC INTOSH, ALEX	BAL	146	1ST WARD
MC INTOSH, EMMA	BAL	367	8TH WARD
MC INTOSH, HELLEN	BAL	324	7TH WARD
MC INTOSH, JOHN	BAL	470	14TH WAR
MC INTOSH, JOSEPH	BAL	440	14TH WAR
MC INTOSH, JOSEPH	FRE	344	MIDDLETO
MC INTOSH, JOSEPHINE	BAL	445	8TH WARD
MC INTOSH, MARGARET JR.	BAL	324	7TH WARD
MC INTOSH, MARIA	FRE	341	MIDDLETO
MC INTOSH, MARY	BAL	310	7TH WARD
MC INTOSH, WILLIAM	BAL	370	13TH WAR
MC INTYRE, ALEXANDER	BAL	080	10TH WAR
MC INTYRE, JANE	BAL	294	3RD WARD
MC INTYRE, JOHN	SOM	461	HANGARY
MC INTYRE, JOHN	SOM	465	HANGARY
MC INTYRE, LEWIS	ALL	130	4TH E.D.
MC INTYRE, MARGARET	BAL	011	2ND DIST
MC INTYRE, MARY	BAL	275	20TH WAR
MC INTYRE, OWEN	BAL	110	10TH WAR
MC INTYRE, PATRICK	BAL	421	14TH WAR
MC INTYRE, SUSAN	BAL	428	14TH WAR
MC ITHANNEY, ELIZABETH	CAR	234	UNION TO
MC IVAIN, MARY M.	WAS	269	1ST DIST
MC IVEN, JAMES	BAL	014	2ND DIST
MC JEEVY, MARY	BAL	317	20TH WAR
MC JEFFERY, WILLIAM	HAR	075	BEL AIR
MC JILLIAN, ROSANNA	BAL	431	14TH WAR
MC JILTON, DANIEL A.	BAL	140	16TH WAR
MC JILTON, JOHN F.	BAL	060	15TH WAR
MC JILTON, JOHN N.	BAL	056	15TH WAR
MC JILTON, MARY E.	BAL	056	15TH WAR
MC JILTON, WESLEY	BAL	323	7TH WARD
MC JITTON, DANIEL REV-	BAL	029	18TH WAR
MC JITTON, THOMAS	BAL	183	2ND WARD
MC JODDEN, JOHN	BAL	052	9TH WARD
MC KAIG, ELIZABETH	BAL	414	14TH WAR
MC KAIG, ISAAC	CEC	088	4TH E DI
MC KAIG, JAMES	BAL	320	12TH WAR
MC KAIG, JHOHN	BAL	051	2ND DIST
MC KAIG, JOHN	CEC	108	3RD E DI
MC KAIG, PATRICK	ALL	155	6TH E.D.
MC KAIG, ROBERT	BAL	095	5TH WARD
MC KAIG, WILLIAM	CEC	088	4TH E DI
MC KAIGG, ROBERT S.	ALL	256	CUMBERLA
MC KAIGG, THOMAS	ALL	207	CUMBERLA
MC KAIGG, WILLIAM W.	ALL	207	CUMBERLA
MC KAIN, ANN	BAL	264	1ST DIST
MC KALE, KITTY	BAL	100	10TH WAR
MC KALL, LOUIS	BAL	472	14TH WAR
MC KALLIP, JAMES	CAR	242	TANEYTOW
MC KANA, ELLEN	BAL	168	11TH WAR
MC KANA, HENRY	BAL	179	11TH WAR
MC KANE, MARY L.	BAL	155	11TH WAR
MC KANNEY, MICHAEL	BAL	387	3RD WARD
MC KARNEY, CHARLES	CEC	179	7TH E DI
MC KAW, JAMES	CEC	057	1ST E DI
MC KAW, WILLIAM	CEC	058	1ST E DI
MC KAY, BENJAMIN	ST	292	2ND E DI
MC KAY, BENJAMIN	ST	310	1ST E DI
MC KAY, BRIDGET	CEC	088	4TH E DI
MC KAY, CECELIA-BLACK	ST	330	4TH E DI
MC KAY, D.	BAL	162	1ST WARD
MC KAY, FRANK	BAL	124	1ST WARD
MC KAY, J.	BAL	150	1ST WARD
MC KAY, J.	BAL	138	1ST WARD
MC KAY, JOANNA	BAL	220	12TH WAR
MC KAY, JOHN	BAL	386	3RD WARD
MC KAY, JOHN	BAL	248	6TH WARD
MC KAY, JOHN	BAL	031	9TH WARD
MC KAY, JOHN	ANN	464	HOWARD D
MC KAY, M.F.	BAL	164	1ST WARD
MC KAY, MARGARET	BAL	033	1ST WARD
MC KAY, MARTHA	ANN	464	HOWARD D
MC KAY, MARY	BAL	055	1ST WARD
MC KAY, MARY A.	BAL	007	1ST WARD
MC KAY, MARY ALICE SIS-	BAL	316	20TH WAR
MC KAY, NELSON	ANN	304	1ST DIST
MC KAY, OLIVER T.	ST	296	2ND E DI
MC KAY, ROBERT	ST	296	2ND E DI
MC KAY, SISTER CORSINA	FRE	197	5TH E DI
MC KAY, THOMAS	CEC	041	CHESAPEA
MC KAY, THOMAS	ST	297	2ND E DI
MC KAY, THOMAS	BAL	092	1ST WARD
MC KAY, WILLIAM	BAL	348	7TH WARD
MC KAY, WILLIAM	ST	310	1ST E DI
MC KEAN, EDWARD	BAL	159	19TH WAR
MC KEAN, JAMES D.	BAL	046	4TH WARD
MC KEAN, JOHN	BAL	159	19TH WAR
MC KEAN, PATRICK	BAL	278	20TH WAR
MC KEAN,MRS.	ALL	263	CUMBERLA
MC KEARNEY, MARY	FRE	056	FREDERIC
MC KEE, AGNES	BAL	174	19TH WAR
MC KEE, ALEXANDER	PRI	067	NOTTINGH
MC KEE, BERNARD	BAL	059	15TH WAR
MC KEE, C.B. REV.	BAL	262	1ST DIST
MC KEE, CHARLES	BAL	430	14TH WAR
MC KEE, CHARLES	BAL	160	11TH WAR
MC KEE, DR. J.B.	WAS	128	HAGERSTO
MC KEE, ELIZA	BAL	412	14TH WAR
MC KEE, ELIZA J.	BAL	169	16TH WAR
MC KEE, GEORGE S.	BAL	094	1ST WARD
MC KEE, HUGH	WAS	286	1ST DIST
MC KEE, JANE F.	BAL	059	15TH WAR
MC KEE, JOHN	BAL	283	12TH WAR
MC KEE, JOHN	BAL	107	15TH WAR
MC KEE, JOHN	WAS	283	1ST DIST
MC KEE, JOHN	WAS	067	2ND SUBD
MC KEE, JOHN F.	KEN	223	2ND DIST
MC KEE, LEANDER	WAS	135	HAGERSTO
MC KEE, MARGARET	BAL	221	12TH WAR
MC KEE, MARGARET	BAL	236	12TH WAR
MC KEE, MARY	BAL	186	19TH WAR
MC KEE, MICHAEL	BAL	124	5TH WARD
MC KEE, PATRICK	ALL	203	CUMBERLA
MC KEE, PATRICK	ALL	031	2ND E.D.
MC KEE, PATRICK	BAL	226	6TH WARD
MC KEE, PATRICK	BAL	342	1ST DIST
MC KEE, SAMUEL	WAS	224	1ST DIST
MC KEE, STEPHEN	WOR	169	6TH E DI
MC KEE, STEPHEN	WOR	168	6TH E DI
MC KEE, THOMAS	ALL	219	CUMBERLA
MC KEE, WILLIAM H.	BAL	189	11TH WAR
MC KEE, WILSON	ANN	469	HOWARD D
MC KEEDEN, D.W.	BAL	261	12TH WAR
MC KEEL, WILLIAM	BAL	352	7TH WARD
MC KEEN, CARMELIA	BAL	137	11TH WAR
MC KEEN, CHARLES	BAL	461	1ST DIST
MC KEEN, JAMES	ALL	088	5TH E.D.
MC KEEN, JOHN	BAL	009	EASTERN
MC KEENER, JOSHUA	CEC	197	7TH E DI
MC KEES, JOHN	BAL	083	18TH WAR
MC KEEVER, ANN	BAL	251	6TH WARD
MC KEEVER, BRIDGET	BAL	260	12TH WAR
MC KEEVER, BRIDGET	BAL	157	11TH WAR
MC KEEVER, DANIEL	BAL	146	1ST WARD
MC KEEVER, ELLEN	BAL	268	20TH WAR
MC KEEVER, ISAAC	BAL	159	11TH WAR
MC KEEVER, JAMES	BAL	252	20TH WAR
MC KEEVER, JAMES	BAL	170	11TH WAR
MC KEEVER, JOHN	BAL	384	8TH WARD
MC KEEVER, MARGARET	BAL	155	11TH WAR
MC KEEVER, NEALY	BAL	143	19TH WAR
MC KEEVER, SUSAN	BAL	201	11TH WAR
MC KEEVERS, ROSE	BAL	080	4TH WARD
MC KEHAN, JAMES	BAL	254	12TH WAR
MC KEHAN, JANE	FRE	163	EMMITTSB
MC KEHAN, SAMUEL	BAL	255	12TH WAR
MC KEIN, SUSANAH	BAL	212	11TH WAR
MC KEIVEN, JOHN	BAL	274	12TH WAR
MC KELDEN, WILLIAM	BAL	080	18TH WAR
MC KELDON, EDWARD M.	CEC	154	PORT DUP
MC KELL, WILLIAM	BAL	120	16TH WAR
MC KELLEY, JAMES	FRE	285	WOODSBOR
MC KELSE, ISABELLA	BAL	234	2ND WARD
MC KELVIN, CAROLIN	BAL	045	18TH WAR
MC KELVIN, JOHN	BAL	132	18TH WAR
MC KELVY, ELIZABETH	BAL	283	12TH WAR
MC KELVY, JOHN	BAL	282	12TH WAR
MC KEN, FRANCS	BAL	256	12TH WAR
MC KENAN, HUGH	BAL	081	10TH WAR
MC KENDICK, GOERGE	PRI	097	SPALDING
MC KENEY, JOSEPH	ANN	403	8TH DIST
MC KENIG, DANIEL	BAL	094	1ST WARD
MC KENLEY, ANN	BAL	332	13TH WAR
MC KENLEY, GEORGE	BAL	305	1ST DIST
MC KENLEY, JOHN *	BAL	341	1ST DIST
MC KENLY, ELIZABETH	BAL	033	1ST WARD
MC KENLY, JAMES	BAL	033	1ST WARD
MC KENNA, ANN	BAL	231	19TH WAR
MC KENNA, ANN	BAL	319	20TH WAR
MC KENNA, ANTHONY	BAL	414	8TH WARD
MC KENNA, BIDDER	BAL	359	8TH WARD
MC KENNA, BRIDGET	BAL	406	8TH WARD
MC KENNA, ELLEN	BAL	150	19TH WAR
MC KENNA, EVERSTON	BAL	215	11TH WAR
MC KENNA, FRANCIS	BAL	164	6TH WARD
MC KENNA, JOHN	BAL	233	6TH WARD
MC KENNA, JOHN	BAL	233	6TH WARD
MC KENNA, MARY	BAL	425	14TH WAR
MC KENNA, MARY MISS-	BAL	315	20TH WAR
MC KENNA, MARY MRS-	BAL	315	20TH WAR
MC KENNA, PATRICK	BAL	170	16TH WAR
MC KENNA, PETER	BAL	209	6TH WARD
MC KENNAN, DANIEL	ALL	234	CUMBERLA
MC KENNER, JOHN	ALL	232	CUMBERLA
MC KENNEY, ANN	KEN	282	3RD DIST
MC KENNEY, E. D.	BAL	320	1ST DIST
MC KENNEY, ELIZABETH	BAL	096	5TH WARD
MC KENNEY, FRANCIS	BAL	442	8TH WARD
MC KENNEY, JEREMIAH	ALL	105	5TH E.D.
MC KENNEY, JOHN	BAL	423	3RD WARD
MC KENNEY, JOHN-COLONEL	QUE	187	3RD E DI
MC KENNEY, JULA	BAL	224	12TH WAR
MC KENNEY, MARGARET	CAL	009	1ST DIST
MC KENNEY, MARY	BAL	107	5TH WARD
MC KENNEY, PETER	BAL	144	1ST WARD
MC KENNEY, SAMUEL	QUE	169	2ND E DI
MC KENNEY, THOMAS	BAL	096	10TH WAR
MC KENNEY, WILLIAM	BAL	106	18TH WAR
MC KENNIN, PATRICK	BAL	300	20TH WAR
MC KENNON W.*	BAL	069	10TH WAR
MC KENNY, ANN	CAR	124	NO TWP L

MC KENNY, ANN M. CHA 222 ALLENS F
MC KENNY, ARY BAL 273 2ND WARD
MC KENNY, ELIZABETH BAL 237 1ST DIST
MC KENNY, JANE BAL 079 4TH WARD
MC KENNY, JESSE CAR 396 2ND DIST
MC KENNY, JOHN BAL 282 20TH WAR
MC KENNY, JOHN BAL 044 15TH WAR
MC KENNY, MARGARET BAL 100 5TH WARD
MC KENNY, MARY BAL 189 11TH WAR
MC KENNY, MARY BAL 376 3RD WARD
MC KENNY, MUGENT ALL 085 5TH E.D.
MC KENNY, R. BAL 168 1ST WARD
MC KENNY, SAVE A. CHA 225 ALLENS F
MC KENNY, WILLIAM BAL 381 1ST DIST
MC KENON, RACHIEL HAR 008 1ST DIST
MC KENREY, PATRICK BAL 090 5TH WARD
MC KENSEN, FRANCIS BAL 168 2ND DIST
MC KENSEY, JAMES BAL 364 3RD WARD
MC KENSEY, SAMUEL BAL 400 1ST DIST
MC KENSIE, A. BAL 439 14TH WAR
MC KENSIE, HELEN BAL 430 14TH WAR
MC KENSIEY, THOMAS BAL 127 11TH WAR
MC KENTRE, THOMAS BAL 108 1ST WARD
MC KENTRY, THOMAS * BAL 400 1ST DIST
MC KENY, THOMAS * BAL 392 1ST DIST
MC KENZIE, AARON ALL 138 6TH E.D.
MC KENZIE, BENJAMIN ALL 151 6TH E.D.
MC KENZIE, CHARLES ALL 151 6TH E.D.
MC KENZIE, CHARLES BAL 051 2ND DIST
MC KENZIE, CANIEL ALL 138 6TH E.D.
MC KENZIE, CANIEL ALL 092 5TH E.D.
MC KENZIE, CAVID ALL 152 6TH E.D.
MC KENZIE, ELIAS FRE 083 FREDERIC
MC KENZIE, EVAN BAL 281 12TH WAR
MC KENZIE, FRANCIS FRE 319 MIDDLETO
MC KENZIE, GEORGE ALL 153 6TH E.D.
MC KENZIE, HENRY ALL 091 5TH E.D.
MC KENZIE, HENRY BAL 124 1ST WARD
MC KENZIE, JANE BAL 271 2ND WARD
MC KENZIE, JEREMIAH ALL 004 3RD E.D.
MC KENZIE, JESSE ALL 151 6TH E.D.
MC KENZIE, JOHN BAL 115 1ST WARD
MC KENZIE, JOHN BAL 013 2ND DIST
MC KENZIE, LEO ALL 004 3RD E.D.
MC KENZIE, MARY CEC 109 4TH E DI
MC KENZIE, MOSES ALL 151 6TH E.D.
MC KENZIE, REBECCA ALL 152 6TH E.D.
MC KENZIE, RUHANNAH BAL 039 9TH WARD
MC KENZIE, SAMUEL ALL 152 6TH E.D.
MC KENZIE, TOBIAS CEC 109 3RD E DI
MC KENZIE, WILLIAM BAL 130 1ST WARD
MC KENZIE, WILLIAM BAL 059 15TH WAR
MC KEON, MARY BAL 008 EASTERN
MC KEONAN, JANE BAL 168 11TH WAR
MC KEOWN, HENRY M. BAL 261 6TH WARD
MC KEOWN, WILLIAM BAL 171 11TH WAR
MC KERBY, MARY BAL 347 3RD WARD
MC KERMY, JAMES PRI 049 AQUASCO
MC KERNAN, ELLEN BAL 120 16TH WAR
MC KERNAN, PATRICK BAL 316 20TH WAR
MC KERNEY, WILLIAM KEN 270 1ST DIST
MC KERR, ANN BAL 383 13TH WAR
MC KERRY, JAMES E. CHA 225 ALLENS F
MC KERRY, THOMAS * BAL 392 1ST DIST
MC KERSHIELD, MATILCA CEC 035 CHESAPEA
MC KERVEN, WILLIAM BAL 178 19TH WAR
MC KERVIN, JOHN BAL 277 12TH WAR
MC KETRICK, THOMAS BAL 345 1ST DIST
MC KEVES, HENRY ALL 104 5TH E.D.
MC KEW, FRANCIS BAL 006 9TH WARD
MC KEW, MICHAEL BAL 208 11TH WAR
MC KEW, PATRICK BAL 109 5TH WARD
MC KEW, THCMAS BAL 034 15TH WAR
MC KEWAN, ANN BAL 215 11TH WAR
MC KEWAN, THOMAS BAL 092 5TH WARD
MC KEWEN, ARCHIBALD BAL 048 15TH WAR
MC KEWEN, AUTHER BAL 361 8TH WARD
MC KEWEN, JOHN BAL 006 18TH WAR
MC KEWEN, SARAH V. BAL 038 9TH WARD
MC KEWON, MARY BAL 177 19TH WAR
MC KEY, ARTHUR ANN 460 HOWARD D
MC KEYS, JAMES BAL 123 11TH WAR
MC KHANEY, ROBERT BAL 048 2ND DIST
MC KHENNY, JAMES BAL 329 13TH WAR
MC KIBBIN, CHARLES BAL 096 10TH WAR
MC KIBBIN, J. G.* BAL 115 11TH WAR
MC KIBBIN, MARGARETTA BAL 149 5TH WARD
MC KIDNAP, JOHN ALL 195 CUMBERLA
MC KIM, ANNE BAL 364 13TH WAR
MC KIM, EMILIE L. BAL 099 10TH WAR
MC KIM, JOHN S. BAL 211 11TH WAR
MC KIM, JOHN T. MGM 427 MEDLEY 3
MC KIM, MARGARET BAL 210 2ND WARD
MC KIM, MARTHA BAL 251 6TH WARD
MC KIM, ROBERT BAL 110 10TH WAR
MC KIM, WILLAIM BAL 155 1ST WARD
MC KIM, WILLIAM BAL 144 11TH WAR
MC KIMM, JCHN BAL 280 7TH WARD
MC KINE, ALEX MRS. BAL 191 11TH WAR
MC KINE, ANN BAL 301 12TH WAR
MC KINE, ANN BAL 301 12TH WAR
MC KINE, JOHN BAL 014 1ST WARD
MC KINLEY, ANN BAL 134 11TH WAR
MC KINLEY, BENJAMIN BAL 045 1ST WARD
MC KINLEY, CATHERINE BAL 352 3RD WARD
MC KINLEY, FRANCIS Y. BAL 398 8TH WARD
MC KINLEY, GOERGE BAL 305 1ST DIST
MC KINLEY, HERBERT WAS 159 2ND DIST
MC KINLEY, HIRAM WAS 162 HAGERSTO
MC KINLEY, JOHN HAR 099 2ND DIST
MC KINLEY, JOHN BAL 242 20TH WAR
MC KINLEY, JOHN * BAL 341 1ST DIST
MC KINLEY, MARGARET ALL 021 2ND E.D.
MC KINLEY, MARY BAL 173 2ND DIST
MC KINLEY, MARY BAL 179 19TH WAR
MC KINLEY, NANCY BAL 094 15TH WAR
MC KINLEY, PRISCILLA C. BAL 253 6TH WARD
MC KINLEY, STEPHEN ALL 012 3RD E.D.
MC KINLEY, THOMAS BAL 162 6TH WARD
MC KINLEY, WILLIAM BAL 269 7TH WARD
MC KINLEY, WILLIAM BAL 269 12TH WAR
MC KINLEY, WILLIAM BAL 006 15TH WAR
MC KINLEY, WILLIAM BAL 235 17TH WAR
MC KINLEY, WILLIAM BAL 154 19TH WAR
MC KINLY, WILLIAM BAL 154 19TH WAR
MC KINN, DAVID BAL 083 2ND DIST
MC KINN, H. BAL 203 11TH WAR
MC KINN, HASLET BAL 203 11TH WAR
MC KINNAN, CATHARINE BAL 215 11TH WAR
MC KINNELL, JOHN C. BAL 250 20TH WAR
MC KINNELL, MARGARET BAL 249 20TH WAR
MC KINNEN, JOHN BAL 004 EASTERN
MC KINNEY, A. BAL 285 20TH WAR
MC KINNEY, ANN E. CEC 092 4TH E DI
MC KINNEY, BRIDGET BAL 191 19TH WAR
MC KINNEY, CHARLES CEC 116 3RD E DI
MC KINNEY, CHARLES BAL 086 4TH WARD
MC KINNEY, CHARLES F. BAL 162 1ST WARD
MC KINNEY, E. D. * BAL 320 1ST DIST
MC KINNEY, ELIZABETH CEC 197 7TH E DI
MC KINNEY, GEORGE CEC 203 6TH E DI
MC KINNEY, HUGH WAS 140 2ND DIST
MC KINNEY, JOHN CEC 171 6TH E DI
MC KINNEY, JOHN CAR 326 1ST DIST
MC KINNEY, JOHN C. QUE 243 5TH E DI
MC KINNEY, MICHAEL BAL 103 5TH WARD
MC KINNEY, OWEN BAL 080 2ND DIST
MC KINNEY, PETER WAS 055 2ND SUBD
MC KINNEY, ROBERT WAS 116 2ND DIST
MC KINNEY, ROBERT CEC 104 4TH E DI
MC KINNEY, ROBERT CEC 196 6TH E DI
MC KINNEY, ROBERT* SOM 358 BRINKLEY
MC KINNEY, SARAH FRE 063 FREDERIC
MC KINNEY, SARAH-BLACK FRE 043 FREDERIC
MC KINNEY, THOMAS BAL 390 8TH WARD
MC KINNEY, THOMAS BAL 297 7TH WARD
MC KINNIE, ANN BAL 258 12TH WAR
MC KINNIE, MARY BAL 108 10TH WAR
MC KINNIG, MARTHA BAL 212 11TH WAR
MC KINNON W.* BAL 069 10TH WAR
MC KINNTZ, JOHN BAL 312 20TH WAR
MC KINNY, GEORGE BAL 396 14TH WAR
MC KINNY, JOSEPH CEC 071 5TH E DI
MC KINNY, MARGARET CEC 077 NORTHEAS
MC KINNY, ROBERT CEC 177 7TH E DI
MC KINNY, SALLY BAL 396 14TH WAR
MC KINNY, SARAH CEC 072 5TH E DI
MC KINNY, THOMAS CEC 068 5TH E DI
MC KINNY, THOMAS B. CEC 067 5TH E DI
MC KINNY, TRELOUS KEN 313 3RD DIST
MC KINS, SARAH BAL 261 17TH WAR
MC KINSEE, ANN SOM 526 QUANTICO
MC KINSEE, MARY F. SOM 531 QUANTICO
MC KINSEY, AARON ANN 466 HOWARD D
MC KINSEY, ANDREW BAL 405 8TH WARD
MC KINSEY, CALIB BAL 361 1ST DIST
MC KINSEY, DANIEL BAL 358 1ST DIST
MC KINSEY, DAVID BAL 286 7TH WARD
MC KINSEY, DAVID ANN 468 HOWARD D
MC KINSEY, ELIZABETH BAL 385 1ST DIST
MC KINSEY, ELLEN BAL 364 3RD WARD
MC KINSEY, GEORGE BAL 382 8TH WARD
MC KINSEY, GEORGE ALL 031 2ND E.D.
MC KINSEY, GEORGE WAS 225 1ST DIST
MC KINSEY, HIRAM ANN 462 HOWARD D
MC KINSEY, JACOB WAS 249 1ST DIST
MC KINSEY, JOHN BAL 304 1ST DIST
MC KINSEY, JOSEPH BAL 298 7TH WARD
MC KINSEY, JOSEPH BAL 363 1ST DIST
MC KINSEY, MARY BAL 365 1ST DIST
MC KINSEY, MARY TAL 112 ST MICHA
MC KINSEY, ORPA BAL 342 1ST DIST
MC KINSEY, STEPHEN A. SOM 531 QUANTICO
MC KINSEY, WILLIAM BAL 357 1ST DIST
MC KINSTRY, EVAN CAR 382 2ND DIST
MC KINSY, ROBERT CEC 033 CHESAPEA
MC KINZEE, ALPHA A. BAL 369 1ST DIST
MC KINZEE, JESSE BAL 369 1ST DIST
MC KINZIE, DAVID ALL 153 6TH E.D.
MC KINZIE, ISRAEL ANN 500 HOWARD D
MC KISSICK, ELIZABETH FRE 195 5TH E DI
MC KITTRICK, PHILIP BAL 405 8TH WARD
MC KLASKEY, ROSEAN BAL 392 1ST DIST
MC KLEIFF, DELILIA WAS 270 1ST DIST
MC KLEMAN, HENRY BAL 259 2ND WARD
MC KLICKLESS, MARY BAL 018 2ND DIST
MC KLIFF, WILLIAM WAS 270 1ST DIST
MC KNEAL, THOMAS CEC 085 5TH E DI
MC KNETT, JOHN CAR 147 NO TWP L
MC KNETT, ROBERT H. CAR 140 NO TWP L
MC KNEW, BASIL ANN 328 2ND DIST
MC KNEW, M. C. ANN 328 2ND DIST
MC KNIGHT, ANN O. BAL 030 15TH WAR
MC KNIGHT, ANNA M. ALL 211 CUMBERLA
MC KNIGHT, CLARA BAL 115 5TH WARD
MC KNIGHT, DAVID ALL 219 CUMBERLA
MC KNIGHT, ELIZABETH MGM 319 CRACKLIN
MC KNIGHT, G.W. BAL 173 1ST WARD
MC KNIGHT, GEORGE CEC 127 5TH E DI
MC KNIGHT, JOHN ALL 136 4TH E.D.
MC KNIGHT, MAGDELINE PRI 032 VANSVILL
MC KNIGHT, MARY BAL 235 12TH WAR
MC KNIGHT, MARY LOUISA ALL 199 CUMBERLA
MC KNIGHT, R. BAL 286 2ND WARD
MC KNIGHT, SAMUEL CEC 127 5TH E DI
MC KNIGHT, SIMEON ALL 198 CUMBERLA
MC KNIGHT, SOPHIA ALL 180 8TH E.D.
MC KNIGHT, THOMAS BAL 444 8TH WARD
MC KNITT, JAMES T.* TAL 056 EASTON D
MC KNOTT, ROBERT H. TAL 058 EASTON D
MC KNOTT, WILLIAM CAR 148 NO TWP L
MC KORKLE, JAMES ALL 177 7TH E.D.
MC KREEVER, MARGARET DOR 448 1ST DIST
MC KRINK, FRANCES HAR 018 1ST DIST
MC KRINSTRY, JOHN CAR 382 2ND DIST
MC KUCE, POLLY BAL 131 5TH WARD
MC KUEN, JOHN ANN 265 ANNAPOLI
MC KUEON, ARTHUR BAL 179 11TH WAR
MC KULLY, GEORGE BAL 382 1ST DIST
MC KURLEY, MARY BAL 375 1ST DIST
MC KUSKEY, ROSE BAL 187 19TH WAR
MC KUSTA, PATRICK BAL 041 1ST WARD
MC KUSTA, THOMAS BAL 041 1ST WARD
MC KUY, SARAH BAL 200 11TH WAR
MC KY, FELIX BAL 463 1ST DIST
MC LACKLEA, JAMES BAL 327 13TH WAR
MC LAIDE, JESSE BAL 173 11TH WAR
MC LAIEN, RANDAULPH BAL 300 17TH WAR
MC LAIN, ALAER F. FRE 259 NEW MARK
MC LAIN, CHARLES CEC 066 1ST E DI
MC LAIN, CHRISTOPHER CEC 070 5TH E DI
MC LAIN, DANIEL BAL 212 6TH WARD
MC LAIN, DAVID BAL 411 1ST DIST
MC LAIN, ELEANOR BAL 192 6TH WARD
MC LAIN, ELIZA CEC 061 1ST E DI
MC LAIN, ELIZABETH BAL 255 6TH WARD
MC LAIN, ESTHER CEC 089 4TH E DI
MC LAIN, JACOB BAL 273 17TH WAR
MC LAIN, JACOB BAL 016 15TH WAR
MC LAIN, JAMES SOM 398 BRINKLEY
MC LAIN, JOHN BAL 368 1ST DIST
MC LAIN, JOHN BAL 008 1ST WARD
MC LAIN, JOHN CEC 070 5TH E DI
MC LAIN, LOUIS CEC 046 1ST E DI
MC LAIN, LUCRETIA FRE 004 FREDERIC
MC LAIN, MORDICAI FRE 261 NEW MARK
MC LAIN, ROBERT BAL 274 17TH WAR
MC LAIN, SARAH CEC 085 5TH E DI
MC LAIN, SARAH SOM 356 BRINKLEY
MC LAIN, THOMAS CEC 154 PORT DUP
MC LAINE, ALEXANDER BAL 285 17TH WAR
MC LAINE, PATRICK BAL 283 17TH WAR
MC LAINE, PHILIS BAL 113 5TH WARD
MC LAMAR, MARGARET ALL 217 CUMBERLA
MC LANAHAN, ALICE R. FRE 012 FREDERIC
MC LANAHAN, ANN BAL 050 9TH WARD
MC LANAHAN, ANN R. FRE 012 FREDERIC
MC LANAHAN, ELIZA BAL 066 10TH WAR
MC LANAHAN, ELIZABETH WAS 296 1ST DIST
MC LANAHAN, GEORGE WAS 296 1ST DIST
MC LANAHAN, JAMES WAS 124 2ND DIST
MC LANAHAN, JOHN M. WAS 160 2ND DIST
MC LANAHAN, JOHNSON ALL 139 6TH E.D.
MC LANAHAN, SAMUEL WAS 143 HAGERSTO
MC LANE, ALFRED BAL 246 20TH WAR
MC LANE, CAROLINE A. BAL 054 15TH WAR
MC LANE, CORNELIUS ANN 282 ANNAPOLI
MC LANE, ELIZA BAL 151 11TH WAR
MC LANE, ELIZABETH FRE 228 BUCKEYST
MC LANE, GEORGE BAL 004 9TH WARD
MC LANE, HANNAH BAL 075 15TH WAR
MC LANE, JAMES FRE 217 BUCKEYST
MC LANE, JAMES BAL 174 19TH WAR
MC LANE, JAMES WOR 233 6TH E DI
MC LANE, JAMES WOR 200 8TH E DI
MC LANE, JAMES L. BAL 033 15TH WAR
MC LANE, JOHN BAL 146 1ST WARD
MC LANE, JOHN BAL 169 1ST WARD
MC LANE, JOHN B. WOR 191 8TH E DI
MC LANE, JOHN E. BAL 032 15TH WAR
MC LANE, LEVIN BAL 032 15TH WAR
MC LANE, LOUIS JR. BAL 153 11TH WAR
MC LANE, MARGARET BAL 215 11TH WAR
MC LANE, MARGARETT BAL 205 11TH WAR
MC LANE, MARY E. BAL 058 15TH WAR
MC LANE, PAT BAL 145 19TH WAR
MC LANE, R. BAL 117 1ST WARD
MC LANE, R.M. BAL 204 11TH WAR
MC LANE, ROBERT BAL 004 9TH WARD
MC LANE, SALLY E. WOR 232 6TH E DI
MC LANE, SAMUEL BAL 018 18TH WAR
MC LANE, WILLIAM FRE 228 BUCKEYST
MC LANE, WILLIAM FRE 004 FREDERIC
MC LANE, WILLIAM WOR 216 4TH E DI
MC LANE, WILLIAM BAL 166 1ST WARD
MC LANE, WILLIAM BAL 271 7TH WARD
MC LANGHLAN, JOHN W. BAL 114 1ST WARD
MC LANHAN, BOBT J. BAL 029 2ND DIST
MC LANNAN, HUGH BAL 449 14TH WAR
MC LAUCHLIN, ROSALIE BAL 085 10TH WAR
MC LAUGH, JOSEPH A. BAL 023 1ST WARD
MC LAUGHAN, J. BAL 322 12TH WAR
MC LAUGHAN, JAMES ALL 073 5TH E.D.
MC LAUGHLAN, SARAH BAL 112 5TH WARD
MC LAUGHLIN, A. J. ALL 163 6TH E.D.
MC LAUGHLIN, ANDREW BAL 108 10TH WAR
MC LAUGHLIN, ANN ALL 181 8TH E.D.
MC LAUGHLIN, ANN BAL 334 1ST DIST
MC LAUGHLIN, ANN BAL 278 7TH WARD
MC LAUGHLIN, ANN BAL 278 7TH WARD
MC LAUGHLIN, ANN BAL 184 11TH WAR
MC LAUGHLIN, ANN BAL 272 12TH WAR
MC LAUGHLIN, ANN BAL 242 20TH WAR
MC LAUGHLIN, AUGUSTUS BAL 108 10TH WAR
MC LAUGHLIN, B. FRE 20 5TH E DI
MC LAUGHLIN, BERREN ALL 175 7TH E.D.
MC LAUGHLIN, BERTILLA SIS BAL 316 20TH WAR
MC LAUGHLIN, BRIDGET BAL 024 9TH WARD
MC LAUGHLIN, BRIDGET BAL 233 6TH WARD
MC LAUGHLIN, CATHERINE BAL 155 11TH WAR
MC LAUGHLIN, CHARLES BAL 394 14TH WAR
MC LAUGHLIN, CHARLES BAL 263 20TH WAR
MC LAUGHLIN, CHARLES BAL 263 20TH WAR
MC LAUGHLIN, CHARLES BAL 075 15TH WAR
MC LAUGHLIN, DANIEL WAS 133 2ND DIST
MC LAUGHLIN, E.K. WAS 021 2ND SUBD
MC LAUGHLIN, EDWARD ALL 042 10TH E.D
MC LAUGHLIN, EDWARD BAL 049 18TH WAR
MC LAUGHLIN, ELIZABETH BAL 167 6TH WARD
MC LAUGHLIN, FRANCIS BAL 209 19TH WAR
MC LAUGHLIN, G. H. BAL 332 1ST DIST
MC LAUGHLIN, GEORGE BAL 073 10TH WAR
MC LAUGHLIN, GEORGE W. BAL 123 5TH WARD
MC LAUGHLIN, HENRY WAS 303 1ST DIST
MC LAUGHLIN, IRVIN BAL 245 12TH WAR
MC LAUGHLIN, ISABELLA BAL 171 11TH WAR
MC LAUGHLIN, JAMES BAL 179 11TH WAR
MC LAUGHLIN, JAMES BAL 281 2ND WARD
MC LAUGHLIN, JAMES BAL 163 6TH WARD
MC LAUGHLIN, JAMES ALL 103 5TH E.D.
MC LAUGHLIN, JAMES BAL 012 2ND DIST
MC LAUGHLIN, JAMES WAS 302 1ST DIST
MC LAUGHLIN, JAMES WAS 136 2ND DIST
MC LAUGHLIN, JAMES HAR 040 1ST DIST
MC LAUGHLIN, JAMES H. BAL 255 6TH WARD
MC LAUGHLIN, JANE WAS 107 2ND DIST
MC LAUGHLIN, JOHN WAS 295 1ST DIST
MC LAUGHLIN, JOHN BAL 149 2ND DIST
MC LAUGHLIN, JOHN ALL 174 7TH E.D.
MC LAUGHLIN, JOHN BAL 024 18TH WAR
MC LAUGHLIN, JOHN BAL 025 18TH WAR
MC LAUGHLIN, JOHN D. WAS 198 1ST DIST
MC LAUGHLIN, JOHN Q. ALL 181 8TH E.D.
MC LAUGHLIN, JOSEPH ALL 163 6TH E.D.
MC LAUGHLIN, JOSEPH BAL 378 8TH WARD
MC LAUGHLIN, JOSEPH BAL 294 12TH WAR
MC LAUGHLIN, LEVIN BAL 152 5TH WARD
MC LAUGHLIN, LEVIN BAL 005 15TH WAR
MC LAUGHLIN, LEWIS E. WAS 303 1ST DIST
MC LAUGHLIN, LUKE BAL 449 1ST DIST
MC LAUGHLIN, MARGARETT BAL 134 11TH WAR
MC LAUGHLIN, MARY BAL 285 20TH WAR
MC LAUGHLIN, MARY BAL 343 13TH WAR
MC LAUGHLIN, MARY BAL 056 15TH WAR
MC LAUGHLIN, MARY WAS 134 HAGERSTO
MC LAUGHLIN, MICHAEL BAL 449 1ST DIST
MC LAUGHLIN, PATRICK BAL 127 5TH WARD
MC LAUGHLIN, PATRICK BAL 069 10TH WAR
MC LAUGHLIN, PERRY B. WAS 289 1ST DIST
MC LAUGHLIN, PHILIP WAS 108 2ND DIST

Name	County	Page	Locality
MC LAUGHLIN, PRISCILLA M.	MGM	420	MEDLEY 3
MC LAUGHLIN, ROBERT	BAL	186	11TH WAR
MC LAUGHLIN, ROGER	ALL	069	5TH E.D.
MC LAUGHLIN, ROSE	BAL	046	15TH WAR
MC LAUGHLIN, ROSE	BAL	049	9TH WARD
MC LAUGHLIN, SAMUEL	WAS	094	2ND SUBD
MC LAUGHLIN, SARAH	BAL	272	12TH WAR
MC LAUGHLIN, SARAH A.	ANN	497	HOWARD D
MC LAUGHLIN, SUSAN	BAL	257	20TH WAR
MC LAUGHLIN, THOMAS	KEN	313	3RD DIST
MC LAUGHLIN, THOMAS J.	BAL	061	15TH WAR
MC LAUGHLIN, THOMAS W.	HAR	040	1ST DIST
MC LAUGHLIN, WILILAM	BAL	270	2ND WARD
MC LAUGHLIN, WILLIAM	BAL	229	2ND WARD
MC LAUGHLIN, WILLIAM	BAL	184	11TH WAR
MC LAUGHLIN, WILLIAM	ALL	165	6TH E.D.
MC LAUGHLIN, WILLIAM	BAL	023	18TH WAR
MC LAUGHLIN, WILLIAM J.	ANN	455	HOWARD D
MC LAUGLIN, EDWARD	BAL	460	1ST DIST
MC LAURE, J.	BAL	127	5TH WARD
MC LEAN, A.	BAL	151	1ST WARD
MC LEAN, A.	BAL	135	1ST WARD
MC LEAN, ALEXANDER	BAL	349	7TH WARD
MC LEAN, ARTHUR	BAL	296	3RD WARD
MC LEAN, AUTHUR	BAL	164	19TH WAR
MC LEAN, CHARLES DR-	BAL	418	1ST DIST
MC LEAN, ED.	BAL	028	18TH WAR
MC LEAN, ELIAS	BAL	036	9TH WARD
MC LEAN, ELISA	BAL	307	3RD WARD
MC LEAN, ELIZABETH	BAL	349	7TH WARD
MC LEAN, GEORGE	BAL	298	12TH WAR
MC LEAN, HARRIOTT	BAL	086	4TH WARD
MC LEAN, JAMES	BAL	160	19TH WAR
MC LEAN, JANE	BAL	319	3RD WARD
MC LEAN, JOHN	BAL	334	7TH WARD
MC LEAN, JOHN	BAL	369	8TH WARD
MC LEAN, JOHN	BAL	114	18TH WAR
MC LEAN, LUCY	CHA	293	BOJANTOW
MC LEAN, MARY	BAL	358	13TH WAR
MC LEAN, MORFIT	BAL	058	2ND DIST
MC LEAN, MOSES	BAL	235	6TH WARD
MC LEAN, ORRICK	BAL	420	1ST DIST
MC LEAN, REBECCA	BAL	039	18TH WAR
MC LEAN, SUSANA	BAL	341	3RD WARD
MC LEAN, THOMAS L.	FRE	304	WOODSBOR
MC LEAN, WILLAM	BAL	463	14TH WAR
MC LEAN, WILLIAM	BAL	276	20TH WAR
MC LEAN, WILLIAM	BAL	327	7TH WARD
MC LEAN, WILLIAM H.	BAL	254	6TH WARD
MC LEAN, WILLLIAM	BAL	197	6TH WARD
MC LEAN,ALLEN	BAL	119	1ST WARD
MC LEAR, ANN	BAL	369	8TH WARD
MC LEAR, ROSINA	BAL	369	8TH WARD
MC LEARNEY, PATRICK	BAL	395	3RD WARD
MC LEARY, ANN	BAL	315	12TH WAR
MC LEARY, DAVID	BAL	179	11TH WAR
MC LEARY, WILLIAM M.	ANN	456	HOWARD D
MC LEASE, MARTHA E.	BAL	210	2ND WARD
MC LEAVY, HUGH	BAL	335	7TH WARD
MC LEAVY, JAMES	BAL	334	7TH WARD
MC LEERY, THOMAS	BAL	313	12TH WAR
MC LELAN, WILLAIM	BAL	200	19TH WAR
MC LELAND, SUSAN	BAL	121	11TH WAR
MC LELLAN, LAURA	BAL	051	15TH WAR
MC LELLAN, RUFUS C.	BAL	051	15TH WAR
MC LELLAND, JANE	FRE	398	JEFFERSO
MC LEMEE, PATRICK	ALL	070	5TH E.D.
MC LEN, ROBERE	BAL	012	2ND DIST
MC LENAHAN, THOMAS J.	MGM	437	CLARKSTR
MC LENNA, AMOS	ALL	199	CUMBERLA
MC LENNARD, ELLEN	BAL	187	19TH WAR
MC LEOD, BERNARD	FRE	065	FREDERIC
MC LEOD, MARTIN	BAL	072	1ST WARD
MC LEOD, MARY H.	BAL	212	11TH WAR
MC LEOD, SUSAN	FRE	340	MIDDLETO
MC LERMEE, HENRY J.	ALL	196	CUMBERLA
MC LERTY, MEED*	BAL	272	20TH WAR
MC LEWCE, CHARLES	ALL	243	CUMBERLA
MC LEWCE, JOHN	ALL	243	CUMBERLA
MC LEWELL, ANN	CEC	006	ELKTON 3
MC LIERENTS, JOHN	CHA	222	ALLENS F
MC LISTER, M. A.	BAL	063	10TH WAR
MC LOANE, RICHARD	BAL	104	18TH WAR
MC LOARLEY, ANN*	BAL	389	3RD WARD
MC LOCKLIN, BIDDY	BAL	152	11TH WAR
MC LOCKLIN, MARGARET	BAL	101	1ST WARD
MC LOFFLIN, CHARLES	WOR	319	1ST E DI
MC LONE, JOHN	BAL	415	8TH WARD
MC LOUGHLIN, BRIDGET	ALL	217	CUMBERLA
MC LOUGHLIN, EDWARD	BAL	022	4TH WARD
MC LOUGHLIN, GEORGE	BAL	064	1ST WARD
MC LOUGHLIN, MARY	BAL	193	11TH WAR
MC LOUGHLIN,JAMES	ALL	219	CUMBERLA
MC LUCAS, ANDREW	WAS	138	2ND DIST
MC LUINER, CHARELS	BAL	308	12TH WAR
MC MACEDE, AUTHER *	BAL	065	18TH WAR
MC MACHEN, JOHN	ANN	468	HOWARD D
MC MACKEN, ELIZABETH	BAL	259	1ST DIST
MC MACKEN, FRANCES	BAL	442	14TH WAR
MC MACKEN, JAMES	MGM	392	ROCKERLE
MC MACKEN, JOHN	BAL	259	1ST DIST
MC MACKEN, ROSE A.	BAL	323	1ST DIST
MC MACKIN, ELLEN B.	BAL	058	10TH WAR
MC MACKIN, EMILY JANE	ANN	420	HOWARD D
MC MACKIN, MICHAEL	BAL	178	2ND DIST
MC MACKIN, PETER	WAS	001	WILLIAMS
MC MACKIN, ROSANNA	BAL	040	9TH WARD
MC MACKIN, WILLIAM	ANN	420	HOWARD D
MC MAGH, BERNARD	BAL	337	3RD WARD
MC MAGH, BRIDGET	BAL	338	3RD WARD
MC MAHAN, BRIDGET	HAR	181	3RD DIST
MC MAHAN, DANIEL	BAL	402	1ST DIST
MC MAHAN, ELIZABETH	BAL	246	2ND WARD
MC MAHAN, ELIZABETH	TAL	038	EASTON D
MC MAHAN, HESTER	TAL	056	EASTON D
MC MAHAN, JAMES T.*	TAL	036	EASTON D
MC MAHAN, JOHN	BAL	384	8TH WARD
MC MAHAN, JOHN	BAL	292	17TH WAR
MC MAHAN, JOHN H.	TAL	052	EASTON D
MC MAHAN, JOSEPH	CAR	152	NO TWP L
MC MAHAN, JOSEPH	BAL	083	1ST WARD
MC MAHAN, MARTIN	CAR	230	5TH DIST
MC MAHAN, MATHIAS J.	TAL	055	EASTON D
MC MAHAN, MICHAEL	BAL	198	2ND WARD
MC MAHAN, PATRICK	BAL	062	18TH WAR
MC MAHAN, PATRICK	BAL	041	18TH WAR
MC MAHAN, REBECCA*	TAL	058	EASTON D
MC MAHAN, RICHARD	TAL	055	EASTON D
MC MAHAN, RICHARD H.	TAL	052	EASTON D
MC MAHAN, ROBERT*	TAL	052	EASTON D
MC MAHAN, SOLLOMAN	TAL	055	EASTON D
MC MAHAN, TIDDA *	BAL	282	1ST DIST
MC MAHAN, WRIGHTSON	TAL	054	EASTON D
MC MAHEN, MICHAEL	BAL	160	11TH WAR
MC MAHON, ANN	BAL	352	7TH WARD
MC MAHON, BARBARA	ALL	220	CUMBERLA
MC MAHON, BIDDY	BAL	220	2ND WARD
MC MAHON, CATHERINE	BAL	010	4TH WARD
MC MAHON, CHARLES	BAL	231	6TH WARD
MC MAHON, CHARLES	BAL	350	7TH WARD
MC MAHON, ELIZABETH	BAL	269	7TH WARD
MC MAHON, ELLEN	BAL	470	14TH WAR
MC MAHON, GEORGE	BAL	169	16TH WAR
MC MAHON, HARRIET	BAL	253	6TH WARD
MC MAHON, HENRY	BAL	265	7TH WARD
MC MAHON, J. V. L.	BAL	470	14TH WAR
MC MAHON, JAMES	DOR	373	1ST DIST
MC MAHON, JAMES	ALL	246	CUMBERLA
MC MAHON, JOHN	BAL	232	6TH WARD
MC MAHON, JOHN	BAL	178	6TH WARD
MC MAHON, JOHN	BAL	178	6TH WARD
MC MAHON, JOHN	BAL	074	4TH WARD
MC MAHON, JOHN	BAL	415	14TH WAR
MC MAHON, JOHN T.	BAL	253	6TH WARD
MC MAHON, JOSEPH	BAL	316	20TH WAR
MC MAHON, KATE	BAL	363	8TH WARD
MC MAHON, MARY	BAL	390	8TH WARD
MC MAHON, MARY	BAL	426	8TH WARD
MC MAHON, MARY	BAL	102	1ST WARD
MC MAHON, MARY	ALL	103	5TH E.D.
MC MAHON, MARY	FRE	021	FREDERIC
MC MAHON, MICHAEL	BAL	220	2ND WARD
MC MAHON, OWEN	BAL	283	17TH WAR
MC MAHON, PATRICK	BAL	403	8TH WARD
MC MAHON, PETER	ALL	149	6TH E.D.
MC MAHON, PHILIP	BAL	369	8TH WARD
MC MAHON, ROSANNA	BAL	066	10TH WAR
MC MAHON, THOMAS W.	ALL	216	CUMBERLA
MC MAHON, WILLIAM	ALL	256	CUMBERLA
MC MAHON, WILLIAM	BAL	454	14TH WAR
MC MAHON, WILLIAM H.	TAL	024	EASTON D
MC MAHUN, MICHELL	HAR	198	3RD DIST
MC MAKEN, MARY	BAL	315	12TH WAR
MC MAKEN, MICHAEL	BAL	185	11TH WAR
MC MAKEN, THOMAS	BAL	305	12TH WAR
MC MAKIN, ALICE	BAL	092	18TH WAR
MC MAKIN, JOHN	WAS	001	WILLIAMS
MC MAKIN, MARY	BAL	101	5TH WARD
MC MAKIN, ROBERT	BAL	206	19TH WAR
MC MAKIN, THOMAS G.	BAL	086	18TH WAR
MC MANA, MARTIN	ALL	053	10TH E.D
MC MANAHA, MICHAEL	ALL	052	10TH E.D
MC MANCE, MATHEW	BAL	364	8TH WARD
MC MANE, J.	BAL	295	12TH WAR
MC MANEY, HUGH	ALL	156	6TH E.D.
MC MANIN, JAMES	BAL	155	2ND DIST
MC MANIS, ELIZA	BAL	387	3RD WARD
MC MANN ,JOHN	KEN	300	3RD DIST
MC MANN, ANN	BAL	249	12TH WAR
MC MANN, FRISBY	BAL	291	1ST DIST
MC MANN, MICHAEL	BAL	192	11TH WAR
MC MANNIS, MRS.	ALL	240	CUMBERLA
MC MANNS, BIDDY	BAL	009	EASTERN
MC MANNS, HUGH	BAL	150	1ST WARD
MC MANUS, BERNARD	BAL	312	12TH WAR
MC MANUS, CATHERINE A.	BAL	382	8TH WARD
MC MANUS, CATHRINE	BAL	205	11TH WAR
MC MANUS, ELIZABETH	BAL	360	8TH WARD
MC MANUS, FELIX R. DR.	BAL	335	13TH WAR
MC MANUS, HUGH	BAL	389	8TH WARD
MC MANUS, JOHN	BAL	279	2ND WARD
MC MANUS, JOHN	BAL	075	10TH WAR
MC MANUS, MARY	BAL	079	10TH WAR
MC MANUS, PATRICK	BAL	281	7TH WARD
MC MANUS, THOMAS	BAL	382	8TH WARD
MC MANUS, WILLIAM	BAL	358	8TH WARD
MC MAON, JOHN	HAR	071	1ST DIST
MC MAREUS, ROBERT-MULATTO	FRE	245	NEW MARK
MC MARNER, CATHARINE	BAL	135	5TH WARD
MC MASTER, ALEXANDER	CEC	156	PORT DUP
MC MASTER, JOHN T.B.	WOR	342	1ST E DI
MC MASTER, SAMUEL	CAR	400	2ND DIST
MC MASTER, SAMUEL T.	WOR	184	6TH E DI
MC MASTERS, JANE	BAL	224	6TH WARD
MC MAUL, MRS.	BAL	001	18TH WAR
MC MEAN, JOSEPH	WAS	037	2ND SUBD
MC MECHINE, THOMAS*	BAL	356	3RD WARD
MC MEIN, MARY*	BAL	355	3RD WARD
MC MELLEN, HENRY	BAL	387	3RD WARD
MC MELSON, BENJAMIN	WOR	211	4TH E DI
MC MERRICK, WILLIAM	FRE	029	FREDERIC
MC MICHAEL, HUGH	ALL	222	CUMBERLA
MC MICHAEL, M.	BAL	109	10TH WAR
MC MICHAEL, WILLIAM	CEC	074	5TH E DI
MC MICHAEL, WILLIAM	DOR	444	1ST DIST
MC MICHEW, MARY A.	BAL	085	4TH WARD
MC MILLAN, ELIZABETH	BAL	377	8TH WARD
MC MILLAN, JAMES	BAL	147	16TH WAR
MC MILLAN, JOHN	BAL	179	11TH WAR
MC MILLAND, MARY *	ANN	337	3RD DIST
MC MILLEN, THOMAS *	BAL	111	2ND DIST
MC MILLIAN, ALEXANDER	BAL	158	1ST WARD
MC MILLIAN, JOHN M.	BAL	110	18TH WAR
MC MILLIN, GEORGE *	BAL	065	18TH WAR
MC MITCHELL, JOHN	CHA	219	ALLENS F
MC MOCKEN, MARY	BAL	304	1ST DIST
MC MOHAN, THOMAS	CEC	041	CHESAPEA
MC MORRIS, GEORGE	BAL	432	1ST DIST
MC MORROW, CHARLES	BAL	013	15TH WAR
MC MULARCHEY, PATRICK	BAL	447	1ST DIST
MC MULLAN, JOHN	BAL	132	2ND DIST
MC MULLAN, MARGARET	BAL	185	16TH WAR
MC MULLEN JOHN	CEC	084	CHARLEST
MC MULLEN, BRIDGET	BAL	259	6TH WARD
MC MULLEN, CHARLES	BAL	165	6TH WARD
MC MULLEN, EDW.	BAL	315	20TH WAR
MC MULLEN, FRANCES A.	HAR	168	3RD DIST
MC MULLEN, HUGH	ALL	104	5TH E.D.
MC MULLEN, JAMES	CEC	199	7TH E DI
MC MULLEN, JAMS	CEC	180	7TH E DI
MC MULLEN, JHON	BAL	353	13TH WAR
MC MULLEN, JOHN	CEC	182	7TH E DI
MC MULLEN, JOHN	BAL	137	11TH WAR
MC MULLEN, JOHN	BAL	084	10TH WAR
MC MULLEN, JOHN	BAL	044	15TH WAR
MC MULLEN, JOSEPH	CEC	155	PORT DUP
MC MULLEN, LEWIS	ALL	108	5TH E.D.
MC MULLEN, LEWIS	ALL	099	5TH E.D.
MC MULLEN, MARGARET	ALL	107	5TH E.D.
MC MULLEN, MARGARET	BAL	291	12TH WAR
MC MULLEN, MARGARET	BAL	231	2ND WARD
MC MULLEN, MARGARET	BAL	123	5TH WARD
MC MULLEN, MARGARET	BAL	362	13TH WAR
MC MULLEN, MARGARET	CEC	149	PORT DUP
MC MULLEN, MARGARET	FRE	043	FREDERIC
MC MULLEN, MARY	BAL	139	19TH WAR
MC MULLEN, MARY	BAL	028	9TH WARD
MC MULLEN, MICHAEL	BAL	262	6TH WARD
MC MULLEN, RICHARD H.	BAL	237	6TH WARD
MC MULLEN, ROBERT	WAS	011	WILLIAMS
MC MULLEN, SALLY	BAL	443	14TH WAR
MC MULLEN, SARAH	CEC	146	PORT DUP
MC MULLEN, SARAH	CEC	146	PORT DUP
MC MULLEN, SARAH	BAL	310	12TH WAR
MC MULLEN, THOMAS	CEC	159	PORT DUP
MC MULLEN, THOMAS	CEC	158	PORT DUP
MC MULLEN, THOMAS	CEC	182	7TH E DI
MC MULLEN, THOMAS	WAS	148	2ND DIST
MC MULLEN, WILLIAM	ALL	106	5TH E.D.
MC MULLER, HANNAH	FRE	098	FREDERIC
MC MULLER, MARGARET	BAL	139	19TH WAR
MC MULLIGAN, MARY	BAL	230	1ST DIST
MC MULLIN, BRIDGET	WAS	122	HAGERSTO
MC MULLIN, DONALD	BAL	181	2ND DIST
MC MULLIN, JOHN	ALL	108	5TH E.D.
MC MULLIN, SILAS	WAS	279	LEITERSB
MC MULLIN, THOMAS	DOR	434	1ST DIST
MC MULLIN, THOMAS	HAR	154	3RD DIST
MC MULLIN, WILLIAM	BAL	077	4TH WARD
MC MULLNE, JAMES	BAL	198	2ND WARD
MC MULLON, ELLEN	WAS	158	2ND DIST
MC MULTY, JAMES	HAR	131	2ND DIST
MC MULTY, MARTHA	BAL	382	8TH WARD
MC MURDIE, HENRY	FRE	20	5TH E DI
MC MURPHY, SILAS D.	BAL	475	14TH WAR
MC MURRAY, ALEXANDER	BAL	165	1ST WARD
MC MURRAY, ANN	BAL	175	2ND WARD
MC MURRAY, ELIZABETH	BAL	175	2ND WARD
MC MURRY, ELIZABETH	WAS	182	BOONSBOR
MC MURRY, ISEBELLA J.	BAL	091	18TH WAR
MC MURRY, JAMES	BAL	064	1ST WARD
MC MURRY, JOHN	BAL	091	18TH WAR
MC MUSTRIA, WILLIAM	FRE	013	FREDERIC
MC MUTT, MARY	HAR	003	1ST DIST
MC NAB, DAVID	HAR	043	1ST DIST
MC NAB, ISAAC	HAR	183	3RD DIST
MC NAB, JOHN	BAL	114	2ND DIST
MC NAB, MARY	HAR	039	1ST DIST
MC NAB, RICHARD *	HAR	196	3RD DIST
MC NABB, CATHERINE	BAL	407	8TH WARD
MC NABB, CHARLES	HAR	081	2ND DIST
MC NABB, JAMES	BAL	256	12TH WAR
MC NABB, JOHN	BAL	407	8TH WARD
MC NABB, OSCAR	HAR	081	2ND DIST
MC NABB, WILLIAM	HAR	081	2ND DIST
MC NAIR, ANN	FRE	333	MIDDLETO
MC NALLEY, THOMAS	HAR	158	3RD DIST
MC NALLY, ANN	BAL	129	11TH WAR
MC NALLY, ELIZA	HAR	088	2ND DIST
MC NALLY, HENRY	BAL	200	11TH WAR
MC NALLY, JAMES	BAL	192	11TH WAR
MC NALLY, JAMES	BAL	182	2ND WARD
MC NALLY, JOHN	BAL	313	12TH WAR
MC NALLY, M.F.	BAL	201	11TH WAR
MC NALLY, PATRICK	BAL	172	11TH WAR
MC NALLY, ROSE	BAL	166	11TH WAR
MC NALT, DANIEL	BAL	082	2ND DIST
MC NALTY, ANN	BAL	I47	11TH WAR
MC NAMAR, MARIA	BAL	125	5TH WARD
MC NAMAR, N.	BAL	166	1ST WARD
MC NAMARA, BRIDGET	BAL	064	15TH WAR
MC NAMARA, BRIDGET	BAL	409	3RD WARD
MC NAMARA, JAMES	BAL	028	9TH WARD
MC NAMARA, JOHN	FRE	065	FREDERIC
MC NAMARA, PATRICK	BAL	005	4TH WARD
MC NAMARA, SALEY A.	DOR	423	1ST DIST
MC NAMARA, SARAH A.	DOR	376	1ST DIST
MC NAMARA, WILLIAM H.	DOR	413	1ST DIST
MC NAME, MARY	BAL	423	3RD WARD
MC NAMEE, JOHN	CEC	154	PORT DUP
MC NAMEE, PETER	CEC	173	6TH E DI
MC NAMEE, ROBERT	KEN	313	3RD DIST
MC NAMMERSON, HUGH	BAL	469	14TH WAR
MC NAMORD, N.	BAL	166	1ST WARD
MC NANCE, JAMES	BAL	177	11TH WAR
MC NARA, JOHN	WOR	340	1ST E DI
MC NASH, CHARLES	CAR	143	NO TWP L
MC NEAF, WILLIAM*	TAL	053	EASTON D
MC NEAL, ALEXANDE	BAL	283	7TH WARD
MC NEAL, ANDREW L.	BAL	338	7TH WARD
MC NEAL, ANTHONY	BAL	143	2ND DIST
MC NEAL, BRIDGET	BAL	439	14TH WAR
MC NEAL, CATHERINE	BAL	264	7TH WARD
MC NEAL, EDWARD	BAL	155	1ST WARD
MC NEAL, ELIZABETH	BAL	070	15TH WAR
MC NEAL, ELIZABETH	BAL	052	9TH WARD
MC NEAL, GEORGE	SOM	482	TRAPP DI
MC NEAL, HUGH	BAL	035	15TH WAR
MC NEAL, JAMES	BAL	192	2ND WARD
MC NEAL, JAMES	BAL	186	5TH DIST
MC NEAL, JAMES H.	BAL	005	15TH WAR
MC NEAL, JAMES H.	TAL	053	EASTON D
MC NEAL, JAMES H.	TAL	033	EASTON D
MC NEAL, JOHN	BAL	075	18TH WAR
MC NEAL, JOSEPH	CEC	010	ELKTON 3
MC NEAL, MARGARETT	BAL	026	4TH WARD
MC NEAL, MARTIN	BAL	134	2ND DIST
MC NEAL, MARY	BAL	025	9TH WARD
MC NEAL, MARY C.	BAL	109	10TH WAR
MC NEAL, MATHEW	BAL	400	1ST DIST
MC NEAL, OWEN	BAL	424	8TH WARD
MC NEAL, PATRICK	BAL	400	1ST DIST
MC NEAL, PATRICK	BAL	349	7TH WARD
MC NEAL, SARAH	SOM	483	TRAPP DI
MC NEAL, WILLIAM	SOM	489	SALISBUR
MC NEAL, WILLIAM A.*	TAL	053	EASTON D
MC NEAL,LOYD	BAL	187	2ND WARD
MC NEALEN, ANTONY	BAL	146	2ND DIST
MC NEALY,ISABELLA	BAL	012	2ND DIST
MC NEAR, JAMES	ALL	250	CUMBERLA
MC NEESE, HORATIO	BAL	061	4TH WARD
MC NEIL, ARCHIBALD	ALL	241	CUMBERLA
MC NEIL, FRANCIS	FRE	202	5TH E DI
MC NEIL, GEORGE	BAL	045	4TH WARD
MC NEIL, JAMES	BAL	357	3RD WARD
MC NEIL, THOMS	ALL	236	CUMBERLA
MC NEIL, WILLAIM	BAL	145	1ST WARD
MC NEILL, EDWARD J.	BAL	161	1ST WARD
MC NEILL, HOBERT	ALL	095	5TH E.D.
MC NEILLE, JOHN	WOR	272	BERLIN 1

MC NEILLE, REBECCA WOR 266 BERLIN 1
MC NEILLY, JOHN BAL 247 20TH WAR
MC NEILLY, MARGARET BAL 298 1ST DIST
MC NEIR, ELIZABETH* BAL 304 3RD WARD
MC NEIR, GOERGE BAL 134 5TH WARD
MC NEIR, J.J. BAL 139 5TH WARD
MC NEIR, WILLIAM BAL 139 5TH WARD
MC NEIR, WILLIAM SR. ANN 278 ANNAPOLI
MC NELLAR, GEORGE QUE 163 2ND E DI
MC NELLY, ANN BAL 002 EASTERN
MC NELLY, ANN BAL 064 15TH WAR
MC NELLY, ARTHUR BAL 334 1ST DIST
MC NELLY, ELIZABETH BAL 305 17TH WAR
MC NELLY, HENRY BAL 201 19TH WAR
MC NELLY, HUGH BAL 304 17TH WAR
MC NELLY, MARIA BAL 109 5TH WARD
MC NELLY, MARY E. BAL 177 19TH WAR
MC NELLY, MATHEW BAL 304 17TH WAR
MC NELLY, PATRICK BAL 020 9TH WARD
MC NELLY, PATRICK BAL 272 1ST DIST
MC NELLY, SARAH BAL 021 9TH WARD
MC NELLY, WILLAIM BAL 463 1ST DIST
MC NELSON, JOHN FRE 320 MIDDLETO
MC NETT, LUCINDA BAL 199 19TH WAR
MC NEVIN, JOHN BAL 326 7TH WARD
MC NEVIN, MARK BAL 087 15TH WAR
MC NEVIN, VIRGINIA A. BAL 326 7TH WARD
MC NEW, AMANDA ALL 158 6TH E.D.
MC NEW, BASIL * BAL 097 18TH WAR
MC NEW, CAROLINE BAL 099 18TH WAR
MC NEW, JAMES BAL 390 8TH WARD
MC NEW, JANES PRI 032 VANSVILL
MC NEW, JOSEPH PRI 021 VANSVILL
MC NEW, MAHALA PRI 038 VANSVILL
MC NEW, THOMAS PRI 038 VANSVILL
MC NEW, THOMAS BAL 099 18TH WAR
MC NEW, THOMAS BAL 117 18TH WAR
MC NEW, WILLIAM PRI 035 VANSVILL
MC NEWAY, FRANCES CEC 210 7TH E DI
MC NICHOL, DANIEL BAL 118 2ND DIST
MC NICHOLES, BERNOO * BAL 114 2ND DIST
MC NICKLE, ELLEN BAL 103 10TH WAR
MC NICKOLLS, GEORGE BAL 292 17TH WAR
MC NICOLS, MARGARET BAL 152 11TH WAR
MC NIER, ANDREW BAL 283 7TH WARD
MC NIER, ELIZABETH* BAL 304 3RD WARD
MC NIER, PERRY CAR 268 WESTMINS
MC NIER, RICHARD BAL 231 6TH WARD
MC NIGHT, BRIDGET ALL 181 8TH E.D.
MC NIGHT, JAMES BAL 419 3RD WARD
MC NINCH, RICHARD BAL 308 7TH WARD
MC NINEMY, JAMES CEC 173 6TH E DI
MC NNAMEE, FRANKLIN CEC 172 6TH E DI
MC NOLAN, WILLIAM ALL 056 10TH E.D
MC NOODEN, CHARLES BAL 282 12TH WAR
MC NULL, ARCHIBALD WAS 298 1ST DIST
MC NULL, JOHN ALL 077 5TH E.D.
MC NULL, JOHN ALL 203 CUMBERLA
MC NULTY, ANDREW HAR 106 2ND DIST
MC NULTY, ANN BAL 145 11TH WAR
MC NULTY, ANNIE* BAL 357 3RD WARD
MC NULTY, BRIDGET BAL 372 3RD WARD
MC NULTY, CATHERINE BAL 120 11TH WAR
MC NULTY, CHARLES FRE 203 5TH E DI
MC NULTY, CORNELIUS FRE 183 5TH E DI
MC NULTY, DENNIS FRE 183 5TH E DI
MC NULTY, ELIZABETH BAL 342 1ST DIST
MC NULTY, ELLEN FRE 066 FREDERIC
MC NULTY, FELIX ALL 078 5TH E.D.
MC NULTY, GEORGE BAL 116 1ST WARD
MC NULTY, HENRY FRE 390 PETERSVI
MC NULTY, HUGH FRE 055 FREDERIC
MC NULTY, JOHN BAL 359 13TH WAR
MC NULTY, MARY BAL 366 13TH WAR
MC NULTY, MARY HAR 088 2ND DIST
MC NULTY, MARY BAL 159 19TH WAR
MC NULTY, MARY BAL 161 16TH WAR
MC NULTY, MARY BAL 264 7TH WARD
MC NULTY, MICHAEL ALL 078 5TH E.D.
MC NULTY, NEILL BAL 037 1ST WARD
MC NULTY, PATRICK ANN 421 HOWARD D
MC NULTY, PATRICK FRE 163 EMMITTSB
MC NULTY, PETER BAL 159 19TH WAR
MC NULTY, THOMAS BAL 397 8TH WARD
MC NULTY, THOMAS BAL 129 16TH WAR
MC NUNAWAY, JOHN CEC 173 6TH E DI
MC NUTT, REBECCA BAL 439 14TH WAR
MC NUTT, SAMUEL G. HAR 033 1ST DIST
MC NUTT, SARAH HAR 003 1ST DIST
MC NUTTY, ANNIE* BAL 357 3RD WARD
MC NUTTY, MARIA BAL 185 11TH WAR
MC OLY, JANE* BAL 371 3RD WARD
MC OMAS, ELLEN BAL 472 14TH WAR
MC ONLEY, ELLICK HAR 071 1ST DIST
MC ONNELL, JOHN ALL 150 6TH E.D.
MC OWEN, THOMAS BAL 143 1ST WARD
MC OWYN, WILLIAM BAL 223 19TH WAR
MC PARLANA, MICHAEL BAL 356 8TH WARD
MC PARLIN, M.C. ANN 286 ANNAPOLI
MC PHAIL, CATHARINE BAL 169 16TH WAR
MC PHAIL, JAMES L. BAL 103 10TH WAR
MC PHAIL, MARY BAL 066 10TH WAR
MC PHAIL, WILLIAM BAL 355 13TH WAR
MC PHEROSN, MATTHEW ALL 088 5TH E.D.
MC PHERSON, ALEXANDER BAL 364 13TH WAR
MC PHERSON, ALPHE FRE 085 FREDERIC
MC PHERSON, ANNE BAL 114 15TH WAR
MC PHERSON, BERSON CHA 259 MIDDLETO
MC PHERSON, CATHERINE D. FRE 041 FREDERIC
MC PHERSON, CHARLES H. PRI 046 AQUASCO
MC PHERSON, DUNCAN BAL 114 1ST WARD
MC PHERSON, DUNKIN BAL 362 1ST DIST
MC PHERSON, EDWARD CHA 217 ALLENS F
MC PHERSON, ELIZABETH BAL 183 2ND WARD
MC PHERSON, GEORGE ANN 388 4TH DIST
MC PHERSON, GEORGE H. ANN 386 4TH DIST
MC PHERSON, H. WAS 021 2ND SUBD
MC PHERSON, H.B. PRI 104 PISCATAW
MC PHERSON, J. BAL 117 1ST WARD
MC PHERSON, JAMES H. WAS 273 RIDGEVIL
MC PHERSON, JOHN ANN 336 3RD DIST
MC PHERSON, JOHN BAL 105 5TH WARD
MC PHERSON, JOHN BAL 261 20TH WAR
MC PHERSON, JOHN FRE 081 FREDERIC
MC PHERSON, JOHN BAL 002 4TH WARD
MC PHERSON, JOHN FRE 277 NEW MARK
MC PHERSON, JOHN W. CHA 276 ALLENS F
MC PHERSON, JOSEPH FRE 101 FREDERIC
MC PHERSON, JOSEPH BAL 092 5TH WARD
MC PHERSON, MARY ANN 406 8TH DIST
MC PHERSON, MARY CHA 260 MIDDLETO
MC PHERSON, MASON L. CHA 263 MIDDLETO
MC PHERSON, MATILDA FRE 070 FREDERIC
MC PHERSON, R. BAL 137 1ST WARD
MC PHERSON, ROBERT BAL 439 14TH WAR
MC PHERSON, SALLY CHA 287 BOJANTOW
MC PHERSON, SAMUEL CHA 259 MIDDLETO
MC PHERSON, SAMUEL ANN 386 4TH DIST
MC PHERSON, SUSAN E. BAL 106 5TH WARD
MC PHERSON, SUSANNA FRE 191 5TH E DI
MC PHERSON, THOMAS-BLACK FRE 208 BUCKEYST
MC PHERSON, W. H. ANN 405 8TH DIST
MC PHERSON, WILLIAM BAL 136 18TH WAR
MC PHERSON, WILLIAM FRE 122 CREAGERS
MC PHIESON, WILLIAM G. BAL 324 12TH WAR
MC PHILLIPS, BIDDY BAL 472 14TH WAR
MC PHILLIPS, MICHAEL BAL 291 17TH WAR
MC PHINNEY, M.J. PRI 077 MARLBROU
MC POLAN, THOMAS BAL 060 15TH WAR
MC POLAND, SUSAN BAL 335 13TH WAR
MC PRICE, ISAAC BAL 183 5TH DIST
MC QUADE, ANN BAL 470 14TH WAR
MC QUADE, ARTHUR FRE 311 MIDDLETO
MC QUADE, MARY BAL 470 14TH WAR
MC QUADE, MORTIMA BAL 212 11TH WAR
MC QUAID, CATHARINE ALL 074 5TH E.D.
MC QUAID, JOSEPH BAL 302 3RD WARD
MC QUAR, WILLIAM TAL 106 ST MICHA
MC QUAY, JAMES CAR 375 9TH DIST
MC QUAY, JOHN TAL 106 ST MICHA
MC QUAY, JOHN H. TAL 106 ST MICHA
MC QUAY, JOHN R. TAL 002 EASTON D
MC QUAY, LEVIN DOR 390 1ST DIST
MC QUAY, MARGARET TAL 007 EASTON D
MC QUAY, MARY TAL 105 ST MICHA
MC QUAY, MARY* TAL 019 EASTON D
MC QUAY, PATRICK TAL 113 ST MICHA
MC QUAY, RUBEN TAL 104 ST MICHA
MC QUDDE, HANNAH ALL 235 CUMBERLA
MC QUEEN, JAMES BAL 003 9TH WARD
MC QUIGGEN, MARY E. BAL 171 6TH WARD
MC QUILER, PATRICK BAL 021 2ND DIST
MC QUILLAN, ANN BAL 143 11TH WAR
MC QUILLAN, JAMES BAL 415 8TH WARD
MC QUILLAN, SISTER C. FRE 198 5TH E DI
MC QUIRTY, HURIA BAL 004 4TH WARD
MC QURK, WILLIAM BAL 008 EASTERN
MC RAY, MARY BAL 179 19TH WAR
MC RAY, MARY PRI 079 MARLBROU
MC REA, HENRY ALL 174 7TH E.D.
MC REA, SAMUEL ALL 159 6TH E.D.
MC REA, THEODORE ALL 136 4TH E.D.
MC READY, SUSAN BAL 310 12TH WAR
MC REYNOLDS, WILLAIM CEC 129 6TH E DI
MC RICHARDS, THOMAS ALL 142 6TH E.D.
MC ROBERTS, MARY A. BAL 182 19TH WAR
MC ROBERTS, WILLIAM BAL 001 EASTERN
MC ROBERTSON, PETER ANN 267 ANNAPOLI
MC ROBIE, ANDREW ALL 065 10TH E.D
MC ROBIE, ELISHA ALL 065 10TH E.D
MC ROBIE, JOHN ALL 046 10TH E.D
MC ROBIE, JOHN ALL 057 10TH E.D
MC ROBIE, PETER ALL 054 10TH E.D
MC ROBIE, WILLIAM ALL 046 10TH E.D
MC ROBIL, SARAH ALL 055 10TH E.D
MC ROY, ANN BAL 183 11TH WAR
MC ROY, ELEXANDER HAR 199 3RD DIST
MC ROY, JOHN BAL 118 18TH WAR
MC RURETRY, SAMUEL CAR 381 2ND DIST
MC RYAN, JAMES BAL 068 1ST WARD
MC SCHSAN, CHARLES BAL 183 11TH WAR
MC SHAE, MARY BAL 170 2ND DIST
MC SHAHEE, JOHN BAL 164 6TH WARD
MC SHANE, BARNARD BAL 402 8TH WARD
MC SHANE, ELIZABETH BAL 014 18TH WAR
MC SHANE, ELIZABETH BAL 033 4TH WARD
MC SHANE, HARRY BAL 098 5TH WARD
MC SHANE, JAMES BAL 192 11TH WAR
MC SHANE, JOHN BAL 368 8TH WARD
MC SHANE, LEWIS BAL 051 1ST WARD
MC SHANE, PAT BAL 099 5TH WARD
MC SHANE, PETER BAL 355 8TH WARD
MC SHANE, ROSA BAL 188 11TH WAR
MC SHANE, WILLIAM BAL 128 5TH WARD
MC SHARE, LAURENCE BAL 234 2ND WARD
MC SHENY, ANN MRS- BAL 315 20TH WAR
MC SHERRY, JOHN BAL 282 12TH WAR
MC SHERRY, SARAH BAL 267 12TH WAR
MC SHURY, JAMES FRE 029 FREDERIC
MC SKIMMER, WILLIAM HAR 300 3RD DIST
MC SLEMONS, JAMES* SOM 505 SALISBUR
MC SOARLEY, ANN* BAL 389 3RD WARD
MC SOPER, WILLAIM BAL 234 1ST DIST
MC SOULA, CATHARINE BAL 192 6TH WARD
MC SPARREN, HENRY BAL 131 1ST WARD
MC SPEDDEN, ROBERT J. BAL 251 2ND WARD
MC STEVENSON, ANN* BAL 369 3RD WARD
MC SWEEN, DANIEL BAL 011 9TH WARD
MC SWEENEY, CATHERINE BAL 314 3RD WARD
MC SWEENEY, JANE BAL 314 3RD WARD
MC SWEENEY, PETER BAL 186 16TH WAR
MC SWENEY, MARY BAL 344 13TH WAR
MC TADDEN, FRANCIS BAL 389 1ST DIST
MC TAGE, BERNARD BAL 044 9TH WARD
MC TAGGART, JAMES BAL 349 7TH WARD
MC TAGUE, ANN BAL 050 15TH WAR
MC TAGUE, CATHARINE BAL 072 15TH WAR
MC TAGUE, JOHN ANN 522 HOWARD D
MC TAGUE, MARY BAL 073 15TH WAR
MC TAVISH, CHARLES C. ANN 483 HOWARD D
MC TEAGUE, ANN BAL 364 8TH WARD
MC TEAGUE, BRIDGET BAL 362 8TH WARD
MC TEAGUE, CATHERINE BAL 362 8TH WARD
MC THEOWN, MARY BAL 171 11TH WAR
MC TIE, MARGARET ANN 451 HOWARD D
MC TRAVRS, WILLIAM* DOR 357 3RD DIVI
MC VANDERBERG, JOHN BAL 200 11TH WAR
MC VEIN, ADLER ANN 287 ANNAPOLI
MC VEIN, CATHARINE ANN 287 ANNAPOLI
MC VETT, JOSEPH E.* DOR 454 1ST DIST
MC VEY, ABSALOM B. CEC 127 5TH E DI
MC VEY, ANDREW CEC 157 PORT DUP
MC VEY, BENJAMIN CEC 173 6TH E DI
MC VEY, FRANCIS CEC 184 7TH E DI
MC VEY, HIRAM CEC 174 6TH E DI
MC VEY, JAMES CEC 135 6TH E DI
MC VEY, JAMES CEC 127 5TH E DI
MC VEY, JAMES K. CEC 129 5TH E DI
MC VEY, JOHN HAR 117 2ND DIST
MC VEY, JOHN BAL 159 1ST WARD
MC VEY, JOHN T. CEC 081 CHARLEST
MC VEY, JONATHAN CEC 130 6TH E DI
MC VEY, JONATHAN CEC 183 7TH E DI
MC VEY, LEVI CEC 152 PORT DUP
MC VEY, LEVY HAR 134 2ND DIST
MC VEY, NATHAN CEC 157 PORT DUP
MC VEY, NATHAN B. CEC 168 6TH E DI
MC VEY, THOMAS CEC 123 3RD E DI
MC VIER, DANIEL BAL 124 1ST WARD
MC VOY, JUDY BAL 361 8TH WARD
MC WADARD, MARGARET BAL 312 12TH WAR
MC WANE, MICHAEL CEC 026 ELKTON 3
MC WELSH, MARY BAL 314 20TH WAR
MC WENIRE, MICHAEL BAL 014 1ST WARD
MC WHINNEY, DAVID BAL 177 19TH WAR
MC WHINNEY, HESTER BAL 384 13TH WAR
MC WHINNY, JAMES BAL 228 19TH WAR
MC WHIRTER, ARCHIBALD BAL 006 15TH WAR
MC WHITE, JAMES BAL 045 9TH WARD
MC WHORTON, JEFFERSON KEN 308 3RD DIST
MC WILLIAM, FRANK CHA 226 ALLENS F
MC WILLIAM, JOHN BAL 361 8TH WARD
MC WILLIAM, JOHN B. CHA 226 ALLENS F
MC WILLIAMS, ANN BAL 147 11TH WAR
MC WILLIAMS, ANN BAL 414 8TH WARD
MC WILLIAMS, ANN BAL 166 11TH WAR
MC WILLIAMS, BENJAMIN DOR 301 1ST DIST
MC WILLIAMS, CATHERINE BAL 051 4TH WARD
MC WILLIAMS, CATHERINE BAL 421 8TH WARD
MC WILLIAMS, CHARLOTTE ST 303 2ND E DI
MC WILLIAMS, DANIEL BAL 188 2ND WARD
MC WILLIAMS, DANIEL ALL 096 5TH E.D.
MC WILLIAMS, DAVID BAL 004 9TH WARD
MC WILLIAMS, DENNIS BAL 421 8TH WARD
MC WILLIAMS, E. BAL 069 10TH WAR
MC WILLIAMS, EMELINE ST 317 4TH E DI
MC WILLIAMS, EZEKIEL DOR 305 1ST DIST
MC WILLIAMS, HENRICK TAL 061 EASTON D
MC WILLIAMS, JAMES WAS 038 2ND SUBD
MC WILLIAMS, JOHN DOR 304 1ST DIST
MC WILLIAMS, JOHN BAL 034 4TH WARD
MC WILLIAMS, JOHN ALL 170 6TH E.D.
MC WILLIAMS, JOSEPH G. ST 317 4TH E DI
MC WILLIAMS, MICHEL BAL 094 2ND DIST
MC WILLIAMS, PATRICK BAL 068 4TH WARD
MC WILLIAMS, ROBERT BAL 326 7TH WARD
MC YARISH, JOHN BAL 146 11TH WAR
MCAPHERSON, MARY R. BAL 439 14TH WAR
MCARTER, CHARLES M. BAL 123 1ST WARD
MCCOMBS, JOHN L. CAR 149 NO TWP L
MCGUIE, ELLEN BAL 183 2ND WARD
MCK HEISTER, THOMAS * WAS 162 HAGERSTO
MCK KEPLER, WILLIAM WAS 164 HAGERSTO
MCKINSEY, COLLIN CAR 184 8TH DIST
MCKINSTREY, HENRY CAR 276 7TH DIST
MCLEREARY, ANN WAS 053 2ND SUBD
MCPHAM, MARY HAR 019 1ST DIST
MCUCBBIN, WILLIAM BAL 125 2ND DIST
ME GEE, SARAH A. BAL 217 11TH WAR
ME, CHARLES L.* DOR 375 1ST DIST
MEABY, DANIEL BAL 016 1ST WARD
MEACH, CONRAD BAL 055 1ST WARD
MEACH, JOHN BAL 055 1ST WARD
MEACHUM, WILLIAM HAR 089 2ND DIST
MEAD, ADAM ANN 451 HOWARD D
MEAD, EVE BAL 047 9TH WARD
MEAD, JAMES R. ANN 446 HOWARD D
MEAD, L. L. BAL 158 1ST WARD
MEAD, LOUIS BAL 199 19TH WAR
MEAD, LOUISA R. BAL 199 19TH WAR
MEAD, MARY BAL 443 8TH WARD
MEAD, MARY PRI 066 NOTTINGH
MEAD, MARY C. BAL 197 6TH WARD
MEAD, PHILIP BAL 240 17TH WAR
MEAD, SAMUEL L. BAL 114 1ST WARD
MEAD, T. L. BAL 154 1ST WARD
MEAD, THOMAS H. BAL 199 19TH WAR
MEAD, WALTER C. FRE 204 BUCKEYST
MEAD, WILLIAM BAL 115 1ST WARD
MEADE, RICHARD FRE 203 5TH E DI
MEADE, WILLIAM CAL 058 3RD DIST
MEADER, ANDREW BAL 094 18TH WAR
MEADER, HENRY BAL 212 17TH WAR
MEADS, AQUILLA BAL 080 2ND DIST
MEADS, BENEDICT WAS 033 2ND SUBD
MEADS, BENJAMIN BAL 114 5TH WARD
MEADS, CHARLOTTE BAL 342 7TH WARD
MEADS, DANIEL BAL 032 1ST WARD
MEADS, ELISHA HAR 017 1ST DIST
MEADS, ELIZA BAL 096 10TH WAR
MEADS, ELIZABETH A. BAL 332 7TH WARD
MEADS, ELLIN HAR 067 1ST DIST
MEADS, GEORGE BAL 349 7TH WARD
MEADS, HENRIETTA BAL 240 17TH WAR
MEADS, HENRY BAL 039 1ST WARD
MEADS, JAMES BAL 458 1ST DIST
MEADS, JAMES BAL 057 2ND DIST
MEADS, JAMES HAR 179 3RD DIST
MEADS, JEFF BAL 443 1ST DIST
MEADS, JEREMIAH WAS 007 WILLIAMS
MEADS, JOHN D. HAR 016 1ST DIST
MEADS, MARY BAL 298 7TH WARD
MEADS, MARY A. BAL 264 2ND WARD
MEADS, MARY C. BAL 267 7TH WARD
MEADS, NATHAN T. BAL 438 1ST DIST
MEADS, RACHEL WAS 034 2ND SUBD
MEADS, SAMUEL BAL 135 5TH WARD
MEADS, WASHINGTON BAL 239 6TH WARD
MEADS, WILLIAM A. BAL 349 7TH WARD
MEADS, WILLIAM W. BAL 264 2ND WARD
MEAEES, A. J. * TAL 086 ST MICHA
MEAGER, L. BAL 319 12TH WAR
MEAGIN, MARTIN BAL 132 2ND DIST
MEAHEL, ABRAHAM FRE 271 NEW MARK
MEAKEN, ANN BAL 279 20TH WAR
MEAKEN, WILLIAM BAL 296 20TH WAR
MEAKIN, SAMUEL BAL 297 20TH WAR
MEAKIN, SARAH J. BAL 297 20TH WAR
MEAKINS, SOPHIA KEN 242 2ND DIST
MEAL, JOHN BAL 160 11TH WAR
MEAL, MARY BAL 163 11TH WAR
MEALER, HARTMAN TAL 109 ST MICHA
MEALEY, ISAIAH FRE 340 MIDDLETO
MEALEY, MARY BAL 104 5TH WARD
MEALY, E.M. WAS 136 HAGERSTO
MEALY, JAMES C. BAL 413 14TH WAR
MEALY, JOHN E. ALL 199 CUMBERLA
MEALY, MELTON FRE 254 NEW MARK
MEALY, MICHAEL ALL 135 4TH E.D.
MEALY, WILLIAM FRE 250 NEW MARK

MEAMS, ELIZABETH CEC 095 4TH E DI
MEANALY, ALEXANDER * BAL 273 1ST DIST
MEANARY, ALEXANDER * BAL 273 1ST DIST
MEANIUS, ADAM BAL 055 1ST WARD
MEANLY, JANE PRI 109 PISCATAW
MEANS, ANN C. BAL 460 1ST DIST
MEANS, HARISON DOR 429 1ST DIST
MEANS, NANCY HAR 048 1ST DIST
MEARES, JOHN CEC 036 CHESAPEA
MEARGUDEN, CARL BAL 047 1ST WARD
MEARIS, GEORGE BAL 105 10TH WAR
MEARIS, JACOB* BAL 031 4TH WARD
MEARITT, JOHN BAL 250 20TH WAR
MEARNIS, MARGARET SR. CEC 125 5TH E DI
MEARNS, ANDREW F. CEC 126 5TH E DI
MEARNS, HUGH CEC 125 5TH E DI
MEARNS, JAMES CEC 128 5TH E DI
MEARNS, JOHN CEC 126 5TH E DI
MEARNS, JOHN CEC 064 1ST E DI
MEARNS, LEVI R. CEC 114 3RD E DI
MEARNS, SAMUEL CEC 127 5TH E DI
MEARNS, WILLIAM CEC 126 5TH E DI
MEARS, DANIEL CEC 038 CHESAPEA
MEARS, EDWARD F. A. BAL 188 6TH WARD
MEARS, HENRY WOR 246 1ST CENS
MEARS, HESTER WOR 186 7TH E DI
MEARS, JAMES H. DOR 411 1ST DIST
MEARS, JOHN DOR 411 1ST DIST
MEARS, JOHN WOR 294 9TH E DI
MEARS, JOHN WOR 283 BERLIN 1
MEARS, JOHN B. BAL 013 4TH WARD
MEARS, LEVIN* DOR 434 1ST DIST
MEARS, LOUIS BAL 458 1ST DIST
MEARS, MARY WOR 185 6TH E DI
MEARS, ROBERT BAL 260 20TH WAR
MEARS, THOMAS H. BAL 304 3RD WARD
MEARS, THOMAS P. BAL 305 3RD WARD
MEARS, WILLIAM BAL 025 1ST WARD
MEARS, WILLIAM* DOR 410 1ST DIST
MEARSELL, ANTON BAL 085 1ST WARD
MEARY, MARIA BAL 006 18TH WAR
MEAS, ANN R. DOR 434 1ST DIST
MEASE, JOHN ALL 007 3RD E.D.
MEASE, SAMUEL ALL 013 3RD E.D.
MEASEL, DANIEL FRE 234 BUCKEYST
MEASEL, ELIZABETH FRE 095 FREDERIC
MEASEL, FREDERICK FRE 098 FREDERIC
MEASEL, GEORGE FRE 091 FREDERIC
MEASEL, JOHN FRE 092 FREDERIC
MEASEL, JOSEPH FRE 093 FREDERIC
MEASEL, MALINDA FRE 088 FREDERIC
MEASEL, MARGARET WAS 162 HAGERSTO
MEASON, JAMES BAL 147 1ST WARD
MEASON, NOAH BAL 253 20TH WAR
MEAUGER, JOHN BAL 373 8TH WARD
MEBER, MICHAEL * BAL 139 19TH WAR
MECANGEN, KIPIAH* DOR 373 1ST DIST
MECARTER, ELIZABETH CAR 123 NO TWP L
MECARTER, MARY CAR 123 NO TWP L
MECHAM, ANTHONY BAL 294 3RD WARD
MECHAM, ISAAC HAR 144 2ND DIST
MECHAN, CATHARINE BAL 213 11TH WAR
MECHEM, GEORGE HAR 113 2ND DIST
MECHEN, FRANK ANN 304 1ST DIST
MECHER, RICHARD HAR 050 1ST DIST
MECKEDEY, ELLEN BAL 304 20TH WAR
MECKET, JOHN BAL 272 7TH WARD
MECKINS, MARY C. CAL 014 1ST DIST
MECKLEY, DANIEL CAR 338 6TH DIST
MECKNIGHT, WILINGTON BAL 212 17TH WAR
MECONKER, LAURA BAL 120 11TH WAR
MECOTTER, JANE DOR 322 1ST DIST
MECRADY, ANDREW DOR 351 3RD DIVI
MECRADY, ELIZA DOR 351 3RD DIVI
MECRADY, JAMES* DOR 351 3RD DIVI
MECRONEY, P. PRI 082 QUEEN AN
MECY, JAMES CEC 181 7TH E DI
MEDAIRY, HARRIETT BAL 215 17TH WAR
MEDAIRY, JACOB BAL 428 14TH WAR
MEDAIRY, JOHN BAL 065 15TH WAR
MEDALTON, THEADORE W. HAR 192 3RD DIST
MEDAN, ELIZABETH * BAL 301 1ST DIST
MEDAVEY, ALEXANDER BAL 427 14TH WAR
MEDCALF, A.P. ANN 273 ANNAPOLI
MEDCALF, CRANKLIN BAL 043 2ND DIST
MEDCALF, ELIZAH BAL 412 8TH WARD
MEDCALF, GEORGE ANN 451 HOWARD D
MEDCALF, JOSHUA CAR 413 2ND DIST
MEDCALF, NICHOLAS FRE 308 WOODSBOR
MEDCALF, THOMAS BAL 087 18TH WAR
MEDCALFE, WILLIAM M. BAL 474 14TH WAR
MEDCALFF, BENJAMIN W. WAS 126 2ND DIST
MEDDIS, GEORGE W. KEN 299 3RD DIST
MEDDLETON, ED. * ALL 096 5TH E.D.
MEDDLETON, WILLIAM ALL 159 6TH E.D.
MEDDUS, JOHN KEN 286 3RD DIST
MEDEILL, JOSEPH M. BAL 282 2ND WARD
MEDELY, JOHN T. MGM 430 CLARKSTR
MEDERETH, LOUISA BAL 177 11TH WAR
MEDERICK, HENRY BAL 146 19TH WAR
MEDERY, JOHN BAL 047 2ND DIST
MEDEWELLER, JOHN BAL 345 3RD WARD
MEDFORD ANN 283 ANNAPOLI
MEDFORD, ANN KEN 296 3RD DIST
MEDFORD, ANNA M. * KEN 246 2ND DIST
MEDFORD, ANSIL DOR 439 1ST DIST
MEDFORD, EDWIN E. DOR 319 1ST DIST
MEDFORD, MARGRETE CAR 125 NO TWP L
MEDFORD, MARIA DOR 453 1ST DIST
MEDFORD, NATHANIEL DOR 310 1ST DIST
MEDFORD, ROBERT M. DOR 311 1ST DIST
MEDFORD, S. ANN 283 ANNAPOLI
MEDFORD, SALLY DOR 320 1ST DIST
MEDFORD, THOMAS B. CAR 126 NO TWP L
MEDFORD, URIA A. DOR 454 1ST DIST
MEDFORD, WILLIAM CAR 124 NO TWP L
MEDFORD, WILLIAM W. CAR 106 NO TWP L
MEDIDITH, AMMON DOR 420 1ST DIST
MEDINGER, ANDREW BAL 428 8TH WARD
MEDINGER, CAROLINE BAL 226 6TH WARD
MEDINGER, CHARLES J. BAL 344 13TH WAR
MEDINGER, CHRISTIANA BAL 081 15TH WAR
MEDINGER, CHRISTOPHER BAL 386 8TH WARD
MEDINGER, FRED BAL 059 2ND DIST
MEDINGER, GEORGE BAL 200 11TH WAR
MEDINGER, GOTLIEB BAL 304 7TH WARD
MEDINGER, JOHN G. BAL 386 8TH WARD
MEDINGER, LOUISA BAL 392 14TH WAR
MEDL, FRANCIS O. PRI 112 PISCATAW
MEDLEY, CHARLES ST 313 1ST E DI
MEDLEY, CLARA ST 283 3RD E DI
MEDLEY, CLARA ST 284 2ND E DI
MEDLEY, GEORGE W. BAL 112 18TH WAR
MEDLEY, LONIS ST 254 3RD E DI
MEDLEY, ROBERT B. ST 277 3RD E DI
MEDLEY, WILLIAM E. BAL 112 18TH WAR
MEDLIAC, WILLIAM CAR 268 WESTMINS
MEDLY, JAMES PRI 113 PISCATAW
MEDLY, JAMES A. PRI 112 PISCATAW
MEDLY, SARAH PRI 113 PISCATAW
MEDSFORD, CHARLES BAL 094 15TH WAR
MEDTART, JESES L. BAL 409 14TH WAR
MEDTART, JESSE BAL 428 14TH WAR
MEDTART, LEWIS FRE 032 FREDERIC
MEE, PETER BAL 458 1ST DIST
MEED, GEORGE BAL 307 1ST DIST
MEED, MARGARET BAL 307 1ST DIST
MEEDEN, GEORGE BAL 344 7TH WARD
MEEDER, PETER BAL 215 19TH WAR
MEEDS, BECKY-BLACK QUE 187 3RD E DI
MEEDS, CHARLES A. CAR 086 NO TWP L
MEEDS, EDWIN M. BAL 158 18TH WAR
MEEDS, EMILY L. BAL 212 11TH WAR
MEEDS, HESTER ANN QUE 208 3RD E DI
MEEDS, JANE C. QUE 210 3RD E DI
MEEDS, JOHN T. QUE 192 3RD E DI
MEEDS, LAURA E. BAL 159 16TH WAR
MEEDS, RICHARD QUE 210 3RD E DI
MEEDS, ROBERT BAL 044 1ST WARD
MEEDS, THOMAS QUE 212 3RD E DI
MEEDS, WILLIAM QUE 215 3RD E DI
MEEDS, WILLIAM-BLACK QUE 147 1ST E DI
MEEHAN, BARTHOLOMEW BAL 039 1ST WARD
MEEHIN, PATRICK BAL 279 7TH WARD
MEEK, DAVID ALL 237 CUMBERLA
MEEK, DAVID B. ANN 388 4TH DIST
MEEK, JAMES ANN 358 3RD DIST
MEEK, JOHN ANN 358 3RD DIST
MEEK, JOHN ANN 329 2ND DIST
MEEK, JOHN FRE 382 PETERSVI
MEEK, MARTHA ANN 324 2ND DIST
MEEK, MOSES H. WAS 150 2ND DIST
MEEKAS, JOHN BAL 141 2ND DIST
MEEKIN, NOAH DOR 355 3RD DIVI
MEEKINS, ANN DOR 332 3RD DIVI
MEEKINS, AUSTIN ANN 310 1ST DIST
MEEKINS, BASIL BAL 354 3RD WARD
MEEKINS, CAROLINE DOR 356 3RD DIVI
MEEKINS, CHARLES CAL 021 2ND DIST
MEEKINS, COLUMBUS DOR 355 3RD DIVI
MEEKINS, DANIEL DOR 361 3RD DIVI
MEEKINS, DENWOOD DOR 327 3RD DIVI
MEEKINS, ELENOR DOR 327 3RD DIVI
MEEKINS, ELIZABETH DOR 334 3RD DIVI
MEEKINS, ELIZABETH DOR 417 1ST DIST
MEEKINS, ELIZABETH BAL 019 15TH WAR
MEEKINS, ELIZABETH BAL 020 15TH WAR
MEEKINS, GEORGE BAL 351 7TH WARD
MEEKINS, GEORGE H. DOR 332 3RD DIVI
MEEKINS, GEORGE J. DOR 433 1ST DIST
MEEKINS, HENERY DOR 331 3RD DIVI
MEEKINS, ISAAC BAL 016 15TH WAR
MEEKINS, ISAAC H. DOR 377 1ST DIST
MEEKINS, JAMES KEN 245 2ND DIST
MEEKINS, JOHN DOR 331 3RD DIVI
MEEKINS, JOHN D. ANN 327 2ND DIST
MEEKINS, JOSEPH ANN 298 1ST DIST
MEEKINS, JOSEPH W. DOR 328 3RD DIVI
MEEKINS, JOSEPH W. SR.* DOR 330 3RD DIVI
MEEKINS, JOSIAH J. DOR 332 3RD DIVI
MEEKINS, LETTITIA DOR 330 3RD DIVI
MEEKINS, MARGARET BAL 352 3RD WARD
MEEKINS, MARIA BAL 019 15TH WAR
MEEKINS, MARTHA A. DOR 329 3RD DIVI
MEEKINS, MARY DOR 355 3RD DIVI
MEEKINS, MARY G. ANN 396 8TH DIST
MEEKINS, MATHIAS DOR 326 3RD DIVI
MEEKINS, PHILLIS DOR 356 3RD DIVI
MEEKINS, ROBERT DOR 329 3RD DIVI
MEEKINS, ROBERT DOR 371 3RD DIVI
MEEKINS, ROBERT DOR 419 1ST DIST
MEEKINS, SAMUEL J. DOR 326 3RD DIVI
MEEKINS, THOMAS DOR 415 1ST DIST
MEEKINS, WILLIAM DOR 419 1ST DIST
MEEKINS, WILLIAM DOR 371 3RD DIVI
MEEKINS, WILLIAM A. ANN 295 1ST DIST
MEEKINS, WILLIAM L. DOR 328 3RD DIVI
MEEKS, ADAMS BAL 161 11TH WAR
MEEKS, AQUILLA KEN 271 1ST DIST
MEEKS, CAROLINE BAL 142 2ND DIST
MEEKS, CATHERINE BAL 063 10TH WAR
MEEKS, JOHN W. BAL 117 18TH WAR
MEEKS, LOUISA ANN 386 4TH DIST
MEEKS, TEMPERANCE KEN 243 2ND DIST
MEEKS, W. * BAL 141 2ND DIST
MEEKS, WILLIAM ANN 427 HOWARD D
MEEKS, WILLIAM BAL 038 4TH WARD
MEEKS, WILLIAM KEN 271 1ST DIST
MEEKS, WILLIAM F. KEN 311 3RD DIST
MEEKS, WILLIAM W. BAL 115 18TH WAR
MEELEY, MARGARET BAL 024 9TH WARD
MEELZBERGER, M. B. BAL 319 12TH WAR
MEEM, JOHN T. BAL 021 18TH WAR
MEEMIRE, WILLIAM BAL 280 7TH WARD
MEER, MARIA BAL 094 18TH WAR
MEERABRAKER, JOHN H. WAS 289 1ST DIST
MEERTON, HENRY * ANN 356 3RD DIST
MEERWOOD, GEROGE* DOR 381 1ST DIST
MEESE, THOMAS BAL 202 19TH WAR
MEESONIER, HARRIET BAL 356 13TH WAR
MEESSYER, JOSEPH FRE 266 NEW MARK
MEETS, WILLIAM BAL 285 12TH WAR
MEFFORD, JOHN FRE 115 CREAGERS
MEFFSKIE, LEWIS ALL 118 5TH E.D.
MEGARDAN, ELY BAL 306 12TH WAR
MEGARDEN, A. BAL 306 12TH WAR
MEGEE, ANNIE BELLE TAYLOR BAL 217 11TH WAR
MEGEE, GEORGE A. BAL 216 11TH WAR
MEGEE, JOHN BAL 159 11TH WAR
MEGEE, SUSANNAH BAL 217 11TH WAR
MEGENHARDT, F. BAL 241 12TH WAR
MEGGS, AUGUSTUS S. BAL 095 15TH WAR
MEGINNESS, BENJAMIN R. KEN 281 3RD DIST
MEGINNESS, MARY KEN 281 3RD DIST
MEGINNESS, SAMUEL D. BAL 058 15TH WAR
MEGINNIS, DANIEL QUE 136 1ST E DI
MEGINNIS, DANIEL T. QUE 136 1ST E DI
MEGINNIS, WILLIAM QUE 127 1ST E DI
MEGLOCKLING, STEPHEN DOR 371 3RD DIVI
MEGRATH, ANN PRI 081 QUEEN AN
MEGREGOR, ANN E. PRI 073 MARLBROU
MEGREGOR, ELIZA PRI 073 MARLBROU
MEGREGOR, RODERICK PRI 075 MARLBROU
MEGUIRE, HENERY DOR 368 3RD DIVI
MEGURE, AQUILLA KEN 280 3RD DIST
MEGURK, GEORGE HAR 010 1ST DIST
MEHAN, AARON BAL 109 1ST WARD
MEHANY, LAURENCE PRI 006 BLADENSB
MEHESSING, JAOCB BAL 248 2ND WARD
MEHIRN, PATRICK ALL 135 4TH E.D.
MEHLER, VALENTINE BAL 052 9TH WARD
MEHLING, JOSEPH BAL 426 8TH WARD
MEHM, GEORGE CAR 332 MANCHEST
MEHRING, JOHN CAR 242 TANEYTOW
MEHUKE, H. BAL 263 2ND WARD
MEIDS, STEPHEN-MULATTO BAL 228 2ND WARD
MEIER, PETER BAL 141 1ST WARD
MEIGASON, BENJAMIN BAL 303 12TH WAR
MEIHALL, JOSEPH H. BAL 445 14TH WAR
MEIL, PEER BAL 249 2ND WARD
MEINICKE, LOUISA CAR 290 7TH DIST
MEIR, MARY E. ANN 449 HOWARD D
MEIS, JOHN BAL 262 20TH WAR
MEISEL, HENRY* BAL 112 15TH WAR
MEISEL, MICHAEL WAS 185 BOONSBOR
MEISER, GEORGE BAL 217 17TH WAR
MEISER, WILLIAM BAL 075 1ST WARD
MEISINGER, CONRAD BAL 148 19TH WAR
MEISNER, ADAM WAS 297 1ST DIST
MEISNER, JACOB WAS 238 CAVETOWN
MEISNER, SAMUEL WAS 244 SMITHSBU
MEISS, BATZER ALL 035 2ND E.D.
MEIST, FREDERICK BAL 230 19TH WAR
MEISTER, PREASA BAL 134 11TH WAR
MEITCHELL, HENRY-BLACK CAR 114 NO TWP L
MEITE, HENRY BAL 214 17TH WAR
MEITZ, ELENOR BAL 188 2ND WARD
MEITZELL, MICHAEL BAL 090 1ST WARD
MEIXSELL, JOHNJ. BAL 259 12TH WAR
MEIZELL, JOSEPH H. BAL 394 14TH WAR
MEK, SARAH CAR 273 WESTMINS
MEKS, MARTHA HAR 114 2ND DIST
MEL, WILLIAM HAR 172 3RD DIST
MELA, CHARLES CEC 055 1ST E DI
MELANEON, PHLEGIE FRE 20 5TH E DI
MELANEY, SOLOMON CAR 118 NO TWP L
MELANEY, WILLIAM CAR 114 NO TWP L
MELBORNE, FRANCIS* SOM 399 BRINKLEY
MELBOURN, SPENCER SOM 389 BRINKLEY
MELBURN, JOHN L. ST 297 2ND E DI
MELBURN, SUSAN ST 307 1ST E DI
MELCHAIR, NATHANIEL BAL 048 9TH WARD
MELCHEL, WASHINGTON FRE 266 NEW MARK
MELCHIER, CAROLINE BAL 413 14TH WAR
MELCHIN, NATHANIEL BAL 103 2ND DIST
MELCHIOR, BERTHA BAL 349 13TH WAR
MELCHLEY, CHRISTIAN BAL 112 2ND DIST
MELCHOIR, CARL BAL 290 1ST DIST
MELCHOR, ELIZABETH WAS 171 FUNKSTOW
MELCOR, JOSHUA ANN 514 HOWARD D
MELDENDER, CASSER BAL 200 5TH DIST
MELDWIN, JAMES MGM 424 MEDLEY 3
MELER, HENRY BAL 253 12TH WAR
MELFORD, SAMUEL MGM 414 MEDLEY 3
MELHOLLAND, ROBERT D. BAL 072 1ST WARD
MELHORN, CHRISTIANA BAL 261 1ST DIST
MELIA, JOHN ALL 195 CUMBERLA
MELINE, MISSM. FRE 200 5TH E DI
MELINGY, FRANCIS BAL 160 19TH WAR
MELIUS, ALEXANDER BAL 407 8TH WARD
MELIUS, CONROD FRE 024 FREDERIC
MELKINK, GEORGE BAL 438 1ST DIST
MELKON, MICHAEL BAL 240 2ND WARD
MELLAN, CATHARINE BAL 363 1ST DIST
MELLAN, CATHARINE BAL 363 1ST DIST
MELLAR, FRANCIS A. BAL 267 12TH WAR
MELLASKIN, HENRY KEN 297 3RD DIST
MELLEN, PATRICK BAL 073 1ST WARD
MELLEN, SUSANA ANN 456 HOWARD D
MELLER, EDMUND ALL 094 5TH E.D.
MELLER, ELIZABETH ALL 148 6TH E.D.
MELLER, H. F. ALL 126 4TH E.D.
MELLER, JOHN BAL 272 7TH WARD
MELLER, LOUISA ALL 113 5TH E.D.
MELLER, MARY BAL 458 8TH WARD
MELLER, PETER ALL 148 6TH E.D.
MELLET, PEGGY BAL 311 1ST DIST
MELLETZER, ERNEST HAR 203 3RD DIST
MELLHOLLAND, THOMAS BAL 292 12TH WAR
MELLHORN, ADA BAL 302 20TH WAR
MELLHORNE, MARY F. BAL 405 8TH WARD
MELLINE, MARY BAL 063 15TH WAR
MELLINGER, JOHN E. WAS 169 FUNKSTOW
MELLON, EDWARD BAL 056 15TH WAR
MELLONROR, HENRY-BLACK ST 294 2ND E DI
MELLOR, MICHAEL BAL 038 9TH WARD
MELLS, ELIZABETH* DOR 365 3RD DIVI
MELLVILLE, JOHN BAL 392 1ST DIST
MELOCK, MARY FRE 001 FREDERIC
MELONEY, EDWARD CAR 132 NO TWP L
MELONEY, JOHN CAR 120 NO TWP L
MELONEY, MARY CAR 148 NO TWP L
MELONEY, MARY CAR 169 NO TWP L
MELONEY, SAMUEL CAR 169 NO TWP L
MELONEY, SAMUEL CAR 076 NO TWP L
MELONEY, WILLIAM CAR 131 NO TWP L
MELRICH, GOTLIEB BAL 370 13TH WAR
MELSON, BENJAMIN S. WOR 212 4TH E DI
MELSON, DANIEL F. WOR 212 4TH E DI
MELSON, ELIJAH WOR 212 4TH E DI
MELSON, ELIZA G. WOR 212 4TH E DI
MELSON, GEORGE WOR 209 4TH E DI
MELSON, JAMES SOM 414 DUBLIN D
MELSON, JOHN SOM 509 BARREN C
MELSON, LEVIN D. SOM 429 PRINCESS
MELSON, MARY SOM 512 BARREN C
MELSON, MARY SOM 509 BARREN C
MELSON, MARY E. SOM 427 PRINCESS
MELSON, SARAH M. SOM 535 QUANTICO
MELSON, SOPHIA WOR 231 6TH E DI
MELSON, W. R. TAL 085 ST MICHA
MELTCHER, CHARLES BAL 349 7TH WARD
MELTEE, HELLEN V.* BAL 049 4TH WARD
MELTEE, MARIA A. BAL 048 4TH WARD
MELTEE, MARTIN* BAL 048 4TH WARD
MELTON, FRANCES WAS 152 HAGERSTO
MELTON, PHILIP ST 322 4TH E DI
MELTON,EMILY ST 299 2ND E DI
MELTONS, JOSEPH* DOR 431 1ST DIST
MELTZGER, MARY BAL 316 12TH WAR

Name	Co.	Page	District
MELTZING, JAMES G.	BAL	314	12TH WAR
MELVEN, CHARLES	ALL	084	5TH E.D.
MELVILLE, MARY	BAL	085	4TH WARD
MELVILLE, SAMUEL	BAL	043	18TH WAR
MELVIN, A. W.	KEN	225	2ND DIST
MELVIN, AGNES	SOM	412	DUBLIN D
MELVIN, ALFORD	WOR	349	1ST E DI
MELVIN, ANN	BAL	186	11TH WAR
MELVIN, ANNA-BLACK	WOR	343	1ST E DI
MELVIN, AVARY	WOR	343	1ST E DI
MELVIN, GEORGE	BAL	120	16TH WAR
MELVIN, GEORGE	CAR	079	NO TWP L
MELVIN, GEORGE W.	BAL	165	1ST WARD
MELVIN, GEORGE W.	BAL	135	1ST WARD
MELVIN, JOHN	WOR	328	1ST E DI
MELVIN, JOHN B.	TAL	011	EASTON D
MELVIN, JOHN B.	SOM	412	DUBLIN D
MELVIN, JOHN F.	KEN	226	2ND DIST
MELVIN, LITTLETON	WOR	344	1ST E DI
MELVIN, LOUISA	TAL	090	ST MICHA
MELVIN, MARY	QUE	246	5TH E DI
MELVIN, MILTON	KEN	226	2ND DIST
MELVIN, PATTY	WOR	326	1ST E DI
MELVIN, SAMUEL	BAL	289	20TH WAR
MELVIN, SARAH-BLACK	WOR	343	1ST E DI
MELVIN, SOPHIA-BLACK	WOR	343	1ST E DI
MELVIN, THOMAS	CAR	109	NO TWP L
MELVIN, THOMAS	BAL	311	1ST DIST
MELVIN, THOMAS B.	WOR	343	1ST E DI
MELVIN, THOMASJ.R	CAR	109	NO TWP L
MELVIN, WHITY	WOR	338	1ST E DI
MELVIN, WILLIAM	WOR	349	1ST E DI
MELVIN, WILLIAM W.	WOR	343	1ST E DI
MELWOOD, MARY H.	TAL	072	EASTON T
MEMAN, DOWLEY	QUE	153	1ST E DI
MEMBLY, JOHN	BAL	006	1ST WARD
MEMMART, CHARLES	BAL	081	10TH WAR
MEMNA, JAMES	ALL	011	3RD E.D.
MEMOFNA, MICHAEL	ALL	177	7TH E.D.
MENABRAKER, FREDERICK	WAS	291	1ST DIST
MENAEBRAKER, FREDERICK	WAS	288	1ST DIST
MENADA, JOHN	CEC	031	CHESAPEA
MENAMAR, ASBURY	DOR	343	3RD DIVI
MENAMAR, CLEMENT	DOR	345	3RD DIVI
MENAMAR, GEORGE S.*	DOR	372	3RD DIVI
MENAMAR, HARIETT	DOR	335	3RD DIVI
MENAMAR, HARIETT	DOR	335	3RD DIVI
MENAMAR, JOHN T.	DOR	336	3RD DIVI
MENAMAR, LEVEN R.	DOR	353	3RD DIVI
MENAMAR, THOMAS	DOR	339	3RD DIVI
MENAMAR, WILL*	DOR	338	3RD DIVI
MENCE, BARBARA	BAL	038	9TH WARD
MENCER, JOHN C.	WAS	115	2ND DIST
MENCER, SUSAN	WAS	116	2ND DIST
MENCHAN, JAMES	ALL	076	5TH E.D.
MENCHEY, SOLOMON *	FRE	099	FREDERIC
MENCHY, JACOB	CAR	345	6TH DIST
MENCKE, HENRY	BAL	041	9TH WARD
MENCKEN, FREDERICK	BAL	191	2ND WARD
MENDY, ANNA-BLACK	ST	317	4TH E DI
MENEHAN, JAMES	ALL	140	6TH E.D.
MENEZRAM, EARNET	BAL	062	1ST WARD
MENGATE, MARGARET D.	CHA	221	ALLENS F
MENGER, A.J.	PRI	053	AQUASCO
MENGES, MATILDA	BAL	204	6TH DIST
MENGLE, JAMES	BAL	005	1ST WARD
MENIKIN, JACOB *	ANN	346	3RD DIST
MENKEN, BURKHARDT	BAL	091	15TH WAR
MENLEY, OTHE	BAL	298	12TH WAR
MENNER, CASPAR	BAL	164	19TH WAR
MENNERLY, JOHN	SOM	518	BARREN C
MENNEY, SARAH	BAL	189	2ND WARD
MENNICK, JOHN *	BAL	304	12TH WAR
MENNICK, JOSEPH	FRE	348	MIDDLETO
MENNINGER, L. F.	BAL	034	4TH WARD
MENNIS, WILLIAM	MGM	386	ROCKERLE
MENON, JOHN	BAL	186	19TH WAR
MENSEL, ALEXANDER	BAL	080	2ND DIST
MENSEL, CHARLES	BAL	080	2ND DIST
MENSER, CONRAD	WAS	263	1ST DIST
MENSER, GEORGE	WAS	115	2ND DIST
MENSER, JAMES W.	WAS	116	2ND DIST
MENSER, JOHN	WAS	277	RIDGEVIL
MENSER, SAMUEL	WAS	272	RIDGEVIL
MENSER, SAMUEL	WAS	248	SMITHSBU
MENSER, SORABABEL	WAS	278	LEITERSB
MENSON, BELINDA	BAL	301	12TH WAR
MENSON, HESTER A.	BAL	421	3RD WARD
MENSOR, JACOB	FRE	249	NEW MARK
MENSOR, THOMAS	BAL	283	1ST DIST
MENSTER, HENRY	BAL	334	7TH WARD
MENT, ADAM	BAL	259	20TH WAR
MENT, PETER F.	BAL	149	19TH WAR
MENTDROP, HENRY	ALL	195	CUMBERLA
MENTELL, GEORGE *	BAL	306	20TH WAR
MENTEN, IRA	BAL	228	12TH WAR
MENTLY, WILLIAM	BAL	139	1ST WARD
MENTY, ELIZA	BAL	269	20TH WAR
MENTZ, ISAAC	WAS	282	1ST DIST
MENTZ, MICHAEL	BAL	459	1ST DIST
MENTZEL, HENRY	BAL	398	14TH WAR
MENTZER, GEORGE	FRE	163	EMMITTSB
MENTZER, SARAH	BAL	243	12TH WAR
MENTZER, SIMON	FRE	166	EMMITTSB
MENYMAN, GEORGE	BAL	066	10TH WAR
MENYON, ELLEN	BAL	243	12TH WAR
MENZE, ALBRECHT	MGM	360	BERRYS D
MENZER, GEORGE	WAS	263	1ST DIST
MENZIE, MARTIN	BAL	149	19TH WAR
MENZIER, JAME	BAL	274	12TH WAR
MENZIES, JAMES	BAL	160	16TH WAR
MEODEMUS, ELIZABETH	CAR	269	WESTMINS
MEODY, JOHN S. *	KEN	252	1ST DIST
MEOLISTER, SAMUEL	DOR	319	1ST DIST
MEOLISTER, SUSAN*	DOR	311	1ST DIST
MEOLLISTER, MEHALY	DOR	323	1ST DIST
MEPARD, JACOB	BAL	036	1ST WARD
MEPHAM, THOMAS	HAR	054	1ST DIST
MEPHELUS, ROBERT	PRI	109	PISCATAW
MEPHERSON, CLARK	ANN	479	HOWARD D
MEQURE, GEROGE	KEN	280	3RD DIST
MERAHAN, PHILIPS	BAL	062	2ND DIST
MERAN, MARY	BAL	296	12TH WAR
MERANDER, JOSEPH	SOM	414	DUBLIN D
MERARVETZ, M.L.	BAL	263	12TH WAR
MERCALF, J. L.	BAL	302	12TH WAR
MERCEIR, AUGUSTA	FRE	202	5TH E DI
MERCENET, JULES	FRE	202	5TH E DI
MERCER, ANDREW	CAR	229	5TH DIST
MERCER, ANDREW	ANN	516	HOWARD D
MERCER, ANN	ANN	500	HOWARD D
MERCER, ANN	BAL	054	4TH WARD
MERCER, ANN E.	BAL	105	18TH WAR
MERCER, ANNA P.	BAL	197	19TH WAR
MERCER, ARCHIBALD	BAL	469	14TH WAR
MERCER, CHARLES	BAL	123	16TH WAR
MERCER, CORNEALOUS	CAR	229	5TH DIST
MERCER, CYRUS T.	ANN	508	HOWARD D
MERCER, ELIZA	ANN	516	HOWARD D
MERCER, FRANCIS	MGM	437	CLARKSTR
MERCER, GEORGE N.	BAL	393	3RD WARD
MERCER, GUSTAVAS	CAR	224	5TH DIST
MERCER, HENRY	FRE	439	8TH E DI
MERCER, HENRY R.	BAL	475	14TH WAR
MERCER, ISAIAH JR.	ANN	453	HOWARD D
MERCER, ISAIAH SR.	ANN	453	HOWARD D
MERCER, JAMES	BAL	059	2ND DIST
MERCER, JAMES	CEC	035	CHESAPEA
MERCER, JAMES	BAL	128	18TH WAR
MERCER, JAMES	FRE	305	WOODSBOR
MERCER, JAMES W.M.	BAL	144	16TH WAR
MERCER, JOHN	CEC	075	NORTHEAS
MERCER, JOHN C.	ANN	510	HOWARD D
MERCER, JOHN W.	ANN	513	HOWARD D
MERCER, JOSEPH	ALL	231	CUMBERLA
MERCER, JOSEPH	MGM	382	ROCKERLE
MERCER, LUTHER O.	ANN	508	HOWARD D
MERCER, MARGARET	BAL	223	6TH WARD
MERCER, MARIA	ANN	507	HOWARD D
MERCER, MILLICENT	CEC	076	NORTHEAS
MERCER, PERRY G.	BAL	423	14TH WAR
MERCER, RICHARD	CAR	227	5TH DIST
MERCER, RICHARD S.	ANN	306	1ST DIST
MERCER, ROBERT	BAL	238	17TH WAR
MERCER, ROBERT	BAL	128	18TH WAR
MERCER, ROBERT S.	CAR	229	5TH DIST
MERCER, SARAH	BAL	049	18TH WAR
MERCER, THOAMS	BAL	098	18TH WAR
MERCER, THOMAS	BAL	103	18TH WAR
MERCER, THOMAS S.	ANN	306	1ST DIST
MERCER, VIRGIL M.	ANN	453	HOWARD D
MERCER, WASHINGTON	ANN	459	HOWARD D
MERCER, WILLIAM	MGM	372	BERRYS D
MERCERET, NALALIE	BAL	314	12TH WAR
MERCHANT, ALEXANDER	QUE	128	1ST E DI
MERCHANT, CAROLINE L.	CEC	137	6TH E DI
MERCHANT, ISAAC	BAL	195	19TH WAR
MERCHANT, JAMES	KEN	228	2ND DIST
MERCHANT, JOHN	MGM	407	MEDLEY 3
MERCHANT, JOHN	MGM	427	MEDLEY 3
MERCHANT, JOHN	ANN	375	4TH DIST
MERCHANT, JOHN	QUE	231	4TH E DI
MERCHANT, JOHN W.	QUE	231	4TH E DI
MERCHANT, JOSEPH	BAL	096	5TH WARD
MERCHANT, JOSEPH L. *	ANN	417	HOWARD D
MERCHANT, MARY	QUE	128	1ST E DI
MERCHANT, MARY	CEC	137	6TH E DI
MERCHANT, NOAH	QUE	134	1ST E DI
MERCHANT, NOAH C.	QUE	127	1ST E DI
MERCHANTS, WILLIAM	BAL	081	1ST WARD
MERCOMIK, ELISA	BAL	120	11TH WAR
MERCYANN, NAPOLEON	ALL	136	4TH E.D.
MERDITH, EDFERD	KEN	253	1ST DIST
MERDMAN, JACOB	BAL	300	12TH WAR
MERORDER, JACOB	BAL	156	19TH WAR
MERE, JOHN	ALL	202	CUMBERLA
MEREDITH, AMANDA	BAL	044	4TH WARD
MEREDITH, ARTHUR C.D.	CAR	411	2ND DIST
MEREDITH, AUGUSTUS	BAL	168	19TH WAR
MEREDITH, BENJAMIN	BAL	386	13TH WAR
MEREDITH, ELIZABETH	DOR	346	3RD DIVI
MEREDITH, ELIZABETH*	DOR	347	3RD DIVI
MEREDITH, ELLEN	BAL	038	2ND DIST
MEREDITH, EUPHRAS	BAL	168	19TH WAR
MEREDITH, JAMES A.	ANN	490	HOWARD D
MEREDITH, JAMES JR.	QUE	173	2ND E DI
MEREDITH, JOHN	BAL	209	6TH WARD
MEREDITH, JOHN F.	BAL	021	4TH WARD
MEREDITH, JOHN Y.	FRE	250	NEW MARK
MEREDITH, JONATHAN	BAL	099	10TH WAR
MEREDITH, JOSEPH P.	BAL	161	19TH WAR
MEREDITH, JOSHUA	CAR	099	NO TWP L
MEREDITH, MARY	BAL	066	4TH WARD
MEREDITH, MARY	BAL	038	2ND DIST
MEREDITH, MARY	BAL	073	15TH WAR
MEREDITH, NATHANIEL	CAR	377	2ND DIST
MEREDITH, SAMUEL	FRE	117	CREAGERS
MEREDITH, SAMUEL	BAL	037	2ND DIST
MEREDITH, SARAH	BAL	166	16TH WAR
MEREDITH, SARAH A.	BAL	059	4TH WARD
MEREDITH, SILVESTER*	DOR	348	3RD DIVI
MEREDITH, THOMAS	BAL	469	14TH WAR
MEREDITH, THOMAS J.	BAL	125	11TH WAR
MEREDITH, WILLIAM B.	BAL	218	19TH WAR
MEREDITH, WILLIAM S.	CAR	097	NO TWP L
MEREGON, BRIDGET	BAL	215	11TH WAR
MEREIDITH, BENJAMIN	QUE	125	1ST E DI
MEREIDITH, MARGARET	BAL	274	12TH WAR
MEREIKEN, ELIZABETH	BAL	334	13TH WAR
MERELING, CONROD	FRE	009	FREDERIC
MERELING, DANIEL	FRE	101	FREDERIC
MERELING, LEWIS	FRE	080	FREDERIC
MERETT, JOSEPH E.*	DOR	454	1ST DIST
MERETTE, A.*	BAL	102	10TH WAR
MERGAN, THOMAS	BAL	122	11TH WAR
MERGHER, CATHRINE *	BAL	140	19TH WAR
MERIAN, ANN	ANN	270	ANNAPOLI
MERICA, ELIZABETH *	SOM	469	TRAPPE D
MERICAN, ELIZA L.	BAL	251	1ST DIST
MERICK, CHARLOTTE	BAL	372	3RD WARD
MERICK, ELIZABETH	CEC	015	ELKTON 3
MERICK, GEORGE	TAL	068	EASTON T
MERICK, MATHIAS	TAL	052	EASTON D
MERICK, MATTHEW	DOR	382	1ST DIST
MERICK, MICHAEL	ALL	242	CUMBERLA
MERICK, SARAH C.	SOM	500	SALISBUR
MERICK, STANBURY	DOR	433	1ST DIST
MERICK, WILLIAM	CEC	026	ELKTON 3
MERIDA, WILLIAM	CEC	034	CHESAPEA
MERIDA, WRITTY *	SOM	452	DAMES QU
MERIDETH, ALEXANDER LAYTH	BAL	114	18TH WAR
MERIDETH, JAMES	BAL	203	17TH WAR
MERIDETH, JOHN	DOR	346	3RD DIVI
MERIDETH, JULIA A.	KEN	224	2ND DIST
MERIDETH, LEVI *	WAS	180	BOONSBOR
MERIDETH, SAMUEL	WAS	181	BOONSBOR
MERIDETH, SOPHIA	BAL	203	17TH WAR
MERIDETH, WILLIAM	CEC	029	CHESAPEA
MERIDICX, HENRY	BAL	220	17TH WAR
MERIDITH, AMUS	DOR	346	3RD DIVI
MERIDITH, AUGUSTUS	BAL	241	17TH WAR
MERIDITH, ELIZABETH*	DOR	347	3RD DIVI
MERIDITH, GEORGE	DOR	452	1ST DIST
MERIDITH, GEORGE	QUE	193	3RD E DI
MERIDITH, JAMES	QUE	197	3RD E DI
MERIDITH, JANE	DOR	348	3RD DIVI
MERIDITH, MARY	DOR	376	1ST DIST
MERIDITH, MARY A.	BAL	348	7TH WARD
MERIDITH, PRITCHET	DOR	422	1ST DIST
MERIDITH, SAMUEL	DOR	348	3RD DIVI
MERIDITH, SAMUEL	BAL	038	18TH WAR
MERIDITH, SARAH A.	QUE	197	3RD E DI
MERIDITH, SETH	TAL	022	EASTON D
MERIDITH, THOMAS	QUE	240	5TH E DI
MERIDITH, THOMAS	DOR	422	1ST DIST
MERIDITH, WILLIAM	CEC	109	4TH E DI
MERIDITH, WILLIAM	QUE	196	3RD E DI
MERIDITH, ZIPPORAH	DOR	355	3RD DIVI
MERIGAN, MINA	BAL	219	17TH WAR
MERIGIRE, ELIZABETH	BAL	250	17TH WAR
MERIKEN, LOUISA	WAS	154	HAGERSTO
MERINDER, EDWARD J.	SOM	415	DUBLIN D
MERINDER, MARGARET	SOM	420	PRINCESS
MERINDER, THOMAS	SOM	419	PRINCESS
MERINDER, WILLIAM	SOM	414	DUBLIN D
MERINE, MARIAH	DOR	363	3RD DIVI
MERINE, WILLIAM	CAR	121	NO TWP L
MERIT, AMANDA	BAL	420	1ST DIST
MERITH, JOHN	CEC	060	1ST E DI
MERITS, KINSEY	BAL	244	20TH WAR
MERKEL, HENRY R.	BAL	145	16TH WAR
MERKER, ANDREW	BAL	261	12TH WAR
MERKET, SALLY	BAL	129	18TH WAR
MERKIN, WILLIAM	PRI	045	VANSVILL
MERKINGS, SUSAN	BAL	023	9TH WARD
MERKLE, JOSEPH	BAL	347	1ST DIST
MERKLIN, GEORGE M.	BAL	058	15TH WAR
MERLES, THOMAS	CAL	058	3RD DIST
MERLIN, NIHCOLAS	FRE	314	MIDDLETO
MERLINBERGER, ELIZABETH	ALL	199	CUMBERLA
MERLY, HENRY	BAL	462	1ST DIST
MERMAN, JACOB	BAL	127	5TH WARD
MERMAN, JOHN B.	BAL	221	2ND WARD
MERNECK, CHARELS	BAL	374	13TH WAR
MERNINGER, HELEN	WAS	026	2ND SUBD
MERNINGER, HENRY	WAS	025	2ND SUBD
MERRAY, EDWARD	BAL	141	1ST WARD
MERRAYMAN, MARTICO	CAR	185	8TH DIST
MERRDITH, GEORGE D.	QUE	239	5TH E DI
MERRELING, GEORGE	FRE	008	FREDERIC
MERREN, GEORGE	BAL	120	1ST WARD
MERRER, DAVID	BAL	295	20TH WAR
MERRER, NICHOLAS	BAL	294	20TH WAR
MERRETT, ELIZA J.	KEN	296	3RD DIST
MERRIAM, CHRIS	BAL	273	12TH WAR
MERRIAM, HENRY A.	BAL	079	15TH WAR
MERRICAN, FRANCES	BAL	311	7TH WARD
MERRICAN, WILLIAM	BAL	432	8TH WARD
MERRICK JAMES 3RD	QUE	160	2ND E DI
MERRICK, ALGERNON	DOR	315	1ST DIST
MERRICK, CAROLINE	DOR	320	1ST DIST
MERRICK, DANIEL	TAL	057	EASTON D
MERRICK, DAVID	TAL	057	EASTON D
MERRICK, DOROTHY T. Q.	TAL	054	EASTON D
MERRICK, ELIZABETH	DOR	311	1ST DIST
MERRICK, ELLEN	BAL	339	13TH WAR
MERRICK, ELLEN	BAL	112	5TH WARD
MERRICK, EZEKIEL T.	QUE	143	1ST E DI
MERRICK, FRANK F.*	DOR	451	1ST DIST
MERRICK, GEORGE	QUE	233	4TH E DI
MERRICK, JACOB B.	MGM	334	CRACKLIN
MERRICK, JESSE T.	BAL	195	6TH WARD
MERRICK, JOHN	DOR	320	1ST DIST
MERRICK, JOSEPH J.	WAS	299	1ST DIST
MERRICK, JOSEPH R.*	TAL	051	EASTON D
MERRICK, LUCY A.	BAL	326	7TH WARD
MERRICK, MICHALL P.	MGM	330	CRACKLIN
MERRICK, MONTGOMMERY	TAL	052	EASTON D
MERRICK, RACHEL	DOR	373	1ST DIST
MERRICK, RICHARD	BAL	167	11TH WAR
MERRICK, ROBERT	BAL	350	7TH WARD
MERRICK, SAMUEL B.	TAL	052	EASTON D
MERRICK, SOLOMON T.*	TAL	052	EASTON D
MERRICK, WASHINGTON	DOR	450	1ST DIST
MERRICK, WILLIAM D.	CHA	218	ALLENS F
MERRICK, ZACHARIAH	DOR	307	1ST DIST
MERRIDETH, JOHN C.	BAL	246	17TH WAR
MERRIDETH, JOHN T.	PRI	043	VANSVILL
MERRIDETH, RICHARD	BAL	203	17TH WAR
MERRIDETH, THOMAS	BAL	037	2ND DIST
MERRIDETH, WILLIAM	BAL	037	2ND DIST
MERRIDITH, BENJAMIN	QUE	149	1ST E DI
MERRIDITH, EDWIN	QUE	177	2ND E DI
MERRIDITH, ELIZABETH	QUE	234	4TH E DI
MERRIDITH, ELIZABETH	BAL	354	7TH WARD
MERRIDITH, JAMES	QUE	147	1ST E DI
MERRIDITH, JOHN T.	QUE	211	3RD E DI
MERRIDITH, MOSES	QUE	203	3RD E DI
MERRIDITH, MOSES	QUE	180	2ND E DI
MERRIDITH, ROBERT	QUE	179	2ND E DI
MERRIDITH, SAMUEL	QUE	156	2ND E DI
MERRIDITH, SOPHIAH	TAL	082	ST MICHA
MERRIDITH, THOMAS	QUE	157	2ND E DI
MERRIDITH, THOMAS R.	QUE	155	2ND E DI
MERRIDITH, WILLIAM	QUE	152	1ST E DI
MERRIDITH, WILLIAM	QUE	177	2ND E DI
MERRIDITH, WILLIAM	QUE	215	3RD E DI
MERRIDITH, WILLIAM	QUE	209	3RD E DI
MERRIDITH, WILLIAM	QUE	193	3RD E DI
MERRIEAN, HESTER	BAL	157	11TH WAR
MERRIK, MATILDA	BAL	162	11TH WAR
MERRIKEN, GEORGE	BAL	137	5TH WARD
MERRIKEN, JAEMS	BAL	347	13TH WAR
MERRIKEN, JOSHUA L.	BAL	358	3RD WARD
MERRIKIN, ANN	ANN	379	4TH DIST
MERRIKIN, ELISABETH	ANN	350	3RD DIST
MERRIKIN, JACOB *	ANN	346	3RD DIST
MERRIKIN, JOHN	ANN	371	4TH DIST
MERRIKIN, JOHN	BAL	027	18TH WAR
MERRIKIN, MARIA	ANN	371	4TH DIST
MERRIKIN, SALLY	ANN	328	2ND DIST
MERRIL, ANNA	WOR	333	1ST E DI
MERRIL, JAMES	WOR	333	1ST E DI
MERRIL, JOSEPH	WOR	330	1ST E DI
MERRIL, LEVI	WOR	334	1ST E DI
MERRIL, LEVI-BLACK	WOR	344	1ST E DI
MERRIL, LEVIN	WOR	334	1ST E DI
MERRIL, LEVIN JR.	WOR	333	1ST E DI
MERRIL, THOMAS	WOR	332	1ST E DI
MERRIL, WILLIAM	WOR	332	1ST E DI

Name	County	Page	District
MERRIL, WILLIAM H.	WOR	342	1ST E DI
MERRILL, DANIEL FEAR	ALL	021	2ND E.D.
MERRILL, ELIZABETH	BAL	085	15TH WAR
MERRILL, GEORGE	SOM	398	BRINKLEY
MERRILL, HENRY	BAL	145	1ST WARD
MERRILL, JAMES H.	BAL	240	12TH WAR
MERRILL, JOHN	ALL	002	3RD E.D.
MERRILL, JOHN	SOM	377	BRINKLEY
MERRILL, JOHN L.	BAL	360	3RD WARD
MERRILL, MARTHA	ALL	021	2ND E.D.
MERRILL, MOSES	BAL	269	7TH WARD
MERRILL, PHILIP	ALL	002	3RD E.D.
MERRILL, STEVEN	ALL	054	10TH E.D
MERRILL, WILLIAM	ALL	020	2ND E.D.
MERRILL, WILLIAM	BAL	241	12TH WAR
MERRILL, WILLIAM H.	BAL	144	1ST WARD
MERRILLION, REBECCA C.	BAL	167	16TH WAR
MERRILY, JACOB	BAL	072	2ND DIST
MERRIMAN, ABNER	FRE	388	PETERSVI
MERRIMAN, ELIZABETH	BAL	287	7TH WARD
MERRIMAN, FANNEY	HAR	009	1ST DIST
MERRIMAN, NELSON	HAR	025	1ST DIST
MERRIMAN, TH. C.	BAL	119	11TH WAR
MERRIMAN, NICHOLAS	BAL	072	2ND DIST
MERRIMIN, NANCY	CEC	147	PORT DUP
MERRIS, JOSEPH *	KEN	280	3RD DIST
MERRISH, WILLIAM H.	TAL	088	ST MICHA.
MERRIT, CALEB	TAL	052	EASTON D
MERRIT, ELIZABETH	TAL	052	EASTON D
MERRIT, GEORGE	BAL	200	6TH WARD
MERRIT, JACOB	BAL	461	14TH WAR
MERRIT, JOSEPH	BAL	027	9TH WARD
MERRIT, JOSEPH	BAL	275	2ND WARD
MERRIT, MARY	MGM	442	CLARKSTR
MERRITT, ABLE	CEC	035	CHESAPEA
MERRITT, ABRAHAM	HAR	086	2ND DIST
MERRITT, ADELINE	KEN	226	2ND DIST
MERRITT, ANN	CEC	042	CHESAPEA
MERRITT, CALEB	BAL	195	2ND WARD
MERRITT, CHARLES	BAL	036	9TH WARD
MERRITT, CHARLES	BAL	198	17TH WAR
MERRITT, CHARLES	CEC	124	5TH E DI
MERRITT, ELIZA	BAL	044	9TH WARD
MERRITT, GE. W.	ANN	339	3RD DIST
MERRITT, GEORGE	BAL	433	14TH WAR
MERRITT, HENRIETTA	BAL	242	17TH WAR
MERRITT, HENRIETTA	KEN	256	1ST DIST
MERRITT, HENRY	BAL	052	9TH WARD
MERRITT, ISAAC H.	BAL	375	3RD WARD
MERRITT, JAMES	BAL	195	2ND WARD
MERRITT, JAMES	HAR	145	3RD DIST
MERRITT, JAMES P.	BAL	174	11TH WAR
MERRITT, JAMES T.	CEC	042	CHESAPEA
MERRITT, JANE	BAL	438	8TH WARD
MERRITT, JOHN	BAL	162	11TH WAR
MERRITT, JOHN	ANN	339	3RD DIST
MERRITT, JOHN	BAL	414	3RD WARD
MERRITT, JOSEPH	CEC	043	CHESAPEA
MERRITT, JOSEPH	BAL	212	17TH WAR
MERRITT, JULIANNA	KEN	234	2ND DIST
MERRITT, MARY	BAL	243	12TH WAR
MERRITT, MARY A.B.	BAL	316	7TH WARD
MERRITT, PHOEBE	HAR	096	2ND DIST
MERRITT, RALPH	BAL	281	12TH WAR
MERRITT, REECE	KEN	290	3RD DIST
MERRITT, SAMUEL	BAL	127	1ST WARD
MERRITT, SOPHIA	BAL	169	19TH WAR
MERRITT, SPENCER	KEN	313	3RD DIST
MERRITT, SUSAN	BAL	249	17TH WAR
MERRITT, THOMAS	KEN	222	2ND DIST
MERRITT, THOMAS H.	ANN	340	3RD DIST
MERRITT, WILLIAM	CEC	216	7TH E DI
MERRITT, WILLIAM	BAL	040	18TH WAR
MERRITT, WILLIAM G.	KEN	310	3RD DIST
MERRITT, WILLIAM K.	BAL	108	10TH WAR
MERRIWETHER, LOUISA A.	MGM	322	CRACKLIN
MERRY, EDWARD	BAL	383	3RD WARD
MERRY, GEORGE	CEC	081	CHARLEST
MERRY, JAMES	CEC	067	5TH E DI
MERRY, JAMES	CEC	073	5TH E DI
MERRY, ROBERT	ALL	217	CUMBERLA
MERRY, MICHAEL	BAL	282	12TH WAR
MERRYMAN, ABERILLA	BAL	458	1ST DIST
MERRYMAN, ADAM	BAL	131	1ST WARD
MERRYMAN, ANN	BAL	429	1ST DIST
MERRYMAN, BENJAMN	BAL	028	2ND DIST
MERRYMAN, CALEB	BAL	294	1ST DIST
MERRYMAN, CHARLES	BAL	194	5TH DIST
MERRYMAN, CHARLES	BAL	095	5TH WARD
MERRYMAN, CLARA	BAL	027	2ND DIST
MERRYMAN, ELIZABETH	BAL	259	1ST DIST
MERRYMAN, ELLNE	BAL	165	2ND DIST
MERRYMAN, FRANCIS	FRE	066	FREDERIC
MERRYMAN, GARHART	BAL	274	1ST DIST
MERRYMAN, GEORGE	BAL	017	2ND DIST
MERRYMAN, GEORGE	BAL	090	10TH WAR
MERRYMAN, H.N.	WAS	021	2ND SUBD
MERRYMAN, HARVEY	BAL	420	1ST DIST
MERRYMAN, JOHN	BAL	450	1ST DIST
MERRYMAN, JOHN	BAL	044	2ND DIST
MERRYMAN, JOHN	BAL	163	6TH WARD
MERRYMAN, JOHN	FRE	289	WOODSBOR
MERRYMAN, JOHN B.	BAL	428	1ST DIST
MERRYMAN, JOHN E.	BAL	415	1ST DIST
MERRYMAN, JOHN JR.	BAL	432	1ST DIST
MERRYMAN, LEVI	BAL	443	1ST DIST
MERRYMAN, MARTICO	CAR	194	4TH DIST
MERRYMAN, MICAJAH	BAL	030	2ND DIST
MERRYMAN, MOSES S.R.	BAL	012	15TH WAR
MERRYMAN, NICHOLAS	BAL	422	1ST DIST
MERRYMAN, NICHOLAS	BAL	429	1ST DIST
MERRYMAN, NICHOLAS	BAL	420	1ST DIST
MERRYMAN, NICHOLAS	BAL	247	20TH WAR
MERRYMAN, NOTICIA	BAL	416	1ST DIST
MERRYMAN, OLIVE P.	BAL	304	12TH WAR
MERRYMAN, OLIVER P.	BAL	010	EASTERN
MERRYMAN, SAMUEL	BAL	304	12TH WAR
MERRYMAN, SAMUEL W.	BAL	014	4TH WARD
MERRYMAN, SARAH	BAL	183	5TH DIST
MERRYMAN, THOMAS	BAL	194	5TH DIST
MERRYMAN, WILLIAM	BAL	252	20TH WAR
MERRYWEATHER, REUBEN	BAL	141	2ND DIST
MERSELL, PHILIP	BAL	143	2ND DIST
MERSER, JACOB	WAS	263	1ST DIST
MERSER, JOHN	BAL	199	6TH WARD
MERSER, SAMUEL	WAS	266	1ST DIST
MERSERILEY, CATHARINE	BAL	249	20TH WAR
MERSERSMITH, E.	BAL	142	19TH WAR
MERSFELDER, SIMON	BAL	236	17TH WAR
MERSING, GEORGE T. *	BAL	140	19TH WAR

Name	County	Page	District
MERSMAN, JOHN	BAL	424	8TH WARD
MERSON, JOHN	MGM	352	BERRYS D
MERSON, JOHN JR.	MGM	352	BERRYS D
MERSON, JONATHAN	MGM	352	BERRYS D
MERSON, KITTY	MGM	352	BERRYS D
MERSON, MARY	BAL	357	1ST DIST
MERSON, REZIN	ANN	455	HOWARD D
MERSON, THOMAS	MGM	383	ROCKERLE
MERSON, WILLAIM	ANN	460	HOWARD D
MERSONIER, ANTOINETTE	BAL	356	13TH WAR
MERST, SUSAN	BAL	230	19TH WAR
MERT, JOHN	FRE	087	FREDERIC
MERTER, THOMAS	WAS	025	2ND SUBD
MERTON, MARTHA	BAL	214	11TH WAR
MERTZ, DANIEL	FRE	280	WOODSBOR
MERTZ, GEORGE D.	FRE	294	WOODSBOR
MERTZ, JOHN N.	WAS	193	1ST DIST
MERUNBUMBER, CATHARINE *	BAL	154	2ND DIST
MERURY, MARGARET *	WAS	160	HAGERSTO
MERVIN, CHARLES	TAL	072	EASTON T
MERVIN, THOMAS A.	TAL	072	EASTON T
MERY, E. A.	BAL	147	1ST WARD
MERYHART, W. SHINGTON	ALL	184	9TH E.D.
MERYTH, CHARLES	BAL	281	12TH WAR
MERZEY, HENRY	BAL	242	20TH WAR
MESBACH, ANDREW	BAL	258	2ND WARD
MESCKE, HENRY	BAL	401	14TH WAR
MESECK, FREDERICKA	BAL	153	16TH WAR
MESEER, JAMES-MULATTO	FRE	451	8TH E DI
MESER, DANIEL	WAS	245	SMITHSBU
MESETT, F.	BAL	135	1ST WARD
MESIER, GEORGE	BAL	217	17TH WAR
MESINER, JOHN	WAS	248	SMITHSBU
MESKILL, DENBNIS	BAL	053	2ND DIST
MESLINGER, ANSEL	BAL	047	1ST WARD
MESME, JACOB	BAL	090	2ND DIST
MESMON, FRANK	ALL	242	CUMBERLA
MESNER, GEORGE	BAL	193	6TH WARD
MESSAMER, VALLENTINE	CAR	337	6TH DIST
MESSAMORE, GEORGE	CAR	330	MANCHEST
MESSE, DAVID	BAL	161	19TH WAR
MESSECKE, FREDERICK	BAL	410	14TH WAR
MESSEE, ABRAHAM	BAL	016	15TH WAR
MESSELTTA, JOHN	FRE	269	NEW MARK
MESSER, EDWARD	FRE	076	FREDERIC
MESSER, JACOB	FRE	076	FREDERIC
MESSER, LAWRENCE D.	BAL	048	18TH WAR
MESSER, PHILIP	BAL	090	2ND DIST
MESSER, SAMUEL	FRE	289	WOODSBOR
MESSER, WILLIAM	FRE	077	FREDERIC
MESSERSMITH, CHARLES	BAL	262	20TH WAR
MESSERSMITH, F.	BAL	261	20TH WAR
MESSERSMITH, GEORGE	BAL	413	8TH WARD
MESSERSMITH, JACOB	BAL	168	16TH WAR
MESSERSMITH, JOHN	BAL	092	10TH WAR
MESSERSMITH, JOHN K.	BAL	261	20TH WAR
MESSICK, FRANCIS	WOR	342	1ST E DI
MESSICK, JAMES	WOR	299	SNOW HIL
MESSICK, JANE	WOR	229	6TH E DI
MESSICK, JOHN W.	WOR	209	4TH E DI
MESSICK, MARY	BAL	173	19TH WAR
MESSIMORE, JOHN	CAR	330	MANCHEST
MESSING, ADAM	BAL	280	17TH WAR
MESSINGER, SAMUEL	CAR	255	3RD DIST
MESSLER, DAVID	CAR	383	2ND DIST
MESSLER, ULRICH	CAR	383	2ND DIST
MESSMAN, MARY	WAS	160	HAGERSTO
MESSONIEF, FRANCIS	BAL	205	11TH WAR
MESSUE, J.	BAL	281	12TH WAR
MEST, HENRY	BAL	002	15TH WAR
MESTER, GEORGE	DOR	347	3RD DIVI
MESTER, LEVISA*	DOR	342	3RD DIVI
MESTER, LOUIS	BAL	320	12TH WAR
MESTER, PLANER*	DOR	342	3RD DIVI
MESTER, SHARLOTT	DOR	354	3RD DIVI
MESTER, WILLIAM*	DOR	371	3RD DIVI
MESTON, DUDLY	BAL	360	3RD WARD
METCALF, JAMES	WAS	272	RIDGEVIL
METCALF, MARTHA	FRE	113	CREAGERS
METCALF, SAMUEL	FRE	023	FREDERIC
METCALF, SUSAN	FRE	021	FREDERIC
METCALF, THOMAS	FRE	127	CREAGERS
METCALF, THOMAS	CAR	285	7TH DIST
METCALF, THOMAS	CAR	285	7TH DIST
METCALF, WILLIAM	FRE	132	CREAGERS
METCALF, WILLIAM	BAL	261	1ST DIST
METEER, SUSAN	BAL	268	7TH WARD
METER, THOMAS	CEC	022	ELKTON 3
METER, THOMAS	CEC	022	ELKTON 3
METGER, BARNARD	BAL	274	1ST DIST
METHELL, CHARLES-BLACK	CAR	126	NO TWP L
METIZINGY, JOHN	BAL	315	12TH WAR
METLER, CHRISTIANA	BAL	412	14TH WAR
METLER, MARY E. MISS-	BAL	315	20TH WAR
METON, HENRY	ALL	196	CUMBERLA
METON, JOHN	ALL	196	CUMBERLA
METS, GEORGE	WAS	296	1ST DIST
METS, J. F.*	BAL	074	10TH WAR
METSAM, GEORGE	BAL	333	3RD WARD
METSDORF, JOHN	BAL	457	8TH WARD
METTAM, JOSEPH REV.	BAL	252	1ST DIST
METTAM, SAMUEL B.	BAL	252	1ST DIST
METTAN, W.H.	BAL	291	12TH WAR
METTART, MATTHIAS	BAL	426	14TH WAR
METTEE, ALBERT	BAL	307	7TH WARD
METTEE, ANNA	BAL	264	2ND WARD
METTEE, GEORGE H.	BAL	473	14TH WAR
METTEE, HELLEN V.*	BAL	049	4TH WARD
METTEE, LEONARD	BAL	204	6TH WARD
METTEE, LEONARD C.	BAL	098	15TH WAR
METTEE, LYDIA A.	BAL	264	7TH WARD
METTEE, MARTIN W.	BAL	264	7TH WARD
METTEE, MARTIN*	BAL	048	4TH WARD
METTEE, MARY A.	BAL	307	7TH WARD
METTEE, WILLIAM	BAL	427	14TH WAR
METTEE, WILLIAM H.	BAL	007	4TH WARD
METTENBERG, HENRY	BAL	253	12TH WAR
METTENDORFF, CHARLES	BAL	464	14TH WAR
METTER, ELIZABETH	BAL	001	18TH WAR
METTERD, E.	ALL	218	CUMBERLA
METTIE, JOHN	BAL	204	6TH WARD
METTIMORE, JAMES	ST	274	3RD E DI
METTIMORE, JAMES	ST	345	5TH E DI
METTONS, JOSEPH*	DOR	431	1ST DIST
METTS, HEZEKIAH	MGM	429	CLARKSTR
METTS, LUCINDA	MGM	380	ROCKERLE
METTS, SARAH V.	MGM	380	ROCKERLE
METYGER, WILLIAM	FRE	342	MIDDLETO
METZ, ABIGAIL	ALL	121	4TH E.D.
METZ, ADAM	WAS	086	2ND SUBD

Name	County	Page	District
METZ, AUGUSTUS	BAL	369	13TH WAR
METZ, BARBARA	BAL	433	8TH WARD
METZ, CATHARINE	WAS	070	2ND SUBD
METZ, CHISTOPHER	FRE	416	8TH E DI
METZ, ELIZA	ALL	013	3RD E.D.
METZ, ELIZABETH	ALL	011	3RD E.D.
METZ, ELIZABETH	ALL	007	3RD E.D.
METZ, ELIZABETH J.	DOR	313	1ST DIST
METZ, ELLEN	ALL	017	3RD E.D.
METZ, EMELY	ALL	123	4TH E.D.
METZ, EMILY	WAS	073	2ND SUBD
METZ, GEORGE	WAS	073	2ND SUBD
METZ, HANNAH	ALL	174	7TH E.D.
METZ, HENRY	WAS	073	2ND SUBD
METZ, ISAAC	ALL	016	3RD E.D.
METZ, JACOB	WAS	071	2ND SUBD
METZ, JACOB	WAS	197	1ST DIST
METZ, JOHN	ALL	042	10TH E.D
METZ, JOHN	BAL	435	8TH WARD
METZ, JOHN	ALL	228	CUMBERLA
METZ, JOHN	FRE	416	8TH E DI
METZ, JOHN F.	DOR	312	1ST DIST
METZ, JOHN F.	ALL	017	3RD E.D.
METZ, JOHN P.	WAS	272	RIDGEVIL
METZ, LYDIA	WAS	272	RIDGEVIL
METZ, MARY	WAS	014	2ND SUBD
METZ, MARYANN	ALL	143	6TH E.D.
METZ, NICHOLAS	FRE	414	8TH E DI
METZ, NOAH	WAS	270	1ST DIST
METZ, PHEBE	FRE	064	FREDERIC
METZ, RACHAEL	ALL	016	3RD E.D.
METZ, RICHARD A.	BAL	346	13TH WAR
METZ, WILLIAM	FRE	008	FREDERIC
METZ, WILLIAM	BAL	299	3RD WARD
METZEL, GEORGE V.	BAL	184	11TH WAR
METZELL, CATHERINE	BAL	131	18TH WAR
METZER, ANDREW	WAS	129	HAGERSTO
METZER, LOUIZA	BAL	112	5TH WARD
METZGAR, GEORGE	FRE	008	FREDERIC
METZGER, AARON	BAL	013	9TH WARD
METZGER, ALICE A.	MGM	413	MEDLEY 3
METZGER, BASTIAN	BAL	323	3RD WARD
METZGER, ELIZABETH	HAR	146	3RD DIST
METZGER, ELIZABETH A.	MGM	407	MEDLEY 3
METZGER, FRANK W.	BAL	292	3RD WARD
METZGER, FREDERICK	BAL	236	2ND WARD
METZGER, JEANETTE	BAL	063	15TH WAR
METZGER, WILLIAM	MGM	412	MEDLEY 3
METZGUE, JACOB	FRE	064	FREDERIC
METZLER, ABRAHAM	BAL	221	1ST DIST
METZLER, CHRISTIAN	BAL	031	15TH WAR
METZLER, FREDERIC	BAL	236	6TH WARD
METZLER, NICHOLAS	CAR	355	6TH DIST
METZUHN, JOSEPH	BAL	032	15TH WAR
MEUSEL, JOANNA	BAL	066	15TH WAR
MEVAY, PENRY	KEN	295	3RD DIST
MEWBERN, PHILIP H.	ANN	366	4TH DIST
MEWBURN, JAMES	ANN	379	4TH DIST
MEWNON, MARY ANN	ALL	247	CUMBERLA
MEWSHAW, CHARLES	ANN	339	3RD DIST
MEWSHAW, JOSEPH	ANN	417	HOWARD D
MEWSHAW, VAN	ANN	342	3RD DIST
MEWSHAW, ZACHARIAH	BAL	073	15TH WAR
MEX, LYODIA	ALL	159	6TH E.D.
MEXSEL, JACOB	BAL	241	12TH WAR
MEXTER, E.	BAL	211	19TH WAR
MEYAFOR, MARY	BAL	110	10TH WAR
MEYER, ANDREW M.	BAL	070	15TH WAR
MEYER, AUGUST	BAL	007	15TH WAR
MEYER, AUGUSTUS	BAL	466	14TH WAR
MEYER, BARTEL	FRE	049	FREDERIC
MEYER, CAROLINE	BAL	042	15TH WAR
MEYER, CHARLES	BAL	155	16TH WAR
MEYER, CHRISTOPHER	BAL	075	1ST WARD
MEYER, CHRISTOPHER	BAL	076	1ST WARD
MEYER, ELIZABETH	BAL	217	6TH WARD
MEYER, FREDERIC G.	BAL	169	6TH WARD
MEYER, GEORGE	BAL	086	1ST WARD
MEYER, GEORGE	BAL	060	15TH WAR
MEYER, GEORGE	BAL	011	9TH WARD
MEYER, HENRY	BAL	070	1ST WARD
MEYER, HENRY	BAL	142	2ND DIST
MEYER, HENRY	FRE	048	FREDERIC
MEYER, HENRY G.	BAL	120	16TH WAR
MEYER, JOHN	BAL	003	EASTERN
MEYER, JOHN	BAL	463	1ST DIST
MEYER, JOHN C.	BAL	117	15TH WAR
MEYER, JOHN H.	BAL	120	16TH WAR
MEYER, JOHN H.	BAL	091	15TH WAR
MEYER, JOSEPH	BAL	076	1ST WARD
MEYER, JOSEPH H.	BAL	031	9TH WARD
MEYER, JULIUS	BAL	458	8TH WARD
MEYER, KERMAN H.	BAL	041	15TH WAR
MEYER, MATTHIAS	FRE	384	PETERSVI
MEYER, PHILIP	BAL	007	4TH WARD
MEYER, RICHARD	BAL	039	15TH WAR
MEYER, THOMAS	BAL	109	1ST WARD
MEYER, WILLIAM	BAL	115	15TH WAR
MEYER, WILLIAM	BAL	115	15TH WAR
MEYER, WILLIAM	BAL	142	16TH WAR
MEYERS, BARBARA	CAR	336	6TH DIST
MEYERS, CAROLINE	BAL	014	9TH WARD
MEYERS, CATHARINE	BAL	143	16TH WAR
MEYERS, JOHN P.	BAL	142	16TH WAR
MEYERS, RICHARD	BAL	120	16TH WAR
MEYERSBRAM, JOHN B.	BAL	220	12TH WAR
MEYICK, GEORGE *	SOM	443	DAMES QU
MEYICK, JAMES*	SOM	549	TYASKIN
MEYICK, NEHEMIAH	SOM	442	DAMES QU
MEYNBURG, SIMON	ST	274	3RD E DI
MEYRERS, HENRY	BAL	275	2ND WARD
MEYSER, JOHN	BAL	056	1ST WARD
MEZICK, BAPTIST	ANN	350	3RD DIST
MEZICK, BENJAMIN	SOM	472	TRAPPE D
MEZICK, DAVID	SOM	454	DAMES QU
MEZICK, ELEANOR	SOM	535	QUANTICO
MEZICK, ELIZABETH J.	WOR	191	8TH E DI
MEZICK, FRANCIS	SOM	537	TYASKIN
MEZICK, GEORGE W.	SOM	547	TYASKIN
MEZICK, HENERETTA	SOM	547	TYASKIN
MEZICK, ISAAC	SOM	540	TYASKIN
MEZICK, JAMES*	SOM	549	TYASKIN
MEZICK, JOHN	SOM	496	SALISBUR
MEZICK, JOHN	SOM	430	PRINCESS
MEZICK, JOHNSON	SOM	455	DAMES QU
MEZICK, JOSHUA	SOM	540	TYASKIN
MEZICK, LEVIN W.	SOM	552	TYASKIN
MEZICK, MALON	SOM	547	TYASKIN
MEZICK, MARGARET	SOM	547	TYASKIN
MEZICK, MARY	SOM	526	QUANTICO

MEZICK, MARY	WOR	197	8TH E DI
MEZICK, MINUS D.	SOM	512	BARREN C
MEZICK, NELSON	SOM	525	QUANTICO
MEZICK, PHILIP N.	SOM	472	TRAPPE D
MEZICK, SAMUEL	SOM	537	TYASKIN
MEZICK, WILLIAM	SOM	552	TYASKIN
MEZICK, WILLIAM H.	SOM	540	TYASKIN
MEZICKS, LEWIS	CAR	117	NO TWP L
MEZICKS, LUCY	CAR	118	NO TWP L
MEZZECK, CATHARINE	DOR	306	1ST DIST
MEZZECK, GEORGE W.	DOR	318	1ST DIST
MEZZECK, HENNERITTA*	DOR	315	1ST DIST
MEZZECK, JAMES	DOR	298	1ST DIST
MEZZECK, MACE	DOR	306	1ST DIST
MEZZECK, TAMER*	DOR	301	1ST DIST
MEZZICK, CAROLINE	DOR	304	1ST DIST
MEZZICK, GEORGE	DOR	301	1ST DIST
MEZZICK, HENNERITTA	DOR	313	1ST DIST
MEZZICK, SARAH N.*	DOR	298	1ST DIST
MEZZICK, SOLOMON	DOR	418	1ST DIST
MHEER, GEORGE *	BAL	012	9TH WARD
MIAS, SAMUEL	CEC	050	1ST E DI
MIBERGER, P.	BAL	216	19TH WAR
MICCE, NICKOLAS	BAL	182	2ND WARD
MICE, GEORGE	ALL	202	CUMBERLA
MICE, WILLIAM	BAL	089	1ST WARD
MICENTEER, JOHN	HAR	151	3RD DIST
MICES, LUIS*	TAL	039	EASTON D
MICES, MARY	TAL	110	ST MICHA
MICHAEL, ADAM	WAS	039	2ND SUBD
MICHAEL, AMANDA	FRE	338	MIDDLETO
MICHAEL, ANDREW	BAL	371	8TH WARD
MICHAEL, ANN C.	FRE	072	FREDERIC
MICHAEL, ANN M.	FRE	337	MIDDLETO
MICHAEL, AUGUGTA	BAL	444	14TH WAR
MICHAEL, BENETT	HAR	167	3RD DIST
MICHAEL, C. ADOLPHUS	BAL	354	7TH WARD
MICHAEL, CALITA *	ALL	125	4TH E.D.
MICHAEL, CATHARINE	FRE	022	FREDERIC
MICHAEL, CATHARINE	WAS	210	1ST DIST
MICHAEL, CHRISTIAN	BAL	279	1ST DIST
MICHAEL, CHRISTIANA	BAL	459	14TH WAR
MICHAEL, CUNROD	FRE	368	CATOCTIN
MICHAEL, DANIEL	FRE	216	BUCKEYST
MICHAEL, DANIEL	FRE	341	MIDDLETO
MICHAEL, DANIEL G.	HAR	163	3RD DIST
MICHAEL, DAVID	BAL	102	18TH WAR
MICHAEL, DAVID	ALL	125	4TH E.D.
MICHAEL, ELI	FRE	338	MIDDLETO
MICHAEL, ELIZABETH	FRE	263	NEW MARK
MICHAEL, ETHAN	BAL	281	20TH WAR
MICHAEL, EZRA	FRE	219	BUCKEYST
MICHAEL, EZRA	FRE	134	CREAGERS
MICHAEL, FRANCIS	BAL	143	16TH WAR
MICHAEL, FREDERICK	FRE	344	MIDDLETO
MICHAEL, GISBERT	FRE	221	BUCKEYST
MICHAEL, HENRY	FRE	326	MIDDLETO
MICHAEL, HENRY	FRE	352	MIDDLETO
MICHAEL, HENRY	BAL	115	15TH WAR
MICHAEL, HENRY	BAL	110	2ND DIST
MICHAEL, HENRY	BAL	297	3RD WARD
MICHAEL, HENRY J.	BAL	169	11TH WAR
MICHAEL, HENRY S.	FRE	219	BUCKEYST
MICHAEL, ISAAC	FRE	323	MIDDLETO
MICHAEL, JACOB	FRE	323	MIDDLETO
MICHAEL, JACOB	FRE	337	MIDDLETO
MICHAEL, JACOB	HAR	186	3RD DIST
MICHAEL, JACOB	CAR	337	6TH DIST
MICHAEL, JAMES	FRE	343	MIDDLETO
MICHAEL, JESSE	ALL	125	4TH E.D.
MICHAEL, JOHN	ALL	125	4TH E.D.
MICHAEL, JOHN	BAL	212	6TH DIST
MICHAEL, JOHN	BAL	055	2ND DIST
MICHAEL, JOHN	BAL	145	16TH WAR
MICHAEL, JOHN	BAL	256	1ST DIST
MICHAEL, JOHN	BAL	173	19TH WAR
MICHAEL, JOHN	FRE	088	FREDERIC
MICHAEL, JOHN G.	WAS	104	2ND DIST
MICHAEL, JOHN H.	CEC	146	PORT DUP
MICHAEL, JOSEPH	CAR	192	4TH DIST
MICHAEL, LAURETTA	FRE	400	JEFFERSO
MICHAEL, LEWIS	FRE	339	MIDDLETO
MICHAEL, LEWIS	FRE	338	MIDDLETO
MICHAEL, LUCIOUS	FRE	023	FREDERIC
MICHAEL, MANUEL H.	BAL	416	8TH WARD
MICHAEL, MARGARET	FRE	022	FREDERIC
MICHAEL, MARGARET	BAL	373	13TH WAR
MICHAEL, MUNDEL	BAL	155	19TH WAR
MICHAEL, OWEN	HAR	112	2ND DIST
MICHAEL, PERRY	FRE	338	MIDDLETO
MICHAEL, PRECIOUS	FRE	215	BUCKEYST
MICHAEL, RAYMOND	BAL	212	6TH DIST
MICHAEL, THEODORE	BAL	441	14TH WAR
MICHAEL, THOMAS	FRE	205	BUCKEYST
MICHAEL, THOMAS	CAR	214	5TH DIST
MICHAEL, WILLIAM	HAR	112	2ND DIST
MICHAEL, WILLIAM	ALL	125	4TH E.D.
MICHAEL, WILLIAM B.	BAL	060	15TH WAR
MICHAEL.ALICE C.	FRE	002	FREDERIC
MICHAEL.ANDREW	FRE	219	BUCKEYST
MICHAELS, ELIZABETH	ALL	003	3RD E.D.
MICHAELS, J.G.	WAS	019	2ND SUBD
MICHAELS, JESSE	ALL	125	4TH E.D.
MICHAELS, JOHN	ALL	124	4TH E.D.
MICHAELS, PHILIP	ALL	125	4TH E.D.
MICHAELS, PHILIP A.	ALL	125	4TH E.D.
MICHAELS, SUSAN	ALL	040	2ND E.D.
MICHAL, JOHN C.	WAS	135	2ND DIST
MICHAM, HENRY	BAL	001	9TH WARD
MICHEAELS, LEWIS	WAS	055	2ND SUBD
MICHEAL, FRANCIS C.	BAL	062	18TH WAR
MICHEL, FREDERICK	BAL	064	1ST WARD
MICHEL, FREDERICK	BAL	353	3RD WARD
MICHEL, GEORGE	BAL	378	8TH WARD
MICHEL, MARGARET	BAL	262	2ND WARD
MICHEL, MARGARET	HAR	044	1ST DIST
MICHEL, MARY	BAL	183	5TH DIST
MICHELL, GEORGE L.	HAR	179	3RD DIST
MICHELL, HANNAH	HAR	182	3RD DIST
MICHELL, HENRY	HAR	163	3RD DIST
MICHELL, HENRY E.	HAR	185	3RD DIST
MICHELL, JAMES W.	HAR	186	3RD DIST
MICHELL, JOHN	BAL	294	17TH WAR
MICHELL, SARAH A.	HAR	176	3RD DIST
MICHELL, WILLIAM H.	HAR	183	3RD DIST
MICHIEL, C.	BAL	129	5TH WARD
MICHIEL, LOUIS	BAL	131	5TH WARD
MICHINGNER, NANCY	HAR	044	1ST DIST
MICHMORE, JAMES	HAR	077	BEL AIR
MICHTOLD, CHARLES J.	BAL	217	17TH WAR

MICKALL, LEWIS	BAL	431	14TH WAR
MICKEL, DANIEL	HAR	163	3RD DIST
MICKEL, HENRY	BAL	134	1ST WARD
MICKEL, REGINA	BAL	085	10TH WAR
MICKELL, JACOB J.	HAR	150	3RD DIST
MICKER, ROBERT	BAL	392	14TH WAR
MICKERSON, CHARLES	BAL	123	1ST WARD
MICKIE, CATHARINE	BAL	247	12TH WAR
MICKLE, ELIZABETH	FRE	164	EMMITTSB
MICKLE, HENRY	BAL	061	1ST WARD
MICKLE, JOHN	WAS	259	1ST DIST
MICKLE, WILLIAM	BAL	170	11TH WAR
MICKLEY, DANIEL	WAS	257	1ST DIST
MICKLEY, DANIEL	WAS	257	1ST DIST
MICKLEY, ELI	FRE	020	FREDERIC
MICKLOON, R.	BAL	153	1ST WARD
MICKLOW, R.	BAL	164	1ST WARD
MICKSELL, GEORGE	FRE	140	CREAGERS
MICKSHANE, ANN	BAL	127	11TH WAR
MICROFT, ANN	BAL	001	EASTERN
MICTCHEL, WILLIAM K.	BAL	296	1ST DIST
MIDDENDEY, HERMAN*	BAL	061	4TH WARD
MIDDENDORF, HARMAN	BAL	274	7TH WARD
MIDDENDORF, HENRY	BAL	004	15TH WAR
MIDDENDORF, HENRY	HAR	097	2ND DIST
MIDDLECAMP, JOHN	ANN	266	ANNAPOLI
MIDDLECOFF, DANIEL	WAS	048	2ND SUBD
MIDDLECOFF, MARY	WAS	049	2ND SUBD
MIDDLECUFF, JOHN C.	WAS	065	2ND SUBD
MIDDLEDITCH, JOHN	HAR	089	2ND DIST
MIDDLEDITCH, SARAH	HAR	111	2ND DIST
MIDDLEGAP, HENRY	BAL	466	14TH WAR
MIDDLEHAUFF, BENJAMIN	WAS	291	1ST DIST
MIDDLEHAUFF, DAVID	WAS	133	HAGERSTO
MIDDLEHAUFF, JACOB	WAS	288	1ST DIST
MIDDLEHAUFF, JOHN D.	WAS	140	HAGERSTO
MIDDLEHAUFF, JOHN G.	WAS	274	RIDGEVIL
MIDDLEHAUFF, JONATHAN	WAS	275	RIDGEVIL
MIDDLEHAUFF, LEONARD	WAS	288	1ST DIST
MIDDLEHAUFF, SAMUEL	WAS	282	1ST DIST
MIDDLEHAUGFF, MARIA	WAS	148	HAGERSTO
MIDDLEKAAFF, E.	ALL	256	CUMBERLA
MIDDLEKARFF, JACOB	WAS	222	1ST DIST
MIDDLEKAUFF, CHRIST.	WAS	187	BOONSBOR
MIDDLEKAUFF, DANIEL	WAS	129	HAGERSTO
MIDDLEKAUFF, DANIEL	WAS	282	1ST DIST
MIDDLEKAUFF, DANIEL G.	WAS	288	1ST DIST
MIDDLEKAUFF, ELIAS	WAS	291	1ST DIST
MIDDLEKAUFF, HENRY	WAS	128	HAGERSTO
MIDDLEKAUFF, HETTA	WAS	047	2ND SUBD
MIDDLEKAUFF, JACOB C.	WAS	190	1ST DIST
MIDDLEKAUFF, JOHN	WAS	032	2ND SUBD
MIDDLEKAUFF, JOSEPH	WAS	266	1ST DIST
MIDDLEKAUFF, LEONARD	WAS	274	RIDGEVIL
MIDDLEKAUFF, MARTHA R.M.	WAS	140	HAGERSTO
MIDDLEKAUFF, MARY	WAS	129	HAGERSTO
MIDDLEKAUFF, PETER	WAS	266	1ST DIST
MIDDLEKAUFF, PETER	WAS	205	1ST DIST
MIDDLEKAUFF, SAMUEL	WAS	110	2ND DIST
MIDDLEKAUFF, SOHIA	WAS	299	1ST DIST
MIDDLEKAUFF, SOLOMON	WAS	281	1ST DIST
MIDDLEKAUFF, SUSAN	WAS	103	2ND DIST
MIDDLEKAUFF, SUSAN	WAS	191	1ST DIST
MIDDLEKOUFF, SIMON	WAS	232	1ST DIST
MIDDLEMIS, THOMAS	BAL	411	1ST DIST
MIDDLEMUNDIG, FRANCIS *	BAL	133	2ND DIST
MIDDLETON, ALEXANDER	PRI	112	PISCATAW
MIDDLETON, BENJAMIN	KEN	229	2ND DIST
MIDDLETON, BETTY	CHA	252	BOJANTOW
MIDDLETON, C.F.	BAL	187	2ND WARD
MIDDLETON, CHARLES	PRI	099	SPALDING
MIDDLETON, DANIEL	ALL	194	9TH E.D.
MIDDLETON, DAVID	CHA	219	ALLENS F
MIDDLETON, E. A.	CHA	218	ALLENS F
MIDDLETON, EDWARD	KEN	232	2ND DIST
MIDDLETON, ELIAS	FRE	051	FREDERIC
MIDDLETON, FANNY	BAL	008	1ST WARD
MIDDLETON, HANNAH	KEN	228	2ND DIST
MIDDLETON, HORATIO	ALL	194	9TH E.D.
MIDDLETON, HUGH	ALL	190	9TH E.D.
MIDDLETON, J. H.	BAL	155	1ST WARD
MIDDLETON, JAMES	KEN	228	2ND DIST
MIDDLETON, JAMES	BAL	259	20TH WAR
MIDDLETON, JAMES	QUE	186	3RD E DI
MIDDLETON, JAMES H. V.	CHA	252	BOJANTOW
MIDDLETON, JASPER	ALL	186	9TH E.D.
MIDDLETON, JOHN	BAL	119	1ST WARD
MIDDLETON, JOHN	KEN	264	1ST DIST
MIDDLETON, JOHN W.	BAL	022	4TH WARD
MIDDLETON, JOSEPH	KEN	227	2ND DIST
MIDDLETON, JOSEPH	BAL	280	2ND WARD
MIDDLETON, JOSEPH T.	CHA	285	BOJANTOW
MIDDLETON, MARY A.	KEN	228	2ND DIST
MIDDLETON, MARY J.	BAL	088	18TH WAR
MIDDLETON, NANCY	ALL	194	9TH E.D.
MIDDLETON, NELSON	ALL	158	6TH E.D.
MIDDLETON, PRESCELLA	ALL	097	5TH E.D.
MIDDLETON, REBECCA	BAL	063	4TH WARD
MIDDLETON, RICHARD	BAL	376	3RD WARD
MIDDLETON, RICHARD	BAL	057	15TH WAR
MIDDLETON, SARAH	KEN	235	2ND DIST
MIDDLETON, THOMAS	BAL	034	9TH WARD
MIDDLETON, URSILLA	BAL	182	11TH WAR
MIDDLETON, W.	BAL	117	1ST WARD
MIDDLETON, WATSON	BAL	167	1ST WARD
MIDDLETON, WILLIAM	BAL	405	1ST DIST
MIDDLETON, WILLIAM	WOR	203	4TH E DI
MIDDLETON, WILLIAM A. L.	WOR	218	4TH E DI
MIDDLETON.JOEL	ALL	190	9TH E.D.
MIDENDORF, HENRY	BAL	290	17TH WAR
MIDFORD, JAMES	CAR	070	NO TWP L
MIDLECAMP, HAM	ANN	319	2ND DIST
MIDLECAMP, HENRY	ANN	318	2ND DIST
MIDLETON, ANN*	TAL	053	EASTON D
MIDLETON, JESSE L.*	TAL	030	EASTON D
MIDLETON, JOHN	TAL	057	EASTON D
MIDMAN, MICHAEL	HAR	096	2ND DIST
MIEGAN, HENRY	BAL	245	2ND WARD
MIELVAY, MICHAEL	ALL	136	4TH E.D.
MIENBERG, BETSEY	BAL	015	9TH WARD
MIER, DAVID B.	ALL	196	CUMBERLA
MIER, JOHN	ALL	120	5TH E.D.
MIER, JOHN	BAL	278	2ND WARD
MIERLY, THOMAS	FRE	190	5TH E DI
MIERS, ALFRED-BLACK	QUE	201	3RD E DI
MIERS, CHARLES-BLACK	QUE	202	3RD E DI
MIERS, HARRISON	QUE	219	3RD E DI
MIERS, HENRIETTA	QUE	216	3RD E DI
MIERS, JAMES-BLACK	QUE	183	3RD E DI
MIERS, JOHN	KEN	260	1ST DIST

MIERS, JOHN-BLACK	QUE	201	3RD E DI
MIERS, SARAH A.	QUE	126	1ST E DI
MIERS, THOMAS	BAL	154	1ST WARD
MIESTER, GEORGE	ALL	226	CUMBERLA
MIFINGER, GOERGE	BAL	055	2ND DIST
MIFLIN, CATHARINE	BAL	394	1ST DIST
MIGAN, MARY	BAL	211	11TH WAR
MIGGS, SARAH*	BAL	366	3RD WARD
MIGROH, ALEXANDER	BAL	054	9TH WARD
MIHLEN, HERMAN	BAL	247	2ND WARD
MIKE, MICHAEL	BAL	282	1ST DIST
MIKESELL, JACOB	CAR	249	3RD DIST
MIKESELL, PETER B.	CAR	251	3RD DIST
MIKESELL, WILLIAM B.	CAR	249	3RD DIST
MILAN, ESTER J.	SOM	401	BRINKLEY
MILAN, JAMES	BAL	030	4TH WARD
MILAN, MICHAEL	ALL	053	10TH E.D
MILAND, ANN	ALL	077	5TH E.D.
MILBERRY, HARRIET J.	FRE	289	WOODSBOR
MILBERRY, RACHAEL-MULATTO	FRE	452	8TH E DI
MILBORN, MARGARET A.	QUE	196	3RD E DI
MILBORN, SAMUEL	KEN	306	3RD DIST
MILBORN, ZACOK T.	WOR	304	SNOW HIL
MILBORNE, CHARLES D.	SOM	402	BRINKLEY
MILBORNE, FRANCIS*	SOM	399	BRINKLEY
MILBORNE, HENRY	SOM	401	BRINKLEY
MILBORNE, JOHN	SOM	400	BRINKLEY
MILBORNE, LANDRICK	SOM	398	BRINKLEY
MILBORNE, LITTLETON	SOM	362	BRINKLEY
MILBORNE, LITTLETON	SOM	411	DUBLIN D
MILBORNE, NATHANIEL	SOM	411	DUBLIN D
MILBORNE, ROBERT	SOM	413	DUBLIN D
MILBORNE, SAMUEL	SOM	398	BRINKLEY
MILBORNE, SAMUEL D.	SOM	399	BRINKLEY
MILBORNE, SARAH	SOM	411	DUBLIN D
MILBORNE, TAMER	SOM	398	BRINKLEY
MILBORNE, WILLIAM	SOM	411	DUBLIN D
MILBORNE, WILLIAM	SOM	412	DUBLIN D
MILBORNE, WILLIAM W.	SOM	400	BRINKLEY
MILBOURN, JAMES-BLACK	QUE	137	1ST E DI
MILBOURN, SUSAN	WOR	221	4TH E DI
MILBOURNE, ELIJAH S.	BAL	003	15TH WAR
MILBOURNE, GEORGE	ANN	317	1ST DIST
MILBOURNE, GEORGE	BAL	177	16TH WAR
MILBOURNE, GILBERT S.	SOM	396	BRINKLEY
MILBOURNE, HARIET	SOM	411	DUBLIN D
MILBOURNE, JAMES	SOM	411	DUBLIN D
MILBOURNE, MARY	SOM	413	DUBLIN D
MILBOWRNE, ALBERT P.	B'L	205	6TH WARD
MILBURN, ARTEMISSA	BAL	178	6TH WARD
MILBURN, BENJAMIN T.	CEC	107	3RD E DI
MILBURN, ELEANOR	ST	303	2ND E DI
MILBURN, ELIAS	ST	313	1ST E DI
MILBURN, ELLEN	ST	299	2ND E DI
MILBURN, GEORGE W.	CEC	007	ELKTON 3
MILBURN, HARRIET	BAL	430	14TH WAR
MILBURN, JAMES A.	BAL	392	3RD WARD
MILBURN, JAMES C.	ST	298	2ND E DI
MILBURN, JAMES T.	ST	310	1ST E DI
MILBURN, JAMES W.P.	ST	321	4TH E DI
MILBURN, JAMES*	BAL	311	3RD WARD
MILBURN, JOHN	ST	309	1ST E DI
MILBURN, JOHN	CEC	080	NORTHEAS
MILBURN, JOHN H.	ST	295	2ND E DI
MILBURN, JOHN H.	ST	300	2ND E DI
MILBURN, JOSEPH	ST	309	1ST E DI
MILBURN, LUCY	BAL	152	16TH WAR
MILBURN, PERMELIA	ST	302	2ND E DI
MILBURN, PETER	CEC	016	ELKTON 3
MILBURN, PETER	CEC	014	ELKTON 3
MILBURN, R. N.	BAL	269	20TH WAR
MILBURN, SARAH E.A.	ST	309	1ST E DI
MILBURN, SUSAN	BAL	432	14TH WAR
MILBURN, SUSAN G.	ST	321	4TH E DI
MILBURN, THOMAS	CEC	125	5TH E DI
MILBURN, WILLIAM	BAL	119	15TH WAR
MILBY, HENRY	QUE	218	3RD E DI
MILBY, SAMUEL	CAR	071	NO TWP L
MILCHENY, CATHARINE *	BAL	099	2ND DIST
MILCHING, COONRAD	BAL	099	2ND DIST
MILCHNOR, JOHN D.	CEC	212	7TH E DI
MILDER, DAVID	CEC	043	CHESAPEA
MILEAN, ALICE	BAL	053	9TH WARD
MILELR, ANN	WAS	156	2ND DIST
MILELR, JESSE	BAL	140	19TH WAR
MILELR, MARGARET	FRE	021	FREDERIC
MILENWORTH, THOMAS	FRE	250	NEW MARK
MILER, DANIEL	TAL	095	ST MICHA
MILER, MARTIN J.	BAL	028	9TH WARD
MILER.VALENTINE	BAL	244	2ND WARD
MILES, ABRAM	BAL	046	2ND DIST
MILES, ADAM	CAR	274	7TH DIST
MILES, AGNELINE	FRE	092	FREDERIC
MILES, ALBERT	BAL	001	9TH WARD
MILES, ALFRED	SOM	425	PRINCESS
MILES, ALICE	CHA	257	MIDDLETO
MILES, ALLEN	MGM	342	CLARKSBU
MILES, ALMUDA *	FRE	273	NEW MARK
MILES, AMELIA	BAL	414	14TH WAR
MILES, ANN	BAL	260	20TH WAR
MILES, ANN	ANN	455	HOWARD D
MILES, ANN	ST	274	3RD E DI
MILES, ARMORY	DOR	407	1ST DIST
MILES, AUGUSTAS W.	BAL	066	18TH WAR
MILES, BANNOMOR*	DOR	404	1ST DIST
MILES, BARR	DOR	387	1ST DIST
MILES, BENJAMIN	CAR	204	4TH DIST
MILES, BENJAMIN G.	BAL	408	8TH WARD
MILES, BETTY	ANN	317	1ST DIST
MILES, CAROLINE E.	ST	306	1ST E DI
MILES, CAROLINE V.	SOM	421	PRINCESS
MILES, CATHARINE	SOM	441	DAMES QU
MILES, CATHERINE	BAL	280	20TH WAR
MILES, CHARITY	BAL	103	15TH WAR
MILES, CHARLES	MGM	344	CLARKSBU
MILES, CHARLES A.	BAL	077	4TH WARD
MILES, CHARLES A.	BAL	199	11TH WAR
MILES, CHARLES P.	FRE	226	BUCKEYST
MILES, CRISY	CAL	028	2ND DIST
MILES, DANIEL	BAL	413	14TH WAR
MILES, DANIEL	SOM	353	BRINKLEY
MILES, DAVID	WOR	331	1ST E DI
MILES, DAVID	KEN	277	1ST DIST
MILES, EASTER	SOM	485	TRAPP DI
MILES, EDWAN R.	SOM	353	BRINKLEY
MILES, EDWARD	CHA	257	MIDDLETO
MILES, ELEN	CHA	274	ALLENS F
MILES, ELI	WAS	148	2ND DIST
MILES, ELIE	WAS	138	HAGERSTO
MILES, ELIJAH	KEN	221	2ND DIST

MILES, ELIZ	BAL	253	12TH WAR
MILES, ELIZABETH	FRE	164	EMMITTSB
MILES, ELIZABETH	DOR	469	1ST DIST
MILES, ELLICK	PRI	038	VANSVILL
MILES, EMMA	BAL	337	13TH WAR
MILES, FREDERICK B.	FRE	086	FREDERIC
MILES, GEORGE	DOR	407	1ST DIST
MILES, GEORGE	SOM	370	BRINKLEY
MILES, GEORGE	SOM	469	TRAPPE D
MILES, GEORGE	BAL	130	1ST WARD
MILES, GRACEN	CHA	257	MIDDLETO
MILES, HANNAH	SOM	388	BRINKLEY
MILES, HANSON	WAS	135	HAGERSTO
MILES, HANSON	MGM	440	CLARKSTR
MILES, HARRIET A.	FRE	238	NEW MARK
MILES, HENRY	MGM	394	ROCKERLE
MILES, HENRY	SOM	387	BRINKLEY
MILES, HENRY	WAS	122	2ND DIST
MILES, HENRY	BAL	093	5TH WARD
MILES, HENRY	BAL	093	5TH WARD
MILES, JACOB	FRE	091	FREDERIC
MILES, JANE SH.	ST	300	2ND E DI
MILES, JAMES	DOR	468	1ST DIST
MILES, JAMES	DOR	467	1ST DIST
MILES, JAMES	SOM	372	BRINKLEY
MILES, JAMES	DOR	387	1ST DIST
MILES, JAMES B.	DOR	378	1ST DIST
MILES, JAMES H.	DOR	391	1ST DIST
MILES, JAMES*	DOR	390	1ST DIST
MILES, JEREMIAH-BLACK	CAR	402	2ND DIST
MILES, JOHN	DOR	425	1ST DIST
MILES, JOHN	DOR	415	1ST DIST
MILES, JOHN	FRE	387	PETERSVI
MILES, JOHN	MGM	433	CLARKSTR
MILES, JOHN	BAL	173	11TH WAR
MILES, JOHN	BAL	317	12TH WAR
MILES, JOHN	BAL	366	3RD WARD
MILES, JOHN H.	SOM	387	BRINKLEY
MILES, JOHN T.	FRE	394	PETERSVI
MILES, JOSEPH	PRI	035	VANSVILL
MILES, JOSHUA H.	SOM	371	BRINKLEY
MILES, LAZARUS	SOM	353	BRINKLEY
MILES, LEVI	ANN	352	3RD DIST
MILES, LOYD	WAS	007	WILLIAMS
MILES, MAHALY*	BAL	421	3RD WARD
MILES, MARTHA B.	BAL	065	18TH WAR
MILES, MARY	BAL	293	20TH WAR
MILES, MARY	DOR	404	1ST DIST
MILES, MARY	DOR	392	1ST DIST
MILES, MARY	SOM	437	PRINCESS
MILES, MARY	MGM	341	CLARKSBU
MILES, MARY	MGM	336	CRACKLIN
MILES, MARY	PRI	035	VANSVILL
MILES, MARY	SOM	484	TRAPP DI
MILES, MARY	DOR	455	1ST DIST
MILES, MARY	BAL	065	2ND DIST
MILES, MARY	BAL	097	10TH WAR
MILES, MATTHIAS	SOM	422	PRINCESS
MILES, MOSES	BAL	058	2ND DIST
MILES, NANCY	DOR	414	1ST DIST
MILES, NATHAN	ANN	447	HOWARD D
MILES, NATHAN E.	MGM	425	MEDLEY 3
MILES, NICHOLAS V.	CHA	268	BOJANTOW
MILES, OSCAR	ST	331	4TH E DI
MILES, PETER	SOM	470	TRAPPE D
MILES, PETER	BAL	093	5TH WARD
MILES, PHILIP	BAL	028	9TH WARD
MILES, POLLY	SOM	378	BRINKLEY
MILES, RACHAEL A.	FRE	048	FREDERIC
MILES, RAMOND	SOM	383	BRINKLEY
MILES, RAPHEAL	PRI	105	PISCATAW
MILES, REBECCA	WAS	206	1ST DIST
MILES, RECHEAL	BAL	013	18TH WAR
MILES, RICHARD	ST	331	4TH E DI
MILES, RICHARD D.	BAL	351	3RD WARD
MILES, RICHARD M.	ANN	403	8TH DIST
MILES, ROBERT	BAL	113	15TH WAR
MILES, ROBERT	CHA	274	ALLENS F
MILES, SALLEY, J.	BAL	341	7TH WARD
MILES, SALLY	CHA	290	BOJANTOW
MILES, SALLY	FRE	164	EMMITTSB
MILES, SAMUEL	DOR	438	1ST DIST
MILES, SAMUEL	BAL	173	19TH WAR
MILES, SAMUEL	SOM	353	BRINKLEY
MILES, SAMUEL G.	BAL	119	15TH WAR
MILES, SOPHIA	BAL	069	15TH WAR
MILES, SOUTHY F.	SOM	365	BRINKLEY
MILES, STEPHEN	SOM	367	BRINKLEY
MILES, STEPHEN	SOM	371	BRINKLEY
MILES, STEPHEN R.P	SOM	390	BRINKLEY
MILES, THOMAS	SOM	366	BRINKLEY
MILES, THOMAS	BAL	262	12TH WAR
MILES, THOMAS	ALL	110	5TH E.D.
MILES, THOMAS H.	ST	306	1ST E DI
MILES, THOMAS-BLACK	CAR	410	2ND DIST
MILES, URIAH	BAL	246	12TH WAR
MILES, URIAH	BAL	245	12TH WAR
MILES, VIRGINIA A.	MGM	442	CLARKSTR
MILES, WAFRY	SOM	383	BRINKLEY
MILES, WASHINGTON	SOM	428	PRINCESS
MILES, WHITTINGTON	SOM	383	BRINKLEY
MILES, WILLIAM	SOM	367	BRINKLEY
MILES, WILLIAM	SOM	395	BRINKLEY
MILES, WILLIAM	PRI	035	VANSVILL
MILES, WILLIAM	SOM	414	DUBLIN D
MILES, WILLIAM	DOR	413	1ST DIST
MILES, WILLIAM	DOR	404	1ST DIST
MILES, WILLIAM F. M.	SOM	421	PRINCESS
MILES, WILLIAM G.	MGM	353	BERRYS D
MILES, WILLIAM T.	CAL	027	2ND DIST
MILES, WILLIAM*	SOM	365	BRINKLEY
MILES.ELEY	BAL	280	12TH WAR
MILES.RHODY E.	FRE	405	JEFFERSO
MILES.ROBERT	BAL	018	1ST WARD
MILESWORTH, MATTHIAS	FRE	251	NEW MARK
MILEY, ELIZABETH	WAS	112	2ND DIST
MILEY, MARTHA	WAS	112	2ND DIST
MILGAN, JOHN	BAL	209	2ND WARD
MILGERS, JOHN	CEC	020	ELKTON 3
MILHAN, WILLIAM	BAL	231	2ND WARD
MILHOLLAND, JOHN V.	ANN	469	HOWARD D
MILIED, HENRY	BAL	166	1ST WARD
MILIGAN, JAMES	HAR	145	3RD DIST
MILIGAN, JULIA	BAL	179	16TH WAR
MILIGAN, WASHINGTON	SOM	419	PRINCESS
MILIUS, FREDERICK	CAR	365	9TH DIST
MILKY, HENRY	BAL	266	2ND WARD
MILL, M.	ANN	274	ANNAPOLI
MILL, WILLIAM	CAR	348	6TH DIST
MILLAGAN, GEORGE	KEN	289	3RD DIST
MILLAGAN, JAMES	BAL	386	1ST DIST
MILLAGE, J.	BAL	333	1ST DIST
MILLAMAN, GEORGE L.	BAL	291	1ST DIST
MILLAN, JOHN	BAL	209	2ND WARD
MILLAR, ALEXANDER	BAL	358	13TH WAR
MILLAR, JANE H.	CHA	233	HILLTOP
MILLAR, JOHN	SOM	428	PRINCESS
MILLAR, JOHN	CHA	292	BOJANTOW
MILLAR, JOHN	BAL	240	2ND WARD
MILLAR, JOHN M.	CEC	188	7TH E DI
MILLAR, JOHN S.	BAL	277	1ST DIST
MILLAR, LAURA	BAL	396	14TH WAR
MILLAR, REBECCA	BAL	393	14TH WAR
MILLAR, REBECCA EMMA	BAL	394	14TH WAR
MILLAR, THOMAS	BAL	088	1ST WARD
MILLAR, THOMAS A.	CHA	244	HILLTOP
MILLARD, CHARLES	PRI	076	MARLBROU
MILLARD, EUGENE	BAL	212	11TH WAR
MILLARD, IGNATIUS	ST	254	3RD E DI
MILLARD, JOHN M.	ST	266	3RD E DI
MILLARD, KATE	BAL	025	4TH WARD
MILLARD, LOUIS-BVLACK	ST	309	1ST E DI
MILLARD, M.F.	BAL	212	11TH WAR
MILLARD, MARY	ST	266	3RD E DI
MILLARD, PAULINE	BAL	212	11TH WAR
MILLARD, ROSA	ST	266	3RD E DI
MILLBERRY, NICHOLAS-MULAT	FRE	421	8TH E DI
MILLBOURN, THOMAS	BAL	352	7TH WARD
MILLBURN, CAROLINE	CEC	006	ELKTON 3
MILLBURN, JOHN H.	BAL	038	4TH WARD
MILLBURN, MARY	CEC	001	ELKTON 3
MILLBURN, MILLY	BAL	044	4TH WARD
MILLBURN, NICHOLAS	CEC	160	PORT DUP
MILLBURN, PERRY	CEC	002	ELKTON 3
MILLBURN, SHADRACK	BAL	378	1ST DIST
MILLEAN, ELIZABETH	CHA	229	MIDDLETO
MILLEARY, WASHINGTON	PRI	016	BLADENSB
MILLEGAN, SARAH	CEC	104	4TH E DI
MILLEMUN, GEORGE	BAL	169	19TH WAR
MILLEMUN, JOHN	BAL	169	19TH WAR
MILLEN, ALICE V.	BAL	460	14TH WAR
MILLEN, BERNARD	BAL	173	11TH WAR
MILLEN, ELIZA	BAL	131	11TH WAR
MILLEN, ELLEN	BAL	147	5TH WARD
MILLEN, FRISBY	BAL	134	2ND DIST
MILLEN, HOTMAN	BAL	291	1ST DIST
MILLEN, JOHN	CEC	037	CHESAPEA
MILLEN, LAURA V.	ANN	456	HOWARD D
MILLEN, RACHEL	ANN	456	HOWARD D
MILLEN, WILHEMINA	BAL	288	1ST DIST
MILLENBERGER, GEORGE W.	BAL	372	13TH WAR
MILLENDER, HENRY	BAL	120	11TH WAR
MILLENDER, RUTHANNA	CEC	200	7TH E DI
MILLENDRATER, MICHAEL	BAL	209	6TH WARD
MILLENNIX, JOHN	BAL	093	18TH WAR
MILLER, *	BAL	192	5TH DIST
MILLER, AARON	KEN	242	2ND DIST
MILLER, ABIJAH	CAR	192	4TH DIST
MILLER, ABRAHAM	CAR	184	8TH DIST
MILLER, ABRAHAM	WAS	057	2ND SUBD
MILLER, ABRAHAM	WAS	146	HAGERSTO
MILLER, ABRAHAM	WAS	129	2ND DIST
MILLER, ADALINE	BAL	167	11TH WAR
MILLER, ADAM	BAL	068	1ST WARD
MILLER, ADAM	BAL	390	3RD WARD
MILLER, ADAM	ANN	276	ANNAPOLI
MILLER, ADAM	CAR	187	4TH DIST
MILLER, ADAM	FRE	339	MIDDLETO
MILLER, ADAM	BAL	017	18TH WAR
MILLER, AEFRED A.	BAL	269	20TH WAR
MILLER, AGUSTUS	KEN	226	2ND DIST
MILLER, AGUUSTINE	FRE	169	5TH E DI
MILLER, ALBERT	BAL	276	17TH WAR
MILLER, ALBERT	BAL	151	1ST WARD
MILLER, ALBERT C.	BAL	293	3RD WARD
MILLER, ALEXANDER	DOR	348	3RD DIVI
MILLER, ALFRED	BAL	405	14TH WAR
MILLER, ALFRED	BAL	141	19TH WAR
MILLER, ALFRED J.	BAL	040	4TH WARD
MILLER, ALICE	WAS	158	2ND DIST
MILLER, ALICE	PRI	032	VANSVILL
MILLER, AMOS	CAR	360	9TH DIST
MILLER, ANDREW	BAL	125	18TH WAR
MILLER, ANDREW	BAL	143	19TH WAR
MILLER, ANDREW	BAL	113	18TH WAR
MILLER, ANDREW	FRE	279	WOODSBOR
MILLER, ANDREW	FRE	120	CREAGERS
MILLER, ANDREW	WAS	256	1ST DIST
MILLER, ANDREW	BAL	323	3RD WARD
MILLER, ANDREW	ALL	117	5TH E.D.
MILLER, ANDREW	ALL	117	5TH E.D.
MILLER, ANDREW	BAL	364	3RD WARD
MILLER, ANDREW	BAL	030	15TH WAR
MILLER, ANDREW	ALL	245	CUMBERLA
MILLER, ANDREW B.	WAS	202	1ST DIST
MILLER, ANDREW D.	BAL	046	9TH WARD
MILLER, ANDREW J.	BAL	015	18TH WAR
MILLER, ANDREW K.	WAS	100	2ND DIST
MILLER, ANDREW*	BAL	024	4TH WARD
MILLER, ANGALINE	BAL	351	1ST DIST
MILLER, ANN	BAL	139	5TH WARD
MILLER, ANN	BAL	152	16TH WAR
MILLER, ANN	BAL	226	19TH WAR
MILLER, ANN	FRE	305	WOODSBOR
MILLER, ANN	WAS	106	2ND DIST
MILLER, ANN	WAS	057	2ND SUBD
MILLER, ANN	WAS	298	1ST DIST
MILLER, ANN C.	CAR	179	8TH DIST
MILLER, ANN E.	BAL	365	3RD WARD
MILLER, ANN M.	BAL	039	4TH WARD
MILLER, ANN M.	BAL	171	19TH WAR
MILLER, ANN M.	WAS	147	HAGERSTO
MILLER, ANNA	WAS	276	RIDGEVIL
MILLER, ANNA	BAL	316	12TH WAR
MILLER, ANNA	ANN	521	HOWARD D
MILLER, ANNE	BAL	178	16TH WAR
MILLER, ANNE	BAL	116	15TH WAR
MILLER, ANNE	BAL	025	15TH WAR
MILLER, ANNE	BAL	005	15TH WAR
MILLER, ANNE	BAL	073	15TH WAR
MILLER, ANTHONY	BAL	436	8TH WARD
MILLER, ANTHONY	BAL	124	16TH WAR
MILLER, ANTON	BAL	098	1ST WARD
MILLER, AREA	BAL	359	13TH WAR
MILLER, ARNOLD	WOR	258	1ST CENS
MILLER, ARNOLD	WOR	280	BERLIN 1
MILLER, ASHBURY	BAL	074	1ST WARD
MILLER, AUGUST	BAL	012	9TH WARD
MILLER, AUGUSTINE	FRE	169	5TH E DI
MILLER, AUGUSTUS	BAL	149	19TH WAR
MILLER, B.	BAL	148	1ST WARD
MILLER, BALSER	WAS	154	HAGERSTO
MILLER, BARBARA	BAL	165	2ND DIST
MILLER, BARBARY	WAS	207	1ST DIST
MILLER, BENJAMIN	WAS	020	2ND SUBD
MILLER, BENJAMIN	BAL	339	1ST DIST
MILLER, BENJAMIN	CEC	115	3RD E DI
MILLER, BENJAMIN F.	HAR	162	3RD DIST
MILLER, BIDEN	BAL	188	19TH WAR
MILLER, C. F.	BAL	307	20TH WAR
MILLER, CALE	ANN	475	HOWARD D
MILLER, CALEB	CEC	014	ELKTON 3
MILLER, CALITA	ALL	116	5TH E.D.
MILLER, CAROLINE	BAL	321	3RD WARD
MILLER, CAROLINE	BAL	460	1ST DIST
MILLER, CAROLINE	BAL	037	4TH WARD
MILLER, CAROLINE	WAS	184	BOONSBOR
MILLER, CAROLINE L.	BAL	039	4TH WARD
MILLER, CASPER	BAL	278	17TH WAR
MILLER, CATHARINE	BAL	207	19TH WAR
MILLER, CATHARINE	FRE	411	8TH E DI
MILLER, CATHARINE	WAS	187	BOONSBOR
MILLER, CATHARINE	WAS	123	HAGERSTO
MILLER, CATHARINE	BAL	114	2ND DIST
MILLER, CATHARINE	BAL	112	2ND DIST
MILLER, CATHARINE	BAL	031	2ND DIST
MILLER, CATHARINE	BAL	005	EASTERN
MILLER, CATHARINE	BAL	095	15TH WAR
MILLER, CATHERINE	BAL	081	10TH WAR
MILLER, CATHERINE	BAL	275	7TH WARD
MILLER, CATHERINE	BAL	031	4TH WARD
MILLER, CATHERINE	BAL	113	18TH WAR
MILLER, CATHERINE	BAL	079	4TH WARD
MILLER, CATHERINE	MGM	430	CLARKSTR
MILLER, CATHERINE E.	CEC	174	6TH E DI
MILLER, CELIA	TAL	008	EASTON D
MILLER, CESAR	CEC	192	5TH E DI
MILLER, CESAR	CEC	215	7TH E DI
MILLER, CHARELS	ALL	085	5TH E.D.
MILLER, CHARELS	BAL	426	8TH WARD
MILLER, CHARLES	BAL	132	1ST WARD
MILLER, CHARLES	BAL	134	1ST WARD
MILLER, CHARLES	BAL	095	15TH WAR
MILLER, CHARLES	BAL	074	2ND DIST
MILLER, CHARLES	BAL	162	2ND DIST
MILLER, CHARLES	BAL	202	2ND WARD
MILLER, CHARLES	FRE	367	CATOCTIN
MILLER, CHARLES	KEN	292	3RD DIST
MILLER, CHARLES	QUE	217	3RD E DI
MILLER, CHARLES	QUE	204	3RD E DI
MILLER, CHARLES	QUE	206	3RD E DI
MILLER, CHARLES E.	BAL	083	4TH WARD
MILLER, CHARLOTT	BAL	276	7TH WARD
MILLER, CHARLOTT-MULATTO	BAL	218	2ND WARD
MILLER, CHARLOTTE	CEC	117	4TH E DI
MILLER, CHAROLOTT B.	BAL	118	18TH WAR
MILLER, CHESTER	TAL	038	EASTON D
MILLER, CHRISTAIN	CAR	223	5TH DIST
MILLER, CHRISTIAN	FRE	360	CATOCTIN
MILLER, CHRISTIAN	CAR	306	1ST DIST
MILLER, CHRISTIAN	BAL	353	13TH WAR
MILLER, CHRISTIAN	BAL	234	17TH WAR
MILLER, CHRISTIAN	FRE	147	10TH E D
MILLER, CHRISTIAN	WAS	298	1ST DIST
MILLER, CHRISTIAN	BAL	356	8TH WARD
MILLER, CHRISTIAN	BAL	281	1ST DIST
MILLER, CHRISTIAN	ALL	230	CUMBERLA
MILLER, CHRISTIAN	BAL	080	10TH WAR
MILLER, CHRISTIAN	BAL	345	7TH WARD
MILLER, CHRISTIAN	BAL	461	1ST DIST
MILLER, CHRISTIAN	BAL	293	3RD WARD
MILLER, CHRISTINA	BAL	136	16TH WAR
MILLER, CHRISTINA	BAL	268	2ND WARD
MILLER, CHRISTINA	BAL	085	4TH WARD
MILLER, CHRISTOPHER	BAL	209	2ND WARD
MILLER, CONBRAD	BAL	068	1ST WARD
MILLER, CONRAD	BAL	044	15TH WAR
MILLER, CONRAD	ALL	086	5TH E.D.
MILLER, CONRAD	BAL	148	19TH WAR
MILLER, CONRADT	BAL	448	8TH WARD
MILLER, CONROD	FRE	054	FREDERIC
MILLER, CORNELIUS F.	PRI	106	PISCATAW
MILLER, CYDNEY	HAR	169	3RD DIST
MILLER, D.	BAL	314	12TH WAR
MILLER, DADENAN	TAL	109	ST MICHA
MILLER, DAIVO S.	TAL	094	ST MICHA
MILLER, DANIEL	WAS	281	1ST DIST
MILLER, DANIEL	WAS	110	2ND DIST
MILLER, DANIEL	WAS	053	2ND SUBD
MILLER, DANIEL	WAS	057	2ND SUBD
MILLER, DANIEL	ALL	133	4TH E.D.
MILLER, DANIEL	BAL	267	2ND WARD
MILLER, DANIEL	BAL	382	1ST DIST
MILLER, DANIEL	FRE	055	FREDERIC
MILLER, DANIEL	FRE	091	FREDERIC
MILLER, DANIEL	FRE	335	MIDDLETO
MILLER, DANIEL	BAL	233	17TH WAR
MILLER, DANIEL	BAL	415	14TH WAR
MILLER, DANIEL	CAR	346	6TH DIST
MILLER, DANIEL M.	WAS	195	1ST DIST
MILLER, DANIEL-BLACK	QUE	191	3RD E DI
MILLER, DANUEL	WAS	119	2ND DIST
MILLER, DAVID	WAS	127	2ND DIST
MILLER, DAVID	WAS	233	1ST DIST
MILLER, DAVID	WAS	084	2ND SUBD
MILLER, DAVID	FRE	134	CREAGERS
MILLER, DAVID	CAR	297	7TH DIST
MILLER, DAVID	BAL	326	1ST DIST
MILLER, DAVID	BAL	277	2ND WARD
MILLER, DAVID A.	FRE	102	FREDERIC
MILLER, DAVID C.	WAS	116	2ND DIST
MILLER, DAVID H.	BAL	102	18TH WAR
MILLER, DAVID L.	WAS	047	2ND SUBD
MILLER, DAVID R.	WAS	060	2ND SUBD
MILLER, DAVID S.	FRE	026	FREDERIC
MILLER, DEBY	ANN	485	HOWARD D
MILLER, DECATER	BAL	383	13TH WAR
MILLER, DENNIOS	BAL	144	1ST WARD
MILLER, DENNIS	BAL	264	2ND WARD
MILLER, DENTON	ANN	475	HOWARD D
MILLER, DINAH	BAL	330	13TH WAR
MILLER, DORATHA	BAL	277	2ND WARD
MILLER, E.	BAL	144	1ST WARD
MILLER, EDWARD	BAL	259	6TH WARD
MILLER, EDWARD	BAL	048	1ST WARD
MILLER, EDWARD	BAL	349	3RD WARD
MILLER, EDWARD	BAL	217	19TH WAR
MILLER, EDWARD A.	BAL	257	12TH WAR
MILLER, EDWARDINA	BAL	205	11TH WAR
MILLER, EELIZA	TAL	094	ST MICHA

Name	County	Page	District
MILLER, EELIZA	TAL	093	ST MICHA
MILLER, ELI	WAS	148	2ND DIST
MILLER, ELI	FRE	346	MIDDLETO
MILLER, ELIJAH E.	KEN	286	3RD DIST
MILLER, ELIZA	WAS	292	1ST DIST
MILLER, ELIZA	WAS	017	2ND SUBD
MILLER, ELIZA	BAL	033	4TH WARD
MILLER, ELIZA	CAR	249	3RD DIST
MILLER, ELIZA	BAL	350	3RD WARD
MILLER, ELIZA	ANN	344	3RD DIST
MILLER, ELIZA J.	BAL	084	18TH WAR
MILLER, ELIZA M.	BAL	194	11TH WAR
MILLER, ELIZA-BLACK	QUE	148	1ST E DI
MILLER, ELIZABETH	HAR	129	2ND DIST
MILLER, ELIZABETH	CAR	250	3RD DIST
MILLER, ELIZABETH	CAR	335	6TH DIST
MILLER, ELIZABETH	CEC	086	4TH E DI
MILLER, ELIZABETH	FRE	346	MIDDLETO
MILLER, ELIZABETH	BAL	439	14TH WAR
MILLER, ELIZABETH	BAL	282	20TH WAR
MILLER, ELIZABETH	BAL	293	20TH WAR
MILLER, ELIZABETH	HAR	060	1ST DIST
MILLER, ELIZABETH	BAL	190	11TH WAR
MILLER, ELIZABETH	BAL	257	12TH WAR
MILLER, ELIZABETH	BAL	173	11TH WAR
MILLER, ELIZABETH	BAL	045	2ND DIST
MILLER, ELIZABETH	BAL	241	1ST DIST
MILLER, ELIZABETH	BAL	277	12TH WAR
MILLER, ELIZABETH	ALL	130	4TH E.D.
MILLER, ELIZABETH	BAL	185	2ND WARD
MILLER, ELIZABETH	WAS	035	2ND SUBD
MILLER, ELIZABETH	WAS	012	WILLIAMS
MILLER, ELIZABETH	WAS	024	2ND SUBD
MILLER, ELIZABETH	PRI	003	BLADENSB
MILLER, ELIZABETH	WAS	207	1ST DIST
MILLER, ELIZABETH	WAS	263	1ST DIST
MILLER, ELIZABETH A.	BAL	205	6TH WARD
MILLER, ELLEN	TAL	049	EASTON T
MILLER, ELLEN	BAL	345	13TH WAR
MILLER, ELLEN	CEC	131	6TH E DI
MILLER, ELLEN	BAL	134	11TH WAR
MILLER, ELSY	BAL	263	20TH WAR
MILLER, EMANUEL	BAL	471	14TH WAR
MILLER, EMELINE	BAL	170	6TH WARD
MILLER, EMILY	BAL	119	15TH WAR
MILLER, EMILY	BAL	077	4TH WARD
MILLER, EMMEANUEL	BAL	074	18TH WAR
MILLER, EMORY	BAL	044	15TH WAR
MILLER, ENOCH	BAL	006	4TH WARD
MILLER, EPHRAIM	CAR	277	7TH DIST
MILLER, EVA	ALL	215	CUMBERLA
MILLER, EVE	WAS	132	2ND DIST
MILLER, EZRA	FRE	084	FREDERIC
MILLER, EZRA	FRE	079	FREDERIC
MILLER, FALTINA	BAL	142	19TH WAR
MILLER, FANNY	BAL	242	20TH WAR
MILLER, FETUS	BAL	171	19TH WAR
MILLER, FRANCES	BAL	023	9TH WARD
MILLER, FRANCIS	BAL	158	2ND DIST
MILLER, FRANCIS	BAL	273	2ND WARD
MILLER, FRANCIS	CEC	009	ELKTON 3
MILLER, FRANCIS	CEC	086	4TH E DI
MILLER, FRANCIS	SOM	523	BARREN C
MILLER, FRANK	BAL	142	1ST WARD
MILLER, FRANK	BAL	154	1ST WARD
MILLER, FRANKLIN	BAL	050	9TH WARD
MILLER, FREDERICK	BAL	268	2ND WARD
MILLER, FREDERICK	BAL	273	2ND WARD
MILLER, FREDERICK	BAL	048	1ST WARD
MILLER, FREDERICK	BAL	182	11TH WAR
MILLER, FREDERICK	BAL	352	7TH WARD
MILLER, FREDERICK	BAL	010	EASTERN
MILLER, FREDERICK	BAL	367	1ST DIST
MILLER, FREDERICK	WAS	122	2ND DIST
MILLER, FREDERICK	WAS	131	HAGERSTO
MILLER, FREDERICK	FRE	401	JEFFERSO
MILLER, FREDERICK D.	FRE	096	FREDERIC
MILLER, FREDERIKC	FRE	143	10TH E D
MILLER, G.	BAL	150	1ST WARD
MILLER, GEORGE	BAL	224	2ND WARD
MILLER, GEORGE	BAL	204	6TH DIST
MILLER, GEORGE	ANN	341	3RD DIST
MILLER, GEORGE	ANN	367	4TH DIST
MILLER, GEORGE	ANN	443	HOWARD D
MILLER, GEORGE	BAL	266	12TH WAR
MILLER, GEORGE	BAL	070	15TH WAR
MILLER, GEORGE	BAL	070	1ST WARD
MILLER, GEORGE	BAL	095	1ST WARD
MILLER, GEORGE	BAL	122	1ST WARD
MILLER, GEORGE	BAL	127	1ST WARD
MILLER, GEORGE	BAL	399	3RD WARD
MILLER, GEORGE	BAL	380	3RD WARD
MILLER, GEORGE	BAL	303	7TH WARD
MILLER, GEORGE	FRE	113	CREAGERS
MILLER, GEORGE	FRE	084	FREDERIC
MILLER, GEORGE	FRE	083	FREDERIC
MILLER, GEORGE	MGM	381	ROCKERLE
MILLER, GEORGE	CAR	242	TANEYTOW
MILLER, GEORGE	BAL	199	19TH WAR
MILLER, GEORGE	CAR	293	7TH DIST
MILLER, GEORGE	BAL	441	14TH WAR
MILLER, GEORGE	WAS	117	2ND DIST
MILLER, GEORGE	PRI	107	PISCATAW
MILLER, GEORGE	WAS	260	1ST DIST
MILLER, GEORGE	WAS	258	1ST DIST
MILLER, GEORGE C.	BAL	034	4TH WARD
MILLER, GEORGE F.	CAR	203	4TH DIST
MILLER, GEORGE H.	BAL	048	18TH WAR
MILLER, GEORGE H.	WAS	004	WILLIAMS
MILLER, GEORGE M.	BAL	361	13TH WAR
MILLER, GEORGE M.	BAL	039	9TH WARD
MILLER, GEORGE N.	ANN	419	HOWARD D
MILLER, GEORGE W.	BAL	139	1ST WARD
MILLER, GEORGE W.	BAL	120	1ST WARD
MILLER, GEORGE W.	CAR	202	4TH DIST
MILLER, GOEBIT	BAL	030	1ST WARD
MILLER, H.	BAL	139	1ST WARD
MILLER, HANNAH	CEC	029	CHESAPEA
MILLER, HANNAH	HAR	033	1ST DIST
MILLER, HANNAH	FRE	173	5TH E DI
MILLER, HANNAH	KEN	242	2ND DIST
MILLER, HARMAN	BAL	142	19TH WAR
MILLER, HARRIET	ANN	462	HOWARD D
MILLER, HARRIET	BAL	115	15TH WAR
MILLER, HARRIET-BLACK	CAR	155	NO TWP L
MILLER, HARRIETT	BAL	211	11TH WAR
MILLER, HARRISON	FRE	101	FREDERIC
MILLER, HARRISON	BAL	457	8TH WARD
MILLER, HENRY	BAL	456	8TH WARD
MILLER, HENRY	BAL	343	7TH WARD
MILLER, HENRY	BAL	166	16TH WAR
MILLER, HENRY	BAL	082	10TH WAR
MILLER, HENRY	ANN	344	3RD DIST
MILLER, HENRY	BAL	082	2ND DIST
MILLER, HENRY	ALL	230	CUMBERLA
MILLER, HENRY	BAL	240	2ND WARD
MILLER, HENRY	BAL	387	3RD WARD
MILLER, HENRY	BAL	134	1ST WARD
MILLER, HENRY	BAL	265	2ND WARD
MILLER, HENRY	BAL	268	2ND WARD
MILLER, HENRY	BAL	283	7TH WARD
MILLER, HENRY	BAL	276	2ND WARD
MILLER, HENRY	BAL	051	1ST WARD
MILLER, HENRY	BAL	176	2ND WARD
MILLER, HENRY	BAL	155	5TH WARD
MILLER, HENRY	BAL	238	6TH WARD
MILLER, HENRY	BAL	331	1ST DIST
MILLER, HENRY	BAL	364	1ST DIST
MILLER, HENRY	BAL	371	1ST DIST
MILLER, HENRY	BAL	460	1ST DIST
MILLER, HENRY	BAL	459	1ST DIST
MILLER, HENRY	BAL	297	3RD WARD
MILLER, HENRY	ALL	117	5TH E.D.
MILLER, HENRY	ALL	019	2ND E.D.
MILLER, HENRY	BAL	309	1ST DIST
MILLER, HENRY	BAL	322	1ST DIST
MILLER, HENRY	ALL	145	6TH E.D.
MILLER, HENRY	ALL	146	6TH E.D.
MILLER, HENRY	FRE	121	CREAGERS
MILLER, HENRY	FRE	143	10TH E D
MILLER, HENRY	CAR	179	8TH DIST
MILLER, HENRY	CAR	187	4TH DIST
MILLER, HENRY	CAR	296	7TH DIST
MILLER, HENRY	BAL	064	4TH WARD
MILLER, HENRY	BAL	205	17TH WAR
MILLER, HENRY	CEC	178	7TH E DI
MILLER, HENRY	BAL	282	17TH WAR
MILLER, HENRY	WAS	287	1ST DIST
MILLER, HENRY	WAS	294	1ST DIST
MILLER, HENRY	WAS	201	1ST DIST
MILLER, HENRY	WAS	253	1ST DIST
MILLER, HENRY	QUE	207	3RD E DI
MILLER, HENRY F.	WAS	180	BOONSBOR
MILLER, HENRY H.	CAR	335	6TH DIST
MILLER, HENRY J.	BAL	368	13TH WAR
MILLER, HENRY P.	ALL	136	4TH E.D.
MILLER, HERMAN	BAL	274	7TH WARD
MILLER, HERNY	BAL	416	1ST DIST
MILLER, HERNY	CAR	335	6TH DIST
MILLER, HESTER	WOR	286	BERLIN 1
MILLER, HESTOR	BAL	115	5TH WARD
MILLER, HORACE	KEN	220	2ND DIST
MILLER, ISAAC	CAR	257	3RD DIST
MILLER, ISAAC	BAL	148	1ST WARD
MILLER, ISAAC	BAL	457	8TH WARD
MILLER, ISAAC	SOM	516	BARREN C
MILLER, ISAAC-BLACK	CAR	085	NO TWP L
MILLER, ISABELLA	WAS	219	1ST DIST
MILLER, ISABELLA	BAL	271	2ND WARD
MILLER, ISRAEL	ALL	123	4TH E.D.
MILLER, ISREAL	FRE	431	8TH E DI
MILLER, J.	BAL	153	1ST WARD
MILLER, J. A.	WAS	093	2ND SUBD
MILLER, J. F.	BAL	333	1ST DIST
MILLER, J. F.	BAL	108	10TH WAR
MILLER, J.W.	ALL	011	3RD E.D.
MILLER, JACOB	ALL	130	4TH E.D.
MILLER, JACOB	ALL	022	2ND E.D.
MILLER, JACOB	BAL	085	10TH WAR
MILLER, JACOB	BAL	089	10TH WAR
MILLER, JACOB	BAL	276	12TH WAR
MILLER, JACOB	BAL	318	3RD WARD
MILLER, JACOB	BAL	160	1ST WARD
MILLER, JACOB	BAL	423	8TH WARD
MILLER, JACOB	BAL	390	3RD WARD
MILLER, JACOB	BAL	139	1ST WARD
MILLER, JACOB	BAL	208	11TH WAR
MILLER, JACOB	BAL	445	8TH WARD
MILLER, JACOB	BAL	433	8TH WARD
MILLER, JACOB	BAL	043	1ST WARD
MILLER, JACOB	BAL	085	1ST WARD
MILLER, JACOB	BAL	167	2ND DIST
MILLER, JACOB	ANN	438	HOWARD D
MILLER, JACOB	WAS	075	2ND SUBD
MILLER, JACOB	WAS	287	1ST DIST
MILLER, JACOB	WAS	296	1ST DIST
MILLER, JACOB	WAS	274	RIDGEVIL
MILLER, JACOB	WAS	023	2ND SUBD
MILLER, JACOB	WAS	043	2ND SUBD
MILLER, JACOB	WAS	256	1ST DIST
MILLER, JACOB	WAS	203	1ST DIST
MILLER, JACOB	WAS	163	2ND DIST
MILLER, JACOB	WAS	132	2ND DIST
MILLER, JACOB	TAL	088	ST MICHA
MILLER, JACOB	BAL	448	14TH WAR
MILLER, JACOB	BAL	465	14TH WAR
MILLER, JACOB	CAR	286	7TH DIST
MILLER, JACOB	CAR	275	7TH DIST
MILLER, JACOB	BAL	060	18TH WAR
MILLER, JACOB	BAL	065	18TH WAR
MILLER, JACOB	FRE	121	CREAGERS
MILLER, JACOB	FRE	120	CREAGERS
MILLER, JACOB	MGM	339	CLARKSBU
MILLER, JACOB	FRE	193	5TH E DI
MILLER, JACOB C.	ALL	101	5TH E.D.
MILLER, JACOB D.	FRE	350	MIDDLETO
MILLER, JACOB F.	FRE	144	10TH E D
MILLER, JACOB F.	BAL	133	1ST WARD
MILLER, JACOB F.	WAS	059	2ND SUBD
MILLER, JACOB H.	FRE	313	MIDDLETO
MILLER, JACOB N.	CAR	330	MANCHEST
MILLER, JACOB P.	BAL	192	11TH WAR
MILLER, JAMES	BAL	459	8TH WARD
MILLER, JAMES	BAL	223	12TH WAR
MILLER, JAMES	BAL	222	12TH WAR
MILLER, JAMES	BAL	141	1ST WARD
MILLER, JAMES	BAL	273	7TH WARD
MILLER, JAMES	ALL	122	4TH E.D.
MILLER, JAMES	ANN	276	ANNAPOLI
MILLER, JAMES	BAL	241	1ST DIST
MILLER, JAMES	BAL	023	1ST WARD
MILLER, JAMES	BAL	028	9TH WARD
MILLER, JAMES	BAL	316	7TH WARD
MILLER, JAMES	BAL	154	16TH WAR
MILLER, JAMES	BAL	473	14TH WAR
MILLER, JAMES	BAL	242	20TH WAR
MILLER, JAMES	HAR	067	1ST DIST
MILLER, JAMES	SOM	416	DUBLIN D
MILLER, JAMES D.	QUE	192	3RD E DI
MILLER, JAMES E.	BAL	302	17TH WAR
MILLER, JAMES H.	HAR	080	2ND DIST
MILLER, JAMES H.	BAL	106	15TH WAR
MILLER, JAMES H. DR.	BAL	339	13TH WAR
MILLER, JAMES M.	ANN	458	HOWARD D
MILLER, JAMES T.	HAR	138	2ND DIST
MILLER, JAMES W.	BAL	387	8TH WARD
MILLER, JANE	BAL	286	12TH WAR
MILLER, JANE	BAL	411	1ST DIST
MILLER, JANE	CAR	303	1ST DIST
MILLER, JANE	TAL	092	ST MICHA
MILLER, JANE A.	FRE	336	MIDDLETO
MILLER, JANEA	HAR	124	2ND DIST
MILLER, JAOCB	CAR	179	8TH DIST
MILLER, JAOCB	BAL	353	13TH WAR
MILLER, JAOCB	CAR	335	6TH DIST
MILLER, JAOCB	ALL	247	CUMBERLA
MILLER, JEREMIAH	BAL	282	7TH WARD
MILLER, JEREMIAH	ALL	123	4TH E.D.
MILLER, JEREMIAH	WAS	249	1ST DIST
MILLER, JESSE	BAL	411	1ST DIST
MILLER, JESSE	HAR	125	2ND DIST
MILLER, JINNEY	WOR	244	1ST CENS
MILLER, JOB	FRE	389	PETERSVI
MILLER, JOHANA	WAS	112	2ND DIST
MILLER, JOHN	WAS	110	2ND DIST
MILLER, JOHN	WAS	092	2ND SUBD
MILLER, JOHN	WAS	033	2ND SUBD
MILLER, JOHN	WAS	036	2ND SUBD
MILLER, JOHN	TAL	103	ST MICHA
MILLER, JOHN	TAL	115	ST MICHA
MILLER, JOHN	WAS	217	1ST DIST
MILLER, JOHN	WAS	210	1ST DIST
MILLER, JOHN	WAS	203	1ST DIST
MILLER, JOHN	TAL	083	ST MICHA
MILLER, JOHN	WAS	147	2ND DIST
MILLER, JOHN	WAS	163	HAGERSTO
MILLER, JOHN	WAS	132	HAGERSTO
MILLER, JOHN	WAS	153	HAGERSTO
MILLER, JOHN	FRE	411	8TH E DI
MILLER, JOHN	FRE	439	8TH E DI
MILLER, JOHN	BAL	286	20TH WAR
MILLER, JOHN	FRE	168	EMMITTSB
MILLER, JOHN	FRE	144	10TH E D
MILLER, JOHN	FRE	196	5TH E DI
MILLER, JOHN	FRE	122	CREAGERS
MILLER, JOHN	FRE	120	CREAGERS
MILLER, JOHN	KEN	229	2ND DIST
MILLER, JOHN	HAR	171	3RD DIST
MILLER, JOHN	CAR	338	6TH DIST
MILLER, JOHN	CAR	326	1ST DIST
MILLER, JOHN	BAL	064	18TH WAR
MILLER, JOHN	CAR	272	WESTMINS
MILLER, JOHN	CEC	110	4TH E DI
MILLER, JOHN	CEC	091	4TH E DI
MILLER, JOHN	BAL	252	17TH WAR
MILLER, JOHN	CEC	174	6TH E DI
MILLER, JOHN	CEC	172	6TH E DI
MILLER, JOHN	BAL	220	17TH WAR
MILLER, JOHN	BAL	384	13TH WAR
MILLER, JOHN	BAL	422	14TH WAR
MILLER, JOHN	BAL	422	14TH WAR
MILLER, JOHN	FRE	363	CATOCTIN
MILLER, JOHN	FRE	345	MIDDLETO
MILLER, JOHN	FRE	339	MIDDLETO
MILLER, JOHN	FRE	354	MIDDLETO
MILLER, JOHN	FRE	287	WOODSBOR
MILLER, JOHN	FRE	301	WOODSBOR
MILLER, JOHN	BAL	121	18TH WAR
MILLER, JOHN	BAL	109	18TH WAR
MILLER, JOHN	FRE	256	NEW MARK
MILLER, JOHN	HAR	071	1ST DIST
MILLER, JOHN	FRE	091	FREDERIC
MILLER, JOHN	BAL	445	14TH WAR
MILLER, JOHN	BAL	115	11TH WAR
MILLER, JOHN	BAL	435	1ST DIST
MILLER, JOHN	BAL	211	6TH DIST
MILLER, JOHN	ALL	122	4TH E.D.
MILLER, JOHN	ALL	122	4TH E.D.
MILLER, JOHN	ANN	288	ANNAPOLI
MILLER, JOHN	ALL	037	2ND E.D.
MILLER, JOHN	ALL	037	2ND E.D.
MILLER, JOHN	ALL	022	2ND E.D.
MILLER, JOHN	ALL	023	2ND E.D.
MILLER, JOHN	BAL	143	1ST WARD
MILLER, JOHN	BAL	129	1ST WARD
MILLER, JOHN	BAL	425	8TH WARD
MILLER, JOHN	BAL	261	2ND WARD
MILLER, JOHN	BAL	241	2ND WARD
MILLER, JOHN	BAL	274	2ND WARD
MILLER, JOHN	ALL	247	CUMBERLA
MILLER, JOHN	ANN	367	4TH DIST
MILLER, JOHN	BAL	060	2ND DIST
MILLER, JOHN	BAL	081	10TH WAR
MILLER, JOHN	BAL	143	5TH WARD
MILLER, JOHN	BAL	200	2ND WARD
MILLER, JOHN	BAL	265	1ST DIST
MILLER, JOHN	BAL	162	2ND DIST
MILLER, JOHN	BAL	084	1ST WARD
MILLER, JOHN	BAL	121	1ST WARD
MILLER, JOHN	BAL	115	1ST WARD
MILLER, JOHN	BAL	354	3RD WARD
MILLER, JOHN	BAL	002	1ST WARD
MILLER, JOHN	BAL	184	5TH DIST
MILLER, JOHN	BAL	072	15TH WAR
MILLER, JOHN	BAL	452	8TH WARD
MILLER, JOHN	BAL	003	9TH WARD
MILLER, JOHN	BAL	452	8TH WARD
MILLER, JOHN	BAL	031	15TH WAR
MILLER, JOHN	BAL	033	15TH WAR
MILLER, JOHN A.	BAL	195	5TH DIST
MILLER, JOHN A.	ALL	061	10TH E.D
MILLER, JOHN A.	KEN	230	2ND DIST
MILLER, JOHN A.	FRE	196	5TH E DI
MILLER, JOHN A.	WAS	107	2ND DIST
MILLER, JOHN B.	CAR	291	7TH DIST
MILLER, JOHN C.	WAS	281	1ST DIST
MILLER, JOHN C.	ANN	438	HOWARD D
MILLER, JOHN CROWN	BAL	074	2ND DIST
MILLER, JOHN D.	BAL	187	19TH WAR
MILLER, JOHN F.	BAL	106	18TH WAR
MILLER, JOHN F.	FRE	005	FREDERIC
MILLER, JOHN G.	WAS	195	1ST DIST
MILLER, JOHN H.	WAS	293	1ST DIST
MILLER, JOHN H.	FRE	383	PETERSVI
MILLER, JOHN H.	CAR	292	7TH DIST
MILLER, JOHN H.	ALL	034	2ND E.D.
MILLER, JOHN H.	BAL	236	6TH WARD
MILLER, JOHN H.	BAL	304	12TH WAR
MILLER, JOHN J.	WAS	131	2ND DIST
MILLER, JOHN JR.	WAS	019	2ND SUBD

Name	County	Page	Locality
MILLER, JOHN JR.	CAR	293	7TH DIST
MILLER, JOHN P.	FRE	120	CREAGERS
MILLER, JOHN P.	FRE	119	CREAGERS
MILLER, JOHN P.	ALL	037	2ND E.D.
MILLER, JOHN Q.	FRE	382	PETERSVI
MILLER, JOHN R.	MGM	378	ROCKERLE
MILLER, JOHN R.	BAL	053	2ND DIST
MILLER, JOHN SR.	CAR	293	7TH DIST
MILLER, JOHN SR.	WAS	019	2ND SUBD
MILLER, JOHN T.	WAS	015	2ND SUBD
MILLER, JOHN W.	WAS	023	2ND SUBD
MILLER, JOHN W.	WAS	110	2ND DIST
MILLER, JOHN W.	FRE	057	FREDERIC
MILLER, JOHN W.	FRE	283	WOODSBOR
MILLER, JOHN W.	CEC	104	4TH E DI
MILLER, JONATHAN	ANN	505	HOWARD D
MILLER, JONOTHAN	WAS	192	1ST DIST
MILLER, JOSEPH	WAS	134	2ND DIST
MILLER, JOSEPH	WAS	279	LEITERSB
MILLER, JOSEPH	ANN	416	HOWARD D
MILLER, JOSEPH	BAL	286	12TH WAR
MILLER, JOSEPH	BAL	231	6TH WARD
MILLER, JOSEPH	BAL	125	1ST WARD
MILLER, JOSEPH	BAL	172	11TH WAR
MILLER, JOSEPH	CEC	091	4TH E DI
MILLER, JOSEPH	BAL	005	18TH WAR
MILLER, JOSEPH	HAR	073	1ST DIST.
MILLER, JOSEPH	HAR	006	1ST DIST
MILLER, JOSEPH	CEC	017	ELKTON 3
MILLER, JOSEPH	KEN	240	2ND DIST
MILLER, JOSEPH	BAL	452	14TH WAR
MILLER, JOSEPH	BAL	234	17TH WAR
MILLER, JOSEPH H.	WOR	244	1ST CENS
MILLER, JOSEPHINE	BAL	148	5TH WARD
MILLER, JOSHUA	BAL	399	1ST DIST
MILLER, JOSHUA H.	BAL	060	4TH WARD
MILLER, JOSIAH	BAL	244	6TH WARD
MILLER, JULIA A.	CAR	379	2ND DIST
MILLER, JULIAN	FRE	022	FREDERIC
MILLER, JULIANN-BLACK	QUE	179	2ND E DI
MILLER, KELLY	BAL	252	20TH WAR
MILLER, LATITIA	BAL	189	19TH WAR
MILLER, LAURA J.	BAL	116	15TH WAR
MILLER, LAURENCE	BAL	249	2ND WARD
MILLER, LAWRENCE	BAL	199	17TH WAR
MILLER, LAWRENCE	CEC	038	CHESAPEA
MILLER, LAWRENCE	CAR	348	6TH DIST
MILLER, LAYFAYETTE	WAS	065	2ND SUBD
MILLER, LEAH	DOR	383	1ST DIST
MILLER, LEONARD	FRE	313	MIDDLETO
MILLER, LEVIN	SOM	421	PRINCESS
MILLER, LEVIN	SOM	416	DUBLIN D
MILLER, LEVINIA	BAL	096	5TH WARD
MILLER, LEWIS	BAL	309	12TH WAR
MILLER, LEWIS	BAL	194	11TH WAR
MILLER, LEWIS	ALL	259	CUMBERLA
MILLER, LEWIS	FRE	067	FREDERIC
MILLER, LEWIS	CAR	337	6TH DIST
MILLER, LEWIS	CAR	293	7TH DIST
MILLER, LEWIS	BAL	246	20TH WAR
MILLER, LEWIS	HAR	184	3RD DIST
MILLER, LOUISA	HAR	157	3RD DIST
MILLER, LOUISA	BAL	285	20TH WAR
MILLER, LOUISA	BAL	147	19TH WAR
MILLER, LOUISA	BAL	119	11TH WAR
MILLER, LOUISA A.	BAL	315	1ST DIST
MILLER, LUCINDA	BAL	423	1ST DIST
MILLER, LUCRETIA	PRI	023	VANSVILL
MILLER, LUCY	BAL	277	12TH WAR
MILLER, LUDWIG	BAL	118	15TH WAR
MILLER, LYCURGUS	FRE	125	CREAGERS
MILLER, LYDIA	CEC	122	4TH E DI
MILLER, LYDIA	ANN	345	3RD DIST
MILLER, M.H.	WAS	144	HAGERSTO
MILLER, MAHLON	FRE	344	MIDDLETO
MILLER, MALINDA	BAL	395	1ST DIST
MILLER, MARGARET	BAL	318	3RD WARD
MILLER, MARGARET	ANN	436	HOWARD D
MILLER, MARGARET	BAL	167	16TH WAR
MILLER, MARGARET	BAL	263	2ND WARD
MILLER, MARGARET	BAL	249	6TH WARD
MILLER, MARGARET	BAL	370	8TH WARD
MILLER, MARGARET	BAL	291	7TH WARD
MILLER, MARGARET	BAL	044	9TH WARD
MILLER, MARGARET	BAL	201	6TH WARD
MILLER, MARGARET	BAL	076	1ST WARD
MILLER, MARGARET	BAL	082	1ST WARD
MILLER, MARGARET	CAR	240	TANEYTOW
MILLER, MARGARET	BAL	257	20TH WAR
MILLER, MARGARET	FRE	032	FREDERIC
MILLER, MARGARET	TAL	003	EASTON D
MILLER, MARGARET	WAS	024	2ND SUBD
MILLER, MARGARET	WAS	205	1ST DIST
MILLER, MARGARET A.	TAL	051	EASTON D
MILLER, MARGARET A.	KEN	215	2ND DIST
MILLER, MARGARET A.	CAR	272	WESTMINS
MILLER, MARGARET E.	FRE	060	FREDERIC
MILLER, MARGARET P.	BAL	002	18TH WAR
MILLER, MARGARETT	BAL	093	18TH WAR
MILLER, MARGARETT	BAL	463	1ST DIST
MILLER, MARGRET	BAL	184	2ND WARD
MILLER, MARGRET	BAL	183	2ND WARD
MILLER, MARIA	BAL	018	2ND DIST
MILLER, MARIA	BAL	357	13TH WAR
MILLER, MARION	KEN	243	2ND DIST
MILLER, MARK	CAR	230	5TH DIST
MILLER, MARRION	FRE	041	FREDERIC
MILLER, MARRY	WAS	067	2ND SUBD
MILLER, MARTHA	BAL	040	4TH WARD
MILLER, MARTHA M.	BAL	367	3RD WARD
MILLER, MARTIN	BAL	189	17TH WAR
MILLER, MARTIN	BAL	312	20TH WAR
MILLER, MARTIN	FRE	095	FREDERIC
MILLER, MARTIN	BAL	417	14TH WAR
MILLER, MARTIN	FRE	266	NEW MARK
MILLER, MARTIN	WAS	266	1ST DIST
MILLER, MARY	WAS	102	2ND DIST
MILLER, MARY	WAS	107	2ND DIST
MILLER, MARY	WAS	114	2ND DIST
MILLER, MARY	WAS	169	FUNKSTOW
MILLER, MARY	WAS	120	2ND DIST
MILLER, MARY	BAL	355	13TH WAR
MILLER, MARY	BAL	346	13TH WAR
MILLER, MARY	CEC	170	6TH E DI
MILLER, MARY	FRE	059	FREDERIC
MILLER, MARY	FRE	344	MIDDLETO
MILLER, MARY	BAL	189	19TH WAR
MILLER, MARY	FRE	133	CREAGERS
MILLER, MARY	FRE	145	10TH E D
MILLER, MARY	CAL	001	1ST DIST
MILLER, MARY	BAL	094	10TH WAR
MILLER, MARY	BAL	164	2ND DIST
MILLER, MARY	BAL	250	1ST DIST
MILLER, MARY	BAL	232	6TH WARD
MILLER, MARY	BAL	195	2ND WARD
MILLER, MARY	BAL	459	1ST DIST
MILLER, MARY	BAL	367	1ST DIST
MILLER, MARY	BAL	100	5TH WARD
MILLER, MARY	BAL	400	8TH WARD
MILLER, MARY	ALL	079	5TH E.D.
MILLER, MARY	BAL	453	8TH WARD
MILLER, MARY A.	BAL	417	8TH WARD
MILLER, MARY A.	BAL	121	5TH WARD
MILLER, MARY A.	BAL	159	6TH WARD
MILLER, MARY A.	BAL	179	16TH WAR
MILLER, MARY A.	FRE	090	FREDERIC
MILLER, MARY A.	PRI	022	VANSVILL
MILLER, MARY ANN	PRI	106	PISCATAW
MILLER, MARY D.	BAL	116	15TH WAR
MILLER, MARY E.	CAR	203	4TH DIST
MILLER, MARY F.	BAL	047	1ST WARD
MILLER, MARYANN	BAL	386	3RD WARD
MILLER, MATHEW	CAR	360	9TH DIST
MILLER, MATILDA	WAS	156	HAGERSTO
MILLER, MATILCA R.	FRE	087	FREDERIC
MILLER, MATTHEW	WAS	164	HAGERSTO
MILLER, MATTHEW	BAL	252	6TH WARD
MILLER, MELTON H.	FRE	101	FREDERIC
MILLER, MELVINA	BAL	353	7TH WARD
MILLER, MERRITT	KEN	235	2ND DIST
MILLER, METILDA	BAL	128	11TH WAR
MILLER, MICHAEL	BAL	216	19TH WAR
MILLER, MICHAEL	BAL	079	4TH WARD
MILLER, MICHAEL	FRE	210	BUCKEYST
MILLER, MICHAEL	BAL	197	11TH WAR
MILLER, MICHAEL	BAL	040	15TH WAR
MILLER, MICHAEL	BAL	280	2ND WARD
MILLER, MICHAEL	WAS	024	2ND SUBD
MILLER, MICHAEL M.	KEN	218	2ND DIST
MILLER, MICHAL	WAS	109	2ND DIST
MILLER, MILTON A.	CAR	266	WESTMINS
MILLER, MOSES	BAL	091	2ND DIST
MILLER, MRS.	BAL	128	5TH WARD
MILLER, N.	BAL	144	1ST WARD
MILLER, NANCY	ALL	204	CUMBERLA
MILLER, NANCY	CEC	115	3RD E DI
MILLER, NANCY	FRE	120	CREAGERS
MILLER, NANCY	WAS	265	1ST DIST
MILLER, NANCY	WAS	225	1ST DIST
MILLER, NATHANIEL C.	SOM	422	PRINCESS
MILLER, NICHOLAS	CAR	348	6TH DIST
MILLER, NICHOLAS	ANN	366	4TH DIST
MILLER, NICHOLAS	BAL	009	15TH WAR
MILLER, NICHOLINA	BAL	077	4TH WARD
MILLER, NOAH	FRE	112	CREAGERS
MILLER, O.	BAL	135	1ST WARD
MILLER, OLIVER	ANN	292	ANNAPOLI
MILLER, OLIVER	BAL	093	18TH WAR
MILLER, OLIVER	WAS	153	HAGERSTO
MILLER, OLIVIA	BAL	112	18TH WAR
MILLER, ORBERT	ANN	349	3RD DIST
MILLER, ORPHY	BAL	357	1ST DIST
MILLER, OTHO	WAS	125	2ND DIST
MILLER, PETER	WAS	118	2ND DIST
MILLER, PETER	WAS	057	2ND SUBD
MILLER, PETER	WAS	092	2ND SUBD
MILLER, PETER	PRI	103	SPALDING
MILLER, PETER	ANN	520	HOWARD D
MILLER, PETER	ANN	324	2ND DIST
MILLER, PETER	BAL	433	14TH WAR
MILLER, PETER	FRE	065	FREDERIC
MILLER, PETER	CAR	186	8TH DIST
MILLER, PHILIP	ALL	118	5TH E.D.
MILLER, PHILIP	ALL	150	6TH E.D.
MILLER, PHILIP	BAL	145	1ST WARD
MILLER, PHILIF H.	CAR	287	7TH DIST
MILLER, PHILLIP	BAL	233	17TH WAR
MILLER, POLLY	FRE	196	5TH E DI
MILLER, POLLY	ALL	112	5TH E.D.
MILLER, POLLY	BAL	370	1ST DIST
MILLER, POLLY	WAS	156	HAGERSTO
MILLER, POMPEY	ANN	356	3RD DIST
MILLER, QANN	BAL	359	1ST DIST
MILLER, R. M.	BAL	289	20TH WAR
MILLER, RACHEL	CEC	115	3RD E DI
MILLER, RACHEL	CEC	056	1ST E DI
MILLER, REBECA	WAS	116	2ND DIST
MILLER, REBECCA	WAS	110	2ND DIST
MILLER, REBECCA	BAL	424	3RD WARD
MILLER, REBECCA	BAL	316	3RD WARD
MILLER, REBECCA	BAL	077	15TH WAR
MILLER, REBECCA A.	BAL	104	15TH WAR
MILLER, RICHARD	BAL	318	1ST DIST
MILLER, RICHARD	BAL	145	1ST WARD
MILLER, RICHARD	BAL	421	8TH WARD
MILLER, RICHARD	BAL	174	1ST WARD
MILLER, RICHARD	BAL	063	1ST WARD
MILLER, RICHARD	BAL	297	20TH WAR
MILLER, RICHARD	HAR	123	2ND DIST
MILLER, ROBERT	BAL	078	4TH WARD
MILLER, ROBERT	BAL	186	5TH DIST
MILLER, ROBERT	BAL	161	1ST WARD
MILLER, ROBERT	BAL	266	2ND WARD
MILLER, ROBERT	BAL	150	16TH WAR
MILLER, ROBERT	BAL	153	16TH WAR
MILLER, ROBERT	BAL	095	5TH WARD
MILLER, ROBERT	WOR	257	1ST CENS
MILLER, ROBERT J.	BAL	120	1ST WARD
MILLER, ROBET	BAL	059	2ND DIST
MILLER, ROSA	BAL	134	16TH WAR
MILLER, ROSA*	BAL	014	4TH WARD
MILLER, ROSE	BAL	210	17TH WAR
MILLER, ROSE ANN	BAL	290	17TH WAR
MILLER, ROSE B.	PRI	106	PISCATAW
MILLER, ROSEANNA	CEC	005	ELKTON 3
MILLER, ROSINA	BAL	276	7TH WARD
MILLER, RUDOLPH	BAL	047	1ST WARD
MILLER, RUHANAH D.	WAS	100	2ND DIST
MILLER, SALLY	QUE	242	5TH E DI
MILLER, SAMUEL	WAS	192	1ST DIST
MILLER, SAMUEL	WAS	101	2ND DIST
MILLER, SAMUEL	WAS	022	2ND SUBD
MILLER, SAMUEL	WAS	249	1ST DIST
MILLER, SAMUEL	BAL	043	2ND DIST
MILLER, SAMUEL	BAL	185	11TH WAR
MILLER, SAMUEL	ALL	132	4TH E.D.
MILLER, SAMUEL	ALL	117	5TH E.D.
MILLER, SAMUEL	CAR	294	7TH DIST
MILLER, SAMUEL	CEC	108	3RD E DI
MILLER, SAMUEL	CEC	107	3RD E DI
MILLER, SAMUEL	CAR	344	6TH DIST
MILLER, SAMUEL	CEC	174	6TH E DI
MILLER, SAMUEL	HAR	167	3RD DIST
MILLER, SAMUEL B.	ALL	115	5TH E.D.
MILLER, SAMUEL-BLACK	CAR	084	NO TWP L
MILLER, SAMUJEL	FRE	120	CREAGERS
MILLER, SARAH	KEN	243	2ND DIST
MILLER, SARAH	ALL	121	4TH E.D.
MILLER, SARAH	ALL	091	5TH E.D.
MILLER, SARAH	BAL	462	1ST DIST
MILLER, SARAH	BAL	435	1ST DIST
MILLER, SARAH	WAS	226	1ST DIST
MILLER, SARAH	PRI	020	VANSVILL
MILLER, SARAH A.	WAS	112	2ND DIST
MILLER, SARAH ANN	BAL	475	14TH WAR
MILLER, SARAH E.	BAL	049	1ST WARD
MILLER, SARAH E.	BAL	205	6TH WARD
MILLER, SARHA	BAL	434	8TH WARD
MILLER, SEBASTIAN	BAL	146	2ND DIST
MILLER, SIDNEY	HAR	160	3RD DIST
MILLER, SIMON	FRE	334	MIDDLETO
MILLER, SOPHIA	CAR	335	6TH DIST
MILLER, SOPHIA	WAS	270	1ST DIST
MILLER, SOPHIA	WAS	137	HAGERSTO
MILLER, SOPHIA	TAL	117	ST MICHA
MILLER, STEPHEN	CEC	100	3RD E DI
MILLER, STEPHEN	BAL	039	2ND DIST
MILLER, STEPHEN	ANN	344	3RD DIST
MILLER, STEPHEN	ALL	192	9TH E.D.
MILLER, SUSAN	HAR	124	2ND DIST
MILLER, SUSAN	BAL	217	19TH WAR
MILLER, SUSAN	WAS	150	HAGERSTO
MILLER, SUSAN	WAS	191	1ST DIST
MILLER, SUSAN	WAS	283	1ST DIST
MILLER, SUSAN	WAS	210	1ST DIST
MILLER, SUSANA	FRE	101	FREDERIC
MILLER, THEODORE	BAL	224	17TH WAR
MILLER, THEODORE	BAL	296	1ST DIST
MILLER, THOMAS	ANN	345	3RD DIST
MILLER, THOMAS	BAL	031	2ND DIST
MILLER, THOMAS	BAL	239	6TH WARD
MILLER, THOMAS	BAL	030	9TH WARD
MILLER, THOMAS	BAL	434	1ST DIST
MILLER, THOMAS	BAL	316	3RD WARD
MILLER, THOMAS	ANN	499	HOWARD D
MILLER, THOMAS	BAL	235	17TH WAR
MILLER, THOMAS	HAR	164	3RD DIST
MILLER, THOMAS	CAR	203	4TH DIST
MILLER, THOMAS	CEC	115	3RD E DI
MILLER, THOMAS	TAL	103	ST MICHA
MILLER, THOMAS A.	FRE	287	WOODSBOR
MILLER, THOMAS B.	HAR	131	2ND DIST
MILLER, THOMAS C.	MGM	337	CRACKLIN
MILLER, THOMAS D.	BAL	339	13TH WAR
MILLER, TOBIAS	WAS	169	FUNKSTOW
MILLER, TOBIAS G.	BAL	293	1ST DIST
MILLER, UPTON	WAS	203	1ST DIST
MILLER, V.	WAS	022	2ND SUBD
MILLER, VALENTINE	WAS	157	2ND DIST
MILLER, VALENTINE	BAL	043	2ND DIST
MILLER, VICTORIA	CEC	039	CHESAPEA
MILLER, VINCENT-BLACK	CAR	101	NO TWP L
MILLER, VIRGINIA	HAR	067	1ST DIST
MILLER, W.H.	BAL	169	1ST WARD
MILLER, WESLEY	HAR	124	2ND DIST
MILLER, WILLIAM	HAR	165	3RD DIST
MILLER, WILLIAM	FRE	091	FREDERIC
MILLER, WILLIAM	CAR	166	NO TWP L
MILLER, WILLIAM	CEC	167	6TH E DI
MILLER, WILLIAM	BAL	078	4TH WARD
MILLER, WILLIAM	BAL	128	18TH WAR
MILLER, WILLIAM	CEC	115	3RD E DI
MILLER, WILLIAM	CAR	323	1ST DIST
MILLER, WILLIAM	CAR	276	7TH DIST
MILLER, WILLIAM	BAL	193	6TH WARD
MILLER, WILLIAM	BAL	205	6TH WARD
MILLER, WILLIAM	BAL	345	3RD WARD
MILLER, WILLIAM	BAL	323	3RD WARD
MILLER, WILLIAM	ALL	117	5TH E.D.
MILLER, WILLIAM	ALL	117	5TH E.D.
MILLER, WILLIAM	BAL	196	11TH WAR
MILLER, WILLIAM	BAL	257	2ND WARD
MILLER, WILLIAM	BAL	140	1ST WARD
MILLER, WILLIAM	BAL	147	1ST WARD
MILLER, WILLIAM	BAL	128	1ST WARD
MILLER, WILLIAM	BAL	282	2ND WARD
MILLER, WILLIAM	BAL	282	2ND WARD
MILLER, WILLIAM	BAL	407	9TH WARD
MILLER, WILLIAM	BAL	191	17TH WAR
MILLER, WILLIAM	BAL	124	16TH WAR
MILLER, WILLIAM	WAS	188	1ST DIST
MILLER, WILLIAM	WAS	147	HAGERSTO
MILLER, WILLIAM	WAS	065	2ND SUBD
MILLER, WILLIAM	WAS	206	1ST DIST
MILLER, WILLIAM	KEN	292	3RD DIST
MILLER, WILLIAM A.	KEN	287	3RD DIST
MILLER, WILLIAM A.	FRE	196	5TH E DI
MILLER, WILLIAM C.	BAL	475	14TH WAR
MILLER, WILLIAM D.	BAL	387	13TH WAR
MILLER, WILLIAM H.	FRE	121	CREAGERS
MILLER, WILLIAM H.	WAS	180	BOONSBOR
MILLER, WILLIAM H.	WAS	162	2ND DIST
MILLER, WILLIAM H.	QUE	226	4TH E DI
MILLER, WILLIAM H.	ALL	061	10TH E.D
MILLER, WILLIAM H.	BAL	231	6TH WARD
MILLER, WILLIAM H.	BAL	139	5TH WARD
MILLER, WILLIAM I.	BAL	133	1ST WARD
MILLER, WILLIAM JR.	FRE	287	WOODSBOR
MILLER, WILLIAM M.	WAS	082	2ND SUBD
MILLER, WILLIAM P.	BAL	306	1ST DIST
MILLER, WILLIAM SR.	FRE	287	WOODSBOR
MILLER.AMELIA	BAL	079	1ST WARD
MILLER.ENGLETY	BAL	043	1ST WARD
MILLER.GEORGE D.	FRE	015	FREDERIC
MILLER.ISAAC	ALL	035	2ND E.D.
MILLER.JACOB	BAL	019	2ND DIST
MILLER.JAOB	BAL	046	2ND DIST
MILLER.MAHALY-BLACK	CAR	071	NO TWP L
MILLER.MARGARET	BAL	256	2ND WARD
MILLER.NICHOLAS	BAL	210	2ND WARD
MILLER.PETER	BAL	192	2ND WARD
MILLER.PHILLIP	BAL	074	1ST WARD
MILLER.SAMUEL	BAL	052	2ND DIST
MILLER.WILLIAM L.	FRE	207	BUCKEYST
MILLES, CHARLES	BAL	053	9TH WARD
MILLES, LAERTES*	BAL	029	4TH WARD
MILLEW, MARY	BAL	373	8TH WARD
MILLHOLLAND, ALLEN	BAL	118	5TH WARD
MILLHOLLAND, JOHN	BAL	132	1ST WARD
MILLHOLLAND, TERESA	BAL	009	18TH WAR

Name	County	Page	District
MILLHOUE, ELIZABETH	CAR	386	2ND DIST
MILLHOUSE, CATHERINE	ALL	247	CUMBERLA
MILLIACK, WILLIAM	FRE	124	CREAGERS
MILLICHOP, LOUIZA	BAL	116	5TH WARD
MILLICOM, JAMES H.	BAL	263	1ST DIST
MILLIFORD, CATHARINE	ST	334	4TH E DI
MILLIGAN, CATHERINE	BAL	441	8TH WARD
MILLIGAN, DAVID	KEN	260	1ST DIST
MILLIGAN, DELIA	BAL	258	6TH WARD
MILLIGAN, ELI	SOM	352	BRINKLEY
MILLIGAN, ELIZABETH	SOM	352	BRINKLEY
MILLIGAN, ELIZABETH	BAL	311	3RD WARD
MILLIGAN, ELIZABETH	KEN	242	2ND DIST
MILLIGAN, ENNALLS*	DOR	305	1ST DIST
MILLIGAN, GEORGE B.	BAL	059	10TH WAR
MILLIGAN, HENRY	SOM	419	PRINCESS
MILLIGAN, HESTERAN	DOR	298	1ST DIST
MILLIGAN, ISAAC	DOR	298	1ST DIST
MILLIGAN, JAMES	WAS	073	2ND SUBD
MILLIGAN, JAMES H.	DOR	296	1ST DIST
MILLIGAN, JOSEPH	ALL	052	10TH E.D
MILLIGAN, JOSES	BAL	117	15TH WAR
MILLIGAN, JOSIAH	SOM	351	BRINKLEY
MILLIGAN, MARY	KEN	242	2ND DIST
MILLIGAN, MARY A.	BAL	107	18TH WAR
MILLIGAN, MICHAEL	ALL	056	10TH E.D
MILLIGAN, SALLY A.	DOR	299	1ST DIST
MILLIGAN, SAMUEL	CEC	096	4TH E DI
MILLIGAN, SARAH	KEN	219	2ND DIST
MILLIGAN, SOLOMON	DOR	298	1ST DIST
MILLIGAN, STANLY	DOR	297	1ST DIST
MILLIGAN, THOMAS	DOR	301	1ST DIST
MILLIGAN, WESLEY	SOM	419	PRINCESS
MILLIGAN, WHALIN	DOR	297	1ST DIST
MILLIKEN, ELSY	BAL	204	19TH WAR
MILLIKEN, FRANCIS	WAS	159	2ND DIST
MILLIKEN, JAMES H.	BAL	015	4TH WARD
MILLIMAN, GEORGE	BAL	088	4TH WARD
MILLIMAN, MARY A.	BAL	423	8TH WARD
MILLIN, REES	HAR	175	3RD DIST
MILLIN, WILLIAM G.	ANN	453	HOWARD D
MILLING, ROBERT H.	BAL	181	2ND DIST
MILLINGAN, NANCY	KEN	238	2ND DIST
MILLINGEN, SUSAN	WAS	134	HAGERSTO
MILLINGTON, GEORGE T.	CAR	149	NO TWP L
MILLINGTON, JOHN N.	BAL	261	6TH WARD
MILLINGTON, RICHARD	KEN	310	3RD DIST
MILLINIS, MARY	BAL	206	19TH WAR
MILLINIX, BASIL	ANN	373	4TH DIST
MILLIR, PROCTOR*	TAL	040	EASTON D
MILLIS, CATHERINE A.*	TAL	032	EASTON D
MILLIS, GEORGE P.	TAL	071	EASTON T
MILLIS, JAMES H.*	TAL	030	EASTON D
MILLIS, JANE*	DOR	380	1ST DIST
MILLIS, JOHN M.	TAL	084	ST MICHA
MILLIS, JOSEPH G.*	TAL	056	EASTON D
MILLIS, MARGARET*	TAL	010	EASTON D
MILLIS, MARY J.	BAL	154	16TH WAR
MILLIS, SARAH	DOR	387	1ST DIST
MILLIS, THOMAS	TAL	106	ST MICHA
MILLMAN, HENRY	ALL	154	6TH E.D.
MILLOM, EDWARD	QUE	153	1ST E DI
MILLOR, SARAH	BAL	035	9TH WARD
MILLR, JOHN	BAL	142	1ST WARD
MILLRE, HARRIET	BAL	463	14TH WAR
MILLRON, WILIAM	WOR	207	4TH E DI
MILLS, AMANDA	SOM	460	HANGARY
MILLS, AMELIA	WOR	178	6TH E DI
MILLS, ANDREW J.	BAL	088	18TH WAR
MILLS, ANN	DOR	349	3RD DIVI
MILLS, ANN M.	FRE	095	FREDERIC
MILLS, ANN M.	SOM	507	BARREN C
MILLS, ANN R.	BAL	029	18TH WAR
MILLS, ANNA	BAL	378	1ST DIST
MILLS, BENJAMIN	SOM	499	SALISBUR
MILLS, BENJAMIN	SOM	532	QUANTICO
MILLS, BENJAMIN-BLACK	WOR	334	1ST E DI
MILLS, CALVIN	DOR	387	1ST DIST
MILLS, CATHRINE	BAL	071	18TH WAR
MILLS, CHANE	CAL	002	1ST DIST
MILLS, CHARLES	BAL	237	17TH WAR
MILLS, CHARLES	SOM	526	QUANTICO
MILLS, CHARLES	ALL	215	CUMBERLA
MILLS, CHARLES W.	MGM	318	CRACKLIN
MILLS, CHARLOTTE	ST	261	3RD E DI
MILLS, CICELY	ST	283	3RD E DI
MILLS, CLEMENT	SOM	513	BARREN C
MILLS, DANIEL H.	WOR	187	7TH E DI
MILLS, DAVID	WOR	228	6TH E DI
MILLS, EDWARD C.	BAL	330	13TH WAR
MILLS, EDWARD-BLACK	WOR	321	1ST E DI
MILLS, ELIZA	BAL	247	17TH WAR
MILLS, ELIZA A.	CEC	088	4TH E DI
MILLS, ELIZABETH	WAS	116	2ND DIST
MILLS, ELIZABETH	WAS	138	2ND DIST
MILLS, ELIZABETH	WAS	162	HAGERSTO
MILLS, ELIZABETH B.	ST	283	3RD E DI
MILLS, ELIZABETH*	DOR	365	3RD DIVI
MILLS, ELIZBETH B.	ST	284	2ND E DI
MILLS, ELLEN	BAL	127	5TH WARD
MILLS, ELLEN G.	ANN	521	HOWARD D
MILLS, ELMIRA	SOM	522	BARREN C
MILLS, ENOCH G.	CAL	029	2ND DIST
MILLS, EVERT	CAL	018	1ST DIST
MILLS, EZEKIEL	ANN	451	HOWARD D
MILLS, GEORGE	BAL	095	18TH WAR
MILLS, GEORGE	SOM	421	PRINCESS
MILLS, GEORGE	WOR	279	BERLIN 1
MILLS, GEORGE A.	ANN	451	HOWARD D
MILLS, GEORGE E.	FRE	063	FREDERIC
MILLS, GEORGE M.	BAL	430	8TH WARD
MILLS, GEORGE W.	SOM	532	QUANTICO
MILLS, HANDY	WOR	343	1ST E DI
MILLS, HENERY	DOR	327	3RD DIVI
MILLS, HENRY	BAL	308	3RD WARD
MILLS, HENRY	BAL	240	6TH WARD
MILLS, HESTER	DOR	341	3RD DIVI
MILLS, HESTER A.	CEC	179	7TH E DI
MILLS, IMOGENE	BAL	186	2ND WARD
MILLS, ISAAC E.	SOM	518	BARREN C
MILLS, IWLLIAM H.	BAL	071	18TH WAR
MILLS, JACOB	WAS	098	2ND DIST
MILLS, JACOB-BLACK	WOR	345	1ST E DI
MILLS, JAMES	WAS	141	2ND DIST
MILLS, JAMES	WOR	184	6TH E DI
MILLS, JAMES	CAL	023	2ND DIST
MILLS, JAMES	BAL	391	1ST DIST
MILLS, JAMES	BAL	099	1ST WARD
MILLS, JAMES B.	BAL	030	18TH WAR
MILLS, JAMES B.*	DOR	326	3RD DIVI

Name	County	Page	District
MILLS, JAMES F.	WOR	257	1ST CENS
MILLS, JAMES P.	BAL	030	18TH WAR
MILLS, JANE	BAL	200	19TH WAR
MILLS, JEHN	SOM	499	SALISBUR
MILLS, JIM-BLACK	WOR	337	1ST E DI
MILLS, JOB	BAL	068	10TH WAR
MILLS, JOHN	BAL	081	15TH WAR
MILLS, JOHN	BAL	118	1ST WARD
MILLS, JOHN	BAL	114	5TH WARD
MILLS, JOHN	SOM	485	TRAPP DI
MILLS, JOHN	TAL	004	EASTON D
MILLS, JOHN	WOR	305	SNOW HIL
MILLS, JOHN	MGM	317	CRACKLIN
MILLS, JOHN	DOR	392	1ST DIST
MILLS, JOHN	FRE	294	WOODSBOR
MILLS, JOHN	CAL	022	2ND DIST
MILLS, JOHN A.	ANN	275	ANNAPOLI
MILLS, JOHN B.	WOR	343	1ST E DI
MILLS, JOHN C.	FRE	211	BUCKEYST
MILLS, JOHN H.	ST	265	3RD E DI
MILLS, JOHN J.	CAL	003	1ST DIST
MILLS, JOHN L.	BAL	008	18TH WAR
MILLS, JOHN L.	MGM	317	CRACKLIN
MILLS, JOSEPH	CEC	038	CHESAPEA
MILLS, JOSEPH	BAL	098	5TH WARD
MILLS, JOSEPH C.	BAL	320	1ST DIST
MILLS, JOSH	DOR	340	3RD DIVI
MILLS, JOSIAH	SOM	522	BARREN C
MILLS, JOSIAH D.	ALL	214	CUMBERLA
MILLS, JULIANN	BAL	300	7TH WARD
MILLS, LAURA	WOR	185	6TH E DI
MILLS, LEAH	SOM	499	SALISBUR
MILLS, LEMUEL M.	WOR	173	6TH E DI
MILLS, LEOANRD C.	DOR	350	3RD DIVI
MILLS, LEVEN	WOR	325	1ST E DI
MILLS, LEVIN	BAL	179	16TH WAR
MILLS, LEVIN	BAL	343	1ST DIST
MILLS, LEVINA	WAS	150	HAGERSTO
MILLS, LEWIS	WOR	301	SNOW HIL
MILLS, LOUISA	SOM	511	BARREN C
MILLS, LOUISA A.	CEC	155	PORT DUP
MILLS, LYDIA	BAL	042	18TH WAR
MILLS, MALIKE	SOM	410	DUBLIN D
MILLS, MARGARET	BAL	327	13TH WAR
MILLS, MARIA	BAL	144	11TH WAR
MILLS, MARY	WAS	142	2ND DIST
MILLS, MARY	WOR	327	1ST E DI
MILLS, MARY A.	FRE	212	BUCKEYST
MILLS, MARY E.	BAL	160	6TH WARD
MILLS, MARY F.	CAL	023	2ND DIST
MILLS, MARY JEAN	SOM	388	BRINKLEY
MILLS, MARY P.	ST	274	3RD E DI
MILLS, MARY T.	FRE	388	PETERSVI
MILLS, MARY-BLACK	ALL	159	6TH E.D.
MILLS, MELVINA	ANN	266	ANNAPOLI
MILLS, MISS E.	WOR	340	1ST E DI
MILLS, NANCY	SOM	507	BARREN C
MILLS, NICHOLAS	WAS	138	2ND DIST
MILLS, OTHO	BAL	028	1ST WARD
MILLS, PENELOPE	DOR	426	1ST DIST
MILLS, POLISH	ST	254	3RD E DI
MILLS, R. M.	BAL	257	20TH WAR
MILLS, REBECCA	BAL	319	3RD WARD
MILLS, RICHARD	DOR	343	3RD DIVI
MILLS, RIGHTSON	SOM	506	BARREN C
MILLS, RINALDO	WAS	122	2ND DIST
MILLS, ROBERT	WAS	123	2ND DIST
MILLS, ROBERT	WOR	302	SNOW HIL
MILLS, ROBERT	BAL	031	1ST WARD
MILLS, ROBERT	BAL	187	16TH WAR
MILLS, ROBERT	BAL	186	2ND WARD
MILLS, ROSA	SOM	500	SALISBUR
MILLS, RUTH	QUE	243	5TH E DI
MILLS, SALLY	DOR	299	1ST DIST
MILLS, SALLY A.	BAL	356	3RD WARD
MILLS, SAMUEL	BAL	464	14TH WAR
MILLS, SAMUEL L.	SOM	413	DUBLIN D
MILLS, SARAH	SOM	500	SALISBUR
MILLS, SELBY	WAS	124	2ND DIST
MILLS, SOLOMAN	SOM	412	DUBLIN D
MILLS, STEPHEN	SOM	468	TRAPPE D
MILLS, STEPHEN D.	WOR	232	6TH E DI
MILLS, SYDMUN H.	WAS	138	2ND DIST
MILLS, THOMAS	SOM	413	DUBLIN D
MILLS, THOMAS	MGM	425	MEDLEY 3
MILLS, THOMAS	BAL	031	1ST WARD
MILLS, THOMAS	BAL	291	1ST DIST
MILLS, THOMAS A.	WOR	187	7TH E DI
MILLS, THOMAS J.	HAR	026	1ST DIST
MILLS, THOMAS W.	ALL	170	6TH E.D.
MILLS, WEBSTER	BAL	178	2ND WARD
MILLS, WILLIAM	BAL	141	1ST WARD
MILLS, WILLIAM	ANN	415	HOWARD D
MILLS, WILLIAM	DOR	341	3RD DIVI
MILLS, WILLIAM	DOR	336	3RD DIVI
MILLS, WILLIAM	DOR	369	3RD DIVI
MILLS, WILLIAM	DOR	315	1ST DIST
MILLS, WILLIAM	BAL	199	19TH WAR
MILLS, WILLIAM	QUE	151	1ST E DI
MILLS, WILLIAM	WAS	139	2ND DIST
MILLS, WILLIAM	ST	257	3RD E DI
MILLS, WILLIAM	WOR	328	1ST E DI
MILLS, WILLIAM	WOR	305	SNOW HIL
MILLS, WILLIAM P.	BAL	069	15TH WAR
MILLS, WILLIAM A.	WOR	239	6TH E DI
MILLS, WILLIAM M.	SOM	521	BARREN C
MILLS, WILLIAM P.	BAL	051	9TH WARD
MILLS, WILLIAM SR.	WOR	175	6TH E DI
MILLS, WILLIAN	BAL	225	12TH WAR
MILLS, WRITSON	DOR	343	3RD DIVI
MILLS, YORK	BAL	056	10TH WAR
MILLS, ZACHARY	BAL	058	18TH WAR
MILLS, ZACK F. F.	DOR	299	1ST DIST
MILLS.ELEANOR	WOR	175	6TH E DI
MILLS.LORENZO W.	WOR	173	6TH E DI
MILLS.MARIAH	WOR	339	1ST E DI
MILLS.MARIAH	WOR	343	1ST E DI
MILLS.WALTER	CAL	033	2ND DIST
MILLSOP, JOHN	BAL	374	8TH WARD
MILLSPAUGH, IRETTA	ANN	441	HOWARD D
MILLSTON, HANSON	ALL	200	CUMBER_A
MILLWE, CORNELIUS	FRE	339	MIDDLETO
MILLY, BENJAMIN	QUE	145	1ST E DI
MILLY, JAMES	KEN	208	2ND DIST
MILNER, FREDERICK	BAL	262	20TH WAR
MILNOR, JAMES P.	BAL	160	16TH WAR
MILNOR, JOHN P.	BAL	159	16TH WAR
MILROY, GRACE	BAL	094	15TH WAR
MILROY, JOHN	BAL	093	15TH WAR
MILS, SOLOMAN	WAS	124	2ND DIST

Name	County	Page	District
MILS, STEPHEN	WOR	301	SNOW HIL
MILSON, MARCELLUS	WOR	291	9TH E DI
MILSTAMOR, BENNETTE	CHA	251	MIDDLETO
MILSTEAD, ALEN B.	CHA	240	HILLTOP
MILSTEAD, HENRY V.	CHA	243	HILLTOP
MILSTEAD, IGNATIUS	CHA	247	HILLTOP
MILSTEAD, JAMES	CHA	237	HILLTOP
MILSTEAD, MARY	CHA	236	HILLTOP
MILSTEAD, MIDDLETON	CHA	264	HILLTOP
MILSTEAD, RICHARD	CHA	235	HILLTOP
MILSTEAD, SUSAN	CHA	237	HILLTOP
MILSTEAD, THOMAS J.	CHA	239	HILLTOP
MILSTEAD, WILLIAM	ANN	437	HOWARD D
MILSTEAD, WILLIAM	BAL	211	6TH WARD
MILSTEAD, WILLIAM F.	BAL	146	1ST WARD
MILSTEDD, WILLIAM	CHA	243	HILLTOP
MILT, HENRY	ALL	260	CUMBERLA
MILT, JOHN	ALL	259	CUMBERLA
MILTAG, SUSAN	WAS	128	HAGERSTO
MILTAG, THOMAS E.	WAS	148	HAGERSTO
MILTEN, WILLIAM	CAR	392	2ND DIST
MILTENBERGE, JOHN *	BAL	112	2ND DIST
MILTENBERGER, ANTHONY	BAL	159	16TH WAR
MILTENBERGER, SARAH	BAL	373	13TH WAR
MILTER, JOHANA	WAS	112	2ND DIST
MILTEVER, JOHN Z.	CHA	276	ALLENS F
MILTIN, MARY A.	WAS	151	HAGERSTO
MILTON, ABRAHAM	PRI	022	VANSVILL
MILTON, ANN E.	BAL	179	19TH WAR
MILTON, EDWARD	BAL	302	17TH WAR
MILTON, ERASTUS	BAL	359	13TH WAR
MILTON, GEORGE *	BAL	111	2ND DIST
MILTON, GEORGE*	BAL	407	3RD WARD
MILTON, JAMES	MGM	342	CLARKSBU
MILVILLE, ELIZABETH	BAL	343	1ST DIST
MILWARD, JAMES	KEN	302	3RD DIST
MILYARD, CHRISTIAN	CAR	382	2ND DIST
MIMER, SARAH	CAR	138	NO TWP L
MIMMICK, DAVID	FRE	345	MIDDLETO
MIMON, THOMAS *	HAR	199	3RD DIST
MIMS, JANE R.	BAL	050	1ST WARD
MIMSEN, WILLIAM	BAL	117	1ST WARD
MIMTAY, FREDENKER	BAL	155	2ND DIST
MINA, EDWARD	BAL	276	12TH WAR
MINAH, HENRY	BAL	332	3RD WARD
MINAHAN, P.	BAL	140	1ST WARD
MINAHAN,MARY	BAL	333	13TH WAR
MINBELY, JOHN	BAL	094	2ND DIST
MINCE, ELIZABETH	BAL	439	8TH WARD
MINCE, GEORGE*	BAL	337	3RD WARD
MINCHER, JOHN	BAL	259	12TH WAR
MINCHER, JOHN	BAL	276	20TH WAR
MINCHER, MARY	BAL	313	12TH WAR
MINOLE, ROBERTUS	MGM	409	MEDLEY 3
MINDONEY, ELIZABETH-BLACK	BAL	214	2ND WARD
MINDONEY, HENRY-BLACK	BAL	214	2ND WARD
MINE, EDWARD	BAL	254	12TH WAR
MINEPT, DANIEL	BAL	032	1ST WARD
MINER, ADVESH *	BAL	306	12TH WAR
MINER, B.	BAL	173	1ST WARD
MINER, CATHERINE-MULATTO	FRE	189	5TH E DI
MINER, FRANCES	WAS	278	LEITERSB
MINER, GEORGE	WAS	269	1ST DIST
MINER, JOHN	BAL	216	19TH WAR
MINER, JOSEPH	ALL	023	2ND E.D.
MINER, MARGARET	BAL	382	13TH WAR
MINER, WILLIAM	CAR	305	1ST DIST
MINERHIMER, HENRY	BAL	056	18TH WAR
MINES, CATHERINE	BAL	371	3RD WARD
MINES, ELIJAH	BAL	335	1ST DIST
MINES, JOHN	BAL	335	1ST DIST
MINES, MARY	MGM	400	ROCKERLE
MINETT, LEWIS	CAR	314	1ST DIST
MINFERD, MILLY*	BAL	392	3RD WARD
MING, ADAM	BAL	198	2ND WARD
MINGAN, ELIZABETH	BAL	234	2ND WARD
MINGED, B.P.	WAS	205	1ST DIST
MINGEL, JOHN	BAL	202	6TH WARD
MINGER, CAROLINE	BAL	417	8TH WARD
MINGER, CHRISTOPHER	BAL	158	11TH WAR
MINGEY, AFSELL	DOR	304	1ST DIST
MINGIN, JOB	BAL	113	2ND DIST
MINGLE, AARON	CEC	089	4TH E DI
MINGLE, SAMUEL	ALL	215	CUMBERLA
MINGLIN, RICHRD	CEC	085	5TH E DI
MINGO, BETSY	WAS	008	WILLIAMS
MINGO, CHARLES	BAL	396	3RD WARD
MINGO, CHARLES	BAL	457	8TH WARD
MINGO, MARY	BAL	129	5TH WARD
MINGOLD, NICHOLAS	BAL	300	1ST DIST
MINGSLEY, JOHN B.	BAL	093	2ND DIST
MINHEART, CASPER	BAL	070	4TH WARD
MINHEART, GEORGE	BAL	070	4TH WARD
MINHENNY, HENRY	BAL	011	9TH WARD
MINICH, GEORGE W.	TAL	083	ST MICHA
MINICK, CHARLES E.	BAL	199	19TH WAR
MINICK, CONRAD	BAL	362	3RD WARD
MINICK, JOHN	BAL	421	8TH WARD
MINICK, MARY J.	CAR	268	WESTMINS
MINICK, WILLIAM P.	BAL	122	1ST WARD
MINIFIE, JAMES	BAL	133	16TH WAR
MINIFIE, WILLIAM	BAL	068	10TH WAR
MINILKELD, CATHARINE	BAL	245	2ND WARD
MINIS, PAUL	CAR	214	5TH DIST
MINISTER, SAMUEL*	BAL	406	3RD WARD
MINK, CHRISTIAN	BAL	269	1ST DIST
MINK, ELIZABETH	BAL	069	1ST WARD
MINKE, FRED	BAL	243	17TH WAR
MINKE, SOPHIA	BAL	162	19TH WAR
MINKEN, ANN	BAL	120	2ND DIST
MINKER, JOHN	HAR	013	1ST DIST
MINKER, MARTHA J.	HAR	014	1ST DIST
MINKER, WILLIAM D.	HAR	053	1ST DIST
MINKEY,W.	BAL	258	12TH WAR
MINKI, CATHARINE	CEC	054	1ST E DI
MINKLE, EDWARD	BAL	016	1ST WARD
MINKY,FREDERICK	ALL	240	CUMBERLA
MINLAN, JULIA	BAL	153	11TH WAR
MINNA, MARY	BAL	278	1ST DIST
MINNAY, JOHN	BAL	163	1ST WARD
MINNCIM, MARY *	BAL	044	18TH WAR
MINNER, EDWAR C.	BAL	007	18TH WAR
MINNER, JOHN	CAR	080	NO TWP L
MINNER, WILLIAM H.	QUE	214	3RD E DI
MINNEX, SAMUEL	BAL	275	7TH WARD
MINNFORD, JOHN	WOR	336	1ST E DI
MINNICK, CATHARINE	FRE	336	MIDDLETO
MINNICK, DANIEL	FRE	319	MIDDLETO
MINNICK, DANIEL	WAS	251	1ST DIST
MINNICK, JACOB	FRE	323	MIDDLETO

MINNICK, JACOB HAR 105 2ND DIST
MINNICK, JOHN WAS 276 RIDGEVIL
MINNICK, JOHN BAL 354 3RD WARD
MINNICK, MARY FRE 315 MIDDLETO
MINNICK, MICHAEL BAL 225 19TH WAR
MINNICK, RACHAEL FRE 315 MIDDLETO
MINNICK, SAMUEL HAR 110 2ND DIST
MINNICK, URIAH BAL 178 6TH WARD
MINNICK, WILLIAM BAL 127 1ST WARD
MINNICKS, JOSEPH BAL 287 20TH WAR
MINNICKS, PATRICK BAL 273 1ST DIST
MINNIE, CATHERINE ALL 230 CUMBERLA
MINNIS, GEORGE ANN 428 HOWARD D
MINNIS, JOHN T. MGM 388 ROCKERLE
MINNIX, JOHN BAL 021 2ND DIST
MINNIX, MARY BAL 027 2ND DIST
MINOF, CHRISTIANA WAS 278 LEITERSB
MINOR, DAVID WAS 284 1ST DIST
MINOR, GIDEON ANN 394 8TH DIST
MINOR, H. P. BAL 147 1ST WARD
MINOR, JACKSON FRE 379 PETERSVI
MINOR, JACOB WAS 285 1ST DIST
MINOF, JOHN WAS 284 1ST DIST
MINOR, JOHN BAL 321 1ST DIST
MINOR, JOHN BAL 163 1ST WARD
MINOR, JOHN H. WAS 265 1ST DIST
MINOR, PHEBE WAS 284 1ST DIST
MINOR, WILLIAM WAS 279 LEITERSB
MINOR, WILSON ALL 053 10TH E.D
MINOW, JAMES KEN 270 1ST DIST
MINPLY, CORNELIUS * BAL 168 2ND DIST
MINRICK, MARY * FRE 314 MIDDLETO
MINRON, THOMAS * HAR 199 3RD DIST
MINSEN, ABSOLAM * ANN 372 4TH DIST
MINSK, HARRIET R. BAL 054 4TH WARD
MINSON, THOMAS CHA 218 ALLENS F
MINSTAN,ROBERT BAL 051 1ST WARD
MINSTER, LAURA BAL 355 3RD WARD
MINSTER, SAMUEL* BAL 406 3RD WARD
MINTDROP, MARY C. ALL 195 CUMBERLA
MINTEN, JOSEPH BAL 061 1ST WARD
MINTER, MARTIN CAR 355 6TH DIST
MINTLINE, LOUIS BAL 321 1ST DIST
MINTLUTT, E. BAL 209 19TH WAR
MINTON, JOSIAH C. BAL 336 7TH WARD
MINTRY, ELISABETH ALL 201 CUMBERLA
MINTZ, ELIZABETH BAL 183 2ND WARD
MINTZER, AMOS CAR 325 1ST DIST
MINZEL, FREDERICK BAL 253 20TH WAR
MINZIE, CATHARINE BAL 253 20TH WAR
MINZY, MARY J. BAL 394 3RD WARD
MIRANE, HARMAN BAL 103 2ND DIST
MIRE, CATHERINE ALL 261 CUMBERLA
MIRE, JOHN ALL 258 CUMBERLA
MIRE, JOSEPH ALL 256 CUMBERLA
MIRES, ELY HAR 019 1ST DIST
MIRES, JOHN L. FRE 103 FREDERIC
MIRES, JOSEPH ALL 250 CUMBERLA
MIRES, MARGARET TAL 039 EASTON D
MIRKLAND, SARAH BAL 183 19TH WAR
MIRRAM, ELIZABETH G. BAL 448 14TH WAR
MIRS, MARY A. CAL 012 1ST DIST
MIRTH, MARY A. BAL 250 6TH WARD
MIRTH, SEBASTIAN * BAL 310 20TH WAR
MISBINGER, JOHN BAL 412 8TH WARD
MISEL, DANE BAL 281 12TH WAR
MISEL, JOHN BAL 322 1ST DIST
MISELWELL, PHILIP BAL 062 18TH WAR
MISENER, HENRY BAL 389 1ST DIST
MISENER, JOSEPH FRE 364 CATOCTIN
MISES, PEGGY TAL 110 ST MICHA
MISEY, HERMAN BAL 262 20TH WAR
MISH, GEORGE WAS 109 2ND DIST
MISHELSER, HENRY WAS 142 2ND DIST
MISINGER, DAVID FRE 136 CREAGERS
MISINGER, DAVID FRE 089 FREDERIC
MISKEL, PATRICK BAL 164 2ND DIST
MISKELLY, HUGH BAL 022 4TH WARD
MISKELLY, JOHN BAL 022 4TH WARD
MISKELLY, JOSEPH BAL 097 10TH WAR
MISKELLY, MARY BAL 332 3RD WARD
MISKEMANOW, THOMAS BAL 362 3RD WARD
MISKIMMORE, WILLIAM T. BAL 332 3RD WARD
MISKIMON, ELIZABETH HAR 074 1ST DIST
MISKIMON, MARY BAL 128 5TH WARD
MISKIMONS, ANDREW BAL 265 17TH WAR
MISKINCN, ROBERT HAR 006 1ST DIST
MISMAN, JOHN BAL 111 10TH WAR
MISNER, EPHRAHAM FRE 095 FREDERIC
MISOCK, JACOB WAS 228 1ST DIST
MISOCK, LEONARD WAS 228 1ST DIST
MISS, LEWIS FRE 082 FREDERIC
MISSEL, CAROLINE ANN 451 HOWARD D
MISSELHOUSE, FREDERICK* BAL 417 3RD WARD
MISSHAM, JAMES P. WOR 236 6TH E DI
MISSICK, PRISCILLA WOR 213 4TH E DI
MISSICK, SABRAH WOR 304 SNOW HIL
MISSICK, THEODORE WOR 300 SNOW HIL
MISSICK, THOMAS WOR 229 6TH E DI
MISSILDINE, ALFORD H. BAL 035 18TH WAR
MISSIMER, CATHARINE M. KEN 208 2ND DIST
MISSLER, JOHN ALL 240 CUMBERLA
MISTER, ABRAHAM BAL 080 15TH WAR
MISTER, CHARLES BAL 293 17TH WAR
MISTER, LEVIN BAL 030 15TH WAR
MISTER, LEVISA* DOR 342 3RD DIVI
MISTER, LOVERN DOR 339 3RD DIVI
MISTER, MANUEL DOR 340 3RD DIVI
MISTER, MARY SOM 452 DAMES QU
MISTER, PERMELIA SOM 452 DAMES QU
MISTER, PLANER* DOR 342 3RD DIVI
MISTER, PRESA BAL 134 11TH WAR
MISTER, R.* DOR 417 1ST DIST
MISTER, SEVERN TAL 097 ST MICHA
MISTER, SEVERN JR. TAL 097 ST MICHA
MITBAUGH, MARY WAS 024 2ND SUBD
MITCHAEL, HENRY DOR 309 1ST DIST
MITCHAEL, SAMUEL CHA 227 ALLENS F
MITCHAEL, WILLIAM BAL 256 12TH WAR
MITCHAELL, WALTER CHA 262 MIDDLETO
MITCHEL, ALBICH BAL 341 1ST DIST
MITCHEL, ALEXANDER BAL 299 7TH WARD
MITCHEL, ALPHRED HAR 048 1ST DIST
MITCHEL, AMANDA BAL 336 1ST DIST
MITCHEL, ANN M. BAL 379 8TH WARD
MITCHEL, ANTHONY BAL 348 3RD WARD
MITCHEL, AUTHER BAL 357 8TH WARD
MITCHEL, CATHARINE BAL 184 2ND WARD
MITCHEL, CORNELIUS BAL 408 8TH WARD
MITCHEL, ELIZA BAL 461 1ST DIST
MITCHEL, ELIZA WAS 019 2ND SUBD
MITCHEL, ELIZABETH BAL 350 7TH WARD
MITCHEL, ELIZABETH ANN 438 HOWARD D
MITCHEL, FRANCES BAL 376 8TH WARD
MITCHEL, GEORGE BAL 376 8TH WARD
MITCHEL, GEORGE BAL 296 1ST DIST
MITCHEL, GEORGEANA BAL 383 8TH WARD
MITCHEL, HANSON MGM 403 ROCKERLE
MITCHEL, HENRIETTA BAL 293 3RD WARD
MITCHEL, HENRY L. CHA 262 MIDDLETO
MITCHEL, ISAAC BAL 291 1ST DIST
MITCHEL, ISAAH TAL 120 ST MICHA
MITCHEL, ISABEL BAL 337 1ST DIST
MITCHEL, JAMES BAL 376 8TH WARD
MITCHEL, JAMES TAL 100 ST MICHA
MITCHEL, JANE BAL 408 8TH WARD
MITCHEL, JANE T. BAL 332 7TH WARD
MITCHEL, JOHN BAL 376 8TH WARD
MITCHEL, JOSEPH BAL 372 8TH WARD
MITCHEL, JOSEPH T. KEN 237 2ND DIST
MITCHEL, LLOYD TAL 099 ST MICHA
MITCHEL, LOYD BAL 375 8TH WARD
MITCHEL, LUCRECIA HAR 147 3RD DIST
MITCHEL, LUTHER BAL 335 1ST DIST
MITCHEL, MARY BAL 377 8TH WARD
MITCHEL, MARY BAL 374 8TH WARD
MITCHEL, MATILDA A. BAL 023 2ND DIST
MITCHEL, NAHTANIEL BAL 095 5TH WARD
MITCHEL, NATHAN BAL 384 8TH WARD
MITCHEL, PETER TAL 099 ST MICHA
MITCHEL, RACHEL CAL 005 1ST DIST
MITCHEL, SAMUE H. JR. BAL 305 7TH WARD
MITCHEL, SAMUEL FRE 266 NEW MARK
MITCHEL, SARAH BAL 336 1ST DIST
MITCHEL, SOLOMON DOR 358 3RD DIVI
MITCHEL, STEPHEN BAL 068 2ND DIST
MITCHEL, THOMAS BAL 337 1ST DIST
MITCHEL, TOFILUS TAL 099 ST MICHA
MITCHEL,ALEXANDER FRE 229 BUCKEYST
MITCHELE, REBECCA* DOR 441 1ST DIST
MITCHELL, AARON DOR 392 1ST DIST
MITCHELL, ADELLE BAL 248 6TH WARD
MITCHELL, AGRIPPA WAS 160 2ND DIST
MITCHELL, AIRY A. MGM 315 CRACKLIN
MITCHELL, ALACE CHA 262 MIDDLETO
MITCHELL, ALEXANDER BAL 042 4TH WARD
MITCHELL, ALEXANDER WAS 291 1ST DIST
MITCHELL, ALEXANDER SOM 527 QUANTICO
MITCHELL, ALFRED HAR 117 2ND DIST
MITCHELL, AMOS A. HAR 169 3RD DIST
MITCHELL, ANN HAR 137 2ND DIST
MITCHELL, ANN HAR 127 2ND DIST
MITCHELL, ANN CEC 170 6TH E DI
MITCHELL, ANN BAL 164 16TH WAR
MITCHELL, ANN A. BAL 214 11TH WAR
MITCHELL, ANN E. BAL 186 6TH WARD
MITCHELL, ANN M. FRE 383 PETERSVI
MITCHELL, ANNA BAL 417 14TH WAR
MITCHELL, ANNA M. ANN 436 HOWARD D
MITCHELL, ANTHONY BAL 012 4TH WARD
MITCHELL, ARTHUR CEC 004 ELKTON 3
MITCHELL, BARNARD HAR 152 3RD DIST
MITCHELL, BEN PRI 081 QUEEN AN
MITCHELL, BENJAMIN WAS 159 2ND DIST
MITCHELL, BENJAMIN ANN 403 8TH DIST
MITCHELL, BURTON G. WOR 215 4TH E DI
MITCHELL, CAROLINE E. BAL 065 10TH WAR
MITCHELL, CAROLINE M. DOR 378 1ST DIST
MITCHELL, CATHARINE DOR 393 1ST DIST
MITCHELL, CATHARINE BAL 470 14TH WAR
MITCHELL, CATHARINE BAL 208 6TH WARD
MITCHELL, CATHERINE BAL 105 10TH WAR
MITCHELL, CHARLES ALL 136 4TH E.D.
MITCHELL, CHARLES HAR 137 2ND DIST
MITCHELL, CHARLES A. DOR 378 1ST DIST
MITCHELL, CHARLES J. B. QUE 239 5TH E DI
MITCHELL, CHARLOTTE BAL 034 4TH WARD
MITCHELL, CHAUNCEY HAR 167 3RD DIST
MITCHELL, CLARA E. BAL 187 16TH WAR
MITCHELL, CLARA L. BAL 187 16TH WAR
MITCHELL, CLEMENCY HAR 164 3RD DIST
MITCHELL, CORBIN L. HAR 169 3RD DIST
MITCHELL, CORNELIA BAL 254 2ND WARD
MITCHELL, CORNELIS CAL 009 1ST DIST
MITCHELL, CORNELIUS CAL 040 3RD DIST
MITCHELL, DANIEL HAR 166 3RD DIST
MITCHELL, DANILE E. HAR 167 3RD DIST
MITCHELL, DAVID CEC 008 ELKTON 3
MITCHELL, DAVID BAL 215 17TH WAR
MITCHELL, EDWARD BAL 034 4TH WARD
MITCHELL, EDWARD HAR 131 2ND DIST
MITCHELL, EDWARD BAL 279 2ND WARD
MITCHELL, ELEANOR B PRI 034 VANSVILL
MITCHELL, ELIJAH WOR 207 4TH E DI
MITCHELL, ELISHA BAL 086 1ST WARD
MITCHELL, ELISHA HAR 117 2ND DIST
MITCHELL, ELIZA BAL 182 6TH WARD
MITCHELL, ELIZABETH BAL 393 3RD WARD
MITCHELL, ELIZABETH HAR 136 2ND DIST
MITCHELL, ELIZABETH CEC 008 ELKTON 3
MITCHELL, ELIZABETH CEC 150 PORT DUP
MITCHELL, ELIZABETH BAL 459 14TH WAR
MITCHELL, ELIZABETH SOM 520 BARREN C
MITCHELL, ELIZABETH WOR 252 1ST CENS
MITCHELL, ELIZABETH A. MGM 410 MEDLEY 3
MITCHELL, ELLEN BAL 243 17TH WAR
MITCHELL, ELLENER BAL 131 11TH WAR
MITCHELL, EMANUEL BAL 207 17TH WAR
MITCHELL, EMELINE BAL 180 16TH WAR
MITCHELL, EMILY BAL 078 1ST WARD
MITCHELL, EPHRAIM BAL 049 4TH WARD
MITCHELL, EUGENE D. C. CHA 263 MIDDLETO
MITCHELL, EVELINE DOR 392 1ST DIST
MITCHELL, EVIN HAR 184 3RD DIST
MITCHELL, EZEKIEL HAR 159 3RD DIST
MITCHELL, FRANCIS HAR 100 2ND DIST
MITCHELL, FRANCIS SOM 554 TYASKIN
MITCHELL, FRANCIS A. SOM 362 BRINKLEY
MITCHELL, FRANCIS J. BAL 088 4TH WARD
MITCHELL, FRANK BAL 215 11TH WAR
MITCHELL, GEORGE HAR 084 2ND DIST
MITCHELL, GEORGE BAL 285 17TH WAR
MITCHELL, GEORGE PRI 043 VANSVILL
MITCHELL, GEORGE KEN 297 3RD DIST
MITCHELL, GEORGE BAL 092 15TH WAR
MITCHELL, GEORGE ANN 346 3RD DIST
MITCHELL, GEORGE A. PRI 084 QUEEN AN
MITCHELL, GEORGE T. WOR 233 6TH E DI
MITCHELL, GEORGE W. BAL 078 15TH WAR
MITCHELL, GEORGE W. BAL 325 3RD WARD
MITCHELL, HANNA HAR 168 3RD DIST
MITCHELL, HANNAH ALL 256 CUMBERLA
MITCHELL, HENRIETTA BAL 053 4TH WARD
MITCHELL, HENRY HAR 150 3RD DIST
MITCHELL, HENRY ALL 234 CUMBERLA
MITCHELL, HENRY ALL 233 CUMBERLA
MITCHELL, HENRY PRI 035 VANSVILL
MITCHELL, HENRY TAL 084 ST MICHA
MITCHELL, HENRY WAS 154 HAGERSTO
MITCHELL, HENRY J. SOM 362 BRINKLEY
MITCHELL, HEZEKIAH MGM 347 BERRYS D
MITCHELL, ISAAC SOM 492 SALISBUR
MITCHELL, ISAAC KEN 303 3RD DIST
MITCHELL, ISAAC BAL 338 3RD WARD
MITCHELL, ISAAC BAL 274 12TH WAR
MITCHELL, ISAAC F. BAL 001 9TH WARD
MITCHELL, ISABELLA BAL 198 6TH WARD
MITCHELL, J. A. BAL 042 4TH WARD
MITCHELL, JACOB ALL 209 CUMBERLA
MITCHELL, JACOB WOR 244 1ST CENS
MITCHELL, JAMES WOR 205 4TH E DI
MITCHELL, JAMES WAS 160 2ND DIST
MITCHELL, JAMES SOM 552 TYASKIN
MITCHELL, JAMES WOR 310 2ND E DI
MITCHELL, JAMES BAL 155 1ST WARD
MITCHELL, JAMES BAL 027 9TH WARD
MITCHELL, JAMES BAL 001 9TH WARD
MITCHELL, JAMES ANN 514 HOWARD D
MITCHELL, JAMES BAL 154 16TH WAR
MITCHELL, JAMES BAL 028 1ST WARD
MITCHELL, JAMES HAR 150 3RD DIST
MITCHELL, JAMES HAR 155 3RD DIST
MITCHELL, JAMES CEC 062 1ST E DI
MITCHELL, JAMES B. BAL 380 3RD WARD
MITCHELL, JAMES F. DOR 378 1ST DIST
MITCHELL, JAMES H. BAL 282 2ND WARD
MITCHELL, JAMES H. WOR 238 6TH E DI
MITCHELL, JAMES H. KEN 286 3RD DIST
MITCHELL, JAMES M. SOM 523 BARREN C
MITCHELL, JANE BAL 257 1ST DIST
MITCHELL, JANE BAL 115 15TH WAR
MITCHELL, JANE BAL 048 15TH WAR
MITCHELL, JANE CEC 008 ELKTON 3
MITCHELL, JANE BAL 118 11TH WAR
MITCHELL, JARRETT HAR 136 2ND DIST
MITCHELL, JESSE CAR 097 NO TWP L
MITCHELL, JOHN HAR 127 2ND DIST
MITCHELL, JOHN HAR 172 3RD DIST
MITCHELL, JOHN BAL 205 19TH WAR
MITCHELL, JOHN DOR 395 1ST DIST
MITCHELL, JOHN DOR 379 1ST DIST
MITCHELL, JOHN BAL 149 19TH WAR
MITCHELL, JOHN BAL 134 18TH WAR
MITCHELL, JOHN BAL 280 17TH WAR
MITCHELL, JOHN BAL 060 4TH WARD
MITCHELL, JOHN CEC 198 7TH E DI
MITCHELL, JOHN BAL 096 10TH WAR
MITCHELL, JOHN BAL 041 9TH WARD
MITCHELL, JOHN BAL 019 9TH WARD
MITCHELL, JOHN BAL 218 6TH WARD
MITCHELL, JOHN ANN 278 ANNAPOLI
MITCHELL, JOHN ANN 340 3RD DIST
MITCHELL, JOHN ANN 349 3RD DIST
MITCHELL, JOHN BAL 108 2ND DIST
MITCHELL, JOHN WOR 238 6TH E DI
MITCHELL, JOHN PRI 084 QUEEN AN
MITCHELL, JOHN WOR 313 2ND E DI
MITCHELL, JOHN F. BAL 215 17TH WAR
MITCHELL, JOHN H. HAR 121 2ND DIST
MITCHELL, JOHN H. BAL 380 3RD WARD
MITCHELL, JOHN JR. HAR 185 3RD DIST
MITCHELL, JOHN S. BAL 216 17TH WAR
MITCHELL, JOHN T. BAL 086 18TH WAR
MITCHELL, JOHN W. BAL 083 18TH WAR
MITCHELL, JOHN W. DOR 395 1ST DIST
MITCHELL, JOSEPH DOR 395 1ST DIST
MITCHELL, JOSEPH BAL 275 2ND WARD
MITCHELL, JOSEPH F. DOR 378 1ST DIST
MITCHELL, JOSHUA BAL 177 6TH WARD
MITCHELL, JOSHUA WOR 205 4TH E DI
MITCHELL, JOSHUA C.-BLACK BAL 225 2ND WARD
MITCHELL, JOSIAH ANN 417 HOWARD D
MITCHELL, JOSIAH BAL 194 17TH WAR
MITCHELL, JOSIAH G. WOR 204 4TH E DI
MITCHELL, JSOEPH G. HAR 163 3RD DIST
MITCHELL, KENDIRCH PRI 091 MARLBROU
MITCHELL, LARY HAR 164 3RD DIST
MITCHELL, LARY HAR 172 3RD DIST
MITCHELL, LEWIS BAL 180 6TH WARD
MITCHELL, LITTLETON WOR 306 2ND E DI
MITCHELL, LOUISA SOM 490 SALISBUR
MITCHELL, LOYD BAL 076 2ND DIST
MITCHELL, LUCINDA ANN 316 1ST DIST
MITCHELL, LUCY ANN 315 1ST DIST
MITCHELL, MARCELLUS A. BAL 075 15TH WAR
MITCHELL, MARGARET BAL 205 19TH WAR
MITCHELL, MARGARET A. BAL 158 19TH WAR
MITCHELL, MARIA BAL 229 6TH WARD
MITCHELL, MARTHA BAL 044 4TH WARD
MITCHELL, MARTHA BAL 082 4TH WARD
MITCHELL, MARTHA PRI 023 VANSVILL
MITCHELL, MARTIN ALL 144 6TH E.D.
MITCHELL, MARY ALL 018 3RD E.D.
MITCHELL, MARY BAL 198 11TH WAR
MITCHELL, MARY BAL 015 1ST WARD
MITCHELL, MARY BAL 355 13TH WAR
MITCHELL, MARY BAL 124 18TH WAR
MITCHELL, MARY BAL 318 20TH WAR
MITCHELL, MATILDA PRI 022 VANSVILL
MITCHELL, MATILDA WOR 208 4TH E DI
MITCHELL, MICHAEL DOR 395 1ST DIST
MITCHELL, MICHAEL BAL 348 1ST DIST
MITCHELL, MILLY WOR 213 4TH E DI
MITCHELL, MISS E. FRE 200 5TH E DI
MITCHELL, MORDICIA PRI 081 QUEEN AN
MITCHELL, MR. BAL 134 5TH WARD
MITCHELL, NATHAN WOR 209 4TH E DI
MITCHELL, NATHANIEL BAL 030 15TH WAR
MITCHELL, NICHOLAS BAL 006 4TH WARD
MITCHELL, OLIVER M. CEC 028 CHESAPEA
MITCHELL, PACA HAR 177 3RD DIST
MITCHELL, PAMELIA HAR 088 2ND DIST
MITCHELL, PATRICK ALL 076 5TH E.D.
MITCHELL, PERRY BAL 098 18TH WAR
MITCHELL, PERRY* DOR 416 1ST DIST
MITCHELL, PETER DOR 389 1ST DIST
MITCHELL, PHEBY CEC 153 PORT DUP
MITCHELL, PRICELLA SOM 499 SALISBUR
MITCHELL, RACHEL WOR 264 BERLIN 1
MITCHELL, RACHEL BAL 365 13TH WAR

Name	County	Page	District
MITCHELL, RAMON	BAL	209	6TH DIST
MITCHELL, REBECCA	BAL	214	11TH WAR
MITCHELL, REBECCA*	DOR	441	1ST DIST
MITCHELL, RICHARD	DOR	393	1ST DIST
MITCHELL, RICHARD	DOR	395	1ST DIST
MITCHELL, RICHARD	BAL	056	4TH WARD
MITCHELL, RICHARD	HAR	178	3RD DIST
MITCHELL, RICHARD	ALL	150	6TH E.D.
MITCHELL, RICHARD	BAL	077	15TH WAR
MITCHELL, RICHARD H.	CHA	219	ALLENS F
MITCHELL, RICHARD JR.	HAR	164	3RD DIST
MITCHELL, RICTOR M.	PRI	001	BLADENSB
MITCHELL, ROBERT	WOR	205	4TH E DI
MITCHELL, ROBERT	BAL	002	4TH WARD
MITCHELL, ROBERT	HAR	103	2ND DIST
MITCHELL, ROBERT	BAL	393	3RD WARD
MITCHELL, ROBERT C.	SOM	533	QUANTICO
MITCHELL, ROBERT-MULATTO	BAL	225	2ND WARD
MITCHELL, RUFUS	BAL	193	17TH WAR
MITCHELL, RUFUS W.	WOR	213	4TH E DI
MITCHELL, SAMUEL	WOR	207	4TH E DI
MITCHELL, SAMUEL	WAS	274	RIDGEVIL
MITCHELL, SAMUEL	BAL	094	15TH WAR
MITCHELL, SAMUEL	ANN	296	1ST DIST
MITCHELL, SAMUEL	HAR	109	2ND DIST
MITCHELL, SAMUEL	FRE	009	FREDERIC
MITCHELL, SAMUEL C.	BAL	050	4TH WARD
MITCHELL, SAMUEL P.	WOR	261	BERLIN 1
MITCHELL, SARAH	WOR	263	BERLIN 1
MITCHELL, SARAH	HAR	125	2ND DIST
MITCHELL, SARAH	CAL	041	3RD DIST
MITCHELL, SARAH	ALL	072	5TH E.D.
MITCHELL, SARAH	BAL	027	15TH WAR
MITCHELL, SARAH A.	BAL	352	3RD WARD
MITCHELL, SARAH E.	HAR	123	2ND DIST
MITCHELL, SARAH*	DOR	438	1ST DIST
MITCHELL, SHADRACK	DOR	378	1ST DIST
MITCHELL, SILBOURN	PRI	008	BLADENSB
MITCHELL, SOLOMON	HAR	152	3RD DIST
MITCHELL, SOMERSET	MGM	331	CRACKLIN
MITCHELL, SOPHIA	BAL	372	3RD WARD
MITCHELL, SOPHIA F.	DOR	378	1ST DIST
MITCHELL, STEPHEN	BAL	139	2ND DIST
MITCHELL, SUSAN	DOR	386	1ST DIST
MITCHELL, SYLVESTER	HAR	176	3RD DIST
MITCHELL, THEODORE	SOM	497	SALISBUR
MITCHELL, THOAMS	BAL	139	19TH WAR
MITCHELL, THOMAS	HAR	149	3RD DIST
MITCHELL, THOMAS	MGM	330	CRACKLIN
MITCHELL, THOMAS	BAL	211	17TH WAR
MITCHELL, THOMAS	MGM	369	BERRYS D
MITCHELL, THOMAS	SOM	425	PRINCESS
MITCHELL, THOMAS	SOM	533	QUANTICC
MITCHELL, THOMAS	PRI	038	VANSVILL
MITCHELL, THOMAS	BAL	106	10TH WAR
MITCHELL, THOMAS	BAL	167	1ST WARD
MITCHELL, THOMAS A.	ANN	281	ANNAPOLI
MITCHELL, THOMAS P.	HAR	179	3RD DIST
MITCHELL, TILGHMAN	MGM	369	BERRYS D
MITCHELL, URIAH	ANN	417	HOWARD D
MITCHELL, W.	DOR	421	1ST DIST
MITCHELL, WILLAIM	PRI	061	NOTTINGH
MITCHELL, WILLAM	WOR	252	1ST CENS
MITCHELL, WILLIAM	WOR	307	2ND E DI
MITCHELL, WILLIAM	SOM	502	SALISBUR
MITCHELL, WILLIAM	SOM	469	TRAPPE D
MITCHELL, WILLIAM	ST	345	5TH E DI
MITCHELL, WILLIAM	HAR	136	2ND DIST
MITCHELL, WILLIAM	BAL	240	17TH WAR
MITCHELL, WILLIAM	BAL	091	15TH WAR
MITCHELL, WILLIAM	BAL	356	3RD WARD
MITCHELL, WILLIAM	BAL	354	3RD WARD
MITCHELL, WILLIAM	BAL	292	3RD WARD
MITCHELL, WILLIAM H.	BAL	163	16TH WAR
MITCHELL, WILLIAM H.	DOR	402	1ST DIST
MITCHELL, WILLIAM H.	BAL	095	18TH WAR
MITCHELL, WILLIAM M.	HAR	164	3RD DIST
MITCHELL, WILLIAM T.	WOR	180	6TH E DI
MITCHELL, ZACHARY	BAL	263	17TH WAR
MITCHELL, ZADOK	MGM	410	MEDLEY 3
MITCHELL, ZEBEDEE	DOR	402	1ST DIST
MITCHELL, ZEBULON	BAL	012	15TH WAR
MITCHELL, ZELEDER	PRI	003	BLADENSB
MITCHELL.JOSEPH P.	BAL	023	2ND DIST
MITCHELL.MARY-BLACK	QUE	185	3RD E DI
MITCHGELL, ANN	BAL	023	1ST WARD
MITCHLING, JOHN	BAL	107	2ND DIST
MITCHNER, J.	BAL	136	1ST WARD
MITCHNER, JOHN	CEC	085	5TH E DI
MITCHNER, SARAH	CEC	086	4TH E DI
MITE, FRANK	BAL	205	17TH WAR
MITELINK, HENRIETTA*	BAL	313	3RD WARD
MITGCHELL, EMMELINE	WOR	205	4TH E DI
MITH, LAVENIA	FRE	247	NEW MARK
MITHCELL MARY	BAL	293	3RD WARD
MITHCELL, ELISHA	WOR	251	1ST CENS
MITHCELL, GEORGE	WOR	256	1ST CENS
MITHCELL, ISAAC	WOR	196	8TH E DI
MITHCELL, JAMES	WOR	214	4TH E DI
MITHCELL, WILLIAM	BAL	142	2ND DIST
MITHCELL, WILLIAM C.	WOR	245	1ST CENS
MITMAN, CATHERINE	FRE	042	FREDERIC
MITONG, LOUISA	ALL	248	CUMBERLA
MITSTREL, NELLY	TAL	087	ST MICHA
MITTAN, JOHN P.	BAL	282	20TH WAR
MITTANER, JOHN	BAL	223	19TH WAR
MITTASE, LAPE	BAL	122	1ST WARD
MITTE, HENRY	WAS	054	2ND SUBD
MITTEEN, HANAH *	BAL	046	18TH WAR
MITTEER, HANAH *	BAL	046	18TH WAR
MITTEN, DANIEL	CAR	275	7TH DIST
MITTEN, GEORGE	CAR	265	WESTMINS
MITTEN, HENRY G.	CAR	265	WESTMINS
MITTEN, LYDIA	CAR	393	2ND DIST
MITTEN, MARY	CAR	096	NO TWP L
MITTEN, MILES	CAR	297	7TH DIST
MITTEN, NELSON	CAR	269	WESTMINS
MITTEN, SUSAN	CAR	272	WESTMINS
MITTENBURG, WILLIAM	BAL	112	2ND DIST
MITTENDORF, META	BAL	156	11TH WAR
MITTENDORFF, HY.	BAL	287	1ST DIST
MITTER, EPHRAIM *	SOM	434	PRINCESS
MITTINGER, IRA	BAL	210	19TH WAR
MITTINGER, MARGARET	BAL	211	19TH WAR
MITTNACHT, HENRY	BAL	075	10TH WAR
MITTON, MAGDELENA	BAL	336	13TH WAR
MITTUR, HANAH *	BAL	046	18TH WAR
MITZ, JOHN	BAL	329	13TH WAR
MITZER, G. L.	BAL	329	13TH WAR
MITZER, SOPHIA	BAL	202	2ND WARD
MITZGER, CATHARINE	HAR	151	3RD DIST
MIX, JOHN	FRE	026	FREDERIC
MIX, THOMAS	BAL	335	13TH WAR
MIXON, ROBERT	BAL	472	14TH WAR
MIXTER, COLUMBUS	QUE	155	2ND E DI
MIXTER, ELIZABETH	BAL	216	19TH WAR
MIXTER, JOHN	BAL	215	19TH WAR
MIZICK, DRAPER	WOR	192	8TH E DI
MIZICK, EBENEZER	WOR	191	8TH E DI
MLLLER, ANN	CAR	112	NO TWP L
MO, RACHEL	BAL	403	1ST DIST
MOAKE, JOHN	BAL	323	1ST DIST
MOAKUR, JOHN	BAL	007	EASTERN
MOALAND, ISAAC	KEN	295	3RD DIST
MOALDEN, ELIAS	MGM	424	MEDLEY 3
MOALE, ELEANOR	BAL	238	1ST DIST
MOALE, GEORGE	BAL	201	6TH WARD
MOALE, JOHN	BAL	200	6TH WARD
MOALE, JOHN T.	BAL	243	1ST DIST
MOALE, JULIA*	BAL	097	10TH WAR
MOALE, R. H.	BAL	167	11TH WAR
MOALE, RANDLE H.	BAL	143	11TH WAR
MOALE, RICHARD	BAL	104	10TH WAR
MOALE, ROBERT N.	BAL	249	1ST DIST
MOALE, SAMUEL	BAL	141	11TH WAR
MOALE, WILLIAM A.	BAL	205	11TH WAR
MOAN, FRANCES	BAL	028	4TH WARD
MOAR, CHARLES *	BAL	323	1ST DIST
MOAR, JOHN D.	WAS	218	1ST DIST
MOAR, SAMUEL	BAL	392	1ST DIST
MOAT, ANN	BAL	093	10TH WAR
MOAT, JAMES	CEC	100	3RD E DI
MOATE, JAMES	CEC	086	4TH E DI
MOATS, DANIEL	WAS	202	1ST DIST
MOATS, ELIAS	WAS	203	1ST DIST
MOATS, JACOB	WAS	276	RIDGEVIL
MOATS, NANCY	WAS	051	2ND SUBD
MOATS, SAMUEL	WAS	051	2ND SUBD
MOATS, SAMUEL	WAS	014	WILLIAMS
MOATZ, JOHN H.	WAS	030	2ND SUBD
MOBARRY, HARRIET	ANN	291	ANNAPOLI
MOBBERBY, ELDRED W.	FRE	238	NEW MARK
MOBBERLEY, LAURA	FRE	053	FREDERIC
MOBBERLEY, LEVI	FRE	053	FREDERIC
MOBBERLEY, MARY C.	FRE	094	FREDERIC
MOBBERLY, DELILA	MGM	444	CLARKSTR
MOBBERLY, EZEKIEL	MGM	439	CLARKSTR
MOBBERLY, LEVI	FRE	060	FREDERIC
MOBBERLY, SALLY	MGM	440	CLARKSTR
MOBBERLY, SAMUEL	MGM	429	CLARKSTR
MOBERLY, ELIZABETH	FRE	407	JEFFERSO
MOBERRY, ELIZA	ANN	298	1ST DIST
MOBERRY, HENRY	CAR	126	NO TWP L
MOBERY, ELIZABETH	DOR	335	3RD DIVI
MOBERY, MOSES	TAL	051	EASTON D
MOBERY, THOMAS	DOR	354	3RD DIVI
MOBLES, JOHN H.	FRE	207	BUCKEYST
MOBLES, WILLIAM T.	FRE	206	BUCKEYST
MOBLEY, AMELIA	CAR	233	5TH DIST
MOBLEY, DELILAH A.	MGM	333	CRACKLIN
MOBLEY, DENNIS-BLACK	FRE	216	BUCKEYST
MOBLEY, E.M.	WAS	125	HAGERSTO
MOBLEY, ELI	WAS	125	HAGERSTO
MOBLEY, GEORGE W.	MGM	323	CRACKLIN
MOBLEY, JOSEPH C.	FRE	233	BUCKEYST
MOBLEY, REAZIN	CAR	233	5TH DIST
MOBLEY, SARAH	CAR	394	2ND DIST
MOBLEY, SUSAN	BAL	217	6TH WARD
MOBLEY, WILLIAM	HAR	005	1ST DIST
MOBLY, ELIZA	ANN	486	HOWARD D
MOBLY, ELIZABETH	CAR	281	7TH DIST
MOBLY, HORACE	FRE	275	NEW MARK
MOBLY, JOHN	ALL	210	CUMBERLA
MOBLY, THOMAS	CAR	283	7TH DIST
MOBRAY, AMY	DOR	393	1ST DIST
MOBRAY, BUD*	DOR	382	1ST DIST
MOBRAY, CELIA	DOR	318	1ST DIST
MOBRAY, EMELINE*	DOR	408	1ST DIST
MOBRAY, GEORGE	DOR	379	1ST DIST
MOBRAY, HENRIETTA	BAL	053	9TH WARD
MOBRAY, JAMES	DOR	318	1ST DIST
MOBRAY, JAMES F.	DOR	382	1ST DIST
MOBRAY, JOHN	DOR	382	1ST DIST
MOBRAY, JOHN	DOR	386	1ST DIST
MOBRAY, JOHN P.	DOR	424	1ST DIST
MOBRAY, JOHN*	DOR	407	1ST DIST
MOBRAY, JOHN*	DOR	379	1ST DIST
MOBRAY, JOSEPH	DOR	317	1ST DIST
MOBRAY, LEVIN*	DOR	422	1ST DIST
MOBRAY, OLIVER*	DOR	375	1ST DIST
MOBRAY, SARAH	DOR	416	1ST DIST
MOBRAY, SETH	DOR	393	1ST DIST
MOBRAY, THOMAS	DOR	394	1ST DIST
MOBRAY, THOMAS	DOR	420	1ST DIST
MOBRAY, WHITE G.*	DOR	416	1ST DIST
MOBRAY, WILLIAM	DOR	309	1ST DIST
MOBRAY, WILLIAM*	DOR	469	1ST DIST
MOCABEE, MATHEW	ANN	322	2ND DIST
MOCK, CAROLINE	WAS	188	1ST DIST
MOCK, GOTLEIB	WAS	263	1ST DIST
MOCK, JACOB	WAS	273	RIDGEVIL
MOCKABEE, JOHN	WAS	094	2ND SUBD
MOCKABEE, JOSEPH	ANN	306	1ST DIST
MOCKABEE, ZACHARIAH	WAS	094	2ND SUBD
MOCKABY, JANE	BAL	411	1ST DIST
MOCKBEE, ELIZABETH	MGM	427	MEDLEY 3
MOCKBEE, OTHIAS	ANN	333	2ND DIST
MOCKBRE, AMANDA	MGM	375	ROCKERLE
MOCKEL, BEALSER	BAL	089	10TH WAR
MOCKELMANAB, ANDREW*	BAL	077	4TH WARD
MOCKER, JOHN	BAL	348	7TH WARD
MOCKLE, JOHN	BAL	411	3RD WARD
MOCKLEY, CHARLES	BAL	441	1ST DIST
MOCLER, THOMAS	PRI	033	VANSVILL
MODFRED, WILLIAM	BAL	005	EASTERN
MODOCK, GEORGE*	DOR	315	1ST DIST
MODOCK, RICHARD B.	FRE	230	BUCKEYST
MODOCK,AUGUSTUS	FRE	230	BUCKEYST
MOEBUS, HENRY	BAL	018	9TH WARD
MOEHLE, ------*	BAL	084	10TH WAR
MOELLING, THEODORE	ANN	522	HOWARD D
MOELY, EVERHART	BAL	297	17TH WAR
MOELY, P.B.	BAL	293	12TH WAR
MOET, RICHARD*	BAL	235	12TH WAR
MOFFAT, ROBERT	BAL	420	14TH WAR
MOFFAT, THOMAS	BAL	035	15TH WAR
MOFFERLY, REGEN	FRE	267	NEW MARK
MOFFET, ROBERT	BAL	023	2ND DIST
MOFFET, THOMAS	BAL	453	1ST DIST
MOFFETT, ELIZABETH	FRE	409	JEFFERSO
MOFFETT, RICHARD	KEN	303	3RD DIST
MOFFETT, WILLIAM	BAL	363	8TH WARD
MOFFIT, AGNESS	BAL	333	7TH WARD
MOFFIT, BENJAMIN	DOR	467	1ST DIST
MOFFIT, DANIEL	BAL	410	1ST DIST
MOFFIT, DANIEL	BAL	410	1ST DIST
MOFFIT, JAMES	HAR	162	3RD DIST
MOFFIT, JAMES T.	QUE	135	1ST E DI
MOFFIT, JOHN	BAL	347	1ST DIST
MOFFIT, JOHN	WAS	163	2ND DIST
MOFFIT, LOUISA	BAL	140	19TH WAR
MOFFIT, MARY A.	CAR	257	WESTMINS
MOFFIT, PATRICK	BAL	143	1ST WARD
MOFFIT, SAMUEL D.	CEC	138	6TH E DI
MOFFIT, THOMAS	QUE	179	2ND E DI
MOFFIT, WILLIAM	BAL	045	2ND DIST
MOFFIT.ELIZAETH	CAR	391	2ND DIST
MOFFITT, AGUSTA S.	BAL	036	18TH WAR
MOFFITT, ANN	QUE	128	1ST E DI
MOFFITT, ANTHONY T.	BAL	212	6TH WARD
MOFFITT, ELIZA	CAR	271	WESTMINS
MOFFITT, ELIZA	KEN	301	3RD DIST
MOFFITT, ENOCK	KEN	298	3RD DIST
MOFFITT, HANAH	BAL	274	7TH WARD
MOFFITT, JAMES	KEN	300	3RD DIST
MOFFITT, JAMES	KEN	312	3RD DIST
MOFFITT, JAMES	KEN	303	3RD DIST
MOFFITT, JOHN	BAL	382	8TH WARD
MOFFITT, JOHN F.	HAR	162	3RD DIST
MOFFITT, JOHN T.	CAR	276	7TH DIST
MOFFITT, JOSEPH	KEN	221	2ND DIST
MOFFITT, LANSLOTT	KEN	303	3RD DIST
MOFFITT, LOUIS M.	BAL	037	18TH WAR
MOFFITT, MARY E.	KEN	304	3RD DIST
MOFFITT, RICHARD	KEN	310	3RD DIST
MOFFITT, ROSE J.	BAL	278	7TH WARD
MOFFITT, SAMUEL	CAR	271	WESTMINS
MOFFITT, THOMAS	BAL	286	7TH WARD
MOFFITT, THOMAS	KEN	311	3RD DIST
MOFFITT, WILLIAM	KEN	285	3RD DIST
MOFFITT, WILLIAM	KEN	258	1ST DIST
MOFFITT, WILLIAM H.	BAL	126	5TH WARD
MOFFITT, WILLIAM R.	BAL	419	14TH WAR
MOFFITT, WILLIAM W.	BAL	114	5TH WARD
MOFFULEY.RACHAEL	FRE	053	FREDERIC
MOGAETTE, NELSON A.	BAL	360	13TH WAR
MOGGANS, SARAH	WAS	240	CAVETOWN
MOGGINS, JACOB	WAS	293	1ST DIST
MOGGINS, JOHN H.	WAS	241	CAVETOWN
MOGGINS, JONOTHAN	WAS	290	1ST DIST
MOGGINS, MARTIN	WAS	262	1ST DIST
MOGUNGAL, CATHARINE	ALL	080	5TH E.D.
MOHAN, JOSEPH	CEC	211	7TH E DI
MOHAN, MARY A.	CEC	142	6TH E DI
MOHAN, THOMAS	ALL	068	5TH E.D.
MOHAN, WILLIAM	CEC	020	ELKTON 3
MOHAY, BUD*	DOR	382	1ST DIST
MOHAY, EMELINE*	DOR	408	1ST DIST
MOHAY, HOOPER R.	DOR	422	1ST DIST
MOHAY, JAMES	DOR	422	1ST DIST
MOHAY, JOHN*	DOR	379	1ST DIST
MOHAY, WHITE G.*	DOR	416	1ST DIST
MOHEFER, MARY	BAL	237	12TH WAR
MOHENEATH, CATERINE	FRE	249	NEW MARK
MOHLER, ANDREW R.	FRE	141	CREAGERS
MOHLER, ANN M.	BAL	421	3RD WARD
MOHLER, EDWARD	BAL	017	1ST WARD
MOHLER, JACOB T.	BAL	410	3RD WARD
MOHLER, JOHN	FRE	101	FREDERIC
MOHLER, MARTIN	BAL	453	8TH WARD
MOHLER, MARY E.	FRE	007	FREDERIC
MOHLER, WILLIAM	WAS	133	HAGERSTO
MOHON, BENJAMIN	HAR	131	2ND DIST
MOHON, EDWIN	HAR	133	2ND DIST
MOHON, ELIZABETH	HAR	131	2ND DIST
MOHON, ELIZABETH	HAR	132	2ND DIST
MOHON, MARGARETT	HAR	133	2ND DIST
MOHON, MARY	HAR	137	2ND DIST
MOHON, WILLIAM	HAR	133	2ND DIST
MOHRMAN, JOHN	FRE	037	FREDERIC
MOHUN, APTRICK	BAL	291	20TH WAR
MOILAN, JOHN	BAL	354	13TH WAR
MOIR, AUGUST	BAL	378	8TH WARD
MOIR, JAMES	BAL	141	16TH WAR
MOIRE, PENELOPE	BAL	303	7TH WARD
MOLANE, HENRY	BAL	358	1ST DIST
MOLAR, RICHARD	BAL	159	1ST WARD
MOLDE, G.M.	BAL	228	19TH WAR
MOLDEN, CAROLINE	ANN	298	1ST DIST
MOLDEN, ELIZABETH	WAS	126	2ND DIST
MOLDEN, GEORGE	ANN	398	8TH DIST
MOLDEN, HENRY W.	FRE	406	JEFFERSO
MOLDEN, JAMES	ANN	408	8TH DIST
MOLDEN, WILLIAM	CHA	250	MIDDLETO
MOLDENHAUER, G.	BAL	347	13TH WAR
MOLDER, MARIAH	ANN	398	8TH DIST
MOLDOORN, MARTIN	ALL	053	10TH E.D
MOLE, FREDERICK	BAL	111	2ND DIST
MOLE, WILLIAM	BAL	228	2ND WARD
MOLEHEIR, THEODORE	BAL	026	4TH WARD
MOLENEUX, CHARLTON D.	MGM	345	CLARKSBU
MOLER, ADAM	WAS	302	1ST DIST
MOLER, GEORGE	CAR	391	2ND DIST
MOLER, JACOB	WAS	037	2ND SUBD
MOLER, JEREMIAH	FRE	306	WOODSBOR
MOLER, MARY C.	WAS	127	2ND DIST
MOLER, SARAH	WAS	037	2ND SUBD
MOLES, ASBUY	CAR	393	2ND DIST
MOLES, FANNY-BLACK	CAR	363	9TH DIST
MOLESMITH, SARAH	FRE	246	NEW MARK
MOLESWORTH, ALFRED	MGM	434	CLARKSTR
MOLESWORTH, CATHARINE	ANN	492	HOWARD D
MOLESWORTH, ELI	ANN	492	HOWARD D
MOLESWORTH, GEORGE	FRE	422	8TH E DI
MOLESWORTH, JOSEPH	FRE	252	NEW MARK
MOLESWORTH, JOSHUA	CAR	371	9TH DIST
MOLESWORTH, SAMUEL *	FRE	251	NEW MARK
MOLESWORTH.RACHAEL	FRE	424	8TH E DI
MOLHERLY, THOMAS	FRE	277	NEW MARK
MOLIN, JAMES	CHA	266	MIDDLETO
MOLINEUX, ASBURY	MGM	345	CLARKSBU
MOLINEUX, JOSHUA	MGM	345	CLARKSBU
MOLINEUX, WILLIAM A.	MGM	345	CLARKSBU
MOLING, CAROLINE	FRE	224	BUCKEYST
MOLING, EDWARD S.	FRE	225	BUCKEYST
MOLING, GEORGE W.	FRE	006	FREDERIC
MOLING, JOHN S.	FRE	403	JEFFERSO
MOLING, SUSAN C.	FRE	225	BUCKEYST
MOLING, WILLIAM	FRE	005	FREDERIC
MOLISER, JOHN A.	BAL	369	8TH WARD

Name	County	Page	District
MOLLAY, MARY*	BAL	346	3RD WARD
MOLLER, ADAM	CAR	319	1ST DIST
MOLLER, BETTY	BAL	037	1ST WARD
MOLLET, PATRICK	ALL	053	10TH E.D
MOLLISON, HENRY	BAL	164	16TH WAR
MOLLONEE, CANIEL	BAL	138	11TH WAR
MOLLOY, THOMAS	BAL	028	9TH WARD
MOLLY, ANN	BAL	287	1ST DIST
MOLLY, HENRY	BAL	062	15TH WAR
MOLLYHOINE, WILLIAM	CHA	225	ALLENS F
MOLLYSON, CATHARINE	BAL	263	1ST DIST
MOLOCK, AHAM	DOR	436	1ST DIST
MOLOCK, EPHRAIM	DOR	436	1ST DIST
MOLOCK, JAMES	BAL	046	1ST WARD
MOLOCK, JOHN	DOR	446	1ST DIST
MOLOCK, JOHN	SOM	507	BARREN C
MOLOCK, LITTLETON	DOR	466	1ST DIST
MOLOCK, MAJOR	DOR	436	1ST DIST
MOLOCK, RICHARD	DOR	436	1ST DIST
MOLOCK, RILEY*	DOR	440	1ST DIST
MOLOCK, RITEY*	DOR	440	1ST DIST
MOLONE, FRANCIS	FRE	327	MIDDLETO
MOLONE, PATRICK	BAL	148	5TH WARD
MOLONG, LEVIN	CAR	161	NO TWP L
MOLTER, JACOB	FRE	162	EMMITTSB
MOLTER, JOSHUA	FRE	163	EMMITTSB
MOLTON, EZEKIEL	HAR	168	3RD DIST.
MOLUCK, MILLY	BAL	168	16TH WAR
MOMEY, E. T. *	BAL	316	12TH WAR
MOMSON, MARY	BAL	439	14TH WAR
MONA, M.	BAL	114	1ST WARD
MONAGAN, THOMAS	BAL	112	1ST WARD
MONAGHAN, ELIZA	WAS	152	HAGERSTO
MONAGHAN, JOHN	BAL	004	4TH WARD
MONAGHAN, MARY	BAL	002	4TH WARD
MONAGHAN, THOMAS	BAL	421	1ST DIST
MONAHAN, HARMAN	ALL	129	4TH E.D.
MONAHAN, JOHN	ALL	129	4TH E.D.
MONAHAN, JOHN	ALL	077	5TH E.D.
MONAHAN, MARY	ANN	412	HOWARD D
MONAHAN, MATHEWS	ALL	052	10TH E.D
MONAHAN, ROSA	ALL	076	5TH E.D.
MONAHAS, CORNELIUS	ALL	184	9TH E.D.
MONAKIN, ANTHONY	ALL	075	5TH E.D.
MONALIN, JOHN	BAL	099	2ND DIST
MONARTY, THOMAS J.	CAL	005	1ST DIST
MONCHAN, THOMAS	ALL	139	6TH E.D.
MONCREIF, ROBERT	FRE	423	8TH E DI
MONDAY, ELLEN	QUE	247	5TH E DI
MONDAY, FRNAS *	WAS	135	2ND DIST
MONDAY, JANE	BAL	402	1ST DIST
MONDAY, JULIA	QUE	251	5TH E DI
MONDAY, RICHARD	QUE	249	5TH E DI
MONDERFLED, POWELL	ALL	019	2ND E.D.
MONDORF, CALIF	BAL	230	1ST DIST
MONDORF, J.H.	BAL	231	1ST DIST
MONDY, CHARLES	WAS	022	2ND SUBD
MONDY, JOHN	WAS	017	2ND SUBD
MONDY, LENCH	WAS	023	2ND SUBD
MONEAND, LOUIS	BAL	253	12TH WAR
MONEGAN, HENRY	CAR	269	WESTMINS
MONEGAN, PATRICK	BAL	029	15TH WAR
MONERT, ANDREW	BAL	009	15TH WAR
MONET, PRISCILLA	CAL	026	2ND DIST
MONET, WILLIAM	CAL	031	2ND DIST
MONETT, EASOM E.	CAL	001	1ST DIST
MONETT, ELIZA J.	CAL	031	2ND DIST
MONETT, ISAAC	CAL	033	2ND DIST
MONETT, JOHN	CAL	007	1ST DIST
MONETT, MOSES	CAL	034	2ND DIST
MONETT, SARAH ANN	CAL	031	2ND DIST
MONEY, CAROLINE	CEC	029	CHESAPEA
MONEY, GEORGE P.	ALL	245	CUMBERLA
MONEY, HUGH	BAL	053	15TH WAR
MONEY, JOHN-BLACK	QUE	154	1ST E DI
MONEY, JOSEPH	KEN	305	3RD DIST
MONEY, JOSEPH A.	KEN	305	3RD DIST
MONEY, MARTINER	CEC	049	1ST E DI
MONEY, MARY	BAL	032	1ST WARD
MONEY, MINTA	CEC	128	5TH E DI
MONG, JOHN	WAS	229	1ST DIST
MONG, JOHN	WAS	290	1ST DIST
MONG, JONATHAN P.	WAS	144	HAGERSTO
MONG, PETER	WAS	260	1ST DIST
MONGER, MAGDALINE	FRE	428	8TH E DI
MONGER, WILLIAM	BAL	076	1ST WARD
MONGOLD, CATHARINE	BAL	300	1ST DIST
MONGOLD, NICHOLAS	BAL	300	1ST DIST
MONGOMERY, JOSEPH	CAR	217	5TH DIST
MONGOMERY, JOSEPH	HAR	173	3RD DIST
MONGOMERY, JOSEPH	CHA	283	BOJANTOW
MONGOMERY, MARY	BAL	458	1ST DIST
MONHOLLAND, DENNIS	ALL	074	5TH E.D.
MONIER,ABRAHAM	BAL	126	1ST WARD
MONIES, CHARLES	BAL	123	1ST WARD
MONIGAN, JOSEPH	WAS	025	2ND SUBD
MONIGN, NOBLE*	DOR	422	1ST DIST
MONITZ, JOSEPH	FRE	161	EMMITTSB
MONK, JOHN C.	CHA	264	MIDDLETO
MONK, MARGARET	BAL	174	2ND DIST
MONK, SALLY	BAL	383	13TH WAR
MONK, THOMAS	BAL	160	1ST WARD
MONK, THOMAS	BAL	166	1ST WARD
MONK, THOMAS	BAL	171	1ST WARD
MONK, WILLIAM	BAL	386	3RD WARD
MONKEFF, ELIZABETH	BAL	346	13TH WAR
MONKS, JAMES	HAR	109	2ND DIST
MONKS, LEWIS	HAR	110	2ND DIST
MONKS, THOMAS	HAR	105	2ND DIST
MONKUR, J.C.S.	BAL	246	2ND WARD
MONKUR, JOHN C.S.	BAL	246	2ND WARD
MONLY, AMANDA	FRE	245	NEW MARK
MONMEN,RUDOLPH	BAL	064	1ST WARD
MONMONEA, CHARLES G.	BAL	057	1ST WARD
MONMONICE, THOMAS C.*	BAL	386	3RD WARD
MONMONIER, THOMAS	BAL	342	3RD WARD
MONMONIER, WILLIAM B.	BAL	357	3RD WARD
MONMOUICE, THOMAS C.*	BAL	386	3RD WARD
MONMOUIER, JOHN	BAL	346	3RD WARD
MONN, WILLIAM-BLACK	CAR	133	NO TWP L
MONNAEE, WILLIAM *	FRE	092	FREDERIC
MONNER, JOHN	BAL	219	19TH WAR
MONNY, WILLIAM T.	CEC	062	1ST E DI
MONOHON, ATTY	HAR	135	2ND DIST
MONOKY, ELIZA	DOR	416	1ST DIST
MONON, JOHN	BAL	264	20TH WAR
MONORY, MILLIE	FRE	011	FREDERIC
MONPOOLEMER, MARGARET	ALL	218	CUMBERLA
MONROE, CATHARINE	WAS	208	1ST DIST
MONROE, GEORGE O.	CHA	259	MIDDLETO
MONROE, GEORGE W.	CAR	214	5TH DIST
MONROE, H.L.	PRI	111	PISCATAW
MONROE, J.W.	PRI	111	PISCATAW
MONROE, JAMES	BAL	145	2ND DIST
MONROE, JAMES	BAL	116	2ND DIST
MONROE, JAMES	BAL	191	17TH WAR
MONROE, JAMES W.	WAS	184	BOONSBOR
MONROE, JAMES W.	BAL	149	11TH WAR
MONROE, JOHN	BAL	471	14TH WAR
MONROE, JOHN	PRI	121	PISCATAW
MONROE, JOHN	PRI	083	QUEEN AN
MONROE, L.	PRI	118	PISCATAW
MONROE, L.B.	PRI	109	PISCATAW
MONROE, LEVI N.	PRI	111	PISCATAW
MONROE, ROBERT W.	BAL	169	16TH WAR
MONROE, SARAH	BAL	260	12TH WAR
MONROE, SUSAN	CHA	259	MIDDLETO
MONROE, THEODORE	CHA	266	MIDDLETO
MONROE, WILLIAM	WAS	184	BOONSBOR
MONROW, ELIZA	BAL	461	1ST DIST
MONRUL, THOMAS	BAL	143	1ST WARD
MONS, ELIZA	FRE	267	NEW MARK
MONSART, NICHOLAS	BAL	066	18TH WAR
MONSAVAT, ISAAC	BAL	206	11TH WAR
MONSBOCK, MARY	BAL	103	1ST WARD
MONSHAW, ROSE	BAL	432	1ST DIST
MONSHOUR, JACOB	FRE	175	5TH E DI
MONSHOUR, JAMES O.	FRE	175	5TH E DI
MONSING, WILLIAM	BAL	254	12TH WAR
MONSONIER, CHARLES	FRE	202	5TH E DI
MONSORATT, OSCAR	BAL	241	2ND WARD
MONT, SAMUEL	FRE	137	CREAGERS
MONTAGUE, CHARLES	BAL	006	9TH WARD
MONTAGUE, ELIZABETH	BAL	281	20TH WAR
MONTAGUE, HENRY P.	TAL	048	EASTON T
MONTAGUE, LOUISA	BAL	226	12TH WAR
MONTAGUE, MICHAEL	BAL	093	2ND DIST
MONTAGUE, PETER	BAL	346	13TH WAR
MONTAGUE, PHILIP	WAS	095	2ND SUBD
MONTAGUE, RICHARD	BAL	001	9TH WARD
MONTAGUE, WILLIAM	BAL	226	12TH WAR
MONTAGUE, WILLIAM	BAL	167	11TH WAR
MONTAGUE, WILLIAM	BAL	167	11TH WAR
MONTANDON, ELENOR	BAL	225	12TH WAR
MONTANDON, MARY	BAL	224	12TH WAR
MONTEBAUGH, JOHN	WAS	200	1ST DIST
MONTEBAUGH, SARAH	WAS	210	1ST DIST
MONTEL, MARY	WAS	166	HAGERSTO
MONTELL, ANTHONY	BAL	133	1ST WARD
MONTELL, GEORGE *	BAL	306	20TH WAR
MONTELL, HENRY H.	BAL	414	1ST DIST
MONTELL, JAMES	BAL	054	4TH WARD
MONTELL, JOHN B.	BAL	088	4TH WARD
MONTELL, MARY	BAL	467	14TH WAR
MONTERAY, GEORGE	BAL	360	3RD WARD
MONTERE, GEORGE	MGM	389	ROCKERLE
MONTGANLY, JOHN *	BAL	214	6TH WARD
MONTGARILY, JOHN *	BAL	214	6TH WARD
MONTGARRETTY, JOSEPH	BAL	305	17TH WAR
MONTGER, BENEDICK J.	CHA	251	MIDDLETO
MONTGILION, JEREMIAH	ANN	426	HOWARD D
MONTGOMERY, ASAHEL	HAR	101	2ND DIST
MONTGOMERY, AUGUSTUS	BAL	366	8TH WARD
MONTGOMERY, CATHERINE	CHA	283	BOJANTOW
MONTGOMERY, CHARLOTTE	HAR	101	2ND DIST
MONTGOMERY, CHRISTPHER	BAL	471	14TH WAR
MONTGOMERY, DELIAH	BAL	024	1ST WARD
MONTGOMERY, ELIZABETH	PRI	030	VANSVILL
MONTGOMERY, FANNY-BLACK	CAR	410	2ND DIST
MONTGOMERY, FRANCIS	CHA	255	MIDDLETO
MONTGOMERY, GEORGE	BAL	300	3RD WARD
MONTGOMERY, GEORGE A.	BAL	294	7TH WARD
MONTGOMERY, H.	BAL	313	12TH WAR
MONTGOMERY, HERNY	BAL	413	8TH WARD
MONTGOMERY, HUGH R.	ALL	186	9TH E.D.
MONTGOMERY, J.	BAL	169	1ST WARD
MONTGOMERY, J.	BAL	163	1ST WARD
MONTGOMERY, JAEMS	BAL	385	13TH WAR
MONTGOMERY, JAMES	CHA	250	MIDDLETO
MONTGOMERY, JAMES	FRE	275	NEW MARK
MONTGOMERY, JAMES	FRE	277	NEW MARK
MONTGOMERY, JAMES	BAL	313	12TH WAR
MONTGOMERY, JANE	CHA	247	HILLTOP
MONTGOMERY, JEREMIAH	CAR	384	2ND DIST
MONTGOMERY, JOHN	FRE	275	NEW MARK
MONTGOMERY, JOHN	HAR	025	1ST DIST
MONTGOMERY, JOHN	BAL	168	1ST WARD
MONTGOMERY, JOHN	BAL	115	1ST WARD
MONTGOMERY, JOHN	ANN	422	HOWARD D
MONTGOMERY, JOHN	WAS	147	2ND DIST
MONTGOMERY, JOSEPH	BAL	134	1ST WARD
MONTGOMERY, JULIAN	CHA	250	MIDDLETO
MONTGOMERY, LEWIS	CEC	089	4TH E DI
MONTGOMERY, LOVEY	HAR	099	2ND DIST
MONTGOMERY, LYDIA	BAL	322	7TH WARD
MONTGOMERY, MARTIN-BLACK	BAL	208	2ND WARD
MONTGOMERY, MARY	BAL	346	13TH WAR
MONTGOMERY, MARY	BAL	188	19TH WAR
MONTGOMERY, MATILDA	BAL	294	7TH WARD
MONTGOMERY, MILLY-BLACK	BAL	222	2ND WARD
MONTGOMERY, NANCY	BAL	387	8TH WARD
MONTGOMERY, NORRIS	BAL	093	5TH WARD
MONTGOMERY, NORTON	BAL	002	15TH WAR
MONTGOMERY, RACHEL	BAL	023	1ST WARD
MONTGOMERY, RICHARD	BAL	387	8TH WARD
MONTGOMERY, ROBERT	BAL	345	1ST DIST
MONTGOMERY, ROBERT	BAL	114	2ND DIST
MONTGOMERY, ROBERT	CEC	158	PORT DUP
MONTGOMERY, SAMUEL-BLACK	BAL	222	2ND WARD
MONTGOMERY, SARA V.	CHA	286	BOJANTOW
MONTGOMERY, SARAH	BAL	074	13TH WAR
MONTGOMERY, SARAH A.-BLAC	BAL	214	2ND WARD
MONTGOMERY, THOMAS	BAL	094	2ND DIST
MONTGOMERY, THOMAS	BAL	319	12TH WAR
MONTGOMERY, THOMAS	CAR	384	2ND DIST
MONTGOMERY, WASHINGTON	ALL	187	9TH E.D.
MONTGOMERY, WILLIAM	BAL	194	17TH WAR
MONTGOMERY, WILLIAM	BAL	209	2ND WARD
MONTGOMERY, WILLIAM L.	BAL	331	7TH WARD
MONTGOMERY, WILLIAM-BLACK	BAL	214	2ND WARD
MONTGOMERY, WORTHINGTON	ALL	186	9TH E.D.
MONTGOMEY, JAMES H.	CHA	292	BOJANTOW
MONTGUE, FRANCES	BAL	326	7TH WARD
MONTIGUE, DARIAS	QUE	200	3RD E DI
MONTIGUE, DAVID	QUE	199	3RD E DI
MONTIGUE, JOHN	QUE	198	3RD E DI
MONTILL, FRANCIS T.*	BAL	088	4TH WARD
MONTITT, FRANCIS T.*	BAL	088	4TH WARD
MONTLE, JOHN	WAS	060	2ND SUBD
MONTLY, ELI *	BAL	335	1ST DIST
MONTOOTH, BARNEY	HAR	009	1ST DIST
MONTOOTH, HENRY	HAR	010	1ST DIST
MONTORY, GERTRUDE	BAL	465	14TH WAR
MONTOUT, EDWARD	BAL	123	11TH WAR
MONY, JACOB *	WAS	107	2ND DIST
MOOD, HEPIAH	CAR	070	NO TWP L
MOOD, JOHN	BAL	068	2ND DIST
MOODEY, CHARLOTTE A.-BLAC	QUE	165	2ND E DI
MOODY, AILSEY	BAL	021	9TH WARD
MOODY, ALICE	BAL	316	3RD WARD
MOODY, ANN	BAL	074	4TH WARD
MOODY, BENJAMIN-BLACK	FRE	052	FREDERIC
MOODY, BETTY-BLACK	QUE	185	3RD E DI
MOODY, CHARLES	ANN	507	HOWARD D
MOODY, CHRISTINA	BAL	058	1ST WARD
MOODY, CHRISTOPHER	BAL	393	1ST DIST
MOODY, EDWIN	BAL	295	20TH WAR
MOODY, GEORGE	MGM	321	CRACKLIN
MOODY, GEORGE	TAL	105	ST MICHA
MOODY, HENRIETTA	QUE	251	5TH E DI
MOODY, ISAAC	CEC	043	CHESAPEA
MOODY, ISABELLA	BAL	128	11TH WAR
MOODY, JACOB	TAL	023	EASTON D
MOODY, JAMES	BAL	226	19TH WAR
MOODY, JOHN	BAL	326	7TH WARD
MOODY, JOHN B.	BAL	054	9TH WARD
MOODY, JOHN S. *	KEN	252	1ST DIST
MOODY, JOHN T.	CEC	108	3RD E DI
MOODY, JONATHAN	CEC	007	ELKTON 3
MOODY, JOSEPH	BAL	074	15TH WAR
MOODY, LEWIS	WAS	020	2ND SUBD
MOODY, LUCY	WAS	007	WILLIAMS
MOODY, MARTHA	ANN	414	HOWARD D
MOODY, OCTAVIA	BAL	340	3RD WARD
MOODY, RACHEL	TAL	105	ST MICHA
MOODY, RACHEL	TAL	106	ST MICHA
MOODY, ROBERT	BAL	368	8TH WARD
MOODY, WILLIAM-BLACK	QUE	180	2ND E DI
MOODY, WILLIAM-BLACK	QUE	180	2ND E DI
MOODY, WILLIAM-BLACK	QUE	164	2ND E DI
MOODY,ADELAIDE	FRE	239	NEW MARK
MOOER, CHARLES H.	BAL	434	14TH WAR
MOOER, EDWIN	CEC	184	7TH E DI
MOOES, LAURA P.	HAR	111	2ND DIST
MOOG, GEORGE	BAL	043	18TH WAR
MOOLOLEY, MICHAEL	ALL	051	10TH E.D
MOOLS, EDWIN	BAL	266	20TH WAR
MOON, A. J.	ALL	132	4TH E.D.
MOON, AARON	BAL	091	2ND DIST
MOON, ABRAHAM	ALL	065	10TH E.D
MOON, ANN	BAL	259	17TH WAR
MOON, ANNA	BAL	438	8TH WARD
MOON, BENJAMIN	ALL	064	10TH E.D
MOON, DAVID	CEC	127	5TH E DI
MOON, EDGAR	CEC	122	4TH E DI
MOON, EDWARD B.	BAL	060	18TH WAR
MOON, FRANCES	BAL	419	14TH WAR
MOON, GARRETT V.	ALL	064	10TH E.D
MOON, HORATIO	BAL	069	4TH WARD
MOON, ISAAC	ALL	064	10TH E.D
MOON, JACOB	ALL	060	10TH E.D
MOON, JOSEPH	CEC	121	4TH E DI
MOON, LAWRENCE	ALL	142	6TH E.D.
MOON, LEVI	ALL	131	4TH E.D.
MOON, MICHAEL*	BAL	423	3RD WARD
MOON, REUBEN	ALL	131	4TH E.D.
MOON, SIMETRA*	TAL	050	EASTON T
MOON, THOMAS	ALL	061	10TH E.D
MOON, WILLIAM	ALL	132	4TH E.D.
MOON, WILLIAM	BAL	277	17TH WAR
MOON, WILLIAM F.	BAL	173	1ST WARD
MOONERY, WANNY	BAL	021	9TH WARD
MOONEY, BRUM	ALL	051	10TH E.D
MOONEY, DAVID	BAL	069	2ND DIST
MOONEY, EDWARD	BAL	133	5TH WARD
MOONEY, FRANCIS	BAL	446	8TH WARD
MOONEY, FRANCIS	BAL	119	1ST WARD
MOONEY, FRANCIS	FRE	20	5TH E DI
MOONEY, H.J.	BAL	044	2ND DIST
MOONEY, ISABELLA	BAL	236	6TH WARD
MOONEY, JAMES	BAL	236	6TH WARD
MOONEY, JAMES	ANN	421	HOWARD D
MOONEY, JAMES	BAL	365	1ST DIST
MOONEY, JAMES	BAL	004	18TH WAR
MOONEY, JAMES	CAL	015	1ST DIST
MOONEY, JANE	BAL	010	4TH WARD
MOONEY, JOHN	BAL	116	11TH WAR
MOONEY, JOHN	BAL	170	1ST WARD
MOONEY, JOHN	BAL	212	6TH WARD
MOONEY, JOHN	BAL	110	10TH WAR
MOONEY, JOSEPH	BAL	044	18TH WAR
MOONEY, KATE	BAL	317	20TH WAR
MOONEY, LORA	BAL	429	1ST DIST
MOONEY, MARIA	BAL	435	8TH WARD
MOONEY, MARY	BAL	302	20TH WAR
MOONEY, MICHAEL	ALL	047	10TH E.D
MOONEY, PAT	BAL	144	5TH WARD
MOONEY, PAT	ANN	347	3RD DIST
MOONEY, PATRICK	ALL	079	5TH E.D.
MOONEY, PATRICK	ALL	142	6TH E.D.
MOONEY, PATRICK	BAL	171	11TH WAR
MOONEY, PATRICK	BAL	299	17TH WAR
MOONEY, PATRICK	BAL	301	17TH WAR
MOONEY, PATRICK	HAR	123	2ND DIST
MOONEY, SARAH	BAL	365	1ST DIST
MOONEY, SARAH	BAL	158	2ND DIST
MOONEY, SOPHIA	QUE	169	2ND E DI
MOONEY, THOMAS	ALL	048	10TH E.D
MOONEY, THOMAS	BAL	231	2ND WARD
MOONEY, VINCENT	FRE	202	5TH E DI
MOONEY, WILLIAM	FRE	167	EMMITTSB
MOONEY, WILLIAM	BAL	027	18TH WAR
MOONEY, WILLIAM	BAL	241	6TH WARD
MOONEY, WINIFER	BAL	029	4TH WARD
MOONLEY, CORMICK	ALL	050	10TH E.D
MOONN, WILLAIM	ALL	061	10TH E.D
MOONSHOWER, JOSEPH	CAR	385	2ND DIST
MOONTZ, JOHN H.	BAL	122	1ST WARD
MOONY, HUGH	ALL	155	6TH E.D.
MOONY, HUGH	BAL	060	2ND DIST
MOONY, JAMES	DOR	313	1ST DIST
MOONY, WILLIAM*	DOR	302	1ST DIST
MOOR, CATHARINE	BAL	224	17TH WAR
MOOR, CHARLES *	BAL	323	1ST DIST
MOOR, ELLEN	BAL	209	17TH WAR
MOOR, FRANCIS	HAR	168	3RD DIST
MOOR, GEORGE	BAL	150	5TH WARD
MOOR, GEORGE	BAL	101	5TH WARD
MOOR, HARRIETT	BAL	122	5TH WARD
MOOR, HENRY A.	CHA	249	MIDDLETO

Name	County	Page	District
MOOR, ISABELLA	ALL	170	6TH E.D.
MOOR, J.D.W.	ALL	241	CUMBERLA
MOOR, JAMES	ALL	205	CUMBERLA
MOOR, JAMES	CAR	283	7TH DIST
MOOR, JAMES N.	BAL	204	17TH WAR
MOOR, JOHN	ALL	215	CUMBERLA
MOOR, JOHN	ALL	169	6TH E.D.
MOOR, JOHN	BAL	114	2ND DIST
MOOR, MARY	BAL	343	1ST DIST
MOOR, MARY	BAL	146	5TH WARD
MOOR, MR.	BAL	201	17TH WAR
MCOR, PHIKIP	BAL	344	1ST DIST
MOOR, REUBEN	ALL	245	CUMBERLA
MOOR, ROBERT P.	CHA	250	MIDDLETO
MOOR, SARAH	BAL	212	17TH WAR
MOOR, SPALDING C.	CHA	249	MIDDLETO
MOOR,LOUISA	ALL	215	CUMBERLA
MOORE AMELIA J.	SOM	365	BRINKLEY
MCORE, ABRAHAM-MULATTO	BAL	222	2ND WARD
MOORE, ADRIANNA	CEC	201	6TH E DI
MOORE, ALEXANDER	HAR	081	2ND DIST
MOORE, ALEXANDER	BAL	113	2ND DIST
MOORE, ALEXANDER	BAL	117	2ND DIST
MOORE, ALEXANDER	WAS	138	2ND DIST
MOORE, AMANDA	CEC	107	3RD E DI
MCORE, AMOS	CEC	209	7TH E DI
MOORE, AMOS	CEC	187	7TH E DI
MCORE, ANDREW	TAL	099	ST MICHA
MOORE, ANN	WAS	118	2ND DIST
MOORE, ANN	KEN	308	3RD DIST
MOORE, ANN	TAL	111	ST MICHA
MOORE, ANN	CEC	207	7TH E DI
MOORE, ANN	DOR	393	1ST DIST
MOORE, ANN E.	BAL	212	11TH WAR
MOORE, ANNA	CEC	015	ELKTON 3
MOORE, ANNA	BAL	066	2ND DIST
MOORE, ANNA E.	BAL	392	14TH WAR
MOORE, ANNA M.	ANN	521	HOWARD D
MOORE, ANTHONY	BAL	079	10TH WAR
MOORE, ARCHIBALD	BAL	267	7TH WARD
MOORE, ARSEMUS	HAR	110	2ND DIST
MOORE, ASSENTH	KEN	270	1ST DIST
MOORE, BALINDY S.	FRE	277	NEW MARK
MCORE, BARNEY	BAL	025	2ND DIST
MOORE, BENJAMIN	BAL	243	20TH WAR
MOORE, BENJAMIN P.	HAR	086	2ND DIST
MOORE, BENJAMIN P. JR.	BAL	001	15TH WAR
MOORE, BETSEY	SOM	513	BARREN C
MOORE, BRANNOCK*	DOR	448	1ST DIST
MOORE, C. B.	BAL	469	14TH WAR
MCORE, CAROLINE	BAL	119	11TH WAR
MOORE, CASANDER	HAR	176	3RD DIST
MOORE, CATHARINE	FRE	163	EMMITTSB
MOORE, CATHARINE	BAL	333	7TH WARD
MOORE, CATHARINE	ANN	429	HOWARD D
MOORE, CELIA A.	HAR	086	2ND DIST
MOORE, CHARLES	ANN	345	3RD DIST
MOORE, CHARLES	BAL	265	12TH WAR
MOORE, CHARLES F.	CEC	042	CHESAPEA
MOORE, CHARLES W.	MGM	374	ROCKERLE
MOORE, CHARLOTT	CEC	064	1ST E DI
MOORE, CHARLOTTE	BAL	213	11TH WAR
MOORE, CHRISTOPHER	BAL	274	20TH WAR
MOORE, COLEGATE C.	BAL	213	11TH WAR
MOORE, COLEGATE C.	BAL	104	10TH WAR
MCORE, CORYDON	BAL	471	14TH WAR
MCORE, CORYDON R.	BAL	471	14TH WAR
MOORE, CYRUS	BAL	141	16TH WAR
MOORE, DANIEL	BAL	195	17TH WAR
MOORE, DANIEL	KEN	309	3RD DIST
MOORE, DANIEL	WAS	041	2ND SUBD
MOORE, DANIEL	WAS	046	2ND SUBD
MOORE, DANIEL*	BAL	271	20TH WAR
MOORE, DAVID	CEC	210	7TH E DI
MOORE, DAVID	CAR	083	NO TWP L
MOORE, DAVID	BAL	106	18TH WAR
MOORE, DAVID	TAL	052	EASTON D
MOORE, DAVID	SOM	382	BRINKLEY
MOORE, DAVID	QUE	229	4TH E DI
MOORE, DAVID	BAL	315	12TH WAR
MOORE, DAVID W.	BAL	431	14TH WAR
MOORE, DEBORAH A.	BAL	174	6TH WARD
MOORE, DENNIS	DOR	346	3RD DIVI
MOORE, EDWARD	BAL	083	4TH WARD
MOORE, EDWARD	CEC	150	PORT DUP
MOORE, EDWARD	QUE	137	1ST E DI
MOORE, EDWARD	BAL	460	1ST DIST
MOORE, EDWARD A.	KEN	209	2ND DIST
MOORE, EDWIN	SOM	425	PRINCESS
MOORE, ELGARE S.	ST	311	1ST E DI
MOORE, ELI	SOM	387	BRINKLEY
MOORE, ELIAS	MGM	349	BERRYS D
MOORE, ELIZA	HAR	080	2ND DIST
MOORE, ELIZA	CEC	210	7TH E DI
MOORE, ELIZA	BAL	029	9TH WARD
MCORE, ELIZA H.	CAR	235	UNION TO
MOORE, ELIZABETH	BAL	040	4TH WARD
MOORE, ELIZABETH	QUE	132	1ST E DI
MOORE, ELIZABETH	CEC	142	6TH E DI
MOORE, ELIZABETH	BAL	358	13TH WAR
MOORE, ELIZABETH	BAL	162	6TH WARD
MOORE, ELIZABETH	BAL	177	2ND WARD
MOORE, ELIZABETH	BAL	331	13TH WAR
MOORE, ELIZABETH	BAL	106	15TH WAR
MOORE, ELIZABETH	BAL	044	2ND DIST
MOORE, ELIZABETH	QUE	178	2ND E DI
MOORE, ELLEN	TAL	105	ST MICHA
MOORE, ELLEN	BAL	214	11TH WAR
MOORE, ELY	BAL	212	19TH WAR
MOORE, EPHRAIM	CEC	171	6TH E DI
MOORE, ESTHER	SOM	386	BRINKLEY
MOORE, F.S.	WAS	021	2ND SUBD
MOORE, FANNY	BAL	072	10TH WAR
MOORE, FRANCES	BAL	106	15TH WAR
MOORE, FRANCIS	BAL	008	9TH WARD
MOORE, FRANCIS M.	ST	298	2ND E DI
MOORE, FREDERICK	KEN	310	3RD DIST
MOORE, FREDERICK	CEC	054	1ST E DI
MOORE, G. S. REV.	WOR	261	BERLIN 1
MCORE, GARRISON	TAL	097	ST MICHA
MOORE, GAY	BAL	062	10TH WAR
MOORE, GEORGE	BAL	331	13TH WAR
MOORE, GEORGE	BAL	065	2ND DIST
MOORE, GEORGE	BAL	242	6TH WARD
MCORE, GEORGE	BAL	256	5TH WARD
MOORE, GEORGE	ST	296	2ND E DI
MOORE, GEORGE	SOM	529	QUANTICO
MOORE, GEORGE	CEC	075	NORTHEAS
MOORE, GEORGE	CEC	061	1ST E DI
MOORE, GEORGE	BAL	086	18TH WAR

Name	County	Page	District
MOORE, GEORGE	CEC	149	PORT DUP
MOORE, GEORGE	CEC	048	1ST E DI
MOORE, GEORGE	FRE	019	FREDERIC
MOORE, GEORGE	BAL	142	19TH WAR
MOORE, GEORGE E.	SOM	480	TRAPP DI
MOORE, GEORGE F.	ST	280	3RD E DI
MOORE, GEORGE L.	BAL	094	18TH WAR
MOORE, GEORGE W.	BAL	322	3RD WARD
MOORE, GIBBONS	ANN	442	HOWARD D
MOORE, GIBBONS P.	CEC	171	6TH E DI
MOORE, GLEDSTANES A.	BAL	043	15TH WAR
MOORE, GRACE	HAR	187	3RD DIST
MOORE, H. A.	BAL	279	20TH WAR
MOORE, HAMILTON	ANN	478	HOWARD D
MOORE, HAMILTON	WAS	118	2ND DIST
MOORE, HAMILTON	SOM	378	BRINKLEY
MOORE, HANNAH	BAL	336	3RD WARD
MOORE, HANNIBAL	BAL	311	3RD WARD
MOORE, HARRIET W.	CEC	100	3RD E DI
MOORE, HARRY	HAR	106	2ND DIST
MOORE, HENERY	DOR	353	3RD DIVI
MOORE, HENRY	BAL	318	3RD WARD
MOORE, HENRY	BAL	270	12TH WAR
MOORE, HENRY	BAL	228	6TH WARD
MOORE, HENRY	BAL	177	2ND WARD
MOORE, HENRY	BAL	224	2ND WARD
MOORE, HENRY	TAL	099	ST MICHA
MOORE, HENRY J.	BAL	083	1ST WARD
MOORE, HENRY L.	MGM	328	CRACKLIN
MOORE, HENRY-BLACK	QUE	125	1ST E DI
MOORE, HORATIC	PRI	021	VANSVILL
MOORE, HUMPHREY	BAL	040	9TH WARD
MOORE, IGNATIUS	ST	309	1ST E DI
MOORE, ISAAC	SOM	378	BRINKLEY
MOORE, ISAAC	BAL	420	8TH WARD
MOORE, ISAAC	MGM	371	BERRYS D
MOORE, ISAACK	DOR	353	3RD DIVI
MOORE, J.	BAL	149	1ST WARD
MOORE, J. L.	ALL	072	5TH E.D.
MOORE, J. W. J.	ST	280	3RD E DI
MOORE, J.W.	BAL	159	1ST WARD
MOORE, JACOB	PRI	074	MARLBROU
MOORE, JACOB	HAR	185	3RD DIST
MOORE, JACOB M.	BAL	102	15TH WAR
MOORE, JAMES	BAL	168	1ST WARD
MOORE, JAMES	BAL	459	8TH WARD
MOORE, JAMES	BAL	342	7TH WARD
MOORE, JAMES	BAL	063	1ST WARD
MOORE, JAMES	BAL	099	2ND DIST
MOORE, JAMES	ANN	452	HOWARD D
MOORE, JAMES	FRE	141	CREAGERS
MOORE, JAMES	DOR	326	3RD DIVI
MOORE, JAMES	HAR	081	2ND DIST
MOORE, JAMES	CEC	091	4TH E DI
MOORE, JAMES	CEC	106	3RD E DI
MOORE, JAMES	CEC	100	3RD E DI
MOORE, JAMES	CEC	100	3RD E DI
MOORE, JAMES	CEC	064	1ST E DI
MOORE, JAMES	CEC	160	6TH E DI
MOORE, JAMES	DOR	305	1ST DIST
MOORE, JAMES	BAL	245	17TH WAR
MOORE, JAMES	DOR	392	1ST DIST
MOORE, JAMES	DOR	407	1ST DIST
MOORE, JAMES	DOR	435	1ST DIST
MOORE, JAMES	CEC	044	CHESAPEA
MOORE, JAMES	BAL	214	11TH WAR
MOORE, JAMES	SOM	389	BRINKLEY
MOORE, JAMES	TAL	053	EASTON D
MOORE, JAMES	WAS	137	2ND DIST
MOORE, JAMES	ST	297	2ND E DI
MOORE, JAMES	TAL	099	ST MICHA
MOORE, JAMES B.	BAL	397	8TH WARD
MOORE, JAMES C.	BAL	073	18TH WAR
MOORE, JAMES E.	BAL	170	1ST WARD
MOORE, JAMES F.	BAL	356	3RD WARD
MOORE, JAMES F.	SOM	539	TYASKIN
MOORE, JAMES H.	DOR	297	1ST DIST
MOORE, JAMES H.	DOR	325	1ST DIST
MOORE, JAMES J.	WOR	185	6TH E DI
MOORE, JAMES S.	KEN	247	2ND DIST
MOORE, JANE	BAL	271	12TH WAR
MOORE, JANE	BAL	207	11TH WAR
MOORE, JANE C.	BAL	230	6TH WARD
MOORE, JANE H.	KEN	273	1ST DIST
MOORE, JAOCB W.	CAR	123	NO TWP L
MOORE, JEMIMA	SOM	381	BRINKLEY
MOORE, JEREMIAH	SOM	378	BRINKLEY
MOORE, JOB	SOM	380	BRINKLEY
MOORE, JOH M.	QUE	175	2ND E DI
MOORE, JOHN	ST	308	1ST E DI
MOORE, JOHN	SOM	471	TRAPPE D
MOORE, JOHN	WAS	159	HAGERSTO
MOORE, JOHN	SOM	392	BRINKLEY
MOORE, JOHN	SOM	517	BARREN C
MOORE, JOHN	SOM	534	QUANTICO
MOORE, JOHN	PRI	029	VANSVILL
MOORE, JOHN	PRI	048	AQUASCO
MOORE, JOHN	TAL	100	ST MICHA
MOORE, JOHN	WOR	253	1ST CENS
MOORE, JOHN	WAS	069	2ND SUBD
MOORE, JOHN	HAR	137	2ND DIST
MOORE, JOHN	DOR	369	3RD DIVI
MOORE, JOHN	CEC	209	7TH E DI
MOORE, JOHN	CEC	202	6TH E DI
MOORE, JOHN	CEC	150	PORT DUP
MOORE, JOHN	CEC	174	6TH E DI
MOORE, JOHN	BAL	061	4TH WARD
MOORE, JOHN	CEC	068	5TH E DI
MOORE, JOHN	BAL	002	18TH WAR
MOORE, JCHN	BAL	184	19TH WAR
MOORE, JOHN	DOR	437	1ST DIST
MOORE, JOHN	HAR	055	1ST DIST
MOORE, JOHN	BAL	158	1ST WARD
MOORE, JOHN	BAL	034	9TH WARD
MOORE, JOHN	BAL	201	6TH WARD
MOORE, JOHN	BAL	017	15TH WAR
MOORE, JOHN	BAL	094	1ST WARD
MOORE, JOHN	BAL	012	1ST WARD
MCORE, JOHN	BAL	145	1ST WARD
MOORE, JOHN	BAL	145	1ST WARD
MOORE, JOHN	BAL	229	2ND WARD
MOORE, JOHN	BAL	089	2ND DIST
MCORE, JOHN	BAL	037	2ND DIST
MOORE, JOHN	BAL	035	2ND DIST
MOORE, JOHN	BAL	093	10TH WAR
MOORE, JOHN	BAL	086	15TH WAR
MOORE, JOHN	BAL	300	3RD WARD
MOORE, JOHN C.	BAL	286	12TH WAR
MOORE, JOHN D.	PRI	090	MARLBROU
MOORE, JOHN E.	SOM	471	TRAPPE D

Name	County	Page	District
MOORE, JOHN J.	BAL	103	15TH WAR
MOORE, JOHN N.	DOR	462	1ST DIST
MOORE, JOHN R.	ANN	479	HOWARD D
MOORE, JOHN R.	BAL	054	15TH WAR
MOORE, JOHN T.	ST	309	1ST E DI
MOORE, JOHN T.	FRE	017	FREDERIC
MOORE, JOHN W.	SOM	444	DAMES QU
MOCRE, JOHN W.	KEN	313	3RD DIST
MOORE, JOHN W.	SOM	536	TYASKIN
MOORE, JOHN WILLIAM	BAL	245	17TH WAR
MOORE, JOSEPH	CAR	388	2ND DIST
MOORE, JOSEPH	CEC	054	1ST E DI
MOORE, JOSEPH	WAS	113	2ND DIST
MOORE, JOSEPHINE	ALL	109	5TH E.D.
MOORE, JOSIAH	PRI	070	MARLBROU
MOORE, JOSIAH	DOR	455	1ST DIST
MOORE, JOSIAH	HAR	003	1ST DIST
MOORE, KESIAH	CAR	124	NO TWP L
MOORE, LAWERANCE	BAL	027	18TH WAR
MOORE, LEMUEL	DOR	345	3RD DIVI
MOORE, LEONARD	ALL	072	5TH E.D.
MOORE, LEVEN	DOR	353	3RD DIVI
MOORE, LEVI	BAL	342	7TH WARD
MOORE, LEVI	WAS	140	2ND DIST
MOORE, LEVIN E.	BAL	128	1ST WARD
MOORE, LLOYD	BAL	376	13TH WAR
MOORE, LOUISA	HAR	017	1ST DIST
MOORE, LOYD	HAR	194	3RD DIST
MOORE, LUCINDA	ALL	204	CUMBERLA
MOORE, LUCRETIA	ANN	442	HOWARD D
MOORE, LYDIA	BAL	191	19TH WAR
MOORE, MARGARET	BAL	361	13TH WAR
MOORE, MARGARET	BAL	007	9TH WARD
MOORE, MARGARET	BAL	283	12TH WAR
MOORE, MARGARET	BAL	084	10TH WAR
MOORE, MARGARET	BAL	067	10TH WAR
MOORE, MARGARET	SOM	537	TYASKIN
MOORE, MARGARETT	BAL	045	4TH WARD
MOORE, MARGARETT E.	KEN	300	3RD DIST
MOORE, MARIA	BAL	106	18TH WAR
MOORE, MARIA	BAL	164	11TH WAR
MOORE, MARIAH	CAL	012	1ST DIST
MOORE, MARIAH	KEN	303	3RD DIST
MOORE, MARSHAM	PRI	071	MARLBROU
MOORE, MARTHA	BAL	434	14TH WAR
MOORE, MARTHA	FRE	163	EMMITTSB
MOORE, MARTHA	BAL	298	12TH WAR
MOORE, MARTHA	BAL	102	15TH WAR
MOORE, MARTHA	BAL	090	15TH WAR
MOORE, MARTHA	BAL	121	2ND DIST
MOORE, MARTHA	BAL	300	7TH WARD
MOORE, MARTHA A.	QUE	151	1ST E DI
MOORE, MARY	BAL	064	4TH WARD
MOORE, MARY	HAR	190	3RD DIST
MOORE, MARY	CEC	011	ELKTON 3
MOORE, MARY	CEC	007	ELKTON 3
MOORE, MARY	CAR	185	8TH DIST
MOORE, MARY	DOR	346	3RD DIVI
MOORE, MARY	DOR	353	3RD DIVI
MOORE, MARY	CEC	211	7TH E DI
MOORE, MARY	DOR	317	1ST DIST
MOORE, MARY	BAL	068	18TH WAR
MOORE, MARY	BAL	137	2ND DIST
MOORE, MARY	BAL	068	10TH WAR
MOORE, MARY	BAL	185	11TH WAR
MOORE, MARY	BAL	181	11TH WAR
MOORE, MARY	BAL	019	9TH WARD
MOORE, MARY	BAL	218	2ND WARD
MOORE, MARY	KEN	288	3RD DIST
MOORE, MARY	ST	298	2ND E DI
MOORE, MARY	TAL	089	ST MICHA
MOORE, MARY	WAS	091	2ND SUBD
MOORE, MARY	WAS	041	2ND SUBD
MOORE, MARY *	ALL	141	6TH E.D.
MOORE, MARY A.	BAL	345	7TH WARD
MOORE, MARY A.	BAL	432	8TH WARD
MOORE, MARY A.	BAL	052	1ST WARD
MOORE, MARY A.	BAL	025	1ST WARD
MOORE, MARY A.	DOR	454	1ST DIST
MOORE, MARY A.	CEC	004	ELKTON 3
MOORE, MARY A.	BAL	112	18TH WAR
MOORE, MARY A.	DOR	300	1ST DIST
MOORE, MARY C.	PRI	029	VANSVILL
MOORE, MARY E.	CEC	207	7TH E DI
MOORE, MARY F.	WAS	115	2ND DIST
MOORE, MARY M.	BAL	014	4TH WARD
MOORE, MARY P.	BAL	097	10TH WAR
MOORE, MARY R.	HAR	149	3RD DIST
MOORE, MARY T.	BAL	068	10TH WAR
MOORE, MATHEW	BAL	344	7TH WARD
MOORE, MATILDA	QUE	152	1ST E DI
MOORE, MATTHEW	BAL	297	20TH WAR
MOORE, MICHAEL	BAL	441	8TH WARD
MOORE, MICHAEL	ALL	139	6TH E.D.
MOORE, MICHAEL	BAL	193	2ND WARD
MOORE, MICHAEL	BAL	147	2ND DIST
MOORE, MORDICA J.	PRI	071	MARLBROU
MOORE, MOSES	CEC	006	ELKTON 3
MOORE, NANCY	BAL	134	11TH WAR
MOORE, NANCY	SOM	496	SALISBUR
MOORE, NANCY	BAL	174	6TH WARD
MOORE, NANCY	BAL	099	10TH WAR
MOORE, NANCY	BAL	127	16TH WAR
MOORE, NATHANIEL	BAL	319	3RD WARD
MOORE, NATHANIEL P.	MGM	366	BERRYS D
MOORE, NED	DOR	420	1ST DIST
MOORE, NELLY	CEC	118	4TH E DI
MOORE, NOAH	SOM	552	TYASKIN
MOORE, P.	BAL	170	1ST WARD
MOORE, PAP *	KEN	282	3RD DIST
MOORE, PATIENCE	SOM	389	BRINKLEY
MOORE, PATRICK	BAL	172	6TH WARD
MOORE, PATRICK	ALL	142	6TH E.D.
MOORE, PATRICK	HAR	120	2ND DIST
MOORE, PATRICK	CEC	142	6TH E DI
MOORE, PEGGY	TAL	104	ST MICHA
MOORE, PERMELIA F.	HAR	166	3RD DIST
MOORE, PERRY	BAL	127	2ND DIST
MOORE, PETER	BAL	037	1ST WARD
MOORE, PHEBE	BAL	053	9TH WARD
MOORE, PHEBE	FRE	095	FREDERIC
MOORE, PHEBY A.	CEC	121	4TH E DI
MOORE, PRECILLA	BAL	292	3RD WARD
MOORE, PRISCILLA	QUE	241	5TH E DI
MOORE, R.	BAL	117	1ST WARD
MOORE, RACHEL A.	BAL	007	1ST WARD
MOORE, REBECCA	WOR	226	4TH E DI
MOORE, REBECCA	CEC	064	1ST E DI
MOORE, REBECCA	CAR	101	NO TWP L
MOORE, REBECCA	CEC	001	ELKTON 3

Name	County	Page	District
MOORE, REUBEN	ALL	067	10TH E.D
MOORE, RICHARD	BAL	317	3RD WARD
MOORE, RICHARD	BAL	288	12TH WAR
MOORE, RICHARD	QUE	236	4TH E DI
MOORE, RICHARD	DOR	453	1ST DIST
MOORE, RICHARD C.	BAL	405	3RD WARD
MOORE, ROBERT	BAL	387	8TH WARD
MOORE, ROBERT	BAL	084	10TH WAR
MOORE, ROBERT	BAL	423	3RD WARD
MOORE, ROBERT	BAL	378	13TH WAR
MOORE, ROBERT	BAL	147	19TH WAR
MOORE, ROBERT R.	MGM	371	BERRYS D
MOORE, RUFUS	SOM	428	PRINCESS
MOORE, SALEY*	DOR	463	1ST DIST
MOORE, SALLY	SOM	480	TRAPP DI
MOORE, SALLY	DOR	306	1ST DIST
MOORE, SALLY A.	WOR	302	SNOW HIL
MOORE, SAMUEL	SOM	537	TYASKIN
MOORE, SAMUEL	SOM	463	HANGARY
MOORE, SAMUEL	FRE	080	FREDERIC
MOORE, SAMUEL	CAR	154	NO TWP L
MOORE, SAMUEL	CEC	062	1ST E DI
MOORE, SAMUEL	BAL	011	18TH WAR
MOORE, SAMUEL	BAL	011	18TH WAR
MOORE, SAMUEL	BAL	083	2ND DIST
MOORE, SAMUEL	BAL	043	9TH WARD
MOORE, SAMUEL H.	QUE	152	1ST E DI.
MOORE, SAMUEL W.	BAL	313	7TH WARD
MOORE, SANO	BAL	054	2ND DIST
MOORE, SARAH	BAL	234	6TH WARD
MOORE, SARAH	BAL	173	16TH WAR
MOORE, SARAH	ALL	094	5TH E.D.
MOORE, SARAH	BAL	103	1ST WARD
MOORE, SARAH	BAL	387	13TH WAR
MOORE, SARAH	HAR	109	2ND DIST
MOORE, SARAH	DOR	424	1ST DIST
MOORE, SARAH	CEC	003	ELKTON 3
MOORE, SARAH	CEC	210	7TH E DI
MOORE, SARAH A.	FRE	065	FREDERIC
MOORE, SARAH E.	BAL	009	15TH WAR
MOORE, SARAH E.	SOM	533	QUANTICO
MOORE, SARAH E.	SOM	528	QUANTICO
MOORE, SARAH J.	BAL	427	14TH WAR
MOORE, SARAH MRS.	BAL	137	11TH WAR
MOORE, SARAH R.	BAL	366	8TH WARD
MOORE, SARHA	BAL	468	14TH WAR
MOORE, SENY *	KEN	280	3RD DIST
MOORE, SEWALL	QUE	166	2ND E DI
MOORE, SHARLOTT	HAR	175	3RD DIST
MOORE, SIDNEY	BAL	184	19TH WAR
MOORE, SOLOMON	SOM	522	BARREN C
MOORE, SOPHIA	WAS	114	2ND DIST
MOORE, SOPHIA	MGM	319	CRACKLIN
MOORE, STEPHEN	DOR	442	1ST DIST
MOORE, SUSAN	FRE	187	5TH E DI
MOORE, SUSAN	BAL	064	4TH WARD
MOORE, SUSAN	BAL	088	4TH WARD
MOORE, SUSAN	BAL	111	15TH WAR
MOORE, SUSAN E.	FRE	358	CATOCTIN
MOORE, T. J.	BAL	150	1ST WARD
MOORE, THEODORE	BAL	302	12TH WAR
MOORE, THERBURNE L.	BAL	357	13TH WAR
MOORE, THOMAS	BAL	110	18TH WAR
MOORE, THOMAS	BAL	118	11TH WAR
MOORE, THOMAS	DOR	344	3RD DIVI
MOORE, THOMAS	DOR	341	3RD DIVI
MOORE, THOMAS	BAL	052	18TH WAR
MOORE, THOMAS	BAL	154	16TH WAR
MOORE, THOMAS	BAL	131	1ST WARD
MOORE, THOMAS	BAL	356	3RD WARD
MOORE, THOMAS	ALL	128	4TH E.D.
MOORE, THOMAS	WOR	283	BERLIN 1
MOORE, THOMAS	SOM	536	TYASKIN
MOORE, THOMAS	SOM	480	TRAPP DI
MOORE, THOMAS	KEN	307	3RD DIST
MOORE, THOMAS	SOM	392	BRINKLEY
MOORE, THOMAS B.	SOM	554	TYASKIN
MOORE, THOMAS G.	ST	308	1ST E DI
MOORE, THOMAS T.	CAR	098	NO TWP L
MOORE, THOMASJ.	BAL	173	1ST WARD
MOORE, UPTON T.	WAS	138	2ND DIST
MOORE, VINCENT P.	DOR	317	1ST DIST
MOORE, W.I.	BAL	165	1ST WARD
MOORE, WALTER	ANN	467	HOWARD D
MOORE, WASHINGTON	CEC	059	1ST E DI
MOORE, WILFORD	PRI	054	AQUASCO
MOORE, WILLIAM	WOR	245	1ST CENS
MOORE, WILLIAM	SOM	508	BARREN C
MOORE, WILLIAM	SOM	519	BARREN C
MOORE, WILLIAM	SOM	504	SALISBUR
MOORE, WILLIAM	TAL	107	ST MICHA
MOORE, WILLIAM	SOM	381	BRINKLEY
MOORE, WILLIAM	WOR	340	1ST E DI
MOORE, WILLIAM	DOR	462	1ST DIST
MOORE, WILLIAM	QUE	172	2ND E DI
MOORE, WILLIAM	KEN	287	3RD DIST
MOORE, WILLIAM	WOR	299	SNOW HIL
MOORE, WILLIAM	WAS	073	2ND SUBD
MOORE, WILLIAM	CEC	075	NORTHEAS
MOORE, WILLIAM	CEC	109	4TH E DI
MOORE, WILLIAM	CEC	099	3RD E DI
MOORE, WILLIAM	DOR	367	3RD DIVI
MOORE, WILLIAM	DOR	353	3RD DIVI
MOORE, WILLIAM	CEC	211	7TH E DI
MOORE, WILLIAM	CAR	098	NO TWP L
MOORE, WILLIAM	BAL	063	4TH WARD
MOORE, WILLIAM	CEC	150	PORT DUP
MOORE, WILLIAM	CEC	128	5TH E DI
MOORE, WILLIAM	CEC	169	6TH E DI
MOORE, WILLIAM	CEC	171	6TH E DI
MOORE, WILLIAM	HAR	130	2ND DIST
MOORE, WILLIAM	SOM	411	DUBLIN D
MOORE, WILLIAM	BAL	174	1ST WARD
MOORE, WILLIAM	BAL	168	6TH WARD
MOORE, WILLIAM	ALL	093	5TH E.D.
MOORE, WILLIAM	BAL	121	1ST WARD
MOORE, WILLIAM	BAL	163	2ND DIST
MOORE, WILLIAM	BAL	282	2ND WARD
MOORE, WILLIAM	BAL	133	16TH WAR
MOORE, WILLIAM	BAL	174	16TH WAR
MOORE, WILLIAM	BAL	290	12TH WAR
MOORE, WILLIAM	BAL	007	15TH WAR
MOORE, WILLIAM	BAL	198	11TH WAR
MOORE, WILLIAM	BAL	178	11TH WAR
MOORE, WILLIAM	BAL	172	11TH WAR
MOORE, WILLIAM	BAL	318	3RD WARD
MOORE, WILLIAM B.	DOR	306	1ST DIST
MOORE, WILLIAM H.	BAL	394	3RD WARD
MOORE, WILLIAM H.	BAL	035	9TH WARD
MOORE, WILLIAM J.	DOR	306	1ST DIST
MOORE, WILLIAM J.H.	BAL	158	1ST WARD
MOORE, WILLIAM M.	CEC	100	3RD E DI
MOORE, WILLIAM N.	ANN	415	HOWARD D
MOORE, WILLIAM W.	CEC	200	7TH E DI
MOORE, WILLIAM W.	ST	306	1ST E DI
MOORE, WILLIAM-MULATTO	BAL	208	2ND WARD
MOORE, WILLIAMANNA*	SOM	536	TYASKIN
MOORE, WILSON	BAL	091	15TH WAR
MOORE, WILSON	BAL	100	10TH WAR
MOORE, ZEDEKIAH	ANN	445	HOWARD D
MOORE, ZEDRICK	ANN	359	3RD DIST
MOORE, ZILLEY	DOR	365	3RD DIVI
MOORE, ZORA	SOM	512	BARREN C
MOORE,MARGARET E.	QUE	153	1ST E DI
MOORE,NANCY	CAR	123	NO TWP L
MOORE,ROSANNA	BAL	208	2ND WARD
MOORE,S.	BAL	172	1ST WARD
MOORE,WILHELM	BAL	126	1ST WARD
MOORES, AQUILLA P.	HAR	110	2ND DIST
MOORES, PARKER	BAL	377	13TH WAR
MOORES, THOMAS H.	BAL	199	11TH WAR
MOORHEAD, JOHN	BAL	018	4TH WARD
MOOSEY, FRANCES	QUE	245	5TH E DI
MOOSTINAN, SISTER M.M.	FRE	198	5TH E DI
MOOTHY, CATHERINE	ALL	227	CUMBERLA
MOOTY, BRIDGET	ALL	233	CUMBERLA
MOOVER, COCKRAN	BAL	104	18TH WAR
MOPBURG, MARY	FRE	401	JEFFERSO
MOPLING, CHRISTIAN N.	MGM	407	MEDLEY 3
MOPLING, HENRY W.	MGM	413	MEDLEY 3
MOPLING, JOHN	MGM	426	MEDLEY 3
MOPLING, PETER K.	MGM	414	MEDLEY 3
MOPPS, ABBY	BAL	225	12TH WAR
MOPPS, EMMA	BAL	245	12TH WAR
MOPPS, WILLIAM	BAL	170	19TH WAR
MOPPS,GEORGE	FRE	443	8TH E DI
MOR, SARAH	KEN	295	3RD DIST
MORA, SIMON	ALL	057	10TH E.D
MORAN, JAMES	FRE	203	5TH E DI
MORAN, MARY J.	BAL	046	4TH WARD
MORAN, ANN	CHA	281	BOJANTOW
MORAN, ANN E.	BAL	074	2ND DIST
MORAN, BIDDY	BAL	470	14TH WAR
MORAN, BRIDGET	FRE	044	FREDERIC
MORAN, CATHARINE	BAL	272	1ST DIST
MORAN, CATHERN	BAL	149	11TH WAR
MORAN, CHARLES L.	BAL	079	4TH WARD
MORAN, CHARLES M.	CHA	282	BOJANTOW
MORAN, DANIEL	ALL	052	10TH E.D
MORAN, ELEANOR	CHA	286	BOJANTOW
MORAN, ELEN	CHA	285	BOJANTOW
MORAN, ELIZA	BAL	187	2ND WARD
MORAN, ELIZABETH	BAL	075	15TH WAR
MORAN, ELIZABETH	CHA	280	BOJANTOW
MORAN, ELIZABETH	BAL	198	19TH WAR
MORAN, GEORGE B.	CHA	280	BOJANTOW
MORAN, GEORGE W.	BAL	046	4TH WARD
MORAN, HARRIET	CHA	282	BOJANTOW
MORAN, HUGH	BAL	185	2ND WARD
MORAN, JAMES	BAL	191	6TH WARD
MORAN, JAMES	BAL	225	12TH WAR
MORAN, JAMES	PRI	091	MARLBROU
MORAN, JOHN	BAL	007	15TH WAR
MORAN, JOHN	BAL	008	9TH WARD
MORAN, JOHN	ALL	051	10TH E.D
MORAN, JOHN	BAL	414	8TH WARD
MORAN, JOHN	BAL	216	11TH WAR
MORAN, JOHN H.	ST	344	5TH E DI
MORAN, JOHN J.	BAL	356	3RD WARD
MORAN, JOHN L.	CHA	286	BOJANTOW
MORAN, JOSEPH J.	BAL	258	6TH WARD
MORAN, MAGUEL	BAL	211	11TH WAR
MORAN, MARGARET	BAL	046	18TH WAR
MORAN, MARY	BAL	006	15TH WAR
MORAN, MARY	BAL	053	9TH WARD
MORAN, MARY	BAL	330	13TH WAR
MORAN, MARY A.	CHA	283	BOJANTOW
MORAN, MARY A.	CHA	280	BOJANTOW
MORAN, MARY A.	FRE	066	FREDERIC
MORAN, MICHAEL	ALL	143	6TH E.D.
MORAN, MICHAEL	BAL	190	6TH WARD
MORAN, PATRICK	ALL	053	10TH E.D
MORAN, PATRICK	ALL	128	4TH E.D.
MORAN, PATRICK	BAL	143	1ST WARD
MORAN, PRICILLA	CHA	281	BOJANTOW
MORAN, RICHARD J.	BAL	187	2ND WARD
MORAN, ROBERT H.	BAL	119	18TH WAR
MORAN, SAMUEL C.	CHA	285	BOJANTOW
MORAN, SISTER CORONA	FRE	197	5TH E DI
MORAN, SISTER M.M.	FRE	198	5TH E DI
MORAN, SISTER M.S.	FRE	198	5TH E DI
MORAN, SUSAN	CHA	281	BOJANTOW
MORAN, TEDDY	ALL	053	10TH E.D
MORAN, THOMAS	ALL	050	10TH E.D
MORAN, THOMAS	ALL	050	10TH E.D
MORAN, THOMAS	BAL	076	15TH WAR
MORAN, WILLIAM	DOR	411	1ST DIST
MORAN, WILLIAM	ST	341	5TH E DI
MORAN, WILLIAM J.	BAL	070	18TH WAR
MORAN,MATTHEW	FRE	203	5TH E DI
MORARIA, SAMUEL	WAS	012	WILLIAMS
MORARTY, JAMES	BAL	385	8TH WARD
MORARTY, MARY	BAL	309	7TH WARD
MORATTY, PATRICK	BAL	007	15TH WAR
MORAWETZ, LEOPORE	BAL	125	5TH WARD
MORBURY, WILLIAM H.	FRE	094	FREDERIC
MORCE, JANE	BAL	141	11TH WAR
MORDEN, PETER	CEC	027	CHESAPEA
MORDEW, ANTHONY	HAR	060	1ST DIST
MORDEW, JANE	HAR	061	1ST DIST
MORDIR, OWEN	BAL	006	9TH WARD
MORE, AGNES A.	CAR	366	9TH DIST
MORE, AMANDA	HAR	164	3RD DIST
MORE, DANIEL H.	ST	267	3RD E DI
MORE, ELIZABETH	CAR	364	9TH DIST
MORE, HENRY	HAR	153	3RD DIST
MORE, JAMES	FRE	233	BUCKEYST
MORE, JAMES	BAL	291	20TH WAR
MORE, JAMES	PRI	118	PISCATAW
MORE, JANE	HAR	156	3RD DIST
MORE, JOHN	FRE	290	WOODSBOR
MORE, JOHN	CAR	364	9TH DIST
MORE, JOSEPH	BAL	385	13TH WAR
MORE, JOSEPH	TAL	097	ST MICHA
MORE, MARGARETTA*	BAL	363	3RD WARD
MORE, NIELD	DOR	372	3RD DIVI
MORE, SISTER M.J.	FRE	198	5TH E DI
MORE, SOPHIA	FRE	342	MIDDLETO
MORE, WILLIAM	HAR	155	3RD DIST
MOREAN, JAMES	BAL	418	1ST DIST
MOREDALE, MARK	CEC	071	5TH E DI
MOREDOCK, HENRY-MULATTO	FRE	436	8TH E DI
MOREFORD, JAMES	BAL	365	8TH WARD
MOREGAN, HENRY	WAS	033	2ND SUBD
MOREHAND, JOSHUA F.*	BAL	395	3RD WARD
MOREHANKER, HENRY	BAL	077	4TH WARD
MOREHEAD, NATHAN-MULATTO	FRE	428	8TH E DI
MOREHEAD, WILLIAM	FRE	159	EMMITTSB
MOREHORE, BIDDEY	BAL	352	7TH WARD
MOREHOUSE, ALANSON	BAL	422	3RD WARD
MOREIGH, MARGARET	DOR	430	1ST DIST
MORELAN, MARGARET	WAS	178	BOONSBOR
MORELAND, E.	PRI	051	AQUASCO
MORELAND, ELIZA J.	FRE	047	FREDERIC
MORELAND, ELIZABETH	BAL	056	15TH WAR
MORELAND, GEORGE	PRI	051	AQUASCO
MORELAND, JAMES	CAL	062	3RD DIST
MORELAND, JOHN	PRI	051	AQUASCO
MORELAND, JOSHUA F.*	BAL	395	3RD WARD
MORELAND, PETER	PRI	050	AQUASCO
MORELAND, S. B.	BAL	105	18TH WAR
MORELAND, WILLIAM	FRE	066	FREDERIC
MORELAND, WILLIAM H.	BAL	335	7TH WARD
MORELANG, ELIZABETH	BAL	145	16TH WAR
MORELL, WILLAIM	BAL	199	19TH WAR
MORELOCK, DEMUS	CAR	295	7TH DIST
MORELOCK, ELIZABETH J.	CAR	297	7TH DIST
MORELOCK, HENRY E.	FRE	453	8TH E DI
MORELOCK, JACOB	CAR	404	2ND DIST
MORELOCK, JERAMIAH	CAR	246	3RD DIST
MORELOCK, MICHAEL	CAR	289	7TH DIST
MORELOCK, MICHAEL JR.	CAR	289	7TH DIST
MORELOCK, URIAH	CAR	403	2ND DIST
MORFATT, ANN	BAL	195	5TH DIST
MORFET, H. M.	BAL	296	1ST DIST
MORFFETT, BENJAMIN	FRE	408	JEFFERSO
MORFIET, CHARLES	BAL	261	20TH WAR
MORFIT, CHARLES	BAL	297	1ST DIST
MORFITT, JOHN	BAL	409	14TH WAR
MORFORD, RUTH A.	BAL	366	8TH WARD
MORFOTT, JOHN	BAL	195	5TH DIST
MORGAL, ADAM	BAL	004	EASTERN
MORGAL, JACOB	BAL	004	EASTERN
MORGAN, ABRAHAM	HAR	003	1ST DIST
MORGAN, ALFORD	ST	308	1ST E DI
MORGAN, AMY	FRE	360	CATOCTIN
MORGAN, ANN PATIENCE SIS-	BAL	316	20TH WAR
MORGAN, AUGUSTUS	BAL	233	20TH WAR
MORGAN, BENJAMIN	CEC	202	6TH E DI
MORGAN, BENJAMIN	HAR	184	3RD DIST
MORGAN, BENJAMIN	ALL	120	5TH E.D.
MORGAN, BENNETT*	DOR	378	1ST DIST
MORGAN, C. HENRY	TAL	027	EASTON D
MORGAN, CAROLINE C.	BAL	307	3RD WARD
MORGAN, CHARELS	BAL	184	5TH DIST
MORGAN, CHARLES	BAL	386	1ST DIST
MORGAN, CHARLES	ST	322	4TH E DI
MORGAN, CHARLES A.	ST	308	1ST E DI
MORGAN, CHARLES H.	CAR	121	NO TWP L
MORGAN, CHARLES W.	FRE	293	WOODSBOR
MORGAN, DANIEL	CAR	160	NO TWP L
MORGAN, DANIEL	MGM	319	CRACKLIN
MORGAN, DANIEL	TAL	088	ST MICHA
MORGAN, DANIEL	BAL	096	5TH WARD
MORGAN, DANIEL	BAL	008	EASTERN
MORGAN, DANIEL T.	ST	270	3RD E DI
MORGAN, DAVID	ANN	453	HOWARD D
MORGAN, DAVID	FRE	349	MIDDLETO
MORGAN, DUNBAR	CEC	010	ELKTON 3
MORGAN, EDWARD	HAR	140	2ND DIST
MORGAN, EDWARD	BAL	138	11TH WAR
MORGAN, EDWARD	BAL	462	1ST DIST
MORGAN, EDWARD	BAL	115	5TH WARD
MORGAN, EDWARD	BAL	111	5TH WARD
MORGAN, EDWARD	WAS	161	HAGERSTO
MORGAN, ELIZA	BAL	184	5TH DIST
MORGAN, ELIZABETH	ANN	454	HOWARD D
MORGAN, ELIZABETH	BAL	281	7TH WARD
MORGAN, ELIZABETH	BAL	006	15TH WAR
MORGAN, ELIZABETH	WAS	173	FUNKSTOW
MORGAN, ELIZABETH	ST	262	3RD E DI
MORGAN, ELLEN	ALL	196	CUMBERLA
MORGAN, EMILY	PRI	032	VANSVILL
MORGAN, ENOCH	TAL	055	EASTON D
MORGAN, ESAW	HAR	105	2ND DIST
MORGAN, EVAN J.	BAL	282	12TH WAR
MORGAN, FRANCIS	TAL	042	EASTON D
MORGAN, FREDERICK *	ALL	100	5TH E.D.
MORGAN, GEORGE	BAL	456	8TH WARD
MORGAN, GEORGE	BAL	087	2ND DIST
MORGAN, GEORGE	BAL	155	1ST WARD
MORGAN, GEORGE	BAL	169	6TH WARD
MORGAN, GEORGE	BAL	227	6TH WARD
MORGAN, GEORGE H.	ST	286	2ND E DI
MORGAN, GEORGE W.	BAL	161	6TH WARD
MORGAN, GEORGE W.	BAL	027	9TH WARD
MORGAN, HENORA	BAL	431	8TH WARD
MORGAN, HENRY	BAL	145	2ND DIST
MORGAN, HENRY	ST	326	4TH E DI
MORGAN, HENRY	WAS	198	1ST DIST
MORGAN, HENRY	BAL	285	17TH WAR
MORGAN, HENRY C.	BAL	384	13TH WAR
MORGAN, HUGH	BAL	143	2ND DIST
MORGAN, HUMPHREY	ALL	179	7TH E.D.
MORGAN, J.	BAL	173	1ST WARD
MORGAN, J.	BAL	063	10TH WAR
MORGAN, J.	BAL	136	1ST WARD
MORGAN, J. STEPHEN	ST	333	4TH E DI
MORGAN, JACOB	CAR	074	NO TWP L
MORGAN, JAMES	CAR	150	NO TWP L
MORGAN, JAMES	BAL	245	17TH WAR
MORGAN, JAMES	CEC	061	1ST E DI
MORGAN, JAMES	SOM	429	PRINCESS
MORGAN, JAMES	BAL	271	20TH WAR
MORGAN, JAMES	TAL	032	EASTON D
MORGAN, JAMES	BAL	302	7TH WARD
MORGAN, JAMES	BAL	142	5TH WARD
MORGAN, JAMES	ALL	195	CUMBERLA
MORGAN, JAMES	BAL	349	7TH WARD
MORGAN, JAMES	BAL	462	1ST DIST
MORGAN, JAMES	ANN	513	HOWARD D
MORGAN, JAMES A.	ST	263	3RD E DI
MORGAN, JAMES B.	BAL	421	1ST DIST
MORGAN, JAMES H.	ST	333	4TH E DI
MORGAN, JAMES H.	CHA	224	ALLENS F
MORGAN, JAMES L.	HAR	114	2ND DIST
MORGAN, JARED	BAL	027	2ND DIST
MORGAN, JERMETT	CAR	074	NO TWP L
MORGAN, JOHN	CAR	117	NO TWP L
MORGAN, JOHN	FRE	086	FREDERIC

Name	Co.	Page	District
MORGAN, JOHN	FRE	085	FREDERIC
MORGAN, JOHN	CEC	061	1ST E DI
MORGAN, JOHN	KEN	220	2ND DIST
MORGAN, JOHN	ANN	507	HOWARD D
MORGAN, JOHN	BAL	272	12TH WAR
MORGAN, JOHN	ALL	067	10TH E.D
MORGAN, JOHN	BAL	243	6TH WARD
MORGAN, JOHN	BAL	144	1ST WARD
MORGAN, JOHN	SOM	393	BRINKLEY
MORGAN, JOHN	WAS	031	2ND SUBD
MORGAN, JOHN	SOM	485	TRAPP DI
MORGAN, JOHN F.	DOR	378	1ST DIST
MORGAN, JOHN R. V.	BAL	100	15TH WAR
MORGAN, JOHN T.	CEC	011	ELKTON 3
MORGAN, JOHN W.	CEC	051	1ST E DI
MORGAN, JOHN-BLACK	CAR	102	NO TWP L
MORGAN, JOHN-BLACK	ST	302	2ND E DI
MORGAN, JOSEPH	ST	254	3RD E DI
MORGAN, JOSEPH	CEC	095	4TH E DI
MORGAN, JOSEPH	BAL	373	8TH WARD
MORGAN, JOSEPH	BAL	337	3RD WARD
MORGAN, JOSEPH-BLACK	CAR	102	NO TWP L
MORGAN, JOSIAS W.	HAR	114	2ND DIST
MORGAN, JOSPEH	ST	324	4TH E DI
MORGAN, JULIA	ANN	291	ANNAPOLI
MORGAN, JULIA A.	QUE	208	3RD E DI
MORGAN, LEWIS	BAL	262	20TH WAR
MORGAN, LORENZO	BAL	050	9TH WARD
MORGAN, LUCINDA	WAS	186	BOONSBOR
MORGAN, LUDWIG	BAL	205	6TH WARD
MORGAN, M. *	BAL	143	2ND DIST
MORGAN, MAHALA	SOM	393	BRINKLEY
MORGAN, MARGARET	CEC	014	ELKTON 3
MORGAN, MARGARET A.C.-BLA	ST	301	2ND E DI
MORGAN, MARTHA	ST	327	4TH E DI
MORGAN, MARTHA	BAL	144	5TH WARD
MORGAN, MARTHA	BAL	265	12TH WAR
MORGAN, MARTHA	BAL	254	1ST DIST
MORGAN, MARY	BAL	229	12TH WAR
MORGAN, MARY	BAL	330	13TH WAR
MORGAN, MARY	BAL	096	10TH WAR
MORGAN, MARY	BAL	096	5TH WARD
MORGAN, MARY	BAL	294	3RD WARD
MORGAN, MARY	PRI	022	VANSVILL
MORGAN, MARY	BAL	303	20TH WAR
MORGAN, MARY	HAR	084	2ND DIST
MORGAN, MARY	KEN	217	2ND DIST
MORGAN, MARY E.	CEC	095	4TH E DI
MORGAN, MATTHEW	CEC	203	6TH E DI
MORGAN, MATTHIAS	QUE	152	1ST E DI
MORGAN, N. J. B.	BAL	324	12TH WAR
MORGAN, NEOMI	BAL	230	1ST DIST
MORGAN, OWEN	CAR	111	NO TWP L
MORGAN, PATRICK	BAL	134	2ND DIST
MORGAN, PHILIP	CAR	112	NO TWP L
MORGAN, PHILIP C.	TAL	032	EASTCN D
MORGAN, R.L.	HAR	159	3RD DIST
MORGAN, RACHAEL	FRE	086	FREDERIC
MORGAN, RACHEL	BAL	043	4TH WARD
MORGAN, RAPHAEL	ST	263	3RD E DI
MORGAN, ROBERT	HAR	006	1ST DIST
MORGAN, ROBERT	BAL	007	4TH WARD
MORGAN, ROMULUS B.	PRI	021	VANSVILL
MORGAN, ROSANNA	ANN	499	HOWARD D
MORGAN, SAMUEL	BAL	057	10TH WAR
MORGAN, SAMUEL	WAS	236	CAVETOWN
MORGAN, SAMUEL C.	WAS	030	2ND SUBD
MORGAN, SARAH	KEN	270	1ST DIST
MORGAN, SARAH	BAL	129	16TH WAR
MORGAN, SARAH	BAL	322	3RD WARD
MORGAN, SARAH	HAR	009	1ST DIST
MORGAN, SARAH	HAR	060	1ST DIST
MORGAN, SARAH	KEN	232	2ND DIST
MORGAN, SARAH A.	TAL	057	EASTON D
MORGAN, SARAH A.-BLACK	ST	301	2ND E DI
MORGAN, SARRAH	DOR	335	3RD DIVI
MORGAN, SCLLOMAN	TAL	054	EASTON D
MORGAN, SOLOMON	CAR	118	NO TWP L
MORGAN, SOLOMON	CAR	070	NO TWP L
MORGAN, SUSAN	HAR	039	1ST DIST
MORGAN, SUSAN	FRE	349	MIDDLETO
MORGAN, SUSAN	SOM	393	BRINKLEY
MORGAN, SUSAN	WAS	014	WILLIAMS
MORGAN, THOAMS	HAR	014	1ST DIST
MORGAN, THOASM	CAL	007	1ST DIST
MORGAN, THOMA SH.	HAR	114	2ND DIST
MORGAN, THOMAS	BAL	450	14TH WAR
MORGAN, THOMAS	CEC	012	ELKTON 3
MORGAN, THOMAS	BAL	384	13TH WAR
MORGAN, THOMAS	BAL	005	18TH WAR
MORGAN, THOMAS	SOM	396	BRINKLEY
MORGAN, THOMAS	QUE	215	3RD E DI
MORGAN, THOMAS	ANN	349	3RD DIST
MORGAN, THOMAS H.	HAR	005	1ST DIST
MORGAN, THOMAS W.	FRE	043	FREDERIC
MORGAN, THOMAS W.	ST	270	3RD E DI
MORGAN, VIRGINIA	BAL	068	18TH WAR
MORGAN, VIRGINIA	BAL	115	5TH WARD
MORGAN, WAKEMAN	HAR	001	1ST DIST
MORGAN, WESTRY	SOM	385	BRINKLEY
MORGAN, WILLAIM	ALL	068	5TH E.D.
MORGAN, WILLIAM	ALL	075	5TH E.D.
MORGAN, WILLIAM	ALL	179	7TH E.D.
MORGAN, WILLIAM	BAL	413	1ST DIST
MORGAN, WILLIAM	BAL	311	12TH WAR
MORGAN, WILLIAM	QUE	216	3RD E DI
MORGAN, WILLIAM	ST	335	4TH E DI
MORGAN, WILLIAM	WAS	076	2ND SUBD
MORGAN, WILLIAM	WAS	076	2ND SUBD
MORGAN, WILLIAM	FRE	091	FREDERIC
MORGAN, WILLIAM	HAR	064	1ST DIST
MORGAN, WILLIAM	BAL	218	17TH WAR
MORGAN, WILLIAM	CEC	019	ELKTON 3
MORGAN, WILLIAM	CAR	084	NO TWP L
MORGAN, WILLIAM B	HAR	146	3RD DIST
MORGAN, WILLIAM F.	HAR	140	2ND DIST
MORGAN, WILLIAM F.	DOR	312	1ST DIST
MORGAN, WILLIAM F.	WAS	159	HAGERSTO
MORGAN, WILLIAM G.	BAL	119	1ST WARD
MORGAN, WILLIAM H.	HAR	039	1ST DIST
MORGAN, WILLIAM J.	ANN	453	HOWARD D
MORGAN, WILLIAM M.	ANN	385	4TH DIST
MORGAN, WILLIAM R.	ST	334	4TH E DI
MORGAN, WILLIAM T.	ST	263	3RD E DI
MORGAN, WILLIAM-BLACK	CAR	145	NO TWP L
MORGAN, WILSON B.	BAL	366	3RD WARD
MORGAN,MARGRET	BAL	068	1ST WARD
MORGANROTH, FREDERICK	ALL	056	10TH E.D
MORGANS, DANIEL	FRE	363	CATOCTIN
MORGANS, JACOB	FRE	360	CATOCTIN
MORGANS, JOHN	FRE	360	CATOCTIN
MORGANS, MARY	FRE	365	CATOCTIN
MORGANSHALL, SUSAN	WAS	166	1ST DIST
MORHEISER, SARAH	BAL	255	6TH WARD
MORHINEY, FREDERICK	BAL	221	2ND WARD
MORHLRAY, WILLIAM	BAL	118	2ND DIST
MORIAITY, PATRICK *	BAL	168	2ND DIST
MORIAN,WILLIAM	BAL	128	1ST WARD
MORIARTY, ANN	BAL	348	13TH WAR
MORIARTY, MARY	BAL	100	2ND DIST
MORIARTZ, JOHN	BAL	110	1ST WARD
MORICKAN, THOMAS	BAL	432	1ST DIST
MORIGN, NOBLE*	DOR	422	1ST DIST
MORIN, DAVID	WAS	025	2ND SUBD
MORIN, GEORGE W.	WAS	031	2ND SUBD
MORIN, UPTON	WAS	030	2ND SUBD
MORINGSTAR, CATHARINE	FRE	427	8TH E DI
MORINGSTAR, LEVI	FRE	282	WOODSBOR
MORININGSTAR, WASHINGTON	CAR	382	2ND DIST
MORINKEY, HENRY	BAL	018	9TH WARD
MORIS, ELIZABETH	DOR	361	3RD DIVI
MORISON, EDWARD	WAS	006	WILLIAMS
MORISON, MARY	WAS	049	2ND SUBD
MORISON, NATHANIEL H.	BAL	098	10TH WAR
MORITZ, FREDERICK	BAL	238	20TH WAR
MORITZ, M.	BAL	045	9TH WARD
MORIY, ISAAC	CEC	169	6TH E DI
MORKET, JAMES	BAL	185	2ND WARD
MORLAND, GEORGE	MGM	390	ROCKERLE
MORLEY, DOMENEEK	ALL	142	6TH E.D.
MORLING, FRANCES	BAL	032	4TH WARD
MORLING, GEORGE W.	TAL	096	ST MICHA
MORLING, HENRY	TAL	014	EASTON D
MORLING, WILLIAM H.	TAL	095	ST MICHA
MORLINGER, JOHN E.	BAL	112	5TH WARD
MORLOCK, FREDERICK	BAL	102	1ST WARD
MORLOCK, SAMUEL	CEC	006	ELKTON 3
MORMAM, CLEMENS	BAL	324	3RD WARD
MORMAN, ANNA E.	QUE	233	4TH E DI
MORMAN, JOHN	ALL	205	CUMBERLA
MORMAN, WASHINGTON	FRE	066	FREDERIC
MORMON, NICHOLAS	BAL	417	3RD WARD
MORN, PATRICK	BAL	304	17TH WAR
MORNER, WILLIAM	BAL	257	12TH WAR
MORNET, JOHN	BAL	143	1ST WARD
MORNING, HENRY	BAL	121	1ST WARD
MORNINGER, WILLIAM	WAS	033	2ND SUBD
MORNINGSTAR, GEORGE D.	FRE	230	BUCKEYST
MORNINGSTAR, HENRY	FRE	105	CREAGERS
MORNINGSTAR, JESSEE	FRE	415	8TH E DI
MORNINGSTAR, JOHN	FRE	288	WOODSBOR
MORNINGSTAR, JOHN M.	FRE	279	WOODSBOR
MORNINGSTAR, PHILLIP	FRE	063	FREDERIC
MORNINGSTAR, WILLIAM	BAL	074	4TH WARD
MORNINGSTON, SARAH	ALL	248	CUMBERLA
MORNINGTON, MICHAEL	FRE	230	BUCKEYST
MORNINGTSTAR, SUSAN	FRE	030	FREDERIC
MORNSLY, FRED	BAL	222	19TH WAR
MOROCCO, SARAH	CEC	035	CHESAPEA
MOROF, GEORGE	ALL	235	CUMBERLA
MOROW, WILEY*	DOR	429	1ST DIST
MORPOE, LEWIS	BAL	146	16TH WAR
MORRA, J.	BAL	100	10TH WAR
MORRAS, JOHN H.	CEC	058	1ST E DI
MORRAYMAN, GEORGE	CAR	173	8TH DIST
MORRE, HARIET	BAL	271	20TH WAR
MORRE, JOSEPH	BAL	117	2ND DIST
MORRE, MARY*	DOR	376	1ST DIST
MORRE, WILLIAM	BAL	167	1ST WARD
MORREL, MARY	DOR	430	1ST DIST
MORRELL, FREDERICK	CAL	027	2ND DIST
MORRELL, GEORGE E.	BAL	096	5TH WARD
MORRELL, HENRY N.	BAL	281	2ND WARD
MORRER, JAMES	BAL	035	2ND DIST
MORRESY, EDWARD	ALL	072	5TH E.D.
MORRICK, DENNIS	WAS	155	2ND DIST
MORRIFIELD, REBECCA	BAL	383	13TH WAR
MORRIL, IRVIN	WOR	342	1ST E DI
MORRILL, HARRISON O.	BAL	383	13TH WAR
MORRILL, S.C.	WAS	021	2ND SUBD
MORRINGSTAR, JOHN	CAR	234	UNION TO
MORRIOSN, EWIN	BAL	301	20TH WAR
MORRIOSN, MARY	FRE	298	WOODSBOR
MORRIS, AARON	SOM	498	SALISBUR
MORRIS, ALBERT	BAL	003	15TH WAR
MORRIS, AMELIA	KEN	223	2ND DIST
MORRIS, ANN	DOR	405	1ST DIST
MORRIS, ANN A H.L.	ANN	521	HOWARD D
MORRIS, ANN E.	BAL	060	4TH WARD
MORRIS, ANNE	BAL	379	13TH WAR
MORRIS, B.	BAL	090	5TH WARD
MORRIS, B.F.	BAL	128	1ST WARD
MORRIS, BARNEY	BAL	081	10TH WAR
MORRIS, BEALE	BAL	059	2ND DIST
MORRIS, BENJAMIN	WOR	174	6TH E DI
MORRIS, BENJAMIN G.	KEN	234	2ND DIST
MORRIS, BLAIR	WAS	023	2ND SUBD
MORRIS, BOB	WOR	290	9TH E DI
MORRIS, BURTON	CEC	038	CHESAPEA
MORRIS, CAROLINE	BAL	319	3RD WARD
MORRIS, CATHARINE	BAL	071	1ST WARD
MORRIS, CATHARINE	BAL	465	14TH WAR
MORRIS, CATHERINE	BAL	171	11TH WAR
MORRIS, CHARLES	BAL	458	8TH WARD
MORRIS, CHARLES	ALL	260	CUMBERLA
MORRIS, CHARLES	CEC	071	5TH E DI
MORRIS, CHARLES	SOM	497	SALISBUR
MORRIS, CHARLES P.	BAL	372	3RD WARD
MORRIS, CHARLOTTE	KEN	224	2ND DIST
MORRIS, CORNELIUS	SOM	512	BARREN C
MORRIS, CURTIS	CAR	108	NO TWP L
MORRIS, CYAE	WOR	247	1ST CENS
MORRIS, D.	BAL	157	1ST WARD
MORRIS, DAVID	SOM	423	PRINCESS
MORRIS, DEBORAH	BAL	183	6TH WARD
MORRIS, DENARD	SOM	485	TRAPP DI
MORRIS, EDWARD	DOR	460	1ST DIST
MORRIS, EDWARD	BAL	134	2ND DIST
MORRIS, EDWARD	CAR	076	NO TWP L
MORRIS, ELIJAH	CAR	106	NO TWP L
MORRIS, ELISHA	BAL	459	8TH WARD
MORRIS, ELIZA	BAL	295	12TH WAR
MORRIS, ELIZA	BAL	181	16TH WAR
MORRIS, ELIZA	CAR	116	NO TWP L
MORRIS, ELIZA	CAR	078	NO TWP L
MORRIS, ELIZA	SOM	510	BARREN C
MORRIS, ELIZA	WOR	198	8TH E DI
MORRIS, ELIZA ANN	CAR	078	NO TWP L
MORRIS, ELIZA Q.	HAR	053	1ST DIST
MORRIS, ELIZABETH	SOM	408	DUBLIN D
MORRIS, ELIZABETH	SOM	485	TRAPP DI
MORRIS, ELIZABETH	BAL	332	13TH WAR
MORRIS, ELLEN	BAL	181	16TH WAR
MORRIS, ELLEN	WOR	259	BERLIN 1
MORRIS, ELLEN	BAL	258	17TH WAR
MORRIS, EZRA	BAL	213	6TH DIST
MORRIS, FRANCIS W.	PRI	078	MARLBROU
MORRIS, GEORGE	WOR	247	1ST CENS
MORRIS, GEORGE	CEC	069	5TH E DI
MORRIS, GEORGE A.	HAR	032	1ST DIST
MORRIS, GEORGE W.	BAL	368	3RD WARD
MORRIS, GEORGIANA	BAL	369	3RD WARD
MORRIS, H. R.	BAL	282	2ND WARD
MORRIS, HANNAH	WOR	279	BERLIN 1
MORRIS, HENRIETTA E.	WOR	224	4TH E DI
MORRIS, HENRY	SOM	474	TRAPPE D
MORRIS, HENRY	BAL	400	3RD WARD
MORRIS, HENRY	SOM	423	PRINCESS
MORRIS, ISAAC	BAL	047	1ST WARD
MORRIS, ISAAC	BAL	292	3RD WARD
MORRIS, ISAAC	WOR	226	4TH E DI
MORRIS, ISAAC	WOR	190	8TH E DI
MORRIS, J.	BAL	148	1ST WARD
MORRIS, J.	BAL	164	1ST WARD
MORRIS, J. D.	BAL	332	1ST DIST
MORRIS, JACOB	BAL	140	1ST WARD
MORRIS, JACOB	KEN	276	1ST DIST
MORRIS, JACOB T.	BAL	420	3RD WARD
MORRIS, JAMES	CEC	036	CHESAPEA
MORRIS, JAMES	HAR	133	2ND DIST
MORRIS, JAMES	BAL	157	19TH WAR
MORRIS, JAMES	CHA	220	ALLENS F
MORRIS, JAMES	WOR	193	8TH E DI
MORRIS, JAMES	BAL	330	3RD WARD
MORRIS, JAMES	BAL	346	3RD WARD
MORRIS, JAMES	BAL	153	1ST WARD
MORRIS, JAMES	ANN	481	HOWARD D
MORRIS, JAMES	ALL	175	7TH E.D.
MORRIS, JAMES A.	BAL	008	1ST WARD
MORRIS, JAMES T.	BAL	130	1ST WARD
MORRIS, JAMES-BLACK	WOR	172	6TH E DI
MORRIS, JAMS	SOM	473	TRAPPE D
MORRIS, JANE	WOR	288	BERLIN 1
MORRIS, JARRET	HAR	025	1ST DIST
MORRIS, JEMIMA	BAL	033	2ND DIST
MORRIS, JEREMIAH	TAL	076	EASTON T
MORRIS, JESSEE	KEN	257	1ST DIST
MORRIS, JOHN	WAS	152	2ND DIST
MORRIS, JOHN	WOR	236	6TH E DI
MORRIS, JOHN	SOM	492	SALISBUR
MORRIS, JOHN	BAL	130	1ST WARD
MORRIS, JOHN	BAL	033	1ST WARD
MORRIS, JOHN	BAL	071	1ST WARD
MORRIS, JOHN	ALL	068	5TH E.D.
MORRIS, JOHN	BAL	156	1ST WARD
MORRIS, JOHN	BAL	026	9TH WARD
MORRIS, JOHN	BAL	217	6TH DIST
MORRIS, JOHN	MGM	376	ROCKERLE
MORRIS, JOHN	CHA	290	BOJANTOW
MORRIS, JOHN	CAR	340	6TH DIST
MORRIS, JOHN	CAR	253	3RD DIST
MORRIS, JOHN	BAL	103	18TH WAR
MORRIS, JOHN	CAR	111	NO TWP L
MORRIS, JOHN B.	BAL	144	11TH WAR
MORRIS, JOHN B.	BAL	144	11TH WAR
MORRIS, JOHN B.	SOM	388	BRINKLEY
MORRIS, JOHN G. REV.	BAL	345	13TH WAR
MORRIS, JOHN H.	CAR	078	NO TWP L
MORRIS, JOHN L.	WOR	173	6TH E DI
MORRIS, JOHN M.	BAL	037	15TH WAR
MORRIS, JOHN Q.	BAL	045	15TH WAR
MORRIS, JOSEPH P.	BAL	268	12TH WAR
MORRIS, JOSHUA	WOR	270	BERLIN 1
MORRIS, JOSHUA	WOR	266	BERLIN 1
MORRIS, JOSIAH	SOM	434	PRINCESS
MORRIS, JULIA	SOM	423	PRINCESS
MORRIS, JULY-BLACK	CAR	079	NO TWP L
MORRIS, JUSTICE	WOR	277	BERLIN 1
MORRIS, KRANSHAW	ALL	156	6TH E.D.
MORRIS, L.	BAL	281	2ND WARD
MORRIS, L.M.	BAL	117	1ST WARD
MORRIS, LAVINIA	WOR	173	6TH E DI
MORRIS, LEAH	WOR	221	4TH E DI
MORRIS, LEAH E.	WOR	230	6TH E DI
MORRIS, LEMUEL	BAL	214	6TH DIST
MORRIS, LEONARD	WOR	173	6TH E DI
MORRIS, LEONRD	WOR	233	6TH E DI
MORRIS, LOUIS	BAL	217	6TH DIST
MORRIS, LOUIS W.	WOR	193	8TH E DI
MORRIS, M.W.	BAL	166	1ST WARD
MORRIS, MARGARET	WOR	316	2ND E DI
MORRIS, MARGARET	BAL	231	19TH WAR
MORRIS, MARGARET B. P.	BAL	455	8TH WARD
MORRIS, MARGARET E.	DOR	460	1ST DIST
MORRIS, MARTHA	BAL	198	17TH WAR
MORRIS, MARTHA	CAR	169	NO TWP L
MORRIS, MARY	FRE	066	FREDERIC
MORRIS, MARY	DOR	404	1ST DIST
MORRIS, MARY	BAL	271	12TH WAR
MORRIS, MARY	BAL	217	6TH DIST
MORRIS, MARY	BAL	037	1ST WARD
MORRIS, MARY	WOR	187	7TH E DI
MORRIS, MARY	SOM	498	SALISBUR
MORRIS, MARY	SOM	501	SALISBUR
MORRIS, MARY	WOR	267	BERLIN 1
MORRIS, MARY A.	SOM	467	TRAPPE D
MORRIS, MARY F.	BAL	330	3RD WARD
MORRIS, MARYANNA	WOR	193	8TH E DI
MORRIS, MATILDA	SOM	491	SALISBUR
MORRIS, MAURICE	BAL	233	6TH WARD
MORRIS, METILDA	HAR	030	1ST DIST
MORRIS, MILES	WAS	162	HAGERSTO
MORRIS, N.	BAL	281	2ND WARD
MORRIS, NANCY	WOR	240	6TH E DI
MORRIS, NANCY	WOR	275	BERLIN 1
MORRIS, NAOMI	WOR	174	6TH E DI
MORRIS, NEHEMIAH	WOR	239	6TH E DI
MORRIS, NOAH	DOR	459	1ST DIST
MORRIS, OLEVIA	CHA	217	ALLENS F
MORRIS, OWEN	BAL	271	12TH WAR
MORRIS, PELOPUS	CEC	077	NORTHEAS
MORRIS, PETER	WOR	168	6TH E DI
MORRIS, PETER L.	WOR	222	4TH E DI
MORRIS, PHILIP H.	BAL	465	14TH WAR
MORRIS, R.	BAL	136	1ST WARD
MORRIS, RACHLIFF	WOR	173	6TH E DI
MORRIS, REBECCA	HAR	162	3RD DIST
MORRIS, RHODA	WOR	276	BERLIN 1
MORRIS, RICHARD	BAL	134	1ST WARD
MORRIS, RILEY W.	WOR	223	4TH E DI

MORRIS, ROBERT BAL 172 1ST WARD
MORRIS, RODAH WOR 243 1ST CENS
MORRIS, RODAY WOR 242 1ST CENS
MORRIS, SABRA-BLACK WOR 322 1ST E DI
MORRIS, SALEM BAL 217 6TH DIST
MORRIS, SALLY A. WOR 206 4TH E DI
MORRIS, SAMUEL WOR 192 8TH E DI
MORRIS, SAMUEL BAL 217 6TH DIST
MORRIS, SAMUEL BAL 210 6TH DIST
MORRIS, SAMUEL CAR 079 NO TWP L
MORRIS, SAMUEL OF JAMES BAL 212 6TH DIST
MORRIS, SAMUEL OF JOHN BAL 213 6TH DIST
MORRIS, SARAH BAL 052 15TH WAR
MORRIS, SARAH BAL 280 20TH WAR
MORRIS, SARAH CEC 049 1ST E DI
MORRIS, SARAH SOM 469 TRAPPE D
MORRIS, STEPHEN BAL 160 1ST WARD
MORRIS, SUSAN BAL 098 5TH WARD
MORRIS, THOAMS BAL 402 1ST DIST
MORRIS, THOAMS BAL 296 20TH WAR
MORRIS, THOMAS BAL 144 11TH WAR
MORRIS, THOMAS HAR 162 3RD DIST
MORRIS, THOMAS BAL 382 8TH WARD
MORRIS, THOMAS C.* BAL 380 3RD WARD
MORRIS, THOMAS H. SOM 424 PRINCESS
MORRIS, THOMAS J. WOR 234 6TH E DI
MORRIS, THOMAS R. BAL 455 8TH WARD.
MORRIS, THOMAS W. ANN 430 HOWARD D
MORRIS, VHOORHIES C.* BAL 380 3RD WARD
MORRIS, VINCENT CAR 112 NO TWP L
MORRIS, WARREN SOM 478 TRAPP DI
MORRIS, WILLIAM DOR 460 1ST DIST
MORRIS, WILLIAM KEN 283 3RD DIST
MORRIS, WILLIAM CAR 122 NO TWP L
MORRIS, WILLIAM HAR 024 1ST DIST
MORRIS, WILLIAM HAR 142 2ND DIST
MORRIS, WILLIAM CHA 234 HILLTOP
MORRIS, WILLIAM CEC 064 1ST E DI
MORRIS, WILLIAM DOR 403 1ST DIST
MORRIS, WILLIAM BAL 271 2ND WARD
MORRIS, WILLIAM BAL 455 8TH WARD
MORRIS, WILLIAM BAL 213 6TH DIST
MORRIS, WILLIAM BAL 189 2ND WARD
MORRIS, WILLIAM BAL 107 10TH WAR
MORRIS, WILLIAM C. WOR 241 1ST CENS
MORRIS, WILLIAM H. BAL 181 16TH WAR
MORRIS, WILLIAM L. CHA 230 BOJANTOW
MORRIS, WILLIAM P. WOR 193 8TH E DI
MORRIS, WILLIAM R. WOR 174 6TH E DI
MORRISEY, DENNIS WAS 113 2ND DIST
MORRISON, ALFRED WAS 048 2ND SUBD
MORRISON, AMBROSE HAR 045 1ST DIST
MORRISON, ANDREW FRE 342 MIDDLETO
MORRISON, ANN D. BAL 308 3RD WARD
MORRISON, ANTHONY ANN 343 3RD DIST
MORRISON, ARTHUR CEC 032 CHESAPEA
MORRISON, AUGUSTUS MGM 319 CRACKLIN
MORRISON, B.T. ALL 248 CUMBERLA
MORRISON, BARNEY ANN 429 HOWARD D
MORRISON, CATHERINE J. BAL 076 18TH WAR
MORRISON, CHARLES CEC 110 4TH E DI
MORRISON, DAIVD BAL 470 14TH WAR
MORRISON, DANIEL HAR 045 1ST DIST
MORRISON, CANIEL BAL 123 1ST WARD
MORRISON, DANIEL F. CEC 208 7TH E DI
MORRISON, CAVID FRE 175 5TH E DI
MORRISON, DAVID BAL 347 3RD WARD
MORRISON, DELIA BAL 063 2ND DIST
MORRISON, E. BAL 139 5TH WARD
MORRISON, E. BAL 057 18TH WAR
MORRISON, ECWARD BAL 035 4TH WARD
MORRISON, ELISHAS HAR 045 1ST DIST
MORRISON, ELIZA BAL 084 2ND DIST
MORRISON, ELIZA G. FRE 383 PETERSVI
MORRISON, ELIZA S. BAL 197 5TH DIST
MORRISON, ELIZABETH CEC 111 4TH E DI
MORRISON, ELLEN BAL 213 6TH WARD
MORRISON, EMMOR HAR 142 2ND DIST
MORRISON, FRANCES BAL 295 20TH WAR
MORRISON, FRANCIS L. BAL 067 18TH WAR
MORRISON, FRANIS WOR 302 SNOW HIL
MORRISON, FRED BAL 164 2ND DIST
MORRISON, FRED BAL 444 1ST DIST
MORRISON, FREDERICK W. BAL 116 1ST WARD
MORRISON, GEORGE BAL 213 6TH WARD
MORRISON, GEORGE SOM 472 TRAPPE D
MORRISON, GEORGE CEC 111 4TH E DI
MORRISON, GEORGE SOM 434 PRINCESS
MORRISON, H.J. BAL 158 6TH WARD
MORRISON, HAORACE BAL 141 11TH WAR
MORRISON, HARRIET BAL 097 10TH WAR
MORRISON, HENRY BAL 233 2ND WARD
MORRISON, HENRY CEC 144 PORT DUP
MORRISON, HENRY WAS 064 2ND SUBD
MORRISON, HENRY L. FRE 391 PETERSVI
MORRISON, HENRY-BLACK BAL 176 2ND WARD
MORRISON, INFANT HAR 135 2ND DIST
MORRISON, ISAAC BAL 285 2ND WAFD
MORRISON, ISSABEL CAR 410 2ND DIST
MORRISON, JAMES BAL 401 14TH WAR
MORRISON, JAMES BAL 094 18TH WAR
MORRISON, JAMES BAL 286 2ND WARD
MORRISON, JAMES BAL 173 1ST WARD
MORRISON, JAMES BAL 115 5TH WARD
MORRISON, JAMES J. HAR 134 2ND DIST
MORRISON, JEFFERSON BAL 197 11TH WAR
MORRISON, JEREMIAH G. FRE 383 PETERSVI
MORRISON, JOHN SOM 417 PRINCESS
MORRISON, JOHN HAR 045 1ST DIST
MORRISON, JOHN MGM 411 MEDLEY 3
MORRISON, JOHN BAL 179 11TH WAR
MORRISON, JOHN BAL 368 8TH WARD
MORRISON, JOHN BAL 146 1ST WARD
MORRISON, JOHN BAL 117 1ST WARD
MORRISON, JOHN ALL 100 5TH E.D.
MORRISON, JOHN E. BAL 237 12TH WAR
MORRISON, JOSEPH BAL 308 7TH WARD
MORRISON, JOSEPH B. HAR 014 1ST DIST
MORRISON, JOSIAH CEC 087 4TH E DI
MORRISON, LUCY ALL 206 CUMBERLA
MOFRISON, MANSFIELD HAR 142 2ND DIST
MORRISON, MARGARET BAL 358 8TH WARD
MORRISON, MARIA BAL 285 2ND WARD
MORRISON, MARIA BAL 197 5TH DIST
MORRISON, MARIA HAR 135 2ND DIST
MORRISON, MARIA BAL 141 11TH WAR
MORRISON, MARTHA FRE 203 5TH E DI
MORRISON, MARTHA BAL 087 4TH WARD
MORRISON, MARY BAL 160 2ND DIST
MORRISON, MARY BAL 238 2ND WARD
MORRISON, MARY BAL 196 2ND WARD
MORRISON, MARY A. BAL 283 2ND WARD
MORRISON, MARY J. BAL 421 8TH WARD
MORRISON, MATHEW BAL 393 1ST DIST
MORRISON, MICHAEL BAL 358 8TH WARD
MORRISON, MOSES CEC 015 ELKTON 3
MORRISON, OTTO BAL 120 1ST WARD
MORRISON, RICHARD BAL 127 1ST WARD
MORRISON, RICHARD G. PRI 023 VANSVILL
MORRISON, ROBERT BAL 197 5TH DIST
MORRISON, ROBERT BAL 178 11TH WAR
MORRISCN, ROBERT BAL 454 8TH WARD
MORRISCN, ROBERT CAR 307 1ST DIST
MORRISON, ROBERT SOM 418 PRINCESS
MORRISON, ROSANA HAR 012 1ST DIST
MORRISON, ROSANNA BAL 173 6TH WARD
MORRISON, ROSEANN BAL 190 6TH WARD
MORRISON, SAMUEL FRE 178 5TH E DI
MORRISON, SARAH BAL 312 1ST DIST
MORRISON, SARAH WAS 124 HAGERSTO
MORRISON, SARAH WAS 222 1ST DIST
MORRISON, SARAH E. BAL 380 3RD WARD
MORRISON, SUSAN FRE 178 5TH E DI
MORRISON, SUSANNA BAL 217 6TH WARD
MORRISON, TALBOT BAL 230 1ST DIST
MORRISON, THOMAS CEC 149 PORT DUP
MORRISON, TOWNSEND CEC 149 PORT DUP
MORRISON, VIRGINIA ALL 100 5TH E.D.
MORRISON, VIRGINIA WAS 003 WILLIAMS
MORRISON, WILLIAM PRI 027 VANSVILL
MORRISON, WILLIAM WAS 063 2ND SUBD
MORRISON, WILLIAM BAL 027 1ST WARD
MORRISON, WILLIAM BAL 230 1ST DIST
MORRISON, WILLIAM HAR 135 2ND DIST
MORRISON, WILLIAM BAL 233 20TH WAR
MORRISON, WILLIAM BAL 028 4TH WARD
MORRISON, WILLIAM BAL 066 18TH WAR
MORRISON, WILLIAM B. FRE 176 5TH E DI
MORRISON,J.B. BAL 139 1ST WARD
MORRISON,M. BAL 133 1ST WARD
MORRISON,MARY ALL 247 CUMBERLA
MORRISS, JACOB BAL 264 17TH WAR
MORRISS, JAMES PRI 047 AQUASCO
MORRISS, JOHN TAL 042 EASTON D
MORRISS, MARY BAL 115 5TH WARD
MORRISSEY, PATRICK BAL 027 4TH WARD
MORRISSON, ANN FRE 192 5TH E DI
MORRISSCN, BARBARA WAS 215 1ST DIST
MORRISSON, DAVID FRE 164 EMMITTSB
MORRISSON, ELIZABETH BAL 010 4TH WARD
MORRISSON, HARRIET FRE 176 5TH E DI
MORRISSCN, HENRY BAL 143 5TH WARD
MORRISSON, JAMES BAL 095 5TH WARD
MORRISSCN, JANE FRE 165 EMMITTSB
MORRISSON, JOHN WAS 215 1ST DIST
MORRISSON, MALINDA WAS 211 1ST DIST
MORRISSON, MARTHA FRE 164 EMMITTSB
MORRISSCN, NANCY CEC 168 6TH E DI
MORRISSON, THOMAS WAS 211 1ST DIST
MORRITT, HENRY BAL 131 1ST WARD
MORRKILL, H. P. BAL 167 11TH WAR
MORRON, SAMUEL BAL 148 19TH WAR
MORROW, A. BAL 152 1ST WARD
MCRROW, ACHSAL BAL 205 6TH WARD
MORROW, ANDREW BAL 292 7TH WARD
MORROW, GEORGE BAL 218 6TH DIST
MORROW, GEORGE ALL 175 7TH E.D.
MORROW, HARRIET BAL 072 15TH WAR
MORROW, JAMES BAL 303 3RD WARD
MORROW, JAMES BAL 146 1ST WARD
MORROW, JOHN BAL 209 6TH DIST
MORROW, JOHN BAL 226 1ST DIST
MORROW, JOHN BAL 072 15TH WAR
MORROW, JOHN BAL 186 19TH WAR
MORROW, MARGARET BAL 029 9TH WARD
MORROW, ROBERT BAL 115 11TH WAR
MORROW, SAMUEL W. BAL 406 3RD WARD
MORROW, TOWNSEND BAL 319 1ST DIST
MORROW, WILLAIM BAL 348 7TH WARD
MORROW, WILLIAM BAL 132 1ST WARD
MORROW, WILLIAM BAL 001 4TH WARD
MORROW, WILLIAM BAL 042 18TH WAR
MORROW, WILLIAM BAL 264 20TH WAR
MORROW, WILLIAM B. WAS 300 1ST DIST
MORROW, WILLIAM H. BAL 258 6TH WARD
MORROW,WILLIAM ALL 218 CUMBERLA
MORRY, JACOB * WAS 107 2ND DIST
MORSBERGER, PAUL BAL 008 15TH WAR
MORSE, CATHARINE CAR 366 9TH DIST
MORSE, CHARLES BAL 214 17TH WAR
MORSE, CHARLES BAL 029 15TH WAR
MORSE, CHARLES BAL 012 2ND DIST
MORSE, ELIZABETH HAR 065 1ST DIST
MORSE, ISABEL BAL 293 12TH WAR
MORSE, JOHN BAL 128 1ST WARD
MORSE, PATRICK BAL 281 12TH WAR
MORSE, R. BAL 157 1ST WARD
MORSE, SARAH WAS 153 2ND DIST
MORSE, SUSANA BAL 423 3RD WARD
MORSE, THOMAS W. BAL 297 7TH WARD
MORSE, WILLIAM BAL 219 19TH WAR
MORSEL, MARGARET CAL 008 1ST DIST
MORSELL, ARRON BAL 132 18TH WAR
MORSELL, BENJAMIN CAL 029 2ND DIST
MORSELL, ELIZANETH CAL 023 2ND DIST
MORSELL, HENRIETTA PRI 066 NOTTINGH
MORSELL, HETTY BAL 145 11TH WAR
MORSELL, JAMES PRI 066 NOTTINGH
MORSELL, JOHN CAL 053 3RD DIST
MORSELL, JOHN CAL 058 3RD DIST
MORSELL, JOHN C. PRI 033 VANSVILL
MORSELL, JOSEPH TAL 054 EASTON D
MORSELL, JOSHUA CAL 023 2ND DIST
MORSELL, JOSHUA ANN 401 8TH DIST
MORSELL, PERRY BAL 125 18TH WAR
MORSELL, SAMUEL PRI 041 VANSVILL
MORSEY, LOUIS BAL 220 19TH WAR
MORSS, J.B. REV. BAL 248 1ST DIST
MORSTER, SARAH CEC 029 CHESAPEA
MORT, GEORGE CAR 316 1ST DIST
MORT, GEORGE CAR 255 3RD DIST
MORT, JOHN BAL 205 2ND WARD
MORT, PETER CAR 256 3RD DIST
MORT, PETER FRE 287 WOODSBOR
MORT, SUSANNA FRE 395 PETERSVI
MORT, WILLIAM FRE 283 WOODSBOR
MORT, WILLIAM FRE 287 WOODSBOR
MORT, WILLIAM FRE 184 5TH E DI
MORTAN, ADALINE CEC 045 1ST E DI
MORTAN, WILLIAM CEC 192 5TH E DI
MORTCO, GEORGE W. CHA 222 ALLENS F
MORTGAGE, GEORGE QUE 218 3RD E DI
MORTGAGE, HESTER QUE 184 3RD E DI
MORTGAGE, JAMES QUE 209 3RD E DI
MORTGAGE, THOMAS QUE 218 3RD E DI
MORTH, JAMES BAL 070 1ST WARD
MORTHLAND, ANN CAR 265 WESTMINS
MORTHLAND, SUSANNAH BAL 381 13TH WAR
MORTHOLCH, RICHARD BAL 009 EASTERN
MORTILL, JACOB WAS 212 1ST DIST
MORTIMER, ELIZABETH BAL 334 3RD WARD
MORTIMER, FRANCIS FRE 436 8TH E DI
MORTIMER, GEORGE BAL 167 1ST WARD
MORTIMER, HENRY H. BAL 107 15TH WAR
MORTIMER, JAMES V. BAL 182 6TH WARD
MORTIMER, JOHN BAL 160 6TH WARD
MORTIMER, JOHN BAL 104 5TH WARD
MORTIMER, JOHN BAL 354 3RD WARD
MORTIMER, JOHN BAL 396 3RD WARD
MORTIMER, JOHN BAL 008 9TH WARD
MORTIMER, JOHN W. BAL 249 12TH WAR
MORTIMER, MARGARET A. BAL 327 7TH WARD
MORTIMER, WILLIAM BAL 129 1ST WARD
MORTIMER, WILLIAM BAL 173 1ST WARD
MORTIMORE, JOHN R. TAL 067 EASTON T
MORTINE, GEORGE ALL 142 6TH E.D.
MORTLAND, WILLIAM BAL 130 1ST WARD
MORTON, BILL ANN 401 8TH DIST
MORTON, BRIDGETT BAL 033 4TH WARD
MORTON, CATHAINE BAL 072 1ST WARD
MORTON, CHARLES DOR 383 1ST DIST
MORTON, DIXON BAL 431 1ST DIST
MORTON, DUDLEY BAL 024 9TH WARD
MORTON, EDWARD CAL 039 2ND DIST
MORTON, EMMA BAL 357 13TH WAR
MORTON, FRANCIS B. BAL 137 11TH WAR
MORTON, GEORGE PRI 047 AQUASCO
MORTON, GEORGE C. BAL 291 12TH WAR
MORTON, GEORGE W. PRI 046 AQUASCO
MORTON, HAMILTON CEC 044 1ST E DI
MORTON, HARRIETT BAL 036 4TH WARD
MORTON, JAMES CEC 185 7TH E DI
MORTON, JAMES CHA 256 MIDDLETO
MORTON, JAMES W. QUE 179 2ND E DI
MORTON, JOHN CEC 055 1ST E DI
MORTON, JULIA A. BAL 139 19TH WAR
MORTON, MARGARET BAL 420 14TH WAR
MORTON, MARGARET BAL 023 9TH WARD
MORTON, MARGARETT BAL 033 4TH WARD
MORTON, MARIA P. CHA 285 BOJANTOW
MORTON, MARY CEC 147 PORT DUP
MORTON, MARY ALL 229 CUMBERLA
MORTON, MARY C. ANN 312 1ST DIST
MORTON, MJOHN BAL 214 6TH WARD
MORTON, MOORE BAL 088 15TH WAR
MORTON, PETER BAL 432 8TH WARD
MORTON, PETER CAR 106 NO TWP L
MORTON, PHILLIP FRE 072 FREDERIC
MORTON, ROBERT BAL 210 6TH WARD
MORTON, ROBERT BAL 048 2ND DIST
MORTON, S. P. DOR 394 1ST DIST
MORTON, T. BAL 281 2ND WARD
MORTON, THOMAS HAR 079 2ND DIST
MORTON, THOMAS M. BAL 393 8TH WARD
MORTON, WILLIAM BAL 105 1ST WARD
MORTON, WILLIAM CAL 037 2ND DIST
MORUAHAN, PATRICK ALL 142 6TH E.D.
MOSBURG, ANDREW FRE 218 BUCKEYST
MOSBURG, EDWARD FRE 209 BUCKEYST
MOSBURG, REBECCA FRE 220 BUCKEYST
MOSBURY, GEORGE D. FRE 074 FREDERIC
MOSE, BAGRIEL WAS 045 2ND SUBD
MOSE, ELIZABETH WAS 039 2ND SUBD
MOSE, FRANKLIN WAS 055 2ND SUBD
MOSE, GEORGE WAS 037 2ND SUBD
MOSE, HENRY WAS 038 2ND SUBD
MOSE, JAMES WAS 066 2ND SUBD
MOSE, JAMES * BAL 291 20TH WAR
MOSE, MARY WAS 039 2ND SUBD
MOSE, SUSAN WAS 061 2ND SUBD
MOSEL, MATILDA BAL 348 13TH WAR
MOSELEY, JOHN HAR 097 2ND DIST
MOSELEY, MISS A. FRE 199 5TH E DI
MOSELY, JOHN SOM 443 DAMES QU
MOSELY, LEAH SOM 427 PRINCESS
MOSEMAN, JOHN HAR 153 3RD DIST
MOSER, AMANDA FRE 370 CATOCTIN
MOSER, AMANDA FRE 357 CATOCTIN
MOSER, CHRISTIAN FRE 349 MIDDLETO
MOSER, DANIEL FRE 433 8TH E DI
MOSER, ELIAS FRE 357 CATOCTIN
MOSER, ELIAS FRE 124 CREAGERS
MOSER, EPHRAIM FRE 147 10TH E D
MOSER, EZRA FRE 154 10TH E D
MOSER, HENRY FRE 147 10TH E D
MOSER, ISAAC FRE 355 MIDDLETO
MOSER, JACOB FRE 351 MIDDLETO
MOSER, JACOB BAL 008 4TH WARD
MOSER, JOHN FRE 341 MIDDLETO
MOSER, JOHN FRE 348 MIDDLETO
MOSER, JOHN FRE 357 CATOCTIN
MOSER, JOHN FRE 348 MIDDLETO
MOSER, JOHN BAL 193 6TH WARD
MOSER, JOSIAH FRE 358 CATOCTIN
MOSER, LAWSON FRE 349 MIDDLETO
MOSER, LEONARD FRE 147 10TH E D
MOSER, MARGARET S. FRE 147 10TH E D
MOSER, MORRIS ANN 291 ANNAPOLI
MOSER, PETER FRE 411 8TH E DI
MOSER, SAMUEL FRE 372 CATOCTIN
MOSER, SARAH FRE 341 MIDDLETO
MOSER, SUSAN FRE 127 CREAGERS
MOSER, WILLIAM WAS 022 2ND SUBD
MOSES, BROTHER BAL 216 11TH WAR
MOSES, CHARLOTT BAL 122 5TH WARD
MOSES, ELIZA BAL 002 EASTERN
MOSES, FELIX BAL 142 1ST WARD
MOSES, FREDERICK BAL 178 2ND WARD
MOSES, GOERGE BAL 144 5TH WARD
MOSES, HERVEY BAL 002 EASTERN
MOSES, LEWIS R. BAL 278 2ND WARD
MOSES, THOMAS BAL 448 8TH WARD
MOSES, THOMAS BAL 084 4TH WARD
MOSH, CATHARINE WAS 126 HAGERSTO
MOSHER, ALICE BAL 111 10TH WAR
MOSHER, CASSANDER BAL 454 1ST DIST
MOSHER, ELIZABETH BAL 059 10TH WAR
MOSHER, H. BAL 247 2ND WARD
MOSHER, JACOB BAL 454 1ST DIST
MOSHER, JOHN BAL 454 1ST DIST

MOSHER, LEOPOLD BAL 076 15TH WAR
MOSHER, MARIA BAL 401 3RD WARD
MOSHER, MARTIN BAL 376 1ST DIST
MOSHER, MARY BAL 192 6TH WARD
MOSHER, NANCY BAL 006 18TH WAR
MOSHER, THOMAS BAL 081 1ST WARD
MOSHER, WILLIAM OR- BAL 370 1ST DIST
MOSHERMAN, JACOB BAL 129 2ND DIST
MOSHIER, WILLIAM FRE 182 5TH E DI
MOSIER, AYRUS * FRE 131 CREAGERS
MOSIER, BENJAMIN FRE 152 10TH E D
MOSIER, HENRY FRE 117 CREAGERS
MOSIER, JOHN ANN 304 1ST DIST
MOSINGER, JOHN P. BAL 432 1ST DIST
MOSLEY, HENRY BAL 159 1ST WARD
MOSLEY, REUBEN M. MGM 433 CLARKSTR
MOSLEY, SUSAN FRE 255 NEW MARK
MOSON, MATILDA S. CHA 227 ALLENS F
MOSS, CHARLES FRE 395 PETERSVI
MOSS, CHARLES S BAL 154 1ST WARD
MOSS, CHARLES SR. FRE 397 PETERSVI
MOSS, HAMILTON P. ANN 350 3RD DIST
MOSS, ISAAC BAL 172 2ND DIST
MOSS, JAMES O. HAR 193 3RD DIST
MOSS, JOHN QUE 153 1ST E DI
MOSS, JOHN A. BAL 382 3RD WARD
MOSS, JOSEPH BAL 162 1ST WARD
MOSS, JOSEPH ALL 192 9TH E.D.
MOSS, MARY BAL 216 6TH WARD
MOSS, ROBERT B. ANN 350 3RD DIST
MOSS, SISTER E. FRE 198 5TH E DI
MOSS.CATHARINE ALL 008 3RD E.D.
MOSSBURGH, NANCY WAS 194 1ST DIST
MOSSER, WILLIAM R. BAL 371 8TH WARD
MOST, HENRY BAL 383 3RD WARD
MOST, JOHN ALL 028 2ND E.D.
MOSTLER, ASA WAS 044 2ND SUBD
MOSTTER, DENNIS WAS 044 2ND SUBD
MOSURE, CHARLES BAL 313 7TH WARD
MOSVELL, G. BAL 167 1ST WARD
MOSVER, C.R. BAL 277 12TH WAR
MOSWOOD, WILLIAM BAL 101 2ND DIST
MOSZEL, JOHN A. BAL 219 6TH WARD
MOTCH, NICHOLAS QUE 251 5TH E DI
MOTE, GEORGE-BLACK CAR 074 NO TWP L
MOTE, MARGARETT-BLACK CAR 168 NO TWP L
MOTE, WILLIAM BAL 109 2ND DIST
MOTELBOCK, JOHN M. BAL 143 19TH WAR
MOTEN, CATHARINE BAL 226 12TH WAR
MOTES, JACOB WAS 130 2ND DIST
MOTHER, ANDREW* TAL 014 EASTON D
MOTHER, MICHAEL CAR 329 MANCHEST
MOTHERLY, SUSAN FRE 243 NEW MARK
MOTIN, OBADIAH SOM 501 SALISBUR
MOTON, EBARNEZER * CAR 217 5TH DIST
MOTON, SAMUEL CAR 217 5TH DIST
MOTON, SAMUEL CAR 217 5TH DIST
MOTSELBAUGH, FREDERICK BAL 239 1ST DIST
MOTT, ABRAHAM G. BAL 220 6TH WARD
MOTT, BENJAMIN CEC 048 1ST E DI
MOTT, EDWARD CHA 225 ALLENS F
MOTT, ELIZABETH A. BAL 264 7TH WARD
MOTT, EMILY BAL 046 18TH WAR
MOTT, JAMES BAL 045 18TH WAR
MOTT, MARY BAL 066 4TH WARD
MOTT, MARY BAL 283 7TH WARD
MOTT, SARAH A. CEC 142 6TH E DI
MOTT, THOMAS BAL 142 2ND DIST
MOTT, THOMAS QUE 163 2ND E DI
MOTT, WILLIAM BAL 394 14TH WAR
MOTTA, FRANCIS M.D. BAL 258 1ST DIST
MOTTAR, JEROME WAS 111 2ND DIST
MOTTER, ABRAHAM WAS 113 2ND DIST
MOTTER, ANDREW CAR 260 3RD DIST
MOTTER, CHARLES W. CAR 331 MANCHEST
MOTTER, EDWARD FRE 20 5TH E DI
MOTTER, ELIZABETH CAR 260 3RD DIST
MOTTER, ELIZABETH WAS 186 BOONSBOR
MOTTER, GEORGE WAS 200 1ST DIST
MOTTER, GEORGE CAR 331 MANCHEST
MOTTER, HENRY CAR 331 MANCHEST
MOTTER, ISAAC WAS 007 WILLIAMS
MOTTER, JACOB WAS 111 2ND DIST
MOTTER, JOHN CAR 257 3RD DIST
MOTTER, JOHN S. FRE 319 MIDDLETO
MOTTER, JOSEPH BAL 257 1ST DIST
MOTTER, JOSHUA WAS 200 1ST DIST
MOTTER, LEWIS M. FRE 164 EMMITTSB
MOTTER, LYDIA BAL 094 10TH WAR
MOTTER, MARY TAL 109 ST MICHA
MOTTER, MARY M. FRE 160 EMMITTSB
MOTTER, NANCY FRE 032 FREDERIC
MOTTER, WILLIAM FRE 178 5TH E DI
MOTTER, WILLIAM CAR 259 3RD DIST
MOTTERN, JOHN FRE 401 JEFFERSO
MOTTO, THEODORE BAL 437 14TH WAR
MOTZ, JOHN BAL 350 7TH WARD
MOUAT, JAMES* BAL 360 3RD WARD
MOUBS, PERRY FRE 247 NEW MARK
MOUDEY, HENRY WAS 111 2ND DIST
MOUDEY, JOHN WAS 122 2ND DIST
MOUDY, ELIE WAS 100 2ND DIST
MOUDY, EVE WAS 012 WILLIAMS
MOUDY, WILLIAM WAS 114 2ND DIST
MOUISE, MARY BAL 236 2ND WARD
MOUL, CONRAD CAR 273 WESTMINS
MOUL, JACOB BAL 341 3RD WARD
MOULDEN, ELIZA A. MGM 377 ROCKERLE
MOULDEN, JOSEPH CAL 052 3RD DIST
MOULDEN, MORTIMER MGM 385 ROCKERLE
MOULDEN, SAMUEL J. MGM 409 MEDLEY 3
MOULDEN, SARAH A. FRE 020 FREDERIC
MOULDEN, WILLIAM CAL 047 3RD DIST
MOULDEN,MC KINNEY FRE 037 FREDERIC
MOULE, JULIA* BAL 097 10TH WAR
MOULL, MARGARET BAL 179 2ND DIST
MOULSON, FRANCIS BAL 054 9TH WARD
MOULTER, SUSAN BAL 208 17TH WAR
MOULTER, THOMAS W. HAR 166 3RD DIST
MOULTON, EDWARD P. BAL 119 15TH WAR
MOULTON, JAMES F. BAL 441 14TH WAR
MOULTON, JOHN BAL 272 12TH WAR
MOULTON, WILLIAM BAL 358 13TH WAR
MOUNE, WILLIAM G. BAL 078 4TH WARD
MOUNT, ELIAS FRE 240 NEW MARK
MOUNT, ELIZA BAL 117 11TH WAR
MOUNT, ELIZABETH FRE 238 NEW MARK
MOUNT, GEORGE BAL 238 20TH WAR
MOUNT, H. BAL 142 1ST WARD
MOUNT, JAMES* BAL 360 3RD WARD
MOUNT, MARTHA BAL 281 1ST DIST
MOUNT, SARAH FRE 277 NEW MARK
MOUNTY, JAMES BAL 174 11TH WAR
MOUNTZ, CATHERINE MGM 382 ROCKERLE
MOUNTZ, JOHN W. ALL 172 7TH E.D.
MOUR, CHRISTIAN BAL 308 7TH WARD
MOURER, WILLIAM CAR 266 WESTMINS
MOURIN, JOHN L. BAL 380 8TH WARD
MOURN, WILLIAM BAL 003 4TH WARD
MOURNE, JAMES BAL 005 4TH WARD
MOUSE, JOHN BAL 150 5TH WARD
MOUSE, PETER WAS 140 2ND DIST
MOUSE, PHILIP WAS 141 2ND DIST
MOUSEY, ANN BAL 265 20TH WAR
MOUSLEY, JOHN CEC 127 5TH E DI
MOUSLEY, JOSEPH CEC 015 ELKTON 3
MOUTAIN, SAAH BAL 230 2ND WARD
MOUTIEN, ROBERT-BLACK CAR 102 NO TWP L
MOUTLY, ELI * BAL 335 1ST DIST
MOUTON, FREDERICK BAL 297 7TH WARD
MOW, DORCTHEA BAL 312 3RD WARD
MOWBERRY, SARAH BAL 074 4TH WARD
MOWBRAY, FREDERICK A. BAL 280 2ND WARD
MOWBRAY, GEORGE W. BAL 126 5TH WARD
MOWBRAY, JOHN BAL 119 5TH WARD
MOWBRAY, MARY BAL 033 1ST WARD
MOWBRAY, RACHAEL BAL 020 15TH WAR
MOWDY, SUSAN WAS 100 2ND DIST
MOWELL, GILBERT WAS 266 1ST DIST
MOWELL, PETER BAL 088 1ST WARD
MOWEN, DAVID WAS 296 1ST DIST
MOWEN, DEWALT WAS 126 2ND DIST
MOWEN, ELIAS WAS 297 1ST DIST
MOWEN, EROWINE WAS 295 1ST DIST
MOWEN, JOHN WAS 297 1ST DIST
MOWEN, JOHN WAS 296 1ST DIST
MOWEN, JOHN WAS 134 2ND DIST
MOWEN, JOHN WAS 133 2ND DIST
MOWEN, LEISHIE WAS 132 2ND DIST
MOWEN, LEONARD WAS 297 1ST DIST
MOWEN, G. WAS 130 2ND DIST
MOWER, MARGARET BAL 158 1ST WARD
MOWERY, HENRY ALL 216 CUMBERLA
MOWL, CROMEL CAR 267 WESTMINS
MOWL, LINCHART BAL 113 2ND DIST
MOWLER, SARAH BAL 112 2ND DIST
MOWLRAY, WILLIAM CAR 390 2ND DIST
MOWON, SAMUEL BAL 117 2ND DIST
MOWRAY, J. WAS 145 2ND DIST
MOWRY, ABRAHAM BAL 171 1ST WARD
MOWRY, DANIEL WAS 280 LEITERSB
MOWRY, ELLEN WAS 199 1ST DIST
MOWRY, JOHN WAS 186 BOONSBOR
MOXLEY, ALLEN WAS 212 1ST DIST
MOXLEY, DANIEL WAS 162 2ND DIST
MOXLEY, ELIZABETH PRI 114 PISCATAW
MOXLEY, ELIZABETH MGM 435 CLARKSTR
MOXLEY, EZEKIEL BAL 095 18TH WAR
MOXLEY, GEORGE M. MGM 433 CLARKSTR
MOXLEY, HANSON MGM 433 CLARKSTR
MOXLEY, HENRY MGM 370 BERRYS D
MOXLEY, JOHN MGM 433 CLARKSTR
MOXLEY, JOHN BAL 145 1ST WARD
MOXLEY, JONAH BAL 163 16TH WAR
MOXLEY, LEAH FRE 395 PETERSVI
MOXLEY, LUTHER FRE 446 8TH E DI
MOXLEY, MAHLON T. ANN 412 HOWARD D
MOXLEY, NANCY MGM 345 CLARKSBU
MOXLEY, NEHEMIAH ANN 478 HOWARD D
MOXLEY, RACHEL MGM 433 CLARKSTR
MOXLEY, RISDON BAL 295 7TH WARD
MOXLEY, SAMUEL MGM 433 CLARKSTR
MOXLEY, SAMUEL WAS 156 2ND DIST
MOXLEY, SOPHIA WAS 163 2ND DIST
MOXLEY, WALTER MGM 346 CLARKSBU
MOXLEY, WILLIAM BAL 249 2ND WARD
MOXLEY, WILLIAM BAL 064 15TH WAR
MOXLY, EMILY MGM 345 CLARKSBU
MOYAN, ROSE BAL 424 14TH WAR
MOYENDARIER, JACOB BAL 272 20TH WAR
MOYER, BARBARY BAL 216 19TH WAR
MOYER, DANIEL WAS 205 1ST DIST
MOYHER, MARY WAS 168 FUNKSTOW
MOYLAN, MICHAEL BAL 064 4TH WARD
MOYLES, BIDDY BAL 186 16TH WAR
MOYLON, CORNELIUS BAL 423 3RD WARD
MOZINGO, ALFRED BAL 355 13TH WAR
MORQUESS, RICHARD BAL 214 6TH WARD
MRABURY, ALEXANDER M. CAL 046 3RD DIST
MRRY, JAMES PRI 114 PISCATAW
MSECKE, FREDERICK BAL 131 1ST WARD
MUAR, SOPHIA A. BAL 107 1ST WARD
MUBERGER, MICHAEL * BAL 051 4TH WARD
MUBREADY, BRIDGET FRE 269 NEW MARK
MUCK, AARON BAL 047 9TH WARD
MUCK, ABRAHAM WAS 136 2ND DIST
MUCK, ELIZABETH WAS 216 1ST DIST
MUCK, ELIZABETH FRE 345 MIDDLETO
MUCK, GEORGE FRE 355 MIDDLETO
MUCK, HENRY FRE 353 MIDDLETO
MUCK, JOHN H. FRE 322 MIDDLETO
MUCK, JOHN W. FRE 334 MIDDLETO
MUCK, THOMAS FRE 367 CATOCTIN
MUCK, THOMAS FRE 324 MIDDLETO
MUCK, THOMAS WAS 171 FUNKSTOW
MUCKELROY, JOHN WAS 030 2ND SUBD
MUCKENER, MARGARET BAL 112 1ST WARD
MUCKETT, MARGARET BAL 162 2ND DIST
MUCKMELLON, JAMES BAL 273 17TH WAR
MUDD, ALFRED ST 266 3RD E DI
MUDD, CATHERINE CHA 253 MIDDLETO
MUDD, DANIEL CHA 293 BOJANTOW
MUDD, DOMNICK CHA 247 HILLTOP
MUDD, ELIZABETH CHA 254 MIDDLETO
MUDD, HENRY J. BAL 022 15TH WAR
MUDD, JULIAN CHA 293 BOJANTOW
MUDD, MACELLUS CHA 254 MIDDLETO
MUDD, MARION FRE 029 FREDERIC
MUDD, MARY E. FRE 066 FREDERIC
MUDD, MARY R. PRI 104 PISCATAW
MUDD, SUSANNAH FRE 065 FREDERIC
MUDD, SYLVESTER PRI 063 NOTTINGH
MUDD, THEADORE CHA 294 BOJANTOW
MUDD, THOMAS CHA 294 BOJANTOW
MUDD, UZ. CHA 291 MIDDLETO
MUDD, WILLIAM V. CHA 247 HILLTOP
MUDDERS, FREDEN * CHA 293 BOJANTOW
MUDDY, ELIZABETH BAL 126 2ND DIST
MUDG, CHARLES F. CEC 035 CHESAPEA
MUDGE, ABNER B. ALL 216 CUMBERLA
MUDGE, EDMUND T. BAL 057 10TH WAR
MUDROCK, DILLEY BAL 057 10TH WAR
MUDY, CHARLOTTE-MULATTO WAS 160 2ND DIST
MUDY, ELIZABETH-MULATTO FRE 233 BUCKEYST
MUELIN, MARK FRE 232 BUCKEYST
MUELLER, ANDREW ALL 214 CUMBERLA
MUELLER, T. W. BAL 034 18TH WAR
MUER, ALEXANDER BAL 296 3RD WARD
MUER, ARNOLD SOM 358 BRINKLEY
MUER, CAROLINE SOM 355 BRINKLEY
MUER, GEORGE T. SOM 354 BRINKLEY
MUER, HAMILTON BAL 223 17TH WAR
MUER, JAMES BAL 339 7TH WARD
MUER, JOHN SOM 440 DAMES QU
MUER, JOHN JR. BAL 184 5TH DIST
MUER, NELLY SOM 357 BRINKLEY
MUER, ROBERT SOM 439 DAMES QU
MUER, ROBERT SOM 441 DAMES QU
MUER, THOMAS SOM 440 DAMES QU
MUER, WILLIAM SOM 430 PRINCESS
MUER, WILLIAM SOM 440 DAMES QU
MUERTON, HENRY * SOM 353 BRINKLEY
MUESHAW, JOHN ANN 356 3RD DIST
MUFFNER, JOHN ANN 298 1ST DIST
MUG, ADAM BAL 137 1ST WARD
MUG, LEWIS BAL 069 1ST WARD
MUGAN, DANIEL ANN 428 HOWARD D
MUGENT, FREDRICK FRE 20 5TH E DI
MUGENT, MICHAEL BAL 035 18TH WAR
MUGG, THOAMS N. ALL 110 5TH E.D.
MUGREE, MARY ST 255 3RD E DI
MUHL, BALLREAR * BAL 109 5TH WARD
MUHL, CONRAD BAL 372 13TH WAR
MUHL, CONRAD BAL 191 19TH WAR
MUHL, G. BAL 459 14TH WAR
MUICA, JAMES BAL 141 1ST WARD
MUIR, ANN WOR 180 6TH E DI
MUIR, HUGH DOR 381 1ST DIST
MUIR, JAMES N. DOR 396 1ST DIST
MUIR, JOHN BAL 115 15TH WAR
MUIR, JOHN BAL 184 5TH DIST
MUIR, REBECCA DOR 396 1ST DIST
MUIR, ROBERT BAL 115 15TH WAR
MUIR, ROBERT H. BAL 280 2ND WARD
MUIR, URIAH DOR 397 1ST DIST
MUIRRAY, CHARELS BAL 328 3RD WARD
MUIRS, ELIZA QUE 210 3RD E DI
MUISH, ELIZABETH TAL 023 EASTON D
MUISH, SOLLOMAN* TAL 010 EASTON D
MUITZ, LAURENCE TAL 009 EASTON D
MUKINGS, SAMUEL BAL 256 2ND WARD
MULATTO BAL 098 10TH WAR
MULBERRY, HANNAH FRE 242 NEW MARK
MULBERRY, HENRY FRE 294 WOODSBOR
MULCARA, ELLEN FRE 108 CREAGERS
MULCONRY, THOMAS PRI 027 VANSVILL
MULCORN, THOMAS BAL 064 15TH WAR
MULCRONE, PATRICK BAL 458 1ST DIST
MULCROWN, MICHAEL BAL 091 5TH WARD
MULDOWNIE, BRIDGET ALL 129 4TH E.D.
MULENDON, DANIEL ALL 219 CUMBERLA
MULENDON, JACOB * WAS 085 2ND SUBD
MULENDON, JOHN WAS 083 2ND SUBD
MULENEX, BASEL WAS 085 2ND SUBD
MULENEX, JOSHUA ALL 008 3RD E.D.
MULES, CHARLES BAL 392 1ST DIST
MULES, ELIZABETH BAL 088 4TH WARD
MULES, SARAH CAL 049 3RD DIST
MULET, CATHARINE CAL 058 3RD DIST
MULEY, THOMAS BAL 333 1ST DIST
MULFINGER, CHARLES BAL 218 19TH WAR
MULFINGER, CHRISTIAN BAL 065 2ND DIST
MULFORD, ARAMINTA MGM 375 ROCKERLE
MULFORD, BENJAMIN CEC 032 CHESAPEA
MULFORD, JOHN CEC 033 CHESAPEA
MULFORD, MARY E. CEC 031 CHESAPEA
MULFORD, WILLIAM S. CEC 079 NORTHEAS
MULGOTTON, JOSEPH KEN 289 3RD DIST
MULGREEN, JOHN BAL 196 6TH WARD
MULGROVE, JOHN BAL 175 19TH WAR
MULHDER, GEORGE BAL 112 1ST WARD
MULHEAR, PATRICK BAL 064 1ST WARD
MULHEARN, JOHN ALL 254 CUMBERLA
MULHEREN, ANN ALL 052 10TH E.D
MULHOFFER, JOHN W. ALL 216 CUMBERLA
MULHOLLAND, JOHN BAL 080 10TH WAR
MULHOLLAND, MARY ALL 264 CUMBERLA
MULHORN, ELLEN KEN 306 3RD DIST
MULHORN, JOHN FRE 052 FREDERIC
MULICAN, JOHN FRE 062 FREDERIC
MULIGAN, DENIS HAR 061 1ST DIST
MULIKIN, BENJAMIN A. BAL 352 1ST DIST
MULINIX, ELIZABETH TAL 043 EASTON D
MULINIX, HENRY H. ANN 493 HOWARD D
MULINIX, JESSE W. ANN 493 HOWARD D
MULINIX, JOHN E. ANN 491 HOWARD D
MULINIX, JONATHAN ANN 366 4TH DIST
MULINIX, ROBERT ANN 492 HOWARD D
MULKERSON, JAMES ANN 493 HOWARD D
MULL, JACOB BAL 309 4TH WARD
MULL, JACOB CAR 314 1ST DIST
MULL, JOHN BAL 066 18TH WAR
MULL, SAMUEL WAS 035 2ND SUBD
MULLAN, JAMES BAL 268 20TH WAR
MULLAN, MARY BAL 288 20TH WAR
MULLAN, MICHAEL BAL 230 19TH WAR
MULLAN, NEAL BAL 272 1ST DIST
MULLAN, OWEN BAL 225 19TH WAR
MULLAN,JOHANNA BAL 034 1ST WARD
MULLAND, HARRIET BAL 045 1ST WARD
MULLAR, WALTER M. BAL 209 19TH WAR
MULLCACHAY, JOHN CHA 233 HILLTOP
MULLEN, ALFRED ANN 413 HOWARD D
MULLEN, ANDREW BAL 287 20TH WAR
MULLEN, ANN ALL 128 4TH E.D.
MULLEN, ANN ALL 221 CUMBERLA
MULLEN, ANN BAL 209 6TH WARD
MULLEN, ANN BAL 200 11TH WAR
MULLEN, ANN BAL 299 7TH WARD
MULLEN, ANN BAL 035 4TH WARD
MULLEN, ANN E. FRE 442 8TH E DI
MULLEN, ANN M. CEC 159 PORT DUP
MULLEN, CATHARINE BAL 250 2ND WARD
MULLEN, CATHERINE BAL 169 11TH WAR
MULLEN, CATHERINE BAL 032 9TH WARD
MULLEN, CESAR CEC 204 6TH E DI
MULLEN, CHARLES CEC 202 6TH E DI
MULLEN, CHARLES FRE 338 MIDDLETO
MULLEN, CHRISTOPHER BAL 123 11TH WAR
MULLEN, DANIEL CEC 014 ELKTON 3

Name	County	Page	District
MULLEN, DANIEL	BAL	279	7TH WARD
MULLEN, DAVID	BAL	230	19TH WAR
MULLEN, DENNIS	BAL	149	2ND DIST
MULLEN, E.	FRE	200	5TH E DI
MULLEN, EDWARD	FRE	403	JEFFERSO
MULLEN, ELIZABETH	BAL	034	4TH WARD
MULLEN, EMELINE N.	FRE	429	8TH E DI
MULLEN, FELIX	BAL	161	11TH WAR
MULLEN, GENNET	BAL	123	11TH WAR
MULLEN, GEORGE	FRE	339	MIDDLETO
MULLEN, GEORGE	CEC	116	3RD E DI
MULLEN, HENRY	BAL	109	1ST WARD
MULLEN, HENRY	BAL	392	3RD WARD
MULLEN, HENRY	WAS	059	2ND SUBD
MULLEN, HIRAM H.	FRE	362	CATOCTIN
MULLEN, HUGH	FRE	098	FREDERIC
MULLEN, HUGH	ALL	050	10TH E.D
MULLEN, ISABEL	BAL	007	EASTERN
MULLEN, ISABELLA	BAL	392	3RD WARD
MULLEN, JACOB H.	CAR	255	3RD DIST
MULLEN, JAMES	CEC	001	ELKTON 3
MULLEN, JAMES	CEC	046	1ST E DI
MULLEN, JAMES	BAL	067	4TH WARD
MULLEN, JAMES	BAL	381	8TH WARD
MULLEN, JAMES	BAL	150	2ND DIST
MULLEN, JAMES	BAL	184	2ND WARD
MULLEN, JAMES	BAL	231	12TH WAR
MULLEN, JAMES H.	BAL	189	11TH WAR
MULLEN, JANE	BAL	381	8TH WARD
MULLEN, JANE	CEC	047	1ST E DI
MULLEN, JOHN	BAL	464	14TH WAR
MULLEN, JOHN	FRE	402	JEFFERSO
MULLEN, JOHN	FRE	450	8TH E DI
MULLEN, JOHN	BAL	257	20TH WAR
MULLEN, JOHN	BAL	189	11TH WAR
MULLEN, JOHN	BAL	172	11TH WAR
MULLEN, JOHN	BAL	456	8TH WARD
MULLEN, JOHN	BAL	177	2ND DIST
MULLEN, JOHN	WAS	063	2ND SUBD
MULLEN, JOHN J.	CAR	281	7TH DIST
MULLEN, JOHN M.	BAL	157	16TH WAR
MULLEN, JOHN P.	BAL	438	8TH WARD
MULLEN, JOHNNA	WAS	061	2ND SUBD
MULLEN, MARGARET	BAL	035	9TH WARD
MULLEN, MARGARET	FRE	318	MIDDLETO
MULLEN, MARGRETT	BAL	071	18TH WAR
MULLEN, MARTHA	BAL	288	20TH WAR
MULLEN, MARTIN	BAL	276	1ST DIST
MULLEN, MARTIN	ALL	053	10TH E.D
MULLEN, MARY	ALL	242	CUMBERLA
MULLEN, MARY	BAL	183	19TH WAR
MULLEN, MARY E.	CAR	364	9TH DIST
MULLEN, MARY J.	BAL	304	7TH WARD
MULLEN, MARY M.	BAL	361	13TH WAR
MULLEN, MATILDA	ANN	459	HOWARD D
MULLEN, MICHAEL	BAL	134	2ND DIST
MULLEN, MICHAEL	ALL	056	10TH E.D
MULLEN, MICHAEL	BAL	276	1ST DIST
MULLEN, MR-	BAL	051	15TH WAR
MULLEN, NEIL	BAL	161	2ND DIST
MULLEN, PETER	BAL	003	18TH WAR
MULLEN, RACHEL	BAL	267	12TH WAR
MULLEN, SARAH	BAL	264	7TH WARD
MULLEN, SARAH	BAL	387	1ST DIST
MULLEN, SUSANNAH	CEC	159	PORT DUP
MULLEN, THOMAS	BAL	124	5TH WARD
MULLEN, THOMAS	BAL	199	2ND WARD
MULLEN, THOMAS	BAL	297	12TH WAR
MULLEN, THOMAS E.	FRE	423	8TH E DI
MULLEN, WILLIAM	CEC	156	PORT DUP
MULLEN, WILLIAM	BAL	046	9TH WARD
MULLEN, WILLIAM	BAL	356	8TH WARD
MULLEN, EDWARC	ALL	252	CUMBERLA
MULLENBROOK, CHARLES	BAL	283	1ST DIST
MULLENBROOK, WILMINA	BAL	283	1ST DIST
MULLENDON, JACOB	WAS	082	2ND SUBD
MULLENIN, ANN M.	FRE	246	NEW MARK
MULLENIX, FRANCIS	CAR	396	2ND DIST
MULLENS, PATRICK	BAL	224	6TH WARD
MULLER, AUGUST	BAL	105	15TH WAR
MULLER, CRAFT	BAL	007	15TH WAR
MULLER, HERMAN	BAL	075	10TH WAR
MULLER, JAMES	BAL	020	2ND DIST
MULLER, JAMES	BAL	110	5TH WARD
MULLER, JAMES	FRE	402	JEFFERSO
MULLER, JAMES N.	BAL	383	3RD WARD
MULLER, JOHN	ALL	148	6TH E.D.
MULLER, JULIUS E.	BAL	321	12TH WAR
MULLER, LEWIS C.	BAL	308	3RD WARD
MULLER, LOUIS	BAL	096	10TH WAR
MULLER, LOUISA	BAL	008	15TH WAR
MULLER, PATRICK	BAL	283	1ST DIST
MULLER, PHILIP H.	BAL	312	3RD WARD
MULLER, SARAH	ALL	115	5TH E.D.
MULLER, VALINTINE	BAL	258	2ND WARD
MULLET, THOMAS	BAL	280	7TH WARD
MULLEY, JOHN M.	BAL	011	18TH WAR
MULLHOFFER, WILLIAM	BAL	453	8TH WARD
MULLIAIN, LEONARD	FRE	270	NEW MARK
MULLICAN, BASIL	MGM	365	BERRYS D
MULLICAN, HENRY	MGM	381	ROCKERLE
MULLICAN, HENRY	MGM	363	BERRYS D
MULLICAN, HENRY C.	MGM	364	BERRYS D
MULLICAN, JOHN	FRE	234	BUCKEYST
MULLICAN, PHILIP	CAR	070	NO TWP L
MULLICAN, SAMUEL	BAL	461	1ST DIST
MULLICAN, SUSAN	FRE	020	FREDERIC
MULLICAN, THOMAS	FRE	232	BUCKEYST
MULLICAN, WILLIAM	MGM	382	ROCKERLE
MULLIDY, BRIDGETT	BAL	019	4TH WARD
MULLIEAN, JOHN	MGM	401	ROCKERLE
MULLIGAN, CATHARINE	FRE	203	5TH E DI
MULLIGAN, CATHERINE	BAL	018	4TH WARD
MULLIGAN, CATHERINE	BAL	031	4TH WARD
MULLIGAN, FANNY-MULATTO	BAL	222	2ND WARD
MULLIGAN, JAMES	BAL	419	8TH WARD
MULLIGAN, JOHN	BAL	424	8TH WARD
MULLIGAN, JOHN	FRE	263	NEW MARK
MULLIGAN, MICHAEL	BAL	409	8TH WARD
MULLIGAN, MICHAEL	BAL	447	8TH WARD
MULLIGAN, PATRICK	BAL	261	2ND WARD
MULLIGAN, ROSE	BAL	003	9TH WARD
MULLIGAN, ROSE	BAL	281	17TH WAR
MULLIGAN, THOMAS	BAL	424	8TH WARD
MULLIGAN, THOMAS	BAL	259	6TH WARD
MULLIGAN, THOMAS	BAL	147	1ST WARD
MULLIGEN, MARY E.	FRE	180	5TH E DI
MULLIHEN, ELIZABETH *	TAL	074	EASTON T
MULLIKAN, MORTIMER H.	BAL	316	1ST DIST
MULLIKEA, O. W.	BAL	344	13TH WAR
MULLIKEN, ASBEL	BAL	423	8TH WARD
MULLIKEN, B.A.	PRI	081	QUEEN AN
MULLIKEN, B.D.	PRI	085	QUEEN AN
MULLIKEN, B.H.	PRI	093	MARLBROU
MULLIKEN, BEN J.	PRI	075	MARLBROU
MULLIKEN, ELIZA	PRI	085	QUEEN AN
MULLIKEN, F.	PRI	120	PISCATAW
MULLIKEN, GEORGE	BAL	345	13TH WAR
MULLIKEN, JAMES	BAL	082	18TH WAR
MULLIKEN, JAMES	PRI	090	MARLBROU
MULLIKEN, JAMES	PRI	120	PISCATAW
MULLIKEN, JAMES	PRI	082	QUEEN AN
MULLIKEN, JEREMIAH	PRI	091	MARLBROU
MULLIKEN, JEREMIAH JR.	PRI	074	MARLBROU
MULLIKEN, JOHN	TAL	041	EASTON D
MULLIKEN, JOHN	QUE	212	3RD E DI
MULLIKEN, JOHN B.	PRI	084	QUEEN AN
MULLIKEN, MARY E.	BAL	012	4TH WARD
MULLIKEN, OWEN J.	PRI	120	PISCATAW
MULLIKEN, R.	PRI	103	SPALDING
MULLIKEN, RICHARD B.	PRI	085	QUEEN AN
MULLIKEN, SOPHIA	PRI	072	MARLBROU
MULLIKEN, SOPHIA	PRI	072	MARLBROU
MULLIKEN, THOMAS	BAL	064	4TH WARD
MULLIKEN, WILLIAM	PRI	120	PISCATAW
MULLIKIN, ADAM	BAL	316	3RD WARD
MULLIKIN, ANN	TAL	034	EASTON D
MULLIKIN, AUTHOR	TAL	107	ST MICHA
MULLIKIN, BENJAMIN O.	ANN	364	4TH DIST
MULLIKIN, BRIDGET	BAL	104	10TH WAR
MULLIKIN, CHARLES F.	TAL	037	EASTON D
MULLIKIN, ELEANORA	BAL	006	15TH WAR
MULLIKIN, GEORGE	QUE	159	2ND E DI
MULLIKIN, GEORGE A.	TAL	049	EASTON T
MULLIKIN, GEORGE W.	TAL	048	EASTON T
MULLIKIN, JAMES	TAL	023	EASTON D
MULLIKIN, JEREMIAH	TAL	041	EASTON D
MULLIKIN, JOHN	TAL	033	EASTON D
MULLIKIN, JOHN F.	TAL	037	EASTON D
MULLIKIN, MARY	TAL	049	EASTON T
MULLIKIN, MARY C.	TAL	063	EASTON O
MULLIKIN, PETER B.	TAL	047	EASTON T
MULLIKIN, PHILIMOR	TAL	047	EASTON T
MULLIKIN, SOLOMAN	TAL	049	EASTON T
MULLIKIN, SOLOMAN JR.	TAL	049	EASTON T
MULLIKIN, WILLIAM N.	TAL	043	EASTON D
MULLIN, ANN	BAL	013	4TH WARD
MULLIN, ANN	BAL	316	20TH WAR
MULLIN, CHARLES	BAL	011	4TH WARD
MULLIN, DANIEL	BAL	264	7TH WARD
MULLIN, EDWARD	ALL	167	6TH E.D.
MULLIN, HUGH	FRE	336	MIDDLETO
MULLIN, JAMES	BAL	094	10TH WAR
MULLIN, JOHN	BAL	093	10TH WAR
MULLIN, JOHN	ANN	286	ANNAPOLI
MULLIN, JOHN	BAL	362	8TH WARD
MULLIN, JOHN	BAL	279	2ND WARD
MULLIN, JOHN	BAL	007	15TH WAR
MULLIN, JOHN	BAL	332	7TH WARD
MULLIN, JOHN	BAL	006	9TH WARD
MULLIN, MARGARET	BAL	354	7TH WARD
MULLIN, MARY A.	BAL	323	7TH WARD
MULLIN, MARY A. MISS-	BAL	315	20TH WAR
MULLIN, MARY E.	BAL	305	3RD WARD
MULLIN, PATRICK	BAL	264	7TH WARD
MULLIN, PATRICK	BAL	281	20TH WAR
MULLIN, PHILIP	BAL	015	9TH WARD
MULLIN, RACHEL A.	BAL	165	16TH WAR
MULLIN, RASE	BAL	079	4TH WARD
MULLIN, SAMUEL	BAL	033	4TH WARD
MULLIN, SARAH	BAL	405	3RD WARD
MULLIN, THOMAS	HAR	086	2ND DIST
MULLIN, WILLIAM	HAR	123	2ND DIST
MULLIN, WILLIAM	CEC	099	3RD E DI
MULLIN, WILLIAM M.	BAL	212	19TH WAR
MULLINAX, SARAH	FRE	021	FREDERIC
MULLINGTON, EMA	KEN	310	3RD DIST
MULLININ, THOMAS	FRE	247	NEW MARK
MULLINISE, BENJAMIN	FRE	250	NEW MARK
MULLLICAN, JOHN T.	MGM	422	MEDLEY 3
MULLOBY, THOMAS	BAL	210	6TH WARD
MULLOCH, ISAAC	BAL	336	3RD WARD
MULLON, ARTHUR	BAL	170	11TH WAR
MULLON, HENRY	WAS	143	2ND DIST
MULLY, FRANCES	BAL	404	14TH WAR
MULLYNER, GEORGE	BAL	181	11TH WAR
MULLYNIX, GEORGE	BAL	077	10TH WAR
MULMACK, CHARLES	BAL	298	17TH WAR
MULMERRICK, MARY	ALL	252	CUMBERLA
MULNAIR, CATHERINE	BAL	009	9TH WARD
MULORY, JAMES	BAL	102	2ND DIST
MULOT, MARIAH	WAS	032	2ND SUBD
MULOY, MICHAEL	BAL	278	1ST DIST
MULRANA, MATTHEW	BAL	272	1ST DIST
MULRAY, MICHAEL	ALL	136	4TH E.D.
MULRAY, PATRICK	ALL	136	4TH E.D.
MULREADY, EDWIN	BAL	042	9TH WARD
MULREADY, THOMAS	ALL	099	5TH E.D.
MULROY, THOMAS	BAL	156	1ST WARD
MULSE, CAHERINE	BAL	404	8TH WARD
MULSEN, MARY	BAL	282	12TH WAR
MULSOY, THOMAS	ALL	052	10TH E.D
MULTER, GEORGE M.	BAL	265	20TH WAR
MULTIN, T.	BAL	258	12TH WAR
MULTS, PHILIP A.	BAL	404	8TH WARD
MULTZ, ELIZABETH	BAL	001	EASTERN
MULTZ, JOHN W.	BAL	378	1ST DIST
MULTZER, JOHN	BAL	012	9TH WARD
MULVAIL, BIDDY*	BAL	094	10TH WAR
MULVANEY, MARIA	BAL	471	14TH WAR
MULVANEY, THOMAS	ALL	110	5TH E.D.
MULVANY, MARTIN	ALL	136	4TH E.D.
MULVEY, OWEN	BAL	028	9TH WARD
MULVOHILL, THOMAS	PRI	031	VANSVILL
MUMA, BARBARA	WAS	036	2ND SUBD
MUMA, BARBARA	WAS	042	2ND SUBD
MUMAN, HENRY	BAL	091	2ND DIST
MUMAN, HENRY	BAL	112	2ND DIST
MUMFORD, ANN	FRE	307	WOODSBOR
MUMFORD, EVANS	WOR	271	BERLIN 1
MUMFORD, GEORGE	WOR	253	1ST CENS
MUMFORD, GEORGE A.	FRE	138	CREAGERS
MUMFORD, HENRY	WOR	265	BERLIN 1
MUMFORD, HENRY	WOR	310	2ND E DI
MUMFORD, JAMES	WOR	271	BERLIN 1
MUMFORD, JAMES	WOR	170	6TH E DI
MUMFORD, JAMES	ANN	493	HOWARD D
MUMFORD, JESSE	WOR	265	BERLIN 1
MUMFORD, JOSEPH	WOR	250	1ST CENS
MUMFORD, JOSHUA	WOR	249	1ST CENS
MUMFORD, LEVINA	WOR	241	1ST CENS
MUMFORD, MAJOR	WOR	309	2ND E DI
MUMFORD, MARGARET	FRE	309	WOODSBOR
MUMFORD, MARY	FRE	310	WOODSBOR
MUMFORD, MARY A.	WOR	171	6TH E DI
MUMFORD, NELLA	WOR	283	BERLIN 1
MUMFORD, RICHARD	FRE	353	MIDDLETO
MUMFORD, SARAH A.	WOR	272	BERLIN 1
MUMFORD, SHADRACH	WOR	170	6TH E DI
MUMFORD, THOMAS	WOR	272	BERLIN 1
MUMFORD, THOMAS M.	WOR	310	2ND E DI
MUMFORD, WILLAIM	WOR	311	2ND E DI
MUMFORD, WILLAIM	WOR	301	SNOW HIL
MUMFORD, WILLIAM	WOR	290	9TH E DI
MUMFORD, WILLIAM	WOR	284	BERLIN 1
MUMFORD, WILLIAM	WOR	282	BERLIN 1
MUMFORD, WILLIAM	WOR	271	BERLIN 1
MUMFORD, WILLIAM	FRE	296	WOODSBOR
MUMFORD, WILLIAM W.	WOR	258	1ST CENS
MUMFORD, ZEBULON	WOR	276	BERLIN 1
MUMMA, A.G.	WAS	144	HAGERSTO
MUMMA, ADAM	BAL	029	2ND DIST
MUMMA, AMANDA	BAL	422	8TH WARD
MUMMA, ANN *	BAL	100	2ND DIST
MUMMA, CYRUS	FRE	179	5TH E DI
MUMMA, DAVID	BAL	006	EASTERN
MUMMA, DAVID	BAL	418	8TH WARD
MUMMA, ELIZA	WAS	147	HAGERSTO
MUMMA, ELIZABETH	BAL	418	8TH WARD
MUMMA, ELIZABETH	BAL	419	8TH WARD
MUMMA, GEORGE	BAL	169	2ND DIST
MUMMA, HARRIET	WAS	282	1ST DIST
MUMMA, JACOB	WAS	042	2ND SUBD
MUMMA, JACOB	BAL	012	2ND DIST
MUMMA, JACOB J.	BAL	416	8TH WARD
MUMMA, JACOB R.	WAS	127	HAGERSTO
MUMMA, JOHN	BAL	103	2ND DIST
MUMMA, MARY	BAL	415	8TH WARD
MUMMA, MARY	WAS	201	1ST DIST
MUMMA, NATHANIEL	WAS	201	1ST DIST
MUMMA, RICHARD	BAL	413	8TH WARD
MUMMA, SAMUEL	WAS	232	1ST DIST
MUMMA, SAMUEL	WAS	042	2ND SUBD
MUMMA, SUSAN	BAL	394	8TH WARD
MUMMA, WILLIAM	BAL	103	2ND DIST
MUMMAUGH, GEORGE	CAR	188	4TH DIST
MUMMER, JOHN	FRE	111	CREAGERS
MUMMERT, WILLIAM	WAS	138	2ND DIST
MUMMET, NANCY	WAS	193	1ST DIST
MUMMET, WILLIAM	WAS	188	1ST DIST
MUMMY, CATHARINE	BAL	214	6TH WARD
MUMMY, THOMAS W.	QUE	194	3RD E DI
MUMMY, WILLIAM	BAL	189	5TH DIST
MUMPBIER, GEORGE*	BAL	398	3RD WARD
MUMPFORD, JAMES W.	WOR	308	2ND E DI
MUMPVIER, GEORGE*	BAL	398	3RD WARD
MUMS, JAMES	KEN	301	3RD DIST
MUMY, THOMAS	BAL	198	2ND WARD
MUN, SARAH *	BAL	334	1ST DIST
MUNAHUN, CATHARINE *	BAL	058	15TH WAR
MUNANY, JULIA	BAL	282	12TH WAR
MUNBRIC, JOHN	BAL	068	1ST WARD
MUNCASTER, EDWIN M.	MGM	317	CRACKLIN
MUNCIR, FREDRICK	CHA	257	MIDDLETO
MUNCK, THEODORE	BAL	405	14TH WAR
MUNCKS, MARGARET	BAL	274	20TH WAR
MUNCY, SARAH ANN	ALL	246	CUMBERLA
MUNCY, WILLIAM	CEC	026	ELKTON 3
MUND, CHARLOTTE	BAL	369	13TH WAR
MUNDAY, BENJAMIN	ANN	420	HOWARD D
MUNDAY, MARGARET	ALL	235	CUMBERLA
MUNDAY, MARY A.	WAS	158	2ND DIST
MUNDAY, PETER W.	WAS	158	2ND DIST
MUNDER, CHARLES	BAL	181	11TH WAR
MUNDER, CHARLES F.	BAL	371	13TH WAR
MUNDER, CHARLES F.	BAL	371	13TH WAR
MUNDER, GEORGE	BAL	253	20TH WAR
MUNDER, LEWIS F.	BAL	061	15TH WAR
MUNDINGHALL, ELI	CEC	014	ELKTON 3
MUNDINGHALL, ELIZABETH	CEC	014	ELKTON 3
MUNDLE, JAMES	CEC	163	6TH E DI
MUNDORA, HORACE	BAL	153	2ND DIST
MUNDORF, JOHN	BAL	231	1ST DIST
MUNDY, BENJAMIN	ANN	432	HOWARD D
MUNDY, FREDERICK	BAL	411	3RD WARD
MUNDY, JOHN	BAL	005	1ST WARD
MUNDY, JOHN	WAS	298	1ST DIST
MUNEY, JOHN	BAL	206	2ND WARD
MUNEY, THOMAS	BAL	358	8TH WARD
MUNFORD, JOHN	WOR	241	1ST CENS
MUNGAN, DENNIS	WAS	202	1ST DIST
MUNGAN, ELIZABETH	BAL	276	20TH WAR
MUNGEN, JOSEPH	WAS	202	1ST DIST
MUNGEN, MARY	WAS	203	1ST DIST
MUNGOMERY, MATILDA	HAR	175	3RD DIST
MUNGUMRA, ELIZA	HAR	175	3RD DIST
MUNGUN, CHRISTIAN	WAS	202	1ST DIST
MUNHOLLAND, STEVEN	ALL	012	3RD E.D.
MUNK, ALLEN*	BAL	320	3RD WARD
MUNK, GEORGE	BAL	127	18TH WAR
MUNK, JACOB	HAR	181	3RD DIST
MUNK, JACOB	HAR	182	3RD DIST
MUNK, MARY JANE	HAR	182	3RD DIST
MUNK, ROBERT	HAR	194	3RD DIST
MUNKMA, CAROLINE	BAL	004	EASTERN
MUNN, SAMUEL E.	BAL	046	9TH WARD
MUNNAHAN, WILLIAM	ALL	135	4TH E.D.
MUNNETT, MARY	ALL	170	7TH E.D.
MUNNICK, GEORGE	FRE	336	MIDDLETO
MUNNIKHYSER, JACOB M.	BAL	095	2ND DIST
MUNNIKLURYSEND, JOHN A.	HAR	092	2ND DIST
MUNNIS, ALEXANDER	BAL	106	5TH WARD
MUNNRA, NICHOLAS	BAL	118	1ST WARD
MUNNS, ELIABETH	BAL	291	12TH WAR
MUNRAY, THOMAS	BAL	056	1ST WARD
MUNRO, RACHEL	BAL	289	20TH WAR
MUNROE, ALI	BAL	280	20TH WAR
MUNROE, ANN	BAL	022	4TH WARD
MUNROE, CATHARINE	ST	327	4TH E DI
MUNROE, CHARCILLA	BAL	146	2ND DIST
MUNROE, ELEANOR	ST	281	3RD E DI
MUNROE, FINLEY	BAL	382	3RD WARD
MUNROE, GRAFTON	ANN	268	ANNAPOLI
MUNROE, HENRY	BAL	305	3RD WARD
MUNROE, ISAAC	BAL	108	10TH WAR
MUNROE, JAMES	BAL	128	1ST WARD
MUNROE, JOHN H.	BAL	079	15TH WAR
MUNROE, JOHN L.	BAL	049	1ST WARD
MUNROE, MARGARET	BAL	205	2ND WARD
MUNROE, MARY	BAL	058	4TH WARD

MUNROE, NATHANIEL BAL 058 15TH WAR
MUNROE, R. L. BAL 127 2ND DIST
MUNROE, WILLIAM BAL 152 1ST WARD
MUNROY, JANE BAL 232 12TH WAR
MUNSEN, FREDERIC KEN 211 2ND DIST
MUNSEN, JACOB FRE 154 10TH E D
MUNSEN, MARY BAL 039 4TH WARD
MUNSER, BETSEY ANN 275 ANNAPOLI
MUNSHIRE, JOHN FRE 106 CREAGERS
MUNSHOUR, JOHN FRE 180 5TH E DI
MUNSON, DANIEL KEN 268 1ST DIST
MUNSON, DAVID J. WAS 217 1ST DIST
MUNSON, EDWIN-BLACK QUE 152 1ST E DI
MUNSON, EZRA WAS 134 2ND DIST
MUNSON, FREDERICK WAS 123 HAGERSTO
MUNSON, GEORGE C. BAL 470 14TH WAR
MUNSON, HARRIET CEC 145 PORT DUP
MUNSON, JAMES KEN 283 3RD DIST
MUNSON, JOSHUA WAS 106 2ND DIST
MUNSON, JOSHUA CEC 038 CHESAPEA
MUNSON, JULIAN L. WAS 134 2ND DIST
MUNSON, LEWIS FRE 153 10TH E D
MUNSON, PERE-BLACK QUE 152 1ST E DI
MUNSON, PHILLAS CEC 143 7TH E DI
MUNSON, ROBERT CEC 200 7TH E DI
MUNSON, WILLIAM KEN 278 1ST DIST
MUNSON, ZACARAH KEN 237 2ND DIST
MUNSOR, JOSHUA CEC 036 CHESAPEA
MUNSTANE, EMMELIA FRE 425 8TH E DI
MUNSTER, GEORGE BAL 070 2ND DIST
MUNTY, ELEN CAR 226 5TH DIST
MUNTY, LUCY CAR 225 5TH DIST
MUNTZ, JOHN WAS 269 1ST DIST
MUPER, P. BAL 165 1ST WARD
MUPH, PATRICK ST 261 3RD E DI
MURAY, CHRISTIANA BAL 053 2ND DIST
MURAY, PATRICK ALL 076 5TH E.D.
MURCH, ALLEN* BAL 320 3RD WARD
MURCHEL, RICHARD Z. * CHA 289 MIDDLETO
MURDOCH, MARGARET BAL 409 3RD WARD
MURDOCK, ALEXANDER BAL 263 1ST DIST
MURDOCK, ALICE BAL 211 11TH WAR
MURDOCK, ARCHABALD FRE 043 FREDERIC
MURDOCK, AUGUSUS BAL 203 2ND WARD
MURDOCK, CATHARINE BAL 330 13TH WAR
MURDOCK, CHARLES BAL 320 20TH WAR
MURDOCK, CONROD ALL 240 CUMBERLA
MURDOCK, E.-BLACK FRE 200 5TH E DI
MURDOCK, ELEANOR CHA 238 HILLTOP
MURDOCK, ELIZABETH CHA 219 ALLENS F
MURDOCK, GEORGE FRE 306 WOODSBOR
MURDOCK, GEORGE* DOR 315 1ST DIST
MURDOCK, HANNAH BAL 123 5TH WARD
MURDOCK, HARRIET-BLACK FRE 048 FREDERIC
MURDOCK, ISAIAH CAR 360 9TH DIST
MURDOCK, JAMES QUE 162 2ND E DI
MURDOCK, JOHN BAL 080 18TH WAR
MURDOCK, JOHN CHA 239 HILLTOP
MURDOCK, JOHN FRE 355 MIDDLETO
MURDOCK, JOHNM. FRE 149 10TH E D
MURDOCK, JOSEPH CHA 244 HILLTOP
MURDOCK, LYDIA CHA 235 HILLTOP
MURDOCK, MARY BAL 023 18TH WAR
MURDOCK, MARY J. CHA 245 HILLTOP
MURDOCK, MATILDA FRE 065 FREDERIC
MURDOCK, RACHAEL-BLACK FRE 190 5TH E DI
MURDOCK, ROBERT BAL 104 18TH WAR
MURDOCK, SAMEUL BAL 318 1ST DIST
MURDOCK, SUSAN CHA 236 HILLTOP
MURDOCK, THOMAS ANN 277 ANNAPOLI
MURDOCK, THOMAS BAL 192 11TH WAR
MURDOCK, THOMAS QUE 162 2ND E DI
MURDOCK, WESLEY-BLACK FRE 042 FREDERIC
MURDOCK, WILLIAM BAL 052 18TH WAR
MURDOCK, WILLIAM QUE 153 1ST E DI
MURDOCK, WILLIAM ANN 288 ANNAPOLI
MURDOCK, WILLIAM ANN 286 ANNAPOLI
MURDOCK, WILLIAM BAL 366 3RD WARD
MURDOCK, WILLIAM T. JR. BAL 210 11TH WAR
MURDYS, THOMAS BAL 190 19TH WAR
MURE, AMANCA TAL 085 ST MICHA
MURENBY, JOHN CEC 216 7TH E DI
MURER, H. S. * BAL 151 1ST WARD
MURGESS, PENNY BAL 312 12TH WAR
MURGRITE, ALFRED C. BAL 132 1ST WARD
MURIS, JOSEPH * KEN 280 3RD DIST
MURK, JOHN H. BAL 296 12TH WAR
MURKHART, CONROD FRE 021 FREDERIC
MURLEIGZE, NICHOLAS * BAL 024 9TH WARD
MUROE, J. * BAL 283 20TH WAR
MURPER, CHRISTIAN ALL 034 2ND E.D.
MURPHEN, CHARLES CEC 035 CHESAPEA
MURPHEY, ANNA QUE 249 5TH E DI
MURPHEY, ARTHUR DOR 343 3RD DIVI
MURPHEY, BRIDGET BAL 065 18TH WAR
MURPHEY, BURZELIA* DOR 342 3RD DIVI
MURPHEY, CHARLES P. FRE 096 FREDERIC
MURPHEY, ELIJA DOR 343 3RD DIVI
MURPHEY, ELIZA BAL 319 7TH WARD
MURPHEY, FRANCIS P. FRE 190 5TH E DI
MURPHEY, GOERGE BAL 320 7TH WARD
MURPHEY, HUGH WAS 026 2ND SUBD
MURPHEY, J. FRE 200 5TH E DI
MURPHEY, JAMES BAL 026 18TH WAR
MURPHEY, JOBE DOR 341 3RD DIVI
MURPHEY, JOHN BAL 404 8TH WARD
MURPHEY, JOHN BAL 114 2ND DIST
MURPHEY, JOHN C. KEN 257 1ST DIST
MURPHEY, JOHN R. FRE 280 WOODSBOR
MURPHEY, JON BAL 220 12TH WAR
MURPHEY, JOSHUA FRE 292 WOODSBOR
MURPHEY, MARGARET FRE 291 WOODSBOR
MURPHEY, MARY FRE 160 EMMITTSB
MURPHEY, PRITCHETT DOR 340 3RD DIVI
MURPHEY, SALLY KEN 208 2ND DIST
MURPHY, AMELIA ANN 490 HOWARD D
MURPHY, ANN BAL 061 10TH WAR
MURPHY, ANN BAL 162 16TH WAR
MURPHY, ANN ALL 140 6TH E.D.
MURPHY, ANN BAL 126 5TH WARD
MURPHY, ANN FRE 230 BUCKEYST
MURPHY, ANN BAL 316 20TH WAR
MURPHY, ANN WAS 094 2ND SUBD
MURPHY, ANN E. ALL 126 4TH E.D.
MURPHY, ANNA BAL 118 5TH WARD
MURPHY, ANTHONY ALL 143 6TH E.D.
MURPHY, BARNEY BAL 008 EASTERN
MURPHY, BART. WAS 064 2ND SUBD
MURPHY, BARTINE BAL 358 8TH WARD
MURPHY, BASIL ANN 476 HOWARD D
MURPHY, BENJAMIN BAL 434 14TH WAR
MURPHY, BIDDY BAL 246 12TH WAR
MURPHY, BIDEGAIL ALL 126 4TH E.D.
MURPHY, CATHARINE ALL 107 5TH E.D.
MURPHY, CATHARINE BAL 249 6TH WARD
MURPHY, CATHARINE BAL 298 20TH WAR
MURPHY, CATHERINE BAL 021 9TH WARD
MURPHY, CHARLES BAL 349 7TH WARD
MURPHY, CHARLES BAL 302 12TH WAR
MURPHY, CHARLES CHA 289 BOJANTOW
MURPHY, CHARLES H. MGM 439 CLARKSTR
MURPHY, CHARLES W. KEN 291 3RD DIST
MURPHY, DANIEL DOR 457 1ST DIST
MURPHY, DANIEL BAL 034 9TH WARD
MURPHY, DANIEL BAL 097 5TH WARD
MURPHY, DENNIS ALL 195 CUMBERLA
MURPHY, DENNIS FRE 045 FREDERIC
MURPHY, DIMMICK ALL 142 6TH E.D.
MURPHY, EDWARD BAL 029 4TH WARD
MURPHY, ELIZA BAL 116 11TH WAR
MURPHY, ELIZABETH CHA 273 ALLENS F
MURPHY, ELLEN BAL 454 14TH WAR
MURPHY, ELLEN FRE 443 8TH E DI
MURPHY, ELLEN CEC 207 7TH E DI
MURPHY, ELLEN BAL 235 6TH WARD
MURPHY, EMELINE DOR 428 1ST DIST
MURPHY, EPHRIM H. HAR 196 3RD DIST
MURPHY, EUJENIA * BAL 427 8TH WARD
MURPHY, EVANS BAL 264 2ND WARD
MURPHY, FRANCES ALL 155 6TH E.D.
MURPHY, FRANCES A. HAR 192 3RD DIST
MURPHY, FRANCIS HAR 145 3RD DIST
MURPHY, FRANCIS BAL 188 2ND WARD
MURPHY, FRANCIS D. CHA 288 BOJANTOW
MURPHY, GARRET ALL 260 CUMBERLA
MURPHY, GEORGE ANN 473 HOWARD D
MURPHY, GEORGE ALL 082 5TH E.D.
MURPHY, GEORGE CAR 118 NO TWP L
MURPHY, GEORGE B. ALL 125 4TH E.D.
MURPHY, GEORGE W. SOM 503 SALISBUR
MURPHY, GREENBURY ANN 477 HOWARD D
MURPHY, HANNAH BAL 383 3RD WARD
MURPHY, HANRY BAL 283 20TH WAR
MURPHY, HENRY BAL 365 13TH WAR
MURPHY, HESTER TAL 009 EASTON D
MURPHY, HEZAKIAH CAR 319 1ST DIST
MURPHY, HUGH ALL 129 4TH E.D.
MURPHY, HUGH BAL 315 7TH WARD
MURPHY, IRA BAL 173 19TH WAR
MURPHY, ISAAC BAL 148 2ND DIST
MURPHY, J. BAL 147 1ST WARD
MURPHY, J. C. BAL 052 9TH WARD
MURPHY, J. THOMAS ANN 517 HOWARD D
MURPHY, JAEMS ALL 110 5TH E.D.
MURPHY, JAMES BAL 057 15TH WAR
MURPHY, JAMES FRE 009 FREDERIC
MURPHY, JAMES CHA 289 BOJANTOW
MURPHY, JAMES HAR 144 2ND DIST
MURPHY, JAMES HAR 145 3RD DIST
MURPHY, JAMES HAR 145 3RD DIST
MURPHY, JAMES DOR 438 1ST DIST
MURPHY, JAMES HAR 005 1ST DIST
MURPHY, JAMES BAL 302 17TH WAR
MURPHY, JAMES WAS 034 2ND SUBD
MURPHY, JAMES SOM 502 SALISBUR
MURPHY, JAMES DOR 457 1ST DIST
MURPHY, JAMES TAL 051 EASTON D
MURPHY, JAMES * BAL 298 12TH WAR
MURPHY, JAMES C. TAL 090 ST MICHA
MURPHY, JAMES E. ALL 126 4TH E.D.
MURPHY, JAMES H. FRE 260 NEW MARK
MURPHY, JAMES T. BAL 347 7TH WARD
MURPHY, JAMES W. BAL 088 15TH WAR
MURPHY, JANE BAL 360 8TH WARD
MURPHY, JANE CHA 267 MIDDLETO
MURPHY, JEREMIAH ALL 214 CUMBERLA
MURPHY, JESSEE D. BAL 427 8TH WARD
MURPHY, JOHANNA BAL 070 15TH WAR
MURPHY, JOHN BAL 181 11TH WAR
MURPHY, JOHN BAL 169 11TH WAR
MURPHY, JOHN BAL 165 11TH WAR
MURPHY, JOHN BAL 165 11TH WAR
MURPHY, JOHN ALL 079 5TH E.D.
MURPHY, JOHN BAL 383 3RD WARD
MURPHY, JOHN BAL 384 8TH WARD
MURPHY, JOHN BAL 108 10TH WAR
MURPHY, JOHN ALL 226 CUMBERLA
MURPHY, JOHN ANN 478 HOWARD D
MURPHY, JOHN BAL 013 2ND DIST
MURPHY, JOHN BAL 020 2ND DIST
MURPHY, JOHN BAL 236 5TH WARD
MURPHY, JOHN BAL 201 6TH WARD
MURPHY, JOHN BAL 275 1ST DIST
MURPHY, JOHN BAL 247 1ST DIST
MURPHY, JOHN BAL 042 1ST WARD
MURPHY, JOHN BAL 113 1ST WARD
MURPHY, JOHN BAL 005 1ST WARD
MURPHY, JOHN HAR 179 3RD DIST
MURPHY, JOHN CEC 083 CHARLEST
MURPHY, JOHN CEC 102 4TH E DI
MURPHY, JOHN FRE 096 FREDERIC
MURPHY, JOHN BAL 201 19TH WAR
MURPHY, JOHN BAL 036 4TH WARD
MURPHY, JOHN CEC 179 7TH E DI
MURPHY, JOHN DOR 300 1ST DIST
MURPHY, JOHN QUE 161 2ND E DI
MURPHY, JOHN QUE 207 3RD E DI
MURPHY, JOHN SOM 519 BARREN C
MURPHY, JOHN PRI 114 PISCATAW
MURPHY, JOHN WAS 284 1ST DIST
MURPHY, JOHN A. CHA 260 MIDDLETO
MURPHY, JOHN B. HAR 172 3RD DIST
MURPHY, JOHN C. HAR 031 1ST DIST
MURPHY, JOHN K. QUE 227 4TH E DI
MURPHY, JOHN N. BAL 043 4TH WARD
MURPHY, JOHN T. QUE 161 2ND E DI
MURPHY, JOSEPH QUE 163 2ND E DI
MURPHY, JOSEPH CEC 156 PORT DUP
MURPHY, JOSEPH CEC 187 7TH E DI
MURPHY, JOSEPH ANN 478 HOWARD D
MURPHY, JOSIAH ALL 055 10TH E.D
MURPHY, JULIA ALL 226 CUMBERLA
MURPHY, JULIA BAL 035 9TH WARD
MURPHY, JULIA BAL 052 15TH WAR
MURPHY, JULIA CAR 244 3RD DIST
MURPHY, JULIA A. MGM 440 CLARKSTR
MURPHY, KATEN BAL 150 2ND DIST
MURPHY, KITTY BAL 097 5TH WARD
MURPHY, LARKIN ANN 489 HOWARD D
MURPHY, LOYD ANN 366 4TH DIST
MURPHY, LYDIA CEC 155 PORT DUP
MURPHY, MARGARET BAL 347 13TH WAR
MURPHY, MARGARET BAL 456 14TH WAR
MURPHY, MARGARET BAL 293 3RD WARD
MURPHY, MARGARET BAL 028 9TH WARD
MURPHY, MARGARET BAL 079 10TH WAR
MURPHY, MARIA QUE 225 4TH E DI
MURPHY, MARTIN BAL 361 8TH WARD
MURPHY, MARY BAL 255 6TH WARD
MURPHY, MARY BAL 090 10TH WAR
MURPHY, MARY BAL 274 12TH WAR
MURPHY, MARY BAL 432 1ST DIST
MURPHY, MARY ALL 232 CUMBERLA
MURPHY, MARY BAL 049 2ND DIST
MURPHY, MARY ANN 449 HOWARD D
MURPHY, MARY BAL 268 12TH WAR
MURPHY, MARY BAL 070 15TH WAR
MURPHY, MARY ALL 077 5TH E.D.
MURPHY, MARY ALL 206 CUMBERLA
MURPHY, MARY BAL 114 11TH WAR
MURPHY, MARY BAL 066 18TH WAR
MURPHY, MARY BAL 205 19TH WAR
MURPHY, MARY A. HAR 010 1ST DIST
MURPHY, MARY A. BAL 140 19TH WAR
MURPHY, MARY C. FRE 065 FREDERIC
MURPHY, MARYANN ALL 126 4TH E.D.
MURPHY, MATILDA DOR 300 1ST DIST
MURPHY, MATTHEW BAL 186 16TH WAR
MURPHY, MICHAEL ANN 478 HOWARD D
MURPHY, MICHAEL BAL 172 2ND DIST
MURPHY, MICHAEL BAL 435 14TH WAR
MURPHY, MICHAEL CAR 195 4TH DIST
MURPHY, MICHAEL BAL 302 17TH WAR
MURPHY, MICHAEL MGM 350 BERRYS D
MURPHY, MICHAEL WAS 164 2ND DIST
MURPHY, MR. BAL 122 5TH WARD
MURPHY, NANCY BAL 177 2ND DIST
MURPHY, NANCY BAL 176 19TH WAR
MURPHY, NAT DOR 457 1ST DIST
MURPHY, NICHOLAS CEC 046 1ST E DI
MURPHY, NOAH CAR 145 NO TWP L
MURPHY, OSBURN CHA 227 ALLENS F
MURPHY, OWEN ALL 129 4TH E.D.
MURPHY, PATRICK ALL 078 5TH E.D.
MURPHY, PATRICK ALL 088 5TH E.D.
MURPHY, PATRICK ALL 052 10TH E.D
MURPHY, PATRICK ALL 049 10TH E.D
MURPHY, PATRICK BAL 177 2ND DIST
MURPHY, PATRICK BAL 033 1ST WARD
MURPHY, PATRICK BAL 279 12TH WAR
MURPHY, PATRICK BAL 014 15TH WAR
MURPHY, PATRICK BAL 349 7TH WARD
MURPHY, PATRICK CEC 020 ELKTON 3
MURPHY, PATRICK BAL 288 17TH WAR
MURPHY, PATRICK PRI 114 PISCATAW
MURPHY, PATRICK* BAL 339 3RD WARD
MURPHY, PETER BAL 460 1ST DIST
MURPHY, PETER ALL 149 6TH E.D.
MURPHY, PETER BAL 285 17TH WAR
MURPHY, PHILIP BAL 148 19TH WAR
MURPHY, PHILLIP FRE 066 FREDERIC
MURPHY, PRICILLA CHA 268 BOJANTOW
MURPHY, PRUCILLA SOM 432 PRINCESS
MURPHY, RACHEL ANN 489 HOWARD D
MURPHY, REBECCA ANN 489 HOWARD D
MURPHY, REBECCA DOR 458 1ST DIST
MURPHY, REUBEN MGM 350 BERRYS D
MURPHY, RICHARD CEC 089 4TH E DI
MURPHY, RICHARD R. TAL 026 EASTON D
MURPHY, ROBERT CEC 159 PORT DUP
MURPHY, ROBINSON TAL 101 ST MICHA
MURPHY, ROSE BAL 467 14TH WAR
MURPHY, SABRA L. WOR 218 4TH E DI
MURPHY, SALLY BAL 471 14TH WAR
MURPHY, SARAH CEC 032 CHESAPEA
MURPHY, SARAH BAL 420 3RD WARD
MURPHY, SARAH CEC 206 7TH E DI
MURPHY, SARAH BAL 321 3RD WARD
MURPHY, SARAH BAL 106 10TH WAR
MURPHY, SARAH BAL 199 6TH WARD
MURPHY, SHADRACK T. DOR 455 1ST DIST
MURPHY, SIMON BAL 131 1ST WARD
MURPHY, SUSAN PRI 029 VANSVILL
MURPHY, TEMPERANCE BAL 299 17TH WAR
MURPHY, THOMAS BAL 292 17TH WAR
MURPHY, THOMAS BAL 410 3RD WARD
MURPHY, THOMAS CEC 042 CHESAPEA
MURPHY, THOMAS CAR 211 5TH DIST
MURPHY, THOMAS CAR 147 NO TWP L
MURPHY, THOMAS BAL 115 11TH WAR
MURPHY, THOMAS BAL 443 14TH WAR
MURPHY, THOMAS BAL 316 20TH WAR
MURPHY, THOMAS FRE 050 FREDERIC
MURPHY, THOMAS QUE 223 4TH E DI
MURPHY, THOMAS BAL 122 5TH WARD
MURPHY, THOMAS ALL 057 10TH E.D
MURPHY, THOMAS ALL 052 10TH E.D
MURPHY, THOMAS BAL 014 15TH WAR
MURPHY, THOMAS BAL 010 15TH WAR
MURPHY, THOMAS BAL 018 1ST WARD
MURPHY, THOMAS BAL 353 3RD WARD
MURPHY, THOMAS BAL 012 2ND DIST
MURPHY, THOMAS * BAL 168 2ND DIST
MURPHY, THOMAS H. BAL 424 14TH WAR
MURPHY, THOMAS J. HAR 186 3RD DIST
MURPHY, THOMAS L. BAL 319 3RD WARD
MURPHY, TIMOTHY BAL 169 2ND DIST
MURPHY, VIRGINIA H. BAL 024 4TH WARD
MURPHY, W. MRS. BAL 470 14TH WAR
MURPHY, W.A. BAL 117 1ST WARD
MURPHY, WILLAIM BAL 144 1ST WARD
MURPHY, WILLIAM BAL 155 2ND DIST
MURPHY, WILLIAM BAL 163 2ND DIST
MURPHY, WILLIAM BAL 369 3RD WARD
MURPHY, WILLIAM BAL 437 1ST DIST
MURPHY, WILLIAM BAL 032 2ND DIST
MURPHY, WILLIAM ALL 055 10TH E.D
MURPHY, WILLIAM ALL 078 5TH E.D.
MURPHY, WILLIAM ALL 076 5TH E.D.
MURPHY, WILLIAM ALL 139 6TH E.D.
MURPHY, WILLIAM ALL 003 3RD E.D.
MURPHY, WILLIAM CAR 116 NO TWP L
MURPHY, WILLIAM HAR 175 3RD DIST
MURPHY, WILLIAM CHA 290 BOJANTOW
MURPHY, WILLIAM CEC 075 NORTHEAS
MURPHY, WILLIAM FRE 436 8TH E DI
MURPHY, WILLIAM HAR 189 3RD DIST
MURPHY, WILLIAM WAS 151 2ND DIST
MURPHY, WILLIAM E. MGM 434 CLARKSTR
MURPHY, MARY A. BAL 045 1ST WARD

MURR, JACOB F. BAL 411 14TH WAR
MURR, SARAH * BAL 334 1ST DIST
MURRAN, SISTER M.D. FRE 198 5TH E DI
MURRAND, JAMES FRE 182 5TH E DI
MURRAY, ABIGAIL BAL 043 15TH WAR
MURRAY, ALEXANDER BAL 071 4TH WARD
MURRAY, AMASA BAL 246 12TH WAR
MURRAY, ANDREW BAL 082 10TH WAR
MURRAY, ANN ALL 191 9TH E.D.
MURRAY, ANN BAL 216 6TH WARD
MURRAY, ANN WAS 022 2ND SUBD
MURRAY, ANN G. DOR 378 1ST DIST
MURRAY, ANTHONY ANN 369 4TH DIST
MURRAY, ARTHUR BAL 246 6TH WARD
MURRAY, AVERY A. BAL 172 11TH WAR
MURRAY, BRIDGET BAL 076 10TH WAR
MURRAY, CAROLINE BAL 106 15TH WAR
MURRAY, CATHARINE CAR 180 8TH DIST
MURRAY, CATHERINE BAL 054 4TH WARD
MURRAY, CATHERINE BAL 088 18TH WAR
MURRAY, CATHERINE BAL 192 11TH WAR
MURRAY, CATHERINE BAL 318 3RD WARD
MURRAY, CECELIA BAL 250 6TH WARD
MURRAY, CHARLES BAL 145 1ST WARD
MURRAY, CHARLES BAL 172 11TH WAR
MURRAY, CHARLES ALL 128 4TH E.D.
MURRAY, CHARLES ALL 100 5TH E.D.
MURRAY, CHARLES BAL 285 17TH WAR
MURRAY, CHARLOTTE QUE 249 5TH E DI
MURRAY, CANIEL WAS 024 2ND SUBD
MURRAY, CAVID WOR 246 1ST CENS
MURRAY, CAVID BAL 071 4TH WARD
MURRAY, CAVID BAL 310 3RD WARD
MURRAY, CAVID BAL 078 15TH WAR
MURRAY, EBENEZER SOM 461 HANGARY
MURRAY, EDWARD BAL 088 10TH WAR
MURRAY, EDWARD ALL 150 6TH E.D.
MURRAY, EDWARD BAL 201 11TH WAR
MURRAY, EDWARD BAL 224 6TH WARD
MURRAY, EDWARD ANN 442 HOWARD D
MURRAY, EDWARD-MULATTO ST 297 2ND E DI
MURRAY, ELISABETH ALL 240 CUMBERLA
MURRAY, ELIZA BAL 180 6TH WARD
MURRAY, ELIZA BAL 140 11TH WAR
MURRAY, ELIZA J. BAL 024 15TH WAR
MURRAY, ELIZABETH BAL 172 11TH WAR
MURRAY, ELIZABETH BAL 349 13TH WAR
MURRAY, ELIZABETH QUE 213 3RD E DI
MURRAY, ELIZABETH WOR 248 1ST CENS
MURRAY, ELIZABETH PRI 058 NOTTINGH
MURRAY, ELLEN M. CAR 266 WESTMINS
MURRAY, ETTY BAL 218 6TH WARD
MURRAY, FRANCIS K. ANN 430 HOWARD D
MURRAY, FRANCISP WOR 327 1ST E DI
MURRAY, FREDERICK BAL 180 19TH WAR
MURRAY, FREDERICK T. BAL 167 16TH WAR
MURRAY, GEORGE BAL 188 6TH WARD
MURRAY, GEORGE BAL 142 5TH WARD
MURRAY, GEORGE BAL 156 11TH WAR
MURRAY, GEORGE-BLACK QUE 156 2ND E DI
MURRAY, H. C. BAL 321 12TH WAR
MURRAY, HENRY BAL 161 16TH WAR
MURRAY, HENRY BAL 179 19TH WAR
MURRAY, HENRY WOR 341 1ST E DI
MURRAY, HENRY M. ANN 426 HOWARD D
MURRAY, HUGH BAL 422 14TH WAR
MURRAY, HUMPHRY BAL 150 11TH WAR
MURRAY, IRA BAL 175 19TH WAR
MURRAY, ISAAC WOR 247 1ST CENS
MURRAY, JACOB CAR 171 8TH DIST
MURRAY, JACOB BAL 337 3RD WARD
MURRAY, JACOB BAL 113 5TH WARD
MURRAY, JAMES BAL 205 6TH WARD
MURRAY, JAMES BAL 247 6TH WARD
MURRAY, JAMES BAL 046 9TH WARD
MURRAY, JAMES BAL 021 15TH WAR
MURRAY, JAMES BAL 184 11TH WAR
MURRAY, JAMES BAL 185 11TH WAR
MURRAY, JAMES BAL 064 15TH WAR
MURRAY, JAMES BAL 019 15TH WAR
MURRAY, JAMES BAL 147 11TH WAR
MURRAY, JAMES BAL 308 20TH WAR
MURRAY, JAMES BAL 072 18TH WAR
MURRAY, JAMES DOR 444 1ST DIST
MURRAY, JAMES BAL 278 20TH WAR
MURRAY, JAMES WOR 327 1ST E DI
MURRAY, JAMES A. BAL 112 18TH WAR
MURRAY, JAMES F. BAL 288 20TH WAR
MURRAY, JAMES H. ANN 297 1ST DIST
MURRAY, JAMES P. BAL 173 11TH WAR
MURRAY, JAMES Y. BAL 214 11TH WAR
MURRAY, JAMES-BLACK QUE 146 1ST E DI
MURRAY, JANE BAL 277 20TH WAR
MURRAY, JANE BAL 120 5TH WARD
MURRAY, JOHN BAL 077 15TH WAR
MURRAY, JOHN BAL 157 2ND DIST
MURRAY, JOHN BAL 116 1ST WARD
MURRAY, JOHN BAL 090 18TH WAR
MURRAY, JOHN CAL 035 2ND DIST
MURRAY, JOHN WOR 248 1ST CENS
MURRAY, JOHN WOR 247 1ST CENS
MURRAY, JOHN H. QUE 211 3RD E DI
MURRAY, JOHN L. CAR 265 WESTMINS
MURRAY, JOHN P. BAL 283 20TH WAR
MURRAY, JOHN T. SOM 475 TRAPPE D
MURRAY, JOHN W. CAR 358 9TH DIST
MURRAY, JOHN W. CAR 184 8TH DIST
MURRAY, JOHN-BLACK QUE 153 1ST E DI
MURRAY, JOSEPH WAS 157 2ND DIST
MURRAY, JOSHUA CAR 207 4TH DIST
MURRAY, JOSHUA B. WOR 246 1ST CENS
MURRAY, JULIA ANN 444 HOWARD D
MURRAY, KENCAL WOR 242 1ST CENS
MURRAY, LAWRENCE BAL 094 5TH WARD
MURRAY, LEVI BAL 248 20TH WAR
MURRAY, LOUISA WAS 013 WILLIAMS
MURRAY, M. ANN 284 ANNAPOLI
MURRAY, MALINDA BAL 230 6TH WARD
MURRAY, MARGARET BAL 312 3RD WARD
MURRAY, MARGARET BAL 213 11TH WAR
MURRAY, MARGARET BAL 348 13TH WAR
MURRAY, MARGARET BAL 316 20TH WAR
MURRAY, MARIA BAL 343 3RD WARD
MURRAY, MARIA BAL 154 5TH WARD
MURRAY, MARIA-BLACK QUE 180 2ND E DI
MURRAY, MARTIN ALL 050 10TH E.D
MURRAY, MARY BAL 135 5TH WARD
MURRAY, MARY ANN 455 HOWARD D
MURRAY, MARY BAL 307 12TH WAR
MURRAY, MARY BAL 383 3RD WARD

MURRAY, MARY WOR 258 1ST CENS
MURRAY, MARY BAL 070 4TH WARD
MURRAY, MARY BAL 048 4TH WARD
MURRAY, MARY CAR 184 8TH DIST
MURRAY, MARY BAL 031 4TH WARD
MURRAY, MARY BAL 234 20TH WAR
MURRAY, MARY A. BAL 193 11TH WAR
MURRAY, MARY E. BAL 256 6TH WARD
MURRAY, MARY E. DOR 378 1ST DIST
MURRAY, MARY J. BAL 040 9TH WARD
MURRAY, MARY MRS- ANN 305 1ST DIST
MURRAY, MATHEW H. BAL 419 3RD WARD
MURRAY, MATILDA WAS 007 WILLIAMS
MURRAY, MICHAEL ALL 052 10TH E.D
MURRAY, MICHAEL BAL 401 3RD WARD
MURRAY, MICHAEL BAL 021 15TH WAR
MURRAY, NANCY WOR 248 1ST CENS
MURRAY, NANCY BAL 212 17TH WAR
MURRAY, NED BAL 411 3RD WARD
MURRAY, OLIVER ANN 284 ANNAPOLI
MURRAY, PATRICK ALL 052 10TH E.D
MURRAY, PATRICK ALL 048 10TH E.D
MURRAY, PATRICK BAL 283 17TH WAR
MURRAY, PERRY BAL 330 13TH WAR
MURRAY, PERRY KEN 258 1ST DIST
MURRAY, PETER BAL 310 12TH WAR
MURRAY, PHILIP BAL 369 3RD WARD
MURRAY, PHILL-BLACK QUE 195 3RD E DI
MURRAY, RACHEL BAL 320 12TH WAR
MURRAY, RACHEL ANN 516 HOWARD D
MURRAY, REBECA BAL 179 16TH WAR
MURRAY, RICHARD BAL 169 19TH WAR
MURRAY, ROBERT CAR 232 5TH DIST
MURRAY, ROBERT BAL 094 5TH WARD
MURRAY, ROBERT ALL 109 5TH E.D.
MURRAY, ROSE BAL 185 11TH WAR
MURRAY, RUEBEN BAL 090 18TH WAR
MURRAY, SAMUEL BAL 197 19TH WAR
MURRAY, SAMUEL BAL 293 20TH WAR
MURRAY, SAMUEL M. BAL 206 19TH WAR
MURRAY, SAMUEL T. ANN 499 HOWARD D
MURRAY, SAMUEL-BLACK QUE 179 2ND E DI
MURRAY, SARAH CAR 196 4TH DIST
MURRAY, SARAH BAL 429 14TH WAR
MURRAY, SARAH A. SOM 475 TRAPPE D
MURRAY, SHEWEY BAL 200 17TH WAR
MURRAY, SPENCER BAL 044 9TH WARD
MURRAY, STANLY BAL 142 5TH WARD
MURRAY, SUSAN BAL 146 16TH WAR
MURRAY, SUSAN WOR 268 BERLIN 1
MURRAY, THOMAS QUE 247 5TH E DI
MURRAY, THOMAS BAL 094 5TH WARD
MURRAY, THOMAS BAL 192 11TH WAR
MURRAY, THOMAS BAL 057 15TH WAR
MURRAY, THOMAS BAL 029 4TH WARD
MURRAY, WALTER BAL 089 18TH WAR
MURRAY, WESLY ANN 266 ANNAPOLI
MURRAY, WILLIAM BAL 154 16TH WAR
MURRAY, WILLIAM BAL 078 10TH WAR
MURRAY, WILLIAM BAL 016 9TH WARD
MURRAY, WILLIAM BAL 210 6TH WARD
MURRAY, WILLIAM BAL 378 13TH WAR
MURRAY, WILLIAM BAL 162 19TH WAR
MURRAY, WILLIAM DOR 441 1ST DIST
MURRAY, WILLIAM WOR 241 1ST CENS
MURRAY, WILLIAM H. TAL 100 ST MICHA
MURRAY, WILLIAM H. BAL 089 15TH WAR
MURRAY, WILLIAM T. BAL 166 16TH WAR
MURRAY, WHEELOR CAR 171 8TH DIST
MURRELL, ELEANOR SOM 489 SALISBUR
MURRELL, GEORGE SOM 471 TRAPPE D
MURRELL, JOHN SOM 471 TRAPPE D
MURREY, CORNELIA BAL 266 7TH WARD
MURREY, DANIEL KEN 232 2ND DIST
MURREY, EMILY KEN 232 2ND DIST
MURREY, FRANCES BAL 406 8TH WARD
MURREY, ISAAC BAL 303 7TH WARD
MURREY, JACOB BAL 408 8TH WARD
MURREY, JAMES BAL 280 7TH WARD
MURREY, JAMES BAL 275 7TH WARD
MURREY, JOHN BAL 457 8TH WARD
MURREY, JOHN KEN 260 1ST DIST
MURREY, JOHN W. BAL 332 7TH WARD
MURREY, JULIA BAL 291 7TH WARD
MURREY, MARY BAL 290 7TH WARD
MURREY, OWEN BAL 370 8TH WARD
MURREY, PATRICK FRE 095 FREDERIC
MURREY, RACHEL BAL 359 8TH WARD
MURREY, ROBERT BAL 458 8TH WARD
MURREY, SAMUEL BAL 365 8TH WARD
MURREY, SIMON KEN 272 1ST DIST
MURREY, THOMAS BAL 333 7TH WARD
MURREY, THOMAS B. FRE 019 FREDERIC
MURREY, VIRGINIA BAL 369 8TH WARD
MURRICKHUYSIN, WILLIAM T. HAR 075 BEL AIR
MURRING, CHRSITIAN CAR 320 1ST DIST
MURRY, ABRAHAM BAL 250 1ST DIST
MURRY, ALICE BAL 441 14TH WAR
MURRY, AMY-BLACK CAR 169 NO TWP L
MURRY, ANDREW WAS 156 2ND DIST
MURRY, ANN CHA 290 BOJANTOW
MURRY, ANN BAL 020 1ST WARD
MURRY, ANN ALL 162 6TH E.D.
MURRY, ANN BAL 459 1ST DIST
MURRY, ANN E. WAS 142 HAGERSTO
MURRY, ANN M. DOR 314 1ST DIST
MURRY, ANN-BLACK CAR 119 NO TWP L
MURRY, ARAH* DOR 314 1ST DIST
MURRY, AUGUSTUS-BLACK CAR 075 NO TWP L
MURRY, EETSEY SOM 475 TRAPPE D
MURRY, BRIDGET BAL 448 1ST DIST
MURRY, C. BAL 151 1ST WARD
MURRY, C. BAL 163 1ST WARD
MURRY, CAROLINE CAL 004 1ST DIST
MURRY, CATHARINE ALL 139 6TH E.D.
MURRY, CHARLES ALL 216 CUMBERLA
MURRY, CHARLES DOR 322 1ST DIST
MURRY, CHARLES WAS 036 2ND SUBD
MURRY, D. BAL 295 1ST DIST
MURRY, DAVID WAS 108 2ND DIST
MURRY, EASAH BAL 030 1ST WARD
MURRY, ELIZA KEN 265 1ST DIST
MURRY, ELIZA FRE 066 FREDERIC
MURRY, ELIZABETH WAS 154 HAGERSTO
MURRY, ELIZABETH BAL 299 1ST DIST
MURRY, ELLEN TAL 039 EASTON D
MURRY, ELLEN-MULATTO ST 294 2ND E DI
MURRY, EVERAT CAL 004 1ST DIST
MURRY, F. BAL 161 1ST WARD
MURRY, FRANCAS-MULATTO BAL 218 2ND WARD

MURRY, FRANCIS BAL 115 1ST WARD
MURRY, FRANCIS T. CAR 269 WESTMINS
MURRY, GEORGE BAL 311 1ST DIST
MURRY, GUSTUS CAL 018 1ST DIST
MURRY, H. BAL 173 1ST WARD
MURRY, HAMILTON BAL 149 1ST WARD
MURRY, HANNAH C. BAL 277 1ST DIST
MURRY, HENRY WAS 221 1ST DIST
MURRY, IGNATIUS-MULATTO ST 293 2ND E DI
MURRY, ISHMAEL BAL 245 1ST DIST
MURRY, J. BAL 164 1ST WARD
MURRY, JACK BAL 283 12TH WAR
MURRY, JAMES ANN 281 ANNAPOLI
MURRY, JAMES BAL 128 1ST WARD
MURRY, JAMES PRI 025 VANSVILL
MURRY, JAMES WAS 157 HAGERSTO
MURRY, JAMES CAR 088 NO TWP L
MURRY, JAMES BAL 117 11TH WAR
MURRY, JAMES SOM 430 PRINCESS
MURRY, JAMES-MULATTO ST 300 2ND E DI
MURRY, JOHN WAS 218 1ST DIST
MURRY, JOHN WAS 297 1ST DIST
MURRY, JOHN BAL 234 2ND WARD
MURRY, JOHN ALL 140 6TH E.D.
MURRY, JOHN BAL 269 1ST DIST
MURRY, JOHN BAL 276 1ST DIST
MURRY, JOHN BAL 036 1ST WARD
MURRY, JOHN BAL 412 1ST DIST
MURRY, JOHN BAL 053 2ND DIST
MURRY, JOHN A. TAL 066 EASTON T
MURRY, JOHN L.-MULATTO ST 295 2ND E DI
MURRY, JOHN W. BAL 099 1ST WARD
MURRY, JOSEPH WOR 246 1ST CENS
MURRY, JOSEPH-BLACK CAR 137 NO TWP L
MURRY, JOSEPH-MULATTO ST 308 1ST E DI
MURRY, LAWRENCE WAS 154 2ND DIST
MURRY, LEVIN DOR 312 1ST DIST
MURRY, M. BAL 163 1ST WARD
MURRY, MALACHI ALL 136 4TH E.D.
MURRY, MARIA BAL 233 1ST DIST
MURRY, MARIA ALL 247 CUMBERLA
MURRY, MARIA BAL 424 14TH WAR
MURRY, MARY BAL 461 1ST DIST
MURRY, MARY PRI 036 VANSVILL
MURRY, MARY C. BAL 318 1ST DIST
MURRY, MICHAEL ALL 085 5TH E.D.
MURRY, MICHAEL BAL 329 1ST DIST
MURRY, MICHAEL WAS 094 2ND SUBD
MURRY, MICHAEL FRE 202 5TH E DI
MURRY, MRS. ALL 240 CUMBERLA
MURRY, NANCY WAS 121 HAGERSTO
MURRY, PATRICK BAL 444 1ST DIST
MURRY, PATRICK BAL 447 1ST DIST
MURRY, PATRICK BAL 252 1ST DIST
MURRY, PETER BAL 444 1ST DIST
MURRY, RACHAEL DOR 318 1ST DIST
MURRY, RHODY-BLACK CAR 075 NO TWP L
MURRY, RICHARD CHA 249 HILLTOP
MURRY, RICHARD WAS 154 2ND DIST
MURRY, ROGER ALL 112 5TH E.D.
MURRY, SAMUEL TAL 040 EASTON D
MURRY, SARAH TAL 094 ST MICHA
MURRY, SARAH ANN DOR 314 1ST DIST
MURRY, SARRAH WAS 301 1ST DIST
MURRY, SISTER M.S. FRE 198 5TH E DI
MURRY, STEVEN WAS 119 2ND DIST
MURRY, SUSAN WAS 045 2ND SUBD
MURRY, T. BAL 135 1ST WARD
MURRY, THOMAS BAL 448 1ST DIST
MURRY, THOMAS BAL 271 1ST DIST
MURRY, THOMAS BAL 099 1ST WARD
MURRY, THOMAS BAL 115 1ST WARD
MURRY, THOMAS QUE 215 3RD E DI
MURRY, THOMAS CEC 093 4TH E DI
MURRY, THOMAS CEC 035 CHESAPEA
MURRY, THOMAS-BLACK CAR 133 NO TWP L
MURRY, WILLAIM ALL 107 5TH E.D.
MURRY, WILLIAM ALL 209 CUMBERLA
MURRY, WILLIAM ALL 217 CUMBERLA
MURRY, WILLIAM BAL 025 2ND DIST
MURRY, WILLIAM BAL 001 9TH WARD
MURRY, WILLIAM CEC 008 ELKTON 3
MURRY, WILLIAM DOR 315 1ST DIST
MURRY.J. BAL 162 1ST WARD
MURRY.JAMES BAL 100 1ST WARD
MURRYT, JOHN BAL 095 1ST WARD
MURSE, WILLIAM L. BAL 224 12TH WAR
MURSEN, ABSOLAM * ANN 372 4TH DIST
MURSEN, DAVID ANN 373 4TH DIST
MURSER, JESSE FRE 183 5TH E DI
MURST, JOH E. BAL 474 14TH WAR
MURTHEW, ANN * ALL 070 5TH E.D.
MURTHORN, J. BAL 090 5TH WARD
MURTON, HENRY * ANN 356 3RD DIST
MURTOUGH, MICGHAEL BAL 018 2ND DIST
MURTTAGH, MARY BAL 019 2ND DIST
MURTY, MARY ALL 216 CUMBERLA
MURY, WILLIAM KEN 215 2ND DIST
MUSAYER, DAVID FRE 266 NEW MARK
MUSCHETT, WALTER BAL 157 11TH WAR
MUSE, ANN DOR 313 1ST DIST
MUSE, BERY-BLACK CAR 158 NO TWP L
MUSE, CAROLINE TAL 072 EASTON T
MUSE, ELY BAL 219 19TH WAR
MUSE, ISAAC BAL 161 19TH WAR
MUSE, J. A. B. BAL 332 1ST DIST
MUSE, JAMES A.* DOR 378 1ST DIST
MUSE, JAMES-BLACK CAR 164 NO TWP L
MUSE, JOHN H. DOR 314 1ST DIST
MUSE, JOSEPH BAL 149 16TH WAR
MUSE, JOSEPH E. DOR 423 1ST DIST
MUSE, JOSEPH E. DOR 379 1ST DIST
MUSE, MARY E. BAL 161 19TH WAR
MUSE, MARY-BLACK CAR 139 NO TWP L
MUSE, MARY-BLACK CAR 141 NO TWP L
MUSE, MOLLY BAL 202 19TH WAR
MUSE, MOSE-BLACK CAR 163 NO TWP L
MUSE, WILLIAM H. DOR 423 1ST DIST
MUSEL, HENRY* BAL 112 15TH WAR
MUSEN, GEORGE CEC 040 CHESAPEA
MUSER, HANNAH CEC 039 CHESAPEA
MUSER, JESSE * FRE 163 EMMITTSB
MUSER, JOHN CEC 040 CHESAPEA
MUSETTER, MARY FRE 446 8TH E DI
MUSGRAME, CHARLES * BAL 355 1ST DIST
MUSGRAVE, ALSE BAL 300 1ST DIST
MUSGRAVE, ANDREW BAL 024 9TH WARD
MUSGRAVE, CATHARINE BAL 322 12TH WAR
MUSGRAVE, CHARLES * BAL 355 1ST DIST
MUSGRAVE, JAMES BAL 089 5TH WARD

NAME	CO	PAGE	DISTRICT
MUSGRAVE, STEPHEN	BAL	453	1ST DIST
MUSGRAVE, STEPHEN	BAL	364	1ST DIST
MUSGROVE, CALEB	MGM	323	CRACKLIN
MUSGROVE, ELIZABETH	BAL	039	4TH WARD
MUSGROVE, EMMA	MGM	335	CRACKLIN
MUSGROVE, GEORGE W.	BAL	129	1ST WARD
MUSGROVE, JAMES	ANN	494	HOWARD D
MUSGROVE, JAMES	FRE	193	5TH E DI
MUSGROVE, JOHN H.	ANN	496	HOWARD D
MUSGROVE, MARY	CEC	128	5TH E DI
MUSGROVE, NANCY	FRE	160	EMMITTSB
MUSGROVE, NATHAN	FRE	437	8TH E DI
MUSGROVE, NICHOLAS	ANN	485	HOWARD D
MUSGROVE, STEPHEN	ANN	498	HOWARD D
MUSGROVE, SUSAN	FRE	289	WOODSBOR
MUSH, JOHN	BAL	368	8TH WARD
MUSH, JOHN*	BAL	089	10TH WAR
MUSH, MARY	WAS	150	HAGERSTO
MUSHAVE, CHARLES H.	BAL	266	17TH WAR
MUSHAVE, SOPHIA	BAL	266	17TH WAR
MUSHAW, ANN L.	ANN	383	4TH DIST
MUSHAW, CHARLES	ANN	383	4TH DIST
MUSHAW, DAVID V.	ANN	383	4TH DIST
MUSHAW, DENIS	BAL	336	1ST DIST
MUSHAW, SAMUEL	ANN	298	1ST DIST
MUSHAW, SARAH	ANN	383	4TH DIST
MUSHETT, ANN K.	CHA	241	HILLTOP
MUSIL, JOHN	BAL	201	2ND WARD
MUSK, CHRISTIAN	WAS	148	HAGERSTO
MUSMAN, MARGARET	BAL	437	14TH WAR
MUSON, WILLIAM	BAL	154	1ST WARD
MUSSALMAN, JACOB	ALL	013	3RD E.D.
MUSSE, CHRISTIAN	BAL	018	9TH WARD
MUSSELLER, CHRISTOPHER	FRE	269	NEW MARK
MUSSELMAN, JACOB	BAL	435	8TH WARD
MUSSELMAN, JOHN	BAL	187	16TH WAR
MUSSELMAN, SARAH	BAL	238	1ST DIST
MUSSEN, ROBERT	BAL	173	1ST WARD
MUSSER, ANN	ALL	008	3RD E.D.
MUSSER, JOSEPH	ALL	008	3RD E.D.
MUSSER, MARY	BAL	370	8TH WARD
MUSSER, WILLIAM	MGM	429	CLARKSTR
MUSSER, WILLIAM H.	MGM	429	CLARKSTR
MUSSETTA, PHILIP	FRE	246	NEW MARK
MUSSETTER, JOEL	ALL	007	3RD E.D.
MUSSLEMAN, DAVID	BAL	251	1ST DIST
MUSSLEMAN, ELIZABETH	BAL	238	1ST DIST
MUSSLEMAN, JOHN	BAL	251	1ST DIST
MUSSMAN, JOHN	BAL	335	13TH WAR
MUST, ELIZABETH	BAL	258	20TH WAR
MUST, HENRY	BAL	258	20TH WAR
MUST, JOHN P.	BAL	257	20TH WAR
MUSTER, MARGARET	BAL	323	12TH WAR
MUSTER, PETER	BAL	239	17TH WAR
MUSTERMAN, ANNY*	BAL	074	4TH WARD
MUSTERMAN, ELIZABETH	BAL	162	2ND DIST
MUSTERS, JOHN F.	ANN	469	HOWARD D
MUSTIER, ISAAC	BAL	220	2ND WARD
MUSY, MARY E.	FRE	390	PETERSVI
MUTH, CATHARINE	BAL	283	2ND WARD
MUTH, GEORGE	BAL	232	6TH WARD
MUTH, JOHN*	BAL	089	10TH WAR
MUTH, PHILIP	BAL	387	13TH WAR
MUTH, SEBASTIAN *	BAL	310	20TH WAR
MUTHI, JOHN C.	BAL	218	19TH WAR
MUTT, JOHN	BAL	226	19TH WAR
MUTTER, FREDERICK	BAL	118	15TH WAR
MUTTER, SAMUEL	CEC	184	7TH E DI
MUTTERSBAUGH, PETER	WAS	281	LEITERSB
MUTZE, ADAM	BAL	417	3RD WARD
MUYEIS, SARAH E. *	BAL	309	20TH WAR
MYAM, ABRAHAM	BAL	271	7TH WARD
MYATT, ALPHEUS	BAL	178	19TH WAR
MYELY, JACOB	CAR	287	7TH DIST
MYENBERGE, BERTHA	BAL	272	7TH WARD
MYER, ADAM	BAL	372	8TH WARD
MYER, ALEXANDER	BAL	103	5TH WARD
MYER, ANTONY	BAL	104	5TH WARD
MYER, AUGUSTUS	HAR	138	2ND DIST
MYER, BARBARA	BAL	350	7TH WARD
MYER, BETSY	BAL	109	15TH WAR
MYER, CHARLES	BAL	411	14TH WAR
MYER, DOFFIT	BAL	141	5TH WARD
MYER, E.	BAL	150	1ST WARD
MYER, ELLEN M. S.	BAL	442	1ST DIST
MYER, FREDERICK	BAL	437	14TH WAR
MYER, FREDERICK	BAL	147	19TH WAR
MYER, GEORGE	BAL	353	13TH WAR
MYER, GEORGE	BAL	312	20TH WAR
MYER, GEORGE	FRE	026	FREDERIC
MYER, GERHARD	BAL	086	10TH WAR
MYER, HANDY	BAL	385	13TH WAR
MYER, HANNAH	BAL	120	5TH WARD
MYER, HENRIETTA	BAL	143	11TH WAR
MYER, HENRY	BAL	443	14TH WAR
MYER, HENRY	BAL	369	13TH WAR
MYER, HENRY	BAL	217	17TH WAR
MYER, HENRY	BAL	060	18TH WAR
MYER, HENRY	BAL	324	7TH WARD
MYER, HENRY	BAL	221	2ND WARD
MYER, HENRY	BAL	049	1ST WARD
MYER, ISAAC	BAL	388	8TH WARD
MYER, JACOB	BAL	127	5TH WARD
MYER, JACOB H.	WAS	257	1ST DIST
MYER, JAMES	BAL	053	15TH WAR
MYER, JOHN	BAL	267	7TH WARD
MYER, JOHN	ALL	120	5TH E.D.
MYER, JOHN	BAL	273	20TH WAR
MYER, JOHN C.	BAL	127	18TH WAR
MYER, LAWRENCE	BAL	369	13TH WAR
MYER, LAWRENCE	BAL	138	2ND DIST
MYER, LOUISA	BAL	370	13TH WAR
MYER, MARGARET	BAL	298	12TH WAR
MYER, MARTHA	BAL	199	17TH WAR
MYER, MARTIN	ALL	113	5TH E.D.
MYER, MARY	BAL	254	20TH WAR
MYER, MARY	BAL	412	14TH WAR
MYER, MARY S.	WAS	257	1ST DIST
MYER, MAYER D.	BAL	111	5TH WARD
MYER, MICHAEL	HAR	095	2ND DIST
MYER, PHILIP	BAL	346	13TH WAR
MYER, PHILLIP	BAL	116	5TH WARD
MYER, SAMUEL	BAL	132	5TH WARD
MYER, SAMUEL ST.	WAS	300	1ST DIST
MYER, SUSANNAH	BAL	053	15TH WAR
MYER, THOMAS	BAL	150	1ST WARD
MYER, THOMAS	HAR	138	2ND DIST
MYER, THOMAS J.	BAL	099	15TH WAR
MYER, WILLIAM	BAL	421	8TH WARD
MYER.S PHILIP	BAL	128	11TH WAR
MYERBECK, M.	BAL	318	12TH WAR
MYERES, JOHN	ALL	210	CUMBERLA
MYERES, MARY	FRE	071	FREDERIC
MYERES, PETER	ALL	225	CUMBERLA
MYERLEY, FREDERICK	FRE	005	FREDERIC
MYERLY, BENJAMIN	CAR	275	7TH DIST
MYERLY, DAVID	CAR	408	2ND DIST
MYERLY, DORATHY	CAR	306	1ST DIST
MYERLY, ELIAS	CAR	339	6TH DIST
MYERLY, EMILY	CAR	290	7TH DIST
MYERLY, GEORGE	CAR	287	7TH DIST
MYERLY, JACOB	CAR	277	7TH DIST
MYERLY, JOHN	CAR	290	7TH DIST
MYERLY, MELISSA J.	CAR	340	6TH DIST
MYERLY, MICAJAH	CAR	278	7TH DIST
MYERLY, SAMUEL	CAR	278	7TH DIST
MYERLY, SOLOMON	CAR	331	MANCHEST
MYERLY, SUSAN	CAR	288	7TH DIST
MYERS, ABRAHAM	CAR	242	TANEYTOW
MYERS, ABRAHAM	CAR	380	2ND DIST
MYERS, ABRAM	BAL	375	1ST DIST
MYERS, ACAM	ANN	515	HOWARD D
MYERS, ADAM	FRE	438	8TH E DI
MYERS, ADAM	WAS	056	2ND SUBD
MYERS, ADAMS	WAS	147	2ND DIST
MYERS, ALEXANDER	WAS	146	2ND DIST
MYERS, ALEXANDER	BAL	231	19TH WAR
MYERS, ALFRED	BAL	053	1ST WARD
MYERS, ALICE	WAS	066	2ND SUBD
MYERS, AMANDA	BAL	172	6TH WARD
MYERS, AMANDA	BAL	003	15TH WAR
MYERS, ANDREW	BAL	265	20TH WAR
MYERS, ANDREW L.	BAL	404	14TH WAR
MYERS, ANN	CAR	250	3RD DIST
MYERS, ANN	CAR	350	6TH DIST
MYERS, ANN	BAL	169	19TH WAR
MYERS, ANN	BAL	137	5TH WARD
MYERS, ANN M.	BAL	101	5TH WARD
MYERS, ANN M.	ANN	422	HOWARD D
MYERS, ANN M.	WAS	234	1ST DIST
MYERS, ANTHONY	WAS	269	1ST DIST
MYERS, ARMINTA	CAR	266	WESTMINS
MYERS, AUGUSTUS	BAL	115	18TH WAR
MYERS, BARBANY	FRE	037	FREDERIC
MYERS, BARBANY	BAL	197	5TH DIST
MYERS, BARBARY	BAL	196	5TH DIST
MYERS, BENJAMIN	WAS	131	2ND DIST
MYERS, BETSEY	BAL	165	16TH WAR
MYERS, C.	BAL	249	12TH WAR
MYERS, CAROLINE	BAL	156	1ST WARD
MYERS, CASPER	BAL	084	1ST WARD
MYERS, CASSIAS	FRE	178	5TH E DI
MYERS, CATHARINE	MGM	386	ROCKERLE
MYERS, CATHARINE	FRE	203	5TH E DI
MYERS, CATHERINE	FRE	305	WOODSBOR
MYERS, CATHRINE	CAR	155	NO TWP L
MYERS, CHARELS	BAL	139	19TH WAR
MYERS, CHARLES	BAL	224	12TH WAR
MYERS, CHARLES	BAL	446	8TH WARD
MYERS, CHARLES	BAL	161	1ST WARD
MYERS, CHARLES	BAL	080	10TH WAR
MYERS, CHARLES	BAL	104	2ND DIST
MYERS, CHARLES	BAL	222	1ST DIST
MYERS, CHARLES	ANN	491	HOWARD D
MYERS, CHARLES	BAL	141	1ST WARD
MYERS, CHARLES	FRE	103	FREDERIC
MYERS, CHARLES	BAL	029	18TH WAR
MYERS, CHARLES	BAL	209	19TH WAR
MYERS, CHARLES	BAL	433	14TH WAR
MYERS, CHARLES L.	HAR	138	2ND DIST
MYERS, CHARLOTT	BAL	245	12TH WAR
MYERS, CHARLOTTE A.	BAL	069	10TH WAR
MYERS, CHESTER	KEN	257	1ST DIST
MYERS, CHRISTIAN	WAS	276	RIDGEVIL
MYERS, CHRISTIAN	WAS	111	2ND DIST
MYERS, CHRISTIAN	CAR	262	3RD DIST
MYERS, CHRISTINA	BAL	292	1ST DIST
MYERS, CONRAD	ALL	005	3RD E.D.
MYERS, CONRAD	ALL	018	3RD E.D.
MYERS, CONRAD	BAL	128	11TH WAR
MYERS, DANIEL	CAR	261	3RD DIST
MYERS, DANIEL	FRE	190	5TH E DI
MYERS, DANIEL	BAL	294	20TH WAR
MYERS, DANIEL	BAL	298	12TH WAR
MYERS, DANIEL	BAL	330	3RD WARD
MYERS, DANIEL	WAS	246	SMITHSBU
MYERS, DANIEL	WAS	144	2ND DIST
MYERS, DANIEL	WAS	118	2ND DIST
MYERS, DANIEL E.	BAL	399	8TH WARD
MYERS, DANIEL H.	WAS	145	2ND DIST
MYERS, DAVID	WAS	116	2ND DIST
MYERS, DAVID	WAS	118	2ND DIST
MYERS, DAVID	WAS	056	2ND SUBD
MYERS, DAVID	BAL	175	11TH WAR
MYERS, DAVID	BAL	127	5TH WARD
MYERS, DAVID	FRE	107	CREAGERS
MYERS, DAVID	CAR	261	3RD DIST
MYERS, DAVID	CAR	403	2ND DIST
MYERS, DAVID	CAR	404	2ND DIST
MYERS, DAVID R.	BAL	215	19TH WAR
MYERS, DEDRICK	ANN	426	HOWARD D
MYERS, DELILA	WAS	071	2ND SUBD
MYERS, DENNIS	FRE	094	FREDERIC
MYERS, E.	BAL	136	1ST WARD
MYERS, EDWARD	BAL	139	1ST WARD
MYERS, EDWARD	BAL	247	6TH WARD
MYERS, EDWARD	BAL	375	3RD WARD
MYERS, EDWARD	CAR	367	9TH DIST
MYERS, EDWARD	BAL	098	18TH WAR
MYERS, EDWARD JR.	BAL	014	2ND DIST
MYERS, EDWARD L.	BAL	014	2ND DIST
MYERS, ELEXANDER	HAR	148	3RD DIST
MYERS, ELI	CAR	341	6TH DIST
MYERS, ELI	WAS	116	2ND DIST
MYERS, ELISHA	CAR	173	8TH DIST
MYERS, ELIZA	CAR	195	4TH DIST
MYERS, ELIZA	BAL	280	20TH WAR
MYERS, ELIZA	BAL	112	5TH WARD
MYERS, ELIZABETH	BAL	150	5TH WARD
MYERS, ELIZABETH	BAL	195	2ND WARD
MYERS, ELIZABETH	BAL	049	9TH WARD
MYERS, ELIZABETH	ANN	413	HOWARD D
MYERS, ELIZABETH	CAR	279	7TH DIST
MYERS, ELIZABETH	CAR	261	3RD DIST
MYERS, ELIZABETH	MGM	346	CLARKSBU
MYERS, ELIZABETH	FRE	106	CREAGERS
MYERS, ELIZABETH	HAR	151	3RD DIST
MYERS, ELIZABETH	BAL	451	14TH WAR
MYERS, ELIZABETH	BAL	471	14TH WAR
MYERS, ELIZABETH	WAS	116	2ND DIST
MYERS, ELIZABETH	WAS	146	2ND DIST
MYERS, ELIZABETH	WAS	129	2ND DIST
MYERS, ELIZABETH	WAS	142	HAGERSTO
MYERS, ELIZABETH	WAS	190	1ST DIST
MYERS, ELIZABETH	WAS	128	HAGERSTO
MYERS, ELIZABETHA.	BAL	361	13TH WAR
MYERS, ELLEN	WAS	047	2ND SUBD
MYERS, ELLEN	BAL	156	16TH WAR
MYERS, EMAIEL	WAS	132	2ND DIST
MYERS, EMANUEL	CAR	245	3RD DIST
MYERS, EMELINE	HAR	202	3RD DIST
MYERS, ENOCH	ALL	123	4TH E.D.
MYERS, EPHRAHAM	FRE	107	CREAGERS
MYERS, EVE	WAS	025	2ND SUBD
MYERS, EXFERRY	FRE	189	5TH E DI
MYERS, EXFERRY	FRE	162	EMMITTSB
MYERS, FANY	BAL	010	EASTERN
MYERS, FARRY	BAL	010	EASTERN
MYERS, FINEY	KEN	212	2ND DIST
MYERS, FLORENCE	BAL	097	10TH WAR
MYERS, FRANCIS	FRE	20	5TH E DI
MYERS, FRANK	ANN	413	HOWARD D
MYERS, FRANK	BAL	239	2ND WARD
MYERS, FREDERICK	BAL	261	2ND WARD
MYERS, FREDERICK	BAL	219	17TH WAR
MYERS, FREDERICK	BAL	265	17TH WAR
MYERS, FREDRICK	CAR	111	NO TWP L
MYERS, G.	BAL	322	12TH WAR
MYERS, GEORGE	BAL	183	16TH WAR
MYERS, GEORGE	BAL	417	8TH WARD
MYERS, GEORGE	BAL	416	8TH WARD
MYERS, GEORGE	ALL	107	5TH E.D.
MYERS, GEORGE	ALL	147	6TH E.D.
MYERS, GEORGE	BAL	419	1ST DIST
MYERS, GEORGE	BAL	346	1ST DIST
MYERS, GEORGE	BAL	291	1ST DIST
MYERS, GEORGE	BAL	351	13TH WAR
MYERS, GEORGE	KEN	235	2ND DIST
MYERS, GEORGE	BAL	058	18TH WAR
MYERS, GEORGE	BAL	029	4TH WARD
MYERS, GEORGE	FRE	094	FREDERIC
MYERS, GEORGE	WAS	055	2ND SUBD
MYERS, GEORGE E.	CAR	180	8TH DIST
MYERS, GUSTAVE	BAL	273	7TH WARD
MYERS, H.	BAL	137	1ST WARD
MYERS, H.	BAL	162	1ST WARD
MYERS, H.	BAL	148	1ST WARD
MYERS, HANNAH	BAL	414	1ST DIST
MYERS, HENRIETTA	BAL	353	3RD WARD
MYERS, HENRIETTA	BAL	109	2ND DIST
MYERS, HENRIETTA	CAR	258	3RD DIST
MYERS, HENRY	CAR	260	3RD DIST
MYERS, HENRY	BAL	137	18TH WAR
MYERS, HENRY	DOR	396	1ST DIST
MYERS, HENRY	BAL	111	2ND DIST
MYERS, HENRY	BAL	131	2ND DIST
MYERS, HENRY	BAL	139	2ND DIST
MYERS, HENRY	BAL	303	1ST DIST
MYERS, HENRY	BAL	413	1ST DIST
MYERS, HENRY	BAL	095	5TH WARD
MYERS, HENRY	BAL	201	2ND WARD
MYERS, HENRY	ALL	106	5TH E.D.
MYERS, HENRY	ANN	389	4TH DIST
MYERS, HENRY	BAL	139	16TH WAR
MYERS, HENRY	BAL	122	16TH WAR
MYERS, HENRY	BAL	428	8TH WARD
MYERS, HENRY	WAS	105	2ND DIST
MYERS, HENRY	WAS	159	HAGERSTO
MYERS, HENRY	WAS	253	1ST DIST
MYERS, HENRY	WAS	211	1ST DIST
MYERS, HENRY-BLACK	CAR	088	NO TWP L
MYERS, HERTY	BAL	248	20TH WAR
MYERS, ISAAC	CAR	407	2ND DIST
MYERS, ISAAC	WAS	212	1ST DIST
MYERS, ISAIAH	BAL	399	14TH WAR
MYERS, J. *	CAR	277	7TH DIST
MYERS, JACK	FRE	257	NEW MARK
MYERS, JACK	WAS	125	HAGERSTO
MYERS, JACOB	WAS	254	1ST DIST
MYERS, JACOB	WAS	252	1ST DIST
MYERS, JACOB	WAS	047	2ND SUBD
MYERS, JACOB	WAS	297	1ST DIST
MYERS, JACOB	WAS	287	1ST DIST
MYERS, JACOB	WAS	298	1ST DIST
MYERS, JACOB	CAR	405	2ND DIST
MYERS, JACOB	BAL	009	9TH WARD
MYERS, JACOB	BAL	331	7TH WARD
MYERS, JACOB	ALL	030	2ND E.D.
MYERS, JACOB	ALL	028	2ND E.D.
MYERS, JACOB	BAL	336	3RD WARD
MYERS, JACOB	BAL	236	1ST DIST
MYERS, JACOB	BAL	252	1ST DIST
MYERS, JACOB	BAL	396	3RD WARD
MYERS, JACOB C.	CAR	261	3RD DIST
MYERS, JACOB H.	ALL	131	4TH E.D.
MYERS, JACOB S.	WAS	147	2ND DIST
MYERS, JAMES	WAS	110	2ND DIST
MYERS, JAMES	BAL	274	2ND WARD
MYERS, JAMES	BAL	291	1ST DIST
MYERS, JAMES	BAL	008	1ST WARD
MYERS, JAMES	BAL	239	6TH WARD
MYERS, JAMES	BAL	461	14TH WAR
MYERS, JAMES	BAL	132	11TH WAR
MYERS, JAMES B.	CEC	122	4TH E DI
MYERS, JAMES B.	WAS	219	1ST DIST
MYERS, JAMES R.	WAS	137	2ND DIST
MYERS, JAMES-BLACK	FRE	196	5TH E DI
MYERS, JANE	WAS	118	2ND DIST
MYERS, JEREMIAH-MULATTO	FRE	245	NEW MARK
MYERS, JEROME	BAL	161	19TH WAR
MYERS, JERRY	BAL	395	14TH WAR
MYERS, JESSE	FRE	426	8TH E DI
MYERS, JESSE	BAL	241	5TH WARD
MYERS, JOHN	BAL	246	6TH WARD
MYERS, JOHN	BAL	154	5TH WARD
MYERS, JOHN	BAL	293	1ST DIST
MYERS, JOHN	BAL	261	1ST DIST
MYERS, JOHN	BAL	237	1ST DIST
MYERS, JOHN	BAL	295	7TH WARD
MYERS, JOHN	BAL	280	2ND WARD
MYERS, JOHN	BAL	095	5TH WARD
MYERS, JOHN	BAL	402	1ST DIST
MYERS, JOHN	BAL	173	11TH WAR
MYERS, JOHN	BAL	181	11TH WAR
MYERS, JOHN	FRE	427	8TH E DI
MYERS, JOHN	FRE	265	NEW MARK
MYERS, JOHN	FRE	257	NEW MARK
MYERS, JOHN	CAR	405	2ND DIST
MYERS, JOHN	CAR	400	2ND DIST
MYERS, JOHN	FRE	306	WOODSBOR

Name	County	Page	District
MYERS, JOHN	FRE	298	WOODSBOR
MYERS, JOHN	HAR	151	3RD DIST
MYERS, JOHN	HAR	141	2ND DIST
MYERS, JOHN	CAR	279	7TH DIST
MYERS, JOHN	CAR	262	3RD DIST
MYERS, JOHN	CEC	090	4TH E DI
MYERS, JOHN	CAR	194	4TH DIST
MYERS, JOHN	BAL	018	4TH WARD
MYERS, JOHN	BAL	198	19TH WAR
MYERS, JOHN	BAL	213	11TH WAR
MYERS, JOHN	HAR	071	1ST DIST
MYERS, JOHN	HAR	018	1ST DIST
MYERS, JOHN	WAS	162	HAGERSTO
MYERS, JOHN	WAS	299	1ST DIST
MYERS, JOHN	WAS	066	2ND SUBD
MYERS, JOHN	WAS	053	2ND SUBD
MYERS, JOHN	WAS	053	2ND SUBD
MYERS, JOHN	WAS	014	2ND SUBD
MYERS, JOHN B.	MGM	379	ROCKERLE
MYERS, JOHN H.	BAL	282	17TH WAR
MYERS, JOHN LEEL	BAL	451	14TH WAR
MYERS, JOHN W.	BAL	112	18TH WAR
MYERS, JOHN W.	BAL	044	18TH WAR
MYERS, JOHN W.-BLACK	FRE	431	8TH E DI
MYERS, JOHN-BLACK	FRE	228	BUCKEYST
MYERS, JOHN-BLACK	QUE	146	1ST E DI
MYERS, JONAS	CAR	412	2ND DIST.
MYERS, JONAS	BAL	314	12TH WAR
MYERS, JONATHAN	WAS	126	2ND DIST
MYERS, JONATHAN	WAS	147	2ND DIST
MYERS, JONATHAN	WAS	147	2ND DIST
MYERS, JONATHAN	WAS	147	2ND DIST
MYERS, JOSEPH	WAS	255	1ST DIST
MYERS, JOSEPH	CAR	404	2ND DIST
MYERS, JOSEPH	BAL	116	18TH WAR
MYERS, JOSEPH	CAR	378	2ND DIST
MYERS, JOSEPH A.	WAS	247	SMITHSBU
MYERS, JOSEPH G.	BAL	168	6TH WARD
MYERS, JOSEPH P.	WAS	109	2ND DIST
MYERS, JOSEPHINE	BAL	317	7TH WARD
MYERS, JOSHUA	BAL	325	3RD WARD
MYERS, JOSHUA	BAL	051	4TH WARD
MYERS, JULIA	BAL	065	10TH WAR
MYERS, JULIA	BAL	053	9TH WARD
MYERS, JULIA	BAL	297	12TH WAR
MYERS, JULIA A.	CAR	350	6TH DIST
MYERS, JULIAN	BAL	336	3RD WARD
MYERS, KITTY	ANN	476	HOWARD D
MYERS, LAMBERT	BAL	152	5TH WARD
MYERS, LEATHER	WAS	112	2ND DIST
MYERS, LENE	FRE	054	FREDERIC
MYERS, LERWIS	BAL	472	14TH WAR
MYERS, LEVI	WAS	042	2ND SUBD
MYERS, LEWIS	WAS	120	2ND DIST
MYERS, LEWIS	CAR	292	7TH DIST
MYERS, LEWIS	ANN	426	HOWARD D
MYERS, LEWIS H.	WAS	279	LEITERSB
MYERS, LOUISA	BAL	045	15TH WAR
MYERS, LOUISA	BAL	144	11TH WAR
MYERS, LUCINDA	WAS	163	2ND DIST
MYERS, LUCINDY	WAS	215	1ST DIST
MYERS, LYDIA	WAS	216	1ST DIST
MYERS, MALINDA	ANN	448	HOWARD D
MYERS, MANDILLA	CAR	348	6TH DIST
MYERS, MARGARET	FRE	055	FREDERIC
MYERS, MARGARET	CAR	408	2ND DIST
MYERS, MARGARET	BAL	273	20TH WAR
MYERS, MARGARET	BAL	397	8TH WARD
MYERS, MARIA	BAL	054	4TH WARD
MYERS, MARIE	BAL	223	12TH WAR
MYERS, MARTHA S.	WAS	132	2ND DIST
MYERS, MARTIN	WAS	147	2ND DIST
MYERS, MARTIN	WAS	103	2ND DIST
MYERS, MARTIN	ALL	184	9TH E.D.
MYERS, MARTIN	HAR	017	1ST DIST
MYERS, MARTIN	FRE	144	10TH E D
MYERS, MARY	BAL	130	18TH WAR
MYERS, MARY	BAL	132	11TH WAR
MYERS, MARY	BAL	231	2ND WARD
MYERS, MARY	BAL	065	2ND DIST
MYERS, MARY	ANN	362	4TH DIST
MYERS, MARY	BAL	459	1ST DIST
MYERS, MARY	BAL	463	1ST DIST
MYERS, MARY	BAL	211	6TH DIST
MYERS, MARY	BAL	063	10TH WAR
MYERS, MARY	BAL	257	1ST DIST
MYERS, MARY	BAL	043	1ST WARD
MYERS, MARY	WAS	113	2ND DIST
MYERS, MARY	WAS	125	2ND DIST
MYERS, MARY A.	BAL	403	1ST DIST
MYERS, MARY ANN	BAL	108	5TH WARD
MYERS, MARY E.	WAS	236	CAVETOWN
MYERS, MARY J.	BAL	373	3RD WARD
MYERS, MARY J.	BAL	051	15TH WAR
MYERS, MARY J.	BAL	212	19TH WAR
MYERS, MARYANN	BAL	421	3RD WARD
MYERS, MICHAEL	BAL	003	15TH WAR
MYERS, MICHAL	WAS	101	2ND DIST
MYERS, MILKY	KEN	212	2ND DIST
MYERS, MOSES	CAR	183	8TH DIST
MYERS, MYERS A.	CAR	412	2ND DIST
MYERS, NATHAN	BAL	319	3RD WARD
MYERS, NATHAN	BAL	154	5TH WARD
MYERS, NATHAN	BAL	164	1ST WARD
MYERS, NIMROD	WAS	134	HAGERSTO
MYERS, OLIVER P.	BAL	394	14TH WAR
MYERS, PETER	CAR	249	3RD DIST
MYERS, PETER	WAS	133	2ND DIST
MYERS, PETER	WAS	205	1ST DIST
MYERS, PETER E.	CAR	253	3RD DIST
MYERS, PHEBE-BLACK	CAR	367	9TH DIST
MYERS, PHEBE-BLACK	QUE	148	1ST E DI
MYERS, PHILIP	FRE	273	NEW MARK
MYERS, PHILIP	BAL	346	1ST DIST
MYERS, PHILIP	BAL	197	11TH WAR
MYERS, PHILIP H.L.	CAR	349	6TH DIST
MYERS, PHILLIP	BAL	305	17TH WAR
MYERS, PHILLIP	BAL	119	11TH WAR
MYERS, PHILLIP	KEN	275	1ST DIST
MYERS, POMPEY-BLACK	QUE	146	1ST E DI
MYERS, PONELL	BAL	202	2ND WARD
MYERS, PRISSILLA	WAS	118	2ND DIST
MYERS, R.	BAL	305	20TH WAR
MYERS, REBECCA	BAL	231	19TH WAR
MYERS, REBECCA	WAS	156	2ND DIST
MYERS, REBECCA	BAL	346	1ST DIST
MYERS, RICHARD	BAL	395	1ST DIST
MYERS, RICHARD	BAL	176	6TH WARD
MYERS, ROBERT	BAL	348	3RD WARD
MYERS, RUTH	BAL	028	18TH WAR
MYERS, SALLY	BAL	190	2ND WARD
MYERS, SALLY	BAL	346	3RD WARD
MYERS, SAMUEL	ANN	516	HOWARD D
MYERS, SAMUEL	BAL	183	5TH DIST
MYERS, SAMUEL	BAL	196	5TH DIST
MYERS, SAMUEL	BAL	249	12TH WAR
MYERS, SAMUEL	CAR	257	3RD DIST
MYERS, SAMUEL	CAR	255	3RD DIST
MYERS, SAMUEL	CEC	061	1ST E DI
MYERS, SAMUEL	CAR	383	2ND DIST
MYERS, SAMUEL	BAL	394	14TH WAR
MYERS, SAMUEL	BAL	398	14TH WAR
MYERS, SAMUEL	CAR	404	2ND DIST
MYERS, SAMUEL	FRE	302	WOODSBOR
MYERS, SAMUEL	WAS	110	2ND DIST
MYERS, SAMUEL	WAS	278	LEITERSB
MYERS, SAMUEL	WAS	075	2ND SUBD
MYERS, SARAH	BAL	124	11TH WAR
MYERS, SARAH	BAL	155	5TH WARD
MYERS, SARAH	BAL	172	16TH WAR
MYERS, SARAH	BAL	394	3RD WARD
MYERS, SARAH J.	BAL	336	3RD WARD
MYERS, SAVILLA	FRE	449	8TH E DI
MYERS, SOLOMON	WAS	285	1ST DIST
MYERS, SOLOMON-BLACK	QUE	178	2ND E DI
MYERS, SOPHIA	BAL	089	1ST WARD
MYERS, SOPHIA	BAL	139	2ND DIST
MYERS, STEPHEN	BAL	290	1ST DIST
MYERS, STEPHEN	BAL	315	12TH WAR
MYERS, SUSAN	BAL	308	12TH WAR
MYERS, SUSAN	BAL	153	5TH WARD
MYERS, SUSAN	WAS	147	2ND DIST
MYERS, SUSAN	CAR	354	6TH DIST
MYERS, THOMANTHY	BAL	117	18TH WAR
MYERS, THOMAS J.	FRE	206	BUCKEYST
MYERS, TOBIAS	BAL	292	7TH WARD
MYERS, UPTON B.	ALL	124	4TH E.D.
MYERS, VINCENT	FRE	196	5TH E DI
MYERS, W. HENRY	BAL	109	10TH WAR
MYERS, WESLAY	CAR	391	2ND DIST
MYERS, WILAM	BAL	441	8TH WARD
MYERS, WILLAIM	BAL	137	5TH WARD
MYERS, WILLIAM	BAL	159	1ST WARD
MYERS, WILLIAM	BAL	168	1ST WARD
MYERS, WILLIAM	ALL	123	4TH E.D.
MYERS, WILLIAM	ALL	020	2ND E.D.
MYERS, WILLIAM	BAL	231	2ND WARD
MYERS, WILLIAM	BAL	258	2ND WARD
MYERS, WILLIAM	BAL	141	1ST WARD
MYERS, WILLIAM	BAL	136	1ST WARD
MYERS, WILLIAM	BAL	089	1ST WARD
MYERS, WILLIAM	CAR	347	6TH DIST
MYERS, WILLIAM	BAL	301	17TH WAR
MYERS, WILLIAM	WAS	131	2ND DIST
MYERS, WILLIAM G.H.	BAL	014	2ND DIST
MYERS, WILLIAM H.	BAL	374	8TH WARD
MYERS, WILLIAM H.	BAL	169	16TH WAR
MYERS, WILLIAM V.	KEN	282	3RD DIST
MYERS, ZACHARIAH	WAS	193	1ST DIST
MYERS, ZACHARIAH	FRE	413	8TH E DI
MYERS.CHARLES	CAR	403	2ND DIST
MYERS.EDWARD	BAL	133	1ST WARD
MYERS.PETER	FRE	215	BUCKEYST
MYERSE, ELLEN	CAR	277	7TH DIST
MYERSE, HENRY	CAR	260	3RD DIST
MYHAN, WILLIAM	WAS	104	2ND DIST
MYLES, CINDERELLA	BAL	214	11TH WAR
MYLES, DANIEL	BAL	143	2ND DIST
MYLES, HENRY	ANN	288	ANNAPOLI
MYLES, JAMES	BAL	170	1ST WARD
MYLES, MARGARET	BAL	148	11TH WAR
MYLES, PATRICK	BAL	013	15TH WAR
MYLIS, SARAH E. *	BAL	309	20TH WAR
MYRES, CHRISTIAN H.	HAR	180	3RD DIST
MYRES, DAVID	ANN	287	ANNAPOLI
MYRES, DAVID	ANN	287	ANNAPOLI
MYRES, ELLEN	ANN	288	ANNAPOLI
MYRES, HENRY	BAL	246	2ND WARD
MYRES, JOHN	KEN	307	3RD DIST
MYRES, JOSEPH	BAL	196	2ND WARD
MYRES, MARGARET	ALL	207	CUMBERLA
MYRES, THOMAS	ALL	233	CUMBERLA
MYRES, WILLIAM	BAL	004	1ST WARD
MYRICK, CAVID *	SOM	454	DAMES QU
MYRICK, GEORGE	SOM	443	DAMES QU
MYRICK, JOHNSON *	SOM	455	DAMES QU
MYRICK, JOSEPH	BAL	053	4TH WARD
MYRICK, NEHEMIAH	SOM	442	DAMES QU
MYRON, CHRISTOPHER	BAL	318	7TH WARD
MYRRY, TIMOTHY	BAL	295	1ST DIST
MYSER, GEORGE	BAL	277	7TH WARD
MYSER, JOHN	BAL	200	2ND WARD
MYSER, MARTIN	BAL	209	2ND WARD
MYSOCK, LEONARD	WAS	227	1ST DIST
MYSTEIN, JOHN	BAL	254	12TH WAR
MYTER, ANNA	BAL	170	19TH WAR
MYVILL, WALTER	CAL	016	1ST DIST
MZFGIN, XZLLY	ANN	397	8TH DIST
N O NEIL, H.	BAL	135	5TH WARD
NAAS, JUSTUS	BAL	370	13TH WAR
NABB, EDWARD H.	TAL	004	EASTON D
NABB, ELIZABETH	BAL	225	6TH WARD
NABB, FRANCIS	TAL	075	EASTON T
NABB, HENRY W.	BAL	255	1ST DIST
NABB, JOHN D.	TAL	025	EASTON D
NABB, LOUISA J.*	TAL	004	EASTON D
NABB, WILLIAM H.	TAL	066	EASTON T
NABE, GEORGE W.	CEC	054	1ST E DI
NABE, GEORGE	CEC	065	1ST E DI
NACE, ALFERD	CAR	184	8TH DIST
NACE, CAROLINE	BAL	430	1ST DIST
NACE, GEORGE	BAL	415	1ST DIST
NACE, JOHN	BAL	214	6TH DIST
NACE, JOHN M.	BAL	201	19TH WAR
NACE, MARTIN *	WAS	055	2ND SUBD
NACE, SOPHIA	BAL	251	1ST DIST
NACE, SUSAN*	DOR	444	1ST DIST
NACE, WILLIAM	BAL	243	1ST DIST
NACE, WILLIAM	BAL	415	1ST DIST
NACE.GEORGE	CAR	399	2ND DIST
NACH, MARGARET	BAL	299	20TH WAR
NACHMAN, ABRIAHAM	BAL	276	17TH WAR
NACK, AUGTS	BAL	162	1ST WARD
NACKMANRA, JACOB A.	BAL	316	3RD WARD
NADALL, BURNARD H.	BAL	186	2ND WARD
NADDE, CATHARINE	ANN	469	HOWARD D
NADIE, MARTIN	ANN	500	HOWARD D
NADLE, ISABELLA	TAL	087	ST MICHA
NADLER, PETER	WAS	211	1ST DIST
NAE, MARGARET	BAL	326	1ST DIST
NAER, JOHN	FRE	390	PETERSVI
NAFAN, PETER *	ALL	050	10TH E.D
NAFE, HENRY	CAR	175	8TH DIST
NAFF, EDWARD H.	BAL	454	14TH WAR
NAFF, JOHN H.	BAL	065	18TH WAR
NAFFELL, JOHN	BAL	178	2ND WARD
NAGAL, EDWARD	BAL	082	18TH WAR
NAGAL, PATRICK	BAL	184	11TH WAR
NAGAL, SOPHIA	BAL	082	18TH WAR
NAGEL, ANDREW	BAL	370	13TH WAR
NAGEL, JACOB	BAL	147	11TH WAR
NAGELSCHMIDT, HENRY	BAL	045	15TH WAR
NAGET, WILLIAM	CEC	076	NORTHEAS
NAGGLE, JACOB	BAL	193	2ND WARD
NAGHEL, SAMUEL*	BAL	386	3RD WARD
NAGLAR, LAWRENCE	BAL	279	1ST DIST
NAGLE, ANTHONY	BAL	380	1ST DIST
NAGLE, ELIZABETH	CAR	275	7TH DIST
NAGLE, EMANUEL	HAR	010	1ST DIST
NAGLE, FREDIK	BAL	116	18TH WAR
NAGLE, GEORGE	BAL	380	1ST DIST
NAGLE, HINDRUS	BAL	221	2ND WARD
NAGLE, HNERY	BAL	436	14TH WAR
NAGLE, JAMES	PRI	003	BLADENSB
NAGLE, LEWIS	BAL	108	1ST WARD
NAGLE, PETER	BAL	181	2ND WARD
NAGLE, WILLIAM H.	BAL	147	16TH WAR
NAGLER, MARY	FRE	223	BUCKEYST
NAHAM, AMBROSE	DOR	429	1ST DIST
NAHAN, DANIEL	FRE	076	FREDERIC
NAID, CHARITY	BAL	036	1ST WARD
NAID, PHILLIP	BAL	031	1ST WARD
NAID, ROBERT *	KEN	222	2ND DIST
NAIGLE, NICHOLAS	BAL	377	8TH WARD
NAIL, ADAM	WAS	284	1ST DIST
NAIL, HENRY	ALL	102	5TH E.D.
NAIL, JOHN	BAL	031	1ST WARD
NAIL, SAMUEL	CAR	240	TANEYTOW
NAIL, WILLIAM	CAR	302	1ST DIST
NAIL, WILLIAM	BAL	280	1ST DIST
NAIL, WILLIAM	BAL	284	1ST DIST
NAILER, JOHN	KEN	260	1ST DIST
NAILER, PATRICK	ALL	154	6TH E.D.
NAILL, DAVID W.	FRE	430	8TH E DI
NAILL, JACOB H.	FRE	422	8TH E DI
NAILL, NATHANIEL H.	FRE	428	8TH E DI
NAILL, PETER	FRE	428	8TH E DI
NAILL, SAMUEL	FRE	447	8TH E DI
NAILL, THEODORE	FRE	430	8TH E DI
NAILL.WASHINGTON M.	FRE	430	8TH E DI
NAILLE, CHRISTIAN	FRE	173	5TH E DI
NAILOR, CECILIA	BAL	397	3RD WARD
NAILOR, ELLEN	WAS	067	2ND SUBD
NAILOR, GEORGE	WAS	067	2ND SUBD
NAILOR, JOHN W.	CAL	018	1ST DIST
NAILOR, JOSEPH	WAS	098	2ND DIST
NAILOR, NATHAN-BLACK	MGM	406	MEDLEY 3
NAILOR, NELSON	BAL	086	18TH WAR
NAILOR, WILLIAM	CHA	277	BOJANTOW
NAIN, ZACHARIA*	DOR	383	1ST DIST
NAIREN, ANNIE	BAL	350	3RD WARD
NAIREN, MAHALAH-BLACK	WOR	172	6TH E DI
NAIREN, PERRIGAN	WOR	201	3RD E DI
NAIREN, ROBERT	WOR	175	6TH E DI
NAIRN, ELIZABETH	SOM	491	SALISBUR
NAIRN, J.C.	BAL	003	18TH WAR
NAISLER, EMAUL *	ALL	169	6TH E.D.
NAITHEN, ANDREW	CHA	218	ALLENS F
NALAGAN, DAVID	BAL	153	2ND DIST
NALE, CHARES	CEC	054	1ST E DI
NALEON, SALLY A.	SOM	526	QUANTICO
NALIN, MICHAEL	BAL	286	1ST DIST
NALLER, SOTT-BLACK	CAR	105	NO TWP L
NALLEY, LEVI	PRI	006	BLADENSB
NALLINGER, FREDERICK	BAL	075	18TH WAR
NALLS, ALBERT	CHA	272	ALLENS F
NALLS, BENJAMIN T.	BAL	068	10TH WAR
NALLS, SUSANNA	BAL	069	10TH WAR
NALLS, URZZIAL	CHA	244	HILLTOP
NALLY, CALISTA	CHA	251	MIDDLETO
NALLY, EZRA	WAS	198	1ST DIST
NALLY, FRANCIS	CHA	227	ALLENS F
NALLY, JOHN	BAL	363	13TH WAR
NALLY, JOHN	PRI	108	PISCATAW
NALLY, JOHN	BAL	264	1ST DIST
NALLY, MARY	CHA	275	ALLENS F
NALLY, RICHARD	KEN	247	2ND DIST
NALLY, RICHARD	BAL	366	13TH WAR
NALLY, RICHARD	BAL	056	4TH WARD
NALLY, ROBERT	PRI	017	BLADENSB
NALLY, SAMUEL	WAS	035	2ND SUBD
NALLY, WILLIAM	BAL	074	2ND DIST
NALLY, WILLIAM G.	CHA	245	HILLTOP
NALLY, ZACHARIAH	PRI	017	BLADENSB
NAME, DAVID M.	WAS	286	1ST DIST
NAMER, JOHN	BAL	194	19TH WAR
NAMER, MARTIN	BAL	229	17TH WAR
NAN, HUGH	BAL	460	1ST DIST
NAN, JOHN	BAL	235	20TH WAR
NANCE, PETER	CAR	393	2ND DIST
NANCY, DELIA D.	BAL	317	12TH WAR
NANKUNS, HENRY	BAL	132	1ST WARD
NANT, JOHN	BAL	442	14TH WAR
NANTON, PATRICK	ALL	051	10TH E.D
NANTS, ANN	BAL	158	6TH WARD
NANTS, JOHN	BAL	269	1ST DIST
NANTZ, ANNA	BAL	239	20TH WAR
NAPIER, WILLIAM	BAL	242	17TH WAR
NAPINGER, DANIEL	BAL	091	2ND DIST
NAPP, HARRIETT	BAL	268	7TH WARD
NAPP, WILLIAM	BAL	222	12TH WAR
NAPPY, MARYANN	BAL	331	3RD WARD
NARAH, HENRY	ANN	292	ANNAPOLI
NARDECAM, DAVID*	DOR	333	3RD DIVI
NARE, ADAM	WAS	014	WILLIAMS
NARE, JOHN	CHA	218	ALLENS F
NARE, JOSEPH	WAS	013	WILLIAMS
NARKS, WILLIAM	BAL	119	1ST WARD
NARLOR, JOHN E.-BLACK	MGM	423	MEDLEY 3
NARMAN, GEORGE	BAL	327	13TH WAR
NARMAN, SAMUEL	BAL	015	9TH WARD
NARNER, CATHARINE	BAL	261	12TH WAR
NARRIS, JENNY *	ANN	396	8TH DIST
NARROTE, JACOB	DOR	388	1ST DIST
NARTHEN, NANCY	CHA	241	HILLTOP
NARTON, THOMAS	ALL	014	3RD E.D.
NARY, CHARLES	ALL	182	8TH E.D.
NARY, MARY F.	ANN	366	4TH DIST
NARY, SAMUEL	ANN	365	4TH DIST
NARY, THOMAS*	BAL	127	5TH WARD

Name	County	Page	District
NASAR, JOHN	BAL	266	12TH WAR
NASE, EMILY	BAL	294	12TH WAR
NASH, ADAM	BAL	012	15TH WAR
NASH, AFFY	BAL	470	14TH WAR
NASH, ANDREW	DOR	446	1ST DIST
NASH, ANN	BAL	260	12TH WAR
NASH, CAROLINE	DOR	387	1ST DIST
NASH, CATHARIEN	BAL	056	15TH WAR
NASH, CHARLES	BAL	127	1ST WARD
NASH, CHARLES	DOR	431	1ST DIST
NASH, ELLEN	BAL	028	1ST WARD
NASH, ELLEN	BAL	229	1ST DIST
NASH, EPHRAIM	BAL	291	17TH WAR
NASH, EVAN	BAL	261	17TH WAR
NASH, EVE A.	BAL	040	4TH WARD
NASH, JAMES	BAL	168	2ND DIST
NASH, JAMES K.	CHA	245	HILLTOP
NASH, JOSEPH	ANN	357	3RD DIST
NASH, M.	BAL	152	1ST WARD
NASH, MARGARET	DOR	433	1ST DIST
NASH, MARY	BAL	213	11TH WAR
NASH, MARY	BAL	211	2ND WARD
NASH, MICHAEL	BAL	020	9TH WARD
NASH, MICHAEL	BAL	143	1ST WARD
NASH, PATRICK	BAL	211	2ND WARD
NASH, ROBERT	BAL	114	11TH WAR
NASH, SAMUEL	DOR	448	1ST DIST
NASH, SAMUEL	BAL	013	2ND DIST
NASH, SARAH	BAL	033	1ST WARD
NASH, THOAMS	BAL	050	18TH WAR
NASH, THOMAS	FRE	326	MIDDLETO
NASH, THOMAS	BAL	013	2ND DIST
NASH, THOMAS	BAL	211	2ND WARD
NASH, THOMAS	BAL	297	7TH WARD
NASH, THOMAS	BAL	324	1ST DIST
NASH, WESTER	BAL	102	1ST WARD
NASH, WILLIAM	BAL	168	2ND DIST
NASH, WILLIAM	BAL	305	12TH WAR
NASH, WILLIAM	BAL	261	17TH WAR
NASON, MARY E.	ANN	288	ANNAPOLI
NASON, WILLIAM	BAL	174	1ST WARD
NATE, HARMON E.	BAL	074	4TH WARD
NATERS, S.H.	BAL	173	1ST WARD
NATERS, S.H.	BAL	115	1ST WARD
NATGRAW, FREDERICK	BAL	257	2ND WARD
NATHAN, ISAAC	ALL	241	CUMBERLA
NATHAN, JAMES	BAL	342	13TH WAR
NATHAN, MARGARET	ALL	021	2ND E.D.
NATHAN, MARIA	BAL	169	11TH WAR
NATHAN, PETER	ALL	021	2ND E.D.
NATHAN, SARAH	BAL	167	2ND DIST
NATHANS, ELIZABETH	BAL	186	11TH WAR
NATINGHAM, JOHN	WAS	145	HAGERSTO
NATINGHAN, THOMAS	WAS	145	HAGERSTO
NATORIDAY, MARY T.	BAL	045	9TH WARD
NATTALI, EDWARD	BAL	037	4TH WARD
NATTEMAYER, DAVID *	FRE	166	EMMITTSB
NATTER, PHILLIS	WOR	192	8TH E DI
NATTERS, SUSAN	BAL	073	1ST WARD
NATTHEWS, ISAAC	BAL	115	1ST WARD
NATTINGLEY, RICHARD	ST	336	4TH E DI
NATTLE, HENRY	BAL	119	2ND DIST
NATURE, RACHAEL	FRE	182	5TH E DI
NAUGHLER, FERDINAND	BAL	080	1ST WARD
NAUGHLIN, LAWRENCE	BAL	448	1ST DIST
NAUGHTER, CWEN	BAL	175	2ND WARD
NAUGHTIN, JOHN	BAL	449	1ST DIST
NAUGHTON, MARY	BAL	034	9TH WARD
NAUGLE, CONRAOT	BAL	426	8TH WARD
NAUGLE, LEWIS	BAL	237	17TH WAR
NAUGLE, MARY A.	BAL	154	16TH WAR
NAUGTON, ELLEN	BAL	048	18TH WAR
NAUIS, JENNY *	ANN	396	8TH DIST
NAUM, JOHN	BAL	060	2ND DIST
NAUMBERG, ALEXANDER	BAL	013	9TH WARD
NAUSHAN, HENRY	BAL	242	2ND WARD
NAUTHANS, JOHN	BAL	196	2ND WARD
NAVILL, MATHEW	BAL	186	11TH WAR
NAVY, HENRY G.	DOR	358	3RD DIVI
NAVY, MOSES	DOR	363	3RD DIVI
NAW, HENRY	BAL	119	18TH WAR
NAX, FRANCIS	FRE	048	FREDERIC
NAX, JACOB	BAL	244	6TH WARD
NAY, JOHN Y	ANN	492	HOWARD D
NAY, PATRICK	WAS	026	2ND SUBD
NAYLAS, JOHN	BAL	131	1ST WARD
NAYLER, FRANCIS	BAL	232	12TH WAR
NAYLOR, ANN	BAL	311	12TH WAR
NAYLOR, B.	PRI	052	AQUASCO
NAYLOR, EMMA	BAL	310	12TH WAR
NAYLOR, EVILINDA	PRI	048	AQUASCO
NAYLOR, HENRY	PRI	096	SPALDING
NAYLOR, JAMES	FRE	244	NEW MARK
NAYLOR, JAMES OF ISAAC	PRI	052	AQUASCO
NAYLOR, JAMES OF JAMES	PRI	051	AQUASCO
NAYLOR, JETSON	PRI	096	SPALDING
NAYLOR, JOHN	BAL	077	15TH WAR
NAYLOR, JOHN	BAL	185	11TH WAR
NAYLOR, LEVI	BAL	185	5TH DIST
NAYLOR, MARGARET*	BAL	071	10TH WAR
NAYLOR, MARTHA	PRI	065	NOTTINGH
NAYLOR, PERRY	CAL	020	2ND DIST
NAYLOR, REBECCA-BLACK	FRE	225	BUCKEYST
NAYLOR, SAMUEL	BAL	196	5TH DIST
NAYLOR, SAMUEL T.	BAL	300	3RD WARD
NAYLOR, SARAH	BAL	185	5TH DIST
NAYLOR, SOPHIA*	BAL	305	3RD WARD
NAYLOR, STEPHEN	ANN	371	4TH DIST
NAYLOR, THOMAS	PRI	048	AQUASCO
NAZAREMUS, FREDERICK	WAS	224	1ST DIST
NCHOLL, GODFRIED	BAL	071	1ST WARD
NCIHOLAS, WILLIAM	BAL	233	2ND WARD
NEABL, WILLIAM *	ALL	159	6TH E.D.
NEAD, EVE	ALL	261	CUMBERLA
NEADIT, GOVANE	DOR	373	1ST DIST
NEADLES, HARRISON	TAL	017	EASTON D
NEADLY, THOMAS	DOR	429	1ST DIST
NEADNER, FREDERICK	BAL	063	15TH WAR
NEAGLE, ELIZABETH	BAL	181	2ND WARD
NEAGLEY, CHRISTIAN	WAS	292	1ST DIST
NEAL, ABNER	CAR	271	WESTMINS
NEAL, AIRY	ANN	470	HOWARD D
NEAL, ALICE	BAL	146	16TH WAR
NEAL, ANN	BAL	270	1ST DIST
NEAL, ANN C.	FRE	044	FREDERIC
NEAL, ANN E.	CHA	225	ALLENS F
NEAL, BENNETT	CHA	219	ALLENS F
NEAL, CATHARINE	DOR	317	1ST DIST
NEAL, CATHERINE	BAL	411	8TH WARD
NEAL, CHARLES A.	CEC	157	PORT DUP
NEAL, CHARLOTT	BAL	125	11TH WAR
NEAL, DANIEL	CAR	151	NO TWP L
NEAL, DAVID	ALL	203	CUMBERLA
NEAL, EBANEZAR	CEC	029	CHESAPEA
NEAL, EDWARD	BAL	274	1ST DIST
NEAL, ELIZA	FRE	060	FREDERIC
NEAL, ELIZABETH A.	CHA	217	ALLENS F
NEAL, ELLEN	BAL	418	14TH WAR
NEAL, FRANCIS	BAL	429	14TH WAR
NEAL, FRANCIS	CHA	218	ALLENS F
NEAL, FREDERICK	KEN	291	3RD DIST
NEAL, GEORGE	DOR	297	1ST DIST
NEAL, GEORGE	KEN	215	2ND DIST
NEAL, HENRY A.	CHA	220	ALLENS F
NEAL, HUGH	DOR	369	3RD DIVI
NEAL, HUGH	BAL	232	1ST DIST
NEAL, HUGH	ALL	202	CUMBERLA
NEAL, IRVIN	BAL	471	14TH WAR
NEAL, ISAAC	BAL	161	1ST WARD
NEAL, J. MISS-	BAL	315	20TH WAR
NEAL, JAMES	DOR	369	3RD DIVI
NEAL, JAMES	BAL	188	2ND WARD
NEAL, JAMES	BAL	069	15TH WAR
NEAL, JAMES	BAL	162	11TH WAR
NEAL, JAMES	WAS	020	2ND SUBD
NEAL, JAMES F.	CHA	217	ALLENS F
NEAL, JAMES H.	CHA	231	HILLTOP
NEAL, JAMES H.	QUE	138	1ST E DI
NEAL, JOHN	QUE	138	1ST E DI
NEAL, JOHN	WAS	132	2ND DIST
NEAL, JOHN	BAL	271	1ST DIST
NEAL, JOHN	BAL	332	13TH WAR
NEAL, JOHN	ANN	516	HOWARD D
NEAL, JOHN O.	BAL	180	11TH WAR
NEAL, JOSEPH	FRE	044	FREDERIC
NEAL, LEONA	BAL	212	11TH WAR
NEAL, LOUISA	BAL	429	14TH WAR
NEAL, LUIS W.	TAL	014	EASTON D
NEAL, MARTHA J.	DOR	323	1ST DIST
NEAL, MARY	BAL	004	18TH WAR
NEAL, MARY	BAL	095	5TH WARD
NEAL, MARY	BAL	317	1ST DIST
NEAL, MARY O.	BAL	011	18TH WAR
NEAL, MILLY-BLACK	MGM	428	CLARKSTR
NEAL, PATRICK	BAL	441	1ST DIST
NEAL, RACHEL	TAL	004	EASTON D
NEAL, RICHARD	ANN	495	HOWARD D
NEAL, RICHARD	BAL	353	1ST DIST
NEAL, RIGBY	SOM	511	BARREN C
NEAL, ROBERT	TAL	035	EASTON D
NEAL, SAMUEL	BAL	069	15TH WAR
NEAL, SARAH	BAL	356	1ST DIST
NEAL, SARAH R.	KEN	246	2ND DIST
NEAL, SUSAN A.	DOR	310	1ST DIST
NEAL, THOAMS	KEN	221	2ND DIST
NEAL, THOMAS	BAL	263	1ST DIST
NEAL, THOMAS	BAL	029	9TH WARD
NEAL, TIMOTHY	CAR	230	5TH DIST
NEAL, TRUMAN	BAL	256	1ST DIST
NEAL, TURPIN W.	DOR	310	1ST DIST
NEAL, WESLEY	ANN	454	HOWARD D
NEAL, WILLIAM	ANN	415	HOWARD D
NEAL, WILLIAM	CHA	270	ALLENS F
NEAL, WILLIAM	BAL	229	17TH WAR
NEAL, WILLIAM	CAR	122	NO TWP L
NEAL, WILLIAM	CAR	410	2ND DIST
NEAL, WILLIAM	TAL	006	EASTON D
NEAL, WINGATE	CAR	117	NO TWP L
NEALE, ABRAHAM	BAL	253	20TH WAR
NEALE, ADBLAIDE	BAL	332	13TH WAR
NEALE, ANN	ST	262	3RD E DI
NEALE, CATHARINE	ST	266	3RD E DI
NEALE, DEIDAMIA	BAL	457	8TH WARD
NEALE, ELIZA A.	ST	323	4TH E DI
NEALE, ELIZABETH	ST	328	4TH E DI
NEALE, ELIZABETH	BAL	201	6TH WARD
NEALE, EMELINE	BAL	087	15TH WAR
NEALE, ENOCH	ST	276	3RD E DI
NEALE, FRANCIS C.	ST	327	4TH E DI
NEALE, GEORGE M.	BAL	063	1ST WARD
NEALE, GEORGEANNA	BAL	159	16TH WAR
NEALE, IGNATIUS-BLACK	ST	336	4TH E DI
NEALE, ISAAC	DOR	437	1ST DIST
NEALE, JAMES-BLACK	ST	316	4TH E DI
NEALE, JOHN	BAL	263	20TH WAR
NEALE, JOHN O.	BAL	188	11TH WAR
NEALE, JOHN WHITE	DOR	393	1ST DIST
NEALE, JOHNH.	ST	271	3RD E DI
NEALE, JOSEPHINE	ST	274	3RD E DI
NEALE, JOSHUA	ST	333	4TH E DI
NEALE, LEONARD	ST	280	3RD E DI
NEALE, LYDIA-BLACK	ST	324	4TH E DI
NEALE, MAJOR	DOR	443	1ST DIST
NEALE, MARGARET C.	ST	281	3RD E DI
NEALE, MARY	BAL	090	15TH WAR
NEALE, MARY E.	ST	313	1ST E DI
NEALE, MARY G.	FRE	065	FREDERIC
NEALE, MARY J.	ST	316	4TH E DI
NEALE, MILLY*	DOR	438	1ST DIST
NEALE, CUTERBRIDGE H.	DOR	392	1ST DIST
NEALE, ROBERT	ST	340	5TH E DI
NEALE, SAMUEL N.	DOR	459	1ST DIST
NEALE, SARAH	ST	281	3RD E DI
NEALE, WILLIA H.	BAL	025	15TH WAR
NEALEY, WILLIAMR.	ALL	021	2ND E.D.
NEALL, GUSTAVUS-BLACK	MGM	401	ROCKERLE
NEALLE, SOPHIA	FRE	184	5TH E DI
NEALS, CHARLES	BAL	398	3RD WARD
NEALY, JOHN REV.	TAL	075	EASTON T
NEALY, MARY	BAL	093	5TH WARD
NEALY, MARY ANN	ALL	026	2ND E.D.
NEALY, WILLIAM	ALL	026	2ND E.D.
NEALY, WILLIAM	BAL	316	7TH WARD
NEAR, J.R.	ALL	217	CUMBERLA
NEARNAY, WILLAIM	ALL	050	10TH E.D
NEARY, ELIZA	FRE	338	MIDDLETO
NEARY, OPPY	ANN	366	4TH DIST
NEAUSBOR, JOSEPH	BAL	293	17TH WAR
NEAVER, HENRY	BAL	074	1ST WARD
NEAWITT, NATHANIEL	QUE	216	3RD E DI
NEBBLING, JACOB	BAL	251	20TH WAR
NEBEL, PETER	BAL	303	20TH WAR
NEBOW, EMILA	BAL	428	1ST DIST
NEBUGE, FREDERICK	ALL	184	9TH E.D.
NECOLL, SARAH J.*	BAL	395	3RD WARD
NEDELIS, ALPHENSE	BAL	297	12TH WAR
NEDHAM, MARGARET	CEC	011	ELKTON 3
NEE, B.	BAL	117	1ST WARD
NEE, JOHN	BAL	140	1ST WARD
NEE, PHILIP	ALL	092	5TH E.D.
NEED, ANN	BAL	271	20TH WAR
NEED, WILLIAM	FRE	360	CATOCTIN
NEEDE, JAMES	BAL	140	1ST WARD
NEEDHAM, ASA	BAL	005	15TH WAR
NEEDHAM, ELIZA	BAL	073	4TH WARD
NEEDLE, LEWIS	BAL	084	4TH WARD
NEEDLER, JOHN	BAL	122	16TH WAR
NEEDLES, EDWARD	BAL	476	14TH WAR
NEEDLES, JANE	BAL	355	3RD WARD
NEEDLES, JOHN	BAL	384	13TH WAR
NEEDLES, SALLIE	BAL	132	16TH WAR
NEEDLES, VINCENT	TAL	028	EASTON D
NEEDY, HENRY	WAS	300	1ST DIST
NEEDY, JACOB	WAS	246	SMITHSBU
NEEDY, MARGARET	WAS	261	1ST DIST
NEEDY, RUTH ANN	WAS	161	HAGERSTO
NEEDY, SAMUEL	WAS	234	1ST DIST
NEEDY, WILLIAM	WAS	125	2ND DIST
NEEHARNAY, AUGUSTUS	BAL	416	14TH WAR
NEEL, MARY	MGM	339	CLARKSBU
NEELE, WILLIAM	BAL	236	20TH WAR
NEELEY, ALEXANDER	ANN	296	1ST DIST
NEELEY, JAMES	BAL	260	20TH WAR
NEELEY, JAMES	BAL	260	20TH WAR
NEELEY, ROBERT F.	ANN	300	1ST DIST
NEELEY, SARAH	BAL	228	19TH WAR
NEELY, ANN	BAL	162	2ND DIST
NEELY, ELIZA	BAL	078	4TH WARD
NEELY, MARY ANN	BAL	346	13TH WAR
NEEN, PETER	BAL	333	1ST DIST
NEEP, JOHN	BAL	388	1ST DIST
NEEP, JOSEPH	BAL	388	1ST DIST
NEEP, LEWIS	BAL	388	1ST DIST
NEEPER, MARY	HAR	042	1ST DIST
NEEPER, MELISSA	HAR	046	1ST DIST
NEEPIER, WILLIAM	BAL	042	15TH WAR
NEES, ERNST	BAL	350	13TH WAR
NEFF, ANDREW	FRE	373	CATOCTIN
NEFF, BENJAMIN C.	ANN	399	8TH DIST
NEFF, CATHARINE	WAS	124	HAGERSTO
NEFF, JACOB	FRE	311	MIDDLETO
NEFF, JOHN	FRE	373	CATOCTIN
NEFF, JOHN	WAS	253	1ST DIST
NEFF, JOHN	WAS	193	1ST DIST
NEFF, JOHN	ALL	099	5TH E.D.
NEFF, JOHN	ALL	028	2ND E.D.
NEFF, JOHN	BAL	379	1ST DIST
NEFF, MARGAREWT	FRE	336	MIDDLETO
NEFF, MARY A.	BAL	041	18TH WAR
NEFF, MICHAEL	ALL	028	2ND E.D.
NEFF, NANCY	ALL	124	4TH E.D.
NEFF, REBECA	CAR	212	5TH DIST
NEFF, SARAHA	ALL	115	5TH E.D.
NEFF, SUSAN	ALL	093	5TH E.D.
NEFF, WILLIAM	ALL	124	4TH E.D.
NEFMAN, HENRY *	BAL	123	2ND DIST
NEGLE, JAMES	BAL	090	15TH WAR
NEGLER, L.P.	BAL	124	1ST WARD
NEGLEY, LAURA	WAS	205	1ST DIST
NEGLEY, PETER	WAS	205	1ST DIST
NEGLY, CATHARINE	WAS	145	HAGERSTO
NEGRO, BECKY	BAL	227	1ST DIST
NEGRO, CLOE	HAR	062	1ST DIST
NEGRO, ELIZA	ANN	343	3RD DIST
NEGRO, ELLEN	ANN	324	2ND DIST
NEGRO, FANNY	ANN	337	3RD DIST
NEGRO, HAGER	HAR	061	1ST DIST
NEGRO, HENRY	ANN	337	3RD DIST
NEGRO, JAMES	ANN	320	2ND DIST
NEGRO, MARY-BLACK	FRE	033	FREDERIC
NEGRO, RACHEL	ANN	337	3RD DIST
NEGROA, NICK	BAL	242	1ST DIST
NEHRMAN, CHARLES*	BAL	112	15TH WAR
NEHRMAN, HENRY	WAS	127	HAGERSTO
NEIBERT, PHILIP	WAS	233	1ST DIST
NEIBERT, PHILIP	WAS	253	1ST DIST
NEIBOLT, JOHN	BAL	312	3RD WARD
NEIBRANDT, JACOB	FRE	080	FREDERIC
NEIBRANDT, JOHN	FRE	080	FREDERIC
NEIDER, JOSEPHINE	BAL	186	6TH WARD
NEIDHARDT, WILLIAM	FRE	034	FREDERIC
NEIDIG, ABRAHAM	FRE	306	WOODSBOR
NEIDING, CHARLES	BAL	143	19TH WAR
NEIDMYER, JOHN H.	BAL	024	18TH WAR
NEIFER, WILLIAM	WAS	264	1ST DIST
NEIGH, SAMUEL	WAS	139	HAGERSTO
NEIGH, SAMUEL	WAS	271	1ST DIST
NEIGHBOURS, MARTHA	FRE	098	FREDERIC
NEIGHBOURS, MARY C.*	TAL	055	EASTON D
NEIGHBOURS, NATHAN P.	FRE	097	FREDERIC
NEIGHBOURS, T. T.	TAL	057	EASTON D
NEIGHBOURS, WILLIAM	TAL	057	EASTON D
NEIGHBUSE, WILLIAM	BAL	398	14TH WAR
NEIGHMEYER, MARTIN	BAL	458	14TH WAR
NEIGHORST, HENRY	BAL	179	2ND WARD
NEIGHT, SAMUEL	WAS	174	FUNKSTOW
NEIGHTRAND, JOSEPH	ALL	263	CUMBERLA
NEIKIRK, CATHARINE	WAS	024	2ND SUBD
NEIKIRK, DAVID	WAS	028	2ND SUBD
NEIKIRK, DAVID	WAS	023	2ND SUBD
NEIKIRK, HENRY	WAS	057	2ND SUBD
NEIKIRK, HENRY F.	WAS	057	2ND SUBD
NEIKIRK, JOHN	WAS	023	2ND SUBD
NEIKIRK, JOHN	WAS	177	1ST DIST
NEIKIRK, JOHN	WAS	210	1ST DIST
NEIKIRK, JOSEPH	WAS	179	BOONSBOR
NEIKIRK, SAMUEL	WAS	211	1ST DIST
NEIKIRK, SUSAN	WAS	211	1ST DIST
NEIL, ANNA O.	BAL	104	5TH WARD
NEIL, BENNET	ANN	287	ANNAPOLI
NEIL, CATHERINE	BAL	002	4TH WARD
NEIL, CHARLOTTE	BAL	082	1ST WARD
NEIL, DICK	ANN	317	1ST DIST
NEIL, EDWIN	BAL	002	4TH WARD
NEIL, ELIZABETH-MULATTO	FRE	038	FREDERIC
NEIL, HARRIET	BAL	144	5TH WARD
NEIL, HENRY	BAL	260	17TH WAR
NEIL, JANE	BAL	395	14TH WAR
NEIL, JOHN	BAL	169	1ST WARD
NEIL, JOHN M.	BAL	164	1ST WARD
NEIL, JONATHAN	FRE	086	FREDERIC
NEIL, JOSEPH	BAL	326	7TH WARD
NEIL, LOUIS	CEC	034	CHESAPEA
NEIL, M.	BAL	090	5TH WARD
NEIL, MARGARET	BAL	042	1ST WARD
NEIL, MARIA T.	BAL	446	8TH WARD
NEIL, MARTHA	BAL	057	18TH WAR
NEIL, MARY	BAL	020	4TH WARD
NEIL, MARY	BAL	135	5TH WARD
NEIL, P.	BAL	173	1ST WARD

NEIL, RICHARD BAL 047 4TH WARD
NEIL, SAMUEL-MULATTO FRE 038 FREDERIC
NEIL, SUSANA BAL 432 8TH WARD
NEIL, THOMAS BAL 162 11TH WAR
NEIL, THOMAS D. BAL 160 11TH WAR
NEIL, WILLIAM BAL 256 17TH WAR
NEIL, WILLIAM BAL 071 1ST WARD
NEILAN, MARIA BAL 006 1ST WARD
NEILENGALL, LEWIS CAR 332 MANCHEST
NEILL, ALEX. JR. WAS 136 HAGERSTO
NEILL, ALEXANDER WAS 140 HAGERSTO
NEILL, DAVID WAS 159 2ND DIST
NEILL, GEORGE BAL 093 10TH WAR
NEILL, JAMES BAL 051 15TH WAR
NEILL, JAMES FRE 139 CREAGERS
NEILL, JOHN BAL 024 1ST WARD
NEILL, JOHN * FRE 125 CREAGERS
NEILL, K. D. BAL 277 20TH WAR
NEILLS, MARY FRE 181 5TH E DI
NEILLY, JOHN J. FRE 170 5TH E DI
NEILSON, CAROLINE BAL 322 12TH WAR
NEILSON, CRAWFORD BAL 180 11TH WAR
NEILSON, ELIZABETH BAL 059 4TH WARD
NEILSON, ELIZABETH BAL 225 19TH WAR
NEILSON, F. BAL 150 1ST WARD
NEILSON, FANNY BAL 249 1ST DIST
NEILSON, GEORGE BAL 440 1ST DIST
NEILSON, HESTER BAL 045 4TH WARD
NEILSON, JOHN BAL 146 1ST WARD
NEILSON, JOHN BAL 265 2ND WARD
NEILSON, O.W. BAL 158 1ST WARD
NEILSON, PETER BAL 234 2ND WARD
NEILSON, ROBERT BAL 014 15TH WAR
NEILSON, THOMAS N. BAL 031 4TH WARD
NEILY, RICHARD W. BAL 394 3RD WARD
NEIMEYER, JOHN H. BAL 103 15TH WAR
NEIMYER, JOHN JR. BAL 146 16TH WAR
NEINMYER, JOHN H. BAL 146 16TH WAR
NEIR, ELIZA BAL 277 20TH WAR
NEIR, MARY M. BAL 131 5TH WARD
NEIS, ELIZABETH BAL 290 12TH WAR
NEIS, JOSHUA BAL 031 4TH WARD
NEISS, HIRAM M. FRE 046 FREDERIC
NEISZ, FREDERICK FRE 051 FREDERIC
NEISZ, SOPHIA FRE 051 FREDERIC
NEITZELL, SAMUEL BAL 090 1ST WARD
NEIVES, FRISBY* TAL 030 EASTON D
NEIVETT, ANN TAL 107 ST MICHA
NEKSON, BIDIAH ST 269 3RD E DI
NELAND, PATRICK ALL 110 5TH E.D.
NELAND, THOMAS ALL 073 5TH E.D.
NELARD, WILLIAM HAR 010 1ST DIST
NELEMS, JOHN BAL 214 17TH WAR
NELL, FREDERICK CEC 057 1ST E DI
NELL, JASPER TAL 118 ST MICHA
NELL, JOSEPH MGM 340 CLARKSBU
NELL, THOMAS H.* DOR 377 1ST DIST
NELLIGAN, THOMAS BAL 036 4TH WARD
NELLIN, LYDIA BAL 435 8TH WARD
NELLS, ALLEN H. ALL 263 CUMBERLA
NELLY, ADAM BAL 027 4TH WARD
NELLY, JACOB WAS 032 2ND SUBD
NELLY, MARGARET BAL 226 19TH WAR
NELSON, ALEXANDER SOM 527 QUANTICO
NELSON, ALMIRA SOM 527 QUANTICO
NELSON, ALONZO SOM 381 BRINKLEY
NELSON, ANDREW SOM 377 BRINKLEY
NELSON, ANDREW K. CEC 099 3RD E DI
NELSON, ANN CECILIA BAL 106 10TH WAR
NELSON, BASEL ALL 153 6TH E.D.
NELSON, BENJAMIN SOM 454 DAMES QU
NELSON, BENNETT HAR 178 3RD DIST
NELSON, BURGESS FRE 315 MIDDLETO
NELSON, CAROLINE BAL 430 1ST DIST
NELSON, CASSANDRA ANN 449 HOWARD D
NELSON, CATHARINE BAL 464 14TH WAR
NELSON, CATHERINE BAL 001 9TH WARD
NELSON, CHAELS BAL 152 1ST WARD
NELSON, CHARLES BAL 150 1ST WARD
NELSON, CHARLES BAL 125 1ST WARD
NELSON, CYRUS SOM 526 QUANTICO
NELSON, DANIEL HAR 170 3RD DIST
NELSON, DAVID SOM 377 BRINKLEY
NELSON, DAVID BAL 046 2ND DIST
NELSON, DAVID BAL 429 1ST DIST
NELSON, ELEYER BAL 222 12TH WAR
NELSON, ELIJAH SOM 381 BRINKLEY
NELSON, ELISHA FRE 452 8TH E DI
NELSON, ELIZA FRE 029 FREDERIC
NELSON, ELIZA FRE 314 MIDDLETO
NELSON, ELIZABETH BAL 192 19TH WAR
NELSON, ELIZABETH BAL 434 14TH WAR
NELSON, ELIZABETH ST 270 3RD E DI
NELSON, ELIZABETH ANN 449 HOWARD D
NELSON, ELIZABETH BAL 106 15TH WAR
NELSON, ELLEN BAL 084 15TH WAR
NELSON, EMILY BAL 058 10TH WAR
NELSON, ESTER-BLACK BAL 223 2ND WARD
NELSON, FRANCIS SOM 362 BRINKLEY
NELSON, G. BAL 166 1ST WARD
NELSON, GARRETT B. HAR 182 3RD DIST
NELSON, GEORGE HAR 181 3RD DIST
NELSON, GEORGE CEC 210 7TH E DI
NELSON, GEORGE BAL 169 1ST WARD
NELSON, GEORGE BAL 180 11TH WAR
NELSON, GEORGE SOM 528 QUANTICO
NELSON, GEORGE L. W. ST 270 3RD E DI
NELSON, GEORGE W. BAL 122 1ST WARD
NELSON, GEORGIANA BAL 259 6TH WARD
NELSON, HANNAH CEC 199 7TH E DI
NELSON, HANS QUE 237 4TH E DI
NELSON, HARRIET BAL 196 11TH WAR
NELSON, HARRIET BAL 071 10TH WAR
NELSON, HARRIET ANN 497 HOWARD D
NELSON, HENRY BAL 088 1ST WARD
NELSON, HENRY WOR 305 2ND E DI
NELSON, HENRY CEC 148 PORT DUP
NELSON, HENRY HAR 192 3RD DIST
NELSON, HENRY FRE 259 NEW MARK
NELSON, HESTER BAL 002 1ST WARD
NELSON, HORATIA* SOM 554 TYASKIN
NELSON, HUGH BAL 040 18TH WAR
NELSON, ISAAC SOM 376 BRINKLEY
NELSON, J. BAL 118 1ST WARD
NELSON, J. BAL 286 2ND WARD
NELSON, J. BAL 169 1ST WARD
NELSON, J. BAL 166 1ST WARD
NELSON, J. BAL 149 1ST WARD
NELSON, J.A. BAL 001 18TH WAR
NELSON, J.H. BAL 169 1ST WARD
NELSON, JACOB BAL 125 1ST WARD
NELSON, JAMES BAL 176 6TH WARD
NELSON, JAMES BAL 167 6TH WARD
NELSON, JAMES BAL 088 2ND DIST
NELSON, JAMES ALL 102 5TH E.D.
NELSON, JAMES CEC 066 1ST E DI
NELSON, JAMES CEC 169 6TH E DI
NELSON, JAMES HAR 189 3RD DIST
NELSON, JAMES HAR 066 1ST DIST
NELSON, JAMES SOM 382 BRINKLEY
NELSON, JAMES C. HAR 026 1ST DIST
NELSON, JAMES S. WOR 300 SNOW HIL
NELSON, JANE BAL 440 1ST DIST
NELSON, JESSE FRE 442 8TH E DI
NELSON, JOB SOM 381 BRINKLEY
NELSON, JOB SOM 377 BRINKLEY
NELSON, JOEL WOR 314 2ND E DI
NELSON, JOHN SOM 375 BRINKLEY
NELSON, JOHN QUE 232 4TH E DI
NELSON, JOHN HAR 071 1ST DIST
NELSON, JOHN FRE 084 FREDERIC
NELSON, JOHN CEC 171 6TH E DI
NELSON, JOHN CEC 188 7TH E DI
NELSON, JOHN BAL 434 14TH WAR
NELSON, JOHN CAR 385 2ND DIST
NELSON, JOHN CAR 285 7TH DIST
NELSON, JOHN BAL 230 1ST DIST
NELSON, JOHN BAL 128 5TH WARD
NELSON, JOHN BAL 105 1ST WARD
NELSON, JOHN BAL 075 1ST WARD
NELSON, JOHN BAL 286 2ND WARD
NELSON, JOHN BAL 060 10TH WAR
NELSON, JOHN BAL 266 2ND WARD
NELSON, JOHN BAL 140 1ST WARD
NELSON, JOHN F. BAL 165 1ST WARD
NELSON, JOHN H. CHA 263 MIDDLETO
NELSON, JOHN JR. SOM 378 BRINKLEY
NELSON, JOSEPH BAL 284 20TH WAR
NELSON, JOSEPH BAL 464 14TH WAR
NELSON, JOSEPH BAL 335 7TH WARD
NELSON, JOSEPH JR. BAL 306 7TH WARD
NELSON, JOSEPH R. FRE 060 FREDERIC
NELSON, JOSEPHENE CEC 134 6TH E DI
NELSON, JOSHUA HAR 071 1ST DIST
NELSON, JOSHUA R. HAR 069 1ST DIST
NELSON, JUDY MGM 439 CLARKSTR
NELSON, JULIA BAL 464 14TH WAR
NELSON, JULIANA BAL 098 10TH WAR
NELSON, LEVI WOR 302 SNOW HIL
NELSON, MADISON FRE 056 FREDERIC
NELSON, MANUEL BAL 076 18TH WAR
NELSON, MARK CEC 169 6TH E DI
NELSON, MARK CEC 197 7TH E DI
NELSON, MARSHALL BAL 397 14TH WAR
NELSON, MARY BAL 152 5TH WARD
NELSON, MARY BAL 030 9TH WARD
NELSON, MARY C. BAL 418 1ST DIST
NELSON, MARY J. CEC 165 6TH E DI
NELSON, MARY J. CEC 148 PORT DUP
NELSON, MUNTA-BLACK ST 333 4TH E DI
NELSON, NANCY SOM 375 BRINKLEY
NELSON, NATHAN HAR 071 1ST DIST
NELSON, NATHAN FRE 264 NEW MARK
NELSON, NATHAN FRE 266 NEW MARK
NELSON, NATHAN BAL 207 6TH DIST
NELSON, NEIL BAL 142 1ST WARD
NELSON, NICHOLAS H. HAR 018 1ST DIST
NELSON, NOAH BAL 136 1ST WARD
NELSON, NOAH BAL 022 9TH WARD
NELSON, OBEDIAH ST 315 4TH E DI
NELSON, P. BAL 164 1ST WARD
NELSON, P. G. BAL 154 1ST WARD
NELSON, PAUL WOR 329 1ST E DI
NELSON, PERRY FRE 355 MIDDLETO
NELSON, PERRY O. SOM 529 QUANTICO
NELSON, PETER BAL 162 1ST WARD
NELSON, PETER BAL 160 1ST WARD
NELSON, PETER BAL 146 1ST WARD
NELSON, PETER BAL 087 1ST WARD
NELSON, PETER BAL 105 1ST WARD
NELSON, PETER BAL 001 1ST WARD
NELSON, RACHAEL CHA 264 MIDDLETO
NELSON, REBECCA BAL 269 17TH WAR
NELSON, REBECCA SOM 552 TYASKIN
NELSON, REBECCA M. FRE 266 NEW MARK
NELSON, RICHARD F. CHA 263 MIDDLETO
NELSON, ROBERT FRE 303 WOODSBOR
NELSON, ROBERT WOR 317 2ND E DI
NELSON, ROBERT ANN 489 HOWARD D
NELSON, SACKER SOM 376 BRINKLEY
NELSON, SACKER JR. SOM 376 BRINKLEY
NELSON, SAMUEL M. WOR 312 2ND E DI
NELSON, SAMUEL-MULATTO FRE 437 8TH E DI
NELSON, SARAH MGM 439 CLARKSTR
NELSON, SARAH SOM 534 QUANTICO
NELSON, SOPHIA BAL 064 2ND DIST
NELSON, THEODORE BAL 040 18TH WAR
NELSON, THOMAS FRE 301 WOODSBOR
NELSON, THOMAS BAL 226 1ST DIST
NELSON, THOMAS BAL 274 1ST DIST
NELSON, THOMAS SOM 376 BRINKLEY
NELSON, THOMAS C. SOM 380 BRINKLEY
NELSON, THOMAS S. FRE 031 FREDERIC
NELSON, THOMAS T. SOM 376 BRINKLEY
NELSON, WASHINGTON BAL 066 10TH WAR
NELSON, WEIGHTMAN BAL 398 1ST DIST
NELSON, WILLIAM BAL 160 6TH WARD
NELSON, WILLIAM BAL 106 1ST WARD
NELSON, WILLIAM BAL 029 1ST WARD
NELSON, WILLIAM BAL 035 2ND DIST
NELSON, WILLIAM SOM 382 BRINKLEY
NELSON, WILLIAM WOR 264 BERLIN 1
NELSON, WILLIAM FRE 377 PETERSVI
NELSON, WILLIAM HAR 169 3RD DIST
NELSON, WILLIAM BAL 428 14TH WAR
NELSON, WILLIAM HAR 026 1ST DIST
NELSON, WILLIAM HAR 018 1ST DIST
NELSON, WILLIAM B. BAL 101 10TH WAR
NELSON, WILLIAM C. WOR 301 SNOW HIL
NELSON, WILLIAM E. BAL 314 7TH WARD
NELSON, WILLIAM T. QUE 249 5TH E DI
NELSON, ZEPHINIAH ST 271 3RD E DI
NELSON,E. BAL 139 1ST WARD
NELSON,JAMESP. CAR 398 2ND DIST
NELSON,JOHN ALL 246 CUMBERLA
NELSON,PETER BAL 116 1ST WARD
NELSON,RICHARD BAL 042 2ND DIST
NELSON,WILLIAM L. FRE 239 NEW MARK
NEMAN, HENRY BAL 224 12TH WAR
NEMEL, JAMES W. HAR 169 3RD DIST
NEMFER, HENRY BAL 210 19TH WAR
NEMIER, JOHN FRE 054 FREDERIC
NEMIES, FREDERICK BAL 307 20TH WAR
NEMINE, WILLIAM HAR 202 3RD DIST
NEMMO, WILLIAM R. BAL 045 4TH WARD
NENINGER, CORNELUS BAL 263 2ND WARD
NENINGER, DANIEL BAL 119 1ST WARD
NENKLEBATCH, ANDREW BAL 077 4TH WARD
NENSLAYER, JOHN F. BAL 423 14TH WAR
NEORN, ADAM* DOR 426 1ST DIST
NEOTHEMAR, JOHN BAL 451 14TH WAR
NEPHKIN, ADAM ALL 042 10TH E.D
NEPHOUT, BALSER BAL 181 2ND WARD
NEPIN, H.L. BAL 228 12TH WAR
NEPOLIAN, VANO HAR 191 3RD DIST
NEPTLER, HENRY ALL 168 6TH E.D.
NEPTON, ELIZABETH BAL 083 15TH WAR
NERBECK, WILLIAM BAL 303 12TH WAR
NERERNAN, REBECCA BAL 283 12TH WAR
NERGENT, JAMES * BAL 316 20TH WAR
NERR, ADAM FRE 027 FREDERIC
NERSSENER, JAMES H. BAL 244 20TH WAR
NERSTIN, ISAAC BAL 182 19TH WAR
NERT, MARRY * BAL 322 12TH WAR
NERTHERS, DAVID CAR 077 NO TWP L
NERWIN, JESSE* DOR 429 1ST DIST
NESBETT, ALEXANDER BAL 053 2ND DIST
NESBETT, JONATHAN CEC 157 PORT DUP
NESBETT, JONATHAN JR. WAS 122 2ND DIST
NESBETT, JOSEPH G. CEC 146 PORT DUP
NESBETT, MOSES CEC 203 6TH E DI
NESBIT, JOSIAH DOR 463 1ST DIST
NESBIT, SAMUEL HAR 034 1ST DIST
NESBITT, ALEXANDER CEC 157 PORT DUP
NESBITT, ALEXANDER H. WAS 021 2ND SUBD
NESBITT, DAVID CEC 157 PORT DUP
NESBITT, ISAAC WAS 154 HAGERSTO
NESBITT, JOHN TAL 111 ST MICHA
NESBITT, JOHN CEC 158 PORT DUP
NESBITT, JOHNATHAN WAS 142 2ND DIST
NESBITT, MARSHAL CEC 207 7TH E DI
NESBITT, MOSES CEC 209 7TH E DI
NESBITT, ROBERT CEC 202 6TH E DI
NESBITT, ROBERT CEC 157 PORT DUP
NESBITT, THOMAS CEC 207 7TH E DI
NESBITT, THOMAS L. WAS 155 HAGERSTO
NESH, EPRAM * WAS 119 2ND DIST
NESITT, THOMAS FRE 005 FREDERIC
NESLINE, JOHN BAL 206 2ND WARD
NESS, MARY A. BAL 218 2ND WARD
NESS, SAMUEL J. BAL 410 1ST DIST
NESS, WILLIAM H. BAL 169 6TH WARD
NESSEN, N. BAL 149 1ST WARD
NESSEY, MARY A. * BAL 348 1ST DIST
NESTON, JOHN BAL 175 2ND WARD
NESWANDER, JOHN WAS 129 2ND DIST
NESWANDER, MARGARET WAS 129 2ND DIST
NESWANGER, TABITHA FRE 405 JEFFERSO
NET, PIN* DOR 431 1ST DIST
NETER, PATRICK HAR 164 3RD DIST
NETHOLER, CHRISTIAN ALL 059 10TH E.D
NETRY, PATRICK ALL 196 CUMBERLA
NETT, HENRY BAL 118 1ST WARD
NETTER, ANNE BAL 096 15TH WAR
NETTER, GATCHELL R. BAL 215 6TH WARD
NETTER, HENRY BAL 152 16TH WAR
NETTER, MARY E. BAL 152 16TH WAR
NETTER, N. BAL 119 11TH WAR
NETTLE, HENRY BAL 129 2ND DIST
NETTLE, MARIA CHA 287 BOJANTOW
NETTLE, MARY QUE 211 3RD E DI
NETTLE, THOMAS D. CHA 287 BOJANTOW
NETTLES, GEORGE ANN 475 HOWARD D
NETTLES, JOHN BAL 121 18TH WAR
NETTS, ELIZABETH WAS 200 1ST DIST
NETTS, ELLEN WAS 199 1ST DIST
NETTS, JOHN WAS 209 1ST DIST
NETTS, SARAH C. WAS 210 1ST DIST
NETTS, WILLIAM H. WAS 196 1ST DIST
NETZDORF, JOHN BAL 269 17TH WAR
NEUBERTH, JOHN BAL 016 15TH WAR
NEUBERTH, LOUIS J. BAL 161 16TH WAR
NEUCOMMER, SUSAN WAS 136 2ND DIST
NEUFER, CHRISTIAN BAL 171 19TH WAR
NEUHAUS, FREDERIC J. BAL 185 6TH WARD
NEUHAUS, JOHN BAL 047 18TH WAR
NEUMYER, W.* BAL 100 10TH WAR
NEUPERT, CHARLES BAL 086 10TH WAR
NEURILLEN, JOHN BAL 140 11TH WAR
NEUSANDER, MARGARET WAS 129 2ND DIST
NEUSE, JOSEPH WAS 069 2ND SUBD
NEUSE, MARGARET WAS 068 2ND SUBD
NEVAN, MARY BAL 204 11TH WAR
NEVEL, CASANDER HAR 031 1ST DIST
NEVEL, ELLEN HAR 202 3RD DIST
NEVEL, JAMES BAL 390 1ST DIST
NEVEL, JOHN CHA 223 ALLENS F
NEVENS, JAMES ALL 262 CUMBERLA
NEVEREAH, PETER BAL 244 17TH WAR
NEVERKAMP, FRANK BAL 174 19TH WAR
NEVET, ROBERT CHA 220 ALLENS F
NEVET, SARA CHA 227 ALLENS F
NEVET, WILLIAM CHA 220 ALLENS F
NEVETT, JAMES BAL 388 8TH WARD
NEVIL, JOHN HAR 031 1ST DIST
NEVIL, RICHARD* DOR 416 1ST DIST
NEVILAID, SARAH CEC 030 CHESAPEA
NEVILL, ANN QUE 123 1ST E DI
NEVILL, HENRIETTA QUE 175 2ND E DI
NEVILL, JAMES QUE 151 1ST E DI
NEVILL, LAVINA CEC 004 ELKTON 3
NEVILL, ROBERT CEC 069 5TH E DI
NEVILL, WILLIAM BAL 420 8TH WARD
NEVILLE, AMELIA BAL 275 2ND WARD
NEVILLE, HONORA BAL 082 4TH WARD
NEVILLE, JERRY BAL 225 12TH WAR
NEVILLE, MARY CEC 009 ELKTON 3
NEVIN, JOHN BAL 040 9TH WARD
NEVING, ELIZABETH BAL 328 13TH WAR
NEVINGER, WILLIAM WAS 063 2ND SUBD
NEVINGER, WILLIAM WAS 038 2ND SUBD
NEVINS, JOHN BAL 091 5TH WARD
NEVINS, LYDIA V. D. MGM 394 ROCKERLE
NEVIT, RICHARD* DOR 415 1ST DIST
NEVITT, ANN M. ST 316 4TH E DI
NEVITT, CHARLES ST 315 4TH E DI
NEVITT, JOSEPH MGM 385 ROCKERLE
NEVITT, REBECCA BAL 041 9TH WARD
NEVITT, VIRGINIA BAL 225 6TH WARD
NEVITT, WILLIMA C. BAL 123 5TH WARD

Name	County	Page	District
NEW, BASIL'M. *	BAL	097	18TH WAR
NEW, DANIEL	BAL	383	8TH WARD
NEWALL, JANETTA	BAL	436	14TH WAR
NEWALL, JOSEPH	BAL	146	5TH WARD
NEWANDER, CHRISTIAN	WAS	129	2ND DIST
NEWBELL, JOHN G.	BAL	035	18TH WAR
NEWBERG, JOHN W.	CHA	244	HILLTOP
NEWBERRY, JOSHUA	ALL	008	3RD E.D.
NEWBERT, JOHN	BAL	269	2ND WARD
NEWBERTH, MICHAEL JR.	BAL	160	16TH WAR
NEWBOLD, MICHAEL	QUE	193	3RD E DI
NEWBRON, C.	BAL	321	20TH WAR
NEWBUNGER, VALENTINE	BAL	169	2ND DIST
NEWBURY, ROBERT	BAL	390	8TH WARD
NEWCANL, ELLEN	BAL	247	12TH WAR
NEWCOMB, LEWIS R.	BAL	019	18TH WAR
NEWCOMB, MARIAH	SOM	353	BRINKLEY
NEWCOMB, MARTHA	KEN	296	3RD DIST
NEWCOMB, MARY	BAL	353	7TH WARD
NEWCOMB, PETER	BAL	092	1ST WARD
NEWCOMB, THOMAS	KEN	304	3RD DIST
NEWCOMBER, SAMUEL	CAR	322	1ST DIST
NEWCOMER, ABRAHAM	WAS	271	1ST DIST
NEWCOMER, ANN	WAS	219	1ST DIST
NEWCOMER, BARBARA	CAR	315	1ST DIST
NEWCOMER, BENJAMIN F.	BAL	430	14TH WAR
NEWCOMER, CHRISTIAN	WAS	219	1ST DIST
NEWCOMER, CHRISTIAN	WAS	260	1ST DIST
NEWCOMER, CHRISTIAN	WAS	277	LEITERSB
NEWCOMER, DAVID	WAS	271	1ST DIST
NEWCOMER, DAVID	WAS	300	1ST DIST
NEWCOMER, DAVID H.	WAS	208	1ST DIST
NEWCOMER, ELIZABETH	WAS	224	1ST DIST
NEWCOMER, HENRIETTA	WAS	269	1ST DIST
NEWCOMER, HENRY	WAS	224	1ST DIST
NEWCOMER, HENRY	WAS	277	RIDGEVIL
NEWCOMER, HENRY	CAR	305	1ST DIST
NEWCOMER, ISAAC	CAR	305	1ST DIST
NEWCOMER, ISAAC	WAS	207	1ST DIST
NEWCOMER, JACOB	WAS	231	1ST DIST
NEWCOMER, JACOB	WAS	251	1ST DIST
NEWCOMER, JACOB	CAR	315	1ST DIST
NEWCOMER, JOEL	WAS	197	1ST DIST
NEWCOMER, JOHN	WAS	197	1ST DIST
NEWCOMER, JOHN	WAS	223	1ST DIST
NEWCOMER, JOHN	WAS	271	1ST DIST
NEWCOMER, JOHN	WAS	138	HAGERSTO
NEWCOMER, JOHN	BAL	020	1ST WARD
NEWCOMER, JONOTHAN	WAS	208	1ST DIST
NEWCOMER, JOSEPH	WAS	150	HAGERSTO
NEWCOMER, JOSHUA	WAS	296	1ST DIST
NEWCOMER, JOSHUA	WAS	038	2ND SUBD
NEWCOMER, MARY J.	CAR	295	7TH DIST
NEWCOMER, MELCON	WAS	208	1ST DIST
NEWCOMER, MICHAEL	WAS	218	1ST DIST
NEWCOMER, MICHAEL	WAS	144	HAGERSTO
NEWCOMER, PETER	WAS	182	BOONSBOR
NEWCOMER, PETER	WAS	262	1ST DIST
NEWCOMER, RHUE	WAS	061	2ND SUBD
NEWCOMER, SIMON	ALL	235	CUMBERLA
NEWCOMER, SUSAN M.	WAS	198	1ST DIST
NEWCOMER, THOMAS	WAS	291	1ST DIST
NEWCOMER, WILLIAM	WAS	030	2ND SUBD
NEWCOMMER, JACOB	WAS	136	2ND DIST
NEWCUM, CHARLES	CAR	113	NO TWP L
NEWCUM, JOHN-BLACK	CAR	140	NO TWP L
NEWCUM, JOSIAH-BLACK	CAR	142	NO TWP L
NEWCUM, POMPY-BLACK	CAR	133	NO TWP L
NEWDEMUS, JOHN T.	FRE	309	WOODSBOR
NEWEL, ALEXANDER	BAL	321	7TH WARD
NEWELL, JAMES	BAL	142	1ST WARD
NEWELL, JAMES	BAL	243	17TH WAR
NEWELL, JOHN	ALL	190	9TH E.D.
NEWELL, LEWIS P.	ALL	190	9TH E.D.
NEWELL, MARY E.	KEN	208	2ND DIST
NEWELL, PETER	BAL	104	15TH WAR
NEWELL, SAMUEL Y.	BAL	393	8TH WARD
NEWELL, SARAH	BAL	322	12TH WAR
NEWELL, WILLIAM E.	KEN	312	3RD DIST
NEWELL, WILLIAM H.	BAL	335	7TH WARD
NEWET, SARAH	BAL	314	1ST DIST
NEWET, WILLIAM	BAL	314	1ST DIST
NEWEY, JOHN	FRE	095	FREDERIC
NEWHAUST, JOHN	BAL	282	17TH WAR
NEWHOLD, JOSEPH	ALL	241	CUMBERLA
NEWHOUSE, J.	BAL	173	1ST WARD
NEWHOUSE, J.	BAL	173	1ST WARD
NEWHOUSE, J.	BAL	149	1ST WARD
NEWHOUSE, MARY	BAL	277	2ND WARD
NEWILL, OLIVER	BAL	184	11TH WAR
NEWITT, JAMES C.	BAL	184	11TH WAR
NEWKIRK, -----	WAS	188	BOONSBOR
NEWKIRK, ISAAC	WAS	102	2ND DIST
NEWKIRK, SOLOMON	WAS	209	1ST DIST
NEWL, JOHN	WAS	047	2ND SUBD
NEWLAND, DANIEL	BAL	271	1ST DIST
NEWLAND, DAVID	BAL	265	1ST DIST
NEWLAND, EDGAR	ALL	254	CUMBERLA
NEWLAND, HENRY	ALL	057	10TH E.D
NEWLAND, JOHN	BAL	251	2ND WARD
NEWLER, WILLIAM	CAR	099	NO TWP L
NEWLIN, ARTEMAS	MGM	320	CRACKLIN
NEWLIN, FERDINAN H.*	TAL	020	EASTON D
NEWLIN, MICHAEL	HAR	142	2ND DIST
NEWLING, GEORGE H.	BAL	243	2ND WARD
NEWLY, WARNER	CAR	099	NO TWP L
NEWMAN, ALEXANDER	ALL	001	3RD E.D.
NEWMAN, ANN	BAL	402	3RD WARD
NEWMAN, ANN	BAL	204	6TH WARD
NEWMAN, ANN E.	FRE	066	FREDERIC
NEWMAN, ANTHONY	BAL	143	2ND DIST
NEWMAN, ANTHONY	BAL	046	1ST WARD
NEWMAN, AUGUSTUS	BAL	273	20TH WAR
NEWMAN, BETSEY	SOM	368	BRINKLEY
NEWMAN, C.M.	QUE	176	2ND E DI
NEWMAN, CASPER	BAL	327	7TH WARD
NEWMAN, CATHERINE	QUE	223	4TH E DI
NEWMAN, CHARLOTT	BAL	215	2ND WARD
NEWMAN, DANIEL	QUE	187	3RD E DI
NEWMAN, DAVID	ALL	215	CUMBERLA
NEWMAN, E.	PRI	108	PISCATAW
NEWMAN, ELIAS R.	BAL	401	14TH WAR
NEWMAN, ELIZA	TAL	088	ST MICHA
NEWMAN, ELIZABETH	QUE	166	2ND E DI
NEWMAN, ELIZABETH	QUE	165	2ND E DI
NEWMAN, ELIZABETH	SOM	441	DAMES QU
NEWMAN, EMMERSON	BAL	325	7TH WARD
NEWMAN, FRANCIS	PRI	096	SPALDING
NEWMAN, FRANCIS L.	PRI	085	QUEEN AN
NEWMAN, GEORGE	PRI	107	PISCATAW
NEWMAN, GEORGE	PRI	001	BLADENSB
NEWMAN, GEORGE	BAL	294	12TH WAR
NEWMAN, GEORGE	DOR	406	1ST DIST
NEWMAN, GEORGE-BLACK	QUE	204	3RD E DI
NEWMAN, HENRY	PRI	055	AQUASCO
NEWMAN, HENRY	BAL	112	5TH WARD
NEWMAN, HETTY	BAL	349	3RD WARD
NEWMAN, HILLARY	PRI	055	AQUASCO
NEWMAN, HORATIO	PRI	006	BLADENSB
NEWMAN, J.	BAL	127	5TH WARD
NEWMAN, J.	BAL	262	12TH WAR
NEWMAN, JACOB	WAS	005	WILLIAMS
NEWMAN, JACOB	WAS	015	2ND SUBD
NEWMAN, JAMES	BAL	168	1ST WARD
NEWMAN, JAMES	ALL	180	8TH E.D.
NEWMAN, JENNEY	BAL	295	7TH WARD
NEWMAN, JOHN	ALL	009	3RD E.D.
NEWMAN, JOHN	ALL	010	3RD E.D.
NEWMAN, JOHN	BAL	177	6TH WARD
NEWMAN, JOHN	WAS	289	1ST DIST
NEWMAN, JOHN	KEN	305	3RD DIST
NEWMAN, JOHN	SOM	383	BRINKLEY
NEWMAN, JOHN	HAR	062	1ST DIST
NEWMAN, JOHN	CAR	121	NO TWP L
NEWMAN, JOHN	BAL	147	11TH WAR
NEWMAN, JOHN	QUE	154	1ST E DI
NEWMAN, JOHN F.	KEN	298	3RD DIST
NEWMAN, JOHN*	DOR	406	1ST DIST
NEWMAN, JOSEPH	BAL	035	18TH WAR
NEWMAN, JOSEPH	TAL	081	ST MICHA
NEWMAN, JOSEPH	TAL	098	ST MICHA
NEWMAN, JOSEPH	WAS	289	1ST DIST
NEWMAN, JOSEPH	BAL	326	7TH WARD
NEWMAN, JOSHUA J.*	BAL	371	3RD WARD
NEWMAN, LOUISA	BAL	219	17TH WAR
NEWMAN, MARY	QUE	139	1ST E DI
NEWMAN, MARY	BAL	096	1ST WARD
NEWMAN, MARY	BAL	007	1ST WARD
NEWMAN, MARY	BAL	241	2ND WARD
NEWMAN, MARY	BAL	101	5TH WARD
NEWMAN, MARY E.	BAL	071	4TH WARD
NEWMAN, MARY E.	KEN	306	3RD DIST
NEWMAN, MARY E.-MULATTO	MGM	409	MEDLEY 3
NEWMAN, MICAHEL	BAL	279	2ND WARD
NEWMAN, MICHAEL	BAL	127	1ST WARD
NEWMAN, MOSES	BAL	316	3RD WARD
NEWMAN, OLIVER	BAL	254	12TH WAR
NEWMAN, P.	PRI	055	AQUASCO
NEWMAN, PURNELL	BAL	026	9TH WARD
NEWMAN, RISDEN	BAL	071	4TH WARD
NEWMAN, ROBERT	TAL	103	ST MICHA
NEWMAN, SALLY	ALL	012	3RD E.D.
NEWMAN, SAMUEL	SOM	504	SALISBUR
NEWMAN, SAMUEL	WAS	126	HAGERSTO
NEWMAN, SAMUEL H.	BAL	154	11TH WAR
NEWMAN, SUSAN	SOM	435	PRINCESS
NEWMAN, SUSANA	BAL	371	3RD WARD
NEWMAN, THOMAS	BAL	080	1ST WARD
NEWMAN, THOMAS	ALL	145	6TH E.D.
NEWMAN, THOMAS	BAL	002	9TH WARD
NEWMAN, THOMAS	BAL	456	8TH WARD
NEWMAN, THOMAS	SOM	482	TRAPP DI
NEWMAN, TIMOTHY	BAL	348	7TH WARD
NEWMAN, WASHINGTON	ALL	012	3RD E.D.
NEWMAN, WILLIAM	BAL	133	5TH WARD
NEWMAN, WILLIAM	BAL	280	12TH WAR
NEWMAN, WILLIAM	TAL	097	ST MICHA
NEWMAN, WILLIAM	CAR	101	NO TWP L
NEWMAN, WILLIAM E. G.	QUE	231	4TH E DI
NEWMAN, WILLIAM K.	ALL	217	CUMBERLA
NEWMAN, WILLIAM-BLACK	QUE	203	3RD E DI
NEWMASTER, GEORGE	BAL	112	2ND DIST
NEWMASTER, HENRY	BAL	108	2ND DIST
NEWMAYER, MARY H.S.	FRE	239	NEW MARK
NEWMILLER, JOHN	BAL	340	3RD WARD
NEWMILLER, WILLIAM	BAL	304	17TH WAR
NEWMYER, W.*	BAL	100	10TH WAR
NEWMYRES, JOSEPH	ALL	225	CUMBERLA
NEWNAM, FANNY	QUE	184	3RD E DI
NEWNAM, GEORGE	TAL	063	EASTON D
NEWNAM, HENRY	TAL	062	EASTON D
NEWNAM, HENRY*	TAL	034	EASTON D
NEWNAM, JAMES H.	TAL	047	EASTON T
NEWNAM, JAMES M.	TAL	053	EASTON D
NEWNAM, JOHN	TAL	042	EASTON D
NEWNAM, JOHN	TAL	041	EASTON D
NEWNAM, JOHN S.	TAL	065	EASTON T
NEWNAM, JULIANNA	QUE	183	3RD E DI
NEWNAM, MOSES	TAL	052	EASTON D
NEWNAM, NECK*	TAL	062	EASTON D
NEWNAM, NED	TAL	060	EASTON D
NEWNAM, RICHARD	TAL	002	EASTON D
NEWNAM, ROSE A.	TAL	063	EASTON D
NEWNAM, SALLY	TAL	049	EASTON T
NEWNAN, JAMES	TAL	025	EASTON D
NEWNAN, MARGARET	QUE	133	1ST E DI
NEWNON, PETER	ALL	143	6TH E.D.
NEWPORT, ADAM	FRE	062	FREDERIC
NEWPORT, ANN	FRE	051	FREDERIC
NEWPORT, MARY	FRE	060	FREDERIC
NEWPORT,MARY	FRE	030	FREDERIC
NEWSHAFFER, LAURENCE	BAL	025	4TH WARD
NEWSHAW, ANN E.	ANN	418	HOWARD D
NEWSOM, H.	BAL	158	1ST WARD
NEWSOME, MARTIN	KEN	280	3RD DIST
NEWSOMER, REBECCA	TAL	029	EASTON D
NEWSON, ABRAHAM	WAS	013	WILLIAMS
NEWSON, THOMAS	CEC	091	4TH E DI
NEWSWANGER, DANIEL	WAS	296	1ST DIST
NEWTON, A. B.	CEC	131	6TH E DI
NEWTON, CHARLES	BAL	106	5TH WARD
NEWTON, CLEMENT	ANN	445	HOWARD D
NEWTON, ELIZABETH	WOR	316	2ND E DI
NEWTON, ELIZABETH A.	BAL	067	18TH WAR
NEWTON, ELLEN R.	ST	261	3RD E DI
NEWTON, FRANCIS	BAL	144	1ST WARD
NEWTON, GEORGE C.	ST	261	3RD E DI
NEWTON, GEORGENNA	BAL	060	18TH WAR
NEWTON, HORACE B.	FRE	347	MIDDLETO
NEWTON, IGNATICUS B.	DOR	296	1ST DIST
NEWTON, ISAAC	BAL	153	19TH WAR
NEWTON, JAMES	QUE	144	1ST E DI
NEWTON, JOHN	DOR	376	1ST DIST
NEWTON, JOHN	DOR	299	1ST DIST
NEWTON, JOHN	PRI	005	BLADENSB
NEWTON, JOSEPH H.	DOR	296	1ST DIST
NEWTON, JOSIAH	KEN	293	3RD DIST
NEWTON, JULIANNA	ANN	436	HOWARD D
NEWTON, KATE	MGM	320	CRACKLIN
NEWTON, LEONE-BLACK	WOR	171	6TH E DI
NEWTON, LEWIS*	DOR	392	1ST DIST
NEWTON, MARTHA	KEN	304	3RD DIST
NEWTON, MARY	BAL	155	19TH WAR
NEWTON, MARY	DOR	296	1ST DIST
NEWTON, MARY J.	ST	263	3RD E DI
NEWTON, MARY J.	ANN	437	HOWARD D
NEWTON, MR-	BAL	061	15TH WAR
NEWTON, NANCY	WOR	287	BERLIN 1
NEWTON, NIMROD	DOR	461	1ST DIST
NEWTON, ROBERT	BAL	384	8TH WARD
NEWTON, ROSETTA	BAL	066	4TH WARD
NEWTON, S.	BAL	307	12TH WAR
NEWTON, SALLY	WOR	263	BERLIN 1
NEWTON, SARAH	DOR	374	1ST DIST
NEWTON, SUSAN A.	WOR	266	BERLIN 1
NEWTON, THOMAS	DOR	422	1ST DIST
NEWTON, THOMAS	BAL	158	16TH WAR
NEWTON, THOMAS	BAL	221	12TH WAR
NEWTON, THOMAS	ANN	425	HOWARD D
NEWTON, WILLIAM	BAL	069	1ST WARD
NEWTON, WILLIAM	BAL	284	1ST DIST
NEWTON, WILLIAM	BAL	109	18TH WAR
NEWTON, WILLIAM	FRE	385	PETERSVI
NEWTON, WILLIAM	FRE	397	PETERSVI
NEWTON, WILLIAM	DOR	296	1ST DIST
NEWTON, WILLIAM	BAL	176	19TH WAR
NEWTON, WILLIAM F.	DOR	319	1ST DIST
NEWTON, WILLIAM J.	BAL	176	19TH WAR
NEWTON, WILLIAM J.	KEN	280	3RD DIST
NEWTON, WILLIAM Q.	ST	261	3RD E DI
NEWWORKS, WILLIAM	BAL	103	15TH WAR
NEWZINK, CHARLES	BAL	147	1ST WARD
NFENZ, LEWIS	FRE	024	FREDERIC
NIADY, JOHN	BAL	147	11TH WAR
NIAL, ELIZABETH	CAR	151	NO TWP L
NIBERT, FREDERICK	BAL	348	13TH WAR
NIBET, CHARLES	BAL	434	8TH WARD
NIBLER, JOSHUA	WOR	227	4TH E DI
NIBLET, CHARELS H.	WOR	238	6TH E DI
NIBLET, HENRY W.	WOR	210	4TH E DI
NIBLET, HESTER E.	WOR	202	4TH E DI
NIBLET, JAMES	WOR	231	6TH E DI
NIBLET, JENKINS H.	WOR	210	4TH E DI
NIBLET, JOHN	BAL	300	7TH WARD
NIBLET, MARY A.	BAL	300	7TH WARD
NIBLET, RICHARD	WOR	211	4TH E DI
NIBLET, WILLIAM J.	WOR	231	6TH E DI
NIBLET, WILSON	WOR	202	4TH E DI
NIBLOCK, JOHN	CEC	156	PORT DUP
NIBLOCK, WILLIAM	BAL	280	2ND WARD
NICADEMUS, SAMUEL	WAS	273	RIDGEVIL
NICAHSON, ELISHA	CAR	123	NO TWP L
NICALS, BENJAMIN	CAR	153	NO TWP L
NICALS, DANIEL	CAR	122	NO TWP L
NICALS, EDWARD	CAR	122	NO TWP L
NICALS, HENRY	CAR	113	NO TWP L
NICALS, JOHN	CAR	138	NO TWP L
NICALS, JOHN	CAR	155	NO TWP L
NICALS, ROBERT	CAR	153	NO TWP L
NICE, AUGUSTSU	BAL	412	8TH WARD
NICE, CATHERINE	BAL	270	7TH WARD
NICE, JANE	BAL	305	20TH WAR
NICE, MARY C.	BAL	426	8TH WARD
NICE, ROBERT V.	BAL	033	1ST WARD
NICELS, RODY	CAR	120	NO TWP L
NICELY, ABRAM	ALL	178	7TH E.D.
NICELY, JULIANN	ALL	247	CUMBERLA
NICELY, REBECCA	ALL	179	7TH E.D.
NICELY, WILLIAM	ALL	127	4TH E.D.
NICERSON, JAMES	CAR	100	NO TWP L
NICH, EBLANE	BAL	237	2ND WARD
NICHADEMUS, CONRAD	WAS	200	1ST DIST
NICHADEMUS, THOMAS	WAS	200	1ST DIST
NICHALES, ANN	MGM	384	ROCKERLE
NICHOLSON, JO. *	BAL	307	20TH WAR
NICHE, JOHN	CEC	084	CHARLEST
NICHELSON, HENRY	BAL	298	7TH WARD
NICHELSON, HENRY	BAL	322	7TH WARD
NICHEOLES, JAMES	HAR	193	3RD DIST
NICHER, ADAM *	BAL	310	12TH WAR
NICHKERSON, SUSAN	BAL	162	11TH WAR
NICHODEMUS, ANDREW	CAR	393	2ND DIST
NICHODEMUS, ANN M.	CAR	358	9TH DIST
NICHODEMUS, HAMILTON	CAR	411	2ND DIST
NICHODEMUS, NANCY	CAR	394	2ND DIST
NICHODEMUS, SUSANNA	FRE	438	8TH E DI
NICHOL, DAVID	BAL	018	1ST WARD
NICHOL, ELIZABETH	BAL	324	3RD WARD
NICHOL, JANE	BAL	143	2ND DIST
NICHOL, MATILDA	BAL	144	2ND DIST
NICHOLAS, AQUILLA	BAL	153	2ND DIST
NICHOLAS, CHARLES A.	BAL	229	6TH WARD
NICHOLAS, CINDERELLA	BAL	150	11TH WAR
NICHOLAS, COL J.	ANN	283	ANNAPOLI
NICHOLAS, COLLIN	CAR	191	4TH DIST
NICHOLAS, D.	BAL	316	12TH WAR
NICHOLAS, ELIZABETH	MGM	426	MEDLEY 3
NICHOLAS, GEORGE	BAL	035	18TH WAR
NICHOLAS, GDEORGE	FRE	217	BUCKEYST
NICHOLAS, HENRY	WAS	255	1ST DIST
NICHOLAS, HERHENA	BAL	332	7TH WARD
NICHOLAS, JAMES	BAL	064	1ST WARD
NICHOLAS, JAMES	BAL	224	1ST DIST
NICHOLAS, JANE	MGM	421	MEDLEY 3
NICHOLAS, JOHN	CAR	192	4TH DIST
NICHOLAS, JOHN	BAL	243	6TH WARD
NICHOLAS, JOHN J.	FRE	210	BUCKEYST
NICHOLAS, JOHN SPEAR	BAL	107	10TH WAR
NICHOLAS, LAVINA	BAL	187	11TH WAR
NICHOLAS, LEWIS	CAR	262	3RD DIST
NICHOLAS, M.S.	BAL	284	12TH WAR
NICHOLAS, MATHIAS	WAS	256	1ST DIST
NICHOLAS, MICHAEL	BAL	241	12TH WAR
NICHOLAS, MICHAEL	BAL	359	13TH WAR
NICHOLAS, PHILIP	BAL	140	19TH WAR
NICHOLAS, REBECCA	FRE	217	BUCKEYST
NICHOLAS, ROBERT	BAL	223	17TH WAR
NICHOLAS, SAMUEL P.	MGM	432	CLARKSTR
NICHOLAS, SARAH	BAL	248	1ST DIST
NICHOLAS, SARAH	BAL	009	EASTERN
NICHOLAS, SEBASTIAN	BAL	304	3RD WARD
NICHOLAS, SIMON SR.	MGM	417	MEDLEY 3
NICHOLAS, THOMAS	FRE	233	BUCKEYST
NICHOLAS, WILLIAM	BAL	122	1ST WARD
NICHOLAS, WILLIAM	ALL	215	CUMBERLA
NICHOLAS, WILLIAM H.	MGM	421	MEDLEY 3
NICHOLAS, WILSON N.	BAL	151	11TH WAR
NICHOLAS,CAMDEN P.	MGM	418	MEDLEY 3
NICHOLASON, DAVID	QUE	235	4TH E DI
NICHOLDEMUS, ISAAC C.	FRE	434	8TH E DI

Name	Co.	No.	District
NICHOLDEMUS, VALENTINE	FRE	437	8TH E DI
NICHOLDEMUS, WASHINGTON	FRE	435	8TH E DI
NICHOLDSON, ELLENER D.	BAL	114	18TH WAR
NICHOLDSON, THOMAS	BAL	113	18TH WAR
NICHOLES, JOSEPH	HAR	200	3RD DIST
NICHOLES, LEAH K.	MGM	441	CLARKSTR
NICHOLES, LEMUEL	MGM	443	CLARKSTR
NICHOLES, THOMAS	ANN	477	HOWARD D
NICHOLL, WILLIAM	BAL	386	8TH WARD
NICHOLLAS, CATHERINE	WOR	199	8TH E DI
NICHOLLS, AUGUSTSU	BAL	361	13TH WAR
NICHOLLS, ELLEN	BAL	340	13TH WAR
NICHOLLS, FANNY	BAL	175	11TH WAR
NICHOLLS, GEORGE	WOR	181	6TH E DI
NICHOLLS, JAMES D.	WOR	172	6TH E DI
NICHOLLS, JAMES K.	MGM	365	BERRYS D
NICHOLLS, JOSEPH	ALL	103	5TH E.D.
NICHOLLS, JOSEPH	ALL	100	5TH E.D.
NICHOLLS, JOSEPH	ALL	100	5TH E.D.
NICHOLLS, LEAH E.	WOR	173	6TH E DI
NICHOLLS, MARY	PRI	029	VANSVILL
NICHOLLS, NANCY	WOR	237	6TH E DI
NICHOLLS, ROBERT	MGM	331	CRACKLIN
NICHOLLS, SALLY	WOR	197	8TH E DI
NICHOLLS, THOMAS	BAL	173	11TH WAR
NICHOLLS, WILLIAM J.	BAL	166	2ND DIST
NICHOLLSON, ELIJAH	WOR	169	6TH E DI.
NICHOLLSON, WILLIAM	WOR	175	6TH E DI
NICHOLS, ABBY	BAL	079	10TH WAR
NICHOLS, ADAM	BAL	386	3RD WARD
NICHOLS, ADOLPH	BAL	287	1ST DIST
NICHOLS, ANDREW	CEC	214	7TH E DI
NICHOLS, ANN	ANN	446	HOWARD D
NICHOLS, ANN	QUE	184	3RD E DI
NICHOLS, ANNA M.	BAL	031	15TH WAR
NICHOLS, ARCHIBALD	MGM	444	CLARKSTR
NICHOLS, ARNOLD	CEC	005	ELKTON 3
NICHOLS, B.	BAL	162	1ST WARD
NICHOLS, BENJAMIN B.	BAL	384	3RD WARD
NICHOLS, CAROLINE	FRE	156	10TH E D
NICHOLS, CASPER	BAL	292	7TH WARD
NICHOLS, CATHERINE	BAL	061	10TH WAR
NICHOLS, CATHERINE	MGM	355	BERRYS D
NICHOLS, CELIA	QUE	216	3RD E DI
NICHOLS, CHARLES	BAL	286	12TH WAR
NICHOLS, CHARLES	BAL	293	3RD WARD
NICHOLS, CHARLES D.	BAL	376	3RD WARD
NICHOLS, CHARLES-MULATTO	BAL	208	2ND WARD
NICHOLS, CONRAD	BAL	402	14TH WAR
NICHOLS, CORNELIUS	BAL	045	4TH WARD
NICHOLS, D.	PRI	122	PISCATAW
NICHOLS, DAVID	BAL	126	1ST WARD
NICHOLS, DEBORAH	ALL	239	CUMBERLA
NICHOLS, DIANAH	BAL	302	7TH WARD
NICHOLS, E.	BAL	148	1ST WARD
NICHOLS, E.H.	BAL	130	1ST WARD
NICHOLS, EASTER	BAL	049	15TH WAR
NICHOLS, ELIAS	SOM	501	SALISBUR
NICHOLS, ELIJA	BAL	126	1ST WARD
NICHOLS, ELIZA	BAL	265	20TH WAR
NICHOLS, ELIZABETH	MGM	381	ROCKERLE
NICHOLS, ELIZABETH	PRI	078	MARLBROU
NICHOLS, F.	BAL	129	1ST WARD
NICHOLS, HANNAH	BAL	310	3RD WARD
NICHOLS, HARRIET	TAL	072	EASTON T
NICHOLS, HECTY	BAL	234	20TH WAR
NICHOLS, HENRY	WAS	257	1ST DIST
NICHOLS, HENRY	BAL	257	6TH WARD
NICHOLS, HENRY	BAL	145	1ST WARD
NICHOLS, HENRY	BAL	029	9TH WARD
NICHOLS, HENRY	ANN	479	HOWARD D
NICHOLS, HENRY	BAL	089	15TH WAR
NICHOLS, HENRY	BAL	305	12TH WAR
NICHOLS, ISAAC	ANN	321	2ND DIST
NICHOLS, ISAAC	SOM	498	SALISBUR
NICHOLS, ISAAC	SOM	489	SALISBUR
NICHOLS, JACOB	MGM	424	MEDLEY 3
NICHOLS, JAMES	CEC	198	7TH E DI
NICHOLS, JAMES	CEC	196	6TH E DI
NICHOLS, JEREMIAH	BAL	123	1ST WARD
NICHOLS, JERRY-BLACK	BAL	245	2ND WARD
NICHOLS, JOHN	ANN	318	2ND DIST
NICHOLS, JOHN	BAL	113	15TH WAR
NICHOLS, JOHN	BAL	201	6TH WARD
NICHOLS, JOHN	CEC	198	7TH E DI
NICHOLS, JOHN B.	ANN	318	2ND DIST
NICHOLS, JONATHAN	SOM	502	SALISBUR
NICHOLS, JOSEPH	FRE	357	CATOCTIN
NICHOLS, JOSHUA	SOM	502	SALISBUR
NICHOLS, LAWRENCE P.	BAL	122	1ST WARD
NICHOLS, M.	BAL	148	1ST WARD
NICHOLS, MARGARET	SOM	431	PRINCESS
NICHOLS, MARGARET MRS-	ANN	372	4TH DIST
NICHOLS, MARTHA	BAL	209	19TH WAR
NICHOLS, MARY	CEC	199	7TH E DI
NICHOLS, MARY	CAL	012	1ST DIST
NICHOLS, MARY	BAL	221	1ST DIST
NICHOLS, MARY A.	BAL	448	8TH WARD
NICHOLS, MATILDA	BAL	343	1ST DIST
NICHOLS, PERE	QUE	216	3RD E DI
NICHOLS, PETGER	FRE	061	FREDERIC
NICHOLS, R.	BAL	159	1ST WARD
NICHOLS, R.	BAL	171	1ST WARD
NICHOLS, RACHAEL A.	BAL	014	15TH WAR
NICHOLS, RICHARD	BAL	174	1ST WARD
NICHOLS, RICHARD	BAL	402	3RD WARD
NICHOLS, RICHARD	SOM	405	DUBLIN D
NICHOLS, RICHARD	CEC	137	6TH E DI
NICHOLS, RICHARD	PRI	072	MARLBROU
NICHOLS, ROBERT	BAL	050	9TH WARD
NICHOLS, ROSETTA	BAL	080	4TH WARD
NICHOLS, SAMUEL	CAR	150	NO TWP L
NICHOLS, SAMUEL	CEC	198	7TH E DI
NICHOLS, SAMUEL	CAR	188	4TH DIST
NICHOLS, SAMUEL	BAL	260	6TH WARD
NICHOLS, SAMUEL	ANN	481	HOWARD D
NICHOLS, SAMUEL	WAS	067	2ND SUBD
NICHOLS, SARAH	BAL	138	11TH WAR
NICHOLS, SARAH	CEC	182	7TH E DI
NICHOLS, SARAH C.	MGM	443	CLARKSTR
NICHOLS, SETH	FRE	035	FREDERIC
NICHOLS, SOPHIA A.	BAL	450	8TH WARD
NICHOLS, THEODORE	FRE	254	NEW MARK
NICHOLS, THOMAS	BAL	162	1ST WARD
NICHOLS, THOMAS	QUE	216	3RD E DI
NICHOLS, THOMAS	QUE	216	3RD E DI
NICHOLS, THOMAS F.	QUE	184	3RD E DI
NICHOLS, WARREN	BAL	060	10TH WAR
NICHOLS, WILLIAM	BAL	105	15TH WAR
NICHOLS, WILLIAM	ANN	319	2ND DIST
NICHOLS, WILLIAM	FRE	039	FREDERIC
NICHOLS, WILLIAM	BAL	315	20TH WAR
NICHOLS, WILLIAM	CEC	198	7TH E DI
NICHOLS, WILLIAM	FRE	100	FREDERIC
NICHOLS, WILLIAM H.-MULAT	BAL	223	2ND WARD
NICHOLS, WILLIAM W.	CEC	199	7TH E DI
NICHOLS,JOHN	FRE	041	FREDERIC
NICHOLS,SETH C.	BAL	164	1ST WARD
NICHOLSON, ALEXANDER	BAL	338	7TH WARD
NICHOLSON, ALEXANDER	BAL	408	14TH WAR
NICHOLSON, ANDREW	BAL	445	14TH WAR
NICHOLSON, ANDREW	BAL	446	14TH WAR
NICHOLSON, ANN E.	BAL	378	3RD WARD
NICHOLSON, ARCHIBALD	BAL	280	7TH WARD
NICHOLSON, ARTHUR	BAL	306	1ST DIST
NICHOLSON, BAKER	MGM	418	MEDLEY 3
NICHOLSON, BENJAMIN	BAL	286	12TH WAR
NICHOLSON, BENJAMIN	QUE	222	4TH E DI
NICHOLSON, BENJAMIN S.	ANN	294	1ST DIST
NICHOLSON, CAROLINE	WAS	257	1ST DIST
NICHOLSON, CAROLINE	BAL	197	19TH WAR
NICHOLSON, CHARLES	BAL	303	7TH WARD
NICHOLSON, CHARLES	BAL	164	1ST WARD
NICHOLSON, CHARLES	BAL	231	6TH WARD
NICHOLSON, CHARLES	BAL	254	1ST DIST
NICHOLSON, EDWIN	BAL	226	19TH WAR
NICHOLSON, EDWIN	BAL	040	4TH WARD
NICHOLSON, ELEY	BAL	220	12TH WAR
NICHOLSON, ELIZABETH	BAL	272	2ND WARD
NICHOLSON, ELIZABETH	BAL	105	10TH WAR
NICHOLSON, ELIZABETH	BAL	136	16TH WAR
NICHOLSON, ELLEN	BAL	318	20TH WAR
NICHOLSON, EMERSON	BAL	051	9TH WARD
NICHOLSON, H. W.	BAL	333	1ST DIST
NICHOLSON, HARRIET	MGM	439	CLARKSTR
NICHOLSON, HENRY	ANN	342	3RD DIST
NICHOLSON, HOPPER	QUE	190	3RD E DI
NICHOLSON, ISAIAH	BAL	083	4TH WARD
NICHOLSON, J.	BAL	139	1ST WARD
NICHOLSON, J.	BAL	129	1ST WARD
NICHOLSON, JACOB C.	BAL	020	4TH WARD
NICHOLSON, JAMES	MGM	430	CLARKSTR
NICHOLSON, JAMES	BAL	116	18TH WAR
NICHOLSON, JAMES	ANN	294	1ST DIST
NICHOLSON, JAMES	MGM	444	CLARKSTR
NICHOLSON, JAMES	SOM	501	SALISBUR
NICHOLSON, JAMES	QUE	228	4TH E DI
NICHOLSON, JOHN	ANN	475	HOWARD D
NICHOLSON, JOHN	BAL	124	16TH WAR
NICHOLSON, JOHN	CEC	032	CHESAPEA
NICHOLSON, JOHN H.	QUE	190	3RD E DI
NICHOLSON, JOHNT.	MGM	421	MEDLEY 3
NICHOLSON, JOSEPH	TAL	017	EASTON D
NICHOLSON, JOSEPH	ANN	328	2ND DIST
NICHOLSON, JOSEPH H.	QUE	209	3RD E DI
NICHOLSON, JOSEPH J. REV-	SOM	425	PRINCESS
NICHOLSON, LAURA	BAL	104	10TH WAR
NICHOLSON, LOTT	ANN	475	HOWARD D
NICHOLSON, LOYD H.	MGM	421	MEDLEY 3
NICHOLSON, MALACHI	BAL	121	16TH WAR
NICHOLSON, MARIA	BAL	197	19TH WAR
NICHOLSON, MARY	BAL	318	20TH WAR
NICHOLSON, MARY A.	MGM	420	MEDLEY 3
NICHOLSON, MIRANDA	MGM	420	MEDLEY 3
NICHOLSON, N.	ANN	283	ANNAPOLI
NICHOLSON, N.	BAL	150	1ST WARD
NICHOLSON, NICHOLAS	ANN	296	1ST DIST
NICHOLSON, NICHOLAS	BAL	148	16TH WAR
NICHOLSON, RICHARD	BAL	389	1ST DIST
NICHOLSON, RICHARD C.	ANN	476	HOWARD D
NICHOLSON, ROBERT	KEN	229	2ND DIST
NICHOLSON, SAMUEL T.	BAL	219	12TH WAR
NICHOLSON, SARAH	BAL	180	6TH WARD
NICHOLSON, SARAH	BAL	258	1ST DIST
NICHOLSON, SARAH	MGM	432	CLARKSTR
NICHOLSON, SARAH	KEN	270	1ST DIST
NICHOLSON, SIMMONS	QUE	226	4TH E DI
NICHOLSON, SOMERVILLE	ANN	295	1ST DIST
NICHOLSON, SUSAN	BAL	053	15TH WAR
NICHOLSON, SUSAN	BAL	081	15TH WAR
NICHOLSON, THADDEUS	BAL	030	4TH WARD
NICHOLSON, THOMAS	BAL	146	19TH WAR
NICHOLSON, THOMAS F.	BAL	303	3RD WARD
NICHOLSON, WILLIAM	BAL	165	16TH WAR
NICHOLSON, WILLIAM	BAL	302	3RD WARD
NICHOLSON, WILLIAM	BAL	031	15TH WAR
NICHOLSON, WILLIAM	BAL	261	12TH WAR
NICHOLSON, WILLIAM	BAL	038	1ST WARD
NICHOLSON, WILLIAM	CEC	032	CHESAPEA
NICHOLSON, WILLIAM	MGM	438	CLARKSTR
NICHOLSON, WILLIAM H.	BAL	210	2ND WARD
NICHOLSON,HENRY	BAL	135	1ST WARD
NICHORSON, JOHN L.	QUE	132	1ST E DI
NICHORSON, NOAH	QUE	132	1ST E DI
NICHORSON, THOMAS-BLACK	QUE	158	2ND E DI
NICHOSEN, MARGARET	QUE	130	1ST E DI
NICHOSON, ADAM	WAS	110	2ND DIST
NICHOSON, JAMES	WAS	110	2ND DIST
NICHOSON, JOHN	QUE	129	1ST E DI
NICHOSON, JOHN JR.	QUE	168	2ND E DI
NICHOSON, JOHN T.	QUE	130	1ST E DI
NICHOSON, LAMBERT	WAS	109	2ND DIST
NICHOSON, MARY E.	QUE	168	2ND E DI
NICHOSON, MARY J.	QUE	178	2ND E DI
NICHOSON, MILLY	WAS	110	2ND DIST
NICHOSON, SAMUEL P.	QUE	131	1ST E DI
NICHOSSON, VINCENT	QUE	128	1ST E DI
NICK, E.A.	BAL	163	1ST WARD
NICK, WILLIAM	WOR	189	7TH E DI
NICKADEMUS, JACOB	WAS	190	1ST DIST
NICKADEMUS, JOHN	WAS	190	1ST DIST
NICKAL, D.	PRI	049	AQUASCO
NICKAM, JAMES H.	FRE	175	5TH E DI
NICKEESON, JOSEPH	BAL	421	14TH WAR
NICKEL, JACOB	FRE	101	FREDERIC
NICKELL, ROBERT	BAL	173	11TH WAR
NICKELLS, AMELIA	BAL	172	11TH WAR
NICKELS, CATHRINE	WOR	242	1ST CENS
NICKELS, JAMES	KEN	286	3RD DIST
NICKELS, JOHN	WAS	084	2ND SUBD
NICKELS, MARRY	WAS	068	2ND SUBD
NICKELS, NANCY	WOR	242	1ST CENS
NICKELS, NATHANIEL	WOR	242	1ST CENS
NICKELSON, JOHNJ.	BAL	406	14TH WAR
NICKELSON, THOMAS	WOR	304	SNOW HIL
NICKERING, E. C. K.	BAL	328	13TH WAR
NICKERS, R.	BAL	169	1ST WARD
NICKERSAN, JOHN H.	BAL	045	9TH WARD
NICKERSEON, WILLIAM	WOR	205	4TH E DI
NICKERSON, CHARLES	BAL	059	10TH WAR
NICKERSON, CHARLES	BAL	121	18TH WAR
NICKERSON, GEORGE	BAL	051	18TH WAR
NICKERSON, GEORGE L.	BAL	060	18TH WAR
NICKERSON, HANNAH	QUE	151	1ST E DI
NICKERSON, HESTER	ANN	265	ANNAPOLI
NICKERSON, JANE	BAL	129	11TH WAR
NICKERSON, JOHN	BAL	060	18TH WAR
NICKERSON, LAMBERT	KEN	303	3RD DIST
NICKERSON, LIDIA	BAL	201	11TH WAR
NICKERSON, PAMELIA A.	BAL	350	13TH WAR
NICKERSON, REBECCA	WAS	007	WILLIAMS
NICKERSON, RIDGELEY	QUE	133	1ST E DI
NICKERSON, T.	BAL	135	1ST WARD
NICKERSON, THOMAS	QUE	153	1ST E DI
NICKERSON, THOMAS	BAL	045	18TH WAR
NICKERSON, WILLIAM H.	BAL	137	1ST WARD
NICKERSON, WILLIAM P.	QUE	139	1ST E DI
NICKERSON, WILLIAM R.	QUE	136	1ST E DI
NICKERSON,MATILDA	QUE	140	1ST E DI
NICKINS, LEVI	CEC	214	7TH E DI
NICKLAS, GEORGE	BAL	223	6TH WARD
NICKLE, ADAM	FRE	015	FREDERIC
NICKLERAN, BERNARD	BAL	231	2ND WARD
NICKLESS, SARAH	BAL	205	11TH WAR
NICKODEMUS, JACOB	WAS	086	2ND SUBD
NICKOFF, JACOB	BAL	174	19TH WAR
NICKOLLS, ANN	BAL	252	17TH WAR
NICKOLLS, FRANK	BAL	099	5TH WARD
NICKOLLS, HENESLEY	BAL	248	17TH WAR
NICKOLLS, J. SMITH	BAL	175	11TH WAR
NICKOLLS, ZACHARAY	BAL	243	17TH WAR
NICKOLLSON, JOHN	WOR	217	4TH E DI
McICKOLS, HENRY	BAL	116	5TH WARD
NICKOLS, JACOB	WAS	070	2ND SUBD
NICKOLS, JAMES	BAL	117	5TH WARD
NICKOLS, MARY	BAL	116	5TH WARD
NICKOLS, MRS.	BAL	116	5TH WARD
NICKOLS, THOMAS	BAL	110	2ND DIST
NICKOLSON, ABRAHAZM	BAL	009	EASTERN
NICKOLSON, CHARLES	BAL	121	5TH WARD
NICKOLSON, ELIZABETH	WAS	077	2ND SUBD
NICKOLSON, FRANCIS	BAL	115	5TH WARD
NICKOLSON, ISAAC	BAL	130	5TH WARD
NICKOLSON, ISAAC	BAL	130	5TH WARD
NICKOLSON, R.	BAL	151	1ST WARD
NICKS, MICHAEL	BAL	235	17TH WAR
NICKSON, JIM*	TAL	010	EASTON D
NICKUL, JOHN	BAL	256	17TH WAR
NICKUM, ELIZA	FRE	160	EMMITTSB
NICKUM, ELIZABETH	FRE	160	EMMITTSB
NICKUM, JOHN D.	FRE	160	EMMITTSB
NICKUM, JOSEPH	FRE	160	EMMITTSB
NICKUM, MARY	FRE	160	EMMITTSB
NICKUM, SOPHIA	FRE	161	EMMITTSB
NICOALS, WASHINGTON	CAR	122	NO TWP L
NICODEMUS, CATHARINE *	CAR	286	7TH DIST
NICODEMUS, DAVID	CAR	286	7TH DIST
NICODEMUS, FREDRICK	WAS	103	2ND DIST
NICODEMUS, HENRY	CAR	285	7TH DIST
NICODEMUS, J.C.	BAL	236	12TH WAR
NICODEMUS, JOHN	FRE	144	10TH E D
NICODEMUS, JOHN	FRE	040	FREDERIC
NICODEMUS, NATHAN	CAR	285	7TH DIST
NICODEMUS, PHILIP	CAR	285	7TH DIST
NICODEMUS, SUSAN	FRE	145	10TH E D
NICODERMUS, JERRY	BAL	235	12TH WAR
NICOL, W.W.	HAR	151	3RD DIST
NICOL, WILLIAM	BAL	333	3RD WARD
NICOLAI, HENRY	BAL	101	15TH WAR
NICOLAI, HENRY JR.	BAL	102	15TH WAR
NICOLAI, MARGARET	BAL	105	15TH WAR
NICOLAS, MARGARET	BAL	403	3RD WARD
NICOLES, ANN J.	TAL	052	EASTON D
NICOLES, ELIZABETH	TAL	061	EASTON D
NICOLES, HARIATE	DOR	413	1ST DIST
NICOLES, ISAAC	DOR	447	1ST DIST
NICOLES, JAMES	DOR	441	1ST DIST
NICOLES, JAMES	TAL	051	EASTON D
NICOLES, JANE	TAL	045	EASTON T
NICOLES, JOHN	TAL	038	EASTON D
NICOLES, JOSEPH M.	DOR	437	1ST DIST
NICOLES, MAHALA	DOR	390	1ST DIST
NICOLES, PRISSY	TAL	022	EASTON D
NICOLES, ROBERT*	DOR	437	1ST DIST
NICOLES, WILLIAM	DOR	445	1ST DIST
NICOLL, NELSON	BAL	280	2ND WARD
NICOLL, WILLIAM	BAL	406	3RD WARD
NICOLLS, ADELINE	HAR	119	2ND DIST
NICOLLS, DANIEL	KEN	294	3RD DIST
NICOLLS, ROBERT*	DOR	437	1ST DIST
NICOLS, CAROLINE	TAL	093	ST MICHA
NICOLS, DANIEL	CAR	145	NO TWP L
NICOLS, E. A.	TAL	069	EASTON T
NICOLS, EDWARD-BLACK	CAR	157	NO TWP L
NICOLS, ELIZA	CAR	158	NO TWP L
NICOLS, ELIZABETH	TAL	051	EASTON D
NICOLS, FLORA	DOR	384	1ST DIST
NICOLS, GABRIEL*	DOR	413	1ST DIST
NICOLS, GEORGE	ANN	389	4TH DIST
NICOLS, GEORGE	BAL	152	2ND DIST
NICOLS, GRACE	TAL	072	EASTON T
NICOLS, HENERITTA	DOR	320	1ST DIST
NICOLS, HENRY M.	TAL	009	EASTON D
NICOLS, HESTER-BLACK	CAR	146	NO TWP L
NICOLS, JAMES	CAR	153	NO TWP L
NICOLS, JAMES	DOR	421	1ST DIST
NICOLS, JAMES H.	CAR	124	NO TWP L
NICOLS, JAMES R.	DOR	308	1ST DIST
NICOLS, JEREMIAH	DOR	315	1ST DIST
NICOLS, JEREMIAH	KEN	262	1ST DIST
NICOLS, JOHN	CAR	125	NO TWP L
NICOLS, JOHN	CAR	157	NO TWP L
NICOLS, JOHN	BAL	169	2ND DIST
NICOLS, JOHN W.	BAL	038	4TH WARD
NICOLS, JONATHAN	CAR	094	NO TWP L
NICOLS, JONES*	DOR	420	1ST DIST
NICOLS, LINDERELLY	CAR	159	NO TWP L
NICOLS, MARGARET	TAL	073	EASTON T
NICOLS, MARGARETT	DOR	297	1ST DIST
NICOLS, MARY	CAR	148	NO TWP L
NICOLS, MARY C.	TAL	041	EASTON D
NICOLS, MARY T.	DOR	318	1ST DIST
NICOLS, MATILDA	BAL	041	4TH WARD
NICOLS, MILLY	DOR	319	1ST DIST
NICOLS, N. E.	TAL	004	EASTON D
NICOLS, NED	DOR	390	1ST DIST
NICOLS, PERE	QUE	245	5TH E DI
NICOLS, PERRY	TAL	034	EASTON D
NICOLS, PRISILLA	TAL	094	ST MICHA
NICOLS, RICHARD	CAR	065	NO TWP L

Name	Co.	Page	Location
NICOLS. RICHARD L.	KEN	256	1ST DIST
NICOLS. ROBERT	CAR	157	NO TWP L
NICOLS. RUTH A.	TAL	046	EASTON T
NICOLS. SARAH	CAR	156	NO TWP L
NICOLS. SENY	CAR	153	NO TWP L
NICOLS. SILAS	CAR	152	NO TWP L
NICOLS. STEPHEN-BLACK	CAR	168	NO TWP L
NICOLS. SUSAN A.	TAL	028	EASTON D
NICOLS. THOMAS	CAR	066	NO TWP L
NICOLS. THOMAS	CAR	120	NO TWP L
NICOLS. THOMAS	DOR	320	1ST DIST
NICOLS. THOMAS-BLACK	CAR	147	NO TWP L
NICOLS. WILLIAM-BLACK	CAR	138	NO TWP L
NICOLS. WILLIAM-BLACK	CAR	167	NO TWP L
NICOLSON, ALBERT	BAL	447	14TH WAR
NICOLSON. CHARLES R.	CAR	149	NO TWP L
NICOLSON. WILLIAM G.	CAR	148	NO TWP L
NIDEN. REBECCA	CEC	195	6TH E DI
NIDER. MARY	BAL	123	2ND DIST
NIEBLING. ELIZA	BAL	349	13TH WAR
NIEBLING. SALINA	BAL	349	13TH WAR
NIEBOHR, C.	BAL	109	10TH WAR
NIEL. RAHCEL	ANN	317	1ST DIST
NIELL, FREDERIC	BAL	219	6TH WARD
NIELL. WILLIAM	FRE	113	CREAGERS
NIELSON, THEOPHILUS	BAL	018	1ST WARD
NIELSON, WILLIAM	BAL	163	1ST WARD
NIEMEYER. BERNARD	BAL	019	9TH WARD
NIER. PERRY M.	CAR	268	WESTMINS
NIERMAN, HENRY	BAL	367	13TH WAR
NIERN, JOSEPH	BAL	081	10TH WAR
NIERUREE. JOHN R.	BAL	356	13TH WAR
NIESHEY, HENRY	BAL	018	9TH WARD
NIET, ABSALOM	WAS	064	2ND SUBD
NIGENT, ANN *	BAL	284	20TH WAR
NIGER. GORGE	BAL	079	2ND DIST
NIGER. MARY	CEC	076	NORTHEAS
NIGER. TABIN *	BAL	306	12TH WAR
NIGH. ARMEAT	BAL	011	18TH WAR
NIGH. GEORGE N.	CEC	069	5TH E DI
NIGHBOURS. MARY C.*	TAL	055	EASTON D
NIGHT. DENNIS	ANN	388	4TH DIST
NIGHT. ELIZA	WAS	174	FUNKSTOW
NIGHT. JAMES	DOR	369	3RD DIVI
NIGHT. JOHN	BAL	460	1ST DIST
NIGHT. NATHAN	BAL	365	1ST DIST
NIGHT. ORMAN	BAL	290	1ST DIST
NIGHTHART. FREDERICK	BAL	267	17TH WAR
NIGHTHEART. GERTRUDE	ALL	244	CUMBERLA
NIGHTINGALE. HARRIET L.	BAL	383	13TH WAR
NIGHTON, E.	ANN	270	ANNAPOLI
NIGHTON, J.	PRI	062	NOTTINGH
NIGHTON, NICHOLAS	BAL	290	17TH WAR
NIGLE. JACOB	BAL	220	2ND WARD
NIHAFER, CASPER	CAR	341	6TH DIST
NIHBERGER. CHARLES	BAL	411	14TH WAR
NIHBURGER. CHRISTIANA	BAL	411	14TH WAR
NIHOFF. GEORGE F.	BAL	010	18TH WAR
NIHOLSON. WALTER	MGM	444	CLARKSTR
NIKEL. ADAM	ALL	210	CUMBERLA
NIKIRK, MARY	WAS	201	1ST DIST
NILE,S JOHNA.	FRE	029	FREDERIC
NILES, ELIZABETH	BAL	423	14TH WAR
NILES. GEORGE W.	FRE	445	8TH E DI
NILES. HARY A.	BAL	014	9TH WARD
NILES. HENRY	BAL	378	13TH WAR
NILES. MARGARET	BAL	207	2ND WARD
NILING. SOLOMON	CAL	012	1ST DIST
NILLEY, JOHN	BAL	022	1ST WARD
NILSON. JOHN	KEN	246	2ND DIST
NILSON. JOHN	FRE	098	FREDERIC
NILSON. SAMUEL	BAL	115	2ND DIST
NIMAKER, JACOB	BAL	251	1ST DIST
NIMBLY, ELLEN	KEN	261	1ST DIST
NIME, ELIZABETH	BAL	248	2ND WARD
NIMLY. JERRY	KEN	256	1ST DIST
NIMMO. JOSEPH*	BAL	112	10TH WAR
NIMMS, JOHN	BAL	046	9TH WARD
NIMMS, JOSEPH*	BAL	112	10TH WAR
NIMMS, THOMAS	BAL	329	13TH WAR
NIMMY, SAMUEL	WAS	159	HAGERSTO
NIMMY, SAMUEL	WAS	157	HAGERSTO
NIMS. WILLIAM G.	BAL	049	1ST WARD
NINCLE. ALBERT	WOR	319	1ST E DI
NINDE. JAMES	BAL	035	9TH WARD
NINE, JEROME	BAL	125	1ST WARD
NINE. JOHN	BAL	204	2ND WARD
NINE. SOPHIE	BAL	300	20TH WAR
NINGERTH, FRED	BAL	180	11TH WAR
NINGLE. E. J.	ANN	337	3RD DIST
NINGLE. J.	BAL	137	1ST WARD
NIPP, CHRISTINE	BAL	185	19TH WAR
NIPPARD. GEORGE	BAL	285	7TH WARD
NIPPARD. GEORGE	BAL	254	6TH WARD
NIPPERJULL, JOHN *	BAL	300	20TH WAR
NIPPERKEN. CHARLES	BAL	193	19TH WAR
NIPPOLD. ANDREW	BAL	155	16TH WAR
NIPPS, MARGARET	BAL	237	17TH WAR
NISBIT, ELIZA	BAL	032	9TH WARD
NISCON, WILLIAM	BAL	119	1ST WARD
NISE. BARBARA	ALL	244	CUMBERLA
NISER. MARY G.	BAL	293	7TH WARD
NISER. WILLIAM	BAL	292	7TH WARD
NISHAFER. CATHERINE	BAL	307	20TH WAR
NISOLS. ANTHONY	TAL	003	EASTON D
NISOLS. ROSE	TAL	072	EASTON T
NISOLS. THOMAS C.	TAL	090	ST MICHA
NISROUERGER. JACOB *	WAS	084	2ND SUBD
NISSON, M.	BAL	318	12TH WAR
NISWANGER. VINCENT	WAS	087	2ND SUBD
NITERHOUSE, MARGARET	WAS	098	2ND DIST
NITZEL, JOHN	WAS	010	WILLIAMS
NITZEL, JOHN	WAS	006	WILLIAMS
NIX. JOHN	BAL	309	7TH WARD
NIX, JOHN	BAL	253	2ND WARD
NIX, JOHN	BAL	205	2ND WARD
NIXDORFF, HENRY	FRE	001	FREDERIC
NIXDORFF, TOEIAS	BAL	016	18TH WAR
NIXON. CHARLES	BAL	114	1ST WARD
NIXON, HUGH	ALL	178	7TH E.D.
NIXON. JACOB	BAL	271	17TH WAR
NIXON. JOHN	MGM	392	ROCKERLE
NIXON. JOHN	BAL	409	8TH WARD
NIXCN. JOSEPH	BAL	200	17TH WAR
NIXON, RICHARD	TAL	052	EASTON D
NIXCN, ROBERT M.	KEN	292	3RD DIST
NLAPORT, JOHN	FRE	264	NEW MARK
NLOSER. JACOB	FRE	351	MIDDLETO
NMOORE, RACHEL A.	DOR	367	3RD DIVI
NOA. BENJAMIN	BAL	281	17TH WAR
NOACK. WILLIAM H.	CEC	051	1ST E DI
NOAN. PATRICK	ALL	053	10TH E.D
NOBB. JOHN H.	BAL	125	1ST WARD
NOBBLE, J. H.	BAL	150	1ST WARD
NOBLE. BENJAMIN	HAR	124	2ND DIST
NOBLE. CHARLES H.	TAL	012	EASTON D
NOBLE. CHRISTIAN	BAL	077	4TH WARD
NOBLE. DANIEL	CAR	164	NO TWP L
NOBLE, DAVID	BAL	278	17TH WAR
NOBLE. ELIZABETH	CAR	078	NO TWP L
NOBLE. FANNY A.	BAL	073	4TH WARD
NOBLE. FRED	BAL	131	2ND DIST
NOBLE. GARY	DOR	320	1ST DIST
NOBLE. HARRIET	BAL	322	7TH WARD
NOBLE. ISAAC	CAR	154	NO TWP L
NOBLE. J.H.	BAL	158	1ST WARD
NOBLE. JAMES	BAL	242	2ND WARD
NOBLE. JAMES	CEC	037	CHESAPEA
NOBLE. JAMES	HAR	166	3RD DIST
NOBLE. JAMES	WOR	238	6TH E DI
NOBLE, JAMES	SOM	510	BARREN C
NOBLE. JOHN	WOR	238	6TH E DI
NOBLE, JOHN	HAR	170	3RD DIST
NOBLE. JOHN	BAL	136	1ST WARD
NOBLE. JOHN	BAL	079	2ND DIST
NOBLE. JOHN H.	BAL	321	7TH WARD
NOBLE. JOSHUA	DOR	322	1ST DIST
NOBLE. MARY	CAL	015	1ST DIST
NOBLE, MARY	BAL	011	9TH WARD
NOBLE. MASON	BAL	190	11TH WAR
NOBLE, NANCY	WOR	238	6TH E DI
NOBLE. NATHAN	CAR	127	NO TWP L
NOBLE. SARAH	HAR	146	3RD DIST
NOBLE, SARAH	SOM	440	DAMES QU
NOBLE. SARAH	SOM	462	HANGARY
NOBLE. SARAH	SOM	470	TRAPPE D
NOBLE. SARAH A.	TAL	012	EASTON D
NOBLE. THOMAS	SOM	488	SALISBUR
NOBLE. THOMAS	CAR	116	NO TWP L
NOBLE, TWIFORD	CAR	155	NO TWP L
NOBLE. WILLIAM	CAR	122	NO TWP L
NOBLE. WILLIAM D.	DOR	316	1ST DIST
NOBLE. WILLIS	CAR	155	NO TWP L
NOBLE,EDWARD	CAR	123	NO TWP L
NOBLES, SAMUEL-BLACK	FRE	219	BUCKEYST
NOBLETT. SARAH	BAL	031	15TH WAR
NOBLETTE. JOHN	BAL	018	15TH WAR
NOCHOLS, J.	BAL	150	1ST WARD
NOCK, SARAH A.	BAL	216	6TH WARD
NOCKEY, JOHN	BAL	125	1ST WARD
NOCKS, JOSEPH	BAL	099	2ND DIST
NOCOCK, JAMES	BAL	119	1ST WARD
NOCODEMUS. JACOB	CAR	284	7TH DIST
NOCTON, THOMAS	ALL	152	6TH E.D.
NODDY. ELEANOR C.	BAL	261	6TH WARD
NODE. JOHN	BAL	133	11TH WAR
NODINE, RICHARD	CEC	047	1ST E DI
NOEL. ANN	BAL	341	13TH WAR
NOEL. E. N. B.	BAL	111	10TH WAR
NOEL. EDWARD	BAL	220	12TH WAR
NOEL. JOHN	BAL	341	13TH WAR
NOEL. MARY L.A.	BAL	205	11TH WAR
NOELS. JACOB	WAS	281	1ST DIST
NOFORD. GABBY	WAS	281	LEITERSB
NOFTIS. PATRICK	BAL	340	1ST DIST
NOGEL. ISAAC	ANN	416	HOWARD D
NOGENGAST. BARBARA	ANN	418	HOWARD D
NOGENGAST. JOHN	ANN	418	HOWARD D
NOGENGAST. MARGARET	ANN	418	HOWARD D
NOGENGAST. MARGARET	ANN	413	HOWARD D
NOGENGAST. MARY	ANN	419	HOWARD D
NOGER. WILLIAM	ANN	416	HOWARD D
NOGERTY. MICHAEL	BAL	270	12TH WAR
NOGLE. JOHN	FRE	146	10TH E D
NOISS. JOHN	BAL	254	2ND WARD
NOIZE. PETER E.	FRE	087	FREDERIC
NOKE. MARIA-BLACK	QUE	182	3RD E DI
NOKE. WILLIAM	QUE	209	3RD E DI
NOKES. CHARLES	KEN	308	3RD DIST
NOKES. GEROGE	KEN	283	3RD DIST
NOKES. MARGARET	FRE	070	FREDERIC
NOKES. MARTHA-BLACK	QUE	124	1ST E DI
NOKES. WILLIAM	MGM	407	MEDLEY 3
NOLAN. CATHERINE	BAL	044	4TH WARD
NOLAN. CHARLES	HAR	016	1ST DIST
NOLAN. ELLEN	BAL	224	12TH WAR
NOLAN. GEORGE A.	BAL	470	14TH WAR
NOLAN. GEORGE H.	BAL	172	1ST WARD
NOLAN. HENRY	BAL	170	2ND DIST
NOLAN. JOHN	BAL	122	1ST WARD
NOLAN. MARY	BAL	160	11TH WAR
NOLAN. MCHAEL	ALL	255	CUMBERLA
NOLAN. PATRICK	BAL	172	11TH WAR
NOLAN. PATRICK	ALL	056	10TH E.D
NOLAN. PATRICK	BAL	026	18TH WAR
NOLAN, THOMAS	ALL	155	6TH E.D.
NOLAND. ALEXANDER-MULATTO	FRE	038	FREDERIC
NOLAND. ANN	ALL	073	5TH E.D.
NOLAND. ANN	BAL	104	10TH WAR
NOLAND. ANN	BAL	292	12TH WAR
NOLAND. BRIDGET	ALL	102	5TH E.D.
NOLAND. BRIDGET	BAL	427	1ST DIST
NOLAND. CAROLINE F.	MGM	360	BERRYS D
NOLAND. CATHERINE	BAL	313	3RD WARD
NOLAND. DANIEL-MULATTO	FRE	025	FREDERIC
NOLAND. DENIS	BAL	312	1ST DIST
NOLAND. EDWARD	BAL	183	16TH WAR
NOLAND. FRANCES	FRE	066	FREDERIC
NOLAND, HENRY	FRE	084	FREDERIC
NOLAND. JAMES	ALL	102	5TH E.D.
NOLAND. JAMES	BAL	028	9TH WARD
NOLAND. JEREMIAH	ALL	183	8TH E.D.
NOLAND. JOHN	ALL	261	CUMBER_A
NOLAND. JOHN	BAL	269	1ST DIST
NOLAND. JOHN C.	BAL	433	8TH WARD
NOLAND. JOHN-BLACK	FRE	041	FREDERIC
NOLAND. MARY M.	BAL	214	11TH WAR
NOLAND. MATTHEW	BAL	367	13TH WAR
NOLAND. MICHAEL	ALL	180	8TH E.D.
NOLAND. RICHARD	BAL	163	1ST WARD
NOLAND. THOAMS	ALL	082	5TH E.D.
NOLAR. RICHARD	BAL	168	1ST WARD
NOLEN, ELIZABETH	BAL	101	2ND DIST
NOLEN. HENRY	BAL	088	15TH WAR
NOLEN. JOHN	BAL	075	10TH WAR
NOLEN. JOSHUA C.	BAL	131	1ST WARD
NOLEN, MICHAEL	WAS	034	2ND SUBD
NOLEN, WILLIAM C.	BAL	039	1ST WARD
NOLER. WILLIAM	BAL	309	20TH WAR
NOLES. BARBARY	WAS	110	2ND DIST
NOLES. THOMAS	CEC	068	5TH E DI
NOLEY. JOHN H.	PRI	115	PISCATAW
NOLIN. HESTER	BAL	118	15TH WAR
NOLIN. MARY	BAL	303	17TH WAR
NOLKA. JOSEPH	BAL	366	13TH WAR
NOLL. GEORGE	CAR	283	7TH DIST
NOLL. SAMUEL H.	BAL	248	12TH WAR
NOLLEY. CHARLES	FRE	307	WOODSBOR
NOLLEY. JOHN	FRE	299	WOODSBOR
NOLLGG. CHARLES	FRE	298	WOODSBOR
NOLLMYER. ANN M.	BAL	427	8TH WARD
NOLLMYER. JOHN F.	BAL	426	8TH WARD
NOLLS. CATHARINE	WAS	136	HAGERSTO
NOLLY. LYDIA	FRE	301	WOODSBOR
NOLS. GEORGE E.	BAL	190	19TH WAR
NOLTE. LEWIS	FRE	055	FREDERIC
NOLTEA. AUGUST	BAL	085	1ST WARD
NOLTEY. FREDERICK	BAL	117	15TH WAR
NOLTZ. HERNY	BAL	090	1ST WARD
NOLY, THOMS	PRI	067	NOTTINGH
NONEMAKER, ANDREW	BAL	228	17TH WAR
NONEMAKER, DANIEL	BAL	413	8TH WARD
NONEMAKER. GEORGE	BAL	413	8TH WARD
NONEMAKER, JONAS	BAL	419	8TH WARD
NONES. HANNAH	BAL	190	6TH WARD
NONES. JOSEPH	BAL	190	6TH WARD
NONIS. JOSEPH*	BAL	305	3RD WARD
NONWOOOD. CATHERINE	FRE	244	NEW MARK
NOODLE, ANN	BAL	275	12TH WAR
NOOL. ADAM	BAL	395	1ST DIST
NOOLEN, EDWARD	BAL	101	5TH WARD
NOON, ANN	BAL	303	3RD WARD
NOON, ANNA	HAR	155	3RD DIST
NOON, HONOR	ALL	049	10TH E.D
NOON, JUDITH	BAL	271	12TH WAR
NOON. OWEN	BAL	273	1ST DIST
NOONAN. CATHERINE	BAL	352	3RD WARD
NOONAN. DENIS	BAL	311	3RD WARD
NOONAN, HANAH	BAL	031	4TH WARD
NOONAN, JOHN	FRE	263	NEW MARK
NOONAN. MARY	BAL	107	10TH WAR
NOONY. MATTHIAS	BAL	400	14TH WAR
NOORE. PATRICK	BAL	299	17TH WAR
NOROMAN, RUDOLPH	BAL	069	10TH WAR
NOROS. GEORGE	BAL	142	2ND DIST
NORE. J.	BAL	148	1ST WARD
NORE. JOHN	BAL	120	1ST WARD
NOREN.MICHEL	BAL	065	2ND DIST
NORFOLK, DINAH	CAL	022	2ND DIST
NORFOLK, ELIZABETH	CAL	021	2ND DIST
NORFOLK, ELIZABETH	CAL	021	2ND DIST
NORFOLK. ELIZABETH	CAL	039	2ND DIST
NORFOLK. GEORGE	CAL	045	3RD DIST
NORFOLK. HEZE	CAL	021	2ND DIST
NORFOLK. JAEMS J.	CAL	021	2ND DIST
NORFOLK. JAMES	CAL	057	3RD DIST
NORFOLK. JAMES	BAL	242	17TH WAR
NORFOLK. JOHN	BAL	261	17TH WAR
NORFOLK. JOHN	CAL	029	2ND DIST
NORFOLK, JOHN	CAL	029	2ND DIST
NORFOLK, JOHN	BAL	408	14TH WAR
NORFOLK. JOHN T.	BAL	294	3RD WARD
NORFOLK. JOHN W.	BAL	035	15TH WAR
NORFOLK. JOSEPH	CAL	063	3RD DIST
NORFOLK, KINSEY	CAL	020	2ND DIST
NORFOLK. MARGARET	CAL	037	2ND DIST
NORFOLK. NATHANIEL	CAL	046	3RD DIST
NORFOLK. OWEN	PRI	091	MARLBROU
NORFOLK. PRINDERWELL	CAL	040	3RD DIST
NORFOLK. RICHARD	ST	349	5TH E DI
NORFOLK. THOMAS H.	BAL	294	3RD WARD
NORFOLK. WILLIAM	ANN	469	HOWARD D
NORINGTON. SARAH	HAR	083	2ND DIST
NORIS, AMELIA G.	BAL	157	11TH WAR
NORIS. KENNEDY O.	BAL	153	11TH WAR
NORIS. MARY	CHA	289	MIDDLETO
NORIS. PENRY	KEN	287	3RD DIST
NORIS. THOMAS	BAL	183	2ND WARD
NORKTON. JOHN	ALL	082	5TH E.D.
NORMA. ADELINE	BAL	118	5TH WARD
NORMAN. A.M.	BAL	015	1ST WARD
NORMAN. BASIL-BLACK	FRE	214	BUCKEYST
NORMAN. CELIA	DOR	434	1ST DIST
NORMAN. ELIZABETH	BAL	217	6TH WARD
NORMAN. GEORGE	BAL	292	17TH WAR
NORMAN. HANNAH	BAL	214	17TH WAR
NORMAN. HENRY	ALL	221	CUMBERLA
NORMAN. HENRY	DOR	461	1ST DIST
NORMAN. HOWARD	CEC	163	6TH E DI
NORMAN. J.D.	BAL	241	12TH WAR
NORMAN. JAMES	ANN	410	8TH DIST
NORMAN. JANE	ANN	406	8TH DIST
NORMAN. JESSE	MGM	403	ROCKERLE
NORMAN. JESSE-BLACK	MGM	415	MEDLEY 3
NORMAN. JOHN	QUE	228	4TH E DI
NORMAN. JOHN R.	BAL	308	3RD WARD
NORMAN. JOSEPH	BAL	220	6TH WARD
NORMAN. MARGARET	BAL	187	11TH WAR
NORMAN. MARY A.	DOR	433	1ST DIST
NORMAN. RICHARD	BAL	099	15TH WAR
NORMAN. RICHARD C.	CHA	238	HILLTOP
NORMAN. SAMUEL	ANN	406	8TH DIST
NORMAN. SAMUEL	BAL	124	5TH WARD
NORMAN. STEPHEN	CEC	194	7TH E DI
NORMAN. SUSAN	DOR	441	1ST DIST
NORMAN. THEOPHILAS	ANN	410	8TH DIST
NORMAN. WALTER	ANN	406	8TH DIST
NORMANY. JULIA A.	CEC	036	CHESAPEA
NORMER. CORNELIUS	BAL	143	1ST WARD
NORMICO. BENJAMIN	BAL	189	2ND WARD
NORMOYLE. THOMAS	BAL	026	18TH WAR
NORON. JOHN*	DOR	425	1ST DIST
NOROTN. PATRICK	ALL	056	10TH E.D
NOROTN. PETER	BAL	346	13TH WAR
NORR. PETER	BAL	131	1ST WARD
NORRFIS. RESHA	HAR	096	2ND DIST
NORRID. DEBORAH	CAR	268	WESTMINS
NORRIS. ABRAHAM-MULATTO	FRE	038	FREDERIC
NORRIS. ALEXANDER	HAR	046	1ST DIST
NORRIS. ALEXANDER	HAR	095	2ND DIST
NORRIS. ALEXANDER	HAR	012	1ST DIST
NORRIS. ALLEN	BAL	373	1ST DIST
NORRIS. AMANDA	WAS	084	2ND SUBD
NORRIS. AMERICA	BAL	436	14TH WAR
NORRIS. ANN	HAR	054	1ST DIST
NORRIS. ANN	WAS	106	2ND DIST
NORRIS. ANN	ST	279	3RD E DI
NORRIS. ANN	BAL	191	11TH WAR
NORRIS. ANN MARIA	CAR	224	5TH DIST
NORRIS. AQUILLA	BAL	432	8TH WARD

NORRIS, ARCHIBALD ANN 467 HOWARD D
NORRIS, ARMON T. FRE 281 WOODSBOR
NORRIS, BARNET T. MGM 406 MEDLEY 3
NORRIS, BASIL FRE 013 FREDERIC
NORRIS, BENJAMIN HAR 024 1ST DIST
NORRIS, BENJAMIN BAL 117 18TH WAR
NORRIS, BENJAMIN BAL 057 2ND DIST
NORRIS, BENJAMIN ANN 519 HOWARD D
NORRIS, BENJAMIN WAS 093 2ND SUBD
NORRIS, BENJAMIN B. BAL 465 14TH WAR
NORRIS, BENJAMIN F. BAL 065 18TH WAR
NORRIS, C. SIDNEY BAL 314 20TH WAR
NORRIS, CALEB P. FRE 238 NEW MARK
NORRIS, CARDIFF HAR 096 2ND DIST
NORRIS, CARLISLE WAS 021 2ND SUBD
NORRIS, CATHARINE FRE 308 WOODSBOR
NORRIS, CECILIA BAL 026 15TH WAR
NORRIS, CELIN BAL 279 12TH WAR
NORRIS, CHARLES ALL 183 8TH E.D.
NORRIS, CHARLES BAL 048 1ST WARD
NORRIS, CHARLES FRE 331 MIDDLETO
NORRIS, CHARLES H. CAR 095 NO TWP L
NORRIS, CHARLOTT BAL 038 4TH WARD
NORRIS, CHARLOTTE BAL 024 18TH WAR
NORRIS, CHARLOTTE ANN 265 ANNAPOLI
NORRIS, CLARISSA BAL 476 14TH WAR
NORRIS, CLEM FRE 135 CREAGERS.
NORRIS, DANIEL HAR 021 1ST DIST
NORRIS, DAVID HAR 100 2ND DIST
NORRIS, DAVID CEC 152 PORT DUP
NORRIS, DAVID BAL 307 1ST DIST
NORRIS, DAVID WAS 091 2ND SUBD
NORRIS, DAVID L. HAR 079 2ND DIST
NORRIS, DAWES FRE 229 BUCKEYST
NORRIS, ED. BAL 024 18TH WAR
NORRIS, EDMOND ST 290 2ND E DI
NORRIS, EDWARD HAR 073 1ST DIST
NORRIS, EDWARD BAL 384 13TH WAR
NORRIS, EDWARD BAL 146 1ST WARD
NORRIS, EDWARD BAL 282 7TH WARD
NORRIS, EDWARD BAL 279 2ND WARD
NORRIS, EDWARD L. BAL 157 11TH WAR
NORRIS, EDWARD O. CAR 326 1ST DIST
NORRIS, ELIJAH BAL 440 1ST DIST
NORRIS, ELINOR CEC 100 3RD E DI
NORRIS, ELIZ BAL 325 12TH WAR
NORRIS, ELIZA BAL 230 12TH WAR
NORRIS, ELIZABETH BAL 313 7TH WARD
NORRIS, ELIZABETH HAR 095 2ND DIST
NORRIS, ELIZABETH HAR 039 1ST DIST
NORRIS, ELIZABETH BAL 167 19TH WAR
NORRIS, ELIZABETH BAL 182 19TH WAR
NORRIS, ELIZABETH TAL 004 EASTON D
NORRIS, ELIZABETH ST 295 2ND E DI
NORRIS, ELIZABETH ST 328 4TH E DI
NORRIS, ELIZABETH S. WAS 106 2ND DIST
NORRIS, ELLEN BAL 180 16TH WAR
NORRIS, ELY BAL 050 2ND DIST
NORRIS, EMILY L. ST 300 2ND E DI
NORRIS, ETAY E.* BAL 115 11TH WAR
NORRIS, FANNY BAL 376 1ST DIST
NORRIS, FRANCIS F. ANN 459 HOWARD D
NORRIS, GEORGE BAL 042 2ND DIST
NORRIS, GEORGE ANN 266 ANNAPOLI
NORRIS, GEORGE CEC 067 5TH E DI
NORRIS, GEORGE WAS 079 2ND SUBD
NORRIS, GEORGE L. BAL 149 11TH WAR
NORRIS, GEORGE W. BAL 339 13TH WAR
NORRIS, GEORGEANNA BAL 162 16TH WAR
NORRIS, GREENBURNS BAL 042 2ND DIST
NORRIS, HAM S. BAL 165 19TH WAR
NORRIS, HANNAH BAL 234 20TH WAR
NORRIS, HANNAH KEN 251 2ND DIST
NORRIS, HARRIET WAS 092 2ND SUBD
NORRIS, HARRIOTT BAL 042 4TH WARD
NORRIS, HENRIETTA ALL 183 8TH E.D.
NORRIS, HENRY CEC 035 CHESAPEA
NORRIS, HENRY FRE 032 FREDERIC
NORRIS, HENRY S. CAR 268 WESTMINS
NORRIS, HETTY BAL 197 17TH WAR
NORRIS, HEZEKIAH WAS 107 2ND DIST
NORRIS, HILLERY FRE 136 CREAGERS
NORRIS, ISAAC FRE 159 EMMITTSB
NORRIS, ISAAC BAL 304 17TH WAR
NORRIS, ISAAC FRE 345 MIDDLETO
NORRIS, ISAAC WAS 076 2ND SUBD
NORRIS, ISAAC BAL 011 2ND DIST
NORRIS, ISAAC H. BAL 380 3RD WARD
NORRIS, ISRAEL HAR 019 1ST DIST
NORRIS, J.C. BAL 250 12TH WAR
NORRIS, J.W. BAL 002 18TH WAR
NORRIS, JACOB BAL 470 14TH WAR
NORRIS, JACOB WAS 186 BOONSBOR
NORRIS, JACOB SR. FRE 389 PETERSVL
NORRIS, JAMES HAR 046 1ST DIST
NORRIS, JAMES FRE 294 WOODSBOR
NORRIS, JAMES PRI 107 PISCATAW
NORRIS, JAMES ALL 250 CUMBERLA
NORRIS, JAMES BAL 041 2ND DIST
NORRIS, JAMES BAL 215 6TH WARD
NORRIS, JAMES H. BAL 195 2ND WARD
NORRIS, JAMES H. CHA 220 ALLENS F
NORRIS, JAMES L. FRE 033 FREDERIC
NORRIS, JANE BAL 067 4TH WARD
NORRIS, JANE BAL 109 15TH WAR
NORRIS, JANE A. BAL 033 2ND DIST
NORRIS, JARRETT FRE 206 BUCKEYST
NORRIS, JESSE WAS 076 2ND SUBD
NORRIS, JOHN WAS 091 2ND SUBD
NORRIS, JOHN WAS 092 2ND SUBD
NORRIS, JOHN FRE 303 WOODSBOR
NORRIS, JOHN HAR 012 1ST DIST
NORRIS, JOHN HAR 005 1ST DIST
NORRIS, JOHN HAR 097 2ND DIST
NORRIS, JOHN BAL 183 19TH WAR
NORRIS, JOHN KEN 250 2ND DIST
NORRIS, JOHN BAL 009 EASTERN
NORRIS, JOHN BAL 135 2ND DIST
NORRIS, JOHN BAL 220 12TH WAR
NORRIS, JOHN B. CHA 292 BOJANTOW
NORRIS, JOHN B. ST 280 3RD E DI
NORRIS, JOHN C. WAS 135 HAGERSTO
NORRIS, JOHN C. BAL 070 15TH WAR
NORRIS, JOHN G. HAR 020 1ST DIST
NORRIS, JOHN H. BAL 163 16TH WAR
NORRIS, JOHN L. HAR 079 2ND DIST
NORRIS, JOHN L. ST 301 2ND E DI
NORRIS, JOHN P. CAR 394 2ND DIST
NORRIS, JOHN PHILIP BAL 466 14TH WAR
NORRIS, JOHN T. ST 331 4TH E DI

NORRIS, JOHN-BLACK MGM 398 ROCKERLE
NORRIS, JONATHAN BAL 210 6TH WARD
NORRIS, JOSEPH* BAL 305 3RD WARD
NORRIS, JOSHUA BAL 085 18TH WAR
NORRIS, JOSHUA WAS 267 1ST DIST
NORRIS, JOSHUA H. BAL 084 4TH WARD
NORRIS, LAYFAYETT FRE 053 FREDERIC
NORRIS, LLOYD HAR 096 2ND DIST
NORRIS, LLOYD HAR 079 2ND DIST
NORRIS, LLOYD M. BAL 146 1ST WARD
NORRIS, LOTT FRE 442 8TH E DI
NORRIS, LOUISA HAR 045 1ST DIST
NORRIS, MAHALA FRE 043 FREDERIC
NORRIS, MARIA BAL 084 4TH WARD
NORRIS, MARTIN CAR 079 NO TWP L
NORRIS, MARTIN FRE 329 MIDDLETO
NORRIS, MARY BAL 424 14TH WAR
NORRIS, MARY BAL 211 17TH WAR
NORRIS, MARY HAR 019 1ST DIST
NORRIS, MARY CHA 223 ALLENS F
NORRIS, MARY CEC 213 7TH E DI
NORRIS, MARY BAL 409 3RD WARD
NORRIS, MARY BAL 303 1ST DIST
NORRIS, MARY ST 300 2ND E DI
NORRIS, MARY WAS 180 BOONSBOR
NORRIS, MARY WAS 077 2ND SUBD
NORRIS, MARY A. BAL 172 16TH WAR
NORRIS, MARY ANN BAL 384 13TH WAR
NORRIS, MARY E. HAR 043 1ST DIST
NORRIS, MARY J. WAS 138 HAGERSTO
NORRIS, MARY M. HAR 121 2ND DIST
NORRIS, MATHIAS B. FRE 448 8TH E DI
NORRIS, MATTHEW HAR 041 1ST DIST
NORRIS, MISS- ANN 407 8TH DIST
NORRIS, MOSES HAR 037 1ST DIST
NORRIS, MOSES HAR 039 1ST DIST
NORRIS, MRS. CHARLOTTE BAL 020 18TH WAR
NORRIS, NATHAN BAL 208 17TH WAR
NORRIS, NELSON BAL 228 6TH WARD
NORRIS, NICHOLAS FRE 437 8TH E DI
NORRIS, NIMROD FRE 436 8TH E DI
NORRIS, NIMROD BAL 317 7TH WARD
NORRIS, OLIVER BAL 384 13TH WAR
NORRIS, OTHO FRE 031 FREDERIC
NORRIS, PATRICK WAS 089 2ND SUBD
NORRIS, R.S. WOR 343 1ST E DI
NORRIS, RACHEL WAS 091 2ND SUBD
NORRIS, REUBEN HAR 036 1ST DIST
NORRIS, RICHARD CAR 080 NO TWP L
NORRIS, RICHARD BAL 154 11TH WAR
NORRIS, RICHARD BAL 421 1ST DIST
NORRIS, RICHARD BAL 188 11TH WAR
NORRIS, ROBERT W. HAR 096 2ND DIST
NORRIS, S. BAL 329 13TH WAR
NORRIS, SALLEY BAL 353 7TH WARD
NORRIS, SAMUEL HAR 041 1ST DIST
NORRIS, SAMUEL CAR 099 NO TWP L
NORRIS, SARAH FRE 001 FREDERIC
NORRIS, SARAH BAL 177 11TH WAR
NORRIS, SARAH A. BAL 353 7TH WARD
NORRIS, SARAH A. BAL 380 3RD WARD
NORRIS, SIDNEY BAL 020 2ND DIST
NORRIS, SILUS A. HAR 096 2ND DIST
NORRIS, SISTER ANN SIMEON FRE 197 5TH E DI
NORRIS, SOLOMON BAL 011 2ND DIST
NORRIS, SOLOMON BAL 456 1ST DIST
NORRIS, SOPHIA WAS 192 1ST DIST
NORRIS, SUSAN WAS 141 HAGERSTO
NORRIS, SYDNEY BAL 380 3RD WARD
NORRIS, THOAMS E. BAL 475 14TH WAR
NORRIS, THOMAS FRE 206 BUCKEYST
NORRIS, THOMAS BAL 041 2ND DIST
NORRIS, THOMAS BAL 186 5TH DIST
NORRIS, THOMAS WAS 152 2ND DIST
NORRIS, THOMAS WAS 152 2ND DIST
NORRIS, THOMAS WAS 151 2ND DIST
NORRIS, THOMAS A. HAR 097 2ND DIST
NORRIS, THOMAS B. FRE 099 FREDERIC
NORRIS, THOMAS F. TAL 004 EASTON D
NORRIS, WALTER BAL 033 2ND DIST
NORRIS, WILLIAM BAL 302 7TH WARD
NORRIS, WILLIAM BAL 229 12TH WAR
NORRIS, WILLIAM BAL 185 6TH WARD
NORRIS, WILLIAM WAS 093 2ND SUBD
NORRIS, WILLIAM WAS 085 2ND SUBD
NORRIS, WILLIAM WAS 134 HAGERSTO
NORRIS, WILLIAM MGM 396 ROCKERLE
NORRIS, WILLIAM FRE 329 MIDDLETO
NORRIS, WILLIAM FRE 244 NEW MARK
NORRIS, WILLIAM CAR 080 NO TWP L
NORRIS, WILLIAM CEC 155 PORT DUP
NORRIS, WILLIAM A. CAR 394 2ND DIST
NORRIS, WILLIAM A. ST 335 4TH E DI
NORRIS, WILLIAM B. BAL 068 15TH WAR
NORRIS, WILLIAM G. ANN 323 2ND DIST
NORRIS, WILLIAM H. KEN 263 1ST DIST
NORRIS, WILLIAM H. BAL 021 18TH WAR
NORRIS, WILLIAM H. BAL 384 13TH WAR
NORRIS, WILLIAM H. BAL 153 11TH WAR
NORRIS, WILLIAM J. ST 289 2ND E DI
NORRIS, Y. BAL 207 19TH WAR
NORRIS,RACHEL BAL 061 2ND DIST
NORRISON, CORNELIUS BAL 002 9TH WARD
NORRISS, ADAM BAL 226 17TH WAR
NORRISS, ANN ST 285 2ND E DI
NORRISS, CHARLES G. ST 280 3RD E DI
NORRISS, CLEMENT ST 280 3RD E DI
NORRISS, CLEMENT ST 280 3RD E DI
NORRISS, ELIZABETH ST 279 3RD E DI
NORRISS, HENRY ST 280 3RD E DI
NORRISS, JAMES ST 287 2ND E DI
NORRISS, JAMES ST 287 2ND E DI
NORRISS, JAMES G. ST 255 3RD E DI
NORRISS, JAMES M. ST 282 3RD E DI
NORRISS, JOEL FRE 254 NEW MARK
NORRISS, JOHN TAL 056 EASTON D
NORRISS, JOSEPHINE ST 267 3RD E DI
NORRISS, LLOYD. L. ST 281 3RD E DI
NORRISS, MARY E. ST 256 3RD E DI
NORRISS, ROBERT ST 280 3RD E DI
NORRISS, SOPHIA ST 279 3RD E DI
NORRISS, WILLIAM ST 279 3RD E DI
NORRUS, ELIZA BAL 140 2ND DIST
NORT, MARY BAL 306 20TH WAR
NORTH, A. BAL 118 1ST WARD
NORTH, CAROLINE BAL 078 10TH WAR
NORTH, CAROLINE DOR 401 1ST DIST
NORTH, EDMUND BAL 265 17TH WAR
NORTH, EDWARD BAL 116 1ST WARD
NORTH, EDWARD BAL 065 1ST WARD

NORTH, EDWARD SOM 541 TYASKIN
NORTH, ELIZABETH BAL 248 17TH WAR
NORTH, GEORGE* BAL 307 3RD WARD
NORTH, HENRY BAL 241 17TH WAR
NORTH, HICKS DOR 397 1ST DIST
NORTH, JAMES DOR 386 1ST DIST
NORTH, JAMES DOR 401 1ST DIST
NORTH, JAMES BAL 138 16TH WAR
NORTH, JAMES BAL 130 1ST WARD
NORTH, JAMES H. BAL 238 17TH WAR
NORTH, JEREMIAH DOR 407 1ST DIST
NORTH, JOBE DOR 359 3RD DIVI
NORTH, JOHN BAL 248 17TH WAR
NORTH, JOHN BAL 251 17TH WAR
NORTH, JOHN BAL 265 17TH WAR
NORTH, JOHN ALL 190 9TH E.D.
NORTH, JOHN SOM 543 TYASKIN
NORTH, MARGRET DOR 362 3RD DIVI
NORTH, MARY ALL 191 9TH E.D.
NORTH, PERRY DOR 405 1ST DIST
NORTH, PRECILLA BAL 400 3RD WARD
NORTH, RICHARD F. TAL 103 ST MICHA
NORTH, THEODORE SOM 550 TYASKIN
NORTH, THOMAS G. BAL 273 17TH WAR
NORTH, WILLIAM DOR 429 1ST DIST
NORTH, WILLIAM SOM 542 TYASKIN
NORTHAM, SARAH BAL 273 17TH WAR
NORTHMUFT, JOHN * BAL 104 2ND DIST
NORTIMAN, HENRY BAL 064 1ST WARD
NORTON, ALEXANDER PRI 009 BLADENSB
NORTON, ANDREW BAL 469 14TH WAR
NORTON, ANN HAR 183 3RD DIST
NORTON, BRIDGET BAL 019 15TH WAR
NORTON, ELLEN BAL 041 15TH WAR
NORTON, ELLEN BAL 006 EASTERN
NORTON, EMMA H. ANN 521 HOWARD D
NORTON, FRANCES HAR 177 3RD DIST
NORTON, FRANCIS HAR 119 2ND DIST
NORTON, FRANCIS BAL 091 15TH WAR
NORTON, GEORGE BAL 456 8TH WARD
NORTON, GEORGE BAL 139 5TH WARD
NORTON, GEORGE MGM 358 BERRYS D
NORTON, HENRIETTA PRI 075 MARLBROU
NORTON, JAMES BAL 213 2ND WARD
NORTON, JAMES ALL 188 9TH E.D.
NORTON, JOHN BAL 005 EASTERN
NORTON, JOHN* DOR 425 1ST DIST
NORTON, LEONARD MGM 358 BERRYS D
NORTON, M. BAL 123 1ST WARD
NORTON, MAGRET BAL 213 2ND WARD
NORTON, MARIA BAL 087 18TH WAR
NORTON, MARY HAR 207 3RD DIST
NORTON, MARY BAL 457 14TH WAR
NORTON, MARY BAL 230 12TH WAR
NORTON, MARY BAL 389 3RD WARD
NORTON, MARY BAL 367 8TH WARD
NORTON, MARY A. ANN 453 HOWARD D
NORTON, MARY A. BAL 130 18TH WAR
NORTON, MICHAEL BAL 029 4TH WARD
NORTON, MICHAEL BAL 409 8TH WARD
NORTON, MICHALS ALL 056 10TH E.D
NORTON, NATHINEAL BAL 129 18TH WAR
NORTON, PATRICK BAL 005 EASTERN
NORTON, PATRICK BAL 244 6TH WARD
NORTON, REBECCA BAL 285 17TH WAR
NORTON, SAMUEL HAR 035 1ST DIST
NORTON, SARAH BAL 077 2ND DIST
NORTON, SOLOMON* DOR 448 1ST DIST
NORTON, SOLOMON* DOR 448 1ST DIST
NORTON, SYLVESTER HAR 027 1ST DIST
NORTON, VIRGINIA ANN 521 HOWARD D
NORTON, WILLIAM MGM 373 BERRYS D
NORTON, WINNY ANN MGM 358 BERRYS D
NORTON,LAURENCE ALL 254 CUMBERLA
NORTON,MARY BAL 111 1ST WARD
NORVILLE, J. BAL 161 1ST WARD
NORVILLE, SARAH A. BAL 275 2ND WARD
NORVILLE, WILLIAM BAL 274 2ND WARD
NORWAL, BROOKE PRI 065 NOTTINGH
NORWAL, BROOKE PRI 065 NOTTINGH
NORWELL, JOHN H. PRI 065 NOTTINGH
NORWOOD, ACHSA BAL 391 14TH WAR
NORWOOD, ALEXANDER BAL 444 1ST DIST
NORWOOD, ANN BAL 176 6TH WARD
NORWOOD, ANNA BAL 119 2ND DIST
NORWOOD, BENJAMIN BAL 397 8TH WARD
NORWOOD, BETT M. FRE 245 NEW MARK
NORWOOD, CHARLES BAL 043 4TH WARD
NORWOOD, EDWARD BAL 130 18TH WAR
NORWOOD, EDWARD BAL 397 8TH WARD
NORWOOD, EDWARD BAL 396 8TH WARD
NORWOOD, EDWARD BAL 130 2ND DIST
NORWOOD, ELISABETH BAL 472 14TH WAR
NORWOOD, ELIZA DOR 401 1ST DIST
NORWOOD, ELIZABETH BAL 269 12TH WAR
NORWOOD, GILES BAL 396 8TH WARD
NORWOOD, ISAIAH FRE 443 8TH E DI
NORWOOD, JANE F. BAL 311 3RD WARD
NORWOOD, JEMIMA ANN 512 HOWARD D
NORWOOD, JEREMIAH MGM 438 CLARKSTR
NORWOOD, JOHN BAL 310 3RD WARD
NORWOOD, JOHN ANN 495 HOWARD D
NORWOOD, JOHN BAL 170 19TH WAR
NORWOOD, JOHN BAL 215 17TH WAR
NORWOOD, JOSEPH BAL 100 5TH WARD
NORWOOD, JOSHUA MGM 346 CLARKSBU
NORWOOD, LAMBERT L. BAL 157 11TH WAR
NORWOOD, MARGARET MGM 436 CLARKSTR
NORWOOD, MARY BAL 026 9TH WARD
NORWOOD, MARY A. MGM 438 CLARKSTR
NORWOOD, MARY L. MGM 434 CLARKSTR
NORWOOD, RICHARD J. BAL 097 1ST WARD
NORWOOD, STEPHEN BAL 124 2ND DIST
NORWOOD, THOMAS BAL 310 3RD WARD
NORWOOD, THOMAS BAL 051 15TH WAR
NORWOOD, THOMAS FRE 245 NEW MARK
NORWOOD,REUBEN FRE 448 8TH E DI
NOSAN, SARAH CEC 084 CHARLEST
NOSE, CATHARINE BAL 189 2ND WARD
NOSIER, JOHN BAL 132 2ND DIST
NOSNER, JOHN BAL 105 1ST WARD
NOSSELL, BARNHARD BAL 448 14TH WAR
NOTA, LEONARD FRE 067 FREDERIC
NOTES, HENRY BAL 441 1ST DIST
NOTES, JAMES CEC 050 1ST E DI
NOTHARD, PHOEBE BAL 166 2ND DIST
NOTMEYER, JOHN BAL 438 14TH WAR
NOTSERIMES, JOHN FRE 080 FREDERIC
NOTT, CHRISTOPHER ALL 256 CUMBERLA
NOTT, CORNELIUS BAL 414 14TH WAR

NOTT, ELIZABETH CHA 221 ALLENS F
NOTT, ELIZABETH CHA 226 ALLENS F
NOTT, MARY BAL 463 1ST DIST
NOTT, MARY WAS 140 HAGERSTO
NOTTING, CHARLES BAL 464 14TH WAR
NOTTINGHAM, WILLIAM BAL 033 15TH WAR
NOTTS, ALEXANDER CAR 086 NO TWP L
NOTTS, JAMES* TAL 023 EASTON D
NOURE, CHARLES H. MGM 412 MEDLEY 3
NOURSE, WILLIAM C. BAL 050 9TH WARD
NOUSE, ELIZA BAL 333 1ST DIST
NOUSE, WILLIAM BAL 152 19TH WAR
NOUVEL, JOSEPH BAL 001 15TH WAR
NOUVELL, MARY BAL 331 13TH WAR
NOVVAL, ROBERT QUE 151 1ST E DI
NOVY, MOSES DOR 358 3RD DIVI
NOW, JAMES ALL 243 CUMBERLA
NOWAN, RICHARD BAL 280 2ND WARD
NOWEL, MARY CAR 076 NO TWP L
NOWEL, WILLIAM L. CAR 079 NO TWP L
NOWELL, GILBERT ANN 407 8TH DIST
NOWELL, HENRY BAL 131 1ST WARD
NOWELL, JOHN WAS 019 2ND SUBD
NOWELL, JOSEPH WAS 031 2ND SUBD
NOWELL, JOSEPH WAS 019 2ND SUBD
NOWELL, MARGARET ST 302 2ND E DI
NOWELL, WILLIAM ANN 306 1ST DIST
NOWELL, WILLIAM CAL 059 3RD DIST
NOWIL, JAMES BAL 049 9TH WARD
NOWLAND, A. C. BAL 332 1ST DIST
NOWLAND, ALFRED C. CEC 054 1ST E DI
NOWLAND, ANDERSON CEC 110 4TH E DI
NOWLAND, ANN CEC 110 4TH E DI
NOWLAND, AUGUSTUS J. KEN 302 3RD DIST
NOWLAND, BENEDICK KEN 291 3RD DIST
NOWLAND, BENNONI CEC 125 5TH E DI
NOWLAND, JAMES KEN 296 3RD DIST
NOWLAND, JANE CEC 095 4TH E DI
NOWLAND, JOHN CEC 126 5TH E DI
NOWLAND, LAMBERT CEC 030 CHESAPEA
NOWLAND, LAMBERT BAL 080 15TH WAR
NOWLAND, LIDIA BAL 462 1ST DIST
NOWLAND, MARY E. CEC 004 ELKTON 3
NOWLAND, NORMAN CEC 150 PORT DUP
NOWLAND, OTHO CEC 124 5TH E DI
NOWLAND, REYNOLDS CEC 125 5TH E DI
NOWLAND, WILLIAM CEC 090 4TH E DI
NOWLAND, WILLIAM H. CEC 057 1ST E DI
NOWLEN, SPENCER BAL 167 11TH WAR
NOWLS, HENRIETTA M. TAL 068 EASTON T
NOWYER, FRANCIS BAL 426 8TH WARD
NOX, GEORGE TAL 008 EASTON D
NOX, JOSEPH WAS 179 BOONSBOR
NOX, WLIZA WAS 178 BOONSBOR
NOYE, CHARLES BAL 430 8TH WARD
NOYES, BENJAMIN BAL 289 3RD WARD
NOYES, CLINTON H. BAL 065 10TH WAR
NOYES, DAVID C. BAL 083 18TH WAR
NOYES, ELIZABETH BAL 458 14TH WAR
NOYES, ENOCH BAL 083 18TH WAR
NOYES, MARY A. BAL 269 20TH WAR
NOYES, WILLIAM BAL 142 1ST WARD
NOYLES, MARTHA A. SOM 518 BARREN C
NRICE, PETER * WAS 064 2ND SUBD
NUBERS, ANN BAL 246 2ND WARD
NUBERT, CASPAR BAL 402 14TH WAR
NUBLE, JACOB BAL 244 2ND WARD
NUBRAY, JAMES BAL 047 1ST WARD
NUBY, CONRAD BAL 455 14TH WAR
NUCE, PETER * WAS 064 2ND SUBD
NUELLER, CHARLES BAL 345 13TH WAR
NUFER, M.A. WAS 018 2ND SUBD
NUFER, MICHAEL WAS 250 1ST DIST
NUFFER, JOHN W. WAS 242 CAVETOWN
NUGANT, ALBERTOS BAL 039 9TH WARD
NUGANT, PATRICK ALL 168 6TH E.D.
NUGAS, JOSEPH BAL 418 14TH WAR
NUGEN, SAMUEL ANN 487 HOWARD D
NUGENT, ANN * BAL 284 20TH WAR
NUGENT, BERNARD BAL 361 8TH WARD
NUGENT, ELIAS BAL 458 8TH WARD
NUGENT, FRANCES BAL 049 15TH WAR
NUGENT, HANNAH ANN 418 HOWARD D
NUGENT, JAMES BAL 262 2ND WARD
NUGENT, JAMES * BAL 316 20TH WAR
NUGENT, JOSEPH MGM 326 CRACKLIN
NUGENT, JOSEPH MGM 322 CRACKLIN
NUGENT, JULIA BAL 244 12TH WAR
NUGENT, MARY BAL 173 16TH WAR
NUGENT, MARY J. ALL 168 6TH E.D.
NUGENT, MICHAEL BAL 401 8TH WARD
NUGENT, NICHOLAS BAL 177 16TH WAR
NUGENT, RACHAEL A. BAL 071 15TH WAR
NUGENT, SAMUEL BAL 191 17TH WAR
NUGENT, SYLVESTER BAL 319 7TH WARD
NUGENT, THOMAS BAL 320 12TH WAR
NUGENT, THOMAS BAL 444 1ST DIST
NUGENT, WILLAM BAL 218 19TH WAR
NUGENT, WILLIAM BAL 218 12TH WAR
NUGEON, LLOYD CAR 227 5TH DIST
NUGEON, SUSAN CAR 228 5TH DIST
NUGER, THOMAS BAL 230 19TH WAR
NUGERT, MICHAEL BAL 042 1ST WARD
NUGHBERGEN, ELIZA BAL 454 14TH WAR
NUGHBOURS, JAMES CAR 164 NO TWP L
NULIN, BRIDGET BAL 118 5TH WARD
NULL, ABRAHAM CAR 380 2ND DIST
NULL, ABSOLUM BAL 007 18TH WAR
NULL, ELIZABETH WAS 131 2ND DIST
NULL, EMILY J. CAR 303 1ST DIST
NULL, GEORGE CAR 302 1ST DIST
NULL, GEORGE CAR 242 TANEYTOW
NULL, GEORGE FRE 338 MIDDLETO
NULL, GEORGE ALL 180 8TH E.D.
NULL, HENRY ALL 219 CUMBERLA
NULL, HENRY FRE 337 MIDDLETO
NULL, HENRY BAL 105 18TH WAR
NULL, HENRY CAR 310 1ST DIST
NULL, HENRY CAR 185 8TH DIST
NULL, HENRY WAS 166 HAGERSTO
NULL, ISABELL ALL 099 5TH E.D.
NULL, JAMES WAS 004 WILLIAMS
NULL, JOHN H. FRE 133 CREAGERS
NULL, JOSEPH ALL 204 CUMBERLA
NULL, JOSHUA FRE 171 5TH E DI
NULL, LEWIS CAR 303 1ST DIST
NULL, MALISSA FRE 108 CREAGERS
NULL, MARGARET CAR 243 TANEYTOW
NULL, MARY FRE 108 CREAGERS
NULL, MARY WAS 184 BOONSBOR
NULL, MARY C. CAR 303 1ST DIST
NULL, MICHAEL CAR 309 1ST DIST
NULL, PETER FRE 338 MIDDLETO
NULL, REBECCA CAR 260 3RD DIST
NULL, ROBERT WAS 166 1ST DIST
NULL, SAMUEL CAR 300 1ST DIST
NULL, SAMUEL S. CAR 300 1ST DIST
NULL, SUSAN WAS 017 2ND SUBD
NULL, WILLIAM WAS 026 2ND SUBD
NULL, WILLIAM WAS 244 SMITHSBU
NULLE, R. BAL 149 1ST WARD
NULT, MICHAEL WAS 068 2ND SUBD
NULT, PHILIP ALL 260 CUMBERLA
NULTY, HENRY BAL 241 1ST DIST
NULTZ, AUTHEN BAL 133 11TH WAR
NUMAN, E. * BAL 320 20TH WAR
NUMAN, JAMES CHA 275 ALLENS F
NUMAN, JAMES BAL 353 13TH WAR
NUMAN, JOHN CHA 278 BOJANTOW
NUMAN, R. BAL 151 1ST WARD
NUMASTER, CHRISTIAN BAL 001 9TH WARD
NUMBER, C.P. BAL 163 1ST WARD
NUMBER, SARAH BAL 110 2ND DIST
NUMBERS, JAMES W. HAR 166 3RD DIST
NUMBERS, THOMAS CAR 132 NO TWP L
NUMBERS, WILLINA HAR 179 3RD DIST
NUMSEN, F. H. BAL 273 20TH WAR
NUMSEN, WILLIAM BAL 038 9TH WARD
NUMSON, WILLIAM BAL 421 14TH WAR
NUMYER, FREDERICK BAL 367 13TH WAR
NUN, JACKSON HAR 197 3RD DIST
NUNABRAKER, HENRY WAS 240 CAVETOWN
NUNAMACHER, DANIEL WAS 208 1ST DIST
NUNAMACKER, HENRY WAS 215 1ST DIST
NUNAMACKER, JOHN WAS 218 1ST DIST
NUNAMAKER, BARNEY WAS 100 2ND DIST
NUNCAN, YANCA BAL 105 1ST WARD
NUNELY, MARY BAL 199 11TH WAR
NUNEMAKE, HENRY CAR 341 6TH DIST
NUNEMAKER, EPHRAIM FRE 164 EMMITTSB
NUNEMAKER, SAMUEL CAR 338 6TH DIST
NUNING, CORNELIUS BAL 031 15TH WAR
NUNMAMACKER, JOHN WAS 126 HAGERSTO
NUNN, ELIZABETH L. HAR 080 2ND DIST
NUNN, STEPHEN BAL 123 2ND DIST
NUNNEMACKER, ELIZABETH WAS 166 HAGERSTO
NUNTY, GEORGE BAL 150 19TH WAR
NUNVILLAR, SAMUEL CEC 187 7TH E DI
NUNVILLER, ELIZABETH CEC 005 ELKTON 3
NUNVILLER, ISAAC CEC 017 ELKTON 3
NUNVILLER, MARY C. CEC 017 ELKTON 3
NUPLE, GEORGE BAL 105 2ND DIST
NUPOCK, CARY BAL 392 1ST DIST
NURATH, ENEST BAL 372 13TH WAR
NURCANN, JAMES BAL 025 9TH WARD
NURRIS, MRS. BAL 465 14TH WAR
NURSE, MARGARET WAS 162 HAGERSTO
NURSE, MRS- WAS 162 HAGERSTO
NURSE, WILLIAM WAS 162 HAGERSTO
NURSER, HENRY FRE 177 5TH E DI
NUSBAUM, ABRAHAM FRE 436 8TH E DI
NUSBAUM, ADAM FRE 421 8TH E DI
NUSBAUM, ANN A. FRE 307 WOODSBOR
NUSBAUM, CATHARINE FRE 435 8TH E DI
NUSBAUM, DANIEL FRE 255 NEW MARK
NUSBAUM, DAVID FRE 430 8TH E DI
NUSBAUM, ELI FRE 298 WOODSBOR
NUSBAUM, ELIZABETH FRE 441 8TH E DI
NUSBAUM, ELIZABETH FRE 435 8TH E DI
NUSBAUM, FREDERICK FRE 445 8TH E DI
NUSBAUM, JACOB FRE 435 8TH E DI
NUSBAUM, JACOB CAR 366 9TH DIST
NUSBAUM, JAOCB FRE 411 8TH E DI
NUSBAUM, JOHN FRE 446 8TH E DI
NUSBAUM, JOHN FRE 264 NEW MARK
NUSBAUM, JOSPEH BAL 107 5TH WARD
NUSBAUM, SAMUEL FRE 300 WOODSBOR
NUSBAUM, SAMUEL FRE 418 8TH E DI
NUSBAUM, SOLOMON FRE 417 8TH E DI
NUSBAUM, SUSAN FRE 239 NEW MARK
NUSBAUN,W ILLIAM CAR 411 2ND DIST
NUSE, ELLEN WAS 057 2ND SUBD
NUSER, LLIZE BAL 253 12TH WAR
NUSEY, SARAH BAL 353 7TH WARD
NUSLIENE, JOHN BAL 306 7TH WARD
NUSSBAUM, JAOCB FRE 032 FREDERIC
NUSSBAUM, JOHN CAR 412 2ND DIST
NUSSUR, ELIZABETH BAL 460 14TH WAR
NUSZ, GEORGE FRE 050 FREDERIC
NUSZ, WILLIAM FRE 060 FREDERIC
NUTE, JOHN P. CAR 136 NO TWP L
NUTHALL, ANN ST 297 2ND E DI
NUTHALL, JOHN W. ST 296 2ND E DI
NUTHALL, SARAH A. ST 274 3RD E DI
NUTHALL, WILLIAM ST 278 3RD E DI
NUTON, HENRIETTA BAL 198 11TH WAR
NUTT, MARY A. BAL 205 2ND WARD
NUTT, THOMAS WAS 036 2ND SUBD
NUTTER, CAROLINE* DOR 384 1ST DIST
NUTTER, EDMUND BAL 077 18TH WAR
NUTTER, EPHRAIM SOM 434 PRINCESS
NUTTER, FINEY SOM 545 TYASKIN
NUTTER, GEORGE SOM 545 TYASKIN
NUTTER, HENRY SOM 550 TYASKIN
NUTTER, HENRY BAL 009 9TH WARD
NUTTER, HEZEKIAH SOM 545 TYASKIN
NUTTER, JESSE SOM 550 TYASKIN
NUTTER, LEVIN BAL 106 10TH WAR
NUTTER, LITTLETON DOR 452 1ST DIST
NUTTER, MARY BAL 134 16TH WAR
NUTTER, MATTY SOM 545 TYASKIN
NUTTER, NEHEMIAH-BLACK CAR 105 NO TWP L
NUTTER, PRISSY DOR 385 1ST DIST
NUTTER, STEPHEN SOM 550 TYASKIN
NUTTER, WILLIAM DOR 385 1ST DIST
NUTTER, WILLIAM W. SOM 545 TYASKIN
NUTTER, ZACHARIAH SOM 545 TYASKIN
NUTTING, BONNER MGM 368 BERRYS D
NUTTING, LOUISA MGM 368 BERRYS D
NUTTLE, ISAAC DOR 306 1ST DIST
NUTTLE, NIMROD CAR 116 NO TWP L
NUTTLE, SARAH CAR 118 NO TWP L
NUTTLE, TILGHMAN CAR 116 NO TWP L
NUTTS, EBENEZER BAL 081 1ST WARD
NUTWELL, GEORGE W. ANN 409 8TH DIST
NUTWELL, JOHN ANN 319 2ND DIST
NUTWELL, JOHN S. E. ANN 409 8TH DIST
NUTWELL, LEVI CHA 282 BOJANTOW
NYBURG, SAMUEL BAL 009 9TH WARD
NYE, GEORGE BAL 080 2ND DIST
NYERS, DANIEL CAR 212 5TH DIST
NYHOFF, CHRISTIAN FRE 052 FREDERIC
NYMAN, D. G. WAS 184 BOONSBOR
NYMAN, ELIZABETH WAS 179 BOONSBOR
NYMAN, GEORGE WAS 187 BOONSBOR
NYMAN, H. G. WAS 185 BOONSBOR
NYMAN, HENRY WAS 184 BOONSBOR
NYMAN, HENRY FRE 033 FREDERIC
NYMAN, JOSEPH WAS 191 1ST DIST
NYMAN, LEWIS B. WAS 181 BOONSBOR
NYMAN, MICHAEL WAS 179 BOONSBOR
O FRE 399 JEFFERSO
O FRE 038 FREDERIC
O CAR 077 NO TWP L
O BACHELOR, CHRISTOPHER BAL 016 1ST WARD
O BARROLL.PETER BAL 122 1ST WARD
O BAURKE, PETRO FRE 202 5TH E DI
O BERRY, HENRY BAL 061 2ND DIST
O BIREN, C. BAL 298 12TH WAR
O BIREN, CHALES BAL 286 2ND WARD
O BIREN, MARY BAL 186 16TH WAR
O BLANCHARD, ROBER BAL 128 1ST WARD
O BRADY, PATRICK BAL 123 18TH WAR
O BREIN, MILY CAR 394 2ND DIST
O BRIAN, BRIDGET BAL 097 1ST WARD
O BRIAN, BRIDGET BAL 032 1ST WARD
O BRIAN, CATHARINE BAL 006 EASTERN
O BRIAN, CATHARINE BAL 105 5TH WARD
O BRIAN, CATHERINE ALL 219 CUMBERLA
O BRIAN, CORNELIUS BAL 291 17TH WAR
O BRIAN, DANIEL BAL 200 17TH WAR
O BRIAN, DENNIS BAL 342 13TH WAR
O BRIAN, EDWARD HAR 157 3RD DIST
O BRIAN, EDWARD ALL 170 7TH E.D.
O BRIAN, FREDERICK ALL 232 CUMBERLA
O BRIAN, GODFREY ALL 033 2ND E.D.
O BRIAN, HANNAH HAR 156 3RD DIST
O BRIAN, JAMES HAR 158 3RD DIST
O BRIAN, JOHN BAL 302 17TH WAR
O BRIAN, JOHN A. FRE 216 BUCKEYST
O BRIAN, MARY HAR 155 3RD DIST
O BRIAN, OWEN HAR 159 3RD DIST
O BRIAN, PATRICK SOM 433 PRINCESS
O BRIAN, SUSAN ALL 040 2ND E.D.
O BRIAN, SUSAN BAL 179 2ND WARD
O BRIAN, THOMAS BAL 179 2ND WARD
O BRIAN, THOMAS BAL 137 1ST WARD
O BRIAN, THOMAS BAL 302 17TH WAR
O BRIEN, BIDDY BAL 053 9TH WARD
O BRIEN, BRIDGET CAL 051 9TH WARD
O BRIEN, CARSANORA * BAL 369 13TH WAR
O BRIEN, CATHERINE BAL 085 10TH WAR
O BRIEN, CATHERINE BAL 171 11TH WAR
O BRIEN, CATHERINE L. BAL 118 11TH WAR
O BRIEN, CELESTINE BAL 212 11TH WAR
O BRIEN, DAVID BAL 356 3RD WARD
O BRIEN, DENNIS BAL 468 14TH WAR
O BRIEN, DENNIS BAL 055 18TH WAR
O BRIEN, EDMOND FRE 410 8TH E DI
O BRIEN, EDWARD BAL 165 11TH WAR
O BRIEN, EDWARD BAL 313 12TH WAR
O BRIEN, EDWARD BAL 299 7TH WARD
O BRIEN, ELIZA BAL 312 3RD WARD
O BRIEN, ELIZABETH BAL 288 20TH WAR
O BRIEN, ELLEN BAL 065 15TH WAR
O BRIEN, ELLEN BAL 161 6TH WARD
O BRIEN, H.-BLACK FRE 200 5TH E DI
O BRIEN, HENRY BAL 021 1ST WARD
O BRIEN, HUGH BAL 358 8TH WARD
O BRIEN, ISEBELLA A. BAL 052 18TH WAR
O BRIEN, JAMES BAL 107 18TH WAR
O BRIEN, JAMES BAL 208 6TH WARD
O BRIEN, JEREMIAH O. BAL 035 4TH WARD
O BRIEN, JOHN CAR 391 2ND DIST
O BRIEN, JOHN BAL 346 13TH WAR
O BRIEN, JOHN BAL 264 2ND WARD
O BRIEN, JOHN BAL 393 3RD WARD
O BRIEN, JOHN BAL 179 2ND DIST
O BRIEN, JOHN BAL 012 1ST WARD
O BRIEN, JOHN BAL 318 3RD WARD
O BRIEN, JOHN BAL 131 16TH WAR
O BRIEN, JOHN BAL 319 7TH WARD
O BRIEN, JOHN ANN 469 HOWARD D
O BRIEN, LARRY BAL 317 3RD WARD
O BRIEN, LAURENCE BAL 243 2ND WARD
O BRIEN, M. P. BAL 053 18TH WAR
O BRIEN, M.-BLACK FRE 200 5TH E DI
O BRIEN, MARGARET BAL 474 14TH WAR
O BRIEN, MARGARET BAL 359 8TH WARD
O BRIEN, MARY BAL 050 9TH WARD
O BRIEN, MARY BAL 037 1ST WARD
O BRIEN, MARY BAL 180 2ND WARD
O BRIEN, MARY BAL 257 12TH WAR
O BRIEN, MARY HAR 144 2ND DIST
O BRIEN, MARY BAL 085 4TH WARD
O BRIEN, MARY BAL 153 19TH WAR
O BRIEN, MARY BAL 252 20TH WAR
O BRIEN, MARY MGM 377 ROCKERLE
O BRIEN, MARY A. BAL 067 18TH WAR
O BRIEN, MATTHEW BAL 050 15TH WAR
O BRIEN, MICHAEL BAL 170 16TH WAR
O BRIEN, MICHAEL BAL 154 19TH WAR
O BRIEN, MICHAEL BAL 469 14TH WAR
O BRIEN, MICHEAL BAL 054 18TH WAR
O BRIEN, MRS. O.* BAL 008 4TH WARD
O BRIEN, NACE-BLACK FRE 196 5TH E DI
O BRIEN, P. BAL 267 20TH WAR
O BRIEN, PATRICK MGM 320 CRACKLIN
O BRIEN, PATRICK BAL 060 18TH WAR
O BRIEN, PATRICK HAR 093 2ND DIST
O BRIEN, PATRICK WAS 064 2ND SUBD
O BRIEN, RACHEL CAR 381 2ND DIST
O BRIEN, RICHARD BAL 186 16TH WAR
O BRIEN, ROSE BAL 205 19TH WAR
O BRIEN, SARAH BAL 225 12TH WAR
O BRIEN, SOLOMON BAL 205 19TH WAR
O BRIEN, SUSAN BAL 083 10TH WAR
O BRIEN, TERRANCE BAL 159 16TH WAR
O BRIEN, TERRENCE FRE 418 8TH E DI
O BRIEN, THOMAS BAL 062 18TH WAR
O BRIEN, TIMOTHY ALL 049 10TH E.D
O BRIEN, WILLIAM BAL 296 12TH WAR
O BRIEN, WILLIAM BAL 274 1ST DIST
O BRIEN, WILLIAM FRE 051 FREDERIC
O BRIEN,MICHAEL BAL 102 1ST WARD
O BRIENS, THOMAS BAL 297 7TH WARD
O BRINE, MICHAEL ALL 196 CUMBERLA
O BRION, WILLIAM WAS 113 2ND DIST
O BROWN, MELVIN BAL 122 1ST WARD
O BRYAN, LUCY PRI 009 BLADENSB

O BRYAN, MATHEW WAS 164 2ND DIST
O BRYAN, MICHAEL KEN 300 3RD DIST
O BRYAN, WILLIAM BAL 143 1ST WARD
O CALLAHAN, JEREMIAH BAL 186 6TH WARD
O CARY, A.D. FRE 039 FREDERIC
O CONE, CYRENIESS BAL 389 13TH WAR
O CONELL, JOHN FRE 379 PETERSVI
O CONNELL, B. CEC 011 ELKTON 3
O CONNELL, BRIDGET ALL 145 6TH E.D.
O CONNELL, HENRY BAL 264 7TH WARD
O CONNELL, JULIA ALL 214 CUMBERLA
O CONNELL, SISTER ANN L. FRE 197 5TH E DI
O CONNELL, THOMAS BAL 032 1ST WARD
O CONNER, BARNEY ALL 070 5TH E.D.
O CONNER, CATHARINE BAL 091 2ND DIST
O CONNER, DANIEL ALL 070 5TH E.D.
O CONNER, DANIEL BAL 361 3RD WARD
O CONNER, DANIEL BAL 367 8TH WARD
O CONNER, DANIEL BAL 323 7TH WARD
O CONNER, ELIZA BAL 387 13TH WAR
O CONNER, ELIZABETH BAL 260 12TH WAR
O CONNER, ELLEN CEC 211 7TH E DI
O CONNER, ELLEN BAL 153 19TH WAR
O CONNER, ELLENOR BAL 403 8TH WARD
O CONNER, JAMES BAL 323 7TH WARD
O CONNER, JAMES BAL 153 19TH WAR
O CONNER, JAMES BAL 177 19TH WAR
O CONNER, JAMES J. ANN 469 HOWARD D
O CONNER, JOHN BAL 138 18TH WAR
O CONNER, JOHN HAR 198 3RD DIST
O CONNER, JOHN H. BAL 209 2ND WARD
O CONNER, MARY ALL 261 CUMBERLA
O CONNER, MARY BAL 473 14TH WAR
O CONNER, MICHAEL BAL 127 5TH WARD
O CONNER, NANCY BAL 425 14TH WAR
O CONNER, PAT BAL 461 1ST DIST
O CONNER, PATRICK MGM 393 ROCKERLE
O CONNER, PETER BAL 360 8TH WARD
O CONNER, REBECCA BAL 148 19TH WAR
O CONNER, TIMOTHY BAL 147 5TH WARD
O CONNOR, BRIDGET BAL 066 18TH WAR
O CONNOR, CHARLES BAL 116 1ST WARD
O CONNOR, CHARLOTTE BAL 177 2ND DIST
O CONNOR, DANIEL ANN 469 HOWARD D
O CONNOR, HERCULES BAL 023 4TH WARD
O CONNOR, HUGH MGM 394 ROCKERLE
O CONNOR, HUGH BAL 442 14TH WAR
O CONNOR, JAMES BAL 377 8TH WARD
O CONNOR, JANE BAL 142 2ND DIST
O CONNOR, JOHN BAL 132 1ST WARD
O CONNOR, MARIAN BAL 074 10TH WAR
O CONNOR, MARTIN HAR 078 2ND DIST
O CONNOR, MARY ANN 441 HOWARD D
O CONNOR, MATTHEW BAL 005 9TH WARD
O CONNOR, MICHAEL BAL 010 EASTERN
O CONNOR, MICHAEL BAL 324 3RD WARD
O CONNOR, PATRICK BAL 041 15TH WAR
O CONNOR, RICHARD BAL 139 11TH WAR
O CONNOR, SARAH BAL 321 12TH WAR
O CONNOR, THOMAS BAL 028 9TH WARD
O DAWSON, LOTT ALL 136 4TH E.D.
O DAY, MICHAEL ALL 127 4TH E.D.
O DAY, PATRICK BAL 147 2ND DIST
O DEAR, ELIJAH * SOM 410 DUBLIN D
O DEAR, ROBERT SOM 410 DUBLIN D
O DELL, JAMES H. BAL 403 8TH WARD
O DERINEER, MARY * BAL 281 20TH WAR
O DONALD, ELIZABETH BAL 223 1ST DIST
O DONALD, JOHN BAL 432 14TH WAR
O DONALHUE, MARY FRE 066 FREDERIC
O DONEL, NATHANIEL BAL 246 2ND WARD
O DONELL, CORNELIUS PRI 003 BLADENSB
O DONNEL, BARNY ALL 219 CUMBERLA
O DONNEL, MICHAEL BAL 067 2ND DIST
O DONNEL, THOMAS CEC 061 1ST E DI
O DONNELL, ANNE BAL 047 9TH WARD
O DONNELL, ANTHONY ALL 052 10TH E.D
O DONNELL, BARNEY ALL 235 CUMBERLA
O DONNELL, BRIDGETT BAL 009 4TH WARD
O DONNELL, CHARLES ALL 221 CUMBERLA
O DONNELL, CHARLES BAL 027 9TH WARD
O DONNELL, D. A. BAL 075 10TH WAR
O DONNELL, E.H. ALL 049 10TH E.D
O DONNELL, EDWARD ALL 140 6TH E.D.
O DONNELL, EDWARD HAR 110 2ND DIST
O DONNELL, ELLEN BAL 300 12TH WAR
O DONNELL, GEORGE HAR 110 2ND DIST
O DONNELL, JAMES HAR 110 2ND DIST
O DONNELL, JAMES BAL 385 13TH WAR
O DONNELL, JAMES BAL 160 19TH WAR
O DONNELL, JOHN HAR 110 2ND DIST
O DONNELL, JOHN ALL 135 4TH E.D.
O DONNELL, JOHN ALL 135 4TH E.D.
O DONNELL, JOHN ANN 484 HOWARD D
O DONNELL, JOHN BAL 060 15TH WAR
O DONNELL, JOSEPH BAL 132 1ST WARD
O DONNELL, MARY ALL 170 7TH E.D.
O DONNELL, MICHAEL ALL 048 10TH E.D
O DONNELL, MICHAEL MGM 332 CRACKLIN
O DONNELL, MISS J. FRE 199 5TH E DI
O DONNELL, NEALE BAL 318 12TH WAR
O DONNELL, SUSAN ALL 082 5TH E.D.
O DONNELL, THOMAS HAR 110 2ND DIST
O DONNELL, THOMAS CEC 058 1ST E DI
O DONNELL, TIMOTHY ANN 495 HOWARD D
O DONNIE, WINEFRED BAL 312 12TH WAR
O FARRELL, FRANCIS BAL 020 9TH WARD
O FARRELL, SARAH BAL 255 20TH WAR
O FARREN, EDWARD BAL 462 1ST DIST
O FARROLL, IGNATIOUS KEN 237 2ND DIST
O FORD, PATRICK ALL 052 10TH E.D
O FRUL, WILLIAM BAL 160 1ST WARD
O GARE, THOMAS BAL 461 1ST DIST
O GARY, PATRICK ALL 140 6TH E.D.
O GREERY, JOHN ALL 070 5TH E.D.
O GRIMES, JAMES MGM 381 ROCKERLE
O HAND, AMOS BAL 123 1ST WARD
O HANNA, JAMES BAL 046 1ST WARD
O HARA, BENJAMIN ANN 309 1ST DIST
O HARA, CHARLES BAL 022 9TH WARD
O HARA, JAMES BAL 009 9TH WARD
O HARA, JAMES BAL 143 2ND DIST
O HARA, JOHN BAL 447 8TH WARD
O HARA, JOHN BAL 020 9TH WARD
O HARA, JOHN BAL 016 9TH WARD
O HARA, JOHN ANN 309 1ST DIST
O HARA, JOHN FRE 261 NEW MARK
O HARA, MARY BAL 052 15TH WAR
O HARA, MICHAEL ALL 053 10TH E.D
O HARA, SARAH BAL 121 2ND DIST
O HARA, WILLIAM ANN 309 1ST DIST
O HARA, WILLIAM BAL 461 14TH WAR
O HARE, MARGARET BAL 162 16TH WAR
O HARRA, MARTIN BAL 202 6TH WARD
O HARROW, JOHN ALL 051 10TH E.D
O HEALY, ANN BAL 262 1ST DIST
O HEARN, MARY BAL 183 2ND WARD
O HORN, MOSES E. HAR 102 2ND DIST
O KANE, JAMES FRE 067 FREDERIC
O KEEF, MICHAEL BAL 356 8TH WARD
O KEEFE, DAVID BAL 026 9TH WARD
O KEIL, JAMES BAL 096 1ST WARD
O KEILLY, JOHN FRE 067 FREDERIC
O KELLY, MARY BAL 394 14TH WAR
O KERNIE, THOMAS BAL 119 11TH WAR
O LAFFERTY, WILLIAM BAL 348 7TH WARD
O LAUGHLIN, FRANCES BAL 342 13TH WAR
O LAUGHLIN, M. BAL 316 12TH WAR
O LAUGHLIN, MATILDA BAL 170 6TH WARD
O LEARY, A. BAL 099 10TH WAR
O LEARY, ARTHUR BAL 346 3RD WARD
O LEARY, BAT BAL 226 1ST DIST
O LEARY, CHARLES FRE 20 5TH E DI
O LEARY, EDWARD BAL 389 3RD WARD
O LEARY, ELIZA BAL 339 3RD WARD
O LEARY, HENRY A. BAL 190 2ND WARD
O LEARY, ISAAC BAL 218 2ND WARD
O LEARY, JOHN BAL 164 2ND DIST
O LEARY, MARY BAL 079 1ST WARD
O LEARY, MARY BAL 340 3RD WARD
O LEARY, RICHARD BAL 176 2ND WARD
O LEARY, THOMAS BAL 311 3RD WARD
O LEARY, THOMAS BAL 389 3RD WARD
O LONEY, M. BAL 268 2ND WARD
O LOVE, SAMUEL BAL 003 9TH WARD
O MALEY, CHARLES BAL 021 9TH WARD
O MALLAY, JOHN BAL 311 1ST DIST
O MALLEY, JAMES BAL 360 8TH WARD
O MARIA, ELOVER BAL 429 1ST DIST
O MEURA, JAMES BAL 305 20TH WAR
O NAIL, HENRY ANN 463 HOWARD D
O NEAL, ANN ANN 430 HOWARD D
O NEAL, BARNEY BAL 165 2ND DIST
O NEAL, BRIDGET BAL 201 6TH WARD
O NEAL, CHARLES C. BAL 358 1ST DIST
O NEAL, DANIEL BAL 448 1ST DIST
O NEAL, DENNIS ALL 239 CUMBERLA
O NEAL, EDWARD ALL 161 6TH E.D.
O NEAL, ELIZA BAL 220 2ND WARD
O NEAL, ELIZA BAL 211 11TH WAR
O NEAL, ELIZABETH ALL 238 CUMBERLA
O NEAL, ELIZABETH A. BAL 356 13TH WAR
O NEAL, ELIZER HAR 154 3RD DIST
O NEAL, FRANCIS ANN 412 HOWARD D
O NEAL, HENRY ANN 437 HOWARD D
O NEAL, HENRY BAL 029 9TH WARD
O NEAL, HOWARD BAL 472 14TH WAR
O NEAL, ISREAL C. FRE 023 FREDERIC
O NEAL, J. H. BAL 470 14TH WAR
O NEAL, J.W.C. BAL 267 20TH WAR
O NEAL, JAMES BAL 448 1ST DIST
O NEAL, JAMES ANN 518 HOWARD D
O NEAL, JAMES BAL 291 12TH WAR
O NEAL, JAMES BAL 182 16TH WAR
O NEAL, JAMES WAS 094 2ND SUBD
O NEAL, JANE BAL 418 14TH WAR
O NEAL, JEREMIAH PRI 003 BLADENSB
O NEAL, JOHN BAL 004 18TH WAR
O NEAL, JOHN FRE 351 MIDDLETO
O NEAL, JOHN ALL 053 10TH E.D
O NEAL, JOHN H. HAR 145 3RD DIST
O NEAL, JOHN J. KEN 249 2ND DIST
O NEAL, MARGARET BAL 255 12TH WAR
O NEAL, MARTIN FRE 067 FREDERIC
O NEAL, MICHAEL BAL 449 1ST DIST
O NEAL, MICHAEL ANN 465 HOWARD D
O NEAL, MICHAEL ALL 227 CUMBERLA
O NEAL, OWEN BAL 087 2ND DIST
O NEAL, OWEN HAR 145 3RD DIST
O NEAL, PAT BAL 449 1ST DIST
O NEAL, PATRICK ANN 430 HOWARD D
O NEAL, PATRICK FRE 069 FREDERIC
O NEAL, Q. L. BAL 331 13TH WAR
O NEAL, ROGER BAL 117 15TH WAR
O NEAL, SAMUEL ANN 461 HOWARD D
O NEAL, SINGLETON FRE 019 FREDERIC
O NEAL, THOMA SH. FRE 042 FREDERIC
O NEAL, THOMAS ANN 443 HOWARD D
O NEAL, WASHINGTON MGM 360 BERRYS D
O NEAL, WILLIAM WAS 067 2ND SUBD
O NEAL, WILLIAM P. BAL 359 13TH WAR
O NEALE, BRIDGET BAL 189 11TH WAR
O NEALE, DANIEL BAL 172 11TH WAR
O NEALE, WILLIAM MGM 359 BERRYS D
O NEALL, WILLIAM MGM 399 ROCKERLE
O NEEL, THOMAS HAR 114 2ND DIST
O NEELE, WILLIAM BAL 184 19TH WAR
O NEIL, ANDREW BAL 358 8TH WARD
O NEIL, ANN BAL 352 7TH WARD
O NEIL, BARNEY BAL 355 8TH WARD
O NEIL, CATHARINE BAL 278 17TH WAR
O NEIL, DANIEL BAL 235 17TH WAR
O NEIL, DANIEL BAL 389 8TH WARD
O NEIL, DENNIS FRE 397 PETERSVI
O NEIL, EUGENE BAL 156 1ST WARD
O NEIL, FRANCIS BAL 359 8TH WARD
O NEIL, JAMES BAL 360 8TH WARD
O NEIL, JAMES BAL 358 8TH WARD
O NEIL, JAMES BAL 373 8TH WARD
O NEIL, JAMES BAL 264 7TH WARD
O NEIL, JESSE BAL 134 2ND DIST
O NEIL, JOHN BAL 368 8TH WARD
O NEIL, JOHN BAL 003 15TH WAR
O NEIL, JOHN BAL 156 16TH WAR
O NEIL, JOHN BAL 326 7TH WARD
O NEIL, JOHN BAL 418 3RD WARD
O NEIL, M. BAL 449 8TH WARD
O NEIL, MARTIN BAL 132 2ND DIST
O NEIL, MARY BAL 360 8TH WARD
O NEIL, MARY BAL 393 8TH WARD
O NEIL, MARY HAR 104 2ND DIST
O NEIL, OWEN BAL 365 8TH WARD
O NEIL, PATRICK BAL 007 15TH WAR
O NEIL, ROBERT BAL 114 1ST WARD
O NEIL, TENANCE BAL 418 8TH WARD
O NEIL, THOMAS ALL 252 CUMBERLA
O NEILE, JOHN BAL 125 1ST WARD
O NEILL, ELLEN BAL 300 20TH WAR
O NEILL, FRANCIS BAL 291 12TH WAR
O NEILL, JAMES BAL 001 4TH WARD
O NEILL, JOHN BAL 181 19TH WAR
O NEILL, JOHN BAL 019 1ST WARD
O NEILL, JOSEPH BAL 269 12TH WAR
O NEILL, JOSEPH WAS 183 BOONSBOR
O NEILL, MARY BAL 181 19TH WAR
O NEILL, MICHAEL BAL 316 20TH WAR
O NEILL, PETER BAL 047 9TH WARD
O NEILL, ROBERT BAL 239 20TH WAR
O NEILL, THOMAS BAL 293 20TH WAR
O NEILL, WILLIAM HAR 101 2ND DIST
O NEILLE, MISS M. FRE 199 5TH E DI
O NIEL, BRIDGET BAL 084 1ST WARD
O NIEL, HUGH ANN 302 1ST DIST
O NIELL, ANN BAL 279 12TH WAR
O OUCE, JOHN BAL 326 12TH WAR
O QUINCHE, ALEXANDER MGM 412 MEDLEY 3
O RAER, ADOLPHUS ALL 236 CUMBERLA
O RAN, JAMES BAL 409 8TH WARD
O RARITAN, WILLIAM ALL 033 2ND E.D.
O REILY, WILLIAM H. MGM 380 ROCKERLE
O RIELY, FRANCIS BAL 079 18TH WAR
O RILEY, CATHARINE BAL 464 14TH WAR
O RILEY, MARTHA J. BAL 267 7TH WARD
O RILEY, MATTHEW BAL 155 5TH WARD
O ROKE, BERNARD ALL 226 CUMBERLA
O ROUKE, ANNA BAL 020 18TH WAR
O ROURK, ELIZABETH BAL 080 15TH WAR
O ROURKE, JAMES BAL 031 9TH WARD
O ROURKE, MARY BAL 067 10TH WAR
O ROWIE, JOHN BAL 338 13TH WAR
O RUKE, MISS A. FRE 199 5TH E DI
O SHEA, THOMAS BAL 394 14TH WAR
O TOOL, EDWARD ALL 209 CUMBERLA
O TOOLE, MARGARET ALL 262 CUMBERLA
O TOOLE, MARY BAL 086 10TH WAR
O TOOLE, MICHAEL ALL 068 5TH E.D.
O TOOLE, THOMAS FRE 188 5TH E DI
O TRILL, EDWARD ALL 243 CUMBERLA
O WILLIAMS, ELISHA MGM 400 ROCKERLE
O//UTER, ZACHARIAH SOM 451 DAMES QU
OACKF, JACOB BAL 069 1ST WARD
OAKE, JOHN * ALL 159 6TH E.D.
OAKER, LEWIS ALL 159 6TH E.D.
OAKINS, ADELA BAL 087 4TH WARD
OAKLEY, ELIZA BAL 375 3RD WARD
OAKLEY, EMELINE BAL 249 12TH WAR
OAKLEY, HANNAH BAL 318 1ST DIST
OAKLEY, J.A. BAL 165 1ST WARD
OAKLEY, JOHN T. ANN 368 4TH DIST
OAKLEY, THOMAS BAL 265 2ND WARD
OAKLY, CATHRINE PRI 056 AQUASCO
OAKS, FRANICS F. TAL 084 ST MICHA
OAKS, JAMES ANN 418 HOWARD D
OAKS, JAOCB BAL 192 2ND WARD
OAKS, JOHN BAL 031 4TH WARD
OALE, ALBERT BAL 284 17TH WAR
OAR, JAMES M. CAR 378 2ND DIST
OAR, PETER* BAL 064 4TH WARD
OARMAN, WILLIAM BAL 280 2ND WARD
OAST, HENRY BAL 041 1ST WARD
OASTELA, ANDREW* BAL 298 3RD WARD
OATES, N. BAL 164 1ST WARD
OATES, WILLIAM BAL 382 1ST DIST
OATMAN, FREDERICK HAR 094 2ND DIST
OATS, ANDREW ANN 389 4TH DIST
OATS, CATHARINE ALL 069 5TH E.D.
OATS, JOHN FRE 038 FREDERIC
OBAL, MARGARET * BAL 271 1ST DIST
OBEDIAH, LEWIS CAR 274 7TH DIST
OBEDORF, BARBET BAL 321 12TH WAR
OBENDORF, C. BAL 258 12TH WAR
OBENDORF, JOHN L. FRE 027 FREDERIC
OBENDORFF, JOSEPH BAL 048 9TH WARD
OBENHEIM, CAROLINE BAL 013 9TH WARD
OBER, CATHARINE BAL 170 16TH WAR
OBER, GUSTAVUS BAL 113 15TH WAR
OBER, KATE BAL 114 15TH WAR
OBER, SOPHIA BAL 272 2ND WARD
OBERNDORF, JULIUS BAL 163 6TH WARD
OBES, ANNA BAL 368 1ST DIST
OBIER, MARY R. CAR 124 NO TWP L
OBIT, JOHN DOR 458 1ST DIST
OBLE, ELIZABETH BAL 312 1ST DIST
OBLE, LEIGHER DOR 361 3RD DIVI
OBRIAN, RICHARD BAL 400 1ST DIST
OBRIEN, PETER ALL 135 4TH E.D.
OBRINE, ELIZABETH BAL 400 1ST DIST
OBRISON, MARTIN BAL 259 1ST DIST
OBURG, HENRY QUE 251 5TH E DI
OBUSHON, MARGARETT BAL 205 11TH WAR
OCHELMAN, JOHN BAL 278 12TH WAR
OCHILTREE, COZIA BAL 212 11TH WAR
OCHILTSEE, COZIA BAL 212 11TH WAR
OCKER, ANN E. CAR 268 WESTMINS
OCKERFORD, GEORGE BAL 105 2ND DIST
OCKES, FRED BAL 411 1ST DIST
OCKMAN, HARRIET* TAL 061 EASTON D
OCKMAY, HENRY* TAL 060 EASTON D
OCLBY, DORATHY CHA 241 HILLTOP
OCOKAMY, SARAH A. BAL 193 17TH WAR
OCOKOMY, JAMES BAL 193 17TH WAR
ODALL, DANIEL TAL 108 ST MICHA
ODARE, JOHN * WAS 053 2ND SUBD
ODAY, JAMES CAR 121 NO TWP L
ODD, JOHN H. ST 278 3RD E DI
ODELL, BENJAMIN SOM 394 BRINKLEY
ODELL, DAVID G. WOR 180 6TH E DI
ODELL, GEORGE E. BAL 327 1ST DIST
ODELL, JUSTUS SOM 370 BRINKLEY
ODELL, MARY WOR 339 1ST E DI
ODELL, PERRY BAL 328 1ST DIST
ODELL, WALTER BAL 327 1ST DIST
ODELL, WALTER J. BAL 083 18TH WAR
ODELL, WILLIAM BAL 327 1ST DIST
ODELL, WILLIAM BAL 374 1ST DIST
ODEMAN, HERMAN BAL 002 1ST WARD
ODEN, ALFRED MGM 416 MEDLEY 3
ODEN, BENJAMIN ANN 370 4TH DIST
ODEN, BENJAMIN ANN 364 4TH DIST
ODEN, CAHTERINE MGM 415 MEDLEY 3
ODEN, CHARLOTTE MGM 443 CLARKSTR
ODEN, ELLEN FRE 032 FREDERIC
ODEN, GEORGE MGM 422 MEDLEY 3
ODEN, HARRIET M. FRE 039 FREDERIC
ODEN, JOHN MGM 444 CLARKSTR
ODEN, JOSEPHINE WAS 126 HAGERSTO
ODEN, LYDIA A. CAR 368 9TH DIST
ODEN, M.A. BAL 159 19TH WAR
ODEN, MALINDA FRE 230 BUCKEYST
ODEN, MARY WAS 149 HAGERSTO

ODEN, MARY PRI 069 MARLBROU
ODEN, WILLIAM ANN 365 4TH DIST
ODEN, WILLIAM Z. FRE 223 BUCKEYST
ODEN, MALINDA FRE 229 BUCKEYST
ODENBERGER, DANIEL WAS 133 2ND DIST
ODENBERGER, PHELIP WAS 134 2ND DIST
ODENSTEIN, GABRIEL BAL 114 5TH WARD
ODENWALD, MICHAEL BAL 408 1ST DIST
ODER, ALFRED MGM 414 MEDLEY 3
ODER, JACOB BAL 271 2ND WARD
ODERY, JAMES TAL 030 EASTON D
ODESLUYS, CHARLES L.* BAL 421 3RD WARD
ODIAR, JOHN BAL 099 5TH WARD
ODONAL, SIMON CAR 223 5TH DIST
ODONALD, DAVID BAL 424 1ST DIST
ODONEN, SARAH * BAL 370 1ST DIST
ODOUEN, SARAH * BAL 370 1ST DIST
ODOUS, LEWIS BAL 030 9TH WARD
ODOWN, SARAH * BAL 370 1ST DIST
ODRISCOLL, ELIZABETH ST 274 3RD E DI
ODWYER, MARY A. BAL 378 1ST DIST
OEHRL, JOHN BAL 038 18TH WAR
OENDOFF, GARRETT BAL 368 8TH WARD
OESTER, ADAM BAL 087 15TH WAR
OETTER, JOHN H. BAL 093 15TH WAR
OFARRY, EDWARD BAL 460 1ST DIST
OFFAL, FANNY BAL 396 3RD WARD
OFFARD, ELIZA BAL 084 18TH WAR
OFFATE, COLBERT MGM 396 ROCKERLE
OFFATE, ELIZABETH MGM 388 ROCKERLE
OFFATE, JAMES MGM 383 ROCKERLE
OFFATE, JOHN MGM 388 ROCKERLE
OFFATE, LUCY MGM 386 ROCKERLE
OFFATE, THOMAS L. MGM 386 ROCKERLE
OFFATT, COLMORE B. FRE 222 BUCKEYST
OFFATT, LEVIN MGM 380 ROCKERLE
OFFATT, LEVIN MGM 380 ROCKERLE
OFFATT, THOMAS W. MGM 380 ROCKERLE
OFFEND, SUSAN BAL 007 1ST WARD
OFFER, BEN ANN 274 ANNAPOLI
OFFER, MARY CAL 062 3RD DIST
OFFER, WILLAIM BAL 301 12TH WAR
OFFERT, CHARLES FRE 185 5TH E DI
OFFITT, BENEDICT BAL 440 8TH WARD
OFFITT, MARY BAL 406 8TH WARD
OFFITT, WILLIAM R.M. BAL 254 17TH WAR
OFFLEY, ELIZA J. BAL 072 10TH WAR
OFFLEY, ELIZABETH-BLACK QUE 152 1ST E DI
OFFLEY, JOHN BAL 378 3RD WARD
OFFLEY, JOHN S. QUE 139 1ST E DI
OFFLEY, JOSEPH W. BAL 297 3RD WARD
OFFLEY, MICHAEL BAL 432 8TH WARD
OFFLY, ISAAC QUE 126 1ST E DI
OFFORD, RICHARD FRE 211 BUCKEYST
OFFUTE, ELIZABETH L. MGM 396 ROCKERLE
OFFUTE, MARIAH MGM 386 ROCKERLE
OFFUTE, NICHOLAS D. MGM 405 ROCKERLE
OFFUTE, THOMAS H. MGM 397 ROCKERLE
OFFUTE, THOMAS M. MGM 386 ROCKERLE
OFFUTT, CALMORE MGM 421 MEDLEY 3
OFFUTT, ELIZABETH A. MGM 422 MEDLEY 3
OFFUTT, J.W. ALL 240 CUMBERLA
OFFUTT, JAMES L. MGM 415 MEDLEY 3
OFFUTT, JOHN F.C. BAL 007 18TH WAR
OFFUTT, JOSHUA W. MGM 398 ROCKERLE
OFFUTT, SARAH J. ALL 240 CUMBERLA
OGDEN, AMBROSE BAL 097 18TH WAR
OGDEN, CATHARINE BAL 349 13TH WAR
OGDEN, EDWARD T. ALL 241 CUMBERLA
OGDEN, ELIZABETH BAL 043 2ND DIST
OGDEN, ELIZABETH CAL 059 3RD DIST
OGDEN, HESTER A. TAL 056 EASTON D
OGDEN, HIRAM BAL 134 1ST WARD
OGDEN, JAMES H. CAL 043 3RD DIST
OGDEN, JOHN J. CAL 025 2ND DIST
OGDEN, LOUIZA BAL 121 5TH WARD
OGDEN, MANN BAL 303 12TH WAR
OGDEN, MARY BAL 365 1ST DIST
OGDEN, MARY E. BAL 072 1ST WARD
OGDEN, MERRIT BAL 280 2ND WARD
OGDEN, SUSAN CAL 024 2ND DIST
OGDEN, USSAN BAL 111 18TH WAR
OGDEN, WILLIAM CAL 042 3RD DIST
OGDEN, LUCRETIA ALL 012 3RD E.D.
OGDON, JOHN PRI 087 SPALDING
OGG, CAROLINE E. CAR 206 4TH DIST
OGG, GEORGE CAR 202 4TH DIST
OGG, JOHN CAR 200 4TH DIST
OGG, LABEN CAR 202 4TH DIST
OGG, LUCRETIA A. BAL 225 1ST DIST
OGG, NICHOLAS CAR 206 4TH DIST
OGG, SAMUEL J. CAR 199 4TH DIST
OGG, WILLIAM ALL 036 2ND E.D.
OGIER, MARY BAL 406 3RD WARD
OGILBY, SAMUEL WAS 164 HAGERSTO
OGILVIE, DOLLY BAL 103 10TH WAR
OGLE, A.M. PRI 057 AQUASCO
OGLE, ALEXANDER FRE 069 FREDERIC
OGLE, ALEXANDER-BLACK FRE 017 FREDERIC
OGLE, ALFRED FRE 449 8TH E DI
OGLE, ANN FRE 031 FREDERIC
OGLE, ANN-BLACK FRE 052 FREDERIC
OGLE, ATKIN S. BAL 245 20TH WAR
OGLE, BENJAMIN FRE 261 NEW MARK
OGLE, CATHARINE BAL 308 7TH WARD
OGLE, DANIEL CAR 388 2ND DIST
OGLE, DAVID CAR 389 2ND DIST
OGLE, DIANA BAL 272 1ST DIST
OGLE, ELIZABETH BAL 208 6TH WARD
OGLE, ELIZABETH BAL 008 18TH WAR
OGLE, ELIZABETH BAL 168 19TH WAR
OGLE, ELLEN CAR 273 WESTMINS
OGLE, GEORGE HAR 080 2ND DIST
OGLE, HENRY FRE 299 WOODSBOR
OGLE, HENRY BAL 094 1ST WARD
OGLE, JAMES BAL 320 3RD WARD
OGLE, JAMES FRE 096 FREDERIC
OGLE, JAMES CAR 386 2ND DIST
OGLE, JOHN CAR 388 2ND DIST
OGLE, JOHN FRE 308 WOODSBOR
OGLE, JOHN FRE 005 FREDERIC
OGLE, JOHN BAL 242 2ND WARD
OGLE, JOSEPH BAL 156 19TH WAR
OGLE, JULIAN FRE 261 NEW MARK
OGLE, MARTHA BAL 220 6TH WARD
OGLE, MARY BAL 285 7TH WARD
OGLE, MARY FRE 009 FREDERIC
OGLE, MARY E.M. FRE 024 FREDERIC
OGLE, MARY J. BAL 194 11TH WAR
OGLE, MARY L. ALL 241 CUMBERLA
OGLE, MRS. BAL 085 4TH WARD
OGLE, R.L. PRI 122 PISCATAW
OGLE, REUBEN FRE 416 8TH E DI
OGLE, RICHARD BAL 098 15TH WAR
OGLE, ROBERT BAL 114 18TH WAR
OGLE, SAMUEL E. CAR 380 2ND DIST
OGLE, SAMUEL V. FRE 016 FREDERIC
OGLE, SARAH FRE 073 FREDERIC
OGLE, SARAH BAL 353 7TH WARD
OGLE, SARAY BAL 056 10TH WAR
OGLE, SOPHIA BAL 097 2ND DIST
OGLE, SUSAN ALL 012 3RD E.D.
OGLE, THEODORE ALL 240 CUMBERLA
OGLE, THOMAS FRE 415 8TH E DI
OGLE, THOMAS-BLACK FRE 038 FREDERIC
OGLE, WILLIAM BAL 056 10TH WAR
OGLE, WILLIAM D. PRI 086 QUEEN AN
OGLE, WILLIAM E. CAR 397 2ND DIST
OGLE, WILLIAM W. FRE 444 8TH E DI
OGLE, YOUST BAL 063 2ND DIST
OGLE, EVAN FRE 415 8TH E DI
OGLE, RICHARD-BLACK FRE 419 8TH E DI
OGLEBY, ELIZABETH BAL 071 4TH WARD
OGLEBY, SOPHIA ALL 212 CUMBERLA
OGLEMAN, ISBELLA BAL 371 3RD WARD
OGLESEY, MARY J. BAL 214 11TH WAR
OGLESY, MARY BAL 296 7TH WARD
OGLETON, JOHN H.-MULATTO FRE 386 PETERSVI
OGLETON, SAMUEL-MULATTO FRE 385 PETERSVI
OGLEVEY, VIRGINIA BAL 214 11TH WAR
OGMAN, RICHARD QUE 238 5TH E DI
OGWAR, HENRY TAL 078 EASTON T
OGY, JAMES ALL 111 5TH E.D.
OGY, WHITTINGTON WOR 180 6TH E DI
OHALEY, PATRICK SOM 434 PRINCESS
OHARE, MICHAEL BAL 254 1ST DIST
OHARRA, MICHAEL BAL 273 1ST DIST
OHHAN, M. DE YATES BAL 212 11TH WAR
OHI, ELLEN E. ANN 509 HOWARD D
OHLE, AUGUST BAL 104 2ND DIST
OHLEMELLER, SEBASTAIN ANN 418 HOWARD D
OHLER, CATHARINE FRE 172 5TH E DI
OHLER, FREDERICK FRE 172 5TH E DI
OHLER, GEORGE FRE 105 CREAGERS
OHLER, GEORGE CAR 312 1ST DIST
OHLER, ISAAC FRE 170 5TH E DI
OHLER, ISAIAH JOSEPH FRE 173 5TH E DI
OHLER, JACOB FRE 176 5TH E DI
OHLER, JAMES FRE 172 5TH E DI
OHLER, JAMES CAR 310 1ST DIST
OHLER, JOHN FRE 170 5TH E DI
OHLER, LEVI FRE 139 CREAGERS
OHLER, LEWIS CAR 220 5TH DIST
OHLER, PETER CAR 311 1ST DIST
OHLER, SAMUEL FRE 170 5TH E DI
OHLER, SAMUEL G. FRE 169 5TH E DI
OHM, MICHAEL BAL 238 17TH WAR
OHR, CHARLES, H. ALL 217 CUMBERLA
OHR, ELIAS J. WAS 083 2ND SUBD
OHR, FREDERICK BAL 370 3RD WARD
OHR, JACOB J. WAS 091 2ND SUBD
OI/U/AMS, SAMUEL SOM 487 SALISBUR
OIKE, IGNATIUS BAL 045 9TH WARD
OILER, ANDREW WAS 267 1ST DIST
OINDORFF, ANNA FRE 034 FREDERIC
OIRTERLY, JOHN BAL 337 13TH WAR
OITER, ANSOR WAS 271 1ST DIST
OITTIS, JOHN BAL 019 2ND DIST
OKEEF, REBECCA BAL 327 1ST DIST
OKER, CAROLINE WAS 139 HAGERSTO
OKER, JOHN WAS 125 HAGERSTO
OKESLEY, CAROLINE BAL 463 8TH WARD
OKLEY, THOMAS BAL 117 1ST WARD
OLAND, HENRY FRE 074 FREDERIC
OLANEL, FREDERICK FRE 076 FREDERIC
OLANGE, SOPHIA FRE 109 CREAGERS
OLD, HUGH BAL 272 2ND WARD
OLD, RICHARD BAL 012 1ST WARD
OLDBRAND, GEORGE BAL 130 1ST WARD
OLDEN, ISA BAL 461 1ST DIST
OLDERICK, H. BAL 150 1ST WARD
OLDFIELD, G.S. BAL 204 11TH WAR
OLDFIELD, JOHN HAR 144 2ND DIST
OLDFIELD, WILLIAM QUE 243 5TH E DI
OLDGOTT, GEORGE P. BAL 444 8TH WARD
OLDHAM, ANN CEC 037 CHESAPEA
OLDHAM, ANN BAL 168 19TH WAR
OLDHAM, C. BAL 173 1ST WARD
OLDHAM, C. W. BAL 148 1ST WARD
OLDHAM, CALEB BAL 174 1ST WARD
OLDHAM, CALEB BAL 155 1ST WARD
OLDHAM, CHARLES W. BAL 161 1ST WARD
OLDHAM, EDWARD BAL 255 17TH WAR
OLDHAM, ELINOR CEC 134 6TH E DI
OLDHAM, GEORGE W. CEC 134 6TH E DI
OLDHAM, GEORGE W. CEC 013 ELKTON 3
OLDHAM, JAMES CEC 139 6TH E DI
OLDHAM, JANE BAL 177 11TH WAR
OLDHAM, JOHN HAR 147 3RD DIST
OLDHAM, JOHN W. CEC 134 6TH E DI
OLDHAM, JOSEPH BAL 047 18TH WAR
OLDHAM, JOSEPH BAL 003 9TH WARD
OLDHAM, MILKY CEC 117 4TH E DI
OLDHAM, REBECCA BAL 047 18TH WAR
OLDHAM, RICHARD CEC 057 1ST E DI
OLDHAM, SARAH BAL 008 15TH WAR
OLDHAM, WILLIAM BAL 116 5TH WARD
OLDHAM, WILLIAM M. BAL 038 18TH WAR
OLDHMAN, JACOB ALL 180 8TH E.D.
OLDHOUSE, CONRAD ALL 104 5TH E.D.
OLDNER, ANN BAL 044 1ST WARD
OLDNER, ANNA BAL 405 3RD WARD
OLDRIDGE, TAYLOR* TAL 037 EASTON D
OLDSON, HORATIO G. TAL 103 ST MICHA
OLDSON, MARY G. TAL 080 ST MICHA
OLDSON, WILLIAM H.C. QUE 143 1ST E DI
OLE, WILLIAM BAL 375 1ST DIST
OLEAL, MARGARET * BAL 271 1ST DIST
OLEAN, MARY BAL 271 20TH WAR
OLEARY, THOMAS WAS 140 HAGERSTO
OLEFER, ROBERT ALL 109 5TH E.D.
OLEM, MARY BAL 015 9TH WARD
OLER, CHARLES BAL 311 20TH WAR
OLER, CHARLOTT BAL 262 1ST DIST
OLER, JACOB BAL 276 1ST DIST
OLER, MARGARET BAL 164 6TH WARD
OLER, ROBERT A. BAL 261 1ST DIST
OLER, W. H. BAL 310 20TH WAR
OLES, CHARLES BAL 103 2ND DIST
OLFNER, SARAH BAL 053 9TH WARD
OLHENWALK, JAMES BAL 141 1ST WARD
OLIER, JAMES CHA 275 ALLENS F
OLIGRATH, ABRAHAM BAL 211 6TH DIST
OLINGER, CATHARINE CAR 250 3RD DIST
OLIPHANT, THOMAS BAL 129 2ND DIST
OLIVAR, JOSEPH CEC 097 4TH E DI
OLIVE, ANN BAL 467 14TH WAR
OLIVE, JANE BAL 075 1ST WARD
OLIVE, JOHN BAL 059 15TH WAR
OLIVE, MARY BAL 340 7TH WARD
OLIVE, MARY J. BAL 340 7TH WARD
OLIVE, NANCY BAL 275 20TH WAR
OLIVE, THOMAS BAL 033 15TH WAR
OLIVER, A. BAL 167 1ST WARD
OLIVER, ALLEN BAL 108 18TH WAR
OLIVER, AMELIA CHA 241 HILLTOP
OLIVER, ANN BAL 240 20TH WAR
OLIVER, BENJAMIN ALL 095 5TH E.D.
OLIVER, CAROLINE ANN 313 1ST DIST
OLIVER, CHARLES BAL 006 15TH WAR
OLIVER, CUFF CEC 144 PORT DUP
OLIVER, DAVID BAL 458 14TH WAR
OLIVER, DENTON WAS 152 2ND DIST
OLIVER, DOMNICK CHA 269 ALLENS F
OLIVER, E. BAL 135 1ST WARD
OLIVER, ELIJAH HAR 106 2ND DIST
OLIVER, ELIZA BAL 076 18TH WAR
OLIVER, ELIZA BAL 330 7TH WARD
OLIVER, ELIZABETH ANN 428 HOWARD D
OLIVER, ELIZABETH CEC 105 3RD E DI
OLIVER, ELLEN WAS 008 WILLIAMS
OLIVER, EZEKIEL ANN 384 4TH DIST
OLIVER, F. BAL 140 1ST WARD
OLIVER, FANNY TAL 001 EASTON D
OLIVER, FRANCIS BAL 012 1ST WARD
OLIVER, FRANCIS BAL 012 1ST WARD
OLIVER, FRANCIS CAR 215 5TH DIST
OLIVER, GEORGE BAL 135 2ND DIST
OLIVER, GEORGE BAL 456 8TH WARD
OLIVER, GEORGE ALL 109 5TH E.D.
OLIVER, GEORGE H. CHA 275 ALLENS F
OLIVER, GREENBRY BAL 160 2ND DIST
OLIVER, GUSTA ANN 363 4TH DIST
OLIVER, HANNAH BAL 321 3RD WARD
OLIVER, HARRY BAL 166 1ST WARD
OLIVER, HELLERY W. ANN 499 HOWARD D
OLIVER, HENRY BAL 150 1ST WARD
OLIVER, HENRY BAL 175 11TH WAR
OLIVER, HENRY BAL 354 13TH WAR
OLIVER, HENRY BAL 165 19TH WAR
OLIVER, HENRY-BLACK BAL 214 2ND WARD
OLIVER, ISAAC ANN 331 2ND DIST
OLIVER, JAMES ALL 127 4TH E.D.
OLIVER, JAMES O. CHA 240 HILLTOP
OLIVER, JAMES W. CHA 275 ALLENS F
OLIVER, JOHN CEC 214 7TH E DI
OLIVER, JOHN ALL 107 5TH E.D.
OLIVER, JOHN BAL 138 5TH WARD
OLIVER, JOHN BAL 290 3RD WARD
OLIVER, JOHN ANN 454 HOWARD D
OLIVER, JOHN BAL 275 7TH WARD
OLIVER, JOHN BAL 177 16TH WAR
OLIVER, JOSEPH N. CHA 275 ALLENS F
OLIVER, JOSHUA WAS 261 1ST DIST
OLIVER, LUKE H. ST 338 4TH E DI
OLIVER, LYDIA BAL 189 17TH WAR
OLIVER, MARIA BAL 319 3RD WARD
OLIVER, MARIA L. CHA 241 HILLTOP
OLIVER, MARIAH WAS 008 WILLIAMS
OLIVER, MARTHA BAL 136 18TH WAR
OLIVER, MARY ALL 108 5TH E.D.
OLIVER, MARY BAL 021 1ST WARD
OLIVER, MATILDA BAL 125 16TH WAR
OLIVER, MATILDA FRE 062 FREDERIC
OLIVER, MICHAEL ALL 142 6TH E.D.
OLIVER, OTHO BAL 222 12TH WAR
OLIVER, OWEN BAL 246 12TH WAR
OLIVER, REBECCA BAL 297 12TH WAR
OLIVER, ROBERT CHA 218 ALLENS F
OLIVER, SAMUEL BAL 254 6TH WARD
OLIVER, SAMUEL WAS 162 2ND DIST
OLIVER, SARAH BAL 120 2ND DIST
OLIVER, SASANER HAR 163 3RD DIST
OLIVER, SOLOMON* TAL 001 EASTON D
OLIVER, SOPHIA BAL 080 15TH WAR
OLIVER, SUSANNA BAL 154 5TH WARD
OLIVER, SUSANNA A. CHA 275 ALLENS F
OLIVER, THOMAS BAL 297 12TH WAR
OLIVER, THOMAS BAL 074 10TH WAR
OLIVER, THOMAS BAL 150 2ND DIST
OLIVER, THOMAS V. CEC 002 ELKTON 3
OLIVER, WILLIAM CHA 279 BOJANTOW
OLIVER, WILLIAM BAL 262 20TH WAR
OLIVER, WILLIAM BAL 154 5TH WARD
OLIVER, WILLIAM BAL 155 1ST WARD
OLIVER, WILLIAM ANN 375 4TH DIST
OLIVER, WILLIAM BAL 246 12TH WAR
OLIVER, WILLIAM BAL 113 1ST WARD
OLLIVER, REBECCA A. BAL 069 15TH WAR
OLLOWAY, SARAH A. QUE 156 2ND E DI
OLMAN, FREDERICK BAL 335 13TH WAR
OLMAY, HENRY BAL 214 19TH WAR
OLMEAR, CLEMENTINA BAL 008 4TH WARD
OLMEAR, SOPHIA BAL 008 4TH WARD
OLMSTEAD, JEREMIAH BAL 127 1ST WARD
OLMSTEAD, WILLIAM M. BAL 004 9TH WARD
OLNY, ELLEN HAR 159 3RD DIST
OLOVER, REBECCA WAS 152 2ND DIST
OLRIGE, OTHO WAS 041 2ND SUBD
OLSER, ALVERDA BAL 433 14TH WAR
OLSUP, THOMAS BAL 206 17TH WAR
OLT, CATHERINE FRE 115 CREAGERS
OLT, ELIZABETH CAR 388 2ND DIST
OLT, GEORGE FRE 123 CREAGERS
OLT, JOHN FRE 135 CREAGERS
OLVER, ISABELLA ALL 107 5TH E.D.
OLVER, JOHN ALL 095 5TH E.D.
OLVIER, ISAAC BAL 151 1ST WARD
OLVIS, JOHN BAL 024 15TH WAR
OLVIS, MARGARET BAL 023 15TH WAR
OLVIS, REYNOLDS BAL 387 3RD WARD
OLWIN, BENJAMIN WAS 035 2ND SUBD
OLWINE, AUGUSTUS H. BAL 359 3RD WARD
OMARGAR, JOSEPH BAL 367 3RD WARD
OMAYER, SUSAN BAL 101 10TH WAR
OMENHEISSER, GOTLEIB F. BAL 128 16TH WAR
OMETRA, BRIDGET BAL 098 1ST WARD
OMEY, WILLIAM BAL 463 1ST DIST
OMLINK, MARY BAL 003 4TH WARD
OMSON, ELIZABETH WAS 274 RIDGEVIL

Name	County	Page	District
OMSTED, M. J. REV.	WOR	304	SNOW HIL
ONAY, SUSAN	BAL	239	6TH WARD
ONBARCH, GEORGE	BAL	348	7TH WARD
ONDENBAUGH, ELIZABETH	BAL	375	8TH WARD
ONEAL, ARTHUR	BAL	276	1ST DIST
ONEAL, ELIZA	BAL	276	1ST DIST
ONEAL, HENRY	ALL	088	5TH E.D.
ONEAL, JOHN	CAR	220	5TH DIST
ONELEY, JOHN-BLACK	FRE	230	BUCKEYST
ONELY, BENJAMIN-BLACK	FRE	230	BUCKEYST
ONELY, WILLIAM	WOR	319	1ST E DI
ONENS, JOHN D.	SOM	494	SALISBUR
ONES, MARY A.	FRE	327	MIDDLETO
ONICK, CHARLES	BAL	121	11TH WAR
ONIEAREA, JULIA	ANN	465	HOWARD D
ONION, EDWARD M.	BAL	355	3RD WARD
ONION, FRANCIS	BAL	098	10TH WAR
ONION, JOHN W.	BAL	126	2ND DIST
ONION, NATHAN	ANN	391	4TH DIST
ONIONS, JOHN	SOM	375	BRINKLEY
ONIONS, LOYD D.	BAL	389	8TH WARD
ONIONS, STEPHEN	PRI	005	BLADENSB
ONLY, JOHN-BLACK	MGM	423	MEDLEY 3
ONLY, LUCY-BLACK	FRE	017	FREDERIC
ONLY, PHILIP	ALL	209	CUMBERLA
ONNEY, STEPHEN	BAL	196	17TH WAR
ONONEAL, SILVEY	BAL	121	16TH WAR
ONSLOW, JOHN	BAL	279	7TH WARD
ONTERBRIDGE, HENRY	BAL	155	1ST WARD
ONTOLS, CATHARINE	BAL	359	13TH WAR
ONWUTTER, CHARLES	BAL	132	16TH WAR
OOLRICH, ANDREW	BAL	072	2ND DIST
OOLRICH, HENRY	BAL	072	2ND DIST
OPEL, JOHN	BAL	369	1ST DIST
OPENHEIMER, HAITZ	BAL	043	1ST WARD
OPHIE, MOSES*	DOR	393	1ST DIST
OPHIR, DREW	DOR	419	1ST DIST
OPLSTEN, FERDINAND	BAL	408	14TH WAR
OPPELMAYER, JOSEPH	BAL	126	16TH WAR
OPPENHEIM, CAROLINE	BAL	063	15TH WAR
OPPENHEIM, EARNEST	BAL	304	7TH WARD
OPPENHEIM, ELLEN	BAL	064	15TH WAR
OPPENHEIMER, DAVID	BAL	090	10TH WAR
OPPENHEIMER, L. B.	BAL	091	10TH WAR
OPPENHEIMER, RICHARD	BAL	106	5TH WARD
OPPENMYER, HENRY	BAL	153	16TH WAR
OPPERHAUSE, JOHN	BAL	408	3RD WARD
OPPILL, CASPER	BAL	208	17TH WAR
OPPOLD, SEBASTIAN	CAR	311	1ST DIST
OPRR, ANASTASIA	BAL	014	2ND DIST
OPT, JOHN	BAL	400	1ST DIST
ORAING, ANN *	BAL	320	12TH WAR
ORAM, BENJAMIN	BAL	381	3RD WARD
ORAM, CALOE	BAL	313	3RD WARD
ORAM, CHARLOT	BAL	302	1ST DIST
ORAM, CUMBERLAND	BAL	407	1ST DIST
ORAM, DANIEL	DOR	415	1ST DIST
ORAM, ELLEN	BAL	170	19TH WAR
ORAM, JAMES	BAL	302	1ST DIST
ORAM, JOHN H.	BAL	165	19TH WAR
ORAM, JOSHUA F.	BAL	414	3RD WARD
ORAM, MARGARET	BAL	244	20TH WAR
ORAM, SMALLWOOD	BAL	407	1ST DIST
ORAM, WILLIAM	BAL	148	1ST WARD
ORAM, WILLIAM W.	BAL	324	3RD WARD
ORBITZ, GEORGE P.	BAL	445	8TH WARD
ORCHARD, ANN	BAL	120	5TH WARD
ORCHARD, CATHARINE	BAL	120	5TH WARD
ORCO, NANCY	ALL	263	CUMBERLA
ORDISCOLL, ELIZABETH	ST	274	3RD E DI
ORDNER, DANIEL	FRE	049	FREDERIC
ORDNER, ELIZA	WAS	199	1ST DIST
ORDNER, PETER	FRE	355	MIDDLETO
ORDNER, SARAH	WAS	186	BOONSBOR
ORDNER, STEPHEN	WAS	186	BOONSBOR
ORE, MARY	CEC	017	ELKTON 3
ORE, MARY	BAL	153	11TH WAR
OREAL, MICHAEL	BAL	339	1ST DIST
OREM, ANDREW	TAL	096	ST MICHA
OREM, ANDREW	TAL	096	ST MICHA
OREM, DANIEL	KEN	247	2ND DIST
OREM, ELLEN	BAL	425	14TH WAR
OREM, GEORGE W.	DOR	393	1ST DIST
OREM, HUGH S.	BAL	241	17TH WAR
OREM, ISAIAH	BAL	273	17TH WAR
OREM, J. C.	BAL	332	1ST DIST
OREM, JAMES	BAL	220	19TH WAR
OREM, JAMES	BAL	078	18TH WAR
OREM, JAMES H.	BAL	047	18TH WAR
OREM, JOHN	BAL	237	17TH WAR
OREM, JOHN	KEN	238	2ND DIST
OREM, JOHN E.	BAL	025	15TH WAR
OREM, JOHN M.	BAL	425	14TH WAR
OREM, JOSHUA	BAL	419	8TH WARD
OREM, JULIA A.	BAL	195	6TH WARD
OREM, LLOYD	BAL	139	16TH WAR
OREM, MARY	BAL	371	8TH WARD
OREM, MARY	DOR	355	3RD DIVI
OREM, NICHOLAS	TAL	103	ST MICHA
OREM, WILLIAM	KEN	272	1ST DIST
OREM, WILLIAM	BAL	191	19TH WAR
OREM, WILLIAM G.	BAL	248	17TH WAR
OREM, WILLIAM H.	BAL	018	15TH WAR
OREM, ZACHARIA	ANN	501	HOWARD D
OREN, SPEADEN *	TAL	095	ST MICHA
ORENDOFF, ARON	CAR	222	5TH DIST
ORENDOFF, CATHARINE	CAR	194	4TH DIST
ORENDOFFER, ANDREW	BAL	277	2ND WARD
ORENDORFF, DAVID	CAR	305	1ST DIST
ORENDORFF, GEORGE	CAR	276	7TH DIST
ORENDORFF, GEORGE A.	CAR	312	1ST DIST
ORENDORFF, JOHN	CAR	279	7TH DIST
ORENDORFF, JOSEPH	CAR	297	7TH DIST
ORENDUTCH, FREDERICK	BAL	274	17TH WAR
ORENSCHAL, CHRISTIAN	BAL	386	13TH WAR
OREARN, JOHN	BAL	355	13TH WAR
ORFF, CHRISTOPHER	BAL	136	16TH WAR
ORFFUTT, LEMUEL	BAL	330	1ST DIST
ORFFUTT, MARIA E.A.	BAL	249	1ST DIST
ORFIELD, JOSHUA*	BAL	337	3RD WARD
ORFUTT, EMILA	BAL	353	1ST DIST
ORGAN, RICHARD	BAL	155	1ST WARD
ORHAL, EDWARD	BAL	066	18TH WAR
ORICK, BARNEY	WAS	160	2ND DIST
ORICK, CRULUM	WAS	154	2ND DIST
ORICK, ELIZABETH	BAL	296	1ST DIST
ORIM, W. M.	BAL	332	1ST DIST
ORKAMAS, ELIZA*	TAL	060	EASTON D
ORKMAN, HARRIET*	TAL	061	EASTON D
ORLE, JOHN	BAL	131	1ST WARD
ORM, CATHARINE	BAL	100	15TH WAR
ORM, ELIZABETH	BAL	226	1ST DIST
ORM, MARY	BAL	309	1ST DIST
ORMA, MISS B.	FRE	199	5TH E DI
ORMAN, LUCRETIA	WAS	050	2ND SUBD
ORME, CHARLES E.	FRE	055	FREDERIC
ORME, CHARLES H.C.	MGM	414	MEDLEY 3
ORME, DENNIS G.	ANN	309	1ST DIST
ORME, GEORGE N.	PRI	052	AQUASCO
ORME, JACOB	FRE	231	BUCKEYST
ORME, JAMES	MGM	318	CRACKLIN
ORME, MARGARET E.	MGM	360	BERRYS D
ORMES, C.	WAS	007	WILLIAMS
ORMSEY, JOHN	BAL	125	1ST WARD
ORNDOFF, CHRISTIAN	ALL	014	3RD E.D.
ORNDOFF, WILLIAM	BAL	404	1ST DIST
ORNDORFF, ARIETTA	BAL	462	14TH WAR
ORNDORFF, DAVID	CAR	265	WESTMINS
ORNDORFF, HENRY	BAL	071	1ST WARD
ORNDORFF, SAMUEL	BAL	470	14TH WAR
ORNDORFF, SAMUEL	BAL	456	14TH WAR
ORNDUFF, JOSEPH	WAS	108	2ND DIST
ORNEY, CATHERINE	BAL	192	11TH WAR
ORNICK, DANIEL	BAL	268	20TH WAR
ORNULT, JOHN	BAL	284	1ST DIST
ORPUT, ELIAS	CAR	285	7TH DIST
ORPUT, ELIZABETH	CAR	285	7TH DIST
ORPUT, RICHARD	CAR	285	7TH DIST
ORR, ADAM	BAL	293	20TH WAR
ORR, ANDREW	CEC	148	PORT DUP
ORR, CATH	BAL	220	12TH WAR
ORR, CHARLES	BAL	344	13TH WAR
ORR, DAVID	CEC	145	PORT DUP
ORR, ELIZA	CEC	098	3RD E DI
ORR, EVAN	CEC	193	5TH E DI
ORR, JAMES	CEC	147	PORT DUP
ORR, JAMES	CAR	225	5TH DIST
ORR, JAMES	ALL	204	CUMBERLA
ORR, JOHANNA	BAL	075	10TH WAR
ORR, JOHN	BAL	114	1ST WARD
ORR, JOHN	BAL	134	1ST WARD
ORR, JOHN A.	WAS	286	1ST DIST
ORR, JOSEPH	CEC	154	PORT DUP
ORR, SARAH	CEC	154	PORT DUP
ORR, SCOTT	ALL	204	CUMBERLA
ORR, SIMON	BAL	105	1ST WARD
ORR, THOMAS	CEC	098	3RD E DI
ORR, WILLIAM	ALL	216	CUMBERLA
ORR, WILLIAM	BAL	254	6TH WARD
ORRAN, RACHEL	BAL	269	2ND WARD
ORRELL, DANIEL	CAR	071	NO TWP L
ORRELL, ROBERT J.	CAR	074	NO TWP L
ORRELL, ZEBOIAL	CAR	079	NO TWP L
ORRENBAUGH, WILLIAM H.	BAL	398	14TH WAR
ORRICH, JOHN C.	BAL	055	2ND DIST
ORRICK, ANN G.	BAL	256	1ST DIST
ORRICK, EDWARD G.	BAL	225	1ST DIST
ORRICK, ELIZA L.	BAL	244	1ST DIST
ORRICK, GEORGE	BAL	100	10TH WAR
ORRICK, GEORGE	WAS	215	1ST DIST
ORRICK, JOHN	BAL	453	1ST DIST
ORRICK, LUCY A.	ANN	521	HOWARD D
ORRICK, SARAH	WAS	215	1ST DIST
ORRICK, WILLIAM K.	BAL	296	20TH WAR
ORRILL, MARY	CAR	082	NO TWP L
ORRISON, ANDREW	FRE	321	MIDDLETO
ORRISON, DAVID	BAL	106	18TH WAR
ORRISON, PRESLEY	FRE	210	BUCKEYST
ORRISON, WILLIAM	FRE	386	PETERSVI
ORSBORN, AMOS	HAR	163	3RD DIST
ORSBORN, GEORGE	ST	348	5TH E DI
ORSBOURN, WILLIAM M.	BAL	392	8TH WARD
ORSBURN, ABIJAH	BAL	241	1ST DIST
ORSBURN, BARBARA	BAL	462	1ST DIST
ORSBURN, DORSEY	BAL	241	1ST DIST
ORSBURN, JOSEPH	BAL	277	1ST DIST
ORSBURN, LIDIA	BAL	462	1ST DIST
ORSBURN, SILAS	BAL	421	1ST DIST
ORSENOOFF, BARNEY	BAL	095	1ST WARD
ORSLER, CATHARINE A.	BAL	234	1ST DIST
ORSLER, JOHN W.	BAL	325	1ST DIST
ORSLER, WESLEY	BAL	228	1ST DIST
ORSLER, WILLIAM	BAL	327	1ST DIST
ORSME, WILLIAM	BAL	029	9TH WARD
ORSTERN, JOHN	BAL	019	15TH WAR
ORT, CONRAD	ALL	087	5TH E.D.
ORT, CONRADT	BAL	271	7TH WARD
ORT, MARY ANN	BAL	354	13TH WAR
ORTERS, FRANCIS	BAL	113	1ST WARD
ORTHER, LOUISA *	KEN	220	2ND DIST
ORTIS, F.	BAL	161	1ST WARD
ORTLISS, SAMUEL	BAL	291	7TH WARD
ORTMAN, MARY	FRE	391	PETERSVI
ORTNER, MARY	FRE	147	10TH E D
ORUM, ROBERT	BAL	183	5TH DIST
ORVENS, AMANDA	BAL	176	19TH WAR
ORWINN, ANN *	WAS	093	2ND SUBD
OSBERTH, LOUIZA	BAL	103	5TH WARD
OSBON, WILLIAM	BAL	036	15TH WAR
OSBOREN, J. H.	ANN	416	HOWARD D
OSBORN, BARNEY	HAR	157	3RD DIST
OSBORN, BENJAMIN	DOR	375	1ST DIST
OSBORN, BENJINON	HAR	201	3RD DIST
OSBORN, BETTY	CHA	254	MIDDLETO
OSBORN, CHARLES	ST	332	4TH E DI
OSBORN, CYRUS	HAR	166	3RD DIST
OSBORN, ELI	CEC	063	1ST E DI
OSBORN, ELIZABETH	HAR	160	3RD DIST
OSBORN, FRANCIS E.	CHA	282	BOJANTOW
OSBORN, GEORGE	HAR	170	3RD DIST
OSBORN, GEORGE H.	WAS	151	HAGERSTO
OSBORN, HARRIETT	HAR	163	3RD DIST
OSBORN, HENRY	HAR	151	3RD DIST
OSBORN, HENRY	WAS	234	1ST DIST
OSBORN, J. F.	BAL	153	1ST WARD
OSBORN, JACOB	HAR	157	3RD DIST
OSBORN, JAMES H.	HAR	161	3RD DIST
OSBORN, JANE	HAR	160	3RD DIST
OSBORN, JOHN	CHA	229	MIDDLETO
OSBORN, KASIAH	BAL	293	17TH WAR
OSBORN, LEVIN	CAL	037	2ND DIST
OSBORN, MARGARET	BAL	079	15TH WAR
OSBORN, MARTHA	BAL	224	6TH WARD
OSBORN, MARTHEW	HAR	163	3RD DIST
OSBORN, MARTHY	HAR	166	3RD DIST
OSBORN, MARY	HAR	181	3RD DIST
OSBORN, MARY E.	HAR	170	3RD DIST
OSBORN, MARY M.	FRE	066	FREDERIC
OSBORN, SAMUEL C.	KEN	269	1ST DIST
OSBORN, SUSAN	BAL	003	1ST WARD
OSBORN, THOMAS	BAL	193	5TH DIST
OSBORNE, ALDRICK	ANN	352	3RD DIST
OSBORNE, ALPHONSO E.	BAL	147	16TH WAR
OSBORNE, ARIANNA	ANN	356	3RD DIST
OSBORNE, BENJAMIN	ANN	345	3RD DIST
OSBORNE, COMFORT	ANN	437	HOWARD D
OSBORNE, ELIZABETH	BAL	150	16TH WAR
OSBORNE, ELIZABETH	BAL	140	11TH WAR
OSBORNE, GARRET	BAL	018	15TH WAR
OSBORNE, GEORGE	HAR	125	2ND DIST
OSBORNE, JOSEPH G.	ANN	345	3RD DIST
OSBORNE, JOSHUA	ANN	348	3RD DIST
OSBORNE, MARIA	HAR	118	2ND DIST
OSBORNE, MARY	ALL	213	CUMBERLA
OSBORNE, MARY A.	ANN	437	HOWARD D
OSBORNE, ROBERT	HAR	125	2ND DIST
OSBORNE, SAMUEL	HAR	136	2ND DIST
OSBORNE, SUSAN	ANN	418	HOWARD D
OSBOUN, EDWARD	BAL	068	18TH WAR
OSBOURN, ANN M.	PRI	001	BLADENSB
OSBOURN, FRANCIS	BAL	008	EASTERN
OSBOURN, GEORGE	BAL	166	19TH WAR
OSBOURN, HENRY	BAL	187	2ND WARD
OSBOURN, ISAAC	BAL	200	19TH WAR
OSBOURN, JAMES	BAL	014	9TH WARD
OSBOURN, JOHN C.	FRE	221	BUCKEYST
OSBOURN, MARY M.	BAL	188	2ND WARD
OSBOURN, MATILDA F.	BAL	019	2ND DIST
OSBOURN, MINERVA	BAL	392	8TH WARD
OSBOURN, W.W.	BAL	173	1ST WARD
OSBOURNE, HENRIETTA	PRI	104	PISCATAW
OSBOURNE, J.W.	BAL	197	11TH WAR
OSBOURNE, JAMES	BAL	286	2ND WARD
OSBOURNE, JOHN	PRI	074	MARLBROU
OSBOURNE, JOHN H.	PRI	105	PISCATAW
OSBOURNE, JOHN H.	PRI	106	PISCATAW
OSBOURNE, LEVI	PRI	075	MARLBROU
OSBOURNE, LEWIS	BAL	196	19TH WAR
OSBOURNE, LUCRETIA	BAL	267	12TH WAR
OSBOURNE, R.H.	PRI	074	MARLBROU
OSBOURNE, RACHEL	PRI	069	MARLBROU
OSBOURNE, RICHARD	PRI	074	MARLBROU
OSBOURNE, RICHARD	BAL	177	11TH WAR
OSBOURNE, SARAH A.	PRI	076	MARLBROU
OSBOURNE, SARAH A.	BAL	015	18TH WAR
OSBOURNE, SUSAN	PRI	074	MARLBROU
OSBOURNE, THOMAS H.	PRI	104	PISCATAW
OSBOURNE, WALTER	PRI	106	PISCATAW
OSBSON, JESSE	HAR	156	3RD DIST
OSBURN, HENRY	BAL	068	4TH WARD
OSBURN, J. F.	BAL	150	1ST WARD
OSBURN, J. F.	BAL	147	1ST WARD
OSBURN, JAMES	CHA	228	ALLENS F
OSBURN, JOHN	CHA	251	MIDDLETO
OSBURN, JOSHUA	ANN	358	3RD DIST
OSBURN, RICHARD	ANN	356	3RD DIST
OSBURN, SARAH	BAL	420	14TH WAR
OSBURN, THEADORE	CEC	149	PORT DUP
OSBURNE, WILLIAM	BAL	048	4TH WARD
OSCHIN, DEIDRICH	BAL	112	10TH WAR
OSEE, CONRAD	BAL	036	18TH WAR
OSENDOFF, MARY	BAL	115	5TH WARD
OSENG, GEORGE	BAL	366	13TH WAR
OSERDORF, GEORGE	BAL	250	2ND WARD
OSGARTH, CHARLOTTE	BAL	372	13TH WAR
OSGOOBY, GEORGE	BAL	296	3RD WARD
OSGOOD, JOHN	HAR	088	2ND DIST
OSGOOD, WILLIAM M.	BAL	155	1ST WARD
OSICH, LEWIS	BAL	009	9TH WARD
OSIS, ANTONIO	BAL	312	12TH WAR
OSKENS, JAMES	BAL	261	2ND WARD
OSKINS, WILLIAM H.	BAL	070	4TH WARD
OSLER, EMANUEL P.	BAL	324	3RD WARD
OSLER, GEORGE B.	BAL	324	3RD WARD
OSLER, JOHN	BAL	433	14TH WAR
OSLER, JOHN	WAS	117	2ND DIST
OSLER, RUBEN	FRE	129	CREAGERS
OSLING, CLINSTOFF	BAL	437	14TH WAR
OSLING, HENRY	BAL	437	14TH WAR
OSMAN, LAINHARDT	BAL	012	9TH WARD
OSMOND, WILLIAM	KEN	290	3RD DIST
OSMOS, DANIEL	BAL	161	16TH WAR
OSPINGER, WOLF	BAL	047	1ST WARD
OSPRIL, D. T.	BAL	291	3RD WARD
OSS, WILLIAM	ALL	106	5TH E.D.
OSSIRE, GEORGE H.	FRE	328	MIDDLETO
OSTENDORF, ALEXANDER	BAL	367	13TH WAR
OSTENDORF, ANTHONY	BAL	353	13TH WAR
OSTENDORF, GEORGE Q.	BAL	020	9TH WARD
OSTER, CATHARINE	BAL	206	11TH WAR
OSTER, DANIEL	WAS	292	1ST DIST
OSTER, J.W.	BAL	206	11TH WAR
OSTER, JACOB	BAL	290	3RD WARD
OSTER, JOHN	WAS	249	1ST DIST
OSTER, JOHN	BAL	423	3RD WARD
OSTER, LEAH	WAS	243	CAVETOWN
OSTER, M.	WAS	002	WILLIAMS
OSTER, MATHIAS	WAS	292	1ST DIST
OSTERDAY, ISAAC	BAL	106	1ST WARD
OSTERMAN, AUGUST	BAL	133	11TH WAR
OSTEROUS, DENI	BAL	214	17TH WAR
OSTLER, JOSEPH	HAR	038	1ST DIST
OSWALD, BENJAMIN F.	WAS	240	CAVETOWN
OSWALD, DAVID	WAS	240	CAVETOWN
OSWALD, JAMES	BAL	290	7TH WARD
OSWALD, MARGARET	WAS	240	CAVETOWN
OSWALD, MARY	BAL	285	20TH WAR
OSWALD, MARY A.	BAL	290	7TH WARD
OSWALD, PHILIP	WAS	238	CAVETOWN
OSWALD, SARAH	WAS	248	SMITHSBU
OSWALD, WILLIAM	BAL	401	8TH WARD
OSWEN, BROTHER	BAL	216	11TH WAR
OSWINKEN, CHRISTIAN	BAL	004	4TH WARD
OSWINKLE, TERESA	BAL	017	4TH WARD
OSWOLD, BROTHER	BAL	216	11TH WAR
OSYOR, H.	BAL	166	1ST WARD
OTELER, GEORGE	BAL	302	17TH WAR
OTENWALT, PHILIP	BAL	368	13TH WAR
OTHE, JOHN	BAL	264	20TH WAR
OTHER, HENRIETTA	BAL	071	1ST WARD
OTHICK, WILLIAM D.	BAL	466	14TH WAR
OTHO, SAMUEL	BAL	286	12TH WAR
OTHOVER, JACOB	BAL	267	2ND WARD
OTIS, JOHN	BAL	227	19TH WAR
OTIS, VALENTINE	FRE	300	WOODSBOR
OTL, JOHN	FRE	112	CREAGERS
OTL, WILLIAM	FRE	135	CREAGERS
OTMER, HENRY	BAL	416	1ST DIST
OTROME, HARTMAN	BAL	262	20TH WAR
OTT, ANDREW	BAL	213	19TH WAR

Name	County	Page	District
OTT, CATHARINE	FRE	171	5TH E DI
OTT, CHARLES	BAL	028	9TH WARD
OTT, CHARLES F.	FRE	048	FREDERIC
OTT, CANIEL	WAS	260	1ST DIST
OTT, ELIZABETH	WAS	207	1ST DIST
OTT, GEORGE	ALL	232	CUMBERLA
OTT, JACOB	WAS	224	1ST DIST
OTT, JOHN	FRE	054	FREDERIC
OTT, JOHN	FRE	171	5TH E DI
OTT, LYDIA	FRE	309	WOODSBOR
CTT, MICHAEL	CAR	300	1ST DIST
OTT, PETER	FRE	001	FREDERIC
OTT, SAMUEL	WAS	231	1ST DIST
OTTA, FRED	BAL	265	1ST DIST
OTTAFORD, WILLIAM *	BAL	275	1ST DIST
OTTE, FREDERICK	BAL	013	4TH WARD
OTTELSPERGER, JOHN	WAS	272	RIDGEVIL
OTTEN, WILLIAM *	BAL	100	18TH WAR
OTTER, ANDREW	BAL	095	1ST WARD
OTTER, CAROLINE	BAL	094	1ST WARD
OTTER, ELIZABETH	BAL	146	19TH WAR
OTTER, HENRY	BAL	095	1ST WARD
OTTER, JAMES	BAL	146	19TH WAR
CTTER, JOHN H.	ANN	427	HOWARD D
OTTER, WILLIAM	BAL	271	12TH WAR
OTTER, WILLIAM *	BAL	100	18TH WAR
CTTERBOL, JOSEPH	BAL	206	19TH WAR
OTTLES, ELIZABETH	BAL	253	12TH WAR
OTTMAN, CHRISTIANA	BAL	245	2ND WARD
CTTMAN, PETER	BAL	003	4TH WARD
OTTMER, FERDINAND	BAL	377	8TH WARD
OTTO, ALBERT	ALL	044	10TH E.D
OTTO, ANDREW	BAL	124	1ST WARD
OTTO, CHRIST	WAS	210	1ST DIST
OTTO, DAVID	CAR	326	1ST DIST
OTTO, ELI	FRE	281	WOODSBOR
OTTO, ELIZABETH	BAL	297	17TH WAR
OTTO, ERNEST	BAL	211	2ND WARD
OTTO, GEORGE	BAL	337	13TH WAR
OTTO, HENRY	WAS	098	2ND DIST
OTTO, JOHN	WAS	060	2ND SUBD
OTTC, JOHN	FRE	281	WOODSBOR
CTTC, JOHN	ALL	016	3RD E.D.
OTTO, JOHN	BAL	292	7TH WARD
OTTO, JOHN E.	ALL	043	10TH E.D
OTTO, LEVI	ALL	043	10TH E.D
OTTO, MARTHA	CAR	327	1ST DIST
CTTO, PETER	CAR	325	1ST DIST
CTTO, SAMUEL	CAR	327	1ST DIST
OTTO, SIMON	BAL	297	17TH WAR
OTUR, HENRY	SOM	393	BRINKLEY
OTWINE, WILLIAM	BAL	209	19TH WAR
CUDEWINE, SARAH	BAL	125	5TH WARD
OUEN, JULIA-BLACK	FRE	013	FREDERIC
OUFERTRIGER, HENRY	BAL	459	14TH WAR
OUFFUTT, JOSEPH	BAL	127	5TH WARD
OULD, GEORGE	BAL	462	14TH WAR
OULD, LANCASTER	BAL	378	1ST DIST
CULEHEN, JOHN	BAL	117	5TH WARD
OUR, JACOB	BAL	314	1ST DIST
OURAND, THCMAS	FRE	305	WOODSBOR
OURSLER, ASARIAH	CAR	198	4TH DIST
OURSLER, BASIL J.	BAL	330	1ST DIST
OURSLER, EDWARD	BAL	185	16TH WAR
OURSLER, ECWARD	CAR	330	MANCHEST
OURSLER, ELIAS	CAR	332	MANCHEST
OURSLER, ELIZABETH	CAR	196	4TH DIST
OURSLER, HERNY	CAR	276	7TH DIST
OURSLER, JOHN	CAR	216	5TH DIST
OURSLER, MARGARET	BAL	173	16TH WAR
OURSLER, RICHARD	CAR	396	2ND DIST
OURSLER, WILLIAM	CAR	270	WESTMINS
OURSPRUNG, AUGUSTA	BAL	279	1ST DIST
OURSPRUNG, CATHARINE	BAL	278	1ST DIST
CURSTER, WILLIAM W.	BAL	184	16TH WAR
OUSTERHOUS, HENRY	BAL	017	15TH WAR
OUSTLAND, HENRY*	BAL	417	3RD WARD
OUTER, NANCY	SOM	393	BRINKLEY
OUTER, POLLY	SOM	410	DUBLIN D
OUTER, SARAH	BAL	298	12TH WAR
OUTH, CATHARINE	BAL	304	7TH WARD
OUTHERISK, MARGARET	ANN	464	HOWARD D
CUTHOUSE, W.	BAL	155	1ST WARD
OUTLAW, BETTIE	ANN	521	HOWARD D
OUTLAW, HARRIET B.	ANN	521	HOWARD D
OUTON, WILLIAM	BAL	194	11TH WAR
OUTT, JOHN	BAL	197	11TH WAR
OUTT, MAY B.	BAL	196	11TH WAR
OUTTEN, EZEKIEL-BLACK	WOR	327	1ST E DI
OUTTEN, PERRY	CAR	108	NO TWP L
OUTTEN, PETER C.	WOR	327	1ST E DI
OUTTEN, WILLIAM	WOR	336	1ST E DI
OUZEST, WILLIAM	BAL	185	2ND WARD
OVELINAN, JOSEPH	FRE	176	5TH E DI
OVELLMAN, GEORGE	FRE	181	5TH E DI
OVELMAN, ABRAHAM	FRE	181	5TH E DI
OVENHAMMER, HENRIETTA	BAL	081	4TH WARD
OVERBACK, CHARLES	BAL	147	5TH WARD
OVERCASH, SOLOMAN	WAS	109	2ND DIST
OVERDEER, CATHARINE	CAR	247	3RD DIST
OVERDEER, SOLOMON	CAR	330	MANCHEST
OVERHOFF, SARAH	BAL	237	6TH WARD
OVERLY, MARTHA	SOM	428	PRINCESS
OVERLY, THOMAS	SOM	427	PRINCESS
OVERMAN, JOHN	BAL	221	17TH WAR
OVERMAN, WILLIAM	CAR	342	6TH DIST
OVERSIDE, CERILLA	BAL	226	2ND WARD
OVERTON, JAMES	BAL	363	8TH WARD
OVRER, FREDRICK LON *	BAL	274	2ND WARD
OWEINGS, THOMAS C. DR.	BAL	338	13TH WAR
OWEN, ALEXANDER	ST	315	4TH E DI
OWEN, ANGELME	BAL	272	12TH WAR
OWEN, BENJAMIN F.	CEC	212	7TH E DI
OWEN, BETSY	CHA	290	BOJANTOW
OWEN, BIDOY	BAL	271	12TH WAR
OWEN, CAROILNE E.	BAL	249	1ST DIST
OWEN, CHARLES W.	CEC	075	NORTHEAS
OWEN, EDWARC W.	MGM	327	CRACKLIN
OWEN, ELIE	WAS	190	1ST DIST
OWEN, ELISHA D.	ANN	302	1ST DIST
OWEN, GEORGE	BAL	316	1ST DIST
OWEN, J.	WAS	021	2ND SUBD
OWEN, JAMES C.	BAL	430	8TH WARD
OWEN, JANE E.	BAL	065	1ST WARD
OWEN, JESSE	CEC	191	5TH E DI
OWEN, JOHN	BAL	272	12TH WAR
OWEN, JOHN	ANN	495	HOWARD D
OWEN, JOHN W.	CHA	290	BOJANTOW
OWEN, JOSEPH F.	CHA	249	HILLTOP
OWEN, JOSHUA	ANN	502	HOWARD D

Name	County	Page	District
OWEN, JULIA	BAL	202	11TH WAR
OWEN, KENELLY R.*	TAL	026	EASTON D
OWEN, MARY B.	CHA	290	BOJANTOW
OWEN, NANCY J.	CHA	221	ALLENS F
OWEN, PATRICK	BAL	384	8TH WARD
OWEN, R.H.	BAL	265	1ST DIST
OWEN, S.	BAL	333	1ST DIST
OWEN, SARAH B.	BAL	413	1ST DIST
OWEN, THCMAS	CHA	219	ALLENS F
OWEN, THCMAS	MGM	367	BERRYS D
OWEN, WASHINGTCN G.	MGM	367	BERRYS D
OWEN, WASHINGTON W.	MGM	367	BERRYS D
OWEN, WILLIAM	CHA	218	ALLENS F
OWEN, WILLIAM J.	BAL	317	12TH WAR
OWENS, ALEXANDER	ANN	395	8TH DIST
OWENS, ALLY	PRI	086	QUEEN AN
OWENS, AMELIA	SOM	503	SALISBUR
OWENS, ANN	BAL	279	7TH WARD
OWENS, ANN	CEC	083	CHARLEST
OWENS, ANTHONY-MULATTO	FRE	010	FREDERIC
OWENS, BARNEY	BAL	350	7TH WARD
OWENS, BASIL	PRI	033	VANSVILL
OWENS, BENJAMIN	SOM	516	BARREN C
OWENS, BEAJAMIN	ANN	374	4TH DIST
OWENS, BENJAMIN	CAL	050	3RD DIST
OWENS, BRIDGETT	BAL	052	4TH WARD
OWENS, C.	BAL	151	1ST WARD
OWENS, CALVERT	ST	332	4TH E DI
OWENS, CHARISILLA	BAL	024	2ND DIST
OWENS, CHARLES	CEC	015	ELKTON 3
OWENS, CHARLOTT	FRE	029	FREDERIC
OWENS, CHARLOTTA	CEC	192	5TH E DI
OWENS, CHARLOTTE	SOM	534	QUANTICO
OWENS, DAVID	CEC	190	5TH E DI
OWENS, DAVID	CEC	125	5TH E DI
OWENS, CAVID	BAL	457	8TH WARD
OWENS, DELIA T.	ST	333	4TH E DI
OWENS, DENNIS	ANN	396	8TH DIST
OWENS, E.	ANN	270	ANNAPOLI
OWENS, E. T.	BAL	471	14TH WAR
OWENS, EBENEZER	SOM	492	SALISBUR
OWENS, EDWARD T.	BAL	447	14TH WAR
OWENS, ELEANOR	SOM	519	BARREN C
OWENS, ELEANORA	BAL	111	15TH WAR
OWENS, ELISHA G.	SOM	534	QUANTICO
OWENS, ELIZA	BAL	321	1ST DIST
OWENS, ELIZA	BAL	378	3RD WARD
OWENS, ELIZA MRS-	ANN	297	1ST DIST
OWENS, ELIZABETH	BAL	022	15TH WAR
OWENS, ELIZABETH	WAS	062	2ND SUBD
OWENS, ELIZABETH	CEC	107	3RD E DI
OWENS, ELIZABETH	MGM	329	CRACKLIN
OWENS, ELLEN	BAL	124	11TH WAR
OWENS, ELLEN	BAL	075	15TH WAR
OWENS, ENOCH	ANN	395	8TH DIST
OWENS, FANNY	BAL	244	6TH WARD
OWENS, FIELDER	ANN	289	ANNAPOLI
OWENS, FRANCES	CEC	083	CHARLEST
OWENS, FRANCIS	BAL	006	9TH WARD
OWENS, FRANCIS	BAL	049	9TH WARD
OWENS, FREDRIC P.	CEC	130	6TH E DI
OWENS, G. F.	ANN	295	1ST DIST
OWENS, GAS. *	ANN	299	1ST DIST
OWENS, GEORGE	BAL	006	9TH WARD
OWENS, GEORGE	BAL	328	3RD WARD
OWENS, GEORGE	BAL	091	5TH WARD
OWENS, GEORGE	BAL	022	1ST WARD
OWENS, GEORGE	DOR	341	3RD DIVI
OWENS, GEORGE	ST	329	4TH E DI
OWENS, GEORGE	KEN	300	3RD DIST
OWENS, GUSTAVIUS	MGM	344	CLARKSBU
OWENS, HASSILET	CEC	178	7TH E DI
OWENS, HENRY	PRI	095	SPALDING
OWENS, HENRY	ANN	305	1ST DIST
OWENS, HORACE	ANN	395	8TH DIST
OWENS, HUGH	FRE	076	FREDERIC
OWENS, IGNATIUS	ST	328	4TH E DI
OWENS, ISAAC	ANN	306	1ST DIST
OWENS, ISAAC	BAL	182	2ND WARD
OWENS, ISAAC B.	ANN	302	1ST DIST
OWENS, JACOB	CEC	068	5TH E DI
OWENS, JAMES	CEC	024	ELKTON 3
OWENS, JAMES	ANN	398	8TH DIST
OWENS, JAMES	BAL	338	7TH WARD
OWENS, JAMES	ST	315	4TH E DI
OWENS, JAMES	PRI	033	VANSVILL
OWENS, JAMES	WAS	143	HAGERSTO
OWENS, JAMES E.	PRI	095	SPALDING
OWENS, JAMES E.	BAL	140	16TH WAR
OWENS, JAMES JR.	ANN	395	8TH DIST
OWENS, JAMES S.	ANN	394	8TH DIST
OWENS, JAMES SR.	ANN	395	8TH DIST
OWENS, JANE	ST	330	4TH E DI
OWENS, JOHN	BAL	084	1ST WARD
OWENS, JOHN	CEC	083	CHARLEST
OWENS, JOHN	BAL	303	17TH WAR
OWENS, JOHN C.	CAR	236	UNION TO
OWENS, JOHN JR.	ANN	311	1ST DIST
OWENS, JOHN JR.	ANN	316	1ST DIST
OWENS, JOHN T.	KEN	222	2ND DIST
OWENS, JOSEPH	PRI	036	VANSVILL
OWENS, JOSEPH	ST	269	3RD E DI
OWENS, JOSEPH JR.	ANN	394	8TH DIST
OWENS, JOSHUA	BAL	176	16TH WAR
OWENS, JOSHUA	ANN	374	4TH DIST
OWENS, JOSHUA	SOM	511	BARREN C
OWENS, JOSIAH	ST	281	3RD E DI
OWENS, JUDITH	BAL	026	1ST WARD
OWENS, LAURA	BAL	423	3RD WARD
OWENS, LAURA A.	BAL	244	6TH WARD
OWENS, LEAR	BAL	387	3RD WARD
OWENS, LOUISA	CEC	017	ELKTON 3
OWENS, LOUISA SR.	SOM	492	SALISBUR
OWENS, MARGARET	BAL	383	3RD WARD
OWENS, MARGARET	BAL	091	5TH WARD
OWENS, MARTHA L.	CAL	051	3RD DIST
OWENS, MARY	CEC	034	CHESAPEA
OWENS, MARY	BAL	228	19TH WAR
OWENS, MARY	BAL	384	3RD WARD
OWENS, MARY	BAL	069	1ST WARD
OWENS, MARY	ANN	374	4TH DIST
OWENS, MARY	ANN	299	1ST DIST
OWENS, MARY	ANN	298	1ST DIST
OWENS, MARY C.	ANN	300	1ST DIST
OWENS, MATTHEW	HAR	108	2ND DIST
OWENS, MITELDA	BAL	040	18TH WAR
OWENS, NATHAN	CEC	014	ELKTON 3
OWENS, NELLY	ANN	289	ANNAPOLI
OWENS, NELLY	BAL	206	11TH WAR
OWENS, NELSON	ST	304	2ND E DI

Name	County	Page	District
OWENS, NESSEY	BAL	216	6TH WARD
OWENS, NICHOLAS	ANN	301	1ST DIST
OWENS, OWEN	BAL	066	10TH WAR
OWENS, PATRICK	BAL	148	5TH WARD
OWENS, PETER	SOM	535	QUANTICO
OWENS, PHILIP	BAL	039	15TH WAR
OWENS, PHILLIS	CEC	181	7TH E DI
OWENS, RICHARD	BAL	154	1ST WARD
OWENS, RICHARD	ANN	382	4TH DIST
OWENS, ROBERT	BAL	083	1ST WARD
OWENS, ROBERT	BAL	112	5TH WARD
OWENS, ROBERT	BAL	378	1ST DIST
OWENS, ROBERT	ST	298	2ND E DI
OWENS, RUSSELL	CEC	126	5TH E DI
OWENS, SAMUEL	MGM	349	BERRYS D
OWENS, SAMUEL	ANN	433	HOWARD D
OWENS, SAMUEL	ANN	301	1ST DIST
OWENS, SARAH	BAL	387	3RD WARD
OWENS, SUSAN	BAL	084	1ST WARD
OWENS, SUSAN E.	ANN	299	1ST DIST
OWENS, T.	BAL	233	12TH WAR
OWENS, THOMAS	ANN	396	8TH DIST
OWENS, THOMAS	CEC	080	NORTHEAS
OWENS, THOMAS	CEC	102	4TH E DI
OWENS, THOMAS F.	ANN	395	8TH DIST
OWENS, THOMAS G.	BAL	002	4TH WARD
OWENS, THOMAS M.	BAL	318	3RD WARD
OWENS, WILLAIM	PRI	095	SPALDING
OWENS, WILLIAM	BAL	261	6TH WARD
OWENS, WILLIAM	BAL	167	1ST WARD
OWENS, WILLIAM	KEN	241	2ND DIST
OWENS, WILLIAM	BAL	342	13TH WAR
OWENS, WILLIAM M.	ALL	127	4TH E.D.
OWENS, WILLIAM P.	BAL	019	4TH WARD
OWENS,MARY A.	BAL	033	1ST WARD
OWENS,T HOMAS	ST	331	4TH E DI
OWESN, PRICILLA	ST	332	4TH E DI
OWING, HENRY H.	ANN	476	HOWARD D
OWING, JAMES	CAR	377	2ND DIST
OWING, JESSE	CAR	378	2ND DIST
OWING, JESSE-BLACK	CAR	382	2ND DIST
OWING, MARY	CAR	378	2ND DIST
OWING, ORREY-BLACK	CAR	398	2ND DIST
OWING, PAUL	BAL	295	12TH WAR
OWING, RICHARD	ANN	433	HOWARD D
OWING,S THOMAS B.	CAR	375	9TH DIST
OWINGS, ABRAHAM	BAL	446	1ST DIST
OWINGS, ACH.	BAL	295	1ST DIST
OWINGS, ALEXANDER	BAL	450	8TH WARD
OWINGS, ANN	BAL	298	1ST DIST
OWINGS, ANN	ANN	458	HOWARD D
OWINGS, ANN	BAL	055	18TH WAR
OWINGS, BARNEY	BAL	249	1ST DIST
OWINGS, BASEL	BAL	319	1ST DIST
OWINGS, BASIL	ANN	508	HOWARD D
OWINGS, BASSIL	BAL	280	17TH WAR
OWINGS, BEAL	BAL	223	1ST DIST
OWINGS, BENJAMIN	BAL	375	1ST DIST
OWINGS, C. HOWARD	BAL	328	1ST DIST
OWINGS, CALIB D.	BAL	329	1ST DIST
OWINGS, CARLIOUS	FRE	424	8TH E DI
OWINGS, CAROLINE	BAL	394	14TH WAR
OWINGS, CATHARINE	BAL	254	1ST DIST
OWINGS, CATHARINE	BAL	131	16TH WAR
OWINGS, CHARLES	BAL	318	1ST DIST
OWINGS, CHARLES	CAR	231	5TH DIST
OWINGS, CHARLES C.	ANN	499	HOWARD D
OWINGS, CHARLES R.	BAL	412	1ST DIST
OWINGS, CHARLOTTE	BAL	441	1ST DIST
OWINGS, DAVID	BAL	230	1ST DIST
OWINGS, DORATHY	BAL	296	1ST DIST
OWINGS, DUNCAN	ANN	494	HOWARD D
OWINGS, EDWIN V.	CAR	226	5TH DIST
OWINGS, ELIZABETH	CAR	201	4TH DIST
OWINGS, ELIZABETH	BAL	323	1ST DIST
OWINGS, GEORGE	BAL	341	1ST DIST
OWINGS, HANNAH	BAL	248	1ST DIST
OWINGS, HARRIET	MGM	320	CRACKLIN
OWINGS, HENRY	BAL	264	1ST DIST
OWINGS, HENRY	BAL	384	1ST DIST
OWINGS, HENRY	BAL	376	1ST DIST
OWINGS, IRIEL	BAL	277	1ST DIST
OWINGS, ISRIEL	BAL	406	1ST DIST
OWINGS, ISRIEL	BAL	387	1ST DIST
OWINGS, JACOB	BAL	391	14TH WAR
OWINGS, JAMES	BAL	402	14TH WAR
OWINGS, JAMES	BAL	469	14TH WAR
OWINGS, JAMES	BAL	026	18TH WAR
OWINGS, JAMES	BAL	448	1ST DIST
OWINGS, JAMES	BAL	384	8TH WARD
OWINGS, JAMES	BAL	384	8TH WARD
OWINGS, JAMES H.	MGM	319	CRACKLIN
OWINGS, JAMES W.	BAL	255	1ST DIST
OWINGS, JESSEE	BAL	100	2ND DIST
OWINGS, JOHN	BAL	190	5TH DIST
OWINGS, JOHN	BAL	449	1ST DIST
OWINGS, JOHN	BAL	083	18TH WAR
OWINGS, JOHN H.	ANN	494	HOWARD D
OWINGS, JOHN-MULATTO	FRE	435	8TH E DI
OWINGS, JOSH	BAL	002	18TH WAR
OWINGS, JOSHUA	CAR	364	9TH DIST
OWINGS, JOSHUA	BAL	268	1ST DIST
OWINGS, L. K.	BAL	039	4TH WARD
OWINGS, LLOYD	ANN	481	HOWARD D
OWINGS, LOUISA	BAL	299	1ST DIST
OWINGS, LYDIA A.	ANN	448	HOWARD D
OWINGS, MARY	BAL	094	18TH WAR
OWINGS, MATILDA	BAL	204	19TH WAR
OWINGS, NANCY H.*	BAL	103	10TH WAR
OWINGS, NATHAN H.	FRE	439	8TH E DI
OWINGS, NICHOLAS	ANN	512	HOWARD D
OWINGS, ORRELLANA H.	FRE	448	8TH E DI
OWINGS, PETER	BAL	377	8TH WARD
OWINGS, PETER S.	BAL	415	1ST DIST
OWINGS, PHILIP R.	BAL	464	1ST DIST
OWINGS, R. H.	BAL	471	14TH WAR
OWINGS, RACHAEL-MULATTO	FRE	442	8TH E DI
OWINGS, RICAHRD	BAL	257	17TH WAR
OWINGS, RICARD	ANN	402	8TH DIST
OWINGS, RICHARD	BAL	189	17TH WAR
OWINGS, RICHARD	BAL	122	1ST WARD
OWINGS, S. S.	BAL	282	2ND WARD
OWINGS, SAMUEL	BAL	416	1ST DIST
OWINGS, SAMUEL	CAL	043	3RD DIST
OWINGS, SAMUEL B.*	BAL	103	10TH WAR
OWINGS, SAMUEL C.	BAL	397	14TH WAR
OWINGS, SAMUEL L.	ANN	486	HOWARD D
OWINGS, SAMUEL L.	ANN	486	HOWARD D
OWINGS, SAMUEL-MULATTO	FRE	429	8TH E DI
OWINGS, SOPHIA	BAL	330	1ST DIST

OWINGS, THOEDORE BAL 439 14TH WAR
OWINGS, THOMAS ANN 402 8TH DIST
OWINGS, THOMAS WOR 196 8TH E DI
OWINGS, THOMAS J. BAL 296 1ST DIST
OWINGS, WASHINGTON FRE 445 8TH E DI
OWINGS, WILLIAM ANN 487 HOWARD D
OWINGS, WILLIAM L. BAL 415 1ST DIST
OWINGTON, CHARLES BAL 129 1ST WARD
OWININGS, JOHN HAR 206 3RD DIST
OWINS, ELISHA DOR 300 1ST DIST
OWINS, MARY BAL 405 8TH WARD
OWL, NATHANIEL WAS 129 2ND DIST
OWLDER, CHARLES BAL 130 11TH WAR
OWLINGS, ELIZABETH BAL 131 16TH WAR
OWMUDA, FRANCIS BAL 106 18TH WAR
OWNEY, CATHRINE BAL 012 18TH WAR
OWREN, DAVID FRE 307 WOODSBOR
OWRSLER, STEPHEN CAR 195 4TH DIST
OXENHAM, ANDRWE C. TAL 091 ST MICHA
OYBORIN, URSULA L. * BAL 302 20TH WAR
OYE, A.-BLACK FRE 200 5TH E DI
OYL, LOUIS BAL 007 15TH WAR
OYLER, BILLY ANN 342 3RD DIST
OYLER, JACOB BAL 287 20TH WAR
OYSTERMAN, JANET BAL 259 20TH WAR
OYSTERMAN, JOHN BAL 259 20TH WAR
OZBORN, LYDIA CAR 382 2ND DIST
OZIER, ELIZABETH BAL 121 16TH WAR
OZIER, JOHN BAL 350 7TH WARD
OZIER, NICHOLAS BAL 345 7TH WARD
OZMON, ANN M. TAL 065 EASTON T
OZMON, HARRIET TAL 072 EASTON T
OZMON, JOHN W. C. TAL 055 EASTON D
OZMON, JONATHAN TAL 069 EASTON T
OZMON, WILLIAM TAL 055 EASTON D
OZMONT, ELIZABETH TAL 065 EASTON T
OZMONT, JOHN* TAL 054 EASTON D
OZURDA, VINCENT BAL 002 18TH WAR
P---, ISAAC ANN 339 3RD DIST
PAAS, CATHERINE BAL 086 10TH WAR
PACA, BENJAMIN KEN 288 3RD DIST
PACA, ED T. QUE 243 5TH E DI
PACA, JACOB W. BAL 214 6TH WARD
PACA, JOHN HAR 083 2ND DIST
PACA, LOUISA KEN 301 3RD DIST
PACA, MARGARET BAL 454 14TH WAR
PACA, MARY J. ANN 415 HOWARD D
PACA, NANCY C. BAL 447 14TH WAR
PACA, SARAH HAR 151 3RD DIST
PACA, SARAH HAR 155 3RD DIST
PACA, THOMAS KEN 305 3RD DIST
PACA, WILLIAM B. QUE 243 5TH E DI
PACAEER, RICHARD * ANN 337 3RD DIST
PACCE, HARRIET BAL 089 5TH WARD
PACCIANINA, BASIL FRE 067 FREDERIC
PACE, ANNA BAL 051 15TH WAR
PACELEY, ARIS R. FRE 096 FREDERIC
PACER, ALICE CEC 057 1ST E DI
PACHELL, JAMES BAL 162 1ST WARD
PACK, KEZIA ANN 360 3RD DIST
PACK, LEVI ANN 358 3RD DIST
PACK, RACHELL BAL 223 17TH WAR
PACK, RUTH BAL 223 17TH WAR
PACK, SUSAN ANN 296 1ST DIST
PACKARD, BENJAMIN F. FRE 028 FREDERIC
PACKARD, M. BAL 118 1ST WARD
PACKER, MARY W. CEC 146 PORT DUP
PACKIE, ALEXANDER BAL 186 6TH WARD
PACKS, GEORGE FRE 128 CREAGERS
PACKWOOD, J. C. BAL 151 1ST WARD
PACKWOOD, JOHN E. BAL 134 1ST WARD
PACKWOOD, RACHAEL BAL 049 1ST WARD
PACO, ELIZA A. HAR 089 2ND DIST
PACO, F.M. BAL 142 1ST WARD
PACO, WILLIAM HAR 088 2ND DIST
PACOCK, ISRAEL BAL 031 2ND DIST
PACOR, JULIANNA QUE 243 5TH E DI
PACT, HARRY BAL 148 19TH WAR
PADDER, MARY ALL 075 5TH E.D.
PADDON, PETER ALL 141 6TH E.D.
PADDY, JAMES CAL 038 2ND DIST
PADDY, JOSHUA CAL 026 2ND DIST
PADELTON, JOHN BAL 081 1ST WARD
PADEN, ALEXANDER WAS 173 FUNKSTOW
PADEN, NELLY WAS 174 FUNKSTOW
PADERSON, ROBERT BAL 162 19TH WAR
PADGET, AZARIAS CHA 290 BOJANTOW
PADGET, CHRISTENA CHA 251 MIDDLETO
PADGET, ELISHA CHA 228 BOJANTOW
PADGET, ELIZABETH FRE 095 FREDERIC
PADGET, GEORGE R. CHA 268 BOJANTOW
PADGET, HARRIET CHA 268 BOJANTOW
PADGET, J. T. CHA 219 ALLENS F
PADGET, JAMES W. CHA 244 HILLTOP
PADGET, JOHN MGM 406 MEDLEY 3
PADGET, JOSEPH CHA 266 MIDDLETO
PADGET, MOSES MGM 387 ROCKERLE
PADGET, OFFA MGM 387 ROCKERLE
PADGET, ROBERT BAL 437 8TH WARD
PADGET, RUFUS CHA 254 MIDDLETO
PADGET, SARA CHA 267 MIDDLETO
PADGET, TERRESA CHA 217 ALLENS F
PADGET, THOMAS H. CHA 293 BOJANTOW
PADGET, THOMAS V. CHA 268 BOJANTOW
PADGET, W.A. ST 334 4TH E DI
PADGET, WILLIAM CHA 229 MIDDLETO
PADGETT, ALEXANDER PRI 017 BLADENSB
PADGETT, ALFRED FRE 216 BUCKEYST
PADGETT, BAKER PRI 055 AQUASCO
PADGETT, BENJAMIN PRI 006 BLADENSB
PADGETT, ELIZABETH PRI 088 SPALDING
PADGETT, GEORGE W. FRE 219 BUCKEYST
PADGETT, GOERGE W. FRE 395 PETERSVI
PADGETT, H. W. BAL 072 10TH WAR
PADGETT, JOHN MGM 354 BERRYS D
PADGETT, MARY FRE 216 BUCKEYST
PADGETT, MARY FRE 216 BUCKEYST
PADGETT, THOMAS PRI 036 VANSVILL
PADGETT, WILLIAM H. BAL 212 6TH WARD
PADUE, P. BAL 122 1ST WARD
PAENRS, AUGSUTUS L. BAL 334 13TH WAR
PAFF, JOHN BAL 216 2ND WARD
PAFLE, JOHN BAL 249 2ND WARD
PAGAN, JANE DOR 356 3RD DIVI
PAGAN, LEVY DOR 358 3RD DIVI
PAGAN, MARY A. BAL 017 15TH WAR
PAGE, ALBERT W. BAL 389 8TH WARD
PAGE, ALEXANDER DOR 424 1ST DIST
PAGE, ANDREW G. HAR 040 1ST DIST
PAGE, ANNA DOR 378 1ST DIST
PAGE, ANTHONY C. PRI 086 QUEEN AN
PAGE, CALVIN FRE 033 FREDERIC
PAGE, CHARELS W. BAL 257 17TH WAR
PAGE, CYRUS BAL 311 3RD WARD
PAGE, DANIEL C. BAL 406 3RD WARD
PAGE, F. M. BAL 136 11TH WAR
PAGE, GEORGE F. BAL 050 18TH WAR
PAGE, GEORGE W. MGM 340 CLARKSBU
PAGE, HENRY KEN 223 2ND DIST
PAGE, HENRY DOR 378 1ST DIST
PAGE, HENRY KEN 276 1ST DIST
PAGE, JACOB KEN 220 2ND DIST
PAGE, JAEMS KEN 266 1ST DIST
PAGE, JAMES KEN 265 1ST DIST
PAGE, JAMES MGM 443 CLARKSTR
PAGE, JAMES CEC 050 1ST E DI
PAGE, JAMES F. MGM 444 CLARKSTR
PAGE, LEWIS BAL 212 19TH WAR
PAGE, LEWIS BAL 454 8TH WARD
PAGE, MARGARET C. BAL 413 3RD WARD
PAGE, MARY J. DOR 324 1ST DIST
PAGE, NATHAN BAL 107 18TH WAR
PAGE, NATHAN KEN 267 1ST DIST
PAGE, NATHAN H. MGM 432 CLARKSTR
PAGE, PUTMAN ALL 206 CUMBERLA
PAGE, ROBERT DOR 466 1ST DIST
PAGE, THOMAS BAL 046 2ND DIST
PAGE, THOMAS FRE 074 FREDERIC
PAGE, THOMAS J. HAR 040 1ST DIST
PAGE, TILVY KEN 232 2ND DIST
PAGE, WASHINGTON A. BAL 013 4TH WARD
PAGE, WILLIAM DOR 323 1ST DIST
PAGE, WILLIAM BAL 401 14TH WAR
PAGE, WILLIAM BAL 160 1ST WARD
PAGE, WILLIAM JOHN BAL 258 17TH WAR
PAGENSTEAD, JOSEPH BAL 135 11TH WAR
PAGER, JAMES N. BAL 282 2ND WARD
PAGET, ELIJAH BAL 012 15TH WAR
PAGHILL, SAMUEL BAL 110 2ND DIST
PAGOS, MARIE* BAL 097 10TH WAR
PAHM, JERRY FRE 091 FREDERIC
PAHNTZ, HENRY P.* BAL 089 10TH WAR
PAIN, BENJAMIN WOR 326 1ST E DI
PAIN, EBEN* DOR 465 1ST DIST
PAIN, ELIJA WOR 295 9TH E DI
PAIN, ELIZ. BAL 043 18TH WAR
PAIN, GEORGE WOR 293 9TH E DI
PAIN, GOERGE B. HAR 153 3RD DIST
PAIN, HESTER J.* DOR 465 1ST DIST
PAIN, JOHN HAR 021 1ST DIST
PAIN, JOHN BAL 272 1ST DIST
PAIN, MOSES WOR 346 1ST E DI
PAIN, WILLEY HAR 074 1ST DIST
PAIN, WILLIAM WAS 136 2ND DIST
PAINE, ALLEN BAL 001 18TH WAR
PAINE, AMELIA BAL 295 17TH WAR
PAINE, AMELIA BAL 053 15TH WAR
PAINE, ANN M. BAL 232 6TH WARD
PAINE, CHARLOTTE BAL 070 15TH WAR
PAINE, CORNELIUS ST 320 4TH E DI
PAINE, D.A. BAL 212 11TH WAR
PAINE, E.E. BAL 135 5TH WARD
PAINE, EMILINE BAL 145 5TH WARD
PAINE, HILLERY FRE 333 MIDDLETO
PAINE, J.F. BAL 165 1ST WARD
PAINE, JAMES BAL 185 11TH WAR
PAINE, JAMES R. BAL 174 16TH WAR
PAINE, JOHN BAL 062 18TH WAR
PAINE, JOHN BAL 095 18TH WAR
PAINE, JOHN WOR 326 1ST E DI
PAINE, JOHN PRI 097 SPALDING
PAINE, LANDY BAL 280 2ND WARD
PAINE, LEAH WOR 326 1ST E DI
PAINE, LITTLETON WOR 298 9TH E DI
PAINE, MARGARET BAL 002 18TH WAR
PAINE, MARGARET BAL 403 14TH WAR
PAINE, MARY BAL 089 5TH WARD
PAINE, RACHEL R. BAL 153 5TH WARD
PAINE, RICHARD ST 331 4TH E DI
PAINE, ROBERT BAL 471 14TH WAR
PAINE, ROBERT E. BAL 248 12TH WAR
PAINE, THOMAS JR. ST 321 4TH E DI
PAINE, THOMAS SR. ST 321 4TH E DI
PAINE, WILLIAM FRE 322 MIDDLETO
PAINE,GEORGE ALL 210 CUMBERLA
PAINETT, JOHN ALL 018 3RD E.D.
PAINEY, JOHN BAL 163 11TH WAR
PAINT, HANAH WAS 056 2ND SUBD
PAINTER, ABRAHAM BAL 197 5TH DIST
PAINTER, CHARLES W. CAR 361 9TH DIST
PAINTER, DAVID BAL 209 6TH DIST
PAINTER, EDWARD BAL 439 1ST DIST
PAINTER, EDWARD BAL 439 1ST DIST
PAINTER, EDWARD HAR 078 2ND DIST
PAINTER, ELIZABETH BAL 402 1ST DIST
PAINTER, ELLEN CAR 269 WESTMINS
PAINTER, ISABELLA BAL 436 14TH WAR
PAINTER, ISRAEL ALL 063 10TH E.D
PAINTER, JACOB WAS 056 2ND SUBD
PAINTER, JEFFERSON ANN 470 HOWARD D
PAINTER, JOHN WAS 158 HAGERSTO
PAINTER, MELKER WAS 129 2ND DIST
PAINTER, MILTON BAL 231 1ST DIST
PAINTER, RICHARD WAS 298 1ST DIST
PAINTER, ROBERT CAR 188 4TH DIST
PAINTER, SARAH BAL 232 1ST DIST
PAINTER, SUSAN BAL 435 14TH WAR
PAINTER, THOMAS BAL 224 1ST DIST
PAINTER, WILLIAM BAL 285 2ND WARD
PAINTON, JAMES CAR 164 NO TWP L
PAINTT, CATHARINE WOR 319 1ST E DI
PAIR, DANIEL* BAL 316 3RD WARD
PAIR, EBEN* DOR 465 1ST DIST
PAIR, HESTER J.* DOR 465 1ST DIST
PAIR, SAMUEL CAR 298 1ST DIST
PAIRLS, JONAS QUE 243 5TH E DI
PAISLEY, DAVID BAL 035 4TH WARD
PAISLEY, RICHARD MGM 321 CRACKLIN
PAISLEY, WILLIAM H. MGM 368 BERRYS D
PAIST, JAMES BAL 141 19TH WAR
PAISTE, MAHLON ANN 467 HOWARD D
PAITNER, ADAM BAL 035 1ST WARD
PALAGARRG, D. BAL 134 11TH WAR
PALE, LLOYD BAL 242 12TH WAR
PALEMR, SAMUEL FRE 372 CATOCTIN
PALES, EDW. BAL 307 20TH WAR
PALING, THOMAS BAL 003 EASTERN
PALL, MAHALA SOM 541 TYASKIN
PALLACE, MARY BAL 118 5TH WARD
PALLERSCN, JOHN * ALL 099 5TH E.D.
PALM, JEREMIAH-BLACK FRE 451 8TH E DI
PALM, JOEPH-BLACK FRE 418 8TH E DI
PALMAR, NANCY BAL 456 14TH WAR
PALMATERRY, GEORGE BAL 170 16TH WAR
PALMEMAN, MARY BAL 183 5TH DIST
PALMENTORY, JOHN KEN 298 3RD DIST
PALMER, ADALINE BAL 059 4TH WARD
PALMER, BENJAMIN WAS 282 1ST DIST
PALMER, BENJAMIN TAL 021 EASTON D
PALMER, BETSY BAL 436 14TH WAR
PALMER, CATHARINE BAL 178 2ND WARD
PALMER, CHARLES BAL 013 1ST WARD
PALMER, CHARLES DOR 335 3RD DIVI
PALMER, CHARLES CEC 211 7TH E DI
PALMER, CHRISTIAN WAS 033 2ND SUBD
PALMER, DANIEL WAS 052 2ND SUBD
PALMER, DANIEL FRE 367 CATOCTIN
PALMER, DAVID CAR 350 6TH DIST
PALMER, DAVID WAS 031 2ND SUBD
PALMER, DELIA BAL 304 3RD WARD
PALMER, DR. BAL 127 11TH WAR
PALMER, E. PRI 119 PISCATAW
PALMER, EDED BAL 236 12TH WAR
PALMER, EDWARD BAL 035 2ND DIST
PALMER, ELIJAH BAL 036 2ND DIST
PALMER, ELLEN FRE 336 MIDDLETO
PALMER, EMMA WAS 124 HAGERSTO
PALMER, EPHRAIM BAL 300 17TH WAR
PALMER, G. BAL 137 1ST WARD
PALMER, GEORGE BAL 296 17TH WAR
PALMER, GEORGE BAL 059 4TH WARD
PALMER, GEORGE FRE 117 CREAGERS
PALMER, GEORGE C. QUE 189 3RD E DI
PALMER, GEORGE S. QUE 170 2ND E DI
PALMER, HARRIET A. ANN 305 1ST DIST
PALMER, HENRIETTA BAL 016 15TH WAR
PALMER, HENRY C. BAL 360 8TH WARD
PALMER, HEZEKIAH FRE 366 CATOCTIN
PALMER, ISAAC BAL 122 1ST WARD
PALMER, ISACK TAL 007 EASTON D
PALMER, JACOB WAS 032 2ND SUBD
PALMER, JACOB FRE 373 CATOCTIN
PALMER, JAMES DOR 359 3RD DIVI
PALMER, JAMES BAL 294 20TH WAR
PALMER, JAMES QUE 190 3RD E DI
PALMER, JAMES E. TAL 078 EASTON T
PALMER, JANE MRS. BAL 127 11TH WAR
PALMER, JANE V. PRI 106 PISCATAW
PALMER, JOHN PRI 117 PISCATAW
PALMER, JOHN QUE 184 3RD E DI
PALMER, JOHN BAL 143 1ST WARD
PALMER, JOHN BAL 034 2ND DIST
PALMER, JOHN BAL 207 6TH DIST
PALMER, JOHN W. KEN 287 3RD DIST
PALMER, JONATHAN FRE 350 MIDDLETO
PALMER, JOSEPH BAL 229 19TH WAR
PALMER, JOSEPH CEC 211 7TH E DI
PALMER, JOSEPH WAS 203 1ST DIST
PALMER, JOSEPH WAS 016 2ND SUBD
PALMER, JOSEPH M. FRE 042 FREDERIC
PALMER, JOSEPH T. BAL 130 5TH WARD
PALMER, JOSEPHINE M. FRE 042 FREDERIC
PALMER, JOSEPHINE-MULATTO FRE 419 8TH E DI
PALMER, JOSHUA BAL 125 2ND DIST
PALMER, KITTY BAL 395 14TH WAR
PALMER, M. BAL 319 20TH WAR
PALMER, M. BAL 252 12TH WAR
PALMER, MAGDELINE BAL 126 2ND DIST
PALMER, MAHLAN HAR 174 3RD DIST
PALMER, MARIA BAL 044 15TH WAR
PALMER, MARY BAL 178 2ND WARD
PALMER, MARY FRE 047 FREDERIC
PALMER, MARY BAL 298 20TH WAR
PALMER, MARY QUE 244 5TH E DI
PALMER, MARY QUE 239 5TH E DI
PALMER, MARY WAS 162 HAGERSTO
PALMER, PENNEL MGM 366 BERRYS D
PALMER, PETER FRE 349 MIDDLETO
PALMER, RHODA BAL 049 15TH WAR
PALMER, S. S. BAL 353 1ST DIST
PALMER, SALLY BAL 458 1ST DIST
PALMER, SAMUEL BAL 293 3RD WARD
PALMER, SAMUEL KEN 211 2ND DIST
PALMER, SAMUEL WAS 061 2ND SUBD
PALMER, SAMUEL WAS 049 2ND SUBD
PALMER, SARAH BAL 273 17TH WAR
PALMER, SARAH BAL 389 8TH WARD
PALMER, SUSAN WAS 144 HAGERSTO
PALMER, THOMAS D. BAL 134 1ST WARD
PALMER, WILLIAM BAL 003 15TH WAR
PALMER, WILLIAM WAS 209 1ST DIST
PALMER, WILLIAM C. BAL 437 1ST DIST
PALMER, WILLIAM F. PRI 106 PISCATAW
PALMER, WILLIAM G. PRI 004 BLADENSB
PALMER, WILLIAM H. KEN 267 1ST DIST
PALMER, WILLIAM H. KEN 208 2ND DIST
PALMER, WILLIAM J. BAL 026 1ST WARD
PALMER, WILLIAM P. MGM 371 BERRYS D
PALMER, WILLIAM R. FRE 349 MIDDLETO
PALMER, WILSON L. QUE 235 4TH E DI
PALNE, CATHAIRNE CAR 269 WESTMINS
PALRININ, SOPHIA FRE 161 EMMITTSB
PALTER, CHARLES* BAL 048 4TH WARD
PALWMAN, BELINDA CAR 183 8TH DIST
PALYMAN, ANN BAL 310 12TH WAR
PAM, CAHRLES FRE 083 FREDERIC
PAMBROKE, BENJAMIN ST 309 1ST E DI
PAMPELL, ELIZABETH FRE 095 FREDERIC
PAMPELL, HENRY FRE 009 FREDERIC
PAMPHILIAN, NICHOLAS BAL 177 16TH WAR
PAMPHILION, WILLIAM J. ANN 420 HOWARD D
PAMPHILON, JAMES BAL 403 1ST DIST
PANAN, HENRY CAL 025 2ND DIST
PANCOAST, JOHN BAL 075 15TH WAR
PANCOAST, JOSPEH BAL 349 13TH WAR
PANCOST, JOHN BAL 461 14TH WAR
PANDY, MARY BAL 152 11TH WAR
PANE*, JAMES CAR 144 NO TWP L
PANE, CHARLES CAR 145 NO TWP L
PANE, DANIEL CAR 155 NO TWP L
PANE, ELEANOR WOR 336 1ST E DI
PANE, ELLEN BAL 038 4TH WARD
PANE, GORY CAR 122 NO TWP L
PANE, JAMES WOR 327 1ST E DI
PANE, JAMES H. FRE 383 PETERSVI
PANE, JAOCB WOR 324 1ST E DI
PANE, JOHN WOR 336 1ST E DI
PANE, JOHN J. WOR 320 1ST E DI
PANE, JOSHUA A. SOM 393 BRINKLEY
PANE, MARY WOR 336 1ST E DI

Name	Co.	Page	District
PANE, MARY	PRI	014	BLADENSB
PANE, SAMUEL	WOR	330	1ST E DI
PANE, STEPHEN	WOR	297	9TH E DI
PANE, WRIXHAM	WOR	336	1ST E DI
PANEBECKER, DAVID	CAR	352	6TH DIST
PANETTI, JOHN P.	BAL	094	10TH WAR
PANIZ, FREDERICK	BAL	209	2ND WARD
PANNELL, JAMES	HAR	119	2ND DIST
PANNELL, JAMES E	HAR	119	2ND DIST
PANNELL, JAMES M.	HAR	118	2ND DIST
PANNELL, WILLIAM	HAR	101	2ND DIST
PANNETT, WILLIAM	ALL	020	2ND E.D.
PANNS, FREDERICK	BAL	198	17TH WAR
PANNS, SAMUEL	BAL	198	17TH WAR
PANOTT, THOMAS	TAL	076	EASTON T
PANSER, SALVADOR	ALL	064	10TH E.D
PANT, PETER	WAS	145	HAGERSTO
PANTIER, M. A.	BAL	082	4TH WARD
PAPE, BERNHARD	BAL	126	1ST WARD
PAPE, J.C.	BAL	024	2ND DIST
PAPEN, MICHAEL	BAL	130	1ST WARD
PAPERMAN, BARNEY	BAL	436	8TH WARD
PAPP, ELIAS	BAL	066	1ST WARD
PAPP, JANE	BAL	158	19TH WAR
PAPP, SOPHIA	BAL	285	2ND WARD
PAPPLER, GEORGE W.	BAL	102	1ST WARD
PAPPLER, JACOB	BAL	077	1ST WARD
PAPPON, WILLIAM	ANN	276	ANNAPOLI
PAPST, JOHN G.	BAL	181	6TH WARD
PAPST, WILLIAM	BAL	180	6TH WARD
PAR--, JIM *	ANN	337	3RD DIST
PARADESE, JOHN	WOR	337	1ST E DI
PARADISE, BENJAMIN	WOR	323	1ST E DI
PARADISE, THOMAS	WOR	311	2ND E DI
PARADISE, WILLIAM	WOR	337	1ST E DI
PARAWAY, JAMES	ANN	424	HOWARD D
PARAWAY, NICHOLAS	CAR	268	WESTMINS
PARAWAY, SUSAN	BAL	057	18TH WAR
PARAWAY, WILLIAM	BAL	316	1ST DIST
PARBLO, AUGUSTA	BAL	136	5TH WARD
PARCE, MARY W.	CEC	049	1ST E DI
PARDEE, ELI S.	QUE	150	1ST E DI
PARDEE, ROBERT*	DOR	420	1ST DIST
PARDIAN, BEE	BAL	043	2ND DIST
PARDIAN, RICHARD	BAL	043	2ND DIST
PARDOE, ANN	CAL	009	1ST DIST
PARDOE, SAMUEL	CAL	011	1ST DIST
PARDOE, WILLIAM	CAL	009	1ST DIST
PARENT, JOHN	FRE	354	MIDDLETO
PARENTE, GEORGE W.	DOR	375	1ST DIST
PAREWELL, JOHN	BAL	203	17TH WAR
PAREWELL, MARIA	BAL	203	17TH WAR
PAREY, CYRUS B.	BAL	050	4TH WARD
PARHAM, ELIZA *	BAL	168	2ND DIST
PARHER, HARRIET	WOR	202	4TH E DI
PARIN, NATHANIEL	BAL	289	3RD WARD
PARINE, LORA	BAL	251	1ST DIST
PARIS, MARY E.	CEC	121	4TH E DI
PARISH, ANN ELIZA	CAR	195	4TH DIST
PARISH, AQUILLA	BAL	331	1ST DIST
PARISH, EDWARD	BAL	231	1ST DIST
PARISH, ELACUM	BAL	330	1ST DIST
PARISH, ELIZABETH	BAL	399	3RD WARD
PARISH, ELIZABETH	FRE	439	8TH E DI
PARISH, ELLEN	ANN	275	ANNAPOLI
PARISH, EUGENE W.	FRE	407	JEFFERSO
PARISH, GEORGE	ANN	274	ANNAPOLI
PARISH, GEORGE W.	CAR	211	5TH DIST
PARISH, GIDEON	BAL	266	1ST DIST
PARISH, JAMES	CAR	208	5TH DIST
PARISH, JAMES	CAR	208	5TH DIST
PARISH, JAMES	CAR	219	5TH DIST
PARISH, JOHN	BAL	226	1ST DIST
PARISH, JOHN W.	CAR	223	5TH DIST
PARISH, JOSEPH	CAR	182	8TH DIST
PARISH, JOSIAH	CAR	326	1ST DIST
PARISH, MARGARET	CAR	188	4TH DIST
PARISH, MARTHA	BAL	308	20TH WAR
PARISH, MORDICA	BAL	439	1ST DIST
PARISH, MOSES	CAR	210	5TH DIST
PARISH, MYRE	CAR	206	4TH DIST
PARISH, N.M.	FRE	406	JEFFERSO
PARISH, NORRIS B.	BAL	042	2ND DIST
PARISH, THOMA SA.	BAL	227	1ST DIST
PARISH, THOMAS	BAL	227	1ST DIST
PARISH, ZEBADIAH	CAR	194	4TH DIST
PARISH,LOUIS	BAL	189	2ND WARD
PARK, ALEXANDER	KEN	251	2ND DIST
PARK, CATHERINE	BAL	137	11TH WAR
PARK, EDWIN D.	BAL	450	1ST DIST
PARK, ELLEN A.	BAL	012	2ND DIST
PARK, FRANCIS G.	CEC	098	4TH E DI
PARK, GEORGE	ALL	092	5TH E.D.
PARK, H. A. L.	FRE	285	WOODSBOR
PARK, JANE	BAL	207	11TH WAR
PARK, JOHN	WAS	067	2ND SUBD
PARK, MARGARET	BAL	435	1ST DIST
PARK, MARY	WAS	180	BOONSBOR
PARK, PETER	BAL	450	1ST DIST
PARK, PETER	BAL	450	1ST DIST
PARK, RUTH	BAL	450	1ST DIST
PARK, SAMUEL	WAS	067	2ND SUBD
PARKE, ISAAC	CAL	014	1ST DIST
PARKE, JOSEPH*	DOR	417	1ST DIST
PARKE, JOSPH M.	CAR	272	WESTMINS
PARKENSON, JOHN T.	SOM	444	DAMES QU
PARKENSON, RICHARD	BAL	088	18TH WAR
PARKER, ABNER	ALL	100	5TH E.D.
PARKER, ABRAM*	DOR	452	1ST DIST
PARKER, ALFRED	ANN	332	2ND DIST
PARKER, AMELIA	ANN	291	ANNAPOLI
PARKER, ANDERSON	TAL	016	EASTON D
PARKER, ANDREW	BAL	010	1ST WARD
PARKER, ANDREW	BAL	180	19TH WAR
PARKER, ANN	BAL	173	16TH WAR
PARKER, ANN	SOM	533	QUANTICO
PARKER, ANN	SOM	503	SALISBUR
PARKER, ANN K.	CHA	292	BOJANTOW
PARKER, ANN M.	BAL	084	18TH WAR
PARKER, ANN V.	BAL	281	7TH WARD
PARKER, ARCHIBALD	ALL	105	5TH E.D.
PARKER, ASA W.	BAL	163	1ST WARD
PARKER, AYRES G.	WOR	226	4TH E DI
PARKER, BEN	ANN	332	2ND DIST
PARKER, BENJAMIN	ALL	086	5TH E.D.
PARKER, BENJAMIN	WOR	239	6TH E DI
PARKER, BENJAMIN	BAL	216	17TH WAR
PARKER, BETTY	ANN	327	2ND DIST
PARKER, BRIDGET	BAL	284	17TH WAR
PARKER, CALETA	ALL	123	4TH E.D.
PARKER, CAMPBELL	BAL	179	19TH WAR
PARKER, CAROLINE	BAL	091	15TH WAR
PARKER, CASANDER	BAL	215	6TH DIST
PARKER, CATHARINE	HAR	122	2ND DIST
PARKER, CATHARINE	SOM	527	QUANTICO
PARKER, CHARELS J.R	WOR	304	SNOW HIL
PARKER, CHARLES	WOR	171	6TH E DI
PARKER, CHARLES	CEC	105	3RD E DI
PARKER, CHARLES	BAL	214	2ND WARD
PARKER, CHARLES	BAL	266	2ND WARD
PARKER, CLEMENT, J. B.	BAL	037	15TH WAR
PARKER, COLUMBUS	ANN	466	HOWARD D
PARKER, DANIEL	BAL	453	14TH WAR
PARKER, DAVID	CEC	128	5TH E DI
PARKER, DAVID	MGM	365	BERRYS D
PARKER, DAVID	BAL	192	17TH WAR
PARKER, E. W.	BAL	349	13TH WAR
PARKER, EDWARD	BAL	422	14TH WAR
PARKER, EDWARD	BAL	423	14TH WAR
PARKER, EDWIN L.	BAL	118	15TH WAR
PARKER, ELIAS	ANN	332	2ND DIST
PARKER, ELIAS	BAL	081	18TH WAR
PARKER, ELIJAH	ANN	312	1ST DIST
PARKER, ELIJAH H.	WOR	240	6TH E DI
PARKER, ELIJAH L.	WOR	212	4TH E DI
PARKER, ELISHA	WOR	192	8TH E DI
PARKER, ELISHA P.	WOR	236	6TH E DI
PARKER, ELIZA	BAL	266	2ND WARD
PARKER, ELIZA	CAL	008	1ST DIST
PARKER, ELIZA	BAL	391	14TH WAR
PARKER, ELIZA	CAL	062	3RD DIST
PARKER, ELIZA J.	SOM	365	BRINKLEY
PARKER, ELIZABETH	WOR	237	6TH E DI
PARKER, ELIZABETH	KEN	282	3RD DIST
PARKER, ELIZABETH	WOR	259	BERLIN 1
PARKER, ELIZABETH	CAR	146	NO TWP L
PARKER, ELIZABETH	DOR	313	1ST DIST
PARKER, ELIZABETH	ALL	100	5TH E.D.
PARKER, ELIZABETH	BAL	312	3RD WARD
PARKER, ELIZABETH	BAL	323	3RD WARD
PARKER, ELIZABETH S.	WOR	171	6TH E DI
PARKER, ELIZABETH-BLACK	WOR	169	6TH E DI
PARKER, ELLEN	SOM	532	QUANTICO
PARKER, ELLEN	ALL	089	5TH E.D.
PARKER, ELLEN	ANN	289	ANNAPOLI
PARKER, ELLEN	BAL	066	10TH WAR
PARKER, ELLEN F.	BAL	346	7TH WARD
PARKER, EMILY V.	BAL	056	15TH WAR
PARKER, EWARD	CAR	223	5TH DIST
PARKER, GEORGE	ALL	089	5TH E.D.
PARKER, GEORGE A.	WOR	260	BERLIN 1
PARKER, GEROGE	SOM	421	PRINCESS
PARKER, HANNAH	WOR	232	6TH E DI
PARKER, HANNAH	PRI	079	QUEEN AN
PARKER, HARIETT	DOR	332	3RD DIVI
PARKER, HARRITT*	BAL	349	3RD WARD
PARKER, HENERY	DOR	327	3RD DIVI
PARKER, HENRY	FRE	222	BUCKEYST
PARKER, HENRY	BAL	121	1ST WARD
PARKER, HENRY	BAL	145	1ST WARD
PARKER, HENRY	BAL	134	5TH WARD
PARKER, HENRY S.	SOM	529	QUANTICO
PARKER, HOOPER	WOR	212	4TH E DI
PARKER, HOWES*	DOR	311	1ST DIST
PARKER, HUGH F.	BAL	320	3RD WARD
PARKER, IGNATIUS	BAL	238	6TH WARD
PARKER, ISAAC	BAL	124	1ST WARD
PARKER, ISAAC	DOR	362	3RD DIVI
PARKER, ISAAC	BAL	130	11TH WAR
PARKER, ISABELLA	WOR	247	1ST CENS
PARKER, ISAC*	HAR	147	3RD DIST
PARKER, ISAIAH	DOR	431	1ST DIST
PARKER, J.	BAL	093	15TH WAR
PARKER, JACOB JR.	BAL	075	18TH WAR
PARKER, JACOB SR.	WOR	239	6TH E DI
PARKER, JAMES	WOR	238	6TH E DI
PARKER, JAMES	WOR	237	6TH E DI
PARKER, JAMES	WOR	182	6TH E DI
PARKER, JAMES	WOR	177	6TH E DI
PARKER, JAMES	CHA	292	BOJANTOW
PARKER, JAMES	HAR	180	3RD DIST
PARKER, JAMES	BAL	152	11TH WAR
PARKER, JAMES	BAL	178	19TH WAR
PARKER, JAMES	BAL	438	14TH WAR
PARKER, JAMES	BAL	332	13TH WAR
PARKER, JAMES	BAL	463	1ST DIST
PARKER, JAMES	ANN	498	HOWARD D
PARKER, JAMES	ALL	092	5TH E.D.
PARKER, JAMES A. L.	ANN	389	4TH DIST
PARKER, JAMES D.	BAL	179	11TH WAR
PARKER, JANE	WOR	235	6TH E DI
PARKER, JANE-BLACK	BAL	350	3RD WARD
PARKER, JESSEE B.	ST	329	4TH E DI
PARKER, JOHN	BAL	431	8TH WARD
PARKER, JOHN	BAL	059	15TH WAR
PARKER, JOHN	BAL	255	12TH WAR
PARKER, JOHN	BAL	323	3RD WARD
PARKER, JOHN	BAL	436	1ST DIST
PARKER, JOHN	BAL	436	1ST DIST
PARKER, JOHN	BAL	192	2ND WARD
PARKER, JOHN	BAL	399	8TH WARD
PARKER, JOHN	BAL	054	2ND DIST
PARKER, JOHN	BAL	058	2ND DIST
PARKER, JOHN	PRI	037	VANSVILL
PARKER, JOHN	WOR	212	4TH E DI
PARKER, JOHN	PRI	101	SPALDING
PARKER, JOHN	WAS	003	WILLIAMS
PARKER, JOHN	SOM	380	BRINKLEY
PARKER, JOHN	BAL	187	19TH WAR
PARKER, JOHN	BAL	187	19TH WAR
PARKER, JOHN	BAL	189	19TH WAR
PARKER, JOHN	CAL	045	3RD DIST
PARKER, JOHN	BAL	453	14TH WAR
PARKER, JOHN	BAL	287	20TH WAR
PARKER, JOHN	BAL	318	20TH WAR
PARKER, JOHN C.	CAL	006	1ST DIST
PARKER, JOHN D.	DOR	370	3RD DIVI
PARKER, JOHN F.	BAL	192	2ND WARD
PARKER, JOHN T.	WOR	211	4TH E DI
PARKER, JOHN W.	WOR	237	6TH E DI
PARKER, JOHN W.	DOR	327	3RD DIVI
PARKER, JOHN-BLACK	FRE	406	JEFFERSO
PARKER, JOHN-BLACK	ST	329	4TH E DI
PARKER, JOHN-BLACK	WOR	172	6TH E DI
PARKER, JONATHAN	BAL	370	13TH WAR
PARKER, JOSEPH	HAR	033	1ST DIST
PARKER, JOSEPH	HAR	122	2ND DIST
PARKER, JOSEPH	PRI	040	VANSVILL
PARKER, JOSEPH	BAL	270	2ND WARD
PARKER, JOSEPH	BAL	108	15TH WAR
PARKER, JOSEPH C.	HAR	128	2ND DIST
PARKER, JOSEPH H.	PRI	104	PISCATAW
PARKER, JOSEPH*	DOR	417	1ST DIST
PARKER, JOSEPH-BLACK	FRE	433	8TH E DI
PARKER, JOSHUA A.-BLACK	WOR	172	6TH E DI
PARKER, JOSHUA R.	WOR	226	4TH E DI
PARKER, KITTY P.	ANN	521	HOWARD D
PARKER, LAUTA	WOR	219	4TH E DI
PARKER, LEAH	SOM	503	SALISBUR
PARKER, LEAH	SOM	388	BRINKLEY
PARKER, LEVIN H.	BAL	264	17TH WAR
PARKER, LEVINA	SOM	504	SALISBUR
PARKER, LEWIS W.	WOR	233	6TH E DI
PARKER, M.	FRE	200	5TH E DI
PARKER, MA+Y	BAL	121	11TH WAR
PARKER, MARIA	FRE	306	WOODSBOR
PARKER, MARY	BAL	168	19TH WAR
PARKER, MARY	BAL	130	11TH WAR
PARKER, MARY	BAL	465	14TH WAR
PARKER, MARY	CAL	010	1ST DIST
PARKER, MARY	BAL	412	3RD WARD
PARKER, MARY	BAL	060	15TH WAR
PARKER, MARY	BAL	042	15TH WAR
PARKER, MARY	ANN	333	2ND DIST
PARKER, MARY E.	ALL	127	4TH E.D.
PARKER, MARY E.	BAL	060	15TH WAR
PARKER, MARY E.	WOR	213	4TH E DI
PARKER, MARY J.	WOR	213	4TH E DI
PARKER, MARY J.	CEC	127	5TH E DI
PARKER, MARY-BLACK	ST	318	4TH E DI
PARKER, MATILDA A.	WOR	193	8TH E DI
PARKER, MICHAEL	BAL	034	15TH WAR
PARKER, MISS S.	FRE	199	5TH E DI
PARKER, MOSES-BLACK	WOR	171	6TH E DI
PARKER, MRS-	ANN	306	1ST DIST
PARKER, NANCY	BAL	413	14TH WAR
PARKER, NANCY-MULATTO	BAL	222	2ND WARD
PARKER, NATHAN	BAL	332	13TH WAR
PARKER, NICHOLAS	BAL	058	2ND DIST
PARKER, OLIVER A.	BAL	060	15TH WAR
PARKER, PENELOPE	BAL	180	2ND DIST
PARKER, PETER	ANN	375	4TH DIST
PARKER, PETER	WOR	250	1ST CENS
PARKER, PHOEBY*	DOR	443	1ST DIST
PARKER, RACHAEL	BAL	302	3RD WARD
PARKER, RACHAEL A.-BLACK	FRE	437	8TH E DI
PARKER, REBECCA	BAL	151	5TH WARD
PARKER, REBECCA-BLACK	FRE	433	8TH E DI
PARKER, RICHARD	BAL	178	19TH WAR
PARKER, RICHARD	BAL	420	1ST DIST
PARKER, RICHARD	SOM	503	SALISBUR
PARKER, ROBERT	BAL	092	2ND DIST
PARKER, ROBERT	DOR	446	1ST DIST
PARKER, ROBERT	CAL	008	1ST DIST
PARKER, ROBERT	HAR	033	1ST DIST
PARKER, ROBERT-BLACK	FRE	443	8TH E DI
PARKER, RUTH	BAL	037	18TH WAR
PARKER, SALLY	BAL	310	3RD WARD
PARKER, SAMPSON	WOR	225	4TH E DI
PARKER, SAMUEL	WOR	237	6TH E DI
PARKER, SAMUEL	WAS	004	WILLIAMS
PARKER, SAMUEL	BAL	058	2ND DIST
PARKER, SAMUEL	HAR	105	2ND DIST
PARKER, SARAH	BAL	453	14TH WAR
PARKER, SARAH	CAL	040	3RD DIST
PARKER, SARAH	BAL	148	11TH WAR
PARKER, SARAH	BAL	356	13TH WAR
PARKER, SARAH	BAL	035	2ND DIST
PARKER, SARAH	BAL	204	6TH WARD
PARKER, SARAH ANN	BAL	262	17TH WAR
PARKER, SCARBOROUGH	WOR	213	4TH E DI
PARKER, SIMON	SOM	405	DUBLIN D
PARKER, SOPHIA	BAL	330	13TH WAR
PARKER, SUSAN	ANN	325	2ND DIST
PARKER, SUSAN	BAL	019	4TH WARD
PARKER, SUSAN	SOM	467	HANGARY
PARKER, SUSANAH	CAR	218	5TH DIST
PARKER, THEODORE	BAL	157	1ST WARD
PARKER, THEODORE W.	WOR	232	6TH E DI
PARKER, THOMAS	WOR	212	4TH E DI
PARKER, THOMAS	WOR	222	4TH E DI
PARKER, THOMAS	BAL	133	16TH WAR
PARKER, THOMAS	BAL	086	15TH WAR
PARKER, THOMAS	BAL	318	20TH WAR
PARKER, THOMAS P.	WOR	171	6TH E DI
PARKER, THOMAS-MULATTO	BAL	239	2ND WARD
PARKER, V.	FRE	200	5TH E DI
PARKER, WALTER B.	CHA	282	BOJANTOW
PARKER, WESLEY	SOM	407	DUBLIN D
PARKER, WESLEY	SOM	412	DUBLIN D
PARKER, WILLIAM	KEN	243	2ND DIST
PARKER, WILLIAM	BAL	187	19TH WAR
PARKER, WILLIAM	BAL	339	13TH WAR
PARKER, WILLIAM	BAL	417	14TH WAR
PARKER, WILLIAM	CEC	146	PORT DUP
PARKER, WILLIAM	BAL	121	11TH WAR
PARKER, WILLIAM	BAL	021	18TH WAR
PARKER, WILLIAM	BAL	162	1ST WARD
PARKER, WILLIAM	BAL	150	1ST WARD
PARKER, WILLIAM	BAL	325	1ST DIST
PARKER, WILLIAM	ALL	101	5TH E.D.
PARKER, WILLIAM	ALL	101	5TH E.D.
PARKER, WILLIAM	BAL	105	1ST WARD
PARKER, WILLIAM	SOM	382	BRINKLEY
PARKER, WILLIAM A.	WOR	224	4TH E DI
PARKER, WILLIAM H.	ALL	094	5TH E.D.
PARKER, WILLIAM H.	HAR	160	3RD DIST
PARKER, WILLIAM-BLACK	FRE	434	8TH E DI
PARKER, WILLIS	BAL	189	11TH WAR
PARKERSON, HENRY	ALL	217	CUMBERLA
PARKES, ABRAM*	DOR	452	1ST DIST
PARKES, ANN	SOM	447	DAMES QU
PARKES, CHALRES	SOM	449	DAMES QU
PARKES, GEORGE	SOM	446	DAMES QU
PARKES, JOHN	SOM	448	DAMES QU
PARKES, JOHN	SOM	464	HANGARY
PARKES, JOHN	ANN	401	8TH DIST
PARKES, JOHN E.	SOM	442	DAMES QU
PARKES, JOHN H.	SOM	464	HANGARY
PARKES, LAWSON	SOM	458	DAMES QU
PARKES, LINTA	BAL	232	2ND WARD
PARKES, LLOYOD	BAL	289	3RD WARD
PARKES, MARY*	DOR	446	1ST DIST
PARKES, SOLOMO	DOR	330	3RD DIVI
PARKES, THOMAS	ANN	405	8TH DIST
PARKES, THOMAS	SOM	457	DAMES QU
PARKETTS, J.	BAL	117	1ST WARD
PARKHILL, HAMILTON	BAL	161	6TH WARD
PARKHURST, ANDREW	BAL	003	EASTERN
PARKHURST, J. JR.	BAL	469	14TH WAR

PARKHURST, SIMON BAL 423 3RD WARD
PARKIND, GEORGE QUE 248 5TH E DI
PARKING, E. BAL 118 1ST WARD
PARKINGSON, R.B. ANN 273 ANNAPOLI
PARKINGSON, RESPA ANN 272 ANNAPOLI
PARKINGSON, THOMAS ANN 271 ANNAPOLI
PARKINS, NICHOLAS A. FRE 272 NEW MARK
PARKINS, THOMAS BAL 420 8TH WARD
PARKINSON, AMELIA BAL 233 6TH WARD
PARKINSON, AMILIA ANN 285 ANNAPOLI
PARKINSON, FRANCIS HAR 097 2ND DIST
PARKINSON, JAMES BAL 192 6TH WARD
PARKINSON, JAMES R. BAL 177 11TH WAR
PARKINSON, JOEL BAL 126 1ST WARD
PARKINSON, JOSEPH ANN 290 ANNAPOLI
PARKINSON, JOSEPH H. ANN 265 ANNAPOLI
PARKINSON, MARIA BAL 176 11TH WAR
PARKINSON, T. BAL 148 1ST WARD
PARKINSON, W. ANN 285 ANNAPOLI
PARKINSON, WILLAIM ANN 265 ANNAPOLI
PARKMAN, A. ANN 270 ANNAPOLI
PARKS, ABRAHAM BAL 439 1ST DIST
PARKS, ADELINE BAL 197 6TH WARD
PARKS, AJMES BAL 314 20TH WAR
PARKS, AQUILLA BAL 142 2ND DIST
PARKS, ARTHUR SOM 388 BRINKLEY
PARKS, B. BAL 168 1ST WARD.
PARKS, BARBARA BAL 374 8TH WARD
PARKS, BENJAMIN DOR 330 3RD DIVI
PARKS, BRIDGET SOM 491 SALISBUR
PARKS, CALEB BAL 288 3RD WARD
PARKS, CHARLOTT BAL 040 4TH WARD
PARKS, EDWIN A. BAL 363 8TH WARD
PARKS, ELIAS BAL 454 1ST DIST
PARKS, ELIAS SOM 356 BRINKLEY
PARKS, ELISHA BAL 450 1ST DIST
PARKS, ELISHA BAL 024 2ND DIST
PARKS, ELISHA BAL 024 2ND DIST
PARKS, ELIZA ANN 417 HOWARD D
PARKS, ELIZABETH BAL 075 15TH WAR
PARKS, ELIZABETH BAL 186 5TH DIST
PARKS, ELIZABETH SOM 357 BRINKLEY
PARKS, ELIZABETH SOM 444 DAMES QU
PARKS, ELLEN ALL 083 5TH E.D.
PARKS, GABRIEL SOM 457 DAMES QU
PARKS, GEORGE BAL 132 11TH WAR
PARKS, GEORGE BAL 269 17TH WAR
PARKS, GEORGE W. KEN 247 2ND DIST
PARKS, GEORGELLA BAL 454 1ST DIST
PARKS, HENRIETTA BAL 127 11TH WAR
PARKS, HENRIETTE BAL 127 11TH WAR
PARKS, HENRY SOM 357 BRINKLEY
PARKS, HENRY O. BAL 146 1ST WARD
PARKS, HEZEKIAH * ANN 405 8TH DIST
PARKS, ISAAC WOR 340 1ST E DI
PARKS, ISAAC H. SOM 361 BRINKLEY
PARKS, ISAAH HAR 198 3RD DIST
PARKS, J. FRE 164 EMMITTSB
PARKS, JAMES SOM 356 BRINKLEY
PARKS, JAMES BAL 142 2ND DIST
PARKS, JAMES D. KEN 301 3RD DIST
PARKS, JAMES F. BAL 458 8TH WARD
PARKS, JAMES S. BAL 454 1ST DIST
PARKS, JEREMIAH SOM 454 DAMES QU
PARKS, JESSE SOM 544 TYASKIN
PARKS, JOANNA* DOR 437 1ST DIST
PARKS, JOHN BAL 237 17TH WAR
PARKS, JOHN DOR 336 3RD DIVI
PARKS, JOHN WAS 202 1ST DIST
PARKS, JOHN SOM 354 BRINKLEY
PARKS, JOHN BAL 450 1ST DIST
PARKS, JOHN BAL 025 15TH WAR
PARKS, JOHN BAL 374 8TH WARD
PARKS, JOHN E. SOM 355 BRINKLEY
PARKS, JOHN W. BAL 354 13TH WAR
PARKS, JOSEPH WAS 058 2ND SUBD
PARKS, JOSEPH BAL 079 2ND DIST
PARKS, JOSEPH B. BAL 363 8TH WARD
PARKS, JOSHUA BAL 096 2ND DIST
PARKS, JOSHUA BAL 202 11TH WAR
PARKS, LILY BAL 284 17TH WAR
PARKS, LUDIA R. BAL 355 13TH WAR
PARKS, M.* DOR 412 1ST DIST
PARKS, MARGARET BAL 006 1ST WARD
PARKS, MARY BAL 127 11TH WAR
PARKS, MARY SOM 360 BRINKLEY
PARKS, MARY SOM 457 DAMES QU
PARKS, MARY A. DOR 423 1ST DIST
PARKS, MARY A. BAL 453 1ST DIST
PARKS, MARY E. DOR 426 1ST DIST
PARKS, MARY J. BAL 404 14TH WAR
PARKS, MARY J. BAL 080 4TH WARD
PARKS, PATTY SOM 396 BRINKLEY
PARKS, PETER BAL 450 1ST DIST
PARKS, POLLY SOM 442 DAMES QU
PARKS, PRICELLA SOM 445 DAMES QU
PARKS, PRISCILLA BAL 232 6TH WARD
PARKS, REUBIN SOM 355 BRINKLEY
PARKS, REVELL SOM 354 BRINKLEY
PARKS, ROBERT SOM 438 DAMES QU
PARKS, SAMUEL W. BAL 044 15TH WAR
PARKS, SARAH BAL 305 3RD WARD
PARKS, SOLOMON SOM 397 BRINKLEY
PARKS, SUSAN A. BAL 386 3RD WARD
PARKS, THOMAS DOR 336 3RD DIVI
PARKS, THOMAS B. BAL 366 1ST DIST
PARKS, THOMAS E. SOM 355 BRINKLEY
PARKS, WASHINGTON ANN 405 8TH DIST
PARKS, WILLIAM ALL 082 5TH E.D.
PARKS, WILLIAM BAL 291 3RD WARD
PARKS, WILLIAM SOM 487 SALISBUR
PARKS, WILLIAM DOR 342 3RD DIVI
PARKS, WILLIAM BAL 212 17TH WAR
PARKS, WILLIAM DOR 388 1ST DIST
PARKS, WILLIAM F. BAL 366 1ST DIST
PARKS, WILLIAM H. SOM 355 BRINKLEY
PARKS, WILLIAM T. DOR 301 1ST DIST
PARKS, WILLIAM W. SOM 452 DAMES QU
PARKS, WILLIAM W. KEN 249 2ND DIST
PARKS, ZACARIAH DOR 330 3RD DIVI
PARKSON, FENTON WAS 164 2ND DIST
PARKUM, HENRY * SOM 436 PRINCESS
PARLER, HANNAH HAR 062 1ST DIST
PARLET, CHARLES HAR 062 1ST DIST
PARLET, JOSHUA BAL 011 2ND DIST
PARLETT, ALBERT BAL 105 2ND DIST
PARLETT, BENJAMIN F. BAL 051 15TH WAR
PARLETT, JAMES B. BAL 374 1ST DIST
PARLETT, JOHN BAL 029 2ND DIST
PARLETT, MARTHA A. BAL 221 6TH WARD
PARLETT, THOMAS BAL 069 2ND DIST
PARLETT, WILLIAM BAL 030 2ND DIST
PARLETTE, ISRAEL BAL 160 2ND DIST
PARLETTE, THOMAS BAL 117 2ND DIST
PARLETTE, WILLIAM BAL 097 2ND DIST
PARLEY, ELLEN BAL 421 8TH WARD
PARLEY, PETER PRI 006 BLADENSB
PARLEY, RICHARD BAL 065 2ND DIST
PARLITT, WILLIAM BAL 036 1ST WARD
PARLONS, JAMES T. BAL 362 3RD WARD
PARLOT, DAVID CAR 233 5TH DIST
PARLOT, MARY BAL 077 2ND DIST
PARLOTT, WASHINGTON HAR 061 1ST DIST
PARMA, WESTLEY* TAL 022 EASTON D
PARMALEE, CATHARINE WAS 187 BOONSBOR
PARMAN, CHARITY BAL 454 14TH WAR
PARMCUTT, ROBERT BAL 026 18TH WAR
PARME, SARAH* DOR 394 1ST DIST
PARMEE, HENRY A.* TAL 044 EASTON D
PARMEE, JOHN TAL 021 EASTON D
PARMEE, WESTLEY* TAL 022 EASTON D
PARMELEE, DANIEL L. BAL 017 18TH WAR
PARMER, AVE TAL 112 ST MICHA
PARMER, BRAMUS SOM 536 TYASKIN
PARMER, EDWARD WOR 201 3RD E DI
PARMER, ELIHU H. WOR 220 4TH E DI
PARMER, GEORGE BAL 217 6TH DIST
PARMER, JENKINS J. WOR 202 4TH E DI
PARMER, JOHN WOR 287 BERLIN 1
PARMER, JOSEPH B. BAL 213 6TH DIST
PARMER, JOSIAH SOM 537 TYASKIN
PARMER, MARY WOR 256 1ST CENS
PARMER, PEACER * TAL 115 ST MICHA
PARMER, PETER J. SOM 537 TYASKIN
PARMER, SABEN B. WOR 269 BERLIN 1
PARMER, SARAH BAL 213 6TH DIST
PARMER, THOASM WOR 253 1ST CENS
PARMER, WILLIAM TAL 113 ST MICHA
PARMES, HENRY A.* TAL 044 EASTON D
PARMEYER, ALEXANDER BAL 175 11TH WAR
PARMEYER, REBECCA BAL 174 11TH WAR
PARMON, HENRY WOR 251 1ST CENS
PARNELL, MARGARET WOR 221 4TH E DI
PARNELL, WILLIAM WAS 143 2ND DIST
PARNIER, THOMAS P. WAS 208 1ST DIST
PARNIN, JOHN* DOR 380 1ST DIST
PARNIP, ISNAL CAR 072 NO TWP L
PARNIP, ISREAL B. CAR 072 NO TWP L
PAROLEY, JAMS BAL 234 12TH WAR
PAROT, JAMES BAL 144 2ND DIST
PARR, AUGUSTA* BAL 414 3RD WARD
PARR, D. PRESTON BAL 026 4TH WARD
PARR, DAVID BAL 040 4TH WARD
PARR, ELIZABETH BAL 232 6TH WARD
PARR, HENRY BAL 233 6TH WARD
PARR, ISRAEL M. BAL 313 3RD WARD
PARR, JAEMS ST 286 2ND E DI
PARR, JAMES L. BAL 063 4TH WARD
PARR, MARGARET BAL 313 3RD WARD
PARR, MARY BAL 314 3RD WARD
PARR, MICHAEL BAL 436 8TH WARD
PARR, WILLIAM BAL 165 6TH WARD
PARRAN, AGNUS CAL 013 1ST DIST
PARRAN, CAROLINE BAL 096 15TH WAR
PARRAN, CHARELS S. CAL 030 2ND DIST
PARRAN, ELIZA CAL 009 1ST DIST
PARRAN, ELIZABETH CAL 018 1ST DIST
PARRAN, HESTER BAL 130 16TH WAR
PARRAN, HORATIO ANN 427 HOWARD D
PARRAN, JAMES BAL 101 15TH WAR
PARRAN, JOHN CAL 010 1ST DIST
PARRAN, JOHN CAL 027 2ND DIST
PARRAN, RICHARD CAL 036 2ND DIST
PARRAN, SARAH BAL 096 2ND DIST
PARRAN, TAWNY CAL 022 2ND DIST
PARRAWAY, ELIZABETH BAL 020 18TH WAR
PARRELL, ELIZA BAL 027 1ST WARD
PARRET, WILLIAM BAL 303 3RD WARD
PARRETT, JOHN S. BAL 122 1ST WARD
PARRIN, HARRIETT DOR 321 1ST DIST
PARRIOTT, LAURA BAL 201 11TH WAR
PARRIS, DANIEL HAR 164 3RD DIST
PARRIS, ELI CAR 110 NO TWP L
PARRIS, JOHN CAR 104 NO TWP L
PARRIS, JOSEPH L. CAR 099 NO TWP L
PARRIS, MATHEW CAR 082 NO TWP L
PARRIS, SARAH A. CAR 110 NO TWP L
PARRIS, THOMAS QUE 138 1ST E DI
PARRIS, WILLIAM QUE 135 1ST E DI
PARRISH, ELAKIN BAL 124 11TH WAR
PARRISH, HESTER A.J. ANN 275 ANNAPOLI
PARRISH, JACOB BAL 182 16TH WAR
PARRISH, LOUIS E. BAL 183 16TH WAR
PARRISH, RICHARD CAR 389 2ND DIST
PARRISH, WILLIAM BAL 184 16TH WAR
PARRISH, WILLIAM BAL 139 5TH WARD
PARRISH, WILLIAM BAL 415 8TH WARD
PARRISH, WILLIAM T. ANN 286 ANNAPOLI
PARRKER, ANN-BLACK ST 317 4TH E DI
PARRON, JESSE BAL 286 1ST DIST
PARRON, THOMAS CAL 007 1ST DIST
PARROT, AARON CEC 179 7TH E DI
PARROT, J. S. BAL 148 1ST WARD
PARROT, WILLIAM CEC 081 CHARLEST
PARROTT, BARNETT TAL 046 EASTON T
PARROTT, ELIZABETH DOR 373 1ST DIST
PARROTT, EMELIE * BAL 314 20TH WAR
PARROTT, GEORGE W. TAL 016 EASTON D
PARROTT, JAMES TAL 027 EASTON D
PARROTT, JAMES M. TAL 062 EASTON D
PARROTT, JAMES W. BAL 172 6TH WARD
PARROTT, JAMES* TAL 005 EASTON D
PARROTT, JOHN B. BAL 020 18TH WAR
PARROTT, JOHN S. BAL 406 3RD WARD
PARROTT, LAURA BAL 314 20TH WAR
PARROTT, MARY BAL 044 4TH WARD
PARROTT, MARY E. ANN 329 2ND DIST
PARROTT, MARY R. KEN 251 2ND DIST
PARROTT, R. ANN 338 3RD DIST
PARROTT, REBECCA J. BAL 068 4TH WARD
PARROTT, SARAH A. BAL 040 15TH WAR
PARROTT, SARAH L. KEN 224 2ND DIST
PARROTT, STEPHEN CEC 007 ELKTON 3
PARROTT, WILLIAM HAR 076 BEL AIR
PARROTT, WILLIAM BAL 039 15TH WAR
PARROTT, WILLIAM TAL 050 EASTON T
PARROTT, WILLIAM E. BAL 408 3RD WARD
PARROTT, WILLIAM F. QUE 189 3RD E DI
PARRY,MARY-BLACK FRE 016 FREDERIC
PARRYVARY, OLIVER BAL 396 14TH WAR
PARSLEY, DAVID MGM 320 CRACKLIN
PARSLEY, MAHALA MGM 336 CRACKLIN
PARSLEY, MARGARET MGM 320 CRACKLIN
PARSNER, FRANCIS BAL 007 9TH WARD
PARSON, ANN B. PRI 056 AQUASCO
PARSON, ARNER HAR 041 1ST DIST
PARSON, BENJAMIN CAL 007 1ST DIST
PARSON, CHARLOTTA R. BAL 286 1ST DIST
PARSON, DARCUS CAL 007 1ST DIST
PARSON, HANNAH FRE 284 WOODSBOR
PARSON, J. BAL 245 20TH WAR
PARSON, JOSEPH F. ANN 517 HOWARD D
PARSON, MAGDALENE BAL 170 19TH WAR
PARSON, MARY A. BAL 412 1ST DIST
PARSON, MOSES HAR 026 1ST DIST
PARSON, THOMAS BAL 180 2ND DIST
PARSONS, AARON WOR 200 8TH E DI
PARSONS, ALLISON C. SOM 493 SALISBUR
PARSONS, AMELIA WOR 234 6TH E DI
PARSONS, ANN J. BAL 387 3RD WARD
PARSONS, BENJAMIN SOM 491 SALISBUR
PARSONS, BENJAMIN H. SOM 490 SALISBUR
PARSONS, BETSEY* TAL 038 EASTON D
PARSONS, CAROLINE WOR 200 8TH E DI
PARSONS, CHARELS W. WOR 217 4TH E DI
PARSONS, CHARLES WOR 230 6TH E DI
PARSONS, CHARLES SOM 503 SALISBUR
PARSONS, CHARLES BAL 116 1ST WARD
PARSONS, CHARLOTTE BAL 221 19TH WAR
PARSONS, CLARRISSA A. WOR 216 4TH E DI
PARSONS, DAVID B. WOR 230 6TH E DI
PARSONS, DENARD SOM 410 DUBLIN D
PARSONS, DRAPER WOR 226 4TH E DI
PARSONS, EDMOND BAL 303 1ST DIST
PARSONS, EDWAD L. WOR 226 4TH E DI
PARSONS, EDWARD ALL 135 4TH E.D.
PARSONS, ELI WOR 252 1ST CENS
PARSONS, ELIJAH WOR 233 6TH E DI
PARSONS, ELIJAH WOR 226 4TH E DI
PARSONS, ELIPHALET BAL 175 16TH WAR
PARSONS, ELISAH C. WOR 211 4TH E DI
PARSONS, ELISHA WOR 225 4TH E DI
PARSONS, ELIZA J. WOR 223 4TH E DI
PARSONS, ELIZABETH WOR 268 BERLIN 1
PARSONS, ELIZABETH BAL 174 16TH WAR
PARSONS, ELIZABETH BAL 100 15TH WAR
PARSONS, ELIZABETH BAL 056 2ND DIST
PARSONS, ELIZABETH BAL 018 2ND DIST
PARSONS, ELIZABETH SOM 413 DUBLIN D
PARSONS, ELIZABETH A. SOM 427 PRINCESS
PARSONS, ELLEN BAL 302 1ST DIST
PARSONS, ELLEN BAL 034 15TH WAR
PARSONS, EMMELINE WOR 203 4TH E DI
PARSONS, EPHRAIM W. WOR 167 6TH E DI
PARSONS, FREEBORN SOM 493 SALISBUR
PARSONS, GEORGE WOR 203 4TH E DI
PARSONS, GEORGE WOR 195 8TH E DI
PARSONS, GEORGE WOR 227 4TH E DI
PARSONS, GEORGE SOM 413 DUBLIN D
PARSONS, GEORGE H. WOR 225 4TH E DI
PARSONS, GEORGE L. WOR 208 4TH E DI
PARSONS, GEORGE M. WOR 203 4TH E DI
PARSONS, GEORGE R. QUE 179 2ND E DI
PARSONS, HANNAH WOR 191 8TH E DI
PARSONS, HANNAH SOM 491 SALISBUR
PARSONS, HENRIETTA WOR 258 1ST CENS
PARSONS, HENRY WOR 223 4TH E DI
PARSONS, HENRY WOR 232 6TH E DI
PARSONS, HESTER E. WOR 235 6TH E DI
PARSONS, ISAAC WOR 252 1ST CENS
PARSONS, ISAAC KEN 242 2ND DIST
PARSONS, ISAAC H. WOR 211 4TH E DI
PARSONS, JAMES L. WOR 211 4TH E DI
PARSONS, JAMES T. WOR 204 4TH E DI
PARSONS, JEHU SOM 504 SALISBUR
PARSONS, JEHU SOM 415 DUBLIN D
PARSONS, JOHN WOR 220 4TH E DI
PARSONS, JOHN WOR 192 8TH E DI
PARSONS, JOHN WOR 229 6TH E DI
PARSONS, JOHN ST 322 4TH E DI
PARSONS, JOHN WOR 346 1ST E DI
PARSONS, JOHN BAL 411 8TH WARD
PARSONS, JOHN C. WOR 246 1ST CENS
PARSONS, JOHN P. WOR 233 6TH E DI
PARSONS, JOHN W. KEN 242 2ND DIST
PARSONS, JONATHAN BAL 174 16TH WAR
PARSONS, JORDAN J. WOR 225 4TH E DI
PARSONS, JOSEPH WOR 232 6TH E DI
PARSONS, JOSEPH BAL 035 15TH WAR
PARSONS, JOSEPH DOR 338 3RD DIVI
PARSONS, JOSHUA BAL 221 19TH WAR
PARSONS, JOSHUA BAL 303 1ST DIST
PARSONS, JOSHUA WOR 233 6TH E DI
PARSONS, JOSHUA J. WOR 210 4TH E DI
PARSONS, JOSIAH WOR 270 BERLIN 1
PARSONS, JULIA J. WOR 223 4TH E DI
PARSONS, KENDAL SOM 441 DAMES QU
PARSONS, LAMBERT SOM 488 SALISBUR
PARSONS, LEVIN WOR 198 8TH E DI
PARSONS, LEWIS BAL 064 2ND DIST
PARSONS, LYDIA BAL 058 2ND DIST
PARSONS, LYDIA KEN 250 2ND DIST
PARSONS, MARIA WOR 233 6TH E DI
PARSONS, MARIAH SOM 437 DAMES QU
PARSONS, MARTHA A. E. WOR 237 6TH E DI
PARSONS, MARY WOR 207 4TH E DI
PARSONS, MARY WOR 272 BERLIN 1
PARSONS, MARY BAL 267 20TH WAR
PARSONS, MARY E. BAL 070 4TH WARD
PARSONS, MARY E. BAL 203 11TH WAR
PARSONS, MARY J. WOR 192 8TH E DI
PARSONS, MASON FRE 284 WOODSBOR
PARSONS, MICHAEL BAL 325 1ST DIST
PARSONS, MILLY SOM 495 SALISBUR
PARSONS, MILTON SOM 494 SALISBUR
PARSONS, MOLLY WOR 299 SNOW HIL
PARSONS, MORDECAI WOR 240 5TH E DI
PARSONS, NANCY WOR 210 4TH E DI
PARSONS, NANCY WOR 200 8TH E DI
PARSONS, NATHANIEL BAL 301 1ST DIST
PARSONS, NOAH D. WOR 286 BERLIN 1
PARSONS, NOAH S. WOR 286 BERLIN 1
PARSONS, PATRICK W. WOR 223 4TH E DI
PARSONS, PETER BAL 035 15TH WAR
PARSONS, PETER E. SOM 415 DUBLIN D
PARSONS, PETER P. WOR 223 4TH E DI
PARSONS, PETER R. WOR 223 4TH E DI
PARSONS, PETER T. WOR 217 4TH E DI
PARSONS, PRECELLA SOM 424 PRINCESS
PARSONS, PRUNELL WOR 254 1ST CENS

Name	County	Page	District
PARSONS, PURNELL W.	WOR	214	4TH E DI
PARSONS, RHODA	WOR	233	6TH E DI
PARSONS, RICHARD	BAL	413	1ST DIST
PARSONS, ROBERT	WOR	233	6TH E DI
PARSONS, ROBERT	WOR	249	1ST CENS
PARSONS, ROBERT H.	WOR	227	4TH E DI
PARSONS, RUFUS M.	WOR	223	4TH E DI
PARSONS, RUFUS M.	SOM	437	DAMES QU
PARSONS, SABRA	WOR	212	4TH E DI
PARSONS, SALLY	WOR	203	4TH E DI
PARSONS, SAMUEL	WOR	255	1ST CENS
PARSONS, SAMUEL	SOM	413	DUBLIN D
PARSONS, SAMUEL	HAR	014	1ST DIST
PARSONS, SAMUEL J.	BAL	379	13TH WAR
PARSONS, SAMUEL T.	WOR	214	4TH E DI
PARSONS, SAMUEL-BLACK	WOR	167	6TH E DI
PARSONS, SARAH	SOM	497	SALISBUR
PARSONS, SARAH	BAL	414	3RD WARD
PARSONS, SARAH	BAL	248	12TH WAR
PARSONS, SARAH A.	WOR	251	1ST CENS
PARSONS, SARAH E.	WOR	195	8TH E DI
PARSONS, SUSAN	BAL	067	10TH WAR
PARSONS, SUSAN	BAL	096	10TH WAR
PARSONS, SYDNEY	SOM	493	SALISBUR
PARSONS, THEODORE	SOM	491	SALISBUR
PARSONS, THOMAS	WOR	219	4TH E DI
PARSONS, THOMAS	TAL	101	ST MICHA
PARSONS, THOMAS	BAL	059	15TH WAR
PARSONS, THOMAS	BAL	226	6TH WARD
PARSONS, THOMAS	CAR	215	5TH DIST
PARSONS, THOMAS	KEN	230	2ND DIST
PARSONS, WILLIAM	SOM	411	DUBLIN D
PARSONS, WILLIAM	BAL	137	18TH WAR
PARSONS, WILLIAM	BAL	437	8TH WARD
PARSONS, WILLIAM	SOM	479	TRAPP DI
PARSONS, WILLIAM	WOR	229	6TH E DI
PARSONS, WILLIAM G.W.	BAL	144	16TH WAR
PARSONS, WILLIAM H.	WOR	220	4TH E DI
PARSONS, WILLIAM L.	BAL	197	11TH WAR
PARSONS, WILLIAM Z. REV-	BAL	062	18TH WAR
PARSONS, ZENA	SOM	413	DUBLIN D
PARSORIS, CHARLES	BAL	178	19TH WAR
PARSTON, WILLIAM P.	BAL	202	11TH WAR
PARTERFIELD, PHILIP T.	TAL	101	ST MICHA
PARTEYER, JACOB	BAL	195	19TH WAR
PARTINGTON, JULIAN	BAL	364	1ST DIST
PARTLET, JACOB	BAL	317	1ST DIST
PARTLETT, RUELMA	BAL	401	14TH WAR
PARTLOW, WILLIAM	BAL	329	13TH WAR
PARTRAGE, JOHN	ST	285	2ND E DI
PARTRAGE, JOHN R.	ST	298	2ND E DI
PARTRIDGE, GEORGE	BAL	180	2ND WARD
PARTRIDGE, HARRIET	BAL	013	1ST WARD
PARTRICGE, JAMES R.	BAL	140	11TH WAR
PARTRIDGE, JOHN	CEC	005	ELKTON 3
PARTRIDGE, LAMBERT W.	BAL	351	1ST DIST
PARTRIDGE, MARGARET R.	BAL	070	15TH WAR
PARTRIDGE, WILLIAM	BAL	351	1ST DIST
PARTRIDGE, WILLIAM	BAL	350	1ST DIST
PARTRIDGE, WILLIAM	DOR	326	3RD DIVI
PARTY, THIMOTHY	FRE	136	CREAGERS
PARUSS, JOHN	BAL	274	2ND WARD
PARVEL, HENRY *	BAL	422	1ST DIST
PARVIN, EDWARD	DOR	321	1ST DIST
PARVLY, CAROLINE	BAL	329	13TH WAR
PARY, JOHN	HAR	046	1ST DIST
PASANE, LEWIS	BAL	068	4TH WARD
PASCAL, EDWARD	BAL	133	1ST WARD
PASCAL, ELIZABETH	BAL	415	3RD WARD
PASCAL, MARGARET	BAL	133	16TH WAR
PASCAL, MARION	BAL	332	7TH WARD
PASCAL, PETER	BAL	143	1ST WARD
PASCAL, T.	BAL	157	1ST WARD
PASCALL, ELIZABETH	BAL	055	1ST WARD
PASCALL, JAMES R.	BAL	025	1ST WARD
PASCAULT, E.	BAL	063	10TH WAR
PASCHAL, CORNELIA	BAL	242	6TH WARD
PASCHAL, PETER	BAL	168	6TH WARD
PASCOE, ISAIH	BAL	088	18TH WAR
PASEY, JAMES	BAL	249	20TH WAR
PASEY, STEPHEN	BAL	121	11TH WAR
PASLETT, DAVID	BAL	112	2ND DIST
PASLETT, HEZEKIAH	BAL	104	2ND DIST
PASQUAY, JACOB	BAL	089	10TH WAR
PASQUEL, BETSEY	BAL	345	7TH WARD
PASQUEL, ELIZABETH	BAL	335	7TH WARD
PASQUEL, MARY	BAL	325	7TH WARD
PASQUELL, MARGARET	BAL	421	8TH WARD
PASS, JOHN	FRE	363	CATOCTIN
PASSA, JAMES B.	CAR	211	5TH DIST
PASSANCH, ALEXANDER A.*	TAL	004	EASTON D
PASSANE, LEONARD*	BAL	021	4TH WARD
PASSANET, ALEXANDER A.*	TAL	004	EASTON D
PASSANO, JOSEPH	BAL	186	2ND WARD
PASSANO, JOSHUA	BAL	035	4TH WARD
PASSANO, MARY	BAL	036	4TH WARD
PASSAUL, LANCHART	BAL	231	2ND WARD
PASSIMORE, WILLIAM	BAL	356	3RD WARD
PASSMORE, ELLIS P.	CEC	167	6TH E DI
PASSMORE, JAMES G.	WAS	019	2ND SUBD
PASSON, RACHEL	MGM	315	CRACKLIN
PASSPAE, JAMES*	BAL	414	3RD WARD
PASTERFIELD, ELIZABETH	TAL	101	ST MICHA
PASTERFIELD, FANNEY	BAL	298	7TH WARD
PASTERFIELD, JOHN*	TAL	046	EASTON T
PASTERFIELD, MARGARET	BAL	430	8TH WARD
PASTERFIELD, MARTHA A.	BAL	310	7TH WARD
PASTERFIELD, WILLIAM H.	BAL	310	7TH WARD
PASTERS, ALICE J.	BAL	161	6TH WARD
PASTERS, FRANCIS	BAL	160	6TH WARD
PASTIMIS, SAMUEL	BAL	163	19TH WAR
PASTLEY, AMANDA	FRE	088	FREDERIC
PASTWIGHT, SARAH	CAR	149	NO TWP L
PASXAULB, LEWIS C.	QUE	235	4TH E DI
PATCHELL, JOSEPH	CAR	155	NO TWP L
PATCHELL, WESLEY	CAR	137	NO TWP L
PATCHERSON, GEORGE	CHA	220	ALLENS F
PATCHETT, ABSALOM	CAR	141	NO TWP L
PATCHETT, NATHAN	CAR	153	NO TWP L
PATCHETT, WILLIAM-BLACK	CAR	080	NO TWP L
PATCHIT, FRANCES	DOR	313	1ST DIST
PATE, CHARLES	BAL	019	1ST WARD
PATE, ISABELLA	BAL	098	1ST WARD
PATE,WILLIAM	BAL	099	1ST WARD
PATELER, MARTHA J.	BAL	302	7TH WARD
PATEN, DAVID	CEC	080	NORTHEAS
PATEN, ELIZABETH-MULATTO	FRE	218	BUCKEYST
PATEN, MARY E.-MULATTO	FRE	218	BUCKEYST
PATEN, PETER	WAS	162	HAGERSTO
PATER, MATHIAS	BAL	359	1ST DIST
PATERSON, ANN	DOR	359	3RD DIVI
PATERSON, ANN J.	CHA	269	ALLENS F
PATERSON, AUGUSTUS	DOR	357	3RD DIVI
PATERSON, GEORGE	WAS	066	2ND SUBD
PATERSON, HENRY H.	BAL	252	17TH WAR
PATERSON, JAMES	DOR	357	3RD DIVI
PATERSON, JOHN	CAL	002	1ST DIST
PATERSON, JOHN	WAS	072	2ND SUBD
PATERSON, JOHN H.	CEC	133	6TH E DI
PATERSON, LEPER	ALL	206	CUMBERLA
PATERSON, MARY	WAS	073	2ND SUBD
PATERSON, MARY A.	BAL	201	19TH WAR
PATERSON, NANCY	WAS	066	2ND SUBD
PATERSON, REVEL	WOR	304	SNOW HIL
PATERSON, SOLOMON	WAS	071	2ND SUBD
PATERSON, THOAMS	HAR	198	3RD DIST
PATERSON, THOMAS	WAS	062	2ND SUBD
PATERSON, WEST	WAS	071	2ND SUBD
PATERSON, WILLIAM	WAS	003	WILLIAMS
PATERSON, WILLIAM P.	HAR	188	3RD DIST
PATERSON, ZACKARIAH	WAS	071	2ND SUBD
PATES, DANIEL	BAL	291	3RD WARD
PATESBERRY, MARY	BAL	291	12TH WAR
PATIENCE, ANN	ALL	084	5TH E.D.
PATINGER, MARY	WAS	133	HAGERSTO
PATISON, JEREMIAH	WAS	003	WILLIAMS
PATON, HENRY	BAL	274	2ND WARD
PATON, STEPHEN	BAL	311	3RD WARD
PATRIC, LOTT	SOM	545	TYASKIN
PATRICK, BROTHER	BAL	216	11TH WAR
PATRICK, G.	ALL	239	CUMBERLA
PATRICK, GEORGANNA E.	FRE	052	FREDERIC
PATRICK, J.	BAL	333	1ST DIST
PATRICK, JAMES	BAL	314	3RD WARD
PATRICK, JAMES	ALL	110	5TH E.D.
PATRICK, JOHN	BAL	025	9TH WARD
PATRICK, JOHN	HAR	119	2ND DIST
PATRICK, LETITIA	BAL	166	19TH WAR
PATRICK, LEWIS	CAR	394	2ND DIST
PATRICK, LORENZO D.	BAL	061	15TH WAR
PATRICK, MARY A.	BAL	137	11TH WAR
PATRICK, NANCY	FRE	447	8TH E DI
PATRICK, NOAH	CAR	103	NO TWP L
PATRICK, PETER	ALL	239	CUMBERLA
PATRICK, PETER	BAL	319	12TH WAR
PATRICK, SAMUEL	BAL	303	12TH WAR
PATRICK, W.	BAL	332	1ST DIST
PATRICK, WILLIAM	BAL	195	2ND WARD
PATRICK, WILLIAM	QUE	135	1ST E DI
PATRICK, WILLIAM H.	CAR	392	2ND DIST
PATRICK, WILLIAM J.	QUE	136	1ST E DI
PATRICKS, SUSAN	FRE	095	FREDERIC
PATRON, THOMAS	CEC	183	7TH E DI
PATTAN, JAMES	CEC	093	4TH E DI
PATTEN, FANNY	BAL	061	15TH WAR
PATTEN, JABEZ	BAL	134	1ST WARD
PATTEN, JOHN	ALL	139	6TH E.D.
PATTEN, LEWIS D.	MGM	389	ROCKERLE
PATTEN, MARGARET	WAS	002	WILLIAMS
PATTEN, RICHARD	BAL	130	5TH WARD
PATTEN, ROBERT	BAL	107	15TH WAR
PATTEN, SARAH	WAS	059	2ND SUBD
PATTEN, WILLIAM	BAL	091	18TH WAR
PATTENGALL, JOHN	FRE	230	BUCKEYST
PATTER, CATHARINE	BAL	155	5TH WARD
PATTEROSN, OWEN	BAL	177	2ND DIST
PATTERSN, CHARELS	BAL	280	2ND WARD
PATTERSON, A.B.	BAL	020	18TH WAR
PATTERSON, AMELIA	BAL	097	15TH WAR
PATTERSON, ANN	BAL	129	11TH WAR
PATTERSON, ARCHABALD	FRE	123	CREAGERS
PATTERSON, CALENDER	BAL	309	7TH WARD
PATTERSON, CASSANDER	BAL	384	8TH WARD
PATTERSON, CATHARINE	CAR	207	4TH DIST
PATTERSON, CHARLES	BAL	336	13TH WAR
PATTERSON, CHARLES	BAL	195	5TH DIST
PATTERSON, CHARLES	BAL	426	1ST DIST
PATTERSON, D.	BAL	221	19TH WAR
PATTERSON, DANIEL	BAL	376	3RD WARD
PATTERSON, DANIEL REV.	WOR	261	BERLIN 1
PATTERSON, DAVID	BAL	322	1ST DIST
PATTERSON, EDWARD	BAL	319	3RD WARD
PATTERSON, EDWARD	BAL	049	9TH WARD
PATTERSON, EDWARD	BAL	124	11TH WAR
PATTERSON, ELEANOR	FRE	170	5TH E DI
PATTERSON, ELIAS	FRE	124	CREAGERS
PATTERSON, ELIZA A.	BAL	322	3RD WARD
PATTERSON, ELIZA J.	BAL	219	19TH WAR
PATTERSON, ELIZABETH	BAL	338	7TH WARD
PATTERSON, ELLEN	BAL	112	5TH WARD
PATTERSON, ELLEN	BAL	385	13TH WAR
PATTERSON, GEORGE	CAR	222	5TH DIST
PATTERSON, GEORGE	ANN	317	1ST DIST
PATTERSON, GEORGE W.	WOR	328	1ST E DI
PATTERSON, GURNEY C.	ANN	312	1ST DIST
PATTERSON, HANAH	BAL	346	7TH WARD
PATTERSON, HANNAH	CEC	185	7TH E DI
PATTERSON, HARRIETT E.	BAL	303	3RD WARD
PATTERSON, HELLEN M.	PRI	003	BLADENSB
PATTERSON, HENRIETTA	BAL	412	14TH WAR
PATTERSON, HENRY	BAL	201	6TH DIST
PATTERSON, HENRY	BAL	069	10TH WAR
PATTERSON, HENRY	BAL	197	17TH WAR
PATTERSON, HETTY	SOM	415	DUBLIN D
PATTERSON, HOLMES A.	WAS	184	BOONSBOR
PATTERSON, JACOB	BAL	063	4TH WARD
PATTERSON, JAMES	BAL	139	19TH WAR
PATTERSON, JAMES	BAL	318	7TH WARD
PATTERSON, JAMES	BAL	061	15TH WAR
PATTERSON, JAMES	BAL	056	15TH WAR
PATTERSON, JAMES	BAL	077	1ST WARD
PATTERSON, JAMES	BAL	407	8TH WARD
PATTERSON, JAMES	BAL	227	6TH WARD
PATTERSON, JANE	BAL	161	2ND DIST
PATTERSON, JANE	BAL	011	15TH WAR
PATTERSON, JANE	BAL	068	4TH WARD
PATTERSON, JANE	BAL	124	11TH WAR
PATTERSON, JANE	PRI	003	BLADENSB
PATTERSON, JANE L.	BAL	323	3RD WARD
PATTERSON, JOHN	BAL	384	1ST DIST
PATTERSON, JOHN	BAL	011	9TH WARD
PATTERSON, JOHN	BAL	198	5TH DIST
PATTERSON, JOHN	BAL	248	1ST DIST
PATTERSON, JOHN	BAL	043	9TH WARD
PATTERSON, JOHN	BAL	027	9TH WARD
PATTERSON, JOHN	BAL	359	8TH WARD
PATTERSON, JOHN	BAL	359	8TH WARD
PATTERSON, JOHN	BAL	267	7TH WARD
PATTERSON, JOHN	BAL	071	10TH WAR
PATTERSON, JOHN	ALL	134	4TH E.D.
PATTERSON, JOHN	ALL	012	3RD E.D.
PATTERSON, JOHN	BAL	144	2ND DIST
PATTERSON, JOHN	BAL	203	19TH WAR
PATTERSON, JOHN	FRE	169	5TH E DI
PATTERSON, JOHN	BAL	275	20TH WAR
PATTERSON, JOHN H.	BAL	197	11TH WAR
PATTERSON, JOHN R.	FRE	046	FREDERIC
PATTERSON, JOHN S.	BAL	208	6TH WARD
PATTERSON, JOSEPH	BAL	028	15TH WAR
PATTERSON, JOSEPH W.	BAL	049	9TH WARD
PATTERSON, KENNADY	CEC	180	7TH E DI
PATTERSON, LEWIS	BAL	376	3RD WARD
PATTERSON, LORENZO	BAL	084	2ND DIST
PATTERSON, LYSANDER	BAL	049	2ND DIST
PATTERSON, M. MRS.	BAL	214	11TH WAR
PATTERSON, MARGARET A.	CAR	396	2ND DIST
PATTERSON, MARGARETT	BAL	022	4TH WARD
PATTERSON, MARY	BAL	216	11TH WAR
PATTERSON, MARY	BAL	146	5TH WARD
PATTERSON, MARY	ANN	312	1ST DIST
PATTERSON, MARY	BAL	294	7TH WARD
PATTERSON, MARY A.	BAL	095	18TH WAR
PATTERSON, MARY E.	BAL	377	13TH WAR
PATTERSON, MARY J.	ANN	417	HOWARD D
PATTERSON, MARY J.	ANN	427	HOWARD D
PATTERSON, MILKY	WOR	328	1ST E DI
PATTERSON, MRS.	BAL	244	17TH WAR
PATTERSON, ORVILLE	HAR	102	2ND DIST
PATTERSON, PETER	BAL	199	5TH DIST
PATTERSON, RACHELL	BAL	189	17TH WAR
PATTERSON, REBECCA J.	BAL	080	15TH WAR
PATTERSON, ROBERT	BAL	151	16TH WAR
PATTERSON, ROBERT	SOM	440	DAMES QU
PATTERSON, ROBERT	FRE	155	10TH E D
PATTERSON, ROBERT	SOM	530	QUANTICO
PATTERSON, SAMEUL	BAL	201	19TH WAR
PATTERSON, SAMUEL	HAR	098	2ND DIST
PATTERSON, SAMUEL	HAR	016	1ST DIST
PATTERSON, SAMUEL	BAL	139	19TH WAR
PATTERSON, SAMUEL	BAL	154	16TH WAR
PATTERSON, SAMUEL	BAL	137	2ND DIST
PATTERSON, SAMUEL J.	BAL	148	16TH WAR
PATTERSON, SARAH	BAL	321	7TH WARD
PATTERSON, SARAH	BAL	404	14TH WAR
PATTERSON, SARAH A.	BAL	196	11TH WAR
PATTERSON, SOPHIA	BAL	376	3RD WARD
PATTERSON, SUSAN	WOR	328	1ST E DI
PATTERSON, THOMAS	BAL	219	19TH WAR
PATTERSON, THOMAS	FRE	124	CREAGERS
PATTERSON, THOMAS	FRE	034	FREDERIC
PATTERSON, WILHILMINA	BAL	322	1ST DIST
PATTERSON, WILLIAM	BAL	257	1ST DIST
PATTERSON, WILLIAM	BAL	074	1ST WARD
PATTERSON, WILLIAM	BAL	342	7TH WARD
PATTERSON, WILLIAM	BAL	320	7TH WARD
PATTERSON, WILLIAM	BAL	079	15TH WAR
PATTERSON, WILLIAM	BAL	070	10TH WAR
PATTERSON, WILLIAM	BAL	027	9TH WARD
PATTERSON, WILLIAM	BAL	245	20TH WAR
PATTERSON, WILLIAM	FRE	122	CREAGERS
PATTERSON, WILLIAM	HAR	111	2ND DIST
PATTERSON, WILLIAM	SOM	417	PRINCESS
PATTERSON, WILLIAM	MGM	363	BERRYS D
PATTERSON, WILLIAM	CEC	186	7TH E DI
PATTERSON, WILLIAM	BAL	026	18TH WAR
PATTERSON, WILLIAM DR.	FRE	159	EMMITTSB
PATTERSON, WILLIAM G.	BAL	097	10TH WAR
PATTERSON, WILLIAM R.	BAL	057	15TH WAR
PATTERSON,AMELIA	BAL	215	2ND WARD
PATTESON, MARY	BAL	052	2ND DIST
PATTESON, MARY	BAL	407	14TH WAR
PATTEY, JOHN	WOR	272	BERLIN 1
PATTEY, MATILDA	WOR	255	1ST CENS
PATTEY, POWELL	WOR	272	BERLIN 1
PATTEYON, FRED	BAL	283	12TH WAR
PATTINGALL, HARRIET	FRE	004	FREDERIC
PATTISON, ACHSAH*	DOR	417	1ST DIST
PATTISON, ANNA	DOR	375	1ST DIST
PATTISON, CHARLES	DOR	446	1ST DIST
PATTISON, CHARLOTTE H.	BAL	083	15TH WAR
PATTISON, JAMES	DOR	448	1ST DIST
PATTISON, JAMES F.	BAL	266	1ST DIST
PATTISON, JEREMIAH	DOR	396	1ST DIST
PATTISON, JEREMIAH	DOR	469	1ST DIST
PATTISON, JOHN	DOR	452	1ST DIST
PATTISON, JOHN R.	DOR	390	1ST DIST
PATTISON, M. F.	DOR	373	1ST DIST
PATTISON, RICHARD	BAL	067	4TH WARD
PATTISON, SAMUEL	DOR	391	1ST DIST
PATTISON, SAMUEL	BAL	073	15TH WAR
PATTISON, SARAH	DOR	413	1ST DIST
PATTISON, SARAH	TAL	087	ST MICHA
PATTISON, SUSAN	DOR	386	1ST DIST
PATTISON, THOMAS	DOR	438	1ST DIST
PATTISON, THOMAS	BAL	078	15TH WAR
PATTISON, THOMAS J.	BAL	172	1ST WARD
PATTISON, WILLIAM A.	HAR	184	3RD DIST
PATTON, ANDREW M.	CEC	155	PORT DUP
PATTON, ANN	BAL	393	8TH WARD
PATTON, BARROTT	CAR	141	NO TWP L
PATTON, CHARLES	BAL	015	1ST WARD
PATTON, CHARLES A.	ANN	518	HOWARD D
PATTON, CHRISTIAN	BAL	212	2ND WARD
PATTON, EBENEZER	BAL	078	10TH WAR
PATTON, ELIZABETH	BAL	454	14TH WAR
PATTON, ELLEN	CEC	156	PORT DUP
PATTON, ELLEN	CEC	204	6TH E DI
PATTON, ELLINOR	CEC	157	PORT DUP
PATTON, HENRY	ALL	017	3RD E.D.
PATTON, ISABELLA	CEC	203	6TH E DI
PATTON, JOHN	HAR	065	1ST DIST
PATTON, JOHN	MGM	413	MEDLEY 3
PATTON, JOHN W.	KEN	259	1ST DIST
PATTON, LEWIS	MGM	354	BERRYS D
PATTON, LYDIA	CAR	144	NO TWP L
PATTON, LYDIA	CAR	144	NO TWP L
PATTON, MARGARET	CEC	169	6TH E DI
PATTON, MARGARETT	BAL	007	4TH WARD
PATTON, MATHEW	CAR	143	NO TWP L
PATTON, MICHAEL	ALL	126	4TH E.D.
PATTON, WILLIAM	BAL	393	8TH WARD
PATTON, WILLIAM	BAL	006	4TH WARD
PATTON, WILLIAM	CEC	159	PORT DUP
PAUDER, HENRIETTA*	BAL	025	4TH WARD
PAUGH, ADELIA	ALL	067	10TH E.D
PAUGH, ANN	ALL	062	10TH E.D
PAUGH, CHARLES	ALL	221	CUMBERLA
PAUGH, HENRY	ALL	132	4TH E.D.
PAUGH, HENRY	ALL	131	4TH E.D.
PAUGH, JACOB	ALL	067	10TH E.D

Name	County	Page	District
PAUGH, JOHN C.	ALL	066	10TH E.D
PAUGH, JOSEPH H.	ALL	067	10TH E.D
PAUGH, LOUIS	ALL	066	10TH E.D
PAUGH, MICHAEL	ALL	067	10TH E.D
PAUGH, NICHOLAS	ALL	066	10TH E.D
PAUGH, PHILLIP H.	ALL	065	10TH E.D
PAUGH, THOMAS	ALL	067	10TH E.D
PAUGH, WILLIAM	ALL	095	5TH E.D.
PAUGH, WILLIAM H.	ALL	224	CUMBERLA
PAUL, ALEXANDER	BAL	137	18TH WAR
PAUL, AMANDA	BAL	018	4TH WARD
PAUL, ANN	DOR	339	3RD DIVI
PAUL, BETSY	DOR	410	1ST DIST
PAUL, CHARLES J.	ST	267	3RD E DI
PAUL, DAVID	CAR	401	2ND DIST
PAUL, ELIZA J.	BAL	078	15TH WAR
PAUL, GEORGE	ALL	008	3RD E.D.
PAUL, GEORGE	BAL	280	1ST DIST
PAUL, GEORGE E.	ST	285	2ND E DI
PAUL, GEORGE E.	ST	284	2ND E DI
PAUL, GEORGE R.	BAL	290	20TH WAR
PAUL, JAMES	HAR	200	3RD DIST
PAUL, JAMES	BAL	210	19TH WAR
PAUL, JANE E.	ST	279	3RD E DI
PAUL, JOHN	CEC	087	4TH E DI
PAUL, JOHN	ALL	102	5TH E.D.
PAUL, JOHN	BAL	077	2ND DIST
PAUL, JOHN S.	BAL	311	20TH WAR
PAUL, JONATHAN	DOR	410	1ST DIST
PAUL, LEVIN	DOR	410	1ST DIST
PAUL, LEVIN	DOR	458	1ST DIST
PAUL, LOUIS	BAL	111	15TH WAR
PAUL, M.*	DOR	410	1ST DIST
PAUL, MARGARET	QUE	252	5TH E DI
PAUL, MARGARET A. L.*	DOR	409	1ST DIST
PAUL, MARGARET E.	ST	279	3RD E DI
PAUL, MARIA A.	BAL	446	14TH WAR
PAUL, MARY	BAL	108	2ND DIST
PAUL, MARY A.	BAL	374	1ST DIST
PAUL, NANCY	DOR	450	1ST DIST
PAUL, NEHSAH*	DOR	410	1ST DIST
PAUL, PHOEBE P.	BAL	150	16TH WAR
PAUL, REBECCA	BAL	094	10TH WAR
PAUL, ROBERT	DOR	420	1ST DIST
PAUL, ROBERT-BLACK	QUE	191	3RD E DI
PAUL, THOMAS	BAL	150	1ST WARD
PAUL, WILLIAM	BAL	284	12TH WAR
PAUL, WILLIAM	BAL	284	1ST DIST
PAUL, WILLIAM	BAL	119	1ST WARD
PAUL, WILLIAM	BAL	406	14TH WAR
PAUL, WILLIAM	DOR	334	3RD DIVI
PAUL, ZACHARIA	DOR	445	1ST DIST
PAULE, STEPHERD	BAL	102	1ST WARD
PAULEY, ELLENOR J.	FRE	003	FREDERIC
PAULEY, HOWARD	FRE	096	FREDERIC
PAULICK, NEAPOLE	BAL	303	7TH WARD
PAULINE, SARAH	BAL	462	14TH WAR
PAULKING, JOHN	CAR	098	NO TWP L
PAULL, SARAH J.	HAR	175	3RD DIST
PAULSON, CAROLIN	BAL	204	2ND WARD
PAULSON, H.	BAL	151	1ST WARD
PAULSON, J.	BAL	135	1ST WARD
PAULSON, JOHN	BAL	169	1ST WARD
PAULSON, JOHN	BAL	409	3RD WARD
PAULSON, RACHAEL	CAR	285	7TH DIST
PAULSON, SARAH J.	BAL	141	11TH WAR
PAULT, WILLIAM H.	TAL	071	EASTON T
PAULUS, JOHN	ALL	243	CUMBERLA
PAUOTT, THOAMS	TAL	076	EASTON T
PAURISE, THOMAS *	BAL	135	18TH WAR
PAURUE, THOMAS *	BAL	135	18TH WAR
PAVER, POLLY	ALL	190	9TH E.D.
PAWBLITA, JOHN	BAL	421	1ST DIST
PAWBLITS, THOMAS	BAL	244	1ST DIST
PAWBLITZ, MARY	BAL	426	1ST DIST
PAWEL, HENRY *	BAL	422	1ST DIST
PAWELL, THOMAS	BAL	261	1ST DIST
PAWLEY, JAMES	BAL	076	4TH WARD
PAWLEY, OPHELIA	BAL	039	4TH WARD
PAWLIN, MARTIN	ALL	057	10TH E.D
PAWLING, FRANCIS	WAS	137	2ND DIST
PAWNELL, JOHN	ALL	221	CUMBERLA
PAWPLETS, WILLIAM	BAL	246	1ST DIST
PAWSON, ELIZA	BAL	467	14TH WAR
PAXLY, MARY B.	BAL	385	13TH WAR
PAXON, WARNER	CEC	128	5TH E DI
PAXTON, ANTHONY C.	CEC	129	6TH E DI
PAXTON, CLARRISA	BAL	042	2ND DIST
PAXTON, D.D.	WAS	012	WILLIAMS
PAXTON, DAVID	ALL	201	CUMBERLA
PAXTON, EASTER	BAL	015	2ND DIST
PAXTON, EMILY	ALL	237	CUMBERLA
PAXTON, HENRY	ALL	156	6TH E.D.
PAXTON, JOHN	CAR	299	1ST DIST
PAXTON, JOSEPH	ALL	167	6TH E.D.
PAXTON, NELSON	ALL	157	6TH E.D.
PAXTON, SAMUEL	ALL	156	6TH E.D.
PAXTON, THOMAS	ALL	151	6TH E.D.
PAXTON, WILLIAM	MGM	392	ROCKERLE
PAXTON,W ILLIAM	FRE	188	5TH E DI
PAYELS, GEORGE H.	BAL	241	12TH WAR
PAYHILL, JOHN	BAL	110	2ND DIST
PAYLES, CHRISTOPHER	BAL	154	2ND DIST
PAYLOR, JOHN	WAS	156	2ND DIST
PAYNE, ANDREW	PRI	098	SPALDING
PAYNE, ANDREW	PRI	099	SPALDING
PAYNE, ANN	WAS	093	2ND SUBD
PAYNE, BENJAMIN N.	BAL	014	2ND DIST
PAYNE, CHARLES	BAL	166	2ND DIST
PAYNE, CHARLES	BAL	284	7TH WARD
PAYNE, CLARISSA E.	MGM	333	CRACKLIN
PAYNE, ELISHA D. DR.	CAR	270	WESTMINS
PAYNE, ELIZA	WAS	094	2ND SUBD
PAYNE, GEORGE	BAL	132	1ST WARD
PAYNE, GEORGE M.	BAL	155	19TH WAR
PAYNE, H.	BAL	169	1ST WARD
PAYNE, HENRIETTA-MULATTO	FRE	447	8TH E DI
PAYNE, HENRY	BAL	161	1ST WARD
PAYNE, HENRY	KEN	272	1ST DIST
PAYNE, HUGH	PRI	099	SPALDING
PAYNE, JAMES	BAL	320	7TH WARD
PAYNE, JOHN	QUE	197	3RD E DI
PAYNE, JOHN	BAL	458	14TH WAR
PAYNE, JOSEPH	DOR	318	1ST DIST
PAYNE, JOSEPH	FRE	055	FREDERIC
PAYNE, JULIA O.	CAR	270	WESTMINS
PAYNE, LEVIN	DOR	310	1ST DIST
PAYNE, LEVY	DOR	313	1ST DIST
PAYNE, MARGARET	FRE	231	BUCKEYST
PAYNE, MARIAH	DOR	310	1ST DIST
PAYNE, MARY J.	BAL	069	15TH WAR
PAYNE, PATTY	WOR	326	1ST E DI
PAYNE, PETER	ALL	094	5TH E.D.
PAYNE, SAMUEL H.	WOR	345	1ST E DI
PAYNE, SARAH	WAS	092	2ND SUBD
PAYNE, WILLAM	ALL	135	4TH E.D.
PAYNE, WILLIAM	BAL	143	16TH WAR
PAYNE, WILLIAM	PRI	115	PISCATAW
PAYNE, WILLIAM	DOR	312	1ST DIST
PAYNE, WILLIAM T.	MGM	347	BERRYS D
PAYNOR, JOHN	HAR	104	2ND DIST
PAYOR, DENNIS	BAL	379	8TH WARD
PAYOR, ELY *	BAL	092	18TH WAR
PAYOT, SARAH	BAL	078	10TH WAR
PAYOTN, WILLIAM	SOM	463	HANGARY
PAYSON, G.	BAL	051	9TH WARD
PAYTHER, ELIZABETH	BAL	350	3RD WARD
PAYTON, ELIZABETH G.	SOM	408	DUBLIN D
PAYTON, JAMES H.	WOR	299	SNOW HIL
PAYTON, JOHN B.	CAL	010	1ST DIST
PAYTON, SUSAN	SOM	405	DUBLIN D
PAYTON, WILLIAM	SOM	461	HANGARY
PAYTON, WILLIAM	WOR	320	1ST E DI
PCKIS, JAMES	CAR	309	1ST DIST
PEA, RASHEL	TAL	088	ST MICHA
PEA, SAMUEL	ALL	180	8TH E.D.
PEABODY, DANIEL H.	ALL	255	CUMBERLA
PEABODY, HURMAN	BAL	279	20TH WAR
PEACA, AQUILLA	HAR	158	3RD DIST
PEACA, JAMES	HAR	157	3RD DIST
PEACA, WILLIAM B.	HAR	185	3RD DIST
PEACE, AMELIA	HAR	150	3RD DIST
PEACE, FRANCIS	HAR	137	2ND DIST
PEACE, ISAAC	KEN	291	3RD DIST
PEACE, SAMUEL	CEC	145	PORT DUP
PEACH, ADAM	BAL	192	17TH WAR
PEACH, CHARLES	BAL	200	6TH WARD
PEACH, DARCUS	BAL	230	17TH WAR
PEACH, DEBORAH-BLACK	FRE	034	FREDERIC
PEACH, JOHN	CEC	041	CHESAPEA
PEACH, JOHN	BAL	122	16TH WAR
PEACH, JOSEPH	BAL	121	2ND DIST
PEACH, JOSEPH	BAL	108	18TH WAR
PEACH, JOSEPH F.	BAL	165	16TH WAR
PEACH, LOYD-BLACK	FRE	243	NEW MARK
PEACH, MARGARET	BAL	249	17TH WAR
PEACH, RICHARD	FRE	276	NEW MARK
PEACH, RICHARD	BAL	121	16TH WAR
PEACH, SUSAN-MULATTO	FRE	241	NEW MARK
PEACH, THOMAS	FRE	272	NEW MARK
PEACH, URIAS	BAL	122	16TH WAR
PEACH, WILLIAM	BAL	253	17TH WAR
PEACH, WILLIAM	BAL	296	17TH WAR
PEACH, WILLIAM E.	PRI	084	QUEEN AN
PEACHY, SUSAN	BAL	133	5TH WARD
PEACHY, THOMAS G.	BAL	024	9TH WARD
PEACKICK, HENREITTA	BAL	232	2ND WARD
PEACO, JIM-BLACK	QUE	183	3RD E DI
PEACOCK, CHARLES	BAL	252	1ST DIST
PEACOCK, E.	PRI	059	NOTTINGH
PEACOCK, ELISHA	SOM	412	DUBLIN D
PEACOCK, ELIZA	BAL	119	11TH WAR
PEACOCK, ELIZABETH	SOM	412	DUBLIN D
PEACOCK, ELIZABETH	PRI	060	NOTTINGH
PEACOCK, ELIZABETH	BAL	162	11TH WAR
PEACOCK, ELLEN	BAL	011	18TH WAR
PEACOCK, GEORGE	BAL	157	6TH WARD
PEACOCK, GEORGE	PRI	060	NOTTINGH
PEACOCK, HENRY	KEN	286	3RD DIST
PEACOCK, INGRAM E.	BAL	131	16TH WAR
PEACOCK, JAMES	BAL	047	9TH WARD
PEACOCK, JAMES	BAL	250	1ST DIST
PEACOCK, JAMES	BAL	276	2ND WARD
PEACOCK, JANE	PRI	059	NOTTINGH
PEACOCK, JOHN	BAL	251	1ST DIST
PEACOCK, JOHN	BAL	167	1ST WARD
PEACOCK, JOHN	BAL	405	1ST DIST
PEACOCK, JULIA	BAL	085	1ST WARD
PEACOCK, LUKE	BAL	386	1ST DIST
PEACOCK, MARY	BAL	373	1ST DIST
PEACOCK, MARY	BAL	330	1ST DIST
PEACOCK, MARY	BAL	024	9TH WARD
PEACOCK, MARY	KEN	286	3RD DIST
PEACOCK, MARY A.	BAL	413	1ST DIST
PEACOCK, NANCY	BAL	405	1ST DIST
PEACOCK, RACHEL	BAL	454	8TH WARD
PEACOCK, RICHARD	BAL	099	1ST WARD
PEACOCK, RICHARD	KEN	297	3RD DIST
PEACOCK, SAMUEL	KEN	309	3RD DIST
PEACOCK, SAMUEL	BAL	368	8TH WARD
PEACOCK, SARAH	BAL	162	11TH WAR
PEACOCK, SARAH	BAL	214	6TH WARD
PEACOCK, THOMAS	BAL	169	1ST WARD
PEACOCK, WILLIAM	BAL	265	2ND WARD
PEACOCK, WILLIAM	BAL	391	8TH WARD
PEACOCK, WILLIAM	BAL	050	1ST WARD
PEACOCK, WILLIAM	KEN	297	3RD DIST
PEACOCK, WILLIAM	BAL	055	18TH WAR
PEACOCK, WILLIAM H.	ST	284	2ND E DI
PEACOCK, WILLIAM H.	ST	283	3RD E DI
PEAD, MAHALA	BAL	177	6TH WARD
PEAK, ANN	BAL	098	5TH WARD
PEAK, BENNETT	WAS	134	HAGERSTO
PEAK, ELIZA	BAL	405	3RD WARD
PEAK, GRANDISON	ANN	311	1ST DIST
PEAK, JOHN	BAL	405	3RD WARD
PEAKE, ALLISIA	ST	268	3RD E DI
PEAKE, ANASTATIA	ST	279	3RD E DI
PEAKE, ANN	ST	258	3RD E DI
PEAKE, ELIZABETH	FRE	065	FREDERIC
PEAKE, JOSHUA	PRI	069	MARLBROU
PEAKE, JULIA A.	ST	256	3RD E DI
PEAKE, LOUIS B.	ST	299	2ND E DI
PEAKE, RICAHRD P.	ST	272	3RD E DI
PEAKE, RICHARD	ST	265	3RD E DI
PEAKE, ROBERT	ST	256	3RD E DI
PEAKE, WILLIAM H.	ANN	303	1ST DIST
PEAKER, CUPID	HAR	033	1ST DIST
PEAKER, FRANCIS	WAS	155	HAGERSTO
PEAKER, JOHN	HAR	034	1ST DIST
PEAKER, MATH N.	BAL	122	11TH WAR
PEAKER, STEPHEN	WAS	155	HAGERSTO
PEAKLE, HENRY	BAL	341	13TH WAR
PEAL, HERMAN	BAL	320	1ST DIST
PEAL, JOHN	BAL	383	1ST DIST
PEAL, MARTHA	BAL	413	3RD WARD
PEAL, MARY A.	BAL	070	18TH WAR
PEALE, JOHN W.	BAL	059	4TH WARD
PEALES, R.	BAL	172	1ST WARD
PEAN, MARGARET	BAL	288	3RD WARD
PEANT, MARY	CHA	294	BOJANTOW
PEAP, GEORGE	BAL	270	12TH WAR
PEARCE, ALEXANDER	BAL	111	10TH WAR
PEARCE, ALFRED	BAL	032	4TH WARD
PEARCE, ANDREW	CEC	050	1ST E DI
PEARCE, ANN	ANN	374	4TH DIST
PEARCE, ANN M.	HAR	078	2ND DIST
PEARCE, ARTHUR	BAL	050	2ND DIST
PEARCE, BENJAMIN	CEC	016	ELKTON 3
PEARCE, CALEB	BAL	185	5TH DIST
PEARCE, CHARLES	CEC	045	1ST E DI
PEARCE, CHARLES R.	BAL	103	10TH WAR
PEARCE, CHARLOTTE	BAL	038	2ND DIST
PEARCE, DANIEL	WAS	015	2ND SUBD
PEARCE, DANIEL L.	BAL	411	14TH WAR
PEARCE, DAVID	BAL	130	2ND DIST
PEARCE, DAVID	BAL	059	2ND DIST
PEARCE, DAVID	BAL	115	1ST WARD
PEARCE, EDWARD	BAL	084	2ND DIST
PEARCE, ELIZA	BAL	048	2ND DIST
PEARCE, ELIZABETH	BAL	215	6TH DIST
PEARCE, ELIZABETH	CAR	082	NO TWP L
PEARCE, ELLEN	BAL	059	2ND DIST
PEARCE, EMILY	BAL	039	9TH WARD
PEARCE, EMILY	PRI	037	VANSVILL
PEARCE, EMILY J.	BAL	342	3RD WARD
PEARCE, GEORGE	BAL	095	2ND DIST
PEARCE, GEORGE	BAL	185	5TH DIST
PEARCE, GEORGE	PRI	049	AQUASCO
PEARCE, GEORGE	BAL	400	14TH WAR
PEARCE, GEORGE R.	CEC	048	1ST E DI
PEARCE, HANSON	WAS	025	2ND SUBD
PEARCE, HENRY	CEC	053	1ST E DI
PEARCE, HENRY	BAL	070	2ND DIST
PEARCE, HETTY-BLACK	QUE	185	3RD E DI
PEARCE, ISAIAH	BAL	032	2ND DIST
PEARCE, J.	BAL	140	1ST WARD
PEARCE, JACOB M.	BAL	020	2ND DIST
PEARCE, JAMES	BAL	113	2ND DIST
PEARCE, JAMES	BAL	127	1ST WARD
PEARCE, JAMES	BAL	185	5TH DIST
PEARCE, JAMES	KEN	270	1ST DIST
PEARCE, JAMES	KEN	267	1ST DIST
PEARCE, JAMES	KEN	285	3RD DIST
PEARCE, JAMES	KEN	242	2ND DIST
PEARCE, JAMES	KEN	243	2ND DIST
PEARCE, JAMES	KEN	234	2ND DIST
PEARCE, JAMES	KEN	229	2ND DIST
PEARCE, JAMES A.	KEN	217	2ND DIST
PEARCE, JAMES-BLACK	CAR	168	NO TWP L
PEARCE, JAMES-BLACK	CAR	138	NO TWP L
PEARCE, JOHANNA	BAL	069	4TH WARD
PEARCE, JOHN	BAL	398	14TH WAR
PEARCE, JOHN	CEC	039	CHESAPEA
PEARCE, JOHN	FRE	241	NEW MARK
PEARCE, JOHN	KEN	242	2ND DIST
PEARCE, JOHN	KEN	231	2ND DIST
PEARCE, JOHN	CEC	055	1ST E DI
PEARCE, JOHN	HAR	058	1ST DIST
PEARCE, JOHN	BAL	252	20TH WAR
PEARCE, JOHN	FRE	390	PETERSVI
PEARCE, JOHN	KEN	263	1ST DIST
PEARCE, JOHN	BAL	050	2ND DIST
PEARCE, JOHN	BAL	050	2ND DIST
PEARCE, JOHN	BAL	045	2ND DIST
PEARCE, JOHN	ALL	105	5TH E.D.
PEARCE, JOHN B.	BAL	048	2ND DIST
PEARCE, JOHN J.	CEC	052	1ST E DI
PEARCE, JOSEPH	FRE	270	NEW MARK
PEARCE, JOSEPH	BAL	049	2ND DIST
PEARCE, JOSEPH	ANN	359	3RD DIST
PEARCE, JOSEPH	BAL	153	2ND DIST
PEARCE, JOSEPH	BAL	403	3RD WARD
PEARCE, JOSEPH	PRI	037	VANSVILL
PEARCE, JOSHUA	BAL	036	2ND DIST
PEARCE, JOSIAH	BAL	209	6TH DIST
PEARCE, JULIUS	BAL	190	6TH WARD
PEARCE, LOYD	WAS	024	2ND SUBD
PEARCE, LUKE	BAL	082	2ND DIST
PEARCE, MADALINE	ANN	381	4TH DIST
PEARCE, MARGARET	BAL	217	6TH DIST
PEARCE, MARGARET	CEC	052	1ST E DI
PEARCE, MARGARET	MGM	407	MEDLEY 3
PEARCE, MARGARET	KEN	242	2ND DIST
PEARCE, MARGARET	BAL	186	19TH WAR
PEARCE, MARTHA	BAL	266	17TH WAR
PEARCE, MARTHA	BAL	070	2ND DIST
PEARCE, MARY	KEN	226	2ND DIST
PEARCE, MARY	KEN	296	3RD DIST
PEARCE, MARY	KEN	298	3RD DIST
PEARCE, MARY A.	BAL	140	16TH WAR
PEARCE, MARY ANN	BAL	324	3RD WARD
PEARCE, MARY E.	CEC	164	6TH E DI
PEARCE, MARY J.	BAL	012	1ST WARD
PEARCE, MARY L.	BAL	045	2ND DIST
PEARCE, MICAJAH	BAL	053	2ND DIST
PEARCE, OBED	BAL	046	4TH WARD
PEARCE, PERRY	BAL	121	16TH WAR
PEARCE, PETER	QUE	219	3RD E DI
PEARCE, PHILIP	BAL	017	2ND DIST
PEARCE, REBECCA	BAL	185	5TH DIST
PEARCE, RICHARD	PRI	037	VANSVILL
PEARCE, RICHARD	KEN	236	2ND DIST
PEARCE, RICHARDSON	BAL	141	2ND DIST
PEARCE, ROSEANNA	CEC	041	CHESAPEA
PEARCE, RUTH	BAL	035	2ND DIST
PEARCE, RUTH	WAS	067	2ND SUBD
PEARCE, SAMUEL	KEN	273	1ST DIST
PEARCE, SAMUEL	MGM	424	MEDLEY 3
PEARCE, SARAH	KEN	228	2ND DIST
PEARCE, SARAH	BAL	036	2ND DIST
PEARCE, SARAH	BAL	209	6TH WARD
PEARCE, SARAH A.	BAL	033	2ND DIST
PEARCE, SIMON	KEN	236	2ND DIST
PEARCE, STEPHEN	TAL	014	EASTON D
PEARCE, STEPHEN A.	BAL	066	4TH WARD
PEARCE, SUSAN A.	KEN	263	1ST DIST
PEARCE, THOMAS	PRI	058	NOTTINGH
PEARCE, THOMAS	CEC	053	1ST E DI
PEARCE, THOMAS	BAL	048	2ND DIST
PEARCE, WILLEMINA	CEC	053	1ST E DI
PEARCE, WILLIAM	HAR	080	2ND DIST
PEARCE, WILLIAM	BAL	048	2ND DIST
PEARCE, WILLIAM	BAL	048	2ND DIST
PEARCE, WILLIAM	BAL	024	2ND DIST
PEARCE, WILLIAM	BAL	086	2ND DIST
PEARCE, WILLIAM	ALL	105	5TH E.D.
PEARCE, WILLIAM	KEN	273	1ST DIST
PEARCE, WILLIAM	QUE	206	3RD E DI
PEARCE, WILLIAM-BLACK	QUE	200	3RD E DI

PEARCY, CHARLES CEC 068 5TH E DI
PEARCY, EDWARD CEC 072 5TH E DI
PEARCY, HENRY CEC 068 5TH E DI
PEARL, WILLIAM FRE 069 FREDERIC
PEARLE, GEORGE JAMES FRE 187 5TH E DI
PEARLE, PETER BAL 143 1ST WARD
PEARLE, THOMAS FRE 119 CREAGERS
PEARMAN, JOHN T. ALL 135 4TH E.D.
PEARN, GEORGE BAL 287 3RD WARD
PEARRE, JAMES MGM 420 MEDLEY 3
PEARRE, WILLIAM MGM 420 MEDLEY 3
PEARSAW, BARTHOLOMEW* HAR 177 3RD DIST
PEARSE, DEBORAH FRE 442 8TH E DI
PEARSE, JAMES FRE 431 8TH E DI
PEARSE, JAMES CEC 041 CHESAPEA
PEARSE, JAMES W. FRE 410 8TH E DI
PEARSE, JOHN BAL 024 2ND DIST
PEARSE, MARGARETT A. FRE 431 8TH E DI
PEARSE, RICHARD FRE 406 JEFFERSO
PEARSE, RICHARD BAL 024 2ND DIST
PEARSE, WALTER BAL 114 2ND DIST
PEARSER, GEORGE A. ALL 254 CUMBERLA
PEARSON, ANDREW BAL 379 13TH WAR
PEARSON, ANN N. BAL 048 1ST WARD
PEARSON, ANN* DOR 361 3RD DIVI
PEARSON, CAROLINE CEC 020 ELKTON 3
PEARSON, CATHARINE BAL 235 17TH WAR
PEARSON, CATHERINE BAL 093 1ST WARD
PEARSON, DAVID BAL 139 1ST WARD
PEARSON, EDWARD DOR 337 3RD DIVI
PEARSON, ELI CEC 020 ELKTON 3
PEARSON, ELIZA HAR 030 1ST DIST
PEARSON, ELIZA ANN 337 3RD DIST
PEARSON, ELIZA QUE 250 5TH E DI
PEARSON, ELIZABETH BAL 048 1ST WARD
PEARSON, ELIZABETH BAL 211 6TH WARD
PEARSON, ELIZABETH BAL 214 11TH WAR
PEARSON, EMELINE BAL 342 3RD WARD
PEARSON, G. BAL 138 1ST WARD
PEARSON, G. BAL 101 10TH WAR
PEARSON, GEORGE BAL 139 1ST WARD
PEARSON, GEORGE BAL 117 1ST WARD
PEARSON, GEORGE DOR 334 3RD DIVI
PEARSON, ISAAC E. FRE 167 EMMITTSB
PEARSON, ISEBELLA CEC 097 4TH E DI
PEARSON, JACOB CEC 020 ELKTON 3.
PEARSON, JOHN CAR 150 NO TWP L
PEARSON, JOHN W. KEN 292 3RD DIST
PEARSON, JOSEPH CAR 169 NO TWP L
PEARSON, JOSEPH BAL 380 13TH WAR
PEARSON, JOSEPH BAL 213 6TH WARD
PEARSON, JULIA BAL 179 6TH WARD
PEARSON, LEVI BAL 286 17TH WAR
PEARSON, MARY DOR 370 3RD DIVI
PEARSON, MARY BAL 176 6TH WARD
PEARSON, MARY A. FRE 065 FREDERIC
PEARSON, MARY C. BAL 380 13TH WAR
PEARSON, MARYANN BAL 339 3RD WARD
PEARSON, MERIAM ANN 521 HOWARD D
PEARSON, NANCY J. BAL 125 16TH WAR
PEARSON, NOAH BAL 021 1ST WARD
PEARSON, PETER CEC 120 3RD E DI
PEARSON, SAMUEL F. KEN 309 3RD DIST
PEARSON, SARAH CAR 134 NO TWP L
PEARSON, SOLOMON BAL 288 17TH WAR
PEARSON, THOMAS BAL 123 1ST WARD
PEARSON, THOMAS BAL 172 1ST WARD
PEARSON, W.G. WAS 021 2ND SUBD
PEARSON, WILLIAM CAR 149 NO TWP L
PEARSON, WILSON CEC 120 3RD E DI
PEARY, ELLEN CEC 090 4TH E DI
PEARY, JOHN CEC 112 4TH E DI
PEARY, MARGARET CEC 182 7TH E DI
PEARY, SARAH J. CEC 090 4TH E DI
PEASA, CATHARINE HAR 157 3RD DIST
PEASE, CHARELS BAL 316 12TH WAR
PEASE, CHARLOTTE BAL 384 13TH WAR
PEASE, FRANCIS BAL 450 14TH WAR
PEASE, LOUIS BAL 182 19TH WAR
PEASE, WILLIAM H. BAL 409 1ST DIST
PEASELY, REBECCA FRE 263 NEW MARK
PEASSER, THOMAS HAR 187 3RD DIST
PEATERS, MARY HAR 034 1ST DIST
PEATZ, WILLIAM BAL 230 2ND WARD
PEAVY, FRANKLIN MGM 394 ROCKERLE
PEBBLE, DANIEL ALL 219 CUMBERLA
PECART, CHARLOTTE H. BAL 051 1ST WARD
PECK, ANN BAL 320 7TH WARD
PECK, ANN M. BAL 135 18TH WAR
PECK, ANN* TAL 009 EASTON D
PECK, BIDDY-BLACK BAL 216 2ND WARD
PECK, BURR BAL 006 4TH WARD
PECK, CATHARINE BAL 431 14TH WAR
PECK, CATHERINE BAL 431 8TH WARD
PECK, DAVIC BAL 430 8TH WARD
PECK, CAVID PRI 063 NOTTINGH
PECK, ELLEN S. FRE 410 8TH E DI
PECK, EMMA BAL 305 7TH WARD
PECK, FREDERIC BAL 055 9TH WARD
PECK, FREDERICK BAL 291 17TH WAR
PECK, GEORGE BAL 157 2ND DIST
PECK, GEORGE QUE 252 5TH E DI
PECK, HENRY WAS 157 2ND DIST
PECK, HENRY BAL 192 17TH WAR
PECK, HENRY BAL 001 15TH WAR
PECK, HENRY ALL 037 2ND E.D.
PECK, JACOB ALL 037 2ND E.D.
PECK, JOHN CAR 296 7TH DIST
PECK, JOHN E. BAL 290 12TH WAR
PECK, LEVI HAR 079 2ND DIST
PECK, LEVIN BAL 216 17TH WAR
PECK, LEWIS BAL 458 8TH WARD
PECK, LEWIS BAL 386 8TH WARD
PECK, MARY HAR 130 2ND DIST
PECK, NATHANIEL BAL 168 11TH WAR
PECK, NELSON BAL 457 8TH WARD
PECK, PAULINE BAL 297 12TH WAR
PECK, ROBERT-MULATTO FRE 010 FREDERIC
PECK, SAMUEL TAL 028 EASTON D
PECK, STEPHEN BAL 065 18TH WAR
PECK, STEPHEN BAL 264 1ST DIST
PECK, THOMAS E. BAL 447 14TH WAR
PECK, WILLAIM ANN 471 HOWARD D
PECKAEREL, MARY CHA 229 MIDDLETO
PECKAEREL, SARA A. CHA 287 BOJANTOW
PECKAERERL, JOHN N. CHA 284 BOJANTOW
PECKAERL, ALFRED CHA 291 MIDDLETO
PECKAREL, CALEB CHA 253 MIDDLETO
PECKAREL, THOMAS H. CHA 253 MIDDLETO
PECKER, EDWARD BAL 349 7TH WARD
PECKER, JOHN BAL 200 19TH WAR
PECKETT, JEROME* BAL 373 3RD WARD
PECKHAM, MARY E. QUE 171 2ND E DI
PECKHAM, WILLIAM O. QUE 170 2ND E DI
PECKOCHECK, MAGDALEN BAL 250 6TH WARD
PECKSCHECK, ANDREW BAL 102 5TH WARD
PECKURN, MARY BAL 246 2ND WARD
PECOCK, JOHN BAL 034 18TH WAR
PECORE, CHARLOTTE BAL 003 EASTERN
PEDDERICK, EMMET BAL 246 17TH WAR
PEDDICORD, ALTHA FRE 194 5TH E DI
PEDDICORD, CALEB ANN 505 HOWARD D
PEDDICORD, J. THEODORE FRE 190 5TH E DI
PEDDICORD, JASPER FRE 191 5TH E DI
PEDDICORD, PERRY FRE 194 5TH E DI
PEDDICORD, WASHINGTON A. ANN 512 HOWARD D
PEDDRICK, JOHN BAL 400 14TH WAR
PEDGEON, JOHN BAL 257 2ND WARD
PEDICARD, JOHN BAL 290 1ST DIST
PEDICORD, ADAM BAL 305 1ST DIST
PEDICORD, ANN BAL 426 1ST DIST
PEDICORD, CALIB BAL 386 1ST DIST
PEDICORD, JANE FRE 191 5TH E DI
PEDICORD, JOHN BAL 377 1ST DIST
PEDICORD, LAYFAYETTE BAL 377 1ST DIST
PEDICORD, NATHAN FRE 191 5TH E DI
PEDICORD, SUSAN BAL 298 1ST DIST
PEDICORD, WILLIAM FRE 191 5TH E DI
PEDRICK, ELIZA BAL 093 10TH WAR
PEDRICK, THOMAS BAL 013 15TH WAR
PEDUCY, CATHERINE BAL 378 3RD WARD
PEDUSIE, FRANCIS BAL 438 8TH WARD
PEDUZZO, WILLIAM BAL 249 2ND WARD
PEE, LILLEY DOR 360 3RD DIVI
PEEDE, ROBERT BAL 292 7TH WARD
PEEL, ELIZABETH BAL 320 3RD WARD
PEEPE, CONRAD PRI 039 VANSVILL
PEERCE, ELEANOR MGM 357 BERRYS D
PEERCE, WILLIAM C. MGM 364 BERRYS D
PEESE, MARY M. * TAL 073 EASTON T
PEFER, CONROD FRE 119 CREAGERS
PEFER, LAURENCE FRE 119 CREAGERS
PEFFER, JOHN A. BAL 178 16TH WAR
PEFLE, MARY A. FRE 044 FREDERIC
PEGANO, JOSE A. BAL 357 13TH WAR
PEGG, JAMES ST 290 2ND E DI
PEGLER, RICHARD BAL 327 13TH WAR
PEICE, ELIZABETH-BLACK CAR 134 NO TWP L
PEIDT, MARY E. BAL 195 2ND WARD
PEIGHTER, CHRISTIAN ALL 056 10TH E.D
PEIGNER, GEORGE BAL 381 8TH WARD
PEINE, ELIZABETH BAL 262 12TH WAR
PEININGTON, HENRY O.H. HAR 179 3RD DIST
PEIRCE, AMELIA BAL 215 11TH WAR
PEIRCE, EPHRIAM BAL 054 18TH WAR
PEIRCE, JOHN BAL 213 11TH WAR
PEIRCE, JOHN WAS 149 2ND DIST
PEIRMAN, RICHARD ANN 378 4TH DIST
PEIRPOINT, GEORGE BAL 297 1ST DIST
PEISLUKE, JOHN CEC 058 1ST E DI
PEITGER, CATHARINE BAL 262 2ND WARD
PEKEN, JAMES CEC 158 PORT DUP
PEKER, CAROLINE CEC 194 7TH E DI
PELCHER, RIXHAM WOR 344 1ST E DI
PELCHER, STEPHEN WOR 330 1ST E DI
PELCHER, WARNER WOR 349 1ST E DI
PELCKER, LEMUEL WOR 348 1ST E DI
PELCKER, MARTIN BAL 215 2ND WARD
PELDER, J. W. BAL 282 2ND WARD
PELET, WILLIAM WAS 066 2ND SUBD
PELFAST, JOHN CEC 196 6TH E DI
PELGRIM,R.C. BAL 164 1ST WARD
PELIGAN, RICHRD CEC 026 ELKTON 3
PELIT, CAROLINE BAL 409 8TH WARD
PELIT, PETER BAL 409 8TH WARD
PELKELTON,MARY ST 324 4TH E DI
PELKER, WILLIAM BAL 401 1ST DIST
PELKILTON, SYLVESTER ST 341 5TH E DI
PELKINGTON, WILLIAM* BAL 375 3RD WARD
PELKINTON, HENRY ST 255 3RD E DI
PELKINTON, JOHN L. ST 286 2ND E DI
PELKINTON, JOSEPH ST 265 3RD E DI
PELKITTEN, JOHN ST 331 4TH E DI
PELL, RACHEL G. CEC 203 6TH E DI
PELL, SARAH CEC 002 ELKTON 3
PELLAR, BRIDGET BAL 371 13TH WAR
PELLERS, SMAUEL BAL 272 12TH WAR
PELPES, JOSEPH CEC 069 5TH E DI
PELTHWOOD, ANN BAL 263 20TH WAR
PELTIT, ISAAC BAL 304 12TH WAR
PELTON, CATHARINE ANN 519 HOWARD D
PELTON, EMORY ALL 237 CUMBERLA
PELTON, JULIA BAL 225 12TH WAR
PELTON, REZIN BAL 092 15TH WAR
PELTON, SARAH BAL 056 10TH WAR
PELTON, SUSAN ALL 226 CUMBERLA
PELTON, THOMAS ALL 112 5TH E.D.
PELTON, WILLIAM ANN 519 HOWARD D
PELTS, HENRY BAL 024 4TH WARD
PELTZ, JOHN WAS 143 HAGERSTO
PELZER, HERNY CAR 180 8TH DIST
PEMBLETON, HARWOOD-BLACK CAR 167 NO TWP L
PEMBLETON, HENRIETTA* TAL 043 EASTON D
PEMBLETON, JOHN BAL 468 14TH WAR
PEMBLETON, JOHN-BLACK CAR 093 NO TWP L
PEMBLETON, PERE QUE 213 3RD E DI
PEMBLETON, RACHEL TAL 029 EASTON D
PEMBROKE, ANNA M. BAL 056 10TH WAR
PEMBROKE, BETSY WAS 042 2ND SUBD
PEMBROKE, GEORGE W. ST 288 2ND E DI
PEMBROKE, JANE-BLACK QUE 195 3RD E DI
PEMBROKE, JOHN-BLACK QUE 199 3RD E DI
PEMBROKE, MARY BAL 292 12TH WAR
PEMBROOK, BAZIL QUE 207 3RD E DI
PEMBROOK, PIPHARY QUE 206 3RD E DI
PEMGA, JAMES L. BAL 023 1ST WARD
PEMGOY, JOHN W. * BAL 272 7TH WARD
PEMJOY, JOSEPH* BAL 305 7TH WARD
PEMJOY, NELSON BAL 294 7TH WARD
PEMM, NANCY FRE 027 FREDERIC
PEMMER, CAROLINE BAL 242 12TH WAR
PEN, SARAH BAL 356 1ST DIST
PENBLETON, THEADORE TAL 006 EASTON D
PENCE, LETITIN BAL 233 12TH WAR
PENDALE, LORINTZ BAL 027 9TH WARD
PENDALL, CELIA BAL 034 18TH WAR
PENDEGRASS, WILLIAM BAL 356 8TH WARD
PENDEL, ELIZABETH BAL 356 13TH WAR
PENDELL, AUGUSTUS CAL 059 3RD DIST
PENDELL, B. T. BAL 140 19TH WAR
PENDELL, EDWARD BAL 341 13TH WAR
PENDELL, MRS. E. L. BAL 125 11TH WAR
PENDER, JOHN W. CAR 074 NO TWP L
PENDER, MARY * KEN 258 1ST DIST
PENDER, WASHINGTON CAR 125 NO TWP L
PENDERGAST, CATHARINE BAL 250 6TH WARD
PENDERGAST, CHARLES BAL 044 4TH WARD
PENDERGAST, MARGARET BAL 101 1ST WARD
PENDEXTER, HENRY BAL 014 4TH WARD
PENDLETON, BENJAMIN WAS 162 2ND DIST
PENDLETON, ELIZABETH TAL 021 EASTON D
PENDLETON, ELIZABETH BAL 465 14TH WAR
PENDLETON, HENRY SOM 420 PRINCESS
PENDLETON, JOE TAL 011 EASTON D
PENDLETON, JOSEPH TAL 016 EASTON D
PENDLETON, KATE BAL 251 12TH WAR
PENDLETON, L. W. BAL 465 14TH WAR
PENDLETON, PHILIP BAL 150 11TH WAR
PENDLETON, ROBERT W. BAL 388 13TH WAR
PENDLETON, TIMOTHY H. BAL 123 18TH WAR
PENDLETON, WILLIAM N. FRE 031 FREDERIC
PENDUM, RUFUS R. FRE 270 NEW MARK
PENEGOY, JAMES BAL 191 5TH DIST
PENEGROY, HENRY BAL 189 5TH DIST
PENER, MICHAEL BAL 064 1ST WARD
PENETT, WILLIAM BAL 031 2ND DIST
PENEWELL, LEAH SOM 498 SALISBUR
PENGH, ELIZABETH ALL 177 7TH E.D.
PENHIND, JAMES R.* TAL 018 EASTON D
PENICK, ANN CEC 070 5TH E DI
PENIJOY, JOSEPH* BAL 305 7TH WARD
PENIMAN, AUGUST BAL 278 1ST DIST
PENINGTON, CHARLES BAL 211 11TH WAR
PENINGTON, ELISHA N. * KEN 222 2ND DIST
PENINGTON, ELIZA CAR 196 4TH DIST
PENINGTON, HENRIETTA BAL 459 1ST DIST
PENINGTON, JAMES W. BAL 284 7TH WARD
PENINGTON, JOHN H. BAL 267 7TH WARD
PENINGTON, JOSHUA BAL 211 11TH WAR
PENINGTON, NOAH FRE 287 WOODSBOR
PENINGTON, OBID CAR 208 5TH DIST
[illegible]NINGTON, ROBERT BAL 458 1ST DIST
P[illegible]NION, WILLIAM BAL 257 20TH WAR
P[illegible]NISON, AGNES BAL 248 20TH WAR
P[illegible]NK, JOSEPH BAL 046 1ST WARD
PE[illegible]KET, ELLEN BAL 260 12TH WAR
PE[illegible]KNAUR, ROSURA BAL 268 12TH WAR
PEN[illegible]TON, WILLIAM BAL 315 20TH WAR
PENA[illegible]N, SAMUEL L. HAR 146 3RD DIST
PENN, ALEXANDER BAL 155 11TH WAR
PENN, ANN FRE 261 NEW MARK
PENN, ANN BAL 002 1ST WARD
PENN, BENJAMIN J. CHA 269 ALLENS F
PENN, BENJAMIN-MULATTO FRE 451 8TH E DI
PENN, CHARLES P. ST 336 4TH E DI
PENN, EDWARD FRE 300 WOODSBOR
PENN, ELIZABETH MGM 333 CRACKLIN
PENN, ELIZABETH D. MGM 333 CRACKLIN
PENN, EMANUEL ST 347 5TH E DI
PENN, ERASTES MGM 323 CRACKLIN
PENN, FRANCIS-MULATTO FRE 438 8TH E DI
PENN, GEORGE W. ANN 497 HOWARD D
PENN, HANSON PRI 005 BLADENSB
PENN, JACOB BAL 351 1ST DIST
PENN, JACOB ANN 416 HOWARD D
PENN, JACOB BAL 283 17TH WAR
PENN, JAMES MGM 445 CLARKSTR
PENN, JAMES D. ST 338 4TH E DI
PENN, JESSE FRE 247 NEW MARK
PENN, JOHN CAR 362 9TH DIST
PENN, JOHN ANN 388 4TH DIST
PENN, LEVI ANN 496 HOWARD D
PENN, MARIA FRE 247 NEW MARK
PENN, MILTON C. ANN 388 4TH DIST
PENN, NANCY BAL 284 17TH WAR
PENN, NICHOLAS-MULATTO FRE 451 8TH E DI
PENN, REUBEN MGM 334 CRACKLIN
PENN, RUTH BAL 361 1ST DIST
PENN, SARAH BAL 016 18TH WAR
PENN, SHARLOTT FRE 289 WOODSBOR
PENN, STEPHEN CAR 362 9TH DIST
PENN, THOMAS CHA 222 ALLENS F
PENN, THOMAS PRI 040 VANSVILL
PENN, WILLIAM CHA 223 ALLENS F
PENN, WILLIAM G. MGM 333 CRACKLIN
PENN, WILLIAM H. CAR 224 5TH DIST
PENN, WILLIAM P. BAL 255 20TH WAR
PENN, WILLIAM S. ALL 205 CUMBERLA
PENNAMAN, SARAH BAL 267 12TH WAR
PENNE, ANN BAL 254 12TH WAR
PENNEL, DAVID WAS 038 2ND SUBD
PENNEL, MARY WAS 037 2ND SUBD
PENNEL, MARY WAS 188 1ST DIST
PENNEL, SARAH CEC 081 CHARLEST
PENNELL, GREENBURY CEC 013 ELKTON 3
PENNELL, JOHN WOR 165 6TH E DI
PENNELL, JOHN-BLACK WOR 172 6TH E DI
PENNELL, MILBY WOR 166 6TH E DI
PENNELL, R.E. BAL 160 1ST WARD
PENNELL, REBECCA CEC 137 6TH E DI
PENNELL, WILLIAM CEC 216 7TH E DI
PENNELLY, JAMES CEC 181 7TH E DI
PENNELTON, SAMUEL C. BAL 113 18TH WAR
PENNEMAN, HENRIETTA BAL 467 14TH WAR
PENNEMAN, WILLIAM BAL 463 14TH WAR
PENNER, ELIZABETH WAS 249 1ST DIST
PENNER, GRAFTON FRE 151 10TH E D
PENNER, JACOB WAS 249 1ST DIST
PENNER, PETER WAS 255 1ST DIST
PENNER, PETER WAS 256 1ST DIST
PENNER, WILLIAM WAS 248 1ST DIST
PENNERWELL, SUSAN WOR 291 9TH E DI
PENNEWELL, WILLIAM H. WOR 255 BERLIN 1
PENNEWILL, JANE WOR 283 BERLIN 1
PENNEWILL, JOHN WOR 273 BERLIN 1
PENNEWILL, LUKE WOR 277 BERLIN 1
PENNEWILL, WESTLY WOR 296 9TH E DI
PENNEWILL, WILLIAM T. WOR 296 9TH E DI
PENNFIELD, THEODOSIA E. MGM 415 MEDLEY 3
PENNICK, JOHN CEC 071 5TH E DI
PENNICK, ROBERT CEC 069 5TH E DI
PENNICK, WILLIAM CEC 071 5TH E DI
PENNICK, WILLIAM* BAL 391 3RD WARD
PENNICKS, CATHARINE BAL 233 20TH WAR
PENNIGTON, JOHN W. BAL 124 1ST WARD
PENNILL, AQUILLA CEC 202 6TH E DI
PENNILL, HENRY B. WOR 166 6TH E DI
PENNIMAN, ABBOT L. BAL 079 4TH WARD
PENNIMAN, AUGUSTUA BAL 205 11TH WAR
PENNIMAN, CHARLES H. BAL 353 7TH WARD

Name	County	Page	District
PENNIMAN, JOHN	BAL	095	5TH WARD
PENNING, CHARLES	BAL	142	16TH WAR
PENNINGTON, A. J.	BAL	333	1ST DIST
PENNINGTON, ARMANIA	CEC	062	1ST E DI
PENNINGTON, AUGUSTINE H.	BAL	069	15TH WAR
PENNINGTON, AZARIAS	CEC	071	5TH E DI
PENNINGTON, DANIEL	CEC	050	1ST E DI
PENNINGTON, DEBORA A.*	BAL	307	3RD WARD
PENNINGTON, EDWARD	CEC	045	1ST E DI
PENNINGTON, EDWARD H.	BAL	058	15TH WAR
PENNINGTON, ELEY	BAL	304	12TH WAR
PENNINGTON, ELIZABETH	CEC	050	1ST E DI
PENNINGTON, ELIZABETH A.	CEC	137	6TH E DI
PENNINGTON, GEORGE B.	CEC	053	1ST E DI
PENNINGTON, GEORGE P.	CEC	052	1ST E DI
PENNINGTON, GOVER	BAL	148	2ND DIST
PENNINGTON, JAMES	BAL	220	6TH WARD
PENNINGTON, JAMES	BAL	234	6TH WARD
PENNINGTON, JAMES H.	KEN	309	3RD DIST
PENNINGTON, JOHN	KEN	286	3RD DIST
PENNINGTON, JOHN	BAL	031	9TH WARD
PENNINGTON, JOHN	BAL	148	2ND DIST
PENNINGTON, JOHN	BAL	116	2ND DIST
PENNINGTON, JOHN	CEC	049	1ST E DI
PENNINGTON, JOHN H.	ANN	413	HOWARD D
PENNINGTON, JOSEPH	QUE	239	5TH E DI
PENNINGTON, JOSEPH L.	ALL	126	4TH E.D.
PENNINGTON, JOSHUA	CEC	063	1ST E DI
PENNINGTON, LEVI	BAL	082	2ND DIST
PENNINGTON, LEWIS	HAR	123	2ND DIST
PENNINGTON, MARTHA E.	BAL	131	16TH WAR
PENNINGTON, MARY C.	BAL	398	14TH WAR
PENNINGTON, NOBLE	CEC	048	1ST E DI
PENNINGTON, PERAGIN	CEC	053	1ST E DI
PENNINGTON, PEREGRIN	TAL	025	EASTON D
PENNINGTON, PERRY	TAL	011	EASTON D
PENNINGTON, RICHARD	BAL	112	10TH WAR
PENNINGTON, ROBERT	CEC	009	ELKTON 3
PENNINGTON, ROBERT	BAL	073	10TH WAR
PENNINGTON, ROBERT	BAL	029	9TH WARD
PENNINGTON, ROBERT	BAL	032	9TH WARD
PENNINGTON, ROSS T.	BAL	043	15TH WAR
PENNINGTON, RUGH	BAL	380	1ST DIST
PENNINGTON, SARAH	KEN	301	3RD DIST
PENNINGTON, SUSAN	BAL	001	1ST WARD
PENNINGTON, WILLIAM	KEN	306	3RD DIST
PENNINGTON, WILLIAM	QUE	180	2ND E DI
PENNINGTON, WILLIAM	CEC	062	1ST E DI
PENNINGTON, WILLIAM C.	HAR	077	BEL AIR
PENNINGTON, WILLIAM H.	ANN	413	HOWARD D
PENNINGTON, WILLIAM P.	DOR	378	1ST DIST
PENNINGTONE, DEBORA A.*	BAL	307	3RD WARD
PENNIWELL, ELIAS	WOR	296	9TH E DI
PENNIWELL, RHODA	WOR	278	BERLIN 1
PENNMAN, SARAH F.	BAL	181	19TH WAR
PENNOCK, DANIEL	CEC	067	5TH E DI
PENNOCK, DANIEL	CEC	068	5TH E DI
PENNOCK, EBER	CEC	210	7TH E DI
PENNOCK, ELIZA	CEC	149	PORT DUP
PENNOCK, ISAAC	CEC	069	5TH E DI
PENNOCK, JOSEPH	CEC	106	3RD E DI
PENNOCK, SOLOMON	CEC	106	3RD E DI
PENNOE, WILLIAM F.	CHA	239	HILLTOP
PENNOE, WILLIAM W.	CHA	238	HILLTOP
PENNWILL, WILLIAM	WOR	265	BERLIN 1
PENNY, HENRY A.	ANN	444	HOWARD D
PENNY, JAMES	CHA	237	HILLTOP
PENNY, LEVI	CHA	257	MIDDLETO
PENNY, SARAH	CEC	068	5TH E DI
PENNY, SARAH	BAL	229	1ST DIST
PENNY, SUSANAH	BAL	265	1ST DIST
PENNYFIELD, GEORGE	MGM	381	ROCKERLE
PENNYFIELD, LEAR	MGM	389	ROCKERLE
PENNYFIELD, THOMAS	MGM	414	MEDLEY 3
PENNYFIELD, ESTHER	MGM	401	ROCKERLE
PENNYWELL, MARGARETT A.	DOR	316	1ST DIST
PENPOLD, CHARLES	BAL	474	14TH WAR
PENRE, JOHN	CAR	362	9TH DIST
PENROSE, ELIAKIN G.	BAL	035	9TH WARD
PENROSE, HENRY	BAL	123	1ST WARD
PENRY, WILLIAM	ALL	254	CUMBERLA
PENSAS, BALY	BAL	396	14TH WAR
PENSIL, ANN M.	CAR	260	3RD DIST
PENSONS, ANN	BAL	322	12TH WAR
PENSONS, J.C.	BAL	224	19TH WAR
PENTER, P.J.	BAL	139	1ST WARD
PENTISS, SAMUEL F. G.	BAL	072	4TH WARD
PENTLAND, JAME	BAL	416	8TH WARD
PENTNEY, JOHN	WAS	113	2ND DIST
PENTY, HENRY L.	BAL	453	8TH WARD
PENTY, JOHN W.	BAL	309	20TH WAR
PENTZ, CHARLES	BAL	305	7TH WARD
PENTZ, CHRISTIAN	WAS	027	2ND SUBD
PENTZ, DANIEL*	BAL	303	3RD WARD
PENTZ, HENRY B.	BAL	341	7TH WARD
PENTZ, JOHN J.	BAL	303	3RD WARD
PENTZ, JOHN W.	BAL	443	8TH WARD
PENTZ, MARGARET E.	BAL	341	7TH WARD
PENTZ, MARION	BAL	341	7TH WARD
PENTZ, MARY	WAS	027	2ND SUBD
PENTZ, P. HENRY	BAL	305	7TH WARD
PENTZ, SAMUEL J.	BAL	416	8TH WARD
PENVIMAN, GEORGE W.	BAL	187	11TH WAR
PENWELL, MATTHIAS	WOR	224	4TH E DI
PENWELL, THOMAS	WOR	224	4TH E DI
PENWELL, WILLIAM H.	WOR	174	6TH E DI
PENWICK, JOHN L.	ST	258	3RD E DI
PENZEL, LOUISE	BAL	371	13TH WAR
PEOAN, ANN	ALL	097	5TH E.D.
PEOCKUM, HENRY *	SOM	436	PRINCESS
PEOCOCK, JOHN L.	ST	257	3RD E DI
PEOCOCK, MARY J.	ST	254	3RD E DI
PEOPLES, JAMES	FRE	171	5TH E DI
PEOPLES, JOHN	FRE	169	5TH E DI
PEOPLES, JOHN	FRE	169	5TH E DI
PEOPLES, REBECCA	FRE	167	EMMITTSB
PEPAR, CHARLES H.	BAL	113	15TH WAR
PEPENO, LOUIS*	BAL	080	10TH WAR
PEPERMINT, RANTINE	ANN	386	4TH DIST
PEPERRINK, CONRAD	ALL	227	CUMBERLA
PEPERS, H.P.	BAL	166	1ST WARD
PEPLE, DAVID	FRE	095	FREDERIC
PEPLER, ALEXANDER	BAL	454	8TH WARD
PEPPELL, DANIEL	ALL	092	5TH E.D.
PEPPER, JOHN H.	BAL	286	20TH WAR
PEPPER, KITTY	BAL	083	4TH WARD
PEPPER, LEVI	SOM	423	PRINCESS
PEPPER, NANCY	SOM	416	DUBLIN D
PEPPER, WILLIAM H.	SOM	484	TRAPP DI
PEPPERSOCH, JOSEPH	BAL	186	6TH WARD
PEPPIE, MARY	BAL	234	12TH WAR
PEPPIN, SOLOMON	CAR	078	NO TWP L
PEPPIN, MARGRETT	CAR	074	NO TWP L
PEPPIN, WILLIAM	CAR	081	NO TWP L
PEPPLE, ABRAHAM	FRE	192	5TH E DI
PEPPLE, JOHN	FRE	193	5TH E DI
PEPPLE, WILLIAM	FRE	160	EMMITTSB
PEPPLER, PHILIP	BAL	062	15TH WAR
PERACE, RACHEL	BAL	178	2ND DIST
PERACE, RALPH	BAL	172	2ND DIST
PERAIL, CHARLES	ALL	240	CUMBERLA
PERCE, CAROLINE	BAL	253	12TH WAR
PERCE, JOHN	BAL	273	12TH WAR
PERCEIL, JAMES	BAL	311	1ST DIST
PERCELT, BARBARY	WAS	125	2ND DIST
PERCELT, JOHN	WAS	131	2ND DIST
PERCELT, MICHAEL	WAS	125	2ND DIST
PERCIVAL, JOSEPH	BAL	120	1ST WARD
PERCIVEL, WILLIAM	PRI	080	QUEEN AN
PERCUSON, THOAMS	HAR	001	1ST DIST
PERCY, CAVID	ALL	086	5TH E.D.
PERCY, DOUGLAS	ALL	099	5TH E.D.
PERCY, JAMES	ALL	150	6TH E.D.
PERCY, MISS J.	FRE	199	5TH E DI
PERDA, MARY T.	CHA	237	HILLTOP
PERDA, WILLIAM	CHA	236	HILLTOP
PERDEER, SANDRA *	ALL	108	5TH E.D.
PERDIN, F.	BAL	233	20TH WAR
PERDT, VALENTINE	BAL	086	10TH WAR
PERDUE, ANN	BAL	033	2ND DIST
PERDUE, JOHN	BAL	048	2ND DIST
PERDUE, RACHELL	BAL	108	5TH WARD
PERDY, SUSAN	ALL	229	CUMBERLA
PEREGAY, J.	BAL	169	19TH WAR
PEREGAY, JAMES C.*	BAL	405	3RD WARD
PEREGORY, SAMUEL H.	BAL	161	1ST WARD
PEREGOY, BENJAMIN	BAL	288	20TH WAR
PEREGOY, CHARLES	BAL	238	12TH WAR
PEREGOY, DANIEL A.	BAL	305	20TH WAR
PEREGOY, ELIZABETH	BAL	186	5TH DIST
PEREGOY, EMILY	BAL	387	8TH WARD
PEREGOY, J. W.	BAL	148	1ST WARD
PEREGOY, JEHU	BAL	382	1ST DIST
PEREGOY, JOHN W.	BAL	383	1ST DIST
PEREGOY, MICHAEL	BAL	200	5TH DIST
PEREGOY, MOSES J.	HAR	138	2ND DIST
PEREGOY, R. H.	BAL	073	10TH WAR
PEREGOY, RUTH	BAL	033	18TH WAR
PEREGOY, S. H.	BAL	148	1ST WARD
PEREGOY, SARAH	BAL	397	1ST DIST
PEREJOY, CHARLES E.	BAL	169	19TH WAR
PEREJOY, JOSEPH	BAL	207	19TH WAR
PERELL, JOHN F.	CEC	060	1ST E DI
PERES, ESTEAM	BAL	330	13TH WAR
PEREZ, FRANCIS	FRE	20	5TH E DI
PERGENTER, HENRY	ANN	418	HOWARD D
PERIGAN, SARAH-BLACK	WOR	345	1ST E DI
PERIGO, BENJAMIN	BAL	042	15TH WAR
PERIGO, NATHAN W.	BAL	315	1ST DIST
PERIMAN, SHARLOTT W.	HAR	186	3RD DIST
PERINE, EDWARD J.	BAL	404	8TH WARD
PERINE, HENRY	BAL	076	2ND DIST
PERINE, JOHN	BAL	440	1ST DIST
PERINE, JOHN T.	BAL	009	18TH WAR
PERINE, LOM	BAL	180	2ND DIST
PERINE, MAULDEN	BAL	049	18TH WAR
PERINE, RICHARD	BAL	011	2ND DIST
PERINE, THOMAS J.	BAL	185	16TH WAR
PERINE, WESLY	BAL	030	2ND DIST
PERINGTCN, ELISHA N. *	KEN	222	2ND DIST
PERISMIDT, HENRY	BAL	233	17TH WAR
PERKEY, IRENA	CAR	182	8TH DIST
PERKG, JAMES	BAL	103	5TH WARD
PERKHAM, MARY	TAL	017	EASTON D
PERKIN, EMILY J.	HAR	056	1ST DIST
PERKINS, BENJAMIN B.	KEN	214	2ND DIST
PERKINS, BETSEY	WOR	278	BERLIN 1
PERKINS, DAVID	BAL	286	2ND WARD
PERKINS, DLLAS. B.	BAL	092	18TH WAR
PERKINS, EBEN	QUE	200	3RD E DI
PERKINS, EDWARD	BAL	290	17TH WAR
PERKINS, EDWARD	BAL	048	4TH WARD
PERKINS, EDWARD	QUE	144	1ST E DI
PERKINS, EDWARD	BAL	282	2ND WARD
PERKINS, ELISHA	BAL	407	14TH WAR
PERKINS, ELIZA	FRE	186	5TH E DI
PERKINS, ELIZA	QUE	249	5TH E DI
PERKINS, ELIZABETH	QUE	144	1ST E DI
PERKINS, ELIZABETH	BAL	316	3RD WARD
PERKINS, ELIZABETH	BAL	076	1ST WARD
PERKINS, EMALINE	SOM	350	BRINKLEY
PERKINS, EMMORY	BAL	199	17TH WAR
PERKINS, F.	BAL	140	1ST WARD
PERKINS, FRANCIS	KEN	213	2ND DIST
PERKINS, GEORGE	BAL	050	1ST WARD
PERKINS, GEORGE W. T.	KEN	209	2ND DIST
PERKINS, HANNAH	BAL	303	12TH WAR
PERKINS, HECTOR	BAL	151	5TH WARD
PERKINS, HENRY	BAL	286	7TH WARD
PERKINS, HENRY	KEN	247	2ND DIST
PERKINS, HENRY	PRI	089	SPALDING
PERKINS, ISAAC	KEN	245	2ND DIST
PERKINS, JAEMS	BAL	461	14TH WAR
PERKINS, JAMES	QUE	144	1ST E DI
PERKINS, JAMES	PRI	041	VANSVILL
PERKINS, JAMES	BAL	138	1ST WARD
PERKINS, JAMES	BAL	166	1ST WARD
PERKINS, JAMES P.	QUE	151	1ST E DI
PERKINS, JOHN	FRE	125	CREAGERS
PERKINS, JOHN	FRE	206	BUCKEYST
PERKINS, JOHN	KEN	260	1ST DIST
PERKINS, JOSEPH	ALL	055	10TH E.D
PERKINS, LOUISA	WAS	075	2ND SUBD
PERKINS, LOUISA J.	BAL	122	18TH WAR
PERKINS, LUCRETIA	BAL	297	3RD WARD
PERKINS, LUCY	BAL	156	11TH WAR
PERKINS, O. S.	BAL	329	13TH WAR
PERKINS, PETER	WAS	065	2ND SUBD
PERKINS, PHATCH. *	BAL	091	18TH WAR
PERKINS, PRISCILLA	BAL	080	15TH WAR
PERKINS, RACHEL	TAL	026	EASTON D
PERKINS, REBECCA	KEN	312	3RD DIST
PERKINS, ROBERT	WOR	268	BERLIN 1
PERKINS, SALLY	BAL	359	13TH WAR
PERKINS, SAMUEL	KEN	212	2ND DIST
PERKINS, SAMUEL	KEN	307	3RD DIST
PERKINS, SARAH	KEN	213	2ND DIST
PERKINS, SARAH	KEN	214	2ND DIST
PERKINS, WASHINGTON	BAL	125	16TH WAR
PERKINS, WESLEY	BAL	100	10TH WAR
PERKINS, WILLIAM	BAL	282	2ND WARD
PERKINS, WILLIAM	KEN	212	2ND DIST
PERKINS, WILLIAM	BAL	421	3RD WARD
PERKINS, WILLIAM C.	BAL	121	18TH WAR
PERL, IGNATIOUS-MULATTO	FRE	408	JEFFERSO
PERL, JACOB-MULATTO	FRE	408	JEFFERSO
PERL, MARY-MULATTO	FRE	408	JEFFERSO
PERLY, GEORGE S.	BAL	144	1ST WARD
PERMAUCKT, CAROLETTON *	BAL	117	2ND DIST
PERMOTT, EMELIE *	BAL	314	20TH WAR
PERNAL, ELIJAH	DOR	306	1ST DIST
PERNELL, ISAAC	QUE	238	5TH E DI
PERNELL, LET	WOR	280	BERLIN 1
PERNELL, MARTHA E.	HAR	150	3RD DIST
PERNELL, SUSAN	WAS	144	2ND DIST
PERNGOY, JOHN W. *	BAL	272	7TH WARD
PERNGOY, WILLIAM C. D. *	BAL	272	7TH WARD
PERNINGER, AMELIA	BAL	187	19TH WAR
PERNINGOTN, JAMES *	BAL	158	2ND DIST
PERNJOY, CORNELIUS H.	BAL	354	7TH WARD
PERNNELL, ANN M.	WOR	201	3RD E DI
PEROGOY, JAMES	BAL	015	18TH WAR
PEROTT, LAWRENCE	BAL	009	4TH WARD
PERPER, CHRISTOPHER	BAL	271	1ST DIST
PERRE, WESTLEY	TAL	021	EASTON D
PERREGOY, NICHOLAS	BAL	287	3RD WARD
PERREY, ANN S.	BAL	289	7TH WARD
PERREY, ELIZABETH SR.	CEC	181	7TH E DI
PERREY, GEORGE	BAL	289	7TH WARD
PERREY, MARY E.	BAL	282	7TH WARD
PERREY, WILLIAM	BAL	422	8TH WARD
PERRICAN, ANN	BAL	027	18TH WAR
PERRIE, EDWARD L.	PRI	064	NOTTINGH
PERRIE, ELISHA	PRI	100	SPALDING
PERRIE, HUGH	PRI	062	NOTTINGH
PERRIEN, WILLIAM	BAL	453	1ST DIST
PERRIGO, CHARLES	BAL	282	7TH WARD
PERRIGO, DANIEL	BAL	023	1ST WARD
PERRIGOY, JOHN W.	BAL	272	7TH WARD
PERRIGOY, WILLIAM C. D. *	BAL	272	7TH WARD
PERRIJOY, ELIZABETH	BAL	315	7TH WARD
PERRIJOY, JOSEPH	BAL	315	7TH WARD
PERRILL, JAMES-MULATTO	FRE	208	BUCKEYST
PERRILL, MARY E.	FRE	208	BUCKEYST
PERRILL, PHILIP	FRE	233	BUCKEYST
PERRILL, THOMAS	FRE	064	FREDERIC
PERRILL, THOMAS-MULATTO	FRE	215	BUCKEYST
PERRIN, JOHN	BAL	152	16TH WAR
PERRINE, ELIZA	BAL	088	10TH WAR
PERRINE, SUSANAH	BAL	077	2ND DIST
PERRION, WILLIAM	BAL	248	12TH WAR
PERRIWINKEL, FRED	KEN	247	2ND DIST
PERRN, BENJAMIN	CAR	370	9TH DIST
PERROY, BILL	HAR	084	2ND DIST
PERRY, ANN	BAL	429	14TH WAR
PERRY, ANN	QUE	243	5TH E DI
PERRY, ANN E.	BAL	276	1ST DIST
PERRY, ANN M.	FRE	045	FREDERIC
PERRY, ARIND	BAL	231	6TH WARD
PERRY, BENJAMIN	WAS	134	2ND DIST
PERRY, BENJAMIN	WAS	161	HAGERSTO
PERRY, BENJAMIN	TAL	113	ST MICHA
PERRY, BENJAMIN J.	MGM	360	BERRYS D
PERRY, CAROLINE	BAL	035	15TH WAR
PERRY, CHARIS	BAL	307	12TH WAR
PERRY, CHARLE SH.-BLACK	FRE	218	BUCKEYST
PERRY, CHARLES	BAL	106	15TH WAR
PERRY, CHARLES	BAL	157	1ST WARD
PERRY, CHIS	BAL	307	12TH WAR
PERRY, CYRUS E.	MGM	391	ROCKERLE
PERRY, DANIEL	BAL	122	1ST WARD
PERRY, EBENEZER	CEC	090	4TH E DI
PERRY, EDMAN	CHA	233	HILLTOP
PERRY, EDWARD	BAL	085	18TH WAR
PERRY, EDWARD	BAL	143	1ST WARD
PERRY, EDWARD R.	CAR	158	NO TWP L
PERRY, EDWIN D.	BAL	401	3RD WARD
PERRY, ELBERT	MGM	387	ROCKERLE
PERRY, ELIZA	BAL	213	11TH WAR
PERRY, ELIZABETH	CHA	223	ALLENS F
PERRY, ELIZABETH	MGM	344	CLARKSBU
PERRY, ELIZABETH	BAL	158	16TH WAR
PERRY, ELIZABETH	BAL	149	2ND DIST
PERRY, ELIZABETH	TAL	090	ST MICHA
PERRY, ELLEN	BAL	188	5TH DIST
PERRY, ELLIS R.	BAL	208	6TH DIST
PERRY, ERASMOUS	MGM	390	ROCKERLE
PERRY, FRANCES A.	BAL	348	3RD WARD
PERRY, FRANK	CHA	285	BOJANTOW
PERRY, GEORGE	BAL	155	1ST WARD
PERRY, GEORGE C.	ALL	240	CUMBERLA
PERRY, HARRIETT*	BAL	050	4TH WARD
PERRY, HARRY	FRE	202	5TH E DI
PERRY, HELLEN	BAL	115	5TH WARD
PERRY, HENRY	FRE	088	FREDERIC
PERRY, HERMAN H.	BAL	039	4TH WARD
PERRY, IRAEL	BAL	092	18TH WAR
PERRY, J.	BAL	163	1ST WARD
PERRY, J.	BAL	171	1ST WARD
PERRY, J.	BAL	135	1ST WARD
PERRY, JACOB	FRE	304	WOODSBOR
PERRY, JACOB SR.	FRE	122	CREAGERS
PERRY, JAMES	BAL	016	9TH WARD
PERRY, JAMES	BAL	115	5TH WARD
PERRY, JAMES	TAL	016	EASTON D
PERRY, JANE	BAL	055	15TH WAR
PERRY, JANE	DOR	436	1ST DIST
PERRY, JOHN	DOR	414	1ST DIST
PERRY, JOHN	FRE	102	FREDERIC
PERRY, JOHN	BAL	403	3RD WARD
PERRY, JOHN	ALL	182	8TH E.D.
PERRY, JOHN	QUE	249	5TH E DI
PERRY, JOHN B.	ST	271	3RD E DI
PERRY, JOHN H.	ANN	351	3RD DIST
PERRY, JOHN W.	QUE	192	3RD E DI
PERRY, JONATHAN	FRE	353	MIDDLETO
PERRY, JOSEPH	BAL	121	1ST WARD
PERRY, LEONARD	BAL	086	4TH WARD
PERRY, LEVI	BAL	246	12TH WAR
PERRY, MAJOR-BLACK	BAL	217	2ND WARD
PERRY, MARGARET-BLACK	MGM	397	ROCKERLE
PERRY, MARRY	ALL	257	CUMBERLA
PERRY, MARTIN	FRE	338	MIDDLETO
PERRY, MARY	FRE	070	FREDERIC
PERRY, MARY	BAL	068	4TH WARD
PERRY, MARY	FRE	101	FREDERIC
PERRY, MARY	BAL	111	5TH WARD
PERRY, MARY	TAL	017	EASTON D
PERRY, MARY	TAL	047	EASTON T
PERRY, MARY	TAL	120	ST MICHA

Name	County	Page	District
PERRY, MARY E.	BAL	304	20TH WAR
PERRY, MARY E.	CHA	233	HILLTOP
PERRY, MATILDA	WAS	252	1ST DIST
PERRY, NANCY	CHA	247	HILLTOP
PERRY, NINIAH	MGM	390	ROCKERLE
PERRY, NOAH	QUE	166	2ND E DI
PERRY, NOAH	BAL	073	15TH WAR
PERRY, OLLIVER	BAL	189	2ND WARD
PERRY, P.	BAL	148	1ST WARD
PERRY, PRECILLA	BAL	005	1ST WARD
PERRY, PRISCILLA S.	BAL	100	15TH WAR
PERRY, R.	BAL	118	1ST WARD
PERRY, RACHAEL	BAL	134	18TH WAR
PERRY, RACHEL-BLACK	QUE	199	3RD E DI
PERRY, REBECCA	ST	348	5TH E DI
PERRY, REBECCA	CHA	247	HILLTOP
PERRY, RICHARD	KEN	216	2ND DIST
PERRY, ROBERT	BAL	072	1ST WARD
PERRY, ROBERT	ANN	404	8TH DIST
PERRY, ROBERT	BAL	140	1ST WARD
PERRY, ROBERT M.	BAL	126	1ST WARD
PERRY, ROGER	BAL	062	10TH WAR
PERRY, RUTH A.	MGM	363	BERRYS D
PERRY, SAMUEL	MGM	395	ROCKERLE
PERRY, SAMUEL	CEC	176	7TH E DI
PERRY, SAMUEL	CAL	014	1ST DIST
PERRY, SAMUEL T.	BAL	119	1ST WARD
PERRY, SARAH	BAL	059	4TH WARD
PERRY, SOPHIA	FRE	349	MIDDLETO
PERRY, SUSAN	HAR	106	2ND DIST
PERRY, THOMAS	ALL	104	5TH E.D.
PERRY, THOMAS	BAL	171	1ST WARD
PERRY, THOMAS	ALL	254	CUMBERLA
PERRY, THOMAS R.	BAL	337	13TH WAR
PERRY, WILLIAM	CAR	158	NO TWP L
PERRY, WILLIAM	CHA	233	HILLTOP
PERRY, WILLIAM	FRE	415	8TH E DI
PERRY, WILLIAM	ALL	215	CUMBERLA
PERRY, WILLIAM	TAL	113	ST MICHA
PERRY, WILLIAM	QUE	251	5TH E DI
PERRY, WILLIAM A.	TAL	059	EASTON D
PERRY, WILLIAM F.	BAL	388	3RD WARD
PERRY, WILLIAM F.	HAR	172	3RD DIST
PERRY, WILLIAM H.	FRE	392	PETERSVI
PERRY, WILLIAM T.	MGM	342	CLARKSBU
PERRY,WILLIAM	BAL	138	1ST WARD
PERRYGORY, LOUISA	CEC	153	PORT DUP
PERRYMAN, ISABOLA A.	HAR	192	3RD DIST
PERSANETT, JOHN	BAL	205	17TH WAR
PERSE, WILLIAM F.	WOR	292	9TH E DI
PERSEY, NATHANIEL *	SOM	421	PRINCESS
PERSLEY, GEORGE O.	BAL	393	14TH WAR
PERSLEY, JAMES	BAL	392	14TH WAR
PERSON, ANN	DOR	469	1ST DIST
PERSON, ISAAC	HAR	194	3RD DIST
PERSON, JOHN B.	BAL	051	9TH WARD
PERSON, ROBERT	ALL	252	CUMBERLA
PERSON, THOMAS	TAL	003	EASTON D
PERSONET, ANGELINE	TAL	079	ST MICHA
PERSONETH, ELIZABETH	QUE	244	5TH E DI
PERSONETTE, JOHN	QUE	242	5TH E DI
PERSONETTE, LORENZO	QUE	239	5TH E DI
PERSONETTE, RACHEL	BAL	204	6TH WARD
PERT, ANN*	TAL	009	EASTON D
PERTE, JOHN	BAL	053	1ST WARD
PERURIEN, J. M.	BAL	429	14TH WAR
PERVAIL, JOHN	BAL	235	12TH WAR
PERVILION, WILLIAM	PRI	103	SPALDING
PERVILLION, JAMES	PRI	078	MARLBROU
PERVILLION, JOHN	PRI	080	QUEEN AN
PERVILSIOR, E.	PRI	122	PISCATAW
PERVIS, HESTER A.	BAL	417	3RD WARD
PERVIS, WILLIAM	BAL	170	1ST WARD
PESST, JOHN	BAL	258	2ND WARD
PESTER, LOUISA	BAL	257	12TH WAR
PESTLER, CHARLES	BAL	244	12TH WAR
PETER, BROTHER	BAL	216	11TH WAR
PETER, CASPER	BAL	280	17TH WAR
PETER, CHARLES	BAL	311	12TH WAR
PETER, DANIEL	BAL	079	10TH WAR
PETER, ERNEST	BAL	265	20TH WAR
PETER, GEORGE	MGM	381	ROCKERLE
PETER, GEORGE H.	MGM	406	MEDLEY 3
PETER, JOHN	BAL	423	14TH WAR
PETER, JOHN	BAL	436	8TH WARD
PETER, JOHN J.	BAL	040	9TH WARD
PETER, JOHNS	CAR	411	2ND DIST
PETER, MARIA	BAL	232	2ND WARD
PETER, MATHIAS	BAL	217	19TH WAR
PETER, PHILIP G.	BAL	213	19TH WAR
PETER, ROBERT	MGM	381	ROCKERLE
PETER, SALLY JOHNS	MGM	412	MEDLEY 3
PETER, SIMON	CAR	400	2ND DIST
PETER, SIMON	CAR	246	3RD DIST
PETER, THOMAS	FRE	230	BUCKEYST
PETER, THOMAS	MGM	412	MEDLEY 3
PETER, THOMAS	WAS	067	2ND SUBD
PETER, WARNER L.	QUE	133	1ST E DI
PETERE, JOSEPH	ALL	201	CUMBERLA
PETEREE, ELIZABETH	BAL	110	18TH WAR
PETERFELF, HENRY	BAL	218	17TH WAR
PETERGREW, GRACE	BAL	411	3RD WARD
PETERKIN, JACOB	BAL	323	7TH WARD
PETERKIN, PRESILLA	BAL	275	7TH WARD
PETERKIN, SUSAN	BAL	208	17TH WAR
PETERKIN, WILLIAM S.	BAL	046	18TH WAR
PETERKING, JACOB	DOR	360	3RD DIVI
PETERMAN, DORCAS	BAL	213	6TH DIST
PETERMAN, ELIZABETH	FRE	203	5TH E DI
PETERMAN, ELIZABETH	CAR	345	6TH DIST
PETERMAN, GEORGE	WAS	055	2ND SUBD
PETERMAN, GEORGE	WAS	036	2ND SUBD
PETERMAN, MARY C.	ALL	211	CUMBERLA
PETERMAN, PETER	CAR	345	6TH DIST
PETERMAN, SARAH	ALL	226	CUMBERLA
PETERMAN, WILLIAM S.	ALL	211	CUMBERLA
PETERS, ANDREW	BAL	268	1ST DIST
PETERS, ANN E.	BAL	127	11TH WAR
PETERS, ANN M.	BAL	114	18TH WAR
PETERS, ANNA A.	QUE	190	3RD E DI
PETERS, ANTHONY	SOM	473	TRAPPE D
PETERS, BELINDA	FRE	189	5TH E DI
PETERS, C.G.	BAL	141	19TH WAR
PETERS, CAROLINE	BAL	142	19TH WAR
PETERS, CAROLINE	SOM	477	TRAPP DI
PETERS, CATHARINE	BAL	247	12TH WAR
PETERS, CEASAR	WAS	008	WILLIAMS
PETERS, CHARLES	BAL	288	7TH WARD
PETERS, CHARLES	BAL	134	11TH WAR
PETERS, CHARLES	CAR	116	NO TWP L
PETERS, CHARLOTTE	SOM	477	TRAPP DI
PETERS, CHRISTIANA	BAL	228	6TH WARD
PETERS, CLARA	BAL	255	12TH WAR
PETERS, CLARA	ANN	377	4TH DIST
PETERS, EDWARD	BAL	009	EASTERN
PETERS, ELIE	WAS	233	1ST DIST
PETERS, ELIZ	BAL	233	12TH WAR
PETERS, ELIZABETH	MGM	430	CLARKSTR
PETERS, ELIZEBETH	HAR	159	3RD DIST
PETERS, EPHRAIM-BLACK	WOR	333	1ST E DI
PETERS, EVA	BAL	336	3RD WARD
PETERS, FANNY	BAL	357	13TH WAR
PETERS, FERDERICK	WAS	143	HAGERSTO
PETERS, FREDREICK	BAL	181	2ND WARD
PETERS, G.C.	BAL	141	19TH WAR
PETERS, GEORGE	BAL	460	1ST DIST
PETERS, GEORGE	BAL	001	9TH WARD
PETERS, GEORGE	SOM	473	TRAPPE D
PETERS, GEROGE	BAL	318	20TH WAR
PETERS, GOERGE	QUE	127	1ST E DI
PETERS, HENRIETTA	QUE	138	1ST E DI
PETERS, HENRY	CEC	175	7TH E DI
PETERS, ISAAC	BAL	346	13TH WAR
PETERS, JACOB	QUE	151	1ST E DI
PETERS, JAMES	CEC	088	4TH E DI
PETERS, JAMES	BAL	133	1ST WARD
PETERS, JAMES	BAL	302	1ST DIST
PETERS, JAMES L.	BAL	121	11TH WAR
PETERS, JANE	SOM	477	TRAPP DI
PETERS, JESSE	BAL	275	12TH WAR
PETERS, JOHN	BAL	371	1ST DIST
PETERS, JOHN	BAL	228	6TH WARD
PETERS, JOHN	HAR	138	2ND DIST
PETERS, JOHN	CEC	177	7TH E DI
PETERS, JOHN	FRE	229	BUCKEYST
PETERS, JOHN	FRE	229	BUCKEYST
PETERS, JOHN C.	BAL	007	9TH WARD
PETERS, JOHN F.	BAL	083	1ST WARD
PETERS, JOHN W.	QUE	129	1ST E DI
PETERS, JOHN W.	HAR	080	2ND DIST
PETERS, JOSEPH	CAL	061	3RD DIST
PETERS, JOSEPHINE	FRE	189	5TH E DI
PETERS, LEAH	SOM	483	TRAPP DI
PETERS, LEVINA	SOM	407	DUBLIN D
PETERS, LEWIS	BAL	337	13TH WAR
PETERS, LEWIS	CAR	311	1ST DIST
PETERS, LIDDY O.	BAL	012	18TH WAR
PETERS, LIDIA-BLACK	WOR	334	1ST E DI
PETERS, LOUIS	BAL	269	2ND WARD
PETERS, LUCY	BAL	280	20TH WAR
PETERS, M.	BAL	072	10TH WAR
PETERS, MARIA	BAL	136	11TH WAR
PETERS, MARTHA A.	QUE	189	3RD E DI
PETERS, MARY	SOM	477	TRAPP DI
PETERS, MARY	BAL	123	16TH WAR
PETERS, MARY	BAL	005	1ST WARD
PETERS, MARY A.	BAL	191	11TH WAR
PETERS, MICHAEL	BAL	313	7TH WARD
PETERS, MILLY	SOM	493	SALISBUR
PETERS, MORDECAI	BAL	442	14TH WAR
PETERS, MRS. J.	BAL	245	12TH WAR
PETERS, P.	ANN	346	3RD DIST
PETERS, PETER	FRE	317	MIDDLETO
PETERS, PETERS	BAL	079	1ST WARD
PETERS, POLLY	BAL	302	12TH WAR
PETERS, PURNELL	SOM	406	DUBLIN D
PETERS, RACHEL	MGM	390	ROCKERLE
PETERS, ROSENIA	BAL	134	11TH WAR
PETERS, ROSETTA-MULATTO	QUE	129	1ST E DI
PETERS, SALLY	SOM	484	TRAPP DI
PETERS, SALLY	SOM	466	HANGARY
PETERS, SAMUEL	WAS	012	WILLIAMS
PETERS, SAMUEL	QUE	135	1ST E DI
PETERS, SANDY	SOM	483	TRAPP DI
PETERS, SARAH A.	HAR	147	3RD DIST
PETERS, SARAH MRS.	BAL	121	11TH WAR
PETERS, SAVILLA	FRE	311	MIDDLETO
PETERS, SCLOMON	BAL	357	8TH WARD
PETERS, SUSAN	CEC	176	7TH E DI
PETERS, SUSAN A.	BAL	147	16TH WAR
PETERS, THOMAS	QUE	123	1ST E DI
PETERS, TOBIAS	BAL	351	13TH WAR
PETERS, W. C.	BAL	279	20TH WAR
PETERS, WILLIAM	QUE	127	1ST E DI
PETERS, WILLIAM	QUE	133	1ST E DI
PETERS, WILLIAM	HAR	161	3RD DIST
PETERS, WILLIAM	BAL	144	19TH WAR
PETERS, WILLIAM	HAR	205	3RD DIST
PETERS, WILLIAM	SOM	446	DAMES QU
PETERS, WILLIAM	BAL	137	1ST WARD
PETERS, WILLIAM	BAL	294	3RD WARD
PETERS, WILLIAM	ALL	168	6TH E.D.
PETERS, WILLIAM A.	FRE	010	FREDERIC
PETERS, WILLIAM B.	BAL	157	1ST WARD
PETERS, WILLIAM H.	BAL	231	12TH WAR
PETERS, WILLIAML.	QUE	127	1ST E DI
PETERS,JESSE P.	BAL	242	12TH WAR
PETERSEN, P.	BAL	161	1ST WARD
PETERSON, ALEXANDER	CEC	059	1ST E DI
PETERSON, ANDREW	BAL	105	1ST WARD
PETERSON, ANNA M.	BAL	215	11TH WAR
PETERSON, ASBURY	CEC	048	1ST E DI
PETERSON, C. H.	BAL	149	1ST WARD
PETERSON, CAROLINE	BAL	065	1ST WARD
PETERSON, CHARLES	BAL	118	1ST WARD
PETERSON, CHARLES	BAL	117	1ST WARD
PETERSON, CHARLES H.	BAL	121	1ST WARD
PETERSON, D.	BAL	163	1ST WARD
PETERSON, DAVID	FRE	288	WOODSBOR
PETERSON, DELIA	BAL	079	2ND DIST
PETERSON, DELILA	SOM	419	PRINCESS
PETERSON, EDWARD	BAL	118	1ST WARD
PETERSON, ELIAS	HAR	080	2ND DIST
PETERSON, ELIZABETH	BAL	159	2ND DIST
PETERSON, ELIZABETH	ANN	273	ANNAPOLI
PETERSON, ELIZABETH	BAL	242	2ND WARD
PETERSON, ERASMUS	BAL	334	3RD WARD
PETERSON, F.	BAL	135	1ST WARD
PETERSON, F.	BAL	167	1ST WARD
PETERSON, GEORGE	BAL	304	12TH WAR
PETERSON, GEORGE	BAL	157	19TH WAR
PETERSON, GEORGE	CEC	098	4TH E DI
PETERSON, GEORGE	CAL	009	1ST DIST
PETERSON, HENRY	BAL	263	2ND WARD
PETERSON, ISAAC	HAR	096	2ND DIST
PETERSON, J.	BAL	151	1ST WARD
PETERSON, JAMES	ANN	289	ANNAPOLI
PETERSON, JAMES	ANN	318	2ND DIST
PETERSON, JAMES	HAR	096	2ND DIST
PETERSON, JOHN	BAL	168	1ST WARD
PETERSON, JOHN	BAL	132	1ST WARD
PETERSON, JOHN	BAL	110	1ST WARD
PETERSON, JOHN	BAL	108	2ND DIST
PETERSON, JOSEPH	BAL	140	1ST WARD
PETERSON, LEVI	SOM	417	PRINCESS
PETERSON, LOUISA	BAL	264	17TH WAR
PETERSON, M.	BAL	140	1ST WARD
PETERSON, MARTHA A.	KEN	237	2ND DIST
PETERSON, MARTIN	BAL	277	2ND WARD
PETERSON, MARY	BAL	183	6TH WARD
PETERSON, P.	BAL	138	1ST WARD
PETERSON, P.G.	BAL	166	1ST WARD
PETERSON, P.H.	BAL	167	1ST WARD
PETERSON, PETER	CEC	096	4TH E DI
PETERSON, S.	BAL	165	1ST WARD
PETERSON, SARAH	CEC	104	4TH E DI
PETERSON, T.	BAL	135	1ST WARD
PETERSON, THOMAS	BAL	133	1ST WARD
PETERSON, THOMAS	BAL	124	1ST WARD
PETERSON, TOBIAS	CEC	094	4TH E DI
PETERSON, TOBIAS	CEC	104	4TH E DI
PETERSON, VIOLET	SOM	429	PRINCESS
PETERSON, VIRGINIA	SOM	430	PRINCESS
PETERSON, WILLIAM	BAL	124	1ST WARD
PETERSON, WILLIAM	BAL	166	1ST WARD
PETERSON, WILLIAM H.	CEC	027	CHESAPEA
PETERSON, WILLIAM J.	BAL	066	1ST WARD
PETERSON, WITHROUT	BAL	105	1ST WARD
PETERSON,AMOS	BAL	118	1ST WARD
PETES, WILLIAM	BAL	306	1ST DIST
PETESON, AMRTIN	BAL	116	1ST WARD
PETESON, J.	BAL	138	1ST WARD
PETGERS, SIMON	BAL	178	2ND DIST
PETHERBRIDGE, EDWARD R.	BAL	039	4TH WARD
PETHERBRIDGE, RICHARD	BAL	293	3RD WARD
PETHERBRIGE, JOHN F.	ANN	399	8TH DIST
PETHERIDGE, FRANCES	BAL	359	3RD WARD
PETINGALE, BENJAMIN H.	FRE	354	MIDDLETO
PETINGALL, ROBERT	FRE	344	MIDDLETO
PETINGALL, SARAH	FRE	316	MIDDLETO
PETINGER, RICHARD	BAL	036	1ST WARD
PETINGILL,ALBERT	BAL	119	1ST WARD
PETIT, DAVID	BAL	171	1ST WARD
PETIT, LUCINDA B.	BAL	026	4TH WARD
PETJICE, HARRIET	BAL	242	2ND WARD
PETKIN, GEORGE MRS.	BAL	195	11TH WAR
PETNY, EPHRAIM	CAR	400	2ND DIST
PETNY,HENRY	CAR	400	2ND DIST
PETRE, GEORGE	WAS	282	1ST DIST
PETRE, JOHN	WAS	189	1ST DIST
PETREY, DAVID	CAR	410	2ND DIST
PETREY, MICHEAL	CAR	399	2ND DIST
PETRICK, ANDREW	ALL	106	5TH E.D.
PETRIE, JOHN F.	BAL	136	11TH WAR
PETRMAN, JOHN W.	ALL	211	CUMBERLA
PETRY, ELIZA	WAS	167	1ST DIST
PETRY, JACOB	CAR	292	7TH DIST
PETRY, PHILIP	BAL	110	15TH WAR
PETT, ANN*	BAL	046	4TH WARD
PETTEBONE, JOHN E.	ANN	356	3RD DIST
PETTEBONE, PHILIP	ANN	355	3RD DIST
PETTECORD, JOHN	BAL	162	6TH WARD
PETTEGREW, JANE	BAL	359	3RD WARD
PETTERS, HENETTA	HAR	206	3RD DIST
PETTERS, PHILIP	HAR	206	3RD DIST
PETTET, ANN	BAL	279	12TH WAR
PETTET, ELI	CHA	243	HILLTOP
PETTEY, SARAH	BAL	295	20TH WAR
PETTICARD, LOUISA J.	BAL	049	2ND DIST
PETTICHORD, S.	FRE	200	5TH E DI
PETTICOAT, KENSEY	BAL	111	2ND DIST
PETTICORD, ASBURY	ANN	503	HOWARD D
PETTICORD, BENJAMIN	ANN	495	HOWARD D
PETTICORD, CHARLES	BAL	214	6TH WARD
PETTICORD, JAMES	BAL	183	6TH WARD
PETTICORD, JANE	BAL	215	6TH WARD
PETTICORD, JARRETS	ANN	425	HOWARD D
PETTICORD, M.	FRE	200	5TH E DI
PETTICORD, THOMAS	ANN	499	HOWARD D
PETTICORD, WILLIAM	ANN	503	HOWARD D
PETTICORD, WILLIAM P.	BAL	049	2ND DIST
PETTIGER, WILLIAM	BAL	262	2ND WARD
PETTIGINE, HARRIET	BAL	277	2ND WARD
PETTIGREN, GRACE	BAL	064	2ND DIST
PETTINESSER, A.	BAL	449	8TH WARD
PETTINGER, JACOB	FRE	179	5TH E DI
PETTINGER, JEREMIAH	FRE	164	EMMITTSB
PETTINGER, JOSHUA	FRE	109	CREAGERS
PETTINGILL, J.	BAL	162	1ST WARD
PETTIS, JAMES	BAL	232	1ST DIST
PETTIS, JAMES	BAL	232	1ST DIST
PETTISH, SUSAN	BAL	230	1ST DIST
PETTIT, AMORY M.	BAL	169	6TH WARD
PETTIT, DAVID	BAL	133	1ST WARD
PETTIT, JAMES	BAL	276	7TH WARD
PETTIT, JANE A.	FRE	043	FREDERIC
PETTIT, MALVINA	BAL	169	6TH WARD
PETTIT, MARY A.	BAL	248	20TH WAR
PETTIT, MOSES	BAL	027	9TH WARD
PETTIT, O.T.	BAL	114	5TH WARD
PETTITT, DAVID	BAL	114	1ST WARD
PETTITT, JOSEPH D.	ANN	416	HOWARD D
PETTMAN, JOHN	ALL	211	CUMBERLA
PETTRERBRIDGE, MARY	BAL	277	7TH WARD
PETTS, BENJAMIN	WOR	277	BERLIN 1
PETTS, ELIZABETH	FRE	029	FREDERIC
PETTS, NICHOLAS H.	FRE	045	FREDERIC
PETTS, RICHARD	ANN	348	3RD DIST
PETTY, CORNELIUS	ANN	414	HOWARD D
PETTY, FREDERICK	BAL	275	17TH WAR
PETTY, JAMES	BAL	314	12TH WAR
PETTY, LEVIN*	DOR	445	1ST DIST
PETZOLD, LOUIS	BAL	162	16TH WAR
PETZT, OTTO	BAL	252	12TH WAR
PEUGH, DAVID L.	MGM	324	CRACKLIN
PEUGH, JESSE T.	ALL	175	7TH E.D.
PEW, BENJAMIN	HAR	009	1ST DIST
PEW, ELZA	HAR	189	3RD DIST
PEW, EMILY	BAL	015	4TH WARD
PEYER, ELIZA	BAL	322	12TH WAR
PEYTON, CAROLINE	BAL	058	10TH WAR
PEYTON, SAMUEL	BAL	159	1ST WARD
PEYTON, WILLIAM	BAL	397	14TH WAR
PFAFF, ELIZABETH	BAL	084	10TH WAR
PFAHL, LISETTA	BAL	087	10TH WAR
PFATZGRAF, HENRY	BAL	354	13TH WAR
PFAUS, JOHN	BAL	220	2ND WARD
PFAUTZ, CHRISTIAN	WAS	175	FUNKSTOW
PFAUTZ, ESTHER	FRE	433	8TH E DI
PFAUTZ, GEORGE	FRE	413	8TH E DI

Name	County	Page	District
PFAUTZ, HANNAH	FRE	176	5TH E DI
PFAUTZ, ISAAC	FRE	415	8TH E DI
PFAUTZ, JOHN	FRE	410	8TH E DI
PFAUTZ, MARTIN	WAS	175	FUNKSTOW
PFAUTZ, PETER	FRE	414	8TH E DI
PFAUTZ, SAMUEL	FRE	433	8TH E DI
PFAUTZ, SOPHIA	FRE	415	8TH E DI
PFEFFER, WILLIAM	BAL	221	1ST DIST
PFEIFER, BENJAMIN	BAL	133	16TH WAR
PFEIFER, CASPAR	FRE	395	PETERSVI
PFEIFER, JOHN	MGM	374	ROCKERLE
PFEIFFER, ADAM	BAL	174	19TH WAR
PFEIFFER, CATHERINE	BAL	318	20TH WAR
PFEIFFER, FREDERICK	BAL	343	1ST DIST
PFEIFFER, JOHN	BAL	152	2ND DIST
PFEIFFER, L.	BAL	148	19TH WAR
PFEIL, AMANDA	BAL	080	10TH WAR
PFEISTER, BARTHOLOMEW	BAL	252	2ND WARD
PFELDY, GEORGE	BAL	131	2ND DIST
PFELMAN, JANE	BAL	096	10TH WAR
PFELTY, MARIA	BAL	087	4TH WARD
PFER, CHRISTIAN	BAL	315	12TH WAR
PFERFER, GEROGE	BAL	312	20TH WAR
PFERFF, ANDRE	BAL	210	17TH WAR
PFIEFF, AUGUST	BAL	048	9TH WARD
PFIEFFER, CHARLES	PRI	107	PISCATAW
PFIEFFER, MARGARET	PRI	064	NOTTINGH
PFIEL, PETER	BAL	038	15TH WAR
PFISTERER, JOSEPH	BAL	247	20TH WAR
PFOCH, GEORGE	WAS	099	2ND DIST
PFONTZ, DAVID	CAR	238	UNION TO
PFORR, CONRAD	BAL	017	9TH WARD
PFORR, GEORGE	BAL	173	6TH WARD
PFOUTS, HANNAH	FRE	175	5TH E DI
PFSTENER, JOSEPH G.	BAL	246	20TH WAR
PFYCLE, GEORGE	BAL	284	17TH WAR
PGE, ELIZA J.	BAL	175	2ND WARD
PHAFF, JACOB	BAL	357	8TH WARD
PHAL, HENRY	BAL	256	2ND WARD
PHAL, SAAH	BAL	062	1ST WARD
PHALE, GERNIAN	BAL	231	2ND WARD
PHALEN, JOHN	BAL	279	2ND WARD
PHANACE, A.	BAL	156	1ST WARD
PHARES, ELIAS	CEC	208	7TH E DI
PHARIS, CALVIN	CEC	015	ELKTON 3
PHEARSON, S.M.	BAL	136	1ST WARD
PHEASANT, SAMUEL	WAS	291	1ST DIST
PHEBACK, ANN	CHA	240	HILLTOP
PHEBUS, ELIZABETH	FRE	011	FREDERIC
PHEBUS, GEORGE	FRE	005	FREDERIC
PHEBUS, JAMES	FRE	016	FREDERIC
PHEBUS, JOHN	FRE	007	FREDERIC
PHEBUS, JOHN	CAR	367	9TH DIST
PHEGAN, SALLY	BAL	109	10TH WAR
PHEIFF, MARTIN*	BAL	126	2ND DIST
PHEIFFEN, WILLIAM	BAL	229	2ND WARD
PHEIFFER, ANDREW	CAR	330	MANCHEST
PHEIFFER, FRANCES	BAL	306	20TH WAR
PHEIFFER, WILLIAM H.	BAL	206	2ND WARD
PHEISNER, JACOB	BAL	064	1ST WARD
PHELAN, EDWARD	BAL	145	1ST WARD
PHELAN, JESSE C.	BAL	221	6TH WARD
PHELIN, ALICE *	ANN	388	4TH DIST
PHELPS, A. H.L. MRS.	ANN	521	HOWARD D
PHELPS, ANN	BAL	301	1ST DIST
PHELPS, ANN	ANN	364	4TH DIST
PHELPS, ANN	PRI	082	QUEEN AN
PHELPS, CAMDEN	ANN	342	3RD DIST
PHELPS, CATHRINE	BAL	052	18TH WAR
PHELPS, EBENISSER T.	BAL	035	18TH WAR
PHELPS, ELISHA	ANN	438	HOWARD D
PHELPS, ELIZABETH	BAL	008	18TH WAR
PHELPS, FRANCIS P.	DOR	412	1ST DIST
PHELPS, GARDNER	BAL	181	19TH WAR
PHELPS, GEORGE	FRE	241	NEW MARK
PHELPS, GEORGE	ANN	433	HOWARD D
PHELPS, GEORGE	BAL	129	5TH WARD
PHELPS, GERARD	PRI	029	VANSVILL
PHELPS, HENRY	BAL	369	13TH WAR
PHELPS, HENRY A.	PRI	120	PISCATAW
PHELPS, JAMES	BAL	210	2ND WARD
PHELPS, JAMES	ANN	367	4TH DIST
PHELPS, JANE	BAL	032	4TH WARD
PHELPS, JOHN	FRE	258	NEW MARK
PHELPS, JOHN	BAL	254	12TH WAR
PHELPS, JOHN	PRI	111	PISCATAW
PHELPS, JOHN B. T.	BAL	252	6TH WARD
PHELPS, JONATHAN D.	ANN	441	HOWARD D
PHELPS, JOSEPH	ANN	276	ANNAPOLI
PHELPS, JOSHUA	ANN	465	HOWARD D
PHELPS, JOSHUA	ANN	512	HOWARD D
PHELPS, JOSHUA	PRI	044	VANSVILL
PHELPS, JULIET	ANN	272	ANNAPOLI
PHELPS, LLOYD	ANN	456	HOWARD D
PHELPS, M.A.	ANN	267	ANNAPOLI
PHELPS, MARIA	ANN	290	ANNAPOLI
PHELPS, MARY	BAL	410	1ST DIST
PHELPS, MARY A.	BAL	309	1ST DIST
PHELPS, MATHUSELADA *	ALL	089	5TH E.D.
PHELPS, NELSON	ANN	385	4TH DIST
PHELPS, NELSON	ANN	472	HOWARD D
PHELPS, RICHARD	ANN	385	4TH DIST
PHELPS, RICHARD	ANN	363	4TH DIST
PHELPS, RICHARD	ANN	388	4TH DIST
PHELPS, RICHARD	ANN	391	4TH DIST
PHELPS, RICHARD	PRI	111	PISCATAW
PHELPS, SAMUEL	BAL	452	8TH WARD
PHELPS, SILAS	BAL	299	7TH WARD
PHELPS, SOPHIA	ANN	437	HOWARD D
PHELPS, SUSAN	BAL	036	18TH WAR
PHELPS, THOMAS	PRI	069	MARLBROU
PHELPS, WALTER	ANN	320	2ND DIST
PHELPS, WALTER W.	BAL	051	18TH WAR
PHELPS, WILLIAM	ANN	291	ANNAPOLI
PHELPS, WILLIAM	ANN	364	4TH DIST
PHELPS, WILLIAM	ANN	372	4TH DIST
PHELPS, WILLIAM	BAL	301	1ST DIST
PHELPS, WILLIAM J.	BAL	084	4TH WARD
PHELPS, WILLIAM T.	ANN	364	4TH DIST
PHELPS,ELISHA B.	ALL	230	CUMBERLA
PHELPS,ROBERT	FRE	033	FREDERIC
PHELTZ, GUSTAINS	BAL	158	2ND DIST
PHENIX, CHARLES	ANN	333	2ND DIST
PHENIX, EUGENIA	ANN	309	1ST DIST
PHEOBUS, EDWARD	BAL	199	17TH WAR
PHEOBUS, FRANCIS A.	BAL	062	18TH WAR
PHEOBUS, PETER	FRE	242	NEW MARK
PHEONEY, E.	BAL	114	1ST WARD
PHEONIX, JAMES H.	QUE	230	4TH E DI
PHEPOE, JOHN	BAL	174	1ST WARD

Name	County	Page	District
PHERFER, JOHNHEARING,WINB	BAL	067	1ST WARD
PHERSEN, GEORGE	BAL	121	1ST WARD
PHERVS, WILLIAM*	ALL	087	5TH E.D.
PHESENT, MARY	CEC	021	ELKTON 3
PHEUBUS, NELLY	SOM	440	DAMES QU
PHEW, WILLIAM	FRE	018	FREDERIC
PHIBBONS, JOHN	CAL	046	3RD DIST
PHIEFFER, JOHN W.	BAL	225	2ND WARD
PHIEFFER, MARY A.	BAL	235	2ND WARD
PHIEN, VALENTINE	BAL	036	1ST WARD
PHIESLER, CHRISTIAN	BAL	214	2ND WARD
PHIFER, ANDREW	HAR	155	3RD DIST
PHIFER, HENRY	BAL	202	2ND WARD
PHILBERT, GEORGE	BAL	382	8TH WARD
PHILBERT, MICHAEL	BAL	194	6TH WARD
PHILBY, MARY A.	FRE	052	FREDERIC
PHILBY, SAMUEL	FRE	033	FREDERIC
PHILEEGER, JOHN	FRE	207	BUCKEYST
PHILEMOR, JOHN	QUE	243	5TH E DI
PHILIP, CHARLES	BAL	317	20TH WAR
PHILIP, ELIAS	CAR	308	1ST DIST
PHILIP, JOHN	FRE	388	PETERSVI
PHILIP, MARY J.	BAL	316	20TH WAR
PHILIPPS, ORSAMES P.	BAL	067	18TH WAR
PHILIPS, LLOYD	BAL	373	3RD WARD
PHILIPS, ABRAHAM A.	BAL	428	8TH WARD
PHILIPS, ADIRE	BAL	262	20TH WAR
PHILIPS, ALEXANDER	CAR	202	4TH DIST
PHILIPS, AMANDA	PRI	030	VANSVILL
PHILIPS, AMY	BAL	265	1ST DIST
PHILIPS, ANN M.	FRE	163	EMMITTSB
PHILIPS, ANNE	BAL	063	15TH WAR
PHILIPS, ASBURY	CAR	211	5TH DIST
PHILIPS, BAZZELL P.	CAR	215	5TH DIST
PHILIPS, BENJAMIN F.	MGM	344	CLARKSBU
PHILIPS, BETSY	BAL	222	17TH WAR
PHILIPS, CHRISTOPHER C.*	BAL	395	3RD WARD
PHILIPS, CLARK	CEC	166	6TH E DI
PHILIPS, DAVID	ANN	266	ANNAPOLI
PHILIPS, DENNIS	WAS	147	2ND DIST
PHILIPS, EDWARD J.	PRI	028	VANSVILL
PHILIPS, EDWIN	BAL	332	7TH WARD
PHILIPS, EDWIN J.	ANN	500	HOWARD D
PHILIPS, ELISHA	CAR	155	NO TWP L
PHILIPS, ELIZA A.	BAL	144	16TH WAR
PHILIPS, ELIZABETH	BAL	178	16TH WAR
PHILIPS, ELIZABETH	BAL	036	15TH WAR
PHILIPS, ELIZABETH	BAL	124	2ND DIST
PHILIPS, ELIZABETH	BAL	136	18TH WAR
PHILIPS, ELLEN	BAL	239	12TH WAR
PHILIPS, ELLIS	CEC	194	7TH E DI
PHILIPS, EMMA	BAL	376	3RD WARD
PHILIPS, FLORMAN	CAR	354	6TH DIST
PHILIPS, FRANCINA	CEC	198	7TH E DI
PHILIPS, GEORGE	BAL	340	7TH WARD
PHILIPS, GEORGE	BAL	335	7TH WARD
PHILIPS, GOTFRIED	BAL	379	1ST DIST
PHILIPS, HANNAH	BAL	386	3RD WARD
PHILIPS, HARRIET A.	CAR	219	5TH DIST
PHILIPS, HARRY R.	BAL	167	1ST WARD
PHILIPS, HARRY T. P.	BAL	405	3RD WARD
PHILIPS, HENRY	PRI	017	BLADENSB
PHILIPS, HENRY	WAS	146	2ND DIST
PHILIPS, HETTY	BAL	196	19TH WAR
PHILIPS, ISAAC	BAL	388	8TH WARD
PHILIPS, ISAAC	BAL	089	5TH WARD
PHILIPS, JAMES	BAL	311	7TH WARD
PHILIPS, JAMES	ANN	389	4TH DIST
PHILIPS, JAMES	CEC	154	PORT DUP
PHILIPS, JAMES	QUE	243	5TH E DI
PHILIPS, JANE	BAL	459	1ST DIST
PHILIPS, JANE	BAL	457	1ST DIST
PHILIPS, JANE	BAL	270	12TH WAR
PHILIPS, JEMIMA	FRE	379	PETERSVI
PHILIPS, JENNETTA A.	BAL	303	3RD WARD
PHILIPS, JESSE	CAR	218	5TH DIST
PHILIPS, JOHN	CEC	194	7TH E DI
PHILIPS, JOHN	CHA	245	HILLTOP
PHILIPS, JOHN	CEC	098	3RD E DI
PHILIPS, JOHN	BAL	462	1ST DIST
PHILIPS, JOHN	BAL	225	1ST DIST
PHILIPS, JOHN	BAL	074	2ND DIST
PHILIPS, JOHN E.	BAL	265	7TH WARD
PHILIPS, JOSEPH	BAL	292	7TH WARD
PHILIPS, JOSEPH	BAL	457	8TH WARD
PHILIPS, JOSEPH	CEC	074	NORTHEAS
PHILIPS, JOSEPH C.-BLACK	CAR	162	NO TWP L
PHILIPS, JULIE	ANN	351	3RD DIST
PHILIPS, LANTER-BLACK	CAR	151	NO TWP L
PHILIPS, LEVIN	BAL	338	3RD WARD
PHILIPS, LEWIS	BAL	069	15TH WAR
PHILIPS, LIDDY	BAL	022	4TH WARD
PHILIPS, MARGARET	CEC	011	ELKTON 3
PHILIPS, MARGARET	BAL	047	15TH WAR
PHILIPS, MARGARET	WAS	152	HAGERSTO
PHILIPS, MARTHA	BAL	102	10TH WAR
PHILIPS, MARY	WAS	134	HAGERSTO
PHILIPS, NATHAN	CAR	218	5TH DIST
PHILIPS, NOAH	FRE	292	WOODSBOR
PHILIPS, PERRY	BAL	368	3RD WARD
PHILIPS, PHEOBE	BAL	270	1ST DIST
PHILIPS, PHILIP	CAR	106	NO TWP L
PHILIPS, RACHEL	BAL	324	12TH WAR
PHILIPS, RACHEL	BAL	296	7TH WARD
PHILIPS, ROSAN	CAR	217	5TH DIST
PHILIPS, SAMUEL	CAR	218	5TH DIST
PHILIPS, SAMUEL	BAL	233	20TH WAR
PHILIPS, SAMUEL	CEC	078	NORTHEAS
PHILIPS, SAMUEL	FRE	396	PETERSVI
PHILIPS, SAMUEL	BAL	037	15TH WAR
PHILIPS, SARAH	MGM	342	CLARKSBU
PHILIPS, SHARLOTT-BLACK	CAR	122	NO TWP L
PHILIPS, STEVIN-BLACK	CAR	123	NO TWP L
PHILIPS, THOMAS	BAL	405	3RD WARD
PHILIPS, THOMAS	BAL	322	12TH WAR
PHILIPS, THOMAS	BAL	356	3RD WARD
PHILIPS, THOMAS	BAL	290	1ST DIST
PHILIPS, URIAH	CAR	218	5TH DIST
PHILIPS, URIAH C.	CAR	218	5TH DIST
PHILIPS, WESLEY	BAL	022	15TH WAR
PHILIPS, WILLIAM	BAL	245	12TH WAR
PHILIPS, WILLIAM	CEC	155	PORT DUP
PHILIPS, WILLIAM B.	FRE	234	BUCKEYST
PHILIPS, WILLIAM B.	BAL	270	7TH WARD
PHILIPS, WILLIAM B.	BAL	288	7TH WARD
PHILIPS, WILLIAM S.	TAL	113	ST MICHA
PHILIPS, WILLIAM-BLACK	CAR	136	NO TWP L
PHILIPS, ZACHARIAH	ANN	351	3RD DIST
PHILISE, MISS	BAL	129	5TH WARD
PHILLING, LOUIS	BAL	191	2ND WARD

Name	County	Page	District
PHILLIP, DANIEL L.	BAL	108	5TH WARD
PHILLIP, SUSAN	WOR	330	1ST E DI
PHILLIPE, PHILLIP	BAL	268	2ND WARD
PHILLIPS, ABRAHAM	BAL	356	13TH WAR
PHILLIPS, ANDREW	BAL	018	1ST WARD
PHILLIPS, ANN	BAL	057	10TH WAR
PHILLIPS, ANN	QUE	236	4TH E DI
PHILLIPS, ANN L.	BAL	084	18TH WAR
PHILLIPS, ANN M.	DOR	320	1ST DIST
PHILLIPS, ASA	SOM	553	TYASKIN
PHILLIPS, ASA L.	SOM	529	QUANTICO
PHILLIPS, BASIL C.	BAL	007	9TH WARD
PHILLIPS, BENJAMIN	WOR	279	BERLIN 1
PHILLIPS, BENJAMIN	DOR	327	3RD DIVI
PHILLIPS, BRISTOR	BAL	178	6TH WARD
PHILLIPS, BYARD	SOM	510	BARREN C
PHILLIPS, CAPT. JOHN	ANN	275	ANNAPOLI
PHILLIPS, CATHARINE	BAL	240	6TH WARD
PHILLIPS, CATHERINE	BAL	018	1ST WARD
PHILLIPS, CATHERINE J.	BAL	092	10TH WAR
PHILLIPS, CECELIA	BAL	184	6TH WARD
PHILLIPS, CHARLES	BAL	151	2ND DIST
PHILLIPS, CHARLES	BAL	107	5TH WARD
PHILLIPS, CHARLES W.	DOR	433	1ST DIST
PHILLIPS, CHARLOTTE A.	BAL	260	6TH WARD
PHILLIPS, CLARKSON	HAR	123	2ND DIST
PHILLIPS, COURSEY	QUE	137	1ST E DI
PHILLIPS, D.	ANN	272	ANNAPOLI
PHILLIPS, DANIEL	BAL	116	5TH WARD
PHILLIPS, DANIEL J.	QUE	130	1ST E DI
PHILLIPS, DORRATHY	BAL	263	17TH WAR
PHILLIPS, EASTER	SOM	524	BARREN C
PHILLIPS, ELIJAH	SOM	506	BARREN C
PHILLIPS, ELIZA	DOR	398	1ST DIST
PHILLIPS, ELIZA	DOR	327	3RD DIVI
PHILLIPS, ELIZABETH	BAL	234	17TH WAR
PHILLIPS, ELIZABETH	QUE	146	1ST E DI
PHILLIPS, ELIZABETH	BAL	019	4TH WARD
PHILLIPS, ELIZABETH	SOM	528	QUANTICO
PHILLIPS, ELIZABETH	SOM	504	SALISBUR
PHILLIPS, ELIZABETH	WOR	348	1ST E DI
PHILLIPS, ELLIOT	DOR	390	1ST DIST
PHILLIPS, EMALINE	SOM	528	QUANTICO
PHILLIPS, F.	BAL	142	1ST WARD
PHILLIPS, F.	BAL	138	1ST WARD
PHILLIPS, GEORGE	BAL	253	6TH WARD
PHILLIPS, GEORGE	SOM	514	BARREN C
PHILLIPS, GEORGE	WOR	209	4TH E DI
PHILLIPS, GEORGE	KEN	241	2ND DIST
PHILLIPS, GEORGE	BAL	259	17TH WAR
PHILLIPS, GEORGE	DOR	330	3RD DIVI
PHILLIPS, GEORGE W.	WOR	238	6TH E DI
PHILLIPS, GEORGE W.	ANN	276	ANNAPOLI
PHILLIPS, GILBERT	WOR	216	4TH E DI
PHILLIPS, GREENBURY	BAL	075	4TH WARD
PHILLIPS, H. R.	BAL	155	1ST WARD
PHILLIPS, HARRIET	QUE	145	1ST E DI
PHILLIPS, HENRIETTA	QUE	174	2ND E DI
PHILLIPS, HENRY	DOR	391	1ST DIST
PHILLIPS, HESTER	BAL	350	3RD WARD
PHILLIPS, HIRAM	WOR	196	8TH E DI
PHILLIPS, HUGH	BAL	252	6TH WARD
PHILLIPS, ISAAC	WOR	222	4TH E DI
PHILLIPS, ISAAC	DOR	312	1ST DIST
PHILLIPS, ISAAC J.	CEC	101	4TH E DI
PHILLIPS, J.	BAL	154	1ST WARD
PHILLIPS, JAEMS	BAL	339	13TH WAR
PHILLIPS, JAMES	BAL	283	17TH WAR
PHILLIPS, JAMES	DOR	402	1ST DIST
PHILLIPS, JAMES	KEN	236	2ND DIST
PHILLIPS, JAMES	CEC	036	CHESAPEA
PHILLIPS, JAMES	BAL	176	6TH WARD
PHILLIPS, JAMES	BAL	378	3RD WARD
PHILLIPS, JAMES	BAL	030	1ST WARD
PHILLIPS, JAMES	BAL	117	5TH WARD
PHILLIPS, JAMES	WOR	292	9TH E DI
PHILLIPS, JAMES A. BYRAD	WOR	266	BERLIN 1
PHILLIPS, JAMES H.	SOM	554	TYASKIN
PHILLIPS, JAMES R.	SOM	512	BARREN C
PHILLIPS, JAMES R.	DOR	446	1ST DIST
PHILLIPS, JAMES T.	BAL	211	6TH WARD
PHILLIPS, JAMES W.	KEN	220	2ND DIST
PHILLIPS, JAMES W.	DOR	307	1ST DIST
PHILLIPS, JANE	BAL	380	13TH WAR
PHILLIPS, JOHN	DOR	327	3RD DIVI
PHILLIPS, JOHN	DOR	327	3RD DIVI
PHILLIPS, JOHN	FRE	443	8TH E DI
PHILLIPS, JOHN	BAL	475	14TH WAR
PHILLIPS, JOHN	BAL	184	2ND WARD
PHILLIPS, JOHN	BAL	279	2ND WARD
PHILLIPS, JOHN	BAL	285	2ND WARD
PHILLIPS, JOHN	SOM	399	BRINKLEY
PHILLIPS, JOHN B.	BAL	283	2ND WARD
PHILLIPS, JOHN E.	DOR	312	1ST DIST
PHILLIPS, JOHN J.	DOR	391	1ST DIST
PHILLIPS, JOHN M.	SOM	528	QUANTICO
PHILLIPS, JOHN SR.	WOR	202	4TH E DI
PHILLIPS, JOSEPH	BAL	166	6TH WARD
PHILLIPS, JOSEPH A.	SOM	515	BARREN C
PHILLIPS, JOSEPH T.	BAL	117	5TH WARD
PHILLIPS, JOSHUA	WOR	270	BERLIN 1
PHILLIPS, JOSHUA W.	SOM	514	BARREN C
PHILLIPS, LARNHARDT	BAL	087	1ST WARD
PHILLIPS, LAVINIA	BAL	223	17TH WAR
PHILLIPS, LETITIA	DOR	334	3RD DIVI
PHILLIPS, LEVIN	DOR	402	1ST DIST
PHILLIPS, LEVIN	SOM	519	BARREN C
PHILLIPS, LLEWELLYN	BAL	169	16TH WAR
PHILLIPS, LOUIS	BAL	093	18TH WAR
PHILLIPS, LYCURGUS *	FRE	288	WOODSBOR
PHILLIPS, MAJOR	WOR	237	6TH E DI
PHILLIPS, MARGARET	QUE	236	4TH E DI
PHILLIPS, MARGARET A.	DOR	445	1ST DIST
PHILLIPS, MARGRETT	DOR	332	3RD DIVI
PHILLIPS, MARIAH	WOR	342	1ST E DI
PHILLIPS, MARK	CEC	102	4TH E DI
PHILLIPS, MARTHA E.	MGM	438	CLARKSTR
PHILLIPS, MARY	WOR	271	BERLIN 1
PHILLIPS, MARY	SOM	514	BARREN C
PHILLIPS, MARY	DOR	333	3RD DIVI
PHILLIPS, MARY	BAL	033	4TH WARD
PHILLIPS, MARY	FRE	087	FREDERIC
PHILLIPS, MARY	ANN	313	1ST DIST
PHILLIPS, MARY	ANN	420	HOWARD D
PHILLIPS, MARY A.	DOR	378	1ST DIST
PHILLIPS, MARY J.	DOR	419	1ST DIST
PHILLIPS, MARY-BLACK	WOR	317	2ND E DI
PHILLIPS, MATILDA	BAL	244	20TH WAR
PHILLIPS, MOSES	KEN	241	2ND DIST
PHILLIPS, N.A.	BAL	167	1ST WARD

PHILLIPS, NANCY SOM 489 SALISBUR
PHILLIPS, NANCY WOR 309 2ND E DI
PHILLIPS, NANCY MC G. * BAL 359 13TH WAR
PHILLIPS, NICHOLAS BAL 087 1ST WARD
PHILLIPS, NOAH SOM 512 BARREN C
PHILLIPS, PERNELL WOR 253 1ST CENS
PHILLIPS, PETER SOM 530 QUANTICO
PHILLIPS, PETER BAL 004 4TH WARD
PHILLIPS, PHEBE ANN WOR 270 BERLIN 1
PHILLIPS, PHILIP L. MGM 414 MEDLEY 3
PHILLIPS, PHILLIS DOR 324 1ST DIST
PHILLIPS, PHOEBY BAL 091 18TH WAR
PHILLIPS, POLLY WOR 315 2ND E DI
PHILLIPS, RACHAEL SOM 521 BARREN C
PHILLIPS, RACHEL DOR 327 3RD DIVI
PHILLIPS, REUBEN DOR 405 1ST DIST
PHILLIPS, RHODA SOM 530 QUANTICO
PHILLIPS, RICHARD QUE 214 3RD E DI
PHILLIPS, RICHARD QUE 144 1ST E DI
PHILLIPS, RICHARD BAL 393 3RD WARD
PHILLIPS, ROZANNA DOR 318 1ST DIST
PHILLIPS, S. BAL 142 1ST WARD
PHILLIPS, S. BAL 129 1ST WARD
PHILLIPS, SAMUEL QUE 144 1ST E DI
PHILLIPS, SAMUEL QUE 134 1ST E DI
PHILLIPS, SAMUEL BAL 476 14TH WAR
PHILLIPS, SARAH DOR 296 1ST DIST
PHILLIPS, SARAH A. BAL 200 6TH WARD
PHILLIPS, SOLOMON ANN 276 ANNAPOLI
PHILLIPS, SOLOMON BAL 420 14TH WAR
PHILLIPS, SOLOMON DOR 333 3RD DIVI
PHILLIPS, SOLONON T. DOR 350 3RD DIVI
PHILLIPS, SUSAN DOR 309 1ST DIST
PHILLIPS, SUSAN BAL 426 14TH WAR
PHILLIPS, THOMAS DOR 318 1ST DIST
PHILLIPS, THOMAS BAL 304 17TH WAR
PHILLIPS, THOMAS H. BAL 187 2ND WARD
PHILLIPS, THOMAS H. SOM 526 QUANTICO
PHILLIPS, THOMAS H. MGM 438 CLARKSTR
PHILLIPS, THOMAS S. BAL 057 10TH WAR
PHILLIPS, THOMAS W. WOR 229 6TH E DI
PHILLIPS, URIAH SOM 554 TYASKIN
PHILLIPS, VACHEL ANN 420 HOWARD D
PHILLIPS, WESLY* DOR 404 1ST DIST
PHILLIPS, WHITTINGTON WOR 350 1ST E DI
PHILLIPS, WHITTY SOM 525 BARREN C
PHILLIPS, WILLIAM SOM 525 BARREN C
PHILLIPS, WILLIAM DOR 398 1ST DIST
PHILLIPS, WILLIAM BAL 232 17TH WAR
PHILLIPS, WILLIAM BAL 340 13TH WAR
PHILLIPS, WILLIAM QUE 137 1ST E DI
PHILLIPS, WILLIAM BAL 157 1ST WARD
PHILLIPS, WILLIAM BAL 218 2ND WARD
PHILLIPS, WILLIAM J. BAL 338 3RD WARD
PHILLIPS, WILLIAM M. BAL 205 6TH WARD
PHILLIPS, WILLIAM M. SOM 506 BARREN C
PHILLIPS, WILLIAM S. BAL 342 3RD WARD
PHILLIPS, WILLY DOR 378 1ST DIST
PHILLIPS,HOLLINS BAL 065 1ST WARD
PHILLIPS,JAMES B. BAL 114 1ST WARD
PHILLIPS,PETER BAL 244 2ND WARD
PHILLIPS,ROBERT BAL 128 1ST WARD
PHILLIPS,THERESA BAL 051 1ST WARD
PHILLIPS,WILLIAM FRE 031 FREDERIC
PHILLPS, JOHN JR. WOR 209 4TH E DI
PHILOPS, JAMES-BLACK CAR 126 NO TWP L
PHILOPT, EDWARD P. BAL 244 1ST DIST
PHILPET, BRIAN JR. FRE 391 PETERSVI
PHILPET, BRIAN SR. FRE 391 PETERSVI
PHILPHINE, MARY BAL 043 1ST WARD
PHILPOT, ELIZABETH BAL 154 11TH WAR
PHILPOT, HANNAH BAL 419 14TH WAR
PHILPOT, HANNAH BAL 041 1ST WARD
PHILPOT, JOHN BAL 049 2ND DIST
PHILPOT, WILLIAM BAL 037 18TH WAR
PHILPOTT, BENJAMIN FRE 379 PETERSVI
PHILPS, W.H. BAL 173 19TH WAR
PHINES, MARTHA BAL 251 12TH WAR
PHINIX, MARTHA BAL 061 10TH WAR
PHINIX, THOMAS BAL 061 10TH WAR
PHIPEN, THOASM C. WOR 238 6TH E DI
PHIPP, ANN BAL 278 12TH WAR
PHIPPEN, ELIJAH* SOM 497 SALISBUR
PHIPPEN, MARGARET SOM 507 BARREN C
PHIPPEN, ROBERT W. SOM 507 BARREN C
PHIPPEN, THOMAS SOM 506 BARREN C
PHIPPS, J. W. ANN 411 8TH DIST
PHIPPS, JOHN ANN 410 8TH DIST
PHIPPS, JOHN E. WOR 231 6TH E DI
PHIPPS, LOUISA BAL 245 6TH WARD
PHIPPS, MARY BAL 251 12TH WAR
PHIPPS, NATHAN ANN 401 8TH DIST
PHIPPS, NEILSON ANN 404 8TH DIST
PHIPPS, RANDOLPH ANN 355 3RD DIST
PHIPPS, RICHARD ANN 404 8TH DIST
PHIPPS, ROGER ANN 307 1ST DIST
PHIPPS, THOMAS ANN 409 8TH DIST
PHIPS, RACHEL L. BAL 454 8TH WARD
PHIPS, SAMUEL S. FRE 283 WOODSBOR
PHISIC, WILLIAM CEC 186 7TH E DI
PHITTER, HENERY HAR 196 3RD DIST
PHLEGER, EDWARD FRE 073 FREDERIC
PHLER, JOHN CAR 301 1ST DIST
PHLUGER, MARY FRE 207 BUCKEYST
PHOEEUS, ADELAD BAL 064 18TH WAR
PHOEBUS, JAMES SOM 441 DAMES QU
PHOEBUS, JAMES A. SOM 430 PRINCESS
PHOEBUS, JANE SOM 458 DAMES QU
PHOEBUS, JOHN BAL 093 18TH WAR
PHOEBUS, SALLY SOM 437 DAMES QU
PHOEBUS, THOMAS SOM 437 DAMES QU
PHOEBUS, THORNTON SOM 439 DAMES QU
PHOELIN, MORRIS ALL 057 10TH E.D
PHOENIX, LAVINIA BAL 056 10TH WAR
PHOENIX, MARY WAS 224 1ST DIST
PHREANER, WILLIAM WAS 296 1ST DIST
PHRIEIG, SARAH BAL 238 2ND WARD
PHRISBY, LUCINDER HAR 184 3RD DIST
PHRISBY, SANDY HAR 206 3RD DIST
PHRODER, FRANCIS FRE 031 FREDERIC
PHUCKER, JOSIAH ALL 061 10TH E.D
PHYFEE, CHRISTIAN BAL 432 8TH WARD
PHYFER, JOHN G. BAL 372 8TH WARD
PHYSIC, EDMUND CEC 182 7TH E DI
PHYSIC, EVALINA CEC 143 7TH E DI
PHYSIC, WASHINGTON CEC 197 7TH E DI
PICCIOLI, GEOSUE * BAL 321 20TH WAR
PICE, JOHN WAS 299 1ST DIST
PICE, WILLIAM HAR 189 3RD DIST
PICHON, FRANCIS BAL 118 1ST WARD
PICHOT, LOUIS PRI 086 QUEEN AN
PICK, CHARLES F. BAL 080 10TH WAR
PICK, EDWARD BAL 079 10TH WAR
PICKAEEREL, WILLIAM B. CHA 291 MIDDLETO
PICKAEREL, JOSEPH CHA 251 MIDDLETO
PICKAEREL, JOSIA CHA 253 MIDDLETO
PICKEL, SELEST BAL 259 2ND WARD
PICKELL, GEORGE BAL 191 2ND WARD
PICKELL, JOHN BAL 257 12TH WAR
PICKELL, JOHN BAL 227 1ST DIST
PICKELLS, PETER PRI 036 VANSVILL
PICKELLS, WHITINGTON CAR 120 NO TWP L
PICKEN, LEONARD FRE 129 CREAGERS
PICKENS, MARY FRE 223 BUCKEYST
PICKENS, THOMAS FRE 385 PETERSVI
PICKENSCHIRT, GEORGE BAL 081 10TH WAR
PICKERAM, SARAH DOR 312 1ST DIST
PICKERELL, A. CHA 289 BOJANTOW
PICKERING, AMANDA BAL 026 1ST WARD
PICKERING, JOHN BAL 026 1ST WARD
PICKERING, JOHN BAL 040 1ST WARD
PICKERING, MARY TAL 065 EASTON T
PICKERING, NANCY CAR 092 NO TWP L
PICKERING, SAMUEL BAL 013 4TH WARD
PICKERING, SAMUEL BAL 176 2ND DIST
PICKERING, WILLIAM BAL 444 14TH WAR
PICKERS, JACOB MGM 431 CLARKSTR
PICKERS, JACOB C. MGM 431 CLARKSTR
PICKERSGALL, MARY BAL 017 4TH WARD
PICKERT, EDWARD BAL 314 12TH WAR
PICKERT, JOHBN BAL 095 1ST WARD
PICKET, AMELIA CAR 230 5TH DIST
PICKET, AMELIA CAR 226 5TH DIST
PICKET, AQUILLA CAR 372 9TH DIST
PICKET, AUGUSTA CAR 228 5TH DIST
PICKET, CHARLES CAR 362 9TH DIST
PICKET, CHARLES W. CAR 226 5TH DIST
PICKET, DANIEL BAL 378 1ST DIST
PICKET, EZEKIAL CAR 271 WESTMINS
PICKET, EZEKIEL CAR 371 9TH DIST
PICKET, JESSE B. H. CAR 226 5TH DIST
PICKET, JOHN B. HAR 147 3RD DIST
PICKET, JOHNATHAN CAR 225 5TH DIST
PICKET, LUCRECY A. CAR 225 5TH DIST
PICKET, ORLANA H. FRE 248 NEW MARK
PICKET, SUSAN WAS 145 HAGERSTO
PICKET, THOMAS CAR 226 5TH DIST
PICKET, THOMAS CAR 359 9TH DIST
PICKET, WARNER CAR 228 5TH DIST
PICKET, WILLIAM CAR 372 9TH DIST
PICKET, WILLIAM CAR 367 9TH DIST
PICKET, WINCHESTER CAR 225 5TH DIST
PICKETT, BERRY C. ANN 506 HOWARD D
PICKETT, BLANCH BAL 176 6TH WARD
PICKETT, CATHERINE BAL 378 8TH WARD
PICKETT, CHARLES ANN 510 HOWARD D
PICKETT, CHARLES BAL 303 20TH WAR
PICKETT, ELIZABETH BAL 306 20TH WAR
PICKETT, HENRY WAS 155 HAGERSTO
PICKETT, JEROME* BAL 373 3RD WARD
PICKETT, JOHN BAL 272 12TH WAR
PICKETT, JOHNZEE ANN 456 HOWARD D
PICKETT, ROBERT BAL 176 6TH WARD
PICKING, JOHN FRE 186 5TH E DI
PICKING, LEWIS BAL 303 20TH WAR
PICKING, MARY A.E. FRE 186 5TH E DI
PICKING, THOMAS FRE 136 CREAGERS
PICKINON, WILLIAM DOR 323 1ST DIST
PICKIRCH, SISTER LYDIA FRE 197 5TH E DI
PICKLE, ELIZABETH CEC 161 6TH E DI
PICKMAN, GILBERT BAL 175 2ND WARD
PICKNELL, J.C. BAL 161 1ST WARD
PICKRELL, JOHN F. BAL 138 18TH WAR
PICKRELL, SARAH MISS- BAL 315 20TH WAR
PIE, CHARLES CAR 288 7TH DIST
PIE, JERIMIAH WAS 143 2ND DIST
PIE, RACHAEL CAR 271 WESTMINS
PIE, ROSSITTA BAL 128 11TH WAR
PIE, SAMUEL WAS 137 2ND DIST
PIEARCE, THOMAS * BAL 270 1ST DIST
PIEPINBRINKER, FRANZ ANN 426 HOWARD D
PIER, DANIEL* BAL 316 3RD WARD
PIER, DANIEL-MULATTO BAL 239 2ND WARD
PIER, LIDIA BAL 461 1ST DIST
PIER, MARY BAL 401 8TH WARD
PIERA, RICHARD BAL 027 9TH WARD
PIERA, WILLIAM H. CEC 052 1ST E DI
PIERCE, ANDREW R. CEC 166 6TH E DI
PIERCE, ANN BAL 463 1ST DIST
PIERCE, ANN ANN 417 HOWARD D
PIERCE, ANN ANN 448 HOWARD D
PIERCE, CATHARINE B. CEC 052 1ST E DI
PIERCE, CHARLES ALL 127 4TH E.D.
PIERCE, DAVID BAL 099 5TH WARD
PIERCE, DAVID BAL 170 1ST WARD
PIERCE, DAVIDSON D. CEC 022 ELKTON 3
PIERCE, ELI QUE 136 1ST E DI
PIERCE, ELIAS QUE 174 2ND E DI
PIERCE, ELIJAH CEC 129 6TH E DI
PIERCE, ELIZABETH HAR 171 3RD DIST
PIERCE, EMANUEL BAL 357 1ST DIST
PIERCE, EMANUEL BAL 267 1ST DIST
PIERCE, GEORGE BAL 196 17TH WAR
PIERCE, GEORGE C. ANN 482 HOWARD D
PIERCE, GEORGE W. BAL 350 7TH WARD
PIERCE, HARRIET ANN 274 ANNAPOLI
PIERCE, HARRIETT BAL 096 5TH WARD
PIERCE, HENRY MGM 349 BERRYS D
PIERCE, HIRAM ALL 128 4TH E.D.
PIERCE, JAMES BAL 224 1ST DIST
PIERCE, JAMES BAL 460 8TH WARD
PIERCE, JAMES L. BAL 423 1ST DIST
PIERCE, JANE BAL 381 13TH WAR
PIERCE, JOHN BAL 095 5TH WARD
PIERCE, JOHN ANN 274 ANNAPOLI
PIERCE, JOHN A. BAL 403 1ST DIST
PIERCE, JOHN W. WAS 149 2ND DIST
PIERCE, JOHN-BLACK QUE 164 2ND E DI
PIERCE, JOHN-BLACK QUE 152 1ST E DI
PIERCE, JOSEPH BAL 363 1ST DIST
PIERCE, JOSEPH ALL 220 CUMBERLA
PIERCE, JOSEPH S. BAL 316 1ST DIST
PIERCE, JOSEPH W. BAL 248 1ST DIST
PIERCE, JOSHUA MGM 331 CRACKLIN
PIERCE, LENOX ALL 187 9TH E.D.
PIERCE, LEVE BAL 377 1ST DIST
PIERCE, LEWIS D. ALL 153 6TH E.D.
PIERCE, MARGARET CEC 166 6TH E DI
PIERCE, MARGARET BAL 213 11TH WAR
PIERCE, MARTHA E.-BLACK QUE 146 1ST E DI
PIERCE, MARY CEC 087 4TH E DI
PIERCE, MARY BAL 150 19TH WAR
PIERCE, MARY BAL 395 1ST DIST
PIERCE, MARY BAL 364 1ST DIST
PIERCE, MARY BAL 095 5TH WARD
PIERCE, MARY BAL 375 8TH WARD
PIERCE, MARY A. ANN 437 HOWARD D
PIERCE, MARY M. BAL 351 7TH WARD
PIERCE, MARY T. FRE 065 FREDERIC
PIERCE, MATTHEW CEC 012 ELKTON 3
PIERCE, MRS. E. BAL 220 17TH WAR
PIERCE, MYERS ANN 433 HOWARD D
PIERCE, RACHEL CEC 166 6TH E DI
PIERCE, RACHEL C. BAL 035 9TH WARD
PIERCE, RACHEL E. BAL 364 1ST DIST
PIERCE, RICHARD BAL 456 8TH WARD
PIERCE, SAMUEL CEC 168 6TH E DI
PIERCE, SARAH BAL 189 19TH WAR
PIERCE, SARAH J. CEC 163 6TH E DI
PIERCE, THOMAS CEC 077 NORTHEAS
PIERCE, THOMAS BAL 442 8TH WARD
PIERCE, THOMAS BAL 028 9TH WARD
PIERCE, THOMAS ALL 209 CUMBERLA
PIERCE, THOMAS BAL 270 1ST DIST
PIERCE, VIOLETTA BAL 364 1ST DIST
PIERCE, WILLIAM BAL 422 8TH WARD
PIERCE, WILLIAM BAL 077 2ND DIST
PIERCE, WILLIAM CEC 087 4TH E DI
PIERCE, WILLIAM CEC 165 6TH E DI
PIERCE, WILLIAM CEC 136 6TH E DI
PIERCE, WILLIAM BAL 016 4TH WARD
PIERCE, WILLIAM HAR 191 3RD DIST
PIERCE, WILLIAM H. BAL 337 7TH WARD
PIERCE, WILLIAM H.H. BAL 204 11TH WAR
PIERCEN, STEPHEN HAR 203 3RD DIST
PIERCESON, JOSEPH BAL 264 1ST DIST
PIERCEY, JACOB H. BAL 413 8TH WARD
PIERCEY, JOHN BAL 425 8TH WARD
PIERCEY, JOHN BAL 323 7TH WARD
PIERCY, ALGERNON DOR 451 1ST DIST
PIERCY, JOSEPH B. F. DOR 411 1ST DIST
PIERCY, RICHARD W. DOR 404 1ST DIST
PIERPOINT, ABALINE BAL 368 1ST DIST
PIERPOINT, GEORGE BAL 462 1ST DIST
PIERPOINT, JAMES BAL 442 14TH WAR
PIERPOINT, JOHN BAL 063 18TH WAR
PIERPOINT, JOSEPH BAL 377 1ST DIST
PIERPOINT, THOMAS BAL 367 1ST DIST
PIERPOINT, WALTER BAL 370 1ST DIST
PIERPOINT, WILLIAM BAL 348 1ST DIST
PIERPONT, BURNS ANN 461 HOWARD D
PIERSBAUGH, HENRY WAS 153 HAGERSTO
PIERSOL, JOHN BAL 053 2ND DIST
PIERSOL, THOMAS BAL 053 2ND DIST
PIERSON, ABERT BAL 037 15TH WAR
PIERSON, ALLEN CEC 127 5TH E DI
PIERSON, AMOS CEC 141 6TH E DI
PIERSON, BENJAMIN CEC 194 7TH E DI
PIERSON, CLOUD CEC 129 6TH E DI
PIERSON, JAMES C. CEC 131 6TH E DI
PIERSON, JESSE CEC 091 4TH E DI
PIERSON, JOHN BAL 128 1ST WARD
PIERSON, JOSEPH CEC 141 6TH E DI
PIERSON, LYDIA CEC 004 ELKTON 3
PIERSON, MARY A. CEC 129 6TH E DI
PIERSON, ROHANNA CEC 141 6TH E DI
PIERSON, SUSANNA CEC 128 5TH E DI
PIERSON, THOMAS BAL 339 7TH WARD
PIERSON, THOMAS J. BAL 020 15TH WAR
PIERSON, WILLIAM BAL 290 12TH WAR
PIERSON, WILLIAM HAR 140 2ND DIST
PIERZIER, ROBERT * CHA 237 HILLTOP
PIES, CHARLES BAL 438 14TH WAR
PIET, JOHN B. BAL 134 11TH WAR
PIFER, JACOB BAL 400 1ST DIST
PIFSER, ELIAS * WAS 052 2ND SUBD
PIGGOT, AUSTIN BAL 299 12TH WAR
PIGGOT, ROBERT BAL 360 3RD WARD
PIGMAN, FANNY ALL 234 CUMBERLA
PIGMAN, HARRIET ALL 262 CUMBERLA
PIGMAN, NATHAN BAL 111 15TH WAR
PIGMAN, SMALLWOOD ALL 262 CUMBERLA
PIGOT, ELIZABETH PRI 056 AQUASCO
PIKE, CALEB-MULATTO FRE 431 8TH E DI
PIKE, FRANCIS WAS 099 2ND DIST
PIKE, FRITZ BAL 145 19TH WAR
PIKE, HENRY BAL 360 13TH WAR
PIKE, JANE M.-BLACK ST 325 4TH E DI
PIKE, MARIA BAL 266 20TH WAR
PIKE, MARTHA BAL 114 1ST WARD
PIKE, MARY BAL 146 19TH WAR
PIKE, MARY FRE 069 FREDERIC
PIKE, ROSA E. BAL 010 4TH WARD
PIKE, SUSAN BAL 293 20TH WAR
PIKER, MICHAEL BAL 211 19TH WAR
PILCELTON, EDWARD BAL 356 8TH WARD
PILCHARD, ERASTUS WOR 350 1ST E DI
PILCHER, DENARD WOR 346 1ST E DI
PILCHER, HENRY WOR 332 1ST E DI
PILE, CONRAD BAL 190 19TH WAR
PILE, ISAAC C. BAL 292 7TH WARD
PILE, LEWIS CEC 133 6TH E DI
PILE, SAMUEL BAL 350 7TH WARD
PILES, CHARLES PRI 011 BLADENSB
PILES, EBEANASOR BAL 304 1ST DIST
PILES, FRANCIS PRI 118 PISCATAW
PILES, FRANK CHA 232 HILLTOP
PILES, H. PRI 117 PISCATAW
PILES, HILEARY MGM 412 MEDLEY 3
PILES, JOHN MGM 421 MEDLEY 3
PILES, JOHN PRI 119 PISCATAW
PILES, MARY BAL 386 8TH WARD
PILES, RICHARD MGM 426 MEDLEY 3
PILES, SARAH ALL 172 7TH E.D.
PILES, THOMAS PRI 099 SPALDING
PILES, WILLIAM H. PRI 098 SPALDING
PILES, WILLIAM H. MGM 390 ROCKERLE
PILES, WILLIAM V. PRI 098 SPALDING
PILIPS, LYDIA BAL 018 2ND DIST
PILKENTON, GEORGE BAL 359 8TH WARD
PILKETON, PETER CEC 104 4TH E DI
PILKILTON, IGNATIUS ST 324 4TH E DI
PILKINGTON, JOSEPH CEC 105 3RD E DI
PILKINGTON, LAWRENCE CEC 105 3RD E DI
PILKINGTON, WILLIAM* BAL 375 3RD WARD
PILKITTON, WILLIAM ST 330 4TH E DI
PILL, ELIZABETH BAL 090 18TH WAR
PILLER, SARAH ALL 215 CUMBERLA
PILLHELFEFE, JOHN BAL 113 2ND DIST
PILLOW, BENJAMIN FRE 013 FREDERIC

PILLSBEE, RICHARD	BAL	214	6TH WARD
PILSBURG, J.	BAL	118	1ST WARD
PILSCH, ELIZABETH	BAL	072	2ND DIST
PILSCH, GOTTIEB	BAL	071	2ND DIST
PILSON, GEORGE	BAL	082	2ND DIST
PILSON, JOHN	BAL	410	8TH WARD
PILSON, MARTHA	BAL	372	1ST DIST
PILSON, ROBERT	PRI	025	VANSVILL
PILSON, SAMUEL	BAL	115	2ND DIST
PILSON,EMMA	BAL	025	2ND DIST
PIMMONDS, THOMAS	QUE	125	1ST E DI
PIMPLE, MARY	BAL	267	7TH WARD
PIN, ELIZABETH	BAL	077	15TH WAR
PINAWELL, MITCHELL	WOR	242	1ST CENS
PINCER, WILLIAM	DOR	431	1ST DIST
PINCHAM, MARTHA	BAL	095	10TH WAR
PINCHER, MARTHA	BAL	194	17TH WAR
PINCHER, MARY	BAL	194	17TH WAR
PINCKFIELD, MARY A.	TAL	024	EASTON D
PINCKNEY, CHARLES	BAL	205	19TH WAR
PINCKNEY, EMILY	BAL	361	13TH WAR
PINCKNEY, FREDERICK	BAL	356	13TH WAR
PINCKNEY, LONDON	ANN	321	2ND DIST
PINCKNEY, SALLY	ANN	322	2ND DIST
PINDALL, THOMAS	BAL	075	4TH WARD
PINCAR, ANN	QUE	231	4TH E DI
PINDAR, JAMES	BAL	342	3RD WARD
PINDAR, WILLIAM	QUE	171	2ND E DI
PINDAR, WILLIAM	QUE	196	3RD E DI
PINDE, CHARLES*	DOR	436	1ST DIST
PINDE, DURNUM	DOR	421	1ST DIST
PINDE, ELI*	DOR	436	1ST DIST
PINDE, JOSEPH*	DOR	435	1ST DIST
PINDE, MARGARET	DOR	434	1ST DIST
PINDE, MARY*	DOR	436	1ST DIST
PINDE, MARY*	DOR	435	1ST DIST
PINDE, NOAH*	DOR	434	1ST DIST
PINDE, THOMAS*	DOR	444	1ST DIST
PINDEL, MATTHEW	BAL	130	16TH WAR
PINDELL, ACI	BAL	178	6TH WARD
PINDELL, ELIZABETH	ANN	277	ANNAPOLI
PINDELL, LAURA V.	BAL	136	18TH WAR
PINDELL, MISSOURI	BAL	214	11TH WAR
PINDELL, RINALDO	ANN	299	1ST DIST
PINDELL, ROBERT G.	ANN	408	8TH DIST
PINDELL, SALLY	BAL	249	2ND WARD
PINDELL, THOMAS M.	ANN	270	ANNAPOLI
PINDELL, WILLIAM	BAL	240	20TH WAR
PINDEN, JOSEPHINE *	BAL	300	12TH WAR
PINDER, ANNA	DOR	424	1ST DIST
PINDER, CHARLES*	DOR	436	1ST DIST
PINDER, ELI*	DOR	436	1ST DIST
PINDER, HENRY	DOR	464	1ST DIST
PINDER, JAMES	DOR	428	1ST DIST
PINDER, JOSEPH*	DOR	435	1ST DIST
PINDER, MARGARETT	DOR	307	1ST DIST
PINDER, MARY	BAL	150	11TH WAR
PINDER, MARY*	DOR	436	1ST DIST
PINDER, MARY*	DOR	435	1ST DIST
PINDER, MARY*	DOR	436	1ST DIST
PINDER, NOAH*	DOR	434	1ST DIST
PINDER, RICHARD*	DOR	436	1ST DIST
PINDER, ROBERT	DOR	435	1ST DIST
PINDER, THOMAS	DOR	307	1ST DIST
PINDER, THOMAS*	DOR	444	1ST DIST
PINDER, WILLIAM	QUE	155	2ND E DI
PINDLE, ADOLPHUS	BAL	383	1ST DIST
PINDLE, CATHERINE	BAL	339	3RD WARD
PINDLE, CHARLOTTE	BAL	216	6TH WARD
PINDLE, ELIJAH	BAL	343	3RD WARD
PINDLE, ELIZABETH	ANN	399	8TH DIST
PINDLE, ELIZABETH	BAL	298	1ST DIST
PINDLE, ELIZABETH	BAL	336	7TH WARD
PINDLE, ISAIAH	BAL	156	5TH WARD
PINDLE, J. N.	ANN	401	8TH DIST
PINDLE, JACOB	BAL	438	14TH WAR
PINDLE, JAMES	BAL	344	3RD WARD
PINDLE, JAMES P.	BAL	319	3RD WARD
PINDLE, JOSEPH	BAL	335	7TH WARD
PINDLE, LEWIS	BAL	215	6TH WARD
PINDLE, RICHARD	BAL	207	6TH WARD
PINDLE, RICHARD	ANN	479	HOWARD D
PINDLE, RICHARD	WAS	126	2ND DIST
PINDLE, WILLIAM	BAL	457	8TH WARD
PINE, CHARLES	BAL	174	1ST WARD
PINE, ELSY	BAL	267	20TH WAR
PINE, JESSE	BAL	286	1ST DIST
PINE, REVERDY	BAL	121	1ST WARD
PINE, ROERDY	BAL	149	1ST WARD
PINE, WILLIAM	KEN	266	1ST DIST
PINER, ELIZABETH	KEN	301	3RD DIST
PINER, GEORGE	CEC	059	1ST E DI
PINER, JAMES	KEN	255	1ST DIST
PINER, MAFORD	KEN	292	3RD DIST
PINER, MARIA JANE	DOR	407	1ST DIST
PINER, MARIA*	DOR	407	1ST DIST
PINER, ORANGE	KEN	297	3RD DIST
PINER, RICHARD	KEN	262	1ST DIST
PINER, SARAH	KEN	285	3RD DIST
PINES, HENTSON	TAL	033	EASTON D
PINES, JANE	BAL	456	14TH WAR
PINES, JANE	BAL	376	1ST DIST
PINES, R.	BAL	172	1ST WARD
PINES, REVEDY	BAL	174	1ST WARD
PINEY, HINTSON	TAL	020	EASTON D
PINFIELD, ELLENOR	TAL	029	EASTON D
PINFIELD, JAMES	QUE	196	3RD E DI
PINFIELD, THOMAS	KEN	259	1ST DIST
PINGLETON, AREY *	BAL	100	18TH WAR
PINHETT, SEANA	TAL	075	EASTON T
PINHIND, BENNETT*	TAL	017	EASTON D
PINHIND, PIRHAL*	TAL	025	EASTON D
PININGTON, N.C.	HAR	155	3RD DIST
PINION, FRANCES A.	HAR	001	1ST DIST
PINION, HARRETT	HAR	150	3RD DIST
PINION, JAMES	HAR	127	2ND DIST
PINION, SUSAN	BAL	253	6TH WARD
PINK, NICKOLAS	BAL	146	5TH WARD
PINK, WILLIAM	CEC	197	7TH E DI
PINKEL, JAMES*	DOR	434	1ST DIST
PINKEON, MILLY *	BAL	124	2ND DIST
PINKERT, ALEXANDER	BAL	025	15TH WAR
PINKERT, CHRLES	BAL	025	15TH WAR
PINKERTON, JANETT	WAS	180	BOONSBOR
PINKERTON, JOHN	BAL	034	4TH WARD
PINKERTON, MARY A.	BAL	055	15TH WAR
PINKERTON, SAMUEL	BAL	228	12TH WAR
PINKERTON, SAMUEL	BAL	109	2ND DIST
PINKET, CHARLES	DOR	460	1ST DIST
PINKET, DANIEL	CAR	159	NO TWP L
PINKET, DRAPER	DOR	466	1ST DIST
PINKET, EBEN	DOR	464	1ST DIST
PINKET, EDWARD	BAL	214	17TH WAR
PINKET, ELIJAH	WOR	230	6TH E DI
PINKET, ELIZA	DOR	413	1ST DIST
PINKET, JAMES*	DOR	434	1ST DIST
PINKET, JOB	DOR	448	1ST DIST
PINKET, JOHN	DOR	389	1ST DIST
PINKET, JOSIAH	BAL	408	8TH WARD
PINKET, MARY	DOR	311	1ST DIST
PINKET, RALF	DOR	451	1ST DIST
PINKET, THOMAS	DOR	319	1ST DIST
PINKET, THOMAS	DOR	448	1ST DIST
PINKETT, ABREHAM	BAL	228	17TH WAR
PINKETT, CHARLES	DOR	311	1ST DIST
PINKETT, CHARLOTTE	SOM	490	SALISBUR
PINKETT, DENARD	SOM	504	SALISBUR
PINKETT, HUGHY	SOM	505	SALISBUR
PINKETT, MARY	SOM	490	SALISBUR
PINKETT, SALLY	SOM	494	SALISBUR
PINKETTE, JOHN*	BAL	315	3RD WARD
PINKFIELD, ELIZA AN	QUE	208	3RD E DI
PINKFIELD, HENRIETTA	QUE	145	1ST E DI
PINKFIELD, WILLIAM J.	QUE	215	3RD E DI
PINKIND, JOHN H.	QUE	249	5TH E DI
PINKIND, MARY E.	TAL	065	EASTON T
PINKINE, MICHAEL	CAR	107	NO TWP L
PINKINE, THOMAS C.	QUE	164	2ND E DI
PINKLEY, JACOB	WAS	171	FUNKSTOW
PINKNEY, ANN	BAL	182	11TH WAR
PINKNEY, ANN	ANN	269	ANNAPOLI
PINKNEY, CAROLNE	BAL	128	2ND DIST
PINKNEY, HAMMOND	BAL	296	1ST DIST
PINKNEY, HENRIETTA	ALL	257	CUMBERLA
PINKNEY, HETTY	BAL	206	19TH WAR
PINKNEY, JAMES	HAR	202	3RD DIST
PINKNEY, JAMES	BAL	346	7TH WARD
PINKNEY, JANE B. MRS-	BAL	315	20TH WAR
PINKNEY, JANE R.	BAL	157	11TH WAR
PINKNEY, JEANNET	BAL	306	12TH WAR
PINKNEY, JOHN	TAL	055	EASTON D
PINKNEY, JOSEPH	TAL	052	EASTON D
PINKNEY, JOSEPH	TAL	091	ST MICHA
PINKNEY, LEWIS	BAL	397	8TH WARD
PINKNEY, MARIA	BAL	127	11TH WAR
PINKNEY, MOSES	BAL	256	20TH WAR
PINKNEY, MRS.	ANN	282	ANNAPOLI
PINKNEY, NINIAN DR. *	TAL	075	EASTON T
PINKNEY, NOAH	WAS	090	2ND SUBD
PINKNEY, PERRY	TAL	079	ST MICHA
PINKNEY, REACHEL	BAL	111	18TH WAR
PINKNEY, REBECCA	BAL	157	11TH WAR
PINKNEY, SAMUEL	TAL	042	EASTON D
PINKNEY, T.	BAL	221	12TH WAR
PINKNEY, WILLIAM	BAL	185	11TH WAR
PINKNEY, WILLIAM	PRI	005	BLADENSB
PINKNY, BARNE-BLACK	CAR	404	2ND DIST
PINLE, MARY	BAL	156	5TH WARD
PINN, ELIZA	BAL	460	1ST DIST
PINNELL, REBECCA	BAL	157	11TH WAR
PINNIN, SARLOTT	HAR	187	3RD DIST
PINNISE, GEORGE W.	BAL	132	1ST WARD
PINO, ANTHONY	BAL	031	4TH WARD
PINTER, BENJAMIN R.	WOR	225	4TH E DI
PINTIEEA, GEORGE *	QUE	238	5TH E DI
PINTO, JOHN V.	SOM	435	PRINCESS
PINTOE, PATTY	SOM	465	HANGARY
PIPE, RACHAEL	BAL	166	11TH WAR
PIPENBRICKER, CAROLINE	BAL	263	1ST DIST
PIPENBROCK, ANNA	ANN	435	HOWARD D
PIPER,	QUE	132	1ST E DI
PIPER, ALFRED	ALL	161	6TH E.D.
PIPER, CAROLINE	BAL	343	1ST DIST
PIPER, D. A.	BAL	057	15TH WAR
PIPER, DANIEL	WAS	052	2ND SUBD
PIPER, DANIEL	WAS	001	WILLIAMS
PIPER, DAVID	WAS	062	2ND SUBD
PIPER, DAVID	WAS	189	1ST DIST
PIPER, ELIAS *	WAS	052	2ND SUBD
PIPER, EVE	WAS	044	2ND SUBD
PIPER, FANNY	BAL	056	15TH WAR
PIPER, HENRY	WAS	060	2ND SUBD
PIPER, JAMES COL-	ANN	412	HOWARD D
PIPER, JOHN	ALL	185	9TH E.D.
PIPER, JOHN	BAL	342	1ST DIST
PIPER, JOHN	WAS	209	1ST DIST
PIPER, JOHN	BAL	139	19TH WAR
PIPER, JOHN	BAL	243	20TH WAR
PIPER, JOHN F.	BAL	127	11TH WAR
PIPER, JOHN G.	CAR	393	2ND DIST
PIPER, M. J.	ALL	173	7TH E.D.
PIPER, MARY	CAR	272	WESTMINS
PIPER,-MARY	WAS	121	HAGERSTO
PIPER, MICHAEL	BAL	084	18TH WAR
PIPER, PETER	BAL	461	1ST DIST
PIPER, PHILIP	BAL	197	19TH WAR
PIPER, RICHARD F.	BAL	106	10TH WAR
PIPER, SUSAN	WAS	094	2ND SUBD
PIPER, THOMAS	WAS	055	2ND SUBD
PIPER, WILLIAM	KEN	265	1ST DIST
PIPER,GODFREY	CAR	393	2ND DIST
PIPERBRING, PETER	ALL	224	CUMBERLA
PIPES, ALFRED	QUE	238	5TH E DI
PIPES, CAROLINE	BAL	093	10TH WAR
PIPES, CAROLINE	BAL	343	3RD WARD
PIPES, CAROLINE	BAL	203	17TH WAR
PIPES, FREDERICK	QUE	238	5TH E DI
PIPES, JAMES	KEN	312	3RD DIST
PIPFER, MATTHIAS	BAL	452	14TH WAR
PIPPEN, JAMES	CAR	073	NO TWP L
PIPPEN, MARY E.	CAR	073	NO TWP L
PIPPIN, ASA	QUE	146	1ST E DI
PIPPIN, JAMES	QUE	160	2ND E DI
PIPPIN, JEANETTE	QUE	161	2ND E DI
PIPPIN, JOHN	QUE	146	1ST E DI
PIPPIN, JOHN D.	CAR	071	NO TWP L
PIPPIN, MILKY	KEN	234	2ND DIST
PIPPIN, ROBERT	CAR	102	NO TWP L
PIPPIN, THOMAS	KEN	313	3RD DIST
PIPPS, BEN	PRI	081	QUEEN AN
PIQUETT, DANIEL	BAL	271	17TH WAR
PIQUETT, JOHN P.	BAL	103	18TH WAR
PIQUETT, MARY	BAL	103	18TH WAR
PIQUIETT, MARY	BAL	103	18TH WAR
PIRCE, JOEL	ANN	459	HOWARD D
PIRCE, LAMIN	BAL	209	19TH WAR
PIRCHINEL, PIRHAL*	TAL	025	EASTON D
PIRELY, JAMES	BAL	290	1ST DIST
PIRIE, GEORGE	BAL	034	18TH WAR
PIRIE, JANE	BAL	034	18TH WAR
PISCUD, EDWARD	BAL	047	9TH WARD
PISEL, CATHARINE	ALL	035	2ND E.D.
PISEL, JACOB	ALL	035	2ND E.D.
PISEL, JOSIAH	ALL	035	2ND E.D.
PISPER, ELIZA	BAL	218	12TH WAR
PISTER, GEORGE	BAL	359	13TH WAR
PISTER, MARY	BAL	265	12TH WAR
PISTON, ANDREW	BAL	006	9TH WARD
PISTON, SAMUEL	BAL	258	12TH WAR
PISTRA, JOHN	BAL	061	4TH WARD
PIT, AMOS	HAR	187	3RD DIST
PIT, MARTHY	HAR	182	3RD DIST
PIT, PETER	HAR	181	3RD DIST
PIT, THOMAS	HAR	203	3RD DIST
PITCHER, ALBERT	CAL	025	2ND DIST
PITCHER, AMANDA	BAL	290	3RD WARD
PITCHER, GABRIEL	CAL	002	1ST DIST
PITCHER, GEORGE	CAL	005	1ST DIST
PITCHER, JAMES	ANN	384	4TH DIST
PITCHER, JOHN	CAL	006	1ST DIST
PITCHER, JOHN	WAS	069	2ND SUBD
PITCHER, MARGARET	CAL	040	3RD DIST
PITCHER, MARGARET E.	ANN	339	3RD DIST
PITCHER, THOAMS C.	ANN	376	4TH DIST
PITCHER, WILLAM	CAL	006	1ST DIST
PITCHER, WILLIMA H.	WAS	128	HAGERSTO
PITCOCK, BENJAMIN	HAR	199	3RD DIST
PITCOCK, JOHN W.	BAL	145	1ST WARD
PITCOCK, JOHNATHAN	HAR	201	3RD DIST
PITE, MARY	DOR	379	1ST DIST
PITEY, LEVIN*	DOR	445	1ST DIST
PITINER, CHARLES H.	ANN	463	HOWARD D
PITMAN, EDWARD	BAL	439	14TH WAR
PITROFF, JOHN	BAL	336	7TH WARD
PITS, ANN	BAL	192	19TH WAR
PITS, ISAAC	HAR	183	3RD DIST
PITS, MARY L.	BAL	281	20TH WAR
PITSINGER, CONRAD	BAL	360	1ST DIST
PITSMYER, CHARLES	BAL	130	11TH WAR
PITT, ADALINE	BAL	128	11TH WAR
PITT, ANN M.	BAL	159	16TH WAR
PITT, ANN*	BAL	046	4TH WARD
PITT, CHARLES F.	BAL	072	15TH WAR
PITT, CHARLES H.	BAL	407	3RD WARD
PITT, ELIZA	CEC	010	ELKTON 3
PITT, ELIZA	DOR	454	1ST DIST
PITT, FRANCES	CEC	175	7TH E DI
PITT, JACOB	CEC	174	6TH E DI
PITT, JOHN E.	WOR	263	BERLIN 1
PITT, MARY	BAL	218	12TH WAR
PITT, MARY	BAL	218	12TH WAR
PITT, MARY	BAL	175	11TH WAR
PITT, THOMAS	BAL	018	1ST WARD
PITT, THOMAS	BAL	410	3RD WARD
PITT, THOMAS	HAR	092	2ND DIST
PITT, THOMAS J.	BAL	020	4TH WARD
PITT, THOMAS N.	WOR	263	BERLIN 1
PITT, WILLIAM	BAL	065	18TH WAR
PITT,S JOHN	WOR	264	BERLIN 1
PITTENGER, ANDERW L.	FRE	293	WOODSBOR
PITTER, CHRISTIAN	BAL	012	9TH WARD
PITTINGER, ANN	FRE	281	WOODSBOR
PITTINGER, HEZEKIAH	FRE	292	WOODSBOR
PITTINGER, JOHN	FRE	288	WOODSBOR
PITTINGER, MARY	FRE	292	WOODSBOR
PITTINGER, SAMUEL	FRE	432	8TH E DI
PITTINUS, LEONARD	FRE	065	FREDERIC
PITTS, AMOS	WOR	288	BERLIN 1
PITTS, ARENA	SOM	485	TRAPP DI
PITTS, BELL	WOR	277	BERLIN 1
PITTS, CHARLES H.	BAL	198	11TH WAR
PITTS, CHARLES H. JR.	BAL	199	11TH WAR
PITTS, EDWARD	WOR	268	BERLIN 1
PITTS, ELIJAH	WOR	280	BERLIN 1
PITTS, ELIZA	WOR	269	BERLIN 1
PITTS, ELIZABETH	BAL	457	8TH WARD
PITTS, ELIZABETH	BAL	144	5TH WARD
PITTS, FANEY	WOR	304	SNOW HIL
PITTS, GEORGE	WOR	271	BERLIN 1
PITTS, H. R.	WOR	261	BERLIN 1
PITTS, HANDY	WOR	277	BERLIN 1
PITTS, JACOB	WOR	249	1ST CENS
PITTS, JAMES	DOR	298	1ST DIST
PITTS, JAMS	WOR	241	1ST CENS
PITTS, JESSE	WOR	268	BERLIN 1
PITTS, JOHN R.	WOR	259	BERLIN 1
PITTS, JOSHUA B.	BAL	431	1ST DIST
PITTS, LOUIS	BAL	183	5TH DIST
PITTS, LSUDY *	WOR	261	BERLIN 1
PITTS, MARTHA	WOR	273	BERLIN 1
PITTS, MILLY	WOR	280	BERLIN 1
PITTS, MILLY	SOM	483	TRAPP DI
PITTS, PLATER	WOR	268	BERLIN 1
PITTS, RHODA	WOR	280	BERLIN 1
PITTS, ROBERT	WOR	263	BERLIN 1
PITTS, THOMAS C.	BAL	048	15TH WAR
PITTS, THOMAS G.	BAL	205	11TH WAR
PITTS, WILLIAM	WOR	259	BERLIN 1
PITTS, WILLIAM	DOR	298	1ST DIST
PITZ, ISAAC	HAR	194	3RD DIST
PIVATY, ANN	BAL	269	20TH WAR
PIWAS, WILLIAM *	BAL	149	1ST WARD
PLACIDE, HENRY S.	BAL	049	4TH WARD
PLACK, LOUISE	BAL	001	18TH WAR
PLAIN, ANN E.	FRE	256	NEW MARK
PLAIN, NANCY	FRE	256	NEW MARK
PLAIN, STEPHEN	FRE	256	NEW MARK
PLAINE, DANIEL	CAR	413	2ND DIST
PLAITE, EPHRAIM	KEN	309	3RD DIST
PLAKIT, JOSHUA	BAL	302	20TH WAR
PLALER, JOHN*	DOR	388	1ST DIST
PLAMMER, ANN	FRE	069	FREDERIC
PLANCIDE, DANIEL	CAR	012	2ND DIST
PLANE, BENAIAH	CAR	390	2ND DIST
PLANE, GEORGE	ANN	508	HOWARD D
PLANE, HIRAM	CAR	391	2ND DIST
PLANE, JONATHAN	CAR	381	2ND DIST
PLANE, LYDIA	CAR	386	2ND DIST
PLANE, SAMUEL	CAR	390	2ND DIST
PLANETSON, MARY	DOR	373	1ST DIST
PLANGEANT, JOHN	BAL	271	2ND WARD
PLANK, EMILY	ALL	203	CUMBERLA
PLANK, JAMES	ALL	203	CUMBERLA
PLANK, MICHAEL	BAL	118	15TH WAR
PLANSEE, ELLEN	BAL	357	13TH WAR
PLANTER, ELIZABETH	BAL	194	11TH WAR
PLANTER, GEORGE	BAL	338	3RD WARD
PLANTER, HESTER	SOM	426	PRINCESS
PLANTER, ISRAEL	SOM	426	PRINCESS
PLANTER, JOHN	SOM	432	PRINCESS

Name	County	Page	District
PLANY, PHILLIP	BAL	212	2ND WARD
PLAPIONS, CHARLES A.	TAL	065	EASTON T
PLARIE, SHARLOTTE M.*	TAL	035	EASTON D
PLARSON, GEORGE	CAR	333	MANCHEST
PLARTNER, JOHN	BAL	009	9TH WARD
PLASKITT, JOHN	BAL	080	2ND DIST
PLASKITT, THOMA	BAL	003	EASTERN
PLASTERFIELD, JAMES	DOR	364	3RD DIVI
PLATER, CHARITY	QUE	253	5TH E DI
PLATER, EDWARD	PRI	064	NOTTINGH
PLATER, HARRIET	ANN	338	3RD DIST
PLATER, HENRY	FRE	295	WOODSBOR
PLATER, HENRYETTA	BAL	175	11TH WAR
PLATER, ISAAC	CAL	061	3RD DIST
PLATER, JOHN*	DOR	388	1ST DIST
PLATER, JOSEPH	BAL	048	15TH WAR
PLATO, CHARLES	BAL	180	11TH WAR
PLATO, HANNAH	BAL	092	15TH WAR
PLATO, HARRIET-BLACK	QUE	177	2ND E DI
PLATO, JOHN	BAL	091	15TH WAR
PLATO, MARY A.	BAL	159	16TH WAR
PLATT, ELIZABETH	FRE	046	FREDERIC
PLATT, JOHN	BAL	332	7TH WARD
PLATT, MARY	FRE	046	FREDERIC
PLATT, WILLIAM	BAL	377	8TH WARD
PLATT, WILLIAM H.	BAL	134	1ST WARD
PLATT, WILLIAM H.	MGM	349	BERRYS D
PLATTEN, CHARLES	BAL	302	17TH WAR
PLATTER, ACALINE	BAL	274	1ST DIST
PLATTER, BARNARD	BAL	274	1ST DIST
PLATTER, ELIZABETH	BAL	274	1ST DIST
PLATTER, JACOB	ALL	118	5TH E.D.
PLAWMAN, SHADRACH	BAL	011	2ND DIST
PLAX, GILBERT *	CAR	210	5TH DIST
PLEASANT, ELIZABETH	MGM	362	BERRYS D
PLEASANTS, BASIL B.	MGM	414	MEDLEY 3
PLEASANTS, BROOK	BAL	403	14TH WAR
PLEASANTS, BROOKE	BAL	142	11TH WAR
PLEASANTS, CANIEL	BAL	105	10TH WAR
PLEASANTS, ELIZA C.	MGM	347	BERRYS D
PLEASANTS, J. HALL	BAL	056	10TH WAR
PLEASANTS, JOHN M.	BAL	246	2ND WARD
PLEASANTS, RICHARD H.	BAL	058	10TH WAR
PLEASANTS, W. L.	BAL	325	12TH WAR
PLEETS, GEORGE	BAL	268	2ND WARD
PLENBOLT, ELIZABETH	BAL	103	1ST WARD
PLENBOLT, FREDERICK	BAL	103	1ST WARD
PLENKETT, BRIDGET	BAL	247	12TH WAR
PLENNER, ABERTUN	BAL	037	1ST WARD
PLENNER, RUDOLPH	BAL	037	1ST WARD
PLER, MARY S.	CAR	321	1ST DIST
PLER, MICHAEL	CAR	324	1ST DIST
PLER, SAMUEL	CAR	320	1ST DIST
PLETCHER, CHARLES	BAL	399	1ST DIST
PLETCHER, RANDOLPH	BAL	400	1ST DIST
PLETZER, ANN	BAL	370	1ST DIST
PLIFF, JOSEPHINE	QUE	187	3RD E DI
PLILIPS, WILLIAM	BAL	272	20TH WAR
PLIMKET, ANN	BAL	136	11TH WAR
PLITT, EMMANUEL	BAL	181	16TH WAR
PLITT, HENRY	BAL	209	17TH WAR
PLIZER, MR.	BAL	304	17TH WAR
PLOKKER, F.	BAL	170	1ST WARD
PLOTNER, BENJAMIN	WAS	119	2ND DIST
PLOUGHMAN, EPHRAIM	PRI	022	VANSVILL
PLOUGHMAN, HENRY E.	PRI	033	VANSVILL
PLOUGHMAN, JONATHAN	PRI	031	VANSVILL
PLOUGHMAN, JONATHAN	PRI	023	VANSVILL
PLOUGHMAN, JOSHUA	BAL	437	1ST DIST
PLOUGHMAN, WILLIAM	BAL	035	2ND DIST
PLOWDEN, CHLOE	WAS	166	HAGERSTO
PLOWDEN, EDMOND	ST	285	2ND E DI
PLOWDEN, EDMUND	ST	330	4TH E DI
PLOWDEN, WILLIAM H.	CHA	256	MIDDLETO
PLOWMAN, ADELINE	CAR	395	2ND DIST
PLOWMAN, ANDREW J.	CAR	236	UNION TO
PLOWMAN, ANN	BAL	389	8TH WARD
PLOWMAN, ELIZA	CAR	173	8TH DIST
PLOWMAN, ELIZA	HAR	095	2ND DIST
PLOWMAN, EPHRAIM	BAL	121	2ND DIST
PLOWMAN, GEORGE	CAR	191	4TH DIST
PLOWMAN, JACOB	CAR	234	UNION TO
PLOWMAN, JAMES	BAL	083	18TH WAR
PLOWMAN, JAMES M.	BAL	289	7TH WARD
PLOWMAN, JESSE	BAL	119	2ND DIST
PLOWMAN, JSOHUA	CAR	354	6TH DIST
PLOWMAN, NICHOLAS	CAR	354	6TH DIST
PLOWMAN, NOAH	CAR	381	2ND DIST
PLOWMAN, RICHARD	BAL	288	7TH WARD
PLOWMAN, SARAH	CAR	279	7TH DIST
PLOWMAN, SUSANAH	CAR	179	8TH DIST
PLOWMAN, WILLIAM	BAL	438	8TH WARD
PLOWNAN, COLUMBUS	CAR	381	2ND DIST
PLUCK, ELY	BAL	141	19TH WAR
PLUCK, JAOB	CEC	015	ELKTON 3
PLUCK, STEPHEN	CEC	015	ELKTON 3
PLUCKE, WASHINGTON	ALL	001	3RD E.D.
PLUCKER, ANDREW	ALL	004	3RD E.D.
PLUCKER, CHRISTIAN	ALL	005	3RD E.D.
PLUCKER, DANIEL	ALL	004	3RD E.D.
PLUCKER, DANIEL	ALL	002	3RD E.D.
PLUCKER, ELIZABETH	ALL	012	3RD E.D.
PLUCKER, JACOB	ALL	008	3RD E.D.
PLUCKER, JEREMIAH	ALL	012	3RD E.D.
PLUCKER, JOHN	ALL	003	3RD E.D.
PLUCKER, JOHN JR.	ALL	004	3RD E.D.
PLUGA, MARY	BAL	144	19TH WAR
PLUM, ANDREW *	WAS	191	1ST DIST
PLUM, JAMES T.	BAL	192	19TH WAR
PLUM, JOSEPH	BAL	104	18TH WAR
PLUMANBURG, JULIUS	BAL	304	3RD WARD
PLUMB, JOHN	BAL	073	1ST WARD
PLUMB, JOHN	WAS	129	2ND DIST
PLUMB, JOHN	WAS	295	1ST DIST
PLUMBER, FRED	BAL	285	20TH WAR
PLUMER, ADAM	PRI	077	MARLBROU
PLUMER, HENRY	BAL	349	7TH WARD
PLUMER, JAMES	WAS	092	2ND SUBD
PLUMER, JAMES	WAS	094	2ND SUBD
PLUMER, JOHN	WAS	253	1ST DIST
PLUMER, LOUISA	WAS	287	1ST DIST
PLUMER, LOUISA	DOR	371	3RD DIVI
PLUMER, MARGARET	BAL	250	17TH WAR
PLUMER, MARY	BAL	294	1ST DIST
PLUMER, ROBERT	HAR	165	3RD DIST
PLUMER, WILLIAM	ALL	217	CUMBERLA
PLUMK, LUDERICK	CAR	204	4TH DIST
PLUMMER, -----*	TAL	009	EASTON D
PLUMMER, ABNER	FRE	256	NEW MARK
PLUMMER, ALLEN	TAL	100	ST MICHA
PLUMMER, ANN	QUE	252	5TH E DI
PLUMMER, ANN	FRE	218	BUCKEYST
PLUMMER, ANN	ANN	505	HOWARD D
PLUMMER, ANNA	QUE	205	3RD E DI
PLUMMER, ANTHONY	PRI	063	NOTTINGH
PLUMMER, BENJAMIN	FRE	071	FREDERIC
PLUMMER, BRICE	ANN	385	4TH DIST
PLUMMER, CATHARINE	TAL	032	EASTON D
PLUMMER, CESAR	MGM	349	BERRYS D
PLUMMER, COMFORT	BAL	267	20TH WAR
PLUMMER, DAVID	MGM	328	CRACKLIN
PLUMMER, E.	ANN	342	3RD DIST
PLUMMER, EDGAR	CAR	077	NO TWP L
PLUMMER, EDWARD	KEN	241	2ND DIST
PLUMMER, EDWARD	DOR	382	1ST DIST
PLUMMER, EDWARD	DOR	382	1ST DIST
PLUMMER, EELIZABETH*	TAL	005	EASTON D
PLUMMER, ELI	QUE	172	2ND E DI
PLUMMER, ELIZA	CEC	022	ELKTON 3
PLUMMER, ELIZABETH	QUE	213	3RD E DI
PLUMMER, ELIZABETH	BAL	005	15TH WAR
PLUMMER, EMILY	TAL	026	EASTON D
PLUMMER, EVE ANNA-BLACK	MGM	416	MEDLEY 3
PLUMMER, GEORGE	ALL	087	5TH E.D.
PLUMMER, GEORGE	BAL	304	7TH WARD
PLUMMER, GEORGE W.	MGM	422	MEDLEY 3
PLUMMER, GERRARD	BAL	082	4TH WARD
PLUMMER, HENRIETTA	CAR	072	NO TWP L
PLUMMER, HENRY	FRE	069	FREDERIC
PLUMMER, HENRY-BLACK	MGM	423	MEDLEY 3
PLUMMER, HENSON	MGM	372	BERRYS D
PLUMMER, HERMAN	BAL	191	17TH WAR
PLUMMER, HIRAM	FRE	102	FREDERIC
PLUMMER, JAEMS	BAL	404	14TH WAR
PLUMMER, JAMES	CEC	041	CHESAPEA
PLUMMER, JAMES	WAS	092	2ND SUBD
PLUMMER, JAMES H.	BAL	051	15TH WAR
PLUMMER, JESSE	FRE	241	NEW MARK
PLUMMER, JOANNA	ANN	332	2ND DIST
PLUMMER, JOHN	CEC	038	CHESAPEA
PLUMMER, JOHN	BAL	404	14TH WAR
PLUMMER, JOHN B.	BAL	302	3RD WARD
PLUMMER, JOHN F.	BAL	249	6TH WARD
PLUMMER, JOHN H.-BLACK	MGM	426	MEDLEY 3
PLUMMER, JOHN W.*	TAL	006	EASTON D
PLUMMER, JOSEPH	MGM	425	MEDLEY 3
PLUMMER, JOSEPH	CAL	060	3RD DIST
PLUMMER, JOSEPH	ANN	505	HOWARD D
PLUMMER, JULIANN	TAL	022	EASTON D
PLUMMER, LAMBERT	BAL	194	19TH WAR
PLUMMER, LETITIA A.	CAR	071	NO TWP L
PLUMMER, LOUIS-MULATTO	MGM	414	MEDLEY 3
PLUMMER, LOUISA	BAL	044	1ST WARD
PLUMMER, MARCELLUS	CAR	073	NO TWP L
PLUMMER, MARGARET-BLACK	FRE	046	FREDERIC
PLUMMER, MARGARET-BLACK	FRE	005	FREDERIC
PLUMMER, MARIA	PRI	077	MARLBROU
PLUMMER, MARION A. B.	BAL	064	10TH WAR
PLUMMER, MARTIN	CAR	105	NO TWP L
PLUMMER, MARY	FRE	241	NEW MARK
PLUMMER, MARY A.	ANN	377	4TH DIST
PLUMMER, MORDECAI	ANN	401	8TH DIST
PLUMMER, MORDICIAS L.	PRI	078	MARLBROU
PLUMMER, NANCY	MGM	424	MEDLEY 3
PLUMMER, NANCY	MGM	325	CRACKLIN
PLUMMER, NICHOLAS	CEC	035	CHESAPEA
PLUMMER, PERRY	TAL	040	EASTON D
PLUMMER, PETER-BLACK	MGM	407	MEDLEY 3
PLUMMER, PHILEMON M.	MGM	422	MEDLEY 3
PLUMMER, PHILIP	CEC	088	4TH E DI
PLUMMER, RACHEL-BLACK	MGM	415	MEDLEY 3
PLUMMER, RICAHRD	BAL	473	14TH WAR
PLUMMER, RICHARD	CAR	066	NO TWP L
PLUMMER, RICHARD	FRE	271	NEW MARK
PLUMMER, RICHARD	TAL	014	EASTON D
PLUMMER, RISDON	QUE	218	3RD E DI
PLUMMER, ROBERT	TAL	014	EASTON D
PLUMMER, ROBERT	TAL	022	EASTON D
PLUMMER, ROBERT	CAL	060	3RD DIST
PLUMMER, ROBERT	MGM	325	CRACKLIN
PLUMMER, ROBERT	FRE	100	FREDERIC
PLUMMER, ROBERT	BAL	145	1ST WARD
PLUMMER, SAMUEL	BAL	043	15TH WAR
PLUMMER, SAMUEL	QUE	245	5TH E DI
PLUMMER, SOLLOMAN	TAL	038	EASTON D
PLUMMER, SOLOMON	TAL	081	ST MICHA
PLUMMER, SOLOMON	MGM	421	MEDLEY 3
PLUMMER, STEPHEN	QUE	208	3RD E DI
PLUMMER, THOMAS	QUE	168	2ND E DI
PLUMMER, THOMAS	TAL	036	EASTON D
PLUMMER, THOMAS	CAL	060	3RD DIST
PLUMMER, THOMAS G.	FRE	243	NEW MARK
PLUMMER, WILLIAM	FRE	241	NEW MARK
PLUMMER, WILLIAM	CAL	061	3RD DIST
PLUMMER, WILLIAM	CAR	071	NO TWP L
PLUMMER, WILLIAM	CEC	041	CHESAPEA
PLUMMER, WILLIAM	BAL	194	19TH WAR
PLUMMER, WILLIAM	TAL	019	EASTON D
PLUMMER, WILLIAM	TAL	100	ST MICHA
PLUMMER, WILLIAM	ANN	401	8TH DIST
PLUMMER, WILLIAM	ALL	230	CUMBERLA
PLUMMER, WILLIAM	BAL	080	15TH WAR
PLUMMER, WILLIAM B.	FRE	256	NEW MARK
PLUMMER, WILLIAM H.	BAL	384	3RD WARD
PLUMMER, WILLIAMS	BAL	302	3RD WARD
PLUMMER,PRISSILLER	FRE	227	BUCKEYST
PLUNK, JOHN	BAL	458	14TH WAR
PLUNKET, ALETHA	ANN	369	4TH DIST
PLUNKET, ELLEN	BAL	070	15TH WAR
PLUNKET, ELLEN	BAL	180	2ND DIST
PLUNKET, MARK	BAL	127	5TH WARD
PLUNKET, THOMAS	BAL	127	5TH WARD
PLUNKETT, JAMES	BAL	032	9TH WARD
PLUNKETT, MARY	BAL	230	19TH WAR
PLUNKETT, PATRICK	ALL	156	6TH E.D.
PLYMAN, JOHN	BAL	082	15TH WAR
PLYTTLE, JANE S.	BAL	058	10TH WAR
POCHLMAN, ADAM *	BAL	394	1ST DIST
POCHOCHECK, MARGARETT	BAL	170	11TH WAR
POCKER, CHARLES F.	BAL	156	19TH WAR
POCOCK, ANN E.	BAL	039	1ST WARD
POCOCK, CHARLES	BAL	038	1ST WARD
POCOCK, DAVID	BAL	032	2ND DIST
POCOCK, FRANKLIN JR.	BAL	057	2ND DIST
POCOCK, GEORGE	BAL	216	6TH WARD
POCOCK, GEORGE H.	ANN	414	HOWARD D
POCOCK, JESSE	HAR	062	1ST DIST
POCOCK, JOHN	BAL	047	2ND DIST
POCOCK, JOHN	BAL	002	EASTERN
POCOCK, THOMAS	ANN	414	HOWARD D
POCOCK, THOMAS	BAL	209	6TH WARD
POCOP, ANTHONY	BAL	372	8TH WARD
PODDINGTON, EDWARD	BAL	260	1ST DIST
PODDINGTON, MARY A.	BAL	263	1ST DIST
PODIRE, CONRAD	BAL	266	12TH WAR
POE, FRANCIS	FRE	20	5TH E DI
POE, GEORGE	BAL	352	1ST DIST
POE, GEORGE	WAS	266	1ST DIST
POE, GEORGE	ST	296	2ND E DI
POE, JAMES	WAS	279	LEITERSB
POE, JOHN	BAL	324	3RD WARD
POE, JOHN	BAL	285	1ST DIST
POE, JOHN	MGM	323	CRACKLIN
POE, JOHN P.	BAL	067	18TH WAR
POE, NELSON	BAL	068	18TH WAR
POE, THOMAS	CEC	119	3RD E DI
POE, TOUMIN	FRE	202	5TH E DI
POE, URIAH	MGM	323	CRACKLIN
POEHLMAN, ADAM *	BAL	394	1ST DIST
POESY, JOHN A.	CAL	033	2ND DIST
POETS, MARY	BAL	014	2ND DIST
POETS, SARAH	BAL	223	19TH WAR
POFENBERGER, SIMON	WAS	028	2ND SUBD
POFF, IRA	BAL	259	12TH WAR
POFF, JACOB	FRE	355	MIDDLETO
POFFEE, THOMAS	ALL	196	CUMBERLA
POFFENBERGER, CALVIN	FRE	375	CATOCTIN
POFFENBERGER, DANIEL	FRE	341	MIDDLETO
POFFENBERGER, DANIEL	WAS	037	2ND SUBD
POFFENBERGER, ELIZABETH	FRE	311	MIDDLETO
POFFENBERGER, ENOS	FRE	342	MIDDLETO
POFFENBERGER, HENRY	FRE	370	CATOCTIN
POFFENBERGER, HENRY	WAS	053	2ND SUBD
POFFENBERGER, HEZEKIAH	FRE	341	MIDDLETO
POFFENBERGER, ISAAC	FRE	340	MIDDLETO
POFFENBERGER, JACOB	FRE	374	CATOCTIN
POFFENBERGER, JACOB	FRE	332	MIDDLETO
POFFENBERGER, JACOB	WAS	052	2ND SUBD
POFFENBERGER, JOHN	WAS	180	BOONSBOR
POFFENBERGER, JOHN R.	WAS	039	2ND SUBD
POFFENBERGER, JOSEPH	WAS	065	2ND SUBD
POFFENBERGER, MARY	WAS	081	2ND SUBD
POFFENBERGER, MARY	FRE	342	MIDDLETO
POFFENBERGER, SAMUEL	WAS	076	2ND SUBD
POFFENBERGER, THOMAS	WAS	078	2ND SUBD
POFFINBERGER, DANIEL	WAS	199	1ST DIST
POFFINBERGER, DAVID	WAS	188	1ST DIST
POFFINBERGER, EEVE	WAS	162	HAGERSTO
POFFINBERGER, JOHN	WAS	057	2ND SUBD
POFFINHERGER, BENJAMIN	WAS	137	HAGERSTO
POFRED, ANDREW *	WAS	177	1ST DIST
POHLE, FREDERICK	BAL	301	7TH WARD
POHLMAN, DANIEL	BAL	037	4TH WARD
POHLMYER, W. R.	BAL	081	10TH WAR
POICE, SUSAN	WAS	014	WILLIAMS
POINDEXTER, LOUISA	BAL	097	10TH WAR
POINTER, ISAAC	WOR	280	BERLIN 1
POINTER, JOHN	KEN	311	3RD DIST
POINTS, SARAH	BAL	143	5TH WARD
POISE, JOHANNA	BAL	347	13TH WAR
POIST, JACOB	BAL	227	1ST DIST
POIST, WILLIAM	BAL	231	1ST DIST
POIST, WILLIAM SR.	BAL	242	1ST DIST
POKE, HENRY	KEN	289	3RD DIST
POKE, PETR	BAL	096	1ST WARD
POLACKS, MAGNES	BAL	027	1ST WARD
POLAID, SARAH E.	WAS	113	2ND DIST
POLAND, ABRAM	ALL	131	4TH E.D.
POLAND, ALEXANDER	ALL	133	4TH E.D.
POLAND, AURON	ALL	131	4TH E.D.
POLAND, JACKSON	ALL	124	4TH E.D.
POLAND, JEMIMA	ALL	134	4TH E.D.
POLAND, JOHN	ALL	134	4TH E.D.
POLAND, JOHN	ALL	136	4TH E.D.
POLAND, MARGARET	ALL	124	4TH E.D.
POLAND, MARGARET	ALL	132	4TH E.D.
POLAND, MOSES	ALL	125	4TH E.D.
POLAND, MOSES	ALL	115	5TH E.D.
POLAND, RACHEL	ALL	124	4TH E.D.
POLAND, SAMUEL	ALL	131	4TH E.D.
POLAND, SAMUEL	ALL	132	4TH E.D.
POLAND, SARAH	ALL	125	4TH E.D.
POLAND, SUSAN	ALL	133	4TH E.D.
POLAND, THOMAS	FRE	074	FREDERIC
POLAND, WILLIAM	ALL	131	4TH E.D.
POLAND, WILLIAM	ALL	133	4TH E.D.
POLE, ANNA	BAL	107	5TH WARD
POLE, F.	BAL	147	1ST WARD
POLE, GEORGE W.	FRE	285	WOODSBOR
POLEHILTON, ROBERT	BAL	326	12TH WAR
POLEMAN, WILLIAM	BAL	185	5TH DIST
POLIAL,LYDIA	QUE	135	1ST E DI
POLINSE, BETSEY	TAL	036	EASTON D
POLITLON, ALEXANDER	BAL	098	18TH WAR
POLK, AARON	SOM	491	SALISBUR
POLK, AARON SR.	WOR	229	6TH E DI
POLK, ALFRED K.	SOM	451	DAMES QU
POLK, ANN	BAL	431	8TH WARD
POLK, CAPTAIN	ANN	265	ANNAPOLI
POLK, DAVID	BAL	190	6TH WARD
POLK, EDWARD J.	HAR	180	3RD DIST
POLK, GILLIS	BAL	460	14TH WAR
POLK, GUSTAVUS	HAR	077	BEL AIR
POLK, HARRY	SOM	491	SALISBUR
POLK, HENRY	SOM	549	TYASKIN
POLK, HERARY	BAL	282	12TH WAR
POLK, JACOB	SOM	537	TYASKIN
POLK, JAMES	SOM	548	TYASKIN
POLK, JAMES	BAL	070	10TH WAR
POLK, JAMES K.	ANN	427	HOWARD D
POLK, JAMES K.	QUE	129	1ST E DI
POLK, JAMES P.	QUE	177	2ND E DI
POLK, JOHN	SOM	487	SALISBUR
POLK, JOHN	CEC	171	6TH E DI
POLK, JOHN C.	HAR	189	3RD DIST
POLK, JOHN M.	BAL	122	11TH WAR
POLK, JOHN P.	BAL	308	12TH WAR
POLK, JOSEPH G.	SOM	436	PRINCESS
POLK, LEAH	SOM	477	TRAPP DI
POLK, LEWIS	BAL	305	12TH WAR
POLK, LITTLETON	BAL	214	17TH WAR
POLK, LITTLETON R.	SOM	485	TRAPP DI
POLK, MARGARET	BAL	081	15TH WAR
POLK, MORRIS	SOM	478	TRAPP DI
POLK, MOSES	BAL	339	3RD WARD
POLK, OLIVER	SOM	488	SALISBUR
POLK, SALLY A.	SOM	506	BARREN C
POLK, SAMUEL	CEC	159	PORT DUP
POLK, SARAH A.	WOR	192	8TH E DI
POLK, SIDNEY	ANN	278	ANNAPOLI

POLK, SOPHIA BAL 040 9TH WARD
POLK, SUSAN SOM 441 DAMES QU
POLK, THOMAS SOM 502 SALISBUR
POLK, WHITTINGTON SOM 412 DUBLIN D
POLK, WILIAM WOR 341 1ST E DI
POLK, WILLIAM BAL 010 18TH WAR
POLK, WILLIAM BAL 167 6TH WARD
POLK, WILLIAM R. KEN 222 2ND DIST
POLK, WILLIAM S. BAL 112 10TH WAR
POLK, WILLIAM T. G. SOM 427 PRINCESS
POLK, ROBERT M. BAL 258 12TH WAR
POLKE, DOWRENZO BAL 214 17TH WAR
POLKE, FERDINAND BAL 076 1ST WARD
POLKELTY, JAMES BAL 141 11TH WAR
POLLARD, DAVID BAL 318 7TH WARD
POLLARD, J. J. BAL 108 10TH WAR
POLLARD, JAMES R. BAL 043 15TH WAR
POLLARD, MARY BAL 459 14TH WAR
POLLARD, PATRICK BAL 459 14TH WAR
POLLARD, PETER BAL 114 5TH WARD
POLLARD, SALLY BAL 398 3RD WARD
POLLARD, SETH BAL 023 4TH WARD
POLLARD, WILLIAM BAL 303 3RD WARD
POLLARD, WILLIAM BAL 318 7TH WARD
POLLET, EDWARD BAL 333 3RD WARD
POLLETT, JAMES A. WOR 194 8TH E DI
POLLETT, JOHN WOR 194 8TH E DI
POLLETT, LOUIS WOR 192 8TH E DI
POLLETT, MARY A. WOR 228 6TH E DI
POLLETT, WILLIAM WOR 228 6TH E DI
POLLEY, ELIZA BAL 387 13TH WAR
POLLEY, MARY BAL 353 7TH WARD
POLLIT, HARRIET BAL 127 16TH WAR
POLLITT, ANN SOM 481 TRAPP DI
POLLITT, BENJAMIN WOR 192 8TH E DI
POLLITT, CHARLES WOR 230 6TH E DI
POLLITT, DANIEL WOR 192 8TH E DI
POLLITT, DRUCILLA SOM 424 PRINCESS
POLLITT, ELIZABETH BAL 333 13TH WAR
POLLITT, ELIZABETH A. WOR 196 8TH E DI
POLLITT, EVE SOM 485 TRAPP DI
POLLITT, FROST SOM 423 PRINCESS
POLLITT, GEORGE SOM 423 PRINCESS
POLLITT, GILLES SOM 525 BARREN C
POLLITT, HECTOR SOM 416 PRINCESS
POLLITT, HENRY SOM 423 PRINCESS
POLLITT, HENRY SOM 407 DUBLIN D
POLLITT, JOB WOR 192 8TH E DI
POLLITT, JOHN SOM 441 DAMES QU
POLLITT, JOHN SOM 435 PRINCESS
POLLITT, JOHN E. SOM 469 TRAPPE D
POLLITT, JONATHAN WOR 197 8TH E DI
POLLITT, JOSIAH M. WOR 194 8TH E DI
POLLITT, LEVIN SOM 423 PRINCESS
POLLITT, LEVIN J. SOM 534 QUANTICO
POLLITT, MARIAH SOM 436 PRINCESS
POLLITT, SANDY WOR 195 8TH E DI
POLLITT, STEPHEN WOR 195 8TH E DI
POLLITT, TAMER SOM 469 TRAPPE D
POLLITT, THOMAS WOR 229 6TH E DI
POLLITT, TITUS WOR 199 8TH E DI
POLLITT, TUBMAN SOM 429 PRINCESS
POLLITT, WILLIAM SOM 488 SALISBUR
POLLITT, ZEBADEE SOM 407 DUBLIN D
POLLOCK, ABRAHAM BAL 457 14TH WAR
POLLOCK, ABRAHAM BAL 120 11TH WAR
POLLOCK, CHASE BAL 471 14TH WAR
POLLOCK, HENRY BAL 052 9TH WARD
POLLOCK, HENRY BAL 015 9TH WARD
POLLOCK, JAMES BAL 309 12TH WAR
POLLOCK, JOSEPH W. ALL 264 CUMBERLA
POLLOCK, MONK BAL 014 9TH WARD
POLLOCK, SARAH J. BAL 111 10TH WAR
POLLOCK, WILLIAM BAL 109 18TH WAR
POLLY, ABIGAIL ANN 285 ANNAPOLI
POLLY, JOHN H. FRE 125 CREAGERS
POLLY, MARY BAL 126 5TH WARD
POLMER, DANIEL WAS 155 2ND DIST
POLOCK, MARCUS S.* BAL 314 3RD WARD
POLTERE, ADDI BAL 035 9TH WARD
POLTON, CHARLES ANN 427 HOWARD D
POLTON, GEORGE H. ANN 518 HOWARD D
POLTON, JAMES BAL 076 18TH WAR
POLTON, JOHN ANN 432 HOWARD D
POLTON, ZACHARIAH ANN 518 HOWARD D
POMEY, SHARLOTT-BLACK CAR 088 NO TWP L
POMPHRY, GEORGE S. BAL 271 1ST DIST
POMPHRY, JOHN BAL 319 1ST DIST
POMPHRY, JOSH BAL 320 1ST DIST
PONCE, A. BAL 281 2ND WARD
PONCE, L. BAL 114 1ST WARD
PONCIA, ANTHONY BAL 030 9TH WARD
POND, CALEB-BLACK WOR 321 1ST E DI
POND, E. A. BAL 101 10TH WAR
PONDER, HENRIETTA* BAL 025 4TH WARD
PONDER, HENRY* BAL 323 3RD WARD
PONDER, LEONARD BAL 248 12TH WAR
PONDER, SOPHIER FRE 227 BUCKEYST
PONDER, WILLIAM P. BAL 359 13TH WAR
PONETLY, CHARLES BAL 118 1ST WARD
PONS, R. T. BAL 349 3RD WARD
PONT, CHARLOTTE WAS 257 1ST DIST
PONTCH, THOMAS * ALL 072 5TH E.D.
PONTICE, EDWARD F. BAL 341 13TH WAR
PONTILER, E. BAL 137 1ST WARD
POOD, CHARLES CEC 004 ELKTON 3
POOHR, FERDINAN BAL 457 8TH WARD
POOL, AARON CAR 366 9TH DIST
POOL, AMOS CAR 368 9TH DIST
POOL, BENJAMIN CAR 319 1ST DIST
POOL, BENJAMIN WOR 302 SNOW HIL
POOL, CHARLES FRE 127 CREAGERS
POOL, CHARLES ANN 495 HOWARD D
POOL, CHARLES A. CAR 397 2ND DIST
POOL, ELI ANN 494 HOWARD D
POOL, ELLEN WAS 049 2ND SUBD
POOL, ELLY BAL 204 17TH WAR
POOL, EMILY WAS 181 BOONSBOR
POOL, ESTHER CAR 397 2ND DIST
POOL, F. BAL 171 1ST WARD
POOL, F. BAL 163 1ST WARD
POOL, FRANCIS CAR 320 1ST DIST
POOL, FRANKLIN BAL 395 3RD WARD
POOL, GEORGE ALL 181 8TH E.D.
POOL, GEORGE FRE 103 FREDERIC
POOL, GEORGE W.* TAL 012 EASTON D
POOL, HARRIET FRE 063 FREDERIC
POOL, HENRY CAR 203 4TH DIST
POOL, HENRY CAR 368 9TH DIST
POOL, HENRY CAR 118 NO TWP L
POOL, HETTY ANN CAR 397 2ND DIST
POOL, JAMES CAR 113 NO TWP L
POOL, JOHN CAR 160 NO TWP L
POOL, JOHN CAR 206 4TH DIST
POOL, JOHN ANN 510 HOWARD D
POOL, JOHN E. PRI 120 PISCATAW
POOL, JOHN G. ANN 492 HOWARD D
POOL, JOHN H. WOR 341 1ST E DI
POOL, JOSEPH CAR 203 4TH DIST
POOL, JOSHUA ANN 510 HOWARD D
POOL, LLOYD CAR 203 4TH DIST
POOL, LLOYD CAR 212 5TH DIST
POOL, MARGARET ANN 502 HOWARD D
POOL, MARY BAL 390 1ST DIST
POOL, MARY BAL 110 1ST WARD
POOL, MARY CAR 131 NO TWP L
POOL, MARY ANN BAL 365 13TH WAR
POOL, NATHAN CAR 202 4TH DIST
POOL, NEAMIAH CAR 370 9TH DIST
POOL, OWEN CAR 227 5TH DIST
POOL, RESIN BAL 238 17TH WAR
POOL, ROBERT BAL 090 5TH WARD
POOL, RUBEN CAR 212 5TH DIST
POOL, RUTH BAL 410 14TH WAR
POOL, SALMON CAR 371 9TH DIST
POOL, SAMUEL CAR 152 NO TWP L
POOL, SAMUEL ALL 008 3RD E.D.
POOL, SARAH J. CAR 169 NO TWP L
POOL, SUSAN ANN 506 HOWARD D
POOL, THOMAS BAL 462 14TH WAR
POOL, THOMAS J. ALL 219 CUMBERLA
POOL, UPTON BAL 224 1ST DIST
POOL, VALINDA CAL 060 3RD DIST
POOL, WALTER FRE 091 FREDERIC
POOL, WALTER BAL 352 1ST DIST
POOL, WASHINGTON FRE 248 NEW MARK
POOL, WESLEY BAL 225 1ST DIST
POOL, WILLIAM FRE 141 CREAGERS
POOL, WILLIAM DOR 322 1ST DIST
POOL, WILLIAM G. ANN 508 HOWARD D
POOL, ZACHARIAH CAR 369 9TH DIST
POOL, MARGARET CAR 396 2ND DIST
POOLAND, JOHN BAL 255 1ST DIST
POOLE, ADAM FRE 337 MIDDLETO
POOLE, ALBINUS CAR 289 7TH DIST
POOLE, ANN E. FRE 301 WOODSBOR
POOLE, ANN W. MGM 407 MEDLEY 3
POOLE, BEALL FRE 444 8TH E DI
POOLE, BUSHROD CAR 244 3RD DIST
POOLE, CATHERINE FRE 438 8TH E DI
POOLE, CATHERINE MGM 355 BERRYS D
POOLE, CONRAD FRE 303 WOODSBOR
POOLE, DANIEL J. FRE 179 5TH E DI
POOLE, DENNIS-MULATTO FRE 434 8TH E DI
POOLE, ELIZA FRE 257 NEW MARK
POOLE, ELIZABETH ALL 182 8TH E.D.
POOLE, EPHRAIM H. FRE 434 8TH E DI
POOLE, FREDERICK S. MGM 406 MEDLEY 3
POOLE, GEORGE W. FRE 263 NEW MARK
POOLE, GREENBERRY MGM 440 CLARKSTR
POOLE, HANNAH BAL 159 11TH WAR
POOLE, HANSON FRE 377 PETERSVI
POOLE, JAMES BAL 162 6TH WARD
POOLE, JOHN FRE 003 FREDERIC
POOLE, JOHN HAR 104 2ND DIST
POOLE, JOHN D. MGM 374 ROCKERLE
POOLE, JOHN R. CEC 028 CHESAPEA
POOLE, JOHN W. MGM 426 MEDLEY 3
POOLE, LEVI FRE 120 CREAGERS
POOLE, LUCRETIA BAL 431 14TH WAR
POOLE, LYDIA A. FRE 377 PETERSVI
POOLE, MARY FRE 423 8TH E DI
POOLE, MARY BAL 119 18TH WAR
POOLE, MARY A. FRE 271 NEW MARK
POOLE, NARCISSA FRE 065 FREDERIC
POOLE, PERRY FRE 316 MIDDLETO
POOLE, PRISCILLA W. MGM 411 MEDLEY 3
POOLE, REBECCA BAL 133 18TH WAR
POOLE, RICHARD FRE 262 NEW MARK
POOLE, SAMUEL FRE 258 NEW MARK
POOLE, SAMUEL FRE 370 CATOCTIN
POOLE, SAMUEL ALL 211 CUMBERLA
POOLE, SAMUEL WAS 152 2ND DIST
POOLE, THOMAS BAL 382 8TH WARD
POOLE, THOMAS MGM 406 MEDLEY 3
POOLE, THOMAS E. FRE 447 8TH E DI
POOLE, THOMAS E.D. FRE 441 8TH E DI
POOLE, THORNTON FRE 422 8TH E DI
POOLE, WALTER MGM 421 MEDLEY 3
POOLE, WARREN MGM 436 CLARKSTR
POOLE, WILLIAM SOM 529 QUANTICO
POOLE, WILLIAM MGM 408 MEDLEY 3
POOLE, WILLIAM FRE 004 FREDERIC
POOLE, WILLIAM FRE 371 CATOCTIN
POOLE, WILLIAM FRE 368 CATOCTIN
POOLE, WILLIAM MGM 342 CLARKSBU
POOLE, WILLIAM CAR 329 MANCHEST
POOLE, WILLIAM BAL 256 1ST DIST
POOLE, WILLIAM D. MGM 415 MEDLEY 3
POOLE, WILLIAM E. BAL 151 16TH WAR
POOLE, DENNIS FRE 029 FREDERIC
POOLE, MARIA FRE 036 FREDERIC
POOLE, MARY A. CAR 393 2ND DIST
POOLER, JOHN BAL 458 14TH WAR
POOLEY, JOHN MGM 348 BERRYS D
POOLY, THOMAS CHA 241 HILLTOP
POOR, DUDLEY ANN 449 HOWARD D
POOR, ELLIOT D. D. BAL 330 13TH WAR
POOR, JOHN F. BAL 469 14TH WAR
POOR, JOHN H. BAL 144 11TH WAR
POOR, VIRGINIA BAL 023 4TH WARD
POORE, JOHN M. CAR 081 NO TWP L
POORE, JOHN-BLACK CAR 080 NO TWP L
POORE, MARY A. CAR 081 NO TWP L
POORE, REUBEN CAR 102 NO TWP L
POORE, WILLIAM JR. CAR 081 NO TWP L
POORE, WILLIAM SR. CAR 082 NO TWP L
POORMAN, BARBARA E. WAS 148 HAGERSTO
POORMAN, CATHARINE A. FRE 186 5TH E DI
POORMAN, GEORGE BAL 159 2ND DIST
POORMAN, LOUISA FRE 148 10TH E D
POOTER, ABRAHAM ANN 453 HOWARD D
POOTER, ANASTASIA ANN 449 HOWARD D
POOTS, ADAM ANN 456 HOWARD D
POOTS, JAMES E. QUE 170 2ND E DI
POOTS, JOHN QUE 158 2ND E DI
POOTS, PHILI QUE 155 2ND E DI
POPE, A. BAL 159 1ST WARD
POPE, AMELIA MGM 375 ROCKERLE
POPE, BARBARA BAL 472 14TH WAR
POPE, BERNARD BAL 269 2ND WARD
POPE, DANIEL HAR 085 2ND DIST
POPE, ELIZABETH BAL 371 3RD WARD
POPE, FOLGER BAL 034 9TH WARD
POPE, FRANKLIN F. BAL 134 5TH WARD
POPE, GEORGE T. MGM 334 CRACKLIN
POPE, GODPEDE BAL 243 2ND WARD
POPE, GOERGE BAL 125 5TH WARD
POPE, HENRIETTA ANN 379 4TH DIST
POPE, HENRY WOR 181 6TH E DI
POPE, JACOB F. BAL 440 14TH WAR
POPE, JOHN FRE 058 FREDERIC
POPE, JOHN C. WOR 188 7TH E DI
POPE, JOHN D. BAL 114 5TH WARD
POPE, JOSEPH O. BAL 124 11TH WAR
POPE, JOSH O. BAL 039 2ND DIST
POPE, LITTLETON D. WOR 178 6TH E DI
POPE, MARGARET BAL 401 14TH WAR
POPE, MARY P. WOR 182 6TH E DI
POPE, NATHANIEL G. ANN 374 4TH DIST
POPE, NICHOLAS ALL 004 3RD E.D.
POPE, RACHEL BAL 341 3RD WARD
POPE, RANDOLPH BAL 181 6TH WARD
POPE, SARAH R. BAL 124 5TH WARD
POPE, SUSAN CEC 060 1ST E DI
POPE, SUSANNAH BAL 124 11TH WAR
POPE, WILLIAM E. WOR 182 6TH E DI
POPED, ANDREW * WAS 177 1ST DIST
POPLACE, WILLIAM BAL 305 7TH WARD
POPLER, HENRY BAL 119 18TH WAR
POPLER, WILLIAM HAR 151 3RD DIST
POPP, CHRISTIAN BAL 166 16TH WAR
POPP, GEORGE BAL 031 4TH WARD
POPP, JOHN BAL 021 2ND DIST
POPP, JOHN WAS 112 2ND DIST
POPP, PHILIP * ALL 115 5TH E.D.
POPP, WILLIAM BAL 101 1ST WARD
POPPF, ROBERT BAL 048 9TH WARD
POPPIN, WILLIAM ANN 411 8TH DIST
POPPLAIN, NICHOLAS BAL 321 20TH WAR
POPPLER, ELIZABETH BAL 313 20TH WAR
POPPLER, GEORGE BAL 312 20TH WAR
POPPLETON, MARY* BAL 074 4TH WARD
POPPLUN, MARY BAL 383 13TH WAR
POPPS, MARGARET BAL 021 2ND DIST
PORADE, PHEOLIE * BAL 321 12TH WAR
PORCELT, JOHN * WAS 131 2ND DIST
PORILT, GEORGE CAR 213 5TH DIST
PORSINGER, GEORGE BAL 007 4TH WARD
PORTER, ABRAHAM MGM 386 ROCKERLE
PORTER, ADAM HAR 044 1ST DIST
PORTER, ADELINE BAL 140 11TH WAR
PORTER, ALEXANDER CAR 361 9TH DIST
PORTER, ALEXANDER BAL 342 1ST DIST
PORTER, AMANDA TAL 027 EASTON D
PORTER, ANDERSON CAR 104 NO TWP L
PORTER, ANN QUE 230 4TH E DI
PORTER, ANN E. BAL 266 1ST DIST
PORTER, ARENA TAL 010 EASTON D
PORTER, ASA BAL 462 1ST DIST
PORTER, AUGUSTUS BAL 117 1ST WARD
PORTER, AUTHER TAL 103 ST MICHA
PORTER, BENJAMIN TAL 029 EASTON D
PORTER, BENJAMIN CEC 020 ELKTON 3
PORTER, BUCK BAL 262 1ST DIST
PORTER, C.T. BAL 002 18TH WAR
PORTER, CAROLINE ANN 494 HOWARD D
PORTER, CASANDRA ANN 442 HOWARD D
PORTER, CATHARINE BAL 226 6TH WARD
PORTER, CATHARINE WAS 154 HAGERSTO
PORTER, CHARLES TAL 029 EASTON D
PORTER, CHARLES BAL 407 14TH WAR
PORTER, CHARLES MGM 370 BERRYS D
PORTER, CHARLOTT CAR 368 9TH DIST
PORTER, CLEMENTINE CAR 104 NO TWP L
PORTER, COMELIA FRE 318 MIDDLETO
PORTER, DANIEL BAL 031 1ST WARD
PORTER, EDWARD MGM 349 BERRYS D
PORTER, EDWARD MGM 437 CLARKSTR
PORTER, EDWARD SOM 485 TRAPP DI
PORTER, EDWARD TAL 117 ST MICHA
PORTER, EDWARD D. BAL 406 14TH WAR
PORTER, EDWARD P. WOR 181 6TH E DI
PORTER, ELIJAH ANN 492 HOWARD D
PORTER, ELIZA BAL 368 8TH WARD
PORTER, ELIZABETH BAL 189 6TH WARD
PORTER, ELIZABETH BAL 149 2ND DIST
PORTER, ELIZABETH WAS 046 2ND SUBD
PORTER, ELIZABETH QUE 174 2ND E DI
PORTER, ELIZABETH CAR 147 NO TWP L
PORTER, ELIZABETH BAL 159 19TH WAR
PORTER, ELIZABETH CEC 137 6TH E DI
PORTER, ELIZABETH FRE 022 FREDERIC
PORTER, ELIZABETH * KEN 285 3RD DIST
PORTER, ELLEN BAL 123 2ND DIST
PORTER, ELLEN BAL 163 11TH WAR
PORTER, EMILY B. BAL 072 1ST WARD
PORTER, ESTHER BAL 068 10TH WAR
PORTER, EZEKIEL WOR 268 BERLIN 1
PORTER, FRANCES MGM 438 CLARKSTR
PORTER, FRANCES A. CAR 109 NO TWP L
PORTER, FRANICS WOR 305 SNOW HIL
PORTER, FRANICS WOR 300 SNOW HIL
PORTER, G. A. BAL 072 10TH WAR
PORTER, GEOREG W. BAL 394 14TH WAR
PORTER, GEORGE BAL 359 13TH WAR
PORTER, GEORGE ALL 097 5TH E.D.
PORTER, GEORGE WOR 302 SNOW HIL
PORTER, GEORGE H. TAL 037 EASTON D
PORTER, GEORGE J. SOM 435 PRINCESS
PORTER, GEORGE T. BAL 063 15TH WAR
PORTER, GEORGE W. ALL 068 5TH E.D.
PORTER, GEORGE W. BAL 195 5TH DIST
PORTER, GEORGE W. SOM 412 DUBLIN D
PORTER, GEORGE W. QUE 225 4TH E DI
PORTER, GEORGE-BLACK WOR 173 6TH E DI
PORTER, GRACE WOR 250 1ST CENS
PORTER, HANNAH M. BAL 222 1ST DIST
PORTER, HARRISON FRE 317 MIDDLETO
PORTER, HENRY BAL 048 4TH WARD
PORTER, HENRY CEC 025 ELKTON 3
PORTER, HENRY BAL 006 4TH WARD
PORTER, HENRY ALL 069 5TH E.D.
PORTER, HENRY BAL 119 2ND DIST
PORTER, HENRY QUE 231 4TH E DI
PORTER, HENRY A. KEN 245 2ND DIST
PORTER, HENRY CORT FRE 249 NEW MARK
PORTER, HUGH BAL 089 18TH WAR
PORTER, HUGH BAL 189 6TH WARD
PORTER, ISAAC CAR 164 NO TWP L

Name	County	Page	District
PORTER, ISAAC	WOR	284	BERLIN 1
PORTER, ISIAH	BAL	208	17TH WAR
PORTER, J.	BAL	154	1ST WARD
PORTER, J. W.	ALL	101	5TH E.D.
PORTER, JACKSON	CEC	188	7TH E DI
PORTER, JAMES	BAL	424	14TH WAR
PORTER, JAMES	CEC	029	CHESAPEA
PORTER, JAMES	CAR	210	5TH DIST
PORTER, JAMES	BAL	457	14TH WAR
PORTER, JAMES	ALL	100	5TH E.D.
PORTER, JAMES	ALL	096	5TH E.D.
PORTER, JAMES	BAL	342	1ST DIST
PORTER, JAMES	BAL	269	12TH WAR
PORTER, JAMES	QUE	207	3RD E DI
PORTER, JAMES	QUE	223	4TH E DI
PORTER, JAMES R.	BAL	104	5TH WARD
PORTER, JANE	BAL	056	10TH WAR
PORTER, JANE	WOR	341	1ST E DI
PORTER, JEMIMA	BAL	142	2ND DIST
PORTER, JIM	BAL	351	7TH WARD
PORTER, JOE-BLACK	WOR	334	1ST E DI
PORTER, JOHN	KEN	300	3RD DIST
PORTER, JOHN	TAL	001	EASTON D
PORTER, JOHN	WAS	090	2ND SUBD
PORTER, JOHN	TAL	103	ST MICHA
PORTER, JOHN	BAL	459	8TH WARD
PORTER, JOHN	ANN	456	HOWARD D
PORTER, JOHN	ANN	428	HOWARD D
PORTER, JOHN	BAL	090	2ND DIST
PORTER, JOHN	ALL	097	5TH E.D.
PORTER, JOHN	ALL	108	5TH E.D.
PORTER, JOHN	BAL	071	1ST WARD
PORTER, JOHN	BAL	127	1ST WARD
PORTER, JOHN	CAR	110	NO TWP L
PORTER, JOHN	CEC	158	PORT DUP
PORTER, JOHN	KEN	230	2ND DIST
PORTER, JOHN	QUE	158	2ND E DI
PORTER, JOHN	FRE	070	FREDERIC
PORTER, JOHN A.	FRE	062	FREDERIC
PORTER, JOHN B.	ALL	097	5TH E.D.
PORTER, JOHN B. DR-	BAL	047	18TH WAR
PORTER, JOHN H.	CEC	170	6TH E DI
PORTER, JOHN H.	ALL	068	5TH E.D.
PORTER, JOHN M.	ALL	060	10TH E.D
PORTER, JOHN T.	WOR	273	BERLIN 1
PORTER, JOHN W.	TAL	007	EASTON D
PORTER, JOHN W.	TAL	085	ST MICHA
PORTER, JOHN W.	ALL	070	5TH E.D.
PORTER, JOHN W.	FRE	303	WOODSBOR
PORTER, JOHNATHAN	BAL	317	7TH WARD
PORTER, JONATHAN	TAL	077	EASTON T
PORTER, JOSEPH	KEN	244	2ND DIST
PORTER, JOSEPHUS	ALL	100	5TH E.D.
PORTER, JOSHUA	CAR	110	NO TWP L
PORTER, JOSHUA	CAR	210	5TH DIST
PORTER, JOSHUA	WOR	297	9TH E DI
PORTER, JOSIAH	ALL	097	5TH E.D.
PORTER, JULIAN	BAL	059	4TH WARD
PORTER, LARRY	ALL	097	5TH E.D.
PORTER, LEMUEL	ANN	442	HOWARD D
PORTER, LEVI	ALL	100	5TH E.D.
PORTER, LEVI	SOM	468	TRAPPE D
PORTER, LEVI R.	ALL	090	5TH E.D.
PORTER, LEVIN	SOM	471	TRAPPE D
PORTER, LEWIS	WAS	041	2ND SUBD
PORTER, LOUIS	BAL	328	1ST DIST
PORTER, LUCRETIA	ALL	122	4TH E.D.
PORTER, MAHALA	BAL	420	14TH WAR
PORTER, MANERVA	BAL	289	3RD WARD
PORTER, MARGARET	BAL	341	3RD WARD
PORTER, MARGARET	ALL	101	5TH E.D.
PORTER, MARGARET	BAL	028	1ST WARD
PORTER, MARGARET	CEC	025	ELKTON 3
PORTER, MARGARET	CAR	362	9TH DIST
PORTER, MARGARET	CEC	214	7TH E DI
PORTER, MARIAH	CAR	103	NO TWP L
PORTER, MARTHA	BAL	441	14TH WAR
PORTER, MARTHA	CEC	158	PORT DUP
PORTER, MARTHA	BAL	463	1ST DIST
PORTER, MARTHA	ANN	472	HOWARD D
PORTER, MARY	BAL	034	1ST WARD
PORTER, MARY	CEC	197	7TH E DI
PORTER, MARY	CEC	019	ELKTON 3
PORTER, MARY	CEC	016	ELKTON 3
PORTER, MARY	WOR	311	2ND E DI
PORTER, MARY	MGM	437	CLARKSTR
PORTER, MARY	QUE	228	4TH E DI
PORTER, MARY	SOM	536	TYASKIN
PORTER, MARY A.	SOM	428	PRINCESS
PORTER, MARY E.	MGM	319	CRACKLIN
PORTER, MARY E.	KEN	310	3RD DIST
PORTER, MARY J.	TAL	019	EASTON D
PORTER, MC KINNEY	WOR	171	6TH E DI
PORTER, MELISSA	BAL	269	12TH WAR
PORTER, MICHAEL	ALL	102	5TH E.D.
PORTER, MOSES	ALL	108	5TH E.D.
PORTER, NANCY	WOR	303	SNOW HIL
PORTER, NANCY	TAL	117	ST MICHA
PORTER, NANCY	FRE	248	NEW MARK
PORTER, NATHAN	CAR	221	5TH DIST
PORTER, NATHAN	QUE	253	5TH E DI
PORTER, NATHAN	ANN	461	HOWARD D
PORTER, NATHANIEL	ANN	510	HOWARD D
PORTER, NOAH	ANN	277	ANNAPOLI
PORTER, OLANDER	CEC	183	7TH E DI
PORTER, OWEN R.	TAL	026	EASTON D
PORTER, P.	BAL	139	1ST WARD
PORTER, PERRY	TAL	085	ST MICHA
PORTER, PETER	BAL	133	11TH WAR
PORTER, PHILIP	FRE	385	PETERSVI
PORTER, PRICELLA	SOM	410	DUBLIN D
PORTER, R. L.	BAL	050	4TH WARD
PORTER, RACHEL A.	CEC	013	ELKTON 3
PORTER, REAZIN	CAR	219	5TH DIST
PORTER, REBECCA	CEC	183	7TH E DI
PORTER, REBECCA	QUE	229	4TH E DI
PORTER, REBECCA	TAL	012	EASTON D
PORTER, RICHARD	ALL	113	5TH E.D.
PORTER, ROBERT	BAL	122	2ND DIST
PORTER, ROBERT B.	BAL	002	18TH WAR
PORTER, SALINA	CAR	362	9TH DIST
PORTER, SALLY	WOR	295	9TH E DI
PORTER, SAMUEL	CAR	330	MANCHEST
PORTER, SAMUEL	ALL	101	5TH E.D.
PORTER, SARAH	BAL	066	2ND DIST
PORTER, SARAH	CAR	361	9TH DIST
PORTER, SARAH P.	SOM	421	PRINCESS
PORTER, SCOTT	ALL	097	5TH E.D.
PORTER, SUSAN M.	QUE	148	1ST E DI
PORTER, THEODORE	SOM	534	QUANTICO
PORTER, THOMAS	TAL	104	ST MICHA
PORTER, THOMAS	ALL	093	5TH E.D.
PORTER, THOMAS	BAL	229	1ST DIST
PORTER, THOMAS B.	CAR	362	9TH DIST
PORTER, THOMAS C.	FRE	271	NEW MARK
PORTER, THOMAS S.	WOR	308	2ND E DI
PORTER, WASHINGTON	BAL	149	5TH WARD
PORTER, WELSEY	CAR	216	5TH DIST
PORTER, WILLIAM	HAR	190	3RD DIST
PORTER, WILLIAM	SOM	419	PRINCESS
PORTER, WILLIAM	BAL	129	1ST WARD
PORTER, WILLIAM	BAL	020	15TH WAR
PORTER, WILLIAM	TAL	018	EASTON D
PORTER, WILLIAM	WOR	281	BERLIN 1
PORTER, WILLIAM E.	QUE	140	1ST E DI
PORTER, WILLIAM M.	MGM	333	CRACKLIN
PORTER, ZADOK	WOR	269	BERLIN 1
PORTER, ZADOK	WOR	297	9TH E DI
PORTER, JOHN	BAL	107	1ST WARD
PORTER, MARY	CAR	165	NO TWP L
PORTER, W ILLIAM H.	QUE	149	1ST E DI
PORTERFIELD, A.	WAS	005	WILLIAMS
PORTERFIELD, A.H.	WAS	005	WILLIAMS
PORTERFIELD, C.T.	WAS	007	WILLIAMS
PORTES, ROBERT J.	CAR	103	NO TWP L
PORTNER, ISAAC	FRE	365	CATOCTIN
PORTS, ABERT T.	CAR	185	8TH DIST
PORTS, DAVID	WAS	199	1ST DIST
PORTS, GEORGE	BAL	196	5TH DIST
PORTS, HARRIET	TAL	042	EASTON D
PORTS, JOHN	CAR	331	MANCHEST
PORTS, MARY W.	CAR	185	8TH DIST
PORTS, WILLIAM F.	CAR	215	5TH DIST
PORTSAL, CONRAD	BAL	192	2ND WARD
PORTZ, CAVID	BAL	442	1ST DIST
PORTZ, EDWARD	BAL	384	1ST DIST
PORTZ, JACOB	BAL	394	1ST DIST
POSEY, ADAM	CHA	244	HILLTOP
POSEY, ADRIAN A.	BAL	055	4TH WARD
POSEY, BOLIVER	WAS	128	HAGERSTO
POSEY, BUDDY	CHA	243	HILLTOP
POSEY, CATHERINE	CHA	289	MIDDLETO
POSEY, CHARLES	ST	261	3RD E DI
POSEY, ELIZA	CHA	243	HILLTOP
POSEY, ELIZABETH	ST	336	4TH E DI
POSEY, ELLEN	BAL	028	9TH WARD
POSEY, F.J.	WAS	150	HAGERSTO
POSEY, FRANCIS	PRI	104	PISCATAW
POSEY, HANDSON H.	CHA	244	HILLTOP
POSEY, HARRIETT	HAR	106	2ND DIST
POSEY, HARRISON	ST	347	5TH E DI
POSEY, HENRY	BAL	418	14TH WAR
POSEY, HESTER	FRE	039	FREDERIC
POSEY, ISAIAH	CHA	224	ALLENS F
POSEY, JAMES	CHA	239	HILLTOP
POSEY, JAMES	BAL	145	1ST WARD
POSEY, JOHN	CHA	249	HILLTOP
POSEY, LAURENCE	CHA	220	ALLENS F
POSEY, LYDIA	CHA	235	HILLTOP
POSEY, MARGARET	BAL	432	14TH WAR
POSEY, MARY A.	BAL	011	4TH WARD
POSEY, MARY A.	CAL	031	2ND DIST
POSEY, MARY U.	CHA	225	ALLENS F
POSEY, PETER D.	MGM	391	ROCKERLE
POSEY, RICHARD	CHA	242	HILLTOP
POSEY, RICHARD B.	CHA	238	HILLTOP
POSEY, RICHARD H.	CHA	238	HILLTOP
POSEY, ROBERT D.	ST	318	4TH E DI
POSEY, SAMUEL	CHA	247	HILLTOP
POSEY, THOMAS	CHA	242	HILLTOP
POSEY, THOMAS	CHA	242	HILLTOP
POSEY, THOMAS	CHA	221	ALLENS F
POSEY, THOMAS	ST	339	5TH E DI
POSEY, THOMAS M.	CHA	248	HILLTOP
POSEY, U. V.	CHA	225	ALLENS F
POSEY, VIRGINIA*	BAL	319	3RD WARD
POSEY, WASHINGTON A.	CHA	218	ALLENS F
POSLEY, ANN	WOR	246	1ST CENS
POSLEY, ELSAY	WOR	244	1ST CENS
POSLEY, GEORGE	WOR	247	1ST CENS
POSLEY, JANE	WOR	247	1ST CENS
POSLEY, LET	WOR	247	1ST CENS
POSLEY, RACHEL	WOR	245	1ST CENS
POSLEY, WILLIAM	WOR	246	1ST CENS
POSLY, CALEB	WOR	243	1ST CENS
POSLY, PETER	WOR	243	1ST CENS
POSSEY, GEORGE	CAL	003	1ST DIST
POST, E. H.	BAL	332	1ST DIST
POST, EUGENE	BAL	296	1ST DIST
POST, G.W.	WAS	137	HAGERSTO
POST, NELSON	BAL	440	14TH WAR
POST, SARAH	WAS	133	HAGERSTO
POST, WILLAIN H.	BAL	275	2ND WARD
POSTEL, CHRISTOPHER	BAL	181	2ND WARD
POSTEN, JAMES	WOR	326	1ST E DI
POSTEN, JAMES	WOR	325	1ST E DI
POSTER, EVELINE	ALL	166	6TH E.D.
POSTLY, LEVIN-BLACK	WOR	347	1ST E DI
POSTLY, MINGO	WOR	267	BERLIN 1
POSTMAN, JOHANNES	BAL	466	14TH WAR
POSTOR, WILLIAM	ALL	094	5TH E.D.
POSWICHS, NICHOLAS	BAL	272	2ND WARD
POSY, IGNATIUS	CHA	247	HILLTOP
POSY, SARA	CHA	274	ALLENS F
POTEC, FRANCIS	BAL	271	1ST DIST
POTEE, ELIZABETH	BAL	412	8TH WARD
POTEE, FRANCES	BAL	277	17TH WAR
POTEE, GEORGE	BAL	129	18TH WAR
POTEE, ISAAC	BAL	120	18TH WAR
POTEE, WILLIAM H.	BAL	127	18TH WAR
POTEET, ELIZABETH	HAR	058	1ST DIST
POTEET, JAMES	HAR	022	1ST DIST
POTEET, SUSAN	BAL	024	2ND DIST
POTER, P. P.	BAL	299	3RD WARD
POTINGER, JOHN F.	BAL	272	2ND WARD
POTINGER, MARGARET S.	WAS	178	BOONSBOR
POTSEL, SAMUEL	BAL	454	14TH WAR
POTT, CATHARINE	BAL	252	2ND WARD
POTT, GEORGE	WOR	229	6TH E DI
POTT, GEORGE C.	BAL	365	13TH WAR
POTT, LYMAN	BAL	163	19TH WAR
POTTER, ANN	BAL	341	13TH WAR
POTTER, ANN	BAL	401	8TH WARD
POTTER, ANN	BAL	401	8TH WARD
POTTER, CEZER	TAL	047	EASTON T
POTTER, D.F.	BAL	162	1ST WARD
POTTER, DANIEL	FRE	202	5TH E DI
POTTER, DAVID G.	WAS	080	2ND SUBD
POTTER, ELIJAH	SOM	384	BRINKLEY
POTTER, ELIJAH	BAL	306	7TH WARD
POTTER, GEORGE	BAL	168	11TH WAR
POTTER, GEORGE	WAS	082	2ND SUBD
POTTER, H.	BAL	147	1ST WARD
POTTER, HAMILTON	FRE	319	MIDDLETO
POTTER, HANNA	TAL	002	EASTON D
POTTER, HENRY	TAL	001	EASTON D
POTTER, HENRY	QUE	228	4TH E DI
POTTER, HENRY	ALL	114	5TH E.D.
POTTER, HUGH	BAL	279	2ND WARD
POTTER, ISAAC	BAL	149	5TH WARD
POTTER, ISAAC	BAL	277	17TH WAR
POTTER, JACOB	FRE	327	MIDDLETO
POTTER, JESSE	BAL	054	1ST WARD
POTTER, JESSE	SOM	364	BRINKLEY
POTTER, JOHN	SOM	392	BRINKLEY
POTTER, JOHN	WAS	124	2ND DIST
POTTER, JOHN	WAS	088	2ND SUBD
POTTER, JOHN	ALL	132	4TH E.D.
POTTER, JOHN	ALL	153	6TH E.D.
POTTER, JOHN	BAL	059	4TH WARD
POTTER, JOHN	BAL	302	17TH WAR
POTTER, JOHN D.	FRE	384	PETERSVI
POTTER, LEVIN A.	SOM	476	TRAPPE D
POTTER, MARY	SOM	365	BRINKLEY
POTTER, MARY A.	BAL	162	6TH WARD
POTTER, PETER	BAL	125	1ST WARD
POTTER, RICHARD	BAL	086	18TH WAR
POTTER, RICHARD-BLACK	CAR	096	NO TWP L
POTTER, SARAH	SOM	385	BRINKLEY
POTTER, SARAH	WAS	085	2ND SUBD
POTTER, SARAH T.	CAR	164	NO TWP L
POTTER, STANFORD-BLACK	CAR	146	NO TWP L
POTTER, STEPHEN	BAL	169	1ST WARD
POTTER, SYDNEY	BAL	137	5TH WARD
POTTER, THOMAS	BAL	179	6TH WARD
POTTER, WILLIAM	BAL	179	6TH WARD
POTTER, WILLIAM	BAL	370	13TH WAR
POTTER, WRIGHT	ALL	040	2ND E.D.
POTTERFIELD, ALBERT	FRE	164	EMMITTSB
POTTERFIELD, MARGARET A.	FRE	193	5TH E DI
POTTINGER, FRANCIS	WAS	136	HAGERSTO
POTTIT, JOHN *	WOR	308	2ND E DI
POTTON, JAMES	BAL	047	9TH WARD
POTTS, AARON	ALL	183	8TH E.D.
POTTS, AARON	ALL	158	6TH E.D.
POTTS, ABRAM-BLACK	QUE	132	1ST E DI
POTTS, ANN M.	QUE	190	3RD E DI
POTTS, ANN MARIA-BLACK	QUE	148	1ST E DI
POTTS, CATHARINE	WAS	232	1ST DIST
POTTS, CATHERINE	MGM	433	CLARKSTR
POTTS, CHARLES	WAS	022	2ND SUBD
POTTS, CHARLES-BLACK	CAR	088	NO TWP L
POTTS, CHARLES-BLACK	FRE	015	FREDERIC
POTTS, ELIZABETH	QUE	211	3RD E DI
POTTS, ELIZABETH-BLACK	QUE	192	3RD E DI
POTTS, ELIZABETH-BLACK	FRE	016	FREDERIC
POTTS, ELLENORA M.	FRE	033	FREDERIC
POTTS, GEORGE	WAS	022	2ND SUBD
POTTS, GEORGE M.	FRE	307	WOODSBOR
POTTS, GEORGE M.	FRE	035	FREDERIC
POTTS, HARRIET	BAL	098	10TH WAR
POTTS, HENRY-BLACK	CAR	075	NO TWP L
POTTS, JAMES	CAR	330	MANCHEST
POTTS, JOHN G.	BAL	370	1ST DIST
POTTS, LEWIS-BLACK	FRE	015	FREDERIC
POTTS, LUCY-BLACK	FRE	220	BUCKEYST
POTTS, MARIA-BLACK	QUE	203	3RD E DI
POTTS, MARY	QUE	208	3RD E DI
POTTS, MARY	CAR	098	NO TWP L
POTTS, MARY R.	QUE	187	3RD E DI
POTTS, PETER	BAL	117	11TH WAR
POTTS, RICHARD	FRE	031	FREDERIC
POTTS, RICHARD	ANN	516	HOWARD D
POTTS, ROBERT	BAL	410	1ST DIST
POTTS, ROBERT	WAS	268	1ST DIST
POTTS, SUSAN-BLACK	FRE	398	JEFFERSO
POTTS, THOMAS	CAR	071	NO TWP L
POTTS, THOMAS H.S.	BAL	161	1ST WARD
POTTS, THOMAS-BLACK	QUE	125	1ST E DI
POTTS, WILLIAM	KEN	241	2ND DIST
POTTS, WILLIAM	WAS	243	CAVETOWN
POTTS, WILLIAM	WAS	249	1ST DIST
POTTS, WILLIAM	WAS	250	1ST DIST
POTTS, WILLIAM	TAL	029	EASTON D
POTTS, WILLIAM-BLACK	QUE	125	1ST E DI
POTTS, WILLIAM-BLACK	QUE	147	1ST E DI
POTTS, WILLIAM-BLACK	CAR	091	NO TWP L
POTTS,MARY	QUE	187	3RD E DI
POTTS,RACHEL-BPOTTS	CAR	088	NO TWP L
POUCH, GEORGE	BAL	202	17TH WAR
POUCH, JOHN T.	ANN	369	4TH DIST
POUDER, HENRY*	BAL	323	3RD WARD
POUDER, MARTHA	BAL	427	14TH WAR
POUEL, SARAH	CAR	364	9TH DIST
POUERS, WILLIAM	FRE	063	FREDERIC
POUEY, MARY	TAL	113	ST MICHA
POUGH, GEORGE	ALL	128	4TH E.D.
POUGH, JOHN D.	ALL	066	10TH E.D
POUGHFF, THOMAS*	BAL	391	3RD WARD
POUITS, CAROLINE	BAL	138	5TH WARD
POULEY, NICOLAS	DOR	341	3RD DIVI
POULEY, SARRAH C.	DOR	342	3RD DIVI
POULS, CARTER	PRI	034	VANSVILL
POULSON, ALEXANDER W.	BAL	014	18TH WAR
POULSON, ELIZABETH	BAL	016	18TH WAR
POULSON, ISABELLA	BAL	405	8TH WARD
POULSON, JOHN	BAL	025	18TH WAR
POULSON, MARGARET	BAL	317	12TH WAR
POULSON, MARY	CAR	285	7TH DIST
POULSON, PAUL	BAL	159	1ST WARD
POULSON, SARAH J.	BAL	187	11TH WAR
POULTNERY, ELIZABETH	BAL	065	15TH WAR
POULTNEY, ANN	BAL	059	10TH WAR
POULTNEY, JANE	BAL	467	14TH WAR
POULTNEY, SAMUEL	BAL	140	11TH WAR
POULTON, CHARLES	BAL	124	18TH WAR
POULTON, JOHN	BAL	123	18TH WAR
POULTON, SUSAN A.	BAL	185	16TH WAR
POULTON, THOMAS	ANN	386	4TH DIST
POUSE, T.	BAL	281	2ND WARD
POWBLITS, EPHRAIM	BAL	246	1ST DIST
POWBLITS, JACOB	BAL	244	1ST DIST
POWBLITS, JOHN	BAL	245	1ST DIST
POWBLITS, MARY	BAL	245	1ST DIST
POWDEN, ISAAC	BAL	112	2ND DIST
POWDER, ANDREW	CAR	272	WESTMINS
POWDER, JACOB	CAR	282	7TH DIST
POWDERS, JOHN	WAS	283	1ST DIST
POWEL, ADAM	MGM	415	MEDLEY 3
POWEL, ANN	CAR	400	2ND DIST

Name	County	Page	District
POWEL, BENJAMIN	BAL	058	2ND DIST
POWEL, BENJAMIN M.	WAS	128	2ND DIST
POWEL, DANIEL	FRE	139	CREAGERS
POWEL, DAVID	CAR	394	2ND DIST
POWEL, DAVID	WAS	114	2ND DIST
POWEL, ELIZA	BAL	458	1ST DIST
POWEL, ESTHER	CAR	295	7TH DIST
POWEL, HILEARY	MGM	404	ROCKERLE
POWEL, JACOB	CAR	257	3RD DIST
POWEL, JACOB	CAR	406	2ND DIST
POWEL, JACOB	CAR	171	8TH DIST
POWEL, JOHN	BAL	154	19TH WAR
POWEL, JOHN	HAR	057	1ST DIST
POWEL, JOHN	BAL	469	14TH WAR
POWEL, THOMAS	HAR	070	1ST DIST
POWEL, UPTON	WAS	133	2ND DIST
POWEL, WILLIAM	CAR	294	7TH DIST
POWEL, WILLIAM	FRE	140	CREAGERS
POWEL, WILLIAM	FRE	139	CREAGERS
POWEL, WILLIAM-BLACK	MGM	412	MEDLEY 3
POWELL, A.	WAS	005	WILLIAMS
POWELL, AMANDA	WOR	182	6TH E DI
POWELL, AMELIA A.	BAL	257	6TH WARD
POWELL, ANANIAS W.	WOR	294	9TH E DI
POWELL, ANANIAS	WOR	275	BERLIN 1
POWELL, ANN	ALL	253	CUMBERLA
POWELL, ANN C.	WAS	114	2ND DIST.
POWELL, ANN E.	BAL	303	3RD WARD
POWELL, ANN M.	WOR	280	BERLIN 1
POWELL, AREY	BAL	179	11TH WAR
POWELL, ARTHUR M.	WOR	349	1ST E DI
POWELL, BASIL	MGM	331	CRACKLIN
POWELL, CALEB	WOR	215	4TH E DI
POWELL, CALEB SR.	WOR	216	4TH E DI
POWELL, CHARLES	MGM	371	BERRYS D
POWELL, CHARLES	BAL	399	14TH WAR
POWELL, CHARLES R.	BAL	024	9TH WARD
POWELL, CLARA	BAL	002	4TH WARD
POWELL, COMFORT E.	WOR	183	6TH E DI
POWELL, CORO HAZAN	WOR	214	4TH E DI
POWELL, DANIEL	BAL	206	2ND WARD
POWELL, DAVID P.	BAL	466	14TH WAR
POWELL, DAVIS	BAL	084	2ND DIST
POWELL, DENNIS	MGM	328	CRACKLIN
POWELL, DENNY	WOR	213	4TH E DI
POWELL, EBE	WOR	271	BERLIN 1
POWELL, EBY	WOR	295	9TH E DI
POWELL, EDWARD	WOR	179	6TH E DI
POWELL, EDWARD	SOM	354	BRINKLEY
POWELL, ELIAS	BAL	382	3RD WARD
POWELL, ELISHA	WOR	311	2ND E DI
POWELL, ELIZA	BAL	207	2ND WARD
POWELL, ELIZA	BAL	333	1ST DIST
POWELL, ELIZA *	BAL	121	2ND DIST
POWELL, ELIZA J.	BAL	194	11TH WAR
POWELL, ELIZA J.	BAL	412	3RD WARD
POWELL, ELIZABETH	ANN	412	HOWARD D
POWELL, ELIZABETH	WOR	317	2ND E DI
POWELL, F.	BAL	172	1ST WARD
POWELL, F.	BAL	169	1ST WARD
POWELL, G. W.	BAL	055	4TH WARD
POWELL, GEORGE	SOM	409	DUBLIN D
POWELL, GEORGE	TAL	031	EASTON D
POWELL, GEORGE W.	SOM	495	SALISBUR
POWELL, GEROGE	FRE	105	CREAGERS
POWELL, HANDY	WOR	172	6TH E DI
POWELL, HENNA	WOR	280	BERLIN 1
POWELL, HENRY	MGM	371	BERRYS D
POWELL, HENRY	DOR	299	1ST DIST
POWELL, HENRY	BAL	024	4TH WARD
POWELL, HENRY	BAL	394	14TH WAR
POWELL, HENRY	BAL	272	20TH WAR
POWELL, HENRY	BAL	255	6TH WARD
POWELL, HENRY	BAL	114	1ST WARD
POWELL, HIRAM J.	WOR	258	1ST CENS
POWELL, IEHU *	WOR	270	BERLIN 1
POWELL, ISAAC	WOR	291	9TH E DI
POWELL, ISAAC	WOR	256	1ST CENS
POWELL, ISAAC	WOR	306	2ND E DI
POWELL, ISAAC F.	SOM	415	DUBLIN D
POWELL, J. C. W.	TAL	066	EASTON T
POWELL, J. REYNOLDS	BAL	138	18TH WAR
POWELL, JACOB R.	WOR	216	4TH E DI
POWELL, JAEMS	WOR	314	2ND E DI
POWELL, JAMES	SOM	416	PRINCESS
POWELL, JAMES	BAL	234	20TH WAR
POWELL, JAMES	ALL	108	5TH E.D.
POWELL, JAMES	BAL	068	15TH WAR
POWELL, JAMES B.	ALL	062	10TH E.D
POWELL, JAMES B.	WOR	196	8TH E DI
POWELL, JAMES M.	WOR	179	6TH E DI
POWELL, JANE	WOR	179	6TH E DI
POWELL, JANE	WOR	296	9TH E DI
POWELL, JANE	MGM	352	BERRYS D
POWELL, JAOCB	BAL	196	5TH DIST
POWELL, JESSE	WOR	264	BERLIN 1
POWELL, JESSE	SOM	400	BRINKLEY
POWELL, JOHN	WOR	285	BERLIN 1
POWELL, JOHN	WOR	260	BERLIN 1
POWELL, JOHN	WOR	311	2ND E DI
POWELL, JOHN	WAS	014	WILLIAMS
POWELL, JOHN	WOR	246	1ST CENS
POWELL, JOHN	BAL	196	5TH DIST
POWELL, JOHN	ALL	156	6TH E.D.
POWELL, JOHN	ANN	302	1ST DIST
POWELL, JOHN	BAL	390	3RD WARD
POWELL, JOHN	BAL	038	9TH WARD
POWELL, JOHN	BAL	062	2ND DIST
POWELL, JOHN	BAL	258	20TH WAR
POWELL, JOHN	BAL	373	13TH WAR
POWELL, JOHN	BAL	274	17TH WAR
POWELL, JOHN A. W.	TAL	008	EASTON D
POWELL, JOHN D.	BAL	374	3RD WARD
POWELL, JOHN W.	SOM	482	TRAPP DI
POWELL, JOHN W.	WOR	335	1ST E DI
POWELL, JORDAN	BAL	173	6TH WARD
POWELL, JOSHUA	BAL	095	15TH WAR
POWELL, JOSIAH D.	WOR	166	6TH E DI
POWELL, JULIA	FRE	060	FREDERIC
POWELL, KATY	MGM	370	BERRYS D
POWELL, L. D.	WOR	259	BERLIN 1
POWELL, LAMBERT C.	WOR	271	BERLIN 1
POWELL, LAMBERT C.	WOR	165	6TH E DI
POWELL, LAURA	BAL	237	6TH WARD
POWELL, LAZARUS	SOM	536	TYASKIN
POWELL, LEVI	WOR	312	2ND E DI
POWELL, LEVIN	WOR	182	6TH E DI
POWELL, LEVIN	WOR	318	2ND E DI
POWELL, LEWIS	FRE	105	CREAGERS
POWELL, LORENZO	WOR	310	2ND E DI
POWELL, LOTTA	WOR	305	2ND E DI
POWELL, LOUISA	BAL	363	8TH WARD
POWELL, LYDIA	BAL	264	17TH WAR
POWELL, MAHALIA-BLACK	WOR	345	1ST E DI
POWELL, MARGARET	WOR	342	1ST E DI
POWELL, MARGARET	BAL	061	10TH WAR
POWELL, MARGARET	BAL	361	3RD WARD
POWELL, MARGARET	BAL	108	2ND DIST
POWELL, MARIA	WOR	181	6TH E DI
POWELL, MARIAH	WOR	340	1ST E DI
POWELL, MARY	CEC	213	7TH E DI
POWELL, MARY A.	WOR	206	4TH E DI
POWELL, MOLLY W.	WOR	215	4TH E DI
POWELL, MORRIS	BAL	045	18TH WAR
POWELL, MOSES	WAS	212	1ST DIST
POWELL, NANCY	WOR	269	BERLIN 1
POWELL, NANCY R.	WOR	271	BERLIN 1
POWELL, P. C.	WOR	260	BERLIN 1
POWELL, PARAGON	SOM	526	QUANTICO
POWELL, PATTY	WOR	268	BERLIN 1
POWELL, PERRY	BAL	412	3RD WARD
POWELL, PETGER	WOR	214	4TH E DI
POWELL, R. W.	BAL	147	1ST WARD
POWELL, RACHEL	WOR	215	4TH E DI
POWELL, REBECCA	WOR	261	BERLIN 1
POWELL, RICHARD	SOM	388	BRINKLEY
POWELL, ROBERT	WOR	311	2ND E DI
POWELL, ROBERT	WOR	189	7TH E DI
POWELL, ROBERT E.	WOR	165	6TH E DI
POWELL, ROBERT H.	WOR	240	6TH E DI
POWELL, ROBERT M.	WOR	289	9TH E DI
POWELL, ROBERT W.	WOR	349	1ST E DI
POWELL, ROBERT W.	BAL	240	2ND WARD
POWELL, ROSINA	CEC	108	3RD E DI
POWELL, ROSSITTA	BAL	190	11TH WAR
POWELL, SAMUEL	MGM	316	CRACKLIN
POWELL, SAMUEL	SOM	405	DUBLIN D
POWELL, SAMUEL	TAL	032	EASTON D
POWELL, SAMUEL R.	ANN	458	HOWARD D
POWELL, SAMUEL-BLACK	FRE	018	FREDERIC
POWELL, SARAH	MGM	372	BERRYS D
POWELL, SARAH	BAL	375	13TH WAR
POWELL, SARAH	BAL	291	7TH WARD
POWELL, SARAH	WOR	274	BERLIN 1
POWELL, SARAH ANN	ALL	092	5TH E.D.
POWELL, SARAH C.	BAL	055	4TH WARD
POWELL, SARAH E.	BAL	005	1ST WARD
POWELL, SOPHRONOUS N.	WOR	319	1ST E DI
POWELL, SUSAN	ANN	397	8TH DIST
POWELL, SUSAN	BAL	259	6TH WARD
POWELL, SUSAN	BAL	249	6TH WARD
POWELL, SUSAN D.	WOR	182	6TH E DI
POWELL, SUSAN H.	BAL	137	18TH WAR
POWELL, THOMAS	FRE	063	FREDERIC
POWELL, THOMAS	BAL	459	8TH WARD
POWELL, THOMAS	BAL	015	15TH WAR
POWELL, THOMAS A.	WOR	218	4TH E DI
POWELL, WALTER	SOM	401	BRINKLEY
POWELL, WASHINGTON	BAL	009	1ST WARD
POWELL, WHITTINGTON	SOM	421	PRINCESS
POWELL, WILLIAM	CEC	196	6TH E DI
POWELL, WILLIAM	BAL	169	2ND DIST
POWELL, WILLIAM	BAL	388	3RD WARD
POWELL, WILLIAM	ANN	397	8TH DIST
POWELL, WILLIAM	ALL	092	5TH E.D.
POWELL, WILLIAM	BAL	074	2ND DIST
POWELL, WILLIAM	BAL	060	2ND DIST
POWELL, WILLIAM	BAL	317	7TH WARD
POWELL, WILLIAM	WOR	179	6TH E DI
POWELL, WILLIAM	WOR	255	1ST CENS
POWELL, WILLIAM	WAS	217	1ST DIST
POWELL, WILLIAM N.	WAS	014	2ND SUBD
POWELL, WILLIAM N.	TAL	044	EASTON T
POWELL, WILLIAM R.	WOR	255	1ST CENS
POWELL, WILLIAM R.	BAL	333	1ST DIST
POWELL, WILLIAM T.	WOR	271	BERLIN 1
POWELL, WILLIAM-BLACK	WOR	173	6TH E DI
POWELL, ZADOCK	WOR	187	7TH E DI
POWELL, ZADOK	WOR	292	9TH E DI
POWELL, R.	BAL	136	1ST WARD
POWELLS, LYDIA	BAL	240	12TH WAR
POWELLS, MARY E.	KEN	300	3RD DIST
POWELS, JACOB	WAS	150	HAGERSTO
POWELS, UPTON	WAS	151	HAGERSTO
POWER, ADELINE	BAL	383	3RD WARD
POWER, ANASTASIA	BAL	076	10TH WAR
POWER, BARBARA	ALL	260	CUMBERLA
POWER, CAROLINE	BAL	069	1ST WARD
POWER, CHALOTTE	BAL	048	1ST WARD
POWER, CHARLES C.	BAL	250	20TH WAR
POWER, CORNELIUS	BAL	401	3RD WARD
POWER, EDWARD J.	QUE	153	1ST E DI
POWER, ELIZABETH	MGM	442	CLARKSTR
POWER, GEORGE	BAL	363	8TH WARD
POWER, HENRY	CAL	035	2ND DIST
POWER, JAMES	CHA	218	ALLENS F
POWER, JAMES	BAL	119	1ST WARD
POWER, JAMES	BAL	236	12TH WAR
POWER, JAMES	BAL	370	1ST DIST
POWER, JAMES M.D.	BAL	239	1ST DIST
POWER, JOHN	BAL	058	1ST WARD
POWER, JOHN	BAL	460	1ST DIST
POWER, JOHN	BAL	224	1ST DIST
POWER, JOSEPH	FRE	316	MIDDLETO
POWER, MAGDALENE	ALL	261	CUMBERLA
POWER, MARY	BAL	314	3RD WARD
POWER, MARY	ALL	072	5TH E.D.
POWER, MARY	HAR	207	3RD DIST
POWER, MARY	BAL	338	13TH WAR
POWER, ROBERT T.	MGM	383	ROCKERLE
POWER, WILLIAM	BAL	107	10TH WAR
POWERA, MICHAEL	BAL	099	5TH WARD
POWERS, ANN	CHA	240	HILLTOP
POWERS, ANN	WAS	300	1ST DIST
POWERS, ANN B.	WAS	143	2ND DIST
POWERS, EDWARD	BAL	256	17TH WAR
POWERS, EDWARD	BAL	423	3RD WARD
POWERS, EDWARD	CAR	192	4TH DIST
POWERS, ELIZA L.	BAL	250	20TH WAR
POWERS, ELIZABETH	BAL	070	10TH WAR
POWERS, GEORGE	ANN	483	HOWARD D
POWERS, HENRY	BAL	056	4TH WARD
POWERS, HIRAM	BAL	079	2ND DIST
POWERS, JAMES	BAL	053	1ST WARD
POWERS, JAMES	BAL	151	1ST WARD
POWERS, JAMES	BAL	153	1ST WARD
POWERS, JAMES	HAR	162	3RD DIST
POWERS, JOHN	HAR	172	3RD DIST
POWERS, JOHN	MGM	352	BERRYS D
POWERS, JOHN	BAL	152	1ST WARD
POWERS, JOHN	BAL	046	1ST WARD
POWERS, JOHN	ALL	155	6TH E.D.
POWERS, JOHN	BAL	141	1ST WARD
POWERS, JOHN	WAS	301	1ST DIST
POWERS, JOHN C.	BAL	358	3RD WARD
POWERS, JOHN W.	BAL	023	1ST WARD
POWERS, MARY	BAL	449	1ST DIST
POWERS, MICHAL	HAR	207	3RD DIST
POWERS, PATRICK	BAL	300	1ST DIST
POWERS, PATRICK	SOM	364	BRINKLEY
POWERS, PETER	BAL	291	1ST DIST
POWERS, PULLUS	BAL	203	2ND WARD
POWERS, THOMAS	BAL	137	1ST WARD
POWERS, THOMAS	BAL	074	2ND DIST
POWERS, THOMAS	BAL	098	2ND DIST
POWERS, THOMAS	CAL	037	2ND DIST
POWERS, WALTER	BAL	230	12TH WAR
POWERS, WILLIAM	BAL	147	1ST WARD
POWERS, WILLIAM	BAL	120	1ST WARD
POWERS, WILLIAM	WAS	253	1ST DIST
POWERS, WILLIAMS	WAS	142	2ND DIST
POWLER, JEREMIAH	FRE	244	NEW MARK
POWLES, ELIZABETH	WAS	275	RIDGEVIL
POWLES, HENRY	WAS	262	1ST DIST
POWLES, HENRY	BAL	355	13TH WAR
POWLES, JOHN	BAL	427	8TH WARD
POWLES, MARY R. *	BAL	064	18TH WAR
POWLEY, HARRIET	BAL	397	8TH WARD
POWNELL, JACOB P.	ALL	222	CUMBERLA
POWNELL, JOHNATHAN	ALL	222	CUMBERLA
POWNELL, JOSEPH	ALL	222	CUMBERLA
PRACHT, AUGUSTUS C.	BAL	213	19TH WAR
PRACHT, GEORGE	BAL	119	15TH WAR
PRACKMAN, WILLIAM	BAL	209	17TH WAR
PRAFF, MARGARET	BAL	405	14TH WAR
PRAGAW, ELIZA	BAL	331	3RD WARD
PRAGEN, V.O.	BAL	117	1ST WARD
PRAGER, HENRY	BAL	199	17TH WAR
PRAITHER, BASELL	WAS	115	2ND DIST
PRAITHER, FRIEND	WAS	122	2ND DIST
PRALER, DOROTHEA	BAL	063	15TH WAR
PRALLE, ANDREW	BAL	181	6TH WARD
PRALLE, ELI	BAL	017	9TH WARD
PRALLE, GEORGE	BAL	017	9TH WARD
PRASCH, JOHN	BAL	387	8TH WARD
PRASER, CYRUS	HAR	187	3RD DIST
PRASER, JOHN	HAR	187	3RD DIST
PRASER, WILLIAM	HAR	187	3RD DIST
PRAT, MARY	BAL	400	14TH WAR
PRATER, ALFRED	BAL	310	20TH WAR
PRATER, JEFFERSON	FRE	309	WOODSBOR
PRATHAN, JAMES	MGM	365	BERRYS D
PRATHER, ANN V.	PRI	013	BLADENSB
PRATHER, DANUEL M.	WAS	124	2ND DIST
PRATHER, EMMA	BAL	223	19TH WAR
PRATHER, HTOMAS	WAS	155	2ND DIST
PRATHER, JEMIMA	MGM	328	CRACKLIN
PRATHER, JEMINIA	WAS	124	2ND DIST
PRATHER, JOHNATHAN	WAS	164	2ND DIST
PRATHER, MARY	PRI	044	VANSVILL
PRATHER, MARY A.	ANN	435	HOWARD D
PRATHER, NATHAN	PRI	045	VANSVILL
PRATHER, RICHARD	WAS	118	2ND DIST
PRATHER, RICHARD	PRI	012	BLADENSB
PRATHER, RICHARD O.	PRI	083	QUEEN AN
PRATHER, SINGLETON	MGM	404	ROCKERLE
PRATHER, ZEPHENIAH	PRI	005	BLADENSB
PRATICE, CHARLES-BLACK	CAR	141	NO TWP L
PRATICE, CHARLES-BLACK	CAR	142	NO TWP L
PRATICE, HENRY-BLACK	CAR	141	NO TWP L
PRATICE, ISAAC-BLACK	CAR	152	NO TWP L
PRATICE, JAMES-BLACK	CAR	142	NO TWP L
PRATICE, JOHN-BLACK	CAR	157	NO TWP L
PRATICE, SOLOMON-BLACK	CAR	139	NO TWP L
PRATICE, STEVIN-BLACK	CAR	134	NO TWP L
PRATICE, WESLEY-BLACK	CAR	143	NO TWP L
PRATICE, WILLIAM-BLACK	CAR	139	NO TWP L
PRATICE, WILLIAM-BLACK	CAR	164	NO TWP L
PRATT, ALSADE*	TAL	006	EASTON D
PRATT, ANN ELIZA	BAL	342	13TH WAR
PRATT, AUGUSTA C.	BAL	049	15TH WAR
PRATT, BENNETT	QUE	131	1ST E DI
PRATT, BIDDY	BAL	455	14TH WAR
PRATT, CEILIA	BAL	025	1ST WARD
PRATT, CHARELS H.	BAL	189	6TH WARD
PRATT, CHARLES	QUE	252	5TH E DI
PRATT, CHRISTOPHER	KEN	229	2ND DIST
PRATT, DAVID	BAL	152	5TH WARD
PRATT, DAVID	BAL	133	1ST WARD
PRATT, DEBORAH-BLACK	QUE	167	2ND E DI
PRATT, EDWIN E.	QUE	239	5TH E DI
PRATT, ELIZABETH	TAL	061	EASTON D
PRATT, ELIZABETH	BAL	448	14TH WAR
PRATT, ELMOTER*	TAL	009	EASTON D
PRATT, EMILY	QUE	183	3RD E DI
PRATT, ENOCH	BAL	150	11TH WAR
PRATT, ENOCH	BAL	438	14TH WAR
PRATT, FRANCIS	BAL	128	18TH WAR
PRATT, HENRY R.	BAL	242	12TH WAR
PRATT, HESLY	BAL	286	12TH WAR
PRATT, HESTER A.	BAL	324	7TH WARD
PRATT, HORACE	BAL	117	5TH WARD
PRATT, ISAAC	ANN	467	HOWARD D
PRATT, J.	BAL	139	1ST WARD
PRATT, JABEZ	BAL	429	14TH WAR
PRATT, JACOB H.	QUE	192	3RD E DI
PRATT, JAMES	ALL	236	CUMBERLA
PRATT, JAMES	BAL	285	1ST DIST
PRATT, JOHN	BAL	166	1ST WARD
PRATT, JOSHUA	TAL	008	EASTON D
PRATT, LOUIZA	BAL	111	5TH WARD
PRATT, LOUIZA	CAR	073	NO TWP L
PRATT, MARY	PRI	032	VANSVILL
PRATT, MARY A.	BAL	149	19TH WAR
PRATT, MARY-BLACK	FRE	049	FREDERIC
PRATT, MISS C.	FRE	199	5TH E DI
PRATT, P. W.	QUE	211	3RD E DI
PRATT, S. H. DR-	BAL	030	18TH WAR
PRATT, SAMUEL	QUE	147	1ST E DI
PRATT, SAMUEL	BAL	242	6TH WARD
PRATT, SIMON	BAL	148	1ST WARD
PRATT, SUSAN	BAL	324	12TH WAR
PRATT, T. T.	BAL	333	1ST DIST
PRATT, THOMAS	BAL	242	12TH WAR
PRATT, THOMAS	QUE	146	1ST E DI
PRATT, THOMAS	QUE	145	1ST E DI
PRATT, THOMAS G.	CAR	143	NO TWP L
PRATT, THOMAS G.	ANN	293	ANNAPOLI
PRATT, THOMAS P.	QUE	168	2ND E DI
PRATT, TRUMAN	BAL	247	20TH WAR

Name	County	Page	Locality
PRATT, WILLAIM	BAL	149	1ST WARD
PRATT, WILLIAM	BAL	176	6TH WARD
PRATT, WILLIAM	BAL	349	13TH WAR
PRATT, WILLIAM	QUE	160	2ND E DI
PRATT, WILLIAM J.	CAR	084	NO TWP L
PRATT, WILLIAM T.	TAL	036	EASTON D
PRATTE, PETER	BAL	207	19TH WAR
PRATTIS, TILGHMAN	BAL	102	15TH WAR
PRAVICE, ELIZABETH	CAR	142	NO TWP L
PRAY, ISIAS	ANN	268	ANNAPOLI
PRCE, ELIZABETH	CAR	287	7TH DIST
PREARSON, SARAH A.	BAL	021	1ST WARD
PREAST, JOHN	BAL	271	1ST DIST
PREBB, WILLIAM	BAL	073	1ST WARD
PREBBLE, SARILLA	FRE	012	FREDERIC
PREBERRY, MARTHA	BAL	340	1ST DIST
PRECHTEL, FREDERICK	BAL	165	16TH WAR
PRECHTEL, G. F.	BAL	080	10TH WAR
PRECHTEL, JOHN	BAL	081	10TH WAR
PREDAL, CHARLES	BAL	081	2ND DIST
PREDIEAUX, ANN	WOR	280	BERLIN 1
PREECE, EDWARD	BAL	147	5TH WARD
PREECE, EDWARD JR.	BAL	147	5TH WARD
PREGG, ROBERT	KEN	292	3RD DIST
PREIS, MICHAEL	BAL	265	12TH WAR
PREISS, ELIZABETH	BAL	241	20TH WAR
PREISS, HERSCH	BAL	317	12TH WAR
PREISS, JOHN	BAL	240	20TH WAR
PREIST, CATHARINE	BAL	014	18TH WAR
PRELL, LEWIS	BAL	362	13TH WAR
PREMER, RACHAEL-BLACK	BAL	216	2ND WARD
PRENOF, LOUISA	BAL	353	7TH WARD
PRENTESS, GEORGE	ALL	110	5TH E.D.
PRENTICE, NANCY	BAL	219	12TH WAR
PRENTION, GEORGE	CHA	236	HILLTOP
PRENTIS, JOHN	BAL	402	1ST DIST
PREPPOINT, WILLAIM	BAL	278	2ND WARD
PRESBARY, DAVID	HAR	060	1ST DIST
PRESBARY, GEORGE	HAR	034	1ST DIST
PRESBARY, HENNAH	HAR	012	1ST DIST
PRESBEY, STEPHEN	HAR	172	3RD DIST
PRESBORY, SARAH A.	HAR	150	3RD DIST
PRESBURY, JESSE	BAL	176	6TH WARD
PRESCO, JAMES *	BAL	348	1ST DIST
PRESCOTT, JANE	BAL	220	6TH WARD
PRESCOTT, RUBEN	BAL	214	6TH WARD
PRESGROVE, BENJAMIN	BAL	107	2ND DIST
PRESLEY, WILLIAM	HAR	199	3RD DIST
PRESTER, MARY	BAL	455	1ST DIST
PRESTMAN, G.	BAL	151	11TH WAR
PRESTMAN, JACOB	BAL	283	20TH WAR
PRESTON, AARON	HAR	132	2ND DIST
PRESTON, ALBERT	CEC	214	7TH E DI
PRESTON, AMOS	CEC	214	7TH E DI
PRESTON, ANN	BAL	457	14TH WAR
PRESTON, AQUILA	HAR	107	2ND DIST
PRESTON, AVARILLA	HAR	114	2ND DIST
PRESTON, BETSY	BAL	054	2ND DIST
PRESTON, BLANCHE L.	HAR	136	2ND DIST
PRESTON, CATHARINE	BAL	258	12TH WAR
PRESTON, CHARLES	BAL	011	2ND DIST
PRESTON, CHARLES	FRE	087	FREDERIC
PRESTON, CHARLES	FRE	034	FREDERIC
PRESTON, CHARLOTTE	HAR	103	2ND DIST
PRESTON, CHRIS	BAL	226	19TH WAR
PRESTON, CRISTIANA A.	BAL	137	18TH WAR
PRESTON, CANIEL	CEC	143	7TH E DI
PRESTON, CAVID	HAR	087	2ND DIST
PRESTON, DEBORAH	MGM	336	CRACKLIN
PRESTON, EDMUND M.	BAL	016	15TH WAR
PRESTON, ELIZA	ANN	384	4TH DIST
PRESTON, ELIZA A.	HAR	052	1ST DIST
PRESTON, ELIZABETH	HAR	105	2ND DIST
PRESTON, ELIZABETH	BAL	127	18TH WAR
PRESTON, FANNY	BAL	409	14TH WAR
PRESTON, FREDERICK	ALL	255	CUMBERLA
PRESTON, GEORGE	BAL	416	8TH WARD
PRESTON, GEORGE	HAR	145	3RD DIST
PRESTON, HANNAH E.	HAR	130	2ND DIST
PRESTON, HARRIET	HAR	089	2ND DIST
PRESTON, HARRIOTT	BAL	106	18TH WAR
PRESTON, HENRIETTA	HAR	106	2ND DIST
PRESTON, HENRY	HAR	030	1ST DIST
PRESTON, HENRY	HAR	116	2ND DIST
PRESTON, HENRY	BAL	237	20TH WAR
PRESTON, HENRY	BAL	011	2ND DIST
PRESTON, HENRY D.	BAL	409	14TH WAR
PRESTON, JACOB	BAL	246	6TH WARD
PRESTON, JACOB A.	HAR	186	3RD DIST
PRESTON, JAMES	HAR	186	3RD DIST
PRESTON, JAMES	HAR	051	1ST DIST
PRESTON, JANE	BAL	046	9TH WARD
PRESTON, JANE	BAL	017	15TH WAR
PRESTON, JOHN	BAL	051	2ND DIST
PRESTON, JOHN	BAL	016	4TH WARD
PRESTON, JOHN H.	BAL	002	15TH WAR
PRESTON, JONAS	BAL	040	2ND DIST
PRESTON, JONAS	CEC	214	7TH E DI
PRESTON, JOSEPH	CEC	171	6TH E DI
PRESTON, JULIA A.	BAL	078	10TH WAR
PRESTON, JUPITER	CEC	181	7TH E DI
PRESTON, LARY	HAR	153	3RD DIST
PRESTON, LOUISA	HAR	109	2ND DIST
PRESTON, MARGARET	BAL	149	11TH WAR
PRESTON, MARGARETT	BAL	093	18TH WAR
PRESTON, MARTHA	BAL	014	4TH WARD
PRESTON, MARTHA	BAL	460	1ST DIST
PRESTON, MARY	BAL	295	12TH WAR
PRESTON, MARY	BAL	022	2ND DIST
PRESTON, MARY	BAL	064	4TH WARD
PRESTON, MARY D.	CEC	200	7TH E DI
PRESTON, MARY O.	BAL	192	6TH WARD
PRESTON, MESHECK	ALL	110	5TH E.D.
PRESTON, MOSES	HAR	103	2ND DIST
PRESTON, MOSES	HAR	134	2ND DIST
PRESTON, NANCY	HAR	143	2ND DIST
PRESTON, OLIVER J.	BAL	019	1ST WARD
PRESTON, PETER	BAL	177	11TH WAR
PRESTON, PETER	TAL	070	EASTON T
PRESTON, REBECCA	HAR	006	1ST DIST
PRESTON, ROGER	HAR	122	2ND DIST
PRESTON, SAMUEL	HAR	115	2ND DIST
PRESTON, SAMUEL B.	FRE	397	PETERSVI
PRESTON, SARAH	HAR	107	2ND DIST
PRESTON, SARAH	HAR	134	2ND DIST
PRESTON, SARAH	ALL	091	5TH E.D.
PRESTON, SHADRACK	ALL	111	5TH E.D.
PRESTON, STEPHEN	HAR	130	2ND DIST
PRESTON, THOMAS	FRE	270	NEW MARK
PRESTON, TIMOTHY	BAL	046	9TH WARD

Name	County	Page	Locality
PRESTON, WESLEY	HAR	110	2ND DIST
PRESTON, WILLIAM	BAL	078	18TH WAR
PRESTON, WILLIAM	BAL	455	14TH WAR
PRESTON, WILLIAM	BAL	277	1ST DIST
PRESTON, WILLIAM	BAL	066	2ND DIST
PRESTON, WILLIAM	BAL	295	12TH WAR
PRESTON, WILLIAM	BAL	140	16TH WAR
PRESTON, WILLIAM H.	BAL	052	9TH WARD
PRESTON, WILLIAM M.	BAL	301	17TH WAR
PRESTON, WILLIAM T.	HAR	103	2ND DIST
PRESTON, SAMUEL	BAL	140	1ST WARD
PRESTON, THOMAS	BAL	030	2ND DIST
PRETLOVE, AMELIA	BAL	300	7TH WARD
PRETSSINAN, LOYD	ANN	488	HOWARD D
PRETT, ANNA	WAS	235	1ST DIST
PRETTONE, CAROLINE*	BAL	389	3RD WARD
PRETTOVE, CAROLINE*	BAL	389	3RD WARD
PRETTYHOOVER, AMELIA	WAS	157	HAGERSTO
PRETTYMAN, INDIANNA	WAS	131	HAGERSTO
PRETTYMAN, JOSEPH	WAS	131	HAGERSTO
PRETTYMAN, LEVIN	KEN	290	3RD DIST
PRETTYMAN, WILLIAM	BAL	226	19TH WAR
PRETYMAN, PETER	WAS	251	1ST DIST
PRETYMAN, SAMUEL	WAS	128	HAGERSTO
PRETYMAN, WILLIAM	WAS	132	HAGERSTO
PRETYMAN, WILLIAM	WAS	132	HAGERSTO
PRETZMAN, DAVID	WAS	270	1ST DIST
PREVOST, A. SR.	BAL	184	19TH WAR
PREVOST, JULIA	BAL	184	19TH WAR
PREWELL, JOHN	SOM	370	BRINKLEY
PREWIT, BENJAMIN	HAR	049	1ST DIST
PRIAN, MARTIN *	HAR	036	1ST DIST
PRICE, ABRAM-BLACK	QUE	179	2ND E DI
PRICE, ALLEN	BAL	315	12TH WAR
PRICE, ALLEN	BAL	227	12TH WAR
PRICE, AMELIA	CEC	098	3RD E DI
PRICE, AMON	CAR	183	8TH DIST
PRICE, AMRIA	CAL	060	3RD DIST
PRICE, ANDREW	BAL	034	15TH WAR
PRICE, ANN	CEC	065	1ST E DI
PRICE, ANN	QUE	245	5TH E DI
PRICE, ANN B.	CEC	062	1ST E DI
PRICE, ANN E.	BAL	128	16TH WAR
PRICE, ANN E.	BAL	242	2ND WARD
PRICE, ANN M.	BAL	172	2ND DIST
PRICE, ARCHABOLD	ST	288	2ND E DI
PRICE, AUGUSTUS M.	BAL	344	13TH WAR
PRICE, EASSEL*	TAL	049	EASTON T
PRICE, BENJAMIN	DOR	454	1ST DIST
PRICE, BENJAMIN	CEC	050	1ST E DI
PRICE, BENJAMIN	BAL	266	1ST DIST
PRICE, BENJAMIN	BAL	439	1ST DIST
PRICE, BENJAMIN	BAL	017	2ND DIST
PRICE, BENJAMIN	ANN	460	HOWARD D
PRICE, BETSEY*	BAL	002	4TH WARD
PRICE, CAROLINE	BAL	289	3RD WARD
PRICE, CAROLINE	BAL	266	2ND WARD
PRICE, CATHAIRNE	CAR	174	8TH DIST
PRICE, CATHARINE	WAS	198	1ST DIST
PRICE, CHARLES	MGM	330	CRACKLIN
PRICE, CHARLES	BAL	268	1ST DIST
PRICE, CHARLOTTE	QUE	201	3RD E DI
PRICE, CHRISTOPHER	CEC	122	4TH E DI
PRICE, CHRITOPHER	QUE	241	5TH E DI
PRICE, D.	BAL	161	1ST WARD
PRICE, DANIEL	BAL	195	5TH DIST
PRICE, DANIEL	BAL	436	1ST DIST
PRICE, DANIEL	MGM	422	MEDLEY 3
PRICE, CAVID	BAL	313	3RD WARD
PRICE, DAVID	BAL	160	1ST WARD
PRICE, DAVID	BAL	005	15TH WAR
PRICE, DAVID B.	BAL	026	18TH WAR
PRICE, CAVID E.	WAS	156	2ND DIST
PRICE, DAVID K.	CEC	054	1ST E DI
PRICE, DAVID W.	BAL	426	1ST DIST
PRICE, DEBORAH	CAR	156	NO TWP L
PRICE, DENNARD	TAL	054	EASTON D
PRICE, DOLLY	CHA	246	HILLTOP
PRICE, DORO*	SOM	493	SALISBUR
PRICE, EAVE	HAR	009	1ST DIST
PRICE, EDWARD	WAS	043	2ND SUBD
PRICE, EDWARD C.	HAR	085	2ND DIST
PRICE, EDWARD P.	QUE	220	3RD E DI
PRICE, EDWARD W.	QUE	171	2ND E DI
PRICE, ELEANOR	WOR	319	1ST E DI
PRICE, ELFRED	QUE	228	4TH E DI
PRICE, ELI	CEC	035	CHESAPEA
PRICE, ELIAS	MGM	326	CRACKLIN
PRICE, ELIJAH	FRE	276	NEW MARK
PRICE, ELIJAH	BAL	425	1ST DIST
PRICE, ELINOR	ANN	503	HOWARD D
PRICE, ELISTH	BAL	174	2ND DIST
PRICE, ELIZA	BAL	076	15TH WAR
PRICE, ELIZA	BAL	019	15TH WAR
PRICE, ELIZA	BAL	253	6TH WARD
PRICE, ELIZA	BAL	393	14TH WAR
PRICE, ELIZA	TAL	033	EASTON D
PRICE, ELIZA-BLACK	QUE	148	1ST E DI
PRICE, ELIZABETH	QUE	151	1ST E DI
PRICE, ELIZABETH	HAR	161	3RD DIST
PRICE, ELIZABETH	BAL	146	11TH WAR
PRICE, ELIZABETH	CEC	053	1ST E DI
PRICE, ELIZABETH	TAL	097	ST MICHA
PRICE, ELIZABETH	BAL	237	1ST DIST
PRICE, ELIZABETH	BAL	426	1ST DIST
PRICE, ELIZABETH	BAL	052	2ND DIST
PRICE, ELLEN	BAL	053	18TH WAR
PRICE, EMARY	BAL	294	1ST DIST
PRICE, EMELINE	BAL	137	16TH WAR
PRICE, EMMA	MGM	423	MEDLEY 3
PRICE, EZEKIEL	TAL	031	EASTON D
PRICE, FRANCES	DOR	342	3RD DIVI
PRICE, FRANCIS	CHA	243	HILLTOP
PRICE, FRANCIS	DOR	380	1ST DIST
PRICE, FRANK	TAL	078	EASTON T
PRICE, FRANKLIN	CEC	015	ELKTON 3
PRICE, FREDERICK	BAL	330	7TH WARD
PRICE, FREDERICK	BAL	049	15TH WAR
PRICE, FREDERICK	BAL	174	1ST WARD
PRICE, FRISBY-BLACK	QUE	152	1ST E DI
PRICE, G.B.M.	ALL	262	CUMBERLA
PRICE, GEORGE	BAL	049	2ND DIST
PRICE, GEORGE	BAL	086	2ND DIST
PRICE, GEORGE	BAL	295	3RD WARD
PRICE, GEORGE	BAL	217	6TH DIST
PRICE, GEORGE	BAL	214	6TH DIST
PRICE, GEORGE	BAL	145	1ST WARD
PRICE, GEORGE	CEC	057	1ST E DI
PRICE, GEORGE	CAR	067	NO TWP L
PRICE, GEORGE	CEC	181	7TH E DI

Name	County	Page	Locality
PRICE, GEORGE	WOR	319	1ST E DI
PRICE, GEORGE	WOR	315	2ND E DI
PRICE, GEORGE	WOR	223	4TH E DI
PRICE, GEORGE	SOM	535	QUANTICO
PRICE, GEORGE B.	BAL	200	19TH WAR
PRICE, GEORGE E.	QUE	156	2ND E DI
PRICE, GEORGE W.	CEC	162	6TH E DI
PRICE, GEORGE W.	BAL	050	4TH WARD
PRICE, GEORGE W.	BAL	042	9TH WARD
PRICE, GEORGE W. *	KEN	223	2ND DIST
PRICE, GEORGE-BLACK	QUE	142	1ST E DI
PRICE, GEORGEW W.	BAL	391	14TH WAR
PRICE, HAGOR	BAL	243	1ST DIST
PRICE, HANNA	BAL	015	4TH WARD
PRICE, HANNAH	FRE	258	NEW MARK
PRICE, HANNAH	CEC	053	1ST E DI
PRICE, HANNAH	BAL	193	5TH DIST
PRICE, HANNAH	BAL	236	1ST DIST
PRICE, HARRY	ANN	268	ANNAPOLI
PRICE, HELEN A.	CEC	125	5TH E DI
PRICE, HENRY	CAR	066	NO TWP L
PRICE, HENRY	BAL	277	12TH WAR
PRICE, HENRY	TAL	033	EASTON D
PRICE, HENRY	TAL	098	ST MICHA
PRICE, HENRY C.	BAL	073	10TH WAR
PRICE, HORATIO	CAR	267	WESTMINS
PRICE, HYLAND	CEC	045	1ST E DI
PRICE, HYLAND B.	KEN	223	2ND DIST
PRICE, ISAAC	BAL	425	1ST DIST
PRICE, ISAAC	SOM	397	BRINKLEY
PRICE, ISAAC L.	KEN	222	2ND DIST
PRICE, ISRAEL	BAL	019	2ND DIST
PRICE, JACOB	BAL	074	15TH WAR
PRICE, JACOB	CAR	244	3RD DIST
PRICE, JACOB	CEC	114	3RD E DI
PRICE, JACOB	WAS	030	2ND SUBD
PRICE, JACOB	PRI	084	QUEEN AN
PRICE, JAMES	TAL	118	ST MICHA
PRICE, JAMES	WOR	199	8TH E DI
PRICE, JAMES	SOM	493	SALISBUR
PRICE, JAMES	TAL	053	EASTON D
PRICE, JAMES	KEN	277	1ST DIST
PRICE, JAMES	ST	326	4TH E DI
PRICE, JAMES	CEC	057	1ST E DI
PRICE, JAMES	CEC	041	CHESAPEA
PRICE, JAMES	CEC	043	CHESAPEA
PRICE, JAMES	CAR	074	NO TWP L
PRICE, JAMES	CAR	109	NO TWP L
PRICE, JAMES	QUE	159	2ND E DI
PRICE, JAMES	BAL	241	20TH WAR
PRICE, JAMES	BAL	206	11TH WAR
PRICE, JAMES	BAL	108	2ND DIST
PRICE, JAMES	BAL	197	5TH DIST
PRICE, JAMES	BAL	145	1ST WARD
PRICE, JAMES	BAL	411	8TH WARD
PRICE, JAMES	BAL	128	1ST WARD
PRICE, JAMES JR.	SOM	495	SALISBUR
PRICE, JAMES M.	ALL	134	4TH E.D.
PRICE, JAMES W.	QUE	179	2ND E DI
PRICE, JAMES W.	CEC	103	4TH E DI
PRICE, JAMES W.	HAR	043	1ST DIST
PRICE, JAMES-BLACK	QUE	150	1ST E DI
PRICE, JAMES-BLACK	QUE	142	1ST E DI
PRICE, JEHU	BAL	426	1ST DIST
PRICE, JESSE	HAR	124	2ND DIST
PRICE, JESSE	TAL	058	EASTON D
PRICE, JOB	FRE	275	NEW MARK
PRICE, JOE	TAL	004	EASTON D
PRICE, JOEL	BAL	426	1ST DIST
PRICE, JOEL E.	BAL	427	1ST DIST
PRICE, JOHN	BAL	435	1ST DIST
PRICE, JOHN	BAL	425	1ST DIST
PRICE, JOHN	BAL	413	1ST DIST
PRICE, JOHN	BAL	217	6TH DIST
PRICE, JOHN	BAL	316	3RD WARD
PRICE, JOHN	BAL	380	1ST DIST
PRICE, JOHN	ANN	293	ANNAPOLI
PRICE, JOHN	BAL	133	1ST WARD
PRICE, JOHN	ANN	477	HOWARD D
PRICE, JOHN	BAL	113	2ND DIST
PRICE, JOHN	BAL	286	2ND WARD
PRICE, JOHN	BAL	459	8TH WARD
PRICE, JOHN	BAL	133	16TH WAR
PRICE, JOHN	BAL	149	1ST WARD
PRICE, JOHN	TAL	054	EASTON D
PRICE, JOHN	QUE	188	3RD E DI
PRICE, JOHN	WAS	208	1ST DIST
PRICE, JOHN	HAR	197	3RD DIST
PRICE, JOHN	HAR	138	2ND DIST
PRICE, JOHN	SOM	432	PRINCESS
PRICE, JOHN	CAR	100	NO TWP L
PRICE, JOHN	CAR	075	NO TWP L
PRICE, JOHN	CAL	060	3RD DIST
PRICE, JOHN	CEC	047	1ST E DI
PRICE, JOHN	CEC	017	ELKTON 3
PRICE, JOHN	CEC	029	CHESAPEA
PRICE, JOHN	CAR	192	4TH DIST
PRICE, JOHN	BAL	056	4TH WARD
PRICE, JOHN	BAL	257	17TH WAR
PRICE, JOHN	BAL	208	17TH WAR
PRICE, JOHN C.	CAR	333	MANCHEST
PRICE, JOHN C.	QUE	198	3RD E DI
PRICE, JOHN F.	HAR	087	2ND DIST
PRICE, JOHN F.	CHA	236	HILLTOP
PRICE, JOHN H.	HAR	122	2ND DIST
PRICE, JOHN H.	TAL	009	EASTON D
PRICE, JOHN H.	BAL	186	2ND WARD
PRICE, JOHN H.	BAL	179	16TH WAR
PRICE, JOHN K.	BAL	019	2ND DIST
PRICE, JOHN L.	BAL	187	5TH DIST
PRICE, JOHN M.	BAL	033	2ND DIST
PRICE, JOHN R.	CEC	048	1ST E DI
PRICE, JOHN S.	QUE	192	3RD E DI
PRICE, JOHN T.	HAR	099	2ND DIST
PRICE, JOHN-BLACK	QUE	145	1ST E DI
PRICE, JOHN-BLACK	QUE	143	1ST E DI
PRICE, JOHN-BLACK	CAR	137	NO TWP L
PRICE, JOSEPH	CAR	107	NO TWP L
PRICE, JOSEPH	HAR	181	3RD DIST
PRICE, JOSEPH	CEC	042	CHESAPEA
PRICE, JOSEPH	CHA	242	HILLTOP
PRICE, JOSEPH	CEC	055	1ST E DI
PRICE, JOSEPH	QUE	211	3RD E DI
PRICE, JOSEPH	KEN	307	3RD DIST
PRICE, JOSEPH	BAL	312	7TH WARD
PRICE, JOSEPH	BAL	425	1ST DIST
PRICE, JOSEPH D.	WAS	246	SMITHSBU
PRICE, JOSEPH R.	TAL	003	EASTON D
PRICE, JOSEPH R.J.	BAL	440	1ST DIST
PRICE, JOSEPHEAN	BAL	255	1ST DIST

Name	Location
PRICE, JOSHUA	BAL 439 1ST DIST
PRICE, JOSIAH	BAL 071 10TH WAR
PRICE, JULIA	CEC 046 1ST E DI
PRICE, JULIA	BAL 153 11TH WAR
PRICE, JULIA A.	HAR 099 2ND DIST
PRICE, JULIA A.	WOR 215 4TH E DI
PRICE, L.	BAL 115 1ST WARD
PRICE, L.	BAL 150 1ST WARD
PRICE, L. F.	BAL 286 2ND WARD
PRICE, L.F.	BAL 171 1ST WARD
PRICE, L.F.	BAL 165 1ST WARD
PRICE, LEVI	BAL 426 1ST DIST
PRICE, LEVIN B.	SOM 472 TRAPPE D
PRICE, LEWIS	BAL 136 2ND DIST
PRICE, LOUIS	CEC 062 1ST E DI
PRICE, LOUISA	BAL 288 3RD WARD
PRICE, LOVICE-BLACK	CAR 134 NO TWP L
PRICE, MAHALA	BAL 127 16TH WAR
PRICE, MAHLON M.D.	BAL 426 1ST DIST
PRICE, MARGARET	BAL 059 10TH WAR
PRICE, MARGARET	BAL 236 1ST DIST
PRICE, MARGARET	ALL 183 8TH E.D.
PRICE, MARGARET	HAR 186 3RD DIST
PRICE, MARGARET	KEN 276 1ST DIST
PRICE, MARGARET	WOR 222 4TH E DI
PRICE, MARGARET	SOM 481 TRAPP DI
PRICE, MARGARET J.	BAL 331 7TH WARD
PRICE, MARGARET V.	BAL 432 14TH WAR
PRICE, MARIA	BAL 257 1ST DIST
PRICE, MARIA*	DOR 380 1ST DIST
PRICE, MARTHA	WOR 311 2ND E DI
PRICE, MARTHA J.	HAR 099 2ND DIST
PRICE, MARTHY	DOR 382 1ST DIST
PRICE, MARTIN	CAR 139 NO TWP L
PRICE, MARY	HAR 143 2ND DIST
PRICE, MARY	BAL 090 18TH WAR
PRICE, MARY	SOM 397 BRINKLEY
PRICE, MARY	BAL 290 1ST DIST
PRICE, MARY	BAL 356 3RD WARD
PRICE, MARY	ALL 090 5TH E.D.
PRICE, MARY	BAL 436 1ST DIST
PRICE, MARY	BAL 045 2ND DIST
PRICE, MARY A.	BAL 025 2ND DIST
PRICE, MARY A.	BAL 426 1ST DIST
PRICE, MARY A.	BAL 085 18TH WAR
PRICE, MARY E.	WAS 182 BOONSBOR
PRICE, MARY E.	QUE 171 2ND E DI
PRICE, MARY R.	HAR 198 3RD DIST
PRICE, MARY-BLACK	CAR 118 NO TWP L
PRICE, MATILDA	CAR 154 NO TWP L
PRICE, MATILDA A.	BAL 154 16TH WAR
PRICE, MILCAH	HAR 181 3RD DIST
PRICE, MILLY	WOR 307 2ND E DI
PRICE, MISS	ANN 280 ANNAPOLI
PRICE, MONTMOREY H.	BAL 035 9TH WARD
PRICE, MORDECAI	BAL 019 2ND DIST
PRICE, MORDECAI	QUE 148 1ST E DI
PRICE, MORDECAI	CAR 267 WESTMINS
PRICE, MORDICA OF SAMUEL	BAL 427 1ST DIST
PRICE, MOSES D.	BAL 427 1ST DIST
PRICE, MR.	BAL 213 17TH WAR
PRICE, N. WESLY	FRE 262 NEW MARK
PRICE, NANCY	TAL 032 EASTON D
PRICE, NATHAN	BAL 146 19TH WAR
PRICE, NEHEMIAH	ST 311 1ST E DI
PRICE, NEHEMIAH	BAL 054 2ND DIST
PRICE, NELSON	BAL 194 5TH DIST
PRICE, NICHOLAS	TAL 042 EASTON D
PRICE, PARPINE-BLACK	WOR 174 6TH E DI
PRICE, PERRY	KEN 252 1ST DIST
PRICE, PETER	SOM 458 DAMES QU
PRICE, PETER	BAL 397 1ST DIST
PRICE, PHILLIS	SOM 493 SALISBUR
PRICE, R.	BAL 147 1ST WARD
PRICE, REBECCA	BAL 216 6TH DIST
PRICE, REBECCA	WAS 042 2ND SUBD
PRICE, REBECCA	BAL 356 13TH WAR
PRICE, RICHARD	BAL 462 14TH WAR
PRICE, RICHARD	CHA 242 HILLTOP
PRICE, RICHARD	BAL 267 20TH WAR
PRICE, ROBERT	CEC 054 1ST E DI
PRICE, ROBERT	SOM 485 TRAPP DI
PRICE, ROBERT	BAL 195 5TH DIST
PRICE, ROBERT G.	QUE 192 3RD E DI
PRICE, ROMAN	BAL 199 11TH WAR
PRICE, ROSETTA	TAL 075 EASTON T
PRICE, SALLY	SOM 535 QUANTICO
PRICE, SALLY	TAL 049 EASTON T
PRICE, SAMUEL	SOM 424 PRINCESS
PRICE, SAMUEL	CEC 057 1ST E DI
PRICE, SAMUEL	CAR 351 6TH DIST
PRICE, SAMUEL	HAR 138 2ND DIST
PRICE, SAMUEL	CEC 039 CHESAPEA
PRICE, SAMUEL	CEC 039 CHESAPEA
PRICE, SAMUEL	CEC 051 1ST E DI
PRICE, SAMUEL	CAR 164 NO TWP L
PRICE, SAMUEL	WAS 278 LEITERSB
PRICE, SAMUEL	TAL 058 EASTON D
PRICE, SAMUEL	BAL 441 8TH WARD
PRICE, SAMUEL	BAL 183 5TH DIST
PRICE, SAMUEL	BAL 208 6TH DIST
PRICE, SAMUEL	BAL 426 1ST DIST
PRICE, SAMUEL	BAL 457 1ST DIST
PRICE, SAMUEL	BAL 051 2ND DIST
PRICE, SAMUEL	ANN 480 HOWARD D
PRICE, SAMUEL C.	BAL 426 1ST DIST
PRICE, SAMUEL D.	BAL 431 1ST DIST
PRICE, SAMUEL J.	CEC 015 ELKTON 3
PRICE, SAMUEL M.	BAL 425 1ST DIST
PRICE, SARAH	BAL 425 1ST DIST
PRICE, SARAH	BAL 069 2ND DIST
PRICE, SARAH	BAL 447 8TH WARD
PRICE, SARAH	BAL 397 3RD WARD
PRICE, SARAH	QUE 157 2ND E DI
PRICE, SARAH	BAL 146 19TH WAR
PRICE, SARAH	TAL 050 EASTON T
PRICE, SARAH A.	WAS 128 HAGERSTO
PRICE, SARAH C.	BAL 399 1ST DIST
PRICE, SARAH G.	TAL 041 EASTON D
PRICE, SAURA	TAL 076 EASTON T
PRICE, SKELTON	BAL 456 1ST DIST
PRICE, SKELTON	BAL 077 2ND DIST
PRICE, SOPHIA	BAL 169 19TH WAR
PRICE, SOPHIA-BLACK	QUE 124 1ST E DI
PRICE, STPEHEN	BAL 023 2ND DIST
PRICE, SULLA	BAL 205 2ND WARD
PRICE, SUSAN	BAL 010 1ST WARD
PRICE, SUSAN-BLACK	QUE 151 1ST E DI
PRICE, THOASM	ST 288 2ND E DI
PRICE, THOMAS	TAL 043 EASTON D
PRICE, THOMAS	SOM 535 QUANTICO
PRICE, THOMAS	CEC 065 1ST E DI
PRICE, THOMAS	CEC 058 1ST E DI
PRICE, THOMAS	MGM 379 ROCKERLE
PRICE, THOMAS	BAL 458 1ST DIST
PRICE, THOMAS	BAL 218 6TH DIST
PRICE, THOMAS E.	TAL 066 EASTON T
PRICE, THOMAS R.	TAL 054 EASTON D
PRICE, THOMAS R.	BAL 423 1ST DIST
PRICE, THOMAS S.	ST 310 1ST E DI
PRICE, THOMAS*	SOM 399 BRINK_EY
PRICE, THOMS	BAL 079 2ND DIST
PRICE, VALENTINE	BAL 216 6TH DIST
PRICE, WALTER	BAL 007 15TH WAR
PRICE, WASHINGTON	TAL 097 ST MICHA
PRICE, WASHINGTON	CEC 146 PORT DUP
PRICE, WASHINGTON	CEC 146 PORT DUP
PRICE, WASHINGTON	CEC 155 PORT DUP
PRICE, WESLEY-BLACK	QUE 142 1ST E DI
PRICE, WILLIAM	QUE 158 2ND E DI
PRICE, WILLIAM	MGM 330 CRACKLIN
PRICE, WILLIAM	DOR 307 1ST DIST
PRICE, WILLIAM	SOM 448 DAMES QU
PRICE, WILLIAM	SOM 453 DAMES QU
PRICE, WILLIAM	HAR 037 1ST DIST
PRICE, WILLIAM	CEC 054 1ST E DI
PRICE, WILLIAM	CEC 056 1ST E DI
PRICE, WILLIAM	CEC 044 CHESAPEA
PRICE, WILLIAM	CEC 045 1ST E DI
PRICE, WILLIAM	CEC 023 ELKTON 3
PRICE, WILLIAM	DOR 342 3RD DIVI
PRICE, WILLIAM	CAR 106 NO TWP L
PRICE, WILLIAM	BAL 456 14TH WAR
PRICE, WILLIAM	WOR 350 1ST E DI
PRICE, WILLIAM	ST 295 2ND E DI
PRICE, WILLIAM	TAL 050 EASTON T
PRICE, WILLIAM	TAL 015 EASTON D
PRICE, WILLIAM	BAL 434 8TH WARD
PRICE, WILLIAM	BAL 439 1ST DIST
PRICE, WILLIAM	BAL 370 1ST DIST
PRICE, WILLIAM	BAL 054 2ND DIST
PRICE, WILLIAM	BAL 029 2ND DIST
PRICE, WILLIAM	BAL 016 2ND DIST
PRICE, WILLIAM	ALL 254 CUMBERLA
PRICE, WILLIAM	BAL 411 8TH WARD
PRICE, WILLIAM	ALL 086 5TH E.D.
PRICE, WILLIAM	ALL 093 5TH E.D.
PRICE, WILLIAM D.	CEC 055 1ST E DI
PRICE, WILLIAM G.	BAL 114 15TH WAR
PRICE, WILLIAM H.	KEN 221 2ND DIST
PRICE, WILLIAM J.	CEC 001 ELKTON 3
PRICE, WILLIAM L.	BAL 189 17TH WAR
PRICE, WILLIAM L.	QUE 240 5TH E DI
PRICE, WILLIAM N.	CAR 163 NO TWP L
PRICE, WILLIAM P.	ST 310 1ST E DI
PRICE, WILLIAM P.	BAL 021 2ND DIST
PRICE, WILLIAM R.	BAL 448 8TH WARD
PRICE, WORRICK	BAL 043 2ND DIST
PRICE,EDWARD	BAL 049 2ND DIST
PRICE,MARY-BLACK	QUE 153 1ST E DI
PRICER, PETER	HAR 145 3RD DIST
PRICHARD, ELIZA	BAL 085 4TH WARD
PRICHARD, JOHN	BAL 145 1ST WARD
PRICHARD, MARGARET H.	CEC 135 6TH E DI
PRICHARD, MARY S.	BAL 140 11TH WAR
PRICHARD, RACHEL	CEC 135 6TH E DI
PRICHETT, CAROLINE	CEC 086 4TH E DI
PRICHETT, HANNAH	CEC 085 5TH E DI
PRICHETT, HENRY	CEC 086 4TH E DI
PRICHETT, MARTHA	CEC 085 5TH E DI
PRICHETT, WILLIAM	BAL 265 17TH WAR
PRICKLE, JACOB	BAL 178 2ND WARD
PRICKUM, LEMUEL *	SOM 422 PRINCESS
PRIDE, JANE	DOR 430 1ST DIST
PRIDGET, HENRY	BAL 348 3RD WARD
PRIDGON, JOHN	BAL 037 15TH WAR
PRIE, CHARLES R. *	ANN 421 HOWARD D
PRIE, HENRY H. *	ANN 412 HOWARD D
PRIEG, MARK *	HAR 190 3RD DIST
PRIES, EMELINE	BAL 330 7TH WARD
PRIEST, WILLIAM	CEC 130 6TH E DI
PRIESTHOFF, KATE	BAL 157 19TH WAR
PRIESTLAR, PETER	BAL 194 6TH WARD
PRIESTLES, WILLIAM	MGM 388 ROCKERLE
PRIESTLEY, EDWARD	BAL 042 4TH WARD
PRIG, ABRAHAM H.	HAR 168 3RD DIST
PRIGG, ALLEN J.	CEC 175 7TH E DI
PRIGG, EDWARD	HAR 032 1ST DIST
PRIGG, ELIZA	HAR 035 1ST DIST
PRIGG, ELIZABETH C.	HAR 115 2ND DIST
PRIGG, HENRY	HAR 034 1ST DIST
PRIGG, JAMES	HAR 033 1ST DIST
PRIGG, JOSEPH	HAR 035 1ST DIST
PRIGG, SARAH	HAR 034 1ST DIST
PRIGLER, HENRY	BAL 094 18TH WAR
PRIGNELL, SAMUEL	BAL 061 18TH WAR
PRILL, THOMAS S.	BAL 286 2ND WARD
PRIM, AMELIA L.	BAL 348 7TH WARD
PRIM, JANE	FRE 062 FREDERIC
PRIME, BENJAMIN *	BAL 114 18TH WAR
PRIME, ELI S.	PRI 001 BLADENSB
PRIME, WILLIAM T.	PRI 001 BLADENSB
PRIMECE, DANIEL	BAL 230 12TH WAR
PRIMES, HEZEKIAH	BAL 260 20TH WAR
PRIMROSE, CATHERINE	BAL 070 10TH WAR
PRIMROSE, GREENBERRY	BAL 130 16TH WAR
PRIMROSE, GREENBURY	BAL 244 6TH WARD
PRIMROSE, HARRIET	TAL 022 EASTON D
PRIMROSE, J.	BAL 135 1ST WARD
PRIMROSE, JAMES W.	QUE 169 2ND E DI
PRIMROSE, JOHN	QUE 167 2ND E DI
PRIMROSE, JOHN	ANN 426 HOWARD D
PRIMROSE, MARY	TAL 020 EASTON D
PRIMROSE, PERRY	ANN 349 3RD DIST
PRIMROSE, RUBIN	KEN 290 3RD DIST
PRIMROSE, SARAH	BAL 247 17TH WAR
PRIMROSE, SUSAN	QUE 167 2ND E DI
PRIMROSE, THOMAS	QUE 165 2ND E DI
PRIMROSE, WILLIAM	QUE 165 2ND E DI
PRIMROSE, WILLIAM	BAL 249 17TH WAR
PRIMROSE, WILLIAM	BAL 022 18TH WAR
PRINCE, ANTHONY	BAL 080 1ST WARD
PRINCE, BENJAMIN F.	BAL 165 1ST WARD
PRINCE, CONRAD	BAL 210 2ND WARD
PRINCE, ELLEN	BAL 042 1ST WARD
PRINCE, HENRIETTA	BAL 027 4TH WARD
PRINCE, ISRAEL M.	BAL 158 1ST WARD
PRINCE, JOHN	BAL 244 2ND WARD
PRINCE, JOHN	BAL 039 18TH WAR
PRINCE, LEMUEL S.	BAL 277 7TH WARD
PRINCE, MARY A. MRS-	BAL 315 20TH WAR
PRINCE, THOMAS	FRE 036 FREDERIC
PRINCE, WILLIAM	BAL 115 5TH WARD
PRINCE, WILLIAM A.	BAL 350 3RD WARD
PRINCE, WILLIAM L.	CEC 163 6TH E DI
PRINE,JAMES	ALL 240 CUMBERLA
PRINGLE, JOHN	ALL 088 5TH E.D.
PRINNELL, JOSHUA-BLACK	WOR 323 1ST E DI
PRINT, ROBERT	WOR 321 1ST E DI
PRINTY, JOHN	BAL 031 15TH WAR
PRINTZ, FREDERICK	BAL 302 20TH WAR
PRIOR, AMELIA	SOM 468 TRAPPE D
PRIOR, BENJAMIN	FRE 364 CATOCTIN
PRIOR, DAVID	FRE 156 10TH E D
PRIOR, DAVID	WOR 231 6TH E DI
PRIOR, DELILA	FRE 341 MIDDLETO
PRIOR, ELEANOR	WOR 198 8TH E DI
PRIOR, ELLWOOD	CEC 167 6TH E DI
PRIOR, F.	BAL 100 15TH WAR
PRIOR, FRANCIS	SOM 483 TRAPP DI
PRIOR, HANNAH	WAS 238 CAVETOWN
PRIOR, HESTER W.	WOR 228 6TH E DI
PRIOR, JACOB	WAS 155 2ND DIST
PRIOR, JACOB	FRE 363 CATOCTIN
PRIOR, JOHN	CEC 079 NORTHEAS
PRIOR, JOHN	SOM 477 TRAPP DI
PRIOR, JOHN	BAL 163 6TH WARD
PRIOR, LAWSON	FRE 362 CATOCTIN
PRIOR, MARGARET	FRE 345 MIDDLETO
PRIOR, MARY	SOM 426 PRINCESS
PRIOR, NAPOLEON	MGM 323 CRACKLIN
PRIOR, SALLY	SOM 468 TRAPPE D
PRIOR, SAMUEL H.	WOR 195 8TH E DI
PRIOR, SOPHIA	WAS 152 2ND DIST
PRIOR, THOMAS	SOM 470 TRAPPE D
PRIOR, WILLIAM	WOR 197 8TH E DI
PRIOR, WILLIAM	WOR 231 6TH E DI
PRIOR, WILLIAM H.	CEC 079 NORTHEAS
PRISBY, WILLIAM	CEC 008 ELKTON 3
PRISH, EDWARD	BAL 258 1ST DIST
PRISKELL, ANN	BAL 033 18TH WAR
PRISTON, PETER	ALL 090 5TH E.D.
PRITCHARD, AMERICA	MGM 442 CLARKSTR
PRITCHARD, ARTHUR A.	PRI 029 VANSVILL
PRITCHARD, ASAEL	HAR 001 1ST DIST
PRITCHARD, E. A.	BAL 049 4TH WARD
PRITCHARD, ELIZA	ANN 323 2ND DIST
PRITCHARD, ELIZABETH	WAS 077 2ND SUBD
PRITCHARD, FLORENCE	BAL 187 2ND WARD
PRITCHARD, HANAH	BAL 342 7TH WARD
PRITCHARD, JAMES	ANN 403 8TH DIST
PRITCHARD, JAMES	ANN 308 1ST DIST
PRITCHARD, JOHN W.	KEN 210 2ND DIST
PRITCHARD, JOSEPH	BAL 252 6TH WARD
PRITCHARD, LEVIN	BAL 170 6TH WARD
PRITCHARD, MARGARET	ANN 277 ANNAPOLI
PRITCHARD, SAMUEL A.	BAL 102 1ST WARD
PRITCHARD, THOMAS	BAL 265 7TH WARD
PRITCHARD, WILLIAM	BAL 159 2ND DIST
PRITCHARD, WILLIAM	BAL 096 10TH WAR
PRITCHARD, WILLIAM	BAL 076 2ND DIST
PRITCHARD, ZEPHARA	BAL 053 9TH WARD
PRITCHELE, CHARLOTTE*	DOR 418 1ST DIST
PRITCHELL, EDWARD	CAR 109 NO TWP L
PRITCHELL, ELIZABETH	CAR 119 NO TWP L
PRITCHELL, HENRIETTA	CAR 119 NO TWP L
PRITCHELL, JOHN-MULATTO	CAR 069 NO TWP L
PRITCHELL, WESLEY	CAR 074 NO TWP L
PRITCHET, ANNN	TAL 044 EASTON T
PRITCHET, CATHARINE	TAL 008 EASTON D
PRITCHET, DANIEL	TAL 061 EASTON D
PRITCHET, FRISBY	TAL 051 EASTON D
PRITCHET, SAMUEL	TAL 068 EASTON T
PRITCHET, THOMAS J.	TAL 025 EASTON D
PRITCHET, WILLIAM A. *.	TAL 099 ST MICHA
PRITCHET, WILLIAM E.	TAL 008 EASTON D
PRITCHETT, A. B.	TAL 068 EASTON T
PRITCHETT, ARTHUR	DOR 335 3RD DIVI
PRITCHETT, ARTHUR H.	DOR 339 3RD DIVI
PRITCHETT, CAROLINE	CAR 077 NO TWP L
PRITCHETT, EDWARD	CAR 148 NO TWP L
PRITCHETT, EDWARD	DOR 340 3RD DIVI
PRITCHETT, EDWARD	DOR 341 3RD DIVI
PRITCHETT, GEORGE	DOR 335 3RD DIVI
PRITCHETT, GEORGE	CAR 067 NO TWP L
PRITCHETT, HENERY	DOR 338 3RD DIVI
PRITCHETT, JAMES	HAR 163 3RD DIST
PRITCHETT, JOHN H.	DOR 341 3RD DIVI
PRITCHETT, JOHN H.	DOR 348 3RD DIVI
PRITCHETT, JULIA E.	DOR 339 3RD DIVI
PRITCHETT, JULIANN	DOR 341 3RD DIVI
PRITCHETT, LOVEY	DOR 344 3RD DIVI
PRITCHETT, PETER B.	CAR 129 NO TWP L
PRITCHETT, SAMUEL-MULATTO	CAR 068 NO TWP L
PRITCHETT, SARRAH	DOR 337 3RD DIVI
PRITCHETT, SUSAN	DOR 341 3RD DIVI
PRITCHETT, THOAMS	SOM 441 DAMES QU
PRITCHETT, THOMAS	CAR 075 NO TWP L
PRITCHETT, THOMAS B.	CAR 098 NO TWP L
PRITCHETT, WILLIAM	HAR 161 3RD DIST
PRITCHETT, WILLIAM H.	CAR 168 NO TWP L
PRITCHETT, WILLIAM T.	BAL 054 15TH WAR
PRITCHETT, ZEBULON	DOR 341 3RD DIVI
PRITCHETT, ZEBULON	DOR 342 3RD DIVI
PRITTENMAN, HENRY	CAR 165 NO TWP L
PRITTS, JOHN	ALL 040 2ND E.D.
PRITTYMAN, L. C.	WOR 252 1ST CENS
PRITZEL, LOUIS	BAL 089 10TH WAR
PROBERSON, JOHNB.	BAL 140 1ST WARD
PROBY, JAMES	ALL 214 CUMBERLA
PROBY, ROBERT-MULATTO	FRE 018 FREDERIC
PROCTER, CAROLINE	BAL 144 5TH WARD
PROCTER, CHARLES	BAL 375 13TH WAR
PROCTER, ISRIEL D.	HAR 197 3RD DIST
PROCTER, JULY A.-BLACK	FRE 218 BUCKEYST
PROCTER, LINAAM *	BAL 123 2ND DIST
PROCTER, MARY D.	BAL 318 7TH WARD
PROCTER, WILSON	BAL 384 13TH WAR
PROCTON, ANN	MGM 378 ROCKERLE
PROCTON, MARY E.	MGM 379 ROCKERLE
PROCTOR, AARON*	DOR 408 1ST DIST
PROCTOR, ABNER	WAS 176 1ST DIST
PROCTOR, ABRAHAM	FRE 155 10TH E D
PROCTOR, ALEXIOUS	PRI 114 PISCATAW
PROCTOR, BENEDICT	PRI 113 PISCATAW
PROCTOR, C.	PRI 089 SPALDING
PROCTOR, CHARLES	CHA 277 BOJANTOW
PROCTOR, CHARLES	CHA 268 BOJANTOW
PROCTOR, E.	PRI 055 AQUASCO
PROCTOR, EDWARD	WAS 008 WILLIAMS

PROCTOR, EDWARD HAR 042 1ST DIST
PROCTOR, ELIZABETH HAR 042 1ST DIST
PROCTOR, ELLEN BAL 032 4TH WARD
PROCTOR, ELLY CHA 284 BOJANTOW
PROCTOR, GEORGE W. CHA 293 BOJANTOW
PROCTOR, HARY* DOR 408 1ST DIST
PROCTOR, HENRY CHA 277 BOJANTOW
PROCTOR, HENRY BAL 416 1ST DIST
PROCTOR, ISAAC PRI 111 PISCATAW
PROCTOR, J. PRI 115 PISCATAW
PROCTOR, JAMES CHA 283 BOJANTOW
PROCTOR, JAMES G. KEN 295 3RD DIST
PROCTOR, JENIFER CHA 275 ALLENS F
PROCTOR, JOANNA CHA 290 BOJANTOW
PROCTOR, JOHN CHA 284 BOJANTOW
PROCTOR, JOHN BAL 128 2ND DIST
PROCTOR, JOHN H. CHA 277 BOJANTOW
PROCTOR, JOHN H. CHA 244 HILLTOP
PROCTOR, JOHN O. WAS 005 WILLIAMS
PROCTOR, JOHN-MULATTO FRE 231 BUCKEYST
PROCTOR, JOHNC. BAL 055 2ND DIST
PROCTOR, JOSEPH CHA 290 BOJANTOW
PROCTOR, JOSEPH-BLACK FRE 016 FREDERIC
PROCTOR, JOSEPH-MULATTO FRE 221 BUCKEYST
PROCTOR, JOSEPHINE BAL 111 18TH WAR
PROCTOR, JOSIAS CHA 278 BOJANTOW
PROCTOR, JULIAN CHA 278 BOJANTOW
PROCTOR, MARY WAS 022 2ND SUBD
PROCTOR, ROBERT HAR 059 1ST DIST
PROCTOR, ROBERT BAL 065 2ND DIST
PROCTOR, THOMAS BAL 046 2ND DIST
PROCTOR, THOMAS CHA 252 BOJANTOW
PROCTOR, THOMAS PRI 092 MARLBROU
PROCTOR, WILLIAM BAL 013 4TH WARD
PROCTOR, WILLIAM BAL 401 14TH WAR
PRODA, DORIUS MARY BAL 058 10TH WAR
PROER, SARAH BAL 204 2ND WARD
PROFATER, ELIZABETH BAL 132 16TH WAR
PROMEL, JOHN T. BAL 476 14TH WAR
PROMELL, ISAAC WOR 262 BERLIN 1
PRONATH, S. BAL 449 8TH WARD
PRONOME, GERESA BAL 320 12TH WAR
PROSEHIRE, CHARLOTTE BAL 044 2ND DIST
PROSHIRE, CATHERINE BAL 044 2ND DIST
PROSINGER, JOHN BAL 007 4TH WARD
PROTCOR, THOMAS BAL 123 2ND DIST
PROTHER, JOSIAH BAL 223 19TH WAR
PROTMAN, SEBASTIAN BAL 318 12TH WAR
PROTZMAN, ELIZABETH FRE 185 5TH E DI
PROTZMAN, FRANCIS WAS 165 HAGERSTO
PROUCE, ELSIN* DOR 309 1ST DIST
PROUCE, THOMAS DOR 309 1ST DIST
PROUD, JOHN G. BAL 014 18TH WAR
PROUDFEET, MARY A. BAL 369 8TH WARD
PROUSE, ASBURSY CAR 090 NO TWP L
PROUSE, ELIJAH CAR 089 NO TWP L
PROUSE, ELIZABETH CAR 133 NO TWP L
PROUSE, GEORGE CAR 089 NO TWP L
PROUSE, JOHN DOR 460 1ST DIST
PROUT, ALBERT BAL 225 17TH WAR
PROUT, CATHARINE BAL 189 17TH WAR
PROUT, CATHARINE BAL 099 2ND DIST
PROUT, CATHOUN BAL 130 11TH WAR
PROUT, DANIEL CAL 046 3RD DIST
PROUT, DIANA BAL 267 7TH WARD
PROUT, ELIZA PRI 087 QUEEN AN
PROUT, GEORGE BAL 044 4TH WARD
PROUT, HARRIET ANN 291 ANNAPOLI
PROUT, HENRY BAL 183 16TH WAR
PROUT, ISAAC-BLACK FRE 026 FREDERIC
PROUT, ISRAEL BAL 098 15TH WAR
PROUT, JAMES FRE 009 FREDERIC
PROUT, JAMES FRE 298 WOODSBOR
PROUT, JAMES-BLACK FRE 005 FREDERIC
PROUT, JANE ANN 291 ANNAPOLI
PROUT, JOHN BAL 208 17TH WAR
PROUT, LETITIA QUE 237 4TH E DI
PROUT, MARGARET-BLACK FRE 218 BUCKEYST
PROUT, MATHIS* TAL 004 EASTON D
PROUT, NACY BAL 065 15TH WAR
PROUT, NANCY PRI 044 VANSVILL
PROUT, PHILIP ANN 363 4TH DIST
PROUT, RACHEL MGM 378 ROCKERLE
PROUT, RICHARD CAL 057 3RD DIST
PROUT, ROBERT CHA 244 HILLTOP
PROUT, ROBERT BAL 183 16TH WAR
PROUT, SARAH BAL 152 5TH WARD
PROUT, VIRGIL M. CAL 055 3RD DIST
PROUT, WILLIAM ANN 318 2ND DIST
PROUT, WILLIAM T. ANN 403 8TH DIST
PROVA, CHARLES BAL 296 7TH WARD
PROVIANCE, JOSEPH G. BAL 302 7TH WARD
PROVIANCE, SAMUEL BAL 364 8TH WARD
PROVIENCE, LOUISA BAL 298 7TH WARD
PRSTON, HENRY C. HAR 110 2ND DIST
PRUDY, ALLEN CEC 059 1ST E DI
PRUEL, HENRY BAL 267 2ND WARD
PRUEL, JAMES BAL 437 8TH WARD
PRUET, ABRAHAM BAL 438 8TH WARD
PRUET, ELIZABETH J. BAL 122 18TH WAR
PRUET, LAURA BAL 044 15TH WAR
PRUETT, HENRY BAL 134 2ND DIST
PRUG, MARK HAR 190 3RD DIST
PRUGH, ABRAHAM CAR 207 4TH DIST
PRUGH, DAVID CAR 213 5TH DIST
PRUGH, FREDERICK CAR 375 9TH DIST
PRUGNER, CHRISTIAN BAL 001 9TH WARD
PRUIT, FRANK BAL 110 5TH WARD
PRUITT, BENJAMIN WOR 323 1ST E DI
PRUITT, DAVID WOR 266 BERLIN 1
PRUITT, EDWARD T. SOM 401 BRINKLEY
PRUITT, ELANOR WOR 311 2ND E DI
PRUITT, ELIZA WOR 237 1ST E DI
PRUITT, FANNEY WOR 309 2ND E DI
PRUITT, GABRIEL SOM 367 BRINKLEY
PRUITT, GEORGE WOR 311 2ND E DI
PRUITT, JANE WOR 316 2ND E DI
PRUITT, JOHN WOR 303 SNOW HIL
PRUITT, JOHN WOR 321 1ST E DI
PRUITT, LAZFOUS WOR 337 1ST E DI
PRUITT, LEMUEL P. WOR 244 1ST CENS
PRUITT, WILLIAM WOR 317 2ND E DI
PRUITT, WILLIAM WOR 324 1ST E DI
PRUITT, WILLIAM WOR 309 2ND E DI
PRUITT, WILLIAM SOM 456 DAMES QU
PRUITY, CHARLES BAL 091 5TH WARD
PRY, C.C. BAL 169 1ST WARD
PRY, JOSEPH BAL 315 1ST DIST
PRY, PHILIP WAS 074 2ND SUBD
PRY, SAMUEL WAS 074 2ND SUBD

PRY, RHODY FRE 406 JEFFERSO
PRYAN, MARGARET HAR 010 1ST DIST
PRYER, JAMES WAS 149 2ND DIST
PRYER, JAMES P. KEN 291 3RD DIST
PRYON, THOMAS BAL 105 5TH WARD
PRYOR, BENJAMIN BAL 090 18TH WAR
PRYOR, CHRISTIAN BAL 458 14TH WAR
PRYOR, EDWARD BAL 184 6TH WARD
PRYOR, GEORGE BAL 278 12TH WAR
PRYOR, GEORGE W. BAL 219 6TH WARD
PRYOR, HESTOR BAL 130 5TH WARD
PRYOR, JOHN H. BAL 263 17TH WAR
PRYOR, MANUAL BAL 114 1ST WARD
PRYOR, RICHARD BAL 130 5TH WARD
PRYOR, SAMUEL WAS 018 2ND SUBD
PSCHMANN, ELI* BAL 084 10TH WAR
PSSALEN, ABBIS BAL 133 11TH WAR
PUBERS, WILLIAM BAL 135 1ST WARD
PUBRAN, CAROLINE MGM 399 ROCKERLE
PUBRAN, SOLOMON MGM 399 ROCKERLE
PUCELEY, WILLIAMS FRE 205 BUCKEYST
PUCKARD, MARY A. BAL 130 11TH WAR
PUCKETT, CHARLES G. ANN 292 ANNAPOLI
PUCKUM, CHARLOTTE SOM 491 SALISBUR
PUCKUM, HENRY SOM 479 TRAPP DI
PUCKUM, HETTY SOM 495 SALISBUR
PUCKUM, LEMUEL * SOM 422 PRINCESS
PUCKUM, NANCY SOM 546 TYASKIN
PUCKUM, NANCY SOM 473 TRAPPE D
PUCKUM, WILLIAM THOMAS SOM 495 SALISBUR
PUE, ARTHUR ANN 465 HOWARD D
PUE, BILL HAR 088 2ND DIST
PUE, CHARLES R. ANN 471 HOWARD D
PUE, CHARLES R. * ANN 421 HOWARD D
PUE, ELIZABETH BAL 349 7TH WARD
PUE, HENRY H. ANN 412 HOWARD D
PUE, MICHAEL ANN 443 HOWARD D
PUE, MICHAEL E. HAR 095 2ND DIST
PUE, MISS M. FRE 199 5TH E DI
PUE, PEGGY BAL 104 10TH WAR
PUE, REBECCA BAL 348 13TH WAR
PUE, ROBERT BAL 078 2ND DIST
PUEE, HANNAH * BAL 381 13TH WAR
PUESY, SARAH CEC 120 4TH E DI
PUFF, ADAM * ALL 111 5TH E.D.
PUFF, THOMAS BAL 390 3RD WARD
PUFFTH, MARTIN BAL 248 12TH WAR
PUGG, SIMON BAL 171 19TH WAR
PUGH, ALFRED CEC 007 ELKTON 3
PUGH, DAVID CAR 357 6TH DIST
PUGH, JAMES CEC 068 5TH E DI
PUGH, JAMES BAL 044 1ST WARD
PUGH, MAGDELINE BAL 403 8TH WARD
PUGH, MARY A. CEC 023 ELKTON 3
PUGH, MARY J. BAL 043 1ST WARD
PUGH, SHARLOTTE ALL 211 CUMBERLA
PUGH, WILLIAM BAL 043 1ST WARD
PUGH, WILLIAM MGM 439 CLARKSTR
PUGOS, MARIE* BAL 097 10TH WAR
PUGSLEY, JOHN H. BAL 095 5TH WARD
PUHL, GEORGE BAL 018 9TH WARD
PUIER, GEORGE BAL 259 2ND WARD
PUIES, BENJAMIN BAL 142 2ND DIST
PUISE, DENELLA BAL 175 2ND WARD
PUISER, CONRAD BAL 181 2ND WARD
PUISER, MARGRET BAL 182 2ND WARD
PUIT, JAMES* DOR 461 1ST DIST
PULAY, ANN * BAL 317 1ST DIST
PULBY, JAMES BAL 012 1ST WARD
PULL, WILLIAM BAL 165 11TH WAR
PULLET, COMFORT BAL 086 15TH WAR
PULLET, HESTER-BLACK WOR 333 1ST E DI
PULLET, MARGARET H. BAL 086 15TH WAR
PULLETT, SAMUEL BAL 173 11TH WAR
PULLEY, CATHARINE BAL 317 7TH WARD
PULLEY, HENRY BAL 317 7TH WARD
PULLEY, JAMES BAL 248 6TH WARD
PULLEY, JOHN P. BAL 442 14TH WAR
PULLIN, WASHINGTON BAL 015 1ST WARD
PULLMAN, IRA KEN 283 3RD DIST
PULLMAN, SUSAN KEN 283 3RD DIST
PULLY, ISAAC ANN 360 3RD DIST
PULLY, WILLIAM BAL 038 1ST WARD
PULTY, CHARLES BAL 161 16TH WAR
PUM, GREENBARY PRI 031 VANSVILL
PUMELTAN, JOHN ALL 236 CUMBERLA
PUMER, CORNELIA HAR 039 1ST DIST
PUMES, DINAH BAL 091 18TH WAR
PUMFREY, ANN BAL 256 20TH WAR
PUMFREY, THOMAS BAL 223 12TH WAR
PUMPHREY, ADALINE ANN 368 4TH DIST
PUMPHREY, ALPHEUS B. ANN 380 4TH DIST
PUMPHREY, ARTHUR PRI 009 BLADENSB
PUMPHREY, CHARLES ANN 341 3RD DIST
PUMPHREY, CHARLES BAL 128 5TH WARD
PUMPHREY, ELIZABETH ANN 345 3RD DIST
PUMPHREY, ELIZABETH PRI 090 MARLBROU
PUMPHREY, ENNIS PRI 070 MARLBROU
PUMPHREY, HENRY A. MGM 417 MEDLEY 3
PUMPHREY, ISAIAH ANN 381 4TH DIST
PUMPHREY, J.G. PRI 069 MARLBROU
PUMPHREY, JOHN PRI 006 BLADENSB
PUMPHREY, JOHN BAL 379 3RD WARD
PUMPHREY, JOHN K. PRI 090 MARLBROU
PUMPHREY, JOHN T. ANN 359 3RD DIST
PUMPHREY, JOHN W. MGM 417 MEDLEY 3
PUMPHREY, MARGARET BAL 298 7TH WARD
PUMPHREY, MARSHA PRI 069 MARLBROU
PUMPHREY, MATHEW ANN 462 HOWARD D
PUMPHREY, NATHAN ANN 341 3RD DIST
PUMPHREY, OSBORN ANN 344 3RD DIST
PUMPHREY, RECOTR PRI 090 MARLBROU
PUMPHREY, SARAH PRI 002 BLADENSB
PUMPHREY, SUSAN ANN 455 HOWARD D
PUMPHREY, SUSAN ANN 461 HOWARD D
PUMPHREY, THOMAS ANN 341 3RD DIST
PUMPHREY, THOMSA ANN 341 3RD DIST
PUMPHREY, V. R. ANN 360 3RD DIST
PUMPHREY, WALTER ANN 347 3RD DIST
PUMPHREY, WILLIAM E. PRI 014 BLADENSB
PUMPHREY, WILLIAM E. MGM 377 ROCKERLE
PUMPHREY, ZACHEUS ANN 359 3RD DIST
PUMPHRY, DAVID BAL 295 17TH WAR
PUMPHRY, JETSON C. PRI 100 SPALDING
PUMPHRY, WILLIAM MGM 416 MEDLEY 3
PUMPREY, GEORGE BAL 286 20TH WAR
PUMPREY, RACHEL BAL 013 18TH WAR
PUMROY, LOVERING * QUE 247 5TH E DI
PUNCE, CYANE MGM 426 MEDLEY 3
PUNILLION, E. PRI 057 AQUASCO

PUNT, DANIEL WAS 270 1ST DIST
PUNT, GEORGE WAS 270 1ST DIST
PUNT, GEORGE WAS 248 1ST DIST
PUNT, LEVI BAL 234 2ND WARD
PUPELT, CHARLES CEC 059 1ST E DI
PUPTMAN, B. C.* BAL 108 10TH WAR
PURCEL, SUSAN BAL 265 17TH WAR
PURCHALL, GEORGE BAL 112 5TH WARD
PURDAY, HENRY HAR 026 1ST DIST
PURDIE, JOHN ALL 241 CUMBERLA
PURDIN, MARY BAL 336 7TH WARD
PURDOM, JAMES W. MGM 316 CRACKLIN
PURDON, CHARLES R. MGM 340 CLARKSBU
PURDON, JOHN MGM 341 CLARKSBU
PURDON, JOSHUA MGM 441 CLARKSTR
PURDON, MARY L. ST 307 1ST E DI
PURDUE, ELIJAH L. WOR 231 6TH E DI
PURDUE, GEORGE K. WOR 232 6TH E DI
PURDUE, GILLIP WOR 168 6TH E DI
PURDUE, JAMES B. WOR 231 6TH E DI
PURDUE, JAMES W. B. WOR 233 6TH E DI
PURDUE, JOHN WOR 222 4TH E DI
PURDUE, JOHN B. WOR 231 6TH E DI
PURDUE, LEMUEL H. WOR 222 4TH E DI
PURDUM, HEPSIBAH MGM 345 CLARKSBU
PURDUM, WESLEY B. MGM 346 CLARKSBU
PURDUN, JOHN L. MGM 434 CLARKSTR
PURDUN, JOSIAH W. MGM 435 CLARKSTR
PURDY, BASEL FRE 265 NEW MARK
PURDY, CAPT- ANN 327 2ND DIST
PURDY, CAROLINE ANN 310 1ST DIST
PURDY, CAROLINE BAL 017 4TH WARD
PURDY, CHARLOTTE ANN 352 3RD DIST
PURDY, EDWARD ALL 233 CUMBERLA
PURDY, EDWEARD TAL 110 ST MICHA
PURDY, GEORGE A. FRE 245 NEW MARK
PURDY, J. BAL 118 1ST WARD
PURDY, JAMES BAL 121 1ST WARD
PURDY, JAMES BAL 298 17TH WAR
PURDY, JOHN BAL 093 18TH WAR
PURDY, JOHN ANN 298 1ST DIST
PURDY, JOHN ANN 311 1ST DIST
PURDY, JOHN ANN 336 3RD DIST
PURDY, JOHN BAL 351 1ST DIST
PURDY, JOHN BAL 140 1ST WARD
PURDY, JOHN H. BAL 053 18TH WAR
PURDY, JOSEPH FRE 352 MIDDLETO
PURDY, JOSEPH ALL 106 5TH E.D.
PURDY, LOUISA BAL 254 20TH WAR
PURDY, MARGARET ANN 310 1ST DIST
PURDY, MARY JANE BAL 345 13TH WAR
PURDY, NANCY WAS 126 HAGERSTO
PURDY, REUBEN ANN 352 3RD DIST
PURDY, RICHARD ANN 295 1ST DIST
PURDY, RICHARD FRE 246 NEW MARK
PURDY, SALLY ANN 268 ANNAPOLI
PURDY, SAMUEL JR. ANN 308 1ST DIST
PURDY, SINGLETON FRE 269 NEW MARK
PURDY, SUSAN-MULATTO FRE 008 FREDERIC
PURDY, THOMAS ANN 311 1ST DIST
PURDY, THOMAS BAL 185 16TH WAR
PURDY, THOMAS D. FRE 019 FREDERIC
PURDY, WILLIAM FRE 204 BUCKEYST
PURGER, CICERO BAL 256 20TH WAR
PURGINSON, THOMAS ANN 277 ANNAPOLI
PURIGHT, LEDIA BAL 167 11TH WAR
PURIN, RUTH WAS 073 2ND SUBD
PURKEY, REBECCA BAL 197 5TH DIST
PURKINS, PERRY-BLACK CAR 138 NO TWP L
PURKINS, SARAH A. HAR 052 1ST DIST
PURMELION, N. ANN 297 1ST DIST
PURNALL, LOUISA* BAL 072 10TH WAR
PURNANCE, ROBERT BAL 194 11TH WAR
PURNEL, THOMAS BAL 348 7TH WARD
PURNELL, ANN BAL 120 5TH WARD
PURNELL, ANN G. HAR 121 2ND DIST
PURNELL, BARBASHIA SOM 388 BRINKLEY
PURNELL, BEN WOR 310 2ND E DI
PURNELL, BILL WOR 282 BERLIN 1
PURNELL, BILL WOR 267 BERLIN 1
PURNELL, BILL WOR 291 9TH E DI
PURNELL, BILL WOR 266 BERLIN 1
PURNELL, CATHARINE WOR 286 BERLIN 1
PURNELL, CATHARINE S. BAL 121 16TH WAR
PURNELL, CHARELS WOR 255 1ST CENS
PURNELL, CHARLES WOR 282 BERLIN 1
PURNELL, CHARLES B. BAL 372 13TH WAR
PURNELL, CHARLES-MULATTO BAL 179 2ND WARD
PURNELL, CHARLOTE WOR 311 2ND E DI
PURNELL, CHARLOTTE WOR 227 4TH E DI
PURNELL, COMFORT WOR 306 2ND E DI
PURNELL, DANIEL WOR 292 9TH E DI
PURNELL, DANIEL WOR 214 4TH E DI
PURNELL, DELIA BAL 348 13TH WAR
PURNELL, DINAH WOR 296 9TH E DI
PURNELL, EBBEN WOR 178 6TH E DI
PURNELL, ELIZABETH WOR 294 9TH E DI
PURNELL, EMILY BAL 177 16TH WAR
PURNELL, EMMELINE W. WOR 209 4TH E DI
PURNELL, G. WASHINGTON WOR 213 4TH E DI
PURNELL, GEORGE SOM 530 QUANTICO
PURNELL, GEORGE WOR 273 BERLIN 1
PURNELL, GEORGE WOR 281 BERLIN 1
PURNELL, GEORGE WOR 305 2ND E DI
PURNELL, GEORGE WOR 327 1ST E DI
PURNELL, GEORGE-BLACK WOR 325 1ST E DI
PURNELL, HANNAH-BLACK WOR 333 1ST E DI
PURNELL, HANNAH-BLACK WOR 343 1ST E DI
PURNELL, HENNA WOR 316 2ND E DI
PURNELL, HENRIATTA WOR 263 BERLIN 1
PURNELL, HENRY WOR 309 2ND E DI
PURNELL, HENRY WOR 295 9TH E DI
PURNELL, HENRY CEC 030 CHESAPEA
PURNELL, HENRY W. QUE 132 1ST E DI
PURNELL, HENRY-BLACK CAR 079 NO TWP L
PURNELL, HET * WOR 269 BERLIN 1
PURNELL, IRVIN WOR 282 BERLIN 1
PURNELL, ISAAC WOR 220 4TH E DI
PURNELL, JACOB WOR 181 6TH E DI
PURNELL, JACOB WOR 290 9TH E DI
PURNELL, JAEMS B. R. WOR 299 SNOW HIL
PURNELL, JAMES KEN 301 3RD DIST
PURNELL, JAMES CEC 002 ELKTON 3
PURNELL, JAMES R. WOR 263 BERLIN 1
PURNELL, JAMES-BLACK WOR 170 6TH E DI
PURNELL, JESSE WOR 295 9TH E DI
PURNELL, JESSE SOM 481 TRAPP DI
PURNELL, JIM WOR 306 2ND E DI
PURNELL, JOEL WOR 293 9TH E DI
PURNELL, JOHN WOR 314 2ND E DI

Name	County	Page	Locality
PURNELL, JOHN	WOR	305	2ND E DI
PURNELL, JOHN	BAL	108	15TH WAR
PURNELL, JOHN A.	WOR	284	BERLIN 1
PURNELL, JOHN F.	WOR	303	SNOW HIL
PURNELL, JOHN H.	SOM	482	TRAPP DI
PURNELL, JOHN S.	WOR	263	BERLIN 1
PURNELL, JOHN W. T.	WOR	289	9TH E DI
PURNELL, JOHN-BLACK	WOR	326	1ST E DI
PURNELL, JOSEPH	WOR	316	2ND E DI
PURNELL, JOSHUA	WOR	283	BERLIN 1
PURNELL, JOSHUA	WOR	287	BERLIN 1
PURNELL, JOSHUA-BLACK	WOR	170	6TH E DI
PURNELL, JUDAH	WOR	287	BERLIN 1
PURNELL, LAURA	WOR	314	2ND E DI
PURNELL, LEVI	WOR	264	BERLIN 1
PURNELL, LEVIN	WOR	306	2ND E DI
PURNELL, LINDA	WOR	272	BERLIN 1
PURNELL, LINDA	WOR	283	BERLIN 1
PURNELL, LITTLETON	WOR	297	9TH E DI
PURNELL, LITTLETON	WOR	255	1ST CENS
PURNELL, LITTLETON R.	WOR	300	SNOW HIL
PURNELL, LOT	WOR	303	SNOW HIL
PURNELL, LOUISA	BAL	283	12TH WAR
PURNELL, LOUISA*	BAL	072	10TH WAR
PURNELL, MAHALAH C.	WOR	220	4TH E DI
PURNELL, MARGARET	WOR	221	4TH E DI
PURNELL, MARIA-BLACK	WOR	170	6TH E DI
PURNELL, MARTHA A.	WOR	214	4TH E DI
PURNELL, MARTHIA	WOR	300	SNOW HIL
PURNELL, MARY	WOR	295	9TH E DI
PURNELL, MARY	WOR	310	2ND E DI
PURNELL, MARY	WOR	304	SNOW HIL
PURNELL, MARY	BAL	413	1ST DIST
PURNELL, MARY J.	WOR	261	BERLIN 1
PURNELL, MINTY	WOR	255	1ST CENS
PURNELL, MOSES	WOR	264	BERLIN 1
PURNELL, MUNNEY REV.	WOR	305	2ND E DI
PURNELL, MURRAY *	WOR	305	SNOW HIL
PURNELL, NANCY	WOR	283	BERLIN 1
PURNELL, NETTY	WOR	298	9TH E DI
PURNELL, PETER	WOR	284	BERLIN 1
PURNELL, RACHEL R.	WOR	261	BERLIN 1
PURNELL, RODY	WOR	247	1ST CENS
PURNELL, SABRA	WOR	291	9TH E DI
PURNELL, SALLY A.	WOR	188	7TH E DI
PURNELL, SALLY-MULATTO	WOR	172	6TH E DI
PURNELL, SARAH	WOR	246	1ST CENS
PURNELL, SARAH	BAL	347	13TH WAR
PURNELL, SERINA-BLACK	BAL	249	2ND WARD
PURNELL, SEVIN	WOR	283	BERLIN 1
PURNELL, STEHEN	WOR	306	2ND E DI
PURNELL, STEPHEN	WOR	292	9TH E DI
PURNELL, STEPHEN S.	BAL	110	5TH WARD
PURNELL, THOAMS	WOR	256	1ST CENS
PURNELL, THOMAS	WOR	310	2ND E DI
PURNELL, THOMAS	CAR	100	NO TWP L
PURNELL, WEALTHY	SOM	489	SALISBUR
PURNELL, WILLIAM	WOR	178	6TH E DI
PURNELL, WILLIAM	WOR	298	9TH E DI
PURNELL, WILLIAM	WOR	303	SNOW HIL
PURNELL, WILLIAM	WOR	304	SNOW HIL
PURNELL, WILLIAM	BAL	284	12TH WAR
PURNELL, WILLIAM M.	WOR	305	2ND E DI
PURNELL, WLLIAM H.	WOR	299	SNOW HIL
PURNELL, ZADOCK	WOR	283	BERLIN 1
PURNELL, ZADOK	WOR	260	BERLIN 1
PURNELL,LEVI-BLACK	WOR	168	6TH E DI
PURNELL,LEVI-BLACK	WOR	169	6TH E DI
PURNELL,LITTLETON-BLACK	WOR	172	6TH E DI
PURNER, JAMES	BAL	361	3RD WARD
PURNER, JEFFERSON	CEC	020	ELKTON 3
PURNER, REBECCA	BAL	025	9TH WARD
PURNER, WILLIAM	CEC	163	6TH E DI
PURNER, WILLIAM	CEC	125	5TH E DI
PURNES, DINAH *	BAL	091	18TH WAR
PURNIMAN, T.	BAL	062	10TH WAR
PURP, JOSEPH	CEC	188	7TH E DI
PURPER, JOHN	BAL	130	18TH WAR
PURPUR, CHARLES	BAL	178	16TH WAR
PURRES, DINAH *	BAL	091	18TH WAR
PURRIANCE, JOHN	BAL	055	9TH WARD
PURROWS, WILLIAM	PRI	038	VANSVILL
PURSE, CHARLES W.	BAL	214	11TH WAR
PURSELL, JAMES	BAL	134	18TH WAR
PURSER, JOSEPH	ALL	073	5TH E.D.
PURSER, MARY ANN	BAL	292	17TH WAR
PURSEY, ISAAC	WOR	188	7TH E DI
PURSLEY, JOHN R.	TAL	079	ST MICHA
PURSLIFF, WILLIAM	BAL	350	7TH WARD
PURT, JOHN	CAR	132	NO TWP L
PURTIANCE, SAMUEL *	BAL	084	2ND DIST
PURTLE, MARY ANN	ALL	238	CUMBERLA
PURTLE, THCMAS	ALL	237	CUMBERLA
PURVEY, AMELIA	BAL	266	12TH WAR
PURVIANCE, EMMA G.*	BAL	103	10TH WAR
PURVIANCE, JOHN	BAL	174	6TH WARD
PURVIANCE, LUCRETIA	BAL	156	16TH WAR
PURVIANCE, WESLEY	BAL	089	15TH WAR
PURVIENCE, WILIAM	BAL	027	2ND DIST
PURVIS, JAMES F.	BAL	453	8TH WARD
PURVIS, MARY L.	BAL	454	8TH WARD
PURWELL, C.	BAL	072	10TH WAR
PUSBY, WILLIAM	BAL	090	1ST WARD
PUSEY, BENJAMIN	SOM	424	PRINCESS
PUSEY, CALEB H.	BAL	189	2ND WARD
PUSEY, DAVID	WOR	188	7TH E DI
PUSEY, EMORY	WOR	187	7TH E DI
PUSEY, EPHRAIM H.	WOR	188	7TH E DI
PUSEY, ISAAC	WOR	186	7TH E DI
PUSEY, ISRAEL	BAL	404	14TH WAR
PUSEY, JAMES D.	WOR	188	7TH E DI
PUSEY, JEPTHA	WOR	193	8TH E DI
PUSEY, JOHN	SOM	422	PRINCESS
PUSEY, JOHN A.	SOM	422	PRINCESS
PUSEY, JOSIAH	SOM	424	PRINCESS
PUSEY, LEVIN	WOR	189	7TH E DI
PUSEY, LITTLETON H.	SOM	416	DUBLIN D
PUSEY, LYDIA	WOR	187	7TH E DI
PUSEY, NATHAN	BAL	340	13TH WAR
PUSEY, NATHANIEL *	SOM	421	PRINCESS
PUSEY, PUCY *	WOR	188	7TH E DI
PUSEY, PURNELL	WOR	186	7TH E DI
PUSEY, PURNELL L.	WOR	188	7TH E DI
PUSEY, PURNELL SR.	WOR	188	7TH E DI
PUSEY, REBECCA L.	WOR	189	7TH E DI
PUSEY, SARAH	SOM	422	PRINCESS
PUSEY, STEPHEN T.	WOR	188	7TH E DI
PUSEY, THOMAS	SOM	429	PRINCESS
PUSEY, THOMAS	CAR	190	4TH DIST
PUSEY, WHITTINGTON	WOR	186	7TH E DI
PUSEY, WILLIAM	WAS	104	2ND DIST
PUSEY, WILLIAM J.	WOR	183	6TH E DI
PUSEY, WILLIAM C.	WOR	188	7TH E DI
PUSSEY, MARGARET ANN	CAR	382	2ND DIST
PUSSY, WILLIAM	BAL	147	19TH WAR
PUTER, ALEXADNER	BAL	147	19TH WAR
PUTER, ELIZABETH *	KEN	285	3RD DIST
PUTMAN, JOHN	FRE	337	MIDDLETO
PUTMAN, JOHN J.	FRE	139	CREAGERS
PUTMAN, POWLESS	BAL	368	8TH WARD
PUTMAN, SAMUEL	FRE	337	MIDDLETO
PUTMAN, SUSAN	WAS	074	2ND SUBD
PUTNEY, DAVID	BAL	330	1ST DIST
PUTNEY, H. A.	ANN	420	HOWARD D
PUTRUFF, MICHAEL	WAS	157	2ND DIST
PUTRVAN, JOSEPH	BAL	171	1ST WARD
PUTT, SARAH	WAS	152	HAGERSTO
PUTZNETT, ANN	FRE	056	FREDERIC
PUVIN, THOMAS*	SOM	490	SALISBUR
PVIRE, JAMES	TAL	075	EASTON T
PWELL, JIM	WOR	306	2ND E DI
PWERS, JAMES	BAL	130	1ST WARD
PYATT, ELIZABETH	BAL	070	4TH WARD
PYE, CAROLINE	CHA	221	ALLENS F
PYE, CHARLES	BAL	472	14TH WAR
PYE, CHARLES A.	CHA	231	HILLTOP
PYE, ISAAC	BAL	351	7TH WARD
PYE, OLIVA	BAL	212	11TH WAR
PYFER, ELIZABETH	BAL	054	9TH WARD
PYFER, GODFREY	BAL	208	11TH WAR
PYFFER, MICHAEL	BAL	422	8TH WARD
PYFFER, RACHAEL	FRE	036	FREDERIC
PYLCRAFT, SAMUEL	HAR	183	3RD DIST
PYLE, DAVID	HAR	044	1ST DIST
PYLE, ELIZABETH	HAR	111	2ND DIST
PYLE, HARLEN	HAR	049	1ST DIST
PYLE, ISAAC	HAR	049	1ST DIST
PYLE, JESSE	CEC	164	6TH E DI
PYLE, JOHN C.	HAR	044	1ST DIST
PYLE, JOSEPH	CEC	142	6TH E DI
PYLE, JOSHUA H.	HAR	111	2ND DIST
PYLE, LOUIS E.	HAR	008	1ST DIST
PYLE, NATHAN	HAR	011	1ST DIST
PYLE, ROBERT	BAL	169	1ST WARD
PYLE, SAMUEL	BAL	117	2ND DIST
PYLE, WILLIAM	BAL	263	17TH WAR
PYLE, WILLIAM	BAL	122	18TH WAR
PYLE,NANCY	HAR	111	2ND DIST
PYLES, ANN	HAR	112	2ND DIST
PYLES, BENJAMIN	PRI	010	BLADENSB
PYLES, ELY	HAR	112	2ND DIST
PYLES, HERMAN	HAR	112	2ND DIST
PYLES, HERMAN	HAR	112	2ND DIST
PYLES, WILLIAM F.	FRE	234	BUCKEYST
PYLIS, SARAH	HAR	096	2ND DIST
PYMAN, MARY E.	BAL	233	12TH WAR
PYNE, H.R.	WAS	021	2ND SUBD
PYPHER, WILLIAM	BAL	437	8TH WARD
PYRELL, WILLIAM	PRI	036	VANSVILL
QERTS, JOHN*	BAL	268	20TH WAR
QIND, DAVID	BAL	159	11TH WAR
QINGLEY, THOMAS J.	CAR	148	NO TWP L
QRIMAN, THOMA SH.	BAL	248	12TH WAR
QUACKEN, CESAR	BAL	084	2ND DIST
QUADE, FRANCIS	CHA	245	HILLTOP
QUAICE, JAMES	ST	328	4TH E DI
QUAIE, CHARLES L.	ST	328	4TH E DI
QUAIGLER, WILLIAM	BAL	047	18TH WAR
QUAIL, GEORGE R.	BAL	412	14TH WAR
QUAIL, JAMES R.	BAL	015	18TH WAR
QUAIL, JOHN	BAL	196	5TH DIST
QUAIL, MARY	CAR	331	MANCHEST
QUAIL, WILLIAM	BAL	237	1ST DIST
QUAILES, CHARLOTTE *	HAR	001	1ST DIST
QUAISH, MARGARETT	BAL	085	4TH WARD
QUAKENBUSH, H.W.	ALL	221	CUMBERLA
QUANELS, FRANCIS	BAL	186	2ND WARD
QUANK, JAMES	BAL	154	1ST WARD
QUANN, JOHN	BAL	021	9TH WARD
QUANTRILL, JESSE D.E.	ALL	254	CUMBERLA
QUARL, JOHN	BAL	265	12TH WAR
QUARLES, CHARLOTT *	HAR	001	1ST DIST
QUARTMAN, JOHN	CAR	266	WESTMINS
QUARTMAN, MARY	BAL	115	5TH WARD
QUARY, PHILIP	CAL	049	3RD DIST
QUAY, CATHERINE	BAL	011	4TH WARD
QUAY, EPHRIM M.	TAL	010	EASTON D
QUAY, JOHN	BAL	267	12TH WAR
QUAY, JOHN C.	BAL	137	18TH WAR
QUAY, JOHN J.	BAL	279	2ND WARD
QUAY, MARY M.*	TAL	019	EASTON D
QUAY, RICHARD	BAL	347	7TH WARD
QUAY, SIDNEY	BAL	280	12TH WAR
QUE, MICHAEL	BAL	169	11TH WAR
QUEALL, JAMES C.	PRI	107	PISCATAW
QUEBECK, ELI	BAL	146	11TH WAR
QUEBECK, HENRY	BAL	146	11TH WAR
QUEEN, ADALINE	ANN	365	4TH DIST
QUEEN, ALEXANDER	CHA	267	BOJANTOW
QUEEN, ANN	BAL	342	13TH WAR
QUEEN, ANN	ANN	445	HOWARD D
QUEEN, ANN	ALL	210	CUMBERLA
QUEEN, ANN	PRI	038	VANSVILL
QUEEN, BEN	PRI	079	QUEEN AN
QUEEN, CHAPMAN	ANN	332	2ND DIST
QUEEN, DANIEL	ANN	331	2ND DIST
QUEEN, E.	ANN	283	ANNAPOLI
QUEEN, ELIAS	ANN	332	2ND DIST
QUEEN, ELIZA	ANN	374	4TH DIST
QUEEN, ELIZA	ANN	377	4TH DIST
QUEEN, ELIZA	BAL	117	15TH WAR
QUEEN, ELIZA	BAL	128	5TH WARD
QUEEN, ELIZA	CHA	241	HILLTOP
QUEEN, ELLEN	ANN	363	4TH DIST
QUEEN, ELLEN R.	MGM	376	ROCKERLE
QUEEN, EMANUEL	BAL	313	3RD WARD
QUEEN, FANNY	BAL	167	16TH WAR
QUEEN, FRANCES A.	BAL	178	16TH WAR
QUEEN, FRANCES E.	BAL	041	15TH WAR
QUEEN, GEORGE	BAL	458	8TH WARD
QUEEN, GEORGIANNA	BAL	191	17TH WAR
QUEEN, HARRIET	BAL	101	15TH WAR
QUEEN, HENRY	BAL	083	2ND DIST
QUEEN, HENRY	BAL	058	2ND DIST
QUEEN, ISAAC	ANN	339	3RD DIST
QUEEN, ISAAC	ANN	332	2ND DIST
QUEEN, JAEMS	BAL	341	13TH WAR
QUEEN, JAMES	BAL	117	15TH WAR
QUEEN, JAMES	BAL	429	1ST DIST
QUEEN, JANE	BAL	121	16TH WAR
QUEEN, JANE	PRI	087	QUEEN AN
QUEEN, JOHN	ST	288	2ND E DI
QUEEN, JOHN	ANN	384	4TH DIST
QUEEN, JOHN	BAL	421	14TH WAR
QUEEN, JOSEPH	ANN	376	4TH DIST
QUEEN, JOSEPH	ANN	321	2ND DIST
QUEEN, JOSEPH	PRI	082	QUEEN AN
QUEEN, JULIUS	BAL	003	15TH WAR
QUEEN, LEWIS	PRI	087	QUEEN AN
QUEEN, LUCRETIA	BAL	117	15TH WAR
QUEEN, MARGARET	ANN	329	2ND DIST
QUEEN, MARGARET	BAL	212	11TH WAR
QUEEN, MARY	BAL	230	17TH WAR
QUEEN, MARY	BAL	121	16TH WAR
QUEEN, MARY	BAL	152	16TH WAR
QUEEN, MARY	PRI	102	SPALDING
QUEEN, MICHAEL	BAL	136	2ND DIST
QUEEN, NANCY	PRI	121	PISCATAW
QUEEN, NANCY	BAL	452	14TH WAR
QUEEN, NOAH	PRI	122	PISCATAW
QUEEN, NOAH	PRI	057	AQUASCO
QUEEN, PATRICK	ALL	141	6TH E.D.
QUEEN, PRISCILLA	ANN	332	2ND DIST
QUEEN, ROBERT	ANN	406	3TH DIST
QUEEN, SALLY	ANN	362	4TH DIST
QUEEN, SARAH	BAL	107	18TH WAR
QUEEN, SOPHIA	BAL	141	16TH WAR
QUEEN, STEPHEN	BAL	028	15TH WAR
QUEEN, STEPHEN	PRI	086	QUEEN AN
QUEEN, SUSAN	PRI	087	QUEEN AN
QUEEN, SUSAN	CHA	262	MIDDLETO
QUEEN, SYLVESTER	PRI	087	QUEEN AN
QUEEN, THOAMS	ANN	339	3RD DIST
QUEEN, THOMAS	ANN	327	2ND DIST
QUEEN, THOMAS	ANN	312	1ST DIST
QUEEN, THOMAS	BAL	101	5TH WARD
QUEEN, THOMAS	PRI	086	QUEEN AN
QUEEN, THOMAS M.	CHA	287	BOJANTOW
QUEEN, WILLIAM	CHA	267	BOJANTOW
QUEEN, WILLIAM	BAL	226	17TH WAR
QUEEN, WILLIAM	BAL	255	17TH WAR
QUEEN, WILLIAM	PRI	085	QUEEN AN
QUEEN, WILLIAM	PRI	086	QUEEN AN
QUEEN, WILLIAM	ANN	327	2ND DIST
QUEEN, WILLIAM	ANN	333	2ND DIST
QUEEN, WILLIAM	BAL	192	17TH WAR
QUEEN, WILLIAM	BAL	167	6TH WARD
QUEEN, WILLIAM	BAL	382	3RD WARD
QUEEN, WINNY A.	ANN	364	4TH DIST
QUEES, ROBERT	CEC	111	4TH E DI
QUEGG, LEWIS	ALL	170	7TH E.D.
QUEGG, MARY	ALL	170	7TH E.D.
QUEHAN, ELIZABETH	BAL	367	8TH WARD
QUEHAN, JEREMIAH	BAL	366	8TH WARD
QUEINT, PETER *	BAL	151	1ST WARD
QUEN, FRANCES	BAL	421	14TH WAR
QUENEY, SARAH	BAL	002	EASTERN
QUENT, MAGDELINE	BAL	379	8TH WARD
QUESSADA, IGNATIO	FRE	202	5TH E DI
QUEST, MOSES	BAL	033	1ST WARD
QUEY, WILLIAM	BAL	070	4TH WARD
QUGLEY, MARY	BAL	183	2ND WARD
QUHN, ABRAHAM	BAL	331	13TH WAR
QUI, WILLIAM	BAL	169	11TH WAR
QUICK, ANASTATIA	BAL	406	3RD WARD
QUICK, GEORGE	BAL	074	2ND DIST
QUICK, H. J.	BAL	276	1ST DIST
QUICK, JOHN	DOR	386	1ST DIST
QUICK, JOHN W.	BAL	258	1ST DIST
QUICK, MARY A.	ANN	432	HOWARD D
QUICK, NICHOLAS	BAL	242	1ST DIST
QUICK, PETER	BAL	104	2ND DIST
QUICK, WILLIAM W.	WOR	301	SNOW HIL
QUICKLEY, DAN	HAR	065	1ST DIST
QUICKLIN, GRAFTON	BAL	088	2ND DIST
QUID, PATRICK	BAL	159	11TH WAR
QUIGBY, ANNIE	BAL	407	14TH WAR
QUIGG, BARBARA	BAL	335	13TH WAR
QUIGG, JAMES	ALL	070	5TH E.D.
QUIGG, SARAH	ALL	071	5TH E.D.
QUIGGS, MARY	BAL	412	3RD WARD
QUIGLEY, PATRICK	BAL	057	15TH WAR
QUIGLEY, ANN	BAL	209	19TH WAR
QUIGLEY, BRIDGET	BAL	319	7TH WARD
QUIGLEY, CATHARINE	BAL	163	16TH WAR
QUIGLEY, CATHARINE	BAL	476	14TH WAR
QUIGLEY, DAN	BAL	446	1ST DIST
QUIGLEY, EDWARD	BAL	186	11TH WAR
QUIGLEY, ELIZA	BAL	049	2ND DIST
QUIGLEY, ELLEN	BAL	467	14TH WAR
QUIGLEY, HUGH	HAR	044	1ST DIST
QUIGLEY, HUGH	BAL	022	18TH WAR
QUIGLEY, JOHN	BAL	262	20TH WAR
QUIGLEY, MARTIN	BAL	387	3RD WARD
QUIGLEY, MICHAEL	BAL	333	7TH WARD
QUIGLEY, ROBERT	WAS	131	HAGERSTO
QUIGLEY, WILLIAM	ALL	048	10TH E.D
QUIGLIN, RACHEL	ANN	416	HOWARD D
QUIGLY, AMOS	CEC	144	PORT DUP
QUIGLY, BIDDY	BAL	141	11TH WAR
QUIGLY, MARY	BAL	462	1ST DIST
QUIGLY, PETER	ALL	243	CUMBERLA
QUIGLY, PETER	BAL	276	1ST DIST
QUIGLY, RACHEL	BAL	462	1ST DIST
QUIKENS, BETSY	ANN	398	8TH DIST
QUIKHAW, JOHN *	BAL	120	18TH WAR
QUILE, JOHN	ANN	500	HOWARD D
QUILL, BENJAMIN	CAL	042	3RD DIST
QUILL, MARTHA	BAL	461	14TH WAR
QUILLAN, JAMES	BAL	263	20TH WAR
QUILLEN, ASA	WOR	270	BERLIN 1
QUILLEN, GEORGE	WOR	281	BERLIN 1
QUILLEN, HENRY	WOR	283	BERLIN 1
QUILLEN, JANE	WOR	264	BERLIN 1
QUILLEN, RACHEL A.	WOR	258	1ST CENS
QUILLEN, THOMAS	WOR	281	BERLIN 1
QUILLEN, WILLIAM H.	WOR	215	4TH E DI
QUILLER, DANIEL-MULATTO	FRE	419	8TH E DI
QUILLER, EDWARD	BAL	064	2ND DIST
QUILLEY, GEORGE P.	BAL	279	2ND WARD
QUILLHIDE, MARY	FRE	131	CREAGERS
QUILLIN, EBE	WOR	261	BERLIN 1
QUILLIN, FANNY	WOR	263	BERLIN 1
QUILLIN, JAMES	WOR	277	BERLIN 1
QUILLIN, JAMES	WOR	279	BERLIN 1
QUILLIN, JOHN	WOR	275	BERLIN 1
QUILLIN, JOSEPH	WOR	276	BERLIN 1
QUILLIN, LAMBERT	WOR	281	BERLIN 1
QUILLIN, LEVI	WOR	280	BERLIN 1
QUILLIN, NATHANIEL	WOR	275	BERLIN 1

QUILLIN, PHILIP HAR 152 3RD DIST
QUILLIN, RACHEL WOR 279 BERLIN 1
QUILLIN, SALLY WOR 270 BERLIN 1
QUILLIN, SARAH WOR 276 BERLIN 1
QUILLIN, THOMAS WOR 283 BERLIN 1
QUILLIN, THOMAS WOR 282 BERLIN 1
QUILLIN, WILLIAM WOR 276 BERLIN 1
QUILLINS, STEPHEN WOR 282 BERLIN 1
QUILLS, THOMSZ BAL 115 2ND DIST
QUIM, CHARLES BAL 288 1ST DIST
QUIM, JOHN BAL 160 1ST WARD
QUIMBLY, ANDREW CEC 115 3RD E DI
QUIMBY, BENJAMIN KEN 312 3RD DIST
QUIMEY, DAVID KEN 209 2ND DIST
QUIMBY, JAMES W. KEN 218 2ND DIST
QUIN, APTRICK BAL 418 1ST DIST
QUIN, BOYD ANN 270 ANNAPOLI
QUIN, FRANCIS BAL 110 10TH WAR
QUIN, HANNAH CAR 381 2ND DIST
QUIN, JAMES ANN 414 HOWARD D
QUIN, JOHN BAL 462 1ST DIST
QUIN, JOHN BAL 318 20TH WAR
QUIN, JOSIAH TAL 023 EASTON D
QUIN, M. BAL 127 5TH WARD
QUIN, MICHAL TAL 022 EASTON D
QUIN, PETER BAL 058 1ST WARD
QUIN, SARAH BAL 213 11TH WAR
QUIN, TERRENCE BAL 131 5TH WARD
QUIN,LUCY BAL 070 1ST WARD
QUINAN, JAMES BAL 090 1ST WARD
QUINCY, ELLEN S. BAL 102 5TH WARD
QUINDON, JAMES * BAL 300 12TH WAR
QUINES, JOHN BAL 054 1ST WARD
QUING, JOHN BAL 038 1ST WARD
QUINHAIR, JASIAH BAL 139 1ST WARD
QUININE, JOHN R. CAL 039 2ND DIST
QUINK,ANDREW BAL 097 1ST WARD
QUINLAIR, JOHN BAL 139 1ST WARD
QUINLAN, ANN BAL 041 9TH WARD
QUINLAN, B. M. BAL 457 8TH WARD
QUINLAN, ELLEN BAL 078 15TH WAR
QUINLAN, JOHN FRE 20 5TH E DI
QUINLAN, LEONARD G. BAL 258 12TH WAR
QUINLAN, THOMAS BAL 298 20TH WAR
QUINLAND, JOHN BAL 396 8TH WARD
QUINLAND, LUCY HAR 109 2ND DIST
QUINLEN, JAMES L. HAR 110 2ND DIST
QUINLEY, ELIJAH KEN 301 3RD DIST
QUINLIN, CHARITY M. HAR 005 1ST DIST
QUINLIN, ISAAC HAR 111 2ND DIST
QUINLIN, LUKE BAL 449 1ST DIST
QUINLIN, MARY BAL 092 2ND DIST
QUINLIN, SUSAN HAR 108 2ND DIST
QUINLY, AGNES BAL 096 2ND DIST
QUINLY, ANN CEC 115 3RD E DI
QUINN, ALEXANDER ALL 053 10TH E.D
QUINN, AMANDA BAL 025 4TH WARD
QUINN, ANN ALL 084 5TH E.D.
QUINN, ANN BAL 352 7TH WARD
QUINN, ARTHUR FRE 20 5TH E DI
QUINN, BARNEY BAL 036 4TH WARD
QUINN, BRIDGET BAL 053 9TH WARD
QUINN, CALAGUE * BAL 287 1ST DIST
QUINN, CAROLINE BAL 097 5TH WARD
QUINN, CATHARINE BAL 180 6TH WARD
QUINN, CATHERINE BAL 014 9TH WARD
QUINN, CHARLES BAL 179 2ND WARD
QUINN, DANIEL BAL 406 1ST DIST
QUINN, EDWARD BAL 029 4TH WARD
QUINN, EDWARD BAL 129 18TH WAR
QUINN, ELIZA BAL 334 3RD WARD
QUINN, ELIZA BAL 385 8TH WARD
QUINN, ELIZABETH BAL 183 2ND WARD
QUINN, ELLEN BAL 380 3RD WARD
QUINN, ELLEN BAL 022 1ST WARD
QUINN, ELLEN BAL 004 4TH WARD
QUINN, FRANCIS BAL 420 8TH WARD
QUINN, HARRIET BAL 364 3RD WARD
QUINN, HENRY BAL 319 7TH WARD
QUINN, HUGH BAL 053 9TH WARD
QUINN, HUGH BAL 423 8TH WARD
QUINN, JAMES BAL 415 8TH WARD
QUINN, JAMES BAL 197 2ND WARD
QUINN, JAMES BAL 342 1ST DIST
QUINN, JAMES ALL 081 5TH E.D.
QUINN, JAMES HAR 186 3RD DIST
QUINN, JANE BAL 057 15TH WAR
QUINN, JOHN ANN 269 ANNAPOLI
QUINN, JOHN BAL 461 1ST DIST
QUINN, JOHN BAL 025 9TH WARD
QUINN, JOHN BAL 162 1ST WARD
QUINN, JOHN BAL 386 8TH WARD
QUINN, JOHN BAL 370 8TH WARD
QUINN, JOHN BAL 017 1ST WARD
QUINN, JOHN HAR 067 1ST DIST
QUINN, JOHN F. BAL 446 8TH WARD
QUINN, JOHN R. BAL 086 18TH WAR
QUINN, JOHN W. WOR 339 1ST E DI
QUINN, JOSEPH BAL 090 5TH WARD
QUINN, JULIA BAL 109 1ST WARD
QUINN, LAURENSON QUE 237 4TH E DI
QUINN, LILA BAL 225 12TH WAR
QUINN, LORREN-BLACK WOR 340 1ST E DI
QUINN, LYDIA WAS 005 WILLIAMS
QUINN, MARGARET BAL 255 6TH WARD
QUINN, MARGARETT BAL 079 4TH WARD
QUINN, MARIA BAL 424 3RD WARD
QUINN, MARIAH-BLACK WOR 343 1ST E DI
QUINN, MARTIN ALL 127 4TH E.D.
QUINN, MARTIN ALL 252 CUMBERLA
QUINN, MARY ALL 081 5TH E.D.
QUINN, MARY BAL 218 12TH WAR
QUINN, MARY BAL 110 10TH WAR
QUINN, MARY BAL 083 10TH WAR
QUINN, MARY QUE 251 5TH E DI
QUINN, MARY BAL 316 20TH WAR
QUINN, MARY HAR 118 2ND DIST
QUINN, MARY ANN BAL 333 13TH WAR
QUINN, MARY J. BAL 049 9TH WARD
QUINN, MICHAEL ALL 172 7TH E.D.
QUINN, MICHAEL BAL 231 6TH WARD
QUINN, NANCY BAL 042 9TH WARD
QUINN, NICHOLAS BAL 439 8TH WARD
QUINN, NOAH-BLACK WOR 349 1ST E DI
QUINN, OWEN ALL 067 10TH E.D
QUINN, PATRICK BAL 049 9TH WARD
QUINN, PATRICK MGM 381 ROCKERLE
QUINN, PRISCILLA-MULATTO BAL 248 2ND WARD
QUINN, R. BAL 139 1ST WARD
QUINN, ROSY BAL 159 6TH WARD

QUINN, SARAH BAL 392 8TH WARD
QUINN, SISTER M.O. FRE 198 5TH E DI
QUINN, STEPHEN WOR 343 1ST E DI
QUINN, WILLIAM WOR 343 1ST E DI
QUINN, WILLIAM BAL 182 11TH WAR
QUINN, WILLIAM H. BAL 333 3RD WARD
QUINNS, BIDDY HAR 118 2ND DIST
QUINNS, PATRICK BAL 177 11TH WAR
QUINSAY, S. BAL 166 1ST WARD
QUINSEY, SAMUEL BAL 171 1ST WARD
QUINSEY, SAMUEL BAL 170 1ST WARD
QUINTIN, CHARLES H. BAL 261 2ND WARD
QUINTON, ABLE WOR 294 9TH E DI
QUINTON, ELIZABETH SOM 508 BARREN C
QUINTON, HENRY SOM 508 BARREN C
QUINTON, HENRY SOM 506 BARREN C
QUINTON, MARTHA BAL 307 12TH WAR
QUINTON, NICY WOR 299 SNOW HIL
QUINTON, RICHARD SOM 513 BARREN C
QUINTON, SOPHIA SOM 506 BARREN C
QUINTY, MARGARET BAL 357 3RD WARD
QUIORICE, GEORGE BAL 084 18TH WAR
QUIRK, JULIA A. BAL 033 1ST WARD
QUIRK, ROSANNA BAL 022 15TH WAR
QUIRLEY, WILLIAM* DOR 354 3RD DIVI
QUISLEY, WILLIAM* DOR 354 3RD DIVI
QUMFREY, JOHN BAL 273 12TH WAR
QUMFREY, MARIA BAL 272 12TH WAR
QUNCY, WILLIAM BAL 160 1ST WARD
QUNN, SARAH-BLACK CAR 082 NO TWP L
QUNTRY, MARY BAL 205 19TH WAR
QUONTZ, CHARLES ALL 231 CUMBERLA
QURAP, JOHN BAL 060 18TH WAR
QUYNER, LOUISA BAL 361 13TH WAR
QUYNN, ALLEN G. FRE 026 FREDERIC
QUYNN, CALVIN FRE 051 FREDERIC
QUYNN, JAMES BAL 274 20TH WAR
QUYNN, JOHN T. FRE 022 FREDERIC
QUYNN, RICHARD BAL 277 20TH WAR
QUYNN, WILLIAM * BAL 273 20TH WAR
QWEESE, JOHN H. BAL 053 1ST WARD
QWIN, SUSAN PRI 080 QUEEN AN
QWINN, WILLIAM A. PRI 064 NOTTINGH
RAABE, DOLPHIN BAL 028 18TH WAR
RAB, EMANUEL BAL 039 9TH WARD
RAB, JOSEPHINE BAL 004 EASTERN
RABAUM, HENRY BAL 310 1ST DIST
RABAWN, PETER BAL 262 1ST DIST
RABB, DAVID CHA 294 BOJANTOW
RABB, JOHN D. BAL 386 13TH WAR
RABB, PHILIP BAL 262 20TH WAR
RABBIT, BRIDGET ALL 227 CUMBERLA
RABBIT, ELIZABETH MGM 400 ROCKERLE
RABBIT, THOMAS ALL 053 10TH E.D
RABBIT, THOMAS H. MGM 400 ROCKERLE
RABBIT, WILLIAM MGM 383 ROCKERLE
RABBITT, JAMES MGM 361 BERRYS D
RABBITT, JOHN MGM 363 BERRYS D
RABBITT, SAMUEL MGM 368 BERRYS D
RABBITT, THOMAS H. MGM 368 BERRYS D
RABBITT, WILLIAM J. MGM 363 BERRYS D
RABE, JOHN T. BAL 108 5TH WARD
RABER, HARRIET BAL 220 1ST DIST
RABES, HENRY* TAL 061 EASTON D
RABES, JOHN* TAL 043 EASTON D
RABES, JULIANN* TAL 051 EASTON D
RABES, LOUISA* TAL 055 EASTON D
RABES, MARY* TAL 056 EASTON D
RABES, MATILDA* TAL 049 EASTON T
RABES, P.* TAL 045 EASTON T
RABES, PETER* TAL 058 EASTON D
RABEY, JAMES TAL 043 EASTON D
RABINE, ANNA BAL 180 2ND DIST
RABINE, GEORGE BAL 179 2ND DIST
RABITT, GEORGE KEN 284 3RD DIST
RABLEIN, MARTHA BAL 034 15TH WAR
RABLEIN, MARTIN BAL 033 15TH WAR
RABNAU, ELIZABETH BAL 038 9TH WARD
RABOLT, GEORGE ALL 221 CUMBERLA
RABOLT, JOHN ALL 221 CUMBERLA
RABOLT, MARY ALL 222 CUMBERLA
RABORG, CHRISTOPHER BAL 131 16TH WAR
RABORG, CHRISTOPHER H. BAL 177 16TH WAR
RABORG, GODDARD BAL 173 16TH WAR
RABORG, HENRIETTA BAL 178 16TH WAR
RABORG, HENRIETTA BAL 179 16TH WAR
RABOS, EPHRIAM BAL 389 1ST DIST
RABOS, HENRY BAL 389 1ST DIST
RABOUCH, HENRY ALL 099 5TH E.D.
RABURG, ANN M. BAL 365 3RD WARD
RABURY, T. BAL 231 19TH WAR
RABY, RICHARD BAL 430 1ST DIST
RACH, PATRICK BAL 082 2ND DIST
RACHES, J. BAL 158 1ST WARD
RACHFORD, THOMAS BAL 053 18TH WAR
RACK, ANN BAL 125 11TH WAR
RACK, JOHN BAL 028 9TH WARD
RACKER, HENRY BAL 130 1ST WARD
RACKES, ELLEN CEC 213 7TH E DI
RACKLIFF, WILL WOR 272 BERLIN 1
RACKS, HARRISON BAL 071 4TH WARD
RACLE, PHILIP * BAL 062 15TH WAR
RACRAFT, PETER ALL 146 6TH E.D.
RADCLIFF, PHILIP CEC 139 6TH E DI
RADCLIFFE, KITTY ANN 314 1ST DIST
RADCLIFFE, SAMUEL J. ANN 456 HOWARD D
RADCLIFFE, SUSAN BAL 361 1ST DIST
RADDASH, ROBERT BAL 465 14TH WAR
RADDICKE, FREDERICK BAL 040 15TH WAR
RADDISH, ANN BAL 371 3RD WARD
RADDON, JAMES BAL 374 13TH WAR
RADECKE, DEDRICK BAL 368 13TH WAR
RADECKE, HENRY C. BAL 367 13TH WAR
RADECKE, MARY L. BAL 367 13TH WAR
RADEN, PHILIP BAL 230 19TH WAR
RADFORD, JOHN BAL 125 1ST WARD
RADFORD, MONECHA ST 268 3RD E DI
RADFORD, MONICHA ST 268 3RD E DI
RADGET, ANN CHA 262 MIDDLETO
RADICEY, EDWARD BAL 172 11TH WAR
RADINGER, JOHN BAL 368 1ST DIST
RADLEY, SAMUEL BAL 027 1ST WARD
RADLIFF, RACHEL BAL 442 14TH WAR
RADNEY, ANAMAIAS WOR 277 BERLIN 1
RADNEY, PHILLIP WOR 277 BERLIN 1
RADRICK, JOHN BAL 112 2ND DIST
RAE, FRANCIS BAL 173 16TH WAR
RAEGER, JOHN BAL 033 15TH WAR
RAEHL, ADOLPH BAL 165 16TH WAR
RAELE, PHILIP * BAL 062 15TH WAR

RAELING, RUDOLPH BAL 013 15TH WAR
RAELTER, HENRY BAL 095 1ST WARD
RAENGLE, CHRISTOPHER FRE 405 JEFFERSO
RAERKER, CHRISTIAN BAL 331 13TH WAR
RAFERTY, DENNIS ALL 119 5TH E.D.
RAFERTY, MICHAEL BAL 168 11TH WAR
RAFEY, HARIETT BAL 192 11TH WAR
RAFFEL, ELIZABETH BAL 331 7TH WARD
RAFFERTY, CATHARINE BAL 001 EASTERN
RAFFERTY, HANNAH BAL 006 9TH WARD
RAFFERTY, HUGH BAL 016 2ND DIST
RAFFERTY, JOHN BAL 161 2ND DIST
RAFFERTY, MARY BAL 045 15TH WAR
RAFFERTY, MARY BAL 231 19TH WAR
RAFFERTY, MARYANN* BAL 413 3RD WARD
RAFFERTY, PATRICK ALL 075 5TH E.D.
RAFFERTY, WILLAIM BAL 231 19TH WAR
RAFFLE, JOSHUA D. BAL 419 3RD WARD
RAFKELLY, WILLIAM BAL 028 18TH WAR
RAFLY, FREDERIC WAS 153 2ND DIST
RAFNER, LEONARD BAL 251 20TH WAR
RAGAN, CHARLES ANN 401 8TH DIST
RAGAN, JANE FRE 031 FREDERIC
RAGAN, JOHN H. WAS 145 HAGERSTO
RAGAN, JOSEPH BAL 119 1ST WARD
RAGAN, MARSHAL A. CEC 165 6TH E DI
RAGAN, MARTIN BAL 062 15TH WAR
RAGAN, MARY BAL 178 16TH WAR
RAGAN, R. SR. WAS 121 HAGERSTO
RAGAN, THOMAS BAL 472 14TH WAR
RAGAN, WILLIAM WAS 121 HAGERSTO
RAGAN, WILLIAM F.-MULATTO FRE 024 FREDERIC
RAGAN,MARY BAL 189 2ND WARD
RAGDER, GEORGE BAL 138 2ND DIST
RAGE, MARGARET TAL 043 EASTON D
RAGEN, RICHARD WAS 268 1ST DIST
RAGEN,JOHANNA ALL 211 CUMBERLA
RAGER, DOROTHIA BAL 002 9TH WARD
RAGER, MICAHEL WAS 028 2ND SUBD
RAGF, ANDRWE BAL 363 13TH WAR
RAGHLIE, DONALD BAL 413 8TH WARD
RAGNER, WILLIAM S. BAL 028 1ST WARD
RAHIL, GEORGE ALL 095 5TH E.D.
RAHITY, HANNAH BAL 044 4TH WARD
RAHLER, CHRISTIAN BAL 250 2ND WARD
RAHN, MATILDA CAR 409 2ND DIST
RAHN, PETER BAL 276 1ST DIST
RAHRMAN, ANN M. FRE 157 10TH E D
RAHRMAN, JOHN BAL 034 9TH WARD
RAHTGEN, JOHN BAL 089 1ST WARD
RAIFF, ISAAC CAL 049 3RD DIST
RAIKES, LIDDY A. BAL 071 4TH WARD
RAILEY, BENEDICT A. ST 256 3RD E DI
RAILEY, CHARLES ST 290 2ND E DI
RAILEY, CHARLES A. ST 265 3RD E DI
RAILEY, DOROTHY ST 264 3RD E DI
RAILEY, ELEANOR ST 286 2ND E DI
RAILEY, GEORGE F. ST 254 3RD E DI
RAILEY, JAMES T. M. ST 260 3RD E DI
RAILEY, JAMES W. ST 285 2ND E DI
RAILEY, JOHN B. ST 264 3RD E DI
RAILEY, WILLIAM A. ST 265 3RD E DI
RAILEY, ZACHARIAH C. ST 265 3RD E DI
RAILING, HENRY FRE 091 FREDERIC
RAIM, WILLIAM BAL 029 9TH WARD
RAIN, BASSETT WOR 216 4TH E DI
RAIN, CATHARINE BAL 137 2ND DIST
RAIN, GILBERT WOR 202 4TH E DI
RAIN, GILLEY WOR 284 BERLIN 1
RAIN, JOHN WOR 217 4TH E DI
RAIN, MARTHA WOR 262 BERLIN 1
RAIN, MICHEL BAL 084 2ND DIST
RAIN, PETER WOR 254 1ST CENS
RAIN, ROBERT QUE 206 3RD E DI
RAIN, SUSAN BAL 069 1ST WARD
RAINALLS, ROBERT BAL 273 2ND WARD
RAINBOW, CHARLES BAL 075 4TH WARD
RAINBOW, ELIZABETH BAL 075 4TH WARD
RAINBOW, ELIZABETH BAL 193 6TH WARD
RAINBOW, EVERLINE BAL 429 1ST DIST
RAINBOW, ISAAC BAL 183 5TH DIST
RAINBOW, ISAIAH BAL 423 1ST DIST
RAINBOW, ISAIAH BAL 421 1ST DIST
RAINBOW, MARTHA BAL 184 19TH WAR
RAINBOW, THOMAS A. BAL 184 19TH WAR
RAINE, DAVID M. BAL 122 18TH WAR
RAINE, FRED BAL 081 10TH WAR
RAINE, JAMES WAS 011 WILLIAMS
RAINE, PETER BAL 137 5TH WARD
RAINE, ROBERT E. BAL 151 1ST WARD
RAINE, WILLIAM BAL 015 9TH WARD
RAINER, BENJAMIN* BAL 115 11TH WAR
RAINER, ROSA BAL 051 4TH WARD
RAINES, ANTONY BAL 001 EASTERN
RAINEY, JANE BAL 124 5TH WARD
RAINIER, ANTON BAL 104 1ST WARD
RAINS, C.H. BAL 166 1ST WARD
RAINS, LEWIS BAL 372 3RD WARD
RAINY, JESSE P. WOR 273 BERLIN 1
RAISEN, JAMES BAL 200 6TH WARD
RAISEN, KITT-BLACK QUE 137 1ST E DI
RAISER, JAOCB FRE 234 BUCKEYST
RAISIN, GEORGE QUE 227 4TH E DI
RAISIN, JANE BAL 300 12TH WAR
RAISIN, RICHARD QUE 216 3RD E DI
RAISON, JOSEPH TAL 067 EASTON T
RAISON, MARTHA-BLACK CAR 098 NO TWP L
RAIT, MARIA BAL 077 10TH WAR
RAITT, CHARLES H. HAR 026 1ST DIST
RAKECAMP, LEWIS ALL 198 CUMBERLA
RAKENSPERG, MARY BAL 239 12TH WAR
RAKENSPORG, D. BAL 238 12TH WAR
RAKER, GEORGE BAL 193 5TH DIST
RAKES, HENRY* TAL 061 EASTON D
RAKES, JOHN* TAL 043 EASTON D
RAKES, JULIANN* TAL 051 EASTON D
RAKES, LOUISA* TAL 055 EASTON D
RAKES, MARY* TAL 056 EASTON D
RAKES, MATILDA* TAL 049 EASTON T
RAKES, PETER* TAL 058 EASTON D
RAKES, THOMAS CEC 134 6TH E DI
RAKLE, JOHN BAL 276 2ND WARD
RALDENBACK, J.E.M. PRI 065 NOTTINGH
RALE, RACHEL* DOR 424 1ST DIST
RALEKER, THOMAS ALL 108 5TH E.D.
RALEY, ATTAWAY ST 326 4TH E DI
RALEY, JAMES R. ST 326 4TH E DI
RALEY, JOHN L. ST 323 4TH E DI
RALEY, PHILLIS QUE 219 3RD E DI
RALEY, RICHARD P. ST 320 4TH E DI

NAME	CO.	PAGE	DISTRICT
RALEY, SARAH	ST	326	4TH E DI
RALEY, WILLIAM	ST	326	4TH E DI
RALL, JOHN	BAL	204	2ND WARD
RALLEN,' JOHN	BAL	252	20TH WAR
RALLENTIN, CAVID	BAL	118	1ST WARD
RALLEY, CANIEL	FRE	151	10TH E D
RALPH, ALEXANDER	CEC	090	4TH E DI
RALPH, ANN	BAL	207	2ND WARD
RALPH, ARCH	WAS	117	2ND DIST
RALPH, BENJAIN	BAL	156	1ST WARD
RALPH, CALEB	CEC	175	7TH E DI
RALPH, CHARLES WESLEY	QUE	129	1ST E DI
RALPH, GEORGE	BAL	162	1ST WARD
RALPH, GEORGE	BAL	167	1ST WARD
RALPH, JOSEPH	BAL	422	14TH WAR
RALPH, MARY	CEC	212	7TH E DI
RALSENKATTER, WILLIAM	BAL	243	2ND WARD
RALY, GEORGE	CEC	062	1ST E DI
RAMAGE, EMILY	BAL	393	3RD WARD
RAMBESY, ELLEN B.	HAR	155	3RD DIST
RAMBO, JACOB	CEC	001	ELKTON 3
RAMBO, JOHN	CEC	097	4TH E DI
RAMBURG, CANIEL	FRE	134	CREAGERS
RAMBURG, LEWIS	FRE	047	FREDERIC
RAMBURG, NELSON	FRE	102	FREDERIC
RAMBY, GEORGE	CAR	333	MANCHEST
RAMBY, SAMUEL H.	CAR	268	WESTMINS
RAMBY, SARAH A. E.	CAR	266	WESTMINS
RAMBY, THOMAS B.	CAR	330	MANCHEST
RAMEEERGER, EDWARD	FRE	090	FREDERIC
RAMER, BENJAMIN*	BAL	115	11TH WAR
RAMER, DANEIL	BAL	210	6TH DIST
RAMER, JOHN	BAL	239	1ST DIST
RAMER, MARY	BAL	041	4TH WARD
RAMICAFF, VALEUS	BAL	106	1ST WARD
RAMLER, JOHN	BAL	079	1ST WARD
RAMNS, CHRISTMA	ALL	209	CUMBERLA
RAMOND, RACHAEL	BAL	268	1ST DIST
RAMPLEY, JAMES	HAR	016	1ST DIST
RAMPLEY, THCMAS	HAR	038	1ST DIST
RAMPLEY, WILLIAM	HAR	016	1ST DIST
RAMPMYER, CHARLES	BAL	308	20TH WAR
RAMSAY, CHARLES	BAL	168	19TH WAR
RAMSAY, CHARLES	BAL	310	3RD WARD
RAMSAY, ELIZA	BAL	310	3RD WARD
RAMSAY, GEORGE A.	BAL	169	19TH WAR
RAMSAY, GUSTAVUS	CAL	032	2ND DIST
RAMSAY, HUGH C.	HAR	042	1ST DIST
RAMSAY, JANE M.	BAL	169	19TH WAR
RAMSAY, MARGARET	BAL	168	19TH WAR
RAMSAY, SAMUEL J.	HAR	001	1ST DIST
RAMSBERG, MARY	FRE	442	8TH E DI
RAMSBERRY, LYDIA	FRE	089	FREDERIC
RAMSBERY, MARY A.	FRE	090	FREDERIC
RAMSBREY, CHRISTIAN	FRE	318	MIDDLETO
RAMSEUR, JOHN *	FRE	320	MIDDLETO
RAMSBURG, AMANDA E.	FRE	071	FREDERIC
RAMSBURG, CATHARINE	FRE	212	BUCKEYST
RAMSBURG, CLEAS	FRE	260	NEW MARK
RAMSBURG, CANIEL	FRE	321	MIDDLETO
RAMSBURG, ELIZABETH	FRE	212	BUCKEYST
RAMSBURG, ELIZABETH	FRE	225	BUCKEYST
RAMSBURG, ELIZABETH	FRE	032	FREDERIC
RAMSBURG, GEORGE A.	FRE	407	JEFFERSO
RAMSBURG, HANSON	FRE	321	MIDDLETO
RAMSBURG, HENRY	FRE	323	MIDDLETO
RAMSBURG, HENRY	FRE	137	CREAGERS
RAMSBURG, HENRY *	FRE	321	MIDDLETO
RAMSBURG, JACOB	FRE	141	CREAGERS
RAMSBURG, JAOCB	FRE	212	BUCKEYST
RAMSBURG, JCHN	FRE	044	FREDERIC
RAMSBURG, JOHN F.	FRE	324	MIDDLETO
RAMSBURG, JOSEPH	FRE	354	MIDDLETO
RAMSBURG, LEVI	FRE	333	MIDDLETO
RAMSBURG, MARY J.	FRE	213	BUCKEYST
RAMSBURG, SAMUEL	FRE	330	MIDDLETO
RAMSBURG, STEVEN	FRE	093	FREDERIC
RAMSBURG, WILLIAM H.	FRE	096	FREDERIC
RAMSBURGH, WILLIAM	WAS	193	1ST DIST
RAMSBURY, DENNIS	FRE	089	FREDERIC
RAMSBURY, ELIZABETH	FRE	314	MIDDLETO
RAMSBURY, ISAAC	WAS	084	2ND SUBD
RAMSBURY, JOSEPH	FRE	355	MIDDLETO
RAMSBURY, JOSIAH	FRE	077	FREDERIC
RAMSBURY, MARY	FRE	136	CREAGERS
RAMSBURY, SAMUEL	FRE	090	FREDERIC
RAMSBURY, WILLIAM M.	FRE	098	FREDERIC
RAMSBUY, DAVID J.	FRE	118	CREAGERS
RAMSEY, ALBERT G.	BAL	020	15TH WAR
RAMSEY, ALBERTA	BAL	148	11TH WAR
RAMSEY, AMANDA	CEC	183	7TH E DI
RAMSEY, ARCHIBALD	HAR	158	3RD DIST
RAMSEY, DAVIC	BAL	084	18TH WAR
RAMSEY, E. A.	ANN	337	3RD DIST
RAMSEY, ELIZA	BAL	049	4TH WARD
RAMSEY, ELIZABETH	BAL	083	10TH WAR
RAMSEY, ISAAC J.	BAL	258	2ND WARD
RAMSEY, JOHN	BAL	229	2ND WARD
RAMSEY, JOHN	BAL	227	2ND WARD
RAMSEY, JCHN	BAL	284	1ST DIST
RAMSEY, JOHN	BAL	147	19TH WAR
RAMSEY, JOSEPH E.	BAL	294	7TH WARD
RAMSEY, JOSHUA A.	BAL	384	3RD WARD
RAMSEY, KENZIA-MULATTO	BAL	184	2ND WARD
RAMSEY, LABERT	WAS	216	1ST DIST
RAMSEY, MARTHA	HAR	118	2ND DIST
RAMSEY, MARY A.	BAL	147	19TH WAR
RAMSEY, MATTHEW	BAL	164	6TH WARD
RAMSEY, MAUIAN	BAL	111	10TH WAR
RAMSEY, MRS.	BAL	085	4TH WARD
RAMSEY, NATHANIEL	HAR	134	2ND DIST
RAMSEY, NEMORE	HAR	182	3RD DIST
RAMSEY, RACHEL	BAL	457	8TH WARD
RAMSEY, RACHELL	BAL	235	17TH WAR
RAMSEY, ROBERT J.	BAL	440	8TH WARD
RAMSEY, THCMAS-BLACK	FRE	018	FREDERIC
RAMSEY, W.	BAL	062	10TH WAR
RAMSEY, WILLIAM	HAR	146	3RD DIST
RAMSEY, WILLIAM M.	BAL	101	10TH WAR
RAMSEY, WILLIAM W.	BAL	196	2ND WARD
RAMSLING, LEWIS *	FRE	368	CATOCTIN
RAMSOMA, MARGARET	MGM	345	CLARKSBU
RAMSON, LOYDE	CAR	368	9TH DIST
RAMSY, ANDREW	CEC	196	6TH E DI
RAMSY, ELIZABETH	CAL	038	2ND DIST
RAMSY, JEFFERSON	CEC	182	7TH E DI
RAMSY, RACHEL	CEC	196	6TH E DI
RAMSY, SARAH	CEC	197	7TH E DI
RAMSY, WARNER	CEC	197	7TH E DI
RAMSY, WILLIAM	CEC	160	PORT DUP
RAMSY, WILLIAM	BAL	464	14TH WAR
RAMUS, MARY	FRE	384	PETERSVI
RAMY, ROBERT A.	QUE	183	3RD E DI
RAN, A.	BAL	104	10TH WAR
RANALLS, CHARLES	BAL	179	2ND WARD
RANARD, MICHAEL	BAL	189	2ND WARD
RANCER, WILLAIM	BAL	128	5TH WARD
RANCH, FREDERICK	BAL	466	14TH WAR
RAND, SOPHONA	BAL	377	1ST DIST
RANDAL, GEORGIANA	BAL	403	3RD WARD
RANDAL, HANNAH	HAR	022	1ST DIST
RANDAL, JAMES	ANN	507	HOWARD D
RANDAL, MARY	HAR	072	1ST DIST
RANDAL, PHILLIP	BAL	188	2ND WARD
RANDALL, AGNES	BAL	103	10TH WAR
RANDALL, ALEXANDER	ANN	281	ANNAPOLI
RANDALL, ANDERW	BAL	003	1ST WARD
RANDALL, ANN	BAL	317	20TH WAR
RANDALL, ANN M.	BAL	394	3RD WARD
RANDALL, BEN	CAL	060	3RD DIST
RANDALL, BENCROTS	BAL	064	1ST WARD
RANDALL, BENLE	BAL	242	12TH WAR
RANDALL, BUEL	BAL	274	20TH WAR
RANDALL, CHARLES	BAL	142	1ST WARD
RANDALL, CONAGUNDA	BAL	067	1ST WARD
RANDALL, DAVID	CAL	050	3RD DIST
RANDALL, DORCAS	BAL	203	19TH WAR
RANDALL, DUDLEY A.	BAL	065	10TH WAR
RANDALL, E.	ANN	296	1ST DIST
RANDALL, ESAW	CAR	358	9TH DIST
RANDALL, GEORGE B.	BAL	308	12TH WAR
RANDALL, GEORGE H.	BAL	062	4TH WARD
RANDALL, HARRIET	CAL	060	3RD DIST
RANDALL, HENRY E.	BAL	050	9TH WARD
RANDALL, JAMES	ANN	510	HOWARD D
RANDALL, JEHU	CAR	393	2ND DIST
RANDALL, JOHN	BAL	053	15TH WAR
RANDALL, JOHN	BAL	273	12TH WAR
RANDALL, JOHN B.	BAL	032	9TH WARD
RANDALL, JOHN F.	BAL	402	3RD WARD
RANDALL, JULIA	BAL	025	1ST WARD
RANDALL, MARGARET	BAL	308	12TH WAR
RANDALL, MARY	BAL	127	16TH WAR
RANDALL, MARY	BAL	212	11TH WAR
RANDALL, MARY A.	BAL	034	15TH WAR
RANDALL, ROBERT	BAL	361	3RD WARD
RANDALL, ROBERT	BAL	387	13TH WAR
RANDALL, ROBERT	BAL	166	19TH WAR
RANDALL, SAMUEL O.	BAL	385	3RD WARD
RANDALL, SARAH	BAL	180	19TH WAR
RANDALL, SUSAN	ANN	492	HOWARD D
RANDALL, THOMAS	BAL	042	4TH WARD
RANDALL, VACHEL	BAL	258	20TH WAR
RANDALL, WILLIAM	BAL	361	3RD WARD
RANDALL, WILLIAM	BAL	190	6TH WARD
RANDAN, SARAH	BAL	324	12TH WAR
RANDANNO, JOHN B.	BAL	312	12TH WAR
RANDEBUSH, JOHN	KEN	214	2ND DIST
RANDELL, DEBORA	ANN	276	ANNAPOLI
RANDELL, EMILY	BAL	046	18TH WAR
RANDELL, JOHN	ANN	405	8TH DIST
RANDELL, JOHN K.	BAL	046	18TH WAR
RANDELL, MARY E.	TAL	094	ST MICHA
RANDELL, SALLY	BAL	340	13TH WAR
RANDELL, WILLIAM	BAL	331	1ST DIST
RANDLE, CAROLINE	CAR	214	5TH DIST
RANDLE, CHARLES	DOR	355	3RD DIVI
RANDLE, CLAGETT W.	WAS	293	1ST DIST
RANDLE, ELISHA	BAL	117	5TH WARD
RANDLE, ENOCH	BAL	324	1ST DIST
RANDLE, JAMES	WAS	048	2ND SUBD
RANDLE, JOHN	CEC	034	CHESAPEA
RANDLE, LANE	WAS	141	HAGERSTO
RANDLE, RICHARD	BAL	285	1ST DIST
RANDLE, SARAH	BAL	120	5TH WARD
RANDLE, THOMAS H.	BAL	312	1ST DIST
RANDLE, WILLIAM	FRE	291	WOODSBOR
RANDLE, WILLIAM H.	BAL	090	15TH WAR
RANDLES, JAMES	BAL	447	1ST DIST
RANDOL, JOHN T.	BAL	277	1ST DIST
RANDOL, LOYD	BAL	325	1ST DIST
RANDOLPH, ANDREW J.	BAL	394	3RD WARD
RANDOLPH, C.	BAL	171	1ST WARD
RANDOLPH, COLUMBUS	BAL	434	14TH WAR
RANDOLPH, ELIZA	BAL	357	13TH WAR
RANDOLPH, GEORGE	BAL	301	17TH WAR
RANDOLPH, GEORGE	WAS	186	BOONSBOR
RANDOLPH, JOHN	BAL	175	6TH WARD
RANDOLPH, JOHN W.	BAL	246	2ND WARD
RANDOLPH, MISS E.	FRE	199	5TH E DI
RANDOLPH, MISS J.	FRE	199	5TH E DI
RANDOLPH, MISS L.	FRE	199	5TH E DI
RANDOLPH, R.	BAL	148	1ST WARD
RANDOLPH, RICHARD	BAL	171	1ST WARD
RANDOLPH, ROBERT-BLACK	FRE	048	FREDERIC
RANDOLPH, VIRGININ	BAL	197	6TH WARD
RANDOLPH, WESLEY	MGM	325	CRACKLIN
RANDOLPH, WILLIAM	BAL	309	12TH WAR
RANDSON, JOHN D.	CHA	217	ALLENS F
RANDUER, CHARLES	BAL	303	12TH WAR
RANE, BRIDGET	BAL	165	2ND DIST
RANE, JAMES	BAL	375	13TH WAR
RANE, JAMES	WOR	259	BERLIN 1
RANE, JEMIMA	BAL	378	13TH WAR
RANE, MARY	WOR	264	BERLIN 1
RANE, R. D.	BAL	147	1ST WARD
RANE, WILLIAM	WOR	259	BERLIN 1
RANER, AUGUSTUS	BAL	101	2ND DIST
RANER, JOHN *	ANN	340	3RD DIST
RANER, SOLOMAN	BAL	133	18TH WAR
RANEY, CATHARINE	WAS	215	1ST DIST
RANEY, JAMES	BAL	112	1ST WARD
RANEY,MICHAEL	ALL	046	10TH E.D
RANEYHILL, MARY E. D.	CAL	026	2ND DIST
RANFOLS, HENRY	BAL	369	13TH WAR
RANFT, JOSEPH	BAL	423	14TH WAR
RANFT, JOSEPH	BAL	156	16TH WAR
RANIS, ISAAC	BAL	270	1ST DIST
RANKEN, SUSAN	BAL	230	19TH WAR
RANKIN, ALEX	BAL	166	1ST WARD
RANKIN, JOHN A.	CEC	002	ELKTON 3
RANKIN, MARY J.	BAL	199	6TH WARD
RANKIN, MOSES	BAL	058	2ND DIST
RANKIN, OWEN	BAL	131	1ST WARD
RANKIN, CWIN	BAL	144	1ST WARD
RANKIN, ROBERT	BAL	381	3RD WARD
RANKIN, SAMUEL	BAL	256	6TH WARD
RANKIN, SAMUEL	BAL	058	2ND DIST
RANKIN, SAMUEL	BAL	356	3RD WARD
RANKIN, SAMUEL	BAL	103	5TH WARD
RANKIN, WILLIAM J.	BAL	212	6TH WARD
RANKIN, WILLIAM W.	CEC	112	4TH E DI
RANKIN,OWEN	BAL	135	1ST WARD
RANKINGS, SARAH	BAL	247	1ST DIST
RANKINS, J.	BAL	147	1ST WARD
RANKLES, BASI.	FRE	248	NEW MARK
RANKLEY, SUSAN	FRE	248	NEW MARK
RANKLY, SAMUEL	FRE	250	NEW MARK
RANLEIGH, ELIZA	DOR	375	1ST DIST
RANLINE, JOHN	BAL	131	1ST WARD
RANNARD, GEORGE	BAL	134	1ST WARD
RANNIE, ANN	MGM	363	BERRYS D
RANNIE, JAMES	MGM	362	BERRYS D
RANNOF, JOAD	BAL	163	1ST WARD
RANNON, MICHAEL	BAL	345	13TH WAR
RANOLDS, THOMAS	BAL	445	1ST DIST
RANOR, MARTHA	CHA	262	MIDDLETO
RANORA, PETER	BAL	368	13TH WAR
RANSALE, JOHN	ST	296	2ND E DI
RANSALE, JOHN	ST	295	2ND E DI
RANSBURG, SEBASTIAN	FRE	407	JEFFERSO
RANSEIN, MARY	BAL	218	2ND WARD
RANSEY, JOHN	BAL	116	1ST WARD
RANSEY, WILLIAM A.	BAL	003	1ST WARD
RANTER, JOHN T.	PRI	092	MARLBROU
RANTIN, SAMUEL	MGM	400	ROCKERLE
RAP, THOMAS*	DOR	386	1ST DIST
RAPE, JOHN	ALL	050	10TH E.D
RAPEHORN, PETER	BAL	286	1ST DIST
RAPENCER, CHRISTIAN	BAL	344	1ST DIST
RAPENCER, DANIEL	BAL	344	1ST DIST
RAPET, MARY*	DOR	410	1ST DIST
RAPETE, NANCY*	DOR	410	1ST DIST
RAPFF, PHILIP LLTT	BAL	435	14TH WAR
RAPHEL, STEPHEN	BAL	120	2ND DIST
RAPHELL, MICHAEL	BAL	289	3RD WARD
RAPINE, SUSANNAH B.	BAL	102	10TH WAR
RAPLE, CONRAD	HAR	158	3RD DIST
RAPP, JOHN	BAL	251	20TH WAR
RAPP, JULIANNA	BAL	184	2ND WARD
RAPP, WILLIAM	BAL	143	2ND DIST
RAPPE, HAENRY	BAL	392	14TH WAR
RAPPELL, JOHN	BAL	319	12TH WAR
RAPPLEY, HANNAH S.	BAL	440	8TH WARD
RAPS, MICHAEL	ALL	148	6TH E.D.
RAPST, ANDREW	BAL	119	18TH WAR
RAPSWORTH, EMMA	PRI	001	BLADENSB
RARADON, RIDGWAY	DOR	367	3RD DIVI
RARDON, EVE	CAR	191	4TH DIST
RARP, ANDERW	BAL	351	13TH WAR
RARR, MARY	WAS	229	1ST DIST
RASALVE, L.	BAL	166	1ST WARD
RASAR, HOSA	BAL	438	1ST DIST
RASBELLEY, ADAM	ALL	238	CUMBERLA
RASBERG, TERESA	BAL	252	12TH WAR
RASBERRY, EZEKIEL-BLACK	QUE	128	1ST E DI
RASBERRY, HENRY-BLACK	QUE	130	1ST E DI
RASBERRY, JAMES-BLACK	QUE	142	1ST E DI
RASBERRY, JONAS-BLACK	QUE	172	2ND E DI
RASBERRY, MARY J.-BLACK	QUE	128	1ST E DI
RASBERRY, NATHANIEL-BLACK	QUE	128	1ST E DI
RASBERRY, ROBERT-BLACK	QUE	137	1ST E DI
RASBERRY, SARAH-BLACK	QUE	154	1ST E DI
RASBERRY, STEPHEN-BLACK	QUE	142	1ST E DI
RASBERRY, STEPHEN-BLACK	QUE	150	1ST E DI
RASCH, CHARLES	BAL	229	6TH WARD
RASCH, CHARLES	BAL	075	10TH WAR
RASCH, MARGARET A.	BAL	004	15TH WAR
RASCHE, BERNARD	BAL	240	17TH WAR
RASH, CHRISTIAN	BAL	423	3RD WARD
RASH, DANIEL	QUE	134	1ST E DI
RASH, JAMES	QUE	124	1ST E DI
RASH, MARTIN	QUE	163	2ND E DI
RASHER, HARRIETT	BAL	184	11TH WAR
RASHLY, SAMUEL-BLACK	QUE	168	2ND E DI
RASIN, ALFRED	KEN	229	2ND DIST
RASIN, AMRY	KEN	246	2ND DIST
RASIN, ANN	KEN	295	3RD DIST
RASIN, EDWARD F.	KEN	313	3RD DIST
RASIN, ELIJAH	KEN	313	3RD DIST
RASIN, EMILY	KEN	214	2ND DIST
RASIN, GEORGE	KEN	282	3RD DIST
RASIN, GEORGE *	KEN	229	2ND DIST
RASIN, JAMES	KEN	236	2ND DIST
RASIN, JAMES A.	KEN	227	2ND DIST
RASIN, JOSEPH	KEN	247	2ND DIST
RASIN, JOSEPH	KEN	270	1ST DIST
RASIN, LOUIS	KEN	273	1ST DIST
RASIN, MARGARET	KEN	223	2ND DIST
RASIN, MARY R.	KEN	302	3RD DIST
RASIN, NANCY	KEN	313	3RD DIST
RASIN, PHEBE W.	KEN	295	3RD DIST
RASIN, PHILIP F.	KEN	226	2ND DIST
RASIN, SARAH	CEC	004	ELKTON 3
RASIN, SOLOMON	KEN	272	1ST DIST
RASIN, WILLIAM B.	KEN	227	2ND DIST
RASON, JOSEPH	CEC	042	CHESAPEA
RASPER, HENRY	BAL	073	2ND DIST
RASSHEL, STEPHANIA	FRE	066	FREDERIC
RASSOM, ABRAHAM	BAL	187	5TH DIST
RASTEAN, WILLIAM	BAL	079	2ND DIST
RASTY, MARGARETT M.	HAR	184	3RD DIST
RATCHT, AUGUSTUS C.	BAL	371	13TH WAR
RATCLICK, GEORGE	BAL	157	1ST WARD
RATCLIFF, CATHERINE	MGM	379	ROCKERLE
RATCLIFF, ELIZA	QUE	190	3RD E DI
RATCLIFF, JAMES*	DOR	403	1ST DIST
RATCLIFF, JOHN	DOR	387	1ST DIST
RATCLIFF, JOHN	CHA	242	HILLTOP
RATCLIFF, JOHN	DOR	470	1ST DIST
RATCLIFF, JOSEPH	FRE	226	BUCKEYST
RATCLIFF, NATHAN	CHA	245	HILLTOP
RATCLIFF, ROBERT	CHA	245	HILLTOP
RATCLIFF, SUSAN	QUE	198	3RD E DI
RATCLIFF, THOMAS	CHA	247	HILLTOP
RATCLIFF, THOMAS	BAL	244	12TH WAR
RATCLIFF, UPTON	FRE	445	8TH E DI
RATCLIFFE, ELIZA	BAL	258	1ST DIST
RATCLIFFE, HENRY	BAL	165	1ST WARD
RATCLIFFE, LUTHER	BAL	032	9TH WARD
RATH, CHARLES	BAL	313	1ST DIST
RATHAFORT, THOMAS	WAS	154	2ND DIST
RATHAL, THOMAS	BAL	049	15TH WAR
RATHBERRY, JAMES	CEC	075	NORTHEAS
RATHEE, EELIZA *	TAL	074	EASTON T
RATHEE, LEVINA	TAL	002	EASTON D
RATHEE, WILLIAM R.*	TAL	068	EASTON T
RATHEL, CHARLES	TAL	014	EASTON D
RATHEL, CHRISTIAN	BAL	334	3RD WARD
RATHEL, GEORGE W.	TAL	097	ST MICHA

Name	County / Page / District
RATHEL, JANE	CAR 128 NO TWP L
RATHFL, JARIFER	CAR 165 NO TWP L
RATHEL, LYDIA	CAR 120 NO TWP L
RATHEL, MAHALY	CAR 166 NO TWP L
RATHEL, PRISCILLE	CAR 122 NO TWP L
RATHELL, JANE	CAR 120 NO TWP L
RATHELL, THOMAS H.	BAL 023 15TH WAR
RATHELL, WILLIAM H.	BAL 023 15TH WAR
RATHEN, MARGARET	PRI 006 BLADENSB
RATHER, ANNIE	PRI 077 MARLBROU
RATHER, JAMES H.	TAL 027 EASTON D
RATHER, SAMUEL	TAL 089 ST MICHA
RATHER, WILLIAM R.*	TAL 068 EASTON T
RATHERDALE, GEORGE	BAL 258 17TH WAR
RATHERS, FRANCES	BAL 341 13TH WAR
RATHWAIT, JOHN	ALL 204 CUMBERLA
RATIGAN, MICHAEL *	BAL 422 1ST DIST
RATIGARE, MICHAEL *	BAL 422 1ST DIST
RATLEDGE, JAMES L.	WOR 317 2ND E DI
RATLEY, WILLIAM	BAL 380 8TH WARD
RATLIFF, CHARLES	MGM 380 ROCKERLE
RATLIFF, THOMAS	TAL 071 EASTON T
RATLIFF, WILLIAM	WAS 164 HAGERSTO
RATRUDE, ANDREW	BAL 028 18TH WAR
RATRYCE, D.	BAL 182 19TH WAR
RATSON, HENRY	BAL 208 2ND WARD
RATTER, ELIZABETH	BAL 371 13TH WAR
RATTER, WILLIAM	QUE 153 1ST E DI
RATTGER, RUDOLPH	BAL 171 2ND DIST
RATTIGAN, JAMES*	DOR 386 1ST DIST
RATTLE, ELIZABETH	BAL 163 6TH WARD
RATTLE, HENRY H.	BAL 015 4TH WARD
RATTLEMILLER, CHRISTIAN*	BAL 320 3RD WARD
RATTRIE, JAMES	MGM 396 ROCKERLE
RATTY, CHRISTY	BAL 469 14TH WAR
RATTY, ROSE	BAL 248 2ND WARD
RATWAY, WILLIAM	BAL 206 11TH WAR
RATWIN, GEORGE	BAL 233 2ND WARD
RATZENBERGER, LEWIS	BAL 352 13TH WAR
RAU, GOTLIEB	BAL 416 8TH WARD
RAUB, MICHAEL	BAL 333 1ST DIST
RAUBENOUR, PHILIP	BAL 239 1ST DIST
RAUBET, CATHARINE	BAL 254 2ND WARD
RAUCH, NICHOLAS	BAL 237 2ND WARD
RAUCHFORD, JOHN	BAL 172 11TH WAR
RAUCHFORD, JOHN	BAL 172 11TH WAR
RAUENSCROFT, WILLIAM *	ALL 118 5TH E.D.
RAUGHLY, THOMAS	ALL 142 6TH E.D.
RAUL, ELIZABETH	BAL 318 1ST DIST
RAULEIGH, ELIZABETH B.*	DOR 375 1ST DIST
RAULEIGH, JES H. C.	DOR 466 1ST DIST
RAULEIGH, MARY S.	DOR 432 1ST DIST
RAULEIGH, NOAH	DOR 434 1ST DIST
RAULEIGH, ROBERT	DOR 465 1ST DIST
RAULEIGH, ROBERT G.	DOR 432 1ST DIST
RAULEIGH, ROBERT W.	DOR 376 1ST DIST
RAULEIGH, W.	DOR 437 1ST DIST
RAULINGS, ELIZABETH	CEC 143 7TH E DI
RAULINGS, JOSEPH-MULATTO	BAL 219 2ND WARD
RAULINGS, MARION	CEC 150 PORT DUP
RAULSON, S. P. M.	CHA 221 ALLENS F
RAUM, GEORGE	BAL 231 2ND WARD
RAUMGARTNER, JOHN	CAR 302 1ST DIST
RAUNAMON, DAVID	BAL 243 1ST DIST
RAURSEY,JOHN	BAL 116 1ST WARD
RAUSER, REINHOLAT	BAL 230 2ND WARD
RAUTIGAN, MICHAEL	DOR 469 1ST DIST
RAUTZONG, JOSEPH	FRE 138 CREAGERS
RAVDALS, HENNY	BAL 271 1ST DIST
RAVEN, DOROTHA	FRE 088 FREDERIC
RAVEN, JAMES L.	BAL 178 6TH WARD
RAVEN, MARY A.	BAL 178 6TH WARD
RAVENCROFT, ELI	ALL 003 3RD E.D.
RAVENCROFT, JAMES	ALL 003 3RD E.D.
RAVENSCROFT, ABNER	ALL 122 4TH E.D.
RAVENSCROFT, CHARLES	ALL 134 4TH E.D.
RAVENSCROFT, ROBERT	ALL 126 4TH E.D.
RAVENSCROFT, WILLIAM	ALL 136 4TH E.D.
RAVLEY, GOERGIANA T.	ANN 488 HOWARD D
RAW, GEORGE	BAL 268 2ND WARD
RAW, JOHN C.	BAL 249 20TH WAR
RAW, JOSHUA	BAL 059 4TH WARD
RAWBRES, FRANCES E.	ALL 109 5TH E.D.
RAWHOUSER, JOSHUA	BAL 431 1ST DIST
RAWLES, ALLISAN	BAL 008 9TH WARD
RAWLEY, LEVIN	DOR 439 1ST DIST
RAWLEY, SAMUEL W.	KEN 219 2ND DIST
RAWLING, ELIZABETH	BAL 205 2ND WARD
RAWLING, PETER	PRI 051 AQUASCO
RAWLINGS, ALFRED	PRI 064 NOTTINGH
RAWLINGS, ALMIRA F.	BAL 156 16TH WAR
RAWLINGS, ANN E.	BAL 069 15TH WAR
RAWLINGS, B.	BAL 111 15TH WAR
RAWLINGS, BARBARA	CAL 026 2ND DIST
RAWLINGS, BENJAMIN	CAL 030 2ND DIST
RAWLINGS, BENJAMIN	PRI 064 NOTTINGH
RAWLINGS, CALEB	PRI 056 AQUASCO
RAWLINGS, CASSYDA	DOR 319 1ST DIST
RAWLINGS, E.	ANN 338 3RD DIST
RAWLINGS, ELEVEN	ANN 396 8TH DIST
RAWLINGS, ELIZABETH	PRI 054 AQUASCO
RAWLINGS, GEORGE A.	BAL 155 16TH WAR
RAWLINGS, HENRY	ANN 337 3RD DIST
RAWLINGS, JAMES	PRI 064 NOTTINGH
RAWLINGS, JAMES A.	PRI 057 NOTTINGH
RAWLINGS, JAMES W.	DOR 319 1ST DIST
RAWLINGS, JOHN V. T.	PRI 057 NOTTINGH
RAWLINGS, JOSHUA	ANN 367 4TH DIST
RAWLINGS, JR. T.	PRI 051 AQUASCO
RAWLINGS, M.	PRI 057 NOTTINGH
RAWLINGS, M.E.	PRI 055 AQUASCO
RAWLINGS, MARY	PRI 050 AQUASCO
RAWLINGS, MARY G.	CAL 048 3RD DIST
RAWLINGS, MARY H.	BAL 362 13TH WAR
RAWLINGS, MOSES	ALL 138 6TH E.D.
RAWLINGS, MOSES	ANN 294 1ST DIST
RAWLINGS, MRS-	ANN 309 1ST DIST
RAWLINGS, PRISCILLA	PRI 052 AQUASCO
RAWLINGS, RICHARD H.	PRI 115 PISCATAW
RAWLINGS, RICHARD H.	CAL 048 3RD DIST
RAWLINGS, SALLY	ANN 289 ANNAPOLI
RAWLINGS, SARAH	ANN 269 ANNAPOLI
RAWLINGS, SARAH	PRI 058 NOTTINGH
RAWLINGS, SUSAN	PRI 091 MARLBROU
RAWLINGS, WILLIAM	QUE 182 3RD E DI
RAWLINGS, WILLIAM	CAL 023 2ND DIST
RAWLINS, ELIZABETH	MGM 405 ROCKERLE
RAWLINS, JAMES	MGM 370 BERRYS D
RAWLINS, MARGARET A.	MGM 439 CLARKSTR
RAWLINS, MARY	MGM 440 CLARKSTR
RAWLINS, THOMAS	MGM 409 MEDLEY 3
RAWLS, WILLIS	BAL 033 15TH WAR
RAWLS, WILLIS C.	BAL 008 9TH WARD
RAWSON, LUCY M.	ANN 521 HOWARD D
RAY, ADAM	BAL 214 17TH WAR
RAY, AGNES	BAL 080 4TH WARD
RAY, ALEXANDER	BAL 330 7TH WARD
RAY, ALFRED	BAL 405 3RD WARD
RAY, ALLEN	BAL 198 17TH WAR
RAY, ALVERDA	BAL 356 1ST DIST
RAY, ANDREW	BAL 375 8TH WARD
RAY, ANGELINA	ANN 370 4TH DIST
RAY, ANN	CEC 159 PORT DUP
RAY, BASIL	BAL 356 1ST DIST
RAY, BENJAMIN	ANN 370 4TH DIST
RAY, BENJAMIN	BAL 222 12TH WAR
RAY, BENJAMIN F.	BAL 355 1ST DIST
RAY, CATHARINE	ANN 271 ANNAPOLI
RAY, CHARITY	BAL 335 13TH WAR
RAY, CHARLES	WAS 064 2ND SUBD
RAY, E.R.	BAL 158 1ST WARD
RAY, EDWARD*	TAL 063 EASTON D
RAY, ELLEN	BAL 353 7TH WARD
RAY, ELLEN*	BAL 014 4TH WARD
RAY, FRANCIS	HAR 200 3RD DIST
RAY, GEORGE M.	BAL 163 19TH WAR
RAY, GERARD	MGM 322 CRACKLIN
RAY, GODFREY	BAL 127 5TH WARD
RAY, GUSTOVIES *	BAL 288 20TH WAR
RAY, HARVY	FRE 395 PETERSVI
RAY, HENRY	BAL 260 1ST DIST
RAY, HESTER	TAL 001 EASTON D
RAY, HUGH	BAL 282 1ST DIST
RAY, ISABELLA	BAL 217 6TH WARD
RAY, JAMES	BAL 048 9TH WARD
RAY, JAMES	WAS 100 2ND DIST
RAY, JAMES	MGM 396 ROCKERLE
RAY, JANE	MGM 391 ROCKERLE
RAY, JIM	ANN 295 1ST DIST
RAY, JOHN	BAL 221 2ND WARD
RAY, JOHN	BAL 001 15TH WAR
RAY, JOHN	BAL 287 3RD WARD
RAY, JOHN	ANN 386 4TH DIST
RAY, JOHN	ANN 416 HOWARD D
RAY, JOHN	BAL 021 2ND DIST
RAY, JOHN	MGM 367 BERRYS D
RAY, JOHN	CAL 046 3RD DIST
RAY, JOHN	BAL 060 18TH WAR
RAY, JOHN B.	BAL 272 7TH WARD
RAY, JOHN C.	HAR 202 3RD DIST
RAY, JOHN T.	ANN 455 HOWARD D
RAY, JOSEPH	BAL 287 3RD WARD
RAY, JOSEPH	BAL 151 19TH WAR
RAY, JOSEPH	BAL 243 20TH WAR
RAY, JOSIAH	ANN 368 4TH DIST
RAY, KATE	ANN 521 HOWARD D
RAY, KELLY L.	ANN 480 HOWARD D
RAY, LOREINER	FRE 395 PETERSVI
RAY, MARGARETT	BAL 101 18TH WAR
RAY, MARSELLAS	BAL 267 17TH WAR
RAY, MARTHY A.	TAL 002 EASTON D
RAY, MARY	CEC 192 5TH E DI
RAY, NICHOLAS	MGM 323 CRACKLIN
RAY, OLIVER	BAL 252 12TH WAR
RAY, REBECCA	TAL 053 EASTON D
RAY, ROBERT	BAL 005 EASTERN
RAY, SUSAN E.	MGM 324 CRACKLIN
RAY, SUSANNAH	CEC 126 5TH E DI
RAY, THOMAS	CAL 046 3RD DIST
RAY, THOMAS	BAL 252 12TH WAR
RAY, WILLIAM	ALL 086 5TH E.D.
RAY, WILLIAM	CEC 126 5TH E DI
RAY, WILLIAM	BAL 205 19TH WAR
RAY, WILLIAM	WAS 120 2ND DIST
RAY, WILLIAM A.	BAL 057 18TH WAR
RAY, WILLIAM A.	BAL 055 18TH WAR
RAY, WILLIAM H.	MGM 341 CLARKSBU
RAY, WILLIAM H.	FRE 398 JEFFERSO
RAY, WILLIMA	WAS 094 2ND SUBD
RAYAN, FRANCIS	BAL 395 14TH WAR
RAYBELLA, VALENTINE	BAL 235 2ND WARD
RAYBURN, MARY	BAL 101 5TH WARD
RAYER, J.	BAL 130 1ST WARD
RAYFIELD, JAMES	SOM 382 BRINKLEY
RAYFIELD, MARGARET	SOM 456 DAMES QU
RAYFOOOSE, MARTIN	CAR 336 6TH DIST
RAYMAN, JULIA A.	BAL 187 11TH WAR
RAYMAN, M. SIS-	BAL 062 18TH WAR
RAYMER, JOHN A.	FRE 372 CATOCTIN
RAYMER, WILLIAM P.	FRE 366 CATOCTIN
RAYMES, E.	BAL 152 1ST WARD
RAYMO, LEWIS	BAL 119 5TH WARD
RAYMOND, CALVIN R.	CAR 271 WESTMINS
RAYMOND, DAVID	BAL 018 18TH WAR
RAYMOND, ELIZA	BAL 137 11TH WAR
RAYMOND, FRANCES	HAR 139 2ND DIST
RAYMOND, GEORGE	BAL 143 1ST WARD
RAYMOND, GILBERT REV.	ANN 469 HOWARD D
RAYMOND, JAMES	CAR 271 WESTMINS
RAYMOND, JOHN W.	BAL 014 15TH WAR
RAYMOND, SAMUEL W.	BAL 090 15TH WAR
RAYMOND, SARAH	BAL 005 4TH WARD
RAYNARD, ADAM	CEC 005 ELKTON 3
RAYNARD, ANDREW	BAL 118 1ST WARD
RAYNARD, JAMES*	DOR 403 1ST DIST
RAYNER, ALETHA	ANN 357 3RD DIST
RAYNER, JOHN	BAL 030 1ST WARD
RAYNER, JOHN	PRI 029 VANSVILL
RAYNER, MARY	BAL 029 15TH WAR
RAYNER, WILLIAM	BAL 016 1ST WARD
RAYNER,HARRIET	BAL 074 1ST WARD
RAYNOLDS, JOSEPH	BAL 305 1ST DIST
RAYNOLDS, MARTIN	BAL 272 1ST DIST
RAYNOLDS, THOMAS	ALL 082 5TH E.D.
RAYNOLL, MARY E.	CAR 282 7TH DIST
RAYNOLS, MARY	BAL 273 1ST DIST
RAYNOLS, WILLIAM	BAL 273 1ST DIST
RAYNOLS, WILLIAM	BAL 273 1ST DIST
RAYNOR, PRISCILLA	BAL 106 15TH WAR
RAYNULL, JACOB	CAR 281 7TH DIST
RAYON, THOMAS	BAL 454 8TH WARD
RAYONS, MODIST*	BAL 071 10TH WAR
RAYS, WILLIAM	ALL 218 CUMBERLA
RAYTON, SUSAN	BAL 112 1ST WARD
RBOREA, WILLIAM	BAL 126 2ND DIST
REA, ANN	BAL 176 16TH WAR
REA, HENRY P.	BAL 105 15TH WAR
REA, JAMES	BAL 165 11TH WAR
REA, JAMES	DOR 381 1ST DIST
REA, JOHN	BAL 164 11TH WAR
REA, MARY J.	DOR 375 1ST DIST
REA, REZIN	FRE 384 PETERSVI
REA, THOMAS F.	DOR 375 1ST DIST
REA, WILLIAM	DOR 375 1ST DIST
REA, WILLIAM V.	BAL 072 15TH WAR
REABSON, CATHARINE	BAL 209 2ND WARD
REACH, ALEX	BAL 156 11TH WAR
REACH, CATHERINE	BAL 157 11TH WAR
REACH, DORCA	BAL 304 12TH WAR
REACH, DORUTHY	BAL 381 13TH WAR
REACH, M.	BAL 316 20TH WAR
REACH, STEPHEN	ALL 259 CUMBERLA
REACHER, CATHERINE	FRE 141 CREAGERS
READ, ALICE	HAR 006 1ST DIST
READ, BENJAMIN	MGM 339 CLARKSBU
READ, BENJAMIN	BAL 158 1ST WARD
READ, BENJAMIN	BAL 142 1ST WARD
READ, CHARITY	ALL 014 3RD E.D.
READ, CHARLES	BAL 117 1ST WARD
READ, E.D.	ALL 241 CUMBERLA
READ, EDWARD	BAL 068 15TH WAR
READ, ELIZABETH	BAL 072 4TH WARD
READ, FRANCIS	BAL 264 2ND WARD
READ, GEORGE	ALL 235 CUMBERLA
READ, GRACE	BAL 071 2ND DIST
READ, GURYNN	ALL 158 6TH E.D.
READ, HENRY	WOR 347 1ST E DI
READ, HENRY	WOR 348 1ST E DI
READ, HENRY C.	BAL 143 11TH WAR
READ, HULDA	WOR 269 BERLIN 1
READ, JAMES	WOR 272 BERLIN 1
READ, JAMES	DOR 313 1ST DIST
READ, JAMES M.	DOR 334 3RD DIVI
READ, JANE	ALL 172 7TH E.D.
READ, JESSE	FRE 202 5TH E DI
READ, JOHN	FRE 202 5TH E DI
READ, JOHN	BAL 072 2ND DIST
READ, JOHN	WOR 267 BERLIN 1
READ, JOHN H.	BAL 220 12TH WAR
READ, JOHN THOMAS	WOR 257 1ST CENS
READ, JOHN W.	BAL 384 3RD WARD
READ, JOHN W.	FRE 392 PETERSVI
READ, JOSHUA	WOR 280 BERLIN 1
READ, LEONARD-MULATTO	FRE 181 5TH E DI
READ, LYDIA M.	BAL 419 3RD WARD
READ, MARIA	PRI 071 MARLBROU
READ, MARIAH	SOM 432 PRINCESS
READ, MARY ANN	FRE 162 EMMITTSB
READ, NATHANIEL	HAR 159 3RD DIST
READ, NELSON C.	ALL 263 CUMBERLA
READ, PAYTON	PRI 027 VANSVILL
READ, PEGGY	WOR 323 1ST E DI
READ, RACHEL	BAL 361 13TH WAR
READ, ROBERT	ALL 255 CUMBERLA
READ, THOMAS	ALL 014 3RD E.D.
READ, THOMAS	FRE 178 5TH E DI
READ, THOMAS	MGM 403 ROCKERLE
READ, THOMAS	WOR 323 1ST E DI
READ, WESLEY	FRE 185 5TH E DI
READ, WILIAM	BAL 147 1ST WARD
READ, WILLIAM	DOR 323 1ST DIST
READ, WILLIAM	WOR 323 1ST E DI
READ, WILLIAM	TAL 022 EASTON D
READ, WILLIAM G.	MGM 412 MEDLEY 3
READ, WILLIAM H.	BAL 249 2ND WARD
READ, WILLIAM P.	TAL 056 EASTON D
READDEN, JAMES	HAR 198 3RD DIST
READDY, THOMAS	BAL 003 9TH WARD
READE, GEORGE W.	FRE 328 MIDDLETO
READER, DANIEL	FRE 323 MIDDLETO
READER, HATMAN	BAL 352 13TH WAR
READER, JOHN	BAL 072 4TH WARD
READER, MARTIN	FRE 326 MIDDLETO
READER, NICHOLAS	BAL 255 20TH WAR
READER, RACHEL	WAS 062 2ND SUBD
READER, RICHARD H.	ST 333 4TH E DI
READER, WILLIAM T.A.	ST 315 4TH E DI
READING, JAMES G.	CAR 108 NO TWP L
READING, PHILIP	WAS 163 HAGERSTO
READLE, FREDERICK	BAL 463 1ST DIST
READLIP, ANNA*	BAL 304 3RD WARD
READLISS, ANNA*	BAL 304 3RD WARD
READON, ELLEN	BAL 352 7TH WARD
READY, ARCHIBALD	BAL 358 8TH WARD
READY, BRIGET	BAL 458 1ST DIST
READY, ELIZABETH	BAL 174 16TH WAR
READY, EMANUEL	BAL 397 8TH WARD
READY, JAMES	ALL 075 5TH E.D.
READY, JAMES	TAL 077 EASTON T
READY, MICHAEL	ALL 075 5TH E.D.
READY, RACHAEL	ANN 265 ANNAPOLI
READY, ROBERT	BAL 160 1ST WARD
READY, SAMUEL	BAL 075 15TH WAR
READY, WILLIAM	BAL 291 12TH WAR
REAGAN, EDWARD	BAL 402 8TH WARD
REAGAN, JAMES	BAL 004 18TH WAR
REAGAN, PATRICK	ALL 172 7TH E.D.
REAGAN, WILLIAM	DOR 439 1ST DIST
REAGRAN, WILLIAM B.	KEN 286 3RD DIST
REAHAN, JOHN L.	BAL 367 13TH WAR
REAHL, JOSEPH	BAL 308 12TH WAR
REAHL, LOUIS	BAL 141 16TH WAR
REAKER, JACOB	BAL 087 10TH WAR
REAKERS, WILLIAM	BAL 185 11TH WAR
REAL, CASPER	BAL 409 8TH WARD
REAL, CATHARINE	BAL 172 2ND DIST
REAL, E.D.	BAL 118 1ST WARD
REAL, JAMES	BAL 293 12TH WAR
REALD, JOHN	ALL 172 7TH E.D.
REALL, MARY E.	FRE 405 JEFFERSO
REALLY, JACOB	CAR 410 2ND DIST
REALLY, JANES	BAL 127 11TH WAR
REALY, SARAH	CEC 041 CHESAPEA
REAM, JAMES	WAS 128 HAGERSTO
REAM, JOHN	WAS 295 1ST DIST
REAM, JOHN	CAR 363 9TH DIST
REAM, JOSEPH H.	BAL 373 13TH WAR
REAMEN, WILLIAM	BAL 230 2ND WARD
REAMORES, MARY	FRE 207 BUCKEYST
REAMS, THOMAS-BLACK	BAL 228 2ND WARD
REANER, EMILY	BAL 136 18TH WAR
REANER, GEORGE	BAL 082 1ST WARD
REANER, JOSEPH *	BAL 105 18TH WAR
REANER, THOMAS	BAL 133 18TH WAR
REANEY, LAURA	BAL 136 18TH WAR
REANEY, WILLIAM	BAL 065 4TH WARD
REANEY, WILLIAM	BAL 065 4TH WARD
REANEY, WILLIAM	BAL 315 20TH WAR
REANING, PHILLIP	BAL 084 1ST WARD
REANNER, ELLEN	BAL 136 18TH WAR

Name	County	Page	District
REANNER, JAMES W.	BAL	133	18TH WAR
REANY, MARY A.	BAL	235	6TH WARD
REARDAN, MICHAEL	BAL	304	20TH WAR
REARDAN, PATRICK	BAL	308	12TH WAR
REARDEN, MARGARET	BAL	446	14TH WAR
REARDING, WILLIAM	WAS	162	HAGERSTO
REARDON, DAVID	ALL	081	5TH E.D.
REARDON, JOHN	BAL	180	2ND DIST
REARDON, MRS-	ANN	303	1ST DIST
REARDON, TIMOTHY	ANN	303	1ST DIST
REARED, MARY	BAL	436	8TH WARD
REARICK, ADAM	HAR	063	1ST DIST
REARRD, GEORGE W.	BAL	095	1ST WARD
REASDON, ANN	BAL	347	13TH WAR
REASDON, JOHN	BAL	348	13TH WAR
REASE, ANN J.	TAL	065	EASTON T
REASE, CHARLES	TAL	051	EASTON D
REASE, CHARLES	BAL	004	18TH WAR
REASE, JANE	TAL	071	EASTON T
REASE, JOHN	TAL	029	EASTON D
REASE, SARAH	BAL	325	12TH WAR
REASE, WILLIAM	TAL	024	EASTON D
REASIN, AMANDA V	HAR	125	2ND DIST
REASIN, JAMES F.	HAR	125	2ND DIST
REASIN, ROBERT W.	BAL	432	8TH WARD
REASIN, WILLIAM	BAL	365	8TH WARD
REASON, BETSEY	BAL	312	3RD WARD
REASON, CAROLINE	CEC	025	ELKTON 3
REASON, CARROLINE	TAL	014	EASTON D
REASON, ELIGAR A.-BLACK	CAR	082	NO TWP L
REASON, JONATHAN	CEC	107	3RD E DI
REASON, MARTHY	HAR	186	3RD DIST
REASON, PERRY	TAL	001	EASTON D
REASON, SAMUEL H.	HAR	150	3RD DIST
REASSON, MARY	BAL	301	3RD WARD
REAT, HARMAN	BAL	108	2ND DIST
REATCH, ANDREW	WAS	034	2ND SUBD
REAUER, JOSEPH *	BAL	105	18TH WAR
REAVER, ISAAC D.	WOR	221	4TH E DI
REAVES, JAMES	BAL	051	18TH WAR
REAVES, JOHN D.	HAR	160	3RD DIST
REAVES, MRS-	ANN	305	1ST DIST
REAVES, ROBERT	WOR	229	6TH E DI
REAVES, ROBERT F.	WOR	221	4TH E DI
REAVES, WILLIAM	BAL	089	1ST WARD
REAY, DAVID	BAL	379	3RD WARD
REBARGER, FRANCIS J.	BAL	443	8TH WARD
REBEL, BENJAMIN	WOR	261	BERLIN 1
REBINE, HENRY	BAL	029	4TH WARD
REBITZ, HENRY	BAL	077	10TH WAR
REBOU, ANN*	BAL	325	3RD WARD
REBOS, ANN*	BAL	325	3RD WARD
RECA, MARGARETT	FRE	410	8TH E DI
RECARR, ROSETTA	PRI	010	BLADENSB
RECELY, DANIEL	BAL	358	13TH WAR
RECHT, ADAM	BAL	326	7TH WARD
RECK, CATHARINE	CAR	237	UNION TO
RECK, ESTHER	FRE	426	8TH E DI
RECK, JOHN	CAR	305	1ST DIST
RECK, LEVI	CAR	410	2ND DIST
RECK, WILLIAM	CAR	377	2ND DIST
RECKARD, JOHN H.	ALL	155	6TH E.D.
RECKINOR, JOSEPH	ALL	028	2ND E.D.
RECKITT, ANN M.	BAL	131	16TH WAR
RECKLE, HENRY	ALL	017	3RD E.D.
RECKLEY, SEBASTIAN	WAS	297	1ST DIST
RECKNER, JAMES	ALL	013	3RD E.D.
RECKNOR, ELISABETH	ALL	028	2ND E.D.
RECKNOR, JAMES	ALL	003	3RD E.D.
RECKNOR, JESSE	ALL	028	2ND E.D.
RECKNUR, JOHN JR.	ALL	002	3RD E.D.
RECKNOR, JOHN SR.	ALL	002	3RD E.D.
RECKNOR, MWILLIAM	ALL	006	3RD E.D.
RECKNOR, WILLIAM	ALL	028	2ND E.D.
RECKROTE, JAMES	WAS	228	1ST DIST
RECKSLOFF, HERMAN	BAL	219	19TH WAR
RECOE, ANN T.	WAS	248	SMITHSBU
RECORD, SEBASTIAN	ALL	228	CUMBERLA
RED, FRANCES	BAL	142	16TH WAR
REDAT, THOMAS	BAL	393	1ST DIST
REDBECKER, JOHN	BAL	351	13TH WAR
REDBERG, JACOB	WAS	153	HAGERSTO
REDBURN, PRISCILLA	WAS	150	2ND DIST
REDDEEN, W .T.	WOR	342	1ST E DI
REDDEN, CATHARINE	WOR	349	1ST E DI
REDDEN, HENRY	SOM	528	QUANTICO
REDDEN, HENRY	BAL	346	13TH WAR
REDDEN, HENRY-BLACK	WOR	337	1ST E DI
REDDEN, JAMES	WOR	321	1ST E DI
REDDEN, JAMES	BAL	161	1ST WARD
REDDEN, JOHN-BLACK	WOR	337	1ST E DI
REDDEN, M.	BAL	161	1ST WARD
REDDEN, MARGARET	SOM	503	SALISBUR
REDDEN, NEHEMIAH	WOR	321	1ST E DI
REDDEN, PURNAL	WOR	339	1ST E DI
REDDEN, STEPHEN	WOR	344	1ST E DI
REDDICK, LEONARD	FRE	443	8TH E DI
REDDIM, NANTZY*	BAL	387	3RD WARD
REDDIN, JOHN	BAL	308	1ST DIST
REDDIN, WILLIAM-BLACK	WOR	317	2ND E DI
REDDING, ANDREW	HAR	121	2ND DIST
REDDING, BENJAMIN	KEN	305	3RD DIST
REDDING, CAROLINE	BAL	382	8TH WARD
REDDING, GEORGE	CEC	008	ELKTON 3
REDDING, JOSEPH	BAL	201	6TH WARD
REDDING, JOSEPH H.	BAL	201	6TH WARD
REDDING, NATHANIEL	KEN	304	3RD DIST
REDDING, OCTAVIA L.	BAL	057	15TH WAR
REDDING, PELAGIA	BAL	212	11TH WAR
REDDING, PHILLIP	KEN	221	2ND DIST
REDDING, WILLIAM	BAL	005	9TH WARD
REDDING, WILLIAM	ANN	446	HOWARD D
REDDING, WILLIAM	KEN	291	3RD DIST
REDDING, WILLIAM	KEN	293	3RD DIST
REDDING, WILLIAM A.	BAL	052	15TH WAR
REDDICN, NANTZY*	BAL	387	3RD WARD
REDDISH, BENJAMIN J.	BAL	389	3RD WARD
REDDISH, HOTTON*	DOR	466	1ST DIST
REDDISH, JOHN	WOR	192	8TH E DI
REDDISH, JOHN	WOR	233	6TH E DI
REDDISH, SARAH E.	BAL	371	3RD WARD
REDDISH, WILLIAM	WOR	195	8TH E DI
REDDISH, WILLIAM	WOR	192	8TH E DI
REDDISH, WILLIAM	DOR	467	1ST DIST
REDDISH, WILLIAM	DOR	467	1ST DIST
REDDIT, JAMES	DOR	396	1ST DIST
REDDON, ANN	CEC	031	CHESAPEA
REDDY, ELEY	ST	257	3RD E DI
REDEP, HETTY	WOR	287	BERLIN I
REDERMAN, ANN	ALL	134	4TH E.D.
REDERMAN, JOHN	ALL	135	4TH E.D.
REDFER, JOHN	BAL	274	20TH WAR
REDGAN, MARGARET A.	BAL	308	7TH WARD
REDGAWAY, MARIA *	BAL	316	12TH WAR
REDGELEY, WILLIAM	ALL	152	6TH E.D.
REDGELY, CHARLES	ALL	160	6TH E.D.
REDGESTER, ANN M.	BAL	139	11TH WAR
REDGNER, ROSENA	BAL	043	18TH WAR
REDGRAVE, ELIZABETH	BAL	435	8TH WARD
REDGRAVE, JAMES	BAL	297	20TH WAR
REDGRAVE, JOHN B.	BAL	162	16TH WAR
REDGRAVE, JOHN G.	BAL	031	18TH WAR
REDGRAVE, JOHN W.	KEN	285	3RD DIST
REDGRAVE, N.	BAL	299	12TH WAR
REDGRAVE, SAMUEL	BAL	282	20TH WAR
REDGRAVE, SAMUEL H	BAL	126	16TH WAR
REDGRAVES, ABRAHAM	KEN	272	1ST DIST
REDGRAVES, ELIZABETH	CEC	046	1ST E DI
REDGRAVES, ISAAC	BAL	055	1ST WARD
REDGRAVES, M.	BAL	299	12TH WAR
REDGRAVES, MARTHA	WAS	162	HAGERSTO
REDHEAD, EDWARD	DOR	375	1ST DIST
REDICORD, WILLIAM	BAL	377	1ST DIST
REDIKER, LAURENC	BAL	067	2ND DIST
REDIN, LOUISA *	KEN	212	2ND DIST
REDING, ANN	BAL	274	12TH WAR
REDING, GEORGE	CAR	254	3RD DIST
REDING, MARGARET	CEC	030	CHESAPEA
REDINGS, EDWARD	BAL	007	4TH WARD
REDIOUT, JEFFERSON-BLACK	CAR	106	NO TWP L
REDISH, ELIZA	SOM	533	QUANTICO
REDISH, ELIZABETH	CAR	192	4TH DIST
REDISH, JAMES	ANN	341	3RD DIST
REDISH, JOHN	SOM	526	QUANTICO
REDISH, PURNEL	ANN	381	4TH DIST
REDISON, ELIZABETH	CAR	297	7TH DIST
REDMAN, ALEXANDER	ST	281	3RD E DI
REDMAN, ANN	ST	296	2ND E DI
REDMAN, ANNA L.	BAL	024	4TH WARD
REDMAN, ARCHABLE	BAL	183	2ND WARD
REDMAN, CATHARINE	WAS	292	1ST DIST
REDMAN, CHAELS	QUE	241	5TH E DI
REDMAN, DAVID D.	BAL	164	6TH WARD
REDMAN, ELLEN	WAS	162	HAGERSTO
REDMAN, GEORGE	ANN	462	HOWARD D
REDMAN, HENRY	BAL	110	5TH WARD
REDMAN, HUGH	BAL	267	17TH WAR
REDMAN, JACOB	BAL	271	1ST DIST
REDMAN, JAMES	BAL	098	2ND DIST
REDMAN, JAMES	TAL	019	EASTON D
REDMAN, JAMES B.	ST	292	2ND E DI
REDMAN, JEFFERSON	ST	266	3RD E DI
REDMAN, JERCASA *	FRE	079	FREDERIC
REDMAN, JESSE	BAL	348	1ST DIST
REDMAN, JOHN	BAL	352	1ST DIST
REDMAN, JOHN	BAL	361	1ST DIST
REDMAN, JOHN	CHA	227	ALLENS F
REDMAN, JOHN B.	ST	285	2ND E DI
REDMAN, JOHN L.	ST	282	3RD E DI
REDMAN, MARY	ST	287	2ND E DI
REDMAN, MATILDA	BAL	348	1ST DIST
REDMAN, PANNY	ST	293	2ND E DI
REDMAN, PATRICK	BAL	074	4TH WARD
REDMAN, PETER	PRI	006	BLADENSB
REDMAN, ROBERT	FRE	099	FREDERIC
REDMAN, SAMUEL	ANN	455	HOWARD D
REDMAN, SAMUEL	BAL	050	15TH WAR
REDMAN, SARAH	WAS	134	HAGERSTO
REDMAN, THEOPHELUS	BAL	344	1ST DIST
REDMAN, THOMAS H.	ST	283	3RD E DI
REDMAN, THOMAS H.	ST	284	2ND E DI
REDMAN, WILLIAM	ST	287	2ND E DI
REDMAN, WILLIAM	BAL	342	1ST DIST
REDMAN, WILLIAM C.	ST	295	2ND E DI
REDMAN, WILLIAM W.	ST	296	2ND E DI
REDMER, LUDWICK	ALL	001	3RD E.D.
REDMILES, JOHN	ANN	364	4TH DIST
REDMON, FRANCIS	ALL	007	3RD E.D.
REDMOND, CATHERINE	BAL	424	3RD WARD
REDMOND, JOHN	BAL	121	1ST WARD
REDMOND, JOHN	BAL	177	2ND DIST
REDMOND, THOMAS	BAL	117	1ST WARD
REDNEY, GEORGE W.	BAL	045	1ST WARD
REDRIER, JOHN	BAL	437	14TH WAR
REDRING, JOHN	FRE	022	FREDERIC
REDSIC, LOUISA	ALL	196	CUMBERLA
REDSTIN, CLARISA *	SOM	454	DAMES QU
REDUE, JOSEPH	KEN	209	2ND DIST
REDUE, LOUISA *	KEN	212	2ND DIST
REDVELL, HARRIET W.	BAL	028	1ST WARD
REDWOOD, WILLIAM H.	BAL	102	10TH WAR
REDYELY, OLIVER	BAL	228	12TH WAR
REE, SARAH	KEN	310	3RD DIST
REECE, ALICE A.	CEC	162	6TH E DI
REECE, CHARLES	CEC	048	1ST E DI
REECE, DAVID	ALL	089	5TH E.D.
REECE, MARGARET	CEC	033	CHESAPEA
REECE, UPTON	ALL	157	6TH E.D.
REECE, WILLIAM	ALL	089	5TH E.D.
REECHER, CATHARINE	FRE	185	5TH E DI
REECHER, HENRY	FRE	186	5TH E DI
REECHER, JOHN	FRE	363	CATOCTIN
REECHER, JONATHAN	FRE	187	5TH E DI
REECKER, JOSEPH	FRE	133	CREAGERS
REED, AGNESS	BAL	225	6TH WARD
REED, ALBERT	KEN	235	2ND DIST
REED, ALBERTINE	DOR	299	1ST DIST
REED, ALEXANDER	QUE	240	5TH E DI
REED, ALFRED	PRI	033	VANSVILL
REED, ALFRED	CAL	038	2ND DIST
REED, AMOS	CAR	372	9TH DIST
REED, AMOS	BAL	120	1ST WARD
REED, ANN	BAL	237	6TH WARD
REED, ANN	BAL	455	14TH WAR
REED, ANN	CEC	028	CHESAPEA
REED, ANN	BAL	188	19TH WAR
REED, ANN	KEN	309	3RD DIST
REED, ANN ALOYSIA SIS-	BAL	316	20TH WAR
REED, ANN B.	SOM	427	PRINCESS
REED, ANN M.	BAL	100	15TH WAR
REED, ANNA	KEN	256	1ST DIST
REED, ATTAWAY-MULATTO	ST	327	4TH E DI
REED, BENEDICK	KEN	281	3RD DIST
REED, BENJAMIN	ST	321	4TH E DI
REED, BENJAMIN	CEC	059	1ST E DI
REED, BENJAMIN	DOR	420	1ST DIST
REED, BERNARD C.	WAS	223	1ST DIST
REED, CATHARINE	CAR	174	8TH DIST
REED, CHARLES	CAR	138	NO TWP L
REED, CHARLES	BAL	344	1ST DIST
REED, CHARLES	BAL	414	1ST DIST
REED, CHARLOTTE	BAL	182	11TH WAR
REED, CHARLOTTE	BAL	189	11TH WAR
REED, CHARLOTTE	KEN	223	2ND DIST
REED, DANIEL	BAL	294	7TH WARD
REED, DAVID	HAR	055	1ST DIST
REED, DAVID	BAL	358	13TH WAR
REED, DELIA	BAL	105	10TH WAR
REED, EDWARD	BAL	155	2ND DIST
REED, EDWARD	CEC	028	CHESAPEA
REED, EDWARD	QUE	156	2ND E DI
REED, EDWARD J.	BAL	222	6TH WARD
REED, ELIAH M. *	BAL	403	14TH WAR
REED, ELIAS	BAL	390	1ST DIST
REED, ELIAS	BAL	317	1ST DIST
REED, ELIAS J.	BAL	390	1ST DIST
REED, ELIZA	BAL	177	6TH WARD
REED, ELIZABETH	BAL	177	6TH WARD
REED, ELIZABETH	BAL	074	15TH WAR
REED, ELIZABETH	FRE	280	WOODSBOR
REED, ELIZABETH	BAL	058	18TH WAR
REED, ELIZABETH	KEN	293	3RD DIST
REED, ELLEN	BAL	193	2ND WARD
REED, EMMA A.	CEC	176	7TH E DI
REED, EMORY	KEN	270	1ST DIST
REED, FANNY	CAR	349	6TH DIST
REED, FEBEE	WAS	136	2ND DIST
REED, FELIX-MULATTO	BAL	217	2ND WARD
REED, FRANCIS	WAS	043	2ND SUBD
REED, FRANCIS P.	BAL	293	12TH WAR
REED, FRANCIS Z.	BAL	105	10TH WAR
REED, FREDERICK	BAL	218	17TH WAR
REED, GEORGE	CAL	054	3RD DIST
REED, GEORGE	CAR	308	1ST DIST
REED, GEORGE	HAR	083	2ND DIST
REED, GEORGE	BAL	406	1ST DIST
REED, GEORGE	BAL	123	1ST WARD
REED, GEORGE	WAS	195	1ST DIST
REED, GEORGE R.	KEN	241	2ND DIST
REED, GEORGE W.	CEC	012	ELKTON 3
REED, GEORGEANNA	BAL	160	16TH WAR
REED, H. C.	BAL	063	10TH WAR
REED, HANSON	CEC	213	7TH E DI
REED, HARRIOTT	BAL	024	4TH WARD
REED, HARRY	BAL	348	3RD WARD
REED, HARRY	KEN	273	1ST DIST
REED, HENRY	WAS	143	2ND DIST
REED, HENRY	BAL	409	1ST DIST
REED, HENRY	CHA	281	BOJANTOW
REED, HENRY	KEN	213	2ND DIST
REED, HENRY-BLACK	ST	345	5TH E DI
REED, ISAAC	DOR	404	1ST DIST
REED, ISAAC	FRE	022	FREDERIC
REED, ISAAC	CAL	057	3RD DIST
REED, ISABELLA	BAL	245	12TH WAR
REED, JACOB	BAL	325	1ST DIST
REED, JACOB	CAR	308	1ST DIST
REED, JACOB	BAL	199	19TH WAR
REED, JACOB	WAS	173	FUNKSTOW
REED, JACOB	WAS	173	FUNKSTOW
REED, JACOB H.	BAL	081	18TH WAR
REED, JAMES	BAL	302	17TH WAR
REED, JAMES	FRE	033	FREDERIC
REED, JAMES	QUE	140	1ST E DI
REED, JAMES	HAR	073	1ST DIST
REED, JAMES	BAL	208	17TH WAR
REED, JAMES	QUE	203	3RD E DI
REED, JAMES	BAL	219	5TH DIST
REED, JAMES	BAL	292	12TH WAR
REED, JAMES	BAL	072	1ST WARD
REED, JAMES	BAL	127	5TH WARD
REED, JAMES	BAL	168	1ST WARD
REED, JAMES	BAL	137	1ST WARD
REED, JAMES A.	BAL	069	10TH WAR
REED, JAMES R.	BAL	391	1ST DIST
REED, JAMES-BLACK	ST	340	5TH E DI
REED, JANE	WAS	248	SMITHSBU
REED, JANE	WAS	143	2ND DIST
REED, JANE	BAL	152	16TH WAR
REED, JANE	BAL	005	EASTERN
REED, JANE	KEN	237	2ND DIST
REED, JESSE	QUE	155	2ND E DI
REED, JOHN	BAL	085	18TH WAR
REED, JOHN	CEC	071	5TH E DI
REED, JOHN	CEC	110	4TH E DI
REED, JOHN	BAL	187	19TH WAR
REED, JOHN	CEC	041	CHESAPEA
REED, JOHN	BAL	151	19TH WAR
REED, JOHN	BAL	160	16TH WAR
REED, JOHN	BAL	229	2ND WARD
REED, JOHN	BAL	184	6TH WARD
REED, JOHN	BAL	259	1ST DIST
REED, JOHN	ALL	157	6TH E.D.
REED, JOHN	BAL	182	11TH WAR
REED, JOHN	DOR	456	1ST DIST
REED, JOHN C.	DOR	383	1ST DIST
REED, JOHN C.	BAL	141	19TH WAR
REED, JOHN C.	BAL	038	4TH WARD
REED, JOHN C.T.	WAS	234	1ST DIST
REED, JOSEPH	WAS	065	2ND SUBD
REED, JOSEPH	CEC	038	CHESAPEA
REED, JOSEPH	BAL	289	17TH WAR
REED, JOSEPH	BAL	183	11TH WAR
REED, JOSEPH	BAL	421	8TH WARD
REED, JOSEPH	ALL	013	3RD E.D.
REED, JOSEPH	BAL	172	1ST WARD
REED, JOSEPH T.	CEC	160	PORT DUP
REED, JOSEPH-BLACK	ST	334	4TH E DI
REED, JOSEPH-BLACK	QUE	199	3RD E DI
REED, JOSHUA	CEC	061	1ST E DI
REED, JOSHUA	BAL	068	15TH WAR
REED, JOSIAH-BLACK	ST	327	4TH E DI
REED, JULIA	BAL	453	14TH WAR
REED, JULIANNE	BAL	252	17TH WAR
REED, LARKIN	BAL	180	2ND DIST
REED, LAURENCE	QUE	171	2ND E DI
REED, LETTY	KEN	243	2ND DIST
REED, LEVI-BLACK	ST	334	4TH E DI
REED, LOUIS	BAL	259	1ST DIST
REED, MARGARET	CAR	242	TANEYTOW
REED, MARGARET	CAR	218	5TH DIST
REED, MARGARETT	BAL	027	18TH WAR
REED, MARTHA	CEC	126	5TH E DI
REED, MARTHA	FRE	253	NEW MARK
REED, MARY	BAL	003	18TH WAR
REED, MARY	BAL	389	13TH WAR
REED, MARY	BAL	171	6TH WARD
REED, MARY	BAL	020	9TH WARD
REED, MARY	BAL	093	15TH WAR
REED, MARY	BAL	122	2ND DIST

REED, MARY	QUE	165	2ND E DI
REED, MARY	WAS	164	2ND DIST
REED, MARY	WAS	125	2ND DIST
REED, MARY A.	BAL	453	14TH WAR
REED, MARY E.	CAR	105	NO TWP L
REED, MATILDA	BAL	065	10TH WAR
REED, MAY J.	BAL	041	18TH WAR
REED, MORDICA	BAL	075	18TH WAR
REED, NATHANIEL	CAL	053	3RD DIST
REED, P. G.	CAR	213	5TH DIST
REED, PERRY	BAL	049	15TH WAR
REED, PETER	BAL	453	14TH WAR
REED, PETER	KEN	270	1ST DIST
REED, PHILIP	BAL	211	19TH WAR
REED, PHILIP	ALL	244	CUMBERLA
REED, REBECCA	CEC	009	ELKTON 3
REED, REUBEN	ANN	490	HOWARD D
REED, RICHARD	BAL	342	13TH WAR
REED, RICHARD	KEN	306	3RD DIST
REED, ROBERT	BAL	180	19TH WAR
REED, ROBERT	BAL	409	1ST DIST
REED, ROBERT	BAL	195	2ND WARD
REED, ROSETTA	BAL	011	1ST WARD
REED, S. P.	BAL	152	1ST WARD
REED, SAMUEL	BAL	157	2ND DIST
REED, SAMUEL	BAL	053	1ST WARD
REED, SAMUEL	CEC	169	6TH E DI
REED, SAMUEL	QUE	124	1ST E DI
REED, SAMUEL	HAR	065	1ST DIST
REED, SAMUEL	KEN	303	3RD DIST
REED, SAMUEL	WAS	132	HAGERSTO
REED, SARAH	KEN	235	2ND DIST
REED, SARAH	BAL	286	20TH WAR
REED, SARAH	BAL	454	8TH WARD
REED, SARAH A.	ANN	436	HOWARD D
REED, SARAH J.	CAR	119	NO TWP L
REED, SARAH R.	BAL	177	6TH WARD
REED, SOPHIA	BAL	141	11TH WAR
REED, SOPHIA	BAL	417	14TH WAR
REED, SUSAN E.-MULATTO	ST	334	4TH E DI
REED, SUSAN-BLACK	ST	295	2ND E DI
REED, SUSAN-MULATTO	ST	346	5TH E DI
REED, SYLVESTER	CAR	137	NO TWP L
REED, TEMPERANCE	BAL	019	18TH WAR
REED, THOAMS	BAL	403	14TH WAR
REED, THOAMS	FRE	114	CREAGERS
REED, THOMAS	CHA	282	BOJANTOW
REED, THOMAS	CAR	099	NO TWP L
REED, THOMAS	CEC	076	NORTHEAS
REED, THOMAS	KEN	270	1ST DIST
REED, THOMAS	WAS	125	2ND DIST
REED, THOMAS	MGM	444	CLARKSTR
REED, THOMAS	ALL	237	CUMBERLA
REED, THOMAS	BAL	065	2ND DIST
REED, THOMAS	BAL	058	15TH WAR
REED, THOMAS	BAL	096	15TH WAR
REED, THOMAS	BAL	100	10TH WAR
REED, THOMAS B.	BAL	164	11TH WAR
REED, THOMAS S.	BAL	146	1ST WARD
REED, WALDON	CEC	124	5TH E DI
REED, WILILAM H.	BAL	164	11TH WAR
REED, WILLIAM	BAL	290	12TH WAR
REED, WILLIAM	BAL	145	2ND DIST
REED, WILLIAM	BAL	259	1ST DIST
REED, WILLIAM	BAL	118	1ST WARD
REED, WILLIAM	CEC	176	7TH E DI
REED, WILLIAM	CEC	160	PORT DUP
REED, WILLIAM	BAL	009	18TH WAR
REED, WILLIAM	CEC	092	4TH E DI
REED, WILLIAM	QUE	140	1ST E DI
REED, WILLIAM	MGM	318	CRACKLIN
REED, WILLIAM	MGM	318	CRACKLIN
REED, WILLIAM	HAR	089	2ND DIST
REED, WILLIAM	SOM	430	PRINCESS
REED, WILLIAM	MGM	372	BERRYS D
REED, WILLIAM	CEC	018	ELKTON 3
REED, WILLIAM	QUE	253	5TH E DI
REED, WILLIAM	KEN	284	3RD DIST
REED, WILLIAM	ST	343	5TH E DI
REED, WILLIAM C.	BAL	352	7TH WARD
REED, WILLIAM L.	BAL	438	8TH WARD
REED, WILLIAM S.	CAR	081	NO TWP L
REED, GEORGE	BAL	344	1ST DIST
REEDE, ANN	HAR	189	3RD DIST
REEDE, CHARLOTT	BAL	311	7TH WARD
REEDE, DAVID	HAR	197	3RD DIST
REEDE, ELLEN	BAL	415	8TH WARD
REEDE, HESTER	HAR	189	3RD DIST
REEDE, JACOB H.	HAR	181	3RD DIST
REEDE, JAMES	HAR	185	3RD DIST
REEDE, JAMES	BAL	178	11TH WAR
REEDE, JOHN	HAR	184	3RD DIST
REEDE, JOSEPH B.	HAR	153	3RD DIST
REEDE, MARTHY	HAR	181	3RD DIST
REEDE, PRISCILLA G.	HAR	203	3RD DIST
REEDE, SUSANER	HAR	184	3RD DIST
REEDE, THOMAS	ALL	162	6TH E.D.
REEDE, UPTON	HAR	202	3RD DIST
REEDE, WILLIAM	HAR	194	3RD DIST
REEDE, WILLIAM	HAR	204	3RD DIST
REEDENHOUR, WILLIAM	WAS	263	1ST DIST
REEDER, ALEXANDER B.	WAS	113	2ND DIST
REEDER, ALLEN	WAS	122	2ND DIST
REEDER, ANDREW J.	BAL	008	15TH WAR
REEDER, ANN	CHA	230	MIDDLETO
REEDER, BENJAMIN	WAS	077	2ND SUBD
REEDER, CHARISTOPHER	BAL	187	11TH WAR
REEDER, CHARLES	BAL	276	17TH WAR
REEDER, CHARLES	BAL	256	17TH WAR
REEDER, CHARLES JR.	BAL	264	17TH WAR
REEDER, DAVID	FRE	332	MIDDLETO
REEDER, FRANCIS	WAS	077	2ND SUBD
REEDER, GEORGE	WAS	078	2ND SUBD
REEDER, GEORGE	BAL	453	8TH WARD
REEDER, GEORGE W.	BAL	251	17TH WAR
REEDER, GEROCE *	KEN	223	2ND DIST
REEDER, HANNAH	BAL	185	2ND WARD
REEDER, HENRY W.	WAS	098	2ND DIST
REEDER, HIRAM	WAS	077	2ND SUBD
REEDER, JACOB	BAL	198	17TH WAR
REEDER, JAMES	WAS	063	2ND SUBD
REEDER, JOHN	BAL	147	2ND DIST
REEDER, JOHN D.	BAL	279	2ND WARD
REEDER, JOHN S.	CHA	221	ALLENS F
REEDER, MARY	FRE	331	MIDDLETO
REEDER, MARY E.	BAL	096	15TH WAR
REEDER, NANCY	WAS	077	2ND SUBD
REEDER, PHILIP	WAS	079	2ND SUBD
REEDER, RICHARD H.	ST	261	3RD E DI
REEDER, ROBERT S.	CHA	289	MIDDLETO
REEDER, SAMUEL	FRE	354	MIDDLETO
REEDER, WILLIAM	ST	261	3RD E DI
REEDER, WILLIAM A.	WAS	102	2ND DIST
REEDER, WILLIAM O.	ST	261	3RD E DI
REEDER, ZACKARIAH	WAS	084	2ND SUBD
REEDMAN, THOMAS	BAL	457	8TH WARD
REEDNER, FREDERICK	BAL	366	13TH WAR
REEDNER, JOHN	BAL	041	4TH WARD
REEDY, DAVID	WAS	302	1ST DIST
REEFMAN, FREDERICK	BAL	066	4TH WARD,
REEFSNIDER, GEORGE	CAR	323	1ST DIST
REEHLER, FRANCES	BAL	335	13TH WAR
REEKENSTAFF, JOHN	BAL	203	11TH WAR
REEL, DAVID	WAS	065	2ND SUBD
REEL, HENRY	WAS	053	2ND SUBD
REEL, HULDY	WAS	054	2ND SUBD
REEL, J. T.	WAS	178	BOONSBOR
REEL, JACOB	ALL	180	8TH E.D.
REEL, JOHN	WAS	089	2ND SUBD
REEL, JOHN	BAL	225	19TH WAR
REEL, NICHOLAS	FRE	272	NEW MARK
REEL, OTHER	BAL	095	18TH WAR
REEL, RHINEHART	BAL	218	17TH WAR
REEL, SAMUEL	WAS	053	2ND SUBD
REELE, JOHN	WAS	232	1ST DIST
REEMS, HENRY	BAL	149	5TH WARD
REEMSY, BENJAMIN	CEC	116	3RD E DI
REEN, MARY	BAL	194	11TH WAR
REEP, CATHARINE	WAS	299	1ST DIST
REEPER, CATHERINE	BAL	421	3RD WARD
REEPERS, ELIZABETH	FRE	162	EMMITTSB
REES, JOHN	BAL	402	1ST DIST
REES, JOSEPHIA	HAR	160	3RD DIST
REESE, ADALINE	CEC	144	PORT DUP
REESE, ADAM	BAL	313	7TH WARD
REESE, ANDREW	BAL	035	15TH WAR
REESE, ANDREW	BAL	315	20TH WAR
REESE, ANDREW	CAR	275	7TH DIST
REESE, ANN	CEC	147	PORT DUP
REESE, ANN	CEC	017	ELKTON 3
REESE, ANNA	QUE	205	3RD E DI
REESE, CATHARINE	CAR	260	3RD DIST
REESE, CATHERINE	BAL	066	10TH WAR
REESE, CHARLES	BAL	065	15TH WAR
REESE, CHARLES S.	BAL	261	6TH WARD
REESE, CORNELIUS C.	WAS	245	SMITHSBU
REESE, DANIEL E.	CAR	265	WESTMINS
REESE, DANIEL M.	BAL	176	16TH WAR
REESE, DAVID	BAL	391	3RD WARD
REESE, DAVID	BAL	342	3RD WARD
REESE, DAVID	CAR	296	7TH DIST
REESE, DAVID F.	WAS	171	FUNKSTOW
REESE, DEBORAH	CAR	139	NO TWP L
REESE, EDWARD	BAL	092	2ND DIST
REESE, EDWARD J.	MGM	341	CLARKSBU
REESE, EDWIN F.	BAL	250	1ST DIST
REESE, ELI Y.	BAL	159	16TH WAR
REESE, ELIZA	BAL	325	3RD WARD
REESE, ELIZA	BAL	188	6TH WARD
REESE, ELIZABETH	BAL	318	3RD WARD
REESE, ELLEN	FRE	442	8TH E DI
REESE, EMMOR	HAR	124	2ND DIST
REESE, EPHRAIN	SOM	404	BRINKLEY
REESE, FREDERICK	BAL	016	1ST WARD
REESE, GEORGE	BAL	010	EASTERN
REESE, GEORGE	HAR	048	1ST DIST
REESE, GEORGE H.-MULATTO	BAL	218	2ND WARD
REESE, HANNAH S.	BAL	451	1ST DIST
REESE, HENRY	BAL	094	2ND DIST
REESE, HENRY	BAL	449	8TH WARD
REESE, HENRY	BAL	115	14TH WAR
REESE, ISAAC	HAR	118	2ND DIST
REESE, ISAIAH	WAS	233	1ST DIST
REESE, JACKSON	WAS	225	1ST DIST
REESE, JACOB	WAS	146	HAGERSTO
REESE, JACOB	FRE	064	FREDERIC
REESE, JACOB	CAR	162	NO TWP L
REESE, JACOB	CAR	275	7TH DIST
REESE, JACOB	CAR	273	WESTMINS
REESE, JACOB	BAL	097	15TH WAR
REESE, JAMES	KEN	254	1ST DIST
REESE, JAMES	DOR	381	1ST DIST
REESE, JOHN	BAL	303	17TH WAR
REESE, JOHN	FRE	090	FREDERIC
REESE, JOHN	BAL	360	13TH WAR
REESE, JOHN	BAL	112	2ND DIST
REESE, JOHN	BAL	362	1ST DIST
REESE, JOHN	BAL	196	6TH WARD
REESE, JOHN A.	QUE	186	3RD E DI
REESE, JOHN A.	BAL	264	20TH WAR
REESE, JOHN A.*	BAL	006	4TH WARD
REESE, JOHN B.G.	ANN	469	HOWARD D
REESE, JOHN D.	ALL	071	5TH E.D.
REESE, JOHN E.	BAL	476	14TH WAR
REESE, JOHN F.	CAR	270	WESTMINS
REESE, JOHN L. JR.	BAL	098	15TH WAR
REESE, JOHN M.	BAL	127	1ST WARD
REESE, JOHN R.	BAL	231	1ST DIST
REESE, JOHN S.	BAL	064	2ND DIST
REESE, JOHN W.	BAL	256	1ST DIST
REESE, JOSEPH	BAL	160	2ND DIST
REESE, JOSEPH	BAL	227	19TH WAR
REESE, JOSHUA	SOM	371	BRINKLEY
REESE, LEWIS	FRE	091	FREDERIC
REESE, LIZZY*	BAL	314	3RD WARD
REESE, LYDIA	WAS	217	1ST DIST
REESE, MARGARET	BAL	211	6TH WARD
REESE, MARGARETT K.	BAL	256	1ST DIST
REESE, MARTHA	BAL	163	19TH WAR
REESE, MARY	BAL	123	11TH WAR
REESE, MARY	BAL	158	16TH WAR
REESE, MARY A.	BAL	162	19TH WAR
REESE, MARY A.E.	BAL	159	16TH WAR
REESE, MARY E.	BAL	218	6TH WARD
REESE, MARY M.	BAL	115	15TH WAR
REESE, MATALINA	BAL	196	6TH WARD
REESE, MICHEAL	WAS	166	1ST DIST
REESE, NEOMA	WAS	252	1ST DIST
REESE, REBECCA	BAL	181	19TH WAR
REESE, RICHARD	CEC	001	ELKTON 3
REESE, S.	BAL	329	13TH WAR
REESE, SAMUEL	BAL	163	19TH WAR
REESE, STEPHEN	BAL	082	18TH WAR
REESE, SUSAN	BAL	165	6TH WARD
REESE, SUSAN	BAL	451	1ST DIST
REESE, SUSANNAH R.	BAL	072	15TH WAR
REESE, THOMAS	BAL	303	17TH WAR
REESE, THOMAS	CAR	139	NO TWP L
REESE, THOMAS	QUE	210	3RD E DI
REESE, THOMAS L.	BAL	118	15TH WAR
REESE, THOMAS M.	BAL	115	15TH WAR
REESE, WASHINGTON	SOM	446	DAMES QU
REESE, WILLIAM	CAR	147	NO TWP L
REESE, WILLIAM	BAL	303	17TH WAR
REESE, WILLIAM	CAR	272	WESTMINS
REESE, WILLIAM	CAR	163	NO TWP L
REESE, WILLIAM	BAL	109	15TH WAR
REESE, WILLIAM	BAL	123	1ST WARD
REESE, WILLIAM	BAL	123	1ST WARD
REESE, WILLIAM	ALL	070	5TH E.D.
REESE, WILLIAM	QUE	206	3RD E DI
REESE, WILLIAM	QUE	189	3RD E DI
REESE, WILLIAM D.	BAL	054	15TH WAR
REESE, WILLIAM H.	SOM	412	DUBLIN D
REESE,ELLEN	BAL	064	2ND DIST
REESER, ELIZABETH *	BAL	119	18TH WAR
REESHOUS, SALLY	BAL	474	14TH WAR
REESTER, THOMAS	ALL	109	5TH E.D.
REEVE, WILLIAM	BAL	172	19TH WAR
REEVELY, NICHOLAS	CAR	356	6TH DIST
REEVER, ELIZABETH *	BAL	119	18TH WAR
REEVER, FREDERICK	CAR	309	1ST DIST
REEVER, FREDERICK	CAR	300	1ST DIST
REEVER, HENRY	CAR	242	TANEYTOW
REEVER, JAMES	FRE	170	5TH E DI
REEVER, JOHN	CAR	300	1ST DIST
REEVER, JOSEPH	CAR	298	1ST DIST
REEVER, SAMUEL	CAR	242	TANEYTOW
REEVER, SOPHIA	WAS	267	1ST DIST
REEVER, WASHINGTON	CAR	300	1ST DIST
REEVES, ABIGALE	CHA	254	MIDDLETO
REEVES, ALFRED	CHA	253	MIDDLETO
REEVES, ANN	ANN	317	1ST DIST
REEVES, GEORGE	BAL	173	1ST WARD
REEVES, HORATIO	CHA	279	BOJANTOW
REEVES, ISAAC	BAL	117	1ST WARD
REEVES, JOHN	BAL	028	4TH WARD
REEVES, JOHN A.	BAL	191	6TH WARD
REEVES, JOHN R. T.	CHA	241	HILLTOP
REEVES, JOSEPH	FRE	193	5TH E DI
REEVES, JOSHUA F.	BAL	052	4TH WARD
REEVES, MARGARET	BAL	304	17TH WAR
REEVES, MARY	QUE	251	5TH E DI
REEVES, MARY R.	BAL	052	4TH WARD
REEVES, NANCY V.	CHA	253	MIDDLETO
REEVES, P.	BAL	149	1ST WARD
REEVES, RICHARD	BAL	374	1ST DIST
REEVES, SAMUEL	QUE	251	5TH E DI
REEVES, THEODORE	BAL	010	1ST WARD
REEVES, WILLIAM	KEN	291	3RD DIST
REEZZARD, JANE	ANN	505	HOWARD D
REFAMER, JOHN JR.	WAS	077	2ND SUBD
REFFMAN, PETER	BAL	061	1ST WARD
REGAN, ARCHIBALD*	DOR	439	1ST DIST
REGAN, CATHARINE	BAL	269	12TH WAR
REGAN, CATHERINE	ALL	253	CUMBERLA
REGAN, DENWOOD*	DOR	432	1ST DIST
REGAN, JAMES	ALL	252	CUMBERLA
REGAN, JOHN	BAL	382	8TH WARD
REGAN, MICHAEL	ALL	053	10TH E.D
REGAN, PETER	ALL	155	6TH E.D.
REGAN, THOMAS	BAL	121	1ST WARD
REGAN, WILLAIM	BAL	147	1ST WARD
REGAN,MICHAEL	BAL	024	2ND DIST
REGANS, CHARLES T.	DOR	362	3RD DIVI
REGANS, JOHN	DOR	361	3RD DIVI
REGESTER, WALTER	CEC	046	1ST E DI
REGET, MARY	ALL	145	6TH E.D.
REGGAN, FREDRICK	BAL	139	11TH WAR
REGGIN, JIM	WOR	291	9TH E DI
REGGS, HENRY	FRE	267	NEW MARK
REGGS, MARY L.	FRE	255	NEW MARK
REGISTER, JOSEPH	BAL	098	5TH WARD
REGISTER, ROBERT W.	BAL	011	15TH WAR
REGISTER, SAMUEL	BAL	099	2ND DIST
REGISTER, SENANCA *	BAL	099	2ND DIST
REGISTER, WILLIAM	KEN	218	2ND DIST
REGLE, ABRAM	CEC	065	1ST E DI
REGNEW, CHARLES	BAL	111	5TH WARD
REGNIER, JOHN	DOR	380	1ST DIST
REHBERGER, H.	BAL	236	2ND WARD
REHRBAUGH, ANN M.	CAR	247	3RD DIST
REHREN, HENRY	BAL	455	8TH WARD
REICH, GEORGE	BAL	051	1ST WARD
REICH, JOHN	FRE	102	FREDERIC
REICH, PHILIP	FRE	102	FREDERIC
REICH, WILLIAM	FRE	021	FREDERIC
REICHAN, JACOB	WAS	032	2ND SUBD
REICHARD, DANIEL	WAS	032	2ND SUBD
REICHARD, DANIEL	WAS	031	2ND SUBD
REICHARD, JOHN	WAS	031	2ND SUBD
REICHARD, VALENTINE	WAS	031	2ND SUBD
REICHART, CATHARINE	CAR	344	6TH DIST
REICHART, JOHN	CAR	348	6TH DIST
REICHBER, HENRY	BAL	070	1ST WARD
REICHER, BARBET	BAL	105	15TH WAR
REICHERT, JOHN	BAL	221	17TH WAR
REICHESTEEN,JANE	BAL	423	14TH WAR
REICHLER, GEORGE W.	CAR	364	9TH DIST
REID, ANDREW	BAL	108	10TH WAR
REID, BENJAMIN	BAL	169	1ST WARD
REID, CHARLES A.	HAR	001	1ST DIST
REID, EDWARD	BAL	034	9TH WARD
REID, GEORGE N.	MGM	426	MEDLEY 3
REID, H.R.	BAL	171	1ST WARD
REID, HERMAN	BAL	008	9TH WARD
REID, JACOB	BAL	390	3RD WARD
REID, JAMES	MGM	430	CLARKSTR
REID, JAMES	CAR	410	2ND DIST
REID, JAMES	BAL	019	4TH WARD
REID, JAMES M.	MGM	377	ROCKERLE
REID, JESSE D.	BAL	366	3RD WARD
REID, JOHN	CAR	356	6TH DIST
REID, JOHN	BAL	362	13TH WAR
REID, JOHN	FRE	391	PETERSVI
REID, JOHN	WAS	266	1ST DIST
REID, JOHN O.	BAL	143	11TH WAR
REID, JOHN W.	BAL	032	1ST WARD
REID, MARY	BAL	006	1ST WARD
REID, MAXY	BAL	404	1ST DIST
REID, MINTY	MGM	432	CLARKSTR
REID, PHILIP	MGM	407	MEDLEY 3
REID, THOMAS	MGM	417	MEDLEY 3
REID, THOMAS	QUE	203	3RD E DI
REID, THOMAS S.	FRE	223	BUCKEYST
REID, WILLIAM	MGM	421	MEDLEY 3
REID, WILLIAM	WAS	012	WILLIAMS
REID, WILLIAM	BAL	171	1ST WARD
REIDASIL, JACOB	BAL	081	10TH WAR
REIDENHORN, SAMUEL	WAS	143	HAGERSTO

REIDENHOUS, DANIEL WAS 302 1ST DIST
REIDSNIDER, DAIVD CAR 317 1ST DIST
REIDSNIDER, DAVID CAR 317 1ST DIST
REIEF, HENRIETTA BAL 235 2ND WARD
REIFF, DAVID WAS 298 1ST DIST
REIFF, JOHN WAS 292 1ST DIST
REIFLE, DAVID BAL 107 2ND DIST
REIFSINDER, WILLIAM BAL 232 12TH WAR
REIFSNIDER, JESSE CAR 266 WESTMINS
REIFSNIDER, JOHN FRE 285 WOODSBOR
REIGART, JOHN BAL 004 15TH WAR
REIGART, MATTHEW BAL 012 15TH WAR
REIGART, PHILLIP FRE 029 FREDERIC
REIGENDOFFER, JAMES BAL 237 2ND WARD
REIGHLFRESH, BARBARA BAL 095 1ST WARD
REIGLE, ELISABETH ANN 330 2ND DIST
REIGLE, WILLIAM HAR 034 1ST DIST
REIGNER, PETER BAL 066 1ST WARD
REIGNER, REDWICK BAL 202 2ND WARD
REIGTFRISH, WILLIAM BAL 095 1ST WARD
REIHM, JOSIAH BAL 458 14TH WAR
REIKLART, VALENTINE BAL 231 2ND WARD
REIL, DAVID BAL 208 19TH WAR
REILERS, PHILIP R. BAL 033 1ST WARD
REILEY, ANN BAL 283 17TH WAR
REILEY, BIDY BAL 091 18TH WAR
REILEY, CANIEL FRE 155 10TH E D
REILEY, ELLENORA FRE 412 8TH E DI
REILEY, GEORGE BAL 251 17TH WAR
REILEY, GEORGE BAL 264 17TH WAR
REILEY, HESTER BAL 196 2ND WARD
REILEY, JAMES FRE 009 FREDERIC
REILEY, JOHN BAL 063 18TH WAR
REILEY, MARGARET BAL 252 17TH WAR
REILEY, MARTHA ANN 444 HOWARD D
REILEY, MARY BAL 379 1ST DIST
REILEY, MARY J. HAR 145 3RD DIST
REILEY, PATRICK BAL 031 15TH WAR
REILHOLTZ, DAVID HAR 146 3RD DIST
REILLEY, BARNABAS FRE 160 EMMITTSB
REILLEY, FRANCIS BAL 115 11TH WAR
REILLEY, GEORGE BAL 019 9TH WARD
REILLY, A. B. BAL 136 11TH WAR
REILLY, ALEXANDER BAL 185 11TH WAR
REILLY, CATHARINE ALL 022 2ND E.D.
REILLY, CHARLES BAL 136 11TH WAR
REILLY, DEDA BAL 204 11TH WAR
REILLY, EDWARD BAL 258 20TH WAR
REILLY, ELIZA BAL 213 11TH WAR
REILLY, ELIZABET BAL 013 18TH WAR
REILLY, ELIZABETH BAL 215 11TH WAR
REILLY, ELLEN BAL 215 11TH WAR
REILLY, JAMES BAL 023 18TH WAR
REILLY, JAMES BAL 211 11TH WAR
REILLY, JOHN BAL 135 11TH WAR
REILLY, JOHN BAL 469 14TH WAR
REILLY, JOHN BAL 156 19TH WAR
REILLY, JOSEPH BAL 035 9TH WARD
REILLY, JULIETT* BAL 115 11TH WAR
REILLY, L.V. BAL 150 19TH WAR
REILLY, MARGARET E. BAL 035 9TH WARD
REILLY, MARTIN BAL 105 18TH WAR
REILLY, MARY A. BAL 131 18TH WAR
REILLY, MORRIS BAL 177 11TH WAR
REILLY, PATRICK BAL 010 18TH WAR
REILLY, PETER BAL 105 18TH WAR
REILLY, ROSE BAL 147 11TH WAR
REILLY, RUBEN REV. BAL 014 18TH WAR
REILLY, SARAH A. BAL 117 18TH WAR
REILLY, SISTER M. FRE 198 5TH E DI
REILLY, SUSAN BAL 176 19TH WAR
REILLY, THOMAS BAL 176 11TH WAR
REILY, ADILIA DOR 382 1ST DIST
REILY, AMANDA J. BAL 192 11TH WAR
REILY, BRANEY BAL 202 11TH WAR
REILY, HINSOR* DOR 403 1ST DIST
REILY, JAMES BAL 158 11TH WAR
REILY, JAMES BAL 375 8TH WARD
REILY, JOHN BAL 395 3RD WARD
REILY, JOHN BAL 050 2ND DIST
REILY, JOHN BAL 027 2ND DIST
REILY, LEE BAL 378 1ST DIST
REILY, M. BAL 155 1ST WARD
REILY, MARGARET BAL 398 3RD WARD
REILY, MARY BAL 174 11TH WAR
REILY, MARY BAL 360 3RD WARD
REILY, MARY BAL 470 14TH WAR
REILY, MARY BAL 088 4TH WARD
REILY, MARY J. BAL 077 4TH WARD
REILY, NANCY WAS 009 WILLIAMS
REILY, PHILIP BAL 159 11TH WAR
REILY, STEVEN ALL 051 10TH E.D
REILY, THOMAS CAR 356 6TH DIST
REIM, HENRITTA BAL 139 11TH WAR
REIMAN, ALEXANDER BAL 001 18TH WAR
REIMAN, ALEXANDER BAL 001 18TH WAR
REIMAN, HENRY CAR 264 WESTMINS
REIMAN, HENRY BAL 436 14TH WAR
REIMAN, JAMES BAL 052 4TH WARD
REIMAN, JOSEPH H. BAL 436 14TH WAR
REIMAN, WILLIAM J. BAL 001 18TH WAR
REIMBY, THOMAS * BAL 131 18TH WAR
REIMILLER, GEORGE BAL 030 1ST WARD
REIMILLER, LEWIS BAL 029 1ST WARD
REIMINGER, WILLIAM BAL 190 19TH WAR
REIMSNIDER, CHARLES ANN 429 HOWARD D
REIN, PHILIP BAL 049 9TH WARD
REINAN, OWEN BAL 402 8TH WARD
REINECK, CONRAD ALL 189 9TH E.D.
REINEMAN, HENRY CAR 322 1ST DIST
REINER, CASPER BAL 061 1ST WARD
REINER, ELIZABETH BAL 468 14TH WAR
REINER, JOHN BAL 049 1ST WARD
REINER, WILLIAM FRE 095 FREDERIC
REINGTON, MICHEL HAR 159 3RD DIST
REINHARDT, CHARLES BAL 307 3RD WARD
REINHARDT, CHARLES C. BAL 055 9TH WARD
REINHARDT, CHARLES F. BAL 112 10TH WAR
REINHARDT, NICHOLAS BAL 173 19TH WAR
REINHARDT, V. BAL 112 10TH WAR
REINHART, ELIZABETH BAL 278 20TH WAR
REINHART, EMANUEL BAL 222 6TH WARD
REINHEART, ABRAM J. CEC 145 PORT DUP
REINHEIMER, FREDERICK BAL 235 2ND WARD
REINHOLT, LOUIS BAL 087 10TH WAR
REINICAR, JOHN BAL 233 17TH WAR
REINICK, FRANK BAL 302 17TH WAR
REINICK, PETER BAL 072 4TH WARD
REINICKER, GEORGE A. BAL 143 11TH WAR
REINICKER, LYDIA CAR 413 2ND DIST
REINICKER, WILLIAM J. BAL 250 12TH WAR
REINKE, AMODEUS FRE 117 CREAGERS
REINMAN, JACOB BAL 102 1ST WARD
REINONT, GEORGE BAL 263 12TH WAR
REINSEMAN, FREDERICK BAL 282 1ST DIST
REINSTADLER, GEORGE BAL 255 1ST DIST
REINTZ, CHRISTOPHER BAL 466 14TH WAR
REIP, ALFRED H. BAL 418 14TH WAR
REIP, CHARLES WAS 164 2ND DIST
REIP, CONRAD BAL 119 18TH WAR
REIP, EDWARD H. BAL 448 14TH WAR
REIP, HENRY BAL 452 14TH WAR
REIP, LAWRENCE BAL 452 14TH WAR
REIP, LULTANA BAL 448 14TH WAR
REIPKER, HENRY BAL 230 17TH WAR
REIPPLE, CATHARINE CAR 334 6TH DIST
REIPSONG, JOHN WAS 182 BOONSBOR
REIPSUM, JOHN BAL 293 17TH WAR
REIRGIER, CHARLES F. BAL 044 1ST WARD
REIRLE, JOHN W.* BAL 312 3RD WARD
REIS, PHILIP BAL 189 19TH WAR
REISCH, JOHN V. BAL 087 1ST WARD
REISE, JOSEPH BAL 274 2ND WARD
REISENBAUGH, HY. BAL 287 1ST DIST
REISHTINE, WILLIAM BAL 130 18TH WAR
REISIDE, WILLIAM BAL 102 2ND DIST
REISINGER, . BAL 253 12TH WAR
REISINGER, DANIEL BAL 241 12TH WAR
REISINGER, GEORGE BAL 003 1ST WARD
REISINGER, GEORGE BAL 198 19TH WAR
REISINGER, HENRY BAL 062 15TH WAR
REISINGER, LOUIS BAL 186 16TH WAR
REISINGER, MARTHA BAL 142 11TH WAR
REISINGER, MARTIN FRE 241 NEW MARK
REISINGER, MARTIN BAL 099 18TH WAR
REISLER, ADAM H. BAL 110 5TH WARD
REISLER, MARIA BAL 290 12TH WAR
REISLER, MARY FRE 420 8TH E DI
REISLER, THOMAS BAL 331 3RD WARD
REISLEY, JOSEPH BAL 125 18TH WAR
REISNER, CATHARINE BAL 282 17TH WAR
REISNER, JOHN BAL 258 6TH WARD
REISNER, JOHN G. FRE 036 FREDERIC
REISNER, REBECCA BAL 345 7TH WARD
REISNER, WILLIAM WAS 244 SMITHSBU
REISS, LOUIS H. BAL 251 12TH WAR
REISSNIDER, LEVI L. BAL 360 13TH WAR
REIST, GEORGE W. * BAL 287 20TH WAR
REISTADDEN, ELIZABETH BAL 360 1ST DIST
REISTER, ABRAM BAL 040 2ND DIST
REISTER, CAROLINE WAS 121 HAGERSTO
REISTER, ELIAS BAL 248 6TH WARD
REISTER, ELIZA BAL 016 2ND DIST
REISTER, HESTER A. BAL 173 16TH WAR
REISTER, JOHN G. BAL 278 12TH WAR
REISTER, LAURENCE BAL 245 2ND WARD
REISTER, MARTHA BAL 184 6TH WARD
REISTER, PHILIP BAL 248 1ST DIST
REITER, HERMAN H. BAL 308 3RD WARD
REITNER, JOSEPH BAL 266 2ND WARD
REITNER, JOSEPH BAL 146 11TH WAR
REITY, FREDRICK BAL 050 18TH WAR
REITZ, FREDERICK BAL 257 17TH WAR
REITZ, HENRY J. BAL 235 2ND WARD
REITZ, JOHN BAL 240 2ND WARD
REITZ, LOUIS BAL 015 15TH WAR
REITZ, THOMAS BAL 015 15TH WAR
REITZELL, JACOB WAS 103 2ND DIST
REIZE, SIMON BAL 240 2ND WARD
REKOE, THOMAS W. BAL 369 13TH WAR
RELAWEN, MATTHEW CEC 181 7TH E DI
RELCKER, GEORGE* BAL 061 4TH WARD
RELDEKER, WILLIAM ALL 173 7TH E.D.
RELEIR, JOHN BAL 320 1ST DIST
RELEY, CORNELIUS HAR 172 3RD DIST
RELEY, GEORGE ALL 128 4TH E.D.
RELING, SOPHIA BAL 210 6TH DIST
RELL, PATRICK BAL 006 9TH WARD
RELLY, GEORGE BAL 346 13TH WAR
RELSE, MARY BAL 381 13TH WAR
RELSO, REBECCA BAL 381 13TH WAR
RELSY, ELIZABETH BAL 288 12TH WAR
REMALT, THOMAS BAL 436 8TH WARD
REMARE, A. BAL 104 10TH WAR
REMBOLD, CARL HAR 085 2ND DIST
REMDOLLAR, JACOB BAL 297 12TH WAR
REMER, JACOB WAS 151 HAGERSTO
REMICH, NICHOLAS BAL 232 1ST DIST
REMICKER, GEORGE BAL 135 11TH WAR
REMINGTON, AVARILLA BAL 404 3RD WARD
REMINGTON, JESSE* BAL 404 3RD WARD
REMLEY, FREDERICK BAL 379 3RD WARD
REMLEY, JACOB A. BAL 290 3RD WARD
REMMA, WILLAIM BAL 249 1ST DIST
REMMAN, S. BAL 238 20TH WAR
REMMER, EDWARD BAL 039 18TH WAR
REMMER, MARY A. BAL 025 18TH WAR
REMMINGTON, JAMES BAL 121 2ND DIST
REMPLY, WILLIAM HAR 054 1ST DIST
REMSBURY, BENJAMIN FRE 323 MIDDLETO
REMYDAY, BETSY DOR 467 1ST DIST
REN, GEORGE BAL 301 7TH WARD
RENACKER, DANIEL CAR 252 3RD DIST
RENACKER, FRANCIS BAL 304 20TH WAR
RENACKER, PAUL CAR 253 3RD DIST
RENACKER, WILLIAM CAR 253 3RD DIST
RENAHAN, MICHAEL BAL 257 2ND WARD
RENALDS, JOHN BAL 342 1ST DIST
RENARD, MARGARET ANN 314 1ST DIST
RENCH, ADAM FRE 379 PETERSVI
RENCH, ELIZABETH WAS 142 HAGERSTO
RENCH, JOHN FRE 378 PETERSVI
RENCH, JOSEPH WAS 142 HAGERSTO
RENCH, K.D. ALL 013 3RD E.D.
RENCH, MARY A. WAS 295 1ST DIST
RENCH,MARY ALL 013 3RD E.D.
RENCHEN, JOSEPH ANN 483 HOWARD D
RENCHER, JOHN SOM 401 BRINKLEY
RENCHER, JOHN SOM 432 PRINCESS
RENCHER, JOHN R. BAL 080 15TH WAR
RENDERRY, MARGARET CEC 069 5TH E DI
RENDHAM, THOMAS W. BAL 184 5TH DIST
RENEHAN, ELLENORA BAL 258 2ND WARD
RENEHAN, JOHN FRE 397 PETERSVI
RENER, FRANK WAS 135 HAGERSTO
RENER, JOHN H. FRE 213 BUCKEYST
RENGART, GEORGE BAL 270 12TH WAR
RENGER, ADAMS ALL 029 2ND E.D.
RENGER, LEWIS BAL 107 1ST WARD
RENGOLD, GEORGE BAL 235 12TH WAR
RENHARD, MARY BAL 046 18TH WAR
RENICKER, JACOB CAR 262 3RD DIST
RENINGTON, ABNER BAL 130 1ST WARD
RENKT, HENRY BAL 260 2ND WARD
RENN, ISAAC FRE 214 BUCKEYST
RENN, LYDIA FRE 221 BUCKEYST
RENNALLS, B.S. BAL 047 1ST WARD
RENNARD, CAROLINE DOR 450 1ST DIST
RENNARD, MOSES DOR 388 1ST DIST
RENNEHAN, EDWARD ANN 500 HOWARD D
RENNELLS, JAMES KEN 312 3RD DIST
RENNER, ADAM FRE 357 CATOCTIN
RENNER, BARBARY WAS 132 HAGERSTO
RENNER, CAROLINE FRE 288 WOODSBOR
RENNER, DANIEL FRE 287 WOODSBOR
RENNER, EDWIN WAS 045 2ND SUBD
RENNER, ELIZABETH BAL 164 11TH WAR
RENNER, FRANCIS BAL 164 11TH WAR
RENNER, GEORGE FRE 109 CREAGERS
RENNER, GEORGE L. BAL 094 18TH WAR
RENNER, JACOB FRE 292 WOODSBOR
RENNER, JACOB FRE 293 WOODSBOR
RENNER, JACOB FRE 357 CATOCTIN
RENNER, JACOB WAS 026 2ND SUBD
RENNER, JACOB WAS 158 HAGERSTO
RENNER, JOHN WAS 025 2ND SUBD
RENNER, JOHN WAS 043 2ND SUBD
RENNER, JOHN FRE 288 WOODSBOR
RENNER, JOHNATHAN FRE 383 PETERSVI
RENNER, JOHNATHAN FRE 389 PETERSVI
RENNER, JOSEPH BAL 161 11TH WAR
RENNER, LEVY FRE 105 CREAGERS
RENNER, MARY WAS 261 1ST DIST
RENNER, PETER WAS 238 CAVETOWN
RENNER, SARAH FRE 111 CREAGERS
RENNER, SARAH CATHARINE WAS 025 2ND SUBD
RENNER, SOLOMON WAS 038 2ND SUBD
RENNER, SUSAN FRE 302 WOODSBOR
RENNER, SUSAN FRE 280 WOODSBOR
RENNER, WALLENTIN WAS 133 HAGERSTO
RENNER, WILLIAM FRE 372 CATOCTIN
RENNERT, ROBERT BAL 094 10TH WAR
RENNEYCK, CATHARINE BAL 404 14TH WAR
RENNICK, WILLIAM* BAL 391 3RD WARD
RENNINGER, LOUISA ALL 263 CUMBERLA
RENNINGTON, GEORGE CEC 193 5TH E DI
RENNNEBERGER, PHILIP FRE 223 BUCKEYST
RENNO, ANDREW BAL 165 6TH WARD
RENNOUS, EDWARD BAL 158 6TH WARD
RENNOUS, JOHN BAL 021 9TH WARD
RENNOUT, TIMOTHY BAL 180 2ND WARD
RENOFF, FREDERIC BAL 206 6TH WARD
RENOFF, MARY E. BAL 207 6TH WARD
RENOLDS, CATHERINE WAS 154 2ND DIST
RENOLDS, ELIZABETH WAS 135 2ND DIST
RENOLDS, MARY WOR 264 BERLIN 1
RENOLDS, MARY J.-BLACK BAL 184 2ND WARD
RENOLDS, POLLY WOR 265 BERLIN 1
RENOLS, JAMES CAR 214 5TH DIST
RENOR, CATHARINE CAR 321 1ST DIST
RENOUFF, FREDERICK BAL 097 5TH WARD
RENOWLS, WILLIAM BAL 400 8TH WARD
RENS, JOHN BAL 380 1ST DIST
RENS, ROSINA* BAL 083 10TH WAR
RENSHAW, ARTHUR CAR 198 4TH DIST
RENSHAW, HARRIET BAL 210 6TH WARD
RENSHAW, HARRY G. HAR 144 2ND DIST
RENSHAW, JOHN BAL 272 12TH WAR
RENSHAW, LEMUEL BAL 069 4TH WARD
RENSHAW, LOUIS M. BAL 105 10TH WAR
RENSHAW, LYDIA BAL 412 14TH WAR
RENSHAW, ROBERT BAL 402 1ST DIST
RENSHAW, WILLIAM MGM 396 ROCKERLE
RENSHOFF, DAVID WAS 277 LEITERSB
RENSHRING, STEPHEN MGM 415 MEDLEY 3
RENSKIE, MARY ALL 196 CUMBERLA
RENSKY, ELIZ BAL 324 12TH WAR
RENSY, JOHN BAL 234 17TH WAR
RENT, DANIEL FRE 352 MIDDLETO
RENTINHOMON, HENRY BAL 451 14TH WAR
RENTLEY, MARY BAL 375 13TH WAR
RENTZ, ANDREW BAL 439 8TH WARD
RENTZ, FRANCIS BAL 438 8TH WARD
RENTZ, JACOB BAL 369 1ST DIST
RENTZELL, GEORGE BAL 352 7TH WARD
RENUF, RICHARD BAL 061 1ST WARD
RENUF, RICHARD A. BAL 062 1ST WARD
RENVILLE, JOHN BAL 389 1ST DIST
RENWICK, ROBERT BAL 207 11TH WAR
RENWICK, WILLIAM H. BAL 117 11TH WAR
RENZ, ROSINA* BAL 083 10TH WAR
REORIDAN, MARY FRE 056 FREDERIC
REP, SARAH WAS 024 2ND SUBD
REP, WILLIAM CAR 392 2ND DIST
REPA, HENRY BAL 313 7TH WARD
REPART, GEORGE BAL 288 17TH WAR
REPHARD, GEORGE BAL 209 2ND WARD
REPOHN, PETER* BAL 112 10TH WAR
REPP, ABBALONA FRE 279 WOODSBOR
REPP, CHRISTIAN FRE 426 8TH E DI
REPP, CONRAD BAL 130 16TH WAR
REPP, EPHRIAM B. FRE 279 WOODSBOR
REPP, HENRY FRE 416 8TH E DI
REPP, HENRY BAL 123 16TH WAR
REPP, HENRY JR. FRE 426 8TH E DI
REPP, JOHN H. FRE 410 8TH E DI
REPP, JOHN S. FRE 410 8TH E DI
REPP, LEWIS P. WAS 172 FUNKSTOW
REPP, MARTHA E. CAR 393 2ND DIST
REPP, MICHAL WAS 135 2ND DIST
REPP, SAMUEL WAS 120 2ND DIST
REPP, SAMUEL FRE 426 8TH E DI
REPPARA, JAMES BAL 321 7TH WARD
REPPELL, JOHN BAL 198 2ND WARD
REPPEN, THOMAS FRE 256 NEW MARK
REPPER, DANIEL FRE 265 NEW MARK
REPPIN, WILLIAM FRE 240 NEW MARK
REPRAHN, PETER* BAL 112 10TH WAR
RERCHENBOUGH, JOHN BAL 256 2ND WARD
RERDON, JOHN BAL 297 1ST DIST
RERGER, VALENTINE BAL 211 19TH WAR
RESBARY, DARE HAR 051 1ST DIST
RESE, ANN BAL 431 8TH WARD
RESH, DANIEL WAS 301 1ST DIST
RESH, JACOB BAL 197 5TH DIST
RESH, JAMES WAS 302 1ST DIST
RESH, MICHAEL * BAL 359 1ST DIST
RESH, MOSES WAS 301 1ST DIST
RESH, PETER WAS 301 1ST DIST
RESH, PHILIP BAL 359 1ST DIST

Name	County	Page	District
RESH, SAMUEL	WAS	301	1ST DIST
RESHER, HARRIET	BAL	218	6TH DIST
RESIDE, JAMES	BAL	103	2ND DIST
RESIDE, MARY	BAL	048	15TH WAR
RESIN, GEORGE	BAL	103	15TH WAR
RESIN, JACOB	CEC	008	ELKTON 3
RESIN, JANE	BAL	274	12TH WAR
RESIN, NATHAN	BAL	213	17TH WAR
RESIN, RACHEL	BAL	097	15TH WAR
RESIN, VELINDA	CHA	241	HILLTOP
RESISTICE, ELEY *	BAL	307	12TH WAR
RESLEY, ANDREW	BAL	101	1ST WARD
RESLEY, CATHARINE	ALL	095	5TH E.D.
RESLEY, HORAC	ALL	212	CUMBERLA
RESORE, CHARLES H.G.	WAS	245	SMITHSBU
RESS, GEORGE	BAL	259	2ND WARD
RESS, JOHN	CHA	292	BOJANTOW
RESSER, REBECCA	WAS	275	RIDGEVIL
RESSING, W.	BAL	314	12TH WAR
RESSLER, JOHN	BAL	192	2ND WARD
REST, ELIZA	BAL	390	3RD WARD
REST, WILLIAM	ALL	103	5TH E.D.
RESTER, WILLIAM	BAL	017	2ND DIST
RESUNNA, LESTER	BAL	312	12TH WAR
RETAN, CHARLES	BAL	004	4TH WARD
RETGORING, SOPHIA	FRE	031	FREDERIC
RETHERFORD, CHARLES	FRE	033	FREDERIC
RETHERFORD, GEORGE	FRE	024	FREDERIC
RETICKER, SOPHIA A.	BAL	069	15TH WAR
RETIRE, MARGARET	BAL	318	20TH WAR
RETMYER, HENMAR	BAL	100	18TH WAR
RETNER, RACHEL	ALL	184	9TH E.D.
RETSON, H.	BAL	159	1ST WARD
RETTER, JOHN	ALL	205	CUMBERLA
RETTER, JOHN	BAL	212	17TH WAR
RETZE, JOHN H.	BAL	055	15TH WAR
REUBEN, HENRY	BAL	174	16TH WAR
REUBENS, CHARLES	BAL	001	15TH WAR
REUTCH, CATHARINE	WAS	032	2ND SUBD
REUTCH, CANIEL S.	WAS	086	2ND SUBD
REUTER, ANDREW	BAL	091	10TH WAR
REUTER, U. *	BAL	125	2ND DIST
REUWER, DIEDRICH	BAL	162	16TH WAR
REVEER, ROBERT	BAL	261	6TH WARD
REVEL, CHARLOT	WOR	281	BERLIN 1
REVEL, JAMES	ANN	302	1ST DIST
REVELL, AURELIA	SOM	394	BRINKLEY
REVELL, CURTIS	SOM	419	PRINCESS
REVELL, CAVID	SOM	359	BRINKLEY
REVELL, DAVID	SOM	359	BRINKLEY
REVELL, EDWARD	SOM	410	DUBLIN D
REVELL, EDWARD A.	SOM	431	PRINCESS
REVELL, ELIZA A.	SOM	425	PRINCESS
REVELL, EMALINE	SOM	356	BRINKLEY
REVELL, GEORGE	SOM	356	BRINKLEY
REVELL, GEORGE	SOM	485	TRAPP DI
REVELL, ISAAC	SOM	355	BRINKLEY
REVELL, JAMES S.	SOM	399	BRINKLEY
REVELL, JOHN	SOM	398	BRINKLEY
REVELL, LEMUEL H.	SOM	410	DUBLIN D
REVELL, MARIAH	SOM	427	PRINCESS
REVELL, MAY A.	ANN	273	ANNAPOLI
REVELL, PETER	BAL	046	18TH WAR
REVELL, W. T. DR-	ANN	347	3RD DIST
REVELL, WILLIAM	SOM	525	BARREN C
REVELL, WILLIAM T.	SOM	411	DUBLIN D
REVERR, ANN R.	BAL	129	16TH WAR
REVERS, HENRY	BAL	135	2ND DIST
REVERSEY, JOHN B.	BAL	119	2ND DIST
REVES, JOHN	CHA	277	BOJANTOW
REVES, THOMAS	ST	343	5TH E DI
REVIL, HENRIETTA	WOR	262	BERLIN 1
REW, JAMES	TAL	079	ST MICHA
REWALL, MARTIN	PRI	009	BLADENSB
REX, ANN C.	BAL	302	7TH WARD
REY, ANN	BAL	125	18TH WAR
REYBRED, THOMAS	BAL	322	12TH WAR
REYBURN, IRA S.	BAL	250	20TH WAR
REYDEMYER, JOHN	BAL	391	14TH WAR
REYLER, MARGARET	BAL	326	12TH WAR
REYLEY, PATRICK	BAL	018	2ND DIST
REYMONSNYDER, JOHN	WAS	247	SMITHSBU
REYNER, LOUIZA	CAR	095	NO TWP L
REYNIELL, SAMUEL	WAS	198	1ST DIST
REYNOCS, ELIZA*	BAL	355	3RD WARD
REYNOLD, HAMMOND H.	WOR	199	8TH E DI
REYNOLD, JACOB	WAS	270	1ST DIST
REYNOLD, NORTON	BAL	141	1ST WARD
REYNOLD, PETER	WAS	270	1ST DIST
REYNOLD, SOLCMON	WAS	271	1ST DIST
REYNOLD.S SARAH	BAL	258	12TH WAR
REYNOLDS, ALDRIDGE	CEC	073	5TH E DI
REYNOLDS, ALFRED	WOR	175	6TH E DI
REYNOLDS, ALFRED H.	BAL	091	5TH WARD
REYNOLDS, ALICE	CEC	072	5TH E DI
REYNOLDS, ALLEN	ANN	416	HOWARD D
REYNOLDS, ANN	ANN	439	HOWARD D
REYNOLDS, ANN	KEN	220	2ND DIST
REYNOLDS, ANN B.	FRE	021	FREDERIC
REYNOLDS, BARNARD	ALL	084	5TH E.D.
REYNOLDS, BENIJAH*	BAL	332	3RD WARD
REYNOLDS, BENJAMIN	CEC	210	7TH E DI
REYNOLDS, BENJAMIN	CEC	022	ELKTON 3
REYNOLDS, BENJAMIN	WAS	147	HAGERSTO
REYNOLDS, BERNARD	BAL	047	9TH WARD
REYNOLDS, BRIDGET	BAL	104	10TH WAR
REYNOLDS, CALEB	CEC	124	5TH E DI
REYNOLDS, CAROLINE	BAL	018	15TH WAR
REYNOLDS, CAROLINE MISS-	BAL	315	20TH WAR
REYNOLDS, CHARLES	ALL	243	CUMBERLA
REYNOLDS, CHARLES E.	BAL	081	18TH WAR
REYNOLDS, CHARLES F.	BAL	347	1ST DIST
REYNOLDS, CHRISTIAN*	BAL	332	3RD WARD
REYNOLDS, CCMFORT E.	WOR	199	8TH E DI
REYNOLDS, D. ESTE	BAL	186	11TH WAR
REYNOLDS, DAVID	CEC	213	7TH E DI
REYNOLDS, DAVID	CEC	208	7TH E DI
REYNOLDS, DE WITT C.	BAL	422	3RD WARD
REYNOLDS, DENNIS	ANN	415	HOWARD D
REYNOLDS, DOMINICK	BAL	128	5TH WARD
REYNOLDS, E. B.	BAL	152	1ST WARD
REYNOLDS, E. W.	BAL	308	20TH WAR
REYNOLDS, EDWARD	BAL	053	2ND DIST
REYNOLDS, ECWARD	BAL	080	15TH WAR
REYNOLDS, ELIJAH	CEC	150	PORT DUP
REYNOLDS, ELIJAH S.	QUE	182	3RD E DI
REYNOLDS, ELIZA	CEC	166	6TH E DI
REYNOLDS, ELIZA	BAL	072	18TH WAR
REYNOLDS, ELIZA*	BAL	355	3RD WARD
REYNOLDS, ELIZABETH	BAL	157	16TH WAR
REYNOLDS, ELIZABETH	BAL	136	16TH WAR
REYNOLDS, ELLEN	BAL	316	20TH WAR
REYNOLDS, ELLENORA	FRE	045	FREDERIC
REYNOLDS, ELLIS	CEC	162	6TH E DI
REYNOLDS, ENEAS	BAL	155	16TH WAR
REYNOLDS, EZRA	WAS	045	2ND SUBD
REYNOLDS, EZRA	WAS	054	2ND SUBD
REYNOLDS, FRANCIS	ALL	083	5TH E.D.
REYNOLDS, FRANK	ALL	135	4TH E.D.
REYNOLDS, FRANKLIN	ALL	206	CUMBERLA
REYNOLDS, G. W.	BAL	080	18TH WAR
REYNOLDS, GARRAWAY	MGM	358	BERRYS D
REYNOLDS, GEORGE	BAL	079	18TH WAR
REYNOLDS, GEORGE	BAL	168	6TH WARD
REYNOLDS, GEORGE	BAL	154	1ST WARD
REYNOLDS, GOVAN	BAL	065	15TH WAR
REYNOLDS, GRAFTON M.	BAL	079	18TH WAR
REYNOLDS, GREENBURY	MGM	364	BERRYS D
REYNOLDS, HAINS	CEC	166	6TH E DI
REYNOLDS, HARRIET	BAL	316	20TH WAR
REYNOLDS, HENRY	HAR	010	1ST DIST
REYNOLDS, HENRY	CEC	167	6TH E DI
REYNOLDS, HENRY	CEC	171	6TH E DI
REYNOLDS, HENRY B.	WAS	258	1ST DIST
REYNOLDS, HENRY R.	BAL	032	4TH WARD
REYNOLDS, HERMAN	HAR	039	1ST DIST
REYNOLDS, HINDFORD	CEC	171	6TH E DI
REYNOLDS, HOSEN	BAL	347	1ST DIST
REYNOLDS, HUGH	BAL	329	7TH WARD
REYNOLDS, ISAAC	CEC	168	6TH E DI
REYNOLDS, ISRAEL	CEC	121	4TH E DI
REYNOLDS, JACOB	CEC	168	6TH E DI
REYNOLDS, JACOB	CEC	166	6TH E DI
REYNOLDS, JACOB	CEC	163	6TH E DI
REYNOLDS, JACOB	WAS	260	1ST DIST
REYNOLDS, JACOB H.	CEC	168	6TH E DI
REYNOLDS, JAMES	MGM	358	BERRYS D
REYNOLDS, JAMES	QUE	176	2ND E DI
REYNOLDS, JAMES	BAL	105	10TH WAR
REYNOLDS, JAMES	BAL	222	6TH WARD
REYNOLDS, JOEL	CEC	181	7TH E DI
REYNOLDS, JOHN	CEC	168	6TH E DI
REYNOLDS, JOHN	BAL	219	17TH WAR
REYNOLDS, JOHN	BAL	432	14TH WAR
REYNOLDS, JOHN	BAL	009	4TH WARD
REYNOLDS, JOHN	BAL	090	15TH WAR
REYNOLDS, JOHN	ALL	069	5TH E.D.
REYNOLDS, JOHN	ALL	083	5TH E.D.
REYNOLDS, JOHN	WAS	196	1ST DIST
REYNOLDS, JOHN	WAS	069	2ND SUBD
REYNOLDS, JOHN	WAS	095	2ND SUBD
REYNOLDS, JOHN	WAS	153	HAGERSTO
REYNOLDS, JOHN A.	BAL	346	7TH WARD
REYNOLDS, JOHN C.	BAL	024	4TH WARD
REYNOLDS, JOHN H.	BAL	281	7TH WARD
REYNOLDS, JOHN M.	BAL	199	19TH WAR
REYNOLDS, JOHN T.	CEC	168	6TH E DI
REYNOLDS, JONATHAN	CEC	165	6TH E DI
REYNOLDS, JOSEPH	CEC	169	6TH E DI
REYNOLDS, JOSEPH	CEC	169	6TH E DI
REYNOLDS, JOSEPH	CEC	169	6TH E DI
REYNOLDS, JOSEPH	BAL	187	11TH WAR
REYNOLDS, JOSIAH	BAL	086	4TH WARD
REYNOLDS, LATITIA J.	BAL	155	16TH WAR
REYNOLDS, LEONARD	BAL	087	18TH WAR
REYNOLDS, LEONARD	CEC	199	7TH E DI
REYNOLDS, LEVI	CEC	117	4TH E DI
REYNOLDS, LINSEY H.	BAL	290	7TH WARD
REYNOLDS, LOUIS	BAL	017	15TH WAR
REYNOLDS, LOUISA	KEN	220	2ND DIST
REYNOLDS, MADISON	BAL	091	15TH WAR
REYNOLDS, MARGARET	BAL	270	12TH WAR
REYNOLDS, MARIA	WAS	164	HAGERSTO
REYNOLDS, MARY	WAS	122	HAGERSTO
REYNOLDS, MARY	BAL	062	15TH WAR
REYNOLDS, MARY	CEC	168	6TH E DI
REYNOLDS, MARY	BAL	470	14TH WAR
REYNOLDS, MARY A.	WAS	261	1ST DIST
REYNOLDS, MARY E.	CEC	119	3RD E DI
REYNOLDS, MARY E.	BAL	197	6TH WARD
REYNOLDS, MICHAEL	BAL	263	20TH WAR
REYNOLDS, N.	BAL	117	1ST WARD
REYNOLDS, NELSON	BAL	057	18TH WAR
REYNOLDS, NORTON	BAL	207	6TH WARD
REYNOLDS, OWEN	PRI	003	BLADENSB
REYNOLDS, PATRICK	BAL	360	8TH WARD
REYNOLDS, PETER	WAS	261	1ST DIST
REYNOLDS, PHILENA	CEC	147	PORT DUP
REYNOLDS, PHILLIP	KEN	276	1ST DIST
REYNOLDS, PIZEME	BAL	278	12TH WAR
REYNOLDS, RACHEL A.	BAL	163	19TH WAR
REYNOLDS, RACHEL M.	CEC	147	PORT DUP
REYNOLDS, REBECCA	CEC	165	6TH E DI
REYNOLDS, RICHARD M.	BAL	083	15TH WAR
REYNOLDS, ROBERT	BAL	009	EASTERN
REYNOLDS, ROBERT	BAL	095	18TH WAR
REYNOLDS, RUBEN	CEC	166	6TH E DI
REYNOLDS, SAMUEL	CEC	166	6TH E DI
REYNOLDS, SAMUEL	CEC	124	5TH E DI
REYNOLDS, SAMUEL	WAS	260	1ST DIST
REYNOLDS, SAMUEL O.	HAR	038	1ST DIST
REYNOLDS, SARAH	CEC	180	7TH E DI
REYNOLDS, SARAH	BAL	282	20TH WAR
REYNOLDS, SARAH A.	CEC	170	6TH E DI
REYNOLDS, SILAS C.	WAS	199	1ST DIST
REYNOLDS, STEPHEN	CEC	168	6TH E DI
REYNOLDS, SUSAN	BAL	373	13TH WAR
REYNOLDS, SYLVESTER	HAR	051	1ST DIST
REYNOLDS, TEMSA	BAL	443	14TH WAR
REYNOLDS, THOMAS	BAL	125	2ND DIST
REYNOLDS, THOMAS	BAL	141	16TH WAR
REYNOLDS, THOMAS	BAL	165	1ST WARD
REYNOLDS, THOMAS	ALL	068	5TH E.D.
REYNOLDS, THOMAS	ALL	155	6TH E.D.
REYNOLDS, WILLIAM	BAL	294	12TH WAR
REYNOLDS, WILLIAM	BAL	035	15TH WAR
REYNOLDS, WILLIAM	BAL	316	20TH WAR
REYNOLDS, WILLIAM	BAL	415	14TH WAR
REYNOLDS, WILLIAM	BAL	340	13TH WAR
REYNOLDS, WILLIAM	BAL	278	20TH WAR
REYNOLDS, WILLIAM	BAL	167	19TH WAR
REYNOLDS, WILLIAM	WAS	051	2ND SUBD
REYNOLDS, WILLIAM	PRI	085	QUEEN AN
REYNOLDS, WILLIAM M.	CEC	167	6TH E DI
REYNOLDS.EDWARD	ST	308	1ST E DI
REYNOLDS.SAULSBURY B.	QUE	193	3RD E DI
REYNOLL, GEORGE	WAS	238	CAVETOWN
REYNOLL, JOHN	WAS	238	CAVETOWN
REYNULL, EVE A.	WAS	227	1ST DIST
REYNULL, SAMUEL	WAS	241	CAVETOWN
REYNULL, WILLIAM	WAS	251	1ST DIST
REYS.	BAL	190	2ND WARD
REYS, ANN O.*	DOR	447	1ST DIST
REYS, MACELINE	ALL	255	CUMBERLA
REYS, PHILIP	ALL	255	CUMBERLA
REYS, PRISSY*	DOR	447	1ST DIST
REYS, ROBERT	DOR	324	1ST DIST
REYSER, SEBASTIAN	BAL	251	2ND WARD
REYSTER, WILLIAM	BAL	459	8TH WARD
REYSTON, NANCY	BAL	189	19TH WAR
REYWORTH, MARIA	BAL	347	13TH WAR
REZER, GEORGE H.	ALL	112	5TH E.D.
REZIN, MARY	QUE	216	3RD E DI
REZIN, WILLIAM	QUE	215	3RD E DI
RGER, JANE	BAL	328	13TH WAR
RHAINE, HENRY	BAL	202	2ND WARD
RHAINE, JOHN	BAL	134	18TH WAR
RHAPP, JOHN	BAL	199	2ND WARD
RHEA, BENJAMIN F.	DOR	399	1ST DIST
RHEA, CAROLINE	BAL	054	9TH WARD
RHEA, MARTHA E.	FRE	161	EMMITTSB
RHEA, WILLIAM*	DOR	399	1ST DIST
RHEAD, WILLIAM	BAL	323	3RD WARD
RHEAKNOR, FRANCIS*	BAL	352	3RD WARD
RHEAM, SARAH	FRE	241	NEW MARK
RHEART, CONRAD E.	BAL	287	3RD WARD
RHEART, CONRAD E.	BAL	287	3RD WARD
RHEICKART, GEORGE *	FRE	326	MIDDLETO
RHEINHART, CHARLES	BAL	427	14TH WAR
RHEMINGSNYDER, GOTILIEB	BAL	268	7TH WARD
RHENWALT, JOHN	BAL	353	13TH WAR
RHETT, THOMAS S.	BAL	302	17TH WAR
RHEY, MATTHIAS	BAL	315	20TH WAR
RHIEL, CATHERINE	FRE	036	FREDERIC
RHIEL, JAOCB	FRE	011	FREDERIC
RHIGNETT, MARY	QUE	216	3RD E DI
RHIMIN, ELIJAH*	BAL	352	3RD WARD
RHIMON, ELIJAH*	BAL	352	3RD WARD
RHINE, ALOYSIUS	FRE	056	FREDERIC
RHINE, ELLEN	BAL	023	18TH WAR
RHINE, GEORGE	BAL	043	10TH WAR
RHINE, JOHN W.	ANN	476	HOWARD D
RHINE, MARIA	BAL	133	18TH WAR
RHINE, MARY	CEC	084	CHARLEST
RHINE, MARY	BAL	201	6TH DIST
RHINEHARDT, BERNARD	BAL	122	11TH WAR
RHINEHARDT, HENRY	BAL	123	11TH WAR
RHINEHARDT, JOHN H.	BAL	229	6TH WARD
RHINEHART, ABSALOM	BAL	028	2ND DIST
RHINEHART, ALICE E.	FRE	243	NEW MARK
RHINEHART, ANN	BAL	464	14TH WAR
RHINEHART, CATHARINE	BAL	025	2ND DIST
RHINEHART, CHARLES	BAL	213	6TH WARD
RHINEHART, CHRISTIAN	FRE	336	MIDDLETO
RHINEHART, DANIEL	WAS	017	2ND SUBD
RHINEHART, DAVID	FRE	243	NEW MARK
RHINEHART, FERDINAND	BAL	188	6TH WARD
RHINEHART, FRED	BAL	215	11TH WAR
RHINEHART, HENRIETTA	BAL	044	4TH WARD
RHINEHART, JACOB	WAS	090	2ND SUBD
RHINEHART, JOHN	BAL	048	2ND DIST
RHINEHART, JOHN	BAL	139	2ND DIST
RHINEHART, PHILIP	BAL	225	6TH WARD
RHINEHART, PHILIP	BAL	224	6TH WARD
RHINEHART, SAMUEL	WAS	080	2ND SUBD
RHINEHART, SAMUEL	WAS	159	2ND DIST
RHINEHART, SARAH A.	BAL	139	16TH WAR
RHINEHEART, JESSE	BAL	025	2ND DIST
RHINEHEART, JOSEPH L.	BAL	028	2ND DIST
RHINEHEART, SAMUEL	WAS	274	RIDGEVIL
RHINEHEART, SAMUEL	BAL	005	4TH WARD
RHINEHEART, SUSAN	WAS	129	HAGERSTO
RHINEHEART, SUSAN	WAS	232	1ST DIST
RHINEHILL, CONRAD	BAL	346	13TH WAR
RHINEMAN, OBEMILLA	BAL	158	11TH WAR
RHINEMAN, PHILIP	BAL	159	11TH WAR
RHINES, THOMAS	BAL	129	11TH WAR
RHINHARDT, W. H.	BAL	139	11TH WAR
RHIREHART, FREDERICK	FRE	266	NEW MARK
RHOAD, FREDERICK	BAL	245	1ST DIST
RHOAD, JOSEPH	BAL	321	1ST DIST
RHOAD, MARGARET	BAL	321	1ST DIST
RHOAD, WILLIAM	BAL	169	16TH WAR
RHOADES, GEORGE	FRE	380	PETERSVI
RHOADES, JAMES	BAL	008	18TH WAR
RHOADES, JEREMIAH	QUE	242	5TH E DI
RHOADES, LUCRETTA	BAL	210	11TH WAR
RHOADES, SARAH	BAL	063	10TH WAR
RHOADS, A.G.	FRE	019	FREDERIC
RHOADS, ELIZABETH	FRE	084	FREDERIC
RHOADS, HENRY	FRE	080	FREDERIC
RHOADS, JOHN	FRE	054	FREDERIC
RHOADS, JOSHUA	FRE	072	FREDERIC
RHOADS, PETER	FRE	383	PETERSVI
RHODA, CHARLES	BAL	405	14TH WAR
RHODA, ZACHARIAH	BAL	363	3RD WARD
RHODAN, FANNY	BAL	214	11TH WAR
RHODE, FRITZ.	BAL	107	2ND DIST
RHODE, JACOB JR.	WAS	006	WILLIAMS
RHODEMAUX, WILLIAM	BAL	377	8TH WARD
RHODEN, HESTER	TAL	063	EASTON D
RHODER, JOHN	BAL	264	7TH WARD
RHODERICK, JOHN	FRE	032	FREDERIC
RHODES, AMALKA	BAL	022	4TH WARD
RHODES, ANN	FRE	390	PETERSVI
RHODES, B.C.	BAL	247	12TH WAR
RHODES, BEACHAM	SOM	530	QUANTICO
RHODES, CHARLES E.	BAL	158	1ST WARD
RHODES, CHARLES S.	TAL	111	ST MICHA
RHODES, CHLOE	MGM	328	CRACKLIN
RHODES, CHRISTA	FRE	399	JEFFERSO
RHODES, DANIEL	WAS	109	2ND DIST
RHODES, DANIEL	WAS	214	1ST DIST
RHODES, DANIEL	ALL	144	6TH E.D.
RHODES, DNAIEL	FRE	357	CATOCTIN
RHODES, ELIZABETH	FRE	405	JEFFERSO
RHODES, FANNY	CAL	035	2ND DIST
RHODES, FRANCES	CAL	032	2ND DIST
RHODES, FRANCES	BAL	267	1ST DIST
RHODES, FREDERICK	ANN	457	HOWARD D
RHODES, FREDERICK	ANN	422	HOWARD D
RHODES, FREDERICK C.	BAL	064	18TH WAR
RHODES, GEORGE	FRE	228	BUCKEYST
RHODES, GEORGE	ALL	060	10TH E.D
RHODES, GEORGE	ALL	060	10TH E.D
RHODES, GEORGE A.	ANN	415	HOWARD D
RHODES, GEORGE C.	BAL	173	6TH WARD
RHODES, HARRIET	ANN	416	HOWARD D
RHODES, HENRY	BAL	021	4TH WARD
RHODES, HENRY G.	FRE	388	PETERSVI

Name	County	Page	District
RHODES, ISAAC	ANN	430	HOWARD D
RHODES, JAMES	ANN	418	HOWARD D
RHODES, JOHN	ANN	341	3RD DIST
RHODES, JOHN	ALL	228	CUMBERLA
RHODES, JOHN	ALL	199	CUMBERLA
RHODES, JOHN	BAL	146	1ST WARD
RHODES, JOHN	ANN	495	HOWARD D
RHODES, JOHN	WAS	193	1ST DIST
RHODES, JOHN H.	BAL	072	15TH WAR
RHODES, JOHN R.	BAL	195	19TH WAR
RHODES, MARGARET	BAL	033	9TH WARD
RHODES, MARGARETT	FRE	409	JEFFERSO
RHODES, MARTIN	ANN	495	HOWARD D
RHODES, MARY	CAL	033	2ND DIST
RHODES, MARY	CAL	025	2ND DIST
RHODES, MARY J.	CAL	036	2ND DIST
RHODES, MILDRED	BAL	316	20TH WAR
RHODES, PATRICK	ALL	075	5TH E.D.
RHODES, PERRY	FRE	324	MIDDLETO
RHODES, PETER	BAL	215	6TH WARD
RHODES, PHILIP	BAL	043	15TH WAR
RHODES, PRISCILLA	CAL	037	2ND DIST
RHODES, RACHEL	ANN	496	HOWARD D
RHODES, REBECCA	ANN	358	3RD DIST
RHODES, REBECCA	DOR	323	1ST DIST
RHODES, ROBERT H.	CAR	098	NO TWP L
RHODES, SAMUEL	CAR	410	2ND DIST
RHODES, WILLIAM	BAL	045	15TH WAR
RHODES, WILLIAM	ALL	074	5TH E.D.
RHODES, WILLIAM	ALL	003	3RD E.D.
RHODES,EMILY	ALL	003	3RD E.D.
RHODDICK, GEORGE	FRE	009	FREDERIC
RHODRICK, BENJAMIN	FRE	326	MIDDLETO
RHODRICK, PERRY	FRE	339	MIDDLETO
RHODRUC, JOSEPH	FRE	404	JEFFERSO
RHODRUC, LEWIS	FRE	407	JEFFERSO
RHODS, JACOB	WAS	115	2ND DIST
RHOES, ELIZA	CAL	037	2ND DIST
RHON, ANN	BAL	462	1ST DIST
RHONER, J.	BAL	449	8TH WARD
RHOODS, WILLIAM	BAL	022	4TH WARD
RHOPP, SOPHIA	CAR	397	2ND DIST
RHORE, FREDRIK	WAS	140	2ND DIST
RHORE, SUSAN	WAS	209	1ST DIST
RHORER, HARRIET	WAS	201	1ST DIST
RHORER, HENRY	WAS	221	1ST DIST
RHORER, HENRY	WAS	166	1ST DIST
RHORER, JOHN	WAS	222	1ST DIST
RHORER, JOSEPH F.	WAS	258	1ST DIST
RHORER, MARY	WAS	176	1ST DIST
RHORER, PHILIP T.	WAS	180	BOONSBOR
RHORER, SOLOMON	WAS	129	HAGERSTO
RHORER, SOLOMON B.	WAS	132	HAGERSTO
RHORER, SUSAN	WAS	174	FUNKSTOW
RHUET, JAMES	CAR	242	TANEYTOW
RHULE, SARAH	BAL	206	6TH DIST
RHUNE, ADOLPH	BAL	374	13TH WAR
RHUPEOCHT, HENRY W.	FRE	057	FREDERIC
RHYAN, FRANCIS	BAL	397	8TH WARD
RHYAN, MARTIAN	BAL	383	8TH WARD
RHYAN, MATHIAS	ANN	483	HOWARD D
RHYAN, THOMAS	BAL	172	11TH WAR
RHYNE, HENRY	ANN	450	HOWARD D
RHYNE, MARGARET	BAL	445	8TH WARD
RHYNE, MARY N.	CAL	024	2ND DIST
RIAB, JAMES*	DOR	440	1ST DIST
RIAB, JOSHUA*	DOR	431	1ST DIST
RIAB, LEAH	DOR	389	1ST DIST
RIAB, MARY	DOR	423	1ST DIST
RIAL, OLIAH *	BAL	378	1ST DIST
RIAL, HENRY	CAR	386	2ND DIST
RIAL, NATHANIEL	DOR	315	1ST DIST
RIAL, SARAH	DOR	312	1ST DIST
RIALER, JOHN	BAL	249	20TH WAR
RIALL, GEORGE	SOM	540	TYASKIN
RIALL, JAMES	FRE	203	5TH E DI
RIALL, JAMES H.	SOM	481	TRAPP DI
RIALL, WILLIAM	SOM	545	TYASKIN
RIALY, ALICE	BAL	215	11TH WAR
RIAN, ELLEN	ALL	241	CUMBERLA
RIAN, JAMES	ALL	240	CUMBERLA
RIAN, PATRICK	BAL	258	2ND WARD
RIANS, MARY	BAL	036	15TH WAR
RIAT, JAMES*	DOR	440	1ST DIST
RIAT, JOSHUA*	DOR	431	1ST DIST
RIBER, EHNRY	ANN	423	HOWARD D
RIBERT, JOHN	BAL	350	13TH WAR
RIBINSON, THOMAS	ANN	518	HOWARD D
RIBLEY, JOHN	ALL	031	2ND E.D.
RICAHRDSON,BENJAMIN-BLACK	FRE	246	NEW MARK
RICAND, JAMES B. *	KEN	214	2ND DIST
RICAND, LAWRENCE M.	KEN	273	1ST DIST
RICARD, JACOB	BAL	227	1ST DIST
RICARDS, JACOB	KEN	281	3RD DIST
RICARDS, JOHN R.	BAL	216	11TH WAR
RICARDSON, CHARLES	WOR	278	BERLIN 1
RICARDSON, JAMES	CAR	089	NC TWP L
RICARDSON, POLLY	WOR	316	2ND E DI
RICARDSON, SAMUEL	QUE	217	3RD E DI
RICARDSON,W ILLIAM	WOR	336	1ST E DI
RICAUD, MARY R.	ANN	521	HOWARD D
RICE, ABRAHAM	BAL	322	12TH WAR
RICE, ABRAHAM	WAS	129	2ND DIST
RICE, ADAM	BAL	280	1ST DIST
RICE, ADAM	FRE	139	CREAGERS
RICE, ADELINE	ANN	467	HOWARD D
RICE, ALEXANDER	BAL	143	5TH WARD
RICE, ANDREW	BAL	029	2ND DIST
RICE, AQUILSEN*	ALL	163	6TH E.D.
RICE, BENJAMIN	CEC	215	7TH E DI
RICE, CASPER	CAR	213	5TH DIST
RICE, CATHAIRNE	BAL	270	2ND WARD
RICE, CATHERINE	FRE	101	FREDERIC
RICE, CATO	BAL	294	20TH WAR
RICE, CHARLES	CEC	012	ELKTON 3
RICE, CHARLES	BAL	033	18TH WAR
RICE, CHARLES	BAL	398	1ST DIST
RICE, CHARLOTT	CEC	053	1ST E DI
RICE, CHARLOTTE	FRE	240	NEW MARK
RICE, CHARLOTTE	CEC	180	7TH E DI
RICE, DANIEL	BAL	462	1ST DIST
RICE, DANIEL	BAL	396	8TH WARD
RICE, DANIEL	WAS	177	1ST DIST
RICE, DANIEL	WAS	288	1ST DIST
RICE, DAVIC	ALL	161	6TH E.D.
RICE, DENNIS	ALL	045	10TH E.D
RICE, EBER	BAL	375	1ST DIST
RICE, EDWAO	HAR	170	3RD DIST
RICE, EDWARD	ALL	166	6TH E.D.
RICE, EDWARD L.	FRE	329	MIDDLETO
RICE, ELI	ALL	166	6TH E.D.
RICE, ELIAS	BAL	302	3RD WARD
RICE, ELIZA	HAR	159	3RD DIST
RICE, ELIZA	BAL	083	4TH WARD
RICE, ELIZABETH	HAR	154	3RD DIST
RICE, ELIZABETH	CEC	095	4TH E DI
RICE, ELIZABETH	FRE	392	PETERSVI
RICE, ELIZABETH	ALL	167	6TH E.D.
RICE, ELIZABETH	ALL	157	6TH E.D.
RICE, EMILY C.	TAL	010	EASTON D
RICE, FRANCIS	CEC	058	1ST E DI
RICE, FREDERICK	BAL	261	1ST DIST
RICE, FREEBORN	HAR	171	3RD DIST
RICE, GEORGE	FRE	136	CREAGERS
RICE, GEORGE	FRE	370	CATOCTIN
RICE, GEORGE	FRE	019	FREDERIC
RICE, GECRGE	BAL	211	19TH WAR
RICE, GEORGE	FRE	061	FREDERIC
RICE, GEORGE	HAR	091	2ND DIST
RICE, GEORGE	ALL	166	6TH E.D.
RICE, GEORGE	ALL	166	6TH E.D.
RICE, GEORGE B.	FRE	405	JEFFERSO
RICE, GOERGE	BAL	150	5TH WARD
RICE, GRAFTON J.	FRE	061	FREDERIC
RICE, HANNAH	CEC	184	7TH E DI
RICE, HARKLESS	HAR	181	3RD DIST
RICE, HENRY	FRE	370	CATOCTIN
RICE, HENRY	FRE	341	MIDDLETO
RICE, HENRY	WAS	129	2ND DIST
RICE, HENRY	WAS	216	1ST DIST
RICE, ISAAC	ALL	157	6TH E.D.
RICE, JACOB	ALL	167	6TH E.D.
RICE, JACOB	BAL	270	2ND WARD
RICE, JACOB	WAS	299	1ST DIST
RICE, JACOB	WAS	298	1ST DIST
RICE, JACOB	FRE	371	CATOCTIN
RICE, JACOB	BAL	309	20TH WAR
RICE, JAMES	WAS	089	2ND SUBD
RICE, JAMES	ALL	235	CUMBERLA
RICE, JESSE L.	MGM	408	MEDLEY 3
RICE, JOHN	HAR	065	1ST DIST
RICE, JOHN	HAR	186	3RD DIST
RICE, JOHN	FRE	374	CATOCTIN
RICE, JOHN	BAL	211	19TH WAR
RICE, JOHN	ALL	157	6TH E.D.
RICE, JOHN	ALL	166	6TH E.D.
RICE, JOHN	BAL	308	1ST DIST
RICE, JOHN	ANN	328	2ND DIST
RICE, JOHN	BAL	150	1ST WARD
RICE, JOHN	BAL	111	5TH WARD
RICE, JOHN	TAL	100	ST MICHA
RICE, JOHN	WAS	164	2ND DIST
RICE, JOHN	WAS	192	1ST DIST
RICE, JOHN HY	FRE	114	CREAGERS
RICE, JOHN M.	TAL	010	EASTON D
RICE, JOHN T.	BAL	341	13TH WAR
RICE, JOSEPH	WAS	273	RIDGEVIL
RICE, JOSEPH	WAS	213	1ST DIST
RICE, JOSHUA	ALL	160	6TH E.D.
RICE, JUDAH	BAL	029	9TH WARD
RICE, KETA	HAR	187	3RD DIST
RICE, LAWRENCE	BAL	261	1ST DIST
RICE, LEVI	ALL	167	6TH E.D.
RICE, LEVIN	FRE	405	JEFFERSO
RICE, LEWIS	FRE	033	FREDERIC
RICE, LEWIS	SOM	399	BRINKLEY
RICE, MARALLIS	BAL	046	9TH WARD
RICE, MARGARET	ALL	220	CUMBERLA
RICE, MARGARET	BAL	176	16TH WAR
RICE, MARGARET	ST	337	4TH E DI
RICE, MARGARET	HAR	178	3RD DIST
RICE, MARTHA	FRE	405	JEFFERSO
RICE, MARTHA	ST	273	3RD E DI
RICE, MARTHA A.	BAL	201	11TH WAR
RICE, MARTHA ANN	ALL	167	6TH E.D.
RICE, MARY	BAL	214	6TH WARD
RICE, MARY	HAR	154	3RD DIST
RICE, MARY	BAL	239	20TH WAR
RICE, MARY	CAR	361	9TH DIST
RICE, MARY JANE	BAL	339	13TH WAR
RICE, MECHOR	BAL	283	1ST DIST
RICE, MICHAEL	BAL	354	3RD WARD
RICE, MICHAEL	BAL	019	9TH WARD
RICE, MICHAEL	BAL	072	2ND DIST
RICE, MICHAEL	BAL	415	14TH WAR
RICE, MINA	ALL	165	6TH E.D.
RICE, MOSES	HAR	170	3RD DIST
RICE, MUHL	FRE	136	CREAGERS
RICE, NELSON	ALL	192	9TH E.D.
RICE, NICHOLAS*	TAL	019	EASTON D
RICE, PERRY	WAS	089	2ND SUBD
RICE, PERRY	FRE	061	FREDERIC
RICE, PETER	BAL	286	17TH WAR
RICE, PETER	TAL	100	ST MICHA
RICE, RACHEL	CEC	153	PORT DUP
RICE, REBECCA	FRE	054	FREDERIC
RICE, RICHARD	HAR	179	3RD DIST
RICE, SAMUEL	FRE	135	CREAGERS
RICE, SAMUEL	WAS	225	1ST DIST
RICE, SAMUEL E.	BAL	409	14TH WAR
RICE, SARAH	WAS	225	1ST DIST
RICE, SARAH	WAS	090	2ND SUBD
RICE, SARAH	BAL	219	12TH WAR
RICE, SEBASTIAN	BAL	302	3RD WARD
RICE, SHARLOTT	HAR	178	3RD DIST
RICE, SOLOMON	HAR	170	3RD DIST
RICE, SOLOMON	ALL	167	6TH E.D.
RICE, SOPHIA	FRE	371	CATOCTIN
RICE, SUSAN	CEC	058	1ST E DI
RICE, THOMAS	BAL	019	1ST WARD
RICE, THOMAS	BAL	113	1ST WARD
RICE, THOMAS H.	BAL	042	15TH WAR
RICE, THOMAS*	SOM	399	BRINKLEY
RICE, WELSEY A.	FRE	136	CREAGERS
RICE, WILLIAM	HAR	181	3RD DIST
RICE, WILLIAM	MGM	427	MEDLEY 3
RICE, WILLIAM	TAL	027	EASTON D
RICE, WILLIAM T.	BAL	381	3RD WARD
RICELAND, ANDREW	ALL	230	CUMBERLA
RICELAND, FREDERICK	ALL	228	CUMBERLA
RICELAND, GEORGE	ALL	230	CUMBERLA
RICELAND, MARGARET	ALL	228	CUMBERLA
RICELAND, MARGARET	ALL	230	CUMBERLA
RICERSON, SOLOMON	CAR	227	5TH DIST
RICESINGER, LOUIS F. *	BAL	040	18TH WAR
RICEY, PETER *	ALL	157	6TH E.D.
RICH, ARMISTEAD	BAL	246	6TH WARD
RICH, ARTHUR	BAL	058	15TH WAR
RICH, ARTHUR DR.	BAL	374	13TH WAR
RICH, BAZIL	BAL	215	6TH WARD
RICH, BENJAMIN-BLACK	CAR	159	NO TWP L
RICH, DANIEL-BLACK	CAR	075	NO TWP L
RICH, CANIEL-BLACK	CAR	167	NO TWP L
RICH, DANIL	DOR	440	1ST DIST
RICH, EDWARD	DOR	423	1ST DIST
RICH, ELIZABETH	WOR	192	8TH E DI
RICH, ENNALS-BLACK	CAR	140	NO TWP L
RICH, GABRIEL*	DOR	406	1ST DIST
RICH, GEORGE	BAL	171	1ST WARD
RICH, GEORGE L.	BAL	227	2ND WARD
RICH, GEORRGE	WOR	195	8TH E DI
RICH, HARRISON	CAR	065	NO TWP L
RICH, HENRIETTA-BLACK	CAR	167	NO TWP L
RICH, JAMES*	DOR	440	1ST DIST
RICH, JOHN	DOR	428	1ST DIST
RICH, JOHN	CAR	108	NO TWP L
RICH, JOHN	BAL	441	8TH WARD
RICH, JOHN	BAL	459	8TH WARD
RICH, JOHN-BLACK	CAR	168	NO TWP L
RICH, JOSEPH	BAL	110	2ND DIST
RICH, JOSEPH-BLACK	CAR	170	NO TWP L
RICH, M.M.	ANN	271	ANNAPOLI
RICH, MARCELLUS-BLACK	CAR	128	NO TWP L
RICH, MARGARET	BAL	407	8TH WARD
RICH, MICHAEL *	BAL	359	1ST DIST
RICH, PETER	CAR	164	NO TWP L
RICH, ROBERT	BAL	122	11TH WAR
RICH, SAMUEL-BLACK	CAR	146	NO TWP L
RICH, SARAH R.	BAL	032	4TH WARD
RICH, SUSAN	BAL	461	1ST DIST
RICH, THOMAS	WOR	198	8TH E DI
RICH, THOMAS J.	CAR	111	NO TWP L
RICH, WILLIAM	SOM	504	SALISBUR
RICHADS, LOGARUS	ALL	086	5TH E.D.
RICHADSON, BENJAMIN A.	CAR	167	NO TWP L
RICHADSON, HENRIETTA*	DOR	378	1ST DIST
RICHADSON, JAMES H.	TAL	086	ST MICHA
RICHADSON, JOSEPH	WOR	307	2ND E DI
RICHARD, ANTHONY	BAL	135	16TH WAR
RICHARD, CATHERINE	CHA	289	MIDDLETO
RICHARD, CHRISTIAN	WAS	257	1ST DIST
RICHARD, DANIEL *	CAR	344	6TH DIST
RICHARD, GEORGE	BAL	337	13TH WAR
RICHARD, GEORGE	WAS	128	2ND DIST
RICHARD, GEORGE	BAL	105	2ND DIST
RICHARD, HARRY	BAL	161	19TH WAR
RICHARD, ISABELLA	BAL	136	5TH WARD
RICHARD, JACOB	WAS	276	RIDGEVIL
RICHARD, JAMES	KEN	270	1ST DIST
RICHARD, JAMES	CEC	135	6TH E DI
RICHARD, JOHN	FRE	077	FREDERIC
RICHARD, JOHN	FRE	004	FREDERIC
RICHARD, JOHN	BAL	100	5TH WARD
RICHARD, JOSEPH	BAL	140	1ST WARD
RICHARD, JOSEPH	BAL	125	1ST WARD
RICHARD, JOSEPH	BAL	129	11TH WAR
RICHARD, JULIAN	WAS	287	1ST DIST
RICHARD, LEWIS	BAL	427	14TH WAR
RICHARD, MARTIN	BAL	144	1ST WARD
RICHARD, MARY	BAL	105	2ND DIST
RICHARD, MARY	BAL	271	20TH WAR
RICHARD, SAMUEL	BAL	188	11TH WAR
RICHARD, STEPHEN	BAL	118	5TH WARD
RICHARD, V.P.	BAL	118	5TH WARD
RICHARDS, ABRAHAM	FRE	400	JEFFERSO
RICHARDS, ADAM	BAL	343	7TH WARD
RICHARDS, AMAN	BAL	235	1ST DIST
RICHARDS, ANN	BAL	062	2ND DIST
RICHARDS, ANN	BAL	321	12TH WAR
RICHARDS, ANN	CEC	199	7TH E DI
RICHARDS, ANN	MGM	438	CLARKSTR
RICHARDS, ANN	PRI	049	AQUASCO
RICHARDS, BRIDGET	BAL	227	2ND WARD
RICHARDS, CATHERINE	CHA	250	MIDDLETO
RICHARDS, CHARLES	BAL	452	14TH WAR
RICHARDS, CHARLES	CAR	175	8TH DIST
RICHARDS, CHARLES E.	BAL	133	1ST WARD
RICHARDS, CHRISTENA	CHA	251	MIDDLETO
RICHARDS, DANIEL	CAR	179	8TH DIST
RICHARDS, DANIEL	BAL	041	9TH WARD
RICHARDS, DAVID	CAR	187	8TH DIST
RICHARDS, DAVID W.	CAR	177	8TH DIST
RICHARDS, E. C.	BAL	471	14TH WAR
RICHARDS, EDRED	BAL	071	2ND DIST
RICHARDS, EDWARD	HAR	188	3RD DIST
RICHARDS, ELIZA	BAL	402	8TH WARD
RICHARDS, ELIZA M.	CHA	273	ALLENS F
RICHARDS, ELIZABETH	BAL	289	12TH WAR
RICHARDS, ELLEN	PRI	053	AQUASCO
RICHARDS, FRANCIS	BAL	272	17TH WAR
RICHARDS, FRANCIS A.	BAL	437	8TH WARD
RICHARDS, GEORGE	BAL	311	7TH WARD
RICHARDS, GEORGE	CAR	181	8TH DIST
RICHARDS, GEORGE	CHA	250	MIDDLETO
RICHARDS, GEORGE	CHA	230	BOJANTOW
RICHARDS, GEORGE	WOR	304	SNOW HIL
RICHARDS, GEORGE	WOR	296	9TH E DI
RICHARDS, GEORGE JR.	CAR	182	8TH DIST
RICHARDS, GEORGE S.	CHA	229	MIDDLETO
RICHARDS, GEORGE W.	BAL	049	18TH WAR
RICHARDS, HARRIET-BLACK	CAR	097	NO TWP L
RICHARDS, HARRIETT	BAL	126	11TH WAR
RICHARDS, HENRY	FRE	382	PETERSVI
RICHARDS, HIRAM	ANN	358	3RD DIST
RICHARDS, ISAAC	ALL	222	CUMBERLA
RICHARDS, J.	BAL	139	1ST WARD
RICHARDS, J.	BAL	227	12TH WAR
RICHARDS, JACOB	FRE	400	JEFFERSO
RICHARDS, JACOB	CEC	171	6TH E DI
RICHARDS, JAMES	FRE	387	PETERSVI
RICHARDS, JAMES	BAL	236	1ST DIST
RICHARDS, JANE	PRI	053	AQUASCO
RICHARDS, JOHN	BAL	395	8TH WARD
RICHARDS, JOHN	BAL	068	10TH WAR
RICHARDS, JOHN	BAL	043	9TH WARD
RICHARDS, JOHN	BAL	021	9TH WARD
RICHARDS, JOHN	ALL	046	10TH E.D
RICHARDS, JOHN	BAL	337	13TH WAR
RICHARDS, JOHN	BAL	212	19TH WAR
RICHARDS, JOHN	CEC	062	1ST E DI
RICHARDS, JOHN A.	BAL	129	18TH WAR
RICHARDS, JOHN H.	BAL	210	11TH WAR
RICHARDS, JOHN L.	BAL	235	1ST DIST
RICHARDS, JOHN S.	WOR	339	1ST E DI
RICHARDS, JOSEPH	MGM	439	CLARKSTR
RICHARDS, JOSEPH H.	BAL	057	18TH WAR
RICHARDS, JUDSON	PRI	102	SPALDING
RICHARDS, LEAH	DOR	317	1ST DIST
RICHARDS, LEWIS	ALL	001	3RD E.D.
RICHARDS, MARTIN	BAL	145	1ST WARD

RICHARDS, MARY BAL 363 8TH WARD
RICHARDS, MARY BAL 235 12TH WAR
RICHARDS, MARY BAL 022 15TH WAR
RICHARDS, MARY BAL 101 10TH WAR
RICHARDS, MARY TAL 069 EASTON T
RICHARDS, MICHAEL ALL 068 5TH E.D.
RICHARDS, NOBLE CHA 249 HILLTOP
RICHARDS, OWEN BAL 277 1ST DIST
RICHARDS, PATRICK BAL 227 2ND WARD
RICHARDS, RACHEL A. BAL 201 6TH WARD
RICHARDS, RICHARD CAR 180 8TH DIST
RICHARDS, ROSE BAL 388 13TH WAR
RICHARDS, RUTH BAL 404 14TH WAR
RICHARDS, SAMUEL BAL 023 15TH WAR
RICHARDS, SAMUEL B. BAL 205 6TH WARD
RICHARDS, SOLOMON BAL 402 8TH WARD
RICHARDS, SOLOMON DOR 317 1ST DIST
RICHARDS, T.H.B. BAL 233 1ST DIST
RICHARDS, TERRENA CHA 230 BOJANTOW
RICHARDS, THOMAS CEC 172 6TH E DI
RICHARDS, THOMAS CEC 172 6TH E DI
RICHARDS, THOMAS BAL 417 1ST DIST
RICHARDS, THOMAS BAL 235 1ST DIST
RICHARDS, THOMAS BAL 171 2ND DIST
RICHARDS, THOMAS ALL 077 5TH E.D.
RICHARDS, THOMAS BAL 075 2ND DIST
RICHARDS, THOMAS J. ALL 085 5TH E.D.
RICHARDS, WASHINGTON CEC 180 7TH E DI
RICHARDS, WILLAIM WOR 311 2ND E DI
RICHARDS, WILLIAM WOR 303 SNOW HIL
RICHARDS, WILLIAM MGM 436 CLARKSTR
RICHARDS, WILLIAM WOR 291 9TH E DI
RICHARDS, WILLIAM WOR 291 9TH E DI
RICHARDS, WILLIAM CEC 171 6TH E DI
RICHARDS, WILLIAM BAL 062 18TH WAR
RICHARDS, WILLIAM BAL 327 3RD WARD
RICHARDS, WILLIAM BAL 127 1ST WARD
RICHARDS, YRISTY BAL 143 11TH WAR
RICHARDSON, A. BAL 115 1ST WARD
RICHARDSON, ADAM DOR 416 1ST DIST
RICHARDSON, ALEXANDER-MUL FRE 452 8TH E DI
RICHARDSON, ALLEN BAL 033 9TH WARD
RICHARDSON, AMANDA BAL 245 6TH WARD
RICHARDSON, AMANDAN FRE 379 PETERSVI
RICHARDSON, ANDREW-BLACK FRE 434 8TH E DI
RICHARDSON, ANN BAL 120 11TH WAR
RICHARDSON, ANN BAL 399 8TH WARD
RICHARDSON, ANN BAL 344 7TH WARD
RICHARDSON, ANN M. WOR 201 3RD E DI
RICHARDSON, ANN-BLACK QUE 143 1ST E DI
RICHARDSON, ARMEL H. WOR 202 4TH E DI
RICHARDSON, ARMSTRONG CEC 196 6TH E DI
RICHARDSON, ARNOLD HAR 107 2ND DIST
RICHARDSON, B. BAL 126 1ST WARD
RICHARDSON, B.C. BAL 236 12TH WAR
RICHARDSON, BEN BAL 281 2ND WARD
RICHARDSON, BENJAMIN BAL 247 12TH WAR
RICHARDSON, BENJAMIN BAL 078 10TH WAR
RICHARDSON, BENJAMIN MGM 396 ROCKERLE
RICHARDSON, BENJAMIN CEC 071 5TH E DI
RICHARDSON, BENJAMIN WOR 309 2ND E DI
RICHARDSON, BENJAMIN WOR 302 SNOW HIL
RICHARDSON, BENJAMIN WOR 322 1ST E DI
RICHARDSON, CATHARINE HAR 077 BEL AIR
RICHARDSON, CATHERINE BAL 115 18TH WAR
RICHARDSON, CATHERINE M. BAL 398 8TH WARD
RICHARDSON, CECELIA BAL 162 6TH WARD
RICHARDSON, CHARLE BAL 072 1ST WARD
RICHARDSON, CHARLES BAL 139 1ST WARD
RICHARDSON, CHARLES BAL 178 16TH WAR
RICHARDSON, CHARLES BAL 257 20TH WAR
RICHARDSON, CHARLES TAL 070 EASTON T
RICHARDSON, CHARLES DR- BAL 311 1ST DIST
RICHARDSON, CHARLOTTA CEC 202 6TH E DI
RICHARDSON, CHARLOTTE PRI 022 VANSVILL
RICHARDSON, CORDELIA FRE 298 WOODSBOR
RICHARDSON, DAVID WOR 299 SNOW HIL
RICHARDSON, DAVID BAL 414 8TH WARD
RICHARDSON, DAVIS FRE 206 BUCKEYST
RICHARDSON, DELEA BAL 301 12TH WAR
RICHARDSON, DOLLY SOM 422 PRINCESS
RICHARDSON, E. CEC 050 1ST E DI
RICHARDSON, EDWARD DOR 416 1ST DIST
RICHARDSON, EDWARD CEC 197 7TH E DI
RICHARDSON, EDWARD BAL 076 4TH WARD
RICHARDSON, EDWARD J. BAL 381 13TH WAR
RICHARDSON, EDWARD V. BAL 088 18TH WAR
RICHARDSON, EDWARD* DOR 417 1ST DIST
RICHARDSON, ELI BAL 250 20TH WAR
RICHARDSON, ELIAS G. HAR 101 2ND DIST
RICHARDSON, ELISHA BAL 094 5TH WARD
RICHARDSON, ELIZ BAL 243 12TH WAR
RICHARDSON, ELIZA BAL 060 10TH WAR
RICHARDSON, ELIZA BAL 108 18TH WAR
RICHARDSON, ELIZA CAR 146 NO TWP L
RICHARDSON, ELIZABETH HAR 085 2ND DIST
RICHARDSON, ELIZABETH MGM 442 CLARKSTR
RICHARDSON, ELLEN BAL 133 5TH WARD
RICHARDSON, EMMANUEL-BLAC QUE 197 3RD E DI
RICHARDSON, EPHRAIM FRE 263 NEW MARK
RICHARDSON, EZEKIEL HAR 054 1ST DIST
RICHARDSON, FRANCIS WOR 303 SNOW HIL
RICHARDSON, FRANCIS SOM 355 BRINKLEY
RICHARDSON, FRISBY KEN 277 1ST DIST
RICHARDSON, GEORGE WOR 287 BERLIN 1
RICHARDSON, GEORGE DOR 419 1ST DIST
RICHARDSON, GEORGE BAL 118 18TH WAR
RICHARDSON, GEORGE BAL 235 20TH WAR
RICHARDSON, GEORGE BAL 161 1ST WARD
RICHARDSON, GEORGE BAL 124 1ST WARD
RICHARDSON, GEORGE P. BAL 280 2ND WARD
RICHARDSON, GEORGE R. BAL 108 10TH WAR
RICHARDSON, GEORGE W. BAL 405 1ST DIST
RICHARDSON, GEORGE W. ANN 482 HOWARD D
RICHARDSON, GEORGE W. BAL 366 13TH WAR
RICHARDSON, GEORGE W. ST 274 3RD E DI
RICHARDSON, H. BAL 114 1ST WARD
RICHARDSON, HAGER FRE 135 CREAGERS
RICHARDSON, HANNAH CEC 016 ELKTON 3
RICHARDSON, HANNAH ANN 272 ANNAPOLI
RICHARDSON, HANNAH WOR 189 7TH E DI
RICHARDSON, HARRIET WOR 312 2ND E DI
RICHARDSON, HARRIET-BLACK QUE 183 3RD E DI
RICHARDSON, HENNA-BLACK WOR 317 2ND E DI
RICHARDSON, HENRIETTA BAL 202 6TH WARD
RICHARDSON, HENRIETTA* DOR 378 1ST DIST
RICHARDSON, HENRY BAL 216 11TH WAR
RICHARDSON, HENRY HAR 115 2ND DIST
RICHARDSON, HENRY CEC 082 CHARLEST
RICHARDSON, HENRY ANN 343 3RD DIST
RICHARDSON, HENRY BAL 417 8TH WARD
RICHARDSON, HENRY WOR 307 2ND E DI
RICHARDSON, HENRY WAS 274 RIDGEVIL
RICHARDSON, HENRY TAL 046 EASTON T
RICHARDSON, HENRY PRI 048 AQUASCO
RICHARDSON, HESTER WOR 349 1ST E DI
RICHARDSON, HESTER-MULATT BAL 245 2ND WARD
RICHARDSON, HUMPHREY SOM 422 PRINCESS
RICHARDSON, ISAAC FRE 169 5TH E DI
RICHARDSON, J.L. ALL 219 CUMBERLA
RICHARDSON, JACOB ANN 438 HOWARD D
RICHARDSON, JACOB BAL 263 1ST DIST
RICHARDSON, JACOB C. QUE 210 3RD E DI
RICHARDSON, JACOB-BLACK QUE 144 1ST E DI
RICHARDSON, JAEMS TAL 101 ST MICHA
RICHARDSON, JAMES WOR 270 BERLIN 1
RICHARDSON, JAMES ST 312 1ST E DI
RICHARDSON, JAMES WOR 186 7TH E DI
RICHARDSON, JAMES CAR 393 2ND DIST
RICHARDSON, JAMES DOR 416 1ST DIST
RICHARDSON, JAMES BAL 244 20TH WAR
RICHARDSON, JAMES BAL 248 20TH WAR
RICHARDSON, JAMES CHA 259 MIDDLETO
RICHARDSON, JAMES CHA 259 MIDDLETO
RICHARDSON, JAMES BAL 142 2ND DIST
RICHARDSON, JAMES BAL 232 2ND WARD
RICHARDSON, JAMES H. BAL 143 16TH WAR
RICHARDSON, JAMES K. BAL 111 5TH WARD
RICHARDSON, JAMES P. QUE 192 3RD E DI
RICHARDSON, JAMES-BLACK BAL 219 2ND WARD
RICHARDSON, JANE ANN 275 ANNAPOLI
RICHARDSON, JANE BAL 222 12TH WAR
RICHARDSON, JANE CAR 271 WESTMINS
RICHARDSON, JARVIS WOR 310 2ND E DI
RICHARDSON, JEMIMA ANN 298 1ST DIST
RICHARDSON, JEMIMA BAL 119 2ND DIST
RICHARDSON, JEROME DOR 416 1ST DIST
RICHARDSON, JESSE DOR 417 1ST DIST
RICHARDSON, JESSE DOR 467 1ST DIST
RICHARDSON, JETSON F. PRI 101 SPALDING
RICHARDSON, JOBE TAL 037 EASTON D
RICHARDSON, JOHN WOR 307 2ND E DI
RICHARDSON, JOHN WOR 300 SNOW HIL
RICHARDSON, JOHN WOR 276 BERLIN 1
RICHARDSON, JOHN WAS 090 2ND SUBD
RICHARDSON, JOHN WOR 332 1ST E DI
RICHARDSON, JOHN DOR 415 1ST DIST
RICHARDSON, JOHN FRE 212 BUCKEYST
RICHARDSON, JOHN CEC 211 7TH E DI
RICHARDSON, JOHN CEC 163 6TH E DI
RICHARDSON, JOHN BAL 444 14TH WAR
RICHARDSON, JOHN BAL 125 2ND DIST
RICHARDSON, JOHN BAL 190 6TH WARD
RICHARDSON, JOHN BAL 094 5TH WARD
RICHARDSON, JOHN BAL 183 16TH WAR
RICHARDSON, JOHN A. MGM 442 CLARKSTR
RICHARDSON, JOHN H. WOR 178 6TH E DI
RICHARDSON, JOHN P. WOR 266 BERLIN 1
RICHARDSON, JOHN R. BAL 320 1ST DIST
RICHARDSON, JOHN T. WOR 207 4TH E DI
RICHARDSON, JOHN T. CEC 108 3RD E DI
RICHARDSON, JOHN W. BAL 021 18TH WAR
RICHARDSON, JOHN W. MGM 357 BERRYS D
RICHARDSON, JOHN W. BAL 252 6TH WARD
RICHARDSON, JOHN W. BAL 359 3RD WARD
RICHARDSON, JOSEPH BAL 132 1ST WARD
RICHARDSON, JOSEPH BAL 113 5TH WARD
RICHARDSON, JOSEPH BAL 198 6TH WARD
RICHARDSON, JOSEPH CEC 103 4TH E DI
RICHARDSON, JOSEPH CAR 089 NO TWP L
RICHARDSON, JOSEPH CEC 122 4TH E DI
RICHARDSON, JOSEPH CEC 210 7TH E DI
RICHARDSON, JOSEPH CEC 214 7TH E DI
RICHARDSON, JOSEPH DOR 396 1ST DIST
RICHARDSON, JOSEPH BAL 236 20TH WAR
RICHARDSON, JOSEPH QUE 213 3RD E DI
RICHARDSON, JOSEPH ST 311 1ST E DI
RICHARDSON, JOSEPH P.W. WOR 299 SNOW HIL
RICHARDSON, JOSEPH T. ANN 298 1ST DIST
RICHARDSON, JOSEPH-BLACK FRE 190 5TH E DI
RICHARDSON, JOSHUA DOR 415 1ST DIST
RICHARDSON, JOSHUA ANN 351 3RD DIST
RICHARDSON, LAURA HAR 006 1ST DIST
RICHARDSON, LEAH SOM 424 PRINCESS
RICHARDSON, LETITIA BAL 114 15TH WAR
RICHARDSON, LEVIN DOR 467 1ST DIST
RICHARDSON, LEVIN WOR 178 6TH E DI
RICHARDSON, LITTLETON WOR 200 8TH E DI
RICHARDSON, LITTLETON WOR 312 2ND E DI
RICHARDSON, LOUISA-BLACK QUE 172 2ND E DI
RICHARDSON, LUCY BAL 108 18TH WAR
RICHARDSON, LUCY B. CAR 169 NO TWP L
RICHARDSON, M.M. ANN 272 ANNAPOLI
RICHARDSON, MARGARET BAL 126 16TH WAR
RICHARDSON, MARGARET HAR 075 BEL AIR
RICHARDSON, MARGARET HAR 164 3RD DIST
RICHARDSON, MARGARET BAL 431 14TH WAR
RICHARDSON, MARGARET WOR 296 9TH E DI
RICHARDSON, MARGARET B. BAL 251 6TH WARD
RICHARDSON, MARGARETT BAL 120 11TH WAR
RICHARDSON, MARGRETT CAR 076 NO TWP L
RICHARDSON, MARIA ANN 343 3RD DIST
RICHARDSON, MARIA WAS 292 1ST DIST
RICHARDSON, MARTHA BAL 163 11TH WAR
RICHARDSON, MARY BAL 109 15TH WAR
RICHARDSON, MARY BAL 110 15TH WAR
RICHARDSON, MARY MGM 440 CLARKSTR
RICHARDSON, MARY WOR 343 1ST E DI
RICHARDSON, MARY WOR 349 1ST E DI
RICHARDSON, MARY SOM 354 BRINKLEY
RICHARDSON, MARY CAR 111 NO TWP L
RICHARDSON, MARY BAL 072 4TH WARD
RICHARDSON, MARY BAL 201 19TH WAR
RICHARDSON, MARY C. BAL 338 13TH WAR
RICHARDSON, MARY C. WOR 309 2ND E DI
RICHARDSON, MARY E. TAL 009 EASTON D
RICHARDSON, MARY E. TAL 083 ST MICHA
RICHARDSON, MARY J. FRE 169 5TH E DI
RICHARDSON, MARY J. FRE 275 NEW MARK
RICHARDSON, MARY-BLACK FRE 191 5TH E DI
RICHARDSON, MARYAN BAL 387 3RD WARD
RICHARDSON, MATTHEW DOR 417 1ST DIST
RICHARDSON, N. BAL 157 1ST WARD
RICHARDSON, NANCY BAL 343 7TH WARD
RICHARDSON, NANCY BAL 251 17TH WAR
RICHARDSON, NANCY TAL 089 ST MICHA
RICHARDSON, NANCY WOR 330 1ST E DI
RICHARDSON, NANCY WOR 297 9TH E DI
RICHARDSON, NANCY WOR 293 9TH E DI
RICHARDSON, NATHANIEL SOM 449 DAMES QU
RICHARDSON, NICHOLAS KEN 221 2ND DIST
RICHARDSON, OLIVER QUE 173 2ND E DI
RICHARDSON, OLIVER BAL 108 15TH WAR
RICHARDSON, ORVILLE BAL 364 13TH WAR
RICHARDSON, PATIENCE BAL 175 16TH WAR
RICHARDSON, PETER DOR 418 1ST DIST
RICHARDSON, RACHAEL BAL 129 11TH WAR
RICHARDSON, RACHEAL BAL 124 18TH WAR
RICHARDSON, RACHEL MGM 327 CRACKLIN
RICHARDSON, RACHEL BAL 251 20TH WAR
RICHARDSON, RACHEL BAL 244 6TH WARD
RICHARDSON, RACHEL ANN 302 1ST DIST
RICHARDSON, REBECCA BAL 060 10TH WAR
RICHARDSON, REBECCA BAL 345 13TH WAR
RICHARDSON, RICHARD FRE 262 NEW MARK
RICHARDSON, RILY WOR 307 2ND E DI
RICHARDSON, ROBERT WAS 130 2ND DIST
RICHARDSON, ROBERT BAL 120 11TH WAR
RICHARDSON, ROBERT CEC 026 ELKTON 3
RICHARDSON, ROBERT CEC 025 ELKTON 3
RICHARDSON, ROBERT BAL 160 1ST WARD
RICHARDSON, ROBERT BAL 035 15TH WAR
RICHARDSON, ROBERT A. BAL 020 18TH WAR
RICHARDSON, ROSETTA BAL 039 4TH WARD
RICHARDSON, SABRAH * WOR 285 BERLIN 1
RICHARDSON, SALLY WOR 310 2ND E DI
RICHARDSON, SAMUEL WOR 301 SNOW HIL
RICHARDSON, SAMUEL QUE 196 3RD E DI
RICHARDSON, SAMUEL BAL 377 13TH WAR
RICHARDSON, SAMUEL BAL 377 13TH WAR
RICHARDSON, SAMUEL BAL 256 12TH WAR
RICHARDSON, SAMUEL BAL 399 8TH WARD
RICHARDSON, SAMUEL ANN 350 3RD DIST
RICHARDSON, SAMUEL ANN 353 3RD DIST
RICHARDSON, SAMUEL M. BAL 304 20TH WAR
RICHARDSON, SAMUEL P. HAR 002 1ST DIST
RICHARDSON, SAMULE WOR 329 1ST E DI
RICHARDSON, SARAH CEC 162 6TH E DI
RICHARDSON, SARAH CAR 079 NO TWP L
RICHARDSON, SARAH E. CAR 126 NO TWP L
RICHARDSON, SARAH E. FRE 060 FREDERIC
RICHARDSON, SARAH J.-BLAC FRE 434 8TH E DI
RICHARDSON, SEWELL CEC 019 ELKTON 3
RICHARDSON, SISTER A.F. FRE 197 5TH E DI
RICHARDSON, SKELTON BAL 049 2ND DIST
RICHARDSON, SKINNER DOR 417 1ST DIST
RICHARDSON, SOPHIA BAL 068 15TH WAR
RICHARDSON, STANLY* DOR 415 1ST DIST
RICHARDSON, STEPHEN BAL 383 3RD WARD
RICHARDSON, SUSAN BAL 255 1ST DIST
RICHARDSON, T.A. PRI 051 AQUASCO
RICHARDSON, TABITHA SOM 422 PRINCESS
RICHARDSON, THOMAS HAR 025 1ST DIST
RICHARDSON, THOMAS FRE 136 CREAGERS
RICHARDSON, THOMAS BAL 038 4TH WARD
RICHARDSON, THOMAS CEC 164 6TH E DI
RICHARDSON, THOMAS CEC 082 CHARLEST
RICHARDSON, THOMAS WOR 188 7TH E DI
RICHARDSON, THOMAS TAL 102 ST MICHA
RICHARDSON, THOMAS QUE 217 3RD E DI
RICHARDSON, THOMAS BAL 124 1ST WARD
RICHARDSON, THOMAS BAL 456 8TH WARD
RICHARDSON, THOMAS BAL 050 2ND DIST
RICHARDSON, THOMAS BAL 059 2ND DIST
RICHARDSON, THOMAS BAL 169 16TH WAR
RICHARDSON, THOMAS E. BAL 287 17TH WAR
RICHARDSON, THOMAS J. ANN 298 1ST DIST
RICHARSON, VACHEL BAL 201 6TH WARD
RICHARDSON, VALLIANT TAL 084 ST MICHA
RICHARDSON, VINCENT HAR 037 1ST DIST
RICHARDSON, VIRGINIA FRE 228 BUCKEYST
RICHARDSON, W. ANN 273 ANNAPOLI
RICHARDSON, W. L. BAL 283 20TH WAR
RICHARDSON, WASHINGTON ALL 263 CUMBERLA
RICHARDSON, WATERMAN CEC 208 7TH E DI
RICHARDSON, WILLIAM CEC 199 7TH E DI
RICHARDSON, WILLIAM CHA 261 MIDDLETO
RICHARDSON, WILLIAM DOR 414 1ST DIST
RICHARDSON, WILLIAM HAR 077 BEL AIR
RICHARDSON, WILLIAM BAL 204 17TH WAR
RICHARDSON, WILLIAM BAL 039 4TH WARD
RICHARDSON, WILLIAM BAL 195 19TH WAR
RICHARDSON, WILLIAM BAL 050 2ND DIST
RICHARDSON, WILLIAM BAL 148 2ND DIST
RICHARDSON, WILLIAM BAL 148 2ND DIST
RICHARDSON, WILLIAM BAL 227 6TH WARD
RICHARDSON, WILLIAM BAL 190 2ND WARD
RICHARDSON, WILLIAM BAL 029 15TH WAR
RICHARDSON, WILLIAM BAL 340 7TH WARD
RICHARDSON, WILLIAM WAS 130 2ND DIST
RICHARDSON, WILLIAM WOR 214 4TH E DI
RICHARDSON, WILLIAM WOR 224 4TH E DI
RICHARDSON, WILLIAM PRI 031 VANSVILL
RICHARDSON, WILLIAM PRI 050 AQUASCO
RICHARDSON, WILLIAM WOR 309 2ND E DI
RICHARDSON, WILLIAM TAL 003 EASTON D
RICHARDSON, WILLIAM E. BAL 383 13TH WAR
RICHARDSON, WILLIAM H. BAL 019 4TH WARD
RICHARSON, WILLIAM H. HAR 080 2ND DIST
RICHARDSON, WILLIAM H. FRE 257 NEW MARK
RICHARDSON, WILLIAM H. TAL 025 EASTON D
RICHARDSON, WILLIAM J. ALL 217 CUMBERLA
RICHARDSON, WILLIAM T. CEC 082 CHARLEST
RICHARDSON, WILLIAM W. PRI 047 AQUASCO
RICHARDSON, WILLIAM W. WOR 329 1ST E DI
RICHARDSON, WILLIAM-BLACK QUE 165 2ND E DI
RICHARDSON, WILLIAM-BLACK FRE 383 PETERSVI
RICHARDSON, WILLIAM-BLACK FRE 189 5TH E DI
RICHARDSON, WILLIAM-BLACK FRE 203 5TH E DI
RICHARDSON, ZACHERIAH ANN 463 HOWARD D
RICHARDSON, ZADCK WOR 309 2ND E DI
RICHARDSON, W ILLIAM FRE 234 BUCKEYST
RICHARES, JOHN ALL 085 5TH E.D.
RICHARSON, ALLEN BAL 155 1ST WARD
RICHASON, MOSES CEC 093 4TH E DI
RICHE, JAMES PRI 062 NOTTINGH
RICHE, THOMAS BAL 163 1ST WARD
RICHEE, ELIZABETH HAR 042 1ST DIST
RICHENBARGH, MARTIN WAS 205 1ST DIST
RICHENBERGER, JOSEPH BAL 006 15TH WAR
RICHER, MARY BAL 008 4TH WARD
RICHERDSON, CASSININ BAL 007 18TH WAR
RICHERS, NICHOLAS BAL 029 15TH WAR
RICHERSON, BENJAMIN HAR 180 3RD DIST
RICHERSON, ELIZABETH R. HAR 195 3RD DIST
RICHERSON, JACOB HAR 191 3RD DIST
RICHERSON, JANE CAR 198 4TH DIST
RICHERSON, NATHANIEL CAR 210 5TH DIST
RICHERSON, SAMUEL DOR 337 3RD DIVI
RICHES, ALEXANDER BAL 303 17TH WAR

RICHEY, CHARLES CEC 175 7TH E DI
RICHEY, ELIZABETH BAL 125 11TH WAR
RICHEY, JOHN CEC 174 6TH E DI
RICHEY, THEODORE BAL 153 2ND DIST
RICHEY, WILLIAM CEC 174 6TH E DI
RICHFIELD, ELIZABETH HAR 179 3RD DIST
RICHFIELD, FRISBY J. BAL 310 3RD WARD
RICHFIELD, MIRANDALE BAL 168 6TH WARD
RICHFIELD, WILLIAM HAR 194 3RD DIST
RICHHAMER, HENRY BAL 263 2ND WARD
RICHIE, JOHN L. BAL 469 14TH WAR
RICHINIS, AMELIA BAL 141 19TH WAR
RICHINSON, HOWARD BAL 134 1ST WARD
RICHINSON, JESSE BAL 267 20TH WAR
RICHIRZON, MARY E. DOR 354 3RD DIVI
RICHLE, CONRAD BAL 177 2ND WARD
RICHLY, EVERHEART ALL 176 7TH E.D.
RICHMAN, HENRY BAL 283 12TH WAR
RICHMAN, HORNET BAL 125 1ST WARD
RICHMAN, WILLIAM BAL 315 1ST DIST
RICHMOND, CAVID BAL 350 7TH WARD
RICHMOND, EPHRAIM FRE 438 8TH E DI
RICHMOND, FRANCIS ALL 027 2ND E.D.
RICHMONC, CEORGE BAL 362 1ST DIST
RICHMOND, HENRY BAL 349 1ST DIST
RICHMOND, HENRY BAL 127 1ST WARD
RICHMOND, JOHN W. BAL 138 16TH WAR
RICHMOND, MARY BAL 217 6TH WARD
RICHMOND, MARY A. BAL 216 6TH WARD
RICHMOND, RICHARD BAL 053 1ST WARD
RICHMOND, SAMUEL BAL 264 20TH WAR
RICHMOND, WILLIAM C. BAL 350 1ST DIST
RICHRADSON, MARY E. CEC 104 4TH E DI
RICHSTEIN, JOHN BAL 030 4TH WARD
RICHTER, CHRISTY MGM 336 CRACKLIN
RICHTER, CAVID BAL 013 15TH WAR
RICHTER, FREDERICK BAL 151 16TH WAR
RICHTER, FREDERICK MGM 417 MEDLEY 3
RICHTER, CEORGE BAL 040 15TH WAR
RICHTER, H. BAL 297 3RD WARD
RICHTER, HENRY BAL 279 1ST DIST
RICHTER, JAMES BAL 144 16TH WAR
RICHTER, JOHN BAL 010 18TH WAR
RICHWIN, HENRY BAL 415 14TH WAR
RICK, ELIAS CAR 378 2ND DIST
RICK, GOERGE BAL 045 1ST WARD
RICK, HENRY CAR 380 2ND DIST
RICK, PHILIP BAL 083 10TH WAR
RICKARD, JOSHUA CAR 229 5TH DIST
RICKARD, P. J. WAS 184 BOONSBOR
RICKARDS, JOHN CAR 224 5TH DIST
RICKARDS, JOHN A. WAS 002 WILLIAMS
RICKARDS, JONATHAN FRE 085 FREDERIC
RICKARDS, MARY DOR 317 1ST DIST
RICKARDS, THOMAS J. DOR 312 1ST DIST
RICKEARD, GREENBURY L. ANN 490 HOWARD D
RICKEL, JOHN BAL 280 17TH WAR
RICKENS, FREDERICK H. BAL 122 1ST WARD
RICKENTON, JONATHAN CEC 035 CHESAPEA
RICKER, ELIAS CAR 333 MANCHEST
RICKER, JAMES BAL 356 3RD WARD
RICKERBY, ALFRED BAL 391 8TH WARD
RICKERDS, WILLIAM MGM 328 CRACKLIN
RICKERMAN, HENRY ALL 120 5TH E.D.
RICKERSON, THOMAS CAR 228 5TH DIST
RICKERT, CEORGE BAL 180 16TH WAR
RICKERT, R.P. BAL 129 1ST WARD
RICKET, LOVRING BAL 230 1ST DIST
RICKET, MARY BAL 278 1ST DIST
RICKETS, ABRAHAM MGM 386 ROCKERLE
RICKETS, CAROLINE FRE 050 FREDERIC
RICKETS, CHARLOTT BAL 458 1ST DIST
RICKETS, CAVID KEN 212 2ND DIST
RICKETS, CAVID C. KEN 278 1ST DIST
RICKETS, EDWARD MGM 417 MEDLEY 3
RICKETS, JAMES MGM 429 CLARKSTR
RICKETS, JAMES HAR 174 3RD DIST
RICKETS, JAOCB MGM 411 MEDLEY 3
RICKETS, JOHN MGM 386 ROCKERLE
RICKETS, JOHN BAL 083 1ST WARD
RICKETS, LEONARD KEN 247 2ND DIST
RICKETS, MARGARET KEN 248 2ND DIST
RICKETS, MARGARET BAL 278 1ST DIST
RICKETS, MARTHA ANN 486 HOWARD D
RICKETS, MERCHANT MGM 404 ROCKERLE
RICKETS, NICHOLAS MGM 429 CLARKSTR
RICKETS, ROBERT MGM 365 BERRYS D
RICKETS, SAMUEL HAR 206 3RD DIST
RICKETS, T. M. HAR 205 3RD DIST
RICKETS, WASHINGTON MGM 430 CLARKSTR
RICKETS, WILLIAM T. MGM 385 ROCKERLE
RICKETT, BARBARA BAL 256 20TH WAR
RICKETT, JOHN BAL 007 4TH WARD
RICKETT, LOUIS BAL 380 8TH WARD
RICKETT, MARGARETT A. BAL 033 4TH WARD
RICKETT, THOMAS BAL 008 4TH WARD
RICKETTS, ACEY BAL 103 18TH WAR
RICKETTS, ANN BAL 120 2ND DIST
RICKETTS, ANNA CEC 049 1ST E DI
RICKETTS, DANIEL FRE 204 BUCKEYST
RICKETTS, DAVID BAL 457 8TH WARD
RICKETTS, DAVID F. BAL 352 7TH WARD
RICKETTS, FRANCES MGM 317 CRACKLIN
RICKETTS, HENSON MGM 317 CRACKLIN
RICKETTS, JIM-BLACK QUE 125 1ST E DI
RICKETTS, JOHN MGM 334 CRACKLIN
RICKETTS, JOHN MGM 315 CRACKLIN
RICKETTS, JOHN BAL 186 6TH WARD
RICKETTS, JOHN BAL 192 2ND WARD
RICKETTS, JOSEPH C. BAL 008 15TH WAR
RICKETTS, LEVIN H. QUE 149 1ST E DI
RICKETTS, MARGARETT BAL 351 7TH WARD
RICKETTS, MARTIN BAL 215 2ND WARD
RICKETTS, MARY CEC 049 1ST E DI
RICKETTS, MARY BAL 031 4TH WARD
RICKETTS, MARY CEC 085 5TH E DI
RICKETTS, MARY A. CEC 155 PORT DUP
RICKETTS, MARY J. BAL 105 18TH WAR
RICKETTS, MARY M. BAL 067 4TH WARD
RICKETTS, PHILIP BAL 380 8TH WARD
RICKETTS, ROBERT FRE 234 BUCKEYST
RICKETTS, THOMAS CEC 099 3RD E DI
RICKETTS, WESLEY BAL 163 16TH WAR
RICKETTS, WILLIAM BAL 271 1ST DIST
RICKETTS, WILLIAM CEC 091 4TH E DI
RICKETTS, WILLIAM CEC 186 7TH E DI
RICKETTS, WILLIAM CEC 017 ELKTON 3
RICKETTS, WILLIAM CEC 024 ELKTON 3
RICKETTS, WILLIAM CEC 003 ELKTON 3
RICKETTS, WILLIAM S. BAL 155 2ND DIST
RICKETTS, WINSTON HAR 119 2ND DIST
RICKEY, SOLOMON CEC 173 6TH E DI
RICKITS, LEAH A. DOR 453 1ST DIST
RICKMAN, BERNARD BAL 105 1ST WARD
RICKMAN, MARY BAL 360 13TH WAR
RICKORD, MARTIN WAS 133 2ND DIST
RICKS, ABERDEEN CEC 124 5TH E DI
RICKS, HEMAN BAL 046 1ST WARD
RICKS, WILLIAM BAL 369 13TH WAR
RICKTER, ALLCINDER BAL 011 18TH WAR
RICKTER, JOHN BAL 111 18TH WAR
RICKTER, JOHN JR. BAL 011 18TH WAR
RICLER, ALEXANDER CAR 273 WESTMINS
RID, ELI BAL 436 1ST DIST
RIDAWAY, MARTHA BAL 310 3RD WARD
RIDD, LCRISA BAL 185 2ND WARD
RIDDE, JOHN BAL 084 2ND DIST
RIDDELL, AGNESS BAL 251 1ST DIST
RIDDELL, ROBERT BAL 251 1ST DIST
RIDDELMOSER, WILLIAM A. WAS 248 SMITHSBU
RIDDEN, LUCY WOR 230 6TH E DI
RIDDER, FREDRICK HAR 200 3RD DIST
RIDDER, JANE BAL 139 2ND DIST
RIDDER, JULIA HAR 192 3RD DIST
RIDDER, SARAH A. HAR 192 3RD DIST
RIDDING, ABRAHAM KEN 251 2ND DIST
RIDDING, ALEXANDER KEN 242 2ND DIST
RIDDING, FRISBY KEN 242 2ND DIST
RIDDING, JAMES R. * KEN 285 3RD DIST
RIDDING, WILLIAM KEN 264 1ST DIST
RIDDINGER, JOHN CAR 340 6TH DIST
RIDDISH, GEORGE W. WOR 198 8TH E DI
RIDDLE, ADAM BAL 088 18TH WAR
RIDDLE, CATHERINE PRI 025 VANSVILL
RIDDLE, CONRADT BAL 417 8TH WARD
RIDDLE, ELISHA BAL 110 5TH WARD
RIDDLE, ELIZABETH PRI 041 VANSVILL
RIDDLE, ELIZABETH WAS 172 FUNKSTOW
RIDDLE, EMILY PRI 045 VANSVILL
RIDDLE, GEORGE BAL 084 1ST WARD
RIDDLE, GEORGE HAR 061 1ST DIST
RIDDLE, HUMPHRY CEC 192 5TH E DI
RIDDLE, JACOB PRI 041 VANSVILL
RIDDLE, JAMES BAL 004 4TH WARD
RIDDLE, JAMES A. ANN 441 HOWARD D
RIDDLE, JOHN CEC 203 6TH E DI
RIDDLE, JOHN CEC 186 7TH E DI
RIDDLE, JOHN CEC 159 PORT DUP
RIDDLE, JOHN PRI 030 VANSVILL
RIDDLE, JOHN W. BAL 316 7TH WARD
RIDDLE, LAWSON PRI 030 VANSVILL
RIDDLE, MARGARET BAL 379 8TH WARD
RIDDLE, MARY BAL 172 16TH WAR
RIDDLE, CTHA CEC 180 7TH E DI
RIDDLE, ROBERT BAL 012 2ND DIST
RIDDLE, SAMUEL PRI 021 VANSVILL
RIDDLE, SARAH BAL 096 2ND DIST
RIDDLE, SOPHIA PRI 020 VANSVILL
RIDDLE, SUSAN PRI 030 VANSVILL
RIDDLE, THOMAS CEC 160 PORT DUP
RIDDLE, WILLIAM CEC 159 PORT DUP
RIDDLE, WILLIAM ANN 441 HOWARD D
RIDDLEMAN, CHARELS G. FRE 264 NEW MARK
RIDDLEMESER, JOSEPH BAL 261 12TH WAR
RIDDLEMORE, JACOB FRE 264 NEW MARK
RIDDLEMOSE, SAMUEL D. FRE 312 MIDDLETO
RIDDLEMCSER, EPHRAIM FRE 079 FREDERIC
RIDDLEMOSER, JAMES L. FRE 419 8TH E DI
RIDDLEMCSER, JOHN D. BAL 454 8TH WARD
RIDE, FRANCIS DOR 448 1ST DIST
RIDEA, JOHN BAL 105 1ST WARD
RIDEANT, LEVIN DOR 440 1ST DIST
RIDEANT, RICHARD DOR 427 1ST DIST
RIDEANT, ROBERT DOR 441 1ST DIST
RIDEAWAY, MARY BAL 349 3RD WARD
RIDEHORN, SOLCMON WAS 240 CAVETOWN
RIDEN, MARGARETT BAL 116 11TH WAR
RIDENAUR, JACOB A. WAS 120 2ND DIST
RIDENBAUGH, ADAM FRE 378 PETERSVI
RIDENBAUGH, MARGARETT FRE 379 PETERSVI
RIDENHOEN, FANNY WAS 224 1ST DIST
RIDENHOUR, ADAM WAS 242 CAVETOWN
RIDENHOUR, CORNELIUS WAS 232 1ST DIST
RIDENHOUR, DANIEL WAS 244 SMITHSBU
RIDENHOUR, HIRAM WAS 204 1ST DIST
RIDENHOUR, ISAAC WAS 287 1ST DIST
RIDENHOUR, MAGDELENE WAS 258 1ST DIST
RIDENHOUR, MARTIN WAS 229 1ST DIST
RIDENHOUR, ROZEN WAS 287 1ST DIST
RIDENCUR, ANDREW FRE 20 5TH E DI
RIDENOUR, BENJAMIN WAS 166 HAGERSTO
RIDENOUR, BENJAMIN WAS 176 1ST DIST
RIDENOUR, CATHARINE WAS 144 HAGERSTO
RIDENOUR, CATHARINE WAS 102 2ND DIST
RIDENOUR, CATHARINE WAS 214 1ST DIST
RIDENOUR, CHARLES FRE 200 5TH E DI
RIDENOUR, DANIEL FRE 026 FREDERIC
RIDENOUR, DANIEL P. WAS 128 2ND DIST
RIDENCUR, DAVID WAS 166 HAGERSTO
RIDENOUR, DAVID WAS 176 1ST DIST
RIDENOUR, DAVID WAS 126 HAGERSTO
RIDENOUR, ELIZABETH WAS 195 1ST DIST
RIDENOUR, ELIZABETH FRE 066 FREDERIC
RIDENOUR, ELIZBETH FRE 153 10TH E D
RIDENOUR, FREDERICK FRE 357 CATOCTIN
RIDENOUR, GEORGE FRE 192 5TH E DI
RIDENOUR, GEORGE * WAS 160 HAGERSTO
RIDENOUR, HARRIET WAS 222 1ST DIST
RIDENOUR, HENRY B. WAS 195 1ST DIST
RIDENOUR, ISAAC WAS 020 2ND SUBD
RIDENOUR, J.W. WAS 010 WILLIAMS
RIDENOUR, JACOB WAS 176 1ST DIST
RIDENOUR, JACOB WAS 161 HAGERSTO
RIDENOUR, JACOB FRE 195 5TH E DI
RIDENOUR, JACOB FRE 332 MIDDLETO
RIDENOUR, JAOCB FRE 20 5TH E DI
RIDENOUR, JOHN WAS 146 HAGERSTO
RIDENOUR, JOHN D. WAS 153 HAGERSTO
RIDENOUR, JOHNATHAN WAS 136 2ND DIST
RIDENOUR, JOSEPH FRE 153 10TH E D
RIDENOUR, LEWIS WAS 159 HAGERSTO
RIDENOUR, MARY WAS 019 2ND SUBD
RIDENOUR, MARY A. * WAS 161 HAGERSTO
RIDENOUR, MICHAEL WAS 148 HAGERSTO
RIDENOUR, REBECCA FRE 374 CATOCTIN
RIDENOUR, REBECCA * WAS 160 HAGERSTO
RIDENOUR, ROSE FRE 315 MIDDLETO
RIDENOUR, SAMUEL WAS 249 1ST DIST
RIDENOUR, SARAH A.E. FRE 187 5TH E DI
RIDENOUR, SOPHIA FRE 192 5TH E DI
RIDENOUR, SUSAN WAS 139 HAGERSTO
RIDENOUR, SUSAN WAS 128 2ND DIST
RIDENOUR, WILLIAM FRE 110 CREAGERS
RIDENOUR, WILLIAM FRE 117 CREAGERS
RIDEOUT, ANN FRE 162 EMMITTSB
RIDEOUT, ASBUEES * TAL 108 ST MICHA
RIDEOUT, BARBARA-BLACK FRE 191 5TH E DI
RIDEOUT, CAOLINE BAL 431 8TH WARD
RIDEOUT, E.-BLACK FRE 200 5TH E DI
RIDEOUT, ELEX* DOR 444 1ST DIST
RIDEOUT, ELISHA DOR 323 1ST DIST
RIDEOUT, ELIZA BAL 294 7TH WARD
RIDEOUT, ELLEN-BLACK CAR 069 NO TWP L
RIDEOUT, HENRY TAL 109 ST MICHA
RIDEOUT, ISAAC FRE 284 WOODSBOR
RIDEOUT, JOHN DOR 444 1ST DIST
RIDEOUT, JOSHUA FRE 285 WOODSBOR
RIDEOUT, JUELY WAS 085 2ND SUBD
RIDEOUT, MARY BAL 149 2ND DIST
RIDEOUT, MARY E. WAS 148 2ND DIST
RIDEOUT, PETER BAL 247 1ST DIST
RIDEOUT, PHILIP-BLACK FRE 189 5TH E DI
RIDEOUT, SANDY DOR 437 1ST DIST
RIDEOUT, SARAH WAS 135 HAGERSTO
RIDEOUT, THOMAS-BLACK CAR 133 NO TWP L
RIDEOUT, THOMAS-BLACK FRE 422 8TH E DI
RIDEOUT, W.H. WAS 014 2ND SUBD
RIDEOUT, WILLIAM WAS 027 2ND SUBD
RIDER, ADALINE BAL 461 1ST DIST
RIDER, ALBERT BAL 250 20TH WAR
RIDER, ALEXANDER BAL 278 12TH WAR
RIDER, ALFRED FRE 130 CREAGERS
RIDER, AMELIA SOM 490 SALISBUR
RIDER, ANDREW CAR 256 3RD DIST
RIDER, ANSON WAS 018 2ND SUBD
RIDER, ARON BAL 081 4TH WARD
RIDER, CHARLES SOM 554 TYASKIN
RIDER, CHARLES E. SOM 528 QUANTICO
RIDER, CONRADT BAL 371 8TH WARD
RIDER, DAN BAL 238 1ST DIST
RIDER, EDWARD BAL 457 1ST DIST
RIDER, EDWARD HAR 068 1ST DIST
RIDER, EDWARD JR. BAL 176 2ND DIST
RIDER, ELIAS BAL 254 20TH WAR
RIDER, ELY BAL 223 12TH WAR
RIDER, EVAN CEC 023 ELKTON 3
RIDER, GEORGE HAR 104 2ND DIST
RIDER, GEORGE CAR 104 NO TWP L
RIDER, GEORGE WAS 146 HAGERSTO
RIDER, GEORGE W. WAS 142 HAGERSTO
RIDER, HENRY HAR 104 2ND DIST
RIDER, JACOB CAR 410 2ND DIST
RIDER, JAMES SOM 495 SALISBUR
RIDER, JAMES BAL 294 12TH WAR
RIDER, JAMES W. WOR 287 BERLIN 1
RIDER, JOHN SOM 489 SALISBUR
RIDER, JOHN BAL 132 18TH WAR
RIDER, JOHN G. BAL 457 1ST DIST
RIDER, JOHN W. SOM 494 SALISBUR
RIDER, MANUEL BAL 257 1ST DIST
RIDER, MARIA BAL 129 5TH WARD
RIDER, MARY BAL 284 20TH WAR
RIDER, MARY BAL 278 20TH WAR
RIDER, MARY E. SOM 516 BARREN C
RIDER, MARY M. BAL 107 15TH WAR
RIDER, MICHAEL FRE 174 5TH E DI
RIDER, NATHAN SOM 491 SALISBUR
RIDER, NOAH SOM 484 TRAPP DI
RIDER, NOAH T. WOR 229 6TH E DI
RIDER, PERRY WOR 191 8TH E DI
RIDER, PETER BAL 291 20TH WAR
RIDER, PHILIP SOM 524 BARREN C
RIDER, SAMUEL CAR 175 8TH DIST
RIDER, SARAH ANN 414 HOWARD D
RIDER, SOLOMON BAL 085 1ST WARD
RIDER, SOLOMON SOM 519 BARREN C
RIDER, STEPHEN CEC 037 CHESAPEA
RIDER, SUSAN SOM 530 QUANTICO
RIDER, THOMAS F. J. SOM 554 TYASKIN
RIDER, THOMAS J. SOM 529 QUANTICO
RIDER, WASHINGTON BAL 104 15TH WAR
RIDER, WILLIAM BAL 085 1ST WARD
RIDER, WILLIAM H. SOM 493 SALISBUR
RIDER, WILLIAM P. SOM 428 PRINCESS
RIDERWIN, GEORGE * WAS 160 HAGERSTO
RIDERWIN, MARY A. * WAS 161 HAGERSTO
RIDERWIN, REBECCA * WAS 160 HAGERSTO
RIDEWAY, JAMES W. BAL 301 3RD WARD
RIDGAWAY, ALEXANDER CAR 098 NO TWP L
RIDGAWAY, CATHARINE BAL 171 16TH WAR
RIDGAWAY, HENRY BAL 005 15TH WAR
RIDGAWAY, JAMES A. TAL 002 EASTON D
RIDGAWAY, JOSIAH BAL 333 7TH WARD
RIDGAWAY, PERRY BAL 173 6TH WARD
RIDGAWAY, PITTA G. TAL 120 ST MICHA
RIDGAWAY, S.C. BAL 241 12TH WAR
RIDGAWAY, SAMUEL S. TAL 102 ST MICHA
RIDGAWAY, SARAH TAL 120 ST MICHA
RIDGAWAY, SARAH CAR 109 NO TWP L
RIDGAWAY, SUSAN CAR 159 NO TWP L
RIDGAWAY, WILLIAM BAL 009 4TH WARD
RIDGAWAY, WILLIAM BAL 060 2ND DIST
RIDGAWAY, WILLIAM H. BAL 178 6TH WARD
RIDGAWAY, WILLIAM H. TAL 107 ST MICHA
RIDGDAN, MARY A. BAL 196 2ND WARD
RIDGDE, MARY ST 288 2ND E DI
RIDGE, CORNELIUS FRE 139 CREAGERS
RIDGE, GREEHBURY * FRE 140 CREAGERS
RIDGE, HENRY BAL 033 18TH WAR
RIDGE, SUSAN FRE 140 CREAGERS
RIDGEAWAY, HERY TAL 102 ST MICHA
RIDGEBY, CAROLINE BAL 149 11TH WAR
RIDGELEY, BETTY ANN 332 2ND DIST
RIDGELEY, DAVID BAL 049 15TH WAR
RIDGELEY, EUGENE BAL 127 1ST WARD
RIDGELEY, HIRAM FRE 314 MIDDLETO
RIDGELEY, J. S. BAL 045 9TH WARD
RIDGELEY, JOHN BAL 023 9TH WARD
RIDGELEY, JOSHUA FRE 345 MIDDLETO
RIDGELEY, SUSAN FRE 073 FREDERIC
RIDGELEY, SUSAN ANN 326 2ND DIST
RIDGELL, JOHATHAN ST 287 2ND E DI
RIDGELL, RICAHRD ST 287 2ND E DI
RIDGELL, URIAH B. ST 300 2ND E DI
RIDGELL, WILLIAM H. ST 288 2ND E DI
RIDGELY, A. G. BAL 143 11TH WAR
RIDGELY, A. T. BAL 324 12TH WAR
RIDGELY, AMELIA ANN 485 HOWARD D
RIDGELY, ANGELINA ANN 431 HOWARD D
RIDGELY, ANN ANN 503 HOWARD D

Name	County	Page	District
RIDGELY, ANN	MGM	332	CRACKLIN
RIDGELY, AUGUSTAS	BAL	202	11TH WAR
RIDGELY, BEAL	ANN	496	HOWARD D
RIDGELY, BENJAMIN	BAL	027	2ND DIST
RIDGELY, BETHENA	FRE	344	MIDDLETO
RIDGELY, CHAPMAN	ANN	501	HOWARD D
RIDGELY, CHARLES	ANN	501	HOWARD D
RIDGELY, CHARLES	ANN	470	HOWARD D
RIDGELY, CHARLES	ANN	448	HOWARD D
RIDGELY, CHARLES	PRI	060	NOTTINGH
RIDGELY, CHARLES C.	ANN	475	HOWARD D
RIDGELY, CHARLES G.	BAL	259	6TH WARD
RIDGELY, CHARLES J.	PRI	093	MARLBROU
RIDGELY, CHARLES W.	BAL	260	12TH WAR
RIDGELY, CHARLOTTE	BAL	241	6TH WARD
RIDGELY, CHRISTIANA	BAL	385	13TH WAR
RIDGELY, DANIEL B.	BAL	096	10TH WAR
RIDGELY, DENNIS R.	BAL	302	1ST DIST
RIDGELY, EDWARD	BAL	071	15TH WAR
RIDGELY, EDWARD P.	ANN	481	HOWARD D
RIDGELY, EHNRY	ANN	326	2ND DIST
RIDGELY, ELIZABETH R.	ANN	412	HOWARD D
RIDGELY, ELLEANOR	ALL	015	3RD E.D.
RIDGELY, EZRA	MGM	332	CRACKLIN
RIDGELY, FANNY	BAL	377	13TH WAR
RIDGELY, FRANKLIN L.	BAL	097	10TH WAR
RIDGELY, GEORGE K.	ANN	497	HOWARD D
RIDGELY, GREENBURY	PRI	092	MARLBROU
RIDGELY, HARRIET	BAL	260	12TH WAR
RIDGELY, HENRY	ANN	419	HOWARD D
RIDGELY, HENRY K.	ANN	512	HOWARD D
RIDGELY, ISAAC	ANN	511	HOWARD D
RIDGELY, J. LEE *	BAL	149	1ST WARD
RIDGELY, JAMES L.	BAL	268	1ST DIST
RIDGELY, JAMES L. JR.	BAL	052	9TH WARD
RIDGELY, JEMIMA	ALL	253	CUMBERLA
RIDGELY, JOHN	BAL	011	2ND DIST
RIDGELY, JOHN	ANN	443	HOWARD D
RIDGELY, JOHN	BAL	033	9TH WARD
RIDGELY, JOHN W.	BAL	276	1ST DIST
RIDGELY, JULIA	BAL	056	10TH WAR
RIDGELY, KITTY	ANN	522	HOWARD D
RIDGELY, LEWIS	ANN	501	HOWARD D
RIDGELY, LLOYD	PRI	060	NOTTINGH
RIDGELY, LOT	BAL	024	9TH WARD
RIDGELY, LOYD	ANN	500	HOWARD D
RIDGELY, MARTHA A.	BAL	081	4TH WARD
RIDGELY, MARY	BAL	242	12TH WAR
RIDGELY, MONICA	MGM	367	BERRYS D
RIDGELY, MRS. DAVID	BAL	207	11TH WAR
RIDGELY, NANCY	ALL	092	5TH E.D.
RIDGELY, NICHOLAS	BAL	129	18TH WAR
RIDGELY, NICHOLAS	PRI	063	NOTTINGH
RIDGELY, NICHOLAS R.	ANN	486	HOWARD D
RIDGELY, NINAM	FRE	347	MIDDLETO
RIDGELY, NOAH	BAL	187	11TH WAR
RIDGELY, PETER	BAL	370	13TH WAR
RIDGELY, RACHEL	BAL	363	13TH WAR
RIDGELY, RICHARD	WAS	008	WILLIAMS
RIDGELY, SAMUEL	ANN	501	HOWARD D
RIDGELY, WILLIAM	WAS	171	FUNKSTOW
RIDGELY, WILLIAM H.	BAL	099	15TH WAR
RIDGEWARY, HARRIET	PRI	012	BLADENSB
RIDGEWAY, ANN	PRI	102	SPALDING
RIDGEWAY, CHARLES	PRI	074	MARLBROU
RIDGEWAY, ELLEN	PRI	071	MARLBROU
RIDGEWAY, J.	BAL	448	1ST DIST
RIDGEWAY, JESSE	PRI	096	SPALDING
RIDGEWAY, JULIET	PRI	065	NOTTINGH
RIDGEWAY, THOMAS	PRI	097	SPALDING
RIDGEWAY, WILLARD	PRI	100	SPALDING
RIDGEY, ALFRED	BAL	252	20TH WAR
RIDGLEY, ANN S.	BAL	098	5TH WARD
RIDGLEY, CHARLES C. JR.	ANN	473	HOWARD D
RIDGLEY, CLARISSA	ANN	489	HOWARD D
RIDGLEY, CORRELLA	CAR	281	7TH DIST
RIDGLEY, F.A.	ANN	271	ANNAPOLI
RIDGLEY, HARRIET	BAL	193	17TH WAR
RIDGLEY, HENRY	ANN	503	HOWARD D
RIDGLEY, JAMES	BAL	064	10TH WAR
RIDGLEY, JOHN S.	ANN	412	HOWARD D
RIDGLEY, MARY	BAL	134	16TH WAR
RIDGLEY, MARY	BAL	109	2ND DIST
RIDGLEY, PHILEMON	ANN	489	HOWARD D
RIDGLEY, RICHARD	ANN	494	HOWARD D
RIDGLEY, ROBERT J.	QUE	158	2ND E DI
RIDGLEY, RUBEN	ANN	503	HOWARD D
RIDGLEY, SINGLETON	BAL	098	5TH WARD
RIDGLEY, WILLIAM R.	CAR	231	5TH DIST
RIDGLY, CHARLES	ANN	475	HOWARD D
RIDGLY, JACOB	HAR	193	3RD DIST
RIDGLY, JAMES	BAL	172	11TH WAR
RIDGLY, JANE	ANN	459	HOWARD D
RIDGLY, SAMUEL	ANN	486	HOWARD D
RIDGLY, SARAH	ANN	481	HOWARD D
RIDGLY, WILLIAM P.	ANN	481	HOWARD D
RIDGON, JAMES	BAL	298	17TH WAR
RIDGSON, WILLIAM A.	BAL	170	1ST WARD
RIDGWAY, ARTHUR P.	PRI	033	VANSVILL
RIDGWAY, DAVID	BAL	133	5TH WARD
RIDGWAY, ELIZABETH	PRI	015	BLADENSB
RIDGWAY, FRED JEROME	BAL	229	17TH WAR
RIDGWAY, JOHN W.	TAL	102	ST MICHA
RIDGWAY, LEONARD	PRI	012	BLADENSB
RIDGWAY, SARAH	BAL	366	3RD WARD
RIDGWAY, WILLIAM	BAL	295	7TH WARD
RIDING, A.G.	BAL	172	1ST WARD
RIDING, ANDREW	BAL	171	1ST WARD
RIDING, CONRAD	BAL	052	4TH WARD
RIDINGER, CATHARINE	CAR	304	1ST DIST
RIDINGER, JOHN	CAR	321	1ST DIST
RIDINGER, SAMUEL	CAR	314	1ST DIST
RIDJAWAY, ANNA*	TAL	048	EASTON T
RIDJAWAY, JAMES H.	TAL	010	EASTON D
RIDKEY, MARY	BAL	020	4TH WARD
RIDLE, BARBARY	BAL	335	13TH WAR
RIDLEY, ELIZABETH	BAL	309	7TH WARD
RIDLUS, ANN	BAL	079	2ND DIST
RIDMAN, DENNIS	BAL	042	1ST WARD
RIDMAUR, JOHN	FRE	088	FREDERIC
RIDNER, THEODORE	BAL	247	2ND WARD
RIDNEY, CATHARINE	BAL	268	1ST DIST
RIDNEY, JOHN *	KEN	266	1ST DIST
RIDNEY, MARGARET	BAL	012	9TH WARD
RIDOUT, ANN	ANN	353	3RD DIST
RIDOUT, ELISABETH	ANN	350	3RD DIST
RIDOUT, ELISABETH N.	ANN	350	3RD DIST
RIDOUT, EMMA	BAL	401	14TH WAR
RIDOUT, HORATIO	ANN	353	3RD DIST
RIDOUT, J.	ANN	270	ANNAPOLI
RIDOUT, JOHN	ANN	350	3RD DIST
RIDOUT, MARTHA	BAL	229	19TH WAR
RIDOUT, MARY	BAL	236	20TH WAR
RIDOUT, PERRY H.	BAL	001	9TH WARD
RIDOUT, SAMUEL	ANN	353	3RD DIST
RIDOUT, WEEMS	ANN	353	3RD DIST
RIDY, DANIEL	HAR	063	1ST DIST
RIEESINGER, LOUIS F. *	BAL	040	18TH WAR
RIEFLE, CAROLINE	BAL	087	4TH WARD
RIEGART, EMMA	BAL	249	6TH WARD
RIEGART, HENRY F.	BAL	248	6TH WARD
RIEL, RHEINHARDT	BAL	049	9TH WARD
RIELEY, MICHAEL	ALL	052	10TH E.D
RIELLY, PATRICK JR.	BAL	007	9TH WARD
RIELY, ALEXANDER	BAL	192	19TH WAR
RIELY, CHARLES	BAL	169	1ST WARD
RIELY, D.	BAL	148	1ST WARD
RIELY, E.S.	ANN	271	ANNAPOLI
RIELY, E.S.JR.	ANN	271	ANNAPOLI
RIELY, ELIZABETH	WOR	283	BERLIN I
RIELY, ELLEN J.	BAL	455	8TH WARD
RIELY, GEORGE	BAL	280	7TH WARD
RIELY, JOHN	ALL	023	2ND E.D.
RIELY, JOHN	ALL	140	6TH E.D.
RIELY, JOHN	ALL	127	4TH E.D.
RIELY, MARGARET	BAL	275	2ND WARD
RIELY, MARTHA	ALL	144	6TH E.D.
RIELY, MILES	ALL	073	5TH E.D.
RIELY, PATRICK	ALL	136	4TH E.D.
RIELY, PATRICK	BAL	358	8TH WARD
RIELY, PETER	ALL	141	6TH E.D.
RIELY, PHILIP	BAL	027	9TH WARD
RIELY, THOMAS	BAL	003	9TH WARD
RIELY, THOMAS	BAL	045	4TH WARD
RIELY, WILLIAM	WOR	226	4TH E DI
RIEMAN, EMMA	BAL	283	12TH WAR
RIEMAN, GOTLEIB	BAL	081	1ST WARD
RIEMAR, PETER	BAL	152	19TH WAR
RIEMAS, ROBERT	BAL	217	19TH WAR
RIEMER, ELIZABETH	BAL	255	2ND WARD
RIENDESILL, CATHARINE	WAS	213	1ST DIST
RIENDESILL, DAVID	WAS	214	1ST DIST
RIENDESILL, MICHAEL	WAS	213	1ST DIST
RIENEKER, MARY J.	BAL	103	5TH WARD
RIEPE, GERHARDT H. *	BAL	209	6TH WARD
RIER, FREDERICK	BAL	384	13TH WAR
RIERLY, JOHN	HAR	068	1ST DIST
RIERLY, WILLIAM *	HAR	049	1ST DIST
RIESSE, GERHARDT H. *	BAL	209	6TH WARD
RIESTER, HESTER A.	BAL	323	7TH WARD
RIFE, JACOB	FRE	147	10TH E D
RIFE, JOHN	WAS	166	1ST DIST
RIFE, MARGARET	BAL	370	8TH WARD
RIFELICH, CASPER	BAL	324	1ST DIST
RIFER, JOHN	BAL	359	13TH WAR
RIFFELL, ELIZABETH	HAR	147	3RD DIST
RIFFLE, JOHN C.	ALL	234	CUMBERLA
RIFFLE, SUSANNA	FRE	348	MIDDLETO
RIFFLE, URIAH	FRE	335	MIDDLETO
RIFHTER, DAVID	CAR	290	7TH DIST
RIGA, MICHAEL	BAL	281	1ST DIST
RIGAR, GEORGE *	BAL	132	18TH WAR
RIGART, CATHARINE	BAL	461	1ST DIST
RIGBES, ISAAC M.	BAL	139	1ST WARD
RIGBEY, EDWARD *	BAL	040	18TH WAR
RIGBS, JAMES P.	TAL	097	ST MICHA
RIGBY, AMILLA A.	CEC	175	7TH E DI
RIGBY, AQUILLA	HAR	029	1ST DIST
RIGBY, CHARLES H.	TAL	094	ST MICHA
RIGBY, ELIZA	BAL	055	15TH WAR
RIGBY, FRANCES	HAR	027	1ST DIST
RIGBY, GEORGE	BAL	361	1ST DIST
RIGBY, HENRY	BAL	319	3RD WARD
RIGBY, HOSEA	CEC	148	PORT DUP
RIGBY, MICHAEL	BAL	067	2ND DIST
RIGBY, PHILIP A.	BAL	173	16TH WAR
RIGBY, SARAH A.	HAR	069	1ST DIST
RIGBY, SUSAN	BAL	302	7TH WARD
RIGBY, WILLIAM	HAR	119	2ND DIST
RIGBYH, JEFFERSON	CEC	175	7TH E DI
RIGDEN, CALEB	BAL	291	20TH WAR
RIGDEN, HENRY	HAR	080	2ND DIST
RIGDEN, SUSANNA L.	BAL	179	6TH WARD
RIGDON, ANN E.	HAR	024	1ST DIST
RIGDON, BAKER	HAR	005	1ST DIST
RIGDON, ELIZABETH N.	HAR	005	1ST DIST
RIGDON, ELY	HAR	005	1ST DIST
RIGDON, FRANKLIN	HAR	005	1ST DIST
RIGDON, GEORGE W. S.	HAR	009	1ST DIST
RIGDON, JAMES	HAR	005	1ST DIST
RIGDON, JOHN	BAL	114	5TH WARD
RIGDON, M.	HAR	053	1ST DIST
RIGDON, MARY	HAR	052	1ST DIST
RIGDON, MARY	HAR	069	1ST DIST
RIGDON, MARY	HAR	052	1ST DIST
RIGDON, MICHAEL	BAL	154	2ND DIST
RIGDON, STEPHEN	HAR	005	1ST DIST
RIGDON, WILLIAM	HAR	023	1ST DIST
RIGELL, OSTEN R.	ST	282	3RD E DI
RIGELL, THOMAS	ST	282	3RD E DI
RIGERT, MARY	ALL	262	CUMBERLA
RIGG, EDWARD	BAL	106	1ST WARD
RIGG, SAMUEL	BAL	229	19TH WAR
RIGGAN, WILLIAM	DOR	303	1ST DIST
RIGGBY, LEVIN	BAL	299	17TH WAR
RIGGEN, ALFRED B.	SOM	428	PRINCESS
RIGGEN, ANN L.	BAL	389	13TH WAR
RIGGEN, ARELIA	SOM	393	BRINKLEY
RIGGEN, CHARLES	SOM	394	BRINKLEY
RIGGEN, EDWARD	SOM	395	BRINKLEY
RIGGEN, ELIJAH	SOM	508	BARREN C
RIGGEN, ELISHA	SOM	447	DAMES QU
RIGGEN, ELIZABETH	SOM	373	BRINKLEY
RIGGEN, EMORY	SOM	370	BRINKLEY
RIGGEN, HANNAH	SOM	374	BRINKLEY
RIGGEN, HENERETTA	SOM	400	BRINKLEY
RIGGEN, HENRY	SOM	422	PRINCESS
RIGGEN, HENRY J.	SOM	411	DUBLIN D
RIGGEN, ISAAC	SOM	378	BRINKLEY
RIGGEN, JASON	SOM	375	BRINKLEY
RIGGEN, JOHN	SOM	373	BRINKLEY
RIGGEN, JOHN	SOM	374	BRINKLEY
RIGGEN, JOHN	SOM	398	BRINKLEY
RIGGEN, JOHN	SOM	471	TRAPPE D
RIGGEN, JONATHAN	SOM	512	BARREN C
RIGGEN, JOSHUA	SOM	358	BRINKLEY
RIGGEN, LEAH	SOM	484	TRAPP DI
RIGGEN, LEANDER	SOM	461	HANGARY
RIGGEN, LEVI	SOM	370	BRINKLEY
RIGGEN, MARY	SOM	386	BRINKLEY
RIGGEN, MARY	SOM	428	PRINCESS
RIGGEN, MATILDA	SOM	371	BRINKLEY
RIGGEN, NANCY	SOM	373	BRINKLEY
RIGGEN, NOAH	SOM	373	BRINKLEY
RIGGEN, NOAH	SOM	400	BRINKLEY
RIGGEN, OBADIAH	SOM	368	BRINKLEY
RIGGEN, PETER	SOM	483	TRAPP DI
RIGGEN, SARAH	SOM	401	BRINKLEY
RIGGEN, SEVERN	SOM	373	BRINKLEY
RIGGEN, TAMER	SOM	477	TRAPP DI
RIGGEN, THOMAS	SOM	373	BRINKLEY
RIGGEN, WILLIAM	SOM	373	BRINKLEY
RIGGEN, WILLIAM	SOM	397	BRINKLEY
RIGGEN, WILLIAM	SOM	506	BARREN C
RIGGEN, WILLIAM H.	SOM	400	BRINKLEY
RIGGEN, WILLIAM W.	SOM	367	BRINKLEY
RIGGEN, ZEDEKIAH	SOM	505	SALISBUR
RIGGER, AUGUSTUS	BAL	002	4TH WARD
RIGGER, LAURENCE	BAL	001	4TH WARD
RIGGER, RODA	BAL	065	1ST WARD
RIGGER, TERESA	BAL	048	4TH WARD
RIGGIN, BYARD	WOR	191	8TH E DI
RIGGIN, CATHARINE A.	BAL	007	15TH WAR
RIGGIN, ELIJAH	WOR	237	6TH E DI
RIGGIN, ELLEN	BAL	104	10TH WAR
RIGGIN, GEORGE W.	WOR	225	4TH E DI
RIGGIN, HENRY J.	WOR	191	8TH E DI
RIGGIN, ISREAL	BAL	258	17TH WAR
RIGGIN, JOHN	WOR	191	8TH E DI
RIGGIN, JOSEPH	WOR	191	8TH E DI
RIGGIN, KELLUM	BAL	002	15TH WAR
RIGGIN, LEMUEL	WOR	187	7TH E DI
RIGGIN, LEVI	WOR	188	7TH E DI
RIGGIN, MARGARET A.	BAL	187	16TH WAR
RIGGIN, MARY A.	BAL	002	15TH WAR
RIGGIN, MARY ANN	BAL	283	17TH WAR
RIGGIN, PATIENCE	WOR	301	SNOW HIL
RIGGIN, SARAH	BAL	085	15TH WAR
RIGGIN, THOMAS	WOR	195	8TH E DI
RIGGIN, WILLIAM	WOR	186	7TH E DI
RIGGIN, WILLIAM D.	WOR	186	7TH E DI
RIGGINS, ELIZABETH	BAL	458	1ST DIST
RIGGINS, JAMES	QUE	248	5TH E DI
RIGGINS, JOSEPH	BAL	236	17TH WAR
RIGGINS, POLLY	WOR	340	1ST E DI
RIGGINS, RUTH	BAL	274	17TH WAR
RIGGLE, DAVID	CAR	277	7TH DIST
RIGGLE, GEORGE	CAR	277	7TH DIST
RIGGLE, GEORGE	BAL	287	1ST DIST
RIGGLE, HARRIET A.	BAL	008	15TH WAR
RIGGLE, HENRY	CAR	329	MANCHEST
RIGGLE, JACOB	CAR	329	MANCHEST
RIGGLE, LEWIS	CAR	332	MANCHEST
RIGGLE, LEWIS	CAR	329	MANCHEST
RIGGLE, LUCY ANN	CAR	277	7TH DIST
RIGGLE, PETER	BAL	289	1ST DIST
RIGGLER, HENRY	BAL	328	3RD WARD
RIGGLES, RICHARD	MGM	388	ROCKERLE
RIGGLES, ROBERT	BAL	088	18TH WAR
RIGGN, BETSY	WOR	292	9TH E DI
RIGGS, AGUSTUS	ANN	498	HOWARD D
RIGGS, ANTHONY-BLACK	FRE	221	BUCKEYST
RIGGS, ARTEMAS W.	ANN	507	HOWARD D
RIGGS, ASBERRY	FRE	306	WOODSBOR
RIGGS, BENJAMIN	BAL	213	17TH WAR
RIGGS, CHRISTIPER M.	BAL	134	18TH WAR
RIGGS, DANIEL T.	BAL	213	17TH WAR
RIGGS, ELISHA	MGM	337	CRACKLIN
RIGGS, ELIZA	FRE	255	NEW MARK
RIGGS, ELIZABETH	FRE	057	FREDERIC
RIGGS, ELIZABETH-BLACK	FRE	017	FREDERIC
RIGGS, ELLEN-BLACK	FRE	039	FREDERIC
RIGGS, EMELINE	MGM	333	CRACKLIN
RIGGS, FRANCES	BAL	080	15TH WAR
RIGGS, GEORGE	BAL	014	1ST WARD
RIGGS, GEORGE	BAL	412	14TH WAR
RIGGS, GEORGE M.	BAL	225	19TH WAR
RIGGS, GEORGE S.	BAL	226	19TH WAR
RIGGS, GEROGE	BAL	291	20TH WAR
RIGGS, HENRY	FRE	301	WOODSBOR
RIGGS, ISAAC	FRE	298	WOODSBOR
RIGGS, ISAAC	FRE	060	FREDERIC
RIGGS, ISABEL	MGM	341	CLARKSBU
RIGGS, JAMES	FRE	231	BUCKEYST
RIGGS, JOHN	BAL	370	13TH WAR
RIGGS, JOHN A.	DOR	374	1ST DIST
RIGGS, JOHN-BLACK	FRE	438	8TH E DI
RIGGS, JOSEPH	CAL	058	3RD DIST
RIGGS, JOSHUA	MGM	341	CLARKSBU
RIGGS, JULIA	MGM	327	CRACKLIN
RIGGS, LUCY-BLACK	FRE	220	BUCKEYST
RIGGS, MARGARET	BAL	107	1ST WARD
RIGGS, MARGARET	WOR	237	6TH E DI
RIGGS, MARY	MGM	341	CLARKSBU
RIGGS, MARY JANE	BAL	258	17TH WAR
RIGGS, MARY-BLACK	FRE	423	8TH E DI
RIGGS, MELLISSA	MGM	343	CLARKSBU
RIGGS, MISS A.	FRE	200	5TH E DI
RIGGS, PRISCILLA	BAL	115	15TH WAR
RIGGS, PRISCILLA	ANN	363	4TH DIST
RIGGS, REMAS	MGM	327	CRACKLIN
RIGGS, SAMUEL	MGM	326	CRACKLIN
RIGGS, SAMUEL	MGM	325	CRACKLIN
RIGGS, SAMUEL	MGM	325	CRACKLIN
RIGGS, WILLIAM	CAL	029	2ND DIST
RIGGS, WILLIAM	CAL	029	2ND DIST
RIGGS, WINNIFRED	ALL	064	10TH E.D
RIGGUS, T.	BAL	007	4TH WARD
RIGHART, JOHN	BAL	059	2ND DIST
RIGHT, GEORGE W.	BAL	256	1ST DIST
RIGHT, JAMES	WAS	127	HAGERSTO
RIGHT, WILLIAM	SOM	423	PRINCESS
RIGHT, MARY M.	FRE	381	PETERSVI
RIGHTER, JACOB	CAR	273	WESTMINS
RIGHTER, MICHAEL	CAR	292	7TH DIST
RIGHTER, SUSAN	FRE	205	BUCKEYST
RIGLE, BARBARY	BAL	037	18TH WAR
RIGLER, ANDREW	WAS	138	HAGERSTO
RIGLER, JOHN H.	ANN	323	2ND DIST
RIGLEY, JOHN	BAL	353	1ST DIST
RIGLEY, THOAMS	KEN	259	1ST DIST
RIGNAW, WILLIAM	WAS	049	2ND SUBD
RIGNER, EDWARD	BAL	031	9TH WARD
RIGNEY, ELLEN	BAL	154	2ND DIST
RIGNEY, JOHN	BAL	216	6TH DIST
RIGNEY, JOHN F.	BAL	361	13TH WAR
RIGNEY, WILLIAM H.	FRE	049	FREDERIC
RIGOUT, CASPER	BAL	358	8TH WARD
RIGS, WASHINGTON-BLACK	FRE	444	8TH E DI
RIGSBY, THOMAS	BAL	146	1ST WARD

RIGSBY, THOMAS BAL 143 1ST WARD
RIGTRY, ELIZA BAL 233 1ST DIST
RIHARDSON, JOE BAL 458 8TH WARD
RIHCARDSON, SAMUEL HAR 025 1ST DIST
RIHLARARD, BERNARD * BAL 269 2ND WARD
RILAND, ANDREW J. ALL 234 CUMBERLA
RILENKROAT, P. BAL 255 20TH WAR
RILEY, ADAM C. BAL 170 6TH WARD
RILEY, ALEXANDER BAL 174 2ND DIST
RILEY, ALEXANDER ANN 413 HOWARD D
RILEY, ALICE BAL 175 2ND WARD
RILEY, ANDREW MGM 396 ROCKERLE
RILEY, ANN BAL 038 9TH WARD
RILEY, ANN BAL 206 6TH WARD
RILEY, ANN BAL 157 6TH WARD
RILEY, ANN BAL 237 12TH WAR
RILEY, ANNA BAL 269 12TH WAR
RILEY, BARNEY BAL 132 2ND DIST
RILEY, BENJAMIN KEN 310 3RD DIST
RILEY, BRIDGET BAL 445 14TH WAR
RILEY, C. M. KEN 262 1ST DIST
RILEY, CAROLINE MGM 395 ROCKERLE
RILEY, CATHARINE BAL 091 18TH WAR
RILEY, CATHARINE ALL 141 6TH E.D.
RILEY, CATHERINE ANN 324 2ND DIST
RILEY, CHARLES CEC 171 6TH E DI
RILEY, CHARLOTTE BAL 055 15TH WAR
RILEY, CHARLOTTE KEN 291 3RD DIST
RILEY, CLEM ANN 337 3RD DIST
RILEY, COLOMBUS BAL 292 7TH WARD
RILEY, DANIEL BAL 082 2ND DIST
RILEY, DANIEL BAL 073 1ST WARD
RILEY, DENNIS BAL 147 2ND DIST
RILEY, EDW. BAL 296 20TH WAR
RILEY, ELIZA BAL 092 2ND DIST
RILEY, ELIZABETH BAL 149 2ND DIST
RILEY, ELIZABETH ANN 415 HOWARD D
RILEY, ELIZABETH BAL 226 6TH WARD
RILEY, ELIZABETH BAL 126 16TH WAR
RILEY, ELIZABETH BAL 291 17TH WAR
RILEY, ELIZABETH BAL 401 14TH WAR
RILEY, ELIZABETH FRE 231 BUCKEYST
RILEY, ELIZABETH HAR 165 3RD DIST
RILEY, ELIZABETH KEN 313 3RD DIST
RILEY, ELIZABETH V. CEC 171 6TH E DI
RILEY, EMELINE E. BAL 077 10TH WAR
RILEY, EMILY BAL 269 12TH WAR
RILEY, FANNY BAL 241 20TH WAR
RILEY, FRANCIS ALL 246 CUMBERLA
RILEY, GEORGE ALL 021 2ND E.D.
RILEY, GEORGE BAL 387 1ST DIST
RILEY, HANNA KEN 294 3RD DIST
RILEY, HENRY BAL 038 2ND DIST
RILEY, HUGH BAL 143 1ST WARD
RILEY, ISAAC MGM 399 ROCKERLE
RILEY, ISMA BAL 303 7TH WARD
RILEY, ISRIEL BAL 271 1ST DIST
RILEY, JAMES BAL 291 7TH WARD
RILEY, JAMES ALL 071 5TH E.D.
RILEY, JAMES BAL 034 15TH WAR
RILEY, JAMES BAL 024 15TH WAR
RILEY, JAMES BAL 452 8TH WARD
RILEY, JAMES BAL 077 10TH WAR
RILEY, JAMES BAL 223 6TH WARD
RILEY, JAMES BAL 257 20TH WAR
RILEY, JAMES KEN 228 2ND DIST
RILEY, JAMES FRE 273 NEW MARK
RILEY, JAMES WOR 316 2ND E DI
RILEY, JAMES W. ST 291 2ND E DI
RILEY, JAMES W. HAR 191 3RD DIST
RILEY, JANE ALL 243 CUMBERLA
RILEY, JANE BAL 103 5TH WARD
RILEY, JAOCB WOR 287 BERLIN 1
RILEY, JAOCB-BLACK WOR 335 1ST E DI
RILEY, JERRY BAL 248 12TH WAR
RILEY, JMARGARET BAL 269 12TH WAR
RILEY, JOHN BAL 012 15TH WAR
RILEY, JOHN BAL 348 7TH WARD
RILEY, JOHN BAL 007 15TH WAR
RILEY, JOHN BAL 061 15TH WAR
RILEY, JOHN BAL 409 1ST DIST
RILEY, JOHN BAL 212 6TH DIST
RILEY, JOHN BAL 436 1ST DIST
RILEY, JOHN BAL 430 1ST DIST
RILEY, JOHN ANN 376 4TH DIST
RILEY, JOHN ALL 141 6TH E.D.
RILEY, JOHN ALL 177 7TH E.D.
RILEY, JOHN BAL 233 2ND WARD
RILEY, JOHN BAL 384 8TH WARD
RILEY, JOHN BAL 272 1ST DIST
RILEY, JOHN BAL 019 1ST WARD
RILEY, JOHN WAS 136 2ND DIST
RILEY, JOHN WAS 106 2ND DIST
RILEY, JOHN HAR 181 3RD DIST
RILEY, JOHN HAR 128 2ND DIST
RILEY, JOHN CEC 170 6TH E DI
RILEY, JOHN BAL 339 13TH WAR
RILEY, JOHN B. ST 280 3RD E DI
RILEY, JOHN D. BAL 211 6TH WARD
RILEY, JOHN H. BAL 411 1ST DIST
RILEY, JOHN J. ANN 415 HOWARD D
RILEY, JOSEPH BAL 429 1ST DIST
RILEY, JOSEPH C. BAL 144 16TH WAR
RILEY, JULIANA BAL 099 10TH WAR
RILEY, LAWRENCE BAL 442 8TH WARD
RILEY, LEE BAL 333 1ST DIST
RILEY, LOUISA KEN 240 2ND DIST
RILEY, MARGARET BAL 395 1ST DIST
RILEY, MARGARET ANN 413 HOWARD D
RILEY, MARGARET J. BAL 144 16TH WAR
RILEY, MARTHA SOM 402 BRINKLEY
RILEY, MARTHA WOR 261 BERLIN 1
RILEY, MARY BAL 052 9TH WARD
RILEY, MARY BAL 108 5TH WARD
RILEY, MARY BAL 438 8TH WARD
RILEY, MATILDA HAR 180 3RD DIST
RILEY, MICHAEL BAL 343 13TH WAR
RILEY, MICHAEL CEC 022 ELKTON 3
RILEY, MICHAEL ALL 143 6TH E.D.
RILEY, MICHAEL BAL 281 1ST DIST
RILEY, MICHAEL BAL 271 1ST DIST
RILEY, MICHEL BAL 040 2ND DIST
RILEY, NANCY BAL 143 2ND DIST
RILEY, NOAH SOM 360 BRINKLEY
RILEY, OWEN ALL 170 7TH E.D.
RILEY, OWEN BAL 020 9TH WARD
RILEY, PATRICK BAL 132 2ND DIST
RILEY, PATRICK ALL 243 CUMBERLA
RILEY, PATRICK BAL 102 2ND DIST
RILEY, PATRICK BAL 103 2ND DIST
RILEY, PATRICK BAL 459 8TH WARD
RILEY, PATRICK BAL 330 13TH WAR
RILEY, PETER ALL 242 CUMBERLA
RILEY, PETER ANN 337 3RD DIST
RILEY, PETER WOR 242 1ST CENS
RILEY, POLYDORE BAL 016 9TH WARD
RILEY, PRISCILLA CEC 169 6TH E DI
RILEY, RBEECCA CAR 066 NO TWP L
RILEY, REBECA WOR 289 9TH E DI
RILEY, ROSE ALL 078 5TH E.D.
RILEY, SAMUEL BAL 437 1ST DIST
RILEY, SAMUEL KEN 294 3RD DIST
RILEY, SAMUEL KEN 293 3RD DIST
RILEY, SAMUEL KEN 296 3RD DIST
RILEY, SAMUEL KEN 232 2ND DIST
RILEY, SAMUEL M. WOR 224 4TH E DI
RILEY, SAMUEL S. BAL 176 16TH WAR
RILEY, SARAH BAL 168 16TH WAR
RILEY, SERNANDA BAL 436 1ST DIST
RILEY, SINTHIA WAS 113 2ND DIST
RILEY, SPENCER WOR 260 BERLIN 1
RILEY, SUSAN KEN 294 3RD DIST
RILEY, THEDORE BAL 141 16TH WAR
RILEY, THOMAS BAL 115 15TH WAR
RILEY, THOMAS BAL 168 1ST WARD
RILEY, THOMAS ALL 258 CUMBERLA
RILEY, THOMAS BAL 038 15TH WAR
RILEY, THCMAS BAL 273 1ST DIST
RILEY, THOMAS BAL 275 7TH WARD
RILEY, THOMAS CAR 190 4TH DIST
RILEY, WILLIAM BAL 171 19TH WAR
RILEY, WILLIAM ALL 251 CUMBERLA
RILEY, WILLIAM BAL 214 6TH WARD
RILEY, WILLIAM BAL 064 10TH WAR
RILEY, WILLIAM ALL 169 6TH E.D.
RILEY, WILLIAM WAS 107 2ND DIST
RILEY, WILLIAM WOR 304 SNOW HIL
RILEY, WILLIAM E. BAL 294 7TH WARD
RILEY, WILLIAM L. BAL 236 6TH WARD
RILEY, ZANY KEN 309 3RD DIST
RILEY,BARNEY BAL 069 2ND DIST
RILEY,OTHO MGM 421 MEDLEY 3
RILHILSNT, FRANCIS * TAL 072 EASTON T
RILL, ANN M. BAL 264 2ND WARD
RILL, HANNAH BAL 276 2ND WARD
RILLAM, JESSEE DOR 373 1ST DIST
RILLAMN, ELIZA DOR 404 1ST DIST
RILLEY, ANN BAL 125 11TH WAR
RILLEY, J. BAL 148 1ST WARD
RILLEY, PETER BAL 124 11TH WAR
RILLMAN, GREENBURY BAL 098 1ST WARD
RILLY, JAMES BAL 057 1ST WARD
RILY, AUTHER WAS 121 HAGERSTO
RILY, ELEN BAL 271 1ST DIST
RILY, ELIZABETH BAL 451 14TH WAR
RILY, JANE CEC 198 7TH E DI
RILY, SARAH CAR 358 9TH DIST
RIMBEIH, JULIUS BAL 048 18TH WAR
RIMBOCH, PETER BAL 078 10TH WAR
RIMBY, JACOB BAL 146 1ST WARD
RIMBY, JUSTINA CAR 268 WESTMINS
RIMELVE, FRANCIS BAL 057 1ST WARD
RIMER, EDDY-BLACK ST 339 4TH E DI
RIMER, SABRY-BLACK ST 307 1ST E DI
RIMITZ, CHARLES * BAL 146 2ND DIST
RIMLEY, CHARLES BAL 394 1ST DIST
RIMLEY, HENRY WAS 131 HAGERSTO
RIMMER, JAMES QUE 241 5TH E DI
RIMMER, ZACARIAH BAL 083 1ST WARD
RIMMOR, WILLIAM BAL 377 3RD WARD
RIMMY, ELSY* DOR 451 1ST DIST
RIMNER, ISAAC BAL 067 2ND DIST
RIMRICH, HENRY BAL 232 1ST DIST
RIMSEY, JACOB BAL 393 1ST DIST
RIMSEY, MICHAEL BAL 394 1ST DIST
RIN, WILLIAM-MULATTO FRE 244 NEW MARK
RINAMON, JACOB BAL 196 5TH DIST
RINAULD, HENRY FRE 151 10TH E D
RINBY, WILLIAM BAL 068 10TH WAR
RINBY, WILLIAM BAL 068 10TH WAR
RINCEKER, ANN BAL 258 1ST DIST
RINCLY, HENRY * BAL 295 1ST DIST
RIND, ELIZABETH BAL 376 1ST DIST
RIND, GEORGE BAL 376 1ST DIST
RINDAR, CHARLES BAL 069 1ST WARD
RINDEDOLLAR, JOHN CAR 300 1ST DIST
RINDLA, MARY * ANN 379 4TH DIST
RINDLER, MARY * ANN 379 4TH DIST
RINDY, MARGARET BAL 017 1ST WARD
RINE, ELIZA BAL 299 20TH WAR
RINE, ELIZABETH FRE 277 NEW MARK
RINE, ELIZABETH BAL 165 11TH WAR
RINE, ELIZABETH J. FRE 245 NEW MARK
RINE, EMANIEL WAS 130 2ND DIST
RINE, JESSE W. FRE 269 NEW MARK
RINE, JOHN FRE 275 NEW MARK
RINE, JOHN CEC 180 7TH E DI
RINE, MARGARET CEC 180 7TH E DI
RINE, MARY FRE 273 NEW MARK
RINE, MARY BAL 325 12TH WAR
RINE, MIDE * TAL 079 ST MICHA
RINE, REUBEN-BLACK FRE 243 NEW MARK
RINE, SAMUEL FRE 245 NEW MARK
RINE, SAMUEL H. FRE 245 NEW MARK
RINE,MARY ALL 261 CUMBERLA
RINECKER, HENRY BAL 413 1ST DIST
RINECKER, HERNY BAL 404 1ST DIST
RINEDOLLAR, HENRY CAR 315 1ST DIST
RINEDOLLAR, WILLIAM CAR 241 TANEYTOW
RINEDOLLER, JAMES CAR 242 TANEYTOW
RINEDOLLER, JOHN CAR 260 3RD DIST
RINEGAN, WILLIAM BAL 074 2ND DIST
RINEHARDT, WILLIAM BAL 045 18TH WAR
RINEHART, ANDREW H. FRE 209 BUCKEYST
RINEHART, CHRISTIAN BAL 458 1ST DIST
RINEHART, CONRAD BAL 419 1ST DIST
RINEHART, CONRAD BAL 280 17TH WAR
RINEHART, DANIEL CAR 343 6TH DIST
RINEHART, DAVID FRE 427 8TH E DI
RINEHART, FRANCIS BAL 240 1ST DIST
RINEHART, G. BAL 151 1ST WARD
RINEHART, G. BAL 163 1ST WARD
RINEHART, GEORGE BAL 152 1ST WARD
RINEHART, GEORGE BAL 242 17TH WAR
RINEHART, GEORGE CAR 171 8TH DIST
RINEHART, ISREAL CAR 382 2ND DIST
RINEHART, JERAMIAH CAR 256 3RD DIST
RINEHART, JEREMIAH CAR 409 2ND DIST
RINEHART, JOHN CAR 407 2ND DIST
RINEHART, JOSEPH CAR 343 6TH DIST
RINEHART, MARIA CAR 411 2ND DIST
RINEHART, MARY CAR 345 6TH DIST
RINEHART, MARY CAR 179 8TH DIST
RINEHART, RACHEL BAL 410 1ST DIST
RINEHART, REBECCA CAR 256 3RD DIST
RINEHART, REBECCA E. FRE 210 BUCKEYST
RINEHART, SARAH CAR 344 6TH DIST
RINEHART, WILLIAM FRE 304 WOODSBOR
RINEHART,EVAN T. FRE 427 8TH E DI
RINEHARTT, HENRY BAL 006 15TH WAR
RINEHEART, BALINDA C. WAS 300 1ST DIST
RINEHEART, HENRY B. WAS 232 1ST DIST
RINEKART, GEORGE BAL 045 18TH WAR
RINEKER, ELIZA BAL 420 14TH WAR
RINEKER, LENA BAL 225 17TH WAR
RINEMAN, CHARLOTE CAR 172 8TH DIST
RINEMAN, JACOB CAR 171 8TH DIST
RINEMAN, JACOB CAR 171 8TH DIST
RINEMAN, SUSANAH CAR 173 8TH DIST
RINER, HORRIS HAR 170 3RD DIST
RINES, EDWARD SOM 386 BRINKLEY
RINES, JAMES BAL 280 2ND WARD
RING, ANNIE BAL 338 13TH WAR
RING, AUGUSTUS T. BAL 002 9TH WARD
RING, CATHARINE BAL 119 15TH WAR
RING, DENIS BAL 310 1ST DIST
RING, ELIZABETH BAL 248 2ND WARD
RING, ELLEN BAL 337 13TH WAR
RING, ELLEN PRI 030 VANSVILL
RING, GEORGE BAL 258 2ND WARD
RING, H. BAL 099 10TH WAR
RING, HEFFENET BAL 421 3RD WARD
RING, J.M. BAL 130 1ST WARD
RING, JAMES BAL 100 10TH WAR
RING, JOHN ALL 067 10TH E.D
RING, JOHN G. BAL 288 12TH WAR
RING, JOSEPH BAL 374 8TH WARD
RING, JOSEPH BAL 097 1ST WARD
RING, MICHAEL BAL 406 8TH WARD
RING, SOFAHIA C. BAL 182 6TH WARD
RING, SUSAN C. BAL 057 18TH WAR
RING, WILLIAM C. BAL 221 19TH WAR
RINGALE, HENRY BAL 223 12TH WAR
RINGAR, CHARLOTT BAL 340 3RD WARD
RINGE, SAMUEL BAL 459 14TH WAR
RINGER, ANN V. WAS 129 HAGERSTO
RINGER, CHARLES ALL 062 10TH E.D
RINGER, DAVID WAS 199 1ST DIST
RINGER, ELIAS WAS 288 1ST DIST
RINGER, HARRIET ALL 040 2ND E.D.
RINGER, HENRY BAL 274 12TH WAR
RINGER, JOHN WAS 199 1ST DIST
RINGER, JOHN FRE 384 PETERSVI
RINGER, JOHN H. WAS 200 1ST DIST
RINGER, JOHN OF R. WAS 199 1ST DIST
RINGER, JOSEPH WAS 199 1ST DIST
RINGER, MAGDALENA FRE 384 PETERSVI
RINGER, MARY A. WAS 290 1ST DIST
RINGER, PETER WAS 199 1ST DIST
RINGER, PETER JR. WAS 199 1ST DIST
RINGER, SAMUEL WAS 281 1ST DIST
RINGEY, SARAH CEC 074 5TH E DI
RINGGOLD, ANTHONY KEN 246 2ND DIST
RINGGOLD, ARENA QUE 235 4TH E DI
RINGGOLD, BENJAMIN BAL 119 2ND DIST
RINGGOLD, CATHARINE BAL 340 13TH WAR
RINGGOLD, CYRUS-BLACK QUE 200 3RD E DI
RINGGOLD, DANIEL BAL 231 6TH WARD
RINGGOLD, EDWARD QUE 234 4TH E DI
RINGGOLD, EDWARD KEN 223 2ND DIST
RINGGOLD, ELIZABETH KEN 230 2ND DIST
RINGGOLD, ELIZABETH KEN 261 1ST DIST
RINGGOLD, FRANCES BAL 080 4TH WARD
RINGGOLD, FRANCIS BAL 172 6TH WARD
RINGGOLD, GEORGE KEN 261 1ST DIST
RINGGOLD, HANNAH A. BAL 242 6TH WARD
RINGGOLD, HARRIET BAL 035 9TH WARD
RINGGOLD, HENRIETTA BAL 241 2ND WARD
RINGGOLD, HEZEKIAH BAL 202 6TH WARD
RINGGOLD, HORACE QUE 191 3RD E DI
RINGGOLD, ISABELLA J. KEN 234 2ND DIST
RINGGOLD, JAMES KEN 244 2ND DIST
RINGGOLD, JAMES QUE 233 4TH E DI
RINGGOLD, JAMES QUE 234 4TH E DI
RINGGOLD, JAMES BAL 176 6TH WARD
RINGGOLD, JAMES B. QUE 234 4TH E DI
RINGGOLD, JANE QUE 233 4TH E DI
RINGGOLD, JOHN BAL 122 1ST WARD
RINGGOLD, JOHN FRE 404 JEFFERSO
RINGGOLD, JOHN FRE 405 JEFFERSO
RINGGOLD, JOHN E. BAL 050 15TH WAR
RINGGOLD, JOHN L. KEN 213 2ND DIST
RINGGOLD, JOSEPH QUE 239 5TH E DI
RINGGOLD, JOSIAH KEN 234 2ND DIST
RINGGOLD, JULIA ANN BAL 385 13TH WAR
RINGGOLD, LOUISA KEN 213 2ND DIST
RINGGOLD, MARY KEN 213 2ND DIST
RINGGOLD, MARY BAL 049 15TH WAR
RINGGOLD, MARY C. ANN 521 HOWARD D
RINGGOLD, MATILDA QUE 239 5TH E DI
RINGGOLD, MOSES BAL 168 6TH WARD
RINGGOLD, PERRY BAL 148 1ST WARD
RINGGOLD, PERRY BAL 030 9TH WARD
RINGGOLD, PHILIP BAL 168 6TH WARD
RINGGOLD, RICHARD BAL 242 6TH WARD
RINGGOLD, RICHARD W. KEN 208 2ND DIST
RINGGOLD, SALLY BAL 122 16TH WAR
RINGGOLD, SAMUEL QUE 222 4TH E DI
RINGGOLD, SARAH J. KEN 221 2ND DIST
RINGGOLD, STEPHEN KEN 278 1ST DIST
RINGGOLD, STEPHEN-BLACK QUE 198 3RD E DI
RINGGOLD, THOMAS W. KEN 231 2ND DIST
RINGGOLD, WILLIAM C. QUE 225 4TH E DI
RINGGOLD, WILLIAM F. QUE 225 4TH E DI
RINGGOLD, WILLIAM-BLACK QUE 153 1ST E DI
RINGGOLD,WALTER S. FRE 019 FREDERIC
RINGGOLDS, WILLIAM-BLACK BAL 250 2ND WARD
RINGHAUSEN, LOUIS BAL 276 1ST DIST
RINGLE, ISAAC BAL 135 18TH WAR
RINGLE, MARY ANN BAL 376 13TH WAR
RINGLE, NATHAN HAR 204 3RD DIST
RINGLE, THOMAS HAR 204 3RD DIST
RINGLEY, HENRY BAL 219 2ND WARD
RINGLEY, HUGH BAL 219 2ND WARD
RINGLOW, MARY BAL 326 12TH WAR
RINGOLA, SUSAN BAL 367 8TH WARD
RINGOLD, AARON WAS 215 1ST DIST
RINGOLD, ALICE CEC 154 PORT DUP
RINGOLD, C. BAL 203 11TH WAR
RINGOLD, CAROLINE BAL 130 16TH WAR

Name	County	Page	District
RINGOLD, CAROLINE	BAL	130	16TH WAR
RINGOLD, CHARLES	BAL	134	11TH WAR
RINGOLD, E.	WAS	020	2ND SUBD
RINGOLD, EDITH ANN	BAL	376	13TH WAR
RINGOLD, EDWARD	BAL	311	12TH WAR
RINGOLD, EDWIN-BLACK	QUE	170	2ND E DI
RINGOLD, ELISHA	CAR	066	NO TWP L
RINGOLD, ELIZA	BAL	267	7TH WARD
RINGOLD, ELIZABETH	BAL	222	17TH WAR
RINGOLD, FREDERICK	WAS	156	HAGERSTO
RINGOLD, GEORGIANA	BAL	153	5TH WARD
RINGOLD, HANNAH	BAL	432	14TH WAR
RINGOLD, ISAAC	BAL	029	15TH WAR
RINGOLD, JACOB	BAL	376	13TH WAR
RINGOLD, JACOB	FRE	324	MIDDLETO
RINGOLD, JAMES	BAL	241	20TH WAR
RINGOLD, JAMES	TAL	028	EASTON D
RINGOLD, JAMESH.	QUE	162	2ND E DI
RINGOLD, JOHN	BAL	207	17TH WAR
RINGOLD, JOHN W.	CAR	067	NO TWP L
RINGOLD, LYDIA-BLACK	QUE	189	3RD E DI
RINGOLD, MARGARET	KEN	296	3RD DIST
RINGOLD, MARGARET MISS-	BAL	315	20TH WAR
RINGOLD, MARIAH	KEN	291	3RD DIST
RINGOLD, MARY	BAL	157	11TH WAR
RINGOLD, MARY	CAR	213	5TH DIST
RINGOLD, MARY	BAL	014	9TH WARD
RINGOLD, P.	BAL	043	18TH WAR
RINGOLD, PERRY	BAL	028	15TH WAR
RINGOLD, PERRY	BAL	144	5TH WARD
RINGOLD, RACHEL	BAL	389	13TH WAR
RINGOLD, RICHARD	BAL	177	11TH WAR
RINGOLD, SAMUEL	BAL	352	7TH WARD
RINGOLD, SAMUEL	BAL	303	7TH WARD
RINGOLD, SAMUEL	BAL	138	16TH WAR
RINGOLD, SAMUEL	BAL	341	13TH WAR
RINGOLD, SAMUEL	KEN	292	3RD DIST
RINGOLD, SAMUEL DR-	BAL	041	18TH WAR
RINGOLD, THOMAS	CEC	146	PORT DUP
RINGOLD, THOMAS	BAL	116	15TH WAR
RINGOLD, THOMAS C.	KEN	313	3RD DIST
RINGOLD, WILLIAM	BAL	105	10TH WAR
RINGOLD, WILLIAM	BAL	143	5TH WARD
RINGOLD, WILLIAM	BAL	211	19TH WAR
RINGOOLD, EDWARD	BAL	207	6TH WARD
RINGROSE, AARON	BAL	237	17TH WAR
RINGROSE, JAMES	BAL	405	3RD WARD
RINGROSE, JAMES	BAL	386	3RD WARD
RINGROSE, JOHN W.	BAL	460	14TH WAR
RINGROSE, REBECCA	BAL	416	3RD WARD
RINGROSE, SAMUEL	BAL	398	3RD WARD
RINGROSE, SUSAN	BAL	386	3RD WARD
RINGROSE, WILLIAM	ANN	432	HOWARD D
RINGROUSE, WALTER	BAL	015	1ST WARD
RINGSTURF, PETER	BAL	009	4TH WARD
RINICH, JAMES	CAR	257	3RD DIST
RINIDOLLAR, GEORGE	CAR	311	1ST DIST
RINKLE, OTTO	HAR	016	1ST DIST
RINLEY, GEORGE	BAL	216	2ND WARD
RINN, JOHN	ALL	197	CUMBERLA
RINNARD, HENRY	BAL	048	9TH WARD
RINNEMAN, THOMAS *	QUE	214	3RD E DI
RINNEY, WILLIAM	ALL	260	CUMBERLA
RINNEY, WILLIAM DR.	BAL	331	13TH WAR
RINNHART, JOHNA.	ALL	259	CUMBERLA
RINNY, JONATHAN*	DOR	426	1ST DIST
RINPLING, HARMAN F.*	BAL	370	1ST DIST
RINTERMAN, FREDERICK	BAL	224	2ND WARD
RINYALINK, HENRY	BAL	070	2ND DIST
RINYALINK, HENRY	BAL	069	2ND DIST
RINZEN, PETER	CHA	235	HILLTOP
RIORDAN, CORNELIUS*	BAL	401	3RD WARD
RIORDAU, CORNELIUS*	BAL	401	3RD WARD
RIOT, B. L. REV.	ANN	460	HOWARD D
RIPER, MARY J.	QUE	145	1ST E DI
RIPLEY, CHARLOTTE	BAL	075	2ND DIST
RIPLEY, JAMES	BAL	102	18TH WAR
RIPLEY, SUSAN A.	BAL	098	18TH WAR
RIPPEN, CATHARINE	FRE	417	8TH E DI
RIPPEN, JOHN F.	FRE	421	8TH E DI
RIPPEY, JAMES	BAL	342	3RD WARD
RIPPLE, LEWIS	WAS	245	SMITHSBU
RIPPLE, SAMUEL	CAR	226	5TH DIST
RIPPLE, SAMUEL L.	CAR	226	5TH DIST
RIPPMAN, CATHERINE	FRE	034	FREDERIC
RIPPOR, JOHN	DOR	355	3RD DIVI
RIPPY, REBECCA S.*	BAL	342	3RD WARD
RIPSONG, JOHN M.	WAS	186	BOONSBOR
RIRACLY, HENRY *	BAL	295	1ST DIST
RIRAELY, HENRY *	BAL	295	1ST DIST
RIRSE, JOHN J.	BAL	165	19TH WAR
RIRWAN, MARY J.	DOR	420	1ST DIST
RISCAY, JAMES	BAL	175	19TH WAR
RISCH, LOUISA	BAL	007	15TH WAR
RISCHTER, THEOBOLD	BAL	035	15TH WAR
RISE, ANTHONY	ALL	261	CUMBERLA
RISE, NICHOLAS*	TAL	019	EASTON D
RISE, SARAH	BAL	173	16TH WAR
RISELL, JACOB	BAL	125	18TH WAR
RISEMAN, GEORGE M.	BAL	144	19TH WAR
RISEN, JOSEPH	CHA	241	HILLTOP
RISENHART, WILLIAM A.	BAL	199	6TH WARD
RISER, EDWARD	QUE	150	1ST E DI
RISER, GEORGE	WAS	152	2ND DIST
RISH, GABRIEL*	DOR	406	1ST DIST
RISH, GEORGE	BAL	157	1ST WARD
RISHER, MARY	WAS	127	HAGERSTO
RISICES, JAMES	BAL	276	1ST DIST
RISIN, ANN	CHA	241	HILLTOP
RISINER, GEORGE	HAR	060	1ST DIST
RISINGER, WILLIAM	BAL	372	8TH WARD
RISK, DAVID	FRE	183	5TH E DI
RISKER, EMMA	BAL	309	12TH WAR
RIST, LEVI	BAL	058	15TH WAR
RISTELL, L	BAL	319	12TH WAR
RISTER, HENRY	BAL	396	14TH WAR
RISTON, BASIL	BAL	290	7TH WARD
RISTON, JESSEE	HAR	072	1ST DIST
RISTON, JOHN T.	BAL	080	10TH WAR
RITCHA, SARAH	SOM	466	HANGARY
RITCHARDS, JOHN	BAL	324	3RD WARD
RITCHE, JAMES	PRI	061	NOTTINGH
RITCHEY, CHARLOTTE	FRE	211	BUCKEYST
RITCHEY, JOSEPH	FRE	223	BUCKEYST
RITCHFIELD, AARON	BAL	153	5TH WARD
RITCHIE, ADAM	FRE	050	FREDERIC
RITCHIE, ALBERT	FRE	028	FREDERIC
RITCHIE, ELEANOR	SOM	466	HANGARY
RITCHIE, MR.	PRI	083	QUEEN AN
RITCHIE, ROBERT	SOM	435	PRINCESS

Name	County	Page	District
RITCHIE, WILLIAM	BAL	329	7TH WARD
RITCHRE, WILLIAM H.	BAL	105	18TH WAR
RITE, ANN	HAR	152	3RD DIST
RITE, JOHN	HAR	152	3RD DIST
RITE, NANCY-BLACK	WOR	322	1ST E DI
RITENGER, JOHN	BAL	441	8TH WARD
RITENHOUR, ANTONE	BAL	294	17TH WAR
RITENHOUSE, CHARLES	BAL	280	1ST DIST
RITEOUT, SARAH	BAL	199	17TH WAR
RITER, GEORGE	BAL	060	2ND DIST
RITER, GEORGE U.	BAL	059	2ND DIST
RITER, JOSEPH	BAL	233	20TH WAR
RITER, MARY A.	BAL	233	20TH WAR
RITES, GEORGE	FRE	441	8TH E DI
RITES, GEORGE D.	CAR	361	9TH DIST
RITNER, JOHN R.	BAL	297	20TH WAR
RITNEY, ELIZABETH	BAL	051	1ST WARD
RITRER, TOBIAS*	BAL	345	3RD WARD
RITSEL, CONRAD	BAL	292	1ST DIST
RITSON, WILLIAM	BAL	211	2ND WARD
RITT, ELIZABETH	FRE	021	FREDERIC
RITTE,R JACOB	CAR	212	5TH DIST
RITTE,R SARAH	CAR	329	MANCHEST
RITTENHOUSE, GEORGE R.	BAL	076	18TH WAR
RITTENHOUSE, MARY	BAL	460	14TH WAR
RITTER, ADAM	ALL	126	4TH E.D.
RITTER, ALFRED A.	FRE	041	FREDERIC
RITTER, BERNARD	BAL	236	17TH WAR
RITTER, ELI	BAL	073	2ND DIST
RITTER, EMANUEL	BAL	295	1ST DIST
RITTER, EZEKIEL	BAL	184	5TH DIST
RITTER, FREDERICK	ALL	208	CUMBERLA
RITTER, FREDERICK	CAR	339	6TH DIST
RITTER, HENRY	BAL	255	1ST DIST
RITTER, HENRY	ALL	242	CUMBERLA
RITTER, JAMES A.	BAL	327	1ST DIST
RITTER, JESSE	HAR	042	1ST DIST
RITTER, JOHN	ALL	145	6TH E.D.
RITTER, JOHN	ALL	062	10TH E.D
RITTER, JOHN	ALL	061	10TH E.D
RITTER, JOHN	BAL	405	1ST DIST
RITTER, JOHNEY	BAL	377	1ST DIST
RITTER, JOSEPH	BAL	404	1ST DIST
RITTER, JULIA	BAL	045	18TH WAR
RITTER, LEWIS	WAS	278	LEITERSB
RITTER, MARY	BAL	196	11TH WAR
RITTER, MICHAEL	CAR	339	6TH DIST
RITTER, OWEN	BAL	408	1ST DIST
RITTER, PETER S.	CAR	339	6TH DIST
RITTER, RINALDO	BAL	247	20TH WAR
RITTER, SYLVESTER	ALL	089	5TH E.D.
RITTER, THOMAS	BAL	277	1ST DIST
RITTER, WILSON	BAL	381	1ST DIST
RITZ, BENJAMIN	HAR	047	1ST DIST
RITZ, EDWARD	BAL	337	13TH WAR
RITZ, ELIZABETH	FRE	374	CATOCTIN
RITZ, JOHN	WAS	176	1ST DIST
RITZ, PAUL	BAL	368	1ST DIST
RITZ, TANHARTS	BAL	427	14TH WAR
RITZELL, JOSEPH	ALL	227	CUMBERLA
RITZER, TOBIAS*	BAL	345	3RD WARD
RIVEL, SISTER M. JOSEPHIN	FRE	197	5TH E DI
RIVER, ELIZABETH	BAL	229	19TH WAR
RIVER, JOHN C.	PRI	014	BLADENSB
RIVERS, CATHARINE M.	ANN	457	HOWARD D
RIVERS, DEBORAH	CEC	100	3RD E DI
RIVERS, J.	BAL	157	1ST WARD
RIX, SARAH	CAR	328	MANCHEST
RIXSE, JOHN A.	BAL	133	16TH WAR
RIXTER, LUDWILL	BAL	142	16TH WAR
RIZART, CATHARINE	BAL	007	15TH WAR
RIZER, GEORGE	ALL	235	CUMBERLA
RIZER, GUSTAVUS	ALL	238	CUMBERLA
RIZER, MARTIN	ALL	238	CUMBERLA
RIZER, MARTIN	ALL	236	CUMBERLA
RIZER, MARTIN	ALL	085	5TH E.D.
RIZER, WILLIAM L.	ALL	236	CUMBERLA
RIZINET, LAWRENCE A.	BAL	339	13TH WAR
RLAY, REBEC	BAL	220	12TH WAR
RLETZLEN, F.	BAL	449	8TH WARD
RNAZ, HENRY	BAL	328	13TH WAR
ROABBECK, GEORGE	BAL	042	1ST WARD
ROACH, ANN	BAL	403	8TH WARD
ROACH, ANN E.	FRE	410	8TH E DI
ROACH, BRIDGES	BAL	146	11TH WAR
ROACH, CAROLINE	BAL	166	2ND DIST
ROACH, CHARLES W.	CEC	076	NORTHEAS
ROACH, DANIEL	ALL	243	CUMBERLA
ROACH, DELIA-BLACK	WOR	322	1ST E DI
ROACH, EDWARD	BAL	064	1ST WARD
ROACH, EDWARD	BAL	143	1ST WARD
ROACH, ELISHA	SOM	425	PRINCESS
ROACH, ELIZA	SOM	367	BRINKLEY
ROACH, EMILY	BAL	244	6TH WARD
ROACH, FANNY	BAL	115	5TH WARD
ROACH, FREDERICK	BAL	202	17TH WAR
ROACH, GEORGE	BAL	166	1ST WARD
ROACH, GEORGE	BAL	094	15TH WAR
ROACH, HENRY	BAL	272	7TH WARD
ROACH, JAMES	BAL	143	1ST WARD
ROACH, JAMES	BAL	091	5TH WARD
ROACH, JAMES	FRE	044	FREDERIC
ROACH, JAMES	CAL	030	2ND DIST
ROACH, JAMES	BAL	129	18TH WAR
ROACH, JAMES	SOM	370	BRINKLEY
ROACH, JAMES	SOM	391	BRINKLEY
ROACH, JAMES J.	BAL	433	14TH WAR
ROACH, JAMES W.	ST	308	1ST E DI
ROACH, JANE	SOM	403	BRINKLEY
ROACH, JANE	ALL	068	5TH E.D.
ROACH, JESSE	BAL	048	2ND DIST
ROACH, JOHANNA	BAL	273	17TH WAR
ROACH, JOHN	BAL	165	1ST WARD
ROACH, JOHN	BAL	063	1ST WARD
ROACH, JOHN	BAL	076	1ST WARD
ROACH, JOHN	WAS	124	2ND DIST
ROACH, JOHN-BLACK	WOR	335	1ST E DI
ROACH, LAWRENCE	WAS	164	2ND DIST
ROACH, LEVY	BAL	129	18TH WAR
ROACH, MAHALIA-BLACK	WOR	338	1ST E DI
ROACH, MARGARET	MGM	335	CRACKLIN
ROACH, MARGARET	BAL	395	1ST DIST
ROACH, MARGRET A.	BAL	182	2ND WARD
ROACH, MARIA	WOR	178	6TH E DI
ROACH, MARY	BAL	019	9TH WARD
ROACH, MARY	FRE	066	FREDERIC
ROACH, NEAMIAH	SOM	418	PRINCESS
ROACH, NICHOLAS	BAL	120	1ST WARD
ROACH, PATRICK	BAL	124	16TH WAR
ROACH, PETER	BAL	169	1ST WARD

Name	County	Page	District
ROACH, PETER	BAL	263	2ND WARD
ROACH, RACHEL	CAR	207	4TH DIST
ROACH, SARAH	BAL	276	2ND WARD
ROACH, THOMAS	BAL	021	9TH WARD
ROACH, THOMAS C.	FRE	040	FREDERIC
ROACH, THOMAS F.	BAL	201	11TH WAR
ROACH, WESTWARD W.	FRE	389	PETERSVI
ROACH, WILLIAM	CAR	207	4TH DIST
ROACH, WILLIAM	CEC	098	3RD E DI
ROACH, WILLIAM	BAL	105	1ST WARD
ROACH, WILLIAM A.	BAL	129	1ST WARD
ROACHE, GEORGE	BAL	030	4TH WARD
ROACHES, MICHAEL	BAL	201	11TH WAR
ROACK, SARAH	WOR	303	SNOW HIL
ROADE, MARTIN	BAL	084	1ST WARD
ROADES, CHARLES	CEC	038	CHESAPEA
ROADHOUPT, GOTLIEB	BAL	409	1ST DIST
ROADIT, JOHN	MGM	381	ROCKERLE
ROADMAN, LAVINIA	BAL	162	16TH WAR
ROADPOUCH, PETER	CAR	244	3RD DIST
ROADS, CONRAD	WAS	256	1ST DIST
ROADS, JAMES	PRI	020	VANSVILL
ROADS, JEREMIAH	WAS	030	2ND SUBD
ROADS, JOHN	BAL	371	1ST DIST
ROADS, JULIAN	WAS	180	BOONSBOR
ROADS, LUCEY	CAL	004	1ST DIST
ROADS, PHILIP	WAS	256	1ST DIST
ROADS, WILLIAM	CEC	056	1ST E DI
ROAK, DANIEL	ALL	135	4TH E.D.
ROAK, FREDERICK	BAL	107	1ST WARD
ROAK, JOHN	ALL	150	6TH E.D.
ROAKE, JAMES	CEC	111	4TH E DI
ROAKE, MICHAEL	ANN	421	HOWARD D
ROAKE, OWEN	BAL	208	11TH WAR
ROALES, WILLIAM	ALL	143	6TH E.D.
ROAN, CHRISTIAN	WAS	291	1ST DIST
ROAP, WILLIAM	BAL	193	2ND WARD
ROARDLEY, SALLY	ANN	272	ANNAPOLI
ROARK, WILLIAM	TAL	051	EASTON D
ROARKE, JAMES	BAL	127	5TH WARD
ROAS, JOSEPH	BAL	316	12TH WAR
ROASE, HENRY	BAL	268	17TH WAR
ROASH, JACOB	BAL	015	9TH WARD
ROATH, JOHN	CEC	060	1ST E DI
ROATS, GEORGE	ALL	128	4TH E.D.
ROAUCK, ADAM	BAL	281	17TH WAR
ROB, HENRY	DOR	453	1ST DIST
ROBACH, ELIZABETH	BAL	240	2ND WARD
ROBANKS, CRISSY	ANN	320	2ND DIST
ROBART, MARY*	BAL	339	3RD WARD
ROBAUGH, GEORGE	ALL	149	6TH E.D.
ROBAUGH, HARMON	ALL	149	6TH E.D.
ROBAUGH, MARY S.	FRE	065	FREDERIC
ROBAY, Z.G.	PRI	108	PISCATAW
ROBB, A.	BAL	148	1ST WARD
ROBB, AMELIA	BAL	342	3RD WARD
ROBB, CORNELIA*	BAL	330	3RD WARD
ROBB, JAMES	BAL	002	1ST WARD
ROBB, JOHN	BAL	157	2ND DIST
ROBB, JOHN	CEC	003	ELKTON 3
ROBB, JOHN A.	BAL	422	3RD WARD
ROBB, JOSEPH	BAL	134	16TH WAR
ROBB, LEWY	HAR	176	3RD DIST
ROBB, MARIA	BAL	319	3RD WARD
ROBB, MOSES	BAL	330	7TH WARD
ROBB, RICHARD	CAR	328	MANCHEST
ROBB, WILLIAM	BAL	394	14TH WAR
ROBBACK, JOHN	WAS	135	2ND DIST
ROBBERTS, HENERETTA	CHA	228	BOJANTOW
ROBBIN, JACOB	BAL	116	5TH WARD
ROBBINS, ASA	WOR	202	4TH E DI
ROBBINS, DAVID	BAL	126	1ST WARD
ROBBINS, ELIZA	BAL	249	12TH WAR
ROBBINS, HENRY R.	BAL	155	16TH WAR
ROBBINS, HORRACE W.	BAL	061	18TH WAR
ROBBINS, HUS	BAL	273	12TH WAR
ROBBINS, JAMES	BAL	213	6TH WARD
ROBBINS, JOHN	BAL	030	15TH WAR
ROBBINS, LEVIN	BAL	108	15TH WAR
ROBBINS, LEWIS	BAL	122	1ST WARD
ROBBINS, MARGARET J.	WOR	202	4TH E DI
ROBBINS, MARY E.	BAL	012	15TH WAR
ROBBINS, MOSES S.	BAL	012	15TH WAR
ROBBINS, O.D.	ALL	216	CUMBERLA
ROBBINS, WILLIAM	BAL	089	1ST WARD
ROBBINS, WILLIAM	BAL	356	3RD WARD
ROBBINS, WILLIAM	BAL	356	3RD WARD
ROBBINS, WILLIAM	BAL	158	1ST WARD
ROBBINS, WILLIAM	BAL	127	1ST WARD
ROBBINSON, JOSEPH	HAR	005	1ST DIST
ROBELET, J. B.	BAL	152	1ST WARD
ROBELET, JOHN B.	BAL	394	3RD WARD
ROBELET, LAURA V.	BAL	395	3RD WARD
ROBELLER, SARAH A.	PRI	026	VANSVILL
ROBENSON, SAMUEL	ALL	163	6TH E.D.
ROBERSON, ABEL	DOR	348	3RD DIVI
ROBERSON, BINNEY	KEN	215	2ND DIST
ROBERSON, CALEP	DOR	343	3RD DIVI
ROBERSON, CATHARINE	CAR	220	5TH DIST
ROBERSON, EBANEZOR	CHA	219	ALLENS F
ROBERSON, EDWARD	KEN	226	2ND DIST
ROBERSON, ELIZA-BLACK	KEN	215	2ND DIST
ROBERSON, ELIZABETH	BAL	222	2ND WARD
ROBERSON, EMILEY	CEC	044	1ST E DI
ROBERSON, HANNAH	DOR	350	3RD DIVI
ROBERSON, HENRIETTER	CEC	044	1ST E DI
ROBERSON, HENRY	FRE	211	BUCKEYST
ROBERSON, HUDSON	KEN	216	2ND DIST
ROBERSON, ISAAC	DOR	347	3RD DIVI
ROBERSON, ISABELLA	DOR	447	1ST DIST
ROBERSON, JAMES	DOR	360	3RD DIVI
ROBERSON, JOHN	SOM	512	BARREN C
ROBERSON, JOHN	KEN	277	1ST DIST
ROBERSON, JOHN	DOR	346	3RD DIVI
ROBERSON, JOHN	DOR	332	3RD DIVI
ROBERSON, JOHN	HAR	164	3RD DIST
ROBERSON, JOHN P.	CEC	067	5TH E DI
ROBERSON, KIZIAH	CHA	290	BOJANTOW
ROBERSON, LAKE	DOR	372	3RD DIVI
ROBERSON, MARCELLUS	DOR	351	3RD DIVI
ROBERSON, MARGARET	DOR	349	3RD DIVI
ROBERSON, MARY A.E.-BLACK	BAL	316	12TH WAR
ROBERSON, PHEBA	BAL	208	2ND WARD
ROBERSON, REBECCA	DOR	336	3RD DIVI
ROBERSON, ROBERT	DOR	346	3RD DIVI
ROBERSON, ROGER C.	CEC	074	5TH E DI
ROBERSON, ROWLAND	DOR	361	3RD DIVI
ROBERSON, SARAH	BAL	004	1ST WARD
ROBERSON, SARRAH	SOM	512	BARREN C
	DOR	360	3RD DIVI

Name	County	Page	District
ROBERSON, SILAS	DOR	336	3RD DIVI
ROBERSON, SOPHIA	HAR	204	3RD DIST
ROBERSON, SUSAN	DOR	340	3RD DIVI
ROBERSON, THOMAS	BAL	123	1ST WARD
ROBERSON, VINCENT	KEN	215	2ND DIST
ROBERSON, WILLIAM	DOR	364	3RD DIVI
ROBERSON, WILLIAM	DOR	328	3RD DIVI
ROBERT, ANN C.	BAL	197	11TH WAR
ROBERT, BRACLEY	BAL	118	11TH WAR
ROBERT, ELIZABETH	KEN	212	2ND DIST
ROBERT, ELIZABETH	BAL	021	1ST WARD
ROBERT, JAMES	BAL	018	1ST WARD
ROBERT, JAMES	BAL	174	11TH WAR
ROBERT, JAMES	QUE	177	2ND E DI
ROBERT, JESSE	BAL	186	19TH WAR
ROBERT, MARGARET	BAL	186	19TH WAR
ROBERT, MARY	BAL	044	9TH WARD
ROBERT, RICHARD	BAL	118	11TH WAR
ROBERT, WILLIAM	BAL	169	2ND DIST
ROBERTS, A.F.	ALL	209	CUMBERLA
ROBERTS, AARON	SOM	397	BRINKLEY
ROBERTS, ABRAHAM	BAL	051	9TH WARD
ROBERTS, ACAMS	QUE	233	4TH E DI
ROBERTS, ALEXANDER	BAL	057	1ST WARD
ROBERTS, ALFRED	BAL	202	19TH WAR
ROBERTS, ALFRED-MULATTO	FRE	452	8TH E DI
ROBERTS, ALFRED-MULATTO	FRE	437	8TH E DI
ROBERTS, ALLY	ANN	318	2ND DIST
ROBERTS, AMELIA	BAL	206	2ND WARD
ROBERTS, AMELIA O.	PRI	013	BLADENSB
ROBERTS, ANDREW	TAL	031	EASTON D
ROBERTS, ANDREW	BAL	303	17TH WAR
ROBERTS, ANN	BAL	473	14TH WAR
ROBERTS, ANN	BAL	154	11TH WAR
ROBERTS, ANN	QUE	182	3RD E DI
ROBERTS, ANN	QUE	184	3RD E DI
ROBERTS, ANN	BAL	168	11TH WAR
ROBERTS, ANNA	CEC	041	CHESAPEA
ROBERTS, ARDELLA	BAL	070	4TH WARD
ROBERTS, ARTHUR	CEC	025	ELKTON 3
ROBERTS, ARTHUR	SOM	416	PRINCESS
ROBERTS, ARZIMMA	BAL	343	3RD WARD
ROBERTS, ASAEL	FRE	232	BUCKEYST
ROBERTS, AUGUSTUS-MULATTO	FRE	038	FREDERIC
ROBERTS, BENJAMIN	CEC	025	ELKTON 3
ROBERTS, BENJAMIN R.	BAL	132	16TH WAR
ROBERTS, BENJAMIN W.	SOM	532	QUANTICO
ROBERTS, BETSEY	BAL	393	8TH WARD
ROBERTS, BETTY	BAL	152	11TH WAR
ROBERTS, CAROLINE	MGM	348	BERRYS D
ROBERTS, CASPER	BAL	180	2ND WARD
ROBERTS, CHARITY	BAL	098	15TH WAR
ROBERTS, CHARLES	BAL	141	16TH WAR
ROBERTS, CHARLES	BAL	234	12TH WAR
ROBERTS, CHARLES	BAL	121	1ST WARD
ROBERTS, CHARLES	BAL	162	19TH WAR
ROBERTS, CHARLES	CEC	059	1ST E DI
ROBERTS, CHARLES	SOM	517	BARREN C
ROBERTS, CHARLES	QUE	184	3RD E DI
ROBERTS, CHARLES	TAL	097	ST MICHA
ROBERTS, CHARLOTTE	WOR	182	6TH E DI
ROBERTS, CHEESMAN	BAL	173	6TH WARD
ROBERTS, CONRAD	BAL	082	1ST WARD
ROBERTS, D.	BAL	155	1ST WARD
ROBERTS, DANIEL	KEN	308	3RD DIST
ROBERTS, DARKEY	QUE	226	4TH E DI
ROBERTS, DAVID	BAL	113	1ST WARD
ROBERTS, DAVVHENY	QUE	237	4TH E DI
ROBERTS, EASTER	WAS	008	WILLIAMS
ROBERTS, EDW.	BAL	307	20TH WAR
ROBERTS, EDWARD	BAL	430	14TH WAR
ROBERTS, EDWARD	BAL	119	1ST WARD
ROBERTS, EDWARD	BAL	403	3RD WARD
ROBERTS, EDWARD P.	BAL	398	8TH WARD
ROBERTS, EDWIN	KEN	301	3RD DIST
ROBERTS, ELEANOR	SOM	450	DAMES QU
ROBERTS, ELI	WOR	185	6TH E DI
ROBERTS, ELIZA	BAL	162	19TH WAR
ROBERTS, ELIZA	BAL	131	11TH WAR
ROBERTS, ELIZA	BAL	080	1ST WARD
ROBERTS, ELIZA	BAL	072	10TH WAR
ROBERTS, ELIZABETH	BAL	329	7TH WARD
ROBERTS, ELIZABETH	BAL	353	7TH WARD
ROBERTS, ELIZABETH	BAL	462	1ST DIST
ROBERTS, ELIZABETH	ALL	193	9TH E.D.
ROBERTS, ELIZABETH-MULATT	FRE	438	8TH E DI
ROBERTS, EMALINE	SOM	462	HANGARY
ROBERTS, EMULY	BAL	319	12TH WAR
ROBERTS, EPHRAHAM-BLACK	FRE	031	FREDERIC
ROBERTS, ERNEST	BAL	100	1ST WARD
ROBERTS, FRANCIS	HAR	179	3RD DIST
ROBERTS, FRANCIS J.	BAL	393	8TH WARD
ROBERTS, GEORGE	ALL	187	9TH E.D.
ROBERTS, GEORGE	ALL	099	5TH E.D.
ROBERTS, GEORGE	BAL	320	3RD WARD
ROBERTS, GEORGE	DOR	347	3RD DIVI
ROBERTS, GEORGE	FRE	089	FREDERIC
ROBERTS, GEORGE	DOR	305	1ST DIST
ROBERTS, GEORGE C. M.	BAL	057	15TH WAR
ROBERTS, GEORGE H.	WOR	189	7TH E DI
ROBERTS, GEORGE W.	WOR	210	4TH E DI
ROBERTS, GREENBURG-MULATT	FRE	451	8TH E DI
ROBERTS, HARRIETT	ALL	159	6TH E.D.
ROBERTS, HELTER	CEC	018	ELKTON 3
ROBERTS, HENRIETTA	WAS	157	2ND DIST
ROBERTS, HENRY	TAL	097	ST MICHA
ROBERTS, HENRY	CEC	176	7TH E DI
ROBERTS, HENRY	SOM	417	PRINCESS
ROBERTS, HENRY	SOM	442	DAMES QU
ROBERTS, HENRY	SOM	446	DAMES QU
ROBERTS, HENRY	SOM	413	DUBLIN D
ROBERTS, HENRY	BAL	191	17TH WAR
ROBERTS, HENRY G.	BAL	457	8TH WARD
ROBERTS, HENRY H.	CAR	193	4TH DIST
ROBERTS, HENRY J.	BAL	339	13TH WAR
ROBERTS, HENRY-BLACK	FRE	412	8TH E DI
ROBERTS, HESTER	DOR	360	3RD DIVI
ROBERTS, HESTER A.	WOR	181	6TH E DI
ROBERTS, HORRACE T.	KEN	301	3RD DIST
ROBERTS, HUGH	ALL	087	5TH E.D.
ROBERTS, HUGH	BAL	052	1ST WARD
ROBERTS, ISAAC	SOM	399	BRINKLEY
ROBERTS, ISAAC	SOM	415	DUBLIN D
ROBERTS, ISAAC G.	BAL	259	6TH WARD
ROBERTS, ISAAC G.	BAL	183	6TH WARD
ROBERTS, ISABELLA	BAL	205	6TH WARD
ROBERTS, J.	BAL	118	1ST WARD
ROBERTS, JACOB	BAL	086	15TH WAR
ROBERTS, JAMES	ALL	090	5TH E.D.
ROBERTS, JAMES	BAL	079	2ND DIST
ROBERTS, JAMES	WOR	329	1ST E DI
ROBERTS, JAMES	WOR	339	1ST E DI
ROBERTS, JAMES H.	TAL	062	EASTON D
ROBERTS, JAMES R.	BAL	275	12TH WAR
ROBERTS, JAMES-BLACK	BAL	250	2ND WARD
ROBERTS, JANE	ALL	072	5TH E.D.
ROBERTS, JANE	BAL	210	11TH WAR
ROBERTS, JANE	BAL	450	8TH WARD
ROBERTS, JANE	BAL	003	4TH WARD
ROBERTS, JANE R.	BAL	450	8TH WARD
ROBERTS, JANE-BLACK	FRE	415	8TH E DI
ROBERTS, JESSE	FRE	301	WOODSBOR
ROBERTS, JINKINS H.	HAR	196	3RD DIST
ROBERTS, JOHN	DOR	336	3RD DIVI
ROBERTS, JOHN	CEC	047	1ST E DI
ROBERTS, JOHN	CAR	235	UNION TO
ROBERTS, JOHN	CEC	145	PORT DUP
ROBERTS, JOHN	CEC	076	NORTHEAS
ROBERTS, JOHN	BAL	388	3RD WARD
ROBERTS, JOHN	BAL	363	3RD WARD
ROBERTS, JOHN	WAS	122	HAGERSTO
ROBERTS, JOHN	WOR	179	6TH E DI
ROBERTS, JOHN P.	TAL	029	EASTON D
ROBERTS, JOHN R.	BAL	262	6TH WARD
ROBERTS, JOHN R.	SOM	436	PRINCESS
ROBERTS, JOHN W.	TAL	062	EASTON D
ROBERTS, JONATHAN M.	CEC	179	7TH E DI
ROBERTS, JOSEPH	CEC	136	6TH E DI
ROBERTS, JOSEPH	BAL	280	17TH WAR
ROBERTS, JOSEPH	BAL	287	17TH WAR
ROBERTS, JOSEPH	WAS	052	2ND SUBD
ROBERTS, JOSEPH	ANN	318	2ND DIST
ROBERTS, JOSEPH	BAL	443	1ST DIST
ROBERTS, JOSEPH K.	PRI	005	BLADENSB
ROBERTS, JOSEPH K.	PRI	013	BLADENSB
ROBERTS, JOSEPH W.	CEC	041	CHESAPEA
ROBERTS, JOSHUA	MGM	338	CRACKLIN
ROBERTS, JOSHUA	BAL	443	8TH WARD
ROBERTS, JOSHUA W.	SOM	554	TYASKIN
ROBERTS, JOSIA	CHA	228	BOJANTOW
ROBERTS, JULIA	BAL	244	20TH WAR
ROBERTS, JULIA	BAL	347	13TH WAR
ROBERTS, JULIA	BAL	206	6TH WARD
ROBERTS, JULIET L.	BAL	297	7TH WARD
ROBERTS, KITTY	BAL	058	10TH WAR
ROBERTS, LAMBERT	BAL	091	2ND DIST
ROBERTS, LEAH	TAL	038	EASTON D
ROBERTS, LEMUEL	QUE	123	1ST E DI
ROBERTS, LEWIS	BAL	176	2ND DIST
ROBERTS, LINDA	BAL	274	2ND WARD
ROBERTS, LORENZO	CEC	215	7TH E DI
ROBERTS, LOUIS	CEC	043	CHESAPEA
ROBERTS, LOUISA-BLACK	WOR	172	6TH E DI
ROBERTS, LOYD-MULATTO	FRE	451	8TH E DI
ROBERTS, LUCINDA	ALL	232	CUMBERLA
ROBERTS, LUICY	QUE	242	5TH E DI
ROBERTS, LUTHER	ANN	414	HOWARD D
ROBERTS, LYDIA	BAL	060	10TH WAR
ROBERTS, MABLE	TAL	043	EASTON D
ROBERTS, MARGARET	BAL	057	1ST WARD
ROBERTS, MARGARET	BAL	256	17TH WAR
ROBERTS, MARGARET	BAL	397	14TH WAR
ROBERTS, MARGARET	CAL	038	2ND DIST
ROBERTS, MARGARETT A.	BAL	046	4TH WARD
ROBERTS, MARGRETT-BLACK	FRE	451	8TH E DI
ROBERTS, MARIA	BAL	272	7TH WARD
ROBERTS, MARY	BAL	101	1ST WARD
ROBERTS, MARY	BAL	150	16TH WAR
ROBERTS, MARY	ALL	146	6TH E.D.
ROBERTS, MARY	BAL	030	9TH WARD
ROBERTS, MARY	BAL	223	12TH WAR
ROBERTS, MARY	CAR	091	NO TWP L
ROBERTS, MARY	CAR	236	UNION TO
ROBERTS, MARY	SOM	416	DUBLIN D
ROBERTS, MARY	WAS	122	HAGERSTO
ROBERTS, MARY A.	BAL	232	6TH WARD
ROBERTS, MARY ANN	FRE	182	5TH E DI
ROBERTS, MARY E.	BAL	390	13TH WAR
ROBERTS, MARY E.	BAL	349	13TH WAR
ROBERTS, MARY E.	BAL	342	3RD WARD
ROBERTS, MARY E.	TAL	105	ST MICHA
ROBERTS, MARY M.	BAL	440	8TH WARD
ROBERTS, MARY-BLACK	WOR	321	1ST E DI
ROBERTS, MASSY	SOM	466	HANGARY
ROBERTS, MATTHEW	SOM	425	PRINCESS
ROBERTS, MICHAEL	FRE	093	FREDERIC
ROBERTS, MOSES	SOM	406	DUBLIN D
ROBERTS, MOSES	HAR	084	2ND DIST
ROBERTS, MOSES-BLACK	FRE	438	8TH E DI
ROBERTS, MUNRCE	BAL	090	2ND DIST
ROBERTS, N.	BAL	164	1ST WARD
ROBERTS, NANCY	QUE	210	3RD E DI
ROBERTS, NANCY	QUE	210	3RD E DI
ROBERTS, NANCY	WOR	272	BERLIN 1
ROBERTS, NANCY	WOR	280	BERLIN 1
ROBERTS, NATHAN	CEC	070	5TH E DI
ROBERTS, NELSCN	SOM	460	HANGARY
ROBERTS, OWEN	TAL	105	ST MICHA
ROBERTS, OWEN	BAL	098	1ST WARD
ROBERTS, P.	BAL	149	1ST WARD
ROBERTS, PHACTCN-BLACK	QUE	130	1ST E DI
ROBERTS, PHAETON-BLACK	QUE	128	1ST E DI
ROBERTS, PHEBE	BAL	052	9TH WARD
ROBERTS, PRECILLA	BAL	402	3RD WARD
ROBERTS, PRISALA	HAR	207	3RD DIST
ROBERTS, RACHAEL	BAL	150	11TH WAR
ROBERTS, RACHELL	BAL	261	17TH WAR
ROBERTS, REBECCA	BAL	092	18TH WAR
ROBERTS, ROBERT	BAL	315	3RD WARD
ROBERTS, ROBERT R.	CAL	024	2ND DIST
ROBERTS, SAMUEL	CEC	156	PORT DUP
ROBERTS, SAMUEL	FRE	031	FREDERIC
ROBERTS, SAMUEL	BAL	280	2ND WARD
ROBERTS, SARAH	BAL	102	18TH WAR
ROBERTS, SARAH	CAR	388	2ND DIST
ROBERTS, SARAH	CEC	070	5TH E DI
ROBERTS, SARAH	CEC	044	CHESAPEA
ROBERTS, SARAH	TAL	073	EASTON T
ROBERTS, SARAH A.	TAL	070	EASTON T
ROBERTS, SARAH-BLACK	WOR	345	1ST E DI
ROBERTS, SARRAH	DOR	333	3RD DIVI
ROBERTS, SUSAN	TAL	077	EASTON T
ROBERTS, SUSAN	BAL	098	10TH WAR
ROBERTS, THOMAS	BAL	309	3RD WARD
ROBERTS, THOMAS	ALL	264	CUMBER_A
ROBERTS, THOMAS	BAL	008	15TH WAR
ROBERTS, THOMAS	QUE	228	4TH E DI
ROBERTS, THOMAS	SOM	462	HANGARY
ROBERTS, THOMAS	SOM	554	TYASKIN
ROBERTS, THOMAS	HAR	010	1ST DIST
ROBERTS, THOMAS A.	CEC	054	1ST E DI
ROBERTS, WASHINGTON	BAL	113	5TH WARD
ROBERTS, WILHELMINA	BAL	170	16TH WAR
ROBERTS, WILIAM	QUE	135	1ST E DI
ROBERTS, WILIAM -BLACK	CAR	166	NO TWP L
ROBERTS, WILLAIM	BAL	409	8TH WARD
ROBERTS, WILLIAM	BAL	271	7TH WARD
ROBERTS, WILLIAM	BAL	143	1ST WARD
ROBERTS, WILLIAM	BAL	152	1ST WARD
ROBERTS, WILLIAM	BAL	154	1ST WARD
ROBERTS, WILLIAM	BAL	162	1ST WARD
ROBERTS, WILLIAM	BAL	229	6TH WARD
ROBERTS, WILLIAM	BAL	179	2ND WARD
ROBERTS, WILLIAM	BAL	213	2ND WARD
ROBERTS, WILLIAM	BAL	106	1ST WARD
ROBERTS, WILLIAM	BAL	255	1ST DIST
ROBERTS, WILLIAM	CEC	029	CHESAPEA
ROBERTS, WILLIAM	CAR	237	UNION TO
ROBERTS, WILLIAM	BAL	028	18TH WAR
ROBERTS, WILLIAM	HAR	010	1ST DIST
ROBERTS, WILLIAM	BAL	472	14TH WAR
ROBERTS, WILLIAM	QUE	186	3RD E DI
ROBERTS, WILLIAM	WAS	182	BOONSBOR
ROBERTS, WILLIAM	SOM	500	SALISBUR
ROBERTS, WILLIAM D.	BAL	186	6TH WARD
ROBERTS, WILLIAM G.	BAL	443	8TH WARD
ROBERTS, WILLIAM H.	HAR	098	2ND DIST
ROBERTS, WILLIAM J.	TAL	069	EASTON T
ROBERTS, WILLIAM R.-BLACK	WOR	172	6TH E DI
ROBERTS, WILLIAM W.	SOM	543	TYASKIN
ROBERTS, WOOLMAN H.	QUE	143	1ST E DI
ROBERTS,MARY	BAL	100	1ST WARD
ROBERTSON, ALEXANDER	SOM	363	BRINKLEY
ROBERTSON, ALEXANDER	WAS	098	2ND DIST
ROBERTSON, ALEXANDER H.	CHA	233	HILLTOP
ROBERTSON, ALFRED	SOM	363	BRINKLEY
ROBERTSON, ALONZO W.	SOM	511	BARREN C
ROBERTSON, BENJAMIN N.	PRI	046	AQUASCO
ROBERTSON, BETSEY	SOM	508	BARREN C
ROBERTSON, BRITTEMHAM*	DOR	464	1ST DIST
ROBERTSON, C. MRS-	BAL	315	20TH WAR
ROBERTSON, CHARLES	SOM	513	BARREN C
ROBERTSON, CHRISTCPHER W.	BAL	031	15TH WAR
ROBERTSON, DANIL	DOR	454	1ST DIST
ROBERTSON, DAVID	BAL	319	7TH WARD
ROBERTSON, EDGAR W.	SOM	363	BRINKLEY
ROBERTSON, ELI	SOM	509	BARREN C
ROBERTSON, ELIJAH	CAR	233	5TH DIST
ROBERTSON, ELIZA	WAS	150	HAGERSTO
ROBERTSON, ELIZA E.	SOM	510	BARREN C
ROBERTSON, ELIZABETH	SOM	470	TRAPPE D
ROBERTSON, ELIZABETH	SOM	554	TYASKIN
ROBERTSON, ELIZABETH	SOM	423	PRINCESS
ROBERTSON, ELIZABETH	BAL	382	13TH WAR
ROBERTSON, FRANCIS	SOM	547	TYASKIN
ROBERTSON, FRANCIS	ST	288	2ND E DI
ROBERTSON, FRANCIS	ALL	186	9TH E.D.
ROBERTSON, GEORGE	BAL	131	1ST WARD
ROBERTSON, GEORGE	DOR	460	1ST DIST
ROBERTSON, GEORGE M.	BAL	027	4TH WARD
ROBERTSON, HANDSCN	CHA	233	HILLTOP
ROBERTSON, HENRY	SOM	426	PRINCESS
ROBERTSON, HENRY	SOM	423	PRINCESS
ROBERTSON, HESTER A.	DOR	447	1ST DIST
ROBERTSON, HESTER-BLACK	MGM	418	MEDLEY 3
ROBERTSON, J.	BAL	129	1ST WARD
ROBERTSON, JAMES	BAL	062	15TH WAR
ROBERTSON, JAMES	BAL	122	1ST WARD
ROBERTSON, JAMES	CHA	249	MIDDLETO
ROBERTSON, JAMES	CHA	234	HILLTOP
ROBERTSON, JAMES	CHA	242	HILLTOP
ROBERTSON, JAMES	WOR	325	1ST E DI
ROBERTSON, JAMES	SOM	541	TYASKIN
ROBERTSON, JAMES	SOM	509	BARREN C
ROBERTSON, JAMES H.	FRE	100	FREDERIC
ROBERTSON, JAMES O.	CAL	028	2ND DIST
ROBERTSON, JESSE	BAL	193	17TH WAR
ROBERTSON, JESSE	BAL	016	2ND DIST
ROBERTSON, JOHN	BAL	133	1ST WARD
ROBERTSON, JOHN	BAL	172	1ST WARD
ROBERTSON, JOHN	CAL	025	2ND DIST
ROBERTSON, JOHN	CHA	242	HILLTOP
ROBERTSON, JOHN	DOR	431	1ST DIST
ROBERTSON, JOHN	SOM	509	BARREN C
ROBERTSON, JOHN	SOM	502	SALISBUR
ROBERTSON, JOHN	SOM	485	TRAPP DI
ROBERTSON, JOHN	WAS	126	2ND DIST
ROBERTSON, JOHN	SOM	362	BRINKLEY
ROBERTSON, JOHN	WOR	348	1ST E DI
ROBERTSON, JOHN E.	WOR	194	8TH E DI
ROBERTSON, JOHN F.	DOR	378	1ST DIST
ROBERTSON, JOHN H.	PRI	088	SPALDING
ROBERTSON, JOHN T.	BAL	360	13TH WAR
ROBERTSON, JOHN-BLACK	MGM	412	MEDLEY 3
ROBERTSON, JOSEPH	DOR	374	1ST DIST
ROBERTSON, JOSEPH	CAL	040	3RD DIST
ROBERTSON, JOSEPH	ALL	106	5TH E.D.
ROBERTSON, JOSEPH B.	DOR	379	1ST DIST
ROBERTSON, LEAH	SOM	544	TYASKIN
ROBERTSON, LEVIN	SOM	423	PRINCESS
ROBERTSON, MARGARET	BAL	052	15TH WAR
ROBERTSON, MARTHY	DOR	382	1ST DIST
ROBERTSON, MARY	CAL	024	2ND DIST
ROBERTSON, MARY	BAL	063	2ND DIST
ROBERTSON, MARY	SOM	539	TYASKIN
ROBERTSON, MARY	SOM	509	BARREN C
ROBERTSON, MARY A.	SOM	511	BARREN C
ROBERTSON, MARY A.	SOM	550	TYASKIN
ROBERTSON, MARY E.	SOM	539	TYASKIN
ROBERTSON, MARY W.R.	CEC	005	ELKTON 3
ROBERTSON, NANCY	SOM	401	BRINKLEY
ROBERTSON, NELLY	SOM	548	TYASKIN
ROBERTSON, PHILLIS H.	MGM	404	ROCKERLE
ROBERTSON, POLLY	CHA	241	HILLTOP
ROBERTSON, PRISCILLA A.	MGM	367	BERRYS D
ROBERTSON, RACHAEL	SOM	510	BARREN C
ROBERTSON, RACHEL T.	MGM	320	CRACKLIN
ROBERTSON, REBECCA	DOR	456	1ST DIST
ROBERTSON, RICHARD	BAL	159	1ST WARD
ROBERTSON, ROBERT	SOM	523	BARREN C
ROBERTSON, ROBERT	SOM	421	PRINCESS
ROBERTSON, ROBERT R.	DOR	373	1ST DIST
ROBERTSON, SAMUEL	MGM	380	ROCKERLE
ROBERTSON, SAMUEL	SOM	547	TYASKIN
ROBERTSON, SAMUEL	BAL	333	13TH WAR
ROBERTSON, SAMUEL F.	DOR	430	1ST DIST
ROBERTSON, SAMUEL W.	SOM	516	BARREN C
ROBERTSON, SIDONIA	BAL	145	16TH WAR
ROBERTSON, SOLOMON	DOR	387	1ST DIST
ROBERTSON, SOPHIA	DOR	376	1ST DIST

Name	County	Page	District
ROBERTSON, SUSAN	CHA	241	HILLTOP
ROBERTSON, SYDNEY	SOM	434	PRINCESS
ROBERTSON, THEODORE	MGM	378	ROCKERLE
ROBERTSON, THOMAS	DOR	431	1ST DIST
ROBERTSON, THOMAS	BAL	063	2ND DIST
ROBERTSON, THOMAS	SOM	531	QUANTICO
ROBERTSON, THOMAS	SOM	506	BARREN C
ROBERTSON, THOMAS	SOM	544	TYASKIN
ROBERTSON, THOMAS	WAS	150	2ND DIST
ROBERTSON, THOMAS F. H.	DOR	430	1ST DIST
ROBERTSON, VANCE	DOR	451	1ST DIST
ROBERTSON, WALTER H.	CHA	231	HILLTOP
ROBERTSON, WILLIAM	MGM	317	CRACKLIN
ROBERTSON, WILLIAM	CEC	025	ELKTON 3
ROBERTSON, WILLIAM	SOM	363	BRINKLEY
ROBERTSON, WILLIAM	WOR	336	1ST E DI
ROBERTSON, WILLIAM	SOM	547	TYASKIN
ROBERTSON, WILLIAM	SOM	550	TYASKIN
ROBERTSON, WILLIAM	BAL	007	1ST WARD
ROBERTSON, WILLIAM B.	PRI	109	PISCATAW
ROBERTSON, WILLIAM G.	MGM	403	ROCKERLE
ROBERTSON,NELSON R.	MGM	404	ROCKERLE
ROBERTSTON, A. H.	BAL	055	9TH WARD
ROBES, ELIZABETH	BAL	006	18TH WAR
ROBESTINE, SAMUEL	BAL	207	6TH DIST
ROBETH, CHARLES	BAL	328	13TH WAR
ROBEY, ANN	CHA	233	HILLTOP
ROBEY, AQUILLA	CHA	251	MIDDLETO
ROBEY, BARTON	CHA	290	BOJANTOW
ROBEY, CAROLINE	CHA	262	MIDDLETO
ROBEY, CATHERINE	CHA	228	ALLENS F
ROBEY, CHARLES C.	CHA	217	ALLENS F
ROBEY, CLOY	PRI	121	PISCATAW
ROBEY, CORNELIUS	CHA	254	MIDDLETO
ROBEY, ELIZABETH M.	PRI	055	AQUASCO
ROBEY, GEORGE	ALL	180	8TH E.D.
ROBEY, HENRY M.	CHA	287	BOJANTOW
ROBEY, JACOBY	ALL	179	7TH E.D.
ROBEY, JOHN	WAS	149	2ND DIST
ROBEY, MARGARET V.	WAS	261	1ST DIST
ROBEY, MARY	CHA	287	BOJANTOW
ROBEY, PHEBY	PRI	109	PISCATAW
ROBEY, RUFUS	CHA	285	BOJANTOW
ROBEY, SARA A.	CHA	228	BOJANTOW
ROBEY, URIAH	CHA	217	ALLENS F
ROBEY, WILLIAM	CHA	266	MIDDLETO
ROBEY, WILLIAM G.	CHA	259	MIDDLETO
ROBEY, WILLIAM S.	CHA	254	MIDDLETO
ROBIE, HEZEKIAH	ALL	024	3RD E.D.
ROBIN, ELIZA	BAL	038	1ST WARD
ROBIN, MARTHA	BAL	142	5TH WARD
ROBIN, MARY	BAL	291	12TH WAR
ROBIN, PATRICK	BAL	209	2ND WARD
ROBIN, S.	BAL	104	10TH WAR
ROBINET, JEREMIAH	WAS	196	1ST DIST
ROBINETT, AMOS	ALL	193	9TH E.D.
ROBINETT, CONRAC A.	ALL	191	9TH E.D.
ROBINETT, DORCAS	ALL	192	9TH E.D.
ROBINETT, ELI	ALL	193	9TH E.D.
ROBINETT, GEORGE	ALL	192	9TH E.D.
ROBINETT, GEORGE	ALL	193	9TH E.D.
ROBINETT, HARRYEN	ALL	185	9TH E.D.
ROBINETT, JAMES	ALL	189	9TH E.D.
ROBINETT, JASPER	ALL	193	9TH E.D.
ROBINETT, JASPER	ALL	185	9TH E.D.
ROBINETT, JEREMIAH	ALL	185	9TH E.D.
ROBINETT, JEROS W.	ALL	192	9TH E.D.
ROBINETT, M.G.	ALL	193	9TH E.D.
ROBINETT, MARTHA	ALL	186	9TH E.D.
ROBINETT, MASRA	ALL	192	9TH E.D.
ROBINETT, MOSES L.	ALL	190	9TH E.D.
ROBINETT, NATHAN	ALL	191	9TH E.D.
ROBINETT, SARAH	ALL	186	9TH E.D.
ROBINETT, WILLIAM	ALL	191	9TH E.D.
ROBINETTE, MOSES	ALL	186	9TH E.D.
ROBINGSN, JOHN T.	CAL	032	2ND DIST
ROBINS, AMBROSE	WOR	201	3RD E DI
ROBINS, AMBROSE	WOR	309	2ND E DI
ROBINS, AMOS	WOR	296	9TH E DI
ROBINS, ANOAZIA	WOR	263	BERLIN 1
ROBINS, ARTHUR	WOR	279	BERLIN 1
ROBINS, BENJAMIN	BAL	321	3RD WARD
ROBINS, EDWARD	WOR	273	BERLIN 1
ROBINS, EDWARD	WOR	189	7TH E DI
ROBINS, ELIZA-BLACK	WOR	326	1ST E DI
ROBINS, EMANUEL	WAS	046	2ND SUBD
ROBINS, GEORG	BAL	066	1ST WARD
ROBINS, HANDY	SOM	502	SALISBUR
ROBINS, HARVEY	SOM	502	SALISBUR
ROBINS, HET	WOR	279	BERLIN 1
ROBINS, ISAAC	WOR	292	9TH E DI
ROBINS, ISABELL	WOR	273	BERLIN 1
ROBINS, ISHMAEL	WOR	296	9TH E DI
ROBINS, JAMES	DOR	343	3RD DIVI
ROBINS, JAMES B.	WOR	299	SNOW HIL
ROBINS, JIM	WOR	282	BERLIN 1
ROBINS, JOHN	WOR	265	BERLIN 1
ROBINS, JOHN	WOR	300	SNOW HIL
ROBINS, JOHN	SOM	554	TYASKIN
ROBINS, JOHN	WOR	329	1ST E DI
ROBINS, LEAH	WOR	307	2ND E DI
ROBINS, LETTY	SOM	501	SALISBUR
ROBINS, LEWIS	BAL	124	1ST WARD
ROBINS, MARGARET	SOM	501	SALISBUR
ROBINS, MARGARET	SOM	554	TYASKIN
ROBINS, MARY	SOM	502	SALISBUR
ROBINS, MOSES	SOM	554	TYASKIN
ROBINS, MRS.*	DOR	454	1ST DIST
ROBINS, RHODA-BLACK	WOR	172	6TH E DI
ROBINS, SAMUEL	WOR	306	2ND E DI
ROBINS, WILLIAM	PRI	022	VANSVILL
ROBINS, WILLIAM	DOR	348	3RD DIVI
ROBINS, YORK	WOR	248	1ST CENS
ROBINSON, ACSHA	BAL	055	15TH WAR
ROBINSON, ADELINE	BAL	031	9TH WARD
ROBINSON, AGNES WIRT	BAL	404	14TH WAR
ROBINSON, AGUSTINE-BLACK	CAR	383	2ND DIST
ROBINSON, ALETHA A.	ANN	359	3RD DIST
ROBINSON, ALEXANDER	BAL	340	7TH WARD
ROBINSON, ALEXANDER	ALL	177	7TH E.D.
ROBINSON, ALEXANDER	BAL	156	16TH WAR
ROBINSON, ALEXANDER	BAL	403	14TH WAR
ROBINSON, ALEXANDER	BAL	177	19TH WAR
ROBINSON, ALEXANDER N.	SOM	513	BARREN C
ROBINSON, ALFRED T.	PRI	111	PISCATAW
ROBINSON, ALPHOUS	BAL	387	8TH WARD
ROBINSON, AMY	ANN	328	2ND DIST
ROBINSON, ANN	BAL	267	7TH WARD
ROBINSON, ANN	BAL	085	15TH WAR
ROBINSON, ANN	BAL	223	6TH WARD
ROBINSON, ANN	BAL	093	1ST WARD
ROBINSON, ANN	CAR	065	NO TWP L
ROBINSON, ANN	BAL	127	11TH WAR
ROBINSON, ANN	CEC	069	5TH E DI
ROBINSON, ANN	CEC	061	1ST E DI
ROBINSON, ANN	MGM	425	MEDLEY 3
ROBINSON, ANN	BAL	137	18TH WAR
ROBINSON, ANN E.	BAL	369	8TH WARD
ROBINSON, ANN J.	BAL	147	19TH WAR
ROBINSON, ANN M.	HAR	112	2ND DIST
ROBINSON, ANN M.	ANN	322	2ND DIST
ROBINSON, ANNA N.	FRE	065	FREDERIC
ROBINSON, ANNE	BAL	060	15TH WAR
ROBINSON, ANNIE	BAL	336	3RD WARD
ROBINSON, ANTHONY	BAL	015	1ST WARD
ROBINSON, ARCHIBALD	ANN	352	3RD DIST
ROBINSON, ARY F.	TAL	075	EASTON T
ROBINSON, AUGSUTSU	BAL	442	8TH WARD
ROBINSON, AUGUSTUS M.	BAL	168	16TH WAR
ROBINSON, BALINDA	BAL	365	3RD WARD
ROBINSON, BECKY	ANN	288	ANNAPOLI
ROBINSON, BENJAMIN	ANN	346	3RD DIST
ROBINSON, BENJAMIN	CAL	033	2ND DIST
ROBINSON, BENJAMIN	BAL	266	20TH WAR
ROBINSON, BRIDGET	BAL	411	3RD WARD
ROBINSON, BRIDGET	BAL	064	2ND DIST
ROBINSON, BROWN	BAL	260	20TH WAR
ROBINSON, C.	BAL	155	1ST WARD
ROBINSON, CAROLINE	BAL	144	19TH WAR
ROBINSON, CATHARINE	ANN	430	HOWARD D
ROBINSON, CATHARINE	BAL	333	13TH WAR
ROBINSON, CATHARINE	BAL	239	12TH WAR
ROBINSON, CATHARINE	WAS	159	HAGERSTO
ROBINSON, CATHARINE	TAL	015	EASTON D
ROBINSON, CATHARINE R.	BAL	077	1ST WARD
ROBINSON, CATHERINE	BAL	190	11TH WAR
ROBINSON, CATHERINE	BAL	185	11TH WAR
ROBINSON, CATHERINE	ALL	251	CUMBERLA
ROBINSON, CATHERINE	BAL	274	7TH WARD
ROBINSON, CHARELS	BAL	150	1ST WARD
ROBINSON, CHARLE	BAL	058	2ND DIST
ROBINSON, CHARLES	BAL	037	2ND DIST
ROBINSON, CHARLES	BAL	222	6TH WARD
ROBINSON, CHARLES	BAL	122	1ST WARD
ROBINSON, CHARLES	BAL	116	1ST WARD
ROBINSON, CHARLES	BAL	297	12TH WAR
ROBINSON, CHARLES	TAL	094	ST MICHA
ROBINSON, CHARLES	TAL	068	EASTON T
ROBINSON, CHARLES	PRI	104	PISCATAW
ROBINSON, CHARLES	HAR	073	1ST DIST
ROBINSON, CHARLES	BAL	033	18TH WAR
ROBINSON, CHARLES	FRE	189	5TH E DI
ROBINSON, CHARLOTT	BAL	371	3RD WARD
ROBINSON, CHARLOTTE	BAL	167	16TH WAR
ROBINSON, CHARLOTTE-BLACK	FRE	046	FREDERIC
ROBINSON, CHRISTIANE	BAL	124	18TH WAR
ROBINSON, CLARA J.	BAL	132	16TH WAR
ROBINSON, CRISSA	SOM	538	TYASKIN
ROBINSON, CYRUS	WAS	248	SMITHSBU
ROBINSON, DALEY	DOR	426	1ST DIST
ROBINSON, DANIEL	BAL	014	18TH WAR
ROBINSON, DANIEL	QUE	236	4TH E DI
ROBINSON, DARKEY	KEN	285	3RD DIST
ROBINSON, DASHREE	BAL	222	12TH WAR
ROBINSON, DAVID	ANN	348	3RD DIST
ROBINSON, DAVID	BAL	129	1ST WARD
ROBINSON, DAVID	ALL	192	9TH E.D.
ROBINSON, DAVID	BAL	246	17TH WAR
ROBINSON, DAVID-BLACK	FRE	042	FREDERIC
ROBINSON, DEBBY	ANN	516	HOWARD D
ROBINSON, DELIA	BAL	141	11TH WAR
ROBINSON, DENNIS	BAL	111	1ST WARD
ROBINSON, DICK	ANN	420	HOWARD D
ROBINSON, DOLLY C.	SOM	549	TYASKIN
ROBINSON, EDWARD	BAL	132	1ST WARD
ROBINSON, EDWARD F.	FRE	150	10TH E D
ROBINSON, EDWARD W.	BAL	378	3RD WARD
ROBINSON, EDWARD W.	BAL	185	2ND WARD
ROBINSON, ELI	ALL	258	CUMBERLA
ROBINSON, ELI	ALL	212	CUMBERLA
ROBINSON, ELIZA	ANN	350	3RD DIST
ROBINSON, ELIZA	BAL	370	8TH WARD
ROBINSON, ELIZA	ANN	514	HOWARD D
ROBINSON, ELIZA	BAL	074	10TH WAR
ROBINSON, ELIZA	FRE	149	10TH E D
ROBINSON, ELIZA	HAR	173	3RD DIST
ROBINSON, ELIZA	KEN	291	3RD DIST
ROBINSON, ELIZA	QUE	222	4TH E DI
ROBINSON, ELIZA MRS-	BAL	315	20TH WAR
ROBINSON, ELIZABETH	BAL	192	19TH WAR
ROBINSON, ELIZABETH	SOM	518	BARREN C
ROBINSON, ELIZABETH	BAL	384	3RD WARD
ROBINSON, ELIZABETH	BAL	392	3RD WARD
ROBINSON, ELIZABETH	BAL	277	2ND WARD
ROBINSON, ELIZABETH	ANN	286	ANNAPOLI
ROBINSON, ELIZABETH	BAL	006	9TH WARD
ROBINSON, ELIZABETH	BAL	003	9TH WARD
ROBINSON, ELIZABETH	BAL	015	9TH WARD
ROBINSON, ELIZABETH G.	BAL	444	8TH WARD
ROBINSON, ELIZABTH	ALL	188	9TH E.D.
ROBINSON, ELLEN M. R.	BAL	087	15TH WAR
ROBINSON, EMELINE	BAL	049	15TH WAR
ROBINSON, EMILY	BAL	191	11TH WAR
ROBINSON, EMILY	BAL	140	19TH WAR
ROBINSON, EMMA	BAL	371	8TH WARD
ROBINSON, FANNY	BAL	165	16TH WAR
ROBINSON, FRANCAS-MULATTO	BAL	223	2ND WARD
ROBINSON, FRANCIS	ANN	455	HOWARD D
ROBINSON, FRANSIS	WAS	056	2ND SUBD
ROBINSON, FREDERICK	QUE	249	5TH E DI
ROBINSON, GEORGANNA	BAL	207	11TH WAR
ROBINSON, GEORGE	BAL	185	11TH WAR
ROBINSON, GEORGE	BAL	053	2ND DIST
ROBINSON, GEORGE	ALL	106	5TH E.D.
ROBINSON, GEORGE	ALL	092	5TH E.D.
ROBINSON, GEORGE	ALL	092	5TH E.D.
ROBINSON, GEORGE	BAL	357	3RD WARD
ROBINSON, GEORGE	BAL	120	1ST WARD
ROBINSON, GEORGE	BAL	152	2ND DIST
ROBINSON, GEORGE	HAR	111	2ND DIST
ROBINSON, GEORGE	CEC	077	NORTHEAS
ROBINSON, GEORGE	BAL	280	17TH WAR
ROBINSON, GEORGE	DOR	346	3RD DIVI
ROBINSON, GEORGE A.*	BAL	311	3RD WARD
ROBINSON, GEORGE W.	BAL	167	11TH WAR
ROBINSON, GEORGE W.	TAL	060	EASTON D
ROBINSON, GEORGE W.	SOM	538	TYASKIN
ROBINSON, GEORGIANA	BAL	088	4TH WARD
ROBINSON, GOERGE	WAS	012	WILLIAMS
ROBINSON, GRAFTON	HAR	083	2ND DIST
ROBINSON, HANNAH R.	BAL	045	18TH WAR
ROBINSON, HARRIET	BAL	084	1ST WARD
ROBINSON, HARRIET	BAL	034	9TH WARD
ROBINSON, HARRIET F.	ANN	521	HOWARD D
ROBINSON, HELEN	ALL	241	CUMBERLA
ROBINSON, HENNERITTA	DOR	309	1ST DIST
ROBINSON, HENRIETTA	BAL	420	3RD WARD
ROBINSON, HENRY	BAL	269	20TH WAR
ROBINSON, HENRY	BAL	046	18TH WAR
ROBINSON, HENRY	DOR	300	1ST DIST
ROBINSON, HENRY	BAL	056	4TH WARD
ROBINSON, HENRY	FRE	046	FREDERIC
ROBINSON, HENRY	CEC	067	5TH E DI
ROBINSON, HENRY	BAL	404	3RD WARD
ROBINSON, HENRY B.	BAL	317	7TH WARD
ROBINSON, HENRY R.	BAL	046	9TH WARD
ROBINSON, HERMAN	PRI	031	VANSVILL
ROBINSON, HESTER	BAL	385	8TH WARD
ROBINSON, HEZAKIAH	WAS	153	HAGERSTO
ROBINSON, HIRAM	BAL	139	1ST WARD
ROBINSON, HUNTER	BAL	266	20TH WAR
ROBINSON, ISABEL	BAL	305	20TH WAR
ROBINSON, J.	BAL	152	1ST WARD
ROBINSON, J.	BAL	265	12TH WAR
ROBINSON, J.	PRI	100	SPALDING
ROBINSON, J.H.	BAL	255	20TH WAR
ROBINSON, JACKSON	BAL	152	2ND DIST
ROBINSON, JACOB	HAR	083	2ND DIST
ROBINSON, JAMES	DOR	346	3RD DIVI
ROBINSON, JAMES	FRE	123	CREAGERS
ROBINSON, JAMES	FRE	122	CREAGERS
ROBINSON, JAMES	BAL	384	13TH WAR
ROBINSON, JAMES	CEC	162	6TH E DI
ROBINSON, JAMES	BAL	179	19TH WAR
ROBINSON, JAMES	BAL	176	19TH WAR
ROBINSON, JAMES	CAL	034	2ND DIST
ROBINSON, JAMES	BAL	121	1ST WARD
ROBINSON, JAMES	BAL	037	1ST WARD
ROBINSON, JAMES	BAL	143	1ST WARD
ROBINSON, JAMES	BAL	131	1ST WARD
ROBINSON, JAMES	BAL	144	16TH WAR
ROBINSON, JAMES	BAL	195	17TH WAR
ROBINSON, JAMES	BAL	011	2ND DIST
ROBINSON, JAMES	ALL	024	3RD E.D.
ROBINSON, JAMES	PRI	072	MARLBROU
ROBINSON, JAMES	PRI	021	VANSVILL
ROBINSON, JAMES	KEN	283	3RD DIST
ROBINSON, JAMES	KEN	281	3RD DIST
ROBINSON, JAMES A.	BAL	216	11TH WAR
ROBINSON, JAMES B.	CAL	053	3RD DIST
ROBINSON, JAMES C.	BAL	078	4TH WARD
ROBINSON, JAMES C.	HAR	195	3RD DIST
ROBINSON, JAMES S.	HAR	006	1ST DIST
ROBINSON, JAMES S.*	TAL	057	EASTON D
ROBINSON, JAMES-BLACK	CAR	084	NO TWP L
ROBINSON, JANE	BAL	279	20TH WAR
ROBINSON, JANE	WAS	157	HAGERSTO
ROBINSON, JANE	BAL	169	6TH WARD
ROBINSON, JANNETTE	BAL	371	13TH WAR
ROBINSON, JEREMIAH	CAR	283	7TH DIST
ROBINSON, JESSE-BLACK	WOR	345	1ST E DI
ROBINSON, JOBE B.A.	CAR	142	NO TWP L
ROBINSON, JOHN	CAL	031	2ND DIST
ROBINSON, JOHN	CAR	283	7TH DIST
ROBINSON, JOHN	CEC	063	1ST E DI
ROBINSON, JOHN	CEC	056	1ST E DI
ROBINSON, JOHN	CEC	120	3RD E DI
ROBINSON, JOHN	BAL	370	13TH WAR
ROBINSON, JOHN	BAL	081	4TH WARD
ROBINSON, JOHN	BAL	246	17TH WAR
ROBINSON, JOHN	HAR	010	1ST DIST
ROBINSON, JOHN	HAR	007	1ST DIST
ROBINSON, JOHN	HAR	050	1ST DIST
ROBINSON, JOHN	HAR	039	1ST DIST
ROBINSON, JOHN	HAR	078	2ND DIST
ROBINSON, JOHN	BAL	180	19TH WAR
ROBINSON, JOHN	WAS	152	HAGERSTO
ROBINSON, JOHN	QUE	225	4TH E DI
ROBINSON, JOHN	WAS	247	SMITHSBU
ROBINSON, JOHN	SOM	511	BARREN C
ROBINSON, JOHN	BAL	159	1ST WARD
ROBINSON, JOHN	ALL	184	9TH E.D.
ROBINSON, JOHN	ALL	177	7TH E.D.
ROBINSON, JOHN	BAL	189	17TH WAR
ROBINSON, JOHN	BAL	079	15TH WAR
ROBINSON, JOHN	BAL	095	10TH WAR
ROBINSON, JOHN	BAL	112	15TH WAR
ROBINSON, JOHN	BAL	143	1ST WARD
ROBINSON, JOHN	BAL	403	3RD WARD
ROBINSON, JOHN	BAL	282	2ND WARD
ROBINSON, JOHN	BAL	282	2ND WARD
ROBINSON, JOHN	BAL	253	2ND WARD
ROBINSON, JOHN	BAL	278	7TH WARD
ROBINSON, JOHN	BAL	115	1ST WARD
ROBINSON, JOHN	BAL	124	1ST WARD
ROBINSON, JOHN	BAL	001	1ST WARD
ROBINSON, JOHN	BAL	032	1ST WARD
ROBINSON, JOHN	BAL	458	8TH WARD
ROBINSON, JOHN C.	BAL	345	13TH WAR
ROBINSON, JOHN H.	ANN	354	3RD DIST
ROBINSON, JOHN H.	BAL	348	3RD WARD
ROBINSON, JOHN M.	BAL	225	6TH WARD
ROBINSON, JOHN M.	QUE	182	3RD E DI
ROBINSON, JOHN Q. A.	TAL	070	EASTON T
ROBINSON, JOHN R.	BAL	053	18TH WAR
ROBINSON, JOHN S.	BAL	233	12TH WAR
ROBINSON, JOHN T.	KEN	290	3RD DIST
ROBINSON, JOHN T.	TAL	009	EASTON D
ROBINSON, JOHN W.	BAL	421	14TH WAR
ROBINSON, JOSEPH	HAR	008	1ST DIST
ROBINSON, JOSEPH	DOR	404	1ST DIST
ROBINSON, JOSEPH	BAL	182	11TH WAR
ROBINSON, JOSEPH	BAL	007	1ST WARD
ROBINSON, JOSEPH	BAL	311	7TH WARD
ROBINSON, JOSEPH	BAL	191	17TH WAR
ROBINSON, JOSEPH	ANN	310	1ST DIST
ROBINSON, JOSEPH B.	HAR	133	2ND DIST
ROBINSON, JOSEPH E.	ALL	106	5TH E.D.
ROBINSON, JOSEPH S.	HAR	042	1ST DIST
ROBINSON, JOSHUA	CAR	267	WESTMINS
ROBINSON, JOSHUA	BAL	100	18TH WAR
ROBINSON, JOSHUA	BAL	412	3RD WARD
ROBINSON, JOSHUA	BAL	397	14TH WAR
ROBINSON, JOSHUA	BAL	102	15TH WAR
ROBINSON, JOSHUA*	BAL	339	3RD WARD
ROBINSON, JOVIN	FRE	128	CREAGERS
ROBINSON, JULIA	BAL	476	14TH WAR
ROBINSON, JULIA	BAL	172	2ND DIST
ROBINSON, JULIA A.	BAL	447	14TH WAR
ROBINSON, JULIANN	BAL	153	5TH WARD

ROBINSON, JULIANN QUE 225 4TH E DI
ROBINSON, L. BAL 151 5TH WARD
ROBINSON, LAURA BAL 397 3RD WARD
ROBINSON, LAVINIA BAL 136 16TH WAR
ROBINSON, LAWSON-MULATTO FRE 028 FREDERIC
ROBINSON, LEAH DOR 299 1ST DIST
ROBINSON, LEVERNIA * TAL 076 EASTON T
ROBINSON, LEVIN CAR 140 NO TWP L
ROBINSON, LEVIN* DOR 425 1ST DIST
ROBINSON, LEVINE BAL 456 8TH WARD
ROBINSON, LEWIS BAL 458 8TH WARD
ROBINSON, LEWIS BAL 256 12TH WAR
ROBINSON, LEWIS BAL 009 1ST WARD
ROBINSON, LOUISA BAL 121 16TH WAR
ROBINSON, LOUISA MGM 392 ROCKERLE
ROBINSON, LOUISA MGM 372 BERRYS D
ROBINSON, LOUISA E. BAL 413 3RD WARD
ROBINSON, LUCINDA BAL 420 3RD WARD
ROBINSON, M. S. ANN 295 1ST DIST
ROBINSON, MABLE BAL 322 7TH WARD
ROBINSON, MAHALA BAL 151 2ND DIST
ROBINSON, MAHALA BAL 031 9TH WARD
ROBINSON, MAHALA BAL 082 18TH WAR
ROBINSON, MAJOR A. SOM 511 BARREN C
ROBINSON, MALINDA WAS 143 HAGERSTO
ROBINSON, MARGARET TAL 069 EASTON T
ROBINSON, MARGARET BAL 087 18TH WAR
ROBINSON, MARGARET FRE 203 5TH E DI
ROBINSON, MARGARET BAL 313 7TH WARD
ROBINSON, MARGARET BAL 302 12TH WAR
ROBINSON, MARGARET S. TAL 048 EASTON T
ROBINSON, MARIA BAL 151 11TH WAR
ROBINSON, MARIA BAL 434 14TH WAR
ROBINSON, MARTHA BAL 102 15TH WAR
ROBINSON, MARTHA M. TAL 093 ST MICHA
ROBINSON, MARTHA W. CAL 053 3RD DIST
ROBINSON, MARTIN CAR 112 NO TWP L
ROBINSON, MARY BAL 136 11TH WAR
ROBINSON, MARY BAL 078 4TH WARD
ROBINSON, MARY BAL 087 4TH WARD
ROBINSON, MARY BAL 063 4TH WARD
ROBINSON, MARY BAL 384 13TH WAR
ROBINSON, MARY HAR 023 1ST DIST
ROBINSON, MARY HAR 070 1ST DIST
ROBINSON, MARY FRE 056 FREDERIC
ROBINSON, MARY BAL 269 20TH WAR
ROBINSON, MARY BAL 261 20TH WAR
ROBINSON, MARY BAL 332 13TH WAR
ROBINSON, MARY BAL 189 17TH WAR
ROBINSON, MARY BAL 160 6TH WARD
ROBINSON, MARY BAL 352 3RD WARD
ROBINSON, MARY BAL 083 1ST WARD
ROBINSON, MARY BAL 396 3RD WARD
ROBINSON, MARY BAL 313 7TH WARD
ROBINSON, MARY BAL 308 3RD WARD
ROBINSON, MARY A. BAL 025 1ST WARD
ROBINSON, MARY A. BAL 044 1ST WARD
ROBINSON, MARY A. BAL 159 19TH WAR
ROBINSON, MARY A. QUE 232 4TH E DI
ROBINSON, MARY E. ANN 322 2ND DIST
ROBINSON, MARY H. SOM 490 SALISBUR
ROBINSON, MARY M. HAR 039 1ST DIST
ROBINSON, MARY-BLACK BAL 215 2ND WARD
ROBINSON, MATILDA BAL 246 2ND WARD
ROBINSON, MATILDA BAL 145 11TH WAR
ROBINSON, MATILDA BAL 209 19TH WAR
ROBINSON, MATTHEW BAL 467 14TH WAR
ROBINSON, MEPHILICA BAL 377 13TH WAR
ROBINSON, MICHAEL BAL 073 1ST WARD
ROBINSON, MISS V. FRE 200 5TH E DI
ROBINSON, MORGAN ALL 004 3RD E.D.
ROBINSON, NANCY DOR 298 1ST DIST
ROBINSON, NATHANIEL BAL 347 3RD WARD
ROBINSON, NICHOLAS BAL 293 7TH WARD
ROBINSON, NICHOLAS MGM 331 CRACKLIN
ROBINSON, NICHOLAS MGM 372 BERRYS D
ROBINSON, OLIVER BAL 115 2ND DIST
ROBINSON, OWEN QUE 222 4TH E DI
ROBINSON, P.* TAL 066 EASTON T
ROBINSON, PERE QUE 233 4TH E DI
ROBINSON, PERRY KEN 285 3RD DIST
ROBINSON, PERRY BAL 424 14TH WAR
ROBINSON, PERRY H. TAL 114 ST MICHA
ROBINSON, PHILIP BAL 316 12TH WAR
ROBINSON, RACHAEL BAL 083 4TH WARD
ROBINSON, RACHEL BAL 101 10TH WAR
ROBINSON, RACHEL BAL 159 16TH WAR
ROBINSON, RACHEL BAL 270 7TH WARD
ROBINSON, RACHEL ANN 329 2ND DIST
ROBINSON, REBECA BAL 297 7TH WARD
ROBINSON, REBECA WAS 122 2ND DIST
ROBINSON, REBECCA BAL 121 2ND DIST
ROBINSON, REBECCA QUE 152 1ST E DI
ROBINSON, REBECCA KEN 215 2ND DIST
ROBINSON, REUBEN CAR 274 7TH DIST
ROBINSON, REZIN H. BAL 247 20TH WAR
ROBINSON, RICHARD CAR 293 7TH DIST
ROBINSON, RICHARD BAL 151 19TH WAR
ROBINSON, RICHARD BAL 290 7TH WARD
ROBINSON, RICHARD BAL 322 7TH WARD
ROBINSON, RICHARD QUE 234 4TH E DI
ROBINSON, ROBERT A. HAR 080 2ND DIST
ROBINSON, ROBERT E. ANN 313 1ST DIST
ROBINSON, RODA BAL 388 13TH WAR
ROBINSON, SAMUEL BAL 463 14TH WAR
ROBINSON, SAMUEL HAR 077 BEL AIR
ROBINSON, SAMUEL HAR 035 1ST DIST
ROBINSON, SAMUEL CAR 274 7TH DIST
ROBINSON, SAMUEL DOR 307 1ST DIST
ROBINSON, SAMUEL ALL 176 7TH E.D.
ROBINSON, SAMUEL BAL 343 3RD WARD
ROBINSON, SAMUEL BAL 420 8TH WARD
ROBINSON, SAMUEL DOR 469 1ST DIST
ROBINSON, SAMUEL A. SOM 538 TYASKIN
ROBINSON, SAMUEL L. BAL 404 3RD WARD
ROBINSON, SAMUEL S. QUE 191 3RD E DI
ROBINSON, SARAH BAL 117 5TH WARD
ROBINSON, SARAH BAL 275 12TH WAR
ROBINSON, SARAH BAL 365 3RD WARD
ROBINSON, SARAH BAL 109 1ST WARD
ROBINSON, SARAH BAL 056 4TH WARD
ROBINSON, SARAH BAL 346 13TH WAR
ROBINSON, SARAH BAL 221 17TH WAR
ROBINSON, SARAH CEC 052 1ST E DI
ROBINSON, SARAH BAL 394 14TH WAR
ROBINSON, SARAH QUE 145 1ST E DI
ROBINSON, SARAH A. BAL 194 19TH WAR
ROBINSON, SARAH-MULATTO FRE 046 FREDERIC
ROBINSON, SEDONIA A. BAL 195 17TH WAR
ROBINSON, SEVENIE * TAL 093 ST MICHA
ROBINSON, SLAYTOR B. CEC 163 6TH E DI
ROBINSON, SOLOMON TAL 041 EASTON D
ROBINSON, SOPHIA WAS 199 1ST DIST
ROBINSON, SOPHIA BAL 375 13TH WAR
ROBINSON, SOPHIA BAL 185 11TH WAR
ROBINSON, STEPHEN BAL 263 12TH WAR
ROBINSON, STEPHEN BAL 296 17TH WAR
ROBINSON, STEPHEN A. BAL 030 1ST WARD
ROBINSON, SUSAN BAL 019 15TH WAR
ROBINSON, SUSAN BAL 084 18TH WAR
ROBINSON, SUSAN BAL 377 13TH WAR
ROBINSON, SUSAN CAR 228 5TH DIST
ROBINSON, SUSAN M. CEC 136 6TH E DI
ROBINSON, SUSANA BAL 293 7TH WARD
ROBINSON, T.A. BAL 135 1ST WARD
ROBINSON, T.G. WAS 126 HAGERSTO
ROBINSON, THEADORE BAL 381 8TH WARD
ROBINSON, THOAMS HAR 026 1ST DIST
ROBINSON, THOMAS HAR 009 1ST DIST
ROBINSON, THOMAS BAL 078 4TH WARD
ROBINSON, THOMAS BAL 204 17TH WAR
ROBINSON, THOMAS BAL 212 19TH WAR
ROBINSON, THOMAS BAL 151 19TH WAR
ROBINSON, THOMAS BAL 033 1ST WARD
ROBINSON, THOMAS BAL 055 9TH WARD
ROBINSON, THOMAS BAL 075 2ND DIST
ROBINSON, THOMAS BAL 019 9TH WARD
ROBINSON, THOMAS BAL 173 1ST WARD
ROBINSON, THOMAS WAS 246 SMITHSBU
ROBINSON, THOMAS TAL 060 EASTON D
ROBINSON, THOMAS B. CAL 053 3RD DIST
ROBINSON, THOMAS R. BAL 416 3RD WARD
ROBINSON, THOMAS W. PRI 111 PISCATAW
ROBINSON, VALENTINE-BLACK QUE 157 2ND E DI
ROBINSON, WASHINGTON H. SOM 538 TYASKIN
ROBINSON, WELRY ANN 277 ANNAPOLI
ROBINSON, WILLAIM BAL 154 19TH WAR
ROBINSON, WILLAIM N. BAL 369 8TH WARD
ROBINSON, WILLIAM BAL 131 1ST WARD
ROBINSON, WILLIAM BAL 281 7TH WARD
ROBINSON, WILLIAM BAL 145 1ST WARD
ROBINSON, WILLIAM ALL 002 3RD E.D.
ROBINSON, WILLIAM ALL 088 5TH E.D.
ROBINSON, WILLIAM BAL 174 1ST WARD
ROBINSON, WILLIAM BAL 157 1ST WARD
ROBINSON, WILLIAM ANN 352 3RD DIST
ROBINSON, WILLIAM BAL 126 16TH WAR
ROBINSON, WILLIAM BAL 025 1ST WARD
ROBINSON, WILLIAM BAL 119 1ST WARD
ROBINSON, WILLIAM BAL 097 1ST WARD
ROBINSON, WILLIAM BAL 016 1ST WARD
ROBINSON, WILLIAM BAL 345 3RD WARD
ROBINSON, WILLIAM DOR 404 1ST DIST
ROBINSON, WILLIAM BAL 203 19TH WAR
ROBINSON, WILLIAM BAL 212 19TH WAR
ROBINSON, WILLIAM CEC 022 ELKTON 3
ROBINSON, WILLIAM DOR 299 1ST DIST
ROBINSON, WILLIAM BAL 058 4TH WARD
ROBINSON, WILLIAM FRE 094 FREDERIC
ROBINSON, WILLIAM FRE 057 FREDERIC
ROBINSON, WILLIAM CEC 052 1ST E DI
ROBINSON, WILLIAM CEC 069 5TH E DI
ROBINSON, WILLIAM BAL 088 18TH WAR
ROBINSON, WILLIAM DOR 343 3RD DIVI
ROBINSON, WILLIAM QUE 228 4TH E DI
ROBINSON, WILLIAM C. BAL 197 11TH WAR
ROBINSON, WILLIAM H. BAL 081 15TH WAR
ROBINSON, WILLIAM H. BAL 128 1ST WARD
ROBINSON, WILLIAM T. BAL 132 1ST WARD
ROBINSON, ZACHARIAH-BLACK BAL 225 2ND WARD
ROBINSON, ZEDOCK PRI 111 PISCATAW
ROBINSON,J. BAL 173 1ST WARD
ROBINSON,JOHN B. BAL 130 1ST WARD
ROBINSON,RICHARD-BLACK QUE 161 2ND E DI
ROBINSON,S ARAH BAL 036 1ST WARD
ROBINSON,W ILLIAM BAL 161 1ST WARD
ROBINSON,W ILLIAM CAR 091 NO TWP L
ROBISON, A. BAL 332 1ST DIST
ROBISON, ADAM-BLACK FRE 051 FREDERIC
ROBISON, ANNA ALL 244 CUMBERLA
ROBISON, CAROLINE BAL 315 1ST DIST
ROBISON, CECELIA BAL 255 1ST DIST
ROBISON, DANEIL BAL 250 1ST DIST
ROBISON, DANIEL BAL 415 1ST DIST
ROBISON, ELIZA BAL 458 1ST DIST
ROBISON, EMILINE BAL 304 1ST DIST
ROBISON, HAMMITAL BAL 328 1ST DIST
ROBISON, HANNAH BAL 227 1ST DIST
ROBISON, HARRY BAL 407 1ST DIST
ROBISON, HENRY ALL 256 CUMBERLA
ROBISON, JAMES BAL 256 1ST DIST
ROBISON, JANE WAS 160 2ND DIST
ROBISON, JOHN BAL 256 1ST DIST
ROBISON, JOHN BAL 304 1ST DIST
ROBISON, JOHN ALL 235 CUMBERLA
ROBISON, JOHN BAL 407 1ST DIST
ROBISON, JOHN BAL 366 1ST DIST
ROBISON, JOHN BAL 330 1ST DIST
ROBISON, JOHN BAL 002 15TH WAR
ROBISON, JOHN A. ALL 243 CUMBERLA
ROBISON, JULIA BAL 257 1ST DIST
ROBISON, LOUISA BAL 403 1ST DIST
ROBISON, MARGARET CAR 199 4TH DIST
ROBISON, MARY BAL 257 1ST DIST
ROBISON, PHILLIS ALL 257 CUMBERLA
ROBISON, RACHAEL BAL 301 1ST DIST
ROBISON, RACHAEL BAL 285 1ST DIST
ROBISON, RICHARD BAL 383 1ST DIST
ROBISON, SAMUEL BAL 364 1ST DIST
ROBISON, SARAH BAL 459 1ST DIST
ROBISON, SARAH BAL 317 1ST DIST
ROBISON, SOPHIA A. BAL 088 15TH WAR
ROBISON, SUSAN BAL 381 1ST DIST
ROBISON, THOMAS BAL 352 1ST DIST
ROBISON, THOMAS BAL 366 1ST DIST
ROBISON, WILLIAM BAL 293 1ST DIST
ROBISON, WILLIAM ALL 209 CUMBERLA
ROBLE, THOMAS FRE 138 CREAGERS
ROBLINGS, JULIA A. BAL 206 11TH WAR
ROBLITZ, HY BAL 199 5TH DIST
ROBORN, DANIEL-MULATTO BAL 234 2ND WARD
ROBORN, DANIEL-MULATTO BAL 234 2ND WARD
ROBOSON, ALEXANDER ALL 037 2ND E.D.
ROBOSON, THOMAS P. ALL 185 9TH E.D.
ROBRECHT, JOHN H.* TAL 065 EASTON T
ROBRETSON, PHILLIP BAL 224 12TH WAR
ROBS, WASHINGTON CAR 220 5TH DIST
ROBSON, JOHN BAL 146 1ST WARD
ROBSON, MARIA L. BAL 074 10TH WAR
ROBSON, SARH M. TAL 090 ST MICHA
ROBSON, THOMAS R. TAL 068 EASTON T
ROBURGH, JOHN BAL 082 1ST WARD
ROBY, ALEXINA PRI 038 VANSVILL
ROBY, ALFRED CHA 228 ALLENS F
ROBY, AMOS-BLACK WOR 320 1ST E DI
ROBY, BASIL MGM 354 BERRYS D
ROBY, CATHARINE-MULATTO WOR 341 1ST E DI
ROBY, DANIEL-BLACK WOR 344 1ST E DI
ROBY, EDGAR PRI 037 VANSVILL
ROBY, ELISHA CHA 228 ALLENS F
ROBY, FRANCIS CHA 260 MIDDLETO
ROBY, HENRY CHA 228 BOJANTOW
ROBY, HENRY M. CHA 261 MIDDLETO
ROBY, ISAAC ALL 180 8TH E.D.
ROBY, JACKSON WAS 154 2ND DIST
ROBY, JAMES WAS 153 2ND DIST
ROBY, JAMES WAS 049 2ND SUBD
ROBY, JOHN C. PRI 037 VANSVILL
ROBY, LEVIN-BLACK WOR 319 1ST E DI
ROBY, MARY WAS 138 2ND DIST
ROBY, MARY CHA 267 MIDDLETO
ROBY, MARY CHA 289 MIDDLETO
ROBY, NANCY CHA 228 ALLENS F
ROBY, NELSON PRI 038 VANSVILL
ROBY, OWEN ALL 180 8TH E.D.
ROBY, SAMUEL G. CHA 261 MIDDLETO
ROBY, SAMUEL H. CHA 229 MIDDLETO
ROBY, SHADRICK-BLACK WOR 323 1ST E DI
ROBY, SIMEON BAL 460 1ST DIST
ROBY, STACY CHA 250 MIDDLETO
ROBY, THEADORE CHA 291 MIDDLETO
ROBY, THEADORE CHA 292 BOJANTOW
ROBY, THOMAS Y. CHA 262 MIDDLETO
ROBY, TOWNLEY B. * BAL 399 8TH WARD
ROBY, WILLAM HAR 076 BEL AIR
ROBY, WILLIAM BAL 405 14TH WAR
ROBY, WILLIAM A. WOR 320 1ST E DI
ROBY, WILLIAM B. CHA 260 MIDDLETO
ROBY, WILLIAM H. WOR 341 1ST E DI
ROBY, WILLIAM Z. CHA 249 MIDDLETO
ROCH, JOHN BAL 237 2ND WARD
ROCH, MORRIS BAL 367 8TH WARD
ROCHE, EDMUND BAL 248 6TH WARD
ROCHE, MARIA J. BAL 062 4TH WARD
ROCHE, P. BAL 159 1ST WARD
ROCHE, P. BAL 162 1ST WARD
ROCHE, PETER BAL 174 1ST WARD
ROCHE,EDWARD BAL 100 1ST WARD
ROCHE,WILLIAM AN. BAL 173 1ST WARD
ROCHESTER, ABRAHAM-BLACK QUE 147 1ST E DI
ROCHESTER, ANN BAL 177 6TH WARD
ROCHESTER, ANN QUE 178 2ND E DI
ROCHESTER, ANN QUE 187 3RD E DI
ROCHESTER, ARTHUR-BLACK QUE 174 2ND E DI
ROCHESTER, BENJAMIN-BLACK CAR 080 NO TWP L
ROCHESTER, DAVID QUE 173 2ND E DI
ROCHESTER, FRANCIS A. QUE 168 2ND E DI
ROCHESTER, FRANCIS H. KEN 284 3RD DIST
ROCHESTER, JOSEPH E. CAR 170 NO TWP L
ROCHESTER, LETITIA QUE 153 1ST E DI
ROCHESTER, MARY-BLACK CAR 081 NO TWP L
ROCHESTER, NANCY-BLACK QUE 158 2ND E DI
ROCHESTER, THOMAS KEN 301 3RD DIST
ROCHESTER, WILLIAM KEN 305 3RD DIST
ROCHESTER, WILLIAM KEN 310 3RD DIST
ROCHIE, E. BAL 449 8TH WARD
ROCHLER, FRANCES BAL 368 13TH WAR
ROCIER, NELSON BAL 033 2ND DIST
ROCK, ANN CEC 118 4TH E DI
ROCK, CATHARINE BAL 125 5TH WARD
ROCK, CHARLES ST 336 4TH E DI
ROCK, ELANOR WOR 314 2ND E DI
ROCK, FRANCIS J. HAR 146 3RD DIST
ROCK, GEORGE CEC 127 5TH E DI
ROCK, HENRY SOM 534 QUANTICO
ROCK, JAMES ST 328 4TH E DI
ROCK, JANE ST 340 5TH E DI
ROCK, JOSEPH BAL 406 8TH WARD
ROCK, LUCY WOR 303 SNOW HIL
ROCK, MARY WOR 228 6TH E DI
ROCK, MARY BAL 041 4TH WARD
ROCK, MARY E. WOR 228 6TH E DI
ROCK, NEAL BAL 360 8TH WARD
ROCK, PATRICK ALL 196 CUMBERLA
ROCK, SARAH TAL 020 EASTON D
ROCK, SCLINE SOM 475 TRAPPE D
ROCK, THOMAS WOR 316 2ND E DI
ROCK, THOMAS BAL 168 2ND DIST
ROCK, THOMAS BAL 137 16TH WAR
ROCK, TIMOTHY BAL 186 11TH WAR
ROCK, WILLIAM WOR 237 6TH E DI
ROCK, WILLIAM CEC 129 5TH E DI
ROCK, WILLIAM BAL 369 13TH WAR
ROCKBACK, LAWRENCE CAR 342 6TH DIST
ROCKE, JOHN H. BAL 382 13TH WAR
ROCKEL, HENRY BAL 352 13TH WAR
ROCKEPEN, CHRISTINA BAL 109 1ST WARD
ROCKETT, EDMOND PRI 058 NOTTINGH
ROCKHOLD, ELIJAH ANN 348 3RD DIST
ROCKHOLD, ELIJAH HAR 059 1ST DIST
ROCKHOLD, ELIZABETH BAL 367 3RD WARD
ROCKHOLD, JOHN WAS 118 2ND DIST
ROCKHOLD, SOLOMAN WAS 113 2ND DIST
ROCKHOLD, SUSAN BAL 032 2ND DIST
ROCKNEY, MATILDA BAL 001 18TH WAR
ROCKS, MICHAEL BAL 359 8TH WARD
ROCKS, PHILIP WAS 257 1ST DIST
ROCKS, THOMSON BAL 274 2ND WARD
ROCKSTEEN, GEORGE BAL 423 14TH WAR
ROCKWELL, ALFRED BAL 065 18TH WAR
ROCKWELL, ELIHU H. FRE 447 8TH E DI
ROCKWELL, JESSE WAS 150 2ND DIST
ROCKWELL, JOHN BAL 303 3RD WARD
ROCKWELL, LANES BAL 354 13TH WAR
ROCKWELL, RICHARD BAL 199 2ND WARD
ROCKWELL, THOMAS R. WAS 120 2ND DIST
ROCKWELL, WILLIAM WAS 131 2ND DIST
ROCKY, WILLIAM HAR 050 1ST DIST
ROCLETT, ROSA BAL 383 13TH WAR
ROCLKEY, PETER FRE 071 FREDERIC
ROD, ADAM BAL 386 13TH WAR
ROD, ANN BAL 421 8TH WARD
RODAMLOK, WILLIAM CEC 139 6TH E DI
RODAN, JAMES BAL 402 3RD WARD
RODDE, L. W. BAL 294 20TH WAR
RODDEN, MARY BAL 268 17TH WAR
RODDY, JOHN FRE 147 10TH E D
RODDY, MARTH FRE 186 5TH E DI
RODE, RUTH BAL 307 20TH WAR
RODEGAN, MICHAEL ALL 135 4TH E.D.

Name	County	Page	District
RODEMER, GEORGE	ALL	120	5TH E.D.
RODEWISER, JOHN	FRE	112	CREAGERS
RODEMYER, ERNEST	BAL	207	19TH WAR
RODEN, BARBARA	BAL	337	3RD WARD
RODEN, MARY J.	BAL	173	6TH WARD
RODEN, PATRICK	BAL	081	10TH WAR
RODEN, PATRICK	BAL	316	20TH WAR
RODEN, WILLIAM	BAL	148	2ND DIST
RODENHEFFER, LAWRENCE	FRE	086	FREDERIC
RODENHIGER, WILLIAM	KEN	237	2ND DIST
RODENKEIGER, GEORGE	KEN	250	2ND DIST
RODENMAYER, HENRY	BAL	193	6TH WARD
RODENMEYER, GEORGE C.	BAL	220	6TH WARD
RODENSTOCK, GERSON	BAL	422	3RD WARD
RODENSTOCK, SAMUEL	BAL	422	3RD WARD
RODER, ANDREW	PRI	092	MARLBROU
RODERICK, GEORGE	WAS	039	2ND SUBD
RODERICK, GEORGE	FRE	298	WOODSBOR
RODERICK, JOHN	FRE	255	NEW MARK
RODERICK, JOSEPH	FRE	265	NEW MARK
RODERICK, MAHLON	FRE	314	MIDDLETO
RODERICK, MARY	WAS	094	2ND SUBD
RODERICK, PHILIP	WAS	040	2ND SUBD
RODERICK, THEADORE	CEC	007	ELKTON 3
RODERICK, THOMAS SPRIGG	ANN	268	ANNAPOLI
RODERICK, WILLIAM	FRE	257	NEW MARK
RODERKE, DEDERICK	BAL	210	17TH WAR
RODERT, JOHN	BAL	034	15TH WAR
RODES, ELIAS	CEC	040	CHESAPEA
RODES, GEORGE	CAR	198	4TH DIST
RODES, JOHN	ANN	336	3RD DIST
RODES, SYLVESTER	DOR	457	1ST DIST
RODET, MARY C.	BAL	013	9TH WARD
RODEWALD, FRED	BAL	003	EASTERN
RODEWALD, FREDERICK	BAL	031	15TH WAR
RODEWALD, HENRY	BAL	351	7TH WARD
RODEWALD, MARGARET A.	BAL	296	3RD WARD
RODEWIG, ERNEST	BAL	060	15TH WAR
RODEY, CLRAN	BAL	230	12TH WAR
RODEYMEYER, ELLA	BAL	391	14TH WAR
RODFORD, JOSIAH	ST	271	3RD E DI
RODGELY, JAMES S.	BAL	050	9TH WARD
RODGER, JOHN	WAS	273	RIDGEVIL
RODGERS, AENER	CEC	136	6TH E DI
RODGERS, ANDREW	BAL	155	2ND DIST
RODGERS, BENJAMIN	BAL	216	6TH DIST
RODGERS, C.H.	BAL	194	11TH WAR
RODGERS, CHARLE	BAL	128	1ST WARD
RODGERS, DEBRA	BAL	192	11TH WAR
RODGERS, ELLEN	BAL	051	2ND DIST
RODGERS, FRANK	ANN	298	1ST DIST
RODGERS, GEORGE	BAL	176	2ND DIST
RODGERS, GEORGE	BAL	128	5TH WARD
RODGERS, GEORGE J.	BAL	405	8TH WARD
RODGERS, GEORGE L.	BAL	066	1ST WARD
RODGERS, HANNAH	BAL	114	5TH WARD
RODGERS, HENRY	BAL	230	17TH WAR
RODGERS, HUGH	BAL	278	7TH WARD
RODGERS, ISAAC	BAL	065	1ST WARD
RODGERS, ISRAEL	CEC	128	5TH E DI
RODGERS, JACOB L.	BAL	405	8TH WARD
RODGERS, JAMES	BAL	216	6TH DIST
RODGERS, JAMES	CAR	242	TANEYTOW
RODGERS, JAMES C.	FRE	202	5TH E DI
RODGERS, JAMES P.	FRE	202	5TH E DI
RODGERS, JANE	BAL	155	2ND DIST
RODGERS, JEREMIAH	CEC	122	4TH E DI
RODGERS, JOHN	BAL	023	18TH WAR
RODGERS, JOHN	FRE	428	8TH E DI
RODGERS, JOHN	BAL	159	2ND DIST
RODGERS, JOHN	BAL	281	1ST DIST
RODGERS, JOHN	BAL	128	5TH WARD
RODGERS, JOHN	BAL	456	8TH WARD
RODGERS, JOHN	BAL	075	10TH WAR
RODGERS, JOHN	WOR	243	1ST CENS
RODGERS, JOHN E.	WAS	010	WILLIAMS
RODGERS, JOHN W.	BAL	065	1ST WARD
RODGERS, JOHN W.	CEC	128	5TH E DI
RODGERS, JOHN-BLACK	FRE	010	FREDERIC
RODGERS, JOSEPH	BAL	435	8TH WARD
RODGERS, JOSEPH	WAS	010	WILLIAMS
RODGERS, JOSEPH JR.	BAL	016	18TH WAR
RODGERS, JOSIAH H.	WOR	242	1ST CENS
RODGERS, L. LOYD	BAL	191	11TH WAR
RODGERS, M. A.	ANN	411	8TH DIST
RODGERS, M. ELIZABETH	BAL	194	11TH WAR
RODGERS, MANVILLE	FRE	202	5TH E DI
RODGERS, MARIA	BAL	184	11TH WAR
RODGERS, MARY	FRE	066	FREDERIC
RODGERS, MICHAEL	CEC	142	6TH E DI
RODGERS, MISS M.	FRE	199	5TH E DI
RODGERS, NATHANIEL	BAL	084	1ST WARD
RODGERS, PATRICK	BAL	176	11TH WAR
RODGERS, PETER	ANN	317	1ST DIST
RODGERS, PHILLIP	FRE	040	FREDERIC
RODGERS, RACHAEL	BAL	213	6TH DIST
RODGERS, ROBERT S.	HAR	171	3RD DIST
RODGERS, ROOT	BAL	014	2ND DIST
RODGERS, ROSANNA	BAL	216	6TH DIST
RODGERS, ROWLAND	BAL	188	11TH WAR
RODGERS, SAMEUL	WAS	011	WILLIAMS
RODGERS, SAMUEL	FRE	121	CREAGERS
RODGERS, SARAH	BAL	136	18TH WAR
RODGERS, SISTER ANN	FRE	198	5TH E DI
RODGERS, SOPHIA	ANN	298	1ST DIST
RODGERS, STEPHEN	ANN	380	4TH DIST
RODGERS, THOMAS	BAL	091	1ST WARD
RODGERS, THOMAS	BAL	104	10TH WAR
RODGERS, THOMAS	CEC	122	4TH E DI
RODGERS, THOMAS	CEC	122	4TH E DI
RODGERS, THOMAS	CEC	136	6TH E DI
RODGERS, TOM	TAL	077	EASTON T
RODGERS, WASHINGTON	CEC	149	PORT DUP
RODGERS, WATLY	WOR	241	1ST CENS
RODGERS, WILLAIM	BAL	122	5TH WARD
RODGERS, WILLIAM	ANN	405	8TH DIST
RODGERS, WILLIAM	BAL	456	8TH WARD
RODGERS, WILLIAM	WOR	242	1ST CENS
RODGERS, WILLIAM	WAS	272	RIDGEVIL
RODGERS, WILLIAM	CEC	136	6TH E DI
RODGERS, WILLIAM	BAL	001	18TH WAR
RODGERS, WILLIAM	CHA	223	ALLENS F
RODGERS, WILLIAM	CHA	223	ALLENS F
RODGERS, WILLIAM R.	ALL	196	CUMBERLA
RODGERSON, MARTHA	CHA	258	MIDDLETO
RODGRONE, ANN	BAL	199	11TH WAR
RODIER, JULIUS	BAL	125	16TH WAR
RODIGAN, MARY	BAL	372	8TH WARD
RODIGAN, THOMAS	BAL	372	8TH WARD
RODIN, GEORGE	BAL	133	2ND DIST
RODIN, SOPHIA	BAL	133	2ND DIST
RODKEY, GEORGE	CAR	413	2ND DIST
RODLEY, LEDORA	CEC	025	ELKTON 3
RODMAN, CHARLES	BAL	127	2ND DIST
RODMAN, WILLIAM	BAL	362	13TH WAR
RODMER, NICHOLAS	BAL	381	8TH WARD
RODNERS, KIRBY	KEN	234	2ND DIST
RODNEY, AMRY	BAL	072	15TH WAR
RODNEY, DINAH	BAL	083	2ND DIST
RODNEY, KIRBY	KEN	273	1ST DIST
RODNEY, MARY	BAL	036	15TH WAR
RODNEY, MARY	BAL	126	16TH WAR
RODNEY, PERRY S.	WOR	277	BERLIN 1
RODNEY, STEPHEN	BAL	039	15TH WAR
RODOLPH, JACOB	BAL	386	13TH WAR
RODOLPH, PHE	BAL	143	19TH WAR
RODWALD, HENRY	BAL	437	14TH WAR
RODY, JOHN	ALL	053	10TH E.D
ROE, ANDREW	CAR	075	NO TWP L
ROE, ANNA	BAL	136	5TH WARD
ROE, BENJAMIN	QUE	155	2ND E DI
ROE, BENNER	BAL	066	4TH WARD
ROE, BILL-BLACK	QUE	134	1ST E DI
ROE, CAFF-BLACK	QUE	125	1ST E DI
ROE, CHARLOTTE	QUE	215	3RD E DI
ROE, CHARLOTTE A.	QUE	188	3RD E DI
ROE, CLAYTON	QUE	241	5TH E DI
ROE, DANIEL-BLACK	QUE	125	1ST E DI
ROE, DEBORAH	CAR	168	NO TWP L
ROE, ELIZABETH	CAR	076	NO TWP L
ROE, ELIZABETH	CAR	105	NO TWP L
ROE, ELIZABETH	KEN	308	3RD DIST
ROE, EMILY	TAL	032	EASTON D
ROE, EMORY T.	QUE	191	3RD E DI
ROE, GEORGE	CHA	239	HILLTOP
ROE, HESTER A.	TAL	018	EASTON D
ROE, JAME SB.	QUE	124	1ST E DI
ROE, JAMES	CAR	106	NO TWP L
ROE, JAMES	CAR	110	NO TWP L
ROE, JAMES	CAR	170	NO TWP L
ROE, JAMES	QUE	197	3RD E DI
ROE, JAMES	QUE	159	2ND E DI
ROE, JAMES	QUE	160	2ND E DI
ROE, JAMES	BAL	194	17TH WAR
ROE, JAMES A.	TAL	018	EASTON D
ROE, JOHN	CAR	078	NO TWP L
ROE, JOHN A.	CAR	073	NO TWP L
ROE, JOHNS	BAL	052	4TH WARD
ROE, LEMUEL W.	CHA	262	MIDDLETO
ROE, MAHALA A.	DOR	449	1ST DIST
ROE, MARTHA	CAR	092	NO TWP L
ROE, MARY E.-BLACK	QUE	126	1ST E DI
ROE, NATHANIEL	CAR	092	NO TWP L
ROE, PARROTT	CAR	094	NO TWP L
ROE, PERRY	TAL	037	EASTON D
ROE, RICHARD W.	TAL	030	EASTON D
ROE, ROBERT	BAL	136	5TH WARD
ROE, SAMUEL	BAL	144	1ST WARD
ROE, SAMUEL	CAR	106	NO TWP L
ROE, SAMUEL	QUE	158	2ND E DI
ROE, SAMUEL B.	QUE	208	3RD E DI
ROE, SARAH	CHA	289	BOJANTOW
ROE, SARAH A.	CAR	076	NO TWP L
ROE, SOLOMON	QUE	155	2ND E DI
ROE, SOLOMON	QUE	218	3RD E DI
ROE, SUSAN	CAR	092	NO TWP L
ROE, THOMAS	CAR	116	NO TWP L
ROE, THOMAS	CAR	111	NO TWP L
ROE, THOMAS	CAR	112	NO TWP L
ROE, THOMAS	CAR	072	NO TWP L
ROE, WILLIAM	CAR	075	NO TWP L
ROE, WILLIAM	QUE	152	1ST E DI
ROE, WILLIAM	KEN	259	1ST DIST
ROE, WILLIAM M.	CAR	072	NO TWP L
ROE, WILLIAM-BLACK	QUE	126	1ST E DI
ROE, MATILDA	CAR	104	NO TWP L
ROEBERRY, JOHN	BAL	163	1ST WARD
ROEDELL, WILLIAM *	WAS	132	2ND DIST
ROEDER, CONRAD	BAL	021	15TH WAR
ROEDER, GEORGE O. F.	KEN	225	2ND DIST
ROEDER, GEORGE R.	KEN	224	2ND DIST
ROEDER, GEROGE *	KEN	223	2ND DIST
ROEGELIN, F.	BAL	238	20TH WAR
ROELKEY, CHRISTIAN	FRE	016	FREDERIC
ROELKEY, HENRY F.W.	FRE	004	FREDERIC
ROELKEY, JOHN	FRE	016	FREDERIC
ROELKEY, WILLIAM	FRE	006	FREDERIC
ROELKY, CHARLES L.	FRE	243	NEW MARK
ROELY, ELIZA	WOR	313	2ND E DI
ROEN, RACHEL	TAL	113	ST MICHA
ROESWICK, F. W.	BAL	269	2ND WARD
ROETHE, CHRISTIAN	BAL	032	15TH WAR
ROETHLINGSHOFER, GEORGE	BAL	146	16TH WAR
ROEVER, FERDINAND	BAL	103	15TH WAR
ROFF, JOHN	BAL	022	2ND DIST
ROFF, JOHN	BAL	378	13TH WAR
ROFFERTY, MARYANN*	BAL	413	3RD WARD
ROFFLER, JAMES	BAL	156	1ST WARD
ROFUS, LEWIS	FRE	074	FREDERIC
ROFWISK, CHRISTIAN *	BAL	275	1ST DIST
ROGAN, JOHN	ALL	049	10TH E.D
ROGAN, JOHN	ALL	184	9TH E.D.
ROGAN, MICHAEL	ALL	140	6TH E.D.
ROGAN, SHIMOTHY	BAL	281	1ST DIST
ROGER, ALBERT A.	ALL	154	6TH E.D.
ROGER, EMANUEL	CAR	300	1ST DIST
ROGER, JACOB	CAR	235	UNION TO
ROGER, JACOB	ALL	154	6TH E.D.
ROGER, MARGARET	ANN	505	HOWARD D
ROGER, RUFUS	WAS	016	2ND SUBD
ROGER, SAMUEL	WAS	272	RIDGEVIL
ROGERS, AARON	BAL	388	1ST DIST
ROGERS, ALEXANDER	BAL	374	1ST DIST
ROGERS, ALEXANDER	BAL	380	1ST DIST
ROGERS, ALEXANDER M.	BAL	111	10TH WAR
ROGERS, AMMI	BAL	161	6TH WARD
ROGERS, ANN	BAL	391	1ST DIST
ROGERS, ANN	BAL	026	1ST WARD
ROGERS, ANN	BAL	239	20TH WAR
ROGERS, ANN B.	BAL	096	10TH WAR
ROGERS, ANNA	BAL	299	3RD WARD
ROGERS, ANNE	BAL	195	6TH WARD
ROGERS, BENJAMIN F.	BAL	100	15TH WAR
ROGERS, CAROLINE	BAL	181	19TH WAR
ROGERS, CAROLINE	BAL	033	4TH WARD
ROGERS, CATHERINE	BAL	071	4TH WARD
ROGERS, CHARELS L.	BAL	250	1ST DIST
ROGERS, CHARLES	BAL	157	1ST WARD
ROGERS, CHARLES	BAL	348	7TH WARD
ROGERS, CLEM	BAL	376	1ST DIST
ROGERS, DANIEL B.	BAL	066	1ST WARD
ROGERS, DOMENICK	ALL	050	10TH E.D
ROGERS, EDWARD H.	BAL	103	10TH WAR
ROGERS, ELIJAH B.	HAR	093	2ND DIST
ROGERS, ELISHA	HAR	131	2ND DIST
ROGERS, ELIZABETH	BAL	351	1ST DIST
ROGERS, ELLEN	BAL	381	1ST DIST
ROGERS, ELLEN	BAL	305	1ST DIST
ROGERS, EMELINE	KEN	216	2ND DIST
ROGERS, FRANKLIN M.	BAL	162	16TH WAR
ROGERS, GARRIT	BAL	236	1ST DIST
ROGERS, GEORGE	BAL	071	15TH WAR
ROGERS, GEORGE	BAL	014	2ND DIST
ROGERS, GEORGE M.	BAL	164	2ND DIST
ROGERS, GEORGE W.	BAL	405	1ST DIST
ROGERS, GILBERT	BAL	166	2ND DIST
ROGERS, H. CLAY	BAL	158	1ST WARD
ROGERS, HARRIET	BAL	067	2ND DIST
ROGERS, HARRIET	BAL	015	15TH WAR
ROGERS, HENRY J.	BAL	162	16TH WAR
ROGERS, HUGH	BAL	207	6TH WARD
ROGERS, HUGH	BAL	127	1ST WARD
ROGERS, ISAAC	HAR	055	1ST DIST
ROGERS, ISAAC S.	KEN	238	2ND DIST
ROGERS, J.	BAL	263	12TH WAR
ROGERS, J.M.	BAL	248	12TH WAR
ROGERS, JAMES	BAL	016	15TH WAR
ROGERS, JAMES	BAL	149	1ST WARD
ROGERS, JAMES	BAL	252	1ST DIST
ROGERS, JAMES	BAL	372	1ST DIST
ROGERS, JAMES	BAL	078	4TH WARD
ROGERS, JAMES A.	BAL	030	15TH WAR
ROGERS, JASON	BAL	227	12TH WAR
ROGERS, JEREMIAH	ALL	196	CUMBERLA
ROGERS, JOHN	BAL	461	1ST DIST
ROGERS, JOHN	BAL	453	1ST DIST
ROGERS, JOHN	BAL	162	2ND DIST
ROGERS, JOHN	BAL	304	1ST DIST
ROGERS, JOHN	BAL	300	12TH WAR
ROGERS, JOHN	BAL	306	12TH WAR
ROGERS, JOHN	ANN	429	HOWARD D
ROGERS, JOHN	HAR	105	2ND DIST
ROGERS, JOHN	SOM	446	DAMES QU
ROGERS, JOHN	KEN	208	2ND DIST
ROGERS, JOHN	BAL	170	19TH WAR
ROGERS, JOHN	BAL	223	19TH WAR
ROGERS, JOHN H.	BAL	179	16TH WAR
ROGERS, JOHN O.	HAR	093	2ND DIST
ROGERS, JOSEPH	ALL	074	5TH E.D.
ROGERS, JOSEPH D.	BAL	014	15TH WAR
ROGERS, JOSEPH SR.	BAL	232	12TH WAR
ROGERS, JULIA	BAL	114	15TH WAR
ROGERS, JULIA ANN	BAL	102	10TH WAR
ROGERS, LEVI	KEN	211	2ND DIST
ROGERS, LLOYD, N.	BAL	439	1ST DIST
ROGERS, LUCY	ALL	253	CUMBERLA
ROGERS, LUCY D.	ANN	467	HOWARD D
ROGERS, M.	BAL	163	1ST WARD
ROGERS, MARGARET	BAL	336	13TH WAR
ROGERS, MARGARETT	BAL	015	4TH WARD
ROGERS, MARIAH	TAL	001	EASTON D
ROGERS, MARTHA A.	BAL	059	15TH WAR
ROGERS, MARY	BAL	249	12TH WAR
ROGERS, MARY	BAL	191	11TH WAR
ROGERS, MARY	BAL	298	12TH WAR
ROGERS, MARY	CAL	048	3RD DIST
ROGERS, MARY ANN	BAL	121	5TH WARD
ROGERS, MARY C.	BAL	057	10TH WAR
ROGERS, MATILDA	BAL	406	14TH WAR
ROGERS, MICAJAH	CAR	219	5TH DIST
ROGERS, MICHAEL	ALL	087	5TH E.D.
ROGERS, MICHAEL W.	BAL	111	15TH WAR
ROGERS, MOSES	BAL	372	1ST DIST
ROGERS, NANCY	BAL	188	2ND WARD
ROGERS, NANCY-BLACK	BAL	188	2ND WARD
ROGERS, NATHAN	BAL	250	12TH WAR
ROGERS, PATRICK	ALL	049	10TH E.D
ROGERS, PATRICK J.	BAL	350	1ST DIST
ROGERS, PHILIP	CAR	273	WESTMINS
ROGERS, REBECCA	BAL	110	10TH WAR
ROGERS, ROBERT	BAL	162	2ND DIST
ROGERS, ROBERT	BAL	259	1ST DIST
ROGERS, ROLAND J.	HAR	114	2ND DIST
ROGERS, SAMUEL	HAR	029	1ST DIST
ROGERS, SAMUEL	KEN	211	2ND DIST
ROGERS, SAMUEL	KEN	208	2ND DIST
ROGERS, SAMUEL	BAL	330	1ST DIST
ROGERS, SAMUEL O.	ANN	466	HOWARD D
ROGERS, SARAH	BAL	223	19TH WAR
ROGERS, SARAH	BAL	263	17TH WAR
ROGERS, SIDNEY	BAL	046	9TH WARD
ROGERS, SUSAN	BAL	180	6TH WARD
ROGERS, TAYLOR *	BAL	363	1ST DIST
ROGERS, TERRENCE	QUE	223	4TH E DI
ROGERS, THOMAS	BAL	353	13TH WAR
ROGERS, THOMAS	MGM	377	ROCKERLE
ROGERS, W.	BAL	322	12TH WAR
ROGERS, W. R.	BAL	033	4TH WARD
ROGERS, WILLIAM	BAL	015	4TH WARD
ROGERS, WILLIAM	BAL	240	20TH WAR
ROGERS, WILLIAM	BAL	313	12TH WAR
ROGERS, WILLIAM	BAL	044	9TH WARD
ROGERS, WILLIAM	BAL	162	1ST WARD
ROGERS, WILLIAM	BAL	012	2ND DIST
ROGERS, WILLIAM	BAL	331	1ST DIST
ROGERS, WILLIAM	ST	292	2ND E DI
ROGERS, WILLIAM	PRI	031	VANSVILL
ROGG, MARTHA	CEC	187	7TH E DI
ROGGEN, WILLIAM	BAL	126	1ST WARD
ROGGERS, CHARLES P.	BAL	030	18TH WAR
ROGGERS, JACOB	WOR	281	BERLIN 1
ROGGS, CHARLES	BAL	259	12TH WAR
ROGLE, JOHN	BAL	073	2ND DIST
ROGUE, FRANCIS	BAL	088	10TH WAR
ROHE, FREDERICK	ALL	086	5TH E.D.
ROHE, GEORGE	BAL	059	18TH WAR
ROHER, STEVEN	ALL	070	5TH E.D.
ROHERER, JOHN W.	BAL	399	8TH WARD
ROHL, JOHN	BAL	051	1ST WARD
ROHLEDER, FRANCES	BAL	058	4TH WARD
ROHNER, ABRAHAM	WAS	078	2ND SUBD
ROHON, ANTHONY	ALL	119	5TH E.D.
ROHR, GEORGE	BAL	206	11TH WAR
ROHR, HANNAH	BAL	230	6TH WARD
ROHR, HENRY	FRE	225	BUCKEYST
ROHR, JACOB	FRE	047	FREDERIC
ROHR, JOHN	MGM	425	MEDLEY 3
ROHRBACK, HENRY	WAS	057	2ND SUBD
ROHRBACK, HENRY B.	WAS	057	2ND SUBD
ROHRBACK, JACOB	WAS	039	2ND SUBD

Name	County	Page	District
ROHRBACK, JOHN	WAS	062	2ND SUBD
ROHRBACK, MARRY	WAS	058	2ND SUBD
ROHRBACK, MARTIN	WAS	039	2ND SUBD
ROHRBACK, WILLIAM	WAS	040	2ND SUBD
ROHRBASH, JOHN	BAL	007	4TH WARD
ROHRER, ABRAHAM *	WAS	078	2ND SUBD
ROHRER, CHRISTIAN	WAS	034	2ND SUBD
ROHRER, DAVID	WAS	083	2ND SUBD
ROHRER, DAVID	WAS	227	1ST DIST
ROHRER, ELIAS E.	WAS	082	2ND SUBD
ROHRER, ELIZABETH	WAS	081	2ND SUBD
ROHRER, EMANUEL	WAS	279	LEITERSB
ROHRER, FREDERICK	WAS	083	2ND SUBD
ROHRER, FREDERICK	WAS	081	2ND SUBD
ROHRER, GEORGE C.	WAS	082	2ND SUBD
ROHRER, HENRY	WAS	072	2ND SUBD
ROHRER, JACOB	WAS	081	2ND SUBD
ROHRER, JACOB	WAS	081	2ND SUBD
ROHRER, JACOB	WAS	226	1ST DIST
ROHRER, JACOB M.	WAS	081	2ND SUBD
ROHRER, JEREMIAH	WAS	083	2ND SUBD
ROHRER, JOHN	WAS	083	2ND SUBD
ROHRER, JOHN	WAS	081	2ND SUBD
ROHRER, JOHN	WAS	081	2ND SUBD
ROHRER, JOHN M.	WAS	081	2ND SUBD
ROHRER, JOSEPH	WAS	081	2ND SUBD
ROHRER, JOSEPH	WAS	032	2ND SUBD
ROHRER, JOSEPH S.	WAS	083	2ND SUBD
ROHRER, JOSIAH	WAS	086	2ND SUBD
ROHRER, MAHLON	FRE	143	10TH E D
ROHRER, MARTIN	WAS	081	2ND SUBD
ROHRER, MARTIN	WAS	082	2ND SUBD
ROHRER, MARTIN	WAS	081	2ND SUBD
ROHRER, MARY MARGARET	FRE	144	10TH E D
ROHRER, SAMUEL	WAS	294	1ST DIST
ROHRER, SARAH	WAS	083	2ND SUBD
ROHRER, SINCLIER	WAS	082	2ND SUBD
ROHRER, SOPHIA	WAS	083	2ND SUBD
ROINS, MOSES S.	BAL	236	2ND WARD
ROIS, AMELIA	BAL	285	20TH WAR
ROITMAN, MARK	HAR	060	1ST DIST
ROKE, MARGARETT	BAL	068	4TH WARD
ROKESS, JOHN	BAL	170	6TH WARD
ROLAN, JAMES N.	BAL	168	1ST WARD
ROLAND, AMELIA	ALL	240	CUMBERLA
ROLAND, EDWARD	ALL	153	6TH E.D.
ROLAND, EVAN J.	ALL	121	4TH E.D.
ROLAND, FREDERICK W.	CHA	251	MIDDLETO
ROLAND, GEORGE	BAL	164	1ST WARD
ROLAND, GEORGE	PRI	117	PISCATAW
ROLAND, JAMES W.	BAL	317	1ST DIST
ROLAND, JOHN	BAL	281	2ND WARD
ROLAND, MARY	BAL	151	11TH WAR
ROLAND, MICHAEL	ALL	119	5TH E.D.
ROLAND, WILLIAM	PRI	118	PISCATAW
ROLB, ELIZABETH	FRE	062	FREDERIC
ROLP, MATHIAS	FRE	110	CREAGERS
ROLBACK, JOHN	WAS	135	2ND DIST
ROLDERS, HENRY J.	BAL	239	2ND WARD
ROLDGER, AUGUSTUS	BAL	109	5TH WARD
ROLE, JAMES	QUE	231	4TH E DI
ROLE, JOHN	BAL	447	8TH WARD
ROLEN, JONATHAN	ALL	172	7TH E.D.
ROLENS, THOMAS	CAR	228	5TH DIST
ROLEPICK, JACOB	BAL	072	2ND DIST
ROLES, ABRAHAM H.	CAR	157	NO TWP L
ROLES, CHARLES-BLACK	FRE	229	BUCKEYST
ROLES, HARY*	DOR	408	1ST DIST
ROLES, ISAAC	DOR	412	1ST DIST
ROLES, JANES	BAL	306	1ST DIST
ROLES, JOHN	BAL	306	1ST DIST
ROLES, JOSEPH	DOR	421	1ST DIST
ROLES, MARTHA	ANN	320	2ND DIST
ROLES, SAMUEL	ANN	314	1ST DIST
ROLETON, MARGARET	BAL	102	18TH WAR
ROLEY, AUTUSTIUS A.	BAL	376	13TH WAR
ROLEY, EDWARD	WOR	315	2ND E DI
ROLEY, EMANUL	WAS	140	2ND DIST
ROLEY, JAMES	WOR	315	2ND E DI
ROLEY, LEAH	SOM	401	BRINKLEY
ROLEY, MATILDA	WOR	302	SNOW HIL
ROLEY, STEPHEN	SOM	401	BRINKLEY
ROLEY, WILLIAM	WOR	316	2ND E DI
ROLEY, WILLIAM	ALL	166	6TH E.D.
ROLEY, WILLIAM H.	WOR	298	9TH E DI
ROLF, JOHN	BAL	005	9TH WARD
ROLFAS, ANTHONY	BAL	283	2ND WARD
ROLFE, CHRISTIAN	BAL	013	2ND DIST
ROLFIERY, EDWARD	ALL	155	6TH E.D.
ROLFINK, HENRY*	BAL	052	4TH WARD
ROLFLEY, GEORGE	BAL	463	1ST DIST
ROLINGS, GASAWAY	CAR	212	5TH DIST
ROLINS, ANGELINA	BAL	397	8TH WARD
ROLINS, FREDERICK	BAL	337	7TH WARD
ROLINS, JOSHUA	BAL	401	8TH WARD
ROLINS, SARAH	BAL	107	5TH WARD
ROLISON, ELIZABETH	BAL	175	11TH WAR
ROLKEY, GEORGE A.	BAL	140	16TH WAR
ROLLAINS, JIM	BAL	267	1ST DIST
ROLLE, FIDDEMAN	TAL	101	ST MICHA
ROLLE, WILLIAM	TAL	110	ST MICHA
ROLLEAN, HENRY	WOR	338	1ST E DI
ROLLEATHER, MARY	BAL	244	17TH WAR
ROLLEE, ROBERT	TAL	101	ST MICHA
ROLLENNAGER, GEORGE	BAL	438	14TH WAR
ROLLENS, DEMUS-BLACK	FRE	405	JEFFERSO
ROLLER, GEORGE	CAR	344	6TH DIST
ROLLER, JOHN	CAR	344	6TH DIST
ROLLERMAN, FRITZE	ANN	288	ANNAPOLI
ROLLES, WILLIAM W.	TAL	021	EASTON D
ROLLEY, HENSON	BAL	086	18TH WAR
ROLLEY, JAMES	BAL	156	1ST WARD
ROLLIN, ANDREW	BAL	116	1ST WARD
ROLLINGS, HENRY	ANN	324	2ND DIST
ROLLINGS, HENRY T.	ANN	323	2ND DIST
ROLLINGS, JACOB	ALL	109	5TH E.D.
ROLLINGS, JANE	ANN	319	2ND DIST
ROLLINGS, MARY	BAL	397	1ST DIST
ROLLINS, ANDREW	BAL	142	1ST WARD
ROLLINS, ANN	FRE	344	MIDDLETO
ROLLINS, ANN M.	BAL	121	16TH WAR
ROLLINS, CHARLES-BLACK	FRE	227	BUCKEYST
ROLLINS, CHARLOTTE	CAL	036	2ND DIST
ROLLINS, DAWSON	FRE	371	CATOCTIN
ROLLINS, EBEN W.	BAL	126	1ST WARD
ROLLINS, EDWARD	BAL	152	5TH WARD
ROLLINS, EDWARD	BAL	009	9TH WARD
ROLLINS, EDWARD	BAL	128	2ND DIST
ROLLINS, ELIZABETH	WAS	162	HAGERSTO
ROLLINS, ELLEN	BAL	353	1ST DIST
ROLLINS, ELLEN	BAL	158	11TH WAR
ROLLINS, ELLEN	FRE	103	FREDERIC
ROLLINS, FRANK	BAL	020	2ND DIST
ROLLINS, H.R.	BAL	108	1ST WARD
ROLLINS, HANNAH A.	SOM	398	BRINKLEY
ROLLINS, HENRY C.	CAR	150	NO TWP L
ROLLINS, ISAAC	BAL	142	2ND DIST
ROLLINS, JAMES	BAL	158	11TH WAR
ROLLINS, JAMES	CAL	036	2ND DIST
ROLLINS, JAMES	CEC	197	7TH E DI
ROLLINS, JANE-BLACK	FRE	031	FREDERIC
ROLLINS, JESSE	FRE	310	WOODSBOR
ROLLINS, JESSE	BAL	151	5TH WARD
ROLLINS, JOHN	BAL	152	2ND DIST
ROLLINS, JOHN H.	FRE	086	FREDERIC
ROLLINS, JOHN-BLACK	FRE	227	BUCKEYST
ROLLINS, JULIAN-MULATTO	BAL	208	2ND WARD
ROLLINS, LAURA L.	BAL	158	11TH WAR
ROLLINS, LEWIS	BAL	133	1ST WARD
ROLLINS, MARY	ANN	499	HOWARD D
ROLLINS, MARY	BAL	420	14TH WAR
ROLLINS, MRS.*	DOR	454	1ST DIST
ROLLINS, RELTY A.	BAL	391	8TH WARD
ROLLINS, RICHARD	BAL	384	1ST DIST
ROLLINS, ROBERT	CEC	214	7TH E DI
ROLLINS, SAMUEL	FRE	369	CATOCTIN
ROLLINS, SOLOM A.	BAL	306	3RD WARD
ROLLINS, THOMAS	BAL	046	15TH WAR
ROLLINS, WILLIAM	CEC	208	7TH E DI
ROLLINS, WILLIAM	BAL	392	14TH WAR
ROLLINS, WILLIAM P.	BAL	179	6TH WARD
ROLLINS, WILLIAM-BLACK	FRE	231	BUCKEYST
ROLLINS, WILLIMA	BAL	153	2ND DIST
ROLLINSON, GEORGE W.	KEN	301	3RD DIST
ROLLINSON, JOHN	KEN	271	1ST DIST
ROLLINSON, MARY A.	BAL	163	11TH WAR
ROLLINSON, PERRY	TAL	012	EASTON D
ROLLINSON, WILLIAM	TAL	066	EASTON T
ROLLINSON, WILLIAM	TAL	104	ST MICHA
ROLLINSON, WILLIAM	KEN	239	2ND DIST
ROLLISON, CATHARIEN	KEN	210	2ND DIST
ROLLISON, HENRY M.	KEN	225	2ND DIST
ROLLISON, JAMES	BAL	406	8TH WARD
ROLLISON, JAMES	BAL	406	8TH WARD
ROLLISON, LUDLOW L.	KEN	223	2ND DIST
ROLLISON, MARGARET E.	QUE	194	3RD E DI
ROLLISON, SARAH A.	QUE	193	3RD E DI
ROLLISON, WILLIAM A.	KEN	255	1ST DIST
ROLLMAN, JOHN	BAL	277	7TH WARD
ROLLMAN, WILLIAM	BAL	271	7TH WARD
ROLLNS, MARY A.	CAL	033	2ND DIST
ROLLS, JOHN	BAL	284	2ND WARD
ROLLY, ELLEN	WOR	299	SNOW HIL
ROLNER, HENRY	WAS	040	2ND SUBD
ROLOSON, HUGH	BAL	169	16TH WAR
ROLOSON, WIDOW	BAL	276	12TH WAR
ROLOSON, WILLIAM H.	BAL	115	15TH WAR
ROLPH, CHARLOTTE A.	QUE	167	2ND E DI
ROLPH, DAVID	QUE	140	1ST E DI
ROLPH, JAMES	QUE	170	2ND E DI
ROLPH, JOHN	QUE	151	1ST E DI
ROLPH, JOHN	CHA	281	BOJANTOW
ROLPH, JOHN	KEN	226	2ND DIST
ROLPH, JOSHUA	QUE	127	1ST E DI
ROLPH, RICHARD S.	KEN	311	3RD DIST
ROLPH, SAMUEL	QUE	167	2ND E DI
ROLPH, SARAH E.	QUE	150	1ST E DI
ROLPH, WILLIAM	KEN	227	2ND DIST
ROLPH, WILLIAM F.	QUE	167	2ND E DI
ROLPH, WALTER	QUE	134	1ST E DI
ROLS, ANDREW	BAL	264	1ST DIST
ROLS, ANDREW	BAL	380	1ST DIST
ROLS, WILLIAM	BAL	368	1ST DIST
ROLSTON, JOHN	BAL	186	6TH WARD
ROMAN, BENJAMIN F.	WAS	117	2ND DIST
ROMAN, CATHARINE	ALL	151	6TH E.D.
ROMAN, CATHARINE	ALL	151	6TH E.D.
ROMAN, HAINS	CEC	212	7TH E DI
ROMAN, J.D.	ALL	216	CUMBERLA
ROMAN, J.D.	WAS	133	HAGERSTO
ROMAN, JAMES P.	WAS	152	2ND DIST
ROMAN, JOHN	BAL	329	3RD WARD
ROMAN, JOHN	BAL	249	1ST DIST
ROMAN, JOHN	BAL	279	2ND WARD
ROMAN, JOSEPH	CEC	206	7TH E DI
ROMAN, JOSEPH	CEC	214	7TH E DI
ROMAN, SAMUEL	CEC	213	7TH E DI
ROMASER, FREDERICK	BAL	210	17TH WAR
ROMAX, THOMAS	BAL	392	14TH WAR
ROMESS, JOHN	BAL	280	1ST DIST
ROMINE, SAMUEL	BAL	208	6TH WARD
ROMISER, JOHN M. *	BAL	140	19TH WAR
ROMLEY, JACOB A.	BAL	425	3RD WARD
ROMM, NICHOLAS	BAL	370	13TH WAR
ROMMEL, FREDERICK	BAL	270	12TH WAR
ROMMELL, E.N.	BAL	269	12TH WAR
ROMOSER, JOHN G.	BAL	090	15TH WAR
ROMOSER, JOHN P.	BAL	094	15TH WAR
ROMSEY, ROBERT	BAL	438	8TH WARD
RON, SAMUEL	CAR	385	2ND DIST
RONBINSON, MARY	BAL	001	1ST WARD
ROND, MARRETTA	BAL	328	13TH WAR
ROND, PHILIP	ALL	234	CUMBERLA
RONE, JOHN	BAL	368	1ST DIST
RONE, ISAAC	BAL	069	2ND DIST
RONER, PETER	BAL	273	20TH WAR
RONESHART, JACOB	BAL	143	2ND DIST
RONEY, ALICE	BAL	141	11TH WAR
RONEY, ANICE	BAL	088	4TH WARD
RONEY, BENJAMIN	ANN	442	HOWARD D
RONEY, BUEN	BAL	175	2ND WARD
RONEY, CATHARINE	BAL	365	13TH WAR
RONEY, DAVID	ALL	100	5TH E.D.
RONEY, EDWARD	BAL	176	2ND WARD
RONEY, JAMES	ALL	075	5TH E.D.
RONEY, JAMES	BAL	033	4TH WARD
RONEY, JAMES H.	WAS	115	2ND DIST
RONEY, JOHN	BAL	192	6TH WARD
RONEY, JOHN	BAL	015	2ND DIST
RONEY, MARY	BAL	431	1ST DIST
RONEY, MARY	BAL	027	4TH WARD
RONEY, MICHAEL	BAL	028	4TH WARD
RONEY, PATRICK	ALL	099	5TH E.D.
RONEY, THOMAS	ALL	085	5TH E.D.
RONEY, THOMAS	ALL	046	10TH E.D
RONEY, WILLAIM	ANN	441	HOWARD D
RONIE, JOHN	BAL	093	1ST WARD
RONS, JAMES H.J.	QUE	156	2ND E DI
RONSAVILLE, DAVID C.L.	BAL	186	16TH WAR
ROOBBS, WILLIAM	BAL	160	1ST WARD
ROOBE, REBECCA	BAL	006	18TH WAR
ROOBOTHAM, MARY	BAL	175	2ND DIST
ROOCH, HENRY	WAS	223	1ST DIST
ROODS, JOHN M.	BAL	190	2ND WARD
ROOF, CHRISTIAN	CAR	402	2ND DIST
ROOF, DANIEL	CAR	403	2ND DIST
ROOF, HIRAM	FRE	413	8TH E DI
ROOF, JACOB	CAR	391	2ND DIST
ROOF, JACOB	BAL	368	1ST DIST
ROOF, JOEL	FRE	435	8TH E DI
ROOF, JOHN	CAR	180	8TH DIST
ROOF, PETER	BAL	071	1ST WARD
ROOF, SAMUEL	FRE	423	8TH E DI
ROOK, C. W.	BAL	147	1ST WARD
ROOK, DANIEL	ALL	056	10TH E.D
ROOK, FREDERICK	BAL	166	1ST WARD
ROOK, HEX	ANN	286	ANNAPOLI
ROOK, JAMES	WOR	174	6TH E DI
ROOK, JOHN	WOR	234	6TH E DI
ROOK, JOSEPH*	DOR	429	1ST DIST
ROOK, JOSHUA	WOR	174	6TH E DI
ROOK, JULIA A.*	DOR	429	1ST DIST
ROOK, PARKER	WOR	170	6TH E DI
ROOK, POLLY	BAL	438	14TH WAR
ROOK, ROBERT*	DOR	448	1ST DIST
ROOK, SAMUEL	WAS	277	RIDGEVIL
ROOK, SAMUEL	WAS	284	1ST DIST
ROOK, ISAAC	WOR	174	6TH E DI
ROOKE, DENNIS	SOM	504	SALISBUR
ROOKE, JOHN	SOM	534	QUANTICO
ROOKE, HERMAN	BAL	252	2ND WARD
ROOKER, REBECCA	BAL	433	14TH WAR
ROOKER, SAMUEL	BAL	145	19TH WAR
ROOKS, ROBERT	BAL	461	1ST DIST
ROONE, G.	BAL	136	1ST WARD
ROONEY, ALICE A.	BAL	261	6TH WARD
ROONEY, ANNA	BAL	072	15TH WAR
ROONEY, JAMES	BAL	132	2ND DIST
ROONEY, JAMES F.	BAL	261	6TH WARD
ROONEY, L.	BAL	140	5TH WARD
ROONEY, LYDIA	BAL	059	15TH WAR
ROONEY, MARY	BAL	377	13TH WAR
ROONEY, MICHAEL	BAL	001	15TH WAR
ROONEY, P. H.	BAL	471	14TH WAR
ROONEY, PATRICK	BAL	139	5TH WARD
ROONEY, PATRICK	BAL	124	16TH WAR
ROONEY, SISTER MARY	FRE	198	5TH E DI
ROONEY, THOMAS	BAL	359	8TH WARD
ROONEY, THOMAS	BAL	001	EASTERN
ROOP, ABRAHAM	CAR	286	7TH DIST
ROOP, CHRISTOPHER	CAR	186	8TH DIST
ROOP, DAVID	CAR	309	1ST DIST
ROOP, DAVID SR.	CAR	296	7TH DIST
ROOP, EWITH	CAR	236	UNION TO
ROOP, JAOCB JR.	FRE	435	8TH E DI
ROOP, JOHN	CAR	402	2ND DIST
ROOP, JOHN JR.	CAR	290	7TH DIST
ROOP, JOHN SR.	CAR	290	7TH DIST
ROOP, JOSEPH	CAR	387	2ND DIST
ROOP, SOPHIA	WAS	126	HAGERSTO
ROOPER, JOHN P.	ALL	207	CUMBERLA
ROORBACK, JACOB	FRE	328	MIDDLETO
ROORBOCK, HANNAH	BAL	180	19TH WAR
ROOS, ROBERT	SOM	438	DAMES QU
ROOS, ROBERT	BAL	100	10TH WAR
ROOSBACK, DANIEL	FRE	367	CATOCTIN
ROOSE, JAMES	ANN	480	HOWARD D
ROOT, AGNESS	FRE	279	WOODSBOR
ROOT, BASIL	BAL	290	20TH WAR
ROOT, CALVIN L.	BAL	022	4TH WARD
ROOT, DANIEL	FRE	452	8TH E DI
ROOT, DANIEL	FRE	279	WOODSBOR
ROOT, DANIEL	WAS	223	1ST DIST
ROOT, HENRY	HAR	124	2ND DIST
ROOT, HENRY	BAL	387	13TH WAR
ROOT, JACOB	FRE	279	WOODSBOR
ROOT, JACOB	WAS	196	1ST DIST
ROOT, JOHN W.	HAR	133	2ND DIST
ROOT, SARAH	BAL	393	8TH WARD
ROOTE, JOHN	BAL	390	8TH WARD
ROOTMAN, SHUMAN	BAL	305	3RD WARD
ROOTS, SAMUEL	PRI	021	VANSVILL
ROPE, HENRY	FRE	082	FREDERIC
ROPE, JOHN	FRE	052	FREDERIC
ROPE, LENHART *	BAL	369	13TH WAR
ROPE, ZADOCK H.	DOR	430	1ST DIST
ROPELEY, A.	BAL	242	20TH WAR
ROPER, CATHERINE	BAL	379	3RD WARD
ROPER, ELLEN L.	WAS	127	HAGERSTO
ROPER, G.B.W.	ALL	235	CUMBERLA
ROPES, ARCHER	BAL	108	10TH WAR
ROPP, SARAH L.	FRE	350	MIDDLETO
RORAN, CATHARINE	BAL	260	12TH WAR
RORHART, ELIZABETH	BAL	048	1ST WARD
RORHBACK, EPHRAIM	CAR	340	6TH DIST
RORICK, MARGARET	WAS	095	2ND SUBD
RORK, JOHN	WAS	071	2ND SUBD
RORK, WILLIAM	BAL	420	14TH WAR
RORKBACK, ADAM	CAR	344	6TH DIST
RORTON, ELIZABETH	BAL	333	13TH WAR
ROSAN, CHARLES W.	BAL	440	1ST DIST
ROSAN, CYLANUS J.	BAL	439	1ST DIST
ROSAN, STERLING D.	CAL	005	1ST DIST
ROSASILVA, F.	BAL	165	1ST WARD
ROSBERD, MATTHEW	WOR	195	8TH E DI
ROSBUSH, JACOB	BAL	239	2ND WARD
ROSCHESTER, WILLIAM-BLACK	CAR	080	NO TWP L
ROSCIER, MARGARET	BAL	032	2ND DIST
ROSE, ADELINE	BAL	074	10TH WAR
ROSE, ALEXANDER	ALL	127	4TH E.D.
ROSE, ANN E.	BAL	205	2ND WARD
ROSE, ANNA	CEC	016	ELKTON 3
ROSE, ARN	BAL	139	1ST WARD
ROSE, BENB	WAS	263	1ST DIST
ROSE, CAROLINE	BAL	063	15TH WAR
ROSE, CATHARINE	BAL	391	14TH WAR
ROSE, CATHERINE	CHA	244	HILLTOP
ROSE, CHARLOTT	BAL	283	17TH WAR
ROSE, CHRISTOPHER	BAL	372	13TH WAR
ROSE, ELIZABETH	BAL	062	18TH WAR
ROSE, ELIZABETH	FRE	169	5TH E DI
ROSE, ELIZABETH	BAL	169	16TH WAR
ROSE, ELLEN	BAL	203	19TH WAR
ROSE, ENOCH	ALL	156	6TH E.D.
ROSE, ENOCH	ALL	247	CUMBERLA
ROSE, F. F.	BAL	447	8TH WARD
ROSE, GEORGE	BAL	281	17TH WAR
ROSE, GEORGE	BAL	281	17TH WAR
ROSE, GEORGE W.	BAL	167	1ST WARD
ROSE, HENRY	BAL	063	15TH WAR

Name	County	Page	District
RCSE, HENRY	BAL	302	17TH WAR
RCSE, HENRY	BAL	072	18TH WAR
ROSE, HERMAN	BAL	118	1ST WARD
ROSE, HESTER	BAL	146	16TH WAR
ROSE, ISREAL	BAL	255	17TH WAR
ROSE, JACKSCN	ALL	029	2ND E.D.
ROSE, JACOB	BAL	270	7TH WARD
ROSE, JACOB	BAL	457	14TH WAR
ROSE, JANE	BAL	001	15TH WAR
ROSE, JOHN	BAL	062	15TH WAR
ROSE, JOHN	BAL	231	12TH WAR
RCSE, JOHN	BAL	455	14TH WAR
ROSE, JOHN	BAL	387	13TH WAR
ROSE, JOHN	BAL	286	20TH WAR
ROSE, JOSEPH	BAL	140	1ST WARD
ROSE, LAURA V.	BAL	072	18TH WAR
ROSE, LEWIS A.	BAL	094	5TH WARD
RCSE, LITMAN	BAL	299	3RD WARD
RCSE, LYDIA	BAL	298	12TH WAR
RCSE, MARTHA A.	KEN	292	3RD DIST
ROSE, MARY	BAL	361	3RD WARD
ROSE, MARY	ANN	472	HOWARD D
ROSE, MARY	BAL	121	11TH WAR
ROSE, MARY	BAL	215	19TH WAR
ROSE, MARY A.	BAL	300	3RD WARD
RCSE, MR.	BAL	122	5TH WARD
ROSE, PETER	BAL	092	5TH WARD
ROSE, PEYTCN R.	BAL	404	14TH WAR
ROSE, SAMUEL	KEN	241	2ND DIST
ROSE, SARAH	BAL	213	11TH WAR
ROSE, SIMION L.	BAL	277	17TH WAR
ROSE, SUSAN	CEC	211	7TH E DI
ROSE, SUSAN	BAL	382	8TH WARD
ROSE, TERESA	BAL	281	17TH WAR
ROSE, W. H.	BAL	074	10TH WAR
ROSE, WILLIAM	BAL	275	2ND WARD
RCSE, WILLIAM	TAL	012	EASTON D
ROSE, WILLIAM F.	WAS	159	HAGERSTO
RCSE,ELIZABETH	BAL	062	1ST WARD
ROSEBAY, JAMES A.	KEN	293	3RD DIST
ROSEBERRY, JOHN	BAL	060	18TH WAR
ROSEGANN, HERMAN	BAL	121	18TH WAR
ROSEL, WILLIAM F.	CEC	031	CHESAPEA
ROSELIEB, CHRIST.	BAL	267	1ST DIST
ROSEMAN, GEORGE	BAL	224	19TH WAR
ROSEMER, JOHN	BAL	091	10TH WAR
ROSEN, EDWARD	BAL	463	1ST DIST
ROSEN, FRANCES V.	BAL	242	2ND WARD
ROSENATH, RACHAEL	BAL	263	2ND WARD
ROSENBAUGH, CAROLINE	BAL	114	5TH WARD
ROSENBAUGH, HENRY	ALL	218	CUMBERLA
ROSENBAUM, BENARD	BAL	107	5TH WARD
ROSENBAUM, CAROLINE	BAL	379	3RD WARD
ROSENBAUM, GEORGE	BAL	206	19TH WAR
ROSENBERG, HENRY	BAL	158	2ND DIST
ROSENBERG, JOHN	BAL	433	8TH WARD
ROSENBERG, MARY	ALL	264	CUMBERLA
ROSENBERGER, B.	ALL	262	CUMBERLA
ROSENBERGER, FREDERICK	BAL	263	20TH WAR
ROSENBERGER, JOSEPH	ANN	452	HOWARD D
ROSENBERGER, PAUL	BAL	283	1ST DIST
ROSENBERRY, JOHN	BAL	140	16TH WAR
ROSENBOUGH, FRANCAS	BAL	239	2ND WARD
RCSENBROOK, CHRISTIAN	BAL	243	17TH WAR
ROSENBURG, GERTRUDE	BAL	239	1ST DIST
ROSENBURG, HARRISON	BAL	113	15TH WAR
ROSENBURG, ISAAC	BAL	457	14TH WAR
ROSENBURG, LEONARD	BAL	239	1ST DIST
ROSENBURG, LEWIS	BAL	045	9TH WARD
ROSENBURGH, LANEHART	CAR	200	4TH DIST
ROSENBURGUR, MOSES	BAL	073	4TH WARD
ROSENBURY, ELIAS	BAL	457	14TH WAR
ROSENCALE, HENRY	BAL	092	10TH WAR
ROSENDOLL, MICHAEL	BAL	038	4TH WARD
ROSENDOWN, SALMON*	BAL	066	4TH WARD
ROSENFELT, LSIGMUND	BAL	045	9TH WARD
ROSENFIELD, ABRAHAM	BAL	300	3RD WARD
ROSENFIELD, MOSES	BAL	228	2ND WARD
ROSENFIELD, SIMON	BAL	022	4TH WARD
ROSENGOING, JOHN	BAL	139	2ND DIST
ROSENHAUPT, JONAS	BAL	086	10TH WAR
ROSENKIRSH, SIMON	BAL	050	1ST WARD
ROSENMENKLE, HENRY	FRE	005	FREDERIC
ROSENMYER, CHRISTOPHER	BAL	089	1ST WARD
RCSENPAVOR, FREDRICK	HAR	207	3RD DIST
ROSENSTED, JOHN	FRE	175	5TH E DI
ROSENSTEEL, GEORGE T.	BAL	135	11TH WAR
ROSENSTEEL, JOSEPH	BAL	195	6TH WARD
ROSENSTEEL, SISTER A.	FRE	198	5TH E DI
ROSENSTEEL, THOMAS	FRE	434	8TH E DI
ROSENSTEIL, JAMES	FRE	184	5TH E DI
ROSENSTEIL, JOSEPH	FRE	182	5TH E DI
ROSENSTEIN, CATHERINE	BAL	038	9TH WARD
ROSENSTOCK, CHRISTIAN	WAS	049	2ND SUBD
ROSENSTOCK, GEORGE	BAL	248	2ND WARD
ROSENSTOCK, PHILIP	FRE	145	10TH E D
ROSENSTOCK, SAMUEL	BAL	248	2ND WARD
ROSENSTOCK, WERUS	BAL	241	2ND WARD
ROSENSWIG, NEWMAN	BAL	002	15TH WAR
ROSENTHAL, LEVI	BAL	207	19TH WAR
ROSENTHAL, LOUIS	BAL	070	15TH WAR
ROSENTHAL, M.	BAL	239	20TH WAR
ROSENTHALL, SIMMON	ANN	291	ANNAPOLI
ROSENTOCK, DAVID	BAL	230	2ND WARD
ROSENWALD, JUDA	BAL	090	10TH WAR
ROSENWIG, ELLIS	BAL	338	13TH WAR
ROSER, GAZELDA C.	CAR	394	2ND DIST
ROSER, WESLEY	BAL	437	1ST DIST
ROSERFELT, BARBARA	BAL	040	1ST WARD
ROSET, WILLIAM A.	BAL	214	6TH WARD
RCSETTA, J.	BAL	149	1ST WARD
ROSETTICER, MARY M.	BAL	244	1ST DIST
ROSEWAY, CHARLES	BAL	188	6TH WARD
ROSEWELL, WILLIAM	BAL	155	1ST WARD
RCSHER, NELSON	BAL	021	2ND DIST
ROSHER, WILLAIM	BAL	217	6TH DIST
ROSIER, HENRY	WAS	013	WILLIAMS
RCSIER, JOHN	BAL	033	2ND DIST
RCSIER, MOSES	BAL	034	2ND DIST
ROSIN, JOSEPH O.	KEN	266	3RD DIST
ROSING, H.	BAL	239	2ND WARD
ROSIS, JOSEPH P.	BAL	243	12TH WAR
RCSMAN, CHARLES	BAL	450	14TH WAR
RCSMAN, J.	BAL	152	1ST WARD
RCSOZER, ROWSANNA	FRE	183	5TH E DI
ROSRELL, S. M.	BAL	019	4TH WARD
ROSS, ABRAHAM	HAR	128	2ND DIST
ROSS, ADAM	BAL	066	4TH WARD
ROSS, ADAM	BAL	102	2ND DIST
ROSS, ALEXANDER	BAL	106	1ST WARD
ROSS, ALFRED	BAL	303	3RD WARD
ROSS, AMELIA	BAL	065	10TH WAR
ROSS, ANN	BAL	316	3RD WARD
ROSS, ANN E.	BAL	026	15TH WAR
ROSS, ANN M.	BAL	189	17TH WAR
ROSS, ANNA	QUE	208	3RD E DI
ROSS, AUTHER P.	TAL	042	EASTON D
ROSS, BENJAMIN B.	BAL	039	9TH WARD
ROSS, BENJAMIN-BLACK	CAR	162	NO TWP L
ROSS, BETSY	CAL	062	3RD DIST
ROSS, CATHARINE	CEC	008	ELKTON 3
ROSS, CATHERINE	CEC	080	NORTHEAS
ROSS, CHARLES	BAL	084	1ST WARD
ROSS, CHARLES	ANN	420	HOWARD D
ROSS, CHARLES H.	BAL	187	2ND WARD
ROSS, CHARLES H.	TAL	051	EASTON D
ROSS, COOCHER-BLACK	FRE	231	BUCKEYST
ROSS, DANIEL	BAL	211	17TH WAR
ROSS, DANIEL	FRE	173	5TH E DI
ROSS, DANIEL	BAL	182	16TH WAR
ROSS, DAVID	BAL	165	1ST WARD
ROSS, DAVID	BAL	051	18TH WAR
ROSS, DAVID J.	HAR	128	2ND DIST
ROSS, DAVID J.	BAL	252	6TH WARD
ROSS, EDWAD	QUE	174	2ND E DI
ROSS, EDWARD	SOM	403	BRINKLEY
ROSS, EDWARD	BAL	295	7TH WARD
ROSS, EDWARD	DOR	314	1ST DIST
ROSS, EDWARD	MGM	366	BERRYS D
ROSS, ELIZA	FRE	099	FREDERIC
ROSS, ELIZABETH	QUE	124	1ST E DI
ROSS, ELIZABETH	DOR	338	3RD DIVI
ROSS, ELIZABETH	CAR	380	2ND DIST
ROSS, ELIZABETH	CAL	037	2ND DIST
ROSS, ELIZABETH	CAR	126	NO TWP L
ROSS, ELIZABETH	BAL	175	2ND WARD
ROSS, ELIZABETH	ALL	124	4TH E.D.
ROSS, ELIZABETH	QUE	181	2ND E DI
ROSS, ELIZABETH	QUE	215	3RD E DI
ROSS, ELLEN	WAS	287	1ST DIST
ROSS, EMILY M.	WAS	258	1ST DIST
ROSS, EMMA L.	DOR	308	1ST DIST
ROSS, ENOCH-BLACK	BAL	252	6TH WARD
ROSS, FRANCIS	CAR	156	NO TWP L
ROSS, G.	SOM	425	PRINCESS
ROSS, GEORGE	BAL	148	1ST WARD
ROSS, GEORGE	BAL	222	1ST DIST
ROSS, GEORGE	BAL	297	17TH WAR
ROSS, GIDDY	FRE	294	WOODSBOR
ROSS, GINNA	WAS	157	HAGERSTO
ROSS, HARRIET	DOR	362	3RD DIVI
ROSS, HARRIET	MGM	370	BERRYS D
ROSS, HARRIET	CAL	054	3RD DIST
ROSS, HARRIET	PRI	007	BLADENSB
ROSS, HARRIET	ALL	127	4TH E.D.
ROSS, HARRIET-BLACK	FRE	048	FREDERIC
ROSS, HARRIET-MULATTO	FRE	018	FREDERIC
ROSS, HENERY*	DOR	331	3RD DIVI
ROSS, HENRIETTA	BAL	322	3RD WARD
ROSS, HENRY	ALL	112	5TH E.D.
ROSS, HENRY	BAL	394	3RD WARD
ROSS, HENRY THOMAS	QUE	195	3RD E DI
ROSS, HERMAN	BAL	144	1ST WARD
ROSS, HUGHETT-BLACK	CAR	136	NO TWP L
ROSS, ISAAC	HAR	169	3RD DIST
ROSS, ISAAK	DOR	370	3RD DIVI
ROSS, J.S.	BAL	116	1ST WARD
ROSS, JACOB	WAS	047	2ND SUBD
ROSS, JAMES	BAL	121	1ST WARD
ROSS, JAMES	BAL	027	1ST WARD
ROSS, JAMES	BAL	302	7TH WARD
ROSS, JAMES	ALL	098	5TH E.D.
ROSS, JAMES	BAL	319	3RD WARD
ROSS, JAMES	BAL	045	9TH WARD
ROSS, JAMES	KEN	237	2ND DIST
ROSS, JAMES	CAL	025	2ND DIST
ROSS, JAMES	DOR	298	1ST DIST
ROSS, JAMES	CAR	164	NO TWP L
ROSS, JAMES B.	SOM	415	DUBLIN D
ROSS, JAMES D.	BAL	123	5TH WARD
ROSS, JAMES E.	BAL	089	1ST WARD
ROSS, JAMES R.	HAR	149	3RD DIST
ROSS, JANE	BAL	094	10TH WAR
ROSS, JEANETTE	BAL	062	2ND DIST
ROSS, JERRY *	ANN	289	ANNAPOLI
ROSS, JOHANNA	BAL	109	1ST WARD
ROSS, JOHN	BAL	026	1ST WARD
ROSS, JOHN	BAL	055	1ST WARD
ROSS, JOHN	ALL	141	6TH E.D.
ROSS, JOHN	BAL	140	1ST WARD
ROSS, JOHN	BAL	160	1ST WARD
ROSS, JOHN	BAL	443	1ST DIST
ROSS, JOHN	DOR	339	3RD DIVI
ROSS, JOHN	DOR	417	1ST DIST
ROSS, JOHN	DOR	391	1ST DIST
ROSS, JOHN	WAS	287	1ST DIST
ROSS, JOHN R.	BAL	246	20TH WAR
ROSS, JOHN T.	BAL	211	17TH WAR
ROSS, JOHN W.	BAL	045	9TH WARD
ROSS, JOHN-BLACK	QUE	123	1ST E DI
ROSS, JOHN-MULATTO	QUE	129	1ST E DI
ROSS, JOHN-MULATTO	QUE	129	1ST E DI
ROSS, JOSEPH	HAR	034	1ST DIST
ROSS, JOSEPH	ALL	126	4TH E.D.
ROSS, JOSEPH	TAL	042	EASTON D
ROSS, JOSEPH A.	BAL	249	6TH WARD
ROSS, JULYANN	CAR	102	NO TWP L
ROSS, L. C.	BAL	120	18TH WAR
ROSS, LETTY	WAS	132	HAGERSTO
ROSS, LEVI	FRE	055	FREDERIC
ROSS, LEVIN	SOM	439	DAMES QU
ROSS, LEVIN	SOM	462	HANGARY
ROSS, LEWIS	DOR	379	1ST DIST
ROSS, LEWIS	DOR	429	1ST DIST
ROSS, LEWIS P.	BAL	219	17TH WAR
ROSS, LLOYD	BAL	189	17TH WAR
ROSS, LOUISA	CAL	043	3RD DIST
ROSS, LUCRETIA	DOR	402	1ST DIST
ROSS, MARGARET	BAL	297	17TH WAR
ROSS, MARGARET A.	BAL	407	8TH WARD
ROSS, MARGRET	BAL	067	18TH WAR
ROSS, MARIA	FRE	101	FREDERIC
ROSS, MARIA	BAL	121	5TH WARD
ROSS, MARIAH	CAR	081	NO TWP L
ROSS, MARIAH	DOR	359	3RD DIVI
ROSS, MARTHA*	BAL	003	4TH WARD
ROSS, MARY	CAR	160	NO TWP L
ROSS, MARY	ALL	098	5TH E.D.
ROSS, MARY	BAL	319	1ST DIST
ROSS, MARY	BAL	229	12TH WAR
ROSS, MARY	DOR	462	1ST DIST
ROSS, MARY	SOM	400	BRINKLEY
ROSS, MARY A.	BAL	108	15TH WAR
ROSS, MARY E.	ALL	115	5TH E.D.
ROSS, MARY E.	BAL	124	5TH WARD
ROSS, MOSES	ANN	407	8TH DIST
ROSS, NANCY	SOM	458	DAMES QU
ROSS, NANCY	FRE	369	CATOCTIN
ROSS, NANCY-BLACK	FRE	231	BUCKEYST
ROSS, NOAH	SOM	404	BRINKLEY
ROSS, PRESTON-BLACK	FRE	196	5TH E DI
ROSS, RACHEL	ALL	113	5TH E.D.
ROSS, RACHIEL	HAR	034	1ST DIST
ROSS, RALPH	WOR	340	1ST E DI
ROSS, REBECCA	BAL	152	11TH WAR
ROSS, RICHARD	CAR	099	NO TWP L
ROSS, RICHARD L.	MGM	358	BERRYS D
ROSS, RICHARD-MULATTO	QUE	159	2ND E DI
ROSS, ROBERT	DOR	469	1ST DIST
ROSS, ROBERT	CAR	083	NO TWP L
ROSS, ROBERT	DOR	357	3RD DIVI
ROSS, ROBERT	DOR	357	3RD DIVI
ROSS, ROBERT	BAL	001	4TH WARD
ROSS, ROBERT	BAL	205	17TH WAR
ROSS, ROBERT	ALL	125	4TH E.D.
ROSS, ROBERT	ALL	123	4TH E.D.
ROSS, ROBERT	BAL	230	12TH WAR
ROSS, ROBERT	BAL	239	12TH WAR
ROSS, ROBERT	BAL	195	11TH WAR
ROSS, ROBERT	BAL	235	6TH WARD
ROSS, ROBERT JR.	ALL	124	4TH E.D.
ROSS, ROBERT R.	BAL	291	7TH WARD
ROSS, ROBERT W.	TAL	057	EASTON D
ROSS, RUHEMAB*	BAL	061	4TH WARD
ROSS, RYLAND	BAL	083	2ND DIST
ROSS, S.	BAL	136	1ST WARD
ROSS, SALLY	SOM	395	BRINKLEY
ROSS, SARAH	QUE	214	3RD E DI
ROSS, SARAH	QUE	216	3RD E DI
ROSS, SARAH	BAL	128	5TH WARD
ROSS, SARAH	BAL	085	4TH WARD
ROSS, SARAH A.	BAL	290	17TH WAR
ROSS, SARAH-BLACK	CAR	156	NO TWP L
ROSS, SIMON	DOR	370	3RD DIVI
ROSS, SIMON	MGM	363	BERRYS D
ROSS, SOPHIA	BAL	247	2ND WARD
ROSS, STOUTON*	SOM	403	BRINKLEY
ROSS, SUSAN	BAL	014	1ST WARD
ROSS, SUSANER	CAL	009	1ST DIST
ROSS, THOMAS	DOR	369	3RD DIVI
ROSS, THOMAS	BAL	267	20TH WAR
ROSS, THOMAS	BAL	136	5TH WARD
ROSS, THOMAS	PRI	080	QUEEN AN
ROSS, THOMAS*	DOR	386	1ST DIST
ROSS, WESTLEY	ALL	174	7TH E.D.
ROSS, WILLAIM	ALL	133	4TH E.D.
ROSS, WILLIAM	ALL	115	5TH E.D.
ROSS, WILLIAM	ALL	150	6TH E.D.
ROSS, WILLIAM	ANN	277	ANNAPOLI
ROSS, WILLIAM	BAL	275	2ND WARD
ROSS, WILLIAM	DOR	313	1ST DIST
ROSS, WILLIAM	SOM	403	BRINKLEY
ROSS, WILLIAM	HAR	119	2ND DIST
ROSS, WILLIAM	FRE	035	FREDERIC
ROSS, WILLIAM	SOM	430	PRINCESS
ROSS, WILLIAM	DOR	305	1ST DIST
ROSS, WILLIAM	WOR	331	1ST E DI
ROSS, WILLIAM	WAS	287	1ST DIST
ROSS, WILLIAM E.	BAL	105	15TH WAR
ROSS, WILLIAM G.	BAL	182	16TH WAR
ROSS, WILLIAM H.	BAL	355	3RD WARD
ROSS, WILLIAM H.	DOR	379	1ST DIST
ROSS, WILLIAM S.	BAL	124	1ST WARD
ROSS, WORTHINGTON	FRE	056	FREDERIC
ROSSDEUSAR, JOHN	BAL	106	18TH WAR
ROSSETICE, EDWARD J.	BAL	244	1ST DIST
ROSSETTA, HANNAH	BAL	211	17TH WAR
ROSSINE, DAVID	CEC	015	ELKTON 3
ROSSINE, GEORGE	CEC	107	3RD E DI
ROSSISSEA, AGUST	BAL	119	1ST WARD
ROSSISTER, JOHN	BAL	349	7TH WARD
ROSSITER, JAMES N.	BAL	041	9TH WARD
ROST, JOHN	BAL	179	2ND WARD
ROST, MARTIN	BAL	212	17TH WAR
ROSTIGAN, M.	BAL	116	1ST WARD
ROSTLEMAN, WILLIAM	BAL	114	1ST WARD
ROSWICK, CHRISTIAN *	BAL	275	1ST DIST
ROSY, GEORGE C.	BAL	135	16TH WAR
ROSZDE, WILLIAM	DOR	373	1ST DIST
ROSZEL, SOPHRONIA *	BAL	340	13TH WAR
ROSZEL, STEPHEN B.	BAL	252	6TH WARD
ROSZELE, JOHN	DOR	404	1ST DIST
ROSZELL, SAMUEL	FRE	043	FREDERIC
ROSZWEG, GODFREY	BAL	087	15TH WAR
ROT, DANIEL	KEN	288	3RD DIST
ROTAN, HARIET	BAL	268	20TH WAR
ROTAN, WILLAIM	BAL	203	19TH WAR
ROTCLIFF, MARIA	PRI	026	VANSVILL
ROTE, JACOB	BAL	270	7TH WARD
ROTE, JAMES	CAR	346	6TH DIST
ROTE, MICHAEL	FRE	060	FREDERIC
ROTE, PETER	BAL	343	7TH WARD
ROTE, THOMAS	CAR	185	8TH DIST
ROTELER, EDWARD	PRI	023	VANSVILL
ROTELER, WILLIAM	PRI	025	VANSVILL
ROTEN, COLUMBUS	BAL	018	15TH WAR
ROTEN, SUSAN	BAL	011	15TH WAR
ROTES, ADAM	BAL	442	14TH WAR
ROTH, E.	BAL	138	5TH WARD
ROTH, FREDERICK	WAS	256	1ST DIST
ROTH, GEORGE	BAL	310	20TH WAR
ROTH, GEORGE	BAL	310	20TH WAR
ROTH, J.	BAL	138	5TH WARD
ROTH, JOHN	BAL	273	20TH WAR
ROTH, NATHAN	CEC	214	7TH E DI
ROTH, NICHOLAS	ALL	223	CUMBERLA
ROTHAM, MARY	BAL	472	14TH WAR
ROTHART, JOHN H.	BAL	169	6TH WARD
ROTHE, J. A.	BAL	322	1ST DIST
ROTHELL, ANN	BAL	004	9TH WARD
ROTHELL, PARRIOTT	ANN	314	1ST DIST
ROTHERMAND, JOHN	BAL	119	18TH WAR
ROTHERY, GEORGE	FRE	384	PETERSVI
ROTHERY, GEORGE	FRE	384	PETERSVI
ROTHIDALE, ROB	BAL	185	2ND WARD
ROTHLET, WILLIAM	BAL	466	14TH WAR
ROTHROCK, JOHN	BAL	034	18TH WAR
ROTHROCK, JOSEPH	BAL	069	18TH WAR
ROTHROCK, WILLIAM	BAL	053	18TH WAR
ROTHSCHILD, LOUIS	BAL	091	10TH WAR

Name	County	Page	District
ROTHTICLE, BIDDY*	DOR	403	1ST DIST
ROTHWAY, DANIEL	ALL	153	6TH E.D.
ROTHWAY, DANIEL	ALL	051	10TH E.D
ROTHWELL, ALEXANDER	CEC	021	ELKTON 3
ROTHWELL, REDDEN	CEC	067	5TH E DI
ROTHWELL, RICHARD	BAL	198	11TH WAR
ROTON, NICHOLAS	BAL	395	3RD WARD
ROTOP, LOUISA	BAL	238	12TH WAR
ROTTEN, BENJAMIN	BAL	268	17TH WAR
ROTTEN, HANNAH	BAL	264	17TH WAR
ROUAKE, ANN C.	BAL	134	11TH WAR
ROUBLE, HENRY	BAL	086	1ST WARD
ROUCE, C. C.	HAR	199	3RD DIST
ROUCE, MARY R.	HAR	199	3RD DIST
ROUCE, WILLIAM C.	HAR	199	3RD DIST
ROUCK, JOHN	BAL	119	1ST WARD
ROUCK, LENOX	BAL	132	18TH WAR
ROUD, ELIZABETH	FRE	057	FREDERIC
ROUF, CATHARINE	WAS	090	2ND SUBD
ROUF, JOHN W.	WAS	090	2ND SUBD
ROUGER, DANIEL	FRE	142	CREAGERS
ROUGH, AGNES	WAS	160	2ND DIST
ROUGHMAN, THOMAS	DOR	385	1ST DIST
ROUKE, MATILDA	BAL	075	1ST WARD
ROULENSON, JOEL H.	QUE	187	3RD E DI
ROULENSON, JOHN H.	QUE	187	3RD E DI
ROULETT, JOHN	WAS	063	2ND SUBD
ROULISON, JESSE JR.	QUE	177	2ND E DI
ROULISON, JESSE SR.	QUE	177	2ND E DI
ROULMAN, FREDERICK	BAL	076	1ST WARD
ROULTON, DAVID	CAR	257	3RD DIST
ROULY, JOSEPH	BAL	016	1ST WARD
ROUND, GEORGE T.	WOR	224	4TH E DI
ROUND, PETER	WOR	226	4TH E DI
ROUND, SALLY A.	WOR	237	6TH E DI
ROUND, WILLIAM	WOR	184	6TH E DI
ROUND, WILLIAM *	WOR	236	6TH E DI
ROUNDS, JAMES R.*	SOM	527	QUANTICO
ROUNDS, JOHN	SOM	514	BARREN C
ROUNDS, MARCELLUS	SOM	515	BARREN C
ROUNDS, MARY	SOM	353	BRINKLEY
ROUNDS, MARY E.	SOM	523	BARREN C
ROUNDS, MORRIS	SOM	396	BRINKLEY
ROUNDS, THOMAS	WOR	309	2ND E DI
ROUNDTREE, CATHARINE	BAL	206	6TH WARD
ROUNDTREE, JOHN	BAL	195	6TH WARD
ROUNDTREE, WILLIAM	BAL	206	6TH WARD
ROUNDTREE, WILLIAM	BAL	011	18TH WAR
ROUNTELL, THOMAS M.	BAL	144	19TH WAR
ROUPE, MARY MISS-	BAL	315	20TH WAR
ROURK, JOHN	BAL	230	19TH WAR
ROURK, JOHN	BAL	199	2ND WARD
ROURK, PATRICK H.	BAL	364	3RD WARD
ROURKE, BRIDGET	BAL	046	9TH WARD
ROURKE, HUGH	BAL	180	16TH WAR
ROURKE, JAMES	BAL	046	9TH WARD
ROURKE, MARY	BAL	006	9TH WARD
ROURMAUN, FRANKLIN *	BAL	095	18TH WAR
ROUS, JOHN G.	BAL	274	20TH WAR
ROUSE, ALMENA	BAL	339	7TH WARD
ROUSE, ANDREW	BAL	190	2ND WARD
ROUSE, BENJAMIN	BAL	407	3RD WARD
ROUSE, CATHARINE	BAL	264	2ND WARD
ROUSE, GEORGE	QUE	157	2ND E DI
ROUSE, JACOB	BAL	354	3RD WARD
ROUSE, JAMES	BAL	165	1ST WARD
ROUSE, JAMES W.	BAL	264	2ND WARD
ROUSE, JANE	QUE	147	1ST E DI
ROUSE, JOHN	BAL	117	18TH WAR
ROUSE, JOHN	BAL	114	11TH WAR
ROUSE, JOHN	BAL	269	17TH WAR
ROUSE, JOHN	BAL	381	8TH WARD
ROUSE, JOHN	BAL	416	8TH WARD
ROUSE, JOHN	BAL	400	8TH WARD
ROUSE, JOSEPH	CAR	094	NO TWP L
ROUSE, MARY	CAR	167	NO TWP L
ROUSE, MARY	BAL	100	18TH WAR
ROUSE, ROBERT	CAR	083	NO TWP L
ROUSE, RUDOLPH	BAL	406	3RD WARD
ROUSE, SAMUEL	TAL	079	ST MICHA
ROUSE, WILLIAM	QUE	157	2ND E DI
ROUSER, ELIZA	FRE	130	CREAGERS
ROUSER, HENRY	FRE	130	CREAGERS
ROUSEY, HANNAH	HAR	031	1ST DIST
ROUSEY, JOHN	HAR	004	1ST DIST
ROUSEY, JOSEPH	HAR	031	1ST DIST
ROUSH, ANNA	ALL	209	CUMBERLA
ROUSHER, SARAH	HAR	145	3RD DIST
ROUSKULP, DANIELS	WAS	135	HAGERSTO
ROUSKULP, UPTON	WAS	124	HAGERSTO
ROUSSE, GEORGE	BAL	120	1ST WARD
ROUSSE, MARY MISS-	BAL	315	20TH WAR
ROUT, ADAM	BAL	200	2ND WARD
ROUT, ISRAEL	FRE	426	8TH E DI
ROUT, WILLIAM	CAR	382	2ND DIST
ROUT, JAMES	FRE	427	8TH E DI
ROUTAKER, CATHARINE *	FRE	315	MIDDLETO
ROUTGAHN, MARIA	FRE	315	MIDDLETO
ROUTGAN, CAROLINE	BAL	218	19TH WAR
ROUTGATIN, NATHANIEL	FRE	312	MIDDLETO
ROUTJOHN, ADAM	FRE	345	MIDDLETO
ROUTJOHN, AMANDA E.	FRE	322	MIDDLETO
ROUTJOHN, CATHARINE	FRE	337	MIDDLETO
ROUTJOHN, CATHARINE	FRE	371	CATOCTIN
ROUTJOHN, CYRUS	FRE	342	MIDDLETO
ROUTJOHN, DANIEL	FRE	321	MIDDLETO
ROUTJOHN, EDWARD	FRE	327	MIDDLETO
ROUTJOHN, ELI	FRE	352	MIDDLETO
ROUTJOHN, ELIAS	FRE	371	CATOCTIN
ROUTJOHN, ENOS	FRE	351	MIDDLETO
ROUTJOHN, GEORGE	FRE	352	MIDDLETO
ROUTJOHN, GEORGE L.	FRE	351	MIDDLETO
ROUTJOHN, HEZEKIAH	FRE	348	MIDDLETO
ROUTJOHN, JACOB	FRE	345	MIDDLETO
ROUTJOHN, JACOB	FRE	371	CATOCTIN
ROUTJOHN, JACOB	FRE	138	CREAGERS
ROUTJOHN, JOHN	FRE	345	MIDDLETO
ROUTJOHN, JOHN E.	FRE	347	MIDDLETO
ROUTJOHN, JONATHAN	FRE	321	MIDDLETO
ROUTJOHN, JOSHUA	FRE	320	MIDDLETO
ROUTJOHN, JOSHUA	FRE	352	MIDDLETO
ROUTJOHN, LEVI *	FRE	314	MIDDLETO
ROUTPOUCH, DANIEL	CAR	401	2ND DIST
ROUTSON, HENRY	CAR	234	UNION TO
ROUTSON, REBECCA	CAR	290	7TH DIST
ROUTSON, SARAH	CAR	388	2ND DIST
ROUTSONG, CATHARINE R.	FRE	281	WOODSBOR
ROUTZAH, MARY A.	FRE	374	CATOCTIN
ROUTZAHN, ELIZABETH	FRE	403	JEFFERSO
ROUTZAHN, EZRA A.	FRE	402	JEFFERSO
ROUTZAHN, JOHN	FRE	333	MIDDLETO
ROUTZAHN, LUCRETIA A.	FRE	065	FREDERIC
ROUTZAHN, PHILIP	FRE	403	JEFFERSO
ROUTZHAN, JOSEPH	FRE	042	FREDERIC
ROUTZHAN, LEWIS	FRE	312	MIDDLETO
ROUTZMAN, BENJAMIN	FRE	403	JEFFERSO
ROUTZON, CATHERINE	FRE	427	8TH E DI
ROUTZONE, MARY	CAR	286	7TH DIST
ROUX, ALFRED	WAS	162	HAGERSTO
ROUX, CAROLINE	WAS	127	HAGERSTO
ROUX, CHARLES	WAS	158	HAGERSTO
ROUX, HANNA	WAS	162	HAGERSTO
ROUY, JOHN	BAL	004	9TH WARD
ROUZAHAN, JAMES	WAS	171	FUNKSTOW
ROUZER, CATHERINE	FRE	118	CREAGERS
ROUZER, URIAS	FRE	128	CREAGERS
ROVERTY, JOHN	BAL	298	17TH WAR
ROVEY, JACOB A.	WAS	231	1ST DIST
ROVIAL, GEORGE	BAL	109	10TH WAR
ROVINSON, ANDREW	BAL	362	8TH WARD
ROW, ABRAHAM	WAS	239	CAVETOWN
ROW, ALFRED S.	CAR	306	1ST DIST
ROW, ALICE S.	CAR	306	1ST DIST
ROW, CONRAD	BAL	068	4TH WARD
ROW, DANIEL	WAS	271	1ST DIST
ROW, DAVID	CAR	385	2ND DIST
ROW, ELIZA	BAL	338	7TH WARD
ROW, FRANCES	CAR	320	1ST DIST
ROW, GEORGE	CAR	385	2ND DIST
ROW, HENRY	CAR	266	WESTMINS
ROW, HENRY	WAS	205	1ST DIST
ROW, HENRY JR.	WAS	205	1ST DIST
ROW, ISAAC	WAS	290	1ST DIST
ROW, ISAAC	CAR	385	2ND DIST
ROW, JACOB	WAS	219	1ST DIST
ROW, JAMES	WAS	282	1ST DIST
ROW, JOHN	CAR	384	2ND DIST
ROW, JOHN	CAR	304	1ST DIST
ROW, JOHN	CAR	305	1ST DIST
ROW, JOHN	FRE	421	8TH E DI
ROW, JOHN	FRE	325	MIDDLETO
ROW, MARY	BAL	198	17TH WAR
ROW, NANCY	WAS	218	1ST DIST
ROW, NANCY	WAS	271	1ST DIST
ROW, SARAH	CAR	385	2ND DIST
ROW, WILLIAM	WAS	171	FUNKSTOW
ROWA, JOHN	BAL	304	7TH WARD
ROWAN, MICHAEL	ALL	106	5TH E.D.
ROWAN, MICHAEL	ALL	073	5TH E.D.
ROWAN, MICHAEL	BAL	161	2ND DIST
ROWAN, SOPHIA	BAL	161	2ND DIST
ROWBOTHAN, HANNAH	BAL	007	4TH WARD
ROWDEN, EDWARD	BAL	001	EASTERN
ROWE, ANN	BAL	170	1ST WARD
ROWE, ANTHONY	FRE	041	FREDERIC
ROWE, BELL	WAS	052	2ND SUBD
ROWE, CHARLES F.	SOM	449	DAMES QU
ROWE, ELIZABETH	FRE	175	5TH E DI
ROWE, EMILY	SOM	450	DAMES QU
ROWE, EVE	BAL	016	2ND DIST
ROWE, EZRA	BAL	390	3RD WARD
ROWE, FRANCIS A.	FRE	062	FREDERIC
ROWE, FREDERICK	CHA	263	MIDDLETO
ROWE, GEORGE	FRE	357	CATOCTIN
ROWE, GEORGE W.	CHA	236	HILLTOP
ROWE, HANNAH	FRE	163	EMMITTSB
ROWE, HANNAH	FRE	161	EMMITTSB
ROWE, HARRIETT	FRE	172	5TH E DI
ROWE, IDA	BAL	082	18TH WAR
ROWE, JACOB	WAS	140	HAGERSTO
ROWE, JAMES	FRE	172	5TH E DI
ROWE, JAMES	BAL	056	2ND DIST
ROWE, JAMES	ALL	248	CUMBERLA
ROWE, JANE L.	BAL	172	1ST WARD
ROWE, JOHN	FRE	172	5TH E DI
ROWE, JOHN K.	BAL	015	2ND DIST
ROWE, JOPSEH	BAL	431	1ST DIST
ROWE, JOSEPH	FRE	163	EMMITTSB
ROWE, JOSEPH	FRE	132	CREAGERS
ROWE, JOSEPH E.	BAL	033	9TH WARD
ROWE, LOUISA	BAL	431	1ST DIST
ROWE, LUCINDA	SOM	492	SALISBUR
ROWE, MALINDA	BAL	214	11TH WAR
ROWE, MARGARET	WAS	194	1ST DIST
ROWE, MARIAH	FRE	142	CREAGERS
ROWE, MARTHA	WAS	029	2ND SUBD
ROWE, MARY	WAS	038	2ND SUBD
ROWE, MARY	CHA	236	HILLTOP
ROWE, MARY	FRE	062	FREDERIC
ROWE, MICHAEL	BAL	053	9TH WARD
ROWE, NATHANIEL	FRE	060	FREDERIC
ROWE, PETER	FRE	162	EMMITTSB
ROWE, RICHARD	BAL	125	18TH WAR
ROWE, RICHARD	CAR	223	5TH DIST
ROWE, RICHARD	BAL	458	8TH WARD
ROWE, SALLY	WAS	033	2ND SUBD
ROWE, SAMUEL	SOM	451	DAMES QU
ROWE, SAMUEL	WAS	162	HAGERSTO
ROWE, SARAH	WAS	231	1ST DIST
ROWE, SARAH	FRE	162	EMMITTSB
ROWE, SPENCER	FRE	173	5TH E DI
ROWE, SUSAN	BAL	308	12TH WAR
ROWE, SYLVESTER	FRE	160	EMMITTSB
ROWE, THOMAS	CEC	042	CHESAPEA
ROWE, VIRGINIA	BAL	056	2ND DIST
ROWE, WALTER	BAL	055	2ND DIST
ROWE, WILLIAM	BAL	020	2ND DIST
ROWE, WILLIAM	BAL	055	2ND DIST
ROWE, WILLIAM	BAL	169	1ST WARD
ROWE, WILLIAM	BAL	159	1ST WARD
ROWE, WILLIAM	BAL	161	1ST WARD
ROWE, WILLIAM	BAL	228	2ND WARD
ROWE, WILLIAM	BAL	263	2ND WARD
ROWE, WILLIAM	BAL	214	11TH WAR
ROWE, WILLIAM	SOM	449	DAMES QU
ROWE, WILLIAM G.	FRE	165	EMMITTSB
ROWE, WILLIAM H.	FRE	128	CREAGERS
ROWE, WILLIAM H.	CHA	263	MIDDLETO
ROWE, WILLIAM N.	BAL	157	16TH WAR
ROWEL, BARNEY	BAL	169	2ND DIST
ROWELL, MARY	BAL	176	19TH WAR
ROWELL, WILLIAM *	WAS	132	2ND DIST
ROWELS, HENRY	BAL	023	1ST WARD
ROWEN, JOHN A.	BAL	272	2ND WARD
ROWEN, KENELLY*	TAL	026	EASTON D
ROWEN, MICHAEL	ALL	156	6TH E.D.
ROWEY, JAMES*	TAL	044	EASTON T
ROWIE, JOHN O.	BAL	338	13TH WAR
ROWIN, JOHN	TAL	065	EASTON T
ROWINS, FRANSIS	TAL	066	EASTON T
ROWINS, MARGARETT	DOR	320	1ST DIST
ROWINS, NANCY	CAR	161	NO TWP L
ROWINS, PETER	CAR	168	NO TWP L
ROWINS, WASHINGTON	CAR	151	NO TWP L
ROWINSM, CHARLES J.	DOR	374	1ST DIST
ROWKES, P.	BAL	148	1ST WARD
ROWLAND, ABRAHAM	WAS	099	2ND DIST
ROWLAND, ANDREW	WAS	176	1ST DIST
ROWLAND, AQUILLA	WAS	029	2ND SUBD
ROWLAND, BARBARY	WAS	149	HAGERSTO
ROWLAND, CHARLES	ALL	013	3RD E.D.
ROWLAND, CHRISTIAN	WAS	206	1ST DIST
ROWLAND, DANIEL	WAS	233	1ST DIST
ROWLAND, DAVID	WAS	029	2ND SUBD
ROWLAND, DAVID	WAS	296	1ST DIST
ROWLAND, ELIZABETH	WAS	102	2ND DIST
ROWLAND, ELY	BAL	156	19TH WAR
ROWLAND, HENRY	WAS	102	2ND DIST
ROWLAND, ISAAC	WAS	177	1ST DIST
ROWLAND, ISAAC	WAS	159	2ND DIST
ROWLAND, ISAAC B.	WAS	031	2ND SUBD
ROWLAND, J.H.	WAS	021	2ND SUBD
ROWLAND, JAMES H.	CEC	147	PORT DUP
ROWLAND, JAMES-BLACK	FRE	420	8TH E DI
ROWLAND, JOHN	WAS	029	2ND SUBD
ROWLAND, JOHN	WAS	157	2ND DIST
ROWLAND, JOHN	WAS	161	2ND DIST
ROWLAND, JOHN	BAL	165	1ST WARD
ROWLAND, JOHN F.	WAS	029	2ND SUBD
ROWLAND, JOHN S.	WAS	030	2ND SUBD
ROWLAND, JONAS	WAS	268	1ST DIST
ROWLAND, JONATHAN	WAS	029	2ND SUBD
ROWLAND, JOSEPH	WAS	162	2ND DIST
ROWLAND, MADISON	CEC	157	PORT DUP
ROWLAND, MARY	WAS	157	2ND DIST
ROWLAND, PETER	WAS	026	2ND SUBD
ROWLAND, SAMUEL	CEC	206	7TH E DI
ROWLAND, SARAH	WAS	155	2ND DIST
ROWLAND, UPTON	WAS	159	2ND DIST
ROWLE, ISAAC	BAL	157	2ND DIST
ROWLES, EDWARD	ANN	429	HOWARD D
ROWLES, HARRIET N.	ANN	417	HOWARD D
ROWLES, ISAAC C.	ANN	517	HOWARD D
ROWLES, JACOB	QUE	248	5TH E DI
ROWLES, JACOB	QUE	247	5TH E DI
ROWLES, JACOB	BAL	257	20TH WAR
ROWLES, JAMES	ANN	426	HOWARD D
ROWLES, JAMES	BAL	044	9TH WARD
ROWLES, JOHN H.	ANN	442	HOWARD D
ROWLES, JOSEPH	BAL	403	3RD WARD
ROWLES, LEVIN	BAL	366	3RD WARD
ROWLES, LEWIS	QUE	251	5TH E DI
ROWLES, MARY A.	ANN	418	HOWARD D
ROWLES, MULTER	BAL	266	20TH WAR
ROWLES, SARAH J.	QUE	247	5TH E DI
ROWLES, THOMAS	BAL	218	19TH WAR
ROWLES, WILLIAM	ANN	426	HOWARD D
ROWLEY, ANN M.	BAL	292	3RD WARD
ROWLEY, CLEMENTINE	CEC	086	4TH E DI
ROWLEY, EDWARD	BAL	324	3RD WARD
ROWLEY, EDWARD	BAL	164	11TH WAR
ROWLEY, JAMES	BAL	292	3RD WARD
ROWLEY, JAMES	ALL	049	10TH E.D
ROWLEY, JOHN	BAL	116	15TH WAR
ROWLINGS, JOHN J.	CAL	007	1ST DIST
ROWLINSON, BENJAMIN	QUE	176	2ND E DI
ROWLISON, BENJAMIN	QUE	176	2ND E DI
ROWLY, EMILY	CEC	086	4TH E DI
ROWLY, WILLIAM*	DOR	414	1ST DIST
ROWNO, ESTHER W.	BAL	083	15TH WAR
ROWSER, CATHARINE	WAS	034	2ND SUBD
ROWSER, MARY	PRI	004	BLADENSB
ROWZER, CATHARINE	FRE	186	5TH E DI
ROWZER, JOEL	FRE	145	10TH E D
ROWZER, WILLIAM	FRE	183	5TH E DI
ROX, HENRY	BAL	455	8TH WARD
ROX, WILLIAM	CEC	158	PORT DUP
ROXBOROUGH, AGNES	SOM	495	SALISBUR
ROXBOROUGH, ELIZABETH	SOM	494	SALISBUR
ROXBOROUGH, ELLEN	SOM	494	SALISBUR
ROXBURG, WILLIAM	WOR	304	SNOW HIL
ROXBURY, JEREMIAH	CEC	162	6TH E DI
ROXBURY, JOHN	CEC	161	6TH E DI
ROY, ELLEN	BAL	355	13TH WAR
ROY, ELLEN*	BAL	014	4TH WARD
ROY, HENRIETTA	QUE	218	3RD E DI
ROY, HENRY	BAL	110	15TH WAR
ROY, JAMES	BAL	046	9TH WARD
ROY, JOHN	BAL	003	15TH WAR
ROY, JOHN	BAL	063	2ND DIST
ROY, JOHN	QUE	212	3RD E DI
ROY, JOHN	BAL	018	4TH WARD
ROY, MARGARET R.	BAL	086	18TH WAR
ROY, MILLY-BLACK	CAR	092	NO TWP L
ROY, WILIAM	BAL	462	14TH WAR
ROYAEL, MARY J.	BAL	092	10TH WAR
ROYAL, NATHAN	TAL	054	EASTON D
ROYAL, PHILIP-BLACK	QUE	181	2ND E DI
ROYAL, POLLY	BAL	177	2ND DIST
ROYAL, W. HENRY	BAL	086	10TH WAR
ROYEN, JOHN	BAL	367	13TH WAR
ROYER, JEHU	CAR	290	7TH DIST
ROYER, JESSE	CAR	290	7TH DIST
ROYER, JESSE	CAR	289	7TH DIST
ROYER, JOHN	CAR	357	6TH DIST
ROYER, JOHN	BAL	162	2ND DIST
ROYER, LUCINDA	CAR	409	2ND DIST
ROYER,CHRISTIAN	CAR	357	6TH DIST
ROYLS, WILLIAM	CHA	234	HILLTOP
ROYS, A. MISS-	ANN	299	1ST DIST
ROYSE, WILLIAM R.*	DOR	323	1ST DIST
ROYSTIN, SARAH	BAL	189	19TH WAR
ROYSTON, BOSLEY	BAL	049	2ND DIST
ROYSTON, CALEB	BAL	051	2ND DIST
ROYSTON, CALEB W.	BAL	437	1ST DIST
ROYSTON, EDWARD	BAL	021	2ND DIST
ROYSTON, ELIZABETH	BAL	193	6TH WARD
ROYSTON, ELLEN	BAL	116	15TH WAR
ROYSTON, EMILY	BAL	050	2ND DIST
ROYSTON, HENRY	BAL	034	4TH WARD
ROYSTON, JAMS	ANN	502	HOWARD D
ROYSTON, JOHN	BAL	195	5TH DIST
ROYSTON, JOHN W.	BAL	184	5TH DIST
ROYSTON, JOHN W.	BAL	048	18TH WAR
ROYSTON, JOSEPH T.	BAL	019	18TH WAR
ROYSTON, JOSHUA	BAL	115	15TH WAR
ROYSTON, JOSHUA D.	BAL	262	1ST DIST
ROYSTON, MOSES	CAR	172	8TH DIST
ROYSTON, ROBERT	BAL	193	5TH DIST
ROYSTON, ROBERT	BAL	058	2ND DIST

ROYSTON, ROSEANN BAL 050 15TH WAR
ROYSTON, SARAH BAL 048 18TH WAR
ROYSTON, SOPHIA BAL 051 2ND DIST
ROYSTON, W. BAL 137 1ST WARD
ROYSTON, W. B. BAL 073 10TH WAR
ROYSTON, WESLEY BAL 051 2ND DIST
ROYTON, JOHN BAL 200 5TH DIST
ROZEL, JOHN CEC 011 ELKTON 3
ROZELL, EBBALI TAL 115 ST MICHA
ROZELL, HARRIET-BLACK CAR 096 NO TWP L
ROZELL, JACOB CAR 100 NO TWP L
ROZENBERG, ABRAHAM BAL 013 9TH WARD
ROZENBERG, JOHN ALL 003 3RD E.D.
ROZENBURG, DR. FRE 385 PETERSVI
ROZETT, HENRY CAR 097 NO TWP L
ROZIER, CHARLOTTE QUE 253 5TH E DI
ROZIER, NATHAN MGM 369 BERRYS D
ROZIER, SOLOMON QUE 253 5TH E DI
RPUST, AUGUST BAL 220 17TH WAR
RRAFT, HENRY BAL 347 13TH WAR
RREID, JOHN BAL 160 1ST WARD
RRIED, LEWIS BAL 014 9TH WARD
RSSES, JOHN BAL 284 1ST DIST
RTAYLOR, JAMES BAL 034 1ST WARD
RUA, REBECA WAS 136 2ND DIST
RUACH, GILES WOR 181 6TH E DI
RUACH, JAMES WOR 175 6TH E DI
RUACH, JOHN WOR 181 6TH E DI
RUACH, JOHNSON WOR 175 6TH E DI
RUACH, WILLIAM WOR 175 6TH E DI
RUACH, WILLIAM T.B. WOR 175 6TH E DI
RUACK, ELIZA WOR 198 8TH E DI
RUAN, ELLEN BAL 344 13TH WAR
RUARCH, EDWARD BAL 222 17TH WAR
RUARD, WILLIAM BAL 081 18TH WAR
RUARK, BRIDGET BAL 016 9TH WARD
RUARK, EASTER SOM 489 SALISBUR
RUARK, EDWARD SOM 481 TRAPP DI
RUARK, EDWARD BAL 440 1ST DIST
RUARK, EDWARD BAL 303 3RD WARD
RUARK, EDWARD BAL 413 3RD WARD
RUARK, HENRY BAL 363 3RD WARD
RUARK, JAMES ANN 411 8TH DIST
RUARK, JOHN BAL 033 1ST WARD
RUARK, MAJOR T. SOM 487 SALISBUR
RUARK, PETER BAL 022 18TH WAR
RUARK, SARRAH DOR 343 3RD DIVI
RUARK, SUSAN BAL 326 7TH WARD
RUARK, THOMAS H. DOR 380 1ST DIST
RUARK, THOMAS* TAL 016 EASTON D
RUARK, WILLIAM DOR 343 3RD DIVI
RUARK, WILLIAM M. SOM 489 SALISBUR
RUARK, WILLIAM T. SOM 487 SALISBUR
RUARKE, ELIZABETH DOR 331 3RD DIVI
RUARKE, LEVEN DOR 363 3RD DIVI
RUASH, JOEL WOR 189 7TH E DI
RUBAN, SUSAN BAL 025 18TH WAR
RUBEN, ELIZABETH ALL 157 6TH E.D.
RUBEN, SALLY BAL 364 13TH WAR
RUBOTTOM, JOHN CAR 209 5TH DIST
RUBOTTOM, RACHEL CAR 232 5TH DIST
RUBY, CLARARY* TAL 058 EASTON D
RUBY, H. BAL 135 1ST WARD
RUBY, JAMES CAR 175 8TH DIST
RUBY, JOHN CAR 357 6TH DIST
RUBY, JOHN ALL 174 7TH E.D.
RUBY, LLOYD CAR 177 8TH DIST
RUBY, MICHAEL CEC 130 6TH E DI
RUBY, NATHAN ALL 189 9TH E.D.
RUBY, THOMAS ALL 174 7TH E.D.
RUBY, URIAH CAR 181 8TH DIST
RUBY, VALENTINE CAR 176 8TH DIST
RUBY, VIRGINIA BAL 013 1ST WARD
RUBYU, HENRY CAR 175 8TH DIST
RUCHT, MELLEYMETT BAL 213 19TH WAR
RUCK, HENRIETTA BAL 049 4TH WARD
RUCK, JOHN BAL 047 1ST WARD
RUCK, PHILIP FRE 251 NEW MARK
RUCKER, THOAMS BAL 288 20TH WAR
RUCKERT, JOHN BAL 112 10TH WAR
RUCKLE, ANN E. BAL 143 19TH WAR
RUCKLE, CHARLES BAL 064 18TH WAR
RUCKLE, GEORGE BAL 310 12TH WAR
RUCKLE, GEORCE W. BAL 187 6TH WARD
RUCKLE, ISABELLA BAL 158 16TH WAR
RUCKLE, JOSEPH N. BAL 142 19TH WAR
RUCKLE, MARY BAL 186 6TH WARD
RUCKLE, SARAH A. BAL 007 EASTERN
RUCKLE, THOMAS BAL 159 11TH WAR
RUCKLE, THOMAS C. BAL 337 13TH WAR
RUCKLER, THOMAS DOR 394 1ST DIST
RUCKLES, WILLIAM FRE 249 NEW MARK
RUCKLY, CATHERINE FRE 249 NEW MARK
RUDALPH, BARBARY BAL 147 5TH WARD
RUCDACH, REBECCA BAL 119 15TH WAR
RUDDEN, ELLEN BAL 202 17TH WAR
RUDDIN, ANN BAL 397 8TH WARD
RUDDOCK, WASHINGTON BAL 138 18TH WAR
RUDENSTEIN, SOPHIA BAL 100 15TH WAR
RUDER, ANN WAS 064 2ND SUBD
RUDER, PETER BAL 217 19TH WAR
RUDESILL, GEORGE WAS 264 1ST DIST
RUDESILL, TOBIAS CAR 241 TANEYTOW
RUDISILL, THOMAS CAR 315 1ST DIST
RUDISILL, WILLIAM CAR 241 TANEYTOW
RUDLEY, CHRISTIAN BAL 280 2ND WARD
RUDLOPH, JOHN BAL 215 2ND WARD
RUDLOPH, MARIA CEC 016 ELKTON 3
RUDOLF, CHRISTIANA CAR 262 3RD DIST
RUDOLF, FRANCIS BAL 091 10TH WAR
RUDOLF, FREDRICA BAL 092 10TH WAR
RUDOLPH, CHARLES BAL 122 2ND DIST
RUDOLPH, DANIEL H. CAR 408 2ND DIST
RUDOLPH, HENRY BAL 024 15TH WAR
RUDOLPH, MARTIN BAL 004 15TH WAR
RUDOLPH, MARY F. BAL 041 9TH WARD
RUDOLPH,JAMES F. BAL 079 1ST WARD
RUDY, C. BAL 172 1ST WARD
RUDY, DANIEL FRE 334 MIDDLETO
RUDY, ELIZABETH WAS 217 1ST DIST
RUDY, EMANUEL WAS 228 1ST DIST
RUDY, FREDERICK FRE 331 MIDDLETO
RUDY, HANSON FRE 325 MIDDLETO
RUDY, JACOB FRE 330 MIDDLETO
RUDY, JOSHUA FRE 331 MIDDLETO
RUDY, MATHREW ALL 052 10TH E.D
RUDY, PATRICK ALL 048 10TH E.D
RUDY, SAMUEL WAS 209 1ST DIST
RUDY, SUSAN HAR 105 2ND DIST
RUDY, WASHINGTON WAS 206 1ST DIST
RUDY, WASHINGTON WAS 192 1ST DIST
RUDY, WILLIAM FRE 386 PETERSVI
RUE, GEORGE DOR 386 1ST DIST
RUE, GEORGE DOR 465 1ST DIST
RUE, JOHN BAL 144 1ST WARD
RUE, MICHAEL WAS 245 SMITHSBU
RUE, MUNDAS BAL 046 1ST WARD
RUE, REBECCA WAS 245 SMITHSBU
RUEL, HENRY BAL 017 4TH WARD
RUENCKEL, JOHN BAL 363 13TH WAR
RUFENSTEEN, WILLIAM BAL 416 14TH WAR
RUFF, BENJAMIN BAL 118 11TH WAR
RUFF, CAPA BAL 059 2ND DIST
RUFF, CHARLES BAL 077 10TH WAR
RUFF, CYRUS N. DOR 376 1ST DIST
RUFF, DAVID WAS 117 2ND DIST
RUFF, ELIZA S. HAR 104 2ND DIST
RUFF, FREDERICK BAL 114 11TH WAR
RUFF, GEORGE BAL 072 2ND DIST
RUFF, HENRY ANN 412 HOWARD D
RUFF, HENRY BAL 002 4TH WARD
RUFF, JAMES HAR 103 2ND DIST
RUFF, JOHN BAL 395 1ST DIST
RUFF, JOHN G. BAL 321 1ST DIST
RUFF, JOHN J. BAL 349 1ST DIST
RUFF, MARGARET BAL 105 2ND DIST
RUFF, NANCY HAR 030 1ST DIST
RUFF, OTTAVIN HAR 207 3RD DIST
RUFF, PAMELIA ANN 295 1ST DIST
RUFF, PHILIP HAR 083 2ND DIST
RUFF, REBECCA HAR 002 1ST DIST
RUFF, REBECCA BAL 128 2ND DIST
RUFF, SAMUEL BAL 129 2ND DIST
RUFF, SARAH BAL 091 5TH WARD
RUFF, SARAH R. HAR 167 3RD DIST
RUFFLER, AMANDA BAL 139 11TH WAR
RUFFNER, HENRY BAL 066 1ST WARD
RUFFY, HENRY BAL 261 1ST DIST
RUGART, HUSTEN BAL 202 2ND WARD
RUGG, EVERET L. CEC 141 6TH E DI
RUGLE, SAMUEL PRI 107 PISCATAW
RUGLE,JACOB BAL 066 2ND DIST
RUHAN, PATRICK ALL 051 10TH E.D
RUHL, ELIZABETH BAL 294 7TH WARD
RUHL, GEORGE BAL 215 6TH WARD
RUHL, JAMES BAL 294 7TH WARD
RUHL, JOSEPH BAL 281 17TH WAR
RUHL, MARY CAR 330 MANCHEST
RUKER, LEWIS ANN 342 3RD DIST
RUKETS, ISAAC MGM 403 ROCKERLE
RUKETS, RHODA MGM 403 ROCKERLE
RUKY, JOHN CAR 296 7TH DIST
RULACK, JOSEPH BAL 328 13TH WAR
RULAN, WILLIAM BAL 202 17TH WAR
RULAUGH, RUDOLPH BAL 269 2ND WARD
RULBET, PETER BAL 104 2ND DIST
RULO, FREDERICK BAL 346 13TH WAR
RULE, ANN E. BAL 277 17TH WAR
RULE, ANNA BAL 438 1ST DIST
RULE, CHRISTOPHER BAL 277 17TH WAR
RULE, HY BAL 206 6TH DIST
RULE, JACOB BAL 209 6TH DIST
RULE, JACOB BAL 209 6TH DIST
RULE, JOHN BAL 119 15TH WAR
RULE, THOMAS ANN 425 HOWARD D
RULE, WILLAIM BAL 210 6TH DIST
RULE, WILLIAM BAL 212 6TH DIST
RULER, J. BAL 319 20TH WAR
RULET, WILLIAM WAS 057 2ND SUBD
RULEY, EDWARD BAL 214 19TH WAR
RULEY, HENRY P. BAL 388 3RD WARD
RULEY, JAMES QUE 131 1ST E DI
RULEY, JOHN CEC 049 1ST E DI
RULEY, MATTHEW W. BAL 202 6TH WARD
RULEY, PENGUIN W. BAL 322 3RD WARD
RULEY, THOMAS BAL 101 1ST WARD
RULEY, THOMAS BAL 100 1ST WARD
RULKER, HENRY ALL 233 CUMBERLA
RULLMAN, CHARLES BAL 351 3RD WARD
RULLMAN, WIGANS BAL 085 10TH WAR
RULLY, MATILDA BAL 183 19TH WAR
RULTER, THOMAS QUE 150 1ST E DI
RULTER, THOMAS BAL 142 1ST WARD
RULY, JAMES CEC 048 1ST E DI
RULY, JOHN BAL 127 5TH WARD
RULY, MARY BAL 283 17TH WAR
RULY, SAMUEL CEC 048 1ST E DI
RUM, AUGUSTUS BAL 211 17TH WAR
RUM, CHARELS BAL 211 17TH WAR
RUM, THOMAS BAL 003 9TH WARD
RUMACK, CHRISTINA BAL 361 13TH WAR
RUMACK, MADELINA BAL 331 13TH WAR
RUMBERGER, PHARAS WAS 172 FUNKSTOW
RUMBLE, JAMES B. CAR 163 NO TWP L
RUMBLY, EDWARD* DOR 400 1ST DIST
RUMBLY, GEORGE DOR 394 1ST DIST
RUMBLY, JANE DOR 400 1ST DIST
RUMBLY, PRISSILEY DOR 411 1ST DIST
RUMBLY, RACHEL DOR 440 1ST DIST
RUMBURG, EDWARD BAL 092 5TH WARD
RUMELL, BARBARA FRE 153 10TH E D
RUMER, PRISCILLA BAL 236 12TH WAR
RUMERE, JOSEPH ALL 093 5TH E.D.
RUMFORD, ROBERT HAR 053 1ST DIST
RUMLER, PERRY CAR 259 3RD DIST
RUMLEY, MARY WAS 155 HAGERSTO
RUMLEY, SHADERICK TAL 027 EASTON D
RUMLEY, WILLIAM DOR 341 3RD DIVI
RUMMEL, PETER WAS 295 1ST DIST
RUMMELL, CHARLES BAL 025 1ST WARD
RUMNEY, JANE BAL 154 16TH WAR
RUMNEY, LUCY BAL 055 4TH WARD
RUMNEY, ROBERT BAL 147 16TH WAR
RUMOSER, JACOB F. BAL 166 11TH WAR
RUMPLER, GABRIEL BAL 147 11TH WAR
RUMSBURG, JOHN W. FRE 233 BUCKEYST
RUMSEY, GEORGE * HAR 205 3RD DIST
RUMSEY, JOHN BAL 301 20TH WAR
RUMSEY, JOHN H. HAR 146 3RD DIST
RUMSEY, LOUISA HAR 174 3RD DIST
RUMSEY, MARY BAL 119 2ND DIST
RUMSEY, PRESILD HAR 187 3RD DIST
RUMSPIRT, WILLIAM CAR 237 UNION TO
RUMSTINE, JOHN T. ANN 458 HOWARD D
RUNALDAS, WILLIAM BAL 325 1ST DIST
RUNBEY, PETER FRE 166 EMMITTSB
RUNCKEL, CONRAD BAL 362 13TH WAR
RUNCUM, FREDERICK BAL 027 4TH WARD
RUNDELL, LEWIS BAL 132 18TH WAR
RUNDLE, JOSEPH BAL 235 17TH WAR
RUNDLE, SARAH BAL 247 17TH WAR
RUNDLE, WILLIAM BAL 085 15TH WAR
RUNDLET, ANDREW J. BAL 127 1ST WARD
RUNEBOLD, JOHN CAR 144 NO TWP L
RUNELL, HUSINE BAL 296 12TH WAR
RUNEY, JOHN WAS 064 2ND SUBD
RUNGE, MARY BAL 006 15TH WAR
RUNISEY, GEORGE * HAR 205 3RD DIST
RUNK,MARTIN ALL 197 CUMBERLA
RUNK,MICHAEL BAL 030 2ND DIST
RUNKLE, JOHN BAL 297 1ST DIST
RUNKLE, WASHINGTON CAR 368 9TH DIST
RUNKLES, BEAL Y. FRE 251 NEW MARK
RUNKLES, JACOB Y. FRE 254 NEW MARK
RUNKLES, JOSEPH FRE 251 NEW MARK
RUNKLES, MARY FRE 441 8TH E DI
RUNKLES, MARY F. CAR 368 9TH DIST
RUNKLES, MOSES FRE 306 WOODSBOR
RUNKLES, SUSANNAH FRE 257 NEW MARK
RUNKT, HENRY BAL 260 2ND WARD
RUNNA, GEORGEANNA BAL 196 2ND WARD
RUNNELS, MARY BAL 359 1ST DIST
RUNNOLDS, ANN WOR 290 9TH E DI
RUNNY, JOHN BAL 137 5TH WARD
RUNPH, JOHN J. BAL 060 1ST WARD
RUNS, MARY* TAL 035 EASTON D
RUNSEY, JAMES HAR 182 3RD DIST
RUNY, BRIAN BAL 273 1ST DIST
RUOULL, ADAM BAL 221 2ND WARD
RUP, MARIAH* SOM 496 SALISBUR
RUPE, JOHN BAL 126 18TH WAR
RUPE, JOHN * BAL 127 18TH WAR
RUPE, WILLIAM BAL 234 20TH WAR
RUPEE, WILLIAM* TAL 008 EASTON D
RUPEER, FRANKLIN * KEN 236 2ND DIST
RUPEL, CLEMENT ANN 472 HOWARD D
RUPER, HENRY BAL 297 1ST DIST
RUPER, JULIA SOM 482 TRAPP DI
RUPERM, JEREMIAH* TAL 041 EASTON D
RUPERT, GEORGE BAL 062 15TH WAR
RUPERT, JOHN BAL 254 1ST DIST
RUPERT, JOHN BAL 314 12TH WAR
RUPERT, JOHN BAL 314 12TH WAR
RUPERT, JOHN H. BAL 254 1ST DIST
RUPERT, JOSEPH BAL 230 2ND WARD
RUPERT, MARY ALL 120 5TH E.D.
RUPERT, W. BAL 314 12TH WAR
RUPERT, WILLIAM BAL 307 7TH WARD
RUPHERT, RUDOLPH BAL 230 2ND WARD
RUPLE, PATRICK BAL 003 EASTERN
RUPP, CHARLES BAL 224 12TH WAR
RUPP, GEORGE WAS 164 HAGERSTO
RUPP, GEORGE CAR 340 6TH DIST
RUPP, HENRY BAL 156 16TH WAR
RUPP, JOHN BAL 148 16TH WAR
RUPP, LEWIS FRE 352 MIDDLETO
RUPP, MARIA CAR 340 6TH DIST
RUPP, MARY CAR 331 MANCHEST
RUPP, SAVILLA CAR 334 6TH DIST
RUPP, YOUNG BAL 219 12TH WAR
RUPPLE, HENRY BAL 241 17TH WAR
RUPUM, SIDNAN* TAL 040 EASTON D
RUPUM, WILLIAM* TAL 042 EASTON D
RURTMAN, DANIEL F. BAL 145 1ST WARD
RURTZ, T. NEWTON BAL 340 13TH WAR
RUSBY, ROBERT BAL 345 13TH WAR
RUSCU, GEORGE * KEN 229 2ND DIST
RUSDLY, RICHARD HAR 160 3RD DIST
RUSE, JOHN CAR 354 6TH DIST
RUSE, JOHN BAL 406 14TH WAR
RUSE, JOHN BAL 004 9TH WARD
RUSEA, PATRICK HAR 172 3RD DIST
RUSEL, JOHN DOR 348 3RD DIVI
RUSEL, JOSEPH BAL 324 1ST DIST
RUSEL, SARAH WAS 058 2ND SUBD
RUSELL, EDWARD PRI 020 VANSVILL
RUSELL, JOHN C.* DOR 302 1ST DIST
RUSELL, R.H. BAL 171 1ST WARD
RUSELO, JOHN BAL 032 18TH WAR
RUSEY, WILLIAM BAL 458 8TH WARD
RUSH, ANDREW ALL 136 4TH E.D.
RUSH, ANDREW BAL 285 1ST DIST
RUSH, BENJAMIN WAS 288 1ST DIST
RUSH, BRIDGET BAL 006 EASTERN
RUSH, CLEMMET* TAL 031 EASTON D
RUSH, DAVID WAS 156 2ND DIST
RUSH, EELIZABETH* TAL 006 EASTON D
RUSH, FRANCIS BAL 162 19TH WAR
RUSH, FREDERICK BAL 293 17TH WAR
RUSH, JACOB HAR 140 2ND DIST
RUSH, JACOB BAL 238 20TH WAR
RUSH, JAMES H. ALL 023 2ND E.D.
RUSH, JOHN BAL 274 12TH WAR
RUSH, JOHN P. WAS 159 2ND DIST
RUSH, JOSEPH BAL 213 19TH WAR
RUSH, JOSEPHINE BAL 149 5TH WARD
RUSH, MARTHA HAR 106 2ND DIST
RUSH, THOMAS WAS 249 1ST DIST
RUSH, THOMASJ. BAL 108 1ST WARD
RUSH, WILLIAM WAS 158 2ND DIST
RUSHE, BARBARA BAL 160 19TH WAR
RUSHE, JOSEPH BAL 160 19TH WAR
RUSHMIRE, WILLIAM BAL 368 13TH WAR
RUSHOM, BARN* BAL 354 3RD WARD
RUSHORN, BARN* BAL 354 3RD WARD
RUSIA, WILLIAM BAL 445 8TH WARD
RUSIN, AJENS KEN 246 2ND DIST
RUSIN, DULANY KEN 245 2ND DIST
RUSIN, EMORY KEN 225 2ND DIST
RUSIN, JOHN W. KEN 244 2ND DIST
RUSIN, SAMUEL KEN 246 2ND DIST
RUSIN, THOMAS KEN 252 1ST DIST
RUSIN, WARNER KEN 248 2ND DIST
RUSINER, PHILIP FRE 313 MIDDLETO
RUSK, ABRAHAM BAL 445 8TH WARD
RUSK, EDWARD BAL 295 17TH WAR
RUSK, EDWIN BAL 416 8TH WARD
RUSK, ELIZABETH A. BAL 369 3RD WARD
RUSK, GEORGE W. BAL 107 1ST WARD
RUSK, JACOB K. BAL 111 1ST WARD
RUSK, JOHN BAL 412 8TH WARD
RUSK, LEMUEL* BAL 415 3RD WARD
RUSK, MARY BAL 332 7TH WARD
RUSK, MARY C. BAL 325 7TH WARD
RUSK, PETER BAL 378 8TH WARD
RUSK, ROBERT BAL 411 8TH WARD
RUSK, ROBERT BAL 442 8TH WARD
RUSK, ROBERT BAL 025 9TH WARD
RUSK, THOMAS BAL 442 8TH WARD
RUSK, WILLIAM BAL 304 7TH WARD

Name	County	Page	District
RUSKELL, JOHN	BAL	148	2ND DIST
RUSKELL, JOHN	BAL	344	13TH WAR
RUSKELL, THOMAS	BAL	267	12TH WAR
RUSLEY, JAMES	WAS	155	2ND DIST
RUSLEY, JOHN	WAS	154	2ND DIST
RUSS, K.	BAL	449	8TH WARD
RUSS, MARIAH*	SOM	496	SALISBUR
RUSSANE, WILLIAM-BLACK	CAR	151	NO TWP L
RUSSEER, FRANKLIN *	KEN	236	2ND DIST
RUSSEL, ALEYZAN	HAR	030	1ST DIST
RUSSEL, CLEM	BAL	211	11TH WAR
RUSSEL, CANIEL	WOR	304	SNOW HIL
RUSSEL, EDWARD	MGM	374	ROCKERLE
RUSSEL, ELELN	WAS	044	2ND SUBD
RUSSEL, ELIZA	FRE	059	FREDERIC
RUSSEL, FRED	BAL	270	1ST DIST
RUSSEL, HENRY	FRE	291	WOODSBOR
RUSSEL, J. A.	BAL	039	18TH WAR
RUSSEL, JACOB	WAS	073	2ND SUBD
RUSSEL, JOHN	WAS	073	2ND SUBD
RUSSEL, JOHN	FRE	385	PETERSVI
RUSSEL, JOHN	BAL	267	1ST DIST
RUSSEL, MARIAH	CAR	152	NO TWP L
RUSSEL, MARY	CAL	045	3RD DIST
RUSSEL, MARY V.	BAL	413	14TH WAR
RUSSEL, MICHAEL	BAL	420	1ST DIST
RUSSEL, PHILIP	BAL	028	2ND DIST
RUSSEL, ROBERT G.	MGM	374	ROCKERLE
RUSSEL, RUTHANDHALL, NANC	BAL	164	11TH WAR
RUSSEL, SALLY	WOR	302	SNOW HIL
RUSSEL, SAMUEL	HAR	146	3RD DIST
RUSSEL, SARAH E.	BAL	402	14TH WAR
RUSSEL, SARAH J.	HAR	032	1ST DIST
RUSSEL, WESTLEY	DOR	353	3RD DIVI
RUSSEL, WILLIAM	BAL	036	18TH WAR
RUSSEL, WILLIAM*	TAL	008	EASTON D
RUSSELL, AARON	BAL	241	6TH WARD
RUSSELL, ABRAHAM	ALL	254	CUMBERLA
RUSSELL, ALEXANDER J.	BAL	361	13TH WAR
RUSSELL, ALEXANDER JR.	BAL	180	16TH WAR
RUSSELL, ALFRED M.	KEN	209	2ND DIST
RUSSELL, AMELIA	SOM	526	QUANTICO
RUSSELL, ANDREW	BAL	439	1ST DIST
RUSSELL, ANN	BAL	228	6TH WARD
RUSSELL, ANN	BAL	048	15TH WAR
RUSSELL, ANN	BAL	040	1ST WARD
RUSSELL, ANN	ST	317	4TH E DI
RUSSELL, ARCHIBALD	BAL	179	19TH WAR
RUSSELL, AVARILLA	HAR	121	2ND DIST
RUSSELL, B.	BAL	144	5TH WARD
RUSSELL, BARBARA	BAL	143	16TH WAR
RUSSELL, BENEDICT	ST	276	3RD E DI
RUSSELL, BENJAMIN	BAL	327	13TH WAR
RUSSELL, CHARLES	BAL	096	1ST WARD
RUSSELL, CHARLES	ANN	277	ANNAPOLI
RUSSELL, CHARLES	ANN	281	ANNAPOLI
RUSSELL, CHARLES A.	ST	324	4TH E DI
RUSSELL, CHARLES J.	BAL	119	1ST WARD
RUSSELL, CHARLES L.	ST	266	3RD E DI
RUSSELL, CHRISTINA	BAL	145	16TH WAR
RUSSELL, CLEN *	BAL	317	12TH WAR
RUSSELL, ELISABETH	ALL	254	CUMBERLA
RUSSELL, ELIZA	BAL	368	3RD WARD
RUSSELL, ELIZA	HAR	105	2ND DIST
RUSSELL, ELIZABETH	SOM	518	BARREN C
RUSSELL, ELIZABETH	WAS	036	2ND SUBD
RUSSELL, ELIZABETH A.	ST	276	3RD E DI
RUSSELL, ESTHER	BAL	380	13TH WAR
RUSSELL, EUGENE	BAL	253	20TH WAR
RUSSELL, EUGENE	BAL	006	1ST WARD
RUSSELL, FANNY	BAL	210	11TH WAR
RUSSELL, FANNY	FRE	045	FREDERIC
RUSSELL, GEORGE	BAL	046	18TH WAR
RUSSELL, GEORGE	FRE	316	MIDDLETO
RUSSELL, GEORGE	CEC	083	CHARLEST
RUSSELL, GEORGE	BAL	116	11TH WAR
RUSSELL, GEORGE	BAL	450	8TH WARD
RUSSELL, GEORGE	BAL	191	6TH WARD
RUSSELL, GEORGE W.	BAL	054	4TH WARD
RUSSELL, HANNAH-MULATTO	FRE	234	BUCKEYST
RUSSELL, HARRIET	BAL	463	14TH WAR
RUSSELL, HENRY	BAL	221	6TH WARD
RUSSELL, HENRY	ALL	061	10TH E.D
RUSSELL, HENRY	ST	254	3RD E DI
RUSSELL, HENRY	WAS	156	HAGERSTO
RUSSELL, HENRY	KEN	266	1ST DIST
RUSSELL, ISAAC L.	FRE	255	NEW MARK
RUSSELL, ISAIAH	ANN	277	ANNAPOLI
RUSSELL, JACOB	BAL	067	1ST WARD
RUSSELL, JAMES	BAL	125	1ST WARD
RUSSELL, JAMES	BAL	097	1ST WARD
RUSSELL, JAMES	BAL	144	1ST WARD
RUSSELL, JAMES	FRE	268	NEW MARK
RUSSELL', JAMES	CEC	159	PORT DUP
RUSSELL, JAMES	SOM	476	TRAPPE D
RUSSELL, JAMES	SOM	518	BARREN C
RUSSELL, JAMES A.	ST	329	4TH E DI
RUSSELL, JAMES A.	ST	278	3RD E DI
RUSSELL, JAMES A.	BAL	388	13TH WAR
RUSSELL, JAMES M	ST	266	3RD E DI
RUSSELL, JAMES P.	DOR	306	1ST DIST
RUSSELL, JANE	BAL	356	13TH WAR
RUSSELL, JANE	CEC	199	7TH E DI
RUSSELL, JEROME	ST	315	4TH E DI
RUSSELL, JOBE G.	DOR	303	1ST DIST
RUSSELL, JOHN	BAL	431	14TH WAR
RUSSELL, JOHN	CEC	189	7TH E DI
RUSSELL, JOHN	BAL	386	13TH WAR
RUSSELL, JOHN	KEN	210	2ND DIST
RUSSELL, JOHN	CEC	052	1ST E DI
RUSSELL, JOHN	MGM	330	CRACKLIN
RUSSELL, JOHN	BAL	420	3RD WARD
RUSSELL, JOHN	BAL	406	8TH WARD
RUSSELL, JOHN	ALL	135	4TH E.D.
RUSSELL, JOHN	BAL	459	8TH WARD
RUSSELL, JOHN	ALL	251	CUMBERLA
RUSSELL, JOHN	ANN	485	HOWARD D
RUSSELL, JOHN	BAL	126	16TH WAR
RUSSELL, JOHN	BAL	380	1ST DIST
RUSSELL, JOHN B.	CEC	134	6TH E DI
RUSSELL, JOHN B.	ST	291	2ND E DI
RUSSELL, JOHN B.	ST	316	4TH E DI
RUSSELL, JOHN H.	HAR	122	2ND DIST
RUSSELL, JOHN J.	BAL	163	19TH WAR
RUSSELL, JOHN W.	BAL	129	1ST WARD
RUSSELL, JOSEPH	CEC	088	4TH E DI
RUSSELL, JOSEPH	BAL	442	14TH WAR
RUSSELL, JOSEPH	ST	328	4TH E DI
RUSSELL, JOSHUA	BAL	415	8TH WARD
RUSSELL, JOSIAH	SOM	367	BRINKLEY
RUSSELL, JULIA	SOM	467	HANGARY
RUSSELL, LAURA	MGM	331	CRACKLIN
RUSSELL, LAVINIA	BAL	437	14TH WAR
RUSSELL, LEWIS	BAL	137	18TH WAR
RUSSELL, LLOYD	BAL	153	2ND DIST
RUSSELL, LORENZO S.	PRI	025	VANSVILL
RUSSELL, MARGARETT	HAR	121	2ND DIST
RUSSELL, MARIA	CEC	077	NORTHEAS
RUSSELL, MARY	BAL	005	4TH WARD
RUSSELL, MARY	BAL	180	16TH WAR
RUSSELL, MARY A.	BAL	013	18TH WAR
RUSSELL, MARY A.	BAL	297	20TH WAR
RUSSELL, NANCY	BAL	024	15TH WAR
RUSSELL, PATRICK	BAL	174	11TH WAR
RUSSELL, PHILIP	PRI	040	VANSVILL
RUSSELL, R.H.	BAL	129	1ST WARD
RUSSELL, RACHEL	BAL	269	2ND WARD
RUSSELL, RAMOND	ST	263	3RD E DI
RUSSELL, REBECCA	MGM	331	CRACKLIN
RUSSELL, REBECCA	FRE	269	NEW MARK
RUSSELL, RICHARD	BAL	180	19TH WAR
RUSSELL, ROBERT	CAR	369	9TH DIST
RUSSELL, ROBERT	SOM	523	BARREN C
RUSSELL, ROBERT	BAL	290	3RD WARD
RUSSELL, ROBERT C.	BAL	314	3RD WARD
RUSSELL, SALLY	BAL	328	13TH WAR
RUSSELL, SAMUEL	BAL	445	14TH WAR
RUSSELL, SARAH	FRE	255	NEW MARK
RUSSELL, SOLOMON	DOR	300	1ST DIST
RUSSELL, SUSAN	BAL	276	12TH WAR
RUSSELL, TELITHA	HAR	143	2ND DIST
RUSSELL, THEODORE, W.	KEN	211	2ND DIST
RUSSELL, THOMAS	DOR	304	1ST DIST
RUSSELL, THOMAS	CEC	125	5TH E DI
RUSSELL, THOMAS	MGM	362	BERRYS D
RUSSELL, THOMAS	BAL	157	16TH WAR
RUSSELL, THOMAS	BAL	146	1ST WARD
RUSSELL, THOMAS	SOM	531	QUANTICO
RUSSELL, THOMAS	PRI	045	VANSVILL
RUSSELL, THOMAS	PRI	020	VANSVILL
RUSSELL, THOMAS	ST	294	2ND E DI
RUSSELL, THOMAS	QUE	171	2ND E DI
RUSSELL, THOMAS G.	BAL	387	13TH WAR
RUSSELL, THOMAS M.	BAL	111	10TH WAR
RUSSELL, WILLIAM	BAL	024	9TH WARD
RUSSELL, WILLIAM	BAL	148	1ST WARD
RUSSELL, WILLIAM	DOR	303	1ST DIST
RUSSELL, WILLIAM	BAL	423	14TH WAR
RUSSELL, WILLIAM	HAR	128	2ND DIST
RUSSELL, WILLIAM T.	ST	274	3RD E DI
RUSSELL, ZACHARIAH H.	ST	335	4TH E DI
RUSSELL,LOUIS	BAL	089	1ST WARD
RUSSELS, JAMES	WOR	195	8TH E DI
RUSSEM, JOHN	CAR	094	NO TWP L
RUSSEUR, ELIZABETH	CAR	095	NO TWP L
RUSSEY, LEWIS	WAS	221	1ST DIST
RUSSIM, JOSEPH C.*	TAL	014	EASTON D
RUSSIM, SYDENHAM T.*	TAL	015	EASTON D
RUSSIN, LYDENHAM T.*	TAL	015	EASTON D
RUSSLE, ANTONY	BAL	140	2ND DIST
RUSSLE, JAMES	BAL	123	2ND DIST
RUSSLE, JAMES T.	HAR	146	3RD DIST
RUSSLE, JOHN	HAR	146	3RD DIST
RUSSLE, JOHN	BAL	024	2ND DIST
RUSSLE, ROBERT	BAL	064	2ND DIST
RUSSLE, ROEBUCK	BAL	055	2ND DIST
RUSSLE, WILLIAM	BAL	052	2ND DIST
RUSSMAN, JOHN J.	FRE	369	CATOCTIN
RUSSUM, ALEXANDER	QUE	211	3RD E DI
RUSSUM, ALIRE	TAL	071	EASTON T
RUSSUM, ELI-BLACK	CAR	127	NO TWP L
RUSSUM, FRANCIS*	TAL	015	EASTON D
RUSSUM, LEAH	BAL	247	6TH WARD
RUSSUM, NATHAN	CAR	107	NO TWP L
RUSSUM, ROBERT	CAR	111	NO TWP L
RUSSUM, SIDNAH*	TAL	040	EASTON D
RUSSUM, WILLIAM	CAR	106	NO TWP L
RUSSUM, WILLIAM*	TAL	042	EASTON D
RUSSUM,EMELINE-BLACK	CAR	127	NO TWP L
RUST, AUSTIN	BAL	237	2ND WARD
RUST, CLEMMET*	TAL	031	EASTON D
RUST, GEORGE	BAL	271	2ND WARD
RUST, GEORGE	BAL	193	2ND WARD
RUST, GEORGE W.	BAL	287	20TH WAR
RUST, HARRIET	BAL	316	1ST DIST
RUST, JACK-BLACK	QUE	200	3RD E DI
RUST, JACKSON	BAL	046	18TH WAR
RUST, JEREMIAH	CAR	105	NO TWP L
RUST, LEVI	BAL	412	14TH WAR
RUST, PATIENCE	BAL	387	1ST DIST
RUST, PAUL	BAL	387	1ST DIST
RUST, PHILLIP	BAL	007	9TH WARD
RUST, SAMUEL	BAL	220	6TH WARD
RUST, THOMAS	MGM	427	MEDLEY 3
RUSTAR, THOMAS	BAL	079	2ND DIST
RUSTEAU, REBECA	BAL	302	7TH WARD
RUSTELL, JOHN	BAL	205	19TH WAR
RUSTER, FREDERICK	BAL	236	2ND WARD
RUSY, MARY E.	HAR	182	3RD DIST
RUTER, GILBERT	CEC	018	ELKTON 3
RUTER, JOHN H.	BAL	319	1ST DIST
RUTH, ABHRAIM *	BAL	048	18TH WAR
RUTH, FRANCIS A.	QUE	171	2ND E DI
RUTH, JACOB	BAL	190	2ND WARD
RUTH, JAES	QUE	246	5TH E DI
RUTH, JOHN	KEN	306	3RD DIST
RUTH, JOHN	BAL	048	18TH WAR
RUTH, JOHN	HAR	131	2ND DIST
RUTH, JOHN C.	QUE	191	3RD E DI
RUTH, JOHN S.	BAL	031	18TH WAR
RUTH, NATHAN	KEN	303	3RD DIST
RUTH, ROBERT	QUE	219	3RD E DI
RUTH, ROBERT	KEN	312	3RD DIST
RUTH, SAMUEL B.	QUE	150	1ST E DI
RUTH, THOMAS D. C.	QUE	218	3RD E DI
RUTH, WILLIAM	WAS	300	1ST DIST
RUTH, WILLIAM	BAL	261	2ND WARD
RUTH, WILLIAM T.	QUE	195	3RD E DI
RUTHBERRY, WILLIAM	ALL	120	5TH E.D.
RUTHELL, EZEKIEL	CAR	091	NO TWP L
RUTHERFORD, ALEXANDER	BAL	048	4TH WARD
RUTHERFORD, ALEXANDER	BAL	179	19TH WAR
RUTHERFORD, ANN M.	BAL	114	15TH WAR
RUTHERFORD, SAMUEL	BAL	448	8TH WARD
RUTHLEDGE, ELIZABETH	BAL	032	2ND DIST
RUTHLIDGE, JOSHUA	BAL	393	8TH WARD
RUTHON, R.	BAL	117	1ST WARD
RUTHRAFF, JACOB	WAS	170	FUNKSTOW
RUTLEDGE, ABRAHAM	HAR	025	1ST DIST
RUTLEDGE, ABRAHAM	HAR	066	1ST DIST
RUTLEDGE, ANN	HAR	111	2ND DIST
RUTLEDGE, BELINDA	BAL	038	2ND DIST
RUTLEDGE, BENJAMIN	BAL	035	2ND DIST
RUTLEDGE, BLANCH	HAR	066	1ST DIST
RUTLEDGE, CECILIA	BAL	035	2ND DIST
RUTLEDGE, EDWARD	HAR	071	1ST DIST
RUTLEDGE, ELIZA	BAL	293	1ST DIST
RUTLEDGE, IGNATIUS	HAR	009	1ST DIST
RUTLEDGE, JACOB	HAR	018	1ST DIST
RUTLEDGE, JARRET	BAL	435	1ST DIST
RUTLEDGE, JOHN	BAL	057	2ND DIST
RUTLEDGE, JOHN	BAL	160	6TH WARD
RUTLEDGE, JOHN W.	HAR	059	1ST DIST
RUTLEDGE, JOSHUA L.	BAL	214	6TH WARD
RUTLEDGE, LEVI	BAL	040	2ND DIST
RUTLEDGE, RUFUS F.	BAL	438	1ST DIST
RUTLEDGE, SOPHIA	HAR	077	BEL AIR
RUTLEDGE, THOMAS	HAR	025	1ST DIST
RUTLEDGE, THOMAS	BAL	438	1ST DIST
RUTLEDGE, WILLIAM	BAL	437	1ST DIST
RUTLEDGE, WILLIAM	BAL	211	6TH WARD
RUTLEGE, GEORGE W.	BAL	295	20TH WAR
RUTLER, FRANCIS	DOR	375	1ST DIST
RUTLER, JOHN	BAL	053	1ST WARD
RUTLER, JOSIAH L.*	BAL	407	3RD WARD
RUTLER, MARGARET	KEN	263	1ST DIST
RUTLER, S. A.*	DOR	375	1ST DIST
RUTLER, SAMUEL	BAL	262	12TH WAR
RUTLIDGE, JOHN	BAL	388	8TH WARD
RUTT, REZIN	FRE	395	PETERSVI
RUTT, RICHARD	BAL	263	2ND WARD
RUTTER, AARON	BAL	463	1ST DIST
RUTTER, ALEXANDER	BAL	010	EASTERN
RUTTER, ANN	CEC	020	ELKTON 3
RUTTER, CAROLINE	BAL	370	1ST DIST
RUTTER, EBONY	CEC	020	ELKTON 3
RUTTER, EDWARD	BAL	137	16TH WAR
RUTTER, ELIZABETH	WOR	262	BERLIN 1
RUTTER, EMIEL	BAL	164	6TH WARD
RUTTER, FRANCES	CEC	013	ELKTON 3
RUTTER, GILBERT	CEC	116	3RD E DI
RUTTER, HARRIET	BAL	184	11TH WAR
RUTTER, HARRIET H. A.	BAL	269	7TH WARD
RUTTER, HENRETTA*	BAL	114	11TH WAR
RUTTER, HOWARD	CEC	020	ELKTON 3
RUTTER, JAMES	CEC	073	5TH E DI
RUTTER, JOHN	CEC	067	5TH E DI
RUTTER, JOHN	BAL	152	1ST WARD
RUTTER, JOHN	BAL	009	1ST WARD
RUTTER, JOHN H.	BAL	269	7TH WARD
RUTTER, JOSEPH	BAL	292	3RD WARD
RUTTER, JOSHUA	HAR	143	2ND DIST
RUTTER, JOSIAH	BAL	263	1ST DIST
RUTTER, JOSIAH L.*	BAL	407	3RD WARD
RUTTER, LAURA V.	FRE	002	FREDERIC
RUTTER, MARTHA	CEC	073	5TH E DI
RUTTER, MARY	BAL	317	20TH WAR
RUTTER, RALPH	BAL	047	4TH WARD
RUTTER, RICHARD	CEC	098	3RD E DI
RUTTER, RICHARD	CEC	190	5TH E DI
RUTTER, SARAH	BAL	146	16TH WAR
RUTTER, SARAH B.	CEC	067	5TH E DI
RUTTER, SARAH J.	CEC	072	5TH E DI
RUTTER, THOMAS	CEC	187	7TH E DI
RUTTER, THOMAS B.	BAL	043	9TH WARD
RUTTER, THOMAS F.	QUE	151	1ST E DI
RUTTER, THOMAS G.	BAL	122	5TH WARD
RUTTER, VIRGINIA O.	BAL	044	9TH WARD
RUTTER, WILLIAM	QUE	153	1ST E DI
RUTTER, WILLIAM	CEC	187	7TH E DI
RUTTER, WILLIAM	CEC	037	CHESAPEA
RUTTER, WILLIS	CEC	004	ELKTON 3
RUTTFRUSH, SIMON	BAL	095	1ST WARD
RUTTLE, WILLIAM	BAL	287	20TH WAR
RUTTZ, BENJAMIN	BAL	362	13TH WAR
RUTVENOLD, HENRY	WAS	034	2ND SUBD
RUTZ, WILLIAM	BAL	084	10TH WAR
RUVEGRANT, SOPHIA	BAL	219	12TH WAR
RYA, JOHN T.	WAS	100	2ND DIST
RYAL, WILLIAM	BAL	143	1ST WARD
RYALS, WILLIAM	BAL	171	1ST WARD
RYAN, ADAULPHUS	BAL	299	17TH WAR
RYAN, ANDREW	BAL	082	10TH WAR
RYAN, ANN	BAL	025	9TH WARD
RYAN, ANN	BAL	002	15TH WAR
RYAN, ANN	ALL	173	7TH E.D.
RYAN, BRIDGET	ANN	438	HOWARD D
RYAN, BRIDGET	BAL	447	14TH WAR
RYAN, CATHERINE	ALL	211	CUMBERLA
RYAN, CHARLES	BAL	457	8TH WARD
RYAN, CORNELIUS	BAL	035	4TH WARD
RYAN, CANIEL	ALL	180	8TH E.D.
RYAN, DANIEL	BAL	187	5TH DIST
RYAN, DANIEL	BAL	338	1ST DIST
RYAN, ELIZA	BAL	241	6TH WARD
RYAN, ELIZA	BAL	119	15TH WAR
RYAN, ELIZABETH	BAL	188	5TH DIST
RYAN, ELIZABETH	MGM	436	CLARKSTR
RYAN, ELLEN	BAL	022	1ST WARD
RYAN, ELLEN	BAL	355	13TH WAR
RYAN, HARRIET	ANN	521	HOWARD D
RYAN, HENRY	BAL	173	6TH WARD
RYAN, HENRY	BAL	450	14TH WAR
RYAN, HUGH	BAL	007	15TH WAR
RYAN, JAMES	BAL	002	15TH WAR
RYAN, JAMES	BAL	002	15TH WAR
RYAN, JAMES	BAL	185	11TH WAR
RYAN, JAMES	BAL	029	9TH WARD
RYAN, JAMES	BAL	172	2ND DIST
RYAN, JAMES	BAL	008	EASTERN
RYAN, JAMES	BAL	062	2ND DIST
RYAN, JAMES S.	BAL	057	18TH WAR
RYAN, JEREMIAH	BAL	143	2ND DIST
RYAN, JEREMIAH	BAL	149	2ND DIST
RYAN, JEREMIAH	BAL	057	15TH WAR
RYAN, JOHN	BAL	022	1ST WARD
RYAN, JOHN	BAL	033	9TH WARD
RYAN, JOHN	BAL	122	16TH WAR
RYAN, JOHN	BAL	085	10TH WAR
RYAN, JOHN	ALL	203	CUMBERLA
RYAN, JOHN	BAL	125	1ST WARD
RYAN, JOHN	BAL	400	14TH WAR
RYAN, JOHN	BAL	357	13TH WAR
RYAN, JOHN	BAL	382	13TH WAR
RYAN, JOHN	BAL	263	20TH WAR
RYAN, JOSEPH	BAL	398	8TH WARD
RYAN, JOSEPH	ANN	469	HOWARD D
RYAN, JOSEPH M.	ALL	253	CUMBERLA
RYAN, LYDIA A.	BAL	180	16TH WAR
RYAN, M.	FRE	200	5TH E DI

Name	County	Page	District
RYAN, MARGARET A.	BAL	407	3RD WARD
RYAN, MARGRETT	BAL	057	18TH WAR
RYAN, MARGRETT	BAL	105	18TH WAR
RYAN, MARTIN	BAL	457	8TH WARD
RYAN, MARY	BAL	058	2ND DIST
RYAN, MARY	BAL	278	7TH WARD
RYAN, MARY	BAL	359	3RD WARD
RYAN, MARY	BAL	411	3RD WARD
RYAN, MARY A.	BAL	267	2ND WARD
RYAN, MARY A.	BAL	339	1ST DIST
RYAN, MARY ANN	BAL	355	13TH WAR
RYAN, MATHEW	ALL	099	5TH E.D.
RYAN, MICHAEL	ALL	146	6TH E.D.
RYAN, MICHAEL	BAL	173	11TH WAR
RYAN, MICHAEL	FRE	058	FREDERIC
RYAN, MICHAEL	FRE	067	FREDERIC
RYAN, OWEN	BAL	148	16TH WAR
RYAN, PATRICK	BAL	445	8TH WARD
RYAN, PATRICK	ALL	050	10TH E.D
RYAN, PETER	WAS	116	2ND DIST
RYAN, PHILLIP	ALL	210	CUMBERLA
RYAN, ROBERT	MGM	426	MEDLEY 3
RYAN, SARAH	BAL	059	4TH WARD
RYAN, SIPHYRION	BAL	208	17TH WAR
RYAN, THOMAS	BAL	005	4TH WARD
RYAN, THOMAS	BAL	446	14TH WAR
RYAN, THOMAS	BAL	269	1ST DIST
RYAN, TIMOTHY	CEC	062	1ST E DI
RYAN, WILLA	ALL	146	6TH E.D.
RYAN, WILLIAM	ALL	108	5TH E.D.
RYAN, WILLIAM	BAL	019	1ST WARD
RYAN, WILLIAM	BAL	001	15TH WAR
RYAN, WILLIAM	BAL	153	1ST WARD
RYAN, WILLIAM	QUE	214	3RD E DI
RYAN, WILLIAM HJ.	BAL	431	14TH WAR
RYAN, WILLIAM J.	BAL	278	7TH WARD
RYAN, WILLIAM W.D.	BAL	175	16TH WAR
RYAN.BRIDGET	FRE	036	FREDERIC
RYANS, ASBURY	BAL	212	17TH WAR
RYANS, EDWARD	BAL	384	1ST DIST
RYCE, ANN WILLIMNE	ALL	235	CUMBERLA
RYDER, B.	BAL	320	12TH WAR
RYDER, PESKET	BAL	246	2ND WARD
RYE, CATHARINE	WAS	036	2ND SUBD
RYE, CATHARINE	WAS	046	2ND SUBD
RYE, CATHARINE	WAS	064	2ND SUBD
RYE, EDWARD R.	CHA	257	MIDDLETO
RYE, ELIZABETH	WAS	037	2ND SUBD
RYE, JANE	CHA	261	MIDDLETO
RYE, JOHN V.	CHA	257	MIDDLETO
RYE, MARGARET E.	CHA	292	BOJANTOW
RYE, ROBERT	CHA	246	HILLTOP
RYE, SAMUEL	CHA	289	BOJANTOW
RYE, WILLS	CHA	247	HILLTOP
RYEL, PATRICK	BAL	451	14TH WAR
RYERS, HENRY	CAR	297	7TH DIST
RYERS, JAMES	BAL	372	1ST DIST
RYERS, TAYLOR *	BAL	363	1ST DIST
RYLAND, A.A.	ALL	033	2ND E.D.
RYLAND, BARBARA	ALL	028	2ND E.D.
RYLAND, CATHARINE	BAL	192	6TH WARD
RYLAND, CATHERINE	BAL	385	8TH WARD
RYLAND, ELIZABETH	BAL	169	19TH WAR
RYLAND, ISAAC	KEN	305	3RD DIST
RYLAND, JAMES	BAL	139	2ND DIST
RYLAND, ROBERT	CEC	015	ELKTON 3
RYLAND, SAMUEL	BAL	220	1ST DIST
RYLAND, SARAH	PRI	041	VANSVILL
RYLAND, SYLVESTER	ALL	027	2ND E.D.
RYLE, ANNORIA	HAR	145	3RD DIST
RYLER, CATHERINE	BAL	439	8TH WARD
RYLER, JOHN	BAL	446	8TH WARD
RYLER, PHILIP	BAL	346	1ST DIST
RYLEY, CLEM	BAL	272	1ST DIST
RYLEY, EDEEN *	BAL	274	1ST DIST
RYLEY, EDWARD *	KEN	280	3RD DIST
RYLEY, ELIZA	BAL	263	1ST DIST
RYLEY, HENRIETTA	KEN	281	3RD DIST
RYLEY, JOHN	PRI	025	VANSVILL
RYLEY, M.	BAL	141	1ST WARD
RYLEY, MARY A.	FRE	389	PETERSVI
RYLEY, MILLA	BAL	445	1ST DIST
RYLEY, MOSES	BAL	447	1ST DIST
RYLIE, GRAFTEN	BAL	370	1ST DIST
RYLIE, MARGARET	BAL	347	1ST DIST
RYLIE, PHILIP *	BAL	346	1ST DIST
RYLY, DENIS	BAL	455	1ST DIST
RYME, PETER	WAS	112	2ND DIST
RYMOND, PETER	PRI	019	VANSVILL
RYNE, FRANKLIN	BAL	367	8TH WARD
RYNE, JAMES	WAS	099	2ND DIST
RYNE, WILLIAM	BAL	367	8TH WARD
RYNHART, CHRISTOPHER	BAL	218	17TH WAR
RYNHART, JOHN	BAL	208	17TH WAR
RYNOLD, DANIEL	WAS	226	1ST DIST
RYON, ANN	PRI	029	VANSVILL
RYON, EDMOND	PRI	001	BLADENSB
RYON, ELIJAH	WOR	248	1ST CENS
RYON, ELIZABETH	PRI	065	NOTTINGH
RYON, ELIZABETH	PRI	073	MARLBROU
RYON, J. J.	BAL	186	11TH WAR
RYON, JOHN	BAL	134	1ST WARD
RYON, M.A.	PRI	067	NOTTINGH
RYON, MARY	PRI	098	SPALDING
RYON, ROBERT	PRI	074	MARLBROU
RYON, SARAH	PRI	064	NOTTINGH
RYON, THOMAS	PRI	069	MARLBROU
RYON, THOMAS P.	PRI	103	SPALDING
RYON, VIOLETTA	PRI	008	BLADENSB
RYON, WALTER	PRI	042	VANSVILL
RYON, WILLIAM G.	PRI	044	VANSVILL
RYORNS, JOHN T. *	BAL	286	1ST DIST
RYSER, JACOB	BAL	343	7TH WARD
S	WOR	230	6TH E DI
S	QUE	177	2ND E DI
SABADIE, JOSEPH	FRE	379	PETERSVI
SABB, GEORGE	BAL	013	1ST WARD
SABEL, JOHN*	BAL	393	3RD WARD
SABELLS, ANDREW J.	BAL	060	1ST WARD
SABEN, JOHN	BAL	136	1ST WARD
SABF, JOHN A.	BAL	079	1ST WARD
SABF, WILLIAM	BAL	079	1ST WARD
SABLE, JOHN	BAL	328	3RD WARD
SABLER, GEORGE W.	MGM	438	CLARKSTR
SABLES, JACKSON	ST	312	1ST E DI
SABRE, WILLIAM	BAL	054	9TH WARD
SACHELL, SUSAN	BAL	223	17TH WAR
SACHERMAN, HENRY	BAL	464	14TH WAR
SACHSE, EDWARD	BAL	081	10TH WAR
SACKARMAN, MICHIEL	BAL	149	5TH WARD
SACKETT, WILLIAM*	BAL	045	4TH WARD
SACKNER, PETER	BAL	192	2ND WARD
SACLARR, JOHN	BAL	114	5TH WARD
SACOMPT, WILLIAM	BAL	299	1ST DIST
SACOTT, HENRY*	ALL	091	5TH E.D.
SADDLE, BELINDA	BAL	225	19TH WAR
SADDLE, PERRY	CAR	281	7TH DIST
SADDLER, CHRISTINA	BAL	028	1ST WARD
SADDLER, ELLEN	BAL	276	12TH WAR
SADDLER, GEORGE	FRE	014	FREDERIC
SADDLER, JOHN	QUE	210	3RD E DI
SADDLER, MARY F.	BAL	025	1ST WARD
SADDLER, PERRY	BAL	098	2ND DIST
SADDLER, SOLOMON	FRE	421	8TH E DI
SADLER, ELIZABETH	FRE	262	NEW MARK
SADLER, GEORGE	BAL	044	15TH WAR
SADLER, GEORGE T.	BAL	139	11TH WAR
SADLER, JAMES M.	BAL	146	1ST WARD
SADLER, JOHN H.	HAR	014	1ST DIST
SADLER, JOSEPH	BAL	236	17TH WAR
SADLER, JULIANNE	BAL	211	17TH WAR
SADLER, MARGARET *	BAL	121	2ND DIST
SADLER, MARTHA A.	BAL	038	15TH WAR
SADLER, MARY	BAL	007	15TH WAR
SADLER, MARY C.	HAR	029	1ST DIST
SADLER, PHILIP	BAL	143	1ST WARD
SADLER, REBECCA	CEC	008	ELKTON 3
SADLER, THOMAS	HAR	146	3RD DIST
SADLER, VALENTINE	BAL	200	19TH WAR
SADLER, WILLIAM	BAL	132	1ST WARD
SADLER, WILLIAM H.	BAL	031	15TH WAR
SADLER, WILLIAM H.	FRE	299	WOODSBOR
SADLTER, MARY E.	BAL	400	8TH WARD
SADMON, LAWRENCE	BAL	434	8TH WARD
SADTLER, ELLEN	BAL	280	7TH WARD
SADTLER, HENRY	BAL	391	8TH WARD
SADTLER, JOHN P.	BAL	274	20TH WAR
SADTLER, PHILIP	BAL	161	2ND DIST
SAESKUM, HENRY	BAL	310	12TH WAR
SAEYTLER, MARY M.	FRE	269	NEW MARK
SAFAHER, HENRY	BAL	230	2ND WARD
SAFAILLE, JOHN	BAL	388	13TH WAR
SAFF, GEORGE	BAL	160	2ND DIST
SAFFELL, ELLEN	BAL	236	17TH WAR
SAFFELL, RACHEL	MGM	336	CRACKLIN
SAFFER, SARAH	BAL	338	13TH WAR
SAFFERED, MARTIN	BAL	023	18TH WAR
SAFFERTY, ISAAC	ALL	145	6TH E.D.
SAFFIELD, CHARLES	ANN	360	3RD DIST
SAFFIELD, JOSHUA	ANN	324	2ND DIST
SAFFIELD, WILLIAM	ANN	359	3RD DIST
SAFFLE, MARIA	BAL	229	1ST DIST
SAFFORD, JOHN	BAL	099	18TH WAR
SAFFRAN, CHARLES*	BAL	028	4TH WARD
SAFRAN, GEORGE	BAL	333	13TH WAR
SAFRON, GEORGE	BAL	433	14TH WAR
SAGE, WILLIAM R.	MGM	400	ROCKERLE
SAGER, BENJAMIN	WAS	233	1ST DIST
SAGER, CASANDRA	WAS	230	1ST DIST
SAGER, DANIEL	WAS	168	FUNKSTOW
SAGER, ELIZABETH	WAS	230	1ST DIST
SAGER, JACOB	WAS	252	1ST DIST
SAGER, JOHN	WAS	230	1ST DIST
SAGER, SOLOMON	WAS	217	1ST DIST
SAGER, SUSAN	WAS	270	1ST DIST
SAGERFOUS, JOHN	BAL	244	17TH WAR
SAGG, STEPHEN	BAL	078	2ND DIST
SAGGS, THOMAS	BAL	078	2ND DIST
SAGLE, THOMAS W.	BAL	280	7TH WARD
SAGMAN, GEORGE	ALL	111	5TH E.D.
SAGRER, SARAH	ALL	158	6TH E.D.
SAGUR, PHOEBE	ALL	164	6TH E.D.
SAHEN, CATHERINE	FRE	007	FREDERIC
SAHLEY, PHILIP	KEN	241	2ND DIST
SAHM, JACOB	FRE	060	FREDERIC
SAHM, JAOCB	FRE	020	FREDERIC
SAHM, MARY	FRE	045	FREDERIC
SAHM, PETER	FRE	062	FREDERIC
SAHM, PETER	FRE	005	FREDERIC
SAIL, JULIA	BAL	020	4TH WARD
SAILLING, GERTRUDE	BAL	416	14TH WAR
SAILOR, ANDREW	CAR	204	4TH DIST
SAILOR, ANDREW	BAL	239	1ST DIST
SAILOR, DAVID	WAS	286	1ST DIST
SAILOR, FREDERICK	BAL	457	8TH WARD
SAILOR, JOHN	WAS	161	HAGERSTO
SAILOR, JOSEPH	WAS	130	HAGERSTO
SAILOR, MARTHA	WAS	113	2ND DIST
SAILOR, SARAH	WAS	065	2ND SUBD
SAINHART, CASPER	BAL	096	1ST WARD
SAINT, ELIZABETH-BLACK	FRE	052	FREDERIC
SAINT, HENRIETTA	FRE	262	NEW MARK
SAINT, ISAAH	FRE	025	FREDERIC
SAINT, MARY	FRE	262	NEW MARK
SAIRELL, THOMAS	ALL	052	10TH E.D
SAKE, JAMES*	DOR	308	1ST DIST
SAKE, JOHN*	DOR	315	1ST DIST
SAKER, SAMUEL *	BAL	365	1ST DIST
SAKS, ANDREW	BAL	178	16TH WAR
SAKS, WILLIAM	BAL	178	16TH WAR
SALBECK, FRANCIS	BAL	201	2ND WARD
SALBY, ARTHUR	ALL	157	6TH E.D.
SALEN, GEORGE	BAL	233	2ND WARD
SALERY, JOHN	BAL	444	8TH WARD
SALES, AARON	BAL	279	7TH WARD
SALES, AARON	BAL	278	7TH WARD
SALES, BENJAMIN	BAL	202	6TH WARD
SALES, ELLEN	BAL	455	1ST DIST
SALES, ELLENER	WAS	122	HAGERSTO
SALES, HENRY	BAL	425	8TH WARD
SALES, JULIA	BAL	229	6TH WARD
SALES, ROBERT	BAL	032	1ST WARD
SALES, SAMUEL	BAL	093	5TH WARD
SALESMAN, LEAPPOLE	BAL	301	7TH WARD
SALEY, MICHAEL	ALL	170	7TH E.D.
SALGEE, JOHN	BAL	217	17TH WAR
SALGUES, ISABELLA O.	BAL	006	15TH WAR
SALGUES, MARGARET	BAL	006	15TH WAR
SALIMORE, ELIZABETH	CHA	276	ALLENS F
SALINGER, ADAM	BAL	303	7TH WARD
SALISBURY, JOHN	SOM	368	BRINKLEY
SALISBURY, RACHEL	BAL	091	10TH WAR
SALLER, DANIEL	QUE	132	1ST E DI
SALLEY, CATHERINE	BAL	166	11TH WAR
SALLEY, HUGH	BAL	381	8TH WARD
SALLNER, AUGUSTUS	ALL	248	CUMBERLA
SALLOWAY, SARAH	QUE	126	1ST E DI
SALLS, HARRIET	BAL	364	13TH WAR
SALLY, AMES	BAL	458	1ST DIST
SALLY, JAMES	BAL	293	12TH WAR
SALLY, JAMES	BAL	113	1ST WARD
SALLY, MARTIN	ALL	140	6TH E.D.
SALLY, THOMAS	BAL	444	1ST DIST
SALLY, WILLIAM	BAL	082	2ND DIST
SALMON, A.	BAL	164	1ST WARD
SALMON, ANTHONY	BAL	012	15TH WAR
SALMON, GEORGE	FRE	056	FREDERIC
SALMON, MARY	ALL	159	6TH E.D.
SALMON, SARAH	FRE	242	NEW MARK
SALMON, SARAH	BAL	127	11TH WAR
SALMON, WADNEL L.*	BAL	423	3RD WARD
SALMON.ALEX	BAL	169	1ST WARD
SALNON, MARY	ALL	237	CUMBERLA
SALNON, THOMAS	ALL	236	CUMBERLA
SALOM, FRANCES*	BAL	031	4TH WARD
SALOM, JOHN	BAL	031	4TH WARD
SALOR, EDWARD	HAR	067	1ST DIST
SALSBERRY, JAMES W.*	TAL	037	EASTON D
SALSBURY, AMANDA	BAL	382	3RD WARD
SALSBURY, ANDREW J.	BAL	001	4TH WARD
SALSBURY, CHADE	CEC	042	CHESAPEA
SALSBURY, ELIZA	CEC	040	CHESAPEA
SALSBURY, ELIZA	BAL	069	2ND DIST
SALSBURY, HENRY	TAL	063	EASTON D
SALSBURY, JERRY	KEN	282	3RD DIST
SALSBURY, MANDY	SOM	393	BRINKLEY
SALSBURY, MATHEW	KEN	271	1ST DIST
SALSBURY, MATILDA	ALL	248	CUMBERLA
SALSBURY, SALLY S.	BAL	425	3RD WARD
SALSBURY, SARAH	BAL	366	3RD WARD
SALSBURY, STEPHEN	CEC	040	CHESAPEA
SALSBURY, STEPHEN	SOM	385	BRINKLEY
SALSOM, CHRISTINA	FRE	395	PETERSVI
SALT, MARK H.	BAL	404	14TH WAR
SALTAR, ELIZA*	BAL	034	4TH WARD
SALTER, A.	BAL	142	1ST WARD
SALTER, CAROLINE	BAL	382	13TH WAR
SALTER, DICK-BLACK	QUE	183	3RD E DI
SALTER, ELIZABETH	BAL	309	3RD WARD
SALTER, JULIA	BAL	035	9TH WARD
SALTER, SAMUEL	QUE	230	4TH E DI
SALTZER, GEORGE	BAL	334	13TH WAR
SALTZGIVER, JOHN H.	FRE	190	5TH E DI
SALTZGIVER, JOHN HENRY	FRE	191	5TH E DI
SALVA, ELLEN J.	BAL	139	5TH WARD
SALVA, JANE	BAL	152	5TH WARD
SALVA, JOHN G.	BAL	139	5TH WARD
SALVADOR, ROSA	BAL	116	15TH WAR
SALVADUE, JAMES	BAL	445	14TH WAR
SALVERY, EUGENE	BAL	031	18TH WAR
SALVESSON, BENJAMIN	BAL	158	1ST WARD
SALYMAN, ANN	BAL	310	12TH WAR
SALYMAN, ELLEN	BAL	208	19TH WAR
SALZELL, SAMUEL	MGM	408	MEDLEY 3
SALZMAN, WILLIAM	BAL	207	19TH WAR
SAMAN, HENRY	TAL	108	ST MICHA
SAMAN, HEZEKIAH	FRE	358	CATOCTIN
SAMBERT, ELIZABETH*	DOR	301	1ST DIST
SAMBRIGHT, BARBARA	BAL	187	2ND WARD
SAMDEN, THOMAS*	SOM	354	BRINKLEY
SAMDIN, DAWSON	TAL	106	ST MICHA
SAMDIN, LUCRETIA	TAL	104	ST MICHA
SAMDIN, ROSE A.	TAL	111	ST MICHA
SAMDIN, THOMAS H. *	TAL	081	ST MICHA
SAMERSON, RACHAEL	FRE	145	10TH E D
SAMERWIN, PETER	BAL	321	12TH WAR
SAMITH, GEORGE	BAL	370	1ST DIST
SAMMELL, JOSHUA	CAR	337	6TH DIST
SAMMILL, JAMES	BAL	144	1ST WARD
SAMMON, CATHARINE	TAL	090	ST MICHA
SAMMONS, ANDREW	CAR	097	NO TWP L
SAMMONS, JOHN	ALL	109	5TH E.D.
SAMMONS, JOHN	ALL	085	5TH E.D.
SAMOND, GEORGE	BAL	114	18TH WAR
SAMONS, BENJAMIN	WAS	043	2ND SUBD
SAMP, THOMAS J.	BAL	122	1ST WARD
SAMPKINS, WILLIAM A.	ALL	250	CUMBERLA
SAMPLE, GEORGE W.	FRE	107	CREAGERS
SAMPLE, JEROME	FRE	112	CREAGERS
SAMPLE, JOHN	FRE	111	CREAGERS
SAMPLE, MARANDA	FRE	168	EMMITTSB
SAMPLER, MATILDA	CAR	320	1ST DIST
SAMPLEY, OLIVER E.*	BAL	071	4TH WARD
SAMPSEL, WILLIAM	MGM	364	BERRYS D
SAMPSHAN,W ILIAM	BAL	126	1ST WARD
SAMPSON, ABRAHAM JR.	BAL	218	6TH DIST
SAMPSON, ABRAM	BAL	034	2ND DIST
SAMPSON, ALEXANDER	BAL	369	1ST DIST
SAMPSON, ALFRED	DOR	455	1ST DIST
SAMPSON, AMOS	CAR	303	1ST DIST
SAMPSON, CAROLINE	BAL	044	4TH WARD
SAMPSON, CHARLES	BAL	269	17TH WAR
SAMPSON, D.	BAL	139	1ST WARD
SAMPSON, DAVID	BAL	437	1ST DIST
SAMPSON, DAVID	BAL	133	16TH WAR
SAMPSON, E.	BAL	133	5TH WARD
SAMPSON, ELIJAH	BAL	057	2ND DIST
SAMPSON, ELIZA	BAL	277	12TH WAR
SAMPSON, ELIZABETH	HAR	008	1ST DIST
SAMPSON, EMALINE	SOM	513	BARREN C
SAMPSON, GEORGE	QUE	216	3RD E DI
SAMPSON, HARIOTT	DOR	459	1ST DIST
SAMPSON, HUGH	ALL	094	5TH E.D.
SAMPSON, ISRAEL	BAL	055	2ND DIST
SAMPSON, JACOB	BAL	167	6TH WARD
SAMPSON, JAMES H.	BAL	273	7TH WARD
SAMPSON, JIM	TAL	055	EASTON D
SAMPSON, JOHN	BAL	033	9TH WARD
SAMPSON, JOHN	DOR	311	1ST DIST
SAMPSON, JOSEPH	BAL	274	17TH WAR
SAMPSON, JOSEPHINE	BAL	162	6TH WARD
SAMPSON, JOSHUA	BAL	365	3RD WARD
SAMPSON, JOSIAH	BAL	443	14TH WAR
SAMPSON, LOUISA	BAL	035	9TH WARD
SAMPSON, MARGARET	ALL	109	5TH E.D.
SAMPSON, MARTHA*	BAL	075	4TH WARD
SAMPSON, MARY	BAL	213	6TH DIST
SAMPSON, MOSES M.*	DOR	375	1ST DIST
SAMPSON, PETER	ALL	088	5TH E.D.
SAMPSON, RACHEL	KEN	215	2ND DIST
SAMPSON, REBECCA	BAL	374	13TH WAR
SAMPSON, SALEY*	DOR	425	1ST DIST
SAMPSON, SAMUEL	BAL	119	1ST WARD
SAMPSON, SAMUEL V.	BAL	033	2ND DIST
SAMPSON, SOPHIA	HAR	008	1ST DIST
SAMPSON, THOMAS	HAR	115	2ND DIST
SAMPSON, THOMAS	CAR	107	NO TWP L
SAMPSON.ELY S.	BAL	034	2ND DIST
SAMPSON.MARY	BAL	057	2ND DIST
SAMPTON, JAMES A.	BAL	291	12TH WAR

Name	County	Page	District
SAMSON, BOB*	DOR	460	1ST DIST
SAMSON, JANE	DOR	459	1ST DIST
SAMSON, WESLY	DOR	462	1ST DIST
SAMUEL, DAVID	BAL	303	17TH WAR
SAMUEL, WILLIAM	ANN	406	8TH DIST
SAMUELS, ADINE	BAL	127	16TH WAR
SAMUELS, ALEXANDER	BAL	131	18TH WAR
SAMUL, EPHRAIM	WAS	079	2ND SUBD
SAMUL, SUSAN	WAS	079	2ND SUBD
SAMULLER, AUGUSTUS*	BAL	085	10TH WAR
SAMUTH, JOSIAH	FRE	179	5TH E DI
SANAN,SARAH	BAL	067	1ST WARD
SANBEL, JACOB	BAL	202	6TH DIST
SANBLE, JOHN M.	BAL	202	6TH DIST
SANBURY, JAMES	BAL	069	2ND DIST
SANCASTER, CHARLOTT	BAL	446	8TH WARD
SANCASTER, ELLEN	ALL	089	5TH E.D.
SANCHARD, ANN	BAL	198	5TH DIST
SANCHARD, FRANCES	BAL	209	6TH DIST
SANCHARD, HY	BAL	198	5TH DIST
SAND, ELIZABETH	BAL	296	12TH WAR
SAND, WILLIAM	BAL	141	1ST WARD
SANDALL, MAGNESS	BAL	187	6TH WARD
SANDBURY, T. T.	BAL	470	14TH WAR
SANDBURY, THEODORE	BAL	359	13TH WAR
SANDEBAY, ELIZA	CAL	040	3RD DIST
SANDELAMA, THOMAS	BAL	116	1ST WARD
SANDELTS, ROBERT	BAL	126	1ST WARD
SANDER, HENRY	BAL	203	19TH WAR
SANDER, ISAAC	CAR	305	1ST DIST
SANDER, LAURENCE	FRE	080	FREDERIC
SANDER, MARGARET	CHA	268	BOJANTOW
SANDER, SAMUEL	BAL	395	8TH WARD
SANDERLAND, A.	BAL	249	20TH WAR
SANDERLAND, MARGARET	CAL	045	3RD DIST
SANDERLAND, ZACHARIAH	CAL	047	3RD DIST
SANDERMAN, H.	BAL	267	20TH WAR
SANDERMAN, HENRY R.*	BAL	422	3RD WARD
SANDERS, A.	BAL	148	1ST WARD
SANDERS, ALEXANDER	CAR	290	7TH DIST
SANDERS, AMELIA ANN	BAL	251	17TH WAR
SANDERS, AMOS	BAL	159	1ST WARD
SANDERS, ANN M.	CHA	264	HILLTOP
SANDERS, BENEDICTA	BAL	212	11TH WAR
SANDERS, BENJAMIN	HAR	138	2ND DIST
SANDERS, BENJAMIN	WAS	112	2ND DIST
SANDERS, BENJAMIN-BLACK	CAR	073	NO TWP L
SANDERS, BEVERLY C.	BAL	104	10TH WAR
SANDERS, CELENIA*	BAL	067	4TH WARD
SANDERS, CHARLES	BAL	145	11TH WAR
SANDERS, CHARLES	BAL	236	20TH WAR
SANDERS, CHARLES	FRE	034	FREDERIC
SANDERS, CHARLES	ALL	251	CUMBERLA
SANDERS, CHARLES	WAS	109	2ND DIST
SANDERS, CHARLES	TAL	078	EASTON T
SANDERS, CHARLES H.	TAL	052	EASTON D
SANDERS, DAVID	WAS	108	2ND DIST
SANDERS, DENNIS	SOM	535	QUANTICO
SANDERS, DOROTHY A.	FRE	395	PETERSVI
SANDERS, EDWARD	WAS	292	1ST DIST
SANDERS, EDWARD J.*	BAL	043	4TH WARD
SANDERS, ELIZA	BAL	055	15TH WAR
SANDERS, ELIZABETH	BAL	062	2ND DIST
SANDERS, ELIZABETH	FRE	054	FREDERIC
SANDERS, ELIZABETH	HAR	147	3RD DIST
SANDERS, EMILY	KEN	303	3RD DIST
SANDERS, EMILY*	BAL	336	3RD WARD
SANDERS, ENOCH-MULATTO	FRE	429	8TH E DI
SANDERS, GEORGE	BAL	310	20TH WAR
SANDERS, GEORGE	FRE	132	CREAGERS
SANDERS, GEORGE	CAR	391	2ND DIST
SANDERS, GEORGE*	BAL	023	4TH WARD
SANDERS, HARMON	ALL	058	10TH E.D
SANDERS, HENRY	BAL	433	1ST DIST
SANDERS, HENRY	BAL	013	1ST WARD
SANDERS, HENRY	FRE	388	PETERSVI
SANDERS, HINDSON	BAL	272	17TH WAR
SANDERS, HOWARD	FRE	302	WOODSBOR
SANDERS, IGNATIUS	FRE	044	FREDERIC
SANDERS, ISAAC	HAR	171	3RD DIST
SANDERS, ISAAC	WAS	007	WILLIAMS
SANDERS, J.	BAL	136	1ST WARD
SANDERS, J.H.	BAL	135	1ST WARD
SANDERS, J.H.	BAL	116	1ST WARD
SANDERS, JACOB *	FRE	124	CREAGERS
SANDERS, JAMES	WAS	252	1ST DIST
SANDERS, JAMES	TAL	052	EASTON D
SANDERS, JAMES H.	ST	288	2ND E DI
SANDERS, JAMES*	BAL	421	3RD WARD
SANDERS, JOHN	FRE	105	CREAGERS
SANDERS, JOHN	FRE	149	10TH E D
SANDERS, JOHN	FRE	055	FREDERIC
SANDERS, JOHN	BAL	121	11TH WAR
SANDERS, JOHN	ALL	155	6TH E.D.
SANDERS, JOHN	BAL	151	5TH WARD
SANDERS, JOHN C.	HAR	153	3RD DIST
SANDERS, JOHN E.	WAS	158	2ND DIST
SANDERS, JOHN H.	BAL	168	1ST WARD
SANDERS, JOHN H.	BAL	115	1ST WARD
SANDERS, JOHN M.	BAL	236	12TH WAR
SANDERS, JOHN W.	BAL	236	12TH WAR
SANDERS, JOHN*	BAL	039	4TH WARD
SANDERS, JOSEPH	BAL	181	19TH WAR
SANDERS, JOSEPH	CHA	267	MIDDLETO
SANDERS, JOSEPH	BAL	251	17TH WAR
SANDERS, JOSEPH	BAL	102	2ND DIST
SANDERS, JOSEPH E.	CHA	264	HILLTOP
SANDERS, JULIA A.-MULATTO	CAR	398	2ND DIST
SANDERS, JULIANNA	BAL	273	17TH WAR
SANDERS, LAURA*	BAL	044	4TH WARD
SANDERS, LEVEN	DOR	370	3RD DIVI
SANDERS, LOUISA	ALL	054	10TH E.D
SANDERS, LUCRETIA	WAS	109	2ND DIST
SANDERS, M.T.	PRI	051	AQUASCO
SANDERS, MARGARET	BAL	211	6TH WARD
SANDERS, MARGARETT	BAL	203	11TH WAR
SANDERS, MARY	CHA	264	HILLTOP
SANDERS, MARY	HAR	035	1ST DIST
SANDERS, MARY V.	CHA	251	MIDDLETO
SANDERS, MATTHEW	PRI	086	QUEEN AN
SANDERS, MC ENDRY	PRI	040	VANSVILL
SANDERS, MISS J.	FRE	199	5TH E DI
SANDERS, NEAL	CAR	326	1ST DIST
SANDERS, NELLY	FRE	286	WOODSBOR
SANDERS, PETER	BAL	297	17TH WAR
SANDERS, PHEBE	CAR	271	WESTMINS
SANDERS, PHILLIP	BAL	220	2ND WARD
SANDERS, PRISCILLA	BAL	236	2ND WARD
SANDERS, RACHEL	ANN	507	HOWARD D
SANDERS, RICHARD	ANN	370	4TH DIST
SANDERS, ROBERT	CAR	324	1ST DIST
SANDERS, ROBERT D.	CAR	317	1ST DIST
SANDERS, SARAH	BAL	280	17TH WAR
SANDERS, SARAH	CEC	209	7TH E DI
SANDERS, SARAH	BAL	256	12TH WAR
SANDERS, SARAH	BAL	299	12TH WAR
SANDERS, SOLOMON	PRI	039	VANSVILL
SANDERS, SOLOMON S.	BAL	182	6TH WARD
SANDERS, SUSAN A.	BAL	243	6TH WARD
SANDERS, THOMAS	WAS	112	2ND DIST
SANDERS, THOMAS	WAS	252	1ST DIST
SANDERS, THOMAS	FRE	232	BUCKEYST
SANDERS, THOMAS	HAR	143	2ND DIST
SANDERS, THOMAS	BAL	237	17TH WAR
SANDERS, TIMOTHY-MULATTO	FRE	429	8TH E DI
SANDERS, WILLIAM	CHA	264	HILLTOP
SANDERS, WILLIAM	KEN	268	1ST DIST
SANDERS, WILLIAM	BAL	156	5TH WARD
SANDERS, WILLIAM	BAL	152	5TH WARD
SANDERS, WILLIAM	BAL	136	5TH WARD
SANDERS, WILLIAM	BAL	062	2ND DIST
SANDERSON, ANN W.	BAL	114	15TH WAR
SANDERSON, ELENORA	BAL	065	15TH WAR
SANDERSON, GEORGE	BAL	129	5TH WARD
SANDERSON, HARRIET	ALL	029	2ND E.D.
SANDERSON, HENRY S.	BAL	130	5TH WARD
SANDERSON, JOHN	BAL	169	11TH WAR
SANDERSON, LAURA	BAL	118	5TH WARD
SANDERSON, MARY A.	BAL	063	4TH WARD
SANDERSON, WILLIAM R.	FRE	029	FREDERIC
SANDES, JAMES W.	MGM	426	MEDLEY 3
SANDES, JOHN	CAR	338	6TH DIST
SANDES, OBADIAH	BAL	075	2ND DIST
SANDES, SARAH	FRE	191	5TH E DI
SANDFORD, ANN E.	BAL	314	20TH WAR
SANDFORD, J.J.	HAR	159	3RD DIST
SANDFORD, JOHN L.	BAL	300	20TH WAR
SANDFORD, MARTHA E.	ANN	521	HOWARD D
SANDIFORD, LEAH	BAL	059	2ND DIST
SANDIS, D. C.*	BAL	052	4TH WARD
SANDIS, HARRY	BAL	262	1ST DIST
SANDLER, GEORGE W.	BAL	095	15TH WAR
SANDO, EDWIN	CAR	304	1ST DIST
SANDREWS, DANIEL*	DOR	364	3RD DIVI
SANDS, AMELIA-BLACK	FRE	049	FREDERIC
SANDS, ANN	ANN	278	ANNAPOLI
SANDS, ANN	KEN	301	3RD DIST
SANDS, ANN*	BAL	061	4TH WARD
SANDS, BENJAMIN F.	MGM	359	BERRYS D
SANDS, BETSEY*	BAL	085	4TH WARD
SANDS, BRIDGET	BAL	289	3RD WARD
SANDS, EDWARD	ANN	291	ANNAPOLI
SANDS, EDWARD	BAL	046	15TH WAR
SANDS, ELIZABETH	WAS	269	1ST DIST
SANDS, GEORGE	WAS	232	1ST DIST
SANDS, GEORGE W.	FRE	007	FREDERIC
SANDS, HARRY	WAS	161	HAGERSTO
SANDS, HENRIETTA-BLACK	FRE	048	FREDERIC
SANDS, HENRY	BAL	044	15TH WAR
SANDS, JANE	ANN	310	1ST DIST
SANDS, JANE*	BAL	053	4TH WARD
SANDS, JOHN	BAL	049	18TH WAR
SANDS, JOHN	ANN	282	ANNAPOLI
SANDS, JOSEPH	BAL	132	5TH WARD
SANDS, MARGARET	WAS	157	HAGERSTO
SANDS, MARY E.	WAS	243	CAVETOWN
SANDS, RICHARD	ANN	275	ANNAPOLI
SANDS, SALLY E.	ANN	272	ANNAPOLI
SANDS, SARAH	BAL	415	8TH WARD
SANDS, SARAH	WAS	269	1ST DIST
SANDS, SARAH H.	WAS	123	HAGERSTO
SANDS, SARAH J.	BAL	351	1ST DIST
SANDS, THOMAS	ANN	276	ANNAPOLI
SANDS, THOMAS	HAR	141	2ND DIST
SANDS, WILLIAM	BAL	128	1ST WARD
SANDS, WILLIAM	BAL	132	1ST WARD
SANDS, WILLIAM	ANN	384	4TH DIST
SANDS, WILLIAM	WAS	279	LEITERSB
SANDSTREET, A.C.	BAL	256	1ST DIST
SANDSTREET, EDWARD	BAL	256	1ST DIST
SANDY, JOHN	CHA	244	HILLTOP
SANE, WILLIAM	BAL	017	1ST WARD
SANENVERT, ELY	BAL	141	19TH WAR
SANENWELL, JOHN	BAL	165	19TH WAR
SANER, JOHN	BAL	189	19TH WAR
SANERWEIN, GEORGE P. *	BAL	293	20TH WAR
SANERWEIN, MARY *	BAL	293	20TH WAR
SANEVER,HERNY	BAL	084	1ST WARD
SANFARE, WILLIAM*	BAL	342	3RD WARD
SANFORD, ALFRED	BAL	027	1ST WARD
SANFORD, DANIEL A.	BAL	027	1ST WARD
SANFORD, GEORGE	BAL	171	2ND DIST
SANFORD, JAMES	ANN	328	2ND DIST
SANFORD, JOHN	ANN	316	1ST DIST
SANFORD, SARAH	CEC	185	7TH E DI
SANFORD, THOMAS H	BAL	260	12TH WAR
SANGLER, NICHOLAS	BAL	061	1ST WARD
SANGREL, JOBE*	DOR	351	3RD DIVI
SANGREL, JOHN*	DOR	345	3RD DIVI
SANGSDALE, HENRY J.	WOR	262	BERLIN I
SANGSTON, CATHERINE	CAR	148	NO TWP L
SANGSTON, JOHN T.	CAR	094	NO TWP L
SANGSTON, LAWRENCE *	BAL	070	15TH WAR
SANGTER, ANN	BAL	273	20TH WAR
SANIKER, EMANUEL	FRE	398	JEFFERSO
SANIKER, MARY E.	FRE	399	JEFFERSO
SANK, CORBIN	BAL	252	17TH WAR
SANK, GEROGE *	BAL	122	18TH WAR
SANK, JAMES	BAL	214	17TH WAR
SANK, JOHN M.	BAL	146	19TH WAR
SANK, NICHOLAS	BAL	262	12TH WAR
SANK, NICHOLAS	ALL	238	CUMBERLA
SANK, PLUMMER	FRE	269	NEW MARK
SANK, SPENCER	BAL	101	15TH WAR
SANKFORD, EUPHAMY*	DOR	299	1ST DIST
SANKFORD, JOHN	DOR	301	1ST DIST
SANKFORD, LEWIS	DOR	298	1ST DIST
SANKFORD, LOVEY*	DOR	306	1ST DIST
SANKFORD, NANCY C.*	SOM	509	BARREN C
SANKFORD, SARAH*	SOM	521	BARREN C
SANKFORD, TULLY	DOR	302	1ST DIST
SANKFORD, TURFIN*	DOR	305	1ST DIST
SANKFORD, WILLIAM H.*	SOM	377	BRINKLEY
SANKS, ABNER D.	BAL	013	18TH WAR
SANKS, AMOS	BAL	212	17TH WAR
SANKS, ANNA	BAL	175	16TH WAR
SANKS, EDWARD	BAL	473	14TH WAR
SANKS, JESSE	BAL	258	17TH WAR
SANKS, JOHN	BAL	213	17TH WAR
SANKS, JOHN	BAL	140	16TH WAR
SANKS, MARY	BAL	022	15TH WAR
SANMINIG, CONRAD	BAL	258	12TH WAR
SANNA, JOHN	BAL	076	1ST WARD
SANNODERT, JOHN	BAL	105	1ST WARD
SANNELER, ELLEN	BAL	276	17TH WAR
SANNER, ABELE	ST	303	2ND E DI
SANNER, ANN	ST	305	1ST E DI
SANNER, JAMES	WAS	212	1ST DIST
SANNER, JOHN	ST	302	2ND E DI
SANNER, JOHN	FRE	324	MIDDLETO
SANNER, JOHN F.	BAL	008	1ST WARD
SANNER, JOHN H.*	BAL	119	15TH WAR
SANNER, JOHN S.	BAL	054	9TH WARD
SANNER, JOHN W.	BAL	238	20TH WAR
SANNER, MARTHA	BAL	281	7TH WARD
SANNER, SAMUEL A.	ST	307	1ST E DI
SANNER, THOMAS	ST	302	2ND E DI
SANOR, LOUISA	BAL	122	2ND DIST
SANPHER, WILLIAM	BAL	133	1ST WARD
SANPHER, WILLIAM	BAL	134	1ST WARD
SANS, WILLIAM	BAL	121	1ST WARD
SANSBERRY, VINSANT	WAS	288	1ST DIST
SANSBURY, E.	PRI	119	PISCATAW
SANSBURY, FRED	PRI	098	SPALDING
SANSBURY, H.	PRI	117	PISCATAW
SANSBURY, JAMES W.	PRI	091	MARLBROU
SANSBURY, JOHN	PRI	103	SPALDING
SANSBURY, THOMAS	PRI	092	MARLBROU
SANSERS, JAMES	ST	272	3RD E DI
SANSERS, JOHN	ALL	058	10TH E.D
SANSLY, CORNELIA *	ANN	302	1ST DIST
SANSON, RICHARD	ALL	071	5TH E.D.
SANTMARE, E. MANUEL	FRE	383	PETERSVI
SANTMYER, LEWIS A.	BAL	249	12TH WAR
SANTON, ANN	ST	279	3RD E DI
SANTREE, ELIZA	BAL	185	11TH WAR
SANTROP, CATHARINE	BAL	227	12TH WAR
SANTY, EZRA	WAS	074	2ND SUBD
SANVIE, JAMES	BAL	185	2ND WARD
SAP, EDWARD *	BAL	135	2ND DIST
SAPER, SAMUEL J.	BAL	249	12TH WAR
SAPER, UNDERWOOD	CHA	253	MIDDLETO
SAPHEL, J.	ANN	347	3RD DIST
SAPINGTON, ANN	ANN	462	HOWARD D
SAPP, ANTHONY	ALL	111	5TH E.D.
SAPP, CHARLES C.	BAL	098	1ST WARD
SAPP, DANIEL*	BAL	371	3RD WARD
SAPP, ELIZABETH	BAL	157	2ND DIST
SAPP, ELIZABETH	BAL	098	10TH WAR
SAPP, JACOB	BAL	076	2ND DIST
SAPP, JACOB*	BAL	077	4TH WARD
SAPP, JAMES	BAL	183	6TH WARD
SAPP, JOHN	BAL	160	2ND DIST
SAPP, JOHN	KEN	246	2ND DIST
SAPP, JOSHUA F.*	BAL	367	3RD WARD
SAPP, MARY	BAL	146	2ND DIST
SAPP, SUSAN	BAL	034	1ST WARD
SAPP, THOMAS	KEN	299	3RD DIST
SAPP, WASHINGTON	BAL	160	2ND DIST
SAPP, WILLIAM	KEN	246	2ND DIST
SAPPARD, ELI	BAL	003	EASTERN
SAPPHEL, M.	ANN	347	3RD DIST
SAPPHUL, W.	ANN	347	3RD DIST
SAPPINGTON, ANN	BAL	105	5TH WARD
SAPPINGTON, ANN E.	KEN	228	2ND DIST
SAPPINGTON, ASBURY W.	ANN	509	HOWARD D
SAPPINGTON, AUGUSTINE	BAL	171	16TH WAR
SAPPINGTON, GERRARD H.	BAL	310	7TH WARD
SAPPINGTON, GREENBERRY R.	FRE	442	8TH E DI
SAPPINGTON, GREENBURY P.	ANN	389	4TH DIST
SAPPINGTON, HARMUTT	HAR	085	2ND DIST
SAPPINGTON, JAMES	KEN	237	2ND DIST
SAPPINGTON, JANE A.	ANN	324	2ND DIST
SAPPINGTON, JOHN	HAR	001	1ST DIST
SAPPINGTON, JOHN R.	HAR	169	3RD DIST
SAPPINGTON, LOT	ANN	378	4TH DIST
SAPPINGTON, MARGARET	HAR	130	2ND DIST
SAPPINGTON, MARY	KEN	245	2ND DIST
SAPPINGTON, NICHOLAS J.	BAL	057	15TH WAR
SAPPINGTON, REBECCA	BAL	366	1ST DIST
SAPPINGTON, RICHARD	BAL	182	6TH WARD
SAPPINGTON, RICHARD	FRE	067	FREDERIC
SAPPINGTON, THOMAS	FRE	448	8TH E DI
SAPPINGTON, THOMAS	FRE	005	FREDERIC
SAPS, JOHN	BAL	069	2ND DIST
SAPWARTZ, MARY	BAL	247	20TH WAR
SARA, JOSIAH*	DOR	433	1ST DIST
SARA, THOMAS*	DOR	433	1ST DIST
SARABLE, MARY	CAR	285	7TH DIST
SARACE, EDWARD	BAL	192	17TH WAR
SARAGUAY, DENNIS	BAL	457	8TH WARD
SARBANCHER, MATILDA	BAL	107	15TH WAR
SARBAUGH, JACOB	BAL	121	11TH WAR
SARBOKEN, JOHN	BAL	428	8TH WARD
SARCABLE, MICHAEL	HAR	102	2ND DIST
SARCER, JOHN	BAL	205	2ND WARD
SARD, JOSIAH*	DOR	433	1ST DIST
SARD, SARAH	BAL	346	1ST DIST
SARD, THOMAS*	DOR	433	1ST DIST
SARD, THOMAS*	DOR	459	1ST DIST
SARDEN, JOHN	BAL	145	1ST WARD
SARF, GOLFRIED *	BAL	444	8TH WARD
SARFRON, FRANCIS	BAL	444	14TH WAR
SARGE, MOSES*	BAL	374	3RD WARD
SARGEANT, L. S.	BAL	332	1ST DIST
SARGENT, BENJAMIN	CEC	162	6TH E DI
SARGENT, GEORGE	CEC	050	1ST E DI
SARGENT, NANCY M.	CEC	025	ELKTON 3
SARGENT, ROBERT	CEC	164	6TH E DI
SARGENT, S. R. REV-	BAL	060	10TH WAR
SARGENT, THOMAS B.	BAL	474	14TH WAR
SARGES, ELIZABETH	CEC	210	7TH E DI
SARGES, FREDERICK	WAS	185	BOONSBOR
SARGES, MARGARET	WAS	186	BOONSBOR
SARGIN, MICHAEL	ALL	119	5TH E.D.
SARGRO, WILLIAM	QUE	243	5TH E DI
SARICK, MARY E.	BAL	297	3RD WARD
SARILLE, MARY A.	BAL	028	2ND DIST
SARMORE, JOHN A.	SOM	429	PRINCESS
SARNDIN, ROBERT *	TAL	081	ST MICHA
SARNER, JOHN	BAL	198	2ND WARD
SARNER, WILLIAM F.	BAL	188	2ND WARD
SARORY, HARRIOT *	KEN	240	2ND DIST
SAROUSKY, JOHN F.	BAL	084	1ST WARD
SARROM, GEORGE	BAL	255	20TH WAR
SARSNIP, JACK-BLACK	FRE	195	5TH E DI
SARSTELL, SIDNEY	FRE	029	FREDERIC
SARTIN, JAMES	QUE	149	1ST E DI
SARTIN, LOUISA	QUE	144	1ST E DI
SARTZBAUGH, VIRGINIA	BAL	426	14TH WAR

Name	County	Page	District
SARVOAN, JOSEPH *	BAL	282	1ST DIST
SASKER, MARY	FRE	035	FREDERIC
SASSON, THOMAS	ALL	139	6TH E.D.
SATCHEL, MARY C.*	TAL	048	EASTON T
SATCHELL, CHARLES	DOR	382	1ST DIST
SATCHELL, JANE	BAL	040	4TH WARD
SATCHERN, THOMASJ.	WOR	319	1ST E DI
SATCHUM, JOHN	WOR	302	SNOW HIL
SATE, JOHN	BAL	206	6TH DIST
SATEE, LEWIS F.	ANN	274	ANNAPOLI
SATER, JOHN	BAL	198	5TH DIST
SATER, JOHN	BAL	192	5TH DIST
SATHERED, JOHN	BAL	064	18TH WAR
SATHERLAND, WILLIAM	MGM	389	ROCKERLE
SATHERLING, THOMAS	BAL	255	20TH WAR
SATHRFIELD, THOMAS	CAR	083	NO TWP L
SATMOLD, C. E.	ALL	139	6TH E.D.
SATSHIL, JOHN*	TAL	038	EASTON D
SATTAR, ELIZA*	BAL	034	4TH WARD
SATTER, GEORGE E.	FRE	032	FREDERIC
SATTER, WILLIAM E.	FRE	031	FREDERIC
SATTERFIELD, ANDREW	TAL	006	EASTON D
SATTERFIELD, ANN*	TAL	016	EASTON D
SATTERFIELD, CALEB-BLACK	CAR	095	NO TWP L
SATTERFIELD, ELIZABETH-BL	CAR	114	NO TWP L
SATTERFIELD, ELIZABETH	CAR	156	NO TWP L
SATTERFIELD, ELIZABETH	BAL	054	15TH WAR
SATTERFIELD, GREEN	CAR	098	NO TWP L
SATTERFIELD, JAMES T.	BAL	185	11TH WAR
SATTERFIELD, JOHN	BAL	185	11TH WAR
SATTERFIELD, JOHN	CAR	113	NO TWP L
SATTERFIELD, JOHN	TAL	066	EASTON T
SATTERFIELD, MARGARET D.	BAL	219	6TH WARD
SATTERFIELD, MARGRETT-BLA	CAR	132	NO TWP L
SATTERFIELD, MARTHA E.	QUE	159	2ND E DI
SATTERFIELD, MARY	CAR	163	NO TWP L
SATTERFIELD, MARY S.	TAL	065	EASTON T
SATTERFIELD, MARY-BLACK	CAR	107	NO TWP L
SATTERFIELD, NATHAN	KEN	309	3RD DIST
SATTERFIELD, NATHANIEL	QUE	174	2ND E DI
SATTERFIELD, SAMPSON-BLAC	CAR	131	NO TWP L
SATTERFIELD, SAMUEL	TAL	066	EASTON T
SATTERFIELD, SAMUEL	TAL	066	EASTON T
SATTERFIELD, SARAH	CAR	156	NO TWP L
SATTERFIELD, THOMAS J.	QUE	192	3RD E DI
SATTERFIELD, WASHINGTON-B	CAR	131	NO TWP L
SATTERFIELD, WEIGHT-BLACK	CAR	095	NO TWP L
SATTERFIELD, WILLIAM	CAR	080	NO TWP L
SATTERFIELD, WILLIAM	CEC	059	1ST E DI
SATTERFIELD, WILLIAM	TAL	072	EASTON T
SATTERFIELD, WILLIAM L.	QUE	146	1ST E DI
SATTERFIELD, WILLIAM M.	TAL	004	EASTON D
SATTERFIELD,LYDIA	QUE	143	1ST E DI
SATTIN, MARY	QUE	238	5TH E DI
SATUR, CHARLES	BAL	457	1ST DIST
SATURDEY, CHARLES	ALL	224	CUMBERLA
SAUCER, MARGARET *	ALL	059	10TH E.D
SAUDER, CHARLES	BAL	218	17TH WAR
SAUDERLAND, WILLIAM	BAL	261	20TH WAR
SAUER, CASPAR	BAL	308	20TH WAR
SAUER, CHRIS	BAL	223	19TH WAR
SAUER, HENRY	BAL	320	20TH WAR
SAUER, JOHN	BAL	223	19TH WAR
SAUERHOFF, JOHN	BAL	015	15TH WAR
SAUERWEIN, GEORGE P.	BAL	293	20TH WAR
SAUERWEIN, MARY	BAL	293	20TH WAR
SAUGER, J. H.	BAL	148	1ST WARD
SAUGHN, JOSEPH	BAL	256	2ND WARD
SAUIER, ALAXANDRIA	BAL	207	11TH WAR
SAUK, CHARLES	BAL	190	17TH WAR
SAUK, GEORGE *	BAL	122	18TH WAR
SAUK, JOSEPH	BAL	065	2ND DIST
SAUL, JOSEPH W.	BAL	476	14TH WAR
SAUL, LOUISA	BAL	468	14TH WAR
SAUL, THOMAS	BAL	354	7TH WARD
SAULBERRY, WILLIAM	BAL	423	1ST DIST
SAULOFF, ELIZA	BAL	188	2ND WARD
SAULSBERRY, JAMES	BAL	272	17TH WAR
SAULSBURRY, ANDREW	BAL	248	17TH WAR
SAULSAURRY, JAMES	BAL	272	17TH WARD
SAULSBURY, ADER	CAR	148	NO TWP L
SAULSBURY, ALEXANDER	CAR	134	NO TWP L
SAULSBURY, ANDREW	BAL	073	15TH WAR
SAULSBURY, ANN	CAR	146	NO TWP L
SAULSBURY, CHARLES	CAR	118	NO TWP L
SAULSBURY, EDWARD H.	BAL	200	17TH WAR
SAULSBURY, HENRY-BLACK	CAR	095	NO TWP L
SAULSBURY, JAMES	CAR	168	NO TWP L
SAULSBURY, JAMES	BAL	117	15TH WAR
SAULSBURY, JAMES W.	CAR	150	NO TWP L
SAULSBURY, JOHN R.T.	CAR	149	NO TWP L
SAULSBURY, JOHN-BLACK	CAR	110	NO TWP L
SAULSBURY, JOHN-BLACK	CAR	108	NO TWP L
SAULSBURY, MATHEW	CAR	089	NO TWP L
SAULSBURY, SAMUEL	BAL	145	16TH WAR
SAULSBURY, THOMAS	CAR	107	NO TWP L
SAULSBURY, THOMAS R.	CAR	069	NO TWP L
SAULSBURY,MARGRETT	CAR	110	NO TWP L
SAULSBURY,WILLIAM E.	CAR	169	NO TWP L
SAULTER, ADAM	BAL	413	8TH WARD
SAULUVEEN, WILLIAM *	BAL	273	20TH WAR
SAUM, ABRAHAM	CAR	382	2ND DIST
SAUM, CHARLES	BAL	247	20TH WAR
SAUM, MARY	FRE	427	8TH E DI
SAUMINICK, WILLIAM *	BAL	120	18TH WAR
SAUMINIG, JACOB	BAL	176	16TH WAR
SAUNACE, FRANCAS	BAL	215	2ND WARD
SAUNDER, BETSEY	BAL	329	7TH WARD
SAUNDERS, AARON	DOR	365	3RD DIVI
SAUNDERS, ABRAHAM	WAS	300	1ST DIST
SAUNDERS, ALFRED	BAL	155	5TH WARD
SAUNDERS, ANN	WAS	298	1ST DIST
SAUNDERS, BENJAMIN	BAL	445	8TH WARD
SAUNDERS, CAROLINE	BAL	032	1ST WARD
SAUNDERS, ED	BAL	130	1ST WARD
SAUNDERS, EDWARD	HAR	129	2ND DIST
SAUNDERS, EDWARD	HAR	121	2ND DIST
SAUNDERS, ELIZA J.	BAL	241	6TH WARD
SAUNDERS, ELIZABETH	BAL	260	6TH WARD
SAUNDERS, GABREL	DOR	363	3RD DIVI
SAUNDERS, GEORGE	BAL	220	19TH WAR
SAUNDERS, GEORGE	BAL	452	8TH WARD
SAUNDERS, GEORGE	BAL	456	8TH WARD
SAUNDERS, GEORGE W.	BAL	272	20TH WAR
SAUNDERS, GEORGE W.	WOR	233	6TH E DI
SAUNDERS, H.	BAL	155	1ST WARD
SAUNDERS, HENRY	BAL	005	1ST WARD
SAUNDERS, HENRY	ANN	423	HOWARD D
SAUNDERS, HONER	BAL	220	19TH WAR
SAUNDERS, J.H.	BAL	129	1ST WARD
SAUNDERS, JACOB	DOR	333	3RD DIVI
SAUNDERS, JAMES	CEC	070	5TH E DI
SAUNDERS, JAMES M.	BAL	450	8TH WARD
SAUNDERS, JANE	DOR	365	3RD DIVI
SAUNDERS, JANE	BAL	381	13TH WAR
SAUNDERS, JOHN	DOR	335	3RD DIVI
SAUNDERS, JOHN	HAR	137	2ND DIST
SAUNDERS, JOHN	HAR	117	2ND DIST
SAUNDERS, JOHN	BAL	288	7TH WARD
SAUNDERS, JOHN	BAL	274	7TH WARD
SAUNDERS, KEZIAH	BAL	228	6TH WARD
SAUNDERS, LEMUEL	BAL	271	7TH WARD
SAUNDERS, LEVIN	BAL	228	6TH WARD
SAUNDERS, MARIA	HAR	115	2ND DIST
SAUNDERS, MARIA	BAL	136	18TH WAR
SAUNDERS, OLIVER	BAL	460	8TH WARD
SAUNDERS, ROBERT	CEC	203	6TH E DI
SAUNDERS, SAMUEL	FRE	261	NEW MARK
SAUNDERS, SARRAH	DOR	357	3RD DIVI
SAUNDERS, THOMAS	QUE	232	4TH E DI
SAUNDERS, THOMAS W.	BAL	159	6TH WARD
SAUNDERS, WILLIAM	BAL	432	8TH WARD
SAUNDERS, WILLIAM	BAL	301	7TH WARD
SAUNDERS, WILLIAM	DOR	365	3RD DIVI
SAUNDERS, WILLIAM	CEC	083	CHARLEST
SAUNDERS, WILLIAM W.	WOR	232	6TH E DI
SAUNDIN, ROBERT*	TAL	117	ST MICHA
SAUNER, GEORGE H.	BAL	122	16TH WAR
SAUNER, JAMES	BAL	183	2ND WARD
SAUNER, JOHN H.*	BAL	119	15TH WAR
SAUNER, ROBERT	BAL	081	1ST WARD
SAUNER, SARAH	BAL	013	1ST WARD
SAUNEY, SAMUEL	ST	290	2ND E DI
SAUNISESH, JONATHAN	BAL	032	1ST WARD
SAUNTREE, JOHN	BAL	180	11TH WAR
SAUOLER, NICHOLAS *	BAL	312	20TH WAR
SAUR, MARTIN	BAL	332	1ST DIST
SAURBAUGH, JACOB	WAS	109	2ND DIST
SAURWINE, CATHARINE	BAL	204	11TH WAR
SAURWINE, ELIZABETH	BAL	204	11TH WAR
SAURYVINE, ELIZA	BAL	117	5TH WARD
SAUSAR, PETER	ANN	281	ANNAPOLI
SAUSAR, SAMUEL H.	ANN	330	2ND DIST
SAUSELL, JOHN	FRE	274	NEW MARK
SAUSLBURY, GORE	CAR	066	NO TWP L
SAUSTER, MARY E.	BAL	237	6TH WARD
SAUTER, BARBARA	BAL	385	1ST DIST
SAUTER, MARGARET A.	BAL	385	1ST DIST
SAUTMAN, JOSEPH	WAS	051	2ND SUBD
SAUTMAN, MARGARET	WAS	047	2ND SUBD
SAUTTE, WILLIAM	BAL	333	13TH WAR
SAUX, AMELIA	BAL	017	9TH WARD
SAUX, JOHN	BAL	017	9TH WARD
SAUX, JOHN	BAL	233	2ND WARD
SAVAGE, AMELIA	BAL	364	8TH WARD
SAVAGE, AMOS W.	ALL	027	2ND E.D.
SAVAGE, AVA	ALL	030	2ND E.D.
SAVAGE, EBE	WOR	244	1ST CENS
SAVAGE, EBE JR.	WOR	245	1ST CENS
SAVAGE, ELIZ	BAL	241	12TH WAR
SAVAGE, ELIZABETH	BAL	037	15TH WAR
SAVAGE, ELIZABETH	SOM	421	PRINCESS
SAVAGE, EMALINE	WOR	345	1ST E DI
SAVAGE, EMILY	BAL	110	5TH WARD
SAVAGE, EVAN	ALL	029	2ND E.D.
SAVAGE, GEORGE	BAL	166	19TH WAR
SAVAGE, GRIFFIN	WOR	185	6TH E DI
SAVAGE, HAVERICK D.	BAL	353	7TH WARD
SAVAGE, HETTY	WOR	319	1ST E DI
SAVAGE, HOLLIDAY	ALL	033	2ND E.D.
SAVAGE, ISAAC	BAL	028	15TH WAR
SAVAGE, ISRAEL	ALL	030	2ND E.D.
SAVAGE, JAMES	WOR	241	1ST CENS
SAVAGE, JAMES	CAL	014	1ST DIST
SAVAGE, JOHN	ALL	030	2ND E.D.
SAVAGE, JOHN	BAL	395	8TH WARD
SAVAGE, JOHN	BAL	062	1ST WARD
SAVAGE, JOHN T.	WOR	241	1ST CENS
SAVAGE, JOSEPH	WOR	245	1ST CENS
SAVAGE, L. E.	BAL	470	14TH WAR
SAVAGE, LEMUEL	ALL	030	2ND E.D.
SAVAGE, LEVIN	SOM	358	BRINKLEY
SAVAGE, LUCY	CAL	014	1ST DIST
SAVAGE, LYDIA	SOM	353	BRINKLEY
SAVAGE, M.	BAL	135	1ST WARD
SAVAGE, M.	BAL	150	1ST WARD
SAVAGE, MARY	WOR	244	1ST CENS
SAVAGE, MRS-	ANN	328	2ND DIST
SAVAGE, NELSON	ALL	045	10TH E.D
SAVAGE, PATRICK	FRE	196	5TH E DI
SAVAGE, PURNELL J.	WOR	209	4TH E DI
SAVAGE, ROBERT	SOM	359	BRINKLEY
SAVAGE, ROBERT	ALL	025	2ND E.D.
SAVAGE, ROBINSON	ALL	026	2ND E.D.
SAVAGE, SARAH	BAL	114	15TH WAR
SAVAGE, SARAH	CHA	232	HILLTOP
SAVAGE, SEVERN	WOR	245	1ST CENS
SAVAGE, THOMAS	ALL	043	10TH E.D
SAVAGE, THOMAS B.	WOR	206	4TH E DI
SAVAGE, WILLIAM	CEC	033	CHESAPEA
SAVAGE, WILLIAM H.	BAL	289	20TH WAR
SAVALL, PATRICK	ALL	142	6TH E.D.
SAVARY, AUGUSTUS	BAL	454	14TH WAR
SAVAY, E.	PRI	049	AQUASCO
SAVEN, AUGUSTINE	CEC	044	1ST E DI
SAVEN, AUGUSTUS	CEC	044	1ST E DI
SAVEN, MARY	CEC	054	1ST E DI
SAVEN, SUSAN	CEC	028	CHESAPEA
SAVEN, THOMAS	CEC	055	1ST E DI
SAVER, LEWIS	BAL	453	8TH WARD
SAVILLE, ANN	BAL	070	10TH WAR
SAVILLE, ANN G.	BAL	021	9TH WARD
SAVILLE, ELSY	BAL	267	20TH WAR
SAVILLE, EMMA	BAL	021	9TH WARD
SAVILLE, THOMAS	BAL	184	19TH WAR
SAVIN, BENJAMIN	CEC	046	1ST E DI
SAVIN, JAMES B.	KEN	291	3RD DIST
SAVIN, MARCUS	BAL	126	5TH WARD
SAVIN, THOMAS L.	KEN	222	2ND DIST
SAVING, EDWARD	WAS	095	2ND SUBD
SAVING, PATRICK	WAS	095	2ND SUBD
SAVORY, E.	PRI	122	PISCATAW
SAVOY, A.	PRI	065	NOTTINGH
SAVOY, ALISON	PRI	070	MARLBROU
SAVOY, BARBARA	FRE	260	NEW MARK
SAVOY, BASSIL	BAL	279	17TH WAR
SAVOY, CAROLINE	BAL	105	15TH WAR
SAVOY, COMFORT	ANN	501	HOWARD D
SAVOY, CORNELIUS	ANN	501	HOWARD D
SAVOY, CREIG	FRE	211	BUCKEYST
SAVOY, FRANCIS	CHA	277	BOJANTOW
SAVOY, H.	PRI	057	NOTTINGH
SAVOY, HAMILTON	FRE	300	WOODSBOR
SAVOY, HENRY	PRI	046	AQUASCO
SAVOY, HENRY	ANN	522	HOWARD D
SAVOY, JANE	ANN	466	HOWARD D
SAVOY, JOHN	PRI	111	PISCATAW
SAVOY, JULIA	BAL	111	15TH WAR
SAVOY, LEWIS	ALL	111	5TH E.D.
SAVOY, MARGARET	PRI	047	AQUASCO
SAVOY, MARY	BAL	094	15TH WAR
SAVOY, RACHEL	BAL	175	16TH WAR
SAVOY, RACHEL	FRE	266	NEW MARK
SAVOY, RICHARD	FRE	266	NEW MARK
SAVOY, STEPHEN	ANN	464	HOWARD D
SAVOY, SUSAN	CAL	052	3RD DIST
SAVOY, THOMAS	ANN	471	HOWARD D
SAVOY, TINGLETON	FRE	310	WOODSBOR
SAVOY, WASHINGTON	FRE	255	NEW MARK
SAVVY, THACY	CHA	264	MIDDLETO
SAW, JOHN*	TAL	026	EASTON D
SAW, WILLIAM	HAR	087	2ND DIST
SAWBAUGHER, FRANCIS	ALL	020	2ND E.D.
SAWBLE, DOROTHY	CAR	287	7TH DIST
SAWBLE, GEORGE	CAR	345	6TH DIST
SAWBLE, JOHN	CAR	288	7TH DIST
SAWBLE, JONAS	CAR	396	2ND DIST
SAWBLE, JOSEPH	CAR	353	6TH DIST
SAWBLE, LYDIA	CAR	344	6TH DIST
SAWBLE, MARGARET	CAR	393	2ND DIST
SAWBLE, MICHAEL	CAR	344	6TH DIST
SAWBLE, MICHAEL JR.	CAR	284	7TH DIST
SAWBLE, PETER	CAR	344	6TH DIST
SAWBLE, SAMUEL	CAR	284	7TH DIST
SAWERS, ELEN	CAR	217	5TH DIST
SAWERS, WILLIAM	CAR	219	5TH DIST
SAWEY, THOMAS*	BAL	110	10TH WAR
SAWKINS, S.	BAL	058	18TH WAR
SAWLER, LAWRENCE*	BAL	387	3RD WARD
SAWNER, RAGINE	BAL	002	18TH WAR
SAWOAN, JOSEPH *	BAL	282	1ST DIST
SAWSLY, CORNELIA *	ANN	302	1ST DIST
SAWSON, AMRY-BLACK	CAR	071	NO TWP L
SAWSON, MOSES	CAR	328	MANCHEST
SAWYE, MARGARET *	BAL	165	2ND DIST
SAWYER, ALICE	TAL	075	EASTON T
SAWYER, CAROLINE	FRE	061	FREDERIC
SAWYER, DARIUS	BAL	213	19TH WAR
SAWYER, DELIA	KEN	229	2ND DIST
SAWYER, EDWARD	FRE	063	FREDERIC
SAWYER, FREDERICK	BAL	306	3RD WARD
SAWYER, HENRY	CAR	248	3RD DIST
SAWYER, JOHN	CAR	246	3RD DIST
SAWYER, JOHN H.	BAL	118	1ST WARD
SAWYER, LEONARD	BAL	167	11TH WAR
SAWYER, MARGARET	BAL	006	18TH WAR
SAWYER, MARY	BAL	049	18TH WAR
SAWYER, MARY	BAL	042	9TH WARD
SAWYER, MARY A.	BAL	034	1ST WARD
SAWYER, MARY A.	BAL	332	7TH WARD
SAWYER, NATHAN	BAL	024	9TH WARD
SAWYER, NATHAN	CAR	249	3RD DIST
SAWYER, SAMUEL	CAR	293	7TH DIST
SAWYER, WILLIAM	CAR	277	7TH DIST
SAWYER, WILLIAM	HAR	094	2ND DIST
SAWYERS, FREDERICK	BAL	305	3RD WARD
SAXE, HENNAW *	BAL	267	2ND WARD
SAXON, JAMES	BAL	209	19TH WAR
SAXON, JAMES-BLACK	ST	294	2ND E DI
SAXONHEIM, JACOB	CAR	310	1ST DIST
SAXTON, ALBANNS L.	CEC	097	4TH E DI
SAXTON, ARABEL	BAL	317	20TH WAR
SAXTON, CATHERINE	BAL	282	20TH WAR
SAXTON, ELIZA	PRI	081	QUEEN AN
SAXTON, GEEORGE	ST	324	4TH E DI
SAXTON, JOHN	CHA	286	BOJANTOW
SAXTON, JOSEPH	CHA	269	ALLENS F
SAXTON, JULIA A.	BAL	250	6TH WARD
SAXTON, OWEN	BAL	281	20TH WAR
SAXTON, RICHARD	BAL	349	13TH WAR
SAXTON, ROBERT	ST	347	5TH E DI
SAXTON, THOMAS J.	DOR	451	1ST DIST
SAY, C.	BAL	224	19TH WAR
SAY, JOHN	BAL	019	2ND DIST
SAY, SARAH	BAL	246	1ST DIST
SAYER, HENRY	BAL	271	2ND WARD
SAYFIELD, CHARLOTTE	BAL	058	1ST WARD
SAYFIELD, ELIZABETH	WOR	302	SNOW HIL
SAYFIELD, GEORGE	SOM	351	BRINKLEY
SAYFIELD, JOHN*	SOM	361	BRINKLEY
SAYFIELD, NANCY*	SOM	360	BRINKLEY
SAYFIELD, SAMPSON	WOR	190	8TH E DI
SAYLE, MARGARET	BAL	209	2ND WARD
SAYLER, ABRAHAM	FRE	413	8TH E DI
SAYLER, DANIEL	FRE	426	8TH E DI
SAYLER, JACOB JR.	FRE	414	8TH E DI
SAYLER, JAOCB	FRE	447	8TH E DI
SAYLER, JOHN	FRE	425	8TH E DI
SAYLER, REUBEN	FRE	425	8TH E DI
SAYLER, SOLOMON JR.	FRE	426	8TH E DI
SAYLOR, ANN*	BAL	375	3RD WARD
SAYLOR, CATHARINE	WAS	064	2ND SUBD
SAYLOR, DANIEL	ALL	238	CUMBERLA
SAYLOR, JACOB	ALL	206	CUMBERLA
SAYLOR, JACOB	CAR	381	2ND DIST
SAYLOR, JESSE*	BAL	350	3RD WARD
SAYLOR, LEAH	WAS	064	2ND SUBD
SAYLOR, SOLOMON SR.	FRE	411	8TH E DI
SAYPOLE, JOHN E.	FRE	377	PETERSVI
SAYR, MARY	MGM	360	BERRYS D
SBEDDET, JOHN	BAL	119	1ST WARD
SBIRD, WILLIAM	ALL	218	CUMBERLA
SBURNS, JOHN	BAL	132	1ST WARD
SCADMAN,WILLIAM	CAR	148	NO TWP L
SCAFFER, DAVID	BAL	068	2ND DIST
SCAFFER, MARGARET	BAL	004	1ST WARD
SCAFFER, MICHAEL	BAL	068	2ND DIST
SCAGGINS, HENRY	BAL	455	14TH WAR
SCAGGS, GEORGE B.	MGM	351	BERRYS D
SCAGGS, SCAGGS	PRI	042	VANSVILL
SCALAIN, ELIZABETH *	BAL	295	20TH WAR
SCALAS, GEORGE*	BAL	405	3RD WARD
SCALES, GEORGE*	BAL	405	3RD WARD
SCALEY, EDWARD	ALL	052	10TH E.D
SCALION, JOHN	BAL	278	1ST DIST
SCALIVAN, MARY	BAL	086	2ND DIST
SCALLY, JAMES	BAL	004	9TH WARD
SCALLY, KETTY	BAL	117	2ND DIST
SCALLY, MARGARET	BAL	266	2ND WARD
SCALLY, MICHAEL	ALL	050	10TH E.D

Name	County	Page	District
SCANDAL, JOHN	BAL	173	19TH WAR
SCANEY, HENRY*	TAL	019	EASTON D
SCANLAN, G. MARY	BAL	059	18TH WAR
SCANLAN, JAMES	BAL	184	16TH WAR
SCANLAN, JOHN	BAL	418	3RD WARD
SCANLIN, JAMES	ALL	050	10TH E.D
SCANNEL, JOHN	BAL	356	3RD WARD
SCANTLEBRUY, C. C.	BAL	047	9TH WARD
SCANTLIN, EDWARD	CEC	031	CHESAPEA
SCAR, ANN M.	CEC	011	ELKTON 3
SCAR, CATHARINE	BAL	355	13TH WAR
SCAR, JOHN	CEC	011	ELKTON 3
SCAR, JULIA	CEC	011	ELKTON 3
SCARBORO, SUSAN	WAS	237	CAVETOWN
SCARBOROUGH, AMOS K.	HAR	041	1ST DIST
SCARBOROUGH, ANN E.	HAR	001	1ST DIST
SCARBOROUGH, ANN E.	CEC	117	4TH E DI
SCARBOROUGH, ARCHY	HAR	030	1ST DIST
SCARBOROUGH, BENJAMIN	HAR	007	1ST DIST
SCARBOROUGH, CHARLES	HAR	005	1ST DIST
SCARBOROUGH, CLARISA	HAR	007	1ST DIST
SCARBOROUGH, EDWARD A.	HAR	013	1ST DIST
SCARBOROUGH, ELIAS	HAR	007	1ST DIST
SCARBOROUGH, ELIZABETH	HAR	012	1ST DIST
SCARBOROUGH, ENIS	HAR	033	1ST DIST
SCARBOROUGH, ENOS	CEC	115	3RD E DI
SCARBOROUGH, ENOS	CEC	176	7TH E DI
SCARBOROUGH, EUCLIDUS	HAR	013	1ST DIST
SCARBOROUGH, EZEAKLE	BAL	296	1ST DIST
SCARBOROUGH, HEZEKIAH	HAR	008	1ST DIST
SCARBOROUGH, HEZEKIAH	HAR	007	1ST DIST
SCARBOROUGH, HUGH T.	CEC	114	3RD E DI
SCARBOROUGH, IRA	BAL	172	19TH WAR
SCARBOROUGH, ISAAC	HAR	043	1ST DIST
SCARBOROUGH, JOHN	CEC	114	3RD E DI
SCARBOROUGH, JOHN A.	SOM	536	TYASKIN
SCARBOROUGH, JOHN W.	HAR	007	1ST DIST
SCARBOROUGH, JOHN W.	HAR	001	1ST DIST
SCARBOROUGH, JOSEPH H.	HAR	047	1ST DIST
SCARBOROUGH, JOSEPH W.	HAR	007	1ST DIST
SCARBOROUGH, JOSIAH	HAR	013	1ST DIST
SCARBOROUGH, MARY	HAR	041	1ST DIST
SCARBOROUGH, PARKER	HAR	047	1ST DIST
SCARBOROUGH, PETER	WOR	273	BERLIN 1
SCARBOROUGH, REBECCA	HAR	032	1ST DIST
SCARBOROUGH, SAMUEL	HAR	047	1ST DIST
SCARBOROUGH, SAMUEL	HAR	007	1ST DIST
SCARBOROUGH, SARAH	CEC	115	3RD E DI
SCARBOROUGH, SILAS	HAR	090	2ND DIST
SCARBOROUGH, THOMAS	CEC	106	3RD E DI
SCARBOROUGH, THOMAS E.	HAR	008	1ST DIST
SCARBOROUGH, WATSON	CEC	115	3RD E DI
SCARBOROUGH, WESLEY	CEC	090	4TH E DI
SCARBOROUGH, WILLIAM	HAR	036	1ST DIST
SCARBROUGH, EDWARD	WOR	312	2ND E DI
SCARBROUGH, KENDAL	WOR	312	2ND E DI
SCARBROUGHS, WILLAM	WOR	302	SNOW HIL
SCARF, ELISHA	BAL	202	11TH WAR
SCARF, ELIZABETH	BAL	021	9TH WARD
SCARF, GEORGE W.	BAL	116	11TH WAR
SCARF, JAMES	BAL	234	20TH WAR
SCARF, JAMES H.	BAL	288	12TH WAR
SCARF, JOHN	BAL	181	2ND WARD
SCARF, JOHN	BAL	156	2ND DIST
SCARF, JOHN	BAL	047	2ND DIST
SCARF, JOSEPH	BAL	156	2ND DIST
SCARF, MARGARET	BAL	064	2ND DIST
SCARF, MARY E.	BAL	021	9TH WARD
SCARF, ROBERT	BAL	153	19TH WAR
SCARF, THOMAS	BAL	057	18TH WAR
SCARF, WILLIAM	BAL	058	18TH WAR
SCARF, WILLIAM W.	BAL	209	19TH WAR
SCARFF, HANNAH	BAL	364	8TH WARD
SCARFF, HENRY	BAL	390	8TH WARD
SCARFF, HENRY	HAR	049	1ST DIST
SCARFF, ISAAC	BAL	100	2ND DIST
SCARFF, JACOB	FRE	208	BUCKEYST
SCARFF, JAMES R.	HAR	062	1ST DIST
SCARFF, JOHN	HAR	044	1ST DIST
SCARFF, JOHN	BAL	360	1ST DIST
SCARFF, JOSHUA H.	HAR	061	1ST DIST
SCARFF, MARY	FRE	073	FREDERIC
SCARFF, MARY A.	FRE	217	BUCKEYST
SCARFF, SAMUEL G.	HAR	050	1ST DIST
SCARFF, WILLIAM	BAL	222	6TH WARD
SCARFFT, CONRAD	BAL	106	2ND DIST
SCARORDUGH	HAR	030	1ST DIST
SCARP, GEORGE W.	BAL	011	1ST WARD
SCARS, ANNE M.*	BAL	115	15TH WAR
SCATE, JOHN*	DOR	462	1ST DIST
SCATHERMAN, DANIEL	FRE	134	CREAGERS
SCATLING, HENRY	BAL	354	13TH WAR
SCAULDING, WILLIAM	BAL	006	9TH WARD
SCAUMBAUM, HENRY	BAL	005	9TH WARD
SCEMET, MARY	BAL	107	1ST WARD
SCENA, DAVID *	KEN	246	2ND DIST
SCEPTER, MARY	FRE	197	5TH E DI
SCERBROUGH, WILLIAM J.	WOR	313	2ND E DI
SCESHLING, JOHN	BAL	055	9TH WARD
SCHAAF, DOROTHY	BAL	112	10TH WAR
SCHAAM, PAUL	ANN	482	HOWARD D
SCHAD, ANGELINE	BAL	079	1ST WARD
SCHAD, CORNELIA	BAL	002	1ST WARD
SCHAD, HENRY	BAL	086	10TH WAR
SCHAD,ENGLEBAT	BAL	079	1ST WARD
SCHADS, MARION	BAL	141	5TH WARD
SCHAEFER, C. J.	BAL	077	10TH WAR
SCHAEFER, FRANCIS M.	BAL	345	13TH WAR
SCHAEFER, JACOB	BAL	062	15TH WAR
SCHAEFER, MATILDA	BAL	388	13TH WAR
SCHAEFER, PHILIP A.	BAL	088	10TH WAR
SCHAEFFER, AUGUSTUS H.	FRE	010	FREDERIC
SCHAEFFER, CARLINE	FRE	036	FREDERIC
SCHAEFFER, DANIEL	FRE	078	FREDERIC
SCHAEFFER, DAVID	BAL	179	6TH WARD
SCHAEFFER, ELLEN A.	BAL	258	6TH WARD
SCHAEFFER, FRANCIS	BAL	007	9TH WARD
SCHAEFFER, GEORGE	BAL	179	6TH WARD
SCHAEFFER, GEORGE	BAL	192	6TH WARD
SCHAEFFER, GEORGE	BAL	078	10TH WAR
SCHAEFFER, GUSTAVUS	FRE	142	CREAGERS
SCHAEFFER, HENRY	FRE	025	FREDERIC
SCHAEFFER, HERMAN	BAL	217	6TH WARD
SCHAEFFER, JOHN	BAL	204	6TH WARD
SCHAEFFER, JOHN	BAL	231	6TH WARD
SCHAEFFER, JOHN	BAL	005	15TH WAR
SCHAEFFER, JOHN F. D.	FRE	137	CREAGERS
SCHAEFFER, JOHN R.	HAR	095	2ND DIST
SCHAEFFER, JOHNH.	FRE	208	BUCKEYST
SCHAEFFER, MARGARET	BAL	005	15TH WAR
SCHAEFFER, MARGARET C.	FRE	042	FREDERIC
SCHAEFFER, MARY	BAL	079	10TH WAR
SCHAEFFER, MARY A.	PRI	107	PISCATAW
SCHAEFFER, MATILDA	FRE	036	FREDERIC
SCHAEFFER, PETER	FRE	094	FREDERIC
SCHAEFFER, RHEINHARDT	BAL	194	6TH WARD
SCHAEFFER, THOMAS	BAL	164	6TH WARD
SCHAEFFER,ELY	FRE	208	BUCKEYST
SCHAEFFNER, HENRY S.	FRE	023	FREDERIC
SCHAEL, AMELIA	BAL	369	13TH WAR
SCHAER, MARY	BAL	003	1ST WARD
SCHAFER, CRISTIAN	BAL	105	18TH WAR
SCHAFER, GEORGE E.	BAL	010	1ST WARD
SCHAFER, HENRY	BAL	235	1ST DIST
SCHAFER, HENRY	BAL	413	1ST DIST
SCHAFFEE, F.	BAL	148	1ST WARD
SCHAFFEE, WILLIAM	BAL	424	8TH WARD
SCHAFFER, A.C.	BAL	199	11TH WAR
SCHAFFER, ABRAM	BAL	068	2ND DIST
SCHAFFER, ADAM	BAL	253	2ND WARD
SCHAFFER, ADCN	BAL	091	5TH WARD
SCHAFFER, ALLEN G.	BAL	091	5TH WARD
SCHAFFER, ANN M.	BAL	034	18TH WAR
SCHAFFER, C. A.	BAL	148	11TH WAR
SCHAFFER, CATHARINE	BAL	147	5TH WARD
SCHAFFER, CONRAD	BAL	241	2ND WARD
SCHAFFER, CONRAD	BAL	023	1ST WARD
SCHAFFER, ELIZABETH	BAL	190	2ND WARD
SCHAFFER, ELIZABETH	BAL	068	2ND DIST
SCHAFFER, ELIZABETH	BAL	135	2ND DIST
SCHAFFER, FREDERICK	BAL	064	1ST WARD
SCHAFFER, GEORGE	BAL	147	5TH WARD
SCHAFFER, GEORGE A.	BAL	246	6TH WARD
SCHAFFER, HENRY	BAL	060	4TH WARD
SCHAFFER, JEMIMA	BAL	267	17TH WAR
SCHAFFER, JOHN	ANN	420	HOWARD D
SCHAFFER, JOHN	BAL	274	7TH WARD
SCHAFFER, JOHN	BAL	296	3RD WARD
SCHAFFER, JOHN D.	KEN	243	2ND DIST
SCHAFFER, JOHN M.	BAL	322	7TH WARD
SCHAFFER, LYDIA	BAL	051	2ND DIST
SCHAFFER, MAHALA	BAL	061	10TH WAR
SCHAFFER, MARTIN	BAL	158	11TH WAR
SCHAFFER, MICHAEL	BAL	258	2ND WARD
SCHAFFER, OLIVER	KEN	243	2ND DIST
SCHAFFER, PHILIP	BAL	074	1ST WARD
SCHAFFER, SOPHIA	BAL	019	4TH WARD
SCHAFFER, THEODORE	BAL	081	1ST WARD
SCHAFFER, THOMAS	BAL	004	1ST WARD
SCHAFFER, THOMAS B.	BAL	172	1ST WARD
SCHAFFER, WILLIAM C.	BAL	091	5TH WARD
SCHAFFNER, ANN M.	FRE	034	FREDERIC
SCHAGER, WILLIAM	BAL	203	2ND WARD
SCHAGOMAN, CATHARINE	CAR	266	WESTMINS
SCHAIFFER, FREDERICK	BAL	049	9TH WARD
SCHALB, SEBASTIAN	BAL	194	6TH WARD
SCHALLER, GOTTLEIB REV-	BAL	307	3RD WARD
SCHALTZE, CONRAD	BAL	366	13TH WAR
SCHANE, JOHN	BAL	083	1ST WARD
SCHANER, MARGARET	BAL	108	1ST WARD
SCHANKLIN, ALLICE	BAL	209	11TH WAR
SCHANPELBEYER, CAROLINE	BAL	283	12TH WAR
SCHANS, A.	BAL	449	8TH WARD
SCHANT, JOHN	BAL	043	9TH WARD
SCHAPER, ADAM	BAL	381	8TH WARD
SCHAPKABEN, JOHN	BAL	069	10TH WAR
SCHAPTER, CONRAD	BAL	080	1ST WARD
SCHARBER, ANDREW	BAL	111	2ND DIST
SCHARBERG, HERMAN	BAL	034	9TH WARD
SCHARDLEMAN, JOHN	BAL	008	15TH WAR
SCHARF, ADAM	BAL	106	2ND DIST
SCHARF, ANN	BAL	061	15TH WAR
SCHARF, ANN M.	BAL	059	18TH WAR
SCHARF, GEORGE	BAL	195	17TH WAR
SCHARF, WILLIAM	BAL	093	10TH WAR
SCHARFERMAN, HERMAN	BAL	282	17TH WAR
SCHARFF, THOMAS	BAL	304	17TH WAR
SCHARLBACK, JOHN H.	BAL	227	2ND WARD
SCHARLEFORD, SAMUEL	BAL	120	1ST WARD
SCHARLER, JOHN	BAL	198	2ND WARD
SCHARRER, JOSEPH	BAL	279	1ST DIST
SCHARRIER, PETER	BAL	036	9TH WARD
SCHARTZ, FREDERICK	BAL	007	4TH WARD
SCHATKA, AUGUSTA	BAL	460	14TH WAR
SCHATKA, CHARLES	BAL	436	14TH WAR
SCHAUB, JOHN	BAL	063	1ST WARD
SCHAUL, ANN	BAL	268	12TH WAR
SCHAULL, HENRY	BAL	056	1ST WARD
SCHAUM, CAROLINE	BAL	010	15TH WAR
SCHAUM, FREDERICK	BAL	010	15TH WAR
SCHAUM, LOUIS	BAL	015	15TH WAR
SCHAUM, LOUIS	BAL	018	15TH WAR
SCHAUM, LOUIS JR.	BAL	016	15TH WAR
SCHAUM, WILLAIM	BAL	009	15TH WAR
SCHAUPEBERGE, J.H.	BAL	283	12TH WAR
SCHAVER, EVE	BAL	257	2ND WARD
SCHAWAKER, CATHARINE	BAL	012	1ST WARD
SCHAWBLA, ELIZAVBETH	BAL	415	14TH WAR
SCHEABLE, CHARLES F.	BAL	036	18TH WAR
SCHEAR, WILLIAM	BAL	470	14TH WAR
SCHEARS, HECTOR	BAL	067	18TH WAR
SCHEBUNDA, HENRY	BAL	429	8TH WARD
SCHEEBLER, LEWIS	BAL	127	5TH WARD
SCHEEL, M.	BAL	449	8TH WARD
SCHEELE, HENRY	BAL	319	3RD WARD
SCHEFFELEIN, ANNIE	BAL	328	3RD WARD
SCHEFFER, CHARLES	BAL	183	19TH WAR
SCHEFFER, S.	BAL	188	19TH WAR
SCHEFFIELD, JOHN	BAL	298	3RD WARD
SCHEIDA, JASSIN	BAL	221	2ND WARD
SCHEIDELMAN, FREDERIC	BAL	217	6TH WARD
SCHEIDT, REV. F.	BAL	276	17TH WAR
SCHEIK, CHRISTOPHER	BAL	196	2ND WARD
SCHEILTZ, AUGUSTUS	BAL	106	1ST WARD
SCHEINHOAF, HENRY	BAL	276	2ND WARD
SCHEINTAL, THOMAS	BAL	236	2ND WARD
SCHEKNEY, WILLIAM R.	BAL	143	1ST WARD
SCHELDT, CATHARINE	BAL	246	2ND WARD
SCHELDT, OTHO	BAL	172	2ND DIST
SCHELER, CONRADT	BAL	300	7TH WARD
SCHELEY, JOHN	ALL	173	7TH E.D.
SCHELL, CHARLES D.	FRE	054	FREDERIC
SCHELL, GEORGE W.	FRE	036	FREDERIC
SCHELL, JOSEPH	FRE	263	NEW MARK
SCHELL, MARY M.M.	FRE	026	FREDERIC
SCHELLEY, GEORGE	BAL	155	1ST WARD
SCHELPFER, RACHEL	BAL	055	9TH WARD
SCHEM, JOHN*	BAL	082	10TH WAR
SCHEMINGER, GEORG	BAL	201	2ND WARD
SCHEMP, JOHN A.	BAL	360	13TH WAR
SCHENBECKER, JOHN	BAL	211	19TH WAR
SCHENBLY, PATRICK	WAS	149	HAGERSTO
SCHENDERBACK, JOSEPH	BAL	229	2ND WARD
SCHENICK, FLORENCE	BAL	156	11TH WAR
SCHENING, JACOB	BAL	079	1ST WARD
SCHENK, A.	BAL	449	8TH WARD
SCHENK, ELIZA A.	FRE	226	BUCKEYST
SCHENK, MARGARET	FRE	278	NEW MARK
SCHENKEL, PHILIP	BAL	096	10TH WAR
SCHENLAST, HENRY	BAL	042	9TH WARD
SCHENLLY, JOHN	WAS	132	2ND DIST
SCHENSTIDER, PHILIP	WAS	155	HAGERSTO
SCHEPELER, CHRISTOPHER	BAL	082	10TH WAR
SCHERBLINE, CHRISTIAN	CAR	336	6TH DIST
SCHERER, CHRISTOH	BAL	040	15TH WAR
SCHERER, CONRAD	BAL	227	2ND WARD
SCHERER, JOHN	BAL	044	9TH WARD
SCHERFF, JOHN	BAL	069	10TH WAR
SCHERICK, MARY	BAL	258	2ND WARD
SCHERICKLEBRE, ELIZA	BAL	066	1ST WARD
SCHERIDER, ADAM	BAL	072	1ST WARD
SCHERK, GEORGE	BAL	237	2ND WARD
SCHERLOCK, JOHN	BAL	278	2ND WARD
SCHERMAN, CONRAD	BAL	086	1ST WARD
SCHERMAN, CONRAD	BAL	088	1ST WARD
SCHERMAN, ELLEN	BAL	062	1ST WARD
SCHERMER, JOHN V.	BAL	061	15TH WAR
SCHERMER, MARGARET	BAL	436	8TH WARD
SCHERMER, RUDOLPH	BAL	131	16TH WAR
SCHERN, JOHN*	BAL	082	10TH WAR
SCHERNINAUT, GEORGE	BAL	264	2ND WARD
SCHERWIDER, JOHN*	BAL	109	2ND DIST
SCHETER, CHARLES	BAL	106	1ST WARD
SCHETLER, CLARA	BAL	003	15TH WAR
SCHEUH, GEORGE	BAL	230	6TH WARD
SCHGMAN, BARNARD	BAL	443	8TH WARD
SCHIA, CHARLES	BAL	362	13TH WAR
SCHIAKIM, H.H.	BAL	079	1ST WARD
SCHIBE, LIZZETTA	BAL	278	1ST DIST
SCHIBE, NICHOLAS	BAL	279	1ST DIST
SCHIBER, JACOB	BAL	132	18TH WAR
SCHICK, MATHIAS	BAL	104	1ST WARD
SCHICKLEY, NELSON	BAL	398	3RD WARD
SCHIDY, PHILIP	QUE	252	5TH E DI
SCHIEBOLD, MARY	BAL	193	2ND WARD
SCHIEFFLAN, JAOCB	BAL	243	2ND WARD
SCHIEFLER, PETER	BAL	164	6TH WARD
SCHIELDS, OWEN	BAL	385	8TH WARD
SCHIELFFLAN, THOMAS	BAL	245	2ND WARD
SCHIER, MAGDALENE	BAL	229	6TH WARD
SCHIGME, MARY	BAL	063	2ND DIST
SCHILDESHIEM, ADOLPH	BAL	127	16TH WAR
SCHILDTKNECHT, WILLIAM *	FRE	374	CATOCTIN
SCHILDTKNECHT, JOSEPH *	FRE	372	CATOCTIN
SCHILDTKNECKT, JACOB	FRE	349	MIDDLETO
SCHILE, JANE	BAL	122	11TH WAR
SCHILHIPH, JOHN *	BAL	086	2ND DIST
SCHILKOFF, MATHIAS	BAL	085	2ND DIST
SCHILL, GEORGE B.	FRE	007	FREDERIC
SCHILL, PHILLIP	FRE	002	FREDERIC
SCHILLA, FREDERICK	BAL	259	2ND WARD
SCHILLER, ANNA	BAL	004	15TH WAR
SCHILLER, CHRISTIAN	WAS	244	SMITHSBU
SCHILLER, JOHN	BAL	278	2ND WARD
SCHILLER, JOHN G.	BAL	221	1ST DIST
SCHILLING, WILLIAM	BAL	066	1ST WARD
SCHILLINGBERGER, GEORGE	BAL	305	7TH WARD
SCHILLINGER, GEROGE	BAL	299	3RD WARD
SCHILLINGER, PHILLIP	BAL	284	17TH WAR
SCHILLINGS, PETER	BAL	094	1ST WARD
SCHILT, SIMON	CAR	257	3RD DIST
SCHIMMER, MICHAEL	BAL	017	4TH WARD
SCHINDER, SAMUEL	WAS	204	1ST DIST
SCHINDLE, DAVID	FRE	343	MIDDLETO
SCHINDLE, GEORGE	WAS	299	1ST DIST
SCHINDLE, JAMES	WAS	299	1ST DIST
SCHINDLE, LEWIS	WAS	299	1ST DIST
SCHINDLER, ELIZABETH	FRE	346	MIDDLETO
SCHINDLER, JOHN JR.	FRE	393	PETERSVI
SCHINDLER, JOHN SR.	FRE	393	PETERSVI
SCHINE, FREDERICK	BAL	459	8TH WARD
SCHINEMER, D.	BAL	256	20TH WAR
SCHINER, JOHN	BAL	061	1ST WARD
SCHINK, ELLEN	BAL	358	8TH WARD
SCHINK, MICHAEL	BAL	208	2ND WARD
SCHINTZ, HENRY	BAL	263	1ST DIST
SCHIRDY, ANN	BAL	066	18TH WAR
SCHIRDY, HENRY	BAL	066	18TH WAR
SCHISSEL, HENRY	BAL	278	1ST DIST
SCHISTER, CATHERINE	FRE	056	FREDERIC
SCHITTKNEEHR, HENRY	FRE	351	MIDDLETO
SCHIVALTY, HERESEY	BAL	252	2ND WARD
SCHIVERS, NICHOLAS	BAL	184	11TH WAR
SCHLAGEL, H.F.	BAL	238	2ND WARD
SCHLAGLE, CHARLES	BAL	273	7TH WARD
SCHLATER, ANTON	BAL	168	16TH WAR
SCHLAVOGT, JOSEPH	BAL	399	1ST DIST
SCHLEE, JOEPH	BAL	410	8TH WARD
SCHLEIGH, DAVID	WAS	159	HAGERSTO
SCHLEIGH, ELIZABETH	WAS	153	HAGERSTO
SCHLEIGH, J.B.	WAS	145	HAGERSTO
SCHLEIGH, JOHN G.	BAL	361	13TH WAR
SCHLEIGH, MARY A.	FRE	031	FREDERIC
SCHLEIGH, PETER	BAL	254	6TH WARD
SCHLEIGH, SARAH	DOR	377	1ST DIST
SCHLEIGH, THOMAS E.	WAS	152	HAGERSTO
SCHLEIMBACK, CHRISTOPH	BAL	038	9TH WARD
SCHLEIN, HENRY	BAL	086	10TH WAR
SCHLESING, MARGARET	BAL	110	10TH WAR
SCHLESS, CONRAD	BAL	048	9TH WARD
SCHLESSENGER, JOHN	BAL	078	1ST WARD
SCHLEY, CATHARINE	WAS	148	2ND DIST
SCHLEY, DAVID	FRE	013	FREDERIC
SCHLEY, EDWARD	FRE	019	FREDERIC
SCHLEY, FAIRFAX	FRE	032	FREDERIC
SCHLEY, HENRY	FRE	023	FREDERIC
SCHLEY, JAMES M.	FRE	135	CREAGERS
SCHLEY, JOHN T.	FRE	028	FREDERIC
SCHLEY, JULIA A.	BAL	223	6TH WARD
SCHLEY, MARY	FRE	013	FREDERIC
SCHLEY,ALFRED	FRE	452	8TH E DI
SCHLICHTER, CONRAD	BAL	231	2ND WARD
SCHLIFER, CHARLES	ANN	386	4TH DIST
SCHLINING, JOHN	BAL	225	1ST DIST
SCHLINKMANN, HARMAN	BAL	113	15TH WAR
SCHLISTER, HENRY	BAL	274	1ST DIST
SCHLOSER, FREDERICK	BAL	314	3RD WARD
SCHLOSS, DAVID	BAL	019	9TH WARD
SCHLOSS, EMANUEL	BAL	048	9TH WARD
SCHLOSS, JACOB A.	BAL	014	9TH WARD

Name	County	Page	District
SCHLOSS, LAZARUS	BAL	053	1ST WARD
SCHLOSS, NATHAN A.	BAL	088	10TH WAR
SCHLOSSER, JOHN W.	WAS	288	1ST DIST
SCHLOSSER, PETER G.	FRE	318	MIDDLETO
SCHLOSSER, TOBIAS	WAS	288	1ST DIST
SCHLOSSTEIN, PHILIP	BAL	057	15TH WAR
SCHLOT, JOHN	BAL	255	20TH WAR
SCHLOTT, C.	BAL	143	19TH WAR
SCHMALZ, HENRY	BAL	128	16TH WAR
SCHMEDT, HENRY	BAL	081	2ND DIST
SCHMELTZ, HENRY	BAL	126	16TH WAR
SCHMELY, H.	BAL	142	19TH WAR
SCHMEMER, MARGARET	BAL	257	20TH WAR
SCHMER, HENRY	BAL	252	12TH WAR
SCHMERLAY, MARGARET	BAL	180	19TH WAR
SCHMICKS, PHILIP	BAL	072	4TH WARD
SCHMID, E.	BAL	449	8TH WARD
SCHMID, H.	BAL	449	8TH WARD
SCHMIDT, ADAM	BAL	021	2ND DIST
SCHMIDT, ANDREW	BAL	103	15TH WAR
SCHMIDT, ANN	BAL	164	6TH WARD
SCHMIDT, ASTOR	BAL	147	11TH WAR
SCHMIDT, AUGUST	BAL	216	17TH WAR
SCHMIDT, AUGUST	BAL	221	17TH WAR
SCHMIDT, BARBARA	BAL	030	9TH WARD
SCHMIDT, CATHARINE	BAL	022	15TH WAR
SCHMIDT, CATHARINE	BAL	276	1ST DIST
SCHMIDT, E. F.	BAL	279	20TH WAR
SCHMIDT, ELIZABETH	BAL	104	15TH WAR
SCHMIDT, FRANZ	BAL	379	13TH WAR
SCHMIDT, GEORGE	BAL	190	2ND WARD
SCHMIDT, GEORGE	BAL	022	2ND DIST
SCHMIDT, HENRY	BAL	048	9TH WARD
SCHMIDT, JOHN	WAS	175	FUNKSTOW
SCHMIDT, LEWIS	BAL	355	13TH WAR
SCHMIDT, MARGRET	BAL	189	2ND WARD
SCHMIDT, PHILIP	BAL	336	13TH WAR
SCHMIDT, STEPHEN	BAL	217	17TH WAR
SCHMIDT, VALENTINE	BAL	267	1ST DIST
SCHMIDT, VALENTINE	BAL	021	15TH WAR
SCHMIDT, WILLIAM	BAL	012	9TH WARD
SCHMILD, FRANCIS	BAL	211	2ND WARD
SCHMILD, MICHAEL	BAL	207	2ND WARD.
SCHMILTD, JOHN	BAL	213	2ND WARD
SCHMINKE, ANN	BAL	054	15TH WAR
SCHMIT, ANTHONY	BAL	288	1ST DIST
SCHMIT, JOHN	BAL	287	1ST DIST
SCHMIT, MATHIAS	BAL	289	1ST DIST
SCHMITD, GUSTAV	BAL	012	9TH WARD
SCHMITD, JOHN	BAL	212	2ND WARD
SCHMITH, J. H.	BAL	153	1ST WARD
SCHMITT, JULIUS	BAL	209	11TH WAR
SCHMITT, L.	BAL	449	8TH WARD
SCHMITTERER, JACOB	BAL	254	2ND WARD
SCHMITZ, HENRY	BAL	038	9TH WARD
SCHMOUDER, ELIZABETH	WAS	155	HAGERSTO
SCHMUCK, GEORGE	BAL	023	15TH WAR
SCHMUCK, LOUIS	BAL	124	16TH WAR
SCHMUDT, JACOB DR.	BAL	370	13TH WAR
SCHMYTH, CHARLES	BAL	073	4TH WARD
SCHNADS, REGANA	BAL	024	9TH WARD
SCHNAGEL, WILHELMINA	BAL	086	10TH WAR
SCHNARR, JOHN	BAL	302	3RD WARD
SCHNATTINGER, SAMUEL	BAL	301	3RD WARD
SCHNAVELY, ISAAC	BAL	247	1ST DIST
SCHNAVELY, JOHN	BAL	248	1ST DIST
SCHNAVELY,J ACOB	BAL	247	1ST DIST
SCHNEBLY, ALFRED	WAS	007	WILLIAMS
SCHNEBLY, DANIEL	WAS	285	1ST DIST
SCHNEBLY, LOUISA	WAS	121	HAGERSTO
SCHNEBLY, MARY	WAS	289	1ST DIST
SCHNECKENBERGER, GEORGE	WAS	251	1ST DIST
SCHNEEDE, JOHN	BAL	053	1ST WARD
SCHNEFFER, ADAM	FRE	221	BUCKEYST
SCHNEIDER, ADAM	BAL	040	9TH WARD
SCHNEIDER, AUGUSTUS	BAL	054	1ST WARD
SCHNEIDER, CATHARINE	BAL	276	17TH WAR
SCHNEIDER, CHRISTINA	BAL	085	10TH WAR
SCHNEIDER, CHRISTOPHER	BAL	256	2ND WARD
SCHNEIDER, CONRAD	BAL	040	9TH WARD
SCHNEIDER, EMMA	BAL	054	1ST WARD
SCHNEIDER, GOTHOLD	BAL	161	16TH WAR
SCHNEIDER, JOHN	BAL	165	16TH WAR
SCHNEIDER, JOHN	BAL	001	9TH WARD
SCHNEIDER, JOHN	BAL	247	17TH WAR
SCHNEIDER, LEWIS	BAL	040	9TH WARD
SCHNEIDER, PIUS	BAL	086	10TH WAR
SCHNEIDER, WENDEL	BAL	199	6TH WARD
SCHNEIDERITH, CHARLES W.	BAL	378	13TH WAR
SCHNEIDT, FREDERICK	BAL	165	16TH WAR
SCHNEIRER, GEORGE	BAL	233	2ND WARD
SCHNEIVER, DORATTA	BAL	230	2ND WARD
SCHNER, HENRY	WAS	143	HAGERSTO
SCHNET, LOUISA	BAL	333	13TH WAR
SCHNEY, CHARLES *	BAL	233	6TH WARD
SCHNIBBE, DEDWICK	BAL	140	16TH WAR
SCHNIVELY, DANIEL H.	WAS	047	2ND SUBD
SCHNOBLET, ANDREW	BAL	458	14TH WAR
SCHNUFF, VALENT	BAL	222	19TH WAR
SCHOANDALEIR, JOHN	ANN	463	HOWARD D
SCHOCKELLS, SAMUEL	CAL	025	2ND DIST
SCHOCKEY, ELIAS	WAS	273	RIDGEVIL
SCHOCKEY, JACOB	WAS	276	RIDGEVIL
SCHOEMAN, OTTO	BAL	082	10TH WAR
SCHOFFER, CHARLOTTE	BAL	075	1ST WARD
SCHOFFER, DILMAN	KEN	257	1ST DIST
SCHOFFER, JOHN D.	KEN	243	2ND DIST
SCHOFIELD, ELIZABETH	BAL	057	10TH WAR
SCHOFIELD, HENRY	BAL	031	4TH WARD
SCHOFIELD, JOHN	ANN	453	HOWARD D
SCHOFIELD, JOHN	BAL	033	9TH WARD
SCHOFIELD, NOAH	BAL	183	5TH DIST
SCHOH, MARY	BAL	036	9TH WARD
SCHOING, S.	BAL	044	9TH WARD
SCHOLDEN, AMELIA	BAL	054	4TH WARD
SCHOLDT, MARGARET *	BAL	172	2ND DIST
SCHOLFAER, PETER *	FRE	344	MIDDLETO
SCHOLFIELD, WILLIAM-MULAT	MGM	398	ROCKERLE
SCHOLL, CHRISTIAN	FRE	057	FREDERIC
SCHOLL, DANIEL	FRE	070	FREDERIC
SCHOLL, DENNIS	FRE	056	FREDERIC
SCHOLL, ELIAS	FRE	307	WOODSBOR
SCHOLL, ELIZBAETH	FRE	020	FREDERIC
SCHOLL, GEORGE	WAS	261	1ST DIST
SCHOLL, HENRY	FRE	272	NEW MARK
SCHOLL, JACOB	FRE	272	NEW MARK
SCHOLL, LOUISA	FRE	022	FREDERIC
SCHOLLY, FRANCES	WAS	154	HAGERSTO
SCHOLY, WILLIAM	ALL	046	10TH E.D
SCHONHOFF, GERHARD	BAL	324	3RD WARD
SCHOOFIELD, ELIJAH C.	WOR	350	1ST E DI
SCHOOFIELD, JAOCB	WOR	298	9TH E DI
SCHOOFIELD, JOSEPH	WOR	349	1ST E DI
SCHOOFIELD, LOYD	WOR	298	9TH E DI
SCHOOFIELD, NATHAN-BLACK	WOR	327	1ST E DI
SCHOOFIELD, WILLIAM	WOR	327	1ST E DI
SCHOOFIELD, WILLIAM	WOR	349	1ST E DI
SCHOOK, JOHN	BAL	133	1ST WARD
SCHOOL, ANNA	BAL	302	12TH WAR
SCHOOL, CHARLES	BAL	302	12TH WAR
SCHOOLEY, JAMES	BAL	162	16TH WAR
SCHOOLFIED, REBECCA	BAL	225	17TH WAR
SCHOOLFIELD, CHARLOTTE	BAL	309	3RC WARD
SCHOOLFIELD, CUDGOE	WOR	350	1ST E DI
SCHOOLFIELD, ELLEN	BAL	001	EASTERN
SCHOOLFIELD, HENRY	WOR	278	BERLIN 1
SCHOOLFIELD, JOHN	CEC	050	1ST E DI
SCHOOLFIELD, VILOX	WOR	301	SNOW HIL
SCHOOLL, LEWIS V.	FRE	261	NEW MARK
SCHOOLT, MARY A.	WAS	108	2ND DIST
SCHOONE, GEORGE	KEN	264	1ST DIST
SCHOPKIN,JOHN	BAL	076	1ST WARD
SCHOPPERT, SAMUEL	WAS	100	2ND DIST
SCHORF, JOHN	HAR	066	1ST DIST
SCHORNE, JOHN	BAL	036	9TH WARD
SCHORP, HENRY	BAL	251	2ND WARD
SCHORTER, JOHN	BAL	111	2ND DIST
SCHOSSER, JOHN D.	WAS	189	1ST DIST
SCHOTT, FRANCIS	BAL	137	16TH WAR
SCHOTT, JOHN	BAL	443	14TH WAR
SCHOTT, MARIA	BAL	401	14TH WAR
SCHOTT, PERRY	BAL	417	14TH WAR
SCHOTT, PHILIP	BAL	304	12TH WAR
SCHOTTA, WILLIAM	BAL	319	1ST DIST
SCHOTTER, PETER	BAL	061	4TH WARD
SCHOTTS, MARTIN	BAL	117	5TH WARD
SCHOUFE, JOHN	BAL	147	19TH WAR
SCHOULBE, MONRITCH	BAL	269	2ND WARD
SCHOUPS, ANDREW	BAL	147	19TH WAR
SCHOUR, JANE	BAL	001	18TH WAR
SCHOW, JOHN L.	BAL	407	3RD WARD
SCHOYER, PETER	BAL	036	15TH WAR
SCHRADER, BANSER	BAL	181	2ND WARD
SCHRADER, ISAAC	FRE	170	5TH E DI
SCHRADER, JACOB	FRE	197	5TH E DI
SCHRAMYER, GEORGE	WAS	112	2ND DIST
SCHRAUM, CHARLES B.	BAL	130	11TH WAR
SCHRAYMYER, SAMUEL H.	WAS	112	2ND DIST
SCHRECK, WILLIAM	BAL	111	1ST WARD
SCHREIBER, PHILIP	BAL	062	15TH WAR
SCHREIBER, WILLIAM	BAL	165	16TH WAR
SCHREPPER, NICHOLAS	BAL	215	2ND WARD
SCHRERMER, CHARLES	BAL	374	8TH WARD
SCHREWES, JULIA	BAL	175	2ND DIST
SCHRIBNER, CATHARINE	BAL	009	18TH WAR
SCHRIBNER, JULIA	BAL	153	5TH WARD
SCHRIBNER, SAMUEL	BAL	060	18TH WAR
SCHRIDER, LEWIS	BAL	288	17TH WAR
SCHRIELBLER, ANDREW	BAL	373	13TH WAR
SCHRIETER, JOHN	BAL	082	1ST WARD
SCHRIFSNYDER, IGNATIUS	BAL	239	17TH WAR
SCHRINER, J.	BAL	218	17TH WAR
SCHRISEE, JACOB	FRE	080	FREDERIC
SCHRISER, REBECCA	FRE	140	CREAGERS
SCHRIVER, CHRISTIAN	BAL	270	17TH WAR
SCHRIVER, CHRISTOPHER *	BAL	209	6TH WARD
SCHRIVER, FREDERICK	FRE	186	5TH E DI
SCHRIVER, JACOB	BAL	279	1ST DIST
SCHRIVER, JOHN	BAL	254	1ST DIST
SCHRIVER, LEWIS	FRE	172	5TH E DI
SCHRIVER, LEWIS	BAL	075	18TH WAR
SCHRIVER, LOUIS	BAL	222	1ST DIST
SCHRIVER, REBECCA	BAL	220	1ST DIST
SCHRIVERS, EDWARD	CAR	390	2ND DIST
SCHRIVNIER, SAMUEL	FRE	421	8TH E DI
SCHRNIVER, COUNDA	BAL	080	1ST WARD
SCHROALLER, SARAH	WAS	188	BOONSBOR
SCHROARTBAGE, JACOB *	CAR	340	6TH DIST
SCHROAT, CATHRINE	BAL	049	18TH WAR
SCHRODER, AIRY	FRE	387	PETERSVI
SCHRODER, BEARNHARDT	MGM	360	BERRYS D
SCHRODER, CATHERINE	BAL	009	9TH WARD
SCHRODER, FREDERIC	MGM	358	BERRYS D
SCHRODER, FREDERICK	ALL	160	6TH E.D.
SCHRODER, JACOB	BAL	418	8TH WARD
SCHRODER, JOHANA	BAL	041	1ST WARD
SCHRODER, JOHN	BAL	132	2ND DIST
SCHRODER, WILLIAM	BAL	356	8TH WARD
SCHRODMYER, HENRY	WAS	112	2ND DIST
SCHROEDER, CATHERINE	MGM	357	BERRYS D
SCHROEDER, FREDERICK	BAL	161	16TH WAR
SCHROEDER, HENRY	BAL	327	13TH WAR
SCHROEDER, PRUDENCE	BAL	145	16TH WAR
SCHROEDER, WILLIAM	BAL	250	12TH WAR
SCHROEPHER, GOLFRIED *	BAL	451	8TH WARD
SCHROER, MARY	BAL	049	18TH WAR
SCHROETER, JOHN	BAL	353	13TH WAR
SCHROETER, PHILIP	BAL	157	16TH WAR
SCHROFFE, CHARLES M.	BAL	073	18TH WAR
SCHRONE, GEORGE *	KEN	264	1ST DIST
SCHROTE, JAMES	BAL	106	18TH WAR
SCHROTE, MATTHEW	BAL	190	19TH WAR
SCHROYER, JOHN	FRE	349	MIDDLETO
SCHRUGUMAN, CATHARINE *	BAL	474	14TH WAR
SCHRUM, JOHN	CAR	291	7TH DIST
SCHRUP, ANN	BAL	119	5TH WARD
SCHRYOCK, LUCRETIA	FRE	182	5TH E DI
SCHUALM, HENRY	FRE	008	FREDERIC
SCHUBEL, CAROLINE*	BAL	097	10TH WAR
SCHUBER, CHARLES	BAL	123	16TH WAR
SCHUBER, CHRISTOPHER JR.	BAL	123	16TH WAR
SCHUBET, FRANCES	BAL	125	2ND DIST
SCHUBOLD, WILLIAM	BAL	193	2ND WARD
SCHUCK, ALBERT	HAR	084	2ND DIST
SCHUEFFER, SUSAN	FRE	136	CREAGERS
SCHUEGHNAY, MICHAEL	ALL	047	10TH E.D
SCHUERER, JOHN	BAL	029	15TH WAR
SCHUERMAN, FRANCIS	BAL	085	10TH WAR
SCHUEY, CHARLES *	BAL	233	6TH WARD
SCHUGAR, CHRISTOPHER	BAL	351	13TH WAR
SCHUH, CARL	BAL	231	2ND WARD
SCHUIH, ALOYSING	BAL	147	11TH WAR
SCHULENBERG, HERMAN	BAL	155	16TH WAR
SCHULER, CHRISTOPHER	BAL	351	13TH WAR
SCHULL, SARAH	WAS	287	1ST DIST
SCHULL, VALENTINE	BAL	247	2ND WARD
SCHULLER, GEORGE	BAL	224	2ND WARD
SCHULLHEIS, HENRY	BAL	315	7TH WARD
SCHULT, FREDERICK	BAL	234	17TH WAR
SCHULTENBACK, MARY *	BAL	313	12TH WAR
SCHULTEY, JOSEPH	BAL	253	20TH WAR
SCHULTHIES, PETER	BAL	221	6TH WARD
SCHULTS, JOHN	FRE	254	NEW MARK
SCHULTZ, ALIAN	FRE	255	NEW MARK
SCHULTZ, ANDREW	BAL	146	11TH WAR
SCHULTZ, CHAUNCY	ALL	013	3RD E.D.
SCHULTZ, COONROD	BAL	171	2ND DIST
SCHULTZ, FREDERICK	BAL	012	9TH WARD
SCHULTZ, JOHN	BAL	110	15TH WAR
SCHULTZ, JOHN	BAL	124	2ND DIST
SCHULTZ, LOUISA	BAL	050	15TH WAR
SCHULTZ, RUDOLPH	BAL	331	13TH WAR
SCHULTZ, WILLIAM	BAL	010	9TH WARD
SCHULTZBERGER, CAROLINE	BAL	248	2ND WARD
SCHULTZE, ARNOLD	BAL	365	13TH WAR
SCHULTZE, AUGUST	BAL	096	10TH WAR
SCHULTZE, VERONICA	BAL	083	15TH WAR
SCHULTZER, AUGUST A.	BAL	194	6TH WARD
SCHUMACHER, FREDERICK	BAL	071	15TH WAR
SCHUMACHER, JAMES	BAL	134	16TH WAR
SCHUMACHER, REINHART	BAL	133	16TH WAR
SCHUMACHER, WILLIAM H.	BAL	104	15TH WAR
SCHUMACKER, CARSON	BAL	009	9TH WARD
SCHUMAN, F.	BAL	066	4TH WARD
SCHUMAN, GEORGE	BAL	213	6TH WARD
SCHUMAN, JOHN	BAL	012	9TH WARD
SCHUMAN, JOHN A.	BAL	428	8TH WARD
SCHUMAN, VALENTINE	BAL	212	6TH WARD
SCHUMIDT, HENRY D.	BAL	442	14TH WAR
SCHUNK, JOHN	BAL	395	3RD WARD
SCHUNK, JOHN	BAL	328	3RD WARD
SCHURBOLD, CATHARINE	BAL	193	2ND WARD
SCHURGART, JOHN *	CAR	289	7TH DIST
SCHURMANN, HENRY T.	BAL	070	15TH WAR
SCHURP, GEORGE	HAR	141	2ND DIST
SCHUSBRADLE, GEORGE	BAL	433	8TH WARD
SCHUSBRADT, ALEXANDER	BAL	434	8TH WARD
SCHUSIGART, JESSE	CAR	296	7TH DIST
SCHUSTER, JOHN	BAL	168	6TH WARD
SCHUT, FRED	BAL	268	12TH WAR
SCHUTT, BARBARA	BAL	094	10TH WAR
SCHUTT, JOHN	BAL	028	1ST WARD
SCHUTT,PETER	BAL	044	1ST WARD
SCHUTTE, HENRY	BAL	430	8TH WARD
SCHUTTER, LOUIS	BAL	266	2ND WARD
SCHUTTLE, JOSEPH	BAL	190	11TH WAR
SCHUTTZ, HENRY	BAL	193	2ND WARD
SCHUTZ, JOHN	BAL	217	6TH WARD
SCHUTZ, JOHN	BAL	103	15TH WAR
SCHUTZ, MARY	BAL	228	2ND WARD
SCHUTZ, PETER	ALL	081	5TH E.D.
SCHUYLER, HANNAH	BAL	414	1ST DIST
SCHUYLER, MALINDA	BAL	414	1ST DIST
SCHVEMAKER, HENRY	BAL	048	9TH WARD
SCHWAB, ADAM	BAL	099	15TH WAR
SCHWAB, AUGUSTA	BAL	016	9TH WARD
SCHWAKE, JOHN	ANN	384	4TH DIST
SCHWAKE, JOHN G.	ANN	425	HOWARD D
SCHWANKOUSKEY, CONRAD	ALL	225	CUMBERLA
SCHWAP, LOUISA	BAL	090	10TH WAR
SCHWARA, GEORGE	ANN	267	ANNAPOLI
SCHWARJOUR, ELIZABETH	BAL	218	17TH WAR
SCHWARTIER, JOHN C.	FRE	280	WOODSBOR
SCHWARTZ, C.	BAL	141	1ST WARD
SCHWARTZ, CONRAD	BAL	029	4TH KARD
SCHWARTZ, DANIEL	BAL	209	17TH WAR
SCHWARTZ, DELILAH	CAR	401	2ND DIST
SCHWARTZ, FREDERIC	BAL	229	6TH WARD
SCHWARTZ, JOSEPH	BAL	355	13TH WAR
SCHWARTZ, JULIUS	BAL	337	13TH WAR
SCHWARTZ, MARY	BAL	337	13TH WAR
SCHWARTZBAUGH, ELIZABETH	CAR	340	6TH DIST
SCHWARTZE, EDWARD	BAL	075	15TH WAR
SCHWARTZE, HARMAN	BAL	168	16TH WAR
SCHWARTZE, JACOB	BAL	087	15TH WAR
SCHWARTZE, L.	BAL	018	15TH WAR
SCHWARTZE, MARIA	BAL	168	16TH WAR
SCHWARTZE, ULDRICKS	ANN	414	HOWARD D
SCHWATKA, JOHN	KEN	302	3RD DIST
SCHWATZ, JOHN*	BAL	419	3RD WARD
SCHWATZBAUM, GABRIEL	BAL	062	15TH WAR
SCHWATZE, HENRIETTA	BAL	420	14TH WAR
SCHWATZE, WILIAM	BAL	448	14TH WAR
SCHWATZENBACK, FREDERICK	BAL	031	15TH WAR
SCHWATZWELDER, MARY	BAL	129	16TH WAR
SCHWEGART, JESSE	CAR	289	7TH DIST
SCHWEICKERT, K.	BAL	449	8TH WARD
SCHWIGART, CYRUS	CAR	295	7TH DIST
SCHWIGART, MARY	CAR	273	WESTMINS
SCHWING, JOHN	BAL	232	2ND WARD
SCHYLER, ELLEN	BAL	249	1ST DIST
SCHYLER, HANNAH	BAL	249	1ST DIST
SCIBEMAN, ALEXANDER	FRE	029	FREDERIC
SCIBES, GEORGE	BAL	264	20TH WAR
SCIBLER, PETER	BAL	038	18TH WAR
SCIBRED, MICHAEL	BAL	170	19TH WAR
SCIDLAY, JOHN	CAR	220	5TH DIST
SCIFT, CHRISTIAN	BAL	261	20TH WAR
SCISELER, LAWRENCE	BAL	267	2ND WARD
SCISH, FRANCS	CAR	153	NO TWP L
SCISSEL, DOROTHY	PRI	036	VANSVILL
SCISSUE, JOSHUA	FRE	246	NEW MARK
SCIVENER, PHILIP	CAL	014	1ST DIST
SCIVIL, RASON	ALL	234	CUMBERLA
SCKESSLER, ZACHARY	FRE	369	CATOCTIN
SCLIBY, JOHN W.	FRE	234	BUCKEYST
SCLIFER, CASPER	ANN	386	4TH DIST
SCLVISTER, ELIZA	BAL	392	14TH WAR
SCNIVLER, ADAM	BAL	042	18TH WAR
SCOANNEGAN, WILLAMI	ALL	053	10TH E.D
SCOAT, JOHN W. *	HAR	190	3RD DIST
SCOAT, WILLIAM H.	HAR	189	3RD DIST
SCOBY, ANN	BAL	429	14TH WAR
SCOBY, ELIZABETH	BAL	430	14TH WAR
SCOCHRIST, WILLIAM	CAR	234	UNION TO
SCOEENEY, JOHN *	BAL	302	20TH WAR
SCOFF, CLEMENT	BAL	158	2ND DIST
SCOFFIELD, WILLIAM	BAL	058	4TH WARD
SCOFIELD, BENJAMIN	BAL	405	14TH WAR
SCOFIELD, HENRY	CEC	163	6TH E DI
SCOFIELD, HENRY	BAL	330	7TH WARD
SCOFIELD, JAMES	BAL	394	1ST DIST
SCOFIELD, JAMES	SOM	446	DAMES QU
SCOFIELD, JAMES	SOM	442	DAMES QU
SCOFIELD, NELLY	SOM	406	DUBLIN D
SCOGGINS, AMELIA	BAL	174	11TH WAR
SCOGGINS, EMILA	BAL	256	1ST DIST
SCOGGINS, GEORGE	BAL	173	11TH WAR
SCOGGINS, RACHAEL-BLACK	FRE	230	BUCKEYST
SCOGGINS, SAMUEL	BAL	390	1ST DIST

Name	County	Page	District
SCOGGINS, SOLLEMAN	FRE	205	BUCKEYST
SCOGGINS, SOPHIA	BAL	266	1ST DIST
SCOGGINS, WILLIAM	BAL	426	1ST DIST
SCOGINGS, ELIZA	BAL	327	7TH WARD
SCOLDFIELD, JOHN	BAL	300	1ST DIST
SCOLLAY, E.S.	ALL	212	CUMBERLA
SCOMES, JOSEPH	TAL	108	ST MICHA
SCONE, JAMES *	BAL	075	15TH WAR
SCOOLFIELD, LEWIS A.	BAL	119	5TH WARD
SCOOLS, JAMES	CAR	372	9TH DIST
SCOOMIS, EDWARD	BAL	080	2ND DIST
SCOONE, CHARLES	KEN	230	2ND DIST
SCOONE, HENIETTA	KEN	228	2ND DIST
SCOONE, JAMES	KEN	234	2ND DIST
SCOONE, WASHINGTON	KEN	265	1ST DIST
SCOOT, ELIZA	BAL	296	12TH WAR
SCOOT, TERRISA	HAR	198	3RD DIST
SCOOT, THOMAS	BAL	301	12TH WAR
SCOOTT, JOHN	KEN	261	1ST DIST
SCORE, JAMES	BAL	251	17TH WAR
SCORE, JAMES	BAL	005	4TH WARD
SCORE, JAMES *	BAL	075	15TH WAR
SCORNA, ROBERT	BAL	445	8TH WARD
SCOT, ANTONY	HAR	151	3RD DIST
SCOT, ELIZABETH	BAL	295	12TH WAR
SCOT, M.	BAL	139	1ST WARD
SCOTE, JOHN A.*	DOR	411	1ST DIST
SCOTE, JOHN*	DOR	462	1ST DIST
SCOTGT, SAMUEL	BAL	156	1ST WARD
SCOTHSCOTT, RHODY	CAR	085	NO TWP L
SCOTIEN, WILLIAM	CEC	077	NORTHEAS
SCOTLAND, WILLIAM	MGM	395	ROCKERLE
SCOTT, AARON	SOM	413	DUBLIN D
SCOTT, ABRAHAM	BAL	077	10TH WAR
SCOTT, ABRAHAM	BAL	422	1ST DIST
SCOTT, ABRAHAM C.	BAL	420	1ST DIST
SCOTT, AGNES	BAL	219	6TH WARD
SCOTT, ALBERT H.	PRI	048	AQUASCO
SCOTT, ALCINDA	BAL	122	16TH WAR
SCOTT, ALEXANDER	BAL	152	16TH WAR
SCOTT, ALEXANDER	FRE	128	CREAGERS
SCOTT, ALVERDA	BAL	116	15TH WAR
SCOTT, AM*	BAL	313	3RD WARD
SCOTT, AMANDA	BAL	282	7TH WARD
SCOTT, AMOS H.	CEC	093	4TH E DI
SCOTT, ANDREW	BAL	359	13TH WAR
SCOTT, ANDREW	BAL	292	7TH WARD
SCOTT, ANDREW	BAL	091	5TH WARD
SCOTT, ANN	BAL	462	1ST DIST
SCOTT, ANN	HAR	198	3RD DIST
SCOTT, ANN	KEN	208	2ND DIST
SCOTT, ANN	BAL	252	20TH WAR
SCOTT, ANN M.	BAL	075	18TH WAR
SCOTT, ANN M.	BAL	134	11TH WAR
SCOTT, ANN M.	KEN	287	3RD DIST
SCOTT, ANNA	CEC	015	ELKTON 3
SCOTT, ANTHONY	BAL	463	1ST DIST
SCOTT, AQUILLA	BAL	408	1ST DIST
SCOTT, AQUILLA	HAR	060	1ST DIST
SCOTT, ARAMINTA	BAL	200	6TH WARD
SCOTT, ARCHIBALD	ALL	203	CUMBERLA
SCOTT, ARNMSTEAD	ST	349	5TH E DI
SCOTT, ASA	WOR	326	1ST E DI
SCOTT, BENJAMIN	HAR	107	2ND DIST
SCOTT, BENJAMIN	CEC	011	ELKTON 3
SCOTT, BENJAMIN	BAL	076	18TH WAR
SCOTT, BENJAMIN	CEC	101	4TH E DI
SCOTT, C.	BAL	103	10TH WAR
SCOTT, CASSA	BAL	288	12TH WAR
SCOTT, CATHARINE	ALL	005	3RD E.D.
SCOTT, CATHERINE	BAL	025	9TH WARD
SCOTT, CATHERINE	BAL	276	7TH WARD
SCOTT, CATHERINE	BAL	458	8TH WARD
SCOTT, CATHERINE J.	CEC	128	5TH E DI
SCOTT, CHARELS	BAL	176	19TH WAR
SCOTT, CHARELS	BAL	199	19TH WAR
SCOTT, CHARELS A.	ALL	085	5TH E.D.
SCOTT, CHARLES	BAL	235	12TH WAR
SCOTT, CHARLES	BAL	280	1ST DIST
SCOTT, CHARLES H.	ANN	303	1ST DIST
SCOTT, CHARLOT	BAL	386	1ST DIST
SCOTT, CHARLOTTE	MGM	363	BERRYS D
SCOTT, CHRISTIAN	BAL	456	1ST DIST
SCOTT, CHRISTIAN	BAL	459	8TH WARD
SCOTT, CLOE	WOR	184	6TH E DI
SCOTT, DANEIL	WAS	291	1ST DIST
SCOTT, DANIEL	BAL	167	1ST WARD
SCOTT, DAVID	BAL	131	1ST WARD
SCOTT, DAVID	BAL	054	2ND DIST
SCOTT, DAVID	CEC	104	4TH E DI
SCOTT, DAVID	CEC	101	4TH E DI
SCOTT, DAVID	CEC	063	1ST E DI
SCOTT, DAVID M.	CAL	017	1ST DIST
SCOTT, DEBORAH	ALL	264	CUMBERLA
SCOTT, DENNIS	BAL	337	3RD WARD
SCOTT, DICK	QUE	238	5TH E DI
SCOTT, DILLY	ANN	378	4TH DIST
SCOTT, DULSENA	DOR	341	3RD DIVI
SCOTT, EDMOND J.	PRI	068	NOTTINGH
SCOTT, EDWARD	PRI	069	MARLBROU
SCOTT, EDWARD	WOR	217	4TH E DI
SCOTT, EDWARD	HAR	029	1ST DIST
SCOTT, EDWARD	BAL	409	1ST DIST
SCOTT, EDWARD	BAL	200	6TH WARD
SCOTT, EDWARD J.	PRI	121	PISCATAW
SCOTT, EDWARD W.	ANN	350	3RD DIST
SCOTT, ELI	BAL	086	2ND DIST
SCOTT, ELICK	BAL	052	2ND DIST
SCOTT, ELISABETH	ALL	024	3RD E.D.
SCOTT, ELISABETH A.	BAL	362	3RD WARD
SCOTT, ELIZ	BAL	241	12TH WAR
SCOTT, ELIZA	BAL	116	15TH WAR
SCOTT, ELIZA	PRI	057	AQUASCO
SCOTT, ELIZA	PRI	007	BLADENSB
SCOTT, ELIZA	MGM	402	ROCKERLE
SCOTT, ELIZA	CEC	089	4TH E DI
SCOTT, ELIZA	BAL	201	19TH WAR
SCOTT, ELIZA G.	BAL	135	11TH WAR
SCOTT, ELIZA J.	BAL	065	15TH WAR
SCOTT, ELIZA J.	BAL	301	7TH WARD
SCOTT, ELIZABETH	BAL	365	3RD WARD
SCOTT, ELIZABETH	BAL	305	3RD WARD
SCOTT, ELIZABETH	BAL	310	3RD WARD
SCOTT, ELIZABETH	SOM	410	DUBLIN D
SCOTT, ELIZABETH	HAR	102	2ND DIST
SCOTT, ELIZABETH	FRE	057	FREDERIC
SCOTT, ELIZABETH	CHA	264	HILLTOP
SCOTT, ELIZABETH	ST	322	4TH E DI
SCOTT, ELIZABETH A.	BAL	084	15TH WAR
SCOTT, ELIZABETH-BLACK	CAR	095	NO TWP L
SCOTT, ELLEN	BAL	072	10TH WAR
SCOTT, ELLEN	BAL	241	12TH WAR
SCOTT, ELLEN	ALL	217	CUMBERLA
SCOTT, EMELY	BAL	328	13TH WAR
SCOTT, EMILA	BAL	286	1ST DIST
SCOTT, EMILY	ANN	320	2ND DIST
SCOTT, EMILY	SOM	449	DAMES QU
SCOTT, EMILY	BAL	357	13TH WAR
SCOTT, EMMA	WAS	150	2ND DIST
SCOTT, EPHRAIM	ANN	468	HOWARD D
SCOTT, ETHELIN D.	HAR	001	1ST DIST
SCOTT, EVANS	ANN	472	HOWARD D
SCOTT, EVEN S.	BAL	281	1ST DIST
SCOTT, FANNY	ANN	519	HOWARD D
SCOTT, FANNY	TAL	086	ST MICHA
SCOTT, FRANCES	MGM	342	CLARKSBU
SCOTT, FRANCIS	BAL	004	9TH WARD
SCOTT, FRANCIS P.	BAL	048	1ST WARD
SCOTT, FRANK	ANN	301	1ST DIST
SCOTT, FRANK	BAL	311	20TH WAR
SCOTT, FREDERICK	BAL	299	20TH WAR
SCOTT, FREDERICK	BAL	180	16TH WAR
SCOTT, GABRIEL L.	SOM	449	DAMES QU
SCOTT, GEORGE	CEC	201	6TH E DI
SCOTT, GEORGE	CEC	200	7TH E DI
SCOTT, GEORGE	CEC	209	7TH E DI
SCOTT, GEORGE	BAL	381	13TH WAR
SCOTT, GEORGE	BAL	083	15TH WAR
SCOTT, GEORGE	BAL	347	7TH WARD
SCOTT, GEORGE	ANN	344	3RD DIST
SCOTT, GEORGE	ANN	422	HOWARD D
SCOTT, GEORGE	BAL	144	1ST WARD
SCOTT, GEORGE	BAL	284	2ND WARD
SCOTT, GEORGE	BAL	165	6TH WARD
SCOTT, GEORGE	WAS	266	1ST DIST
SCOTT, GEORGE A.	WOR	185	7TH E DI
SCOTT, GEORGE W.	TAL	030	EASTON D
SCOTT, GEORGE W.	ANN	449	HOWARD D
SCOTT, GEORGE W.	BAL	378	13TH WAR
SCOTT, GIDEON	CEC	092	4TH E DI
SCOTT, GREENBURY	BAL	141	2ND DIST
SCOTT, HANNAH	CEC	087	4TH E DI
SCOTT, HANNAH	CEC	098	3RD E DI
SCOTT, HARRIET	BAL	358	13TH WAR
SCOTT, HARRIET	KEN	218	2ND DIST
SCOTT, HARRIETT	BAL	342	13TH WAR
SCOTT, HENRIETTA	BAL	179	6TH WARD
SCOTT, HENRY	BAL	082	15TH WAR
SCOTT, HENRY	BAL	050	1ST WARD
SCOTT, HENRY	BAL	293	1ST DIST
SCOTT, HENRY	CAR	103	NO TWP L
SCOTT, HENRY	KEN	294	3RD DIST
SCOTT, HENRY	SOM	394	BRINKLEY
SCOTT, HENRY H.	BAL	128	1ST WARD
SCOTT, HENRY R.	CAL	029	2ND DIST
SCOTT, HENRY T.	PRI	002	BLADENSB
SCOTT, HESTER-BLACK	CAR	110	NO TWP L
SCOTT, HEZEKIAH	BAL	035	9TH WARD
SCOTT, HORACE	BAL	175	6TH WARD
SCOTT, HORATIC	PRI	092	MARLBROU
SCOTT, HORATIO M.	PRI	091	MARLBROU
SCOTT, ISAAC	MGM	371	BERRYS D
SCOTT, ISAAC-BLACK	CAR	097	NO TWP L
SCOTT, ISAAC-BLACK	WOR	327	1ST E DI
SCOTT, ISAIAH	BAL	108	15TH WAR
SCOTT, JAMES	BAL	172	16TH WAR
SCOTT, JAMES	BAL	291	12TH WAR
SCOTT, JAMES	BAL	336	7TH WARD
SCOTT, JAMES	BAL	133	1ST WARD
SCOTT, JAMES	BAL	302	7TH WARD
SCOTT, JAMES	BAL	233	2ND WARD
SCOTT, JAMES	BAL	257	6TH WARD
SCOTT, JAMES	BAL	286	1ST DIST
SCOTT, JAMES	BAL	434	8TH WARD
SCOTT, JAMES	ANN	285	ANNAPOLI
SCOTT, JAMES	BAL	300	3RD WARD
SCOTT, JAMES	WOR	317	2ND E DI
SCOTT, JAMES	QUE	245	5TH E DI
SCOTT, JAMES	KEN	297	3RD DIST
SCOTT, JAMES	HAR	100	2ND DIST
SCOTT, JAMES	CHA	246	HILLTOP
SCOTT, JAMES	HAR	130	2ND DIST
SCOTT, JAMES	HAR	138	2ND DIST
SCOTT, JAMES	CEC	015	ELKTON 3
SCOTT, JAMES	BAL	039	4TH WARD
SCOTT, JAMES A.	HAR	140	2ND DIST
SCOTT, JAMES B.	BAL	131	1ST WARD
SCOTT, JAMES H.	CAR	080	NO TWP L
SCOTT, JAMES H.	QUE	244	5TH E DI
SCOTT, JAMES JR.	WOR	317	2ND E DI
SCOTT, JAMES M.	CEC	097	4TH E DI
SCOTT, JANE	BAL	014	18TH WAR
SCOTT, JANE	CHA	246	HILLTOP
SCOTT, JANE	BAL	121	18TH WAR
SCOTT, JANE	TAL	019	EASTON D
SCOTT, JANE	BAL	033	9TH WARD
SCOTT, JANE	BAL	151	5TH WARD
SCOTT, JANE	ANN	420	HOWARD D
SCOTT, JEREMIAH	CEC	092	4TH E DI
SCOTT, JESSE	TAL	017	EASTON D
SCOTT, JETSON	PRI	074	MARLBROU
SCOTT, JOANA	BAL	404	1ST DIST
SCOTT, JOANNA	CEC	113	4TH E DI
SCOTT, JOHANTHAN	BAL	251	17TH WAR
SCOTT, JOHN	BAL	207	17TH WAR
SCOTT, JOHN	CEC	100	3RD E DI
SCOTT, JOHN	CEC	201	6TH E DI
SCOTT, JOHN	BAL	243	20TH WAR
SCOTT, JOHN	CAR	111	NO TWP L
SCOTT, JOHN	CAL	055	3RD DIST
SCOTT, JOHN	FRE	193	5TH E DI
SCOTT, JOHN	CEC	010	ELKTON 3
SCOTT, JOHN	CEC	016	ELKTON 3
SCOTT, JOHN	BAL	217	6TH WARD
SCOTT, JOHN	BAL	169	1ST WARD
SCOTT, JOHN	BAL	282	2ND WARD
SCOTT, JOHN	BAL	144	1ST WARD
SCOTT, JOHN	BAL	423	8TH WARD
SCOTT, JOHN	BAL	164	11TH WAR
SCOTT, JOHN	BAL	022	15TH WAR
SCOTT, JOHN	BAL	067	1ST WARD
SCOTT, JOHN	BAL	190	17TH WAR
SCOTT, JOHN	PRI	080	QUEEN AN
SCOTT, JOHN	SOM	397	BRINKLEY
SCOTT, JOHN A.*	DOR	411	1ST DIST
SCOTT, JOHN B.	BAL	416	3RD WARD
SCOTT, JOHN B.	BAL	096	10TH WAR
SCOTT, JOHN C. C.	TAL	016	EASTON D
SCOTT, JOHN D.	SOM	444	DAMES QU
SCOTT, JOHN H.	BAL	097	5TH WARD
SCOTT, JOHN J.	PRI	001	BLADENSB
SCOTT, JOHN J.	WOR	254	1ST CENS
SCOTT, JOHN JR.	CEC	100	3RD E DI
SCOTT, JOHN M.	WAS	121	HAGERSTO
SCOTT, JOHN T.	BAL	422	1ST DIST
SCOTT, JOHN W.	BAL	279	2ND WARD
SCOTT, JOHN W.	PRI	006	BLADENSB
SCOTT, JOHN W.	FRE	202	5TH E DI
SCOTT, JOHN*	DOR	462	1ST DIST
SCOTT, JOSEP	BAL	133	1ST WARD
SCOTT, JOSEPH	BAL	279	2ND WARD
SCOTT, JOSEPH	CHA	269	ALLENS F
SCOTT, JOSEPH A.	BAL	142	1ST WARD
SCOTT, JOSEPH R.	BAL	012	15TH WAR
SCOTT, JOSEPH R.	BAL	165	1ST WARD
SCOTT, JOSHUA-BLACK	WOR	350	1ST E DI
SCOTT, JULIA MISS-	BAL	315	20TH WAR
SCOTT, JULIANNA	CEC	089	4TH E DI
SCOTT, JULIANNA	KEN	263	1ST DIST
SCOTT, JULIET A.	CAL	061	3RD DIST
SCOTT, KITTY	BAL	134	16TH WAR
SCOTT, LANCY	BAL	275	7TH WARD
SCOTT, LEAH	SOM	451	DAMES QU
SCOTT, LENA	BAL	062	4TH WARD
SCOTT, LEVI	BAL	180	6TH WARD
SCOTT, LEWIS	BAL	051	1ST WARD
SCOTT, LILA	ANN	355	3RD DIST
SCOTT, LLOYD	PRI	049	AQUASCO
SCOTT, LORENZO	PRI	005	BLADENSB
SCOTT, LOUIS	BAL	121	16TH WAR
SCOTT, LUCY	ANN	486	HOWARD D
SCOTT, MAJOR	CAL	045	3RD DIST
SCOTT, MANLOVE	CAR	120	NO TWP L
SCOTT, MARGARET	CEC	136	6TH E DI
SCOTT, MARGARET	MGM	385	ROCKERLE
SCOTT, MARGARET	CEC	089	4TH E DI
SCOTT, MARGARET	KEN	238	2ND DIST
SCOTT, MARGARET	BAL	299	20TH WAR
SCOTT, MARGARET	BAL	313	3RD WARD
SCOTT, MARGARET	BAL	101	15TH WAR
SCOTT, MARGARET	ALL	088	5TH E.D.
SCOTT, MARGARET A.	BAL	397	8TH WARD
SCOTT, MARGRET	BAL	067	1ST WARD
SCOTT, MARGRETT	CAR	147	NO TWP L
SCOTT, MARGRETT	CAR	147	NO TWP L
SCOTT, MARIA	BAL	319	20TH WAR
SCOTT, MARIA	ALL	045	10TH E.D
SCOTT, MARIA	BAL	132	16TH WAR
SCOTT, MARIA	KEN	297	3RD DIST
SCOTT, MARIAH-BLACK	WOR	327	1ST E DI
SCOTT, MARIETTA	BAL	142	11TH WAR
SCOTT, MARION	PRI	008	BLADENSB
SCOTT, MARLBOROUGH	BAL	409	1ST DIST
SCOTT, MARTHA	BAL	151	2ND DIST
SCOTT, MARTHA	HAR	089	2ND DIST
SCOTT, MARTHA A.	BAL	377	13TH WAR
SCOTT, MARY	BAL	340	13TH WAR
SCOTT, MARY	BAL	252	17TH WAR
SCOTT, MARY	HAR	083	2ND DIST
SCOTT, MARY	CEC	212	7TH E DI
SCOTT, MARY	CEC	211	7TH E DI
SCOTT, MARY	CEC	008	ELKTON 3
SCOTT, MARY	BAL	139	19TH WAR
SCOTT, MARY	BAL	167	19TH WAR
SCOTT, MARY	BAL	073	1ST WARD
SCOTT, MARY	BAL	118	15TH WAR
SCOTT, MARY	BAL	190	17TH WAR
SCOTT, MARY	BAL	105	10TH WAR
SCOTT, MARY	ANN	301	1ST DIST
SCOTT, MARY	BAL	397	8TH WARD
SCOTT, MARY	ANN	378	4TH DIST
SCOTT, MARY	ANN	465	HOWARD D
SCOTT, MARY	ANN	442	HOWARD D
SCOTT, MARY	BAL	257	12TH WAR
SCOTT, MARY	QUE	246	5TH E DI
SCOTT, MARY	WAS	162	HAGERSTO
SCOTT, MARY	WAS	163	HAGERSTO
SCOTT, MARY	WAS	179	BOONSBOR
SCOTT, MARY	ST	341	5TH E DI
SCOTT, MARY A.	BAL	388	8TH WARD
SCOTT, MARY A.	BAL	133	16TH WAR
SCOTT, MARY E.	BAL	338	3RD WARD
SCOTT, MARY E.	KEN	262	1ST DIST
SCOTT, MARY E.	MGM	442	CLARKSTR
SCOTT, MARY E.	WOR	219	4TH E DI
SCOTT, MARY E.	BAL	357	13TH WAR
SCOTT, MARY J.	WAS	166	1ST DIST
SCOTT, MATILDA	BAL	247	12TH WAR
SCOTT, MATTHEW	BAL	255	20TH WAR
SCOTT, MICHAEL	ANN	487	HOWARD D
SCOTT, MILLY	CAL	043	3RD DIST
SCOTT, MILTON	BAL	260	20TH WAR
SCOTT, MISS M.H.	FRE	198	5TH E DI
SCOTT, MOSES	BAL	357	8TH WARD
SCOTT, MRS.	BAL	203	11TH WAR
SCOTT, N.B.	WAS	121	HAGERSTO
SCOTT, NANCY	KEN	282	3RD DIST
SCOTT, NANCY	ANN	270	ANNAPOLI
SCOTT, NANCY	CEC	100	3RD E DI
SCOTT, NANCY	BAL	295	17TH WAR
SCOTT, NAPOLEON	KEN	213	2ND DIST
SCOTT, NATHAN	ANN	442	HOWARD D
SCOTT, NOAH	KEN	256	1ST DIST
SCOTT, OLIVER	ANN	470	HOWARD D
SCOTT, OTHO	HAR	094	2ND DIST
SCOTT, PAT	BAL	195	19TH WAR
SCOTT, PERRY	WAS	292	1ST DIST
SCOTT, PETER	WOR	254	1ST CENS
SCOTT, PETER	BAL	020	2ND DIST
SCOTT, PHILIP	BAL	312	7TH WARD
SCOTT, POLYOORE E.	PRI	065	NOTTINGH
SCOTT, PRICILLA	CHA	292	BOJANTOW
SCOTT, R. H. T.	BAL	151	1ST WARD
SCOTT, RACHAEL	ALL	070	5TH E.D.
SCOTT, RACHEL	ANN	394	8TH DIST
SCOTT, RACHEL	CEC	169	6TH E DI
SCOTT, REBECCA	CEC	005	ELKTON 3
SCOTT, REBECCA	CEC	096	4TH E DI
SCOTT, REBECCA	FRE	384	PETERSVI
SCOTT, REESE P.	BAL	059	15TH WAR
SCOTT, REZIN	BAL	175	6TH WARD
SCOTT, RICHARD	ALL	070	5TH E.D.
SCOTT, RICHARD	BAL	134	1ST WARD
SCOTT, RICHARD	BAL	416	1ST DIST
SCOTT, RICHARD	PRI	071	MARLBROU
SCOTT, RICHARD	QUE	252	5TH E DI
SCOTT, RICHARD J.	PRI	069	MARLBROU
SCOTT, ROBERT	QUE	244	5TH E DI
SCOTT, ROBERT	BAL	259	6TH WARD
SCOTT, ROBERT	BAL	335	7TH WARD

Name	County	Page	District
SCOTT, ROBERT	BAL	073	1ST WARD
SCOTT, ROBERT	BAL	364	3RD WARD
SCOTT, ROBERT	CEC	016	ELKTON 3
SCOTT, ROBERT	BAL	192	19TH WAR
SCOTT, ROBERT	HAR	106	2ND DIST
SCOTT, ROBERT	SOM	449	DAMES QU
SCOTT, ROSETTA	QUE	177	2ND E DI
SCOTT, ROSS	HAR	082	2ND DIST
SCOTT, SALLY	BAL	053	15TH WAR
SCOTT, SAM J.	BAL	155	1ST WARD
SCOTT, SAMUEL	BAL	199	11TH WAR
SCOTT, SAMUEL	BAL	196	11TH WAR
SCOTT, SAMUEL	BAL	058	1ST WARD
SCOTT, SAMUEL	BAL	005	1ST WARD
SCOTT, SAMUEL	BAL	352	1ST DIST
SCOTT, SAMUEL	ANN	308	1ST DIST
SCOTT, SAMUEL	ANN	280	ANNAPOLI
SCOTT, SAMUEL	ANN	333	2ND DIST
SCOTT, SAMUEL	ALL	110	5TH E.D.
SCOTT, SAMUEL	SOM	448	DAMES QU
SCOTT, SAMUEL	HAR	029	1ST DIST
SCOTT, SAMUEL	CEC	008	ELKTON 3
SCOTT, SAMUEL	CAR	166	NO TWP L
SCOTT, SAMUEL	BAL	251	20TH WAR
SCOTT, SAMUEL	CEC	213	7TH E DI
SCOTT, SAMUEL	CEC	214	7TH E DI
SCOTT, SAMUEL	CEC	187	7TH E DI
SCOTT, SAMUEL	CAR	095	NO TWP L
SCOTT, SAMUEL	KEN	291	3RD DIST
SCOTT, SAMUEL	KEN	285	3RD DIST
SCOTT, SAMUEL	SOM	471	TRAPPE D
SCOTT, SAMUEL J.	SOM	450	DAMES QU
SCOTT, SAMUEL W.	BAL	121	1ST WARD
SCOTT, SAMUEL W.	BAL	283	7TH WARD
SCOTT, SARAH	BAL	259	6TH WARD
SCOTT, SARAH	BAL	460	1ST DIST
SCOTT, SARAH	BAL	134	16TH WAR
SCOTT, SARAH	ANN	455	HOWARD D
SCOTT, SARAH A.	SOM	395	BRINKLEY
SCOTT, SARAH E.	SOM	401	BRINKLEY
SCOTT, SARAH J.	BAL	369	3RD WARD
SCOTT, SARAH L.	BAL	097	10TH WAR
SCOTT, SARAH-BLACK	CAR	097	NO TWP L
SCOTT, SERENA	BAL	014	18TH WAR
SCOTT, SHADRACH	BAL	181	16TH WAR
SCOTT, SIDNEY	BAL	416	1ST DIST
SCOTT, SIDNEY	WAS	296	1ST DIST
SCOTT, STEPHEN	WOR	293	9TH E DI
SCOTT, SUSAN	WAS	163	HAGERSTO
SCOTT, SUSAN	ANN	437	HOWARD D
SCOTT, SUSAN	CAR	065	NO TWP L
SCOTT, SUSANNA	ANN	437	HOWARD D
SCOTT, T. PARKIN	BAL	060	10TH WAR
SCOTT, THOASM H.	BAL	185	5TH DIST
SCOTT, THOMAS	BAL	122	16TH WAR
SCOTT, THOMAS	ANN	363	4TH DIST
SCOTT, THOMAS	BAL	422	1ST DIST
SCOTT, THOMAS	BAL	379	8TH WARD
SCOTT, THOMAS	ANN	331	2ND DIST
SCOTT, THOMAS	ALL	088	5TH E.D.
SCOTT, THOMAS	CEC	140	5TH E DI
SCOTT, THOMAS	CAR	166	NO TWP L
SCOTT, THOMAS J.	PRI	006	BLADENSB
SCOTT, THOMAS M.	BAL	420	1ST DIST
SCOTT, TOWSEND	BAL	194	11TH WAR
SCOTT, UPTON	CAR	316	1ST DIST
SCOTT, UZACH	CHA	246	HILLTOP
SCOTT, VILLA M.	CAL	016	1ST DIST
SCOTT, VIRGINIA	BAL	160	6TH WARD
SCOTT, VIRGINIA*	BAL	340	3RD WARD
SCOTT, W.	ALL	247	CUMBERLA
SCOTT, WALTER	HAR	088	2ND DIST
SCOTT, WHIT	WOR	254	1ST CENS
SCOTT, WILLAIM	BAL	193	19TH WAR
SCOTT, WILLAIM	BAL	373	13TH WAR
SCOTT, WILLIAM	CEC	018	ELKTON 3
SCOTT, WILLIAM	FRE	382	PETERSVI
SCOTT, WILLIAM	HAR	199	3RD DIST
SCOTT, WILLIAM	PRI	001	BLADENSB
SCOTT, WILLIAM	TAL	017	EASTON D
SCOTT, WILLIAM	TAL	042	EASTON D
SCOTT, WILLIAM	QUE	244	5TH E DI
SCOTT, WILLIAM	ST	341	5TH E DI
SCOTT, WILLIAM	ST	327	4TH E DI
SCOTT, WILLIAM	PRI	091	MARLBROU
SCOTT, WILLIAM	ANN	464	HOWARD D
SCOTT, WILLIAM	BAL	060	2ND DIST
SCOTT, WILLIAM	BAL	408	1ST DIST
SCOTT, WILLIAM	BAL	399	1ST DIST
SCOTT, WILLIAM	BAL	159	6TH WARD
SCOTT, WILLIAM	BAL	164	11TH WAR
SCOTT, WILLIAM	ALL	143	6TH E.D.
SCOTT, WILLIAM	ALL	109	5TH E.D.
SCOTT, WILLIAM	ANN	270	ANNAPOLI
SCOTT, WILLIAM	BAL	260	6TH WARD
SCOTT, WILLIAM	BAL	275	7TH WARD
SCOTT, WILLIAM	BAL	093	15TH WAR
SCOTT, WILLIAM	BAL	176	2ND DIST
SCOTT, WILLIAM	BAL	285	1ST DIST
SCOTT, WILLIAM	BAL	276	1ST DIST
SCOTT, WILLIAM C.	WOR	315	2ND E DI
SCOTT, WILLIAM H.	BAL	341	3RD WARD
SCOTT, WILLIAM J.	SOM	414	DUBLIN D
SCOTT, WILLIAM N.	CAR	106	NO TWP L
SCOTT, WILLIAM T.	CEC	090	4TH E DI
SCOTT, WILLIAMA.	FRE	050	FREDERIC
SCOTT, WILSON	MGM	371	BERRYS D
SCOTT, WINFIEL	HAR	063	1ST DIST
SCOTT, WINFIELD	HAR	076	BEL AIR
SCOTTE, MARY	CHA	239	HILLTOP
SCOTTEN, JAMES	CEC	065	1ST E DI
SCOTTEN, JAMES	CEC	063	1ST E DI
SCOTTEN, JOSEPH E.	HAR	001	1ST DIST
SCOTTEN, PHEBY	CEC	114	3RD E DI
SCOTTI, LEWIS F.*	BAL	031	4TH WARD
SCOTTON, ELLRIDGE	BAL	037	2ND DIST
SCOVIN, FRANCES	BAL	132	16TH WAR
SCOVINS, PHEBE	BAL	176	6TH WARD
SCOWDRICKS, THOMAS*	DOR	313	1ST DIST
SCRADER, HENRIETTA	BAL	010	9TH WARD
SCRADER, WILLIAM	FRE	170	5TH E DI
SCRAGAN, THOMAS	ANN	339	3RD DIST
SCRAGGANS, HENRY	BAL	389	1ST DIST
SCRAGGS, JAMES	CEC	148	PORT DUP
SCRAGGS, JANE	BAL	024	9TH WARD
SCRAPER, HENRY	HAR	063	1ST DIST
SCREAVES, RACHAEL	BAL	113	18TH WAR
SCREVNER, ALLEN	ANN	495	HOWARD D
SCRIBNER, CATHRINE	BAL	206	11TH WAR
SCRIBNER, ELLEN	BAL	461	1ST DIST
SCRIBNER, ELLEN-BLACK	CAR	086	NO TWP L
SCRIBNER, JOHN-BLACK	CAR	078	NO TWP L
SCRIBNER, PERRY-BLACK	CAR	086	NO TWP L
SCRIBNER, SARAH	BAL	089	15TH WAR
SCRIBNER, WILLIAM	BAL	092	15TH WAR
SCRIVEN, CHARLES J.	BAL	267	12TH WAR
SCRIVENER, CHARLES	CAL	060	3RD DIST
SCRIVENER, DINAH	CAL	044	3RD DIST
SCRIVENER, ELIZA S.	ANN	403	8TH DIST
SCRIVENER, GEORGE	CAL	044	3RD DIST
SCRIVENER, IWLLIAM	ANN	404	8TH DIST
SCRIVENER, JOHN H.	CAL	059	3RD DIST
SCRIVENER, S. W.	ANN	403	8TH DIST
SCRIVENER, SAMUEL	CAL	051	3RD DIST
SCRIVENER, SANDY	CAL	063	3RD DIST
SCRIVENER, WALTER	CAL	044	3RD DIST
SCRIVENER, WILLIAM	CAL	044	3RD DIST
SCRIVENER, WILLIAM B.	ANN	403	8TH DIST
SCRIVINER, THOMAS	CAL	039	2ND DIST
SCRIVNER, JOSHUA	ANN	503	HOWARD D
SCRIVNER, LEWIS	CAR	232	5TH DIST
SCRIVNER, WASHINGTON	ANN	496	HOWARD D
SCRIVNER, WILLIAM	BAL	208	17TH WAR
SCRIVNER, WILLIAM W.	ANN	503	HOWARD D
SCRIWINN, GEORGE	BAL	350	13TH WAR
SCROADER, JOHN	BAL	117	5TH WARD
SCROGGIN, HENRY	CHA	266	MIDDLETO
SCROGGINS, ANN	BAL	412	14TH WAR
SCROGGINS, CHARLES H.	BAL	412	14TH WAR
SCROGGINS, MATILDA	FRE	256	NEW MARK
SCROGGINS, NATHANIEL	ALL	208	CUMBERLA
SCROGGINS, NELSON	FRE	256	NEW MARK
SCROGGINS, SAMUEL	BAL	005	4TH WARD
SCROGGON, LUKE	CHA	218	ALLENS F
SCRONA, WILLIAM	BAL	445	8TH WARD
SCROONG, ELIZA	BAL	243	12TH WAR
SCROPE, CATHERINE	FRE	014	FREDERIC
SCRUIENER, HENRY *	CAL	024	2ND DIST
SCRUTON, JESSE*	TAL	061	EASTON D
SCRUTOR, JESSE*	TAL	061	EASTON D
SCUFFIELL, OTHO	PRI	031	VANSVILL
SCUFFINS, CHARLES H.	WAS	208	1ST DIST
SCUFNER, HENRY	BAL	272	7TH WARD
SCUGGS, ALFRED	ANN	477	HOWARD D
SCUGGS, CHARLES	ANN	441	HOWARD D
SCUGGS, MARY	PRI	020	VANSVILL
SCULLION, SIDNEY	BAL	032	9TH WARD
SCULLY, LAWRENCE	BAL	445	1ST DIST
SCULLY, MATIN	QUE	245	5TH E DI
SCULLY, TIMOTHY B.	BAL	064	4TH WARD
SCUNY, FALLIS*	DOR	409	1ST DIST
SCUYLER, FRED	BAL	261	20TH WAR
SCWARTY, PETER	BAL	051	18TH WAR
SCWARTZ, B.	BAL	356	13TH WAR
SCYAS, SAMUEL	FRE	337	MIDDLETO
SCYLER, CATHERINE*	BAL	391	3RD WARD
SEABOLD, J. C. H.	BAL	450	8TH WARD
SEABOLD, LAWRENCE	BAL	090	1ST WARD
SEABOR, ELIZAH	WAS	124	2ND DIST
SEABORN, MARY	PRI	122	PISCATAW
SEABOY, CATHARINE	BAL	457	14TH WAR
SEABREESE, RICHARD*	BAL	403	3RD WARD
SEABRIGHT, JOHN	BAL	170	16TH WAR
SEABRIGHT, SAMUEL	BAL	445	14TH WAR
SEABROOK, HENRY	BAL	138	2ND DIST
SEABROOK, THOMAS	BAL	040	9TH WARD
SEABROOK, WILLIAM	ANN	520	HOWARD D
SEABROOKS, JOSEPH	CAR	354	6TH DIST
SEABROOKS, WILLIAM C.	FRE	190	5TH E DI
SEABUR, ISREAL	BAL	276	7TH WARD
SEABURN, CHARLOTTE	PRI	053	AQUASCO
SEABURN, G.	PRI	050	AQUASCO
SEABURN, GEORGE N.	PRI	059	NOTTINGH
SEABURN, JAMES	PRI	085	QUEEN AN
SEABURN, KITTY	PRI	053	AQUASCO
SEABURN, MARY	PRI	057	AQUASCO
SEABURN, ROBERT	PRI	053	AQUASCO
SEABURY, SAMUEL	BAL	121	1ST WARD
SEABUS, CHARLES	BAL	468	14TH WAR
SEAFOURS, RICHARD	BAL	080	18TH WAR
SEAFUS, EMORY	BAL	126	18TH WAR
SEAFUS, SAMUEL	BAL	082	18TH WAR
SEAFUS, SARAH J.	BAL	136	18TH WAR
SEAFUS, SUSAN	BAL	066	18TH WAR
SEAFUSS, EVE	WAS	297	1ST DIST
SEAFUSS, ISAAC	WAS	298	1ST DIST
SEAGER, THOMAS	BAL	378	13TH WAR
SEAGGERS, NATHAN	CEC	175	7TH E DI
SEAGLE, JOHN G.B.	BAL	131	5TH WARD
SEAGMAN, ELIZABETH	WAS	242	CAVETOWN
SEAGMAN, JOHN	WAS	300	1ST DIST
SEAGMAN, MARY	WAS	286	1ST DIST
SEAGMAN, WILLIAM	WAS	300	1ST DIST
SEAKIN, GEORGE A.	BAL	343	3RD WARD
SEAL, THOMAS-BLACK	QUE	149	1ST E DI
SEALAIN, ELIZABETH *	BAL	295	20TH WAR
SEALEY, JAMES	BAL	054	1ST WARD
SEALEY, JANE	BAL	054	1ST WARD
SEALLAN, ELLEN	BAL	170	11TH WAR
SEAMAN, MARGARET	BAL	068	1ST WARD
SEAMAN, MARIAH	WAS	050	2ND SUBD
SEAMAN, RACHEL	BAL	063	4TH WARD
SEAMAN, T.	BAL	007	4TH WARD
SEAMAN, WILLIAM	BAL	231	17TH WAR
SEAMAN, WILLIAM	WAS	050	2ND SUBD
SEAMICK, HENRY	BAL	126	18TH WAR
SEAMORE, JOHN	KEN	219	2ND DIST
SEANDER, PETER	CAR	278	7TH DIST
SEANER, SARAH	BAL	303	12TH WAR
SEAPOLT, NICHOLAS	FRE	177	5TH E DI
SEAPOLT, PETER JR.	FRE	175	5TH E DI
SEAPOLT, PETER SR.	FRE	200	5TH E DI
SEARALT, MATHIAS *	WAS	138	2ND DIST
SEARCEY, ELIZABETH	BAL	175	11TH WAR
SEARCH, GRIFFITH M.	MGM	353	BERRYS D
SEARES, EDWORD	HAR	145	3RD DIST
SEARKEY, WILLIAM	ALL	106	5TH E.D.
SEARL, INGEBE	ALL	248	CUMBERLA
SEARLE, JAMES	BAL	149	1ST WARD
SEARLE, JULIA*	BAL	062	4TH WARD
SEARLES, JAMES	ANN	402	8TH DIST
SEARLEY, JANE	BAL	406	3RD WARD
SEARLY, JANE	BAL	080	1ST WARD
SEARS, AMANDA	CEC	171	6TH E DI
SEARS, ANNE M.*	BAL	115	15TH WAR
SEARS, BENJAMIN	CAL	020	2ND DIST
SEARS, CAREY C.	WOR	342	1ST E DI
SEARS, CATHARINE	ANN	458	HOWARD D
SEARS, DANIEL	ALL	085	5TH E.D.
SEARS, EDWARD	TAL	112	ST MICHA
SEARS, EELIZETH	TAL	117	ST MICHA
SEARS, ELIZABET	CAL	054	3RD DIST
SEARS, GEORGE	CEC	210	7TH E DI
SEARS, GEORGE T.	BAL	069	18TH WAR
SEARS, H. E.	BAL	058	10TH WAR
SEARS, HENRY	ANN	490	HOWARD D
SEARS, HENRY	CAL	063	3RD DIST
SEARS, HIRAM	BAL	312	7TH WARD
SEARS, JAMES	QUE	252	5TH E DI
SEARS, JESSE	CAL	053	3RD DIST
SEARS, JOHN	WOR	255	1ST CENS
SEARS, JOHN S.	TAL	111	ST MICHA
SEARS, JULIA	BAL	347	1ST DIST
SEARS, LEVI	CEC	176	7TH E DI
SEARS, MARIA	BAL	073	10TH WAR
SEARS, MARTHA A.*	BAL	084	4TH WARD
SEARS, MARY	BAL	070	15TH WAR
SEARS, MARY	SOM	382	BRINKLEY
SEARS, ROBERT H.-BLACK	BAL	225	2ND WARD
SEARS, SARAH E.	HAR	185	3RD DIST
SEARS, SYDNEY	CAL	051	3RD DIST
SEARS, THOMAS	CAL	050	3RD DIST
SEARS, THOMAS	BAL	069	18TH WAR
SEARS, THOMAS	FRE	391	PETERSVI
SEARS, THOMAS	BAL	054	9TH WARD
SEARS, THOMAS	BAL	102	15TH WAR
SEARS, TOMSY	CAL	041	3RD DIST
SEARS, WILLIAM	CAR	372	9TH DIST
SEARS, WILLIAM	FRE	182	5TH E DI
SEARS, WILLIAM	HAR	157	3RD DIST
SEARS, WILLIAM	CEC	143	7TH E DI
SEARS, WILLIAM	MGM	390	ROCKERLE
SEARS, WILLIAM	BAL	238	6TH WARD
SEARS, WILLIAM	ANN	396	8TH DIST
SEARS, WILLIAM	ANN	301	1ST DIST
SEARS, WILLIAM	SOM	376	BRINKLEY
SEARSON, SAMUEL	CEC	207	7TH E DI
SEARY, JEREMIAH	BAL	361	3RD WARD
SEASE, MARY	ALL	260	CUMBERLA
SEASNOPS, HENRY	ALL	138	6TH E.D.
SEASOR, CHARLES	BAL	249	1ST DIST
SEATHERMAN, CHRISTOPHER *	ALL	154	6TH E.D.
SEATON, JACOB	BAL	398	3RD WARD
SEATON, JAMES	QUE	173	2ND E DI
SEATON, SARAH	QUE	173	2ND E DI
SEATON,PAMELA	QUE	173	2ND E DI
SEATS, LOUIS	ALL	030	2ND E.D.
SEAVALT, MATHIAS *	WAS	138	2ND DIST
SEAVIS, SARAH	TAL	118	ST MICHA
SEAWARD, JOHN	BAL	132	1ST WARD
SEBALER, FREDERICK	BAL	060	1ST WARD
SEBBLE, MARY .A	BAL	177	2ND WARD
SEBEL, JOHN	BAL	148	19TH WAR
SEBER, MARGARET	BAL	166	11TH WAR
SEBERGER, FRANCIS	BAL	210	6TH DIST
SEBIGEL, CATHARINE	BAL	072	1ST WARD
SEBORNS, JOHN	WAS	139	2ND DIST
SEBOSEA, WILLIAM	BAL	376	13TH WAR
SEBUSBAY, RADOIUS	ALL	170	6TH E.D.
SECCOMBE, THOMAS	BAL	230	6TH WARD
SECHRIST, ABRAHAM	BAL	438	1ST DIST
SECHRIST, DAVID	CAR	399	2ND DIST
SECKE, JOSEPH *	BAL	303	12TH WAR
SECKEE, DOROTHEA	BAL	312	20TH WAR
SECKEL, JOSEPH	BAL	334	7TH WARD
SECKEY, ALEXANDER	BAL	148	1ST WARD
SECOMPT, JAMES	WOR	300	SNOW HIL
SECOMPTS, WILLIAM *	WOR	305	SNOW HIL
SECOUR, GIDEON	WAS	234	1ST DIST
SECOUR, GIDEON	WAS	234	1ST DIST
SECOUR, MATILDA A.V.	WAS	232	1ST DIST
SECOUR, WILLIAM	WAS	231	1ST DIST
SECTIVEIN, MARY	BAL	166	11TH WAR
SECTS, HERNY	BAL	080	1ST WARD
SEDENHAM, JESSE A.*	TAL	010	EASTON D
SEDENHAM, NANCY*	TAL	060	EASTON D
SEDGEN, JOSHUA	TAL	105	ST MICHA
SEDGEWICK, JOSEPH	FRE	267	NEW MARK
SEDGEWICK, M.	BAL	237	20TH WAR
SEDGMAN, JOHN	WAS	195	1ST DIST
SEDGWICK, AMY	FRE	060	FREDERIC
SEDGWICK, CHARLOTTE	BAL	300	12TH WAR
SEDGWICK, DANIEL	BAL	253	20TH WAR
SEDGWICK, ELIZA ANN	BAL	001	15TH WAR
SEDGWICK, FRANK	BAL	157	2ND DIST
SEDGWICK, HESTER	MGM	340	CLARKSBU
SEDGWICK, HORACE	MGM	370	BERRYS D
SEDGWICK, JARRIT	MGM	362	BERRYS D
SEDGWICK, JOHN	BAL	301	17TH WAP
SEDGWICK, SUSAN J.	BAL	001	15TH WAP
SEDGWICK, WILLIAM	CEC	033	CHESAPEA
SEDLER, GEORGE	BAL	376	13TH WAR
SEDLER, GEORGE	BAL	208	2ND WARD
SEDONS, LEAH	CAR	285	7TH DIST
SEDORILS, CATHERINE	BAL	327	3RD WARD
SEDRICK, LYDIA-MULATTO	FRE	418	8TH E DI
SEDRICK, PETER	WAS	143	2ND DIST
SEDRICKS, ELLEN	BAL	030	9TH WARD
SEDRICKS, OLIVER	FRE	099	FREDERIC
SEDWICK, ELIZA	CAL	008	1ST DIST
SEDWICK, JOHN A.	CAL	009	1ST DIST
SEDWICKS, JOHN C.	CAL	003	1ST DIST
SEE, EDWARD*	TAL	059	EASTON D
SEE, ELIZA A.-BLACK	BAL	217	2ND WARD
SEE, ELLEN	BAL	237	12TH WAR
SEE, JOHN*	TAL	007	EASTON D
SEE, WILLIAM T.*	TAL	021	EASTON D
SEE, WILLIAM*	DOR	424	1ST DIST
SEEALD, CHARLES	BAL	076	18TH WAR
SEEBOCH, HENRY	BAL	187	16TH WAR
SEEBREESE, JOHN	SOM	525	BARREN C
SEEBREESE, JOHN*	SOM	523	BARREN C
SEEBREESE, THOMAS	SOM	527	QUANTICO
SEEBREESE, WILLIAM	SOM	496	SALISBUR
SEEBRIGHT, JAMES	BAL	103	18TH WAR
SEEBROOK, JOHN	FRE	023	FREDERIC
SEECH, MARY A. F.*	BAL	096	10TH WAR
SEEDES, CYRUS	CEC	079	NORTHEAS
SEEDS, JAMES	BAL	060	18TH WAR
SEEDS, S.C.	BAL	160	1ST WARD
SEEGAR, BENJAMIN	QUE	226	4TH E DI
SEEGAR, ELIZABETH-BLACK	QUE	139	1ST E DI
SEEGAR, JAMES	QUE	211	3RD E DI
SEEGAR, JOHN	QUE	126	1ST E DI
SEEGAR, JOSEPH-BLACK	QUE	134	1ST E DI
SEEGAR, PHILIPPINA	BAL	333	13TH WAR
SEEGAR, RICHARD	QUE	138	1ST E DI
SEEGAR, SUSANNA	QUE	226	4TH E DI
SEEGAR, THOMAS	QUE	206	3RD E DI
SEEGROOPE, JOHN	BAL	021	2ND DIST

SEEK, ADAM BAL 384 1ST DIST
SEELING, CHARLES BAL 070 2ND DIST
SEELS, THOMAS-BLACK QUE 124 1ST E DI
SEEMAN, ANN HAR 068 1ST DIST
SEEMAN, CHRISTIAN FRE 031 FREDERIC
SEENEY, JAMES-BLACK QUE 200 3RD E DI
SEENEY, JOSHUA G. QUE 177 2ND E DI
SEENEY, REBECCA A.-BLACK QUE 164 2ND E DI
SEENEY, SAMUEL QUE 176 2ND E DI
SEENY, DENNIS PRI 099 SPALDING
SEENY, JOHSUA-BLACK QUE 192 3RD E DI
SEEP, CATHARINE BAL 288 12TH WAR
SEERS, MARY BAL 433 14TH WAR
SEESE, CHARLES BAL 327 3RD WARD
SEETS, GEORGE BAL 052 18TH WAR
SEEVER, HENRY BAL 227 19TH WAR
SEFFLER, PETER BAL 010 9TH WARD
SEFTEN, CHARLES FRE 342 MIDDLETO
SEFTON, JOHN* BAL 089 10TH WAR
SEFUS, HENRY TAL 074 EASTON T
SEGABCOSE, WILLIAM CAR 238 UNION TO
SEGAFOORE, ANN FRE 409 JEFFERSO
SEGAFOOS, HENRY FRE 378 PETERSVI
SEGAN, ANN* BAL 341 3RD WARD
SEGAN, BARBARA BAL 397 14TH WAR
SEGAN, JAMES-BLACK BAL 217 2ND WARD
SEGAR, FREDERICK J. BAL 361 3RD WARD
SEGARS, FRANCIS BAL 268 7TH WARD
SEGARS, RUBIN CEC 094 4TH E DI
SEGER, JOSEPH KEN 306 3RD DIST
SEGESTER, CATHARINE BAL 236 6TH WARD
SEGLER, ANN BAL 237 12TH WAR
SEGLER, JOHN ALL 144 6TH E.D.
SEGLER, OTHO ALL 126 4TH E.D.
SEGLER, PHILIP JR. ALL 124 4TH E.D.
SEGLER, WILLIAM ALL 121 4TH E.D.
SEGNOR, JOSEPH BAL 371 8TH WARD
SEHLEY, FREDERICK A. FRE 033 FREDERIC
SEHLEY, GEORGE WAS 133 HAGERSTO
SEHOLAR, HENRY ALL 104 5TH E.D.
SEHRINER, JOHN CAR 377 2ND DIST
SEIB, LEWIS BAL 272 2ND WARD
SEIBART, ADAM BAL 067 1ST WARD
SEIBART, GENET BAL 067 1ST WARD
SEIBER, JOSEPH PRI 025 VANSVILL
SEIBERS, DANIEL WAS 097 2ND DIST
SEIBERT, CATHARINE WAS 134 2ND DIST
SEIBERT, ERNEST BAL 102 1ST WARD
SEIBERT, GEORGE WAS 130 2ND DIST
SEIBERT, GEORGE FRE 050 FREDERIC
SEIBERT, HENRY BAL 033 9TH WARD
SEIBERT, JOHN BAL 327 3RD WARD
SEIBERT, JOHN WAS 134 2ND DIST
SEIBERT, JOSEPH WAS 109 2ND DIST
SEIBERT, MARY E. WAS 302 1ST DIST
SEIBERT, MICHAEL WAS 302 1ST DIST
SEIBERT, MICHAL WAS 134 2ND DIST
SEIBLE, ANDREW BAL 248 2ND WARD
SEIBLE, HENRY BAL 030 1ST WARD
SEIBLE, JOHN BAL 093 1ST WARD
SEIBLER, PETER * BAL 038 18TH WAR
SEIBRET, ADAM BAL 095 18TH WAR
SEICK, A.G. ALL 242 CUMBERLA
SEIDENSTRICKER, FREDERIC BAL 222 6TH WARD
SEIDENSTRICKER, JOHN BAL 025 1ST WARD
SEIDER, FREDERICK* BAL 031 4TH WARD
SEIFERD, FRANCIS CAR 331 MANCHEST
SEIFERT, HARRIETT CAR 330 MANCHEST
SEIFERT, LANHART BAL 104 2ND DIST
SEIGEL, SAMUEL BAL 114 5TH WARD
SEIGERMAN, HENRY BAL 222 2ND WARD
SEIGERT, JOHN BAL 103 1ST WARD
SEIGMUND, HERMAN BAL 246 6TH WARD
SEIGNAN, WILLIAM BAL 043 1ST WARD
SEIGNHARDT, JOHN BAL 236 2ND WARD
SEIK, ISAAC BAL 236 2ND WARD
SEIKER, EDWARD A. BAL 193 6TH WARD
SEILAR, EIAHART WAS 155 2ND DIST
SEILHORST, CASPER BAL 068 1ST WARD
SEILOR, GOOFREY BAL 109 5TH WARD
SEIM, HENRY BAL 104 5TH WARD
SEIMET, MARGARET BAL 097 1ST WARD
SEIMON, CAROLINE BAL 123 16TH WAR
SEINBERG, JACOB BAL 105 1ST WARD
SEIP, CHRISTINA BAL 071 1ST WARD
SEIP, EDWARD BAL 273 2ND WARD
SEIP, JOHN F. BAL 272 2ND WARD
SEIPLE, B. BAL 235 17TH WAR
SEIPP, CHRISTOPHER BAL 004 15TH WAR
SEIPP, CONRAD BAL 054 2ND DIST
SEIPP, JOHN BAL 225 17TH WAR
SEIPP, MOORY E. BAL 054 2ND DIST
SEIPPLE, HENRY BAL 268 2ND WARD
SEIPT, LAURA BAL 227 2ND WARD
SEISE, ADAM BAL 087 1ST WARD
SEISE, JACOB BAL 232 17TH WAR
SEISMAN, HENRY BAL 222 17TH WAR
SEISS, CAROLINE FRE 157 10TH E D
SEISS, DANIEL FRE 181 5TH E DI
SEISS, JOHN FRE 185 5TH E DI
SEISS, JOSEPH ALL 208 CUMBERLA
SEISS, JOSHUA FRE 194 5TH E DI
SEISS, MARY BAL 083 1ST WARD
SEISS, NATHANIEL FRE 157 10TH E D
SEISS, SAMUEL FRE 188 5TH E DI
SEISS, SOPHIA FRE 150 10TH E D
SEITER, GEORGE BAL 235 2ND WARD
SEITS, WILLIAM CAR 337 6TH DIST
SEITZ, C. BAL 239 20TH WAR
SEITZ, CHARLOTTE BAL 026 1ST WARD
SEITZ, JOHN BAL 094 1ST WARD
SEITZS, EDWARD BAL 176 2ND WARD
SEKERMAN, JOHN BAL 208 6TH DIST
SEKINFELDER, ANN* BAL 269 20TH WAR
SEKOFRISKE, FRANK BAL 256 17TH WAR
SELAR, CHARLES BAL 290 17TH WAR
SELASINGER, DAVID FRE 032 FREDERIC
SELBY, ALLAN MGM 322 CRACKLIN
SELBY, ALLEN MGM 385 ROCKERLE
SELBY, ANDREW M. WOR 217 4TH E DI
SELBY, ANN A. MGM 384 ROCKERLE
SELBY, ASA WOR 199 8TH E DI
SELBY, BOB WOR 278 BERLIN 1
SELBY, CAROLINE CAR 227 5TH DIST
SELBY, CATHRINE WOR 324 1ST E DI
SELBY, CHARITY WOR 310 2ND E DI
SELBY, COVINGTON * WOR 177 6TH E DI
SELBY, EBBEN WOR 179 6TH E DI
SELBY, ELIZA S. WOR 227 4TH E DI
SELBY, ELIZABETH WOR 241 1ST CENS
SELBY, ELIZABETH ANN 510 HOWARD D
SELBY, ENOCH ANN 502 HOWARD D
SELBY, GEORGE W. BAL 047 15TH WAR
SELBY, HANDY M. WOR 217 4TH E DI
SELBY, HENRY PRI 062 NOTTINGH
SELBY, HENRY ANN 502 HOWARD D
SELBY, HENRY SOM 423 PRINCESS
SELBY, ISAAC WOR 210 4TH E DI
SELBY, ISAAC WOR 348 1ST E DI
SELBY, JACOB WOR 277 BERLIN 1
SELBY, JAMES WOR 300 SNOW HIL
SELBY, JAMES P. KEN 297 3RD DIST
SELBY, JAOCB-BLACK WOR 322 1ST E DI
SELBY, JENNY-BLACK WOR 322 1ST E DI
SELBY, JESSE WOR 276 BERLIN 1
SELBY, JOHN SOM 421 PRINCESS
SELBY, JOHN E. MGM 355 BERRYS D
SELBY, JOHN H. PRI 071 MARLBROU
SELBY, JOHN N. HAR 180 3RD DIST
SELBY, JOHN W. WOR 214 4TH E DI
SELBY, JOHN W. WOR 319 1ST E DI
SELBY, JOHN-BLACK WOR 328 1ST E DI
SELBY, JOHNSEY CAR 213 5TH DIST
SELBY, JOSHUA PRI 041 VANSVILL
SELBY, JSOHUA-BLACK WOR 172 6TH E DI
SELBY, LEAH WOR 323 1ST E DI
SELBY, LEMUEL WOR 242 1ST CENS
SELBY, LEVIN WOR 309 2ND E DI
SELBY, LEVIN SOM 426 PRINCESS
SELBY, M.J. PRI 052 AQUASCO
SELBY, MARDICA CAR 215 5TH DIST
SELBY, MARY BAL 232 17TH WAR
SELBY, MARY WOR 276 BERLIN 1
SELBY, MARY J. WOR 227 4TH E DI
SELBY, NAKAN MGM 404 ROCKERLE
SELBY, NANCY BAL 073 15TH WAR
SELBY, NANCY-BLACK WOR 323 1ST E DI
SELBY, NANTZY BAL 317 3RD WARD
SELBY, PARKER WOR 314 2ND E DI
SELBY, PATTY WOR 278 BERLIN 1
SELBY, PETER WOR 278 BERLIN 1
SELBY, PETER WOR 322 1ST E DI
SELBY, PURNELL WOR 298 9TH E DI
SELBY, PURNELL WOR 306 2ND E DI
SELBY, RACHEL ANN 506 HOWARD D
SELBY, REBECCA ANN 488 HOWARD D
SELBY, REBECCA BAL 191 6TH WARD
SELBY, RICHARD BAL 191 6TH WARD
SELBY, RICHARD ALL 026 2ND E.D.
SELBY, RICHARD CAR 227 5TH DIST
SELBY, RICHARD JR. MGM 397 ROCKERLE
SELBY, SAMUEL PRI 048 AQUASCO
SELBY, SARAH A. BAL 073 15TH WAR
SELBY, THOMAS PRI 053 AQUASCO
SELBY, THOMAS WOR 241 1ST CENS
SELBY, VIOLETT WOR 304 SNOW HIL
SELBY, VIRGINIA PRI 048 AQUASCO
SELBY, WAISSA-BLACK WOR 176 6TH E DI
SELBY, WELTHY WOR 242 1ST CENS
SELBY, WESLEY CAL 018 1ST DIST
SELBY, WILLAIM MGM 358 BERRYS D
SELBY, WILLIAM WOR 243 1ST CENS
SELBY, WILLIAM WOR 302 SNOW HIL
SELBY, WILLIAM H. MGM 397 ROCKERLE
SELBY, WILLIAM R. MGM 429 CLARKSTR
SELBY, ZACOK WOR 243 1ST CENS
SELBY, ZADOCK BAL 061 15TH WAR
SELBY, ZADOCK P. WOR 313 2ND E DI
SELBY, ZADOCK T. WOR 299 SNOW HIL
SELDNER, ABRAHAM BAL 112 10TH WAR
SELEMAN, CAROLINE ANN 515 HOWARD D
SELEVAGE, FREDERICK BAL 145 1ST WARD
SELHARTY, JOHN CAR 138 NO TWP L
SELICKMEN, SIMON BAL 177 2ND WARD
SELIKANAM, HANNAH BAL 245 2ND WARD
SELIMAN, HERNY ALL 146 6TH E.D.
SELL, DANIEL CAR 319 1ST DIST
SELL, EDWIN FRE 292 WOODSBOR
SELL, EMANUEL CAR 411 2ND DIST
SELL, JACOB CAR 411 2ND DIST
SELL,PETER FRE 171 5TH E DI
SELLAN, CHARLES BAL 232 2ND WARD
SELLAN, JOHANNAS BAL 232 2ND WARD
SELLARS, ELIABETH FRE 187 5TH E DI
SELLARS, JACOB BAL 399 14TH WAR
SELLER, CATHARINE CAR 331 MANCHEST
SELLER, CHRISTINE BAL 214 19TH WAR
SELLER, FRED BAL 270 12TH WAR
SELLER, JOHN BAL 174 2ND DIST
SELLER, JOHN BAL 214 19TH WAR
SELLER, JOHN BAL 224 19TH WAR
SELLERS, CATHERINE BAL 307 20TH WAR
SELLERS, ELIZABETH BAL 178 11TH WAR
SELLERS, EMANUEL BAL 152 19TH WAR
SELLERS, GEORGE WAS 027 2ND SUBD
SELLERS, GEORGE JR. CAR 355 6TH DIST
SELLERS, GEORGE SR. CAR 355 6TH DIST
SELLERS, HARVEY BAL 181 11TH WAR
SELLERS, HENRY F. PRI 032 VANSVILL
SELLERS,.JACOB BAL 129 16TH WAR
SELLERS, JACOB CAR 357 6TH DIST
SELLERS, JACOB CAR 330 MANCHEST
SELLERS, JACOB BAL 152 19TH WAR
SELLERS, JACOB C. BAL 153 19TH WAR
SELLERS, JAMES E. DOR 451 1ST DIST
SELLERS, JOHN CAR 351 6TH DIST
SELLERS, JOHN BAL 238 20TH WAR
SELLERS, JOHN BAL 255 1ST DIST
SELLERS, MARY CAR 254 3RD DIST
SELLERS, NAOMI BAL 319 12TH WAR
SELLERS, PETER CAR 352 6TH DIST
SELLERS, PETER CAR 292 7TH DIST
SELLERS, PETERS CAR 333 MANCHEST
SELLERS, SAMUEL CAR 351 6TH DIST
SELLERS, THOMAS DOR 451 1ST DIST
SELLEY, REBECCA WOR 310 2ND E DI
SELLMAN, ALEXANDER BAL 341 13TH WAR
SELLMAN, ALFRED ANN 316 1ST DIST
SELLMAN, BENJAMIN ANN 436 HOWARD D
SELLMAN, DAVDI BAL 311 12TH WAR
SELLMAN, ELISA BAL 003 18TH WAR
SELLMAN, ELIZA CAR 219 5TH DIST
SELLMAN, GASSAWY MGM 422 MEDLEY 3
SELLMAN, GEORGE BAL 061 1ST WARD
SELLMAN, HENRY CAR 358 9TH DIST
SELLMAN, JOHN ANN 408 8TH DIST
SELLMAN, JOHN H. ANN 316 1ST DIST
SELLMAN, JOHN S. ANN 294 1ST DIST
SELLMAN, JSOHUA CAR 374 9TH DIST
SELLMAN, LOYD CAR 370 9TH DIST
SELLMAN, MARTHA CAR 219 5TH DIST
SELLMAN, MARY ALL 223 CUMBERLA
SELLMAN, MARY C. CAR 287 7TH DIST
SELLMAN, MARY T. ANN 447 HOWARD D
SELLMAN, RICHARD ANN 309 1ST DIST
SELLMAN, RUFUS FRE 248 NEW MARK
SELLMAN, SARAH E. ANN 435 HOWARD D
SELLMAN, WALTER ANN 504 HOWARD D
SELLMAN, WILLIAM BAL 195 11TH WAR
SELLMAN,R OBERT MGM 431 CLARKSTR
SELLY, JOHN T.* BAL 071 4TH WARD
SELLY, MARANDA CAR 375 9TH DIST
SELLY, MICHAEL BAL 174 11TH WAR
SELLY, WILLIAM CAR 393 2ND DIST
SELLY, Z. BAL 205 2ND WARD
SELLZNER, JOHN BAL 278 2ND WARD
SELMAKER, HENRY BAL 164 1ST WARD
SELMAN, ELLEN BAL 416 1ST DIST
SELMAN, GEORGE MGM 429 CLARKSTR
SELMAN, JOHN J.M. MGM 424 MEDLEY 3
SELMAN, LOUIS BAL 325 1ST DIST
SELMAN, LUDWICK BAL 334 1ST DIST
SELMAN, THOMAS BAL 415 1ST DIST
SELMAN, WILLIAM MGM 431 CLARKSTR
SELMAN, WILLIAM D. MGM 423 MEDLEY 3
SELOR, JOHN BAL 091 5TH WARD
SELRAY, ANN BAL 278 12TH WAR
SELSAN, CATHARINE FRE 314 MIDDLETO
SELSAN, DAVID * FRE 325 MIDDLETO
SELSBY, JULIA BAL 435 14TH WAR
SELSOM, ELLEN FRE 403 JEFFERSO
SELT, JAMES M. TAL 111 ST MICHA
SELT, PARNELL C. FRE 009 FREDERIC
SELTNER, HENRIETTA BAL 222 6TH WARD
SELTYER, MARY BAL 312 20TH WAR
SELTZER, ELIZABETH BAL 006 9TH WARD
SELTZER, LEWIS BAL 304 20TH WAR
SELTZER, MARY E. BAL 292 7TH WARD
SELTZER, NICHOLAS FRE 167 EMMITTSB
SELVAGE, ELIZABETH BAL 188 11TH WAR
SELVAGE, GEORGE BAL 344 13TH WAR
SELVAGE, THOMAS BAL 033 4TH WARD
SELVAGE, WILLIAM BAL 136 5TH WARD
SELVEY, JOSEPH PRI 039 VANSVILL
SELVEY, SARAH BAL 045 4TH WARD
SELVY, JOHN S. BAL 053 4TH WARD
SELWAY, ROBERT BAL 227 19TH WAR
SELWY, HAMILTON FRE 234 BUCKEYST
SEMAN, MARY BAL 142 11TH WAR
SEMANS, GEORGE KEN 291 3RD DIST
SEMANS, MENA KEN 289 3RD DIST
SEMANS, PHILIP KEN 261 1ST DIST
SEMANS, RICHARD KEN 292 3RD DIST
SEMANS, SARAH KEN 218 2ND DIST
SEMANS, WILLIAM KEN 291 3RD DIST
SEMAR, SARAH CAR 100 NO TWP L
SEMELLER, ALBRIGHT BAL 124 18TH WAR
SEMERING, C. BAL 252 12TH WAR
SEMERING, DANIEL BAL 125 18TH WAR
SEMERING, PHILIP* BAL 029 4TH WARD
SEMIN, ELIZABETH BAL 199 2ND WARD
SEMKEN, HENRY BAL 356 13TH WAR
SEMKINS, JOHN ST 296 2ND E DI
SEMLER, JACOB WAS 147 HAGERSTO
SEMMES, JAMES * ALL 086 5TH E.D.
SEMMES, JANE PRI 070 MARLBROU
SEMMES, SUSAN PRI 070 MARLBROU
SEMMLER, CONRADT WAS 129 HAGERSTO
SEMMON, CHRISTOPHER ALL 169 6TH E.D.
SEMONE, WILLAIM BAL 147 16TH WAR
SEMOOR, L. BAL 134 5TH WARD
SEMOUR, J.H. ALL 217 CUMBERLA
SEMOUT, FREDERICK BAL 283 17TH WAR
SEMPSON, MOSES M.* DOR 375 1ST DIST
SENACKS, HENRY BAL 245 20TH WAR
SENAMS,ALFRED BAL 107 1ST WARD
SENATE, THOMAS ALL 170 6TH E.D.
SENBAUGH, JOHN J. HAR 102 2ND DIST
SENBERT, GOLBERT BAL 106 1ST WARD
SENCE, SOLOMON BAL 194 5TH DIST
SENCY, ROBERT CAR 139 NO TWP L
SEND, WILLIAM KEN 241 2ND DIST
SENDER, ANTON BAL 237 2ND WARD
SENEER, MICHAEL * ALL 119 5TH E.D.
SENEIDER, VALENTINE BAL 254 2ND WARD
SENEILL, ANDREW FRE 010 FREDERIC
SENEILL, MARGARET FRE 010 FREDERIC
SENER, JOSEPH CAR 362 9TH DIST
SENEY, ANNE BAL 101 15TH WAR
SENFEL, RICHARD FRE 013 FREDERIC
SENFT, HENRY BAL 182 19TH WAR
SENGER, CATHARINE WAS 275 RIDGEVIL
SENGER, DANIEL WAS 271 1ST DIST
SENGER, GEORGE WAS 275 RIDGEVIL
SENGER, REBECCA WAS 273 RIDGEVIL
SENLINE, NATHAN* BAL 073 4TH WARD
SENNA, JOSEPH BAL 023 1ST WARD
SENNA, THOMAS BAL 252 2ND WARD
SENNETT, CAHERINE QUE 135 1ST E DI
SENNETT, JAMES B. QUE 135 1ST E DI
SENNETT, SOLOMON D. QUE 161 2ND E DI
SENNETT, WILLIAM WAS 122 2ND DIST
SENNETT, WILLIAM J. QUE 161 2ND E DI
SENNRORE, JULIAN* DOR 468 1ST DIST
SENNY, LEVIN * SOM 436 PRINCESS
SENPLEY, JOHN M. BAL 070 1ST WARD
SENSANBAUGH, JOHN FRE 361 CATOCTIN
SENSANBAUSE, MAGDALIN FRE 361 CATOCTIN
SENSENAY, JANE * BAL 204 6TH WARD
SENSENEY, CHARLES FRE 428 8TH E DI
SENSENY, ANN CAR 390 2ND DIST
SENSENY, ANNA CAR 390 2ND DIST
SENSENY, HANSON CAR 383 2ND DIST
SENSENY, JAMES CAR 390 2ND DIST
SENSENY, PETER CAR 389 2ND DIST
SENSENY, WASHINGTON CAR 390 2ND DIST
SENSKY, MAXE * ALL 143 6TH E.D.
SENSLEY, CATHERINE FRE 023 FREDERIC
SENTE, JOSHUA* BAL 026 4TH WARD
SENTER, ALVIN MGM 394 ROCKERLE
SENTER, JOSEPH KEN 269 1ST DIST
SENTER, JOSEPH B. BAL 171 1ST WARD
SENTER, STEPHEN BAL 119 15TH WAR
SENTMAN, SOLOMON CAR 242 TANEYTOW
SENTMAN, SUSAN* CEC 102 4TH E DI
SENTON, JOSEPH * KEN 234 2ND DIST
SENTRY, HENRY BAL 195 2ND WARD
SENTRY, VOLENTINE BAL 085 1ST WARD
SENTS, DAVID WAS 249 1ST DIST
SENTS, MARGARET CAR 264 WESTMINS

SENTZ, DANIEL CAR 256 3RD DIST
SENTZ, DAVID CAR 311 1ST DIST
SENTZ, FREDERICK BAL 079 1ST WARD
SENTZ, JACOB CAR 306 1ST DIST
SENTZ, JAMES CAR 181 8TH DIST
SENTZ, JOSHUA CAR 248 3RD DIST
SENTZ, LOUISA FRE 427 8TH E DI
SENTZ, LOUISA BAL 273 12TH WAR
SENTZ, SOLOMON BAL 236 1ST DIST
SENTZ.ELLEN CAR 400 2ND DIST
SENTZER, JAMES BAL 237 12TH WAR
SEOY, WILLIAM * BAL 267 1ST DIST
SEPP, DANIEL BAL 160 2ND DIST
SEPP, RUBEN BAL 117 18TH WAR
SEPPIS, WILLIAM BAL 279 20TH WAR
SEPPO, CATHARINE CAR 294 7TH DIST
SEPPO, DANIEL CAR 252 3RD DIST
SEPPY, WILLIAM CAR 278 7TH DIST
SEPRION, JOHN BAL 350 13TH WAR
SEPT, JOHN ALL 040 2ND E.D.
SEPT, MICHAEL BAL 117 1ST WARD
SEPTEN, JOHN CEC 063 1ST E DI
SEPTEF, FRANKLIN FRE 164 EMMITTSB
SEPTER, JOHN FRE 191 5TH E DI
SERCATA, CLARA * BAL 087 18TH WAR
SERCH, CONRAD FRE 022 FREDERIC
SERCH, MARY A. F.* BAL 096 10TH WAR
SERCUE, DAVID BAL 115 5TH WARD
SERDEIS, MARY BAL 271 12TH WAR
SEREATA, CLARA * BAL 087 18TH WAR
SEREDAY, WILLIAM* TAL 004 EASTON D
SERELING, GEORGE BAL 198 2ND WARD
SERELING, H. BAL 198 2ND WARD
SEREM, CASPER ALL 248 CUMBERLA
SERFF, ABRAHAM CAR 338 6TH DIST
SERFF, CHARLES ALL 196 CUMBERLA
SERGEANT, JAMES BAL 035 4TH WARD
SERGECKS, PHILLIP BAL 255 17TH WAR
SERGLE, JOHN BAL 284 2ND WARD
SERICKLER, MILES CEC 073 5TH E DI
SERIGLE, JOE BAL 141 5TH WARD
SERINNES, CHARLOTTE PRI 019 VANSVILL
SERIT, JESSEE PRI 036 VANSVILL
SERIVENER, JIM ANN 280 ANNAPOLI
SERMAN, MARY DOR 432 1ST DIST
SERMAN, THOMAS* DOR 341 3RD DIVI
SERN, MICHEAL CAR 408 2ND DIST
SERP, ELIZA BAL 265 12TH WAR
SERRANT, SARAH ANN 268 ANNAPOLI
SERRICKILLER, EDWARC BAL 111 5TH WARD
SERRIN, DANIEL BAL 169 19TH WAR
SERRIN, ELIZA FRE 203 5TH E DI
SERUG, MARY BAL 242 12TH WAR
SERUTON, JAMES* TAL 006 EASTON D
SERUTON, MARGARET* TAL 016 EASTON D
SERUTON, MARY A.* TAL 007 EASTON D
SERUTON, MARY* TAL 006 EASTON D
SERVANT, JANE ANN 309 1ST DIST
SERVANT, JANE ANN 278 ANNAPOLI
SERVANT, NOTLEY ALL 159 6TH E.D.
SERVANT, SARAH ALL 208 CUMBERLA
SERVANY, LOUIS BAL 253 12TH WAR
SERVER, ELIZABETH BAL 271 7TH WARD
SERVER, WILLIAM BAL 311 7TH WARD
SERVERY, ACHSA BAL 439 14TH WAR
SERVESON, MARY BAL 103 5TH WARD
SERVICE, A. BAL 306 12TH WAR
SERVIES, SOPHIA CEC 169 6TH E DI
SERVING, M. BAL 269 12TH WAR
SERVISON, BENJAMIN CEC 058 1ST E DI
SERVISON, ISAAC CEC 043 CHESAPEA
SERVISON, SAMUEL CEC 064 1ST E DI
SERVISON, SAMUEL CEC 082 CHARLEST
SERVOIL, WILLIAM ANN 320 2ND DIST
SERVOY, SARAH BAL 277 12TH WAR
SESE, JOHN WAS 043 2ND SUBD
SESFORD, GEORGE BAL 042 9TH WARD
SESSENDER, WILLIAM BAL 128 1ST WARD
SESSMENHAUSEN, JOHN BAL 145 16TH WAR
SESSONS, AUGUSTUS BAL 287 17TH WAR
SETENHAUREN, CLEMOT BAL 174 11TH WAR
SETH, ALEXANDER H. TAL 102 ST MICHA
SETH, CHARLES QUE 155 2ND E DI
SETH, CHARLES-BLACK CAR 070 NO TWP L
SETH, ELIZABETH* BAL 059 4TH WARD
SETH, GEORGE-BLACK CAR 149 NO TWP L
SETH, JOHN-BLACK CAR 110 NO TWP L
SETH, ROBERT D. BAL 037 9TH WARD
SETH, SARAH TAL 085 ST MICHA
SETH, THOMAS CEC 087 4TH E DI
SETH, THOMAS CEC 088 4TH E DI
SETH, THOMAS B.* BAL 082 4TH WARD
SETHEE, JANE* BAL 074 4TH WARD
SETHES, CHARLES FRE 411 8TH E DI
SETKELL, HENRY BAL 241 2ND WARD
SETLIF, EDWARD QUE 180 2ND E DI
SETMATE, WILLIAM * BAL 366 13TH WAR
SETMOUGH, JOHN BAL 210 2ND WARD
SETREDKER, FREDERICK BAL 244 2ND WARD
SETRICK, GEORGE ALL 037 2ND E.D.
SETRICK, GEORGE ALL 038 2ND E.D.
SETTEN, JAMES* BAL 084 4TH WARD
SETTENGER, MARGARET ALL 098 5TH E.D.
SETTLE, ANDREW BAL 452 8TH WARD
SETTLER, SAMUEL BAL 193 17TH WAR
SEVAIN, JAMES F. BAL 166 1ST WARD
SEVAL, EDWARD FRE 267 NEW MARK
SEVALL, THOMAS B. BAL 256 12TH WAR
SEVAN, JAMES CAR 066 NO TWP L
SEVAN, MARTHA S. ST 326 4TH E DI
SEVEGGETT, MARRY CAR 128 NO TWP L
SEVEING, MOSES T. WOR 229 6TH E DI
SEVEIR, MARY A. ANN 322 2ND DIST
SEVELL, RACHEL * BAL 358 1ST DIST
SEVELLER, PETER ALL 076 5TH E.D.
SEVENCY, ROBERT W. PRI 007 BLADENSB
SEVENS, HENRY HAR 191 3RD DIST
SEVER, ANN BAL 061 1ST WARD
SEVER, JOEL G. BAL 030 9TH WARD
SEVERD, JOHN W. BAL 006 1ST WARD
SEVERE, CHARLES BAL 077 1ST WARD
SEVERE, HARRIET BAL 372 1ST DIST
SEVERE, JAMES BAL 270 7TH WARD
SEVERING, FANNY * BAL 282 20TH WAR
SEVERING.CLINTON BAL 332 13TH WAR
SEVERN, JESSE ANN 514 HOWARD D
SEVERN, JOHN ANN 514 HOWARD D
SEVERN, NICHOLAS ANN 515 HOWARD D
SEVERN, WILLIAM BAL 203 6TH DIST
SEVERS, HENRY BAL 314 1ST DIST
SEVERSON, GEORGE BAL 160 19TH WAR
SEVERSON, STEPHEN HAR 117 2ND DIST
SEVETZER, JOSEPH ALL 145 6TH E.D.
SEVIER, GAMES * BAL 151 1ST WARD
SEVIFT, WILLAIM BAL 104 1ST WARD
SEVILL, ARCHOBALD WAS 154 2ND DIST
SEVUTON, JESSE* TAL 061 EASTON D
SEVY, MARGARETT FRE 411 8TH E DI
SEWALL, EDWARD H. QUE 226 4TH E DI
SEWALL, FRANCIS B. CEC 075 NORTHEAS
SEWALL, GEORGE H. ST 272 3RD E DI
SEWALL, HENRY ST 304 2ND E DI
SEWALL, HENRY CEC 060 1ST E DI
SEWALL, HENRY-BLACK QUE 158 2ND E DI
SEWALL, JACOB CEC 048 1ST E DI
SEWALL, JAMES M. BAL 383 13TH WAR
SEWALL, JOHN CEC 048 1ST E DI
SEWALL, JOHN CEC 059 1ST E DI
SEWALL, JOHN BAL 471 14TH WAR
SEWALL, JOHN F. BAL 016 1ST WARD
SEWALL, JULIA E. BAL 321 20TH WAR
SEWALL, MARY BAL 377 13TH WAR
SEWALL, MARY QUE 251 5TH E DI
SEWALL, PHILIP-BLACK QUE 159 2ND E DI
SEWALL, THOMAS QUE 219 3RD E DI
SEWALL, THOMAS BAL 016 1ST WARD
SEWALL, WILLIAM QUE 185 3RD E DI
SEWALL, WILLIAM ST 265 3RD E DI
SEWALL, WILLIAM ST 271 3RD E DI
SEWARAL, GEORGE CAR 076 NO TWP L
SEWARD, ANN BAL 300 7TH WARD
SEWARD, ANN BAL 016 15TH WAR
SEWARD, ANN E. CAR 078 NO TWP L
SEWARD, CHARLES DOR 397 1ST DIST
SEWARD, GEORGE QUE 155 2ND E DI
SEWARD, HENRY DOR 398 1ST DIST
SEWARD, JAME SH. BAL 171 1ST WARD
SEWARD, JAMES BAL 044 1ST WARD
SEWARD, JAMES BAL 048 1ST WARD
SEWARD, JAMES QUE 137 1ST E DI
SEWARD, JAMES CAR 078 NO TWP L
SEWARD, JANE DOR 391 1ST DIST
SEWARD, JOHN CAR 078 NO TWP L
SEWARD, JOHN CAR 078 NO TWP L
SEWARD, JOHN A. BAL 030 15TH WAR
SEWARD, JOHN C. TAL 022 EASTON D
SEWARD, JOHN H. CAR 096 NO TWP L
SEWARD, JOHN S. DOR 373 1ST DIST
SEWARD, LEVI BAL 060 1ST WARD
SEWARD, LEVIN DOR 398 1ST DIST
SEWARD, LEVIN DOR 400 1ST DIST
SEWARD, LEVIN DOR 405 1ST DIST
SEWARD, MARTHA-BLACK ST 338 4TH E DI
SEWARD, MARY QUE 220 3RD E DI
SEWARD, MARY CAR 066 NO TWP L
SEWARD, MATILDA A. BAL 003 1ST WARD
SEWARD, RICHARD DOR 400 1ST DIST
SEWARD, SOLOMON BAL 287 3RD WARD
SEWARD, THOMAS DOR 400 1ST DIST
SEWARD, WILLIAM CAR 078 NO TWP L
SEWARD, WILLIAM BAL 023 15TH WAR
SEWARD, WILLIAM QUE 219 3RD E DI
SEWART, JAMES QUE 167 2ND E DI
SEWARTY, JOHN BAL 221 2ND WARD
SEWARY, PETER BAL 197 19TH WAR
SEWEL, ANN-BLACK CAR 076 NO TWP L
SEWEL, HARRIET BAL 157 2ND DIST
SEWEL, SAMUEL DOR 459 1ST DIST
SEWELL, ALEXANDER-MULATTO CAR 092 NO TWP L
SEWELL, AMERITTE CAR 108 NO TWP L
SEWELL, ANN M. BAL 148 16TH WAR
SEWELL, ANN R.* DOR 464 1ST DIST
SEWELL, ASARIAH BAL 128 1ST WARD
SEWELL, AUGUSTA ANN 378 4TH DIST
SEWELL, CHARLOTTE ANN 345 3RD DIST
SEWELL, CHESTER TAL 063 EASTON D
SEWELL, DORA SOM 520 BARREN C
SEWELL, EDWARD KEN 268 1ST DIST
SEWELL, EELIZA TAL 118 ST MICHA
SEWELL, ELIZA ANN 328 2ND DIST
SEWELL, ELIZA H. BAL 179 16TH WAR
SEWELL, ELIZABETH BAL 174 16TH WAR
SEWELL, ELIZABETH BAL 069 15TH WAR
SEWELL, ELIZABETH TAL 116 ST MICHA
SEWELL, ELIZABETH PRI 024 VANSVILL
SEWELL, GARRETSON DOR 448 1ST DIST
SEWELL, GEORGE TAL 040 EASTON D
SEWELL, GEORGE ANN 444 HOWARD D
SEWELL, GEORGE T. KEN 268 1ST DIST
SEWELL, HARIOTT DOR 459 1ST DIST
SEWELL, HENRIETTA BAL 109 15TH WAR
SEWELL, HENRY BAL 061 10TH WAR
SEWELL, HENRY ANN 376 4TH DIST
SEWELL, HENRY TAL 063 EASTON D
SEWELL, HESTER A. TAL 074 EASTON T
SEWELL, JAMES TAL 087 ST MICHA
SEWELL, JAMES BAL 132 1ST WARD
SEWELL, JAMES BAL 143 1ST WARD
SEWELL, JAMES BAL 223 19TH WAR
SEWELL, JAMES CEC 019 ELKTON 3
SEWELL, JAMES BAL 272 20TH WAR
SEWELL, JAMES KEN 224 2ND DIST
SEWELL, JEREMIAH TAL 087 ST MICHA
SEWELL, JIM TAL 039 EASTON D
SEWELL, JOHN TAL 045 EASTON T
SEWELL, JOHN CEC 011 ELKTON 3
SEWELL, JOHN CAL 039 2ND DIST
SEWELL, JOHN BAL 400 14TH WAR
SEWELL, JOSEPH BAL 072 18TH WAR
SEWELL, JULIA BAL 204 11TH WAR
SEWELL, JULIA A. BAL 250 6TH WARD
SEWELL, LYON BAL 149 11TH WAR
SEWELL, MARANDA ANN 276 ANNAPOLI
SEWELL, MARY CAR 113 NO TWP L
SEWELL, MARY BAL 058 4TH WARD
SEWELL, MARY TAL 062 EASTON D
SEWELL, MARY KEN 289 3RD DIST
SEWELL, MARY A. BAL 097 15TH WAR
SEWELL, MARY F. TAL 111 ST MICHA
SEWELL, MARY J. WAS 161 HAGERSTO
SEWELL, MAZEY TAL 082 ST MICHA
SEWELL, PERRY BAL 192 17TH WAR
SEWELL, REBECCA BAL 017 4TH WARD
SEWELL, RICHARD BAL 250 20TH WAR
SEWELL, RICHARD T. BAL 279 2ND WARD
SEWELL, ROBERT D. PRI 069 MARLBROU
SEWELL, ROBERT F. TAL 112 ST MICHA
SEWELL, ROBERT R. TAL 116 ST MICHA
SEWELL, ROSE A. TAL 110 ST MICHA
SEWELL, SALLY WAS 161 HAGERSTO
SEWELL, SAMUEL ANN 313 1ST DIST
SEWELL, SARAH CAR 092 NO TWP L
SEWELL, THOAMS BAL 321 20TH WAR
SEWELL, THOMAS BAL 309 20TH WAR
SEWELL, THOMAS BAL 309 20TH WAR
SEWELL, THOMAS TAL 116 ST MICHA
SEWELL, THOMAS H. BAL 088 15TH WAR
SEWELL, THOMAS R. BAL 220 17TH WAR
SEWELL, TRUSTUM F.* BAL 371 3RD WARD
SEWELL, WASHINGTON* TAL 062 EASTON D
SEWELL, WILLIAM TAL 023 EASTON D
SEWELL, WILLIAM BAL 191 17TH WAR
SEWELL, WILLIAM BAL 246 17TH WAR
SEWELL, WILLIAM MGM 379 ROCKERLE
SEWELL, WILLIAM H. BAL 071 4TH WARD
SEWELL.ROBERT BAL 120 1ST WARD
SEWELLYER, JOHN * ALL 112 5TH E.D.
SEWELY, WILLIAM BAL 437 14TH WAR
SEWER, JOHN BAL 046 1ST WARD
SEWERS, FOSTER* DOR 310 1ST DIST
SEXTGON, MICHAEL BAL 164 2ND DIST
SEXTON, BRIDGET BAL 047 9TH WARD
SEXTON, EDWARD BAL 138 5TH WARD
SEXTON, J. BAL 151 1ST WARD
SEXTON, JOHN BAL 063 1ST WARD
SEXTON, JOHN BAL 048 9TH WARD
SEXTON, MARGARET BAL 372 8TH WARD
SEXTON, SAMUEL B. BAL 171 16TH WAR
SEYAS, WILLIAM H. FRE 337 MIDDLETO
SEYBOURN, WILLIAM BAL 394 8TH WARD
SEYDER, CHRISTIAN FRE 239 NEW MARK
SEYH, SARAH* TAL 061 EASTON D
SEYHART, SAMUEL BAL 185 19TH WAR
SEYHLER, HENRY * FRE 263 NEW MARK
SEYLE, SALLY BAL 156 11TH WAR
SEYLER, CATHERINE* BAL 391 3RD WARD
SEYLER, FREDERICK BAL 346 13TH WAR
SEYLRO, ADAM ALL 182 8TH E.D.
SEYMIA, JOHN H. BAL 250 20TH WAR
SEYMOND, ELIZA BAL 144 2ND DIST
SEYMOR, CONRAD H. BAL 123 18TH WAR
SEYMORE, AMANDA TAL 046 EASTON T
SEYMORE, CHARLES TAL 046 EASTON T
SEYMORE, DAVID BAL 181 16TH WAR
SEYMORE, ELIZA TAL 036 EASTON D
SEYMORE, EMILY A. TAL 029 EASTON D
SEYMORE, GEORGE TAL 010 EASTON D
SEYMORE, HARRIET BAL 182 16TH WAR
SEYMORE, HUGH TAL 090 ST MICHA
SEYMORE, JEREMIAH TAL 101 ST MICHA
SEYMORE, JOSEPH TAL 044 EASTON T
SEYMORE, LEVIN TAL 024 EASTON D
SEYMORE, LEVIN S. TAL 052 EASTON D
SEYMORE, MARGARET TAL 024 EASTON D
SEYMORE, SARAH TAL 019 EASTON D
SEYMORE, SPEDDEN* TAL 048 EASTON T
SEYMORE, T. T.* TAL 038 EASTON D
SEYMORE, WILLIAM KEN 275 1ST DIST
SEYMORE, WILLIAM S. TAL 085 ST MICHA
SEYMORE, WILLIAM F. BAL 129 18TH WAR
SEYMORE, WILLIAM H. TAL 024 EASTON D
SEYMORE, WILLIAM N. TAL 045 EASTON T
SEYMOUR, ANN ANN 452 HOWARD D
SEYMOUR, CATHARINE ANN 470 HOWARD D
SEYMOUR, CHARLES DOR 468 1ST DIST
SEYMOUR, EDWARD BAL 460 14TH WAR
SEYMOUR, ELIZA BAL 060 2ND DIST
SEYMOUR, JOHN ALL 111 5TH E.D.
SEYMOUR, JOHN QUE 243 5TH E DI
SEYMOUR, JOHN H. BAL 001 4TH WARD
SEYMOUR, LOUISA BAL 339 3RD WARD
SEYMOUR, M.* DOR 373 1ST DIST
SEYMOUR, MARY A. BAL 009 18TH WAR
SEYMOUR, PETER BAL 119 15TH WAR
SEYMOUR, SARAH BAL 097 1ST WARD
SEYMOUR, WILLIAM BAL 154 1ST WARD
SEYMOUR, WILLIAM BAL 009 18TH WAR
SEYMOUR, ZACRIAS BAL 341 3RD WARD
SEYMOURE, FRISBY* TAL 006 EASTON D
SEYMOURE, THOMAS TAL 093 ST MICHA
SEYNING, BELLE * BAL 350 13TH WAR
SEYPOLD, ALLWIN BAL 116 11TH WAR
SEYS, REV J. BAL 019 18TH WAR
SFREEMAN, SUSAN CAR 105 NO TWP L
SFWEADOUR, MARY CAR 289 7TH DIST
SGETTINGS, DAVID BAL 058 2ND DIST
SHAAFF, ARTHUR BAL 105 10TH WAR
SHAASTER, MARY FRE 431 8TH E DI
SHABAKER, GEORGE FRE 050 FREDERIC
SHACK, JACOB ALL 152 6TH E.D.
SHACKELFORD, COLEMAN WAS 047 2ND SUBD
SHACKELFORD, JOHN FRE 387 PETERSVI
SHACKELFORD, LEWIS BAL 085 1ST WARD
SHACKELFORD, LYNNE CHA 219 ALLENS F
SHACKEY, JACOB CAR 379 2ND DIST
SHACKS, ELIZA * ANN 397 8TH DIST
SHAD, ANN M. BAL 126 16TH WAR
SHADD, SAMPSON BAL 279 17TH WAR
SHADDEN, MABLE TAL 104 ST MICHA
SHADDEN, MARINA @ TAL 104 ST MICHA
SHADDUCK, HENRY ALL 216 CUMBERLA
SHADE, GEORGE CAR 295 7TH DIST
SHADE, JOHN ALL 249 CUMBERLA
SHADER, STEPHEN BAL 013 2ND DIST
SHADESON, NANCY CEC 026 ELKTON 3
SHADLE, HENRY BAL 383 1ST DIST
SHADLE, PETER BAL 329 3RD WARD
SHADOCK, JAMES BAL 159 1ST WARD
SHADOLLER, PHILIP BAL 444 8TH WARD
SHADRACH, MARY BAL 024 15TH WAR
SHADRACK, THOMAS ST 297 2ND E DI
SHADRICK, JOHN SR. ST 293 2ND E DI
SHADRICK, WILLIAM BAL 319 1ST DIST
SHADWICK, DAVID BAL 115 1ST WARD
SHADWICK, J. BAL 149 1ST WARD
SHAEFE, SAMUEL FRE 374 CATOCTIN
SHAEFER, DANIEL HAR 064 1ST DIST
SHAEFER, ELIZABETH FRE 318 MIDDLETO
SHAEFER, HANSON FRE 334 MIDDLETO
SHAEFER, THOMAS FRE 321 MIDDLETO
SHAEFFER, AMELIA BAL 257 12TH WAR
SHAEFFER, B. BAL 176 19TH WAR
SHAEFFER, EDIS BAL 146 19TH WAR
SHAEFFER, ELIZABETH A. HAR 076 BEL AIR
SHAEFFER, ELIZABTH BAL 261 12TH WAR
SHAEFFER, GEORGE BAL 255 20TH WAR
SHAEFFER, H. BAL 220 19TH WAR
SHAEFFER, H. BAL 261 12TH WAR
SHAEFFER, JAMES BAL 283 20TH WAR
SHAEFFER, JOHN BAL 181 19TH WAR

Name	County	Page	District
SHAEFFER, JOHN	BAL	146	19TH WAR
SHAEFFER, JOHN	BAL	307	20TH WAR
SHAEFFER, L. C.	BAL	301	20TH WAR
SHAEFFER, LISETTE	BAL	176	19TH WAR
SHAEFFER, MICHAEL	BAL	240	20TH WAR
SHAEFFER, REBEC	BAL	237	12TH WAR
SHAEFFER, SAMUEL	BAL	146	19TH WAR
SHAEFFER, THEODORE	BAL	164	19TH WAR
SHAEFFER, WILLIAM	FRE	133	CREAGERS
SHAEFFER, WILLIAM A.	BAL	066	18TH WAR
SHAEFFER, WILLIAM G.	BAL	475	14TH WAR
SHAER, NOAH	ALL	092	5TH E.D.
SHAFAR, DANIEL	BAL	092	18TH WAR
SHAFAR, EMANUEL	CAR	346	6TH DIST
SHAFER, ABRAHAM	CAR	275	7TH DIST
SHAFER, ABRAHAM	BAL	215	6TH DIST
SHAFER, ADAM	WAS	248	1ST DIST
SHAFER, AMOS	CAR	277	7TH DIST
SHAFER, ANDREW	BAL	385	1ST DIST
SHAFER, ANDREW	BAL	389	1ST DIST
SHAFER, ANN C.	PRI	028	VANSVILL
SHAFER, CAROLINE	BAL	371	13TH WAR
SHAFER, CATHARINE	WAS	150	HAGERSTO
SHAFER, CORNELIUS	ANN	491	HOWARD D
SHAFER, DANIEL	ANN	356	3RD DIST
SHAFER, DANIEL	FRE	133	CREAGERS
SHAFER, DANIEL	CAR	296	7TH DIST
SHAFER, DAVID	CAR	351	6TH DIST
SHAFER, DAVID	CAR	407	2ND DIST
SHAFER, DAVID	BAL	195	5TH DIST
SHAFER, DAVID	WAS	105	2ND DIST
SHAFER, DAVID F.	CAR	328	MANCHEST
SHAFER, ELIZABETH	CAR	271	WESTMINS
SHAFER, ELIZABETH	TAL	062	EASTON D
SHAFER, ELIZABETH	BAL	215	6TH DIST
SHAFER, ELLEN	WAS	159	HAGERSTO
SHAFER, ELLEN	CAR	274	7TH DIST
SHAFER, EMANUEL	CAR	343	6TH DIST
SHAFER, FRANTZ	CAR	337	6TH DIST
SHAFER, GEORGE	CAR	339	6TH DIST
SHAFER, GEORGE	CAR	296	7TH DIST
SHAFER, GEORGE	FRE	402	JEFFERSO
SHAFER, GEORGE	WAS	130	HAGERSTO
SHAFER, GEORGE	WAS	172	FUNKSTOW
SHAFER, GEORGE	WAS	300	1ST DIST
SHAFER, GEORGE	BAL	343	1ST DIST
SHAFER, GEORGE	BAL	307	1ST DIST
SHAFER, HENRY	BAL	397	1ST DIST
SHAFER, HENRY	WAS	172	FUNKSTOW
SHAFER, HENRY	WAS	267	1ST DIST
SHAFER, HENRY	FRE	386	PETERSVI
SHAFER, JACOB	CAR	275	7TH DIST
SHAFER, JACOB	CAR	289	7TH DIST
SHAFER, JACOB	CAR	276	7TH DIST
SHAFER, JACOB	CAR	338	6TH DIST
SHAFER, JACOB	CAR	355	6TH DIST
SHAFER, JACOB	CAR	352	6TH DIST
SHAFER, JACOB	WAS	286	1ST DIST
SHAFER, JACOB	BAL	210	6TH DIST
SHAFER, JOHN	WAS	177	1ST DIST
SHAFER, JOHN	CAR	274	7TH DIST
SHAFER, JOHN SR.	WAS	032	2ND SUBD
SHAFER, JOSEPH	CAR	267	WESTMINS
SHAFER, JOSEPH	FRE	403	JEFFERSO
SHAFER, JOSHUA	CAR	274	7TH DIST
SHAFER, LAVINA	WAS	196	1ST DIST
SHAFER, LUCY	WAS	140	HAGERSTO
SHAFER, LYDIA	WAS	268	1ST DIST
SHAFER, LYDIA	CAR	296	7TH DIST
SHAFER, LYDIA	BAL	214	6TH DIST
SHAFER, LYDIA	BAL	216	6TH DIST
SHAFER, MAGDALINE	BAL	022	2ND DIST
SHAFER, MARGARET	CAR	349	6TH DIST
SHAFER, MARGARET	FRE	115	CREAGERS
SHAFER, MARGARETTA	BAL	337	13TH WAR
SHAFER, MARTIN	BAL	301	1ST DIST
SHAFER, MARY	CAR	290	7TH DIST
SHAFER, MARYBELLE	WAS	131	HAGERSTO
SHAFER, MICHAEL	CAR	354	6TH DIST
SHAFER, NICHOLAS	CAR	271	WESTMINS
SHAFER, PETER	FRE	403	JEFFERSO
SHAFER, ROBERT J.	WAS	178	BOONSBOR
SHAFER, SAMUEL	WAS	049	2ND SUBD
SHAFER, SAMUEL	CAR	352	6TH DIST
SHAFER, SAMUEL	CAR	339	6TH DIST
SHAFER, SAMUEL	FRE	125	CREAGERS
SHAFER, SARHA	CAR	332	MANCHEST
SHAFER, WILLIAM	BAL	359	13TH WAR
SHAFER, WILLIAM	CEC	015	ELKTON 3
SHAFER, WILLIAM	WAS	301	1ST DIST
SHAFER, WILLIAM	WAS	227	1ST DIST
SHAFF, ABRAHAM	FRE	399	JEFFERSO
SHAFF, GEORGE	FRE	403	JEFFERSO
SHAFF, MARGARET	FRE	391	PETERSVI
SHAFFE, VALENTINE	BAL	088	2ND DIST
SHAFFEN, HENRIETTA	BAL	137	11TH WAR
SHAFFER, ADAM	CAR	180	8TH DIST
SHAFFER, AMOS	BAL	268	1ST DIST
SHAFFER, ANDREW	CAR	181	8TH DIST
SHAFFER, ANDREW	CAR	174	8TH DIST
SHAFFER, ANDREW	CAR	227	5TH DIST
SHAFFER, BARBARY	CAR	178	8TH DIST
SHAFFER, BATTSON	BAL	043	18TH WAR
SHAFFER, CATHARINE	CAR	173	8TH DIST
SHAFFER, CHARLES H.	BAL	132	18TH WAR
SHAFFER, DANIEL	FRE	367	CATOCTIN
SHAFFER, DANIEL	BAL	103	18TH WAR
SHAFFER, ELISABETH	ALL	229	CUMBERLA
SHAFFER, ELIZABETH	BAL	319	12TH WAR
SHAFFER, EMANUEL	BAL	187	5TH DIST
SHAFFER, EMANUEL	CAR	220	5TH DIST
SHAFFER, FRANK	ANN	413	HOWARD D
SHAFFER, FREDERICK L.	BAL	329	3RD WARD
SHAFFER, GEORGE	ALL	198	CUMBERLA
SHAFFER, GEORGE	ALL	241	CUMBERLA
SHAFFER, GEORGE	CAR	191	4TH DIST
SHAFFER, GEORGE	BAL	043	18TH WAR
SHAFFER, GEORGE	BAL	242	17TH WAR
SHAFFER, HENRY	HAR	061	1ST DIST
SHAFFER, HENRY	BAL	134	2ND DIST
SHAFFER, HENRY	ALL	197	CUMBERLA
SHAFFER, HENRY	ALL	054	10TH E.D
SHAFFER, JACOB	ALL	094	5TH E.D.
SHAFFER, JACOB	BAL	021	2ND DIST
SHAFFER, JACOB	CAR	172	8TH DIST
SHAFFER, JACOB	CAR	208	4TH DIST
SHAFFER, JACOB	CAR	339	6TH DIST
SHAFFER, JACOB	CAR	400	2ND DIST
SHAFFER, JAMES	BAL	129	2ND DIST
SHAFFER, JAMES W.	HAR	081	2ND DIST
SHAFFER, JOHN	BAL	106	18TH WAR
SHAFFER, JOHN	CAR	173	8TH DIST
SHAFFER, JOHN	ALL	031	2ND E.D.
SHAFFER, JOHN	KEN	287	3RD DIST
SHAFFER, JOHN HL	ALL	060	10TH E.D
SHAFFER, JOHN S.	CAR	172	8TH DIST
SHAFFER, JOHN W.	HAR	081	2ND DIST
SHAFFER, JOSEPH	BAL	129	1ST WARD
SHAFFER, MARGARET	BAL	125	18TH WAR
SHAFFER, MARY	CAR	229	5TH DIST
SHAFFER, MOSES	CAR	178	8TH DIST
SHAFFER, MOSES	CAR	182	8TH DIST
SHAFFER, PETER	ALL	073	5TH E.D.
SHAFFER, PHILIP	CAR	172	8TH DIST
SHAFFER, POLLY	ALL	263	CUMBERLA
SHAFFER, REBECCA	ALL	263	CUMBERLA
SHAFFER, SARAH A.	CAR	204	4TH DIST
SHAFFER, SARAH F.	BAL	244	17TH WAR
SHAFFER, SOPHIA	BAL	371	8TH WARD
SHAFFER, VALENTINE	BAL	428	8TH WARD
SHAFFER, WILLAIM	ALL	070	5TH E.D.
SHAFFER, WILLIAM	HAR	195	3RD DIST
SHAFFER, WILLIAM F.	CAR	178	8TH DIST
SHAFFERMAN, HENRY	ALL	168	6TH E.D.
SHAFFNER, CHARLES M.	WAS	181	BOONSBOR
SHAFFNER, JACOB	BAL	096	10TH WAR
SHAFFNER, SAMUEL	BAL	382	13TH WAR
SHAFFNER, SAMUEL C.	WAS	180	BOONSBOR
SHAFFNER, WILLIAM C.	BAL	191	17TH WAR
SHAFTER, MARTIN	BAL	332	13TH WAR
SHAGUIRE, THOMAS	ALL	048	10TH E.D
SHAID, DAVID	BAL	114	18TH WAR
SHAIN, EDWARD	BAL	277	1ST DIST
SHAIN, GEORGE H.	HAR	059	1ST DIST
SHAK, OTHO A.	FRE	310	WOODSBOR
SHAKESPEAR, BENJAMIN	BAL	231	2ND WARD
SHAKESPEAR, JOHNATHAN	BAL	292	1ST DIST
SHAKESPEARE, JOHN	BAL	014	15TH WAR
SHALER, NICHOLAS	BAL	459	8TH WARD
SHALK, PETER	BAL	213	6TH DIST
SHALL, MARY	BAL	183	5TH DIST
SHALLCROSS, JOHN	BAL	198	6TH WARD
SHALLER, THEODORE	BAL	415	14TH WAR
SHALON, THOMAS	BAL	150	2ND DIST
SHAMBER, ELISABETH	BAL	391	8TH WARD
SHAMBER, GEORGE	BAL	391	8TH WARD
SHAMBERGER, FRED	BAL	176	19TH WAR
SHAMBERGER, ISAAC	BAL	187	5TH DIST
SHAMBERGER, JACOB	BAL	201	6TH DIST
SHAMBERGER, JOHN	BAL	201	6TH DIST
SHAMBERGER, JOHN F.	BAL	177	19TH WAR
SHAMBURG, DANIEL	FRE	384	PETERSVI
SHAMBURG, JOHN	BAL	361	13TH WAR
SHAMBURG, WILLIAM	BAL	373	13TH WAR
SHAMEL, HENRY	WAS	036	2ND SUBD
SHAMER, HENRY	CAR	307	1ST DIST
SHAMER, JAOCB	CAR	181	8TH DIST
SHAMER, JOHN	WAS	073	2ND SUBD
SHAMER, JOHN	BAL	237	1ST DIST
SHAMER, VIRGINIA	BAL	011	9TH WARD
SHAMER, WILLIAM	BAL	097	15TH WAR
SHAMLAFER, MARGARET	BAL	240	1ST DIST
SHAMLAFER, NICHOLAS	BAL	240	1ST DIST
SHAMON, AARON	BAL	001	9TH WARD
SHAMPEINN, REBECCA	BAL	047	9TH WARD
SHAMPER, C.C.	BAL	130	1ST WARD
SHAMWELL, JAMES	ST	335	4TH E DI
SHAMWELL, JOSEPH	ST	335	4TH E DI
SHAMWELL, WILLIAM	ST	319	4TH E DI
SHAMWELL.W ILLIAM	ST	338	4TH E DI
SHANABROOK, DANIEL	BAL	334	7TH WARD
SHANAHAN, MARY	BAL	252	6TH WARD
SHANAHAN, MATHEW	BAL	408	1ST DIST
SHANAHAN, MICHAEL	BAL	262	6TH WARD
SHANAHON, PATRICK	FRE	380	PETERSVI
SHANAN, PAT	BAL	449	1ST DIST
SHANAR, WILLIAM G. *	BAL	140	19TH WAR
SHANBER, JOHN	BAL	091	1ST WARD
SHANBERT, BARBARA	BAL	284	2ND WARD
SHANE, ANNIE T.	BAL	057	15TH WAR
SHANE, DANIEL	BAL	109	1ST WARD
SHANE, EDWARD M.	BAL	003	15TH WAR
SHANE, ELIZABETH	BAL	189	11TH WAR
SHANE, GEORGE R.	ANN	421	HOWARD D
SHANE, HENRY W.	HAR	073	1ST DIST
SHANE, JOHN	BAL	362	8TH WARD
SHANE, JOHN	ALL	215	CUMBERLA
SHANE, JOHN T.	ANN	469	HOWARD D
SHANE, JOSEPH	BAL	165	16TH WAR
SHANE, MARGARET	HAR	073	1ST DIST
SHANE, MARY	ALL	217	CUMBERLA
SHANE, MARY J.	CEC	100	3RD E DI
SHANE, MICHAEL	BAL	400	1ST DIST
SHANE, MORICE	BAL	356	8TH WARD
SHANE, PATRICK	ALL	258	CUMBERLA
SHANE, PETER M.	BAL	355	8TH WARD
SHANE, SARAH	BAL	188	11TH WAR
SHANE, SARAH B.	HAR	073	1ST DIST
SHANE, THOMAS	CEC	197	7TH E DI
SHANE, WESLEY	BAL	122	5TH WARD
SHANEBROCK, JOSEPH	CAR	354	6TH DIST
SHANEBURG, JACOB	ALL	014	3RD E.D.
SHANEDOLLER, CHARLES	BAL	453	8TH WARD
SHANEFELT, J. B.	ALL	139	6TH E.D.
SHANEFELTER, ELIZABETH	BAL	054	15TH WAR
SHANEFELTZ, JOHN	FRE	366	CATOCTIN
SHANELAN, AMI	BAL	236	2ND WARD
SHANER, DANIEL	BAL	203	6TH DIST
SHANER, JOSEPH	CAR	242	TANEYTOW
SHANER, LAVINA	CAR	326	1ST DIST
SHANER, MATHEW	BAL	283	2ND WARD
SHANETTS, ELIZABETH *	BAL	140	19TH WAR
SHANEY, ALEXANDER*	BAL	028	4TH WARD
SHANEY, BERNARD	BAL	096	15TH WAR
SHANEY, ELIZA	BAL	096	15TH WAR
SHANEY, JOHN	BAL	028	4TH WARD
SHANEY, JOSHUA*	BAL	028	4TH WARD
SHANFER, WILLIAM P.	ALL	135	4TH E.D.
SHANGGANLARY, HENRY	BAL	367	13TH WAR
SHANGLER, JOHN	WAS	291	1ST DIST
SHANING, JOHN	HAR	191	3RD DIST
SHANK, ABRAHAM	WAS	259	1ST DIST
SHANK, ADAM	WAS	262	1ST DIST
SHANK, ADAM	WAS	259	1ST DIST
SHANK, ADAM	WAS	279	LEITERSB
SHANK, ADAM	WAS	162	HAGERSTO
SHANK, ALFRED	BAL	122	5TH WARD
SHANK, ANDREW	WAS	217	1ST DIST
SHANK, ANDREW	WAS	262	1ST DIST
SHANK, BARBARA	WAS	263	1ST DIST
SHANK, BENB	WAS	263	1ST DIST
SHANK, CATHERINE	WAS	119	2ND DIST
SHANK, CHRISTIAN	WAS	119	2ND DIST
SHANK, CHRISTIAN	WAS	287	1ST DIST
SHANK, CYRUS	WAS	283	1ST DIST
SHANK, DANIEL	CAR	386	2ND DIST
SHANK, DAVID	WAS	119	2ND DIST
SHANK, GEORGE	FRE	284	WOODSBOR
SHANK, GEORGE W.	FRE	292	WOODSBOR
SHANK, GEORGE W.	FRE	109	CREAGERS
SHANK, GILBERT	BAL	342	1ST DIST
SHANK, HENRY	ALL	001	3RD E.D.
SHANK, HENRY	WAS	119	2ND DIST
SHANK, HENRY	WAS	263	1ST DIST
SHANK, HESTER	WAS	259	1ST DIST
SHANK, JACOB	WAS	113	2ND DIST
SHANK, JACOB	FRE	350	MIDDLETO
SHANK, JACOB	FRE	350	MIDDLETO
SHANK, JACOB OF J.	WAS	263	1ST DIST
SHANK, JOHN	FRE	200	5TH E DI
SHANK, JOHN P.	WAS	195	1ST DIST
SHANK, JONATHAN	WAS	113	2ND DIST
SHANK, JOSEPH	FRE	286	WOODSBOR
SHANK, MARY	FRE	302	WOODSBOR
SHANK, MARY	FRE	286	WOODSBOR
SHANK, MARY	WAS	147	HAGERSTO
SHANK, MARY C.	WAS	218	1ST DIST
SHANK, MICHAEL	FRE	294	WOODSBOR
SHANK, NANCY	WAS	162	HAGERSTO
SHANK, PETER	WAS	228	1ST DIST
SHANK, PETER	WAS	113	2ND DIST
SHANK, PETER	FRE	284	WOODSBOR
SHANK, PETER	FRE	349	MIDDLETO
SHANK, PHEBE ETTA	FRE	310	WOODSBOR
SHANK, WILLIAM	FRE	284	WOODSBOR
SHANK,EZRA	FRE	031	FREDERIC
SHANKEY, MICHAEL	BAL	247	12TH WAR
SHANKLE, JONATHAN	FRE	082	FREDERIC
SHANKLE, JOSHUA	FRE	324	MIDDLETO
SHANKLE, JULIANN	FRE	305	WOODSBOR
SHANKLE, MARY A.	FRE	052	FREDERIC
SHANKLE, PHILLIP	FRE	082	FREDERIC
SHANKLE, SARAH	FRE	090	FREDERIC
SHANKLE, SUSANNA	FRE	337	MIDDLETO
SHANKLIN, JOHN	BAL	078	2ND DIST
SHANKLINE, ELIZABETH	BAL	076	2ND DIST
SHANKS, CHARLES G.	MGM	396	ROCKERLE
SHANKS, JAMES K.	MGM	397	ROCKERLE
SHANKS, MARTHA M.	ST	319	4TH E DI
SHANKS, MORRIS	ST	319	4TH E DI
SHANKS, PERRY	ST	319	4TH E DI
SHANKS, RACHEL	BAL	338	1ST DIST
SHANKS, ROBERT M.	ST	348	5TH E DI
SHANLEY, FRANKLIN	ALL	047	10TH E.D
SHANLEY, JAMES	BAL	112	15TH WAR
SHANLEY, MARIA	BAL	164	6TH WARD
SHANLEY, SISTER MARY JAME	FRE	197	5TH E DI
SHANLIES, ELISABETH	ALL	225	CUMBERLA
SHANLY, TEMP.	ALL	150	6TH E.D.
SHANLY.MCHAEL	ALL	243	CUMBERLA
SHANN, FRANCIS	CHA	248	HILLTOP
SHANNAHAN, BRIDGET	BAL	312	3RD WARD
SHANNAHAN, CATHERINE	BAL	017	4TH WARD
SHANNAHAN, CHARLES L.	TAL	114	ST MICHA
SHANNAHAN, J. H. K.	TAL	068	EASTON T
SHANNAHAN, JAMES	BAL	032	15TH WAR
SHANNAHAN, JAMES S.	TAL	114	ST MICHA
SHANNAHAN, JESSE E.	TAL	090	ST MICHA
SHANNAHAN, MARY E.	TAL	066	EASTON T
SHANNAHAN, NATHAN	CAR	139	NO TWP L
SHANNAHAN, SAMUEL	TAL	072	EASTON T
SHANNAN, PETER	ALL	136	4TH E.D.
SHANNEMORE, ADELINE*	BAL	308	3RD WARD
SHANNER, GEORGE	BAL	440	8TH WARD
SHANNIN, MARY	HAR	187	3RD DIST
SHANNINGTON, ELIZABETH	BAL	034	1ST WARD
SHANNON, ANDREW	BAL	384	8TH WARD
SHANNON, BRIDGET	BAL	018	1ST WARD
SHANNON, CATHERINE A.	BAL	156	11TH WAR
SHANNON, GEORGE	CEC	159	PORT DUP
SHANNON, HENRY B.	CHA	269	ALLENS F
SHANNON, JAMES	BAL	014	9TH WARD
SHANNON, JANE	BAL	062	10TH WAR
SHANNON, JANE	BAL	067	18TH WAR
SHANNON, JANE	BAL	003	18TH WAR
SHANNON, JOHN	BAL	122	5TH WARD
SHANNON, JOHN	BAL	047	9TH WARD
SHANNON, JOSEPH P.	BAL	010	4TH WARD
SHANNON, MARY	BAL	310	20TH WAR
SHANNON, MARY	BAL	065	10TH WAR
SHANNON, NATH.	BAL	278	20TH WAR
SHANNON, NATHANIEL*	BAL	358	3RD WARD
SHANNON, NICHOLAS	BAL	097	18TH WAR
SHANNON, PATRICK	FRE	393	PETERSVI
SHANNON, THOMAS	HAR	088	2ND DIST
SHANNON, THOMAS	ALL	136	4TH E.D.
SHANNON, WILLIAM	BAL	385	8TH WARD
SHANNON, WILLIAM	BAL	137	1ST WARD
SHANNON, WILLIAM	BAL	014	9TH WARD
SHANNON, WILLIAM	BAL	075	2ND DIST
SHANNY, DAVID	CHA	249	HILLTOP
SHANNY, UZ.	CHA	248	HILLTOP
SHANOCK, CAHTARINE	BAL	059	1ST WARD
SHANON, AUGUST	BAL	294	17TH WAR
SHANS, GASSON*	BAL	327	3RD WARD
SHAPE, GEORGE B.	FRE	036	FREDERIC
SHAPP, ELIZABETH	ALL	013	3RD E.D.
SHAPPER, WILLIAM A.	BAL	002	4TH WARD
SHAPS, ELIZABETH	DOR	332	3RD DIVI
SHARCUT, MARY	BAL	359	8TH WARD
SHARE, BUSTIAN	BAL	068	1ST WARD
SHARE, ISAIAH	BAL	241	17TH WAR
SHARE, RICHARD	BAL	387	3RD WARD
SHARE, SERAPHIM	BAL	237	6TH WARD
SHARER, ANN J.	CAR	264	WESTMINS
SHARER, CATHARINE	CAR	309	1ST DIST
SHARER, CRAWFORD	ALL	109	5TH E.D.
SHARER, DANIEL	FRE	008	FREDERIC
SHARER, FRANCIS A.	CAR	271	WESTMINS
SHARER, FREDERICK	BAL	108	1ST WARD
SHARER, GEORGE	FRE	005	FREDERIC
SHARER, GEORGE	FRE	311	MIDDLETO
SHARER, HENRY	WAS	295	1ST DIST
SHARER, JACOB	CAR	339	6TH DIST
SHARER, JACOB	CAR	355	6TH DIST
SHARER, JACOB	CAR	354	6TH DIST
SHARER, JACOB	BAL	203	6TH DIST
SHARER, JERAMIAH	CAR	309	1ST DIST
SHARER, JOHN *	FRE	100	FREDERIC
SHARER, LYDIA	CAR	335	6TH DIST

Name	County	Page	District
SHARER, MARGARET	BAL	205	6TH DIST
SHARER, MARY	BAL	463	1ST DIST
SHARER, MARY	BAL	333	7TH WARD
SHARER, MARY	CAR	313	1ST DIST
SHARER, MARY A.	CAR	309	1ST DIST
SHARER, PETER	CAR	335	6TH DIST
SHARER, PHILIP	MGM	398	ROCKERLE
SHARER, WILLIAM *	WAS	058	2ND SUBD
SHARETTS, WILLIAM L.	BAL	140	19TH WAR
SHARFELL, MARY	BAL	117	18TH WAR
SHARFLE, RANDOLPH	FRE	321	MIDDLETO
SHARIVER, ALFRED	CAR	266	WESTMINS
SHARK, DANIEL	BAL	422	14TH WAR
SHARKER, JOHN	BAL	242	12TH WAR
SHARKEY, B.	BAL	293	12TH WAR
SHARKEY, CHARLES	BAL	295	7TH WARD
SHARKEY, JOHN	BAL	259	12TH WAR
SHARKEY, JOHN	BAL	047	9TH WARD
SHARKEY, JOHN	BAL	373	13TH WAR
SHARKEY, JOHN J.	BAL	024	9TH WARD
SHARKEY, LARANCE	BAL	025	18TH WAR
SHARKEY, MARGARET	BAL	199	11TH WAR
SHARKEY, MARY ANN	BAL	359	13TH WAR
SHARKEY, MICHAEL	BAL	324	1ST DIST
SHARKEY, PATRICK	BAL	432	8TH WARD
SHARKEY, SINGLETON	BAL	472	14TH WAR
SHARKEY, WILLIAM	BAL	045	15TH WAR
SHARKLAND, HENRY R.	BAL	121	1ST WARD
SHARKLEY, ELLEN	BAL	050	9TH WARD
SHARLEP, JOHN *	WAS	136	2ND DIST
SHARLING, EVA	BAL	120	11TH WAR
SHARMAN, CONRAD	BAL	239	1ST DIST
SHARMAN, HARRIET	BAL	299	20TH WAR
SHARNEL, HANSON	PRI	105	PISCATAW
SHAROE, ELIZBAETH	FRE	046	FREDERIC
SHARON, MARY J.	HAR	110	2ND DIST
SHARON, SKINNER	HAR	136	2ND DIST
SHAROW, ELIZA	HAR	110	2ND DIST
SHARP, ABRAM W.	QUE	137	1ST E DI
SHARP, ADAM	ANN	513	HOWARD D
SHARP, ALPHEUS P.	BAL	128	16TH WAR
SHARP, ANGELINE	CAR	155	NO TWP L
SHARP, C. M. K.	BAL	066	10TH WAR
SHARP, CELISTIA	ST	339	5TH E DI
SHARP, CHARLES	ALL	107	5TH E.D.
SHARP, CHARLES H.	BAL	118	1ST WARD
SHARP, DANIEL J.	TAL	008	EASTON D
SHARP, DAVES	CEC	167	6TH E DI
SHARP, DAVID	ALL	146	6TH E.D.
SHARP, ELIZABETH	BAL	025	1ST WARD
SHARP, ELIZABETH	BAL	204	6TH DIST
SHARP, ELIZABETH	CAR	105	NO TWP L
SHARP, ELLEN-BLACK	CAR	133	NO TWP L
SHARP, FRANCES	BAL	031	1ST WARD
SHARP, G. W.	ALL	128	4TH E.D.
SHARP, HENRY	BAL	325	3RD WARD
SHARP, HENRY	BAL	024	9TH WARD
SHARP, HENRY	CAR	179	8TH DIST
SHARP, HENRY W.	CEC	150	PORT DUP
SHARP, HORATIO	CAR	131	NO TWP L
SHARP, JACOB	BAL	010	1ST WARD
SHARP, JACOB	BAL	108	2ND DIST
SHARP, JAMES	BAL	111	2ND DIST
SHARP, JAMES	CEC	170	6TH E DI
SHARP, JOHN	ALL	107	5TH E.D.
SHARP, JOHN	ALL	146	6TH E.D.
SHARP, JOHN	BAL	199	17TH WAR
SHARP, JOHN G.	BAL	069	4TH WARD
SHARP, JONATHAN	BAL	017	4TH WARD
SHARP, JOSEPH	BAL	228	2ND WARD
SHARP, JOSEPH-BLACK	CAR	162	NO TWP L
SHARP, LARA F.	BAL	066	10TH WAR
SHARP, M.	ALL	094	5TH E.D.
SHARP, MARTHA	ST	343	5TH E DI
SHARP, MARTHA-BLACK	CAR	094	NO TWP L
SHARP, MARY	BAL	105	10TH WAR
SHARP, MARY A.	BAL	094	5TH WARD
SHARP, MARY R.	BAL	320	3RD WARD
SHARP, RACHEL	CAR	123	NO TWP L
SHARP, REBECCA	ALL	186	9TH E.D.
SHARP, REBECCA	BAL	168	6TH WARD
SHARP, RICHARD-BLACK	CAR	136	NO TWP L
SHARP, RICHARD-BLACK	CAR	148	NO TWP L
SHARP, ROBERT	BAL	071	4TH WARD
SHARP, SAMUEL	ALL	001	3RD E.D.
SHARP, SAMUEL	TAL	075	EASTON T
SHARP, SARAH	BAL	458	1ST DIST
SHARP, SARAH	BAL	112	5TH WARD
SHARP, SHARLOTT	CAR	149	NO TWP L
SHARP, SIDNEY	BAL	238	6TH WARD
SHARP, SYLVINA	BAL	391	8TH WARD
SHARP, T. R.	BAL	329	13TH WAR
SHARP, THOMAS	BAL	232	1ST DIST
SHARP, THOMAS B.	BAL	308	7TH WARD
SHARP, WILLIAM	ALL	067	10TH E.D
SHARP, WILLIAM	CAR	158	NO TWP L
SHARP, WILLIAM-BLACK	CAR	158	NO TWP L
SHARP, WILLIAM-BLACK	BAL	221	2ND WARD
SHARP, WILLOUGHBY-BLACK	CAR	092	NO TWP L
SHARP, WILLOUGHTEY-BLACK	CAR	162	NO TWP L
SHARP,MARY-BLACK	CAR	156	NO TWP L
SHARPE, J.G.	BAL	258	20TH WAR
SHARPE, ROSINA	BAL	175	19TH WAR
SHARPER, EWELINO	BAL	058	10TH WAR
SHARPER, GOERGE	BAL	093	5TH WARD
SHARPER, LLOYD	BAL	093	5TH WARD
SHARPLESS, ELIZABETH	BAL	097	10TH WAR
SHARPLESS, ELIZABETH	WAS	022	2ND SUBD
SHARPLESS, ISAAC	WAS	022	2ND SUBD
SHARPLESS, JOHN	WAS	007	WILLIAMS
SHARPLESS, JOHN	TAL	079	ST MICHA
SHARPLESS, JOHN	BAL	065	1ST WARD
SHARPLEY, JOHN	BAL	012	4TH WARD
SHARPLEY, JOHN	BAL	449	14TH WAR
SHARPLEY, JOSEPH	WOR	300	SNOW HIL
SHARPLEY, SAMUEL	BAL	225	6TH WARD
SHARPLY, DAVID	WOR	323	1ST E DI
SHARPS, ANN	ANN	320	2ND DIST
SHARPS, FRED	ANN	275	ANNAPOLI
SHARPS, JANE P.	ST	256	3RD E DI
SHARRELLS, JACOB	CAR	324	1ST DIST
SHARRER, JACOB	CAR	196	4TH DIST
SHARRER, JOHN	BAL	029	15TH WAR
SHARRETTS, ELIZABETH *	BAL	140	19TH WAR
SHARROW, MARY	FRE	162	EMMITTSB
SHARROW, MARY	FRE	197	5TH E DI
SHARROW, WILLIAM	FRE	179	5TH E DI
SHART, JULIANNA	BAL	305	17TH WAR
SHARTER, HENRY	WAS	211	1ST DIST
SHARTLEY, MARTHA	CAR	361	9TH DIST
SHARTZER, CHRISTIAN	WAS	254	1ST DIST
SHARTZER, JACOB	WAS	263	1ST DIST
SHARVETTS, BENJAMIN	FRE	431	8TH E DI
SHARY, MARGARET	BAL	269	2ND WARD
SHASE, LEAH	SOM	427	PRINCESS
SHATE, PETER	ALL	209	CUMBERLA
SHATENHELM, JOHN	FRE	258	NEW MARK
SHATER, CHARLES H.	BAL	144	1ST WARD
SHATER, SARAH	BAL	026	1ST WARD
SHATSER, JOHN	ALL	159	6TH E.D.
SHATSER, JOHN	WAS	273	RIDGEVIL
SHATZER, JOHN	WAS	148	2ND DIST
SHATZLEY, LYMON	WAS	128	2ND DIST
SHATZLY, MARY	WAS	125	HAGERSTO
SHAUAHANNEN, JOHN *	BAL	118	2ND DIST
SHAUB, HENRY	BAL	021	15TH WAR
SHAUB, JACOB	BAL	281	1ST DIST
SHAUB, JACOB	BAL	399	1ST DIST
SHAUCK, JARRETT	BAL	216	6TH DIST
SHAUCK, JARRETT	BAL	204	6TH DIST
SHAUCK, JOHN N.	BAL	216	6TH DIST
SHAUCK, PETER F.	BAL	218	6TH DIST
SHAUCK, ROSANNA	BAL	216	6TH DIST
SHAUCKER, JARETT	BAL	003	4TH WARD
SHAUEN, GRAFTON	FRE	006	FREDERIC
SHAUEN, SAMUEL F.	FRE	404	JEFFERSO
SHAUGHNESSY, ELLEN	BAL	054	9TH WARD
SHAUK, GEORGE	BAL	304	3RD WARD
SHAUL, NOAH	BAL	190	5TH DIST
SHAUL, RACHAEL	BAL	190	5TH DIST
SHAUL, SAMUEL	BAL	184	5TH DIST
SHAULK, JOSEPH	BAL	433	1ST DIST
SHAUM, ADAM	BAL	089	2ND DIST
SHAUM, JOHN	FRE	411	8TH E DI
SHAUM, JOHN A.	FRE	439	8TH E DI
SHAUN, JOHN	QUE	149	1ST E DI
SHAUN, SAMUEL	QUE	188	3RD E DI
SHAUNABROOK, FRANCIS *	BAL	107	2ND DIST
SHAUNESSEY, JOHN	HAR	076	BEL AIR
SHAUR, LEWIS	FRE	101	FREDERIC
SHAVEN, CORNELIUS	FRE	013	FREDERIC
SHAVEN, SHEDRICK	FRE	209	BUCKEYST
SHAVER, JOSEPH	CAR	277	7TH DIST
SHAVER, WILLIAM *	WAS	058	2ND SUBD
SHAW, ANDREW	BAL	293	7TH WARD
SHAW, ANN	BAL	077	2ND DIST
SHAW, ANN	MGM	442	CLARKSTR
SHAW, ANN	BAL	121	11TH WAR
SHAW, ANN J.	HAR	031	1ST DIST
SHAW, BENJAMIN	ALL	029	2ND E.D.
SHAW, CALEB C.	BAL	098	15TH WAR
SHAW, CATHARINE	WAS	142	2ND DIST
SHAW, CHANDLER T.	PRI	050	AQUASCO
SHAW, CHARLES	PRI	057	AQUASCO
SHAW, CHARLES	PRI	122	PISCATAW
SHAW, CHARLES	ST	315	4TH E DI
SHAW, CHARLES	CHA	288	BOJANTOW
SHAW, CHARLES H.	BAL	350	1ST DIST
SHAW, DANIEL	BAL	119	1ST WARD
SHAW, DANIEL	BAL	226	2ND WARD
SHAW, DANIEL	BAL	226	2ND WARD
SHAW, DANIEL	BAL	188	2ND WARD
SHAW, DAVID	BAL	077	2ND DIST
SHAW, DAVID	BAL	117	2ND DIST
SHAW, DAVID	BAL	109	2ND DIST
SHAW, DAVID	BAL	288	7TH WARD
SHAW, DAVID	BAL	122	5TH WARD
SHAW, DAVID T.	BAL	349	13TH WAR
SHAW, DEBORAH	MGM	333	CRACKLIN
SHAW, E.	KEN	218	2ND DIST
SHAW, EELIZABETH	TAL	001	EASTON D
SHAW, ELBERT	MGM	324	CRACKLIN
SHAW, ELENORA	BAL	134	18TH WAR
SHAW, ELIAS	BAL	425	14TH WAR
SHAW, ELIJAH	FRE	139	CREAGERS
SHAW, ELIZA	CHA	288	BOJANTOW
SHAW, ELIZA	WAS	117	2ND DIST
SHAW, ELIZA	ANN	278	ANNAPOLI
SHAW, ELIZABETH	BAL	372	8TH WARD
SHAW, ELIZABETH	WAS	179	BOONSBOR
SHAW, ELIZABETH	WAS	217	1ST DIST
SHAW, ELIZABETH	BAL	201	17TH WAR
SHAW, ELIZABETH	BAL	153	11TH WAR
SHAW, ELIZABETH B. T.	BAL	336	3RD WARD
SHAW, EMMA J.	BAL	416	3RD WARD
SHAW, ERASMUS M.	BAL	170	16TH WAR
SHAW, EVAN	PRI	045	VANSVILL
SHAW, FRANCES	FRE	285	WOODSBOR
SHAW, GEORGE	CEC	157	PORT DUP
SHAW, GEORGE	ST	275	3RD E DI
SHAW, GEORGE W.	BAL	350	1ST DIST
SHAW, GREENBURG W.	BAL	397	3RD WARD
SHAW, HENRY	ALL	122	4TH E.D.
SHAW, HENRY L.	CHA	289	BOJANTOW
SHAW, HEZEKIAH	FRE	137	CREAGERS
SHAW, HUGH	BAL	293	12TH WAR
SHAW, ISABELLA	BAL	398	3RD WARD
SHAW, ISABELLA	WAS	186	BOONSBOR
SHAW, ISAIAH	BAL	194	17TH WAR
SHAW, J.	BAL	147	1ST WARD
SHAW, JACOB	WAS	140	2ND DIST
SHAW, JAMES	PRI	011	BLADENSB
SHAW, JAMES	BAL	132	1ST WARD
SHAW, JAMES	BAL	282	12TH WAR
SHAW, JAMES	ALL	126	4TH E.D.
SHAW, JAMES	BAL	091	2ND DIST
SHAW, JAMES	BAL	154	5TH WARD
SHAW, JAMES	BAL	157	1ST WARD
SHAW, JAMES	BAL	125	1ST WARD
SHAW, JAMES A.	MGM	379	ROCKERLE
SHAW, JAMES L.	MGM	362	BERRYS D
SHAW, JAMS	BAL	139	1ST WARD
SHAW, JOHN	BAL	006	1ST WARD
SHAW, JOHN	BAL	042	1ST WARD
SHAW, JOHN	BAL	070	10TH WAR
SHAW, JOHN	HAR	071	1ST DIST
SHAW, JOHN	FRE	137	CREAGERS
SHAW, JOHN	FRE	160	EMMITTSB
SHAW, JOHN	BAL	437	14TH WAR
SHAW, JOHN	CEC	189	7TH E DI
SHAW, JOHN	FRE	384	PETERSVI
SHAW, JOHN	BAL	296	20TH WAR
SHAW, JOHN E.F.	ST	347	5TH E DI
SHAW, JOHN W.	MGM	431	CLARKSTR
SHAW, JOSEPH	ALL	123	4TH E.D.
SHAW, JOSEPH	BAL	022	15TH WAR
SHAW, JOSEPH F.	ST	347	5TH E DI
SHAW, JOSEPH T.	BAL	201	17TH WAR
SHAW, JOSEPHINE	BAL	362	8TH WARD
SHAW, JOSHUA M.	BAL	394	3RD WARD
SHAW, LAURA V.	BAL	022	15TH WAR
SHAW, LEONARD D.	MGM	441	CLARKSTR
SHAW, LEVI	WAS	048	2ND SUBD
SHAW, LEVI	ALL	259	CUMBERLA
SHAW, LEVI	MGM	316	CRACKLIN
SHAW, LOUISA	ALL	171	7TH E.D.
SHAW, LOUISA	BAL	008	1ST WARD
SHAW, LYDIA	BAL	197	11TH WAR
SHAW, LYDNEE *	ALL	122	4TH E.D.
SHAW, MARIA A.	MGM	355	BERRYS D
SHAW, MARINDA	BAL	425	1ST DIST
SHAW, MARTHA	BAL	353	7TH WARD
SHAW, MARY	BAL	329	3RD WARD
SHAW, MARY	WAS	116	2ND DIST
SHAW, MARY	WAS	121	2ND DIST
SHAW, MARY C.	ANN	434	HOWARD D
SHAW, MARY J.	BAL	408	3RD WARD
SHAW, MATHEW	BAL	134	18TH WAR
SHAW, MATHEW	BAL	099	5TH WARD
SHAW, MATHIAS	PRI	010	BLADENSB
SHAW, MOSES	CAR	387	2ND DIST
SHAW, MRS. W.C.	BAL	205	11TH WAR
SHAW, NATHAN	ANN	442	HOWARD D
SHAW, NATHAN	MGM	349	BERRYS D
SHAW, NICHOLAS	MGM	353	BERRYS D
SHAW, NICHOLAS	HAR	069	1ST DIST
SHAW, NICHOLAS	BAL	324	3RD WARD
SHAW, PETER	BAL	121	1ST WARD
SHAW, PETER	BAL	133	1ST WARD
SHAW, R.	BAL	235	12TH WAR
SHAW, REZIN	PRI	016	BLADENSB
SHAW, RICHARD	BAL	247	2ND WARD
SHAW, RICHARD	BAL	156	2ND DIST
SHAW, RICHARD	BAL	416	3RD WARD
SHAW, RICHARD J.	KEN	232	2ND DIST
SHAW, ROBERT	BAL	401	1ST DIST
SHAW, ROBERT	BAL	140	16TH WAR
SHAW, SAMUEL	BAL	025	2ND DIST
SHAW, SAMUEL	CHA	266	MIDDLETO
SHAW, SAMUEL H.	BAL	036	4TH WARD
SHAW, SARAH	MGM	362	BERRYS D
SHAW, SARAH	ALL	162	6TH E.D.
SHAW, SARAH A.	WAS	117	2ND DIST
SHAW, SARAH C.	FRE	205	BUCKEYST
SHAW, SARAH W.	CAR	081	NO TWP L
SHAW, SUSAN	HAR	017	1ST DIST
SHAW, SUSAN	BAL	334	13TH WAR
SHAW, SUSANA	BAL	305	1ST DIST
SHAW, THOMAS	BAL	128	1ST WARD
SHAW, THOMAS	FRE	176	5TH E DI
SHAW, THOMAS	WAS	178	BOONSBOR
SHAW, THOMAS B.	HAR	027	1ST DIST
SHAW, WASHINGTON	BAL	255	2ND WARD
SHAW, WILLIAM	BAL	394	3RD WARD
SHAW, WILLIAM	ALL	131	4TH E.D.
SHAW, WILLIAM	ALL	012	3RD E.D.
SHAW, WILLIAM	BAL	443	1ST DIST
SHAW, WILLIAM	BAL	220	12TH WAR
SHAW, WILLIAM	MGM	432	CLARKSTR
SHAW, WILLIAM	CAR	308	1ST DIST
SHAW, WILLIAM	CAR	236	UNION TO
SHAW, WILLIAM	PRI	038	VANSVILL
SHAW, WILLIAM H.	FRE	137	CREAGERS
SHAW, WILLIAM J.	TAL	007	EASTON D
SHAW, WILLIAM S.	CHA	255	MIDDLETO
SHAW, WILLIAM S.	BAL	216	6TH WARD
SHAW, WILLIAM T.	BAL	066	1ST WARD
SHAW, WILLIAM W.	BAL	332	3RD WARD
SHAW, ZACHARIAH	FRE	205	BUCKEYST
SHAW, ZACHARIAH	PRI	003	BLADENSB
SHAWB, JOHN	BAL	221	1ST DIST
SHAWBARGER, LAURENCE	BAL	381	1ST DIST
SHAWEN, JOSEPH	FRE	404	JEFFERSO
SHAWEN, JOSEPH	FRE	403	JEFFERSO
SHAWEN, RICHARD	FRE	070	FREDERIC
SHAWER, JOHN	WAS	052	2ND SUBD
SHAWLEY, ANN E.	QUE	213	3RD E DI
SHAWMAN, DAVID	WAS	061	2ND SUBD
SHAWMAN, GEORGE	WAS	050	2ND SUBD
SHAWMAN, MELVILLE	WAS	082	2ND SUBD
SHAWMAN, SARAH	WAS	082	2ND SUBD
SHAWN, AQYUILLA	BAL	148	2ND DIST
SHAWN, MARY E.	PRI	106	PISCATAW
SHAWN, PERE	QUE	173	2ND E DI
SHAWN, WILLIAM	BAL	149	2ND DIST
SHAY, BARNETT	HAR	186	3RD DIST
SHAY, CATHERINE	BAL	104	10TH WAR
SHAY, CORNEALIUS	BAL	273	1ST DIST
SHAY, JAMES	BAL	097	2ND DIST
SHAY, JAMES	HAR	186	3RD DIST
SHAY, JAMES K.	BAL	022	2ND DIST
SHAY, JOHN	BAL	444	1ST DIST
SHAY, JOHN	WAS	041	2ND SUBD
SHAY, MARY	BAL	043	1ST WARD
SHAY, PATRICK	BAL	158	2ND DIST
SHAY, THOMAS	WAS	041	2ND SUBD
SHAY, WILLIAM	KEN	218	2ND DIST
SHAY, WILLIAM C.	BAL	022	2ND DIST
SHAYER, JOHN	BAL	267	1ST DIST
SHAYS, M.	BAL	292	12TH WAR
SHCAFFER, ELIZABETH	BAL	193	2ND WARD
SHCLEIGH, JOHN	WAS	128	HAGERSTO
SHCRAUMYER, SUSAN	WAS	112	2ND DIST
SHCUEEN, JACOB	BAL	166	2ND DIST
SHEA, DANIEL	BAL	083	10TH WAR
SHEA, DAVID Q.	BAL	332	7TH WARD
SHEA, ESTHER	SOM	548	TYASKIN
SHEA, GEORGE D.	BAL	001	9TH WARD
SHEA, HENERETTA	SOM	414	DUBLIN D
SHEA, JOHN	BAL	308	3RD WARD
SHEA, JULIA	BAL	258	20TH WAR
SHEAF, HENRY	BAL	446	8TH WARD
SHEAF, JOSEPH	BAL	175	6TH WARD
SHEAF, PERRY	BAL	174	6TH WARD
SHEAF, ROSETTA	BAL	414	14TH WAR
SHEAFER, JOHN H.	WAS	137	HAGERSTO
SHEAFFER, HENRY	BAL	459	14TH WAR
SHEAKLES, JOHN	BAL	086	18TH WAR
SHEAKLES, RICHARD W.	BAL	043	18TH WAR
SHEAKLIS, MARY	BAL	101	18TH WAR
SHEAN, JOHN	CAR	395	2ND DIST
SHEAN, JULIA ANN	CAR	400	2ND DIST
SHEAN, MATILDA	CAR	392	2ND DIST
SHEAN, MELIA	FRE	411	8TH E DI
SHEAN, PATRICK	BAL	400	1ST DIST
SHEAN,ELIZA E.	CAR	397	2ND DIST
SHEANAN, JOHN P.	BAL	404	3RD WARD
SHEAR, JOHN	BAL	371	3RD WARD
SHEAR, MARY	BAL	372	3RD WARD
SHEAR, WILLIAM	BAL	397	3RD WARD

Name	County	Page	District
SHEAR, WILLIAM*	DOR	456	1ST DIST
SHEARDEN, SARAH	BAL	029	2ND DIST
SHEARDON, ASBURY	HAR	128	2ND DIST
SHEARDON, MARY	HAR	084	2ND DIST
SHEARDON, RICHARD	HAR	125	2ND DIST
SHEARER, JAMES	ALL	105	5TH E.D.
SHEARER, MARGARET	CEC	111	4TH E DI
SHEARER, MARTHA	CEC	140	5TH E DI
SHEARER, SARAH J.	CEC	136	6TH E DI
SHEARER, THOMAS	CEC	195	6TH E DI
SHEARER, WILLIAM	CEC	128	5TH E DI
SHEARMAN, OTHO	FRE	030	FREDERIC
SHEARN, RICHARD	BAL	313	1ST DIST
SHEARON, ROBERT	CEC	117	4TH E DI
SHEARS, EDWARD	CEC	008	ELKTON 3
SHEARS, HERMAN	BAL	285	17TH WAR
SHEARS, LEONORA*	BAL	021	4TH WARD
SHEATENHOLM, MARY	FRE	257	NEW MARK
SHEATH, JAMES W.	BAL	169	6TH WARD
SHEATHLAND, HANNAH	HAR	045	1ST DIST
SHEAVES, THOMAS	SOM	442	DAMES QU
SHEAW, ISABELLA	CAR	358	9TH DIST
SHEAW, JOHN	HAR	121	2ND DIST
SHEEA, BOWEL	BAL	396	8TH WARD
SHEBAN, BENJAMIN	BAL	367	3RD WARD
SHEBDON, WILLIAM	BAL	251	17TH WAR
SHEBE, BRIAN	ALL	249	CUMBERLA
SHEBEL, JOSEPH	BAL	043	1ST WARD
SHEBUNN, CHARLES H.	CHA	288	BOJANTOW
SHEBY, GEORGE	CEC	137	6TH E DI
SHECK, JAMES	BAL	242	20TH WAR
SHECKEE, ANN W.	HAR	195	3RD DIST
SHECKELL, ABRAHAM	MGM	344	CLARKSBU
SHECKELL, LEVI	ANN	360	3RD DIST
SHECKELLS, ANN	CAL	021	2ND DIST
SHECKELLS, ASA	MGM	344	CLARKSBU
SHECKELLS, CHARLES	PRI	009	BLADENSB
SHECKELLS, ELIZABETH	PRI	012	BLADENSB
SHECKELLS, EZRA	ANN	318	2ND DIST
SHECKELLS, FRANCIS	ANN	301	1ST DIST
SHECKELLS, JOHN	BAL	160	16TH WAR
SHECKELLS, JULIA	PRI	009	BLADENSB
SHECKELLS, RICHARD	ANN	301	1ST DIST
SHECKELLS, THEODORE	PRI	010	BLADENSB
SHECKELLS, THEODORE	PRI	010	BLADENSB
SHECKELS, OTIS SKINER	BAL	374	1ST DIST
SHECKELS, THOMAS	BAL	023	15TH WAR
SHECKLAND, JULIA	BAL	067	15TH WAR
SHECKLES, BENJAMIN	BAL	236	17TH WAR
SHECKLES, CALEB	PRI	076	MARLBROU
SHECKLES, ENOCH	ANN	399	8TH DIST
SHECKLES, HORACE	CAR	366	9TH DIST
SHECKLES, MARY	BAL	302	17TH WAR
SHECKLES, RICHARD	WAS	151	HAGERSTO
SHECKLES, THOAMS	BAL	084	18TH WAR
SHECKLES, WILLIAM	BAL	302	17TH WAR
SHECKTER, JOHN	BAL	273	20TH WAR
SHED, JOHN H.	BAL	247	20TH WAR
SHEDDEIN, JOHN N.*	DOR	375	1ST DIST
SHEDDEN, JOHN M.*	BAL	378	3RD WARD
SHEDDEN, ROBERT	BAL	375	3RD WARD
SHEDDER, JOHN M.*	BAL	378	3RD WARD
SHEDDIN, EMILY	DOR	380	1ST DIST
SHEDEL, JACOB	BAL	194	19TH WAR
SHEDERS, CATHARINE	WAS	280	LEITERSB
SHEDERS, JOHN R.	WAS	280	LEITERSB
SHEDIE, MARGARET	BAL	195	19TH WAR
SHEDLE, SILVESTER	BAL	370	8TH WARD
SHEDMAN, CATHARINE	WAS	149	HAGERSTO
SHEDMAN, JOHN	WAS	149	HAGERSTO
SHEDMOLD, JOSEPH	ALL	112	5TH E.D.
SHEDRICK, JAMES	MGM	441	CLARKSTR
SHEDRICK, JOHN	BAL	421	3RD WARD
SHEDRICK, MICHAL	WAS	140	2ND DIST
SHEDRICK, NANCEY	WAS	140	2ND DIST
SHEDRICK, RICHARD H.	BAL	407	3RD WARD
SHEDRY, PHILIP	WAS	162	HAGERSTO
SHEEHAN, GEORGE	BAL	449	14TH WAR
SHEEHAN, TIMOTHY	BAL	199	6TH WARD
SHEEHAN, WILLIAM	BAL	054	18TH WAR
SHEEKELLS, JOHN	MGM	342	CLARKSBU
SHEEKER, CHARLES *	BAL	273	20TH WAR
SHEEKLES, W. P.	BAL	064	18TH WAR
SHEELER, ANTHONY	BAL	387	8TH WARD
SHEELER, CATHERINE	BAL	387	8TH WARD
SHEELER, GEORGE*	BAL	412	3RD WARD
SHEELER, JOHN	BAL	119	5TH WARD
SHEELES, AMELIA	WAS	146	HAGERSTO
SHEELEY, JACOB	FRE	179	5TH E DI
SHEELEY, JOHN	FRE	179	5TH E DI
SHEELY, EDWARD .	PRI	075	MARLBROU
SHEENAN, ANN	BAL	034	9TH WARD
SHEER, WILLIAM	BAL	092	5TH WARD
SHEERAN, APTRICK	HAR	001	1ST DIST
SHEERBUT, GEORGE W.	PRI	080	QUEEN AN
SHEERIN, JAMES	FRE	067	FREDERIC
SHEERIN, THOMAS	FRE	067	FREDERIC
SHEES, LOUISA	BAL	289	1ST DIST
SHEETENHELM, THOMAS	FRE	258	NEW MARK
SHEETENHOLEN, ARTHUR	FRE	258	NEW MARK
SHEETS, ABRAHAM	CAR	306	1ST DIST
SHEETS, AMELIA	FRE	044	FREDERIC
SHEETS, ANN	FRE	191	5TH E DI
SHEETS, ANN M.	FRE	130	CREAGERS
SHEETS, CANIEL	CAR	353	6TH DIST
SHEETS, DORATHY	CAR	245	3RD DIST
SHEETS, ELI ERB	CAR	258	3RD DIST
SHEETS, ELIZA	BAL	164	16TH WAR
SHEETS, ELIZABETH	BAL	128	16TH WAR
SHEETS, ELIZABETH	FRE	166	EMMITTSB
SHEETS, ELIZABETH	WAS	280	LEITERSB
SHEETS, GEORGE	FRE	171	5TH E DI
SHEETS, GEORGE	CAR	270	WESTMINS
SHEETS, GEORGE	BAL	201	19TH WAR
SHEETS, HANNAH	ANN	512	HOWARD D
SHEETS, HANNAH E.	FRE	183	5TH E DI
SHEETS, HENRY	BAL	143	19TH WAR
SHEETS, HENRY C.	BAL	207	11TH WAR
SHEETS, JACOB	FRE	165	EMMITTSB
SHEETS, JACOB	CAR	258	3RD DIST
SHEETS, JACOBV	FRE	183	5TH E DI
SHEETS, JAMES	CAR	288	7TH DIST
SHEETS, JAOCB	CAR	282	7TH DIST
SHEETS, JOHN*	BAL	328	3RD WARD
SHEETS, JOSEPH	WAS	147	HAGERSTO
SHEETS, MARGARET	ALL	008	3RD E.D.
SHEETS, MARY	WAS	237	CAVETOWN
SHEETS, MARY C.	CAR	261	3RD DIST
SHEETS, NUTON	WAS	098	2ND DIST
SHEETS, PETER	CAR	292	7TH DIST
SHEETS, REUBEN	WAS	281	LEITERSB
SHEETS, SARAH	CAR	268	WESTMINS
SHEETS, SARAH	FRE	039	FREDERIC
SHEETS, SMAUEL	BAL	267	12TH WAR
SHEETS, THOMAS	WAS	102	2ND DIST
SHEETS, THOMAS A.*	BAL	322	3RD WARD
SHEETS, WILLIAM	ALL	018	3RD E.D.
SHEETS, WILLIAM	BAL	129	16TH WAR
SHEFE, EMORY	CEC	057	1ST E DI
SHEFFELEIN, GEORGE*	BAL	328	3RD WARD
SHEFFER, ALEXANDER	BAL	118	15TH WAR
SHEFFER, CHRISTIANA	BAL	420	14TH WAR
SHEFFER, DANIEL	FRE	352	MIDDLETO
SHEFFER, JONAS	FRE	333	MIDDLETO
SHEFFER, PHILIP	FRE	335	MIDDLETO
SHEFFER, SARAH	FRE	322	MIDDLETO
SHEFFERD, BENJAMIN	BAL	241	20TH WAR
SHEFFIELD, WILLIAM R.	BAL	261	20TH WAR
SHEFFLER, DAVID A.	BAL	034	18TH WAR
SHEFFRAN, POLLY	BAL	201	19TH WAR
SHEFLER, CHARLES	FRE	101	FREDERIC
SHEHAN, JEREMIAH	ALL	214	CUMBERLA
SHEHAN, WILLIAM	BAL	248	6TH WARD
SHEHARD, EDWARD	WAS	013	WILLIAMS
SHEHAUN, WILLIAM	BAL	053	18TH WAR
SHEHEE, WILLIAM*	DOR	448	1ST DIST
SHEHON, MASON	TAL	059	EASTON D
SHEHOON, JOHN	DOR	419	1ST DIST
SHEHORN, LEAH	DOR	418	1ST DIST
SHEHOUSE, WILLIAM	BAL	038	4TH WARD
SHEHREN, WILLIAM	DOR	415	1ST DIST
SHEID, WALTER H.	FRE	338	MIDDLETO
SHEIF, ANN E.	BAL	158	6TH WARD
SHEILDS, CHARLES	BAL	171	11TH WAR
SHEILDS, THOMAS	BAL	165	11TH WAR
SHEILE, DANE	BAL	238	12TH WAR
SHEILEY, WILLIAM	BAL	301	17TH WAR
SHEIP, A.	BAL	470	14TH WAR
SHEIPPLING, FETIS	BAL	250	2ND WARD
SHEKELY, MARY	ALL	217	CUMBERLA
SHELABERGER, ANN A.	WAS	291	1ST DIST
SHELAN, CATHRZINE	CAR	273	WESTMINS
SHELAN, JAMES	BAL	106	5TH WARD
SHELBY, MARTHA	CEC	168	6TH E DI
SHELDEN, JOHN	FRE	384	PETERSVI
SHELDON, BETTY	BAL	322	3RD WARD
SHELDON, JAMES	BAL	266	17TH WAR
SHELDON, JOHN	BAL	333	7TH WARD
SHELDON, LUCIS	BAL	056	4TH WARD
SHELDON, MARGARET	BAL	296	7TH WARD
SHELOT, C.	BAL	255	6TH WARD
SHELDY, JAMES	CEC	041	CHESAPEA
SHELER, FREDERICK	BAL	226	17TH WAR
SHELER, WILLAIM	BAL	081	2ND DIST
SHELEY, CALEB	WAS	241	CAVETOWN
SHELEY, FRANCIS A.	WAS	242	CAVETOWN
SHELEY, JOSEPH	WAS	261	1ST DIST
SHELEY, JOSHUA	WAS	242	CAVETOWN
SHELHORN, JACOB	ALL	195	CUMBERLA
SHELL, HELEN	BAL	045	15TH WAR
SHELL, JOHN	BAL	208	19TH WAR
SHELL, MARGARETT	BAL	017	4TH WARD
SHELLAMN, JAMES M.	CAR	271	WESTMINS
SHELLBRANK, HENRY	FRE	080	FREDERIC
SHELLENBERGER, DOMINICK	BAL	120	18TH WAR
SHELLENBERGER, HENRY	BAL	121	18TH WAR
SHELLENGER, HENRY	BAL	181	11TH WAR
SHELLER, CHRISTIAN	WAS	293	1ST DIST
SHELLEY, JOHN	BAL	018	2ND DIST
SHELLEY, JOHN	BAL	293	12TH WAR
SHELLEY, JOHN	BAL	211	19TH WAR
SHELLEY, PETER L.	BAL	350	7TH WARD
SHELLEY, SARAH	BAL	318	12TH WAR
SHELLHOUSE, JOHN	ALL	201	CUMBERLA
SHELLHOUSE, PETER	ALL	201	CUMBERLA
SHELLING, FREDERICK	ALL	216	CUMBERLA
SHELLMAN, JAMSE M.	CAR	271	WESTMINS
SHELLMAN, WILLIAM	FRE	028	FREDERIC
SHELLS, WILLIAM	FRE	263	NEW MARK
SHELLY, CATHERINE	BAL	376	3RD WARD
SHELLY, DANIEL	BAL	081	2ND DIST
SHELLY, EDWARD M.	BAL	231	1ST DIST
SHELLY, FREDERICK	BAL	415	3RD WARD
SHELLY, JOHN	CEC	166	6TH E DI
SHELLY, JOHN	WOR	290	9TH E DI
SHELLY, JOHN T.	BAL	248	1ST DIST
SHELLY, LEVIN	WOR	299	SNOW HIL
SHELLY, WILLAIM	BAL	248	1ST DIST
SHELLY, WILLIAM	BAL	376	3RD WARD
SHELLY, WILLIAM	CEC	166	6TH E DI
SHELMAN, ADOLPHUS	FRE	188	5TH E DI
SHELMAN, DANIEL	FRE	210	BUCKEYST
SHELOIN, ELIZABETH	BAL	285	20TH WAR
SHELP, FREDERICK	ALL	149	6TH E.D.
SHELT, SAMUEL	CAR	310	1ST DIST
SHELTENA, FREDRICK *	HAR	197	3RD DIST
SHELTER, HENRY	BAL	327	7TH WARD
SHELTON, ANGELINE	FRE	304	WOODSBOR
SHELTON, CATHERINE	BAL	350	3RD WARD
SHELTON, CHARLES-BLACK	FRE	441	8TH E DI
SHELTON, JAMES	FRE	064	FREDERIC
SHELTON, JOHN	BAL	115	2ND DIST
SHELTON, LEAH	SOM	439	DAMES QU
SHELTON, THOMAS	FRE	419	8TH E DI
SHELTON, WILLIAM	SOM	439	DAMES QU
SHELY, MICHAEL	CEC	136	6TH E DI
SHEMAKER, JOHN	CAR	321	1ST DIST
SHEMAS, PRISCILLA	BAL	178	19TH WAR
SHEMERS, WILLIAM	ALL	122	4TH E.D.
SHEN, THOMAS C.	CAR	394	2ND DIST
SHENABECK, S.C.	WAS	005	WILLIAMS
SHENCER, EASTER	WAS	009	WILLIAMS
SHENER, MARI A*	BAL	289	1ST DIST
SHENK, JOHN	FRE	115	CREAGERS
SHENLER, ROBERT	BAL	351	13TH WAR
SHENNESSY, JAMES	BAL	394	14TH WAR
SHENNY, JAMES	BAL	198	2ND WARD
SHENTON, ANN	DOR	327	3RD DIVI
SHENTON, CHARLES	DOR	333	3RD DIVI
SHENTON, GEORGE W.	CAL	017	1ST DIST
SHENTON, HENERY	DOR	372	3RD DIVI
SHENTON, JOHN	DOR	326	3RD DIVI
SHENTON, MOSES	DOR	333	3RD DIVI
SHENTON, ROBERT	DOR	356	3RD DIVI
SHENTON, ROSE	DOR	356	3RD DIVI
SHENTON, WILLIAM	CAL	017	1ST DIST
SHENTOR, DOROTHEY	DOR	372	3RD DIVI
SHENTOR, HENERY	DOR	353	3RD DIVI
SHENTOR, MARGRET	DOR	353	3RD DIVI
SHEOFFER, WILLIAM	BAL	455	14TH WAR
SHEOFNER, SAMUEL	BAL	471	14TH WAR
SHEOKETTS, SUSAN	MGM	342	CLARKSBU
SHEPARD, CHARLES	CEC	136	6TH E DI
SHEPARD, DAVID	CEC	131	6TH E DI
SHEPARD, HARRIET	CEC	121	4TH E DI
SHEPARD, JOEL	FRE	029	FREDERIC
SHEPARD, JOHN	CEC	118	4TH E DI
SHEPARD, MARY A.	BAL	396	1ST DIST
SHEPES, ELIZA	DOR	388	1ST DIST
SHEPHARD, LAURA	BAL	059	10TH WAR
SHEPHEARD, AARON-BLACK	CAR	166	NO TWP L
SHEPHEARD, ADAM-BLACK	CAR	127	NO TWP L
SHEPHEARD, ARY-BLACK	CAR	124	NO TWP L
SHEPHEARD, ELI	CAR	125	NO TWP L
SHEPHEARD, ELLENDER	CAR	086	NO TWP L
SHEPHEARD, GEORGE	BAL	337	13TH WAR
SHEPHEARD, GEORGE-BLACK	CAR	074	NO TWP L
SHEPHEARD, GEORGE-BLACK	CAR	070	NO TWP L
SHEPHEARD, JACOB-BLACK	CAR	127	NO TWP L
SHEPHEARD, JOHN	CAR	089	NO TWP L
SHEPHEARD, MARY ANN	BAL	338	13TH WAR
SHEPHEARD, RHODY-BLACK	CAR	127	NO TWP L
SHEPHEARD, SARAH	CAR	065	NO TWP L
SHEPHEARD, THOMAS-BLACK	CAR	127	NO TWP L
SHEPHERD, A.F.	ALL	188	9TH E.D.
SHEPHERD, AMANDA	QUE	186	3RD E DI
SHEPHERD, ANN	BAL	183	6TH WARD
SHEPHERD, CALEB	DOR	386	1ST DIST
SHEPHERD, CHRISTIAN	WAS	132	HAGERSTO
SHEPHERD, DOLLY	QUE	225	4TH E DI
SHEPHERD, EDWARD	DOR	373	1ST DIST
SHEPHERD, ELIZA	BAL	057	10TH WAR
SHEPHERD, EVE	DOR	452	1ST DIST
SHEPHERD, FINEY	SOM	426	PRINCESS
SHEPHERD, GEORGE	ALL	213	CUMBERLA
SHEPHERD, H.	PRI	117	PISCATAW
SHEPHERD, ISRAEL	BAL	096	1ST WARD
SHEPHERD, LEAKIN	ANN	495	HOWARD D
SHEPHERD, PRICELLA	SOM	359	BRINKLEY
SHEPHERD, PRISCILLA C.	CAL	049	3RD DIST
SHEPHERD, RICHARD	QUE	178	2ND E DI
SHEPHERD, RICHARD	QUE	170	2ND E DI
SHEPHERD, SAMUEL	ANN	502	HOWARD D
SHEPHERD, SOPHIA	ANN	317	1ST DIST
SHEPHERD, THOMAS	ANN	502	HOWARD D
SHEPHERD, WILLIAM	ANN	302	1ST DIST
SHEPLEY, ANN	BAL	226	12TH WAR
SHEPLEY, ELIZABETH	MGM	420	MEDLEY 3
SHEPLEY, JOHN	ALL	127	4TH E.D.
SHEPLEY, RICHARD	ALL	181	8TH E.D.
SHEPP, GOERGE	ALL	039	2ND E.D.
SHEPPAN, ROBERT	BAL	251	20TH WAR
SHEPPARD, ANDREW	BAL	208	11TH WAR
SHEPPARD, ANN	BAL	265	2ND WARD
SHEPPARD, ANN C.	FRE	064	FREDERIC
SHEPPARD, BENJAMIN	WOR	204	4TH E DI
SHEPPARD, CATHARINE	ALL	159	6TH E.D.
SHEPPARD, CHARLES	BAL	136	18TH WAR
SHEPPARD, DAVID	KEN	254	1ST DIST
SHEPPARD, ELIZA	BAL	127	11TH WAR
SHEPPARD, ELIZA	BAL	259	17TH WAR
SHEPPARD, ELIZABETH	BAL	311	12TH WAR
SHEPPARD, ELIZABETH	WAS	158	2ND DIST
SHEPPARD, GEORGE	ANN	455	HOWARD D
SHEPPARD, GEORGE	KEN	255	1ST DIST
SHEPPARD, GEORGE	BAL	299	17TH WAR
SHEPPARD, GEORGE	BAL	301	17TH WAR
SHEPPARD, HENRY	CAR	387	2ND DIST
SHEPPARD, HENRY	BAL	464	14TH WAR
SHEPPARD, HENRY	WAS	139	2ND DIST
SHEPPARD, JAMES	BAL	283	17TH WAR
SHEPPARD, JAMES	BAL	058	2ND DIST
SHEPPARD, JAMES	BAL	115	1ST WARD
SHEPPARD, JANE	KEN	261	1ST DIST
SHEPPARD, JOHN	KEN	276	1ST DIST
SHEPPARD, JOHN	WAS	152	2ND DIST
SHEPPARD, JOHN	BAL	097	1ST WARD
SHEPPARD, JOHN	BAL	250	5TH WARD
SHEPPARD, JOHN	BAL	047	15TH WAR
SHEPPARD, JOHN	BAL	221	12TH WAR
SHEPPARD, JOHN	BAL	274	17TH WAR
SHEPPARD, JOHN D.	WOR	207	4TH E DI
SHEPPARD, JOHN W.	BAL	042	15TH WAR
SHEPPARD, JOSEPH H.	BAL	163	19TH WAR
SHEPPARD, LEWIS	BAL	252	20TH WAR
SHEPPARD, MARGARET	KEN	215	2ND DIST
SHEPPARD, MARY	BAL	164	19TH WAR
SHEPPARD, MARY	BAL	189	19TH WAR
SHEPPARD, MIRANDA	BAL	283	20TH WAR
SHEPPARD, MOSES	BAL	357	13TH WAR
SHEPPARD, NATHANIEL	BAL	035	2ND DIST
SHEPPARD, NICHOLAS A.	BAL	043	15TH WAR
SHEPPARD, RACHEL	BAL	024	2ND DIST
SHEPPARD, RESIN	BAL	132	11TH WAR
SHEPPARD, SARAH	BAL	045	2ND DIST
SHEPPARD, SARAH	WOR	246	1ST CENS
SHEPPARD, SARAH	TAL	066	EASTON T
SHEPPARD, SIMON	KEN	220	2ND DIST
SHEPPARD, THOMAS	CAR	413	2ND DIST
SHEPPARD, THOMAS	BAL	082	18TH WAR
SHEPPARD, THOMAS J.	ANN	497	HOWARD D
SHEPPARD, THOMAS P.	CAR	403	2ND DIST
SHEPPARD, WILLIA	BAL	097	1ST WARD
SHEPPARD, WILLIAM	ANN	502	HOWARD D
SHEPPARD, WILLIAM	BAL	296	12TH WAR
SHEPPARD, WILLIAM	CAR	388	2ND DIST
SHEPPARD, WILLIAM	TAL	031	EASTON D
SHEPPARD, WILLIAM	TAL	031	EASTON D
SHEPPARD, WILLIAM H.	TAL	067	EASTON T
SHEPPERD, BASIL	ANN	282	ANNAPOLI
SHEPPERD, BASIL	ANN	265	ANNAPOLI
SHEPPERD, JOSIAH	BAL	045	2ND DIST
SHEPPERD, JOSIAH JR.	BAL	045	2ND DIST
SHEPPERD, PETER	BAL	044	9TH WARD
SHEPPERD, THOMAS	WAS	140	2ND DIST
SHEPPERD, WILLIAM	ANN	301	1ST DIST
SHEPPEY, FREDRICK	BAL	130	18TH WAR
SHEPREY, JANE	MGM	409	MEDLEY 3
SHEPS, JOHN *	BAL	087	15TH WAR
SHEPSON, CHARLES H.	HAR	165	3RD DIST
SHER, JOHN	FRE	047	FREDERIC
SHERA, DAVID M.	CEC	116	3RD E DI
SHERADEN, PATRICK	WAS	164	2ND DIST
SHERAR, ELIZA	HAR	001	1ST DIST
SHERBERT, JOSEPH	ANN	308	1ST DIST
SHERBERT, JOSEPH *	ANN	396	8TH DIST
SHERBERT, WILLIAM	ANN	307	1ST DIST
SHERBOARD, THOMAS	ANN	360	3RD DIST
SHERBORD, JOHN P.	ANN	360	3RD DIST
SHERBORD, WILLIE ANN	ANN	360	3RD DIST

Name	County	Page	District
SHERBUT, JOSEPH *	ANN	396	8TH DIST
SHERCLIFF, WILIAM	ALL	218	CUMBERLA
SHERCLIFFE, JOHN T.	ST	269	3RD E DI
SHERCLIFFE, LEONARD	ALL	179	7TH E.D.
SHERD, ANN	BAL	397	8TH WARD
SHERDAN, EMILA	BAL	456	1ST DIST
SHERDEN, JAMES	BAL	058	18TH WAR
SHERDEN, NANCY MRS-	BAL	098	18TH WAR
SHERDEN, REZEN	BAL	081	2ND DIST
SHERDINE, CONRAD	BAL	060	1ST WARD
SHERDON, DANIEL	BAL	015	2ND DIST
SHERDON, GEORGE	BAL	128	16TH WAR
SHERDON, KESIAH	BAL	273	7TH WARD
SHERDONG, JOHN *	BAL	100	2ND DIST
SHEREDEN, MICHAEL	BAL	303	17TH WAR
SHEREFELTER, M. A.	BAL	057	10TH WAR
SHEREFF, DIONYSIUS	PRI	002	BLADENSB
SHERELIN, BRYAN*	BAL	079	10TH WAR
SHERENSKY, A.	BAL	288	12TH WAR
SHERER, CHRISTIAN	BAL	089	10TH WAR
SHERER, ELIZABETH D.	BAL	041	15TH WAR
SHERF, CHARLES	BAL	313	20TH WAR
SHERFIELD, FREDERICK	BAL	333	7TH WARD
SHERFY, COLUMBUS	CAR	405	2ND DIST
SHERICK, JOSEPH	WAS	060	2ND SUBD
SHERICAN, ANTHONY	ALL	143	6TH E.D.
SHERIDAN, DANIEL	ANN	520	HOWARD D
SHERIDAN, DANIEL	FRE	20	5TH E DI
SHERICAN, ELISABETH	ALL	215	CUMBERLA
SHERIDAN, JAMES	ALL	209	CUMBERLA
SHERICAN, JAMES	BAL	082	2ND DIST
SHERICAN, JOHN	BAL	098	2ND DIST
SHERIDAN, JOHN	BAL	081	2ND DIST
SHERIDAN, JOHN	BAL	081	2ND DIST
SHERIDAN, JOHN	ALL	052	10TH E.D
SHERIDAN, MARTIN	ALL	053	10TH E.D
SHERIDAN, THOMAS	ALL	209	CUMBERLA
SHERICAN, WILLIAM	ALL	049	10TH E.D
SHERICAN,E DWARD	ALL	209	CUMBERLA
SHERIDEN, GEORGE	ANN	472	HOWARD D
SHERIDON, T.P.	BAL	163	1ST WARD
SHERIDON, THOMAS	BAL	445	1ST DIST
SHERIFF, ELIZABETH	WAS	162	2ND DIST
SHERIFF, NANCY	ALL	153	6TH E.D.
SHERIFF, SUSAN B.	PRI	013	BLADENSB
SHERIFFE, ADELAIDE	PRI	113	PISCATAW
SHERIFFE, J.	PRI	118	PISCATAW
SHERIFFE, J.B.	PRI	112	PISCATAW
SHERIKLE, PETER	BAL	212	17TH WAR
SHERIN, WILLIAM	WAS	015	2ND SUBD
SHERING, BERNARD	BAL	198	2ND WARD
SHERK, MARTIN	CEC	084	CHARLEST
SHERKLIFF, ALLEY O.	ST	326	4TH E DI
SHERLER, ANN	ALL	238	CUMBERLA
SHERLER, JOSEPHUS	CAR	267	WESTMINS
SHERLEY, JOHN	FRE	184	5TH E DI
SHERLIN, MATTHEW	CHA	227	ALLENS F
SHERLOCK, ANN	BAL	140	11TH WAR
SHERLOCK, ANN	BAL	331	13TH WAR
SHERLOCK, E.S.	PRI	090	MARLBROU
SHERLOCK, MARY E.	BAL	271	7TH WARD
SHERLOCK, RACHEL	PRI	093	MARLBROU
SHERLOCK, SARAH	CAL	040	3RD DIST
SHERLOCK, WILLIAM	BAL	098	15TH WAR
SHERM, JOHN	FRE	178	5TH E DI
SHERMAN, ADOLPHUS	BAL	270	7TH WARD
SHERMAN, CARAT	BAL	274	1ST DIST
SHERMAN, CHARLES K.	MGM	319	CRACKLIN
SHERMAN, DAVID	CAR	235	UNION TO
SHERMAN, DAVID A.	DOR	376	1ST DIST
SHERMAN, EMELINE	DOR	450	1ST DIST
SHERMAN, GEORGE	CAR	357	6TH DIST
SHERMAN, HENRY	CAR	351	6TH DIST
SHERMAN, JACOB	CAR	341	6TH DIST
SHERMAN, JACOB	BAL	077	2ND DIST
SHERMAN, JARUS N.	DOR	459	1ST DIST
SHERMAN, JEREMAIH	CAR	235	UNION TO
SHERMAN, JOHN	BAL	059	1ST WARD
SHERMAN, JOHN	ANN	320	2ND DIST
SHERMAN, MARGARET	BAL	301	7TH WARD
SHERMAN, MARGARET	BAL	205	6TH DIST
SHERMAN, MARY	DOR	469	1ST DIST
SHERMAN, MARY A.	BAL	365	8TH WARD
SHERMAN, MITCHELL	DOR	435	1ST DIST
SHERMAN, PEGGY	BAL	206	6TH DIST
SHERMAN, RICHARD	DOR	455	1ST DIST
SHERMAN, THOMAS	BAL	076	2ND DIST
SHERMAN, THOMAS B.	DOR	452	1ST DIST
SHERMAN, WILEY	DOR	463	1ST DIST
SHERMAN, WILLEANINA	MGM	424	MEDLEY 3
SHERMAN, WILLIAM	BAL	209	6TH DIST
SHERMAN, WILLIAM A.	DOR	450	1ST DIST
SHERMAN, WILLIAM H.	BAL	051	18TH WAR
SHERMANTINE, COLUMBUS	ST	289	2ND E DI
SHERMANTINE, ELIZABETH	ST	303	2ND E DI
SHERMANTINE, MARGARET	BAL	353	7TH WARD
SHERMANTINE, WILLIAM	ST	307	1ST E DI
SHERNING, JANE R.	BAL	340	1ST DIST
SHEROD, JAMES	ALL	053	10TH E.D
SHERON, PETER	BAL	003	9TH WARD
SHEROTT, HENRY	BAL	274	1ST DIST
SHERPIN, MORRIS	BAL	355	8TH WARD
SHERRAM, M.	ANN	284	ANNAPOLI
SHERRARD, SARAH	BAL	309	3RD WARD
SHERRETT, SARAH A.	BAL	185	16TH WAR
SHERREY, JAEMS	BAL	424	8TH WARD
SHERREY, MILES	BAL	145	5TH WARD
SHERRIFFE, ALFRED	PRI	088	SPALDING
SHERRIFFE, THOMAS	PRI	089	SPALDING
SHERRIN,MARY	FRE	203	5TH E DI
SHERRY, JAMES	BAL	041	9TH WARD
SHERRY, JOHN	BAL	151	19TH WAR
SHERRY, MICHAEL	ALL	007	3RD E.D.
SHERRY, PETER	BAL	197	2ND WARD
SHERTZ, PETER	BAL	083	2ND DIST
SHERWOD, MARGARETT	BAL	114	18TH WAR
SHERWOOD, ANN	BAL	408	14TH WAR
SHERWOOD, BENJAMIN	BAL	107	5TH WARD
SHERWOOD, BENJAMIN	QUE	244	5TH E DI
SHERWOOD, CHARLES	TAL	061	EASTON D
SHERWOOD, CORNELIUS	TAL	019	EASTON D
SHERWOOD, E.	PRI	118	PISCATAW
SHERWOOD, ELIZABETH	TAL	106	ST MICHA
SHERWOOD, ELIZABETH	BAL	256	6TH WARD
SHERWOOD, F. A.	BAL	156	1ST WARD
SHERWOOD, G.	BAL	279	20TH WAR
SHERWOOD, GEORGE	CAR	091	NO TWP L
SHERWOOD, H. N.	TAL	086	ST MICHA
SHERWOOD, HELLEN	CAR	091	NO TWP L
SHERWOOD, HENRY	TAL	072	EASTON T
SHERWOOD, HENRY A.	BAL	387	3RD WARD
SHERWOOD, HUGH	TAL	003	EASTON D
SHERWOOD, JESSIE A.	BAL	310	3RD WARD
SHERWOOD, JOHN	BAL	161	1ST WARD
SHERWOOD, JOHN W.	ANN	463	HOWARD D
SHERWOOD, JOSEPH	BAL	192	6TH WARD
SHERWOOD, JOSEPH	ALL	158	6TH E.D.
SHERWOOD, JOSHUA	BAL	316	3RD WARD
SHERWOOD, LEWIS	PRI	117	PISCATAW
SHERWOOD, LOUISA	BAL	344	13TH WAR
SHERWOOD, MARGARET	BAL	198	6TH WARD
SHERWOOD, MARY	TAL	044	EASTON D
SHERWOOD, PERRY*	TAL	042	EASTON D
SHERWOOD, PHILIP	BAL	394	3RD WARD
SHERWOOD, PHILLIP	BAL	028	1ST WARD
SHERWOOD, REBECA A.	BAL	296	7TH WARD
SHERWOOD, RICHARD	BAL	038	4TH WARD
SHERWOOD, RICHARD P.	BAL	090	10TH WAR
SHERWOOD, ROBERT	BAL	073	4TH WARD
SHERWOOD, SAMUEL	DOR	452	1ST DIST
SHERWOOD, THOMAS J.	TAL	112	ST MICHA
SHERWOOD, WILLIAM	PRI	074	MARLBROU
SHERWOOD, WILLIAM	BAL	073	4TH WARD
SHERWOOD, WILLIAM	BAL	348	13TH WAR
SHERWOOD, WILLIAM	QUE	124	1ST E DI
SHERWOOD, WILLIAM	BAL	099	15TH WAR
SHERWOOD, WILLIAM	BAL	318	12TH WAR
SHERWOOD, WILLIAM	BAL	188	6TH WARD
SHERWOOD, WILLIAM	BAL	173	6TH WARD
SHERWOOD, WILLIAM	BAL	461	1ST DIST
SHERWOOD, WILLIAM	ALL	159	6TH E.D.
SHERWOOD, WILLIAM	BAL	323	1ST DIST
SHERWOOD,RICHARD	CAR	164	NO TWP L
SHESARD, WILLIAM	WAS	266	1ST DIST
SHESSARD, ANN E.	WAS	232	1ST DIST
SHESSARD, SAMUEL H.	WAS	242	CAVETOWN
SHETERS, CATHARINE	WAS	284	1ST DIST
SHETLER, ADELADE	BAL	357	8TH WARD
SHETTEN, ELLEN	BAL	010	EASTERN
SHETTEN, FREDERICK	BAL	009	EASTERN
SHETTER, WILEMENA	BAL	291	17TH WAR
SHETTERTON, ELISHA H.	BAL	354	7TH WARD
SHETTZ, OSCAR	BAL	014	2ND DIST
SHEUABECK, FREDERICK	WAS	005	WILLIAMS
SHEUER, MARIA *	BAL	289	1ST DIST
SHEVELIN, BRYAN*	BAL	079	10TH WAR
SHEVEY, B.	BAL	308	12TH WAR
SHEW, GEORGE L.	HAR	063	1ST DIST
SHEW, HENRY	CAR	374	9TH DIST
SHEW, LYDIA A.	CAR	374	9TH DIST
SHEW, PETER	WAS	244	SMITHSBU
SHEWMAKER, EDWARD	CEC	080	NORTHEAS
SHEWS, HENRY	HAR	062	1ST DIST
SHEYTT, GODFREY	BAL	215	17TH WAR
SHIBBELY, EARNEST	CEC	147	PORT DUP
SHIBBETTS, HENRY	FRE	368	CATOCTIN
SHIBBETTS, WILLIAM	FRE	345	MIDDLETO
SHIBLINE, BARBARA	BAL	307	1ST DIST
SHICK, HENRY	ALL	211	CUMBERLA
SHICK, HENRY	BAL	326	12TH WAR
SHICK, JOSEPH	BAL	450	14TH WAR
SHICKELS, ENOCK	ANN	398	8TH DIST
SHICKELS, MARY	BAL	098	5TH WARD
SHICKILES, RICHARD W.	MGM	433	CLARKSTR
SHIEBER, PHILIP	BAL	438	14TH WAR
SHIEDS, ABSALOM *	BAL	140	19TH WAR
SHIEF, ANN M.	BAL	116	5TH WARD
SHIEL, MICHAEL	BAL	027	9TH WARD
SHIELD, EDWARD	BAL	359	13TH WAR
SHIELD, GEORGE	CEC	031	CHESAPEA
SHIELD, GEORGE	BAL	404	8TH WARD
SHIELD, JOHN	BAL	161	6TH WARD
SHIELD, LANA	FRE	059	FREDERIC
SHIELD, MARY	CEC	031	CHESAPEA
SHIELD, WILLIAM	BAL	463	1ST DIST
SHIELDS, ABRAHAM-BLACK	QUE	153	1ST E DI
SHIELDS, ANN	BAL	008	EASTERN
SHIELDS, BARNEY	BAL	008	EASTERN
SHIELDS, BARNEY	BAL	135	11TH WAR
SHIELDS, BARNEY	BAL	469	14TH WAR
SHIELDS, DAVID	HAR	012	1ST DIST
SHIELDS, DORIS*	BAL	392	3RD WARD
SHIELDS, EDWARD	BAL	064	10TH WAR
SHIELDS, ELIZABETH	BAL	442	14TH WAR
SHIELDS, ELLEN	BAL	050	9TH WARD
SHIELDS, ELLEN	BAL	242	6TH WARD
SHIELDS, FRANCIS	CAR	167	NO TWP L
SHIELDS, GEORGE	CEC	150	PORT DUP
SHIELDS, GEORGE C.	BAL	420	8TH WARD
SHIELDS, GEORGE D.	BAL	018	18TH WAR
SHIELDS, GOERGE	BAL	310	7TH WARD
SHIELDS, HANNAH	CEC	155	PORT DUP
SHIELDS, HENRIETTA	BAL	068	10TH WAR
SHIELDS, HENRY	HAR	121	2ND DIST
SHIELDS, HENRY	FRE	099	FREDERIC
SHIELDS, JAMES	BAL	424	3RD WARD
SHIELDS, JAMES	CAR	084	NO TWP L
SHIELDS, JAMES	BAL	181	2ND WARD
SHIELDS, JEFFERSON	FRE	023	FREDERIC
SHIELDS, JEFFERSON	WAS	247	SMITHSBU
SHIELDS, JOHN	FRE	192	5TH E DI
SHIELDS, JOHN	BAL	002	15TH WAR
SHIELDS, JOHN J.	BAL	451	14TH WAR
SHIELDS, JULIA	BAL	183	2ND WARD
SHIELDS, LUKE	ANN	441	HOWARD D
SHIELDS, MARY	BAL	201	6TH WARD
SHIELDS, MARY	HAR	128	2ND DIST
SHIELDS, MARY A.	BAL	095	1ST WARD
SHIELDS, MARY J.	BAL	457	14TH WAR
SHIELDS, MAX	FRE	169	5TH E DI
SHIELDS, MICHAEL	BAL	395	1ST DIST
SHIELDS, MICHAEL	ALL	050	10TH E.D
SHIELDS, PATRICK	BAL	205	2ND WARD
SHIELDS, PHILIP	BAL	086	4TH WARD
SHIELDS, R.D.	BAL	260	12TH WAR
SHIELDS, RACHAEL	BAL	020	4TH WARD
SHIELDS, RICHARD	BAL	439	14TH WAR
SHIELDS, SALLY	BAL	020	4TH WARD
SHIELDS, SARAH	CEC	119	3RD E DI
SHIELDS, SOPHIA	HAR	030	1ST DIST
SHIELDS, WILLIAM	CEC	119	3RD E DI
SHIELDS, WILLIAM	DOR	305	1ST DIST
SHIELMAN, OTHO	WAS	201	1ST DIST
SHIERLIN, MICHAEL	BAL	002	9TH WARD
SHIES, MICHAEL	BAL	257	20TH WAR
SHIESS, FRANCES C.	WAS	278	LEITERSB
SHIESS, GEORGE	WAS	284	1ST DIST
SHIESS, GEORGE	WAS	265	1ST DIST
SHIESS, LEWIS	WAS	241	CAVETOWN
SHIESS, OLIVER	WAS	242	CAVETOWN
SHIETER, LOUISA	BAL	246	20TH WAR
SHIFF, MENVER *	BAL	309	12TH WAR
SHIFF, MEYER	BAL	309	12TH WAR
SHIFLER, GEROGE	WAS	191	1ST DIST
SHIFLER, JEREMIAH	WAS	276	RIDGEVIL
SHIFLER, JOHN	WAS	078	2ND SUBD
SHIFLER, SAMUEL	WAS	075	2ND SUBD
SHIFT, M. C.	BAL	308	12TH WAR
SHIGLAND, PETER	PRI	028	VANSVILL
SHILCOTE,WILLIAM	CAR	162	NO TWP L
SHILCOTT, JOHN E.	CAR	136	NO TWP L
SHILD, JACOB	CEC	034	CHESAPEA
SHILDS, MAHALY	DOR	310	1ST DIST
SHILOT, HENRY	CAR	310	1ST DIST
SHILE, ANN	ALL	069	5TH E.D.
SHILENT, MARY	TAL	068	EASTON T
SHILENT, MARY A.	TAL	065	EASTON T
SHILER, C.	BAL	302	20TH WAR
SHILGER, ANDREW	KEN	311	3RD DIST
SHILING, FREDERICK	WAS	174	FUNKSTOW
SHILLDS, CAROLINE	BAL	321	12TH WAR
SHILLEN, GEORGE	FRE	222	BUCKEYST
SHILLEN, JOHN	FRE	232	BUCKEYST
SHILLENBERGER, ISAAC	BAL	122	18TH WAR
SHILLER, ANN	BAL	090	2ND DIST
SHILLER, CONRAD	ALL	205	CUMBERLA
SHILLIG, GEORGE	BAL	008	4TH WARD
SHILLIG, MARY	BAL	009	4TH WARD
SHILLING, COLUMBUS	BAL	102	1ST WARD
SHILLING, DAVID	WAS	174	FUNKSTOW
SHILLING, FAIRO	WAS	250	1ST DIST
SHILLING, FREDERICK	WAS	194	1ST DIST
SHILLING, HENRY	WAS	171	FUNKSTOW
SHILLING, JOACHAM	WAS	236	CAVETOWN
SHILLING, JOHN	WAS	170	FUNKSTOW
SHILLING, JOSIAH	CAR	191	4TH DIST
SHILLING, MARY	BAL	135	11TH WAR
SHILLING, MURRAY F.	CAR	254	3RD DIST
SHILLING, NIHCOLAS	CAR	254	3RD DIST
SHILLING, PETER	BAL	375	8TH WARD
SHILLING, WILIAM	CAR	195	4TH DIST
SHILLING, WILLIAM	CAR	194	4TH DIST
SHILLING, WILLIAM	BAL	297	7TH WARD
SHILLING, WILLIAM	WAS	172	FUNKSTOW
SHILLING, WILLIAM	WAS	061	2ND SUBD
SHILLMAN, JACOB	BAL	337	13TH WAR
SHILMAN, JACOB	BAL	242	1ST DIST
SHILTCUM, THEODORE	BAL	297	1ST DIST
SHIMBEL, FREDERICK	BAL	050	4TH WARD
SHIMEL, JOSIAH	WAS	203	1ST DIST
SHIMEL, PETER H.	WAS	203	1ST DIST
SHIMMEL, BENJAMIN	WAS	144	2ND DIST
SHIMMELL, JACOB	WAS	145	2ND DIST
SHIMP, THOMPSON	ALL	051	10TH E.D
SHINBARGER, JOHN	HAR	053	1ST DIST
SHINBAUGH, JACOB	WAS	130	HAGERSTO
SHINDLE, DAVID	WAS	196	1ST DIST
SHINDLE, PHILIP	WAS	024	2ND SUBD
SHINDLE, SAMUEL E.	WAS	132	HAGERSTO
SHINDLEDECKER, CAHARINE	FRE	192	5TH E DI
SHINDLER, JOHNATHAN	BAL	419	1ST DIST
SHINDLER, SARAH A.	BAL	420	1ST DIST
SHINE, BRIGET	BAL	459	1ST DIST
SHINE, THOMAS	ALL	051	10TH E.D
SHINEDOLLER, GEORGE	BAL	347	1ST DIST
SHINER, JOSEPH	BAL	102	18TH WAR
SHINER, SUSAN	CAR	299	1ST DIST
SHINGHFER, AUGUST	BAL	459	8TH WARD
SHINGLE, ANDREW	WAS	099	2ND DIST
SHINGLE, C.	BAL	175	19TH WAR
SHINGLE, JACOB	BAL	267	1ST DIST
SHINGLE, JOHN	ALL	260	CUMBERLA
SHINGLE, JOHN	BAL	219	17TH WAR
SHINGLE, JOHNATHAN	WAS	128	2ND DIST
SHINGLE, LUCY	BAL	348	7TH WARD
SHINGLE, PHILIP	BAL	155	19TH WAR
SHINGLEDECKER, JACOB	FRE	192	5TH E DI
SHINGLEDECKER, JOHN	FRE	193	5TH E DI
SHINGLEDECKER, WILLIAM	BAL	224	1ST DIST
SHINGLEY, JOHN A.	BAL	154	19TH WAR
SHININGHAM, PETER	BAL	285	2ND WARD
SHINKEL, SUSAN	FRE	059	FREDERIC
SHINKLE, HARRIET	BAL	267	12TH WAR
SHINLER, R.D.	PRI	093	MARLBROU
SHINLEY, J.H.	BAL	160	19TH WAR
SHINLEY, SARAH J.	BAL	161	19TH WAR
SHINNICK, JOHN D.	FRE	037	FREDERIC
SHINTAL, FREDERICK*	BAL	050	4TH WARD
SHIP	CAR	228	5TH DIST
SHIP, GROVE A.	CAR	209	5TH DIST
SHIP,LEY, ELIZA	PRI	029	VANSVILL
SHIPE, ADAM	ALL	219	CUMBERLA
SHIPELY, WESLY	BAL	200	11TH WAR
SHIPHERD, ELLENER	DOR	317	1ST DIST
SHIPHERD, LOUEZA	DOR	317	1ST DIST
SHIPLER, JOSEPH	BAL	104	5TH WARD
SHIPLER, WILLIAM	WAS	208	1ST DIST
SHIPLEY, ADAM	BAL	229	1ST DIST
SHIPLEY, ADAM	BAL	292	12TH WAR
SHIPLEY, ALANSON F.	BAL	221	1ST DIST
SHIPLEY, ALFRED	BAL	146	11TH WAR
SHIPLEY, ALLEN	BAL	334	1ST DIST
SHIPLEY, AMELIA	ANN	519	HOWARD D
SHIPLEY, AMON	CAR	211	5TH DIST
SHIPLEY, AMON	CAR	210	5TH DIST
SHIPLEY, AMOS	ANN	427	HOWARD D
SHIPLEY, ANN	BAL	432	1ST DIST
SHIPLEY, ANN C.	BAL	009	18TH WAR
SHIPLEY, ANN G.	FRE	277	NEW MARK
SHIPLEY, ANN M.	BAL	376	1ST DIST
SHIPLEY, ARCHIMEDIES	BAL	295	20TH WAR
SHIPLEY, ARMEALA	BAL	047	18TH WAR
SHIPLEY, ARTAMAS	BAL	389	1ST DIST
SHIPLEY, BENJAMIN O.	BAL	081	18TH WAR
SHIPLEY, BRICE	CAR	212	5TH DIST
SHIPLEY, CALEB	ANN	499	HOWARD D
SHIPLEY, CALEB JR.	ANN	504	HOWARD D
SHIPLEY, CAROLINE	BAL	070	18TH WAR
SHIPLEY, CASEY	BAL	099	18TH WAR
SHIPLEY, CATHARINE	BAL	144	19TH WAR
SHIPLEY, CHALRE	ALL	218	CUMBERLA
SHIPLEY, CHARELS	BAL	251	1ST DIST
SHIPLEY, CHARLES	BAL	381	1ST DIST
SHIPLEY, CHARLES	BAL	073	18TH WAR
SHIPLEY, COLUMBIA	BAL	105	18TH WAR
SHIPLEY, COLUMBUS	BAL	357	13TH WAR
SHIPLEY, COLUMBUS	BAL	331	1ST DIST
SHIPLEY, CORDELIA	BAL	356	1ST DIST
SHIPLEY, CORNEALOUS	CAR	221	5TH DIST
SHIPLEY, DANIEL E.	BAL	014	18TH WAR

Name	County	Page	District
SHIPLEY, DAVID	CAR	217	5TH DIST
SHIPLEY, DENNISS	FRE	255	NEW MARK
SHIPLEY, DENTON R.	CAR	392	2ND DIST
SHIPLEY, E. G.	BAL	475	14TH WAR
SHIPLEY, EDEN	CAR	231	5TH DIST
SHIPLEY, EDWARD G.	BAL	046	9TH WARD
SHIPLEY, ELIEAZEE	CAR	221	5TH DIST
SHIPLEY, ELIZABETH	CAR	212	5TH DIST
SHIPLEY, ELIZABETH	BAL	106	18TH WAR
SHIPLEY, ELIZABETH	BAL	297	20TH WAR
SHIPLEY, ELIZABETH	BAL	387	1ST DIST
SHIPLEY, EMILY	MGM	366	BERRYS D
SHIPLEY, ENOS	ANN	386	4TH DIST
SHIPLEY, EPHRAIM	ALL	247	CUMBERLA
SHIPLEY, EVELINE	ALL	254	CUMBERLA
SHIPLEY, EVEN H.	CAR	227	5TH DIST
SHIPLEY, EZEKEL	CAR	219	5TH DIST
SHIPLEY, FRANCIS	CAR	202	4TH DIST
SHIPLEY, FRANCIS M.	ANN	494	HOWARD D
SHIPLEY, FREDERICK	ALL	243	CUMBERLA
SHIPLEY, FREDERICK	FRE	371	CATOCTIN
SHIPLEY, FREDERICK	FRE	258	NEW MARK
SHIPLEY, GEORGE	CAR	211	5TH DIST
SHIPLEY, GEORGE	BAL	365	13TH WAR
SHIPLEY, GEORGE	BAL	304	12TH WAR
SHIPLEY, GEORGE	BAL	071	10TH WAR
SHIPLEY, GEORGE S.	BAL	221	1ST DIST
SHIPLEY, GEORGE S. D.	WOR	228	6TH E DI
SHIPLEY, GREENBURY	ANN	416	HOWARD D
SHIPLEY, GREENBURY	CAR	229	5TH DIST
SHIPLEY, GROVE	CAR	209	5TH DIST
SHIPLEY, GUSTAVUS W.	BAL	171	16TH WAR
SHIPLEY, HAMMOND	BAL	419	8TH WARD
SHIPLEY, HANAH	CAR	283	7TH DIST
SHIPLEY, HANSON	ANN	447	HOWARD D
SHIPLEY, HENRY	FRE	319	MIDDLETO
SHIPLEY, HENRY D.	CAR	228	5TH DIST
SHIPLEY, HENRY K.	BAL	278	1ST DIST
SHIPLEY, HOWEL	FRE	257	NEW MARK
SHIPLEY, ISAAC	FRE	207	BUCKEYST
SHIPLEY, JACKSON	BAL	228	19TH WAR
SHIPLEY, JACKSON	BAL	331	1ST DIST
SHIPLEY, JACOB	BAL	389	1ST DIST
SHIPLEY, JACOB L.	BAL	182	16TH WAR
SHIPLEY, JAMES	ANN	412	HOWARD D
SHIPLEY, JAMES	BAL	012	15TH WAR
SHIPLEY, JANE	BAL	096	18TH WAR
SHIPLEY, JOHN	CAR	210	5TH DIST
SHIPLEY, JOHN	CAR	202	4TH DIST
SHIPLEY, JOHN	BAL	281	20TH WAR
SHIPLEY, JOHN	BAL	343	7TH WARD
SHIPLEY, JOHN	BAL	037	2ND DIST
SHIPLEY, JOHN F.	BAL	443	1ST DIST
SHIPLEY, JOHN H.	BAL	391	8TH WARD
SHIPLEY, JOHN S.	BAL	206	19TH WAR
SHIPLEY, JOHNSEY	CAR	210	5TH DIST
SHIPLEY, JOSEPH	BAL	144	19TH WAR
SHIPLEY, JOSEPH	BAL	129	18TH WAR
SHIPLEY, JOSEPH	MGM	336	CRACKLIN
SHIPLEY, JOSEPH T.	ANN	499	HOWARD D
SHIPLEY, JOSHUA	ANN	510	HOWARD D
SHIPLEY, JOSHUA	BAL	385	1ST DIST
SHIPLEY, JOSHUA	BAL	037	2ND DIST
SHIPLEY, JOSHUA	BAL	180	19TH WAR
SHIPLEY, JOSHUA	CAR	280	7TH DIST
SHIPLEY, JOSHUA	FRE	093	FREDERIC
SHIPLEY, JOSHUA H.	CAR	233	5TH DIST
SHIPLEY, L.G.	BAL	268	12TH WAR
SHIPLEY, LARKIN	ANN	374	4TH DIST
SHIPLEY, LARKIN	ANN	491	HOWARD D
SHIPLEY, LARKIN	CAR	224	5TH DIST
SHIPLEY, LEVINA	BAL	105	18TH WAR
SHIPLEY, LEWIS	CAR	232	5TH DIST
SHIPLEY, LLOYD	CAR	203	4TH DIST
SHIPLEY, LLOYD G.	BAL	146	19TH WAR
SHIPLEY, LOUISA A.	ANN	387	4TH DIST
SHIPLEY, LOVIST	BAL	015	18TH WAR
SHIPLEY, LYDIA	WAS	158	2ND DIST
SHIPLEY, MAHALA	FRE	257	NEW MARK
SHIPLEY, MARANDY	CAR	219	5TH DIST
SHIPLEY, MARGARET	CAR	206	4TH DIST
SHIPLEY, MARGARET A.	ANN	474	HOWARD D
SHIPLEY, MARIA	BAL	187	11TH WAR
SHIPLEY, MARIAH	CAR	213	5TH DIST
SHIPLEY, MARTHA	FRE	223	BUCKEYST
SHIPLEY, MARY	BAL	070	18TH WAR
SHIPLEY, MARY	ANN	516	HOWARD D
SHIPLEY, MARY	BAL	299	1ST DIST
SHIPLEY, MARY	BAL	189	5TH DIST
SHIPLEY, MARY E.	FRE	077	FREDERIC
SHIPLEY, MARY J.	BAL	221	1ST DIST
SHIPLEY, MICHA	ANN	412	HOWARD D
SHIPLEY, MILLY	ANN	449	HOWARD D
SHIPLEY, MOSES	BAL	263	1ST DIST
SHIPLEY, NATHAN	ANN	505	HOWARD D
SHIPLEY, OTHO	CAR	270	WESTMINS
SHIPLEY, OWEN	BAL	224	1ST DIST
SHIPLEY, PEOLA	BAL	295	1ST DIST
SHIPLEY, PERRYGRINE	BAL	250	1ST DIST
SHIPLEY, PRUDENCE	CAR	211	5TH DIST
SHIPLEY, RACHAEL	BAL	326	1ST DIST
SHIPLEY, REBECCA	ANN	508	HOWARD D
SHIPLEY, RICHARD	FRE	077	FREDERIC
SHIPLEY, RICHARD A.	ANN	386	4TH DIST
SHIPLEY, ROBERT	BAL	224	1ST DIST
SHIPLEY, ROBERT	BAL	238	12TH WAR
SHIPLEY, ROBERT	BAL	209	19TH WAR
SHIPLEY, ROBERT T.	CAR	221	5TH DIST
SHIPLEY, RODERICK	ANN	506	HOWARD D
SHIPLEY, RUTH	BAL	277	1ST DIST
SHIPLEY, RUTH	CAR	207	4TH DIST
SHIPLEY, SAMUEL	FRE	259	NEW MARK
SHIPLEY, SAMUEL	BAL	419	1ST DIST
SHIPLEY, SAMUEL	BAL	453	1ST DIST
SHIPLEY, SAMUEL	ALL	248	CUMBERLA
SHIPLEY, SAMUEL	PRI	032	VANSVILL
SHIPLEY, SAMUEL	WAS	218	1ST DIST
SHIPLEY, SAMUEL H.	CAR	226	5TH DIST
SHIPLEY, SARAH	CAR	211	5TH DIST
SHIPLEY, SARAH	BAL	051	18TH WAR
SHIPLEY, SUSANAH	CAR	192	4TH DIST
SHIPLEY, TALBOT G.	ANN	510	HOWARD D
SHIPLEY, THERESEA	BAL	388	1ST DIST
SHIPLEY, THOMAS	BAL	252	1ST DIST
SHIPLEY, THOMAS	BAL	222	6TH WARD
SHIPLEY, THOMAS	WAS	050	2ND SUBD
SHIPLEY, THOMAS B.	ANN	518	HOWARD D
SHIPLEY, UPTON W.	MGM	426	MEDLEY 3
SHIPLEY, UPTON, M.	BAL	336	1ST DIST
SHIPLEY, URIAH	BAL	196	19TH WAR
SHIPLEY, WASHINGTON	BAL	033	18TH WAR
SHIPLEY, WESLEY	BAL	165	11TH WAR
SHIPLEY, WILLIAM E.	ANN	470	HOWARD D
SHIPLEY, WILLIAM	ANN	377	4TH DIST
SHIPLEY, WILLIAM	ANN	439	HOWARD D
SHIPLEY, WILLIAM	BAL	391	1ST DIST
SHIPLEY, WILLIAM	CAR	190	4TH DIST
SHIPLEY, WILLIAM G.	FRE	243	NEW MARK
SHIPLEY, WILLIAM H.	BAL	020	18TH WAR
SHIPLEY, ZACHARIAH	BAL	172	19TH WAR
SHIPLEY,MICAH	BAL	027	2ND DIST
SHIPLEY,NATHANIEL	FRE	442	8TH E DI
SHIPLY, BASIL	CAR	387	2ND DIST
SHIPLY, FERDINAND	CAR	330	MANCHEST
SHIPLY, MARY A.	BAL	006	18TH WAR
SHIPLY, NICHOLAS H.	PRI	084	QUEEN AN
SHIPLY, PETER	FRE	262	NEW MARK
SHIPLY, WILLIAM	FRE	273	NEW MARK
SHIPLY,NAPOLEON	FRE	239	NEW MARK
SHIPMAN, MESANDER	FRE	036	FREDERIC
SHIPP, JACOB	WAS	293	1ST DIST
SHIPP, JAMES	WAS	290	1ST DIST
SHIPPER, ISABELLA*	BAL	307	3RD WARD
SHIPPEY, JOSEPH	BAL	245	20TH WAR
SHIPPLEY, ISAAC	BAL	225	17TH WAR
SHIPPLEY, JOSEPH B. *	BAL	129	18TH WAR
SHIPPY, HENRY	BAL	141	1ST WARD
SHIPS, JOHN *	BAL	087	15TH WAR
SHIPTON, PRUDENCE	FRE	033	FREDERIC
SHIRAH, JOHN	BAL	008	4TH WARD
SHIRCLEY, PETER	ALL	061	10TH E.D
SHIRDEN, CHARELS	BAL	208	6TH DIST
SHIRDEN, JULIA	BAL	229	6TH WARD
SHIRE, FREDERICK	BAL	080	1ST WARD
SHIRES, ROBERT	WAS	144	2ND DIST
SHIREY, GIDEON	WAS	236	CAVETOWN
SHIREY, GIDEON	WAS	236	CAVETOWN
SHIREY, JACOB	WAS	129	HAGERSTO
SHIRIFF, JOHN R.	BAL	079	18TH WAR
SHIRK, ELIZA	BAL	111	1ST WARD
SHIRK, FRANCIS	BAL	213	19TH WAR
SHIRKEY, ANNA	CEC	127	5TH E DI
SHIRKEY, CHARLES	FRE	167	EMMITTSB
SHIRLEY, CHARLES	BAL	112	10TH WAR
SHIRLEY, EDWARD	BAL	152	19TH WAR
SHIRLEY, ELIAS	ALL	240	CUMBERLA
SHIRLEY, ELIZABETH	WAS	134	HAGERSTO
SHIRLEY, NANCY	BAL	205	11TH WAR
SHIRLEY, WILLIAM	BAL	045	9TH WARD
SHIRLEY, WILLIAM-BLACK	ST	298	2ND E DI
SHIRLY, CONSTANT	BAL	174	19TH WAR
SHIRNER, PETER	CAR	322	1ST DIST
SHIRVE, RICHARD	CAL	007	1ST DIST
SHISERS, GEORGE	FRE	291	WOODSBOR
SHISLER, CHRISTIANA	BAL	386	1ST DIST
SHISLER, GEORGE	BAL	265	1ST DIST
SHISLER, HENRY	BAL	385	1ST DIST
SHISLER, JOHN	BAL	265	1ST DIST
SHITE, ABRAHAM	WAS	287	1ST DIST
SHITE, JOHN	WAS	283	1ST DIST
SHITHISER, ANDREW	BAL	307	1ST DIST
SHITHISER, CHRISTIANA	BAL	308	1ST DIST
SHITZ, JOSEPH	BAL	212	2ND WARD
SHIVELY, BENNET	BAL	384	1ST DIST
SHIVELY, MATHIAS	BAL	324	1ST DIST
SHIVER, JESSE	CAR	386	2ND DIST
SHIVERS, CORNELIOUS	FRE	422	8TH E DI
SHIVERS, JOHN	FRE	440	8TH E DI
SHIVERS, JOHN	FRE	255	NEW MARK
SHIVERY, ADAM	CEC	021	ELKTON 3
SHIVERY, ADAM	CEC	020	ELKTON 3
SHIVERY, ANN	CEC	038	CHESAPEA
SHIVERY, GEORGE	CEC	020	ELKTON 3
SHIVERY, ISABELLA	CEC	115	3RD E DI
SHIVES, DANIEL	WAS	148	2ND DIST
SHIVES, JACOB	WAS	144	2ND DIST
SHIVES, JACOB	WAS	148	2ND DIST
SHIVES, JOHN	WAS	148	2ND DIST
SHIVES, PETER	WAS	148	2ND DIST
SHIVES, ROBERT	WAS	144	2ND DIST
SHIVORY, WILLIAM	CEC	101	4TH E DI
SHJOPLEY, GROVE A.	CAR	209	5TH DIST
SHLEMAN, WILLIAM B. E. *	HAR	040	1ST DIST
SHMIDT, GEORGE	BAL	242	20TH WAR
SHMIDT, JOHN	BAL	297	12TH WAR
SHNEBLY, JOSEPH	WAS	132	HAGERSTO
SHOAL, MICHAEL *	ANN	386	4TH DIST
SHOAP, DAVID	ALL	091	5TH E.D.
SHOAP, JOHN	CAR	176	8TH DIST
SHOBE, MARY C.	FRE	065	FREDERIC
SHOBER, FREDERICK	BAL	463	1ST DIST
SHOBER, JOHN	BAL	460	1ST DIST
SHOBERT, MICHEAL	BAL	137	18TH WAR
SHOCK, FREDERICK	WAS	149	HAGERSTO
SHOCK, GEORGE	BAL	360	3RD WARD
SHOCK, GEORGE W.	BAL	264	7TH WARD
SHOCK, GRANVILLE	CEC	193	5TH E DI
SHOCK, HARRIET	BAL	346	7TH WARD
SHOCK, JACOB	BAL	043	2ND DIST
SHOCK, JACOB-BLACK	BAL	215	2ND WARD
SHOCK, JAMES	BAL	347	7TH WARD
SHOCK, JOHN	BAL	048	2ND DIST
SHOCK, JOHN	BAL	176	2ND DIST
SHOCK, JOHN	DOR	387	1ST DIST
SHOCK, JOSEPH C.	CEC	031	CHESAPEA
SHOCK, LIBBY	BAL	116	5TH WARD
SHOCK, MORDICA	BAL	346	7TH WARD
SHOCK, NICKOLAS	BAL	047	2ND DIST
SHOCK, SUSANA	BAL	012	4TH WARD
SHOCKALEUR, CHRISTIAN	WAS	274	RIDGEVIL
SHOCKEY, ABRAHAM	WAS	273	RIDGEVIL
SHOCKEY, CATHARINE	WAS	269	1ST DIST
SHOCKEY, CHARLES	ALL	173	7TH E.D.
SHOCKEY, CHRISTIAN	WAS	259	1ST DIST
SHOCKEY, DAVID	WAS	259	1ST DIST
SHOCKEY, SARAH E.	ALL	253	CUMBERLA
SHOCKEY, SOLOMON	WAS	259	1ST DIST
SHOCKLEY, ALISON A.	WOR	235	6TH E DI
SHOCKLEY, AMELIA	WOR	175	6TH E DI
SHOCKLEY, DANIEL	WOR	218	4TH E DI
SHOCKLEY, DAVID	WOR	218	4TH E DI
SHOCKLEY, ELIJAH	WOR	166	6TH E DI
SHOCKLEY, ELIJAH P.	WOR	170	6TH E DI
SHOCKLEY, ELIZABETH	WOR	174	6TH E DI
SHOCKLEY, GEORGE	WOR	174	6TH E DI
SHOCKLEY, GEORGE W.	WOR	170	6TH E DI
SHOCKLEY, GEORGE W.	WOR	226	4TH E DI
SHOCKLEY, GILLET M.	WOR	221	4TH E DI
SHOCKLEY, HENRY	WOR	193	8TH E DI
SHOCKLEY, HESTER-BLACK	WOR	167	6TH E DI
SHOCKLEY, HEZEKIAH G.	SOM	503	SALISBUR
SHOCKLEY, ISAAC	WOR	225	4TH E DI
SHOCKLEY, ISAAC	WOR	171	6TH E DI
SHOCKLEY, JAMES T.	WOR	234	6TH E DI
SHOCKLEY, JOHN	WOR	223	4TH E DI
SHOCKLEY, JOSHUA	WOR	235	6TH E DI
SHOCKLEY, JOSHUA J.	WOR	171	6TH E DI
SHOCKLEY, LEVIN	CEC	100	3RD E DI
SHOCKLEY, MARIA	WOR	234	6TH E DI
SHOCKLEY, MARTHA	SOM	496	SALISBUR
SHOCKLEY, NANCY	WOR	240	6TH E DI
SHOCKLEY, PALMER	CEC	100	3RD E DI
SHOCKLEY, PETER	BAL	461	1ST DIST
SHOCKLEY, RACHEL	WOR	221	4TH E DI
SHOCKLEY, REBECCA	CEC	091	4TH E DI
SHOCKLEY, SALLY	WOR	221	4TH E DI
SHOCKLEY, SAMPSON	WOR	174	6TH E DI
SHOCKLEY, SAMPSON D.	WOR	199	8TH E DI
SHOCKLEY, SARAH A.	WOR	200	8TH E DI
SHOCKLEY, SOLOMON B.	WOR	170	6TH E DI
SHOCKLEY, WALTY	WOR	347	1ST E DI
SHOCKLEY, WASHINGTON	WOR	229	6TH E DI
SHOCKLEY, WILLAIM K.	WOR	168	6TH E DI
SHOCKLEY, WILLIAM K.	WOR	169	6TH E DI
SHOCKLEY, WILLIAM SR.	WOR	173	6TH E DI
SHOCKLEY,WILLIAM	WOR	171	6TH E DI
SHOCKLY, HEZAKIAH D.	WOR	235	6TH E DI
SHOCKLY, JAMES H.	WOR	192	8TH E DI
SHOCKLY, JAMES M.	SOM	505	SALISBUR
SHOCKLY, STEWART	SOM	494	SALISBUR
SHOCKLY, WILLIAM	SOM	514	BARREN C
SHOCKNEY, LOUIS	BAL	324	1ST DIST
SHOCKNEY, SAMUEL	BAL	123	5TH WARD
SHOCKNEY, STEPHEN	CAR	206	4TH DIST
SHOCKY, PATRICK	ALL	196	CUMBERLA
SHOE, HUGH	WAS	150	2ND DIST
SHOEAKER, PHILIP	ALL	189	9TH E.D.
SHOEBROOK, EDWARD	CAR	100	NO TWP L
SHOEBROOKS, HARRIET	QUE	197	3RD E DI
SHOEBROOKS, JOHN	QUE	209	3RD E DI
SHOEBROOKS, MARGARET	QUE	186	3RD E DI
SHOEBROOKS, THOMAS	QUE	185	3RD E DI
SHOEBROOKS, WILLIAM	QUE	205	3RD E DI
SHOEBROOKS,ISAAC	QUE	196	3RD E DI
SHOEHARROW, DANIEL	BAL	408	1ST DIST
SHOEKEY, WILLIAM	ALL	001	3RD E.D.
SHOEMAKER, ABRAHAM	CAR	306	1ST DIST
SHOEMAKER, AMERICUS	CAR	304	1ST DIST
SHOEMAKER, ANN	CAR	317	1ST DIST
SHOEMAKER, BARBARA	CAR	321	1ST DIST
SHOEMAKER, BARBARY	CAR	196	4TH DIST
SHOEMAKER, CHARLES	MGM	391	ROCKERLE
SHOEMAKER, DANIEL	FRE	352	MIDDLETO
SHOEMAKER, DANIEL	FRE	172	5TH E DI
SHOEMAKER, DENNIS	FRE	282	WOODSBOR
SHOEMAKER, EDWARD	MGM	391	ROCKERLE
SHOEMAKER, ELIZABETH	FRE	281	WOODSBOR
SHOEMAKER, FRANCIS	FRE	075	FREDERIC
SHOEMAKER, FREDERICK	CAR	378	2ND DIST
SHOEMAKER, GEORGE	FRE	310	WOODSBOR
SHOEMAKER, GEORGE	CAR	409	2ND DIST
SHOEMAKER, GEORGE W.	BAL	202	17TH WAR
SHOEMAKER, GRANVILLE	BAL	210	6TH DIST
SHOEMAKER, ISAAC	MGM	391	ROCKERLE
SHOEMAKER, JACOB	CAR	325	1ST DIST
SHOEMAKER, JACOB	FRE	171	5TH E DI
SHOEMAKER, JACOB	WAS	163	2ND DIST
SHOEMAKER, JESSE	MGM	391	ROCKERLE
SHOEMAKER, JOHN	CAR	378	2ND DIST
SHOEMAKER, JOHN	BAL	205	17TH WAR
SHOEMAKER, JOHN	FRE	288	WOODSBOR
SHOEMAKER, JOHN	BAL	267	20TH WAR
SHOEMAKER, JOHN	WAS	145	2ND DIST
SHOEMAKER, JOHN M.	FRE	172	5TH E DI
SHOEMAKER, JOHN W.	FRE	410	8TH E DI
SHOEMAKER, JOHN W.	FRE	310	WOODSBOR
SHOEMAKER, JOSEPH	ALL	248	CUMBERLA
SHOEMAKER, LOIS	BAL	146	16TH WAR
SHOEMAKER, MAGDALIN	FRE	353	MIDDLETO
SHOEMAKER, MANNA	BAL	207	19TH WAR
SHOEMAKER, MARY	CAR	327	1ST DIST
SHOEMAKER, MATILDA	BAL	221	17TH WAR
SHOEMAKER, MICHAEL	WAS	273	RIDGEVIL
SHOEMAKER, RACHEL	BAL	159	19TH WAR
SHOEMAKER, RACHELL	BAL	205	17TH WAR
SHOEMAKER, SAMUEL	MGM	391	ROCKERLE
SHOEMAKER, SAMUEL	BAL	099	10TH WAR
SHOEMAKER, SAMUEL	BAL	202	11TH WAR
SHOEMAKER, SARAH	CAR	410	2ND DIST
SHOEMAKER, THOMAS	BAL	066	2ND DIST
SHOEMAKER, WILLIAM	FRE	282	WOODSBOR
SHOEMAKER, WILLIAM	CAR	303	1ST DIST
SHOEMAKER, WILLIAM L.	BAL	394	3RD WARD
SHOEMAN, JOHN	FRE	138	CREAGERS
SHOEUMAN, MARY J. *	FRE	132	CREAGERS
SHOFF, JOHN	CAR	320	1ST DIST
SHOFFER, JESSE	CAR	197	4TH DIST
SHOLL, DANIEL	CAR	252	3RD DIST
SHOLL, GEORGE	BAL	423	3RD WARD
SHOLL, GEORGE A.	WAS	279	LEITERSB
SHOLL, MATILDA	CAR	277	7TH DIST
SHOLL, MICHAEL	CAR	252	3RD DIST
SHOLL, PHILIP	CAR	252	3RD DIST
SHOLTEN, ROBERT	FRE	268	NEW MARK
SHOLTS, DANIEL	BAL	298	3RD WARD
SHOLTZ, CHARLES T.	BAL	044	9TH WARD
SHOMAKER, EDWARD	HAR	152	3RD DIST
SHOMAKER, JOHN F.	HAR	153	3RD DIST
SHOMATH, JOHN	CHA	235	HILLTOP
SHOMMAR, CHARLES	BAL	178	2ND WARD
SHONARD, ANN	WOR	167	6TH E DI
SHONE, HENRY	BAL	276	2ND WARD
SHONE, JOHN G.	BAL	015	15TH WAR
SHONE, JOHN H.	BAL	122	16TH WAR
SHONEFEVER, G.	BAL	320	12TH WAR
SHONEHAN, WILLIAM	ALL	049	10TH E.D
SHONESSEY, JOHN	BAL	134	2ND DIST
SHONHARD, HENRY	BAL	336	7TH WARD
SHONTON, DENNIS	BAL	459	8TH WARD
SHONTZE, LOUISA	BAL	425	14TH WAR
SHOOF, JOHN	FRE	072	FREDERIC
SHOOF, JUSTUS	ANN	370	4TH DIST
SHOOK, ALBERT	BAL	198	19TH WAR
SHOOK, DANIEL	FRE	080	FREDERIC
SHOOK, ELIZABETH	BAL	231	12TH WAR
SHOOK, HENRY	FRE	115	CREAGERS
SHOOK, HENRY	FRE	103	FREDERIC
SHOOK, JACOB	FRE	141	CREAGERS
SHOOK, JOHN J.	FRE	116	CREAGERS
SHOOK, MARY A.	FRE	088	FREDERIC

Name	County	Page	District
SHOOK, PETER	FRE	081	FREDERIC
SHOOK, RACHEL	WAS	018	2ND SUBD
SHOOK, SAMUEL B.	FRE	080	FREDERIC
SHOOK, SUSAN	BAL	198	19TH WAR
SHOOK, WILLIAM	FRE	140	CREAGERS
SHOOLBRED, J.	BAL	332	1ST DIST
SHOONSHUGH, MARGARET *	WAS	100	2ND DIST
SHOOP, ABRAHAM	WAS	111	2ND DIST
SHOOP, ABRAHAM	WAS	110	2ND DIST
SHOOP, ADAM	WAS	004	WILLIAMS
SHOOP, CALVIN	WAS	244	SMITHSBU
SHOOP, CATHARINE	WAS	262	1ST DIST
SHOOP, CATHARINE	WAS	154	HAGERSTO
SHOOP, CHRIST	WAS	110	2ND DIST
SHOOP, ELIZABETH	FRE	081	FREDERIC
SHOOP, HENRY	WAS	108	2ND DIST
SHOOP, HENRY	WAS	135	2ND DIST
SHOOP, JACOB	WAS	219	1ST DIST
SHOOP, JOHN	WAS	220	1ST DIST
SHOOP, JOHN	WAS	110	2ND DIST
SHOOP, JOSEPH	WAS	230	1ST DIST
SHOOP, MARGARET	WAS	135	2ND DIST
SHOOP, SALLY	WAS	153	HAGERSTO
SHOOP, SAMUEL H.	WAS	181	BOONSBOR
SHOOTER, ARNOLD	ANN	440	HOWARD D
SHOOTER, JOHN	BAL	171	2ND DIST
SHOP, MATILDA	BAL	051	15TH WAR
SHOPE, ELIZA	BAL	458	1ST DIST
SHOPE, JOHN	BAL	208	17TH WAR
SHOPE, WILLIAM B.	BAL	425	14TH WAR
SHOPER, GEORGE	ALL	060	10TH E.D
SHOPLEY, ALEXANDRIA	CAR	189	4TH DIST
SHOPLEY, FREDERICK	CAR	207	4TH DIST
SHOPLEY, WILLIAM A.	CAR	272	WESTMINS
SHOPP, JOHN	WAS	214	1ST DIST
SHOPP, MARGARET	KEN	220	2ND DIST
SHOPPY, JOHN A.	BAL	367	3RD WARD
SHORAN, JOHN *	ALL	057	10TH E.D
SHORB, CATHARINE	CAR	308	1ST DIST
SHORB, DAVID	CAR	306	1ST DIST
SHORB, JAMES	CAR	308	1ST DIST
SHORB, JAMES	CAR	260	3RD DIST
SHORB, PETER	FRE	188	5TH E DI
SHORB, WILLIAM	CAR	240	TANEYTOW
SHORDEN, MARY	BAL	229	2ND WARD
SHORE, CATHARINE	BAL	288	17TH WAR
SHORE, DANIEL F.	HAR	033	1ST DIST
SHORE, FREDRICK	BAL	009	4TH WARD
SHORE, MARY	BAL	177	2ND WARD
SHORE, THEDERICK	BAL	176	2ND WARD
SHOREBAKER, ADAM	FRE	052	FREDERIC
SHOREMAKER, BERNARD	CAR	311	1ST DIST
SHORES, ASTELL	SOM	443	DAMES QU
SHORES, BALLARD	TAL	103	ST MICHA
SHORES, BETSEY	SOM	455	DAMES QU
SHORES, EMILY	SOM	438	DAMES QU
SHORES, JAMES	BAL	035	9TH WARD
SHORES, JOHN	SOM	458	DAMES QU
SHORES, JOHN E.	SOM	548	TYASKIN
SHORES, LAMBERT	SOM	452	DAMES QU
SHORES, LEVIN	SOM	446	DAMES QU
SHORES, LEVIN	SOM	444	DAMES QU
SHORES, LEWIS	SOM	439	DAMES QU
SHORES, ROBERT	SOM	447	DAMES QU
SHORES, SEVERN	SOM	441	DAMES QU
SHORES, SOLOMON	SOM	548	TYASKIN
SHORES, SYLUS	SOM	442	DAMES QU
SHORES, TABITHA	SOM	444	DAMES QU
SHORES, THOMAS	SOM	441	DAMES QU
SHORES, THOMAS	SOM	438	DAMES QU
SHORES, THOMAS	SOM	440	DAMES QU
SHORES, WILLIAM	SOM	444	DAMES QU
SHOREY, ANN	BAL	206	6TH WARD
SHORLE, WILLIAM	FRE	281	WOODSBOR
SHORMAKER, SOPHIA	CAR	303	1ST DIST
SHORNE, JACOB	FRE	117	CREAGERS
SHORP, JOHN	BAL	071	4TH WARD
SHORT, ABRAM	ANN	426	HOWARD D
SHORT, ANN	BAL	346	3RD WARD
SHORT, AUGUSTUS	BAL	129	1ST WARD
SHORT, BETTY	CHA	295	HILLTOP
SHORT, CANNON R.	WOR	181	6TH E DI
SHORT, CATHARINE	BAL	214	11TH WAR
SHORT, CHARLES	BAL	339	13TH WAR
SHORT, CONRATT	CAR	308	1ST DIST
SHORT, DAVID	CAR	306	1ST DIST
SHORT, EBEN	DOR	450	1ST DIST
SHORT, ELIJAH	CEC	118	4TH E DI
SHORT, EMELINE	DOR	301	1ST DIST
SHORT, FRANCIS	CEC	118	4TH E DI
SHORT, FRANCIS J.	FRE	167	EMMITTSB
SHORT, GEORGE	BAL	121	18TH WAR
SHORT, GEORGE	ALL	236	CUMBERLA
SHORT, HENRY A.	CHA	270	ALLENS F
SHORT, HETTY*	DOR	457	1ST DIST
SHORT, HICKS	BAL	307	7TH WARD
SHORT, HY.	BAL	198	5TH DIST
SHORT, JAMES	WOR	299	SNOW HIL
SHORT, JAMES A.	FRE	183	5TH E DI
SHORT, JAMES R.	TAL	066	EASTON T
SHORT, JANE	BAL	006	18TH WAR
SHORT, JOHN	CEC	020	ELKTON 3
SHORT, JOHN	CHA	242	HILLTOP
SHORT, JOHN	FRE	379	PETERSVI
SHORT, JOHN	CHA	226	ALLENS F
SHORT, JOHN	BAL	129	1ST WARD
SHORT, JOHN	ANN	381	4TH DIST
SHORT, JOHN	ANN	388	4TH DIST
SHORT, JOHN D.	CAR	307	1ST DIST
SHORT, JOHN R.	PRI	022	VANSVILL
SHORT, JONATHAN	CEC	118	4TH E DI
SHORT, JOSEPH	FRE	177	5TH E DI
SHORT, JOSHUA	FRE	160	EMMITTSB
SHORT, LEVICY	DOR	449	1ST DIST
SHORT, MARIA	CHA	231	HILLTOP
SHORT, MARY A.	CEC	125	5TH E DI
SHORT, MARY C.	CAR	307	1ST DIST
SHORT, MARY M.	CEC	118	4TH E DI
SHORT, MARY*	DOR	457	1ST DIST
SHORT, MISS N.	FRE	199	5TH E DI
SHORT, PERRY	CEC	196	6TH E DI
SHORT, RACHAEL	CHA	223	ALLENS F
SHORT, RICHARD	ANN	388	4TH DIST
SHORT, ROBERT	ANN	368	4TH DIST
SHORT, ROBERT	BAL	162	11TH WAR
SHORT, SAMUEL-BLACK	CAR	145	NO TWP L
SHORT, SARAH	BAL	258	1ST DIST
SHORT, SOPHIA	CEC	001	ELKTON 3
SHORT, THOMAS	FRE	114	CREAGERS
SHORT, WILLIAM	CEC	098	3RD E DI
SHORT, WILLIAM	BAL	153	19TH WAR
SHORT, WILLIAM	BAL	162	11TH WAR
SHORT, WILLIAM	ANN	381	4TH DIST
SHORT, WILLIAM	BAL	103	2ND DIST
SHORT, WILLIAM	ANN	324	2ND DIST
SHORT, WILLIAM	DOR	450	1ST DIST
SHORT, WILLIAM	WOR	278	BERLIN 1
SHORT, WILLIAM C.	BAL	173	16TH WAR
SHORT, MARGARET	BAL	039	1ST WARD
SHORTE, JOHN	BAL	246	20TH WAR
SHORTELL, EDWARD	BAL	141	5TH WARD
SHORTELL, MARY J.	BAL	227	1ST DIST
SHORTEN, JAMS	BAL	052	9TH WARD
SHORTEN, JOHN	BAL	135	11TH WAR
SHORTEN, MARY	BAL	171	2ND DIST
SHORTEN, SILVESTER	BAL	118	11TH WAR
SHORTER WILLIAM	DOR	410	1ST DIST
SHORTER, A.	PRI	108	PISCATAW
SHORTER, ANN	BAL	063	15TH WAR
SHORTER, ARCHY	PRI	034	VANSVILL
SHORTER, BENEDICT-MULATTO	ST	321	4TH E DI
SHORTER, CAIN	DOR	348	3RD DIVI
SHORTER, CATHARINE	WAS	139	HAGERSTO
SHORTER, CATHARINE	WAS	139	HAGERSTO
SHORTER, CHARITY	SOM	544	TYASKIN
SHORTER, CHARLES	BAL	310	3RD WARD
SHORTER, CHARLES	ANN	287	ANNAPOLI
SHORTER, CHLOE	PRI	060	NOTTINGH
SHORTER, ELEANOR	CHA	225	ALLENS F
SHORTER, ELI	PRI	111	PISCATAW
SHORTER, ELIZA	PRI	060	NOTTINGH
SHORTER, ELIZA A.	BAL	002	4TH WARD
SHORTER, GERARD*	DOR	411	1ST DIST
SHORTER, HANNAH	BAL	038	15TH WAR
SHORTER, HENRY	BAL	449	8TH WARD
SHORTER, HENRY	MGM	388	ROCKERLE
SHORTER, HENRY-BLACK	ST	326	4TH E DI
SHORTER, JACOB	PRI	063	NOTTINGH
SHORTER, JAMES	WAS	128	2ND DIST
SHORTER, JIM	BAL	256	1ST DIST
SHORTER, JOHN	BAL	328	7TH WARD
SHORTER, JOHN-BLACK	ST	322	4TH E DI
SHORTER, JULIA	BAL	378	13TH WAR
SHORTER, KITTY J.	PRI	067	NOTTINGH
SHORTER, MARIA	MGM	360	BERRYS D
SHORTER, MARY	WAS	178	BOONSBOR
SHORTER, MATILDA	BAL	043	2ND DIST
SHORTER, NATHAN	PRI	022	VANSVILL
SHORTER, PHEBE	MGM	442	CLARKSTR
SHORTER, PRISCILLA	PRI	060	NOTTINGH
SHORTER, RACHEL	BAL	453	14TH WAR
SHORTER, RICHARD	DOR	348	3RD DIVI
SHORTER, RICHARD	PRI	034	VANSVILL
SHORTER, SARA E.	CHA	269	ALLENS F
SHORTER, SOLOSON	CHA	225	ALLENS F
SHORTER, STEPHEN-BLACK	FRE	220	BUCKEYST
SHORTER, SYRUS-BLACK	FRE	218	BUCKEYST
SHORTER, TERESA	BAL	280	20TH WAR
SHORTER, TERRESA	CHA	229	MIDDLETO
SHORTER, THOMAS	CHA	269	ALLENS F
SHORTER, WESLEY-BLACK	ST	322	4TH E DI
SHORTER, WILLAM	WAS	006	WILLIAMS
SHORTER, WILLIAM	CHA	267	MIDDLETO
SHORTER, WILLIAM	CHA	222	ALLENS F
SHORTER, WILLIAM	DOR	410	1ST DIST
SHORTER, WILLIAM H.-BLACK	FRE	216	BUCKEYST
SHORTER, WILLIAM W.	MGM	386	ROCKERLE
SHORTER, WILLIAM-BLACK	ST	326	4TH E DI
SHORTERS, JOHN	WAS	040	2ND SUBD
SHORTEY, SOPHIA	BAL	153	5TH WARD
SHORTON, JOHN	BAL	418	8TH WARD
SHORTS, GRACE	HAR	084	2ND DIST
SHORTS, JOHN	ANN	500	HOWARD D
SHORTS, WILLIAM	FRE	217	BUCKEYST
SHORTT, MARY M.	BAL	350	3RD WARD
SHOSTER, LOUISA	BAL	043	2ND DIST
SHOSTER, THOMAS	BAL	043	2ND DIST
SHOT, JOSHUA	BAL	023	4TH WARD
SHOT, WILLIAM	TAL	039	EASTON D
SHOTROW, WILLIAM	BAL	388	1ST DIST
SHOTT, JOHN	BAL	282	1ST DIST
SHOTT, JOHN	BAL	312	20TH WAR
SHOTTS, ELIZABETH	BAL	028	4TH WARD
SHOTTS, ISRAEL	BAL	372	8TH WARD
SHOTTS, LEWIS	MGM	375	ROCKERLE
SHOUELL, MARIAH	WOR	244	1ST CENS
SHOUFER, ELIE	WAS	168	FUNKSTOW
SHOUFER, PETER	WAS	169	FUNKSTOW
SHOUK, SUSAN	WAS	210	1ST DIST
SHOULAND, PATRICK	BAL	272	1ST DIST
SHOULTZ, CHARLES	BAL	368	8TH WARD
SHOULTZ, GEORGE	BAL	366	8TH WARD
SHOUP, HENRY	BAL	319	1ST DIST
SHOUP, JOHN	WAS	202	1ST DIST
SHOUPER, JONATHAN	WAS	167	1ST DIST
SHOUSE, DAVID R.	FRE	392	PETERSVI
SHOUSE, JOHN W.	ALL	054	10TH E.D
SHOUT, ARTHUR	CEC	154	PORT DUP
SHOUTS, MARY	BAL	303	3RD WARD
SHOUTS, MARY	BAL	126	2ND DIST
SHOVER, CATHARINE	WAS	212	1ST DIST
SHOVER, ELIZA J.	FRE	355	MIDDLETO
SHOVER, FREDERICK	FRE	354	MIDDLETO
SHOVER, HESTER	WAS	102	2ND DIST
SHOVER, JACOB	WAS	212	1ST DIST
SHOW, CATHARINE	FRE	344	MIDDLETO
SHOW, CHRISTIAN	BAL	131	2ND DIST
SHOW, ELIZABETH	WAS	074	2ND SUBD
SHOW, FRANCES*	BAL	002	4TH WARD
SHOW, HENRY	FRE	369	CATOCTIN
SHOW, HENRY	WAS	048	2ND SUBD
SHOW, JACOB	WAS	053	2ND SUBD
SHOW, JACOB	WAS	052	2ND SUBD
SHOW, JOHN	WAS	203	1ST DIST
SHOW, MARTHA E.	WAS	203	1ST DIST
SHOW, SAMUEL	FRE	369	CATOCTIN
SHOW, THOMAS	WAS	202	1ST DIST
SHOWACRE, CATHARINE E.	BAL	150	16TH WAR
SHOWACRE, JOHN	BAL	150	16TH WAR
SHOWARD, JOSEPH	WOR	224	4TH E DI
SHOWELL, HET	WOR	277	BERLIN 1
SHOWELL, JOSIAH	WOR	271	BERLIN 1
SHOWELL, SAMUEL	WOR	270	BERLIN 1
SHOWELL, WILLIAM	WOR	271	BERLIN 1
SHOWER, ADAM	CAR	333	MANCHEST
SHOWER, CASPER	BAL	384	1ST DIST
SHOWER, GOERGE	CAR	346	6TH DIST
SHOWER, JACOB	CAR	333	MANCHEST
SHOWER, MARTIN	BAL	417	3RD WARD
SHOWER, SARAH	CAR	333	MANCHEST
SHOWERS, HESTOR M.	BAL	234	17TH WAR
SHOWERS, JAMES	BAL	197	5TH DIST
SHOWERS, JOHN	BAL	098	5TH WARD
SHOWERS, MISS C.	FRE	198	5TH E DI
SHOWMAN, AARON G.	WAS	201	1ST DIST
SHOWMAN, GEORGE	BAL	238	17TH WAR
SHOWMAN, MARY	BAL	237	17TH WAR
SHOWMAN, PETER	WAS	201	1ST DIST
SHOYE, MATHIAS	ALL	201	CUMBERLA
SHPATES, ALFRED	BAL	334	13TH WAR
SHRADER, GEORGE	WAS	125	2ND DIST
SHRADER, GEORGE	WAS	125	2ND DIST
SHRAL, MICHAEL *	ANN	386	4TH DIST
SHRATER, HENRY	CAR	191	4TH DIST
SHRATER, MARY V.	CAR	192	4TH DIST
SHRE, COONRODE	HAR	199	3RD DIST
SHRECK, JACOB	BAL	250	6TH WARD
SHRECK, LUCRETIA H.	BAL	040	4TH WARD
SHRECK, MARGARET	BAL	280	7TH WARD
SHREDER, JULIUS	BAL	253	12TH WAR
SHREEVE, DAVID	CAR	190	4TH DIST
SHREEVE, WILLIAM	CAR	265	WESTMINS
SHREEVES, JOSHUA B.	BAL	387	8TH WARD
SHREINE, CONRAD	BAL	206	19TH WAR
SHREUS, GEORGE	BAL	003	9TH WARD
SHREVE, SAMUEL	MGM	356	BERRYS D
SHREVER, BENJAMIN	MGM	415	MEDLEY 3
SHREVER, F. W.	ALL	002	3RD E.D.
SHREVES, JESSE	TAL	065	EASTON T
SHREVES, JULIA	BAL	072	15TH WAR
SHRIBER, HENRY	ALL	168	6TH E.D.
SHRIBER, VERA	ALL	168	6TH E.D.
SHRICK, JOHN	BAL	415	14TH WAR
SHRICK, WILLIAM	HAR	161	3RD DIST
SHRIDEL, FREDRICK*	BAL	001	4TH WARD
SHRIDEN, PATRICK	BAL	171	6TH WARD
SHRIEVER, ELIZABETH	BAL	402	8TH WARD
SHRIFOLE, WILLIAM	BAL	288	3RD WARD
SHRIGLEY, ENOCH M.	FRE	381	PETERSVI
SHRIMP, AWANT	ALL	223	CUMBERLA
SHRINE, CATHARINE	BAL	393	14TH WAR
SHRINER, ANN E.	FRE	065	FREDERIC
SHRINER, ANNA	CAR	321	1ST DIST
SHRINER, ANNA S.	FRE	452	8TH E DI
SHRINER, CATHARINE	CAR	314	1ST DIST
SHRINER, CORLEIUS	FRE	306	WOODSBOR
SHRINER, DAVID	CAR	322	1ST DIST
SHRINER, ELIZA	CAR	304	1ST DIST
SHRINER, HENRY	CAR	313	1ST DIST
SHRINER, ISAAC	CAR	315	1ST DIST
SHRINER, JACOB	CAR	322	1ST DIST
SHRINER, JACOB	CAR	413	2ND DIST
SHRINER, JAMES	CAR	321	1ST DIST
SHRINER, JOANNA	TAL	026	EASTON D
SHRINER, JOHN	CAR	303	1ST DIST
SHRINER, JOHN	CAR	237	UNION TO
SHRINER, JOHN	FRE	012	FREDERIC
SHRINER, JOHN	BAL	014	15TH WAR
SHRINER, JOSEPH	WAS	014	2ND SUBD
SHRINER, PETER	BAL	273	12TH WAR
SHRINER, PETER	CAR	382	2ND DIST
SHRINER, SAMUEL	CAR	322	1ST DIST
SHRINK, WILLIAM	BAL	211	6TH DIST
SHRIPSON, JOHN A.	BAL	271	2ND WARD
SHRISBEY, STEPHEN	HAR	146	3RD DIST
SHRIVE, ALEXANDER	CAL	001	1ST DIST
SHRIVE, ELIZABETH R.	CAL	001	1ST DIST
SHRIVE, JAMES	CAL	024	2ND DIST
SHRIVE, MARTHA	BAL	007	EASTERN
SHRIVEL, MARGARET	BAL	138	16TH WAR
SHRIVER, ABRAHAM	CAR	386	2ND DIST
SHRIVER, ALFORD	ALL	235	CUMBERLA
SHRIVER, ANDREW K.	CAR	260	3RD DIST
SHRIVER, ANN	FRE	447	8TH E DI
SHRIVER, BENJAMIN	FRE	034	FREDERIC
SHRIVER, CH. H.	BAL	269	20TH WAR
SHRIVER, DANIEL	WAS	172	FUNKSTOW
SHRIVER, DAVID	KEN	256	1ST DIST
SHRIVER, DAVID	FRE	279	WOODSBOR
SHRIVER, DAVID	ALL	196	CUMBERLA
SHRIVER, EDWARD	FRE	029	FREDERIC
SHRIVER, EDWARD T.	ALL	234	CUMBERLA
SHRIVER, ELIZABETH	FRE	432	8TH E DI
SHRIVER, ELIZABETH	FRE	311	MIDDLETO
SHRIVER, ELLEN	WAS	082	2ND SUBD
SHRIVER, EVE	ALL	196	CUMBERLA
SHRIVER, HARMAN	WAS	294	1ST DIST
SHRIVER, HENRY	WAS	283	1ST DIST
SHRIVER, HENRY	WAS	205	1ST DIST
SHRIVER, HENRY	WAS	187	BOONSBOR
SHRIVER, HENRY	BAL	421	8TH WARD
SHRIVER, HENRY C.	BAL	160	16TH WAR
SHRIVER, ISAAC	CAR	267	WESTMINS
SHRIVER, JACOB	BAL	339	7TH WARD
SHRIVER, JAMES	BAL	099	15TH WAR
SHRIVER, JOHN	ALL	206	CUMBERLA
SHRIVER, JOHN	BAL	074	2ND DIST
SHRIVER, JOHN	BAL	325	3RD WARD
SHRIVER, JOHN	WAS	187	BOONSBOR
SHRIVER, JOHN S.	BAL	233	12TH WAR
SHRIVER, JOSEPH	ALL	253	CUMBERLA
SHRIVER, JOSEPH	KEN	262	1ST DIST
SHRIVER, JULIA	ALL	220	CUMBERLA
SHRIVER, MARY	CAR	413	2ND DIST
SHRIVER, NANCY	CAR	388	2ND DIST
SHRIVER, NELSON	CAR	379	2ND DIST
SHRIVER, REBECCA	FRE	117	CREAGERS
SHRIVER, THOMAS	ALL	234	CUMBERLA
SHRIVER, VALENT	BAL	292	12TH WAR
SHRIVER, WILLIAM	CAR	244	3RD DIST
SHRIVER, WILLIAM JR.	CAR	260	3RD DIST
SHRIVERS, JSOHUA	FRE	432	8TH E DI
SHRIVERS, MARY J.	BAL	029	9TH WARD
SHRIVERY, GEORGE	CEC	093	4TH E DI
SHRIVERY, SARAH H.	CEC	093	4TH E DI
SHRIVIN, THOMAS	WAS	049	2ND SUBD
SHRIVLE, SUSAN	WAS	141	HAGERSTO
SHRJOCK, HENRY	FRE	107	CREAGERS
SHROCK, JOHN	ALL	038	2ND E.D.
SHROCK, YOST	ALL	022	2ND E.D.
SHRODER, JOHN	BAL	378	8TH WARD
SHRODES, CHARLES	HAR	023	1ST DIST
SHRODES, COONRAD	HAR	048	1ST DIST
SHRODES, JAMES	ALL	207	CUMBERLA
SHRODES, JOHN W.	ALL	207	CUMBERLA
SHROEDER, FREDERICK *	FRE	058	FREDERIC
SHROEDER, HENRY	BAL	063	2ND DIST
SHROEDER, MARGARETT	BAL	030	4TH WARD
SHROFF, JOSEPH	HAR	006	1ST DIST
SHROTE, JOHN	BAL	191	19TH WAR

SHROTER, HENRY CAR 191 4TH DIST
SHROUD, JOHN BAL 442 8TH WARD
SHROUD, WILLIAM BAL 442 8TH WARD
SHROYER, ADAM ALL 032 2ND E.D.
SHROYER, BENJAMIN ALL 102 5TH E.D.
SHROYER, DORATHY CAR 245 3RD DIST
SHROYER, JOHN FRE 359 CATOCTIN
SHROYER, PETER FRE 358 CATOCTIN
SHROYER, SOLOMON FRE 097 FREDERIC
SHROYER, SUSAN FRE 358 CATOCTIN
SHRUM, HENRY WAS 002 WILLIAMS
SHRYACK, SARAH BAL 157 6TH WARD
SHRYE, CATHARINE BAL 218 6TH WARD
SHRYER, ELLEN BAL 128 5TH WARD
SHRYER, GEORGE F. ALL 218 CUMBERLA
SHRYER, THOMAS W. ALL 240 CUMBERLA
SHRYOCK, G.W. BAL 228 12TH WAR
SHRYOCK, GEORGE WAS 167 1ST DIST
SHRYOCK, HENRIETTA ALL 014 3RD E.D.
SHRYOCK, HENRY S. BAL 068 10TH WAR
SHRYOCK, JOHN WAS 167 1ST DIST
SHRYOCK, LENOX M. ALL 175 7TH E.D.
SHRYOCK, LEWIS G. ALL 174 7TH E.D.
SHRYOCK, MARGARET FRE 140 CREAGERS
SHUBART, WILLIAM BAL 095 2ND DIST
SHUBER, FRANCIS BAL 291 12TH WAR
SHUBERT, BENJAMIN ANN 396 8TH DIST
SHUBERT, CHRISTIAN BAL 004 4TH WARD
SHUBERT, ELIZABETH BAL 242 20TH WAR
SHUBERT, ELIZABETH ANN 398 8TH DIST
SHUBERT, JOHN BAL 017 9TH WARD
SHUBERT, JOSEPH * ANN 396 8TH DIST
SHUBRIDGE, ROSINA BAL 100 18TH WAR
SHUCART, WILLIAM BAL 131 5TH WARD
SHUCK, ADAM BAL 383 8TH WARD
SHUCK, CATHARINE ALL 015 3RD E.D.
SHUCK, GEORGE ALL 259 CUMBERLA
SHUCK, HENRY BAL 389 8TH WARD
SHUCK, JACOB BAL 383 8TH WARD
SHUCK, JACOB ALL 212 CUMBERLA
SHUCK, JOHNT. ALL 262 CUMBERLA
SHUCK, JOSEPH ALL 231 CUMBERLA
SHUCK, JUSTUS ANN 380 4TH DIST
SHUCK, MARIA ALL 222 CUMBERLA
SHUCK, MARIA ALL 205 CUMBERLA
SHUCK, MARY ANN ALL 251 CUMBERLA
SHUCK, THOMAS ALL 231 CUMBERLA
SHUCK, WILLIAM ALL 238 CUMBERLA
SHUCK, WILLIAM ALL 212 CUMBERLA
SHUCK,MARY M. ALL 212 CUMBERLA
SHUCKART, HENRY BAL 368 13TH WAR
SHUCKLE, CHARLES W. BAL 250 20TH WAR
SHUCKLES, NELSON CEC 158 PORT DUP
SHUCKLEY, ELEANOR WOR 233 6TH E DI
SHUCY, CATHARINE CAR 395 2ND DIST
SHUCY, JEREMIAH L. CAR 394 2ND DIST
SHUCY, LEWIS CAR 395 2ND DIST
SHUDSON, JAMES BAL 050 1ST WARD
SHUE, ELIZABETH BAL 208 6TH DIST
SHUE, JACOB J. BAL 101 18TH WAR
SHUE, JOHN CAR 337 6TH DIST
SHUE, MELINDA BAL 101 18TH WAR
SHUE, MICHAEL BAL 101 18TH WAR
SHUE, SAMUEL CAR 337 6TH DIST
SHUEE, DAVID * CAR 286 7TH DIST
SHUEY, JACOB K. CAR 397 2ND DIST
SHUFF, BENJAMIN FRE 365 CATOCTIN
SHUFF, CATHERINE FRE 121 CREAGERS
SHUFF, GEORGE FRE 116 CREAGERS
SHUFF, THOMAS FRE 122 CREAGERS
SHUFF, URIAH FRE 126 CREAGERS
SHUFF, WILLIAM FRE 131 CREAGERS
SHUFORD, MORTIMER T. FRE 309 WOODSBOR
SHUGARS, ANDREW BAL 369 1ST DIST
SHUGARS, BENJAMIN BAL 381 1ST DIST
SHUGARS, CATHARINE BAL 234 1ST DIST
SHUGARS, DANIEL BAL 239 1ST DIST
SHUGARS, HANNAH BAL 352 1ST DIST
SHUGARS, JAMES BAL 222 1ST DIST
SHUGARS, MATILDA BAL 317 1ST DIST
SHUGH, ALICE CAR 359 9TH DIST
SHUGH, JOHN A. CAR 358 9TH DIST
SHUGSARS, SAMUEL BAL 317 1ST DIST
SHUHAN, CORNELIUS BAL 025 9TH WARD
SHUINE, EUGENE * BAL 334 13TH WAR
SHULE, FREDERICK BAL 260 1ST DIST
SHULE, JOHN BAL 217 19TH WAR
SHULEER, JAMES BAL 362 8TH WARD
SHULER, CAROLINE BAL 091 5TH WARD
SHULER, CONRAD BAL 066 15TH WAR
SHULER, ELIZABETH CAR 253 3RD DIST
SHULER, GEORGE* BAL 412 3RD WARD
SHULER, HENRY CAR 323 1ST DIST
SHULER, JACOB CAR 303 1ST DIST
SHULER, JESSE CAR 301 1ST DIST
SHULER, JOHN CAR 304 1ST DIST
SHULER, JOHN BAL 091 5TH WARD
SHULER, MARIA CAR 262 3RD DIST
SHULER, MARTIN BAL 279 1ST DIST
SHULL, DAVID WAS 285 1ST DIST
SHULL, JACOB WAS 284 1ST DIST
SHULTER, HENRY BAL 236 20TH WAR
SHULTHERS, JOHN BAL 234 12TH WAR
SHULTS, ELEANOR ALL 108 5TH E.D.
SHULTS, JAMES L. CEC 030 CHESAPEA
SHULTS, MARIA E. FRE 001 FREDERIC
SHULTY, CHRISTIAN ALL 137 4TH E.D.
SHULTY, DAVID BAL 239 1ST DIST
SHULTZ, ABRAHAM CAR 378 2ND DIST
SHULTZ, ANDREW BAL 311 20TH WAR
SHULTZ, ANDREW BAL 065 15TH WAR
SHULTZ, BARBARA BAL 393 3RD WARD
SHULTZ, CHARLES BAL 313 12TH WAR
SHULTZ, DAVID CAR 322 1ST DIST
SHULTZ, DAVID CAR 331 MANCHEST
SHULTZ, EARNEST BAL 379 3RD WARD
SHULTZ, ELIZABETH BAL 308 20TH WAR
SHULTZ, ELLENORA CAR 377 2ND DIST
SHULTZ, EPHRAIM BAL 222 1ST DIST
SHULTZ, ERHOST * BAL 099 18TH WAR
SHULTZ, FERNANDIS BAL 087 18TH WAR
SHULTZ, FREDERICK CAR 171 8TH DIST
SHULTZ, FREDERICK BAL 060 2ND DIST
SHULTZ, GEORGE BAL 345 3RD WARD
SHULTZ, GEORGE BAL 433 1ST DIST
SHULTZ, GEORGE BAL 298 17TH WAR
SHULTZ, GEORGE BAL 081 4TH WARD
SHULTZ, GEORGE FRE 096 FREDERIC
SHULTZ, HENRIETTA BAL 359 3RD WARD
SHULTZ, HENRY FRE 054 FREDERIC
SHULTZ, HENRY FRE 200 5TH E DI
SHULTZ, HENRY BAL 250 20TH WAR
SHULTZ, JESSE CAR 331 MANCHEST
SHULTZ, JOHN CAR 330 MANCHEST
SHULTZ, JOHN BAL 287 17TH WAR
SHULTZ, JOHN CAR 184 8TH DIST
SHULTZ, JOHN CAR 234 UNION TO
SHULTZ, JOHN BAL 167 19TH WAR
SHULTZ, JOHN BAL 187 5TH DIST
SHULTZ, JOSEPH FRE 174 5TH E DI
SHULTZ, JOSEPH C. FRE 150 10TH E D
SHULTZ, MARY BAL 271 20TH WAR
SHULTZ, MARY BAL 196 5TH DIST
SHULTZ, MARY BAL 197 5TH DIST
SHULTZ, MATILDA CAR 385 2ND DIST
SHULTZ, NANCY WAS 168 FUNKSTOW
SHULTZ, NICHOLAS BAL 417 3RD WARD
SHULTZ, PERRY ALL 020 2ND E.D.
SHULTZ, PETER CAR 333 MANCHEST
SHULTZ, PHILLIP ALL 224 CUMBERLA
SHULTZ, REBECCA BAL 183 5TH DIST
SHULTZ, SAMUEL BAL 293 1ST DIST
SHULTZ, THOMAS BAL 289 3RD WARD
SHULTZ,ADAM ALL 013 3RD E.D.
SHULTZE, CHARLES BAL 451 14TH WAR
SHULTZE, CONRAD BAL 442 14TH WAR
SHULTZE, MATTHIAS BAL 392 14TH WAR
SHULTZE, WILLIAM BAL 451 14TH WAR
SHULY, HENRY BAL 249 20TH WAR
SHUM, FREDERICK BAL 288 17TH WAR
SHUMACHER, F. BAL 333 1ST DIST
SHUMAKER, ELIZA D. BAL 354 7TH WARD
SHUMAN, AUGUSTUS BAL 272 17TH WAR
SHUMAN, ELLEN BAL 185 11TH WAR
SHUMAN, HENRY BAL 295 17TH WAR
SHUMAN, MARY BAL 152 11TH WAR
SHUMAN, W.R. ALL 219 CUMBERLA
SHUMAT, LUCRETIA CHA 237 HILLTOP
SHUMEL, GERTURDE BAL 178 2ND WARD
SHUMERL, BENARD BAL 177 2ND WARD
SHUMES, ANN BAL 153 19TH WAR
SHUMO, E. WAS 005 WILLIAMS
SHUMYER, HENRY BAL 279 12TH WAR
SHUMYER, HENRY BAL 278 12TH WAR
SHUN,SAMUEL QUE 182 3RD E DI
SHUNK, ANDREW M. WAS 262 1ST DIST
SHUNK, BENJAMIN CAR 313 1ST DIST
SHUNK, CATHERINE BAL 403 3RD WARD
SHUNK, DANIEL WAS 250 1ST DIST
SHUNK, ELIZABETH BAL 101 2ND DIST
SHUNK, FANNEY FRE 285 WOODSBOR
SHUNK, GEORGE CAR 396 2ND DIST
SHUNK, HENRY WAS 250 1ST DIST
SHUNK, JACOB WAS 262 1ST DIST
SHUNK, JERAMIAH CAR 240 TANEYTOW
SHUNK, MARGARET BAL 101 2ND DIST
SHUNK, MICHAEL WAS 027 2ND SUBD
SHUNK, SAMUEL CAR 235 UNION TO
SHUNK, SOPHIA BAL 203 6TH WARD
SHUNNEBERGER, ANTONE BAL 007 9TH WARD
SHUP, JOHN WAS 134 2ND DIST
SHUP, LOUISA BAL 402 14TH WAR
SHUPGAGLE, WILLIAM CAR 184 8TH DIST
SHUPLEY, GEORGE B. CAR 193 4TH DIST
SHUPLEY, JOSHUA BAL 292 12TH WAR
SHUPLEY, PETER BAL 252 20TH WAR
SHUPP, HENRY BAL 270 7TH WARD
SHUPP, MARGARET FRE 095 FREDERIC
SHURB, JACOB BAL 051 18TH WAR
SHURBUT, SAMUEL ANN 395 8TH DIST
SHURDIN, JAMES BAL 110 10TH WAR
SHURIGLE, L. BAL 272 20TH WAR
SHURLER, E.G. BAL 163 1ST WARD
SHURMEL, STEPHEN BAL 041 9TH WARD
SHURPHY, JOHN ALL 045 10TH E.D
SHURPHY, WILLIAM P. BAL 131 1ST WARD
SHURRAY, JOHN ALL 075 5TH E.D.
SHURRY, S. F. BAL 034 18TH WAR
SHURTIE, JACOB BAL 369 8TH WARD
SHURTZ, CATHARINE BAL 212 19TH WAR
SHURTZ, WILLIAM D. BAL 320 20TH WAR
SHUSSER, NICHOLAS ALL 036 2ND E.D.
SHUSTER, EVE CAR 349 6TH DIST
SHUSTER, JACOB-BLACK CAR 364 9TH DIST
SHUSTER, JOHN BAL 017 18TH WAR
SHUSTER, JOSEPH BAL 063 15TH WAR
SHUSTER, JOSEPH BAL 024 15TH WAR
SHUTE, FREDERICK BAL 047 1ST WARD
SHUTE, JOSHUA BAL 156 2ND DIST
SHUTER, JOHN BAL 285 17TH WAR
SHUTER, THOMAS BAL 233 20TH WAR
SHUTHOFF, CHARLOTTE BAL 265 20TH WAR
SHUTHOWER, HENRY BAL 042 18TH WAR
SHUTLEY, JOHN BAL 039 1ST WARD
SHUTON, THOMAS BAL 127 5TH WARD
SHUTS, GEORGE BAL 362 1ST DIST
SHUTS, JOHN* BAL 328 3RD WARD
SHUTS, MILDRED BAL 363 1ST DIST
SHUTS, THOMAS A. BAL 322 3RD WARD
SHUTT, AMELIA BAL 304 20TH WAR
SHUTT, AUGUSTUS JAMES P. BAL 085 10TH WAR
SHUTT, AUGUSTUS P. BAL 085 10TH WAR
SHUTT, CATHARINE FRE 360 CATOCTIN
SHUTT, CHRISTOPHER BAL 303 20TH WAR
SHUTT, FREDERICK BAL 143 19TH WAR
SHUTT, JAMES BAL 155 2ND DIST
SHUTT, JAOCB FRE 360 CATOCTIN
SHUTT, MARGARET BAL 288 17TH WAR
SHUTT, MATHIAS BAL 183 11TH WAR
SHUTT, PHILIP BAL 224 12TH WAR
SHUTTLE, HENRY BAL 280 17TH WAR
SHUTZ, AUGUSTUS D. BAL 429 8TH WARD
SHUTZ, LEWIS ANN 463 HOWARD D
SHUTZE, SAMUEL BAL 394 14TH WAR
SHVAL, MICHAEL * ANN 386 4TH DIST
SHWUEER, AUGUSTUS CAR 287 7TH DIST
SHYE, MARY BAL 189 11TH WAR
SHYER, MARY C. ALL 228 CUMBERLA
SHYERS, JOHN ALL 027 2ND E.D.
SHYLER, AMANDA TAL 046 EASTON T
SHYLER, JOHN TAL 055 EASTON D
SHYLER, JULIA TAL 060 EASTON D
SHYLER, SAMUEL TAL 062 EASTON D
SHYOCK, ELIZABETH BAL 315 1ST DIST
SHYROCK, C. D. BAL 408 14TH WAR
SHYROCK, JACOB BAL 051 18TH WAR
SIALS, JOHN* BAL 369 3RD WARD
SIAR, JOHN CAR 176 8TH DIST
SIBBLE, MARY BAL 247 2ND WARD
SIBEL, CATHRINE BAL 048 18TH WAR
SIBEL, JOHN* BAL 027 4TH WARD
SIBENA, LEWIS * BAL 309 12TH WAR
SIBER, JOHN WAS 273 RIDGEVIL
SIBERT, AUGUST BAL 319 3RD WARD
SIBERT, BENJAMIN G. WAS 289 1ST DIST
SIBERT, CHARLES BAL 048 4TH WARD
SIBERT, JACOB WAS 056 2ND SUBD
SIBERT, SAMPSON B. ALL 015 3RD E.D.
SIBERT, SOLOMON ALL 016 3RD E.D.
SIBERTS, GERARD* BAL 349 3RD WARD
SIBLEY, EDWARD T. PRI 032 VANSVILL
SIBLEY, ELIZABETH PRI 012 BLADENSB
SIBLEY, JOHN T. PRI 029 VANSVILL
SIBLEY, JONATHAN MGM 342 CLARKSBU
SIBLEY, JONATHAN MGM 341 CLARKSBU
SIBLEY, JSOEPH ALL 020 2ND E.D.
SIBLEY, MARY BAL 264 20TH WAR
SIBLEY, R.S. ALL 205 CUMBERLA
SIBLEY, THOMAS FRE 274 NEW MARK
SIBLEY, THOMAS W. PRI 032 VANSVILL
SIBRET, FRANCIS BAL 242 17TH WAR
SIBTEA, MARTIN BAL 050 1ST WARD
SICCO, JAMES CEC 057 1ST E DI
SICKBERGER, ELIZABETH BAL 006 1ST WARD
SICKEL, GEORGE G. BAL 160 6TH WARD
SICKEL, JOHN L. BAL 337 13TH WAR
SICKER, HENRY BAL 140 5TH WARD
SICKIN, CHARLES BAL 470 14TH WAR
SICKKIN, CHARLES BAL 455 14TH WAR
SICKLE, EPHRAIM ALL 030 2ND E.D.
SICKLE, HENRY ALL 030 2ND E.D.
SICKLE, JACOB ALL 030 2ND E.D.
SICKLE, LEWIS ALL 051 10TH E.D
SICKLE, MOSES FRE 319 MIDDLETO
SICKS, CYRUS FRE 131 CREAGERS
SICKS, THOMAS FRE 176 5TH E DI
SICOE, EDWARD-MULATTO BAL 212 2ND WARD
SICRICK, MARGARET WAS 138 2ND DIST
SIDCO, CHARLES F. BAL 052 9TH WARD
SIDDEL, MICHAEL BAL 283 1ST DIST
SIDDON, JACOB * BAL 110 2ND DIST
SIDDON, RACHAEL BAL 434 14TH WAR
SIDDONS, MARY BAL 311 20TH WAR
SIDEBOARD, FLORA BAL 295 17TH WAR
SIDEL, JOHN BAL 090 2ND DIST
SIDENCE, WILLIAM H.* BAL 298 3RD WARD
SIDERS, MICHAEL WAS 276 RIDGEVIL
SIDERSTICK, ELIZABETH WAS 174 FUNKSTOW
SIDES, ANN BAL 093 18TH WAR
SIDES, ANNIE BAL 353 3RD WARD
SIDES, CATO CAR 358 9TH DIST
SIDES, DANIEL BAL 233 17TH WAR
SIDES, FREDERIC CAR 288 7TH DIST
SIDES, FREDERICK BAL 137 11TH WAR
SIDES, GEORGE CAR 359 9TH DIST
SIDES, GEORGE BAL 093 18TH WAR
SIDES, GEORGE BAL 254 2ND WARD
SIDES, GEORGE W. BAL 239 1ST DIST
SIDES, JOHN BAL 112 2ND DIST
SIDES, JOHN BAL 112 2ND DIST
SIDES, JOHN-BLACK CAR 397 2ND DIST
SIDES, MARGARETT* BAL 030 4TH WARD
SIDES, MENEY BAL 314 20TH WAR
SIDES, SAMUEL BAL 074 10TH WAR
SIDES, SOPHIA BAL 265 20TH WAR
SIDES, WILLIAM* BAL 029 4TH WARD
SIDESTICK, SOLOMON WAS 222 1ST DIST
SIDINGER, ANN ALL 099 5TH E.D.
SIDINGER, PETER BAL 088 1ST WARD
SIDINGS, SUSAN BAL 078 2ND DIST
SIDNEY, ELIZABETH A. BAL 247 2ND WARD
SIDNEY, JOHN * KEN 266 1ST DIST
SIDNEY, JOHN R. BAL 247 2ND WARD
SIDNGS, ELIZABETH BAL 078 2ND DIST
SIDON, JACOB CAR 278 7TH DIST
SIDWELL, ABRAHAM CEC 199 7TH E DI
SIDWELL, MARGARET CEC 165 6TH E DI
SIDWELL, NELSON CEC 161 6TH E DI
SIDWELL, REUBEN FRE 410 8TH E DI
SIDWELL, RUTH CEC 113 4TH E DI
SIEBART, FERDINAND BAL 050 15TH WAR
SIECKS, HENRY BAL 082 15TH WAR
SIEGAMUND, JOHN BAL 206 6TH WARD
SIEGART, GEORGE BAL 180 16TH WAR
SIEGEL, JOHN BAL 254 12TH WAR
SIEGMANN, CONRAD BAL 206 6TH WARD
SIEGNER, MARTHA E. BAL 071 10TH WAR
SIEGRIST, CAROLINE BAL 101 5TH WARD
SIEM, CHARLES BAL 022 15TH WAR
SIER, BEALE CAR 250 3RD DIST
SIER, JANE CAR 260 3RD DIST
SIER, MESS BAL 266 20TH WAR
SIESON, AMANDA ALL 235 CUMBERLA
SIETRICK, LEWIS BAL 475 14TH WAR
SIETZ, JOHN BAL 082 15TH WAR
SIFER, MARY BAL 177 19TH WAR
SIFERT, FREDERICK BAL 458 14TH WAR
SIFFER, ZUNE BAL 204 2ND WARD
SIFFORD, JOHN FRE 031 FREDERIC
SIFONG, JACOB * BAL 418 1ST DIST
SIFORD, JOSHIA BAL 071 18TH WAR
SIFTON, JAMES ANN 291 ANNAPOLI
SIFTON, JOHN* BAL 089 10TH WAR
SIFTON, MARTHA ANN 292 ANNAPOLI
SIFTON, REBECCA ANN 356 3RD DIST
SIGAFOOS, WILLIAM FRE 378 PETERSVI
SIGE, BRIDGET BAL 296 12TH WAR
SIGLE, ELIZA ALL 127 4TH E.D.
SIGLER, EVAN ALL 133 4TH E.D.
SIGLER, JHN BAL 287 12TH WAR
SIGLER, JOHN ALL 123 4TH E.D.
SIGLER, JOHN BAL 209 6TH DIST
SIGLER, MARGARET BAL 088 10TH WAR
SIGLER, MARTIN BAL 060 18TH WAR
SIGLER, PETER WAS 093 2ND SUBD
SIGLER, PHILIP ALL 124 4TH E.D.
SIGLER, THOMAS WAS 080 2ND SUBD
SIGLER, WILLIAM WAS 080 2ND SUBD
SIGLMAN, LUCY BAL 087 4TH WARD
SIGMOND, ALBERT BAL 339 3RD WARD
SIGMUND, FREDERICA BAL 213 19TH WAR
SIGNER, CHARLES BAL 036 15TH WAR
SIGNOR, CHARLES BAL 372 8TH WARD
SIGOUNEY, ANDREW BAL 093 10TH WAR
SIGRIST, CHARLES BAL 003 EASTERN
SIHEVAL, J. BAL 247 2ND WARD
SIKES, ADAM ALL 174 7TH E.D.
SIKES, CALEP BAL 106 18TH WAR
SIKES, CONSTANTIA BAL 318 1ST DIST
SIKES, GOERGE BAL 195 17TH WAR

Name	County	Page	District
SIKES, SERCELIA	BAL	064	18TH WAR
SIKKEN, MARGARET	BAL	208	19TH WAR
SILAHUNT, HENRIETTA	BAL	409	3RD WARD
SILAKEN, HENRY	BAL	134	1ST WARD
SILAMAN, JOHN	CEC	044	CHESAPEA
SILANCE, SUSAN	BAL	027	18TH WAR
SILANCE, SUSAN	BAL	300	7TH WARD
SILAR, ISAAC	WAS	088	2ND SUBD
SILAS, SOPHIA	ALL	199	CUMBERLA
SILCOX, SPENCER	QUE	166	2ND E DI
SILE, SAMUEL	BAL	294	1ST DIST
SILENCE, BAKER T.	MGM	424	MEDLEY 3
SILENCE, ELIZABETH	ST	289	2ND E DI
SILENCE, RICHARD	FRE	233	BUCKEYST
SILENCE, WILLIAM S.	FRE	230	BUCKEYST
SILENCE, WILLIAM T.	FRE	211	BUCKEYST
SILER, MICHAEL	BAL	378	8TH WARD
SILERT, ELIZA	BAL	462	14TH WAR
SILES, JACOB	ST	254	3RD E DI
SILES, MARTHA	KEN	263	1ST DIST
SILES, RICAHRED *	FRE	272	NEW MARK
SILIVAN, PARKER	WOR	250	1ST CENS
SILK, JAMES F.	BAL	420	14TH WAR
SILK, JOHN	BAL	302	17TH WAR
SILK, JOHN	ALL	198	CUMBERLA
SILK, THOMAS R.	BAL	101	1ST WARD
SILKS, ELIZA	BAL	020	2ND DIST
SILKS, JACOB	PRI	040	VANSVILL
SILLMAN, LEAH J.	BAL	053	9TH WARD
SILLS, ANN	BAL	018	4TH WARD
SILLY, MARTHA J.	MGM	355	BERRYS D
SILMAN, ROBERT	BAL	459	1ST DIST
SILS, JOHN W.	HAR	154	3RD DIST
SILSES, BENJAMIN	WAS	231	1ST DIST
SILSOR, CHARLES H.*	DOR	341	3RD DIVI
SILVA, D.	BAL	169	1ST WARD
SILVA, F.	BAL	171	1ST WARD
SILVE, JOHN	BAL	170	1ST WARD
SILVER, AARON	BAL	056	4TH WARD
SILVER, BENJAMIN	HAR	178	3RD DIST
SILVER, ELIZABETH	HAR	171	3RD DIST
SILVER, HENRY A.	HAR	004	1ST DIST
SILVER, JAMES	HAR	026	1ST DIST
SILVER, JOSEPH	HAR	051	1ST DIST
SILVER, MARGARET	HAR	002	1ST DIST
SILVER, MICHAEL	BAL	148	5TH WARD
SILVER, PETER	BAL	099	1ST WARD
SILVER, PHILIP W.	HAR	001	1ST DIST
SILVER, SAMUEL B.	HAR	171	3RD DIST
SILVER, SILVESTER	BAL	128	18TH WAR
SILVER, WILLIAM	HAR	159	3RD DIST
SILVER, WILLIAM Z.	HAR	170	3RD DIST
SILVERISEN, M. MARY *	BAL	105	18TH WAR
SILVERISEN, MILLAY *	BAL	105	18TH WAR
SILVERS, CHARITY	HAR	128	2ND DIST
SILVERS, DAVID	HAR	120	2ND DIST
SILVERS, ELIZABETH	HAR	118	2ND DIST
SILVERS, JOHN	WAS	232	1ST DIST
SILVERS, JOHN A.	HAR	128	2ND DIST
SILVERS, MARTHA	WAS	113	2ND DIST
SILVERS, SILUS B.	HAR	128	2ND DIST
SILVERS, THOMAS	WAS	112	2ND DIST
SILVERSTINE, MARKS	BAL	386	13TH WAR
SILVESTER, HENRY	TAL	008	EASTON D
SILVESTER, MARTN	TAL	107	ST MICHA
SILVESTHAM, HENRY	WOR	229	6TH E DI
SILVEY, ELIZABETH	QUE	186	3RD E DI
SIM, ROBERT	ALL	233	CUMBERLA
SIMAN, CHARLES*	BAL	396	3RD WARD
SIMAN, GEORGE	BAL	278	1ST DIST
SIMCOE, GEORGE	CEC	083	CHARLEST
SIMCOE, WILLIAM	CEC	076	NORTHEAS
SIMENMAN, BENJAMIN *	WAS	080	2ND SUBD
SIMER, HENRY	BAL	070	1ST WARD
SIMER, JOSEPH G.	BAL	240	2ND WARD
SIMES, MARY E.	TAL	001	EASTON D
SIMES, SAMUEL	CEC	046	1ST E DI
SIMME, JOHN W.	CHA	223	ALLENS F
SIMMELL,LEWIS E.	FRE	225	BUCKEYST
SIMMENS, WILLIAM	CAL	035	2ND DIST
SIMMERMAN, CHARLES	BAL	214	17TH WAR
SIMMERS, EDWARD	CHA	245	HILLTOP
SIMMERS, ELIAS	BAL	028	1ST WARD
SIMMERS, EMILY	BAL	027	1ST WARD
SIMMERS, JAMES	WAS	149	2ND DIST
SIMMES, ALEXANDER	ALL	135	4TH E.D.
SIMMON, BENJAMIN	CHA	234	HILLTOP
SIMMON, JOSEPH V.	CHA	235	HILLTOP
SIMMON, LIDDY	ST	275	3RD E DI
SIMMON, MARK	BAL	248	6TH WARD
SIMMON, ROBERT	BAL	026	9TH WARD
SIMMOND, GEORGE	BAL	176	11TH WAR
SIMMOND, RACHEL	CEC	174	6TH E DI
SIMMONDS, CAROLINE	BAL	022	4TH WARD
SIMMONDS, EMELINE	KEN	214	2ND DIST
SIMMONDS, H.S.	BAL	122	1ST WARD
SIMMONDS, J.M.	BAL	136	1ST WARD
SIMMONDS, JAMES M.	BAL	078	15TH WAR
SIMMONDS, JOHN	BAL	203	11TH WAR
SIMMONDS, MARIA	KEN	216	2ND DIST
SIMMONDS, WILLIAM	BAL	087	18TH WAR
SIMMONDS, WILLIAM	BAL	009	15TH WAR
SIMMONDS, WILLIAM	BAL	155	1ST WARD
SIMMONS, A.H.	FRE	227	BUCKEYST
SIMMONS, ABRAHAM R.	FRE	230	BUCKEYST
SIMMONS, ALICE K.	ST	307	1ST E DI
SIMMONS, BAKER H.	FRE	234	BUCKEYST
SIMMONS, BARBARA A.	CAL	017	1ST DIST
SIMMONS, BENJAMIN	CEC	044	1ST E DI
SIMMONS, BENJAMIN	BAL	350	3RD WARD
SIMMONS, C.	BAL	140	1ST WARD
SIMMONS, CATHARIEN	WOR	315	2ND E DI
SIMMONS, CHARELS	BAL	143	1ST WARD
SIMMONS, CHARLES	BAL	268	20TH WAR
SIMMONS, CHARLES S.	FRE	437	8TH E DI
SIMMONS, CLVEY	CHA	263	MIDDLETO
SIMMONS, DRUSELLA	CAL	012	1ST DIST
SIMMONS, ELIJAH	CEC	008	ELKTON 3
SIMMONS, ELIZA A.	WAS	102	2ND DIST
SIMMONS, ELIZABETH	MGM	341	CLARKSBU
SIMMONS, ELIZABETH	FRE	256	NEW MARK
SIMMONS, ELIZABETH	CEC	173	6TH E DI
SIMMONS, ELIZABETH	CEC	157	PORT DUP
SIMMONS, ELIZABETH *	HAR	199	3RD DIST
SIMMONS, ELIZABETH A.	BAL	341	3RD WARD
SIMMONS, ELLENOR H.	FRE	232	BUCKEYST
SIMMONS, FRANCES	BAL	129	16TH WAR
SIMMONS, FRANK	CHA	238	HILLTOP
SIMMONS, FREDERICK	CHA	289	MIDDLETO
SIMMONS, GEORGE	CHA	234	HILLTOP
SIMMONS, GEORGE	MGM	357	BERRYS D
SIMMONS, GEORGE	BAL	142	1ST WARD
SIMMONS, GEORGE	BAL	247	2ND WARD
SIMMONS, GEORGE	ALL	073	5TH E.D.
SIMMONS, GEORGE	ALL	039	2ND E.D.
SIMMONS, H. B.	ALL	160	6TH E.D.
SIMMONS, HANNAH M.	CAL	054	3RD DIST
SIMMONS, HENRY	TAL	093	ST MICHA
SIMMONS, HESEKIAH	BAL	300	1ST DIST
SIMMONS, ISAAC	BAL	261	2ND WARD
SIMMONS, ISAAC	BAL	255	12TH WAR
SIMMONS, J. M.	BAL	155	1ST WARD
SIMMONS, JAMES	WOR	245	1ST CENS
SIMMONS, JAMES	CHA	237	HILLTOP
SIMMONS, JAMES	HAR	157	3RD DIST
SIMMONS, JAMES	KEN	250	2ND DIST
SIMMONS, JAMES A.	HAR	157	3RD DIST
SIMMONS, JAMES H.	FRE	232	BUCKEYST
SIMMONS, JAMES S.	FRE	224	BUCKEYST
SIMMONS, JAMES W.	FRE	230	BUCKEYST
SIMMONS, JAMES-BLACK	QUE	129	1ST E DI
SIMMONS, JESSE	FRE	245	NEW MARK
SIMMONS, JOHN	FRE	408	JEFFERSO
SIMMONS, JOHN	CEC	007	ELKTON 3
SIMMONS, JOHN	WOR	315	2ND E DI
SIMMONS, JOHN	WAS	042	2ND SUBD
SIMMONS, JOHN	BAL	213	6TH WARD
SIMMONS, JOHN	ALL	173	7TH E.D.
SIMMONS, JOHN	ALL	037	2ND E.D.
SIMMONS, JOHN	ALL	074	5TH E.D.
SIMMONS, JOHN A.	FRE	001	FREDERIC
SIMMONS, JOHN F.	FRE	234	BUCKEYST
SIMMONS, JOHN W.	CAL	033	2ND DIST
SIMMONS, JOHN-MULATTO	ST	324	4TH E DI
SIMMONS, JOSEPH	CEC	213	7TH E DI
SIMMONS, JOSHUA	CEC	059	1ST E DI
SIMMONS, JOSIAH	DOR	373	1ST DIST
SIMMONS, JULIA	CEC	006	ELKTON 3
SIMMONS, KINZY	CAL	037	2ND DIST
SIMMONS, LAWRENCE	CEC	040	CHESAPEA
SIMMONS, LAWRENCE	CEC	030	CHESAPEA
SIMMONS, LEVIN	DOR	394	1ST DIST
SIMMONS, MARGARET	CAL	036	2ND DIST
SIMMONS, MARY	CHA	238	HILLTOP
SIMMONS, MARY	ALL	038	2ND E.D.
SIMMONS, MIRANDAH	BAL	158	6TH WARD
SIMMONS, NANCY	ANN	289	ANNAPOLI
SIMMONS, NEG	CHA	236	HILLTOP
SIMMONS, NICHOLAS	BAL	126	1ST WARD
SIMMONS, PHILIP-BLACK	QUE	143	1ST E DI
SIMMONS, RACHEL M.	BAL	284	7TH WARD
SIMMONS, RICHARD	BAL	425	8TH WARD
SIMMONS, RICHARD	ANN	410	8TH DIST
SIMMONS, RICHARD	CEC	057	1ST E DI
SIMMONS, RICHARD	MGM	418	MEDLEY 3
SIMMONS, RICHARD-BLACK	QUE	175	2ND E DI
SIMMONS, ROBERT M.	CEC	166	6TH E DI
SIMMONS, SAMUEL	FRE	231	BUCKEYST
SIMMONS, SAMUEL F.	ANN	508	HOWARD D
SIMMONS, SARAH	BAL	400	1ST DIST
SIMMONS, SARAH	BAL	243	6TH WARD
SIMMONS, SARAH	CAL	037	2ND DIST
SIMMONS, SARAH	CEC	030	CHESAPEA
SIMMONS, SOPHIER	FRE	230	BUCKEYST
SIMMONS, STEPHEN	BAL	265	2ND WARD
SIMMONS, SUSAN	BAL	352	7TH WARD
SIMMONS, TERESA	BAL	212	11TH WAR
SIMMONS, THOMAS F.	CAL	014	1ST DIST
SIMMONS, WESTLY E.	CHA	282	BOJANTOW
SIMMONS, WILLIAM	CHA	236	HILLTOP
SIMMONS, WILLIAM	CEC	213	7TH E DI
SIMMONS, WILLIAM	BAL	293	7TH WARD
SIMMONS, WILLIAM H.	ST	319	4TH E DI
SIMMONS,HENRY	BAL	121	1ST WARD
SIMMORE, MARGRET	BAL	183	2ND WARD
SIMMS, A.	BAL	162	1ST WARD
SIMMS, A. B.	CHA	225	ALLENS F
SIMMS, ADALINE	BAL	051	18TH WAR
SIMMS, ALEXANDER *	BAL	122	2ND DIST
SIMMS, ANN	BAL	152	11TH WAR
SIMMS, ANNA	BAL	302	17TH WAR
SIMMS, CAROLINE-BLACK	BAL	198	2ND WARD
SIMMS, CHARLES	BAL	245	6TH WARD
SIMMS, CHARLES	ANN	303	1ST DIST
SIMMS, DANIEL	ANN	312	1ST DIST
SIMMS, ELIZA	BAL	197	19TH WAR
SIMMS, ELIZABETH	BAL	015	2ND DIST
SIMMS, ELLEN	ANN	302	1ST DIST
SIMMS, ELLEN	CAL	043	3RD DIST
SIMMS, ELLEN	BAL	257	20TH WAR
SIMMS, FRANCIS-MULATTO	BAL	214	2ND WARD
SIMMS, FRANCIS-MULATTO	BAL	214	2ND WARD
SIMMS, GEORGE	BAL	408	3RD WARD
SIMMS, HENRIETTA	BAL	239	6TH WARD
SIMMS, HENRY	FRE	425	8TH E DI
SIMMS, JACOB	BAL	426	1ST DIST
SIMMS, JAMES	SOM	475	TRAPPE D
SIMMS, JANE	ANN	310	1ST DIST
SIMMS, JESSE	SOM	463	HANGARY
SIMMS, JOHN	BAL	242	6TH WARD
SIMMS, JOHN	BAL	238	6TH WARD
SIMMS, JOHN	BAL	080	2ND DIST
SIMMS, JOHN E.	ST	254	3RD E DI
SIMMS, JOSEPH	ST	258	3RD E DI
SIMMS, JOSEPH	BAL	110	15TH WAR
SIMMS, JOSEPH E.	CHA	293	BOJANTOW
SIMMS, JOSEPH JR.	BAL	137	16TH WAR
SIMMS, LEMUEL M.	CHA	266	MIDDLETO
SIMMS, MARGARET A.	BAL	038	2ND DIST
SIMMS, MARIA	BAL	288	3RD WARD
SIMMS, MARTHA	BAL	391	8TH WARD
SIMMS, MARY	BAL	017	2ND DIST
SIMMS, MARY	ANN	316	1ST DIST
SIMMS, MARY	BAL	345	13TH WAR
SIMMS, MARY A.	ST	277	3RD E DI
SIMMS, MARY C.	BAL	001	4TH WARD
SIMMS, MARY E.	BAL	280	7TH WARD
SIMMS, MATILDA	SOM	434	PRINCESS
SIMMS, NANCY	ANN	301	1ST DIST
SIMMS, PETER	BAL	133	1ST WARD
SIMMS, RACHEL	BAL	070	10TH WAR
SIMMS, ROBERT	BAL	055	9TH WARD
SIMMS, ROBERT	BAL	458	8TH WARD
SIMMS, SAMUEL	SOM	462	HANGARY
SIMMS, SARAH A.	ST	258	3RD E DI
SIMMS, SMITH	SOM	463	HANGARY
SIMMS, SOPHIA	SOM	459	HANGARY
SIMMS, SUSAN	BAL	055	9TH WARD
SIMMS, THOMAS	BAL	147	2ND DIST
SIMMS, THOMAS	BAL	175	6TH WARD
SIMMS, THOMAS W.	BAL	391	8TH WARD
SIMMS, WESLEY	BAL	459	8TH WARD
SIMMS, WILLIAM	BAL	458	8TH WARD
SIMMS, WILLIAM	BAL	250	6TH WARD
SIMMS, WILLIAM	SOM	463	HANGARY
SIMMS, WILLIAM	BAL	247	17TH WAR
SIMMS, WILLIAM	CAL	051	3RD DIST
SIMMY, JOHANA	ALL	102	5TH E.D.
SIMNS, WESLEY	BAL	022	18TH WAR
SIMON, ADAM	BAL	381	8TH WARD
SIMON, BIDGET	BAL	421	1ST DIST
SIMON, CHARLES	BAL	323	12TH WAR
SIMON, ELI	BAL	090	10TH WAR
SIMON, HERMAN	BAL	457	14TH WAR
SIMON, JOHN	FRE	009	FREDERIC
SIMON, JOHN	BAL	131	16TH WAR
SIMON, JOHN	BAL	124	2ND DIST
SIMON, JOHN A.	BAL	435	8TH WARD
SIMON, JOSHUA	BAL	380	3RD WARD
SIMON, MATHIAS	BAL	038	9TH WARD
SIMON, PETER	BAL	145	1ST WARD
SIMON, PETER	BAL	314	7TH WARD
SIMON, PHILIP	BAL	381	8TH WARD
SIMON, THOMAS B.	BAL	305	7TH WARD
SIMONDS, JOHN	BAL	196	2ND WARD
SIMONS, EDWARD C.	DOR	360	3RD DIVI
SIMONS, GEORGE	BAL	126	5TH WARD
SIMONS, JACOB	DOR	328	3RD DIVI
SIMONS, JAMES	SOM	528	QUANTICO
SIMONS, JOHNW.	BAL	027	1ST WARD
SIMONS, LEVI	BAL	439	8TH WARD
SIMONS, LEWIS	BAL	064	4TH WARD
SIMONS, LUCY	DOR	348	3RD DIVI
SIMONS, MARY	DOR	348	3RD DIVI
SIMONS, N. G.	BAL	152	1ST WARD
SIMONS, REACHEAL	BAL	211	11TH WAR
SIMONS, SALLY	BAL	166	11TH WAR
SIMONS, SARAH A.	BAL	012	1ST WARD
SIMONS, STOKLY	DOR	466	1ST DIST
SIMONS, SUSAN	DOR	332	3RD DIVI
SIMONS, THOMAS	DOR	348	3RD DIVI
SIMONS, THOMAS	DOR	332	3RD DIVI
SIMONS, THOMAS	DOR	332	3RD DIVI
SIMONS, THOMAS	DOR	348	3RD DIVI
SIMONS, WILLIAM*	DOR	328	3RD DIVI
SIMONS,E.W.	BAL	158	1ST WARD
SIMONSON, JOHN	BAL	042	15TH WAR
SIMONSON, JOSEPH	BAL	110	15TH WAR
SIMONSON, MARGARET A.	BAL	110	15TH WAR
SIMONSON, WILLIAM C.	BAL	286	17TH WAR
SIMOSON, SARAH	BAL	123	11TH WAR
SIMPERS, ADELAIDE	CEC	075	NORTHEAS
SIMPERS, AMANDA	CEC	087	4TH E DI
SIMPERS, ANN	CEC	090	4TH E DI
SIMPERS, ANNY	CEC	116	3RD E DI
SIMPERS, DARIUS	CEC	107	3RD E DI
SIMPERS, ELLEN	CEC	107	3RD E DI
SIMPERS, GEORGE	CEC	016	ELKTON 3
SIMPERS, GEORGE	CAR	173	8TH DIST
SIMPERS, HANNAH	CEC	109	4TH E DI
SIMPERS, HENRY	CEC	087	4TH E DI
SIMPERS, HENRY	CAR	278	7TH DIST
SIMPERS, HENRY D.	CEC	107	3RD E DI
SIMPERS, HENRY G.	CEC	076	NORTHEAS
SIMPERS, HUGH B.	QUE	218	3RD E DI
SIMPERS, JAMES B.	QUE	218	3RD E DI
SIMPERS, JESSE H.	CEC	115	3RD E DI
SIMPERS, JOHN	CEC	079	NORTHEAS
SIMPERS, JOHN	CEC	022	ELKTON 3
SIMPERS, JOHN B.	CEC	073	5TH E DI
SIMPERS, JOHN E.	CEC	010	ELKTON 3
SIMPERS, JOHN R.	CEC	099	3RD E DI
SIMPERS, JOHN W.	CEC	090	4TH E DI
SIMPERS, JOHNSON	CEC	076	NORTHEAS
SIMPERS, JOSEPH	CEC	076	NORTHEAS
SIMPERS, JOSEPH	CEC	119	3RD E DI
SIMPERS, MARCH	CEC	019	ELKTON 3
SIMPERS, MARY	CEC	088	4TH E DI
SIMPERS, MARY	CEC	073	5TH E DI
SIMPERS, MARY A.	CEC	119	3RD E DI
SIMPERS, NATHAN	CEC	078	NORTHEAS
SIMPERS, RACHEL	CEC	015	ELKTON 3
SIMPERS, REBECCA	CEC	047	1ST E DI
SIMPERS, RICHARD	CAR	331	MANCHEST
SIMPERS, RUTH	CEC	085	5TH E DI
SIMPERS, SARAH A.	CEC	119	3RD E DI
SIMPERS, SARAH E.	CEC	116	3RD E DI
SIMPERS, THOMAS	CEC	079	NORTHEAS
SIMPERS, THOMAS	CEC	079	NORTHEAS
SIMPERS, THOMAS W.	CEC	075	NORTHEAS
SIMPERS, WILLIAM	CEC	113	4TH E DI
SIMPERS, WILLIAM	CEC	079	NORTHEAS
SIMPERS, WILLIAM	CEC	120	3RD E DI
SIMPERS, WILLIAM H.	CEC	123	3RD E DI
SIMPIN, WILLIAM	WAS	055	2ND SUBD
SIMPKINS, JESSE	SOM	464	HANGARY
SIMPKINS, JOHN	SOM	464	HANGARY
SIMPKINS, JOHN	ALL	232	CUMBERLA
SIMPKINS, MARIA	BAL	075	15TH WAR
SIMPKINS, MATILDA	SOM	464	HANGARY
SIMPKINS, MOLLY	SOM	352	BRINKLEY
SIMPLE, CATHARINE	BAL	290	17TH WAR
SIMPSOM, EMILINE	BAL	276	17TH WAR
SIMPSON, AGNES	BAL	124	16TH WAR
SIMPSON, ALEXANDER	BAL	255	17TH WAR
SIMPSON, ALICE A.	BAL	326	7TH WARD
SIMPSON, ANDREW	BAL	385	3RD WARD
SIMPSON, ANN	BAL	137	16TH WAR
SIMPSON, ANN	BAL	208	11TH WAR
SIMPSON, BASIL F.	FRE	422	8TH E DI
SIMPSON, BENJAMIN L.	BAL	048	4TH WARD
SIMPSON, BETTY	CHA	286	BOJANTOW
SIMPSON, BRADLY	ANN	381	4TH DIST
SIMPSON, CAROLINE	CHA	228	ALLENS F
SIMPSON, CATHARINE	PRI	033	VANSVILL
SIMPSON, CATHERINE	CHA	259	ALLENS F
SIMPSON, CHARLES B.	FRE	428	8TH E DI
SIMPSON, CHARLES R.	ANN	473	HOWARD D
SIMPSON, DAMES	CAR	072	NO TWP L
SIMPSON, DAVID	ALL	107	5TH E.D.
SIMPSON, DAVID R.	CEC	186	7TH E DI
SIMPSON, E.	BAL	151	1ST WARD
SIMPSON, EDWARD	BAL	449	14TH WAR
SIMPSON, EDWARD G.	BAL	346	7TH WARD
SIMPSON, ELISABETH	FRE	252	NEW MARK
SIMPSON, ELIZA	BAL	055	9TH WARD
SIMPSON, ELIZA	ANN	515	HOWARD D
SIMPSON, ELIZABETH	CAR	079	NO TWP L
SIMPSON, FRANCIS	FRE	450	8TH E DI
SIMPSON, FRANCIS	CHA	272	ALLENS F

Name	County	Page	District
SIMPSON, FRANCIS	CHA	272	ALLENS F
SIMPSON, FREDERICK	BAL	202	17TH WAR
SIMPSON, FRITZ	BAL	052	1ST WARD
SIMPSON, GEORGE	BAL	057	1ST WARD
SIMPSON, GEORGE	BAL	118	1ST WARD
SIMPSON, GEORGE	BAL	081	10TH WAR
SIMPSON, GEORGE	ST	338	4TH E DI
SIMPSON, GEORGE H.	CHA	269	ALLENS F
SIMPSON, GUSTAVUS	CHA	269	ALLENS F
SIMPSON, HANNAH	BAL	075	18TH WAR
SIMPSON, HANNAH MRS-	BAL	315	20TH WAR
SIMPSON, HARRIET	CEC	145	PORT DUP
SIMPSON, HARRISON	DOR	323	1ST DIST
SIMPSON, HARRY	TAL	094	ST MICHA
SIMPSON, HENRY	ANN	453	HOWARD D
SIMPSON, HORACE	BAL	323	7TH WARD
SIMPSON, ISAAC	BAL	020	9TH WARD
SIMPSON, J.	BAL	084	10TH WAR
SIMPSON, JAMES	BAL	096	15TH WAR
SIMPSON, JAMES	ANN	473	HOWARD D
SIMPSON, JAMES	BAL	101	2ND DIST
SIMPSON, JAMES	BAL	463	1ST DIST
SIMPSON, JAMES	CEC	120	4TH E DI
SIMPSON, JAMES	BAL	449	14TH WAR
SIMPSON, JAMES	BAL	123	11TH WAR
SIMPSON, JAMES	BAL	178	19TH WAR
SIMPSON, JAMES	CAR	228	5TH DIST
SIMPSON, JAMES F.	BAL	066	4TH WARD
SIMPSON, JAMES M.	PRI	010	BLADENSB
SIMPSON, JANE	ANN	441	HOWARD D
SIMPSON, JOHN	BAL	173	1ST WARD
SIMPSON, JOHN	BAL	057	1ST WARD
SIMPSON, JOHN	BAL	270	1ST DIST
SIMPSON, JOHN	BAL	353	7TH WARD
SIMPSON, JOHN	BAL	125	1ST WARD
SIMPSON, JOHN	BAL	178	19TH WAR
SIMPSON, JOHN	CAR	066	NO TWP L
SIMPSON, JOHN	DOR	316	1ST DIST
SIMPSON, JOHN A.	FRE	004	FREDERIC
SIMPSON, JOHN D.	BAL	069	10TH WAR
SIMPSON, JOHN F.	BAL	311	1ST DIST
SIMPSON, JOHN R.	BAL	214	6TH WARD
SIMPSON, JOSEPH	BAL	020	9TH WARD
SIMPSON, JOSEPH	DOR	322	1ST DIST
SIMPSON, JOSEPH	BAL	249	17TH WAR
SIMPSON, JOSEPH	MGM	338	CRACKLIN
SIMPSON, JOSEPH W.-MULATT	FRE	446	8TH E DI
SIMPSON, LEVIN	BAL	135	16TH WAR
SIMPSON, LLOYD	PRI	071	MARLBROU
SIMPSON, LOUISA	ANN	489	HOWARD D
SIMPSON, LYDY	FRE	106	CREAGERS
SIMPSON, MARGARET	ALL	108	5TH E.D.
SIMPSON, MARIA	BAL	364	8TH WARD
SIMPSON, MARSHAL	BAL	332	13TH WAR
SIMPSON, MARTHA A.	BAL	181	16TH WAR
SIMPSON, MARY	BAL	242	1ST DIST
SIMPSON, MARY	BAL	310	20TH WAR
SIMPSON, MARY	CHA	232	HILLTOP
SIMPSON, MARY	CEC	123	3RD E DI
SIMPSON, MARY J.	CHA	279	BOJANTOW
SIMPSON, MOSES	BAL	306	3RD WARD
SIMPSON, NANCY	FRE	153	10TH E D
SIMPSON, NANCY	FRE	437	8TH E DI
SIMPSON, NANCY	QUE	203	3RD E DI
SIMPSON, PETER JR.-BLACK	CAR	162	NO TWP L
SIMPSON, PETER-BLACK	CAR	161	NO TWP L
SIMPSON, PHILIP-MULATTO	FRE	242	NEW MARK
SIMPSON, RACHAEL	BAL	068	15TH WAR
SIMPSON, REBECCA	BAL	398	14TH WAR
SIMPSON, REZIN B.	BAL	017	18TH WAR
SIMPSON, RICHARD	FRE	437	8TH E DI
SIMPSON, RICHARD-MULATTO	FRE	445	8TH E DI
SIMPSON, ROBERT	PRI	093	MARLBROU
SIMPSON, ROBERT S.	PRI	028	VANSVILL
SIMPSON, SAMUEL	FRE	023	FREDERIC
SIMPSON, SOPHIA A.	CEC	124	5TH E DI
SIMPSON, STAFFORD	FRE	105	CREAGERS
SIMPSON, STEPHEN	FRE	153	10TH E D
SIMPSON, THOMAS	CAR	149	NO TWP L
SIMPSON, THOMAS	PRI	093	MARLBROU
SIMPSON, THOMAS	BAL	386	3RD WARD
SIMPSON, THOMAS	BAL	237	6TH WARD
SIMPSON, THOMAS D.	CHA	221	ALLENS F
SIMPSON, THOMAS P.	MGM	357	BERRYS D
SIMPSON, WARFIELD	FRE	437	8TH E DI
SIMPSON, WILIAM	BAL	273	2ND WARD
SIMPSON, WILLIAM	BAL	263	2ND WARD
SIMPSON, WILLIAM	BAL	351	3RD WARD
SIMPSON, WILLIAM	BAL	159	2ND DIST
SIMPSON, WILLIAM	BAL	323	7TH WARD
SIMPSON, WILLIAM	ANN	480	HOWARD D
SIMPSON, WILLIAM	CHA	227	ALLENS F
SIMPSON, WILLIAM	FRE	063	FREDERIC
SIMPSON, WILLIAM	BAL	111	10TH WAR
SIMPSON, WILLIAM	BAL	310	20TH WAR
SIMPSON, WILLIAM	CEC	132	6TH E DI
SIMPSON, WILLIAM	BAL	076	18TH WAR
SIMPSON, WILLIAM	DOR	425	1ST DIST
SIMPSON, WILLIAM J.	PRI	068	NOTTINGH
SIMPSON, WILLIAM P.	BAL	075	18TH WAR
SIMPSON, ZABARA	QUE	130	1ST E DI
SIMPSON,AMELIA	BAL	054	1ST WARD
SIMPTER, ALEXANDER	BAL	276	17TH WAR
SIMS, ALVERTA	HAR	188	3RD DIST
SIMS, ANDREW	HAR	073	1ST DIST
SIMS, ANDREW	BAL	116	2ND DIST
SIMS, CHARITY	BAL	166	11TH WAR
SIMS, DANIEL-BLACK	FRE	425	8TH E DI
SIMS, EDGAR C.	BAL	131	5TH WARD
SIMS, ELEZ	BAL	324	12TH WAR
SIMS, EVA	BAL	223	12TH WAR
SIMS, GEORGE H.	HAR	190	3RD DIST
SIMS, HENRY	BAL	434	14TH WAR
SIMS, HENRY	BAL	204	17TH WAR
SIMS, HENRY	BAL	443	1ST DIST
SIMS, HUGH	BAL	122	2ND DIST
SIMS, ISAAC	KEN	237	2ND DIST
SIMS, ISAAC L.	BAL	255	1ST DIST
SIMS, JACOB	HAR	194	3RD DIST
SIMS, JAMES	DOR	312	1ST DIST
SIMS, JAMES	BAL	119	11TH WAR
SIMS, JAMES	BAL	186	5TH DIST
SIMS, JAMES	BAL	422	1ST DIST
SIMS, JOHN	ANN	475	HOWARD D
SIMS, JOHN	ANN	369	4TH DIST
SIMS, JOHN	BAL	119	11TH WAR
SIMS, JOHN	BAL	267	20TH WAR
SIMS, JOHN	TAL	093	ST MICHA
SIMS, LEWIS	BAL	223	12TH WAR
SIMS, MABLE	KEN	215	2ND DIST
SIMS, MARTHA	BAL	257	20TH WAR
SIMS, MARY	BAL	223	12TH WAR
SIMS, MINTA	BAL	426	1ST DIST
SIMS, REBEC	BAL	235	12TH WAR
SIMS, REBECCA	KEN	227	2ND DIST
SIMS, SOLOMON-BLACK	FRE	052	FREDERIC
SIMS, SUSAN	BAL	243	1ST DIST
SIMS, THOMAS	BAL	038	1ST WARD
SIMS, WESLY	WAS	088	2ND SUBD
SIMSON, BEN	ANN	350	3RD DIST
SIMSON, BENEDICK	CHA	269	ALLENS F
SIMSON, MARY	WAS	094	2ND SUBD
SIMSON, WILLIAM	WAS	110	2ND DIST
SIMSTRON, ROBERT C.	BAL	154	16TH WAR
SIMTD, CHRISTIAN	BAL	056	1ST WARD
SIMTRIX, DAFFARY	TAL	118	ST MICHA
SIMUS, HENRY*	SOM	497	SALISBUR
SIN, WILLIAM	BAL	165	16TH WAR
SINBERRY, ISAAC	BAL	050	9TH WARD
SINBURN, D. VAN*	BAL	271	20TH WAR
SINCH, BELSORA*	TAL	065	EASTON T
SINCH, JAMES W.*	DOR	319	1ST DIST
SINCH, WILLIAM*	TAL	065	EASTON T
SINCK, WILLIAM*	BAL	027	4TH WARD
SINCLAIR, A. B.	TAL	113	ST MICHA
SINCLAIR, ALBERT	BAL	227	2ND WARD
SINCLAIR, ALEXANDER	QUE	198	3RD E DI
SINCLAIR, ALICE	BAL	386	3RD WARD
SINCLAIR, AMANDA	BAL	180	2ND WARD
SINCLAIR, ANN E.	BAL	041	15TH WAR
SINCLAIR, CATHARINE	BAL	002	1ST WARD
SINCLAIR, CATHARINE	QUE	251	5TH E DI
SINCLAIR, CATHARINE	WAS	044	2ND SUBD
SINCLAIR, CHARLES	QUE	205	3RD E DI
SINCLAIR, CYRUS	DOR	388	1ST DIST
SINCLAIR, EDWARD	BAL	041	15TH WAR
SINCLAIR, EDWIN	TAL	081	ST MICHA
SINCLAIR, ELSY	BAL	255	20TH WAR
SINCLAIR, EVA	QUE	175	2ND E DI
SINCLAIR, G.	BAL	129	1ST WARD
SINCLAIR, GEORGE	BAL	140	1ST WARD
SINCLAIR, JAMES	BAL	377	1ST DIST
SINCLAIR, JAMES	TAL	114	ST MICHA
SINCLAIR, JANE	BAL	053	4TH WARD
SINCLAIR, JOHN	BAL	398	3RD WARD
SINCLAIR, JOHN C.	BAL	389	3RD WARD
SINCLAIR, LAURA F.	BAL	386	3RD WARD
SINCLAIR, MARGARET	ANN	521	HOWARD D
SINCLAIR, MARGARET	TAL	114	ST MICHA
SINCLAIR, MARGARET	QUE	243	5TH E DI
SINCLAIR, MARIA	ST	335	4TH E DI
SINCLAIR, MARY A.	BAL	319	3RD WARD
SINCLAIR, PERE T.	QUE	205	3RD E DI
SINCLAIR, PERRY	BAL	387	3RD WARD
SINCLAIR, POLLY	BAL	067	4TH WARD
SINCLAIR, PRISCILIA	BAL	180	2ND WARD
SINCLAIR, ROBERT	BAL	099	2ND DIST
SINCLAIR, ROBERT H.	BAL	157	6TH WARD
SINCLAIR, ROBERT JR.	BAL	113	15TH WAR
SINCLAIR, SARAH	QUE	189	3RD E DI
SINCLAIR, SUSAN	BAL	044	1ST WARD
SINCLAIR, SUSAN	BAL	038	1ST WARD
SINCLAIR, THOMAS	ANN	315	1ST DIST
SINCLAIR, VIRGINA	BAL	004	1ST WARD
SINCLAIR, WILLIAM	QUE	233	4TH E DI
SINCLAIR, WILLIAM	BAL	294	20TH WAR
SINCLAR, HENRY	ST	325	4TH E DI
SINCLAR, MARGARET	BAL	082	2ND DIST
SINCLARE, ANN	BAL	353	7TH WARD
SINCLARE, CHRISTIAN	BAL	264	7TH WARD
SINCLARE, EVE	BAL	436	8TH WARD
SINCLARE, FRANCIS	BAL	422	8TH WARD
SINCLARE, JOHN	ST	278	3RD E DI
SINCLAVEN, GUSTAVE	BAL	050	1ST WARD
SINCOMB, JOHN	BAL	405	14TH WAR
SINDALL, CATHARINE	BAL	224	6TH WARD
SINDALL, DAVID	BAL	062	2ND DIST
SINDALL, SAMUEL	BAL	206	6TH WARD
SINDALL, SARAH	BAL	227	6TH WARD
SINDEL, GEORGE	CAR	354	6TH DIST
SINDEL, THOAMS	BAL	049	18TH WAR
SINDELL, WILLIAM	BAL	071	2ND DIST
SINDEN, ALEXANDER	BAL	034	1ST WARD
SINDER, ELIZABETH	BAL	016	1ST WARD
SINDLE, JOHN	BAL	282	7TH WARD
SINDLE, PHILIP	BAL	390	8TH WARD
SINDLE, THEADORE	BAL	273	7TH WARD
SINDLE, WILLIAM M.	BAL	301	1ST DIST
SINDNER, JOHN	BAL	272	2ND WARD
SINDOLLBACK, HENRY	BAL	221	2ND WARD
SINE, EAPHRO	BAL	123	11TH WAR
SINE, JOHN	BAL	282	1ST DIST
SINERCA, DORIES	HAR	147	3RD DIST
SINES, CLARISSA	ALL	045	10TH E.D
SINEWEVER, JACOB	CAR	331	MANCHEST
SINEWEVER, SARAH	CAR	343	6TH DIST
SINGALES, JAMES*	DOR	302	1ST DIST
SINGANO, LEOPOLD	BAL	179	16TH WAR
SINGCLAIR, WILLIAM	BAL	154	5TH WARD
SINGENFELDER, FREDERICK	BAL	258	17TH WAR
SINGER, ALEXANDER	BAL	202	17TH WAR
SINGER, BETSEY	QUE	249	5TH E DI
SINGER, CHARLOTTE	BAL	274	20TH WAR
SINGER, ELIZABETH	BAL	075	1ST WARD
SINGER, FRANCIS	BAL	313	7TH WARD
SINGER, HERRIETTA *	QUE	253	5TH E DI
SINGER, ISAAC	BAL	237	20TH WAR
SINGER, JOHN	FRE	175	5TH E DI
SINGER, JOHN	CAR	409	2ND DIST
SINGER, JULIA-BLACK	QUE	126	1ST E DI
SINGER, LOUISA-BLACK	QUE	127	1ST E DI
SINGER, MARY	BAL	139	19TH WAR
SINGER, MARY	QUE	249	5TH E DI
SINGER, NANCY	BAL	141	5TH WARD
SINGER, SLONGAR	BAL	313	7TH WARD
SINGER, SUSAN	BAL	198	11TH WAR
SINGER, ZORICK	BAL	139	16TH WAR
SINGERVALD, GOTLIP	BAL	108	5TH WARD
SINGLE, ANDREW	BAL	051	1ST WARD
SINGLE, DANIEL	BAL	279	12TH WAR
SINGLE, JERMEIAH	CAR	405	2ND DIST
SINGLE, THOMAS J. *	HAR	194	3RD DIST
SINGLEDECKER, H.	ALL	093	5TH E.D.
SINGLETON, AMOS	HAR	160	3RD DIST
SINGLETON, ANN A.	HAR	167	3RD DIST
SINGLETON, CHARLES F.	BAL	191	11TH WAR
SINGLETON, EVANS	HAR	045	1ST DIST
SINGLETON, FRANCIS	HAR	045	1ST DIST
SINGLETON, HENRY	HAR	119	2ND DIST
SINGLETON, ISAAC	BAL	027	1ST WARD
SINGLETON, JACOB	HAR	160	3RD DIST
SINGLETON, JAMES	HAR	045	1ST DIST
SINGLETON, JAMES	CAR	268	WESTMINS
SINGLETON, JOHN	HAR	152	3RD DIST
SINGLETON, JOHN	BAL	248	6TH WARD
SINGLETON, MARY	BAL	331	13TH WAR
SINGLETON, MARY	BAL	131	5TH WARD
SINGLETON, MARY	BAL	299	17TH WAR
SINGLETON, NICHOLAS	HAR	093	2ND DIST
SINGLETON, RICHARD	HAR	054	1ST DIST
SINGLETON, ROBERT	CAR	210	5TH DIST
SINGLETON, SARAH	HAR	055	1ST DIST
SINGLETON, THOMAS D.	TAL	016	EASTON D
SINGLETON, WILLIAM	HAR	010	1ST DIST
SINGLETON, WILLIAM	BAL	387	3RD WARD
SINGLETON, WILLIAM B.	BAL	081	10TH WAR
SINGO, CHARLES-BLACK	QUE	188	3RD E DI
SINGRELL, ELERAZENE*	DOR	302	1ST DIST
SINK, GEORGE	ALL	258	CUMBERLA
SINKS, JOHN	BAL	284	2ND WAR
SINN, CATHERINE	FRE	047	FREDERIC
SINN, CHARLES W.	MGM	443	CLARKSTR
SINN, EDWARD	FRE	047	FREDERIC
SINN, ISABELLA	FRE	039	FREDERIC
SINN, JOHN G.	MGM	442	CLARKSTR
SINN, JOHN T.	FRE	014	FREDERIC
SINN, JOSEPH	CAR	391	2ND DIST
SINN, PHILLIP H	FRE	060	FREDERIC
SINNER, LANDEN	BAL	022	1ST WARD
SINNERMAN, BENJAMIN	BAL	376	1ST DIST
SINNERS, ALEXANDER	BAL	089	1ST WARD
SINNERS, ELIJAH R.	BAL	362	8TH WARD
SINNETT, JOHN	CEC	147	PORT DUP
SINS, ANN M.*	TAL	034	EASTON D
SINS, BENJAMIN*	TAL	029	EASTON D
SINS, RACHEL*	TAL	031	EASTON D
SINSEL, JANE	BAL	051	15TH WAR
SINSTEAD, JAMES	BAL	149	1ST WARD
SINTON, FRANCIS	CEC	177	7TH E DI
SINTON, JOSEPH	KEN	234	2ND DIST
SINTON, JOSEPH	BAL	032	9TH WARD
SINTON, JOSEPH	KEN	273	1ST DIST
SINTS, PHILIP	BAL	276	1ST DIST
SINTSAY, ANNA J.	BAL	184	11TH WAR
SINTZER, GEORGE	BAL	210	6TH DIST
SINVILL, JAMES	BAL	114	5TH WARD
SINYNS, JOSEPH M.	HAR	155	3RD DIST
SIPE, ASA	BAL	462	1ST DIST
SIPE, CATHARINE	BAL	256	20TH WAR
SIPE, ELIZABETH	CAR	178	8TH DIST
SIPE, EMILINE	BAL	198	17TH WAR
SIPE, JOHN	BAL	207	6TH DIST
SIPE, JOHN	ALL	104	5TH E.D.
SIPE, MARY	CAR	196	4TH DIST
SIPE, PHILIP	CAR	180	8TH DIST
SIPEL, WILLIAM	CEC	215	7TH E DI
SIPENCOT, CATHERINE	BAL	390	8TH WARD
SIPES, ELLEN	ST	328	4TH E DI
SIPES, EPHRAIM	BAL	266	1ST DIST
SIPES, JOHN	BAL	225	19TH WAR
SIPES, JOHN	FRE	189	5TH E DI
SIPES, JOSHUA	BAL	309	20TH WAR
SIPES, ROLLAND	ALL	242	CUMBERLA
SIPES, WILLIAM	FRE	115	CREAGERS
SIPES, WILLIAM H.	BAL	440	1ST DIST
SIPLMAN, THOMAS	BAL	422	14TH WAR
SIPP, FREDERICK	BAL	350	13TH WAR
SIPP, JOSEPH	BAL	226	12TH WAR
SIPPE, ELLEN	CAR	265	WESTMINS
SIPPEL, CONRAD	BAL	017	9TH WARD
SIPPLE, DOROTHEA	BAL	273	12TH WAR
SIPPLE, JAMES	CEC	098	3RD E DI
SIPPLE, LOUISA	BAL	104	18TH WAR
SIPPLE, MADALINE	BAL	239	2ND WARD
SIPPLE, MARY R.C.	CAR	149	NO TWP L
SIPPLE, MATTHEW	BAL	213	2ND WARD
SIPPLE, WILLIAM-BLACK	QUE	190	3RD E DI
SIPPO, PETER	CAR	253	3RD DIST
SIPPY, BARBARY	CAR	249	3RD DIST
SIPPY, DAVID	CAR	332	MANCHEST
SIPPY, GEORGE	CAR	294	7TH DIST
SIPPY, JOSEPH	CAR	250	3RD DIST
SIPPY, REBECCA	CAR	329	MANCHEST
SIPTON, ANDREW	FRE	130	CREAGERS
SIQURT, HEW	HAR	193	3RD DIST
SIRAT, MISS V.	FRE	199	5TH E DI
SIRATE, MISS E.	FRE	199	5TH E DI
SIRE, FREDEIRCK	ALL	096	5TH E.D.
SIRES, JAMES	ALL	204	CUMBERLA
SIRESERY, WILLAIM	CAR	237	UNION TO
SIRILY, JAMES	BAL	142	5TH WARD
SIRMAN, ANN W.	SOM	496	SALISBUR
SIRMAN, GEORGE*	SOM	493	SALISBUR
SIRMAN, SARAH	SOM	359	BRINKLEY
SIRMAN, WILLIAM	SOM	538	TYASKIN
SIRTZLER, C.	BAL	214	19TH WAR
SISCO, ANDREW	CEC	006	ELKTON 3
SISCO, AQUILLA	ANN	303	1ST DIST
SISCO, EMORY	CEC	062	1ST E DI
SISCO, HARRIET	BAL	086	18TH WAR
SISCO, JAMES	CEC	055	1ST E DI
SISCO, JAMES	CEC	055	1ST E DI
SISCO, JOHN	CEC	203	6TH E DI
SISCO, MARGARET	BAL	161	19TH WAR
SISCOE, PERRIE	CEC	065	1ST E DI
SISE, JOSEPH	WAS	043	2ND SUBD
SISELBERGER, ELIZABETH	BAL	159	11TH WAR
SISELBERGER, LEWIS	BAL	200	11TH WAR
SISELLENGER, MARTIN	BAL	159	11TH WAR
SISER, SAMUEL	ANN	303	1ST DIST
SISK, WILLIAM*	DOR	312	1ST DIST
SISLE, JAMES	CEC	152	PORT DUP
SISLER, ELIZABETH	WAS	061	2ND SUBD
SISLER, WILLIAM	WAS	032	2ND SUBD
SISONG, JACOB *	BAL	418	1ST DIST
SISSFORD, MARY E.	BAL	122	5TH WARD
SISSLEBURGER, JAMES	BAL	451	1ST DIST
SISSON, ELIZABETH J.	BAL	220	6TH WARD
SISSON, HUGH	BAL	390	8TH WARD
SISSON, MARTIN	BAL	390	8TH WARD
SISTANCE, ELIZABETH	BAL	169	6TH WARD
SITCHNALL, GEORGE	ALL	055	10TH E.D
SITERDING, JOHN	BAL	036	9TH WARD
SITES, GEORGE	BAL	463	1ST DIST
SITHINGWELL, SARAH	ANN	308	1ST DIST
SITLER, CAROLINE	BAL	155	16TH WAR
SITLER, ELIZABETH	BAL	206	6TH WARD
SITLER, SAMUEL	BAL	242	12TH WAR
SITTIG, AUGUSTUS*	BAL	057	4TH WARD
SITTIG, PHILIP*	BAL	321	3RD WARD

Name	County	Page	District
SITTLE, DANIEL *	WAS	191	1ST DIST
SITTOW, ELIZABETH *	FRE	312	MIDDLETO
SITZ, AGUSTUS	BAL	212	2ND WARD
SITZBAUGH, PETER	BAL	043	18TH WAR
SITZLER, MARTHA E.	BAL	191	19TH WAR
SIVAN, JAMES	BAL	042	15TH WAR
SIVANN, JAMES	BAL	153	11TH WAR
SIVENG, MARY	BAL	269	12TH WAR
SIVENS, HENRY *	HAR	191	3RD DIST
SIX, EDWARD	FRE	129	CREAGERS
SIX, HARRIETT	CAR	326	1ST DIST
SIX, HENRY	CAR	309	1ST DIST
SIX, JAMES	ANN	459	HOWARD D
SIX, JOHN	CAR	319	1ST DIST
SIX, JOSEPH	CAR	308	1ST DIST
SIX, PHILIP	CAR	308	1ST DIST
SIX, SAMUEL	FRE	126	CREAGERS
SIX, SARAH	CAR	321	1ST DIST
SIX, WILLFORD	FRE	116	CREAGERS
SIX, WILLIAM	FRE	127	CREAGERS
SIX, WILLIAM	CAR	309	1ST DIST
SIXON, JOHN	BAL	120	18TH WAR
SIZE, ALEXANDER	BAL	349	13TH WAR
SIZER, JONAS	WAS	280	LEITERSB
SJENKINS, THOMS	BAL	120	1ST WARD
SKAAGS, BEN	PRI	080	QUEEN AN
SKAGGS, LEMUEL	KEN	270	1ST DIST
SKATES, JOHN W.	MGM	375	ROCKERLE
SKEGGS, ELIZA	KEN	294	3RD DIST
SKEGGS, HENRY	FRE	348	MIDDLETO
SKEGGS, HEZEKIAH	FRE	338	MIDDLETO
SKEGGS, WILLIAM G.	KEN	300	3RD DIST
SKELHARST, JOHN	BAL	180	2ND DIST
SKELLENSLAGER, MATHIAS	BAL	324	7TH WARD
SKELLERY, ANN	BAL	097	18TH WAR
SKELLEY, JOHN	BAL	293	12TH WAR
SKELLEY, JOHN	ALL	048	10TH E.D
SKELLEY, MARTIN	BAL	049	2ND DIST
SKELLMAN, CHARTOLL	FRE	074	FREDERIC
SKELLMAN, JOSIAH	BAL	412	1ST DIST
SKELTON, JOHN	BAL	128	2ND DIST
SKELY, SARAH	HAR	145	3RD DIST
SKEMPER, HENRY	PRI	039	VANSVILL
SKENK, JOHN	ALL	232	CUMBERLA
SKENNINGTON, JOHN	BAL	132	1ST WARD
SKERWOOD, GEORGE	BAL	339	13TH WAR
SKIDENER, NOAH	ALL	001	3RD E.D.
SKIDMORE, ANDREW	CAR	371	9TH DIST
SKIDMORE, ANN	PRI	100	SPALDING
SKIFER, CATHERINE	ALL	174	7TH E.D.
SKILER, ROBERT	QUE	144	1ST E DI
SKILER,ELIZA E.	QUE	144	1ST E DI
SKILES, F. W.	FRE	159	EMMITTSB
SKILES, HOPKINS	FRE	193	5TH E DI
SKILES, JOHN	ALL	027	2ND E.D.
SKILES, PERRY H.	FRE	194	5TH E DI
SKILL, JOHN	BAL	083	2ND DIST
SKILLING, JOH	BAL	071	2ND DIST
SKILLY, WILLIAM	CAR	098	NO TWP L
SKILMAN, GEORGE	BAL	059	4TH WARD
SKILMAN, ROBERT	BAL	113	18TH WAR
SKILS, ANDREW	BAL	386	1ST DIST
SKINER, JARRETT	HAR	146	3RD DIST
SKINER, JOHN	HAR	146	3RD DIST
SKINER,WILLIAM E.	FRE	447	8TH E DI
SKINK, SOLOMON	HAR	130	2ND DIST
SKINKSNER, JOHN	BAL	133	11TH WAR
SKINNEBERGER, JACOB	WAS	172	FUNKSTOW
SKINNER, A. MRS.	BAL	152	11TH WAR
SKINNER, A.P.	BAL	259	12TH WAR
SKINNER, ANN	TAL	070	EASTON T
SKINNER, ANN E. *	KEN	222	2ND DIST
SKINNER, BATCHELOR	CAR	096	NO TWP L
SKINNER, BENJAMIN	QUE	206	3RD E DI
SKINNER, BENSON	BAL	430	8TH WARD
SKINNER, BLANE E.	QUE	212	3RD E DI
SKINNER, CAROLINE	BAL	104	5TH WARD
SKINNER, CHARITY	BAL	195	11TH WAR
SKINNER, CHARLES	BAL	003	EASTERN
SKINNER, CHARLES E.	QUE	222	4TH E DI
SKINNER, CLEMENT	CHA	244	HILLTOP
SKINNER, CYTHA	CHA	239	HILLTOP
SKINNER, D. H. DR.	BAL	337	13TH WAR
SKINNER, EDWARD	BAL	431	8TH WARD
SKINNER, ELIZA C.	TAL	092	ST MICHA
SKINNER, ELIZABETH	DOR	469	1ST DIST
SKINNER, ELIZABETH	CAL	036	2ND DIST
SKINNER, EMMA	BAL	168	16TH WAR
SKINNER, EMORY	BAL	067	10TH WAR
SKINNER, ERI	BAL	152	11TH WAR
SKINNER, FRANCES	QUE	187	3RD E DI
SKINNER, FREDERICCA	PRI	062	NOTTINGH
SKINNER, GABRIEL	CAL	024	2ND DIST
SKINNER, GEORGE	BAL	147	1ST WARD
SKINNER, GEORGE W.	BAL	043	15TH WAR
SKINNER, GEORGE WASHINGTO	KEN	276	1ST DIST
SKINNER, GURTAVUS A.	TAL	092	ST MICHA
SKINNER, H.	WAS	021	2ND SUBD
SKINNER, HANNAH J.	BAL	214	11TH WAR
SKINNER, HARRIOTT	BAL	076	4TH WARD
SKINNER, HENRY	FRE	322	MIDDLETO
SKINNER, HESTER ANN	BAL	330	13TH WAR
SKINNER, ISAAC	FRE	426	8TH E DI
SKINNER, ISAAC-MBLACK	FRE	038	FREDERIC
SKINNER, J.	WAS	021	2ND SUBD
SKINNER, J. THOMAS	KEN	240	2ND DIST
SKINNER, JAMES	TAL	003	EASTON D
SKINNER, JAMES	QUE	193	3RD E DI
SKINNER, JAMES	BAL	196	17TH WAR
SKINNER, JAMES	BAL	282	12TH WAR
SKINNER, JAMES	BAL	172	11TH WAR
SKINNER, JAMES A.	BAL	062	15TH WAR
SKINNER, JAMES A.	FRE	344	MIDDLETO
SKINNER, JAMES W.	KEN	240	2ND DIST
SKINNER, JEREMIAH	BAL	027	15TH WAR
SKINNER, JOEL	TAL	076	EASTON T
SKINNER, JOHN	TAL	091	ST MICHA
SKINNER, JOHN	TAL	098	ST MICHA
SKINNER, JOHN	BAL	085	15TH WAR
SKINNER, JOHN	FRE	323	MIDDLETO
SKINNER, JOHN	BAL	250	17TH WAR
SKINNER, JOHN H.	PRI	064	NOTTINGH
SKINNER, JOHN J.	BAL	094	15TH WAR
SKINNER, JOHN K.	TAL	084	ST MICHA
SKINNER, JOHN L.	PRI	062	NOTTINGH
SKINNER, JOHN R.	TAL	027	EASTON D
SKINNER, JOHN R.	FRE	381	PETERSVI
SKINNER, JOHN S.	CHA	263	MIDDLETO
SKINNER, JOHN S.	CHA	263	MIDDLETO
SKINNER, JOHN S.	QUE	238	5TH E DI
SKINNER, JOSEPH A.	WAS	128	HAGERSTO
SKINNER, JOSEPH P.	BAL	048	15TH WAR
SKINNER, LEVIN	DOR	392	1ST DIST
SKINNER, LEWIS	CAL	029	2ND DIST
SKINNER, LILA	FRE	343	MIDDLETO
SKINNER, LLOYD	FRE	318	MIDDLETO
SKINNER, LOUISA	KEN	216	2ND DIST
SKINNER, MARGARET	PRI	061	NOTTINGH
SKINNER, MARIA	BAL	112	5TH WARD
SKINNER, MARIA L.	ANN	521	HOWARD D
SKINNER, MARY	KEN	212	2ND DIST
SKINNER, MARY	FRE	312	MIDDLETO
SKINNER, MARY	CAR	229	5TH DIST
SKINNER, MORDICA	CAR	087	NO TWP L
SKINNER, MOSES	KEN	275	1ST DIST
SKINNER, MR-	BAL	051	15TH WAR
SKINNER, NANCY	BAL	351	7TH WARD
SKINNER, NANCY	BAL	292	7TH WARD
SKINNER, NANCY	WAS	178	BOONSBOR
SKINNER, PEYTON	WAS	192	1ST DIST
SKINNER, PHILEMON	BAL	047	15TH WAR
SKINNER, PHILOMON	KEN	235	2ND DIST
SKINNER, R. S.	ALL	097	5TH E.D.
SKINNER, RACHEL	CAL	038	2ND DIST
SKINNER, RACHELL	BAL	253	17TH WAR
SKINNER, REBERTA	BAL	214	11TH WAR
SKINNER, RICHARD	QUE	155	2ND E DI
SKINNER, RICHARD W.	QUE	202	3RD E DI
SKINNER, RICHARD*	TAL	015	EASTON D
SKINNER, ROBERT	TAL	074	EASTON T
SKINNER, RUTH	TAL	081	ST MICHA
SKINNER, S.*	TAL	043	EASTON D
SKINNER, SAMUEL	CAL	032	2ND DIST
SKINNER, SAMUEL T.	BAL	076	10TH WAR
SKINNER, SARAH	FRE	382	PETERSVI
SKINNER, SLAD*	DOR	296	1ST DIST
SKINNER, SOPHIA E.	QUE	155	2ND E DI
SKINNER, SUSANNAH	BAL	351	7TH WARD
SKINNER, THOMAS	BAL	078	15TH WAR
SKINNER, THOMAS	BAL	103	15TH WAR
SKINNER, THOMAS	BAL	081	1ST WARD
SKINNER, THOMAS	BAL	253	17TH WAR
SKINNER, THOMAS	CHA	239	HILLTOP
SKINNER, THOMAS	CHA	238	HILLTOP
SKINNER, THOMAS	BAL	153	19TH WAR
SKINNER, WASHINGTON H.	DOR	392	1ST DIST
SKINNER, WILLAIM	BAL	343	13TH WAR
SKINNER, WILLIAM	KEN	210	2ND DIST
SKINNER, WILLIAM	CHA	236	HILLTOP
SKINNER, WILLIAM	CAL	036	2ND DIST
SKINNER, WILLIAM	BAL	192	17TH WAR
SKINNER, WILLIAM	BAL	043	15TH WAR
SKINNER, WILLIAM	TAL	014	EASTON D
SKINNER, WILLIAM	TAL	094	ST MICHA
SKINNER, WILLIAM	TAL	091	ST MICHA
SKINNER, WILLIAM	QUE	246	5TH E DI
SKINNER, WILLIAM *	KEN	273	1ST DIST
SKINNER, WILLIAM H.	TAL	075	EASTON T
SKINNER, WILLIAM H.	BAL	272	17TH WAR
SKINNER, ZACHARIA	DOR	392	1ST DIST
SKINNER, ZACHARIA	DOR	393	1ST DIST
SKINNEY, MICHAEL	BAL	267	17TH WAR
SKINNMAN, BARBARA	ALL	261	CUMBERLA
SKIPER, HENRY	WAS	132	2ND DIST
SKIPPER, ELISHA	BAL	308	1ST DIST
SKIPPER, ESTHER	BAL	192	6TH WARD
SKIPPER, JOHN	BAL	419	1ST DIST
SKIPPER, M.	BAL	244	20TH WAR
SKIPPER, NIMROD	BAL	412	1ST DIST
SKIPPER, THOAMS	BAL	355	1ST DIST
SKIPPER, THOMAS	BAL	209	11TH WAR
SKIPPER, THOMAS	BAL	244	1ST DIST
SKIPPER, WILLIAM	BAL	361	1ST DIST
SKIRRIN, WILLIAM *	KEN	273	1ST DIST
SKIRVIN, GEORGE	BAL	129	16TH WAR
SKRINER, BASIL	FRE	100	FREDERIC
SKULLEY, WILLIAM	QUE	146	1ST E DI
SKUSTLE, MARY	BAL	130	11TH WAR
SLACH, JOHN*	BAL	318	3RD WARD
SLACK, ABNER	ANN	519	HOWARD D
SLACK, CHARLES	BAL	210	11TH WAR
SLACK, CHARLOTT	BAL	342	3RD WARD
SLACK, CORDELIA L.	BAL	210	11TH WAR
SLACK, CORN.	ALL	090	5TH E.D.
SLACK, EDWARD	ALL	090	5TH E.D.
SLACK, EDWARD	ALL	090	5TH E.D.
SLACK, ELLEN	BAL	293	1ST DIST
SLACK, JOHN*	BAL	318	3RD WARD
SLACK, MARY	CEC	205	7TH E DI
SLACK, PATRICK	BAL	189	11TH WAR
SLACK, RACHAEL A.	BAL	147	11TH WAR
SLACK, SARAH	CAR	216	5TH DIST
SLACK, SARAH E.	FRE	385	PETERSVI
SLACK, WILLIAM B.	BAL	179	16TH WAR
SLACK, WILLIAM H.	BAL	162	11TH WAR
SLACK, WILLIAM H.	BAL	147	11TH WAR
SLACOM, ANDREW J.	DOR	337	3RD DIVI
SLACOM, BARZILIA*	DOR	360	3RD DIVI
SLACOM, HESTER	DOR	354	3RD DIVI
SLACOM, JAMES	DOR	372	3RD DIVI
SLACOM, LEVEN	DOR	358	3RD DIVI
SLACOM, WASHINGTON	DOR	336	3RD DIVI
SLACUM, EDWARD*	DOR	465	1ST DIST
SLACUM, JOHN G.	DOR	439	1ST DIST
SLACUM, JOSEPH	BAL	265	17TH WAR
SLACUM, MARCELLUS*	DOR	438	1ST DIST
SLACUM, MARGARET E.	DOR	440	1ST DIST
SLADE, ABRAHAM	HAR	071	1ST DIST
SLADE, ABRAHAM	HAR	067	1ST DIST
SLADE, ABRAM	BAL	036	2ND DIST
SLADE, ABURY	BAL	036	2ND DIST
SLADE, ANN	BAL	046	2ND DIST
SLADE, ANN	BAL	038	2ND DIST
SLADE, BASEL	BAL	039	2ND DIST
SLADE, BENJAMIN	BAL	042	2ND DIST
SLADE, BENJAMIN	BAL	441	1ST DIST
SLADE, CROTON	HAR	019	1ST DIST
SLADE, DAVID	BAL	229	1ST DIST
SLADE, DAVID L.	BAL	231	1ST DIST
SLADE, DIXON	HAR	072	1ST DIST
SLADE, EDWARD	BAL	299	12TH WAR
SLADE, ELIZABETH	BAL	050	2ND DIST
SLADE, EZEKIEL	HAR	026	1ST DIST
SLADE, EZEKIEL	HAR	020	1ST DIST
SLADE, HANNAH	HAR	069	1ST DIST
SLADE, JAMES	BAL	084	2ND DIST
SLADE, JANE	HAR	069	1ST DIST
SLADE, JEMIMA	BAL	257	12TH WAR
SLADE, JOHN	HAR	060	1ST DIST
SLADE, JOHN	HAR	065	1ST DIST
SLADE, JOSHUA	BAL	033	2ND DIST
SLADE, LEVI	BAL	045	2ND DIST
SLADE, LEWIS	BAL	127	1ST WARD
SLADE, MARGARET	BAL	040	2ND DIST
SLADE, MARIA	BAL	248	1ST DIST
SLADE, NELSON	BAL	004	1ST WARD
SLADE, THOMAS	BAL	038	2ND DIST
SLADE, VAN RANSELAER	BAL	036	2ND DIST
SLADE, WASHINGTON M.	HAR	197	3RD DIST
SLADE, WILLIAM	HAR	069	1ST DIST
SLADE, WILLIAM	BAL	036	2ND DIST
SLADE, WILLIAM	BAL	050	2ND DIST
SLADE,ASBURY	BAL	042	2ND DIST
SLADER, ANN M.	BAL	165	11TH WAR
SLAFF, PHILLIP	BAL	226	17TH WAR
SLAGAR, MARY	BAL	308	1ST DIST
SLAGENHAUPT, JACOB	CAR	321	1ST DIST
SLAGENHAUPT, JOHN	CAR	321	1ST DIST
SLAGER, POWELL	BAL	297	17TH WAR
SLAGGATER, MICHAEL	BAL	220	2ND WARD
SLAGHEL, JACOB	WAS	155	2ND DIST
SLAGLE, FREDERICK	FRE	381	PETERSVI
SLAGLE, HENRY	FRE	381	PETERSVI
SLAGLE, MARY	CAR	282	7TH DIST
SLAGLE, WILLIAM	CAR	346	6TH DIST
SLAGLER, PETER	CAR	294	7TH DIST
SLAGMAN, PETER J.	FRE	222	BUCKEYST
SLAGMIRE, WILLIAM H.	BAL	012	2ND DIST
SLAHART, ANDREW	BAL	297	17TH WAR
SLAHN, CHRISTIAN	CAR	384	2ND DIST
SLAHN, DAVID	CAR	378	2ND DIST
SLAMBAUGH, SARAH	CAR	345	6TH DIST
SLAMNER, CATHARIN	CAR	390	2ND DIST
SLANE, FRANCIS	BAL	385	8TH WARD
SLANE,AMANDA	ALL	236	CUMBERLA
SLANEY, JAMES	BAL	061	4TH WARD
SLANK, GEORGE	ALL	230	CUMBERLA
SLANLY, JOSEPH-BLACK	CAR	128	NO TWP L
SLAPE, JOHN	CAR	381	2ND DIST
SLAPRAGIAL, JOSEPH	BAL	386	8TH WARD
SLAPTFORT, WILLIAM	DOR	357	3RD DIVI
SLAREGENHAUP, BARBARA	CAR	322	1ST DIST
SLARK, GEORGE	QUE	246	5TH E DI
SLAROP, JACOB	CAR	190	4TH DIST
SLASS, JOHN	FRE	172	5TH E DI
SLASS, MICHAEL	FRE	172	5TH E DI
SLASSER, DANIEL	WAS	180	BOONSBOR
SLATA, JAMES	BAL	145	1ST WARD
SLATE, CHARLES	BAL	355	8TH WARD
SLATER, ABRAHAM	BAL	089	18TH WAR
SLATER, ANN	BAL	191	2ND WARD
SLATER, BETTY	CAL	040	3RD DIST
SLATER, CATHARINE	KEN	212	2ND DIST
SLATER, CHARITY	BAL	421	3RD WARD
SLATER, ELIZA	BAL	381	3RD WARD
SLATER, GEORGE	BAL	141	1ST WARD
SLATER, GEORGE	BAL	013	18TH WAR
SLATER, GEORGE W.	BAL	399	3RD WARD
SLATER, HAMILTON	BAL	154	11TH WAR
SLATER, HARRIET	BAL	381	3RD WARD
SLATER, HENRY	BAL	357	8TH WARD
SLATER, HENRY	BAL	242	2ND WARD
SLATER, HENRY	BAL	190	2ND WARD
SLATER, HENRY	PRI	092	MARLBROU
SLATER, J. B.	BAL	384	13TH WAR
SLATER, JAMES	BAL	381	3RD WARD
SLATER, JENNY	BAL	424	14TH WAR
SLATER, JOB	BAL	086	15TH WAR
SLATER, JOHN	BAL	108	1ST WARD
SLATER, JOHN	DOR	388	1ST DIST
SLATER, KITTY*	DOR	423	1ST DIST
SLATER, MARIA	PRI	112	PISCATAW
SLATER, MARY	BAL	050	9TH WARD
SLATER, MARY A.	BAL	212	11TH WAR
SLATER, MARY M.	BAL	059	15TH WAR
SLATER, MARY S.	BAL	217	6TH WARD
SLATER, MILLE	FRE	070	FREDERIC
SLATER, NOAMI	BAL	006	9TH WARD
SLATER, PETER	TAL	004	EASTON D
SLATER, ROBERT	BAL	183	6TH WARD
SLATER, ROBERT	BAL	086	15TH WAR
SLATER, WASHINGTON F.	BAL	242	2ND WARD
SLATER, WILLIAM	BAL	067	2ND DIST
SLATERY, CATHARINE	BAL	143	2ND DIST
SLATES, SARAH-BLACK	CAR	371	9TH DIST
SLATES, WENDEL	CAR	249	3RD DIST
SLATFEILD, BENJAMIN	CAR	370	9TH DIST
SLATFEILD, ELIZA	CAR	370	9TH DIST
SLATHER, HENRY	ALL	257	CUMBERLA
SLATHERTY, PETER	ANN	473	HOWARD D
SLATON, DAVID	BAL	265	7TH WARD
SLATON, MARGARET *	KEN	262	1ST DIST
SLATON, MOSES *	SOM	428	PRINCESS
SLATOR, WILLIAM	DOR	364	3RD DIVI
SLATTEN, HARRIET	FRE	137	CREAGERS
SLATTER, A.	BAL	116	1ST WARD
SLATTER, MARY	BAL	286	17TH WAR
SLATTER, PATRICK	BAL	297	20TH WAR
SLAUGH, WILLIAM K.	BAL	036	18TH WAR
SLAUGHENHAIPT, SARAH A.	CAR	298	1ST DIST
SLAUGHENHARPT, SAMUEL	CAR	298	1ST DIST
SLAUGHLER, DAVID	CAR	095	NO TWP L
SLAUGHTER, ANSON A.	TAL	062	EASTON D
SLAUGHTER, CATHERINE	CAR	095	NO TWP L
SLAUGHTER, DANIEL	TAL	034	EASTON D
SLAUGHTER, DANIEL	WAS	013	WILLIAMS
SLAUGHTER, EDWARD	KEN	300	3RD DIST
SLAUGHTER, ELIZABETH	BAL	032	9TH WARD
SLAUGHTER, FRANCIS H.	BAL	097	15TH WAR
SLAUGHTER, HENRY B.	KEN	300	3RD DIST
SLAUGHTER, J. M.	BAL	471	14TH WAR
SLAUGHTER, JAMES	TAL	028	EASTON D
SLAUGHTER, JAMES M.	BAL	045	18TH WAR
SLAUGHTER, JAMES*	BAL	117	15TH WAR
SLAUGHTER, JANE	BAL	035	9TH WARD
SLAUGHTER, JOHN	BAL	138	16TH WAR
SLAUGHTER, JOHNATHAN	KEN	300	3RD DIST
SLAUGHTER, PHILIMON	TAL	062	EASTON D
SLAUGHTER, ROBERT	TAL	052	EASTON D
SLAUGHTER, SAMUEL-BLACK	CAR	167	NO TWP L
SLAUGHTER, SUSAN	TAL	016	EASTON D
SLAUGHTER, THOMAS	QUE	152	1ST E DI
SLAUGHTER, THOMAS H.	CAR	149	NO TWP L
SLAUGHTER, TILGHMAN	TAL	062	EASTON D
SLAUGHTER, TURBLT K.	TAL	023	EASTON D
SLAUGHTER, WILLIAM	TAL	052	EASTON D
SLAUGHTER, WILLIAM	BAL	333	1ST DIST
SLAUGHTON, GARRETTSON	BAL	030	9TH WARD
SLAUN, DAVID R.	BAL	418	14TH WAR
SLAVEHOFF, EMILA	BAL	457	1ST DIST

SLAVEN, CHARLES BAL 429 1ST DIST
SLAVEN, DRUCILLA CHA 232 HILLTOP
SLAVEN, WILLIAM CHA 231 HILLTOP
SLAW, JOHN ALL 121 4TH E.D.
SLAYBAUGH, EMANUEL FRE 176 5TH E DI
SLAYBAUGH, SOLOMON FRE 173 5TH E DI
SLAYLE, JOHN W. BAL 243 12TH WAR
SLAYMAKER, HENRIETTA BAL 453 8TH WARD
SLAYMAKER, JOHN H. ANN 267 ANNAPOLI
SLAYMER, FREDERICK BAL 120 11TH WAR
SLAYSMAN, ALEXANDER BAL 223 6TH WARD
SLAYSMAN, WILLIAM BAL 226 6TH WARD
SLAYSMAYER, ELIZABETH BAL 455 8TH WARD
SLAYTON, JOSEPH * BAL 200 6TH WARD
SLAYTOR, MICHAEL CEC 024 ELKTON 3
SLAZEN, MARY BAL 424 3RD WARD
SLCK, HENRY CAR 331 MANCHEST
SLEAR, ALFRED * ALL 102 5TH E.D.
SLEASMAN, GEORGE FRE 150 10TH E D
SLEASMAN, GEORGE H. FRE 150 10TH E D
SLEATHERLAND, ELIZABETH ST 306 1ST E DI
SLECH, MARY* BAL 109 10TH WAR
SLECK, MARY A. WAS 280 LEITERSB
SLECUSKI, FRANK BAL 202 2ND WARD
SLEDE, LENAY FRE 253 NEW MARK
SLEDE, MARTHA WAS 131 HAGERSTO
SLEED, JERUSHE BAL 211 17TH WAR
SLEEGER, DANIEL BAL 210 17TH WAR
SLEEGER, HENRY * ANN 376 4TH DIST
SLEEK, MARGARET FRE 292 WOODSBOR
SLEEPER, GEORGE BAL 302 17TH WAR
SLEEPER, GEORGIANNA* BAL 029 4TH WARD
SLEEPER, HENRY * ANN 376 4TH DIST
SLEER, WILLIAM H. FRE 253 NEW MARK
SLEET, JOHN BAL 356 8TH WARD
SLEET, WILLIAM BAL 391 3RD WARD
SLEETTER, GODFRITS BAL 211 17TH WAR
SLEEVINSKER, AUGUST ALL 084 5TH E.D.
SLEFER, WILLIAM FRE 332 MIDDLETO
SLEIBER, AUGUSTUS BAL 285 2ND WARD
SLEICHKING, LAURA BAL 063 1ST WARD
SLEICHTKING, HENRY BAL 063 1ST WARD
SLEIGH, THOMAS B. ST 343 5TH E DI
SLEINGER, ELIZABETH BAL 311 12TH WAR
SLEINGER, JULIA BAL 251 2ND WARD
SLEMMER, FREDERICK BAL 086 10TH WAR
SLEMMER, LLOYD* BAL 415 3RD WARD
SLEMMONS, ROBERT W. SOM 436 PRINCESS
SLEMNON, JAMES ALL 147 6TH E.D.
SLEMONS, JOHN B.* SOM 505 SALISBUR
SLENDER, HENRY HAR 206 3RD DIST
SLENMER, MARY C. BAL 213 2ND WARD
SLERTH, JOHN BAL 022 2ND DIST
SLETHOUR, JOHN BAL 458 1ST DIST
SLETTER, MARY A. BAL 140 16TH WAR
SLETTINE, GEORGE BAL 254 2ND WARD
SLEVENS, ELENORA BAL 095 18TH WAR
SLEY, JACOB BAL 422 14TH WAR
SLEY, LYDIA BAL 421 14TH WAR
SLEY, WILLIAM BAL 421 14TH WAR
SLICE, AMELIA WAS 291 1ST DIST
SLICE, SAMUEL WAS 268 1ST DIST
SLICER, ANDREW ANN 275 ANNAPOLI
SLICER, ANREW BAL 092 5TH WARD
SLICER, EDWARD A. BAL 420 3RD WARD
SLICER, EMMA BAL 092 5TH WARD
SLICER, GEORGE ALL 191 9TH E.D.
SLICER, HENRY BAL 273 12TH WAR
SLICER, JACOB CEC 198 7TH E DI
SLICER, JAMES ALL 238 CUMBERLA
SLICER, JOHN ALL 027 2ND E.D.
SLICER, LEWIS E. BAL 162 6TH WARD
SLICER, SAMUEL CEC 133 6TH E DI
SLICER, SARAH BAL 092 5TH WARD
SLICER, THOMAS J. CEC 133 6TH E DI
SLICER, WILLIAM J. ALL 213 CUMBERLA
SLICK, ED. BAL 035 18TH WAR
SLICK, FRANCIS CAR 298 1ST DIST
SLICK, JEREMIAH WAS 283 1ST DIST
SLICK, JOHN WAS 264 1ST DIST
SLICK, PEGGY FRE 191 5TH E DI
SLICK, ROBERT CAR 327 1ST DIST
SLICK, SAMUEL CAR 305 1ST DIST
SLICKFOOT, JOSEPH BAL 092 15TH WAR
SLIDER, ANN ALL 248 CUMBERLA
SLIDER, JOHN ALL 179 7TH E.D.
SLIDER, M.W. ALL 179 7TH E.D.
SLIDER, WILLIAM ALL 179 7TH E.D.
SLIFER, ANDREW WAS 019 2ND SUBD
SLIFER, CATHARINE FRE 396 PETERSVI
SLIFER, CECILLA E. FRE 404 JEFFERSO
SLIFER, EZRA FRE 396 PETERSVI
SLIFER, ISRAEL WAS 076 2ND SUBD
SLIFER, JACOB FRE 393 PETERSVI
SLIFER, JOHN FRE 380 PETERSVI
SLIFER, JOHN WAS 186 BOONSBOR
SLIFER, JOSHUA FRE 353 MIDDLETO
SLIFER, MA. WAS 019 2ND SUBD
SLIFER, MARGARET WAS 185 BOONSBOR
SLIFER, MARTIN WAS 188 BOONSBOR
SLIFER, SAMUEL FRE 408 JEFFERSO
SLIGGINS, C. BAL 170 1ST WARD
SLIGH, DANIEL W. ST 280 3RD E DI
SLIGH, MARY A. ST 339 5TH E DI
SLIMMER, CHRISTIAN FRE 414 8TH E DI
SLIMMER, PHILIP FRE 425 8TH E DI
SLIMY, BENJAMIN BAL 455 14TH WAR
SLINGER, HENRY BAL 130 11TH WAR
SLINGLAND, JACOB PRI 024 VANSVILL
SLINGLUFF, CHARLES D. BAL 425 14TH WAR
SLINGLUFF, UPTON BAL 431 14TH WAR
SLINGLUFF, ISAAC CAR 393 2ND DIST
SLINING, MARGARET BAL 460 14TH WAR
SLINMER, MARGRET BAL 213 2ND WARD
SLINST, JOSEPH BAL 239 2ND WARD
SLIPE, GIDEON FRE 353 MIDDLETO
SLISLER, CONRADT BAL 436 8TH WARD
SLITTZ, NICHOLAS BAL 055 2ND DIST
SLIVER, ABRAHAM BAL 375 8TH WARD
SLIVER, JANE HAR 044 1ST DIST
SLIVER, WILLIAM BAL 281 12TH WAR
SLNODDEN, PRISCELLA BAL 222 12TH WAR
SLOAGERBIER, WILLIAM BAL 177 2ND WARD
SLOAN, ALEXANDER ALL 099 5TH E.D.
SLOAN, DAVID ALL 089 5TH E.D.
SLOAN, DAVID ALL 017 3RD E.D.
SLOAN, DAVID WAS 194 1ST DIST
SLOAN, ELISABETH ALL 014 3RD E.D.
SLOAN, ELIZABETH BAL 227 19TH WAR
SLOAN, FREDERICK BAL 263 17TH WAR
SLOAN, GEORGE F. BAL 443 14TH WAR
SLOAN, HARRIET BAL 066 15TH WAR
SLOAN, HUGH BAL 090 5TH WARD
SLOAN, JAMES BAL 174 11TH WAR
SLOAN, JAMES BAL 019 9TH WARD
SLOAN, JAMES BAL 047 4TH WARD
SLOAN, JAMES T. BAL 079 18TH WAR
SLOAN, JOHN BAL 006 9TH WARD
SLOAN, JOHN ALL 014 3RD E.D.
SLOAN, JOHN ALL 099 5TH E.D.
SLOAN, JOHN ALL 103 5TH E.D.
SLOAN, MARY BAL 003 1ST WARD
SLOAN, MARY A. BAL 418 14TH WAR
SLOAN, MATTHEW ALL 105 5TH E.D.
SLOAN, PATRICK BAL 390 3RD WARD
SLOAN, ROBERT BAL 051 9TH WARD
SLOAN, THOMAS BAL 121 2ND DIST
SLOAN, WILLIAM J. BAL 418 14TH WAR
SLOAN, WILLIAM S. BAL 234 6TH WARD
SLOAN,MICHE BAL 246 12TH WAR
SLOAP, GEORGE ALL 115 5TH E.D.
SLOARP, DOROTHY BAL 409 14TH WAR
SLOBAUGH, DANIEL ALL 016 3RD E.D.
SLOCKER, MOSES BAL 292 12TH WAR
SLOCOMB, SAMUEL WOR 330 1ST E DI
SLOCUM, HENRY BAL 026 15TH WAR
SLOCUM, JOHN W. BAL 258 17TH WAR
SLOCUM, NABOTH* DOR 416 1ST DIST
SLOCUMB, JOHN BAL 198 2ND WARD
SLODENSLAGER, GEORGE BAL 237 1ST DIST
SLODER, FREDERICK BAL 204 2ND WARD
SLOFER, ANN BAL 320 7TH WARD
SLOFFER, PHILIP BAL 096 10TH WAR
SLOLTEN, SIDNEY-BLACK CAR 398 2ND DIST
SLONAKER, ANDREW CAR 237 UNION TO
SLONAKER, JACOB CAR 237 UNION TO
SLONAKER, JOHN CAR 237 UNION TO
SLONE, JOHN BAL 338 1ST DIST
SLONEBACK, WILLIAM BAL 331 7TH WARD
SLONER, ELIZABETH CAR 266 7TH DIST
SLONER, ISAAC CEC 053 1ST E DI
SLORP, CATHARINE BAL 355 1ST DIST
SLORP, JEMIAH * CAR 282 7TH DIST
SLOSER, HENRY WAS 057 2ND SUBD
SLOSSER, ELIZABETH WAS 199 1ST DIST
SLOTHERVER, GEORGE BAL 141 19TH WAR
SLOTHFELT, FREDERICK BAL 289 1ST DIST
SLOTHOUR, ELIZABETH FRE 172 5TH E DI
SLOTHOUR, MICHAEL CAR 388 2ND DIST
SLOTTEMEYER, ELIZABETH FRE 362 CATOCTIN
SLOTTER, DANIEL BAL 210 17TH WAR
SLOUCH, CHRISTENA BAL 375 8TH WARD
SLOUFFER, JAMES T. FRE 304 WOODSBOR
SLOUTSEMBURG, MARGARET CEC 144 PORT DUP
SLOW, HENRIETTA BAL 332 3RD WARD
SLOW, TENET* TAL 040 EASTON D
SLOWE, WILLIAM BAL 079 15TH WAR
SLOYAL, CATHARINE BAL 406 14TH WAR
SLTREELER, HENRY * BAL 048 18TH WAR
SLUBBERFIELD, GEORGE ALL 238 CUMBERLA
SLUCKEYSER, PETER FRE 023 FREDERIC
SLUE, GEORGE W. HAR 117 2ND DIST
SLUGER, C. BAL 228 19TH WAR
SLUKER, M. BAL 449 8TH WARD
SLUNKEL, SOPHIAR FRE 234 BUCKEYST
SLUNT, ELIZABETH BAL 291 1ST DIST
SLUNT, PETER BAL 291 1ST DIST
SLUSCHER, HENRY BAL 203 2ND WARD
SLUSCHER, HENRY BAL 203 2ND WARD
SLUSER, NANCY WAS 107 2ND DIST
SLUSHER, MR. BAL 214 17TH WAR
SLUSSER, CATHARINE WAS 015 2ND SUBD
SLUSSER, GEORGE FRE 138 CREAGERS
SLUSSER, MARTHA WAS 057 2ND SUBD
SLUSSER, MICHAEL FRE 192 5TH E DI
SLUSSMAN, CATHARINE WAS 038 2ND SUBD
SLUSSNOGLE, CHARLES ALL 038 2ND E.D.
SLUSSNOGLE, MICHAEL ALL 038 2ND E.D.
SLUTHAUN, JOHN FRE 416 8TH E DI
SLUTHAUR, STEPHEN FRE 433 8TH E DI
SLUTTER, JOHN CAR 315 1ST DIST
SLUTTER, WILLIAM BAL 060 18TH WAR
SLUVENSKIR, MARTIN * ALL 084 5TH E.D.
SLWEWLLYN, THOMAS BAL 156 2ND DIST
SLY, HENRY CEC 182 7TH E DI
SLY, WILLIAM CEC 181 7TH E DI
SLYCE, JOHN BAL 190 2ND WARD
SLYDER, BARNABAS CAR 246 3RD DIST
SLYDER, FREDERIC CAR 335 6TH DIST
SLYDER, JONAS CAR 256 3RD DIST
SLYDER, MAGADALENA CAR 304 1ST DIST
SLYDER, WILLIAM CAR 256 3RD DIST
SLYE, BENJAMIN CAL 038 2ND DIST
SLYE, GEORGE CAL 025 2ND DIST
SLYE, JOHN CAL 045 3RD DIST
SLYE, RICHARD CAL 044 3RD DIST
SLYGINS, MARGARET BAL 205 19TH WAR
SLYNA, DAN-BLACK QUE 134 1ST E DI
SLYNA, FRANCIS-BLACK QUE 172 2ND E DI
SLYTOR, BENJAMIN CEC 036 CHESAPEA
SMACH, HENRY WOR 320 1ST E DI
SMACK, ANDREW CAR 349 6TH DIST
SMACK, ANN WOR 292 9TH E DI
SMACK, CATHERINE WOR 216 4TH E DI
SMACK, DAVID CEC 032 CHESAPEA
SMACK, ELIZABETH WOR 217 4TH E DI
SMACK, FRANCIS WOR 282 BERLIN 1
SMACK, HENRY WOR 292 9TH E DI
SMACK, HIRAM J. WOR 206 4TH E DI
SMACK, HOWELL CEC 038 CHESAPEA
SMACK, HULDA WOR 285 BERLIN 1
SMACK, JAMES WOR 281 BERLIN 1
SMACK, JAMES WOR 254 1ST CENS
SMACK, JAMES M. WOR 283 BERLIN 1
SMACK, JANE WOR 298 9TH E DI
SMACK, JESSE WOR 285 BERLIN 1
SMACK, JOHN WOR 281 BERLIN 1
SMACK, KENDAL WOR 284 BERLIN 1
SMACK, LAMBERT WOR 292 9TH E DI
SMACK, LEAH C. WOR 216 4TH E DI
SMACK, MARY A. WOR 293 9TH E DI
SMACK, MC KIRNA WOR 324 1ST E DI
SMACK, PETER E. WOR 171 6TH E DI
SMACK, RILEY WOR 281 BERLIN 1
SMACK, SAMUEL B. CEC 039 CHESAPEA
SMACK, WILLIAM WOR 255 1ST CENS
SMACK, WILLIAM WOR 165 6TH E DI
SMACTINER, PETER BAL 193 2ND WARD
SMALCOM, JACOB CEC 186 7TH E DI
SMALE, N. DOR 413 1ST DIST
SMALL, AJESM BAL 313 20TH WAR
SMALL, ANN BAL 300 20TH WAR
SMALL, ANN BAL 182 2ND WARD
SMALL, ANN BAL 161 2ND DIST
SMALL, ANN-MULATTO FRE 039 FREDERIC
SMALL, C. H. BAL 047 9TH WARD
SMALL, CAROLINE BAL 184 11TH WAR
SMALL, CATHARINE BAL 249 1ST DIST
SMALL, CHARLOTTE WAS 097 2ND DIST
SMALL, CHARTOLL FRE 100 FREDERIC
SMALL, CRISTIAN ALL 205 CUMBERLA
SMALL, EDWARD BAL 454 14TH WAR
SMALL, ELI FRE 036 FREDERIC
SMALL, ELIZABETH FRE 066 FREDERIC
SMALL, ELIZABETH R. BAL 321 3RD WARD
SMALL, ELLEN BAL 143 16TH WAR
SMALL, FANNY ALL 135 4TH E.D.
SMALL, GEORGE BAL 108 10TH WAR
SMALL, GEORGE BAL 381 3RD WARD
SMALL, GEORGE BAL 280 7TH WARD
SMALL, GEORGE BAL 378 13TH WAR
SMALL, GEORGE SOM 360 BRINKLEY
SMALL, HANNAH BAL 396 14TH WAR
SMALL, HARRIET J. FRE 023 FREDERIC
SMALL, J. BAL 154 1ST WARD
SMALL, JACOB BAL 155 5TH WARD
SMALL, JAMES HAR 128 2ND DIST
SMALL, JAOCB BAL 374 13TH WAR
SMALL, JESSE W. BAL 008 18TH WAR
SMALL, JOHN BAL 300 20TH WAR
SMALL, JOHN BAL 409 14TH WAR
SMALL, JOHN BAL 131 11TH WAR
SMALL, JOHN BAL 380 3RD WARD
SMALL, JOHN BAL 332 13TH WAR
SMALL, JOHN TAL 056 EASTON D
SMALL, JOHN WAS 246 SMITHSBU
SMALL, JOHN S. BAL 326 1ST DIST
SMALL, JOSIAH BAL 456 14TH WAR
SMALL, L. BAL 159 1ST WARD
SMALL, LAURA J. FRE 037 FREDERIC
SMALL, LOUISA BAL 125 11TH WAR
SMALL, MARTIN BAL 105 2ND DIST
SMALL, MARY BAL 073 4TH WARD
SMALL, MOSES BAL 058 10TH WAR
SMALL, NATHANIEL WAS 262 1ST DIST
SMALL, NOAH HAR 129 2ND DIST
SMALL, P.R. WAS 127 HAGERSTO
SMALL, ROBERT SOM 360 BRINKLEY
SMALL, ROBERT WAS 106 2ND DIST
SMALL, SAMUEL WAS 161 2ND DIST
SMALL, SIMON BAL 321 3RD WARD
SMALL, THOMAS BAL 160 1ST WARD
SMALL, WILLAIM BAL 353 7TH WARD
SMALL, WILLIAM BAL 108 5TH WARD
SMALL, WILLIAM ALL 212 CUMBERLA
SMALL, WILLIAM BAL 305 7TH WARD
SMALL,WILLIAM BAL 012 2ND DIST
SMALLBACK, ANDREW BAL 125 2ND DIST
SMALLBOCK, C. BAL 240 20TH WAR
SMALLBROOK, HENRY BAL 259 2ND WARD
SMALLEN, HARIET SOM 478 TRAPP DI
SMALLEN, NANCY * SOM 421 PRINCESS
SMALLEN, SARAH BAL 072 15TH WAR
SMALLS, FREDRICK W. BAL 008 4TH WARD
SMALLWOOD, CHARLES ANN 423 HOWARD D
SMALLWOOD, CATHERINE-BLAC FRE 016 FREDERIC
SMALLWOOD, CHARLES BAL 086 15TH WAR
SMALLWOOD, DAVID BAL 251 20TH WAR
SMALLWOOD, ELIZA S. KEN 255 1ST DIST
SMALLWOOD, ELIZABETH CHA 255 MIDDLETO
SMALLWOOD, ELLEN BAL 374 3RD WARD
SMALLWOOD, EMERY TAL 092 ST MICHA
SMALLWOOD, FRANCIS BAL 233 6TH WARD
SMALLWOOD, FRANCIS L. CHA 264 HILLTOP
SMALLWOOD, GEORGE ANN 394 8TH DIST
SMALLWOOD, GEORGE BAL 459 1ST DIST
SMALLWOOD, GRACY ST 290 2ND E DI
SMALLWOOD, HENRIETTA PRI 070 MARLBROU
SMALLWOOD, HENRY CHA 229 MIDDLETO
SMALLWOOD, JAMES WAS 094 2ND SUBD
SMALLWOOD, JAMES BAL 020 2ND DIST
SMALLWOOD, JANE CHA 263 MIDDLETO
SMALLWOOD, JOHN BAL 240 6TH WARD
SMALLWOOD, JOHN D. ANN 423 HOWARD D
SMALLWOOD, JOHN R. PRI 111 PISCATAW
SMALLWOOD, JOSEPH ANN 423 HOWARD D
SMALLWOOD, KATY QUE 215 3RD E DI
SMALLWOOD, MARY E. BAL 134 11TH WAR
SMALLWOOD, MATILDA BAL 246 20TH WAR
SMALLWOOD, MORGAN FRE 204 BUCKEYST
SMALLWOOD, NICHOLAS BAL 086 15TH WAR
SMALLWOOD, PEGGY-BLACK FRE 407 JEFFERSO
SMALLWOOD, PHILIP ANN 478 HOWARD D
SMALLWOOD, R. L. CHA 254 MIDDLETO
SMALLWOOD, RACHEL ANN 428 HOWARD D
SMALLWOOD, RACHEL TAL 092 ST MICHA
SMALLWOOD, REZIN MGM 348 BERRYS D
SMALLWOOD, RICHARD CHA 264 HILLTOP
SMALLWOOD, ROSANNA FRE 022 FREDERIC
SMALLWOOD, ROSE TAL 018 EASTON D
SMALLWOOD, SALLY BAL 380 13TH WAR
SMALLWOOD, SERENA BAL 167 19TH WAR
SMALLWOOD, SOPHIA ANN 451 HOWARD D
SMALLWOOD, THOMAS PRI 045 VANSVILL
SMALLWOOD, W. BAL 233 20TH WAR
SMALLWOOD, WILLIAM CHA 253 MIDDLETO
SMALLWOOD, WILLIAM C. FRE 159 EMMITTSB
SMALLWOODS, ELIZABETH BAL 258 2ND WARD
SMALLY, NOBLE FRE 271 NEW MARK
SMALSOM, MARTIN* BAL 068 4TH WARD
SMALTZELL, CATHARINE BAL 214 11TH WAR
SMALWOOD, WILLIAM PRI 073 MARLBROU
SMAMEL, FRED * ANN 406 8TH DIST
SMAN, SAMUEL ALL 125 4TH E.D.
SMANNERING, JERRY BAL 020 2ND DIST
SMAPSON, ELLEN BAL 052 9TH WARD
SMARDIN, RICHARD BAL 219 19TH WAR
SMART, JANE DOR 425 1ST DIST
SMART, MARY TAL 067 EASTON T
SMART, THOMAS BAL 021 9TH WARD
SMART, W. DOR 425 1ST DIST
SMART, WILLIAM TAL 047 EASTON T
SMATHER, ISAAC BAL 023 2ND DIST
SMATTER, JOHN BAL 068 4TH WARD
SMATTHIAS,ELIZABETH BAL 274 12TH WAR
SMAUELS, THOMAS BAL 374 8TH WARD
SMAUR, SAMUEL ALL 132 4TH E.D.
SMC CLELLAND, ALLICE BAL 072 1ST WARD
SMEACH, DAVID CAR 267 WESTMINS
SMEACH, ELIZABETH CAR 356 6TH DIST

Name	County	Page	District
SMEACH, LYDIA	CAR	347	6TH DIST
SMEAD, SAMUEL R.	QUE	233	4TH E DI
SMEARMAN, JOHN	ALL	037	2ND E.D.
SMEARMUNT, JOHN	BAL	294	17TH WAR
SMEEDAN, JAMES	BAL	216	6TH DIST
SMELSER, JOHN	CAR	397	2ND DIST
SMELSER, NATHANIEL	CAR	394	2ND DIST
SMELSER, RACHEAL	CAR	397	2ND DIST
SMELSER, UPTON	CAR	397	2ND DIST
SMELTY, GEORGE W.	BAL	008	18TH WAR
SMELTZ, ELIZABETH	FRE	138	CREAGERS
SMELTZ, HENRY	ALL	091	5TH E.D.
SMELTZ, MARY	FRE	308	WOODSBOR
SMELTZ, MARY T.	BAL	007	9TH WARD
SMELTZER, ADAM R.	FRE	322	MIDDLETO
SMELTZER, DANIEL	FRE	329	MIDDLETO
SMELTZER, DAVID	CAR	401	2ND DIST
SMELTZER, HENRY R.	FRE	312	MIDDLETO
SMELTZER, JACOB	FRE	228	BUCKEYST
SMELTZER, JCHN	CAR	392	2ND DIST
SMELTZER, JOSIAH K.	FRE	384	PETERSVI
SMELTZER, WILLIAM H.	FRE	228	BUCKEYST
SMENNER, DANIEL	ALL	224	CUMBERLA
SMENNER, JOHN	ALL	206	CUMBERLA
SMENY, HENRY	BAL	261	20TH WAR
SMEVELIN, DANIEL	FRE	057	FREDERIC
SMIACH, NOAH	CAR	275	7TH DIST
SMICH, RACHEL	BAL	437	14TH WAR
SMICK, HENRY	BAL	101	1ST WARD
SMICK, JOHN	BAL	076	1ST WARD
SMICK, JOHN J.	BAL	124	1ST WARD
SMICK, LEWIS	BAL	293	7TH WARD
SMICK, PETER U.	BAL	390	8TH WARD
SMICK, PHILIP A.	BAL	162	6TH WARD
SMICK, SARAH E.	BAL	391	8TH WARD
SMICK, THOMS	BAL	182	2ND WARD
SMIDT, ANNA M.	BAL	037	15TH WAR
SMIDT, FRED	BAL	109	10TH WAR
SMIDT, MR.	BAL	222	17TH WAR
SMIDT, PETER	BAL	012	4TH WARD
SMIHT, ACAM	FRE	269	NEW MARK
SMIHT, ANNA	BAL	472	14TH WAR
SMIHT, CHARLES H.	BAL	435	14TH WAR
SMIHT, CAVID N.	QUE	207	3RD E DI
SMIHT, HENRY	FRE	327	MIDDLETO
SMIHT, MARTH AJ.	BAL	408	14TH WAR
SMIHT, RACHEL	QUE	207	3RD E DI
SMIHT, SAMUEL	QUE	209	3RD E DI
SMIHT, THOMAS L.	QUE	205	3RD E DI
SMIHT, WILLIAM	TAL	109	ST MICHA
SMILD, ELIZABETH	BAL	189	2ND WARD
SMILD, FREDERICK	BAL	201	2ND WARD
SMILD, JOSHUA	BAL	224	2ND WARD
SMILD, PETER	BAL	083	1ST WARD
SMILD, PHILIP	BAL	087	1ST WARD
SMILD.MICHAEL	BAL	201	2ND WARD
SMILEE, AARON	TAL	021	EASTON D
SMILEE, PHILIP	TAL	003	EASTON D
SMILER, CHARLES	TAL	019	EASTON D
SMILER, HENRY	TAL	019	EASTON D
SMILER, HENRY	TAL	098	ST MICHA
SMILER, MATILDA	TAL	072	EASTON T
SMILES, GEORGE	BAL	394	8TH WARD
SMILES, WILLIAM O.	BAL	402	8TH WARD
SMILEY, J.	BAL	154	1ST WARD
SMILEY, JANE	BAL	010	4TH WARD
SMILEY, MARGARET	BAL	159	11TH WAR
SMILEY, MARGARET	BAL	038	9TH WARD
SMILEY, PRICELLA	BAL	304	3RD WARD
SMILEY, RACHEL	BAL	175	6TH WARD
SMILEY, ROBERT	BAL	010	4TH WARD
SMILEY, ROBERT	BAL	067	18TH WAR
SMILSON, CHARLES A.	BAL	114	5TH WARD
SMILT, JOHN	BAL	104	1ST WARD
SMINK, ECEKARD	BAL	385	1ST DIST
SMINK, JACCB	BAL	386	1ST DIST
SMINK, JOSEPH	BAL	047	1ST WARD
SMIRIK, CHARLES	BAL	094	5TH WARD
SMIRK, CHARLES	BAL	094	5TH WARD
SMISER, HESTER	BAL	456	14TH WAR
SMITD, CATHARINE	BAL	273	2ND WARD
SMITD, JOHN A.	BAL	268	2ND WARD
SMITGH, JAMES E.	CAL	027	2ND DIST
SMITH, A.	BAL	164	1ST WARD
SMITH, A.	BAL	160	1ST WARD
SMITH, A.	BAL	172	1ST WARD
SMITH, A. S.	BAL	282	2ND WARD
SMITH, A.A.	WAS	001	WILLIAMS
SMITH, A.W.	BAL	258	12TH WAR
SMITH, ABIJAH	WAS	209	1ST DIST
SMITH, ABRAHAM	WAS	073	2ND SUBD
SMITH, ABRAHAM	WAS	043	2ND SUBD
SMITH, ABRAHAM	ANN	503	HOWARD D
SMITH, ABRAHAM	ANN	503	HOWARD D
SMITH, ABRAHAM	CAR	393	2ND DIST
SMITH, ABRAHAM	CAR	368	9TH DIST
SMITH, ABRAHAM	BAL	128	18TH WAR
SMITH, ABRAHAM	FRE	427	8TH E DI
SMITH, ABRAM	BAL	102	2ND DIST
SMITH, ACY	PRI	022	VANSVILL
SMITH, ADALINE	BAL	393	3RD WARD
SMITH, ADAM	ALL	224	CUMBERLA
SMITH, ADAM	BAL	178	2ND WARD
SMITH, ADAM	BAL	028	18TH WAR
SMITH, ACAM	CEC	042	CHESAPEA
SMITH, ADELINE MISS-	BAL	315	20TH WAR
SMITH, AGNES	CEC	002	ELKTON 3
SMITH, AGNESS	BAL	350	1ST DIST
SMITH, AHSALOM	FRE	173	5TH E DI
SMITH, AIELSEY	BAL	003	9TH WARD
SMITH, ALBERT	BAL	165	1ST WARD
SMITH, ALBERT	BAL	164	1ST WARD
SMITH, ALBERT	BAL	089	2ND DIST
SMITH, ALEXANDER	BAL	284	12TH WAR
SMITH, ALEXANDER	ANN	331	2ND DIST
SMITH, ALEXANDER	HAR	152	3RD DIST
SMITH, ALEXANDER	HAR	146	3RD DIST
SMITH, ALEXANDER	BAL	212	19TH WAR
SMITH, ALEXANDER	BAL	227	17TH WAR
SMITH, ALEXANDER	QUE	166	2ND E DI
SMITH, ALEXANDER	ST	262	3RD E DI
SMITH, ALEXANDER A.	BAL	447	14TH WAR
SMITH, ALEXANDER B.	PRI	027	VANSVILL
SMITH, ALEXANDER H.	TAL	043	EASTON D
SMITH, ALEY*	DOR	438	1ST DIST
SMITH, ALFRED	QUE	150	1ST E DI
SMITH, ALFRED-MULATTO	QUE	188	3RD E DI
SMITH, ALGIER	CAR	127	NO TWP L
SMITH, ALGIER	CAR	146	NO TWP L
SMITH, ALICE	BAL	191	17TH WAR
SMITH, ALSE	HAR	206	3RD DIST
SMITH, AMANDA	BAL	120	16TH WAR
SMITH, AMANDA	BAL	011	1ST WARD
SMITH, AMANDA E.	FRE	182	5TH E DI
SMITH, AMANDA L.	BAL	169	6TH WARD
SMITH, AMELIA	BAL	102	15TH WAR
SMITH, AMELIA	HAR	142	2ND DIST
SMITH, AMELIA M.	WOR	211	4TH E DI
SMITH, AMONINIAN	BAL	209	17TH WAR
SMITH, AMOS	WAS	299	1ST DIST
SMITH, AMOS	BAL	016	2ND DIST
SMITH, AMRY	BAL	361	13TH WAR
SMITH, AMRY	BAL	403	14TH WAR
SMITH, ANASTALIE *	ST	287	2ND E DI
SMITH, ANDERSON	BAL	205	19TH WAR
SMITH, ANDREW	BAL	445	14TH WAR
SMITH, ANDREW	BAL	445	14TH WAR
SMITH, ANDREW	BAL	445	14TH WAR
SMITH, ANDREW	BAL	081	4TH WARD
SMITH, ANDREW	BAL	119	18TH WAR
SMITH, ANDREW	BAL	140	19TH WAR
SMITH, ANDREW	FRE	297	WOODSBOR
SMITH, ANDREW	BAL	102	18TH WAR
SMITH, ANDREW	FRE	078	FREDERIC
SMITH, ANDREW	HAR	025	1ST DIST
SMITH, ANDREW	HAR	026	1ST DIST
SMITH, ANDREW	BAL	174	16TH WAR
SMITH, ANDREW	BAL	093	15TH WAR
SMITH, ANDREW	BAL	173	1ST WARD
SMITH, ANDREW	BAL	224	2ND WARD
SMITH, ANDREW	BAL	020	9TH WARD
SMITH, ANDREW	BAL	203	6TH WARD
SMITH, ANDREW	BAL	316	1ST DIST
SMITH, ANDREW	BAL	185	11TH WAR
SMITH, ANDREW	BAL	336	3RD WARD
SMITH, ANGELINE	BAL	012	2ND DIST
SMITH, ANN	BAL	066	2ND DIST
SMITH, ANN	BAL	333	1ST DIST
SMITH, ANN	BAL	458	1ST DIST
SMITH, ANN	BAL	377	1ST DIST
SMITH, ANN	BAL	190	11TH WAR
SMITH, ANN	BAL	268	12TH WAR
SMITH, ANN	BAL	167	11TH WAR
SMITH, ANN	ALL	105	5TH E.D.
SMITH, ANN	BAL	209	6TH WARD
SMITH, ANN	BAL	175	6TH WARD
SMITH, ANN	BAL	137	5TH WARD
SMITH, ANN	BAL	106	15TH WAR
SMITH, ANN	BAL	279	12TH WAR
SMITH, ANN	BAL	278	12TH WAR
SMITH, ANN	BAL	314	12TH WAR
SMITH, ANN	BAL	143	16TH WAR
SMITH, ANN	BAL	047	1ST WARD
SMITH, ANN	BAL	048	1ST WARD
SMITH, ANN	BAL	270	1ST DIST
SMITH, ANN	BAL	305	7TH WARD
SMITH, ANN	BAL	296	7TH WARD
SMITH, ANN	MGM	378	ROCKERLE
SMITH, ANN	KEN	214	2ND DIST
SMITH, ANN	BAL	357	13TH WAR
SMITH, ANN	BAL	043	4TH WARD
SMITH, ANN	BAL	397	14TH WAR
SMITH, ANN	BAL	135	11TH WAR
SMITH, ANN	CAL	051	3RD DIST
SMITH, ANN	BAL	213	11TH WAR
SMITH, ANN	CEC	023	ELKTON 3
SMITH, ANN	BAL	171	19TH WAR
SMITH, ANN	CAR	194	4TH DIST
SMITH, ANN	HAR	182	3RD DIST
SMITH, ANN	BAL	243	20TH WAR
SMITH, ANN	BAL	240	20TH WAR
SMITH, ANN	CEC	210	7TH E DI
SMITH, ANN	TAL	095	ST MICHA
SMITH, ANN	TAL	074	EASTON T
SMITH, ANN	TAL	065	EASTON T
SMITH, ANN	PRI	009	BLADENSB
SMITH, ANN	WAS	092	2ND SUBD
SMITH, ANN	KEN	311	3RD DIST
SMITH, ANN A M.	WAS	136	HAGERSTO
SMITH, ANN C.	BAL	064	10TH WAR
SMITH, ANN DELIA	BAL	428	14TH WAR
SMITH, ANN E.	BAL	140	11TH WAR
SMITH, ANN E.	MGM	428	CLARKSTR
SMITH, ANN E.	BAL	002	9TH WARD
SMITH, ANN E.	WAS	117	2ND DIST
SMITH, ANN J.	BAL	022	9TH WARD
SMITH, ANN L.-BLACK	BAL	214	2ND WARD
SMITH, ANN M.	BAL	341	3RD WARD
SMITH, ANN M.	WAS	123	HAGERSTO
SMITH, ANN M.	SOM	471	TRAPPE D
SMITH, ANN M.	FRE	088	FREDERIC
SMITH, ANN M.	BAL	053	4TH WARD
SMITH, ANN M.	FRE	119	CREAGERS
SMITH, ANN MARIA	BAL	387	13TH WAR
SMITH, ANN R.	BAL	050	18TH WAR
SMITH, ANN R.	WAS	195	1ST DIST
SMITH, ANNA	BAL	142	19TH WAR
SMITH, ANNA	BAL	386	1ST DIST
SMITH, ANNA	BAL	003	15TH WAR
SMITH, ANNA	BAL	298	1ST DIST
SMITH, ANNA E.	FRE	071	FREDERIC
SMITH, ANNA M.	BAL	409	1ST DIST
SMITH, ANNA M.-BLACK	QUE	128	1ST E DI
SMITH, ANNA-BLACK	QUE	157	2ND E DI
SMITH, ANNE	BAL	238	12TH WAR
SMITH, ANNE	BAL	096	15TH WAR
SMITH, ANNE	BAL	111	10TH WAR
SMITH, ANNE	BAL	093	10TH WAR
SMITH, ANNIE	BAL	415	3RD WARD
SMITH, ANTHONY	FRE	262	WOODSBOR
SMITH, ANTHONY	CAL	059	3RD DIST
SMITH, ANTHONY	ANN	461	HOWARD D
SMITH, ANTONY	BAL	400	8TH WARD
SMITH, ARAT	QUE	170	2ND E DI
SMITH, ARCHIBLD	BAL	096	2ND DIST
SMITH, ARTHUR	DOR	411	1ST DIST
SMITH, ARTHUR	KEN	239	2ND DIST
SMITH, ARUNDLE	PRI	008	BLADENSB
SMITH, ASA	DOR	311	1ST DIST
SMITH, ASA	BAL	192	5TH DIST
SMITH, ASA H.	BAL	441	14TH WAR
SMITH, AUGSUTUS	BAL	472	14TH WAR
SMITH, AUGUST	ALL	207	CUMBERLA
SMITH, AUGUSTINE	ALL	136	4TH E.D.
SMITH, AUGUSTUS	BAL	122	11TH WAR
SMITH, AUGUSTUS	BAL	222	17TH WAR
SMITH, AUGUSTUS	CEC	018	ELKTON 3
SMITH, AZA	ALL	002	3RD E.D.
SMITH, AZZITTA C.*	DOR	316	1ST DIST
SMITH, BARBARA	CAR	248	3RD DIST
SMITH, BARBARA	WAS	297	1ST DIST
SMITH, BARBARA M.	FRE	164	EMMITTSB
SMITH, BARRA	BAL	179	2ND WARD
SMITH, BARZILLA	DOR	420	1ST DIST
SMITH, BASIL	BAL	256	20TH WAR
SMITH, BASIL	ANN	384	4TH DIST
SMITH, BASIL D.	ANN	377	4TH DIST
SMITH, BATLZELL	FRE	347	MIDDLETO
SMITH, BENARD	BAL	110	5TH WARD
SMITH, BENJAMIN	BAL	376	1ST DIST
SMITH, BENJAMIN	BAL	029	2ND DIST
SMITH, BENJAMIN	BAL	190	17TH WAR
SMITH, BENJAMIN	BAL	100	15TH WAR
SMITH, BENJAMIN	BAL	432	8TH WARD
SMITH, BENJAMIN	FRE	285	WOODSBOR
SMITH, BENJAMIN	CHA	284	BOJANTOW
SMITH, BENJAMIN	BAL	417	14TH WAR
SMITH, BENJAMIN	CAL	043	3RD DIST
SMITH, BENJAMIN	FRE	077	FREDERIC
SMITH, BENJAMIN	SOM	420	PRINCESS
SMITH, BENJAMIN C.	WAS	178	BOONSBOR
SMITH, BENJAMIN-BLACK	CAR	165	NO TWP L
SMITH, BENJAMIN-BLACK	FRE	016	FREDERIC
SMITH, BENJIMAN	HAR	171	3RD DIST
SMITH, BERNARD	BAL	269	12TH WAR
SMITH, BESS	BAL	202	17TH WAR
SMITH, BETSEY	BAL	009	EASTERN
SMITH, BETSEY	SOM	470	TRAPPE D
SMITH, BETSY	BAL	003	EASTERN
SMITH, BETTY	ST	274	3RD E DI
SMITH, BETTY	BAL	029	4TH WARD
SMITH, BIDDY	BAL	350	13TH WAR
SMITH, BIDDY	SOM	527	QUANTICO
SMITH, BILL	ANN	404	8TH DIST
SMITH, BODOOTTO	BAL	015	15TH WAR
SMITH, BRIDGET	ANN	265	ANNAPOLI
SMITH, BRISTER	BAL	176	2ND DIST
SMITH, BUEL J.	HAR	020	1ST DIST
SMITH, BURTON	WOR	250	1ST CENS
SMITH, C.	BAL	163	1ST WARD
SMITH, C.	BAL	147	1ST WARD
SMITH, CAHRELS	ALL	152	6TH E.D.
SMITH, CAHRLES	BAL	147	1ST WARD
SMITH, CAROLINE	BAL	249	6TH WARD
SMITH, CAROLINE	BAL	216	6TH WARD
SMITH, CAROLINE	BAL	045	9TH WARD
SMITH, CAROLINE	BAL	067	15TH WAR
SMITH, CAROLINE	ALL	245	CUMBERLA
SMITH, CAROLINE	ANN	507	HOWARD D
SMITH, CAROLINE L.	BAL	242	6TH WARD
SMITH, CARROLL	BAL	122	1ST WARD
SMITH, CATHARIEN	BAL	298	12TH WAR
SMITH, CATHARIEN	FRE	283	WOODSBOR
SMITH, CATHARINE	FRE	296	WOODSBOR
SMITH, CATHARINE	FRE	319	MIDDLETO
SMITH, CATHARINE	BAL	220	17TH WAR
SMITH, CATHARINE	BAL	208	19TH WAR
SMITH, CATHARINE	BAL	244	20TH WAR
SMITH, CATHARINE	FRE	433	8TH E DI
SMITH, CATHARINE	FRE	425	8TH E DI
SMITH, CATHARINE	BAL	397	14TH WAR
SMITH, CATHARINE	CAR	388	2ND DIST
SMITH, CATHARINE	CAR	283	7TH DIST
SMITH, CATHARINE	BAL	157	16TH WAR
SMITH, CATHARINE	BAL	244	6TH WARD
SMITH, CATHARINE	BAL	459	1ST DIST
SMITH, CATHARINE	BAL	046	2ND DIST
SMITH, CATHARINE	BAL	353	7TH WARD
SMITH, CATHARINE	KEN	262	1ST DIST
SMITH, CATHARINE	WAS	086	2ND SUBD
SMITH, CATHERIN-BLACK	CAR	089	NO TWP L
SMITH, CATHERINE	WAS	107	2ND DIST
SMITH, CATHERINE	QUE	191	3RD E DI
SMITH, CATHERINE	QUE	206	3RD E DI
SMITH, CATHERINE	BAL	184	11TH WAR
SMITH, CATHERINE	BAL	291	3RD WARD
SMITH, CATHERINE	BAL	045	9TH WARD
SMITH, CATHERINE	BAL	386	3RD WARD
SMITH, CATHERINE E.	FRE	117	CREAGERS
SMITH, CATHERINE V.	CHA	245	HILLTOP
SMITH, CECELIA	BAL	276	20TH WAR
SMITH, CECELIA	BAL	115	15TH WAR
SMITH, CHARELS	BAL	146	1ST WARD
SMITH, CHARELS	BAL	197	19TH WAR
SMITH, CHARES	ANN	469	HOWARD D
SMITH, CHARITY	ANN	346	3RD DIST
SMITH, CHARLES	ANN	385	4TH DIST
SMITH, CHARLES	BAL	019	2ND DIST
SMITH, CHARLES	BAL	141	2ND DIST
SMITH, CHARLES	BAL	111	2ND DIST
SMITH, CHARLES	BAL	281	2ND WARD
SMITH, CHARLES	BAL	280	2ND WARD
SMITH, CHARLES	BAL	258	6TH WARD
SMITH, CHARLES	BAL	255	6TH WARD
SMITH, CHARLES	BAL	136	1ST WARD
SMITH, CHARLES	BAL	136	1ST WARD
SMITH, CHARLES	BAL	137	1ST WARD
SMITH, CHARLES	BAL	130	1ST WARD
SMITH, CHARLES	BAL	129	1ST WARD
SMITH, CHARLES	BAL	329	7TH WARD
SMITH, CHARLES	BAL	031	9TH WARD
SMITH, CHARLES	BAL	243	6TH WARD
SMITH, CHARLES	BAL	165	1ST WARD
SMITH, CHARLES	BAL	173	1ST WARD
SMITH, CHARLES	BAL	210	2ND WARD
SMITH, CHARLES	BAL	136	5TH WARD
SMITH, CHARLES	BAL	343	3RD WARD
SMITH, CHARLES	ANN	503	HOWARD D
SMITH, CHARLES	BAL	428	8TH WARD
SMITH, CHARLES	BAL	014	15TH WAR
SMITH, CHARLES	BAL	460	8TH WARD
SMITH, CHARLES	BAL	118	1ST WARD
SMITH, CHARLES	BAL	107	1ST WARD
SMITH, CHARLES	BAL	122	1ST WARD
SMITH, CHARLES	BAL	003	1ST WARD
SMITH, CHARLES	BAL	067	1ST WARD
SMITH, CHARLES	BAL	093	1ST WARD
SMITH, CHARLES	BAL	124	1ST WARD
SMITH, CHARLES	ANN	398	8TH DIST
SMITH, CHARLES	ALL	114	5TH E.D.
SMITH, CHARLES	HAR	183	3RD DIST
SMITH, CHARLES	QUE	149	1ST E DI
SMITH, CHARLES	FRE	146	10TH E D
SMITH, CHARLES	BAL	348	13TH WAR
SMITH, CHARLES	FRE	301	WOODSBOR
SMITH, CHARLES	MGM	425	MEDLEY 3
SMITH, CHARLES	FRE	044	FREDERIC
SMITH, CHARLES	SOM	496	SALISBUR
SMITH, CHARLES	PRI	089	SPALDING
SMITH, CHARLES	TAL	094	ST MICHA

Name	County	Page	District
SMITH, CHARLES A.	WAS	292	1ST DIST
SMITH, CHARLES A.	BAL	091	18TH WAR
SMITH, CHARLES C.	FRE	019	FREDERIC
SMITH, CHARLES C.	BAL	049	1ST WARD
SMITH, CHARLES H.	BAL	354	1ST DIST
SMITH, CHARLES H.	BAL	271	7TH WARD
SMITH, CHARLES JR.	SOM	479	TRAPP DI
SMITH, CHARLES L.	SOM	479	TRAPP DI
SMITH, CHARLES T.	BAL	145	1ST WARD
SMITH, CHARLES T.	DOR	316	1ST DIST
SMITH, CHARLES W.	BAL	029	18TH WAR
SMITH, CHARLES W.	FRE	073	FREDERIC
SMITH, CHARLES W.	BAL	391	14TH WAR
SMITH, CHARLES W.	CAR	092	NO TWP L
SMITH, CHARLOTT	FRE	076	FREDERIC
SMITH, CHARLOTT	BAL	462	1ST DIST
SMITH, CHARLOTTA	BAL	156	11TH WAR
SMITH, CHARLOTTE	SOM	435	PRINCESS
SMITH, CHARLOTTE	BAL	309	3RD WARD
SMITH, CHARLOTTE	BAL	248	12TH WAR
SMITH, CHARLOTTE	BAL	068	2ND DIST
SMITH, CHRELS T.	CEC	094	4TH E DI
SMITH, CHRISTIAN	FRE	078	FREDERIC
SMITH, CHRISTIAN	BAL	367	13TH WAR
SMITH, CHRISTIAN	BAL	233	17TH WAR
SMITH, CHRISTIAN	BAL	279	1ST DIST
SMITH, CHRISTIAN	ALL	168	6TH E.D.
SMITH, CHRISTIAN	BAL	127	5TH WARD
SMITH, CHRISTIAN	WAS	123	HAGERSTO
SMITH, CHRISTIANA	BAL	264	1ST DIST
SMITH, CHRISTIANA	CAR	237	UNION TO
SMITH, CHRISTINA	CAR	331	MANCHEST
SMITH, CHRISTY A.	FRE	229	BUCKEYST
SMITH, CLARANCY	BAL	179	11TH WAR
SMITH, CLEMENT	ALL	046	10TH E.D
SMITH, CLOTILDA	BAL	212	11TH WAR
SMITH, CONRAD	BAL	285	2ND WARD
SMITH, CONRAD	BAL	138	5TH WARD
SMITH, CONRAD	BAL	370	1ST DIST
SMITH, CONRAD	BAL	254	2ND WARD
SMITH, CONRAD	BAL	226	17TH WAR
SMITH, CONRAD	FRE	188	5TH E DI
SMITH, CONRADT	BAL	368	8TH WARD
SMITH, CCONROD	BAL	139	2ND DIST
SMITH, CORA	CEC	178	7TH E DI
SMITH, CORA E.	ST	306	1ST E DI
SMITH, CORDELIA	BAL	369	8TH WARD
SMITH, CORELLA H.	FRE	243	NEW MARK
SMITH, CORNELIUS	CEC	146	PORT DUP
SMITH, CRESTIAN	BAL	050	18TH WAR
SMITH, CUNROD	FRE	339	MIDDLETO
SMITH, CYNTHIA	CEC	005	ELKTON 3
SMITH, CYRUS	BAL	119	5TH WARD
SMITH, D.	BAL	151	1ST WARD
SMITH, D.*	TAL	036	EASTON D
SMITH, D.H.	WAS	127	HAGERSTO
SMITH, CANIEL	WAS	202	1ST DIST
SMITH, CANIEL	WAS	054	2ND SUBD
SMITH, DANIEL	WAS	182	BOONSBOR
SMITH, DANIEL	QUE	235	4TH E DI
SMITH, CANIEL	BAL	161	1ST WARD
SMITH, CANIEL	BAL	147	1ST WARD
SMITH, DANIEL	BAL	138	1ST WARD
SMITH, DANIEL	BAL	084	2ND DIST
SMITH, DANIEL	ANN	297	1ST DIST
SMITH, DANIEL	FRE	327	MIDDLETO
SMITH, CANIEL	FRE	335	MIDDLETO
SMITH, DANIEL	BAL	155	19TH WAR
SMITH, DANIEL	QUE	124	1ST E DI
SMITH, DANIEL	HAR	171	3RD DIST
SMITH, DANIEL	FRE	118	CREAGERS
SMITH, DANIEL	FRE	083	FREDERIC
SMITH, DANIEL	FRE	071	FREDERIC
SMITH, CANIEL	HAR	043	1ST DIST
SMITH, DANIEL R.	HAR	206	3RD DIST
SMITH, DARKNESS	BAL	021	18TH WAR
SMITH, DAVID	KEN	208	2ND DIST
SMITH, DAVID	FRE	325	MIDDLETO
SMITH, CAVID	FRE	357	CATOCTIN
SMITH, DAVID	FRE	351	MIDDLETO
SMITH, DAVID	FRE	364	CATOCTIN
SMITH, CAVID	CAR	307	1ST DIST
SMITH, CAVID	CEC	122	4TH E DI
SMITH, CAVID	FRE	029	FREDERIC
SMITH, DAVID	BAL	246	20TH WAR
SMITH, CAVID	FRE	395	PETERSVI
SMITH, DAVID	DOR	337	3RD DIVI
SMITH, CAVID	BAL	051	2ND DIST
SMITH, DAVID	BAL	159	1ST WARD
SMITH, DAVID	BAL	097	1ST WARD
SMITH, DAVID	BAL	020	1ST WARD
SMITH, DAVID	WOR	328	1ST E DI
SMITH, DAVID	WAS	042	2ND SUBD
SMITH, CAVID	WAS	255	1ST DIST
SMITH, DEBORAH	CAR	168	NO TWP L
SMITH, DENIS A.	BAL	277	1ST DIST
SMITH, DENNIS	FRE	171	5TH E DI
SMITH, DENNIS	TAL	077	EASTON T
SMITH, DENNIS	TAL	074	EASTON T
SMITH, DEVORIX	DOR	318	1ST DIST
SMITH, DIANNA	BAL	191	5TH DIST
SMITH, DOLLY	CAL	037	2ND DIST
SMITH, DORCAS	BAL	048	4TH WARD
SMITH, E.	BAL	117	1ST WARD
SMITH, E.	BAL	141	5TH WARD
SMITH, E. J.	KEN	218	2ND DIST
SMITH, E.G.	BAL	142	1ST WARD
SMITH, EASTER	BAL	181	16TH WAR
SMITH, EASTHEN	WOR	326	1ST E DI
SMITH, EBENEZER	WOR	201	3RD E DI
SMITH, EBENEZER	BAL	416	3RD WARD
SMITH, EDMUND	BAL	121	5TH WARD
SMITH, EDMUND	BAL	118	2ND DIST
SMITH, EDWARD	BAL	011	2ND DIST
SMITH, EDWARD	BAL	121	16TH WAR
SMITH, EDWARC	BAL	155	1ST WARD
SMITH, EDWARD	BAL	124	1ST WARD
SMITH, EDWARD	BAL	171	2ND DIST
SMITH, EDWARD	BAL	383	1ST DIST
SMITH, EDWARD	BAL	343	3RD WARD
SMITH, EDWARD	BAL	209	11TH WAR
SMITH, EDWARD	BAL	359	13TH WAR
SMITH, EDWARD	FRE	380	PETERSVI
SMITH, EDWARC	CHA	293	BOJANTOW
SMITH, EELIZA	TAL	072	EASTON T
SMITH, ELEANOR	MGM	382	ROCKERLE
SMITH, ELEXANDER	HAR	167	3RD DIST
SMITH, ELEXANDER	HAR	157	3RD DIST
SMITH, ELI	FRE	165	EMMITTSB
SMITH, ELI	FRE	040	FREDERIC
SMITH, ELI	FRE	298	WOODSBOR
SMITH, ELI	BAL	143	11TH WAR
SMITH, ELI	BAL	067	18TH WAR
SMITH, ELI	CAR	374	9TH DIST
SMITH, ELIAS	SOM	399	BRINKLEY
SMITH, ELIAS	WAS	022	2ND SUBD
SMITH, ELIAS	BAL	133	1ST WARD
SMITH, ELIAS J.	BAL	414	3RD WARD
SMITH, ELIHU	BAL	390	1ST DIST
SMITH, ELIJAH	BAL	353	7TH WARD
SMITH, ELIJAH	ANN	358	3RD DIST
SMITH, ELIJAH	ANN	318	2ND DIST
SMITH, ELIJAH	CAR	209	5TH DIST
SMITH, ELIJAH	BAL	009	4TH WARD
SMITH, ELIJAH	QUE	140	1ST E DI
SMITH, ELIJAH	PRI	091	MARLBROU
SMITH, ELIJAH S.	PRI	003	BLADENSB
SMITH, ELIJAH-BLACK	CAR	170	NO TWP L
SMITH, ELISA	KEN	210	2ND DIST
SMITH, ELISA C.	BAL	419	14TH WAR
SMITH, ELISABETH	BAL	422	14TH WAR
SMITH, ELISABETH	ALL	229	CUMBERLA
SMITH, ELISABETH	BAL	056	10TH WAR
SMITH, ELISHA	CEC	130	6TH E DI
SMITH, ELISHA	HAR	188	3RD DIST
SMITH, ELIZ	BAL	240	12TH WAR
SMITH, ELIZA	BAL	346	7TH WARD
SMITH, ELIZA	ALL	032	2ND E.D.
SMITH, ELIZA	ANN	513	HOWARD D
SMITH, ELIZA	BAL	361	8TH WARD
SMITH, ELIZA	BAL	107	1ST WARD
SMITH, ELIZA	BAL	384	13TH WAR
SMITH, ELIZA	FRE	321	MIDDLETO
SMITH, ELIZA	CAR	287	7TH DIST
SMITH, ELIZA	BAL	445	14TH WAR
SMITH, ELIZA	BAL	443	14TH WAR
SMITH, ELIZA	CAL	017	1ST DIST
SMITH, ELIZA	HAR	027	1ST DIST
SMITH, ELIZA	ST	286	2ND E DI
SMITH, ELIZA A.	BAL	311	7TH WARD
SMITH, ELIZA A.	BAL	173	6TH WARD
SMITH, ELIZA A.-BLACK	BAL	208	2ND WARD
SMITH, ELIZA BOSTIC	CEC	094	4TH E DI
SMITH, ELIZA J.	BAL	021	4TH WARD
SMITH, ELIZA S.	CAR	285	7TH DIST
SMITH, ELIZABETH	CAR	384	2ND DIST
SMITH, ELIZABETH	BAL	012	4TH WARD
SMITH, ELIZABETH	FRE	346	MIDDLETO
SMITH, ELIZABETH	FRE	346	MIDDLETO
SMITH, ELIZABETH	BAL	214	11TH WAR
SMITH, ELIZABETH	BAL	205	19TH WAR
SMITH, ELIZABETH	SOM	438	DAMES QU
SMITH, ELIZABETH	BAL	465	14TH WAR
SMITH, ELIZABETH	CAR	107	NO TWP L
SMITH, ELIZABETH	CAL	049	3RD DIST
SMITH, ELIZABETH	FRE	311	MIDDLETO
SMITH, ELIZABETH	BAL	157	19TH WAR
SMITH, ELIZABETH	FRE	230	BUCKEYST
SMITH, ELIZABETH	FRE	230	BUCKEYST
SMITH, ELIZABETH	CEC	146	PORT DUP
SMITH, ELIZABETH	HAR	162	3RD DIST
SMITH, ELIZABETH	BAL	254	20TH WAR
SMITH, ELIZABETH	FRE	426	8TH E DI
SMITH, ELIZABETH	BAL	126	5TH WARD
SMITH, ELIZABETH	BAL	219	6TH WARD
SMITH, ELIZABETH	BAL	047	9TH WARD
SMITH, ELIZABETH	BAL	268	2ND WARD
SMITH, ELIZABETH	BAL	250	6TH WARD
SMITH, ELIZABETH	BAL	162	2ND DIST
SMITH, ELIZABETH	BAL	373	3RD WARD
SMITH, ELIZABETH	BAL	075	1ST WARD
SMITH, ELIZABETH	BAL	403	1ST DIST
SMITH, ELIZABETH	BAL	411	1ST DIST
SMITH, ELIZABETH	BAL	410	1ST DIST
SMITH, ELIZABETH	BAL	391	1ST DIST
SMITH, ELIZABETH	BAL	445	1ST DIST
SMITH, ELIZABETH	ALL	114	5TH E.D.
SMITH, ELIZABETH	BAL	250	12TH WAR
SMITH, ELIZABETH	BAL	014	9TH WARD
SMITH, ELIZABETH	BAL	432	8TH WARD
SMITH, ELIZABETH	BAL	173	16TH WAR
SMITH, ELIZABETH	BAL	080	10TH WAR
SMITH, ELIZABETH	ANN	461	HOWARD D
SMITH, ELIZABETH	WAS	131	HAGERSTO
SMITH, ELIZABETH	WAS	039	2ND SUBD
SMITH, ELIZABETH	WAS	113	2ND DIST
SMITH, ELIZABETH	WAS	096	2ND SUBD
SMITH, ELIZABETH	WOR	178	6TH E DI
SMITH, ELIZABETH	PRI	059	NOTTINGH
SMITH, ELIZABETH	WAS	249	1ST DIST
SMITH, ELIZABETH	WAS	123	HAGERSTO
SMITH, ELIZABETH A.	BAL	368	3RD WARD
SMITH, ELIZABETH A.	CEC	154	PORT DUP
SMITH, ELIZABETH B.	PRI	032	VANSVILL
SMITH, ELIZABETH P.	BAL	119	15TH WAR
SMITH, ELIZABETH W.	KEN	223	2ND DIST
SMITH, ELIZBETH	BAL	171	11TH WAR
SMITH, ELLEN	BAL	166	11TH WAR
SMITH, ELLEN	BAL	022	1ST WARD
SMITH, ELLEN	ANN	327	2ND DIST
SMITH, ELLEN	ANN	398	8TH DIST
SMITH, ELLEN	ANN	519	HOWARD D
SMITH, ELLEN	BAL	105	5TH WARD
SMITH, ELLEN	BAL	463	1ST DIST
SMITH, ELLEN	BAL	298	7TH WARD
SMITH, ELLEN	BAL	160	6TH WARD
SMITH, ELLEN	BAL	141	5TH WARD
SMITH, ELLEN	BAL	415	14TH WAR
SMITH, ELLEN	FRE	012	FREDERIC
SMITH, ELLEN	BAL	129	11TH WAR
SMITH, ELLEN	FRE	342	MIDDLETO
SMITH, ELLEN	CAR	167	NO TWP L
SMITH, ELLEN W.	MGM	415	MEDLEY 3
SMITH, ELLEN-BLACK	QUE	187	3RD E DI
SMITH, ELLEN-MULATTO	FRE	383	PETERSVI
SMITH, ELLIS	BAL	202	11TH WAR
SMITH, ELNORA	SOM	552	TYASKIN
SMITH, ELSY	BAL	263	20TH WAR
SMITH, ELY	HAR	111	2ND DIST
SMITH, ELY	BAL	211	19TH WAR
SMITH, EM.	FRE	308	WOODSBOR
SMITH, EMANUEL	BAL	007	EASTERN
SMITH, EMELIA *	TAL	096	ST MICHA
SMITH, EMELINE	BAL	073	15TH WAR
SMITH, EMELINE	BAL	111	15TH WAR
SMITH, EMELINE*	BAL	034	4TH WARD
SMITH, EMILY	BAL	007	4TH WARD
SMITH, EMILY	CAR	227	5TH DIST
SMITH, EMILY	DOR	312	1ST DIST
SMITH, EMILY	FRE	162	EMMITTSB
SMITH, EMILY	BAL	125	5TH WARD
SMITH, EMILY L.J.	BAL	323	7TH WARD
SMITH, EMMA	ALL	245	CUMBERLA
SMITH, EMMA	BAL	192	19TH WAR
SMITH, EMMELINE	WOR	204	4TH E DI
SMITH, EMMERY	PRI	001	BLADENSB
SMITH, EMORY	BAL	119	1ST WARD
SMITH, EPHRAIM	WAS	076	2ND SUBD
SMITH, ERESSUM	WOR	256	1ST CENS
SMITH, ESTHER	BAL	172	2ND DIST
SMITH, EUGENE J.	ALL	095	5TH E.D.
SMITH, EVELINE	BAL	105	15TH WAR
SMITH, EZEKIEL	QUE	150	1ST E DI
SMITH, EZRA	FRE	297	WOODSBOR
SMITH, EZRA	FRE	296	WOODSBOR
SMITH, EZRA	FRE	320	MIDDLETO
SMITH, EZRA	WAS	231	1ST DIST
SMITH, F.B.	CAL	050	3RD DIST
SMITH, FAINY	BAL	114	5TH WARD
SMITH, FANNEY	BAL	342	7TH WARD
SMITH, FANNY	BAL	368	3RD WARD
SMITH, FANNY	BAL	140	2ND DIST
SMITH, FANNY	BAL	123	5TH WARD
SMITH, FANNY	BAL	419	3RD WARD
SMITH, FANNY	TAL	068	EASTON T
SMITH, FANNY V.	BAL	397	3RD WARD
SMITH, FERDINAND	BAL	320	1ST DIST
SMITH, FERDINAND	BAL	317	1ST DIST
SMITH, FERDINAND	BAL	145	19TH WAR
SMITH, FERNETTA F.	HAR	164	3RD DIST
SMITH, FLORA	BAL	183	11TH WAR
SMITH, FLORA	BAL	114	15TH WAR
SMITH, FRANCEANER	CAR	231	5TH DIST
SMITH, FRANCES	BAL	202	19TH WAR
SMITH, FRANCES	DOR	313	1ST DIST
SMITH, FRANCES	BAL	283	20TH WAR
SMITH, FRANCES	BAL	055	4TH WARD
SMITH, FRANCES	BAL	094	10TH WAR
SMITH, FRANCES	BAL	168	16TH WAR
SMITH, FRANCES ANNA	DOR	317	1ST DIST
SMITH, FRANCIS	BAL	338	13TH WAR
SMITH, FRANCIS	BAL	213	11TH WAR
SMITH, FRANCIS	FRE	167	EMMITTSB
SMITH, FRANCIS	FRE	334	MIDDLETO
SMITH, FRANCIS	CAR	375	9TH DIST
SMITH, FRANCIS	BAL	027	18TH WAR
SMITH, FRANCIS	BAL	285	17TH WAR
SMITH, FRANCIS	BAL	206	11TH WAR
SMITH, FRANCIS	BAL	026	2ND DIST
SMITH, FRANCIS	BAL	351	3RD WARD
SMITH, FRANCIS	BAL	124	1ST WARD
SMITH, FRANCIS	BAL	121	1ST WARD
SMITH, FRANCIS	BAL	102	5TH WARD
SMITH, FRANCIS	BAL	227	6TH WARD
SMITH, FRANCIS	WAS	152	HAGERSTO
SMITH, FRANCIS	ST	309	1ST E DI
SMITH, FRANCIS A.	BAL	209	6TH WARD
SMITH, FRANCIS H.	BAL	150	11TH WAR
SMITH, FRANCIS L.	ST	304	2ND E DI
SMITH, FRANCIS P.	CEC	175	7TH E DI
SMITH, FRANK	BAL	165	2ND DIST
SMITH, FRANKLIN	BAL	127	18TH WAR
SMITH, FRANKLIN	HAR	167	3RD DIST
SMITH, FRANKLING J.	CAR	183	8TH DIST
SMITH, FRANNY	BAL	142	11TH WAR
SMITH, FRED	BAL	449	1ST DIST
SMITH, FREDERIC	BAL	173	6TH WARD
SMITH, FREDERIC	BAL	029	2ND DIST
SMITH, FREDERICK	BAL	443	1ST DIST
SMITH, FREDERICK	BAL	167	2ND DIST
SMITH, FREDERICK	BAL	171	2ND DIST
SMITH, FREDERICK	BAL	079	10TH WAR
SMITH, FREDERICK	HAR	176	3RD DIST
SMITH, FREDERICK	BAL	157	19TH WAR
SMITH, FRIDOLIN M.	WAS	189	1ST DIST
SMITH, FRISBY	KEN	256	1ST DIST
SMITH, FRISBY	BAL	048	9TH WARD
SMITH, FRISBY	BAL	165	1ST WARD
SMITH, G. F.	BAL	293	3RD WARD
SMITH, G.W.	ALL	049	10TH E.D
SMITH, G.W.	WAS	123	HAGERSTO
SMITH, GABRIEL	BAL	065	4TH WARD
SMITH, GAMABEL *	BAL	290	20TH WAR
SMITH, GARRISON	BAL	401	14TH WAR
SMITH, GASPER	HAR	156	3RD DIST
SMITH, GEORGE	FRE	151	10TH E D
SMITH, GEORGE	CHA	283	BOJANTOW
SMITH, GEORGE	BAL	293	20TH WAR
SMITH, GEORGE	CEC	194	7TH E DI
SMITH, GEORGE	FRE	001	FREDERIC
SMITH, GEORGE	DOR	368	3RD DIVI
SMITH, GEORGE	DOR	368	3RD DIVI
SMITH, GEORGE	FRE	271	NEW MARK
SMITH, GEORGE	BAL	163	19TH WAR
SMITH, GEORGE	FRE	284	WOODSBOR
SMITH, GEORGE	FRE	296	WOODSBOR
SMITH, GEORGE	FRE	320	MIDDLETO
SMITH, GEORGE	CAR	204	4TH DIST
SMITH, GEORGE	BAL	199	19TH WAR
SMITH, GEORGE	BAL	197	19TH WAR
SMITH, GEORGE	BAL	420	3RD WARD
SMITH, GEORGE	BAL	416	3RD WARD
SMITH, CEORGE	BAL	004	4TH WARD
SMITH, GEORGE	FRE	346	MIDDLETO
SMITH, GEORGE	CAR	252	3RD DIST
SMITH, GEORGE	CEC	056	1ST E DI
SMITH, GEORGE	FRE	079	FREDERIC
SMITH, GEORGE	FRE	079	FREDERIC
SMITH, GEORGE	FRE	098	FREDERIC
SMITH, GEORGE	ST	303	2ND E DI
SMITH, GEORGE	WAS	239	CAVETOWN
SMITH, GEORGE	WAS	238	CAVETOWN
SMITH, GEORGE	WAS	209	1ST DIST
SMITH, GEORGE	KEN	270	1ST DIST
SMITH, GEORGE	WAS	193	1ST DIST
SMITH, GEORGE	WAS	183	BOONSBOR
SMITH, GEORGE	ST	263	3RD E DI
SMITH, GEORGE	WAS	087	2ND SUBD
SMITH, GEORGE	TAL	019	EASTON D
SMITH, GEORGE	ANN	299	1ST DIST
SMITH, GEORGE	ALL	169	6TH E.D.
SMITH, GEORGE	ALL	215	CUMBERLA
SMITH, GEORGE	BAL	387	1ST DIST
SMITH, GEORGE	BAL	388	1ST DIST
SMITH, GEORGE	BAL	305	3RD WARD
SMITH, GEORGE	BAL	161	1ST WARD
SMITH, GEORGE	BAL	165	1ST WARD
SMITH, GEORGE	BAL	168	1ST WARD
SMITH, GEORGE	BAL	178	2ND WARD
SMITH, GEORGE	BAL	138	16TH WAR

SMITH, GEORGE BAL 292 1ST DIST
SMITH, GEORGE ALL 241 CUMBERLA
SMITH, GEORGE BAL 106 2ND DIST
SMITH, GEORGE BAL 100 2ND DIST
SMITH, GEORGE BAL 010 15TH WAR
SMITH, GEORGE BAL 341 7TH WARD
SMITH, GEORGE BAL 060 15TH WAR
SMITH, GEORGE BAL 045 15TH WAR
SMITH, GEORGE BAL 140 1ST WARD
SMITH, GEORGE BAL 303 7TH WARD
SMITH, GEORGE BAL 282 2ND WARD
SMITH, GEORGE BAL 401 8TH WARD
SMITH, GEORGE A. BAL 392 8TH WARD
SMITH, GEORGE A. BAL 034 18TH WAR
SMITH, GEORGE A. CAR 375 9TH DIST
SMITH, GEORGE A. F. DOR 447 1ST DIST
SMITH, GEORGE C. BAL 401 1ST DIST
SMITH, GEORGE D. BAL 010 4TH WARD
SMITH, GEORGE E. FRE 402 JEFFERSO
SMITH, GEORGE G. FRE 283 WOODSBOR
SMITH, GEORGE H. ST 290 2ND E DI
SMITH, GEORGE H. ST 311 1ST E DI
SMITH, GEORGE M. BAL 079 15TH WAR
SMITH, GEORGE P. WOR 303 SNOW HIL
SMITH, GEORGE R. WOR 200 3RD E DI
SMITH, GEORGE W. WOR 192 8TH E DI
SMITH, GEORGE W. WAS 183 BOONSBOR
SMITH, GEORGE W. BAL 407 1ST DIST
SMITH, GEORGE W. BAL 120 1ST WARD
SMITH, GEORGE W. BAL 114 1ST WARD
SMITH, GEORGE W. BAL 159 1ST WARD
SMITH, GEORGE W. BAL 181 19TH WAR
SMITH, GEORGE W. CAR 209 5TH DIST
SMITH, GEORGE W. BAL 080 18TH WAR
SMITH, GEORGE W. BAL 445 14TH WAR
SMITH, GEORGE W. BAL 445 14TH WAR
SMITH, GEORGE W. L. BAL 007 9TH WARD
SMITH, GEORGE* SOM 479 TRAPP DI
SMITH, GEORGEANA BAL 054 4TH WARD
SMITH, GEORGIANNA BAL 363 13TH WAR
SMITH, GEORGIANNA BAL 192 17TH WAR
SMITH, GEORGIANNA BAL 014 2ND DIST
SMITH, CEROGE W. HAR 008 1ST DIST
SMITH, GIDAN HAR 032 1ST DIST
SMITH, GIDEON B. BAL 250 12TH WAR
SMITH, GILBERT BAL 178 2ND WARD
SMITH, GIZZY* BAL 301 3RD WARD
SMITH, GOERGE BAL 138 5TH WARD
SMITH, GRAFTON ANN 371 4TH DIST
SMITH, GRIFFIN BAL 011 1ST WARD
SMITH, GUSTAVUS V. ANN 412 HOWARD D
SMITH, H. BAL 166 1ST WARD
SMITH, H. BAL 130 1ST WARD
SMITH, H. BAL 136 1ST WARD
SMITH, H. BAL 233 20TH WAR
SMITH, H.C. BAL 138 1ST WARD
SMITH, HAGEC BAL 175 11TH WAR
SMITH, HAMILTON BAL 251 12TH WAR
SMITH, HAMILTON J. ANN 299 1ST DIST
SMITH, HAMPDEN SOM 468 TRAPPE D
SMITH, HANNA-BLACK FRE 044 FREDERIC
SMITH, HANNA-BLACK QUE 143 1ST E DI
SMITH, HANNAH SOM 409 DUBLIN D
SMITH, HANNAH BAL 217 19TH WAR
SMITH, HANNAH CEC 144 PORT DUP
SMITH, HANNAH BAL 395 14TH WAR
SMITH, HANNAH BAL 166 19TH WAR
SMITH, HANNAH BAL 166 19TH WAR
SMITH, HANNAH KEN 213 2ND DIST
SMITH, HANNAH ALL 037 2ND E.D.
SMITH, HANNAH BAL 170 11TH WAR
SMITH, HANNAH BAL 020 15TH WAR
SMITH, HANNAH BAL 427 1ST DIST
SMITH, HANNAH C. BAL 249 12TH WAR
SMITH, HARIET BAL 090 18TH WAR
SMITH, HARIOTT DOR 412 1ST DIST
SMITH, HARRIET BAL 395 14TH WAR
SMITH, HARRIET CEC 215 7TH E DI
SMITH, HARRIET BAL 008 15TH WAR
SMITH, HARRIET ANN 507 HOWARD D
SMITH, HARRIET ANN 278 ANNAPOLI
SMITH, HARRIET BAL 183 5TH DIST
SMITH, HARRIET BAL 107 15TH WAR
SMITH, HARRIET PRI 078 MARLBROU
SMITH, HARRIET TAL 120 ST MICHA
SMITH, HARRIET A. BAL 161 6TH WARD
SMITH, HARRIETT QUE 234 4TH E DI
SMITH, HARRIS BAL 447 14TH WAR
SMITH, HARRY SOM 433 PRINCESS
SMITH, HARRY WAS 123 HAGERSTO
SMITH, HARRY TAL 005 EASTON D
SMITH, HARTMAN BAL 443 8TH WARD
SMITH, HEIRAM BAL 118 1ST WARD
SMITH, HENDERSON CEC 172 6TH E DI
SMITH, HENERETTA BAL 332 13TH WAR
SMITH, HENERY DOR 339 3RD DIVI
SMITH, HENNEY BAL 412 8TH WARD
SMITH, HENR BAL 145 1ST WARD
SMITH, HENRIETTA BAL 167 11TH WAR
SMITH, HENRIETTA BAL 110 2ND DIST
SMITH, HENRIETTA CAR 315 1ST DIST
SMITH, HENRIETTA TAL 022 EASTON D
SMITH, HENRIETTA WAS 244 SMITHSBU
SMITH, HENRY WAS 202 1ST DIST
SMITH, HENRY WAS 093 2ND SUBD
SMITH, HENRY WAS 078 2ND SUBD
SMITH, HENRY WOR 265 BERLIN 1
SMITH, HENRY TAL 049 EASTON T
SMITH, HENRY TAL 088 ST MICHA
SMITH, HENRY FRE 354 MIDDLETO
SMITH, HENRY CAR 204 4TH DIST
SMITH, HENRY FRE 027 FREDERIC
SMITH, HENRY HAR 039 1ST DIST
SMITH, HENRY FRE 075 FREDERIC
SMITH, HENRY FRE 071 FREDERIC
SMITH, HENRY DOR 431 1ST DIST
SMITH, HENRY HAR 205 3RD DIST
SMITH, HENRY FRE 274 NEW MARK
SMITH, HENRY BAL 156 19TH WAR
SMITH, HENRY FRE 247 NEW MARK
SMITH, HENRY BAL 072 18TH WAR
SMITH, HENRY BAL 039 18TH WAR
SMITH, HENRY FRE 169 5TH E DI
SMITH, HENRY FRE 151 10TH E D
SMITH, HENRY BAL 314 20TH WAR
SMITH, HENRY HAR 183 3RD DIST
SMITH, HENRY MGM 346 CLARKSBU
SMITH, HENRY HAR 124 2ND DIST
SMITH, HENRY MGM 352 BERRYS D
SMITH, HENRY BAL 143 2ND DIST

SMITH, HENRY BAL 118 2ND DIST
SMITH, HENRY ANN 360 3RD DIST
SMITH, HENRY ALL 245 CUMBERLA
SMITH, HENRY BAL 067 2ND DIST
SMITH, HENRY BAL 340 7TH WARD
SMITH, HENRY BAL 234 12TH WAR
SMITH, HENRY BAL 458 8TH WARD
SMITH, HENRY BAL 197 11TH WAR
SMITH, HENRY BAL 180 11TH WAR
SMITH, HENRY BAL 138 1ST WARD
SMITH, HENRY BAL 393 8TH WARD
SMITH, HENRY BAL 125 1ST WARD
SMITH, HENRY BAL 250 2ND WARD
SMITH, HENRY BAL 293 7TH WARD
SMITH, HENRY BAL 322 7TH WARD
SMITH, HENRY BAL 280 12TH WAR
SMITH, HENRY BAL 302 12TH WAR
SMITH, HENRY BAL 118 1ST WARD
SMITH, HENRY BAL 123 1ST WARD
SMITH, HENRY BAL 088 1ST WARD
SMITH, HENRY BAL 256 1ST DIST
SMITH, HENRY BAL 275 1ST DIST
SMITH, HENRY BAL 159 1ST WARD
SMITH, HENRY BAL 173 6TH WARD
SMITH, HENRY BAL 306 1ST DIST
SMITH, HENRY ANN 320 2ND DIST
SMITH, HENRY ANN 334 2ND DIST
SMITH, HENRY BAL 104 5TH WARD
SMITH, HENRY BAL 105 5TH WARD
SMITH, HENRY ANN 518 HOWARD D
SMITH, HENRY ANN 512 HOWARD D
SMITH, HENRY C. BAL 198 11TH WAR
SMITH, HENRY CLAY BAL 124 1ST WARD
SMITH, HENRY H. BAL 018 9TH WARD
SMITH, HENRY J. WOR 209 4TH E DI
SMITH, HENSON BAL 065 4TH WARD
SMITH, HERMAN A. BAL 403 14TH WAR
SMITH, HESEKIAH BAL 320 7TH WARD
SMITH, HESTER ANN 278 ANNAPOLI
SMITH, HESTER DOR 297 1ST DIST
SMITH, HESTER BAL 340 13TH WAR
SMITH, HESTER WOR 180 6TH E DI
SMITH, HETTY BAL 025 9TH WARD
SMITH, HEZEKIAH SOM 551 TYASKIN
SMITH, HIRAM J. WAS 268 1ST DIST
SMITH, HORACE BAL 235 6TH WARD
SMITH, HORACE ANN 272 ANNAPOLI
SMITH, HORACE BAL 139 1ST WARD
SMITH, HORATIO ANN 324 2ND DIST
SMITH, HORRACE BAL 112 18TH WAR
SMITH, HUGH BAL 179 11TH WAR
SMITH, HUGH BAL 015 15TH WAR
SMITH, HUGH ALL 259 CUMBERLA
SMITH, HUGH ANN 441 HOWARD D
SMITH, HUTCHENS H. QUE 135 1ST E DI
SMITH, IGNATIUS BAL 052 2ND DIST
SMITH, IRA BAL 122 11TH WAR
SMITH, IRA BAL 189 19TH WAR
SMITH, IRRA WAS 071 2ND SUBD
SMITH, ISAAC PRI 027 VANSVILL
SMITH, ISAAC CAR 229 5TH DIST
SMITH, ISAAC CAL 015 1ST DIST
SMITH, ISAAC FRE 263 WOODSBOR
SMITH, ISAAC CAR 382 2ND DIST
SMITH, ISAAC CEC 106 3RD E DI
SMITH, ISAAC BAL 448 8TH WARD
SMITH, ISAAC BAL 342 7TH WARD
SMITH, ISAAC ALL 193 9TH E.D.
SMITH, ISAAC BAL 169 1ST WARD
SMITH, ISAAC BAL 163 2ND DIST
SMITH, ISAAC H. BAL 282 20TH WAR
SMITH, ISABEL CAL 038 2ND DIST
SMITH, ISABELLA BAL 367 13TH WAR
SMITH, ISACK TAL 033 EASTON D
SMITH, ISRAEL WAS 040 2ND SUBD
SMITH, ISREAL FRE 057 FREDERIC
SMITH, J. BAL 201 19TH WAR
SMITH, J. BAL 117 1ST WARD
SMITH, J. BAL 118 1ST WARD
SMITH, J. BAL 165 1ST WARD
SMITH, J. BAL 138 1ST WARD
SMITH, J. B. BAL 320 1ST DIST
SMITH, J. BN. BAL 329 13TH WAR
SMITH, J. BOWEN BAL 364 13TH WAR
SMITH, J. D. BAL 065 4TH WARD
SMITH, J. F. ALL 161 6TH E.D.
SMITH, J. G. BAL 154 1ST WARD
SMITH, J. IRWIN BAL 300 20TH WAR
SMITH, J. L. H. BAL 470 14TH WAR
SMITH, J. SPEAR BAL 284 12TH WAR
SMITH, J.A. BAL 163 1ST WARD
SMITH, J.H. BAL 159 1ST WARD
SMITH, J.H. BAL 160 1ST WARD
SMITH, J.H. BAL 160 1ST WARD
SMITH, J.H. BAL 287 12TH WAR
SMITH, JACOB BAL 081 10TH WAR
SMITH, JACOB BAL 140 5TH WARD
SMITH, JACOB BAL 273 2ND WARD
SMITH, JACOB BAL 348 7TH WARD
SMITH, JACOB BAL 271 12TH WAR
SMITH, JACOB BAL 198 11TH WAR
SMITH, JACOB BAL 030 15TH WAR
SMITH, JACOB BAL 054 2ND DIST
SMITH, JACOB BAL 212 6TH DIST
SMITH, JACOB BAL 116 5TH WARD
SMITH, JACOB FRE 402 JEFFERSO
SMITH, JACOB FRE 012 FREDERIC
SMITH, JACOB BAL 239 20TH WAR
SMITH, JACOB BAL 275 17TH WAR
SMITH, JACOB BAL 216 19TH WAR
SMITH, JACOB FRE 346 MIDDLETO
SMITH, JACOB FRE 357 CATOCTIN
SMITH, JACOB FRE 348 MIDDLETO
SMITH, JACOB FRE 362 CATOCTIN
SMITH, JACOB FRE 071 FREDERIC
SMITH, JACOB CAR 386 2ND DIST
SMITH, JACOB CAR 247 3RD DIST
SMITH, JACOB FRE 330 MIDDLETO
SMITH, JACOB CAR 404 2ND DIST
SMITH, JACOB WAS 077 2ND SUBD
SMITH, JACOB WAS 087 2ND SUBD
SMITH, JACOB WAS 185 BOONSBOR
SMITH, JACOB WAS 134 HAGERSTO
SMITH, JACOB D. BAL 221 6TH WARD
SMITH, JAEMS BAL 153 1ST WARD
SMITH, JAMES BAL 174 6TH WARD
SMITH, JAMES BAL 149 1ST WARD
SMITH, JAMES BAL 245 6TH WARD
SMITH, JAMES BAL 150 5TH WARD
SMITH, JAMES BAL 151 5TH WARD

SMITH, JAMES BAL 151 5TH WARD
SMITH, JAMES BAL 164 1ST WARD
SMITH, JAMES BAL 155 1ST WARD
SMITH, JAMES BAL 171 1ST WARD
SMITH, JAMES BAL 173 1ST WARD
SMITH, JAMES BAL 169 1ST WARD
SMITH, JAMES BAL 189 6TH WARD
SMITH, JAMES BAL 105 5TH WARD
SMITH, JAMES BAL 208 6TH DIST
SMITH, JAMES ANN 506 HOWARD D
SMITH, JAMES BAL 341 3RD WARD
SMITH, JAMES BAL 337 3RD WARD
SMITH, JAMES BAL 394 1ST DIST
SMITH, JAMES ANN 340 3RD DIST
SMITH, JAMES ALL 244 CUMBERLA
SMITH, JAMES ANN 395 8TH DIST
SMITH, JAMES BAL 109 2ND DIST
SMITH, JAMES BAL 124 2ND DIST
SMITH, JAMES ANN 470 HOWARD D
SMITH, JAMES BAL 089 2ND DIST
SMITH, JAMES BAL 209 11TH WAR
SMITH, JAMES BAL 178 11TH WAR
SMITH, JAMES BAL 264 12TH WAR
SMITH, JAMES BAL 162 11TH WAR
SMITH, JAMES BAL 456 8TH WARD
SMITH, JAMES BAL 279 2ND WARD
SMITH, JAMES BAL 280 2ND WARD
SMITH, JAMES BAL 140 1ST WARD
SMITH, JAMES BAL 141 1ST WARD
SMITH, JAMES BAL 145 1ST WARD
SMITH, JAMES BAL 132 1ST WARD
SMITH, JAMES BAL 129 1ST WARD
SMITH, JAMES BAL 363 8TH WARD
SMITH, JAMES BAL 389 3RD WARD
SMITH, JAMES BAL 284 12TH WAR
SMITH, JAMES BAL 329 7TH WARD
SMITH, JAMES BAL 186 16TH WAR
SMITH, JAMES ALL 207 CUMBERLA
SMITH, JAMES BAL 114 1ST WARD
SMITH, JAMES BAL 348 3RD WARD
SMITH, JAMES BAL 123 1ST WARD
SMITH, JAMES BAL 083 1ST WARD
SMITH, JAMES BAL 024 1ST WARD
SMITH, JAMES SOM 403 BRINKLEY
SMITH, JAMES WAS 079 2ND SUBD
SMITH, JAMES TAL 017 EASTON D
SMITH, JAMES TAL 019 EASTON D
SMITH, JAMES SOM 553 TYASKIN
SMITH, JAMES SOM 466 HANGARY
SMITH, JAMES ST 305 1ST E DI
SMITH, JAMES KEN 258 1ST DIST
SMITH, JAMES PRI 089 SPALDING
SMITH, JAMES WOR 228 6TH E DI
SMITH, JAMES BAL 012 18TH WAR
SMITH, JAMES CAR 283 7TH DIST
SMITH, JAMES FRE 075 FREDERIC
SMITH, JAMES SOM 428 PRINCESS
SMITH, JAMES HAR 030 1ST DIST
SMITH, JAMES HAR 014 1ST DIST
SMITH, JAMES CAR 305 1ST DIST
SMITH, JAMES CAR 314 1ST DIST
SMITH, JAMES BAL 062 4TH WARD
SMITH, JAMES CEC 143 7TH E DI
SMITH, JAMES CEC 122 4TH E DI
SMITH, JAMES DOR 362 3RD DIVI
SMITH, JAMES CEC 204 6TH E DI
SMITH, JAMES CAL 006 1ST DIST
SMITH, JAMES BAL 161 11TH WAR
SMITH, JAMES CAL 035 2ND DIST
SMITH, JAMES BAL 158 11TH WAR
SMITH, JAMES MGM 350 BERRYS D
SMITH, JAMES HAR 173 3RD DIST
SMITH, JAMES KEN 250 2ND DIST
SMITH, JAMES KEN 251 2ND DIST
SMITH, JAMES KEN 226 2ND DIST
SMITH, JAMES A. HAR 114 2ND DIST
SMITH, JAMES B. BAL 168 19TH WAR
SMITH, JAMES C. BAL 405 14TH WAR
SMITH, JAMES D. BAL 181 19TH WAR
SMITH, JAMES E. SOM 436 PRINCESS
SMITH, JAMES E. BAL 283 7TH WARD
SMITH, JAMES F. BAL 033 1ST WARD
SMITH, JAMES F. BAL 003 EASTERN
SMITH, JAMES H. BAL 184 6TH WARD
SMITH, JAMES H. BAL 149 1ST WARD
SMITH, JAMES H. SOM 399 BRINKLEY
SMITH, JAMES H. QUE 236 4TH E DI
SMITH, JAMES JR. BAL 211 6TH DIST
SMITH, JAMES M. ALL 240 CUMBERLA
SMITH, JAMES M. BAL 132 1ST WARD
SMITH, JAMES N. BAL 182 19TH WAR
SMITH, JAMES P. CHA 287 BOJANTOW
SMITH, JAMES P. BAL 334 3RD WARD
SMITH, JAMES R. BAL 174 1ST WARD
SMITH, JAMES-BLACK BAL 223 2ND WARD
SMITH, JAMES-MULATTO BAL 176 2ND WARD
SMITH, JAMS BAL 167 1ST WARD
SMITH, JAMSE ALL 119 5TH E.D.
SMITH, JANE ANN 405 8TH DIST
SMITH, JANE BAL 172 6TH WARD
SMITH, JANE BAL 040 9TH WARD
SMITH, JANE BAL 107 1ST WARD
SMITH, JANE BAL 056 10TH WAR
SMITH, JANE KEN 225 2ND DIST
SMITH, JANE HAR 182 3RD DIST
SMITH, JANE SOM 435 PRINCESS
SMITH, JANE BAL 477 14TH WAR
SMITH, JANE CAL 002 1ST DIST
SMITH, JANE BAL 363 13TH WAR
SMITH, JANE WAS 186 BOONSBOR
SMITH, JANE WOR 201 3RD E DI
SMITH, JANE WAS 245 SMITHSBU
SMITH, JANE E. ST 317 4TH E DI
SMITH, JANE-MULATTO FRE 040 FREDERIC
SMITH, JANE-MULATTO FRE 038 FREDERIC
SMITH, JAOCB FRE 20 5TH E DI
SMITH, JAPHET ANN 340 3RD DIST
SMITH, JEMMINA BAL 052 4TH WARD
SMITH, JEREMIAH CAR 359 9TH DIST
SMITH, JEREMIAH BAL 031 2ND DIST
SMITH, JEREMIAH SOM 493 SALISBUR
SMITH, JESSE TAL 031 EASTON D
SMITH, JESSE BAL 146 16TH WAR
SMITH, JESSE BAL 293 1ST DIST
SMITH, JESSE BAL 175 19TH WAR
SMITH, JESSE BAL 258 20TH WAR
SMITH, JIM TAL 021 EASTON D
SMITH, JM BAL 149 1ST WARD
SMITH, JOAB ANN 377 4TH DIST
SMITH, JOB BAL 119 5TH WARD

Name	County	Page	District
SMITH, JOE	BAL	418	1ST DIST
SMITH, JOEL	BAL	281	12TH WAR
SMITH, JOEL	CAR	290	7TH DIST
SMITH, JOEPH	BAL	052	2ND DIST
SMITH, JOHN	BAL	035	2ND DIST
SMITH, JOHN	ANN	385	4TH DIST
SMITH, JOHN	ANN	379	4TH DIST
SMITH, JOHN	ANN	346	3RD DIST
SMITH, JOHN	ALL	262	CUMBERLA
SMITH, JOHN	ALL	223	CUMBERLA
SMITH, JOHN	ALL	228	CUMBERLA
SMITH, JOHN	BAL	106	2ND DIST
SMITH, JOHN	BAL	138	2ND DIST
SMITH, JOHN	ANN	429	HOWARD D
SMITH, JOHN	BAL	164	16TH WAR
SMITH, JOHN	BAL	153	16TH WAR
SMITH, JOHN	BAL	325	7TH WARD
SMITH, JOHN	BAL	441	1ST DIST
SMITH, JOHN	BAL	107	5TH WARD
SMITH, JOHN	BAL	111	5TH WARD
SMITH, JOHN	BAL	105	5TH WARD
SMITH, JOHN	BAL	204	6TH DIST
SMITH, JOHN	ANN	503	HOWARD D
SMITH, JOHN	BAL	339	3RD WARD
SMITH, JOHN	BAL	461	1ST DIST
SMITH, JOHN	BAL	038	9TH WARD
SMITH, JOHN	BAL	166	1ST WARD
SMITH, JOHN	BAL	169	1ST WARD
SMITH, JOHN	BAL	169	1ST WARD
SMITH, JOHN	BAL	181	2ND WARD
SMITH, JOHN	BAL	169	1ST WARD
SMITH, JOHN	BAL	221	2ND WARD
SMITH, JOHN	BAL	196	2ND WARD
SMITH, JOHN	BAL	193	6TH WARD
SMITH, JOHN	BAL	157	1ST WARD
SMITH, JOHN	BAL	159	1ST WARD
SMITH, JOHN	BAL	162	1ST WARD
SMITH, JOHN	BAL	162	1ST WARD
SMITH, JOHN	BAL	151	5TH WARD
SMITH, JOHN	BAL	220	6TH WARD
SMITH, JOHN	BAL	021	1ST WARD
SMITH, JOHN	BAL	113	1ST WARD
SMITH, JOHN	BAL	116	1ST WARD
SMITH, JOHN	BAL	121	1ST WARD
SMITH, JOHN	BAL	118	1ST WARD
SMITH, JOHN	BAL	114	1ST WARD
SMITH, JOHN	BAL	116	1ST WARD
SMITH, JOHN	BAL	107	1ST WARD
SMITH, JOHN	BAL	120	1ST WARD
SMITH, JOHN	BAL	113	1ST WARD
SMITH, JOHN	BAL	094	1ST WARD
SMITH, JOHN	BAL	094	1ST WARD
SMITH, JOHN	BAL	364	3RD WARD
SMITH, JOHN	BAL	355	3RD WARD
SMITH, JOHN	BAL	267	1ST DIST
SMITH, JOHN	BAL	276	1ST DIST
SMITH, JOHN	BAL	194	5TH DIST
SMITH, JOHN	BAL	016	1ST WARD
SMITH, JOHN	BAL	042	1ST WARD
SMITH, JOHN	BAL	060	1ST WARD
SMITH, JOHN	BAL	068	1ST WARD
SMITH, JOHN	ALL	139	6TH E.D.
SMITH, JOHN	ALL	126	4TH E.D.
SMITH, JOHN	ANN	317	1ST DIST
SMITH, JOHN	ANN	337	3RD DIST
SMITH, JOHN	BAL	323	1ST DIST
SMITH, JOHN	ANN	310	1ST DIST
SMITH, JOHN	ANN	280	ANNAPOLI
SMITH, JOHN	ANN	277	ANNAPOLI
SMITH, JOHN	BAL	130	1ST WARD
SMITH, JOHN	BAL	130	1ST WARD
SMITH, JOHN	BAL	136	1ST WARD
SMITH, JOHN	BAL	129	1ST WARD
SMITH, JOHN	BAL	132	1ST WARD
SMITH, JOHN	BAL	131	1ST WARD
SMITH, JOHN	BAL	289	7TH WARD
SMITH, JOHN	BAL	384	3RD WARD
SMITH, JOHN	BAL	400	3RD WARD
SMITH, JOHN	BAL	281	2ND WARD
SMITH, JOHN	BAL	281	2ND WARD
SMITH, JOHN	BAL	370	8TH WARD
SMITH, JOHN	BAL	146	1ST WARD
SMITH, JOHN	BAL	142	1ST WARD
SMITH, JOHN	BAL	141	1ST WARD
SMITH, JOHN	BAL	138	1ST WARD
SMITH, JOHN	BAL	141	1ST WARD
SMITH, JOHN	BAL	139	1ST WARD
SMITH, JOHN	BAL	137	1ST WARD
SMITH, JOHN	BAL	138	1ST WARD
SMITH, JOHN	BAL	146	1ST WARD
SMITH, JOHN	BAL	123	5TH WARD
SMITH, JOHN	BAL	141	1ST WARD
SMITH, JOHN	BAL	145	1ST WARD
SMITH, JOHN	BAL	273	2ND WARD
SMITH, JOHN	BAL	280	2ND WARD
SMITH, JOHN	BAL	279	2ND WARD
SMITH, JOHN	BAL	271	2ND WARD
SMITH, JOHN	BAL	247	2ND WARD
SMITH, JOHN	BAL	456	8TH WARD
SMITH, JOHN	BAL	459	8TH WARD
SMITH, JOHN	BAL	002	9TH WARD
SMITH, JOHN	BAL	001	9TH WARD
SMITH, JOHN	BAL	186	11TH WAR
SMITH, JOHN	BAL	190	11TH WAR
SMITH, JOHN	BAL	036	15TH WAR
SMITH, JOHN	BAL	034	15TH WAR
SMITH, JOHN	BAL	003	15TH WAR
SMITH, JOHN	BAL	253	12TH WAR
SMITH, JOHN	BAL	221	12TH WAR
SMITH, JOHN	BAL	026	18TH WAR
SMITH, JOHN	BAL	034	18TH WAR
SMITH, JOHN	CEC	110	4TH E DI
SMITH, JOHN	CEC	092	4TH E DI
SMITH, JOHN	CEC	092	4TH E DI
SMITH, JOHN	BAL	073	18TH WAR
SMITH, JOHN	BAL	096	18TH WAR
SMITH, JOHN	CAR	394	2ND DIST
SMITH, JOHN	BAL	239	20TH WAR
SMITH, JOHN	BAL	249	20TH WAR
SMITH, JOHN	BAL	242	20TH WAR
SMITH, JOHN	CEC	204	6TH E DI
SMITH, JOHN	CEC	215	7TH E DI
SMITH, JOHN	DOR	334	3RD DIVI
SMITH, JOHN	FRE	443	8TH E DI
SMITH, JOHN	FRE	445	8TH E DI
SMITH, JOHN	FRE	412	8TH E DI
SMITH, JOHN	FRE	390	PETERSVI
SMITH, JOHN	BAL	300	20TH WAR
SMITH, JOHN	FRE	029	FREDERIC
SMITH, JOHN	CAR	211	5TH DIST
SMITH, JOHN	CAR	236	UNION TO
SMITH, JOHN	CAR	216	5TH DIST
SMITH, JOHN	FRE	361	CATOCTIN
SMITH, JOHN	BAL	224	19TH WAR
SMITH, JOHN	FRE	348	MIDDLETO
SMITH, JOHN	FRE	359	CATOCTIN
SMITH, JOHN	BAL	029	4TH WARD
SMITH, JOHN	CEC	042	CHESAPEA
SMITH, JOHN	CEC	122	4TH E DI
SMITH, JOHN	BAL	267	17TH WAR
SMITH, JOHN	BAL	210	17TH WAR
SMITH, JOHN	HAR	173	3RD DIST
SMITH, JOHN	HAR	178	3RD DIST
SMITH, JOHN	FRE	183	5TH E DI
SMITH, JOHN	FRE	129	CREAGERS
SMITH, JOHN	FRE	126	CREAGERS
SMITH, JOHN	FRE	154	10TH E D
SMITH, JOHN	CHA	279	BOJANTOW
SMITH, JOHN	HAR	037	1ST DIST
SMITH, JOHN	SOM	425	PRINCESS
SMITH, JOHN	HAR	112	2ND DIST
SMITH, JOHN	HAR	111	2ND DIST
SMITH, JOHN	FRE	079	FREDERIC
SMITH, JOHN	FRE	078	FREDERIC
SMITH, JOHN	FRE	075	FREDERIC
SMITH, JOHN	FRE	071	FREDERIC
SMITH, JOHN	SOM	408	DUBLIN D
SMITH, JOHN	MGM	424	MEDLEY 3
SMITH, JOHN	BAL	466	14TH WAR
SMITH, JOHN	BAL	400	14TH WAR
SMITH, JOHN	BAL	392	14TH WAR
SMITH, JOHN	BAL	399	14TH WAR
SMITH, JOHN	CAL	030	2ND DIST
SMITH, JOHN	BAL	458	14TH WAR
SMITH, JOHN	FRE	280	WOODSBOR
SMITH, JOHN	CAR	398	2ND DIST
SMITH, JOHN	FRE	207	BUCKEYST
SMITH, JOHN	FRE	327	MIDDLETO
SMITH, JOHN	FRE	295	WOODSBOR
SMITH, JOHN	FRE	319	MIDDLETO
SMITH, JOHN	FRE	318	MIDDLETO
SMITH, JOHN	FRE	225	BUCKEYST
SMITH, JOHN	FRE	247	NEW MARK
SMITH, JOHN	KEN	209	2ND DIST
SMITH, JOHN	TAL	022	EASTON D
SMITH, JOHN	WAS	104	2ND DIST
SMITH, JOHN	WAS	076	2ND SUBD
SMITH, JOHN	WAS	039	2ND SUBD
SMITH, JOHN	WOR	316	2ND E DI
SMITH, JOHN	PRI	001	BLADENSB
SMITH, JOHN	PRI	030	VANSVILL
SMITH, JOHN	PRI	007	BLADENSB
SMITH, JOHN	WOR	254	1ST CENS
SMITH, JOHN	WAS	022	2ND SUBD
SMITH, JOHN	PRI	040	VANSVILL
SMITH, JOHN	SOM	528	QUANTICO
SMITH, JOHN	WAS	252	1ST DIST
SMITH, JOHN	WAS	210	1ST DIST
SMITH, JOHN	WAS	202	1ST DIST
SMITH, JOHN	KEN	308	3RD DIST
SMITH, JOHN	SOM	350	BRINKLEY
SMITH, JOHN	QUE	195	3RD E DI
SMITH, JOHN	WAS	186	BOONSBOR
SMITH, JOHN	QUE	252	5TH E DI
SMITH, JOHN	TAL	061	EASTON D
SMITH, JOHN A.	BAL	422	3RD WARD
SMITH, JOHN A.	BAL	332	3RD WARD
SMITH, JOHN B.	BAL	037	4TH WARD
SMITH, JOHN B.	QUE	149	1ST E DI
SMITH, JOHN B.	BAL	262	17TH WAR
SMITH, JOHN C.	BAL	334	1ST DIST
SMITH, JOHN C.	BAL	250	12TH WAR
SMITH, JOHN C.	BAL	386	8TH WARD
SMITH, JOHN C.	KEN	287	3RD DIST
SMITH, JOHN C. E.	BAL	063	4TH WARD
SMITH, JOHN D.	BAL	419	14TH WAR
SMITH, JOHN D.	BAL	228	1ST DIST
SMITH, JOHN D.	BAL	398	1ST DIST
SMITH, JOHN D.	BAL	264	1ST DIST
SMITH, JOHN D.	BAL	117	1ST WARD
SMITH, JOHN E.	FRE	074	FREDERIC
SMITH, JOHN F.	BAL	161	19TH WAR
SMITH, JOHN F.M.	BAL	317	7TH WARD
SMITH, JOHN G.	BAL	286	2ND WARD
SMITH, JOHN G.	BAL	105	18TH WAR
SMITH, JOHN G.	FRE	022	FREDERIC
SMITH, JOHN G.	FRE	424	8TH E DI
SMITH, JOHN H.	CAR	072	NO TWP L
SMITH, JOHN H.	BAL	006	15TH WAR
SMITH, JOHN H.	BAL	318	7TH WARD
SMITH, JOHN H.	BAL	350	3RD WARD
SMITH, JOHN H.	BAL	096	1ST WARD
SMITH, JOHN H.	BAL	269	2ND WARD
SMITH, JOHN H.	BAL	124	5TH WARD
SMITH, JOHN H.	BAL	391	3RD WARD
SMITH, JOHN H.	BAL	202	2ND WARD
SMITH, JOHN H.	WAS	132	HAGERSTO
SMITH, JOHN H.	WOR	186	7TH E DI
SMITH, JOHN J.	ANN	413	HOWARD D
SMITH, JOHN J.	FRE	335	MIDDLETO
SMITH, JOHN K.	BAL	320	1ST DIST
SMITH, JOHN L.	ALL	169	6TH E.D.
SMITH, JOHN L.	WAS	159	HAGERSTO
SMITH, JOHN L.	WAS	164	HAGERSTO
SMITH, JOHN M.	WAS	159	HAGERSTO
SMITH, JOHN M.	WOR	214	4TH E DI
SMITH, JOHN M.	WAS	255	1ST DIST
SMITH, JOHN M.	BAL	280	2ND WARD
SMITH, JOHN M.	BAL	128	1ST WARD
SMITH, JOHN M.	BAL	009	EASTERN
SMITH, JOHN M.	BAL	192	19TH WAR
SMITH, JOHN M.	BAL	085	18TH WAR
SMITH, JOHN M.	BAL	011	18TH WAR
SMITH, JOHN M.-BLACK	QUE	143	1ST E DI
SMITH, JOHN N.	BAL	144	1ST WARD
SMITH, JOHN P.	BAL	364	8TH WARD
SMITH, JOHN P.	KEN	268	1ST DIST
SMITH, JOHN PETER	BAL	219	17TH WAR
SMITH, JOHN Q.	BAL	391	8TH WARD
SMITH, JOHN R.	CEC	052	1ST E DI
SMITH, JOHN R.	BAL	087	18TH WAR
SMITH, JOHN S.	BAL	232	2ND WARD
SMITH, JOHN S.	BAL	160	1ST WARD
SMITH, JOHN S.	TAL	102	ST MICHA
SMITH, JOHN SR.	FRE	320	MIDDLETO
SMITH, JOHN T.	CAR	368	9TH DIST
SMITH, JOHN T.	BAL	124	5TH WARD
SMITH, JOHN T.	BAL	162	16TH WAR
SMITH, JOHN T.	BAL	178	16TH WAR
SMITH, JOHN TANNY	BAL	211	17TH WAR
SMITH, JOHN W.	BAL	473	14TH WAR
SMITH, JOHN W.	DOR	313	1ST DIST
SMITH, JOHN W.	ANN	337	3RD DIST
SMITH, JOHN W.	ALL	200	CUMBERLA
SMITH, JOHN W.	PRI	069	MARLBROU
SMITH, JOHN-BLACK	ST	322	4TH E DI
SMITH, JOHN-BLACK	QUE	159	2ND E DI
SMITH, JOHN-BLACK	QUE	172	2ND E DI
SMITH, JOHN-BLACK	BAL	136	1ST WARD
SMITH, JOHN-BLACK	BAL	223	2ND WARD
SMITH, JOHN-BLACK	BAL	223	2ND WARD
SMITH, JOHN-BLACK	BAL	176	2ND WARD
SMITH, JOHN-BLACK	CAR	136	NO TWP L
SMITH, JOHN-BLACK	QUE	143	1ST E DI
SMITH, JOHN-MULATTO	FRE	407	JEFFERSO
SMITH, JOHN-MULATTO	QUE	183	3RD E DI
SMITH, JOHNA	BAL	257	6TH WARD
SMITH, JOHNATHAN	BAL	208	6TH DIST
SMITH, JONAS	WAS	266	1ST DIST
SMITH, JONAS	FRE	335	MIDDLETO
SMITH, JONOTHAN	WAS	239	CAVETOWN
SMITH, JOSEPH	QUE	162	2ND E DI
SMITH, JOSEPH	WOR	216	4TH E DI
SMITH, JOSEPH	QUE	234	4TH E DI
SMITH, JOSEPH	WAS	128	2ND DIST
SMITH, JOSEPH	WAS	006	WILLIAMS
SMITH, JOSEPH	PRI	024	VANSVILL
SMITH, JOSEPH	WAS	078	2ND SUBD
SMITH, JOSEPH	WAS	112	2ND DIST
SMITH, JOSEPH	WAS	300	1ST DIST
SMITH, JOSEPH	FRE	335	MIDDLETO
SMITH, JOSEPH	BAL	111	18TH WAR
SMITH, JOSEPH	CAR	401	2ND DIST
SMITH, JOSEPH	DOR	432	1ST DIST
SMITH, JOSEPH	DOR	317	1ST DIST
SMITH, JOSEPH	DOR	316	1ST DIST
SMITH, JOSEPH	FRE	433	8TH E DI
SMITH, JOSEPH	FRE	155	10TH E D
SMITH, JOSEPH	FRE	146	10TH E D
SMITH, JOSEPH	CAR	067	NO TWP L
SMITH, JOSEPH	BAL	338	13TH WAR
SMITH, JOSEPH	BAL	077	18TH WAR
SMITH, JOSEPH	FRE	085	FREDERIC
SMITH, JOSEPH	BAL	203	6TH DIST
SMITH, JOSEPH	BAL	284	7TH WARD
SMITH, JOSEPH	BAL	236	2ND WARD
SMITH, JOSEPH	BAL	400	8TH WARD
SMITH, JOSEPH	BAL	394	8TH WARD
SMITH, JOSEPH	BAL	281	2ND WARD
SMITH, JOSEPH	BAL	176	6TH WARD
SMITH, JOSEPH	BAL	153	1ST WARD
SMITH, JOSEPH	ANN	407	8TH DIST
SMITH, JOSEPH	ANN	303	1ST DIST
SMITH, JOSEPH	ANN	306	1ST DIST
SMITH, JOSEPH	ALL	109	5TH E.D.
SMITH, JOSEPH	ALL	092	5TH E.D.
SMITH, JOSEPH	BAL	066	10TH WAR
SMITH, JOSEPH	BAL	075	10TH WAR
SMITH, JOSEPH	BAL	102	15TH WAR
SMITH, JOSEPH	ANN	339	3RD DIST
SMITH, JOSEPH	BAL	086	2ND DIST
SMITH, JOSEPH	BAL	103	1ST WARD
SMITH, JOSEPH	BAL	123	1ST WARD
SMITH, JOSEPH	BAL	122	1ST WARD
SMITH, JOSEPH	BAL	167	2ND DIST
SMITH, JOSEPH	BAL	427	8TH WARD
SMITH, JOSEPH A.	BAL	438	1ST DIST
SMITH, JOSEPH B.	WAS	113	2ND DIST
SMITH, JOSEPH F.	SOM	428	PRINCESS
SMITH, JOSEPH H.	SOM	428	PRINCESS
SMITH, JOSEPH H.	BAL	151	11TH WAR
SMITH, JOSEPH M.	QUE	161	2ND E DI
SMITH, JOSEPH T.	BAL	088	4TH WARD
SMITH, JOSEPH-BLACK	QUE	199	3RD E DI
SMITH, JOSEPHEEN	BAL	461	1ST DIST
SMITH, JOSEPHINE	BAL	378	3RD WARD
SMITH, JOSEPHINE	BAL	086	15TH WAR
SMITH, JOSEPHINE	CEC	145	PORT DUP
SMITH, JOSEPHINE	BAL	036	18TH WAR
SMITH, JOSEPINE	FRE	065	FREDERIC
SMITH, JOSHUA	CEC	176	7TH E DI
SMITH, JOSHUA	FRE	149	10TH E D
SMITH, JOSHUA	FRE	332	MIDDLETO
SMITH, JOSHUA	CAR	296	7TH DIST
SMITH, JOSHUA	BAL	260	1ST DIST
SMITH, JOSHUA	BAL	385	1ST DIST
SMITH, JOSHUA	BAL	457	8TH WARD
SMITH, JOSHUA	BAL	037	2ND DIST
SMITH, JOSHUA	TAL	015	EASTON D
SMITH, JOSHUA	WOR	191	8TH E DI
SMITH, JOSHUA H.	SOM	490	SALISBUR
SMITH, JOSIAH *	ALL	095	5TH E.D.
SMITH, JOSIAH K.	BAL	370	1ST DIST
SMITH, JSEPH B.P	QUE	188	3RD E DI
SMITH, JSOHUA	BAL	037	2ND DIST
SMITH, JULIA	BAL	414	14TH WAR
SMITH, JULIA	BAL	356	13TH WAR
SMITH, JULIA A.	KEN	258	1ST DIST
SMITH, JULIA A.	SOM	493	SALISBUR
SMITH, JULIAN	FRE	072	FREDERIC
SMITH, JULIANN	WAS	244	SMITHSBU
SMITH, KIMPSON	CEC	176	7TH E DI
SMITH, L	PRI	061	NOTTINGH
SMITH, L.	BAL	154	1ST WARD
SMITH, L. F.	BAL	052	9TH WARD
SMITH, L. MRS.	BAL	157	11TH WAR
SMITH, L. W.	BAL	145	11TH WAR
SMITH, L.R.	PRI	090	MARLBROU
SMITH, LANA	BAL	330	13TH WAR
SMITH, LAREL	BAL	171	2ND DIST
SMITH, LAURA	BAL	317	20TH WAR
SMITH, LAURA C.	ALL	219	CUMBERLA
SMITH, LAURA O.	BAL	010	4TH WARD
SMITH, LAURENCE	BAL	401	3RD WARD
SMITH, LAVINA	FRE	148	10TH E D
SMITH, LAWRENCE	BAL	023	18TH WAR
SMITH, LEAH	CAR	213	5TH DIST
SMITH, LEAH	BAL	376	13TH WAR
SMITH, LEAH-MULATTO	WOR	334	1ST E DI
SMITH, LEEDS	BAL	141	11TH WAR
SMITH, LEMUEL	QUE	170	2ND E DI
SMITH, LEONA	BAL	213	11TH WAR
SMITH, LEONARD	ALL	164	6TH E.D.
SMITH, LEOPOLD, J.	FRE	202	5TH E DI
SMITH, LETITIA	WAS	178	BOONSBOR
SMITH, LEVI	WAS	184	BOONSBOR
SMITH, LEVI G.	CEC	094	4TH E DI
SMITH, LEVIN	SOM	408	DUBLIN D
SMITH, LEVIN	WOR	181	6TH E DI
SMITH, LEVIN C.	SOM	551	TYASKIN

Name	County	Page	District
SMITH, LEVIN L. H.	WOR	210	4TH E DI
SMITH, LEVY	HAR	152	3RD DIST
SMITH, LEWIS	FRE	071	FREDERIC
SMITH, LEWIS	CAL	063	3RD DIST
SMITH, LEWIS	BAL	211	17TH WAR
SMITH, LEWIS	FRE	297	WOODSBOR
SMITH, LEWIS	WOR	313	2ND E DI
SMITH, LEWIS	SOM	475	TRAPPE D
SMITH, LEWIS	BAL	385	3RD WARD
SMITH, LEWIS	ALL	245	CUMBERLA
SMITH, LEWIS	BAL	163	1ST WARD
SMITH, LEWIS	BAL	149	1ST WARD
SMITH, LEWIS	BAL	298	3RD WARD
SMITH, LEWIS H.	WAS	225	1ST DIST
SMITH, LEWIS W.	FRE	300	WOODSBOR
SMITH, LEWIS-BLACK	MGM	426	MEDLEY 3
SMITH, LIDIA	HAR	109	2ND DIST
SMITH, LINNA	TAL	091	ST MICHA
SMITH, LITTLETON	SOM	460	HANGARY
SMITH, LLOYD	QUE	225	4TH E DI
SMITH, LLOYD	QUE	225	4TH E DI
SMITH, LLOYD	BAL	373	1ST DIST
SMITH, LONDON	BAL	242	6TH WARD
SMITH, LOUIS	ST	309	1ST E DI
SMITH, LOUIS	BAL	054	4TH WARD
SMITH, LOUISA	BAL	045	4TH WARD
SMITH, LOUISA	BAL	066	4TH WARD
SMITH, LOUISA	HAR	033	1ST DIST
SMITH, LOUISA	BAL	308	20TH WAR
SMITH, LOUISA	CHA	279	BOJANTOW
SMITH, LOUISA	WAS	088	2ND SUBD
SMITH, LOUISA	BAL	243	6TH WARD
SMITH, LOUISA	BAL	090	5TH WARD
SMITH, LOUISA	BAL	228	1ST DIST
SMITH, LOUISA	BAL	345	1ST DIST
SMITH, LOUISA SR.	BAL	079	10TH WAR
SMITH, LUCINDA	CAR	185	8TH DIST
SMITH, LUCINDA-BLACK	FRE	397	PETERSVI
SMITH, LUCRETIA	WOR	208	4TH E DI
SMITH, LUCY-BLACK	FRE	049	FREDERIC
SMITH, LYDIA	CEC	115	3RD E DI
SMITH, LYDIA	WAS	264	1ST DIST
SMITH, LYDIA A.	BAL	243	6TH WARD
SMITH, LYDIA-BLACK	FRE	428	8TH E DI
SMITH, LYNTHA	BAL	353	7TH WARD
SMITH, M.	BAL	281	2ND WARD
SMITH, M.	ANN	281	ANNAPOLI
SMITH, M.A.	BAL	050	2ND DIST
SMITH, M.A.	WAS	010	WILLIAMS
SMITH, MAHALA	BAL	452	14TH WAR
SMITH, MAJOR	BAL	300	12TH WAR
SMITH, MALVINA	BAL	453	14TH WAR
SMITH, MANUEL	BAL	014	2ND DIST
SMITH, MARAND	BAL	409	1ST DIST
SMITH, MARGARET	BAL	047	2ND DIST
SMITH, MARGARET	BAL	275	12TH WAR
SMITH, MARGARET	BAL	058	10TH WAR
SMITH, MARGARET	BAL	109	15TH WAR
SMITH, MARGARET	BAL	166	16TH WAR
SMITH, MARGARET	ALL	100	5TH E.D.
SMITH, MARGARET	BAL	266	2ND WARD
SMITH, MARGARET	BAL	151	5TH WARD
SMITH, MARGARET	BAL	157	6TH WARD
SMITH, MARGARET	BAL	046	9TH WARD
SMITH, MARGARET	BAL	275	1ST DIST
SMITH, MARGARET	BAL	005	1ST WARD
SMITH, MARGARET	BAL	470	14TH WAR
SMITH, MARGARET	CEC	094	4TH E DI
SMITH, MARGARET	BAL	026	18TH WAR
SMITH, MARGARET	CAR	248	3RD DIST
SMITH, MARGARET	HAR	032	1ST DIST
SMITH, MARGARET	FRE	070	FREDERIC
SMITH, MARGARET	BAL	417	3RD WARD
SMITH, MARGARET	BAL	223	19TH WAR
SMITH, MARGARET	BAL	201	17TH WAR
SMITH, MARGARET	BAL	154	19TH WAR
SMITH, MARGARET	WAS	071	2ND SUBD
SMITH, MARGARET	WAS	284	1ST DIST
SMITH, MARGARET	PRI	023	VANSVILL
SMITH, MARGARET A.	DOR	454	1ST DIST
SMITH, MARGARET E.	FRE	310	WOODSBOR
SMITH, MARGARET F.	ST	297	2ND E DI
SMITH, MARGARET M.	TAL	043	EASTON D
SMITH, MARGARET-BLACK	BAL	222	2ND WARD
SMITH, MARGARETT	BAL	307	3RD WARD
SMITH, MARGARETT A.	BAL	063	4TH WARD
SMITH, MARIA	BAL	043	4TH WARD
SMITH, MARIA	BAL	071	18TH WAR
SMITH, MARIA	BAL	264	20TH WAR
SMITH, MARIA	BAL	111	5TH WARD
SMITH, MARIA	WAS	184	BOONSBOR
SMITH, MARIA C.	MGM	426	MEDLEY 3
SMITH, MARIA H.	CAR	287	7TH DIST
SMITH, MARIAH	SOM	527	QUANTICO
SMITH, MARK	ALL	152	6TH E.D.
SMITH, MARLD*	BAL	354	3RD WARD
SMITH, MARSHALL	BAL	199	11TH WAR
SMITH, MARSHALL	WOR	204	4TH E DI
SMITH, MARTHA	KEN	308	3RD DIST
SMITH, MARTHA	BAL	044	15TH WAR
SMITH, MARTHA	BAL	013	1ST WARD
SMITH, MARTHA	BAL	053	1ST WARD
SMITH, MARTHA	ALL	190	9TH E.D.
SMITH, MARTHA	BAL	311	3RD WARD
SMITH, MARTHA	BAL	242	6TH WARD
SMITH, MARTHA	BAL	474	14TH WAR
SMITH, MARTHA C.	FRE	066	FREDERIC
SMITH, MARTIN	CAR	251	3RD DIST
SMITH, MARTIN	BAL	171	6TH WARD
SMITH, MARTIN	BAL	454	8TH WARD
SMITH, MARTIN	BAL	435	8TH WARD
SMITH, MARY	BAL	436	8TH WARD
SMITH, MARY	BAL	043	15TH WAR
SMITH, MARY	BAL	186	11TH WAR
SMITH, MARY	BAL	073	15TH WAR
SMITH, MARY	BAL	219	6TH WARD
SMITH, MARY	BAL	022	9TH WARD
SMITH, MARY	BAL	228	6TH WARD
SMITH, MARY	BAL	310	3RD WARD
SMITH, MARY	BAL	102	5TH WARD
SMITH, MARY	BAL	297	3RD WARD
SMITH, MARY	BAL	391	1ST DIST
SMITH, MARY	BAL	410	1ST DIST
SMITH, MARY	BAL	386	1ST DIST
SMITH, MARY	BAL	333	1ST DIST
SMITH, MARY	BAL	203	6TH WARD
SMITH, MARY	BAL	461	1ST DIST
SMITH, MARY	BAL	411	1ST DIST
SMITH, MARY	BAL	180	2ND DIST
SMITH, MARY	BAL	352	3RD WARD
SMITH, MARY	BAL	071	1ST WARD
SMITH, MARY	BAL	081	1ST WARD
SMITH, MARY	BAL	293	1ST DIST
SMITH, MARY	BAL	242	2ND WARD
SMITH, MARY	BAL	247	2ND WARD
SMITH, MARY	BAL	242	2ND WARD
SMITH, MARY	BAL	250	6TH WARD
SMITH, MARY	BAL	255	6TH WARD
SMITH, MARY	BAL	113	15TH WAR
SMITH, MARY	BAL	105	15TH WAR
SMITH, MARY	BAL	105	15TH WAR
SMITH, MARY	BAL	090	15TH WAR
SMITH, MARY	BAL	301	12TH WAR
SMITH, MARY	BAL	301	12TH WAR
SMITH, MARY	BAL	289	12TH WAR
SMITH, MARY	BAL	296	12TH WAR
SMITH, MARY	BAL	310	12TH WAR
SMITH, MARY	BAL	072	10TH WAR
SMITH, MARY	BAL	325	7TH WARD
SMITH, MARY	ALL	243	CUMBERLA
SMITH, MARY	ANN	447	HOWARD D
SMITH, MARY	CAR	272	WESTMINS
SMITH, MARY	FRE	079	FREDERIC
SMITH, MARY	FRE	040	FREDERIC
SMITH, MARY	HAR	095	2ND DIST
SMITH, MARY	FRE	095	FREDERIC
SMITH, MARY	BAL	472	14TH WAR
SMITH, MARY	BAL	443	14TH WAR
SMITH, MARY	BAL	116	11TH WAR
SMITH, MARY	BAL	287	20TH WAR
SMITH, MARY	BAL	278	20TH WAR
SMITH, MARY	FRE	444	8TH E DI
SMITH, MARY	DOR	368	3RD DIVI
SMITH, MARY	CHA	221	ALLENS F
SMITH, MARY	BAL	384	13TH WAR
SMITH, MARY	CEC	188	7TH E DI
SMITH, MARY	DOR	307	1ST DIST
SMITH, MARY	BAL	346	13TH WAR
SMITH, MARY	FRE	314	MIDDLETO
SMITH, MARY	FRE	264	NEW MARK
SMITH, MARY	HAR	204	3RD DIST
SMITH, MARY	BAL	118	18TH WAR
SMITH, MARY	BAL	202	19TH WAR
SMITH, MARY	BAL	176	19TH WAR
SMITH, MARY	BAL	017	4TH WARD
SMITH, MARY	BAL	021	4TH WARD
SMITH, MARY	CEC	011	ELKTON 3
SMITH, MARY	KEN	253	1ST DIST
SMITH, MARY	QUE	196	3RD E DI
SMITH, MARY	WOR	233	6TH E DI
SMITH, MARY	WAS	002	WILLIAMS
SMITH, MARY	WAS	012	WILLIAMS
SMITH, MARY	WAS	026	2ND SUBD
SMITH, MARY A	BAL	157	19TH WAR
SMITH, MARY A.	BAL	213	11TH WAR
SMITH, MARY A.	HAR	055	1ST DIST
SMITH, MARY A.	BAL	081	18TH WAR
SMITH, MARY A.	BAL	135	16TH WAR
SMITH, MARY A.	BAL	286	7TH WARD
SMITH, MARY A.	BAL	194	2ND WARD
SMITH, MARY A.	BAL	157	6TH WARD
SMITH, MARY A.	BAL	055	15TH WAR
SMITH, MARY A.H.	ANN	521	HOWARD D
SMITH, MARY B.	FRE	162	EMMITTSB
SMITH, MARY C.	FRE	164	EMMITTSB
SMITH, MARY C.	ALL	229	CUMBERLA
SMITH, MARY C.	BAL	349	3RD WARD
SMITH, MARY C.	WOR	272	BERLIN 1
SMITH, MARY D.-BLACK	ST	326	4TH E DI
SMITH, MARY E.	BAL	072	1ST WARD
SMITH, MARY E.	ANN	493	HOWARD D
SMITH, MARY E.	BAL	073	15TH WAR
SMITH, MARY E.	BAL	281	7TH WARD
SMITH, MARY E.	BAL	138	16TH WAR
SMITH, MARY E.	MGM	352	BERRYS D
SMITH, MARY E.F.	CAL	063	3RD DIST
SMITH, MARY ELLEN	BAL	392	14TH WAR
SMITH, MARY G.	CHA	279	BOJANTOW
SMITH, MARY H.	BAL	413	1ST DIST
SMITH, MARY J.	BAL	250	6TH WARD
SMITH, MARY J.	BAL	186	11TH WAR
SMITH, MARY J.	SOM	457	DAMES QU
SMITH, MARY J.	TAL	100	ST MICHA
SMITH, MARY L.	MGM	317	CRACKLIN
SMITH, MARY L.-BLACK	FRE	017	FREDERIC
SMITH, MARY M.	ANN	379	4TH DIST
SMITH, MARY R.	SOM	553	TYASKIN
SMITH, MARY THEOTRINE SIS	BAL	316	20TH WAR
SMITH, MARY W.	KEN	290	3RD DIST
SMITH, MARY-MULATTO	FRE	452	8TH E DI
SMITH, MARYANN	FRE	411	8TH E DI
SMITH, MATHEW	BAL	380	13TH WAR
SMITH, MATHEW	BAL	425	8TH WARD
SMITH, MATHIAS	FRE	412	8TH E DI
SMITH, MATILDA	BAL	086	4TH WARD
SMITH, MATILDA	MGM	380	ROCKERLE
SMITH, MATILDA	CHA	283	BOJANTOW
SMITH, MATILDA	BAL	214	11TH WAR
SMITH, MATILDA	KEN	210	2ND DIST
SMITH, MATILDA-MULATTO	FRE	041	FREDERIC
SMITH, MATTHEW	DOR	308	1ST DIST
SMITH, MATTHIAS	BAL	104	1ST WARD
SMITH, MATTISMORE	ST	333	4TH E DI
SMITH, MELINDA	ALL	200	CUMBERLA
SMITH, MELVINA	BAL	046	4TH WARD
SMITH, MERREL D.	WOR	254	1ST CENS
SMITH, MESSA	FRE	254	NEW MARK
SMITH, MICHAEL	HAR	029	1ST DIST
SMITH, MICHAEL	BAL	312	20TH WAR
SMITH, MICHAEL	FRE	142	CREAGERS
SMITH, MICHAEL	CAR	251	3RD DIST
SMITH, MICHAEL	WAS	112	2ND DIST
SMITH, MICHAEL	ALL	219	CUMBERLA
SMITH, MICHAEL	BAL	031	15TH WAR
SMITH, MICHAEL	BAL	045	15TH WAR
SMITH, MICHAEL P.	WAS	116	2ND DIST
SMITH, MILKEY	BAL	343	7TH WARD
SMITH, MILLA	BAL	166	11TH WAR
SMITH, MILLY	ANN	294	1ST DIST
SMITH, MIRANDAH	BAL	031	9TH WARD
SMITH, MITCHEL	BAL	114	18TH WAR
SMITH, MORRIS	BAL	221	17TH WAR
SMITH, MOSES	BAL	170	11TH WAR
SMITH, MOSES	ANN	340	3RD DIST
SMITH, MOSES	BAL	141	2ND DIST
SMITH, MOSES	BAL	422	1ST DIST
SMITH, MOSES	BAL	099	5TH WARD
SMITH, MOSES	BAL	317	7TH WARD
SMITH, MOSES	BAL	177	16TH WAR
SMITH, MOSES	QUE	216	3RD E DI
SMITH, MOSES C.	SOM	428	PRINCESS
SMITH, MOSES-BLACK	CAR	134	NO TWP L
SMITH, MRS.	BAL	235	17TH WAR
SMITH, MRS.	BAL	187	19TH WAR
SMITH, MRS-	ANN	411	8TH DIST
SMITH, MRY	CAR	148	NO TWP L
SMITH, N.	BAL	157	1ST WARD
SMITH, N. N.	ANN	338	3RD DIST
SMITH, NACY W.	MGM	442	CLARKSTR
SMITH, NANCY	WAS	065	2ND SUBD
SMITH, NANCY	WAS	038	2ND SUBD
SMITH, NANCY	WOR	343	1ST E DI
SMITH, NANCY	BAL	071	10TH WAR
SMITH, NANCY	CAL	043	3RD DIST
SMITH, NANCY	SOM	437	DAMES QU
SMITH, NANCY	DOR	380	1ST DIST
SMITH, NANCY	HAR	134	2ND DIST
SMITH, NANIE	CHA	281	BOJANTOW
SMITH, NANTZY	BAL	309	3RD WARD
SMITH, NATHAN	BAL	373	1ST DIST
SMITH, NATHAN	BAL	180	16TH WAR
SMITH, NATHAN R.	BAL	145	11TH WAR
SMITH, NATHANIEL	CAL	054	3RD DIST
SMITH, NATHANIEL	HAR	128	2ND DIST
SMITH, NATHANIEL	BAL	301	3RD WARD
SMITH, NATHANIEL	ALL	217	CUMBERLA
SMITH, NATHANIEL	BAL	243	6TH WARD
SMITH, NATHANIEL-BLACK	BAL	219	2ND WARD
SMITH, NATHANIEL-BLACK	CAR	080	NO TWP L
SMITH, NELSON	BAL	424	1ST DIST
SMITH, NERI	ALL	164	6TH E.D.
SMITH, NICHOLAS	BAL	385	1ST DIST
SMITH, NICHOLAS	BAL	260	1ST DIST
SMITH, NICHOLAS	BAL	119	1ST WARD
SMITH, NICHOLAS	BAL	390	8TH WARD
SMITH, NICHOLAS	BAL	222	19TH WAR
SMITH, NICHOLAS	BAL	266	20TH WAR
SMITH, NICHOLAS	BAL	266	20TH WAR
SMITH, NIMROD	CAR	231	5TH DIST
SMITH, NOAH	WAS	078	2ND SUBD
SMITH, NOAH-BLACK	FRE	018	FREDERIC
SMITH, NOAH-BLACK	CAR	110	NO TWP L
SMITH, NORRIS	PRI	119	PISCATAW
SMITH, O.	BAL	117	1ST WARD
SMITH, O.E.A.	ALL	250	CUMRERLA
SMITH, OBADIAH	CAR	306	1ST DIST
SMITH, OLEVIA	HAR	082	2ND DIST
SMITH, OLISEM M.	BAL	114	18TH WAR
SMITH, OWEN	BAL	153	11TH WAR
SMITH, OWEN K.	BAL	320	1ST DIST
SMITH, P.	BAL	165	1ST WARD
SMITH, PAT	BAL	109	2ND DIST
SMITH, PAT	BAL	155	19TH WAR
SMITH, PATRICK	BAL	272	17TH WAR
SMITH, PATRICK	BAL	098	18TH WAR
SMITH, PATRICK	BAL	103	2ND DIST
SMITH, PATRICK	BAL	157	6TH WARD
SMITH, PATRICK	ALL	195	CUMBERLA
SMITH, PATRICK	ALL	047	10TH E.D
SMITH, PATRICK	BAL	272	1ST DIST
SMITH, PATRICK	BAL	401	8TH WARD
SMITH, PATRICK	BAL	441	1ST DIST
SMITH, PATRICK	BAL	172	11TH WAR
SMITH, PATRICK	BAL	068	15TH WAR
SMITH, PATRICK	BAL	059	15TH WAR
SMITH, PATSY	BAL	128	11TH WAR
SMITH, PAULINE	BAL	369	8TH WARD
SMITH, PEGGY	SOM	513	BARREN C
SMITH, PEGGY	TAL	115	ST MICHA
SMITH, PERE	QUE	225	4TH E DI
SMITH, PERRY	KEN	208	2ND DIST
SMITH, PERRY G.	FRE	085	FREDERIC
SMITH, PERRY-BLACK	CAR	082	NO TWP L
SMITH, PERRY-BLACK	CAR	069	NO TWP L
SMITH, PETER	FRE	296	WOODSBOR
SMITH, PETER	BAL	427	14TH WAR
SMITH, PETER	BAL	012	4TH WARD
SMITH, PETER	FRE	352	MIDDLETO
SMITH, PETER	FRE	432	8TH E DI
SMITH, PETER	MGM	318	CRACKLIN
SMITH, PETER	WOR	216	4TH E DI
SMITH, PETER	WAS	074	2ND SUBD
SMITH, PETER	BAL	434	8TH WARD
SMITH, PETER	BAL	443	1ST DIST
SMITH, PETER	BAL	117	1ST WARD
SMITH, PETER	BAL	105	1ST WARD
SMITH, PETER	BAL	350	3RD WARD
SMITH, PETER	ALL	168	6TH E.D.
SMITH, PETER	BAL	046	2ND DIST
SMITH, PETER	BAL	053	9TH WARD
SMITH, PETER B.	CAR	174	8TH DIST
SMITH, PETER M.	BAL	109	15TH WAR
SMITH, PETER P.	ST	314	1ST E DI
SMITH, PHEBE	BAL	396	3RD WARD
SMITH, PHEBE	HAR	100	2ND DIST
SMITH, PHILEMON	MGM	437	CLARKSTR
SMITH, PHILEMON M.	FRE	245	NEW MARK
SMITH, PHILIP	CAR	306	1ST DIST
SMITH, PHILIP	BAL	044	4TH WARD
SMITH, PHILIP	BAL	144	1ST WARD
SMITH, PHILIP	BAL	105	2ND DIST
SMITH, PHILIP B.	BAL	057	18TH WAR
SMITH, PHILIP L.	BAL	423	3RD WARD
SMITH, PHILIPPA	BAL	275	12TH WAR
SMITH, PHILLIP	FRE	290	WOODSBOR
SMITH, PHILLIP	KEN	231	2ND DIST
SMITH, PHOEBE	SOM	492	SALISBUR
SMITH, POLLY	SOM	533	QUANTICO
SMITH, POLLY	BAL	443	14TH WAR
SMITH, POLLY	BAL	389	13TH WAR
SMITH, POLLY	ANN	300	1ST DIST
SMITH, POWLES	BAL	409	8TH WARD
SMITH, PRICILLA	BAL	306	7TH WARD
SMITH, PRICILLA	BAL	150	5TH WARD
SMITH, R.	BAL	241	20TH WAR
SMITH, RACHAEL	BAL	148	11TH WAR
SMITH, RACHAEL	CAR	139	NO TWP L
SMITH, RACHEAL	CAR	404	2ND DIST
SMITH, RACHEL	QUE	156	2ND E DI
SMITH, RACHEL	BAL	233	20TH WAR
SMITH, RACHEL	BAL	210	6TH WARD
SMITH, RACHEL	BAL	387	8TH WARD
SMITH, RACHEL	BAL	376	3RD WARD
SMITH, RACHEL	BAL	160	2ND DIST
SMITH, RACHEL	BAL	265	12TH WAR
SMITH, RACHEL A.	BAL	169	16TH WAR
SMITH, RACHEL A.	MGM	377	ROCKERLE
SMITH, RACHIEL	HAR	034	1ST DIST
SMITH, RANDOLPH A.	MGM	394	ROCKERLE
SMITH, REBECA	BAL	281	20TH WAR

Name	County	Page	District
SMITH, REBECCA	FRE	012	FREDERIC
SMITH, REBECCA	FRE	079	FREDERIC
SMITH, REBECCA	CHA	286	BOJANTOW
SMITH, REBECCA	CHA	281	BOJANTOW
SMITH, REBECCA	FRE	309	WOODSBOR
SMITH, REBECCA	BAL	373	13TH WAR
SMITH, REBECCA	BAL	157	16TH WAR
SMITH, REBECCA	BAL	201	11TH WAR
SMITH, REBECCA	BAL	205	11TH WAR
SMITH, REBECCA	BAL	219	2ND WARD
SMITH, REBECCA	BAL	094	2ND DIST
SMITH, REBECCA	BAL	320	3RD WARD
SMITH, REBECCA	PRI	032	VANSVILL
SMITH, REBECCA J.	BAL	423	3RD WARD
SMITH, RENNIS*	TAL	001	EASTON D
SMITH, RENSALEAR	BAL	101	15TH WAR
SMITH, REUBEN	QUE	164	2ND E DI
SMITH, RHEUBEN	HAR	003	1ST DIST
SMITH, RICHARD	HAR	118	2ND DIST
SMITH, RICHARD	BAL	433	14TH WAR
SMITH, RICHARD	CHA	281	BOJANTOW
SMITH, RICHARD	DOR	321	1ST DIST
SMITH, RICHARD	CAR	374	9TH DIST
SMITH, RICHARD	CAR	395	2ND DIST
SMITH, RICHARD	TAL	009	EASTON D
SMITH, RICHARD	WOR	284	BERLIN 1
SMITH, RICHARD	BAL	094	15TH WAR
SMITH, RICHARD	BAL	288	3RD WARD
SMITH, RICHARD	BAL	286	2ND WARD
SMITH, RICHARD	BAL	183	5TH DIST
SMITH, RICHARD	BAL	276	7TH WARD
SMITH, RICHARD	ANN	297	1ST DIST
SMITH, RICHARD	BAL	311	1ST DIST
SMITH, RICHARD S.*	TAL	043	EASTON D
SMITH, RICHARDSON	SOM	552	TYASKIN
SMITH, RINGOLD	ANN	502	HOWARD D
SMITH, RISDON S. J.	DOR	297	1ST DIST
SMITH, ROBERT	BAL	425	14TH WAR
SMITH, ROBERT	CEC	155	PORT DUP
SMITH, ROBERT	CEC	116	3RD E DI
SMITH, ROBERT	FRE	034	FREDERIC
SMITH, ROBERT	BAL	290	20TH WAR
SMITH, ROBERT	BAL	292	20TH WAR
SMITH, ROBERT	CHA	252	BOJANTOW
SMITH, ROBERT	BAL	309	20TH WAR
SMITH, ROBERT	HAR	175	3RD DIST
SMITH, ROBERT	BAL	179	19TH WAR
SMITH, ROBERT	BAL	041	4TH WARD
SMITH, ROBERT	CAR	134	NO TWP L
SMITH, ROBERT	CAR	068	NO TWP L
SMITH, ROBERT	CAR	120	NO TWP L
SMITH, ROBERT	ALL	073	5TH E.D.
SMITH, ROBERT	BAL	144	1ST WARD
SMITH, ROBERT	BAL	164	11TH WAR
SMITH, ROBERT	BAL	115	2ND DIST
SMITH, ROBERT	BAL	077	2ND DIST
SMITH, ROBERT	BAL	026	9TH WARD
SMITH, ROBERT	TAL	007	EASTON D
SMITH, ROBERT	WAS	076	2ND SUBD
SMITH, ROBERT	DOR	455	1ST DIST
SMITH, ROBERT	WOR	204	4TH E DI
SMITH, RODA	BAL	199	11TH WAR
SMITH, ROSA	BAL	064	10TH WAR
SMITH, ROSA	BAL	088	4TH WARD
SMITH, ROSE	BAL	268	17TH WAR
SMITH, ROSE	BAL	411	3RD WARD
SMITH, ROSE	FRE	203	5TH E DI
SMITH, ROSINDA	CAR	396	2ND DIST
SMITH, RUTH	BAL	407	14TH WAR
SMITH, RUTH	BAL	062	10TH WAR
SMITH, RUTH A.	CEC	205	7TH E DI
SMITH, S.	ANN	284	ANNAPOLI
SMITH, S.	BAL	117	1ST WARD
SMITH, S. C.	BAL	286	2ND WARD
SMITH, S.A.	BAL	140	1ST WARD
SMITH, SABINA	HAR	182	3RD DIST
SMITH, SALLY	BAL	251	20TH WAR
SMITH, SAMUEL	BAL	242	20TH WAR
SMITH, SAMUEL	FRE	159	EMMITTSB
SMITH, SAMUEL	CAL	051	3RD DIST
SMITH, SAMUEL	HAR	204	3RD DIST
SMITH, SAMUEL	DOR	433	1ST DIST
SMITH, SAMUEL	FRE	348	MIDDLETO
SMITH, SAMUEL	CEC	023	ELKTON 3
SMITH, SAMUEL	BAL	418	14TH WAR
SMITH, SAMUEL	CAR	374	9TH DIST
SMITH, SAMUEL	BAL	298	17TH WAR
SMITH, SAMUEL	HAR	118	2ND DIST
SMITH, SAMUEL	HAR	114	2ND DIST
SMITH, SAMUEL	BAL	145	1ST WARD
SMITH, SAMUEL	BAL	138	1ST WARD
SMITH, SAMUEL	BAL	406	3RD WARD
SMITH, SAMUEL	BAL	455	8TH WARD
SMITH, SAMUEL	ANN	305	1ST DIST
SMITH, SAMUEL	ALL	159	6TH E.D.
SMITH, SAMUEL	ANN	399	8TH DIST
SMITH, SAMUEL	BAL	192	17TH WAR
SMITH, SAMUEL	BAL	102	15TH WAR
SMITH, SAMUEL	BAL	104	10TH WAR
SMITH, SAMUEL	BAL	160	6TH WARD
SMITH, SAMUEL	ANN	394	8TH DIST
SMITH, SAMUEL	BAL	345	3RD WARD
SMITH, SAMUEL	BAL	307	3RD WARD
SMITH, SAMUEL	BAL	390	1ST DIST
SMITH, SAMUEL	BAL	404	1ST DIST
SMITH, SAMUEL	BAL	386	1ST DIST
SMITH, SAMUEL	BAL	393	1ST DIST
SMITH, SAMUEL	BAL	460	1ST DIST
SMITH, SAMUEL	WAS	195	1ST DIST
SMITH, SAMUEL	WAS	079	2ND SUBD
SMITH, SAMUEL	PRI	023	VANSVILL
SMITH, SAMUEL	WAS	125	2ND DIST
SMITH, SAMUEL	WAS	189	1ST DIST
SMITH, SAMUEL	WAS	134	2ND DIST
SMITH, SAMUEL A.	CEC	130	6TH E DI
SMITH, SAMUEL A.	KEN	209	2ND DIST
SMITH, SAMUEL B.	FRE	229	BUCKEYST
SMITH, SAMUEL B.	BAL	352	1ST DIST
SMITH, SAMUEL B.	ANN	398	8TH DIST
SMITH, SAMUEL C.	BAL	380	3RD WARD
SMITH, SAMUEL C.	WOR	253	1ST CENS
SMITH, SAMUEL E.	BAL	247	12TH WAR
SMITH, SAMUEL E. *	ANN	397	8TH DIST
SMITH, SAMUEL G.	BAL	135	1ST WARD
SMITH, SAMUEL G.	CAR	119	NO TWP L
SMITH, SAMUEL H.	BAL	299	17TH WAR
SMITH, SAMUEL H.	BAL	400	3RD WARD
SMITH, SAMUEL H.	WAS	182	BOONSBOR
SMITH, SAMUEL J.	BAL	248	12TH WAR
SMITH, SAMUEL JR.	BAL	258	6TH WARD

Name	County	Page	District
SMITH, SAMUEL R.	BAL	065	18TH WAR
SMITH, SAMUEL S.	SOM	479	TRAPP DI
SMITH, SAMUEL W.	KEN	241	2ND DIST
SMITH, SARAH	FRE	150	10TH E D
SMITH, SARAH	HAR	173	3RD DIST
SMITH, SARAH	BAL	017	18TH WAR
SMITH, SARAH	CAL	061	3RD DIST
SMITH, SARAH	BAL	385	13TH WAR
SMITH, SARAH	BAL	392	14TH WAR
SMITH, SARAH	BAL	472	14TH WAR
SMITH, SARAH	HAR	194	3RD DIST
SMITH, SARAH	BAL	075	4TH WARD
SMITH, SARAH	SOM	414	DUBLIN D
SMITH, SARAH	SOM	410	DUBLIN D
SMITH, SARAH	BAL	195	19TH WAR
SMITH, SARAH	CAR	167	NO TWP L
SMITH, SARAH	BAL	036	4TH WARD
SMITH, SARAH	CEC	211	7TH E DI
SMITH, SARAH	PRI	119	PISCATAW
SMITH, SARAH	WAS	120	2ND DIST
SMITH, SARAH	KEN	293	3RD DIST
SMITH, SARAH	BAL	253	12TH WAR
SMITH, SARAH	ALL	021	2ND E.D.
SMITH, SARAH	ALL	210	CUMBERLA
SMITH, SARAH	BAL	066	2ND DIST
SMITH, SARAH	BAL	147	5TH WARD
SMITH, SARAH	BAL	020	9TH WARD
SMITH, SARAH	BAL	244	6TH WARD
SMITH, SARAH	BAL	163	16TH WAR
SMITH, SARAH A.	BAL	137	5TH WARD
SMITH, SARAH A.	BAL	029	9TH WARD
SMITH, SARAH A.	ANN	463	HOWARD D
SMITH, SARAH A.	BAL	068	15TH WAR
SMITH, SARAH A.	BAL	051	15TH WAR
SMITH, SARAH A.	SOM	464	HANGARY
SMITH, SARAH A.	SOM	359	BRINKLEY
SMITH, SARAH A.	BAL	053	4TH WARD
SMITH, SARAH A.	CEC	090	4TH E DI
SMITH, SARAH ANN	BAL	092	10TH WAR
SMITH, SARAH E.	DOR	454	1ST DIST
SMITH, SARAH J.	PRI	064	NOTTINGH
SMITH, SARAH J.	BAL	346	3RD WARD
SMITH, SARAH J.	HAR	114	2ND DIST
SMITH, SARAH J.*	BAL	070	10TH WAR
SMITH, SARAH R.	BAL	380	13TH WAR
SMITH, SARAHA	BAL	353	3RD WARD
SMITH, SAVANAH	BAL	458	1ST DIST
SMITH, SCOTT	FRE	202	5TH E DI
SMITH, SERENA-BLACK	FRE	015	FREDERIC
SMITH, SETH	BAL	360	3RD WARD
SMITH, SETH	WOR	232	6TH E DI
SMITH, SHADE	BAL	148	2ND DIST
SMITH, SHADRACK	DOR	427	1ST DIST
SMITH, SHEDRICK	BAL	314	3RD WARD
SMITH, SIDNEY	ANN	307	1ST DIST
SMITH, SIMON	WAS	260	1ST DIST
SMITH, SISTER M.M.	FRE	198	5TH E DI
SMITH, SISTER M.R.	FRE	197	5TH E DI
SMITH, SMAUEL	FRE	043	FREDERIC
SMITH, SOLOMON	HAR	182	3RD DIST
SMITH, SOLOMON	BAL	183	19TH WAR
SMITH, SOLOMON	FRE	357	CATOCTIN
SMITH, SOLOMON	WAS	190	1ST DIST
SMITH, SOLOMON	BAL	300	3RD WARD
SMITH, SOLOMON-BLACK	QUE	146	1ST E DI
SMITH, SOPHIA	QUE	151	1ST E DI
SMITH, SOPHIA	DOR	427	1ST DIST
SMITH, SOPHIA	BAL	429	14TH WAR
SMITH, SOPHIA	BAL	203	17TH WAR
SMITH, SOPHIA	BAL	401	14TH WAR
SMITH, SOPHIA	WAS	137	HAGERSTO
SMITH, SOPHIA	TAL	002	EASTON D
SMITH, SRAH	CAR	279	7TH DIST
SMITH, STEPHEN	BAL	138	11TH WAR
SMITH, STEPHEN	MGM	426	MEDLEY 3
SMITH, STEPHEN	SOM	480	TRAPP DI
SMITH, STEPHEN	BAL	039	15TH WAR
SMITH, STEPHEN H.-BLACK	ST	326	4TH E DI
SMITH, STERLING	BAL	405	14TH WAR
SMITH, STEVEN	FRE	087	FREDERIC
SMITH, SUSAN	BAL	061	18TH WAR
SMITH, SUSAN	BAL	434	14TH WAR
SMITH, SUSAN	FRE	240	NEW MARK
SMITH, SUSAN	FRE	296	WOODSBOR
SMITH, SUSAN	CHA	278	BOJANTOW
SMITH, SUSAN	CAR	319	1ST DIST
SMITH, SUSAN	CHA	217	ALLENS F
SMITH, SUSAN	WAS	089	2ND SUBD
SMITH, SUSAN	BAL	119	5TH WARD
SMITH, SUSAN	BAL	137	5TH WARD
SMITH, SUSAN B.	FRE	298	WOODSBOR
SMITH, SUSAN-BLACK	CAR	168	NO TWP L
SMITH, SUSAN-BLACK	CAR	391	2ND DIST
SMITH, SUSANNA-MULATTO	FRE	436	8TH E DI
SMITH, SUSANNAH	BAL	147	16TH WAR
SMITH, SYLVESTER H.	DOR	316	1ST DIST
SMITH, SYMS	BAL	245	17TH WAR
SMITH, T. A.	CHA	244	HILLTOP
SMITH, T. C.	BAL	329	13TH WAR
SMITH, TABITAH	WOR	307	2ND E DI
SMITH, TABITHA	WOR	189	7TH E DI
SMITH, TANNEY	BAL	273	7TH WARD
SMITH, TELGHMAN	BAL	342	13TH WAR
SMITH, TEMPEY	BAL	276	7TH WARD
SMITH, TERESSA*	BAL	314	3RD WARD
SMITH, THOMAS	BAL	106	5TH WARD
SMITH, THOMAS	BAL	427	1ST DIST
SMITH, THOMAS	BAL	126	1ST WARD
SMITH, THOMAS	BAL	126	1ST WARD
SMITH, THOMAS	BAL	121	5TH WARD
SMITH, THOMAS	BAL	311	7TH WARD
SMITH, THOMAS	BAL	251	2ND WARD
SMITH, THOMAS	BAL	083	10TH WAR
SMITH, THOMAS	BAL	084	15TH WAR
SMITH, THOMAS	BAL	207	2ND WARD
SMITH, THOMAS	BAL	204	6TH WARD
SMITH, THOMAS	BAL	162	1ST WARD
SMITH, THOMAS	BAL	171	1ST WARD
SMITH, THOMAS	BAL	167	1ST WARD
SMITH, THOMAS	BAL	286	2ND WARD
SMITH, THOMAS	BAL	003	9TH WARD
SMITH, THOMAS	BAL	262	12TH WAR
SMITH, THOMAS	ANN	320	2ND DIST
SMITH, THOMAS	ALL	148	6TH E.D.
SMITH, THOMAS	BAL	066	2ND DIST
SMITH, THOMAS	BAL	131	2ND DIST
SMITH, THOMAS	BAL	085	2ND DIST
SMITH, THOMAS	BAL	010	EASTERN
SMITH, THOMAS	BAL	125	1ST WARD
SMITH, THOMAS	BAL	114	1ST WARD

Name	County	Page	District
SMITH, THOMAS	BAL	007	1ST WARD
SMITH, THOMAS	BAL	253	17TH WAR
SMITH, THOMAS	CEC	143	7TH E DI
SMITH, THOMAS	CAR	392	2ND DIST
SMITH, THOMAS	CEC	074	5TH E DI
SMITH, THOMAS	BAL	057	18TH WAR
SMITH, THOMAS	BAL	084	18TH WAR
SMITH, THOMAS	CEC	092	4TH E DI
SMITH, THOMAS	CEC	081	CHARLEST
SMITH, THOMAS	CAR	359	9TH DIST
SMITH, THOMAS	CAR	200	4TH DIST
SMITH, THOMAS	FRE	246	NEW MARK
SMITH, THOMAS	DOR	433	1ST DIST
SMITH, THOMAS	FRE	220	BUCKEYST
SMITH, THOMAS	BAL	132	18TH WAR
SMITH, THOMAS	FRE	152	10TH E D
SMITH, THOMAS	CAL	048	3RD DIST
SMITH, THOMAS	WOR	204	4TH E DI
SMITH, THOMAS	SOM	488	SALISBUR
SMITH, THOMAS	SOM	491	SALISBUR
SMITH, THOMAS	SOM	534	QUANTICO
SMITH, THOMAS	TAL	117	ST MICHA
SMITH, THOMAS	WAS	084	2ND SUBD
SMITH, THOMAS	PRI	017	BLADENSB
SMITH, THOMAS	TAL	019	EASTON D
SMITH, THOMAS	WOR	285	BERLIN 1
SMITH, THOMAS	WAS	295	1ST DIST
SMITH, THOMAS	ST	308	1ST E DI
SMITH, THOMAS	WAS	183	BOONSBOR
SMITH, THOMAS	WAS	148	2ND DIST
SMITH, THOMAS B.	WOR	233	6TH E DI
SMITH, THOMAS B.	CHA	277	BOJANTOW
SMITH, THOMAS C.	BAL	033	9TH WARD
SMITH, THOMAS D.	BAL	253	12TH WAR
SMITH, THOMAS E.	CAL	015	1ST DIST
SMITH, THOMAS E.	FRE	411	8TH E DI
SMITH, THOMAS E.	WAS	178	BOONSBOR
SMITH, THOMAS F.	BAL	017	15TH WAR
SMITH, THOMAS H.	BAL	016	15TH WAR
SMITH, THOMAS H.	CAR	109	NO TWP L
SMITH, THOMAS J.	ALL	210	CUMBERLA
SMITH, THOMAS O.	MGM	368	BERRYS D
SMITH, THOMAS R.	DOR	453	1ST DIST
SMITH, THOMAS T.	BAL	332	13TH WAR
SMITH, THOMAS W.	DOR	451	1ST DIST
SMITH, THOMAS-BLACK	FRE	234	BUCKEYST
SMITH, TOM	QUE	220	3RD E DI
SMITH, TOM	ANN	342	3RD DIST
SMITH, TRACY	WAS	126	HAGERSTO
SMITH, TUKIEL	CAR	088	NO TWP L
SMITH, VACHAEL	BAL	271	1ST DIST
SMITH, VALENTINE	BAL	104	2ND DIST
SMITH, VAN	MGM	391	ROCKERLE
SMITH, VAUGHN	SOM	359	BRINKLEY
SMITH, VIRGINIA	SOM	360	BRINKLEY
SMITH, VIRGINIA	ALL	227	CUMBERLA
SMITH, VIRGINIA E.	FRE	015	FREDERIC
SMITH, W.	ANN	282	ANNAPOLI
SMITH, W.	BAL	149	1ST WARD
SMITH, W.D.	BAL	138	1ST WARD
SMITH, W.H.	ANN	270	ANNAPOLI
SMITH, WALTER	CAL	018	1ST DIST
SMITH, WALTER	PRI	081	QUEEN AN
SMITH, WASHINGTON	CAR	115	NO TWP L
SMITH, WASHINGTON DOCTOR	DOR	359	3RD DIVI
SMITH, WASHINGTON-BLACK	ST	326	4TH E DI
SMITH, WEST	BAL	093	15TH WAR
SMITH, WESTER	BAL	043	9TH WARD
SMITH, WHITTINGTON	BAL	011	15TH WAR
SMITH, WILIAM	BAL	270	2ND WARD
SMITH, WILIAM	FRE	263	NEW MARK
SMITH, WILIAM-BLACK	CAR	169	NO TWP L
SMITH, WILLAIM	BAL	180	2ND DIST
SMITH, WILLAIM	KEN	297	3RD DIST
SMITH, WILLAIM	PRI	092	MARLBROU
SMITH, WILLIAM	SOM	479	TRAPP DI
SMITH, WILLIAM	SOM	530	QUANTICO
SMITH, WILLIAM	WOR	176	6TH E DI
SMITH, WILLIAM	PRI	037	VANSVILL
SMITH, WILLIAM	KEN	302	3RD DIST
SMITH, WILLIAM	ST	333	4TH E DI
SMITH, WILLIAM	QUE	195	3RD E DI
SMITH, WILLIAM	SOM	456	DAMES QU
SMITH, WILLIAM	SOM	469	TRAPPE D
SMITH, WILLIAM	SOM	475	TRAPPE D
SMITH, WILLIAM	WAS	267	1ST DIST
SMITH, WILLIAM	QUE	165	2ND E DI
SMITH, WILLIAM	ST	334	4TH E DI
SMITH, WILLIAM	WAS	137	2ND DIST
SMITH, WILLIAM	QUE	238	5TH E DI
SMITH, WILLIAM	QUE	250	5TH E DI
SMITH, WILLIAM	WOR	259	BERLIN 1
SMITH, WILLIAM	WAS	085	2ND SUBD
SMITH, WILLIAM	BAL	251	1ST DIST
SMITH, WILLIAM	BAL	108	1ST WARD
SMITH, WILLIAM	BAL	351	3RD WARD
SMITH, WILLIAM	BAL	150	2ND DIST
SMITH, WILLIAM	BAL	166	2ND DIST
SMITH, WILLIAM	BAL	279	2ND WARD
SMITH, WILLIAM	BAL	262	2ND WARD
SMITH, WILLIAM	BAL	249	2ND WARD
SMITH, WILLIAM	BAL	148	1ST WARD
SMITH, WILLIAM	BAL	143	1ST WARD
SMITH, WILLIAM	BAL	137	1ST WARD
SMITH, WILLIAM	BAL	137	1ST WARD
SMITH, WILLIAM	BAL	147	1ST WARD
SMITH, WILLIAM	BAL	140	1ST WARD
SMITH, WILLIAM	BAL	139	1ST WARD
SMITH, WILLIAM	BAL	306	7TH WARD
SMITH, WILLIAM	BAL	123	1ST WARD
SMITH, WILLIAM	BAL	125	1ST WARD
SMITH, WILLIAM	BAL	126	1ST WARD
SMITH, WILLIAM	BAL	127	1ST WARD
SMITH, WILLIAM	BAL	136	1ST WARD
SMITH, WILLIAM	BAL	135	1ST WARD
SMITH, WILLIAM	BAL	135	1ST WARD
SMITH, WILLIAM	BAL	385	8TH WARD
SMITH, WILLIAM	BAL	396	8TH WARD
SMITH, WILLIAM	BAL	231	12TH WAR
SMITH, WILLIAM	BAL	059	15TH WAR
SMITH, WILLIAM	BAL	042	15TH WAR
SMITH, WILLIAM	BAL	202	11TH WAR
SMITH, WILLIAM	BAL	351	7TH WARD
SMITH, WILLIAM	BAL	002	15TH WAR
SMITH, WILLIAM	BAL	153	1ST WARD
SMITH, WILLIAM	BAL	167	1ST WARD
SMITH, WILLIAM	BAL	172	1ST WARD
SMITH, WILLIAM	BAL	172	1ST WARD
SMITH, WILLIAM	BAL	157	1ST WARD
SMITH, WILLIAM	BAL	137	5TH WARD

SMITH, WILLIAM	BAL	158	6TH WARD
SMITH, WILLIAM	BAL	021	9TH WARD
SMITH, WILLIAM	BAL	085	15TH WAR
SMITH, WILLIAM	BAL	076	10TH WAR
SMITH, WILLIAM	BAL	136	16TH WAR
SMITH, WILLIAM	BAL	328	7TH WARD
SMITH, WILLIAM	BAL	323	7TH WARD
SMITH, WILLIAM	BAL	113	15TH WAR
SMITH, WILLIAM	BAL	119	15TH WAR
SMITH, WILLIAM	BAL	286	12TH WAR
SMITH, WILLIAM	ANN	313	1ST DIST
SMITH, WILLIAM	ALL	091	5TH E.D.
SMITH, WILLIAM	ALL	220	CUMBERLA
SMITH, WILLIAM	ALL	228	CUMBERLA
SMITH, WILLIAM	ANN	473	HOWARD D
SMITH, WILLIAM	BAL	007	EASTERN
SMITH, WILLIAM	BAL	140	2ND DIST
SMITH, WILLIAM	BAL	067	2ND DIST
SMITH, WILLIAM	BAL	013	2ND DIST
SMITH, WILLIAM	BAL	457	1ST DIST
SMITH, WILLIAM	BAL	343	3RD WARD
SMITH, WILLIAM	BAL	338	1ST DIST
SMITH, WILLIAM	ANN	512	HOWARD D
SMITH, WILLIAM	BAL	409	3RD WARD
SMITH, WILLIAM	CAR	235	UNION TO
SMITH, WILLIAM	CAR	227	5TH DIST
SMITH, WILLIAM	BAL	171	19TH WAR
SMITH, WILLIAM	BAL	134	18TH WAR
SMITH, WILLIAM	CAR	396	2ND DIST
SMITH, WILLIAM	DOR	410	1ST DIST
SMITH, WILLIAM	FRE	309	WOODSBOR
SMITH, WILLIAM	KEN	218	2ND DIST
SMITH, WILLIAM	DOR	391	1ST DIST
SMITH, WILLIAM	DOR	351	3RD DIVI
SMITH, WILLIAM	FRE	369	CATOCTIN
SMITH, WILLIAM	CHA	244	HILLTOP
SMITH, WILLIAM	CAL	018	1ST DIST
SMITH, WILLIAM	BAL	464	14TH WAR
SMITH, WILLIAM	CAL	040	3RD DIST
SMITH, WILLIAM	HAR	073	1ST DIST
SMITH, WILLIAM	SOM	438	DAMES QU
SMITH, WILLIAM	FRE	073	FREDERIC
SMITH, WILLIAM	CHA	284	BOJANTOW
SMITH, WILLIAM	HAR	181	3RD DIST
SMITH, WILLIAM	CHA	294	BOJANTOW
SMITH, WILLIAM	FRE	118	CREAGERS
SMITH, WILLIAM	CEC	099	3RD E DI
SMITH, WILLIAM	BAL	029	18TH WAR
SMITH, WILLIAM	BAL	102	18TH WAR
SMITH, WILLIAM	BAL	091	18TH WAR
SMITH, WILLIAM	CEC	145	PORT DUP
SMITH, WILLIAM	BAL	275	17TH WAR
SMITH, WILLIAM	BAL	434	14TH WAR
SMITH, WILLIAM	BAL	074	4TH WARD
SMITH, WILLIAM	BAL	359	13TH WAR
SMITH, WILLIAM A.	HAR	161	3RD DIST
SMITH, WILLIAM A.	FRE	161	EMMITTSB
SMITH, WILLIAM A.	BAL	142	19TH WAR
SMITH, WILLIAM A. C.	FRE	297	WOODSBOR
SMITH, WILLIAM B.	CHA	262	MIDDLETO
SMITH, WILLIAM C.	BAL	302	17TH WAR
SMITH, WILLIAM E.	BAL	158	1ST WARD
SMITH, WILLIAM F.	BAL	320	3RD WARD
SMITH, WILLIAM F.	WAS	188	BOONSBOR
SMITH, WILLIAM F.	KEN	310	3RD DIST
SMITH, WILLIAM G.	BAL	164	1ST WARD
SMITH, WILLIAM G.	BAL	152	1ST WARD
SMITH, WILLIAM G.	BAL	150	1ST WARD
SMITH, WILLIAM H.	BAL	021	9TH WARD
SMITH, WILLIAM H.	BAL	171	1ST WARD
SMITH, WILLIAM H.	BAL	171	1ST WARD
SMITH, WILLIAM H.	ALL	246	CUMBERLA
SMITH, WILLIAM H.	ALL	122	4TH E.D.
SMITH, WILLIAM H.	ANN	405	8TH DIST
SMITH, WILLIAM H.	BAL	003	9TH WARD
SMITH, WILLIAM H.	BAL	071	1ST WARD
SMITH, WILLIAM H.	ST	305	1ST E DI
SMITH, WILLIAM H.	CEC	092	4TH E DI
SMITH, WILLIAM H.	BAL	085	18TH WAR
SMITH, WILLIAM H.	FRE	318	MIDDLETO
SMITH, WILLIAM H.	FRE	217	BUCKEYST
SMITH, WILLIAM H.	HAR	162	3RD DIST
SMITH, WILLIAM H.	HAR	119	2ND DIST
SMITH, WILLIAM J.	DOR	449	1ST DIST
SMITH, WILLIAM J.	BAL	150	1ST WARD
SMITH, WILLIAM J.	BAL	321	7TH WARD
SMITH, WILLIAM JR.	SOM	438	DAMES QU
SMITH, WILLIAM K.	BAL	354	1ST DIST
SMITH, WILLIAM L.	ST	313	1ST E DI
SMITH, WILLIAM M.	BAL	237	6TH WARD
SMITH, WILLIAM P.	BAL	130	1ST WARD
SMITH, WILLIAM P.	BAL	124	5TH WARD
SMITH, WILLIAM R.	HAR	204	3RD DIST
SMITH, WILLIAM S.	BAL	097	15TH WAR
SMITH, WILLIAM T.	TAL	083	ST MICHA
SMITH, WILLIAM W.	TAL	023	EASTON D
SMITH, WILLIAM W.	PRI	068	NOTTINGH
SMITH, WILLIAM-BLACK	QUE	183	3RD E DI
SMITH, WILLIAM-BLACK	QUE	203	3RD E DI
SMITH, WILLIAM-BLACK	CAR	401	2ND DIST
SMITH, WILLIAM-BLACK	CAR	167	NO TWP L
SMITH, WILLIAM-MULATTO	FRE	207	BUCKEYST
SMITH, WILLIAM-MULATTO	FRE	427	8TH E DI
SMITH, WILLIAMINE	BAL	137	2ND DIST
SMITH, WILSCN	BAL	085	15TH WAR
SMITH, YOST	ALL	159	6TH E.D.
SMITH, ZACHARA	BAL	016	15TH WAR
SMITH, ZEPHENIER	FRE	116	CREAGERS
SMITH, ZEPORA	CAR	109	NO TWP L
SMITH, ZOROBEBLE*	DOR	428	1ST DIST
SMITH,EMERY	BAL	174	1ST WARD
SMITH,F RANCIS	BAL	116	1ST WARD
SMITH,F.	BAL	173	1ST WARD
SMITH,FENDER-BLACK	FRE	409	JEFFERSO
SMITH,GEORGE	BAL	085	1ST WARD
SMITH,H.S.	BAL	115	1ST WARD
SMITH,J.	BAL	163	1ST WARD
SMITH,JESSE L.	CAR	413	2ND DIST
SMITH,LEONARD-BLACK	FRE	002	FREDERIC
SMITH,LEWIS	FRE	401	JEFFERSO
SMITH,LEWIS	BAL	133	1ST WARD
SMITH,LUCY A.	BAL	183	2ND WARD
SMITH,M.	BAL	121	1ST WARD
SMITH,MARIA	BAL	062	1ST WARD
SMITH,MARY	BAL	066	2ND DIST
SMITH,MARY	CAR	385	2ND DIST
SMITH,MICHAEL	CAR	382	2ND DIST
SMITH,MICHAEL	FRE	417	8TH E DI
SMITH,MICHEAL	QUE	151	1ST E DI
SMITH,NATHANIEL	QUE	142	1ST E DI
SMITH,RACHEAL A.	CAR	395	2ND DIST
SMITH,RAPHAEL J.	FRE	20	5TH E DI
SMITH,ROSY	WOR	343	1ST E DI
SMITH,SUSNA	FRE	416	8TH E DI
SMITH,T.	BAL	137	1ST WARD
SMITH,THEODORE W.	FRE	389	PETERSVI
SMITH,WALTER C.	ALL	216	CUMBERLA
SMITH,WILLIAM	BAL	138	1ST WARD
SMITHEN, MARY	BAL	370	3RD WARD
SMITHERS, BETSY	BAL	124	5TH WARD
SMITHERS, E. F.*	DOR	447	1ST DIST
SMITHERS, LEWELLA	BAL	396	14TH WAR
SMITHERS, R.	ANN	272	ANNAPOLI
SMITHERS, VIRGINIA	BAL	130	5TH WARD
SMITHING, WILLIAM	BAL	137	1ST WARD
SMITHMAN, CHARLES A.	TAL	083	ST MICHA
SMITHSON, ALISON	PRI	105	PISCATAW
SMITHSON, GABRIEL	HAR	068	1ST DIST
SMITHSON, GEORGE A.	HAR	068	1ST DIST
SMITHSON, HENRIETTA	BAL	043	9TH WARD
SMITHSON, JOHN	BAL	397	3RD WARD
SMITHSON, JOHN	HAR	068	1ST DIST
SMITHSON, JOHN	HAR	068	1ST DIST
SMITHSON, JOHN	PRI	040	VANSVILL
SMITHSON, JOHN F.	HAR	080	2ND DIST
SMITHSON, LUTHER	HAR	074	1ST DIST
SMITHSON, MARGARET	HAR	035	1ST DIST
SMITHSON, NATHANIEL	BAL	459	1ST DIST
SMITHSON, THOMAS	HAR	023	1ST DIST
SMITHSON, THOMAS	BAL	463	14TH WAR
SMITHSON, THOMAS E.	HAR	092	2ND DIST
SMITHSON, WILLIAM	HAR	112	2ND DIST
SMITHSON, WILLIAM	HAR	137	2ND DIST
SMITHSON, WILLIAM B.	HAR	106	2ND DIST
SMITHSON, WILLIAM L.	HAR	085	2ND DIST
SMITLE, R.	ANN	284	ANNAPOLI
SMITSON, HENRY	CEC	183	7TH E DI
SMITSON, HEZEKIAH	MGM	330	CRACK_IN
SMITSON, WABBY	CHA	249	HILLTOP
SMITSON, WABLER	CHA	223	ALLENS F
SMITT, HENRY	BAL	141	2ND DIST
SMITTY, ANN	KEN	266	1ST DIST
SMITZ, THEODORE	BAL	063	15TH WAR
SMIYENS, LYDIA	BAL	221	19TH WAR
SMOCK, MARGARET	PRI	074	MARLBROU
SMOLEWOOD, PERRY*	DOR	443	1ST DIST
SMOLLEY, CATHARINE	ALL	045	10TH E.D
SMOLLEY, JOHN A.	ALL	055	10TH E.D
SMOLLEY, JULIAN	ALL	055	10TH E.D
SMOLLEY, LANSCR	ALL	042	10TH E.D
SMOLT, CHARLES	BAL	153	1ST WARD
SMOOK, SOLOMON	BAL	408	8TH WARD
SMOOOT, THOMAS	ST	267	3RD E DI
SMOOT, ALEXANDER	CHA	289	MIDDLETO
SMOOT, ANN E.	DOR	447	1ST DIST
SMOOT, AUTHER D.	CHA	274	ALLENS F
SMOOT, BENJAMIN	CHA	268	BOJANTOW
SMOOT, CATHERINE	BAL	140	11TH WAR
SMOOT, CHARLES	BAL	295	12TH WAR
SMOOT, CHARLES T.	DOR	305	1ST DIST
SMOOT, ELLEN	BAL	140	11TH WAR
SMOOT, EMMA	BAL	317	12TH WAR
SMOOT, G.A.	PRI	101	SPALDING
SMOOT, G.W.	PRI	067	NOTTINGH
SMOOT, HANDSON	CHA	274	ALLENS F
SMOOT, JAMES	ANN	466	HOWARD D
SMOOT, JAOCB G.	MGM	415	MEDLEY 3
SMOOT, JOHN M.	CHA	217	ALLENS F
SMOOT, JOHN N.	ST	298	2ND E DI
SMOOT, JOSEPH	PRI	089	SPALDING
SMOOT, MARY	CHA	225	ALLENS F
SMOOT, S. W.	CHA	221	ALLENS F
SMOOT, SAMUEL	CHA	286	BOJANTOW
SMOOT, THEOPHILIUS	CHA	292	BOJANTOW
SMOOT, THOMAS	CHA	223	ALLENS F
SMOOT, THOMAS	DOR	299	1ST DIST
SMOOT, THOMAS W.	PRI	073	MARLBROU
SMOOT, WILLIAM	CHA	284	BOJANTOW
SMOOT, WILLIAM	CHA	268	BOJANTOW
SMOOTH, SARAH	SOM	512	BARREN C
SMOOTH, THOMAS B.	DOR	305	1ST DIST
SMOOTH, WILLIAM	DOR	305	1ST DIST
SMOOTHERS, MARGARET	BAL	267	1ST DIST
SMORT, JANE	CHA	245	HILLTOP
SMORY, WILLIAM	BAL	261	20TH WAR
SMOTHER, OFFA	ANN	406	8TH DIST
SMOTHER, SARARH	ANN	406	8TH DIST
SMOTHERS, ANNA	ANN	303	1ST DIST
SMOTHERS, ANNA	ANN	305	1ST DIST
SMOTHERS, CATHERINE	BAL	060	10TH WAR
SMOTHERS, HAMILTON-BLACK	FRE	021	FREDERIC
SMOTHERS, HENRY	CHA	285	BOJANTOW
SMOTHERS, JAMES	CAL	059	3RD DIST
SMOTHERS, JHN	FRE	319	MIDDLETO
SMOTHERS, JOHN	CAL	054	3RD DIST
SMOTHERS, JOHN	CAL	044	3RD DIST
SMOTHERS, L.	ANN	296	1ST DIST
SMOTHERS, LUCY-BLACK	FRE	393	PETERSVI
SMOTHERS, MARY	FRE	075	FREDERIC
SMOTHERS, P.	ANN	398	8TH DIST
SMOTHERS, POLLY	ANN	308	1ST DIST
SMOTHERS, ROBERT	FRE	072	FREDERIC
SMOTHERS, SARAH-MULATTO	ST	319	4TH E DI
SMOTHERS, THOMAS J.	FRE	085	FREDERIC
SMOTHERS, THOMAS-MULATTO	FRE	017	FREDERIC
SMOTHERS, WILLIAM	FRE	072	FREDERIC
SMOTHERS, WILLIAM	ANN	319	2ND DIST
SMOTOT, MARY S.	CHA	219	ALLENS F
SMOTOT, WILLIAM H.	CHA	274	ALLENS F
SMOUSE, CATHARINE	ALL	013	3RD E.D.
SMOUSE, CATHARINE	ALL	166	6TH E.D.
SMOUSE, DANIEL	ALL	166	6TH E.D.
SMOUSE, DANIEL	ALL	166	6TH E.D.
SMOUSE, DANIEL	ALL	018	3RD E.D.
SMOUSE, GEORGE	ALL	018	3RD E.D.
SMOUSE, HY	ALL	012	3RD E.D.
SMOUSE, JOHN	ALL	166	6TH E.D.
SMOUSE, MATHIAS	BAL	292	7TH WARD
SMOUSE, THOMAS	ALL	018	3RD E.D.
SMTH, J.S.	BAL	169	1ST WARD
SMTH, SAMUEL	BAL	262	12TH WAR
SMTIH, ANTONY	BAL	158	2ND DIST
SMTIH, GEORGE	BAL	263	2ND WARD
SMTIH, HERNY	BAL	412	1ST DIST
SMTIH, J. G.	BAL	154	1ST WARD
SMTIH, JOHN W.	WOR	304	SNOW HIL
SMTIH, MARGARET	BAL	403	14TH WAR
SMTIH, MARY	BAL	204	2ND WARD
SMULL, AMANDA E.	BAL	019	4TH WARD
SMULL, DAVID B.*	BAL	019	4TH WARD
SMULL, JAMES H.	TAL	087	ST MICHA
SMULLEN, EDWARD	WOR	197	8TH E DI
SMULLEN, ELEANOR	WOR	197	8TH E DI
SMULLEN, ELI	WOR	190	8TH E DI
SMULLEN, HENRY J.	SOM	433	PRINCESS
SMULLEN, ISAAC	WOR	188	7TH E DI
SMULLEN, JOHNH.	WOR	174	6TH E DI
SMULLEN, NANCY	WOR	188	7TH E DI
SMULLEN, NANCY *	SOM	421	PRINCESS
SMULLEN, SARAH *	BAL	072	15TH WAR
SMULLIN, JULIUS	WOR	339	1ST E DI
SMULLIN, ZROABABLE	WOR	339	1ST E DI
SMUNNER, HENRY	ALL	201	CUMBERLA
SMURDEN, ELIZABETH	BAL	134	16TH WAR
SMUSE, BERNARD	BAL	266	17TH WAR
SMUSE, CALEB	BAL	266	17TH WAR
SMUT, SAMUEL	BAL	225	12TH WAR
SMUTE, JOSEPH	ANN	475	HOWARD D
SMUTHERS, ANN	FRE	207	BUCKEYST
SMUTHERS, HENRIETTA	BAL	077	15TH WAR
SMUTHERS, ISAIAH-BLACK	FRE	392	PETERSVI
SMUTHERS, JACOB-BLACK	FRE	213	BUCKEYST
SMUTHERS, L.	ANN	272	ANNAPOLI
SMUTHERS, REBECCA	BAL	096	15TH WAR
SMUTHERS, SARAH A.	BAL	065	15TH WAR
SMUTHEY, PERCY *	ANN	397	8TH DIST
SMVOIT, THOMAS *	QUE	253	5TH E DI
SMYKE, CHARLES	BAL	299	17TH WAR
SMYKE, HARRIETT	BAL	300	17TH WAR
SMYRDEN, ELIAS *	BAL	280	1ST DIST
SMYRE, LEWIS	BAL	370	3RD WARD
SMYRK, SARAH A.	BAL	011	4TH WARD
SMYRK, THOMAS	BAL	141	5TH WARD
SMYSER, ADAM	BAL	409	8TH WARD
SMYSER, ELIZABETH	BAL	008	EASTERN
SMYTH, GEORGE B.	CEC	125	5TH E DI
SMYTH, ISMON	BAL	472	14TH WAR
SMYTH, JAMES H.	KEN	312	3RD DIST
SMYTH, JOHN	BAL	062	4TH WARD
SMYTH, JOSEPH	BAL	160	1ST WARD
SMYTH, JOSEPH	BAL	156	1ST WARD
SMYTH, REBECCA	KEN	228	2ND DIST
SMYTH, RICHARD	KEN	228	2ND DIST
SMYTH, WILLIAM F.	KEN	312	3RD DIST
SMYTHE, ELIZABETH T.	TAL	043	EASTON D
SMYTHE, JAMES H.	TAL	066	EASTON T
SNACK, WILLIAM	BAL	255	20TH WAR
SNACTNER, WILLIAM	BAL	194	2ND WARD
SNADEN, J.	BAL	152	1ST WARD
SNADERS, ALEXANDER-MULATT	FRE	429	8TH E DI
SNADERS, SEPTIMUS	ANN	317	1ST DIST
SNAGLEBAR, HARMCN *	ALL	114	5TH E.D.
SNALL, PATRICK	ALL	143	6TH E.D.
SNANBLE, JOHN	BAL	093	1ST WARD
SNAPP, GEORGE	BAL	094	18TH WAR
SNAPP, JOSEPH	BAL	092	18TH WAR
SNAREEN, DAVID	CEC	049	1ST E DI
SNARELY, WASHINGTON *	WAS	065	2ND SUBD
SNAUTER, MARY	BAL	256	2ND WARD
SNAVELY, CATHARINE	WAS	051	2ND SUBD
SNAVELY, JACOB	WAS	075	2ND SUBD
SNAVELY, JOHN	WAS	050	2ND SUBD
SNAVELY, JOHN	BAL	301	20TH WAR
SNAVELY, JOSEPH	WAS	080	2ND SUBD
SNAVELY, MARY	WAS	075	2ND SUBD
SNAVELY, ROBERT	FRE	208	BUCKEYST
SNAVELY, WASHINGTON *	WAS	065	2ND SUBD
SNAYOE, WILLIAM	BAL	144	1ST WARD
SNCAE, H. F. *	BAL	312	12TH WAR
SNEAD, JOHN E.	BAL	061	15TH WAR
SNEAD, RICHARD	BAL	099	15TH WAR
SNEAD, SARAH A.	BAL	047	18TH WAR
SNEADER, JACOB	CAR	359	9TH DIST
SNEADER, LEVI	CAR	395	2ND DIST
SNEADER, PHILIP	CAR	359	9TH DIST
SNEADS, ARTHUR	BAL	268	1ST DIST
SNEADS, HENRIETTA	BAL	369	1ST DIST
SNEADS, PHEBE	BAL	077	15TH WAR
SNEARY, JOHN K.	WAS	149	HAGERSTO
SNECK, JOHN	CAR	349	6TH DIST
SNECK, JOHN	CAR	334	6TH DIST
SNECKENBERGER, SAMUEL	WAS	251	1ST DIST
SNEDEN, CELIA R.-MULATTO	FRE	225	BUCKEYST
SNEDEN, CHARLES	BAL	126	18TH WAR
SNEDEN, RICHARD	BAL	124	18TH WAR
SNEDO, PETER	BAL	186	2ND WARD
SNEE, CATHERINE	BAL	411	8TH WARD
SNEED, AARON	TAL	066	EASTON T
SNEED, ANN E.	TAL	072	EASTON T
SNEED, ELIZABETH	SOM	449	DAMES QU
SNEED, JOHN	BAL	285	20TH WAR
SNEED, MOSES	KEN	228	2ND DIST
SNEED, RICHARD	HAR	080	2ND DIST
SNEED, RICHARD	BAL	119	2ND DIST
SNEED, SAMUEL	TAL	069	EASTON T
SNEED, SMITH	ANN	339	3RD DIST
SNEED, THOAMS	WOR	207	4TH E DI
SNEED, WILLIAM	SOM	449	DAMES QU
SNEED, WILLIAM	BAL	286	20TH WAR
SNEEDS, ELIZA	BAL	309	20TH WAR
SNEEDS, IRA	BAL	176	19TH WAR
SNEERS, MOSES	BAL	046	9TH WARD
SNEIDE, CASPER	BAL	180	2ND WARD
SNEIDE, JOHN	BAL	177	2ND WARD
SNEIDE, WALTER	BAL	221	2ND WARD
SNEIDER, CAHRLES	BAL	275	2ND WARD
SNEIDER, CARL	BAL	055	1ST WARD
SNEIDER, CHRISTOPHER	BAL	268	2ND WARD
SNEIDER, FREDRICA	BAL	270	2ND WARD
SNEIDER, HENRY	BAL	239	2ND WARD
SNEIDER, JOHN	BAL	261	2ND WARD
SNEIDER, LAURNA	BAL	270	2ND WARD
SNEIDER, MARY	CAL	062	3RD DIST
SNEIKSNEIDER, ELIZABETH	BAL	231	2ND WARD
SNEIKSNEIDER, FRANCAS	BAL	228	2ND WARD
SNELBAUGH, JOHN	BAL	340	7TH WARD
SNELL, ANN	MGM	437	CLARKSTR
SNELL, CONRAD	CAR	179	8TH DIST
SNELL, DENNIS	ANN	445	HOWARD D
SNELL, ELIZA	BAL	459	8TH WARD
SNELL, ELLEN	ANN	457	HOWARD D
SNELL, ELLEN	BAL	077	15TH WAR
SNELL, ELLEN	WAS	152	HAGERSTO
SNELL, FRED	BAL	259	20TH WAR
SNELL, GEORGE	WAS	138	HAGERSTO
SNELL, GEORGE	WAS	162	HAGERSTO
SNELL, GEORGE	WAS	154	2ND DIST
SNELL, GEORGE	MGM	437	CLARKSTR
SNELL, HENRY	BAL	237	20TH WAR
SNELL, HENRY	BAL	221	6TH WARD

SNELL, JAMES ANN 445 HOWARD D
SNELL, JOHN BAL 247 2ND WARD
SNELL, JOHN WAS 162 HAGERSTO
SNELL, KITTY ANN 438 HOWARD D
SNELL, KITTY BAL 162 16TH WAR
SNELL, MARTHA A. ANN 518 HOWARD D
SNELL, MARY BAL 459 8TH WARD
SNELL, MARY A. ANN 457 HOWARD D
SNELL, MOSES BAL 130 16TH WAR
SNELL, ROSE TAL 045 EASTON T
SNELL, SAMUEL ANN 457 HOWARD D
SNELL, SAMUEL ANN 445 HOWARD D
SNELL, TOBIAS ANN 428 HOWARD D
SNELL, WILLIAM FRE 254 NEW MARK
SNELL,ISAAC-BLACK FRE 241 NEW MARK
SNELLER, JOHN ALL 240 CUMBERLA
SNELLING, RICHARD SOM 468 TRAPPE D
SNEULLEN, ELIZA * WOR 189 7TH E DI
SNIBLY, EVE WAS 154 2ND DIST
SNIBLY, GEORGE W. WAS 162 2ND DIST
SNIBLY, JACOB WAS 162 2ND DIST
SNICKE, JOHN ANN 419 HOWARD D
SNIDE, GEORGE ALL 120 5TH E.D.
SNIDER, ABRAHAM FRE 417 8TH E DI
SNIDER, ABRAHAM FRE 422 8TH E DI
SNIDER, ANN M. ALL 230 CUMBERLA
SNIDER, CATHARINE HAR 074 1ST DIST
SNIDER, CHARLES D. WAS 160 2ND DIST
SNIDER, CHRISTIAN WAS 072 2ND SUBD
SNIDER, CHRISTIAN WAS 072 2ND SUBD
SNIDER, CHRISTIAN ANN 491 HOWARD D
SNIDER, DAVID A. CAR 352 6TH DIST
SNIDER, ELIZABETH CAR 368 9TH DIST
SNIDER, ELIZABETH FRE 007 FREDERIC
SNIDER, ELIZABETH ANN 515 HOWARD D
SNIDER, EZRA WAS 076 2ND SUBD
SNIDER, EZRA WAS 080 2ND SUBD
SNIDER, GEORGE FRE 138 CREAGERS
SNIDER, HENRY FRE 413 8TH E DI
SNIDER, HENRY HAR 074 1ST DIST
SNIDER, HENRY TAL 009 EASTON D
SNIDER, HIRAM WAS 189 1ST DIST
SNIDER, JACCB WAS 080 2ND SUBD
SNIDER, JACCB WAS 072 2ND SUBD
SNIDER, JACOB FRE 291 WOODSBOR
SNIDER, JACOB H. FRE 134 CREAGERS
SNIDER, JAMES FRE 095 FREDERIC
SNIDER, JAMES WAS 063 2ND SUBD
SNIDER, JAOCB MGM 417 MEDLEY 3
SNIDER, JOHN FRE 210 BUCKEYST
SNIDER, JOHN FRE 420 8TH E DI
SNIDER, JOHN CAL 040 3RD DIST
SNIDER, JOHN BAL 070 4TH WARD
SNIDER, JOHN BAL 421 14TH WAR
SNIDER, JOHN WAS 061 2ND SUBD
SNIDER, JOHN ALL 232 CUMBERLA
SNIDER, JOHN ALL 223 CUMBERLA
SNIDER, JOHN ALL 247 CUMBERLA
SNIDER, JOHN H. BAL 218 19TH WAR
SNIDER, JOHN J. CAR 369 9TH DIST
SNIDER, JOHN P. BAL 194 5TH DIST
SNIDER, JOHN SR. FRE 414 8TH E DI
SNIDER, JOSEPH H. WAS 075 2ND SUBD
SNIDER, JULIANA BAL 438 14TH WAR
SNIDER, LEWIS FRE 440 8TH E DI
SNIDER, MARTIN BAL 450 14TH WAR
SNIDER, MARTIN WAS 075 2ND SUBD
SNIDER, MARY WAS 065 2ND SUBD
SNIDER, MATTHIAS WAS 138 HAGERSTO
SNIDER, NICHOLAS FRE 118 CREAGERS
SNIDER, PHILIP HAR 034 1ST DIST
SNIDER, REBECCA WAS 064 2ND SUBD
SNIDER, ROSANA WAS 081 2ND SUBD
SNIDER, SARAH WAS 053 2ND SUBD
SNIDER, SARAH FRE 096 FREDERIC
SNIDER, SARAH FRE 433 8TH E DI
SNIDER, SIMON WAS 216 1ST DIST
SNIDER, SISTER M.R. FRE 198 5TH E DI
SNIDER, SISTER P. FRE 198 5TH E DI
SNIDER, SMAUEL FRE 024 FREDERIC
SNIDER, WILLIAM BAL 423 14TH WAR
SNIDER, ZACHARIAH T. ANN 486 HOWARD D
SNIDLEY, HENRY BAL 176 2ND WARD
SNIEW, GEORGE * FRE 317 MIDDLETO
SNIGGLEFRITTER, JULIANN ALL 252 CUMBERLA
SNIPE, MARTHA ELLEN BAL 140 5TH WARD
SNIPLEY, ABSALOM CAR 272 WESTMINS
SNIRELY, REBECCA-MULATTO FRE 033 FREDERIC
SNISELEY, MICHAEL-BLACK FRE 010 FREDERIC
SNISELEY, REBECCA-BLACK FRE 030 FREDERIC
SNISELEY, WILLIAM-BLACK FRE 010 FREDERIC
SNIVELY, EDWARD ALL 217 CUMBERLA
SNIVELY, ELIAS WAS 094 2ND SUBD
SNIVELY, HENRY WAS 284 1ST DIST
SNIVELY, HENRY ALL 256 CUMBERLA
SNIVELY, JACOB BAL 038 15TH WAR
SNIVELY, JACOB C. WAS 080 2ND SUBD
SNIVELY, JOHN H. WAS 080 2ND SUBD
SNIVELY, JOSEPH WAS 053 2ND SUBD
SNIVELY, JOSIAH WAS 303 1ST DIST
SNIVELY, MARY WAS 053 2ND SUBD
SNIVELY, MICHAEL ALL 203 CUMBERLA
SNIVELY, REBECCA WAS 190 1ST DIST
SNIXON, WILLIAM QUE 212 3RD E DI
SNODDEN, GEORGE HAR 193 3RD DIST
SNODDEN, MARY HAR 193 3RD DIST
SNODEN, ASBERRY-BLACK FRE 423 8TH E DI
SNODEN, ELIZA-BLACK FRE 435 8TH E DI
SNODEN, JESY HAR 193 3RD DIST
SNODEN, JOHN-BLACK FRE 218 BUCKEYST
SNODEN, PATIENCE WAS 029 2ND SUBD
SNODEN, PHILIP WAS 026 2ND SUBD
SNODEN, SAMUEL WAS 031 2ND SUBD
SNODEN, SUSAN BAL 124 18TH WAR
SNODEN, WESLEY-MULATTO FRE 435 8TH E DI
SNODER, HANRA HAR 190 3RD DIST
SNODER, JOHN BAL 345 13TH WAR
SNODERLY, GEORGE A. WAS 275 RIDGEVIL
SNODGRASS, J.E. BAL 132 5TH WARD
SNODGRASS, WILLIAM BAL 309 1ST DIST
SNOOON, ANN HAR 025 1ST DIST
SNOENCAMAN, JOSEPH CAR 266 WESTMINS
SNOFFER, ELISABETH BAL 298 3RD WARD
SNOFFER, JOSHUA ALL 230 CUMBERLA
SNOOK, ANN FRE 108 CREAGERS
SNOOK, CATHARINE CAR 325 1ST DIST
SNOOK, CANIEL FRE 112 CREAGERS
SNOOK, DANIEL J. FRE 090 FREDERIC
SNOCK, HENERITTA FRE 097 FREDERIC
SNOOK, JACOE FRE 141 CREAGERS
SNOOK, JACOB H. FRE 090 FREDERIC
SNOOK, JEROME FRE 097 FREDERIC
SNOOK, JOHN CAR 316 1ST DIST
SNOOK, JOSIAH FRE 108 CREAGERS
SNOOK, MARY WAS 161 2ND DIST
SNOOK, SIMON FRE 089 FREDERIC
SNOOK, WILLIAM BAL 267 17TH WAR
SNOOK, WILLIAM FRE 253 NEW MARK
SNOOK, WILLIAM FRE 281 WOODSBOR
SNOOKS, ELENOR ANN 267 ANNAPO_I
SNOOKS, FREDERICK FRE 105 CREAGERS
SNOOKS, JOHN BAL 248 17TH WAR
SNOOKS, JOHN ANN 266 ANNAPOLI
SNOOKS, JOHN BAL 354 7TH WARD
SNOOKS, JOHN BAL 354 7TH WARD
SNOOKS, JOHN WAS 156 2ND DIST
SNOOKS, MARIA ANN 317 1ST DIST
SNOOKS, PETER BAL 077 1ST WARD
SNOOKS, SAMUEL BAL 268 17TH WAR
SNOOKS,HENRY BAL 075 2ND DIST
SNORMITS, CATHERINE BAL 292 3RD WARD
SNOSELEY, JOHN FRE 009 FREDERIC
SNOTERLY, HENRY WAS 284 1ST DIST
SNOUDEN, HENRY-BLACK FRE 012 FREDERIC
SNOUDEN, SOLOMON FRE 063 FREDERIC
SNOUFFER, B.J. FRE 219 BUCKEYST
SNOUFFER, ELIZABETH FRE 223 BUCKEYST
SNOUFFER, GEORGE W. FRE 221 BUCKEYST
SNOUFFER, JAOCB FRE 167 EMMITTSB
SNOUFFER, JOHN B. FRE 223 BUCKEYST
SNOUFFER, JOSEPH FRE 167 EMMITTSB
SNOUFFER, RICHARD FRE 052 FREDERIC
SNOUFFER, WILLIAM FRE 178 5TH E DI
SNOVEL, CATHARINE CAR 242 TANEYTOW
SNOVEL, DANIE CAR 242 TANEYTOW
SNOVEL, JOHN A. FRE 305 WOODSBOR
SNOVELL, JOHN A. CAR 241 TANEYTOW
SNOW, ALONZO CEC 147 PORT DUP
SNOW, DAVID WAS 245 SMITHSBU
SNOW, EDWARD BAL 160 1ST WARD
SNOW, EUNICE E. BAL 413 3RD WARD
SNOW, FRANCES* BAL 002 4TH WARD
SNOW, JAMES WAS 156 2ND DIST
SNOW, JOHN CAR 089 NO TWP L
SNOW, JOHN H. BAL 294 7TH WARD
SNOW, LAURA WAS 245 SMITHSBU
SNOW, LUCRETIA DOR 378 1ST DIST
SNOW, MARIA J. BAL 294 7TH WARD
SNOW, MARY BAL 304 7TH WARD
SNOW, MARY BAL 071 10TH WAR
SNOW, PHILIP BAL 027 4TH WARD
SNOW, RISEN BAL 439 8TH WARD
SNOW, SAMUEL TAL 027 EASTON D
SNOW, SARAH TAL 027 EASTON D
SNOW, THCMAS BAL 459 1ST DIST
SNOW, URIAH* BAL 210 19TH WAR
SNOW, W.F. BAL 013 18TH WAR
SNOW, WALTER R. WOR 300 SNOW HIL
SNOWDEN, ABAGAIL FRE 305 WOODSBOR
SNOWDEN, ACSAH MGM 441 CLARKSTR
SNOWDEN, ALEC ANN 348 3RD DIST
SNOWDEN, ALICE BAL 116 15TH WAR
SNOWDEN, ALICE A. ANN 459 HOWARD D
SNOWDEN, ANDREW ANN 448 HOWARD D
SNOWDEN, ANN ANN 355 3RD DIST
SNOWDEN, ANN BAL 325 12TH WAR
SNOWDEN, BEN ANN 438 HOWARD D
SNOWDEN, BENJAMIN ANN 379 4TH DIST
SNOWDEN, BENJAMIN ANN 348 3RD DIST
SNOWDEN, BENJAMIN BAL 030 2ND DIST
SNOWDEN, BENJAMIN HAR 102 2ND DIST
SNOWDEN, CAROLINE BAL 430 14TH WAR
SNOWDEN, CAROLINE ANN 482 HOWARD D
SNOWDEN, CHARLES BAL 228 1ST DIST
SNOWDEN, DARUS BAL 155 11TH WAR
SNOWDEN, DE WILTON PRI 092 MARLBROU
SNOWDEN, DENIS BAL 118 11TH WAR
SNOWDEN, ELIZA BAL 383 13TH WAR
SNOWDEN, ELIZA A. ANN 494 HOWARD D
SNOWDEN, ELIZABETH ANN 497 HOWARD D
SNOWDEN, ELIZABETH PRI 038 VANSVILL
SNOWDEN, ELIZABETH WAS 154 HAGERSTO
SNOWDEN, EPHRAIM ANN 454 HOWARD D
SNOWDEN, FANNY BAL 154 5TH WARD
SNOWDEN, FANNY BAL 170 19TH WAR
SNOWDEN, HANNAH BAL 244 6TH WARD
SNOWDEN, HARRIET FRE 244 NEW MARK
SNOWDEN, HENRY BAL 149 2ND DIST
SNOWDEN, HENRY BAL 172 2ND DIST
SNOWDEN, HENRY ALL 085 5TH E.D.
SNOWDEN, IRA BAL 196 19TH WAR
SNOWDEN, ISAAC PRI 045 VANSVILL
SNOWDEN, J. H. BAL 332 1ST DIST
SNOWDEN, JAMES BAL 311 12TH WAR
SNOWDEN, JANE BAL 143 5TH WARD
SNOWDEN, JEMIMA ANN 482 HOWARD D
SNOWDEN, JOHN ANN 516 HOWARD D
SNOWDEN, JOHN PRI 092 MARLBROU
SNOWDEN, JOHN FRE 307 WOODSBOR
SNOWDEN, JOHN B. CAR 279 7TH DIST
SNOWDEN, JOHN J. ANN 274 ANNAPOLI
SNOWDEN, LEONARD BAL 459 8TH WARD
SNOWDEN, LUCY BAL 170 19TH WAR
SNOWDEN, LYDIA MGM 333 CRACKLIN
SNOWDEN, MARCELUS D. ANN 350 3RD DIST
SNOWDEN, MARGARET ANN 320 2ND DIST
SNOWDEN, MARGARET HAR 103 2ND DIST
SNOWDEN, MARIA BAL 078 4TH WARD
SNOWDEN, MARIA BAL 243 6TH WARD
SNOWDEN, MARTHA BAL 180 16TH WAR
SNOWDEN, MARY BAL 177 16TH WAR
SNOWDEN, MARY BAL 280 12TH WAR
SNOWDEN, MARY CAR 268 WESTMINS
SNOWDEN, MARY E. BAL 131 18TH WAR
SNOWDEN, MARY E. ANN 386 4TH DIST
SNOWDEN, MILLY MGM 324 CRACKLIN
SNOWDEN, NATHAN BAL 370 1ST DIST
SNOWDEN, NATHANIEL HAR 102 2ND DIST
SNOWDEN, PATIENCE BAL 398 1ST DIST
SNOWDEN, PETER BAL 107 18TH WAR
SNOWDEN, PHEBE BAL 347 3RD WARD
SNOWDEN, PURNY BAL 231 19TH WAR
SNOWDEN, RAZIN BAL 030 9TH WARD
SNOWDEN, REBECCA BAL 229 1ST DIST
SNOWDEN, REBECCA BAL 382 13TH WAR
SNOWDEN, REZIN H. ANN 371 4TH DIST
SNOWDEN, RICHARD N. ANN 372 4TH DIST
SNOWDEN, RICHARD-BLACK FRE 244 NEW MARK
SNOWDEN, SAMUEL BAL 133 2ND DIST
SNOWDEN, SAMUEL ANN 488 HOWARD D
SNOWDEN, SAMUEL PRI 045 VANSVILL
SNOWDEN, SAMUEL-MULATTO FRE 025 FREDERIC
SNOWDEN, THOMAS BAL 251 20TH WAR
SNOWDEN, WILLIAM BAL 459 8TH WARD
SNOWDEN, WILLIAM S. MGM 319 CRACKLIN
SNOWDER, MARY WAS 141 HAGERSTO
SNOWDER, RICHARD FRE 347 MIDDLETO
SNOWDER, WILLIAM FRE 276 NEW MARK
SNOWDIN, FRANCES HAR 168 3RD DIST
SNOWDIN, WASHINGTON CEC 082 CHARLEST
SNOWDON, RICHARD FRE 318 MIDDLETO
SNOWMAN, CHARLES BAL 413 8TH WARD
SNUASR, HENRY * FRE 320 MIDDLETO
SNUCKS, MARGARET BAL 022 9TH WARD
SNUGLER, CONNA BAL 238 2ND WARD
SNUIGLER, JOHN BAL 237 2ND WARD
SNYDER, ABRAHAM WAS 286 1ST DIST
SNYDER, ADAM BAL 368 1ST DIST
SNYDER, ADAM BAL 333 7TH WARD
SNYDER, ADDISON CHA 261 MIDDLETO
SNYDER, AMELIA WAS 056 2ND SUBD
SNYDER, AMRTIN B. FRE 286 WOODSBOR
SNYDER, ANDREW WAS 055 2ND SUBD
SNYDER, ANDREW BAL 346 1ST DIST
SNYDER, ANDREW BAL 147 2ND DIST
SNYDER, ANDRWE CAR 334 6TH DIST
SNYDER, ANN E. MGM 337 CRACKLIN
SNYDER, ANN M. BAL 096 5TH WARD
SNYDER, ANTHONY WAS 280 LEITERSB
SNYDER, ASBURY M. BAL 009 15TH WAR
SNYDER, BARBARY BAL 072 2ND DIST
SNYDER, BARBARY BAL 115 11TH WAR
SNYDER, BETSY WAS 049 2ND SUBD
SNYDER, CASPER BAL 294 17TH WAR
SNYDER, CATHARINE WAS 232 1ST DIST
SNYDER, CATHARINE WAS 200 1ST DIST
SNYDER, CHARLES BAL 075 18TH WAR
SNYDER, CHARLES BAL 313 20TH WAR
SNYDER, CHARLES W. ANN 488 HOWARD D
SNYDER, CHRISTIAN WAS 017 2ND SUBD
SNYDER, CHRISTIAN JR. ANN 492 HOWARD D
SNYDER, CHRISTIAN L. WAS 014 WILLIAMS
SNYDER, DANIEL WAS 028 2ND SUBD
SNYDER, DANIEL WAS 226 1ST DIST
SNYDER, DANIEL BAL 202 6TH DIST
SNYDER, DAVID ALL 004 3RD E.D.
SNYDER, E. BAL 255 6TH WARD
SNYDER, EDWARD WAS 031 2ND SUBD
SNYDER, ELIZA BAL 344 13TH WAR
SNYDER, ELIZABETH WAS 158 2ND DIST
SNYDER, ELIZABETH WAS 189 1ST DIST
SNYDER, ELIZABETH WAS 123 2ND DIST
SNYDER, FLORANCE BAL 047 18TH WAR
SNYDER, FRANCES MGM 336 CRACKLIN
SNYDER, FRANCIS CAR 289 7TH DIST
SNYDER, FREDERIC BAL 199 6TH WARD
SNYDER, FREDERICK BAL 286 17TH WAR
SNYDER, FREDERICK JR. BAL 285 17TH WAR
SNYDER, FREDRICK B. WAS 099 2ND DIST
SNYDER, GEORGE WAS 013 WILLIAMS
SNYDER, GEORGE WAS 158 2ND DIST
SNYDER, GEORGE BAL 297 17TH WAR
SNYDER, GEORGE CAR 322 1ST DIST
SNYDER, GEORGE FRE 303 WOODSBOR
SNYDER, GEORGE BAL 226 1ST DIST
SNYDER, GEORGE BAL 299 3RD WARD
SNYDER, GEORGE BAL 147 2ND DIST
SNYDER, GEORGE D. BAL 202 19TH WAR
SNYDER, GEORGE N. WAS 191 1ST DIST
SNYDER, HAMMONTS* BAL 345 3RD WARD
SNYDER, HANAH BAL 411 8TH WARD
SNYDER, HARRIET BAL 216 6TH WARD
SNYDER, HARRIET BAL 234 12TH WAR
SNYDER, HARRIET WAS 303 1ST DIST
SNYDER, HARRIET WAS 262 1ST DIST
SNYDER, HELENA BAL 012 9TH WARD
SNYDER, HELENA BAL 409 1ST DIST
SNYDER, HENRY BAL 101 5TH WARD
SNYDER, HENRY BAL 364 1ST DIST
SNYDER, HENRY BAL 318 3RD WARD
SNYDER, HENRY ANN 391 4TH DIST
SNYDER, HENRY BAL 120 16TH WAR
SNYDER, HENRY BAL 080 10TH WAR
SNYDER, HENRY BAL 237 1ST DIST
SNYDER, HENRY WAS 158 2ND DIST
SNYDER, HENRY WAS 139 2ND DIST
SNYDER, HENRY CAR 355 6TH DIST
SNYDER, HENRY BAL 290 20TH WAR
SNYDER, HENRY M. FRE 238 NEW MARK
SNYDER, J. M. BAL 332 1ST DIST
SNYDER, JACOB BAL 189 6TH WARD
SNYDER, JACOB BAL 160 19TH WAR
SNYDER, JACOB FRE 333 MIDDLETO
SNYDER, JACOB CAR 322 1ST DIST
SNYDER, JACOB CAR 278 7TH DIST
SNYDER, JACOB CAR 288 7TH DIST
SNYDER, JACOB CAR 305 1ST DIST
SNYDER, JACOB CAR 174 8TH DIST
SNYDER, JACOB BAL 275 17TH WAR
SNYDER, JACOB WAS 139 2ND DIST
SNYDER, JACOB WAS 243 CAVETOWN
SNYDER, JACOB WAS 195 1ST DIST
SNYDER, JAMES BAL 421 8TH WARD
SNYDER, JAMES V. BAL 164 1ST WARD
SNYDER, JANE R. BAL 049 4TH WARD
SNYDER, JOHN CAR 287 7TH DIST
SNYDER, JOHN CAR 336 6TH DIST
SNYDER, JOHN BAL 281 17TH WAR
SNYDER, JOHN BAL 232 6TH WARD
SNYDER, JOHN BAL 026 9TH WARD
SNYDER, JOHN BAL 340 7TH WARD
SNYDER, JOHN BAL 326 3RD WARD
SNYDER, JOHN BAL 369 1ST DIST
SNYDER, JOHN BAL 345 3RD WARD
SNYDER, JOHN BAL 277 12TH WAR
SNYDER, JOHN BAL 092 15TH WAR
SNYDER, JOHN WAS 229 1ST DIST
SNYDER, JOHN WAS 268 1ST DIST
SNYDER, JOHN WAS 139 2ND DIST
SNYDER, JOHN WAS 169 FUNKSTOW
SNYDER, JOHN WAS 014 WILLIAMS
SNYDER, JOHN H. BAL 083 15TH WAR
SNYDER, JOHN P. BAL 192 5TH DIST
SNYDER, JOHN T. WAS 099 2ND DIST
SNYDER, JONAS BAL 018 4TH WARD
SNYDER, JONATHAN BAL 246 1ST DIST
SNYDER, JOSEPH ANN 489 HOWARD D
SNYDER, JOSEPH R. BAL 188 11TH WAR
SNYDER, JOSEPHINE WAS 036 2ND SUBD
SNYDER, JOSHUA WAS 248 SMITHSBU

SNYDER, JOSHUA BAL 017 4TH WARD
SNYDER, JOSHUA FRE 372 CATOCTIN
SNYDER, JOSIAH BAL 237 12TH WAR
SNYDER, JULIUS BAL 047 18TH WAR
SNYDER, JUSTUS BAL 257 12TH WAR
SNYDER, LEOPOLD MGM 401 ROCKERLE
SNYDER, LEWIS ALL 189 9TH E.D.
SNYDER, LEWIS WAS 302 1ST DIST
SNYDER, LEWIS F. BAL 225 17TH WAR
SNYDER, LORA BAL 300 1ST DIST
SNYDER, LOUISA BAL 293 17TH WAR
SNYDER, LUTHER W. MGM 333 CRACKLIN
SNYDER, MARGARET BAL 326 3RD WARD
SNYDER, MARGARET BAL 202 6TH DIST
SNYDER, MARGARET WAS 291 1ST DIST
SNYDER, MARGARET WAS 159 HAGERSTO
SNYDER, MARK BAL 261 1ST DIST
SNYDER, MARTIN BAL 067 15TH WAR
SNYDER, MARTIN BAL 312 12TH WAR
SNYDER, MARTIN FRE 351 MIDDLETO
SNYDER, MARY BAL 008 9TH WARD
SNYDER, MARY BAL 108 5TH WARD
SNYDER, MARY BAL 101 5TH WARD
SNYDER, MARY ANN 383 4TH DIST
SNYDER, MARY ANN ALL 038 2ND E.D.
SNYDER, MARY J. WAS 160 2ND DIST
SNYDER, MICHAEL WAS 243 CAVETOWN
SNYDER, MICHEAL CAR 174 8TH DIST
SNYDER, MOSES F. FRE 342 MIDDLETO
SNYDER, MR- WAS 162 HAGERSTO
SNYDER, MRS- ANN 392 4TH DIST
SNYDER, NELSON WAS 145 2ND DIST
SNYDER, NEWTON, W. BAL 236 6TH WARD
SNYDER, O. H. WAS 168 FUNKSTOW
SNYDER, OTHO WAS 159 HAGERSTO
SNYDER, PETER WAS 138 2ND DIST
SNYDER, PETER WAS 114 2ND DIST
SNYDER, PETER WAS 027 2ND SUBD
SNYDER, PETER WAS 029 2ND SUBD
SNYDER, PETER WAS 097 2ND DIST
SNYDER, PETER BAL 412 8TH WARD
SNYDER, PETER CAR 259 3RD DIST
SNYDER, PHILIP WAS 108 2ND DIST
SNYDER, PHILIP WAS 139 2ND DIST
SNYDER, REBECA WAS 104 2ND DIST
SNYDER, REBECCA WAS 152 HAGERSTO
SNYDER, REBECCA CAR 302 1ST DIST
SNYDER, REMAS MGM 323 CRACKLIN
SNYDER, RISAN BAL 271 12TH WAR
SNYDER, ROMULAS MGM 334 CRACKLIN
SNYDER, SAMUEL CAR 294 7TH DIST
SNYDER, SAMUEL FRE 259 NEW MARK
SNYDER, SAMUEL BAL 237 1ST DIST
SNYDER, SAMUEL WAS 288 1ST DIST
SNYDER, SARAH FRE 239 NEW MARK
SNYDER, SARAH CAR 343 6TH DIST
SNYDER, SARAH P. CAR 305 1ST DIST
SNYDER, SMAUEL CAR 174 8TH DIST
SNYDER, SOLOMON CAR 299 1ST DIST
SNYDER, SUSAN WAS 124 2ND DIST
SNYDER, THOMAS WAS 143 2ND DIST
SNYDER, WESLEY WAS 143 2ND DIST
SNYDER, WILLIAM WAS 170 FUNKSTOW
SNYDER, WILLIAM WAS 017 2ND SUBD
SNYDER, WILLIAM WAS 006 WILLIAMS
SNYDER, WILLIAM BAL 389 3RD WARD
SNYDER, WILLIAM BAL 329 1ST DIST
SNYDER, WILLIAM C. BAL 262 1ST DIST
SNYDER, WILLIAM H. BAL 309 20TH WAR
SNYDER, WILLIAM H. L. BAL 167 11TH WAR
SNYDER, WILLIAM J. FRE 241 NEW MARK
SNYDER, WILLIAM W. WAS 281 LEITERSB
SNYDER,RACHAEL CAR 382 2ND DIST
SOAKE, RANONDE BAL 078 1ST WARD
SOAN, JACOB ALL 116 5TH E.D.
SOANE, GEORGE* BAL 035 4TH WARD
SOAPER, PRESCILLA MGM 440 CLARKSTR
SOBER, GEORGE* BAL 113 15TH WAR
SOBRAL, ANTONIA BAL 136 1ST WARD
SOCKMAN, HENRY BAL 312 20TH WAR
SOCKS, ANDREW ST 303 2ND E DI
SOCKS, CHRISTIANA ALL 214 CUMBERLA
SOCTT, SALLY TAL 073 EASTON T
SOCTT, WILLIAM BAL 001 1ST WARD
SOD, HOSSA BAL 189 17TH WAR
SODAM, WILLAIM BAL 108 5TH WARD
SODEN, JANE BAL 071 15TH WAR
SODERS, DANIEL WAS 043 2ND SUBD
SODIN, WILLIAM BAL 152 1ST WARD
SOFFLER, GEORGE FRE 041 FREDERIC
SOFTUS, PATRICK ALL 140 6TH E.D.
SOGELER, JACOB BAL 275 17TH WAR
SOGRDEN, ANTHONY ALL 098 5TH E.D.
SOHL, ADAM BAL 352 13TH WAR
SOHMANGER, FELIX BAL 178 2ND WARD
SOHNES, CHAELS BAL 370 13TH WAR
SOIB, JACOB BAL 435 14TH WAR
SOISLER, SAMUEL ALL 250 CUMBERLA
SOLAN, ALFRED ANN 336 3RD DIST
SOLAWAY, JOHN KEN 305 3RD DIST
SOLAWAY, JOHN V. KEN 283 3RD DIST
SOLEATTA, MINER BAL 181 11TH WAR
SOLER, CATHARINE BAL 380 13TH WAR
SOLERNS, JOHN BAL 402 1ST DIST
SOLLARS, ANN CAL 015 1ST DIST
SOLLARS, BASEL BAL 096 1ST WARD
SOLLARS, ELIZABETH CAL 012 1ST DIST
SOLLARS, ELIZABETH CAL 007 1ST DIST
SOLLARS, MARY E. ST 307 1ST E DI
SOLLARS, WILLIAM BAL 259 1ST DIST
SOLLER, JOHN QUE 163 2ND E DI
SOLLERER, GEORGE CAR 254 3RD DIST
SOLLERS, AUGUSTUS R. CAL 037 2ND DIST
SOLLERS, BASIL D. BAL 109 1ST WARD
SOLLERS, BENJAMIN BAL 007 18TH WAR
SOLLERS, CHARLES BAL 227 17TH WAR
SOLLERS, JAMES BAL 138 2ND DIST
SOLLERS, JAMES* BAL 308 3RD WARD
SOLLERS, JANE BAL 040 9TH WARD
SOLLERS, JOHN BAL 434 14TH WAR
SOLLERS, JOHN BAL 150 19TH WAR
SOLLERS, PHEBE BAL 243 6TH WARD
SOLLERS, SARAH BAL 204 6TH WARD
SOLLERS, SARAH FRE 446 8TH E DI
SOLLERS, SUSANNA BAL 220 6TH WARD
SOLLERS, THOMAS ANN 345 3RD DIST
SOLLERS, THOMAS E. FRE 421 8TH E DI
SOLLERS, THOMAS O. BAL 456 8TH WARD
SOLLOMON, GEORGE W. HAR 047 1ST DIST
SOLLOWAY, CHARLES QUE 140 1ST E DI
SOLLOWAY, JAMES QUE 126 1ST E DI
SOLLOWAY, NAOMI QUE 127 1ST E DI
SOLLOWAY, SARAH QUE 154 1ST E DI
SOLLOWAY, SUSAN QUE 151 1ST E DI
SOLLOWAY, THOMAS QUE 150 1ST E DI
SOLLOWAY,EORY QUE 168 2ND E DI
SOLLR, PATRICK QUE 179 2ND E DI
SOLLUS, THOMAS ANN 345 3RD DIST
SOLMON, S.B. BAL 001 18TH WAR
SOLNAS, A. BAL 137 1ST WARD
SOLOMAN, ANN BAL 265 7TH WARD
SOLOMAN, JOHN BAL 242 2ND WARD
SOLOMAN, WILHELM BAL 252 2ND WARD
SOLOMAN, WILLIAM BAL 252 2ND WARD
SOLOMON, CHARLES WAS 219 1ST DIST
SOLOMON, EDNA BAL 001 18TH WAR
SOLOMON, EDWARD BAL 288 3RD WARD
SOLOMON, ELIZABETH WAS 218 1ST DIST
SOLOMON, FREADERICK BAL 327 3RD WARD
SOLOMON, ISAAC BAL 261 6TH WARD
SOLOMON, SARAH A. HAR 047 1ST DIST
SOLOMON, SOLOMON BAL 327 3RD WARD
SOLOMON, WILLIAM T. BAL 162 6TH WARD
SOLOMONS, JAMES HAR 102 2ND DIST
SOLONE, MARY BAL 224 12TH WAR
SOLOWAY, JAMES CEC 151 PORT DUP
SOLSBURRY, JAMES W.* TAL 037 EASTON D
SOLSBURY, ARAMINTA CEC 035 CHESAPEA
SOLSBURY, JAMES CEC 043 CHESAPEA
SOLSBURY, MARY CEC 005 ELKTON 3
SOLSBURY, PERRY CEC 008 ELKTON 3
SOLSBURY, REBECCA CEC 089 4TH E DI
SOLSBURY, SARAH CEC 041 CHESAPEA
SOLSBURY, STANLY TAL 095 ST MICHA
SOLSBURY, THOMAS CEC 012 ELKTON 3
SOLTER, CHRISTIAN BAL 171 6TH WARD
SOLUNS, JOHN * BAL 402 1ST DIST
SOLZE, CAROLINE BAL 347 13TH WAR
SOLZE, JOHN BAL 347 13TH WAR
SOMAN, WILLIAM QUE 134 1ST E DI
SOMER, JACOB CEC 005 ELKTON 3
SOMER, JOHN BAL 254 2ND WARD
SOMERFETTA, LEWIS * BAL 268 2ND WARD
SOMERFIELD, T. BAL 281 2ND WARD
SOMERLAND, ELIZABETH ALL 109 5TH E.D.
SOMERS, ABRAHAM FRE 375 CATOCTIN
SOMERS, ADAM FRE 350 MIDDLETO
SOMERS, FREDERICK FRE 350 MIDDLETO
SOMERS, GEORGE FRE 372 CATOCTIN
SOMERS, GEORGE W. FRE 337 MIDDLETO
SOMERS, HENRY W. FRE 319 MIDDLETO
SOMERS, J. BAL 157 1ST WARD
SOMERS, JACOB FRE 372 CATOCTIN
SOMERS, JAMES QUE 250 5TH E DI
SOMERS, JAOCB FRE 338 MIDDLETO
SOMERS, JOHN FRE 339 MIDDLETO
SOMERS, MAGDALEN FRE 372 CATOCTIN
SOMERS, MARGARET FRE 371 CATOCTIN
SOMERS, MARY M. FRE 343 MIDDLETO
SOMERS, WILLIAM BAL 146 1ST WARD
SOMERSVILLE, JOHN T. ST 268 3RD E DI
SOMERTHER, JAMES ANN 279 ANNAPOLI
SOMERVELL, JAMES CAL 048 3RD DIST
SOMERVELL, JOHN CAL 045 3RD DIST
SOMERVILER, WILLIAM N.-MU ST 292 2ND E DI
SOMERVILLE, ABNER ALL 164 6TH E.D.
SOMERVILLE, ALEXANDER ST 290 2ND E DI
SOMERVILLE, ALEXANDER CAL 013 1ST DIST
SOMERVILLE, ANN BAL 216 11TH WAR
SOMERVILLE, ANN ST 268 3RD E DI
SOMERVILLE, ANN R.-MULATT ST 302 2ND E DI
SOMERVILLE, ANTHONY BAL 378 3RD WARD
SOMERVILLE, C. S. BAL 332 1ST DIST
SOMERVILLE, ELIZA A. ST 285 2ND E DI
SOMERVILLE, ELIZA J. MGM 330 CRACKLIN
SOMERVILLE, ELIZABETH CAL 048 3RD DIST
SOMERVILLE, ELIZABETH ST 277 3RD E DI
SOMERVILLE, GEORGE W. BAL 302 12TH WAR
SOMERVILLE, HENRY ST 279 3RD E DI
SOMERVILLE, HENRY-BLACK ST 293 2ND E DI
SOMERVILLE, JAMES PRI 066 NOTTINGH
SOMERVILLE, JAMES BAL 203 6TH WARD
SOMERVILLE, JANE-BLACK ST 292 2ND E DI
SOMERVILLE, JOHN ST 289 2ND E DI
SOMERVILLE, JOHN H. ANN 405 8TH DIST
SOMERVILLE, JOHN H.-BLACK ST 323 4TH E DI
SOMERVILLE, JOHN-BLACK ST 304 2ND E DI
SOMERVILLE, JOSEPH ST 290 2ND E DI
SOMERVILLE, JOSEPH-BLACK ST 307 1ST E DI
SOMERVILLE, JUDY ST 271 3RD E DI
SOMERVILLE, LETTY ST 290 2ND E DI
SOMERVILLE, LUCINDA ST 285 2ND E DI
SOMERVILLE, LUCY ST 323 4TH E DI
SOMERVILLE, MARGARET A. ST 290 2ND E DI
SOMERVILLE, MARGARET L. PRI 056 AQUASCO
SOMERVILLE, MARIA ST 290 2ND E DI
SOMERVILLE, MARY E. ST 307 1ST E DI
SOMERVILLE, MARY E. BAL 053 4TH WARD
SOMERVILLE, MATHA A.-BLAC ST 303 2ND E DI
SOMERVILLE, PETER-MULATTO ST 307 1ST E DI
SOMERVILLE, PRISCILLA-MUL ST 291 2ND E DI
SOMERVILLE, ROBERT ST 256 3RD E DI
SOMERVILLE, ROBERT-BLACK ST 320 4TH E DI
SOMERVILLE, SAMUEL-BLACK ST 303 2ND E DI
SOMERVILLE, SARAH A.-BLAC ST 293 2ND E DI
SOMERVILLE, SOMERSELL BAL 108 18TH WAR
SOMERVILLE, SOPHIA ST 281 3RD E DI
SOMERVILLE, SUSAN BAL 368 3RD WARD
SOMERVILLE, SUSAN-BLACK ST 299 2ND E DI
SOMERVILLE, SUSAN-BLACK ST 291 2ND E DI
SOMERVILLE, THOMAS ST 270 3RD E DI
SOMERVILLE, THOMAS T. PRI 056 AQUASCO
SOMERVILLE, THOMAS-BLACK ST 296 2ND E DI
SOMERVILLE, WILLIAM ST 289 2ND E DI
SOMERVILLE, WILLIAM ST 279 3RD E DI
SOMERVILLE, WILLIAM-BLACK ST 298 2ND E DI
SOMERVILLE, WILLIAM-BLACK ST 333 4TH E DI
SOMERVILLE, WILLIAM-BLACK ST 294 2ND E DI
SOMERVILLE,MCNTA-BLACK ST 329 4TH E DI
SOMERVILLE,W ILLIAM BAL 270 12TH WAR
SOMETHING, JANE CEC 146 PORT DUP
SOMMER, JACOB BAL 112 5TH WARD
SOMMER, JACOB JR. BAL 144 16TH WAR
SOMMER, JOHN BAL 159 16TH WAR
SOMMER, MICHAEL BAL 302 17TH WAR
SOMMER, SAMUEL BAL 153 16TH WAR
SOMMERCAMP, CHARLES ALL 218 CUMBERLA
SOMMERKAMP, SOPHIA BAL 078 15TH WAR
SOMMERMAN, J. BAL 138 5TH WARD
SOMMERS, DAVID J. KEN 222 2ND DIST
SOMMERS, F. BAL 151 1ST WARD
SOMMERS, GEORGE BAL 251 17TH WAR
SOMMERS, JAOCB BAL 420 14TH WAR
SOMMERS, JOHN ST 303 2ND E DI
SOMMERS, JOSEPH BAL 113 5TH WARD
SOMMERS, JOSIAH QUE 243 5TH E DI
SOMMERS, SALLY MOORE QUE 252 5TH E DI
SOMMERS, SEVERN* SOM 359 BRINKLEY
SOMMERS, SUSAN QUE 249 5TH E DI
SOMMERS, WILLIAM QUE 252 5TH E DI
SOMMERVILL, ROBERT BAL 198 17TH WAR
SOMOURE, PETER * ALL 164 6TH E.D.
SOMVERVILLE, ANN ST 290 2ND E DI
SON, MOORITCH* BAL 326 3RD WARD
SONBURCN, ALBERT BAL 244 20TH WAR
SONDER, CONROD BAL 208 2ND WARD
SONDER, MARY BAL 015 9TH WARD
SONDHEIMER, BENEDICT BAL 169 6TH WARD
SONDHEIMER, SAMUEL BAL 251 6TH WARD
SONERFIELD, ANDREW BAL 161 2ND DIST
SONG, MARY* SOM 550 TYASKIN
SONG, STEPHEN DOR 396 1ST DIST
SONG, THOMAS FRE 426 8TH E DI
SONICE, MARY* BAL 422 3RD WARD
SONOHO, GEORGE BAL 410 14TH WAR
SONTE, JOHN CAR 279 7TH DIST
SONTIER, CHARLES H. BAL 129 5TH WARD
SOOHY, ANN* BAL 027 4TH WARD
SOOTHER, ELENORA BAL 437 8TH WARD
SOP, CATHERINE ALL 199 CUMBERLA
SOPE, CONRAD ALL 199 CUMBERLA
SOPE, JACOB SOM 399 BRINKLEY
SOPE, JOHN SOM 399 BRINKLEY
SOPER, A. PRI 097 SPALDING
SOPER, ADDY PRI 087 SPALDING
SOPER, ALEXANDER E. MGM 406 MEDLEY 3
SOPER, ALPIO BAL 112 1ST WARD
SOPER, E. PRI 094 SPALDING
SOPER, ELIZABETH PRI 097 SPALDING
SOPER, FRANCIS M. PRI 090 MARLBROU
SOPER, JAMES CAL 062 3RD DIST
SOPER, JESSE PRI 096 SPALDING
SOPER, JOSEPH PRI 097 SPALDING
SOPER, NATHAN PRI 094 SPALDING
SOPER, NATHAN PRI 102 SPALDING
SOPER, NATHAN PRI 071 MARLBROU
SOPER, NATHAN ANN 394 8TH DIST
SOPER, PHIL PRI 097 SPALDING
SOPER, THOMAS W. PRI 096 SPALDING
SOPER, WILIAM C. MGM 405 ROCKERLE
SOPER, WILLAIM PRI 090 MARLBROU
SOPER, WILLAIM PRI 090 MARLBROU
SOPER, WILLIAM PRI 096 SPALDING
SOPER, WILLIAM BAL 233 1ST DIST
SOPHIA, E.* BAL 109 1CTH WAR
SOPKE, AUGUST BAL 038 9TH WARD
SOPNNLLER, JACOB * FRE 260 NEW MARK
SOPPY, CAROLINE* BAL 008 4TH WARD
SOPRANIS, FELIX FRE 067 FREDERIC
SORAN, JOHN BAL 328 3RD WARD
SORDEN, ALEXANDER P. CAR 089 NO TWP L
SOREL, CARTNEY BAL 082 18TH WAR
SORGELER, AUGUSTUS BAL 158 6TH WARD
SORMWALT, JACOB L. CAR 257 3RD DIST
SORN, STEPLER BAL 192 17TH WAR
SORREL, ROBERT * BAL 398 1ST DIST
SORRELL, ALEXANDER BAL 215 6TH WARD
SORRELL, DARKEY BAL 093 15TH WAR
SORRELL, HENRY BAL 074 15TH WAR
SORRELL, WALTER BAL 085 15TH WAR
SORRELLS, ASHBURN ALL 184 9TH E.D.
SORRILL, CHARLES BAL 031 9TH WARD
SORTER, JOHN BAL 004 18TH WAR
SOSSER, CHARLES BAL 338 1ST DIST
SOSTEN, CHRISTINA BAL 187 11TH WAR
SOTHE, HENRY BAL 448 14TH WAR
SOTHEREON, RICHARD C. ST 348 5TH E DI
SOTHERON, ZACHARIAH CAL 060 3RD DIST
SOTHORON, JAMES P. ST 334 4TH E DI
SOTHORON, JOHN H. ST 348 5TH E DI
SOTHORON, JOHN T. H. ANN 394 8TH DIST
SOTHORON, JOHNT.H. ST 334 4TH E DI
SOTHORON, MARGARET H. ST 307 1ST E DI
SOTHORON, MARY S. ST 345 5TH E DI
SOTHORON, ZACHARIAH H. ANN 394 8TH DIST
SOTNE, BENNET ST 281 3RD E DI
SOTNE, ELLEN C. ST 286 2ND E DI
SOTNE, EVE A. CAR 267 WESTMINS
SOTNE, JOSEPH FRE 088 FREDERIC
SOTNESIFER, AUGUSTUS CAR 258 3RD DIST
SOTON, JOHN ALL 103 5TH E.D.
SOTTEN, PATRICK ALL 159 6TH E.D.
SOUCKS, LITTLE BAL 146 11TH WAR
SOUDERS, GEORGE FRE 408 JEFFERSO
SOUDERS, WILLIAM WAS 212 1ST DIST
SOUERS, MARY FRE 013 FREDERIC
SOUFNER, ADOLPHUS BAL 341 1ST DIST
SOUNEY, WILLIAM BAL 195 2ND WARD
SOUNN, B. MRS- * BAL 315 20TH WAR
SOUR, CATHARINE ALL 013 3RD E.D.
SOUR, ELI CAR 298 1ST DIST
SOUR, THEODORE CAR 353 6TH DIST
SOURDERS, THOMAS ANN 448 HOWARD D
SOURHOOF, HENRY BAL 245 17TH WAR
SOURSBAUGH, GEORGE WAS 126 HAGERSTO
SOURWALT, JACOB BAL 413 14TH WAR
SOURWALT, MARGARET BAL 426 14TH WAR
SOUSTRUM, WILLIAM BAL 278 17TH WAR
SOUTH, BARBARA WAS 289 1ST DIST
SOUTH, BENJAMIN WAS 195 1ST DIST
SOUTH, BENJAMIN WAS 170 FUNKSTOW
SOUTH, CHARLES WAS 171 FUNKSTOW
SOUTH, DANIEL WAS 132 HAGERSTO
SOUTH, DAVID WAS 170 FUNKSTOW
SOUTH, GERA WAS 195 1ST DIST
SOUTH, MARTHA WAS 170 FUNKSTOW
SOUTH, THOMAS WAS 170 FUNKSTOW
SOUTH, WASHINGTON WAS 170 FUNKSTOW
SOUTH, WILLIAM WAS 142 HAGERSTO
SOUTHALL, MARY BAL 296 12TH WAR
SOUTHALND, ELIZABETH BAL 013 18TH WAR
SOUTHCOMB, CAREY BAL 281 7TH WARD
SOUTHCOMB, ELIZABETH BAL 328 3RD WARD
SOUTHCOMB, ELIZABETH BAL 329 3RD WARD
SOUTHCOMB, H. BAL 233 20TH WAR
SOUTHCOMB, JOANA BAL 321 7TH WARD
SOUTHCOMB, MARGARETT BAL 074 4TH WARD
SOUTHCOMB, MARY H.* BAL 328 3RD WARD
SOUTHCOMB, PETER H. BAL 078 4TH WARD
SOUTHEN, JAMES BAL 362 8TH WARD

SOUTHERCOMB, ELMIRA COMBS BAL 258 1ST DIST
SOUTHEREN, ELLEN-BLACK CAR 403 2ND DIST
SOUTHERLAND, JAMES CHA 237 HILLTOP
SOUTHERLAND, JOHN BAL 315 7TH WARD
SOUTHERLAND, WALTER CHA 236 HILLTOP
SOUTHERLAND, WILLIAM CHA 239 HILLTOP
SOUTHERLAND, WILLIAM BAL 148 1ST WARD
SOUTHERLAND, ZEE CHA 259 MIDDLETO
SOUTHGATE, ALFRED BAL 353 3RD WARD
SOUTHGATE, REUBEN CAR 383 2ND DIST
SOUTHGATE, SARAH CAR 385 2ND DIST
SOUTHGATE, WASHINGTON CAR 323 1ST DIST
SOUTHWICK, ROCY HAR 013 1ST DIST
SOUTHWOOD, LEAH BAL 338 13TH WAR
SOUTTS, BENJAMIN F. CEC 174 6TH E DI
SOWARD, ELIZA BAL 240 17TH WAR
SOWDERS, CATHARINE WAS 145 2ND DIST
SOWDERS, MARY J. WAS 144 2ND DIST
SOWE, WILLIAM* BAL 387 3RD WARD
SOWELL, ROBERT * BAL 398 1ST DIST
SOWER, ELIZA ST 317 4TH E DI
SOWER, ELIZABETH CAR 348 6TH DIST
SOWER, JOHN BAL 206 2ND WARD
SOWER, OVERTON G. ALL 182 8TH E.D.
SOWERMAN, FREDERICK W. FRE 209 BUCKEYST
SOWERS, ADAM WAS 098 2ND DIST
SOWERS, CHARLOTTE BAL 103 18TH WAR
SOWERS, DAVID FRE 281 WOODSBOR
SOWERS, ELI WAS 113 2ND DIST
SOWERS, ELIZA FRE 394 PETERSVI
SOWERS, ELIZABETH FRE 099 FREDERIC
SOWERS, ELLEN WAS 079 2ND SUBD
SOWERS, ISAAC ALL 181 8TH E.D.
SOWERS, JACOB WAS 099 2ND DIST
SOWERS, JEREMIAH FRE 170 5TH E DI
SOWERS, JOHN ALL 046 10TH E.D
SOWERS, JOSEPH FRE 101 FREDERIC
SOWERS, JOSEPH TAL 107 ST MICHA
SOWERS, LEVI FRE 095 FREDERIC
SOWERS, MARY WAS 104 2ND DIST
SOWERS, MARY ALL 182 8TH E.D.
SOWERS, MARY E. TAL 108 ST MICHA
SOWERS, PETER WAS 112 2ND DIST
SOWERS, PHILLIP FRE 300 WOODSBOR
SOWMAN, JOHN ALL 201 CUMBERLA
SOWNDS, CHARLES* TAL 027 EASTON D
SOWS, RACHAEL BAL 219 2ND WARD
SOX, BENJAMIN FRE 256 NEW MARK
SOYSTER, SOLOMON ALL 092 5TH E.D.
SPACHT, DAVID FRE 218 BUCKEYST
SPACHT, JACOB FRE 218 BUCKEYST
SPADD, JOHN WAS 142 HAGERSTO
SPADE, JOHN G CAR 290 7TH DIST
SPADE, MICHAEL BAL 024 2ND DIST
SPADIE, ANN BAL 266 12TH WAR
SPAEDING, JANE BAL 233 12TH WAR
SPAFFORD, ANN BAL 329 3RD WARD
SPAFFORD, GEORGE L. BAL 329 3RD WARD
SPAGNLER, JOHN L. BAL 158 19TH WAR
SPAINE, VALENTINE BAL 045 1ST WARD
SPAIR, JOHN BAL 157 2ND DIST
SPALDING, A. ST 255 3RD E DI
SPALDING, ANN F. ST 263 3RD E DI
SPALDING, B. D. CHA 255 MIDDLETO
SPALDING, B. N. BAL 155 11TH WAR
SPALDING, C. C. ST 254 3RD E DI
SPALDING, CAROLINE ST 347 5TH E DI
SPALDING, CATHERINE MGM 423 MEDLEY 3
SPALDING, CHARLES FRE 093 FREDERIC
SPALDING, CLEMENT ST 320 4TH E DI
SPALDING, COMMILLA CHA 261 MIDDLETO
SPALDING, CORNELIA BAL 413 3RD WARD
SPALDING, DAVID BAL 051 9TH WARD
SPALDING, ELIAS FRE 234 BUCKEYST
SPALDING, ELISABETH BAL 297 3RD WARD
SPALDING, ELIZA ST 267 3RD E DI
SPALDING, ELIZABETH WAS 146 HAGERSTO
SPALDING, FRANCIS W. FRE 194 5TH E DI
SPALDING, GEORGE CHA 254 MIDDLETO
SPALDING, GEORGE BAL 107 2ND DIST
SPALDING, GEORGE J. ST 274 3RD E DI
SPALDING, GEORGE W. BAL 412 3RD WARD
SPALDING, JAMES BAL 200 17TH WAR
SPALDING, JOHN BAL 017 15TH WAR
SPALDING, JOHN B. PRI 114 PISCATAW
SPALDING, JOHN R. PRI 047 AQUASCO
SPALDING, JOSEPH FRE 189 5TH E DI
SPALDING, JOSEPHINE FRE 234 BUCKEYST
SPALDING, LURCELIA * ST 260 3RD E DI
SPALDING, MARGARET WAS 140 2ND DIST
SPALDING, MARIA BAL 250 20TH WAR
SPALDING, MARIA BAL 250 20TH WAR
SPALDING, MARTHA BAL 133 5TH WARD
SPALDING, MARY BAL 184 19TH WAR
SPALDING, MARY ST 272 3RD E DI
SPALDING, NANIE BAL 155 11TH WAR
SPALDING, PETER ALL 089 5TH E.D.
SPALDING, REBECCA BAL 060 4TH WARD
SPALDING, RICHARD PRI 047 AQUASCO
SPALDING, RICHARD L. BAL 074 4TH WARD
SPALDING, ROBERT BAL 133 5TH WARD
SPALDING, SAMUEL ST 266 3RD E DI
SPALDING, SYLVESTER ST 273 3RD E DI
SPALDING, THEADORE FRE 176 5TH E DI
SPALDING, WILLIAM BAL 183 19TH WAR
SPALDING, WILLIAM ST 255 3RD E DI
SPALMAN, EDWARD P. ALL 008 3RD E.D.
SPALMAR, CHRISTIAN BAL 181 2ND WARD
SPAMER, CHARLES BAL 328 13TH WAR
SPAMER, HENRY BAL 155 16TH WAR
SPAMER, LUDWIG* BAL 010 4TH WARD
SPANARD, P.H. BAL 166 1ST WARD
SPANCE, JOSHUA QUE 159 2ND E DI
SPANCER, LUDWIG* BAL 010 4TH WARD
SPANCK, CATHERINE BAL 110 10TH WAR
SPANEY, JOSHUA* BAL 028 4TH WARD
SPANGLE, CHARLES* BAL 048 4TH WARD
SPANGLE, GEORGE ALL 127 4TH E.D.
SPANGLER, CHARLES WAS 130 HAGERSTO
SPANGLER, ELIZABETH WAS 272 RIDGEVIL
SPANGLER, FRANKLIN ALL 128 4TH E.D.
SPANGLER, GARDNER BAL 354 7TH WARD
SPANGLER, GEORGE WAS 009 WILLIAMS
SPANGLER, JAMES WAS 269 1ST DIST
SPANGLER, JOHN BAL 177 19TH WAR
SPANGLER, JOHN BAL 148 19TH WAR
SPANGLER, OGELETH WAS 130 HAGERSTO
SPANSEN, JOHN BAL 105 1ST WARD
SPANYON, JOHN BAL 456 8TH WARD
SPARE, ISAAC BAL 022 1ST WARD
SPARE, REBECCA A. HAR 145 3RD DIST
SPARGLE, CHARLES* BAL 048 4TH WARD
SPARHAWK, STEARNS BAL 034 9TH WARD
SPARING, ELIZABETH BAL 238 6TH WARD
SPARKES, ALVERETTA QUE 178 2ND E DI
SPARKES, ANN QUE 196 3RD E DI
SPARKES, CHARLES QUE 161 2ND E DI
SPARKES, CHRISTOPHER QUE 171 2ND E DI
SPARKES, ELIZABETH QUE 165 2ND E DI
SPARKES, GEORGE QUE 173 2ND E DI
SPARKES, GEORGE QUE 173 2ND E DI
SPARKES, HESTER QUE 180 2ND E DI
SPARKES, ISAAC QUE 174 2ND E DI
SPARKES, ISAAC QUE 172 2ND E DI
SPARKES, JAMES QUE 173 2ND E DI
SPARKES, JAMES QUE 177 2ND E DI
SPARKES, JOHN QUE 164 2ND E DI
SPARKES, JOHN QUE 208 3RD E DI
SPARKES, JOHN D. QUE 164 2ND E DI
SPARKES, JOHN M. QUE 174 2ND E DI
SPARKES, JOSEPH QUE 151 1ST E DI
SPARKES, KENT QUE 179 2ND E DI
SPARKES, LODI QUE 176 2ND E DI
SPARKES, LOUISA QUE 202 3RD E DI
SPARKES, LUTHER QUE 177 2ND E DI
SPARKES, MARY E. QUE 192 3RD E DI
SPARKES, NANCY QUE 174 2ND E DI
SPARKES, REBECCA QUE 146 1ST E DI
SPARKES, SAMUEL QUE 197 3RD E DI
SPARKES, SARAH A. QUE 148 1ST E DI
SPARKES, SARAH-BLACK QUE 171 2ND E DI
SPARKES, SLIDER QUE 161 2ND E DI
SPARKES,SARAH E. QUE 191 3RD E DI
SPARKLIN, ANN KEN 305 3RD DIST
SPARKLIN, BARTON J. BAL 283 7TH WARD
SPARKLIN, ELIZABETH BAL 405 8TH WARD
SPARKLIN, SAMUEL BAL 404 8TH WARD
SPARKLIN, SAMUEL TAL 029 EASTON D
SPARKLIN, THOMAS DOR 308 1ST DIST
SPARKLIN, TILGHMAN W. BAL 222 6TH WARD
SPARKLIN, WILLIAM* TAL 007 EASTON D
SPARKLING, DANIEL CAR 162 NO TWP L
SPARKLING, DELEHAY CAR 146 NO TWP L
SPARKS, ABSALOM W. KEN 227 2ND DIST
SPARKS, ALFRED BAL 186 5TH DIST
SPARKS, ALFRED BAL 129 16TH WAR
SPARKS, ANNA MARIA QUE 183 3RD E DI
SPARKS, ARON BAL 041 2ND DIST
SPARKS, ARON BAL 043 2ND DIST
SPARKS, BATHSHEBA BAL 429 1ST DIST
SPARKS, CHARITY-BLACK WOR 340 1ST E DI
SPARKS, DANIEL QUE 205 3RD E DI
SPARKS, EDWARD ANN 269 ANNAPOLI
SPARKS, ELENN BAL 291 12TH WAR
SPARKS, ELIJAH BAL 055 2ND DIST
SPARKS, ELIZA BAL 132 11TH WAR
SPARKS, ELIZABETH BAL 225 19TH WAR
SPARKS, ELIZABETH QUE 183 3RD E DI
SPARKS, FRANCIS BAL 048 2ND DIST
SPARKS, HENRIETTA-BLACK CAR 105 NO TWP L
SPARKS, HESTER QUE 194 3RD E DI
SPARKS, JAMES QUE 195 3RD E DI
SPARKS, JAMES QUE 191 3RD E DI
SPARKS, JAMES BAL 282 2ND WARD
SPARKS, JOHN-BLACK CAR 077 NO TWP L
SPARKS, LABAN BAL 052 2ND DIST
SPARKS, MARY-BLACK CAR 087 NO TWP L
SPARKS, MATHEW BAL 048 2ND DIST
SPARKS, MATILDA-BLACK CAR 077 NO TWP L
SPARKS, NANCY KEN 270 1ST DIST
SPARKS, NATHANIEL QUE 195 3RD E DI
SPARKS, NICHOLAS BAL 189 11TH WAR
SPARKS, OLIVER P. TAL 079 ST MICHA
SPARKS, RACHAEL BAL 193 5TH DIST
SPARKS, REBECCA TAL 092 ST MICHA
SPARKS, REBECCA BAL 127 11TH WAR
SPARKS, ROBERT CAR 096 NO TWP L
SPARKS, ROBERT QUE 196 3RD E DI
SPARKS, SAMUEL TAL 083 ST MICHA
SPARKS, SAMUEL BAL 133 11TH WAR
SPARKS, SARAH A. BAL 249 12TH WAR
SPARKS, SHADRACK BAL 052 2ND DIST
SPARKS, SOLOMON CAR 076 NO TWP L
SPARKS, SOLOMON KEN 260 1ST DIST
SPARKS, SUSAN QUE 193 3RD E DI
SPARKS, THOMAS BAL 133 11TH WAR
SPARKS, WALTER TAL 079 ST MICHA
SPARKS, WILLIAM BAL 036 18TH WAR
SPARKS, WILLIAM P. CAR 076 NO TWP L
SPARKS,RISDEN QUE 144 1ST E DI
SPARLINE, CONRAD ALL 039 2ND E.D.
SPARNER, WILLIAM BAL 226 12TH WAR
SPARROW, ALLEN FRE 316 MIDDLETO
SPARROW, AMANDA WAS 159 HAGERSTO
SPARROW, AMANDA WAS 131 2ND DIST
SPARROW, ANNA BAL 415 14TH WAR
SPARROW, BENJAMIN MGM 387 ROCKERLE
SPARROW, CATHARINE BAL 273 12TH WAR
SPARROW, DEBORAH BAL 375 13TH WAR
SPARROW, ELIZABETH BAL 128 16TH WAR
SPARROW, FRANCIS MGM 387 ROCKERLE
SPARROW, JOHN CAL 060 3RD DIST
SPARROW, JOHN ANN 314 1ST DIST
SPARROW, JOHN W. FRE 400 JEFFERSO
SPARROW, MARTHA BAL 119 11TH WAR
SPARROW, MICHAEL CAL 061 3RD DIST
SPARROW, PATTY BAL 146 11TH WAR
SPARROW, SARAH J. CAL 060 3RD DIST
SPARROW, SOPHIA A. BAL 309 3RD WARD
SPARROW, WILLIAM BAL 174 6TH WARD
SPARROW, WILLIAM WAS 063 2ND SUBD
SPARROW, WILSON L. FRE 399 JEFFERSO
SPARTER, CAUSIN-MULATTO ST 326 4TH E DI
SPATE, FRANCIS ALL 091 5TH E.D.
SPATES, ANN MGM 395 ROCKERLE
SPATES, CHARLES MGM 379 ROCKERLE
SPATES, GEORGE W. MGM 411 MEDLEY 3
SPATES, JOHN S. BAL 274 17TH WAR
SPATES, MARGARET BAL 440 14TH WAR
SPATES, RICHARD P. MGM 407 MEDLEY 3
SPATES, ROBERT N. MGM 393 ROCKERLE
SPATES, THOMAS S. ALL 055 10TH E.D
SPATOZER, PHILIP BAL 058 1ST WARD
SPAUGLER, SASANNAH * BAL 365 13TH WAR
SPAULDING, CHARLES BAL 222 1ST DIST
SPAULDING, GEORGE CAR 302 1ST DIST
SPAULDING, MICHAEL BAL 273 1ST DIST
SPAULDING, WILLIAM BAL 106 2ND DIST
SPAULING, J. BAL 150 1ST WARD
SPAVIN, ALEXANDER BAL 017 15TH WAR
SPAVIN, WILLIAM BAL 274 17TH WAR
SPAWN, JOHN WAS 046 2ND SUBD
SPAWN, JOHN WAS 054 2ND SUBD
SPEACHEL, AUGUSTA BAL 294 1ST DIST
SPEAD, JAMES BAL 002 1ST WARD
SPEAGLE, FREDERICK CAR 175 8TH DIST
SPEAK, ANN E. FRE 110 CREAGERS
SPEAK, ELIAS A. FRE 113 CREAGERS
SPEAK, EMILY E. CHA 233 HILLTOP
SPEAK, F. R. CHA 245 HILLTOP
SPEAK, HENERIETTA CHA 274 ALLENS F
SPEAK, MARY E. CHA 246 HILLTOP
SPEAK, SARAH FRE 109 CREAGERS
SPEAK, THOMAS J. CHA 245 HILLTOP
SPEAK, THOMAS T. CHA 238 HILLTOP
SPEAK, WILLAIM FRE 116 CREAGERS
SPEAKE, ADAM FRE 142 CREAGERS
SPEAKE, JOHN FRE 109 CREAGERS
SPEAKER, CATHERINE BAL 082 4TH WARD
SPEAKER, FREDERICK WAS 013 WILLIAMS
SPEAKER, HENRY WAS 028 2ND SUBD
SPEAKER, JOSEPH FRE 072 FREDERIC
SPEAKER, SAMUEL WAS 093 2ND SUBD
SPEAKER, WASHINGTON WAS 230 1ST DIST
SPEAKER, WILLIAM WAS 087 2ND SUBD
SPEAKES, JAMES H. BAL 304 12TH WAR
SPEAKMAN, ROBERT BAL 116 1ST WARD
SPEAKMAN, ROBERT BAL 140 1ST WARD
SPEAKS, ALLEN FRE 317 MIDDLETO
SPEAKS, ANN A.-MULATTO FRE 392 PETERSVI
SPEAKS, DANIEL FRE 312 MIDDLETO
SPEAKS, EMELINE-BLACK FRE 392 PETERSVI
SPEAKS, EMMA FRE 343 MIDDLETO
SPEAKS, JOSEPH-BLACK FRE 401 JEFFERSO
SPEAKS, LEONARD FRE 317 MIDDLETO
SPEAKS, LEONARD FRE 321 MIDDLETO
SPEAKS, MATILDA BAL 197 6TH WARD
SPEAKS, NICHOALS BAL 093 18TH WAR
SPEAKS, WILLIAM FRE 315 MIDDLETO
SPEALMAN, ADALINE WAS 032 2ND SUBD
SPEALMAN, DAVID FRE 173 5TH E DI
SPEALMAN, EMANUEL WAS 051 2ND SUBD
SPEALMAN, JOSEPH WAS 016 2ND SUBD
SPEALMAN, OTHO WAS 034 2ND SUBD
SPEALMAN, SAVILLA WAS 051 2ND SUBD
SPEALS, JAMES BAL 365 13TH WAR
SPEAR, A. BAL 139 1ST WARD
SPEAR, A. BAL 130 1ST WARD
SPEAR, AMBROSE CEC 066 1ST E DI
SPEAR, ANNA BAL 029 9TH WARD
SPEAR, BARCLAY BAL 213 17TH WAR
SPEAR, BENINGLE BAL 225 17TH WAR
SPEAR, DEWITT C. KEN 306 3RD DIST
SPEAR, JAMES KEN 306 3RD DIST
SPEAR, JAMES JR. KEN 294 3RD DIST
SPEAR, JOHN KEN 309 3RD DIST
SPEAR, JOHN CEC 182 7TH E DI
SPEAR, JOHN CEC 032 CHESAPEA
SPEAR, MARY E. SOM 511 BARREN C
SPEAR, NICHOLAS BAL 254 2ND WARD
SPEAR, OTIS BAL 439 14TH WAR
SPEAR, REBECCA BAL 263 20TH WAR
SPEAR, ROSE BAL 263 20TH WAR
SPEAR, RUTHERFORD BAL 162 1ST WARD
SPEAR, SARAH A. KEN 308 3RD DIST
SPEAR, SOLOMON KEN 234 2ND DIST
SPEAR, THERESA C. BAL 093 10TH WAR
SPEAR, THOMAS BAL 052 1ST WARD
SPEAR, WILLIAM BAL 093 10TH WAR
SPEAR, WILLIAM KEN 309 3RD DIST
SPEAR, WILLIAM* DOR 456 1ST DIST
SPEARES, MARY HAR 206 3RD DIST
SPEARKER, C. WAS 016 2ND SUBD
SPEARS, AUGUST BAL 163 1ST WARD
SPEARS, FRANCES ANN 469 HOWARD D
SPEARS, JAMES BAL 288 3RD WARD
SPEARS, JOHN ANN 365 4TH DIST
SPEARS, JOHN BAL 119 1ST WARD
SPEARS, MARGARET ANN 484 HOWARD D
SPEARS, MARY C. BAL 080 4TH WARD
SPEARS, WILLIAM BAL 220 1ST DIST
SPECARD, DAVID ALL 060 10TH E.D
SPECARD, GEORGE ALL 060 10TH E.D
SPECK, ANDREW ALL 214 CUMBERLA
SPECK, CATHERINE BAL 017 4TH WARD
SPECK, DAVID WAS 194 1ST DIST
SPECK, FREDERICK WAS 285 1ST DIST
SPECK, FREDERICK BAL 260 20TH WAR
SPECK, LAURA A. WAS 270 1ST DIST
SPECK, MARTAIN WAS 127 2ND DIST
SPECK, MARTIN WAS 264 1ST DIST
SPECK, MARY CHA 237 HILLTOP
SPECK, PETER WAS 269 1ST DIST
SPECKER, HENRY WAS 135 2ND DIST
SPECKER, MILLY WAS 133 2ND DIST
SPECKLEMYER, GEORGE BAL 210 17TH WAR
SPECKMAN, ROBERT BAL 280 2ND WARD
SPEDDAN, JOSEPH BAL 321 3RD WARD
SPEDDEN, DANIEL E. HAR 083 2ND DIST
SPEDDEN, EDWARD BAL 159 16TH WAR
SPEDDEN, EDWARD BAL 052 15TH WAR
SPEDDEN, GEORGE BAL 066 15TH WAR
SPEDDEN, JAMES DOR 390 1ST DIST
SPEDDEN, JOHN BAL 040 18TH WAR
SPEDDEN, MARTHA BAL 459 1ST DIST
SPEDDEN, P.M. BAL 137 1ST WARD
SPEDDEN, ROBERT BAL 055 18TH WAR
SPEDDEN, SARAH BAL 357 13TH WAR
SPEDDEN, THOMAS BAL 042 18TH WAR
SPEDDEN, VINCENT BAL 042 18TH WAR
SPEDDEN, VINCENT BAL 058 18TH WAR
SPEDDEN, WILLIAM BAL 069 15TH WAR
SPEDDIN, ALEXANDER DOR 399 1ST DIST
SPEDDIN, ANN* DOR 393 1ST DIST
SPEDDIN, ELIZABETH DOR 397 1ST DIST
SPEDDIN, EMPY DOR 396 1ST DIST
SPEDDIN, IMPY DOR 398 1ST DIST
SPEDDIN, JANE DOR 397 1ST DIST
SPEDDIN, JOHN DOR 397 1ST DIST
SPEDDIN, JOHN M. DOR 378 1ST DIST
SPEDDIN, MARGARET DOR 399 1ST DIST
SPEDDIN, MARGARET DOR 397 1ST DIST
SPEDDIN, MARY J.* DOR 395 1ST DIST
SPEDDIN, ROBERT DOR 396 1ST DIST
SPEDDIN, ROBERT R. DOR 397 1ST DIST
SPEDDIN, SALEY* DOR 396 1ST DIST
SPEDDIN, THOMAS DOR 398 1ST DIST
SPEDDIN, TIMOTHY DOR 397 1ST DIST
SPEDDIN, WILLIAM DOR 395 1ST DIST
SPEDDIN, WILLIAM H. DOR 404 1ST DIST

NAME	CO	PAGE	DISTRICT
SPEDDY, JOHN H.	BAL	214	11TH WAR
SPEDIN, RALF*	DOR	399	1ST DIST
SPEDWINIDY, MARY	BAL	352	7TH WARD
SPEED, CHARLES	BAL	131	1ST WARD
SPEEDY, ELLEN	BAL	214	11TH WAR
SPEELMAN, DANIEL	ALL	120	5TH E.D.
SPEELMAN, JACOB	ALL	205	CUMBERLA
SPEELMAN, JAMES H.	ALL	205	CUMBERLA
SPEELMAN, JONAS	WAS	105	2ND DIST
SPEELMAN, MICHAEL	ALL	211	CUMBERLA
SPEELMAN, PETER	ALL	113	5TH E.D.
SPEELMAN, WILLIAM H.	WAS	074	2ND SUBD
SPEHAN, THOMAS	BAL	274	20TH WAR
SPEICK, CONRAD	BAL	247	2ND WARD
SPEICK, PHILLIP	BAL	247	2ND WARD
SPEIGHT, MARTIN	BAL	112	1ST WARD
SPEIGHTS, EVELINE	BAL	059	4TH WARD
SPEIGHTS, J. T.	BAL	059	4TH WARD
SPEILKER, W. *	BAL	311	20TH WAR
SPEILL, HENRY	BAL	191	2ND WARD
SPEILMAN, BARBARA MRS- *	BAL	315	20TH WAR
SPEILMAN, DAVID	ALL	114	5TH E.D.
SPEILMAN, JOHN	WAS	180	BOONSBOR
SPEILMAN, JOHN H.	CAR	289	7TH DIST
SPEILMAN, JON	WAS	149	HAGERSTO
SPEILMAN, LAWRENCE	ALL	148	6TH E.D.
SPEILMAN, MARTHA	ALL	148	6TH E.D.
SPEIRS, P.	BAL	174	1ST WARD
SPEKER, CATHARINE	WAS	109	2ND DIST
SPEKER, HYRUM	WAS	135	2ND DIST
SPEKER, PHIL	ALL	110	5TH E.D.
SPEKS, SUSAN	FRE	076	FREDERIC
SPELDON, WILLIAM	ALL	106	5TH E.D.
SPELL, JOHN	BAL	124	2ND DIST
SPELL, MARTIN	BAL	067	2ND DIST
SPELLMAN, BARBARA MRS- *	BAL	315	20TH WAR
SPELLMAN, JOHN	HAR	100	2ND DIST
SPELLMAN, JOHN	BAL	029	4TH WARD
SPELLMAN, MARY A.	CAL	021	2ND DIST
SPELLMAN, MICHAEL	BAL	002	15TH WAR
SPELLMAN, WILLIAM	BAL	113	1ST WARD
SPELMAN, ANN	BAL	243	12TH WAR
SPELMAN, ELIZA A.	BAL	382	3RD WARD
SPELMAN, JOHN	BAL	276	12TH WAR
SPELMAN, PATRICK	BAL	276	2ND WARD
SPELT, ADAM	BAL	307	1ST DIST
SPEN, WILLIAM T.	BAL	130	1ST WARD
SPENCE, AMY	SOM	482	TRAPP DI
SPENCE, ANN E.	DOR	317	1ST DIST
SPENCE, ANN M.	BAL	210	2ND WARD
SPENCE, ARA	WOR	299	SNOW HIL
SPENCE, ARA	WOR	307	2ND E DI
SPENCE, ARNOLD	WOR	176	6TH E DI
SPENCE, BENJAMIN	BAL	402	3RD WARD
SPENCE, CARROLL	BAL	312	1ST DIST
SPENCE, COMPTON	BAL	307	20TH WAR
SPENCE, EDWARD	CEC	115	3RD E DI
SPENCE, EELIZA C.	TAL	016	EASTON D
SPENCE, ELIZA	WOR	181	6TH E DI
SPENCE, ELIZA	WOR	181	6TH E DI
SPENCE, EPHRAIM	CEC	095	4TH E DI
SPENCE, FRISBY	BAL	190	17TH WAR
SPENCE, GEORGE P.	WOR	300	SNOW HIL
SPENCE, GEORGE W.	BAL	114	1ST WARD
SPENCE, GEORGE-MULATTC	WOR	171	6TH E DI
SPENCE, HARMAN	BAL	130	18TH WAR
SPENCE, HARRIET	WOR	295	9TH E DI
SPENCE, HELEN A.	ANN	267	ANNAPOLI
SPENCE, HENRY	HAR	007	1ST DIST
SPENCE, HESTER	CEC	114	3RD E DI
SPENCE, IRVIN	WOR	313	2ND E DI
SPENCE, ISAAC	BAL	228	17TH WAR
SPENCE, ISAAC	BAL	227	17TH WAR
SPENCE, JAMES	CEC	091	4TH E DI
SPENCE, JAMES	BAL	145	1ST WARD
SPENCE, JAMES	ANN	345	3RD DIST
SPENCE, JOHN	ANN	321	2ND DIST
SPENCE, JOHN	BAL	297	12TH WAR
SPENCE, JOHN	CEC	099	3RD E DI
SPENCE, JOHN	CEC	029	CHESAPEA
SPENCE, JOHN H.	CEC	105	3RD E DI
SPENCE, JOHN Y.	CAR	090	NO TWP L
SPENCE, JOSEPH	HAR	042	1ST DIST
SPENCE, LITTLETON	WOR	296	9TH E DI
SPENCE, LYDIA	BAL	170	16TH WAR
SPENCE, LYDIA	BAL	324	7TH WARD
SPENCE, MARGARET	WOR	313	2ND E DI
SPENCE, MARGARET	HAR	040	1ST DIST
SPENCE, MARIA	WOR	263	BERLIN 1
SPENCE, MARIA	WOR	221	4TH E DI
SPENCE, MARIA	BAL	069	10TH WAR
SPENCE, MARTHA	BAL	327	7TH WARD
SPENCE, MARY	BAL	316	7TH WARD
SPENCE, MARY E.	BAL	330	3RD WARD
SPENCE, MARY J.	BAL	316	7TH WARD
SPENCE, MARY T.	CEC	001	ELKTON 3
SPENCE, PHEBE	WOR	254	1ST CENS
SPENCE, PHOEBA	ANN	269	ANNAPOLI
SPENCE, REBECCA	BAL	405	1ST DIST
SPENCE, REESE	CEC	009	ELKTON 3
SPENCE, ROBERT	CEC	105	3RD E DI
SPENCE, ROBERT H.	BAL	005	EASTERN
SPENCE, SAMUEL	BAL	166	1ST WARD
SPENCE, SARAH	BAL	331	13TH WAR
SPENCE, SHARLOTTA	CEC	111	4TH E DI
SPENCE, THEADORE	HAR	007	1ST DIST
SPENCE, THERESA	BAL	101	5TH WARD
SPENCE, THOMAS	CEC	105	3RD E DI
SPENCE, THOMAS A.	WOR	307	2ND E DI
SPENCE, THOMAS A.	WOR	189	7TH E DI
SPENCE, WILLIAM	CEC	105	3RD E DI
SPENCE, WILLIAM	HAR	034	1ST DIST
SPENCE, WILLIAM	CEC	134	6TH E DI
SPENCE, WILLIAM	CEC	157	PORT DUP
SPENCE, WILLIAM W.	BAL	107	10TH WAR
SPENCER, ADAM	BAL	209	2ND WARD
SPENCER, ALEXANDER S.	ST	303	2ND E DI
SPENCER, ANN	TAL	059	EASTON D
SPENCER, ANN	BAL	285	12TH WAR
SPENCER, ANN	CAR	196	4TH DIST
SPENCER, ANNA	KEN	298	3RD DIST
SPENCER, BENJAMIN	KEN	292	3RD DIST
SPENCER, BENJAMIN	SOM	412	DUBLIN D
SPENCER, BENJAMIN	KEN	236	2ND DIST
SPENCER, BETSEY	SOM	456	DAMES QU
SPENCER, CHARLES	CAR	190	4TH DIST
SPENCER, CHARLES	CAR	079	NO TWP L
SPENCER, CHARLOTTE	BAL	433	14TH WAR
SPENCER, CHARLOTTE	BAL	259	20TH WAR
SPENCER, CHARLOTTE	BAL	063	10TH WAR
SPENCER, DAVID	BAL	266	20TH WAR
SPENCER, DOLLY	KEN	240	2ND DIST
SPENCER, EDWARD*	TAL	024	EASTON D
SPENCER, ELEY	BAL	219	12TH WAR
SPENCER, ELI	CEC	150	PORT DUP
SPENCER, ELIZA	BAL	232	12TH WAR
SPENCER, ELIZA	BAL	328	3RD WARD
SPENCER, ELIZABETH	BAL	252	1ST DIST
SPENCER, ELIZABETH	WAS	257	1ST DIST
SPENCER, ELIZABETH	QUE	206	3RD E DI
SPENCER, ELLEN	BAL	034	9TH WARD
SPENCER, ELLEN	BAL	387	13TH WAR
SPENCER, ELLEN A.	BAL	140	19TH WAR
SPENCER, ELLEN A.	BAL	093	15TH WAR
SPENCER, ENOCH	BAL	035	1ST WARD
SPENCER, FIELDER	ANN	269	ANNAPOLI
SPENCER, FRANCIS	ST	303	2ND E DI
SPENCER, G.D.	BAL	236	12TH WAR
SPENCER, GEORGE	BAL	174	11TH WAR
SPENCER, GEORGE	BAL	038	9TH WARD
SPENCER, GEORGE	PRI	113	PISCATAW
SPENCER, GEORGE	HAR	117	2ND DIST
SPENCER, GEORGE D.	MGM	365	BERRYS D
SPENCER, GEORGE F.	BAL	045	9TH WARD
SPENCER, GEORGE W.	KEN	295	3RD DIST
SPENCER, H.	BAL	170	1ST WARD
SPENCER, H.	BAL	172	1ST WARD
SPENCER, HELLEN	KEN	312	3RD DIST
SPENCER, HENRY	KEN	289	3RD DIST
SPENCER, HUGH	BAL	215	17TH WAR
SPENCER, HUGH E.	HAR	050	1ST DIST
SPENCER, IRVIN	WOR	221	4TH E DI
SPENCER, ISAAC	KEN	300	3RD DIST
SPENCER, JAMES	TAL	059	EASTON D
SPENCER, JAMES	BAL	150	16TH WAR
SPENCER, JAMES	BAL	372	8TH WARD
SPENCER, JAMES*	TAL	059	EASTON D
SPENCER, JAMES-BLACK	FRE	224	BUCKEYST
SPENCER, JANE	BAL	107	5TH WARD
SPENCER, JARVIS	WAS	136	HAGERSTO
SPENCER, JERES	TAL	087	ST MICHA
SPENCER, JOHN	KEN	296	3RD DIST
SPENCER, JOHN	QUE	170	2ND E DI
SPENCER, JOHN	WOR	312	2ND E DI
SPENCER, JOHN	BAL	454	1ST DIST
SPENCER, JOHN	BAL	161	1ST WARD
SPENCER, JOHN	BAL	119	1ST WARD
SPENCER, JOHN	CAR	109	NO TWP L
SPENCER, JOHN B.	QUE	193	3RD E DI
SPENCER, JOHN E.	WOR	201	3RD E DI
SPENCER, JOHN M.	BAL	402	14TH WAR
SPENCER, JOHN M.	HAR	078	2ND DIST
SPENCER, JOHN T.-BLACK	QUE	175	2ND E DI
SPENCER, JOHN W.	HAR	125	2ND DIST
SPENCER, JOSEPH	CEC	060	1ST E DI
SPENCER, JOSEPH	TAL	038	EASTON D
SPENCER, JOSEPH	BAL	232	6TH WARD
SPENCER, JOSEPH P.	BAL	083	18TH WAR
SPENCER, LELIA	BAL	182	6TH WARD
SPENCER, LYDIA	BAL	238	12TH WAR
SPENCER, LYDIA-BLACK	MGM	423	MEDLEY 3
SPENCER, MARIA	ANN	459	HOWARD D
SPENCER, MARIA-BLACK	QUE	131	1ST E DI
SPENCER, MARTHA	BAL	248	17TH WAR
SPENCER, MARTHA-BLACK	QUE	175	2ND E DI
SPENCER, MARY	BAL	139	19TH WAR
SPENCER, MARY	BAL	205	2ND WARD
SPENCER, MARY	BAL	023	1ST WARD
SPENCER, MARY E.	BAL	016	18TH WAR
SPENCER, MARY E.	CAL	036	2ND DIST
SPENCER, MARY-BLACK	FRE	220	BUCKEYST
SPENCER, MARY-MULATTO	FRE	042	FREDERIC
SPENCER, MATILDA	FRE	029	FREDERIC
SPENCER, MATTHEW	SOM	484	TRAPP DI
SPENCER, MISS J.	FRE	199	5TH E DI
SPENCER, NANCY	BAL	202	17TH WAR
SPENCER, NANCY	BAL	004	15TH WAR
SPENCER, P.K.*	BAL	242	12TH WAR
SPENCER, PERRIGRINE	BAL	059	18TH WAR
SPENCER, PHILIP	CEC	185	7TH E DI
SPENCER, PHILIP-BLACK	MGM	423	MEDLEY 3
SPENCER, R.H.	WAS	021	2ND SUBD
SPENCER, REDDINGFIELD	BAL	060	10TH WAR
SPENCER, RICHARD H.	TAL	044	EASTON D
SPENCER, ROBERT F.	FRE	388	PETERSVI
SPENCER, SAMUEL C.	BAL	437	1ST DIST
SPENCER, SAMUEL W.	KEN	239	2ND DIST
SPENCER, SOPHIA D.	BAL	027	18TH WAR
SPENCER, SUSANNAH	BAL	023	15TH WAR
SPENCER, THOASM O.	ST	285	2ND E DI
SPENCER, THOMAS	BAL	062	1ST WARD
SPENCER, THOMAS	BAL	385	3RD WARD
SPENCER, THOMAS	FRE	247	NEW MARK
SPENCER, THOMAS	CAR	197	4TH DIST
SPENCER, THOMAS-MULATTO	FRE	219	BUCKEYST
SPENCER, VALENTINE	HAR	089	2ND DIST
SPENCER, WILLIAM	MGM	353	BERRYS D
SPENCER, WILLIAM	BAL	458	1ST DIST
SPENCER, WILLIAM	ALL	139	6TH E.D.
SPENCER, WILLIAM	TAL	100	ST MICHA
SPENCER, WILLIAM	KEN	313	3RD DIST
SPENCER, WILLIAM A.	QUE	219	3RD E DI
SPENCER, WILLIAM P.	BAL	306	3RD WARD
SPENCER, WILLIAM S.	FRE	406	JEFFERSO
SPENCER, WILLIAM-BLACK	QUE	126	1ST E DI
SPENCER, WYNDHAM	BAL	246	12TH WAR
SPEND, CHARLES	BAL	087	1ST WARD
SPENDEN, DANIEL	BAL	248	17TH WAR
SPENERD, AMOS	HAR	152	3RD DIST
SPENK, CASPAR	BAL	057	1ST WARD
SPENKS, JEN	BAL	227	12TH WAR
SPENKS, WILLIAM C.	BAL	161	1ST WARD
SPENNY, VIRGINIA	BAL	220	12TH WAR
SPENUBE, J. REV.	TAL	094	ST MICHA
SPERGLHOUSE, AUGUSTUS *	BAL	367	1ST DIST
SPERIKEN, JOHN	BAL	352	7TH WARD
SPERR, REACHEL	BAL	209	11TH WAR
SPERRIER, GEORGE	BAL	430	8TH WARD
SPERROW, ANN E.	BAL	119	11TH WAR
SPERRY, BENJAMIN W.	BAL	454	14TH WAR
SPERRY, JOHN	TAL	018	EASTON D
SPERRY, MARGARET	CAR	329	MANCHEST
SPERRY, PETER	BAL	164	16TH WAR
SPERRY, WILLIAM	BAL	056	10TH WAR
SPESSARD, CATHARINE	WAS	232	1ST DIST
SPESSARD, CHRISTAIAN	WAS	242	CAVETOWN
SPESSARD, DANIEL D.	WAS	250	1ST DIST
SPESSARD, JOHN	WAS	232	1ST DIST
SPESSARD, JOHN JR.	WAS	252	1ST DIST
SPESSARD, MARIA	WAS	236	CAVETOWN
SPESSARD, MARY E.	WAS	243	CAVETOWN
SPESSARD, MARY J.	WAS	252	1ST DIST
SPESSARD, MATILDA	WAS	253	1ST DIST
SPESSARD, RACHAEL	WAS	234	1ST DIST
SPEY, KATRINA	BAL	185	19TH WAR
SPICE, POLLY	BAL	151	11TH WAR
SPICER, ABRAHAM	HAR	086	2ND DIST
SPICER, AMOS	HAR	200	3RD DIST
SPICER, CHARLES	BAL	244	20TH WAR
SPICER, ELIZA A.	BAL	301	17TH WAR
SPICER, ELIZA J.	BAL	168	16TH WAR
SPICER, ELIZA JANE	BAL	409	14TH WAR
SPICER, GEORGE W.	HAR	201	3RD DIST
SPICER, HIRAM	BAL	094	18TH WAR
SPICER, JAMES	HAR	200	3RD DIST
SPICER, JAMES	BAL	373	1ST DIST
SPICER, JEFFYRSON	HAR	200	3RD DIST
SPICER, JEREMIAH	BAL	045	15TH WAR
SPICER, JOHN	BAL	162	19TH WAR
SPICER, JOHN	BAL	301	17TH WAR
SPICER, MARY	BAL	269	12TH WAR
SPICER, NATHANIEL	BAL	083	10TH WAR
SPICER, PRICILLA	BAL	242	17TH WAR
SPICER, SAMUEL	BAL	314	7TH WARD
SPICER, STANTON	MGM	388	ROCKERLE
SPICER, THOMAS	BAL	448	14TH WAR
SPICER, THOMAS	BAL	268	12TH WAR
SPICER, TRAVERS	DOR	359	3RD DIVI
SPICER, WELMIRA	BAL	214	11TH WAR
SPICKER, HENRY	BAL	003	4TH WARD
SPICKGH, JACOB	BAL	104	1ST WARD
SPICKING, JOSEPH	CEC	186	7TH E DI
SPICKLER, MATILDA	WAS	126	2ND DIST
SPICKNALL, CHARLES	CAL	041	3RD DIST
SPICKNALL, MARTHA	CAL	041	3RD DIST
SPICKNALL, THOMAS J.	CAL	041	3RD DIST
SPICKNALL, WILLIAM H.	CAL	060	3RD DIST
SPICKNELL, JAMES	PRI	065	NOTTINGH
SPIDMAN, JACOB	WAS	200	1ST DIST
SPIEGLER, JOHN	BAL	005	EASTERN
SPIELMAN, DANIEL	WAS	194	1ST DIST
SPIELMAN, DAVID	WAS	210	1ST DIST
SPIELMAN, DAVID	WAS	200	1ST DIST
SPIELMAN, EMANUEL	WAS	201	1ST DIST
SPIELMAN, EZRA	WAS	193	1ST DIST
SPIELMAN, HIRAM	WAS	025	2ND SUBD
SPIELMAN, HYRAM	WAS	149	HAGERSTO
SPIELMAN, INA	WAS	004	WILLIAMS
SPIELMAN, JACOB	WAS	292	1ST DIST
SPIELMAN, JACOB	ALL	148	6TH E.D.
SPIELMAN, JOHN	WAS	191	1ST DIST
SPIELMAN, JONATHAN	WAS	105	2ND DIST
SPIELMAN, JOSEPH	ALL	148	6TH E.D.
SPIELMAN, MALINDA	WAS	185	BOONSBOR
SPIELMAN, SAMUEL	WAS	149	HAGERSTO
SPIES, ANDREW	BAL	276	20TH WAR
SPIES, EDWARD	BAL	274	12TH WAR
SPIES, ELSY	BAL	264	20TH WAR
SPIES, FREDERIC	BAL	017	9TH WARD
SPIES, GEORGE C.	BAL	109	5TH WARD
SPIES, GEORGE W.	BAL	042	15TH WAR
SPIES, JOHN G.	BAL	027	15TH WAR
SPIES, MARGARET	BAL	088	15TH WAR
SPIES, REBECCA	BAL	063	15TH WAR
SPIES, WILLIAM	BAL	243	12TH WAR
SPIES, WILLIAM	BAL	087	15TH WAR
SPIGLER, DAVID	WAS	126	2ND DIST
SPIGLER, ELLENORA L.	WAS	293	1ST DIST
SPIGLER, JOHN N.	WAS	109	2ND DIST
SPIGLER, SAMUEL	WAS	295	1ST DIST
SPIGLER, SUSN	WAS	274	RIDGEVIL
SPIGLER, THOMAS B.	WAS	274	RIDGEVIL
SPIGLER, TILGHMAN	WAS	295	1ST DIST
SPIKER, AUSTIN	ALL	036	2ND E.D.
SPIKER, BENJAMIN	ALL	046	10TH E.D
SPIKER, CATHARINE	ALL	003	3RD E.D.
SPIKER, HENRY	ALL	121	4TH E.D.
SPIKER, ISAAC	ALL	007	3RD E.D.
SPIKER, JACOB	ALL	046	10TH E.D
SPIKER, JOHN	ALL	058	10TH E.D
SPIKER, JOSEPH	ALL	039	2ND E.D.
SPIKER, JOSEPH	ALL	036	2ND E.D.
SPIKER, JOSEPH	ALL	041	2ND E.D.
SPIKER, LEWIS	ALL	032	2ND E.D.
SPIKER, SOLOMON	ALL	034	2ND E.D.
SPIKER, WILLIAM	ALL	017	3RD E.D.
SPILCKER, CHARLES W.	BAL	065	10TH WAR
SPILER, HANNAH	CEC	034	CHESAPEA
SPILHEIM, P.	BAL	219	19TH WAR
SPILKER, CHARLES	BAL	083	15TH WAR
SPILLAM, JAMES	BAL	299	17TH WAR
SPILLARDS, OTHER	HAR	202	3RD DIST
SPILLARDS, SARAH	HAR	200	3RD DIST
SPILLER, E. C.	BAL	099	10TH WAR
SPILLER, E. N.	BAL	470	14TH WAR
SPILLMAN, ALEXANDER B.	BAL	050	15TH WAR
SPILLMAN, CONRAD	BAL	161	16TH WAR
SPILLMAN, DOMINICK	BAL	165	11TH WAR
SPILLMAN, ELIZABETH	BAL	111	18TH WAR
SPILLMAN, FREDERICK	BAL	086	18TH WAR
SPILLMAN, JOHN	BAL	045	4TH WARD
SPILLMAN, MARY	BAL	125	5TH WARD
SPILLS, HENRY	BAL	162	1ST WARD
SPILMAN, A.	BAL	060	10TH WAR
SPILMAN, CONRAD	BAL	423	14TH WAR
SPILMAN, GEORGE	BAL	244	12TH WAR
SPILMAN, HENRY	BAL	182	2ND WARD
SPILMAN, LAURA	BAL	183	2ND WARD
SPILMAN, LEWIS	MGM	378	ROCKERLE
SPINABACK, BEN AGE *	BAL	289	20TH WAR
SPINDLER, BETHEA	BAL	081	4TH WARD
SPINDLER, ENOCH G.	BAL	433	1ST DIST
SPINDLER, FREDERIC	BAL	018	9TH WARD
SPINDLER, JOHN	BAL	150	5TH WARD
SPINDLER, JOSHUA	BAL	432	1ST DIST
SPINDLER, KASIAH	BAL	433	1ST DIST
SPINDLER, MARY	BAL	100	5TH WARD
SPINDLER, SUSAN C.	BAL	162	6TH WARD
SPINER, HESTER	BAL	217	19TH WAR
SPING, HENRY	BAL	004	15TH WAR
SPINGER, MARY	HAR	153	3RD DIST
SPINISTER, MICHAEL	ALL	139	6TH E.D.
SPINKLE, FRANCIS	BAL	215	11TH WAR
SPINKS, EDWARD-BLACK	ST	317	4TH E DI
SPINKS, JOHN E.-BLACK	ST	320	4TH E DI
SPINKS, REBECCA	BAL	355	1ST DIST
SPINKS, WILLIAM F.	MGM	381	ROCKERLE
SPINKS, WILLIAM-BLACK	ST	319	4TH E DI
SPINSTER, MARY	BAL	289	20TH WAR
SPIRES, ANN	BAL	337	7TH WARD

Name	Co.	Page	Location
SPIRES, ELSY	BAL	256	20TH WAR
SPIRES, MARY J.	BAL	337	7TH WARD
SPIRES, RICHARD	PRI	092	MARLBROU
SPITINGTON, SAMUEL	QUE	166	2ND E DI
SPITLER, GEORGE	ALL	210	CUMBERLA
SPITZNAGGLE, GEORGE	WAS	287	1ST DIST
SPLUM, NORA	BAL	213	11TH WAR
SPOAR, HENRY	WAS	126	HAGERSTO
SPOCK, JOANNA	CAR	329	MANCHEST
SPOHN, JOHN H.	ANN	507	HOWARD D
SPOKER, ELIZABETH	FRE	314	MIDDLETO
SPOLANDER, C.R.	BAL	206	11TH WAR
SPOLT, JOHN	BAL	223	19TH WAR
SPONG, MATHIAS *	WAS	045	2ND SUBD
SPONSOLER, JOHN JACOB	FRE	268	NEW MARK
SPONSELER, FREDERICK	WAS	105	2ND DIST
SPONSELLER, ADAM	FRE	260	NEW MARK
SPONSELLER, ALFRED	CAR	237	UNION TO
SPONSELLER, FREDERICK	WAS	159	2ND DIST
SPONSELLER, ISAAC	FRE	190	5TH E DI
SPONSELLER, JACOB N.	WAS	102	2ND DIST
SPONSELLER, JOSEPH N.	FRE	444	8TH E DI
SPONSELLER, M.	FRE	200	5TH E DI
SPONSLER, JOHN	BAL	174	11TH WAR
SPOOF, A.	BAL	172	1ST WARD
SPOOF, A.	BAL	166	1ST WARD
SPOONER, PHILLIP	BAL	137	1ST WARD
SPOORE, JAMES	CAL	052	3RD DIST
SPORG, DAVID	WAS	044	2ND SUBD
SPORTWOOD, ESTHER	BAL	142	11TH WAR
SPOTTS, JACOB	WAS	055	2ND SUBD
SPOTTS, JACOB	WAS	054	2ND SUBD
SPOUG, MATHIAS *	WAS	045	2ND SUBD
SPOUSALLER, WILLIAM F.	FRE	258	NEW MARK
SPOUSELLER, HENRITTA	FRE	264	NEW MARK
SPOUSELLER, J. CYRUS	FRE	260	NEW MARK
SPOUSELLER, MARY C.	FRE	166	EMMITTSB
SPOUSSLER, MICHAEL	FRE	166	EMMITTSB
SPOUSWOODS, JOHN H.	BAL	458	8TH WARD
SPRAGUE, ELISKA B.	BAL	476	14TH WAR
SPRAGUE, GEORGE	BAL	332	7TH WARD
SPRAGUE, JOHN	CEC	154	PORT DEP
SPRAGUE, WILLIAM	BAL	128	1ST WARD
SPRAGUES, CHARLES	BAL	456	8TH WARD
SPRANG, ELIZABETH	BAL	056	1ST WARD
SPRANG, GEORGE	BAL	056	1ST WARD
SPRANG, HUGH	BAL	055	1ST WARD
SPRANG, LEWIS	BAL	056	1ST WARD
SPRANKLIN, JOHN	BAL	164	6TH WARD
SPRANKLINGS, JOHN*	BAL	415	3RD WARD
SPRATT, SAMUEL	CEC	149	PORT DEP
SPRAUGE, DANIEL	BAL	291	17TH WAR
SPRECHER, CATHARINE	WAS	023	2ND SUBD
SPRECHER, DANUEL	WAS	107	2ND DIST
SPRECHER, DAVID	WAS	023	2ND SUBD
SPRECHER, ELIE	WAS	023	2ND SUBD
SPRECHER, GEORGE	WAS	023	2ND SUBD
SPRECHER, JACOB	WAS	020	2ND SUBD
SPRECHER, PHILIP	WAS	294	1ST DIST
SPRECHT, SAMUEL	ALL	035	2ND E.D.
SPRENKLE, GEORGE	BAL	243	1ST DIST
SPRENKLE, HENRY	BAL	228	1ST DIST
SPREY, BETSY	BAL	406	14TH WAR
SPREY, C.	BAL	295	12TH WAR
SPRICKLER, MARTHA C.	WAS	126	2ND DIST
SPRIDDLE, ELIZA	BAL	073	15TH WAR
SPRIDDLE, JESSE	BAL	155	5TH WARD
SPRIDDLE, MARTIN	BAL	190	17TH WAR
SPRIDDLE, MOTROND	BAL	141	16TH WAR
SPRIDLE, THOMAS	BAL	223	17TH WAR
SPRIG, CHARLES	BAL	401	1ST DIST
SPRIGG, CATHERINE	BAL	126	18TH WAR
SPRIGG, CATHERINE-BLACK	FRE	242	NEW MARK
SPRIGG, DANIEL	BAL	280	20TH WAR
SPRIGG, ELIZA	PRI	007	BLADENSB
SPRIGG, GEORGE	BAL	094	5TH WARD
SPRIGG, HARRIET	BAL	239	12TH WAR
SPRIGG, HARRIETT	BAL	116	18TH WAR
SPRIGG, HARRY	FRE	084	FREDERIC
SPRIGG, HORACE	BAL	159	16TH WAR
SPRIGG, HORACE	ALL	256	CUMBERLA
SPRIGG, J.	ANN	282	ANNAPOLI
SPRIGG, JAMES	ALL	216	CUMBERLA
SPRIGG, JAMES	ALL	206	CUMBERLA
SPRIGG, JAMES	BAL	155	5TH WARD
SPRIGG, JOSPEH	ALL	263	CUMBERLA
SPRIGG, MARY	ALL	206	CUMBERLA
SPRIGG, MARY	BAL	289	12TH WAR
SPRIGG, MARY L.	BAL	156	5TH WARD
SPRIGG, RACHEL-MULATTO	FRE	239	NEW MARK
SPRIGG, RACHELL	BAL	216	17TH WAR
SPRIGG, SAM	PRI	082	QUEEN AN
SPRIGG, SAMUEL	ANN	506	HOWARD D
SPRIGG, THOMAS	BAL	020	18TH WAR
SPRIGG, UPTON	FRE	254	NEW MARK
SPRIGG, WILLIAM	BAL	166	1ST WARD
SPRIGG, WILLIAM	BAL	167	1ST WARD
SPRIGG, WILLIAM J.	BAL	163	1ST WARD
SPRIGG, WILLIAM G.	ALL	216	CUMBERLA
SPRIGG, WILLIAM O.	ALL	255	CUMBERLA
SPRIGG, W.J.S.	BAL	162	1ST WARD
SPRIGGS, BENJAMIN	ANN	322	2ND DIST
SPRIGGS, BETTY	CAL	061	3RD DIST
SPRIGGS, CHARLES	BAL	153	19TH WAR
SPRIGGS, DAVID	BAL	171	1ST WARD
SPRIGGS, GEORGE	ANN	400	8TH DIST
SPRIGGS, GEORGE	BAL	017	4TH WARD
SPRIGGS, GEORGINA	BAL	024	18TH WAR
SPRIGGS, GREENBERY	BAL	024	18TH WAR
SPRIGGS, HARRIETT	BAL	137	11TH WAR
SPRIGGS, HARRY	BAL	196	19TH WAR
SPRIGGS, HENRY	FRE	413	8TH E DI
SPRIGGS, HENRY	BAL	174	6TH WARD
SPRIGGS, JAMES	ANN	356	3RD DIST
SPRIGGS, JAMES	BAL	312	12TH WAR
SPRIGGS, JAMES W.	BAL	130	18TH WAR
SPRIGGS, JANE	BAL	196	11TH WAR
SPRIGGS, M.	BAL	144	11TH WAR
SPRIGGS, MARY	BAL	049	9TH WARD
SPRIGGS, OLIVIA	BAL	194	17TH WAR
SPRIGGS, OLIVIA	BAL	191	11TH WAR
SPRIGGS, SALLEY	BAL	108	18TH WAR
SPRIGGS, THOMAS	FRE	254	NEW MARK
SPRIGGS, WILLIAM	BAL	110	18TH WAR
SPRIGGS, WILLIAM	BAL	136	18TH WAR
SPRIGGS, WILLIAM	BAL	021	18TH WAR
SPRIGGS, PHILIP-MULATTO	FRE	453	8TH E DI
SPRIGHT, JOHN	BAL	164	1ST WARD
SPRIGS, DAVID	WAS	108	2ND DIST
SPRIGS, EPHRAIM	CAR	215	5TH DIST
SPRIGS, JESSE	CAL	005	1ST DIST
SPRIGS, KITTY	BAL	380	1ST DIST
SPRIGS, SUSAN	ST	286	2ND E DI
SPRIGS, VIRGINIA E.-MULAT	FRE	399	JEFFERSO
SPRIKER, CHARITY	ALL	003	3RD E.D.
SPRIKER, MICHAEL	ALL	003	3RD E.D.
SPRINER, CARL	BAL	261	1ST DIST
SPRING, JOHN	BAL	166	2ND DIST
SPRING, JOHN	BAL	058	18TH WAR
SPRING, PETER M.	WAS	127	HAGERSTO
SPRINGEL, OTTO	BAL	102	15TH WAR
SPRINGER, ANN	BAL	468	14TH WAR
SPRINGER, BENJAMIN	CEC	210	7TH E DI
SPRINGER, D.C.	HAR	184	3RD DIST
SPRINGER, DANIEL	FRE	011	FREDERIC
SPRINGER, DAVID	BAL	068	4TH WARD
SPRINGER, DAVID	WAS	166	1ST DIST
SPRINGER, EDWARD	FRE	190	5TH E DI
SPRINGER, EMANUEL	WAS	247	SMITHSBU
SPRINGER, GEORGE	BAL	269	1ST DIST
SPRINGER, JAMES	BAL	112	5TH WARD
SPRINGER, JOHN	BAL	253	1ST DIST
SPRINGER, JOHN	WAS	058	2ND SUBD
SPRINGER, JOHN	BAL	230	17TH WAR
SPRINGER, MARTHA	CEC	146	PORT DEP
SPRINGER, MARTHA J.	WAS	125	HAGERSTO
SPRINGER, MARY D.	CEC	016	ELKTON 3
SPRINGER, SAMUEL	WAS	109	2ND DIST
SPRINGER, SAMUEL E.	WAS	295	1ST DIST
SPRINGER, SOPHIA	BAL	068	4TH WARD
SPRINGER, THOMAS	FRE	008	FREDERIC
SPRINGER, THOMAS	FRE	311	MIDDLETO
SPRINGLER, JONAS	CAR	304	1ST DIST
SPRINGSTEAD, JOHN	ALL	189	9TH E.D.
SPRINGSTEEL, BENJAMIN	BAL	110	1ST WARD
SPRINKLE, CHARLES	BAL	311	3RD WARD
SPRINKLE, EDWARD	BAL	228	1ST DIST
SPRINKLE, ISAAC	WAS	223	1ST DIST
SPRINKLEY, WILL-BLACK	QUE	168	2ND E DI
SPRNKLE, JANAN	CAR	283	7TH DIST
SPROGLE, DANIEL	ANN	285	ANNAPOLI
SPROGLER, SUSAN	ANN	320	2ND DIST
SPROLE, ANN	BAL	098	2ND DIST
SPROLE, CATHARINE	ANN	285	ANNAPOLI
SPROLE, ELLEN	BAL	407	14TH WAR
SPROLE, JAMES	BAL	098	2ND DIST
SPROLE, JOHN	BAL	315	7TH WARD
SPROLE, THOMAS	BAL	407	14TH WAR
SPROLE, WILLIAM	BAL	287	7TH WARD
SPRONTON, JOHN T.	CEC	140	5TH E DI
SPROTSON, JANE	BAL	447	14TH WAR
SPROUS, ANTHONY	BAL	152	5TH WARD
SPROUSE, ANTHONEY	TAL	073	EASTON T
SPROUSE, JANE	TAL	077	EASTON T
SPROUSE, PERRY	TAL	075	EASTON T
SPROUSE, PHILL	TAL	077	EASTON T
SPROUSE, THOMAS	TAL	077	EASTON T
SPROUTS, R.-BLACK	BAL	184	2ND WARD
SPRUILL, MARY F.	ANN	521	HOWARD D
SPRY, ADALINE	DOR	466	1ST DIST
SPRY, ADELINE	QUE	161	2ND E DI
SPRY, CALESS W.	KEN	299	3RD DIST
SPRY, DAVID	QUE	153	1ST E DI
SPRY, DAVID	QUE	154	1ST E DI
SPRY, ELIZABETH	QUE	136	1ST E DI
SPRY, GEORGE	QUE	177	2ND E DI
SPRY, GEORGE T.	KEN	251	2ND DIST
SPRY, HENRY	QUE	168	2ND E DI
SPRY, JAMES	TAL	097	ST MICHA
SPRY, JANE	QUE	165	2ND E DI
SPRY, JOSEPH	CAR	223	5TH DIST
SPRY, PRISCILLA	QUE	180	2ND E DI
SPRY, WILLIAM T.	KEN	296	3RD DIST
SPUCHER, CHRISTIAN	WAS	108	2ND DIST
SPUCK, ALBERT	BAL	113	1ST WARD
SPUNIER, MADORA	BAL	374	13TH WAR
SPUR, B. R.	BAL	287	1ST DIST
SPUR, JOHN	BAL	300	1ST DIST
SPURECELL, HENRY *	FRE	260	NEW MARK
SPURINER, HARRIET	FRE	253	NEW MARK
SPURNEY, AMANDA	CEC	182	7TH E DI
SPURRIER, BEAL	FRE	443	8TH E DI
SPURRIER, BENNET	CAR	362	9TH DIST
SPURRIER, CHARLOTTE	ANN	485	HOWARD D
SPURRIER, ELIJAH	BAL	338	1ST DIST
SPURRIER, ELIZABETH	FRE	444	8TH E DI
SPURRIER, GREENBERY	BAL	040	18TH WAR
SPURRIER, JOSEPH	CAR	367	9TH DIST
SPURRIER, NESON	BAL	012	18TH WAR
SPURRIER, PHILLIP	ANN	428	HOWARD D
SPURRIER, POLLY	ANN	428	HOWARD D
SPURRIN, JANE *	BAL	269	2ND WARD
SPURRIOR, JOHN	CAR	216	5TH DIST
SPURRY, GEORGE M.	CAR	065	NO TWP L
SPURRY, MATILDA	CAR	148	NO TWP L
SPURUE, THOMAS *	FRE	247	NEW MARK
SQUASH, MARY	BAL	258	1ST DIST
SQUBB, SAMUEL	CEC	103	4TH E DI
SQUIAL, SIDNEY	CAR	351	6TH DIST
SQUIRE, BENJAMIN	CAR	280	7TH DIST
SQUIRE, ISAAC	BAL	371	1ST DIST
SQUIRE, SINGLETON	CAR	281	7TH DIST
SQUIRE, WILLIAM	ANN	330	2ND DIST
SQUIRES, CHARLOTTE	ANN	422	HOWARD D
SQUIRES, GEORGE W.	BAL	110	18TH WAR
SQUIRES, JOHN	BAL	279	2ND WARD
SQUIRES, PHILAMINA	BAL	297	1ST DIST
SQUIRES, REBECCA	BAL	169	6TH WARD
SQUIRL, GEORGE	BAL	446	14TH WAR
SQUIRL, ISAAC	BAL	297	1ST DIST
SQUIRNELL, ROBERT	BAL	311	12TH WAR
SQUIRREL, NELSON	MGM	369	BERRYS D
SQUIRREL, POLLY	MGM	371	BERRYS D
SQUREL, JANE	CAR	204	4TH DIST
SQURIL, NOAH	CAR	208	5TH DIST
SRETT, BENJAMN	BAL	072	1ST WARD
SRIM, GEORG	BAL	040	2ND DIST
SROCENEY, JOHN *	BAL	302	20TH WAR
SROY, WILLIAM *	BAL	267	1ST DIST
SRULMAN, HENRY M. *	FRE	141	CREAGERS
ST BAINER, JOHN	BAL	103	1ST WARD
ST BAKER, WILLIAM	BAL	014	1ST WARD
ST BOOKS, B.	BAL	116	1ST WARD
ST CALAGHAN, W.	BAL	162	1ST WARD
ST CLAIR, BENJAMIN	HAR	058	1ST DIST
ST CLAIR, ELEN B.	CHA	272	ALLENS F
ST CLAIR, IONETTE	ALL	239	CUMBERLA
ST CLAIR, JOHN	CHA	232	HILLTOP
ST CLAIR, JOHN	CEC	134	6TH E DI
ST CLAIR, MARIA	WAS	178	BOONSBOR
ST CLAIR, REBECCA	BAL	398	1ST DIST
ST CLAIR, ROBERT	CHA	271	ALLENS F
ST CLAIR, SILVA	WAS	056	2ND SUBD
ST CLAIR, THOMAS	HAR	057	1ST DIST
ST CLAIR, WILLIAM	HAR	056	1ST DIST
ST CLARE, GEORGE T.	CHA	270	ALLENS F
ST DAWSON, WILLIAM	BAL	014	1ST WARD
ST FRY, JOHN	BAL	010	1ST WARD
ST GEARD, WILLIAM	BAL	016	1ST WARD
ST GROSS, G.	BAL	115	1ST WARD
ST JOHN, CHRISTOPHER	BAL	159	11TH WAR
ST JOHN, MARGARET	BAL	142	11TH WAR
ST JOHNS, GEORGE	BAL	377	8TH WARD
ST JOHNS, REBECCA	BAL	094	10TH WAR
ST JOHNSON, JOHN	BAL	030	1ST WARD
ST JONES, JAMES	BAL	010	1ST WARD
ST JONES, JAMES	BAL	010	1ST WARD
ST JONES, WILLIAM	BAL	037	1ST WARD
ST KINSON, WILLIAM H.	BAL	127	1ST WARD
ST MANKIN, J.	BAL	115	1ST WARD
ST MYER, JAMES M.	BAL	225	12TH WAR
ST PRICHARD, WILLIAM	BAL	037	1ST WARD
ST RARICK, JOHN	BAL	007	1ST WARD
ST TUCKER, JOHN	BAL	103	1ST WARD
ST WATSON, REBECCA	BAL	011	1ST WARD
ST WILLIAMS, J.	BAL	115	1ST WARD
ST WISE, ROBERT	BAL	062	1ST WARD
ST. CLAIR, ANN	HAR	065	1ST DIST
ST. CLAIR, CRISTIANA	BAL	215	11TH WAR
ST. CLAIR, ELIZABETH	HAR	066	1ST DIST
ST. CLAIR, ELIZABETH	HAR	063	1ST DIST
ST. CLAIR, HENRY	BAL	440	14TH WAR
ST. CLAIR, JAMES	HAR	056	1ST DIST
ST. CLAIR, VARNEY	HAR	064	1ST DIST
ST. CLARI, JAMES	CAL	004	1ST DIST
ST. CLURE, JOHN	ALL	094	5TH E.D.
ST. COLE, GEORGE	BAL	002	1ST WARD
ST. JOHN, EVE	WAS	003	WILLIAMS
ST. JOHN, ISAAC	ALL	127	4TH E.D.
ST. MYER, GEORGE W.	BAL	442	1ST DIST
ST. THOMPSON, CHARLES	BAL	143	1ST WARD
STAARA, JERAMIAH	CAR	250	3RD DIST
STABERTS, WILLIAM	ANN	425	HOWARD D
STABLER, ADAM	BAL	035	2ND DIST
STABLER, ANNA	MGM	347	BERRYS D
STABLER, CALEB	MGM	349	BERRYS D
STABLER, CATHERINE	MGM	348	BERRYS D
STABLER, CHRISTIAN	BAL	016	2ND DIST
STABLER, DANIEL	BAL	033	2ND DIST
STABLER, EDWARD	MGM	347	BERRYS D
STABLER, EDWARD H.	BAL	110	15TH WAR
STABLER, FRANCES D.	MGM	347	BERRYS D
STABLER, FRANCIS	BAL	423	14TH WAR
STABLER, GEORGE	MGM	316	CRACKLIN
STABLER, GEORGE	BAL	033	2ND DIST
STABLER, HENRY	BAL	035	2ND DIST
STABLER, HERNY	MGM	331	CRACKLIN
STABLER, JOHN	BAL	139	2ND DIST
STABLER, JOSEPH	MGM	316	CRACKLIN
STABLER, SARAH B.	BAL	319	20TH WAR
STABLER, SUSAN	MGM	347	BERRYS D
STABLER, THOMAS L.	BAL	255	17TH WAR
STABLER, THOMAS P.	MGM	347	BERRYS D
STABLER, WILLIAM D.	MGM	321	CRACKLIN
STABLER, WILLIAM HENRY	MGM	347	BERRYS D
STABLES, EDMUND	MGM	349	BERRYS D
STABLICK, HARMIN	BAL	055	2ND DIST
STABLINGS, PETER	CEC	034	CHESAPEA
STABLINGS, SAMUEL	BAL	120	18TH WAR
STACK, CATHARINE	BAL	120	18TH WAR
STACK, CATHARINE	BAL	149	5TH WARD
STACK, CHARLES	BAL	147	5TH WARD
STACK, ELIZA	DOR	453	1ST DIST
STACK, JACOB	CAR	143	NO TWP L
STACK, JAMES	BAL	120	18TH WAR
STACK, JAMES	DOR	321	1ST DIST
STACK, JOHN R.	BAL	232	6TH WARD
STACK, LEVIN	CAR	085	NO TWP L
STACK, LEVIN	DOR	317	1ST DIST
STACK, MARTHA	CAR	167	NO TWP L
STACK, MARY E.	CAR	093	NO TWP L
STACK, PATRICK	CAR	168	NO TWP L
STACK, PETER C.	DOR	297	1ST DIST
STACK, SELEY	DOR	297	1ST DIST
STACK, SHARTOLL	CAR	137	NO TWP L
STACK, THOMAS	CAR	125	NO TWP L
STACK, WILLIAM	CAR	124	NO TWP L
STACK, WILLIAM	CAR	125	NO TWP L
STACKHOUSE, CATHARINE	QUE	247	5TH E DI
STACKHOUSE, GEORGE	ANN	509	HOWARD D
STACKS, JOSEPH	CEC	205	7TH E DI
STACKS, WILLIAM	MGM	315	CRACKLIN
STACUM, MARY	HAR	015	1ST DIST
STACY, ANNA	BAL	349	13TH WAR
STACY, THOMAS	CAR	282	7TH DIST
STADFFORD, JOSEPH	CAR	290	7TH DIST
STADT, ELIZABETH	DOR	387	1ST DIST
STADT, JACOB	WAS	285	1ST DIST
STAEFER, MARY	BAL	206	2ND WARD
STAEFFER, DANIEL	FRE	029	FREDERIC
STAFFEY, WILLIAM	FRE	099	FREDERIC
STAFFORD, ALEXANDER	WAS	002	WILLIAMS
STAFFORD, ANN E.	BAL	301	17TH WAR
STAFFORD, BEN*	BAL	007	1ST WARD
STAFFORD, CATHARINE	DOR	384	1ST DIST
STAFFORD, CHARLES	BAL	107	1ST WARD
STAFFORD, ELENORA	BAL	218	6TH WARD
STAFFORD, EMILY	BAL	264	2ND WARD
STAFFORD, HARISON	BAL	065	10TH WAR
STAFFORD, HARREIT	DOR	384	1ST DIST
STAFFORD, JAMES	BAL	424	8TH WARD
STAFFORD, JAMES	BAL	457	8TH WARD
STAFFORD, JAMES	BAL	302	17TH WAR
STAFFORD, JOHN	CAR	108	NO TWP L
STAFFORD, JOHN	CAR	119	NO TWP L
STAFFORD, JOHN	CAR	105	NO TWP L
STAFFORD, JOSEPH	QUE	137	1ST E DI
STAFFORD, JOSEPH	ALL	023	2ND E.D.
STAFFORD, LUTHER	TAL	030	EASTON D
STAFFORD, MAHALA	TAL	026	EASTON D
STAFFORD, MARY E.	DOR	389	1ST DIST
STAFFORD, MARY J.	BAL	392	14TH WAR
STAFFORD, MOSES	BAL	392	14TH WAR
STAFFORD, NICHOLAS	BAL	421	8TH WARD
STAFFORD, NICHOLAS	BAL	418	8TH WARD
STAFFORD, RICHARD	BAL	169	2ND DIST
STAFFORD, SARAH	BAL	291	3RD WARD
STAFFORD, THEADON	CAR	115	NO TWP L
STAFFORD, W.H.	CAR	167	NO TWP L
	BAL	158	1ST WARD

Name	County	Page	District
STAFFORD, W.J.	BAL	167	1ST WARD
STAFFORD, WILLIAM	SOM	541	TYASKIN
STAFFORD, WILLIAM	TAL	103	ST MICHA
STAFFORD, WILLIAM W.	BAL	004	1ST WARD
STAFFORT, F.	BAL	449	8TH WARD
STAFNORD, JOHN	CAR	151	NO TWP L
STAGEMAN, CHRISTOPHER	CEC	101	4TH E DI
STAGEMAN, MICHAEL	CEC	101	4TH E DI
STAGEN, JOHN	BAL	180	2ND WARD
STAGER, ISAAC	BAL	383	3RD WARD
STAGGERS, JOHN	BAL	052	18TH WAR
STAGGERS, JOSEPH	BAL	021	18TH WAR
STAGMIRE, BETSY	BAL	013	2ND DIST
STAHL, ALEXANDER	BAL	266	20TH WAR
STAHL, CHARLES G.	BAL	344	7TH WARD
STAHL, ELIZABETH	BAL	441	8TH WARD
STAHL, JACOB	BAL	270	7TH WARD
STAHL, JACOB	BAL	127	16TH WAR
STAHL, JACOB JR.	BAL	294	7TH WARD
STAHL, JOHN	BAL	464	14TH WAR
STAHL, JOHN	WAS	034	2ND SUBD
STAHL, JOSEPH	BAL	203	19TH WAR
STAHL, MARGARET C.	BAL	217	19TH WAR
STAHL, MARY	WAS	024	2ND SUBD
STAHL, SUSAN	BAL	165	6TH WARD
STAHLEY, ALFRED	FRE	145	10TH E D
STAIN, WILLIAM S.	BAL	280	2ND WARD
STAINER, WILLIAM H.	CAR	390	2ND DIST
STAINKICE, HENRY	ST	299	2ND E DI
STAINS, CALEB	BAL	454	1ST DIST
STAINS, ELLEN	BAL	003	1ST WARD
STAINS, MARY	BAL	387	8TH WARD
STAIR, GEORGE	BAL	432	8TH WARD
STAIR, GEORGE	WAS	116	2ND DIST
STAIR, JAMES	BAL	119	2ND DIST
STAIR, JOHN	CAR	312	1ST DIST
STAIRY, EMAUNUE *	CAR	319	1ST DIST
STAITMAN, ABDIAL *	FRE	054	FREDERIC
STAKE, A.K.	WAS	002	WILLIAMS
STAKE, CATHARINE	WAS	008	WILLIAMS
STAKE, E.M.	WAS	012	WILLIAMS
STAKE, ELIS OF A.	WAS	013	WILLIAMS
STAKE, JOHN	WAS	001	WILLIAMS
STAKE, JOHN M.	WAS	013	WILLIAMS
STAKE, ROMAN	BAL	275	17TH WAR
STAKE, WILLIAM	WAS	003	WILLIAMS
STAKER, GEORGE	BAL	255	17TH WAR
STAKLE, ADAM	BAL	364	13TH WAR
STAKLE, STALLMAN	KEN	210	2ND DIST
STAKLE, STEPHEN	KEN	269	1ST DIST
STALCUP, REBECCA	CEC	114	3RD E DI
STALCUP, WILLIAM H.	CEC	151	PORT DUP
STALDS, GEORGE	BAL	007	EASTERN
STALE, HINER	BAL	003	EASTERN
STALER, FRANCES	BAL	302	12TH WAR
STALER, JOHN	BAL	110	18TH WAR
STALEY, ABRAHAM	FRE	073	FREDERIC
STALEY, ABRAHAM	WAS	137	2ND DIST
STALEY, ABRAHAM T.	FRE	088	FREDERIC
STALEY, ALFRED	FRE	139	CREAGERS
STALEY, ANDREW	WAS	289	1ST DIST
STALEY, ANN S.	FRE	382	PETERSVI
STALEY, CATHARINE	FRE	396	PETERSVI
STALEY, CHARLES	BAL	351	13TH WAR
STALEY, CORNELIUS	FRE	083	FREDERIC
STALEY, DANIEL	HAR	063	1ST DIST
STALEY, DANIEL	WAS	300	1ST DIST
STALEY, DAVID	FRE	080	FREDERIC
STALEY, ELIZABETH	FRE	084	FREDERIC
STALEY, ELLEN	FRE	287	WOODSBOR
STALEY, EZRA	FRE	103	FREDERIC
STALEY, FLEET	FRE	322	MIDDLETO
STALEY, FREDERICK	FRE	087	FREDERIC
STALEY, GEORGE	FRE	090	FREDERIC
STALEY, GEORGE	FRE	081	FREDERIC
STALEY, HAMNER	FRE	293	WOODSBOR
STALEY, HENRY	FRE	084	FREDERIC
STALEY, JACOB	BAL	212	6TH DIST
STALEY, JACOB H.	FRE	090	FREDERIC
STALEY, JOHN	FRE	083	FREDERIC
STALEY, JOHN	FRE	083	FREDERIC
STALEY, JOHN A.	FRE	083	FREDERIC
STALEY, JOHN A.	FRE	082	FREDERIC
STALEY, JONATHAN	FRE	215	BUCKEYST
STALEY, JOSEPH E.	FRE	085	FREDERIC
STALEY, JOSHUA	FRE	084	FREDERIC
STALEY, JOSHUA	FRE	083	FREDERIC
STALEY, LEWIS	FRE	382	PETERSVI
STALEY, LUCRITIA	FRE	090	FREDERIC
STALEY, MAHLON T.	FRE	096	FREDERIC
STALEY, MARY V.	WAS	293	1ST DIST
STALEY, NICHOLAS	FRE	085	FREDERIC
STALEY, PETER	FRE	088	FREDERIC
STALEY, SOLOMON	FRE	293	WOODSBOR
STALEY, SUSAN	WAS	253	1ST DIST
STALEY, TOBIAS	FRE	083	FREDERIC
STALEY, WARFIELD	WAS	162	HAGERSTO
STALEY, WILLIAM	WAS	127	2ND DIST
STALEY, WILLIAM	FRE	089	FREDERIC
STALEY, WILLIAM	BAL	213	6TH DIST
STALFORD, GEORGE	BAL	369	13TH WAR
STALFORT, FREDERICK	BAL	423	14TH WAR
STALINGS, WESLEY	BAL	111	18TH WAR
STALL, BENEDICT	BAL	299	7TH WARD
STALL, DANIEL	BAL	100	18TH WAR
STALL, EMMA	BAL	100	5TH WARD
STALL, GEORGE	BAL	093	18TH WAR
STALL, HENRY G.	BAL	050	9TH WARD
STALL, JACOB	BAL	056	18TH WAR
STALL, JACOB	HAR	055	1ST DIST
STALL, JOHN	BAL	165	16TH WAR
STALL, JOSEPH	HAR	055	1ST DIST
STALL, MARY	BAL	310	3RD WARD
STALL, MARY	WAS	261	1ST DIST
STALL, MARY JANE	BAL	204	17TH WAR
STALL, SARAH J.	BAL	192	17TH WAR
STALL, WALTER	BAL	094	18TH WAR
STALL, WILLIAM	FRE	185	5TH E DI
STALL, WILLIAM	ANN	348	3RD DIST
STALLER, CRISTOPHER	BAL	230	17TH WAR
STALLER, JOHN	CAR	288	7TH DIST
STALLER, JOHN	FRE	347	MIDDLETO
STALLINGS, ABRAHAM	MGM	423	MEDLEY 3
STALLINGS, AGUELLA J.	BAL	373	8TH WARD
STALLINGS, CAROLANUS	CAL	044	3RD DIST
STALLINGS, CAROLINE	CAL	061	3RD DIST
STALLINGS, CHARLES	ALL	174	7TH E.D.
STALLINGS, CORNELIA	BAL	325	3RD WARD
STALLINGS, DELILAH R.	FRE	273	NEW MARK
STALLINGS, EDWARD	CAL	047	3RD DIST
STALLINGS, EDWARD	ANN	306	1ST DIST
STALLINGS, ELIJAH	CAL	043	3RD DIST
STALLINGS, ELIZA	CAL	009	1ST DIST
STALLINGS, ELIZABETH	FRE	055	FREDERIC
STALLINGS, EZEKIEL	ALL	178	7TH E.D.
STALLINGS, HENRY	ANN	276	ANNAPOLI
STALLINGS, JAMES	ANN	405	8TH DIST
STALLINGS, JAMES	ANN	357	3RD DIST
STALLINGS, JAMES	BAL	203	11TH WAR
STALLINGS, JEMIMA	BAL	128	18TH WAR
STALLINGS, JOHN	ANN	359	3RD DIST
STALLINGS, JOHN	ANN	408	8TH DIST
STALLINGS, JOHN	ALL	174	7TH E.D.
STALLINGS, JOHN	ALL	171	7TH E.D.
STALLINGS, JOSEPH	CAL	027	2ND DIST
STALLINGS, JOSPEH	BAL	161	6TH WARD
STALLINGS, KITTY	ANN	359	3RD DIST
STALLINGS, LEWIS	BAL	127	18TH WAR
STALLINGS, LLOYD	ALL	171	7TH E.D.
STALLINGS, MARY	BAL	031	9TH WARD
STALLINGS, MARY	CAL	059	3RD DIST
STALLINGS, NELSON	ANN	308	1ST DIST
STALLINGS, PERRY	CAL	020	2ND DIST
STALLINGS, PRISCILLA	CAL	024	2ND DIST
STALLINGS, REBECCA	CAL	060	3RD DIST
STALLINGS, RICHARD	FRE	272	NEW MARK
STALLINGS, RICHARD	MGM	412	MEDLEY 3
STALLINGS, SAMUEL	BAL	377	8TH WARD
STALLINGS, SARAH	ALL	185	9TH E.D.
STALLINGS, SOPHIA	ANN	300	1ST DIST
STALLINGS, VIRGINIA	ANN	299	1ST DIST
STAULINGS, WILLIAM	CAL	012	1ST DIST
STALLINGS, WILLIAM C.	BAL	214	6TH WARD
STALLINGS, WILLIAM M.	CAL	048	3RD DIST
STALLINGS, WILSON	ANN	409	8TH DIST
STALLINGS,WILLIAM	CAL	055	3RD DIST
STALOR, JOHN J.	BAL	373	8TH WARD
STALS, JOHN D.	ALL	059	10TH E.D
STALY, STEPHEN	WAS	278	LEITERSB
STAM, JOHN L.	KEN	211	2ND DIST
STAMBAUGH, ANN E.	FRE	419	8TH E DI
STAMBAUGH, JAMES	CAR	411	2ND DIST
STAMBAUGH, MARY	FRE	179	5TH E DI
STAMER, HENRY	CEC	170	6TH E DI
STAMER, JACOB	CAR	347	6TH DIST
STAMERY, HENRY G.	BAL	263	2ND WARD
STAMMAR, JOHN B.	BAL	445	14TH WAR
STAMMEN, MARIA L.	BAL	210	6TH WARD
STAMMERS, EMILY	BAL	058	10TH WAR
STAMMOS, SHEPARD	BAL	150	2ND DIST
STAMN, SAMUEL	HAR	078	2ND DIST
STAMP, ANN	BAL	356	13TH WAR
STAMP, GEORGE	PRI	049	AQUASCO
STAMP, JOHN	PRI	058	NOTTINGH
STAMP, JOHN	PRI	090	MARLBROU
STAMP, JOHN T.	PRI	065	NOTTINGH
STAMP, JULIA	PRI	090	MARLBROU
STAMP, STEPHEN	CAL	051	3RD DIST
STAMP, THOMAS	BAL	135	18TH WAR
STAMPS, WILIAM	BAL	416	8TH WARD
STAMTON, THOMAS	BAL	286	2ND WARD
STANAMAN, BENARD	BAL	068	1ST WARD
STANARD, JOHN	BAL	393	8TH WARD
STANBER, CHARELS	BAL	276	2ND WARD
STANBERGER, DAVID D.	BAL	269	20TH WAR
STANBROUGH, JOSHUA	BAL	041	9TH WARD
STANBURY, JAMES B.	BAL	262	2ND WARD
STANBURY, LOUISA	BAL	395	14TH WAR
STANBURY, MARY	BAL	064	4TH WARD
STANBURY, MOSES	BAL	434	14TH WAR
STANBURY, RICHARD	BAL	306	3RD WARD
STANBURY, SMITH	BAL	101	10TH WAR
STANBY, GREENBERRY	DOR	315	1ST DIST
STANDBACK, MARGARET	WAS	046	2ND SUBD
STANDEFORD, JAMES	BAL	438	1ST DIST
STANDEFORD, JOSHUA	BAL	437	1ST DIST
STANDEFCRD, WILLAIM	BAL	438	1ST DIST
STANDFORD, CORDELIA	BAL	416	8TH WARD
STANDFORD, GEORGEAN	BAL	380	1ST DIST
STANDFORD, ISAAC	HAR	201	3RD DIST
STANDFORD, MARY	BAL	389	8TH WARD
STANDFORD, MARY E.	BAL	351	7TH WARD
STANDFORD, PHILIPP	BAL	069	18TH WAR
STANDFORD, SARAH	BAL	238	12TH WAR
STANDFORD, THOMAS	BAL	351	7TH WARD
STANDIFON, CLEMENT	BAL	034	2ND DIST
STANDIFORD, BENJAMIN	BAL	031	2ND DIST
STANDIFORD, BENJIMON	HAR	201	3RD DIST
STANDIFORD, CHALRSE	BAL	129	2ND DIST
STANDIFORD, CLAUDIUS	HAR	069	1ST DIST
STANDIFORD, CORDELIA	BAL	197	6TH WARD
STANDIFORD, DELILAH	BAL	042	2ND DIST
STANDIFCRD, JACOB	BAL	208	6TH WARD
STANDIFORD, JAMES	BAL	031	2ND DIST
STANDIFORD, JAMES	BAL	139	16TH WAR
STANDIFORD, LLOYD	HAR	108	2ND DIST
STANDIFORD, WILLIAM	HAR	061	1ST DIST
STANDIFORD,DELIA	BAL	047	2ND DIST
STANDISH, JOHN	ALL	106	5TH E.D.
STANDISH, WILLIAM	CEC	087	4TH E DI
STANDLY, JOHN	CEC	049	1ST E DI
STANDS, LUCY	BAL	128	16TH WAR
STANDSBURY, EDWARD	BAL	131	2ND DIST
STANDSBURY, ELIJAH	ANN	268	ANNAPOLI
STANDSBURY, JCHN	ANN	292	ANNAPOLI
STANDSBURY, MARIA	ANN	290	ANNAPOLI
STANDT, LAFFER	BAL	065	1ST WARD
STANDURY, THOMAS	BAL	066	2ND DIST
STANER, CHARLES	BAL	050	1ST WARD
STANER, IMMOGENE	BAL	164	16TH WAR
STANFER, CAHRLES	BAL	404	14TH WAR
STANFIELD, JOHN M.	TAL	093	ST MICHA
STANFIELD, WILLIAM	BAL	113	15TH WAR
STANFIFCRD, MARGARET	BAL	060	10TH WAR
STANFOED, JAMES	WOR	309	2ND E DI
STANFORD, ADAM	SOM	513	BARREN C
STANFORD, CATHARINE	BAL	147	5TH WARD
STANFORD, CONSTANT D.	SOM	471	TRAPPE D
STANFORD, DARKY	SOM	469	TRAPPE D
STANFORD, E.	PRI	121	PISCATAW
STANFORD, EDWARD-MULATTO	CAR	135	NO TWP L
STANFORD, ELI-BLACK	CAR	135	NO TWP L
STANFORD, ELIZA-BLACK	CAR	137	NO TWP L
STANFORD, HANDY	SOM	472	TRAPPE D
STANFORD, HARRY	SOM	480	TRAPP DI
STANFORD, HENRY	HAR	154	3RD DIST
STANFORD, HENRY-BLACK	CAR	059	NO TWP L
STANFORD, J. H. W.	SOM	496	SALISBUR
STANFORD, JAMES	WOR	194	8TH E DI
STANFORD, JAMES	TAL	033	EASTON D
STANFORD, JOHN	CAR	065	NO TWP L
STANFORD, JOHN	BAL	069	18TH WAR
STANFORD, JOHN	BAL	185	5TH DIST
STANFORD, JOHN-BLACK	CAR	136	NO TWP L
STANFORD, JOHN-BLACK	CAR	095	NO TWP L
STANFORD, LEAH	SOM	478	TRAPP DI
STANFORD, MARY E.	BAL	199	11TH WAR
STANFORD, RICHARD	ANN	337	3RD DIST
STANFORD, RICHARD	CAL	007	1ST DIST
STANFORD, STEPHEN-BLACK	CAR	133	NO TWP L
STANFORD, WILLIAM	WOR	309	2ND E DI
STANFORTH, JOHN	CAL	020	2ND DIST
STANFORTH, LEVIN	CAL	039	2ND DIST
STANG, JOHN	MGM	417	MEDLEY 3
STANGHUN, JULY	CAR	079	NO TWP L
STANGTHUN, ELIZABETH	CAR	079	NO TWP L
STANHOPE, LEWIS	WAS	018	2ND SUBD
STANILS, WILLIAM	ALL	021	2ND E.D.
STANKEY, ROBERT	BAL	192	2ND WARD
STANLEY, ABRAHAM	KEN	281	3RD DIST
STANLEY, ANN	BAL	241	6TH WARD
STANLEY, CHARLES	BAL	028	15TH WAR
STANLEY, CHARLES	KEN	211	2ND DIST
STANLEY, CHRISTINE	BAL	236	12TH WAR
STANLEY, DANIEL	BAL	097	15TH WAR
STANLEY, ELIZABETH	BAL	457	1ST DIST
STANLEY, ELIZABETH	BAL	180	19TH WAR
STANLEY, ELIZABETH	SOM	513	BARREN C
STANLEY, HARVEY	ST	295	2ND E DI
STANLEY, HENRIETTA	QUE	125	1ST E DI
STANLEY, JAMES	KEN	280	3RD DIST
STANLEY, JAMES	BAL	128	16TH WAR
STANLEY, JAMES	BAL	299	12TH WAR
STANLEY, JOSEPH	BAL	178	6TH WARD
STANLEY, JOSEPH	BAL	180	19TH WAR
STANLEY, MARY A.	BAL	039	15TH WAR
STANLEY, MARY JANE	DOR	407	1ST DIST
STANLEY, NANCY	BAL	103	15TH WAR
STANLEY, PHINEAS	BAL	041	9TH WARD
STANLEY, PRISSY	DOR	406	1ST DIST
STANLEY, ROBERT-BLACK	FRE	215	BUCKEYST
STANLEY, SARAH	HAR	091	2ND DIST
STANLEY, SMART	BAL	273	7TH WARD
STANLEY, STEPHEN	SOM	524	BARREN C
STANLEY, SUSAN R.	BAL	061	18TH WAR
STANLEY, TEMPERANCE	BAL	326	3RD WARD
STANLEY, WILLIAM	BAL	180	19TH WAR
STANLEY, WILLIAM T.	KEN	249	2ND DIST
STANLING, PETER N.	BAL	035	9TH WARD
STANLY, ALEX	DOR	383	1ST DIST
STANLY, ALGY	DOR	464	1ST DIST
STANLY, ALICE	BAL	196	17TH WAR
STANLY, ANN M.	DOR	429	1ST DIST
STANLY, CATE	DOR	411	1ST DIST
STANLY, CHARLES	DOR	421	1ST DIST
STANLY, CHARLES	KEN	211	2ND DIST
STANLY, DAVID	DOR	428	1ST DIST
STANLY, DAVIE*	DOR	427	1ST DIST
STANLY, EBEN	DOR	436	1ST DIST
STANLY, ELBERT	DOR	435	1ST DIST
STANLY, ELIZA	DOR	422	1ST DIST
STANLY, ELIZA	DOR	421	1ST DIST
STANLY, ELIZABETH	CEC	056	1ST E DI
STANLY, ELIZABETH	DOR	299	1ST DIST
STANLY, EZEKIEL	DOR	429	1ST DIST
STANLY, GARRETSON	DOR	408	1ST DIST
STANLY, GEORGE	BAL	131	16TH WAR
STANLY, HARISON	DOR	425	1ST DIST
STANLY, HENRY	DOR	429	1ST DIST
STANLY, HENRY	SOM	508	BARREN C
STANLY, J.E.E.	BAL	199	11TH WAR
STANLY, JAME SC.V.	BAL	132	1ST WARD
STANLY, JAMES	DOR	428	1ST DIST
STANLY, JAMES	DOR	429	1ST DIST
STANLY, JAMES T.	BAL	255	17TH WAR
STANLY, JANE	DOR	413	1ST DIST
STANLY, JEFFERY	DOR	454	1ST DIST
STANLY, JESE	DOR	465	1ST DIST
STANLY, JESE	DOR	427	1ST DIST
STANLY, JESE*	DOR	424	1ST DIST
STANLY, JESSE	DOR	425	1ST DIST
STANLY, JIM*	DOR	422	1ST DIST
STANLY, JOHN	DOR	437	1ST DIST
STANLY, JOHN	DOR	408	1ST DIST
STANLY, JOSEPH	DOR	437	1ST DIST
STANLY, JOSHUA	BAL	250	17TH WAR
STANLY, JOSHUA	DOR	462	1ST DIST
STANLY, JOSIAH	DOR	409	1ST DIST
STANLY, JOSIAH	DOR	426	1ST DIST
STANLY, LEVIN	DOR	440	1ST DIST
STANLY, LOUISA	DOR	436	1ST DIST
STANLY, MAJOR	DOR	464	1ST DIST
STANLY, MARY	BAL	085	4TH WARD
STANLY, MARY	BAL	132	16TH WAR
STANLY, MOSES	DOR	431	1ST DIST
STANLY, NATHAN	DOR	425	1ST DIST
STANLY, RITEY*	DOR	405	1ST DIST
STANLY, ROBERT	DOR	440	1ST DIST
STANLY, ROBERT	DOR	437	1ST DIST
STANLY, STEPHEN	DOR	437	1ST DIST
STANLY, STEPHEN	SOM	513	BARREN C
STANLY, WILLIAM	DOR	436	1ST DIST
STANLY, WILLIAM	DOR	426	1ST DIST
STANLY, WILLIAM	DOR	305	1ST DIST
STANLY, WILLIAM	KEN	248	2ND DIST
STANLY,LEVIN-BLACK	CAR	141	NO TWP L
STANLY,SAMUEL	BAL	121	1ST WARD
STANMAN, SAMUEL	CEC	187	7TH E DI
STANNARD, ABHRIAM	BAL	078	18TH WAR
STANNARD, GEORGE P.	BAL	106	10TH WAR
STANNARD, MICHAEL	FRE	200	5TH E DI
STANNIS, SAMUEL	BAL	101	1ST WARD
STANONLEYER, WILLIAM	BAL	423	14TH WAR
STANPLIN, JOHN	BAL	245	2ND WARD
STANSBERRRY, AUGUSTUS	BAL	357	8TH WARD
STANSBERRY, ABRAM	HAR	174	3RD DIST
STANSBERRY, ABRAM	HAR	174	3RD DIST
STANSBERRY, CATHARINE	FRE	412	8TH E DI
STANSBERRY, CHRISTIANNA-M	FRE	411	8TH E DI
STANSBERRY, ELIZA A.	FRE	286	WOODSBOR
STANSBERRY, JAMES	CAR	329	MANCHEST
STANSBERRY, JOSHUA	CAR	335	6TH DIST
STANSBERRY, LUCRETIA	CAR	340	6TH DIST
STANSBERRY, PERE	QUE	237	4TH E DI
STANSBERRY, RICHARD	CAR	340	6TH DIST
STANSBERRY, SARAH-MULATTO	FRE	412	8TH E DI
STANSBERRY, WILLAIM G.	CAR	331	MANCHEST
STANSBERRY, WILLIAM L.	CAR	278	7TH DIST
STANSBERY, DANIEL R.	BAL	091	18TH WAR
STANSBERY, ELIZABETH	HAR	203	3RD DIST

Name	County	Page	District
STANSBERY, CEORGE	HAR	201	3RD DIST
STANSBERY, MARY A.	HAR	202	3RD DIST
STANSBERY, SARAH	BAL	302	20TH WAR
STANSBURG, MARY J.	BAL	208	2ND WARD
STANSBURRY, JACOB	BAL	172	16TH WAR
STANSBURRY, NOAH	CAR	262	3RD DIST
STANSBURRY, RICHARD	BAL	185	5TH DIST
STANSBURRY, ROBERT	BAL	185	5TH DIST
STANSBURRY, WILLIAM	BAL	244	2ND WARD
STANSBURY, ABRAHAM	FRE	177	5TH E DI
STANSBURY, ABRAM	BAL	148	2ND DIST
STANSBURY, ALBERT	BAL	293	7TH WARD
STANSBURY, AMELIA	BAL	053	9TH WARD
STANSBURY, ANN	BAL	464	14TH WAR
STANSBURY, ANNA-BLACK	QUE	182	3RD E DI
STANSBURY, BENJAMIN	TAL	014	EASTON D
STANSBURY, BENJAMIN	BAL	236	1ST DIST
STANSBURY, CAROLINE	BAL	258	6TH WARD
STANSBURY, CASANDRA	HAR	068	1ST DIST
STANSBURY, CHALES	BAL	065	2ND DIST
STANSBURY, CHARLOTTE	BAL	208	19TH WAR
STANSBURY, CHARRITY	BAL	113	5TH WARD
STANSBURY, CORVILLE	BAL	067	2ND DIST
STANSBURY, CANIEL	BAL	229	6TH WARD
STANSBURY, CANIEL R.	ANN	420	HOWARD D
STANSBURY, CEBORAH	BAL	366	8TH WARD
STANSBURY, EDWARD	BAL	058	2ND DIST
STANSBURY, EDWARD D.	ANN	378	4TH DIST
STANSBURY, ELIJAH	BAL	175	2ND WARD
STANSBURY, ELIJAH M.	ANN	443	HOWARD D
STANSBURY, ELIZA	BAL	038	4TH WARD
STANSBURY, ELIZABETH	BAL	132	2ND DIST
STANSBURY, ELIZABETH	BAL	418	8TH WARD
STANSBURY, ELIZABETH	BAL	330	3RD WARD
STANSBURY, ELIZABETH	BAL	255	1ST DIST
STANSBURY, ELIZABETH J.	BAL	203	6TH WARD
STANSBURY, ELLEN	BAL	159	2ND DIST
STANSBURY, EMANUEL	BAL	085	10TH WAR
STANSBURY, EPHRAIM	CAR	177	8TH DIST
STANSBURY, GEORGE	BAL	303	20TH WAR
STANSBURY, CEORGE	ANN	346	3RD DIST
STANSBURY, GEORGE	ANN	337	3RD DIST
STANSBURY, GOERGE	BAL	127	16TH WAR
STANSBURY, HARRIETT	BAL	459	8TH WARD
STANSBURY, HENRIETTA	BAL	294	7TH WARD
STANSBURY, HENRY	CAR	186	8TH DIST
STANSBURY, ISAAC	CAR	201	4TH DIST
STANSBURY, ISAAC	HAR	053	1ST DIST
STANSBURY, ISAAC	BAL	231	6TH WARD
STANSBURY, ISAAC	BAL	113	5TH WARD
STANSBURY, ISAAC L.	BAL	237	1ST DIST
STANSBURY, JACOB	BAL	217	2ND WARD
STANSBURY, JAMES	BAL	189	2ND WARD
STANSBURY, JAMES	BAL	029	15TH WAR
STANSBURY, JAMES	ANN	357	3RD DIST
STANSBURY, JAMES	BAL	096	2ND DIST
STANSBURY, JESSE	BAL	431	8TH WARD
STANSBURY, JOHN	BAL	224	12TH WAR
STANSBURY, JOHN	BAL	133	2ND DIST
STANSBURY, JOHN	BAL	157	2ND DIST
STANSBURY, JOHN	CAR	235	UNION TO
STANSBURY, JOHN	CAR	356	6TH DIST
STANSBURY, JOHN E.	BAL	431	8TH WARD
STANSBURY, JOHN E.	BAL	252	2ND WARD
STANSBURY, JOHN H.	BAL	126	5TH WARD
STANSBURY, JOHN H.	PRI	014	BLADENSB
STANSBURY, JOHN H.	PRI	075	MARLBROU
STANSBURY, JOSEPH	BAL	152	2ND DIST
STANSBURY, JOSEPH	BAL	388	13TH WAR
STANSBURY, JOSPEHINE	BAL	136	11TH WAR
STANSBURY, JSOHUA	CAR	404	2ND DIST
STANSBURY, L.	PRI	118	PISCATAW
STANSBURY, LUCINDA	BAL	127	16TH WAR
STANSBURY, M.	PRI	118	PISCATAW
STANSBURY, MARGARET	QUE	231	4TH E DI
STANSBURY, MARY	BAL	364	8TH WARD
STANSBURY, MARY	HAR	054	1ST DIST
STANSBURY, MARY J.	BAL	097	5TH WARD
STANSBURY, NATHANIEL	BAL	219	6TH WARD
STANSBURY, NICHOLAS	CAR	320	1ST DIST
STANSBURY, NICKOLAS	BAL	119	5TH WARD
STANSBURY, NOAH	BAL	308	20TH WAR
STANSBURY, PHEBE	BAL	174	6TH WARD
STANSBURY, PHIPAPINE	BAL	257	1ST DIST
STANSBURY, PUSSY	BAL	278	20TH WAR
STANSBURY, REBECA	CAR	197	4TH DIST
STANSBURY, RICHARD	BAL	455	1ST DIST
STANSBURY, RICHARD	BAL	029	2ND DIST
STANSBURY, ROBERT	BAL	144	19TH WAR
STANSBURY, SAMUEL	CAR	198	4TH DIST
STANSBURY, SAMUEL	BAL	350	3RD WARD
STANSBURY, SARAH	BAL	104	10TH WAR
STANSBURY, SUSAN	BAL	192	5TH DIST
STANSBURY, SUSAN	BAL	097	5TH WARD
STANSBURY, TALITHA	BAL	157	2ND DIST
STANSBURY, THOMAS	BAL	321	7TH WARD
STANSBURY, TOBIAS	BAL	159	2ND DIST
STANSBURY, TOBIAS	HAR	066	1ST DIST
STANSBURY, WALTER J.	BAL	069	2ND DIST
STANSBURY, WALTER P.	BAL	380	13TH WAR
STANSBURY, WILLIAM	BAL	066	2ND DIST
STANSBURY, WILLIAM	BAL	384	3RD WARD
STANSBURY, WILLIAM	BAL	440	8TH WARD
STANSBURY, WILLIAM T.	BAL	354	13TH WAR
STANSBURY, WINEFRED	BAL	368	8TH WARD
STANSBURY,MICHAEL	BAL	120	1ST WARD
STANSFIELD, BENJAMINE	BAL	326	1ST DIST
STANSFIELD, GEORGE W.	BAL	327	1ST DIST
STANSFIELD, JAMES	BAL	327	1ST DIST
STANSFIELD, JOHN	BAL	327	1ST DIST
STANSFIELD, THOMAS	BAL	327	1ST DIST
STANSFORD, JAMES R.	BAL	448	8TH WARD
STANSLEY, JAMES *	BAL	155	2ND DIST
STANSLINER, RICHARD	BAL	147	2ND DIST
STANSLRUY, CANIEL	BAL	157	2ND DIST
STANSMAN, CHARLES	CAR	165	NO TWP L
STANSON, G.H.	BAL	164	1ST WARD
STANT, JOHN	QUE	128	1ST E DI
STANT, JOHN W.	QUE	165	2ND E DI
STANTLY, ALEXANDER	TAL	038	EASTON D
STANTON, ANN	TAL	047	EASTON T
STANTON, ANTONET	BAL	293	1ST DIST
STANTON, BARNEY	BAL	128	5TH WARD
STANTON, CATHERINE	CAR	120	NO TWP L
STANTON, CHARLES	BAL	311	1ST DIST
STANTON, EDWARD	ANN	473	HOWARD D
STANTON, HARRIET-MULATTO	FRE	438	8TH E DI
STANTON, HENRIETTA-MULATT	CAR	167	NO TWP L
STANTON, HENRY	BAL	325	7TH WARD
STANTON, JANE	TAL	077	EASTON T
STANTON, JOHN	PRI	106	PISCATAW
STANTON, JOHN	BAL	168	11TH WAR
STANTON, JOHN	BAL	238	2ND WARD
STANTON, JOHN	BAL	367	13TH WAR
STANTON, LYDIA	CAR	134	NO TWP L
STANTON, MARIA	FRE	262	NEW MARK
STANTON, MARY	PRI	106	PISCATAW
STANTON, PERRY	WAS	079	2ND SUBD
STANTON, REBECCA	BAL	291	1ST DIST
STANTON, ROBERT	TAL	061	EASTON D
STANTON, SALEY*	DOR	459	1ST DIST
STANTON, SOPHIA	FRE	017	FREDERIC
STANTON, THOMAS	CAR	120	NO TWP L
STANTON, THOMAS	BAL	006	15TH WAR
STANTON, THOMAS	BAL	453	1ST DIST
STANTON, WARNER	FRE	253	NEW MARK
STANTON, WILLIAM	FRE	253	NEW MARK
STANTON, WILLIAM	WAS	173	FUNKSTOW
STANZ, VALENTINE	CAR	292	7TH DIST
STAPEFORD, WINLOCK*	BAL	406	3RD WARD
STAPF, CHRISTIAN	BAL	087	10TH WAR
STAPH, ROBERT	BAL	153	1ST WARD
STAPLEFOOT, LEVINIA*	DOR	417	1ST DIST
STAPLEFORD, JAMES W.	HAR	188	3RD DIST
STAPLEFORD, JULIA A.	BAL	406	3RD WARD
STAPLEFORD, NATHANIEL	QUE	125	1ST E DI
STAPLEFORD, ROBERT	TAL	003	EASTON D
STAPLEFORD, WINLOCK*	BAL	406	3RD WARD
STAPLEFORT, WILLIAM T.	BAL	094	15TH WAR
STAPLES, HARRIET	CEC	036	CHESAPEA
STAPLES, MRS.	CEC	002	ELKTON 3
STAPLES, REBEC	BAL	302	12TH WAR
STAPLETON, ELLEN	ALL	235	CUMBERLA
STAPLETON, JOHN	BAL	272	1ST DIST
STAPLETON, JOSEPH K.	BAL	068	15TH WAR
STAPLETON, LAERTES	BAL	055	15TH WAR
STAPLETON, MARGARET	BAL	283	20TH WAR
STAPLETON, MARY W.	BAL	152	16TH WAR
STAPLETON, REGINALD E.	BAL	080	4TH WARD
STAPLFORT, TRAVERS*	DOR	359	3RD DIVI
STAPTFORT, JOHN S.	DOR	355	3RD DIVI
STAR, AGNESS	BAL	407	1ST DIST
STAR, ANNA	BAL	410	14TH WAR
STAR, EDWIN	FRE	256	NEW MARK
STAR, ELIZABETH	BAL	049	18TH WAR
STAR, GEORGE *	SOM	469	TRAPPE D
STAR, JOHN	BAL	311	1ST DIST
STAR, JOSEPH	BAL	265	1ST DIST
STAR, MENERVA	BAL	303	1ST DIST
STAR, ROBERT	BAL	430	14TH WAR
STARETT, JOHN	CEC	159	PORT DUP
STARIN, PAT.	BAL	156	2ND DIST
STARK, ADAM	ALL	038	2ND E.D.
STARK, GEORGE	ALL	038	2ND E.D.
STARK, GEORGE	ALL	081	5TH E.D.
STARK, HANNAH	BAL	419	3RD WARD
STARK, JOANNA	BAL	074	10TH WAR
STARK, JOSEPHEEN	BAL	351	1ST DIST
STARK, JOSHUA	BAL	336	1ST DIST
STARK, PHEOBE	BAL	349	1ST DIST
STARK,G EORGE	ALL	016	3RD E.D.
STARKE, SIMON	ANN	451	HOWARD D
STARKER, EDWRAD	BAL	288	1ST DIST
STARKER, JOHN	BAL	099	15TH WAR
STARKER, SARAH	BAL	119	5TH WARD
STARKER, SARAH A.*	TAL	115	ST MICHA
STARKEY, ANN	QUE	173	2ND E DI
STARKEY, ANN	QUE	216	3RD E DI
STARKEY, ELIZABETH	QUE	202	3RD E DI
STARKEY, ELIZABETH	QUE	136	1ST E DI
STARKEY, ISABEL W.	CAR	069	NO TWP L
STARKEY, JAMES F.	QUE	137	1ST E DI
STARKEY, JAMES T.	BAL	127	11TH WAR
STARKEY, JASON	TAL	120	ST MICHA
STARKEY, JOHN	BAL	127	11TH WAR
STARKEY, JOHN G.	QUE	182	3RD E DI
STARKEY, JOSEPH-BLACK	QUE	162	2ND E DI
STARKEY, JOSEPH-BLACK	QUE	154	1ST E DI
STARKEY, MAHALA-BLACK	QUE	163	2ND E DI
STARKEY, MARY H.-BLACK	QUE	142	1ST E DI
STARKEY, NATHANIEL	QUE	123	1ST E DI
STARKEY, SAMUEL	QUE	127	1ST E DI
STARKEY, SARAH A.	QUE	178	2ND E DI
STARKEY, SARAH A.	TAL	115	ST MICHA
STARKEY, SEWALL-BLACK	QUE	141	1ST E DI
STARKEY, THOMAS	QUE	140	1ST E DI
STARKEY, THOMAS	QUE	213	3RD E DI
STARKEY, WILLIAM	BAL	295	3RD WARD
STARKEY, WILLIAM L.	QUE	218	3RD E DI
STARKEY, WILLIAM M.	QUE	123	1ST E DI
STARKIN, TOM	BAL	141	5TH WARD
STARKS, ALFRED	BAL	351	1ST DIST
STARLIN, ANN	CEC	042	CHESAPEA
STARLING, CHARLOTTE	BAL	268	12TH WAR
STARLING, JAMES	KEN	293	3RD DIST
STARLING, ROBERT	KEN	218	2ND DIST
STARLING, WILLIAM	KEN	294	3RD DIST
STARLINGS, JOHN T.	ANN	403	8TH DIST
STARLMAN, JOHN	BAL	139	1ST WARD
STARLY, EZEKIEL	DOR	421	1ST DIST
STARN, JOHN L. *	KEN	211	2ND DIST
STARNBAUGH, JOHN	CAR	320	1ST DIST
STARNER, DAVID F.	CAR	293	7TH DIST
STARNER, JACOB	CAR	292	7TH DIST
STARNER, JOHN D.	CAR	251	3RD DIST
STARNER, JOHNATHAN	CAR	252	3RD DIST
STARNER, MARY J.	CAR	296	7TH DIST
STARNER, NATHAN	CAR	293	7TH DIST
STARNER, WILLIAM D.	CAR	252	3RD DIST
STARR, ANN	BAL	155	19TH WAR
STARR, AUGTS	BAL	279	2ND WARD
STARR, BENJAMIN F.	BAL	179	16TH WAR
STARR, BOSNET*	BAL	236	12TH WAR
STARR, CAROLINE	BAL	289	3RD WARD
STARR, CAROLINE	BAL	209	6TH WARD
STARR, CHARLES	HAR	137	2ND DIST
STARR, EDWARD G.	BAL	013	4TH WARD
STARR, ELIZABETH	HAR	139	2ND DIST
STARR, ELIZABETH	BAL	317	20TH WAR
STARR, GEORGE	BAL	271	17TH WAR
STARR, GEORGE W.	BAL	284	20TH WAR
STARR, HERNY	BAL	119	1ST WARD
STARR, ISAIAH	CEC	099	3RD E DI
STARR, JAMES	BAL	091	5TH WARD
STARR, JOHN	BAL	018	18TH WAR
STARR, JOHN	BAL	174	19TH WAR
STARR, JOHN E.	CAR	237	UNION TO
STARR, JOHN M.	CAR	410	2ND DIST
STARR, JOSEPH	BAL	114	5TH WARD
STARR, JOSEPH	BAL	009	15TH WAR
STARR, MARY	BAL	219	12TH WAR
STARR, MARY C.	BAL	114	5TH WARD
STARR, MAURICE F.	FRE	437	8TH E DI
STARR, MOSES	BAL	153	5TH WARD
STARR, MR. S.	BAL	197	19TH WAR
STARR, ROBERT	BAL	371	13TH WAR
STARR, SUSAN	WAS	116	2ND DIST
STARR, THOMAS	DOR	431	1ST DIST
STARR, WESLEY	BAL	473	14TH WAR
STARR, WILLIAM M.	BAL	461	14TH WAR
STARRET, ELIZABETH	BAL	427	1ST DIST
STARRETT, CELIA	BAL	175	11TH WAR
STARRETT, JAMES R.	BAL	170	11TH WAR
STARRS, PATRICK	BAL	231	6TH WARD
STARRY, CHRISTINA	CAR	271	WESTMINS
STARS, PETTER	HAR	198	3RD DIST
START, BENJAMINE	BAL	283	7TH WARD
START, EBENEZER	QUE	152	1ST E DI
START, ELIZABETH	QUE	244	5TH E DI
START, JAMES	QUE	178	2ND E DI
START, JOHN	BAL	090	1ST WARD
START, LYDIA	BAL	042	15TH WAR
START, MARCELLUS	QUE	152	1ST E DI
START, SARAH	BAL	099	5TH WARD
START, SOLOMON R.	BAL	042	15TH WAR
START, THOMAS M.	TAL	067	EASTON T
START, WELSEY	BAL	412	14TH WAR
START, WILLIAM	BAL	412	14TH WAR
START, WILLIAM	QUE	203	3RD E DI
START, WILLIAM F.	QUE	138	1ST E DI
STARTER, GEORGE	BAL	417	8TH WARD
STARTER, JOHN	BAL	270	12TH WAR
STARTIAN, DICK-BLACK	QUE	125	1ST E DI
STARTT, BENJAMIN H.	KEN	260	1ST DIST
STARTT, JOHN	KEN	256	1ST DIST
STARTT, MARTHA	KEN	273	1ST DIST
STARTT, RICHARD	KEN	254	1ST DIST
STARTZMAN, ABRAHAM	BAL	292	3RD WARD
STARTZMAN, DANIEL	WAS	204	1ST DIST
STARTZMAN, DAVID	WAS	205	1ST DIST
STARTZMAN, ELIAS	WAS	103	2ND DIST
STARTZMAN, ISAAC	BAL	051	9TH WARD
STARTZMAN, MARTIN	WAS	205	1ST DIST
STARTZMAN, PETER	ALL	251	CUMBERLA
STARTZMAN, SARAH	WAS	204	1ST DIST
STARTZMAN, WILLIAM L.	ALL	264	CUMBERLA
STARWITE, JOHN	BAL	290	1ST DIST
STARY, JOSIAH	CAR	291	7TH DIST
STARYLY, MINTA	KEN	218	2ND DIST
STASBURRY, PETER	HAR	175	3RD DIST
STASHA, SEVERN	SOM	396	BRINKLEY
STATE, JAMES B. JR.	CAR	166	NC TWP L
STATER, ARTHUR	BAL	228	2ND WARD
STATES, JOHN	QUE	162	2ND E DI
STATES, MILKY	QUE	127	1ST E DI
STATES, WILLIAM H.	QUE	135	1ST E DI
STATIA, ELIZA	WOR	321	1ST E DI
STATING, WILLIAM	DOR	430	1ST DIST
STATON, GEORGE	SOM	446	DAMES QU
STATON, GEORGE W.	SOM	490	SALISBUR
STATON, JOHN	WOR	300	SNOW HIL
STATON, MARGARET *	KEN	262	1ST DIST
STATON, MARIA	KEN	232	2ND DIST
STATON, MOSES *	SOM	428	PRINCESS
STATON, ROBERT T.	WOR	195	8TH E DI
STATON, SARAH	SOM	435	PRINCESS
STATON, WARNER	WOR	197	8TH E DI
STATOR, HARRY	DOR	363	3RD DIVI
STATRA, JOHN	WOR	335	1ST E DI
STATTEN, JEREH	BAL	160	2ND DIST
STATTEN, WILLIAM	BAL	120	1ST WARD
STATTER, JAMES	BAL	159	2ND DIST
STATTLEMYHER, NANCY	FRE	340	MIDDLETO
STATTY, DAVID	CEC	065	1ST E DI
STATZE, ELELINE	ANN	274	ANNAPOLI
STATZEE, MARY	BAL	206	19TH WAR
STATZEE, MICHAEL	BAL	206	19TH WAR
STAUB, CHARLOTT	FRE	091	FREDERIC
STAUB, DANIEL	FRE	302	WOODSBOR
STAUB, DAVID	FRE	121	CREAGERS
STAUB, GEORGE	FRE	139	CREAGERS
STAUB, GEORGE	BAL	282	1ST DIST
STAUB, HENRY W.	FRE	111	CREAGERS
STAUB, JACOB	FRE	075	FREDERIC
STAUB, JEROMIE *	FRE	075	FREDERIC
STAUB, JOHN	FRE	107	CREAGERS
STAUB, JOHN	BAL	183	19TH WAR
STAUB, MARY	FRE	121	CREAGERS
STAUB, MARY	FRE	142	CREAGERS
STAUB, MARY ANN	BAL	183	19TH WAR
STAUB, RUTH ANN	FRE	140	CREAGERS
STAUB, SOLOMON	FRE	108	CREAGERS
STAUB, SOLOMON	FRE	089	FREDERIC
STAUBB, JOHN	BAL	255	2ND WARD
STAUBER, NICKOLAS	BAL	105	5TH WARD
STAUBS, GEORGE	WAS	190	1ST DIST
STAUBS, JAMES	WAS	197	1ST DIST
STAUBS, MARY	WAS	289	1ST DIST
STAUDRAUGH, CHARLES	BAL	227	2ND WARD
STAUFFER, HENRY	FRE	127	CREAGERS
STAUFFER, WILLIAM	FRE	118	CREAGERS
STAUM, JOHN	BAL	141	16TH WAR
STAUNTON, BENJAMIN	ALL	016	3RD E.D.
STAUNTON, CECILIA	BAL	101	1ST WARD
STAUNTON, EDWARD	BAL	371	8TH WARD
STAUNTON, ELIZABETH	WAS	137	HAGERSTO
STAUNTON, JOHN	BAL	382	8TH WARD
STAUNTON, MICHAEL	ALL	048	10TH E.D
STAUNTON, WILLIAM	ALL	016	3RD E.D.
STAUNTOR, EMMA	BAL	281	20TH WAR
STAUP, DANIEL	FRE	111	CREAGERS
STAUP, EVE	FRE	111	CREAGERS
STAUP, GEORGE A.	FRE	111	CREAGERS
STAUP, JACOB	ALL	117	5TH E.D.
STAUP, JOHN	BAL	426	8TH WARD
STAUP, JOHN W.	FRE	111	CREAGERS
STAUP, LYDDIA	ALL	115	5TH E.D.
STAUP, MARYANN	ALL	115	5TH E.D.
STAUP, PETER	ALL	115	5TH E.D.
STAUP, SARAH E.	ALL	118	5TH E.D.
STAUSS, MATTHIAS	BAL	277	2ND WARD
STAVELEY, JAMES R.	KEN	246	2ND DIST
STAVELY, ANNA	KEN	217	2ND DIST
STAVELY, LAURA	BAL	107	15TH WAR
STAVELY, WILLIAM F.	KEN	221	2ND DIST
STAVER, JOHN	BAL	408	3RD WARD
STAVER, MARGARET	CEC	202	6TH E DI
STAWISKI, FELIX	BAL	199	11TH WAR
STAWSHAUGH, MATILDA	FRE	168	EMMITTSB
STAY, PETER	BAL	266	12TH WAR

Name	County	Page	District
STAYBENAN, ELIZABETH	BAL	273	2ND WARD
STAYDEN, BENJAMIN	BAL	118	2ND DIST
STAYLER, HENRY	BAL	217	19TH WAR
STAYLER, WILLIAM	BAL	153	1ST WARD
STAYLEY, H.	BAL	156	1ST WARD
STAYLON, EMILY	BAL	121	11TH WAR
STAYLOR, DOROTHEA	BAL	047	15TH WAR
STAYLOR, HENRY	BAL	070	1ST WARD
STAYLOR, HENRY M. V.	BAL	218	6TH WARD
STAYLOR, JOHN	BAL	179	2ND WARD
STAYLOR, JOHN	BAL	229	17TH WAR
STAYLOR, THOMAS	BAL	132	1ST WARD
STAYLOR, WILLIAM	BAL	251	2ND WARD
STAYLOR, WILLIAM	BAL	145	5TH WARD
STAYNER, MICHAEL	BAL	012	1ST WARD
STAYSHAUE, ANN	BAL	238	17TH WAR
STAYTON, JOSEPH *	BAL	200	6TH WARD
STCHESON, WILLIAM	BAL	396	1ST DIST
STCLAIR, JANE	HAR	020	1ST DIST
STEADMAN, ADELINE	BAL	157	6TH WARD
STEADMAN, J.	BAL	147	1ST WARD
STEADMAN, JOHN	BAL	169	1ST WARD
STEADMAN, MARGARET	BAL	166	2ND DIST
STEADY, BENJAMIN	BAL	042	9TH WARD
STEAHFREE, J. *	BAL	305	12TH WAR
STEANETT, ANN	CAL	006	1ST DIST
STEANEY, LOUISA	BAL	178	19TH WAR
STEARHUFF, JOHN	BAL	252	1ST DIST
STEARN, MYER	BAL	226	2ND WARD
STEARN, SEIPHEN	BAL	064	1ST WARD
STEARNEN, B.	BAL	268	2ND WARD
STEARNS, GEORGE	BAL	115	15TH WAR
STEARS, GEORGE	BAL	372	13TH WAR
STEAVANS, J.	BAL	174	1ST WARD
STEAVELL, CRESTIRIA *	BAL	109	18TH WAR
STEAVENS, ELIZABETH	BAL	349	1ST DIST
STEAVENS, MARY	BAL	340	1ST DIST
STEAVENS, RUTH	BAL	362	1ST DIST
STEAVENS, WILLIAM G.	BAL	416	1ST DIST
STEAVENSON, AIRAN	BAL	427	1ST DIST
STEAVENSON, GEORGE	BAL	422	1ST DIST
STEAVENSON, HENRY	BAL	416	1ST DIST
STEAVENSON, MERRYMAN	BAL	429	1ST DIST
STEBALL, ELIZA	BAL	197	11TH WAR
STEBBINS, SAMUEL	BAL	061	1ST WARD
STEBEN, GEORGE	BAL	282	2ND WARD
STECKEL, FRANCES	BAL	079	18TH WAR
STECKMAN, MARY *	BAL	220	6TH WARD
STECKMIRE, GEORGE	BAL	261	20TH WAR
STECKPE, FRED	BAL	281	12TH WAR
STED, MARY JANE	BAL	014	18TH WAR
STEDDING, CHRISTIAN	BAL	413	14TH WAR
STEDDING, LEWIS	BAL	264	12TH WAR
STEDMAN, ANDREW J.	FRE	380	PETERSVI
STEDMAN, JAMES	BAL	181	16TH WAR
STEDMER, PETER	CEC	077	NORTHEAS
STEDYMAN, WILLIAM	FRE	129	CREAGERS
STEEBE, AUGUSTUS	BAL	219	19TH WAR
STEEFE, JOHN	BAL	154	19TH WAR
STEEK, CHARLES	BAL	335	7TH WARD
STEEL, ABRAHAM	ALL	033	2ND E.D.
STEEL, ABRAHAM W.	FRE	255	NEW MARK
STEEL, ADAM	BAL	143	2ND DIST
STEEL, ALEXANDER	CEC	117	4TH E DI
STEEL, ANN J.	CEC	122	4TH E DI
STEEL, BASIL	FRE	437	8TH E DI
STEEL, CATHERINE	CEC	197	7TH E DI
STEEL, CHARLES	CEC	188	7TH E DI
STEEL, DANIEL	FRE	018	FREDERIC
STEEL, DAVID	CEC	117	4TH E DI
STEEL, ELIZABETH	CEC	118	4TH E DI
STEEL, FRANK	ANN	287	ANNAPOLI
STEEL, GEORG EH.	FRE	018	FREDERIC
STEEL, GEORGE	CEC	028	CHESAPEA
STEEL, GEORGE	HAR	040	1ST DIST
STEEL, HARRIET	BAL	449	14TH WAR
STEEL, HENRY M.	ANN	287	ANNAPOLI
STEEL, HESTER	CEC	156	PORT DUP
STEEL, HUGH	CEC	158	PORT DUP
STEEL, HUGH	CEC	027	CHESAPEA
STEEL, JAMES	CEC	141	6TH E DI
STEEL, JAMES	HAR	042	1ST DIST
STEEL, JAMES	CEC	117	4TH E DI
STEEL, JAMES	BAL	399	1ST DIST
STEEL, JAMES N.	DOR	381	1ST DIST
STEEL, JANE	CEC	117	4TH E DI
STEEL, JEREMIAH	CEC	114	3RD E DI
STEEL, JOHN	CEC	118	4TH E DI
STEEL, JOHN	CEC	156	PORT DUP
STEEL, JOHN	CAR	224	5TH DIST
STEEL, JOHN	BAL	291	1ST DIST
STEEL, JOSEPH	CAR	213	5TH DIST
STEEL, JOSEPH	CEC	098	4TH E DI
STEEL, MARIA	FRE	255	NEW MARK
STEEL, MARIA	WAS	274	RIDGEVIL
STEEL, PHILIP M.	CEC	136	6TH E DI
STEEL, ROBERT	BAL	294	1ST DIST
STEEL, SAMUEL	BAL	407	1ST DIST
STEEL, SUSANA L.	CEC	136	6TH E DI
STEEL, THOMAS J.	BAL	339	13TH WAR
STEEL, VERLINDA	MGM	426	MEDLEY 3
STEEL, WILLIAM	CEC	031	CHESAPEA
STEELE, ARTHUR	DOR	383	1ST DIST
STEELE, CHARLES H. DR-	ANN	314	1ST DIST
STEELE, D. REV.	BAL	096	10TH WAR
STEELE, DAVID	WAS	126	HAGERSTO
STEELE, EBENEZAR	WAS	111	2ND DIST
STEELE, ELIZABETH	WAS	121	HAGERSTO
STEELE, ISSABELLA	DOR	386	1ST DIST
STEELE, JAMES H.	CAR	362	9TH DIST
STEELE, JOHN	WAS	124	2ND DIST
STEELE, JOHN N.	DOR	449	1ST DIST
STEELE, JOHN N. JR.	DOR	449	1ST DIST
STEELE, JOSEPH	FRE	253	NEW MARK
STEELE, JOSEPH	FRE	113	CREAGERS
STEELE, LOUISA	DOR	381	1ST DIST
STEELE, MARY	BAL	221	6TH WARD
STEELE, SAMUEL	BAL	296	12TH WAR
STEELE, SAMUEL	BAL	006	9TH WARD
STEELE, SAMUEL	WAS	125	HAGERSTO
STEELE, WILLIAM	BAL	296	12TH WAR
STEELEMAN, JOHN	BAL	235	2ND WARD
STEELL, CHRISTIAN	FRE	116	CREAGERS
STEELMAN, JOHN S.	BAL	035	9TH WARD
STEEN, CHARLES-BLACK	CAR	371	9TH DIST
STEEN, GEORGE W.	BAL	050	15TH WAR
STEEPE, DAVID	FRE	072	FREDERIC
STEEPE, SAMUEL	FRE	098	FREDERIC
STEEPER, REGINA	BAL	214	11TH WAR
STEER, GRACE	BAL	434	8TH WARD
STEER, JOHN	BAL	273	2ND WARD
STEER, SAMULE L.	BAL	151	16TH WAR
STEER, WILLIAM H.	FRE	253	NEW MARK
STEERS, AUGUSTUS	ALL	250	CUMBERLA
STEET, EHART	BAL	416	8TH WARD
STEETNER, JOHN	BAL	224	2ND WARD
STEEVER, DANIEL	BAL	277	7TH WARD
STEEVER, EDMUND P.	BAL	081	18TH WAR
STEEVER, FRANCIS	BAL	259	6TH WARD
STEEVER, JOHN	CAR	341	6TH DIST
STEEVER, MICHAEL	BAL	437	8TH WARD
STEEWARRT, CAHTERINE	BAL	131	11TH WAR
STEFFENBERGER, CORNELIUS	BAL	098	1ST WARD
STEFFEY, E.E.	WAS	002	WILLIAMS
STEFFEY, GEORGE	BAL	304	12TH WAR
STEFFEY, PETER	WAS	002	WILLIAMS
STEFFMAN, JOHN	BAL	196	2ND WARD
STEFFON, JACOB	CAR	339	6TH DIST
STEFFT, LEWIS	BAL	161	19TH WAR
STEFFY, ANDREW	WAS	265	1ST DIST
STEFFY, CATHARINE	WAS	265	1ST DIST
STEFFY, CATHARINE	WAS	262	1ST DIST
STEFFY, DANIEL	WAS	250	1ST DIST
STEFFY, HENRY	CAR	334	6TH DIST
STEFFY, JOHN D.	WAS	240	CAVETOWN
STEFFY, MALINDA	WAS	269	1ST DIST
STEFFY, MICHAEL	CAR	330	MANCHEST
STEFFY, MICHAEL	CAR	343	6TH DIST
STEFFY, SAMUEL	WAS	262	1ST DIST
STEFFY, SOLOMON	WAS	279	LEITERSB
STEFFY, SUSAN	WAS	280	LEITERSB
STEFFY, WILLIAM	WAS	287	1ST DIST
STEGNER, CATHARINE	CAR	347	6TH DIST
STEGNER, ELI	CAR	343	6TH DIST
STEGNER, GEORGE	CAR	347	6TH DIST
STEGNER, JACOB	CAR	347	6TH DIST
STEGNER, PETER	CAR	347	6TH DIST
STEHENS, SAMUEL	FRE	449	8TH E DI
STEHNER, JOHN	BAL	082	10TH WAR
STEIBING, CHRISTIAN	BAL	070	1ST WARD
STEIDNER, GEORGE	BAL	081	10TH WAR
STEIFEL, FRANCES	BAL	015	9TH WARD
STEIFF, CHARLES M.	BAL	379	13TH WAR
STEIGARS, JOHN	BAL	112	1ST WARD
STEIGER, M.	BAL	449	8TH WARD
STEIGERS, SUGUSTA	BAL	315	1ST DIST
STEIGERS, SUSAN	BAL	206	6TH WARD
STEIGERWALT, JOHN	BAL	233	17TH WAR
STEIGLEMAN, ABRAHAM	BAL	277	7TH WARD
STEIGLEMAN, COLUMBUS	BAL	278	7TH WARD
STEIGLEMAN, JEFFERSON A.	BAL	209	6TH WARD
STEIGLEMAN, JOHN L.	BAL	210	6TH WARD
STEIKENWALD, MYER	BAL	082	1ST WARD
STEILHOFF, MARGARET	BAL	273	7TH WARD
STEILMAN, JOHN	BAL	193	2ND WARD
STEIMMEL, LEWIS	BAL	249	20TH WAR
STEINSS, P.	BAL	090	5TH WARD
STEIN, AGNES	BAL	272	2ND WARD
STEIN, CONRAD	BAL	263	2ND WARD
STEIN, EDWARD	BAL	040	4TH WARD
STEIN, ELIAS	FRE	074	FREDERIC
STEIN, ELIZABETH	FRE	034	FREDERIC
STEIN, ELIZABETH	FRE	337	MIDDLETO
STEIN, ELIZABETH	BAL	225	2ND WARD
STEIN, ELLEN	BAL	073	4TH WARD
STEIN, FREDERICK	BAL	166	16TH WAR
STEIN, FREDERICK	BAL	113	15TH WAR
STEIN, GEORGE	BAL	272	7TH WARD
STEIN, HENRY	BAL	287	1ST DIST
STEIN, HENRY	BAL	062	4TH WARD
STEIN, HENRY	FRE	339	MIDDLETO
STEIN, JAMES T.	BAL	140	5TH WARD
STEIN, JOHN	BAL	297	3RD WARD
STEIN, JOHN	FRE	074	FREDERIC
STEIN, JOHN	FRE	086	FREDERIC
STEIN, JOHN	FRE	086	FREDERIC
STEIN, LEWIS	BAL	132	5TH WARD
STEIN, MARY	BAL	412	8TH WARD
STEIN, MARY A.	BAL	028	1ST WARD
STEIN, MATHEW	BAL	258	2ND WARD
STEIN, MICHAEL	FRE	344	MIDDLETO
STEIN, PETER	BAL	098	1ST WARD
STEIN, PHILLIP	BAL	246	6TH WARD
STEIN, ROBERT	PRI	107	PISCATAW
STEIN, WILLIAM H.	FRE	358	CATOCTIN
STEINBACK, MARGARET	BAL	149	19TH WAR
STEINBECK, SOPHIA F.	MGM	377	ROCKERLE
STEINBERG, JOHN	BAL	262	12TH WAR
STEINBERGER, FANNY	FRE	019	FREDERIC
STEINBERGER, MARKS	FRE	019	FREDERIC
STEINBETZ, GEORGE	BAL	327	3RD WARD
STEINBRICK, FREDERICK	BAL	301	17TH WAR
STEINE, CASPER	ALL	195	CUMBERLA
STEINE, GEORGE	WAS	077	2ND SUBD
STEINE, JOHN B.	WAS	084	2ND SUBD
STEINER, ANDREW	BAL	082	10TH WAR
STEINER, CHRISTIAN	FRE	032	FREDERIC
STEINER, DAVID	CAR	387	2ND DIST
STEINER, DAVID E.	BAL	230	19TH WAR
STEINER, DAVID R.	FRE	171	5TH E DI
STEINER, ELIZABETH	BAL	091	10TH WAR
STEINER, FRANCIS	FRE	366	CATOCTIN
STEINER, FREDERICK	BAL	371	13TH WAR
STEINER, GEORGE	HAR	137	2ND DIST
STEINER, GEORGE	CAR	410	2ND DIST
STEINER, HENRY	HAR	099	2ND DIST
STEINER, HENRY C.	FRE	055	FREDERIC
STEINER, JACOB	FRE	094	FREDERIC
STEINER, JACOB	FRE	096	FREDERIC
STEINER, JOHNA.	FRE	036	FREDERIC
STEINER, M.	BAL	090	10TH WAR
STEINER, M.	BAL	449	8TH WARD
STEINER, MATTHEW	BAL	091	10TH WAR
STEINER, MICHAEL	BAL	226	17TH WAR
STEINER, SOLOLMON	ALL	013	3RD E.D.
STEINFELT, FREDERICK	BAL	033	2ND DIST
STEINFELT, JOHN *	BAL	166	2ND DIST
STEINFIELD, ELIZA	BAL	201	2ND WARD
STEINGLE, JOHN	BAL	276	7TH WARD
STEINHAGAN, CHRISTOPHER	BAL	397	1ST DIST
STEINHAGAN, MARY	BAL	268	1ST DIST
STEINHAGAN, RICHARD	BAL	451	1ST DIST
STEINHARDT, TINA	BAL	092	10TH WAR
STEINHOFER, CHRISTIAN	BAL	020	15TH WAR
STEINHOFFER,LEWIS	BAL	258	12TH WAR
STEINLEIN, GEORGE	BAL	213	2ND WARD
STEINMETZ, GEORGE	WAS	157	HAGERSTO
STEINMETZ, HENRY	WAS	005	WILLIAMS
STEINMITZ, NICHOLAS	BAL	037	15TH WAR
STEIR, CHRISTIANA	CAR	255	3RD DIST
STEIR, JOHN G.	BAL	064	1ST WARD
STEIR, MICHAEL	CAR	256	3RD DIST
STEIREM, REUBEN	CAR	388	2ND DIST
STEITLEBLA, ALEXANDER	BAL	178	2ND WARD
STEITLEBLA, MARGRET	BAL	178	2ND WARD
STEIVER, GEORGE	BAL	218	12TH WAR
STEL, WILLIAM	HAR	178	3RD DIST
STELCHER, JOHN	BAL	316	12TH WAR
STELDLEN, JOHN	BAL	129	11TH WAR
STELHAN, JOHN	BAL	313	1ST DIST
STELHAN, PHILIP	BAL	313	1ST DIST
STELL, LYDIA	FRE	254	NEW MARK
STEM, HENRY W.	FRE	143	10TH E D
STEM, HIRAM	FRE	143	10TH E D
STEM, JOHN	FRE	143	10TH E D
STEM, MARYANN	FRE	415	8TH E DI
STEM, PETER	FRE	143	10TH E D
STEMBLER, GEORGE	BAL	058	18TH WAR
STEMBLER, JOHN	BAL	017	18TH WAR
STEMBLER, NICHOLAS	BAL	404	14TH WAR
STEMBLER, WILLIAM H. *	BAL	049	18TH WAR
STEMER, AGEST	BAL	230	2ND WARD
STEMICK, HENRY	BAL	460	1ST DIST
STEMMAL, LEWIS	BAL	408	14TH WAR
STEMMER, ANN A.	CAR	388	2ND DIST
STEMMER, AVERHART	ALL	096	5TH E.D.
STEMMON, SUSAN	BAL	296	7TH WARD
STEMPH, MICHAEL *	ALL	081	5TH E.D.
STEMPLE, JOHN	WAS	152	HAGERSTO
STEMPLE, JOHN	WAS	152	HAGERSTO
STEMPLE, WILLIAM	WAS	153	HAGERSTO
STENBECK, ELIZABETH	BAL	415	14TH WAR
STENBEKER, SOPHIA	BAL	130	11TH WAR
STENBES, CONRAD	BAL	051	1ST WARD
STENCECUM, ELIZABETH	BAL	254	1ST DIST
STENER, ARCHIBALD	ALL	013	3RD E.D.
STENETT, GEORGANNA	BAL	066	1ST WARD
STENEYER, AMANDA	WAS	215	1ST DIST
STENGER, NICHOLAS	ALL	098	5TH E.D.
STENGIL, FREDERICK	CAR	249	3RD DIST
STENKER, MARTIN	BAL	216	2ND WARD
STENNER, MATTHEW	BAL	260	20TH WAR
STENSON, MARY	BAL	316	20TH WAR
STENTOR, MARGRET	DOR	359	3RD DIVI
STENY, JOHN *	BAL	287	1ST DIST
STEON, WILLIAM W.	FRE	143	10TH E D
STEOYES, JOHN *	WOR	308	2ND E DI
STEPERSON, J.	BAL	130	1ST WARD
STEPHANS, JOHN	CEC	055	1ST E DI
STEPHANS, JOSIAH	CEC	063	1ST E DI
STEPHANS, NICHOLAS	CEC	040	CHESAPEA
STEPHANS, SAMUEL	CEC	052	1ST E DI
STEPHANS, SAMUEL	CEC	052	1ST E DI
STEPHANS, SYLVESTER	CEC	053	1ST E DI
STEPHANS, THOMAS	CEC	061	1ST E DI
STEPHANS, WESLEY	CEC	056	1ST E DI
STEPHEANSON, EMILY	CEC	213	7TH E DI
STEPHEN, EDWARD B.	PRI	006	BLADENSB
STEPHEN, GEORGE	CAR	355	6TH DIST
STEPHEN, HENRY	BAL	433	14TH WAR
STEPHEN, MARY	MGM	375	ROCKERLE
STEPHEN, NICHOLAS C.	PRI	006	BLADENSB
STEPHEN, THOMAS B.	PRI	006	BLADENSB
STEPHENES, LOUISA	DOR	375	1ST DIST
STEPHENS, ALLEN	CEC	151	PORT DUP
STEPHENS, ANN R.	BAL	347	7TH WARD
STEPHENS, AQUILLA	HAR	141	2ND DIST
STEPHENS, BENJAMIN	BAL	116	15TH WAR
STEPHENS, BILL	WOR	315	2ND E DI
STEPHENS, CECELIA	BAL	057	4TH WARD
STEPHENS, CHARLOTTE	CEC	064	1ST E DI
STEPHENS, DAVID	WOR	190	8TH E DI
STEPHENS, ELIZABETH	BAL	122	2ND DIST
STEPHENS, EMILY	KEN	266	1ST DIST
STEPHENS, GEORGE	BAL	122	2ND DIST
STEPHENS, GEORGE W.	PRI	002	BLADENSB
STEPHENS, HACKETT	DOR	299	1ST DIST
STEPHENS, HARRIETT	HAR	181	3RD DIST
STEPHENS, JAMES	QUE	149	1ST E DI
STEPHENS, JAMES	DOR	426	1ST DIST
STEPHENS, JAMES	DOR	434	1ST DIST
STEPHENS, JAMES-BLACK	WOR	322	1ST E DI
STEPHENS, JESSE	ANN	463	HOWARD D
STEPHENS, JESSEE	DOR	312	1ST DIST
STEPHENS, JOHN	DOR	316	1ST DIST
STEPHENS, JOHN	QUE	158	2ND E DI
STEPHENS, JOHN	HAR	181	3RD DIST
STEPHENS, JOHN	BAL	418	14TH WAR
STEPHENS, JOHN	BAL	145	2ND DIST
STEPHENS, JOHN A.	BAL	104	15TH WAR
STEPHENS, JOHN D.	DOR	453	1ST DIST
STEPHENS, JOHN T.	KEN	230	2ND DIST
STEPHENS, JOSHUA	HAR	129	2ND DIST
STEPHENS, LANSAN*	DOR	392	1ST DIST
STEPHENS, LAURA	ANN	521	HOWARD D
STEPHENS, LEVI	DOR	403	1ST DIST
STEPHENS, LINAH	WOR	189	7TH E DI
STEPHENS, LIT-BLACK	WOR	317	2ND E DI
STEPHENS, MARY	WOR	198	8TH E DI
STEPHENS, MARY	DOR	452	1ST DIST
STEPHENS, MARY	WOR	258	1ST CENS
STEPHENS, MARY A.	BAL	119	11TH WAR
STEPHENS, MARY E.	DOR	296	1ST DIST
STEPHENS, NANCY	ANN	506	HOWARD D
STEPHENS, PERRY	BAL	058	4TH WARD
STEPHENS, RUTH	BAL	148	11TH WAR
STEPHENS, SALLY	BAL	450	14TH WAR
STEPHENS, SALLY	QUE	184	3RD E DI
STEPHENS, SAMUEL	KEN	266	1ST DIST
STEPHENS, SAMUEL	KEN	266	1ST DIST
STEPHENS, SAMUEL	WAS	162	2ND DIST
STEPHENS, SAMUEL	FRE	239	NEW MARK
STEPHENS, SEPTIMUS	WAS	187	BOONSBOR
STEPHENS, SUSAN C.	KEN	231	2ND DIST
STEPHENS, THOMAS	KEN	243	2ND DIST
STEPHENS, VANCE*	DOR	462	1ST DIST
STEPHENS, W. H.	BAL	471	14TH WAR
STEPHENS, WASHINGTON	BAL	354	1ST DIST
STEPHENS, WESLEY-BLACK	QUE	139	1ST E DI
STEPHENS, WILLIAM	DOR	298	1ST DIST
STEPHENS, WILLIAM	DOR	316	1ST DIST
STEPHENS, WILLIAM	BAL	011	4TH WARD
STEPHENS, WILLIAM	BAL	321	7TH WARD
STEPHENS, WILLIAM	BAL	180	6TH WARD
STEPHENS, WILLIAM	SOM	504	SALISBUR
STEPHENS, WILLIAM D.	BAL	036	15TH WAR
STEPHENS, WILLIAM H.*	DOR	448	1ST DIST
STEPHENS, WILLIAM W.	KEN	229	2ND DIST
STEPHENS,WILLIAM	BAL	140	1ST WARD
STEPHENSON, ACE	BAL	017	2ND DIST

STEPHENSON, ANDREW M. MGM 422 MEDLEY 3
STEPHENSON, BASIL MGM 361 BERRYS D
STEPHENSON, ELIZA CEC 150 PORT DUP
STEPHENSON, ELIZABETH SOM 368 BRINKLEY
STEPHENSON, ELLEN BAL 396 14TH WAR
STEPHENSON, GEORGE HAR 126 2ND DIST
STEPHENSON, GEORGE HAR 194 3RD DIST
STEPHENSON, HARRIET CEC 150 PORT DUP
STEPHENSON, HARRIET BAL 435 14TH WAR
STEPHENSON, ISAIAH CEC 206 7TH E DI
STEPHENSON, JAMES HAR 127 2ND DIST
STEPHENSON, JAMES SOM 468 TRAPPE D
STEPHENSON, JAMES W. SOM 408 DUBLIN D
STEPHENSON, JEREMIAH CEC 161 6TH E DI
STEPHENSON, JESSE WAS 238 CAVETOWN
STEPHENSON, JOHN MGM 424 MEDLEY 3
STEPHENSON, JOSEPH WAS 249 1ST DIST
STEPHENSON, LORD HAR 170 3RD DIST
STEPHENSON, MILKY A.* SOM 366 BRINKLEY
STEPHENSON, NELSON CEC 201 6TH E DI
STEPHENSON, PATIENCE HAR 185 3RD DIST
STEPHENSON, PRISCILLA HAR 127 2ND DIST
STEPHENSON, RACHEL BAL 017 2ND DIST
STEPHENSON, ROBERT CEC 146 PORT DUP
STEPHENSON, ROBERT SOM 371 BRINKLEY
STEPHENSON, SARAH SOM 412 DUBLIN D
STEPHENSON, WILLIAM SOM 366 BRINKLEY
STEPHENSON, WILLIAM WOR 255 1ST CENS
STEPHENSON, WILLIAM ALL 080 5TH E.D.
STEPHENSON, ZADOCK WOR 191 8TH E DI
STEPHINS, MARGRET DOR 372 3RD DIVI
STEPHON, JOHN CAR 355 6TH DIST
STEPLER, WILLIAM H. CEC 011 ELKTON 3
STEPLINE, MARY FRE 414 8TH E DI
STEPLINE, SUSAN CAR 280 7TH DIST
STEPNES, HORACE BAL 244 1ST DIST
STEPNEY, ANN M. ANN 355 3RD DIST
STEPNEY, CHARLES ANN 351 3RD DIST
STEPNEY, HENRY ANN 355 3RD DIST
STEPNEY, JOHN ANN 356 3RD DIST
STEPNEY, JULIA * ANN 289 ANNAPOLI
STEPNEY, MARGARET ANN 355 3RD DIST
STEPNEY, SUSAN ANN 356 3RD DIST
STEPNEY, THOMAS ANN 354 3RD DIST
STEPNEY, WILLIAM H. ANN 290 ANNAPOLI
STEPNY, HAGAR BAL 268 1ST DIST
STEPP, FREDRICK BAL 130 18TH WAR
STEPPHON, NICHOLAS CAR 360 9TH DIST
STEPPLER, ADOLPHUS BAL 198 2ND WARD
STERART, GEORGE F. BAL 240 17TH WAR
STERCK, FREDERICK BAL 270 2ND WARD
STERELLS, GETLIEB BAL 405 14TH WAR
STERENS, CHRISTIAN FRE 005 FREDERIC
STERENS, JOSEPH FRE 004 FREDERIC
STERGENWALC, ADAM BAL 344 7TH WARD
STERGERS, HENRY BAL 220 12TH WAR
STERIOS, SAMUEL BAL 092 5TH WARD
STERIT, JOSHUA HAR 074 1ST DIST
STERKEL, DAVID FRE 171 5TH E DI
STERLING, AARON SOM 372 BRINKLEY
STERLING, AARON SOM 380 BRINKLEY
STERLING, ARCHIBALD BAL 196 11TH WAR
STERLING, ARON SOM 377 BRINKLEY
STERLING, BETSEY SOM 365 BRINKLEY
STERLING, BETSEY SOM 389 BRINKLEY
STERLING, CAROLINE SOM 375 BRINKLEY
STERLING, CHARLES L. BAL 196 11TH WAR
STERLING, CHRISTOPHER SOM 381 BRINKLEY
STERLING, CLEMENT SOM 382 BRINKLEY
STERLING, DAVID SOM 374 BRINKLEY
STERLING, DORATHA C.* SOM 382 BRINKLEY
STERLING, ELIJAH SOM 381 BRINKLEY
STERLING, ELIZABETH SOM 380 BRINKLEY
STERLING, ELIZABETH SOM 382 BRINKLEY
STERLING, EPHRAIM SOM 379 BRINKLEY
STERLING, GEORGE SOM 377 BRINKLEY
STERLING, GEORGE W. TAL 072 EASTON T
STERLING, GILBERT SOM 382 BRINKLEY
STERLING, GRACE SOM 380 BRINKLEY
STERLING, HANDY SOM 381 BRINKLEY
STERLING, HENERETTA SOM 376 BRINKLEY
STERLING, HENRY SOM 380 BRINKLEY
STERLING, HENRY SOM 377 BRINKLEY
STERLING, HENRY SOM 377 BRINKLEY
STERLING, HENRY SOM 544 TYASKIN
STERLING, ISAAC SOM 372 BRINKLEY
STERLING, ISAAC SOM 374 BRINKLEY
STERLING, ISAAC SOM 377 BRINKLEY
STERLING, JAMES SOM 374 BRINKLEY
STERLING, JAMES SOM 374 BRINKLEY
STERLING, JAMES CEC 093 4TH E DI
STERLING, JESSE SOM 379 BRINKLEY
STERLING, JESSE SOM 380 BRINKLEY
STERLING, JOHN SOM 372 BRINKLEY
STERLING, JOHN SOM 373 BRINKLEY
STERLING, JOHN SOM 380 BRINKLEY
STERLING, JOHN SOM 377 BRINKLEY
STERLING, JOHN BAL 347 3RD WARD
STERLING, JOHN BAL 302 3RD WARD
STERLING, JOHN E. SOM 382 BRINKLEY
STERLING, JOHN F. BAL 297 17TH WAR
STERLING, JOSEPH SOM 379 BRINKLEY
STERLING, JOSEPH SOM 389 BRINKLEY
STERLING, JOSEPH SOM 374 BRINKLEY
STERLING, JOSIAH SOM 382 BRINKLEY
STERLING, LEVIN SOM 382 BRINKLEY
STERLING, LITTLETON SOM 378 BRINKLEY
STERLING, MALON SOM 380 BRINKLEY
STERLING, MARY SOM 377 BRINKLEY
STERLING, MARY SOM 381 BRINKLEY
STERLING, MARY BAL 336 13TH WAR
STERLING, MARY E. BAL 321 3RD WARD
STERLING, MARY E. BAL 037 2ND DIST
STERLING, MARY J. BAL 027 1ST WARD
STERLING, NANCY SOM 376 BRINKLEY
STERLING, NATHAN SOM 379 BRINKLEY
STERLING, NOAH SOM 373 BRINKLEY
STERLING, NOAH SOM 379 BRINKLEY
STERLING, NOAH SOM 372 BRINKLEY
STERLING, RICHARD SOM 381 BRINKLEY
STERLING, RICHARD DOR 468 1ST DIST
STERLING, ROBERT BAL 036 2ND DIST
STERLING, ROSINA BAL 457 14TH WAR
STERLING, SAMUEL BAL 210 11TH WAR
STERLING, SAMUEL SOM 384 BRINKLEY
STERLING, SAMUEL WAS 026 2ND SUBD
STERLING, SARAH SOM 388 BRINKLEY
STERLING, SARAH E. BAL 277 7TH WARD
STERLING, SOUTHY SOM 374 BRINKLEY
STERLING, THOMAS SOM 387 BRINKLEY
STERLING, TRAVES SOM 380 BRINKLEY
STERLING, TRAVIS JR. SOM 380 BRINKLEY
STERLING, TRAVIS SR. SOM 380 BRINKLEY
STERLING, WHITTINGTON SOM 380 BRINKLEY
STERLING, WILLIAM SOM 381 BRINKLEY
STERLING, WILLIAM SOM 378 BRINKLEY
STERLING, WILLIAM SOM 372 BRINKLEY
STERLING, WILLIAM SOM 380 BRINKLEY
STERLING, WILLIAM ALL 104 5TH E.D.
STERLING, WILLIAM BAL 320 7TH WARD
STERLING, WILLIAM T. SOM 379 BRINKLEY
STERM, EMMANUEL BAL 062 15TH WAR
STERM, JACOB BAL 061 15TH WAR
STERM, WILLIAM WAS 003 WILLIAMS
STERN, BOWET BAL 300 7TH WARD
STERN, DAVID WAS 158 HAGERSTO
STERN, ELIE WAS 166 1ST DIST
STERN, HANNAH BAL 013 9TH WARD
STERN, JACOB CAR 360 9TH DIST
STERN, JOSEPH FRE 055 FREDERIC
STERN, MARY CAR 380 2ND DIST
STERN, MICHAEL CAR 407 2ND DIST
STERN, NATHAN CAR 380 2ND DIST
STERN, RACHEL BAL 229 19TH WAR
STERN, REUBEN CAR 388 2ND DIST
STERN, SOPHIA BAL 013 9TH WARD
STERNELL, JOHN ANN 438 HOWARD D
STERNER, C. BAL 264 20TH WAR
STERNER, DANIEL BAL 003 9TH WARD
STERNER, ELIZABETH BAL 171 19TH WAR
STERRET, FRANCIS M. ALL 238 CUMBERLA
STERRET, GEORGE A. HAR 073 1ST DIST
STERRET, HENRY-BLACK BAL 217 2ND WARD
STERRET, JESSE BAL 017 2ND DIST
STERRET, PETER ANN 370 4TH DIST
STERRET, RACHEL BAL 017 2ND DIST
STERRET, REBECCA ALL 253 CUMBERLA
STERRET, WILLIAM ALL 240 CUMBERLA
STERRETT, ELIZA BAL 248 6TH WARD
STERRETT, HANAH BAL 043 2ND DIST
STERRETT, HARRIET BAL 045 2ND DIST
STERRETT, ISSAC S. BAL 174 2ND DIST
STERRETT, PRISCILLA BAL 122 16TH WAR
STERRETT, RACHELL WAS 015 2ND SUBD
STERRETT, SAMUEL BAL 043 2ND DIST
STERRETT, SCIPIO BAL 122 16TH WAR
STERRICK, HENRY BAL 164 19TH WAR
STERRITT, JAMES FRE 188 5TH E DI
STERRITT, JAMES BAL 085 2ND DIST
STERRITT, JOHN G. HAR 072 1ST DIST
STERRY, HENRY CAR 198 4TH DIST
STERTIN, BENJAMIN HAR 195 3RD DIST
STERTZMAN, HARRISON ALL 222 CUMBERLA
STERTZMAN, JOHN ALL 251 CUMBERLA
STERVICH, HENRY CAR 341 6TH DIST
STERZMAN, WILLIAM P. ALL 222 CUMBERLA
STESLEY, ELIZA KEN 300 3RD DIST
STETELY, SUSAN E. FRE 289 WOODSBOR
STETER, HENRY HAR 199 3RD DIST
STETLER, ANGELINE CAR 241 TANEYTOW
STETSON, HARRIET T. BAL 073 15TH WAR
STETZENBACH, HENRY BAL 123 16TH WAR
STEUART, CHARLES BAL 032 4TH WARD
STEUART, GLENDY BAL 059 4TH WARD
STEUART, ISAAC BAL 067 4TH WARD
STEUART, JAMES BAL 088 4TH WARD
STEUART, MARY A. BAL 418 14TH WAR
STEUART, R.* BAL 099 10TH WAR
STEUART, ROBERT T. J. BAL 088 4TH WARD
STEUBENFELT, CHRISTIAN FRE 360 CATOCTIN
STEVANS, ANN TAL 029 EASTON D
STEVANS, BETSEY TAL 099 ST MICHA
STEVANS, BETSEY TAL 067 EASTON T
STEVANS, CATER TAL 018 EASTON D
STEVANS, CHARLES TAL 033 EASTON D
STEVANS, CHARLES R. TAL 050 EASTON T
STEVANS, EDWARD TAL 066 EASTON T
STEVANS, EDWARD J. TAL 039 EASTON D
STEVANS, EDWIN J. TAL 049 EASTON T
STEVANS, HOOPA B. TAL 034 EASTON D
STEVANS, ISACK TAL 043 EASTON D
STEVANS, ISREAL BAL 169 1ST WARD
STEVANS, JOHN TAL 066 EASTON T
STEVANS, JOHN R. TAL 008 EASTON D
STEVANS, JOHN T. TAL 042 EASTON D
STEVANS, JULIANN TAL 048 EASTON T
STEVANS, MARGARET TAL 033 EASTON D
STEVANS, NANCY TAL 051 EASTON D
STEVANS, PERRY G. TAL 023 EASTON D
STEVANS, PETER TAL 024 EASTON D
STEVANS, PETER JR. TAL 040 EASTON D
STEVANS, RICHARD A. TAL 008 EASTON D
STEVANS, SAMUEL TAL 049 EASTON T
STEVANS, SARAH R. TAL 042 EASTON D
STEVANS, THOMAS J. TAL 068 EASTON T
STEVANS, VIRGINIA TAL 043 EASTON D
STEVANS, WILLIAM TAL 065 EASTON T
STEVANS, WILLIAM C. TAL 051 EASTON D
STEVANS, REBECCA FRE 431 8TH E DI
STEVANSON, JOHN S.* TAL 041 EASTON D
STEVEDER, ANDREW BAL 122 2ND DIST
STEVELER, JHN BAL 080 1ST WARD
STEVEN S, HENERETTA SOM 407 DUBLIN D
STEVENISON, JOSEPH BAL 102 2ND DIST
STEVENS, A. BAL 063 10TH WAR
STEVENS, ALEXANDER BAL 026 4TH WARD
STEVENS, ALEXANDER-MULATT BAL 214 2ND WARD
STEVENS, ALEXANDER-MULATT BAL 215 2ND WARD
STEVENS, ALFRED SOM 491 SALISBUR
STEVENS, ANDREW ALL 249 CUMBERLA
STEVENS, ANDREW BAL 042 1ST WARD
STEVENS, ANDREW CAR 179 8TH DIST
STEVENS, ANN BAL 125 11TH WAR
STEVENS, ANN BAL 352 7TH WARD
STEVENS, ANN BAL 338 3RD WARD
STEVENS, ANNA TAL 088 ST MICHA
STEVENS, B. BAL 137 1ST WARD
STEVENS, BENJAMIN BAL 189 11TH WAR
STEVENS, BENJAMIN BAL 176 19TH WAR
STEVENS, BENJAMIN DOR 392 1ST DIST
STEVENS, BESTEY TAL 075 EASTON T
STEVENS, CAROLINE WOR 270 BERLIN 1
STEVENS, CASH BAL 271 20TH WAR
STEVENS, CHARELS FRE 111 CREAGERS
STEVENS, CHARLES BAL 136 18TH WAR
STEVENS, CHARLES FRE 239 NEW MARK
STEVENS, CHARLES QUE 222 4TH E DI
STEVENS, CHARLES BAL 120 1ST WARD
STEVENS, CHARLES BAL 170 1ST WARD
STEVENS, CHARLOTT BAL 102 18TH WAR
STEVENS, CHARLOTTE BAL 204 11TH WAR
STEVENS, CHARLOTTE QUE 225 4TH E DI
STEVENS, CLAYLAND QUE 227 4TH E DI
STEVENS, D.D.L. BAL 161 1ST WARD
STEVENS, E. BAL 142 1ST WARD
STEVENS, EDUARD BAL 242 2ND WARD
STEVENS, ELIJAH DOR 462 1ST DIST
STEVENS, ELIZA BAL 306 7TH WARD
STEVENS, ELIZABETH ALL 207 CUMBERLA
STEVENS, ELIZABETH DOR 459 1ST DIST
STEVENS, ELIZABETH DOR 433 1ST DIST
STEVENS, ELLEN BAL 262 12TH WAR
STEVENS, ELLEN ANN 459 HOWARD D
STEVENS, FANNY BAL 279 17TH WAR
STEVENS, FERDINAND BAL 348 1ST DIST
STEVENS, FRANCIS CAL 055 3RD DIST
STEVENS, GEORGE BAL 039 15TH WAR
STEVENS, H. BAL 277 12TH WAR
STEVENS, HARRY-BLACK QUE 131 1ST E DI
STEVENS, HENERETTA J. SOM 412 DUBLIN D
STEVENS, HENRY CAR 202 4TH DIST
STEVENS, HENRY ALL 087 5TH E.D.
STEVENS, HENRY H. BAL 347 3RD WARD
STEVENS, HENRY-BLACK BAL 250 2ND WARD
STEVENS, HESTER BAL 015 18TH WAR
STEVENS, IDA BAL 170 19TH WAR
STEVENS, ISAAC SOM 494 SALISBUR
STEVENS, ISABELLA BAL 077 1ST WARD
STEVENS, ISRAEL-BLACK BAL 224 2ND WARD
STEVENS, JACOB BAL 005 1ST WARD
STEVENS, JACOB KEN 266 1ST DIST
STEVENS, JAMES DOR 460 1ST DIST
STEVENS, JAMES KEN 310 3RD DIST
STEVENS, JAMES ALL 110 5TH E.D.
STEVENS, JAMES BAL 303 12TH WAR
STEVENS, JAMES ANN 348 3RD DIST
STEVENS, JAMES FRE 315 MIDDLETO
STEVENS, JAMES CAL 059 3RD DIST
STEVENS, JAMES BAL 298 20TH WAR
STEVENS, JAMES BAL 284 20TH WAR
STEVENS, JAMES BAL 384 13TH WAR
STEVENS, JAMES B. BAL 004 18TH WAR
STEVENS, JAMES M. QUE 235 4TH E DI
STEVENS, JAMES W. BAL 006 15TH WAR
STEVENS, JAMES-BLACK QUE 125 1ST E DI
STEVENS, JANE BAL 241 6TH WARD
STEVENS, JESSEE DOR 460 1ST DIST
STEVENS, JOHN QUE 202 3RD E DI
STEVENS, JOHN QUE 235 4TH E DI
STEVENS, JOHN WAS 049 2ND SUBD
STEVENS, JOHN BAL 168 1ST WARD
STEVENS, JOHN BAL 323 12TH WAR
STEVENS, JOHN BAL 067 1ST WARD
STEVENS, JOHN BAL 146 1ST WARD
STEVENS, JOHN B. TAL 085 ST MICHA
STEVENS, JOHN E. BAL 328 7TH WARD
STEVENS, JOHN E. DOR 423 1ST DIST
STEVENS, JOHN G. ALL 217 CUMBERLA
STEVENS, JOHN N. CAR 284 7TH DIST
STEVENS, JOHN S. SOM 407 DUBLIN D
STEVENS, JOHN T. BAL 109 18TH WAR
STEVENS, JOHN T. CAL 058 3RD DIST
STEVENS, JOHN W. DOR 380 1ST DIST
STEVENS, JOHN W. BAL 044 15TH WAR
STEVENS, JOSEPH BAL 005 9TH WARD
STEVENS, JOSEPH BAL 260 17TH WAR
STEVENS, JOSEPH H. BAL 385 13TH WAR
STEVENS, KESSIAH SOM 527 QUANTICO
STEVENS, LEAH BAL 376 13TH WAR
STEVENS, LEWIS CAL 051 3RD DIST
STEVENS, LINER* DOR 394 1ST DIST
STEVENS, LOUISA BAL 385 1ST DIST
STEVENS, LYDIA BAL 245 12TH WAR
STEVENS, MALACHI BAL 241 6TH WARD
STEVENS, MARGARET CAL 055 3RD DIST
STEVENS, MARIA BAL 136 18TH WAR
STEVENS, MARTHA DOR 299 1ST DIST
STEVENS, MARTHA QUE 159 2ND E DI
STEVENS, MARY BAL 249 17TH WAR
STEVENS, MARY BAL 237 17TH WAR
STEVENS, MARY CAR 145 NO TWP L
STEVENS, MARY SOM 407 DUBLIN D
STEVENS, MARY BAL 084 18TH WAR
STEVENS, MARY BAL 297 20TH WAR
STEVENS, MARY BAL 080 15TH WAR
STEVENS, MARY BAL 242 2ND WARD
STEVENS, MARY BAL 272 2ND WARD
STEVENS, MARY BAL 048 1ST WARD
STEVENS, MARY A. FRE 056 FREDERIC
STEVENS, MARY A. BAL 351 13TH WAR
STEVENS, MARY J. BAL 033 1ST WARD
STEVENS, MERRIL BAL 002 4TH WARD
STEVENS, MOSES ALL 068 5TH E.D.
STEVENS, ORLANDO WAS 039 2ND SUBD
STEVENS, PERRY BAL 113 1ST WARD
STEVENS, POLLY WOR 277 BERLIN 1
STEVENS, R. BAL 160 1ST WARD
STEVENS, RACHEL A. BAL 078 10TH WAR
STEVENS, RESIN FRE 419 8TH E DI
STEVENS, REVERDY BAL 283 2ND WARD
STEVENS, REZIN CAR 283 7TH DIST
STEVENS, RHODA BAL 371 3RD WARD
STEVENS, RHODA BAL 049 15TH WAR
STEVENS, RICHARD BAL 282 2ND WARD
STEVENS, RICHARD ANN 354 3RD DIST
STEVENS, RICHARD ANN 465 HOWARD D
STEVENS, RICHARD CAR 222 5TH DIST
STEVENS, RICHARD DOR 404 1ST DIST
STEVENS, ROBERT QUE 250 5TH E DI
STEVENS, ROBERT A. BAL 420 8TH WARD
STEVENS, ROBERT W. CAL 051 3RD DIST
STEVENS, RUBIN KEN 313 3RD DIST
STEVENS, S. BAL 134 5TH WARD
STEVENS, SALLY QUE 200 3RD E DI
STEVENS, SAMUEL S. BAL 080 15TH WAR
STEVENS, SARAH BAL 275 12TH WAR
STEVENS, SARAH E. BAL 349 3RD WARD
STEVENS, SOLOMON-BLACK QUE 194 3RD E DI
STEVENS, SOPHY ANN 355 3RD DIST
STEVENS, SUSAN BAL 133 5TH WARD
STEVENS, SUSANNA FRE 419 8TH E DI
STEVENS, THOMAS BAL 172 1ST WARD
STEVENS, THOMAS BAL 306 7TH WARD
STEVENS, THOMAS ALL 068 5TH E.D.
STEVENS, THOMAS QUE 199 3RD E DI
STEVENS, THOMAS H. SOM 397 BRINKLEY
STEVENS, UPTON H. BAL 037 4TH WARD
STEVENS, WASHINGTON BAL 325 12TH WAR
STEVENS, WILLIAM SOM 469 TRAPPE D
QUE 190 3RD E DI

STEVENS, WILLIAM BAL 155 1ST WARD
STEVENS, WILLIAM BAL 163 1ST WARD
STEVENS, WILLIAM BAL 150 1ST WARD
STEVENS, WILLIAM BAL 158 2ND DIST
STEVENS, WILLIAM BAL 169 11TH WAR
STEVENS, WILLIAM BAL 334 3RD WARD
STEVENS, WILLIAM BAL 292 3RD WARD
STEVENS, WILLIAM FRE 333 MIDDLETO
STEVENS, WILLIAM DOR 394 1ST DIST
STEVENS, WILLIAM BAL 005 18TH WAR
STEVENS, WILLIAM H. QUE 230 4TH E DI
STEVENS, WILLIAM J. QUE 227 4TH E DI
STEVENS, WILLIAM* DOR 462 1ST DIST
STEVENS.NATHAN FRE 239 NEW MARK
STEVENSON, A. BAL 114 1ST WARD
STEVENSON, ANN M.* BAL 369 3RD WARD
STEVENSON, AVARILLA BAL 165 16TH WAR
STEVENSON, BENJAMIN T.* SOM 366 BRINKLEY
STEVENSON, CATHARINE BAL 046 15TH WAR
STEVENSON, CATHARINE BAL 213 11TH WAR
STEVENSON, EASTHER BAL 351 7TH WARD
STEVENSON, EDWARD BAL 011 2ND DIST
STEVENSON, ELIZA-BLACK WOR 333 1ST E DI
STEVENSON, ELIZABETH WOR 340 1ST E DI
STEVENSON, ELIZABETH BAL 295 17TH WAR
STEVENSON, ELIZABETH FRE 447 8TH E DI
STEVENSON, ELIZABETH BAL 211 17TH WAR
STEVENSON, ELLEN BAL 123 5TH WARD
STEVENSON, EMILY BAL 043 2ND DIST
STEVENSON, ERATH BAL 119 5TH WARD
STEVENSON, FRANK WAS 263 1ST DIST
STEVENSON, GEORGE BAL 297 7TH WARD
STEVENSON, GEORGE W. BAL 167 11TH WAR
STEVENSON, HANA BAL 023 4TH WARD
STEVENSON, HANNAH BAL 046 2ND DIST
STEVENSON, HARRIET WOR 263 BERLIN 1
STEVENSON, HENRIETTA FRE 421 8TH E DI
STEVENSON, HENRY BAL 046 2ND DIST
STEVENSON, HENRY M. WOR 342 1ST E DI
STEVENSON, HESTER ANN 461 HOWARD D
STEVENSON, HETTY HAR 128 2ND DIST
STEVENSCN, HONER BAL 433 1ST DIST
STEVENSON, HUE S. WOR 300 SNOW HIL
STEVENSON, HUGH M. WOR 314 2ND E DI
STEVENSON, ISAIH-MULATTO FRE 232 BUCKEYST
STEVENSON, JACK BAL 082 18TH WAR
STEVENSON, JAMES DOR 356 3RD DIVI
STEVENSON, JAMES HAR 081 2ND DIST
STEVENSON, JAMES WOR 342 1ST E DI
STEVENSON, JAMES WAS 249 1ST DIST
STEVENSON, JAMES BAL 112 5TH WARD
STEVENSON, JAMES BAL 002 EASTERN
STEVENSON, JAMES BAL 184 2ND WARD
STEVENSON, JEMIMA CAR 234 UNION TO
STEVENSON, JOHN BAL 051 18TH WAR
STEVENSON, JOHN BAL 145 1ST WARD
STEVENSON, JOHN BAL 141 16TH WAR
STEVENSON, JOHN BAL 086 15TH WAR
STEVENSON, JOHN BAL 190 5TH DIST
STEVENSON, JOHN ALL 120 5TH E.D.
STEVENSON, JOHN WOR 341 1ST E DI
STEVENSON, JOHN B. SOM 367 BRINKLEY
STEVENSON, JOHN E. WOR 329 1ST E DI
STEVENSON, JOHN E. BAL 143 16TH WAR
STEVENSON, JOSHUA BAL 154 5TH WARD
STEVENSON, JOSHUA BAL 010 EASTERN
STEVENSON, JULIA BAL 230 17TH WAR
STEVENSON, LEMUEL WOR 322 1ST E DI
STEVENSON, LEVI-MULATTO FRE 218 BUCKEYST
STEVENSON, LOUISA BAL 062 15TH WAR
STEVENSON, MARGARET WOR 260 BERLIN 1
STEVENSON, MARY WOR 316 2ND E DI
STEVENSON, MARY SOM 366 BRINKLEY
STEVENSON, MARY ANN BAL 281 17TH WAR
STEVENSON, MINJO BAL 076 4TH WARD
STEVENSON, MOLLY WOR 342 1ST E DI
STEVENSON, MOSES SOM 407 DUBLIN D
STEVENSON, NANCY SOM 491 SALISBUR
STEVENSON, NIMROD CAR 274 7TH DIST
STEVENSCN, O.P. BAL 236 12TH WAR
STEVENSON, PLEASANT BAL 189 5TH DIST
STEVENSON, RACHEL BAL 019 4TH WARD
STEVENSON, ROBERT ALL 088 5TH E.D.
STEVENSCN, ROBERT BAL 325 3RD WARD
STEVENSON, SAMUEL ANN 418 HOWARD D
STEVENSON, SAMUEL HAR 049 1ST DIST
STEVENSON, SARAH WOR 256 1ST CENS
STEVENSON, SARAH C. CAR 382 2ND DIST
STEVENSON, SIDNEY HAR 117 2ND DIST
STEVENSON, SOLOMAN BAL 287 7TH WARD
STEVENSON, STEPHEN BAL 047 15TH WAR
STEVENSON, STEPHEN SOM 430 PRINCESS
STEVENSON, SUSAN CAR 268 WESTMINS
STEVENSON, SUSAN BAL 154 5TH WARD
STEVENSON, THOMAS BAL 005 9TH WARD
STEVENSON, THOMAS CAR 285 7TH DIST
STEVENSON, THOMAS H. FRE 445 8TH E DI
STEVENSON, THOMAS S. WOR 304 SNOW HIL
STEVENSON, TIMOTHY BAL 083 2ND DIST
STEVENSON, WESLEY BAL 284 12TH WAR
STEVENSON, WILLIAM BAL 054 9TH WARD
STEVENSON, WILLIAM ALL 106 5TH E.D.
STEVENSON, WILLIAM WOR 303 SNOW HIL
STEVENSON, WILLIAM HAR 128 2ND DIST
STEVENSON, WILLIAM BAL 148 11TH WAR
STEVENSON, WILLIAM W. BAL 161 6TH WARD
STEVENSONS, ROBERT BAL 110 2ND DIST
STEVENTON, CHARLES BAL 123 1ST WARD
STEVENY, GEORGE S.* TAL 053 EASTON D
STEVER, DANIEL BAL 111 1ST WARD
STEVER, GEORGEANN CAR 219 5TH DIST
STEVER, MARYANN BAL 375 3RD WARD
STEVER, WILLIAM CAR 244 3RD DIST
STEVESN, WILLIAM BAL 385 13TH WAR
STEVESON, JOHN WOR 304 SNOW HIL
STEVIL, JACOB BAL 327 3RD WARD
STEVINS, DANIL CAR 141 NO TWP L
STEVINS, ELIJAH CAR 128 NO TWP L
STEVINS, ELIZABETH CAR 158 NO TWP L
STEVINS, ELLEN CAR 115 NO TWP L
STEVINS, JOHN CAR 109 NO TWP L
STEVINS, JOSHUA R. CAR 108 NO TWP L
STEVINS, MARTHA CAR 156 NO TWP L
STEVINS, WILLIAM CAR 163 NO TWP L
STEVNIS, GONTY CAR 118 NO TWP L
STEWAERT, JOHN H. DOR 452 1ST DIST
STEWAR, DAVID BAL 240 1ST DIST
STEWARD, ALEXANDRIA CAR 192 4TH DIST
STEWARD, ANN BAL 458 1ST DIST
STEWARD, ANN ST 258 3RD E DI
STEWARD, ANN M. BAL 061 15TH WAR
STEWARD, AUGUSTUS BAL 413 1ST DIST
STEWARD, CECELIA E. CHA 254 MIDDLETO
STEWARD, CHARLES CHA 260 MIDDLETO
STEWARD, CHARLES BAL 134 1ST WARD
STEWARD, CHARLES QUE 161 2ND E DI
STEWARD, CHARLES-BLACK CAR 384 2ND DIST
STEWARD, EDWARD BAL 226 12TH WAR
STEWARD, EMANUEL BAL 244 1ST DIST
STEWARD, GEORGE BAL 420 1ST DIST
STEWARD, GEORGE BAL 168 1ST WARD
STEWARD, GEORGEANNA CHA 218 ALLENS F
STEWARD, HANDSON CHA 235 HILLTOP
STEWARD, HENRY ALL 069 5TH E.D.
STEWARD, J. BAL 149 1ST WARD
STEWARD, J.G. BAL 174 1ST WARD
STEWARD, JAMES ALL 103 5TH E.D.
STEWARD, JANE CAR 232 5TH DIST
STEWARD, JOHN ALL 069 5TH E.D.
STEWARD, JOHN BAL 108 2ND DIST
STEWARD, JOHN P. ALL 069 5TH E.D.
STEWARD, JOSEPH ALL 233 CUMBERLA
STEWARD, KATE BAL 209 19TH WAR
STEWARD, M. BAL 137 1ST WARD
STEWARD, MARGARET CEC 098 3RD E DI
STEWARD, MARTHA BAL 370 1ST DIST
STEWARD, MARY CHA 292 BOJANTOW
STEWARD, MARY A. ST 275 3RD E DI
STEWARD, MARY-BLACK QUE 125 1ST E DI
STEWARD, RHEUBEN BAL 405 1ST DIST
STEWARD, RHUBEN BAL 260 1ST DIST
STEWARD, RICHARD BAL 159 1ST WARD
STEWARD, ROBERT BAL 449 1ST DIST
STEWARD, SAMUEL R. ST 295 2ND E DI
STEWARD, SARAH BAL 366 1ST DIST
STEWARD, SUSAN CHA 217 ALLENS F
STEWARD, WILLIAM BAL 133 1ST WARD
STEWARD, WILLIAM KEN 290 3RD DIST
STEWARD, WILLIAM ST 275 3RD E DI
STEWARD, WILLIAM H. ALL 069 5TH E.D.
STEWART, A.A. ANN 281 ANNAPOLI
STEWART, ADALINE BAL 046 4TH WARD
STEWART, ADAM PRI 090 MARLBROU
STEWART, AGNES BAL 054 4TH WARD
STEWART, AGNES BAL 343 13TH WAR
STEWART, ALECE TAL 025 EASTON D
STEWART, ALEXANDER CAR 149 NO TWP L
STEWART, ALEXANDER BAL 099 2ND DIST
STEWART, ALEXANDER BAL 440 8TH WARD
STEWART, ALFRED HAR 101 2ND DIST
STEWART, AMANDA BAL 119 11TH WAR
STEWART, AMANDA SOM 472 TRAPPE D
STEWART, AMELIA ANN 314 1ST DIST
STEWART, AMELIA M. CHA 262 MIDDLETO
STEWART, ANDREW CEC 007 ELKTON 3
STEWART, ANN BAL 293 20TH WAR
STEWART, ANN BAL 272 20TH WAR
STEWART, ANN FRE 214 BUCKEYST
STEWART, ANN BAL 166 19TH WAR
STEWART, ANN BAL 426 8TH WARD
STEWART, ANN BAL 234 2ND WARD
STEWART, ANN BAL 391 8TH WARD
STEWART, ANN BAL 182 2ND WARD
STEWART, ANN BAL 301 12TH WAR
STEWART, ANN E. BAL 337 1ST DIST
STEWART, ANN M. DOR 376 1ST DIST
STEWART, ANNA SOM 421 PRINCESS
STEWART, ANNE ANN 294 1ST DIST
STEWART, ARCHIBALD BAL 353 7TH WARD
STEWART, ARCHIBALD FRE 323 MIDDLETO
STEWART, BEN PRI 079 QUEEN AN
STEWART, BENJAIMN CAL 010 1ST DIST
STEWART, BENJAMIN FRE 274 NEW MARK
STEWART, BENJAMIN FRE 223 BUCKEYST
STEWART, BENJAMIN BAL 241 6TH WARD
STEWART, BENJAMIN E. PRI 058 NOTTINGH
STEWART, BETSEY BAL 139 11TH WAR
STEWART, C. BAL 319 12TH WAR
STEWART, CALEB ANN 350 3RD DIST
STEWART, CAROLINE WAS 169 FUNKSTOW
STEWART, CAROLINE-BLACK ST 325 4TH E DI
STEWART, CATH BAL 148 2ND DIST
STEWART, CATHARINE BAL 049 2ND DIST
STEWART, CHALES BAL 055 2ND DIST
STEWART, CHARLES ANN 351 3RD DIST
STEWART, CHARLES BAL 124 16TH WAR
STEWART, CHARLES BAL 102 10TH WAR
STEWART, CHARLES BAL 221 12TH WAR
STEWART, CHARLES BAL 459 8TH WARD
STEWART, CHARLES BAL 040 15TH WAR
STEWART, CHARLES ANN 312 1ST DIST
STEWART, CHARLES BAL 395 8TH WARD
STEWART, CHARLES BAL 269 7TH WARD
STEWART, CHARLES WAS 179 BOONSBOR
STEWART, CHARLES BAL 162 19TH WAR
STEWART, CHARLES FRE 317 MIDDLETO
STEWART, CHARLES BAL 303 20TH WAR
STEWART, CHARLES BAL 263 20TH WAR
STEWART, CHARLES BAL 178 19TH WAR
STEWART, CHARLES A. BAL 363 3RD WARD
STEWART, CHARLES C. ANN 308 1ST DIST
STEWART, CHARLES H. TAL 068 EASTON T
STEWART, CHARLES J. BAL 080 4TH WARD
STEWART, CHARLES R. TAL 005 EASTON D
STEWART, CHARLES R. ANN 449 HOWARD D
STEWART, CHARLES S. DOR 424 1ST DIST
STEWART, COMFORT WAS 150 HAGERSTO
STEWART, D. L. BAL 471 14TH WAR
STEWART, DANIEL R. CAR 096 NO TWP L
STEWART, DAVID BAL 082 4TH WARD
STEWART, DAVID BAL 230 19TH WAR
STEWART, DAVID WAS 009 WILLIAMS
STEWART, DAVID ANN 415 HOWARD D
STEWART, DAVID BAL 320 12TH WAR
STEWART, DAVID BAL 179 6TH WARD
STEWART, DAVID B. KEN 282 3RD DIST
STEWART, DAVID JR. BAL 468 14TH WAR
STEWART, DONALDSON ALL 127 4TH E.D.
STEWART, DORSEY ANN 341 3RD DIST
STEWART, E. ANN 344 3RD DIST
STEWART, EBENEZER BAL 175 16TH WAR
STEWART, EBENEZER C. BAL 172 16TH WAR
STEWART, EDWARD ANN 471 HOWARD D
STEWART, EDWARD ANN 325 2ND DIST
STEWART, EDWARD TAL 068 EASTON T
STEWART, EDWARD H. ANN 318 2ND DIST
STEWART, EDWARD H. BAL 002 15TH WAR
STEWART, ELEANER CHA 294 BOJANTOW
STEWART, ELEANOR BAL 349 13TH WAR
STEWART, ELIJAH BAL 257 20TH WAR
STEWART, ELIJAH HAR 115 2ND DIST
STEWART, ELIJAH HAR 116 2ND DIST
STEWART, ELIRA A. BAL 295 3RD WARD
STEWART, ELIZA BAL 068 15TH WAR
STEWART, ELIZA ANN 275 ANNAPOLI
STEWART, ELIZA BAL 167 2ND DIST
STEWART, ELIZA BAL 024 1ST WARD
STEWART, ELIZA BAL 448 14TH WAR
STEWART, ELIZA BAL 389 13TH WAR
STEWART, ELIZA WAS 154 HAGERSTO
STEWART, ELIZA A. PRI 091 MARLBROU
STEWART, ELIZA JANE BAL 176 2ND WARD
STEWART, ELIZABETH BAL 182 2ND WARD
STEWART, ELIZABETH BAL 041 15TH WAR
STEWART, ELIZABETH BAL 051 2ND DIST
STEWART, ELIZABETH BAL 144 16TH WAR
STEWART, ELIZABETH TAL 053 EASTON D
STEWART, ELIZABETH KEN 311 3RD DIST
STEWART, ELIZANN BAL 224 17TH WAR
STEWART, ELLEN BAL 374 13TH WAR
STEWART, ELLEN SOM 434 PRINCESS
STEWART, ELLENOR BAL 091 5TH WARD
STEWART, EMELINE MGM 325 CRACKLIN
STEWART, EPHRAIM BAL 049 15TH WAR
STEWART, EVERLINE H.-BLAC FRE 228 BUCKEYST
STEWART, FINLEY HAR 044 1ST DIST
STEWART, FRANCIS R. BAL 349 13TH WAR
STEWART, FREDERICK BAL 131 11TH WAR
STEWART, FREDERICK ANN 409 8TH DIST
STEWART, GEORGE BAL 028 15TH WAR
STEWART, GEORGE BAL 039 15TH WAR
STEWART, GEORGE BAL 010 15TH WAR
STEWART, GEORGE BAL 116 15TH WAR
STEWART, GEORGE BAL 001 EASTERN
STEWART, GEORGE BAL 242 6TH WARD
STEWART, GEORGE BAL 075 4TH WARD
STEWART, GEORGE CAR 336 6TH DIST
STEWART, GEORGE * BAL 149 2ND DIST
STEWART, GEORGE B. ANN 299 1ST DIST
STEWART, GEORGE F. BAL 132 11TH WAR
STEWART, GEORGIANNA BAL 096 5TH WARD
STEWART, HAMILTON WAS 067 2ND SUBD
STEWART, HANNA BAL 140 2ND DIST
STEWART, HANNAH BAL 229 12TH WAR
STEWART, HANNAH A. CEC 086 4TH E DI
STEWART, HARRIET BAL 305 3RD WARD
STEWART, HARRIOTT BAL 332 3RD WARD
STEWART, HARRIS W. ALL 229 CUMBERLA
STEWART, HENRIETTA BAL 245 17TH WAR
STEWART, HENRITTA ANN 291 ANNAPOLI
STEWART, HENRY BAL 175 2ND WARD
STEWART, HENRY BAL 395 14TH WAR
STEWART, HENRY TAL 040 EASTON D
STEWART, HENRY H. BAL 330 13TH WAR
STEWART, HENRY-BLACK FRE 017 FREDERIC
STEWART, HESTER BAL 347 7TH WARD
STEWART, HETTY BAL 310 20TH WAR
STEWART, IGNETIUS FRE 274 NEW MARK
STEWART, ISAAC SOM 425 PRINCESS
STEWART, ISAAC BAL 078 10TH WAR
STEWART, ISAAC ANN 310 1ST DIST
STEWART, ISABELLA BAL 011 9TH WARD
STEWART, ISABELLA PRI 021 VANSVILL
STEWART, J.N. WAS 021 2ND SUBD
STEWART, JAMES WAS 282 1ST DIST
STEWART, JAMES SOM 472 TRAPPE D
STEWART, JAMES PRI 090 MARLBROU
STEWART, JAMES BAL 459 8TH WARD
STEWART, JAMES BAL 018 15TH WAR
STEWART, JAMES ANN 328 2ND DIST
STEWART, JAMES BAL 139 16TH WAR
STEWART, JAMES BAL 158 1ST WARD
STEWART, JAMES BAL 212 6TH WARD
STEWART, JAMES BAL 040 2ND DIST
STEWART, JAMES BAL 332 3RD WARD
STEWART, JAMES BAL 383 8TH WARD
STEWART, JAMES BAL 248 20TH WAR
STEWART, JAMES BAL 473 14TH WAR
STEWART, JAMES BAL 051 4TH WARD
STEWART, JAMES H. BAL 383 3RD WARD
STEWART, JAMES M. BAL 345 7TH WARD
STEWART, JAMES R. DOR 324 1ST DIST
STEWART, JAMES V. D. BAL 057 15TH WAR
STEWART, JANE BAL 453 14TH WAR
STEWART, JANE BAL 144 11TH WAR
STEWART, JANE R. BAL 121 16TH WAR
STEWART, JOEL BAL 184 5TH DIST
STEWART, JOHN BAL 356 3RD WARD
STEWART, JOHN BAL 361 3RD WARD
STEWART, JOHN BAL 116 15TH WAR
STEWART, JOHN BAL 135 16TH WAR
STEWART, JOHN BAL 066 10TH WAR
STEWART, JOHN BAL 073 10TH WAR
STEWART, JOHN BAL 329 7TH WARD
STEWART, JOHN BAL 081 15TH WAR
STEWART, JOHN BAL 345 7TH WARD
STEWART, JOHN BAL 351 7TH WARD
STEWART, JOHN BAL 228 12TH WAR
STEWART, JOHN BAL 398 8TH WARD
STEWART, JOHN BAL 281 7TH WARD
STEWART, JOHN BAL 364 8TH WARD
STEWART, JOHN ANN 352 3RD DIST
STEWART, JOHN ANN 452 HOWARD D
STEWART, JOHN BAL 207 2ND WARD
STEWART, JOHN ANN 326 2ND DIST
STEWART, JOHN ANN 272 ANNAPOLI
STEWART, JOHN ALL 134 4TH E.D.
STEWART, JOHN ALL 110 5TH E.D.
STEWART, JOHN BAL 266 20TH WAR
STEWART, JOHN FRE 384 PETERSVI
STEWART, JOHN BAL 050 4TH WARD
STEWART, JOHN MGM 381 ROCKERLE
STEWART, JOHN SOM 409 DUBLIN D
STEWART, JOHN FRE 274 NEW MARK
STEWART, JOHN DOR 416 1ST DIST
STEWART, JOHN MGM 351 BERRYS D
STEWART, JOHN FRE 183 5TH E DI
STEWART, JOHN BAL 222 19TH WAR
STEWART, JOHN PRI 046 AQUASCO
STEWART, JOHN DOR 452 1ST DIST
STEWART, JOHN TAL 060 EASTON D
STEWART, JOHN WAS 169 FUNKSTOW
STEWART, JOHN B. KEN 311 3RD DIST
STEWART, JOHN G. ALL 153 6TH E.D.
STEWART, JOHN H. ANN 290 ANNAPOLI
STEWART, JOHN H. ANN 520 HOWARD D
STEWART, JOHN H. BAL 037 4TH WARD
STEWART, JOHN H. SOM 425 PRINCESS
STEWART, JOHN N. ANN 319 2ND DIST
STEWART, JOHN R. BAL 100 1ST WARD

STEWART, JOHN S. FRE 185 5TH E DI
STEWART, JOHN S. TAL 017 EASTON D
STEWART, JOHN T. DOR 386 1ST DIST
STEWART, JOHN-BLACK BAL 218 2ND WARD
STEWART, JONATHAN ANN 491 HOWARD D
STEWART, JOSEPH BAL 089 1ST WARD
STEWART, JOSEPH ALL 053 10TH E.D
STEWART, JOSEPH BAL 125 16TH WAR
STEWART, JOSEPH FRE 173 5TH E DI
STEWART, JOSEPH CAR 089 NO TWP L
STEWART, JOSEPH B. BAL 175 16TH WAR
STEWART, JOSEPH J. BAL 210 6TH WARD
STEWART, JOSEPH R. DOR 407 1ST DIST
STEWART, JOSEPH W. BAL 181 6TH WARD
STEWART, JOSHUA ANN 339 3RD DIST
STEWART, JOSHUA ANN 341 3RD DIST
STEWART, JOSHUA MGM 323 CRACKLIN
STEWART, JUDSON ANN 273 ANNAPOLI
STEWART, JUDY DOR 464 1ST DIST
STEWART, JULIA BAL 098 2ND DIST
STEWART, KITTY ANN 360 3RD DIST
STEWART, LEAH SOM 427 PRINCESS
STEWART, LEANDER WAS 181 BOONSBOR
STEWART, LEMUEL BAL 223 19TH WAR
STEWART, LEMUEL ANN 397 8TH DIST
STEWART, LESLIE M. ANN 327 2ND DIST
STEWART, LETITIA * BAL 374 13TH WAR
STEWART, LEVIN DOR 345 3RD DIVI
STEWART, LEWIS BAL 408 8TH WARD
STEWART, LIONESS* BAL 361 3RD WARD
STEWART, LITTLETON DOR 464 1ST DIST
STEWART, LLOYD BAL 240 20TH WAR
STEWART, LOUIS A.* DOR 379 1ST DIST
STEWART, LUCY PRI 066 NOTTINGH
STEWART, LUCY A. BAL 131 16TH WAR
STEWART, LUTHER HAR 161 3RD DIST
STEWART, LVAINA ALL 153 6TH E.D.
STEWART, LYDIA BAL 119 15TH WAR
STEWART, MAHLOA-BLACK FRE 241 NEW MARK
STEWART, MARGARET BAL 444 8TH WARD
STEWART, MARGARET SOM 483 TRAPP DI
STEWART, MARIA BAL 359 8TH WARD
STEWART, MARIA DOR 383 1ST DIST
STEWART, MARIAH TAL 077 EASTON T
STEWART, MARINE BAL 147 16TH WAR
STEWART, MARTHA BAL 365 8TH WARD
STEWART, MARTHA D. BAL 003 15TH WAR
STEWART, MARY BAL 187 11TH WAR
STEWART, MARY BAL 375 8TH WARD
STEWART, MARY BAL 403 8TH WARD
STEWART, MARY BAL 289 12TH WAR
STEWART, MARY BAL 068 10TH WAR
STEWART, MARY ANN 405 8TH DIST
STEWART, MARY BAL 365 3RD WARD
STEWART, MARY BAL 218 2ND WARD
STEWART, MARY PRI 079 QUEEN AN
STEWART, MARY KEN 287 3RD DIST
STEWART, MARY WAS 273 RIDGEVIL
STEWART, MARY BAL 082 4TH WARD
STEWART, MARY BAL 066 18TH WAR
STEWART, MARY A. TAL 065 EASTON T
STEWART, MARY E. BAL 107 18TH WAR
STEWART, MARY J. BAL 375 13TH WAR
STEWART, MARY J. BAL 130 11TH WAR
STEWART, MARY-BLACK FRE 017 FREDERIC
STEWART, MARY-BLACK FRE 039 FREDERIC
STEWART, METELDA BAL 116 18TH WAR
STEWART, MICHAEL A. BAL 134 11TH WAR
STEWART, MIRAN* DOR 378 1ST DIST
STEWART, MISS- ANN 296 1ST DIST
STEWART, MORDICA BAL 316 7TH WARD
STEWART, NACE PRI 066 NOTTINGH
STEWART, NELLY G. H. SOM 424 PRINCESS
STEWART, NELSON ALL 112 5TH E.D.
STEWART, NICHOLAS ANN 314 1ST DIST
STEWART, PERRY W. TAL 065 EASTON T
STEWART, PERRY W. JR. TAL 062 EASTON D
STEWART, PETER BAL 350 7TH WARD
STEWART, PHEBE BAL 142 2ND DIST
STEWART, PHILIP ANN 356 3RD DIST
STEWART, PHILLIS QUE 204 3RD E DI
STEWART, PLOWMAN, JANTHE CAR 387 2ND DIST
STEWART, PRISSY DOR 440 1ST DIST
STEWART, RACHAEL KEN 270 1ST DIST
STEWART, RACHEL BAL 311 12TH WAR
STEWART, REBECCA ANN 317 1ST DIST
STEWART, REBECCA KEN 272 1ST DIST
STEWART, REZIN BAL 251 20TH WAR
STEWART, RICHAEL ANN 275 ANNAPOLI
STEWART, RICHARD A. BAL 106 10TH WAR
STEWART, RICHARD A. BAL 123 1ST WARD
STEWART, RICHARD B. BAL 147 16TH WAR
STEWART, RICHARD F. DOR 379 1ST DIST
STEWART, ROBERT BAL 047 4TH WARD
STEWART, ROBERT HAR 124 2ND DIST
STEWART, ROBERT CAR 164 NO TWP L
STEWART, ROBERT BAL 329 7TH WARD
STEWART, ROBERT ANN 329 2ND DIST
STEWART, ROBERT BAL 187 6TH WARD
STEWART, ROBERT BAL 222 6TH WARD
STEWART, ROBERT BAL 335 1ST DIST
STEWART, ROBERT H. PRI 107 PISCATAW
STEWART, SALLY BAL 095 15TH WAR
STEWART, SAMUEL ANN 278 ANNAPOLI
STEWART, SAMUEL ANN 376 4TH DIST
STEWART, SAMUEL BAL 004 EASTERN
STEWART, SAMUEL BAL 285 2ND WARD
STEWART, SAMUEL TAL 095 ST MICHA
STEWART, SARAH BAL 135 2ND DIST
STEWART, SARAH BAL 374 8TH WARD
STEWART, SARAH BAL 346 13TH WAR
STEWART, SARAH A. BAL 154 16TH WAR
STEWART, SARHA A. TAL 077 EASTON T
STEWART, SOLOMON BAL 154 2ND DIST
STEWART, SOPHIA J. CAL 013 1ST DIST
STEWART, STEPHEN CEC 007 ELKTON 3
STEWART, SUSAN FRE 228 BUCKEYST
STEWART, SUSAN BAL 185 5TH DIST
STEWART, SUSAN BAL 280 12TH WAR
STEWART, SUSAN L. DOR 466 1ST DIST
STEWART, SUSAN-BLACK FRE 434 8TH E DI
STEWART, THOMAS DOR 349 3RD DIVI
STEWART, THOMAS DOR 423 1ST DIST
STEWART, THOMAS BAL 043 4TH WARD
STEWART, THOMAS KEN 311 3RD DIST
STEWART, THOMAS KEN 313 3RD DIST
STEWART, THOMAS KEN 268 1ST DIST
STEWART, THOMAS WAS 031 2ND SUBD
STEWART, THOMAS J. DOR 423 1ST DIST
STEWART, THOMAS R. CAR 147 NO TWP L
STEWART, THORNTON-MULATTO FRE 228 BUCKEYST
STEWART, WASH KEN 257 1ST DIST
STEWART, WASHINGTON BAL 245 17TH WAR
STEWART, WILLIAM BAL 277 17TH WAR
STEWART, WILLIAM FRE 224 BUCKEYST
STEWART, WILLIAM CAR 121 NO TWP L
STEWART, WILLIAM CAR 102 NO TWP L
STEWART, WILLIAM BAL 210 19TH WAR
STEWART, WILLIAM HAR 131 2ND DIST
STEWART, WILLIAM MGM 329 CRACKLIN
STEWART, WILLIAM BAL 067 18TH WAR
STEWART, WILLIAM BAL 030 18TH WAR
STEWART, WILLIAM HAR 034 1ST DIST
STEWART, WILLIAM HAR 047 1ST DIST
STEWART, WILLIAM HAR 085 2ND DIST
STEWART, WILLIAM WAS 016 2ND SUBD
STEWART, WILLIAM WAS 011 WILLIAMS
STEWART, WILLIAM WAS 272 RIDGEVIL
STEWART, WILLIAM SOM 548 TYASKIN
STEWART, WILLIAM WAS 135 HAGERSTO
STEWART, WILLIAM SOM 531 QUANTICO
STEWART, WILLIAM BAL 168 2ND DIST
STEWART, WILLIAM BAL 356 3RD WARD
STEWART, WILLIAM BAL 356 3RD WARD
STEWART, WILLIAM BAL 393 8TH WARD
STEWART, WILLIAM BAL 399 3RD WARD
STEWART, WILLIAM BAL 306 7TH WARD
STEWART, WILLIAM ANN 470 HOWARD D
STEWART, WILLIAM ANN 422 HOWARD D
STEWART, WILLIAM BAL 003 15TH WAR
STEWART, WILLIAM BAL 008 9TH WARD
STEWART, WILLIAM BAL 460 8TH WARD
STEWART, WILLIAM ANN 314 1ST DIST
STEWART, WILLIAM BAL 202 6TH WARD
STEWART, WILLIAM B. BAL 202 6TH WARD
STEWART, WILLIAM H. BAL 235 12TH WAR
STEWART, WILLIAM H. BAL 067 15TH WAR
STEWART, WILLIAM H. ANN 356 3RD DIST
STEWART, WILLIAM H. BAL 100 18TH WAR
STEWART, WILLIAM H. BAL 064 4TH WARD
STEWART, WILLIAM H. BAL 082 4TH WARD
STEWART, WILLIAM J. BAL 049 4TH WARD
STEWART, WILLIAM J. BAL 349 13TH WAR
STEWART, WILLIAM R. BAL 155 11TH WAR
STEWART, WILLIAM S. BAL 175 2ND WARD
STEWART, WILLIAM S. BAL 187 16TH WAR
STEWART, WILLIM WAS 007 WILLIAMS
STEWART,E DWARD-BLACK ST 325 4TH E DI
STEWEL, GUSTAV BAL 209 11TH WAR
STEWERT, ASBURY DOR 377 1ST DIST
STEWRAT, ALICE A. PRI 058 NOTTINGH
STEWRAT, C.G. WAS 021 2ND SUBD
STEYER, HENRY BAL 293 3RD WARD
STEYNSEN, THOMAS B. * KEN 210 2ND DIST
STHALE, H. ROSEN BAL 117 11TH WAR
STHEELER, HENRY * BAL 048 18TH WAR
STHUNAN, CHARLES BAL 092 10TH WAR
STIBEL, ALFORD BAL 078 18TH WAR
STICHTENCTH, WILLIAM BAL 146 16TH WAR
STICK, ABEDNEGO CAR 317 1ST DIST
STICK, CHARLES BAL 343 7TH WARD
STICK, MARTHA BAL 207 19TH WAR
STICK, PAUL CAR 351 6TH DIST
STICK, WILLIAMS BAL 208 19TH WAR
STICKEL, DUBRICK BAL 461 1ST DIST
STICKEL, H.R. WAS 002 WILLIAMS
STICKEL, SUSAN WAS 003 WILLIAMS
STICKEL, WILLIAM WAS 002 WILLIAMS
STICKER, CHRISTIAN BAL 273 2ND WARD
STICKET, WILLIAM BAL 354 1ST DIST
STICKHAILS, F. BAL 224 19TH WAR
STICKLE, CARLINE FRE 031 FREDERIC
STICKLE, GEORGE FRE 075 FREDERIC
STICKLE, MARY E. FRE 042 FREDERIC
STICKLE, THERESA FRE 007 FREDERIC
STICKLER, DAVID BAL 385 8TH WARD
STICKLETS, CONRAD BAL 256 2ND WARD
STICKLEY, ANTONIUS BAL 061 4TH WARD
STICKMAN, MARY * BAL 220 6TH WARD
STICKNELL, CHARLES BAL 212 2ND WARD
STICKNEY, HENRY BAL 140 5TH WARD
STICKNEY, J. H. BAL 108 10TH WAR
STICKNEY, PETER BAL 013 4TH WARD
STICKS, WILLIAM CAR 095 NO TWP L
STIDHAM, CORNELIUS CEC 153 PORT DUP
STIDHAM, JOHN BAL 335 13TH WAR
STIDHAM, WILLIAM CEC 105 3RD E DI
STIEF, C. A. BAL 082 10TH WAR
STIEFEL, JULIUS BAL 015 9TH WARD
STIEN, JOSEPH WAS 191 1ST DIST
STIER, FREDERICK BAL 272 2ND WARD
STIER, HAMILTON FRE 238 NEW MARK
STIER, MARGRET BAL 066 1ST WARD
STIER, MARY S. FRE 238 NEW MARK
STIERKWELL, MARGARET BAL 370 8TH WARD
STIES, HESTON ANN* BAL 096 5TH WARD
STIFF, JOSEPHINE BAL 012 9TH WARD
STIFFEY, SAMUEL BAL 331 7TH WARD
STIFFLER, JACOB BAL 436 1ST DIST
STIFFLER, JOHN BAL 436 1ST DIST
STIFFLER, JOHN BAL 436 1ST DIST
STIFFLER, JOHN N. BAL 436 1ST DIST
STIFFY, DAVID BAL 228 12TH WAR
STIFLER, GEORGE BAL 435 1ST DIST
STIFLER, GEORGE WAS 041 2ND SUBD
STIFLER, HARMA WAS 041 2ND SUBD
STIFLER, HY BAL 211 6TH DIST
STIFLER, L. WAS 019 2ND SUBD
STIFLER, PETER BAL 434 1ST DIST
STIFLER, SARAH BAL 056 2ND DIST
STIGER, BALTUS WAS 155 2ND DIST
STIKER, JOHN BAL 401 8TH WARD
STIKLER, JACOB BAL 209 17TH WAR
STIL, CASANDER HAR 178 3RD DIST
STILE, C. BAL 273 20TH WAR
STILELEY, SOLOMON CAR 325 1ST DIST
STILELY, SUSAN FRE 288 WOODSBOR
STILES, ABRAM DOR 438 1ST DIST
STILES, ABRAM DOR 389 1ST DIST
STILES, AHAM DOR 428 1ST DIST
STILES, ARY BAL 231 17TH WAR
STILES, C. BAL 150 1ST WARD
STILES, CHARLES MGM 388 ROCKERLE
STILES, GEORGE DOR 438 1ST DIST
STILES, HARY DOR 429 1ST DIST
STILES, HENRY CEC 192 5TH E DI
STILES, JOHN BAL 240 12TH WAR
STILES, JONATHAN DOR 414 1ST DIST
STILES, MARGARET BAL 321 3RD WARD
STILES, MARIA DOR 433 1ST DIST
STILES, MARTHA TAL 067 EASTON T
STILES, MARY MGM 388 ROCKERLE
STILES, MARY A. DOR 450 1ST DIST
STILES, MARY K. MGM 426 MEDLEY 3
STILES, RICH BAL 355 1ST DIST
STILES, RICHARD ALL 184 9TH E.D.
STILES, SARAH E. BAL 380 1ST DIST
STILES, WILLIAM BAL 101 10TH WAR
STILL, SARAH E. BAL 210 2ND WARD
STILLARDS, MARIA HAR 202 3RD DIST
STILLEY, ANDREW BAL 324 3RD WARD
STILLMAN, JOHN BAL 194 11TH WAR
STILLS, AUGUSTUS BAL 459 8TH WARD
STILLWAGER, ERNEST BAL 086 1ST WARD
STILLWELL, SARAH ALL 209 CUMBERLA
STILLWELL, WILLIAM WAS 159 2ND DIST
STILMAN, JOSEPH B. BAL 397 8TH WARD
STILSIG, EGNALL BAL 147 11TH WAR
STILTZ, JARED BAL 021 2ND DIST
STIM, JOSEPH BAL 205 19TH WAR
STIMEL, SUSAN FRE 416 8TH E DI
STIMEPHLER, JACOBS BAL 221 2ND WARD
STIMMEL, EDWARD H. FRE 283 WOODSBOR
STIMMELL, DAVID FRE 117 CREAGERS
STIMMELL, ELIZABETH FRE 020 FREDERIC
STIMMELL, FREDERICK FRE 225 BUCKEYST
STIMMELL, HENRY FRE 139 CREAGERS
STIMMELL, JACOB FRE 178 5TH E DI
STIMMELL, JOSEPH FRE 226 BUCKEYST
STIMMELL, MITILDA FRE 085 FREDERIC
STIMNEL, JOHN B. FRE 294 WOODSBOR
STIMP, CASPAR BAL 464 14TH WAR
STIMPSON, ANN E. BAL 369 3RD WARD
STIMPSON, JAMES BAL 129 1ST WARD
STIMPSON, JAMES BAL 012 18TH WAR
STINAMENS, JAMES BAL 463 1ST DIST
STINCAMP, JOHN BAL 206 2ND WARD
STINCECUM, PHILIP BAL 288 1ST DIST
STINCHBOMB, NOAH BAL 205 17TH WAR
STINCHCOM, THOMAS HAR 204 3RD DIST
STINCHCOMB, ALFRED ANN 355 3RD DIST
STINCHCOMB, CHARLES ANN 385 4TH DIST
STINCHCOMB, ELIZABETH ANN 518 HOWARD D
STINCHCOMB, GEORGE ANN 469 HOWARD D
STINCHCOMB, JANE BAL 116 11TH WAR
STINCHCOMB, JOHN BAL 036 18TH WAR
STINCHCOMB, JOHN ANN 384 4TH DIST
STINCHCOMB, JOHN BAL 131 1ST WARD
STINCHCOMB, JOHN BAL 030 15TH WAR
STINCHCOMB, JOSHUA BAL 114 15TH WAR
STINCHCOMB, LEVI BAL 035 18TH WAR
STINCHCOMB, NELSON ANN 343 3RD DIST
STINCHCOMB, SARAH ANN 348 3RD DIST
STINCHCOMB, SUSANNAH BAL 119 15TH WAR
STINCHCOMB, THOMAS BAL 011 9TH WARD
STINCHCOMB, THOMAS W. ANN 356 3RD DIST
STINCHCOMB, WILLIAM ANN 355 3RD DIST
STINCHCOMB, WILLIAM T. ANN 352 3RD DIST
STINCHCUMB, SUSAN BAL 282 20TH WAR
STINCHECUM, BEAL BAL 376 1ST DIST
STINCHECUM, JOHN BAL 384 1ST DIST
STINCHECUM, MAGDALINE BAL 376 1ST DIST
STINCHICUM, ALEXANDER BAL 384 1ST DIST
STINCHOMB, A. O. BAL 031 18TH WAR
STINCICUM, CATHARINE BAL 296 1ST DIST
STINCUMB, JAMES BAL 117 5TH WARD
STINCYCUM, ABSALUM BAL 335 1ST DIST
STINCYCUM, AIRA BAL 349 1ST DIST
STINCYCUM, BELILA BAL 301 1ST DIST
STINCYCUM, CALIB BAL 390 1ST DIST
STINCYCUM, JOHN BAL 309 1ST DIST
STINCYCUM, RUTH BAL 387 1ST DIST
STINCYCUM, WESLEY BAL 374 1ST DIST
STINCYCUMB, CHARLES BAL 309 1ST DIST
STINDAY, GEORGE BAL 299 12TH WAR
STINDICCMB, JOSHUA ANN 423 HOWARD D
STINE, ALEXANDER WAS 143 2ND DIST
STINE, CHRISTIAN BAL 180 19TH WAR
STINE, ELIZA BAL 297 12TH WAR
STINE, GEORGE BAL 454 8TH WARD
STINE, GEORGE HAR 012 1ST DIST
STINE, HARRIET FRE 406 JEFFERSO
STINE, HULDA FRE 391 PETERSVI
STINE, JACOB WAS 082 2ND SUBD
STINE, JOHN WAS 081 2ND SUBD
STINE, JOHN WAS 153 2ND DIST
STINE, JOHN WAS 125 2ND DIST
STINE, JOHN WAS 125 2ND DIST
STINE, JOHN HAR 011 1ST DIST
STINE, JOHN HAR 064 1ST DIST
STINE, JOHN BAL 331 1ST DIST
STINE, JOHN C. BAL 238 20TH WAR
STINE, MARGARETT FRE 447 8TH E DI
STINE, MARIAH WAS 089 2ND SUBD
STINE, MARY BAL 286 20TH WAR
STINE, NANCY WAS 198 1ST DIST
STINE, NICKOLAS WAS 080 2ND SUBD
STINE, PETER BAL 210 11TH WAR
STINE, PHILEMON BAL 220 19TH WAR
STINE, PHILIP FRE 404 JEFFERSO
STINE, PHILIP BAL 322 1ST DIST
STINE, SAMUEL ALL 252 CUMBERLA
STINE, SOPHIA BAL 459 1ST DIST
STINE,JOSEPH BAL 053 1ST WARD
STINEACKER, GODFRED BAL 313 1ST DIST
STINEBAUGH, STEPHEN ALL 197 CUMBERLA
STINEBETS, JOHN WAS 162 HAGERSTO
STINECUM, HENRY ALL 228 CUMBERLA
STINEEKE, HENRY A. DR. BAL 333 13TH WAR
STINEHART, CAROLINE BAL 387 8TH WARD
STINEHOFFER, CHARLES BAL 181 11TH WAR
STINEMAN, OLRICH ALL 243 CUMBERLA
STINEMETZ, SOLOMAN WAS 101 2ND DIST
STINEMYER, JOHN BAL 414 8TH WARD
STINEMYER, MARY L. D. BAL 414 8TH WARD
STINER, ANDREW ALL 224 CUMBERLA
STINER, DANIEL CAR 387 2ND DIST
STINER, ELIZABETH BAL 429 14TH WAR
STINER, GENET BAL 407 1ST DIST
STINER, HENRY FRE 306 WOODSBOR
STINER, JOHN BAL 359 1ST DIST
STINER, JOSHUA ALL 245 CUMBERLA
STINER, SARHA BAL 460 14TH WAR
STINER, SOCRATE BAL 225 12TH WAR
STINES, BENJAMIN BAL 429 14TH WAR
STINETT, S. BAL 060 10TH WAR
STING, GEORGE BAL 199 2ND WARD
STING, JOHN * BAL 287 1ST DIST
STINGER, CHRISTOPHER BAL 193 2ND WARD
STINGER, DANIEL FRE 346 MIDDLETO

Name	County	Page	Locality
STINGER, ELIZABETH	WAS	210	1ST DIST
STINGER, GEORGE	BAL	018	4TH WARD
STINGER, JEREMIAH	FRE	345	MIDDLETO
STINGER, JONAS	FRE	315	MIDDLETO
STINGER, MARTIN	FRE	346	MIDDLETO
STINGER, SAMUEL	WAS	173	FUNKSTOW
STINGER, STEVEN	FRE	320	MIDDLETO
STINGER, WILLIAM	FRE	337	MIDDLETO
STINGH, FREDERICK	BAL	199	2ND WARD
STINGLE, GOTLIEB	BAL	101	2ND DIST
STINGLE, MARK	HAR	074	1ST DIST
STINGLIFF, HARTMAN	BAL	126	11TH WAR
STINGLIFF, JESSE	BAL	263	1ST DIST
STINK, JOHN	BAL	451	1ST DIST
STINKEIM, HENRY	BAL	020	9TH WARD
STINLEY, EZEKIEL	BAL	306	20TH WAR
STINLING, EMELY	BAL	269	20TH WAR
STINN, ROBERT	BAL	174	19TH WAR
STINNER, CHARLES	BAL	103	5TH WARD
STINNET, GEORGE W.	CAL	030	2ND DIST
STINNETT, ELIZABETH	CAL	035	2ND DIST
STINNETT, JESSE	CAL	031	2ND DIST
STINOR, WILLIAM	WAS	063	2ND SUBD
STINSON, ARNOLD-BLACK	QUE	134	1ST E DI
STINSON, HARRIET	CAR	070	NO TWP L
STINSON, MARGARET	QUE	219	3RD E DI
STINSON, PHILIP	BAL	460	8TH WARD
STINSON, R.P.	BAL	158	1ST WARD
STINSON, RICHARD	BAL	097	10TH WAR
STINSON, RUFUS P.	BAL	167	1ST WARD
STINSON, SAMUEL G.	QUE	123	1ST E DI
STINSON, WILLIAM	QUE	188	3RD E DI
STINSON, WILLIAM H.	BAL	045	9TH WARD
STINSON, WILLIAM-BLACK	QUE	198	3RD E DI
STINSTON, ISABELLA	CEC	114	3RD E DI
STINTAIN, J. M.	BAL	471	14TH WAR
STINTS, WELHELMM	BAL	268	2ND WARD
STIPES, CATHARINE	WAS	043	2ND SUBD
STIRCH, CHRISTOPHER	BAL	255	20TH WAR
STIRN, LEWIS	BAL	033	18TH WAR
STIRRAT, JAMES	BAL	182	6TH WARD
STIRRATT, DAVID	BAL	217	6TH WARD
STITCHBERRY, MARGARET	TAL	062	EASTON D
STITCHBERRY, MARTHA	TAL	035	EASTON D
STITCHBURY, NICHOLAS P.	TAL	067	EASTON T
STITCHBURY, STEPHEN*	TAL	006	EASTON D
STITCHBURY, WILLIAM T.	TAL	010	EASTON D
STITCHER, ELLEN	BAL	316	12TH WAR
STITELER, HANNAH E.	FRE	132	CREAGERS
STITELEY, ELIZABETH	FRE	292	WOODSBOR
STITELEY, JACOB	FRE	128	CREAGERS
STITELY, ADALINE	FRE	280	WOODSBOR
STITELY, ANN A.	FRE	410	8TH E DI
STITELY, GEORGE	FRE	410	8TH E DI
STITELY, GEORGE	WAS	034	2ND SUBD
STITELY, JACOB	FRE	414	8TH E DI
STITELY, JACOB	FRE	283	WOODSBOR
STITELY, JOHN	FRE	290	WOODSBOR
STITELY, JOHN	FRE	410	8TH E DI
STITELY, JOSIAH	FRE	280	WOODSBOR
STITELY, SAMUEL	FRE	414	8TH E DI
STITELY, SOLOMON	FRE	289	WOODSBOR
STITELY, SOPHIAH	FRE	289	WOODSBOR
STITELY, SUSAN	FRE	289	WOODSBOR
STITELY, WILLIAM	FRE	305	WOODSBOR
STITELY, WILLIAM H.	CAR	364	9TH DIST
STITER, ELIZABETH	BAL	182	2ND WARD
STITHBURY, ROBINSON *	TAL	074	EASTON T
STITLER, GEORGE	FRE	131	CREAGERS
STITLEY, ELEXEMA	FRE	420	8TH E DI
STITTER, CATHARINE	BAL	010	EASTERN
STITTLE, MARY A.	WAS	204	1ST DIST
STITTS, AMOS	BAL	055	2ND DIST
STITZ, ALBERT	BAL	180	6TH WARD
STIVER, CRISTIAN	BAL	097	18TH WAR
STIVER, FREDRICK	WAS	101	2ND DIST
STIVER, JOHN	BAL	127	1ST WARD
STIVERS, ANN	KEN	308	3RD DIST
STIVERS, HENRY	ANN	421	HOWARD D
STIVERS, JAMES	ALL	243	CUMBERLA
STIVERS, WILLIAM S.	BAL	128	1ST WARD
STKINSON, JANE	HAR	050	1ST DIST
STOAKES, WILLIAM	BAL	135	16TH WAR
STOAM, JOHN	BAL	281	1ST DIST
STOBER, ELLEN	BAL	010	EASTERN
STOCK, E.	BAL	012	9TH WARD
STOCK, HENERITTA	BAL	378	13TH WAR
STOCK, JOHN	BAL	293	1ST DIST
STOCK, JOHN	BAL	226	1ST DIST
STOCK, LOUIS	BAL	107	5TH WARD
STOCK, MARIA C.	WAS	169	FUNKSTOW
STOCK, MARTHA J.	BAL	293	1ST DIST
STOCKBRIDGE, JASON JR.	BAL	047	9TH WARD
STOCKDALE, CLARISSA	ANN	471	HOWARD D
STOCKDALE, EDWARD	ANN	466	HOWARD D
STOCKDALE, JESSE	BAL	229	1ST DIST
STOCKDALE, JOSHUA H.	BAL	160	6TH WARD
STOCKDALE, JULIA A.	BAL	149	11TH WAR
STOCKDALE, MARGARET	BAL	077	1ST WARD
STOCKDALE, NOAH	BAL	033	18TH WAR
STOCKDALE, SAMUEL	ANN	459	HOWARD D
STOCKDALE, SARAH	ANN	459	HOWARD D
STOCKDALE, SARAH	HAR	084	2ND DIST
STOCKDALE, THOAMS	BAL	069	18TH WAR
STOCKDEN, RICHARD H.	BAL	194	11TH WAR
STOCKER, ANN E.	HAR	065	1ST DIST
STOCKER, HENRY	BAL	173	2ND DIST
STOCKESLAGER, JOHN	WAS	232	1ST DIST
STOCKET, ANN L.	ANN	269	ANNAPOLI
STOCKETT, AUGUST	BAL	045	15TH WAR
STOCKETT, BENJAMIN	PRI	090	MARLBROU
STOCKETT, EMMANUEL	BAL	076	4TH WARD
STOCKETT, FRANK H.	ANN	268	ANNAPOLI
STOCKETT, GEORGE A.	ANN	296	1ST DIST
STOCKETT, HENRY	BAL	024	1ST WARD
STOCKETT, J. SCHAAF	BAL	061	10TH WAR
STOCKETT, JAMES P.	BAL	089	18TH WAR
STOCKETT, JOSEPH N.	ANN	314	1ST DIST
STOCKETT, LEWIS	BAL	089	18TH WAR
STOCKETT, LOUISA	ANN	311	1ST DIST
STOCKETT, LUCRETIA	ANN	438	HOWARD D
STOCKETT, MARTHA	ANN	311	1ST DIST
STOCKETT, MARY	ANN	313	1ST DIST
STOCKETT, MARY	QUE	163	2ND E DI
STOCKETT, MARY A.	ANN	290	ANNAPOLI
STOCKETT, MRS-	ANN	320	2ND DIST
STOCKETT, RICHARD G.	ANN	522	HOWARD D
STOCKETT, SARAH	ANN	312	1ST DIST
STOCKETT, THOMAS R.	ANN	270	ANNAPOLI
STOCKETT, WILLIAM	QUE	163	2ND E DI
STOCKHAM, JOHN	HAR	183	3RD DIST
STOCKING, ELLEN	BAL	010	1ST WARD
STOCKING, HENRY	BAL	009	1ST WARD
STOCKLAIN, CHARLES	BAL	255	2ND WARD
STOCKLEY, JAMES	SOM	407	DUBLIN D
STOCKLIN, WILLIAM	BAL	274	2ND WARD
STOCKLY, JAMES	SOM	436	PRINCESS
STOCKMAN, AMRTHA	FRE	400	JEFFERSO
STOCKMAN, CHARLES D.	BAL	431	1ST DIST
STOCKMAN, CHARLOTTE	FRE	071	FREDERIC
STOCKMAN, CHRISTIAN	FRE	406	JEFFERSO
STOCKMAN, DANIEL	FRE	406	JEFFERSO
STOCKMAN, DAVID	FRE	399	JEFFERSO
STOCKMAN, ELIZABETH	FRE	400	JEFFERSO
STOCKMAN, ELIZABETH	FRE	072	FREDERIC
STOCKMAN, ELVIRA N.	BAL	045	1ST WARD
STOCKMAN, FREDERICK W.	BAL	044	1ST WARD
STOCKMAN, HENRY	FRE	408	JEFFERSO
STOCKMAN, JOHN	FRE	214	BUCKEYST
STOCKMAN, JOHN J.	FRE	401	JEFFERSO
STOCKMAN, JOSEPH	BAL	285	7TH WARD
STOCKMAN, THEODORE L.	FRE	400	JEFFERSO
STOCKSDAH, NELSON	BAL	016	9TH WARD
STOCKSDALE, AIRY	CAR	361	9TH DIST
STOCKSDALE, ARON	CAR	183	8TH DIST
STOCKSDALE, DOROTHY	BAL	234	1ST DIST
STOCKSDALE, EDMOND	CAR	194	4TH DIST
STOCKSDALE, ELIAS	CAR	215	5TH DIST
STOCKSDALE, ELIAS	BAL	262	6TH WARD
STOCKSDALE, JOHN T.	CAR	195	4TH DIST
STOCKSDALE, LUCRETIA N.	CAR	203	4TH DIST
STOCKSDALE, MARY	CAR	179	8TH DIST
STOCKSDALE, MARY W.	BAL	017	9TH WARD
STOCKSDALE, NATHAN B.	CAR	372	9TH DIST
STOCKSDALE, NOAH	CAR	194	4TH DIST
STOCKSDALE, SARAH K.	CAR	192	4TH DIST
STOCKSDALE, SOLOMON	CAR	193	4TH DIST
STOCKSDALE, SOLOMON	CAR	207	4TH DIST
STOCKSDALE, THOMAS E.	CAR	194	4TH DIST
STOCKSLAGER, JACOB	CAR	305	1ST DIST
STOCKSLAGER, PETER	WAS	206	1ST DIST
STOCKSON, THOMAS	HAR	183	3RD DIST
STOCKTON, AARON W.	BAL	384	3RD WARD
STOCKTON, LUCIUS	BAL	072	10TH WAR
STOCKTON, MARGARET D. L.	BAL	385	3RD WARD
STOCKTON, THOMAS J.	BAL	402	3RD WARD
STOCKWELL, SAMUEL	WAS	125	2ND DIST
STOCKWERTZ, MARGARET	BAL	108	1ST WARD
STODDARD, ALBERT M.	BAL	108	10TH WAR
STODDARD, ISAIAH T.	BAL	179	16TH WAR
STODDARD, JAMES	BAL	053	9TH WARD
STODDARD, JAMES	ALL	199	CUMBERLA
STODDARD, JOHN H.	BAL	033	9TH WARD
STODDARD, JOHN T.	CHA	224	ALLENS F
STODDARD, JOSEPH	ALL	077	5TH E.D.
STODDARD, MARY	BAL	031	9TH WARD
STODDARD, NATHANIEL	BAL	092	18TH WAR
STODDARD, WILLIAM	BAL	251	6TH WARD
STOEBAUGH, DANIEL	ALL	014	3RD E.D.
STOEBAUGH, JOSEPH	ALL	014	3RD E.D.
STOELFFER, JACOB	FRE	304	WOODSBOR
STOESER, MATTIAS	BAL	171	19TH WAR
STOFER, SUSANNA R.	HAR	059	1ST DIST
STOFFEL, CATHERINE	BAL	068	10TH WAR
STOFFEL, DANIEL	BAL	008	18TH WAR
STOFFEL, EGANNAX*	BAL	072	4TH WARD
STOFFEL, EGANNOY*	BAL	072	4TH WARD
STOFFEL, MARY	BAL	206	6TH DIST
STOFFELL, HENRY	BAL	239	17TH WAR
STOFFELL, JOHN	BAL	203	11TH WAR
STOFFER, HENRY	BAL	087	2ND DIST
STOFFER, HENRY	BAL	210	17TH WAR
STOFFER, SAMULE	BAL	213	17TH WAR
STOFNEY, AMELIA	BAL	435	14TH WAR
STOHL, CHARLES	BAL	147	11TH WAR
STOHMAN, H.	BAL	282	2ND WARD
STOHMAN, H.	BAL	158	1ST WARD
STOKDEN, HENRY	BAL	153	2ND DIST
STOKEL, DANIEL *	KEN	243	2ND DIST
STOKELEY, HENRY	BAL	156	16TH WAR
STOKELY, EMELINE	BAL	066	10TH WAR
STOKELY, JACOB	BAL	046	4TH WARD
STOKELY, JOHN	BAL	205	2ND WARD
STOKELY, THOMAS	BAL	391	3RD WARD
STOKEMAN, CONRAD	BAL	215	17TH WAR
STOKEMAN, JOHN H.	BAL	020	9TH WARD
STOKER, ANN	ANN	273	ANNAPOLI
STOKER, H.	BAL	164	1ST WARD
STOKER, HARRISON	TAL	084	ST MICHA
STOKER, JOHN	ANN	273	ANNAPOLI
STOKER, MICHAEL	BAL	023	15TH WAR
STOKER, PHILLIP	BAL	224	2ND WARD
STOKER, TRISTRAM*	TAL	053	EASTON D
STOKERS, MARTIN	BAL	163	11TH WAR
STOKES, ADISON C.	FRE	133	CREAGERS
STOKES, ANDREW	HAR	176	3RD DIST
STOKES, ANDREW	BAL	007	18TH WAR
STOKES, ANN	CEC	151	PORT DUP
STOKES, BENJAMIN	BAL	042	1ST WARD
STOKES, CHARLES	ANN	343	3RD DIST
STOKES, DARIUS	BAL	149	5TH WARD
STOKES, DAVID	HAR	047	1ST DIST
STOKES, ELIZABETH	DOR	431	1ST DIST
STOKES, FRANCIS	HAR	192	3RD DIST
STOKES, HANNAH	BAL	175	6TH WARD
STOKES, HARVY	HAR	013	1ST DIST
STOKES, HENRY	CEC	158	PORT DUP
STOKES, HENRY	FRE	164	EMMITTSB
STOKES, JAMES	BAL	279	2ND WARD
STOKES, JOHN R.	HAR	053	1ST DIST
STOKES, JOSEPH	BAL	207	6TH WARD
STOKES, JOSHUA	FRE	132	CREAGERS
STOKES, LUCINDA	BAL	118	5TH WARD
STOKES, MAJOR	CAR	110	NO TWP L
STOKES, NANCY	DOR	304	1ST DIST
STOKES, NATHAN R.	HAR	043	1ST DIST
STOKES, R. T.	FRE	306	WOODSBOR
STOKES, RACHAEL	BAL	079	4TH WARD
STOKES, SARAH	BAL	120	5TH WARD
STOKES, SARAH	BAL	118	5TH WARD
STOKES, SARAH	BAL	261	6TH WARD
STOKES, THOMAS	DOR	301	1ST DIST
STOKES, TRISTRAM*	TAL	053	EASTON D
STOKES, WILLIAM	BAL	053	15TH WAR
STOKES, WILLIAM B.	BAL	190	11TH WAR
STOKES, WILLIAM H.	BAL	105	10TH WAR
STOKES, WILLIAM J.	PRI	107	PISCATAW
STOKESLAGER, CONRAD	WAS	176	1ST DIST
STOKESLAGER, JACOB	WAS	232	1ST DIST
STOKESLAGER, JOHN	WAS	176	1ST DIST
STOKEY, MATHEW	BAL	102	1ST WARD
STOLAPER, CATHARINE	WAS	138	2ND DIST
STOLELMYER, JAMES	FRE	156	10TH E D
STOLENGER, MARY	CEC	188	7TH E DI
STOLER, CHRISTIAN	ALL	156	6TH E.D.
STOLL, AMELIA C.	BAL	010	9TH WARD
STOLL, JOHN	BAL	391	14TH WAR
STOLLEMYER, JONATHAN	FRE	370	CATOCTIN
STOLLEMYER, JOSEPH	ALL	181	8TH E.D.
STOLLER, JACOB	ALL	153	6TH E.D.
STOLLER, NANCY	WAS	185	BOONSBOR
STOLLIPER, GEORGE	WAS	138	2ND DIST
STOLMIRE, HENRY	CEC	126	5TH E DI
STOLPP, BARBARA *	BAL	231	6TH WARD
STOLSS, J. L.	BAL	315	12TH WAR
STOM, GEORGE	BAL	021	1ST WARD
STOM, JOHN	BAL	287	1ST DIST
STOMFLEE, MARY	BAL	343	7TH WARD
STONARD, JUDITH	CEC	063	1ST E DI
STONBREAKER, MARY	WAS	229	1ST DIST
STONE, AARON A.	BAL	073	10TH WAR
STONE, ADAM	CAR	278	7TH DIST
STONE, ANN	BAL	139	16TH WAR
STONE, ANN-BLACK	WOR	350	1ST E DI
STONE, BENJAMIN	WAS	191	1ST DIST
STONE, CATHARIEN	WAS	191	1ST DIST
STONE, CATHARINE	FRE	439	8TH E DI
STONE, CHARLES	PRI	093	MARLBROU
STONE, CHARLES W.	BAL	010	18TH WAR
STONE, DANIEL	CAR	279	7TH DIST
STONE, DAVID	WAS	056	2ND SUBD
STONE, DAVID N.	BAL	010	18TH WAR
STONE, ELIZA	BAL	350	13TH WAR
STONE, ELIZABETH	FRE	098	FREDERIC
STONE, ELIZABETH	BAL	379	3RD WARD
STONE, EZRA	WAS	191	1ST DIST
STONE, FRANCIS	ST	272	3RD E DI
STONE, FRANCIS	MGM	388	ROCKERLE
STONE, FRANCIS J.	ST	317	4TH E DI
STONE, FREDERICK	PRI	017	BLADENSB
STONE, FREDERICK	FRE	402	JEFFERSO
STONE, GEORGE	BAL	299	17TH WAR
STONE, GEORGE	CAR	339	6TH DIST
STONE, GEORGE	BAL	170	1ST WARD
STONE, GEORGE *	SOM	469	TRAPPE D
STONE, GEORGE B.	PRI	100	SPALDING
STONE, GEORGE R.	BAL	221	1ST DIST
STONE, GEORGE T.	ST	280	3RD E DI
STONE, HARRIET S.	ALL	228	CUMBERLA
STONE, HENRY	ANN	344	3RD DIST
STONE, HENRY	KEN	277	1ST DIST
STONE, HENRY	MGM	357	BERRYS D
STONE, HENRY	FRE	098	FREDERIC
STONE, HEZEKIAH	CHA	217	ALLENS F
STONE, JACOB	CAR	294	7TH DIST
STONE, JAMES	SOM	459	HANGARY
STONE, JAMES E.	BAL	397	14TH WAR
STONE, JAMES F.	CHA	218	ALLENS F
STONE, JAMES H.	MGM	372	BERRYS D
STONE, JAMES H.	BAL	425	3RD WARD
STONE, JANE	CHA	233	HILLTOP
STONE, JOHN	BAL	007	15TH WAR
STONE, JOHN A.	FRE	090	FREDERIC
STONE, JOHN F.	ST	255	3RD E DI
STONE, JOHN G.	WAS	113	2ND DIST
STONE, JOHN H.	ST	334	4TH E DI
STONE, JOHN H.	FRE	065	FREDERIC
STONE, JOHN L.	FRE	098	FREDERIC
STONE, JOHN T.	ST	265	3RD E DI
STONE, JOSEPH	ST	257	3RD E DI
STONE, JOSEPH	CHA	289	BOJANTOW
STONE, JOSEPHINE B.	BAL	473	14TH WAR
STONE, JOSEPHINE B.	BAL	462	14TH WAR
STONE, JOSHUA	ST	256	3RD E DI
STONE, LEVI	FRE	084	FREDERIC
STONE, MARCELLUS L.	ST	256	3RD E DI
STONE, MARTHA	CAL	012	1ST DIST
STONE, MARTHA	BAL	378	1ST DIST
STONE, MARTHA	BAL	301	1ST DIST
STONE, MARTHA A.	ST	280	3RD E DI
STONE, MARY	BAL	228	1ST DIST
STONE, MARY	FRE	097	FREDERIC
STONE, MARY	FRE	345	MIDDLETO
STONE, MATTHEW A.	ST	260	3RD E DI
STONE, MIAH	PRI	017	BLADENSB
STONE, MICHAEL J.	PRI	046	AQUASCO
STONE, PETER H.	ST	272	3RD E DI
STONE, PHILIP	MGM	388	ROCKERLE
STONE, REBECCA	BAL	093	10TH WAR
STONE, ROSAA	ST	307	1ST E DI
STONE, SAMUEL	ST	254	3RD E DI
STONE, SAMUEL	BAL	415	1ST DIST
STONE, SAMUEL	BAL	090	2ND DIST
STONE, SARA M.	CHA	292	BOJANTOW
STONE, SARAH	BAL	343	13TH WAR
STONE, SARAH	WAS	286	1ST DIST
STONE, SARAH A.	WAS	194	1ST DIST
STONE, SARAH E.	MGM	425	MEDLEY 3
STONE, SETH	BAL	074	10TH WAR
STONE, SOPHIA	BAL	249	17TH WAR
STONE, SUSAN	BAL	209	17TH WAR
STONE, SUSAN	BAL	222	19TH WAR
STONE, SUSAN	WAS	201	1ST DIST
STONE, SUSANA	BAL	404	3RD WARD
STONE, THOMAS	SOM	460	HANGARY
STONE, THOMAS	PRI	097	SPALDING
STONE, THOMAS	BAL	262	17TH WAR
STONE, THOMAS J.	ST	270	3RD E DI
STONE, THOMAS L.L.	PRI	056	AQUASCO
STONE, W. J.	BAL	332	1ST DIST
STONE, WALTER	BAL	120	5TH WARD
STONE, WALTER	CHA	264	HILLTOP
STONE, WASHINGTON	FRE	380	PETERSVI
STONE, WILLIAM	DOR	445	1ST DIST
STONE, WILLIAM	BAL	209	6TH WARD
STONE, WILLIAM B.	CHA	264	HILLTOP
STONE, WILLIAM H.	FRE	421	8TH E DI
STONE, WILLIAM H.	ST	272	3RD E DI
STONE, WILLIAM J.	KEN	273	1ST DIST
STONE, WILLIAM W.	BAL	231	17TH WAR
STONEBRAKER, ANN	CAR	236	UNION TO
STONEBRAKER, CHRISTIAN	WAS	096	2ND SUBD
STONEBRAKER, ELIZABETH	WAS	051	2ND SUBD
STONEBRAKER, ELIZABETH	BAL	384	13TH WAR
STONEBRAKER, HUYETT	WAS	235	1ST DIST
STONEBRAKER, JOHN	WAS	098	2ND DIST
STONEBRAKER, JOHN	HAR	106	2ND DIST
STONEBRAKER, JOSEPH	WAS	051	2ND SUBD
STONEBRAKER, MARY	FRE	433	8TH E DI
STONEBRAKER, MARY A.	FRE	052	FREDERIC

Name	County	Page	District
STONEBRAKER, SAMUEL	WAS	050	2ND SUBD
STONEBRAKER, SUSAN	WAS	052	2ND SUBD
STONEBRAKER, WASHINGTON	HAR	118	2ND DIST
STONEBRAKER, WILLIAM	WAS	171	FUNKSTOW
STONEBREAKER, ELIZABETH	CAR	403	2ND DIST
STONEBREAKER, GARRETT	WAS	221	1ST DIST
STONEBREAKER, HENRY	WAS	173	FUNKSTOW
STONEBREAKER, JOSEPH	CAR	399	2ND DIST
STONEBREAKER, PERRY G.	WAS	232	1ST DIST
STONEBRECKER, SAMUEL	BAL	426	14TH WAR
STONEHEIL, BOLEVAR	CHA	269	ALLENS F
STONER, ABRAHAM	FRE	426	8TH E DI
STONER, AUGUSTUS	FRE	432	8TH E DI
STONER, BENJAMIN	WAS	269	1ST DIST
STONER, CATHARINE	WAS	005	WILLIAMS
STONER, CHARLOTT	FRE	003	FREDERIC
STONER, DAVID	FRE	282	WOODSBOR
STONER, DAVID	CAR	379	2ND DIST
STONER, ELIZABETH	WAS	269	1ST DIST
STONER, EPHRAIM	CAR	320	1ST DIST
STONER, GEORGE	CAR	294	7TH DIST
STONER, GEORGE	CAR	293	7TH DIST
STONER, HENRY	CAR	382	2ND DIST
STONER, JACOB	FRE	426	8TH E DI
STONER, JACOB	FRE	117	CREAGERS
STONER, JACOB	WAS	269	1ST DIST
STONER, JOHN	WAS	270	1ST DIST
STONER, JOHN	CAR	379	2ND DIST
STONER, JOHN D.	FRE	428	8TH E DI
STONER, JOHN L.	BAL	284	12TH WAR
STONER, JOHN R.	FRE	117	CREAGERS
STONER, JOHN SR.	CAR	382	2ND DIST
STONER, JOHN W.	FRE	420	8TH E DI
STONER, JOSEPH	CAR	377	2ND DIST
STONER, JULIA	ANN	499	HOWARD D
STONER, MAGDALINE	FRE	414	8TH E DI
STONER, MARY	FRE	053	FREDERIC
STONER, SAMUEL	FRE	429	8TH E DI
STONER, SAMUEL	ANN	499	HOWARD D
STONER, SAMUEL	WAS	008	WILLIAMS
STONER, SAMUEL	WAS	091	2ND SUBD
STONER, SARAH	FRE	299	WOODSBOR
STONER, SOLOMON	FRE	428	8TH E DI
STONER, SUSAN	FRE	046	FREDERIC
STONER, UPTON	FRE	429	8TH E DI
STONER, WILLIAM	FRE	406	JEFFERSO
STONER, WILLIAM	FRE	117	CREAGERS
STONESHIEL, SAMUEL T.	MGM	375	ROCKERLE
STONESIFER, ABRAHAM	CAR	247	3RD DIST
STONESIFER, ABRAHAM	CAR	247	3RD DIST
STONESIFER, ANN	CAR	268	WESTMINS
STONESIFER, CYRUS	CAR	253	3RD DIST
STONESIFER, DANIEL	CAR	253	3RD DIST
STONESIFER, EDWARD	CAR	256	3RD DIST
STONESIFER, HERNY	CAR	295	7TH DIST
STONESIFER, ISAAC	CAR	254	3RD DIST
STONESIFER, ISAAC	CAR	254	3RD DIST
STONESIFER, ISAAC	CAR	398	2ND DIST
STONESIFER, JARRAD	FRE	414	8TH E DI
STONESIFER, JOHN	CAR	291	7TH DIST
STONESIFER, JOHN	CAR	262	3RD DIST
STONESIFER, JOHN	WAS	179	BOONSBOR
STONESIFER, JOSEPH	CAR	254	3RD DIST
STONESIFER, JOSIAH	CAR	247	3RD DIST
STONESIFER, LEVI	CAR	408	2ND DIST
STONESIFER, MARY A.	CAR	247	3RD DIST
STONESIFER, MICAJAH	CAR	294	7TH DIST
STONESIFER, NOAH	CAR	352	6TH DIST
STONESIFER, RACHEL	CAR	247	3RD DIST
STONESIFER, SAMUEL	CAR	260	3RD DIST
STONESIFER, SEVILLA	CAR	248	3RD DIST
STONESIFER, URIAS	CAR	307	1ST DIST
STONESIFER, WILLIAM	CAR	354	6TH DIST
STONESTREET, CHARLES H.	FRE	065	FREDERIC
STONESTREET, EDWARD	MGM	321	CRACKLIN
STONESTREET, EDWARD N.	CHA	231	HILLTOP
STONESTREET, N.E.	PRI	078	MARLBROU
STONESTREET, NICHOLAS	CHA	231	HILLTOP
STONESTREET, THOMAS	PRI	120	PISCATAW
STONESTREET, WILLIAM	CHA	269	ALLENS F
STONESTRET, ANN	CHA	230	MIDDLETO
STONETIREHER, OLIVER	WAS	195	1ST DIST
STONG, JOSEPH	BAL	314	1ST DIST
STONISIFER, DANIEL	CAR	353	6TH DIST
STONISIFER, EPHRAIM	CAR	313	1ST DIST
STONKANNA, FRANCIS	BAL	127	1ST WARD
STONKUG, FRANCIS	BAL	128	1ST WARD
STONSIFER, JOSHUA	CAR	277	7TH DIST
STONSIFER, NELSON	CAR	276	7TH DIST
STONSIFER, PATIENCE	CAR	354	6TH DIST
STONSIFER, WILLIAM	CAR	296	7TH DIST
STOOK, CHRISTIAN	ALL	211	CUMBERLA
STOOKLEY, MARY	BAL	111	5TH WARD
STOOKS, ROBERT-BLACK	CAR	068	NO TWP L
STOONBRAKER, AARON C. *	WAS	102	2ND DIST
STOONGLE, JOSEPH	BAL	434	8TH WARD
STOOPES, BENJAMIN	CEC	021	ELKTON 3
STOOPES, GEORGE-BLACK	FRE	220	BUCKEYST
STOOPS, AARON	BAL	062	15TH WAR
STOOPS, ANN	CEC	049	1ST E DI
STOOPS, ANN	CEC	006	ELKTON 3
STOOPS, AUGUSTUS	CEC	021	ELKTON 3
STOOPS, BENJAMIN	CEC	049	1ST E DI
STOOPS, JAMES	WAS	114	2ND DIST
STOOPS, JAMES	KEN	259	1ST DIST
STOOPS, JAMES	KEN	258	1ST DIST
STOOPS, JOHN	BAL	068	18TH WAR
STOOPS, JOHN W.	KEN	303	3RD DIST
STOOPS, MARGARET	KEN	275	1ST DIST
STOOPS, SARAH	BAL	333	3RD WARD
STOOPS, SOLOMAN	WAS	114	2ND DIST
STOOPS, THOAMS	ANN	315	1ST DIST
STOOPS, WILLIAM D.	KEN	311	3RD DIST
STOPHER, FREDERICK	BAL	207	6TH DIST
STOPP, GEORGE	ALL	055	10TH E.D
STOPS, JACOB	WAS	058	2ND SUBD
STORCH, ADOLPH	BAL	105	5TH WARD
STORCH, JOHN	BAL	300	7TH WARD
STORCH, MARGARETT	BAL	105	5TH WARD
STORDT, GEORGE	BAL	238	20TH WAR
STORE, HENRY	BAL	220	12TH WAR
STORES, MARY	BAL	431	14TH WAR
STORFF, ARON	BAL	073	4TH WARD
STORK, CHARLES	BAL	007	15TH WAR
STORK, G. M.	ALL	120	5TH E.D.
STORK, JOHN M.	ALL	120	5TH E.D.
STORK, JOHN T.	BAL	085	18TH WAR
STORK, MARY W.	BAL	087	18TH WAR
STORK, WILLIAM L.	FRE	409	JEFFERSO
STORKS, LANGHORN	BAL	252	6TH WARD
STORKS, RICHARD B.	BAL	204	6TH WARD
STORKS, SARAH A.	SOM	366	BRINKLEY
STORM, CATHERINE	BAL	398	8TH WARD
STORM, CHRISTIAN	BAL	144	16TH WAR
STORM, EDWIN L.	BAL	374	1ST DIST
STORM, GEORGE	BAL	200	5TH DIST
STORM, JAMES	FRE	160	EMMITTSB
STORM, JEREMIAH	BAL	444	14TH WAR
STORM, JOHN	WAS	273	RIDGEVIL
STORM, JOHN	WAS	254	1ST DIST
STORM, MARY A.	CAR	259	3RD DIST
STORM, MARY M.	FRE	020	FREDERIC
STORM, PETER L.	FRE	020	FREDERIC
STORM, PHILIP	WAS	179	BOONSBOR
STORM, SAMUEL P.	BAL	464	1ST DIST
STORMES, CATHARINE	CAR	176	8TH DIST
STORMES, ELIZABETH	CAR	181	8TH DIST
STORMES, HENRY	CAR	175	8TH DIST
STORMES, JACOB	CAR	185	8TH DIST
STORMES, JACOB	CAR	181	8TH DIST
STORMES, THOMAS	CAR	175	8TH DIST
STORMM, JACOB	HAR	050	1ST DIST
STORMM, SARAH	HAR	050	1ST DIST
STORMS, ANN	BAL	266	17TH WAR
STORMS, AUTHOR	CAR	139	NO TWP L
STORMS, ELLEN	BAL	187	5TH DIST
STORMS, MARY	BAL	446	14TH WAR
STORMS, REGIN	FRE	256	NEW MARK
STORREY, JOHN	WAS	130	2ND DIST
STORSBERGER, SAMUEL	BAL	369	8TH WARD
STORSER, GEORGE	ALL	253	CUMBERLA
STORT, ANDREW	BAL	111	18TH WAR
STORTSBERGER, JOHN	BAL	440	8TH WARD
STORY, ANN J.	BAL	105	18TH WAR
STORY, ANNA	BAL	034	9TH WARD
STORY, ANNA	QUE	192	3RD E DI
STORY, GEORGE	BAL	298	20TH WAR
STORY, JAMES W.	QUE	190	3RD E DI
STORY, JOHN	QUE	194	3RD E DI
STORY, JONATHAN	PRI	025	VANSVILL
STORY, JOSHUA	QUE	158	2ND E DI
STORY, LUTHER W.C.	QUE	188	3RD E DI
STORY, MARY H.	QUE	184	3RD E DI
STORY, MARY J.	BAL	034	9TH WARD
STORY, SILAS	CAR	140	NO TWP L
STORY, WALTER	BAL	115	18TH WAR
STOSH, JEREMIAH	ALL	063	10TH E.D
STOT, JOHN	ALL	214	CUMBERLA
STOTELMYER, GEORGE W.	FRE	151	10TH E D
STOTLER, BENJAMIN	FRE	137	CREAGERS
STOTLER, CHRISTIAN	WAS	234	1ST DIST
STOTLER, DAVID	WAS	301	1ST DIST
STOTLER, JOHN H.	WAS	234	1ST DIST
STOTSENBURG, GEORGE	CEC	010	ELKTON 3
STOTT, JAMES	CEC	087	4TH E DI
STOTT, JAMES	ALL	182	8TH E.D.
STOTT, LEROY	ALL	092	5TH E.D.
STOTT, LOUISA C.	BAL	011	4TH WARD
STOTTELMEYER, PETER	FRE	196	5TH E DI
STOTTER, JACOB	WAS	176	1ST DIST
STOTTER, JOHN	WAS	234	1ST DIST
STOTTER, SAMUEL	WAS	241	CAVETOWN
STOTTLEMGER, JOSEPH	FRE	364	CATOCTIN
STOTTLEMYER, COSTLY	FRE	373	CATOCTIN
STOTTLEMYER, DANIEL	FRE	365	CATOCTIN
STOTTLEMYER, DAVID	FRE	365	CATOCTIN
STOTTLEMYER, GEORGE	FRE	365	CATOCTIN
STOTTLEMYER, HIRAM	FRE	087	FREDERIC
STOTTLEMYER, JACOB	FRE	367	CATOCTIN
STOTTLEMYER, JEMIMA	FRE	363	CATOCTIN
STOTTLEMYER, JOHN	FRE	364	CATOCTIN
STOTTLEMYER, JOHN M.*	FRE	361	CATOCTIN
STOTTLEMYER, JOHN P.	FRE	366	CATOCTIN
STOTTLEMYER, JOHN W.	FRE	374	CATOCTIN
STOTTLEMYER, MARY	FRE	347	MIDDLETO
STOTTLEMYER, MARY	FRE	363	CATOCTIN
STOTTLEMYER, NELSON	FRE	365	CATOCTIN
STOTTLEMYER, PETER	ALL	182	8TH E.D.
STOTTLEMYER, SUSAN	FRE	367	CATOCTIN
STOTTMEYER, DEVAL	WAS	162	2ND DIST
STOTTS, REBECCA	KEN	274	1ST DIST
STOUBS, ELIZABETH	WAS	210	1ST DIST
STOUCH, HENRY	WAS	298	1ST DIST
STOUFER, ABRAHAM	WAS	214	1ST DIST
STOUFER, ABRAHAM	WAS	258	1ST DIST
STOUFER, ABRAHAM	WAS	270	1ST DIST
STOUFER, CHRISTIAN	WAS	263	1ST DIST
STOUFER, DANIEL	WAS	230	1ST DIST
STOUFER, JACOB	WAS	232	1ST DIST
STOUFER, JACOB	WAS	231	1ST DIST
STOUFER, JOHN	WAS	254	1ST DIST
STOUFER, JOHN	WAS	254	1ST DIST
STOUFER, SAMUEL	WAS	161	HAGERSTO
STOUFER, SOLOMON	WAS	287	1ST DIST
STOUFFEN, PETER W.	FRE	384	PETERSVI
STOUFFER, ANN C.	BAL	459	14TH WAR
STOUFFER, C. J.	BAL	470	14TH WAR
STOUFFER, DAVID	CAR	237	UNION TO
STOUFFER, ELI	FRE	185	5TH E DI
STOUFFER, ELIAS	BAL	291	12TH WAR
STOUFFER, GEORGE	FRE	186	5TH E DI
STOUFFER, HENRY	FRE	305	WOODSBOR
STOUFFER, JACOB	BAL	150	19TH WAR
STOUFFER, JAMES	WAS	215	1ST DIST
STOUFFER, JOHN	FRE	299	WOODSBOR
STOUFFER, JOHN	FRE	186	5TH E DI
STOUFFER, JOHN	CAR	240	TANEYTOW
STOUFFER, JOHN	BAL	078	4TH WARD
STOUFFER, JOSEPH	FRE	305	WOODSBOR
STOUFFER, JOSEPH	CAR	392	2ND DIST
STOUFFER, MARIA	FRE	188	5TH E DI
STOUFFER, MARY	WAS	029	2ND SUBD
STOUFFER, MARY	WAS	035	2ND SUBD
STOUFFER, SIMON W.	FRE	305	WOODSBOR
STOUFFER, WILLIAM	WAS	029	2ND SUBD
STOUFFI, SAMUEL	CAR	381	2ND DIST
STOUGHT, WILLIAMS	WAS	142	2ND DIST
STOUK, GEORGE*	BAL	334	3RD WARD
STOUK, LARKIN	WAS	236	CAVETOWN
STOUPES, CHRISTIAN	WAS	243	CAVETOWN
STOUT, CONRAD	BAL	274	20TH WAR
STOUT, ANDREW	BAL	171	6TH WARD
STOUT, ANELICA	BAL	059	10TH WAR
STOUT, ANNA	WAS	188	1ST DIST
STOUT, BENJAMIN	KEN	295	3RD DIST
STOUT, CATHARINE	BAL	315	7TH WARD
STOUT, DANIEL	KEN	310	3RD DIST
STOUT, DAVID	KEN	293	3RD DIST
STOUT, ELIZA	FRE	063	FREDERIC
STOUT, ELIZABETH	CAR	294	7TH DIST
STOUT, EMORY	BAL	168	6TH WARD
STOUT, GEORGE	BAL	275	20TH WAR
STOUT, HENEY	BAL	059	10TH WAR
STOUT, ISABELLA	BAL	170	6TH WARD
STOUT, JAMES M.	FRE	283	WOODSBOR
STOUT, JOHN	CEC	130	6TH E DI
STOUT, JOHN	BAL	038	9TH WARD
STOUT, JOHN	WAS	211	1ST DIST
STOUT, JOHN A.	BAL	113	18TH WAR
STOUT, JOSEPH	CAR	288	7TH DIST
STOUT, JOSEPH	CEC	038	CHESAPEA
STOUT, JOSEPH W.	BAL	113	18TH WAR
STOUT, LOUIS	BAL	131	1ST WARD
STOUT, MARTHA	WAS	182	BOONSBOR
STOUT, RICHARD	TAL	115	ST MICHA
STOUT, SAMUEL	CEC	039	CHESAPEA
STOUT, SARAH	WAS	180	BOONSBOR
STOUT, WESLEY	CEC	133	6TH E DI
STOUTS, ANTHONY	BAL	095	1ST WARD
STOVER, ALFRED	WAS	224	1ST DIST
STOVER, DANIEL	WAS	225	1ST DIST
STOVER, DAVID	WAS	253	1ST DIST
STOVER, DAVID	WAS	220	1ST DIST
STOVER, ELIAS	WAS	284	1ST DIST
STOVER, FRANCIS	HAR	049	1ST DIST
STOVER, FREDERICK	WAS	137	HAGERSTO
STOVER, FREDERICK	ALL	221	CUMBERLA
STOVER, FRISBY	WAS	225	1ST DIST
STOVER, GEORGE	BAL	276	17TH WAR
STOVER, GEORGE W.	BAL	098	18TH WAR
STOVER, HANNAH	BAL	095	2ND DIST
STOVER, HENRY	BAL	120	1ST WARD
STOVER, HENRY	WAS	194	1ST DIST
STOVER, JACOB	WAS	219	1ST DIST
STOVER, JACOB	BAL	088	2ND DIST
STOVER, JAMES	WAS	219	1ST DIST
STOVER, JEREMIAH	WAS	216	1ST DIST
STOVER, JOHN	WAS	284	1ST DIST
STOVER, JOHN	ALL	205	CUMBERLA
STOVER, JOHN H.	BAL	356	3RD WARD
STOVER, L.M.	WAS	155	HAGERSTO
STOVER, MARGARET	BAL	051	2ND DIST
STOVER, MARGARET	CAR	336	6TH DIST
STOVER, MARGARET	FRE	011	FREDERIC
STOVER, MARGARETT	BAL	257	17TH WAR
STOVER, MARY	BAL	084	2ND DIST
STOVER, MARY T.	TAL	112	ST MICHA
STOVER, PHILIP	FRE	219	BUCKEYST
STOVER, SAMUEL	WAS	294	1ST DIST
STOVER, SAMUEL	WAS	206	1ST DIST
STOVER, SARAH	WAS	231	1ST DIST
STOVER, SOLLOMON	FRE	223	BUCKEYST
STOVER, WILLIAM	WAS	252	1ST DIST
STOVER,ELLENORE	FRE	223	BUCKEYST
STOVES, SUSAN	WAS	152	2ND DIST
STOVEY, WILLIAM	TAL	112	ST MICHA
STOW, G.	BAL	317	12TH WAR
STOW, OLIVER	BAL	472	14TH WAR
STOW, TENET*	TAL	040	EASTON D
STOYER, GEORGE	ALL	114	5TH E.D.
STOYER, JOHN	ALL	114	5TH E.D.
STOYER, JOHN	ALL	054	10TH E.D
STOYER, SAMUEL	CAR	252	3RD DIST
STOYKES, GEORGE	FRE	128	CREAGERS
STPHEANSON, ISAAC	CEC	157	PORT DUP
STPHENS, JOHN L.	FRE	299	WOODSBOR
STRABE, NICHOLAS	BAL	382	3RD WARD
STRACK, JOHN	BAL	084	10TH WAR
STRACK, JOHN	BAL	089	10TH WAR
STRACKE, MORICE	BAL	453	8TH WARD
STRADLERS, SAMUEL *	KEN	230	2ND DIST
STRADLEY, BENJAMIN	KEN	301	3RD DIST
STRADLEY, DORCAS	KEN	306	3RD DIST
STRADLEY, HARRIET	BAL	084	10TH WAR
STRADLEY, ISAIAH	QUE	185	3RD E DI
STRADLEY, SAMUEL *	KEN	230	2ND DIST
STRADLEY, WILLIAM	BAL	285	17TH WAR
STRADLY, ELIZA	KEN	262	1ST DIST
STRADLY, SAMUEL	KEN	261	1ST DIST
STRADLY, THOMAS	CEC	049	1ST E DI
STRADWIG, MAGDELEN	ANN	460	HOWARD D
STRAHAM, MARTHA	CEC	104	4TH E DI
STRAHN, EBENEZER*	BAL	366	3RD WARD
STRAILMAN, GEORGE	FRE	004	FREDERIC
STRAIN, JOHN	BAL	132	1ST WARD
STRAIN,JOHN	BAL	119	1ST WARD
STRAIT, MARY	WAS	149	2ND DIST
STRAITLY, JANE	CAL	034	2ND DIST
STRAKMANN, WILLIAM	BAL	037	15TH WAR
STRALER, LUDWICK	BAL	394	1ST DIST
STRALER, REBECCA	BAL	395	1ST DIST
STRALLARD, CAREL	BAL	283	2ND WARD
STRALLS, HENRY *	BAL	291	20TH WAR
STRALY, SARAH A.	WAS	256	1ST DIST
STRAMPE, J.	BAL	174	19TH WAR
STRAN, ANN*	BAL	396	3RD WARD
STRAN, GEORGE	BAL	007	EASTERN
STRAN, JAMES H.	BAL	007	EASTERN
STRAN, WILLIAM H.	BAL	329	3RD WARD
STRANBURGH, MARTIN	BAL	086	1ST WARD
STRANDBERG, HENRY J.	BAL	003	15TH WAR
STRANDBERG, SUSANNA	BAL	003	15TH WAR
STRANDBERY, CARL L.	KEN	208	2ND DIST
STRANEY, EDWARD	BAL	150	19TH WAR
STRANGHAN, HENRY	CAR	072	NO TWP L
STRANING, CATHARINE	BAL	260	2ND WARD
STRANN, EBENEZER*	BAL	365	3RD WARD
STRANS, CHRISTOPHER	BAL	277	2ND WARD
STRANS, HENRY	BAL	229	2ND WARD
STRANS, RACHAEL	BAL	241	2ND WARD
STRANSBERGER, KAUFMAN	BAL	222	6TH WARD
STRANSBURGER, AARON	BAL	221	6TH WARD
STRANSBURGH, STEPHEN	BAL	238	2ND WARD
STRANTMAN, HENRY	BAL	006	9TH WARD
STRAPER, JACOB	ALL	037	2ND E.D.
STRAPER, SARAH	BAL	232	2ND WARD
STRAPPER, HEMAN	BAL	045	1ST WARD
STRASBERGER, JACOB	FRE	424	8TH E DI
STRASBERGER, JOHN F.	FRE	411	8TH E DI
STRASBERGER, MARY	FRE	427	8TH E DI
STRASBERGER, WILLIAM	FRE	424	8TH E DI
STRASBURGH, HANNAH	BAL	209	6TH DIST
STRASBURUGH, AMOS H.	BAL	213	6TH DIST
STRASEN, FREDERICKA	BAL	078	15TH WAR
STRATMEYER, FREDERICK	BAL	011	15TH WAR
STRATMEYER, FREDERICK	BAL	011	15TH WAR
STRATON, BETSA	WOR	304	SNOW HIL
STRATTON, GEORGE	BAL	132	11TH WAR
STRATTON, JAMES	ANN	415	HOWARD D
STRATTON, MARY E.	BAL	359	13TH WAR

STRATTON, MARY M. ALL 212 CUMBERLA
STRATTON, ROBERT BAL 359 13TH WAR
STRATTON, ROSE BAL 284 12TH WAR
STRATTON, T. B. ALL 096 5TH E.D.
STRATTON, THOMAS BAL 091 5TH WARD
STRAU, ANN* BAL 396 3RD WARD
STRAUB, ADAM BAL 434 14TH WAR
STRAUB, SOPHIA BAL 434 14TH WAR
STRAUGHEN, THOMAS CAR 080 NO TWP L
STRAUGHER, SAMUEL ANN 496 HOWARD D
STRAUGHN, DAVID* DOR 377 1ST DIST
STRAUGHN, ELIZA KEN 311 3RD DIST
STRAUGHN, HARRIET M. QUE 201 3RD E DI
STRAUGHN, JAMES DOR 374 1ST DIST
STRAUGHN, JAMES H. QUE 172 2ND E DI
STRAUGHN, JANE BAL 088 15TH WAR
STRAUGHN, THEODORE R. QUE 201 3RD E DI
STRAUGHN, THOMAS QUE 172 2ND E DI
STRAUL, M. BAL 449 8TH WARD
STRAUS, CATHERINE BAL 393 3RD WARD
STRAUS, MARY L. BAL 156 16TH WAR
STRAUS, MATILDA BAL 330 7TH WARD
STRAUS, NANI BAL 020 9TH WARD
STRAUS, WILLIAM BAL 338 7TH WARD
STRAUSBORGER, CHARLES BAL 088 10TH WAR
STRAUSBURG, ELIZABETH WAS 232 1ST DIST
STRAUSBURG, SOLOMON WAS 230 1ST DIST
STRAUSE, CATHERINE FRE 032 FREDERIC
STRAUSS, E. BAL 141 5TH WARD
STRAUSS, GEORGE BAL 250 17TH WAR
STRAUSS, LEWIS BAL 260 2ND WARD
STRAUSS, SAMUEL BAL 256 2ND WARD
STRAUT, PETER BAL 125 18TH WAR
STRAW, CHRIST. WAS 185 BOONSBOR
STRAW, DANIEL BAL 190 5TH DIST
STRAW, JOHN ANN 300 1ST DIST
STRAW, LOUISA WAS 185 BOONSBOR
STRAW, MICHAEL BAL 190 5TH DIST
STRAW, NICHOLAS BAL 238 2ND WARD
STRAWBERRY, POMPY DOR 437 1ST DIST
STRAWBERRY, ROBERT DOR 431 1ST DIST
STRAWBERY, MARY BAL 153 11TH WAR
STRAWBRIDGE, ISAAC ANN 451 HOWARD D
STRAWBRIDGE, JOSEPH HAR 021 1ST DIST
STRAWHAN, JOHN TAL 036 EASTON D
STRAWHON, JOHN TAL 018 EASTON D
STRAWHON, T. * TAL 070 EASTON T
STRAWHORN, BENNETT* TAL 028 EASTON D
STRAWHORN, GEORGE W. TAL 028 EASTON D
STRAWHORN, WILLIAM* TAL 068 EASTON T
STRAWN, MARY A. BAL 295 3RD WARD
STRAWS, ISAAC BAL 296 7TH WARD
STRAWS, ISAAK BAL 303 7TH WARD
STRAWS, SAMUEL BAL 314 12TH WAR
STRAWYER, MARY BAL 189 5TH DIST
STRAYHORN, JONATHAN CEC 103 4TH E DI
STRAYSINGER, CHRISTIAN BAL 006 EASTERN
STREAFFER, JOHN FRE 040 FREDERIC
STREAKER, AUGUSTAS CAR 229 5TH DIST
STREAKER, JACOB ANN 487 HOWARD D
STREAKER, JOHN ANN 490 HOWARD D
STREAKER, LYDIA ANN 489 HOWARD D
STREAKER, MARY ANN 512 HOWARD D
STREAKER, WILLIAM ANN 501 HOWARD D
STREAM, GEORGE S. FRE 388 PETERSVI
STREAMS, DOLLY-BLACK FRE 393 PETERSVI
STREAMS, ISRAEL FRE 380 PETERSVI
STREAMS, MARY A. V. FRE 381 PETERSVI
STREANEY, JOHN BAL 170 19TH WAR
STREB, PETER BAL 051 18TH WAR
STREBECK, MARGARET BAL 172 16TH WAR
STREBLIN, FRANCIS ALL 209 CUMBERLA
STREBOST, WILLIAM BAL 042 9TH WARD
STRECBER, JOHN * BAL 267 2ND WARD
STRECH, EMMA BAL 132 16TH WAR
STREEL, LUTHER M.* DOR 377 1ST DIST
STREEPER, HARRIET BAL 051 1ST WARD
STREES, ADAM BAL 285 2ND WARD
STREET, ARTHUR CEC 154 PORT DUP
STREET, BENJAMIN T. SOM 463 HANGARY
STREET, CATHARINE HAR 044 1ST DIST
STREET, CHARLOTTE V. SOM 538 TYASKIN
STREET, DAVID BAL 086 18TH WAR
STREET, EDWARD* DOR 377 1ST DIST
STREET, ELIZ. * BAL 068 18TH WAR
STREET, HARIET SOM 542 TYASKIN
STREET, JAMES B. BAL 099 15TH WAR
STREET, JANE SOM 544 TYASKIN
STREET, JANE DOR 416 1ST DIST
STREET, JOHN C. BAL 119 5TH WARD
STREET, LUTHER M.* DOR 377 1ST DIST
STREET, MANSFIELD SOM 546 TYASKIN
STREET, MARY SOM 540 TYASKIN
STREET, MARY BAL 095 5TH WARD
STREET, MARY BAL 033 15TH WAR
STREET, MILKEY BAL 422 1ST DIST
STREET, RICHARD TAL 115 ST MICHA
STREET, S. BAL 295 1ST DIST
STREET, SAMUEL SOM 461 HANGARY
STREET, SAMUEL HAR 006 1ST DIST
STREET, SARAH HAR 052 1ST DIST
STREET, STCLAIR HAR 010 1ST DIST
STREET, THOMAS BAL 009 18TH WAR
STREET, THOMAS SOM 539 TYASKIN
STREET, THOMAS BAL 095 5TH WARD
STREET, THOMAS ALL 185 9TH E.D.
STREET, WILLIAM BAL 019 18TH WAR
STREET, ZACHEUS SOM 540 TYASKIN
STREETER S. F.* BAL 097 10TH WAR
STREETS, GEORGE W. ANN 460 HOWARD D
STREETS, JOHN BAL 105 15TH WAR
STREETT, ABRAHAM HAR 055 1ST DIST
STREETT, ABRAHAM Q. HAR 066 1ST DIST
STREETT, ANN HAR 066 1ST DIST
STREETT, CHUZZIA HAR 051 1ST DIST
STREETT, CORBIN HAR 057 1ST DIST
STREETT, CORBIN G. HAR 056 1ST DIST
STREETT, HANNAH HAR 053 1ST DIST
STREETT, JAMOS HAR 037 1ST DIST
STREETT, JOHN HAR 058 1ST DIST
STREETT, JOHN HAR 011 1ST DIST
STREETT, JOHN HAR 025 1ST DIST
STREETT, JOHN C. HAR 053 1ST DIST
STREETT, JOHN W. HAR 065 1ST DIST
STREETT, JOSHUA HAR 045 1ST DIST
STREETT, MERRIMAN HAR 025 1ST DIST
STREETT, ROGERS HAR 053 1ST DIST
STREETT, SAMUEL HAR 057 1ST DIST
STREETT, SHADARACK HAR 066 1ST DIST
STREETT, ST. CLAIR HAR 061 1ST DIST

STREETT, THOMAS HAR 056 1ST DIST
STREETT, THOMAS HAR 057 1ST DIST
STREETT, THOMAS HAR 044 1ST DIST
STREETT, THOMAS HAR 036 1ST DIST
STREETT, WILLIAM HAR 057 1ST DIST
STREETT, WILLIAM HAR 056 1ST DIST
STREETT, WILLIAM HAR 066 1ST DIST
STREETT, WILLIAM HAR 025 1ST DIST
STREETT, WILLIAM C. HAR 037 1ST DIST
STREHMEYER, WILHELMINA BAL 379 13TH WAR
STREICKER, MARY HAR 123 2ND DIST
STRELING, THOMAS BAL 289 17TH WAR
STREMMEL, DAVID CAR 346 6TH DIST
STREMMEL, REBECCA CAR 390 2ND DIST
STRENGER, MARGARET BAL 059 1ST WARD
STRENKUCK, CATHERINE FRE 058 FREDERIC
STRETCH, ELIZABETH BAL 423 3RD WARD
STREVEN, LINHARD* BAL 080 10TH WAR
STREVICH, JOHN CAR 342 6TH DIST
STREVICK, GEORGE CAR 412 2ND DIST
STREW, WILLIAM BAL 293 17TH WAR
STRIBBLING, CORNELIUS E.M ANN 283 ANNAPOLI
STRIBECK, GEORGE BAL 429 14TH WAR
STRIBECK, JOHN BAL 002 1ST WARD
STRIBEL, GEORGE BAL 253 6TH WARD
STRIBLING, JOHN BAL 465 14TH WAR
STRICKER, CATHARIEN BAL 261 2ND WARD
STRICKER, CATHERINE BAL 104 10TH WAR
STRICKER, JOHN HAR 123 2ND DIST
STRICKEY, MARGARET BAL 154 19TH WAR
STRICKLAND, CECELIA BAL 041 15TH WAR
STRICKLAND, DAVID T. CEC 010 ELKTON 3
STRICKLAND, HENRY BAL 423 3RD WARD
STRICKLAND, HENRY CAL 060 3RD DIST
STRICKLAND, JESSE BAL 023 15TH WAR
STRICKLAND, JESSE BAL 394 1ST DIST
STRICKLAND, JOHN CAL 055 3RD DIST
STRICKLAND, JOHN S. CEC 090 4TH E DI
STRICKLAND, JOHNATHAN HAR 068 1ST DIST
STRICKLAND, PALMER CEC 011 ELKTON 3
STRICKLAND, PRICE CEC 010 ELKTON 3
STRICKLAND, REBECCA CEC 004 ELKTON 3
STRICKLAND, SAMUEL FRE 192 5TH E DI
STRICKLAND, SAMUEL BAL 103 15TH WAR
STRICKLAND, SARAH CAL 057 3RD DIST
STRICKLAND, SARAH CAL 055 3RD DIST
STRICKLAND, SARAH A. CAL 038 2ND DIST
STRICKLAND, THOMAS CEC 101 4TH E DI
STRICKLAND, WILLIAM PRI 077 MARLBROU
STRICKLEY, JAMES BAL 108 1ST WARD
STRICKLIN, ELIZABETH CAR 262 3RD DIST
STRICKLIN, HENRY BAL 013 2ND DIST
STRICKLIN, JOHN B. HAR 179 3RD DIST
STRICKLING, JOSHUA CAR 173 8TH DIST
STRICKLING, MARTHA CAR 184 8TH DIST
STRICKNEY, AMANDA BAL 205 19TH WAR
STRIDE, CATHARINE FRE 071 FREDERIC
STRIDE, JOHN FRE 075 FREDERIC
STRIDER, JOHN BAL 401 14TH WAR
STRIDER, JOHN ANN 420 HOWARD D
STRIDER, JULIAN FRE 032 FREDERIC
STRIDER, MARIA F. BAL 264 1ST DIST
STRIELLIZ, WILLIAM BAL 283 2ND WARD
STRIESBOCH, JACOB BAL 267 12TH WAR
STRIFFER, ESTER FRE 085 FREDERIC
STRIFFEY, JOHN WAS 117 2ND DIST
STRIGERT, CHARLES BAL 233 17TH WAR
STRIGLER, ANDREW BAL 086 1ST WARD
STRIGLER, ERNEST BAL 032 18TH WAR
STRIKLER, JOHN BAL 018 9TH WARD
STRIMMER, LEWIS BAL 295 20TH WAR
STRIMNER, MARTIN BAL 256 2ND WARD
STRIMP, MARY * BAL 278 20TH WAR
STRINCHCOMB, NATHANIEL ANN 507 HOWARD D
STRINE, BENJAMIN FRE 291 WOODSBOR
STRINE, JOHN FRE 413 8TH E DI
STRINE, SUSAN FRE 112 CREAGERS
STRINE, SUSANNA FRE 416 8TH E DI
STRINE, WILLIAM BAL 459 1ST DIST
STRINEL, JOHN * CAR 258 3RD DIST
STRINER, CLEMENTINE CAR 378 2ND DIST
STRING, ALEXANDER BAL 179 19TH WAR
STRINGER, ELIZABETH ANN 486 HOWARD D
STRINGER, ELLEANOR ANN 473 HOWARD D
STRINGER, PETER W. BAL 037 9TH WARD
STRINKMAN, FREDERICK BAL 025 15TH WAR
STRIPE, MICHAEL BAL 269 12TH WAR
STRIPPLE, AMENA BAL 297 7TH WARD
STRIPPLE, HARRIETT BAL 130 11TH WAR
STRIPPLE, WILLIAM BAL 248 17TH WAR
STRITE, CHRISTIAN WAS 285 1ST DIST
STRITE, JOHN WAS 292 1ST DIST
STRITE, JOSEPH WAS 285 1ST DIST
STRITE, SAMUEL WAS 131 2ND DIST
STRITEHOFF, MARY HAR 049 1ST DIST
STRITEHOFF, JOHN HAR 012 1ST DIST
STRITEHOOF, PETER HAR 051 1ST DIST
STRITEHOOF, SUSAN HAR 069 1ST DIST
STROBB, HENRY BAL 168 1ST WARD
STROBEL, FERDINAND BAL 080 10TH WAR
STROBEL, JOHN G. BAL 373 13TH WAR
STROBEL, JOHN P. BAL 283 2ND WARD
STROBEL, MICHAEL BAL 201 2ND WARD
STROBEY, HENRY BAL 224 17TH WAR
STROBLE, GEORGE BAL 112 2ND DIST
STROBLE, HENRY BAL 248 2ND WARD
STROBLE, LEWIS BAL 223 17TH WAR
STROBLE, MRS. BAL 223 17TH WAR
STROBLE, ZACHARIAH HAR 074 1ST DIST
STROBURT, MARY BAL 037 18TH WAR
STROCK, HENRY WAS 295 1ST DIST
STROCK, MICHAEL WAS 288 1ST DIST
STROCK, REBECCA WAS 288 1ST DIST
STROCK, YOST WAS 295 1ST DIST
STROCKER, DANIEL WAS 013 WILLIAMS
STRODE, ELIZA FRE 386 PETERSVI
STRODMAN, HARMAN HAR 080 2ND DIST
STRODMAN, JOHN BAL 099 2ND DIST
STRODTMAN, HENRY BAL 031 9TH WARD
STRODTMAN, JOHN BAL 316 1ST DIST
STRODTMAN, JOHN J. BAL 031 9TH WARD
STROFFER, AMELIA C. BAL 209 2ND WARD
STROFFER, CHARLES BAL 074 1ST WARD
STROGLE, MICHAEL ALL 159 6TH E.D.
STROH, CONRAD BAL 133 16TH WAR
STROH, JOHN HAR 119 2ND DIST
STROH, MAGDALENA BAL 169 6TH WARD
STROHEFFER, GEORGE BAL 225 19TH WAR
STROHEFFER, JOHN BAL 225 19TH WAR
STROHM, J. F. BAL 064 10TH WAR

STROHMBERGER, HENRY BAL 207 6TH WARD
STROHMEYER, GEORGE BAL 043 9TH WARD
STROINGER, GEORGE ALL 224 CUMBERLA
STROKES, CAROLINE BAL 066 4TH WARD
STROKS, PHILIP BAL 081 1ST WARD
STROLE, PHILIP WAS 174 FUNKSTOW
STROMBERGER, GEORGE BAL 237 6TH WARD
STROMENGER, JOHN BAL 043 15TH WAR
STROMICH, ELIZABETH BAL 388 1ST DIST
STRONBEL, WILLIAM BAL 103 1ST WARD
STROND, JOHN R. KEN 269 1ST DIST
STRONG, BARBARA ALL 170 7TH E.D.
STRONG, DANIEL ALL 170 6TH E.D.
STRONG, DIMAS HAR 074 1ST DIST
STRONG, ELEN HAR 205 3RD DIST
STRONG, HENRY PRI 034 VANSVILL
STRONG, HORASIC O. HAR 206 3RD DIST
STRONG, JOHN KEN 267 1ST DIST
STRONG, JOSEPH M. ALL 212 CUMBERLA
STRONG, JOSEPH W. HAR 073 1ST DIST
STRONG, LAWRENCE MILLER KEN 252 1ST DIST
STRONG, MARY BAL 134 2ND DIST
STRONG, REBECCA BAL 235 6TH WARD
STRONG, THOMAS KEN 267 1ST DIST
STRONG, WILLIAM QUE 147 1ST E DI
STROPES, JOHN ALL 037 2ND E.D.
STROSSER, ELISABETH ALL 038 2ND E.D.
STROTE, ELIZABETH BAL 258 20TH WAR
STROUBT, GEORGE BAL 241 2ND WARD
STROUP, CHARLES QUE 251 5TH E DI
STROUP, GEORGE BAL 298 17TH WAR
STROUP, JACOB BAL 314 1ST DIST
STROUS, FANNEY BAL 330 7TH WARD
STROUSE, GEORGE WAS 208 1ST DIST
STROUSE, JOHN BAL 369 1ST DIST
STROUSS, MARTIN ANN 482 HOWARD D
STROYER, WILLIAM ALL 043 10TH E.D
STRREEVE, LEVI CAR 270 WESTMINS
STRUBLE, AUGUSTUS BAL 194 17TH WAR
STRUBLE, JOHN WAS 157 2ND DIST
STRUBLE, JOHN H. WAS 158 2ND DIST
STRUBY, CATHARINE BAL 454 14TH WAR
STRUGHN, CHARLES P. DOR 376 1ST DIST
STRUGIS, LOUISA M. WOR 251 1ST CENS
STRUGIS, PETGER W. WOR 221 4TH E DI
STRUGIS, ROBERT WOR 298 9TH E DI
STRUKELEN, MARY BAL 203 17TH WAR
STRUMP, JOHN R. HAR 119 2ND DIST
STRUMP, SAMUEL E. HAR 124 2ND DIST
STRUMP, THOMAS C. HAR 119 2ND DIST
STRUMPS, MICHAEL BAL 288 1ST DIST
STRUP, PETER BAL 094 18TH WAR
STRUT, EDWARD* DOR 377 1ST DIST
STRUTER, S. F.* BAL 097 10TH WAR
STRUTHOOF, ELIZABETH BAL 133 5TH WARD
STRVESTRECKER, M. BAL 214 19TH WAR
STRYKER, JAMES E. BAL 033 15TH WAR
STTOOKS, JOHN-BLACK CAR 089 NO TWP L
STUARD, ANN M. ST 258 3RD E DI
STUARD, CHARLES HAR 184 3RD DIST
STUARD, ISAAC HAR 163 3RD DIST
STUARD, JOHN L.-BLACK ST 338 4TH E DI
STUARD, JOSEPH A. ST 255 3RD E DI
STUARD, MARY HAR 165 3RD DIST
STUARD, WILLIAM L. HAR 171 3RD DIST
STUART, ALEXANDER BAL 208 11TH WAR
STUART, CAROLINE BAL 165 11TH WAR
STUART, CATHARINE BAL 259 17TH WAR
STUART, CHARLES CAL 035 2ND DIST
STUART, CHARLES BAL 071 18TH WAR
STUART, COLUMBUS G. BAL 081 18TH WAR
STUART, DAVID CAL 063 3RD DIST
STUART, EDA BAL 175 11TH WAR
STUART, EDWARD BAL 137 18TH WAR
STUART, ELIZA BAL 140 11TH WAR
STUART, ELIZABETH BAL 160 11TH WAR
STUART, ELIZABETH BAL 154 11TH WAR
STUART, ELIZABETH BAL 168 11TH WAR
STUART, ELLEN BAL 338 13TH WAR
STUART, ENNELS BAL 224 17TH WAR
STUART, FRANCIS BAL 167 11TH WAR
STUART, GEORGE BAL 163 11TH WAR
STUART, GEORGE BAL 095 5TH WARD
STUART, GEORGE A. BAL 137 18TH WAR
STUART, GEORGE H. BAL 060 18TH WAR
STUART, HAMMOND CAL 063 3RD DIST
STUART, HENRY D. BAL 320 3RD WARD
STUART, ISAAC BAL 252 17TH WAR
STUART, ISEBELLA E. BAL 078 18TH WAR
STUART, JAMES BAL 208 11TH WAR
STUART, JOHN BAL 159 1ST WARD
STUART, JOHN WAS 164 2ND DIST
*STUART, JOHN H. WOR 182 6TH E DI
STUART, JOSEPH BAL 168 11TH WAR
STUART, JULIA BAL 135 18TH WAR
STUART, LOUISA BAL 213 11TH WAR
STUART, LYDIA BAL 309 3RD WARD
STUART, M. L. BAL 144 11TH WAR
STUART, MARGARET CAL 034 2ND DIST
STUART, MARIAH CAL 063 3RD DIST
STUART, MARY BAL 146 11TH WAR
STUART, MRS. SOPHIA BAL 016 18TH WAR
STUART, NELLY BAL 122 18TH WAR
STUART, PERE QUE 209 3RD E DI
STUART, POLLY BAL 257 1ST DIST
STUART, R. S. BAL 145 11TH WAR
STUART, REBECCA BAL 153 11TH WAR
STUART, REBECCA BAL 190 11TH WAR
STUART, SALLY BAL 151 11TH WAR
STUART, SARAH BAL 033 18TH WAR
STUART, SARAH BAL 170 11TH WAR
STUART, SUSAN BAL 211 11TH WAR
STUART, WILLIAM BAL 225 17TH WAR
STUART, WILLIAM TAL 118 ST MICHA
STUART, WILLIAM W. BAL 135 5TH WARD
STUART,ALEXANDER-BLACK QUE 169 2ND E DI
STUBBENS, GEORGE CEC 153 PORT DUP
STUBBINS, ANN SOPHIA BAL 074 18TH WAR
STUBBINS, ANNE BAL 346 13TH WAR
STUBBINS, CHARLES BAL 084 18TH WAR
STUBBINS, CHARLES BAL 291 20TH WAR
STUBBINS, JOSEPH FRE 205 BUCKEYST
STUBBINS, RANDOLPH BAL 157 6TH WARD
STUBBINS, WILLIAM BAL 077 18TH WAR
STUBBLEFIELD, SUSAN BAL 216 11TH WAP
STUBBONS, CHARLES BAL 414 1ST DIST
STUBBONS, JOSEPH T. BAL 293 1ST DIST
STUBBONS, WILLIAM CEC 158 PORT DUP
STUBBS, DANIEL WEBSTER BAL 105 15TH WAR
STUBBS, DEBORA BAL 047 4TH WARD

Name	County	Page	District
STUBBS, EDWARD	MGM	364	BERRYS D
STUBBS, JOSEPH	BAL	105	15TH WAR
STUBBS, PHILIP	CEC	060	1ST E DI
STUBBS, SLAYTER B.	CEC	162	6TH E DI
STUBBS, WILLIAM E.	MGM	364	BERRYS D
STUBERING, FREDERICK	ANN	471	HOWARD D
STUBMAN, JOHN T.	BAL	291	3RD WARD
STUBS, HENRY	CAR	084	NO TWP L
STUBS, JOHN	CAR	095	NO TWP L
STUBS, LEVIN	CAR	122	NO TWP L
STUBS, THOMAS H.	CAR	123	NO TWP L
STUCK, F.F.	FRE	217	BUCKEYST
STUCK, FREDERICK	WAS	033	2ND SUBD
STUCK, GEORGE	BAL	098	10TH WAR
STUCK.JACOB	ALL	024	3RD E.D.
STUCKLAND, MARY	CEC	148	PORT DUP
STUCKMAN, HENRY	BAL	237	2ND WARD
STUDD, WILLAIM	BAL	226	17TH WAR
STUDDEN, EDWARD	BAL	185	11TH WAR
STUDLE, CATHARINE	BAL	260	2ND WARD
STUDLEN, JOHN	BAL	144	1ST WARD
STUDLEY, ELIPHALET	WOR	289	9TH E DI
STUDMAN, JOHN	ALL	226	CUMBERLA
STUDT, JOHN H.	BAL	259	2ND WARD
STUDY, DAVID	CAR	255	3RD DIST
STUDY, JACOB	CAR	246	3RD DIST
STUDY, JOHN	CAR	254	3RD DIST
STUESNER, CATHARINE *	BAL	067	15TH WAR
STUFF, HEZEKIAH	WAS	012	WILLIAMS
STUFFLE, ALEXANDER	ALL	256	CUMBERLA
STUFLER, LENIAH	BAL	231	1ST DIST
STUITT, LEMEUL L.	WOR	206	4TH E DI
STUKER, JAMES	BAL	267	2ND WARD
STULFORT, SAILFORD *	BAL	093	2ND DIST
STULL, ADAM	FRE	097	FREDERIC
STULL, BENJAMIN	FRE	280	WOODSBOR
STULL, BENJAMIN	WAS	154	HAGERSTO
STULL, CATHERIN	FRE	014	FREDERIC
STULL, CHARLES	WAS	301	1ST DIST
STULL, CHRISTIAN	FRE	116	CREAGERS
STULL, DANIEL	CAR	188	4TH DIST
STULL, DAVID	CAR	384	2ND DIST
STULL, DAVID F.	FRE	082	FREDERIC
STULL, DEBY	FRE	116	CREAGERS
STULL, DENNIS	FRE	101	FREDERIC
STULL, GEORGE	FRE	089	FREDERIC
STULL, GEORGE	FRE	087	FREDERIC
STULL, HIRAM	WAS	269	1ST DIST
STULL, JACOB	FRE	089	FREDERIC
STULL, JACOB	FRE	103	FREDERIC
STULL, JACOB	FRE	116	CREAGERS
STULL, JOHN	FRE	114	CREAGERS
STULL, JOHN	FRE	178	5TH E DI
STULL, JOHN	FRE	089	FREDERIC
STULL, JOHN	FRE	090	FREDERIC
STULL, JOHN	FRE	215	BUCKEYST
STULL, JOHN	BAL	235	1ST DIST
STULL, JOSHUA	FRE	083	FREDERIC
STULL, LEWIS	FRE	292	WOODSBOR
STULL, LEWIS E.	FRE	127	CREAGERS
STULL, LOUISA	FRE	292	WOODSBOR
STULL, MARGARET A.	HAR	010	1ST DIST
STULL, MICHAEL	FRE	090	FREDERIC
STULL, WILLIAM	FRE	110	CREAGERS
STULL, WILLIAM	FRE	182	5TH E DI
STULLER, CHRISTIAN	CAR	406	2ND DIST
STULLER, CONRAD	CAR	409	2ND DIST
STULLER, DANIEL	CAR	296	7TH DIST
STULLER, DAVID	CAR	314	1ST DIST
STULLER, GEORGE	BAL	222	19TH WAR
STULLER, HENRY	CAR	404	2ND DIST
STULLER, JACOB	CAR	411	2ND DIST
STULLER, JOSHUA	CAR	297	7TH DIST
STULLER, REBECCA	CAR	289	7TH DIST
STULLERY, JOHN J.	BAL	011	9TH WARD
STULLS, MARGARET	CAR	340	6TH DIST
STULTER, MARY	BAL	121	5TH WARD
STULTZ, ABRAHAM	CAR	235	UNION TO
STULTZ, ANN M.	CAR	386	2ND DIST
STULTZ, DANIEL	CAR	381	2ND DIST
STULTZ, DANIEL	BAL	153	19TH WAR
STULTZ, ELIZABETH	FRE	069	FREDERIC
STULTZ, EPHRAIM	FRE	069	FREDERIC
STULTZ, FREDERICK	FRE	187	5TH E DI
STULTZ, HENRY	CAR	378	2ND DIST
STULTZ, JAMES	FRE	027	FREDERIC
STULTZ, JOHN F.	CAR	388	2ND DIST
STULTZ, MARGARET	CAR	399	2ND DIST
STULTZ, MARGARET E.	CAR	236	UNION TO
STULTZ, WILLIAM	CAR	387	2ND DIST
STULTZER, CHARLES	BAL	048	9TH WARD
STULTZHEIN, FRITZ	BAL	146	19TH WAR
STULZ, J.	BAL	449	8TH WARD
STUM, JOHN	BAL	277	1ST DIST
STUMAN, W. R.*	DOR	452	1ST DIST
STUMB, PETER	FRE	067	FREDERIC
STUMBAUGH, MARY	WAS	153	2ND DIST
STUMBAUGH, PETER	WAS	153	2ND DIST
STUMMELL, CORNELIUS	FRE	138	CREAGERS
STUMNER, DANIEL	ANN	419	HOWARD D
STUMP, A. W.	BAL	082	18TH WAR
STUMP, ANN	HAR	175	3RD DIST
STUMP, BARBARY	CAR	172	8TH DIST
STUMP, BENTON	BAL	270	12TH WAR
STUMP, CASANDER	HAR	170	3RD DIST
STUMP, CHRISTIAN	BAL	204	6TH DIST
STUMP, COLEY	BAL	073	10TH WAR
STUMP, CONRAD	BAL	266	20TH WAR
STUMP, DANIEL	BAL	206	6TH DIST
STUMP, DUCKET	HAR	123	2ND DIST
STUMP, ELIZABETH	BAL	139	19TH WAR
STUMP, FREDERICK	BAL	302	7TH WARD
STUMP, HENRY	BAL	221	1ST DIST
STUMP, HENRY	BAL	108	10TH WAR
STUMP, HENRY	BAL	242	6TH WARD
STUMP, HENRY	HAR	184	3RD DIST
STUMP, HERMAN	HAR	124	2ND DIST
STUMP, JACOB	HAR	188	3RD DIST
STUMP, JACOB	ALL	174	7TH E.D.
STUMP, JAMES	BAL	404	3RD WARD
STUMP, JOHN	BAL	454	8TH WARD
STUMP, JOHN	CAR	339	6TH DIST
STUMP, JOHN	CEC	084	CHARLEST
STUMP, JOHN W.	HAR	142	2ND DIST
STUMP, LAVINIA	BAL	242	6TH WARD
STUMP, LEVINA	BAL	346	7TH WARD
STUMP, MARGARETT	HAR	120	2ND DIST
STUMP, MARY	BAL	071	15TH WAR
STUMP, MARY *	BAL	278	20TH WAR
STUMP, PAULINE P.	BAL	243	17TH WAR
STUMP, PETER	CAR	171	8TH DIST
STUMP, PRISCILLA	BAL	003	15TH WAR
STUMP, SAMUEL	BAL	205	6TH DIST
STUMP, SAMUEL	BAL	403	14TH WAR
STUMP, SENVESER *	CAL	017	1ST DIST
STUMP, VALENT	BAL	261	20TH WAR
STUMP,BMARGARET	HAR	030	1ST DIST
STUMPF, FREDERICK C.	BAL	034	15TH WAR
STUMPF, GOERGE	BAL	133	16TH WAR
STUMPHT, CAROLINE	BAL	232	1ST DIST
STUMPS, MARTHA	ALL	174	7TH E.D.
STUNG, LOUISA	ANN	429	HOWARD D
STUNKEL, CHARLES H.	FRE	234	BUCKEYST
STUNKEL, FREDERICK	FRE	220	BUCKEYST
STUNKLE, HENRY	FRE	051	FREDERIC
STUNS, CONRAD	CAR	265	WESTMINS
STUNS, FREDERICK*	BAL	082	10TH WAR
STUNZ, FREDERICK*	BAL	082	10TH WAR
STUP, GEORGE L.	FRE	050	FREDERIC
STUPE, JAOCB	FRE	075	FREDERIC
STUPE, JOSEPH	FRE	078	FREDERIC
STUPLEY, RICHARD	BAL	146	19TH WAR
STURBEN, RACHEL	CEC	051	1ST E DI
STURBOCH, J.	BAL	254	12TH WAR
STURDIVANT, JAMES	BAL	139	11TH WAR
STURGEM, THOMAS	CEC	076	NORTHEAS
STURGEN, CATHARINE	BAL	212	19TH WAR
STURGEON, EDWARD G.	BAL	100	15TH WAR
STURGEON, FREDERIC	BAL	259	6TH WARD
STURGEON, LINDSEY	BAL	216	6TH WARD
STURGEON, SARAH D.	FRE	389	PETERSVI
STURGERS, FLASUS	FRE	023	FREDERIC
STURGES, ELIZABETH	WOR	322	1ST E DI
STURGES, HETTY	WOR	349	1ST E DI
STURGES, JAMES	WOR	322	1ST E DI
STURGES, JOHN	WOR	319	1ST E DI
STURGES, JULIANA	BAL	344	13TH WAR
STURGES, MARGARET	WOR	323	1ST E DI
STURGES, NANCY	WOR	308	2ND E DI
STURGESS, ANN	BAL	189	11TH WAR
STURGESS, BETSEY	SOM	415	DUBLIN D
STURGESS, JOHN R.	SOM	406	DUBLIN D
STURGESS, LITTLETON	SOM	413	DUBLIN D
STURGESS, SAMUEL W.	PRI	079	MARLBROU
STURGESS, SAMUEL W.	PRI	079	MARLBROU
STURGESS, WILLIAM	BAL	309	3RD WARD
STURGIS, ARA	WOR	298	9TH E DI
STURGIS, CHESTER	WOR	203	4TH E DI
STURGIS, ELEANOR	WOR	309	2ND E DI
STURGIS, EPHRAIM	WOR	301	SNOW HIL
STURGIS, GEORGE	WOR	309	2ND E DI
STURGIS, HENRY	WOR	224	4TH E DI
STURGIS, JACOB	WOR	306	2ND E DI
STURGIS, JAMES	WOR	339	1ST E DI
STURGIS, JAMES W.	WOR	259	BERLIN 1
STURGIS, JAOCB	WOR	306	2ND E DI
STURGIS, JOHN	WOR	259	BERLIN 1
STURGIS, JOHN	WOR	214	4TH E DI
STURGIS, JOHN D.	WOR	314	2ND E DI
STURGIS, JOSHUA	WOR	343	1ST E DI
STURGIS, JOSHUA	WOR	175	6TH E DI
STURGIS, JOSHUA-BLACK	WOR	345	1ST E DI
STURGIS, LEAH	WOR	314	2ND E DI
STURGIS, MARY	WOR	308	2ND E DI
STURGIS, NATHAN	WOR	312	2ND E DI
STURGIS, NOAH	WOR	329	1ST E DI
STURGIS, PETER	WOR	298	9TH E DI
STURGIS, SCHEDRICK	WOR	305	2ND E DI
STURGIS, THOMAS	WOR	309	2ND E DI
STURGIS, THOMAS	WOR	313	2ND E DI
STURGIS, THOMAS	WOR	313	2ND E DI
STURGIS, THOMAS	SOM	415	DUBLIN D
STURGIS, THOMAS L.	WOR	235	6TH E DI
STURGIS, WILLIAM	WOR	316	2ND E DI
STURGIS, WILLIAM	WOR	307	2ND E DI
STURGIS, WILLIAM	WOR	308	2ND E DI
STURGIS, WILLIAM	WOR	340	1ST E DI
STURGIS, WILLMON	WOR	300	SNOW HIL
STURGUS, PLEASANT	BAL	263	2ND WARD
STURM, ISABELLA	BAL	317	1ST DIST
STURR, THOMAS	WAS	165	HAGERSTO
STURTT, WILLIAM	BAL	171	19TH WAR
STUTCHZ, OLVIS	BAL	288	3RD WARD
STUTLTZ, MARY E.	CAR	266	WESTMINS
STUTT, HESTER	BAL	161	2ND DIST
STUTTER, SAVILLA	CAR	409	2ND DIST
STUTTS, HENRY	CAR	226	5TH DIST
STUTZ, CASSANDRA	BAL	047	2ND DIST
STUTZ, MARY	CAR	377	2ND DIST
STUVART, ABRAHAM	BAL	149	16TH WAR
STVENSON, JOSHUA J.	FRE	133	CREAGERS
STWART, JOHN	CAR	254	3RD DIST
STWEEVE, JOSEPH	CAR	265	WESTMINS
STWESER, FRANCIS *	CAR	273	WESTMINS
STWINER, DAVID H.	CAR	287	7TH DIST
STYER, FREDERICK	BAL	341	1ST DIST
STYER, JOHN	BAL	341	1ST DIST
STYLER, WILLIAM	BAL	332	7TH WARD
STYLES, REBECCA	MGM	380	ROCKERLE
STYLES, ROBERT	BAL	223	17TH WAR
STYLES, THOMAS	MGM	393	ROCKERLE
STYMITCHS, ELIZABETH	BAL	030	4TH WARD
STYNAX, WILLIAM	ANN	514	HOWARD D
STYNCICUM, DAVID	BAL	371	1ST DIST
STYNCICUM, THOMAS	BAL	296	1ST DIST
STYRN, FRANCIS	BAL	167	1ST WARD
STYSHERS, THOMAS K.	KEN	287	3RD DIST
STYTES, JAMES	BAL	328	7TH WARD
SUAN, GODFREY	FRE	002	FREDERIC
SUARA, ELLEN	BAL	214	6TH DIST
SUBBONS, ELIZA	FRE	092	FREDERIC
SUBERT, JOHN	BAL	271	2ND WARD
SUBLICK, MARCUS	BAL	457	14TH WAR
SUCCHESI, FREDERICK*	BAL	071	10TH WAR
SUCCHISI, FREDERICK*	BAL	071	10TH WAR
SUCH, TEMPERANCE	BAL	416	1ST DIST
SUCHTENS, JAMES*	ALL	217	CUMBERLA
SUCK, GEORGE	BAL	189	5TH DIST
SUD, FRANCES H.*	BAL	073	4TH WARD
SUDDER, JOSEPH	KEN	308	3RD DIST
SUDDLER, TUBMAN W.	SOM	351	BRINKLEY
SUDENSTROUKE, JOHN B.	BAL	142	11TH WAR
SUDERY, JAMES	BAL	389	1ST DIST
SUDLAR, CALEB	SOM	362	BRINKLEY
SUDLAR, CHARLOTTE	SOM	353	BRINKLEY
SUDLAR, THOMAS	SOM	362	BRINKLEY
SUDLAR, WILLIAM C.	SOM	361	BRINKLEY
SUDLER, ARTHUR E.	QUE	123	1ST E DI
SUDLER, CALEB	SOM	363	BRINKLEY
SUDLER, CHARLES	CHA	263	MIDDLETO
SUDLER, CHARLOTTE	SOM	363	BRINKLEY
SUDLER, EDWARD	QUE	234	4TH E DI
SUDLER, EDWARD	QUE	134	1ST E DI
SUDLER, EDWARD-BLACK	QUE	146	1ST E DI
SUDLER, EMORY	KEN	213	2ND DIST
SUDLER, EMORY	KEN	310	3RD DIST
SUDLER, HARRIET-BLACK	QUE	143	1ST E DI
SUDLER, HENERETTA	SOM	427	PRINCESS
SUDLER, JOHN	SOM	420	PRINCESS
SUDLER, JOHN	KEN	305	3RD DIST
SUDLER, JOSEPH	SOM	428	PRINCESS
SUDLER, JOSHUA	CAR	080	NO TWP L
SUDLER, JOSHUA-BLACK	CAR	082	NO TWP L
SUDLER, JSOHUA-BLAKC	CAR	082	NO TWP L
SUDLER, MARY	QUE	174	2ND E DI
SUDLER, MATTHIAS	SOM	428	PRINCESS
SUDLER, THOMAS	QUE	132	1ST E DI
SUDLER, WILLIAM J.	QUE	173	2ND E DI
SUDLER, WILLIAN-BLACK	QUE	165	2ND E DI
SUDMANN, MARY	BAL	125	16TH WAR
SUDMEYER, LOUISA	BAL	063	15TH WAR
SUDORS, MARY	CEC	002	ELKTON 3
SUDROW, ESTER*	BAL	053	4TH WARD
SUDS, LEWIS	BAL	266	2ND WARD
SUEIYSTON, WILLIAM R.	BAL	326	12TH WAR
SUELL, CHRISTIAN-BLACK	FRE	218	BUCKEYST
SUELL, ISAAC	FRE	211	BUCKEYST
SUEMAN, ELLEN	FRE	186	5TH E DI
SUEMAN, EZRA	FRE	152	10TH E D
SUEMRWALT, ANDREW J.	BAL	255	17TH WAR
SUFBOROUGH, JOHN	MGM	361	BERRYS D
SUFFER, WILLIAM S.	ALL	216	CUMBERLA
SUGAR, JACOB	BAL	333	13TH WAR
SUGARS, JOHN	ANN	471	HOWARD D
SUGARS, MARGARET	MGM	331	CRACKLIN
SUGDEN, GEORGE	BAL	062	15TH WAR
SUGER, JOHN	BAL	019	9TH WARD
SUGGANS, MARGARET *	BAL	336	1ST DIST
SUGGISH, MARIA*	BAL	111	10TH WAR
SUIAR, JOHN A.	BAL	202	2ND WARD
SUINN, J.W.	BAL	213	2ND WARD
SUIRE, MARIA*	BAL	041	4TH WARD
SUIRK, GOERGE	BAL	063	1ST WARD
SUIS, BENJAMIN*	TAL	029	EASTON D
SUIT, BASIL	PRI	083	QUEEN AN
SUIT, BENJAMIN S.	ANN	300	1ST DIST
SUIT, CALVERT	ST	321	4TH E DI
SUIT, EDWARD	PRI	004	BLADENSB
SUIT, EDWARD	ANN	315	1ST DIST
SUIT, FIELDER	PRI	091	MARLBROU
SUIT, GRAFTON	PRI	004	BLADENSB
SUIT, JOHN L.	PRI	001	BLADENSB
SUIT, JOHN L.	PRI	083	QUEEN AN
SUIT, JOSIAH	PRI	013	BLADENSB
SUIT, KELITA	CHA	282	BOJANTOW
SUIT, MARTHA A.	ANN	315	1ST DIST
SUIT, MRS-	ANN	299	1ST DIST
SUIT, NATHANIEL	PRI	013	BLADENSB
SUIT, OLIVER R.	PRI	005	BLADENSB
SUIT, SAMUEL	ST	342	5TH E DI
SUIT, THOMAS A.R.	ST	321	4TH E DI
SUIT, WILLIAM	PRI	012	BLADENSB
SUITER, SARAH	WAS	162	2ND DIST
SUITER, WILLIAM	WAS	148	2ND DIST
SUITZ, MARTIN	BAL	178	2ND WARD
SUKLE, LEWIS	ALL	029	2ND E.D.
SUKLE, ZACHARIAH	ALL	029	2ND E.D.
SULAMAN, HIRAM	BAL	461	1ST DIST
SULENDER, EDWARD	DOR	341	3RD DIVI
SULICK, JACOB	FRE	022	FREDERIC
SULISAN, DANIEL	FRE	C24	FREDERIC
SULISAN, JAMES	FRE	024	FREDERIC
SULIVAN, ANN S.*	DOR	381	1ST DIST
SULIVAN, ARMELIA	BAL	201	11TH WAR
SULIVAN, EDWARD	ALL	219	CUMBERLA
SULIVAN, ELIZA C.	DOR	378	1ST DIST
SULIVAN, ELIZABETH	BAL	333	1ST DIST
SULIVAN, EPHRAIM	WAS	287	1ST DIST
SULIVAN, GEORGE*	DOR	439	1ST DIST
SULIVAN, JAMES	WOR	239	6TH E DI
SULIVAN, JANE	SOM	499	SALISBUR
SULIVAN, JOHN	TAL	113	ST MICHA
SULIVAN, LYDIA	WOR	197	8TH E DI
SULIVAN, MALON	ANN	498	HOWARD D
SULIVAN, MICHAEL	BAL	270	2ND WARD
SULIVAN, NELSON	CAR	227	5TH DIST
SULIVAN, SUSAN	BAL	431	14TH WAR
SULIVAN, WILLIAM A.*	DOR	378	1ST DIST
SULIVAN,MATHEW	ALL	217	CUMBERLA
SULIVANE, GEORGE*	DOR	439	1ST DIST
SULIVANE, JAMES*	DOR	455	1ST DIST
SULIVANE, POLLY*	DOR	460	1ST DIST
SULIVANE, WILLIAM A.*	DOR	378	1ST DIST
SULIVANN, ANN S.*	DOR	381	1ST DIST
SULL, LEVI	WOR	350	1ST E DI
SULL, MARTHA	BAL	027	2ND DIST
SULLAVIN, DAVID	KEN	284	3RD DIST
SULLAVIN, JOSEPH	KEN	291	3RD DIST
SULLENS, DAVID	BAL	149	2ND DIST
SULLERMAN, HANNAH	CEC	148	PORT DUP
SULLERS, MARY J.*	DOR	297	1ST DIST
SULLEVAN, ANN	CEC	144	PORT DUP
SULLIVAN, ABNER	ANN	504	HOWARD D
SULLIVAN, ABRAHAM	CAR	333	MANCHEST
SULLIVAN, AMANDA	BAL	075	18TH WAR
SULLIVAN, AMELIA	BAL	081	4TH WARD
SULLIVAN, ANN	BAL	065	4TH WARD
SULLIVAN, ANN	BAL	031	4TH WARD
SULLIVAN, ANN	BAL	351	3RD WARD
SULLIVAN, ANN	BAL	126	16TH WAR
SULLIVAN, ARTEMAS	ANN	512	HOWARD D
SULLIVAN, BARNEY	BAL	398	3RD WARD
SULLIVAN, BENJAMIN T.	ANN	498	HOWARD D
SULLIVAN, BENSON	BAL	034	2ND DIST
SULLIVAN, CATHARINE	BAL	277	12TH WAR
SULLIVAN, CATHERINE	BAL	143	11TH WAR
SULLIVAN, CHARLES	BAL	409	8TH WARD
SULLIVAN, CHARLES A.	ANN	279	ANNAPOLI
SULLIVAN, CLEMENT	CAR	130	NO TWP L
SULLIVAN, DANIEL	CAR	382	2ND DIST
SULLIVAN, DANIEL	CAR	403	2ND DIST
SULLIVAN, DANIEL	BAL	073	1ST WARD
SULLIVAN, DAVID	BAL	195	19TH WAR
SULLIVAN, DAVID	TAL	071	EASTON T
SULLIVAN, DENNIS	BAL	202	19TH WAR
SULLIVAN, DENNIS	BAL	001	18TH WAR
SULLIVAN, DENNIS	MGM	370	BERRYS D
SULLIVAN, DENNIS	BAL	164	2ND DIST
SULLIVAN, EDWARD	BAL	006	1ST WARD
SULLIVAN, EDWARD	BAL	287	7TH WARD

Name	County	Page	District
SULLIVAN, EDWARD	BAL	286	7TH WARD
SULLIVAN, EDWARD	BAL	174	1ST WARD
SULLIVAN, ELIJAH	MGM	316	CRACKLIN
SULLIVAN, ELIZA	TAL	055	EASTON D
SULLIVAN, ELIZA	QUE	183	3RD E DI
SULLIVAN, ELIZABETH	BAL	451	1ST DIST
SULLIVAN, ELLEN	BAL	010	9TH WARD
SULLIVAN, ELLEN	BAL	215	11TH WAR
SULLIVAN, ELLEN	BAL	149	11TH WAR
SULLIVAN, ELVIRA	BAL	330	7TH WARD
SULLIVAN, EUGENE	BAL	146	1ST WARD
SULLIVAN, EUGINE	BAL	189	11TH WAR
SULLIVAN, F.	BAL	173	1ST WARD
SULLIVAN, F.	BAL	152	11TH WAR
SULLIVAN, FELIX R.	BAL	152	11TH WAR
SULLIVAN, FRANCIS	CAR	279	7TH DIST
SULLIVAN, GEORGE W.	CAR	108	NO TWP L
SULLIVAN, HANNAH R.	MGM	336	CRACKLIN
SULLIVAN, HENRIETTA	BAL	312	7TH WARD
SULLIVAN, HENRIETTA	BAL	312	7TH WARD
SULLIVAN, HENRY	BAL	338	3RD WARD
SULLIVAN, HENRY	BAL	303	3RD WARD
SULLIVAN, HESTER	BAL	195	17TH WAR
SULLIVAN, ISAAC	CAR	399	2ND DIST
SULLIVAN, JACOB	CAR	394	2ND DIST
SULLIVAN, JAMES	BAL	165	19TH WAR
SULLIVAN, JAMES	KEN	242	2ND DIST
SULLIVAN, JAMES	CAR	130	NO TWP L
SULLIVAN, JAMES	CAR	128	NO TWP L
SULLIVAN, JAMES	BAL	033	4TH WARD
SULLIVAN, JAMES	CEC	044	CHESAPEA
SULLIVAN, JAMES	BAL	096	10TH WAR
SULLIVAN, JAMES	BAL	191	2ND WARD
SULLIVAN, JAMES	BAL	211	6TH WARD
SULLIVAN, JAMES	BAL	022	15TH WAR
SULLIVAN, JAMES	ALL	214	CUMBERLA
SULLIVAN, JAMES	QUE	198	3RD E DI
SULLIVAN, JAMES L.	HAR	149	3RD DIST
SULLIVAN, JAMES W.	ANN	266	ANNAPOLI
SULLIVAN, JEREMIAH	CAR	100	NO TWP L
SULLIVAN, JEREMIAH	BAL	065	4TH WARD
SULLIVAN, JEREMIAH	BAL	423	14TH WAR
SULLIVAN, JESSE	CAR	286	7TH DIST
SULLIVAN, JESSE	CAR	294	7TH DIST
SULLIVAN, JOHN	CAR	279	7TH DIST
SULLIVAN, JOHN	BAL	029	4TH WARD
SULLIVAN, JOHN	BAL	199	19TH WAR
SULLIVAN, JOHN	BAL	188	11TH WAR
SULLIVAN, JOHN	BAL	041	9TH WARD
SULLIVAN, JOHN	BAL	144	1ST WARD
SULLIVAN, JOHN	BAL	145	1ST WARD
SULLIVAN, JOHN	BAL	289	7TH WARD
SULLIVAN, JOHN	BAL	179	2ND DIST
SULLIVAN, JOHN	BAL	119	1ST WARD
SULLIVAN, JOHN	KEN	277	1ST DIST
SULLIVAN, JOHN	TAL	030	EASTON D
SULLIVAN, JOHN C.	BAL	019	4TH WARD
SULLIVAN, JOHN F.	CAR	130	NO TWP L
SULLIVAN, JOHN P.	BAL	112	15TH WAR
SULLIVAN, JOHN T.	ANN	469	HOWARD D
SULLIVAN, JOSIAH	BAL	231	1ST DIST
SULLIVAN, LEVIN S.	TAL	113	ST MICHA
SULLIVAN, MARGARET	BAL	449	1ST DIST
SULLIVAN, MARGARET	BAL	298	3RD WARD
SULLIVAN, MARGARET	BAL	164	2ND DIST
SULLIVAN, MARGARET	BAL	003	9TH WARD
SULLIVAN, MARGARET	BAL	059	15TH WAR
SULLIVAN, MARGARET	CAR	293	7TH DIST
SULLIVAN, MARGARET	BAL	163	19TH WAR
SULLIVAN, MARGARETT	BAL	019	18TH WAR
SULLIVAN, MARY	CAR	288	7TH DIST
SULLIVAN, MARY	CAR	130	NO TWP L
SULLIVAN, MARY	BAL	294	3RD WARD
SULLIVAN, MARY	ANN	278	ANNAPOLI
SULLIVAN, MARY ANN	ALL	245	CUMBERLA
SULLIVAN, MARY E.	BAL	370	8TH WARD
SULLIVAN, MARY E.	CAR	395	2ND DIST
SULLIVAN, MARY-BLACK	BAL	218	2ND WARD
SULLIVAN, MICHAEL	BAL	266	2ND WARD
SULLIVAN, MICHAEL	BAL	059	15TH WAR
SULLIVAN, MICHAEL	BAL	176	11TH WAR
SULLIVAN, MICHAEL	CAR	352	6TH DIST
SULLIVAN, MICHAEL C.	FRE	065	FREDERIC
SULLIVAN, OWEN	BAL	351	3RD WARD
SULLIVAN, PATRICK	BAL	445	1ST DIST
SULLIVAN, PATRICK H.	BAL	053	15TH WAR
SULLIVAN, PETER	CAR	131	NO TWP L
SULLIVAN, PETER W.	TAL	022	EASTON D
SULLIVAN, PETER-BLACK	CAR	074	NO TWP L
SULLIVAN, PETR	BAL	254	12TH WAR
SULLIVAN, PHILIP	BAL	309	7TH WARD
SULLIVAN, RACHEL	BAL	037	2ND DIST
SULLIVAN, RICHARD	MGM	370	BERRYS D
SULLIVAN, ROBERT	MGM	371	BERRYS D
SULLIVAN, SARAH	BAL	149	19TH WAR
SULLIVAN, SARAH E.	CAR	329	MANCHEST
SULLIVAN, SARAH P.	BAL	422	3RD WARD
SULLIVAN, SUSAN	BAL	099	5TH WARD
SULLIVAN, SYLVESTER	CAR	126	NO TWP L
SULLIVAN, THADDEUS	KEN	209	2ND DIST
SULLIVAN, THADEUS	BAL	333	7TH WARD
SULLIVAN, THOMAS	BAL	064	10TH WAR
SULLIVAN, THOMAS	CEC	044	CHESAPEA
SULLIVAN, THOMAS	BAL	213	17TH WAR
SULLIVAN, THOMAS H.	BAL	005	4TH WARD
SULLIVAN, TILGHMAN	CAR	140	NO TWP L
SULLIVAN, URIAH	CAR	345	6TH DIST
SULLIVAN, VINEY	TAL	073	EASTON T
SULLIVAN, W. W.	ANN	396	8TH DIST
SULLIVAN, WILLAIM	ANN	497	HOWARD D
SULLIVAN, WILLIAM	BAL	096	10TH WAR
SULLIVAN, WILLIAM	BAL	125	16TH WAR
SULLIVAN, WILLIAM	CAR	295	7TH DIST
SULLIVAN, WILLIAM	CAR	126	NO TWP L
SULLIVAN, WILLIAM	CAL	049	3RD DIST
SULLIVAN,DAVID	BAL	048	2ND DIST
SULLIVAN,DENNIS	BAL	128	1ST WARD
SULLIVAN,JAMES	BAL	120	1ST WARD
SULLIVAN,JOHN	BAL	139	1ST WARD
SULLIVAN,JOHN	ALL	231	CUMBERLA
SULLIVAN,MICHAEL	BAL	128	1ST WARD
SULLIVAN,PETER	CAR	136	NO TWP L
SULLIVER, WILLIAM	HAR	149	3RD DIST
SULLIVIN, ANDREW	TAL	061	EASTON D
SULLIVIN, BATEMAN	TAL	044	EASTON T
SULLIVIN, ELIJAH	TAL	046	EASTON T
SULLIVIN, JOHN	TAL	056	EASTON D
SULLIVIN, JOSEPH	TAL	066	EASTON T
SULLY,M.	BAL	288	12TH WAR
SULSER, JACKSON	FRE	361	CATOCTIN
SULSER, REBECCA	FRE	404	JEFFERSO
SULTREN, THOMAS D.*	BAL	084	4TH WARD
SULTZER, ANDREW	BAL	030	9TH WARD
SULTZER, BENJAMIN	ANN	425	HOWARD D
SULTZER, ELIZABETH	FRE	214	BUCKEYST
SULTZER, EMMA	FRE	403	JEFFERSO
SULTZER, FREDERICK	BAL	178	2ND WARD
SULTZER, HENRY C.	BAL	359	3RD WARD
SULTZER, MARGARET	BAL	097	1ST WARD
SULTZER, MATILDA	BAL	333	7TH WARD
SULTZER, SUSAN	BAL	411	3RD WARD
SULTZER, SUSAN M.	BAL	360	3RD WARD
SULVAN, MARY	WOR	219	4TH E DI
SULZBACER, MOSES	BAL	079	1ST WARD
SULZNER, EDWARD	BAL	340	7TH WARD
SULZNER, JOHN C.	BAL	341	7TH WARD
SULZNER, PAULINE	BAL	340	7TH WARD
SUMALT, GEORGE W.	BAL	287	17TH WAR
SUMALT, WILLIAM M.	BAL	237	17TH WAR
SUMAN, CECELIA	FRE	022	FREDERIC
SUMAN, ELIZABETH	FRE	030	FREDERIC
SUMAN, GARRETT	FRE	317	MIDDLETO
SUMAN, GEORGE	FRE	350	MIDDLETO
SUMAN, ISRAEL W.	FRE	022	FREDERIC
SUMAN, JOHN	FRE	234	BUCKEYST
SUMAN, JOHN W.	FRE	358	CATOCTIN
SUMAN, MARY	FRE	348	MIDDLETO
SUMAN, MARY A.	FRE	002	FREDERIC
SUMAN, MARY J.	FRE	204	BUCKEYST
SUMAN, SARAH E.	WAS	123	HAGERSTO
SUMAN, WILLIAM	WAS	181	BOONSBOR
SUMANUS, JACOB H.	BAL	011	18TH WAR
SUMAS, EDGAR	ALL	095	5TH E.D.
SUMER, HENRY A.	BAL	128	1ST WARD
SUMER, MICHAEL	BAL	093	1ST WARD
SUMER, NANCY	BAL	028	15TH WAR
SUMERLINE, F.	ANN	270	ANNAPOLI
SUMERS, CATHARINE	WAS	045	2ND SUBD
SUMERS, CHRISTINA	WAS	062	2ND SUBD
SUMERS, DELANIE,	WAS	058	2ND SUBD
SUMERS, HERMAN	BAL	372	13TH WAR
SUMERS, JACOBENA	ANN	391	4TH DIST
SUMERS, MARY E.	BAL	275	2ND WARD
SUMERS, WILLIAM	WAS	062	2ND SUBD
SUMES, EDWARD	BAL	196	19TH WAR
SUMJOON, LEWIS	ALL	243	CUMBERLA
SUMKMERS, CEPHAS	MGM	436	CLARKSTR
SUMLLEN, JANE *	WOR	188	7TH E DI
SUMMER, ELIZA	BAL	041	4TH WARD
SUMMER, ELIZABETH	BAL	319	7TH WARD
SUMMER, JOHN	BAL	077	18TH WAR
SUMMER, JOHN S.	BAL	061	10TH WAR
SUMMER, MARTIN	BAL	236	2ND WARD
SUMMER, MARY	BAL	111	18TH WAR
SUMMER, SUSAN	BAL	460	1ST DIST
SUMMERFIELD, JAMES	CEC	156	PORT DUP
SUMMERILL, PAUL	BAL	187	6TH WARD
SUMMERILL, PAUL	BAL	187	6TH WARD
SUMMERS, A. H.	MGM	374	ROCKERLE
SUMMERS, ABRAHAM JR.	SOM	382	BRINKLEY
SUMMERS, ABRAHAM SR.	SOM	378	BRINKLEY
SUMMERS, ALICE	FRE	267	NEW MARK
SUMMERS, ALLICE	WAS	028	2ND SUBD
SUMMERS, AMELIA	SOM	387	BRINKLEY
SUMMERS, AMELIA	SOM	427	PRINCESS
SUMMERS, ANDREW	WAS	023	2ND SUBD
SUMMERS, ANDREW	WAS	298	1ST DIST
SUMMERS, ANN	BAL	296	20TH WAR
SUMMERS, ARNOLD	WAS	028	2ND SUBD
SUMMERS, BENJAMIN	SOM	373	BRINKLEY
SUMMERS, BENJAMIN	SOM	374	BRINKLEY
SUMMERS, CAROLINE	BAL	395	8TH WARD
SUMMERS, CHARLOTTE	SOM	367	BRINKLEY
SUMMERS, DAVID	WAS	023	2ND SUBD
SUMMERS, DAVID	ALL	057	10TH E.D
SUMMERS, EDWARD	TAL	033	EASTON D
SUMMERS, ELIJAH	SOM	374	BRINKLEY
SUMMERS, ELIZABETH	WAS	210	1ST DIST
SUMMERS, EPHRAIM	SOM	379	BRINKLEY
SUMMERS, FANNY	SOM	373	BRINKLEY
SUMMERS, GEORGE	SOM	383	BRINKLEY
SUMMERS, GEORGE	WAS	227	1ST DIST
SUMMERS, GEORGE	BAL	262	2ND WARD
SUMMERS, GRACE	SOM	383	BRINKLEY
SUMMERS, HARRIET	TAL	003	EASTON D
SUMMERS, HENERETTA	SOM	388	BRINKLEY
SUMMERS, HENRY	SOM	373	BRINKLEY
SUMMERS, HENRY	ANN	391	4TH DIST
SUMMERS, HESTER	SOM	419	PRINCESS
SUMMERS, HORSEY	SOM	380	BRINKLEY
SUMMERS, ISAAC	SOM	465	HANGARY
SUMMERS, ISAAC	SOM	411	DUBLIN D
SUMMERS, JACOB	WAS	298	1ST DIST
SUMMERS, JACOB	ANN	414	HOWARD D
SUMMERS, JAMES	BAL	033	9TH WARD
SUMMERS, JAMES	SOM	373	BRINKLEY
SUMMERS, JAMES	PRI	097	SPALDING
SUMMERS, JAMES T.P.	WAS	210	1ST DIST
SUMMERS, JESSE	SOM	390	BRINKLEY
SUMMERS, JOHN	SOM	375	BRINKLEY
SUMMERS, JOHN	SOM	383	BRINKLEY
SUMMERS, JOHN	SOM	373	BRINKLEY
SUMMERS, JOHN	SOM	373	BRINKLEY
SUMMERS, JOHN	WAS	023	2ND SUBD
SUMMERS, JOHN	ALL	057	10TH E.D
SUMMERS, JOHN	BAL	246	1ST DIST
SUMMERS, JOHN	HAR	159	3RD DIST
SUMMERS, JOHN F.	PRI	052	AQUASCO
SUMMERS, JOHN G.	PRI	052	AQUASCO
SUMMERS, JOHN H.	TAL	060	EASTON D
SUMMERS, JOHN H.	SOM	438	DAMES QU
SUMMERS, JOHN W.	WAS	150	2ND DIST
SUMMERS, JOSEPH G.	BAL	094	5TH WARD
SUMMERS, LEA	WAS	023	2ND SUBD
SUMMERS, LOUISA	PRI	073	MARLBROU
SUMMERS, LUDWICK	BAL	458	14TH WAR
SUMMERS, LYDIA	ALL	057	10TH E.D
SUMMERS, MARY	BAL	170	6TH WARD
SUMMERS, MARY	BAL	074	15TH WAR
SUMMERS, MARY	SOM	403	BRINKLEY
SUMMERS, MARY	SOM	365	BRINKLEY
SUMMERS, MARY	SOM	376	BRINKLEY
SUMMERS, MARY	SOM	356	BRINKLEY
SUMMERS, MARY	SOM	382	BRINKLEY
SUMMERS, MARY	SOM	375	BRINKLEY
SUMMERS, MARY F.	PRI	073	MARLBROU
SUMMERS, NANCY-BLACK	FRE	046	FREDERIC
SUMMERS, NATHANIEL	WAS	149	2ND DIST
SUMMERS, NICHOLAS	SOM	374	BRINKLEY
SUMMERS, NICHOLAS	WAS	124	HAGERSTO
SUMMERS, PATIENCE	WAS	138	HAGERSTO
SUMMERS, PRICILLA	SOM	372	BRINKLEY
SUMMERS, RACHAEL	SOM	374	BRINKLEY
SUMMERS, RHEUBEN	SOM	366	BRINKLEY
SUMMERS, SAMUEL	SOM	382	BRINKLEY
SUMMERS, SAMUEL	SOM	353	BRINKLEY
SUMMERS, SAMUEL	SOM	480	TRAPP DI
SUMMERS, SAMUEL	BAL	084	10TH WAR
SUMMERS, SAMUEL S.	SOM	365	BRINKLEY
SUMMERS, SARAH	SOM	367	BRINKLEY
SUMMERS, SARAH	TAL	061	EASTON D
SUMMERS, SARAH	PRI	079	MARLBROU
SUMMERS, SARAH	HAR	044	1ST DIST
SUMMERS, SIMON P.	WAS	193	1ST DIST
SUMMERS, SOPHIA	MGM	404	ROCKERLE
SUMMERS, STEPHEN	WAS	131	HAGERSTO
SUMMERS, THOMAS	SOM	402	BRINKLEY
SUMMERS, THOMAS	SOM	372	BRINKLEY
SUMMERS, WILLIAM	SOM	382	BRINKLEY
SUMMERS, WILLIAM	SOM	374	BRINKLEY
SUMMERS, WILLIAM	BAL	075	15TH WAR
SUMMERS, WILLIAM H.	SOM	403	BRINKLEY
SUMMERS,PETER	BAL	022	2ND DIST
SUMMERT, JOHN B.	CAR	281	7TH DIST
SUMMERVELT, LUDWIG	BAL	042	9TH WARD
SUMMERVILE, WILLIAM	BAL	432	8TH WARD
SUMMERVILL, JAMES H.	BAL	358	1ST DIST
SUMMERVILL, SUSAN	BAL	358	1ST DIST
SUMMERVILLE, CATHARINE	BAL	410	1ST DIST
SUMMERVILLE, CHARLOTTE	BAL	175	16TH WAR
SUMMERVILLE, JOHN A.	CAR	384	2ND DIST
SUMMERVILLE, RICHARD	BAL	053	9TH WARD
SUMMERVILLE, THOMAS	BAL	371	8TH WARD
SUMMERVILLE, W. T.	BAL	380	1ST DIST
SUMMERVILLE,PETER	BAL	168	1ST WARD
SUMMES, PETER	BAL	267	20TH WAR
SUMMET, CLOVISA	BAL	292	20TH WAR
SUMMINS, ELIZA *	BAL	223	12TH WAR
SUMMONS, CEPHAS	PRI	035	VANSVILL
SUMMONS, HIRAM	PRI	031	VANSVILL
SUMMVALT, DAVID *	BAL	165	2ND DIST
SUMMVALT, G.	BAL	318	12TH WAR
SUMNER, AMELINE	TAL	085	ST MICHA
SUMNER, F.A.	BAL	017	18TH WAR
SUMNER, F.L.	BAL	017	18TH WAR
SUMNER, FREDERICK	BAL	269	2ND WARD
SUMNER, JOSEPH	BAL	230	19TH WAR
SUMPMAN, CONRADT	BAL	397	8TH WARD
SUMPTSON, THOMAS	QUE	182	3RD E DI
SUMS, GRACE	TAL	031	EASTON D
SUMULLER, AUGUSTUS*	BAL	085	10TH WAR
SUMWALT, GEORGE B.	BAL	256	17TH WAR
SUMWALT, J.	BAL	228	1ST DIST
SUMWALT, JESSE	BAL	300	20TH WAR
SUMWALT, JOHN T.	BAL	107	15TH WAR
SUMWALT, MARGARET	BAL	220	1ST DIST
SUMWALT, MARGARET	BAL	117	11TH WAR
SUMWALT, MARTHA G.	BAL	301	20TH WAR
SUMWALT, ROSEANNA	BAL	030	15TH WAR
SUMWALT, THOMAS S.	BAL	107	15TH WAR
SUMWALT, WILLIAM H.	BAL	475	14TH WAR
SUNBARY, GUSTAVUS	BAL	134	1ST WARD
SUNBOWER, ADAM	ALL	022	2ND E.D.
SUNDBERG, S.	BAL	151	1ST WARD
SUNDER, HENRY	BAL	100	10TH WAR
SUNDERCALL, MARY A.	BAL	194	6TH WARD
SUNDERGILE, JOHN	CAR	281	7TH DIST
SUNDERLAND, BASIL*	BAL	371	3RD WARD
SUNDERLAND, BENJAMIN	ANN	412	HOWARD D
SUNDERLAND, BENJAMIN	HAR	084	2ND DIST
SUNDERLAND, COSMO	CAL	050	3RD DIST
SUNDERLAND, HENRY	CAL	056	3RD DIST
SUNDERLAND, JOHN	BAL	289	7TH WARD
SUNDERLAND, JOHN G.	BAL	289	7TH WARD
SUNDERLAND, MARGARET	CAL	045	3RD DIST
SUNDERLAND, PHEBE	BAL	474	14TH WAR
SUNDERLAND, RICHARD H.	ANN	397	8TH DIST
SUNDERLAND, RICHARD H.	ANN	398	8TH DIST
SUNDERLAND, ROSANNA	BAL	234	6TH WARD
SUNDERLAND, SAMUEL	CAL	027	2ND DIST
SUNDERLAND, ZACHARIAH	CAL	047	3RD DIST
SUNDERMAN, WILLIAM	BAL	059	2ND DIST
SUNDERVALT, AMBROSE	BAL	258	6TH WARD
SUNENLIDER, JOHN	BAL	035	15TH WAR
SUNINS, JOHN	BAL	186	2ND WARD
SUNKFORD, EUPHAMY*	DOR	299	1ST DIST
SUNLIN, JAMES	BAL	349	1ST DIST
SUNMERS, JOSEPH	BAL	289	20TH WAR
SUNMET, MARIE	BAL	273	20TH WAR
SUNNAMAN, ROBERT	BAL	329	13TH WAR
SUNNAP, SYLVESTER*	BAL	411	3RD WARD
SUNNONLEITER, JOHN	BAL	119	18TH WAR
SUNODEN, SUSAN	BAL	259	12TH WAR
SUNRISE, LETTA	BAL	203	2ND WARD
SUNS, ABRAM	BAL	234	12TH WAR
SUNS, MARY*	TAL	035	EASTON D
SUODA, HENRY	BAL	225	2ND WARD
SUOLER, BRIDGET	SOM	359	BRINKLEY
SUPE, ALLEN-MULATTO	CAR	403	2ND DIST
SUPE, DANIEL-BLACK	CAR	411	2ND DIST
SUPER, DANIEL	BAL	035	9TH WARD
SUPER, FREDERICK	BAL	228	19TH WAR
SUPER, HENRY	BAL	176	19TH WAR
SUPERSPER, GEORGE *	BAL	313	20TH WAR
SUPERWELCH, ARNOLD	BAL	109	1ST WARD
SUPLE, MARY V.	BAL	132	16TH WAR
SUPPELYTE, HALVIN*	BAL	119	15TH WAR
SUPPERT, HENRY	FRE	144	10TH E D
SUPPLE, G.	BAL	142	1ST WARD
SUPPLE, JAMES	ANN	473	HOWARD D
SURAS, VIN*	TAL	034	EASTON D
SURDEN, MARY A.	BAL	016	1ST WARD
SURGE,R FREDERICK	BAL	084	1ST WARD
SURGERT, FREDERICK	FRE	343	MIDDLETO
SURGIS, ROSE	WOR	308	2ND E DI
SURGMAN, MARY	BAL	014	18TH WAR
SURITY, ANN M.	BAL	144	11TH WAR
SURKIRK, SUSAN	BAL	126	5TH WARD
SURLINE, MARY	BAL	320	1ST DIST
SURNAN, MARGARET	FRE	015	FREDERIC
SUROY, SOLOMON	BAL	309	1ST DIST
SURREY, MATILDA	ANN	329	2ND DIST
SURT, BRIDGETT*	BAL	062	4TH WARD
SURT, ELIZABETH	MGM	394	ROCKERLE
SURTEY, THERESA	BAL	369	8TH WARD
SURVEY, ELIZABTH-MULATTO	FRE	445	8TH E DI
SURVEY, MATILDA *	ANN	329	2ND DIST
SUSCLELECT, ELLEN	CAR	358	9TH DIST
SUSCLELECT, JOHN	CAR	365	9TH DIST
SUSCLELECT, RICHARD	CAR	365	9TH DIST

Name	County	Page	District
SUSCO, JOSEPH	KEN	233	2ND DIST
SUSNE, CHARLES	BAL	132	1ST WARD
SUSPINE, JAOCB	BAL	244	2ND WARD
SUSTER, ROBERT *	BAL	275	20TH WAR
SUTEMAN, GARRETT	ALL	154	6TH E.D.
SUTER, AMELIA	WAS	153	HAGERSTO
SUTER, CATHARINE	WAS	153	HAGERSTO
SUTER, DANIEL	BAL	268	7TH WARD
SUTER, ELIZA	BAL	400	14TH WAR
SUTER, GEORGE	BAL	209	19TH WAR
SUTER, HENRY	FRE	390	PETERSVI
SUTER, HENRY	BAL	233	6TH WARD
SUTER, JOHN	FRE	425	8TH E DI
SUTER, MARTIN	BAL	304	20TH WAR
SUTER, REBECCA	WAS	157	HAGERSTO
SUTER, SAMUEL	BAL	304	20TH WAR
SUTER, SAMUEL	FRE	388	PETERSVI
SUTER, SEBASTIAN	BAL	316	3RD WARD
SUTER, WILLIAM	FRE	388	PETERSVI
SUTER, WILLIAM	WAS	146	HAGERSTO
SUTERS, SAMUEL	BAL	054	18TH WAR
SUTHERD, JOSEPH	BAL	022	18TH WAR
SUTHERLAND, CATHARINE	BAL	413	1ST DIST
SUTHERLAND, ELICK	HAR	021	1ST DIST
SUTHERLAND, ELLEN	BAL	316	7TH WARD
SUTHERLAND, JOHN	BAL	143	1ST WARD
SUTHERLAND, MARY	QUE	185	3RD E DI
SUTHERLAND, SILAS B.	QUE	184	3RD E DI
SUTHNERLAND, ISABELLA	HAR	024	1ST DIST
SUTLER, REBECCA	CAR	409	2ND DIST
SUTLIFF, HENRY	BAL	441	14TH WAR
SUTLIFF, WILLIAM	BAL	390	8TH WARD
SUTMAN, HANORE *	ALL	149	6TH E.D.
SUTMER, ELIZABETH	BAL	004	15TH WAR
SUTON, ANN	BAL	159	11TH WAR
SUTOR, ALEXANDER	BAL	236	17TH WAR
SUTOR, GEORGE	BAL	039	18TH WAR
SUTOR, NICHOLAS	HAR	146	3RD DIST
SUTOR, THOMAS	HAR	154	3RD DIST
SUTPHER, FREDERICK	BAL	012	1ST WARD
SUTRO, BERNHARD*	BAL	403	3RD WARD
SUTTER, SAMUEL	ALL	040	2ND E.D.
SUTTERFIELD, NATHAN	KEN	268	1ST DIST
SUTTES, REBECCA	BAL	218	17TH WAR
SUTTLE, NANCY	MGM	335	CRACKLIN
SUTTMANN, WILLIAM	TAL	067	EASTON T
SUTTON, ALEXANDER	BAL	146	5TH WARD
SUTTON, ANDREW	BAL	037	2ND DIST
SUTTON, ANDREW	KEN	234	2ND DIST
SUTTON, ARIANA	QUE	209	3RD E DI
SUTTON, BENJAMIN	BAL	438	1ST DIST
SUTTON, BENJAMIN F.	BAL	373	8TH WARD
SUTTON, BETSEY	BAL	398	8TH WARD
SUTTON, CHARLES	BAL	334	1ST DIST
SUTTON, CHARLES	KEN	222	2ND DIST
SUTTON, CLARA	KEN	253	1ST DIST
SUTTON, CAVID	CEC	026	ELKTON 3
SUTTON, DAVID	BAL	057	2ND DIST
SUTTON, EBANEZER	CEC	091	4TH E DI
SUTTON, ELIZABETH	BAL	036	2ND DIST
SUTTON, ELIZABETH	BAL	283	7TH WARD
SUTTON, ELIZABETH	WAS	153	2ND DIST
SUTTON, ELLEN	ST	289	2ND E DI
SUTTON, FLORA	BAL	150	11TH WAR
SUTTON, GEORGE B.	BAL	374	13TH WAR
SUTTON, HIRAM	ALL	110	5TH E.D.
SUTTON, JACOB	KEN	224	2ND DIST
SUTTON, JAMES L.	BAL	034	4TH WARD
SUTTON, JANE	CEC	010	ELKTON 3
SUTTON, JOHN	BAL	242	6TH WARD
SUTTON, JOHN	BAL	185	5TH DIST
SUTTON, JOHN	PRI	102	SPALDING
SUTTON, JOHN B.	KEN	289	3RD DIST
SUTTON, JOHN C.	KEN	296	3RD DIST
SUTTON, JOHN R.	BAL	037	9TH WARD
SUTTON, JOHN W.	BAL	037	9TH WARD
SUTTON, JOHNATHAN	HAR	179	3RD DIST
SUTTON, JOSEPH J.	BAL	319	7TH WARD
SUTTON, JULIA A.	KEN	230	2ND DIST
SUTTON, JULIA A.	KEN	261	1ST DIST
SUTTON, JULIANN	BAL	218	6TH DIST
SUTTON, LEWIS JR.	BAL	065	10TH WAR
SUTTON, LOUIS J.	ST	333	4TH E DI
SUTTON, LUCRETIA	BAL	218	6TH DIST
SUTTON, LUTHER	BAL	042	2ND DIST
SUTTON, LYDIA	CAL	011	1ST DIST
SUTTON, MARDICA	BAL	319	7TH WARD
SUTTON, MARIA	BAL	373	8TH WARD
SUTTON, MARIA	BAL	382	13TH WAR
SUTTON, MARTHA H.	ST	289	2ND E DI
SUTTON, MARY	BAL	472	14TH WAR
SUTTON, MARY	CAR	175	8TH DIST
SUTTON, MARY C.	BAL	226	6TH WARD
SUTTON, OLIVER	HAR	179	3RD DIST
SUTTON, ORLANDER F.	KEN	286	3RD DIST
SUTTON, PHILIP D.	ANN	408	8TH DIST
SUTTON, RACHAEL	BAL	110	2ND DIST
SUTTON, REBECCA	KEN	229	2ND DIST
SUTTON, RICAHRD	BAL	140	19TH WAR
SUTTON, RICHARD	BAL	244	20TH WAR
SUTTON, ROBERT	CEC	106	3RD E DI
SUTTON, SAMUEL	HAR	177	3RD DIST
SUTTON, SAMUEL	CAL	016	1ST DIST
SUTTON, SAMUEL	BAL	020	2ND DIST
SUTTON, SAMUEL	BAL	285	1ST DIST
SUTTON, SAMUEL V.	CEC	010	ELKTON 3
SUTTON, SARAH	CEC	005	ELKTON 3
SUTTON, SARAH	BAL	074	4TH WARD
SUTTON, SARAH	QUE	209	3RD E DI
SUTTON, SARAH C.	KEN	229	2ND DIST
SUTTON, SOLOMON C.	BAL	190	6TH WARD
SUTTON, SOPHIA	CEC	090	4TH E DI
SUTTON, SUSAN	BAL	213	17TH WAR
SUTTON, THERESA	BAL	086	2ND DIST
SUTTON, THOMAS	BAL	320	3RD WARD
SUTTON, THOMAS	QUE	206	3RD E DI
SUTTON, THOMAS J.	BAL	146	5TH WARD
SUTTON, THOMAS P.	CEC	101	4TH E DI
SUTTON, WESTLY	HAR	072	1ST DIST
SUTTON, WILLIAM	BAL	137	11TH WAR
SUTTON, WILLIAM	BAL	321	3RD WARD
SUTTON, WILLIAM	BAL	074	15TH WAR
SUTTON, WILLIAM	QUE	185	3RD E DI
SUTTON, WILLIAM T.	QUE	209	3RD E DI
SUTTON, ABRAM-BLACK	QUE	136	1ST E DI
SUTTON, NICHOLAS	BAL	037	2ND DIST
SUTTZER, HENRY	BAL	317	3RD WARD
SUTTZER, HENRY	BAL	186	2ND WARD
SUTTZER, WILLIAM T.	FRE	078	FREDERIC
SUTWICK, CHARLES	BAL	463	1ST DIST
SUTZ, JAMES	BAL	212	2ND WARD
SUTZ, PETER	BAL	212	2ND WARD
SUVALL, RACHEAL	BAL	126	18TH WAR
SUVELL, ANN	BAL	092	5TH WARD
SUVOY, DANIEL	BAL	310	1ST DIST
SUWELLEN, JOHN	ALL	070	5TH E.D.
SUYER, JOHN	BAL	220	19TH WAR
SUZAN, PETER	BAL	216	2ND WARD
SWAAB, CHARLES	BAL	095	15TH WAR
SWACY, ADELINE	PRI	056	AQUASCO
SWAGER, JACOB	BAL	092	5TH WARD
SWAILES, ALEXANDRIA	CAR	213	5TH DIST
SWAILS, JAMES	WAS	285	1ST DIST
SWAIM, HOWARD	BAL	351	1ST DIST
SWAIN, ALEXANDER	BAL	290	7TH WARD
SWAIN, BENJAMIN	WAS	055	2ND SUBD
SWAIN, CHARLES H.	BAL	123	18TH WAR
SWAIN, CCLMORE A.	PRI	086	QUEEN AN
SWAIN, DAVID	BAL	061	18TH WAR
SWAIN, DORCAS	PRI	010	BLADENSB
SWAIN, EDW.	BAL	299	20TH WAR
SWAIN, GEORGE	WAS	048	2ND SUBD
SWAIN, ISAAC	PRI	062	NOTTINGH
SWAIN, ISAIH	TAL	100	ST MICHA
SWAIN, JARRETT	BAL	201	17TH WAR
SWAIN, JOHN	BAL	412	8TH WARD
SWAIN, JOHN K.	BAL	108	15TH WAR
SWAIN, JOHN T.	PRI	008	BLADENSB
SWAIN, MARY E.	PRI	002	BLADENSB
SWAIN, SAMUEL	WAS	046	2ND SUBD
SWAIN, WILLAIM	PRI	066	NOTTINGH
SWAIN, WILLIAM	WAS	065	2ND SUBD
SWAIN, WILLIAM	BAL	412	8TH WARD
SWAIN, WILLIAM	BAL	412	3RD WARD
SWAINT, FERDINAND	BAL	143	5TH WARD
SWAINY, ELIZABETH *	FRE	314	MIDDLETO
SWALES, CAROLINE	MGM	349	BERRYS D
SWALLENBERG, P.	BAL	207	19TH WAR
SWALLOP, JOHN	ALL	036	2ND E.D.
SWALLOP, LOUIS	ALL	036	2ND E.D.
SWALLUNURGH, WILLIAM	BAL	259	2ND WARD
SWALP, CATHARINE	ALL	036	2ND E.D.
SWALP, ELISABETH	ALL	035	2ND E.D.
SWALP, MARY	ALL	039	2ND E.D.
SWAM, CATHARINE	BAL	410	1ST DIST
SWAM, JOHN	BAL	379	1ST DIST
SWAM, WILLIAM	PRI	088	SPALDING
SWAMLEY, ASA	FRE	240	NEW MARK
SWAMLEY, DANIEL	FRE	255	NEW MARK
SWAMLEY, ELISHA	FRE	259	NEW MARK
SWAN, ANN	BAL	201	17TH WAR
SWAN, ATTAWAY C.A.	ST	335	4TH E DI
SWAN, BENJAMIN-BLACK	FRE	409	JEFFERSO
SWAN, CHARLOTTA	BAL	301	1ST DIST
SWAN, EDWARD	QUE	212	3RD E DI
SWAN, ISAAC	BAL	433	8TH WARD
SWAN, JAMES	ST	332	4TH E DI
SWAN, JOEL	ANN	429	HOWARD D
SWAN, LEWILLEN	ST	339	4TH E DI
SWAN, LEWIS	BAL	209	11TH WAR
SWAN, LOUISA	ALL	254	CUMBERLA
SWAN, LYDIA	BAL	183	19TH WAR
SWAN, MARGARETT-MULATTO	FRE	451	8TH E DI
SWAN, MARIA	BAL	395	8TH WARD
SWAN, MART	BAL	291	12TH WAR
SWAN, MARY	BAL	369	8TH WARD
SWAN, MARY	BAL	020	4TH WARD
SWAN, MARY	CAR	071	NO TWP L
SWAN, OSWALD J.	BAL	281	7TH WARD
SWAN, POLLY	WAS	132	HAGERSTO
SWAN, RICHARD	ANN	282	ANNAPOLI
SWAN, ROBERT	ALL	256	CUMBERLA
SWAN, SAIRETTER	CAR	066	NO TWP L
SWAN, SAMUEL	CAR	076	NO TWP L
SWAN, SAMUEL	BAL	268	17TH WAR
SWAN, SOLOMON	CEC	034	CHESAPEA
SWAN, SUSAN	QUE	213	3RD E DI
SWAN, WALTER	BAL	291	12TH WAR
SWAN, WILLIAM	BAL	237	12TH WAR
SWAN, WILLIAM	WAS	133	HAGERSTO
SWAN, WILLIAM A.	ST	337	4TH E DI
SWAN, JSOHUA	CAR	105	NO TWP L
SWANE, MARGARET	BAL	094	18TH WAR
SWANE, MARTHA	WAS	148	2ND DIST
SWANELY, LYDIA A.	FRE	238	NEW MARK
SWANER, STEPHEN N.	FRE	389	PETERSVI
SWANN, ALEXANDER	CHA	226	ALLENS F
SWANN, ANN	BAL	100	5TH WARD
SWANN, BEN	CHA	272	ALLENS F
SWANN, BENEDICT	ST	336	4TH E DI
SWANN, BENJAMIN	PRI	065	NOTTINGH
SWANN, BETSEY	CHA	230	MIDDLETO
SWANN, BRISCOE	CHA	246	HILLTOP
SWANN, CATE	CHA	227	ALLENS F
SWANN, CATHRINE	PRI	085	QUEEN AN
SWANN, CHARLES	BAL	140	1ST WARD
SWANN, DEBBY	CHA	220	ALLENS F
SWANN, ELIZABETH	CHA	224	ALLENS F
SWANN, ELIZABETH	CHA	234	HILLTOP
SWANN, HENRY	CHA	220	ALLENS F
SWANN, HORACE D.	BAL	182	6TH WARD
SWANN, HUSE	CHA	230	BOJANTOW
SWANN, JAMES	CHA	220	ALLENS F
SWANN, JAMES	CHA	264	MIDDLETO
SWANN, JOHN	CHA	288	BOJANTOW
SWANN, JOHN	CHA	221	ALLENS F
SWANN, JOHN E.	ST	336	4TH E DI
SWANN, JOHN F.	CHA	292	BOJANTOW
SWANN, JOHN S.	CHA	264	MIDDLETO
SWANN, JOHN W.	ST	326	4TH E DI
SWANN, LAURA	PRI	096	SPALDING
SWANN, MAT	CHA	295	HILLTOP
SWANN, PHILIP	BAL	017	4TH WARD
SWANN, PHILY	CHA	271	ALLENS F
SWANN, SAMUEL T.	CHA	276	ALLENS F
SWANN, SAMUEL T.	CHA	276	ALLENS F
SWANN, THOMAS	BAL	153	11TH WAR
SWANN, THOMAS	PRI	116	PISCATAW
SWANN, U.	CHA	283	BOJANTOW
SWANN, WARREN	CHA	242	HILLTOP
SWANN, WILALIM	PRI	096	SPALDING
SWANN, WILLIAM	CHA	271	ALLENS F
SWANN, WILLIE	PRI	085	QUEEN AN
SWAPE, HENRY	FRE	449	8TH E DI
SWAPS, BARBARY	BAL	075	18TH WAR
SWAPS, NENDIES *	BAL	073	18TH WAR
SWARCE, ELIZABETH	BAL	328	7TH WARD
SWARER, GEORGE	BAL	284	7TH WARD
SWARER, GEORGE ANNA	BAL	283	7TH WARD
SWARF, CAROLINE	BAL	292	7TH WARD
SWARINGER, ELIZABETH	MGM	384	ROCKERLE
SWARP, AMMEN	BAL	375	8TH WARD
SWART, ADAM	BAL	298	7TH WARD
SWART, EPHRAIM	HAR	168	3RD DIST
SWARTS, BENJAMIN F.	FRE	226	BUCKEYST
SWARTY, DANIEL	KEN	267	1ST DIST
SWARTY, JOHN	WAS	145	HAGERSTO
SWARTZ, ANN C.	WAS	142	HAGERSTO
SWARTZ, ANN E.	KEN	268	1ST DIST
SWARTZ, CAROLINE	BAL	082	1ST WARD
SWARTZ, CLEMENCE	ALL	202	CUMBERLA
SWARTZ, FRANCIS	ALL	208	CUMBERLA
SWARTZ, GEORGE	WAS	142	HAGERSTO
SWARTZ, H.	BAL	153	1ST WARD
SWARTZ, HENRY	BAL	243	1ST DIST
SWARTZ, HENRY	BAL	246	1ST DIST
SWARTZ, JACOB	ALL	011	3RD E.D.
SWARTZ, JAMES	HAR	100	2ND DIST
SWARTZ, JOHN	BAL	075	2ND DIST
SWARTZ, LAWRENCE	BAL	012	9TH WARD
SWARTZ, MARGARET	WAS	121	HAGERSTO
SWARTZ, MARY	BAL	441	1ST DIST
SWARTZ, MICHAEL	BAL	093	1ST WARD
SWARTZ, MICHAEL	BAL	093	1ST WARD
SWARTZ, NATHAN	BAL	259	2ND WARD
SWARTZ, SIMON	BAL	237	2ND WARD
SWARTZ, WILLIAM	BAL	131	1ST WARD
SWARTZ, WILLIAM	BAL	028	1ST WARD
SWARTZADDER, SARAH	ALL	216	CUMBERLA
SWARTZBAUGH, JOHN W.	CAR	195	4TH DIST
SWARTZENGROVE, FREDERICK	ALL	006	3RD E.D.
SWARTZENGROVER, CHRISTIAN	ALL	009	3RD E.D.
SWARTZENGROVER, JACOB	ALL	006	3RD E.D.
SWARTZENGROVER, JOHN	ALL	005	3RD E.D.
SWARTZENGROVER, JOHN	ALL	006	3RD E.D.
SWARTZENGROVER, JOSEPH	ALL	006	3RD E.D.
SWARTZENGROVER, JOSEPH	ALL	017	3RD E.D.
SWARTZENGROVER, PETER	ALL	017	3RD E.D.
SWARTZERGROVE, CHRISTIAN	ALL	005	3RD E.D.
SWARTZWELDEN, WILLIAM	ALL	046	10TH E.D
SWARTZWELDER, PETER	WAS	121	HAGERSTO
SWARZ, WILLIAM	BAL	221	6TH WARD
SWAT, JOHN W. *	HAR	190	3RD DIST
SWAT, WILLIAM H.	HAR	189	3RD DIST
SWATRZ, SOPHIA	BAL	316	1ST DIST
SWATZ, ANDREW	WAS	127	HAGERSTO
SWATZ, EMERY	BAL	284	1ST DIST
SWATZBENAUGH, JOHN *	TAL	069	EASTON T
SWAUBY, HENRY	BAL	261	1ST DIST
SWAY, WILLIAM	ANN	352	3RD DIST
SWAYNE, BENJAMIN	BAL	179	16TH WAR
SWAYS, MARY A.	BAL	426	8TH WARD
SWEAANER, BASIL	FRE	449	8TH E DI
SWEADNER, DANIEL	FRE	444	8TH E DI
SWEADNER, DANIEL JR.	FRE	444	8TH E DI
SWEADNER, LOUISA	FRE	445	8TH E DI
SWEADNER, WILLIAM	FRE	449	8TH E DI
SWEADNEW, DENNIS	FRE	434	8TH E DI
SWEAMER, ASHLOCK	BAL	014	9TH WARD
SWEAN, CHARLES	BAL	125	1ST WARD
SWEAR, JACOB	BAL	205	6TH DIST
SWEAREIGH, JOHN	BAL	042	9TH WARD
SWEARENGIN, JAEMS	ALL	153	6TH E.D.
SWEARER, GEORGE P.	BAL	098	5TH WARD
SWEARER, MARTHA-BLACK	BAL	219	2ND WARD
SWEARINGEN, SARAH	ALL	264	CUMBERLA
SWEARINGER, ELIZABETH	FRE	044	FREDERIC
SWEARN, BERNARD	FRE	050	FREDERIC
SWEAT, HENRY	BAL	169	1ST WARD
SWEATING, MARY	BAL	288	7TH WARD
SWEDEN, BENJAMIN	BAL	143	1ST WARD
SWEDEN, BENJAMIN	HAR	154	3RD DIST
SWEDEN, JAMES	HAR	153	3RD DIST
SWEDEN, JOHN	CAR	199	4TH DIST
SWEDING, C.	BAL	155	1ST WARD
SWEENEY, ANN	BAL	348	13TH WAR
SWEENEY, BENJAMIN	ANN	316	1ST DIST
SWEENEY, DENNIS	BAL	313	7TH WARD
SWEENEY, EDWARD	BAL	176	2ND DIST
SWEENEY, EUGENE	FRE	025	FREDERIC
SWEENEY, FREDERICK	BAL	047	4TH WARD
SWEENEY, GARRETT	WAS	026	2ND SUBD
SWEENEY, ISREAL	FRE	119	CREAGERS
SWEENEY, JAMES	FRE	169	5TH E DI
SWEENEY, JAMES	BAL	345	7TH WARD
SWEENEY, JOHN	BAL	140	1ST WARD
SWEENEY, JOHN	BAL	104	5TH WARD
SWEENEY, JOHN	BAL	002	4TH WARD
SWEENEY, JOHN	PRI	011	BLADENSB
SWEENEY, JOSEPH	ALL	152	6TH E.D.
SWEENEY, MARTIN	FRE	159	EMMITTSB
SWEENEY, MARY	BAL	177	2ND DIST
SWEENEY, MICHAEL	BAL	177	2ND DIST
SWEENEY, MICHAEL	BAL	210	17TH WAR
SWEENEY, MORDECAI B.	BAL	304	3RD WARD
SWEENEY, P.W.	BAL	162	1ST WARD
SWEENEY, RALPH K.	BAL	180	2ND DIST
SWEENEY, ROSA	BAL	014	2ND DIST
SWEENY, ADY	PRI	068	NOTTINGH
SWEENY, ALFRED	BAL	119	18TH WAR
SWEENY, AMRY	BAL	292	20TH WAR
SWEENY, BIDDY	BAL	472	14TH WAR
SWEENY, FELICIA	PRI	007	BLADENSB
SWEENY, GEORGE	PRI	070	MARLBROU
SWEENY, JOHN	PRI	069	MARLBROU
SWEENY, JOHN	BAL	159	19TH WAR
SWEENY, L.	PRI	101	SPALDING
SWEENY, NOTLEY	PRI	079	QUEEN AN
SWEENY, OWEN	ALL	141	6TH E.D.
SWEENY, SMITH	PRI	122	PISCATAW
SWEENY, THOMAS	PRI	119	PISCATAW
SWEENY, THOMAS	PRI	122	PISCATAW
SWEENY, THOMAS	PRI	057	AQUASCO
SWEENY, WILLIAM	BAL	292	20TH WAR
SWEEPER, MARY	BAL	048	2ND DIST
SWEET, BENJAMIN B.	CEC	138	6TH E DI
SWEET, HARTFORD	BAL	291	12TH WAR
SWEET, ISAAC	ALL	009	3RD E.D.
SWEETE, ARTHER	FRE	083	FREDERIC
SWEETING, JOHN Y.	HAR	205	3RD DIST
SWEETNER, CAROLINE	BAL	207	2ND WARD
SWEETZER, JOSEPH	ANN	343	3RD DIST
SWEETZER, T. H.	ALL	092	5TH E.D.
SWEGLER, AMELIA	BAL	348	7TH WARD
SWEGLER, PETER	BAL	348	7TH WARD
SWEITSER, JEREMIAH	WAS	239	CAVETOWN
SWEITZAR, ANDREW	BAL	177	2ND WARD
SWEITZER, CAROLINE	ALL	045	10TH E.D
SWEITZER, JAMES	BAL	215	2ND WARD
SWEITZER, JOHN	FRE	123	CREAGERS

Name	County	Page	District
SWEITZER, LEVI	ALL	025	2ND E.D.
SWEITZER, MARGARET	WAS	275	RIDGEVIL
SWEITZER, PETER	BAL	240	2ND WARD
SWEITZER, REBECCA	WAS	288	1ST DIST
SWELL, ANDREW	BAL	009	9TH WARD
SWELL, RACHEL	BAL	358	1ST DIST
SWELLYER, JOHN	ALL	116	5TH E.D.
SWELTZER, MARY	BAL	008	9TH WARD
SWEM, CATARINE	BAL	223	1ST DIST
SWEM, ELIZABETH	BAL	247	1ST DIST
SWEM, GEORGE	BAL	246	1ST DIST
SWEM, LOIUSA	BAL	242	1ST DIST
SWEMAN, MATTHEW	ALL	135	4TH E.D.
SWEMBERG, J.	BAL	129	1ST WARD
SWENAGER, GEORGE	BAL	299	1ST DIST
SWENEY, ANN	WAS	157	2ND DIST
SWENEY, FRANCES	BAL	230	12TH WAR
SWENEY, JAMES	BAL	282	2ND WARD
SWENEY, JOHN	BAL	005	9TH WARD
SWENEY, JOHN	ALL	047	10TH E.D
SWENEY, JOHN	WAS	151	2ND DIST
SWENEY, THOMAS	BAL	005	9TH WARD
SWENEY, WILLIAM F.	BAL	169	1ST WARD
SWENK, FREDERICK	CAR	214	5TH DIST
SWERER, SAMUEL	HAR	197	3RD DIST
SWERT, THOAMS B.	HAR	201	3RD DIST
SWERTZER, PETER D.	ALL	039	2ND E.D.
SWETE, EDWARD	ALL	173	7TH E.D.
SWETTINGTON, JOHN	BAL	051	1ST WARD
SWEZEL, MARY	BAL	306	20TH WAR
SWICK, THOMAS	BAL	255	2ND WARD
SWIDENSKY, JOHN	BAL	452	14TH WAR
SWIETZER, CATHERINE	BAL	026	9TH WARD
SWIFT, ADELINE	KEN	254	1ST DIST
SWIFT, ALFRED	HAR	205	3RD DIST
SWIFT, ALFRED	SOM	405	DUBLIN D
SWIFT, BRUAN	BAL	372	3RD WARD
SWIFT, DANIEL	HAR	204	3RD DIST
SWIFT, DANIEL M.	HAR	159	3RD DIST
SWIFT, ELISHA	BAL	108	2ND DIST
SWIFT, ELISHA	BAL	145	16TH WAR
SWIFT, HENRY	SOM	362	BRINKLEY
SWIFT, JAMES	HAR	029	1ST DIST
SWIFT, JAMES W.	HAR	001	1ST DIST
SWIFT, JOHN	BAL	166	1ST WARD
SWIFT, JOHN T.*	SOM	362	BRINKLEY
SWIFT, MARIA A.	QUE	197	3RD E DI
SWIFT, MARTHA	BAL	029	9TH WARD
SWIFT, MARY	HAR	030	1ST DIST
SWIFT, MARY	KEN	243	2ND DIST
SWIFT, MERIDITH	QUE	197	3RD E DI
SWIFT, SARAH	HAR	029	1ST DIST
SWIFT, SARAH	BAL	459	1ST DIST
SWIFT, STEPHEN	SOM	350	BRINKLEY
SWIFT, WILLIAM	BAL	064	15TH WAR
SWIFT, WILLIAM	HAR	013	1ST DIST
SWIFT, WILLIAM	SOM	409	DUBLIN D
SWIFT, WILLIAM	HAR	205	3RD DIST
SWIFT, WILLIAM H.	HAR	176	3RD DIST
SWIGART, CASPAR	ANN	517	HOWARD D
SWIGART, GEORGE	ANN	443	HOWARD D
SWIGART, JOHN	ANN	484	HOWARD D
SWIGART, MARY	ANN	444	HOWARD D
SWIGERT, FREDERICK	FRE	347	MIDDLETO
SWIGERT, FREDERICK	BAL	282	17TH WAR
SWIGERT, MARGARET	BAL	281	17TH WAR
SWIGGET, SAMUEL	DOR	375	1ST DIST
SWIGGETT, ANN	BAL	046	4TH WARD
SWILER, JOSEPHINE	BAL	099	10TH WAR
SWILTZER, ELIZABETH	FRE	415	8TH E DI
SWINDELL, ANNA	BAL	443	1ST DIST
SWINDELLS, SAMUEL	HAR	081	2ND DIST
SWINDLE, MARGARET	BAL	121	2ND DIST
SWINDLE, WILLIAM	BAL	257	17TH WAR
SWING, ELIZABETH	BAL	224	19TH WAR
SWINGER, ANDREW	WAS	142	HAGERSTO
SWINGER, BARBARY	WAS	125	HAGERSTO
SWINGER, CATHARINE	WAS	142	HAGERSTO
SWINGER, DANIEL	WAS	156	HAGERSTO
SWINGLE, MARY	WAS	129	HAGERSTO
SWINNY, JOHN	BAL	140	1ST WARD
SWINTING, EDWORD	HAR	197	3RD DIST
SWINZER, JOHN	BAL	298	12TH WAR
SWISLER, ANTONE	BAL	297	17TH WAR
SWITZENBERGER, NICHOLAS	BAL	350	7TH WARD
SWITZER, CHARLES	BAL	293	7TH WARD
SWITZER, DANIEL	BAL	314	7TH WARD
SWITZER, ELIZA ANN	CAR	198	4TH DIST
SWITZER, ELIZABETH M.	CAR	197	4TH DIST
SWITZER, FRED	BAL	287	20TH WAR
SWITZER, GEORGE	BAL	217	19TH WAR
SWITZER, GEORGE	ALL	182	8TH E.D.
SWITZER, HENRY	WAS	162	HAGERSTO
SWITZER, HENRY	WAS	151	2ND DIST
SWITZER, IRA	BAL	218	12TH WAR
SWITZER, ISAAC	BAL	241	1ST DIST
SWITZER, ISREAL	CAR	381	2ND DIST
SWITZER, JACOB	CAR	388	2ND DIST
SWITZER, JACOB	BAL	209	19TH WAR
SWITZER, JACOB C.	CAR	383	2ND DIST
SWITZER, JAMES	CAR	198	4TH DIST
SWITZER, JAMES L.	CAR	387	2ND DIST
SWITZER, JOHN	CAR	387	2ND DIST
SWITZER, JOHN	CAR	198	4TH DIST
SWITZER, JOHN	BAL	261	1ST DIST
SWITZER, JOHN	BAL	108	2ND DIST
SWITZER, JOHN A.	ALL	189	9TH E.D.
SWITZER, JOHN S.	BAL	007	18TH WAR
SWITZER, JOSEPH	BAL	365	13TH WAR
SWITZER, MARGARET	BAL	107	5TH WARD
SWITZER, MARY	BAL	390	3RD WARD
SWITZER, MARY	WAS	002	WILLIAMS
SWITZER, OLIVER	BAL	296	3RD WARD
SWITZER, PRISCILLA	ALL	189	9TH E.D.
SWITZER, SAMUEL J.	CAR	388	2ND DIST
SWITZER, WILLIAM	BAL	262	1ST DIST
SWITZER, WILLIAM	WAS	198	1ST DIST
SWITZER, WILLIAM A.	CAR	199	4TH DIST
SWOPE, BARBARA	ALL	215	CUMBERLA
SWOPE, BENJAMIN	WAS	156	HAGERSTO
SWOPE, CASPER	WAS	138	HAGERSTO
SWOPE, CATAHRINE	FRE	351	MIDDLETO
SWOPE, CATHARINE A.	WAS	133	HAGERSTO
SWOPE, CORNELIUS E.	WAS	021	2ND SUBD
SWOPE, DANIEL	WAS	134	HAGERSTO
SWOPE, ELIJAH	WAS	249	1ST DIST
SWOPE, ELIZABETH	WAS	230	1ST DIST
SWOPE, GASPER	WAS	163	2ND DIST
SWOPE, IGNATIUS	WAS	233	1ST DIST
SWOPE, JACOB T.	FRE	364	CATOCTIN
SWOPE, JOHN	CAR	243	TANEYTOW
SWOPE, JOHN	FRE	095	FREDERIC
SWOPE, JOHN	WAS	236	CAVETOWN
SWOPE, JOHN	WAS	233	1ST DIST
SWOPE, JOHN	BAL	112	15TH WAR
SWOPE, MARY	WAS	234	1ST DIST
SWOPE, MARY	WAS	091	2ND SUBD
SWOPE, MARY	FRE	152	10TH E D
SWOPE, MICHAEL	FRE	154	10TH E D
SWOPE, MICHAEL	WAS	252	1ST DIST
SWOPE, SAMUEL	CAR	315	1ST DIST
SWOPE, SUSAN	FRE	332	MIDDLETO
SWOPE, THOMAS	WAS	234	1ST DIST
SWOPE, WARNER	FRE	002	FREDERIC
SWOPES, NOAH	WAS	239	CAVETOWN
SWOPLE, MARANDA	FRE	166	EMMITTSB
SWORD, ALEXANDER	BAL	406	3RD WARD
SWORD, CATHARINE	WAS	097	2ND DIST
SWORD, JACOB	WAS	128	2ND DIST
SWORD, JACOB	WAS	120	2ND DIST
SWORD, MARY	WAS	023	2ND SUBD
SWORD, WILLIAM	BAL	385	3RD WARD
SWORDS, JAMES	BAL	022	9TH WARD
SWORMSTEAD, SAMUEL L. DR.	CAR	268	WESTMINS
SWORMSTEDT, FRANCES	ANN	404	8TH DIST
SWUIRREL, MARY	MGM	370	BERRYS D
SWUNGHOUSE, HENRY	ALL	223	CUMBERLA
SWYER, CHRISTOPHER	BAL	361	1ST DIST
SWYER, MARY	BAL	361	1ST DIST
SYAS, ABRAHAM	FRE	252	NEW MARK
SYAS, JACOB	FRE	336	MIDDLETO
SYAS, MICAJAH	CAR	288	7TH DIST
SYAS, NOAH	CAR	277	7TH DIST
SYAS, SARAH	CAR	352	6TH DIST
SYBER, JOHN	BAL	258	2ND WARD
SYBERT, RUDRICK	HAR	196	3RD DIST
SYBES, RACHAEL	BAL	266	1ST DIST
SYBLE, THOMAS	BAL	191	2ND WARD
SYBREY, EDWARD	BAL	079	2ND DIST
SYE, ANN E.	DOR	464	1ST DIST
SYE, CHARLES*	DOR	423	1ST DIST
SYE, DENNIS	DOR	446	1ST DIST
SYE, HARY	DOR	446	1ST DIST
SYE, LEVICY	DOR	455	1ST DIST
SYE, LUCY	DOR	464	1ST DIST
SYENK, GEORGE	BAL	077	1ST WARD
SYERS, BENJAMIN	FRE	252	NEW MARK
SYESTER, DAVID	WAS	066	2ND SUBD
SYFER, JOSEPH	BAL	428	8TH WARD
SYFERT, CHRISTOPHER	CAR	353	6TH DIST
SYFORD, HENRY	BAL	179	6TH WARD
SYFRED, FREDERICKA *	BAL	067	15TH WAR
SYKES, CATHARINE	CAR	272	WESTMINS
SYKES, CHARLES	BAL	307	20TH WAR
SYKES, CHARLES	BAL	017	4TH WARD
SYKES, HARRIETT	BAL	332	13TH WAR
SYKES, J.	BAL	153	1ST WARD
SYKES, JAMES	ANN	515	HOWARD D
SYKES, JOHN	CAR	183	8TH DIST
SYKES, JOHN	BAL	261	17TH WAR
SYKES, JOHN T.	CAR	352	6TH DIST
SYKES, LEWIS	CAR	171	8TH DIST
SYKES, MARGARET	MGM	399	ROCKERLE
SYKES, SYLVANIS	ANN	455	HOWARD D
SYKES, THOMAS	BAL	154	1ST WARD
SYKES, VIRGINIA	BAL	262	17TH WAR
SYLENCE, MARY	PRI	098	SPALDING
SYLER, GEORGE	FRE	354	MIDDLETO
SYLES, HARIETT	BAL	369	13TH WAR
SYLES, HENRY*	BAL	025	4TH WARD
SYLES, JAMES	MGM	443	CLARKSTR
SYLES, MARTHA A.	BAL	026	4TH WARD
SYLES, MARY	BAL	196	11TH WAR
SYLPH, MICHAEL	BAL	005	18TH WAR
SYLTER, CHARLES	CEC	063	1ST E DI
SYLVA, SABASTIAN	BAL	204	11TH WAR
SYLVER, ANDREW	BAL	428	8TH WARD
SYLVESTER, BENNETT	QUE	214	3RD E DI
SYLVESTER, DAVID	CAR	082	NO TWP L
SYLVESTER, ELIZABETH	QUE	157	2ND E DI
SYLVESTER, JAMES	QUE	142	1ST E DI
SYLVESTER, JAMES	CAR	078	NO TWP L
SYLVESTER, JAMES	BAL	240	12TH WAR
SYLVESTER, JOHN	CAR	137	NO TWP L
SYLVESTER, JOHN W.	CAR	082	NO TWP L
SYLVESTER, MARY	CAR	078	NO TWP L
SYLVESTER, MARY	BAL	411	1ST DIST
SYLVESTER, MARY ANN	QUE	218	3RD E DI
SYLVESTER, ROBERT H.	CAR	098	NO TWP L
SYLVESTER, THOMAS	CAR	092	NO TWP L
SYLVESTER, THOMAS	BAL	049	15TH WAR
SYLVESTER, WILLIAM	QUE	161	2ND E DI
SYLWAND, HENRY *	BAL	067	18TH WAR
SYLWRIGHT, WILLIAM	BAL	142	1ST WARD
SYMINGTON, MARGARET	MGM	319	CRACKLIN
SYMINGTON, NELLY A.	SOM	492	SALISBUR
SYMINGTON, THOMAS	BAL	298	20TH WAR
SYMMES, JOHN H.	ALL	212	CUMBERLA
SYMNS, ROBERT	BAL	172	1ST WARD
SYMONDS, JOSEPH	HAR	189	3RD DIST
SYMONDS, SUSANER	HAR	189	3RD DIST
SYMS, JACOB	HAR	186	3RD DIST
SYNK, ADAM	BAL	193	2ND WARD
SYNK, BERNARD	BAL	066	1ST WARD
SYPLE, MICHAEL	BAL	209	17TH WAR
SYPOLE, NANCY	ALL	156	6TH E.D.
SYPPLE, M.	BAL	203	2ND WARD
SYRES, JACOB	BAL	362	13TH WAR
SYRK, LEWIS	BAL	193	2ND WARD
SYRUS, WILLIAM	ALL	243	CUMBERLA
SYSLIM, WILLIAM	BAL	214	11TH WAR
SYSON, GEORGE*	BAL	033	4TH WARD
SYTES, SAMUEL	BAL	276	17TH WAR
SYTHE, EDWARD	BAL	175	11TH WAR
SYTHIE, GEORGE	WAS	121	2ND DIST
SZINIMINGE, EARNEST	BAL	444	14TH WAR
T	BAL	067	1ST WARD
TABB, JOHN T. W.	BAL	382	13TH WAR
TABB, JOHN W.	BAL	364	13TH WAR
TABB, MARY	BAL	062	15TH WAR
TABBER, JOHN	BAL	284	2ND WARD
TABBOTT, JOSEPH C.	QUE	183	3RD E DI
TABELMAN, JOHN G.	BAL	063	1ST WARD
TABER, CHARLES L.	BAL	170	1ST WARD
TABERRY, D.	BAL	281	2ND WARD
TABERT, JAMES E.	BAL	459	8TH WARD
TABLE, ELIZA	BAL	288	12TH WAR
TABLER, ADAM J. P.	WAS	103	2ND DIST
TABLER, CHARLOTT	FRE	079	FREDERIC
TABLER, HARRIET	FRE	275	NEW MARK
TABLER, MARY	FRE	275	NEW MARK
TABLER, MARY A.C.	FRE	391	PETERSVI
TABLER, MARY C.	MGM	438	CLARKSTR
TABLER, WILLIAM	FRE	275	NEW MARK
TABLER, WILLIAM B.	FRE	390	PETERSVI
TABLES, LEWIS	FRE	231	BUCKEYST
TABMAN, SAM	CHA	247	HILLTOP
TABS, EMILINE	ST	276	3RD E DI
TABS, JOHN M.	ST	277	3RD E DI
TACHARIAS, SUSAN	CAR	279	7TH DIST
TACHENBERG, MARY	BAL	036	15TH WAR
TACHLER, LOUIS	BAL	109	5TH WARD
TACKEY, CATHERINE	BAL	131	11TH WAR
TADER, JOSEPH	BAL	130	11TH WAR
TADINGS, MARY	BAL	417	8TH WARD
TAFFERTY, WILLIAM	BAL	419	14TH WAR
TAFT, HENRY	BAL	109	18TH WAR
TAGANT, SAMUEL S.	BAL	167	11TH WAR
TAGART, CARDIFF	BAL	248	1ST DIST
TAGART, ENOCH D.	CEC	088	4TH E DI
TAGART, FREDERICK	BAL	270	7TH WARD
TAGART, JACOB	CEC	088	4TH E DI
TAGART, JANE	BAL	451	8TH WARD
TAGART, WILLIAM	BAL	176	2ND DIST
TAGART, WILLIAM	CEC	092	4TH E DI
TAGE, WALTER	BAL	476	14TH WAR
TAGERT, JESSE	WAS	255	1ST DIST
TAGERT, JESSE	WAS	255	1ST DIST
TAGG, ALFRED	BAL	066	2ND DIST
TAGG, ETHEBERT	BAL	078	2ND DIST
TAGG, GEORGIAN	BAL	078	2ND DIST
TAGG, JULIA	ALL	207	CUMBERLA
TAGG, LYDIA	BAL	079	2ND DIST
TAGG, REBECCA	BAL	076	2ND DIST
TAGG, WILLIAM	CAR	245	3RD DIST
TAGGARCE, JAMES	BAL	151	1ST WARD
TAGGART, HUGH	WAS	135	HAGERSTO
TAGHA, OWEN	BAL	449	1ST DIST
TAGUE, CHARLES	ALL	078	5TH E.D.
TAGUE, GEORGE	ALL	221	CUMBERLA
TAGUE, MARGARET	BAL	378	8TH WARD
TAGUE, PHILIP	ALL	250	CUMBERLA
TAGUE, SOLOMON J.	ALL	219	CUMBERLA
TAGUES, GEORGE	SOM	542	TYASKIN
TAHL, DAVID	BAL	160	16TH WAR
TAHN, ELIZABETH	CAR	292	7TH DIST
TAHN, FREDERICK	CAR	291	7TH DIST
TAHN, JOHN	CAR	291	7TH DIST
TAILER, ASA	HAR	174	3RD DIST
TAILER, ASA	HAR	174	3RD DIST
TAILER, PATHIA	HAR	174	3RD DIST
TAILER, PATHIA	HAR	174	3RD DIST
TAILOR, FRANCIS	CHA	276	ALLENS F
TAILOR, GEORGE	CHA	295	HILLTOP
TAILOR, JAMES F.	HAR	174	3RD DIST
TAILOR, JOHN W.	BAL	296	3RD WARD
TAILOR, LETTY	CHA	284	BOJANTOW
TAILOR, RICHARD	CHA	280	BOJANTOW
TAILOR, WILLIAM A.	HAR	174	3RD DIST
TAINBEALL, WILLIAM	FRE	266	NEW MARK
TAINE, JOHN	BAL	130	18TH WAR
TAINE, SOPHIA	BAL	129	18TH WAR
TAINOUR, WILLIAM *	BAL	067	18TH WAR
TALBERT, BASIL	PRI	019	VANSVILL
TALBERT, ELISHA	BAL	439	1ST DIST
TALBERT, EPHRAIM	PRI	015	BLADENSB
TALBERT, GEORGE	PRI	015	BLADENSB
TALBERT, JEREMIAH	BAL	438	1ST DIST
TALBERT, LORENZO-BLACK	ST	338	4TH E DI
TALBERT, MARGARET	BAL	439	1ST DIST
TALBERT, MARTHA	PRI	032	VANSVILL
TALBERT, MARY A.	PRI	005	BLADENSB
TALBERT, OVERTON	PRI	015	BLADENSB
TALBERT, SARAH	HAR	033	1ST DIST
TALBORT, HENRY	CEC	128	5TH E DI
TALBOT, ALEN	BAL	008	EASTERN
TALBOT, ANN	BAL	046	4TH WARD
TALBOT, ANN E.	PRI	088	SPALDING
TALBOT, ANNA M.	ANN	413	HOWARD D
TALBOT, AQUILLA	BAL	027	2ND DIST
TALBOT, BARBARY	BAL	032	18TH WAR
TALBOT, BENJAMIN	BAL	297	20TH WAR
TALBOT, BENJAMIN	BAL	093	2ND DIST
TALBOT, CAROLINE	BAL	303	12TH WAR
TALBOT, CHARLES	BAL	353	7TH WARD
TALBOT, CHARLES	PRI	089	SPALDING
TALBOT, EDWARD	ANN	460	HOWARD D
TALBOT, EDWARD C.	BAL	455	1ST DIST
TALBOT, ELEAZER	PRI	066	NOTTINGH
TALBOT, ELLEN	BAL	065	18TH WAR
TALBOT, GOERGE	BAL	076	18TH WAR
TALBOT, HENRY	ANN	490	HOWARD D
TALBOT, HENRY F.	CAL	030	2ND DIST
TALBOT, ISAIAH	BAL	374	3RD WARD
TALBOT, J.F.C.	BAL	024	2ND DIST
TALBOT, J.F.C. JR.	BAL	024	2ND DIST
TALBOT, J.K.	BAL	024	2ND DIST
TALBOT, JAMES	BAL	065	10TH WAR
TALBOT, JEFFERSON	ANN	322	2ND DIST
TALBOT, JESSE	BAL	107	10TH WAR
TALBOT, JOHN	PRI	087	SPALDING
TALBOT, JULIA A.	BAL	247	6TH WARD
TALBOT, LEVI	BAL	162	2ND DIST
TALBOT, LUCRETIA	BAL	178	19TH WAR
TALBOT, MARGARET E.	ANN	413	HOWARD D
TALBOT, MARY	BAL	458	1ST DIST
TALBOT, MARY	BAL	430	8TH WARD
TALBOT, MARY A.	BAL	293	20TH WAR
TALBOT, MARYAN*	BAL	374	3RD WARD
TALBOT, NATHANIEL	BAL	145	1ST WARD
TALBOT, PAUL	MGM	394	ROCKERLE
TALBOT, PAUL	PRI	060	NOTTINGH
TALBOT, PRUDENCE	BAL	299	1ST DIST
TALBOT, SARAH	ANN	421	HOWARD D
TALBOT, SARAH	PRI	076	MARLBROU
TALBOT, SARAH	BAL	145	11TH WAR
TALBOT, SARAH W.	BAL	205	6TH WARD
TALBOT, SUSAN P.	PRI	060	NOTTINGH
TALBOT, THOMAS	PRI	079	MARLBROU
TALBOT, THOMAS	BAL	400	1ST DIST
TALBOT, THOMAS	BAL	184	19TH WAR
TALBOT, THOMAS J.	ANN	412	HOWARD D
TALBOT, WILLAIM	PRI	089	SPALDING
TALBOT, WILLIAM	PRI	079	MARLBROU
TALBOT, WILLIAM	PRI	076	MARLBROU
TALBOT, WILLIAM	BAL	436	1ST DIST
TALBOTT, ABEL	BAL	101	2ND DIST
TALBOTT, ADAM	MGM	358	BERRYS D
TALBOTT, ADELAIDE	BAL	250	12TH WAR
TALBOTT, BENJAMIN K.	CAL	052	3RD DIST

Name	County	Page	District
TALBOTT, EDWARD	BAL	189	6TH WARD
TALBOTT, EDWIN	KEN	302	3RD DIST
TALBOTT, ELIZA	MGM	398	ROCKERLE
TALBOTT, ELIZABETH	BAL	212	6TH DIST
TALBOTT, FRANCIS C.	BAL	043	9TH WARD
TALBOTT, HENRIETTA	MGM	358	BERRYS D
TALBOTT, HENRY W.	MGM	415	MEDLEY 3
TALBOTT, JAMES	CAL	002	1ST DIST
TALBOTT, JOHN	CAR	089	NO TWP L
TALBOTT, JOHN	FRE	240	NEW MARK
TALBOTT, JOHN	BAL	093	2ND DIST
TALBOTT, JOHN	BAL	118	15TH WAR
TALBOTT, JOHN	KEN	302	3RD DIST
TALBOTT, MAHLON	BAL	258	12TH WAR
TALBOTT, MEFORD	QUE	186	3RD E DI
TALBOTT, REBECCA B.	BAL	157	16TH WAR
TALBOTT, ROBERT	QUE	201	3RD E DI
TALBOTT, SAMUEL	BAL	082	15TH WAR
TALBOTT, SAMUEL	BAL	113	2ND DIST
TALBOTT, SAMUEL	FRE	238	NEW MARK
TALBOTT, SOPHIA A.	BAL	192	6TH WARD
TALBOTT, THOMAS	ANN	295	1ST DIST
TALBOTT, THOMAS	PRI	063	NOTTINGH
TALBOTT, WILLIAM	BAL	093	2ND DIST
TALBOTT, WILLIAM	BAL	015	15TH WAR
TALBOTT, WILLIAM	BAL	071	15TH WAR
TALBOTT, WILLIAM	CAR	090	NO TWP L
TALBOTT, ZACOK	MGM	398	ROCKERLE
TALBOTT, ANDREW	BAL	070	2ND DIST
TALBUT, JOSEPH	BAL	407	14TH WAR
TALBUT, LEVI	BAL	469	14TH WAR
TALBUT, WILLAIM R.	BAL	407	14TH WAR
TALBY, JOHN	BAL	188	5TH DIST
TALGHMAN, CATHARINE	BAL	245	6TH WARD
TALIAFERRO, G. B.	BAL	063	10TH WAR
TALIOFERRO, EMILY F.	ANN	521	HOWARD D
TALL, ANN	FRE	351	MIDDLETO
TALL, ANN	DOR	367	3RD DIVI
TALL, ANTONY	CAL	011	1ST DIST
TALL, COLUMBUS	BAL	263	17TH WAR
TALL, DEBORAH	CAR	151	NO TWP L
TALL, ELIZABETH*	DOR	368	3RD DIVI
TALL, ELYA	DOR	356	3RD DIVI
TALL, J. A.	BAL	157	1ST WARD
TALL, JAMES*	BAL	313	3RD WARD
TALL, JOHN	DOR	336	3RD DIVI
TALL, JOSEPH	BAL	068	15TH WAR
TALL, JOSEPH L.	BAL	265	7TH WARD
TALL, LEVIN W.	BAL	052	15TH WAR
TALL, MRS.	BAL	266	17TH WAR
TALL, PETER	TAL	066	EASTON T
TALL, RASMUSS	FRE	016	FREDERIC
TALL, RENNA	BAL	350	7TH WARD
TALL, RICHARD	DOR	364	3RD DIVI
TALL, SARAH	WAS	158	HAGERSTO
TALL, SUSAN	DOR	370	3RD DIVI
TALL, TABBY	BAL	237	20TH WAR
TALL, WILLIAM	WAS	029	2ND SUBD
TALL, WILLIAM R.	DOR	364	3RD DIVI
TALL, YOUNG	BAL	258	17TH WAR
TALLANT, MARY	BAL	351	1ST DIST
TALLBOTT, SAMUEL	BAL	123	16TH WAR
TALLERSALL, W.W.	BAL	170	1ST WARD
TALLEY, GEORGE P.	BAL	143	1ST WARD
TALLEY, TOBY	KEN	266	1ST DIST
TALLEY, WILLIAM	BAL	072	1ST WARD
TALLON, PETER	ALL	243	CUMBERLA
TALLOT, J.	BAL	149	1ST WARD
TALLOTT, MARY	BAL	097	2ND DIST
TALLY, ELIZA	BAL	474	14TH WAR
TALLY, MARGARET	ALL	128	4TH E.D.
TALLY, MARY	BAL	134	11TH WAR
TALLY, WILLIAM	CEC	073	5TH E DI
TALLY, WILLIAM	CEC	073	5TH E DI
TALMAN, BYARD	CEC	026	ELKTON 3
TALOBOTT, SUSANNAH	FRE	240	NEW MARK
TALOR, CORBIN	HAR	020	1ST DIST
TAMAMUS, JACOB	BAL	387	1ST DIST
TAMANS, LUTHER	BAL	266	1ST DIST
TAMANUS, C. F.	BAL	333	1ST DIST
TAMBLER, JOHN	BAL	448	14TH WAR
TAME, SARAH A.	ANN	441	HOWARD D
TAMEBOLL, JOHN	BAL	394	14TH WAR
TAMEYHILL, ELIZABETH	BAL	291	3RD WARD
TAMLIN, JOHN	ALL	046	10TH E.D
TAMSY, WILLIAM	CEC	208	7TH E DI
TAMTE, JOHN *	WOR	311	2ND E DI
TAMUS, ISRIEL	BAL	267	1ST DIST
TANBB, WILLIAM	BAL	079	1ST WARD
TANBLE, CHRISTOPHER	BAL	080	1ST WARD
TANE, EMILY	BAL	290	20TH WAR
TANER, GEORGE	BAL	348	13TH WAR
TANEY, ABJCUL	CAR	291	7TH DIST
TANEY, AUGUSTINE	FRE	160	EMMITTSB
TANEY, FELIX B.	FRE	180	5TH E DI
TANEY, FREDERICK	CAR	404	2ND DIST
TANEY, FREDERICK	CAR	314	1ST DIST
TANEY, HARRIET	FRE	448	8TH E DI
TANEY, JACOB	BAL	038	15TH WAR
TANEY, JOHN	CAR	407	2ND DIST
TANEY, JOSEPH A.	MGM	426	MEDLEY 3
TANEY, PATRICK J.	BAL	214	6TH WARD
TANEY, REBECCA	CAR	405	2ND DIST
TANEY, SARHA	FRE	181	5TH E DI
TANEY, WILLIAM	BAL	110	10TH WAR
TANEYHILL, ELIZABETH	CAL	060	3RD DIST
TANEYHILL, S.	BAL	081	10TH WAR
TANEZ, ROGER B.	BAL	099	10TH WAR
TANK, HENRY	BAL	006	1ST WARD
TANKEREY, JOHN	BAL	044	4TH WARD
TANKERFIELD, WILLIAM-BLAC	FRE	216	BUCKEYST
TANKERLY, MARY	BAL	339	13TH WAR
TANNAR, GEORGE W. *	QUE	216	3RD E DI
TANNER, ARMSTRONG	CAL	009	1ST DIST
TANNER, BARBARA	ALL	201	CUMBERLA
TANNER, CAHARINE	BAL	073	1ST WARD
TANNER, CATHARINE	WAS	212	1ST DIST
TANNER, JAMES	BAL	249	17TH WAR
TANNER, JAMES H.*	BAL	305	3RD WARD
TANNER, JOHN	ALL	135	4TH E.D.
TANNER, JOHN	ALL	218	CUMBERLA
TANNER, JOHN	QUE	218	3RD E DI
TANNER, JOHN	WAS	098	2ND DIST
TANNER, JOHN B.	BAL	375	13TH WAR
TANNER, JOHN DR.	BAL	374	13TH WAR
TANNER, JOHN H.	CAL	012	1ST DIST
TANNER, MARY	BAL	372	13TH WAR
TANNER, MARY A. E.	PRI	026	VANSVILL
TANNER, MARY D.	BAL	291	7TH WARD
TANNER, MARY R.	BAL	250	6TH WARD
TANNER, SOPHIA	WAS	208	1ST DIST
TANNER, THOMAS	QUE	229	4TH E DI
TANNER, WILLIAM	QUE	236	4TH E DI
TANNERS, GEORGE J.*	BAL	349	3RD WARD
TANNEY, JAMES	BAL	144	1ST WARD
TANNEY, JOHN F.	ST	258	3RD E DI
TANNING, FREDERICK	BAL	039	15TH WAR
TANNYHILL, HANAH	WAS	061	2ND SUBD
TANOR, MARGARET	BAL	053	15TH WAR
TANSBEY, THOMAS	BAL	006	9TH WARD
TANSEY, JOHN	BAL	448	1ST DIST
TANSEY, JOHN	BAL	448	1ST DIST
TANSEY, MARIA	BAL	076	15TH WAR
TANTMAN, JACOB	FRE	327	MIDDLETO
TANYHILL, ELZIABETH-MULAT	FRE	012	FREDERIC
TAPE, HENRY	BAL	063	2ND DIST
TAPERS, JOANNA	BAL	035	4TH WARD
TAPKIN, FREDERICK	BAL	079	1ST WARD
TAPMAN, ANN	BAL	140	16TH WAR
TAPMAN, ISAAC	WOR	346	1ST E DI
TAPMAN, JAMES	WOR	338	1ST E DI
TAPMAN, JESSE	WOR	330	1ST E DI
TAPMAN, JOHN	WOR	340	1ST E DI
TAPMAN, JOHN	BAL	238	17TH WAR
TAPMAN, NANCY	WOR	328	1ST E DI
TAPMAN, SALLY	WOR	350	1ST E DI
TAPMAN, SAMUEL	BAL	262	17TH WAR
TAPP, SARAH	BAL	089	18TH WAR
TAPPAN, MARGARET	BAL	157	19TH WAR
TAPPAN, WILLIAM C.	BAL	233	6TH WARD
TAPTT, MARY	HAR	029	1ST DIST
TAR, DEBORAH	BAL	476	14TH WAR
TARABULL, EVELINA *	BAL	382	13TH WAR
TARBEY, CHARLES	BAL	175	6TH WARD
TARBUTTA, WILLIAM	QUE	128	1ST E DI
TARBUTTER, ELISHA	QUE	198	3RD E DI
TARBUTTON, EDWARD*	TAL	005	EASTON D
TARBUTTON, ELLEN R.	TAL	021	EASTON D
TARBUTTON, GEORGE	TAL	050	EASTON T
TARBUTTON, JAMES	TAL	021	EASTON D
TARBUTTON, SAMUEL	QUE	176	2ND E DI
TARBUTTON, SUSAN A.	TAL	068	EASTON T
TARBUTTON, THOMAS	TAL	056	EASTON D
TARBUTTON, VIRGINIA	BAL	401	14TH WAR
TARBUTTON, WILLIAM	BAL	400	14TH WAR
TARBUTTON, WILLIAM	TAL	014	EASTON D
TARCXY, OHN L.	BAL	443	14TH WAR
TARDY, JOHN T.	BAL	046	9TH WARD
TARE, JOHN	TAL	082	ST MICHA
TARE, RICHARD	TAL	081	ST MICHA
TARE, WESTLY	HAR	044	1ST DIST
TARKER, WILLIAM-BLACK	FRE	226	BUCKEYST
TARLETON, MARY	BAL	355	3RD WARD
TARLOR, JOSEPH	HAR	174	3RD DIST
TARLTON, ALFORD	ST	296	2ND E DI
TARLTON, ANN	BAL	173	16TH WAR
TARLTON, BASIL	ST	308	1ST E DI
TARLTON, ELIZABETH	BAL	157	16TH WAR
TARLTON, GEORGE	ST	319	4TH E DI
TARLTON, GEORGE C.	ST	272	3RD E DI
TARLTON, HENRIETTA	BAL	263	17TH WAR
TARLTON, JOHN H.T.	ST	320	4TH E DI
TARLTON, JOHN R.	ST	313	1ST E DI
TARLTON, MARY E.	ST	297	2ND E DI
TARLTON, SARAH	ST	254	3RD E DI
TARLTON, WILLIAM T.	ST	302	2ND E DI
TARMAN, JOHN	MGM	388	ROCKERLE
TARMAN, JOHN	BAL	399	1ST DIST
TARMER, HILEARY-BLACK	MGM	408	MEDLEY 3
TARMON, Z.	BAL	329	13TH WAR
TARPIN, SARAH JANE	BAL	347	13TH WAR
TARR, ANN	BAL	022	18TH WAR
TARR, ANN	TAL	011	EASTON D
TARR, CHARLES	WOR	344	1ST E DI
TARR, DAVID	WOR	336	1ST E DI
TARR, EDWIN S.	BAL	071	15TH WAR
TARR, GEORGE	WOR	330	1ST E DI
TARR, GEORGE	WOR	311	2ND E DI
TARR, ISAAC	WOR	287	BERLIN 1
TARR, ISAAC	WOR	288	BERLIN 1
TARR, JAMES	WOR	297	9TH E DI
TARR, JAMES	WOR	324	1ST E DI
TARR, JAMES	CAR	149	NO TWP L
TARR, JOHN	WOR	330	1ST E DI
TARR, JOSEPH H.	CAR	167	NO TWP L
TARR, LAURA	BAL	017	15TH WAR
TARR, LEAH	WOR	330	1ST E DI
TARR, LEVI	WOR	289	9TH E DI
TARR, MARY	WOR	338	1ST E DI
TARR, NANCY	SOM	413	DUBLIN D
TARR, PETER	WOR	283	BERLIN 1
TARR, ROSETTA	BAL	249	6TH WARD
TARR, SAMUEL	BAL	009	1ST WARD
TARR, SARAH	BAL	001	1ST WARD
TARR, THOMAS	BAL	135	1ST WARD
TARR, THOMAS	WOR	337	1ST E DI
TARR, THOMAS	QUE	199	3RD E DI
TARR, WESLEY B.*	BAL	085	10TH WAR
TARR, WILLIAM	QUE	219	3RD E DI
TARR, WILLIAM E.	WOR	301	SNOW HIL
TARR, WILLIAM H.	BAL	224	6TH WARD
TARR, NANCY	WOR	348	1ST E DI
TARRALL, JOHN	BAL	153	1ST WARD
TARRELL, MARTIN	BAL	003	EASTERN
TARREN, MICHAEL	BAL	149	2ND DIST
TARRING, EDWARD H.	CEC	149	PORT DUP
TARRING, WILLIAM	BAL	143	16TH WAR
TARRING, WILLIAM JR.	BAL	139	16TH WAR
TARRY, ROBERT	WAS	137	2ND DIST
TARTER, ELIZA	BAL	439	8TH WARD
TARWAY, MARGARET	BAL	053	1ST WARD
TASCA, WILLIAM H.	HAR	158	3RD DIST
TASCO, ANNA-BLACK	FRE	050	FREDERIC
TASCO, BETSY	CAL	062	3RD DIST
TASCO, CHALRES	CAL	054	3RD DIST
TASCO, CHARLOTTE	CAL	062	3RD DIST
TASCO, ELLEN	BAL	364	1ST DIST
TASCO, FRANCIS	HAR	172	3RD DIST
TASCO, HARRIET	BAL	176	6TH WARD
TASCO, JACOB	CAL	061	3RD DIST
TASCO, JANE	CAL	058	3RD DIST
TASCO, MARY	CAL	062	3RD DIST
TASCO, MARY	BAL	353	1ST DIST
TASCO, RACHAEL	BAL	280	20TH WAR
TASCO, SALLY	CAL	052	3RD DIST
TASCO, SUSAN	HAR	156	3RD DIST
TASCO, WESLEY	BAL	050	9TH WARD
TASCOE, NANCY	BAL	020	18TH WAR
TASE, MARY A.	WAS	276	RIDGEVIL
TASK, STEPHEN	ANN	485	HOWARD D
TASKER, ARCHABALD	ALL	066	10TH E.D
TASKER, BENJAMIN	ALL	045	10TH E.D
TASKER, GEORGE	ANN	289	ANNAPOLI
TASKER, HENRY	ALL	066	10TH E.D
TASKER, LOUISA	ANN	320	2ND DIST
TASKER, LUCY	ANN	481	HOWARD D
TASKER, MARTHA	ANN	278	ANNAPOLI
TASKER, RICHARD	ANN	268	ANNAPOLI
TASKER, WILLIAM	ANN	291	ANNAPOLI
TASKS, ELIZABETH	DOR	304	1ST DIST
TASQUO, GEORGE	BAL	352	1ST DIST
TASSEL, FREDERICK	BAL	009	9TH WARD
TASSEL, JOSEPH	BAL	107	18TH WAR
TASSELL, JAMES	CEC	108	3RD E DI
TASSY, MARY	BAL	408	14TH WAR
TASTE, JACOB	FRE	345	MIDDLETO
TASTO, HENRY	CAR	186	8TH DIST
TATAM, DANIEL	BAL	014	15TH WAR
TATAM, JAMES	BAL	008	15TH WAR
TATAM, JOSEPH	BAL	012	15TH WAR
TATAM, MARY	BAL	014	15TH WAR
TATAM, MARY	BAL	009	15TH WAR
TATE, DANIEL	CAR	385	2ND DIST
TATE, ELIZABETH	BAL	077	2ND DIST
TATE, ELIZABETH	ANN	350	3RD DIST
TATE, ELIZABETH A.	BAL	394	3RD WARD
TATE, HIRAM	BAL	092	15TH WAR
TATE, JAMES	HAR	010	1ST DIST
TATE, JAMES	HAR	052	1ST DIST
TATE, JOHN-BLACK	CAR	070	NO TWP L
TATE, JOSEPH	ALL	224	CUMBERLA
TATE, MISS E.	FRE	199	5TH E DI
TATE, PETER	ALL	079	5TH E.D.
TATE, RACHEL A.	QUE	248	5TH E DI
TATE, RICHARD	CAR	072	NO TWP L
TATE, ROBERT	BAL	051	15TH WAR
TATE, ROBERT-BLACK	CAR	069	NO TWP L
TATE, SAMUEL	HAR	065	1ST DIST
TATE, SARAH	BAL	230	6TH WARD
TATE, SIMON	BAL	175	6TH WARD
TATE, THOMAS	BAL	147	1ST WARD
TATE, THOMAS	CAR	275	7TH DIST
TATE, WALTER	ALL	136	4TH E.D.
TATE, WASHINGTON	CAR	321	1ST DIST
TATE, WILLIAM	FRE	163	EMMITTSB
TATE, ELLENORA	CAR	382	2ND DIST
TATEEMAN, RACHEL	BAL	031	9TH WARD
TATEM, VIRGINIA *	BAL	250	6TH WARD
TATEMAN, GEORGE	BAL	279	2ND WARD
TATERN, VIRGINIA *	BAL	250	6TH WARD
TATES, MARY C.	ST	254	3RD E DI
TATHAM, JOHN	BAL	391	14TH WAR
TATMAN, COLINS	KEN	228	2ND DIST
TATMAN, HENRY	WOR	182	6TH E DI
TATTE, CHRISTOPHER	BAL	139	2ND DIST
TATTERSALLS, W.	BAL	170	1ST WARD
TATTLER, AMERICA	MGM	411	MEDLEY 3
TATTY, MARY E.	FRE	066	FREDERIC
TATUM, JOEL H.	BAL	067	10TH WAR
TAUDTE, LORENZO	BAL	089	10TH WAR
TAULLER, JOHN	CAR	288	7TH DIST
TAUNEY, JOSEPH	WAS	114	2ND DIST
TAUNEY, MONICHA	ST	259	3RD E DI
TAUSTY, JOHN	BAL	381	3RD WARD
TAVEN, AMELIA J.	BAL	438	8TH WARD
TAVERNER, JOSEPH W.	BAL	443	8TH WARD
TAVILLEY, HENRY	BAL	107	5TH WARD
TAVIS, JOHN	BAL	123	1ST WARD
TAW, ANN W. *	ANN	417	HOWARD D
TAWES, JOHN	SOM	373	BRINKLEY
TAWES, JOHN E.	SOM	376	BRINKLEY
TAWES, JOHN E.	SOM	375	BRINKLEY
TAWNEY, DAVID	BAL	192	5TH DIST
TAWNEY, ELIZABETH	CAR	188	4TH DIST
TAWNEY, ETHELBERT	WAS	161	2ND DIST
TAWNEY, REBECA	CAR	190	4TH DIST
TAWNEY, THOMAS	BAL	184	5TH DIST
TAWNEY, THOMAS	BAL	184	5TH DIST
TAWNEY, THOMSA	BAL	192	5TH DIST
TAWNEYHILL, JAMES	WAS	070	2ND SUBD
TAWS, JAMES	SOM	375	BRINKLEY
TAWS, JOHN	SOM	374	BRINKLEY
TAWS, KENNEY	SOM	376	BRINKLEY
TAWS, KISSIAH	SOM	377	BRINKLEY
TAWS, LEAH A.	SOM	376	BRINKLEY
TAWS, MATILDA	SOM	376	BRINKLEY
TAWS, NOAH	SOM	375	BRINKLEY
TAX, SUSAN	BAL	019	2ND DIST
TAY, ELIZA	WAS	045	2ND SUBD
TAYARD, GEORGE	BAL	133	1ST WARD
TAYARS, ELLECK	BAL	037	2ND DIST
TAYER, JOHN J.	BAL	134	18TH WAR
TAYLAN, JOHN *	BAL	167	2ND DIST
TAYLER, ALFRED	BAL	107	18TH WAR
TAYLER, ALLEN	BAL	280	20TH WAR
TAYLER, ELLEN	BAL	375	13TH WAR
TAYLER, JOHN W.	ALL	090	5TH E.D.
TAYLER, JOSIAH C.	KEN	272	1ST DIST
TAYLER, JULIA A.	BAL	140	19TH WAR
TAYLER, MARY C.	FRE	427	8TH E DI
TAYLER, THOAMS	BAL	277	20TH WAR
TAYLOR, A. P.	BAL	046	9TH WARD
TAYLOR, A. W.	WOR	260	BERLIN 1
TAYLOR, ABRAHAM	KEN	266	1ST DIST
TAYLOR, ABRAHAM	BAL	229	6TH WARD
TAYLOR, ABRAHAM	BAL	356	1ST DIST
TAYLOR, ABRAHAM	CAR	381	2ND DIST
TAYLOR, ABRAHAN	CEC	216	7TH E DI
TAYLOR, ACSHA*	BAL	118	15TH WAR
TAYLOR, ADALIJA	WOR	272	BERLIN 1
TAYLOR, AGUSTUS	BAL	179	2ND WARD
TAYLOR, ALBERT G.	CEC	163	6TH E DI
TAYLOR, ALEXANDER	BAL	157	1ST WARD
TAYLOR, ALEXANDER	BAL	091	5TH WARD
TAYLOR, ALFRED	BAL	290	7TH WARD
TAYLOR, AMANDA	BAL	413	8TH WARD
TAYLOR, AMANDA	BAL	332	13TH WAR
TAYLOR, AMANDA	SOM	521	BARREN C
TAYLOR, AMBROSE	BAL	161	6TH WARD
TAYLOR, AMELIA	BAL	335	3RD WARD
TAYLOR, AMELIA	BAL	320	20TH WAR
TAYLOR, AMOS	TAL	031	EASTON D
TAYLOR, ANN	PRI	023	VANSVILL
TAYLOR, ANN	PRI	119	PISCATAW
TAYLOR, ANN	ST	302	2ND E DI
TAYLOR, ANN	HAR	107	2ND DIST
TAYLOR, ANN	BAL	248	17TH WAR
TAYLOR, ANN	BAL	129	11TH WAR
TAYLOR, ANN	BAL	459	1ST DIST
TAYLOR, ANN	BAL	177	6TH WARD

Name	County	Page	Locality
TAYLOR, ANN	BAL	225	2ND WARD
TAYLOR, ANN	BAL	382	8TH WARD
TAYLOR, ANN	BAL	069	15TH WAR
TAYLOR, ANN E.	KEN	292	3RD DIST
TAYLOR, ANN M.	BAL	056	10TH WAR
TAYLOR, ANN R.	HAR	077	BEL AIR
TAYLOR, ANN*	BAL	375	3RD WARD
TAYLOR, ANNA	ANN	331	2ND DIST
TAYLOR, ANNE	BAL	111	15TH WAR
TAYLOR, ANTHONY	BAL	031	2ND DIST
TAYLOR, ARTRIDGE-BLACK	MGM	433	CLARKSTR
TAYLOR, AUGUSTUS	WOR	302	SNOW HIL
TAYLOR, AVERY	SOM	420	PRINCESS
TAYLOR, B. F.	BAL	333	1ST DIST
TAYLOR, BARNABAS	WOR	345	1ST E DI
TAYLOR, BEN	PRI	088	SPALDING
TAYLOR, BENJAMIN	SOM	532	QUANTICO
TAYLOR, BENJAMIN	ANN	291	ANNAPOLI
TAYLOR, BENJAMIN	HAR	195	3RD DIST
TAYLOR, BENJAMIN	CAR	208	4TH DIST
TAYLOR, BENJAMIN	BAL	028	4TH WARD
TAYLOR, BENJAMIN M.	FRE	229	BUCKEYST
TAYLOR, BENNETT	CAR	090	NO TWP L
TAYLOR, BETSEY	BAL	356	1ST DIST
TAYLOR, BETSEY	WOR	277	BERLIN 1
TAYLOR, BETSEY	WOR	278	BERLIN 1
TAYLOR, BONEPART-BLACK	CAR	165	NO TWP L
TAYLOR, BURGESS	ALL	095	5TH E.D.
TAYLOR, CAROLINE	PRI	090	MARLBROU
TAYLOR, CATHARINE	WAS	152	HAGERSTO
TAYLOR, CATHARINE	ST	309	1ST E DI
TAYLOR, CATHARINE	BAL	234	12TH WAR
TAYLOR, CATHARINE	BAL	246	2ND WARD
TAYLOR, CATHARINE	BAL	150	5TH WARD
TAYLOR, CATHARINE	CAR	178	8TH DIST
TAYLOR, CATHARINE	CAR	209	5TH DIST
TAYLOR, CATHARINE	CAR	197	4TH DIST
TAYLOR, CATHERINE	CHA	280	BOJANTOW
TAYLOR, CHARLES	CAL	004	1ST DIST
TAYLOR, CHARLES	MGM	382	ROCKERLE
TAYLOR, CHARLES	BAL	180	11TH WAR
TAYLOR, CHARLES	ANN	272	ANNAPOLI
TAYLOR, CHARLES	PRI	051	AQUASCO
TAYLOR, CHARLES W.	BAL	277	7TH WARD
TAYLOR, CHRISTIANA	MGM	381	ROCKERLE
TAYLOR, CHRISTOPHER	MGM	423	MEDLEY 3
TAYLOR, CYRUS W.	WOR	260	BERLIN 1
TAYLOR, DANIEL	ST	306	1ST E DI
TAYLOR, DANIEL	FRE	279	WOODSBOR
TAYLOR, DANIEL	BAL	250	6TH WARD
TAYLOR, DANIEL	BAL	158	1ST WARD
TAYLOR, DANIEL P.	FRE	279	WOODSBOR
TAYLOR, DAVID	CEC	022	ELKTON 3
TAYLOR, DAVID	ALL	206	CUMBERLA
TAYLOR, DAVID	BAL	233	12TH WAR
TAYLOR, DAVID	BAL	280	12TH WAR
TAYLOR, DEBBY	BAL	363	13TH WAR
TAYLOR, DEBORAH	CEC	160	PORT DUP
TAYLOR, DORCAS	BAL	412	14TH WAR
TAYLOR, E.C.	ANN	283	ANNAPOLI
TAYLOR, EBEN	SOM	524	BARREN C
TAYLOR, EDMUND	ANN	451	HOWARD D
TAYLOR, EDWARD	ANN	268	ANNAPOLI
TAYLOR, EDWARD	BAL	164	1ST WARD
TAYLOR, EDWARD	BAL	170	2ND DIST
TAYLOR, EDWARD	PRI	036	VANSVILL
TAYLOR, EDWARD	WOR	281	BERLIN 1
TAYLOR, EDWARD	WOR	310	2ND E DI
TAYLOR, EDWARD	BAL	107	18TH WAR
TAYLOR, EDWARD C.	BAL	382	3RD WARD
TAYLOR, EDWARD-BLACK	WOR	172	6TH E DI
TAYLOR, EDWARD-BLACK	WOR	325	1ST E DI
TAYLOR, ELDY	WOR	305	SNOW HIL
TAYLOR, ELIAS	WOR	345	1ST E DI
TAYLOR, ELIAS	WOR	206	4TH E DI
TAYLOR, ELIJAH	WOR	339	1ST E DI
TAYLOR, ELISH P.	WOR	242	1ST CENS
TAYLOR, ELISHA	WOR	242	1ST CENS
TAYLOR, ELIZA	WOR	346	1ST E DI
TAYLOR, ELIZA	WOR	304	SNOW HIL
TAYLOR, ELIZA	SOM	456	DAMES QU
TAYLOR, ELIZA	BAL	277	7TH WARD
TAYLOR, ELIZA	BAL	062	2ND DIST
TAYLOR, ELIZA	CEC	180	7TH E DI
TAYLOR, ELIZABETH	BAL	219	17TH WAR
TAYLOR, ELIZABETH	BAL	246	17TH WAR
TAYLOR, ELIZABETH	KEN	217	2ND DIST
TAYLOR, ELIZABETH	BAL	013	4TH WARD
TAYLOR, ELIZABETH	BAL	179	19TH WAR
TAYLOR, ELIZABETH	BAL	459	14TH WAR
TAYLOR, ELIZABETH	BAL	259	20TH WAR
TAYLOR, ELIZABETH	BAL	195	6TH WARD
TAYLOR, ELIZABETH	BAL	457	1ST DIST
TAYLOR, ELIZABETH	SOM	468	TRAPPE D
TAYLOR, ELIZABETH	ST	306	1ST E DI
TAYLOR, ELLEN J.	HAR	148	3RD DIST
TAYLOR, EMANUEL	FRE	292	WOODSBOR
TAYLOR, EMANUEL	WAS	225	1ST DIST
TAYLOR, EMILY	BAL	024	1ST WARD
TAYLOR, EMMA	BAL	054	4TH WARD
TAYLOR, ENFAMY	SOM	454	DAMES QU
TAYLOR, EPHRAIM-BLACK	WOR	345	1ST E DI
TAYLOR, EVA	BAL	141	11TH WAR
TAYLOR, EVELINE	BAL	249	12TH WAR
TAYLOR, EZRA	FRE	301	WOODSBOR
TAYLOR, EZRA	WAS	137	2ND DIST
TAYLOR, FARY MRS.	BAL	137	11TH WAR
TAYLOR, FENWICK	ST	313	1ST E DI
TAYLOR, FRANCES	BAL	383	3RD WARD
TAYLOR, FRANCIS	BAL	171	2ND DIST
TAYLOR, FRANCIS	TAL	024	EASTON D
TAYLOR, FRANCIS A.	SOM	535	QUANTICO
TAYLOR, FRANCIS X.	BAL	060	15TH WAR
TAYLOR, FRANICS-BLACK	CAR	167	NO TWP L
TAYLOR, FRANKLIN	CEC	075	NORTHEAS
TAYLOR, FREDERICK	CEC	087	4TH E DI
TAYLOR, FREDERICK	BAL	417	14TH WAR
TAYLOR, FRISBY	BAL	417	14TH WAR
TAYLOR, FRISBY	KEN	258	1ST DIST
TAYLOR, G.A.	BAL	113	1ST WARD
TAYLOR, G.S.	BAL	141	1ST WARD
TAYLOR, GEORGANNA A.	BAL	130	18TH WAR
TAYLOR, GEORGE	FRE	301	WOODSBOR
TAYLOR, GEORGE	BAL	166	19TH WAR
TAYLOR, GEORGE	CEC	177	7TH E DI
TAYLOR, GEORGE	CEC	177	7TH E DI
TAYLOR, GEORGE	BAL	024	15TH WAR
TAYLOR, GEORGE	BAL	236	20TH WAR
TAYLOR, GEORGE	BAL	001	4TH WARD
TAYLOR, GEORGE	FRE	160	EMMITTSB
TAYLOR, GEORGE	BAL	030	1ST WARD
TAYLOR, GEORGE	BAL	078	1ST WARD
TAYLOR, GEORGE	BAL	002	15TH WAR
TAYLOR, GEORGE	BAL	287	3RD WARD
TAYLOR, GEORGE	BAL	214	6TH DIST
TAYLOR, GEORGE	BAL	166	6TH WARD
TAYLOR, GEORGE	BAL	017	9TH WARD
TAYLOR, GEORGE	ANN	467	HOWARD D
TAYLOR, GEORGE	ANN	267	ANNAPOLI
TAYLOR, GEORGE	ANN	311	1ST DIST
TAYLOR, GEORGE	BAL	332	7TH WARD
TAYLOR, GEORGE	SOM	474	TRAPPE D
TAYLOR, GEORGE	QUE	153	2ND E DI
TAYLOR, GEORGE	TAL	041	EASTON D
TAYLOR, GEORGE E.	BAL	255	6TH WARD
TAYLOR, GEORGE H.	WAS	028	2ND SUBD
TAYLOR, GEORGE I.	BAL	073	1ST WARD
TAYLOR, GEORGE W.	BAL	385	8TH WARD
TAYLOR, GEORGE W.	ALL	236	CUMBERLA
TAYLOR, GEORGE W.	TAL	016	EASTON D
TAYLOR, GEORGE W.	CEC	138	6TH E DI
TAYLOR, GEORGE W.	BAL	363	13TH WAR
TAYLOR, GRIFFEN	FRE	221	BUCKEYST
TAYLOR, H. L.	BAL	178	11TH WAR
TAYLOR, HANNAH	HAR	127	2ND DIST
TAYLOR, HANNAH	HAR	089	2ND DIST
TAYLOR, HANNAH	WOR	200	3RD E DI
TAYLOR, HARRIET V.	BAL	330	3RD WARD
TAYLOR, HARRY	BAL	009	EASTERN
TAYLOR, HENRIETTA	CAR	149	NO TWP L
TAYLOR, HENRY	SOM	423	PRINCESS
TAYLOR, HENRY	KEN	249	2ND DIST
TAYLOR, HENRY	KEN	242	2ND DIST
TAYLOR, HENRY	KEN	248	2ND DIST
TAYLOR, HENRY	FRE	099	FREDERIC
TAYLOR, HENRY	FRE	290	WOODSBOR
TAYLOR, HENRY	BAL	236	20TH WAR
TAYLOR, HENRY	CAR	197	4TH DIST
TAYLOR, HENRY	BAL	178	19TH WAR
TAYLOR, HENRY	BAL	070	18TH WAR
TAYLOR, HENRY	BAL	009	EASTERN
TAYLOR, HENRY	BAL	195	6TH WARD
TAYLOR, HENRY	WOR	321	1ST E DI
TAYLOR, HENRY B.	WOR	258	1ST CENS
TAYLOR, HENRY S.	HAR	195	3RD DIST
TAYLOR, HESIHIAH	BAL	052	16TH WAR
TAYLOR, HESSIKIAH	BAL	008	18TH WAR
TAYLOR, HETTY	WOR	271	BERLIN 1
TAYLOR, HIRAM	CEC	145	PORT DUP
TAYLOR, HOLMES	BAL	475	14TH WAR
TAYLOR, ICHABOD	SOM	504	SALISBUR
TAYLOR, IRCILLA	ST	284	2ND E DI
TAYLOR, IRCILLA	ST	283	3RD E DI
TAYLOR, ISAAC	SOM	509	BARREN C
TAYLOR, ISAAC	SOM	514	BARREN C
TAYLOR, ISAAC	WOR	201	3RD E DI
TAYLOR, ISAAC	QUE	216	3RD E DI
TAYLOR, ISAAC	BAL	423	3RD WARD
TAYLOR, ISAAC	BAL	179	19TH WAR
TAYLOR, ISAAC	BAL	232	6TH WARD
TAYLOR, ISAAC	BAL	176	6TH WARD
TAYLOR, ISAAC	BAL	010	EASTERN
TAYLOR, ISAAC	ANN	445	HOWARD D
TAYLOR, ISAAC	BAL	063	2ND DIST
TAYLOR, ISAAC	BAL	229	2ND WARD
TAYLOR, ISAAC R.	CEC	163	6TH E DI
TAYLOR, ISABEL	BAL	242	12TH WAR
TAYLOR, ISABELLA	BAL	062	15TH WAR
TAYLOR, J.	BAL	165	1ST WARD
TAYLOR, J. H.	BAL	268	7TH WARD
TAYLOR, J.M.	BAL	142	1ST WARD
TAYLOR, JACOB	BAL	053	15TH WAR
TAYLOR, JACOB	BAL	455	8TH WARD
TAYLOR, JACOB	ALL	113	5TH E.D.
TAYLOR, JACOB	CEC	146	PORT DUP
TAYLOR, JACOB	CEC	018	ELKTON 3
TAYLOR, JACOB	FRE	282	WOODSBOR
TAYLOR, JACOB	QUE	216	3RD E DI
TAYLOR, JACOB	WAS	063	2ND SUBD
TAYLOR, JACOB H.	BAL	235	6TH WARD
TAYLOR, JACOB-BLACK	WOR	325	1ST E DI
TAYLOR, JACOB-BLACK	CAR	149	NO TWP L
TAYLOR, JAMES	CAL	020	2ND DIST
TAYLOR, JAMES	CAL	054	3RD DIST
TAYLOR, JAMES	CAL	024	2ND DIST
TAYLOR, JAMES	CAR	397	2ND DIST
TAYLOR, JAMES	BAL	144	19TH WAR
TAYLOR, JAMES	CEC	039	CHESAPEA
TAYLOR, JAMES	CEC	120	4TH E DI
TAYLOR, JAMES	HAR	145	3RD DIST
TAYLOR, JAMES	FRE	190	5TH E DI
TAYLOR, JAMES	WOR	332	1ST E DI
TAYLOR, JAMES	WOR	322	1ST E DI
TAYLOR, JAMES	WOR	277	BERLIN 1
TAYLOR, JAMES	WOR	289	9TH E DI
TAYLOR, JAMES	TAL	029	EASTON D
TAYLOR, JAMES	WAS	049	2ND SUBD
TAYLOR, JAMES	SOM	460	HANGARY
TAYLOR, JAMES	ST	344	5TH E DI
TAYLOR, JAMES	SOM	509	BARREN C
TAYLOR, JAMES	PRI	036	VANSVILL
TAYLOR, JAMES	BAL	244	6TH WARD
TAYLOR, JAMES	BAL	149	1ST WARD
TAYLOR, JAMES	BAL	125	5TH WARD
TAYLOR, JAMES	BAL	195	2ND WARD
TAYLOR, JAMES	ANN	269	ANNAPOLI
TAYLOR, JAMES	BAL	454	8TH WARD
TAYLOR, JAMES	BAL	002	9TH WARD
TAYLOR, JAMES	BAL	037	15TH WAR
TAYLOR, JAMES	BAL	252	2ND WARD
TAYLOR, JAMES	BAL	132	1ST WARD
TAYLOR, JAMES	BAL	134	1ST WARD
TAYLOR, JAMES	BAL	338	3RD WARD
TAYLOR, JAMES	BAL	007	1ST WARD
TAYLOR, JAMES	BAL	187	16TH WAR
TAYLOR, JAMES G.R.	BAL	203	19TH WAR
TAYLOR, JAMES H.	ANN	277	ANNAPOLI
TAYLOR, JAMES L.	BAL	355	8TH WARD
TAYLOR, JAMES L.	CEC	192	5TH E DI
TAYLOR, JAMES T.	SOM	395	BRINKLEY
TAYLOR, JANE	CHA	260	BOJANTOW
TAYLOR, JANE	BAL	473	14TH WAR
TAYLOR, JANE	ALL	098	5TH E.D.
TAYLOR, JANE	BAL	066	15TH WAR
TAYLOR, JANE	BAL	353	7TH WARD
TAYLOR, JANE	BAL	222	6TH WARD
TAYLOR, JANE R.	BAL	229	6TH WARD
TAYLOR, JERRY-BLACK	CAR	168	NO TWP L.
TAYLOR, JESSE	FRE	130	PETERSVI
TAYLOR, JESSE	FRE	270	NEW MARK
TAYLOR, JESSE*	BAL	350	3RD WARD
TAYLOR, JOHN	BAL	363	3RD WARD
TAYLOR, JOHN	BAL	033	1ST WARD
TAYLOR, JOHN	BAL	121	1ST WARD
TAYLOR, JOHN	BAL	118	1ST WARD
TAYLOR, JOHN	BAL	258	1ST DIST
TAYLOR, JOHN	BAL	181	6TH WARD
TAYLOR, JOHN	BAL	055	15TH WAR
TAYLOR, JOHN	ALL	090	5TH E.D.
TAYLOR, JOHN	ALL	208	CUMBERLA
TAYLOR, JOHN	ANN	311	1ST DIST
TAYLOR, JOHN	ALL	022	2ND E.D.
TAYLOR, JOHN	BAL	146	1ST WARD
TAYLOR, JOHN	BAL	266	7TH WARD
TAYLOR, JOHN	BAL	323	7TH WARD
TAYLOR, JOHN	BAL	100	10TH WAR
TAYLOR, JOHN	BAL	304	12TH WAR
TAYLOR, JOHN	BAL	277	12TH WAR
TAYLOR, JOHN	BAL	274	12TH WAR
TAYLOR, JOHN	BAL	356	1ST DIST
TAYLOR, JOHN	BAL	394	1ST DIST
TAYLOR, JOHN	BAL	426	1ST DIST
TAYLOR, JOHN	BAL	126	18TH WAR
TAYLOR, JOHN	CEC	194	7TH E DI
TAYLOR, JOHN	CAR	166	NO TWP L
TAYLOR, JOHN	CAR	198	4TH DIST
TAYLOR, JOHN	CEC	024	ELKTON 3
TAYLOR, JOHN	BAL	019	4TH WARD
TAYLOR, JOHN	BAL	040	4TH WARD
TAYLOR, JOHN	CEC	001	ELKTON 3
TAYLOR, JOHN	CAL	020	2ND DIST
TAYLOR, JOHN	HAR	160	3RD DIST
TAYLOR, JOHN	CEC	066	1ST E DI
TAYLOR, JOHN	BAL	067	4TH WARD
TAYLOR, JOHN	SOM	450	DAMES QU
TAYLOR, JOHN	HAR	024	1ST DIST
TAYLOR, JOHN	HAR	009	1ST DIST
TAYLOR, JOHN	WOR	326	1ST E DI
TAYLOR, JOHN	WAS	133	2ND DIST
TAYLOR, JOHN	WOR	345	1ST E DI
TAYLOR, JOHN	PRI	049	AQUASCO
TAYLOR, JOHN	SOM	504	SALISBUR
TAYLOR, JOHN	WOR	226	4TH E DI
TAYLOR, JOHN	PRI	098	SPALDING
TAYLOR, JOHN	PRI	116	PISCATAW
TAYLOR, JOHN	QUE	188	3RD E DI
TAYLOR, JOHN	KEN	310	3RD DIST
TAYLOR, JOHN	TAL	031	EASTON D
TAYLOR, JOHN	WOR	294	9TH E DI
TAYLOR, JOHN	WOR	290	9TH E DI
TAYLOR, JOHN	WAS	017	2ND SUBD
TAYLOR, JOHN B.	SOM	513	BARREN C
TAYLOR, JOHN E.	SOM	514	BARREN C
TAYLOR, JOHN E.	FRE	010	FREDERIC
TAYLOR, JOHN F.	CAR	166	NO TWP L
TAYLOR, JOHN F.	WOR	192	8TH E DI
TAYLOR, JOHN G.	ANN	271	ANNAPOLI
TAYLOR, JOHN H.	BAL	017	2ND DIST
TAYLOR, JOHN H.	KEN	248	2ND DIST
TAYLOR, JOHN J.	WOR	308	2ND E DI
TAYLOR, JOHN K.	SOM	528	QUANTICO
TAYLOR, JOHN M.	HAR	176	3RD DIST
TAYLOR, JOHN M.	BAL	203	19TH WAR
TAYLOR, JOHN P.	WOR	303	SNOW HIL
TAYLOR, JOHN P.	BAL	426	1ST DIST
TAYLOR, JOHN S.	PRI	004	BLADENSB
TAYLOR, JOHN T.	WOR	183	6TH E DI
TAYLOR, JOHN T.	WOR	189	7TH E DI
TAYLOR, JOHN T.	ANN	277	ANNAPOLI
TAYLOR, JOHN T.	MGM	423	MEDLEY 3
TAYLOR, JOHN W.	SOM	528	QUANTICO
TAYLOR, JOHN W.	MGM	444	CLARKSTR
TAYLOR, JOHN-BLACK	WOR	172	6TH E DI
TAYLOR, JOSEPH	BAL	221	19TH WAR
TAYLOR, JOSEPH	CEC	010	ELKTON 3
TAYLOR, JOSEPH	CEC	088	4TH E DI
TAYLOR, JOSEPH	BAL	473	14TH WAR
TAYLOR, JOSEPH	BAL	462	14TH WAR
TAYLOR, JOSEPH	FRE	270	NEW MARK
TAYLOR, JOSEPH	ANN	281	ANNAPOLI
TAYLOR, JOSEPH	BAL	365	1ST DIST
TAYLOR, JOSEPH	ALL	248	CUMBERLA
TAYLOR, JOSEPH E.	HAR	177	3RD DIST
TAYLOR, JOSEPH P. COLONEL	BAL	070	10TH WAR
TAYLOR, JOSEPHINE	CEC	010	ELKTON 3
TAYLOR, JOSHUA	CEC	181	7TH E DI
TAYLOR, JOSHUA	ANN	323	2ND DIST
TAYLOR, JOSHUA	BAL	306	7TH WARD
TAYLOR, JOSHUA	WOR	289	9TH E DI
TAYLOR, JOSHUA-BLACK	WOR	323	1ST E DI
TAYLOR, JOSIAH	SOM	503	SALISBUR
TAYLOR, JOSIAH	WOR	200	3RD E DI
TAYLOR, JOSIAH S.	SOM	506	BARREN C
TAYLOR, JULIA	BAL	305	1ST DIST
TAYLOR, JULIA A.	SOM	525	BARREN C
TAYLOR, KINDALE	WOR	313	2ND E DI
TAYLOR, KINSEY	CAR	198	4TH DIST
TAYLOR, L.	PRI	111	PISCATAW
TAYLOR, LAVINA	BAL	456	14TH WAR
TAYLOR, LAVINA	ALL	244	CUMBERLA
TAYLOR, LEANDER	WOR	228	6TH E DI
TAYLOR, LEMUEL	WOR	278	BERLIN 1
TAYLOR, LEMUEL	BAL	184	2ND WARD
TAYLOR, LEMUEL G.	ANN	349	3RD DIST
TAYLOR, LEMUEL K.	BAL	367	3RD WARD
TAYLOR, LEONARD	PRI	068	NOTTINGH
TAYLOR, LEVI	SOM	508	BARREN C
TAYLOR, LEVI	ALL	001	3RD E.D.
TAYLOR, LEVI	BAL	060	15TH WAR
TAYLOR, LEVI	CAR	381	2ND DIST
TAYLOR, LEVIN	SOM	484	TRAPP DI
TAYLOR, LEVIN J.	SOM	554	TYASKIN
TAYLOR, LEVIN W.	SOM	483	TRAPP DI
TAYLOR, LEVIN-BLACK	WOR	343	1ST E DI
TAYLOR, LEVINA	BAL	012	2ND DIST
TAYLOR, LITTLETON	SOM	378	BRINKLEY
TAYLOR, LORENZO	BAL	192	6TH WARD
TAYLOR, LORENZO D.	CEC	192	5TH E DI
TAYLOR, LOUISA	BAL	036	4TH WARD
TAYLOR, LOUISA	SOM	411	DUBLIN D
TAYLOR, LOUISA	BAL	219	2ND WARD
TAYLOR, LOVELESS	CAR	191	4TH DIST
TAYLOR, LUKE	WAS	002	1ST DIST
TAYLOR, LURENA	BAL	068	4TH WARD
TAYLOR, LYDIA	WOR	187	7TH E DI
TAYLOR, M.	BAL	161	1ST WARD
TAYLOR, M.	BAL	156	1ST WARD
TAYLOR, M.	BAL	317	12TH WAR
TAYLOR, MAJOR	BAL	205	6TH WARD
TAYLOR, MANCY	WOR	256	1ST CENS

TAYLOR, MARGARET WOR 349 1ST E DI
TAYLOR, MARGARET BAL 219 6TH WARD
TAYLOR, MARGARET BAL 061 15TH WAR
TAYLOR, MARGARET BAL 177 11TH WAR
TAYLOR, MARGARET BAL 016 1ST WARD
TAYLOR, MARGARET BAL 403 14TH WAR
TAYLOR, MARGARET J. BAL 115 5TH WARD
TAYLOR, MARIA BAL 128 5TH WARD
TAYLOR, MARIA BAL 471 14TH WAR
TAYLOR, MARIA BAL 017 4TH WARD
TAYLOR, MARIA WOR 258 1ST CENS
TAYLOR, MARIAH SOM 524 BARREN C
TAYLOR, MARIE * BAL 319 12TH WAR
TAYLOR, MARTHA BAL 230 6TH WARD
TAYLOR, MARTHA BAL 234 12TH WAR
TAYLOR, MARTHA WOR 325 1ST E DI
TAYLOR, MARTHA QUE 216 3RD E DI
TAYLOR, MARTHA MGM 425 MEDLEY 3
TAYLOR, MARTHA E. WOR 235 6TH E DI
TAYLOR, MARY SOM 532 QUANTICO
TAYLOR, MARY WOR 188 7TH E DI
TAYLOR, MARY WOR 265 BERLIN 1
TAYLOR, MARY MGM 381 ROCKERLE
TAYLOR, MARY CAR 197 4TH DIST
TAYLOR, MARY CAL 010 1ST DIST
TAYLOR, MARY CEC 178 7TH E DI
TAYLOR, MARY CEC 186 7TH E DI
TAYLOR, MARY BAL 195 2ND WARD
TAYLOR, MARY BAL 026 9TH WARD
TAYLOR, MARY BAL 109 10TH WAR
TAYLOR, MARY BAL 001 1ST WARD
TAYLOR, MARY ANN 276 ANNAPOLI
TAYLOR, MARY BAL 266 7TH WARD
TAYLOR, MARY A. BAL 150 16TH WAR
TAYLOR, MARY A. BAL 014 15TH WAR
TAYLOR, MARY A. BAL 309 3RD WARD
TAYLOR, MARY A. FRE 070 FREDERIC
TAYLOR, MARY A. HAR 145 3RD DIST
TAYLOR, MARY E. FRE 216 BUCKEYST
TAYLOR, MARY E. SOM 515 BARREN C
TAYLOR, MARY G. HAR 187 3RD DIST
TAYLOR, MARY J. BAL 069 4TH WARD
TAYLOR, MARY J. ANN 514 HOWARD D
TAYLOR, MARY J. BAL 243 6TH WARD
TAYLOR, MARY L.* BAL 076 10TH WAR
TAYLOR, MARY T. FRE 279 WOODSBOR
TAYLOR, MASON FRE 223 BUCKEYST
TAYLOR, MATILDA WOR 340 1ST E DI
TAYLOR, MATTHEW BAL 287 12TH WAR
TAYLOR, MATTHIAS WOR 228 6TH E DI
TAYLOR, MILKY SOM 386 BRINKLEY
TAYLOR, MILLICENT CEC 197 7TH E DI
TAYLOR, MILTON N. BAL 266 7TH WARD
TAYLOR, MISS A. FRE 199 5TH E DI
TAYLOR, MORTIMER BAL 397 8TH WARD
TAYLOR, MRS- BAL 334 1ST DIST
TAYLOR, NANCY BAL 161 19TH WAR
TAYLOR, NANCY CEC 188 7TH E DI
TAYLOR, NANCY BAL 361 13TH WAR
TAYLOR, NANCY BAL 244 17TH WAR
TAYLOR, NANCY BAL 178 19TH WAR
TAYLOR, NANCY SOM 391 BRINKLEY
TAYLOR, NANCY SOM 378 BRINKLEY
TAYLOR, NANCY SOM 517 BARREN C
TAYLOR, NELLY ANN 514 HOWARD D
TAYLOR, NELSON BAL 193 6TH WARD
TAYLOR, OLIVE ST 286 2ND E DI
TAYLOR, OWEN M. ANN 277 ANNAPOLI
TAYLOR, PATRICK BAL 177 2ND WARD
TAYLOR, PERNELL * WOR 182 6TH E DI
TAYLOR, PERRY BAL 281 12TH WAR
TAYLOR, PERRY D. CAR 144 NO TWP L
TAYLOR, PETER BAL 146 1ST WARD
TAYLOR, PETER DOR 468 1ST DIST
TAYLOR, PHILIP BAL 078 2ND DIST
TAYLOR, PHILIP CAR 067 NO TWP L
TAYLOR, PHILL-BLACK QUE 185 3RD E DI
TAYLOR, POLLY SOM 498 SALISBUR
TAYLOR, POLLY WOR 347 1ST E DI
TAYLOR, PURNELL SOM 474 TRAPPE D
TAYLOR, R. A. BAL 019 4TH WARD
TAYLOR, R. Q. BAL 102 10TH WAR
TAYLOR, RACHAEL FRE 232 BUCKEYST
TAYLOR, RACHEL BAL 365 13TH WAR
TAYLOR, RACHEL BAL 400 8TH WARD
TAYLOR, RACHEL-BLACK CAR 113 NO TWP L
TAYLOR, REBECCA BAL 105 18TH WAR
TAYLOR, REBECCA FRE 241 NEW MARK
TAYLOR, REBECCA CEC 095 4TH E DI
TAYLOR, REBECCA E. SOM 508 BARREN C
TAYLOR, REUBEN ALL 147 6TH E.D.
TAYLOR, RICHARD BAL 372 8TH WARD
TAYLOR, RICHARD BAL 313 12TH WAR
TAYLOR, RICHARD BAL 197 6TH WARD
TAYLOR, RICHARD BAL 003 9TH WARD
TAYLOR, RICHARD BAL 177 2ND DIST
TAYLOR, RICHARD W. PRI 069 MARLBROU
TAYLOR, RINGOLD CEC 129 6TH E DI
TAYLOR, ROBERT BAL 017 4TH WARD
TAYLOR, ROBERT WOR 269 BERLIN 1
TAYLOR, ROBERT WAS 015 2ND SUBD
TAYLOR, ROBERT TAL 017 EASTON D
TAYLOR, ROBERT BAL 067 15TH WAR
TAYLOR, ROBERT BAL 169 1ST WARD
TAYLOR, ROBERT BAL 316 1ST DIST
TAYLOR, ROBERT ANN 444 HOWARD D
TAYLOR, ROBERT BAL 343 1ST DIST
TAYLOR, ROBERT A. BAL 210 11TH WAR
TAYLOR, ROBERT M. ANN 292 ANNAPOLI
TAYLOR, ROBERT R. BAL 181 16TH WAR
TAYLOR, ROBERT W. SOM 529 QUANTICO
TAYLOR, RODY PRI 067 NOTTINGH
TAYLOR, ROSE BAL 186 11TH WAR
TAYLOR, RUBEN CEC 017 ELKTON 3
TAYLOR, RUBEN FRE 287 WOODSBOR
TAYLOR, S. G WOR 277 BERLIN 1
TAYLOR, SALLIE PRI 063 NOTTINGH
TAYLOR, SALLIE E. ANN 521 HOWARD D
TAYLOR, SALLY SOM 524 BARREN C
TAYLOR, SALLY SOM 416 DUBLIN D
TAYLOR, SALLY M. WOR 274 BERLIN 1
TAYLOR, SAMUE BAL 330 13TH WAR
TAYLOR, SAMUEL BAL 181 16TH WAR
TAYLOR, SAMUEL BAL 332 7TH WARD
TAYLOR, SAMUEL BAL 367 3RD WARD
TAYLOR, SAMUEL BAL 259 1ST DIST
TAYLOR, SAMUEL WOR 258 1ST CENS
TAYLOR, SAMUEL WAS 050 2ND SUBD
TAYLOR, SAMUEL WOR 186 7TH E DI
TAYLOR, SAMUEL WOR 234 6TH E DI
TAYLOR, SAMUEL KEN 304 3RD DIST
TAYLOR, SAMUEL WOR 329 1ST E DI
TAYLOR, SAMUEL WOR 329 1ST E DI
TAYLOR, SAMUEL SOM 397 BRINKLEY
TAYLOR, SAMUEL MGM 425 MEDLEY 3
TAYLOR, SAMUEL CAR 198 4TH DIST
TAYLOR, SAMUEL CAR 197 4TH DIST
TAYLOR, SAMUEL CEC 167 6TH E DI
TAYLOR, SAMUEL B. BAL 037 9TH WARD
TAYLOR, SAMUEL J. BAL 267 7TH WARD
TAYLOR, SAMUEL J. FRE 216 BUCKEYST
TAYLOR, SAMUEL* BAL 058 4TH WARD
TAYLOR, SARAH BAL 217 11TH WAR
TAYLOR, SARAH BAL 420 3RD WARD
TAYLOR, SARAH CEC 075 NORTHEAS
TAYLOR, SARAH CEC 193 5TH E DI
TAYLOR, SARAH BAL 298 1ST DIST
TAYLOR, SARAH BAL 073 1ST WARD
TAYLOR, SARAH BAL 463 1ST DIST
TAYLOR, SARAH BAL 256 12TH WAR
TAYLOR, SARAH WOR 194 8TH E DI
TAYLOR, SARAH WOR 314 2ND E DI
TAYLOR, SARAH E. CEC 168 6TH E DI
TAYLOR, SARAH E. BAL 136 18TH WAR
TAYLOR, SARAH J. BAL 434 14TH WAR
TAYLOR, SARAH JANE BAL 012 2ND DIST
TAYLOR, SARHA BAL 070 2ND DIST
TAYLOR, SEVERN SOM 367 BRINKLEY
TAYLOR, SHARLOTT CAR 067 NO TWP L
TAYLOR, SIDNEY ANN 275 ANNAPOLI
TAYLOR, SIMON FRE 20 5TH E DI
TAYLOR, SMITHY* DOR 396 1ST DIST
TAYLOR, SOPHIA BAL 070 10TH WAR
TAYLOR, SOPHIA WAS 008 WILLIAMS
TAYLOR, SOPHY BAL 430 14TH WAR
TAYLOR, STAFFORD PRI 048 AQUASCO
TAYLOR, STANRY CHA 292 BOJANTOW
TAYLOR, STEPHEN CEC 150 PORT DUP
TAYLOR, STEPHEN SOM 385 BRINKLEY
TAYLOR, STOHLEY WOR 205 4TH E DI
TAYLOR, SUSAN SOM 503 SALISBUR
TAYLOR, SUSAN WOR 347 1ST E DI
TAYLOR, SUSAN CEC 179 7TH E DI
TAYLOR, SUSAN BAL 068 10TH WAR
TAYLOR, SUSAN BAL 027 2ND DIST
TAYLOR, SUSAN BAL 130 2ND DIST
TAYLOR, SUSAN BAL 190 11TH WAR
TAYLOR, SUSAN BAL 214 6TH DIST
TAYLOR, TANER WOR 304 SNOW HIL
TAYLOR, TEMPERANCE SOM 472 TRAPPE D
TAYLOR, THADEUS BAL 114 15TH WAR
TAYLOR, THEODORE ANN 299 1ST DIST
TAYLOR, THOAMS BAL 045 15TH WAR
TAYLOR, THOAMS CAR 197 4TH DIST
TAYLOR, THOMAS CEC 148 PORT DUP
TAYLOR, THOMAS BAL 205 17TH WAR
TAYLOR, THOMAS QUE 132 1ST E DI
TAYLOR, THOMAS HAR 139 2ND DIST
TAYLOR, THOMAS KEN 249 2ND DIST
TAYLOR, THOMAS QUE 159 2ND E DI
TAYLOR, THOMAS CEC 081 CHARLEST
TAYLOR, THOMAS ANN 342 3RD DIST
TAYLOR, THOMAS ALL 230 CUMBERLA
TAYLOR, THOMAS BAL 412 8TH WARD
TAYLOR, THOMAS BAL 194 2ND WARD
TAYLOR, THOMAS WOR 264 BERLIN 1
TAYLOR, THOMAS WAS 063 2ND SUBD
TAYLOR, THOMAS WOR 319 1ST E DI
TAYLOR, THOMAS WOR 323 1ST E DI
TAYLOR, THOMAS WOR 183 6TH E DI
TAYLOR, THOMAS PRI 119 PISCATAW
TAYLOR, THOMAS B. SOM 516 BARREN C
TAYLOR, THOMAS G. BAL 409 8TH WARD
TAYLOR, THOMASMC FOLES. A BAL 128 1ST WARD
TAYLOR, TIMRA CEC 162 6TH E DI
TAYLOR, VINCENT WAS 013 WILLIAMS
TAYLOR, VIRGAL CAL 004 1ST DIST
TAYLOR, W. JR. ANN 286 ANNAPOLI
TAYLOR, WARREN BAL 365 8TH WARD
TAYLOR, WESLEY WAS 098 2ND DIST
TAYLOR, WILKERSON BAL 010 EASTERN
TAYLOR, WILLAIM PRI 088 SPALDING
TAYLOR, WILLIAM SOM 508 BARREN C
TAYLOR, WILLIAM PRI 118 PISCATAW
TAYLOR, WILLIAM PRI 114 PISCATAW
TAYLOR, WILLIAM WOR 182 6TH E DI
TAYLOR, WILLIAM WOR 194 8TH E DI
TAYLOR, WILLIAM SOM 483 TRAPP DI
TAYLOR, WILLIAM SOM 478 TRAPP DI
TAYLOR, WILLIAM WAS 028 2ND SUBD
TAYLOR, WILLIAM WAS 002 WILLIAMS
TAYLOR, WILLIAM WOR 317 2ND E DI
TAYLOR, WILLIAM SOM 378 BRINKLEY
TAYLOR, WILLIAM SOM 393 BRINKLEY
TAYLOR, WILLIAM SOM 474 TRAPPE D
TAYLOR, WILLIAM QUE 166 2ND E DI
TAYLOR, WILLIAM BAL 133 1ST WARD
TAYLOR, WILLIAM ALL 147 6TH E.D.
TAYLOR, WILLIAM BAL 174 1ST WARD
TAYLOR, WILLIAM BAL 021 9TH WARD
TAYLOR, WILLIAM BAL 020 9TH WARD
TAYLOR, WILLIAM BAL 164 1ST WARD
TAYLOR, WILLIAM BAL 158 1ST WARD
TAYLOR, WILLIAM BAL 229 12TH WAR
TAYLOR, WILLIAM BAL 187 16TH WAR
TAYLOR, WILLIAM BAL 231 1ST DIST
TAYLOR, WILLIAM BAL 459 1ST DIST
TAYLOR, WILLIAM BAL 298 1ST DIST
TAYLOR, WILLIAM BAL 246 17TH WAR
TAYLOR, WILLIAM BAL 227 17TH WAR
TAYLOR, WILLIAM BAL 335 13TH WAR
TAYLOR, WILLIAM BAL 257 17TH WAR
TAYLOR, WILLIAM CAR 393 2ND DIST
TAYLOR, WILLIAM CAR 283 7TH DIST
TAYLOR, WILLIAM QUE 152 1ST E DI
TAYLOR, WILLIAM CEC 024 ELKTON 3
TAYLOR, WILLIAM BAL 167 19TH WAR
TAYLOR, WILLIAM BAL 240 20TH WAR
TAYLOR, WILLIAM SOM 439 DAMES QU
TAYLOR, WILLIAM HAR 009 1ST DIST
TAYLOR, WILLIAM A. BAL 388 13TH WAR
TAYLOR, WILLIAM A. BAL 392 3RD WARD
TAYLOR, WILLIAM A. PRI 115 PISCATAW
TAYLOR, WILLIAM B. ST 296 2ND E DI
TAYLOR, WILLIAM B. FRE 233 BUCKEYST
TAYLOR, WILLIAM H. BAL 017 4TH WARD
TAYLOR, WILLIAM H. BAL 056 4TH WARD
TAYLOR, WILLIAM H. SOM 548 TYASKIN
TAYLOR, WILLIAM H. BAL 121 5TH WARD
TAYLOR, WILLIAM H. BAL 060 15TH WAR
TAYLOR, WILLIAM H. BAL 435 8TH WARD
TAYLOR, WILLIAM J. FRE 122 CREAGERS
TAYLOR, WILLIAM L. HAR 207 3RD DIST
TAYLOR, WILLIAM M. ST 313 1ST E DI
TAYLOR, WILLIAM P. SOM 527 QUANTICO
TAYLOR, WILLIAM P. HAR 196 3RD DIST
TAYLOR, WILLIAM S. BAL 134 16TH WAR
TAYLOR, WILLIAM T. WOR 274 BERLIN 1
TAYLOR, WILLIAM W. BAL 328 7TH WARD
TAYLOR, WILLIAM W. BAL 202 11TH WAR
TAYLOR, WILLIAM W. HAR 079 2ND DIST
TAYLOR, WILLIAM-BLACK CAR 170 NO TWP L
TAYLOR, WILLIAM-BLACK CAR 092 NO TWP L
TAYLOR, WINIFRED FRE 385 PETERSVI
TAYLOR, ZACARIAH BAL 381 3RD WARD
TAYLOR, ZACHARY* TAL 049 EASTON T
TAYLOR, ZACKARY WAS 017 2ND SUBD
TAYLOR, ZEPORAH SOM 393 BRINKLEY
TAYLOR,JOHNH. FRE 231 BUCKEYST
TAYLOR,LEAH-BLACK WOR 172 6TH E DI
TAYLOR,LEWIS ALL 208 CUMBERLA
TAYLOR,MISS M. FRE 199 5TH E DI
TAYLOR,PERMELIA ST 305 1ST E DI
TAYLRE, CHARLES R. BAL 087 4TH WARD
TAYLSON, DANIEL HAR 090 2ND DIST
TAYMAN, AMELIA M. ANN 321 2ND DIST
TAYMAN, ANN BAL 365 1ST DIST
TAYMAN, HENRY A. ANN 409 8TH DIST
TAYMAN, JOHN H. ANN 407 8TH DIST
TAYMAN, RICHARD ANN 330 2ND DIST
TAYMAN, WILLIAM BAL 268 7TH WARD
TAYMON, MARGRET PRI 062 NOTTINGH
TAYMON, SAMUEL PRI 063 NOTTINGH
TAZEWELL, OLIVER ANN 421 HOWARD D
TEABREASE, SHILES C. WOR 228 6TH E DI
TEACH, MARY WAS 297 1ST DIST
TEACHE, CAROLINE* DOR 425 1ST DIST
TEACHER, CAROLINE* DOR 425 1ST DIST
TEACKLE, ELIZABETH BAL 160 16TH WAR
TEACKLE, ST GEORGE W. BAL 060 10TH WAR
TEACKLE, THOMAS N. BAL 106 10TH WAR
TEADER, PERRY BAL 157 2ND DIST
TEAFER, PETER BAL 158 2ND DIST
TEAGAN, J.J. PRI 092 MARLBROU
TEAGLE, GEORGE WOR 295 9TH E DI
TEAGLE, LITTLETON SOM 458 DAMES QU
TEAGLE, MARTIN * BAL 095 15TH WAR
TEAGLE, WESTLY-BLACK WOR 328 1ST E DI
TEAGUE, JAMES WOR 309 2ND E DI
TEAKLE, CHERUBINA BAL 345 13TH WAR
TEAL, ARCHABAL BAL 014 1ST WARD
TEAL, ELIZABETH BAL 047 15TH WAR
TEAL, GEORGE BAL 182 6TH WARD
TEAL, SUSANNA BAL 162 6TH WARD
TEAL, WILLIAM ANN 464 HOWARD D
TEAL, WILLIAM BAL 352 13TH WAR
TEALE, SAMUEL W. BAL 162 6TH WARD
TEALL, OTHO FRE 264 NEW MARK
TEALL, PHILIP BAL 066 4TH WARD
TEAR, BENJAMIN F. BAL 050 15TH WAR
TEARDOCK, W. BAL 291 12TH WAR
TEARLEY, SAMUEL J. BAL 248 12TH WAR
TEARLEY, THOMAS E. BAL 248 12TH WAR
TEARMAN, WILLIAM W. WOR 219 4TH E DI
TEARNY, SARAH BAL 460 1ST DIST
TEAS, JOHN BAL 391 14TH WAR
TEAS, REBECCA BAL 146 16TH WAR
TEAS, SARAH BAL 146 16TH WAR
TEASH, JOHN CEC 202 6TH E DI
TEAT, BENJAMIN KEN 295 3RD DIST
TEAT, JAMES KEN 295 3RD DIST
TEAT, JAMES E. QUE 140 1ST E DI
TEAT, JOHN QUE 217 3RD E DI
TEAT, JOSHUA QUE 137 1ST E DI
TEAT, SARAH QUE 142 1ST E DI
TEAT, STEPHEN-BLACK QUE 200 3RD E DI
TEAT, WILLIAM QUE 139 1ST E DI
TEATAIN, HENRY L. WAS 247 SMITHSBU
TEATE, MARGARET ALL 216 CUMBERLA
TEBBS, THOMAS BAL 356 3RD WARD
TEBBY, WILLIAM G. BAL 317 12TH WAR
TEBER, MARY G. BAL 022 4TH WARD
TEBET, RICHARD CEC 058 1ST E DI
TEBUS, JOHN BAL 173 2ND DIST
TECHEN, JOHN ALL 241 CUMBERLA
TECHNALL, MOSES ALL 130 4TH E.D.
TECHUELY, SAMUEL BAL 267 12TH WAR
TEDDEN, ISAAC WOR 338 1ST E DI
TEDEFIN, DARKIE ANN * BAL 346 13TH WAR
TEDLAR, MICHAEL BAL 075 1ST WARD
TEDRICK, PETER WAS 143 2ND DIST
TEDWICK, JAMES C. CAL 003 1ST DIST
TEDWICK, LUVESER * CAL 003 1ST DIST
TEEKER, JOSEPH WAS 248 1ST DIST
TEEN, AMY BAL 434 14TH WAR
TEEN, WILLIAM R. BAL 434 14TH WAR
TEENER, SINDERILLA BAL 458 8TH WARD
TEEP, WILLIAM BAL 353 13TH WAR
TEFTON, SUSAN ANN 285 ANNAPOLI
TEGELER, DORATHA BAL 099 18TH WAR
TEGELER, GEORGE BAL 103 15TH WAR
TEGUE, JOHN ALL 141 6TH E.D.
TEGUE, MICHAEL ALL 079 5TH E.D.
TEHAN, JOHN FRE 057 FREDERIC
TEHAN, JOHN * FRE 056 FREDERIC
TEHAN, WILLIAM FRE 033 FREDERIC
TEHART, ANTHONY BAL 198 2ND WARD
TEHLA, FREDERICK BAL 458 14TH WAR
TEHREN, JOHN BAL 053 1ST WARD
TEHRIPNER, ADAM BAL 072 1ST WARD
TEIF, ANTHONY BAL 128 5TH WARD
TEISHMAN, WILLIAMMA BAL 444 8TH WARD
TEISTEL, JOHN BAL 135 2ND DIST
TELDS, ALLY ANN 275 ANNAPOLI
TELGHMAN, LETITIA-BLACK CAR 087 NO TWP L
TELHER, ELIJAH WOR 327 1ST E DI
TELICK, ELIZA ALL 251 CUMBERLA
TELL, CHARLES BAL 128 2ND DIST
TELL, JOSEPH BAL 172 19TH WAR
TELL, WILLIAM J. BAL 431 1ST DIST
TELLER, REBECCA BAL 405 3RD WARD
TELLER, STEPHEN BAL 405 3RD WARD
TELSEY, JACOB * ALL 058 10TH E.D
TELSEY, JOHN * ALL 059 10TH E.D
TELTER, HENRY ALL 197 CUMBERLA
TELWAY, THOMAS BAL 058 1ST WARD
TEMPERLY, N. W. BAL 279 2ND WARD
TEMPLE, HANNAH HAR 035 1ST DIST
TEMPLE, AMOS H. * HAR 051 1ST DIST
TEMPLE, ELISABETH ALL 229 CUMBERLA

NAME	CO	PAGE	DISTRICT
TEMPLE, FREDERICK	BAL	323	1ST DIST
TEMPLE, JOHN	BAL	186	19TH WAR
TEMPLE, JOSEPH	HAR	091	2ND DIST
TEMPLE, MARGARET	BAL	082	1ST WARD
TEMPLE, MARY	BAL	186	2ND WARD
TEMPLE, THOMAS	BAL	009	9TH WARD
TEMPLE, THOMAS O.	HAR	112	2ND DIST
TEMPLE, WILLIAM	HAR	089	2ND DIST
TEMPLER, DAVID	CEC	049	1ST E DI
TEMPLES, EMALINE	CEC	007	ELKTON 3
TEMPLES, JAMES	QUE	134	1ST E DI
TEMPLES, JAMES H.	QUE	135	1ST E DI
TEMPLES, JOHN W.	CAR	100	NO TWP L
TEMPLES, SAMUEL	CEC	008	ELKTON 3
TEMPLES, WILLIAM	QUE	135	1ST E DI
TEMPLES, WILLIAM	QUE	135	1ST E DI
TEMPLES, WILLIAM S.	BAL	010	18TH WAR
TEMPLETON, HARRIET	BAL	451	1ST DIST
TEMPLETON, JAMES	BAL	092	18TH WAR
TEMPLETON, RICHARD	BAL	078	2ND DIST
TEMPNLY, THOMAS *	BAL	144	1ST WARD
TEMPSON, ANDREW	FRE	408	JEFFERSO
TEMPTE, AMOS H. *	HAR	051	1ST DIST
TEMPTO, GEORGE*	BAL	101	10TH WAR
TEMSON, FRANCIS *	BAL	218	12TH WAR
TEN EYCK, FREDERICK	CEC	128	5TH E DI
TENANB, ROBERT *	ALL	089	5TH E.D.
TENANT, ALEXANDER	ALL	089	5TH E.D.
TENANT, EDWARD	TAL	110	ST MICHA
TENANT, GEORGE	ALL	088	5TH E.D.
TENANT, JAMES	ALL	101	5TH E.D.
TENANT, JAMES	WAS	016	2ND SUBD
TENANT, MARGARET	HAR	114	2ND DIST
TENANT, MICHAEL	WAS	051	2ND SUBD
TENANT, THOMAS	TAL	090	ST MICHA
TENANT, WILLAIM	WAS	016	2ND SUBD
TENANT, WILLIAM	BAL	287	7TH WARD
TENDAE, JOSHUA	WOR	270	BERLIN 1
TENDALL, MARY J.	WOR	212	4TH E DI
TENDBEY, PHILLIS	WOR	271	BERLIN 1
TENDER, AUGUSTUS	BAL	132	16TH WAR
TENDER, FRISBY	BAL	058	4TH WARD
TENDER, JAMES	BAL	348	3RD WARD
TENDER, JAMES*	BAL	343	3RD WARD
TENDER, LEWIS*	TAL	035	EASTON D
TENDER, RUTH	BAL	002	EASTERN
TENDER, RUTH A.	HAR	123	2ND DIST
TENER, LEREINA	BAL	113	2ND DIST
TENERT, JOSEPH	BAL	149	2ND DIST
TENEY, CATHARINE	HAR	147	3RD DIST
TENEY, RARY	HAR	161	3RD DIST
TENHARDT, NICHOLAS	BAL	089	10TH WAR
TENHER, JAMES*	TAL	043	EASTON D
TENIFORD, WILLIAM	CAR	121	NO TWP L
TENISON, CATHARINE	BAL	297	7TH WARD
TENISON, JOHN E.	ST	269	3RD E DI
TENISON, OLIVER G.	BAL	297	7TH WARD
TENISON, SABASTIAN	ST	266	3RD E DI
TENISON, WILLIAM H.	ST	279	3RD E DI
TENKEN, MARYAN	BAL	360	3RD WARD
TENLEY, GEORGE M.	PRI	007	BLADENSB
TENLEY, HORATIO	PRI	007	BLADENSB
TENLY, HENRY	HAR	106	2ND DIST
TENNANT, ELIZA D.	BAL	020	4TH WARD
TENNANT, GEORGE T.	BAL	174	6TH WARD
TENNANT, MARY C.	BAL	108	10TH WAR
TENNANT, RICHARD	BAL	073	1ST WARD
TENNANT, THOMAS	BAL	074	10TH WAR
TENNELL, JOSEPH S.	CEC	091	4TH E DI
TENNER, GEORGE	CAR	189	4TH DIST
TENNER, JACOB	CAR	189	4TH DIST
TENNER, SUSANAH	CAR	190	4TH DIST
TENNEY, G.W.	ALL	038	2ND E.D.
TENNEY, SALLY	PRI	094	SPALDING
TENNIS, AUGUSTUS	BAL	002	4TH WARD
TENNIS, SAMUEL	WAS	143	HAGERSTO
TENNISON, ABSALOM	CHA	288	BOJANTOW
TENNISON, ABSALOM C.	ST	310	1ST E DI
TENNISON, ANN L.	BAL	378	8TH WARD
TENNISON, EDWARD T.	ST	266	3RD E DI
TENNISON, GEORGE W.	ST	336	4TH E DI
TENNISON, MARY	BAL	259	17TH WAR
TENNISON, SARAH C.	CHA	294	BOJANTOW
TENNSSON, JAMES M.	FRE	044	FREDERIC
TENNY, MICHAEL P.	ALL	136	4TH E.D.
TENOR, ELLEN	ALL	086	5TH E.D.
TENPANY, ELIZABETH*	TAL	037	EASTON D
TENSFIELD, ARNOLD	BAL	046	4TH WARD
TENSFIELD, CHARLES M.	BAL	132	1ST WARD
TENSFIELD, WILLIAM	CAR	195	4TH DIST
TENSFIELD, WILLIAM	CAR	212	5TH DIST
TENSON, ELIZABETH	BAL	386	8TH WARD
TENSOULER, GEORGE *	BAL	312	20TH WAR
TENY, WILLIAM	CEC	062	1ST E DI
TEPH, MARY J.	ANN	510	HOWARD D
TEPP, GEORGE	CAR	341	6TH DIST
TEPP, LAWRENCE	CAR	271	WESTMINS
TEPP, LEONARD	CAR	272	WESTMINS
TEPP, PETER	CAR	295	7TH DIST
TEPP, WILLIAM	CAR	341	6TH DIST
TEPPELLL, URIAH	ST	297	2ND E DI
TERANCE, ADAM	BAL	172	11TH WAR
TERAR, JETTY	BAL	382	13TH WAR
TERASSE, ANNE	BAL	388	13TH WAR
TEREL, JAMES	CAR	214	5TH DIST
TERICK, CHRISTIAN P.	CAR	334	6TH DIST
TERICK, MICHAEL *	BAL	275	1ST DIST
TERIN, BARTHOLOMEW	BAL	349	13TH WAR
TERRELL, ANN	CHA	236	HILLTOP
TERRELL, JAMES	ALL	134	4TH E.D.
TERRELL, JANE	CEC	096	4TH E DI
TERRELL, PATRICK	ALL	057	10TH E.D
TERRY, ALEXANDER	ANN	282	ANNAPOLI
TERRY, HANNAH	CEC	078	NORTHEAS
TERRY, ISAIAH	BAL	164	16TH WAR
TERRY, JAMES E.	BAL	182	6TH WARD
TERRY, JOHN	CEC	092	4TH E DI
TERRY, JOHN	CEC	195	6TH E DI
TERRY, OSEPH	HAR	103	2ND DIST
TERRY, SARAH	CEC	133	6TH E DI
TERRY, THOMAS	CEC	124	5TH E DI
TERRY, THOMAS	FRE	202	5TH E DI
TERRY, THOMAS	ANN	285	ANNAPOLI
TERRY, UPTON	CEC	133	6TH E DI
TERSEEN, WILLIAM	ALL	206	CUMBERLA
TERSH, WILLIAM	CEC	202	6TH E DI
TERTING, JAMES J.	ST	261	3RD E DI
TERUE, MARY	ALL	212	CUMBERLA
TERVIN, JAMES M.	BAL	268	12TH WAR
TESSEE, FREDERICK	BAL	322	12TH WAR
TESSENG, JOHN	BAL	192	19TH WAR
TESST, LUCRETIA	ANN	510	HOWARD D
TETAIN, ALEXANDER B.	WAS	244	SMITHSBU
TETCHELL, MARY *	BAL	291	20TH WAR
TETE, JACOB	CAR	086	NO TWP L
TETER, GEORGE	ALL	170	6TH E.D.
TETRICK, DANIEL	WAS	140	2ND DIST
TETTOW, ANN R.	FRE	264	NEW MARK
TEUEN, WILLIAM	ALL	023	2ND E.D.
TEUNER, WILLIAM	FRE	276	NEW MARK
TEVIET, OLIVER	BAL	350	13TH WAR
TEVIFORD, MARGARET	WOR	284	BERLIN 1
TEVILEY, THOMAS T.	DOR	324	1ST DIST
TEVILLER, HENRY	BAL	136	1ST WARD
TEVIS, JOSEPH	BAL	078	18TH WAR
TEWKSBURY, GEORGE D.	BAL	075	15TH WAR
TEYLER, MOSES	ALL	070	5TH E.D.
TEYOTT, JACOB	TAL	024	EASTON D
THACKARA, OWEN P.	PRI	043	VANSVILL
THACKARY, THOMAS	CEC	007	ELKTON 3
THACKERY, ROBERT	CEC	070	5TH E DI
THACKERY, THOMAS W.	CEC	007	ELKTON 3
THADES, ELIZA	HAR	146	3RD DIST
THALHEIMER, JOHN	BAL	232	6TH WARD
THALLAN, JOHN	BAL	065	1ST WARD
THANE, MISS M.	FRE	199	5TH E DI
THANER, ROSANNA	CAR	313	1ST DIST
THANSEN, WILLIAM W.	HAR	195	3RD DIST
THAPMAN, PEARCIN	CHA	257	MIDDLETO
THARE, ROBERT	TAL	059	EASTON D
THARINGTON, THOMAS	HAR	041	1ST DIST
THARNBY, CHARLES N.	CAR	077	NO TWP L
THARP, ANN	QUE	151	1ST E DI
THARP, ANNA	QUE	141	1ST E DI
THARP, BIXLEY H.	QUE	141	1ST E DI
THARP, HENRY W.	CEC	150	PORT DUP
THARP, JAMES	CAR	148	NO TWP L
THARP, JOHN	WAS	264	1ST DIST
THARP, RUBEN	TAL	075	EASTON T
THARP, SUSANNA	WAS	237	CAVETOWN
THASHER, AUGUSTA	BAL	170	11TH WAR
THASHER, PARSLEY	ALL	172	7TH E.D.
THATCHER, CALIB	BAL	424	1ST DIST
THATER, CHARLES	BAL	164	16TH WAR
THATER, GODLIP	BAL	116	18TH WAR
THATER, PHILIP	BAL	328	13TH WAR
THAWER, MELKI	FRE	279	WOODSBOR
THAWLER, THOMAS	TAL	068	EASTON T
THAWLEY, ANN E.	TAL	022	EASTON D
THAWLEY, JOHN	QUE	201	3RD E DI
THAWLEY, JOHN	CAR	167	NO TWP L
THAWLEY, MARY	QUE	159	2ND E DI
THAWLEY, ROBERT	CAR	166	NO TWP L
THAWLEY, SAMUEL	QUE	145	1ST E DI
THAWLEY, WILLIAM E.	QUE	160	2ND E DI
THAWLY, HENIRETTA	CAR	074	NO TWP L
THAWLY, HENRY	CAR	108	NO TWP L
THAWLY, JOHN	CAR	108	NO TWP L
THAWLY, JOHN JR.	CAR	072	NO TWP L
THAYACE, A.	BAL	156	1ST WARD
THAYER, HANNAH	ALL	058	10TH E.D
THAYER, HENRY C.	BAL	362	8TH WARD
THAYER, LEBAN	BAL	418	3RD WARD
THAYER, N. O.	BAL	139	19TH WAR
THAYER, NATHANIEL C.	BAL	074	4TH WARD
THAYER, RALPH	ALL	024	3RD E.D.
THAYER, SHUNAY	ALL	045	10TH E.D
THAYER, STEPHEN	ALL	027	2ND E.D.
THEDE, JACKSON	MGM	328	CRACKLIN
THEELAN, M. SIS- *	BAL	062	18TH WAR
THEFFORD, JAMES	BAL	356	3RD WARD
THEGRIMER, HARRIET	BAL	250	12TH WAR
THEILMAN, WILLIAM	BAL	340	3RD WARD
THEIM, PHILIP	BAL	048	9TH WARD
THEISY, CONRAD	BAL	044	9TH WARD
THELLER, CATHARINE	BAL	459	1ST DIST
THENY, SUSAN*	TAL	061	EASTON D
THEODORE, LESTER	BAL	312	12TH WAR
THEORNDS, J. O. *	BAL	321	20TH WAR
THERM, MICHAEL	BAL	019	1ST WARD
THERRCLIFFE, WILLIAM	ALL	179	7TH E.D.
THERURAG, ISAAC	BAL	186	2ND WARD
THERVAG, ENENA	BAL	187	2ND WARD
THEYE, HARMAN	BAL	115	15TH WAR
THEYE, HERMAN H.	BAL	041	15TH WAR
THGOMAS, STEPHEN S.	BAL	071	1ST WARD
THICY, MARY*	BAL	418	3RD WARD
THIEMYER, JOHN	BAL	353	13TH WAR
THIERLOW, JOHN	BAL	387	3RD WARD
THIERLOW, LYDIA	BAL	388	3RD WARD
THIEY, MARY*	BAL	418	3RD WARD
THIGH, THOMAS	BAL	275	1ST DIST
THIGHES, ANN	BAL	293	12TH WAR
THILKER, CHARLES F.	BAL	023	9TH WARD
THIMPSON, T.W.	BAL	162	1ST WARD
THINADIN, ELIZABETH *	BAL	321	20TH WAR
THINK, T.	BAL	259	12TH WAR
THISKELD, JOHN	BAL	294	3RD WARD
THISTLE, GEORGE P.	ALL	241	CUMBERLA
THISTLE, MARGARET ANN	ALL	242	CUMBERLA
THISTLE, THOMAS	ALL	009	3RD E.D.
THMAS, ELY A.	BAL	101	18TH WAR
THOAMS, BENJAMIN	ALL	087	5TH E.D.
THOAMS, BRIAN M.	BAL	042	15TH WAR
THOAMS, CATHARINE	QUE	250	5TH E DI
THOAMS, CHARLES H.	BAL	341	13TH WAR
THOAMS, DAVID	WAS	191	1ST DIST
THOAMS, JOHN	QUE	216	3RD E DI
THOAMS, JOSEPH	BAL	448	14TH WAR
THOAMS, MARTHA	BAL	088	18TH WAR
THOAMS, MICHAEWL	ALL	087	5TH E.D.
THOAMS, RACHAEL	ST	264	3RD E DI
THOAMS, WILLIAM H.	ST	261	3RD E DI
THOASM, P.	BAL	148	1ST WARD
THOASM, WILLIAM	HAR	206	3RD DIST
THODES, JAMES	BAL	268	20TH WAR
THOLE, JOHN	BAL	364	13TH WAR
THOLER, CHARLES	BAL	303	12TH WAR
THOMA, JAMES	BAL	431	14TH WAR
THOMA, JOHN	CAL	027	2ND DIST
THOMA.S ADAM	WAS	131	HAGERSTO
THOMA.S ASBURY	BAL	305	17TH WAR
THOMA.S BABYLON	BAL	243	17TH WAR
THOMALAN, E.L.	BAL	003	18TH WAR
THOMALAN, MARY F.	BAL	003	18TH WAR
THOMAN, HERMAN	BAL	033	15TH WAR
THOMAN, SARAH	WAS	186	BOONSBOR
THOMAS, AARON	BAL	363	13TH WAR
THOMAS, AARON	CAR	066	NO TWP L
THOMAS, AARON	DOR	438	1ST DIST
THOMAS, ABRAHAM	CAR	228	5TH DIST
THOMAS, ABRAHAM	BAL	288	1ST DIST
THOMAS, ABRAHAM W.	FRE	208	BUCKEYST
THOMAS, ADAM	BAL	001	4TH WARD
THOMAS, ADAM	BAL	374	3RD WARD
THOMAS, ADELADE	FRE	217	BUCKEYST
THOMAS, ADELINE	BAL	458	8TH WARD
THOMAS, ALBERT	CAL	007	1ST DIST
THOMAS, ALEX	DOR	405	1ST DIST
THOMAS, ALEX	DOR	405	1ST DIST
THOMAS, ALEXANDER	DOR	402	1ST DIST
THOMAS, ALEXANDER	CAR	081	NO TWP L
THOMAS, ALEXANDER	ALL	028	2ND E.D.
THOMAS, ALEXANDER	BAL	401	8TH WARD
THOMAS, ALEXANDER C.	BAL	242	20TH WAR
THOMAS, ALEXANDER-BLACK	CAR	099	NO TWP L
THOMAS, ALEXANDER-BLACK	CAR	110	NO TWP L
THOMAS, ALEXINA	BAL	160	6TH WARD
THOMAS, ALFRED	KEN	243	2ND DIST
THOMAS, ALFRED B.	CEC	055	1ST E DI
THOMAS, ALFRED-BLACK	FRE	017	FREDERIC
THOMAS, ALGEMON*	DOR	315	1ST DIST
THOMAS, ALICE	BAL	105	10TH WAR
THOMAS, ALICE	TAL	117	ST MICHA
THOMAS, ALLEN	ANN	423	HOWARD D
THOMAS, ALLEN-BLACK	QUE	135	1ST E DI
THOMAS, ALOLPHUS	KEN	278	1ST DIST
THOMAS, AMANDA	HAR	043	1ST DIST
THOMAS, AMISA-BLACK	BAL	233	2ND WARD
THOMAS, AMOS	BAL	255	12TH WAR
THOMAS, AMOS P.	HAR	047	1ST DIST
THOMAS, ANDREW	BAL	321	20TH WAR
THOMAS, ANDREW	BAL	443	8TH WARD
THOMAS, ANDREW C.	BAL	293	1ST DIST
THOMAS, ANN	BAL	077	1ST WARD
THOMAS, ANN	BAL	240	1ST DIST
THOMAS, ANN	BAL	141	16TH WAR
THOMAS, ANN	BAL	089	15TH WAR
THOMAS, ANN	BAL	029	9TH WARD
THOMAS, ANN	ANN	501	HOWARD D
THOMAS, ANN	BAL	136	11TH WAR
THOMAS, ANN	PRI	074	MARLBROU
THOMAS, ANN	TAL	095	ST MICHA
THOMAS, ANN	ST	274	3RD E DI
THOMAS, ANN	PRI	001	BLADENSB
THOMAS, ANN	TAL	001	EASTON D
THOMAS, ANN B.	BAL	057	15TH WAR
THOMAS, ANN C.	QUE	209	3RD E DI
THOMAS, ANN E.	ST	310	1ST E DI
THOMAS, ANN E.	BAL	344	7TH WARD
THOMAS, ANN ELIZA	ALL	081	5TH E.D.
THOMAS, ANN M.	BAL	123	5TH WARD
THOMAS, ANN M.	FRE	209	BUCKEYST
THOMAS, ANN S.	SOM	546	TYASKIN
THOMAS, ANN-BLACK	CAR	114	NO TWP L
THOMAS, ANNA	BAL	247	6TH WARD
THOMAS, ANNA M.	QUE	212	3RD E DI
THOMAS, ANTHONY	QUE	216	3RD E DI
THOMAS, ARNOLD-MULATTO	BAL	214	2ND WARD
THOMAS, ASBURY	SOM	466	HANGARY
THOMAS, AUGUS	BAL	409	14TH WAR
THOMAS, B. GORDON	BAL	004	EASTERN
THOMAS, BAKER-BLACK	FRE	038	FREDERIC
THOMAS, BARBARA A.	BAL	188	6TH WARD
THOMAS, BARBARY	FRE	406	JEFFERSO
THOMAS, BARTON	BAL	072	1ST WARD
THOMAS, BEN	PRI	103	SPALDING
THOMAS, BENEDICT	BAL	343	3RD WARD
THOMAS, BENJAMIN	BAL	379	3RD WARD
THOMAS, BENJAMIN	BAL	249	2ND WARD
THOMAS, BENJAMIN	ALL	087	5TH E.D.
THOMAS, BENJAMIN	ALL	104	5TH E.D.
THOMAS, BENJAMIN	BAL	333	13TH WAR
THOMAS, BENJAMIN	SOM	375	BRINKLEY
THOMAS, BENJAMIN	BAL	108	18TH WAR
THOMAS, BENJAMIN	CEC	036	CHESAPEA
THOMAS, BENJAMIN B.	CEC	118	4TH E DI
THOMAS, BENJAMIN F.	BAL	127	1ST WARD
THOMAS, BENJAMIN M.	ANN	395	8TH DIST
THOMAS, BENJAMIN R.	FRE	219	BUCKEYST
THOMAS, BETSY	DOR	399	1ST DIST
THOMAS, BETSY	ANN	325	2ND DIST
THOMAS, BETTY	BAL	348	3RD WARD
THOMAS, BETTY	BAL	250	20TH WAR
THOMAS, BETTY	CAL	046	3RD DIST
THOMAS, BRUCE	BAL	382	13TH WAR
THOMAS, C.	ANN	269	ANNAPOLI
THOMAS, C. K.	BAL	471	14TH WAR
THOMAS, CAROLINE	ANN	425	HOWARD D
THOMAS, CAROLINE	TAL	038	EASTON D
THOMAS, CAROLINE M.	ANN	337	3RD DIST
THOMAS, CATHARINE	BAL	148	16TH WAR
THOMAS, CATHARINE	BAL	347	1ST DIST
THOMAS, CATHARINE	BAL	147	5TH WARD
THOMAS, CATHARINE	BAL	058	15TH WAR
THOMAS, CATHARINE	BAL	044	15TH WAR
THOMAS, CATHARINE	WAS	018	2ND SUBD
THOMAS, CATHARINE	TAL	085	ST MICHA
THOMAS, CATHARINE	FRE	218	BUCKEYST
THOMAS, CATHARINE E.	TAL	091	ST MICHA
THOMAS, CATHERIN	FRE	239	NEW MARK
THOMAS, CATHERINE	CAR	067	NO TWP L
THOMAS, CATHERINE	FRE	034	FREDERIC
THOMAS, CATHERINE	QUE	171	2ND E DI
THOMAS, CATHERINE	BAL	001	9TH WARD
THOMAS, CATHERINE-BLACK	QUE	171	2ND E DI
THOMAS, CATHERINE-BLACK	QUE	171	2ND E DI
THOMAS, CATHRINE	BAL	136	18TH WAR
THOMAS, CECELIA	CHA	277	BOJANTOW
THOMAS, CHARITY	ANN	294	1ST DIST
THOMAS, CHARLE-BLACK	FRE	028	FREDERIC
THOMAS, CHARLES	BAL	152	11TH WAR
THOMAS, CHARLES	BAL	426	14TH WAR
THOMAS, CHARLES	CAR	368	9TH DIST
THOMAS, CHARLES	ANN	290	ANNAPOLI
THOMAS, CHARLES	BAL	459	8TH WARD
THOMAS, CHARLES	BAL	245	6TH WARD
THOMAS, CHARLES	BAL	175	6TH WARD
THOMAS, CHARLES	BAL	259	1ST DIST
THOMAS, CHARLES	TAL	087	ST MICHA
THOMAS, CHARLES	TAL	038	EASTON D
THOMAS, CHARLES E.	FRE	398	JEFFERSO
THOMAS, CHARLES E.	FRE	220	BUCKEYST
THOMAS, CHARLES H.	BAL	152	11TH WAR
THOMAS, CHARLES-BLACK	FRE	433	8TH E DI
THOMAS, CHARLOTT	BAL	006	18TH WAR
THOMAS, CHARLOTTE	PRI	067	NOTTINGH
THOMAS, CHARLOTTE	BAL	030	9TH WARD
THOMAS, CHARLOTTE	ANN	501	HOWARD D
THOMAS, CHARLSE	CAL	020	2ND DIST

Name	County	Page	Location
THOMAS, CHRISTIAN	FRE	067	FREDERIC
THOMAS, CHRISTIAN	ALL	007	3RD E.D.
THOMAS, CHRISTIAN	WAS	142	HAGERSTO
THOMAS, CHRISTIANA	BAL	461	1ST DIST
THOMAS, CHRISTOPHER	FRE	389	PETERSVI
THOMAS, CINDERILLA	CAL	045	3RD DIST
THOMAS, CLARISSA	BAL	468	14TH WAR
THOMAS, CLARISSA	QUE	223	4TH E DI
THOMAS, COLISTA	TAL	072	EASTON T
THOMAS, CONRAD	BAL	390	3RD WARD
THOMAS, DANIEL	WAS	132	HAGERSTO
THOMAS, DANIEL	WAS	200	1ST DIST
THOMAS, DANIEL	KEN	213	2ND DIST
THOMAS, DANIEL	BAL	307	20TH WAR
THOMAS, DANIEL	BAL	409	3RD WARD
THOMAS, DANIEL N.	ANN	471	HOWARD D
THOMAS, DANIEL P.	HAR	047	1ST DIST
THOMAS, DANIEL W.	HAR	186	3RD DIST
THOMAS, DANIEL-BLACK	QUE	157	2ND E DI
THOMAS, DAVID	HAR	160	3RD DIST
THOMAS, DAVID	CEC	019	ELKTON 3
THOMAS, DAVID	CEC	013	ELKTON 3
THOMAS, DAVID	FRE	225	BUCKEYST
THOMAS, DAVID	BAL	252	6TH WARD
THOMAS, DAVID	BAL	233	1ST DIST
THOMAS, DAVID	ALL	090	5TH E.D.
THOMAS, DAVID	BAL	087	1ST WARD
THOMAS, DAVID	BAL	004	1ST WARD
THOMAS, DAVID	BAL	030	1ST WARD
THOMAS, DAVID	WAS	162	HAGERSTO
THOMAS, DAVID	TAL	056	EASTON D
THOMAS, DAVID	TAL	112	ST MICHA
THOMAS, DAVID	TAL	006	EASTON D
THOMAS, DAVID E.	BAL	251	6TH WARD
THOMAS, DAVID O.	FRE	100	FREDERIC
THOMAS, DAVID-BLACK	CAR	114	NO TWP L
THOMAS, DAVID-BLACK	QUE	170	2ND E DI
THOMAS, DAVIDS	CAR	242	TANEYTOW
THOMAS, DAWSON	BAL	031	1ST WARD
THOMAS, DEALY	TAL	033	EASTON D
THOMAS, DEBORAH	CEC	075	NORTHEAS
THOMAS, DEERO	BAL	130	11TH WAR
THOMAS, DENNIS	MGM	328	CRACKLIN
THOMAS, DENNIS	KEN	297	3RD DIST
THOMAS, DOROTHY	TAL	051	EASTON D
THOMAS, E.M.	BAL	138	1ST WARD
THOMAS, EATHA	BAL	297	3RD WARD
THOMAS, ED.	BAL	035	18TH WAR
THOMAS, EDWARD	DOR	398	1ST DIST
THOMAS, EDWARD	MGM	369	BERRYS D
THOMAS, EDWARD	BAL	138	2ND DIST
THOMAS, EDWARD	QUE	209	3RD E DI
THOMAS, EDWARD	TAL	042	EASTON D
THOMAS, EDWARD C.	BAL	016	18TH WAR
THOMAS, EDWARD L.	BAL	072	15TH WAR
THOMAS, EDWARD-BLACK	CAR	115	NO TWP L
THOMAS, EDWIN	BAL	219	2ND WARD
THOMAS, EDWIN	QUE	224	4TH E DI
THOMAS, EDWIN S.	BAL	225	6TH WARD
THOMAS, ELANOR*	DOR	444	1ST DIST
THOMAS, ELEANOR	BAL	346	13TH WAR
THOMAS, ELEXERNA	CAL	008	1ST DIST
THOMAS, ELI	BAL	086	18TH WAR
THOMAS, ELIAS	ALL	217	CUMBERLA
THOMAS, ELIAS	ALL	025	2ND E.D.
THOMAS, ELIJAH	DOR	313	1ST DIST
THOMAS, ELIKJAH	TAL	085	ST MICHA
THOMAS, ELISHA	DOR	351	3RD DIVI
THOMAS, ELISHA	SOM	452	DAMES QU
THOMAS, ELISHA C.	QUE	178	2ND E DI
THOMAS, ELIZA	ST	325	4TH E DI
THOMAS, ELIZA	FRE	380	PETERSVI
THOMAS, ELIZA	BAL	410	14TH WAR
THOMAS, ELIZA	FRE	234	BUCKEYST
THOMAS, ELIZA	BAL	012	15TH WAR
THOMAS, ELIZA	BAL	131	16TH WAR
THOMAS, ELIZA S.	FRE	029	FREDERIC
THOMAS, ELIZABETH	DOR	370	3RD DIVI
THOMAS, ELIZABETH	BAL	274	20TH WAR
THOMAS, ELIZABETH	FRE	271	NEW MARK
THOMAS, ELIZABETH	BAL	403	14TH WAR
THOMAS, ELIZABETH	FRE	055	FREDERIC
THOMAS, ELIZABETH	BAL	032	18TH WAR
THOMAS, ELIZABETH	CEC	119	3RD E DI
THOMAS, ELIZABETH	MGM	333	CRACKLIN
THOMAS, ELIZABETH	BAL	077	15TH WAR
THOMAS, ELIZABETH	BAL	205	11TH WAR
THOMAS, ELIZABETH	BAL	210	2ND WARD
THOMAS, ELIZABETH	BAL	125	5TH WARD
THOMAS, ELIZABETH	BAL	003	1ST WARD
THOMAS, ELIZABETH	BAL	009	1ST WARD
THOMAS, ELIZABETH	KEN	271	1ST DIST
THOMAS, ELIZABETH	KEN	297	3RD DIST
THOMAS, ELIZABETH	DOR	456	1ST DIST
THOMAS, ELIZABETH	QUE	224	4TH E DI
THOMAS, ELIZABETH	WAS	083	2ND SUBD
THOMAS, ELIZABETH A.	WAS	185	BOONSBOR
THOMAS, ELIZABETH B.	BAL	353	7TH WARD
THOMAS, ELIZABETH L.	ST	341	5TH E DI
THOMAS, ELIZABETH T.	ANN	425	HOWARD D
THOMAS, ELLEN	BAL	181	2ND DIST
THOMAS, ELLEN	CAL	045	3RD DIST
THOMAS, ELLEN J.	WAS	196	1ST DIST
THOMAS, ELLEN-BLACK	FRE	016	FREDERIC
THOMAS, ELLENOR	BAL	194	11TH WAR
THOMAS, ELY	BAL	149	19TH WAR
THOMAS, EMELINE	BAL	112	15TH WAR
THOMAS, EMELINE	BAL	107	15TH WAR
THOMAS, EMILY	BAL	030	18TH WAR
THOMAS, EMILY	DOR	454	1ST DIST
THOMAS, EMILY	WAS	018	2ND SUBD
THOMAS, EMILY V.	BAL	073	15TH WAR
THOMAS, ENNALS	TAL	002	EASTON D
THOMAS, EPHRAIM	BAL	344	3RD WARD
THOMAS, EPHRAIM	DOR	413	1ST DIST
THOMAS, EVAN H.	BAL	354	7TH WARD
THOMAS, EVY	FRE	210	BUCKEYST
THOMAS, EZRA M.	FRE	406	JEFFERSO
THOMAS, FATHER	BAL	382	3RD WARD
THOMAS, FLORA	BAL	067	15TH WAR
THOMAS, FLORA	BAL	289	17TH WAR
THOMAS, FLORA	PRI	087	QUEEN AN
THOMAS, FRANCES	BAL	344	7TH WARD
THOMAS, FRANCIS	BAL	036	9TH WARD
THOMAS, FRANCIS	ALL	034	2ND E.D.
THOMAS, FRANCIS	TAL	020	EASTON D
THOMAS, FRANCIS	FRE	381	PETERSVI
THOMAS, FRANCIS	FRE	019	FREDERIC
THOMAS, FRANCIS A.	CEC	085	5TH E DI
THOMAS, FRANK	BAL	404	14TH WAR
THOMAS, FRANK	BAL	252	12TH WAR
THOMAS, FRANKL	TAL	096	ST MICHA
THOMAS, FREDERICK	WAS	194	1ST DIST
THOMAS, FREDERICK	HAR	097	2ND DIST
THOMAS, FRISBY	WAS	199	1ST DIST
THOMAS, G.A.	ANN	273	ANNAPOLI
THOMAS, GABREL	DOR	342	3RD DIVI
THOMAS, GABRIEL	FRE	208	BUCKEYST
THOMAS, GARRETTSON	KEN	213	2ND DIST
THOMAS, GARRISON	BAL	132	16TH WAR
THOMAS, GARRISON	QUE	215	3RD E DI
THOMAS, GEORGE	WAS	199	1ST DIST
THOMAS, GEORGE	ST	341	5TH E DI
THOMAS, GEORGE	ST	348	5TH E DI
THOMAS, GEORGE	TAL	086	ST MICHA
THOMAS, GEORGE	ST	262	3RD E DI
THOMAS, GEORGE	WAS	154	2ND DIST
THOMAS, GEORGE	WAS	082	2ND SUBD
THOMAS, GEORGE	PRI	045	VANSVILL
THOMAS, GEORGE	ALL	029	2ND E.D.
THOMAS, GEORGE	ALL	120	5TH E.D.
THOMAS, GEORGE	BAL	129	5TH WARD
THOMAS, GEORGE	BAL	168	1ST WARD
THOMAS, GEORGE	BAL	124	5TH WARD
THOMAS, GEORGE	BAL	310	7TH WARD
THOMAS, GEORGE	BAL	452	1ST DIST
THOMAS, GEORGE	BAL	115	1ST WARD
THOMAS, GEORGE	ANN	351	3RD DIST
THOMAS, GEORGE	FRE	212	BUCKEYST
THOMAS, GEORGE	DOR	432	1ST DIST
THOMAS, GEORGE	FRE	224	BUCKEYST
THOMAS, GEORGE	DOR	398	1ST DIST
THOMAS, GEORGE	DOR	402	1ST DIST
THOMAS, GEORGE	FRE	081	FREDERIC
THOMAS, GEORGE	CEC	082	CHARLEST
THOMAS, GEORGE	MGM	331	CRACKLIN
THOMAS, GEORGE	CHA	277	BOJANTOW
THOMAS, GEORGE	CHA	263	MIDDLETO
THOMAS, GEORGE	BAL	203	17TH WAR
THOMAS, GEORGE	BAL	052	4TH WARD
THOMAS, GEORGE	BAL	060	4TH WARD
THOMAS, GEORGE	CAR	308	1ST DIST
THOMAS, GEORGE E.	BAL	122	1ST WARD
THOMAS, GEORGE F.	FRE	398	JEFFERSO
THOMAS, GEORGE H.	BAL	379	13TH WAR
THOMAS, GEORGE W.	CAL	017	1ST DIST
THOMAS, GEORGE W.	PRI	046	AQUASCO
THOMAS, GEORGE-BLACK	QUE	140	1ST E DI
THOMAS, GEORGE-BLACK	FRE	181	5TH E DI
THOMAS, GEORGE-BLACK	CAR	392	2ND DIST
THOMAS, GEORGEW	WOR	310	2ND E DI
THOMAS, GIDEON	WAS	082	2ND SUBD
THOMAS, GOERGE	BAL	030	15TH WAR
THOMAS, GREEN	DOR	392	1ST DIST
THOMAS, GREENBURG	DOR	468	1ST DIST
THOMAS, H.	BAL	118	1ST WARD
THOMAS, H.	BAL	139	1ST WARD
THOMAS, H. M.	TAL	042	EASTON D
THOMAS, HANAH	CAR	307	1ST DIST
THOMAS, HANAH A.	BAL	333	7TH WARD
THOMAS, HANAH-BLACK	CAR	139	NO TWP L
THOMAS, HANNAH	BAL	189	6TH WARD
THOMAS, HANNAH/BLACK	QUE	183	3RD E DI
THOMAS, HARIET	PRI	108	PISCATAW
THOMAS, HARRIET	BAL	204	2ND WARD
THOMAS, HARRIET	BAL	366	8TH WARD
THOMAS, HARRIET	BAL	411	1ST DIST
THOMAS, HARRIET	KEN	215	2ND DIST
THOMAS, HARRIET-BLACK	QUE	140	1ST E DI
THOMAS, HARRIET-BLACK	QUE	199	3RD E DI
THOMAS, HARRIETT	BAL	123	11TH WAR
THOMAS, HARRIETT A.	DOR	309	1ST DIST
THOMAS, HARRIOTT	BAL	071	4TH WARD
THOMAS, HARRISON	QUE	211	3RD E DI
THOMAS, HARRISON	QUE	216	3RD E DI
THOMAS, HARRY	DOR	432	1ST DIST
THOMAS, HARY	DOR	418	1ST DIST
THOMAS, HASEL	BAL	398	14TH WAR
THOMAS, HENRIET	BAL	265	12TH WAR
THOMAS, HENRIETTA	DOR	468	1ST DIST
THOMAS, HENRY	QUE	212	3RD E DI
THOMAS, HENRY	PRI	107	PISCATAW
THOMAS, HENRY	TAL	007	EASTON D
THOMAS, HENRY	TAL	101	ST MICHA
THOMAS, HENRY	WAS	158	2ND DIST
THOMAS, HENRY	QUE	225	4TH E DI
THOMAS, HENRY	TAL	066	EASTON T
THOMAS, HENRY	BAL	116	5TH WARD
THOMAS, HENRY	BAL	233	1ST DIST
THOMAS, HENRY	BAL	399	8TH WARD
THOMAS, HENRY	BAL	275	12TH WAR
THOMAS, HENRY	BAL	184	16TH WAR
THOMAS, HENRY	BAL	122	1ST WARD
THOMAS, HENRY	CAL	005	1ST DIST
THOMAS, HENRY	FRE	290	WOODSBOR
THOMAS, HENRY	FRE	033	FREDERIC
THOMAS, HENRY	BAL	300	20TH WAR
THOMAS, HENRY	BAL	239	20TH WAR
THOMAS, HENRY	BAL	411	3RD WARD
THOMAS, HENRY	CAR	225	5TH DIST
THOMAS, HENRY	BAL	036	4TH WARD
THOMAS, HENRY E.	BAL	470	14TH WAR
THOMAS, HENRY J.	BAL	044	4TH WARD
THOMAS, HENRY L.	MGM	390	ROCKERLE
THOMAS, HENRY P.	BAL	403	14TH WAR
THOMAS, HENRY S.	BAL	069	18TH WAR
THOMAS, HENRY W.	BAL	062	10TH WAR
THOMAS, HENRY-BLACK	CAR	168	NO TWP L
THOMAS, HERNY	CAR	400	2ND DIST
THOMAS, HESTER	BAL	097	10TH WAR
THOMAS, HESTER	BAL	039	15TH WAR
THOMAS, HESTER	BAL	019	15TH WAR
THOMAS, HESTER-BLACK	CAR	097	NO TWP L
THOMAS, HEZEKIAH	BAL	071	1ST WARD
THOMAS, HORACE	BAL	365	3RD WARD
THOMAS, HORATIO-BLACK	CAR	152	NO TWP L
THOMAS, HUGH	DOR	401	1ST DIST
THOMAS, ISAAC	CEC	003	ELKTON 3
THOMAS, ISAAC	BAL	006	9TH WARD
THOMAS, ISAAC	BAL	318	3RD WARD
THOMAS, ISAAC-MULATTO	CAR	113	NO TWP L
THOMAS, ISABELLA	CEC	044	1ST E DI
THOMAS, ISACK	TAL	055	EASTON D
THOMAS, ISRAEL	BAL	374	3RD WARD
THOMAS, ISREAL J.	BAL	354	7TH WARD
THOMAS, J. D. *	BAL	321	20TH WAR
THOMAS, J.H.	BAL	137	1ST WARD
THOMAS, JACOB	BAL	180	6TH WARD
THOMAS, JACOB	ALL	055	10TH E.D
THOMAS, JACOB	CEC	017	ELKTON 3
THOMAS, JACOB	FRE	320	MIDDLETO
THOMAS, JACOB	BAL	346	13TH WAR
THOMAS, JACOB	WAS	194	1ST DIST
THOMAS, JACOB	WAS	035	2ND SUBD
THOMAS, JACOB A.	WAS	200	1ST DIST
THOMAS, JACOB A.	ALL	029	2ND E.D.
THOMAS, JAMES	ANN	273	ANNAPOLI
THOMAS, JAMES	BAL	142	5TH WARD
THOMAS, JAMES	BAL	165	1ST WARD
THOMAS, JAMES	BAL	385	8TH WARD
THOMAS, JAMES	BAL	453	8TH WARD
THOMAS, JAMES	BAL	125	1ST WARD
THOMAS, JAMES	BAL	117	1ST WARD
THOMAS, JAMES	BAL	271	1ST DIST
THOMAS, JAMES	BAL	193	17TH WAR
THOMAS, JAMES	BAL	121	16TH WAR
THOMAS, JAMES	DOR	451	1ST DIST
THOMAS, JAMES	ST	341	5TH E DI
THOMAS, JAMES	TAL	055	EASTON.D
THOMAS, JAMES	PRI	060	NOTTINGH
THOMAS, JAMES	TAL	116	ST MICHA
THOMAS, JAMES	FRE	301	WOODSBOR
THOMAS, JAMES	DOR	391	1ST DIST
THOMAS, JAMES	DOR	401	1ST DIST
THOMAS, JAMES	DOR	403	1ST DIST
THOMAS, JAMES	DOR	441	1ST DIST
THOMAS, JAMES	CEC	008	ELKTON 3
THOMAS, JAMES	HAR	005	1ST DIST
THOMAS, JAMES	CAR	121	NO TWP L
THOMAS, JAMES	CAR	130	NO TWP L
THOMAS, JAMES	CAL	059	3RD DIST
THOMAS, JAMES	BAL	033	18TH WAR
THOMAS, JAMES	BAL	098	18TH WAR
THOMAS, JAMES	CAR	320	1ST DIST
THOMAS, JAMES	CHA	285	BOJANTOW
THOMAS, JAMES B.	ALL	080	5TH E.D.
THOMAS, JAMES E.	CHA	285	BOJANTOW
THOMAS, JAMES F.	BAL	129	16TH WAR
THOMAS, JAMES H.	BAL	472	14TH WAR
THOMAS, JAMES H.	ST	262	3RD E DI
THOMAS, JAMES M.	BAL	034	18TH WAR
THOMAS, JAMES W.	KEN	295	3RD DIST
THOMAS, JAMES-BLACK	CAR	155	NO TWP L
THOMAS, JAMES-BLACK	CAR	168	NO TWP L
THOMAS, JAMES-MULATTO	BAL	208	2ND WARD
THOMAS, JAMESB.	BAL	226	2ND WARD
THOMAS, JANE	BAL	170	6TH WARD
THOMAS, JANE	BAL	297	12TH WAR
THOMAS, JANE	BAL	311	12TH WAR
THOMAS, JANE	BAL	099	5TH WARD
THOMAS, JANE	BAL	195	19TH WAR
THOMAS, JANE	BAL	165	19TH WAR
THOMAS, JANE	CEC	216	7TH E DI
THOMAS, JANE	SOM	457	DAMES QU
THOMAS, JANE	ST	291	2ND E DI
THOMAS, JANE	WAS	154	2ND DIST
THOMAS, JANE	TAL	112	ST MICHA
THOMAS, JANE	TAL	101	ST MICHA
THOMAS, JANE	TAL	039	EASTON D
THOMAS, JANE*	DOR	407	1ST DIST
THOMAS, JANE-BLACK	FRE	431	8TH E DI
THOMAS, JEREMIAH	CAL	004	1ST DIST
THOMAS, JESE*	DOR	398	1ST DIST
THOMAS, JESSE	CEC	085	5TH E DI
THOMAS, JESSE	BAL	282	2ND WARD
THOMAS, JIM	TAL	010	EASTON D
THOMAS, JOE	TAL	052	EASTON D
THOMAS, JOEL	WAS	267	1ST DIST
THOMAS, JOEL	QUE	147	1ST E DI
THOMAS, JOHN	CHA	277	BOJANTOW
THOMAS, JOHN	KEN	229	2ND DIST
THOMAS, JOHN	MGM	331	CRACKLIN
THOMAS, JOHN	FRE	102	FREDERIC
THOMAS, JOHN	FRE	202	5TH E DI
THOMAS, JOHN	MGM	347	BERRYS D
THOMAS, JOHN	BAL	283	17TH WAR
THOMAS, JOHN	CAR	359	9TH DIST
THOMAS, JOHN	DOR	401	1ST DIST
THOMAS, JOHN	BAL	162	19TH WAR
THOMAS, JOHN	BAL	106	18TH WAR
THOMAS, JOHN	FRE	239	NEW MARK
THOMAS, JOHN	BAL	135	18TH WAR
THOMAS, JOHN	CAR	141	NO TWP L
THOMAS, JOHN	CAL	059	3RD DIST
THOMAS, JOHN	BAL	400	14TH WAR
THOMAS, JOHN	CEC	198	7TH E DI
THOMAS, JOHN	CHA	225	ALLENS F
THOMAS, JOHN	CHA	226	ALLENS F
THOMAS, JOHN	DOR	370	3RD DIVI
THOMAS, JOHN	CEC	003	ELKTON 3
THOMAS, JOHN	CEC	033	CHESAPEA
THOMAS, JOHN	CAR	308	1ST DIST
THOMAS, JOHN	BAL	237	20TH WAR
THOMAS, JOHN	BAL	228	19TH WAR
THOMAS, JOHN	HAR	005	1ST DIST
THOMAS, JOHN	BAL	075	4TH WARD
THOMAS, JOHN	DOR	300	1ST DIST
THOMAS, JOHN	BAL	214	17TH WAR
THOMAS, JOHN	SOM	454	DAMES QU
THOMAS, JOHN	DOR	456	1ST DIST
THOMAS, JOHN	QUE	210	3RD E DI
THOMAS, JOHN	QUE	189	3RD E DI
THOMAS, JOHN	TAL	097	ST MICHA
THOMAS, JOHN	SOM	359	BRINKLEY
THOMAS, JOHN	SOM	359	BRINKLEY
THOMAS, JOHN	WAS	058	2ND SUBD
THOMAS, JOHN	WAS	054	2ND SUBD
THOMAS, JOHN	PRI	062	NOTTINGH
THOMAS, JOHN	BAL	138	1ST WARD
THOMAS, JOHN	BAL	140	1ST WARD
THOMAS, JOHN	BAL	306	3RD WARD
THOMAS, JOHN	BAL	305	3RD WARD
THOMAS, JOHN	BAL	392	1ST DIST
THOMAS, JOHN	BAL	389	1ST DIST
THOMAS, JOHN	BAL	454	1ST DIST
THOMAS, JOHN	BAL	330	13TH WAR
THOMAS, JOHN	BAL	329	13TH WAR
THOMAS, JOHN	BAL	300	12TH WAR
THOMAS, JOHN	BAL	110	10TH WAR
THOMAS, JOHN	BAL	155	5TH WARD
THOMAS, JOHN	BAL	171	1ST WARD
THOMAS, JOHN	BAL	184	2ND WARD
THOMAS, JOHN	BAL	037	9TH WARD
THOMAS, JOHN	ALL	092	5TH E.D.
THOMAS, JOHN	ANN	268	ANNAPOLI
THOMAS, JOHN	ALL	028	2ND E.D.
THOMAS, JOHN	ALL	013	3RD E.D.
THOMAS, JOHN	ANN	301	1ST DIST
THOMAS, JOHN	ANN	302	1ST DIST
THOMAS, JOHN	ANN	322	2ND DIST

THOMAS, JOHN	ALL	183	8TH E.D.
THOMAS, JOHN	ALL	158	6TH E.D.
THOMAS, JOHN	BAL	116	1ST WARD
THOMAS, JOHN	BAL	356	3RD WARD
THOMAS, JOHN	BAL	125	1ST WARD
THOMAS, JOHN	BAL	349	7TH WARD
THOMAS, JOHN	BAL	460	8TH WARD
THOMAS, JOHN	BAL	041	15TH WAR
THOMAS, JOHN	BAL	250	12TH WAR
THOMAS, JOHN	ANN	344	3RD DIST
THOMAS, JOHN	ANN	397	8TH DIST
THOMAS, JOHN	BAL	148	2ND DIST
THOMAS, JOHN A.	BAL	425	3RD WARD
THOMAS, JOHN B.	QUE	208	3RD E DI
THOMAS, JOHN C.	PRI	046	AQUASCO
THOMAS, JOHN C.	BAL	400	14TH WAR
THOMAS, JOHN CHEW DR.	BAL	333	13TH WAR
THOMAS, JOHN D.	ANN	412	HOWARD D
THOMAS, JOHN D.	CHA	284	BOJANTOW
THOMAS, JOHN F.	BAL	038	9TH WARD
THOMAS, JOHN G. L.	QUE	222	4TH E DI
THOMAS, JOHN H.	SOM	515	BARREN C
THOMAS, JOHN H.	BAL	196	11TH WAR
THOMAS, JOHN H.	BAL	317	3RD WARD
THOMAS, JOHN H.	BAL	243	17TH WAR
THOMAS, JOHN J.	BAL	041	9TH WARD
THOMAS, JOHN L.	ALL	252	CUMBERLA
THOMAS, JOHN R.	ANN	337	3RD DIST
THOMAS, JOHN R.	QUE	166	2ND E DI
THOMAS, JOHN S.	DOR	374	1ST DIST
THOMAS, JOHN T.	QUE	206	3RD E DI
THOMAS, JOHN W.	SOM	464	HANGARY
THOMAS, JOHN W.	PRI	112	PISCATAW
THOMAS, JOHN-BLACK	QUE	183	3RD E DI
THOMAS, JOHN-BLACK	QUE	186	3RD E DI
THOMAS, JOHN-BLACK	CAR	138	NO TWP L
THOMAS, JOHN-BLACK	CAR	089	NO TWP L
THOMAS, JOHNSON P.	BAL	139	11TH WAR
THOMAS, JONAS	FRE	103	FREDERIC
THOMAS, JOSEPH	BAL	448	14TH WAR
THOMAS, JOSEPH	DOR	315	1ST DIST
THOMAS, JOSEPH	BAL	274	17TH WAR
THOMAS, JOSEPH	CEC	127	5TH E DI
THOMAS, JOSEPH	BAL	133	18TH WAR
THOMAS, JOSEPH	BAL	162	19TH WAR
THOMAS, JOSEPH	FRE	219	BUCKEYST
THOMAS, JOSEPH	WAS	058	2ND SUBD
THOMAS, JOSEPH	TAL	085	ST MICHA
THOMAS, JOSEPH	BAL	461	1ST DIST
THOMAS, JOSEPH	BAL	043	15TH WAR
THOMAS, JOSEPH	BAL	261	12TH WAR
THOMAS, JOSEPH	BAL	309	1ST DIST
THOMAS, JOSEPH	ANN	279	ANNAPOLI
THOMAS, JOSEPH	ALL	085	5TH E.D.
THOMAS, JOSEPH	ALL	119	5TH E.D.
THOMAS, JOSEPH	BAL	141	16TH WAR
THOMAS, JOSEPH	BAL	374	3RD WARD
THOMAS, JOSEPH	BAL	120	1ST WARD
THOMAS, JOSEPH B.	BAL	123	1ST WARD
THOMAS, JOSEPH B.	BAL	036	18TH WAR
THOMAS, JOSEPH R.	CEC	193	5TH E DI
THOMAS, JOSEPH S.	CAL	040	3RD DIST
THOMAS, JOSHUA	BAL	120	2ND DIST
THOMAS, JOSHUA	SOM	453	DAMES QU
THOMAS, JOSHUA-BLACK	QUE	146	1ST E DI
THOMAS, JOSIAH	DOR	401	1ST DIST
THOMAS, JOSIAH	DOR	456	1ST DIST
THOMAS, JOSIAH	WAS	189	1ST DIST
THOMAS, JOSIAH S.	FRE	212	BUCKEYST
THOMAS, JULES A. M.	FRE	333	MIDDLETO
THOMAS, JULIA	TAL	032	EASTON D
THOMAS, JULIANN	ALL	196	CUMBERLA
THOMAS, KINSEY	KEN	262	1ST DIST
THOMAS, KINSLEY	BAL	128	1ST WARD
THOMAS, KITZELDLA	CAR	236	UNION TO
THOMAS, L.M.	PRI	046	AQUASCO
THOMAS, LABAN	SOM	449	DAMES QU
THOMAS, LAHAH ANN	ALL	256	CUMBERLA
THOMAS, LAURA	MGM	321	CRACKLIN
THOMAS, LAURA T.	BAL	103	5TH WARD
THOMAS, LAURENCE	BAL	064	2ND DIST
THOMAS, LEAH	BAL	396	14TH WAR
THOMAS, LEANDER	CEC	084	CHARLEST
THOMAS, LESIN-BLACK	FRE	022	FREDERIC
THOMAS, LETTY	CAL	045	3RD DIST
THOMAS, LEVENIA	TAL	054	EASTON D
THOMAS, LEVI	DOR	429	1ST DIST
THOMAS, LEVI	BAL	435	1ST DIST
THOMAS, LEVIN	DOR	395	1ST DIST
THOMAS, LEVIN	FRE	379	PETERSVI
THOMAS, LEVINA	DOR	305	1ST DIST
THOMAS, LEWIS	DOR	392	1ST DIST
THOMAS, LEWIS	CAR	338	6TH DIST
THOMAS, LEWIS	BAL	054	1ST WARD
THOMAS, LEWIS M.	FRE	100	FREDERIC
THOMAS, LEWIS*	DOR	462	1ST DIST
THOMAS, LILEY	PRI	067	NOTTINGH
THOMAS, LINTON	FRE	312	MIDDLETO
THOMAS, LLOYD	FRE	381	PETERSVI
THOMAS, LONDON	CAL	032	2ND DIST
THOMAS, LOUISA	BAL	055	4TH WARD
THOMAS, LOUISA	BAL	237	20TH WAR
THOMAS, LOUISA	BAL	185	19TH WAR
THOMAS, LOUISA	BAL	366	8TH WARD
THOMAS, LUCINDA	PRI	093	MARLBROU
THOMAS, LUCRETIA	TAL	007	EASTON D
THOMAS, LUCY	PRI	043	VANSVILL
THOMAS, LUCY-BLACK	ST	320	4TH E DI
THOMAS, LYDIA	QUE	218	3RD E DI
THOMAS, M.	BAL	309	12TH WAR
THOMAS, M.W.	BAL	143	1ST WARD
THOMAS, MARGARET	BAL	297	1ST DIST
THOMAS, MARGARET	BAL	179	6TH WARD
THOMAS, MARGARET	PRI	074	MARLBROU
THOMAS, MARGARET	CAL	001	1ST DIST
THOMAS, MARGARET	FRE	100	FREDERIC
THOMAS, MARGARETH	BAL	370	13TH WAR
THOMAS, MARIA	PRI	084	QUEEN AN
THOMAS, MARIA	PRI	084	QUEEN AN
THOMAS, MARIA	KEN	270	1ST DIST
THOMAS, MARIA	QUE	188	3RD E DI
THOMAS, MARIA	BAL	186	6TH WARD
THOMAS, MARIA	BAL	180	16TH WAR
THOMAS, MARIA	ANN	473	HOWARD D
THOMAS, MARIA	BAL	074	15TH WAR
THOMAS, MARIAH	WOR	307	2ND E DI
THOMAS, MARIAH	DOR	366	3RD DIVI
THOMAS, MARIAN	CEC	093	4TH E DI
THOMAS, MARTHA	BAL	075	4TH WARD
THOMAS, MARTHA	BAL	322	12TH WAR
THOMAS, MARTHA A.*	DOR	320	1ST DIST
THOMAS, MARTHA E.	BAL	165	19TH WAR
THOMAS, MARTHA J.	TAL	041	EASTON D
THOMAS, MARTHA-BLACK	CAR	132	NO TWP L
THOMAS, MARTIN	BAL	134	2ND DIST
THOMAS, MARTIN-MULATTO	BAL	216	2ND WARD
THOMAS, MARY	BAL	175	6TH WARD
THOMAS, MARY	ANN	337	3RD DIST
THOMAS, MARY	BAL	102	10TH WAR
THOMAS, MARY	BAL	262	12TH WAR
THOMAS, MARY	BAL	342	7TH WARD
THOMAS, MARY	BAL	031	1ST WARD
THOMAS, MARY	BAL	006	1ST WARD
THOMAS, MARY	BAL	013	1ST WARD
THOMAS, MARY	BAL	262	2ND WARD
THOMAS, MARY	DOR	396	1ST DIST
THOMAS, MARY	KEN	220	2ND DIST
THOMAS, MARY	DOR	321	1ST DIST
THOMAS, MARY	BAL	269	20TH WAR
THOMAS, MARY	CHA	226	ALLENS F
THOMAS, MARY	BAL	252	20TH WAR
THOMAS, MARY	BAL	088	4TH WARD
THOMAS, MARY	BAL	359	13TH WAR
THOMAS, MARY	CEC	182	7TH E DI
THOMAS, MARY	CHA	284	BOJANTOW
THOMAS, MARY	CAR	226	5TH DIST
THOMAS, MARY	CEC	024	ELKTON 3
THOMAS, MARY	HAR	034	1ST DIST
THOMAS, MARY	TAL	019	EASTON D
THOMAS, MARY	WAS	060	2ND SUBD
THOMAS, MARY	WAS	203	1ST DIST
THOMAS, MARY	PRI	071	MARLBROU
THOMAS, MARY	PRI	043	VANSVILL
THOMAS, MARY	PRI	046	AQUASCO
THOMAS, MARY	PRI	093	MARLBROU
THOMAS, MARY	TAL	079	ST MICHA
THOMAS, MARY	TAL	096	ST MICHA
THOMAS, MARY A.	BAL	015	18TH WAR
THOMAS, MARY A.	BAL	097	15TH WAR
THOMAS, MARY E.	BAL	104	18TH WAR
THOMAS, MARY F.	KEN	212	2ND DIST
THOMAS, MARY J.	BAL	025	9TH WARD
THOMAS, MARY J.-MULATTO	FRE	243	NEW MARK
THOMAS, MARY R.	KEN	244	2ND DIST
THOMAS, MARY-BLACK	BAL	222	2ND WARD
THOMAS, MARY-BLACK	ST	339	4TH E DI
THOMAS, MATHEW	PRI	086	QUEEN AN
THOMAS, MATHEW	WAS	057	2ND SUBD
THOMAS, MATILDA	TAL	118	ST MICHA
THOMAS, MATILDA	TAL	097	ST MICHA
THOMAS, MATILDA	BAL	160	6TH WARD
THOMAS, MATILDA	BAL	147	11TH WAR
THOMAS, MAYARA	BAL	289	1ST DIST
THOMAS, MELVIRA	BAL	038	1ST WARD
THOMAS, MICHAEL	FRE	348	MIDDLETO
THOMAS, MICHAEL	CEC	138	6TH E DI
THOMAS, MICHAEL	WAS	059	2ND SUBD
THOMAS, MICHAEL	WAS	289	1ST DIST
THOMAS, MIKE-BLACK	QUE	185	3RD E DI
THOMAS, MILES	ALL	001	3RD E.D.
THOMAS, MILEY*	DOR	468	1ST DIST
THOMAS, MINTY	HAR	119	2ND DIST
THOMAS, MISS M.	ANN	267	ANNAPOLI
THOMAS, MORDECAI	HAR	047	1ST DIST
THOMAS, MOSES	DOR	470	1ST DIST
THOMAS, MR.	BAL	165	11TH WAR
THOMAS, MRS.*	DOR	375	1ST DIST
THOMAS, NANCY	BAL	476	14TH WAR
THOMAS, NANCY	DOR	389	1ST DIST
THOMAS, NANCY	DOR	398	1ST DIST
THOMAS, NANCY	ALL	029	2ND E.D.
THOMAS, NANCY	WAS	058	2ND SUBD
THOMAS, NANCY	QUE	240	5TH E DI
THOMAS, NANNY	QUE	217	3RD E DI
THOMAS, NATHAN	BAL	013	1ST WARD
THOMAS, NELLY	ANN	332	2ND DIST
THOMAS, NELLY	MGM	367	BERRYS D
THOMAS, NICHOLAS	MGM	320	CRACKLIN
THOMAS, OLIVER	WAS	074	2ND SUBD
THOMAS, OLIVER H.	HAR	076	BEL AIR
THOMAS, ORRIS-BLACK	CAR	154	NO TWP L
THOMAS, OSCAR	BAL	307	20TH WAR
THOMAS, OTHO	FRE	220	BUCKEYST
THOMAS, OWEN	BAL	157	6TH WARD
THOMAS, P. E.	BAL	333	1ST DIST
THOMAS, PARKER C.	BAL	300	17TH WAR
THOMAS, PAUL	BAL	392	14TH WAR
THOMAS, PAUL	BAL	445	14TH WAR
THOMAS, PAUL	BAL	445	14TH WAR
THOMAS, PAUL	BAL	270	1ST DIST
THOMAS, PERRY	BAL	374	3RD WARD
THOMAS, PERRY	BAL	047	9TH WARD
THOMAS, PERRY	BAL	307	12TH WAR
THOMAS, PERRY	BAL	075	4TH WARD
THOMAS, PERRY	TAL	046	EASTON T
THOMAS, PERRY	TAL	056	EASTON D
THOMAS, PERRY G.	FRE	400	JEFFERSO
THOMAS, PERRY-BLACK	CAR	087	NO TWP L
THOMAS, PERRY-BLACK	CAR	073	NO TWP L
THOMAS, PERRY-BLACK	CAR	094	NO TWP L
THOMAS, PETER	CAL	051	3RD DIST
THOMAS, PETER	SOM	380	BRINKLEY
THOMAS, PETER	WAS	058	2ND SUBD
THOMAS, PETER	ALL	219	CUMBERLA
THOMAS, PHIL*	TAL	049	EASTON T
THOMAS, PHILIP	BAL	387	1ST DIST
THOMAS, PHILIP	BAL	221	1ST DIST
THOMAS, PHILIP	CEC	084	CHARLEST
THOMAS, PHILIP	FRE	232	BUCKEYST
THOMAS, PHILIP	CEC	047	1ST E DI
THOMAS, PHILIP E.	BAL	476	14TH WAR
THOMAS, PHILIP F. GOV-	ANN	293	ANNAPOLI
THOMAS, PHILIP H.	FRE	311	MIDDLETO
THOMAS, PHILIP J.	ANN	302	1ST DIST
THOMAS, PHILIP SIX	CAR	308	1ST DIST
THOMAS, PHILISTINE	BAL	083	15TH WAR
THOMAS, PHILLIP	BAL	141	1ST WARD
THOMAS, PHILLIP P.	BAL	103	5TH WARD
THOMAS, PHILLIS	BAL	034	9TH WARD
THOMAS, PIERCE	BAL	043	9TH WARD
THOMAS, RACHAEL	BAL	344	3RD WARD
THOMAS, RACHEL	BAL	255	6TH WARD
THOMAS, RACHEL	TAL	045	EASTON T
THOMAS, RACHEL A.-MULATTO	FRE	243	NEW MARK
THOMAS, RACHELL	BAL	118	5TH WARD
THOMAS, RAGIS	BAL	198	6TH WARD
THOMAS, REBECCA	BAL	374	3RD WARD
THOMAS, REBECCA	CEC	119	3RD E DI
THOMAS, REBECCA	HAR	058	1ST DIST
THOMAS, REBECCA-BLACK	CAR	148	NO TWP L
THOMAS, REBECCA-BLACK	QUE	164	2ND E DI
THOMAS, RESIN	BAL	261	17TH WAR
THOMAS, RICHARD	CEC	145	PORT DUP
THOMAS, RICHARD	BAL	240	17TH WAR
THOMAS, RICHARD	CAL	025	2ND DIST
THOMAS, RICHARD	BAL	300	17TH WAR
THOMAS, RICHARD	CEC	076	NORTHEAS
THOMAS, RICHARD	FRE	223	BUCKEYST
THOMAS, RICHARD	BAL	222	19TH WAR
THOMAS, RICHARD	CEC	012	ELKTON 3
THOMAS, RICHARD	MGM	338	CRACKLIN
THOMAS, RICHARD	TAL	066	EASTON T
THOMAS, RICHARD	ANN	501	HOWARD D
THOMAS, RICHARD H.	BAL	380	13TH WAR
THOMAS, RICHARD S.	KEN	230	2ND DIST
THOMAS, RICHARD T.	BAL	299	17TH WAR
THOMAS, RICHARD-BLACK	CAR	099	NO TWP L
THOMAS, ROBERT	CAR	138	NO TWP L
THOMAS, ROBERT	BAL	069	18TH WAR
THOMAS, ROBERT	CEC	157	PORT DUP
THOMAS, ROBERT	CEC	022	ELKTON 3
THOMAS, ROBERT	FRE	316	MIDDLETO
THOMAS, ROBERT	ANN	323	2ND DIST
THOMAS, ROBERT	ANN	449	HOWARD D
THOMAS, ROBERT	BAL	459	8TH WARD
THOMAS, ROBERT	QUE	164	2ND E DI
THOMAS, ROBERT JAMES	QUE	148	1ST E DI
THOMAS, ROBERT L.	BAL	185	16TH WAR
THOMAS, ROBERT W.-BLACK	ST	321	4TH E DI
THOMAS, ROBERT-MULATTO	CAR	139	NO TWP L
THOMAS, RODOPH	BAL	288	1ST DIST
THOMAS, ROSANNA	BAL	144	16TH WAR
THOMAS, ROSETTA	BAL	081	15TH WAR
THOMAS, ROSS-BLACK	FRE	435	8TH E DI
THOMAS, ROUSLY	ANN	396	8TH DIST
THOMAS, RUSSELL	CEC	077	NORTHEAS
THOMAS, RUTH	BAL	137	18TH WAR
THOMAS, S.J.	BAL	118	1ST WARD
THOMAS, SALLY	TAL	038	EASTON D
THOMAS, SALLY A.	TAL	002	EASTON D
THOMAS, SAMUEL	WAS	076	2ND SUBD
THOMAS, SAMUEL	BAL	293	1ST DIST
THOMAS, SAMUEL	ANN	397	8TH DIST
THOMAS, SAMUEL	ANN	338	3RD DIST
THOMAS, SAMUEL	BAL	250	12TH WAR
THOMAS, SAMUEL	BAL	144	5TH WARD
THOMAS, SAMUEL	FRE	232	BUCKEYST
THOMAS, SAMUEL	DOR	390	1ST DIST
THOMAS, SAMUEL	DOR	399	1ST DIST
THOMAS, SAMUEL	CEC	056	1ST E DI
THOMAS, SAMUEL	CHA	225	ALLENS F
THOMAS, SAMUEL	DOR	314	1ST DIST
THOMAS, SAMUEL	CAR	138	NO TWP L
THOMAS, SAMUEL	CAR	080	NO TWP L
THOMAS, SAMUEL	CEC	019	ELKTON 3
THOMAS, SAMUEL	BAL	440	14TH WAR
THOMAS, SAMUEL	SOM	445	DAMES QU
THOMAS, SAMUEL	FRE	083	FREDERIC
THOMAS, SAMUEL H.	FRE	221	BUCKEYST
THOMAS, SAMUEL K.	BAL	439	8TH WARD
THOMAS, SAMUEL R.	BAL	132	1ST WARD
THOMAS, SARAH	BAL	171	11TH WAR
THOMAS, SARAH	BAL	061	10TH WAR
THOMAS, SARAH	BAL	114	5TH WARD
THOMAS, SARAH	ANN	512	HOWARD D
THOMAS, SARAH	DOR	379	1ST DIST
THOMAS, SARAH	KEN	215	2ND DIST
THOMAS, SARAH	MGM	361	BERRYS D
THOMAS, SARAH	BAL	205	17TH WAR
THOMAS, SARAH	BAL	340	13TH WAR
THOMAS, SARAH	BAL	359	13TH WAR
THOMAS, SARAH	CEC	026	ELKTON 3
THOMAS, SARAH	CAL	030	2ND DIST
THOMAS, SARAH	WAS	082	2ND SUBD
THOMAS, SARAH	QUE	232	4TH E DI
THOMAS, SARAH A.	WAS	158	2ND DIST
THOMAS, SARAH A.	FRE	221	BUCKEYST
THOMAS, SARAH E.	BAL	449	14TH WAR
THOMAS, SARAH-BLACK	CAR	154	NO TWP L
THOMAS, SCIPIO-BLACK	QUE	200	3RD E DI
THOMAS, SECEAR	BAL	112	18TH WAR
THOMAS, SEIPIO *	QUE	240	5TH E DI
THOMAS, SETH	BAL	344	7TH WARD
THOMAS, SHADRACK	BAL	028	15TH WAR
THOMAS, SIDNEY	BAL	236	12TH WAR
THOMAS, SIDNEY M. H.	BAL	175	6TH WARD
THOMAS, SOLOMAN	ALL	250	CUMBERLA
THOMAS, SOPHIE	BAL	280	20TH WAR
THOMAS, SOPHRONIA	KEN	215	2ND DIST
THOMAS, STEPHEN	CEC	013	ELKTON 3
THOMAS, STEPHEN	HAR	034	1ST DIST
THOMAS, STEPHEN	BAL	101	15TH WAR
THOMAS, STEPHEN	BAL	356	3RD WARD
THOMAS, STEPHEN	BAL	374	3RD WARD
THOMAS, STEPHEN	BAL	356	3RD WARD
THOMAS, STEPHEN A.	FRE	222	BUCKEYST
THOMAS, STERLING	BAL	455	8TH WARD
THOMAS, STPEHEN-BLACK	CAR	070	NO TWP L
THOMAS, SURRETIA*	TAL	044	EASTON D
THOMAS, SUSAN	TAL	053	EASTON D
THOMAS, SUSAN	WAS	145	HAGERSTO
THOMAS, SUSAN	ST	307	1ST E DI
THOMAS, SUSAN	QUE	180	2ND E DI
THOMAS, SUSAN	CAL	020	2ND DIST
THOMAS, SUSAN	FRE	046	FREDERIC
THOMAS, SUSAN	CEC	002	ELKTON 3
THOMAS, SUSAN	BAL	175	19TH WAR
THOMAS, SUSAN	BAL	254	17TH WAR
THOMAS, SUSAN	CEC	113	4TH E DI
THOMAS, SUSAN	BAL	197	17TH WAR
THOMAS, SUSANNAH	FRE	212	BUCKEYST
THOMAS, SUSINER	HAR	151	3RD DIST
THOMAS, TACEY	BAL	437	8TH WARD
THOMAS, THOMAS	ALL	248	CUMBERLA
THOMAS, THOMAS	ALL	074	5TH E.D.
THOMAS, THOMAS	DOR	307	1ST DIST
THOMAS, THOMAS	CEC	024	ELKTON 3
THOMAS, THOMAS	KEN	263	1ST DIST
THOMAS, THOMAS	PRI	093	MARLBROU
THOMAS, THOMAS C.	CAL	017	1ST DIST
THOMAS, THOMAS J.	DOR	398	1ST DIST
THOMAS, THOMAS R.	DOR	398	1ST DIST
THOMAS, THOMAS S.	CEC	073	5TH E DI
THOMAS, THOMAS W.	DOR	391	1ST DIST
THOMAS, THOMAS-BLACK	QUE	197	3RD E DI
THOMAS, THOMAS-BLACK	BAL	214	2ND WARD
THOMAS, THONE	BAL	022	2ND DIST
THOMAS, TIMOTHY	ALL	089	5TH E.D.
THOMAS, VALENTINE	FRE	012	FREDERIC
THOMAS, VERRNON *	HAR	189	3RD DIST

THOMAS, VIRGINIA MGM 322 CRACKLIN
THOMAS, VIRGINIA BAL 243 6TH WARD
THOMAS, VIRGINIA PRI 092 MARLBROU
THOMAS, W. PRI 102 SPALDING
THOMAS, W. PRI 070 MARLBROU
THOMAS, W. BAL 161 1ST WARD
THOMAS, WALTER BAL 164 16TH WAR
THOMAS, WARNER BAL 233 12TH WAR
THOMAS, WASHINGTON BAL 239 17TH WAR
THOMAS, WASHINGTON-MULATT ST 307 1ST E DI
THOMAS, WELSEY BAL 227 17TH WAR
THOMAS, WESLEY-BLACK CAR 154 NO TWP L
THOMAS, WESLY CEC 075 NORTHEAS
THOMAS, WESTEY * QUE 251 5TH E DI
THOMAS, WESTLEY BAL 343 3RD WARD
THOMAS, WILIAM WAS 017 2ND SUBD
THOMAS, WILLIAM WOR 257 1ST CENS
THOMAS, WILLIAM TAL 091 ST MICHA
THOMAS, WILLIAM ST 324 4TH E DI
THOMAS, WILLIAM QUE 217 3RD E DI
THOMAS, WILLIAM QUE 204 3RD E DI
THOMAS, WILLIAM QUE 199 3RD E DI
THOMAS, WILLIAM QUE 208 3RD E DI
THOMAS, WILLIAM QUE 213 3RD E DI
THOMAS, WILLIAM QUE 164 2ND E DI
THOMAS, WILLIAM WAS 122 HAGERSTO
THOMAS, WILLIAM WOR 201 3RD E DI
THOMAS, WILLIAM BAL 462 1ST DIST
THOMAS, WILLIAM BAL 456 8TH WARD
THOMAS, WILLIAM BAL 079 15TH WAR
THOMAS, WILLIAM BAL 095 15TH WAR
THOMAS, WILLIAM BAL 289 12TH WAR
THOMAS, WILLIAM BAL 163 1ST WARD
THOMAS, WILLIAM BAL 159 6TH WARD
THOMAS, WILLIAM BAL 043 9TH WARD
THOMAS, WILLIAM ALL 082 5TH E.D.
THOMAS, WILLIAM ANN 321 2ND DIST
THOMAS, WILLIAM BAL 319 1ST DIST
THOMAS, WILLIAM ALL 018 3RD E.D.
THOMAS, WILLIAM ALL 126 4TH E.D.
THOMAS, WILLIAM BAL 289 1ST DIST
THOMAS, WILLIAM BAL 019 1ST WARD
THOMAS, WILLIAM BAL 030 1ST WARD
THOMAS, WILLIAM BAL 134 1ST WARD
THOMAS, WILLIAM BAL 140 1ST WARD
THOMAS, WILLIAM BAL 082 18TH WAR
THOMAS, WILLIAM BAL 452 14TH WAR
THOMAS, WILLIAM BAL 453 14TH WAR
THOMAS, WILLIAM CAL 029 2ND DIST
THOMAS, WILLIAM BAL 118 11TH WAR
THOMAS, WILLIAM BAL 128 11TH WAR
THOMAS, WILLIAM CEC 139 6TH E DI
THOMAS, WILLIAM BAL 054 4TH WARD
THOMAS, WILLIAM BAL 076 4TH WARD
THOMAS, WILLIAM KEN 250 2ND DIST
THOMAS, WILLIAM QUE 127 1ST E DI
THOMAS, WILLIAM QUE 130 1ST E DI
THOMAS, WILLIAM DOR 412 1ST DIST
THOMAS, WILLIAM DOR 400 1ST DIST
THOMAS, WILLIAM DOR 401 1ST DIST
THOMAS, WILLIAM FRE 232 BUCKEYST
THOMAS, WILLIAM BAL 164 19TH WAR
THOMAS, WILLIAM BAL 160 19TH WAR
THOMAS, WILLIAM DOR 310 1ST DIST
THOMAS, WILLIAM DOR 320 1ST DIST
THOMAS, WILLIAM CEC 036 CHESAPEA
THOMAS, WILLIAM BAL 192 19TH WAR
THOMAS, WILLIAM BAL 192 19TH WAR
THOMAS, WILLIAM CAR 165 NO TWP L
THOMAS, WILLIAM MGM 370 BERRYS D
THOMAS, WILLIAM B. BAL 110 1ST WARD
THOMAS, WILLIAM C. QUE 206 3RD E DI
THOMAS, WILLIAM D. BAL 104 5TH WARD
THOMAS, WILLIAM G. BAL 138 18TH WAR
THOMAS, WILLIAM H. FRE 209 BUCKEYST
THOMAS, WILLIAM H. ST 331 4TH E DI
THOMAS, WILLIAM H. ST 325 4TH E DI
THOMAS, WILLIAM H. TAL 069 EASTON T
THOMAS, WILLIAM H.-BLACK ST 347 5TH E DI
THOMAS, WILLIAM H.-BLACK QUE 156 2ND E DI
THOMAS, WILLIAM J. MGM 371 BERRYS D
THOMAS, WILLIAM J. DOR 316 1ST DIST
THOMAS, WILLIAM J. BAL 436 14TH WAR
THOMAS, WILLIAM M. BAL 412 3RD WARD
THOMAS, WILLIAM P. MGM 347 BERRYS D
THOMAS, WILLIAM S. SOM 453 DAMES QU
THOMAS, WILLIAM T. BAL 034 9TH WARD
THOMAS, WILLIAM W. CEC 093 4TH E DI
THOMAS, WILLIAM* BAL 223 12TH WAR
THOMAS, WILLIAM-BLACK FRE 393 PETERSVI
THOMAS, WILLIAM-BLACK CAR 091 NO TWP L
THOMAS, WILLY BAL 251 12TH WAR
THOMAS, WILSON BAL 169 11TH WAR
THOMAS, ZEREMIAH FRE 299 WOODSBOR
THOMAS,ARMSTEAD, CAROLINE FRE 232 BUCKEYST
THOMAS,CHARLOTTE FRE 208 BUCKEYST
THOMAS,MARTH J. FRE 209 BUCKEYST
THOMAS,MARY CAR 150 NO TWP L
THOMEN, ARAMINTA CEC 072 5TH E DI
THOMITZ, ANDREW BAL 042 9TH WARD
THOMPHEART, JOSEPH ALL 203 CUMBERLA
THOMPCN, LOUISA HAR 053 1ST DIST
THOMPON, RICHARD H. HAR 065 1ST DIST
THOMPOSN, EEN PRI 073 MARLBROU
THOMPOSN, EMMA BAL 327 13TH WAR
THOMPOSN, WILLIAM BAL 146 1ST WARD
THOMPSING, JOHN BAL 281 2ND WARD
THOMPSNO, ST. JOHN PRI 035 VANSVILL
THOMPSON, A. PRI 095 SPALDING
THOMPSON, A. C. C. TAL 087 ST MICHA
THOMPSON, ABERTAS BAL 004 1ST WARD
THOMPSON, ABRAHAM CAR 229 5TH DIST
THOMPSON, ABRAHAM-BLACK ST 294 2ND E DI
THOMPSON, ACHILLES BAL 195 19TH WAR
THOMPSON, AGNES BAL 456 14TH WAR
THOMPSON, AGNESS BAL 155 11TH WAR
THOMPSON, ALBERT CAR 184 8TH DIST
THOMPSON, ALCY CHA 218 ALLENS F
THOMPSON, ALEXANDER BAL 229 17TH WAR
THOMPSON, ALEXANDER BAL 124 1ST WARD
THOMPSON, ALEXANDER BAL 385 3RD WARD
THOMPSON, ALEXANDER BAL 335 7TH WARD
THOMPSON, ALEXANDER ALL 073 5TH E.D.
THOMPSON, ALEXANDER BAL 173 6TH WARD
THOMPSON, ALEXANDER BAL 339 7TH WARD
THOMPSON, ALEXANDER A. BAL 307 7TH WARD
THOMPSON, ALEXANDER W. QUE 225 4TH E DI
THOMPSON, ALFRED BAL 211 19TH WAR
THOMPSON, ALINIA HAR 207 3RD DIST
THOMPSON, ALOYSINS ST 276 3RD E DI
THOMPSON, AMAND M. BAL 220 6TH WARD
THOMPSON, AMANCA BAL 200 6TH WARD
THOMPSON, AMELIA HAR 166 3RD DIST
THOMPSON, AMOS BAL 391 8TH WARD
THOMPSON, AMRY MGM 431 CLARKSTR
THOMPSON, ANDREW HAR 099 2ND DIST
THOMPSON, ANDREW CEC 087 4TH E DI
THOMPSON, ANDREW BAL 145 1ST WARD
THOMPSON, ANDRW BAL 109 1ST WARD
THOMPSON, ANN BAL 115 1ST WARD
THOMPSON, ANN BAL 050 1ST WARD
THOMPSON, ANN BAL 275 2ND WARD
THOMPSON, ANN BAL 215 6TH WARD
THOMPSON, ANN BAL 216 6TH WARD
THOMPSON, ANN BAL 234 6TH WARD
THOMPSON, ANN BAL 187 6TH WARD
THOMPSON, ANN BAL 042 15TH WAR
THOMPSON, ANN BAL 081 15TH WAR
THOMPSON, ANN BAL 093 5TH WARD
THOMPSON, ANN BAL 315 3RD WARD
THOMPSON, ANN ANN 448 HOWARD D
THOMPSON, ANN MGM 338 CRACKLIN
THOMPSON, ANN BAL 135 18TH WAR
THOMPSON, ANN CEC 194 7TH E DI
THOMPSON, ANN BAL 117 11TH WAR
THOMPSON, ANN ST 259 3RD E DI
THOMPSON, ANN PRI 065 NOTTINGH
THOMPSON, ANN E. BAL 125 11TH WAR
THOMPSON, ANN E. BAL 002 4TH WARD
THOMPSON, ANN J. ST 266 3RD E DI
THOMPSON, ANN L. BAL 346 3RD WARD
THOMPSON, ANN M. TAL 043 EASTON D
THOMPSON, ANN M. BAL 013 4TH WARD
THOMPSON, ANN-WIDOW QUE 130 1ST E DI
THOMPSON, ANNA BAL 212 19TH WAR
THOMPSON, ANNE BAL 172 11TH WAR
THOMPSON, ANNIAS CEC 057 1ST E DI
THOMPSON, ANTHONY CEC 195 6TH E DI
THOMPSON, ANTHONY DOR 429 1ST DIST
THOMPSON, ANTHONY ANN 312 1ST DIST
THOMPSON, ANTHONY PRI 095 SPALDING
THOMPSON, ARCHIBALD WAS 276 RIDGEVIL
THOMPSON, ARCHIBALD BAL 362 8TH WARD
THOMPSON, ARDELLA DOR 302 1ST DIST
THOMPSON, ARTHUR BAL 028 18TH WAR
THOMPSON, ARTHUR BAL 407 3RD WARD
THOMPSON, ARTHUR BAL 271 12TH WAR
THOMPSON, ARTHUR D. BAL 423 3RD WARD
THOMPSON, ASABEL MGM 365 BERRYS D
THOMPSON, AUGUSTUS BAL 423 3RD WARD
THOMPSON, BAKER MGM 431 CLARKSTR
THOMPSON, BARNARD CEC 058 1ST E DI
THOMPSON, BENJAMIN MGM 377 ROCKERLE
THOMPSON, BENJAMIN CEC 046 1ST E DI
THOMPSON, BENJAMIN CEC 191 5TH E DI
THOMPSON, BENJAMIN CEC 192 5TH E DI
THOMPSON, BENJAMIN ANN 420 HOWARD D
THOMPSON, C. BAL 156 1ST WARD
THOMPSON, C. BAL 169 1ST WARD
THOMPSON, C. PRI 096 SPALDING
THOMPSON, C. P. BAL 158 1ST WARD
THOMPSON, CABET CEC 075 NORTHEAS
THOMPSON, CAROLINE KEN 213 2ND DIST
THOMPSON, CASANDRA-MULATT FRE 419 8TH E DI
THOMPSON, CATHARINE BAL 156 16TH WAR
THOMPSON, CATHERINE BAL 095 10TH WAR
THOMPSON, CATHERINE MGM 431 CLARKSTR
THOMPSON, CATHERINE-BLACK FRE 041 FREDERIC
THOMPSON, CHARLES CAR 219 5TH DIST
THOMPSON, CHARLES BAL 350 13TH WAR
THOMPSON, CHARLES HAR 158 3RD DIST
THOMPSON, CHARLES BAL 160 1ST WARD
THOMPSON, CHARLES BAL 151 5TH WARD
THOMPSON, CHARLES BAL 280 2ND WARD
THOMPSON, CHARLES BAL 091 5TH WARD
THOMPSON, CHARLES BAL 118 1ST WARD
THOMPSON, CHARLES ST 268 3RD E DI
THOMPSON, CHARLES ST 277 3RD E DI
THOMPSON, CHARLES KEN 287 3RD DIST
THOMPSON, CHARLES E. FRE 202 5TH E DI
THOMPSON, CHARLES H. BAL 114 1ST WARD
THOMPSON, CHARLES H. BAL 155 1ST WARD
THOMPSON, CHARLES H. BAL 096 15TH WAR
THOMPSON, CHARLES J. HAR 162 3RD DIST
THOMPSON, CHARLES P. BAL 153 1ST WARD
THOMPSON, CHARLES ST. BAL 143 1ST WARD
THOMPSON, CHARLOTTE BAL 068 15TH WAR
THOMPSON, CIRIRO BAL 190 11TH WAR
THOMPSON, CLARE B. CHA 230 BOJANTOW
THOMPSON, CLEMENT PRI 113 PISCATAW
THOMPSON, CLEMENT PRI 113 PISCATAW
THOMPSON, CLEMENT A. ST 315 4TH E DI
THOMPSON, CLIENY BAL 061 1ST WARD
THOMPSON, CONRAD BAL 118 1ST WARD
THOMPSON, CORNELIUS BAL 366 13TH WAR
THOMPSON, DAIVD BAL 281 2ND WARD
THOMPSON, DANIEL BAL 200 6TH WARD
THOMPSON, DANIEL DOR 363 3RD DIVI
THOMPSON, DANIEL HAR 109 2ND DIST
THOMPSON, DANIEL HAR 057 1ST DIST
THOMPSON, DANIEL HAR 003 1ST DIST
THOMPSON, DANIEL PRI 059 NOTTINGH
THOMPSON, DANIEL WAS 050 2ND SUBD
THOMPSON, DAVID CAR 259 3RD DIST
THOMPSON, DAVID BAL 126 1ST WARD
THOMPSON, DAVID BAL 122 1ST WARD
THOMPSON, DAVID BAL 014 15TH WAR
THOMPSON, DAVIS BAL 106 10TH WAR
THOMPSON, DOLLY DOR 315 1ST DIST
THOMPSON, DOLLY BAL 458 14TH WAR
THOMPSON, DORCAS BAL 077 2ND DIST
THOMPSON, DOWELL-BLACK QUE 153 1ST E DI
THOMPSON, E. Y. BAL 097 10TH WAR
THOMPSON, EBENZER BAL 118 1ST WARD
THOMPSON, ED BAL 146 1ST WARD
THOMPSON, EDER BAL 159 19TH WAR
THOMPSON, EDWARD BAL 119 18TH WAR
THOMPSON, EDWARD CEC 188 7TH E DI
THOMPSON, EDWARD BAL 342 1ST DIST
THOMPSON, EDWARD KEN 301 3RD DIST
THOMPSON, EDWARD B. BAL 054 15TH WAR
THOMPSON, EDWARD J. BAL 311 3RD WARD
THOMPSON, EDWARD T. CEC 148 PORT DUP
THOMPSON, EDWARD-BLACK FRE 011 FREDERIC
THOMPSON, ELIAS BAL 391 8TH WARD
THOMPSON, ELIJAH HAR 166 3RD DIST
THOMPSON, ELIJAH KEN 234 2ND DIST
THOMPSON, ELIJAH MGM 428 CLARKSTR
THOMPSON, ELIJAH SOM 495 SALISBUR
THOMPSON, ELIZA MGM 317 CRACKLIN
THOMPSON, ELIZA FRE 432 8TH E DI
THOMPSON, ELIZA BAL 145 19TH WAR
THOMPSON, ELIZA BAL 307 7TH WARD
THOMPSON, ELIZA BAL 335 3RD WARD
THOMPSON, ELIZA BAL 343 1ST DIST
THOMPSON, ELIZA BAL 163 16TH WAR
THOMPSON, ELIZA A. ALL 111 5TH E.D.
THOMPSON, ELIZABETH BAL 070 15TH WAR
THOMPSON, ELIZABETH BAL 089 15TH WAR
THOMPSON, ELIZABETH BAL 312 3RD WARD
THOMPSON, ELIZABETH BAL 042 1ST WARD
THOMPSON, ELIZABETH BAL 349 3RD WARD
THOMPSON, ELIZABETH BAL 257 1ST DIST
THOMPSON, ELIZABETH ANN 485 HOWARD D
THOMPSON, ELIZABETH BAL 115 18TH WAR
THOMPSON, ELIZABETH MGM 317 CRACKLIN
THOMPSON, ELIZABETH MGM 350 BERRYS D
THOMPSON, ELIZABETH MGM 398 ROCKERLE
THOMPSON, ELIZABETH BAL 247 17TH WAR
THOMPSON, ELIZABETH BAL 237 17TH WAR
THOMPSON, ELIZABETH BAL 465 14TH WAR
THOMPSON, ELIZABETH BAL 021 4TH WARD
THOMPSON, ELIZABETH BAL 016 4TH WARD
THOMPSON, ELIZABETH ST 317 4TH E DI
THOMPSON, ELIZABETH ST 286 2ND E DI
THOMPSON, ELLEN ALL 218 CUMBERLA
THOMPSON, ELLEN H. BAL 423 3RD WARD
THOMPSON, EMELINE HAR 088 2ND DIST
THOMPSON, EMERSON CAL 059 3RD DIST
THOMPSON, EMERSON ANN 401 8TH DIST
THOMPSON, EMILY ALL 146 6TH E.D.
THOMPSON, EMILY BAL 036 9TH WARD
THOMPSON, EMILY F. SOM 418 PRINCESS
THOMPSON, EMORY HAR 092 2ND DIST
THOMPSON, ENOCH CHA 269 ALLENS F
THOMPSON, ENOCH BAL 351 1ST DIST
THOMPSON, EVAN FRE 273 NEW MARK
THOMPSON, EZECLO KEN 288 3RD DIST
THOMPSON, EZEKIEL CEC 191 5TH E DI
THOMPSON, FANNY ANN 316 1ST DIST
THOMPSON, FRANCES M. HAR 174 3RD DIST
THOMPSON, FRANCES M. HAR 174 3RD DIST
THOMPSON, FRANCIS CHA 290 BOJANTOW
THOMPSON, FRANCIS BAL 017 4TH WARD
THOMPSON, FRANCIS BAL 189 17TH WAR
THOMPSON, FRANCIS ST 334 4TH E DI
THOMPSON, FRANCIS A. BAL 071 18TH WAR
THOMPSON, FRED BAL 144 19TH WAR
THOMPSON, G.C. PRI 117 PISCATAW
THOMPSON, GEORGE PRI 082 QUEEN AN
THOMPSON, GEORGE ST 315 4TH E DI
THOMPSON, GEORGE ST 267 3RD E DI
THOMPSON, GEORGE FRE 305 WOODSBOR
THOMPSON, GEORGE CEC 110 4TH E DI
THOMPSON, GEORGE CEC 198 7TH E DI
THOMPSON, GEORGE HAR 003 1ST DIST
THOMPSON, GEORGE BAL 046 9TH WARD
THOMPSON, GEORGE BAL 157 1ST WARD
THOMPSON, GEORGE ANN 468 HOWARD D
THOMPSON, GEORGE ANN 338 3RD DIST
THOMPSON, GEORGE BAL 110 1ST WARD
THOMPSON, GEORGE BAL 186 5TH DIST
THOMPSON, GEORGE BAL 283 7TH WARD
THOMPSON, GEORGE C. BAL 046 9TH WARD
THOMPSON, GEORGE F. ST 260 3RD E DI
THOMPSON, GEORGE H. PRI 104 PISCATAW
THOMPSON, GEORGE W. QUE 238 5TH E DI
THOMPSON, GEORGE W. ST 256 3RD E DI
THOMPSON, GEORGE W. ANN 485 HOWARD D
THOMPSON, GEORGE W. BAL 346 1ST DIST
THOMPSON, GEORGE-BLACK QUE 157 2ND E DI
THOMPSON, GEROGE KEN 253 1ST DIST
THOMPSON, GEROGE BAL 415 1ST DIST
THOMPSON, GEROGE BAL 236 6TH WARD
THOMPSON, GILES G. PRI 105 PISCATAW
THOMPSON, GUSTABUS A. BAL 473 14TH WAR
THOMPSON, GUSTAVUS A. BAL 473 14TH WAR
THOMPSON, H. BAL 203 19TH WAR
THOMPSON, H. BAL 158 1ST WARD
THOMPSON, H. BAL 154 1ST WARD
THOMPSON, H.C. BAL 172 1ST WARD
THOMPSON, HAMET BAL 391 14TH WAR
THOMPSON, HAMILTON FRE 244 NEW MARK
THOMPSON, HANNAH CEC 197 7TH E DI
THOMPSON, HANNAH CEC 192 5TH E DI
THOMPSON, HANNAH CEC 192 5TH E DI
THOMPSON, HANNAH CEC 075 NORTHEAS
THOMPSON, HARRIET BAL 169 6TH WARD
THOMPSON, HARRIET BAL 256 6TH WARD
THOMPSON, HARRIET A. ST 304 2ND E DI
THOMPSON, HARRIOT BAL 352 3RD WARD
THOMPSON, HARRISON BAL 121 16TH WAR
THOMPSON, HARRISON BAL 285 20TH WAR
THOMPSON, HARRISON CHA 290 BOJANTOW
THOMPSON, HARY LEE DOR 437 1ST DIST
THOMPSON, HENRIETTA BAL 366 13TH WAR
THOMPSON, HENRIETTA BAL 259 6TH WARD
THOMPSON, HENRIETTA BAL 043 9TH WARD
THOMPSON, HENRY BAL 035 9TH WARD
THOMPSON, HENRY BAL 160 1ST WARD
THOMPSON, HENRY BAL 159 1ST WARD
THOMPSON, HENRY BAL 125 1ST WARD
THOMPSON, HENRY BAL 140 1ST WARD
THOMPSON, HENRY BAL 089 1ST WARD
THOMPSON, HENRY ALL 064 10TH E.D
THOMPSON, HENRY ANN 266 ANNAPOLI
THOMPSON, HENRY BAL 343 7TH WARD
THOMPSON, HENRY DOR 431 1ST DIST
THOMPSON, HENRY MGM 318 CRACKLIN
THOMPSON, HENRY CAR 230 5TH DIST
THOMPSON, HENRY CEC 051 1ST E DI
THOMPSON, HENRY FRE 081 FREDERIC
THOMPSON, HENRY ST 334 4TH E DI
THOMPSON, HENRY QUE 213 3RD E DI
THOMPSON, HENRY A. BAL 085 4TH WARD
THOMPSON, HENRY J. ANN 315 1ST DIST
THOMPSON, HENRY* DOR 462 1ST DIST
THOMPSON, HERNIETTA * FRE 252 NEW MARK
THOMPSON, HESTER KEN 283 3RD DIST
THOMPSON, HESTER KEN 283 3RD DIST
THOMPSON, HEZEKIAH BAL 240 6TH WARD
THOMPSON, HORACE MGM 431 CLARKSTR
THOMPSON, HUGH CEC 159 PORT DUP
THOMPSON, HUGH CAR 240 TANEYTOW
THOMPSON, IGNATIUS ST 260 3RD E DI
THOMPSON, IGNATIUS ST 271 3RD E DI
THOMPSON, ISAAC WAS 001 WILLIAMS
THOMPSON, ISABELLA BAL 297 7TH WARD
THOMPSON, ISABELLA BAL 363 8TH WARD
THOMPSON, ISRAEL ALL 063 10TH E.D

Name	County	Page	District
THOMPSON, J.	BAL	142	1ST WARD
THOMPSON, J.	BAL	147	1ST WARD
THOMPSON, J.	BAL	156	1ST WARD
THOMPSON, J.	BAL	157	1ST WARD
THOMPSON, J.	FRE	164	EMMITTSB
THOMPSON, J. J.	BAL	149	1ST WARD
THOMPSON, J.A.	BAL	170	1ST WARD
THOMPSON, J.M.	BAL	152	19TH WAR
THOMPSON, JACOB	BAL	112	18TH WAR
THOMPSON, JACOB	BAL	168	1ST WARD
THOMPSON, JACOB-BLACK	FRE	008	FREDERIC
THOMPSON, JAMES	CEC	216	7TH E DI
THOMPSON, JAMES	DOR	308	1ST DIST
THOMPSON, JAMES	DOR	358	3RD DIVI
THOMPSON, JAMES	FRE	271	NEW MARK
THOMPSON, JAMES	DOR	431	1ST DIST
THOMPSON, JAMES	CHA	269	ALLENS F
THOMPSON, JAMES	HAR	173	3RD DIST
THOMPSON, JAMES	BAL	007	4TH WARD
THOMPSON, JAMES	CAR	300	1ST DIST
THOMPSON, JAMES	BAL	230	17TH WAR
THOMPSON, JAMES	HAR	100	2ND DIST
THOMPSON, JAMES	HAR	059	1ST DIST
THOMPSON, JAMES	HAR	054	1ST DIST
THOMPSON, JAMES	CEC	065	1ST E DI
THOMPSON, JAMES	CEC	059	1ST E DI
THOMPSON, JAMES	BAL	149	1ST WARD
THOMPSON, JAMES	BAL	135	5TH WARD
THOMPSON, JAMES	BAL	204	6TH WARD
THOMPSON, JAMES	BAL	147	1ST WARD
THOMPSON, JAMES	ALL	202	CUMBERLA
THOMPSON, JAMES	BAL	061	15TH WAR
THOMPSON, JAMES	BAL	451	8TH WARD
THOMPSON, JAMES	BAL	046	1ST WARD
THOMPSON, JAMES	BAL	042	1ST WARD
THOMPSON, JAMES	BAL	315	7TH WARD
THOMPSON, JAMES	BAL	319	7TH WARD
THOMPSON, JAMES	BAL	460	1ST DIST
THOMPSON, JAMES	BAL	340	3RD WARD
THOMPSON, JAMES	ANN	468	HOWARD D
THOMPSON, JAMES	BAL	067	2ND DIST
THOMPSON, JAMES	ST	272	3RD E DI
THOMPSON, JAMES	ST	270	3RD E DI
THOMPSON, JAMES	QUE	239	5TH E DI
THOMPSON, JAMES	DOR	452	1ST DIST
THOMPSON, JAMES	DOR	450	1ST DIST
THOMPSON, JAMES	ST	343	5TH E DI
THOMPSON, JAMES A.	BAL	148	16TH WAR
THOMPSON, JAMES B.	DOR	456	1ST DIST
THOMPSON, JAMES B.	FRE	202	5TH E DI
THOMPSON, JAMES B.	BAL	269	20TH WAR
THOMPSON, JAMES H.	KEN	219	2ND DIST
THOMPSON, JAMES M.	ANN	491	HOWARD D
THOMPSON, JAMES R.	BAL	023	2ND DIST
THOMPSON, JAMES R.	ST	286	2ND E DI
THOMPSON, JAMES W.	QUE	184	3RD E DI
THOMPSON, JAMES W.	BAL	023	2ND DIST
THOMPSON, JAMES W.	ANN	474	HOWARD D
THOMPSON, JAMES W.	BAL	033	9TH WARD
THOMPSON, JAMES W.	DOR	448	1ST DIST
THOMPSON, JANE	DOR	421	1ST DIST
THOMPSON, JANE	CEC	112	4TH E DI
THOMPSON, JANE	BAL	041	4TH WARD
THOMPSON, JANE	BAL	107	10TH WAR
THOMPSON, JANE	BAL	083	15TH WAR
THOMPSON, JANE	BAL	186	11TH WAR
THOMPSON, JANE	BAL	261	6TH WARD
THOMPSON, JEFFERSON	MGM	431	CLARKSTR
THOMPSON, JEROME A.	ANN	484	HOWARD D
THOMPSON, JESE	DOR	464	1ST DIST
THOMPSON, JOHN	DOR	459	1ST DIST
THOMPSON, JOHN	QUE	223	4TH E DI
THOMPSON, JOHN	ST	300	2ND E DI
THOMPSON, JOHN	WAS	017	2ND SUBD
THOMPSON, JOHN	WAS	034	2ND SUBD
THOMPSON, JOHN	PRI	012	BLADENSB
THOMPSON, JOHN	ANN	469	HOWARD D
THOMPSON, JOHN	BAL	144	1ST WARD
THOMPSON, JOHN	BAL	282	2ND WARD
THOMPSON, JOHN	BAL	132	1ST WARD
THOMPSON, JOHN	BAL	452	8TH WARD
THOMPSON, JOHN	BAL	219	12TH WAR
THOMPSON, JOHN	BAL	460	8TH WARD
THOMPSON, JOHN	BAL	167	1ST WARD
THOMPSON, JOHN	BAL	170	1ST WARD
THOMPSON, JOHN	BAL	162	1ST WARD
THOMPSON, JOHN	BAL	363	1ST DIST
THOMPSON, JOHN	BAL	305	3RD WARD
THOMPSON, JOHN	ANN	516	HOWARD D
THOMPSON, JOHN	BAL	120	1ST WARD
THOMPSON, JOHN	BAL	122	1ST WARD
THOMPSON, JOHN	BAL	119	1ST WARD
THOMPSON, JOHN	BAL	027	1ST WARD
THOMPSON, JOHN	ALL	187	9TH E.D.
THOMPSON, JOHN	ANN	400	8TH DIST
THOMPSON, JOHN	HAR	065	1ST DIST
THOMPSON, JOHN	CAR	314	1ST DIST
THOMPSON, JOHN	CAR	200	4TH DIST
THOMPSON, JOHN	BAL	103	18TH WAR
THOMPSON, JOHN	DOR	448	1ST DIST
THOMPSON, JOHN	BAL	159	19TH WAR
THOMPSON, JOHN	FRE	274	NEW MARK
THOMPSON, JOHN	BAL	124	18TH WAR
THOMPSON, JOHN	FRE	323	MIDDLETO
THOMPSON, JOHN	CEC	191	5TH E DI
THOMPSON, JOHN	CEC	194	7TH E DI
THOMPSON, JOHN	CEC	195	6TH E DI
THOMPSON, JOHN	CHA	220	ALLENS F
THOMPSON, JOHN	HAR	166	3RD DIST
THOMPSON, JOHN	HAR	150	3RD DIST
THOMPSON, JOHN	HAR	138	2ND DIST
THOMPSON, JOHN	CEC	152	PORT DUP
THOMPSON, JOHN	CEC	126	5TH E DI
THOMPSON, JOHN	CEC	179	7TH E DI
THOMPSON, JOHN	BAL	337	13TH WAR
THOMPSON, JOHN	BAL	131	11TH WAR
THOMPSON, JOHN A.	BAL	237	12TH WAR
THOMPSON, JOHN A.	BAL	275	7TH WARD
THOMPSON, JOHN A.	BAL	296	7TH WARD
THOMPSON, JOHN B.	ST	291	2ND E DI
THOMPSON, JOHN B.	ST	254	3RD E DI
THOMPSON, JOHN B.	ST	263	3RD E DI
THOMPSON, JOHN F.	CHA	273	ALLENS F
THOMPSON, JOHN H.	MGM	324	CRACKLIN
THOMPSON, JOHN H.	QUE	184	3RD E DI
THOMPSON, JOHN H.	PRI	046	AQUASCO
THOMPSON, JOHN H.	BAL	032	1ST WARD
THOMPSON, JOHN H.	BAL	115	1ST WARD
THOMPSON, JOHN J.	CHA	273	ALLENS F
THOMPSON, JOHN L.	PRI	089	SPALDING
THOMPSON, JOHN P.	FRE	033	FREDERIC
THOMPSON, JOHN T.	BAL	026	9TH WARD
THOMPSON, JOHN W.	BAL	103	15TH WAR
THOMPSON, JOHN W.	HAR	085	2ND DIST
THOMPSON, JOHN W.	PRI	109	PISCATAW
THOMPSON, JOHN-BLACK	QUE	153	1ST E DI
THOMPSON, JOHNH.	ALL	220	CUMBERLA
THOMPSON, JOSEPH	BAL	165	1ST WARD
THOMPSON, JOSEPH	BAL	158	2ND DIST
THOMPSON, JOSEPH	BAL	363	8TH WARD
THOMPSON, JOSEPH	CHA	292	BOJANTOW
THOMPSON, JOSEPH	MGM	318	CRACKLIN
THOMPSON, JOSEPH	MGM	402	ROCKERLE
THOMPSON, JOSEPH	HAR	097	2ND DIST
THOMPSON, JOSEPH	BAL	268	20TH WAR
THOMPSON, JOSEPH	BAL	144	19TH WAR
THOMPSON, JOSEPH	CAR	240	TANEYTOW
THOMPSON, JOSEPH	KEN	306	3RD DIST
THOMPSON, JOSEPH	ST	281	3RD E DI
THOMPSON, JOSEPH A.	BAL	191	6TH WARD
THOMPSON, JOSEPH A.J.	MGM	420	MEDLEY 3
THOMPSON, JOSHAWAY	HAR	207	3RD DIST
THOMPSON, JOSHUA	CEC	195	6TH E DI
THOMPSON, JOSHUA	MGM	325	CRACKLIN
THOMPSON, JOSHUA	BAL	238	6TH WARD
THOMPSON, JOSHUA	ST	269	3RD E DI
THOMPSON, JOSHUA	ST	269	3RD E DI
THOMPSON, JOSHUA A.	ANN	494	HOWARD D
THOMPSON, JOSHUA T.	ST	268	3RD E DI
THOMPSON, JOSIAH J.	ST	315	4TH E DI
THOMPSON, JULIA	BAL	096	5TH WARD
THOMPSON, JULIA A.	ANN	401	8TH DIST
THOMPSON, JULIA B.	BAL	356	13TH WAR
THOMPSON, JULIET	FRE	223	BUCKEYST
THOMPSON, KENEDY	BAL	093	5TH WARD
THOMPSON, KETTY	ST	281	3RD E DI
THOMPSON, L. A.	BAL	269	20TH WAR
THOMPSON, LAURA	BAL	317	20TH WAR
THOMPSON, LAWRENCE	BAL	429	14TH WAR
THOMPSON, LEVIN	DOR	407	1ST DIST
THOMPSON, LEWIS	DOR	303	1ST DIST
THOMPSON, LEWIS	CAR	221	5TH DIST
THOMPSON, LEWIS	BAL	047	2ND DIST
THOMPSON, LEWIS S. B.	BAL	184	11TH WAR
THOMPSON, LLOYD	BAL	078	18TH WAR
THOMPSON, LOUIS	ALL	058	10TH E.D
THOMPSON, LOUISA	BAL	364	8TH WARD
THOMPSON, LOUISA	BAL	275	7TH WARD
THOMPSON, LUCINDA	BAL	064	4TH WARD
THOMPSON, LUCRETIA	CHA	273	ALLENS F
THOMPSON, LUCY	CAR	217	5TH DIST
THOMPSON, LUCY	BAL	200	6TH WARD
THOMPSON, LUCY-BLACK	FRE	042	FREDERIC
THOMPSON, LYDIA	MGM	443	CLARKSTR
THOMPSON, M.	BAL	117	1ST WARD
THOMPSON, MARGARET	ANN	467	HOWARD D
THOMPSON, MARGARET	BAL	096	2ND DIST
THOMPSON, MARGARET	MGM	341	CLARKSBU
THOMPSON, MARGARET	KEN	230	2ND DIST
THOMPSON, MARGARET	BAL	238	17TH WAR
THOMPSON, MARGARET A.	FRE	046	FREDERIC
THOMPSON, MARGARET A.	ANN	466	HOWARD D
THOMPSON, MARGARET A.	DOR	459	1ST DIST
THOMPSON, MARGRETT F.	BAL	068	18TH WAR
THOMPSON, MARIA	BAL	111	1ST WARD
THOMPSON, MARIA	BAL	048	15TH WAR
THOMPSON, MARIA C.	CHA	293	BOJANTOW
THOMPSON, MARIA-BLACK	BAL	229	2ND WARD
THOMPSON, MARIA-BLACK	ST	294	2ND E DI
THOMPSON, MARIAH	BAL	052	9TH WARD
THOMPSON, MARIAH L.*	TAL	025	EASTON D
THOMPSON, MARK	BAL	123	2ND DIST
THOMPSON, MARSHAL	CEC	074	NORTHEAS
THOMPSON, MARTHA	BAL	304	3RD WARD
THOMPSON, MARTHA E.	MGM	335	CRACKLIN
THOMPSON, MARTHA O.	BAL	217	6TH WARD
THOMPSON, MARTIN	MGM	382	ROCKERLE
THOMPSON, MARY	HAR	013	1ST DIST
THOMPSON, MARY	HAR	079	2ND DIST
THOMPSON, MARY	HAR	056	1ST DIST
THOMPSON, MARY	CHA	273	ALLENS F
THOMPSON, MARY	HAR	186	3RD DIST
THOMPSON, MARY	CEC	065	1ST E DI
THOMPSON, MARY	BAL	068	18TH WAR
THOMPSON, MARY	BAL	206	19TH WAR
THOMPSON, MARY	BAL	181	19TH WAR
THOMPSON, MARY	BAL	298	20TH WAR
THOMPSON, MARY	BAL	127	11TH WAR
THOMPSON, MARY	BAL	047	9TH WARD
THOMPSON, MARY	BAL	123	2ND DIST
THOMPSON, MARY	BAL	053	9TH WARD
THOMPSON, MARY	BAL	102	10TH WAR
THOMPSON, MARY	BAL	093	10TH WAR
THOMPSON, MARY	BAL	325	12TH WAR
THOMPSON, MARY	BAL	132	16TH WAR
THOMPSON, MARY	BAL	367	8TH WARD
THOMPSON, MARY	BAL	244	12TH WAR
THOMPSON, MARY	BAL	017	15TH WAR
THOMPSON, MARY	BAL	175	11TH WAR
THOMPSON, MARY	BAL	296	1ST DIST
THOMPSON, MARY	PRI	010	BLADENSB
THOMPSON, MARY	SOM	551	TYASKIN
THOMPSON, MARY	KEN	309	3RD DIST
THOMPSON, MARY	KEN	305	3RD DIST
THOMPSON, MARY	ST	263	3RD E DI
THOMPSON, MARY	SOM	521	BARREN C
THOMPSON, MARY A.	BAL	173	2ND DIST
THOMPSON, MARY A.	BAL	335	7TH WARD
THOMPSON, MARY A.	BAL	158	6TH WARD
THOMPSON, MARY A.	BAL	129	11TH WAR
THOMPSON, MARY A.	BAL	034	18TH WAR
THOMPSON, MARY A.	BAL	009	18TH WAR
THOMPSON, MARY A.	BAL	160	19TH WAR
THOMPSON, MARY C.	MGM	422	MEDLEY 3
THOMPSON, MARY E.	ST	286	2ND E DI
THOMPSON, MARY J.	BAL	219	6TH WARD
THOMPSON, MARY L.	ST	272	3RD E DI
THOMPSON, MARY V.	MGM	318	CRACKLIN
THOMPSON, MATHEW	ALL	148	6TH E.D.
THOMPSON, MATILDA-BLACK	QUE	186	3RD E DI
THOMPSON, MATTHEW	ALL	146	6TH E.D.
THOMPSON, MERRITT	WAS	027	2ND SUBD
THOMPSON, METTY	BAL	426	14TH WAR
THOMPSON, MICHAEL	BAL	144	1ST WARD
THOMPSON, MIDLETON	ANN	500	HOWARD D
THOMPSON, MILLICENT	CEC	065	1ST E DI
THOMPSON, MILLY	DOR	459	1ST DIST
THOMPSON, MISS E.	FRE	199	5TH E DI
THOMPSON, MITCHELE*	DOR	455	1ST DIST
THOMPSON, MORRIS	MGM	362	BERRYS D
THOMPSON, MR.*	DOR	459	1ST DIST
THOMPSON, MRS.	PRI	086	QUEEN AN
THOMPSON, MRS. H.	BAL	195	19TH WAR
THOMPSON, NACY W.	MGM	442	CLARKSTR
THOMPSON, NANCY	PRI	117	PISCATAW
THOMPSON, NANCY*	DOR	437	1ST DIST
THOMPSON, NANTZY	BAL	305	3RD WARD
THOMPSON, NATHAN	BAL	186	11TH WAR
THOMPSON, NELSON	MGM	431	CLARKSTR
THOMPSON, NERMA	BAL	212	11TH WAR
THOMPSON, NERMA	BAL	212	11TH WAR
THOMPSON, NICHOLAS	ANN	414	HOWARD D
THOMPSON, NICHOLAS	BAL	177	16TH WAR
THOMPSON, NICHOLAS-MULATT	FRE	033	FREDERIC
THOMPSON, OLOVER	BAL	356	1ST DIST
THOMPSON, OLOVER	BAL	284	1ST DIST
THOMPSON, OWEN	BAL	128	18TH WAR
THOMPSON, P.	BAL	151	1ST WARD
THOMPSON, PARKER	BAL	309	3RD WARD
THOMPSON, PARKER	HAR	059	1ST DIST
THOMPSON, PERRY	KEN	301	3RD DIST
THOMPSON, PERRY	SOM	355	BRINKLEY
THOMPSON, POLLY	BAL	412	14TH WAR
THOMPSON, PRISCILLA	CEC	137	6TH E DI
THOMPSON, R.	BAL	171	1ST WARD
THOMPSON, RACHEL	ANN	364	4TH DIST
THOMPSON, RACHEL	QUE	209	3RD E DI
THOMPSON, REBECCA	ST	306	1ST E DI
THOMPSON, REBECCA	CEC	088	4TH E DI
THOMPSON, RICHARD	BAL	343	13TH WAR
THOMPSON, RICHARD	MGM	430	CLARKSTR
THOMPSON, RICHARD	QUE	123	1ST E DI
THOMPSON, RICHARD	MGM	323	CRACKLIN
THOMPSON, RICHARD	KEN	288	3RD DIST
THOMPSON, RICHARD	DOR	459	1ST DIST
THOMPSON, RICHARD	ANN	485	HOWARD D
THOMPSON, RICHARD	ANN	280	ANNAPOLI
THOMPSON, RICHARD A.	ANN	495	HOWARD D
THOMPSON, RICHARD T.	FRE	229	BUCKEYST
THOMPSON, RICHARD W.	BAL	012	4TH WARD
THOMPSON, RICHARD W.	ANN	495	HOWARD D
THOMPSON, RICHARDSON	DOR	305	1ST DIST
THOMPSON, ROBERT	CEC	154	PORT DUP
THOMPSON, ROBERT	BAL	229	17TH WAR
THOMPSON, ROBERT	BAL	214	11TH WAR
THOMPSON, ROBERT	HAR	046	1ST DIST
THOMPSON, ROBERT	BAL	289	17TH WAR
THOMPSON, ROBERT	CEC	198	7TH E DI
THOMPSON, ROBERT	BAL	392	14TH WAR
THOMPSON, ROBERT	ALL	107	5TH E.D.
THOMPSON, ROBERT	BAL	150	1ST WARD
THOMPSON, ROBERT	BAL	235	6TH WARD
THOMPSON, ROBERT	BAL	053	1ST WARD
THOMPSON, ROBERT	BAL	147	1ST WARD
THOMPSON, ROBERT	ST	304	2ND E DI
THOMPSON, ROBERT	PRI	065	NOTTINGH
THOMPSON, ROBERT	WAS	017	2ND SUBD
THOMPSON, ROBERT	WAS	085	2ND SUBD
THOMPSON, ROBERT A.	BAL	011	4TH WARD
THOMPSON, ROBERT G.	ANN	397	8TH DIST
THOMPSON, ROSETTA	BAL	245	6TH WARD
THOMPSON, RUTH	CEC	098	3RD E DI
THOMPSON, S.	BAL	141	1ST WARD
THOMPSON, S.T.	BAL	204	11TH WAR
THOMPSON, SALLEY	BAL	456	8TH WARD
THOMPSON, SAMUEL	BAL	257	1ST DIST
THOMPSON, SAMUEL	ANN	308	1ST DIST
THOMPSON, SAMUEL	CEC	065	1ST E DI
THOMPSON, SAMUEL	CEC	065	1ST E DI
THOMPSON, SAMUEL	CEC	057	1ST E DI
THOMPSON, SAMUEL	CEC	041	CHESAPEA
THOMPSON, SAMUEL	CEC	194	7TH E DI
THOMPSON, SAMUEL	BAL	248	17TH WAR
THOMPSON, SAMUEL	CEC	160	6TH E DI
THOMPSON, SAMUEL	HAR	122	2ND DIST
THOMPSON, SAMUEL	PRI	095	SPALDING
THOMPSON, SAMUEL C.	MGM	325	CRACKLIN
THOMPSON, SAMUEL-BLACK	FRE	425	8TH E DI
THOMPSON, SARAH	CEC	152	PORT DUP
THOMPSON, SARAH	MGM	429	CLARKSTR
THOMPSON, SARAH	HAR	013	1ST DIST
THOMPSON, SARAH	FRE	066	FREDERIC
THOMPSON, SARAH	BAL	237	12TH WAR
THOMPSON, SARAH A.	BAL	061	18TH WAR
THOMPSON, SARAH A.	DOR	452	1ST DIST
THOMPSON, SARAH E.	BAL	114	18TH WAR
THOMPSON, SARAH E.	BAL	212	6TH WARD
THOMPSON, SARAH-BLACK	QUE	157	2ND E DI
THOMPSON, SEBASTAIN	ST	269	3RD E DI
THOMPSON, SETTIMUS	BAL	178	2ND DIST
THOMPSON, SHADE	KEN	288	3RD DIST
THOMPSON, SHADICK	KEN	284	3RD DIST
THOMPSON, SHADRICK	KEN	302	3RD DIST
THOMPSON, SHARAH	TAL	067	EASTON T
THOMPSON, SINIS	BAL	196	17TH WAR
THOMPSON, SMALLWOOD	FRE	026	FREDERIC
THOMPSON, SNOWDEN	ANN	469	HOWARD D
THOMPSON, SOLOMON	CAL	027	2ND DIST
THOMPSON, SOPHIA	BAL	167	16TH WAR
THOMPSON, SOPHIA	ST	268	3RD E DI
THOMPSON, SOPHIA	DOR	465	1ST DIST
THOMPSON, SOPHIA	WAS	022	2ND SUBD
THOMPSON, STEPHEN J.	HAR	160	3RD DIST
THOMPSON, STEWART	BAL	100	1ST WARD
THOMPSON, STEWART	BAL	101	1ST WARD
THOMPSON, SUSAN	BAL	247	12TH WAR
THOMPSON, SUSAN	MGM	318	CRACKLIN
THOMPSON, SUSAN	CEC	194	7TH E DI
THOMPSON, SUSAN	PRI	110	PISCATAW
THOMPSON, SUSANNA	ST	332	4TH E DI
THOMPSON, SUSANNA O.	HAR	183	3RD DIST
THOMPSON, TAZEWELL	WAS	021	2ND SUBD
THOMPSON, THOMAS	PRI	110	PISCATAW
THOMPSON, THOMAS	MGM	324	CRACKLIN
THOMPSON, THOMAS	CHA	218	ALLENS F
THOMPSON, THOMAS	DOR	357	3RD DIVI
THOMPSON, THOMAS	CEC	065	1ST E DI
THOMPSON, THOMAS	CEC	082	CHARLEST
THOMPSON, THOMAS	BAL	042	4TH WARD
THOMPSON, THOMAS	CAR	236	UNION TO
THOMPSON, THOMAS	BAL	186	5TH DIST
THOMPSON, THOMAS	BAL	186	5TH DIST
THOMPSON, THOMAS	BAL	122	1ST WARD
THOMPSON, THOMAS	ALL	071	5TH E.D.
THOMPSON, THOMAS	BAL	397	3RD WARD
THOMPSON, THOMAS	BAL	201	6TH DIST
THOMPSON, THOMAS	BAL	219	6TH DIST
THOMPSON, THOMAS E.	ANN	500	HOWARD D
THOMPSON, THOMAS H.	PRI	117	PISCATAW
THOMPSON, THOMAS J.	BAL	294	7TH WARD

Name	County	Page	District
THOMPSON, THOMAS O.	PRI	104	PISCATAW
THOMPSON, TOBY-BLACK	QUE	156	2ND E DI
THOMPSON, VACHEL R.	FRE	252	NEW MARK
THOMPSON, VIRGINIA	DOR	424	1ST DIST
THOMPSON, W. W.*	DOR	470	1ST DIST
THOMPSON, W.H.	WAS	021	2ND SUBD
THOMPSON, W.H.	BAL	115	1ST WARD
THOMPSON, WALTER	ST	274	3RD E DI
THOMPSON, WALTER H.	TAL	067	EASTON T
THOMPSON, WASHINGTON	MGM	324	CRACKLIN
THOMPSON, WAT	BAL	194	2ND WARD
THOMPSON, WESBY	DOR	302	1ST DIST
THOMPSON, WILLIAM	CEC	153	PORT DUP
THOMPSON, WILLIAM	CEC	187	7TH E DI
THOMPSON, WILLIAM	MGM	318	CRACKLIN
THOMPSON, WILLIAM	CHA	263	MIDDLETO
THOMPSON, WILLIAM	CHA	289	MIDDLETO
THOMPSON, WILLIAM	CHA	275	ALLENS F
THOMPSON, WILLIAM	CHA	264	MIDDLETO
THOMPSON, WILLIAM	HAR	135	2ND DIST
THOMPSON, WILLIAM	HAR	151	3RD DIST
THOMPSON, WILLIAM	HAR	135	2ND DIST
THOMPSON, WILLIAM	MGM	349	BERRYS D
THOMPSON, WILLIAM	HAR	122	2ND DIST
THOMPSON, WILLIAM	BAL	135	18TH WAR
THOMPSON, WILLIAM	BAL	131	18TH WAR
THOMPSON, WILLIAM	BAL	021	4TH WARD
THOMPSON, WILLIAM	BAL	010	18TH WAR
THOMPSON, WILLIAM	BAL	103	18TH WAR
THOMPSON, WILLIAM	CHA	221	ALLENS F
THOMPSON, WILLIAM	CEC	193	5TH E DI
THOMPSON, WILLIAM	CEC	192	5TH E DI
THOMPSON, WILLIAM	CEC	192	5TH E DI
THOMPSON, WILLIAM	CEC	190	5TH E DI
THOMPSON, WILLIAM	BAL	157	11TH WAR
THOMPSON, WILLIAM	HAR	029	1ST DIST
THOMPSON, WILLIAM	MGM	431	CLARKSTR
THOMPSON, WILLIAM	MGM	391	ROCKERLE
THOMPSON, WILLIAM	MGM	375	ROCKERLE
THOMPSON, WILLIAM	MGM	375	ROCKERLE
THOMPSON, WILLIAM	HAR	106	2ND DIST
THOMPSON, WILLIAM	HAR	105	2ND DIST
THOMPSON, WILLIAM	SOM	418	PRINCESS
THOMPSON, WILLIAM	BAL	243	6TH WARD
THOMPSON, WILLIAM	BAL	021	9TH WARD
THOMPSON, WILLIAM	BAL	151	1ST WARD
THOMPSON, WILLIAM	BAL	170	1ST WARD
THOMPSON, WILLIAM	BAL	161	1ST WARD
THOMPSON, WILLIAM	BAL	114	1ST WARD
THOMPSON, WILLIAM	BAL	245	1ST DIST
THOMPSON, WILLIAM	BAL	003	1ST WARD
THOMPSON, WILLIAM	BAL	098	1ST WARD
THOMPSON, WILLIAM	BAL	042	1ST WARD
THOMPSON, WILLIAM	BAL	155	2ND DIST
THOMPSON, WILLIAM	BAL	356	3RD WARD
THOMPSON, WILLIAM	BAL	136	1ST WARD
THOMPSON, WILLIAM	BAL	316	3RD WARD
THOMPSON, WILLIAM	BAL	356	1ST DIST
THOMPSON, WILLIAM	ALL	092	5TH E.D.
THOMPSON, WILLIAM	ANN	304	1ST DIST
THOMPSON, WILLIAM	BAL	286	2ND WARD
THOMPSON, WILLIAM	BAL	317	7TH WARD
THOMPSON, WILLIAM	BAL	133	2ND DIST
THOMPSON, WILLIAM	BAL	058	2ND DIST
THOMPSON, WILLIAM	DOR	462	1ST DIST
THOMPSON, WILLIAM	KEN	302	3RD DIST
THOMPSON, WILLIAM	PRI	103	SPALDING
THOMPSON, WILLIAM A.	BAL	312	7TH WARD
THOMPSON, WILLIAM A.	BAL	399	3RD WARD
THOMPSON, WILLIAM B.	BAL	269	20TH WAR
THOMPSON, WILLIAM C.	KEN	275	1ST DIST
THOMPSON, WILLIAM F.	ST	305	1ST E DI
THOMPSON, WILLIAM F.	PRI	109	PISCATAW
THOMPSON, WILLIAM H.	HAR	013	1ST DIST
THOMPSON, WILLIAM H.	BAL	196	19TH WAR
THOMPSON, WILLIAM H.	FRE	251	NEW MARK
THOMPSON, WILLIAM H.	ANN	340	3RD DIST
THOMPSON, WILLIAM H.	BAL	354	3RD WARD
THOMPSON, WILLIAM J.	CHA	235	HILLTOP
THOMPSON, WILLIAM K.	TAL	020	EASTON D
THOMPSON, WILLIAM L.	QUE	223	4TH E DI
THOMPSON, WILLIAM L.	QUE	168	2ND E DI
THOMPSON, WILLIAM M.	FRE	385	PETERSVI
THOMPSON, WILLIAM N.	ALL	252	CUMBERLA
THOMPSON, WILLIAM R.	ANN	265	ANNAPOLI
THOMPSON, WILLIAM R.	DOR	437	1ST DIST
THOMPSON, WILLIAM-BLACK	FRE	240	NEW MARK
THOMPSON, WILLIAM-BLACK	QUE	155	2ND E DI
THOMPSON, WILLIS	BAL	244	6TH WARD
THOMPSON, ZACH	KEN	288	3RD DIST
THOMPSON, ZACHARIAH	MGM	342	CLARKSBU
THOMPSON, ZENA	BAL	356	1ST DIST
THOMPSON,A NN E.	ST	310	1ST E DI
THOMPSON,ANN	ST	276	3RD E DI
THOMPSON,MARY	BAL	063	2ND DIST
THOMPSON,MARY W.	BAL	246	12TH WAR
THOMPSON,W ILLIAM	BAL	113	1ST WARD
THOMPSON,W ILLIAM	BAL	128	1ST WARD
THOMS, DANIEL	WAS	189	1ST DIST
THOMS, GEORGE	FRE	401	JEFFERSO
THOMS, WILLIAM	BAL	162	1ST WARD
THOMSA, GEORGE P.	BAL	475	14TH WAR
THOMSEN, CHRISTOPHER	BAL	209	2ND WARD
THOMSER, L.	BAL	153	11TH WAR
THOMSON, ABRAM	BAL	056	2ND DIST
THOMSON, AMY	WAS	252	1ST DIST
THOMSON, CATHARINE	CAR	288	7TH DIST
THOMSON, CHARLES	BAL	028	2ND DIST
THOMSON, CONRAD	WAS	186	BOONSBOR
THOMSON, DAVID	WAS	212	1ST DIST
THOMSON, DERRY	BAL	257	1ST DIST
THOMSON, EDWARD D.	CAR	163	NO TWP L
THOMSON, ELIZA	WAS	138	HAGERSTO
THOMSON, ELIZABETH	CAR	241	TANEYTOW
THOMSON, ELIZABETH	BAL	451	1ST DIST
THOMSON, ELIZABETH *	BAL	321	20TH WAR
THOMSON, FEALDIER	FRE	387	PETERSVI
THOMSON, H. G.	BAL	102	10TH WAR
THOMSON, HAGAR	ANN	317	1ST DIST
THOMSON, HANNAH C.	WAS	276	RIDGEVIL
THOMSON, HENRY	CAR	283	7TH DIST
THOMSON, HORATIO	MGM	347	BERRYS D
THOMSON, JOHN	BAL	284	12TH WAR
THOMSON, JOHN	BAL	130	1ST WARD
THOMSON, JOHN H.	CAR	158	NO TWP L
THOMSON, MARY	WAS	127	HAGERSTO
THOMSON, MARY E.	WAS	138	HAGERSTO
THOMSON, RACHEAL	WAS	190	1ST DIST
THOMSON, SAMUEL	CAR	288	7TH DIST
THOMSON, SARAH	CAR	154	NO TWP L
THOMSON, THOMAS	WAS	167	1ST DIST
THOMSON, VICTOR	WAS	124	HAGERSTO
THOMSON, WILLIAM	WAS	124	HAGERSTO
THOMSON, WILLIAM	WAS	126	2ND DIST
THOMSON, WILLIAM	BAL	158	1ST WARD
THOMSON, WILLIAM S.	BAL	027	2ND DIST
THOMSON,MARY	BAL	027	2ND DIST
THOMSON,MARY	CAR	391	2ND DIST
THOMSPON, CHARLES T.	BAL	156	1ST WARD
THOMSPON, DAVID	BAL	115	1ST WARD
THOMSPON, DAVID-BLACK	QUE	131	1ST E DI
THOMSPON, E.	BAL	281	2ND WARD
THOMSPON, JULIA ANN	BAL	337	13TH WAR
THOMSPON, JULY ANN-MULATT	FRE	231	BUCKEYST
THOMSPON, KINSEY	BAL	279	2ND WARD
THOMSPON, MARIAH-MULATTO	FRE	437	8TH E DI
THOMSPON, MARY J.	BAL	377	13TH WAR
THOMTON, M.	BAL	127	5TH WARD
THONIAS, STEPHEN *	HAR	034	1ST DIST
THONSTICN, ROBERT *	HAR	206	3RD DIST
THOOPER, J.T.	BAL	003	18TH WAR
THORINGTON, JOSEPH	BAL	391	8TH WARD
THORINGTON, RACHAEL *	BAL	412	8TH WARD
THORINGTON, SAMUEL	BAL	290	7TH WARD
THORINGTON, WILLIAM W.	BAL	290	3RD WARD
THORMAN, HENRY	BAL	366	13TH WAR
THORN, ANN	ANN	455	HOWARD D
THORN, ANN M.	ST	336	4TH E DI
THORN, HENRY C.	PRI	109	PISCATAW
THORN, HORACE	BAL	167	1ST WARD
THORN, JOHN	ANN	342	3RD DIST
THORN, KETTY ANN	BAL	353	13TH WAR
THORN, MARY A.	BAL	138	11TH WAR
THORN, SAMUEL	CAL	038	2ND DIST
THORN, SAMUEL-MULATTO	FRE	388	PETERSVI
THORN, THOMAS	BAL	102	18TH WAR
THORN, THOMAS	PRI	108	PISCATAW
THORN, THOMAS E.	PRI	119	PISCATAW
THORN, WASHINGTON	PRI	119	PISCATAW
THORN, WILLAIM	PRI	109	PISCATAW
THORN, WILLAIM	PRI	119	PISCATAW
THORN, WILLIAM	PRI	117	PISCATAW
THORNBEAN, BROTHER	BAL	216	11TH WAR
THORNBURG, ELIZABETH	BAL	437	8TH WARD
THORNBURGH, MARGARET	BAL	381	13TH WAR
THORNBURGH, S.	ALL	134	4TH E.D.
THORNE, FRANCIS	BAL	281	7TH WARD
THORNE, JOHN	BAL	055	18TH WAR
THORNS, JOHN	BAL	186	11TH WAR
THORNSBURGH, GEORGE	WAS	133	HAGERSTO
THORNSBURGH, GEORGE T.	WAS	134	HAGERSTO
THORNSBURGH, ROBERT C.	WAS	161	HAGERSTO
THORNSON, A.	BAL	138	1ST WARD
THORNTON, A. W.	BAL	037	9TH WARD
THORNTON, AARON	BAL	121	18TH WAR
THORNTON, ANN	BAL	162	2ND DIST
THORNTON, BRIDGET	BAL	287	12TH WAR
THORNTON, CAROLINE	BAL	355	13TH WAR
THORNTON, CATHARINE	BAL	213	11TH WAR
THORNTON, DAVID-MULATTO	FRE	452	8TH E DI
THORNTON, EDWARD-BLACK	MGM	421	MEDLEY 3
THORNTON, ELIZABETH	BAL	077	2ND DIST
THORNTON, FRANCES	BAL	134	2ND DIST
THORNTON, HARRIET	ST	292	2ND E DI
THORNTON, HULDY	HAR	112	2ND DIST
THORNTON, JAREY	HAR	070	1ST DIST
THORNTON, JOHN	QUE	125	1ST E DI
THORNTON, JOHN	MGM	348	BERRYS D
THORNTON, JOHN	BAL	127	1ST WARD
THORNTON, MARTHA	BAL	272	17TH WAR
THORNTON, MARTIN	BAL	188	11TH WAR
THORNTON, MARY ANN	FRE	162	EMMITTSB
THORNTON, MARY R.	FRE	065	FREDERIC
THORNTON, P.A.	BAL	173	1ST WARD
THORNTON, PATRICK	ANN	426	HOWARD D
THORNTON, PEGGY	BAL	091	2ND DIST
THORNTON, SAMUEL	BAL	133	2ND DIST
THORNTON, STEPHEN	BAL	385	13TH WAR
THORNTON, STEVEN	BAL	161	2ND DIST
THORNTON, THOMAS	BAL	462	1ST DIST
THORNTON, THOMAS	WOR	281	BERLIN 1
THORNTON, WASHINGTON	ALL	236	CUMBERLA
THORNTON, WILLIAM	ANN	344	3RD DIST
THORNTON, WILLIAM	BAL	257	1ST DIST
THORNTON, WILLIAM	BAL	262	17TH WAR
THORP, ANNA	WAS	222	1ST DIST
THORP, JAMES	BAL	292	12TH WAR
THORPE, CHARLES J.R.	BAL	173	19TH WAR
THORPE, JOHN	BAL	154	19TH WAR
THORPE, WILLIAM	BAL	388	13TH WAR
THORPE, WILLIAM J.	BAL	148	19TH WAR
THORPS, JOSHUA	BAL	009	4TH WARD
THRALL, CHALRES	BAL	116	18TH WAR
THRASHER, ENOCH	ALL	138	6TH E.D.
THRASHER, HARRIET	FRE	381	PETERSVI
THRASHER, ISAAC	ALL	152	6TH E.D.
THRASHER, ROBERT K.	FRE	407	JEFFERSO
THRASHER, THADDEUS	FRE	391	PETERSVI
THRASHER, THOMAS R.L.	FRE	404	JEFFERSO
THRASHER,W.A.	ALL	172	7TH E.D.
THRAUTZ, JACOB	BAL	238	2ND WARD
THRAVER, BENIT	BAL	135	11TH WAR
THRAWLEY, MARY	KEN	286	3RD DIST
THREENES, THOMAS	FRE	276	NEW MARK
THRIFT, CHARITY D.	MGM	432	CLARKSTR
THRIFT, COLMORE	MGM	383	ROCKERLE
THRIFT, JOHN L.	BAL	164	1ST WARD
THRIFT, MARY	BAL	255	20TH WAR
THRIFT, REBECCA	MGM	429	CLARKSTR
THRIFT, SAMUEL	MGM	402	ROCKERLE
THRISBY, LEWIS	BAL	082	1ST WARD
THROE, SAMUEL C.	MGM	358	BERRYS D
THRONG, TRACY	BAL	055	18TH WAR
THRONTON, FRANCIS A.	BAL	446	14TH WAR
THROUGH, MARGARET	BAL	034	2ND DIST
THROUGH, MARY A.	BAL	034	2ND DIST
THROW, MARGARET	BAL	025	2ND DIST
THRUSH, GEORGE	BAL	149	5TH WARD
THRUSH, MARY J.	BAL	157	16TH WAR
THRUST, JOH	ALL	230	CUMBERLA
THUMB, BENJAMIN	WAS	253	1ST DIST
THUMB, DAVID	WAS	105	2ND DIST
THUMB, JACOB	WAS	105	2ND DIST
THUMLERT, JAMES E.	BAL	262	17TH WAR
THUMLERT, MARGARET A.	BAL	264	17TH WAR
THUMLERT, WILLIAM H.	BAL	047	15TH WAR
THUMMER, HENRY	BAL	276	17TH WAR
THUNDER, HENRY G.	BAL	073	10TH WAR
THUNDS, JAMES	BAL	290	20TH WAR
THUNE, CHARLES*	BAL	111	10TH WAR
THUNN, CHARLES*	BAL	111	10TH WAR
THURFMAN, CATHARINE	WAS	293	1ST DIST
THURL, RICHARD	ANN	373	4TH DIST
THURLES, GEORGE W.	ANN	373	4TH DIST
THURMAN, HENRY	BAL	475	14TH WAR
THURSBY, SARAH	BAL	145	16TH WAR
THURSDAY, JOHN	ALL	127	4TH E.D.
THURSH, NICHOLAS	BAL	141	16TH WAR
THURSTIN, DAVID J.	BAL	271	20TH WAR
THURSTON, EDWAR	ANN	460	HOWARD D
THURSTON, ELIZA	BAL	120	5TH WARD
THURSTON, ISAAC	BAL	394	1ST DIST
THURSTON, JOHN B.	WAS	134	HAGERSTO
THURSTON, PHINEAS	BAL	047	9TH WARD
THURSTON, SARAH	WAS	134	HAGERSTO
THUSTON, CHARLES M.	ALL	207	CUMBERLA
THUSTON, SCOTT	ALL	208	CUMBERLA
TIBBALS, SAMUEL A.	BAL	129	16TH WAR
TIBBET, HAMILTON	ALL	099	5TH E.D.
TIBBET, JAMES	HAR	198	3RD DIST
TIBBET, RANSOM	ALL	099	5TH E.D.
TIBBETS, MARTHA	BAL	440	14TH WAR
TIBBETS, THOMAS	BAL	170	1ST WARD
TIBBETT, HIRAM	ALL	099	5TH E.D.
TIBBETT, JAMES	BAL	002	4TH WARD
TIBBETT, JOHN	ALL	099	5TH E.D.
TIBBETT, WILLIAM	ALL	099	5TH E.D.
TIBBITT, J.	BAL	142	1ST WARD
TIBBS, WILLIAM	BAL	145	1ST WARD
TIBBULS, EMMA	BAL	244	20TH WAR
TIBBULS, THOMAS	BAL	244	20TH WAR
TIBER, EBERHART	BAL	339	7TH WARD
TIBER, JOHN F.	BAL	339	7TH WARD
TIBERS, WILLIAM	CEC	065	1ST E DI
TIBET, SAMUEL	CEC	051	1ST E DI
TIBETT, JOHN	BAL	058	1ST WARD
TIBSON, JOHN	BAL	160	1ST WARD
TICE, DANUEL	WAS	119	2ND DIST
TICE, ELIZABETH	FRE	024	FREDERIC
TICE, EMANUEL	WAS	116	2ND DIST
TICE, H.H.	WAS	148	HAGERSTO
TICE, JOHN *	BAL	354	1ST DIST
TICE, JOHN M.	WAS	141	HAGERSTO
TICE, SAMUEL	WAS	111	2ND DIST
TICE, WILLIAM	BAL	395	1ST DIST
TICE,R ELIZABETH	ST	344	5TH E DI
TICER, J.C.	ST	344	5TH E DI
TICHTENWALTER, ADAM	CAR	314	1ST DIST
TICKEL, FRANCIS	FRE	254	NEW MARK
TICKNER, WILLIAM	BAL	056	15TH WAR
TIDBALL, R.M.	WAS	133	HAGERSTO
TIDDEN, MARY*	BAL	351	3RD WARD
TIDEY, WILLIAM	FRE	301	WOODSBOR
TIDINGS, ELIZABETH	BAL	378	3RD WARD
TIDINGS, MARY	BAL	384	3RD WARD
TIDINGS, MARY	PRI	028	VANSVILL
TIDINGS, SAMUEL	ANN	275	ANNAPOLI
TIDINGS, SAMUEL *	BAL	082	2ND DIST
TIDINGS, SUSAN	BAL	414	8TH WARD
TIDINGS, THOAMS	CAL	016	1ST DIST
TIDINSG, SAMUEL R.	CAL	011	1ST DIST
TIDY, JOHN	BAL	288	20TH WAR
TIEGNOR, JOHN	HAR	127	2ND DIST
TIEL, THOMAS A.	BAL	071	1ST WARD
TIELMAN, JSOEPH	BAL	258	6TH WARD
TIERLEY, JAMES	ALL	050	10TH E.D
TIERMAN, WILLIAM	BAL	059	10TH WAR
TIERNAN, PATRICK	BAL	361	8TH WARD
TIERNAN, THOMAS	BAL	409	3RD WARD
TIFFANY, GEORGE	BAL	203	11TH WAR
TIFFANY, HENRY	BAL	314	20TH WAR
TIFFANY, OSMOND C.	BAL	153	11TH WAR
TIFFANY, WILLIAM	BAL	202	11TH WAR
TIFTON, ANN	BAL	415	1ST DIST
TIG, JANE M.	WOR	181	6TH E DI
TIG, LOUISA	WOR	201	3RD E DI
TIGELBOMB, RACHEL	BAL	334	7TH WARD
TIGEMAN, VINCENT	BAL	175	2ND DIST
TIGERT, WILLIAM	WAS	255	1ST DIST
TIGHAM, THOMAS *	ANN	356	3RD DIST
TIGHE, JAMES	BAL	138	1ST WARD
TIGHLMAN, ELIZA	CEC	022	ELKTON 3
TIGHMAN, MICHEAL	BAL	246	6TH WARD
TIGHMAN, RICHARD	BAL	330	7TH WARD
TIGHT, ELIZABETH	WOR	185	7TH E DI
TIGHT, WILLIAM	WOR	186	7TH E DI
TIGLIN, ANDREW	BAL	163	19TH WAR
TIGLMAN, ANN	BAL	342	7TH WARD
TIGLMAN, MACE	BAL	397	8TH WARD
TIGNER, THOMAS	SOM	448	DAMES QU
TIGUE, CATHAINE	BAL	391	14TH WAR
TIHLMAN, THOMAS	WAS	139	HAGERSTO
TILDEN, ANNA M.	QUE	252	5TH E DI
TILDEN, ANNA M.	QUE	245	5TH E DI
TILDEN, CAHRLES	KEN	248	2ND DIST
TILDEN, EDWARD	HAR	175	3RD DIST
TILDEN, EDWARD	CAR	092	NO TWP L
TILDEN, LAURA	KEN	245	2ND DIST
TILDEN, LOUISA	BAL	035	4TH WARD
TILDEN, MARY E.	BAL	397	14TH WAR
TILDEN, MARY E.	QUE	170	2ND E DI
TILDEN, MARY*	BAL	351	3RD WARD
TILDEN, REBECCA B.	KEN	234	2ND DIST
TILDEN, SOPHIA	HAR	180	3RD DIST
TILDEN, THOMAS	HAR	078	2ND DIST
TILDERMAN, ELIZA	BAL	093	5TH WARD
TILE, JOHN	CAR	285	7TH DIST
TILEMAN, HARRIET	BAL	420	3RD WARD
TILES, RACHEL A.	ANN	519	HOWARD D
TILETSON, CELA	TAL	094	ST MICHA
TILGARD, JOHN W.	BAL	059	10TH WAR
TILGHAM, JOSHUA	WOR	174	6TH E DI
TILGHAM, LEVI-BLACK	CAR	169	NO TWP L
TILGHAM, NOAH J.	WOR	174	6TH E DI
TILGHANAN, ROBERT*	BAL	110	10TH WAR
TILGHMAN, ALEXANDER-BLACK	CAR	167	NO TWP L
TILGHMAN, ANN M.	TAL	026	EASTON D
TILGHMAN, ANNA	TAL	026	EASTON D
TILGHMAN, ANNA	BAL	234	6TH WARD
TILGHMAN, ANNA B.	ALL	257	CUMBERLA
TILGHMAN, ARTHUR	BAL	252	6TH WARD
TILGHMAN, CATHARINE	DOR	298	1ST DIST
TILGHMAN, CHARLES	DOR	457	1ST DIST
TILGHMAN, CLOA *	SOM	420	PRINCESS
TILGHMAN, DANIEL	CAR	155	NO TWP L
TILGHMAN, DANIEL	TAL	043	EASTON D
TILGHMAN, DANIEL	TAL	063	EASTON D
TILGHMAN, DAVID	BAL	151	16TH WAR
TILGHMAN, ELI	TAL	102	ST MICHA
TILGHMAN, ELI	TAL	110	ST MICHA

TILGHMAN, ELIZA TAL 039 EASTON D
TILGHMAN, ELIZABETH WOR 167 6TH E DI
TILGHMAN, ELIZABETH KEN 290 3RD DIST
TILGHMAN, ELIZABETH BAL 417 14TH WAR
TILGHMAN, ELIZABETH DOR 318 1ST DIST
TILGHMAN, ELIZABETH* TAL 007 EASTON D
TILGHMAN, FAYETT TAL 076 EASTON T
TILGHMAN, FRANCIS BAL 173 6TH WARD
TILGHMAN, FRISBY WAS 033 2ND SUBD
TILGHMAN, GEORGE TAL 028 EASTON D
TILGHMAN, GEORGE BAL 332 1ST DIST
TILGHMAN, GEORGE-BLACK WOR 327 1ST E DI
TILGHMAN, HARRIET TAL 026 EASTON D
TILGHMAN, HARRIET BAL 057 10TH WAR
TILGHMAN, HARRIET KEN 216 2ND DIST
TILGHMAN, HENRIETTA KEN 290 3RD DIST
TILGHMAN, HENRIETTA M. TAL 025 EASTON D
TILGHMAN, HENRY SOM 394 BRINKLEY
TILGHMAN, HENRY C. TAL 002 EASTON D
TILGHMAN, HENRY* TAL 017 EASTON D
TILGHMAN, HENRY-BLACK QUE 168 2ND E DI
TILGHMAN, HENRY-BLACK CAR 144 NO TWP L
TILGHMAN, IMANUEL-BLACK CAR 087 NO TWP L
TILGHMAN, ISAIAH BAL 028 15TH WAR
TILGHMAN, JACOB KEN 221 2ND DIST
TILGHMAN, JAMES QUE 190 3RD E DI
TILGHMAN, JAMES SOM 399 BRINKLEY
TILGHMAN, JERRY-MULATTO CAR 138 NO TWP L
TILGHMAN, JIM TAL 030 EASTON D
TILGHMAN, JOHN TAL 030 EASTON D
TILGHMAN, JOHN SOM 401 BRINKLEY
TILGHMAN, JOHN QUE 190 3RD E DI
TILGHMAN, JOHN WOR 174 6TH E DI
TILGHMAN, JOHN KEN 239 2ND DIST
TILGHMAN, JOSEPH B. SOM 408 DUBLIN D
TILGHMAN, LEVIN BAL 174 6TH WARD
TILGHMAN, LITTLETON P. WOR 234 6TH E DI
TILGHMAN, LOUISA BAL 197 11TH WAR
TILGHMAN, MARY BAL 071 15TH WAR
TILGHMAN, MARY BAL 077 15TH WAR
TILGHMAN, MARY WOR 234 6TH E DI
TILGHMAN, MARY WAS 140 HAGERSTO
TILGHMAN, MARY QUE 241 5TH E DI
TILGHMAN, MARY J. WOR 331 1ST E DI
TILGHMAN, MARY J. TAL 028 EASTON D
TILGHMAN, MATTHEW W. QUE 219 3RD E DI
TILGHMAN, MIKE TAL 007 EASTON D
TILGHMAN, MONICA-MULATTO FRE 221 BUCKEYST
TILGHMAN, NATHANIEL KEN 244 2ND DIST
TILGHMAN, OLIVER P. SOM 494 SALISBUR
TILGHMAN, PERE QUE 205 3RD E DI
TILGHMAN, PERE KEN 212 2ND DIST
TILGHMAN, PETER KEN 254 1ST DIST
TILGHMAN, PETER KEN 268 1ST DIST
TILGHMAN, PETER WOR 193 8TH E DI
TILGHMAN, ROBERT BAL 294 17TH WAR
TILGHMAN, ROBERT BAL 090 10TH WAR
TILGHMAN, SAMUEL FRE 267 NEW MARK
TILGHMAN, SAMUEL BAL 389 13TH WAR
TILGHMAN, SARAH TAL 074 EASTON T
TILGHMAN, SHARLET TAL 070 EASTON T
TILGHMAN, STEPHEN-BLACK QUE 163 2ND E DI
TILGHMAN, SUSAN TAL 098 ST MICHA
TILGHMAN, SUSAN ANN 351 3RD DIST
TILGHMAN, TENET GEN.* TAL 039 EASTON D
TILGHMAN, THOMAS DOR 457 1ST DIST
TILGHMAN, WILLIAM TAL 098 ST MICHA
TILGHMAN, WILLIAM SOM 395 BRINKLEY
TILGHMAN, WILLIAM BAL 417 14TH WAR
TILGHMAN, WILLIAM DOR 299 1ST DIST
TILGHMAN, WILLIAM B. QUE 188 3RD E DI
TILGHMAN, WILLIAM B. WOR 197 8TH E DI
TILGHMAN, WILLIAM H. TAL 069 EASTON T
TILGHMAN, WILLIAM-BLACK QUE 154 1ST E DI
TILGHONAN, PATIENCE DOR 297 1ST DIST
TILGHURAN, WILLIAM* DOR 316 1ST DIST
TILGLNMAN, JOHN C. * QUE 238 5TH E DI
TILGLNMAN, WILLIAM C. * QUE 238 5TH E DI
TILGLRMAN, CHALES C. QUE 242 5TH E DI
TILGLRMAN, EDWARD QUE 238 5TH E DI
TILGLRMAN, JAMES C. QUE 238 5TH E DI
TILGLRMAN, SAMUEL P. QUE 248 5TH E DI
TILGMAN, ELIZA BAL 204 11TH WAR
TILGMAN, SUSAN-BLACK FRE 038 FREDERIC
TILGTRAMAN, RICHARD * QUE 238 5TH E DI
TILGTRMAN, JAMES QUE 242 5TH E DI
TILLARD, ESTEP E. * ANN 408 8TH DIST
TILLER, F. W. BAL 013 4TH WARD
TILLER, MARTHA-BLACK QUE 132 1ST E DI
TILLER, PERRE-BLACK QUE 142 1ST E DI
TILLER, SHADRACK-BLACK QUE 147 1ST E DI
TILLER, WESLEY-BLACK QUE 145 1ST E DI
TILLERY, JOHN BAL 017 9TH WARD
TILLET, GEORGE BAL 112 2ND DIST
TILLETT, D.H. WAS 021 2ND SUBD
TILLETT, HARRIET A. BAL 055 15TH WAR
TILLGHMAN, EDWARD J. BAL 214 17TH WAR
TILLGHMAN, JULIANN BAL 201 17TH WAR
TILLGHMAN, WILLIAM BAL 214 17TH WAR
TILLGMAN, SARAH BAL 124 5TH WARD
TILLILOW, EUPHELIA WAS 139 HAGERSTO
TILLINGHAST, FRANCIS QUE 147 1ST E DI
TILLIS, A. BAL 154 1ST WARD
TILLISON, GEORGE CEC 008 ELKTON 3
TILLISON, ISAAC CEC 107 3RD E DI
TILLISON, MATILDA KEN 224 2ND DIST
TILLISON, PERRY CEC 008 ELKTON 3
TILLISON, SUSAN G. CEC 148 PORT DUP
TILLISSON, MARY J. BAL 224 17TH WAR
TILLMAN, CALEB BAL 241 17TH WAR
TILLMAN, CATHARINE BAL 022 1ST WARD
TILLMAN, HARRIET* BAL 312 3RD WARD
TILLMAN, HENRY SOM 483 TRAPP DI
TILLMAN, JOHN CAR 193 4TH DIST
TILLMAN, MARY ANN 303 1ST DIST
TILLMAN, ROBERT SOM 402 BRINKLEY
TILLMAN, SAMUEL H. SOM 402 BRINKLEY
TILLMAN, SARAH BAL 113 1ST WARD
TILLMAN, WILLIAM BAL 130 2ND DIST
TILLOTT, COLEMAN HAR 110 2ND DIST
TILLOTTSON, JOHN CAR 092 NO TWP L
TILLOW, E. WAS 197 1ST DIST
TILLSON, MARGARET FRE 259 NEW MARK
TILMAN, GEORGE WOR 312 2ND E DI
TILMAN, HENRY ANN 356 3RD DIST
TILMAN, JACOB BAL 231 1ST DIST
TILMAN, JAMES BAL 436 14TH WAR
TILMAN, JANE CEC 037 CHESAPEA
TILMAN, JOHN BAL 337 1ST DIST
TILMAN, JOHN BAL 126 2ND DIST

TILMAN, JOHN PRI 119 PISCATAW
TILMAN, LJODUP * ANN 290 ANNAPOLI
TILMAN, MARY A. ANN 356 3RD DIST
TILMAN, NANCY PRI 118 PISCATAW
TILMAN, PRISCILLA ST 290 2ND E DI
TILMAN, RACHEL ANN 336 3RD DIST
TILMAN, ROBERT CEC 037 CHESAPEA
TILMAN, SOPHIA BAL 297 1ST DIST
TILMAN, SUSAN BAL 459 1ST DIST
TILMAN, ZELER BAL 384 8TH WARD
TILP, EVA ALL 239 CUMBERLA
TILP, GEORGE ALL 245 CUMBERLA
TILP, HENRY ALL 244 CUMBERLA
TILSON, MARGARET BAL 346 7TH WARD
TILTER, ISAAC CEC 026 ELKTON 3
TILTON, CATHARINE WAS 219 1ST DIST
TILTON, JOSEPHINE ANN 285 ANNAPOLI
TILTON, LENT E. ANN 285 ANNAPOLI
TILTONE, CARLINE V. FRE 057 FREDERIC
TILTONE, MARGARET FRE 064 FREDERIC
TILYARD, ANNA BAL 207 6TH WARD
TILYARD, ASEY P. BAL 352 7TH WARD
TILZMAN, MATHER BAL 076 2ND DIST
TIM, ELLEN BAL 006 1ST WARD
TIM, MICHAEL ALL 152 6TH E.D.
TIMANANS, CHARLES BAL 339 1ST DIST
TIMANS, JOHN HAR 200 3RD DIST
TIMANUS, JACOB ANN 458 HOWARD D
TIMANUS, WILLIAM J. ANN 457 HOWARD D
TIMBLE, G. W. BAL 038 4TH WARD
TIMFELLOW, WILLIAM CEC 048 1ST E DI
TIMM, ROSINA BAL 028 18TH WAR
TIMMERMAN, FREDERIC BAL 208 6TH WARD
TIMMNOS, JOHN BAL 257 17TH WAR
TIMMONS, BENJAMIN WOR 284 BERLIN 1
TIMMONS, CALEB WOR 220 4TH E DI
TIMMONS, CHARLOTTE WOR 177 6TH E DI
TIMMONS, EDWARD WOR 201 3RD E DI
TIMMONS, ELIZABETH WOR 255 1ST CENS
TIMMONS, ELIZABETH HAR 199 3RD DIST
TIMMONS, EZEKIEL WOR 190 8TH E DI
TIMMONS, HANNAH BAL 320 1ST DIST
TIMMONS, ISAAC SOM 527 QUANTICO
TIMMONS, JAMES WOR 284 BERLIN 1
TIMMONS, JOHN WOR 217 4TH E DI
TIMMONS, JOHN H. WOR 292 9TH E DI
TIMMONS, JOHN S. WOR 263 BERLIN 1
TIMMONS, KENDAL WOR 285 BERLIN 1
TIMMONS, LEAH WOR 256 1ST CENS
TIMMONS, MARGARET BAL 026 9TH WARD
TIMMONS, MOLLY WOR 309 2ND E DI
TIMMONS, NANCY WOR 283 BERLIN 1
TIMMONS, RHODA J. WOR 217 4TH E DI
TIMMONS, SAMUEL WOR 255 1ST CENS
TIMMONS, SARAH SOM 539 TYASKIN
TIMMONS, STEPHEN WOR 268 BERLIN 1
TIMMONS, THOAMS WOR 262 BERLIN 1
TIMMONS, THOMAS WOR 286 BERLIN 1
TIMMONS, THOMAS SOM 538 TYASKIN
TIMMONS, THOMAS BAL 024 9TH WARD
TIMMONS, WILIAM WOR 255 1ST CENS
TIMMONS, WILLIAM WOR 287 BERLIN 1
TIMMONS, WILLIAM WOR 295 9TH E DI
TIMMONS, WILLIAM WOR 204 4TH E DI
TIMMOSN, ELIJAH WOR 286 BERLIN 1
TIMMOSN, JAMES WOR 286 BERLIN 1
TIMMOSN, JAMES BAL 425 8TH WARD
TIMMOSN, JANE WOR 257 1ST CENS
TIMMOSN, MC KINNA WOR 254 1ST CENS
TIMMOSN, WILLIAM E. WOR 299 SNOW HIL
TIMMS, CHARLES* BAL 105 10TH WAR
TIMMS, THOMAS ALL 177 7TH E.D.
TIMMY, LOUIS BAL 165 16TH WAR
TIMNS, FRANCIS ST 346 5TH E DI
TIMONS, THOMAS HAR 198 3RD DIST
TIMONUS, JOHN BAL 469 14TH WAR
TIMOTHY, BROTHER BAL 216 11TH WAR
TIMS, EDWARD QUE 235 4TH E DI
TIMS, JOHN ALL 237 CUMBERLA
TIMS, PATRICK ALL 184 9TH E.D.
TINCE, EMILY A. CEC 144 PORT DUP
TINCE, EWSON CEC 144 PORT DUP
TINCE, MARY CEC 048 1ST E DI
TINCEY, GENEVA BAL 145 19TH WAR
TINCHT, CHARLES BAL 268 20TH WAR
TINDAL, ANN L. BAL 432 1ST DIST
TINDAL, HARRIET WOR 267 BERLIN 1
TINDAL, HETTY WOR 300 SNOW HIL
TINDAL, LUCINDA BAL 038 4TH WARD
TINDALL, ANN BAL 071 18TH WAR
TINDALL, SALLY E. WOR 212 4TH E DI
TINDALY, CHARLES WOR 286 BERLIN 1
TINDEL, DANIEL CEC 029 CHESAPEA
TINDEL, JOSENE CEC 030 CHESAPEA
TINDEL, ROBERT W. BAL 016 15TH WAR
TINDEL, WILLIAM H. BAL 016 15TH WAR
TINDLE, ELEANORA BAL 034 15TH WAR
TINDLE, JAMES BAL 439 14TH WAR
TINDLY, BEN WOR 246 1ST CENS
TINE, CHARLOTTE * BAL 274 20TH WAR
TINERMAN, GEORGE H. FRE 297 WOODSBOR
TINGES, GEORGE W. BAL 162 2ND DIST
TINGES, LEWIS ANN 402 8TH DIST
TINGLE, C. W. WOR 260 BERLIN 1
TINGLE, HENRY BAL 273 12TH WAR
TINGLE, HENRY D. WOR 282 BERLIN 1
TINGLE, JACOB WOR 315 2ND E DI
TINGLE, JOHN WOR 286 BERLIN 1
TINGLE, JOSEPH BAL 215 19TH WAR
TINGLE, STUARD WOR 305 SNOW HIL
TINGLE, T. WOR 260 BERLIN 1
TINGLE, WILLIAM WOR 302 SNOW HIL
TINGLE, ZADOK WOR 286 BERLIN 1
TINGLETON, AREY * BAL 100 18TH WAR
TINGLING, BENJAMIN CAR 269 WESTMINS
TINGLING, BENJAMIN FRE 292 WOODSBOR
TINGLING, CYRUS CAR 275 7TH DIST
TINGLING, DANIEL FRE 111 CREAGERS
TINGLING, DAVID CAR 339 6TH DIST
TINGLING, EDWARD CAR 310 1ST DIST
TINGLING, ELIZA CAR 276 7TH DIST
TINGLING, EMANUEL CAR 278 7TH DIST
TINGLING, EPHRIAM BAL 113 18TH WAR
TINGLING, GEORGE CAR 327 1ST DIST
TINGLING, GEORGE CAR 297 7TH DIST
TINGLING, ISAAC FRE 289 WOODSBOR
TINGLING, JACOB CAR 301 1ST DIST
TINGLING, JOHN M. CAR 269 WESTMINS
TINGLING, LEAH CAR 332 MANCHEST
TINGLING, LYDIA CAR 273 WESTMINS

TINGLING, MARGARET S. FRE 107 CREAGERS
TINGLING, PRECILLA CAR 277 7TH DIST
TINGLING, RICHARD CAR 278 7TH DIST
TINGLING, SOPHIAH FRE 292 WOODSBOR
TINGLING, SURRANDA CAR 276 7TH DIST
TINGLING, WILLIAM CAR 279 7TH DIST
TINGLINGER, JOHN CAR 302 1ST DIST
TINGO, JOHN ALL 219 CUMBERLA
TINGSTROM, FREDERICK FRE 219 BUCKEYST
TINIS, EDWARD N. BAL 327 7TH WARD
TINKEN, GEORGE BAL 423 14TH WAR
TINKEN, GEROGE BAL 137 18TH WAR
TINKER, FRED BAL 227 12TH WAR
TINKER, H. BAL 150 1ST WARD
TINKER, MARGARET BAL 423 14TH WAR
TINKINS, ANN CHA 242 HILLTOP
TINKLE, GEORGE ALL 197 CUMBERLA
TINLONG, SARAH BAL 320 20TH WAR
TINNEY, CLEMENTINE CEC 086 4TH E DI
TINNEY, MARGARET CEC 086 4TH E DI
TINNEY, WILLIAM BAL 190 17TH WAR
TINSON, CHARLES HAR 177 3RD DIST
TINSON, JUDY BAL 276 7TH WARD
TINSTY, ENOCH BAL 320 20TH WAR
TINSTY, WILLIAM J. * BAL 273 7TH WARD
TINTEMAN, JACOB FRE 086 FREDERIC
TINTERMAN, LEWIS WAS 227 1ST DIST
TINTERMAN, WILLIAM FRE 140 CREAGERS
TINTON, ELIZA ALL 137 4TH E.D.
TINY, JOSEPH BAL 046 2ND DIST
TINY, MARY BAL 461 1ST DIST
TIPERT, ALBERT BAL 316 1ST DIST
TIPETT, MARY PRI 090 MARLBROU
TIPPELL, MARY C. ST 305 1ST E DI
TIPPELL, THOMAS ST 270 3RD E DI
TIPPET, AMELIA PRI 090 MARLBROU
TIPPET, GEORGE ALL 218 CUMBERLA
TIPPET, GEORGE ALL 253 CUMBERLA
TIPPETT, EMMA M. ST 275 3RD E DI
TIPPETT, JOHN ST 274 3RD E DI
TIPPETT, JOSHUA PRI 050 AQUASCO
TIPPETT, MARIA ST 334 4TH E DI
TIPPETT, MARY ST 255 3RD E DI
TIPPETT, ROBERT ST 330 4TH E DI
TIPPETT, ROBERT F. CHA 291 MIDDLETO
TIPPETT, ROSE E. CHA 291 MIDDLETO
TIPPETT, SABRA ST 255 3RD E DI
TIPPETT, SAMUEL ST 319 4TH E DI
TIPPETT, SUSAN ST 327 4TH E DI
TIPPETT, WALTER ST 334 4TH E DI
TIPPETT, ZACHARIAH ST 333 4TH E DI
TIPPETT, ZACHUS ST 274 3RD E DI
TIPPETTS, CHARLES B. FRE 041 FREDERIC
TIPPING, ROBERT BAL 174 19TH WAR
TIPPITT, DANIEL T.G BAL 091 5TH WARD
TIPPLES, ISAAC J. BAL 471 14TH WAR
TIPPTON, MOSES BAL 405 1ST DIST
TIPTON, ALFRED BAL 016 2ND DIST
TIPTON, AMON BAL 414 14TH WAR
TIPTON, BENJAMIN CAR 186 8TH DIST
TIPTON, BENJAMIN BAL 303 1ST DIST
TIPTON, DAVID C. BAL 428 1ST DIST
TIPTON, EDWARD BAL 022 15TH WAR
TIPTON, EMILINE BAL 439 1ST DIST
TIPTON, GREENBURY CAR 180 8TH DIST
TIPTON, HANNAH E. BAL 016 2ND DIST
TIPTON, JOHN BAL 124 2ND DIST
TIPTON, JOHN CAR 184 8TH DIST
TIPTON, JOSHUA CAR 183 8TH DIST
TIPTON, JOSHUA A. BAL 431 1ST DIST
TIPTON, PATIENCE BAL 269 17TH WAR
TIPTON, REBECCA BAL 451 1ST DIST
TIPTON, RUTH CAR 186 8TH DIST
TIPTON, SAMUEL * BAL 124 2ND DIST
TIPTON, SOLOMON BAL 044 2ND DIST
TIPTON, STEPHEN BAL 419 1ST DIST
TIPTON, SUSAN BAL 037 2ND DIST
TIPTON, WALTER BAL 421 1ST DIST
TIPTON, WESLEY HAR 080 2ND DIST
TIPTON, WILLIAM BAL 016 2ND DIST
TIPTON, WILLIAM PRI 030 VANSVILL
TIRALDA, J. F.* BAL 089 10TH WAR
TIRCE, BENJAMIN BAL 323 12TH WAR
TIRE, PEGGY F. WOR 204 4TH E DI
TIRENAN, CHARLES BAL 187 11TH WAR
TIRES, CLEMENT F. * KEN 250 2ND DIST
TIRHAUCH, FREDERICK WAS 249 1ST DIST
TIRMAER, JOHN T. * WOR 196 8TH E DI
TIRMAN, SARAH WOR 238 6TH E DI
TIRRELL, ANDREW ALL 001 3RD E.D.
TISCAL, GEORGE WAS 303 1ST DIST
TISCHMAYER, LEVI BAL 385 8TH WARD
TISCHMYER, FREDERICK BAL 384 8TH WARD
TISDAL, LUCIUS BAL 075 1ST WARD
TISHER, MARGARET ANN 387 4TH DIST
TISSUE, SARAH ALL 097 5TH E.D.
TITCOMB, BENAIAH BAL 185 6TH WARD
TITCOMB, JAMES BAL 413 8TH WARD
TITISON, SHARLOT TAL 074 EASTON T
TITLONE, DANIEL FRE 025 FREDERIC
TITLOW, DANSEL FRE 257 NEW MARK
TITLOW, HENRY WAS 022 2ND SUBD
TITLOW, MATILDA WAS 185 BCONSBOR
TITO, FREDERICK-BLACK CAR 111 NO TWP L
TITTER, LEWIS M. KEN 253 1ST DIST
TITTER, MORRIS BAL 329 13TH WAR
TITTER, SARAH A. KEN 255 1ST DIST
TITTERT, TACEY BAL 076 1ST WARD
TITTLE, ALEXANDER CAR 300 1ST DIST
TITTLE, ANN BAL 429 1ST DIST
TITTLE, ANNIE HAR 070 1ST DIST
TITTLE, ANTHONY BAL 426 1ST DIST
TITTLE, CATHARINE BAL 039 2ND DIST
TITTLE, CHARITY BAL 429 1ST DIST
TITTLE, HESTER A. BAL 096 10TH WAR
TITTLE, SAMUEL BAL 425 1ST DIST
TITTLE, THOMAS BAL 429 1ST DIST
TITTLE, THOMAS BAL 021 15TH WAR
TITTLE, WILLIAM CHA 295 HILLTOP
TITTLOE, JOHN BAL 007 18TH WAR
TITTO, LYDIA A. FRE 307 WOODSBOR
TITUS, CHALRES C. KEN 271 1ST DIST
TITUS, GEORGE KEN 271 1ST DIST
TITZ, PETER FRE 415 8TH E DI
TIVNER, HESTER A. * BAL 121 18TH WAR
TO ST 334 4TH E DI
TOAD, LEVI CEC 108 3RD E DI
TOADVINE, ALEXANDER SOM 470 TRAPPE D
TOADVINE, ELIJAH WOR 198 8TH E DI
TOADVINE, ESTHER P. ANN 521 HOWARD D

Name	County	Page	District
TOADVINE, GRACE	WOR	195	8TH E DI
TOADVINE, HENRY	SOM	470	TRAPPE D
TOADVINE, JOHN	WOR	195	8TH E DI
TOADVINE, MATTHIAS O.	SOM	503	SALISBUR
TOADVINE, MELVIN	SOM	482	TRAPP DI
TOADVINE, PURNELL	SOM	494	SALISBUR
TOADVINE, ROBERT*	SOM	479	TRAPP DI
TOADVINE, THOMAS	WOR	194	8TH E DI
TOADVINE, UNIS	SOM	489	SALISBUR
TOAP, ELEN	CAR	232	5TH DIST
TOBAN, MARY J.	BAL	138	5TH WARD
TOBEN, ELIZABETH	ALL	148	6TH E.D.
TOBEREY, WILLIAM	FRE	267	NEW MARK
TOBERTY, PATRICK	ALL	252	CUMBERLA
TOBF, JOHN *	BAL	283	1ST DIST
TOBIAS, ELIZABETH	WAS	121	HAGERSTO
TOBIN, CANIEL	BAL	112	18TH WAR
TOBIN, ELIZA	BAL	379	3RD WARD
TOBIN, JOHN	BAL	209	2ND WARD
TOBIN, MARY MISS-	BAL	315	20TH WAR
TOBIN, PATRICK	BAL	104	1ST WARD
TOBIN, PATRICK	BAL	404	3RD WARD
TOBIN, THOMAS W.	BAL	261	6TH WARD
TOBIN, THOMAS W.	BAL	065	10TH WAR
TOBS, ANDREW	QUE	226	4TH E DI
TOBT, JOHN *	BAL	283	1ST DIST
TOBY, ANNA	BAL	398	1ST DIST
TOBY, MICAHEL	ALL	155	6TH E.D.
TOD, LOUISA-MULATTO	FRE	421	8TH E DI
TOD, OWEN-MULATTO	FRE	421	8TH E DI
TODD, ALEXANDER	CAR	224	5TH DIST
TODD, ANDREW	CAR	132	NO TWP L
TODD, ANDREW	BAL	327	7TH WARD
TODD, ANDREW J.	ALL	236	CUMBERLA
TODD, ANDREW J.	DOR	317	1ST DIST
TODD, ANN	BAL	446	8TH WARD
TODD, ANN M.*	DOR	382	1ST DIST
TODD, ANTHONY R.	CAR	153	NO TWP L
TODC, BASIL	BAL	350	1ST DIST
TODD, BENJAMIN	FRE	248	NEW MARK
TODD, BENJAMIN	DOR	355	3RD DIVI
TODD, BENJAMIN	DOR	346	3RD DIVI
TODD, BENJAMIN	BAL	350	13TH WAR
TODD, BENJAMIN	BAL	350	13TH WAR
TODD, BENNETT	CAR	128	NO TWP L
TODD, BRITANIA	CAR	116	NO TWP L
TODD, CELESTE	BAL	224	12TH WAR
TODD, CHARLES	BAL	008	9TH WARD
TODD, CHARLES	CAR	136	NO TWP L
TODD, DAVID	CAR	157	NO TWP L
TODD, DENNIS	WAS	043	2ND SUBD
TODD, EBEN	DOR	317	1ST DIST
TODD, EDWARD	CEC	098	4TH E DI
TODD, ELI	CAR	119	NO TWP L
TODD, ELIAZABETH	CAR	120	NO TWP L
TODD, ELIZABETH	FRE	248	NEW MARK
TODD, ELIZABETH	CAR	165	NO TWP L
TODD, ELIZABETH	BAL	218	19TH WAR
TODD, G. WASHINGTON	ANN	509	HOWARD D
TODD, GEORGE	DOR	345	3RD DIVI
TODD, GEORGE	SOM	491	SALISBUR
TODD, GRAFTON-BLACK	FRE	450	8TH E DI
TODD, HAAAH	BAL	327	7TH WARD
TODD, HENRY	BAL	375	13TH WAR
TODD, HUGH	BAL	408	1ST DIST
TODD, ISABELLA	BAL	149	2ND DIST
TODC, JABEZ	DOR	343	3RD DIVI
TODD, JACOB	DOR	346	3RD DIVI
TODD, JAMES	DOR	340	3RD DIVI
TODD, JAMES	DOR	345	3RD DIVI
TODD, JAMES	CEC	159	PORT DUP
TODD, JAMES	FRE	112	CREAGERS
TODD, JAMES	SOM	444	DAMES QU
TODD, JANE	BAL	357	1ST DIST
TODD, JEREMIAH	CAR	137	NO TWP L
TODD, JOHN	CAR	141	NO TWP L
TODD, JOHN	DOR	335	3RD DIVI
TODD, JOHN	BAL	131	1ST WARD
TODD, JOHN A.	TAL	068	EASTON T
TODD, JOHN H.	CEC	168	6TH E DI
TODD, JOHN M.	CHA	288	BOJANTOW
TODD, JOHN P.	CEC	191	5TH E DI
TODD, JOSEPH	MGM	330	CRACKLIN
TODD, JOSHUA F.	BAL	027	2ND DIST
TODD, JULIA A.	BAL	045	4TH WARD
TODD, LATITIA	BAL	167	16TH WAR
TODC, LEVIN	CAR	164	NO TWP L
TODD, LEVIN W.	DOR	419	1ST DIST
TODD, LEWIS	CEC	156	PORT DUP
TODD, LOUIS	CEC	206	7TH E DI
TODD, MAJOR	DOR	341	3RD DIVI
TODD, MAJOR	DOR	347	3RD DIVI
TODD, MALLISON A.	TAL	070	EASTON T
TODD, MANUEL	DOR	346	3RD DIVI
TODD, MARCELLA	BAL	104	10TH WAR
TODD, MARGARET	BAL	068	2ND DIST
TODD, MARGRETT	DOR	347	3RD DIVI
TODD, MARTIN	DOR	346	3RD DIVI
TODD, MARY	CEC	183	7TH E DI
TODD, MARY	BAL	149	2ND DIST
TODD, MARY	BAL	006	1ST WARD
TODD, MARY A.	BAL	438	14TH WAR
TODD, MARY C.	TAL	059	EASTON D
TODD, MARY E.	BAL	288	17TH WAR
TODD, MARY L.	DOR	342	3RD DIVI
TODD, MARY-BLACK	FRE	449	8TH E DI
TODD, MICHAEL	SOM	546	TYASKIN
TODD, NATHAN	CAR	111	NO TWP L
TODD, NATHANIEL	SOM	447	DAMES QU
TODC, PETER	TAL	068	EASTON T
TODD, PHOEBE	SOM	493	SALISBUR
TODD, PURNELL	CAR	140	NO TWP L
TODD, RICHARD	BAL	149	2ND DIST
TODD, RICHARD	ANN	358	3RD DIST
TODD, RICHARD-BLACK	FRE	451	8TH E DI
TODD, RICHARD-MULATTO	FRE	452	8TH E DI
TODD, RITTA	DOR	346	3RD DIVI
TODD, ROBERT	CEC	183	7TH E DI
TODD, ROBERT M.	BAL	350	13TH WAR
TODD, ROBERT S.	SOM	494	SALISBUR
TODD, RUTH	DOR	342	3RD DIVI
TODD, S.	BAL	222	19TH WAR
TODD, SAMUEL	CAR	163	NO TWP L
TODD, SAMUEL	FRE	246	NEW MARK
TODD, SAMUEL	PRI	028	VANSVILL
TODD, SAMUEL	BAL	144	1ST WARD
TODD, SARRAH	DOR	368	3RD DIVI
TODD, SOLOMON	DOR	338	3RD DIVI
TODD, SOPHIA	DOR	335	3RD DIVI
TODD, SUSAN	CEC	159	PORT DUP
TODD, SUSANAH	BAL	062	2ND DIST
TODD, THOMAS	BAL	015	15TH WAR
TODD, THOMAS	DOR	341	3RD DIVI
TODD, THOMAS	CAR	129	NO TWP L
TODD, THOMAS J.	BAL	114	15TH WAR
TODD, UPTON-BLACK	FRE	418	8TH E DI
TODD, VACHEL B.	MGM	437	CLARKSTR
TODD, WILHAM W.	DOR	317	1ST DIST
TODD, WILLIAM	DOR	341	3RD DIVI
TODD, WILLIAM	CAR	130	NO TWP L
TODD, WILLIAM	CAR	164	NO TWP L
TODD, WILLIAM	BAL	327	7TH WARD
TODD, WILLIAM	ANN	509	HOWARD D
TODD, WILLIAM H.	DOR	366	3RD DIVI
TODD, WILLIAM J.	BAL	152	1ST WARD
TODD, WILLIAM L.	CEC	158	PORT DUP
TODD, WILLIAM T.	TAL	018	EASTON D
TODD, WINDFIELD-MULATTO	FRE	434	8TH E DI
TODD, ZACHARIAH	BAL	025	15TH WAR
TODD, ZEBULON	DOR	346	3RD DIVI
TODDD, CALEP	DOR	346	3RD DIVI
TODDE, ABRAM	ANN	472	HOWARD D
TODER, BENJAMIN	BAL	437	14TH WAR
TODER, JOHN	BAL	317	7TH WARD
TODER, MARGARET	BAL	303	7TH WARD
TODER, ROBERT	BAL	316	7TH WARD
TODER, WILLIAM L.	BAL	011	9TH WARD
TODHUNTER, ELIZABETH	ANN	425	HOWARD D
TODHUNTER, ISAAC E.	ANN	425	HOWARD D
TODHUNTER, MRS.	BAL	105	10TH WAR
TODRICK, SARAH	ANN	356	3RD DIST
TODRIN, ROBERT	BAL	463	1ST DIST
TODVEN, SARAH	BAL	060	15TH WAR
TODVINE, GRACE	WOR	246	1ST CENS
TODWIN, SARAH	BAL	462	1ST DIST
TODYWARE, LEWIS *	BAL	261	2ND WARD
TOE, ISAAC D.	CAL	010	1ST DIST
TOE, JAMES	CAL	018	1ST DIST
TOEMAN, EVALINE	CEC	178	7TH E DI
TOFLING, JOHN	BAL	261	1ST DIST
TOFT, FRANCES A.	BAL	299	20TH WAR
TOFT, JOHN	BAL	288	20TH WAR
TOFT, RICHARD	HAR	082	2ND DIST
TOFT, THOMAS	BAL	431	1ST DIST
TOFT, WILLIAM	BAL	258	20TH WAR
TOFTER, JONATHAN	ALL	122	4TH E.D.
TOGLISON, JACOB	BAL	290	17TH WAR
TOGOOD, NANCY	BAL	261	12TH WAR
TOKER, WILLIAM J.	BAL	125	1ST WARD
TOLAN, JOHN	BAL	426	14TH WAR
TOLAN, JOHN	FRE	160	EMMITTSB
TOLAND, ADAM	HAR	022	1ST DIST
TOLAND, WILLIAM	BAL	092	5TH WARD
TOLAND, WILLIAM	BAL	134	5TH WARD
TOLBERT, GEORGE	CEC	084	CHARLEST
TOLBERT, MARGARET A.	WAS	218	1ST DIST
TOLBERT, NATHAN T.	FRE	224	BUCKEYST
TOLBERT, ROBERT E.	BAL	007	1ST WARD
TOLBERT, WASHINGTON	CEC	139	6TH E DI
TOLBORT, RIELY	WOR	299	SNOW HIL
TOLBOT, CHARLES C.	BAL	349	7TH WARD
TOLBOT, MARYAN*	BAL	374	3RD WARD
TOLEN, MICHAEL	ALL	141	6TH E.D.
TOLEN, WILLIAM*	DOR	340	3RD DIVI
TOLENGER, MARY C.	FRE	048	FREDERIC
TOLESOS, ----*	BAL	087	10TH WAR
TOLEY, JOHN	BAL	145	1ST WARD
TOLEY, TRAVERSE B.*	DOR	470	1ST DIST
TOLFEILD, HENRY	BAL	029	18TH WAR
TOLHINER, MICHAEL	BAL	106	2ND DIST
TOLIBERT, H. H.	BAL	148	1ST WARD
TOLLENGER, EVEN	HAR	172	3RD DIST
TOLLEY, ALEX	BAL	206	2ND WARD
TOLLEY, ALEXANDER*	DOR	328	3RD DIVI
TOLLEY, HENRY*	DOR	329	3RD DIVI
TOLLEY, JAMES W.	HAR	060	1ST DIST
TOLLEY, JANE	BAL	377	3RD WARD
TOLLEY, JERREY	DOR	328	3RD DIVI
TOLLEY, MARY*	DOR	358	3RD DIVI
TOLLEY, SARAH E.	CAL	014	1ST DIST
TOLLINGER, DANIEL	HAR	126	2ND DIST
TOLLINGER, ELIZABETH	BAL	045	18TH WAR
TOLLINGER, JAMES L.	HAR	126	2ND DIST
TOLLS, ELISABETH	ANN	367	4TH DIST
TOLLY, MARGARET	BAL	389	13TH WAR
TOLLY, TRAVERSE B.*	DOR	470	1ST DIST
TOLLY, WILLIAM	BAL	133	2ND DIST
TOLMAN, NACE	PRI	118	PISCATAW
TOLMAN, WILLIAM	BAL	244	17TH WAR
TOLON, JOHN *	BAL	276	20TH WAR
TOLON, JULIA A.	BAL	276	20TH WAR
TOLSIN, GEORGE	BAL	129	1ST WARD
TOLSON, A.H.	PRI	094	SPALDING
TOLSON, BENJAMIN	QUE	225	4TH E DI
TOLSON, BENJAMIN	QUE	224	4TH E DI
TOLSON, CAROLINE	QUE	233	4TH E DI
TOLSON, CHARLES E.	QUE	226	4TH E DI
TOLSON, DANIEL	QUE	226	4TH E DI
TOLSON, GEORGE L.	PRI	099	SPALDING
TOLSON, HENRIETTA	QUE	225	4TH E DI
TOLSON, HENRIETTA	QUE	174	2ND E DI
TOLSON, HENRY	PRI	099	SPALDING
TOLSON, HENRY	ANN	314	1ST DIST
TOLSON, HIRAM	BAL	077	10TH WAR
TOLSON, JACOB	QUE	236	4TH E DI
TOLSON, JACOB C.	ANN	290	ANNAPOLI
TOLSON, JAMES	QUE	224	4TH E DI
TOLSON, JAMES	QUE	226	4TH E DI
TOLSON, JAMES B.	QUE	151	1ST E DI
TOLSON, JAMES-BLACK	QUE	171	2ND E DI
TOLSON, JOHN	QUE	224	4TH E DI
TOLSON, JOHN	QUE	228	4TH E DI
TOLSON, JOHN	QUE	231	4TH E DI
TOLSON, JOHN C.	QUE	223	4TH E DI
TOLSON, JOHN M.	QUE	164	2ND E DI
TOLSON, JOSEPH	BAL	109	1ST WARD
TOLSON, LYDIA C.	QUE	239	5TH E DI
TOLSON, M.E.	PRI	089	SPALDING
TOLSON, MARTHA	BAL	120	2ND DIST
TOLSON, NANCY J.	BAL	173	6TH WARD
TOLSON, PERE	QUE	236	4TH E DI
TOLSON, RACHEL	QUE	164	2ND E DI
TOLSON, RICHARD	QUE	170	2ND E DI
TOLSON, SARAH	BAL	268	7TH WARD
TOLSON, THOMAS	QUE	230	4TH E DI
TOLSON, WILLIAM	QUE	226	4TH E DI
TOLSON, WILLIAM	QUE	166	2ND E DI
TOLSON, WILLIAM	PRI	099	SPALDING
TOLSON, WILLIAM	BAL	056	10TH WAR
TOLSON, WILLIAM	BAL	092	15TH WAR
TOLSON, WILLIAM	BAL	239	17TH WAR
TOLSON,W ILLIAM J.	QUE	175	2ND E DI
TOLVERT, ELIZABETH	BAL	229	2ND WARD
TOMALAUN, JOHN	BAL	195	6TH WARD
TOMAN, MICHAEL	BAL	089	5TH WARD
TOMAS, ANN	SOM	449	DAMES QU
TOMAS, JOHN	BAL	127	1ST WARD
TOMAS, JOHN H.	TAL	080	ST MICHA
TOMAS, NOAH	SOM	397	BRINKLEY
TOMAS, SARAH	BAL	071	1ST WARD
TOMB, NANCY	WAS	281	LEITERSB
TOMBS, ABRAHAM	FRE	152	10TH E D
TOMBS, ABRAHAM	FRE	156	10TH E D
TOMBS, BARBARA	WAS	275	RIDGEVIL
TOMBS, DANIEL	FRE	154	10TH E D
TOMBS, ELIZABETH	WAS	184	BOONSBOR
TOMBS, JACOB	WAS	200	1ST DIST
TOMBS, SAMUEL	FRE	149	10TH E D
TOMBS, SAMUEL	FRE	152	10TH E D
TOMBS, WILLIAM	FRE	152	10TH E D
TOME, CAROLINE M.	CEC	145	PORT DUP
TOME, JACOB	CEC	145	PORT DUP
TOMEY, MATHIAS	BAL	427	8TH WARD
TOMHEART, GEORGE *	PRI	031	VANSVILL
TOMKINS, SAM	PRI	095	SPALDING
TOMLENSON, E.	ALL	138	6TH E.D.
TOMLEY, FRANCIS	BAL	418	8TH WARD
TOMLIN, H.W.	PRI	078	MARLBROU
TOMLIN, R.M.	PRI	064	NOTTINGH
TOMLINSON, BENNETT	TAL	069	EASTON T
TOMLINSON, EDWARD	ANN	419	HOWARD D
TOMLINSON, FREDERICK*	BAL	311	3RD WARD
TOMLINSON, HARRIET	MGM	393	ROCKERLE
TOMLINSON, INA	PRI	055	AQUASCO
TOMLINSON, JESSE	ALL	115	5TH E.D.
TOMLINSON, JOSHUA	ANN	419	HOWARD D
TOMLINSON, SAMUEL	KEN	215	2ND DIST
TOMLINSON, SARAH	ALL	115	5TH E.D.
TOMLINSON, T. W.	BAL	002	4TH WARD
TOMLINSON, WILLIAM	KEN	222	2ND DIST
TOMLINSON, WILLIAM	MGM	393	ROCKERLE
TOMON, HENRY	ALL	195	CUMBERLA
TOMPKINS, EVAN P.	FRE	202	5TH E DI
TOMPKINS, JOHN	HAR	021	1ST DIST
TOMPSON, JAMES	DOR	368	3RD DIVI
TOMPSON, JOHN	CAR	231	5TH DIST
TOMPSON, MARIA	BAL	418	8TH WARD
TOMPSON, MARY	ALL	147	6TH E.D.
TOMS, JOSHUA	WAS	215	1ST DIST
TOMS, SOLOMON	FRE	117	CREAGERS
TOMS, WILLIAM J.	BAL	045	1ST WARD
TOMSON, HENRY	ANN	340	3RD DIST
TOMSON, MARY	ANN	340	3RD DIST
TOMSON, ODOLPHUS	ANN	340	3RD DIST
TOMY, MICHAEL *	BAL	354	1ST DIST
TON, MOORITCH*	BAL	326	3RD WARD
TONA, WILLIAM	CEC	064	1ST E DI
TONER, ANN	CEC	072	5TH E DI
TONER, JAMES	FRE	202	5TH E DI
TONER, JAMES	BAL	161	16TH WAR
TONER, JOHN	BAL	078	10TH WAR
TONER, JOHN	CAR	293	7TH DIST
TONER, JOSEPH	BAL	257	12TH WAR
TONER, MARGARET	BAL	151	2ND DIST
TONER, MICHAEL	BAL	161	16TH WAR
TONER, RICHARD	BAL	090	5TH WARD
TONER, THOMAS E.	BAL	145	1ST WARD
TONER, WILLIAM	BAL	316	7TH WARD
TONEY, ISAAC	BAL	230	17TH WAR
TONEY, JOHN	CEC	177	7TH E DI
TONEY, JOSEPH	BAL	214	19TH WAR
TONG, ADAM	BAL	441	8TH WARD
TONG, JAMES	FRE	298	WOODSBOR
TONG, WILIAM	FRE	309	WOODSBOR
TONGS, JAMES	CEC	098	4TH E DI
TONGS, THOMAS	CEC	106	3RD E DI
TONGUE, AMY	ANN	300	1ST DIST
TONGUE, ANN	ANN	459	HOWARD D
TONGUE, BENJAMIN	ANN	409	8TH DIST
TONGUE, GIDEON G.	CAL	012	1ST DIST
TONGUE, JAMES C.	CAL	012	1ST DIST
TONGUE, JAMES L.	CAL	016	1ST DIST
TONGUE, MARY	FRE	172	5TH E DI
TONGUE, THOMAS R.	CAL	012	1ST DIST
TONGUE,E.B.	BAL	173	1ST WARD
TONIZ, JOSEPH	BAL	202	2ND WARD
TONKINS, JOHN	FRE	330	MIDDLETO
TONKINS, MARTHA E.	CEC	156	PORT DUP
TONNY, ELENER	BAL	234	12TH WAR
TONSOLE, THOMAS	MGM	404	ROCKERLE
TONSON, HENRY	FRE	095	FREDERIC
TONSON, JOHN	FRE	117	CREAGERS
TONSON, PETER	FRE	096	FREDERIC
TONY, KASEY	BAL	111	5TH WARD
TOOD, ANN M.*	DOR	382	1ST DIST
TOOD, ELIJAH-MULATTO	FRE	428	8TH E DI
TOODLE, JESSE	FRE	093	FREDERIC
TOOELL, HENERITTA	HAR	200	3RD DIST
TOOGOOD, ALEXANDER	ANN	329	2ND DIST
TOOGOOD, CALE-MULATTO	FRE	038	FREDERIC
TOOGOOD, CALEB	BAL	413	14TH WAR
TOOGOOD, CALIP	WAS	034	2ND SUBD
TOOGOOD, ENOCH	BAL	310	1ST DIST
TOOGOOD, GEORGIANNA	ANN	391	4TH DIST
TOOGOOD, HAD	FRE	260	NEW MARK
TOOGOOD, JAMES	ANN	299	1ST DIST
TOOGOOD, JANE	BAL	321	1ST DIST
TOOGOOD, JOHN	BAL	434	14TH WAR
TOOGOOD, JULIA	BAL	167	16TH WAR
TOOGOOD, MARGARET J.	BAL	168	16TH WAR
TOOGOOD, MARIA A.	ANN	337	3RD DIST
TOOGOOD, MARTHA	FRE	262	NEW MARK
TOOGOOD, MARY M.	MGM	318	CRACKLIN
TOOGOOD, PEGGY	ANN	497	HOWARD D
TOOGOOD, PHILIP	ANN	498	HOWARD D
TOOGOOD, PHILLIP E.	BAL	245	6TH WARD
TOOGOOD, WILLIAM	BAL	337	3RD WARD
TOOGOOD, WILLIAM	BAL	374	1ST DIST
TOOK, SAMUEL	CEC	167	6TH E DI
TOOKTEN, DANIEL	ANN	317	1ST DIST
TOOL, ELISABETH	BAL	363	3RD WARD
TOOL, ELIZABETH	BAL	159	6TH WARD
TOOL, MORY N.	BAL	047	9TH WARD
TOOL, OWEN C.	BAL	417	8TH WARD
TOOL, PETER	ANN	275	ANNAPOLI
TOOL, TIMOTHY	ALL	119	5TH E.D.
TOOL,MARY	CAR	084	NO TWP L
TOOLAY, ANTHONY	ALL	245	CUMBERLA
TOOLE, JOHN	BAL	245	20TH WAR
TOOLE, MARY O.*	BAL	404	3RD WARD

TOOLE, MICHAEL ANN 440 HOWARD D
TOOLE, MICHAEL ANN 432 HOWARD D
TOOLE, MICHEAL BAL 117 18TH WAR
TOOMAN, JOSEPH BAL 096 15TH WAR
TOOMAY, FREDERICK BAL 066 15TH WAR
TOOMBS, ANNA BAL 114 5TH WARD
TOOMEY, DANIEL T. BAL 183 16TH WAR
TOOMEY, GEORGE BAL 078 10TH WAR
TOOMEY, JACOB BAL 091 15TH WAR
TOOMEY, JOSIAH H.G. BAL 150 16TH WAR
TOONEY, LEMUEL ANN 516 HOWARD D
TOOP, DENNIS A.-MULATTO FRE 428 8TH E DI
TOOTHECAR, SAMUEL BAL 471 14TH WAR
TOOTLE, JOSIAH BAL 115 18TH WAR
TOPIER, BERNARD CEC 116 3RD E DI
TOPP, GEORGE BAL 200 17TH WAR
TOPPER, ANTHONY J. FRE 037 FREDERIC
TOPPER, JOHN FRE 026 FREDERIC
TOPPER, JOHN J. CAR 312 1ST DIST
TOPPER, MARY FRE 057 FREDERIC
TOPPING, CHARLES BAL 252 20TH WAR
TOPPING, MARY BAL 260 20TH WAR
TOPPINGS, REBECCA BAL 248 20TH WAR
TOPPINS, ANNA BAL 023 4TH WARD
TOPPOLES, JAMES BAL 109 5TH WARD
TOPTEN, HENRY * CEC 207 7TH E DI
TOPTON, JAMES QUE 153 1ST E DI
TORBECKER, COONROD BAL 131 2ND DIST
TORBERT, HANNAH CEC 122 4TH E DI
TORBERT, JOHN CEC 001 ELKTON 3
TORBERT, MARTHA CEC 002 ELKTON 3
TORBERT, PAUL CEC 126 5TH E DI
TORBERT, WILLIAM CEC 001 ELKTON 3
TORBORG, GEORGE BAL 346 13TH WAR
TORENCE, ADELINE BAL 092 1ST WARD
TORENCE, ANN BAL 009 1ST WARD
TORESSON, SARAH A. CEC 170 6TH E DI
TORESTELLY, BARNARD BAL 283 1ST DIST
TOREY, SUSAN * KEN 247 2ND DIST
TORFT, JAMES BAL 225 1ST DIST
TORFT, JAMES BAL 229 1ST DIST
TORGOOD, JAMES-BLACK FRE 010 FREDERIC
TORIER, FRANCIS * KEN 253 1ST DIST
TORINGTON, JOHN BAL 275 7TH WARD
TORMAY, P.A. BAL 147 5TH WARD
TORN, MARY BAL 115 5TH WARD
TORNARD, BENJAMIN BAL 141 1ST WARD
TORNECE, JAMES BAL 248 12TH WAR
TORNEY, C. BAL 247 17TH WAR
TORNEY, PAT BAL 463 1ST DIST
TORNEY, WINEY BAL 046 9TH WARD
TORNNER, JOHN BAL 125 1ST WARD
TORNY, MICHAEL * BAL 354 1ST DIST
TORPHY, MARY BAL 175 16TH WAR
TORRANCE, CHARLES A. BAL 069 10TH WAR
TORRANCE, GEORGE BAL 234 12TH WAR
TORRANCE, MARY BAL 109 10TH WAR
TORRANCE, WILLIAM BAL 011 9TH WARD
TORRENCE, JAMES BAL 414 1ST DIST
TORRENCE, MARY S. BAL 255 12TH WAR
TORREY, WINEY ALL 212 CUMBERLA
TORRINGTON, JAMES BAL 038 2ND DIST
TORRY, WILLIAM HAR 063 1ST DIST
TORSCH, HENRY F. BAL 029 15TH WAR
TOSH, LOUIS CEC 202 6TH E DI
TOSSET, JAMES ALL 220 CUMBERLA
TOTLE, ROBERT BAL 132 11TH WAR
TOTLING, CATHARIEN WAS 131 2ND DIST
TOTTLE, JAMES BAL 349 13TH WAR
TOTTSON, JAMES-BLACK CAR 084 NO TWP L
TOUCH, AMOUS BAL 101 18TH WAR
TOUCHSTONE, AGNES CEC 162 6TH E DI
TOUCHSTONE, HENRY E. CEC 142 6TH E DI
TOUCHSTONE, THOMAS CEC 116 3RD E DI
TOUCHTON, ANN S. BAL 322 3RD WARD
TOUCHTON, NATHAN BAL 322 3RD WARD
TOUCHTOR, FRANCIS A. BAL 082 2ND DIST
TOUER, THOMAS BAL 247 17TH WAR
TOUGHMON, FRANCIS ALL 200 CUMBERLA
TOUGHT, J. K. BAL 087 18TH WAR
TOUGHTON, MARY BAL 221 6TH WARD
TOULSON, JAMES CEC 149 PORT DUP
TOULSON, JAMES A. KEN 250 2ND DIST
TOULSON, STEPHEN K. KEN 250 2ND DIST
TOULSON, THOMAS * KEN 242 2ND DIST
TOUNGE, JOHN W. * BAL 063 18TH WAR
TOUNSAND, AUTHOR WOR 245 1ST CENS
TOUNSAND, ELIZA WOR 247 1ST CENS
TOUNSAND, LEVIN WOR 303 SNOW HIL
TOUNSAND, LOUIS WOR 303 SNOW HIL
TOUNSAND, SAMUEL TAL 046 EASTON T
TOUNSAND, SOPHIAH WOR 249 1ST CENS
TOUNSEND, JANE DOR 382 1ST DIST
TOUNSEND, JOSEPH* SOM 481 TRAPP DI
TOURGER, RICHARD * BAL 091 18TH WAR
TOUS, POLLY SOM 364 BRINKLEY
TOUSLY, PETER CEC 020 ELKTON 3
TOUSON, EPHRAIM CEC 173 6TH E DI
TOUSON, MERCY BAL 267 12TH WAR
TOUSON, ROBERT * KEN 229 2ND DIST
TOUSON, WILLIAM FRE 117 CREAGERS
TOUTCHSTONE, MARY J. CEC 131 6TH E DI
TOUTCHSTONE, SARAH C. CEC 142 6TH E DI
TOUTCHTON, JANE HAR 188 3RD DIST
TOUTSON, HENRY CAR 259 3RD DIST
TOVELL, CALEB BAL 133 2ND DIST
TOVEY, MARGARET ALL 239 CUMBERLA
TOWART, REUBEN * BAL 123 2ND DIST
TOWAY, THOMAS BAL 043 18TH WAR
TOWBLE, JOHN CAR 186 8TH DIST
TOWELL, H.W. BAL 138 1ST WARD
TOWENSEND, CHARLES BAL 117 18TH WAR
TOWENSEND, SARAH B. BAL 059 18TH WAR
TOWER, CLARICE CAR 109 NO TWP L
TOWER, F.B. ALL 208 CUMBERLA
TOWER, JAEMS CAR 113 NO TWP L
TOWER, N. BAL 329 13TH WAR
TOWERS, ANDREW CAR 145 NO TWP L
TOWERS, ANDREW CAR 162 NO TWP L
TOWERS, CURTIS CAR 152 NO TWP L
TOWERS, ELIJAH CAR 164 NO TWP L
TOWERS, ELIZABETH CAR 139 NO TWP L
TOWERS, HENRY CAR 168 NO TWP L
TOWERS, HESTER CAR 129 NO TWP L
TOWERS, JAMES CAR 145 NO TWP L
TOWERS, JAMES BAL 130 1ST WARD
TOWERS, SARAH CAR 145 NO TWP L
TOWERS, SOLOMON CAR 145 NO TWP L
TOWERS, TAMSEY CAR 143 NO TWP L
TOWERS, WESLEY CAR 140 NO TWP L
TOWERS, WILLIAM CAR 108 NO TWP L
TOWLER, MATILDA BAL 361 3RD WARD
TOWN, ELIZA BAL 323 12TH WAR
TOWNER, JOHN F. BAL 463 14TH WAR
TOWNER, MELISSA J. BAL 464 14TH WAR
TOWNERY, CHRISTIAN BAL 070 1ST WARD
TOWNEY, HANAH BAL 419 8TH WARD
TOWNEY, MARY ALL 142 6TH E.D.
TOWNEY, PATRICK ALL 142 6TH E.D.
TOWNEY, WILLIAM * BAL 189 5TH DIST
TOWNLEY, JAMES HAR 078 2ND DIST
TOWNS, AMOS BAL 115 5TH WARD
TOWNSAND, HENRY TAL 095 ST MICHA
TOWNSAND, MRS.* TAL 044 EASTON T
TOWNSAND, WILLIAM TAL 094 ST MICHA
TOWNSARD, EDWARD QUE 238 5TH E DI
TOWNSEO, LEVIN WOR 187 7TH E DI
TOWNSEND, ALFRED W. MGM 361 BERRYS D
TOWNSEND, CATHARINE CEC 085 5TH E DI
TOWNSEND, CATHERINE MGM 361 BERRYS D
TOWNSEND, CHARELS WOR 188 7TH E DI
TOWNSEND, CHARLES SOM 422 PRINCESS
TOWNSEND, CHARLOT WOR 342 1ST E DI
TOWNSEND, CUTTER SOM 489 SALISBUR
TOWNSEND, DAVID BAL 392 1ST DIST
TOWNSEND, DAVID BAL 155 2ND DIST
TOWNSEND, EDWARD BAL 345 3RD WARD
TOWNSEND, EDWARD WOR 258 1ST CENS
TOWNSEND, EDWARD SOM 424 PRINCESS
TOWNSEND, ELEANOR-BLACK WOR 166 6TH E DI
TOWNSEND, ELIJA BAL 008 9TH WARD
TOWNSEND, ELIZA WOR 251 1ST CENS
TOWNSEND, ELIZABETH SOM 491 SALISBUR
TOWNSEND, ELIZABETH WOR 327 1ST E DI
TOWNSEND, GEORGE C. WOR 176 6TH E DI
TOWNSEND, GERTRUDE WOR 179 6TH E DI
TOWNSEND, HANNAH-BLACK WOR 172 6TH E DI
TOWNSEND, HENNA WOR 345 1ST E DI
TOWNSEND, HENRY WOR 328 1ST E DI
TOWNSEND, HENRY BAL 312 1ST DIST
TOWNSEND, HESTER WOR 300 SNOW HIL
TOWNSEND, HESTER A. WOR 188 7TH E DI
TOWNSEND, ISAAC WOR 188 7TH E DI
TOWNSEND, ISAAC WOR 299 SNOW HIL
TOWNSEND, ISAAC SR. WOR 178 6TH E DI
TOWNSEND, ISAAC-BLACK WOR 172 6TH E DI
TOWNSEND, ISERAL WOR 246 1ST CENS
TOWNSEND, JACOB KEN 274 1ST DIST
TOWNSEND, JACOB KEN 276 1ST DIST
TOWNSEND, JACOB QUE 130 1ST E DI
TOWNSEND, JACOB A. J. WOR 177 6TH E DI
TOWNSEND, JAMES KEN 281 3RD DIST
TOWNSEND, JAMES WOR 308 2ND E DI
TOWNSEND, JAMES TAL 081 ST MICHA
TOWNSEND, JAMES MGM 330 CRACKLIN
TOWNSEND, JAMES BAL 289 17TH WAR
TOWNSEND, JESSE SOM 554 TYASKIN
TOWNSEND, JOHN CAR 257 3RD DIST
TOWNSEND, JOHN BAL 023 15TH WAR
TOWNSEND, JOHN ANN 340 3RD DIST
TOWNSEND, JOSEPH C. MGM 347 BERRYS D
TOWNSEND, JOSEPH H. WOR 166 6TH E DI
TOWNSEND, JOSEPH* SOM 481 TRAPP DI
TOWNSEND, JOSIAH WOR 175 6TH E DI
TOWNSEND, KITTY ANN 343 3RD DIST
TOWNSEND, LEAH WOR 173 6TH E DI
TOWNSEND, LEVIN H. SOM 491 SALISBUR
TOWNSEND, LEVIN JR. WOR 183 6TH E DI
TOWNSEND, LEVIN SR. WOR 183 6TH E DI
TOWNSEND, LEWIS H. WOR 302 SNOW HIL
TOWNSEND, LITTLETON WOR 335 1ST E DI
TOWNSEND, M. A. P. WOR 255 1ST CENS
TOWNSEND, MAHALA BAL 174 2ND DIST
TOWNSEND, MAJOR D. WOR 187 7TH E DI
TOWNSEND, MARGARET WOR 341 1ST E DI
TOWNSEND, MARGARET WOR 171 6TH E DI
TOWNSEND, MARIA WOR 188 7TH E DI
TOWNSEND, MARY WOR 197 8TH E DI
TOWNSEND, MARY WOR 181 6TH E DI
TOWNSEND, MARY WOR 200 3RD E DI
TOWNSEND, MARY WOR 187 7TH E DI
TOWNSEND, MARY WOR 173 6TH E DI
TOWNSEND, MARY BAL 008 9TH WARD
TOWNSEND, MARY J. CAR 292 7TH DIST
TOWNSEND, MATHIAS BAL 143 2ND DIST
TOWNSEND, MITCHELL WOR 173 6TH E DI
TOWNSEND, NANCY WOR 194 8TH E DI
TOWNSEND, NANCY WOR 251 1ST CENS
TOWNSEND, NEWMAN KEN 286 3RD DIST
TOWNSEND, PERRY BAL 234 12TH WAR
TOWNSEND, PETER SOM 483 TRAPP DI
TOWNSEND, PHOEBE SOM 490 SALISBUR
TOWNSEND, REBECCA WOR 349 1ST E DI
TOWNSEND, REBECCA BAL 042 1ST WARD
TOWNSEND, RICHARD BAL 052 2ND DIST
TOWNSEND, RICHARD H. BAL 088 4TH WARD
TOWNSEND, ROBERT WOR 173 6TH E DI
TOWNSEND, SALLY WOR 187 7TH E DI
TOWNSEND, SAMUEL BAL 334 13TH WAR
TOWNSEND, SAMUEL BAL 452 14TH WAR
TOWNSEND, SAMUEL BAL 389 1ST DIST
TOWNSEND, SARAH ANN 459 HOWARD D
TOWNSEND, SARAH CEC 195 6TH E DI
TOWNSEND, SILAS ANN 474 HOWARD D
TOWNSEND, STEPHEN KEN 212 2ND DIST
TOWNSEND, SUSAN CAR 258 3RD DIST
TOWNSEND, TEAGLE WOR 300 SNOW HIL
TOWNSEND, THOMAS CAR 393 2ND DIST
TOWNSEND, THOMAS BAL 054 1ST WARD
TOWNSEND, THOMAS ALL 176 7TH E.D.
TOWNSEND, THOMAS BAL 196 2ND WARD
TOWNSEND, THOMAS B. BAL 195 2ND WARD
TOWNSEND, THOMAS J. BAL 008 9TH WARD
TOWNSEND, THOMAS J. WOR 183 6TH E DI
TOWNSEND, WILLIAM WOR 254 1ST CENS
TOWNSEND, WILLIAM WOR 341 1ST E DI
TOWNSEND, WILLIAM WOR 321 1ST E DI
TOWNSEND, WILLIAM D. BAL 387 13TH WAR
TOWNSEND, WILLIAM E. WOR 203 4TH E DI
TOWNSEND, WILLIAM J. WOR 188 7TH E DI
TOWNSEND, WILLIAM M. BAL 285 1ST DIST
TOWNSEND, ZADOC SOM 430 PRINCESS
TOWNSHEAD, CATHARINE ALL 054 10TH E.D
TOWNSHEND, FIDELIA BAL 171 16TH WAR
TOWNSHEND, GEORGE L. PRI 060 NOTTINGH
TOWNSHEND, JEREMIAH PRI 116 PISCATAW
TOWNSHEND, JOHN PRI 062 NOTTINGH
TOWNSHEND, M.M. ALL 263 CUMBERLA
TOWNSHEND, MARY PRI 116 PISCATAW
TOWNSHEND, WILLIAM B. PRI 111 PISCATAW
TOWNSHEND, WILLIAM S. S. MGM 374 ROCKERLE
TOWNSLEY, JOHN L. HAR 146 3RD DIST
TOWNSLEY, SUSAN HAR 201 3RD DIST
TOWNSON, JOHN HAR 044 1ST DIST
TOWSEL, EDA KEN 230 2ND DIST
TOWSEND, BRIDGET A. BAL 405 14TH WAR
TOWSEND, DAVID QUE 125 1ST E DI
TOWSEND, JSOHUA WOR 342 1ST E DI
TOWSEND, WILLIAM BAL 106 18TH WAR
TOWSER, ANN ALL 180 8TH E.D.
TOWSER, BENJAMIN KEN 278 1ST DIST
TOWSON, ANNY H. HAR 043 1ST DIST
TOWSON, CHARLES * BAL 293 20TH WAR
TOWSON, DAVID BAL 171 1ST WARD
TOWSON, ELLEN BAL 170 2ND DIST
TOWSON, J. G. BAL 300 20TH WAR
TOWSON, JAMES F. BAL 379 8TH WARD
TOWSON, JOHN FRE 390 PETERSVI
TOWSON, JOHN C. BAL 212 6TH DIST
TOWSON, JOHNP. BAL 131 1ST WARD
TOWSON, JOSEPH BAL 328 3RD WARD
TOWSON, MATILDA BAL 258 17TH WAR
TOWSON, ROSE HAR 149 3RD DIST
TOWSON, SAMUEL J. HAR 044 1ST DIST
TOWSON, SAMUEL T. BAL 166 16TH WAR
TOWSON, SARAH BAL 137 16TH WAR
TOWSON, SARAH BAL 404 8TH WARD
TOWSON, THOMAS W. BAL 449 8TH WARD
TOWSON, WILLIAM O. BAL 042 4TH WARD
TOY, JOHN D. HAR 104 2ND DIST
TOY, SAMUEL D. * BAL 301 20TH WAR
TOY, WALTER BAL 124 16TH WAR
TOY, WILLIAM HAR 105 2ND DIST
TOYCE, JOHN FRE 014 FREDERIC
TOYER, BARTON-BLACK CAR 386 2ND DIST
TOYER, PHILIP CAR 384 2ND DIST
TOZIER, LORENY MGM 414 MEDLEY 3
TRABERS, BENAJMIN BAL 133 1ST WARD
TRABON, ELIZABETH BAL 261 12TH WAR
TRABREY, JAMES BAL 035 1ST WARD
TRABUT, WILLIAM BAL 391 8TH WARD
TRACE, GEORGE CAR 343 6TH DIST
TRACEY, ALEXANDER BAL 296 7TH WARD
TRACEY, ALMIA BAL 158 19TH WAR
TRACEY, ANDREW BAL 160 1ST WARD
TRACEY, ASBURY BAL 296 7TH WARD
TRACEY, BARNEY BAL 423 8TH WARD
TRACEY, BENJAMIN BAL 028 2ND DIST
TRACEY, ELIZA ALL 263 CUMBERLA
TRACEY, ELIZABETH BAL 027 2ND DIST
TRACEY, ELLEN BAL 003 4TH WARD
TRACEY, EPHRAIM BAL 025 2ND DIST
TRACEY, GENEVA BAL 334 3RD WARD
TRACEY, GEORGE B. BAL 227 19TH WAR
TRACEY, GILSON BAL 051 2ND DIST
TRACEY, ISAAC BAL 040 2ND DIST
TRACEY, JANE BAL 051 2ND DIST
TRACEY, JOHN BAL 049 2ND DIST
TRACEY, JOSHUA BAL 056 2ND DIST
TRACEY, JSOH BAL 039 2ND DIST
TRACEY, JUDY BAL 278 7TH WARD
TRACEY, MARGARET BAL 052 2ND DIST
TRACEY, MARGARET BAL 300 20TH WAR
TRACEY, MARTIN BAL 005 9TH WARD
TRACEY, MARY BAL 005 9TH WARD
TRACEY, MARY BAL 024 2ND DIST
TRACEY, MARY ALL 136 4TH E.D.
TRACEY, MARY A. BAL 132 16TH WAR
TRACEY, MICHAEL ALL 049 10TH E.D
TRACEY, MISS A. FRE 199 5TH E DI
TRACEY, PLEASANT BAL 035 2ND DIST
TRACEY, RESIN BAL 326 7TH WARD
TRACEY, RICHARD BAL 037 2ND DIST
TRACEY, SAMUEL BAL 049 2ND DIST
TRACEY, SOLOM BAL 034 2ND DIST
TRACEY, TEASA BAL 247 12TH WAR
TRACEY, THOMAS BAL 038 2ND DIST
TRACEY, THOMAS BAL 278 12TH WAR
TRACEY, WILLIAM BAL 045 2ND DIST
TRACEY, WILLIAM BAL 296 7TH WARD
TRACEY, WILLIAM A. BAL 191 2ND WARD
TRACK, MATHIAS BAL 065 2ND DIST
TRACKLER, GEORGE HAR 156 3RD DIST
TRACY, ANN R. ANN 488 HOWARD D
TRACY, CATHERINE BAL 372 8TH WARD
TRACY, CATHERINE E. FRE 018 FREDERIC
TRACY, CHARLES HAR 017 1ST DIST
TRACY, CHARLES H. BAL 028 18TH WAR
TRACY, CURTIS BAL 207 6TH DIST
TRACY, EDWARD BAL 215 6TH DIST
TRACY, EDWARD PRI 107 PISCATAW
TRACY, ELIAS L. FRE 076 FREDERIC
TRACY, ELIZABETH HAR 017 1ST DIST
TRACY, ELIZABETH CAR 304 1ST DIST
TRACY, ELIZABETH FRE 320 MIDDLETO
TRACY, ELIZABETH ANN 465 HOWARD D
TRACY, ELIZABETH ANN 439 HOWARD D
TRACY, ELLENOR C. ST 335 4TH E DI
TRACY, EPHRAIM CAR 344 6TH DIST
TRACY, GEORGE BAL 189 5TH DIST
TRACY, HIRAM ALL 171 7TH E.D.
TRACY, JAMES BAL 214 6TH DIST
TRACY, JAMES BAL 218 6TH DIST
TRACY, JAMES BAL 181 6TH WARD
TRACY, JAMES BAL 159 11TH WAR
TRACY, JAMES L. WAS 021 2ND SUBD
TRACY, JARRETT BAL 005 18TH WAR
TRACY, JOHN BAL 084 18TH WAR
TRACY, JOHN FRE 317 MIDDLETO
TRACY, JOHN WAS 256 1ST DIST
TRACY, JOHN BAL 214 6TH DIST
TRACY, JOHN BAL 097 1ST WARD
TRACY, JOHN H. ST 335 4TH E DI
TRACY, JOHN M. BAL 201 6TH DIST
TRACY, JOHN P. BAL 051 18TH WAR
TRACY, JOHNATHAN BAL 191 5TH DIST
TRACY, JOSHUA BAL 214 6TH DIST
TRACY, JOSHUA HAR 023 1ST DIST
TRACY, MARGARET CAR 345 6TH DIST
TRACY, MARGARET WAS 170 FUNKSTOW
TRACY, MARGARET WAS 135 HAGERSTO
TRACY, MARTHA BAL 194 5TH DIST
TRACY, MARY BAL 186 2ND WARD
TRACY, MATHEW BAL 145 11TH WAR
TRACY, MATTHEW WAS 259 1ST DIST
TRACY, MICAJA BAL 201 6TH DIST
TRACY, MICAJAI BAL 215 6TH DIST
TRACY, MICHAEL ALL 053 10TH E.D
TRACY, MICHAEL ALL 129 4TH E.D.
TRACY, MONROW HAR 066 1ST DIST

TRACY, RICHARD	BAL	191	5TH DIST
TRACY, RICHARD M.	HAR	070	1ST DIST
TRACY, SAMUEL G.	ALL	227	CUMBERLA
TRACY, SARAH	BAL	025	2ND DIST
TRACY, SARAH	BAL	140	11TH WAR
TRACY, SEWEL	BAL	045	2ND DIST
TRACY, SUSAN	ALL	097	5TH E.D.
TRACY, THOMAS	BAL	186	5TH DIST
TRACY, WASHINGTON *	BAL	321	1ST DIST
TRACY, WILLIAM	BAL	186	5TH DIST
TRACY, WILLIAM	BAL	087	18TH WAR
TRACY, WILLIAM	BAL	029	4TH WARD
TRACY, WILLIAM N.	HAR	022	1ST DIST
TRACY, WINFORD	BAL	269	17TH WAR
TRADER, ADELINE	WOR	230	6TH E DI
TRADER, CHRISTOPHER	BAL	157	2ND DIST
TRADER, CLARRISSA	WOR	237	6TH E DI
TRADER, ELIZABETH-BLACK	WOR	347	1ST E DI
TRADER, GEORGE	WOR	237	6TH E DI
TRADER, JOHN	BAL	090	5TH WARD
TRADER, JOHN	CEC	148	PORT DUP
TRADER, JOHN A.	WOR	233	6TH E DI
TRADER, JOSHUA S. H.	SOM	501	SALISBUR
TRADER, LEAH	SOM	501	SALISBUR
TRADER, LEVIN W.	SOM	460	HANGARY
TRADER, LITTLETON	WOR	326	1ST E DI
TRADER, LITTLETON P.	WOR	177	6TH E DI
TRADER, ROSE A.	WOR	176	6TH E DI
TRADER, RUFUS K.	WOR	218	4TH E DI
TRADER, SAMUEL T.	WOR	185	6TH E DI
TRADER, THOMAS	BAL	090	10TH WAR
TRADER, THOMAS R. B.	SOM	537	TYASKIN
TRADER, WILLIAM B.	WOR	200	8TH E DI
TRAELE, JAMES S.	ALL	184	9TH E.D.
TRAELE, NATHAN	ALL	183	8TH E.D.
TRAFFORD, GEORGE	BAL	105	2ND DIST
TRAFFORD, JAMES	BAL	144	1ST WARD
TRAGER, SARAH A.	HAR	178	3RD DIST
TRAGO, PASCAL	HAR	127	2ND DIST
TRAGO, TASCAL	HAR	131	2ND DIST
TRAGO, WILLIAM	HAR	127	2ND DIST
TRAGO, WILLIAM	FRE	006	FREDERIC
TRAHEAM, ANN	WOR	178	6TH E DI
TRAHEY, MARY	BAL	035	1ST WARD
TRAIL, ABIGAIL	MGM	424	MEDLEY 3
TRAIL, ANN	FRE	233	BUCKEYST
TRAIL, EDWARD	FRE	045	FREDERIC
TRAIL, EDWARD	MGM	339	CLARKSBU
TRAIL, EDWARD L.	MGM	381	ROCKERLE
TRAIL, HANNAH	MGM	409	MEDLEY 3
TRAIL, HENRY	MGM	397	ROCKERLE
TRAIL, HEZEKIAH	MGM	428	CLARKSTR
TRAIL, JAMES L.	FRE	273	NEW MARK
TRAIL, JAMES R.	ANN	458	HOWARD D
TRAIL, LOUISA T.	BAL	108	15TH WAR
TRAIL, MARY A.S.	MGM	403	ROCKERLE
TRAIL, NOTLEY	MGM	330	CRACKLIN
TRAIL, PERRY	MGM	403	ROCKERLE
TRAIL, REBECCA	BAL	204	19TH WAR
TRAIL, SARAH	BAL	204	19TH WAR
TRAIL, SUSANNA	MGM	337	CRACKLIN
TRAIL, VERBINDA	MGM	336	CRACKLIN
TRAIL, WILLIAM E.	MGM	429	CLARKSTR
TRAILE, CASRA	ALL	183	8TH E.D.
TRAILE, DAVID	ALL	183	8TH E.D.
TRAILE, E. H.	ALL	126	4TH E.D.
TRAILE, JAMES S.	ALL	184	9TH E.D.
TRAILE, JOHN	ALL	183	8TH E.D.
TRAILE, WILLIAM	ALL	183	8TH E.D.
TRAILEN, JOSEPH H.	ANN	336	3RD DIST
TRAILY, BARNHART	BAL	103	5TH WARD
TRAIN, ALEXNADER	ANN	515	HOWARD D
TRAINER, ARTHUR	BAL	271	17TH WAR
TRAINER, BERNARD	BAL	365	13TH WAR
TRAINER, EDWARD	BAL	348	7TH WARD
TRAINER, GEORGE	BAL	086	18TH WAR
TRAINER, HUGH	BAL	264	20TH WAR
TRAINER, JAMES	BAL	039	1ST WARD
TRAINER, JAMES	BAL	127	5TH WARD
TRAINER, JANE	FRE	122	CREAGERS
TRAINER, JOHN	FRE	113	CREAGERS
TRAINER, JOHN	BAL	172	11TH WAR
TRAINER, LOUISA	FRE	278	NEW MARK
TRAINER, MARGARET	BAL	319	7TH WARD
TRAINER, MARSELLAS	BAL	092	18TH WAR
TRAINER, MARY ANN	BAL	365	13TH WAR
TRAINER, OWEN	BAL	056	15TH WAR
TRAINER, OWEN	BAL	421	1ST DIST
TRAINER, ROSE	ALL	071	5TH E.D.
TRAINER, THOMAS	BAL	371	8TH WARD
TRAINOR, ANTHONY	BAL	079	10TH WAR
TRAKEL, SARAH	BAL	337	7TH WARD
TRALLINGER, JACOB *	ALL	133	4TH E.D.
TRAMMEL, JOHN	MGM	385	ROCKERLE
TRAMMEL, REBECCA	BAL	344	3RD WARD
TRAMMER, VIRGINIA*	BAL	345	3RD WARD
TRAMPER, LEAHART	BAL	292	1ST DIST
TRANDER, HEZEKIAH W.	MGM	416	MEDLEY 3
TRANER, JOSEPH	BAL	225	1ST DIST
TRANER, PATRICK	BAL	423	3RD WARD
TRANGUA, CEASOR *	BAL	353	1ST DIST
TRAPNELL, JOSEPH	BAL	082	4TH WARD
TRAPNELL, JOSEPH	FRE	027	FREDERIC
TRAPPNELL, GEORGE	BAL	137	5TH WARD
TRASY, REBECCA	CAR	183	8TH DIST
TRATTER, JOHN R.	WOR	335	1ST E DI
TRAVELLA, ANN E.	BAL	400	14TH WAR
TRAVER, FREEMAN	FRE	123	CREAGERS
TRAVER, JOHN	WAS	211	1ST DIST
TRAVER, SUSAN	FRE	362	CATOCTIN
TRAVER, ZACHARIAH	WAS	217	1ST DIST
TRAVERS, ANN	BAL	210	2ND WARD
TRAVERS, ANNA	BAL	052	15TH WAR
TRAVERS, ARELIA	SOM	534	QUANTICO
TRAVERS, ARINA	BAL	043	15TH WAR
TRAVERS, BENJAMIN	DOR	329	3RD DIVI
TRAVERS, BENJAMIN*	DOR	330	3RD DIVI
TRAVERS, BOYLE	FRE	081	FREDERIC
TRAVERS, CATHARINE	HAR	081	2ND DIST
TRAVERS, CHARITY	DOR	350	3RD DIVI
TRAVERS, CHARLES W.	BAL	274	17TH WAR
TRAVERS, CHARLES W. JR.	BAL	274	17TH WAR
TRAVERS, DENNARD	BAL	273	17TH WAR
TRAVERS, DORICK D.	BAL	069	1ST WARD
TRAVERS, DRAPER	DOR	372	3RD DIVI
TRAVERS, EDWARD	BAL	194	17TH WAR
TRAVERS, ELIZA	BAL	274	17TH WAR
TRAVERS, ELIZABETH	BAL	104	10TH WAR
TRAVERS, ELIZABETH	SOM	457	DAMES QU
TRAVERS, ELIZABETH A.	BAL	100	15TH WAR
TRAVERS, EMILA	DOR	357	3RD DIVI
TRAVERS, FRANCES A.	BAL	083	15TH WAR
TRAVERS, FRANCIS	BAL	086	15TH WAR
TRAVERS, FRANCIS	BAL	077	15TH WAR
TRAVERS, FREDERICK	FRE	359	CATOCTIN
TRAVERS, HENERY	DOR	331	3RD DIVI
TRAVERS, HENERY	DOR	330	3RD DIVI
TRAVERS, HENRY	BAL	236	17TH WAR
TRAVERS, HESTER	BAL	043	15TH WAR
TRAVERS, J.	BAL	149	1ST WARD
TRAVERS, JACOB	DOR	357	3RD DIVI
TRAVERS, JEREMIAH T.	BAL	054	15TH WAR
TRAVERS, JOHN	BAL	026	15TH WAR
TRAVERS, JOHN	BAL	165	1ST WARD
TRAVERS, JOHN	BAL	080	15TH WAR
TRAVERS, JOHN	DOR	332	3RD DIVI
TRAVERS, JOHN	DOR	330	3RD DIVI
TRAVERS, JOHN	BAL	262	17TH WAR
TRAVERS, JOHN W. D.	DOR	359	3RD DIVI
TRAVERS, LAKE	DOR	333	3RD DIVI
TRAVERS, LEVY	DOR	357	3RD DIVI
TRAVERS, MARY	DOR	357	3RD DIVI
TRAVERS, MARY	DOR	331	3RD DIVI
TRAVERS, MARY	BAL	104	1ST WARD
TRAVERS, MARY J.	SOM	539	TYASKIN
TRAVERS, MARY-MULATTO	BAL	224	2ND WARD
TRAVERS, MATHEW	DOR	332	3RD DIVI
TRAVERS, MATTHIAS	SOM	543	TYASKIN
TRAVERS, RICHARD	DOR	357	3RD DIVI
TRAVERS, SAMUEL	DOR	358	3RD DIVI
TRAVERS, SAMUEL H.	BAL	100	15TH WAR
TRAVERS, SILAS	DOR	333	3RD DIVI
TRAVERS, THOMAS	BAL	018	15TH WAR
TRAVERS, THOMAS B.	BAL	165	1ST WARD
TRAVERS, THOMAS B.	DOR	356	3RD DIVI
TRAVERS, VACHEL	DOR	330	3RD DIVI
TRAVERS, WILLIAM	BAL	260	17TH WAR
TRAVERS, WILLIAM D.	DOR	356	3RD DIVI
TRAVERS, WILLIAM H.	BAL	069	1ST WARD
TRAVERS, WILLIAM K.	DOR	357	3RD DIVI
TRAVERSE, ARTHUR	DOR	387	1ST DIST
TRAVERSE, ARTHUR	DOR	406	1ST DIST
TRAVERSE, DEVERAUX	DOR	448	1ST DIST
TRAVERSE, FRANCES M.	DOR	376	1ST DIST
TRAVERSE, GEORGE W.	WAS	219	1ST DIST
TRAVERSE, MARY	DOR	414	1ST DIST
TRAVERSE, JANE	DOR	324	1ST DIST
TRAVERSE, MARTHA J.*	DOR	375	1ST DIST
TRAVERSE, MARY	BAL	329	13TH WAR
TRAVERSE, MARY A.	DOR	390	1ST DIST
TRAVERSE, MASHACK*	DOR	444	1ST DIST
TRAVERSE, MATTHEW	DOR	387	1ST DIST
TRAVERSE, THOMAS	DOR	405	1ST DIST
TRAVERSE, WILLIAM	DOR	308	1ST DIST
TRAVICE, SARAH	CAR	092	NO TWP L
TRAVIS, ANN	BAL	402	14TH WAR
TRAVIS, EDWARD	BAL	459	8TH WARD
TRAVIS, JAME SL.	ST	262	3RD E DI
TRAVIS, T.H.	BAL	172	1ST WARD
TRAVIS, WILLIAM	BAL	155	1ST WARD
TRAVIS, WILLIAM	BAL	134	11TH WAR
TRAVIS, WILLIAM R.	BAL	182	11TH WAR
TRAVOR, MARY	DOR	357	3RD DIVI
TRAXEL, GEORGE W.	FRE	164	EMMITTSB
TRAY, ABRAM	BAL	207	19TH WAR
TRAY, JACOB	BAL	007	4TH WARD
TRAY, MARGARETT*	BAL	039	4TH WARD
TRAY, MARY	BAL	127	18TH WAR
TRAYER, JACOB	FRE	239	NEW MARK
TRAYER, THOMAS B.	FRE	239	NEW MARK
TRAYSE, MICHAEL	BAL	258	6TH WARD
TRAZEL, NICHOLAS	BAL	125	1ST WARD
TREACEY, JAMES	BAL	380	1ST DIST
TREACLE, MARY	MGM	327	CRACKLIN
TREACLE, MICHE	BAL	407	1ST DIST
TREACY, CATHARINE	BAL	437	1ST DIST
TREACY, DARCUS L.	BAL	434	1ST DIST
TREACY, EDWARD	BAL	431	1ST DIST
TREACY, JAMES	BAL	433	1ST DIST
TREACY, JAMES	BAL	436	1ST DIST
TREACY, JEFFERSON	BAL	334	1ST DIST
TREACY, JOHN	BAL	418	1ST DIST
TREACY, JOHN	BAL	436	1ST DIST
TREACY, JOHN H.	BAL	419	1ST DIST
TREACY, JOSHUA	BAL	433	1ST DIST
TREACY, MARY	BAL	419	1ST DIST
TREACY, NICHOLAS	BAL	419	1ST DIST
TREACY, OWEN	BAL	434	1ST DIST
TREACY, STARRET	BAL	430	1ST DIST
TREACY, THOMAS C.	BAL	441	1ST DIST
TREACY, WILLIAM	BAL	428	1ST DIST
TREACY, WILLIAM F.	BAL	434	1ST DIST
TREACY, WILLIAM R.	BAL	381	1ST DIST
TREADAWAY, CHRNSWITH	BAL	158	2ND DIST
TREADAWAY, ELLEN	BAL	052	2ND DIST
TREADFEDER, HENRY	BAL	073	2ND DIST
TREADWAWAY, LYDIA	BAL	074	2ND DIST
TREADWAY, ANN	HAR	166	3RD DIST
TREADWAY, CARVILLE	HAR	105	2ND DIST
TREADWAY, DANIEL	BAL	032	2ND DIST
TREADWAY, ELIFLIT	BAL	318	7TH WARD
TREADWAY, ELLEN	BAL	211	5TH DIST
TREADWAY, LEWIS	BAL	299	20TH WAR
TREADWAY, MARY	BAL	042	2ND DIST
TREADWAY, NICHOLAS	BAL	299	20TH WAR
TREADWAY, SARAH	BAL	454	14TH WAR
TREADWAY, THOMAS	BAL	299	20TH WAR
TREADWAY, THOMAS	HAR	114	2ND DIST
TREADWAY, ZADOCK	HAR	122	2ND DIST
TREADWELL, ELIZABETH	HAR	115	2ND DIST
TREADWELL, JAMES	HAR	115	2ND DIST
TREADWELL, JOHN W.	HAR	060	1ST DIST
TREADWELL, OLIVER W.	MGM	377	ROCKERLE
TREADWELL, WILLIAM	HAR	109	2ND DIST
TREAGER, BENJAMIN	BAL	107	2ND DIST
TREAKLE, EZEKIEL*	BAL	336	3RD WARD
TREAKLE, GEORGE	ANN	485	HOWARD D
TREAKLE, JAMES	ANN	483	HOWARD D
TREAKLE, MARY A.	BAL	165	19TH WAR
TREAN, W.H.	BAL	116	1ST WARD
TREANER, RACHAEL	FRE	125	CREAGERS
TREBERS, GUSTA	ALL	245	CUMBER_A
TREBERS, LAURA	ALL	245	CUMBERLA
TREBERS, THEODORE	ALL	244	CUMBERLA
TRECY, MARY	ALL	206	CUMBERLA
TREDAWAY, JOHN	HAR	017	1ST DIST
TREDEWAY, AMOS	HAR	172	3RD DIST
TREDWELL, STEPHENSON	BAL	096	2ND DIST
TREEMAN, SAMUEL B.	BAL	277	20TH WAR
TREEPOCK, CHARLES	ALL	197	CUMBERLA
TREFFENBERG, WILLIAM	BAL	083	15TH WAR
TREGARE, THOMAS	QUE	250	5TH E DI
TREGER, ALICE	HAR	183	3RD DIST
TREGO, ELIZABETH*	DOR	368	3RD DIVI
TREGO, GEORGE W.	BAL	198	17TH WAR
TREGO, WILLIAM	ALL	216	CUMBERLA
TREGO, WILLIAM	BAL	052	15TH WAR
TREHEARN, GATTY	SOM	460	HANGARY
TREHEARN, LEAH	SOM	422	PRINCESS
TREHEARN, THOASM	SOM	416	DUBLIN D
TREIBEAS, J.G.	WAS	127	HAGERSTO
TREICH, JOSEPH	BAL	448	14TH WAR
TREIR, DEBORAH *	KEN	261	1ST DIST
TRELEVIN, MARY	WOR	314	2ND E DI
TREMBER, WILLIAM	BAL	142	1ST WARD
TREMBLE, ELIZA	ALL	257	CUMBERLA
TREMBLE, GEORGE	BAL	020	2ND DIST
TREMBLE, W.	BAL	020	2ND DIST
TREMMEA, THOMAS H.	BAL	412	3RD WARD
TREMONLET, HENRY	FRE	202	5TH E DI
TREMONTEL, BERNARD	FRE	202	5TH E DI
TREMTH, ADAM	BAL	083	1ST WARD
TRENCHARD, ANN	KEN	282	3RD DIST
TRENCHARD, GEORGE O.	QUE	156	2ND E DI
TRENDELL, HENRY	BAL	228	19TH WAR
TRENDOLPH, ADAM	BAL	167	19TH WAR
TRENETT, PANDELON *	BAL	315	20TH WAR
TRENT, ANN	HAR	088	2ND DIST
TRENT, JOHNS.	ALL	040	2ND E.D.
TRENT, SMAUEL	ALL	040	2ND E.D.
TRENTON, JOHN	BAL	023	9TH WARD
TREPFASTERS, JACK	BAL	105	1ST WARD
TRESBURY, CLEMENTINE	BAL	282	12TH WAR
TRESE, H.J.	BAL	118	1ST WARD
TRESELL, THOMAS	BAL	269	20TH WAR
TRESLER, CHRISTIAN	BAL	333	3RD WARD
TRESS, JACOB	CEC	027	CHESAPEA
TRESS, NELSO *	BAL	136	2ND DIST
TRESSEL, JOHN	BAL	215	2ND WARD
TRETTENER, MARY	BAL	205	2ND WARD
TREULIB, PETER	BAL	358	3RD WARD
TREULIEB, FREDERICA	BAL	221	6TH WARD
TREVET, W.R.B.	BAL	123	1ST WARD
TREVETT, BENJAMIN G.	BAL	261	6TH WARD
TREVIS, JAMES	BAL	178	6TH WARD
TREVOTT, RUSSELL	WAS	019	2ND SUBD
TREXEL, CATHARIEN	FRE	161	EMMITTSB
TREXEL, NANCY	FRE	145	10TH E D
TREXLER, CATHERINE	BAL	386	8TH WARD
TREXLER, MARY	BAL	217	19TH WAR
TREYER, WILIAM	BAL	076	1ST WARD
TREZZARD, JOHN T.	QUE	189	3RD E DI
TRIAN, ANNA	BAL	307	1ST DIST
TRIBERT, HENRY	BAL	037	18TH WAR
TRIBLE, FREDERICK	BAL	155	19TH WAR
TRICE, ALAXANDER	DOR	314	1ST DIST
TRICE, CHARLES	CAR	128	NO TWP L
TRICE, CHARLES E.	BAL	407	3RD WARD
TRICE, CLEMENT	DOR	319	1ST DIST
TRICE, EDWARD	CAR	108	NO TWP L
TRICE, ELISHA	DOR	320	1ST DIST
TRICE, GEORGE W.	BAL	407	3RD WARD
TRICE, JAMES	CAR	138	NO TWP L
TRICE, JOHN	CAR	129	NO TWP L
TRICE, JOHN W.	DOR	313	1ST DIST
TRICE, SARAH	CAR	151	NO TWP L
TRICE, SPENCER	DOR	321	1ST DIST
TRICE, THOMAS	CAR	152	NO TWP L
TRICE, THOMAS	WAS	005	WILLIAMS
TRICE, THOMAS*	DOR	312	1ST DIST
TRICE, WILLIAM	CAR	117	NO TWP L
TRICK, JOHN	CEC	050	1ST E DI
TRIEN, JOHN	CAR	175	8TH DIST
TRIER, ELIZABETH	CAR	133	NO TWP L
TRIER, NELLY	BAL	348	3RD WARD
TRIER, WILLIAM	CAR	127	NO TWP L
TRIESE, HENRY	BAL	303	12TH WAR
TRIEST, JOHN C.	CAR	353	6TH DIST
TRIFORD, MARY	KEN	228	2ND DIST
TRIGANT, SISTER M.C.	FRE	197	5TH E DI
TRIGER, DALILAH	BAL	442	14TH WAR
TRIGG, SAMUEL T.	BAL	351	1ST DIST
TRILIER, MARY	ALL	234	CUMBERLA
TRILLEY, SISTER BRIDGET	FRE	198	5TH E DI
TRILSON, JOSHUA	BAL	306	3RD WARD
TRIMBLE, ANNA	CEC	121	4TH E DI
TRIMBLE, ARCHOBALD	WAS	117	2ND DIST
TRIMBLE, CATHARINE	BAL	244	2ND WARD
TRIMBLE, CHARLES	BAL	062	18TH WAR
TRIMBLE, ELIZ	BAL	254	12TH WAR
TRIMBLE, ELIZABETH	HAR	112	2ND DIST
TRIMBLE, ELIZABETH S.	FRE	065	FREDERIC
TRIMBLE, FALDEN	BAL	003	EASTERN
TRIMBLE, HARRIET	BAL	285	1ST DIST
TRIMBLE, HENRY	BAL	426	1ST DIST
TRIMBLE, HENRY	ALL	098	5TH E.D.
TRIMBLE, HENRY H.	BAL	340	3RD WARD
TRIMBLE, J. R.	BAL	151	11TH WAR
TRIMBLE, JAMES	CEC	135	6TH E DI
TRIMBLE, JAMES	CEC	141	6TH E DI
TRIMBLE, JAMES W.	BAL	447	14TH WAR
TRIMBLE, JAMES R.	CEC	188	7TH E DI
TRIMBLE, JOSEPH	HAR	112	2ND DIST
TRIMBLE, NANCY	BAL	433	8TH WARD
TRIMBLE, REBECCA B.	BAL	038	4TH WARD
TRIMBLE, SAMUEL	BAL	021	4TH WARD
TRIMBLE, THOMAS	BAL	016	4TH WARD
TRIMBLE, WILLIAM	BAL	060	4TH WARD
TRIMBLE, WILLIAM	PRI	100	SPALDING
TRIMBLE, WILLIAM P.	BAL	151	11TH WAR
TRIMBLE, MARY	BAL	244	2ND WARD
TRIMBLES, ROBERT	SOM	464	HANGARY
TRIMBS, WILLIAM	BAL	051	1ST WARD
TRIMELL, ELLEN	BAL	025	1ST WARD
TRIMIBLE, ANN M.	BAL	215	11TH WAR
TRIMINGHAM, RALPH	BAL	054	4TH WARD
TRIMMERMAN, HENRY S.	BAL	008	15TH WAR
TRIMP, HERMAN	BAL	019	9TH WARD
TRIMPIN, MARY	BAL	034	15TH WAR
TRINDER, VALENTINE	BAL	213	6TH DIST
TRINE, EMANUEL	CAR	355	6TH DIST
TRINE, SAMUEL	CAR	275	7TH DIST
TRINGER, JACOB	CAR	279	7TH DIST
TRINSSTOL, J.	BAL	271	12TH WAR
TRIP, CORNELIUS	BAL	461	1ST DIST
TRIP, FREDERIC-BLACK	CAR	069	NO TWP L
TRIPHAM, SUSAN	BAL	059	10TH WAR
TRIPLER, SUSAN	FRE	094	FREDERIC
TRIPLETT, WILLIAM S.	ALL	218	CUMBERLA
TRIPOLET, EDWARD	BAL	325	1ST DIST

Name	County	Page	District
TRIPOLET, EPHRAIM	BAL	229	1ST DIST
TRIPOLET, JOHN W.	BAL	229	1ST DIST
TRIPP, ELIZA	BAL	036	4TH WARD
TRIPP, HENRY	BAL	167	16TH WAR
TRIPP, JOHN	BAL	299	17TH WAR
TRIPP, MARY	BAL	058	4TH WARD
TRIPP, MARY	BAL	059	4TH WARD
TRIPP, REBECCA	BAL	254	17TH WAR
TRIPP, RIDELY A.	BAL	067	4TH WARD
TRIPP, SARAH J.	BAL	052	9TH WARD
TRIPP, TILGHMAN	BAL	052	15TH WAR
TRIPPE, CATHERINE D.	MGM	316	CRACKLIN
TRIPPE, FREDERICK	QUE	205	3RD E DI
TRIPPE, HANNAH	BAL	471	14TH WAR
TRIPPE, HENRIETTA	DOR	403	1ST DIST
TRIPPE, HENRY	BAL	046	15TH WAR
TRIPPE, J. E.	BAL	085	4TH WARD
TRIPPE, JONAS	DOR	379	1ST DIST
TRIPPE, JULIANA	BAL	101	10TH WAR
TRIPPE, JULIANNA	TAL	041	EASTON D
TRIPPE, MARY W.	BAL	003	15TH WAR
TRIPPE, NICHOLUS H.	TAL	037	EASTON D
TRIPPE, RACHEL	TAL	045	EASTON T
TRIPPE, RICHARD	BAL	107	18TH WAR
TRIPPE, SALLY	TAL	036	EASTON D
TRIPPE, SAMUEL	TAL	041	EASTON D
TRIPPE, WILLIAM	QUE	209	3RD E DI
TRIPPE, WILLIAM	BAL	108	18TH WAR
TRIPPE, WILLIAM J.	TAL	037	EASTON D
TRIPPE, WILLIAM R.	TAL	042	EASTON D
TRIPPS, E.	BAL	449	8TH WARD
TRISCOTT, GEORGE	FRE	018	FREDERIC
TRISE, WILLIAM MC D.*	TAL	058	EASTON D
TRISKINS, PETER	BAL	170	11TH WAR
TRITCH, BENJAMIN	WAS	190	1ST DIST
TRITCH, HENRY	WAS	169	FUNKSTOW
TRITCH, JACOB	WAS	165	HAGERSTO
TRITE, ANN	BAL	232	12TH WAR
TRITE, JOHN H.	BAL	232	12TH WAR
TRITLE, JACOB	WAS	258	1ST DIST
TRITLE, LEWIS	WAS	248	SMITHSBU
TRITLES, JACOB	WAS	277	RIDGEVIL
TRITT, EDWARD	FRE	397	PETERSVI
TRIUST, FRANCIS	BAL	377	13TH WAR
TRIUTT, MARY	WOR	304	SNOW HIL
TROATH, JOHN	DOR	371	3RD DIVI
TROCKENBROD, JOHN	BAL	200	11TH WAR
TROGLE, GEORGE	BAL	171	2ND DIST
TROHAM, SAMUEL	WOR	301	SNOW HIL
TROLL, FREDERICK	BAL	335	13TH WAR
TRONE, ABRAHAM	WAS	296	1ST DIST
TRONE, ADAM	CAR	401	2ND DIST
TRONE, ADAM	CAR	245	3RD DIST
TRONE, GEORGE	CAR	342	6TH DIST
TRONE, JOHN	FRE	138	CREAGERS
TRONE, LEWIS	WAS	271	1ST DIST
TRONE, MICHAEL	CAR	342	6TH DIST
TRONTFELLER, JOHN	BAL	335	13TH WAR
TROOP, CAROLINE M.	BAL	054	15TH WAR
TROOP, SAMUEL	BAL	093	2ND DIST
TROT, ELIZA	BAL	461	1ST DIST
TROT, HENRY	BAL	249	1ST DIST
TROT, MARGARET A.	BAL	308	7TH WARD
TROT, SOPHIA	BAL	178	11TH WAR
TROT, WILLIAM	CAR	217	5TH DIST
TROTT, ELEAZER	CAL	060	3RD DIST
TROTT, ELIZA	BAL	407	3RD WARD
TROTT, ELLEN *	ANN	396	8TH DIST
TROTT, FRANCIS A.	CAL	063	3RD DIST
TROTT, JACOB	ANN	405	8TH DIST
TROTT, JESSEE	CAL	054	3RD DIST
TROTT, M. E.	ANN	400	8TH DIST
TROTT, MARY	BAL	134	5TH WARD
TROTT, MARY	CAL	060	3RD DIST
TROTT, MC KENDREE	CAL	050	3RD DIST
TROTT, ROBERT H.	TAL	102	ST MICHA
TROTT, SABREC	CAL	062	3RD DIST
TROTT, SAMUEL	CAL	036	2ND DIST
TROTT, SAMUEL E.	BAL	100	15TH WAR
TROTT, SYBERT	BAL	250	6TH WARD
TROTT, THOMAS	BAL	377	3RD WARD
TROTT, THOMAS J.	CAL	058	3RD DIST
TROTT, WILLIAM	CAL	047	3RD DIST
TROTT, WILLIAM	CAL	050	3RD DIST
TROTTON, THOMAS	BAL	359	3RD WARD
TROUDNER, JOHN	BAL	229	6TH WARD
TROUGHT, ROBERT	BAL	372	1ST DIST
TROUMPOUR, JOSHUUA	WAS	139	2ND DIST
TROUP, ADAM	CEC	167	6TH E DI
TROUP, DAVID	WAS	105	2ND DIST
TROUP, DAVID	WAS	218	1ST DIST
TROUP, ELEIA	WAS	136	2ND DIST
TROUP, ELIZABETH	WAS	132	2ND DIST
TROUP, HENRY	WAS	131	2ND DIST
TROUP, JACOB	WAS	125	2ND DIST
TROUP, JOHN	WAS	294	1ST DIST
TROUP, JOHN	BAL	059	2ND DIST
TROUP, MARY	WAS	124	2ND DIST
TROUP, MARY E.	WAS	132	2ND DIST
TROUP, PHILIP	CEC	168	6TH E DI
TROUP, SARAH	WAS	135	2ND DIST
TROUP, SOLOMAN	WAS	111	2ND DIST
TROUT, ABRAHAM	HAR	057	1ST DIST
TROUT, BARBARA	WAS	271	1ST DIST
TROUT, CHARLOTTE	FRE	259	NEW MARK
TROUT, DAVID	HAR	022	1ST DIST
TROUT, HARRIET E.	FRE	230	BUCKEYST
TROUT, JACOB	BAL	043	2ND DIST
TROUT, JOHN	FRE	231	BUCKEYST
TROUT, JOHN	FRE	301	WOODSBOR
TROUT, JOHN	FRE	013	FREDERIC
TROUT, JOSEPH H.	WAS	156	2ND DIST
TROUT, JULIAN	FRE	105	CREAGERS
TROUT, MARY	WAS	275	RIDGEVIL
TROUT, MARY E.	BAL	127	18TH WAR
TROUT, NATHAN	BAL	229	12TH WAR
TROUT, PAUL	WAS	259	1ST DIST
TROUT, REBECCA	FRE	260	NEW MARK
TROUT, RICHARD W.	HAR	022	1ST DIST
TROUT, SARAH	BAL	044	2ND DIST
TROUTMAN, SARAH	BAL	212	6TH DIST
TROUTMAN,HENRY	ALL	246	CUMBERLA
TROUTNER, JAMES	HAR	027	1ST DIST
TROUTNEY, FRANCES	HAR	015	1ST DIST
TROUTWINE, ADAM	CAR	338	6TH DIST
TROUTZ, MARGARET *	TAL	069	EASTON T
TROVINGER, DANIEL	WAS	289	1ST DIST
TROVINGER, JOHN	WAS	267	1ST DIST
TROVINGER, JOSEPH	WAS	267	1ST DIST
TROVINGER, SAMUEL	WAS	267	1ST DIST
TROVINGER, SAMUEL	WAS	268	1ST DIST
TROWBRIDGE, DANIEL	BAL	014	18TH WAR
TROWBRIDGE, LUBIN	BAL	299	12TH WAR
TROWER, JESSE	BAL	133	1ST WARD
TROWNFETTER, JOSHUA	CAR	262	3RD DIST
TROXAL, FREDERICK	FRE	114	CREAGERS
TROXAL, JOHN	FRE	112	CREAGERS
TROXALL, J.	BAL	254	12TH WAR
TROXEL, ALFRED D.	WAS	014	2ND SUBD
TROXEL, AMANDA	FRE	161	EMMITTSB
TROXEL, ANN C.	FRE	180	5TH E DI
TROXEL, ANN M.	FRE	162	EMMITTSB
TROXEL, FELIX J.	FRE	163	EMMITTSB
TROXEL, HARRIET	FRE	161	EMMITTSB
TROXEL, JACOB	FRE	168	EMMITTSB
TROXEL, JACOB	BAL	416	1ST DIST
TROXEL, JOHN	FRE	175	5TH E DI
TROXEL, JOHN	FRE	181	5TH E DI
TROXEL, JOHN	CAR	346	6TH DIST
TROXEL, JOSEPH	FRE	179	5TH E DI
TROXEL, JOSEPH P.	FRE	160	EMMITTSB
TROXEL, JOSHUA	FRE	161	EMMITTSB
TROXEL, MOSES	CAR	248	3RD DIST
TROXEL, PHILIP	BAL	252	1ST DIST
TROXELL, ALFRED	CAR	268	WESTMINS
TROXELL, DANIEL	WAS	157	2ND DIST
TROXELL, DAVID	FRE	117	CREAGERS
TROXELL, ELIZABETH	WAS	147	2ND DIST
TROXELL, JACOB	CAR	260	3RD DIST
TROXELL, JOHN	CAR	259	3RD DIST
TROXELL, JOHN	WAS	162	2ND DIST
TROXELL, JOHN	WAS	159	2ND DIST
TROXELL, JOHN	ALL	193	9TH E.D.
TROXELL, LEVI	WAS	174	FUNKSTOW
TROXELL, MARY	CAR	390	2ND DIST
TROXELL, PHILIP	WAS	154	HAGERSTO
TROXELL, RUTH	CAR	268	WESTMINS
TROXWELL, ABRAHAM	WAS	160	2ND DIST
TROY, FREDERICK	BAL	425	8TH WARD
TROY, HENRY	TAL	046	EASTON T
TROY, JOHN	CEC	172	6TH E DI
TROY, SOLOMAN	TAL	046	EASTON T
TROY, THOMAS	BAL	011	15TH WAR
TROYER, HANSON A.	BAL	047	2ND DIST
TROYER, JACOB	CAR	187	4TH DIST
TROYER, RUBEN	CAR	187	4TH DIST
TROZEL, ALFRED	FRE	153	10TH E D
TRSOP, ELIZABETH	BAL	387	13TH WAR
TRUAX, ELY	BAL	237	20TH WAR
TRUCKS, WILLIAM	MGM	360	BERRYS D
TRUCMAN, JAMES	MGM	382	ROCKERLE
TRUDALE, FREDRICK	ALL	148	6TH E.D.
TRUE, JOHN T.	CAL	017	1ST DIST
TRUE, MARY	BAL	252	20TH WAR
TRUEMAN, HENRY B.R.	PRI	050	AQUASCO
TRUEMAN, JARRETT	WAS	122	2ND DIST
TRUEMAN, NATHANIEL	WAS	099	2ND DIST
TRUEMAN, PETER	WAS	116	2ND DIST
TRUEMAN, SOPHIA	PRI	062	NOTTINGH
TRUEMAN, THOMAS	ANN	317	1ST DIST
TRUEMAN, WILLIAM	CEC	137	6TH E DI
TRUET, OLIVER	BAL	279	7TH WARD
TRUETT, ANN	TAL	087	ST MICHA
TRUETT, CATHARINE	KEN	290	3RD DIST
TRUETT, EDWARD M.	WOR	205	4TH E DI
TRUETT, GEORGE	WOR	167	6TH E DI
TRUETT, ISAAC W.	WOR	193	8TH E DI
TRUETT, JOSIAH	DOR	302	1ST DIST
TRUETT, MARY	WOR	202	4TH E DI
TRUETT, MATTHIAS J.	WOR	206	4TH E DI
TRUETT, SOLOMON	CAR	095	NO TWP L
TRUETT, WILLIAM	KEN	313	3RD DIST
TRUETT, WILLIAM *	BAL	282	2ND WARD
TRUETT, WILLIAM R.	BAL	071	15TH WAR
TRUGEN, EDWARD	BAL	012	15TH WAR
TRUIHELLER, GOTFRIED	BAL	386	8TH WARD
TRUITT, AMELIA	WOR	174	6TH E DI
TRUITT, BENJAMIN	SOM	527	QUANTICO
TRUITT, CALEB P.	WOR	219	4TH E DI
TRUITT, DAVID J.	WOR	261	BERLIN 1
TRUITT, DAVID S.	CAR	095	NO TWP L
TRUITT, EDWARD	WOR	277	BERLIN 1
TRUITT, ELIZABETH	WOR	225	4TH E DI
TRUITT, GEORGE	WOR	274	BERLIN 1
TRUITT, GEORGE H.	WOR	207	4TH E DI
TRUITT, HENRIETTA	WOR	306	2ND E DI
TRUITT, HENRIETTA *	WOR	208	4TH E DI
TRUITT, HENRY S.	WOR	235	6TH E DI
TRUITT, JAMES	WOR	219	4TH E DI
TRUITT, JAMES	WOR	300	SNOW HIL
TRUITT, JAMES	WOR	328	1ST E DI
TRUITT, JESSA	WOR	311	2ND E DI
TRUITT, JESSE	WOR	293	9TH E DI
TRUITT, JOANNA E. C.	WOR	206	4TH E DI
TRUITT, JOB	WOR	215	4TH E DI
TRUITT, JOB L.	WOR	215	4TH E DI
TRUITT, JOHN	WOR	224	4TH E DI
TRUITT, JOHN	WOR	206	4TH E DI
TRUITT, JOHN	WOR	258	1ST CENS
TRUITT, JOHN	WOR	260	BERLIN 1
TRUITT, JOHNO.	WOR	206	4TH E DI
TRUITT, JULIA A.	WOR	219	4TH E DI
TRUITT, MAJOR-BLACK	WOR	323	1ST E DI
TRUITT, MARIA	WOR	218	4TH E DI
TRUITT, MARTHA J.	WOR	224	4TH E DI
TRUITT, MARY	WOR	302	SNOW HIL
TRUITT, MARY J.	WOR	255	1ST CENS
TRUITT, MC KINNA	WOR	255	1ST CENS
TRUITT, MINUS P.	SOM	470	TRAPPE D
TRUITT, PETER	WOR	292	9TH E DI
TRUITT, ROBERT D.	WOR	209	4TH E DI
TRUITT, RODAH	WOR	342	1ST E DI
TRUITT, RUFUS	SOM	493	SALISBUR
TRUITT, RUFUS M	WOR	207	4TH E DI
TRUITT, SAMUEL P.	WOR	211	4TH E DI
TRUITT, SELBY P.	WOR	316	2ND E DI
TRUITT, SILAS J.	WOR	209	4TH E DI
TRUITT, SOTHEY L.	WOR	209	4TH E DI
TRUITT, THOMAS	WOR	232	6TH E DI
TRUITT, THOMAS J.	WOR	207	4TH E DI
TRUITT, WILLIAM	WOR	202	4TH E DI
TRUITT, WILLIAM	WOR	298	9TH E DI
TRUITT, WILLIAM T.	WOR	204	4TH E DI
TRUITT, ZADOK	WOR	309	2ND E DI
TRUITT, ZEDAKIAH	WOR	223	4TH E DI
TRULEY, LEVI	BAL	279	12TH WAR
TRULL, ANNA	BAL	063	10TH WAR
TRULLINGER, JOSEPH *	ALL	132	4TH E.D.
TRULY, CATHERINE	FRE	081	FREDERIC
TRULY, DOLLY	BAL	316	1ST DIST
TRUMAN, FRANCIS	ANN	286	ANNAPOLI
TRUMAN, JOHN	WAS	158	HAGERSTO
TRUMAN, MARY	BAL	154	16TH WAR
TRUMAN, MARY-MULATTO	FRE	038	FREDERIC
TRUMBLE, SARAH	BAL	139	11TH WAR
TRUMBO, AUGUSTUS *	BAL	294	20TH WAR
TRUMBO, CHARLOTTE	BAL	294	20TH WAR
TRUMBO, ELLEN	BAL	005	15TH WAR
TRUMBO, GEORGE	BAL	443	8TH WARD
TRUMBO, GEORGE	CAR	204	4TH DIST
TRUMBO, HENRY	BAL	161	16TH WAR
TRUMBO, LEWIS	CAR	272	WESTMINS
TRUMER, GEROGE	BAL	036	15TH WAR
TRUMP, CHRISTIAN	CAR	381	2ND DIST
TRUMP, DAVID	CAR	409	2ND DIST
TRUMP, GEOREG	CAR	333	MANCHEST
TRUMP, GRANVILLE A.	BAL	148	16TH WAR
TRUMP, HENRY	BAL	420	14TH WAR
TRUMP, JOHN	CAR	345	6TH DIST
TRUMP, MARY J.	CAR	176	8TH DIST
TRUMP, REBECCA	CAR	392	2ND DIST
TRUMP, ROBERT	CEC	205	7TH E DI
TRUMP,SAMUEL	BAL	020	2ND DIST
TRUMPH, JACOB	FRE	439	8TH E DI
TRUMPOUR, GEORGE	WAS	139	2ND DIST
TRUMPOUR, JAMES	WAS	139	2ND DIST
TRUMPOUR, LENARD	WAS	143	2ND DIST
TRUMPS, MARGARET	BAL	151	11TH WAR
TRUNBULL, JOHN	BAL	472	14TH WAR
TRUNDER, DONSILLA	MGM	416	MEDLEY 3
TRUNDLE, EMILY A.	MGM	416	MEDLEY 3
TRUNDLE, ESTHER	MGM	415	MEDLEY 3
TRUNDLE, HEZEKIAH	MGM	414	MEDLEY 3
TRUNDLE, JAMES	FRE	017	FREDERIC
TRUNDLE, JOHN G.	FRE	220	BUCKEYST
TRUNDLE, LAWSON	MGM	405	ROCKERLE
TRUNDLE, LEAH	MGM	374	ROCKERLE
TRUNDLE, OTHO W.	FRE	220	BUCKEYST
TRUNDLE, ROSETTER	FRE	227	BUCKEYST
TRUNDLE, SARAH F.	MGM	322	CRACKLIN
TRUNDLE, SUSAN E.	MGM	409	MEDLEY 3
TRUNDLE, THOMAS	FRE	409	JEFFERSO
TRUNDLE, WILLIAM	MGM	351	BERRYS D
TRUNDLE, WILLIAM H.	MGM	422	MEDLEY 3
TRUNDLE, ZADOCK	FRE	234	BUCKEYST
TRUNDLE,HORATIO	MGM	410	MEDLEY 3
TRUNDLER, CLARISSA	MGM	415	MEDLEY 3
TRUNER, ELIZABETH	BAL	223	19TH WAR
TRUNEY, BRIDGET	BAL	360	3RD WARD
TRUNNELL, JAMES L.	HAR	076	BEL AIR
TRUSEDLE, JOHN A.	FRE	219	BUCKEYST
TRUSHY, JAMES	BAL	028	9TH WARD
TRUSON, ROBERT *	KEN	229	2ND DIST
TRUST, ANDREW	BAL	051	18TH WAR
TRUST, HERMAN	BAL	027	15TH WAR
TRUST, JACOB	BAL	337	13TH WAR
TRUST, JOHN	BAL	183	19TH WAR
TRUSTA, VIOLET	BAL	453	14TH WAR
TRUSTEY, SAMUEL	BAL	400	8TH WARD
TRUSTRINE, JOHN	ALL	228	CUMBERLA
TRUSTY, BECKY-BLACK	QUE	187	3RD E DI
TRUSTY, CHARLOTTA	BAL	322	3RD WARD
TRUSTY, DORCAS-BLACK	QUE	147	1ST E DI
TRUSTY, ELI	CEC	061	1ST E DI
TRUSTY, ELI	CEC	061	1ST E DI
TRUSTY, JACOB	CEC	061	1ST E DI
TRUSTY, JANE R.	BAL	134	5TH WARD
TRUSTY, JOHN	KEN	296	3RD DIST
TRUSTY, JONATHAN	BAL	381	3RD WARD
TRUSTY, JULIA	KEN	214	2ND DIST
TRUSTY, M.	BAL	129	5TH WARD
TRUSTY, MANCES	BAL	301	12TH WAR
TRUSTY, MARTHA-BLACK	QUE	202	3RD E DI
TRUSTY, MARY	KEN	296	3RD DIST
TRUSTY, PERRY	KEN	310	3RD DIST
TRUSTY, REBECCA-BLACK	QUE	201	3RD E DI
TRUSTY, STEPHEN	BAL	130	1ST WARD
TRUSTY, STEPHEN	BAL	377	3RD WARD
TRUSTY, WILLIAM	CEC	021	ELKTON 3
TRUTT, SAMUEL	WOR	177	6TH E DI
TRUTT, WILLIAM L.	WOR	203	4TH E DI
TRUXEL, ELIAS	BAL	259	1ST DIST
TRUXEN, JAMES-BLACK	CAR	144	NO TWP L
TRUXEN, WILLIAM-BLACK	CAR	140	NO TWP L
TRUXWORTH, DAVID H.	BAL	376	8TH WARD
TRUZEN, ANTHONY	BAL	413	8TH WARD
TRWITT, JAMES P.	WOR	205	4TH E DI
TRY, ISRAEL	WAS	045	2ND SUBD
TRYAN, PATRICK	BAL	183	11TH WAR
TRYOR, JOSEPH B.	BAL	315	12TH WAR
TSAFFERY, JOHN	BAL	128	1ST WARD
TSCHUDDY, MARTHA	QUE	162	2ND E DI
TSCHUDDY, MARTIN	QUE	161	2ND-E DI
TSCHUDY, DAVID	WAS	123	HAGERSTO
TSCHUDY, JOST	BAL	006	15TH WAR
TTO	ST	291	2ND E DI
TTO	FRE	452	8TH E DI
TUBAUGH, CHARLES	BAL	295	1ST DIST
TUBAUGH, SIMON	BAL	295	1ST DIST
TUBB, JAMES	WOR	322	1ST E DI
TUBBLE, ROBERT	BAL	422	1ST DIST
TUBBLE, RUTH	BAL	422	1ST DIST
TUBBS, AMY A.	WOR	350	1ST E DI
TUBBS, HERNIETTA	WOR	222	4TH E DI
TUBBS, JAMES H.	CAR	097	NO TWP L
TUBBS, JAMES W.	WOR	271	BERLIN 1
TUBBS, LLOYD	BAL	030	1ST WARD
TUBBS, MARGARET	WOR	281	BERLIN 1
TUBBS, MARIA	ST	303	2ND E DI
TUBBS, MOLLY	WOR	277	BERLIN 1
TUBBS, MOSES	WOR	242	1ST CENS
TUBBS, SAMUEL	WOR	317	2ND E DI
TUBLE, GEORGE	BAL	418	1ST DIST
TUBMAN, ANN	DOR	332	3RD DIVI
TUBMAN, BENJAMIN	CHA	258	MIDDLETO
TUBMAN, BETSY	CHA	247	HILLTOP
TUBMAN, CHARLES	DOR	336	3RD DIVI
TUBMAN, ELINOR	PRI	048	AQUASCO
TUBMAN, EMALINE	DOR	367	3RD DIVI
TUBMAN, EVANS-MULATTO	BAL	179	2ND WARD
TUBMAN, GEORGE	DOR	390	1ST DIST
TUBMAN, HENRY	PRI	048	AQUASCO
TUBMAN, JOHN	DOR	406	1ST DIST
TUBMAN, JOHN	BAL	174	6TH WARD
TUBMAN, MARIA	DOR	390	1ST DIST
TUBMAN, MARY	DOR	335	3RD DIVI
TUBMAN, NEARSE*	DOR	380	1ST DIST
TUBMAN, NOAH	DOR	372	3RD DIVI
TUBMAN, PETER	CHA	246	HILLTOP
TUBMAN, RICHARD H.	DOR	333	3RD DIVI

TUBMAN, RICHARD L.	CHA	258	MIDDLETO
TUBMAN, ROBERT F.	DOR	385	1ST DIST
TUBMAN, SARA E.	CHA	256	MIDDLETO
TUBMAN, SUSAN	DOR	334	3RD DIVI
TUBMAN, THEODORE	ANN	419	HOWARD D
TUBMAN, THOMAS	DOR	363	3RD DIVI
TUBMAN, THOMAS	DOR	469	1ST DIST
TUCE, THOMAS*	DOR	312	1ST DIST
TUCHSTONE, GEORGE T.	CEC	114	3RD E DI
TUCHTON, RATCHELL	HAR	169	3RD DIST
TUCK, CHARLES H.	BAL	121	1ST WARD
TUCK, M.	ANN	282	ANNAPOLI
TUCK, RACHEL A.	BAL	393	14TH WAR
TUCK, WILLIAM H.	PRI	093	MARLBROU
TUCKEN, GASSAWAY*	BAL	371	3RD WARD
TUCKER, AARON	BAL	264	1ST DIST
TUCKER, AARON	ANN	466	HOWARD D
TUCKER, AARON H.	BAL	056	18TH WAR
TUCKER, ALFRED	QUE	198	3RD E DI
TUCKER, ANDREW	FRE	075	FREDERIC
TUCKER, ANN	WAS	089	2ND SUBD
TUCKER, ANN T.	BAL	087	4TH WARD
TUCKER, BASIL	FRE	299	WOODSBOR
TUCKER, BENJAMIN	BAL	294	17TH WAR
TUCKER, BENJAMIN	CAL	004	1ST DIST
TUCKER, BENJAMIN	BAL	137	1ST WARD
TUCKER, BROOKE	CAL	056	3RD DIST
TUCKER, CHARITY	BAL	286	1ST DIST
TUCKER, CHARLES	BAL	045	9TH WARD
TUCKER, CHARLES	CAL	058	3RD DIST
TUCKER, CHARLES	MGM	331	CRACKLIN
TUCKER, CINTHE	BAL	372	1ST DIST
TUCKER, DANIEL	FRE	079	FREDERIC
TUCKER, DAVID	CEC	186	7TH E DI
TUCKER, ELI	BAL	265	20TH WAR
TUCKER, ELIZABETH	DOR	325	1ST DIST
TUCKER, ELIZABETH	CAL	056	3RD DIST
TUCKER, ELIZABETH	PRI	028	VANSVILL
TUCKER, ELLEN	QUE	131	1ST E DI
TUCKER, ELLEN	ANN	315	1ST DIST
TUCKER, ELLEN-BLACK	FRE	028	FREDERIC
TUCKER, EMELINE	CHA	267	MIDDLETO
TUCKER, EMILY W.	BAL	073	4TH WARD
TUCKER, ENOCH G.	BAL	044	9TH WARD
TUCKER, ENOCH G.	WAS	131	HAGERSTO
TUCKER, FRANCIS A.	PRI	007	BLADENSB
TUCKER, GEORGE	BAL	160	1ST WARD
TUCKER, GEORGE	CAL	032	2ND DIST
TUCKER, GEORGE	CAR	395	2ND DIST
TUCKER, GEORGE M.	BAL	037	4TH WARD
TUCKER, GUST	BAL	223	1ST DIST
TUCKER, HARRIET	BAL	422	1ST DIST
TUCKER, HARRIET	BAL	408	14TH WAR
TUCKER, HENRIETTA	BAL	265	7TH WARD
TUCKER, HENRIETTA	TAL	024	EASTON D
TUCKER, HENRY	ANN	299	1ST DIST
TUCKER, HENRY	CAL	039	2ND DIST
TUCKER, HENRY R.	BAL	323	12TH WAR
TUCKER, ISRIEL	BAL	443	1ST DIST
TUCKER, JAMES	ANN	510	HOWARD D
TUCKER, JAMES	ANN	507	HOWARD D
TUCKER, JAMES	BAL	068	2ND DIST
TUCKER, JAMES	CAL	028	2ND DIST
TUCKER, JAMES	BAL	437	14TH WAR
TUCKER, JAMES	CEC	189	7TH E DI
TUCKER, JAMES	HAR	104	2ND DIST
TUCKER, JAMES	PRI	016	BLADENSB
TUCKER, JAMES	QUE	212	3RD E DI
TUCKER, JAMES H.	BAL	184	19TH WAR
TUCKER, JANE	BAL	278	17TH WAR
TUCKER, JOHN	CAR	363	9TH DIST
TUCKER, JOHN	BAL	408	3RD WARD
TUCKER, JOHN	BAL	240	17TH WAR
TUCKER, JOHN	QUE	140	1ST E DI
TUCKER, JOHN	KEN	298	3RD DIST
TUCKER, JOHN	PRI	003	BLADENSB
TUCKER, JOHN	ANN	360	3RD DIST
TUCKER, JOHN	ANN	320	2ND DIST
TUCKER, JOHN	BAL	159	1ST WARD
TUCKER, JOHN	BAL	020	1ST WARD
TUCKER, JOHN	BAL	007	9TH WARD
TUCKER, JOHN H.	BAL	234	6TH WARD
TUCKER, JOHN H.	BAL	068	10TH WAR
TUCKER, JOHN R.	BAL	101	5TH WARD
TUCKER, JOHN T.	BAL	184	19TH WAR
TUCKER, JOSEPH	BAL	067	10TH WAR
TUCKER, JOSEPH	ALL	217	CUMBERLA
TUCKER, JULIANNA	ANN	466	HOWARD D
TUCKER, LOUZA	CAR	083	NO TWP L
TUCKER, MARGARET	BAL	273	12TH WAR
TUCKER, MARTHA	BAL	442	1ST DIST
TUCKER, MARY	ANN	472	HOWARD D
TUCKER, MARY	BAL	388	3RD WARD
TUCKER, MARY A.	CAL	045	3RD DIST
TUCKER, MARY A.	PRI	007	BLADENSB
TUCKER, MARY E.	ANN	311	1ST DIST
TUCKER, MILEY	CAL	040	3RD DIST
TUCKER, MORTON	BAL	432	8TH WARD
TUCKER, NANCY	BAL	423	8TH WARD
TUCKER, NANCY	MGM	390	ROCKERLE
TUCKER, NATHAN	MGM	350	BERRYS D
TUCKER, NATHAN	PRI	101	SPALDING
TUCKER, NELSON	FRE	071	FREDERIC
TUCKER, PATRICK	ALL	153	6TH E.D.
TUCKER, PETER	FRE	299	WOODSBOR
TUCKER, RACHEL	BAL	227	19TH WAR
TUCKER, REBECCA	BAL	196	19TH WAR
TUCKER, RICHARD	MGM	349	BERRYS D
TUCKER, RICHARD	BAL	280	2ND WARD
TUCKER, RICHARD	BAL	026	9TH WARD
TUCKER, RICHARD	QUE	192	3RD E DI
TUCKER, S.L.	BAL	005	EASTERN
TUCKER, SALLY	QUE	186	3RD E DI
TUCKER, SAMUEL	TAL	065	EASTON T
TUCKER, SAMUEL	KEN	238	2ND DIST
TUCKER, SAMUEL	FRE	146	10TH E D
TUCKER, SAMUEL	FRE	122	CREAGERS
TUCKER, SAMUEL	BAL	285	20TH WAR
TUCKER, SAMUEL	DOR	325	1ST DIST
TUCKER, SARAH	BAL	351	1ST DIST
TUCKER, SARAH A.	CAL	020	2ND DIST
TUCKER, SARAH A.	QUE	186	3RD E DI
TUCKER, SEABORN	BAL	137	16TH WAR
TUCKER, STARRY	CHA	279	BOJANTOW
TUCKER, SUSANA	BAL	433	8TH WARD
TUCKER, THOAMS	CAL	012	1ST DIST
TUCKER, THOAMS H.	HAR	197	3RD DIST
TUCKER, THOMAS	CAR	371	9TH DIST
TUCKER, THOMAS	BAL	164	16TH WAR
TUCKER, THOMAS	BAL	159	1ST WARD
TUCKER, THOMAS	BAL	157	1ST WARD
TUCKER, THOMAS	BAL	148	1ST WARD
TUCKER, THOMAS	ANN	304	1ST DIST
TUCKER, THOMAS	WAS	088	2ND SUBD
TUCKER, THOMAS	WAS	061	2ND SUBD
TUCKER, THOMAS J.	QUE	175	2ND E DI
TUCKER, THOMAS W.	CHA	267	MIDDLETO
TUCKER, W. T.	BAL	155	1ST WARD
TUCKER, WALTER	CAL	063	3RD DIST
TUCKER, WILILAM H.	CAL	025	2ND DIST
TUCKER, WILLIAM	CAL	010	1ST DIST
TUCKER, WILLIAM	BAL	390	13TH WAR
TUCKER, WILLIAM	FRE	013	FREDERIC
TUCKER, WILLIAM	ANN	311	1ST DIST
TUCKER, WILLIAM	ANN	315	1ST DIST
TUCKER, WILLIAM	ANN	466	HOWARD D
TUCKER, WILLIAM	PRI	080	QUEEN AN
TUCKER, WILLIAM E.	PRI	073	MARLBROU
TUCKER, WILLIAM H.	HAR	113	2ND DIST
TUCKER, ZACHARIAH	CAL	037	2ND DIST
TUCKER, ZEANDER	FRE	297	WOODSBOR
TUCKERMAN, EDWARD	QUE	190	3RD E DI
TUCKERMAN, ELIZA	QUE	161	2ND E DI
TUCKERMAN, WILLIAM	QUE	188	3RD E DI
TUCKERR, GASSAWAY*	BAL	371	3RD WARD
TUCKERTMON, MARY	CEC	086	4TH E DI
TUCKET, HESEKIAH	FRE	124	CREAGERS
TUCKETT, AMELIA	CHA	241	HILLTOP
TUCKETT, GEORGE	CHA	240	HILLTOP
TUCKETT, HEZEKIAH	CHA	294	BOJANTOW
TUCKETT, LOUISA	CHA	217	ALLENS F
TUCKETT, MARCUS	CHA	260	MIDDLETO
TUCKETT, WALTER	CHA	239	HILLTOP
TUCKEY, WILLIAM E.	BAL	333	3RD WARD
TUCKRAY, JOHN	BAL	215	19TH WAR
TUCKS, IGNATIUS	MGM	401	ROCKERLE
TUCOS, ANN	CHA	255	MIDDLETO
TUDDEWICK, JOHN	BAL	227	1ST DIST
TUDER, ROBERT	BAL	259	17TH WAR
TUDOR, ELIZABETH	BAL	432	14TH WAR
TUDOR, HENRY C.	BAL	015	18TH WAR
TUDOR, HENRY C.	BAL	399	14TH WAR
TUDOR, JOHN	BAL	401	14TH WAR
TUDOR, WILLIAM B.	BAL	399	14TH WAR
TUE, FRANCIS	QUE	225	4TH E DI
TUE, HENRY-BLACK	QUE	191	3RD E DI
TUER, JAMES	BAL	270	17TH WAR
TUER, MARY A.	BAL	299	7TH WARD
TUFFARD, CHARLES	ALL	231	CUMBERLA
TUFFER, MICHAL REV.*	TAL	020	EASTON D
TUFFIT, LOUISA	BAL	298	20TH WAR
TUFFIT, WILLAIM	BAL	284	20TH WAR
TUFT, WILLIAM	CEC	093	4TH E DI
TUFTS, WILLIAM	BAL	236	12TH WAR
TUGEN, CORNELIUS	BAL	156	2ND DIST
TUGGER, SUSANER G.	HAR	184	3RD DIST
TUHAY, JOHN	BAL	102	2ND DIST
TULE, NANCY	BAL	203	11TH WAR
TULER, HENRY *	WAS	064	2ND SUBD
TULER, OLOVER H.	BAL	402	1ST DIST
TULL, AGNES	SOM	416	PRINCESS
TULL, ANN	BAL	164	19TH WAR
TULL, BENJAMIN	WOR	331	1ST E DI
TULL, DANIEL	DOR	300	1ST DIST
TULL, DICEY-BLACK	WOR	331	1ST E DI
TULL, EDWARD W.	DOR	297	1ST DIST
TULL, EDWARD-BLACK	WOR	330	1ST E DI
TULL, ELIZA*	DOR	296	1ST DIST
TULL, ELIZABETH	DOR	297	1ST DIST
TULL, ELIZABETH	CEC	090	4TH E DI
TULL, ELIZABETH SR.	CEC	090	4TH E DI
TULL, ELZA*	DOR	296	1ST DIST
TULL, F. A.	SOM	350	BRINKLEY
TULL, FRISBY	CEC	090	4TH E DI
TULL, GEORGE	WOR	185	6TH E DI
TULL, GEORGE W.	WOR	331	1ST E DI
TULL, GIDEON	WOR	325	1ST E DI
TULL, HARRY	SOM	495	SALISBUR
TULL, HENRY	SOM	386	BRINKLEY
TULL, HENRY	SOM	476	TRAPPE D
TULL, HENRY	SOM	417	PRINCESS
TULL, HENRY	DOR	323	1ST DIST
TULL, HENRY J.	SOM	365	BRINKLEY
TULL, HENRY J.	WOR	177	6TH E DI
TULL, HITTA F.	WOR	245	1ST CENS
TULL, JACOB	DOR	299	1ST DIST
TULL, JAMES	WOR	332	1ST E DI
TULL, JOE-BLACK	WOR	332	1ST E DI
TULL, JOHN	SOM	356	BRINKLEY
TULL, JOHN	DOR	304	1ST DIST
TULL, JOHN A.	SOM	402	BRINKLEY
TULL, JOHN C.	SOM	350	BRINKLEY
TULL, JOHN H.	WOR	185	7TH E DI
TULL, JOHN H.	SOM	403	BRINKLEY
TULL, JOHN W.	DOR	305	1ST DIST
TULL, JOSEPH	SOM	387	BRINKLEY
TULL, JOSHUA	SOM	384	BRINKLEY
TULL, JOSHUA W.	SOM	384	BRINKLEY
TULL, LEVI	WOR	328	1ST E DI
TULL, LEVIN	WOR	322	1ST E DI
TULL, LEVIN	SOM	351	BRINKLEY
TULL, LEVIN	SOM	363	BRINKLEY
TULL, LEVIN	DOR	324	1ST DIST
TULL, LOVEY	SOM	525	BARREN C
TULL, MARY	SOM	390	BRINKLEY
TULL, MARY	SOM	427	PRINCESS
TULL, MARY	SOM	427	PRINCESS
TULL, MILES	WOR	348	1ST E DI
TULL, MRS-	BAL	316	1ST DIST
TULL, NANCY	SOM	364	BRINKLEY
TULL, NANCY	SOM	480	TRAPP DI
TULL, NATHANIEL T.	SOM	386	BRINKLEY
TULL, ORANCY	WOR	325	1ST E DI
TULL, PEGGY	SOM	485	TRAPP DI
TULL, PEGGY	SOM	469	TRAPPE D
TULL, RICHARD	DOR	319	1ST DIST
TULL, RICHARD E.	SOM	353	BRINKLEY
TULL, SARAH	SOM	354	BRINKLEY
TULL, SARAH	SOM	353	BRINKLEY
TULL, SARAH	BAL	270	7TH WARD
TULL, SOLOMON	WOR	347	1ST E DI
TULL, SOLOMON	SOM	350	BRINKLEY
TULL, SOPHIAH	WOR	248	1ST CENS
TULL, STINTON	DOR	306	1ST DIST
TULL, THOMAS	SOM	362	BRINKLEY
TULL, VILET*	BAL	338	3RD WARD
TULL, WESLEY S.	SOM	359	BRINKLEY
TULL, WILLIAM	WOR	325	1ST E DI
TULL, WILLIAM F.	SOM	364	BRINKLEY
TULL, WILLIAM J. H.	SOM	354	BRINKLEY
TULLEY, WILLIAM A.	DOR	305	1ST DIST
TULLIGMAN, ANTONE	BAL	170	19TH WAR
TULLY, CHARLES	FRE	247	NEW MARK
TULLY, MARGARET	BAL	186	19TH WAR
TULLY, MARGARET	BAL	458	1ST DIST
TULLY, MICHAEL	ALL	128	4TH E.D.
TULLY, PATRICK	ALL	135	4TH E.D.
TULTY, HENRY	WAS	249	1ST DIST
TULYLICK, ERNEST	BAL	250	20TH WAR
TUMBAN, HY *	BAL	188	5TH DIST
TUMBAN, JOHN	BAL	188	5TH DIST
TUMBAUGH, JOHN	BAL	191	5TH DIST
TUMBLESON, CHARLES H.	BAL	266	17TH WAR
TUMBLINSON, WILLIAM	BAL	075	15TH WAR
TUMBLINSON, WILLIAM P.	BAL	172	16TH WAR
TUMEY, JOHN	BAL	297	20TH WAR
TUMMILL, LOUIZA	BAL	098	5TH WARD
TUMNEY, WILLIAM	BAL	356	3RD WARD
TUMP, CHARLES	BAL	020	4TH WARD
TUMY, HENRY	BAL	312	1ST DIST
TUNBY, ELIZABETH P.	WOR	207	4TH E DI
TUNIS, ALEXANDER	BAL	216	6TH WARD
TUNIS, ALFRED	SOM	492	SALISBUR
TUNIS, ANN	DOR	372	3RD DIVI
TUNIS, NOAH	DOR	362	3RD DIVI
TUNIS, SAMUEL	BAL	190	6TH WARD
TUNIX, BENJAMIN	WAS	054	2ND SUBD
TUNK, LYDIA	ALL	245	CUMBERLA
TUNLOW, DAVID	ALL	143	6TH E.D.
TUNNEL, HENRY	WOR	315	2ND E DI
TUNNEL, JAMES-BLACK	WOR	340	1ST E DI
TUNNELL, MARY	WOR	185	6TH E DI
TUNNY, JOHN	BAL	418	3RD WARD
TUNOR, DENNIS *	BAL	089	18TH WAR
TUOGOOD, BENJAMIN *	ANN	319	2ND DIST
TUPE, SARAH E.-BLACK	CAR	398	2ND DIST
TUPEE, ALICE	BAL	225	12TH WAR
TUPPLE, MARY	BAL	360	13TH WAR
TUPS, JOHN	BAL	239	12TH WAR
TURBEE, THOMAS J.*	TAL	046	EASTON T
TURBERT, SUSAN	TAL	077	EASTON T
TURBETT, WILLIAM B.	KEN	304	3RD DIST
TURBOTT, SAMUEL D.	WOR	303	SNOW HIL
TURBURG, JOHN	BAL	115	15TH WAR
TURBUTT, WILLIAM	TAL	005	EASTON D
TURFIELD, MARY	BAL	155	16TH WAR
TURFIELD, PHILIP T.	BAL	155	16TH WAR
TURFLE, BARBARA	CAR	400	2ND DIST
TURFLE, CATHARINE	CAR	275	7TH DIST
TURFLE, HENRY	CAR	274	7TH DIST
TURFLE, JOSEPH	CAR	274	7TH DIST
TURGOOD, BENJAMIN *	ANN	319	2ND DIST
TURITT, MARY	WOR	261	BERLIN I
TURK, NICHOLAS	ST	288	2ND E DI
TURKINGTON, JUILA	BAL	125	5TH WARD
TURLEY, HENRY	ALL	230	CUMBERLA
TURLLUGER, MATHALINA *	ALL	132	4TH E.D.
TURMAN, ELIZA	BAL	220	12TH WAR
TURMAN, WILLAIM	BAL	377	13TH WAR
TURMER, SARAH	BAL	223	19TH WAR
TURN, OLIVER	BAL	294	12TH WAR
TURNAN, MARY	BAL	053	9TH WARD
TURNBALL, ANN	BAL	263	1ST DIST
TURNBOLT, ALBERIAN	WAS	101	2ND DIST
TURNBOLT, DARLINGTON	WAS	101	2ND DIST
TURNBOLT, SARAH	WAS	101	2ND DIST
TURNBULL, ALEXANDER	BAL	167	11TH WAR
TURNBULL, DANIEL	HAR	060	1ST DIST
TURNBULL, HENRY C.	BAL	012	2ND DIST
TURNBULL, JOHN	BAL	029	1ST WARD
TURNDLE, PERRY L.	MGM	409	MEDLEY 3
TURNEN, FRANCIS M.	BAL	161	11TH WAR
TURNER, ABHRAIM	BAL	049	18TH WAR
TURNER, ABRAHAM	MGM	358	BERRYS D
TURNER, ABRAHAM	BAL	122	16TH WAR
TURNER, ABRAHAM	BAL	330	3RD WARD
TURNER, ACLVELLE	CHA	279	BOJANTOW
TURNER, ALEXANDER	BAL	200	17TH WAR
TURNER, ALMEDIA	FRE	404	JEFFERSO
TURNER, ANDREW	HAR	018	1ST DIST
TURNER, ANN	BAL	331	3RD WARD
TURNER, ANN	BAL	140	2ND DIST
TURNER, ANN B.	BAL	462	14TH WAR
TURNER, ANN E.	BAL	442	14TH WAR
TURNER, ANN E.	ST	281	3RD E DI
TURNER, ANN H.	ST	337	4TH E DI
TURNER, ANN MARIA-BLACK	QUE	145	1ST E DI
TURNER, ANN R.	FRE	051	FREDERIC
TURNER, AQUILLA	CHA	252	BOJANTOW
TURNER, ARAMINTA	BAL	200	6TH WARD
TURNER, ARR	ST	342	5TH E DI
TURNER, ASA	SOM	469	TRAPPE D
TURNER, ASAHEL	FRE	276	NEW MARK
TURNER, BARBARA	CAL	023	2ND DIST
TURNER, BENJAMIN	CAR	095	NO TWP L
TURNER, BENJAMIN	BAL	257	2ND WARD
TURNER, BETSEY	SOM	481	TRAPP DI
TURNER, BYARD	CEC	210	7TH E DI
TURNER, CALOP	TAL	083	ST MICHA
TURNER, CATHARINE	WAS	170	FUNKSTOW
TURNER, CATHARINE	BAL	074	2ND DIST
TURNER, CATHERINE	ALL	231	CUMBERLA
TURNER, CATHERINE	FRE	110	CREAGERS
TURNER, CELIA M.	QUE	192	3RD E DI
TURNER, CHARLES	ST	333	4TH E DI
TURNER, CHARLES	TAL	046	EASTON T
TURNER, CHARLES	MGM	440	CLARKSTR
TURNER, CHARLES	BAL	079	15TH WAR
TURNER, CHARLES	BAL	290	1ST DIST
TURNER, CHARLES	BAL	232	12TH WAR
TURNER, CHARLES	ANN	412	HOWARD D
TURNER, CHARLES H.	BAL	232	12TH WAR
TURNER, CHRISTIANNA	CHA	264	HILLTOP
TURNER, CLEMENTINE	SOM	488	SALISBUR
TURNER, DANIEL	BAL	217	2ND WARD
TURNER, DAVID*	TAL	052	EASTON D
TURNER, DEBORAH	KEN	245	2ND DIST
TURNER, DENNIS	TAL	062	EASTON D
TURNER, EBAN	CEC	056	1ST E DI
TURNER, EDMUND	BAL	329	3RD WARD
TURNER, EDWARD	CHA	276	ALLENS F
TURNER, EDWARD	CAR	068	NO TWP L
TURNER, EDWARD J.	KEN	305	3RD DIST
TURNER, EILHELMINA	BAL	442	14TH WAR
TURNER, ELISA	BAL	075	18TH WAR
TURNER, ELISHA	BAL	240	6TH WARD
TURNER, ELIZA	BAL	070	4TH WARD
TURNER, ELIZA	DOR	454	1ST DIST
TURNER, ELIZA	WAS	002	WILLIAMS
TURNER, ELIZA A.	TAL	084	ST MICHA

TURNER, ELIZA A. CAR 122 NO TWP L
TURNER, ELIZA A. BAL 417 3RD WARD
TURNER, ELIZA A. BAL 101 2ND DIST
TURNER, ELIZABETH ANN 447 HOWARD D
TURNER, ELIZABETH BAL 212 6TH WARD
TURNER, ELIZABETH BAL 153 5TH WARD
TURNER, ELIZABETH CAL 005 1ST DIST
TURNER, ELIZABETH FRE 312 MIDDLETO
TURNER, ELIZABETH HAR 198 3RD DIST
TURNER, ELIZABETH PRI 027 VANSVILL
TURNER, ELIZABETH KEN 297 3RD DIST
TURNER, ELIZABETH M. QUE 240 5TH E DI
TURNER, ELLECK KEN 296 3RD DIST
TURNER, ELLEN BAL 127 18TH WAR
TURNER, ELLEN CEC 009 ELKTON 3
TURNER, ELLEN BAL 421 14TH WAR
TURNER, ELLICK HAR 051 1ST DIST
TURNER, ELY HAR 017 1ST DIST
TURNER, EMILY ST 274 3RD E DI
TURNER, EMILY BAL 208 6TH WARD
TURNER, EMILY F. BAL 402 3RD WARD
TURNER, EMORY BAL 195 11TH WAR
TURNER, EMORY BAL 209 11TH WAR
TURNER, EPRAIM W. CAR 184 8TH DIST
TURNER, FANNY BAL 057 18TH WAR
TURNER, FRACIS BAL 351 1ST DIST
TURNER, FRANCES BAL 205 2ND WARD
TURNER, FRANCES BAL 185 6TH WARD
TURNER, FRANCES BAL 027 1ST WARD
TURNER, FRANCES BAL 396 14TH WAR
TURNER, FRANCIS BAL 356 3RD WARD
TURNER, FRANCIS M. BAL 084 1ST WARD
TURNER, FRANKLIN WAS 065 2ND SUBD
TURNER, FRECERICK CHA 271 ALLENS F
TURNER, G. ANN 268 ANNAPOLI
TURNER, GEORGE BAL 334 3RD WARD
TURNER, GEORGE CEC 056 1ST E DI
TURNER, GEORGE BAL 293 17TH WAR
TURNER, GEORGE BAL 028 4TH WARD
TURNER, GEORGE CEC 051 1ST E DI
TURNER, GEORGE TAL 114 ST MICHA
TURNER, GEORGE A. BAL 471 14TH WAR
TURNER, GEORGE A. BAL 474 14TH WAR
TURNER, GEORGE A. BAL 457 8TH WARD
TURNER, GEORGE A. M. PRI 046 AQUASCO
TURNER, GEORGE M.-BLACK CAR 154 NO TWP L
TURNER, GEORGE W. ALL 252 CUMBERLA
TURNER, GEORGEAN BAL 101 2ND DIST
TURNER, GEORGEANNA BAL 155 16TH WAR
TURNER, GERTRUDE ALL 165 6TH E.D.
TURNER, HANNAH BAL 033 2ND DIST
TURNER, HARREY F. BAL 341 7TH WARD
TURNER, HARRIET ANN 304 1ST DIST
TURNER, HARRIET BAL 240 6TH WARD
TURNER, HARRIET CAR 095 NO TWP L
TURNER, HARRISON T. CAL 045 3RD DIST
TURNER, HENRY CAR 081 NO TWP L
TURNER, HENRY CEC 033 CHESAPEA
TURNER, HENRY CEC 057 1ST E DI
TURNER, HENRY HAR 101 2ND DIST
TURNER, HENRY ALL 120 5TH E.D.
TURNER, HENRY ANN 343 3RD DIST
TURNER, HENRY BAL 114 1ST WARD
TURNER, HESTER DOR 424 1ST DIST
TURNER, HESTER A. * BAL 121 18TH WAR
TURNER, HORRACE TAL 092 ST MICHA
TURNER, ISAAC KEN 246 2ND DIST
TURNER, ISAAC BAL 329 3RD WARD
TURNER, ISAAC BAL 127 1ST WARD
TURNER, ISABELLA MGM 404 ROCKERLE
TURNER, J. BAL 172 1ST WARD
TURNER, J. C. BAL 147 1ST WARD
TURNER, J. F. BAL 147 1ST WARD
TURNER, J.L. ALL 231 CUMBERLA
TURNER, J.L. PRI 052 AQUASCO
TURNER, JACKSON BAL 205 2ND WARD
TURNER, JACOB C. CAR 183 8TH DIST
TURNER, JAMES HAR 126 2ND DIST
TURNER, JAMES HAR 127 2ND DIST
TURNER, JAMES DOR 446 1ST DIST
TURNER, JAMES BAL 003 18TH WAR
TURNER, JAMES CEC 129 6TH E DI
TURNER, JAMES ALL 233 CUMBERLA
TURNER, JAMES ANN 384 4TH DIST
TURNER, JAMES BAL 438 1ST DIST
TURNER, JAMES ALL 054 10TH E.D
TURNER, JAMES BAL 155 16TH WAR
TURNER, JAMES QUE 226 4TH E DI
TURNER, JAMES MGM 440 CLARKSTR
TURNER, JAMES QUE 192 3RD E DI
TURNER, JAMES FILMORE CHA 272 ALLENS F
TURNER, JAMES H. BAL 229 6TH WARD
TURNER, JAMES J. MGM 365 BERRYS D
TURNER, JAMES JR. CAL 037 2ND DIST
TURNER, JAMES R. CAL 003 1ST DIST
TURNER, JANE BAL 136 11TH WAR
TURNER, JANE CHA 255 MIDDLETO
TURNER, JANE E. CHA 252 BOJANTOW
TURNER, JANE L. HAR 090 2ND DIST
TURNER, JANE-BLACK CAR 082 NO TWP L
TURNER, JEMIMA TAL 088 ST MICHA
TURNER, JESSE WOR 274 BERLIN 1
TURNER, JOANNA BAL 287 17TH WAR
TURNER, JOANNA BAL 072 15TH WAR
TURNER, JOHN ALL 055 10TH E.D
TURNER, JOHN ALL 135 4TH E.D.
TURNER, JOHN ALL 118 5TH E.D.
TURNER, JOHN BAL 337 1ST DIST
TURNER, JOHN BAL 340 1ST DIST
TURNER, JOHN ANN 380 4TH DIST
TURNER, JOHN BAL 144 1ST WARD
TURNER, JOHN BAL 114 1ST WARD
TURNER, JOHN BAL 362 3RD WARD
TURNER, JOHN CEC 075 NORTHEAS
TURNER, JOHN CAL 008 1ST DIST
TURNER, JOHN CAR 154 NO TWP L
TURNER, JOHN SOM 433 PRINCESS
TURNER, JOHN BAL 106 18TH WAR
TURNER, JOHN BAL 023 4TH WARD
TURNER, JOHN PRI 042 VANSVILL
TURNER, JOHN SOM 542 TYASKIN
TURNER, JOHN B. CHA 260 MIDDLETO
TURNER, JOHN C. BAL 054 15TH WAR
TURNER, JOHN E. PRI 046 AQUASCO
TURNER, JOHN F. CHA 236 HILLTOP
TURNER, JOHN H. ST 283 3RD E DI
TURNER, JOHN H. ST 276 3RD E DI
TURNER, JOHN P. CHA 270 ALLENS F
TURNER, JOHN T. CAL 046 3RD DIST
TURNER, JOHN W. BAL 280 2ND WARD
TURNER, JOHN W. ANN 506 HOWARD D
TURNER, JOHNH. ST 315 4TH E DI
TURNER, JONATHAN CHA 250 MIDDLETO
TURNER, JOSEPH CAL 061 3RD DIST
TURNER, JOSEPH CAR 147 NO TWP L
TURNER, JOSEPH PRI 022 VANSVILL
TURNER, JOSEPH WAS 113 2ND DIST
TURNER, JOSEPH TAL 028 EASTON D
TURNER, JOSEPH C. CAR 097 NO TWP L
TURNER, JOSEPH D. MGM 356 BERRYS D
TURNER, JOSHUA FRE 190 5TH E DI
TURNER, JOSHUA BAL 016 4TH WARD
TURNER, JOSHUA ALL 165 6TH E.D.
TURNER, JOSHUA J. BAL 419 8TH WARD
TURNER, JUBE HAR 121 2ND DIST
TURNER, JUDY BAL 151 2ND DIST
TURNER, JULIA KEN 302 3RD DIST
TURNER, JULIA N. PRI 036 VANSVILL
TURNER, JULIANN FRE 406 JEFFERSO
TURNER, JUPITER HAR 126 2ND DIST
TURNER, KESIAH QUE 233 4TH E DI
TURNER, KITTY V. CHA 250 MIDDLETO
TURNER, LAURETTA DOR 448 1ST DIST
TURNER, LESTER BAL 404 1ST DIST
TURNER, LETTICE C. BAL 180 16TH WAR
TURNER, LEWIS HAR 113 2ND DIST
TURNER, LOUIS BAL 256 1ST DIST
TURNER, LOUIS E. ST 331 4TH E DI
TURNER, LOUISA ALL 259 CUMBERLA
TURNER, LOUISA BAL 087 4TH WARD
TURNER, LUCY CHA 280 BOJANTOW
TURNER, M. SUSANNAH BAL 145 16TH WAR
TURNER, MABLE TAL 116 ST MICHA
TURNER, MAHALA BAL 111 1ST WARD
TURNER, MARGARET HAR 017 1ST DIST
TURNER, MARGARET CEC 047 1ST E DI
TURNER, MARGARET A. BAL 067 15TH WAR
TURNER, MARGARETT BAL 012 4TH WARD
TURNER, MARIA BAL 170 11TH WAR
TURNER, MARIA-BLACK CAR 088 NO TWP L
TURNER, MARIAH KEN 298 3RD DIST
TURNER, MARSELUS TAL 015 EASTON D
TURNER, MARTHA BAL 067 15TH WAR
TURNER, MARTHA BAL 457 1ST DIST
TURNER, MARTHA A. TAL 111 ST MICHA
TURNER, MARY PRI 062 NOTTINGH
TURNER, MARY TAL 028 EASTON D
TURNER, MARY PRI 026 VANSVILL
TURNER, MARY KEN 288 3RD DIST
TURNER, MARY KEN 301 3RD DIST
TURNER, MARY BAL 463 1ST DIST
TURNER, MARY BAL 313 12TH WAR
TURNER, MARY ALL 247 CUMBERLA
TURNER, MARY ALL 217 CUMBERLA
TURNER, MARY ANN 304 1ST DIST
TURNER, MARY ANN 290 ANNAPOLI
TURNER, MARY ALL 196 CUMBERLA
TURNER, MARY BAL 229 6TH WARD
TURNER, MARY HAR 125 2ND DIST
TURNER, MARY BAL 311 20TH WAR
TURNER, MARY FRE 032 FREDERIC
TURNER, MARY B. FRE 051 FREDERIC
TURNER, MARY C. CAR 163 NO TWP L
TURNER, MARY C. BAL 037 4TH WARD
TURNER, MARY ELLEN BAL 360 13TH WAR
TURNER, MARY J. FRE 056 FREDERIC
TURNER, MARY J. BAL 230 6TH WARD
TURNER, MARY J. BAL 336 3RD WARD
TURNER, MARY L. MGM 336 CRACKLIN
TURNER, MARY L. BAL 287 17TH WAR
TURNER, MARY P. KEN 287 3RD DIST
TURNER, MARY T. BAL 029 1ST WARD
TURNER, MARY-BLACK CAR 087 NO TWP L
TURNER, MATILCA BAL 158 6TH WARD
TURNER, MAURACE BAL 334 1ST DIST
TURNER, MAYBURY, J. BAL 112 1ST WARD
TURNER, MECTER BAL 143 19TH WAR
TURNER, MERTON ALL 259 CUMBERLA
TURNER, MILLIMINTA KEN 226 2ND DIST
TURNER, MILLY ANN 430 HOWARD D
TURNER, MORRIS BAL 170 11TH WAR
TURNER, MRS- ANN 343 3RD DIST
TURNER, NAAMAN P. SOM 531 QUANTICO
TURNER, NATHAN BAL 365 3RD WARD
TURNER, NATHAN G.C. BAL 341 7TH WARD
TURNER, NELLY BAL 108 15TH WAR
TURNER, NERO QUE 228 4TH E DI
TURNER, NOAH CAR 066 NO TWP L
TURNER, PAMELIA ANN 509 HOWARD D
TURNER, PEGGY SOM 423 PRINCESS
TURNER, PETER CEC 199 7TH E DI
TURNER, PETER WOR 228 6TH E DI
TURNER, PHILIP ST 328 4TH E DI
TURNER, PHILIP A. BAL 286 1ST DIST
TURNER, POLLY SOM 548 TYASKIN
TURNER, RACHEL QUE 213 3RD E DI
TURNER, REBECCA KEN 299 3RD DIST
TURNER, REBECCA BAL 109 15TH WAR
TURNER, REBECCA BAL 068 15TH WAR
TURNER, REBECCA BAL 069 15TH WAR
TURNER, REBECCA BAL 055 15TH WAR
TURNER, REBECCA CAL 053 3RD DIST
TURNER, REZIN BAL 175 2ND DIST
TURNER, RICHARD BAL 339 1ST DIST
TURNER, RICHARD HAR 164 3RD DIST
TURNER, RICHARD CEC 086 4TH E DI
TURNER, RICHARD PRI 027 VANSVILL
TURNER, RICHARD A. KEN 276 1ST DIST
TURNER, RICHARD B. MGM 410 MEDLEY 3
TURNER, RICHARD J. BAL 457 8TH WARD
TURNER, RICHARD T. BAL 163 16TH WAR
TURNER, ROBERT BAL 185 19TH WAR
TURNER, RODWELL BAL 105 10TH WAR
TURNER, ROSANNA BAL 074 2ND DIST
TURNER, SAMUEL HAR 048 1ST DIST
TURNER, SAMUEL CAL 007 1ST DIST
TURNER, SAMUEL WAS 218 1ST DIST
TURNER, SAMUEL WOR 242 1ST CENS
TURNER, SAMUEL E. BAL 056 10TH WAR
TURNER, SARAH BAL 063 10TH WAR
TURNER, SARAH ANN 370 4TH DIST
TURNER, SARAH TAL 005 EASTON D
TURNER, SARAH WAS 149 HAGERSTO
TURNER, SARAH CAR 156 NO TWP L
TURNER, SUSAN BAL 127 18TH WAR
TURNER, SUSAN A. CAL 061 3RD DIST
TURNER, SUSANA BAL 318 3RD WARD
TURNER, SUSANNA BAL 114 5TH WARD
TURNER, SUSANNA M. BAL 105 10TH WAR
TURNER, TABITHA SOM 544 TYASKIN
TURNER, THOMA CAL 052 3RD DIST
TURNER, THOMAS BAL 016 4TH WARD
TURNER, THOMAS BAL 237 20TH WAR
TURNER, THOMAS CHA 251 MIDDLETO
TURNER, THOMAS SOM 467 TRAPPE D
TURNER, THOMAS BAL 318 7TH WARD
TURNER, THOMAS BAL 288 12TH WAR
TURNER, THOMAS BAL 074 15TH WAR
TURNER, THOMAS ALL 165 6TH E.D.
TURNER, THOMAS B. QUE 212 3RD E DI
TURNER, THOMAS B. BAL 468 14TH WAR
TURNER, THOMAS H. TAL 034 EASTON D
TURNER, THOMAS J. PRI 092 MARLBROU
TURNER, THOMAS K. BAL 107 5TH WARD
TURNER, THOMAS P. PRI 035 VANSVILL
TURNER, THOMAS W. BAL 171 16TH WAR
TURNER, V. S. CHA 224 ALLENS F
TURNER, VIRGINIA C. BAL 171 16TH WAR
TURNER, WALER WOR 266 BERLIN 1
TURNER, WASHINGTON-BLACK CAR 087 NC TWP L
TURNER, WILLIAM CAR 156 NO TWP L
TURNER, WILLIAM CHA 250 MIDDLETO
TURNER, WILLIAM HAR 114 2ND DIST
TURNER, WILLIAM MGM 372 BERRYS D
TURNER, WILLIAM MGM 359 BERRYS D
TURNER, WILLIAM HAR 177 3RD DIST
TURNER, WILLIAM HAR 126 2ND DIST
TURNER, WILLIAM SOM 481 TRAPP DI
TURNER, WILLIAM SOM 470 TRAPPE D
TURNER, WILLIAM KEN 259 1ST DIST
TURNER, WILLIAM WAS 149 HAGERSTO
TURNER, WILLIAM BAL 309 3RD WARD
TURNER, WILLIAM BAL 380 1ST DIST
TURNER, WILLIAM BAL 011 9TH WARD
TURNER, WILLIAM BAL 075 2ND DIST
TURNER, WILLIAM BAL 036 9TH WARD
TURNER, WILLIAM BAL 036 9TH WARD
TURNER, WILLIAM B. ST 340 5TH E DI
TURNER, WILLIAM E. CHA 250 MIDDLETO
TURNER, WILLIAM H. BAL 393 14TH WAR
TURNER, WILLIAM H. H. BAL 398 8TH WARD
TURNER, WILLIAM* DOR 462 1ST DIST
TURNER, WILSON ANN 394 8TH DIST
TURNER, WILSON CHA 271 ALLENS F
TURNER, Y. CHA 224 ALLENS F
TURNER, ZABDIAL CAR 156 NO TWP L
TURNER, ZACARIAH BAL 341 3RD WARD
TURNER, ZACHARIAH ANN 379 4TH DIST
TURNER.JACKSON BAL 198 2ND WARD
TURNEY, CATHAINE ALL 020 2ND E.D.
TURNEY, CATHARINE KEN 212 2ND DISTA
TURNEY, HENRY BAL 241 20TH WAR
TURNEY, HENRY BAL 144 2ND DIST
TURNEY, JACOB ALL 038 2ND E.D.
TURNEY, JOHN WAS 137 HAGERSTO
TURNEY, MICHAEL BAL 403 8TH WARD
TURNEY, SOLOMON ALL 032 2ND E.D.
TURNING, JOANNA BAL 112 1ST WARD
TURNNER, ELIZA FRE 445 8TH E DI
TURNOR, DENNIS * BAL 089 18TH WAR
TURNPAUGH, PETER BAL 242 1ST DIST
TURNPAUGH, SARAH BAL 243 1ST DIST
TURNPAUGH, WILLIAM BAL 432 1ST DIST
TURNPAW, CONRAD BAL 433 1ST DIST
TURNTOLT, DARLINGTON WAS 101 2ND DIST
TURPFLE, WILIAM CAR 282 7TH DIST
TURPIN, AARON-BLACK CAR 169 NO TWP L
TURPIN, ELIJAH WOR 306 2ND E DI
TURPIN, ELIZABETH QUE 217 3RD E DI
TURPIN, EMILY L. HAR 140 2ND DIST
TURPIN, FRANCES B. C. DOR 305 1ST DIST
TURPIN, GEORGE SOM 362 BRINKLEY
TURPIN, HANNAH SOM 406 DUBLIN D
TURPIN, HENRY SOM 363 BRINKLEY
TURPIN, HENRY SOM 351 BRINKLEY
TURPIN, ISAAC SOM 394 BRINKLEY
TURPIN, JOHN * WOR 290 9TH E DI
TURPIN, JOHN W. SOM 351 BRINKLEY
TURPIN, JOSEPH DOR 300 1ST DIST
TURPIN, JOSHUA BAL 346 13TH WAR
TURPIN, MARIA H. BAL 032 9TH WARD
TURPIN, MARTHA SOM 403 BRINKLEY
TURPIN, NANCY SOM 440 DAMES QU
TURPIN, NELSON H. BAL 273 7TH WARD
TURPIN, SARAH BAL 052 18TH WAR
TURPIN, THOMAS SOM 404 BRINKLEY
TURPIN, THOMAS WOR 340 1ST E DI
TURPIN, TITUS WOR 310 2ND E DI
TURPIN, WALTER S. QUE 190 3RD E DI
TURPIN, WILLIAM SOM 352 BRINKLEY
TURPIN, WILLIAM SOM 493 SALISBUR
TURPIN, WILLIAM SOM 415 DUBLIN D
TURR, LETITIA * BAL 317 20TH WAR
TURTON, BENJAMIN F. PRI 061 NOTTINGH
TURTON, E. PRI 101 SPALDING
TURTON, RICHEL W. PRI 065 NOTTINGH
TURTON, THOMAS G. PRI 065 NOTTINGH
TURTON, WILLIAM H. ANN 322 2ND DIST
TURTON, WILLIAM L. PRI 059 NOTTINGH
TURVOY, THOMSA CAL 010 1ST DIST
TURY, ANDREW F. CEC 126 5TH E DI
TUSCHNER, FREDERICKA BAL 371 13TH WAR
TUSSEL, HENRY BAL 256 1ST DIST
TUSSELBAUGH, WILLIAM H.B. BAL 098 5TH WARD
TUSTIN, SAMUEL BAL 314 7TH WARD
TUSTIN, SEPTIMUS WAS 123 HAGERSTO
TUTCHET, ELIZABETH L. WAS 151 2ND DIST
TUTCHTON, HERMAN HAR 169 3RD DIST
TUTHILL, D.M. ALL 249 CUMBERLA
TUTLE, JACOB WAS 258 1ST DIST
TUTLE, JOHN CAR 257 3RD DIST
TUTTLE, ALFRED BAL 299 3RD WARD
TUTTLE, COLUMBUS BAL 146 19TH WAR
TUTTLE, DAVID BAL 145 19TH WAR
TUTTLE, DAVID BAL 145 1ST WARD
TUTTLE, ELIZABETH MGM 406 MEDLEY 3
TUTTLE, JANE BAL 347 13TH WAR
TUTTLE, JOHN BAL 009 15TH WAR
TUTTLE, MARY BAL 299 3RD WARD
TUTTLE, MARY BAL 322 12TH WAR
TUTTLE, SARAH BAL 250 6TH WARD
TUTTLE, WALTER A. PRI 004 BLADENSB
TUTTLE, WILLIAM BAL 330 1ST DIST
TUTWILER, CATHARINE WAS 165 HAGERSTO
TUTWILER, EVE WAS 122 HAGERSTO
TUTWILER, ROBERT P. WAS 126 HAGERSTO
TUXALL, ALEXANDER BAL 276 20TH WAR
TUXFORD, MARTIN BAL 023 18TH WAR
TUY, JAMES ST 271 3RD E DI
TUZMOTTEN, ANDREW BAL 190 11TH WAR

Name	County	Page	District
TVANE, JOSEPH	BAL	251	12TH WAR
TWADDELL, JOHN	CEC	142	6TH E DI
TWEED, JAMES	CEC	097	4TH E DI
TWEEDIE, JOHN	BAL	244	12TH WAR
TWEEDY, SAMUEL A.	BAL	174	16TH WAR
TWENY, RUBEN	CEC	021	ELKTON 3
TWIFORD, ALFRED W.	SOM	513	BARREN C
TWIFORD, ELIZABETH	SOM	512	BARREN C
TWIFORD, A.S.	ALL	208	CUMBERLA
TWIG, ANN	WOR	197	8TH E DI
TWIG, HESTER	WOR	187	7TH E DI
TWIG, JAMES H.	WOR	170	6TH E DI
TWIG, JOHN	WOR	194	8TH E DI
TWIG, LOUISA	WOR	192	8TH E DI
TWIG, ROBERT	WOR	192	8TH E DI
TWIGG, ABRAM	ALL	188	9TH E.D.
TWIGG, AMAND C.	ALL	171	7TH E.D.
TWIGG, ANGEL	ALL	191	9TH E.D.
TWIGG, ANGEL	ALL	191	9TH E.D.
TWIGG, ASA	ALL	157	6TH E.D.
TWIGG, BRICE	ALL	171	7TH E.D.
TWIGG, CATHARINE	ALL	158	6TH E.D.
TWIGG, CHARLES	ALL	179	7TH E.D.
TWIGG, DAVID	ALL	191	9TH E.D.
TWIGG, DAVID D.	ALL	191	9TH E.D.
TWIGG, ELI	ALL	178	7TH E.D.
TWIGG, ELIAS	ALL	171	7TH E.D.
TWIGG, ELIZABETH	ALL	171	7TH E.D.
TWIGG, ELIZABETH	ALL	179	7TH E.D.
TWIGG, FRANCES	ALL	189	9TH E.D.
TWIGG, GEORGE	ALL	193	9TH E.D.
TWIGG, GREENBARG	ALL	190	9TH E.D.
TWIGG, GRIFFEN	ALL	179	7TH E.D.
TWIGG, GRIFFIN	ALL	179	7TH E.D.
TWIGG, HAMSON	ALL	190	9TH E.D.
TWIGG, HARNSON	ALL	190	9TH E.D.
TWIGG, JAMES	ALL	174	7TH E.D.
TWIGG, JAMES	ALL	178	7TH E.D.
TWIGG, JAMES	ALL	168	6TH E.D.
TWIGG, JAMES	SOM	470	TRAPPE D
TWIGG, JAMES M.	ALL	190	9TH E.D.
TWIGG, JESSE	ALL	104	5TH E.D.
TWIGG, JOHN	ALL	193	9TH E.D.
TWIGG, LEVI	ALL	178	7TH E.D.
TWIGG, MARYANN	ALL	104	5TH E.D.
TWIGG, MICHAEL	ALL	175	7TH E.D.
TWIGG, OLIVER	ALL	191	9TH E.D.
TWIGG, RACHEL	ALL	173	7TH E.D.
TWIGG, REBECCA	ALL	194	9TH E.D.
TWIGG, ROBERT	ALL	189	9TH E.D.
TWIGG, SARAH	ALL	185	9TH E.D.
TWIGG, SIMEON	ALL	173	7TH E.D.
TWIGG, THOMAS	ALL	191	9TH E.D.
TWIGG, THOMAS	BAL	127	16TH WAR
TWIGG, THOMAS M.	SOM	528	QUANTICO
TWIGG, ZIMERLY	ALL	236	CUMBERLA
TWIGGINS, JACOB-BLCK	CAR	128	NO TWP L
TWILEY, BENJAMIN F.	DOR	433	1ST DIST
TWILEY, JAMES D.	DOR	433	1ST DIST
TWILEY, JESSE	DOR	374	1ST DIST
TWILEY, JOHN	DOR	426	1ST DIST
TWILEY, PRISSY	DOR	387	1ST DIST
TWILEY, SLEIGHTER	DOR	431	1ST DIST
TWILEY, THOMAS	DOR	434	1ST DIST
TWILEY, W. D.	DOR	430	1ST DIST
TWILEY, WILLIAM A.	DOR	412	1ST DIST
TWILLEY, ELLEN	BAL	096	5TH WARD
TWILLEY, ROBERT	WOR	192	8TH E DI
TWILLEY, SAMUEL	DOR	300	1ST DIST
TWILLEY, SAMUEL	DOR	301	1ST DIST
TWILLEY, WILLIAM	WOR	192	8TH E DI
TWILLY, ALPHEUS	SOM	528	QUANTICO
TWILLY, CALEB D.	SOM	471	TRAPPE D
TWILLY, ELEANOR	SOM	549	TYASKIN
TWILLY, ELIZABETH	SOM	494	SALISBUR
TWILLY, GEORGE W.	SOM	529	QUANTICO
TWILLY, GEORGENER*	SOM	550	TYASKIN
TWILLY, JOHN W.	SOM	507	BARREN C
TWILLY, JOSHUA T.	SOM	488	SALISBUR
TWILLY, SAMUEL	SOM	529	QUANTICO
TWILLY, WILLIAM	SOM	550	TYASKIN
TWILLY, WILLIAM B.	SOM	529	QUANTICO
TWINEY, THOMAS	CEC	172	6TH E DI
TWINING, HORRIS B.	HAR	050	1ST DIST
TWINING, ISAAC	HAR	049	1ST DIST
TWINING, JULIA E.	HAR	049	1ST DIST
TWINY, MARY	CEC	068	5TH E DI
TWIPOIN, THOMAS S.	WOR	296	9TH E DI
TWIPSON, JOHN	WOR	296	9TH E DI
TWIST, HELERY	BAL	367	1ST DIST
TWIST, HENRY B.	BAL	006	9TH WARD
TWIST, REBECCA	BAL	370	1ST DIST
TWIST, STEPHEN F.	BAL	008	9TH WARD
TWIST, WILLIAM	BAL	301	1ST DIST
TWOGOOD, MARY	BAL	077	15TH WAR
TWYFORD, JOHN	CAR	097	NO TWP L
TYALOR, HARACE	KEN	256	1ST DIST
TYALOR, NE	ANN	397	8TH DIST
TYANSKY, JOHN	BAL	078	1ST WARD
TYCEN, NATHANIEL	WOR	276	BERLIN 1
TYDING, CHARLES *	BAL	319	12TH WAR
TYDINGS, CRETIA A.	ANN	355	3RD DIST
TYDINGS, EDWARD	BAL	184	6TH WARD
TYDINGS, HENRY	ANN	356	3RD DIST
TYDINGS, HENRY	ANN	410	8TH DIST
TYDINGS, HORATIO	ANN	357	3RD DIST
TYDINGS, JAMES	ANN	294	1ST DIST
TYDINGS, JOHN K.	ANN	356	3RD DIST
TYDINGS, JOHN L.	ANN	357	3RD DIST
TYDINGS, JOHN W.	ANN	275	ANNAPOLI
TYDINGS, JOSEPH	ANN	350	3RD DIST
TYDINGS, KINSEY	ANN	357	3RD DIST
TYDINGS, LEWIS	ANN	266	ANNAPOLI
TYDINGS, LEWIS	BAL	191	6TH WARD
TYDINGS, RICHARD	BAL	237	6TH WARD
TYDINGS, RICHARD	ANN	294	1ST DIST
TYDINGS, RICHARD	ANN	410	8TH DIST
TYDINGS, RICHARD	ANN	356	3RD DIST
TYDINGS, RICHARD	ANN	356	3RD DIST
TYDINGS, ROGER	ANN	294	1ST DIST
TYDINGS, SARAH	ANN	291	ANNAPOLI
TYDINGS, WILLIAM H.	BAL	316	7TH WARD
TYE, ANNE	BAL	371	13TH WAR
TYE, MARY ANN	BAL	355	13TH WAR
TYE, PATRICK	BAL	348	7TH WARD
TYEHOLM, WILLIAM	BAL	168	1ST WARD
TYER, ELLEN-BLACK	CAR	384	2ND DIST
TYERMAN, JOHN	BAL	094	1ST WARD
TYGAIT, JAMES	ALL	055	10TH E.D
TYGHT, THOMAS	BAL	002	1ST WARD

Name	County	Page	District
TYGIST, H. R.	ALL	053	10TH E.D
TYLAND, JOHN	BAL	056	18TH WAR
TYLAND, JOSEPHINE	BAL	096	18TH WAR
TYLAR, ELIZA*	DOR	298	1ST DIST
TYLAR, MILLY	DOR	297	1ST DIST
TYLARD, ELIZABETH	BAL	443	14TH WAR
TYLARD, HENRY W.	BAL	443	14TH WAR
TYLARD, WILLIAM	BAL	102	18TH WAR
TYLER, AGNES	BAL	237	20TH WAR
TYLER, AHEGAIL	FRE	268	NEW MARK
TYLER, ALEXANDER	BAL	120	1ST WARD
TYLER, ALEXANDER	SOM	457	DAMES QU
TYLER, ANN	BAL	187	2ND WARD
TYLER, ANN	FRE	017	FREDERIC
TYLER, BASIL	BAL	253	1ST DIST
TYLER, CAROLINE	FRE	009	FREDERIC
TYLER, CAROLINE	FRE	274	NEW MARK
TYLER, CHARLES	BAL	126	18TH WAR
TYLER, CHARLES	MGM	372	BERRYS D
TYLER, CHARLES	BAL	037	1ST WARD
TYLER, CHARLES	BAL	187	2ND WARD
TYLER, CYLUS	SOM	453	DAMES QU
TYLER, EDWARD	BAL	102	2ND DIST
TYLER, ELEN	CHA	247	HILLTOP
TYLER, ELIAS	FRE	300	WOODSBOR
TYLER, ELISA*	BAL	053	4TH WARD
TYLER, ELIZA	BAL	107	18TH WAR
TYLER, GEORGE	BAL	268	17TH WAR
TYLER, GEORGE	BAL	152	1ST WARD
TYLER, GEORGE	BAL	087	1ST WARD
TYLER, GEORGE	BAL	157	2ND DIST
TYLER, GEORGE	BAL	009	9TH WARD
TYLER, GEORGE K.	BAL	120	5TH WARD
TYLER, GEORGE M.	FRE	041	FREDERIC
TYLER, GRACE C.	PRI	074	MARLBROU
TYLER, GRAFTON	PRI	086	QUEEN AN
TYLER, HANSON	ANN	490	HOWARD D
TYLER, HARRIET	FRE	077	FREDERIC
TYLER, ISAIAH	BAL	192	17TH WAR
TYLER, JAMES	BAL	354	3RD WARD
TYLER, JOHN	BAL	374	13TH WAR
TYLER, JOHN	BAL	126	18TH WAR
TYLER, JOHN A.	BAL	301	17TH WAR
TYLER, JULIAN	MGM	347	BERRYS D
TYLER, LEONARD	ANN	453	HOWARD D
TYLER, LEVIN	SOM	400	BRINKLEY
TYLER, LYDIA	ANN	323	2ND DIST
TYLER, MARGARET	BAL	387	13TH WAR
TYLER, MARIAH	FRE	275	NEW MARK
TYLER, MARTHA	BAL	116	18TH WAR
TYLER, MARTHA	BAL	253	1ST DIST
TYLER, MARY	BAL	057	18TH WAR
TYLER, MARY	BAL	039	18TH WAR
TYLER, MARY E.	BAL	352	7TH WARD
TYLER, MARY J.	BAL	277	7TH WARD
TYLER, NANCY	BAL	025	9TH WARD
TYLER, NANCY	WAS	044	2ND SUBD
TYLER, NELLY	CHA	246	HILLTOP
TYLER, NICHOLAS	MGM	334	CRACKLIN
TYLER, PRISCILLA	ANN	453	HOWARD D
TYLER, RACHEL A.	FRE	275	NEW MARK
TYLER, RICHARD	ANN	453	HOWARD D
TYLER, RICHARD-BLACK	FRE	242	NEW MARK
TYLER, ROBERT	MGM	403	ROCKERLE
TYLER, ROBERT	PRI	083	QUEEN AN
TYLER, RUGHT A.	BAL	126	18TH WAR
TYLER, SAMUEL	MGM	357	BERRYS D
TYLER, SAMUEL	FRE	030	FREDERIC
TYLER, SAMUEL	BAL	195	11TH WAR
TYLER, SARAH	BAL	443	14TH WAR
TYLER, SOLOMON F.	BAL	013	15TH WAR
TYLER, SUSAN	TAL	003	EASTON D
TYLER, THOMAS	PRI	029	VANSVILL
TYLER, THOMAS	SOM	438	DAMES QU
TYLER, THOMAS	FRE	256	NEW MARK
TYLER, THOMAS	BAL	208	17TH WAR
TYLER, VIOLETTA	PRI	084	QUEEN AN
TYLER, WILLIAM	BAL	184	19TH WAR
TYLER, WILLIAM B.	FRE	041	FREDERIC
TYLER, WILLIAM C.	ANN	325	2ND DIST
TYLER, WILLIAM JR.	FRE	059	FREDERIC
TYLER, WILLIAM SR.	FRE	030	FREDERIC
TYLER, ZARIAH	BAL	024	18TH WAR
TYLOR, CAVID	DOR	356	3RD DIVI
TYLOR, DAVID	SOM	456	DAMES QU
TYLOR, DAVID W.	DOR	337	3RD DIVI
TYLOR, EDWARD	SOM	439	DAMES QU
TYLOR, EPHRAIM	SOM	454	DAMES QU
TYLOR, GEORGE	DOR	332	3RD DIVI
TYLOR, HENERY	DOR	337	3RD DIVI
TYLOR, JAMES	DOR	334	3RD DIVI
TYLOR, JAMES E.	DOR	354	3RD DIVI
TYLOR, JOHN	DOR	338	3RD DIVI
TYLOR, JOHN	SOM	448	DAMES QU
TYLOR, JOHN B.	BAL	188	5TH DIST
TYLOR, JOHN L.	SOM	457	DAMES QU
TYLOR, JOSIAH	SOM	456	DAMES QU
TYLOR, LITTELTON	DOR	355	3RD DIVI
TYLOR, MARY	DOR	333	3RD DIVI
TYLOR, MARY	DOR	330	3RD DIVI
TYLOR, MARY	SOM	456	DAMES QU
TYLOR, ROSEAM	DOR	338	3RD DIVI
TYLOR, SARAH	ANN	406	8TH DIST
TYLOR, SOLOMON	DOR	298	1ST DIST
TYLOR, SOLOMON F.	DOR	348	3RD DIVI
TYLOR, THOMAS	DOR	337	3RD DIVI
TYLOR, THOMAS	SOM	455	DAMES QU
TYLOR, THOMAS	SOM	380	BRINKLEY
TYLOR, WILLIAM	SOM	455	DAMES QU
TYLOR, WILLIAM	TAL	115	ST MICHA
TYLOR, WILLIAM	DOR	336	3RD DIVI
TYLOR, WILLIAM	SOM	448	DAMES QU
TYLOR, WILLIAM H.	DOR	297	1ST DIST
TYLOR, WILLIAM JR.	SOM	448	DAMES QU
TYMAN, GEORGE	BAL	201	2ND WARD
TYMAN, J. C.	BAL	151	1ST WARD
TYNEE, TIMOTHY	ALL	253	CUMBERLA
TYON, THOMAS	WOR	245	1ST CENS
TYRE, BENJAMIN	WOR	217	4TH E DI
TYRE, MILLEY	WOR	311	2ND E DI
TYRE, NICHOLAS	HAR	056	1ST DIST
TYRE, PURNELL	WOR	243	1ST CENS
TYRE, SETH W.	WOR	206	4TH E DI
TYRES, JAMES H.	BAL	005	9TH WARD
TYRREL, EDWARD	BAL	044	2ND DIST
TYSER, HENRY	BAL	242	17TH WAR
TYSON, A.H.	BAL	030	2ND DIST
TYSON, ANN	CEC	099	3RD E DI
TYSON, ANNA	BAL	063	15TH WAR
TYSON, BENJAMIN	CEC	133	6TH E DI

Name	County	Page	District
TYSON, BENNET	FRE	160	EMMITTSB
TYSON, CECELIA V.	CHA	280	BOJANTOW
TYSON, CHARLES B.	BAL	260	12TH WAR
TYSON, ELIZABETH	BAL	430	14TH WAR
TYSON, ELIZABETH	CEC	087	4TH E DI
TYSON, ELMIRA	CEC	087	4TH E DI
TYSON, EMILY	CEC	124	5TH E DI
TYSON, G.	BAL	152	1ST WARD
TYSON, GEORGE	BAL	058	2ND DIST
TYSON, GEORGE	BAL	038	2ND DIST
TYSON, GEORGE M.	CEC	064	1ST E DI
TYSON, GEORGE*	BAL	033	4TH WARD
TYSON, HANNAH	CEC	086	4TH E DI
TYSON, HARRIET	BAL	141	16TH WAR
TYSON, HARRIET E.	CEC	160	6TH E DI
TYSON, HENRY	BAL	122	2ND DIST
TYSON, ISAAC	BAL	357	13TH WAR
TYSON, ISAAC	CEC	192	5TH E DI
TYSON, ISAAC JR.	BAL	317	20TH WAR
TYSON, ISRAEL	CEC	165	6TH E DI
TYSON, JAMES	FRE	071	FREDERIC
TYSON, JAMES	BAL	468	14TH WAR
TYSON, JESSE	CEC	141	6TH E DI
TYSON, JOE W.	ANN	483	HOWARD D
TYSON, JOHN	CEC	140	5TH E DI
TYSON, JOHN L.	ANN	458	HOWARD D
TYSON, JOHN W.	CEC	120	3RD E DI
TYSON, JONATHAN	FRE	012	FREDERIC
TYSON, JONATHAN C.	BAL	409	14TH WAR
TYSON, JOSEPH	CEC	141	6TH E DI
TYSON, JOSEPH	BAL	447	1ST DIST
TYSON, LANCY	CEC	122	4TH E DI
TYSON, LETHA	FRE	268	NEW MARK
TYSON, LEVI	CEC	194	7TH E DI
TYSON, MARGARET	BAL	067	15TH WAR
TYSON, MARGARET	BAL	444	8TH WARD
TYSON, MARGARETT	BAL	055	4TH WARD
TYSON, MARIA	CEC	014	ELKTON 3
TYSON, MARTHA	BAL	040	2ND DIST
TYSON, MARTHA A.	FRE	071	FREDERIC
TYSON, MARY	HAR	079	2ND DIST
TYSON, MARY	CEC	136	6TH E DI
TYSON, MARY E.	BAL	031	18TH WAR
TYSON, NATHAN	CEC	140	5TH E DI
TYSON, NATHAN	BAL	419	14TH WAR
TYSON, NATHAN	BAL	244	1ST DIST
TYSON, PHILIP S.	BAL	020	2ND DIST
TYSON, REBECCA A.	CEC	140	5TH E DI
TYSON, RICHARD	BAL	140	11TH WAR
TYSON, RICHARD	BAL	437	1ST DIST
TYSON, SAMUEL	CEC	109	3RD E DI
TYSON, SARAH	BAL	035	2ND DIST
TYSON, SUSAN	BAL	033	2ND DIST
TYSON, THOMAS	CEC	116	3RD E DI
TYSON, THOMAS	CEC	160	6TH E DI
TYSON, THOMAS	MGM	348	BERRYS D
TYSON, WILLIAM	FRE	165	EMMITTSB
TYSON, WILLIAM	CEC	116	3RD E DI
TYSON, WILLIAM	CEC	099	3RD E DI
TYSON, WILLIAM	CEC	020	ELKTON 3
TYSON, WILLIAM	BAL	095	15TH WAR
TYSON, WILLIAM	BAL	158	1ST WARD
TYTUS, RICHARD	ANN	356	3RD DIST
UAIER, JOHN	BAL	376	8TH WARD
UALE, THOMAS U.	BAL	458	8TH WARD
UBER, FREDERICK	FRE	311	MIDDLETO
UBICK, HENRY	BAL	257	20TH WAR
UBOCKE, JAMES E.	BAL	458	8TH WARD
UEANT, CHRISTINA	CAR	320	1ST DIST
UELDON, JOHN	WOR	248	1ST CENS
UENKHAIS, HENRY *	BAL	316	12TH WAR
UENNSON, SARAH *	BAL	223	12TH WAR
UERDERMAN, DEDRICK	BAL	367	13TH WAR
UERS, EDWARD	BAL	157	2ND DIST
UERSE, THOMAS*	DOR	327	3RD DIVI
UHL, ANDREW	BAL	113	18TH WAR
UHL, ELIZABETH	BAL	327	7TH WARD
UHL, FRANCIS A.	BAL	005	9TH WARD
UHL, PETER *	ALL	095	5TH E.D.
UHL, PHILIP	BAL	454	14TH WAR
UHLENBRAGH, ADELAIDE	BAL	106	10TH WAR
UHLER, ANDREW	BAL	246	1ST DIST
UHLER, CALEB	BAL	234	1ST DIST
UHLER, CONRAD	BAL	233	1ST DIST
UHLER, ELIZABETH	WAS	272	RIDGEVIL
UHLER, ERASMUS	BAL	118	5TH WARD
UHLER, GEORGE W.	BAL	254	12TH WAR
UHLER, JACOB	BAL	223	1ST DIST
UHLER, JOHNSON	BAL	418	1ST DIST
UHLER, WILLIAM	BAL	295	1ST DIST
UHLEY, JOSEPH	BAL	211	19TH WAR
UHLEY, SUSAN	BAL	211	19TH WAR
UHLHORN, ANNA S.	BAL	067	15TH WAR
UHLHORN, DOROTHEA	BAL	109	15TH WAR
UHLHORN, RANDEW	BAL	354	13TH WAR
UHNRINE, LOUISA	BAL	134	16TH WAR
UHRIG, B.	BAL	449	8TH WARD
UICE, WILLIAM	BAL	112	2ND DIST
UIERDOSH, GEORGE *	BAL	035	18TH WAR
UINRATH, JOHN	BAL	121	1ST WARD
UINTER, GEORGE	CAR	377	2ND DIST
UKLE, DAVID	ALL	029	2ND E.D.
ULBERT, JOHN*	BAL	018	4TH WARD
ULD, HENRY	BAL	024	15TH WAR
ULD, JACOB	BAL	024	15TH WAR
ULD, PHILIP	BAL	024	15TH WAR
ULDERWA, MATILDA	BAL	076	4TH WARD
ULEHARN, BERNARD	BAL	274	1ST DIST
ULER, JOHN	CAR	189	4TH DIST
ULER, WILLIAM	CAR	189	4TH DIST
ULERICK, SAMUEL	CAR	177	8TH DIST
ULERT, MATHEWS	BAL	066	4TH WARD
ULLRICH, WILLAIM	BAL	124	16TH WAR
ULLUM, JANE	WAS	075	2ND SUBD
ULM, FREDERICK	BAL	294	17TH WAR
ULMER, JOHN	BAL	076	2ND DIST
ULMO, E. E.	BAL	393	14TH WAR
ULRICH, GEORGE	BAL	079	1ST WARD
ULRICH, GOERGE W.	FRE	050	FREDERIC
ULRICH, HENRY	BAL	079	1ST WARD
ULRICH, HUMPHREY	WAS	297	1ST DIST
ULRICH, PHILIP	WAS	145	HAGERSTO
ULRICH, SAMUEL	WAS	144	HAGERSTO
ULRICK, ERNEST	BAL	454	14TH WAR
ULRIETS, GEORGE*	BAL	022	4TH WARD
ULUM, ANDREW *	WAS	191	1ST DIST
UMBACK, MAGDALENE	BAL	239	12TH WAR
UMBAUGH, JANE	ALL	235	CUMBERLA
UMBAUGH, MICHAEL	WAS	123	HAGERSTO
UMBEGER, COLEMAN	CEC	172	6TH E DI

Name	County	Page	District
UMBERGER, HENRY M.	FRE	270	NEW MARK
UMBINE, ANDREW	BAL	449	8TH WARD
UMBLE, ISAAC	ALL	030	2ND E.D.
UMER, SAMUEL	FRE	437	8TH E DI
UMPHENALL, JOHN	ALL	152	6TH E.D.
UMPHETSER, ELIZABETH	BAL	219	17TH WAR
UMPHREY, JAMES	ALL	165	6TH E.D.
UMPSHIRE, JOHN	BAL	011	2ND DIST
UMPSTADOT, ALFRED	MGM	418	MEDLEY 3
UMPSTADOT, JACOB	MGM	418	MEDLEY 3
UMPSTADOT, RICHARD S.	MGM	437	CLARKSTR
UMPTEAD, BARBARA	BAL	259	1ST DIST
UNAGST, URIAS	WAS	246	SMITHSBU
UNBRESHT, GABRIEL	BAL	061	18TH WAR
UNCLE, AUGUST	BAL	287	1ST DIST
UNCLES, BEN	MGM	326	CRACKLIN
UNCLES, PHEBE J.	BAL	122	16TH WAR
UNDER, MICHAEL	ALL	156	6TH E.D.
UNDERBACK, P.	BAL	220	19TH WAR
UNDERDONK, HENRY	BAL	318	1ST DIST
UNDERHALL, JANE	SOM	436	PRINCESS
UNDERHILL, ANN	BAL	048	15TH WAR
UNDERHILL, JINNY	SOM	420	PRINCESS
UNDERHILL, MARY A.	BAL	067	18TH WAR
UNDERHILL, SAMUEL	BAL	212	19TH WAR
UNDERHILL, WILLIAM	SOM	400	BRINKLEY
UNDERSTOOD, BENJAMIN	BAL	052	2ND DIST
UNDERWOOD, ALBERT	BAL	038	1ST WARD
UNDERWOOD, ALFRED	BAL	266	7TH WARD
UNDERWOOD, AMELIA A.	TAL	001	EASTON D
UNDERWOOD, ANN	BAL	068	10TH WAR
UNDERWOOD, BENJAMIN	CEC	097	4TH E DI
UNDERWOOD, CHARLES	CEC	113	4TH E DI
UNDERWOOD, CHARLES	BAL	131	1ST WARD
UNDERWOOD, CHARLES	TAL	031	EASTON D
UNDERWOOD, CHARLES T.	PRI	112	PISCATAW
UNDERWOOD, CHESTER W.	ANN	277	ANNAPOLI
UNDERWOOD, GEORGE	BAL	137	2ND DIST
UNDERWOOD, H.	PRI	114	PISCATAW
UNDERWOOD, HENRY	TAL	054	EASTON D
UNDERWOOD, HENRY	BAL	218	19TH WAR
UNDERWOOD, J.J.	WAS	128	HAGERSTO
UNDERWOOD, JACOB	BAL	425	1ST DIST
UNDERWOOD, JANE	BAL	067	4TH WARD
UNDERWOOD, JOHN	CEC	086	4TH E DI
UNDERWOOD, JOHN	PRI	108	PISCATAW
UNDERWOOD, JOSEPH	CEC	097	4TH E DI
UNDERWOOD, JOSEPH	BAL	210	11TH WAR
UNDERWOOD, JOSHUA	BAL	160	6TH WARD
UNDERWOOD, LOUISA	BAL	237	6TH WARD
UNDERWOOD, LUCY A.	BAL	313	20TH WAR
UNDERWOOD, M.	PRI	110	PISCATAW
UNDERWOOD, MARGARET	BAL	233	6TH WARD
UNDERWOOD, MARIA	BAL	426	1ST DIST
UNDERWOOD, MARY	BAL	003	EASTERN
UNDERWOOD, MARY C.	TAL	061	EASTON D
UNDERWOOD, RACHEL	BAL	213	6TH WARD
UNDERWOOD, THOMAS	BAL	139	2ND DIST
UNDERWOOD, THOMAS	PRI	112	PISCATAW
UNDERWOOD, THOMAS	CEC	130	6TH E DI
UNDERWOOD, WILLIAM	PRI	114	PISCATAW
UNDERWOOD, WILLIAM	BAL	185	5TH DIST
UNDUCH, CHARLOTTE	BAL	126	16TH WAR
UNDUFE, SINCENE	WAS	035	2ND SUBD
UNDUTCH, NICHOLAS	BAL	039	18TH WAR
UNEON, MICHAEL	BAL	153	2ND DIST
UNFREZER, HERMAN	BAL	249	6TH WARD
UNGER, AUGUSTINE*	BAL	350	3RD WARD
UNGER, FREDERICK	WAS	254	1ST DIST
UNGER, GEORGE	WAS	255	1ST DIST
UNGER, JOHN	BAL	089	10TH WAR
UNGER, JOHN	BAL	041	18TH WAR
UNGER, MARY	WAS	249	1ST DIST
UNGER, SAMUEL	CAR	409	2ND DIST
UNGLEBEE, JULIAN	FRE	400	JEFFERSO
UNGLEBOUER, ADAM	FRE	005	FREDERIC
UNIOM, MOSES	BAL	305	3RD WARD
UNION, JULIET	BAL	062	4TH WARD
UNICN, ROBERT	BAL	095	15TH WAR
UNION, THOMAS	BAL	062	4TH WARD
UNKEFER, ABDIEL	FRE	449	8TH E DI
UNKEFER, FRANCIS	FRE	450	8TH E DI
UNKEFER, LYDIA R.	FRE	449	8TH E DI
UNKLE, FREDERICK	BAL	100	15TH WAR
UNKLE, HENRY	BAL	321	1ST DIST
UNKLES, BENJAMIN	BAL	003	18TH WAR
UNKLES, LORENZO	BAL	183	16TH WAR
UNKLESBEE, WILILAM	WAS	191	1ST DIST
UNKNOON-, PATRICK *	BAL	058	18TH WAR
UNKNOWN-, CAROLINE *	BAL	042	18TH WAR
UNKNOWN-, CATHRINE *	BAL	138	18TH WAR
UNKNOWN-, CHARLES *	BAL	076	18TH WAR
UNKNOWN-, DANIEL *	BAL	051	18TH WAR
UNKNOWN-, DANIEL *	BAL	059	18TH WAR
UNKNOWN-, DIDA *	BAL	082	18TH WAR
UNKNOWN-, ELLEN *	BAL	061	18TH WAR
UNKNOWN-, FREDRICK *	BAL	130	18TH WAR
UNKNOWN-, HANAH	BAL	098	18TH WAR
UNKNOWN-, JAMES *	BAL	132	18TH WAR
UNKNOWN-, JOHN	BAL	126	18TH WAR
UNKNOWN-, JOHN *	BAL	112	18TH WAR
UNKNOWN-, LEWIS *	BAL	074	18TH WAR
UNKNOWN-, MARGARETT *	BAL	137	18TH WAR
UNKNOWN-, MARY *	BAL	138	18TH WAR
UNKNOWN-, REBECCA *	BAL	052	18TH WAR
UNKNOWN-, RUFUSS *	BAL	076	18TH WAR
UNKNOWN-, SARAH *	BAL	061	18TH WAR
UNKNOWN-, WILLIAM *	BAL	045	18TH WAR
UNSCHURCH, LEWIS	ANN	466	HOWARD D
UNSHER, BEN	PRI	077	MARLBROU
UONSON, LEVINA	KEN	260	1ST DIST
UOODEN, WILLIAM	BAL	425	8TH WARD
UPDEGRAFF, GEORGE	WAS	121	HAGERSTO
UPDEGRAFF, SAMUEL	WAS	125	HAGERSTO
UPDEGROVE, JESSE	CEC	015	ELKTON 3
UPDERGRAFF, SARAH	BAL	122	2ND DIST
UPENLENDER, FREDERICK	WAS	277	LEITERSB
UPERCOO, FREDERICK	BAL	240	1ST DIST
UPERCOO, JACOB	BAL	235	1ST DIST
UPERCOO, SARAH	BAL	264	1ST DIST
UPERCOO, THOMAS	BAL	235	1ST DIST
UPHOLD, GEORGE	ALL	189	9TH E.D.
UPHOLD, GEORGE	ALL	026	2ND E.D.
UPHOLD, MARIA	ALL	191	9TH E.D.
UPHOLD, WASHINGTON	ALL	040	2ND E.D.
UPJOHN, CANTER*	SOM	486	TRAPP DI
UPMAN, BARBAR	BAL	188	2ND WARD
UPMAN, GEORGE	BAL	370	1ST DIST
UPMAN, HARMAN	BAL	370	1ST DIST
UPP, CHRISTIAN	BAL	222	17TH WAR
UPPENKEN, S.	BAL	233	20TH WAR
UPPER, CONROD	BAL	048	18TH WAR
UPPERMAN, ADAM	BAL	211	17TH WAR
UPPERMAN, ANN M.	BAL	030	18TH WAR
UPPERMAN, CORDELIA	WAS	140	HAGERSTO
UPPERMAN, JEMMIRIAH	BAL	056	18TH WAR
UPPERMAN, JOHN	ALL	119	5TH E.D.
UPPERMAN, JOHN C.	BAL	036	18TH WAR
UPPERMAN, JOSEPH	BAL	455	14TH WAR
UPPERMAN, SARAH	BAL	036	18TH WAR
UPSHAM, WILLIAM	BAL	034	9TH WARD
UPSHER, EMILEY L.*	DOR	386	1ST DIST
UPSHER, GEORGE	WOR	303	SNOW HIL
UPSHM, CANTER*	SOM	486	TRAPP DI
UPSHUR, ANN E.	SOM	472	TRAPPE D
UPTON, BENJAMIN	BAL	033	9TH WARD
UPTON, CATHARIEN	BAL	366	1ST DIST
UPTON, ELEANOR	FRE	273	NEW MARK
UPTON, ELISABETH	BAL	297	3RD WARD
UPTON, HARMAN	BAL	370	1ST DIST
UPTON, HARRIET A.	ANN	379	4TH DIST
UPTON, JAMES	BAL	327	1ST DIST
UPTON, JEHU	BAL	079	18TH WAR
UPTON, JOHN	BAL	376	1ST DIST
UPTON, JOSHUA	BAL	371	1ST DIST
UPTON, MARTHA	ANN	449	HOWARD D
UPTON, SUSAN	BAL	254	6TH WARD
UPTON, THOEDORE	ANN	383	4TH DIST
UPTON, THOMS	ANN	378	4TH DIST
UPTON, WILLIAM	BAL	371	1ST DIST
URARD, ROBERT *	KEN	222	2ND DIST
URBAN, FRANCES	BAL	099	15TH WAR
URBAUGH, HENRY	BAL	038	9TH WARD
URBINE, GEORGE	BAL	190	2ND WARD
URBIS, BROTHER	BAL	216	11TH WAR
URGUHART, HENRY H. *	ANN	308	1ST DIST
URGUHART, ROBERT *	ANN	349	3RD DIST
URICHASCN, MATHA J.	BAL	192	17TH WAR
URIE, HENRY	KEN	243	2ND DIST
URIE, HENRY JR.	KEN	266	1ST DIST
URIE, HENRYU	KEN	266	1ST DIST
URIE, JAMES	KEN	257	1ST DIST
URIE, JAMES	KEN	232	2ND DIST
URIE, JOHN	BAL	134	1ST WARD
URIXON, SARAH	BAL	454	8TH WARD
URKER, CHRISTY *	HAR	199	3RD DIST
URLAUH, EDWARD *	BAL	384	13TH WAR
URLSON, ALEXANDER *	KEN	221	2ND DIST
URNER, JCNAS	FRE	437	8TH E DI
URRY, HENRY	CAR	116	NO TWP L
URRY, THOMAS	CAR	147	NO TWP L
URTNER, CHARLES	WAS	200	1ST DIST
URVIN, JAMES	HAR	055	1ST DIST
URVIN, JOHN	HAR	055	1ST DIST
URWERZAGT, CHRISTAIN	CAR	200	4TH DIST
USEN, SUSEN	BAL	376	1ST DIST
USEN, WILLIAM	BAL	376	1ST DIST
USETON, JOSEPH	KEN	281	3RD DIST
USHANG, ELIE	BAL	033	9TH WARD
USHER, ELIAS	BAL	030	1ST WARD
USHER, ELIZABETH	BAL	313	20TH WAR
USHER, JOHN P.	BAL	003	4TH WARD
USHER, JOHN P.	BAL	127	1ST WARD
USHER, RACHEL	BAL	104	15TH WAR
USHER, T.L.	ALL	247	CUMBERLA
USILLON, AQUILLA *	KEN	218	2ND DIST
USILTEN, JOHN N. *	KEN	212	2ND DIST
USILTER, LEWIS *	KEN	240	2ND DIST
USILTON, JOSEPH	KEN	260	1ST DIST
USILTCN, ROBERT *	KEN	242	2ND DIST
USILTON, ROBERT JR. *	KEN	242	2ND DIST
USILTCN, SAMUEL L. *	KEN	218	2ND DIST
USILTON, SARAH	KEN	218	2ND DIST
USILTON, TEMPERANCE	KEN	218	2ND DIST
USLEBERGER, PETER *	BAL	284	2ND WARD
USSAN, JOHN D.	BAL	068	1ST WARD
USSLETON, AQUILLA	QUE	195	3RD E DI
USTERHOUSE, HERMAN	BAL	350	7TH WARD
USTERLOW, ANSEY	BAL	074	4TH WARD
UTERMHLE, AUGUST	BAL	290	3RD WARD
UTHMAN, CATHARINE	BAL	197	19TH WAR
UTHMAN, CATHARINE S.	BAL	197	19TH WAR
UTT, WILLIAM H.	FRE	148	10TH E D
UTTE, CHRISTIAN	ALL	005	3RD E.D.
UTTE, DAVID	ALL	215	CUMBERLA
UTTE, JACOB	ALL	005	3RD E.D.
UTTER, ELIZABETH	BAL	269	17TH WAR
UTTER, JOHN	BAL	269	17TH WAR
UTTER, JOHN	BAL	060	2ND DIST
UTTOO, DANIEL	ALL	010	3RD E.D.
UTZ, CATHARINE	CAR	265	WESTMINS
UTZ, DANIEL	CAR	346	6TH DIST
UTZ, DANIEL	CAR	319	1ST DIST
UTZ, DAVID	CAR	173	8TH DIST
UTZ, ELIZABETH	CAR	186	8TH DIST
UTZ, ELIZABETH	CAR	344	6TH DIST
UTZ, FREDERICK	CAR	295	7TH DIST
UTZ, GEORGE	CAR	353	6TH DIST
UTZ, JOHN	CAR	278	7TH DIST
UTZ, JOHN	FRE	447	8TH E DI
UTZ, PETER	FRE	432	8TH E DI
UTZ, SAMUEL	FRE	411	8TH E DI
UTZ, SARAH	CAR	319	1ST DIST
UVILLER, LEWIS *	BAL	028	18TH WAR
VADLER, HENRY	ANN	425	HOWARD D
VAGLE, ELLEN	BAL	069	1ST WARD
VAGON, DANIEL	BAL	115	1ST WARD
VAHN, ELIZAVBETH	CAR	332	MANCHEST
VAIL, BENJAMIN	BAL	372	13TH WAR
VAIL, EDWARD	BAL	415	3RD WARD
VAILE, DAVID	ALL	183	8TH E.D.
VAIN, A.	BAL	162	1ST WARD
VAIN, EMORY	QUE	135	1ST E DI
VAIN, JAMES*	DOR	455	1ST DIST
VAIN, SAMUEL	DOR	308	1ST DIST
VAINE, WILLIAM H.	KEN	222	2ND DIST
VALANINGHAM, JAMES L.	SOM	483	TRAPP DI
VALDEMAN, FRANCIS	MGM	365	BERRYS D
VALDEMAN, ANN	MGM	365	BERRYS D
VALDERNAN, MARY	MGM	355	BERRYS D
VALENTINE, ALEXANDER	BAL	175	2ND WARD
VALENTINE, ALEXINA	BAL	076	10TH WAR
VALENTINE, CALVIN	FRE	141	CREAGERS
VALENTINE, CATHERINE	BAL	015	9TH WARD
VALENTINE, CHARLES	BAL	134	1ST WARD
VALENTINE, CHARLES	BAL	133	1ST WARD
VALENTINE, DANIEL	ALL	167	6TH E.D.
VALENTINE, DICK-BLACK	FRE	437	8TH E DI
VALENTINE, ELIZABETH	BAL	119	11TH WAR
VALENTINE, EMANUEL-MULATT	FRE	452	8TH E DI
VALENTINE, F.	BAL	148	1ST WARD
VALENTINE, F.	BAL	164	1ST WARD
VALENTINE, GEORGE	FRE	110	CREAGERS
VALENTINE, GEORGE R.	ALL	165	6TH E.D.
VALENTINE, GIBSON	CEC	106	3RD E DI
VALENTINE, HENRY	ALL	166	6TH E.D.
VALENTINE, JACOB	CAR	379	2ND DIST
VALENTINE, JAMES	CEC	105	3RD E DI
VALENTINE, JOHN	FRE	110	CREAGERS
VALENTINE, JOHN	BAL	123	11TH WAR
VALENTINE, JOHN	ALL	165	6TH E.D.
VALENTINE, JOHN	ALL	198	CUMBERLA
VALENTINE, JOHN	BAL	076	10TH WAR
VALENTINE, JOHN	ANN	446	HOWARD D
VALENTINE, JOHN J.	FRE	140	CREAGERS
VALENTINE, JOSIAH	CAR	379	2ND DIST
VALENTINE, JOSPHEAN	BAL	254	1ST DIST
VALENTINE, JULIUS	BAL	338	7TH WARD
VALENTINE, LEVI	FRE	442	8TH E DI
VALENTINE, MARY	FRE	123	CREAGERS
VALENTINE, MARY	FRE	095	FREDERIC
VALENTINE, MARY A.	FRE	114	CREAGERS
VALENTINE, NANCY	ALL	164	6TH E.D.
VALENTINE, PHILIP-BLACK	FRE	434	8TH E DI
VALENTINE, PHILLIP	BAL	190	2ND WARD
VALENTINE, SAMUEL	ALL	165	6TH E.D.
VALENTINE, SAMUEL	FRE	171	5TH E DI
VALENTINE, SARAH	BAL	133	11TH WAR
VALENTINE, SARAH	ANN	435	HOWARD D
VALENTINE, SOLOMON	FRE	187	5TH E DI
VALENTINE, SUSAN	FRE	110	CREAGERS
VALENTINE, THOMAS-BLACK	FRE	420	8TH E DI
VALENTINE, URIAH	FRE	106	CREAGERS
VALENTINE, WILLIAM	FRE	110	CREAGERS
VALENTINE, WILLIAM	ALL	158	6TH E.D.
VALENTINE, ZADOCK	ALL	165	6TH E.D.
VALENTINE, HONIE-MULATTO	FRE	412	8TH E DI
VALERANT, SALEY	DOR	389	1ST DIST
VALERANT, SAMUEL R.	TAL	112	ST MICHA
VALEY, MARY	BAL	443	8TH WARD
VALIANT, HENRY	BAL	004	15TH WAR
VALIANT, HENRY	BAL	258	6TH WARD
VALIANT, JAMES H.	BAL	261	6TH WARD
VALIANT, JANE	BAL	155	11TH WAR
VALIANT, JOHN	BAL	342	3RD WARD
VALIANT, JOHN F.	BAL	370	3RD WARD
VALIANT, JULIA A.	BAL	190	6TH WARD
VALIANT, MARIA	BAL	107	5TH WARD
VALIANT, MARY	DOR	398	1ST DIST
VALIANT, SAMUEL	BAL	009	EASTERN
VALIANT, SUSAN	BAL	107	5TH WARD
VALIANT, WILLIAM H.	BAL	001	9TH WARD
VALIART, WILLIAM T.	BAL	327	13TH WAR
VALIENT, GOERGE	BAL	308	7TH WARD
VALIENT, JOHN	QUE	208	3RD E DI
VALIENT, ZEDOCK	DOR	366	3RD DIVI
VALLEE, JOSEPH A.	BAL	215	6TH WARD
VALLEE, MARY A.	BAL	278	7TH WARD
VALLENTINE, ELIE	WAS	181	BOONSBOR
VALLENTINNO, A. C.	BAL	190	11TH WAR
VALLER, WILLAIM	BAL	241	17TH WAR
VALLETTE, MISS-	ANN	296	1ST DIST
VALLETTE, VICTOR	BAL	067	10TH WAR
VALLIANT, AMANDA	TAL	116	ST MICHA
VALLIANT, HUGH	TAL	089	ST MICHA
VALLIANT, JAMES	TAL	083	ST MICHA
VALLIANT, JAMES	DOR	429	1ST DIST
VALLIANT, JEREMIAH	TAL	115	ST MICHA
VALLIANT, JOHN	TAL	113	ST MICHA
VALLIANT, JOHN	BAL	458	1ST DIST
VALLIANT, JOHN JR.	TAL	113	ST MICHA
VALLIANT, NICHOLAS	TAL	113	ST MICHA
VALLIANT, RIGBY	TAL	099	ST MICHA
VALLIANT, THEORDORE D.	KEN	217	2ND DIST
VALLIANT, THOMAS	CAR	142	NO TWP L
VALLIANT, WILLIAM H.	TAL	040	EASTON D
VALLIANT, WILLIAM W.	TAL	080	ST MICHA
VALLIENT, NICKOLAS	KEN	286	3RD DIST
VALTER, BERNARD	BAL	430	8TH WARD
VALTER, LEWIS	BAL	325	7TH WARD
VALTSMITH, LEWIS	BAL	307	7TH WARD
VAMER, CONRAD	BAL	243	17TH WAR
VAMORT, WILLIAM *	KEN	244	2ND DIST
VAMPREY, FRANK	ALL	173	7TH E.D.
VAN AMBURG, R. R.	BAL	063	10TH WAR
VAN ARDIN, GEORGE	BAL	059	10TH WAR
VAN BAERLE, MARY	BAL	001	18TH WAR
VAN BEBBER, LUCRETIA	BAL	235	1ST DIST
VAN BIBBER, W. CHEW DR.	BAL	356	13TH WAR
VAN BIBBER, WILLIAM	BAL	251	1ST DIST
VAN BITTEN, G. L.	BAL	157	11TH WAR
VAN BITTEN, MRS.	BAL	156	11TH WAR
VAN BOKKELEN, J. E. REV-	BAL	332	1ST DIST
VAN BOKKELEN, L. REV-	BAL	332	1ST DIST
VAN BOKKELEN, W. A. M.	BAL	332	1ST DIST
VAN BUREN, JACKSON	BAL	125	11TH WAR
VAN BUREN, MARTIN	BAL	213	17TH WAR
VAN BUSON, WILLIAM	BAL	370	13TH WAR
VAN CLEVE, JOSEPH P.	WAS	135	2ND DIST
VAN DANAKER, C.	BAL	258	20TH WAR
VAN DANAKER, GEORGE	BAL	265	20TH WAR
VAN DANAKER, JOSEPH	BAL	313	20TH WAR
VAN DANAKER, MARGARET	BAL	265	20TH WAR
VAN DARRIS, CHARLES	BAL	168	1ST WARD
VAN DIKE, MARGARET	BAL	015	1ST WARD
VAN DROUF, WILLIAM	WAS	026	2ND SUBD
VAN FELT, JOHN	CEC	066	1ST E DI
VAN FEPEN, NATHANIEL	WAS	174	FUNKSTOW
VAN GILDER, ISAAC	BAL	114	1ST WARD
VAN GILDER, SARAH	ALL	210	CUMBERLA
VAN HARTEN, MARGARET	BAL	378	8TH WARD
VAN HOLLAND, AMELIA	BAL	164	16TH WAR
VAN HOLLEN, HENRY	BAL	155	16TH WAR
VAN HORN, ALFRED	BAL	089	5TH WARD
VAN HORN, E.	WAS	020	2ND SUBD
VAN HORN, JAMES	BAL	298	7TH WARD
VAN HORN, JAMES G.	CEC	039	CHESAPEA
VAN HORN, JOHN	HAR	188	3RD DIST
VAN KNIGHTON, JOHN	BAL	099	1ST WARD
VAN LEAR, GEORGE W.	WAS	038	2ND SUBD
VAN LEAR, JOHN	WAS	024	2ND SUBD
VAN LEAR, MARIA	ALL	238	CUMBERLA
VAN LEAR, WILLIAM	ALL	216	CUMBERLA
VAN LION, ANN	BAL	011	2ND DIST
VAN LION, BENJAMIN	BAL	011	2ND DIST
VAN NESS, WILLIAM J.	BAL	016	9TH WARD
VAN NEWKIRK, JOSEPH	BAL	433	8TH WARD
VAN POSEN, WILLIAM	FRE	412	8TH E DI
VAN REDWICK, JOHN T.	ST	284	2ND E DI
VAN RESWICK, JOHN T.	ST	285	2ND E DI

Name	County	Page	District
VAN RISWICK, JOSEPH	ST	254	3RD E DI
VAN ROSSUM, ANN E.	BAL	159	6TH WARD
VAN SANT, AMANDA	BAL	188	2ND WARD
VAN SANT, ELIZABETH	QUE	190	3RD E DI
VAN SANT, GEORGE	CEC	066	1ST E DI
VAN SANT, HENRY	QUE	174	2ND E DI
VAN SANT, JOHN V.	QUE	152	1ST E DI
VAN SANT, JOSHUA	BAL	167	1ST WARD
VAN SANT, MARY E.	QUE	175	2ND E DI
VAN SANT, MOSES	FRE	451	8TH E DI
VAN SANT, NICHOLAS	QUE	125	1ST E DI
VAN SANT, SAMUEL	QUE	163	2ND E DI
VAN SCHALKERYCK, MISS T.	FRE	199	5TH E DI
VAN SCHALKWYCK, ADRIAN	FRE	203	5TH E DI
VAN SCHALKWYCK, HENRY	FRE	20	5TH E DI
VAN SCHALKWYCK, MISS A.	FRE	199	5TH E DI
VAN SHANOK, H. C.	BAL	047	9TH WARD
VAN STAVIN, REBECCA	QUE	131	1ST E DI
VAN WICK, JOHN C	BAL	013	18TH WAR
VAN WYCK, BARLOW	BAL	186	16TH WAR
VAN WYK, S.	BAL	115	1ST WARD
VAN ZANT, WILLIAM	BAL	267	12TH WAR
VAN, LUKE	ALL	178	7TH E.D.
VAN, MARY	BAL	235	20TH WAR
VANAMER, ADELE	BAL	203	11TH WAR
VANANDA, HIRAM	FRE	316	MIDDLETO
VANANDA, JOHN	FRE	316	MIDDLETO
VANASURE, J.T.	ANN	271	ANNAPOLI
VANBEBBER, THOMAS E.	CAR	288	7TH DIST
VANBEBBERT, EURNET	CAR	288	7TH DIST
VANBERGER, MARTIN	BAL	031	18TH WAR
VANBIBBER, JULIANNA	ANN	418	HOWARD D
VANBUREN, MARGARET	BAL	292	1ST DIST
VANCE, ADAM	WAS	014	2ND SUBD
VANCE, CHARLES	MGM	361	BERRYS D
VANCE, DAVID	SOM	490	SALISBUR
VANCE, ELLEN	BAL	383	3RD WARD
VANCE, EUGENE	BAL	463	14TH WAR
VANCE, HETTY	FRE	166	EMMITTSB
VANCE, HUGH	BAL	172	1ST WARD
VANCE, JAMES	CEC	031	CHESAPEA
VANCE, JAMES	KEN	286	3RD DIST
VANCE, JAMES H.	BAL	066	4TH WARD
VANCE, JOHN	BAL	463	1ST DIST
VANCE, JULIA	BAL	141	19TH WAR
VANCE, MARY	MGM	405	ROCKERLE
VANCE, MARY	BAL	331	13TH WAR
VANCE, ROBERT	HAR	069	1ST DIST
VANCE, WILLIAM C.	BAL	048	2ND DIST
VANCHASTINE, MATILDA	BAL	462	14TH WAR
VANCNAT, MARY	BAL	446	14TH WAR
VANCOT, FRANCES	BAL	296	1ST DIST
VANCOTT, DANIEL	BAL	309	7TH WARD
VANCOTT, WILLIAM P.	BAL	309	7TH WARD
VANCOUNT, WILLIAM	CEC	127	5TH E DI
VANCOUNT, WILLIAM	CEC	195	6TH E DI
VANDALEN, SARAH	FRE	076	FREDERIC
VANDARSDALL, AARON	BAL	359	13TH WAR
VANDAWORD, LEWIS	PRI	086	QUEEN AN
VANDEGRAFT, JHN	ALL	160	6TH E.D.
VANDEGRAFT, MARY	BAL	307	1ST DIST
VANDEGREFF, MARY	CEC	030	CHESAPEA
VANDEN, ROBERT R.	HAR	149	3RD DIST
VANDENBERGH, SARAH	BAL	112	5TH WARD
VANDER FORD, ANN E.	QUE	185	3RD E DI
VANDERER, LEWIS N.	BAL	396	8TH WARD
VANDERFORD, CHARLESS K.	CEC	005	ELKTON 3
VANDERFORD, JOHN	QUE	253	5TH E DI
VANDERFORD, LARINIA	KEN	226	2ND DIST
VANDERFORD, SARAH	QUE	204	3RD E DI
VANDERGRIFT, JANE	BAL	165	11TH WAR
VANDERSLICE, ELIZABETH	CEC	141	6TH E DI
VANDERWERKER, HENRY	BAL	371	13TH WAR
VANDERWOOE, GEORGE	BAL	422	14TH WAR
VANDESTICE, RUTH	BAL	207	6TH DIST
VANDESTRICK, H.H.	BAL	164	1ST WARD
VANDEVER, THOMAS	PRI	030	VANSVILL
VANDIFORD, HENRY	CEC	004	ELKTON 3
VANDIGRIFF, JOHN	CEC	039	CHESAPEA
VANDIGRIFF, JOHN J.	CEC	039	CHESAPEA
VANDIGRIFF, THOMAS	CEC	030	CHESAPEA
VANDIVER, WILLIAM	CEC	146	PORT DUP
VANDOM, ELIZA	WOR	271	BERLIN 1
VANDOM, GEORGE	WOR	249	1ST CENS
VANDORN, JOHN W.	BAL	468	14TH WAR
VANDYKE, JAMES	KEN	251	2ND DIST
VANE, DEBORAH	CAR	131	NO TWP L
VANE, ELIZABETH	DOR	455	1ST DIST
VANE, ELIZABETH	ANN	328	2ND DIST
VANE, HENRY	CAR	168	NO TWP L
VANE, JAMES	DOR	430	1ST DIST
VANE, JAMES*	DOR	455	1ST DIST
VANE, JOSEPH T.	DOR	415	1ST DIST
VANE, MARGARET	DOR	456	1ST DIST
VANE, MARY	CAR	118	NO TWP L
VANE, SAMUEL	DOR	458	1ST DIST
VANE, SAMUEL	DOR	458	1ST DIST
VANE, WILLIAM J.	DOR	430	1ST DIST
VANERDER, DAVID	BAL	450	14TH WAR
VANEY, DOUGLAS	BAL	056	15TH WAR
VANFOLSEN, ARNOLD	FRE	305	WOODSBOR
VANFOSSEN, DAVID	BAL	326	7TH WARD
VANFOSSEN, ELIE	FRE	261	NEW MARK
VANFOSSEN, LEVI	FRE	057	FREDERIC
VANFOSSEN, MARY	FRE	101	FREDERIC
VANGANT, JOHN *	HAR	004	1ST DIST
VANHERM, LEWIS *	KEN	256	1ST DIST
VANHOM, WILLIAM*	BAL	406	3RD WARD
VANHORN, AERAHAM	MGM	364	BERRYS D
VANHORN, ALBERT	BAL	265	17TH WAR
VANHORN, ISAAC	ANN	513	HOWARD D
VANHORN, JAMES	BAL	299	1ST DIST
VANHORN, JOHN	WAS	158	2ND DIST
VANHORN, SAMUEL	BAL	265	17TH WAR
VANHORN, WILLIAM*	BAL	406	3RD WARD
VANICE, AUGUSTUS	BAL	184	2ND WARD
VANKIRK, JOHN	WAS	142	2ND DIST
VANLEAN, ROBERT	ALL	110	5TH E.D.
VANLEAR, ANN B.	WAS	198	1ST DIST
VANLEAR, GEORGE	WAS	161	HAGERSTO
VANLEAR, SUSAN M.	WAS	161	HAGERSTO
VANLILL, STEPHEN J.	BAL	170	16TH WAR
VANLILL, WILLIAM T.	BAL	182	16TH WAR
VANLINE, JOHN	BAL	123	16TH WAR
VANNEKER, CHARLES	BAL	021	9TH WARD
VANNER, WILLIAM	BAL	100	1ST WARD
VANNETS, ABRAHAM	BAL	013	9TH WARD
VANNISCK, LOUISA	BAL	100	2ND DIST
VANNORT, ADIN *	KEN	245	2ND DIST
VANNORT, JOHN	CEC	155	PORT DUP
VANNORT, WILLIAM *	KEN	244	2ND DIST
VANORTHEN, JOHN	BAL	209	17TH WAR
VANPELT, AMELIA	ANN	435	HOWARD D
VANRINELLE, MARY	BAL	214	11TH WAR
VANSANT, ANN	KEN	286	3RD DIST
VANSANT, ANNA	BAL	305	1ST DIST
VANSANT, FREDUS	KEN	226	2ND DIST
VANSANT, GEORGE R.	KEN	294	3RD DIST
VANSANT, HANAH	BAL	094	18TH WAR
VANSANT, IRA	KEN	297	3RD DIST
VANSANT, J. JR.	BAL	286	2ND WARD
VANSANT, JAMES	CEC	054	1ST E DI
VANSANT, JOHN	ANN	457	HOWARD D
VANSANT, JOHN	BAL	142	16TH WAR
VANSANT, JOHN D.	KEN	293	3RD DIST
VANSANT, JOSHUA	BAL	305	1ST DIST
VANSANT, JOSHUA	BAL	111	5TH WARD
VANSANT, JOSHUA	CEC	050	1ST E DI
VANSANT, JOSHUA	BAL	260	17TH WAR
VANSANT, JOSHUA JR.	BAL	112	5TH WARD
VANSANT, LAWRENCE L.	KEN	295	3RD DIST
VANSANT, NATH.	BAL	328	1ST DIST
VANSANT, NICHOLSON	BAL	311	1ST DIST
VANSANT, THOMAS	KEN	291	3RD DIST
VANSANT, THOMAS	CEC	054	1ST E DI
VANSANT, W.H.	BAL	233	1ST DIST
VANSANT, WILLIAM	KEN	285	3RD DIST
VANSELL, LEWIS	CAR	203	4TH DIST
VANSELL, RANDEL	CEC	205	7TH E DI
VANSTAVCREN, WILLIAM	KEN	303	3RD DIST
VANWYCK, CATHARINE	BAL	154	16TH WAR
VANZANT, M.	BAL	229	19TH WAR
VAR, PETER*	BAL	064	4TH WARD
VARDEN, ROBERT B.	BAL	234	6TH WARD
VARDY, REBECCA A.	BAL	399	3RD WARD
VARFORSEN, WILLIAM	FRE	243	NEW MARK
VARINA, EDWARD C.	BAL	134	18TH WAR
VARINS, THOMAS	BAL	193	17TH WAR
VARLOW, ASBURY	KEN	289	3RD DIST
VARLOW, JANE	KEN	283	3RD DIST
VARLOW, MARY	KEN	288	3RD DIST
VARMANY, CORNELIUS	CEC	060	1ST E DI
VARMORT, ADIN *	KEN	245	2ND DIST
VARNER, ROSANNA	BAL	121	11TH WAR
VARNES, LETTY	BAL	108	18TH WAR
VARNEY, MITCHELL	BAL	172	6TH WARD
VARNEY, SARAH	HAR	066	1ST DIST
VARNIN, ELIZABETH	CAR	232	5TH DIST
VARNORT, WILLIAM *	KEN	244	2ND DIST
VARRENT, PRINTERTON	BAL	457	8TH WARD
VARS, ELIZABETH	MGM	404	ROCKERLE
VARY, THOMAS*	BAL	127	5TH WARD
VASH, CHARLES	BAL	299	3RD WARD
VASHERILL, H. H.	BAL	153	1ST WARD
VASINGER, STEPHEN	ALL	223	CUMBERLA
VASS, DOUGLASS	PRI	006	BLADENSB
VASSABERE, JOHNB	BAL	060	1ST WARD
VASSETT, ELIZABETH	BAL	099	2ND DIST
VASSETT, HENRY	BAL	099	2ND DIST
VASTERLING, HY.	BAL	288	1ST DIST
VAUGHAN, HENRY	BAL	392	3RD WARD
VAUGHAN, JULIET	BAL	280	1ST DIST
VAUGHAN, MARY	BAL	409	3RD WARD
VAUGHAN, SUSANA	BAL	387	3RD WARD
VAUGHBAUGH, AGUSTA	BAL	213	11TH WAR
VAUGHN, CHARLES H.	BAL	114	11TH WAR
VAUGHN, D. F.	BAL	147	1ST WARD
VAUGHN, ELIZABETH	BAL	218	6TH WARD
VAUGHN, ELIZABETH	DOR	397	1ST DIST
VAUGHN, GIST	BAL	039	2ND DIST
VAUGHN, JAMES	BAL	136	11TH WAR
VAUGHN, JAMES	BAL	404	14TH WAR
VAUGHN, JOHN	BAL	136	11TH WAR
VAUGHN, JOHN	BAL	377	1ST DIST
VAUGHN, JOHN	BAL	325	1ST DIST
VAUGHN, JONATHAN	DOR	305	1ST DIST
VAUGHN, JONATHAN	DOR	303	1ST DIST
VAUGHN, JOSEPH	DOR	419	1ST DIST
VAUGHN, JOSHUA	FRE	450	8TH E DI
VAUGHN, MARY	DOR	301	1ST DIST
VAUGHN, R. W.	BAL	147	1ST WARD
VAUGHN, RACHAEL	BAL	197	11TH WAR
VAUGHN, RACHEL	BAL	377	1ST DIST
VAUGHN, SAMUEL	BAL	325	1ST DIST
VAUGHN, THOMAS	BAL	020	2ND DIST
VAUGHN, WILLIAM	DOR	419	1ST DIST
VAUGHTAN, JANE	BAL	021	2ND DIST
VAVIER, JOHN	BAL	244	17TH WAR
VAXMAN, AUGUST	BAL	320	1ST DIST
VAYLOR, SOPHIA*	BAL	305	3RD WARD
VEACH, EDWARD	BAL	102	2ND DIST
VEALLA, EUGENE	BAL	264	1ST DIST
VEASAY, JOHN	BAL	354	13TH WAR
VEASEL, A.	BAL	072	18TH WAR
VEASEL, ANN M.	BAL	071	18TH WAR
VEASEY, CATHARINE	BAL	202	6TH WARD
VEASEY, JOHN	BAL	176	16TH WAR
VEASY, ANN W.	BAL	438	14TH WAR
VEAZEY, MARY	BAL	278	2ND WARD
VEAZEY, WILLIAM	CEC	079	NORTHEAS
VEAZY, CALEB	CEC	076	NORTHEAS
VEAZY, EDWARD	CEC	045	1ST E DI
VEAZY, GEORGE	CEC	045	1ST E DI
VEAZY, GEORGE	BAL	364	13TH WAR
VEAZY, HENRY	CEC	049	1ST E DI
VEAZY, JAMES	WAS	151	2ND DIST
VEAZY, JOHN	CEC	075	NORTHEAS
VEAZY, JOHN	CEC	058	1ST E DI
VEAZY, JOSEPH	CEC	048	1ST E DI
VEAZY, WILLIAM	CEC	048	1ST E DI
VEAZY, WILLIAM	CEC	080	NORTHEAS
VECKER, SARAH M.	ALL	132	4TH E.D.
VEDERS, SUSANER	CAL	017	1ST DIST
VEDHOLT, JOHN	ALL	202	CUMBERLA
VEDI, HENRY	BAL	376	1ST DIST
VEDIDO, MARY	BAL	194	19TH WAR
VEEDER, SIMON	BAL	372	1ST DIST
VEHEALT, BENJAMIN	BAL	040	1ST WARD
VEIDEN, WILLIAM W.	HAR	153	3RD DIST
VEILL, WILLIAM	BAL	118	1ST WARD
VEINER, MICHAEL	BAL	235	2ND WARD
VEIRS, EDWARD M.	MGM	399	ROCKERLE
VEIRS, FRANKLIN	MGM	407	MEDLEY 3
VEIRS, HEZEKIAH	MGM	428	CLARKSTR
VEIRS, JESSE	MGM	413	MEDLEY 3
VEIRS, JOHN T.	MGM	412	MEDLEY 3
VEIRS, SAMUEL C.	MGM	374	ROCKERLE
VEIRS, SUSAN	MGM	412	MEDLEY 3
VEIRS, WILLIAM A.W.	MGM	412	MEDLEY 3
VEIRS, WILLIAM F.	MGM	413	MEDLEY 3
VEITCH, JOHN	PRI	006	BLADENSB
VELCHER, WILLIAM	BAL	141	1ST WARD
VELEGAR, CHARLES	BAL	104	5TH WARD
VELLEVER, LEVI	ALL	221	CUMBERLA
VEMAN, VOLENTINE	BAL	080	1ST WARD
VENABLE, HENRY	WOR	238	6TH E DI
VENABLE, JAMES A.	WOR	229	6TH E DI
VENABLE, WILLIAM	WOR	232	6TH E DI
VENABLES, ELIZABETH	SOM	498	SALISBUR
VENABLES, ELIZABETH E.	SOM	499	SALISBUR
VENABLES, GEORGE B.	SOM	530	QUANTICO
VENABLES, HYRAM	SOM	519	BARREN C
VENABLES, JAMES	SOM	508	BARREN C
VENABLES, JOHN	SOM	549	TYASKIN
VENABLES, JOHN	DOR	434	1ST DIST
VENABLES, JOHN F.	DOR	447	1ST DIST
VENABLES, MARY	SOM	506	BARREN C
VENABLES, MATILDA	SOM	519	BARREN C
VENABLES, NANCY	SOM	517	BARREN C
VENABLES, RICHARD	SOM	519	BARREN C
VENABLES, SETH D.	SOM	482	TRAPP DI
VENABLES, SOPHIA	SOM	524	BARREN C
VENABLES, WILLIAM	SOM	516	BARREN C
VENCIR, CATHERINE	CHA	234	HILLTOP
VENDER, ANDREW	BAL	063	4TH WARD
VENEDEAR, CAROLINE	BAL	281	20TH WAR
VENER, GEORGE	BAL	358	3RD WARD
VENER, MARGARET	WOR	231	6TH E DI
VENERSDALE, ISAAC	CEC	130	6TH E DI
VENIBLE, DEBBY	PRI	054	AQUASCO
VENING, THOMAS	ALL	227	CUMBERLA
VENNER, HENRY	BAL	099	1ST WARD
VENNER, WILLIA	BAL	101	1ST WARD
VENNILLION, ELIJAH	ANN	279	ANNAPOLI
VENNIMAN, CLARISSA D.	CEC	145	PORT DUP
VENNIMAN, HARRIET E.	CEC	145	PORT DUP
VENNIMAN, JOHN P.	CEC	145	PORT DUP
VENT, JOHN	BAL	080	1ST WARD
VERAKER, JOHN	BAL	076	1ST WARD
VERBECK, AUGUST	BAL	072	4TH WARD
VERDEN, JOHN	BAL	149	1ST WARD
VERDING, MARY	WOR	198	8TH E DI
VERHNER, GOTLIEB	BAL	204	6TH WARD
VERLANDER, JULIA A.	BAL	171	6TH WARD
VERLINDEN, ELIZABETH	HAR	004	1ST DIST
VERMILLION, ELEANOR	PRI	043	VANSVILL
VERMILLION, JOHN	PRI	043	VANSVILL
VERMILLION, LAWSON	PRI	076	MARLBROU
VERMILLION, NICHOLAS	PRI	045	VANSVILL
VERMILLION, ROSY	ANN	298	1ST DIST
VERMULLION, HENRY	CEC	166	6TH E DI
VERNAN, EDGAR E.	CHA	259	MIDDLETO
VERNAN, WALTER G.	CHA	258	MIDDLETO
VERNAY, JOHN	ANN	483	HOWARD D
VERNER, CATHARINE	WAS	133	HAGERSTO
VERNER, JOHN	BAL	318	7TH WARD
VERNER, MARY A.	BAL	267	2ND WARD
VERNETSON, SARAH	BAL	030	4TH WARD
VERNETSON, WILLIAM	BAL	064	4TH WARD
VERNHAIT, CHRISTINA	BAL	069	4TH WARD
VERNIGEN, AUGUSTUS	FRE	119	CREAGERS
VERNOIT, ANGUSTINE	BAL	313	12TH WAR
VERNON, FAIRFAX F.	BAL	119	15TH WAR
VERNON, FREDERIC F.	BAL	042	9TH WARD
VERNON, HENRY	BAL	320	1ST DIST
VERNON, NATHANIEL	FRE	030	FREDERIC
VERNON, PATRICK	WAS	033	2ND SUBD
VERNON, JOSEPH	BAL	103	1ST WARD
VERNON, WILLIAM	BAL	119	1ST WARD
VERNUM, JOHN	QUE	212	3RD E DI
VERNUM, JOHN A.	BAL	328	13TH WAR
VERNUM, WILLIAM K.	BAL	327	13TH WAR
VERONEY, LANEY *	BAL	183	6TH WARD
VERRETT, PENELTON	BAL	162	11TH WAR
VERSAILES, LOUIS	BAL	114	1ST WARD
VERT, JOHN	WAS	067	2ND SUBD
VERTEL, MARNNELIAN	BAL	133	11TH WAR
VERTRIS, HERMAN	WAS	020	2ND SUBD
VESPAL, WILLIAM	PRI	039	VANSVILL
VESPIE, MARTHA G.	BAL	361	3RD WARD
VESSER, MARGARET	BAL	376	13TH WAR
VESSEY, SARAH	BAL	166	6TH WARD
VESSUP, CHAERLS	BAL	319	12TH WAR
VESTEN, JAMES	ALL	221	CUMBERLA
VESTERS, JOHN	BAL	128	1ST WARD
VESTLING, JOHN H.	BAL	354	1ST DIST
VESTRY, JOSEPH	SOM	462	HANGARY
VETRA, WILLIS	SOM	463	HANGARY
VETRE, MARY F.	SOM	531	QUANTICO
VETRY, GEORGE	SOM	462	HANGARY
VETRY, HENRY	SOM	465	HANGARY
VETRY, JAMES S.	SOM	463	HANGARY
VETTER, JOHN	BAL	233	17TH WAR
VETYGOSER, JOHN	BAL	230	2ND WARD
VEXIUM, HENRY	BAL	038	9TH WARD
VEY, HENRY	BAL	261	20TH WAR
VEYL, MARONS	BAL	227	2ND WARD
VEZEY, WILLIAM	WOR	339	1ST E DI
VEZEY, WILLIAM	WOR	336	1ST E DI
VHL, JOSEPH	ALL	146	6TH E.D.
VIAL, JOHN	CAR	214	5TH DIST
VICCINANZER, CAMILLUS	FRE	067	FREDERIC
VICHERS, MARY	TAL	075	EASTON T
VICK, CORDERY	BAL	420	8TH WARD
VICK, ELIZA J.	BAL	420	8TH WARD
VICKARS, AMANDA	DOR	450	1ST DIST
VICKARS, CHARLES	DOR	391	1ST DIST
VICKARS, EDWARD	DOR	437	1ST DIST
VICKARS, ELIZABETH	DOR	454	1ST DIST
VICKARS, ELLEN	DOR	455	1ST DIST
VICKARS, EMELINE	DOR	392	1ST DIST
VICKARS, JAMES	DOR	407	1ST DIST
VICKARS, JOHN	DOR	469	1ST DIST
VICKARS, KITTY*	DOR	406	1ST DIST
VICKARS, MALACHI	DOR	455	1ST DIST
VICKARS, MILEY	DOR	413	1ST DIST
VICKARS, STEWART	DOR	469	1ST DIST
VICKARS, THOMAS	DOR	431	1ST DIST
VICKARS, THOMAS	DOR	390	1ST DIST
VICKARS, WILLIAM	DOR	391	1ST DIST
VICKARS, WILLIAM	DOR	391	1ST DIST
VICKARS, WILLIAM F.	DOR	446	1ST DIST
VICKER, SOPHIA	BAL	465	14TH WAR
VICKERS, ARCHIBALD	CAR	327	1ST DIST
VICKERS, B. ALBERT	BAL	067	15TH WAR
VICKERS, CELIA	DOR	305	1ST DIST
VICKERS, CHARLES	DOR	303	1ST DIST
VICKERS, DENNIS	KEN	267	1ST DIST
VICKERS, GEORGE	KEN	217	2ND DIST
VICKERS, GEORGE R.	BAL	064	15TH WAR

Name	County	Page	District
VICKERS, GREENBURY	BAL	122	16TH WAR
VICKERS, JEMIMA	BAL	187	6TH WARD
VICKERS, JESSE	BAL	355	3RD WARD
VICKERS, JOEL	BAL	067	15TH WAR
VICKERS, JOHN	DOR	310	1ST DIST
VICKERS, JOHN E.	KEN	263	1ST DIST
VICKERS, JOSEPH	DOR	389	1ST DIST
VICKERS, MARGARETT	BAL	060	4TH WARD
VICKERS, MARY	DOR	362	3RD DIVI
VICKERS, MARY	DOR	362	3RD DIVI
VICKERS, MARY	BAL	099	10TH WAR
VICKERS, MARY	BAL	411	1ST DIST
VICKERS, MARY H.	DOR	305	1ST DIST
VICKERS, NATHAN	DOR	319	1ST DIST
VICKERS, OBADIAH	QUE	205	3RD E DI
VICKERS, PETER	DOR	318	1ST DIST
VICKERS, PRUCILLA	SOM	494	SALISBUR
VICKERS, SALLY A.	DOR	298	1ST DIST
VICKERS, SAMUEL	QUE	187	3RD E DI
VICKERS, SAMUEL R.	BAL	065	15TH WAR
VICKERS, THOMAS	KEN	263	1ST DIST
VICKERS, WASHINGTON H.	DOR	310	1ST DIST
VICKERS, WILLIAM	DOR	363	3RD DIVI
VICKERS, WILLIAM	KEN	218	2ND DIST
VICKERS, WILLIAM	WAS	066	2ND SUBD
VICKERS, WILLIAM	BAL	078	15TH WAR
VICKERS, YEKEEL*	DOR	370	3RD DIVI
VICKERT, CHARLES	BAL	146	19TH WAR
VICKERY, ELIZABETH	BAL	024	4TH WARD
VICKERY, MARY	BAL	088	1ST WARD
VICKINY, G.W.	ALL	216	CUMBERLA
VICKORS, THOMAS	WOR	306	2ND E DI
VICKORY, MARY	CAR	103	NO TWP L
VICKRELL, Z W.	BAL	046	9TH WARD
VICKROY, MARY	ALL	166	6TH E.D.
VICTOR, ANSEN	BAL	303	7TH WARD
VICTOR, EMILY S.	BAL	045	9TH WARD
VICTOR, ISAAC K.	WOR	176	6TH E DI
VICTORIA, ANN	BAL	203	17TH WAR
VICTORY, CHARLES	BAL	179	2ND WARD
VICTORY, EDWARD	BAL	001	15TH WAR
VICTORY, THOMAS	BAL	041	1ST WARD
VIELEY, JOHN	BAL	118	1ST WARD
VIENNE, JULIAN	FRE	202	5TH E DI
VIER, SAMUEL C.	ALL	143	6TH E.D.
VIERS, H. FRANKLIN	MGM	374	ROCKERLE
VIESTLAND, HENRY*	BAL	417	3RD WARD
VIETEHEN, SARAH	MGM	378	ROCKERLE
VIGER, MARTIN	BAL	219	17TH WAR
VIGERS, ISAAC	WOR	260	BERLIN 1
VIGITANTE, LEWIS	ST	276	3RD E DI
VILENBECKER, DANIEL	BAL	379	8TH WARD
VILHELM, DAVID	BAL	199	5TH DIST
VILLET, N. H.	BAL	305	20TH WAR
VILLIANS, MARGARET	PRI	083	QUEEN AN
VILRE, JOHN	PRI	039	VANSVILL
VINAGALE, WILLIAM	CEC	053	1ST E DI
VINAGOLE, STEPHEN	CEC	209	7TH E DI
VINCEN, WILLIAM	WOR	304	SNOW HIL
VINCENDEER, VICTORIA	FRE	044	FREDERIC
VINCENT, ANN R.	DOR	383	1ST DIST
VINCENT, BENJAMIN	WOR	193	8TH E DI
VINCENT, CATHERINE	QUE	174	2ND E DI
VINCENT, CATHERINE H.	QUE	142	1ST E DI
VINCENT, CHRISTOPHER	CAR	090	NO TWP L
VINCENT, COLLINS	DOR	303	1ST DIST
VINCENT, ELIZA	DOR	455	1ST DIST
VINCENT, ELIZA A.	SOM	498	SALISBUR
VINCENT, ELIZABETH	CAR	095	NO TWP L
VINCENT, EPHRAIM	SOM	507	BARREN C
VINCENT, GEORGE V.	BAL	091	18TH WAR
VINCENT, GEORGE W.	CAR	167	NO TWP L
VINCENT, HARVEY	SOM	492	SALISBUR
VINCENT, HENRY	BAL	321	1ST DIST
VINCENT, HENRY	BAL	425	1ST DIST
VINCENT, ISAAC	SOM	502	SALISBUR
VINCENT, ISAAC	SOM	498	SALISBUR
VINCENT, JAMES	SOM	512	BARREN C
VINCENT, JAMES	SOM	487	SALISBUR
VINCENT, JAMES	BAL	170	1ST WARD
VINCENT, JAMES	BAL	194	2ND WARD
VINCENT, JANE	BAL	193	11TH WAR
VINCENT, JENNY	DOR	383	1ST DIST
VINCENT, JESSE	BAL	080	18TH WAR
VINCENT, JOHN	DOR	404	1ST DIST
VINCENT, JOHN	CAR	094	NO TWP L
VINCENT, JOHN	DOR	338	3RD DIVI
VINCENT, JOHN	BAL	119	1ST WARD
VINCENT, JOHN F. H..	DOR	430	1ST DIST
VINCENT, LEVIN	DOR	428	1ST DIST
VINCENT, LUCY	BAL	019	15TH WAR
VINCENT, MARCELINA	BAL	086	4TH WARD
VINCENT, MARGARET	DOR	452	1ST DIST
VINCENT, MARY	BAL	213	11TH WAR
VINCENT, MARY J.	SOM	492	SALISBUR
VINCENT, PERRY	BAL	400	14TH WAR
VINCENT, ROBERT	DOR	427	1ST DIST
VINCENT, VIRGINIA	DOR	373	1ST DIST
VINCENT, WILLIAM	BAL	385	13TH WAR
VINCENT, WILLIAM	BAL	258	6TH WARD
VINCENT, WILLIAM N.	SOM	550	TYASKIN
VINCENT, WILLIAM S.	DOR	424	1ST DIST
VINCENTA, VIRGINIA	BAL	111	5TH WARD
VINCENTZ, EDWARD V.	BAL	168	11TH WAR
VINCIENT, SARAH	BAL	208	11TH WAR
VINE, CHARLES	BAL	129	1ST WARD
VINE, CHARLES	BAL	152	1ST WARD
VINE, MITCHELL	ANN	397	8TH DIST
VINEGAR, JACOB	BAL	158	2ND DIST
VINEGAR, LEWIS	BAL	101	2ND DIST
VINERETA, MARY	BAL	327	3RD WARD
VINERITE, HENRY	BAL	326	3RD WARD
VINEY, CHARLES	TAL	073	EASTON T
VINEY, JANE	TAL	074	EASTON T
VINEYARD, LOUISA	BAL	354	3RD WARD
VINEYARD, RACHEL	BAL	177	19TH WAR
VING, JOSEPH T.*	TAL	042	EASTON D
VINHAM, VALENTINE	BAL	133	11TH WAR
VINK, CATHARINE	BAL	120	16TH WAR
VINK, WILLIAM	ANN	424	HOWARD D
VINKLER, JANE	BAL	066	4TH WARD
VINOR, EMILY M.	ALL	237	CUMBERLA
VINSARS, MARY	TAL	038	EASTON D
VINSEN, WILLIAM	TAL	053	EASTON D
VINSENTGHT, JAMES	CAR	125	NO TWP L
VINSON, ANN	MGM	409	MEDLEY 3
VINSON, ANN	BAL	157	16TH WAR
VINSON, I.C.	BAL	139	1ST WARD
VINSON, JAMES	BAL	087	15TH WAR
VINSON, JAMES	TAL	065	EASTON T
VINSON, JAMES	WOR	192	8TH E DI
VINSON, JAMES H.	BAL	156	16TH WAR
VINSON, JOHN T.	MGM	384	ROCKERLE
VINSON, MARY	WOR	239	6TH E DI
VINSON, MARY	PRI	028	VANSVILL
VINSON, NANCY	WOR	238	6TH E DI
VINSON, NAPOLEON B.	MGM	409	MEDLEY 3
VINSON, NATHANIEL	PRI	028	VANSVILL
VINSON, NEAMIAH	TAL	110	ST MICHA
VINSON, THOMAS T.	BAL	125	1ST WARD
VINSON, WILLIAM B.	MGM	406	MEDLEY 3
VINSON, WILLIAM BENJAMIN	MGM	396	ROCKERLE
VINSON, WILLIAM H.	MGM	382	ROCKERLE
VINSOR, MARTHA	TAL	104	ST MICHA
VINTON, PERRY S.	BAL	022	15TH WAR
VINTON, ROBERT L.	BAL	038	4TH WARD
VINTON, ROBERT S.	BAL	220	1ST DIST
VINTON, SAMUEL R.*	DOR	378	1ST DIST
VINTOR, SAMUEL R.*	DOR	378	1ST DIST
VINTROUGH, ELIZA	BAL	401	1ST DIST
VINTTER, MARATS F.	BAL	322	1ST DIST
VINUP, RUDOLPH	BAL	358	3RD WARD
VINZANT, GEORGE	BAL	136	16TH WAR
VINZANT, HENRY	BAL	171	16TH WAR
VIRDIN, WILLIAM W.	BAL	311	3RD WARD
VIRGIN, WILLIAM	BAL	175	2ND DIST
VIRTS, CORNELIUS	FRE	388	PETERSVI
VIRTUE, WILLIAM	BAL	163	6TH WARD
VIRTZ, GEORGE	WAS	138	HAGERSTO
VISAGE, ANN	BAL	270	12TH WAR
VISGUUER, JOHN	BAL	192	2ND WARD
VISHER, JOHN	BAL	238	17TH WAR
VISHERS, SARAH	TAL	076	EASTON T
VISTA, BEAUNO *	BAL	133	18TH WAR
VISTAL, JULIAN	BAL	402	1ST DIST
VIVAL, SUSAN	FRE	203	5TH E DI
VLUM, ANDREW *	WAS	191	1ST DIST
VNCE, DAVID	BAL	101	10TH WAR
VOCHELL, SAMUEL	CAR	102	NO TWP L
VOCK, S. J.C.	BAL	292	12TH WAR
VOCKE, ELIAS	BAL	263	1ST DIST
VODENEY, MARY	PRI	088	SPALDING
VODNEY, JOHN	PRI	087	SPALDING
VOEY, JOSHUA	CAR	162	NO TWP L
VOFFLEY, KITTY*	BAL	048	4TH WARD
VOGEL, ANTHONY	BAL	092	10TH WAR
VOGEL, ELIZABETH	BAL	456	1ST DIST
VOGELGESCNG, JACOB	BAL	004	15TH WAR
VOGELSANG, DOROTHEA	BAL	133	16TH WAR
VOGER, J.	BAL	126	1ST WARD
VOGHT, JOSEPH	BAL	089	1ST WARD
VOGLE, CONRAD	BAL	463	1ST DIST
VOGLEMAN, CHARLES	BAL	463	1ST DIST
VOGLEMAN, WILLIAM	BAL	291	12TH WAR
VOGLESANG, EDWARD	BAL	056	15TH WAR
VOGLESANG, HENRY	BAL	057	15TH WAR
VOGLESONG, ELIZABETH	CAR	364	9TH DIST
VOGLESONG, HENRY	CAR	384	2ND DIST
VOGLESONG, MARTIN	CAR	382	2ND DIST
VOGT, FREDERICK	BAL	109	15TH WAR
VOGT, GEORGE A.	BAL	243	12TH WAR
VOGT, HARMAN	BAL	109	15TH WAR
VOGTS, JOHN P.	BAL	104	1ST WARD
VOHERS, CAPT	ANN	270	ANNAPOLI
VOICE, GEORGE	BAL	281	17TH WAR
VOICE, T.	BAL	115	1ST WARD
VOIER, JOHNSON	BAL	182	2ND WARD
VOIGD, LEWIS	BAL	312	3RD WARD
VOINHAIT, FRITZ*	BAL	069	4TH WARD
VOLANDT, JOHN	BAL	191	6TH WARD
VOLANDT, WILLIAM	BAL	106	1ST WARD
VOLANT, AUGUST C.	BAL	396	8TH WARD
VOLANT, CHRISTIAN	BAL	396	8TH WARD
VOLANT, FREDERICK	BAL	428	8TH WARD
VOLANT, HENRY	BAL	072	4TH WARD
VOLARD, MARGARET	CEC	172	6TH E DI
VOLFET, CHRISTIAN	BAL	123	1ST WARD
VOLGAR, CHRISTIAN	BAL	281	1ST DIST
VOLIVER, TRAMBERT	CHA	219	ALLENS F
VOLK, FRANCIS	BAL	386	13TH WAR
VOLK, JOHN	BAL	179	11TH WAR
VOLK, PETER	BAL	070	2ND DIST
VOLKART, MARY	BAL	036	9TH WARD
VOLKER, FRITZ	BAL	203	6TH WARD
VOLKER, MICHAEL	BAL	172	11TH WAR
VOLKMAN, CHARLES	BAL	084	10TH WAR
VOLKMAN, G. D.	BAL	208	19TH WAR
VOLKMAR, CHARLES	BAL	208	19TH WAR
VOLKMAR, HENRY	BAL	208	19TH WAR
VOLLENTINE, DANIEL	WAS	028	2ND SUBD
VOLLMER, C. LOUIS	BAL	082	10TH WAR
VOLRATH, CHRISTOPHER	BAL	246	2ND WARD
VOLTEN, EMANUEL	BAL	188	2ND WARD
VOLTS, PETER	ANN	452	HOWARD D
VOLTZ, GEORGE	BAL	089	18TH WAR
VOLTZ, JAMES	BAL	290	1ST DIST
VOLTZMAN, HERMAN	BAL	029	18TH WAR
VOLUNT, MAYDE	BAL	227	2ND WARD
VOLVINA, PETER	BAL	271	1ST DIST
VOLY, PETER	BAL	132	11TH WAR
VON AMSBERG, VICTOR	BAL	095	10TH WAR
VON CHAELWAYORCK, AUGUSTU	BAL	301	20TH WAR
VON HOLLEN, GEORGE	BAL	079	15TH WAR
VON KASSFF, FRED	BAL	151	11TH WAR
VON KASSFF, SAMUEL	BAL	151	11TH WAR
VON POST, ALBERT H.	BAL	110	15TH WAR
VON SPRINKELSON, GEORGE A	BAL	447	14TH WAR
VON WATER, AMELIA	BAL	418	14TH WAR
VONO, MARY	PRI	118	PISCATAW
VONDERHEIDE, JOHN H. G.	BAL	111	10TH WAR
VONDERHORST, HENRY	BAL	115	15TH WAR
VONDERSMITH, DANIEL	BAL	447	14TH WAR
VONDERSMITH, PETER	BAL	226	1ST DIST
VONDULEHERE, JACOB	ANN	469	HOWARD D
VONDYKE, JULIA	BAL	284	2ND WARD
VONLESS, HENRY	BAL	422	14TH WAR
VONN, CHARLES B.	KEN	299	3RD DIST
VONOHY, ANNA	BAL	447	14TH WAR
VOP, WILLIAM	CAR	167	NO TWP L
VOQWEA, JOHN	BAL	180	11TH WAR
VORD, MARY	ST	283	3RD E DI
VORE, SUSAN A.	BAL	336	3RD WARD
VORGT, HENRY*	BAL	238	12TH WAR
VORIEN, MARY	BAL	140	11TH WAR
VORMAN, JOHN	BAL	400	1ST DIST
VORMAN, MARY	BAL	374	3RD WARD
VORNAFELT, JOHN	CAR	201	4TH DIST
VORNHART, FRITZ*	BAL	069	4TH WARD
VOSCHELL, JOHN	KEN	271	1ST DIST
VOSHAELL, DAVID	TAL	023	EASTON D
VOSHELL, DRAPER	KEN	272	1ST DIST
VOSHELL, NATHAN	KEN	271	1ST DIST
VOSS, B.F.	BAL	207	11TH WAR
VOSS, HOLADY	CAR	147	NO TWP L
VOSS, MARY	KEN	218	2ND DIST
VOSS, WILLIAM E.	BAL	188	11TH WAR
VOTSOCK, HANNAH E.	BAL	029	15TH WAR
VOTZ, PHILIP	BAL	362	1ST DIST
VOUSE, GEORGE	BAL	372	8TH WARD
VOWAN, ROBERT	WAS	095	2ND SUBD
VOYCE, CHARLES	BAL	229	17TH WAR
VOYCE, THOMAS	BAL	229	17TH WAR
VOYCE, THOMAS	BAL	218	6TH WARD
VOYT, DAVID	BAL	165	19TH WAR
VOYT, FREDERICK	BAL	187	19TH WAR
VOYT, FREDERICK	BAL	187	19TH WAR
VOYT, IRA	BAL	187	19TH WAR
VOYT, MARY	BAL	187	19TH WAR
VOYT, MARY	BAL	269	2ND WARD
VREELAND, PRILLA*	BAL	076	10TH WAR
VROMAN, ELISABETH	ALL	214	CUMBERLA
VROMAN, SAMUEL V.	ALL	214	CUMBERLA
VROOMAN, REBECCA	ALL	109	5TH E.D.
VROSS, JAMES	ALL	079	5TH E.D.
VROSS, RICHARD	BAL	023	2ND DIST
VUISTMEAR, AROWN *	BAL	261	2ND WARD
VULTE, SEBASTIAN	BAL	062	15TH WAR
VUNBERRY, JOSEPH	BAL	181	11TH WAR
VURNS, THOMAS	BAL	442	14TH WAR
VUTSELBERGER, CATHERINE	BAL	373	8TH WARD
VYMIER, HESTER	MGM	423	MEDLEY 3
W. SIGLER, JOHN	ALL	123	4TH E.D.
WABBACH, GEN JOHN B.	BAL	253	1ST DIST
WABLE, HANNAH	ANN	426	HOWARD D
WABLE, SUSANNA	ALL	022	2ND E.D.
WACHLER, MARIAH	FRE	283	WOODSBOR
WACHORE, CATHARINE *	FRE	287	WOODSBOR
WACHTEL, BENJAMIN	WAS	124	2ND DIST
WACHTEL, DANIEL	FRE	372	CATOCTIN
WACHTEL, ELIZABETH	WAS	301	1ST DIST
WACHTEL, JOHN	WAS	301	1ST DIST
WACHTEL, LEONARD	FRE	348	MIDDLETO
WACHTEL, MARY	FRE	350	MIDDLETO
WACHTEL, OTHO	WAS	125	2ND DIST
WACHTEL, SOLOMON	FRE	342	MIDDLETO
WACHTEL, VALENTINE	WAS	125	2ND DIST
WACHTER, GOERGE	FRE	001	FREDERIC
WACHTER, ISAAC	FRE	059	FREDERIC
WACHTER, JOHN	FRE	105	CREAGERS
WACHTER, MARY A.	FRE	090	FREDERIC
WACHTER, MICHAEL	WAS	245	SMITHSBU
WACKMAN, A. D.	BAL	270	2ND WARD
WACKNEY, MARY	BAL	220	12TH WAR
WAD, JOHN W.	BAL	078	1ST WARD
WAD, RUTH	BAL	071	1ST WARD
WAD, SAMUEL	CEC	209	7TH E DI
WADALL, WILLIAM	BAL	061	2ND DIST
WADDEL, JAMES	BAL	355	8TH WARD
WADDEL, MARY J.	BAL	426	8TH WARD
WADDELE, DANIEL	DOR	374	1ST DIST
WADDELL, C.	BAL	129	1ST WARD
WADDELL, CHARLOTTE	BAL	246	12TH WAR
WADDELL, HANNAH	BAL	101	10TH WAR
WADDELL, HANNAH	BAL	101	10TH WAR
WADDELL, JOHN	BAL	281	7TH WARD
WADDELL, MRS.	ANN	266	ANNAPOLI
WADDELL, WILLIAM A.	BAL	412	3RD WARD
WADDER, JANE	BAL	062	2ND DIST
WADDEY, MARY A.	BAL	039	4TH WARD
WADDINGTON, SAMUEL	CEC	087	4TH E DI
WADDLE, COLLISON	CAR	158	NO TWP L
WADDLE, DAVID	CAR	162	NO TWP L
WADDLE, DAVID	BAL	178	19TH WAR
WADDLE, FREDERICK W.	WAS	260	1ST DIST
WADDLE, JAMES	DOR	446	1ST DIST
WADDLE, JOSEPH	DOR	325	1ST DIST
WADDLE, MARIA J.	DOR	446	1ST DIST
WADDLE, THOMAS	TAL	062	EASTON D
WADDLER, JOSEPH	FRE	175	5TH E DI
WADDLES, CAHARINE	FRE	177	5TH E DI
WADDLES, HENRIETTA	FRE	162	EMMITTSB
WADDLES, JEFFERSON	FRE	173	5TH E DI
WADDY, ADDISON	BAL	093	15TH WAR
WADDY, CATHARINE	ANN	469	HOWARD D
WADDY, L.	BAL	150	1ST WARD
WADE, ANNA	BAL	309	1ST DIST
WADE, HAMPTON	BAL	124	2ND DIST
WADE, HENRY	ALL	094	5TH E.D.
WADE, HENRY	ALL	094	5TH E.D.
WADE, HENRY	BAL	102	1ST WARD
WADE, ISAIAH	ALL	149	6TH E.D.
WADE, J. MRS.	BAL	105	10TH WAR
WADE, JAMES P.	MGM	397	ROCKERLE
WADE, JOHN	BAL	105	10TH WAR
WADE, JOHN	BAL	163	2ND DIST
WADE, JOHN	ANN	383	4TH DIST
WADE, JOHN	WAS	057	2ND SUBD
WADE, LANKIN	BAL	310	1ST DIST
WADE, LEO	MGM	431	CLARKSTR
WADE, MARY	CAL	053	3RD DIST
WADE, NANCY	WAS	066	2ND SUBD
WADE, NELSON	BAL	132	5TH WARD
WADE, OLIVER	BAL	089	18TH WAR
WADE, REBECCA	FRE	216	BUCKEYST
WADE, RICHARD	CHA	258	MIDDLETO
WADE, ROBERT	CHA	257	MIDDLETO
WADE, ROBERT P.	MGM	432	CLARKSTR
WADE, ROBERT P. JR.	MGM	430	CLARKSTR
WADE, THOMAS	FRE	019	FREDERIC
WADE, THOMAS	ANN	344	3RD DIST
WADE, UPTON	ANN	513	HOWARD D
WADE, UZEPHENIAH	CHA	257	MIDDLETO
WADE, WILLIAM	ANN	341	3RD DIST
WADE, WILLIAM	BAL	259	2ND WARD
WADE, WILLIAM B.	WAS	149	2ND DIST
WADHEN, ARGELINA	FRE	267	NEW MARK
WADLEIGH, FRANCES	BAL	053	4TH WARD
WADLINE, JOHN	BAL	139	2ND DIST
WADLOE, JAYBEL	BAL	037	2ND DIST
WADLONS, WILLIAM	BAL	204	2ND WARD
WADLOW, JOHN	CAR	213	5TH DIST
WADLOW, PHILOMON	HAR	005	1ST DIST
WADLOW, SOLOMON F.	HAR	069	1ST DIST
WADOH, ANN	BAL	103	1ST WARD
WADSWORTH, CAROLINE	FRE	387	PETERSVI
WADSWORTH, HENRY	FRE	383	PETERSVI
WADSWORTH, MARY	FRE	382	PETERSVI
WADSWORTH, MOSES	ALL	222	CUMBERLA
WADULL, THOMAS*	TAL	029	EASTON D
WAESCHE, GEORGE G.	BAL	141	19TH WAR

NAME	CO.	PAGE	DIST.
WAGAN, ANN	BAL	294	12TH WAR
WAGECHANNY, HENRY	BAL	195	2ND WARD
WAGEL, LARD	ALL	056	10TH E.D
WAGERCHANNY, GEORGE	BAL	195	2ND WARD
WAGERMAN, JACOB	WAS	270	1ST DIST
WAGERMAN, SUSAN	WAS	271	1ST DIST
WAGERS, BARBARA	FRE	270	NEW MARK
WAGERS, LUKE	CAR	202	4TH DIST
WAGERS, NANCY	CAR	200	4TH DIST
WAGGENER, EDMUND	FRE	227	BUCKEYST
WAGGERS, HARMON	ALL	101	5TH E.D.
WAGGIMAN, RICHARD	FRE	145	10TH E D
WAGGIMAN, WILLIAM	FRE	192	5TH E DI
WAGGNER, WILLIAM*	BAL	413	3RD WARD
WAGGOMAN, DAVID	FRE	145	10TH E D
WAGGOMON, ELIZA*	DOR	378	1ST DIST
WAGGONER, ACAM	BAL	281	1ST DIST
WAGGONER, ANN	BAL	459	1ST DIST
WAGGONER, CARL F.	BAL	261	1ST DIST
WAGGONER, CATHERINE	CEC	138	6TH E DI
WAGGONER, CHARLES	BAL	281	1ST DIST
WAGGONER, EDWARD	BAL	251	1ST DIST
WAGGONER, ELIZABETH	CEC	089	4TH E DI
WAGGONER, FRANCIS*	BAL	357	3RD WARD
WAGGONER, GEORGE	BAL	460	1ST DIST
WAGGONER, HENRY	BAL	253	1ST DIST
WAGGONER, JACOB	FRE	082	FREDERIC
WAGGONER, JAMES W.	FRE	073	FREDERIC
WAGGONER, JOHN	FRE	023	FREDERIC
WAGGONER, JOHN	FRE	026	FREDERIC
WAGGONER, JOHN	BAL	279	1ST DIST
WAGGONER, JOHN	BAL	276	1ST DIST
WAGGONER, JOHN	BAL	294	1ST DIST
WAGGONER, JOHN J.	BAL	269	1ST DIST
WAGGONER, MARGARET	ALL	239	CUMBERLA
WAGGONER, MARGARET	FRE	258	NEW MARK
WAGGONER, MARGARET	FRE	260	NEW MARK
WAGGONER, MARY	ALL	261	CUMBERLA
WAGGONER, PHILIP	BAL	336	1ST DIST
WAGGONER, POLLY	FRE	180	5TH E DI
WAGGONER, SAMUEL	BAL	449	1ST DIST
WAGGONER, SAMUEL L.	ALL	174	7TH E.D.
WAGGONER, SAMUELH.	BAL	159	1ST WARD
WAGLIGHT, HENRY	BAL	065	2ND DIST
WAGNER, ADALINE	FRE	309	WOODSBOR
WAGNER, ADAM	CEC	029	CHESAPEA
WAGNER, ALICE	BAL	316	20TH WAR
WAGNER, AMELIA	BAL	284	17TH WAR
WAGNER, ANN	ANN	430	HOWARD D
WAGNER, ANN	ALL	011	3RD E.D.
WAGNER, ARCHIBALD	ALL	042	10TH E.D
WAGNER, AUGUSTAS	BAL	094	18TH WAR
WAGNER, AUGUSTE	BAL	258	12TH WAR
WAGNER, AUGUSTUS	BAL	458	14TH WAR
WAGNER, AUSTIN	BAL	251	2ND WARD
WAGNER, BALTZELL	BAL	240	17TH WAR
WAGNER, BARBARA	BAL	012	18TH WAR
WAGNER, BAREARY	BAL	262	17TH WAR
WAGNER, BASIL	BAL	375	13TH WAR
WAGNER, BENJAMIN	WAS	044	2ND SUBD
WAGNER, CATHARINE	BAL	238	20TH WAR
WAGNER, CATHARINE	FRE	449	8TH E DI
WAGNER, CATHARINE	BAL	190	2ND WARD
WAGNER, CATHERINE	BAL	085	10TH WAR
WAGNER, CHARLES	BAL	081	10TH WAR
WAGNER, CHARLES	BAL	329	13TH WAR
WAGNER, CHARLES	BAL	232	2ND WARD
WAGNER, CHARLES	BAL	210	19TH WAR
WAGNER, CHRIS	BAL	226	19TH WAR
WAGNER, CHRISTIANA	BAL	126	16TH WAR
WAGNER, CONRAD	BAL	001	4TH WARD
WAGNER, DANIEL	FRE	433	8TH E DI
WAGNER, DAVID	FRE	285	WOODSBOR
WAGNER, DAVID	BAL	110	18TH WAR
WAGNER, DENNIS D.	BAL	046	4TH WARD
WAGNER, ELIAS	ALL	244	CUMBERLA
WAGNER, ELIZABETH	BAL	271	2ND WARD
WAGNER, ELIZABETH	BAL	075	1ST WARD
WAGNER, ELIZABETH	BAL	120	18TH WAR
WAGNER, FERDINAND	BAL	013	15TH WAR
WAGNER, FRANCIS	ALL	080	5TH E.D.
WAGNER, FRANK	BAL	400	8TH WARD
WAGNER, FREDERIC	CAR	266	WESTMINS
WAGNER, FREDERICK	BAL	043	18TH WAR
WAGNER, FREDERICK	BAL	074	1ST WARD
WAGNER, FREDERICK	BAL	084	10TH WAR
WAGNER, FREDERICK	ANN	520	HOWARD D
WAGNER, FREDRICKER	BAL	034	18TH WAR
WAGNER, GEORGE	FRE	429	8TH E DI
WAGNER, GEORGE	BAL	402	14TH WAR
WAGNER, GEORGE	BAL	358	3RD WARD
WAGNER, GEORGE	BAL	018	1ST WARD
WAGNER, GEORGE	BAL	043	1ST WARD
WAGNER, GEORGE	BAL	170	6TH WARD
WAGNER, GEORGE L.	BAL	144	1ST WARD
WAGNER, HAM	BAL	213	17TH WAR
WAGNER, HENRY	BAL	134	11TH WAR
WAGNER, HENRY	CAR	285	7TH DIST
WAGNER, HENRY	CAR	401	2ND DIST
WAGNER, HENRY	CAR	173	8TH DIST
WAGNER, HENRY	ALL	009	3RD E.D.
WAGNER, HENRY	ALL	001	3RD E.D.
WAGNER, HENRY	BAL	006	15TH WAR
WAGNER, HENRY C.	BAL	405	14TH WAR
WAGNER, JACK	BAL	130	1ST WARD
WAGNER, JACOB	BAL	281	12TH WAR
WAGNER, JAMES BV.	BAL	470	14TH WAR
WAGNER, JAMES F.	BAL	077	4TH WARD
WAGNER, JESSE	ALL	172	7TH E.D.
WAGNER, JOHN	ALL	041	2ND E.D.
WAGNER, JOHN	BAL	129	1ST WARD
WAGNER, JOHN	BAL	274	7TH WARD
WAGNER, JOHN	BAL	062	15TH WAR
WAGNER, JOHN	BAL	189	2ND WARD
WAGNER, JOHN	BAL	070	2ND DIST
WAGNER, JOHN	BAL	448	14TH WAR
WAGNER, JOHN	CAR	403	2ND DIST
WAGNER, JOHN	CAR	412	2ND DIST
WAGNER, JOHN	FRE	273	NEW MARK
WAGNER, JOSEPH	BAL	221	19TH WAR
WAGNER, JOSEPH	BAL	265	2ND WARD
WAGNER, JOSEPH L.	FRE	448	8TH E DI
WAGNER, JOSEPH T.	ALL	002	3RD E.D.
WAGNER, JULIAN	BAL	302	3RD WARD
WAGNER, LEWIS	BAL	096	1ST WARD
WAGNER, LEWIS	BAL	119	18TH WAR
WAGNER, MARGARET	FRE	066	FREDERIC
WAGNER, MARGARETT	FRE	448	8TH E DI
WAGNER, MARY E.	FRE	349	MIDDLETO
WAGNER, MICHAEL	BAL	239	17TH WAR
WAGNER, MICHAEL	BAL	404	8TH WARD
WAGNER, MICHAEL	BAL	239	2ND WARD
WAGNER, MICHAEL	BAL	033	15TH WAR
WAGNER, MISS C.	FRE	199	5TH E DI
WAGNER, NICHOLAS	FRE	256	NEW MARK
WAGNER, PAULINE	BAL	015	15TH WAR
WAGNER, PETER	ALL	012	3RD E.D.
WAGNER, PETER	BAL	331	13TH WAR
WAGNER, PHILIP	BAL	153	16TH WAR
WAGNER, PHILIP	BAL	306	20TH WAR
WAGNER, PHILIP	BAL	048	18TH WAR
WAGNER, PHILIP	BAL	392	14TH WAR
WAGNER, PHILIP	BAL	406	14TH WAR
WAGNER, PHILIP	BAL	080	18TH WAR
WAGNER, PHILLIP	BAL	231	17TH WAR
WAGNER, POWLES	BAL	276	7TH WARD
WAGNER, REBECCA	BAL	221	19TH WAR
WAGNER, RHINARD	BAL	406	14TH WAR
WAGNER, SAMUEL	BAL	058	1ST WARD
WAGNER, SAMUEL	WAS	122	2ND DIST
WAGNER, SISTER MARY	FRE	198	5TH E DI
WAGNER, SUSAN	ANN	272	ANNAPOLI
WAGNER, THOMAS	ALL	225	CUMBERLA
WAGNER, WILLIAM	BAL	232	2ND WARD
WAGNER, WILLIAM	BAL	306	20TH WAR
WAGNER, WILLIAM	CAR	281	7TH DIST
WAGNER, WILLIAM	FRE	449	8TH E DI
WAGNER, WILLIAM	WAS	011	WILLIAMS
WAGONELY, MARTHA B.	CAR	310	1ST DIST
WAGONER, ANDREW	WAS	267	1ST DIST
WAGONER, ANN S.	WAS	042	2ND SUBD
WAGONER, CATHARINE	WAS	192	1ST DIST
WAGONER, CATHARINE	FRE	203	5TH E DI
WAGONER, CHRITIAN	CAR	323	1ST DIST
WAGONER, DANIEL	CAR	360	9TH DIST
WAGONER, DANIEL	FRE	326	MIDDLETO
WAGONER, ELIJAH	CAR	268	WESTMINS
WAGONER, FRANCIS	CAR	359	9TH DIST
WAGONER, FREDERICK	CAR	394	2ND DIST
WAGONER, HENRY	FRE	187	5TH E DI
WAGONER, HENRY	WAS	145	HAGERSTO
WAGONER, J.H.	ANN	272	ANNAPOLI
WAGONER, JACOB	CAR	281	7TH DIST
WAGONER, JOHN	CAR	305	1ST DIST
WAGONER, JOHN	WAS	150	HAGERSTO
WAGONER, JOHN	WAS	147	HAGERSTO
WAGONER, JOHN A.	WAS	132	HAGERSTO
WAGONER, JONAS	FRE	188	5TH E DI
WAGONER, JOSEPH G.	BAL	238	1ST DIST
WAGONER, JULIAN	WAS	245	SMITHSBU
WAGONER, MARY	CAR	396	2ND DIST
WAGONER, MICHEAL	CAR	400	2ND DIST
WAGONER, ROBERT	BAL	375	1ST DIST
WAGONER, SAMUEL	WAS	201	1ST DIST
WAGONER, SARAH	FRE	203	5TH E DI
WAGONER, SCHNEBLY	WAS	219	1ST DIST
WAGONER, SUSAN	CAR	360	9TH DIST
WAGONER, WILLIAM*	BAL	413	3RD WARD
WAGONHOUSER, MARTIN	CAR	310	1ST DIST
WAGUIRE, JOHN	BAL	159	11TH WAR
WAHL, ADM	BAL	428	8TH WARD
WAHL, BENA	BAL	006	15TH WAR
WAHL, CHRISTAIN	CAR	213	5TH DIST
WAHL, JOHN	BAL	107	5TH WARD
WAHL, PERRY	BAL	144	5TH WARD
WAHLE, MARTIN	BAL	132	5TH WARD
WAHN, FRANCIS	BAL	362	13TH WAR
WAICE, T.	BAL	173	1ST WARD
WAIDEMAN, D.	BAL	137	1ST WARD
WAIFIELD, GANETTSON	FRE	276	NEW MARK
WAIHLER, JAMES	FRE	359	CATOCTIN
WAILE, ASHFORD	ALL	183	8TH E.D.
WAILES, BIDDY	SOM	516	BARREN C
WAILES, ONISMUS	SOM	515	BARREN C
WAILES, RACHEL	BAL	228	6TH WARD
WAILES, SARAH A.	WOR	228	6TH E DI
WAILES, WILLIAM	SOM	500	SALISBUR
WAILES, WILLIAM JOHN	SOM	514	BARREN C
WAILEY, BARBARA	BAL	044	9TH WARD
WAILOR, JAMES	BAL	114	1ST WARD
WAINER, JOHN	BAL	380	8TH WARD
WAINES, LAWRENCE	BAL	129	18TH WAR
WAINRIGHT, BIDDY	SOM	548	TYASKIN
WAINRIGHT, CANNON	SOM	547	TYASKIN
WAINRIGHT, EDWARD J.	SOM	428	PRINCESS
WAINRIGHT, ELIZA A.	SOM	538	TYASKIN
WAINRIGHT, GEORGE	WOR	232	6TH E DI
WAINRIGHT, GEORGE H.	SOM	540	TYASKIN
WAINRIGHT, HAMILTON B. G.	SOM	538	TYASKIN
WAINRIGHT, JANE B.	ST	338	4TH E DI
WAINRIGHT, JESSE	SOM	537	TYASKIN
WAINRIGHT, JOB	SOM	538	TYASKIN
WAINRIGHT, JOHN	SOM	539	TYASKIN
WAINRIGHT, M. D.	SOM	544	TYASKIN
WAINRIGHT, MINERVA	SOM	539	TYASKIN
WAINRIGHT, PHILIP	SOM	511	BARREN C
WAINRIGHT, WILLIAM C.	SOM	538	TYASKIN
WAINRIGHT, WILLIAM H.	SOM	538	TYASKIN
WAINSON, WILIAM *	BAL	300	12TH WAR
WAINWRIGHT, JAMES B.	BAL	429	1ST DIST
WAINWRIGHT, JOHN	BAL	429	1ST DIST
WAINWRIGHT,RICHARD	ST	340	5TH E DI
WAIREN, HENRY	ALL	019	2ND E.D.
WAIT, CHARLES	BAL	174	1ST WARD
WAIT, EDE-BLACK	WOR	347	1ST E DI
WAIT, GEORGE*	BAL	337	3RD WARD
WAIT, JAMES	WOR	279	BERLIN I
WAIT, JOSEPH	BAL	462	1ST DIST
WAIT, MINUS	WOR	291	9TH E DI
WAITE, RICHARD B.	BAL	062	15TH WAR
WAITE, RICHARD C.	BAL	027	15TH WAR
WAITENBOCK, GEORGE	BAL	128	1ST WARD
WAITER, JOHN *	BAL	285	20TH WAR
WAITES, JOSEPH	BAL	043	18TH WAR
WAITMAN, ELIZABETH	WAS	007	WILLIAMS
WAITS, SARAH	BAL	073	1ST WARD
WAITT, HENRY	BAL	109	15TH WAR
WAKEFIELD,ROBERT	ALL	040	2ND E.D.
WAKEHART, JOHN	BAL	276	20TH WAR
WAKELAND, BENJAMIN	HAR	136	2ND DIST
WAKELAND, JOHN	HAR	117	2ND DIST
WAKEMAN, JOHN	ALL	253	CUMBERLA
WAKEMAN, JOSEPH	ALL	253	CUMBERLA
WAKENEIGHT, MARY M.	WAS	185	BOONSBOR
WAKENIGHT, DANIEL	WAS	212	1ST DIST
WAKENIGHT, JOHN	WAS	211	1ST DIST
WAKENIGHT, MARGARET	WAS	199	1ST DIST
WAKENIGHT, MARGARET	WAS	178	BOONSBOR
WAKENIGHT, ROBERT C.	WAS	213	1ST DIST
WAKENIGHT, SUSAN	WAS	213	1ST DIST
WAKERMAN, ROSWELL	CEC	148	PORT DUP
WAKLAND, WILLIAM	HAR	136	2ND DIST
WAKLEN, ELLENOR	ST	330	4TH E DI
WAKMAN, JOSEH *	ALL	103	5TH E.D.
WALACE, ELLEN	BAL	151	11TH WAR
WALARD, GEORGE	CAR	193	4TH DIST
WALBACH, GEORGE	BAL	046	9TH WARD
WALBACUH, JOHN	BAL	389	13TH WAR
WALBECK, VALENTINE	BAL	234	2ND WARD
WALBER, WILLIAM	BAL	172	1ST WARD
WALCH, JOHN C.	HAR	202	3RD DIST
WALCH, SARAH	ALL	216	CUMBERLA
WALCOTT, D. W.	BAL	151	1ST WARD
WALD, THOMAS A.	FRE	386	PETERSVI
WALDAMER, MOSES	BAL	422	14TH WAR
WALDASHOVER, CHRISTIAN	BAL	367	13TH WAR
WALDBICK, WILLIAM	BAL	273	2ND WARD
WALDECK, A.	BAL	173	19TH WAR
WALDECK, JOHN	FRE	331	MIDDLETO
WALDECK, MARY	FRE	332	MIDDLETO
WALDECT, ANTONE	BAL	173	19TH WAR
WALDEFORD, DAVID J.	BAL	103	15TH WAR
WALDEMAN, CATHARINE	BAL	342	13TH WAR
WALDEMANN, W.	BAL	088	10TH WAR
WALDEN, FREDERICK	BAL	270	12TH WAR
WALDER, ANDREW	SOM	492	SALISBUR
WALDFERD, MICHAEL	BAL	112	2ND DIST
WALDING, EDWARD	BAL	107	1ST WARD
WALDING, PHILIP	CHA	242	HILLTOP
WALDMAN, DANIEL J.	BAL	090	15TH WAR
WALDMAN, ELIZA*	BAL	001	4TH WARD
WALDNER, FRANK	BAL	263	2ND WARD
WALDO, SIMON	BAL	218	2ND WARD
WALDO, THOMAS	BAL	014	1ST WARD
WALDON, JAMES	ALL	052	10TH E.D
WALDON, WILLIAM H.	BAL	283	7TH WARD
WALDRON, THOMAS	BAL	400	1ST DIST
WALDSMITH, LOUIS	BAL	082	10TH WAR
WALE, ELIZABETH	ANN	434	HOWARD D
WALEIS, EMILINE	DOR	455	1ST DIST
WALER, MARY A.	CAR	235	UNION TO
WALES, CHARLOTT	BAL	377	3RD WARD
WALES, DAFFANY	CEC	151	PORT DUP
WALES, ELLEN	ANN	315	1ST DIST
WALES, FRANCIS L.	KEN	259	1ST DIST
WALES, GEORGE	QUE	189	3RD E DI
WALES, JAMES C.	BAL	149	16TH WAR
WALES, PHILIP S.	BAL	150	16TH WAR
WALES, SALLY	TAL	038	EASTON D
WALES, SAMUEL	TAL	101	ST MICHA
WALES, SHADE	KEN	225	2ND DIST
WALEY, MATHEW	HAR	184	3RD DIST
WALFE, ROXANN *	BAL	312	12TH WAR
WALFORD, ELIZA	WAS	132	HAGERSTO
WALFORD, ISAAC-BLACK	CAR	162	NO TWP L
WALFRAM, BENEDICT*	BAL	400	3RD WARD
WALFRAM, HELENORA*	BAL	401	3RD WARD
WALGIN, HENRY	BAL	391	14TH WAR
WALICE, ISAAC	CAL	018	1ST DIST
WALIS, LUKE	PRI	036	VANSVILL
WALK, JAMES	BAL	134	1ST WARD
WALKANT, JOHN	BAL	089	10TH WAR
WALKEN, HUGH H.*	BAL	366	3RD WARD
WALKER, ABRAHAM	MGM	338	CRACKLIN
WALKER, ALEX E.	ANN	421	HOWARD D
WALKER, ALFRED	MGM	316	CRACKLIN
WALKER, ANN	BAL	115	11TH WAR
WALKER, ANN	WAS	150	2ND DIST
WALKER, ARA	BAL	459	1ST DIST
WALKER, AUGUSTA	BAL	008	9TH WARD
WALKER, BENJAMIN*	BAL	096	10TH WAR
WALKER, BENNET	BAL	291	1ST DIST
WALKER, C. W.	BAL	109	10TH WAR
WALKER, CASPER	BAL	100	18TH WAR
WALKER, CATHARINE	CAR	337	6TH DIST
WALKER, CATHARINE	BAL	048	15TH WAR
WALKER, CATHERINE	BAL	357	1ST DIST
WALKER, CECELIA	BAL	055	1ST WARD
WALKER, CHARLES	BAL	458	8TH WARD
WALKER, CHARLES	MGM	353	BERRYS D
WALKER, CHARLES	BAL	045	4TH WARD
WALKER, CHARLES	WAS	186	BOONSBOR
WALKER, CHARLES	WAS	209	1ST DIST
WALKER, CHARLES *	BAL	280	2ND WARD
WALKER, CHARLES G.	BAL	134	1ST WARD
WALKER, CHARLES L.	BAL	133	1ST WARD
WALKER, CHARLES W.	FRE	291	WOODSBOR
WALKER, CHARLOTT	BAL	119	11TH WAR
WALKER, CHARLOTTE	ANN	338	3RD DIST
WALKER, CHRISTOPHER	BAL	248	1ST DIST
WALKER, CRAVEN S.	FRE	230	BUCKEYST
WALKER, D.	BAL	137	1ST WARD
WALKER, DANIEL	CAR	337	6TH DIST
WALKER, DANIL	DOR	465	1ST DIST
WALKER, DAVID	ALL	209	CUMBERLA
WALKER, E.	BAL	149	1ST WARD
WALKER, E.	BAL	173	1ST WARD
WALKER, E.	BAL	163	1ST WARD
WALKER, EDWARD	BAL	159	1ST WARD
WALKER, EDWARD	BAL	122	1ST WARD
WALKER, EDWARD	BAL	201	11TH WAR
WALKER, EDWARD	HAR	130	2ND DIST
WALKER, EDWARD	BAL	006	4TH WARD
WALKER, ELIAS	MGM	323	CRACKLIN
WALKER, ELISHA	ANN	441	HOWARD D
WALKER, ELIZA	CAR	162	NO TWP L
WALKER, ELIZA	CEC	197	7TH E DI
WALKER, ELIZABETH	KEN	215	2ND DIST
WALKER, ELIZABETH	BAL	388	13TH WAR
WALKER, ELIZABETH	BAL	056	4TH WARD
WALKER, ELIZABETH	BAL	049	4TH WARD
WALKER, ELIZABETH	BAL	350	3RD WARD
WALKER, ELIZABETH	BAL	269	7TH WARD
WALKER, ELIZABETH	BAL	423	8TH WARD
WALKER, ELIZABETH	BAL	326	3RD WARD
WALKER, ELIZABETH	BAL	322	3RD WARD
WALKER, ELIZABETH	PRI	041	VANSVILL
WALKER, ELIZABETH A.	MGM	320	CRACKLIN
WALKER, ELLEN	BAL	398	8TH WARD
WALKER, EMORY	KEN	263	1ST DIST
WALKER, ERASMUS	FRE	329	MIDDLETO
WALKER, EVAN	BAL	038	15TH WAR
WALKER, F.A.	BAL	161	1ST WARD
WALKER, FANNEY	BAL	433	8TH WARD
WALKER, FAWNEY	BAL	010	4TH WARD
WALKER, FRANCIS	HAR	126	2ND DIST
WALKER, FRANCIS	BAL	206	17TH WAR
WALKER, FRANCIS	BAL	007	18TH WAR
WALKER, FRANCIS	BAL	362	8TH WARD
WALKER, FRANCIS	BAL	319	3RD WARD

Name	County	Page	District
WALKER, FRANCIS	PRI	069	MARLBROU
WALKER, FRANCIS J.	ANN	485	HOWARD D
WALKER, FREDERICK	BAL	279	17TH WAR
WALKER, GEORGE	HAR	177	3RD DIST
WALKER, GEORGE	HAR	181	3RD DIST
WALKER, GEORGE	BAL	206	6TH DIST
WALKER, GEORGE	BAL	147	1ST WARD
WALKER, GEORGE	BAL	150	1ST WARD
WALKER, GEORGE	ALL	106	5TH E.D.
WALKER, GEORGE	PRI	097	SPALDING
WALKER, GEORGE B.	MGM	434	CLARKSTR
WALKER, GEORGE J.	KEN	214	2ND DIST
WALKER, GEORGE T.	BAL	023	2ND DIST
WALKER, GEORGE W.	FRE	301	WOODSBOR
WALKER, GEROGE H.	FRE	385	PETERSVI
WALKER, HANAH	BAL	071	2ND DIST
WALKER, HANNAH	ANN	289	ANNAPOLI
WALKER, HENRIETTA	ST	285	2ND E DI
WALKER, HENRIETTA	ST	284	2ND E DI
WALKER, HENRY	PRI	033	VANSVILL
WALKER, HENRY	KEN	275	1ST DIST
WALKER, HENRY	KEN	261	1ST DIST
WALKER, HENRY	BAL	300	7TH WARD
WALKER, HENRY	CEC	205	7TH E DI
WALKER, HENRY	KEN	230	2ND DIST
WALKER, HENRY	KEN	238	2ND DIST
WALKER, HENRY-BLACK	CAR	387	2ND DIST
WALKER, HORACE	ANN	352	3RD DIST
WALKER, HUGH H.*	BAL	366	3RD WARD
WALKER, HUGH L.	BAL	424	3RD WARD
WALKER, INHAM	TAL	062	EASTON D
WALKER, ISAAC	KEN	258	1ST DIST
WALKER, ISAAC	FRE	305	WOODSBOR
WALKER, J.	BAL	140	1ST WARD
WALKER, J.	BAL	136	1ST WARD
WALKER, J.E.	BAL	140	1ST WARD
WALKER, JACOB	FRE	307	WOODSBOR
WALKER, JAMES	CEC	025	ELKTON 3
WALKER, JAMES	HAR	183	3RD DIST
WALKER, JAMES	BAL	141	1ST WARD
WALKER, JAMES	BAL	122	1ST WARD
WALKER, JAMES	ALL	103	5TH E.D.
WALKER, JAMES	BAL	165	1ST WARD
WALKER, JAMES	ANN	515	HOWARD D
WALKER, JAMES R.	ALL	241	CUMBERLA
WALKER, JAMES R.	QUE	231	4TH E DI
WALKER, JEREMIAH W.	SOM	518	BARREN C
WALKER, JERMIMA	FRE	243	NEW MARK
WALKER, JESSE	HAR	060	1ST DIST
WALKER, JOEL	ANN	340	3RD DIST
WALKER, JOHN	ANN	441	HOWARD D
WALKER, JOHN	BAL	370	1ST DIST
WALKER, JOHN	BAL	290	3RD WARD
WALKER, JOHN	BAL	174	1ST WARD
WALKER, JOHN	BAL	243	6TH WARD
WALKER, JOHN	BAL	311	1ST DIST
WALKER, JOHN	ALL	168	6TH E.D.
WALKER, JOHN	ALL	088	5TH E.D.
WALKER, JOHN	BAL	122	1ST WARD
WALKER, JOHN	BAL	119	1ST WARD
WALKER, JOHN	BAL	267	7TH WARD
WALKER, JOHN	HAR	146	3RD DIST
WALKER, JOHN	MGM	320	CRACKLIN
WALKER, JOHN	BAL	002	18TH WAR
WALKER, JOHN	BAL	200	17TH WAR
WALKER, JOHN	BAL	270	17TH WAR
WALKER, JOHN	BAL	243	17TH WAR
WALKER, JOHN	SOM	512	BARREN C
WALKER, JOHN	PRI	097	SPALDING
WALKER, JOHN A.	FRE	131	CREAGERS
WALKER, JOHN B.	PRI	104	PISCATAW
WALKER, JOHN C.	SOM	367	BRINKLEY
WALKER, JOHN D.*	DOR	449	1ST DIST
WALKER, JOHN E.	BAL	252	17TH WAR
WALKER, JOHN H.	BAL	453	14TH WAR
WALKER, JOHN H.	BAL	165	16TH WAR
WALKER, JOHN M.	BAL	269	20TH WAR
WALKER, JOHN R.	CAR	225	5TH DIST
WALKER, JOHN R.	PRI	092	MARLBROU
WALKER, JOHN R.	PRI	002	BLADENSB
WALKER, JOHN W.	BAL	282	20TH WAR
WALKER, JOHN W.	BAL	250	20TH WAR
WALKER, JOSEPH	SOM	517	BARREN C
WALKER, JOSEPH	BAL	095	10TH WAR
WALKER, JOSEPH	BAL	186	2ND WARD
WALKER, JOSEPH	BAL	206	6TH DIST
WALKER, JOSEPH	BAL	240	12TH WAR
WALKER, JOSEPH S.	BAL	157	16TH WAR
WALKER, JOSEPHINE E.	BAL	101	18TH WAR
WALKER, JOSHUA	BAL	056	4TH WARD
WALKER, JOSHUA	BAL	321	7TH WARD
WALKER, JOSIAH	BAL	437	1ST DIST
WALKER, JUBA	ANN	339	3RD DIST
WALKER, JULIANNA	MGM	318	CRACKLIN
WALKER, L.	PRI	118	PISCATAW
WALKER, LEVIN	CAR	140	NO TWP L
WALKER, MARGARET	BAL	260	20TH WAR
WALKER, MARGARET	WOR	295	9TH E DI
WALKER, MARGARET	ANN	433	HOWARD D
WALKER, MARGARET	BAL	158	16TH WAR
WALKER, MARGARET	BAL	028	1ST WARD
WALKER, MARGARET A.	TAL	051	EASTON D
WALKER, MARGARET A.	CEC	159	PORT DUP
WALKER, MARGARET A.	BAL	410	3RD WARD
WALKER, MARGARET R.	MGM	319	CRACKLIN
WALKER, MARIA	CAR	315	1ST DIST
WALKER, MARIA	BAL	008	9TH WARD
WALKER, MARK	SOM	518	BARREN C
WALKER, MARTHY E.*	DOR	375	1ST DIST
WALKER, MARTIN	ALL	142	6TH E.D.
WALKER, MARY	BAL	153	2ND DIST
WALKER, MARY	BAL	080	10TH WAR
WALKER, MARY	FRE	007	FREDERIC
WALKER, MARY	BAL	236	20TH WAR
WALKER, MARY	FRE	108	CREAGERS
WALKER, MARY	BAL	364	13TH WAR
WALKER, MARY	SOM	509	BARREN C
WALKER, MARY	SOM	512	BARREN C
WALKER, MARY A.	BAL	357	13TH WAR
WALKER, MARY A.	BAL	104	18TH WAR
WALKER, MARY A.	BAL	316	1ST DIST
WALKER, MARY C.	FRE	223	BUCKEYST
WALKER, MARY E.	BAL	353	7TH WARD
WALKER, MARY J.	ANN	445	HOWARD D
WALKER, MARYETTA	DOR	300	1ST DIST
WALKER, MATALINA	BAL	254	6TH WARD
WALKER, MATHIAS	CAR	172	8TH DIST
WALKER, MATILDA	BAL	213	6TH WARD
WALKER, NANCY	ANN	320	2ND DIST
WALKER, NANCY	DOR	303	1ST DIST
WALKER, NATHAN J.	MGM	317	CRACKLIN
WALKER, NOAH	BAL	262	6TH WARD
WALKER, OWEN	CAR	358	9TH DIST
WALKER, OWEN	CAR	285	7TH DIST
WALKER, PATRICK	BAL	181	16TH WAR
WALKER, PERRY-MULATTO	FRE	051	FREDERIC
WALKER, PETER	BAL	259	17TH WAR
WALKER, PETER	BAL	179	19TH WAR
WALKER, PHEBE	HAR	151	3RD DIST
WALKER, PHILIP	BAL	036	9TH WARD
WALKER, PRISCILLA	ALL	220	CUMBERLA
WALKER, PRISCILLA	PRI	035	VANSVILL
WALKER, PRISILLA	PRI	039	VANSVILL
WALKER, RACHEL	FRE	292	WOODSBOR
WALKER, REBECCA	MGM	323	CRACKLIN
WALKER, REBECCA	BAL	014	18TH WAR
WALKER, REBECCA	ALL	214	CUMBERLA
WALKER, RICHARD	ANN	325	2ND DIST
WALKER, RICHARD	ANN	325	2ND DIST
WALKER, RICHARD	BAL	024	9TH WARD
WALKER, RICHARD	BAL	194	2ND WARD
WALKER, RICHARD	BAL	285	1ST DIST
WALKER, RICHARD	BAL	055	4TH WARD
WALKER, RICHARD T.	PRI	109	PISCATAW
WALKER, RICHRAD B.	PRI	035	VANSVILL
WALKER, ROBERT	TAL	114	ST MICHA
WALKER, ROBERT	HAR	132	2ND DIST
WALKER, ROBERT	ANN	344	3RD DIST
WALKER, ROBERT	BAL	423	8TH WARD
WALKER, ROBERT	BAL	313	3RD WARD
WALKER, ROBERT H.	BAL	366	3RD WARD
WALKER, ROSET	BAL	301	1ST DIST
WALKER, SAMUEL	BAL	287	7TH WARD
WALKER, SAMUEL	BAL	134	16TH WAR
WALKER, SAMUEL	FRE	329	MIDDLETO
WALKER, SAMUEL	CEC	203	6TH E DI
WALKER, SAMUEL	SOM	511	BARREN C
WALKER, SAMUEL D.	FRE	299	WOODSBOR
WALKER, SAMUEL H.	BAL	164	1ST WARD
WALKER, SAMUEL T.	BAL	425	3RD WARD
WALKER, SAMUEL T.	QUE	235	4TH E DI
WALKER, SARAH	BAL	069	4TH WARD
WALKER, SARAH	BAL	078	4TH WARD
WALKER, SARAH	HAR	012	1ST DIST
WALKER, SARAH	CAR	161	NO TWP L
WALKER, SARAH	BAL	302	7TH WARD
WALKER, SARAH B.	BAL	112	15TH WAR
WALKER, SARAH E.	ANN	287	ANNAPOLI
WALKER, SARAH E.	FRE	244	NEW MARK
WALKER, SOLOMON-BLACK	CAR	384	2ND DIST
WALKER, SOPHIA	PRI	105	PISCATAW
WALKER, SUSAN	WOR	198	8TH E DI
WALKER, SUSAN	CAR	159	NO TWP L
WALKER, SUSAN	BAL	209	6TH DIST
WALKER, SUSAN A.	BAL	341	3RD WARD
WALKER, SUSANNA	ANN	421	HOWARD D
WALKER, TABITHA	WOR	346	1ST E DI
WALKER, TERESA	BAL	343	13TH WAR
WALKER, THOAMS	BAL	027	18TH WAR
WALKER, THOMAS	BAL	135	11TH WAR
WALKER, THOMAS	HAR	059	1ST DIST
WALKER, THOMAS	MGM	362	BERRYS D
WALKER, THOMAS	PRI	118	PISCATAW
WALKER, THOMAS	KEN	313	3RD DIST
WALKER, THOMAS C. DR.	BAL	249	1ST DIST
WALKER, THOMAS W.	BAL	112	15TH WAR
WALKER, TRUMAN	BAL	255	12TH WAR
WALKER, VIRGINIA P.	BAL	345	13TH WAR
WALKER, WALTER	BAL	214	6TH DIST
WALKER, WALTER	SOM	517	BARREN C
WALKER, WASHINGTON G.	ST	256	3RD E DI
WALKER, WESLEY	BAL	305	7TH WARD
WALKER, WILLIAM	BAL	255	6TH WARD
WALKER, WILLIAM	BAL	141	1ST WARD
WALKER, WILLIAM	ANN	295	1ST DIST
WALKER, WILLIAM	BAL	157	1ST WARD
WALKER, WILLIAM	BAL	157	1ST WARD
WALKER, WILLIAM	BAL	167	1ST WARD
WALKER, WILLIAM	BAL	237	6TH WARD
WALKER, WILLIAM	TAL	059	EASTON D
WALKER, WILLIAM	BAL	056	4TH WARD
WALKER, WILLIAM	CEC	159	PORT DUP
WALKER, WILLIAM	BAL	035	18TH WAR
WALKER, WILLIAM	HAR	146	3RD DIST
WALKER, WILLIAM	FRE	170	5TH E DI
WALKER, WILLIAM T.	ALL	223	CUMBERLA
WALKER, WILLIAM W.	FRE	266	NEW MARK
WALKER, WILSON	FRE	031	FREDERIC
WALKER, ZOE	BAL	274	12TH WAR
WALKER,LEVY	WOR	346	1ST E DI
WALKERS, PETER	ALL	089	5TH E.D.
WALKIN, JAMES	BAL	164	1ST WARD
WALKING, JOHNS	CAR	102	NO TWP L
WALKINS, ELIZABETH	BAL	379	8TH WARD
WALKINS, EVANS	BAL	307	12TH WAR
WALKLAND, FRANCIS	BAL	323	3RD WARD
WALKLAND, FRANCIS*	BAL	323	3RD WARD
WALKS, ELIZABETH	BAL	016	1ST WARD
WALL, ANNA S.	ST	307	1ST E DI
WALL, CATHARINE	DOR	299	1ST DIST
WALL, CRISTIAN	BAL	120	11TH WAR
WALL, DANIEL	BAL	198	19TH WAR
WALL, ELIZABETH	ALL	003	3RD E.D.
WALL, EPHRAIM	BAL	258	12TH WAR
WALL, GEORGE	ANN	411	8TH DIST
WALL, GEORGE N.	PRI	059	NOTTINGH
WALL, JACOB	BAL	092	18TH WAR
WALL, JACOB E.	BAL	091	18TH WAR
WALL, JAMES	BAL	121	1ST WARD
WALL, JAMES T.	CAL	007	1ST DIST
WALL, JESSE D.	PRI	044	VANSVILL
WALL, JOHN	WAS	014	WILLIAMS
WALL, JOHN	BAL	333	13TH WAR
WALL, JOHN	DOR	423	1ST DIST
WALL, JOHN	BAL	152	1ST WARD
WALL, JOHN P.	ANN	434	HOWARD D
WALL, JOSEPH	BAL	380	3RD WARD
WALL, JOSEPH W.	BAL	069	18TH WAR
WALL, MARGARETT	BAL	012	4TH WARD
WALL, MARTEN L.	DOR	335	3RD DIVI
WALL, MARTIN	DOR	308	1ST DIST
WALL, MARY	BAL	263	20TH WAR
WALL, MARY	FRE	262	NEW MARK
WALL, MARY	BAL	272	2ND WARD
WALL, NANCY	SOM	509	BARREN C
WALL, RICHARD P.	CHA	285	BOJANTOW
WALL, ROBERT A.	BAL	045	9TH WARD
WALL, RUTH	BAL	344	13TH WAR
WALL, SALLY	CHA	286	BOJANTOW
WALL, SAMUEL	BAL	108	1ST WARD
WALL, SOPHIA	DOR	423	1ST DIST
WALL, THEODORE	PRI	079	MARLBROU
WALL, WILLIAM B.	PRI	059	NOTTINGH
WALL, WILLIAM C. SR.	BAL	085	10TH WAR
WALL, WILLIAM L.	PRI	058	NOTTINGH
WALL,MITCHELL	BAL	194	2ND WARD
WALLACE, A. V.	MGM	380	ROCKERLE
WALLACE, AARON	DOR	356	3RD DIVI
WALLACE, AARTHUR	DOR	333	3RD DIVI
WALLACE, ABIGAIL	SOM	551	TYASKIN
WALLACE, ADAM	SOM	476	TRAPPE D
WALLACE, ADAM	SOM	429	PRINCESS
WALLACE, ADOLPHUS	KEN	298	3RD DIST
WALLACE, AGNES	BAL	147	16TH WAR
WALLACE, ALEXANDER	ALL	109	5TH E.D.
WALLACE, ALEXANDER	CEC	097	4TH E DI
WALLACE, AMELIA	SOM	452	DAMES QU
WALLACE, ANN	BAL	239	2ND WARD
WALLACE, ANNA	BAL	049	9TH WARD
WALLACE, ANTHONY R.	BAL	080	15TH WAR
WALLACE, ARCHABALD	HAR	037	1ST DIST
WALLACE, ARNOLD	SOM	457	DAMES QU
WALLACE, AUGUSTA	BAL	429	1ST DIST
WALLACE, BENJAMIN	CEC	047	1ST E DI
WALLACE, BENJAMIN	CEC	018	ELKTON 3
WALLACE, BENJAMIN L.	BAL	037	9TH WARD
WALLACE, BETSEY-MULATTO	MGM	398	ROCKERLE
WALLACE, BRISTER	SOM	452	DAMES QU
WALLACE, CATHARINE	BAL	217	11TH WAR
WALLACE, CATHARINE	BAL	144	5TH WARD
WALLACE, CATHERINE-BLACK	QUE	180	2ND E DI
WALLACE, CESAR	BAL	152	2ND DIST
WALLACE, CHARLE	BAL	192	17TH WAR
WALLACE, CHARLES	TAL	020	EASTON D
WALLACE, CHARLES	SOM	446	DAMES QU
WALLACE, CHARLES H.	BAL	311	3RD WARD
WALLACE, DANIEL	HAR	027	1ST DIST
WALLACE, DAVID	QUE	128	1ST E DI
WALLACE, DAVID	BAL	246	6TH WARD
WALLACE, ELIZA	BAL	167	11TH WAR
WALLACE, ELIZABETH	MGM	340	CLARKSBU
WALLACE, ELIZABETH	CEC	070	5TH E DI
WALLACE, ELIZABETH	DOR	355	3RD DIVI
WALLACE, ELIZABETH	QUE	190	3RD E DI
WALLACE, ELIZABETH	WAS	194	1ST DIST
WALLACE, ELLEN	SOM	442	DAMES QU
WALLACE, EVELINE	MGM	371	BERRYS D
WALLACE, EZEKIEL	SOM	452	DAMES QU
WALLACE, FRANCES	BAL	464	14TH WAR
WALLACE, GEORGE	DOR	356	3RD DIVI
WALLACE, GEORGE	CEC	005	ELKTON 3
WALLACE, GEORGE	CEC	035	CHESAPEA
WALLACE, GEORGE	BAL	068	4TH WARD
WALLACE, GEORGE	BAL	324	3RD WARD
WALLACE, GEORGE F.	BAL	071	15TH WAR
WALLACE, GEORGE L.	FRE	110	CREAGERS
WALLACE, GRACE A.	BAL	379	3RD WARD
WALLACE, HAMMELTON	WAS	127	2ND DIST
WALLACE, HANNAH	CEC	036	CHESAPEA
WALLACE, HARRIET	MGM	396	ROCKERLE
WALLACE, HARRIETT	BAL	061	4TH WARD
WALLACE, HENRIETTA	BAL	196	11TH WAR
WALLACE, HENRIETTA	BAL	173	6TH WARD
WALLACE, HENRY	BAL	314	3RD WARD
WALLACE, HENRY	ANN	301	1ST DIST
WALLACE, HENRY	ANN	394	8TH DIST
WALLACE, HENRY	BAL	372	13TH WAR
WALLACE, HENRY	HAR	124	2ND DIST
WALLACE, HENSON	BAL	241	17TH WAR
WALLACE, HORATIO	BAL	401	3RD WARD
WALLACE, ISABELLA	BAL	192	17TH WAR
WALLACE, JACOB	BAL	436	14TH WAR
WALLACE, JAMES	MGM	396	ROCKERLE
WALLACE, JAMES	DOR	355	3RD DIVI
WALLACE, JAMES	DOR	379	1ST DIST
WALLACE, JAMES	BAL	086	15TH WAR
WALLACE, JAMES	TAL	091	ST MICHA
WALLACE, JAMES J.	BAL	063	4TH WARD
WALLACE, JAMES T.	DOR	303	1ST DIST
WALLACE, JARRET	BAL	429	1ST DIST
WALLACE, JOHN	BAL	095	5TH WARD
WALLACE, JOHN	BAL	270	2ND WARD
WALLACE, JOHN	BAL	270	2ND WARD
WALLACE, JOHN	ALL	242	CUMBERLA
WALLACE, JOHN	BAL	163	1ST WARD
WALLACE, JOHN	BAL	294	1ST DIST
WALLACE, JOHN	BAL	203	17TH WAR
WALLACE, JOHN	DOR	355	3RD DIVI
WALLACE, JOHN	FRE	202	5TH E DI
WALLACE, JOHN	CEC	109	3RD E DI
WALLACE, JOSEPH	HAR	051	1ST DIST
WALLACE, JOSEPH	CEC	006	ELKTON 3
WALLACE, JOSEPH	BAL	034	9TH WARD
WALLACE, JOSEPH W.	HAR	003	1ST DIST
WALLACE, LEVIN	SOM	445	DAMES QU
WALLACE, LEWIS	BAL	173	6TH WARD
WALLACE, LYTTLETON	CEC	037	CHESAPEA
WALLACE, M.	BAL	147	1ST WARD
WALLACE, MAHALA	SOM	442	DAMES QU
WALLACE, MARGARET	BAL	445	14TH WAR
WALLACE, MARGARET	BAL	445	14TH WAR
WALLACE, MARGARET	BAL	107	1ST WARD
WALLACE, MARGARET E.	HAR	039	1ST DIST
WALLACE, MARIA	MGM	360	BERRYS D
WALLACE, MARTHA	BAL	242	2ND WARD
WALLACE, MARY	BAL	338	1ST DIST
WALLACE, MARY	BAL	229	12TH WAR
WALLACE, MARY	HAR	027	1ST DIST
WALLACE, MARY	HAR	124	2ND DIST
WALLACE, MARY J.	BAL	118	18TH WAR
WALLACE, MATHEW	DOR	328	3RD DIVI
WALLACE, MICHAEL	BAL	309	3RD WARD
WALLACE, MILLICENT	CEC	001	ELKTON 3
WALLACE, NACE	ANN	343	3RD DIST
WALLACE, NELLY	CEC	099	3RD E DI
WALLACE, OLIVIA	BAL	343	3RD WARD
WALLACE, PATRICK	ALL	052	10TH E.D
WALLACE, POLLY	ANN	376	4TH DIST
WALLACE, RACHEL	HAR	100	2ND DIST
WALLACE, RICHARD	BAL	126	18TH WAR
WALLACE, RICHARD	BAL	402	14TH WAR
WALLACE, RICHARD D.	BAL	138	18TH WAR
WALLACE, RICHARD D.	SOM	445	DAMES QU
WALLACE, ROBERT	DOR	328	3RD DIVI
WALLACE, ROBERT	BAL	265	17TH WAR
WALLACE, ROBERT	BAL	127	1ST WARD
WALLACE, ROBERT	KEN	297	3RD DIST
WALLACE, ROBERT	SOM	537	TYASKIN
WALLACE, SAMUEL	TAL	087	ST MICHA
WALLACE, SAMUEL	ANN	308	1ST DIST

WALLACE, SAMUEL BAL 327 3RD WARD
WALLACE, SAMUEL BAL 110 5TH WARD
WALLACE, SAMUEL BAL 372 13TH WAR
WALLACE, SAMUEL HAR 090 2ND DIST
WALLACE, SAMUEL HAR 038 1ST DIST
WALLACE, SAMUEL-BLACK FRE 180 5TH E DI
WALLACE, SARAH J. BAL 136 18TH WAR
WALLACE, SUSAN CEC 002 ELKTON 3
WALLACE, TABITHA SOM 458 DAMES QU
WALLACE, THOMAS SOM 526 QUANTICO
WALLACE, THOMAS CEC 024 ELKTON 3
WALLACE, THOMAS DOR 302 1ST DIST
WALLACE, THOMAS BAL 426 1ST DIST
WALLACE, THOMAS ALL 074 5TH E.D.
WALLACE, THOMAS BAL 023 9TH WARD
WALLACE, THOMAS BAL 147 16TH WAR
WALLACE, WANE * BAL 183 5TH DIST
WALLACE, WASHINGTON SOM 452 DAMES QU
WALLACE, WESLEY BAL 017 2ND DIST
WALLACE, WHITTENTON DOR 355 3RD DIVI
WALLACE, WILLAIM BAL 155 1ST WARD
WALLACE, WILLIAM BAL 125 1ST WARD
WALLACE, WILLIAM ALL 181 8TH E.D.
WALLACE, WILLIAM BAL 061 4TH WARD
WALLACE, WILLIAM BAL 134 18TH WAR
WALLACE, WILLIAM BAL 117 18TH WAR
WALLACE, WILLIAM CAL 036 2ND DIST
WALLACE, WILLIAM BAL 014 18TH WAR
WALLACE, WILLIAM SOM 545 TYASKIN
WALLACE, WILLIAM TAL 092 ST MICHA
WALLACE, WILLIAM C. QUE 123 1ST E DI
WALLACE, WILLIAM D. SOM 446 DAMES QU
WALLACE, WILLIAM H. CEC 099 3RD E DI
WALLACE, WILLIAM H. SOM 541 TYASKIN
WALLACE, WILLIAM H.-MULAT BAL 208 2ND WARD
WALLACE, WILLIAM JR. BAL 075 18TH WAR
WALLACE, WILLIAM R. BAL 470 14TH WAR
WALLACE, WILLIAM S. BAL 113 5TH WARD
WALLACE, WILLIAM T. BAL 062 4TH WARD
WALLACE, WINGATE DOR 404 1ST DIST
WALLACK, GEORGE WAS 212 1ST DIST
WALLACK, JOHN WAS 267 1ST DIST
WALLAN, GEORGE BAL 131 1ST WARD
WALLAN, JAMES BAL 149 1ST WARD
WALLENER, BAIL BAL 008 1ST WARD
WALLENFELTS, ELIZABETH BAL 360 13TH WAR
WALLENSON, GEORGE BAL 185 11TH WAR
WALLENTINE, SARAH WAS 291 1ST DIST
WALLER, ABNER* BAL 152 19TH WAR
WALLER, ABRAHAM BAL 005 9TH WARD
WALLER, ALEXANDER SOM 475 TRAPPE D
WALLER, ATALINE SOM 498 SALISBUR
WALLER, BIDDY BAL 163 16TH WAR
WALLER, EBENEZER H. SOM 514 BARREN C
WALLER, ELIZABETH SOM 499 SALISBUR
WALLER, ELIZABETH BAL 199 17TH WAR
WALLER, ELIZABETH* SOM 493 SALISBUR
WALLER, ELLEN SOM 432 PRINCESS
WALLER, EMMELINE WOR 229 6TH E DI
WALLER, GEORGE SOM 499 SALISBUR
WALLER, GEORGE SOM 432 PRINCESS
WALLER, GEORGE SOM 451 DAMES QU
WALLER, GEORGE BAL 245 1ST DIST
WALLER, GEORGE * BAL 131 2ND DIST
WALLER, HENRY WAS 170 FUNKSTOW
WALLER, ISHA SOM 501 SALISBUR
WALLER, JACK SOM 499 SALISBUR
WALLER, JAMES WOR 230 6TH E DI
WALLER, JOHN SOM 489 SALISBUR
WALLER, JOHN BAL 178 2ND WARD
WALLER, JOHN BAL 223 1ST DIST
WALLER, JOHN A. J. SOM 516 BARREN C
WALLER, JOHN B. SOM 427 PRINCESS
WALLER, JOHN T. SOM 435 PRINCESS
WALLER, LEVIN* SOM 551 TYASKIN
WALLER, LEWIS BAL 031 1ST WARD
WALLER, LUTHER SOM 523 BARREN C
WALLER, PERRY H. SOM 521 BARREN C
WALLER, PRICELLA WOR 230 6TH E DI
WALLER, ROBERT J. SOM 432 PRINCESS
WALLER, SAMUEL SOM 529 QUANTICO
WALLER, SARAH BAL 223 1ST DIST
WALLER, STEPHEN SOM 521 BARREN C
WALLER, WASHINGTON SOM 432 PRINCESS
WALLER, WILLIAM SOM 491 SALISBUR
WALLER, WILLIAM TAL 063 EASTON D
WALLER, WILLIAM BAL 160 1ST WARD
WALLER, WILLIAM BAL 005 9TH WARD
WALLER, WILLIAM S. SOM 553 TYASKIN
WALLER, WILLIAM T. SOM 432 PRINCESS
WALLERS, T. BAL 157 1ST WARD
WALLES, BASIL CAL 002 1ST DIST
WALLES, BEALA BAL 424 1ST DIST
WALLES, FRANCES CEC 206 7TH E DI
WALLEY, ELIZA BAL 078 1ST WARD
WALLEY, HARRIET BAL 430 8TH WARD
WALLEY, JANE BAL 204 6TH WARD
WALLEY, JOHN QUE 252 5TH E DI
WALLEY, ROBERT QUE 251 5TH E DI
WALLEY, SUSAN-BLACK QUE 130 1ST E DI
WALLEY, RICHARD-BLACK QUE 161 2ND E DI
WALLFISCH, SALMON BAL 066 4TH WARD
WALLIAMS, GEORGE* SOM 394 BRINKLEY
WALLICE, BERTHA * CAL 016 1ST DIST
WALLICE, HENNA TAL 054 EASTON D
WALLICE, MARTHA-BLACK FRE 451 8TH E DI
WALLICH, CHRISTIAN ANN 505 HOWARD D
WALLICK, JOHN WAS 302 1ST DIST
WALLICK, MATTHIAS WAS 212 1ST DIST
WALLING, CAROLINE E. FRE 217 BUCKEYST
WALLING, JAMES FRE 217 BUCKEYST
WALLINSFORD, GEORGE N. PRI 102 SPALDING
WALLIS, ANN BAL 293 12TH WAR
WALLIS, ASA BAL 220 19TH WAR
WALLIS, CAROLINE BAL 343 3RD WARD
WALLIS, CHRISTIANE CAL 015 1ST DIST
WALLIS, DAVID BAL 310 20TH WAR
WALLIS, GARRETSON BAL 172 16TH WAR
WALLIS, GEORGE BAL 201 19TH WAR
WALLIS, HANNAH BAL 175 16TH WAR
WALLIS, HARRISON PRI 001 BLADENSB
WALLIS, HENRY BAL 029 15TH WAR
WALLIS, HESTER BAL 382 3RD WARD
WALLIS, HUGH KEN 225 2ND DIST
WALLIS, ISAAC PRI 007 BLADENSB
WALLIS, JAMES BAL 116 15TH WAR
WALLIS, JERRY QUE 245 5TH E DI
WALLIS, JOHN BAL 224 12TH WAR
WALLIS, LANSWELL* DOR 408 1ST DIST
WALLIS, LOUISA HAR 003 1ST DIST
WALLIS, MARY J. BAL 027 15TH WAR
WALLIS, MATTHEW BAL 027 15TH WAR
WALLIS, MRS. BAL 104 10TH WAR
WALLIS, REASON PRI 013 BLADENSB
WALLIS, REBECCA DOR 430 1ST DIST
WALLIS, ROBERT BAL 278 12TH WAR
WALLIS, RUBIN BAL 136 1ST WARD
WALLIS, S. TEACKLE BAL 062 10TH WAR
WALLIS, SARAH BAL 272 20TH WAR
WALLIS, SYLVIA PRI 013 BLADENSB
WALLIS, URIA PRI 013 BLADENSB
WALLIS, WESLEY BAL 172 16TH WAR
WALLIS, WILLIAM DOR 417 1ST DIST
WALLIS, WILLIAM H. HAR 006 1ST DIST
WALLMORE, ANNA BAL 299 17TH WAR
WALLOP, SARAH A. BAL 058 10TH WAR
WALLOP, SOTTY-BLACK WOR 341 1ST E DI
WALLS, ANN QUE 173 2ND E DI
WALLS, DANIEL QUE 182 3RD E DI
WALLS, DANIEL CEC 142 6TH E DI
WALLS, DANIEL CEC 141 6TH E DI
WALLS, EDWARD QUE 148 1ST E DI
WALLS, ELIZABETH CAR 067 NO TWP L
WALLS, ELIZABETH PRI 059 NOTTINGH
WALLS, FRANCES A. QUE 174 2ND E DI
WALLS, GEORGE W. QUE 148 1ST E DI
WALLS, HENRY QUE 145 1ST E DI
WALLS, JAMES QUE 149 1ST E DI
WALLS, JAMES QUE 139 1ST E DI
WALLS, JAMES QUE 150 1ST E DI
WALLS, JAMES CEC 159 PORT DUP
WALLS, JAMES SOM 425 PRINCESS
WALLS, JAMES H. QUE 174 2ND E DI
WALLS, JOHN KEN 306 3RD DIST
WALLS, JOHN QUE 139 1ST E DI
WALLS, JOHN W. QUE 147 1ST E DI
WALLS, JOSEPH W. QUE 129 1ST E DI
WALLS, JOSHUA QUE 151 1ST E DI
WALLS, JULIAN QUE 174 2ND E DI
WALLS, LOUISA QUE 148 1ST E DI
WALLS, MARGARETT A. KEN 286 3RD DIST
WALLS, MARY A. BAL 342 13TH WAR
WALLS, MARY A. CEC 111 4TH E DI
WALLS, NANCY SOM 425 PRINCESS
WALLS, SAMUEL QUE 160 2ND E DI
WALLS, SAMUEL QUE 176 2ND E DI
WALLS, SAMUEL C. QUE 161 2ND E DI
WALLS, SAMUEL S. QUE 174 2ND E DI
WALLS, SARAH CEC 095 4TH E DI
WALLS, SARAH SR. CEC 120 4TH E DI
WALLS, WARREN QUE 129 1ST E DI
WALLS, WILLAIM PRI 082 QUEEN AN
WALLS, WILLIAM QUE 138 1ST E DI
WALLS, WILLIAM CEC 205 7TH E DI
WALLS, WILLIAM S. QUE 177 2ND E DI
WALLS, WILLIAM-BLACK QUE 147 1ST E DI
WALLS, GEORGE QUE 171 2ND E DI
WALLY, CHARLE SR. BAL 290 12TH WAR
WALLY, ISACK TAL 063 EASTON D
WALMSLEY, ELINOR BAL 408 14TH WAR
WALMSLEY, JAMES BAL 245 12TH WAR
WALMSLEY, LOUISA CEC 014 ELKTON 3
WALMSLEY, LUCRETIA BAL 375 3RD WARD
WALMSLY, GEORGE CEC 053 1ST E DI
WALMSLY, JOHN KEN 299 3RD DIST
WALMSLY, JOHN H. CEC 063 1ST E DI
WALMSLY, LAURA BAL 013 4TH WARD
WALMSLY, MARTHY BAL 068 18TH WAR
WALMSLY, MARY CEC 026 ELKTON 3
WALMSLY, ROBERT CEC 065 1ST E DI
WALMSLY, SARAH CEC 052 1ST E DI
WALMSLY, SARAH CEC 057 1ST E DI
WALRAVEN, JOSEPH KEN 245 2ND DIST
WALSEN, JOHN BAL 025 18TH WAR
WALSH, ALIAN BAL 441 14TH WAR
WALSH, ANDREW ALL 051 10TH E.D
WALSH, ANNA BAL 207 11TH WAR
WALSH, ARON BAL 315 3RD WARD
WALSH, BIDDY BAL 307 3RD WARD
WALSH, BRIDGET BAL 360 3RD WARD
WALSH, BRIGET BAL 275 17TH WAR
WALSH, CATHARINE ALL 056 10TH E.D
WALSH, CATHARINE BAL 232 2ND WARD
WALSH, CATHERINE BAL 383 3RD WARD
WALSH, CHARLES BAL 080 4TH WARD
WALSH, CHARLOTT BAL 348 3RD WARD
WALSH, CHARLOTTE BAL 327 3RD WARD
WALSH, DAVID BAL 127 5TH WARD
WALSH, EDWARD ALL 130 4TH E.D.
WALSH, ELIZA J. BAL 080 4TH WARD
WALSH, ELIZABETH BAL 046 4TH WARD
WALSH, EUPHEMIA BAL 420 3RD WARD
WALSH, FRANCIS BAL 341 7TH WARD
WALSH, JAMES BAL 153 1ST WARD
WALSH, JAMES BAL 181 6TH WARD
WALSH, JOHN ALL 141 6TH E.D.
WALSH, JOHN ALL 048 10TH E.D
WALSH, JOHN ALL 052 10TH E.D
WALSH, JOHN ALL 046 10TH E.D
WALSH, JOHN ALL 155 6TH E.D.
WALSH, JOHN BAL 097 5TH WARD
WALSH, JOHN BAL 402 3RD WARD
WALSH, JOSEPH ALL 092 5TH E.D.
WALSH, JOSEPH BAL 019 9TH WARD
WALSH, JOSEPH BAL 348 3RD WARD
WALSH, JOSIAH WAS 135 HAGERSTO
WALSH, JULIA BAL 396 3RD WARD
WALSH, LAURENCE BAL 060 4TH WARD
WALSH, LAWRENCE J. BAL 122 11TH WAR
WALSH, MARGARET BAL 439 14TH WAR
WALSH, MARTHA BAL 044 4TH WARD
WALSH, MARTIN ALL 156 6TH E.D.
WALSH, MARTIN ALL 130 4TH E.D.
WALSH, MARY BAL 404 3RD WARD
WALSH, MARY BAL 291 12TH WAR
WALSH, MARY ALL 253 CUMBERLA
WALSH, MICHAEL ALL 129 4TH E.D.
WALSH, MICHAEL ALL 082 5TH E.D.
WALSH, MICHAEL ALL 052 10TH E.D
WALSH, MICHAEL ALL 053 10TH E.D
WALSH, MICHAEL ALL 049 10TH E.D
WALSH, MICHAEL BAL 029 4TH WARD
WALSH, MICHAEL QUE 219 3RD E DI
WALSH, MISS A. FRE 198 5TH E DI
WALSH, PATRICK ALL 056 10TH E.D
WALSH, PATRICK ALL 076 5TH E.D.
WALSH, PHILIP BAL 162 11TH WAR
WALSH, ROBERT H. BAL 385 3RD WARD
WALSH, SIMON BAL 368 3RD WARD
WALSH, SNOWDEN BAL 442 14TH WAR
WALSH, SUSAN BAL 053 9TH WARD
WALSH, T. YATES BAL 205 11TH WAR
WALSH, THOMAS BAL 125 5TH WARD
WALSH, THOMAS ALL 048 10TH E.D
WALSH, THOMAS ALL 141 6TH E.D.
WALSH, THOMAS ALL 256 CUMBERLA
WALSH, TIMOTHY BAL 201 11TH WAR
WALSH, VALENTINE ANN 419 HOWARD D
WALSH, WILLIAM BAL 127 5TH WARD
WALSH, WILLIAM BAL 045 18TH WAR
WALSH, YETTA BAL 006 EASTERN
WALSINGHAM, JOHN BAL 101 10TH WAR
WALSON, ISAAC ALL 187 9TH E.D.
WALSON, JESSE ALL 187 9TH E.D.
WALSON, THOMAS H. ALL 189 9TH E.D.
WALSTINE, MARY BAL 321 7TH WARD
WALSTON, CHARLES G. SOM 503 SALISBUR
WALSTON, CLEMENT* DOR 303 1ST DIST
WALSTON, ELEANOR SOM 400 BRINKLEY
WALSTON, ELIZA SOM 547 TYASKIN
WALSTON, GEORGE WOR 232 6TH E DI
WALSTON, GREENBURY SOM 496 SALISBUR
WALSTON, ISAAC SOM 397 BRINKLEY
WALSTON, JAMES SOM 443 DAMES QU
WALSTON, JAMES SOM 435 PRINCESS
WALSTON, JAMES E. SOM 357 BRINKLEY
WALSTON, JOHN T. SOM 357 BRINKLEY
WALSTON, LEAH SOM 396 BRINKLEY
WALSTON, MARY SOM 541 TYASKIN
WALSTON, RILEY Q. WOR 202 4TH E DI
WALSTON, ZEPORA SOM 394 BRINKLEY
WALSTON, ZEPORA SOM 385 BRINKLEY
WALSTROM, SARAH J. HAR 007 1ST DIST
WALSTRUM, PETER BAL 047 15TH WAR
WALSTRUM, PETER BAL 061 15TH WAR
WALT, ARMETA BAL 022 18TH WAR
WALT, JOHN PRI 030 VANSVILL
WALT, THOMAS TAL 040 EASTON D
WALTAMYER, MARY A. BAL 271 1ST DIST
WALTE,R JOHN CAR 223 5TH DIST
WALTEMEYER, CHRISTIAN BAL 204 6TH DIST
WALTEMYER, ADAM BAL 270 1ST DIST
WALTEMYER, JOSEPH WAS 238 CAVETOWN
WALTEMYER, SAMUEL BAL 435 1ST DIST
WALTENNBRICK, JOHN BAL 147 11TH WAR
WALTER, AMBROSE BAL 033 9TH WARD
WALTER, ANDREW BAL 399 1ST DIST
WALTER, ANN ALL 234 CUMBERLA
WALTER, ANN BAL 431 14TH WAR
WALTER, ANN M. BAL 062 4TH WARD
WALTER, ANNA M. BAL 232 1ST DIST
WALTER, ASBURY BAL 275 7TH WARD
WALTER, AUGUST BAL 274 7TH WARD
WALTER, BENARD BAL 065 1ST WARD
WALTER, BENJAMIN BAL 225 19TH WAR
WALTER, CATHARIEN BAL 354 13TH WAR
WALTER, EDWARD BAL 075 4TH WARD
WALTER, EDWARD BAL 075 4TH WARD
WALTER, ELIZABETH SOM 544 TYASKIN
WALTER, ELIZABETH* SOM 493 SALISBUR
WALTER, ELLEN SOM 494 SALISBUR
WALTER, EMELIA BAL 352 1ST DIST
WALTER, FRANCIS SOM 521 BARREN C
WALTER, GEORGE WAS 138 HAGERSTO
WALTER, GEORGE BAL 385 8TH WARD
WALTER, GEORGE BAL 431 14TH WAR
WALTER, GEORGE A. C. SOM 544 TYASKIN
WALTER, GEORGE D. SOM 544 TYASKIN
WALTER, GEORGE R. SOM 519 BARREN C
WALTER, HANDY J. * TAL 072 EASTON T
WALTER, HANSON ALL 021 2ND E.D.
WALTER, HENRY ALL 021 2ND E.D.
WALTER, HENRY BAL 072 1ST WARD
WALTER, HENRY BAL 238 1ST DIST
WALTER, HENRY BAL 221 12TH WAR
WALTER, HENRY BAL 247 20TH WAR
WALTER, HENRY BAL 120 18TH WAR
WALTER, HERMAN BAL 012 4TH WARD
WALTER, HIRAM C. BAL 402 14TH WAR
WALTER, ISAAC BAL 311 12TH WAR
WALTER, ISSAKER DOR 431 1ST DIST
WALTER, J. R. BAL 048 9TH WARD
WALTER, JACOB BAL 313 12TH WAR
WALTER, JACOB BAL 271 12TH WAR
WALTER, JAMES BAL 137 1ST WARD
WALTER, JAMES SOM 449 DAMES QU
WALTER, JAMES H. SOM 547 TYASKIN
WALTER, JAMES N. SOM 548 TYASKIN
WALTER, JANE PRI 078 MARLBROU
WALTER, JESSE SOM 533 QUANTICO
WALTER, JOHN FRE 009 FREDERIC
WALTER, JOHN DOR 342 3RD DIVI
WALTER, JOHN FRE 407 JEFFERSO
WALTER, JOHN CAR 344 6TH DIST
WALTER, JOHN FRE 180 5TH E DI
WALTER, JOHN FRE 117 CREAGERS
WALTER, JOHN BAL 305 7TH WARD
WALTER, JOHN BAL 008 15TH WAR
WALTER, JOHN BAL 122 1ST WARD
WALTER, JOHN BAL 333 3RD WARD
WALTER, JOHN F. WAS 246 SMITHSBU
WALTER, JOHN G. BAL 336 7TH WARD
WALTER, JOHN H. BAL 313 12TH WAR
WALTER, JOSEPH BAL 153 2ND DIST
WALTER, JOSEPH BAL 359 13TH WAR
WALTER, JOSEPH CEC 181 7TH E DI
WALTER, LEVIN SOM 545 TYASKIN
WALTER, LEVIN A. H. SOM 548 TYASKIN
WALTER, LEVIN* SOM 551 TYASKIN
WALTER, MARGARET SOM 545 TYASKIN
WALTER, MARGARET CAR 386 2ND DIST
WALTER, MARGARET FRE 090 FREDERIC
WALTER, MARGARET BAL 304 1ST DIST
WALTER, MARIA BAL 099 5TH WARD
WALTER, MARY BAL 186 16TH WAR
WALTER, MARY BAL 271 12TH WAR
WALTER, MARY SOM 451 DAMES QU
WALTER, MICHAEL BAL 021 9TH WARD
WALTER, PHILIP BAL 333 3RD WARD
WALTER, ROBERT SOM 545 TYASKIN
WALTER, ROBERT B. BAL 374 1ST DIST
WALTER, SALLY SOM 541 TYASKIN
WALTER, SARAH A. BAL 367 3RD WARD
WALTER, SUSAN SOM 539 TYASKIN
WALTER, SUSAN SOM 520 BARREN C
WALTER, THOMAS MGM 416 MEDLEY 3
WALTER, WILLAIM BAL 286 2ND WARD
WALTER, WILLIAM BAL 313 7TH WARD
WALTER, WILLIAM ALL 023 2ND E.D.
WALTER, WILLIAM ALL 184 9TH E.D.

Name	County	Page	District
WALTER, WILLIAM	MGM	407	MEDLEY 3
WALTER, WILLIAM	FRE	212	BUCKEYST
WALTER, WILLIAM	BAL	143	11TH WAR
WALTER, WILLIAM	SOM	544	TYASKIN
WALTER, WILLIAM	QUE	198	3RD E DI
WALTER, WILLIAM	WAS	163	2ND DIST
WALTER, MAHALEY	FRE	224	BUCKEYST
WALTERMYER, DANFORD *	BAL	057	18TH WAR
WALTERS, AGNES	BAL	215	11TH WAR
WALTERS, ALEXANDER K.	BAL	229	1ST DIST
WALTERS, ANN	BAL	175	2ND DIST
WALTERS, ANN	CHA	292	BOJANTOW
WALTERS, ARTHUR	BAL	066	1ST WARD
WALTERS, BENJAMIN	ANN	424	HOWARD D
WALTERS, CHARLES	BAL	164	1ST WARD
WALTERS, CHARLES *	HAR	195	3RD DIST
WALTERS, ELIZA	BAL	169	19TH WAR
WALTERS, ELIZABETH	BAL	330	1ST DIST
WALTERS, EPINALLS*	DOR	319	1ST DIST
WALTERS, FERDINAND	BAL	277	1ST DIST
WALTERS, GEORGE	BAL	142	2ND DIST
WALTERS, GEORGE K.	ANN	482	HOWARD D
WALTERS, GEORGE W.	BAL	147	11TH WAR
WALTERS, HENRY	BAL	032	4TH WARD
WALTERS, HENRY	ALL	065	10TH E.D
WALTERS, HENRY	BAL	164	1ST WARD
WALTERS, HENRY	BAL	133	1ST WARD
WALTERS, HETTA	BAL	378	1ST DIST
WALTERS, JACOB	BAL	270	2ND WARD
WALTERS, JACOB	ALL	064	10TH E.D
WALTERS, JACOB	BAL	174	2ND DIST
WALTERS, JACOB T.	QUE	224	4TH E DI
WALTERS, JAMES H.	BAL	320	3RD WARD
WALTERS, JOHN	BAL	001	15TH WAR
WALTERS, JOHN	BAL	129	11TH WAR
WALTERS, JOHN	BAL	047	4TH WARD
WALTERS, JOHN S.	QUE	168	2ND E DI
WALTERS, JOSEPH	BAL	265	1ST DIST
WALTERS, JOSEPH	ANN	337	3RD DIST
WALTERS, JOSEPHINE	BAL	146	11TH WAR
WALTERS, MAHALY *	HAR	195	3RD DIST
WALTERS, MARGARET	BAL	456	14TH WAR
WALTERS, MARY	BAL	156	11TH WAR
WALTERS, MARY	BAL	164	11TH WAR
WALTERS, NANCY	ANN	425	HOWARD D
WALTERS, P.	BAL	281	2ND WARD
WALTERS, ROBERT	BAL	161	1ST WARD
WALTERS, ROBERT	QUE	179	2ND E DI
WALTERS, SAMUEL	BAL	330	1ST DIST
WALTERS, SAMUEL	BAL	048	4TH WARD
WALTERS, SAMUEL	QUE	154	1ST E DI
WALTERS, SARAH E.	FRE	113	CREAGERS
WALTERS, SUSAN	BAL	277	1ST DIST
WALTERS, THOMAS	BAL	171	1ST WARD
WALTERS, WILLIAM	BAL	163	1ST WARD
WALTERS, WILLIAM	BAL	320	1ST DIST
WALTERS, WILLIAM	BAL	127	1ST WARD
WALTERS, WILLIAM	BAL	138	11TH WAR
WALTERS, WILLIAM	HAR	098	2ND DIST
WALTHAM, ALICE A.	HAR	100	2ND DIST
WALTHAM, ELIZABETH	BAL	094	15TH WAR
WALTHAN, WILLIAM A.	FRE	134	CREAGERS
WALTHEIMER, HENRY	CAR	328	MANCHEST
WALTING, ELLEN F.	BAL	272	2ND WARD
WALTING, SOPHIA	BAL	272	2ND WARD
WALTING, TUOK*	BAL	296	12TH WAR
WALTINGER, HENRY	BAL	165	19TH WAR
WALTJEN, AUGUST	BAL	268	7TH WARD
WALTJEN, FREDERICK	BAL	268	7TH WARD
WALTMAN, HANNAH	FRE	450	8TH E DI
WALTMAN, JACOB	FRE	246	NEW MARK
WALTMAN, JOHN E.	FRE	450	8TH E DI
WALTMYER, JOHN	BAL	216	19TH WAR
WALTNER, EMORY	BAL	141	2ND DIST
WALTON, ANN	BAL	242	6TH WARD
WALTON, ANN	BAL	092	5TH WARD
WALTON, CATHARINE	BAL	195	11TH WAR
WALTON, E.	BAL	044	4TH WARD
WALTON, EDWARD	HAR	083	2ND DIST
WALTON, EDWARD H.	HAR	083	2ND DIST
WALTON, ELIJAH	BAL	256	12TH WAR
WALTON, ELIJAH	BAL	331	13TH WAR
WALTON, EMMA J.	CEC	001	ELKTON 3
WALTON, HENRIETTA	HAR	121	2ND DIST
WALTON, HESTER	BAL	256	20TH WAR
WALTON, HWESTER	HAR	190	3RD DIST
WALTON, J. L. F.	BAL	147	1ST WARD
WALTON, JAMES	BAL	041	9TH WARD
WALTON, JAMES	CEC	001	ELKTON 3
WALTON, JAMES B.	ALL	244	CUMBERLA
WALTON, JANE	BAL	246	20TH WAR
WALTON, JESSE	BAL	161	6TH WARD
WALTON, JOHN	ALL	155	6TH E.D.
WALTON, JOHN	HAR	017	1ST DIST
WALTON, JOHN	BAL	289	17TH WAR
WALTON, JOHN SR.	ANN	266	ANNAPOLI
WALTON, JOSEPH	BAL	302	17TH WAR
WALTON, PRUSILLA	SOM	539	TYASKIN
WALTON, RAPHAEL	BAL	050	9TH WARD
WALTON, RICHARD	BAL	207	19TH WAR
WALTON, SAMUEL	BAL	278	17TH WAR
WALTON, SAMUEL B.	HAR	085	2ND DIST
WALTON, THEADDORE	BAL	117	1ST WARD
WALTON, THOMAS	ANN	266	ANNAPOLI
WALTON, THOMAS	HAR	111	2ND DIST
WALTON, THOMAS	BAL	469	14TH WAR
WALTON, THORNTON	HAR	083	2ND DIST
WALTON, WILLIAM	CAR	193	4TH DIST
WALTON, WILLIAM	BAL	129	2ND DIST
WALTON, WILLIAM	BAL	264	2ND WARD
WALTS, CHARLES	BAL	459	8TH WARD
WALTS, FRANCIS A.	FRE	226	BUCKEYST
WALTS, GEORGE	QUE	128	1ST E DI
WALTS, HESTER A.	BAL	397	3RD WARD
WALTS, HETTY*	BAL	402	3RD WARD
WALTS, JEMIMA	BAL	172	2ND DIST
WALTUN, AGUSTUS	HAR	196	3RD DIST
WALTZ, ANTONY	BAL	132	2ND DIST
WALTZ, CHRISTIANN	ALL	059	10TH E.D
WALTZ, ELIAS	FRE	421	8TH E DI
WALTZ, ELIZABETH	FRE	413	8TH E DI
WALTZ, ELIZABETH	WAS	235	1ST DIST
WALTZ, ENOCH J.	FRE	410	8TH E DI
WALTZ, HANNAH	ALL	124	4TH E.D.
WALTZ, JACOB	FRE	420	8TH E DI
WALTZ, JAMES	WAS	205	1ST DIST
WALTZ, JOHN	WAS	235	1ST DIST
WALTZ, JOHN	BAL	166	16TH WAR
WALTZ, JOHN L.	FRE	255	NEW MARK
WALTZ, LEWIS	CAR	383	2ND DIST
WALTZ, MARGARET	WAS	155	HAGERSTO
WALTZ, MARTIN	WAS	241	CAVETOWN
WALTZ, SUSAN	WAS	235	1ST DIST
WALTZ, SUSANNA	WAS	241	CAVETOWN
WALTZ, WILLAIM	ALL	061	10TH E.D
WALZBERGER, SIMON	BAL	319	12TH WAR
WAMBACH, AUGUST	BAL	131	16TH WAR
WAMBACH, WILLIAM	BAL	139	16TH WAR
WAMBACK, CHARLES	BAL	214	17TH WAR
WAMBACK, EMMANUEL	BAL	396	8TH WARD
WAMBAUGH, JOHN	HAR	102	2ND DIST
WAMBERGHER, PETER	ALL	153	6TH E.D.
WAMBISKEN, FREDERICK	BAL	268	2ND WARD
WAMES, WILLIAM *	ANN	353	3RD DIST
WAMME, FRANCIS L.	BAL	313	12TH WAR
WAMP, JOSEPH	ALL	172	7TH E.D.
WAMPLER, ABRAHAM	CAR	275	7TH DIST
WAMPLER, ELIZABETH	CAR	264	WESTMINS
WAMPLER, HENRY H.	CAR	272	WESTMINS
WAMPLER, J. L.	BAL	159	11TH WAR
WAMPLER, JEREMIAH	WAS	274	RIDGEVIL
WAMPLER, LEWIS	CAR	274	7TH DIST
WAMPLER, WILLIAM	CAR	348	6TH DIST
WAMPS, MARY	ALL	173	7TH E.D.
WAMS, ANN *	BAL	042	18TH WAR
WAMSLEY, BENJAMIN	BAL	278	2ND WARD
WAMSLEY, GEORGE	CEC	049	1ST E DI
WAMSLEY, JAMES	BAL	447	8TH WARD
WAMSLEY, JOHN F.	BAL	283	2ND WARD
WAMSLEY, LAURA	BAL	070	18TH WAR
WAMSLEY, SARAH	BAL	098	2ND DIST
WAMSLY, MARGARET	CEC	063	1ST E DI
WAMSLY, ROBERT	CEC	001	ELKTON 3
WANDEL, MARY	FRE	032	FREDERIC
WANDER, GEORGE	BAL	372	13TH WAR
WANDER, GEORGE	BAL	428	8TH WARD
WANDERER, LEWIS	BAL	395	8TH WARD
WANE, LOUIS	BAL	294	1ST DIST
WANE, MARY	BAL	236	1ST DIST
WANER, ADAM C.	ANN	491	HOWARD D
WANER, ANN J.*	BAL	269	7TH WARD
WANER, FRANCIS	FRE	024	FREDERIC
WANER, JOSEPH	WAS	041	2ND SUBD
WANEY, ELIZA	BAL	225	12TH WAR
WANGER, SANE	BAL	277	12TH WAR
WANGUS, JENKIN	BAL	135	16TH WAR
WANHAM, ANN*	TAL	008	EASTON D
WANIPLER, GEORGE E.	CAR	272	WESTMINS
WANISH, JIM*	TAL	008	EASTON D
WANK, SARAH	BAL	226	12TH WAR
WANN, ABRAHAM	HAR	062	1ST DIST
WANN, BENJAMIN	BAL	119	2ND DIST
WANN, CHARLES	BAL	124	2ND DIST
WANN, HANNAH	BAL	119	2ND DIST
WANN, JACOB	HAR	113	2ND DIST
WANN, JAMES	HAR	113	2ND DIST
WANN, JOHN	HAR	104	2ND DIST
WANN, MARGARETT P.	HAR	110	2ND DIST
WANN, WILLIAM	HAR	113	2ND DIST
WANN, WILLIAM J.	HAR	093	2ND DIST
WANNAL, JOSEPH F.	BAL	033	15TH WAR
WANNAL, MARY A.	ANN	465	HOWARD D
WANNALL, WILLIAM H.	BAL	204	17TH WAR
WANNE, FRANCIS	BAL	353	13TH WAR
WANNELL, JAMES	WOR	189	7TH E DI
WANNER, GUTLIP	WAS	098	2ND DIST
WANNER, HENRY *	ALL	119	5TH E.D.
WANNER, LEWIS	WAS	102	2ND DIST
WANSE, CATHARINE	BAL	354	13TH WAR
WANSY, JOHN	WAS	130	HAGERSTO
WANTLAND, HENRY	BAL	423	1ST DIST
WANTON, MACK	MGM	398	ROCKERLE
WANTON, RICHARD	MGM	379	ROCKERLE
WANTS, ALLICE	WAS	266	1ST DIST
WANTS, GEORGE	CAR	337	6TH DIST
WANTWITH, GEORGE	BAL	167	1ST WARD
WANTY, LEVENIA *	BAL	091	18TH WAR
WANTZ, CATHARINE	CAR	379	2ND DIST
WANTZ, DANIEL	WAS	172	FUNKSTOW
WANTZ, DAVID	CAR	267	WESTMINS
WANTZ, DAVID	CAR	293	7TH DIST
WANTZ, ELIZABETH	BAL	257	20TH WAR
WANTZ, HENRY	BAL	323	12TH WAR
WANTZ, JACOB	BAL	432	1ST DIST
WANTZ, JOHN	BAL	257	20TH WAR
WANTZ, JOHN C.	CAR	267	WESTMINS
WANTZ, LEVENIA *	BAL	091	18TH WAR
WANTZE, MARY	CAR	186	8TH DIST
WANTZNAN, FREDERICK	BAL	244	2ND WARD
WANWICK, JOSEPH	CEC	035	CHESAPEA
WANZAL, CONRAD	ALL	257	CUMBERLA
WAP, GEORGE	BAL	141	1ST WARD
WAPLES, WILLIAM A.	WOR	180	6TH E DI
WAPPINS, MARY W.-BLACK	CAR	364	9TH DIST
WAPPINS, SARAH-BLACK	CAR	382	2ND DIST
WAPPINS, WILFORD	CAR	361	9TH DIST
WAR, JOHN	MGM	408	MEDLEY 3
WARBINHURST, RANDOLPH	BAL	253	1ST DIST
WARBLE, JACOB D.	WAS	231	1ST DIST
WARBURTON, THOMAS	CEC	122	4TH E DI
WARCAM, ELIZABETH *	BAL	357	1ST DIST
WARCHAND, ELIAS	WAS	001	WILLIAMS
WARD, , ROBERT	KEN	273	1ST DIST
WARD, A.	FRE	200	5TH E DI
WARD, AARON	SOM	390	BRINKLEY
WARD, AARON	BAL	454	1ST DIST
WARD, ABE-BLACK	QUE	125	1ST E DI
WARD, ABRAHAM	KEN	306	3RD DIST
WARD, ALEXANDER	KEN	226	2ND DIST
WARD, ALLEN	BAL	030	18TH WAR
WARD, ANN	BAL	042	9TH WARD
WARD, ANN E.	CAL	054	3RD DIST
WARD, ANNA M.	BAL	051	18TH WAR
WARD, ASA	FRE	252	NEW MARK
WARD, B. C.	BAL	146	11TH WAR
WARD, BARBARY	BAL	204	11TH WAR
WARD, BARNY	BAL	002	EASTERN
WARD, BEN	PRI	110	PISCATAW
WARD, BENJAMIN	SOM	382	BRINKLEY
WARD, BENJAMIN	CAL	016	1ST DIST
WARD, BETSEY	SOM	374	BRINKLEY
WARD, BRIDGET	BAL	144	11TH WAR
WARD, CAROLINE	BAL	071	15TH WAR
WARD, CATHARINE	WAS	086	2ND SUBD
WARD, CATHERINE	BAL	047	9TH WARD
WARD, CECELIA	KEN	308	3RD DIST
WARD, CEPHES	CAL	017	1ST DIST
WARD, CHARLES	BAL	469	14TH WAR
WARD, CHARLES	HAR	032	1ST DIST
WARD, CHARLES	SOM	384	BRINKLEY
WARD, CHARLES	BAL	373	3RD WARD
WARD, CHARLES	BAL	313	12TH WAR
WARD, CHARLES H.	SOM	361	BRINKLEY
WARD, CHARLOTTE	SOM	450	DAMES QU
WARD, CHRISTIANNA S.	CHA	261	MIDDLETO
WARD, DANIEL	FRE	335	MIDDLETO
WARD, DANIEL	CEC	016	ELKTON 3
WARD, DANIEL	SOM	370	BRINKLEY
WARD, DAVID	SOM	367	BRINKLEY
WARD, DAVID A.	CAL	032	2ND DIST
WARD, E. GEORGE	MGM	339	CLARKSBU
WARD, EDWARD V.	BAL	390	13TH WAR
WARD, ELISABETH	BAL	302	3RD WARD
WARD, ELISHA	SOM	383	BRINKLEY
WARD, ELIZA	WAS	252	1ST DIST
WARD, ELIZA	CEC	058	1ST E DI
WARD, ELIZA A.	WOR	209	4TH E DI
WARD, ELIZA-MULATTO	MGM	429	CLARKSTR
WARD, ELIZABETH	BAL	259	17TH WAR
WARD, ELIZABETH	ANN	400	8TH DIST
WARD, ELIZABETH *	BAL	317	20TH WAR
WARD, ELIZABETH A.	WOR	191	8TH E DI
WARD, ELLINER	CEC	032	CHESAPEA
WARD, EMELINE	CHA	263	MIDDLETO
WARD, EMER	BAL	136	11TH WAR
WARD, EMILY J.	BAL	027	15TH WAR
WARD, F.A.	PRI	053	AQUASCO
WARD, FARY	BAL	016	2ND DIST
WARD, FENTON	BAL	381	1ST DIST
WARD, FRANKLIN	CAL	059	3RD DIST
WARD, GEORGE	CAR	196	4TH DIST
WARD, GEORGE	BAL	005	EASTERN
WARD, GEORGE	WOR	344	1ST E DI
WARD, GEORGE F.	SOM	395	BRINKLEY
WARD, GEORGE M.	HAR	112	2ND DIST
WARD, GEORGE R.	BAL	387	13TH WAR
WARD, GEORGE W.	DOR	382	1ST DIST
WARD, GEORGE W.	BAL	205	11TH WAR
WARD, GEORGE-BLACK	QUE	125	1ST E DI
WARD, H.M.	PRI	118	PISCATAW
WARD, HANDY	WOR	246	1ST CENS
WARD, HANNAH	BAL	340	13TH WAR
WARD, HARRIET	KEN	244	2ND DIST
WARD, HENRY	KEN	235	2ND DIST
WARD, HENRY	CHA	291	MIDDLETO
WARD, HENRY	BAL	465	14TH WAR
WARD, HENRY	WOR	235	6TH E DI
WARD, HENRY	SOM	371	BRINKLEY
WARD, HENRY	SOM	370	BRINKLEY
WARD, HENRY	WOR	314	2ND E DI
WARD, HENRY	ANN	340	3RD DIST
WARD, HENRY	BAL	156	1ST WARD
WARD, HENRY C.	BAL	470	14TH WAR
WARD, HENRY C.	BAL	384	13TH WAR
WARD, HOPE	SOM	383	BRINKLEY
WARD, HORACE	MGM	339	CLARKSBU
WARD, HUGH	HAR	115	2ND DIST
WARD, IGNATIUS	MGM	324	CRACKLIN
WARD, IRA	BAL	205	19TH WAR
WARD, ISAAC	SOM	388	BRINKLEY
WARD, ISAAC	WOR	328	1ST E DI
WARD, ISAAC W.	SOM	377	BRINKLEY
WARD, JACOB	SOM	384	BRINKLEY
WARD, JACOB-BLACK	WOR	349	1ST E DI
WARD, JAEMS	BAL	100	2ND DIST
WARD, JAMES	ALL	245	CUMBERLA
WARD, JAMES	ALL	232	CUMBERLA
WARD, JAMES	ALL	233	CUMBERLA
WARD, JAMES	BAL	163	1ST WARD
WARD, JAMES	BAL	447	1ST DIST
WARD, JAMES	BAL	193	17TH WAR
WARD, JAMES	BAL	122	1ST WARD
WARD, JAMES	BAL	180	2ND DIST
WARD, JAMES	BAL	361	8TH WARD
WARD, JAMES	SOM	362	BRINKLEY
WARD, JAMES	SOM	390	BRINKLEY
WARD, JAMES	WAS	164	2ND DIST
WARD, JAMES	WAS	083	2ND SUBD
WARD, JAMES	WOR	231	6TH E DI
WARD, JAMES	BAL	198	19TH WAR
WARD, JAMES	CEC	032	CHESAPEA
WARD, JAMES	FRE	161	EMMITTSB
WARD, JAMES	CAL	054	3RD DIST
WARD, JAMES R.	WAS	098	2ND DIST
WARD, JARRETT E.	HAR	170	3RD DIST
WARD, JENKINS	WOR	166	6TH E DI
WARD, JENKINS H.	WOR	235	6TH E DI
WARD, JESSE	BAL	218	6TH DIST
WARD, JOHN	BAL	217	6TH DIST
WARD, JOHN	BAL	448	1ST DIST
WARD, JOHN	BAL	119	1ST WARD
WARD, JOHN	BAL	158	1ST WARD
WARD, JOHN	ANN	441	HOWARD D
WARD, JOHN	ANN	442	HOWARD D
WARD, JOHN	BAL	117	2ND DIST
WARD, JOHN	BAL	206	11TH WAR
WARD, JOHN	ALL	048	10TH E.D
WARD, JOHN	ANN	402	8TH DIST
WARD, JOHN	PRI	031	VANSVILL
WARD, JOHN	KEN	256	1ST DIST
WARD, JOHN	SOM	368	BRINKLEY
WARD, JOHN	SOM	389	BRINKLEY
WARD, JOHN	WOR	346	1ST E DI
WARD, JOHN	QUE	236	4TH E DI
WARD, JOHN	HAR	163	3RD DIST
WARD, JOHN	BAL	160	11TH WAR
WARD, JOHN	CEC	038	CHESAPEA
WARD, JOHN	HAR	075	BEL AIR
WARD, JOHN	FRE	325	MIDDLETO
WARD, JOHN	BAL	053	18TH WAR
WARD, JOHN	FRE	389	PETERSVI
WARD, JOHN W.	ANN	400	8TH DIST
WARD, JOHN D.	CAL	052	3RD DIST
WARD, JOHN E.	FRE	241	NEW MARK
WARD, JOHN E.	BAL	138	16TH WAR
WARD, JOHN G.	SOM	388	BRINKLEY
WARD, JOHN J.	BAL	055	18TH WAR
WARD, JOHN P.	BAL	381	1ST DIST
WARD, JOHN S.	CAL	049	3RD DIST
WARD, JOHN S.	CAL	056	3RD DIST
WARD, JOHN T.	CAR	281	7TH DIST
WARD, JOHN T.	CEC	016	ELKTON 3
WARD, JOHN W.	BAL	177	2ND DIST
WARD, JOHN W.	PRI	105	PISCATAW
WARD, JOSEPH	ALL	248	CUMBERLA
WARD, JOSEPH	BAL	215	6TH WARD
WARD, JOSEPH	CAR	200	4TH DIST
WARD, JOSEPH	HAR	111	2ND DIST
WARD, JOSEPH W.	BAL	057	15TH WAR
WARD, JOSHUA	BAL	155	2ND DIST

Name	County	Page	District
WARD, JOSHUA-BLACK	WOR	337	1ST E DI
WARD, JOSPHUS	FRE	353	MIDDLETO
WARD, LAVINIA	BAL	202	6TH WARD
WARD, LEAH C.	WOR	236	6TH E DI
WARC, LEMUEL	BAL	328	1ST DIST
WARD, LEVI	WOR	317	2ND E DI
WARD, LEVIN	SOM	387	BRINKLEY
WARC, LEVINA	BAL	239	1ST DIST
WARD, LIDDY-MULATTO	BAL	223	2ND WARD
WARD, LOAF	WAS	114	2ND DIST
WARD, LOUIS	BAL	030	18TH WAR
WARD, LOUISA	BAL	042	9TH WARD
WARD, LOVEY	WOR	206	4TH E DI
WARD, LYDIA	CEC	058	1ST E DI
WARD, LYDIA	FRE	353	MIDDLETO
WARD, M.	FRE	200	5TH E DI
WARD, MAR A. C.	CHA	242	HILLTOP
WARD, MARGARET	BAL	345	13TH WAR
WARD, MARGARET	BAL	250	17TH WAR
WARD, MARGARET	BAL	002	9TH WARD
WARD, MARGARET E.	CAL	057	3RD DIST
WARD, MARIA	BAL	082	2ND DIST
WARD, MARTIN	ALL	049	10TH E.D
WARD, MARY	ALL	094	5TH E.D.
WARD, MARY	BAL	242	12TH WAR
WARD, MARY	BAL	127	5TH WARD
WARD, MARY	BAL	299	12TH WAR
WARD, MARY	BAL	110	10TH WAR
WARD, MARY	BAL	374	8TH WARD
WARD, MARY	BAL	278	7TH WARD
WARD, MARY	BAL	371	13TH WAR
WARD, MARY	BAL	087	4TH WARD
WARD, MARY	HAR	114	2ND DIST
WARD, MARY	MGM	379	ROCKERLE
WARD, MARY	SOM	380	BRINKLEY
WARD, MARY	SOM	373	BRINKLEY
WARD, MARY	ST	348	5TH E DI
WARD, MARY	WAS	233	1ST DIST
WARD, MARY	WAS	082	2ND SUBD
WARD, MARY *	BAL	313	20TH WAR
WARC, MARY A.	CAL	024	2ND DIST
WARD, MARY ANN	BAL	333	3RD WARD
WARD, MARY E.	CAL	045	3RD DIST
WARD, MARY S.	CAL	044	3RD DIST
WARD, MICHAEL	HAR	175	3RD DIST
WARD, MICHAEL	BAL	413	1ST DIST
WARD, MICHAEL	KEN	295	3RD DIST
WARD, MILLY	SOM	371	BRINKLEY
WARD, MOSES	WOR	345	1ST E DI
WARD, MRS.	BAL	139	5TH WARD
WARD, NATHAN	CAL	056	3RD DIST
WARD, NATHAN	DOR	390	1ST DIST
WARD, NATHANIEL	BAL	263	17TH WAR
WARD, NED-BLACK	WOR	338	1ST E DI
WARD, NELSON	CAR	217	5TH DIST
WARD, NOAH	SOM	369	BRINKLEY
WARD, OLIVER-BLACK	WOR	349	1ST E DI
WARD, OWEN	BAL	365	13TH WAR
WARD, OWEN	HAR	114	2ND DIST
WARD, OWEN	BAL	319	7TH WARD
WARD, PATRICK	BAL	420	8TH WARD
WARD, PATRICK	HAR	014	1ST DIST
WARD, PATRICK	HAR	177	3RD DIST
WARD, PERRY	CEC	118	4TH E DI
WARD, PLUMMER	CAL	044	3RD DIST
WARC, REBECCA	BAL	326	1ST DIST
WARD, RICHARD	ANN	301	1ST DIST
WARD, RICHARD	CAL	055	3RD DIST
WARD, RICHARD	FRE	332	MIDDLETO
WARD, RICHARD S.	BAL	301	3RD WARD
WARD, ROBERT	BAL	326	1ST DIST
WARD, ROBERT	FRE	415	8TH E DI
WARD, ROBERT *	KEN	222	2ND DIST
WARD, ROBERT H.	BAL	054	9TH WARD
WARC, SAMUEL	BAL	277	1ST DIST
WARD, SAMUEL	CAL	046	3RD DIST
WARD, SAMUEL	CAL	055	3RD DIST
WARD, SAMUEL	WAS	075	2ND SUBD
WARD, SAMUEL	PRI	106	PISCATAW
WARD, SAMUEL W.	CAL	047	3RD DIST
WARD, SAMUL	WAS	115	2ND DIST
WARD, SARAH	ST	295	2ND E DI
WARD, SARAH	BAL	105	15TH WAR
WARD, SARAH	BAL	025	15TH WAR
WARD, SARAH	BAL	042	15TH WAR
WARD, SILAS	MGM	425	MEDLEY 3
WARD, SISTER CATHARINE	FRE	203	5TH E DI
WARD, SISTER MARY CYRIL	FRE	203	5TH E DI
WARD, STEPHEN	SOM	401	BRINKLEY
WARD, STEPHEN-BLACK	WOR	339	1ST E DI
WARD, SUSAN-BLACK	QUE	193	3RD E DI
WARD, THERESA	BAL	109	10TH WAR
WARD, THOMAS	BAL	441	1ST DIST
WARD, THOMAS	BAL	234	6TH WARD
WARD, THOMAS	BAL	022	9TH WARD
WARD, THOMAS	BAL	371	8TH WARD
WARD, THOMAS	WOR	331	1ST E DI
WARD, THOMAS	SOM	366	BRINKLEY
WARD, THOMAS	SOM	369	BRINKLEY
WARD, THOMAS	MGM	403	ROCKERLE
WARD, THOMAS	MGM	421	MEDLEY 3
WARD, THOMAS	HAR	111	2ND DIST
WARD, THOMAS	HAR	108	2ND DIST
WARD, THOMAS	FRE	330	MIDDLETO
WARD, THOMAS	BAL	117	18TH WAR
WARD, THOMAS	DOR	330	3RD DIVI
WARD, THOMAS	CEC	058	1ST E DI
WARD, THOMAS	CAR	192	4TH DIST
WARD, THOMAS C.	ST	348	5TH E DI
WARD, THOMAS JR.	SOM	367	BRINKLEY
WARD, THOMAS M.	BAL	073	15TH WAR
WARD, THOMAS Z.	BAL	361	13TH WAR
WARD, W. H.	BAL	469	14TH WAR
WARD, W.H.	BAL	224	1ST DIST
WARD, WALTER	ANN	303	1ST DIST
WARD, WALTON	SOM	389	BRINKLEY
WARD, WILLAIN	ALL	137	4TH E.D.
WARD, WILLAIM	BAL	027	15TH WAR
WARD, WILLIAM	ALL	113	5TH E.D.
WARD, WILLIAM	ANN	404	8TH DIST
WARD, WILLIAM	ANN	520	HOWARD D
WARD, WILLIAM	BAL	345	3RD WARD
WARD, WILLIAM	BAL	162	1ST WARD
WARD, WILLIAM	BAL	124	16TH WAR
WARD, WILLIAM	BAL	069	10TH WAR
WARD, WILLIAM	BAL	078	1ST WARD
WARD, WILLIAM	BAL	039	2ND DIST
WARD, WILLIAM	SOM	370	BRINKLEY
WARD, WILLIAM	SOM	370	BRINKLEY
WARD, WILLIAN	SOM	370	BRINKLEY
WARD, WILLIAM	SOM	372	BRINKLEY
WARD, WILLIAM	WAS	115	2ND DIST
WARD, WILLIAM	QUE	172	2ND E DI
WARD, WILLIAM	WOR	186	7TH E DI
WARD, WILLIAM	CAR	196	4TH DIST
WARD, WILLIAM	CEC	084	CHARLEST
WARD, WILLIAM	HAR	108	2ND DIST
WARD, WILLIAM	MGM	403	ROCKERLE
WARD, WILLIAM	FRE	200	5TH E DI
WARD, WILLIAM	CHA	288	BOJANTOW
WARD, WILLIAM H.	BAL	235	6TH WARD
WARD, WILLIAM J.	BAL	060	10TH WAR
WARD, WILLIAM M.	BAL	069	10TH WAR
WARD, WILLIAM T.	BAL	147	16TH WAR
WARD, WCRITTA*	SOM	381	BRINKLEY
WARDEBAUGH, JOHN *	BAL	315	12TH WAR
WARDECKER, JOSEPHINE	BAL	352	7TH WARD
WARDECKER, LOUISA	BAL	318	20TH WAR
WARDELL, JOHN A.	BAL	078	18TH WAR
WARDELL, L.	BAL	138	5TH WARD
WARDELL, SAMUEL	BAL	137	5TH WARD
WARDELL, SAMUEL B.	BAL	041	15TH WAR
WARDEN, CATHARINE	BAL	105	2ND DIST
WARDEN, HUGH	BAL	088	4TH WARD
WARDEN, JAMES	BAL	087	4TH WARD
WARDEN, JAMES	BAL	356	3RD WARD
WARDEN, JAMES	BAL	451	1ST DIST
WARDEN, LY	BAL	195	5TH DIST
WARDEN, WILLIAM	BAL	451	1ST DIST
WARDER, ANGELINE	CAR	104	NO TWP L
WARDGELL, JAMES	BAL	382	1ST DIST
WARDIN, SAMUEL S.	CAR	334	MANCHEST
WARDINER, JOHN	ALL	069	5TH E.D.
WARDLE, ISAAC	CEC	185	7TH E DI
WARDNBURGH, WILLIAM	BAL	069	1ST WARD
WARDS, JOHN	BAL	361	8TH WARD
WARDS, JOHN W.	BAL	139	11TH WAR
WARDS, THOMAS	BAL	361	8TH WARD
WARDSWORTH, G.	BAL	101	10TH WAR
WARDWELL, S.W.	ALL	011	3RD E.D.
WARE, AARON	BAL	029	15TH WAR
WARE, ADAM	BAL	287	1ST DIST
WARE, ADDISON B.	CHA	273	ALLENS F
WARE, ALICE	BAL	203	17TH WAR
WARE, ALICE	BAL	081	15TH WAR
WARE, ANDREW	CEC	181	7TH E DI
WARE, ANN	ANN	421	HOWARD D
WARE, ANNE	BAL	091	18TH WAR
WARE, CATHARINE	BAL	391	1ST DIST
WARE, CHARELS	BAL	384	13TH WAR
WARE, CHARLES	BAL	324	1ST DIST
WARE, CHARLES R.	BAL	456	1ST DIST
WARE, CHRISTINA	FRE	326	MIDDLETO
WARE, ELIAS	BAL	038	18TH WAR
WARE, ELIZABETH	CAR	214	5TH DIST
WARE, ELIZABETH	BAL	392	1ST DIST
WARE, ELIZABETH *	BAL	317	20TH WAR
WARE, ELLEN	CEC	028	CHESAPEA
WARE, ETHANAH	CHA	273	ALLENS F
WARE, EVELINA	BAL	404	1ST DIST
WARE, HENRY	BAL	110	1ST WARD
WARE, HENRY	BAL	286	17TH WAR
WARE, JAMES	BAL	378	1ST DIST
WARE, JAMES	BAL	365	1ST DIST
WARE, JAMES	BAL	364	1ST DIST
WARE, JAMES	BAL	202	11TH WAR
WARE, JOHN	BAL	419	8TH WARD
WARE, JOHN	BAL	153	1ST WARD
WARE, JOHN	CAR	223	5TH DIST
WARE, JCHN	BAL	414	3RD WARD
WARE, JOHN	CEC	187	7TH E DI
WARE, JOHN T.	CEC	016	ELKTON 3
WARE, JOHN W.	HAR	065	1ST DIST
WARE, LOUIS	CEC	188	7TH E DI
WARE, LYDIA	BAL	006	EASTERN
WARE, MARGARET	BAL	024	9TH WARD
WARE, MARY	BAL	006	EASTERN
WARE, MARY	BAL	379	1ST DIST
WARE, MARY	CHA	273	ALLENS F
WARE, MARY	CEC	205	7TH E DI
WARE, MARY	BAL	281	20TH WAR
WARE, MARY *	BAL	313	20TH WAR
WARE, MATTHEW	CEC	199	7TH E DI
WARE, MICHAEL	BAL	198	6TH WARD
WARE, NATHAN H.	BAL	456	1ST DIST
WARE, PETER	BAL	217	6TH WARD
WARE, PETER	BAL	434	8TH WARD
WARE, PETER	BAL	312	7TH WARD
WARE, PHILIP	CHA	273	ALLENS F
WARE, RCBERT	CEC	184	7TH E DI
WARE, WILLIAM	CAR	220	5TH DIST
WARE, WILLIAM	BAL	348	7TH WARD
WARE, WILLIAM	BAL	292	1ST DIST
WAREAM, ELIZABETH *	BAL	357	1ST DIST
WAREFIELD, ALBERT H.	CAR	372	9TH DIST
WAREFIELD, BENJAMIN	CAR	366	9TH DIST
WAREFIELD, CARVIL	HAR	176	3RD DIST
WAREFIELD, HENRY	HAR	175	3RD DIST
WAREFIELD, HORATIO S.	CAR	360	9TH DIST
WAREFIELD, JAMES	HAR	174	3RD DIST
WAREFIELD, JSCHUA	CAR	360	9TH DIST
WAREFIELD, SARAH	HAR	174	3RD DIST
WAREFIELD, SUSANER	HAR	176	3RD DIST
WAREFIELD, WESLY T.	CAR	361	9TH DIST
WAREHAM, ABRAM	CEC	072	5TH E DI
WAREHAM, GEORGE	CAR	277	7TH DIST
WAREHAM, JAMES	CEC	029	CHESAPEA
WAREHAM, JOHN G.	CAR	335	6TH DIST
WAREHAM, WILLIAM	BAL	381	8TH WARD
WAREHAME, EPHRAIM	CAR	353	6TH DIST
WAREHARN, ISAAC*	BAL	345	3RD WARD
WAREHARN, JAMES	BAL	345	3RD WARD
WAREHEIM, GEORGE	CAR	335	6TH DIST
WAREHEIM, JOHN	CAR	307	1ST DIST
WAREHEIME, HENRY	CAR	352	6TH DIST
WAREHIEM, SAMUEL	CAR	407	2ND DIST
WAREHIME, JOHN	CAR	172	8TH DIST
WARELONG, MILDRED	BAL	382	13TH WAR
WARENBERGER, MATHIAS	BAL	218	17TH WAR
WARENFELTZ, URIAH	FRE	127	CREAGERS
WARENR, JOHN A.	CAR	392	2ND DIST
WARES, MARGARET	ANN	277	ANNAPOLI
WARF	PRI	028	VANSVILL
WARFE, DANIEL	BAL	093	2ND DIST
WARFEILD, AUGUSTAS	BAL	078	18TH WAR
WARFEILD, JOSEPH G.	BAL	054	18TH WAR
WARFEILD, L.	BAL	151	1ST WARD
WARFEILD, SARAH J.	BAL	048	18TH WAR
WARFFEILD, THOMAS	BAL	034	18TH WAR
WARFIELD, AARON	DOR	403	1ST DIST
WARFIELD, AARON	DOR	387	1ST DIST
WARFIELD, ACSLIA	BAL	129	16TH WAR
WARFIELD, ADAM	BAL	010	1ST WARD
WARFIELD, ALAXANDER	FRE	289	WOODSBOR
WARFIELD, ALBERT G.	ANN	488	HOWARD D
WARFIELD, ALEXANDER	CAR	281	7TH DIST
WARFIELD, ALEXANDER	FRE	443	8TH E DI
WARFIELD, ALFRED	ANN	511	HOWARD D
WARFIELD, ALFRED	BAL	067	10TH WAR
WARFIELD, ALLEN	ANN	358	3RD DIST
WARFIELD, ALLEN	ANN	367	4TH DIST
WARFIELD, AMANDA	ANN	379	4TH DIST
WARFIELD, ANDERSON	BAL	249	12TH WAR
WARFIELD, ANN	ANN	297	1ST DIST
WARFIELD, ANN J.	BAL	013	18TH WAR
WARFIELD, ANNA	BAL	169	6TH WARD
WARFIELD, ASHNY *	MGM	440	CLARKSTR
WARFIELD, AZEL	ANN	512	HOWARD D
WARFIELD, AZEL	ANN	505	HOWARD D
WARFIELD, B.N.	BAL	289	12TH WAR
WARFIELD, BASEL	BAL	321	1ST DIST
WARFIELD, BASIL	CAR	237	UNION TO
WARFIELD, BELA	ANN	511	HOWARD D
WARFIELD, BENI	CAR	223	5TH DIST
WARFIELD, BETSEY	MGM	322	CRACKLIN
WARFIELD, BETSEY	BAL	333	1ST DIST
WARFIELD, C. H.	BAL	429	14TH WAR
WARFIELD, CALEB	FRE	444	8TH E DI
WARFIELD, CALEB	BAL	147	16TH WAR
WARFIELD, CAROLINE	ANN	482	HOWARD D
WARFIELD, CAROLINE	DOR	468	1ST DIST
WARFIELD, CATHARIEN	ALL	085	5TH E.D.
WARFIELD, CHARLES D.	ANN	498	HOWARD D
WARFIELD, CHARLES H.	CAR	229	5TH DIST
WARFIELD, CLARISSA	ANN	484	HOWARD D
WARFIELD, CLAUDIUS	ANN	344	3RD DIST
WARFIELD, DANIEL	BAL	056	10TH WAR
WARFIELD, DANIEL JR.	BAL	056	10TH WAR
WARFIELD, DEBORAH G.	ANN	508	HOWARD D
WARFIELD, DENNIS	ANN	377	4TH DIST
WARFIELD, EDWARD	ANN	500	HOWARD D
WARFIELD, EDWARD	ANN	491	HOWARD D
WARFIELD, EDWIN	MGM	318	CRACKLIN
WARFIELD, ELEY	BAL	223	12TH WAR
WARFIELD, ELIZABETH	ANN	513	HOWARD D
WARFIELD, ELIZABETH	BAL	447	1ST DIST
WARFIELD, ELIZABETH	PRI	028	VANSVILL
WARFIELD, ELIZABETH	MGM	434	CLARKSTR
WARFIELD, ELLEN B.	MGM	329	CRACKLIN
WARFIELD, EPHRAIM	ANN	491	HOWARD D
WARFIELD, FANNY	BAL	392	14TH WAR
WARFIELD, GEORGE	BAL	128	16TH WAR
WARFIELD, GEORGE T.	ANN	391	4TH DIST
WARFIELD, GEORGE W.	ANN	505	HOWARD D
WARFIELD, GEORGE W.	FRE	254	NEW MARK
WARFIELD, GUSTAVUS	ANN	497	HOWARD D
WARFIELD, H.	BAL	101	10TH WAR
WARFIELD, HARRY	ANN	473	HOWARD D
WARFIELD, HENRY	ANN	476	HOWARD D
WARFIELD, HENRY	BAL	364	1ST DIST
WARFIELD, HENRY M.	BAL	314	20TH WAR
WARFIELD, HETTY M.	ANN	512	HOWARD D
WARFIELD, HONOR	CAR	396	2ND DIST
WARFIELD, HORRACE	MGM	435	CLARKSTR
WARFIELD, ISAAC	HAR	127	2ND DIST
WARFIELD, ISAAC	HAR	014	1ST DIST
WARFIELD, ISAAC	BAL	227	6TH WARD
WARFIELD, ISAAC D.	BAL	436	14TH WAR
WARFIELD, ISRAEL G.	MGM	325	CRACKLIN
WARFIELD, JAMES	ANN	456	HOWARD D
WARFIELD, JANE-BLACK	FRE	428	8TH E DI
WARFIELD, JEMIMA	ANN	497	HOWARD D
WARFIELD, JESSE L. DR.	CAR	273	WESTMINS
WARFIELD, JOHN	MGM	433	CLARKSTR
WARFIELD, JOHN	DOR	396	1ST DIST
WARFIELD, JOHN A.	FRE	442	8TH E DI
WARFIELD, JOHN D.	ANN	491	HOWARD D
WARFIELD, JOHN OF JOSHUA	ANN	448	HOWARD D
WARFIELD, JOHNATHAN	BAL	131	11TH WAR
WARFIELD, JONATHAN S.	ANN	343	3RD DIST
WARFIELD, JOSHUA D.	ANN	490	HOWARD D
WARFIELD, JULIANA	ANN	518	HOWARD D
WARFIELD, LEMUEL	ANN	505	HOWARD D
WARFIELD, LEMUEL A.	PRI	030	VANSVILL
WARFIELD, LEWIS M.	MGM	319	CRACKLIN
WARFIELD, LORENZO G.	ANN	494	HOWARD D
WARFIELD, LOT	ANN	367	4TH DIST
WARFIELD, LYDIA D.	ANN	490	HOWARD D
WARFIELD, M. W.	CAR	223	5TH DIST
WARFIELD, MAHLON H.	MGM	441	CLARKSTR
WARFIELD, MARTHA L.	ALL	245	CUMBERLA
WARFIELD, MARY	ANN	357	3RD DIST
WARFIELD, MARY A.	BAL	300	3RD WARD
WARFIELD, MILLY	BAL	078	4TH WARD
WARFIELD, MOSES	HAR	124	2ND DIST
WARFIELD, MOSES	BAL	302	3RD WARD
WARFIELD, NANCY	ANN	357	3RD DIST
WARFIELD, NANCY	BAL	143	16TH WAR
WARFIELD, NATHAN	BAL	338	1ST DIST
WARFIELD, NICHOLAS D.	ANN	506	HOWARD D
WARFIELD, NICHOLAS D.	MGM	383	ROCKERLE
WARFIELD, NICHOLAS R.	ANN	489	HOWARD D
WARFIELD, OSS-BLACK	FRE	451	8TH E DI
WARFIELD, PHILEMCN	ANN	384	4TH DIST
WARFIELD, PHILEMON D.	ANN	506	HOWARD D
WARFIELD, PHILIP	WAS	262	1ST DIST
WARFIELD, R. J.	BAL	473	14TH WAR
WARFIELD, RACHEL	ANN	487	HOWARD D
WARFIELD, RACHEL D.	ANN	447	HOWARD D
WARFIELD, REBECCA	CAR	223	5TH DIST
WARFIELD, REUBEN	ANN	511	HOWARD D
WARFIELD, RICHARD	ANN	340	3RD DIST
WARFIELD, RICHARD	BAL	079	18TH WAR
WARFIELD, RICHARD E.	ANN	475	HOWARD D
WARFIELD, RITTY	DOR	396	1ST DIST
WARFIELD, ROBERT	ALL	264	CUMBERLA
WARFIELD, RUFUS	PRI	024	VANSVILL
WARFIELD, SALVADOR	MGM	349	BERRYS D
WARFIELD, SAMUEL	BAL	325	1ST DIST
WARFIELD, SARAH	ANN	490	HOWARD D
WARFIELD, SARRATT JR.	FRE	416	8TH E DI
WARFIELD, SETH H.	ANN	494	HOWARD D
WARFIELD, SETH W.	ANN	447	HOWARD D
WARFIELD, SIMON	DOR	406	1ST DIST
WARFIELD, SINGLETON	BAL	178	16TH WAR
WARFIELD, SURRETT D. SR.	FRE	453	8TH E DI
WARFIELD, THOMAS	BAL	113	18TH WAR
WARFIELD, THOMAS	MGM	348	BERRYS D
WARFIELD, THOMAS B.	ANN	387	4TH DIST
WARFIELD, WARNER W.	CAR	230	5TH DIST

WARFIELD, WILLIAM CAR 407 2ND DIST
WARFIELD, WILLIAM FRE 438 8TH E DI
WARFIELD, WILLIAM DOR 350 3RD DIVI
WARFIELD, WILLIAM ANN 377 4TH DIST
WARFIELD, WILLIAM ALL 233 CUMBERLA
WARFIELD, WILLIAM H. BAL 171 16TH WAR
WARFIELD, WILLIAM H. MGM 430 CLARKSTR
WARFIELD, WILLIAM R. ANN 489 HOWARD D
WARFIELD, WILLIAM W. ANN 513 HOWARD D
WARFIELD, WILSON D. ANN 490 HOWARD D
WARFORD, JOHN ALL 236 CUMBERLA
WARFORD, RACHEL J. BAL 425 3RD WARD
WARGRER, GEORGE C.* BAL 047 4TH WARD
WARHAM, GEORGE P. QUE 180 2ND E DI
WARHAN, MARTHA A. QUE 180 2ND E DI
WARHEIM, DANIEL CAR 407 2ND DIST
WARICK, FREDERICK BAL 275 17TH WAR
WARICK, JOSEPH CAR 193 4TH DIST
WARINCK, DAVID BAL 289 12TH WAR
WARING, BENJAMIN B. ANN 309 1ST DIST
WARING, CECELIA ANN 354 3RD DIST
WARING, DEBORAH PRI 014 BLADENSB
WARING, ELISABETH ANN 323 2ND DIST
WARING, ELIZABETH BAL 147 11TH WAR
WARING, HENRY MGM 429 CLARKSTR
WARING, HENRY MGM 360 BERRYS D
WARING, HENRY H. PRI 010 BLADENSB
WARING, JAMES ST 333 4TH E DI
WARING, JAMES M. ANN 354 3RD DIST
WARING, JANE R. PRI 041 VANSVILL
WARING, MARSHAM PRI 015 BLADENSB
WARING, MARY PRI 011 BLADENSB
WARING, RACHEL M. ANN 362 4TH DIST
WARING, RICHARD M. ANN 353 3RD DIST
WARING, SARAH A. PRI 010 BLADENSB
WARKER, JOHN BAL 336 1ST DIST
WARKER, W. BAL 115 1ST WARD
WARKEY, GEORGE W. FRE 209 BUCKEYST
WARKIN, RICHARD BAL 386 3RD WARD
WARLEY, FREDERICK FRE 20 5TH E DI
WARLEY, IGNATUIS ST 265 3RD E DI
WARLEY, JOHN BAL 011 18TH WAR
WARLILD, WILLIAM BAL 325 12TH WAR
WARMER, JACOB CAR 341 6TH DIST
WARMLING, ADAULPHUS BAL 255 17TH WAR
WARMLING, MARY BAL 255 17TH WAR
WARMSLEY, L. BAL 150 1ST WARD
WARMSLEY, MRS- ANN 339 3RD DIST
WARMUCK, ASHFORD ALL 144 6TH E.D.
WARN, DAVID KEN 253 1ST DIST
WARNBUCK, LOUISA BAL 140 16TH WAR
WARNE, JAMES CAR 223 5TH DIST
WARNE,P WILLIAM CAR 291 7TH DIST
WARNECK, ANDREW ALL 130 4TH E.D.
WARNECK, HENRY ALL 132 4TH E.D.
WARNECK, JAMES ALL 134 4TH E.D.
WARNECK, JOHN ALL 131 4TH E.D.
WARNECK, JOHN ALL 130 4TH E.D.
WARNECK, JOSEPH ALL 131 4TH E.D.
WARNECK, WILLIAM ALL 131 4TH E.D.
WARNECK, WILLIAM ALL 130 4TH E.D.
WARNEK, JESIAH * ALL 130 4TH E.D.
WARNER, -----* BAL 093 10TH WAR
WARNER, ADAM W. CAR 336 6TH DIST
WARNER, ALBERT TAL 045 EASTON T
WARNER, ALEXANDER TAL 025 EASTON D
WARNER, ANDREW FRE 138 CREAGERS
WARNER, ANDREW CAR 103 NO TWP L
WARNER, ANDREW E. BAL 075 10TH WAR
WARNER, ANN TAL 024 EASTON D
WARNER, ANN L. CAR 260 3RD DIST
WARNER, ANN-BLACK BAL 228 2ND WARD
WARNER, ASA BAL 085 18TH WAR
WARNER, AUGUST FRE 314 MIDDLETO
WARNER, BARBARA FRE 298 WOODSBOR
WARNER, BRINTON HAR 055 1ST DIST
WARNER, CAROLINE K. ANN 521 HOWARD D
WARNER, CATHARINE BAL 273 17TH WAR
WARNER, CATHARINE KEN 260 1ST DIST
WARNER, CHRISTOPHER FRE 014 FREDERIC
WARNER, CLARINDA TAL 024 EASTON D
WARNER, CYPERIAN BAL 215 11TH WAR
WARNER, DAVID WAS 167 1ST DIST
WARNER, DAVID C. FRE 287 WOODSBOR
WARNER, EDWARD BAL 157 19TH WAR
WARNER, EDWARD TAL 029 EASTON D
WARNER, EDWARD M. BAL 426 14TH WAR
WARNER, ELI CAR 341 6TH DIST
WARNER, ELIAS CAR 382 2ND DIST
WARNER, ELIPHALET-BLACK QUE 152 1ST E DI
WARNER, ELIZA ANN QUE 218 3RD E DI
WARNER, ELIZABETH BAL 088 18TH WAR
WARNER, ELIZABETH CAR 403 2ND DIST
WARNER, ELIZABETH CAR 413 2ND DIST
WARNER, ELIZABETH FRE 427 8TH E DI
WARNER, ELIZABETH BAL 401 8TH WARD
WARNER, ELLEN CAR 413 2ND DIST
WARNER, ELLEN-BLACK CAR 072 NO TWP L
WARNER, EMANUEL CAR 326 1ST DIST
WARNER, EMELA FRE 428 8TH E DI
WARNER, FAYETT TAL 078 EASTON T
WARNER, FRANCIS CAR 341 6TH DIST
WARNER, FRANCIS A. BAL 187 6TH WARD
WARNER, FRANKLIN BAL 038 9TH WARD
WARNER, FREDERICK WAS 131 HAGERSTO
WARNER, G. K. BAL 333 1ST DIST
WARNER, GEORG A. BAL 362 13TH WAR
WARNER, GEORGE CAR 333 MANCHEST
WARNER, GEORGE CAR 259 3RD DIST
WARNER, GEORGE CAR 412 2ND DIST
WARNER, GEORGE CAR 234 UNION TO
WARNER, GEORGE WAS 240 CAVETOWN
WARNER, GEORGE JR. BAL 167 16TH WAR
WARNER, GEORGE K. BAL 065 15TH WAR
WARNER, GILES BAL 428 14TH WAR
WARNER, HANNAH FRE 097 FREDERIC
WARNER, HARRISON TAL 017 EASTON D
WARNER, HENRY TAL 016 EASTON D
WARNER, HENRY WAS 166 1ST DIST
WARNER, HENRY CAR 386 2ND DIST
WARNER, HENRY FRE 398 JEFFERSO
WARNER, HENRY KEN 253 1ST DIST
WARNER, HENRY BAL 008 15TH WAR
WARNER, HENRY BAL 441 1ST DIST
WARNER, HENRY BAL 443 1ST DIST
WARNER, HERNY FRE 169 5TH E DI
WARNER, HERNY CAR 282 7TH DIST
WARNER, J. BAL 141 1ST WARD
WARNER, J. E. BAL 182 6TH WARD
WARNER, JACOB BAL 211 11TH WAR

WARNER, JACOB CAR 291 7TH DIST
WARNER, JACOB CAR 344 6TH DIST
WARNER, JACOB CAR 309 1ST DIST
WARNER, JACOB FRE 287 WOODSBOR
WARNER, JAMES CEC 035 CHESAPEA
WARNER, JAMES CAR 258 3RD DIST
WARNER, JAMES CAR 099 NO TWP L
WARNER, JAMES KEN 310 3RD DIST
WARNER, JAMES JR. TAL 073 EASTON T
WARNER, JAMES M. TAL 030 EASTON D
WARNER, JAMES M. TAL 031 EASTON D
WARNER, JAMES M. BAL 069 4TH WARD
WARNER, JANE TAL 071 EASTON T
WARNER, JANE BAL 054 1ST WARD
WARNER, JEHU CAR 384 2ND DIST
WARNER, JERRY KEN 283 3RD DIST
WARNER, JESSE CAR 329 MANCHEST
WARNER, JOHN CAR 341 6TH DIST
WARNER, JOHN FRE 364 CATOCTIN
WARNER, JOHN CAR 402 2ND DIST
WARNER, JOHN FRE 183 5TH E DI
WARNER, JOHN QUE 217 3RD E DI
WARNER, JOHN TAL 054 EASTON D
WARNER, JOHN TAL 044 EASTON T
WARNER, JOHN WAS 103 2ND DIST
WARNER, JOHN WAS 054 2ND SUBD
WARNER, JOHN BAL 123 1ST WARD
WARNER, JOHN BAL 440 1ST DIST
WARNER, JOHN H. CAR 259 3RD DIST
WARNER, JONATHAN HAR 092 2ND DIST
WARNER, JOSEPH CAR 245 3RD DIST
WARNER, JOSEPH FRE 367 CATOCTIN
WARNER, JOSEPH P. BAL 123 1ST WARD
WARNER, JOSEPH P. BAL 103 10TH WAR
WARNER, LEANDER A. BAL 304 7TH WARD
WARNER, LEEDS* TAL 024 EASTON D
WARNER, LETTY CAR 099 NO TWP L
WARNER, LEVINIA TAL 054 EASTON D
WARNER, LEWIS M. BAL 167 11TH WAR
WARNER, LITTLETON BAL 024 1ST WARD
WARNER, LOUISA BAL 254 20TH WAR
WARNER, MARGARET HAR 011 1ST DIST
WARNER, MARGARET BAL 382 3RD WARD
WARNER, MARTHA A. CAR 382 2ND DIST
WARNER, MARY BAL 226 2ND WARD
WARNER, MARY TAL 048 EASTON T
WARNER, MARY ANN BAL 103 10TH WAR
WARNER, MARY J. BAL 188 6TH WARD
WARNER, MARY* DOR 376 1ST DIST
WARNER, MATILDA BAL 165 2ND DIST
WARNER, MICAHEL BAL 447 14TH WAR
WARNER, NEWTON CAR 104 NO TWP L
WARNER, NICHOLAS BAL 088 1ST WARD
WARNER, PERNAL TAL 054 EASTON D
WARNER, PETER CAR 336 6TH DIST
WARNER, PHILIP FRE 287 WOODSBOR
WARNER, RACHEAL CAR 413 2ND DIST
WARNER, RICHARD BAL 401 14TH WAR
WARNER, RICHARD CEC 176 7TH E DI
WARNER, RICHARD TAL 036 EASTON D
WARNER, ROBERT TAL 029 EASTON D
WARNER, ROBERT TAL 014 ST MICHA
WARNER, ROBERT BAL 196 17TH WAR
WARNER, ROBERT H. TAL 029 EASTON D
WARNER, RUTH BAL 025 15TH WAR
WARNER, RUTH A. HAR 013 1ST DIST
WARNER, SALINA FRE 348 MIDDLETO
WARNER, SALLY A. TAL 043 EASTON D
WARNER, SALLY A. TAL 010 EASTON D
WARNER, SAMUEL KEN 292 3RD DIST
WARNER, SAMUEL KEN 305 3RD DIST
WARNER, SAMUEL FRE 113 CREAGERS
WARNER, SAMUEL BAL 140 16TH WAR
WARNER, SARAH BAL 202 6TH WARD
WARNER, SARAH BAL 204 6TH DIST
WARNER, SARAH HAR 057 1ST DIST
WARNER, SARAH HAR 031 1ST DIST
WARNER, SHERIDEN BAL 144 11TH WAR
WARNER, SILAS HAR 013 1ST DIST
WARNER, SUSAN C. BAL 188 16TH WAR
WARNER, SUSQANNA CAR 238 UNION TO
WARNER, THOMAS CAR 253 3RD DIST
WARNER, THOMAS BAL 422 1ST DIST
WARNER, THOMAS BAL 202 6TH WARD
WARNER, THOMAS B. BAL 402 14TH WAR
WARNER, V.C. PRI 075 MARLBROU
WARNER, W. H. BAL 333 1ST DIST
WARNER, WASHINGTON TAL 009 EASTON D
WARNER, WESLEY QUE 217 3RD E DI
WARNER, WILLIAM BAL 107 2ND DIST
WARNER, WILLIAM BAL 087 18TH WAR
WARNER, WILLIAM CAR 385 2ND DIST
WARNER, WILLIAM F. CEC 193 5TH E DI
WARNER, WILLIAM H. FRE 439 8TH E DI
WARNER, WILLIAM H. TAL 017 EASTON D
WARNER, WILLIAM J. CAR 153 NO TWP L
WARNER, WILLIAM R. TAL 004 EASTON D
WARNER, WILLIAM S. BAL 184 6TH WARD
WARNERWITCH, FREDERICK BAL 282 17TH WAR
WARNES, BERNARD * BAL 041 18TH WAR
WARNETT, MARY BAL 312 12TH WAR
WARNICK, HENRY BAL 312 1ST DIST
WARNICK, JOHN ALL 144 6TH E.D.
WARNICK, JOHN BAL 386 8TH WARD
WARNICK, JOHN BAL 385 8TH WARD
WARNICK, JOHN BAL 252 17TH WAR
WARNICK, JOSEPH BAL 224 1ST DIST
WARNICK, SAMUEL ALL 046 10TH E.D
WARNICK, WILLIAM BAL 254 17TH WAR
WARNICK, WILLIAM BAL 147 11TH WAR
WARNKEN, LUHR BAL 182 16TH WAR
WARNKEY, FREDERICK BAL 124 1ST WARD
WARNKEY, JOSEPH BAL 124 1ST WARD
WARNNER, DAVID FRE 413 8TH E DI
WARNOCK, MARY HAR 128 2ND DIST
WARNS, ANN * BAL 042 18TH WAR
WARNS, BENNET BAL 089 18TH WAR
WARNS, CLEMENT ANN 414 HOWARD D
WARRALL, DAVID BAL 160 1ST WARD
WARRAN, JAMES CAL 017 1ST DIST
WARRELL, GRACE CEC 112 4TH E DI
WARREN, ADAM BAL 167 16TH WAR
WARREN, ALLEN BAL 254 6TH WARD
WARREN, ANN BAL 190 11TH WAR
WARREN, ANN WOR 206 4TH E DI
WARREN, ARCHABALD BAL 223 1ST DIST
WARREN, CATHARINE BAL 089 1ST WARD
WARREN, CATHARINE WAS 010 WILLIAMS
WARREN, CHARLES BAL 018 9TH WARD
WARREN, DINAH ANN 300 1ST DIST

WARREN, EDWIN T. HAR 080 2ND DIST
WARREN, ELEN BAL 194 11TH WAR
WARREN, ELIZABETH-MULATTO FRE 240 NEW MARK
WARREN, GEORGE BAL 322 7TH WARD
WARREN, HAMILTON KEN 228 2ND DIST
WARREN, HARPER FRE 251 NEW MARK
WARREN, ISAAC CAR 098 NO TWP L
WARREN, JAMES BAL 441 8TH WARD
WARREN, JAMES ALL 096 5TH E.D.
WARREN, JAMES ALL 071 5TH E.D.
WARREN, JAMES BAL 222 1ST DIST
WARREN, JAMES SOM 479 TRAPP DI
WARREN, JAMES-BLACK FRE 038 FREDERIC
WARREN, JOHN HAR 161 3RD DIST
WARREN, JOHN HAR 165 3RD DIST
WARREN, JOHN BAL 221 1ST DIST
WARREN, JOHN BAL 171 1ST WARD
WARREN, JOHN ALL 236 CUMBERLA
WARREN, JOHN-MULATTO FRE 239 NEW MARK
WARREN, JONATHAN QUE 253 5TH E DI
WARREN, JOSIAH WOR 207 4TH E DI
WARREN, LAFAYETTE SOM 479 TRAPP DI
WARREN, MARGARET MGM 378 ROCKERLE
WARREN, MARTHA SOM 525 QUANTICO
WARREN, MARY QUE 204 3RD E DI
WARREN, MILLY SOM 477 TRAPP DI
WARREN, POLLY MGM 379 ROCKERLE
WARREN, REBECCA BAL 444 8TH WARD
WARREN, SAMUEL FRE 277 NEW MARK
WARREN, SENNA QUE 125 1ST E DI
WARREN, STERRET CAR 236 UNION TO
WARREN, SUSAN TAL 021 EASTON D
WARREN, THOMAS QUE 205 3RD E DI
WARREN, THOMAS BAL 154 1ST WARD
WARREN, WILLIAM ALL 103 5TH E.D.
WARREN, ABRAHAM-BLACK ST 332 4TH E DI
WARREN, W ILLIAM H.-MULATT ST 325 4TH E DI
WARRENFELTS, PHILIP FRE 370 CATOCTIN
WARRENFELTS, JACOB FRE 362 CATOCTIN
WARRENFELTS, JOHN FRE 362 CATOCTIN
WARRENFELTS, JOSIAH FRE 362 CATOCTIN
WARRENFELTZ, DANIEL FRE 361 CATOCTIN
WARRENFELTZ, JACOB FRE 374 CATOCTIN
WARRENFETTS, HEZEKIAH FRE 333 MIDDLETO
WARRICH, JIM* TAL 008 EASTON D
WARRICK, BENJAMIN QUE 217 3RD E DI
WARRICK, JOHN BAL 323 7TH WARD
WARRICK, JOHN BAL 288 7TH WARD
WARRICK, NANCY BAL 454 1ST DIST
WARRICK, ROBERT BAL 169 1ST WARD
WARRIN, GEORGE DOR 431 1ST DIST
WARRING, ELIZABETH M. PRI 068 NOTTINGH
WARRING, GEORGE W. BAL 353 1ST DIST
WARRING, J. T. BAL 152 1ST WARD
WARRING, JOHN BAL 286 2ND WARD
WARRING, JOHN H. PRI 067 NOTTINGH
WARRING, MARY-BLACK ST 341 5TH E DI
WARRING, MILLY PRI 079 MARLBROU
WARRING, PETER ST 341 5TH E DI
WARRING, PRISCILLA ANN 521 HOWARD D
WARRING, RICHARD PRI 077 MARLBROU
WARRING, SARAH PRI 077 MARLBROU
WARRING, SARAH BAL 129 16TH WAR
WARRING, SPENCER M. BAL 129 16TH WAR
WARRING, VIOLETTA PRI 061 NOTTINGH
WARRING, WILLIAM CEC 200 7TH E DI
WARRINGOTN, ALEXANDER WOR 246 1ST CENS
WARRINGOTN, ELIZA WOR 217 4TH E DI
WARRINGOTN, MARY E. WOR 247 1ST CENS
WARRINGOTN, RICHARX WOR 247 1ST CENS
WARRINGTON, CATHARINE BAL 208 6TH WARD
WARRINGTON, CATHERINE CAR 138 NO TWP L
WARRINGTON, JAMES ANN 422 HOWARD D
WARRINGTON, JANE WOR 270 BERLIN 1
WARRINGTON, JOHN BAL 022 1ST WARD
WARRINGTON, LEAH WOR 194 8TH E DI
WARRINGTON, PALLAMORE* BAL 380 3RD WARD
WARRINGTON, SAMUEL WOR 267 BERLIN 1
WARRINGTON, SARAH BAL 012 1ST WARD
WARRINGTON, SOTHY WOR 330 1ST E DI
WARRINGTON, THOMAS J. BAL 380 3RD WARD
WARRINGTON, WILLIAM T. ANN 359 3RD DIST
WARRINGTON, ZENO * WOR 247 1ST CENS
WARRNING, THOMAS H. DOR 429 1ST DIST
WARROCK, ROBERT KEN 310 3RD DIST
WARRSFEN, ELIZABETH BAL 160 11TH WAR
WART, GEORGE* BAL 337 3RD WARD
WARTENBURG, MARYANN BAL 397 3RD WARD
WARTER, WILLIAM QUE 238 5TH E DI
WARTERS, CHARLOTT WOR 313 2ND E DI
WARTERS, ELIZABETH WOR 312 2ND E DI
WARTERS, JOHN WOR 313 2ND E DI
WARTERS, SWEWL D. CAL 004 1ST DIST
WARTHAN, GEORGE FRE 203 5TH E DI
WARTHAN, HENRIETTA FRE 184 5TH E DI
WARTHAN, HENRY FRE 066 FREDERIC
WARTHEE, JOHN F. FRE 268 NEW MARK
WARTHEN, CECILIA MGM 423 MEDLEY 3
WARTHEN, GEORGE CHA 272 ALLENS F
WARTHEN, MARGERY-BLACK MGM 403 ROCKERLE
WARTHEN, SUSAN ANN 336 3RD DIST
WARTLEY, THOMAS ALL 080 5TH E.D.
WARTMAN, MICHAEL BAL 310 1ST DIST
WARTONS, HENRY WOR 314 2ND E DI
WARVER, DANIEL WAS 034 2ND SUBD
WARVICK, C.* BAL 101 10TH WAR
WARWICK, ANNA BAL 207 11TH WAR
WARWICK, BENJAMIN CEC 041 CHESAPEA
WARWICK, C.* BAL 101 10TH WAR
WARWICK, HARRIET BAL 388 13TH WAR
WARWICK, HARRIET J. BAL 364 13TH WAR
WARWICK, JAMES-BLACK QUE 155 2ND E DI
WARWICK, NELLA TAL 012 EASTON D
WARWICK, RICHARD QUE 199 3RD E DI
WARWICK, ROBERT BAL 116 1ST WARD
WARWICK, ROBERT BAL 171 1ST WARD
WARWICK, SARAH KEN 308 3RD DIST
WARWICK, SIMEON-BLACK QUE 158 2ND E DI
WARY, SARAH BAL 362 1ST DIST
WASCAR, ELIZABETH BAL 255 20TH WAR
WASE, CHRISTIAN ALL 184 9TH E.D.
WASEN, MARY A. BAL 211 2ND WARD
WASETELL, ELIZABETH WAS 108 2ND DIST
WASH, JOHN W. BAL 033 1ST WARD
WASHABAUGH, WILLIAM WAS 289 1ST DIST
WASHAIME, CONRAD CAR 349 6TH DIST
WASHBORN, JOHN T. BAL 197 6TH WARD
WASHBORN, GEORGE SOM 479 TRAPP DI
WASHBURN, H. BAL 281 2ND WARD
WASHBURN, HENRY ALL 196 CUMBERLA

Name	County	Page	District
WASHBURN, HENRY	SOM	479	TRAPP DI
WASHBURN, HENRY	SOM	475	TRAPPE D
WASHBURN, JAMES	SOM	473	TRAPPE D
WASHBURN, REUBEN	SOM	473	TRAPPE D
WASHBURN, THOMAS G.	WAS	151	2ND DIST
WASHBURN, WILLIAM H.	SOM	476	TRAPPE D
WASHBURN, WYMAN F.	BAL	109	15TH WAR
WASHCUPS, GEORGE	BAL	170	2ND DIST
WASHEN, ELIJAH	BAL	145	11TH WAR
WASHER, AARON	TAL	016	EASTON D
WASHEY, HENRY	FRE	034	FREDERIC
WASHIINGTON, LEWIS	BAL	019	9TH WARD
WASHINGOTN, ELISHA	BAL	137	2ND DIST
WASHINGTON, ADAM-BLACK	ST	318	4TH E DI
WASHINGTON, ANNA	BAL	217	6TH WARD
WASHINGTON, AQUILLA	HAR	002	1ST DIST
WASHINGTON, AUGUST*	BAL	107	10TH WAR
WASHINGTON, BETSEY	BAL	453	1ST DIST
WASHINGTON, C.	BAL	174	1ST WARD
WASHINGTON, C.	BAL	138	1ST WARD
WASHINGTON, CHARLES	BAL	376	13TH WAR
WASHINGTON, CHLOE	PRI	059	NOTTINGH
WASHINGTON, CORBIN	BAL	164	1ST WARD
WASHINGTON, CORBIN	BAL	156	1ST WARD
WASHINGTON, DANIEL N.	ST	341	5TH E DI
WASHINGTON, ELIE	WAS	209	1ST DIST
WASHINGTON, ELIZA	WAS	046	2ND SUBD
WASHINGTON, ELIZA	BAL	204	11TH WAR
WASHINGTON, FAIRFAX	BAL	080	4TH WARD
WASHINGTON, FANNEY	HAR	030	1ST DIST
WASHINGTON, FREDERICK	BAL	155	5TH WARD
WASHINGTON, FREDERICK	BAL	328	7TH WARD
WASHINGTON, FREDERICK	BAL	173	2ND DIST
WASHINGTON, GEORGE	BAL	304	1ST DIST
WASHINGTON, GEORGE	BAL	161	1ST WARD
WASHINGTON, GEORGE	BAL	457	8TH WARD
WASHINGTON, GEORGE	CEC	185	7TH E DI
WASHINGTON, GEORGE	BAL	040	18TH WAR
WASHINGTON, GEORGE	HAR	191	3RD DIST
WASHINGTON, GEORGE	PRI	088	SPALDING
WASHINGTON, GEORGE	QUE	247	5TH E DI
WASHINGTON, GEORGE	QUE	246	5TH E DI
WASHINGTON, GEORGE C.	MGM	405	ROCKERLE
WASHINGTON, GEORGE-BLACK	QUE	185	3RD E DI
WASHINGTON, GEROGE	KEN	271	1ST DIST
WASHINGTON, HAMPTON	HAR	165	3RD DIST
WASHINGTON, HENRY	BAL	155	5TH WARD
WASHINGTON, HEWRILLA B.	BAL	353	7TH WARD
WASHINGTON, ISAAC	HAR	032	1ST DIST
WASHINGTON, JACOB	WAS	045	2ND SUBD
WASHINGTON, JAME	BAL	120	1ST WARD
WASHINGTON, JAMES	WAS	065	2ND SUBD
WASHINGTON, JAMES	BAL	050	4TH WARD
WASHINGTON, JAMES H.	BAL	011	4TH WARD
WASHINGTON, JOHN	DOR	311	1ST DIST
WASHINGTON, JOHN	WAS	054	2ND SUBD
WASHINGTON, JOSEPH	TAL	050	EASTON T
WASHINGTON, JOSEPH	KEN	263	1ST DIST
WASHINGTON, JULIA	BAL	263	12TH WAR
WASHINGTON, LEVI-BLACK	CAR	141	NO TWP L
WASHINGTON, LOUISA	BAL	002	9TH WARD
WASHINGTON, LOUISA	ANN	490	HOWARD D
WASHINGTON, LUCY-BLACK	FRE	042	FREDERIC
WASHINGTON, MARGARET-MULA	FRE	436	8TH E DI
WASHINGTON, NANCY	BAL	153	5TH WARD
WASHINGTON, PHENOS	BAL	213	17TH WAR
WASHINGTON, REBECCA	DOR	364	3RD DIVI
WASHINGTON, RICHARD	BAL	199	11TH WAR
WASHINGTON, ROBERT	BAL	119	1ST WARD
WASHINGTON, ROSANNA	WAS	190	1ST DIST
WASHINGTON, ROSETTA	DOR	316	1ST DIST
WASHINGTON, SAMUEL-BLACK	CAR	164	NO TWP L
WASHINGTON, SARAH A.	ANN	491	HOWARD D
WASHINGTON, THOMAS	BAL	457	8TH WARD
WASHINGTON, THOMAS	TAL	113	ST MICHA
WASHINGTON, THOMAS F.	TAL	113	ST MICHA
WASHINGTON, VIOLET	CEC	110	4TH E DI
WASHINGTON, WESLEY	HAR	123	2ND DIST
WASHINGTON, WILLIAM-MULAT	CAR	077	NO TWP L
WASHLER, DANIEL	FRE	374	CATOCTIN
WASHLER, HENRY	FRE	372	CATOCTIN
WASHLER, JOHN	FRE	358	CATOCTIN
WASHMILLER, JOHN	ALL	208	CUMBERLA
WASHTLER, JOSEPH	FRE	375	CATOCTIN
WASKEY, AUGUSTUS	FRE	213	BUCKEYST
WASKEY, JULIAN	FRE	399	JEFFERSO
WASKEY, MARY J.	FRE	214	BUCKEYST
WASKEY, PERRY	FRE	408	JEFFERSO
WASON, J.B.	WAS	133	HAGERSTO
WASON, ROBERT	WAS	162	2ND DIST
WASP, ELIZA	BAL	099	15TH WAR
WASS, WILLIAM	ALL	022	2ND E.D.
WASSERMAN, J.L.	BAL	301	7TH WARD
WASSMAN, FRED	BAL	262	12TH WAR
WASSO, FRANCES	BAL	226	12TH WAR
WASSON, ABRAHAM	ANN	317	1ST DIST
WAST, SARAH	BAL	154	5TH WARD
WASTERS, K.F.	BAL	188	2ND WARD
WASTLER, JACOB	FRE	128	CREAGERS
WASTSLER, JACOB	FRE	375	CATOCTIN
WASY, JOHN T.	CAR	226	5TH DIST
WATCHER, DANIEL M.	BAL	119	1ST WARD
WATCHER, ROBERT	CEC	028	CHESAPEA
WATCHMAN, GEORGE	BAL	009	15TH WAR
WATCHMAN, HENRY	BAL	159	2ND DIST
WATCHMAN, JOHN	BAL	017	15TH WAR
WATCHSON, THOMAS	CEC	180	7TH E DI
WATE, PRESTON	BAL	302	12TH WAR
WATEAHAHER, GEORGE *	FRE	267	NEW MARK
WATER, DERMIS	BAL	312	12TH WAR
WATER, JOHN H.	TAL	079	ST MICHA
WATER, MARYANN*	BAL	335	3RD WARD
WATERFORD, SARAH H.	BAL	048	18TH WAR
WATERMAN, G.H.	BAL	162	1ST WARD
WATERMAN, HENRY	BAL	300	7TH WARD
WATERMAN, PHILLIPINA	BAL	156	16TH WAR
WATERMAN, SAMUEL	BAL	363	8TH WARD
WATERMAN, SUSAN	BAL	301	7TH WARD
WATERMAN, THOMAS	BAL	267	17TH WAR
WATERMAN, WILLIAM	BAL	339	13TH WAR
WATERMYER, CHARLES T.H.	ANN	458	HOWARD D
WATERMYER, WILLIAM H.	BAL	058	18TH WAR
WATERS, -----*	BAL	073	10TH WAR
WATERS, ABNER	WOR	298	9TH E DI
WATERS, ADAM	SOM	417	PRINCESS
WATERS, ADAMSON	MGM	340	CLARKSBU
WATERS, AGATTA-BLACK	BAL	208	2ND WARD
WATERS, AGUSTUS	FRE	299	WOODSBOR
WATERS, ALEXANDER	CHA	239	HILLTOP
WATERS, ALEXANDER G.	HAR	048	1ST DIST
WATERS, ALFRED	MGM	360	BERRYS D
WATERS, AMOS	HAR	140	2ND DIST
WATERS, ANDREW G.	BAL	321	20TH WAR
WATERS, ANN	HAR	139	2ND DIST
WATERS, ANN	FRE	278	NEW MARK
WATERS, ANN	BAL	026	4TH WARD
WATERS, ANN	ANN	325	2ND DIST
WATERS, ANN	PRI	081	QUEEN AN
WATERS, ANN J.	BAL	194	11TH WAR
WATERS, ANNA	CEC	056	1ST E DI
WATERS, ANSLEM	WAS	179	BOONSBOR
WATERS, ANTHONY	SOM	549	TYASKIN
WATERS, AQUILLA	ANN	365	4TH DIST
WATERS, ARAMINTA	BAL	111	15TH WAR
WATERS, ARAMINTA	KEN	297	3RD DIST
WATERS, ARNOLD	SOM	462	HANGARY
WATERS, ARNOLD	MGM	366	BERRYS D
WATERS, ARTERIDGE	PRI	042	VANSVILL
WATERS, ARTRIDGE	ANN	372	4TH DIST
WATERS, BASIL W.	MGM	338	CRACKLIN
WATERS, BENJAMIN	HAR	139	2ND DIST
WATERS, BENJAMIN	CEC	049	1ST E DI
WATERS, BENJAMIN	BAL	376	13TH WAR
WATERS, BENJAMIN	BAL	110	10TH WAR
WATERS, BETSY	CHA	276	ALLENS F
WATERS, BETSY	DOR	388	1ST DIST
WATERS, BRIDGET	SOM	485	TRAPP DI
WATERS, C.	BAL	236	20TH WAR
WATERS, C. L.	TAL	072	EASTON T
WATERS, C.W.	QUE	185	3RD E DI
WATERS, CARLINA	BAL	119	11TH WAR
WATERS, CAROLINE	TAL	069	EASTON T
WATERS, CATHERINE	CEC	178	7TH E DI
WATERS, CHARLES	DOR	413	1ST DIST
WATERS, CHARLES	SOM	437	PRINCESS
WATERS, CHARLES	TAL	008	EASTON D
WATERS, CHARLES	BAL	163	2ND DIST
WATERS, CHARLES A.	ANN	322	2ND DIST
WATERS, CHARLES E.	BAL	177	2ND DIST
WATERS, CHARLES H.	BAL	111	5TH WARD
WATERS, CHARLOTTE	BAL	077	10TH WAR
WATERS, CHARLOTTE	SOM	549	TYASKIN
WATERS, CHARLOTTE	MGM	322	CRACKLIN
WATERS, CHARLOTTE E. J.	SOM	418	PRINCESS
WATERS, CLARA J.	BAL	144	19TH WAR
WATERS, CLEMENT	DOR	377	1ST DIST
WATERS, CYRUS	MGM	330	CRACKLIN
WATERS, DANIEL	TAL	033	EASTON D
WATERS, DANIEL	SOM	351	BRINKLEY
WATERS, DAVID	TAL	041	EASTON D
WATERS, DORSEY	FRE	254	NEW MARK
WATERS, E.	PRI	102	SPALDING
WATERS, E. J.	BAL	106	10TH WAR
WATERS, EDWARD	BAL	092	15TH WAR
WATERS, EDWARD	BAL	084	4TH WARD
WATERS, EDWARD M.	CHA	277	BOJANTOW
WATERS, EDWARD M.	SOM	361	BRINKLEY
WATERS, EDWIN	MGM	432	CLARKSTR
WATERS, ELEANOR	BAL	070	15TH WAR
WATERS, ELIAS-BLACK	FRE	452	8TH E DI
WATERS, ELIZA	SOM	434	PRINCESS
WATERS, ELIZA	BAL	236	17TH WAR
WATERS, ELIZA	SOM	354	BRINKLEY
WATERS, ELIZA A.	ANN	508	HOWARD D
WATERS, ELIZABETH	BAL	305	3RD WARD
WATERS, ELIZABETH	BAL	210	2ND WARD
WATERS, ELIZABETH	SOM	428	PRINCESS
WATERS, ELIZABETH D.	BAL	080	15TH WAR
WATERS, ELIZABETH-BLACK	FRE	017	FREDERIC
WATERS, ELSY	BAL	256	20TH WAR
WATERS, EMERY	BAL	403	3RD WARD
WATERS, EMILY	CEC	044	1ST E DI
WATERS, ESTER	HAR	052	1ST DIST
WATERS, EZRA	BAL	130	16TH WAR
WATERS, F.	BAL	101	10TH WAR
WATERS, F.A.	BAL	147	5TH WARD
WATERS, FRANCES	BAL	257	20TH WAR
WATERS, FRANCES	FRE	004	FREDERIC
WATERS, FRANCIS	BAL	325	12TH WAR
WATERS, FRANK	ANN	511	HOWARD D
WATERS, FRANKLIN	MGM	426	MEDLEY 3
WATERS, FRANKLIN	PRI	040	VANSVILL
WATERS, FREEBORN G.	BAL	321	20TH WAR
WATERS, G. W.	BAL	039	4TH WARD
WATERS, GEORGE	HAR	055	1ST DIST
WATERS, GEORGE	BAL	252	17TH WAR
WATERS, GEORGE	CHA	284	BOJANTOW
WATERS, GEORGE	SOM	547	TYASKIN
WATERS, GEORGE	PRI	029	VANSVILL
WATERS, GEORGE	BAL	032	9TH WARD
WATERS, GEORGE	ANN	376	4TH DIST
WATERS, GEORGE	BAL	029	2ND DIST
WATERS, GEORGE H.	PRI	048	AQUASCO
WATERS, GEORGE H.	BAL	228	17TH WAR
WATERS, GEORGE P.	ST	319	4TH E DI
WATERS, GEORGE T.	BAL	284	17TH WAR
WATERS, GEORGIANNA	BAL	228	17TH WAR
WATERS, GEROGE	BAL	341	13TH WAR
WATERS, GILBERT-BLACK	WOR	329	1ST E DI
WATERS, GREENBARY	MGM	340	CLARKSBU
WATERS, H.	BAL	129	1ST WARD
WATERS, HANNAH	BAL	227	19TH WAR
WATERS, HARIET	ANN	406	8TH DIST
WATERS, HARIET	SOM	477	TRAPP DI
WATERS, HARIET	SOM	485	TRAPP DI
WATERS, HARRIET	BAL	026	9TH WARD
WATERS, HARRIET	BAL	315	3RD WARD
WATERS, HARRIET	BAL	168	19TH WAR
WATERS, HENRY	CEC	044	1ST E DI
WATERS, HENRY	SOM	417	PRINCESS
WATERS, HENRY	SOM	420	PRINCESS
WATERS, HENRY	BAL	140	1ST WARD
WATERS, HENRY	BAL	036	1ST WARD
WATERS, HENRY	SOM	459	HANGARY
WATERS, HESTER A.	BAL	124	16TH WAR
WATERS, HESTY	BAL	197	19TH WAR
WATERS, HETTY	BAL	109	15TH WAR
WATERS, HETTY-BLACK	FRE	044	FREDERIC
WATERS, HEZEKIAH	BAL	081	1ST WARD
WATERS, HORATIA	FRE	064	FREDERIC
WATERS, HOWARD	HAR	057	1ST DIST
WATERS, IGNATIOUS JR.	FRE	446	8TH E DI
WATERS, IGNATIUS	ANN	495	HOWARD D
WATERS, IRENAH *	WOR	314	2ND E DI
WATERS, ISAAC	BAL	246	6TH WARD
WATERS, ISAAC	BAL	197	11TH WAR
WATERS, ISAAC	BAL	119	11TH WAR
WATERS, ISAAC	BAL	471	14TH WAR
WATERS, ISABELL	WOR	274	BERLIN 1
WATERS, JACOB	HAR	097	2ND DIST
WATERS, JACOB	BAL	293	1ST DIST
WATERS, JAMES	BAL	271	1ST DIST
WATERS, JAMES	ANN	337	3RD DIST
WATERS, JAMES	ANN	478	HOWARD D
WATERS, JAMES	FRE	343	MIDDLETO
WATERS, JAMES	WAS	016	2ND SUBD
WATERS, JAMES B.	BAL	359	3RD WARD
WATERS, JAMES H.	BAL	191	17TH WAR
WATERS, JAMES M.	WOR	177	6TH E DI
WATERS, JAMES S.	BAL	313	20TH WAR
WATERS, JAMES W.	BAL	061	15TH WAR
WATERS, JAMES-MULATTO	FRE	420	8TH E DI
WATERS, JANE	PRI	038	VANSVILL
WATERS, JANE C.	CHA	240	HILLTOP
WATERS, JANE F.	FRE	165	EMMITTSB
WATERS, JESSE	SOM	478	TRAPP DI
WATERS, JESSE	BAL	249	1ST DIST
WATERS, JOB	DOR	435	1ST DIST
WATERS, JOE	SOM	460	HANGARY
WATERS, JOHN	SOM	463	HANGARY
WATERS, JOHN	PRI	033	VANSVILL
WATERS, JOHN	SOM	363	BRINKLEY
WATERS, JOHN	SOM	359	BRINKLEY
WATERS, JOHN	MGM	350	BERRYS D
WATERS, JOHN	BAL	050	4TH WARD
WATERS, JOHN	BAL	007	15TH WAR
WATERS, JOHN	ALL	050	10TH E.D
WATERS, JOHN	BAL	205	2ND WARD
WATERS, JOHN	BAL	249	2ND WARD
WATERS, JOHN C.	CEC	154	PORT DUP
WATERS, JOHN F.	HAR	052	1ST DIST
WATERS, JOHN H.	BAL	351	1ST DIST
WATERS, JOHN M.	ANN	495	HOWARD D
WATERS, JOHN W.	BAL	048	4TH WARD
WATERS, JOHN-MULATTO	FRE	445	8TH E DI
WATERS, JOHNATHAN	ANN	431	HOWARD D
WATERS, JONAS	BAL	096	2ND DIST
WATERS, JONAS	DOR	443	1ST DIST
WATERS, JOSEPH	WOR	273	BERLIN 1
WATERS, JOSEPH	SOM	548	TYASKIN
WATERS, JOSEPH G.	BAL	188	16TH WAR
WATERS, JOSHUA	SOM	353	BRINKLEY
WATERS, JOSHUA T.	BAL	359	3RD WARD
WATERS, JOSIAH	WAS	202	1ST DIST
WATERS, JULIA	BAL	305	7TH WARD
WATERS, JULIA	FRE	065	FREDERIC
WATERS, JULIA	SOM	419	PRINCESS
WATERS, JULIANA	ANN	432	HOWARD D
WATERS, LAMBERT	SOM	360	BRINKLEY
WATERS, LEAH N.	BAL	013	4TH WARD
WATERS, LEANDER	MGM	328	CRACKLIN
WATERS, LEAR	BAL	032	4TH WARD
WATERS, LEVIN	BAL	197	17TH WAR
WATERS, LEVIN L.	SOM	436	PRINCESS
WATERS, LITTLETON	SOM	406	DUBLIN D
WATERS, LITTLETON	SOM	354	BRINKLEY
WATERS, LOUISA	BAL	348	3RD WARD
WATERS, LOUISIA-BLACK	BAL	219	2ND WARD
WATERS, LUCY	SOM	359	BRINKLEY
WATERS, LYDIA	FRE	214	BUCKEYST
WATERS, MAGER	WOR	312	2ND E DI
WATERS, MAJOR	SOM	433	PRINCESS
WATERS, MARGARET	SOM	422	PRINCESS
WATERS, MARGARET	BAL	385	13TH WAR
WATERS, MARGARET	BAL	053	1ST WARD
WATERS, MARGARET	BAL	111	15TH WAR
WATERS, MARGARETT	KEN	297	3RD DIST
WATERS, MARIA	BAL	045	9TH WARD
WATERS, MARIA	BAL	316	3RD WARD
WATERS, MARIA	ANN	330	2ND DIST
WATERS, MARIAH	SOM	362	BRINKLEY
WATERS, MARTHA E.	ANN	495	HOWARD D
WATERS, MARY	BAL	462	1ST DIST
WATERS, MARY	BAL	081	15TH WAR
WATERS, MARY	BAL	251	6TH WARD
WATERS, MARY	PRI	049	AQUASCO
WATERS, MARY	PRI	052	AQUASCO
WATERS, MARY	FRE	041	FREDERIC
WATERS, MARY	DOR	448	1ST DIST
WATERS, MARY	BAL	021	4TH WARD
WATERS, MARY A.	BAL	352	13TH WAR
WATERS, MARY A.	PRI	031	VANSVILL
WATERS, MARY A. E.	SOM	418	PRINCESS
WATERS, MARY ANN	MGM	315	CRACKLIN
WATERS, MARY B.	BAL	108	15TH WAR
WATERS, MARY E.	BAL	025	15TH WAR
WATERS, MARY E.	MGM	340	CLARKSBU
WATERS, MARY J.	TAL	020	EASTON D
WATERS, MARY L.-MULATTO	BAL	214	2ND WARD
WATERS, MARY-BLACK	FRE	048	FREDERIC
WATERS, MARY-BLACK	FRE	023	FREDERIC
WATERS, MOSES	KEN	298	3RD DIST
WATERS, MRS.	BAL	142	19TH WAR
WATERS, NANCY	CEC	065	1ST E DI
WATERS, NANCY	PRI	086	QUEEN AN
WATERS, NANCY	BAL	270	1ST DIST
WATERS, NANCY	BAL	280	1ST DIST
WATERS, NATHAN OF H.	PRI	044	VANSVILL
WATERS, NATHANIEL	MGM	323	CRACKLIN
WATERS, NELSON	SOM	363	BRINKLEY
WATERS, NICHOLAS	MGM	362	BERRYS D
WATERS, PATRICK	BAL	109	2ND DIST
WATERS, PETER	BAL	123	18TH WAR
WATERS, PETER	SOM	362	BRINKLEY
WATERS, PETER	SOM	350	BRINKLEY
WATERS, PLUMMER	PRI	033	VANSVILL
WATERS, PRESTON	SOM	363	BRINKLEY
WATERS, PRISSY*	DOR	465	1ST DIST
WATERS, PRUDENCE J.	FRE	254	NEW MARK
WATERS, RACHAEL	SOM	534	QUANTICO
WATERS, RACHEL	FRE	250	NEW MARK
WATERS, RACHEL A.	ANN	437	HOWARD D
WATERS, REBECCA	ANN	438	HOWARD D
WATERS, REBECCA	BAL	357	3RD WARD
WATERS, REBECCA	BAL	285	12TH WAR
WATERS, REUBEN	WAS	202	1ST DIST
WATERS, REUBEN	WAS	202	1ST DIST
WATERS, RICHARD	ANN	369	4TH DIST
WATERS, RICHARD	BAL	009	EASTERN
WATERS, RICHARD D.	ANN	422	HOWARD D
WATERS, RICHARD E.	SOM	360	BRINKLEY
WATERS, RICHARD H.	ANN	421	HOWARD D
WATERS, RICHARD H. REV.	ANN	440	HOWARD D
WATERS, RICHARD R.	MGM	322	CRACKLIN
WATERS, RISDEN	BAL	068-	4TH WARD
WATERS, ROBERT	HAR	038	1ST DIST
WATERS, ROBERT	BAL	275	20TH WAR
WATERS, ROBERT	BAL	167	1ST WARD
WATERS, ROBERT H.	SOM	418	PRINCESS
WATERS, ROSEY	SOM	462	HANGARY

WATERS, S. B.	BAL	332	1ST DIST
WATERS, S.R.	BAL	228	12TH WAR
WATERS, SAMUEL	ANN	476	HOWARD D
WATERS, SAMUEL	BAL	173	16TH WAR
WATERS, SAMUEL	BAL	197	17TH WAR
WATERS, SAMUEL	BAL	267	1ST DIST
WATERS, SAMUEL	SOM	353	BRINKLEY
WATERS, SAMUEL	BAL	204	17TH WAR
WATERS, SAMUEL D.	MGM	350	BERRYS D
WATERS, SARAH	BAL	440	14TH WAR
WATERS, SARAH	SOM	447	DAMES QU
WATERS, SARAH	BAL	063	18TH WAR
WATERS, SARAH	SOM	364	BRINKLEY
WATERS, SARAH	SOM	551	TYASKIN
WATERS, SARAH	TAL	005	EASTON D
WATERS, SARAH	BAL	126	2ND DIST
WATERS, SARAH	BAL	228	12TH WAR
WATERS, SARAH-BLACK	QUE	129	1ST E DI
WATERS, SPENCER	BAL	348	3RD WARD
WATERS, SPENCER	BAL	245	6TH WARD
WATERS, STEPHEN	SOM	431	PRINCESS
WATERS, STEPHEN	SOM	436	PRINCESS
WATERS, STEPHEN	SOM	418	PRINCESS
WATERS, STEPHEN	SOM	406	DUBLIN D
WATERS, STEPHEN	SOM	459	HANGARY
WATERS, SUAN	BAL	239	17TH WAR
WATERS, SUSAN	SOM	427	PRINCESS
WATERS, SUSAN	SOM	356	BRINKLEY
WATERS, SUSAN	SOM	485	TRAPP DI
WATERS, SUSAN	BAL	025	15TH WAR
WATERS, SUSAN	BAL	382	3RD WARD
WATERS, TELMON	MGM	430	CLARKSTR
WATERS, THEADORE	TAL	024	EASTON D
WATERS, THOMAS	PRI	045	VANSVILL
WATERS, THOMAS	SOM	360	BRINKLEY
WATERS, THOMAS	MGM	350	BERRYS D
WATERS, THOMAS	BAL	023	9TH WARD
WATERS, THOMAS	ANN	369	4TH DIST
WATERS, THOMAS-BLACK	CAR	162	NO TWP L
WATERS, ULYSSES	FRE	243	NEW MARK
WATERS, VACHEL	ANN	366	4TH DIST
WATERS, WALTER	HAR	057	1ST DIST
WATERS, WASH	ANN	420	HOWARD D
WATERS, WASHINGTON	MGM	339	CLARKSBU
WATERS, WILLIAM	FRE	167	EMMITTSB
WATERS, WILLIAM	MGM	432	CLARKSTR
WATERS, WILLIAM	SOM	445	DAMES QU
WATERS, WILLIAM	FRE	045	FREDERIC
WATERS, WILLIAM	FRE	299	WOODSBOR
WATERS, WILLIAM	BAL	226	19TH WAR
WATERS, WILLIAM	BAL	226	19TH WAR
WATERS, WILLIAM	CEC	026	ELKTON 3
WATERS, WILLIAM	CAL	041	3RD DIST
WATERS, WILLIAM	ANN	369	4TH DIST
WATERS, WILLIAM	BAL	066	2ND DIST
WATERS, WILLIAM	BAL	118	1ST WARD
WATERS, WILLIAM	BAL	362	1ST DIST
WATERS, WILLIAM	QUE	247	5TH E DI
WATERS, WILLIAM	SOM	536	TYASKIN
WATERS, WILLIAM	SOM	538	TYASKIN
WATERS, WILLIAM	SOM	466	HANGARY
WATERS, WILLIAM A.	FRE	045	FREDERIC
WATERS, WILLIAM C.	BAL	048	15TH WAR
WATERS, WILLIAM E.	SOM	431	PRINCESS
WATERS, WILLIAM H.	BAL	425	8TH WARD
WATERS, WILLIAM H.	BAL	231	6TH WARD
WATERS, WILLIAM HENRY	MGM	362	BERRYS D
WATERS, WILLIAM S.	SOM	428	PRINCESS
WATERS, WILLIAM SR.	SOM	362	BRINKLEY
WATERS, WILLIAM T.	BAL	032	4TH WARD
WATERS, WILLIAM W.	BAL	411	1ST DIST
WATERS, ZACHARIAH	MGM	430	CLARKSTR
WATERS, ZACHARIAH D.	FRE	039	FREDERIC
WATERS, ZACOCK M.	CAR	227	5TH DIST
WATERS, ZEBULON	BAL	417	8TH WARD
WATERSON, AUTHER R.	BAL	294	7TH WARD
WATERSON, GEORGE T.	BAL	433	8TH WARD
WATERSON, JOHN	BAL	031	15TH WAR
WATERSON, WILSON	BAL	162	1ST WARD
WATERTON, ANN	BAL	292	17TH WAR
WATES, ANN	BAL	359	13TH WAR
WATES, SOLOMON	BAL	471	14TH WAR
WATESR, COHNE	PRI	086	QUEEN AN
WATESR, E.F.	WAS	016	2ND SUBD
WATHAM, WILLIAM	HAR	205	3RD DIST
WATHAN, ANN	ALL	217	CUMBERLA
WATHEA, MARY	MGM	345	CLARKSBU
WATHEA, WILLIAM	MGM	345	CLARKSBU
WATHEN, BENJAMIN H.	MGM	323	CRACKLIN
WATHEN, CLEMENT	ST	266	3RD E DI
WATHEN, FRANKLIN	ST	271	3RD E DI
WATHEN, GEORGE	ST	266	3RD E DI
WATHEN, JAMES F.	ST	270	3RD E DI
WATHEN, JAMES H.	ST	277	3RD E DI
WATHEN, JOHN F.	ST	273	3RD E DI
WATHEN, LUNICDA	ST	270	3RD E DI
WATHEN, ROBERT H.	ST	266	3RD E DI
WATHEW, MARTIN	ST	266	3RD E DI
WATHEW, MARY A.	ST	267	3RD E DI
WATHING, SOPHIA	ANN	473	HOWARD D
WATHON, JAMES H.	FRE	022	FREDERIC
WATKIN, REBECCA	ANN	278	ANNAPOLI
WATKINS, ALEXANDER	QUE	225	4TH E DI
WATKINS, ALFRED	BAL	240	12TH WAR
WATKINS, ALPHA	MGM	341	CLARKSBU
WATKINS, ANN	BAL	255	12TH WAR
WATKINS, ANN	BAL	208	6TH WARD
WATKINS, ANN E.	BAL	028	15TH WAR
WATKINS, ANN E.-MULATTO	FRE	040	FREDERIC
WATKINS, ANN J.	MGM	435	CLARKSTR
WATKINS, ANN R.	BAL	203	19TH WAR
WATKINS, ANNA	BAL	168	16TH WAR
WATKINS, ARCHIBALD	BAL	051	15TH WAR
WATKINS, ARCHIBALD W.	BAL	105	15TH WAR
WATKINS, BEDFORD-BLACK	MGM	423	MEDLEY 3
WATKINS, BENJAMIN	ANN	295	1ST DIST
WATKINS, BENJAMIN DR-	ANN	327	2ND DIST
WATKINS, BETSEY	BAL	201	11TH WAR
WATKINS, CALEB	MGM	345	CLARKSBU
WATKINS, CAROLINE	BAL	112	5TH WARD
WATKINS, CATHARINE	BAL	159	16TH WAR
WATKINS, CHARLES	ANN	320	2ND DIST
WATKINS, CHARLES	ANN	315	1ST DIST
WATKINS, CHARLES	ANN	452	HOWARD D
WATKINS, DANIEL	ANN	309	1ST DIST
WATKINS, DANIEL	BAL	082	15TH WAR
WATKINS, DANIEL	QUE	222	4TH E DI
WATKINS, EDWARD	WAS	204	1ST DIST
WATKINS, EDWARD	ANN	276	ANNAPOLI
WATKINS, ELIZABETH	BAL	165	6TH WARD
WATKINS, ELIZABETH	CEC	200	7TH E DI
WATKINS, ELIZABETH	BAL	459	14TH WAR
WATKINS, ELIZABETH J.	BAL	145	16TH WAR
WATKINS, EMANUEL	BAL	065	4TH WARD
WATKINS, FRANCIS	BAL	093	5TH WARD
WATKINS, GARRAWAY	MGM	321	CRACKLIN
WATKINS, GASSAWAY	MGM	346	CLARKSBU
WATKINS, GEORGE	BAL	154	5TH WARD
WATKINS, GEORGE	BAL	172	11TH WAR
WATKINS, GEORGE W.	BAL	289	20TH WAR
WATKINS, GRAFTON	MGM	346	CLARKSBU
WATKINS, GREENBERRY M.	MGM	392	ROCKERLE
WATKINS, HANAH	BAL	112	18TH WAR
WATKINS, HARRIET A.	ANN	291	ANNAPOLI
WATKINS, HENRIETTA	BAL	198	6TH WARD
WATKINS, HESTER A.	BAL	418	14TH WAR
WATKINS, HORATIO	WAS	204	1ST DIST
WATKINS, IRA	BAL	243	20TH WAR
WATKINS, ISAAC	BAL	155	5TH WARD
WATKINS, ISAIAH	BAL	096	2ND DIST
WATKINS, ISIAH*	DOR	368	3RD DIVI
WATKINS, JAMES	BAL	119	1ST WARD
WATKINS, JAMES	WAS	204	1ST DIST
WATKINS, JAMES B.	TAL	087	ST MICHA
WATKINS, JAMES H.	ANN	315	1ST DIST
WATKINS, JAMES W.	BAL	227	12TH WAR
WATKINS, JANE	ANN	336	3RD DIST
WATKINS, JANE	ANN	507	HOWARD D
WATKINS, JANE	BAL	183	16TH WAR
WATKINS, JANE	CAL	060	3RD DIST
WATKINS, JOHN	FRE	018	FREDERIC
WATKINS, JOHN	FRE	378	PETERSVI
WATKINS, JOHN	HAR	066	1ST DIST
WATKINS, JOHN	BAL	188	19TH WAR
WATKINS, JOHN	BAL	384	1ST DIST
WATKINS, JOHN	BAL	365	3RD WARD
WATKINS, JOHN	BAL	095	2ND DIST
WATKINS, JOHN	MGM	435	CLARKSTR
WATKINS, JOHN G.	ANN	446	HOWARD D
WATKINS, JOHN G.	BAL	142	16TH WAR
WATKINS, JOHN N.	ANN	266	ANNAPOLI
WATKINS, JOHN N.	ANN	270	ANNAPOLI
WATKINS, JOHN S.	ANN	483	HOWARD D
WATKINS, JOHN T.	BAL	032	9TH WARD
WATKINS, JOHN T.	MGM	435	CLARKSTR
WATKINS, JOHN W.	MGM	344	CLARKSBU
WATKINS, JOHONATHAN	BAL	112	18TH WAR
WATKINS, JOSEPH	BAL	460	1ST DIST
WATKINS, JOSEPH S.	MGM	435	CLARKSTR
WATKINS, JOSIAH	CAR	120	NO TWP L
WATKINS, JULIANA	BAL	066	10TH WAR
WATKINS, KATE	ANN	327	2ND DIST
WATKINS, LAURA	BAL	122	18TH WAR
WATKINS, LEVIN B.	MGM	346	CLARKSBU
WATKINS, LLOYD	BAL	143	16TH WAR
WATKINS, LORENZO	MGM	436	CLARKSTR
WATKINS, LOUIS	BAL	331	1ST DIST
WATKINS, LUCRETIA A.	MGM	345	CLARKSBU
WATKINS, LUCY	ANN	327	2ND DIST
WATKINS, LUCY	BAL	260	12TH WAR
WATKINS, LYDIA A.	BAL	430	8TH WARD
WATKINS, MANELIA E.	MGM	321	CRACKLIN
WATKINS, MARIA	ANN	291	ANNAPOLI
WATKINS, MARY	BAL	383	1ST DIST
WATKINS, MARY	BAL	167	19TH WAR
WATKINS, MARY	BAL	223	17TH WAR
WATKINS, MARY L.	BAL	212	11TH WAR
WATKINS, MATILDA	BAL	049	9TH WARD
WATKINS, MUNRCE	BAL	010	9TH WARD
WATKINS, N.J.	ANN	279	ANNAPOLI
WATKINS, NELLY	PRI	005	BLADENSB
WATKINS, NICHOLAS	ANN	340	3RD DIST
WATKINS, NICHOLAS E.	BAL	046	4TH WARD
WATKINS, NOBLE G.	BAL	145	16TH WAR
WATKINS, NOBLE G.	BAL	153	16TH WAR
WATKINS, PETER	TAL	083	ST MICHA
WATKINS, PRUDENCE	BAL	250	17TH WAR
WATKINS, RACHEL	MGM	346	CLARKSBU
WATKINS, RACHEL	HAR	066	1ST DIST
WATKINS, RACHEL	BAL	331	1ST DIST
WATKINS, RICHARD	MGM	344	CLARKSBU
WATKINS, RICHARD	MGM	439	CLARKSTR
WATKINS, RICHARD G.	ANN	432	HOWARD D
WATKINS, RICHARD R.	BAL	125	16TH WAR
WATKINS, RICHARD R.	WAS	205	1ST DIST
WATKINS, ROBERT	CEC	063	1ST E DI
WATKINS, ROSANNA	WAS	204	1ST DIST
WATKINS, RUTH	BAL	095	2ND DIST
WATKINS, SALLY	BAL	074	18TH WAR
WATKINS, SAMUEL	BAL	373	13TH WAR
WATKINS, SAMUEL	BAL	135	18TH WAR
WATKINS, SAMUEL	CAR	229	5TH DIST
WATKINS, SAMUEL	BAL	095	2ND DIST
WATKINS, SAMUEL	ANN	507	HOWARD D
WATKINS, SAMUEL	BAL	221	12TH WAR
WATKINS, SAMUEL B.	MGM	435	CLARKSTR
WATKINS, SARAH	ST	263	3RD E DI
WATKINS, SARAH	ANN	450	HOWARD D
WATKINS, SARAH	BAL	348	3RD WARD
WATKINS, SARAH	BAL	284	20TH WAR
WATKINS, SARAH E.	CEC	146	PORT DUP
WATKINS, SILAS B.	MGM	346	CLARKSBU
WATKINS, SUNNAN	ANN	336	3RD DIST
WATKINS, SUSANA	BAL	342	3RD WARD
WATKINS, THOASM	BAL	179	2ND DIST
WATKINS, THOMAS	ANN	460	HOWARD D
WATKINS, THOMAS	ANN	464	HOWARD D
WATKINS, THOMAS	ANN	422	HOWARD D
WATKINS, THOMAS	BAL	327	13TH WAR
WATKINS, THOMAS	BAL	024	9TH WARD
WATKINS, THOMAS	BAL	173	6TH WARD
WATKINS, THOMAS	BAL	144	1ST WARD
WATKINS, THOMAS	MGM	398	ROCKERLE
WATKINS, THOMAS	CAL	048	3RD DIST
WATKINS, THOMAS	WAS	094	2ND SUBD
WATKINS, THOMAS B.	BAL	028	15TH WAR
WATKINS, THOMAS C.	BAL	081	15TH WAR
WATKINS, THOMAS F.	BAL	356	3RD WARD
WATKINS, THOMAS J.	DOR	323	1ST DIST
WATKINS, W.	ANN	271	ANNAPOLI
WATKINS, WALTER C.	ANN	292	ANNAPOLI
WATKINS, WILLIAM	ANN	314	1ST DIST
WATKINS, WILLIAM	ANN	313	1ST DIST
WATKINS, WILLIAM	BAL	124	16TH WAR
WATKINS, WILLIAM	BAL	158	16TH WAR
WATKINS, WILLIAM	BAL	456	8TH WARD
WATKINS, WILLIAM	BAL	294	7TH WARD
WATKINS, WILLIAM	BAL	180	2ND WARD
WATKINS, WILLIAM	ANN	456	HOWARD D
WATKINS, WILLIAM	FRE	409	JEFFERSO
WATKINS, WILLIAM	CEC	200	7TH E DI
WATKINS, WILLIAM	MGM	346	CLARKSBU
WATKINS, WILLIAM	MGM	345	CLARKSBU
WATKINS, WILLIAM	BAL	347	13TH WAR
WATKINS, WILLIAM	BAL	047	4TH WARD
WATKINS, WILLIAM	BAL	119	18TH WAR
WATKINS, WILLIAM	BAL	028	18TH WAR
WATKINS, WILLIAM	QUE	236	4TH E DI
WATKINS, WILLIAM H.	CAR	122	NO TWP L
WATKINS, WILLIAM N.	ANN	483	HOWARD D
WATKINS, WILLIAM W.	BAL	134	16TH WAR
WATKINS, WILLIAM W.	BAL	468	14TH WAR
WATLER, WILLIAM	BAL	120	1ST WARD
WATLES, ELLEN	BAL	129	11TH WAR
WATS, MARTHA	BAL	215	11TH WAR
WATS, WILLIAM	CAL	014	1ST DIST
WATSBERGHER	BAL	221	6TH WARD
WATSIFER, ANTON	BAL	369	8TH WARD
WATSON, ABRAHAM	CEC	178	7TH E DI
WATSON, AGNELL	PRI	052	AQUASCO
WATSON, ALEXANDER	PRI	058	NOTTINGH
WATSON, ALEXANDER S.	ALL	209	CUMBERLA
WATSON, ALEXANDER-BLACK	QUE	132	1ST E DI
WATSON, AMANDA	WAS	071	2ND SUBD
WATSON, ANN	BAL	065	15TH WAR
WATSON, ANN E.	BAL	005	18TH WAR
WATSON, ANNA	BAL	416	8TH WARD
WATSON, ARON	BAL	339	3RD WARD
WATSON, BENJAMIN	BAL	110	2ND DIST
WATSON, BENJAMIN	PRI	051	AQUASCO
WATSON, BENJAMIN R.	BAL	339	3RD WARD
WATSON, BILL	PRI	091	MARLBROU
WATSON, CHARLES	BAL	459	8TH WARD
WATSON, CHARLES	BAL	079	15TH WAR
WATSON, CHRISTIAN	WAS	097	2ND DIST
WATSON, DANIEL	PRI	110	PISCATAW
WATSON, DANIEL-BLACK	ST	340	5TH E DI
WATSON, DAVID	BAL	122	16TH WAR
WATSON, DAVID	BAL	225	6TH WARD
WATSON, DAVID B.	BAL	304	17TH WAR
WATSON, EBENEZAR	CEC	095	4TH E DI
WATSON, EDWARD	BAL	038	1ST WARD
WATSON, ELIZA	BAL	212	6TH WARD
WATSON, ELIZABETH	BAL	080	4TH WARD
WATSON, ELIZABETH	PRI	058	NOTTINGH
WATSON, EMRET	WOR	344	1ST E DI
WATSON, FANNY	BAL	248	12TH WAR
WATSON, FIELDER	PRI	051	AQUASCO
WATSON, FREDERICK	BAL	203	2ND WARD
WATSON, FREDERICK	BAL	269	2ND WARD
WATSON, GEORGE	BAL	456	8TH WARD
WATSON, GEORGE W.	BAL	104	5TH WARD
WATSON, HAMPTON J.	BAL	343	13TH WAR
WATSON, HARRY	BAL	153	2ND DIST
WATSON, HENLEY-BLACK	ST	346	5TH E DI
WATSON, HENRY	BAL	051	15TH WAR
WATSON, HENRY	ANN	346	3RD DIST
WATSON, HENRY	BAL	469	14TH WAR
WATSON, HUGH	BAL	005	9TH WARD
WATSON, HUGH	BAL	239	12TH WAR
WATSON, HUGH	BAL	218	6TH WARD
WATSON, HUGH	ALL	152	6TH E.D.
WATSON, ISAAC C.	FRE	092	FREDERIC
WATSON, J.	BAL	149	1ST WARD
WATSON, J.	BAL	163	1ST WARD
WATSON, J.	BAL	163	1ST WARD
WATSON, JAMES	BAL	158	1ST WARD
WATSON, JAMES	BAL	220	6TH WARD
WATSON, JAMES	BAL	211	2ND WARD
WATSON, JAMES	BAL	172	1ST WARD
WATSON, JAMES	ALL	183	8TH E.D.
WATSON, JAMES	CAL	047	3RD DIST
WATSON, JAMES	CEC	084	CHARLEST
WATSON, JAMES	BAL	225	19TH WAR
WATSON, JAMES	PRI	050	AQUASCO
WATSON, JAMES T.	BAL	172	16TH WAR
WATSON, JAMES-BLACK	QUE	132	1ST E DI
WATSON, JANE	BAL	175	11TH WAR
WATSON, JANE	BAL	353	7TH WARD
WATSON, JOHN	BAL	455	8TH WARD
WATSON, JOHN	ALL	088	5TH E.D.
WATSON, JOHN	BAL	188	6TH WARD
WATSON, JOHN	BAL	027	9TH WARD
WATSON, JOHN	BAL	135	5TH WARD
WATSON, JOHN	BAL	122	1ST WARD
WATSON, JOHN	BAL	287	3RD WARD
WATSON, JOHN	BAL	280	2ND WARD
WATSON, JOHN	BAL	361	8TH WARD
WATSON, JOHN	BAL	127	1ST WARD
WATSON, JOHN	FRE	091	FREDERIC
WATSON, JOHN	SOM	425	PRINCESS
WATSON, JOHN	QUE	191	3RD E DI
WATSON, JOHN	KEN	274	1ST DIST
WATSON, JOHN D.	CEC	111	4TH E DI
WATSON, JOHN D.	CEC	113	4TH E DI
WATSON, JOHN E.	CHA	271	ALLENS F
WATSON, JOHN F.	ST	342	5TH E DI
WATSON, JOSEPH	WAS	189	1ST DIST
WATSON, JOSEPH W.	QUE	195	3RD E DI
WATSON, JOSHUA	PRI	050	AQUASCO
WATSON, JOSHUA	PRI	062	NOTTINGH
WATSON, JOSHUA	BAL	210	2ND WARD
WATSON, KEZIAH	BAL	116	2ND DIST
WATSON, KIMBALL G.	FRE	242	NEW MARK
WATSON, LACKEY	BAL	442	1ST DIST
WATSON, LAVINA	CEC	114	3RD E DI
WATSON, LEVI	BAL	150	11TH WAR
WATSON, LEWIS	BAL	147	1ST WAR
WATSON, LEWIS	BAL	147	1ST WARD
WATSON, LEWIS	WAS	183	BOONSBOR
WATSON, LITTLETON	SOM	389	BRINKLEY
WATSON, LYDIA	CAR	242	TANEYTOW
WATSON, MARARET	PRI	057	NOTTINGH
WATSON, MARGARET	CAL	047	3RD DIST
WATSON, MARGARET J.	BAL	242	2ND WARD
WATSON, MARIAH	WOR	342	1ST E DI
WATSON, MARTHA	SOM	398	BRINKLEY
WATSON, MARTHA A.	ST	266	3RD E DI
WATSON, MARTHA-BLACK	CAR	157	NO TWP L
WATSON, MARY	FRE	080	FREDERIC
WATSON, MARY	CEC	185	7TH E DI
WATSON, MARY	BAL	269	20TH WAR
WATSON, MARY	PRI	050	AQUASCO
WATSON, MARY	PRI	054	AQUASCO
WATSON, MARY	SOM	544	TYASKIN
WATSON, MARY	BAL	300	3RD WARD
WATSON, MARY	BAL	317	3RD WARD
WATSON, MARY	ANN	420	HOWARD D
WATSON, MARY	BAL	002	9TH WARD
WATSON, MARY	BAL	070	10TH WAR

WATSON, MARY A. BAL 033 15TH WAR
WATSON, MARY A. WAS 141 HAGERSTO
WATSON, MARY E. CEC 090 4TH E DI
WATSON, MARY J. BAL 348 1ST DIST
WATSON, MINTY WAS 071 2ND SUBD
WATSON, MISS A.M. BAL 137 5TH WARD
WATSON, MITCHEL WOR 337 1ST E DI
WATSON, NAPOLEON BAL 371 3RD WARD
WATSON, NATHAN QUE 166 2ND E DI
WATSON, NATHAN CAL 061 3RD DIST
WATSON, NEHEMIAH WOR 268 BERLIN 1
WATSON, PATTY WOR 344 1ST E DI
WATSON, PETER DOR 311 1ST DIST
WATSON, ROBERT HAR 101 2ND DIST
WATSON, ROBERT WOR 214 4TH E DI
WATSON, ROBERT BAL 174 11TH WAR
WATSON, SAMUEL CAL 048 3RD DIST
WATSON, SARAH BAL 141 11TH WAR
WATSON, SARAH BAL 054 4TH WARD
WATSON, SARAH BAL 001 15TH WAR
WATSON, SARAH A. BAL 306 7TH WARD
WATSON, SARAH J. CAL 048 3RD DIST
WATSON, STEPHEN ANN 341 3RD DIST
WATSON, SUSAN BAL 094 5TH WARD
WATSON, SUSAN CEC 139 6TH E DI
WATSON, SUTTON CAL 061 3RD DIST
WATSON, T. H. BAL 333 1ST DIST
WATSON, THOMAS BAL 241 2ND WARD
WATSON, THOMAS BAL 426 14TH WAR
WATSON, THOMAS C. ANN 334 2ND DIST
WATSON, THOMAS O. BAL 300 3RD WARD
WATSON, THOMS BAL 199 2ND WARD
WATSON, URIANDA WAS 080 2ND SUBD
WATSON, W. BAL 305 20TH WAR
WATSON, W. J. BAL 147 1ST WARD
WATSON, WEST WOR 347 1ST E DI
WATSON, WILLAIM BAL 145 5TH WARD
WATSON, WILLIAM BAL 185 2ND WARD
WATSON, WILLIAM BAL 402 3RD WARD
WATSON, WILLIAM ANN 394 8TH DIST
WATSON, WILLIAM BAL 177 11TH WAR
WATSON, WILLIAM WOR 348 1ST E DI
WATSON, WILLIAM CAR 156 NO TWP L
WATSON, WILLIAM CEC 084 CHARLEST
WATSON, WILLIAM FRE 241 NEW MARK
WATSON, WILLIAM CEC 035 CHESAPEA
WATSON, WILLIAM H. BAL 169 11TH WAR
WATSON, WILLIAM H. ANN 289 ANNAPOLI
WATSON, WILLIAM H. BAL 114 1ST WARD
WATSON, WILLIAM J. BAL 080 4TH WARD
WATSON, WILLIAM T. HAR 002 1ST DIST
WATSON, WILLIAM T. PRI 050 AQUASCO
WATT, DEWANNER ALL 230 CUMBERLA
WATT, EDWARD SOM 554 TYASKIN
WATT, ELIZABETH HAR 064 1ST DIST
WATT, GEORGE BAL 182 16TH WAR
WATT, HUGH BAL 116 1ST WARD
WATT, JAMES BAL 177 19TH WAR
WATT, JAMS HAR 026 1ST DIST
WATT, NICHOLAS HAR 069 1ST DIST
WATT, REBECCA HAR 068 1ST DIST
WATT, THOMAS ALL 172 7TH E.D.
WATT, WILLIAM FRE 015 FREDERIC
WATT, WILLIAM L. BAL 089 5TH WARD
WATTENTON, NATHAN A.-BLAC ST 338 4TH E DI
WATTER, ADAM ALL 208 CUMBERLA
WATTER, CATHARINE ANN 390 4TH DIST
WATTER, GEORGE ANN 390 4TH DIST
WATTERMYER, DANFORD * BAL 057 18TH WAR
WATTERMYER, JACOB BAL 058 18TH WAR
WATTERS, ABRAM HAR 202 3RD DIST
WATTERS, BENEKRICK F. * HAR 206 3RD DIST
WATTERS, CHARLES HAR 195 3RD DIST
WATTERS, EPINALLS* DOR 319 1ST DIST
WATTERS, FREDERICK BAL 174 2ND DIST
WATTERS, HENRY HAR 204 3RD DIST
WATTERS, HENRY HAR 169 3RD DIST
WATTERS, HENRY G. HAR 109 2ND DIST
WATTERS, ISAAC HAR 089 2ND DIST
WATTERS, JAMES HAR 079 2ND DIST
WATTERS, MAHALY HAR 195 3RD DIST
WATTERS, NICHOLAS HAR 089 2ND DIST
WATTERS, WILLIAM HAR 083 2ND DIST
WATTES, IRAD ALL 217 CUMBERLA
WATTIMORE, HORY DOR 430 1ST DIST
WATTING, ELIZABETH ST 347 5TH E DI
WATTLES, JAMES BAL 250 20TH WAR
WATTLES, JAMES L. BAL 289 20TH WAR
WATTMAN, JOSEPH FRE 387 PETERSVI
WATTS, ABRAHAM N. WAS 030 2ND SUBD
WATTS, ALBERT BAL 071 18TH WAR
WATTS, ALEXANDER BAL 081 15TH WAR
WATTS, ALLEN BAL 106 18TH WAR
WATTS, AMOS BAL 103 18TH WAR
WATTS, ANN ST 305 2ND E DI
WATTS, ANNA BAL 185 6TH WARD
WATTS, BARTON ST 290 2ND E DI
WATTS, BENJAMIN BAL 251 1ST DIST
WATTS, BENJAMIN BAL 123 18TH WAR
WATTS, BENJAMIN BAL 210 19TH WAR
WATTS, BENJAMIN B. * KEN 245 2ND DIST
WATTS, CALEB-BLACK ST 336 4TH E DI
WATTS, CECELIA BAL 369 8TH WARD
WATTS, CHARLES R. BAL 351 3RD WARD
WATTS, CUMBERLAND A. BAL 274 7TH WARD
WATTS, DANIEL BAL 191 17TH WAR
WATTS, DANIEL J. BAL 410 14TH WAR
WATTS, DAVID CAL 024 2ND DIST
WATTS, EBEN KEN 283 3RD DIST
WATTS, ELEANOR A. ST 302 2ND E DI
WATTS, ELENORA C. BAL 186 2ND WARD
WATTS, ELIZABETH ST 274 3RD E DI
WATTS, ELIZABETH A. BAL 013 18TH WAR
WATTS, ELLEN BAL 472 14TH WAR
WATTS, EMILINE ST 290 2ND E DI
WATTS, EMILY BAL 047 15TH WAR
WATTS, FRANCIS A. BAL 122 1ST WARD
WATTS, FREDERICK ALL 214 CUMBERLA
WATTS, FREDERICK J. BAL 305 7TH WARD
WATTS, GEORGE BAL 340 7TH WARD
WATTS, GEORGE BAL 415 14TH WAR
WATTS, GEORGE BAL 240 17TH WAR
WATTS, GEORGE H. BAL 359 8TH WARD
WATTS, GERARD S. ALL 212 CUMBERLA
WATTS, GEROGE KEN 274 1ST DIST
WATTS, GERRARD P. BAL 188 16TH WAR
WATTS, HARRIET BAL 175 16TH WAR
WATTS, HARRIET ANN 351 3RD DIST
WATTS, HARRIET ANN 376 4TH DIST
WATTS, HENRY ANN 368 4TH DIST
WATTS, HENRY ANN 376 4TH DIST
WATTS, HENRY ST 295 2ND E DI
WATTS, HENRY WAS 299 1ST DIST
WATTS, HENRY A. ST 301 2ND E DI
WATTS, HETTY* BAL 402 3RD WARD
WATTS, ISAAC ANN 457 HOWARD D
WATTS, ISAAC BAL 220 12TH WAR
WATTS, ISAIAH ANN 375 4TH DIST
WATTS, JAMES ANN 453 HOWARD D
WATTS, JAMES BAL 154 16TH WAR
WATTS, JAMES KEN 274 1ST DIST
WATTS, JAMIMA BAL 172 2ND DIST
WATTS, JANE BAL 105 10TH WAR
WATTS, JESIAH BAL 359 8TH WARD
WATTS, JOHN BAL 342 7TH WARD
WATTS, JOHN BAL 350 7TH WARD
WATTS, JOHN BAL 347 1ST DIST
WATTS, JOHN BAL 401 1ST DIST
WATTS, JOHN MGM 350 BERRYS D
WATTS, JOHN A. HAR 204 3RD DIST
WATTS, JOHN-BLACK BAL 224 2ND WARD
WATTS, JOHN-BLACK BAL 223 2ND WARD
WATTS, JOSEPH ANN 382 4TH DIST
WATTS, JOSHUA ST 265 3RD E DI
WATTS, JOSHUA S. ANN 366 4TH DIST
WATTS, JSOHUA ST 293 2ND E DI
WATTS, JULIA ANN 339 3RD DIST
WATTS, JULIA A. BAL 149 16TH WAR
WATTS, MARTHA E. BAL 171 16TH WAR
WATTS, MARY ST 265 3RD E DI
WATTS, MARY BAL 096 18TH WAR
WATTS, MARY F. BAL 066 4TH WARD
WATTS, MARYANN* BAL 335 3RD WARD
WATTS, MICHAEL WAS 123 HAGERSTO
WATTS, NANCY* DOR 461 1ST DIST
WATTS, NATH. BAL 307 20TH WAR
WATTS, NELSON BAL 254 17TH WAR
WATTS, OLIVIA ST 302 2ND E DI
WATTS, PATTY WOR 283 BERLIN 1
WATTS, PETER ANN 368 4TH DIST
WATTS, PETER BAL 373 3RD WARD
WATTS, PRISSY* DOR 465 1ST DIST
WATTS, R. BAL 282 2ND WARD
WATTS, RACHAEL BAL 130 11TH WAR
WATTS, REBECCA ALL 092 5TH E.D.
WATTS, REBECCA WOR 272 BERLIN 1
WATTS, REVERDY H. BAL 080 15TH WAR
WATTS, RICHARD ANN 380 4TH DIST
WATTS, RICHARD BAL 333 3RD WARD
WATTS, RICHARD BAL 452 14TH WAR
WATTS, ROBERT ST 289 2ND E DI
WATTS, ROBERT J.-BLACK ST 294 2ND E DI
WATTS, ROBERT-MULATTO FRE 190 5TH E DI
WATTS, SAMUEL BAL 375 13TH WAR
WATTS, SAMUEL WAS 156 HAGERSTO
WATTS, SAMUEL ANN 390 4TH DIST
WATTS, SAMUEL BAL 121 16TH WAR
WATTS, SARAH BAL 078 15TH WAR
WATTS, SARAH BAL 117 5TH WARD
WATTS, SARAH BAL 298 1ST DIST
WATTS, SARAH BAL 127 5TH WARD
WATTS, SARAH QUE 246 5TH E DI
WATTS, SOPHIA ST 287 2ND E DI
WATTS, SOPHIA WAS 232 1ST DIST
WATTS, SOPHIA BAL 081 15TH WAR
WATTS, SUSAN ANN 368 4TH DIST
WATTS, SUSAN MGM 355 BERRYS D
WATTS, SUSANNA BAL 195 6TH WARD
WATTS, THOMAS BAL 298 1ST DIST
WATTS, THOMAS BAL 254 6TH WARD
WATTS, THOMAS DOR 297 1ST DIST
WATTS, THOMAS BAL 228 17TH WAR
WATTS, THOMAS MGM 353 BERRYS D
WATTS, THOMAS B. BAL 408 1ST DIST
WATTS, THOMAS B. WAS 171 FUNKSTOW
WATTS, TILLA WAS 120 2ND DIST
WATTS, WILLIAM ST 297 2ND E DI
WATTS, WILLIAM BAL 311 7TH WARD
WATTS, WILLIAM ANN 268 ANNAPOLI
WATTS, WILLIAM KEN 247 2ND DIST
WATTS, WILLIAM HAR 045 1ST DIST
WATTS, WILLIAM J. BAL 413 3RD WARD
WATTS, WILLIAM W. BAL 408 14TH WAR
WATTY, THOMAS BAL 011 4TH WARD
WATUR, HIMAN F. BAL 012 4TH WARD
WATZ, BENJAMIN P. HAR 189 3RD DIST
WAUGH, B. A. REV- BAL 058 10TH WAR
WAUGH, BEVERLY BAL 476 14TH WAR
WAUGH, FANNY ALL 229 CUMBERLA
WAUGH, JAMES C. WAS 126 HAGERSTO
WAUGH, MARY ALL 227 CUMBERLA
WAUGH, WARREN PRI 095 SPALDING
WAUGH, WILLIAM T. BAL 456 8TH WARD
WAUGHE, GEORGE BAL 385 8TH WARD
WAUNEY, CATHARINE ST 282 3RD E DI
WAWARING, ELIZABETH PRI 016 BLADENSB
WAXLER, SUSAN ALL 135 4TH E.D.
WAXMOUTH, AUGUSTUS BAL 025 4TH WARD
WAXMULD, CHARLES BAL 011 18TH WAR
WAXMUTH, CATHERINE BAL 025 4TH WARD
WAY, CALEB HAR 109 2ND DIST
WAY, CATHERINE BAL 396 3RD WARD
WAY, ELIZABETH A. CEC 147 PORT DUP
WAY, ELON J. TAL 003 EASTON D
WAY, FRANCIS HAR 048 1ST DIST
WAY, GEORGE HAR 023 1ST DIST
WAY, H. BAL 169 1ST WARD
WAY, HESTER HAR 023 1ST DIST
WAY, JACOB BAL 205 6TH DIST
WAY, JAMES CEC 207 7TH E DI
WAY, JAMES B. TAL 080 ST MICHA
WAY, JOHN HAR 050 1ST DIST
WAY, JOHN C. CEC 213 7TH E DI
WAY, MARY HAR 023 1ST DIST
WAY, N. BAL 173 1ST WARD
WAY, THOMAS CEC 206 7TH E DI
WAYBRIGHT, WILLIAM FRE 148 10TH E D
WAYCHE, MARGARET BAL 141 19TH WAR
WAYENING, ELIZABETH BAL 185 2ND WARD
WAYLAND, DAVID BAL 459 8TH WARD
WAYLAND, JAMES BAL 459 8TH WARD
WAYLAND, SARAH BAL 031 9TH WARD
WAYMAN, BENJAMIN-BLACK CAR 167 NO TWP L
WAYMAN, CHARLES-BLACK CAR 169 NO TWP L
WAYMAN, CHARLES-BLACK CAR 084 NO TWP L
WAYMAN, HENRY FRE 338 MIDDLETO
WAYMAN, HENRY ANN 494 HOWARD D
WAYMAN, JOHN W. ANN 513 HOWARD D
WAYMAN, JOSEPH-BLACK FRE 018 FREDERIC
WAYMAN, SARAH BAL 377 13TH WAR
WAYMAN, SERRUME-BLACK CAR 113 NO TWP L
WAYMAN, THOMAS TAL 108 ST MICHA
WAYMAN, THOMAS S. TAL 108 ST MICHA
WAYMAN, WILLIAM-BLACK CAR 091 NO TWP L
WAYMANN, FRANCIS-BLACK CAR 093 NO TWP L
WAYMOUTH, FRANCES BAL 063 4TH WARD
WAYNER, JOSEPH ALL 120 5TH E.D.
WAYPLES, LEMUEL* TAL 014 EASTON D
WAYS, C. BAL 168 1ST WARD
WAYS, FREDERICK HAR 159 3RD DIST
WAYS, GEORGE ALL 252 CUMBERLA
WAYS, GEORGE W. ANN 499 HOWARD D
WAYS, JOHN ALL 217 CUMBERLA
WAYS, JOSEPH ALL 219 CUMBERLA
WAYS, MATTHIAS FRE 261 NEW MARK
WAYS, MICHAEL ALL 072 5TH E.D.
WAYS, SAMUEL D. ALL 218 CUMBERLA
WAYSON, ANDREW BAL 397 8TH WARD
WAYSON, AUGUSTUS BAL 144 1ST WARD
WAYSON, EDWARD* DOR 381 1ST DIST
WAYSON, ELIZABETH ANN 286 ANNAPOLI
WAYSON, G. E. W. ANN 411 8TH DIST
WAYSON, JOHN ANN 407 8TH DIST
WAYSON, N. ANN 271 ANNAPOLI
WAYSON, WARNER ANN 257 ANNAPOLI
WAYSON, WILLIAM ANN 407 8TH DIST
WAYSOND, JULIA * ANN 407 8TH DIST
WEAB, HENRY BAL 437 14TH WAR
WEADER, JACOB BAL 104 1ST WARD
WEADLY, THOMAS* DOR 429 1ST DIST
WEAGBY, GEORGE BAL 259 1ST DIST
WEAGLEY, ANDREW WAS 250 1ST DIST
WEAGLEY, GEORGE WAS 260 1ST DIST
WEAGLEY, SAMUEL C. WAS 260 1ST DIST
WEAGLEY, THOMAS-BLACK FRE 174 5TH E DI
WEAKLEY, CHARLES FRE 194 5TH E DI
WEAKLEY, HENRY-MULATTO CAR 176 8TH DIST
WEAKLEY, JAMES P. BAL 264 7TH WARD
WEAKLEY, JOHN BAL 354 7TH WARD
WEAKLEY, ROBERT M. BAL 387 13TH WAR
WEAKLEY, THOMAS FRE 194 5TH E DI
WEAKLEY, WILLIAM CAR 176 8TH DIST
WEAKLEY, WILLIAM JR.-MULT CAR 176 8TH DIST
WEAKLIN, JOSEPH ST 332 4TH E DI
WEAKLIN, THOMAS ST 269 3RD E DI
WEAKLLY, E.A. HAR 062 1ST DIST
WEAKS, HENRY BAL 450 1ST DIST
WEALTY, CATHARINE WAS 183 BOONSBOR
WEALTY, CATHARINE WAS 260 1ST DIST
WEALTY, DANIEL WAS 222 1ST DIST
WEALTY, ELIZABETH WAS 260 1ST DIST
WEALTY, GEORGE WAS 182 BOONSBOR
WEALTY, HAMMON WAS 201 1ST DIST
WEALTY, HENERY WAS 263 1ST DIST
WEALTY, HENRY G. WAS 222 1ST DIST
WEALTY, JACK WAS 162 HAGERSTO
WEALTY, JACOB WAS 260 1ST DIST
WEALTY, JOHN WAS 260 1ST DIST
WEALTY, LOUISA WAS 283 1ST DIST
WEALTY, MAGDELANE WAS 178 BOONSBOR
WEALTY, MARY WAS 248 1ST DIST
WEALTY, MICHAEL WAS 220 1ST DIST
WEALTY, SUSAN WAS 260 1ST DIST
WEALTY, TICE WAS 185 BOONSBOR
WEANER, JOHN BAL 274 2ND WARD
WEANING, MARY M. FRE 378 PETERSVI
WEANT, CATHARINE FRE 161 EMMITTSB
WEANT, JOHN FRE 176 5TH E DI
WEANT, JOHN CAR 308 1ST DIST
WEANT, SAMUEL FRE 172 5TH E DI
WEAR, ABRAHAM CAR 077 NO TWP L
WEARHAM, JOHN HAR 147 3RD DIST
WEARLEY, JOHN BAL 111 18TH WAR
WEAS, FRANK BAL 110 5TH WARD
WEASEL, MARGARET FRE 366 CATOCTIN
WEASLE, FRANCIS FRE 367 CATOCTIN
WEASNER, MICHAEL BAL 220 2ND WARD
WEAST, CONRADT WAS 147 HAGERSTO
WEAST, GEORGE WAS 131 HAGERSTO
WEAST, HENRY WAS 210 1ST DIST
WEAST, HIRAM WAS 181 BOONSBOR
WEAST, SUSAN WAS 182 BOONSBOR
WEASY, CATHARINE BAL 438 14TH WAR
WEAT, JAMES C. WAS 140 HAGERSTO
WEATHERBY, ANN M. * SOM 460 HANGARY
WEATHERBY, JOSEPH DOCTOR DOR 354 3RD DIVI
WEATHERBY, LEAH SOM 513 BARREN C
WEATHERBY, LEAH SR.* SOM 509 BARREN C
WEATHERBY, NACMI BAL 027 15TH WAR
WEATHERBY, PETER* SOM 499 SALISBUR
WEATHERBY, SAMUEL* SOM 509 BARREN C
WEATHERBY, THOMAS* SOM 509 BARREN C
WEATHEREL, GEORGE HAR 206 3RD DIST
WEATHEREL, M. J. HAR 192 3RD DIST
WEATHERLY, ANN M. * SOM 460 HANGARY
WEATHERLY, JAMES SOM 549 TYASKIN
WEATHERLY, JOSEPH SOM 516 BARREN C
WEATHERLY, LEAH SR.* SOM 509 BARREN C
WEATHERLY, PETER* SOM 499 SALISBUR
WEATHERLY, SAMUEL* SOM 509 BARREN C
WEATHERLY, SUSAN SOM 533 QUANTICO
WEATHERLY, THOMAS* SOM 509 BARREN C
WEATHERS, JOSHUA BAL 322 3RD WARD
WEATHERTY, EDWARD K. WOR 229 6TH E DI
WEATHLEY, WILLIAM L. ST 285 2ND E DI
WEATZ, WILLIAM FRE 171 5TH E DI
WEAVEL, REBECCA WAS 260 1ST DIST
WEAVEL, WILLIAM WAS 142 HAGERSTO
WEAVER, ABRAHAM BAL 417 3RD WARD
WEAVER, ABRAHAN CAR 400 2ND DIST
WEAVER, ADAM BAL 407 3RD WARD
WEAVER, ADAM BAL 253 2ND WARD
WEAVER, ALEXANDER FRE 318 MIDDLETO
WEAVER, AMANDA WAS 014 WILLIAMS
WEAVER, AMBROSE BAL 037 4TH WARD
WEAVER, ANDREW BAL 093 1ST WARD
WEAVER, ANDREW N. BAL 076 1ST WARD
WEAVER, ANN R.S. BAL 077 1ST WARD
WEAVER, ANNA WAS 258 1ST DIST
WEAVER, BALDERSON BAL 236 2ND WARD
WEAVER, BENJAMIN BAL 465 14TH WAR
WEAVER, BLANSINA BAL 121 2ND DIST
WEAVER, CAROLINE BAL 361 13TH WAR
WEAVER, CASPER BAL 266 17TH WAR
WEAVER, CASPER BAL 129 18TH WAR
WEAVER, CASPER W. WAS 090 2ND SUBD
WEAVER, CATHARINE BAL 341 13TH WAR
WEAVER, CATHARINE CAR 344 6TH DIST
WEAVER, CATHERINE FRE 062 FREDERIC
WEAVER, CHARLES CEC 120 4TH E DI

Name	County	Page	District
WEAVER, CHARLES	BAL	095	1ST WARD
WEAVER, CHARLES P.	CAR	340	6TH DIST
WEAVER, CHRISTIAN	FRE	399	JEFFERSO
WEAVER, CHRISTIAN	BAL	222	1ST DIST
WEAVER, CCNRADT	BAL	407	8TH WARD
WEAVER, CORNELEAS	BAL	096	18TH WAR
WEAVER, D.C.	BAL	282	12TH WAR
WEAVER, DANIEL	BAL	225	1ST DIST
WEAVER, DANIEL	BAL	355	1ST DIST
WEAVER, DANIEL	BAL	371	3RD WARD
WEAVER, DANIEL	BAL	095	18TH WAR
WEAVER, CAVID	CAR	347	6TH DIST
WEAVER, DAVID	CAR	269	WESTMINS
WEAVER, CAVIC	BAL	135	2ND DIST
WEAVER, DAVIC	WAS	271	1ST DIST
WEAVER, DORTHEA	BAL	112	1ST WARD
WEAVER, E.	PRI	095	SPALDING
WEAVER, EDWARD	QUE	249	5TH E DI
WEAVER, EDWARD T.	BAL	025	9TH WARD
WEAVER, ELIZABETH	BAL	125	16TH WAR
WEAVER, ELIZABETH	QUE	248	5TH E DI
WEAVER, ELIZABETH	WAS	295	1ST DIST
WEAVER, ELIZABETH	CAR	183	8TH DIST
WEAVER, ELLEN	CAR	398	2ND DIST
WEAVER, FERDINAND	WAS	277	RIDGEVIL
WEAVER, FIAT	BAL	225	17TH WAR
WEAVER, FLORA L.	BAL	199	11TH WAR
WEAVER, FRANCES	BAL	262	12TH WAR
WEAVER, FRANCIS	BAL	114	1ST WARD
WEAVER, FRANCIS	BAL	121	11TH WAR
WEAVER, FREDERICK	BAL	036	15TH WAR
WEAVER, GACSSED	BAL	285	2ND WARD
WEAVER, GEORGE	BAL	201	11TH WAR
WEAVER, GEORGE	BAL	076	1ST WARD
WEAVER, GEORGE	BAL	107	5TH WARD
WEAVER, GEORGE	ALL	181	8TH E.D.
WEAVER, GEORGE	CEC	170	6TH E DI
WEAVER, GEORGE	CAR	269	WESTMINS
WEAVER, GEORGE	CAR	342	6TH DIST
WEAVER, GEORGE	CAR	328	MANCHEST
WEAVER, GEORGE	BAL	279	17TH WAR
WEAVER, GECRGE A.	WAS	148	HAGERSTO
WEAVER, GEORGE C.	CEC	119	3RD E DI
WEAVER, GECRGE S.	WAS	143	2ND DIST
WEAVER, GRAFTON	ANN	375	4TH DIST
WEAVER, HARMAN	FRE	047	FREDERIC
WEAVER, HARMAN D.	BAL	162	16TH WAR
WEAVER, HARRIET	FRE	078	FREDERIC
WEAVER, HARRIET E.	PRI	002	BLADENSB
WEAVER, HARRISON	CAR	236	UNION TO
WEAVER, HARRY	ALL	146	6TH E.D.
WEAVER, HENRY	BAL	151	16TH WAR
WEAVER, HENRY	BAL	193	5TH DIST
WEAVER, HENRY	BAL	239	17TH WAR
WEAVER, HENRY	BAL	335	13TH WAR
WEAVER, HENRY	WAS	268	1ST DIST
WEAVER, HESTER	QUE	246	5TH E DI
WEAVER, IDA	BAL	336	3RD WARD
WEAVER, J. W.	ALL	111	5TH E.D.
WEAVER, JACOB	BAL	139	16TH WAR
WEAVER, JACOB	BAL	027	2ND DIST
WEAVER, JACOB B.	BAL	308	3RD WARD
WEAVER, JAMES	BAL	445	14TH WAR
WEAVER, JANE	CEC	007	ELKTON 3
WEAVER, JANE	BAL	193	19TH WAR
WEAVER, JESSE	CAR	403	2ND DIST
WEAVER, JHN	QUE	249	5TH E DI
WEAVER, JOHN	QUE	245	5TH E DI
WEAVER, JOHN	WAS	167	1ST DIST
WEAVER, JOHN	CAR	402	2ND DIST
WEAVER, JOHN	FRE	312	MIDDLETO
WEAVER, JOHN	BAL	106	18TH WAR
WEAVER, JOHN	BAL	245	17TH WAR
WEAVER, JOHN	BAL	416	14TH WAR
WEAVER, JOHN	CAR	349	6TH DIST
WEAVER, JCHN	BAL	071	18TH WAR
WEAVER, JOHN	BAL	368	1ST DIST
WEAVER, JOHN	BAL	236	1ST DIST
WEAVER, JOHN	ALL	218	CUMBERLA
WEAVER, JOHN	BAL	085	15TH WAR
WEAVER, JOHN	ALL	210	CUMBERLA
WEAVER, JOHN	BAL	251	12TH WAR
WEAVER, JOHN	BAL	126	5TH WARD
WEAVER, JCHN	BAL	274	2ND WARD
WEAVER, JOHN A.	WAS	174	FUNKSTOW
WEAVER, JOHN H.	BAL	093	10TH WAR
WEAVER, JONOTHAN	WAS	131	HAGERSTO
WEAVER, JOSEPH	ANN	426	HOWARD D
WEAVER, JOSEPH	ANN	429	HOWARD D
WEAVER, JOSEPH	ANN	418	HOWARD D
WEAVER, JOSEPH	BAL	092	1ST WARD
WEAVER, JOSEPH	BAL	001	18TH WAR
WEAVER, JOSEPH	BAL	223	17TH WAR
WEAVER, JOSEPH	CEC	178	7TH E DI
WEAVER, JOSEPHEEN	BAL	355	1ST DIST
WEAVER, JULIA A.	CAR	350	6TH DIST
WEAVER, JUSTICE	BAL	230	2ND WARD
WEAVER, LEVI	BAL	346	13TH WAR
WEAVER, LEWIS H.	CAR	313	1ST DIST
WEAVER, LOUIS	BAL	237	1ST DIST
WEAVER, MARCH	BAL	211	17TH WAR
WEAVER, MARGARET	CAR	187	4TH DIST
WEAVER, MARY	CAR	270	WESTMINS
WEAVER, MARY	BAL	236	2ND WARD
WEAVER, MARY	BAL	054	15TH WAR
WEAVER, MARY	WAS	248	SMITHSBU
WEAVER, MARY A.	BAL	165	16TH WAR
WEAVER, MELCHOIR	BAL	238	6TH WARD
WEAVER, MICHAEL	WAS	289	1ST DIST
WEAVER, MRS.	BAL	123	5TH WARD
WEAVER, NANCY	BAL	240	1ST DIST
WEAVER, NICHOLAS	QUE	248	5TH E DI
WEAVER, PETER	BAL	252	2ND WARD
WEAVER, PETER	BAL	179	2ND WARD
WEAVER, PETER	BAL	371	13TH WAR
WEAVER, PHILIP	CAR	396	2ND DIST
WEAVER, PHILIP D.	WAS	122	HAGERSTO
WEAVER, PHILLIP	BAL	255	2ND WARD
WEAVER, POLLY	CAR	270	WESTMINS
WEAVER, REBECCA	BAL	074	15TH WAR
WEAVER, RENEGIUS	BAL	073	2ND DIST
WEAVER, ROBERT	BAL	282	12TH WAR
WEAVER, ROSANNA	CAR	235	UNION TO
WEAVER, RUTH	BAL	245	20TH WAR
WEAVER, SAMUEL	CEC	091	4TH E DI
WEAVER, SAMUEL	CAR	403	2ND DIST
WEAVER, SAMUEL	WAS	195	1ST DIST
WEAVER, SARAH	KEN	293	3RD DIST
WEAVER, SARAH	BAL	089	15TH WAR
WEAVER, SARAH	BAL	252	6TH WARD
WEAVER, SOPHIA	CAR	340	6TH DIST
WEAVER, SUSAN	WAS	275	RIDGEVIL
WEAVER, THOMAS	QUE	243	5TH E DI
WEAVER, WILLAM	WAS	264	1ST DIST
WEAVER, WILLIAM	BAL	041	4TH WARD
WEAVER, WILLIAM	BAL	213	17TH WAR
WEAVER, WILLIAM	BAL	335	3RD WARD
WEAVER, WILLIAM H.	BAL	309	3RD WARD
WEAVER, WILLIAM H.	BAL	281	17TH WAR
WEAVER, WILLULM	BAL	232	1ST DIST
WEAVERLY, MARCUS	ALL	245	CUMBERLA
WEAVIL, JOHN	ALL	226	CUMBERLA
WEBB, ABNER	BAL	251	12TH WAR
WEBB, ALBERT L.	BAL	360	13TH WAR
WEBB, ALFRED	SOM	413	DUBLIN D
WEBB, ANG P.	BAL	248	12TH WAR
WEBB, ARIANA	BAL	179	6TH WARD
WEBB, ASA	FRE	165	EMMITTSB
WEBB, ASBURY-BLACK	CAR	144	NO TWP L
WEBB, AUGUSTA-BLACK	CAR	157	NO TWP L
WEBB, BACHUS-BLACK	CAR	146	NO TWP L
WEBB, BENJAMIN	FRE	165	EMMITTSB
WEBB, CATHARINE	FRE	175	5TH E DI
WEBB, CATHARINE	BAL	345	13TH WAR
WEBB, CHARLES	BAL	219	6TH WARD
WEBB, CLARISSA	BAL	197	6TH WARD
WEBB, CLARISSA	ANN	380	4TH DIST
WEBB, CLEY	BAL	323	12TH WAR
WEBB, CONRAD	BAL	167	19TH WAR
WEBB, DAVID	WOR	330	1ST E DI
WEBB, EDMOND J.	BAL	381	13TH WAR
WEBB, EDWARD	WOR	226	4TH E DI
WEBB, ELIZA	KEN	254	1ST DIST
WEBB, ELIZABETH	ANN	402	8TH DIST
WEBB, ELLEN	FRE	410	8TH E DI
WEBB, EMMA	BAL	407	14TH WAR
WEBB, EMMA	WOR	293	9TH E DI
WEBB, FLOYD N.	WAS	245	SMITHSBU
WEBB, FRANCIS	BAL	097	5TH WARD
WEBB, FRANKEY	WOR	338	1ST E DI
WEBB, GALLAWAY	TAL	054	EASTON D
WEBB, GALLOWAY	DOR	430	1ST DIST
WEBB, GEORGE	FRE	238	NEW MARK
WEBB, GEORGE	BAL	304	7TH WARD
WEBB, GEORGE R.	ANN	362	4TH DIST
WEBB, GECRGE W.	BAL	142	11TH WAR
WEBB, HAMILTON	CAL	044	3RD DIST
WEBB, HANSON	CAR	271	WESTMINS
WEBB, HANSON F.	FRE	410	8TH E DI
WEBB, HARRISCN-	CAR	161	NO TWP L
WEBB, HENRY	BAL	071	15TH WAR
WEBB, HENRY A.	BAL	190	19TH WAR
WEBB, HENRY W.	BAL	156	16TH WAR
WEBB, HESTER-BLACK	CAR	161	NO TWP L
WEBB, ISAAC	WOR	350	1ST E DI
WEBB, ISABELLA	TAL	046	EASTON T
WEBB, IWLLIAM-BLACK	CAR	157	NO TWP L
WEBB, JACOB	BAL	149	16TH WAR
WEBB, JAMES	BAL	402	8TH WARD
WEBB, JAMES	BAL	221	6TH WARD
WEBB, JAMES	BAL	034	9TH WARD
WEBB, JAMES	CEC	050	1ST E DI
WEBB, JAMES	BAL	037	4TH WARD
WEBB, JAMES	DOR	409	1ST DIST
WEBB, JAMES	DOR	409	1ST DIST
WEBB, JAMES F.	DOR	448	1ST DIST
WEBB, JAMES W.	BAL	060	1ST WARD
WEBB, JAMES-BLACK	CAR	160	NO TWP L
WEBB, JANE	DOR	448	1ST DIST
WEBB, JANE	BAL	058	18TH WAR
WEBB, JOHN	BAL	199	19TH WAR
WEBB, JCHN	DOR	319	1ST DIST
WEBB, JOHN	SOM	413	DUBLIN D
WEBB, JOHN	BAL	316	7TH WARD
WEBB, JOHN	BAL	220	12TH WAR
WEBB, JOHN	BAL	296	3RD WARD
WEBB, JOHN	KEN	308	3RD DIST
WEBB, JOHN	TAL	114	ST MICHA
WEBB, JOHN H.	WOR	338	1ST E DI
WEBB, JOHN H.	BAL	387	3RD WARD
WEBB, JOHN-BLACK	CAR	162	NO TWP L
WEBB, JOSEPH	KEN	221	2ND DIST
WEBB, JOSEPH B.	MGM	318	CRACKLIN
WEBB, JOSEPH-BLACK	CAR	142	NO TWP L
WEBB, JOSHUA	BAL	390	3RD WARD
WEBB, JOSIAH	DOR	450	1ST DIST
WEBB, JULIAN	WAS	224	1ST DIST
WEBB, LAURA	BAL	056	10TH WAR
WEBB, LAURA J.	BAL	145	11TH WAR
WEBB, LEVI	BAL	200	19TH WAR
WEBB, LEWIS	ALL	126	4TH E.D.
WEBB, LOUISA	BAL	345	13TH WAR
WEBB, LOUIZA-BLACK	CAR	142	NO TWP L
WEBB, MARANDA	WOR	208	4TH E DI
WEBB, MARGARET	HAR	004	1ST DIST
WEBB, MARGARETT	DOR	309	1ST DIST
WEBB, MARTHA	CEC	182	7TH E DI
WEBB, MARTHA	WOR	202	4TH E DI
WEBB, MARY	WOR	217	4TH E DI
WEBB, MARY	KEN	265	1ST DIST
WEBB, MARY	KEN	307	3RD DIST
WEBB, MARY	BAL	274	12TH WAR
WEBB, MARY G.	WOR	286	BERLIN 1
WEBB, MATHEW	FRE	125	CREAGERS
WEBB, MILLY	WOR	254	1ST CENS
WEBB, MILTON	BAL	265	17TH WAR
WEBB, MINTZ	TAL	070	EASTON T
WEBB, MINUS	WOR	292	9TH E DI
WEBB, MCLLY	WOR	285	BERLIN 1
WEBB, MYANDER W.	BAL	407	14TH WAR
WEBB, NANCY	FRE	189	5TH E DI
WEBB, NANCY	WOR	291	9TH E DI
WEBB, NATHAN	BAL	251	12TH WAR
WEBB, PETER	TAL	087	ST MICHA
WEBB, PETER-MULATTO	CAR	162	NO TWP L
WEBB, PHINIAS A.	CEC	155	PORT DUP
WEBB, RICHARD	BAL	114	15TH WAR
WEBB, RGBERT	BAL	226	12TH WAR
WEBB, ROBERT	TAL	049	EASTON T
WEBB, ROSE	DOR	363	3RD DIVI
WEBB, SALLY	WOR	350	1ST E DI
WEBB, SAMUEL	DOR	448	1ST DIST
WEBB, SAMUEL	DOR	447	1ST DIST
WEBB, SAMUEL	BAL	163	16TH WAR
WEBB, SAMUEL	BAL	395	1ST DIST
WEBB, SAMUEL D.	BAL	164	16TH WAR
WEBB, SAMUEL-BLACK	CAR	160	NO TWP L
WEBB, SAMUEL-BLACK	CAR	158	NO TWP L
WEBB, SARAH	BAL	473	14TH WAR
WEBB, SARAH	BAL	081	1ST WARD
WEBB, SARAH J.	CEC	050	1ST E DI
WEBB, SIDNEY	BAL	204	6TH WARD
WEBB, STEPHEN	BAL	168	1ST WARD
WEBB, SUSAN	FRE	125	CREAGERS
WEBB, THOMAS	BAL	363	1ST DIST
WEBB, THOMAS H.	DOR	448	1ST DIST
WEBB, THOMAS S.	ANN	406	8TH DIST
WEBB, WASHINGTON	CEC	155	PORT DUP
WEBB, WILLIAM	CEC	174	6TH E DI
WEBB, WILLIAM	BAL	051	4TH WARD
WEBB, WILLIAM	BAL	223	17TH WAR
WEBB, WILLIAM	KEN	212	2ND DIST
WEBB, WILLIAM	FRE	161	EMMITTSB
WEBB, WILLIAM	SOM	411	DUBLIN D
WEBB, WILLIAM	CEC	055	1ST E DI
WEBB, WILLIAM	BAL	020	1ST WARD
WEBB, WILLIAM	BAL	075	15TH WAR
WEBB, WILLIAM	WOR	295	9TH E DI
WEBB, WILLIAM	KEN	311	3RD DIST
WEBB, WILLIAM M.	CAL	044	3RD DIST
WEBB, WILLIAM W.	WOR	226	4TH E DI
WEBB, WILLIAM-BLACK	CAR	141	NO TWP L
WEBB,PETER-BLACK	CAR	144	NO TWP L
WEBB.SALLY	WOR	285	BERLIN 1
WEBBER, CONRAD	BAL	064	18TH WAR
WEBBER, JACKSON	BAL	127	1ST WARD
WEBBER, JOEL	BAL	125	1ST WARD
WEBBER, JOHN	BAL	329	3RD WARD
WEBBER, JOSEPH	BAL	139	1ST WARD
WEBBER, SUSAN	BAL	098	1ST WARD
WEBBER, W.P.	ALL	218	CUMBERLA
WEBBER, WILLIAM	CAR	092	NO TWP L
WEBBS, GEORGE	CEC	005	ELKTCN 3
WEBDON, EBY	SOM	469	TRAPPE D
WEBER, ADAM	BAL	368	13TH WAR
WEBER, ANDREW	BAL	321	7TH WARD
WEBER, CATHARINE	BAL	300	7TH WARD
WEBER, CHARLES	BAL	050	9TH WARD
WEBER, CHARLES	BAL	040	15TH WAR
WEBER, ELIZABETH	BAL	087	1CTH WAR
WEBER, GEORGE	ALL	26C	CUMBERLA
WEBER, HENRY	BAL	094	1CTH WAR
WEBER, HENRY	BAL	182	6TH WARD
WEBER, JOHN	BAL	300	7TH WARD
WEBER, JOHN	BAL	034	18TH WAR
WEBER, LOUIS	BAL	086	10TH WAR
WEBER, MARY	BAL	04C	15TH WAR
WEBER, MICHAEL	ALL	234	CUMBERLA
WEBER, MICHAEL	CAR	358	9TH DIST
WEBER, SAMUEL	WAS	291	1ST DIST
WEBLE, MARTIN*	BAL	370	3RD WARD
WEBLER, JOHN	CAR	294	7TH DIST
WEBLEY, CHARLOTT	HAR	006	1ST DIST
WEBLEY, HANNAH	HAR	007	1ST DIST
WEBNER, HWNRY C.	BAL	061	18TH WAR
WEBSTER, A.	BAL	114	1ST WARD
WEBSTER, A.	BAL	130	1ST WARD
WEBSTER, A.	BAL	153	1ST WARD
WEBSTER, A.C.	PRI	090	MARLBROU
WEBSTER, ALBERT M.	ANN	299	1ST DIST
WEBSTER, ALEXANDER	SOM	449	DAMES QU
WEBSTER, ALFRED	BAL	073	1ST WARD
WEBSTER, ALFRED	BAL	286	2ND WARD
WEBSTER, ALGENONE	BAL	221	17TH WAR
WEBSTER, AMANDA	HAR	027	1ST DIST
WEBSTER, AMOS	CEC	123	3RD E DI
WEBSTER, ANGELINE	SOM	451	DAMES QU
WEBSTER, ANNB.	ST	264	3RD E DI
WEBSTER, ANNE	BAL	107	10TH WAR
WEBSTER, BENJAMIN	BAL	075	2ND DIST
WEBSTER, CAROLINE	BAL	146	11TH WAR
WEBSTER, CATHERINE	BAL	044	9TH WARD
WEBSTER, CHARELS W.	CAR	273	WESTMINS
WEBSTER, CHARLOT	BAL	193	17TH WAR
WEBSTER, CONELIA	HAR	185	3RD DIST
WEBSTER, CYRUS	MGM	347	BERRYS D
WEBSTER, DANIEL	CHA	281	BOJANTOW
WEBSTER, DAVID	SOM	458	DAMES QU
WEBSTER, E.	PRI	119	PISCATAW
WEBSTER, EDWARD	BAL	020	2ND DIST
WEBSTER, ELIZA	BAL	020	2ND DIST
WEBSTER, ELIZA	DOR	456	1ST DIST
WEBSTER, ELIZA	MGM	318	CRACKLIN
WEBSTER, ELIZA	HAR	018	1ST DIST
WEBSTER, ELIZA	BAL	263	17TH WAR
WEBSTER, ELIZABETH	SOM	444	DAMES QU
WEBSTER, ELIZABETH	BAL	037	4TH WARD
WEBSTER, ELIZABETH	BAL	055	15TH WAR
WEBSTER, ELLEN	BAL	127	5TH WARD
WEBSTER, FANNY	BAL	204	6TH WARD
WEBSTER, FREDERICK	BAL	124	1ST WARD
WEBSTER, G.	BAL	130	1ST WARD
WEBSTER, GEORGE	BAL	098	10TH WAR
WEBSTER, GEORGE	BAL	088	15TH WAR
WEBSTER, GEORGE	CAR	264	WESTMINS
WEBSTER, GEORGE	PRI	055	AQUASCO
WEBSTER, GEORGE D.	FRE	079	FREDERIC
WEBSTER, GEORGE S.	HAR	100	2ND DIST
WEBSTER, GEORGE T.	ALL	245	CUMBERLA
WEBSTER, GEORGIA*	BAL	032	4TH WARD
WEBSTER, GOERGE	FRE	206	BUCKEYST
WEBSTER, GOERGE	BAL	120	1ST WARD
WEBSTER, HAMILTCN	SOM	448	DAMES QU
WEBSTER, HAMILTCN S.	SOM	450	DAMES QU
WEBSTER, HANNAH	HAR	100	2ND DIST
WEBSTER, HANNAH	MGM	370	BERRYS D
WEBSTER, HENRY	HAR	10C	2ND DIST
WEBSTER, HENRY	FRE	077	FREDERIC
WEBSTER, HENRY	BAL	215	17TH WAR
WEBSTER, HENRY	PRI	095	SPALDING
WEBSTER, HENRY W.	BAL	003	15TH WAR
WEBSTER, ISAAC	BAL	194	17TH WAR
WEBSTER, ISAAC	BAL	011	18TH WAR
WEBSTER, ISAAC	BAL	011	18TH WAR
WEBSTER, ISAAC REV.	CAR	267	WESTMINS
WEBSTER, JACOB	SOM	451	DAMES QU
WEBSTER, JAMES	SOM	451	DAMES QU
WEBSTER, JAMES	HAR	101	2ND DIST
WEBSTER, JAMES	FRE	277	NEW MARK
WEBSTER, JAMES	BAL	115	1ST WARD
WEBSTER, JAMES	BAL	124	1ST WARD
WEBSTER, JAMES	PRI	088	SPALDING
WEBSTER, JAMES	PRI	071	MARLBROU
WEBSTER, JAMES A.	HAR	012	1ST DIST
WEBSTER, JAMES R.	BAL	031	18TH WAR
WEBSTER, JAMES R.	DOR	457	1ST DIST
WEBSTER, JANE	BAL	450	8TH WARD
WEBSTER, JESSE	SOM	451	DAMES QU
WEBSTER, JOHN	BAL	035	18TH WAR
WEBSTER, JOHN	BAL	273	17TH WAR

WEBSTER, JOHN MGM 321 CRACKLIN
WEBSTER, JOHN HAR 136 2ND DIST
WEBSTER, JOHN HAR 140 2ND DIST
WEBSTER, JOHN BAL 395 14TH WAR
WEBSTER, JCHN DOR 325 1ST DIST
WEBSTER, JOHN BAL 423 8TH WARD
WEBSTER, JOHN PRI 054 AQUASCO
WEBSTER, JOHN A. HAR 140 2ND DIST
WEBSTER, JOHN B. FRE 076 FREDERIC
WEBSTER, JOHN D. BAL 050 9TH WARD
WEBSTER, JOHN L. BAL 144 11TH WAR
WEBSTER, JOHN T. FRE 077 FREDERIC
WEBSTER, JOHN W. HAR 115 2ND DIST
WEBSTER, JOSEPH BAL 470 14TH WAR
WEBSTER, JOSEPH BAL 196 17TH WAR
WEBSTER, JOSEPH C. SOM 463 HANGARY
WEBSTER, JULIUS D. SOM 451 DAMES QU
WEBSTER, L. ANN 348 3RD DIST
WEBSTER, LAURA BAL 244 17TH WAR
WEBSTER, LEAH SOM 450 DAMES QU
WEBSTER, LETITIA SOM 552 TYASKIN
WEBSTER, LUCRETIA SOM 464 HANGARY
WEBSTER, LUCY A. FRE 292 WOODSBOR
WEBSTER, LUSTRE HAR 136 2ND DIST
WEBSTER, MARGARET BAL 078 1ST WARD
WEBSTER, MARGARET A. BAL 381 13TH WAR
WEBSTER, MARIA BAL 153 16TH WAR
WEBSTER, MARIA BAL 143 16TH WAR
WEBSTER, MARY HAR 191 3RD DIST
WEBSTER, MARY CAL 053 3RD DIST
WEBSTER, MARY BAL 274 20TH WAR
WEBSTER, MARY PRI 117 PISCATAW
WEBSTER, MARY A. FRE 077 FREDERIC
WEBSTER, MARY E. MGM 439 CLARKSTR
WEBSTER, MARY J. BAL 173 16TH WAR
WEBSTER, MICHAEL SOM 450 DAMES QU
WEBSTER, MOSE HAR 034 1ST DIST
WEBSTER, N. BAL 281 2ND WARD
WEBSTER, NATHANIEL BAL 146 1ST WARD
WEBSTER, NATHANIEL SOM 453 DAMES QU
WEBSTER, NOAH SOM 450 DAMES QU
WEBSTER, NOAH HAR 100 2ND DIST
WEBSTER, ORASHA SOM 452 DAMES QU
WEBSTER, PHILIP PRI 071 MARLBROU
WEBSTER, REBECCA FRE 046 FREDERIC
WEBSTER, REBECCA HAR 003 1ST DIST
WEBSTER, REBECCA C. KEN 283 3RD DIST
WEBSTER, RICHARD HAR 101 2ND DIST
WEBSTER, RCADEN BAL 221 17TH WAR
WEBSTER, ROBERT BAL 252 12TH WAR
WEBSTER, SAMUEL SOM 452 DAMES QU
WEBSTER, SARAH CEC 066 1ST E DI
WEBSTER, SARAH PRI 072 MARLBROU
WEBSTER, SARAH A. WAS 213 1ST DIST
WEBSTER, SOPHIA SOM 452 DAMES QU
WEBSTER, SOPHIA HAR 030 1ST DIST
WEBSTER, SOPHIA BAL 171 11TH WAR
WEBSTER, STEPHEN BAL 210 19TH WAR
WEBSTER, SUSAN SOM 447 DAMES QU
WEBSTER, THOMAS FRE 075 FREDERIC
WEBSTER, THOMAS CAR 112 NO TWP L
WEBSTER, THOMAS BAL 115 11TH WAR
WEBSTER, THOMAS BAL 029 9TH WARD
WEBSTER, TUBMAN SOM 451 DAMES QU
WEBSTER, WALLACE SOM 451 DAMES QU
WEBSTER, WILLIAM SOM 451 DAMES QU
WEBSTER, WILLIAM SOM 451 DAMES QU
WEBSTER, WILLIAM HAR 034 1ST DIST
WEBSTER, WILLIAM CAR 192 4TH DIST
WEBSTER, WILLIAM CEC 070 5TH E DI
WEBSTER, WILLIAM CEC 066 1ST E DI
WEBSTER, WILLIAM BAL 423 8TH WARD
WEBSTER, WILLIAM BAL 119 15TH WAR
WEBSTER, WILLIAM DOR 457 1ST DIST
WEBSTER, WILLIAM PRI 050 AQUASCO
WEBSTER, WILLIAM A. BAL 266 2ND WARD
WEBSTER, WILLIAM T. MGM 438 CLARKSTR
WEBSTER, WILLIAM T. FRE 210 BUCKEYST
WEBSTER, ZACH CHA 281 BOJANTOW
WEBSTOCK, CHARELS BAL 256 17TH WAR
WECHLEY, ELISHA P. * BAL 182 6TH WARD
WECK, CHARLOT WAS 033 2ND SUBD
WECK, ELIAS WAS 035 2ND SUBD
WECK, HENRY WAS 035 2ND SUBD
WECKLER, FREDERICK WAS 185 BOONSBOR
WECKSTINE, EASLER BAL 270 2ND WARD
WED, JOHN Y. BAL 251 20TH WAR
WEDDING, CALEB CHA 291 MIDDLETO
WEDDING, ISACH CHA 266 MIDDLETO
WEDDING, JUDSON CHA 230 MIDDLETO
WEDDLE, ELIZABETH FRE 344 MIDDLETO
WEDDLE, GEORGE FRE 336 MIDDLETO
WEDDLE, JACOB FRE 320 MIDDLETO
WEDDLE, JAEMS FRE 339 MIDDLETO
WEDDLE, JAMES FRE 372 CATOCTIN
WEDDLE, JAMES FRE 122 CREAGERS
WEDDLE, JAMES FRE 137 CREAGERS
WEDDLE, JOHN FRE 344 MIDDLETO
WEDDLE, JOHN FRE 358 CATOCTIN
WEDDLE, JOHN D. FRE 077 FREDERIC
WEDDLE, LAWSON B. FRE 320 MIDDLETO
WEDDLE, MARY E. FRE 320 MIDDLETO
WEDDLE, WILLIAM FRE 407 JEFFERSO
WEDEL, JAMES CAR 321 1ST DIST
WEDELLE, HENRY FRE 127 CREAGERS
WEDGE, ADLINE CHA 234 HILLTOP
WEDGE, ANN M. M. BAL 076 4TH WARD
WEDGE, FRANCIS CHA 233 HILLTOP
WEDGE, GEORGE ANN 396 8TH DIST
WEDGE, GEORGE PRI 112 PISCATAW
WEDGE, JOHN PRI 076 MARLBROU
WEDGE, WILLIAM PRI 073 MARLBROU
WEDGE, WILLIAM PRI 075 MARLBROU
WEDGE, WILLIAM BAL 024 4TH WARD
WEDNER, ANDREW BAL 256 20TH WAR
WEDUM, GEORGE HAR 147 3RD DIST
WEE, STEPHEN BAL 218 17TH WAR
WEEAVER, REACHAEL KEN 214 2ND DIST
WEEB, CLARK BAL 345 1ST DIST
WEEB, HENRY BAL 362 1ST DIST
WEEB, JOHN BAL 345 1ST DIST
WEEB, WILLIAM BAL 344 1ST DIST
WEECH, ELENOR * WOR 305 2ND E DI
WEEDEN, CAROLINE BAL 246 17TH WAR
WEEDEN, DANIEL TAL 092 ST MICHA
WEEDEN, ELIZA BAL 249 17TH WAR
WEEDEN, JOHN H. TAL 095 ST MICHA
WEEDEN, JOSEPH ANN 271 ANNAPOLI
WEEDEN, TRISTRAM QUE 151 1ST E DI
WEEDEN, WILLIAM TAL 083 ST MICHA
WEEDON, CHARLES ANN 304 1ST DIST
WEEDON, CLEMENT ANN 321 2ND DIST
WEEDON, HENRY QUE 230 4TH E DI
WEEDON, J. H. BAL 072 10TH WAR
WEEDON, JOHN ANN 350 3RD DIST
WEEDON, MRS- ANN 308 1ST DIST
WEEDON, THOAMS QUE 230 4TH E DI
WEEDON, TRISTRAN QUE 227 4TH E DI
WEEDON, WILLIAM ANN 321 2ND DIST
WEEDS, CHARLES BAL 368 13TH WAR
WEEK, AMANDA WAS 032 2ND SUBD
WEEK, JOHN WAS 032 2ND SUBD
WEEK, MARY WAS 032 2ND SUBD
WEEKER, JOHN BAL 336 13TH WAR
WEEKES, JEMS BAL 156 1ST WARD
WEEKHAM, HENRY BAL 065 4TH WARD
WEEKLEY, CHARLES H. QUE 169 2ND E DI
WEEKLEY, ELISHA P. * BAL 182 6TH WARD
WEEKS, ALFRED BAL 099 18TH WAR
WEEKS, AMANDA BAL 455 8TH WARD
WEEKS, AMANDA QUE 170 2ND E DI
WEEKS, ANN BAL 285 12TH WAR
WEEKS, ANN M. CEC 018 ELKTON 3
WEEKS, ARAMNITA CEC 099 3RD E DI
WEEKS, AUGUSTA BAL 058 10TH WAR
WEEKS, BENJAMIN HAR 041 1ST DIST
WEEKS, CALEB BAL 320 7TH WARD
WEEKS, CALEB BAL 164 1ST WARD
WEEKS, CALEB BAL 115 1ST WARD
WEEKS, CATHARINE BAL 280 12TH WAR
WEEKS, CHARLES E.V. CEC 005 ELKTON 3
WEEKS, ELIZABETH-BLACK QUE 185 3RD E DI
WEEKS, EZEKIEL BAL 374 8TH WARD
WEEKS, FRANCIS A. CHA 219 ALLENS F
WEEKS, HENRY BAL 220 12TH WAR
WEEKS, HEZEKIAH ANN 514 HOWARD D
WEEKS, ISAAC BAL 180 6TH WARD
WEEKS, J. BAL 158 1ST WARD
WEEKS, JAMES BAL 293 7TH WARD
WEEKS, JAMES CEC 122 4TH E DI
WEEKS, JAMES HAR 146 3RD DIST
WEEKS, JAMES-BLACK QUE 185 3RD E DI
WEEKS, JEREMIAH BAL 453 14TH WAR
WEEKS, JOHN BAL 151 1ST WARD
WEEKS, JOHN H. BAL 457 8TH WARD
WEEKS, LEWIS CHA 219 ALLENS F
WEEKS, LIDDY BAL 138 11TH WAR
WEEKS, LUCRETIA BAL 169 2ND DIST
WEEKS, MARIA-BLACK QUE 185 3RD E DI
WEEKS, MARTHA BAL 138 11TH WAR
WEEKS, MARY HAR 161 3RD DIST
WEEKS, MARY BAL 121 5TH WARD
WEEKS, MARY BAL 092 5TH WARD
WEEKS, OLIVER CEC 062 1ST E DI
WEEKS, PETER BAL 224 12TH WAR
WEEKS, PETER BAL 284 12TH WAR
WEEKS, REBECCA BAL 243 12TH WAR
WEEKS, ROBERT BAL 170 6TH WARD
WEEKS, SAMUEL BAL 170 6TH WARD
WEEKS, SARAH BAL 354 13TH WAR
WEEKS, SARAH A. KEN 271 1ST DIST
WEEKS, SCLOMON PRI 015 BLADENSB
WEEKS, WILLIAM BAL 101 18TH WAR
WEELLS, WILLIAM CAL 011 1ST DIST
WEEMANN, A. BAL 153 5TH WARD
WEEMS, A.B. ANN 274 ANNAPOLI
WEEMS, CHARLES CAL 041 3RD DIST
WEEMS, CHARLES H. W. CAL 021 2ND DIST
WEEMS, D. RICHARD ANN 310 1ST DIST
WEEMS, DAVID CAL 029 2ND DIST
WEEMS, DAVID G. ANN 406 8TH DIST
WEEMS, GEORGE ANN 404 8TH DIST
WEEMS, GEORGE L. M. CAL 003 1ST DIST
WEEMS, GEORGE W. CAL 057 3RD DIST
WEEMS, GUSTA ANN 406 8TH DIST
WEEMS, HANNAH BAL 053 15TH WAR
WEEMS, JAMES J. CAL 009 1ST DIST
WEEMS, JAMES K. CAL 041 3RD DIST
WEEMS, JOHN MGM 393 ROCKERLE
WEEMS, JOHN C. ANN 409 8TH DIST
WEEMS, JULIA A. ANN 411 8TH DIST
WEEMS, JULIET BAL 177 16TH WAR
WEEMS, L. L. CAL 011 1ST DIST
WEEMS, LEVIN C. CAL 033 2ND DIST
WEEMS, M. L. BAL 415 14TH WAR
WEEMS, MARGARET E. ST 307 1ST E DI
WEEMS, MARTHA BAL 144 5TH WARD
WEEMS, MARY A. CAL 048 3RD DIST
WEEMS, MARY E. CAL 039 2ND DIST
WEEMS, MILLY CAL 028 2ND DIST
WEEMS, PHILIP BAL 143 1ST WARD
WEEMS, SARAH BAL 078 15TH WAR
WEEMS, SUSANNA BAL 072 15TH WAR
WEEMS, THOMAS KEN 274 1ST DIST
WEEMS, WILLIAM ANN 411 8TH DIST
WEEMS, WILLIAM CAL 026 2ND DIST
WEEMS, WILLIAM M. CAL 049 3RD DIST
WEEN, GEORGE BAL 078 15TH WAR
WEENES, FRANCIS W. CAR 292 7TH DIST
WEEP, LYDIA CHA 223 ALLENS F
WEER, JAMES BAL 152 11TH WAR
WEER, LEONARD KEN 258 1ST DIST
WEESH, ALARON MGM 330 CRACKLIN
WEGLEIN, AARON BAL 144 11TH WAR
WEGLEIN, GEORGE* BAL 331 3RD WARD
WEGLEIN, HANNAH BAL 401 3RD WARD
WEGNER, CAROLINE BAL 332 3RD WARD
WEGNER, CONRAD BAL 285 12TH WAR
WEGNER, JOHN BAL 089 10TH WAR
WEGUNT, HENRY BAL 285 12TH WAR
WEHAGE, HENRY BAL 303 20TH WAR
WEHARVEN, JOHN BAL 131 16TH WAR
WEHENCH, CONRADT BAL 370 8TH WARD
WEHER, FRANCIS BAL 349 7TH WARD
WEHN, HENRY BAL 193 19TH WAR
WEHN, JACOB BAL 180 6TH WARD
WEHN, PHILIP BAL 181 16TH WAR
WEHNER, CATHARINE BAL 123 16TH WAR
WEHOFFER, HENRY BAL 385 13TH WAR
WEHRMAN, FREDERICK BAL 198 6TH WARD
WEIBLE, JOHN BAL 221 17TH WAR
WEICKER, JOHN FRE 194 5TH E DI
WEICKLE, WILLIAM BAL 256 6TH WARD
WEIDEMEYER, ADAM BAL 178 2ND WARD
WEIDENWEAN, GOTTFIED * BAL 034 18TH WAR
WEIDIKINE, FREDERICK BAL 397 14TH WAR
WEIGAL, HENRY BAL 246 2ND WARD
WEIGAN, FERDINAND BAL 034 9TH WARD
WEIGAND, AUGUST BAL 234 12TH WAR
WEIGART, CHARLES BAL 040 15TH WAR
WEIGART, GEORGE BAL 416 14TH WAR
WEIGART, GEROGE BAL 283 12TH WAR
WEIGART, HENRY B. BAL 318 20TH WAR
WEIGART, MARY J. BAL 165 16TH WAR
WEIGART, PETER BAL 315 1ST DIST
WEIGHT, DAVID BAL 185 2ND WARD
WEIGHT, WILLIAM A. BAL 042 1ST WARD
WEIGHTMAN, MARY MISS- BAL 305 7TH WARD
WEIGLE, MARY BAL 315 20TH WAR
WEIGLEY, LOUISA C. FRE 034 FREDERIC
WEIHNER, SISTER L. BAL 262 17TH WAR
WEIKTER, JOHN FRE 198 5TH E DI
WEIL, JACOB BAL 273 2ND WARD
WEIL, JOHN * BAL 007 15TH WAR
WEIL, JONATHAN BAL 318 20TH WAR
WEILAGE, JOHN BAL 013 9TH WARD
WEILAND, GODLIP BAL 123 16TH WAR
WEILEY, RACHEL BAL 132 18TH WAR
WEILLEMBUCK, AUGUSTUS BAL 079 2ND DIST
WEIMAN, CHARLES FRE 022 FREDERIC
WEIMAN, JOSEPH BAL 086 10TH WAR
WEIMAR, LEWIS BAL 092 10TH WAR
WEIMER, ERNEST ALL 261 CUMBERLA
WEIMER, GEORGE BAL 157 19TH WAR
WEIMERT, JACOB FRE 009 FREDERIC
WEIMERT, PETER CAR 266 WESTMINS
WEIMERT, SARAH CAR 293 7TH DIST
WEIMILLER, JOHN CAR 266 WESTMINS
WEIN, MARY CAR 316 1ST DIST
WEINBERG, JOSEPH BAL 205 2ND WARD
WEINER, MARTIN BAL 106 5TH WARD
WEINHOLDT, GEORGE BAL 080 1ST WARD
WEINHOLT, BERNARD BAL 179 6TH WARD
WEINHOLT, CHRISTOPHER BAL 250 2ND WARD
WEINSILL, MARY BAL 250 2ND WARD
WEINSTOCK, BARLETT BAL 013 9TH WARD
WEIR, J. W. BAL 232 2ND WARD
WEIR, JOHN A. BAL 147 1ST WARD
WEIR, SARAH BAL 282 20TH WAR
WEIR, W. ANN 302 1ST DIST
WEIR, WACHELIN BAL 158 1ST WARD
WEIR, WAHSINGTON BAL 167 1ST WARD
WEIR, WASHINGTON BAL 286 2ND WARD
WEIR, WASHINGTON BAL 169 1ST WARD
WEIR, WILLIAM BAL 121 1ST WARD
WEIRCHTH, NORRIS BAL 151 1ST WARD
WEIRHANE, CONRAD CAR 377 2ND DIST
WEIS, ANN C. BAL 259 17TH WAR
WEIS, DANIEL WAS 126 HAGERSTO
WEIS, ELIZABETH WAS 188 1ST DIST
WEIS, EZRA BAL 315 7TH WARD
WEIS, GEORGE WAS 150 HAGERSTO
WEIS, GEORGE WAS 264 1ST DIST
WEIS, HENRY WAS 285 1ST DIST
WEIS, JOHN WAS 125 HAGERSTO
WEIS, LUCINDA WAS 126 HAGERSTO
WEIS, LUCINDA WAS 200 1ST DIST
WEIS, MARY WAS 193 1ST DIST
WEIS, RICHARD BAL 124 5TH WARD
WEISDYKAMPER, KATE WAS 137 HAGERSTO
WEISE, GODFREY BAL 383 13TH WAR
WEISE, JACOB BAL 270 7TH WARD
WEISE, JACOB P. BAL 290 17TH WAR
WEISE, JOHN BAL 182 6TH WARD
WEISEL, D. BAL 107 1ST WARD
WEISEL, MARY WAS 133 HAGERSTO
WEISEL, SAMUEL ALL 262 CUMBERLA
WEISENBACK, LEWIS WAS 002 WILLIAMS
WEISENFIELD, M. BAL 269 2ND WARD
WEISENGER, CHARLES BAL 268 2ND WARD
WEISENHANER, JOHN BAL 216 2ND WARD
WEISHAMPEL, BARBARA BAL 259 12TH WAR
WEISHAMPEL, CHRISTIAN BAL 005 9TH WARD
WEISHAMPEL, J. F. BAL 247 1ST DIST
WEISHELL, JAMES BAL 421 14TH WAR
WEISHENKEIM, MARY G. FRE 099 FREDERIC
WEISLER, ABRAHAM BAL 048 9TH WARD
WEISMAN, EVE BAL 060 1ST WARD
WEISMAN, FRANCIS BAL 262 12TH WAR
WEISMAN, HENRY BAL 212 17TH WAR
WEISMILLER, FREDERICK BAL 113 5TH WARD
WEISMILLER, JACOB ALL 249 CUMBERLA
WEISMILLER, MARGARET ALL 249 CUMBERLA
WEISNER, MICHAEL ALL 249 CUMBERLA
WEISS, CONRAD FRE 101 FREDERIC
WEISS, GEORGE BAL 266 2ND WARD
WEISS, K. BAL 187 16TH WAR
WEISS, MARGARET A. BAL 449 8TH WARD
WEISSEL, HARRIET BAL 263 17TH WAR
WEIST, JOHN WAS 154 HAGERSTO
WEIST, LEWIS BAL 361 13TH WAR
WEITE, WILLIAM W.* WAS 124 HAGERSTO
WEITEN, DAVID BAL 406 3RD WARD
WEITLAND, JOHN BAL 003 1ST WARD
WEITMAN, CHARLES BAL 298 17TH WAR
WEITZEL, JACOB BAL 267 2ND WARD
WEITZELL, HENRY BAL 315 3RD WARD
WEITZELL, THOMAS BAL 203 2ND WARD
WEKINS, ANDREW J. BAL 228 6TH WARD
WEKINSON, CATHERINE ALL 262 CUMBERLA
WELAND, JEREMIAH BAL 306 20TH WAR
WELAND, MARY ANN ALL 010 3RD E.D.
WELAND, ROSANA ALL 011 3RD E.D.
WELAYND, JOEL ALL 007 3RD E.D.
WELB, HENRY ALL 010 3RD E.D.
WELB, MARY FRE 268 NEW MARK
WELB, SAMUEL WAS 237 CAVETOWN
WELB, THOMAS BAL 078 2ND DIST
WELB, WILLIAM FRE 268 NEW MARK
WELBORN, SAMUEL ANN 507 HOWARD D
WELBY, NANCY WOR 294 9TH E DI
WELBY, SAMUEL * PRI 089 SPALDING
WELCH, ABRAHGAM WAS 161 HAGERSTO
WELCH, ALONZO ALL 028 2ND E.D.
WELCH, ANTANY BAL 027 9TH WARD
WELCH, BARTLEY HAR 199 3RD DIST
WELCH, BENAJMIN F.-BLACK BAL 424 8TH WARD
WELCH, BENEDICT MGM 433 CLARKSTR
WELCH, BENJAMIN CHA 264 HILLTOP
WELCH, BENJAMIN CHA 232 HILLTOP
WELCH, CAROLINE-MULATTO ANN 299 1ST DIST
WELCH, CATHERINE MGM 422 MEDLEY 3
WELCH, CECELIA ALL 206 CUMBERLA
WELCH, CHARLES CHA 231 HILLTOP
WELCH, CHARLES CAR 226 5TH DIST
WELCH, CHARLOTT KEN 308 3RD DIST
WELCH, COLLY MRS- KEN 294 3RD DIST
WELCH, D. A. G. * ANN 394 8TH DIST
WELCH, DYSON D. ANN 320 2ND DIST
CHA 270 ALLENS F

Name	County	Page	District
WELCH, EBEN	KEN	282	3RD DIST
WELCH, EDWARD	MGM	434	CLARKSTR
WELCH, EDWARD	CHA	234	HILLTOP
WELCH, ELIZABETH	BAL	004	18TH WAR
WELCH, ELIZABETH	BAL	002	EASTERN
WELCH, ELIZABETH	BAL	420	8TH WARD
WELCH, ELLEN	BAL	008	18TH WAR
WELCH, ELLEN	BAL	215	11TH WAR
WELCH, EMELY	ANN	292	ANNAPOLI
WELCH, EMMA	BAL	262	2ND WARD
WELCH, EVA	ALL	028	2ND E.D.
WELCH, FRANK	ANN	304	1ST DIST
WELCH, FREDERICK	CEC	182	7TH E DI
WELCH, HENRY	ANN	289	ANNAPOLI
WELCH, HENRY C.	ANN	395	8TH DIST
WELCH, JAMES	BAL	132	1ST WARD
WELCH, JAMES	KEN	312	3RD DIST
WELCH, JAMES CAPT.	BAL	331	13TH WAR
WELCH, JAMES W.	KEN	305	3RD DIST
WELCH, JAMES W.	ST	341	5TH E DI
WELCH, JARRETT	HAR	174	3RD DIST
WELCH, JOHN	BAL	422	3RD WARD
WELCH, JOHN	BAL	368	8TH WARD
WELCH, JOHN	ALL	226	CUMBERLA
WELCH, JOHN	BAL	133	2ND DIST
WELCH, JOHN	ALL	107	5TH E.D.
WELCH, JOHN	BAL	162	1ST WARD
WELCH, JOHN	BAL	006	1ST WARD
WELCH, JOHN B.	BAL	292	3RD WARD
WELCH, JOHN D.	KEN	297	3RD DIST
WELCH, JOHN H.	CHA	266	MIDDLETO
WELCH, JOHN M.	BAL	298	7TH WARD
WELCH, JONA	KEN	292	3RD DIST
WELCH, JOSEPH H.	BAL	178	16TH WAR
WELCH, JOSEPH-BLACK	QUE	188	3RD E DI
WELCH, JUDY	BAL	366	8TH WARD
WELCH, MARTHA E.-BLACK	MGM	423	MEDLEY 3
WELCH, MARTICO	CAR	200	4TH DIST
WELCH, MARTIN	HAR	053	1ST DIST
WELCH, MARTIN	BAL	194	2ND WARD
WELCH, MARTIN	ALL	047	10TH E.D
WELCH, MARY	BAL	256	6TH WARD
WELCH, MARY	HAR	053	1ST DIST
WELCH, MARY	CHA	241	HILLTOP
WELCH, MARY	CHA	241	HILLTOP
WELCH, MARY E.	TAL	004	EASTON D
WELCH, MEHALEY	KEN	312	3RD DIST
WELCH, MICHAEL	CEC	179	7TH E DI
WELCH, MICHAEL	BAL	367	8TH WARD
WELCH, MICHAEL	BAL	126	1ST WARD
WELCH, MICHAEL	BAL	174	2ND DIST
WELCH, MORDECAI D.	ANN	352	3RD DIST
WELCH, MOSES	BAL	198	17TH WAR
WELCH, MRS.	ANN	265	ANNAPOLI
WELCH, NANCY	ANN	265	ANNAPOLI
WELCH, NICHOLAS	BAL	135	16TH WAR
WELCH, P.	BAL	157	1ST WARD
WELCH, P.	BAL	171	1ST WARD
WELCH, PATICK	BAL	160	1ST WARD
WELCH, PATRICK	BAL	018	1ST WARD
WELCH, PATRICK	HAR	061	1ST DIST
WELCH, PHEBA A.	CHA	264	HILLTOP
WELCH, PHILOMON	CAR	225	5TH DIST
WELCH, R.A.	BAL	172	1ST WARD
WELCH, REBECCA	BAL	186	6TH WARD
WELCH, RICHAD	BAL	063	1ST WARD
WELCH, RICHARD	CHA	235	HILLTOP
WELCH, ROB A.	BAL	170	1ST WARD
WELCH, ROBERT	HAR	052	1ST DIST
WELCH, ROBERT D.	BAL	167	1ST WARD
WELCH, ROBERT OF BEN	ANN	268	ANNAPOLI
WELCH, ROBERT T.	TAL	050	EASTON T
WELCH, S.	BAL	117	1ST WARD
WELCH, SAMUEL	ALL	028	2ND E.D.
WELCH, SAMUEL	CAR	200	4TH DIST
WELCH, SARAH	HAR	117	2ND DIST
WELCH, SARAH	BAL	373	13TH WAR
WELCH, SARAH	CAL	057	3RD DIST
WELCH, SARAH	BAL	204	2ND WARD
WELCH, SARAH	BAL	356	8TH WARD
WELCH, SARAH	BAL	250	12TH WAR
WELCH, SELLMAN	ANN	320	2ND DIST
WELCH, STEPHEN	BAL	417	8TH WARD
WELCH, STEPHEN	HAR	178	3RD DIST
WELCH, THEODORE H.	HAR	105	2ND DIST
WELCH, THOAMS	ANN	325	2ND DIST
WELCH, VIOLET	HAR	174	3RD DIST
WELCH, VIOLET	HAR	174	3RD DIST
WELCH, WARNER	MGM	438	CLARKSTR
WELCH, WILLIAM	KEN	297	3RD DIST
WELCH, WILLIAM	HAR	117	2ND DIST
WELCH, WILLIAM	BAL	267	7TH WARD
WELCH, WILLIAM	BAL	240	2ND WARD
WELCH, WILLIAM	BAL	226	12TH WAR
WELCH, WILLIAM H.	BAL	241	12TH WAR
WELCH, WILLIAM W.	ST	312	1ST E DI
WELCH,AMEELIA	BAL	207	2ND WARD
WELCOXEN, ELIZA	MGM	325	CRACKLIN
WELDBARGAR, HENRY *	BAL	314	1ST DIST
WELDE, GEORGE	BAL	249	6TH WARD
WELDEN, MICHAEL	BAL	432	1ST DIST
WELDER, MARY E.	BAL	039	4TH WARD
WELDER, SUSAN	BAL	059	15TH WAR
WELDON, CORNELUS	WOR	249	1ST CENS
WELDON, ELIZABETH	WOR	250	1ST CENS
WELDON, FANNY	ALL	212	CUMBERLA
WELDON, HIRAM	ALL	221	CUMBERLA
WELDON, JAMES	CEC	090	4TH E DI
WELDON, JOHN	CEC	133	6TH E DI
WELDON, MARY	BAL	228	6TH WARD
WELDON, MARY A.	CEC	165	6TH E DI
WELDON, MARY E.	BAL	231	6TH WARD
WELDON, SARAH	ALL	212	CUMBERLA
WELDON, SARAH M.	WOR	169	6TH E DI
WELDON, WILLIAM	CEC	164	6TH E DI
WELDON, WILLIAM	CEC	052	1ST E DI
WELDRUN, HENRY	MGM	442	CLARKSTR
WELFONG, DOROTHEA	BAL	169	19TH WAR
WELFORD, SAMUEL	ALL	162	6TH E.D.
WELHELM, SAMUEL	ALL	083	5TH E.D.
WELHEM, SUSANNAH	FRE	272	NEW MARK
WELHIDE, BENJAMIN	FRE	146	10TH E D
WELISHELM, CATHARINE	BAL	210	2ND WARD
WELK, JOHN	WAS	180	BOONSBOR
WELK, LAWSON	WAS	181	BOONSBOR
WELK, SARAH	WAS	180	BOONSBOR
WELK, SARAH	WAS	066	2ND SUBD
WELKA, CHRISTOPHER	BAL	454	14TH WAR
WELKAGER, GEORGE	BAL	361	13TH WAR
WELKER, COLLUMBUS	FRE	289	WOODSBOR

Name	County	Page	District
WELKER, JOHN	FRE	290	WOODSBOR
WELKER, JOHN W.	FRE	303	WOODSBOR
WELKER, MARGARET	FRE	314	MIDDLETO
WELKER, WILLIAM	FRE	204	BUCKEYST
WELKINSON, JACOB	FRE	357	CATOCTIN
WELKINSON, MARGARET*	BAL	347	3RD WARD
WELKS, CAROLINE	BAL	365	13TH WAR
WELKS, JOSEPH	BAL	229	12TH WAR
WELKS, LOUISA	CAR	293	7TH DIST
WELL, CONRAD	BAL	304	3RD WARD
WELL, JOHN	WAS	227	1ST DIST
WELL, JOHN *	BAL	318	20TH WAR
WELLARD, JULIA	BAL	025	2ND DIST
WELLBURN, VIRGINIA	BAL	332	13TH WAR
WELLEN, FRANCIS	CAR	149	NO TWP L
WELLER, ADAM	WAS	146	2ND DIST
WELLER, ADAM	WAS	146	2ND DIST
WELLER, ALFRED	BAL	193	19TH WAR
WELLER, CATHARINE	FRE	186	5TH E DI
WELLER, CATHARINE	WAS	148	2ND DIST
WELLER, CATHERINE	FRE	125	CREAGERS
WELLER, DAVID	FRE	127	CREAGERS
WELLER, EDWARD	FRE	125	CREAGERS
WELLER, EDWARD	BAL	473	14TH WAR
WELLER, ELIAS	FRE	116	CREAGERS
WELLER, ELIAS C.	FRE	124	CREAGERS
WELLER, ELIZABETH	FRE	129	CREAGERS
WELLER, ELMIRA	FRE	116	CREAGERS
WELLER, FREDERICK	FRE	127	CREAGERS
WELLER, HEZEKIAH	FRE	375	CATOCTIN
WELLER, ISAAC	FRE	133	CREAGERS
WELLER, JACOB	FRE	375	CATOCTIN
WELLER, JACOB	WAS	146	2ND DIST
WELLER, JACOB P.	WAS	146	2ND DIST
WELLER, JEREMIAH	FRE	127	CREAGERS
WELLER, JOHN	FRE	133	CREAGERS
WELLER, JOHN	FRE	121	CREAGERS
WELLER, JOHN	FRE	195	5TH E DI
WELLER, JOHN	WAS	146	2ND DIST
WELLER, JOHN	BAL	158	16TH WAR
WELLER, JOHNATHAN	WAS	144	2ND DIST
WELLER, JOSEPH	BAL	227	1ST DIST
WELLER, JOSIAH P.	FRE	132	CREAGERS
WELLER, JULIAN	WAS	146	2ND DIST
WELLER, MARGARET	WAS	146	2ND DIST
WELLER, MARIA	FRE	20	5TH E DI
WELLER, MARTIN D.	FRE	185	5TH E DI
WELLER, MATILDA	FRE	133	CREAGERS
WELLER, PHILIP	BAL	076	10TH WAR
WELLER, ROSANNA	FRE	142	CREAGERS
WELLER, RUBEN	BAL	281	7TH WARD
WELLER, SAMUEL	FRE	133	CREAGERS
WELLER, SAMUEL	FRE	134	CREAGERS
WELLER, SAMUEL	WAS	145	2ND DIST
WELLER, SOPHIA	FRE	128	CREAGERS
WELLER, THOMAS	FRE	186	5TH E DI
WELLER, THOMAS	WAS	146	2ND DIST
WELLER, THOMAS P.	WAS	146	2ND DIST
WELLER, VALINDA	ALL	217	CUMBERLA
WELLER, WILLIAM	BAL	165	1ST WARD
WELLER, WILLIAM	CAR	359	9TH DIST
WELLERS, CLEMENCE	HAR	146	3RD DIST
WELLHAM, HESIKAH	BAL	113	18TH WAR
WELLHOUSE, JOHN P.	ALL	200	CUMBERLA
WELLING, AMOS L.	FRE	204	BUCKEYST
WELLING, FREDERICK	BAL	219	2ND WARD
WELLING, GEORGE*	SOM	539	TYASKIN
WELLING, HENRY	ANN	481	HOWARD D
WELLING, J.M.	BAL	013	18TH WAR
WELLING, POLLY	ANN	476	HOWARD D
WELLING, SARAH	ANN	475	HOWARD D
WELLING, TERRESA*	DOR	363	3RD DIVI
WELLING, THOMAS	WAS	286	1ST DIST
WELLING, WILLIAM	ANN	475	HOWARD D
WELLING, ZACHARIAH	CAR	377	2ND DIST
WELLING,COLUMBUS	FRE	205	BUCKEYST
WELLINGHOFF, ANNA	BAL	328	13TH WAR
WELLINGHOFF, HENRY F.	BAL	328	13TH WAR
WELLINGTON, ADAM	ALL	205	CUMBERLA
WELLINGTON, HANER	HAR	146	3RD DIST
WELLINGTON, JOHN	BAL	364	3RD WARD
WELLINGTON, MICHAEL	BAL	436	8TH WARD
WELLINGTON, WILLIAM	BAL	114	1ST WARD
WELLINGTON, WILLIAM-BLACK	ST	333	4TH E DI
WELLIS, ANN	BAL	001	1ST WARD
WELLIS, PHILIP *	TAL	083	ST MICHA
WELLIS,TUACERIAH	CAR	144	NO TWP L
WELLISON, ANN	ALL	225	CUMBERLA
WELLISON, ASA	ALL	216	CUMBERLA
WELLISON, JAMES	ALL	193	9TH E.D.
WELLIT, GEORGE S.	CHA	249	MIDDLETO
WELLMAN, ERNST	BAL	147	2ND DIST
WELLMER, JOHN	BAL	434	1ST DIST
WELLMEW, ELLEN	BAL	380	13TH WAR
WELLPER, DORETHA	BAL	201	2ND WARD
WELLS, AFFEY	BAL	267	7TH WARD
WELLS, ALFRED H.	PRI	007	BLADENSB
WELLS, ALIN	BAL	019	9TH WARD
WELLS, ANN	BAL	307	12TH WAR
WELLS, ANN	PRI	083	QUEEN AN
WELLS, ANN	BAL	019	18TH WAR
WELLS, ANNA E.	CEC	044	CHESAPEA
WELLS, APPY*	BAL	193	6TH WARD
WELLS, ARAH A.	BAL	347	3RD WARD
WELLS, B. FRANK	BAL	396	1ST DIST
WELLS, BENJAMIN	ANN	410	8TH DIST
WELLS, CANNON	BAL	092	2ND DIST
WELLS, CAROLINE	WOR	205	4TH E DI
WELLS, CAROLINE	CAR	209	5TH DIST
WELLS, CATHARINE	BAL	408	3RD WARD
WELLS, CATHARINE C.	BAL	218	6TH WARD
WELLS, CHARLES	BAL	023	2ND DIST
WELLS, CHARLES C.	ANN	461	HOWARD D
WELLS, CHARLES H.	BAL	026	1ST WARD
WELLS, CHARLOTT	CHA	255	MIDDLETO
WELLS, DANIEL	BAL	136	11TH WAR
WELLS, DANIEL	ANN	485	HOWARD D
WELLS, DANIEL	ANN	338	3RD DIST
WELLS, DAVID	ANN	517	HOWARD D
WELLS, DAVID	BAL	101	2ND DIST
WELLS, DAVID	BAL	102	2ND DIST
WELLS, DEBORAH	TAL	024	EASTON D
WELLS, DENNIS	BAL	169	6TH WARD
WELLS, DINA-BLACK	PRI	121	PISCATAW
WELLS, DORCUS	FRE	046	FREDERIC
WELLS, E.	HAR	154	3RD DIST
WELLS, EDWARD	CHA	220	ALLENS F
WELLS, ELEY	BAL	121	5TH WARD
WELLS, ELIJAH	BAL	219	12TH WAR
	ANN	278	ANNAPOLI

Name	County	Page	District
WELLS, ELIZA	BAL	004	EASTERN
WELLS, ELIZA	BAL	246	2ND WARD
WELLS, ELIZA	CEC	005	ELKTON 3
WELLS, ELIZA	HAR	192	3RD DIST
WELLS, ELIZABETH	PRI	020	VANSVILL
WELLS, ELIZABETH A.	BAL	004	EASTERN
WELLS, ELIZABETH-WELLS	QUE	159	2ND E DI
WELLS, EPHRAIM	TAL	095	ST MICHA
WELLS, FALLS	TAL	104	ST MICHA
WELLS, FREDERICK	BAL	012	9TH WARD
WELLS, FRIELY	QUE	241	5TH E DI
WELLS, GEORGE	ANN	297	ANNAPOLI
WELLS, GEORGE	BAL	229	6TH WARD
WELLS, GEORGE	BAL	119	11TH WAR
WELLS, GEORGE	BAL	063	4TH WARD
WELLS, GJERGE	PRI	079	QUEEN AN
WELLS, HARMAN	HAR	171	3RD DIST
WELLS, HARRETT	HAR	171	3RD DIST
WELLS, HARRY	BAL	053	9TH WARD
WELLS, HENRY	BAL	034	9TH WARD
WELLS, HENRY	ANN	305	1ST DIST
WELLS, HENRY	BAL	456	8TH WARD
WELLS, HENRY	WAS	161	2ND DIST
WELLS, HENRY S.	BAL	359	3RD WARD
WELLS, HESTER	TAL	070	EASTON T
WELLS, HEZEKIAH	PRI	078	MARLBROU
WELLS, HURNEY	BAL	271	20TH WAR
WELLS, IRA	QUE	190	3RD E DI
WELLS, IRENA	WOR	204	4TH E DI
WELLS, ISAAC	BAL	247	6TH WARD
WELLS, JACOB R.	ANN	461	HOWARD D
WELLS, JAMES	BAL	105	10TH WAR
WELLS, JAMES	WOR	205	4TH E DI
WELLS, JAMES	KEN	259	1ST DIST
WELLS, JAMES	TAL	023	EASTON D
WELLS, JAMES	HAR	161	3RD DIST
WELLS, JAMES	BAL	061	4TH WARD
WELLS, JAMES	CEC	144	PORT DUP
WELLS, JAMES	BAL	023	18TH WAR
WELLS, JAMES N.	ANN	294	1ST DIST
WELLS, JANE P.	BAL	143	11TH WAR
WELLS, JEREMIAH	ANN	436	HOWARD D
WELLS, JOHN	ANN	397	8TH DIST
WELLS, JOHN	ANN	342	3RD DIST
WELLS, JOHN	ANN	291	ANNAPOLI
WELLS, JOHN	ANN	409	8TH DIST
WELLS, JOHN	ALL	198	CUMBERLA
WELLS, JOHN	BAL	192	6TH WARD
WELLS, JOHN	BAL	194	2ND WARD
WELLS, JOHN	BAL	344	1ST DIST
WELLS, JOHN	PRI	004	BLADENSB
WELLS, JOHN	QUE	239	5TH E DI
WELLS, JOHN J.	BAL	052	9TH WARD
WELLS, JOHN K.	WAS	083	2ND SUBD
WELLS, JOHN W.	HAR	184	3RD DIST
WELLS, JOSEPH	BAL	245	17TH WAR
WELLS, JOSEPH	CEC	005	ELKTON 3
WELLS, JOSEPH	BAL	211	5TH WARD
WELLS, JOSEPH	BAL	110	2ND DIST
WELLS, JOSEPH	BAL	156	2ND DIST
WELLS, JOSEPHINE	BAL	118	5TH WARD
WELLS, JOSHUA	BAL	004	EASTERN
WELLS, LEUIN	BAL	136	2ND DIST
WELLS, LEWIS	TAL	095	ST MICHA
WELLS, LLOYD	PRI	093	MARLBROU
WELLS, LUCY	BAL	190	6TH WARD
WELLS, M.A.	PRI	119	PISCATAW
WELLS, MAHALA	CAL	012	1ST DIST
WELLS, MAHALA-BLACK	CAR	398	2ND DIST
WELLS, MARANDY	CAR	180	8TH DIST
WELLS, MARGARET	PRI	081	QUEEN AN
WELLS, MARY	BAL	151	19TH WAR
WELLS, MARY	BAL	383	13TH WAR
WELLS, MARY	BAL	074	4TH WARD
WELLS, MARY	ANN	365	4TH DIST
WELLS, MARY	ANN	291	ANNAPOLI
WELLS, MARY B.	BAL	367	3RD WARD
WELLS, MARY C.	BAL	150	16TH WAR
WELLS, MARY J.	BAL	164	16TH WAR
WELLS, MARY J.	BAL	175	11TH WAR
WELLS, MARY*	BAL	405	3RD WARD
WELLS, MILLY	ALL	102	5TH E.D.
WELLS, MINOR	ALL	185	9TH E.D.
WELLS, MINTA	BAL	102	2ND DIST
WELLS, MOSES-BLACK	FRE	392	PETERSVI
WELLS, NACKY	BAL	187	5TH DIST
WELLS, NANCY	BAL	425	14TH WAR
WELLS, NANCY	TAL	095	ST MICHA
WELLS, NATHANIEL B.	BAL	422	3RD WARD
WELLS, NICHOLAS	BAL	343	1ST DIST
WELLS, OTHO	ANN	371	4TH DIST
WELLS, PETER	BAL	371	3RD WARD
WELLS, PRISCILLA	BAL	185	16TH WAR
WELLS, RACHAEL	FRE	315	MIDDLETO
WELLS, REBECCA J.	CEC	011	ELKTON 3
WELLS, RICHARD	FRE	261	NEW MARK
WELLS, RICHARD	CAL	014	1ST DIST
WELLS, RICHARD	ANN	417	HOWARD D
WELLS, RICHARD	ANN	267	ANNAPOLI
WELLS, RICHARD	BAL	219	12TH WAR
WELLS, RICHARD C.*	BAL	415	3RD WARD
WELLS, RICHARD JR.	ANN	448	HOWARD D
WELLS, ROBERT H.	BAL	323	3RD WARD
WELLS, ROBERT R.	BAL	309	3RD WARD
WELLS, ROMULAS	FRE	325	MIDDLETO
WELLS, RUFUS	HAR	156	3RD DIST
WELLS, SARAH	CEC	122	4TH E DI
WELLS, SARAH	ANN	496	HOWARD D
WELLS, SARAH	BAL	315	7TH WARD
WELLS, SARAH	WAS	161	2ND DIST
WELLS, THOMAS	TAL	111	ST MICHA
WELLS, THOMAS	BAL	193	17TH WAR
WELLS, THOMAS	BAL	138	2ND DIST
WELLS, THOMAS	ALL	171	7TH E.D.
WELLS, THOMAS	BAL	240	17TH WAR
WELLS, THOMAS A.	PRI	074	MARLBROU
WELLS, THOMAS W.	CAR	183	8TH DIST
WELLS, TRISTRAM	TAL	099	ST MICHA
WELLS, WELLS	CAR	360	9TH DIST
WELLS, WESLEY	BAL	013	1ST WARD
WELLS, WELLAIM	BAL	137	16TH WAR
WELLS, WILLIAM	BAL	259	1ST DIST
WELLS, WILLIAM	ANN	302	1ST DIST
WELLS, WILLIAM	ANN	404	8TH DIST
WELLS, WILLIAM	BAL	250	17TH WAR
WELLS, WILLIAM	HAR	160	3RD DIST
WELLS, WILLIAM	BAL	475	14TH WAR
WELLS, WILLIAM	PRI	078	MARLBROU
WELLS, WILLIAM	QUE	249	5TH E DI
WELLS, WILLIAM B.	TAL	087	ST MICHA

Name	County	Page	District
WELLS, WILLIAM H.	HAR	167	3RD DIST
WELLS, WILLIAM M.	WOR	208	4TH E DI
WELLS, WILLIAM V.	CHA	268	BOJANTOW
WELLS, WILLY	CAL	055	3RD DIST
WELLS, WILSON L.	ANN	319	2ND DIST
WELLSLAGER, STEPHEN	BAL	232	2ND WARD
WELLSLAGER, STEPHEN D.	BAL	232	2ND WARD
WELLSLINGER, ELIZABETH	DOR	365	3RD DIVI
WELP, NANCY *	ALL	159	6TH E.D.
WELRAGE, HERMAN H.	BAL	165	16TH WAR
WELS, JAMES B.	HAR	153	3RD DIST
WELSCHOLD, THEODORE	BAL	352	13TH WAR
WELSH, AMOS W.	ANN	447	HOWARD D
WELSH, ANN	ALL	103	5TH E.D.
WELSH, ANN	BAL	054	1ST WARD
WELSH, B. A.	ANN	299	1ST DIST
WELSH, BARTHOLOMEW	ANN	468	HOWARD D
WELSH, BENJAIN	BAL	473	14TH WAR
WELSH, BRUNETTE	ANN	441	HOWARD D
WELSH, CATHARINE	ALL	102	5TH E.D.
WELSH, CATHARINE	ALL	092	5TH E.D.
WELSH, CATHARINE	BAL	009	18TH WAR
WELSH, CATHERINE	BAL	134	11TH WAR
WELSH, COLUMBUS	ANN	520	HOWARD D
WELSH, CORNELIUS	BAL	017	1ST WARD
WELSH, CUPLENIA	BAL	123	2ND DIST
WELSH, DANIEL D.	BAL	194	19TH WAR
WELSH, DAVID	BAL	194	19TH WAR
WELSH, DAVID	BAL	010	18TH WAR
WELSH, E.	BAL	058	10TH WAR
WELSH, E. JACOB	BAL	188	19TH WAR
WELSH, ELIZABETH	BAL	058	10TH WAR
WELSH, ELIZABETH	WAS	056	2ND SUBD
WELSH, ELLEN	BAL	293	1ST DIST
WELSH, ELLEN	BAL	001	15TH WAR
WELSH, ELVIRA	BAL	380	1ST DIST
WELSH, EPHRAIM	PRI	031	VANSVILL
WELSH, FERDNAND	BAL	409	1ST DIST
WELSH, FRANCIS A.	BAL	379	13TH WAR
WELSH, GEORGE	BAL	409	1ST DIST
WELSH, GEORGE	ANN	355	3RD DIST
WELSH, GEORGE	PRI	031	VANSVILL
WELSH, HENRY	WAS	198	1ST DIST
WELSH, HENRY	ANN	491	HOWARD D
WELSH, HENRY	ALL	138	6TH E.D.
WELSH, ICHABOD *	ALL	094	5TH E.D.
WELSH, JAMES	ALL	079	5TH E.D.
WELSH, JAMES	BAL	100	2ND DIST
WELSH, JAMES	BAL	328	13TH WAR
WELSH, JAMES	BAL	278	12TH WAR
WELSH, JAMES	BAL	209	19TH WAR
WELSH, JAMES	FRE	055	FREDERIC
WELSH, JANE	BAL	304	12TH WAR
WELSH, JOHN	ALL	076	5TH E.D.
WELSH, JOHN	ALL	138	6TH E.D.
WELSH, JOHN	ALL	157	6TH E.D.
WELSH, JOHN	ALL	166	6TH E.D.
WELSH, JOHN	BAL	382	1ST DIST
WELSH, JOHN	ANN	517	HOWARD D
WELSH, JOHN	BAL	461	1ST DIST
WELSH, JOHN	BAL	164	11TH WAR
WELSH, JOHN	BAL	279	2ND WARD
WELSH, JOHN	BAL	302	17TH WAR
WELSH, JOHN W.	BAL	102	10TH WAR
WELSH, JUDAH	BAL	164	2ND DIST
WELSH, JULIA	ANN	424	HOWARD D
WELSH, LAURENCE	BAL	020	9TH WARD
WELSH, LIDDY	BAL	091	18TH WAR
WELSH, LUTHER	ANN	470	HOWARD D
WELSH, LYCURGUS G.	ANN	373	4TH DIST
WELSH, M. W.	BAL	104	18TH WAR
WELSH, MARCELLA O.	FRE	240	NEW MARK
WELSH, MARGARET	BAL	454	14TH WAR
WELSH, MARGARET	BAL	251	12TH WAR
WELSH, MARGARET	TAL	086	ST MICHA
WELSH, MARTIN	WAS	022	2ND SUBD
WELSH, MARTIN	BAL	001	1ST WARD
WELSH, MARTIN	ALL	049	10TH E.D
WELSH, MARY	BAL	263	12TH WAR
WELSH, MARY	BAL	167	6TH WARD
WELSH, MARY	BAL	110	10TH WAR
WELSH, MARY A.	BAL	312	7TH WARD
WELSH, MARY A.	ANN	508	HOWARD D
WELSH, MICHAEL	WAS	034	2ND SUBD
WELSH, MILTN	ANN	492	HOWARD D
WELSH, MILTSA M.	FRE	240	NEW MARK
WELSH, PATRICK	BAL	317	20TH WAR
WELSH, PATRICK	BAL	442	1ST DIST
WELSH, PATRICK	BAL	003	9TH WARD
WELSH, PATRICK	BAL	056	15TH WAR
WELSH, PATRICK	BAL	157	2ND DIST
WELSH, PHILIP	BAL	171	6TH WARD
WELSH, R.	ANN	296	1ST DIST
WELSH, RICHARD	BAL	372	13TH WAR
WELSH, RICHARD	WAS	022	2ND SUBD
WELSH, RICHARD	WAS	195	1ST DIST
WELSH, ROBERT	ALL	088	5TH E.D.
WELSH, ROBERT H.	ANN	320	2ND DIST
WELSH, RUTH	ANN	299	1ST DIST
WELSH, SAMUEL	BAL	417	14TH WAR
WELSH, SARAH E.	QUE	151	1ST E DI
WELSH, THOMAS	FRE	096	FREDERIC
WELSH, THOMAS	BAL	318	1ST DIST
WELSH, THOMAS	BAL	176	11TH WAR
WELSH, THOMAS	BAL	280	2ND WARD
WELSH, THOMAS H.	FRE	164	EMMITTSB
WELSH, THOMAS J. H.	PRI	027	VANSVILL
WELSH, UPTON D.	ANN	516	HOWARD D
WELSH, VALENTINE	BAL	462	1ST DIST
WELSH, WARREN	ANN	440	HOWARD D
WELSH, WILLIAM	BAL	354	1ST DIST
WELSH, WILLIAM	ALL	159	6TH E.D.
WELSH, WILLIAM	BAL	198	19TH WAR
WELSH, WILLIAM	FRE	033	FREDERIC
WELSH, WILLIAM O.	BAL	291	12TH WAR
WELSHOOVER, ELIZABETH	BAL	202	11TH WAR
WELSHOOVER, WILLIAM *	BAL	290	20TH WAR
WELSHOWER, WILLIAM *	BAL	290	20TH WAR
WELSLAKER, MARTHA	BAL	003	1ST WARD
WELSON, HARINA	ALL	187	9TH E.D.
WELSON, JAMES	ALL	186	9TH E.D.
WELSON, JOHN	ALL	173	7TH E.D.
WELSON, JOHN	ALL	103	5TH E.D.
WELSTER, GEORGE	FRE	032	FREDERIC
WELSTER, HENRY	BAL	381	13TH WAR
WELT, DAVID	ALL	062	10TH E.D
WELT, FREDERICK	ALL	125	4TH E.D.
WELT, THEOPH*	ALL	143	6TH E.D.
WELTER, JOHN	TAL	071	EASTON T
WELTERLEY, MARY	BAL	406	8TH WARD
WELTLEY, CHARLES	BAL	292	17TH WAR
WELTNER, THOMAS	BAL	028	1ST WARD
WELTY, ANTHONY	FRE	183	5TH E DI
WELTY, BARBAR	FRE	176	5TH E DI
WELTY, BERNARD	FRE	190	5TH E DI
WELTY, CASPER	FRE	179	5TH E DI
WELTY, DANIEL	WAS	014	WILLIAMS
WELTY, EICHELBERGER	FRE	190	5TH E DI
WELTY, HENRY	WAS	014	WILLIAMS
WELTY, JACOB	WAS	034	2ND SUBD
WELTY, JAMES S.	FRE	163	EMMITTSB
WELTY, JOHN H.	WAS	034	2ND SUBD
WELTY, JOSEPH	CAR	311	1ST DIST
WELTY, JOSPEHINE	CAR	311	1ST DIST
WELTY, SAMUEL	FRE	147	10TH E D
WELTY, SAMUEL *	WAS	161	HAGERSTO
WELTY, WILLIAM	FRE	203	5TH E DI
WELTZ, ABRAHAM	FRE	160	EMMITTSB
WELTZ, ANDREW	FRE	166	EMMITTSB
WELTZ, CHRISTINA	FRE	166	EMMITTSB
WELTZ, ELIZABETH	WAS	014	WILLIAMS
WELTZ, HARRIET	BAL	465	14TH WAR
WELTZ, JACOB	BAL	253	12TH WAR
WELTZ, JOHN J.	FRE	179	5TH E DI
WELTZY, JOSEPH	FRE	175	5TH E DI
WELZBACKER, AUGUSTUS *	BAL	202	6TH WARD
WEMAN, HENRY	BAL	090	2ND DIST
WEMBS, JAMES	SOM	400	BRINKLEY
WEMIS, JAMES	FRE	097	FREDERIC
WEMPART, IGNATIUS	BAL	226	12TH WAR
WEMPON, MARIA	BAL	257	2ND WARD
WEMPSEY, FRANCIS*	BAL	311	3RD WARD
WENABLE, JOHN	WOR	292	9TH E DI
WENBERG, ABRAHAM	BAL	015	9TH WARD
WENDER, JOHN*	BAL	352	3RD WARD
WENDER, WILLIAM	QUE	205	3RD E DI
WENDERKNECHT, AUGUST	BAL	169	6TH WARD
WENDWORTH, JOHN	BAL	062	2ND DIST
WENER, JAMES	BAL	283	2ND WARD
WENER, JOHN	BAL	205	2ND WARD
WENET, SARAH	BAL	006	1ST WARD
WENFIELD, IRANA	FRE	369	CATOCTIN
WENFLINGER, JONATHAN	FRE	350	MIDDLETO
WENING, ELIZA	FRE	379	PETERSVI
WENINGER, ELIZA	BAL	108	1ST WARD
WENIT, JAMES H.	BAL	009	1ST WARD
WENKE, MARY	BAL	263	12TH WAR
WENKS, SAMUEL*	BAL	394	3RD WARD
WENKWIN, GEORGE	BAL	221	2ND WARD
WENLY, HUGH	BAL	041	1ST WARD
WENN, WILLIAM	BAL	297	12TH WAR
WENNER, JOHN	ALL	039	2ND E.D.
WENNER, JOHN G.	BAL	206	2ND WARD
WENNER, JOHN*	BAL	390	3RD WARD
WENNET, LUCUS	BAL	236	20TH WAR
WENNING, JOHN	BAL	285	12TH WAR
WENNING, JOSEPH	BAL	286	12TH WAR
WENRICH, SUSAN	WAS	295	1ST DIST
WENRICK, DANIEL B.	FRE	204	BUCKEYST
WENRICK, JOHN A.	FRE	206	BUCKEYST
WENRICK, REBECCA	FRE	305	WOODSBOR
WENRICK, SAMEUL	WAS	291	1ST DIST
WENRICK, WILLIAM	FRE	204	BUCKEYST
WENSKER, GEORGE	BAL	092	1ST WARD
WENTBRENNER, ISAAC	ALL	098	5TH E.D.
WENTER, ANN	CHA	239	HILLTOP
WENTER, JULIET	CHA	238	HILLTOP
WENTWORTH, GEORGE W.	BAL	012	15TH WAR
WENTY, GEORGE	BAL	115	11TH WAR
WENTZ, BENJAMIN	CAR	252	3RD DIST
WENTZ, CATHARINE	CAR	335	6TH DIST
WENTZ, CHARLES	BAL	003	15TH WAR
WENTZ, ELIZA	BAL	144	16TH WAR
WENTZ, FREDERICK	CAR	406	2ND DIST
WENTZ, GEORGE	CAR	406	2ND DIST
WENTZ, GEORGE	CAR	267	WESTMINS
WENTZ, JACOB	CAR	274	7TH DIST
WENTZ, JOHN	CAR	346	6TH DIST
WENTZ, JOHN	CAR	408	2ND DIST
WENTZ, JOHN B.	BAL	052	1ST WARD
WENTZ, LYDIA	CAR	407	2ND DIST
WENTZ, PHAMUEL	CAR	343	6TH DIST
WENTZ, PHILIP	CAR	252	3RD DIST
WENTZ, PHILIP	BAL	010	15TH WAR
WENTZ, PHILIP	BAL	019	9TH WARD
WENTZ, RACHEAL	CAR	407	2ND DIST
WENTZ, SAMUEL	CAR	293	7TH DIST
WENTZ, SELINA	BAL	084	18TH WAR
WENTZ, VALENTINE	CAR	294	7TH DIST
WENTZ, VALENTINE	CAR	405	2ND DIST
WENTZ, VALENTINE	CAR	295	7TH DIST
WENTZE, SAMUEL	BAL	393	14TH WAR
WENTZEL, THOMAS	BAL	049	1ST WARD
WENTZEL, VALENTINE	BAL	260	2ND WARD
WENTZELL, ADAM	BAL	056	1ST WARD
WENTZELL, CHARLES	BAL	108	5TH WARD
WENTZELL, HENRY	BAL	212	17TH WAR
WENWOOD, JANE	BAL	226	12TH WAR
WEPLER, JOHN	BAL	278	17TH WAR
WERBLE, FREDERICK	CAR	268	WESTMINS
WEROAN, AMILIA	BAL	288	20TH WAR
WEROAN, WILLIAM	BAL	288	20TH WAR
WERONER, CHARLES	BAL	254	20TH WAR
WERONER, CHARLES	BAL	254	20TH WAR
WERONER, PAUL	BAL	270	12TH WAR
WERE, JOHN	CHA	263	MIDDLETO
WEREGORDEN, AARON	BAL	457	14TH WAR
WERHART, WILLIAM	ALL	198	CUMBERLA
WERKENMILLER, JOHN	MGM	394	ROCKERLE
WERL, GEORGE	BAL	089	18TH WAR
WERLEIN, CATHARINE	BAL	032	15TH WAR
WERLEIN, JOHN	BAL	031	15TH WAR
WERLICH, WILLIAM	BAL	037	15TH WAR
WERLINGS, JOSEPH	BAL	372	13TH WAR
WERMAN, MARY	WOR	305	SNOW HIL
WERMER, GEORGE	ALL	225	CUMBERLA
WERMETH, RUTHERTON	BAL	163	11TH WAR
WERMS, THOMAS	BAL	133	2ND DIST
WERNDING, HERMAN	BAL	031	9TH WARD
WERNER, ALFRED L.	BAL	190	19TH WAR
WERNER, ANN J. *	BAL	269	7TH WARD
WERNER, CHARLES	ALL	217	CUMBERLA
WERNER, HENRY H.	BAL	026	15TH WAR
WERNER, JACOB	BAL	124	2ND DIST
WERNER, JOHN	BAL	088	1ST WARD
WERNER, MARY E.	BAL	265	2ND WARD
WERNER, PETER	BAL	203	2ND WARD
WERNER, PHILLIP	BAL	203	2ND WARD
WERNER, SISTER M.P.	FRE	198	5TH E DI
WERNEY, C. *	BAL	308	12TH WAR
WERNISH, FRANCIS	BAL	422	8TH WARD
WERNS, CHARLOTTE	BAL	035	15TH WAR
WERREN, DAVID	BAL	264	12TH WAR
WERRETT, SAMUEL	WAS	172	FUNKSTOW
WERRICK, MARY A.	CEC	149	PORT DUP
WERRY, JEREMIAH	BAL	172	16TH WAR
WERSING, CATHERINE	BAL	031	9TH WARD
WERT, JOHN	BAL	006	4TH WARD
WERTER, JOHN C.	BAL	366	1ST DIST
WERTH, CHRISTIAN	BAL	207	2ND WARD
WERTON, ELIZA	ALL	153	6TH E.D.
WERTON, JACKSON	ALL	138	6TH E.D.
WERTON, NATHANE *	ALL	138	6TH E.D.
WERTRON, LEWIS*	DOR	392	1ST DIST
WERTS, JESSE	CAR	336	6TH DIST
WERTS, MRS. OF WILLIAM	ANN	281	ANNAPOLI
WES, OTTO	BAL	092	10TH WAR
WESAT, SOPHIA	WAS	179	BOONSBOR
WESBOTT, JAMES	BAL	008	9TH WARD
WESCOTT, CHILENGWORTH	ALL	103	5TH E.D.
WESE, HENRY*	BAL	403	3RD WARD
WESH, HENRY	BAL	297	3RD WARD
WESHER, HESTER	BAL	005	4TH WARD
WESLER, GERTRUDE	BAL	297	3RD WARD
WESLETT, SAMUEL M. C.	CEC	145	PORT DUP
WESLEY, DENNIS	ANN	367	4TH DIST
WESLEY, JACOB	BAL	137	18TH WAR
WESLEY, JAMES	BAL	278	12TH WAR
WESLEY, JIM-BLACK	QUE	129	1ST E DI
WESLEY, JOHN	CAR	080	NO TWP L
WESLEY, JOHN	CAL	058	3RD DIST
WESLEY, JOHN	BAL	192	17TH WAR
WESLEY, JOHN	ANN	371	4TH DIST
WESLEY, JOHN	BAL	105	2ND DIST
WESLEY, JOHN	ANN	497	HOWARD D
WESLEY, JOHN	BAL	459	8TH WARD
WESLEY, JOHN-BLACK	QUE	185	3RD E DI
WESLEY, LOIUS	BAL	186	16TH WAR
WESLEY, LOYD	ANN	367	4TH DIST
WESLEY, MARTHA	BAL	052	18TH WAR
WESLEY, MARY	ANN	367	4TH DIST
WESLEY, MARY A.	CEC	091	4TH E DI
WESLEY, SARAH	BAL	265	20TH WAR
WESLEY, SYLVESTER	BAL	012	4TH WARD
WESLEY, WAKEMAN	CEC	173	6TH E DI
WESLEY, WILLIAM	HAR	119	2ND DIST
WESLEY, WILLIAM	BAL	171	16TH WAR
WESLEY, WILLIAM	BAL	223	12TH WAR
WESLEY, WILLIAM	BAL	244	2ND WARD
WESLTEY, JAMES	FRE	174	5TH E DI
WESLY, JOHN	WAS	146	2ND DIST
WESLY, JOHN	WAS	117	2ND DIST
WESLY, LOUISA	BAL	306	1ST DIST
WESMATT, GEORGE	BAL	379	13TH WAR
WESNER, JOHN	WAS	247	SMITHSBU
WESNER, RICHARD	CAR	278	7TH DIST
WESONG, WILLIAM	BAL	269	12TH WAR
WESSBAUGH, WILLIAM L.*	BAL	349	3RD WARD
WESSEL, MICHAEL	ALL	262	CUMBERLA
WESSELL, HENRY W.	KEN	249	2ND DIST
WESSEY, HANNAH	BAL	463	1ST DIST
WESSSNEDURF, JOSEPH	FRE	205	BUCKEYST
WEST, ABIGALE J.	BAL	068	18TH WAR
WEST, ADDER	SOM	381	BRINKLEY
WEST, AIMESTEAD	MGM	383	ROCKERLE
WEST, AMOS	HAR	079	2ND DIST
WEST, ANN	BAL	293	17TH WAR
WEST, ANN	FRE	417	8TH E DI
WEST, ANN	BAL	266	12TH WAR
WEST, ANNA	BAL	389	13TH WAR
WEST, ANTONEY	BAL	222	12TH WAR
WEST, ARTHUR	PRI	074	MARLBROU
WEST, ARTHUR P.	PRI	060	NOTTINGH
WEST, BENJAMIN	BAL	213	6TH WARD
WEST, BENJAMIN C.	ANN	471	HOWARD D
WEST, BETSY	BAL	470	14TH WAR
WEST, CATHARINE	BAL	229	17TH WAR
WEST, CATHARINE V.	BAL	058	15TH WAR
WEST, CHARLES	BAL	188	11TH WAR
WEST, CHARLES	BAL	312	1ST DIST
WEST, CHARLES	TAL	036	EASTON D
WEST, CHARLOTTE	QUE	147	1ST E DI
WEST, CLARKSON H.	HAR	091	2ND DIST
WEST, CLOTILLIA R.	BAL	187	6TH WARD
WEST, COLUMBUS	BAL	362	3RD WARD
WEST, DANIEL	BAL	314	7TH WARD
WEST, DANIEL	WAS	036	2ND SUBD
WEST, DAVID	WAS	246	SMITHSBU
WEST, DENNIS	FRE	099	FREDERIC
WEST, EBENEZER	BAL	146	1ST WARD
WEST, EDITH	BAL	407	3RD WARD
WEST, EDWARD	CEC	150	PORT DUP
WEST, ELIAS B.	WOR	166	6TH E DI
WEST, ELIZA	BAL	232	17TH WAR
WEST, ELIZA	BAL	361	13TH WAR
WEST, ELIZA	BAL	127	5TH WARD
WEST, ELIZA	BAL	039	2ND DIST
WEST, ELIZABETH	BAL	158	16TH WAR
WEST, ELIZABETH	BAL	109	15TH WAR
WEST, ELIZABETH	BAL	425	1ST DIST
WEST, ELIZABETH	BAL	050	4TH WARD
WEST, ELIZABETH	BAL	082	4TH WARD
WEST, ELIZABETH	FRE	066	FREDERIC
WEST, ELIZABETH A.	MGM	383	ROCKERLE
WEST, ELLEN	WAS	101	2ND DIST
WEST, ERASMUS	MGM	401	ROCKERLE
WEST, EUGENE	FRE	029	FREDERIC
WEST, FANNY	BAL	311	12TH WAR
WEST, GARRISON	TAL	080	ST MICHA
WEST, GEORGE	TAL	080	ST MICHA
WEST, GEORGE	HAR	071	1ST DIST
WEST, GEORGE	BAL	135	18TH WAR
WEST, GEORGE	BAL	166	19TH WAR
WEST, GEORGE W.	FRE	380	PETERSVI
WEST, GEORGE W.-MULATTO	FRE	417	8TH E DI
WEST, H. B.	BAL	279	2ND WARD
WEST, HARRIET	BAL	275	2ND WARD
WEST, HARRIET J.	BAL	138	5TH WARD
WEST, HENRY	BAL	168	1ST WARD
WEST, HENRY	BAL	372	8TH WARD
WEST, HENRY	BAL	053	2ND DIST
WEST, HENRY	MGM	378	ROCKERLE
WEST, HENRY T.	FRE	097	FREDERIC
WEST, ISAAC	WOR	208	4TH E DI
WEST, ISAAC-BLACK	BAL	233	2ND WARD
WEST, ISABELLA	BAL	319	3RD WARD
WEST, ISABELLA	BAL	323	3RD WARD
WEST, ISABELLA	FRE	061	FREDERIC
WEST, ISABELLA	FRE	100	FREDERIC
WEST, JACOB	BAL	378	13TH WAR

Name	Co.	Page	District
WEST, JAMES	HAR	071	1ST DIST
WEST, JAMES	BAL	128	11TH WAR
WEST, JAMES	BAL	208	6TH DIST
WEST, JAMES	BAL	383	8TH WARD
WEST, JAMES	BAL	131	1ST WARD
WEST, JAMES A.	WOR	209	4TH E DI
WEST, JAMES L.	BAL	005	15TH WAR
WEST, JAMES-BLACK	QUE	162	2ND E DI
WEST, JANE	BAL	413	1ST DIST
WEST, JEREMIAH	WAS	104	2ND DIST
WEST, JEREMIAH	CAR	141	NO TWP L
WEST, JIM	ANN	294	1ST DIST
WEST, JOEL	QUE	172	2ND E DI
WEST, JOHN	BAL	448	1ST DIST
WEST, JOHN	BAL	131	1ST WARD
WEST, JOHN	BAL	280	2ND WARD
WEST, JOHN	CAR	234	UNION TO
WEST, JOHN B.	MGM	347	BERRYS D
WEST, JOHN G.	HAR	162	3RD DIST
WEST, JOHN J.	WAS	158	HAGERSTO
WEST, JOHN L.	BAL	141	11TH WAR
WEST, JOHN T.	CEC	010	ELKTON 3
WEST, JOHN T.	BAL	076	15TH WAR
WEST, JOHN W.	FRE	380	PETERSVI
WEST, JOHN W.	WOR	210	4TH E DI
WEST, JOSEPH	BAL	071	18TH WAR
WEST, JOSEPH	BAL	276	7TH WARD
WEST, JULIUS	MGM	374	ROCKERLE
WEST, KENDALL B.	WOR	177	6TH E DI
WEST, LEVIN	FRE	381	PETERSVI
WEST, LORETTA	BAL	305	7TH WARD
WEST, LUCINDA	BAL	318	20TH WAR
WEST, MARIA	BAL	448	14TH WAR
WEST, MARIA	PRI	070	MARLBROU
WEST, MARIA	PRI	069	MARLBROU
WEST, MARIA L.	BAL	026	9TH WARD
WEST, MARY	BAL	037	9TH WARD
WEST, MARY	BAL	205	11TH WAR
WEST, MARY	BAL	296	12TH WAR
WEST, MARY A.	BAL	022	2ND DIST
WEST, MASSEY	QUE	143	1ST E DI
WEST, MINOR	WOR	175	6TH E DI
WEST, NATHAN G.	WOR	208	4TH E DI
WEST, PETER	WOR	210	4TH E DI
WEST, PHEBY	CEC	175	7TH E DI
WEST, RACHEAL	ANN	289	ANNAPOLI
WEST, REBECCA	BAL	355	1ST DIST
WEST, REBECCA	CEC	153	PORT DUP
WEST, RICHARD	MGM	397	ROCKERLE
WEST, SALLY	SOM	420	PRINCESS
WEST, SAMUEL	MGM	397	ROCKERLE
WEST, SAMUEL	BAL	268	17TH WAR
WEST, SAMUEL	QUE	129	1ST E DI
WEST, SAMUEL	CEC	076	NORTHEAS
WEST, SARAH A.	BAL	407	8TH WARD
WEST, SARAH E.	ALL	108	5TH E.D.
WEST, SHADRICK	CAR	094	NO TWP L
WEST, SHARY	ALL	018	3RD E.D.
WEST, SIMSON	CAR	082	NO TWP L
WEST, SLATER	BAL	120	1ST WARD
WEST, SSARAH	CAR	098	NO TWP L
WEST, STACY	HAR	056	1ST DIST
WEST, STEPHEN	ANN	385	4TH DIST
WEST, SWEEMAN	ALL	040	2ND E.D.
WEST, THOMAS	BAL	158	16TH WAR
WEST, THOMAS	WOR	208	4TH E DI
WEST, THOMAS	KEN	282	3RD DIST
WEST, TILMON	MGM	383	ROCKERLE
WEST, VINEY	PRI	077	MARLBROU
WEST, W.	ANN	285	ANNAPOLI
WEST, WILLIAM	ANN	294	1ST DIST
WEST, WILLIAM	ANN	285	ANNAPOLI
WEST, WILLIAM	BAL	016	1ST WARD
WEST, WILLIAM	BAL	133	1ST WARD
WEST, WILLIAM	BAL	330	3RD WARD
WEST, WILLIAM	BAL	235	12TH WAR
WEST, WILLIAM	KEN	280	3RD DIST
WEST, WILLIAM	WAS	164	HAGERSTO
WEST, WILLIAM	WAS	088	2ND SUBD
WEST, WILLIAM	QUE	146	1ST E DI
WEST, WILLIAM	CEC	214	7TH E DI
WEST, WILLIAM	BAL	021	4TH WARD
WEST, WILLIAM	FRE	215	BUCKEYST
WEST, WILLIAM H.	BAL	021	4TH WARD
WEST, WILLIAM T.	WOR	208	4TH E DI
WEST, WILLIAMN	FRE	426	8TH E DI
WEST,FRANCELIA	FRE	417	8TH E DI
WESTCOLL, GEORGE B.	KEN	217	2ND DIST
WESTCOLL, JANE	KEN	217	2ND DIST
WESTCOLL, NICHOLAS G.	KEN	214	2ND DIST
WESTEBERGER, JOHN	WAS	170	FUNKSTOW
WESTEN, CORNELIUS	BAL	280	20TH WAR
WESTENBERGER, MARGARETT	BAL	034	18TH WAR
WESTER, HENRY	BAL	258	12TH WAR
WESTER, SARAH	BAL	268	1ST DIST
WESTERFIELD, BEN	PRI	092	MARLBROU
WESTERHOUSE, HARMON	WAS	098	2ND DIST
WESTERMAN, ALICE	BAL	052	2ND DIST
WESTERMAN, BERNARD	ALL	017	3RD E.D.
WESTERMAN, ELIZABETH	MGM	388	ROCKERLE
WESTERMAN, EMILA	BAL	462	1ST DIST
WESTERMAN, HANNAH	BAL	295	3RD WARD
WESTERMAN, PRESILLA	BAL	165	11TH WAR
WESTERMAN, WILHELMANA	BAL	262	2ND WARD
WESTERN, ELLEN	BAL	174	19TH WAR
WESTERN, JAMES	QUE	235	4TH E DI
WESTFALL, HENRY	BAL	290	7TH WARD
WESTHERSS, ROBERT	BAL	258	2ND WARD
WESTLEY, CHARELS	ALL	099	5TH E.D.
WESTLEY, HENRY	CEC	174	6TH E DI
WESTLY, MARY T.	CEC	174	6TH E DI
WESTMAN, JOHN	FRE	090	FREDERIC
WESTON, EDWARD	QUE	230	4TH E DI
WESTON, ELEANOR	BAL	276	12TH WAR
WESTON, G.	BAL	138	1ST WARD
WESTON, HANNAH A.	BAL	458	14TH WAR
WESTON, JOHN W.	QUE	230	4TH E DI
WESTON, LEWIS	ANN	357	3RD DIST
WESTON, MARY	TAL	038	EASTON D
WESTON, MARY J.	TAL	056	EASTON D
WESTON, MILLY	ANN	305	1ST DIST
WESTON, NANCY	QUE	235	4TH E DI
WESTON, PETER	BAL	305	12TH WAR
WESTON, STEPHEN	ANN	304	1ST DIST
WESTON, SUSAN	TAL	076	EASTON T
WESTWOOD, GEORGE W.	BAL	398	8TH WARD
WESTWOOD, JOHN H.	BAL	259	6TH WARD
WESTWOOD, JOHN S.	BAL	279	2ND WARD
WESTZELL, HENRY	BAL	088	1ST WARD
WETERHOLT, EDWARD	BAL	357	8TH WARD
WETHENT, WILLIAM H.	TAL	072	EASTON T
WETHERAL, ED.	BAL	158	1ST WARD
WETHERAL, JEMIRE	HAR	195	3RD DIST
WETHERALD, ANN	MGM	372	BERRYS D
WETHERALL, JAMES	BAL	012	1ST WARD
WETHERALL, PHEBE	BAL	010	4TH WARD
WETHERALL, WILLIAM G.	BAL	070	15TH WAR
WETHERBY, SAMUEL	WOR	261	BERLIN 1
WETHERED, CHARLES E.	BAL	150	11TH WAR
WETHERED, E.	BAL	150	11TH WAR
WETHERED, ELIZABETH	BAL	447	14TH WAR
WETHERED, GEORGE	BAL	105	10TH WAR
WETHERED, PERE *	KEN	222	2ND DIST
WETHEREL, JOHN	BAL	391	1ST DIST
WETHEREL, PERE *	KEN	222	2ND DIST
WETHERILL, ANNA	HAR	078	2ND DIST
WETHERILL, JANE	FRE	066	FREDERIC
WETHERLY, JOHN	BAL	298	17TH WAR
WETHERS, HANNAH	BAL	030	2ND DIST
WETHERSPOON, ANGLEY	ALL	106	5TH E.D.
WETHERSTINE, ELIZABETH *	BAL	213	6TH WARD
WETHERWICH, CHARLES	BAL	261	1ST DIST
WETHLY, HARRIET	BAL	092	2ND DIST
WETLER, CUET *	BAL	218	12TH WAR
WETMER, CHARLES	ALL	192	9TH E.D.
WETMORE, EDWARD	BAL	237	12TH WAR
WETMORE, SIMON	WAS	230	1ST DIST
WETNIGHT, M.	WAS	004	WILLIAMS
WETNIGHT, SAMUEL *	FRE	327	MIDDLETO
WETNIGHT, WILLIAM	WAS	003	WILLIAMS
WETRICH, HENRY	BAL	270	12TH WAR
WETS, JOHN A.*	BAL	397	3RD WARD
WETSEL, ADALINE	FRE	160	EMMITTSB
WETSEL, ANN M.	FRE	181	5TH E DI
WETSEL, BARBARA	FRE	290	WOODSBOR
WETSEL, CATHARINE	FRE	167	EMMITTSB
WETSEL, DANIEL	FRE	193	5TH E DI
WETSEL, JAMES	FRE	176	5TH E DI
WETSEL, JOHN	FRE	191	5TH E DI
WETSEL, JOSEPH	FRE	191	5TH E DI
WETSEL, LUCINDA	FRE	177	5TH E DI
WETSEL, MARGARET J.	FRE	173	5TH E DI
WETSEL, MARY J.	FRE	176	5TH E DI
WETSEY, MARY J.	BAL	193	11TH WAR
WETSTINE, CATHERINE	ALL	211	CUMBERLA
WETTLE, CATHARINE	FRE	183	5TH E DI
WETTLE, HENER	BAL	282	12TH WAR
WETTMERRSHAUSEN, F	BAL	261	12TH WAR
WETTNER, JOSEPH	BAL	028	1ST WARD
WETTZ, CATHARINE	BAL	248	2ND WARD
WETTZHEIMER, ANN M.	FRE	045	FREDERIC
WETWRIGHT, JACOB	WAS	009	WILLIAMS
WETZ, AMANDA	CAR	345	6TH DIST
WETZ, JOHN A.*	BAL	397	3RD WARD
WETZEL, JACOB	FRE	412	8TH E DI
WETZEL, SOPHIAM	FRE	413	8TH E DI
WETZELL, ELIAS	ALL	002	3RD E.D.
WETZELLS, JOHN	ALL	170	6TH E.D.
WEUKNER, BERNARD	BAL	255	2ND WARD
WEVER, CASPER	BAL	033	9TH WARD
WEVER, DORA	BAL	109	2ND DIST
WEVER, HENRY	BAL	109	2ND DIST
WEVER, JACOB	PRI	008	BLADENSB
WEYANT, DAVID	CAR	302	1ST DIST
WEYBRIGH, JOHN	CAR	319	1ST DIST
WEYE, SILAS	TAL	049	EASTON T
WEYFFARTH, CHARLES C.	BAL	452	14TH WAR
WEYFFARTH, PHILIP	BAL	452	14TH WAR
WEYFFORTH, BETHSHR*	BAL	018	4TH WARD
WEYMILLER, POLLY	FRE	170	5TH E DI
WEYSHAM, THOMAS	BAL	203	19TH WAR
WEZELADIER, VOLENTINE	BAL	092	1ST WARD
WEZKIN, FRANK	BAL	225	2ND WARD
WHAINE, WILLIAM *	BAL	264	2ND WARD
WHALAM, ANTONY	BAL	081	2ND DIST
WHALAN, CATHERINE	BAL	457	8TH WARD
WHALAN, HANNAH	BAL	459	1ST DIST
WHALAN, HOOPER	SOM	477	TRAPP DI
WHALAN, JOHN	ANN	417	HOWARD D
WHALAN, JOSEPH	SOM	467	TRAPPE D
WHALAN, LUKE	BAL	144	2ND DIST
WHALAN, MARY	SOM	468	TRAPPE D
WHALAN, MICHAEL	BAL	103	2ND DIST
WHALAN, THOMAS	BAL	240	17TH WAR
WHALAN, WILLIAM J.	SOM	478	TRAPP DI
WHALAN,JOHN	ALL	050	10TH E.D
WHALAND, ANN	BAL	304	1ST DIST
WHALAND, ANN	SOM	478	TRAPP DI
WHALAND, JOHN W.	KEN	260	1ST DIST
WHALAND, MARGARET	CEC	158	PORT DUP
WHALAND, ROBERT W.	HAR	077	BEL AIR
WHALASE, D.	ALL	155	6TH E.D.
WHALEING, WILLIAM	CAR	215	5TH DIST
WHALEN, ANDREW	BAL	276	1ST DIST
WHALEN, ARIANNA D.	ANN	519	HOWARD D
WHALEN, BEAL	ANN	517	HOWARD D
WHALEN, CATHERINE	MGM	365	BERRYS D
WHALEN, DANIEL	MGM	319	CRACKLIN
WHALEN, GEORGE	BAL	234	2ND WARD
WHALEN, JAMES	BAL	101	1ST WARD
WHALEN, JAMES	ALL	198	CUMBERLA
WHALEN, JANE	BAL	449	1ST DIST
WHALEN, JOHN	BAL	238	2ND WARD
WHALEN, LUCY	WAS	045	2ND SUBD
WHALEN, MARGARET	BAL	239	2ND WARD
WHALEN, MARGARET	MGM	388	ROCKERLE
WHALEN, MARIA	BAL	002	18TH WAR
WHALEN, MARTIN	MGM	405	ROCKERLE
WHALEN, MCIHAEL	BAL	101	1ST WARD
WHALEN, MICHAEL	BAL	449	1ST DIST
WHALEN, MICHAEL	MGM	382	ROCKERLE
WHALEN, NICHOLAS	MGM	416	MEDLEY 3
WHALEN, NICHOLAS	MGM	408	MEDLEY 3
WHALEN, SARAH	MGM	400	ROCKERLE
WHALEN, SERENER-BLACK	FRE	220	BUCKEYST
WHALEN, STEPHEN	BAL	403	14TH WAR
WHALEN, THOMAS	MGM	406	MEDLEY 3
WHALEN, THOMAS	BAL	041	1ST WARD
WHALEN, THOMAS J.	SOM	477	TRAPPE D
WHALEN, WESLEY	ANN	517	HOWARD D
WHALEN, WILLIAM	BAL	364	1ST DIST
WHALEN, WILLIAM	MGM	382	ROCKERLE
WHALEN,MICHAEL	BAL	100	1ST WARD
WHALER, ABRAHAM	CAR	362	9TH DIST
WHALER, CATHARINE	BAL	443	14TH WAR
WHALER, MARIA	BAL	112	1ST WARD
WHALER, THOMAS	ALL	072	5TH E.D.
WHALES, SUSAN	DOR	396	1ST DIST
WHALEY, CATHARINE	WOR	287	BERLIN 1
WHALEY, ELIZA	WOR	256	1ST CENS
WHALEY, GEORGE W.	FRE	234	BUCKEYST
WHALEY, PETER	WOR	287	BERLIN 1
WHALEY, RACHEL	BAL	351	13TH WAR
WHALEY, SETH M.	WOR	266	BERLIN 1
WHALEY, THOMAS	KEN	313	3RD DIST
WHALEY, WILLIAM	TAL	009	EASTON D
WHALEY, ZADOCK	BAL	326	3RD WARD
WHALING, STEPHEN	BAL	364	1ST DIST
WHALING, STEPHEN	CAR	220	5TH DIST
WHALING, WILLIAM	CAR	220	5TH DIST
WHALL, JACOB	BAL	261	2ND WARD
WHALL, PHILLIPINA	BAL	259	2ND WARD
WHALLER, HANNAH	BAL	002	9TH WARD
WHALLEY, CATHERINE	QUE	137	1ST E DI
WHALON, JOE	ANN	467	HOWARD D
WHALON, MARGARET	BAL	114	15TH WAR
WHALON, PATRICK	ANN	475	HOWARD D
WHALTS, JAMES J.	BAL	273	7TH WARD
WHALY, ISAAC	CEC	037	CHESAPEA
WHAN, LOUISEA	BAL	277	2ND WARD
WHAN, WILLIAM	CAR	304	1ST DIST
WHANN, ADAM	CEC	085	5TH E DI
WHANN, SAMUEL	HAR	006	1ST DIST
WHANNA, MICHAEL	BAL	202	2ND WARD
WHAPPING, DEBORAH	CAR	398	2ND DIST
WHARETT, SARAH	CAR	131	NO TWP L
WHARTON, ANTHONY	CEC	078	NORTHEAS
WHARTON, BENJAMIN	WOR	257	1ST CENS
WHARTON, BENJAMIN	TAL	051	EASTON D
WHARTON, DOLLY	WAS	154	HAGERSTO
WHARTON, ELIZABETH	WAS	141	HAGERSTO
WHARTON, JESSE B.	MGM	319	CRACKLIN
WHARTON, JOHN	WOR	255	1ST CENS
WHARTON, JOHN O.	WAS	140	HAGERSTO
WHARTON, PARKER	WOR	266	BERLIN 1
WHARTON, REBECCA	WAS	237	CAVETOWN
WHARTON, WILLIAM	BAL	290	7TH WARD
WHARTON, WILLIAM H. C.	BAL	054	15TH WAR
WHARY, CAROLINE	ANN	465	HOWARD D
WHASKEY, BENJAMIN	BAL	032	4TH WARD
WHAT, MARIA R.	FRE	084	FREDERIC
WHAT, MICHAEL	FRE	091	FREDERIC
WHATKINS, CATHARINE	BAL	260	1ST DIST
WHATKINS, LOUISA	BAL	390	1ST DIST
WHATS, THOAMS	WAS	113	2ND DIST
WHATSOM, ISAAC	WAS	134	2ND DIST
WHATSON, JOHN N.	WAS	162	2ND DIST
WHATTS, JAMES J. *	BAL	273	7TH WARD
WHEADEN, CHARLE	BAL	072	1ST WARD
WHEALAN, EMILY J.	BAL	349	7TH WARD
WHEALAN, LAGLEN	BAL	348	7TH WARD
WHEALAN, MARY	BAL	349	7TH WARD
WHEALAN, WILLIAM	BAL	394	8TH WARD
WHEALER, BENNIT	HAR	012	1ST DIST
WHEAT, ALEXANDER	KEN	273	1ST DIST
WHEAT, EDWARD	BAL	137	18TH WAR
WHEAT, ELIZA	KEN	218	2ND DIST
WHEAT, JOHN B.	BAL	182	6TH WARD
WHEAT, JOHN M.	BAL	304	1ST DIST
WHEAT, JONATHAN	ANN	389	4TH DIST
WHEAT, MARY C.	WAS	140	HAGERSTO
WHEAT, NATHANIEL	BAL	095	18TH WAR
WHEAT, NOAH	ANN	322	2ND DIST
WHEAT, SAMUEL	KEN	235	2ND DIST
WHEAT, THOMAS	KEN	236	2ND DIST
WHEAT, WILLIAM	BAL	323	12TH WAR
WHEATE, JESSE	BAL	304	1ST DIST
WHEATER, HENRY	BAL	124	1ST WARD
WHEATIN, FRANCIS	FRE	317	MIDDLETO
WHEATLEY, ADELINE	BAL	252	17TH WAR
WHEATLEY, ADELINE	BAL	016	15TH WAR
WHEATLEY, ANN E.	ST	309	1ST E DI
WHEATLEY, ARTHUR B.	KEN	269	1ST DIST
WHEATLEY, AUGUSTUR*	DOR	304	1ST DIST
WHEATLEY, BENNETT	TAL	042	EASTON D
WHEATLEY, DANIEL	BAL	342	7TH WARD
WHEATLEY, EDWARD	DOR	304	1ST DIST
WHEATLEY, EDWARD	DOR	304	1ST DIST
WHEATLEY, EDWARD	DOR	366	3RD DIVI
WHEATLEY, ELIZA J.	BAL	270	17TH WAR
WHEATLEY, ELIZABETH	DOR	303	1ST DIST
WHEATLEY, ELIZABETH	DOR	305	1ST DIST
WHEATLEY, ELIZABETH	BAL	076	1ST WARD
WHEATLEY, ELIZABETH	SOM	362	BRINKLEY
WHEATLEY, EZEKIEL	DOR	304	1ST DIST
WHEATLEY, EZEKIEL	DOR	304	1ST DIST
WHEATLEY, GEORGE	DOR	304	1ST DIST
WHEATLEY, ISAAC	BAL	243	6TH WARD
WHEATLEY, JAMES	DOR	305	1ST DIST
WHEATLEY, JAMES	QUE	203	3RD E DI
WHEATLEY, JAMES E.	BAL	315	3RD WARD
WHEATLEY, JAMES R.	DOR	303	1ST DIST
WHEATLEY, JAMES T.	DOR	304	1ST DIST
WHEATLEY, JANE	ST	311	1ST E DI
WHEATLEY, JESSEE	DOR	304	1ST DIST
WHEATLEY, JOHN	DOR	338	3RD DIVI
WHEATLEY, JOHN	ST	305	1ST E DI
WHEATLEY, KITTY	DOR	303	1ST DIST
WHEATLEY, LEVIN	BAL	315	3RD WARD
WHEATLEY, MAGER	DOR	304	1ST DIST
WHEATLEY, MARTHA A.	ST	305	1ST E DI
WHEATLEY, MARY	BAL	055	1ST WARD
WHEATLEY, MARY A.	BAL	096	10TH WAR
WHEATLEY, MATTHEW	ST	311	1ST E DI
WHEATLEY, NERINE	BAL	143	5TH WARD
WHEATLEY, SARAH	DOR	323	1ST DIST
WHEATLEY, SILAS	DOR	304	1ST DIST
WHEATLEY, WILLIAM	ANN	428	HOWARD D
WHEATLEY, WILLIAM C.	ST	308	1ST E DI
WHEATLEY, WILLIAM H.	QUE	136	1ST E DI
WHEATLY, ALFRED	DOR	300	1ST DIST
WHEATLY, BETTY	CHA	253	MIDDLETO
WHEATLY, DEMYA	BAL	038	1ST WARD
WHEATLY, ELIHU	DOR	453	1ST DIST
WHEATLY, HENRY	SOM	480	TRAPP DI
WHEATLY, ISAAC	DOR	424	1ST DIST
WHEATLY, JAMES	DOR	405	1ST DIST
WHEATLY, JAMES	DOR	390	1ST DIST
WHEATLY, JAMES F.	CHA	253	MIDDLETO
WHEATLY, JOHN H.	CAL	012	1ST DIST
WHEATLY, JOSEPH	DOR	462	1ST DIST
WHEATLY, LEVIN	DOR	426	1ST DIST
WHEATLY, PETER	SOM	405	DUBLIN D
WHEATLY, RACHAEL	CHA	274	ALLENS F
WHEATLY, RALF	DOR	405	1ST DIST
WHEATLY, RICHARD	DOR	460	1ST DIST
WHEATLY, SALLY	BAL	197	11TH WAR
WHEATLY, SPENCER	DOR	301	1ST DIST
WHEATLY, WILLIAM	DOR	299	1ST DIST
WHEATLY, WILLIAM	DOR	400	1ST DIST

WHEATLY, WILLIAM ALLENS F
WHEATON, MARY A. PORT DUP
WHEATON, SAMUEL C. 1 PORT DUP
WHEATS, ANDREW 2 HOWARD D
WHEATSTONE, CHARLOT 08 3RD E.D.
WHEATSTONE, JOSEPH 08 3RD E.D.
WHEATY, JOSEPH 427 PRINCESS
WHEBBITTE, ELIZAB 017 18TH WAR
WHEDLETON, ELIZA 125 NO TWP L
WHEDLETON, THOM 127 NO TWP L
WHEDLETON, WILL R 159 NO TWP L
WHEEDEN, HARRI AL 265 7TH WARD
WHEEDEN, MARY AL 011 1ST WARD
WHEEDON, HORAT BAL 262 12TH WAR
WHEEDON, MADIS BAL 382 3RD WARD
WHEELAN, BRID WAS 013 WILLIAMS
WHEELAN, DAN BAL 003 9TH WARD
WHEELAN, MA BAL 177 2ND DIST
WHEELAND, WOR 229 6TH E DI
WHEELEN, T BAL 116 11TH WAR
WHEELEN, DOR 394 1ST DIST
WHEELER, BAL 168 1ST WARD
WHEELER BAL 105 15TH WAR
WHEELER BAL 091 18TH WAR
WHEELER MGM 352 BERRYS D
WHEELE BAL 258 6TH WARD
WHEELE BAL 427 1ST DIST
WHEELE BAL 266 2ND WARD
WHEELE BAL 458 14TH WAR
WHEELE Y A. KEN 218 2ND DIST
WHEELE BAL 160 6TH WARD
WHEELE AIN BAL 062 2ND DIST
WHEEL AMIN BAL 055 2ND DIST
WHEEL NETT BAL 161 6TH WARD
WHEEL IDGET WOR 299 SNOW HIL
WHEE RISON BAL 194 5TH DIST
WHE BRISTER BAL 046 2ND DIST
WHE BRYAN M. BAL 199 5TH DIST
WHE CAROLINE ST 332 4TH E DI
WHE ER, CATHARINE ANN 413 HOWARD D
WHE ER, CATHERINE FRE 065 FREDERIC
WH LER, CHARLES BAL 204 6TH WARD
WH ELER, CHARLES BAL 203 6TH WARD
WHEELER, CHARLES BAL 417 1ST DIST
WHEELER, CHARLES H. ALL 208 CUMBERLA
WHEELER, CHARLES H. CHA 219 ALLENS F
WHEELER, CHRISTIANA ANN 437 HOWARD D
WHEELER, CLARE CHA 266 MIDDLETO
WHEELER, CYRUS CHA 238 HILLTOP
WHEELER, DARIUS BAL 173 16TH WAR
WHEELER, DAVID ALL 055 10TH E.D
WHEELER, DAVID BAL 246 17TH WAR
WHEELER, DEDRICK ANN 413 HOWARD D
WHEELER, DENTON ANN 379 4TH DIST
WHEELER, EBEN DOR 394 1ST DIST
WHEELER, EDUARD R. CAL 051 3RD DIST
WHEELER, EDWARD DOR 386 1ST DIST
WHEELER, EDWIN TAL 050 EASTON T
WHEELER, ELISHA BAL 195 5TH DIST
WHEELER, ELIZA BAL 176 11TH WAR
WHEELER, ELIZA DOR 401 1ST DIST
WHEELER, ELIZABETH CAR 208 5TH DIST
WHEELER, ELIZABETH BAL 011 9TH WARD
WHEELER, ELIZABETH BAL 027 15TH WAR
WHEELER, ELIZABETH BAL 176 2ND DIST
WHEELER, ELIZABETH BAL 065 2ND DIST
WHEELER, ELLEN SOM 387 BRINKLEY
WHEELER, EUGENE BAL 203 19TH WAR
WHEELER, FRANCES CAL 016 1ST DIST
WHEELER, FRANCES BAL 153 16TH WAR
WHEELER, FRANK CHA 259 MIDDLETO
WHEELER, GEORGE BAL 249 17TH WAR
WHEELER, GEORGE BAL 249 17TH WAR
WHEELER, GEORGE SOM 437 PRINCESS
WHEELER, GEORGE ANN 440 HOWARD D
WHEELER, GEORGE BAL 441 1ST DIST
WHEELER, GEORGE ST 287 2ND E DI
WHEELER, GEORGE H. BAL 428 1ST DIST
WHEELER, GRAFTON ANN 390 4TH DIST
WHEELER, GUSTAVUS ANN 431 HOWARD D
WHEELER, HARKLES BAL 133 16TH WAR
WHEELER, HENRY BAL 288 7TH WARD
WHEELER, HENRY BAL 224 17TH WAR
WHEELER, HENRY P. BAL 353 7TH WARD
WHEELER, HESTER A. BAL 182 2ND WARD
WHEELER, HESTER A. BAL 280 17TH WAR
WHEELER, ISAAC BAL 340 7TH WARD
WHEELER, ISAAC BAL 186 5TH DIST
WHEELER, ISAAC BAL 108 1ST WARD
WHEELER, J. BAL 295 12TH WAR
WHEELER, JAMES BAL 164 2ND DIST
WHEELER, JAMES BAL 176 11TH WAR
WHEELER, JAMES BAL 181 11TH WAR
WHEELER, JAMES BAL 070 2ND DIST
WHEELER, JAMES BAL 053 2ND DIST
WHEELER, JAMES BAL 004 18TH WAR
WHEELER, JAMES BAL 216 17TH WAR
WHEELER, JAMES BAL 262 17TH WAR
WHEELER, JAMES DOR 403 1ST DIST
WHEELER, JAMES ST 287 2ND E DI
WHEELER, JAMES H. KEN 312 3RD DIST
WHEELER, JAMES R. BAL 009 18TH WAR
WHEELER, JANE CHA 219 ALLENS F
WHEELER, JANE MRS- BAL 315 20TH WAR
WHEELER, JOHN BAL 288 17TH WAR
WHEELER, JOHN WAS 220 1ST DIST
WHEELER, JOHN BAL 192 5TH DIST
WHEELER, JOHN BAL 097 15TH WAR
WHEELER, JOHN ALL 127 4TH E.D.
WHEELER, JOHN D. BAL 154 16TH WAR
WHEELER, JOHN M. ST 278 3RD E DI
WHEELER, JOHN T. BAL 238 17TH WAR
WHEELER, JOHN W. BAL 385 3RD WARD
WHEELER, JOHNR. BAL 019 2ND DIST
WHEELER, JOSEPH BAL 204 6TH WARD
WHEELER, JOSEPH BAL 177 6TH WARD
WHEELER, JOSEPH FRE 044 FREDERIC
WHEELER, JOSEPH CAR 208 5TH DIST
WHEELER, JOSEPH WAS 206 1ST DIST
WHEELER, JOSEPH A. HAR 104 2ND DIST
WHEELER, JOSEPH O. HAR 109 2ND DIST
WHEELER, JOSHUA BAL 200 5TH DIST
WHEELER, JOSHUA BAL 304 1ST DIST
WHEELER, JOSIAH BAL 194 5TH DIST
WHEELER, JOSIAH B. BAL 186 5TH DIST
WHEELER, LEAH J. SOM 352 BRINKLEY
WHEELER, LENSEANE* SOM 484 TRAPP DI
WHEELER, LEVIN ANN 349 3RD DIST
WHEELER, LORA ST 275 3RD E DI
WHEELER, LOUISA ST 256 3RD E DI

WHEELER, LOVICEY HAR 109 2ND DIST
WHEELER, M. A. ANN 339 3RD DIST
WHEELER, MAJOR BAL 046 9TH WARD
WHEELER, MARGARET BAL 188 5TH DIST
WHEELER, MARGARET CHA 246 HILLTOP
WHEELER, MARGARET DOR 400 1ST DIST
WHEELER, MARIAH L. CAR 230 5TH DIST
WHEELER, MARRY BAL 189 5TH DIST
WHEELER, MARY BAL 018 1ST WARD
WHEELER, MARY BAL 176 6TH WARD
WHEELER, MARY BAL 174 6TH WARD
WHEELER, MARY BAL 020 9TH WARD
WHEELER, MARY ANN 429 HOWARD D
WHEELER, MARY BAL 184 11TH WAR
WHEELER, MARY BAL 298 17TH WAR
WHEELER, MARY BAL 139 11TH WAR
WHEELER, MARY PRI 020 VANSVILL
WHEELER, MARY A. SOM 422 PRINCESS
WHEELER, MARY A. BAL 018 2ND DIST
WHEELER, MARY ANN BAL 187 5TH DIST
WHEELER, MARY E. BAL 053 9TH WARD
WHEELER, MARY J. BAL 476 14TH WAR
WHEELER, MATTHEW DOR 398 1ST DIST
WHEELER, MILLY BAL 121 16TH WAR
WHEELER, MINERVA BAL 061 15TH WAR
WHEELER, MRS. BAL 142 11TH WAR
WHEELER, NANCY BAL 082 15TH WAR
WHEELER, NANCY BAL 220 1ST DIST
WHEELER, NECKEL-BLACK WOR 338 1ST E DI
WHEELER, OLIVIA BAL 050 4TH WARD
WHEELER, ORIS BAL 139 1ST WARD
WHEELER, PATIENCE BAL 063 2ND DIST
WHEELER, PETER DOR 405 1ST DIST
WHEELER, PETER CHA 238 HILLTOP
WHEELER, POLLY SOM 485 TRAPP DI
WHEELER, PRICILLA BAL 245 17TH WAR
WHEELER, RACHAEL BAL 200 5TH DIST
WHEELER, RACHEL BAL 133 2ND DIST
WHEELER, REBECCA BAL 027 18TH WAR
WHEELER, RICHARD BAL 134 18TH WAR
WHEELER, RICHARD ANN 447 HOWARD D
WHEELER, RICHARD B. PRI 040 VANSVILL
WHEELER, RICHARD D. BAL 423 1ST DIST
WHEELER, RICHARD-BLACK BAL 224 2ND WARD
WHEELER, SAMUEL BAL 368 3RD WARD
WHEELER, SAMUEL BAL 334 13TH WAR
WHEELER, SAMUEL E. BAL 219 6TH WARD
WHEELER, SAMUEL J. BAL 209 17TH WAR
WHEELER, SARAH BAL 036 18TH WAR
WHEELER, SARAH BAL 216 11TH WAR
WHEELER, SARAH BAL 196 6TH WARD
WHEELER, SARAH ANN 379 4TH DIST
WHEELER, SARAH BAL 299 12TH WAR
WHEELER, SARAH E. ANN 449 HOWARD D
WHEELER, SISON BAL 125 1ST WARD
WHEELER, SLICER BAL 388 8TH WARD
WHEELER, THOMAS BAL 293 7TH WARD
WHEELER, THOMAS ANN 383 4TH DIST
WHEELER, THOMAS BAL 294 12TH WAR
WHEELER, THOMAS BAL 197 5TH DIST
WHEELER, THOMAS BAL 269 17TH WAR
WHEELER, THOMAS BAL 043 4TH WARD
WHEELER, THOMAS DOR 399 1ST DIST
WHEELER, THOMAS CAL 008 1ST DIST
WHEELER, THOMAS SOM 365 BRINKLEY
WHEELER, THOMAS H. BAL 264 17TH WAR
WHEELER, THOMPSON CHA 241 HILLTOP
WHEELER, W.L. ANN 265 ANNAPOLI
WHEELER, WILIAM J. WOR 329 1ST E DI
WHEELER, WILLIAM BAL 299 1ST DIST
WHEELER, WILLIAM BAL 167 16TH WAR
WHEELER, WILLIAM ANN 377 4TH DIST
WHEELER, WILLIAM ANN 437 HOWARD D
WHEELER, WILLIAM BAL 130 2ND DIST
WHEELER, WILLIAM BAL 019 2ND DIST
WHEELER, WILLIAM BAL 410 1ST DIST
WHEELER, WILLIAM BAL 349 1ST DIST
WHEELER, WILLIAM FRE 311 MIDDLETO
WHEELER, WILLIAM BAL 101 18TH WAR
WHEELER, WILLIAM CAR 333 MANCHEST
WHEELER, WILLIAM B. TAL 068 EASTON T
WHEELER, WILLIAM H. BAL 019 2ND DIST
WHEELER, ZIBEDEE DOR 401 1ST DIST
WHEELER.CATHARINE BAL 205 2ND WARD
WHEELER.EMILY BAL 018 1ST WARD
WHEELLER, RACHEL BAL 377 3RD WARD
WHEELLRIG, CATHERINE BAL 436 8TH WARD
WHEELOR, AARON CAR 208 5TH DIST
WHEELOR, EDWARD CAR 193 4TH DIST
WHEELOR, ELIZABETH CAR 171 8TH DIST
WHEELTON, JAMES R. WOR 324 1ST E DI
WHEELTON, JOHN SOM 380 BRINKLEY
WHEELTON, THOMAS WOR 330 1ST E DI
WHEELTON, WILLIAM WOR 333 1ST E DI
WHEELTON, WILLIAM SOM 379 BRINKLEY
WHEELTON, WILLIAM P. WOR 335 1ST E DI
WHEELWRIGHT, JEREMIAH BAL 118 15TH WAR
WHEET, BERNARD BAL 267 2ND WARD
WHEET, HANNAH BAL 265 2ND WARD
WHEETHELS, NANCY * TAL 113 ST MICHA
WHEHELIM, WI. BAL 075 18TH WAR
WHEIL, ABRAHAM BAL 113 1ST WARD
WHEIL, JAMES BAL 113 1ST WARD
WHEINER, JACOB WAS 151 HAGERSTO
WHEIP, JOSEPH BAL 211 19TH WAR
WHEISEL, GEORGE BAL 212 2ND WARD
WHEISTLER, BENEDICT BAL 063 1ST WARD
WHEISTLER, EMERICH BAL 042 9TH WARD
WHEIT, LEWIS BAL 265 2ND WARD
WHELAN, AGNES BAL 255 12TH WAR
WHELAN, CATHARINE BAL 213 11TH WAR
WHELAN, DANIEL FRE 20 5TH E DI
WHELAN, ELLEN BAL 314 20TH WAR
WHELAN, GEORGE BAL 266 12TH WAR
WHELAN, J. BAL 157 1ST WARD
WHELAN, JAMES BAL 026 2ND DIST
WHELAN, JOHN ANN 500 HOWARD D
WHELAN, MARIE BAL 247 12TH WAR
WHELAN, MARY BAL 375 3RD WARD
WHELAN, MARY BAL 012 4TH WARD
WHELAN, MARY BAL 156 19TH WAR
WHELAN, PATRICK BAL 203 6TH WARD
WHELAN, PATRICK BAL 277 2ND WARD
WHELAN, SARAH BAL 250 6TH WARD
WHELAN, T. BAL 116 1ST WARD
WHELAN, THOMAS BAL 389 13TH WAR
WHELAN, WILLIAM BAL 265 20TH WAR
WHELAND, HENRY ANN 413 HOWARD D
WHELAR, JOSEPH BAL 156 19TH WAR
WHELARD, MARGARET BAL 315 12TH WAR

WHELBY, RACHIEL CAR 154 NO TWP L
WHELEN, SIMON R. BAL 125 1ST WARD
WHELER, ANN CAR 165 NO TWP L
WHELER, CATE CHA 225 ALLENS F
WHELFR, DOLLY CAR 092 NO TWP L
WHELER, JAMES-BLACK CAR 113 NO TWP L
WHELER, LEVIN CAR 153 NO TWP L
WHELER, MARY E. CAR 168 NO TWP L
WHELER, WILLIAM CAR 164 NO TWP L
WHELER, EMELINE CAR 147 NO TWP L
WHELIEM, SAMUEL BAL 076 18TH WAR
WHELL, JACOB BAL 181 2ND WARD
WHELR, SARAH CAR 143 NO TWP L
WHELTON, MIKEL R. WOR 326 1ST E DI
WHELTY, THOMAS CEC 015 ELKTON 3
WHENETT, THOMAS BAL 153 19TH WAR
WHERE, JOHN BAL 185 2ND WARD
WHERETT, EMILY BAL 153 19TH WAR
WHEREY, CATHA * FRE 267 NEW MARK
WHERL, HENRY WAS 054 2ND SUBD
WHERL, JESSE WAS 054 2ND SUBD
WHERRET, ANN M.* TAL 047 EASTON T
WHERRET, WILLIAM DOR 373 1ST DIST
WHERRETT, RICHARD CAR 133 NO TWP L
WHERRIT, JOHN C. ST 292 2ND E DI
WHERRITT, GEORGE BAL 139 16TH WAR
WHERRY, DAVID CEC 112 4TH E DI
WHERRY, JOHN CEC 140 5TH E DI
WHERTON, BENJAMIN ALL 138 6TH E.D.
WHESLOR, GEORGE WOR 305 SNOW HIL
WHESNER, JOSEPH BAL 270 2ND WARD
WHESTONE, JACOB WAS 123 2ND DIST
WHETSEL, ABRAHAM ALL 058 10TH E.D
WHETSEL, CONRAD ALL 058 10TH E.D
WHETSEL, GEORGE WAS 153 2ND DIST
WHETSONE, ALFRED ALL 020 2ND E.D.
WHETSTON, DANIEL WAS 141 2ND DIST
WHETSTON, HENRY WAS 142 2ND DIST
WHETSTONE, JOHN WAS 141 2ND DIST
WHETSTONE, SAMUEL ALL 020 2ND E.D.
WHETTER, IGNATILS FRE 311 MIDDLETO
WHETTIER, JOHN H. FRE 202 5TH E DI
WHETTON, CORNEALOUS CAR 215 5TH DIST
WHEVRING, MATTHEW BAL 172 19TH WAR
WHEWLETT, JOHN Q. * BAL 316 1ST DIST
WHICKLEY, CHARLES F. BAL 002 18TH WAR
WHICKLEY, WILLIAM BAL 020 18TH WAR
WHIONEY, ELIZA C. BAL 395 8TH WARD
WHIG, ANN M. BAL 250 17TH WAR
WHIGBY, ANANNA* TAL 029 EASTON D
WHIGBY, JOHN TAL 005 EASTON D
WHIGBY, SAMUEL TAL 016 EASTON D
WHIGBY, SAMUEL TAL 029 EASTON D
WHIGBY, THOMAS* TAL 004 EASTON D
WHIGHT, EVE BAL 252 2ND WARD
WHILBY, MARY A. CAR 153 NO TWP L
WHILBY, NATHAN CAR 072 NO TWP L
WHILDE, FRANCIS BAL 121 18TH WAR
WHILE, MARY A. DOR 297 1ST DIST
WHILES, WILLIAM BAL 057 18TH WAR
WHILFIELD, MATHEW BAL 015 4TH WARD
WHILHELM, LYDA BAL 150 11TH WAR
WHILL, COLUMBUS BAL 074 1ST WARD
WHILLEY, JAMES M. CAR 106 NO TWP L
WHILLHIDE, DAVID FRE 126 CREAGERS
WHILOCK, JAMES CEC 051 1ST E DI
WHILTON, CHARLES BAL 472 14TH WAR
WHILTON, THOMAS PRI 109 PISCATAW
WHIMS, ASHBURY HAR 175 3RD DIST
WHIMS, JOHN-BLACK FRE 017 FREDERIC
WHIMTLE, ANN CEC 020 ELKTON 3
WHINEBRUNNER, CHRISTIAN FRE 310 WOODSBOR
WHINIS, MARY A. BAL 094 5TH WARD
WHIP, FANNY WAS 178 BOONSBOR
WHIP, GEORGE T. FRE 327 MIDDLETO
WHIP, JOHN FRE 210 BUCKEYST
WHIP, MARY FRE 399 JEFFERSO
WHIP, PETE FRE 392 PETERSVI
WHIP, RUTH FRE 386 PETERSVI
WHIP, SAMUEL T. FRE 210 BUCKEYST
WHIP, SUSAN FRE 338 MIDDLETO
WHIP, THEOPHILUS FRE 336 MIDDLETO
WHIPER, BENJIMON HAR 201 3RD DIST
WHIPLEY, MARY BAL 238 6TH WARD
WHIPLEY, J. BAL 138 1ST WARD
WHIPP, ARCHABLAD FRE 079 FREDERIC
WHIPP, LOYD FRE 075 FREDERIC
WHIPPAMAN, JOHN BAL 157 2ND DIST
WHIPPER, CATHARINE BAL 353 1ST DIST
WHIPPLE, ELIZA BAL 041 1ST WARD
WHIPPLE, ISAAC BAL 167 6TH WARD
WHIPPS, GEORGE BAL 026 18TH WAR
WHIPS, WILLIAM ANN 444 HOWARD D
WHIRL, SAMUEL ALL 184 9TH E.D.
WHIRL, WILLIAM FRE 324 MIDDLETO
WHISLINE, MARY BAL 061 18TH WAR
WHISLOCK, BARBET BAL 317 12TH WAR
WHISNER, HENRY WAS 123 HAGERSTO
WHISON, JAMES M. BAL 353 7TH WARD
WHISPER, JOHN BAL 379 1ST DIST
WHISTLER, CHARLES BAL 250 2ND WARD
WHISTLER, DAVID BAL 185 6TH WARD
WHISTLER, KITTY BAL 114 2ND DIST
WHISTLER, SAMUEL HAR 098 2ND DIST
WHISTLER, WILLIAM S. BAL 177 6TH WARD
WHITACRE, DORSEY H. BAL 454 1ST DIST
WHITACRE, JOHN CAR 081 NO TWP L
WHITAKER, CATHARINE BAL 401 14TH WAR
WHITAKER, DANIEL CEC 183 7TH E DI
WHITAKER, ELIZA BAL 114 15TH WAR
WHITAKER, FRANKLIN HAR 095 2ND DIST
WHITAKER, GEORGE P. CEC 143 7TH E DI
WHITAKER, HOWARD HAR 090 2ND DIST
WHITAKER, ISAAC HAR 091 2ND DIST
WHITAKER, ISAAC HAR 105 2ND DIST
WHITAKER, JOSEPH CEC 062 1ST E DI
WHITAKER, JOSHUA HAR 052 1ST DIST
WHITAKER, MATILDA BAL 296 12TH WAR
WHITAKER, SAMUEL BAL 159 1ST WARD
WHITAKER, SAMUEL HAR 051 1ST DIST
WHITAKER, SUSAN BAL 076 10TH WAR
WHITAKER, THOAMS KEN 230 2ND DIST
WHITBY, DANIEL CAR 154 NO TWP L
WHITBY, EDWARD CAR 142 NO TWP L
WHITBY, J. BAL 063 10TH WAR
WHITBY, JOHN CAR 073 NO TWP L
WHITCAME, JOHN BAL 246 1ST DIST
WHITCOMB, EZEKIAL CEC 133 6TH E DI
WHITCOMB, MR. BAL 033 15TH WAR
WHITCOMB, WESLEY BAL 078 15TH WAR

Name	County	No.	District
WHITCOME, RICHARD	BAL	456	1ST DIST
WHITE, A.	BAL	140	1ST WARD
WHITE, ABBRIN	BAL	121	1ST WARD
WHITE, ABRAHAM-MULATTO	FRE	444	8TH E DI
WHITE, ABRAM	WAS	169	FUNKSTOW
WHITE, ABSALOM K.	CEC	136	6TH E DI
WHITE, ACHSAH G.	ANN	445	HOWARD D
WHITE, ADDISON	FRE	232	BUCKEYST
WHITE, AFFEY	BAL	331	3RD WARD
WHITE, ALEXANDER	BAL	098	5TH WARD
WHITE, ALEXANDER	BAL	152	1ST WARD
WHITE, ALEXANDER	BAL	165	19TH WAR
WHITE, ALEXANDER	QUE	253	5TH E DI
WHITE, ALEXANDER	SOM	546	TYASKIN
WHITE, ALEXANDER J.	SOM	443	DAMES QU
WHITE, ALICE	BAL	202	11TH WAR
WHITE, AMBROSE A.	BAL	274	12TH WAR
WHITE, AMBROSE M.	MGM	426	MEDLEY 3
WHITE, AMELIA	BAL	097	2ND DIST
WHITE, AMORY	WOR	263	BERLIN 1
WHITE, ANDREW	BAL	177	16TH WAR
WHITE, ANDREW	HAR	193	3RD DIST
WHITE, ANDREW	BAL	120	18TH WAR
WHITE, ANDREW	BAL	469	14TH WAR
WHITE, ANN	MGM	379	ROCKERLE
WHITE, ANN	MGM	327	CRACKLIN
WHITE, ANN	BAL	009	18TH WAR
WHITE, ANN	BAL	296	12TH WAR
WHITE, ANN	BAL	102	2ND DIST
WHITE, ANN	BAL	192	11TH WAR
WHITE, ANN	BAL	236	12TH WAR
WHITE, ANN	BAL	050	1ST WARD
WHITE, ANN	ALL	064	10TH E.D
WHITE, ANN	PRI	109	PISCATAW
WHITE, ANN L.	BAL	068	10TH WAR
WHITE, ANN L.	BAL	212	11TH WAR
WHITE, ANN S.	BAL	226	2ND WARD
WHITE, ANNE	BAL	007	15TH WAR
WHITE, ANNE	TAL	003	EASTON D
WHITE, AQUILER	HAR	197	3RD DIST
WHITE, ARTHUR	QUE	234	4TH E DI
WHITE, ARTHUR	BAL	091	15TH WAR
WHITE, ASA	SOM	540	TYASKIN
WHITE, AUGUSTUS R.	WOR	230	6TH E DI
WHITE, AUGUSTUSA	BAL	317	12TH WAR
WHITE, BARRARD*	DOR	456	1ST DIST
WHITE, BELZY	CAL	006	1ST DIST
WHITE, BEN	WOR	273	BERLIN 1
WHITE, BENAJAMIN S.	MGM	410	MEDLEY 3
WHITE, BENJAMIN	WOR	231	6TH E DI
WHITE, BENJAMIN R.	MGM	415	MEDLEY 3
WHITE, BENJAMIN S.	MGM	416	MEDLEY 3
WHITE, BEUCHAM	SOM	475	TRAPPE D
WHITE, BUDDY	CEC	180	7TH E DI
WHITE, CAROLINE	QUE	210	3RD E DI
WHITE, CAROLINE	BAL	204	2ND WARD
WHITE, CATHARINE	BAL	201	6TH WARD
WHITE, CATHARINE	BAL	285	12TH WAR
WHITE, CATHARINE	ANN	453	HOWARD D
WHITE, CATHARINE	SOM	442	DAMES QU
WHITE, CATHARINE	SOM	447	DAMES QU
WHITE, CATHARINE	FRE	311	MIDDLETO
WHITE, CATHARINE L.	BAL	182	6TH WARD
WHITE, CATHERINE	BAL	250	12TH WAR
WHITE, CATHERINE	BAL	320	20TH WAR
WHITE, CATHERINE	QUE	210	3RD E DI
WHITE, CAWLIN	CAR	090	NO TWP L
WHITE, CECELIA	BAL	235	20TH WAR
WHITE, CERINDA	SOM	531	QUANTICO
WHITE, CHARELS H.	BAL	363	13TH WAR
WHITE, CHARITY	BAL	241	1ST DIST
WHITE, CHARLES	BAL	156	2ND DIST
WHITE, CHARLES	BAL	156	1ST WARD
WHITE, CHARLES	BAL	333	7TH WARD
WHITE, CHARLES	BAL	375	1ST DIST
WHITE, CHARLES	ANN	495	HOWARD D
WHITE, CHARLES	HAR	040	1ST DIST
WHITE, CHARLES B.	BAL	080	15TH WAR
WHITE, CHARLES H.	BAL	134	16TH WAR
WHITE, CHARLES W.	ALL	213	CUMBERLA
WHITE, CHARLES-MULATTO	FRE	434	8TH E DI
WHITE, CHARLOTT	WOR	313	2ND E DI
WHITE, CHARLOTTE	BAL	162	2ND DIST
WHITE, CHERRY L.	BAL	062	4TH WARD
WHITE, CHRISTOPHER	CEC	033	CHESAPEA
WHITE, CHRISTOPHER	CEC	032	CHESAPEA
WHITE, CLARA-BLACK	BAL	223	2ND WARD
WHITE, CLEMMENT	DOR	296	1ST DIST
WHITE, CLINTON B.	CEC	185	7TH E DI
WHITE, CORNELIA	BAL	073	15TH WAR
WHITE, CYLUS	SOM	432	PRINCESS
WHITE, CYNTHIA	WAS	167	1ST DIST
WHITE, DANIEL	WAS	253	1ST DIST
WHITE, DANIEL	CEC	071	5TH E DI
WHITE, DANIEL	BAL	025	1ST WARD
WHITE, DANIEL	BAL	294	3RD WARD
WHITE, DANIEL C.	CEC	133	6TH E DI
WHITE, DANILE	BAL	399	14TH WAR
WHITE, DAVID	CEC	145	PORT DUP
WHITE, DAVID	BAL	244	20TH WAR
WHITE, DAVID	ALL	105	5TH E.D.
WHITE, DAVID	KEN	295	3RD DIST
WHITE, DAVID G.	SOM	490	SALISBUR
WHITE, DAVID H.	BAL	165	19TH WAR
WHITE, DEBORA	BAL	138	5TH WARD
WHITE, DENARD	WOR	229	6TH E DI
WHITE, EDWARD	CEC	133	6TH E DI
WHITE, EDWARD	CEC	180	7TH E DI
WHITE, EDWARD	SOM	417	PRINCESS
WHITE, EDWARD	BAL	215	11TH WAR
WHITE, EDWARD DR.	BAL	340	13TH WAR
WHITE, ELEANOR	BAL	361	3RD WARD
WHITE, ELEANORA	BAL	337	3RD WARD
WHITE, ELENOR	ANN	268	ANNAPOLI
WHITE, ELENORA	BAL	062	4TH WARD
WHITE, ELIJAH	WOR	194	8TH E DI
WHITE, ELISHA	SOM	357	BRINKLEY
WHITE, ELISHA	CEC	126	5TH E DI
WHITE, ELIZA	CAL	034	2ND DIST
WHITE, ELIZA	BAL	283	17TH WAR
WHITE, ELIZA	BAL	033	1ST WARD
WHITE, ELIZA	BAL	215	6TH WARD
WHITE, ELIZA	ANN	363	4TH DIST
WHITE, ELIZA	BAL	011	2ND DIST
WHITE, ELIZA	BAL	400	3RD WARD
WHITE, ELIZA C.	ALL	205	CUMBERLA
WHITE, ELIZABETH	BAL	302	1ST DIST
WHITE, ELIZABETH	BAL	067	15TH WAR
WHITE, ELIZABETH	BAL	289	12TH WAR
WHITE, ELIZABETH	BAL	274	12TH WAR
WHITE, ELIZABETH	CAR	084	NO TWP L
WHITE, ELIZABETH	BAL	052	4TH WARD
WHITE, ELIZABETH	BAL	266	17TH WAR
WHITE, ELIZABETH	BAL	202	17TH WAR
WHITE, ELIZABETH	FRE	206	BUCKEYST
WHITE, ELIZABETH	BAL	314	20TH WAR
WHITE, ELIZABETH	QUE	229	4TH E DI
WHITE, ELIZABETH	TAL	074	EASTON T
WHITE, ELIZABETH	SOM	479	TRAPP DI
WHITE, ELIZABETH	PRI	072	MARLBROU
WHITE, ELIZABETH	WOR	263	BERLIN 1
WHITE, ELLEN	SOM	528	QUANTICO
WHITE, ELLEN	CAR	092	NO TWP L
WHITE, ELLEN	SOM	442	DAMES QU
WHITE, ELLEN	BAL	239	12TH WAR
WHITE, ELLEN	BAL	003	9TH WARD
WHITE, ELLEN	BAL	132	5TH WARD
WHITE, ELLNE	BAL	205	2ND WARD
WHITE, EPHRAIM	BAL	266	1ST DIST
WHITE, EVAN	CEC	023	ELKTON 3
WHITE, EVELINE	MGM	419	MEDLEY 3
WHITE, FAITHY	BAL	333	1ST DIST
WHITE, FISHER A.	CEC	004	ELKTON 3
WHITE, FLETCHER	CEC	194	7TH E DI
WHITE, FRANCIS	BAL	168	19TH WAR
WHITE, FREDERICK	FRE	129	CREAGERS
WHITE, FREDERICK	ANN	432	HOWARD D
WHITE, G.	BAL	323	12TH WAR
WHITE, GABRIEAL	FRE	307	WOODSBOR
WHITE, GABRIEL	CAL	034	2ND DIST
WHITE, GAYLOR	BAL	411	14TH WAR
WHITE, GEORGE	CAR	183	8TH DIST
WHITE, GEORGE	BAL	077	4TH WARD
WHITE, GEORGE	BAL	149	16TH WAR
WHITE, GEORGE	BAL	328	7TH WARD
WHITE, GEORGE	ALL	252	CUMBERLA
WHITE, GEORGE	BAL	354	1ST DIST
WHITE, GEORGE	BAL	341	3RD WARD
WHITE, GEORGE	BAL	408	1ST DIST
WHITE, GEORGE	BAL	125	1ST WARD
WHITE, GEORGE	BAL	058	1ST WARD
WHITE, GEORGE	BAL	018	9TH WARD
WHITE, GEORGE	BAL	397	8TH WARD
WHITE, GEORGE	BAL	289	7TH WARD
WHITE, GEORGE	PRI	028	VANSVILL
WHITE, GEORGE	PRI	025	VANSVILL
WHITE, GEORGE	MGM	443	CLARKSTR
WHITE, GEORGE A.	BAL	306	7TH WARD
WHITE, GEORGE F.	ANN	363	4TH DIST
WHITE, GEORGE H.	SOM	548	TYASKIN
WHITE, GEORGE H.	SOM	445	DAMES QU
WHITE, GEORGE N.	ST	310	1ST E DI
WHITE, GEORGE W.	MGM	379	ROCKERLE
WHITE, GEORGEINNA	BAL	180	2ND DIST
WHITE, GILBERT	BAL	116	1ST WARD
WHITE, GILBERT	BAL	142	1ST WARD
WHITE, GCERGE	BAL	066	18TH WAR
WHITE, GOLLIB*	BAL	304	3RD WARD
WHITE, GOTLIB*	BAL	304	3RD WARD
WHITE, GRIFFITH A.	BAL	052	4TH WARD
WHITE, HAMILTCN	SOM	443	DAMES QU
WHITE, HAMILTCN	ALL	156	6TH E.D.
WHITE, HANNAH	BAL	003	15TH WAR
WHITE, HANNY	BAL	340	13TH WAR
WHITE, HARRIET	TAL	071	EASTON T
WHITE, HARRIET A.	BAL	121	16TH WAR
WHITE, HENERETTA	SOM	490	SALISBUR
WHITE, HENRIETTA	QUE	241	5TH E DI
WHITE, HENRIETTA	ANN	356	3RD DIST
WHITE, HENRIETTA	DOR	374	1ST DIST
WHITE, HENRY	DOR	300	1ST DIST
WHITE, HENRY	SOM	442	DAMES QU
WHITE, HENRY	CEC	041	CHESAPEA
WHITE, HENRY	BAL	471	14TH WAR
WHITE, HENRY	BAL	084	15TH WAR
WHITE, HENRY	BAL	018	15TH WAR
WHITE, HENRY	BAL	145	1ST WARD
WHITE, HENRY	BAL	131	1ST WARD
WHITE, HENRY	BAL	115	1ST WARD
WHITE, HENRY	BAL	116	1ST WARD
WHITE, HENRY	BAL	212	2ND WARD
WHITE, HENRY	SOM	538	TYASKIN
WHITE, HENRY	SOM	498	SALISBUR
WHITE, HENRY	SOM	552	TYASKIN
WHITE, HENRY A.	SOM	430	PRINCESS
WHITE, HENRY B.	ALL	063	10TH E.D
WHITE, HENRY P.	SOM	443	DAMES QU
WHITE, HENRY SR.	WOR	234	6TH E DI
WHITE, HENRY W.	SOM	553	TYASKIN
WHITE, HESTER	BAL	503	14TH WAR
WHITE, HETTY-BLACK	WOR	331	1ST E DI
WHITE, HIRAM	FRE	102	FREDERIC
WHITE, HORACE B.C.	BAL	161	1ST WARD
WHITE, HUGH	BAL	068	1ST WARD
WHITE, HUGH	BAL	160	11TH WAR
WHITE, IRA	CEC	201	6TH E DI
WHITE, IRA R.	CHA	289	BOJANTOW
WHITE, ISAAC	CAL	029	2ND DIST
WHITE, ISAAC	WOR	293	9TH E DI
WHITE, ISAAC	SOM	474	TRAPPE D
WHITE, J.	BAL	149	1ST WARD
WHITE, J.	BAL	223	12TH WAR
WHITE, J. M.*	DOR	410	1ST DIST
WHITE, J.W.	ANN	268	ANNAPOLI
WHITE, JACBO R.	BAL	474	14TH WAR
WHITE, JACOB	CEC	024	ELKTON 3
WHITE, JACOB	BAL	214	2ND WARD
WHITE, JACOB	BAL	282	2ND WARD
WHITE, JACOB	WAS	167	1ST DIST
WHITE, JACOB	WOR	229	6TH E DI
WHITE, JAMES	SOM	479	TRAPP DI
WHITE, JAMES	SOM	492	SALISBUR
WHITE, JAMES	WOR	212	4TH E DI
WHITE, JAMES	KEN	298	3RD DIST
WHITE, JAMES	KEN	303	3RD DIST
WHITE, JAMES	SOM	554	TYASKIN
WHITE, JAMES	BAL	306	7TH WARD
WHITE, JAMES	BAL	165	6TH WARD
WHITE, JAMES	BAL	152	5TH WARD
WHITE, JAMES	ALL	064	10TH E.D
WHITE, JAMES	BAL	322	1ST DIST
WHITE, JAMES	ANN	288	ANNAPOLI
WHITE, JAMES	BAL	120	1ST WARD
WHITE, JAMES	BAL	154	2ND DIST
WHITE, JAMES	BAL	318	12TH WAR
WHITE, JAMES	ALL	251	CUMBERLA
WHITE, JAMES	BAL	067	2ND DIST
WHITE, JAMES	BAL	369	1ST DIST
WHITE, JAMES	ANN	513	HOWARD D
WHITE, JAMES	BAL	157	11TH WAR
WHITE, JAMES	BAL	395	14TH WAR
WHITE, JAMES	DOR	331	3RD DIVI
WHITE, JAMES	BAL	101	18TH WAR
WHITE, JAMES B.	BAL	030	4TH WARD
WHITE, JAMES C.	SOM	474	TRAPPE D
WHITE, JAMES D.	BAL	162	16TH WAR
WHITE, JAMES E.	SOM	401	BRINKLEY
WHITE, JAMES H.	SOM	401	BRINKLEY
WHITE, JAMES R.	ANN	279	ANNAPOLI
WHITE, JAMES S.	FRE	331	MIDDLETO
WHITE, JAMES T.	TAL	018	EASTON D
WHITE, JAMES W.	BAL	059	16TH WAR
WHITE, JANE	CEC	081	CHARLEST
WHITE, JANE	BAL	211	17TH WAR
WHITE, JANE	BAL	317	12TH WAR
WHITE, JELIA	BAL	315	12TH WAR
WHITE, JERMIAH-BLACK	FRE	453	8TH E DI
WHITE, JEROME	BAL	333	3RD WARD
WHITE, JERRY-MULATTO	FRE	433	8TH E DI
WHITE, JIM	ANN	340	3RD DIST
WHITE, JOB	BAL	159	1ST WARD
WHITE, JOHN	BAL	205	2ND WARD
WHITE, JOHN	BAL	031	2ND DIST
WHITE, JOHN	ANN	444	HOWARD D
WHITE, JOHN	BAL	123	2ND DIST
WHITE, JOHN	ALL	220	CUMBERLA
WHITE, JOHN	BAL	065	10TH WAR
WHITE, JOHN	BAL	081	10TH WAR
WHITE, JOHN	ALL	062	10TH E.D
WHITE, JOHN	BAL	055	1ST WARD
WHITE, JOHN	BAL	353	3RD WARD
WHITE, JOHN	BAL	357	3RD WARD
WHITE, JOHN	BAL	070	1ST WARD
WHITE, JOHN	BAL	131	1ST WARD
WHITE, JOHN	BAL	144	1ST WARD
WHITE, JOHN	BAL	125	1ST WARD
WHITE, JOHN	BAL	395	3RD WARD
WHITE, JOHN	BAL	260	2ND WARD
WHITE, JOHN	BAL	007	15TH WAR
WHITE, JOHN	BAL	017	15TH WAR
WHITE, JOHN	BAL	283	20TH WAR
WHITE, JOHN	BAL	385	13TH WAR
WHITE, JOHN	CEC	129	6TH E DI
WHITE, JOHN	CEC	185	7TH E DI
WHITE, JOHN	CEC	162	6TH E DI
WHITE, JOHN	CEC	058	1ST E DI
WHITE, JOHN	FRE	207	BUCKEYST
WHITE, JOHN	CEC	033	CHESAPEA
WHITE, JOHN	CEC	017	ELKTON 3
WHITE, JOHN	BAL	198	19TH WAR
WHITE, JOHN	BAL	418	3RD WARD
WHITE, JOHN	CAR	316	1ST DIST
WHITE, JOHN	BAL	405	14TH WAR
WHITE, JOHN	CAR	152	NO TWP L
WHITE, JOHN	BAL	143	11TH WAR
WHITE, JOHN	MGM	360	BERRYS D
WHITE, JOHN	MGM	399	ROCKERLE
WHITE, JOHN	MGM	419	MEDLEY 3
WHITE, JOHN	PRI	014	BLADENSB
WHITE, JOHN	WOR	332	1ST E DI
WHITE, JOHN	SOM	457	DAMES QU
WHITE, JOHN	SOM	458	DAMES QU
WHITE, JOHN	QUE	211	3RD E DI
WHITE, JOHN	KEN	313	3RD DIST
WHITE, JOHN	WAS	266	1ST DIST
WHITE, JOHN	WOR	223	4TH E DI
WHITE, JOHN	SOM	494	SALISBUR
WHITE, JOHN	WOR	236	6TH E DI
WHITE, JOHN	WOR	235	6TH E DI
WHITE, JOHN	SOM	479	TRAPP DI
WHITE, JOHN	PRI	058	NOTTINGH
WHITE, JOHN	PRI	034	VANSVILL
WHITE, JOHN C.	WAS	013	WILLIAMS
WHITE, JOHN C.	BAL	312	12TH WAR
WHITE, JOHN D.	BAL	283	7TH WARD
WHITE, JOHN M.	DOR	317	1ST DIST
WHITE, JOHN O.	SOM	546	TYASKIN
WHITE, JOHN T.	BAL	019	15TH WAR
WHITE, JOHN T.	BAL	317	3RD WARD
WHITE, JOHN W.	FRE	317	MIDDLETO
WHITE, JOHNJR.	CAR	154	NO TWP L
WHITE, JOSEPH	BAL	119	18TH WAR
WHITE, JOSEPH	BAL	109	18TH WAR
WHITE, JOSEPH	BAL	280	20TH WAR
WHITE, JOSEPH	MGM	413	MEDLEY 3
WHITE, JOSEPH	SOM	443	DAMES QU
WHITE, JOSEPH	BAL	111	5TH WARD
WHITE, JOSEPH	BAL	383	8TH WARD
WHITE, JOSEPH	BAL	181	16TH WAR
WHITE, JOSEPH	BAL	077	1ST WARD
WHITE, JOSEPH	BAL	254	1ST DIST
WHITE, JOSEPH	BAL	025	1ST WARD
WHITE, JOSEPH	ANN	421	HOWARD D
WHITE, JOSEPH C.	MGM	412	MEDLEY 3
WHITE, JOSEPH G.	MGM	390	ROCKERLE
WHITE, JOSEPH K.	BAL	252	12TH WAR
WHITE, JOSEPH L.	BAL	008	1ST WARD
WHITE, JOSEPHINE	BAL	269	12TH WAR
WHITE, JOSHUA	CAL	030	2ND DIST
WHITE, JOSHUA	WOR	224	4TH E DI
WHITE, JOSHUA-BLACK	CAR	367	9TH DIST
WHITE, JOSIAH	TAL	003	EASTON D
WHITE, JOSIAH	ANN	330	2ND DIST
WHITE, JUDITH	CAL	030	2ND DIST
WHITE, JULIA	SOM	450	DAMES QU
WHITE, JULIA	BAL	400	3RD WARD
WHITE, JULIANA	BAL	363	1ST DIST
WHITE, L.	BAL	320	12TH WAR
WHITE, L.L.	PRI	108	PISCATAW
WHITE, LAVINA	ANN	297	1ST DIST
WHITE, LEAH	SOM	401	BRINKLEY
WHITE, LEAH E.	WOR	198	8TH E DI
WHITE, LEANNER-BLACK	CAR	108	NO TWP L
WHITE, LEMUEL	WOR	191	8TH E DI
WHITE, LERCY	CEC	030	CHESAPEA
WHITE, LEVI	CAR	221	5TH DIST
WHITE, LEVI	QUE	234	4TH E DI
WHITE, LEVI	QUE	234	4TH E DI
WHITE, LEVI	ANN	436	HOWARD D
WHITE, LEVI S.	BAL	272	7TH WARD
WHITE, LEVI-BLACK	CAR	147	NO TWP L
WHITE, LEVIN C.	SOM	432	PRINCESS
WHITE, LEVIN P.	SOM	491	SALISBUR
WHITE, LEWIS	BAL	275	17TH WAR
WHITE, LEWIS	BAL	160	1ST WARD
WHITE, LITTLETON S.	SOM	437	PRINCESS
WHITE, LITTLETON S.	SOM	484	TRAPP DI
WHITE, LITTLETON T.	WOR	187	7TH E DI
WHITE, LOUISA	BAL	019	4TH WARD
WHITE, LOUISA	BAL	333	1ST DIST

WHITE, LUCRETIA M. BAL 357 13TH WAR
WHITE, LYDIA BAL 198 19TH WAR
WHITE, M. BAL 135 1ST WARD
WHITE, MAGDALENE FRE 405 JEFFERSO
WHITE, MAJOR SOM 458 DAMES QU
WHITE, MARGARET BAL 394 14TH WAR
WHITE, MARGARET BAL 343 1ST DIST
WHITE, MARGARET BAL 221 6TH WARD
WHITE, MARGARET ALL 222 CUMBERLA
WHITE, MARGARET BAL 235 12TH WAR
WHITE, MARGARET BAL 057 15TH WAR
WHITE, MARGARET A. BAL 362 1ST DIST
WHITE, MARGARETT BAL 097 18TH WAR
WHITE, MARGARETTA BAL 277 1ST DIST
WHITE, MARIA BAL 206 11TH WAR
WHITE, MARIA L. MGM 374 ROCKERLE
WHITE, MARIE BAL 297 20TH WAR
WHITE, MARMADUKE QUE 235 4TH E DI
WHITE, MARTH ALL 059 10TH E.D
WHITE, MARTHA BAL 228 12TH WAR
WHITE, MARTHA E. SOM 452 DAMES QU
WHITE, MARY SOM 421 PRINCESS
WHITE, MARY BAL 319 20TH WAR
WHITE, MARY BAL 390 13TH WAR
WHITE, MARY FRE 354 MIDDLETO
WHITE, MARY CEC 179 7TH E DI
WHITE, MARY HAR 161 3RD DIST
WHITE, MARY BAL 027 1ST WARD
WHITE, MARY BAL 068 1ST WARD
WHITE, MARY ANN 482 HOWARD D
WHITE, MARY BAL 242 6TH WARD
WHITE, MARY BAL 032 9TH WARD
WHITE, MARY BAL 286 7TH WARD
WHITE, MARY BAL 308 12TH WAR
WHITE, MARY BAL 077 10TH WAR
WHITE, MARY BAL 078 15TH WAR
WHITE, MARY BAL 285 12TH WAR
WHITE, MARY A. BAL 018 15TH WAR
WHITE, MARY G. SOM 384 BRINKLEY
WHITE, MESSY BAL 275 12TH WAR
WHITE, MICHAEL BAL 276 1ST DIST
WHITE, MICHAEL BAL 085 1ST WARD
WHITE, MICHAEL K. BAL 123 18TH WAR
WHITE, MICHEAL QUE 123 1ST E DI
WHITE, MILES BAL 380 13TH WAR
WHITE, MILLEMINA A. MGM 422 MEDLEY 3
WHITE, MILLY CAL 026 2ND DIST
WHITE, MILLY CAL 027 2ND DIST
WHITE, MILTON CEC 130 6TH E DI
WHITE, MRS. BAL 203 11TH WAR
WHITE, NACE ANN 283 ANNAPOLI
WHITE, NANCY WOR 194 8TH E DI
WHITE, NAPCLEAN CEC 151 PORT DUP
WHITE, NATHAN S. MGM 409 MEDLEY 3
WHITE, NATHANIEL SOM 446 DAMES QU
WHITE, NEIL-BLACK FRE 042 FREDERIC
WHITE, NELLY SOM 470 TRAPPE D
WHITE, NELY ANN 498 HOWARD D
WHITE, NICHOLAS BAL 394 1ST DIST
WHITE, NICHOLAS CAR 291 7TH DIST
WHITE, NOAH BAL 051 4TH WARD
WHITE, NOAH SOM 480 TRAPP DI
WHITE, OZE PRI 070 MARLBROU
WHITE, P. H. BAL 099 10TH WAR
WHITE, PARKE ANN 339 3RD DIST
WHITE, PATRICK BAL 448 1ST DIST
WHITE, PEGGY BAL 136 11TH WAR
WHITE, PENELTON BAL 045 18TH WAR
WHITE, PETER SOM 421 PRINCESS
WHITE, PETER BAL 138 18TH WAR
WHITE, POLLY SOM 487 SALISBUR
WHITE, R. M. BAL 475 14TH WAR
WHITE, RACHAEL BAL 137 11TH WAR
WHITE, RACHAEL SOM 495 SALISBUR
WHITE, RACHEL WOR 229 6TH E DI
WHITE, RACHEL CEC 081 CHARLEST
WHITE, RATCHELL HAR 192 3RD DIST
WHITE, REBECCA BAL 305 7TH WARD
WHITE, REBEL BAL 158 19TH WAR
WHITE, REUBEN BAL 113 15TH WAR
WHITE, REVECCA BAL 361 1ST DIST
WHITE, RICHARD BAL 096 10TH WAR
WHITE, RICHARD BAL 154 16TH WAR
WHITE, RICHARD BAL 003 9TH WARD
WHITE, RICHARD BAL 180 2ND DIST
WHITE, RICHARD BAL 154 2ND DIST
WHITE, RICHARD QUE 216 3RD E DI
WHITE, RICHARD WAS 057 2ND SUBD
WHITE, RICHARD D. BAL 409 3RD WARD
WHITE, RICHARD-BLACK CAR 089 NO TWP L
WHITE, RICHARD-MULATTC BAL 228 2ND WARD
WHITE, ROBERT BAL 014 1ST WARD
WHITE, ROBERT BAL 106 1ST WARD
WHITE, ROBERT BAL 115 1ST WARD
WHITE, ROBERT BAL 190 17TH WAR
WHITE, ROBERT BAL 162 1ST WARD
WHITE, ROBERT BAL 190 6TH WARD
WHITE, ROBERT BAL 171 19TH WAR
WHITE, ROBERT CEC 191 5TH E DI
WHITE, ROSANNA BAL 013 1ST WARD
WHITE, ROSE BAL 268 12TH WAR
WHITE, ROSINA MGM 316 CRACKLIN
WHITE, ROWAN ALL 059 10TH E.D
WHITE, RUFUS WOR 226 4TH E DI
WHITE, RUTH BAL 175 11TH WAR
WHITE, RUTH A. BAL 068 10TH WAR
WHITE, S.B. ALL 261 CUMBERLA
WHITE, SAAH C. ST 312 1ST E DI
WHITE, SALLY SOM 484 TRAPP DI
WHITE, SALLY BAL 228 12TH WAR
WHITE, SALLY ANN SOM 492 SALISBUR
WHITE, SAMUEL SOM 538 TYASKIN
WHITE, SAMUEL SOM 537 TYASKIN
WHITE, SAMUEL QUE 226 4TH E DI
WHITE, SAMUEL BAL 078 2ND DIST
WHITE, SAMUEL BAL 118 15TH WAR
WHITE, SAMUEL ANN 290 ANNAPOLI
WHITE, SAMUEL ANN 280 ANNAPOLI
WHITE, SAMUEL BAL 131 5TH WARD
WHITE, SAMUEL BAL 403 14TH WAR
WHITE, SAMUEL FRE 309 WOODSBOR
WHITE, SAMUEL FRE 204 BUCKEYST
WHITE, SAMUEL BAL 381 13TH WAR
WHITE, SAMUEL J. BAL 188 6TH WARD
WHITE, SAMUEL J. BAL 284 7TH WARD
WHITE, SAMUEL Q. WOR 238 6TH E DI
WHITE, SARAH SOM 478 TRAPP DI
WHITE, SARAH WOR 235 6TH E DI
WHITE, SARAH BAL 218 2ND WARD
WHITE, SARAH BAL 232 6TH WARD

WHITE, SARAH BAL 109 5TH WARD
WHITE, SARAH CEC 132 6TH E DI
WHITE, SARAH BAL 361 13TH WAR
WHITE, SARAH BAL 395 14TH WAR
WHITE, SARAH SOM 432 PRINCESS
WHITE, SARAH MGM 360 BERRYS D
WHITE, SARAH A. C. BAL 417 8TH WARD
WHITE, SARAH J. BAL 228 6TH WARD
WHITE, SIDNEY W. BAL 002 4TH WARD
WHITE, SIMON P. WAS 167 1ST DIST
WHITE, SOPHIA WOR 211 4TH E DI
WHITE, SPICER M. WOR 208 4TH E DI
WHITE, STEPHEN N. MGM 414 MEDLEY 3
WHITE, STEPHEN N.C. MGM 415 MEDLEY 3
WHITE, STEPHEN P. BAL 002 4TH WARD
WHITE, SUAAN BAL 136 11TH WAR
WHITE, SUSAN WOR 350 1ST E DI
WHITE, SUSAN WAS 266 1ST DIST
WHITE, SUSAN BAL 204 2ND WARD
WHITE, SUSAN BAL 318 12TH WAR
WHITE, SUSAN J. BAL 106 10TH WAR
WHITE, SUSAN-BLACK DOR 374 1ST DIST
WHITE, SUSAN-MULATTO FRE 049 FREDERIC
WHITE, SYDNEY BAL 223 2ND WARD
WHITE, TEITHY SOM 480 TRAPP DI
WHITE, THOAMS BAL 395 14TH WAR
WHITE, THOASM BAL 132 2ND DIST
WHITE, THCMAS SOM 446 DAMES QU
WHITE, THOMAS CAR 066 NO TWP L
WHITE, THOMAS BAL 244 20TH WAR
WHITE, THCMAS CEC 030 CHESAPEA
WHITE, THOMAS BAL 365 13TH WAR
WHITE, THOMAS BAL 049 4TH WARD
WHITE, THCMAS DOR 298 1ST DIST
WHITE, THOMAS BAL 119 18TH WAR
WHITE, THCMAS ANN 432 HOWARD D
WHITE, THCMAS BAL 020 9TH WARD
WHITE, THOMAS BAL 150 1ST WARD
WHITE, THCMAS BAL 290 12TH WAR
WHITE, THCMAS BAL 050 9TH WARD
WHITE, THOMAS ANN 280 ANNAPOLI
WHITE, THOMAS WOR 236 6TH E DI
WHITE, THOMAS SOM 502 SALISBUR
WHITE, THOMAS PRI 109 PISCATAW
WHITE, THCMAS B. WOR 294 9TH E DI
WHITE, THCMAS D. WOR 183 6TH E DI
WHITE, THOMAS F. BAL 010 1ST WARD
WHITE, THOMAS J. ALL 226 CUMBERLA
WHITE, THOMAS J. ANN 440 HOWARD D
WHITE, THOMAS J. BAL 040 9TH WARD
WHITE, THOMAS P. CEC 129 6TH E DI
WHITE, THCMAS R. P. L. BAL 085 18TH WAR
WHITE, THOMAS W. WOR 180 6TH E DI
WHITE, THOMAS W. BAL 312 12TH WAR
WHITE, THOMAS-BLACK BAL 187 16TH WAR
WHITE, THOMS CAR 128 NO TWP L
WHITE, TIMOTHY ANN 355 3RD DIST
WHITE, TINNEY FRE 211 BUCKEYST
WHITE, TITUS BAL 216 11TH WAR
WHITE, TITUS SOM 449 DAMES QU
WHITE, TCNY * SOM 391 BRINK_EY
WHITE, TORY * KEN 273 1ST DIST
WHITE, TUBMAN KEN 248 2ND DIST
WHITE, V. A. M.* SOM 357 BRINKLEY
WHITE, VINA TAL 005 EASTON D
WHITE, W.J. PRI 053 AQUASCO
WHITE, WALTER BAL 173 1ST WARD
WHITE, WALTER K. FRE 216 BUCKEYST
WHITE, WANELL QUE 233 4TH E DI
WHITE, WASHINGTON BAL 300 12TH WAR
WHITE, WESLEY HAR 165 3RD DIST
WHITE, WESLEY BAL 017 15TH WAR
WHITE, WESLEY SOM 546 TYASKIN
WHITE, WILLAIM SOM 457 DAMES QU
WHITE, WILLIAM WOR 349 1ST E DI
WHITE, WILLIAM WOR 342 1ST E DI
WHITE, WILLIAM SOM 371 BRINKLEY
WHITE, WILLIAM SOM 453 DAMES QU
WHITE, WILLIAM SOM 457 DAMES QU
WHITE, WILLIAM WOR 233 6TH E DI
WHITE, WILLIAM WOR 261 BERLIN I
WHITE, WILLIAM BAL 159 1ST WARD
WHITE, WILLIAM BAL 156 1ST WARD
WHITE, WILLIAM ANN 379 4TH DIST
WHITE, WILLIAM BAL 005 1ST WARD
WHITE, WILLIAM ALL 058 10TH E.D
WHITE, WILLIAM ALL 057 10TH E.D
WHITE, WILLIAM ALL 064 10TH E.D
WHITE, WILLIAM BAL 305 7TH WARD
WHITE, WILLIAM BAL 135 1ST WARD
WHITE, WILLIAM BAL 136 1ST WARD
WHITE, WILLIAM BAL 279 2ND WARD
WHITE, WILLIAM BAL 140 1ST WARD
WHITE, WILLIAM BAL 365 8TH WARD
WHITE, WILLIAM HAR 168 3RD DIST
WHITE, WILLIAM FRE 129 CREAGERS
WHITE, WILLIAM MGM 345 CLARKSBU
WHITE, WILLIAM HAR 189 3RD DIST
WHITE, WILLIAM HAR 036 1ST DIST
WHITE, WILLIAM FRE 093 FREDERIC
WHITE, WILLIAM CEC 050 1ST E DI
WHITE, WILLIAM BAL 445 14TH WAR
WHITE, WILLIAM DOR 300 1ST DIST
WHITE, WILLIAM DOR 313 1ST DIST
WHITE, WILLIAM B. ALL 063 10TH E.D
WHITE, WILLIAM B. WOR 211 4TH E DI
WHITE, WILLIAM F. T. T. QUE 222 4TH E DI
WHITE, WILLIAM H. BAL 013 1ST WARD
WHITE, WILLIAM H. BAL 232 12TH WAR
WHITE, WILLIAM H. BAL 341 3RD WARD
WHITE, WILLIAM H. BAL 240 20TH WAR
WHITE, WILLIAM H. SOM 444 DAMES QU
WHITE, WILLIAM J. BAL 115 1ST WARD
WHITE, WILLIAM J. C. SOM 443 DAMES QU
WHITE, WILLIAM L. SOM 447 DAMES QU
WHITE, WILLIAM L. QUE 216 3RD E DI
WHITE, WILLIAM M. WOR 165 6TH E DI
WHITE, WILLIAM R. ANN 333 2ND DIST
WHITE, WILLIAM R. BAL 288 7TH WARD
WHITE, WILLIAM T. M. WOR 212 4TH E DI
WHITE, WILLIAM W. WOR 184 6TH E DI
WHITE, WISEMAN PRI 010 BLADENSB
WHITE, ZACHARIAH DOR 317 1ST DIST
WHITE,ALEXANDER BAL 173 1ST WARD
WHITE,ANN BAL 210 2ND WARD
WHITE,MARY BAL 268 12TH WAR
WHITE,RICHARD ALL 025 2ND E.D.
WHITE,STEPHEN-BLACK WOR 331 1ST E DI
WHITE,WILLIAM BAL 166 1ST WARD
WHITEBECKER, JOHN BAL 202 17TH WAR

WHITEBY, WILLIAM W. TAL 015 EASTON D
WHITECKER, DENIS BAL 440 1ST DIST
WHITEE, MARY BAL 371 3RD WARD
WHITEFIELD, MARY ALL 087 5TH E.D.
WHITEFORD, ANN BAL 455 1ST DIST
WHITEFORD, ANN WAS 087 2ND SUBD
WHITEFORD, CHARLES BAL 455 1ST DIST
WHITEFORD, CHARLES BAL 135 2ND DIST
WHITEFORD, DANIEL HAR 038 1ST DIST
WHITEFORD, DAVID BAL 424 14TH WAR
WHITEFORD, DODDRIDGE HAR 045 1ST DIST
WHITEFORD, DORCUS BAL 225 1ST DIST
WHITEFORD, ELITH BAL 135 2ND DIST
WHITEFORD, ELIZABETH BAL 442 1ST DIST
WHITEFORD, ELIZABETH HAR 046 1ST DIST
WHITEFORD, HUGH HAR 038 1ST DIST
WHITEFORD, HUGH HAR 012 1ST DIST
WHITEFORD, HUGH C. HAR 063 1ST DIST
WHITEFORD, JAMES HAR 023 1ST DIST
WHITEFORD, JAMES BAL 210 6TH WARD
WHITEFORD, JAMES W. HAR 044 1ST DIST
WHITEFORD, JEREMIAH HAR 165 3RD DIST
WHITEFORD, JOHN HAR 038 1ST DIST
WHITEFORD, JOHN J. BAL 158 19TH WAR
WHITEFORD, JOHN CF JOHN BAL 442 1ST DIST
WHITEFORD, JOSHUA BAL 177 19TH WAR
WHITEFORD, MICHAEL HAR 012 1ST DIST
WHITEFORD, MICHAEL HAR 012 1ST DIST
WHITEFORD, ROBERT HAR 087 2ND DIST
WHITEFORD, SAMUEL HAR 012 1ST DIST
WHITEFORD, SAMUEL BAL 177 19TH WAR
WHITEFORD, SAMUEL BAL 190 19TH WAR
WHITEFORD, SAMUEL BAL 133 2ND DIST
WHITEFORD, SARAH E. HAR 046 1ST DIST
WHITEFORD, THOMAS WAS 212 1ST DIST
WHITEFORD, WILLIAM HAR 038 1ST DIST
WHITEFORD, WILLIAM HAR 102 2ND DIST
WHITEHAND, ROBERT BAL 311 1ST DIST
WHITEHEAD, ANDREW BAL 006 15TH WAR
WHITEHEAD, ANDREW BAL 143 1ST WARD
WHITEHEAD, BARZILLIA ANN 366 4TH DIST
WHITEHEAD, JOHN CEC 102 4TH E DI
WHITEHEAD, REZIN ANN 370 4TH DIST
WHITEHEAD, SAMUEL ANN 371 4TH DIST
WHITEHEAD, SUSAN ANN 371 4TH DIST
WHITEHEAD, THOMAS K. ANN 371 4TH DIST
WHITEHILL, LEWIS BAL 305 7TH WARD
WHITEHILL, MARY BAL 307 7TH WARD
WHITEHILL,JOHN C. FRE 442 8TH E DI
WHITEHILL,MARY FRE 428 8TH F DI
WHITEHOUSE, DANIEL BAL 087 18TH WAR
WHITEHOUSE, DAVRETT HAR 183 3RD DIST
WHITEHOUSE, GEORGE BAL 001 15TH WAR
WHITEHOUSE, GEORGE BAL 189 6TH WARD
WHITEHOUSE, JAMES MGM 402 ROCKERLE
WHITEKER, CHARLOTT BAL 418 8TH WARD
WHITEKER, ELLEN R. HAR 155 3RD DIST
WHITEKER, GEORGE S. HAR 159 3RD DIST
WHITEKER, THOMAS BAL 417 8TH WARD
WHITEKOPP, HENRY BAL 062 15TH WAR
WHITELEATHER, CATHARINE CAR 331 MANCHEST
WHITELEATHER, DAVID S. CAR 329 MANCHEST
WHITELEATHIER, MARTIN CAR 236 UNION TO
WHITELEY, ALEXANDER DOR 313 1ST DIST
WHITELEY, ARTHUR QUE 177 2ND E DI
WHITELEY, ASBURY QUE 218 3RD E DI
WHITELEY, ELIZABETH BAL 454 1ST DIST
WHITELEY, GEORGE A. QUE 177 2ND E DI
WHITELEY, SAMUEL ANN 307 1ST DIST
WHITELEY, THOAMS E. BAL 066 15TH WAR
WHITELEY, WILLIAM BAL 066 15TH WAR
WHITELEY, WILLIAM QUE 212 3RD E DI
WHITELGY, WILLIAM JAMES QUE 211 3RD E DI
WHITELOCK, AMMOND BAL 328 13TH WAR
WHITELOCK, CHARLES BAL 016 4TH WARD
WHITELOCK, CHARLES CEC 156 PORT DUP
WHITELOCK, ELEANOR H. SOM 418 PRINCESS
WHITELOCK, ELIZABETH HAR 187 3RD DIST
WHITELOCK, HENRY HAR 129 2ND DIST
WHITELOCK, J. BAL 138 1ST WARD
WHITELOCK, JAMES CEC 155 PORT DUP
WHITELOCK, JOHN CEC 180 7TH E DI
WHITELOCK, JOHN HAR 129 2ND DIST
WHITELOCK, JOHN BAL 137 1ST WARD
WHITELOCK, JOSHUA SOM 458 DAMES QU
WHITELOCK, ROBERT BAL 398 1ST DIST
WHITELOCK, SAMUEL CEC 185 7TH E DI
WHITELOCK, SAMUEL CEC 181 7TH E DI
WHITELOCK, SARAH BAL 083 15TH WAR
WHITELOCK, THCMAS CEC 183 7TH E DI
WHITELOCK, WILLIAM CEC 186 7TH E DI
WHITELOCK, WILLIAM CEC 150 PORT DUP
WHITELOCK, WILLIAM HAR 134 2ND DIST
WHITELOCK, WILLIAM CEC 212 7TH E DI
WHITELOCK, WILLIAM L. HAR 129 2ND DIST
WHITELY, ALEXANDER CAR 148 NO TWP L
WHITELY, ARTHER J. BAL 362 13TH WAR
WHITELY, ARTHUR DOR 403 1ST DIST
WHITELY, CHARLES-BLACK CAR 113 NC TWP L
WHITELY, JOHN CEC 144 PORT DUP
WHITELY, JOHN BAL 278 7TH WARD
WHITELY, MAJOR DOR 461 1ST DIST
WHITELY, MARGARET DOR 399 1ST DIST
WHITELY, MERNMORY A. DOR 394 1ST DIST
WHITELY, STANSBURY KEN 214 2ND DIST
WHITELY, THOMAS DOR 394 1ST DIST
WHITELY, WILLIAM CAR 085 NO TWP L
WHITEMAN, ANDREW WAS 281 1ST DIST
WHITEMAN, CHARLES A. BAL 287 17TH WAR
WHITEMAN, GEORGE BAL 293 3RD WARD
WHITEMAN, MARGARET BAL 349 3RD WARD
WHITEMAN, WILLAIM PRI 088 SPALDING
WHITEMARSH, ELLA BAL 457 14TH WAR
WHITEMARSH, GEORGE BAL 456 14TH WAR
WHITEMARSH, JOHN BAL 137 1ST WARD
WHITEMORE, JOHN BAL 001 1ST WARD
WHITEMORE, W.H. BAL 138 1ST WARD
WHITEN, RACHEL BAL 305 1ST DIST
WHITENER, JOHN BAL 063 4TH WARD
WHITENEY, JOHN BAL 156 1ST WARD
WHITER, JAEMS BAL 343 1ST DIST
WHITER, JOHN HAR 181 3RD DIST
WHITERDGE, HORATIO BAL 360 13TH WAR
WHITESEL, WILLIAM BAL 426 1ST DIST
WHITESELL, ADAM BAL 283 1ST DIST
WHITESELL, JAMES BAL 095 5TH WARD
WHITESIDE, JAMES F. REV. BAL 234 1ST DIST
WHITESIDE, JOHN MGM 319 CRACKLIN
WHITESIDE, JOHN BAL 175 19TH WAR
WHITESIDE, JOHN W. PRI 025 VANSVILL

Name	County	Page	District
WHITESIDE, ROBERT	BAL	137	2ND DIST
WHITESIDE, ROBERT	BAL	129	2ND DIST
WHITESIDE, RUTH	BAL	190	19TH WAR
WHITESIDE, WILLIAM	BAL	230	19TH WAR
WHITESIDES, JAMES	ANN	486	HOWARD D
WHITESON, WILLIAM	BAL	156	1ST WARD
WHITEWORTH, MARY	BAL	142	19TH WAR
WHITFIED, WILLIAM *	BAL	127	18TH WAR
WHITFIELD, REBECCA	BAL	030	9TH WARD
WHITFORD, SUSANA	HAR	188	3RD DIST
WHITFORD, WILLIAM	BAL	146	1ST WARD
WHITFORD, WILLIAM	BAL	450	8TH WARD
WHITHAM, CHARELS	BAL	282	2ND WARD
WHITICO, JAMES	QUE	234	4TH E DI
WHITING, BENJAMIN	FRE	076	FREDERIC
WHITING, DANIEL R.	BAL	014	2ND DIST
WHITING, CAVID	BAL	452	8TH WARD
WHITING, J. N.	BAL	153	1ST WARD
WHITING, JAMES	BAL	039	4TH WARD
WHITING, JCHN	FRE	346	MIDDLETO
WHITING, LYDIA	BAL	457	14TH WAR
WHITING, SAMUEL	QUE	205	3RD E DI
WHITING, SARAH A.	BAL	451	8TH WARD
WHITING, W.	DOR	432	1ST DIST
WHITING, WILLIAM B.	BAL	037	9TH WARD
WHITINGHAM, GRACE	BAL	211	11TH WAR
WHITINGHAM, H.	WAS	022	2ND SUBD
WHITINGTON, ELIZA	BAL	461	1ST DIST
WHITINGTON, FRANCES N.	BAL	267	1ST DIST
WHITINGTON, HESTER	PRI	075	MARLBROU
WHITINGTON, JAMES	ANN	402	8TH DIST
WHITINGTON, JOHN	WOR	304	SNOW HIL
WHITINGTON, PEN *	ANN	403	8TH DIST
WHITINGTON, SALLY	BAL	103	10TH WAR
WHITLER, CHARLES	BAL	268	7TH WARD
WHITLER, JOHN *	WAS	075	2ND SUBD
WHITLESTON, JAMES	BAL	001	1ST WARD
WHITLEY, AUTHER	BAL	052	18TH WAR
WHITLEY, ROSEANN	BAL	365	8TH WARD
WHITLEY, WILLIAM-BLACK	CAR	113	NO TWP L
WHITLOCK, CHARLES	SOM	490	SALISBUR
WHITLOCK, EMILY	BAL	145	5TH WARD
WHITLOCK, GUMBERRY	CEC	062	1ST E DI
WHITLOCK, JOHN	FRE	090	FREDERIC
WHITLOCK, JOHN	BAL	422	8TH WARD
WHITLOCK, MATHEW	BAL	332	7TH WARD
WHITLOCK, SAMUEL	BAL	145	5TH WARD
WHITLOCK, WILLIAM	BAL	114	5TH WARD
WHITMAN, ASFER	BAL	398	1ST DIST
WHITMAN, COLUMBUS	SOM	375	BRINKLEY
WHITMAN, EVE	BAL	057	1ST WARD
WHITMAN, GEORGE D.	FRE	119	CREAGERS
WHITMAN, JOHN	BAL	002	4TH WARD
WHITMAN, JOHN	BAL	008	4TH WARD
WHITMAN, JOHN H.	BAL	133	5TH WARD
WHITMAN, JOHN W.	TAL	110	ST MICHA
WHITMAN, MARGARET	TAL	111	ST MICHA
WHITMAN, SAMUEL	BAL	043	9TH WARD
WHITMAN,JOHN	BAL	138	1ST WARD
WHITMARSH, JAMES	BAL	096	10TH WAR
WHITMORE, ANER L.	FRE	179	5TH E DI
WHITMORE, ANNA M.	FRE	195	5TH E DI
WHITMORE, BENJAMIN	FRE	178	5TH E DI
WHITMORE, BENJAMIN	FRE	110	CREAGERS
WHITMORE, BENJAMIN	FRE	176	5TH E DI
WHITMORE, CHRISTIAN	FRE	178	5TH E DI
WHITMORE, JACOPB	FRE	183	5TH E DI
WHITMORE, JOHN	FRE	292	WOODSBOR
WHITMORE, LANE	FRE	186	5TH E DI
WHITMORE, LEAR	FRE	180	5TH E DI
WHITMORE, LUCINDA	FRE	181	5TH E DI
WHITMORE, NICHOLAS	FRE	097	FREDERIC
WHITMORE, SUSAN	FRE	097	FREDERIC
WHITMORE, WILLIAM	FRE	450	8TH E DI
WHITMORE, WILLIAM	BAL	206	2ND WARD
WHITNEY, ALFRED	SOM	426	PRINCESS
WHITNEY, CHARLES B.	BAL	178	16TH WAR
WHITNEY, DANIEL	BAL	013	2ND DIST
WHITNEY, DANIEL	SOM	474	TRAPPE D
WHITNEY, DAVID	BAL	266	20TH WAR
WHITNEY, ELIZABETH	SOM	421	PRINCESS
WHITNEY, FLCRENCE	BAL	342	13TH WAR
WHITNEY, HARIET	SOM	465	HANGARY
WHITNEY, HENRY	SOM	432	PRINCESS
WHITNEY, ISAAC	SOM	485	TRAPP DI
WHITNEY, JAMES	SOM	462	HANGARY
WHITNEY, JESSE	SOM	437	DAMES QU
WHITNEY, MARGARET	BAL	088	18TH WAR
WHITNEY, MARY E.	ALL	213	CUMBERLA
WHITNEY, POLLY	SOM	441	DAMES QU
WHITNEY, RICHARD	BAL	147	19TH WAR
WHITNEY, T. C.	BAL	152	1ST WARD
WHITRIDGE, JOHN DR.	BAL	069	10TH WAR
WHITRIDGE, THOMAS	BAL	260	1ST DIST
WHITSEL, JOHN	BAL	325	7TH WARD
WHITSEL, LEONARD	BAL	338	7TH WARD
WHITSELL, JACOB	BAL	177	2ND WARD
WHITSON, DAVID	BAL	185	16TH WAR
WHITSON, DAVID A.	HAR	086	2ND DIST
WHITSCN, JOHN	BAL	205	2ND WARD
WHITSON, JOSEPH	HAR	086	2ND DIST
WHITSON, MARGARETT	HAR	087	2ND DIST
WHITSON, WILLIAM	HAR	085	2ND DIST
WHITSCN, WILLIAM E.	BAL	178	16TH WAR
WHITTAKER, ARM M.	BAL	176	16TH WAR
WHITTAKER, CHARLES-BLACK	QUE	180	2ND E DI
WHITTAKER, ESAW	BAL	180	6TH WARD
WHITTAKER, FREDERIC	MGM	367	BERRYS D
WHITTAKER, GEORGE	BAL	104	15TH WAR
WHITTAKER, IWLLIAM	BAL	242	6TH WARD
WHITTAKER, LEVINY	MGM	355	BERRYS D
WHITTAKER, LUCY ANNA	ALL	244	CUMBERLA
WHITTAKER, WILLIAM	ALL	244	CUMBERLA
WHITTEKEN, ELIZA	BAL	374	8TH WARD
WHITTEMAN, JOHN	BAL	324	12TH WAR
WHITTEMORE, ADAM	BAL	165	19TH WAR
WHITTEMORE, CALEB	BAL	229	19TH WAR
WHITTEMORE, ELIZABETH	BAL	166	19TH WAR
WHITTEMORE, HENRY	HAR	102	2ND DIST
WHITTEMORE, JAMES	BAL	290	12TH WAR
WHITTEN, GEORGE	BAL	211	2ND WARD
WHITTEN, GECRGE	HAR	186	3RD DIST
WHITTENKEN, GEORGE	BAL	291	17TH WAR
WHITTER, GABRIEL	FRE	224	BUCKEYST
WHITTER, HELLEN	FRE	231	BUCKEYST
WHITTER, JOHN *	WAS	075	2ND SUBD
WHITTER, LEONARD	FRE	009	FREDERIC
WHITTER, SARAH E.	FRE	025	FREDERIC
WHITTER, SUSANB E.	FRE	035	FREDERIC
WHITTER,MARY J.	FRE	206	BUCKEYST
WHITTERS, MARY C.	WAS	144	HAGERSTO
WHITTHILL, JAMES	FRE	024	FREDERIC
WHITTICO, ARTHUR	QUE	219	3RD E DI
WHITTIER, AUGUSTA	BAL	099	10TH WAR
WHITTIER, JIM-BLACK	QUE	182	3RD E DI
WHITTIKER, J.	BAL	211	17TH WAR
WHITTING, CHARLE	BAL	051	1ST WARD
WHITTING, WILLIAM	BAL	232	2ND WARD
WHITTINGHAM, WILLIAM R.	BAL	280	20TH WAR
WHITTINGCN, JOSEPH	WOR	179	6TH E DI
WHITTINGOTN, JOHNR.	WOR	254	1ST CENS
WHITTINGTON, BENJAMIN	SOM	393	BRINKLEY
WHITTINGTON, CATHARINE E.	BAL	278	2ND WARD
WHITTINGTON, EDWARD	ANN	329	2ND DIST
WHITTINGTON, EDWARD	WOR	350	1ST E DI
WHITTINGTON, GEORGE	SOM	393	BRINKLEY
WHITTINGTCN, GEORGE	KEN	303	3RD DIST
WHITTINGTCN, GEORGE	ANN	269	ANNAPOLI
WHITTINGTON, H. W.	BAL	281	2ND WARD
WHITTINGTON, HARVEY	CAL	030	2ND DIST
WHITTINGTCN, HENRY	SOM	389	BRINKLEY
WHITTINGTON, ISAAC	SOM	385	BRINKLEY
WHITTINGTON, J.W.	ANN	286	ANNAPOLI
WHITTINGTON, JAMES	ANN	400	8TH DIST
WHITTINGTON, JAMES	SOM	389	BRINKLEY
WHITTINGTCN, JAMES	SOM	390	BRINKLEY
WHITTINGTCN, JANE	BAL	217	6TH WARD
WHITTINGTON, JANE L.	SOM	489	SALISBUR
WHITTINGTON, JOHN	SOM	363	BRINKLEY
WHITTINGTON, JOHN	KEN	306	3RD DIST
WHITTINGTON, JOHN	QUE	220	4TH E DI
WHITTINGTON, JOHN	ANN	402	8TH DIST
WHITTINGTCN, JOHN	BAL	382	3RD WARD
WHITTINGTCN, JOHN	BAL	369	3RD WARD
WHITTINGTON, JOHN	BAL	153	2ND DIST
WHITTINGTON, JOHN A.	CAL	061	3RD DIST
WHITTINGTON, JOHN N.*	SOM	399	BRINKLEY
WHITTINGTON, JOHN W.	CAL	037	2ND DIST
WHITTINGTON, JOYCE	SOM	390	BRINKLEY
WHITTINGTON, JOYCE	SOM	391	BRINKLEY
WHITTINGTON, KING	CAL	063	3RD DIST
WHITTINGTON, KITTY	ANN	302	1ST DIST
WHITTINGTON, LEAH	SOM	385	BRINKLEY
WHITTINGTON, LEME*	DOR	450	1ST DIST
WHITTINGTON, LEVIN	SOM	363	BRINKLEY
WHITTINGTON, LEWIS	DOR	403	1ST DIST
WHITTINGTON, LITTLETON	SOM	390	BRINKLEY
WHITTINGTON, M.A.	ANN	272	ANNAPOLI
WHITTINGTON, MARY	BAL	059	10TH WAR
WHITTINGTON, MATTHIAS	SOM	552	TYASKIN
WHITTINGTON, PETER	SOM	385	BRINKLEY
WHITTINGTON, PETER	ANN	329	2ND DIST
WHITTINGTON, REBECCA	CAL	058	3RD DIST
WHITTINGTON, RICHARD	ANN	407	8TH DIST
WHITTINGTON, ROBERT	ANN	407	8TH DIST
WHITTINGTCN, ROBERT	SOM	390	BRINKLEY
WHITTINGTON, SAMUEL	SOM	385	BRINKLEY
WHITTINGTON, SAMUEL	CAL	046	3RD DIST
WHITTINGTON, SAMUEL H.	BAL	291	3RD WARD
WHITTINGTCN, STEPHEN	SOM	387	BRINKLEY
WHITTINGTON, STEPHENSON	SOM	390	BRINKLEY
WHITTINGTON, STOUTON	SOM	385	BRINKLEY
WHITTINGTON, WILLIAM	KEN	307	3RD DIST
WHITTINGTON, WILLIAM	QUE	210	3RD E DI
WHITTINGTON, WILLIAM	BAL	243	20TH WAR
WHITTINGTON, WILLIAM	BAL	002	4TH WARD
WHITTINGTON, WILLIAM C.	SOM	390	BRINKLEY
WHITTINGTON, WILLIAM F.	ANN	362	4TH DIST
WHITTINGTON, WILLIAM H.	CAL	047	3RD DIST
WHITTINGTON, WILLIAM T.	BAL	169	19TH WAR
WHITTINGTON, WILLIAM-BLAC	BAL	208	2ND WARD
WHITTLE, BENJAMIN	ANN	417	HOWARD D
WHITTLE, CHARLES W.	ANN	416	HOWARD D
WHITTLE, FRANCIS	CHA	257	MIDDLETO
WHITTLE, JAMES	CHA	257	MIDDLETO
WHITTLE, JEREMIAH	BAL	127	2ND DIST
WHITTLE, JOHN	BAL	116	2ND DIST
WHITTLE, JOHN M.	CAR	284	7TH DIST
WHITTLE, THOMA	BAL	066	2ND DIST
WHITTLER, FREDERICK	BAL	176	2ND WARD
WHITTLER, THECDORE	BAL	176	2ND WARD
WHITTLER, WILLIAM	BAL	081	18TH WAR
WHITTMYER, MARY	BAL	131	5TH WARD
WHITTNG, JOHN	BAL	074	1ST WARD
WHITTON, GRACE	BAL	175	11TH WAR
WHITTTINGTON, WILLIAM	ANN	329	2ND DIST
WHITWELL, ANN J.	CEC	010	ELKTON 3
WHITWELL, ELIZABETH	BAL	339	13TH WAR
WHITWELL, RICHARD	PRI	024	VANSVILL
WHITWITH, CHARLES	HAR	051	1ST DIST
WHITWORTH, MARTHA	BAL	393	1ST DIST
WHITWORTH, SUSAN	BAL	142	19TH WAR
WHOAM, MARGARET	BAL	111	1ST WARD
WHOIS, GEORGE	ALL	168	6TH E.D.
WHOLAND, THOMAS H.	KEN	217	2ND DIST
WHOLEY, WILLIAM	BAL	100	18TH WAR
WHORLEY, ELIZABETH	BAL	098	18TH WAR
WHORLEY, JOSEPH	BAL	098	18TH WAR
WHORP, FRANCES	BAL	199	2ND WARD
WHORT, SAMUEL	WAS	152	2ND DIST
WHORTON, JAMES H.*	TAL	025	EASTON D
WHORTON, MARY A.	TAL	046	EASTON T
WHORTON, WILLIAM	TAL	088	ST MICHA
WHORTON, WILLIAM H.	BAL	279	2ND WARD
WHORTOR, JAMES H.*	TAL	025	EASTON D
WHRIGHT, LOUISA	BAL	128	11TH WAR
WHRIGHT, RESIN	BAL	125	11TH WAR
WHTIE, JOHN	ANN	395	8TH DIST
WHTIE, MARY	BAL	383	13TH WAR
WHTIER, WASHINGTON	BAL	369	1ST DIST
WHUET, ROSINA	BAL	002	4TH WARD
WHYLE, AIDWHAT*	BAL	037	4TH WARD
WHYTHE, WILLIAM P.	BAL	192	11TH WAR
WIANT, ADAM	WAS	006	WILLIAMS
WIANT, AURELIA	WAS	081	2ND SUBD
WIANT, CHRISTIAN	WAS	072	2ND SUBD
WIANT, DAVID	WAS	082	2ND SUBD
WIANT, JOHN	WAS	031	2ND SUBD
WIANT, SIMON	WAS	080	2ND SUBD
WIANT, YOST	FRE	154	10TH E D
WIBBURN, THOMAS	ALL	019	2ND E.D.
WIBEE, GEROGE	BAL	313	20TH WAR
WIBLAS, JOHN	CEC	131	6TH E DI
WIBLE, CAROLINE	BAL	298	7TH WARD
WIBLE, GOERGE	BAL	139	5TH WARD
WIBLE, MARTIN	ST	273	3RD E DI
WIBLE, MARTIN*	BAL	370	3RD WARD
WIBLE, SAMUEL	BAL	301	7TH WARD
WIBLING, CHARLES	CAR	250	3RD DIST
WICK, CHRISTOPHER	BAL	019	9TH WARD
WICK, RICHARD	BAL	330	13TH WAR
WICKAM, JAMES W.	BAL	264	7TH WARD
WICKARD, LEWIS	ALL	220	CUMBERLA
WICKARD, MARY	ALL	245	CUMBERLA
WICKARD, WILLIAM	ALL	231	CUMBERLA
WICKERSHAM, JOHN	BAL	323	3RD WARD
WICKERT, HENRY	BAL	307	20TH WAR
WICKERT, JACOB	CAR	196	4TH DIST
WICKERT, MADGALEN	CAR	266	WESTMINS
WICKES, ANNA M.	KEN	259	1ST DIST
WICKES, BURTON	QUE	222	4TH E DI
WICKES, CHARLES	QUE	232	4TH E DI
WICKES, CHARLES	QUE	236	4TH E DI
WICKES, CHARLES	QUE	236	4TH E DI
WICKES, CHARLES E.	QUE	235	4TH E DI
WICKES, DENNIS	BAL	192	6TH WARD
WICKES, EDWARD	BAL	023	9TH WARD
WICKES, ELIZABETH	KEN	209	2ND DIST
WICKES, JOHN	BAL	017	4TH WARD
WICKES, JOSEPH	KEN	213	2ND DIST
WICKES, JOSEPH A.	KEN	209	2ND DIST
WICKES, LCRINDA W	QUE	223	4TH E DI
WICKES, MARIA	QUE	206	3RD E DI
WICKES, MARY	KEN	214	2ND DIST
WICKES, REBECCA	KEN	216	2ND DIST
WICKES, SARAH	BAL	269	20TH WAR
WICKES, SARAH R.	KEN	269	1ST DIST
WICKES, SIMEN	KEN	208	2ND DIST
WICKES, TINY	KEN	253	1ST DIST
WICKES, WILLIAM	BAL	249	20TH WAR
WICKES, WILLIAM	KEN	267	1ST DIST
WICKES, WILLIAM H.	CAL	061	3RD DIST
WICKESER, ANNA E.	BAL	269	1ST DIST
WICKETT, HIRAM	CAR	132	NO TWP L
WICKEWORTH, JOHN	BAL	301	1ST DIST
WICKEYE, JOHN	BAL	290	20TH WAR
WICKHAM, JACOB	WAS	142	2ND DIST
WICKHAM, JOHN B.	FRE	308	WOODSBOR
WICKHAM, JOSEPH	BAL	261	6TH WARD
WICKHAM, LEWIS A.	FRE	305	WOODSBOR
WICKHAM, WILLIAM	ANN	295	1ST DIST
WICKINS, CATHARIEN	BAL	355	13TH WAR
WICKINS, WILLIAM	BAL	185	2ND WARD
WICKLESS, JOHN	FRE	073	FREDERIC
WICKLEY, N.D.	BAL	002	18TH WAR
WICKLIE, JOHN	FRE	269	NEW MARK
WICKLIFF, CHARLES A.	FRE	029	FREDERIC
WICKLINE, CHARLES	BAL	291	17TH WAR
WICKLOFF, ELIZABETH	BAL	205	2ND WARD
WICKMAN, CAROLINE	BAL	269	2ND WARD
WICKMAN, CHARLES	BAL	178	2ND WARD
WICKMAN, EUSILA	BAL	215	11TH WAR
WICKS, AMUEL J.	KEN	264	1ST DIST
WICKS, DAVID H.	CEC	158	PORT DUP
WICKS, GARDNER	CEC	149	PORT DUP
WICKS, HANNAH	CEC	193	5TH E DI
WICKS, JACKSON	CEC	194	7TH E DI
WICKS, JOHN	WOR	178	6TH E DI
WICKS, LAURA	KEN	313	3RD DIST
WICKS, MARY	KEN	262	1ST DIST
WICKS, SAMUEL J.	KEN	264	1ST DIST
WICKS, TILLY	BAL	255	12TH WAR
WICKS, WILLIAM	TAL	014	EASTON D
WIDAN, MARY	BAL	210	2ND WARD
WIDDLE, JAMES	FRE	343	MIDDLETO
WIDDLEDUGH, HENRY	HAR	197	3RD DIST
WIDDOWFIELD, FRANCIS	BAL	452	8TH WARD
WIDE, JOHN	BAL	128	1ST WARD
WIDE, JOHN	WAS	132	2ND DIST
WIDEAMAN, GEORGE	BAL	371	1ST DIST
WIDEAMAN, SAMUEL *	BAL	371	1ST DIST
WIDEDMAN, SAMUEL *	BAL	371	1ST DIST
WIDEKAMPER, CLARA	BAL	286	17TH WAR
WIDEKIND, GEORGE	BAL	404	14TH WAR
WIDEMAN, AUGUST	BAL	267	20TH WAR
WIDEMAN, CAROLINE	BAL	031	18TH WAR
WIDEMAN, GEORGE	BAL	376	1ST DIST
WIDEMAN, HANNAH	BAL	375	1ST DIST
WIDEMAN, WILLIAM	BAL	386	1ST DIST
WIDEMIRE, ELIZABETH	BAL	306	20TH WAR
WIDEMYER, ADAM	BAL	385	1ST DIST
WIDEMYER, ADOLPHUS	BAL	385	1ST DIST
WIDEMYER, ELIZABETH	BAL	385	1ST DIST
WIDENECH, JOSEPH	BAL	246	1ST DIST
WIDENER, JOHN B.	ALL	258	CUMBERLA
WIDERFIELD, EDUARD	BAL	069	2ND DIST
WIDERFIELD, MARY A.	BAL	092	5TH WARD
WIDMANN, MARIA	BAL	161	16TH WAR
WIDNER, JOSEPH	BAL	240	2ND WARD
WIDRICK, ELIZABETH	FRE	049	FREDERIC
WIDRICK, JACOB	FRE	071	FREDERIC
WIDTERS, ISAAC	WAS	161	HAGERSTO
WIE, SOPHIA	BAL	276	12TH WAR
WIEBB, SARAH	ANN	454	HOWARD D
WIEDER, CHARELS	BAL	032	15TH WAR
WIEGAN, LOUISA	BAL	214	11TH WAR
WIEGAND, JOSEPH	BAL	140	16TH WAR
WIEGART, GEORGE	BAL	316	3RD WARD
WIEGERS, JOHN W.	HAR	087	2ND DIST
WIEGUND, JOHN	BAL	183	16TH WAR
WIEL, MAURICE	BAL	345	3RD WARD
WIEMAN, WILLAIM	ANN	265	ANNAPOLI
WIENDAHL, HENRY	FRE	20	5TH E DI
WIENDAHL, MISS AD.	FRE	198	5TH E DI
WIENDAHL, MISS AG.	FRE	199	5TH E DI
WIENECKE, WILLIAM	BAL	113	15TH WAR
WIENER, MICHAEL	FRE	395	PETERSVI
WIENER, MORRIS	BAL	071	10TH WAR
WIENFELTZ, EZRA	FRE	126	CREAGERS
WIER, COMFERT	BAL	035	2ND DIST
WIER, ELIZA	BAL	283	7TH WARD
WIER, JEANNET	ALL	074	5TH E.D.
WIER, JOHN	BAL	420	8TH WARD
WIER, RACHEL	BAL	291	20TH WAR
WIER, ROBERT	BAL	372	3RD WARD
WIER, WILLIAM H.	BAL	021	2ND DIST
WIERAUCH, MARIA C.	BAL	085	10TH WAR
WIERFUSS, JOSHUA	FRE	194	5TH E DI
WIERMAN, THOMAS	FRE	184	5TH E DI
WIERMAN, WILLIAM	BAL	108	10TH WAR
WIESE, JOHN	BAL	326	7TH WARD
WIESEMANER, CATHRIN	BAL	036	18TH WAR
WIEST, ANTONY	BAL	209	17TH WAR
WIESTLING,MARIAH R.	FRE	447	8TH E DI
WIETSELL, CATHERINE	BAL	366	3RD WARD
WIETY, ELLEN	BAL	319	12TH WAR
WIETZ, JOHN A.	BAL	433	8TH WARD
WIGALL, M.*	BAL	114	11TH WAR
WIGAN, ELIZABETH	BAL	107	10TH WAR
WIGANT, GEORGE	BAL	406	8TH WARD

Name	County	Page	District
WIGAR, CATHARINE	BAL	143	5TH WARD
WIGAR, FRANCIS	ALL	159	6TH E.D.
WIGAR, GEORGE	BAL	143	5TH WARD
WIGAR, PETER	BAL	060	4TH WARD
WIGART, CATAHRIE	BAL	354	7TH WARD
WIGART, DORETY	BAL	136	18TH WAR
WIGART, ELIZABETH	BAL	217	6TH WARD
WIGART, JULIA	BAL	432	14TH WAR
WIGER, JOHN	BAL	251	6TH WARD
WIGFIELD, JOSEPH	ALL	189	9TH E.D.
WIGGAN, SARAH L.	BAL	261	1ST DIST
WIGGENS, ELIZABETH	BAL	366	13TH WAR
WIGGIN, JOHN	WOR	247	1ST CENS
WIGGIN, LEVI	WOR	250	1ST CENS
WIGGIN, MARY	WOR	243	1ST CENS
WIGGIN, MARY A.	PRI	025	VANSVILL
WIGGIN, REUBEN H.	BAL	161	16TH WAR
WIGGINS, ABRAHAM	WAS	128	HAGERSTO
WIGGINS, BETHAN	BAL	301	1ST DIST
WIGGINS, CHARLES	QUE	172	2ND E DI
WIGGINS, CORNELIUS	QUE	172	2ND E DI
WIGGINS, DANIEL	ANN	288	ANNAPOLI
WIGGINS, EDWARD	BAL	028	2ND DIST
WIGGINS, ELIZABETH J.	QUE	215	3RD E DI
WIGGINS, GRASON	QUE	166	2ND E DI
WIGGINS, HARRIET	BAL	471	14TH WAR
WIGGINS, HENRY	BAL	260	17TH WAR
WIGGINS, JAMES	QUE	201	3RD E DI
WIGGINS, JOHN T.	PRI	025	VANSVILL
WIGGINS, JOHN W.	QUE	160	2ND E DI
WIGGINS, JULANNA	KEN	286	3RD DIST
WIGGINS, JULIA A.	QUE	166	2ND E DI
WIGGINS, RAISIN	QUE	154	1ST E DI
WIGGINS, SAMUEL	QUE	247	5TH E DI
WIGGINS, SARAH J.	BAL	138	18TH WAR
WIGGINS, THOMAS	QUE	162	2ND E DI
WIGGINS, THOMAS	QUE	165	2ND E DI
WIGGINS, WILLIAM	QUE	162	2ND E DI
WIGGINTON, WILLIAM	BAL	023	4TH WARD
WIGGLESWORTH, RACHAEL	BAL	301	1ST DIST
WIGGS, SARAH*	BAL	366	3RD WARD
WIGH, H.	BAL	157	1ST WARD
WIGHT, EZEKIEL	ALL	221	CUMBERLA
WIGHT, JOHN L.	BAL	275	12TH WAR
WIGHT, LOUISA	BAL	066	15TH WAR
WIGHT, LOUISA	BAL	284	20TH WAR
WIGHT, OLIVER B.	BAL	006	18TH WAR
WIGHT, SAMUEL	BAL	088	15TH WAR
WIGHT, WILLIAM J.	BAL	003	15TH WAR
WIGHT,PRICILLE	CAR	116	NO TWP L
WIGHTER,CAROLINE	BAL	237	2ND WARD
WIGHTMAN, ARMA	ALL	206	CUMBERLA
WIGHTMAN, GEORGE H.	BAL	328	3RD WARD
WIGHTMAN, WILLIAM H.	BAL	177	16TH WAR
WIGLEY, EDWARD	BAL	270	12TH WAR
WIGLING,WILLIAM	BAL	211	2ND WARD
WIGNE, CHRISTOPHER	BAL	185	19TH WAR
WIGNER, MARY	BAL	283	12TH WAR
WIGRAT, ANDREW	BAL	158	11TH WAR
WIKE, JACOB	FRE	360	CATOCTIN
WIKEN, CATHERINE	ALL	202	CUMBERLA
WIKEN, JOHN	ALL	201	CUMBERLA
WIKER, CHRISTY *	HAR	199	3RD DIST
WIKER, JOHN	BAL	412	1ST DIST
WIKES, JOHN	WAS	296	1ST DIST
WILAN, JOHN	BAL	343	13TH WAR
WILAN, SAMUEL C.	WAS	146	HAGERSTO
WILAND, VALENTINE K.	ALL	169	6TH E.D.
WILARY, BROTHER	BAL	216	11TH WAR
WILBEL, WILLIAM	BAL	147	11TH WAR
WILBER, MICHAEL	BAL	098	2ND DIST
WILBER, SARAH *	WAS	067	2ND SUBD
WILBETT, RODGE N.	WAS	189	1ST DIST
WILBORN, JOSEPH	PRI	C09	BLADENSB
WILBOURNE, SARAH	CAL	064	3RD DIST
WILBUR, HARRISON OTIS	BAL	181	2ND DIST
WILBUR, MARY E.	BAL	086	18TH WAR
WILBURN, ARON	MGM	399	ROCKERLE
WILBURN, HANSON	ALL	034	2ND E.D.
WILBURN, HENRY	CAL	046	3RD DIST
WILBURN, JOHN	ALL	040	2ND E.D.
WILBURN, JOSEPH	BAL	441	8TH WARD
WILBURN, SILAS J.	BAL	444	14TH WAR
WILBURN, WILLIAM	ALL	020	2ND E.D.
WILBURN, WILLIAM	PRI	082	QUEEN AN
WILBURN,WALTER	ALL	041	2ND E.D.
WILCH, MICHAEL	BAL	272	1ST DIST
WILCH, PATRICK	BAL	272	1ST DIST
WILCHRISSEN, WILLIAM	BAL	167	16TH WAR
WILCOX, ANNA	CEC	138	6TH E DI
WILCOX, DANIEL	BAL	236	6TH WARD
WILCOX, GEORGE	BAL	163	1ST WARD
WILCOX, GEORGE	BAL	137	1ST WARD
WILCOX, HENRY	BAL	203	11TH WAR
WILCOX, JANE	BAL	191	17TH WAR
WILCOX, JANE E.	DOR	423	1ST DIST
WILCOX, JOHN	ANN	501	HOWARD D
WILCOX, JOHN G.	BAL	319	7TH WARD
WILCOX, JOHN H.	BAL	223	6TH WARD
WILCOX, JOHN T.	BAL	406	3RD WARD
WILCOX, MARTIMA A.	DOR	376	1ST DIST
WILCOX, MARY	BAL	299	20TH WAR
WILCOX, MARY	BAL	358	13TH WAR
WILCOX, MARY	BAL	250	6TH WARD
WILCOX, PETER	BAL	444	8TH WARD
WILCOX, THOMAS S.	BAL	091	5TH WARD
WILCOX, WILLIAM	BAL	170	1ST WARD
WILCOX, WILLIMA	BAL	320	7TH WARD
WILCOXEN, AMOS	MGM	331	CRACKLIN
WILCOXEN, JESSE	MGM	365	BERRYS D
WILCOXEN, NATHAN P.	PRI	034	VANSVILL
WILCOXON, HANSON T.	WAS	100	2ND DIST
WILCOXON, JOHN	FRE	077	FREDERIC
WILCOXON, MELICENT R.	MGM	377	ROCKERLE
WILCOXON, WILLIAM	FRE	007	FREDERIC
WILD, GEORGE	BAL	010	15TH WAR
WILD, JACOB	BAL	113	5TH WARD
WILD, JOHNF.	BAL	252	12TH WAR
WILDANER, JOHN	BAL	174	19TH WAR
WILDAY, THOMAS	BAL	089	5TH WARD
WILDBARGAR, HENRY *	BAL	314	1ST DIST
WILDBECKEN, FREDERICK	BAL	375	8TH WARD
WILDE, J. W. F.	BAL	305	3RD WARD
WILDEN, ELLIOT C.	BAL	128	1ST WARD
WILDEN, MICHAEL	BAL	421	1ST DIST
WILDENER, JOHN	BAL	393	14TH WAR
WILDER, AVIS-BLACK	ST	337	4TH E DI
WILDERMAN, IRA	BAL	184	19TH WAR
WILDERMAN, JULIA *	BAL	312	12TH WAR
WILDERMAN, THOMAS S.	BAL	039	18TH WAR
WILDERSON, SAMUEL	CAR	192	4TH DIST
WILDES, JOHNA .	FRE	089	FREDERIC
WILDGOSS, EMILY	BAL	054	4TH WARD
WILDMAN, JOSEPH	BAL	033	18TH WAR
WILDMAN, JOSEPH	CEC	115	3RD E DI
WILDMAN, MARGARET A.	ST	259	3RD E DI
WILDMAN, ROBERT	BAL	033	18TH WAR
WILDMAN, SAMUEL V.	BAL	028	18TH WAR
WILDS, JOHN	WAS	137	HAGERSTO
WILDS, JOHN L.	BAL	300	7TH WARD
WILDS, SUSAN	WAS	215	1ST DIST
WILDS, SUSAN	WAS	219	1ST DIST
WILDT, GEORGE	WAS	127	HAGERSTO
WILE, ERNST	BAL	126	2ND DIST
WILEBY, DANIEL	TAL	032	EASTON D
WILEIS, DOROTHY	DOR	418	1ST DIST
WILEIS, JOHN*	DOR	418	1ST DIST
WILEIS, MARGARET	DOR	374	1ST DIST
WILEIS, THOMAS*	DOR	418	1ST DIST
WILENFELDT, FRED	BAL	119	18TH WAR
WILER, DAVID	FRE	174	5TH E DI
WILER, JOHN	FRE	174	5TH E DI
WILERS, NATHANIEL	KEN	214	2ND DIST
WILES, AMANDA	FRE	214	BUCKEYST
WILES, AQUILLA	HAR	015	1ST DIST
WILES, CORILLA	FRE	045	FREDERIC
WILES, DANIEL	FRE	095	FREDERIC
WILES, GEORGE	FRE	139	CREAGERS
WILES, HENERETTA	FRE	141	CREAGERS
WILES, JACOB	FRE	372	CATOCTIN
WILES, JAMES	QUE	145	1ST E DI
WILES, JAMES	HAR	162	3RD DIST
WILES, JAMES	HAR	133	2ND DIST
WILES, JOHN	BAL	084	2ND DIST
WILES, JOHN M.	MGM	381	ROCKERLE
WILES, JOHN T.	FRE	402	JEFFERSO
WILES, LYDIA A.	FRE	210	BUCKEYST
WILES, MARGARET	FRE	136	CREAGERS
WILES, MARY	HAR	133	2ND DIST
WILES, PETER	FRE	339	MIDDLETO
WILES, SARAH A.	HAR	027	1ST DIST
WILES, THOMAS	FRE	337	MIDDLETO
WILES, THOMAS V.	DOR	403	1ST DIST
WILES, TILGHMAN	FRE	213	BUCKEYST
WILES, WILLIAM	HAR	124	2ND DIST
WILET, ANN	CHA	254	MIDDLETO
WILEY, ABRAHAM	HAR	054	1ST DIST
WILEY, AGNES	BAL	278	20TH WAR
WILEY, ANN B.	BAL	214	11TH WAR
WILEY, CAROLINE	HAR	019	1ST DIST
WILEY, CHARLES	BAL	299	3RD WARD
WILEY, CHARLES W.	BAL	080	4TH WARD
WILEY, DAVID	HAR	020	1ST DIST
WILEY, DAVID	DOR	439	1ST DIST
WILEY, DAVID N.	HAR	022	1ST DIST
WILEY, ELIZABETH	HAR	125	2ND DIST
WILEY, ELIZABETH	BAL	207	6TH DIST
WILEY, EMILY	DOR	443	1ST DIST
WILEY, EMILY	DOR	435	1ST DIST
WILEY, FRANCES	BAL	373	3RD WARD
WILEY, HARRIS	ALL	017	3RD E.D.
WILEY, HIRAM	WAS	121	2ND DIST
WILEY, JACOB	DOR	432	1ST DIST
WILEY, JAMES	HAR	022	1ST DIST
WILEY, JAMES	CEC	169	6TH E DI
WILEY, JAMES	FRE	389	PETERSVI
WILEY, JAMES	BAL	004	9TH WARD
WILEY, JAMES R.	CEC	175	7TH E DI
WILEY, JOHN	HAR	019	1ST DIST
WILEY, JOHN	DOR	427	1ST DIST
WILEY, JOHN	CEC	051	1ST E DI
WILEY, JOHN	CEC	048	1ST E DI
WILEY, JOHN	ALL	018	3RD E.D.
WILEY, JOHN	WAS	134	2ND DIST
WILEY, JOHN T.	QUE	132	1ST E DI
WILEY, JOHN W.	HAR	022	1ST DIST
WILEY, JOSEPH	HAR	019	1ST DIST
WILEY, LEVIN	DOR	410	1ST DIST
WILEY, LOUISA A.	BAL	237	6TH WARD
WILEY, LYDIA	CEC	087	4TH E DI
WILEY, MALEACHI*	DOR	440	1ST DIST
WILEY, MALLACHI*	DOR	440	1ST DIST
WILEY, MARGARET	CEC	167	6TH E DI
WILEY, MARTHA	ALL	008	3RD E.D.
WILEY, MARY ANN	BAL	084	10TH WAR
WILEY, MARY E.	QUE	133	1ST E DI
WILEY, MATTHEW	HAR	073	1ST DIST
WILEY, MATTHEW W. N.	HAR	019	1ST DIST
WILEY, MATTHIAS	DOR	440	1ST DIST
WILEY, PARKINSON	BAL	302	3RD WARD
WILEY, ROBERT	BAL	406	1ST DIST
WILEY, ROBERT	DOR	410	1ST DIST
WILEY, ROBERT	DOR	439	1ST DIST
WILEY, ROBERT	BAL	029	4TH WARD
WILEY, SALEY	DOR	438	1ST DIST
WILEY, SAMUEL	BAL	372	13TH WAR
WILEY, SARAH	BAL	310	3RD WARD
WILEY, SARAH J.	BAL	020	4TH WARD
WILEY, SILUS*	DOR	439	1ST DIST
WILEY, SOLOMON	DOR	438	1ST DIST
WILEY, SUSAN	BAL	343	3RD WARD
WILEY, THOMAS	BAL	207	2ND WARD
WILEY, THOMAS	BAL	161	19TH WAR
WILEY, WILAIM	BAL	148	1ST WARD
WILEY, WILLAIM	BAL	171	19TH WAR
WILEY, WILLIAM	BAL	233	20TH WAR
WILEY, WILLIAM	CEC	167	6TH E DI
WILEY, WILLIAM	BAL	001	1ST WARD
WILEY, WILLIAM	BAL	137	1ST WARD
WILEY, WILLIAM	BAL	146	1ST WARD
WILEY, WILLIAM	BAL	280	2ND WARD
WILEY, ZEDEKIAH	DOR	427	1ST DIST
WILEY,JOHN	ALL	020	2ND E.D.
WILFING, HENRY	BAL	169	19TH WAR
WILFRUT, CHARLES	PRI	039	VANSVILL
WILGIS, SARAH	HAR	179	3RD DIST
WILGIST, ANNE	BAL	042	2ND DIST
WILGOOSE, SUSAN	HAR	060	1ST DIST
WILGOOSE, WILLIAM	HAR	114	2ND DIST
WILHAM, J.	ANN	342	3RD DIST
WILHAM, JOHN	ANN	341	3RD DIST
WILHAM, JOHN	ANN	341	3RD DIST
WILHAMS, LAURA	BAL	030	9TH WARD
WILHAMS, N.	BAL	149	1ST WARD
WILHEID, ANN	WAS	134	HAGERSTO
WILHEID, LEWIS	WAS	134	HAGERSTO
WILHELIEM, LOUISA	BAL	076	18TH WAR
WILHELM, ABRAHAM	BAL	195	5TH DIST
WILHELM, ALEXANDER	ALL	033	2ND E.D.
WILHELM, ANDREW	BAL	203	6TH DIST
WILHELM, ANN E.	ST	277	3RD E DI
WILHELM, BENJAMIN	BAL	431	1ST DIST
WILHELM, CATHARINE	BAL	202	6TH DIST
WILHELM, CHARLES	BAL	219	6TH DIST
WILHELM, CHARLES	BAL	100	10TH WAR
WILHELM, DANIEL	BAL	202	6TH DIST
WILHELM, DANIEL	ALL	004	3RD E.D.
WILHELM, DAVID	WAS	047	2ND SUBD
WILHELM, ELIZABETH	ALL	085	5TH E.D.
WILHELM, ELIZABETH	BAL	199	5TH DIST
WILHELM, GEORGE	BAL	186	5TH DIST
WILHELM, GEORGE W.	BAL	412	3RD WARD
WILHELM, HENRY	BAL	002	9TH WARD
WILHELM, HY B.	BAL	219	6TH DIST
WILHELM, HYB.	BAL	202	6TH DIST
WILHELM, JACOB B.	BAL	213	6TH DIST
WILHELM, JACOB H.	BAL	294	20TH WAR
WILHELM, JOHN	BAL	214	19TH WAR
WILHELM, JOHN	BAL	199	5TH DIST
WILHELM, JOHN	ALL	006	3RD E.D.
WILHELM, JOHN M.	BAL	358	3RD WARD
WILHELM, MARGARET A.	BAL	419	3RD WARD
WILHELM, MARY M.	BAL	359	3RD WARD
WILHELM, PETER B.	BAL	212	6TH DIST
WILHELM, PHILIP	ALL	085	5TH E.D.
WILHELM, SAMUEL	BAL	216	6TH DIST
WILHELM, SAMUEL	CAR	335	6TH DIST
WILHELM, SARAH C.	BAL	401	1ST DIST
WILHELM, THOMAS	BAL	189	5TH DIST
WILHELSON, SUSANAN	ALL	114	5TH E.D.
WILHERSON, JAMES	WOR	202	4TH E DI
WILHIDE, ALEXANDER	FRE	156	10TH E D
WILHIDE, ELLIZA	WAS	280	LEITERSB
WILHIDE, HENRY	FRE	145	10TH E D
WILHIDE, JACOB	FRE	165	EMMITTSB
WILHIDE, JACOB	FRE	287	WOODSBOR
WILHIDE, JACOB	FRE	281	WOODSBOR
WILHIDE, SAMUEL	FRE	165	EMMITTSB
WILHIDE, SAMUEL	FRE	197	5TH E DI
WILHIDE, SUSAN	FRE	285	WOODSBOR
WILHWLM, GEORGE	BAL	199	5TH DIST
WILIAMS, JOHN	PRI	033	VANSVILL
WILIAMS, MARIA	MGM	348	BERRYS D
WILIAMS, NATHANIEL	BAL	066	10TH WAR
WILIAMS, REZIN	PRI	044	VANSVILL
WILILAMS, RACHEL	PRI	026	VANSVILL
WILIMAS, ALEXANDER	BAL	314	12TH WAR
WILIS, ELIZABETH	FRE	067	FREDERIC
WILISON, JOHN	WOR	341	1ST E DI
WILISON, SAMUEL E.	HAR	161	3RD DIST
WILISOR, WILLIAM H.	HAR	161	3RD DIST
WILK, CATHARINE A.	BAL	054	1ST WARD
WILK, JOHN	BAL	053	1ST WARD
WILK, MARGARET	BAL	372	8TH WARD
WILKAM, JOHN	BAL	236	2ND WARD
WILKELM, DANIEL	BAL	200	5TH DIST
WILKELM,JACOB	BAL	245	2ND WARD
WILKENS, MARY	BAL	469	14TH WAR
WILKENS, SARAH	WAS	185	BOONSBOR
WILKENSON, GEORGE F.	CHA	278	BOJANTOW
WILKENSON, GEORGE W.	ST	255	3RD E DI
WILKENSON, ROBERT	BAL	414	1ST DIST
WILKER, ELIZA	FRE	334	MIDDLETO
WILKERSON, JAMES	KEN	246	2ND DIST
WILKERSON, JAMES	BAL	083	10TH WAR
WILKERSON, JOHN	WOR	204	4TH E DI
WILKERSON, JOHN	WOR	236	6TH E DI
WILKERSON, MARIA A.	WOR	219	4TH E DI
WILKERSON, MARTHY J.	HAR	193	3RD DIST
WILKERSON, MARY	BAL	361	8TH WARD
WILKERSON, SAMUEL	BAL	133	2ND DIST
WILKERSON, STEPHEN	WOR	210	4TH E DI
WILKERSON, THOMAS	BAL	135	2ND DIST
WILKERSON, THOMAS	HAR	203	3RD DIST
WILKERSON, WILLIAM	BAL	135	2ND DIST
WILKERSON, WILLIAM	BAL	134	2ND DIST
WILKES, SOL.	BAL	221	12TH WAR
WILKES, SUSAN	BAL	221	12TH WAR
WILKESON, JESSIE	WOR	326	1ST E DI
WILKIN, JOHN	BAL	147	1ST WARD
WILKIN, JOHN	BAL	147	1ST WARD
WILKIN, JOHN	BAL	134	1ST WARD
WILKINGON, PATRICK	BAL	104	1ST WARD
WILKINS, ACHSACK	BAL	149	11TH WAR
WILKINS, ANNA	BAL	282	1ST DIST
WILKINS, BARTUS	BAL	058	4TH WARD
WILKINS, CATHERINE	BAL	088	18TH WAR
WILKINS, CHRISTOPHER	BAL	302	3RD WARD
WILKINS, EDWARD	BAL	059	4TH WARD
WILKINS, EDWARD	KEN	234	2ND DIST
WILKINS, ELIZABETH	BAL	363	3RD WARD
WILKINS, ELIZABETH	BAL	205	2ND WARD
WILKINS, GEORGE	CEC	018	ELKTON 3
WILKINS, GEORGE W.	BAL	256	17TH WAR
WILKINS, GEORGE W.	WOR	206	4TH E DI
WILKINS, HENRIETTA	BAL	373	3RD WARD
WILKINS, HENRY	BAL	218	17TH WAR
WILKINS, HENRY	BAL	464	14TH WAR
WILKINS, HENRY	BAL	137	11TH WAR
WILKINS, ISAAC	BAL	129	18TH WAR
WILKINS, JAMES	BAL	232	17TH WAR
WILKINS, JAMES	BAL	336	7TH WARD
WILKINS, JAMES	WOR	292	9TH E DI
WILKINS, JAMES F.	KEN	262	1ST DIST
WILKINS, JAMES-BLACK	QUE	199	3RD E DI
WILKINS, JOHN	BAL	287	1ST DIST
WILKINS, JOHN	BAL	137	1ST WARD
WILKINS, JOHN	BAL	141	1ST WARD
WILKINS, JOHN	BAL	142	1ST WARD
WILKINS, JOHN J.	BAL	386	3RD WARD
WILKINS, JOHN R.	BAL	142	1ST WARD
WILKINS, JOSEPH JR.	BAL	153	11TH WAR
WILKINS, JULIA A.	KEN	215	2ND DIST
WILKINS, LAMBERT	WOR	292	9TH E DI
WILKINS, LUCINDA	WAS	054	2ND SUBD
WILKINS, MAGARET	ANN	435	HOWARD D
WILKINS, MARY	PRI	039	VANSVILL
WILKINS, MARY	WAS	143	HAGERSTO
WILKINS, NANCY	WOR	215	4TH E DI
WILKINS, PATIENCE	BAL	122	16TH WAR
WILKINS, RICHARD G.	BAL	415	3RD WARD
WILKINS, ROBERT E.	SOM	427	PRINCESS
WILKINS, SARAH	BAL	450	8TH WARD
WILKINS, SARAH	QUE	242	5TH E DI
WILKINS, SETH	SOM	403	BRINKLEY
WILKINS, STEPHEN J.	WOR	166	6TH E DI
WILKINS, TALITHA	WOR	215	4TH E DI
WILKINS, THOMAS	BAL	298	3RD WARD
WILKINS, WALLACE	BAL	002	9TH WARD
WILKINS, WILLIAM	ANN	462	HOWARD D

Name	Co.	No.	District
WILKINS, WILLIAM	BAL	288	1ST DIST
WILKINS, WILLIAM	WOR	167	6TH E DI
WILKINS, WILLIAM	CAR	224	5TH DIST
WILKINS, WILLIAM	CAR	232	5TH DIST
WILKINS, WILLIAM	CEC	201	6TH E DI
WILKINS, WILLIAM H. J.	KEN	256	1ST DIST
WILKINSON, ALEXANDER	BAL	143	1ST WARD
WILKINSON, ANN G.	CHA	285	BOJANTOW
WILKINSON, ANN H.	BAL	419	3RD WARD
WILKINSON, CAROLINE	HAR	111	2ND DIST
WILKINSON, CATHERINE	BAL	041	4TH WARD
WILKINSON, CHARLOTTE M.	CAL	021	2ND DIST
WILKINSON, CHRISTOPHER	QUE	217	3RD E DI
WILKINSON, DANIEL	BAL	293	3RD WARD
WILKINSON, EDWARD H.	BAL	069	1ST WARD
WILKINSON, ELIZABETH	BAL	287	3RD WARD
WILKINSON, ELIZABETH	BAL	382	8TH WARD
WILKINSON, ELIZABETH	BAL	148	11TH WAR
WILKINSON, ELIZABETH	CAL	006	1ST DIST
WILKINSON, ELIZABETH	CHA	255	MIDDLETO
WILKINSON, ELIZABETH A.	WAS	126	HAGERSTO
WILKINSON, GEORGE	FRE	350	MIDDLETO
WILKINSON, GEORGE	ANN	400	8TH DIST
WILKINSON, J. B.	BAL	047	18TH WAR
WILKINSON, JACOB	ALL	186	9TH E.D.
WILKINSON, JAMES	BAL	159	11TH WAR
WILKINSON, JAMES	ST	258	3RD E DI
WILKINSON, JAMES T.	BAL	198	6TH WARD
WILKINSON, JARVIS	ALL	207	CUMBERLA
WILKINSON, JESSE	KEN	239	2ND DIST
WILKINSON, JOHN	BAL	121	11TH WAR
WILKINSON, JOHN	BAL	250	17TH WAR
WILKINSON, JOHN	CAR	232	5TH DIST
WILKINSON, JOHN	BAL	153	1ST WARD
WILKINSON, JOHN	ST	256	3RD E DI
WILKINSON, JOHN B.	CHA	253	MIDDLETO
WILKINSON, JOHN V.	ST	264	3RD E DI
WILKINSON, JOSEPH	CAL	028	2ND DIST
WILKINSON, JOSEPH	HAR	135	2ND DIST
WILKINSON, JOSEPH	BAL	019	15TH WAR
WILKINSON, LEWIS	BAL	193	2ND WARD
WILKINSON, LEWIS	BAL	192	2ND WARD
WILKINSON, MARGARET	BAL	215	11TH WAR
WILKINSON, MARGARET*	BAL	347	3RD WARD
WILKINSON, MARTHA	BAL	047	18TH WAR
WILKINSON, MARY	HAR	137	2ND DIST
WILKINSON, MARY	BAL	126	11TH WAR
WILKINSON, MARY	BAL	054	15TH WAR
WILKINSON, MARY	BAL	104	1ST WARD
WILKINSON, NATHAN-BLACK	QUE	146	1ST E DI
WILKINSON, NATHANIEL	WOR	286	BERLIN 1
WILKINSON, PRISCILLA	CAL	029	2ND DIST
WILKINSON, ROBERT	CAL	020	2ND DIST
WILKINSON, ROBERT	BAL	126	1ST WARD
WILKINSON, ROBERT	BAL	135	1ST WARD
WILKINSON, ROBERT T.	BAL	333	3RD WARD
WILKINSON, SAMUEL	BAL	132	2ND DIST
WILKINSON, SAMUEL T.	DOR	324	1ST DIST
WILKINSON, SARAH A.-BLACK	QUE	135	1ST E DI
WILKINSON, SARAH J.	BAL	006	4TH WARD
WILKINSON, SARAH J.	HAR	099	2ND DIST
WILKINSON, SOPHIA	BAL	295	3RD WARD
WILKINSON, SUSAN	BAL	059	10TH WAR
WILKINSON, T.	BAL	281	2ND WARD
WILKINSON, THERESA B.	BAL	212	11TH WAR
WILKINSON, THOAMS	WAS	162	HAGERSTO
WILKINSON, THOMAS	ST	256	3RD E DI
WILKINSON, THOMAS	HAR	081	2ND DIST
WILKINSON, THOMAS	BAL	399	8TH WARD
WILKINSON, THOMAS	ALL	207	CUMBERLA
WILKINSON, THOMAS H.	CAL	047	3RD DIST
WILKINSON, URIAH W.	CAL	001	1ST DIST
WILKINSON, WALTER V.	CHA	255	MIDDLETO
WILKINSON, WILLIAM	CAL	013	1ST DIST
WILKINSON, WILLIAM	BAL	417	3RD WARD
WILKINSON, WILLIAM	BAL	347	7TH WARD
WILKINSON, WILLIAM	BAL	128	5TH WARD
WILKINSON, WILLIAM A.	CHA	255	MIDDLETO
WILKINSON, WILLIAM H.	BAL	220	6TH WARD
WILKINSON, WILLIAM H.	BAL	382	8TH WARD
WILKINSON, WILLIAM J.	BAL	096	18TH WAR
WILKINSON, WILSON	CHA	255	MIDDLETO
WILKINSON, JOHN H.	QUE	184	3RD E DI
WILKISON, BENJAMIN	CEC	064	1ST E DI
WILKISON, ELIZABETH	WOR	343	1ST E DI
WILKISON, HENRY	WOR	302	SNOW HIL
WILKISON, IRVING	WOR	248	1ST CENS
WILKISON, JAMES	CAR	101	NO TWP L
WILKISON, JAMES-BLACK	CAR	099	NO TWP L
WILKISON, JANE T.-BLACK	CAR	100	NO TWP L
WILKISON, LAMBERT	WOR	298	9TH E DI
WILKISON, MARGARET	WOR	328	1ST E DI
WILKISON, ORLANDAS A.	BAL	445	14TH WAR
WILKISON, STINER-BLACK	CAR	088	NO TWP L
WILKISON, WILLIAM	CAR	090	NO TWP L
WILKISSON, FANNY	BAL	058	10TH WAR
WILKMER, MARY J.	BAL	150	11TH WAR
WILKS, FREDERICK	WAS	106	2ND DIST
WILKS, G.	BAL	139	1ST WARD
WILKS, JAMES JR.	BAL	475	14TH WAR
WILKS, JOHN	BAL	331	1ST DIST
WILKS, MARY A.	FRE	065	FREDERIC
WILKS, SARAH	BAL	014	18TH WAR
WILKS, SUSAN	WAS	229	1ST DIST
WILL, ANDREW	BAL	118	15TH WAR
WILL, ARY M.	FRE	188	5TH E DI
WILL, CAROLINE	BAL	322	12TH WAR
WILL, JACOB	BAL	200	2ND WARD
WILL, JOHN	BAL	236	2ND WARD
WILL, MICHEL	BAL	075	2ND DIST
WILL, SARAH *	BAL	281	20TH WAR
WILL, W.	ANN	336	3RD DIST
WILLAIMS, GEORGE	BAL	256	12TH WAR
WILLAIMS, SARAH C.	ANN	478	HOWARD D
WILLAR, ANDREW	BAL	238	12TH WAR
WILLAR, WILLIAM A.	BAL	236	12TH WAR
WILLARD, DAVID	WAS	113	2ND DIST
WILLARD, FLORENCE	ALL	094	5TH E.D.
WILLARD, HENRY D.	BAL	458	8TH WARD
WILLARD, JAMES	FRE	399	JEFFERSO
WILLARD, JOHN	FRE	405	JEFFERSO
WILLARD, JULIUS	BAL	058	15TH WAR
WILLARD, LAWRENCE	FRE	146	10TH E D
WILLARD, MARY C.	FRE	392	PETERSVI
WILLARD, NANCY	FRE	391	PETERSVI
WILLARD, ORRICE	BAL	383	8TH WARD
WILLAY, JAMES	BAL	098	1ST WARD
WILLAY, ALEXANDER	BAL	098	1ST WARD
WILLBAUME, JOHN	BAL	026	4TH WARD
WILLBETT, SUSAN	WAS	189	1ST DIST

Name	Co.	No.	District
WILLCOX, WILLIAM L.	BAL	096	5TH WARD
WILLEHAN, HINSON	CAR	100	NO TWP L
WILLEN, ELLEN	BAL	011	15TH WAR
WILLEN, JOHNW.	MGM	419	MEDLEY 3
WILLENT, MARY	TAL	065	EASTON T
WILLER, CRISTPHOR	BAL	034	18TH WAR
WILLER, DOROTHY*	BAL	109	10TH WAR
WILLER, JAOCB P.	FRE	029	FREDERIC
WILLER, PRESILLA	BAL	034	18TH WAR
WILLERHOUSER, CATHERINE	BAL	336	3RD WARD
WILLERKIN, FRANCIS	BAL	029	18TH WAR
WILLERY, EDWARD	DOR	353	3RD DIVI
WILLERY, JULIAN	DOR	337	3RD DIVI
WILLES, ELIZABETH	BAL	320	1ST DIST
WILLES, JOHN	BAL	424	1ST DIST
WILLESON, ALFRED	ALL	191	9TH E.D.
WILLESON, JACOB	ALL	148	6TH E.D.
WILLESON, RHODA	ALL	191	9TH E.D.
WILLET, ANN R.	CHA	254	MIDDLETO
WILLET, BRUGESS	MGM	399	ROCKERLE
WILLET, CEPHAS	MGM	398	ROCKERLE
WILLET, CHARLES	CHA	251	MIDDLETO
WILLET, F.	PRI	118	PISCATAW
WILLET, FIELDER	PRI	108	PISCATAW
WILLET, JACOB	CAR	257	3RD DIST
WILLET, JAMES	CHA	291	MIDDLETO
WILLET, JAMES S.	CHA	223	ALLENS F
WILLET, JOHN H.	CHA	225	ALLENS F
WILLET, LOUISA V.	CHA	253	MIDDLETO
WILLET, LYDDA	CAL	036	2ND DIST
WILLET, MARY A.	WOR	296	9TH E DI
WILLET, RICHARD	CHA	255	MIDDLETO
WILLET, SALLY M.	CHA	260	MIDDLETO
WILLET, TOWER	CAL	036	2ND DIST
WILLET, WILLIAM H.	CHA	254	MIDDLETO
WILLETS, CASANDER	HAR	027	1ST DIST
WILLETT, ALLEN W.	BAL	301	3RD WARD
WILLETT, CAROLINE	FRE	272	NEW MARK
WILLETT, CHRISTIAN	WAS	126	HAGERSTO
WILLETT, ISAAC	BAL	025	15TH WAR
WILLETT, JOHN	BAL	072	10TH WAR
WILLETT, JOHN	PRI	034	VANSVILL
WILLETT, JOHN	MGM	343	CLARKSBU
WILLETT, JOHN S.	BAL	259	17TH WAR
WILLETT, RACHEL	BAL	471	14TH WAR
WILLETT, ROBERT W.	MGM	375	ROCKERLE
WILLETT, SARAH	PRI	024	VANSVILL
WILLETT, SARAH A.	PRI	004	BLADENSB
WILLEY, ANN	DOR	350	3RD DIVI
WILLEY, DAVID	DOR	345	3RD DIVI
WILLEY, EMALENE	DOR	349	3RD DIVI
WILLEY, GEORGE	DOR	350	3RD DIVI
WILLEY, GEORGE	DOR	354	3RD DIVI
WILLEY, GEORGE	DOR	410	1ST DIST
WILLEY, GOODMAN	DOR	338	3RD DIVI
WILLEY, HENETTA	DOR	334	3RD DIVI
WILLEY, IRA	BAL	146	1ST WARD
WILLEY, JANE	DOR	351	3RD DIVI
WILLEY, JANE	BAL	248	17TH WAR
WILLEY, JERAMIAH	DOR	360	3RD DIVI
WILLEY, JOHN	SOM	546	TYASKIN
WILLEY, JOHN A.	DOR	348	3RD DIVI
WILLEY, JOSEPH	BAL	319	12TH WAR
WILLEY, JOSEPH	BAL	164	6TH WARD
WILLEY, JULIA	BAL	310	3RD WARD
WILLEY, LEMUEL	DOR	354	3RD DIVI
WILLEY, LEVEN	DOR	353	3RD DIVI
WILLEY, LUTHER	BAL	103	18TH WAR
WILLEY, MARCILUS	DOR	361	3RD DIVI
WILLEY, MARY ANN	HAR	145	3RD DIST
WILLEY, MEHALY	DOR	296	1ST DIST
WILLEY, NEWTON	DOR	344	3RD DIVI
WILLEY, PETER	DOR	355	3RD DIVI
WILLEY, RICHARD	BAL	026	1ST WARD
WILLEY, ROBERT	DOR	343	3RD DIVI
WILLEY, ROBERT	DOR	344	3RD DIVI
WILLEY, SAMUEL	DOR	337	3RD DIVI
WILLEY, SAMULE	BAL	018	15TH WAR
WILLEY, SOLOMON	DOR	355	3RD DIVI
WILLEY, T. J.	BAL	333	1ST DIST
WILLEY, THOMAS H.	TAL	083	ST MICHA
WILLEY, TITIA	BAL	018	15TH WAR
WILLEY, WILLIAM	BAL	102	1ST WARD
WILLEY, WILLIAM	BAL	260	6TH WARD
WILLEY, WILLIAM	DOR	349	3RD DIVI
WILLEY, WILLIAM	DOR	354	3RD DIVI
WILLEY, WILLIAM	HAR	145	3RD DIST
WILLEY, WRIGHTSON	DOR	353	3RD DIVI
WILLEY, ZEBULON	DOR	355	3RD DIVI
WILLFULL, JOHN	BAL	430	8TH WARD
WILLGER, WILLIAM	ALL	158	6TH E.D.
WILLHAM, GODFRY	BAL	132	18TH WAR
WILLHELM, ANDREW J.	CAR	204	4TH DIST
WILLHELM, CATHERINE	BAL	381	8TH WARD
WILLHELM, CHARLES	BAL	380	8TH WARD
WILLHELM, JOHN	CAR	171	8TH DIST
WILLHELM, MARGARET	CAR	222	5TH DIST
WILLHELM, NICHILAS V.	BAL	286	20TH WAR
WILLHELMS, ANNA	BAL	310	7TH WARD
WILLHER, MARY	BAL	149	19TH WAR
WILLHIDE, EDWARD	FRE	133	CREAGERS
WILLHIDE, FREDERICK	FRE	117	CREAGERS
WILLHIDE, FREDERICK	FRE	128	CREAGERS
WILLHIDE, HENRY	FRE	136	CREAGERS
WILLHIDE, HENRY	FRE	112	CREAGERS
WILLHIDE, HENRY	FRE	120	CREAGERS
WILLHIDE, JOHN	FRE	125	CREAGERS
WILLHIDE, JOHN	FRE	126	CREAGERS
WILLHIDE, LUCY	FRE	137	CREAGERS
WILLHIDE, MARIA	FRE	134	CREAGERS
WILLHIDE, MARY	FRE	115	CREAGERS
WILLHIDE, MARY	FRE	119	CREAGERS
WILLHIDE, MARY E.	FRE	128	CREAGERS
WILLHIDE, SARAH	FRE	126	CREAGERS
WILLHIDE, WILLIAM	FRE	132	CREAGERS
WILLHIDE, WILLIAM	FRE	122	CREAGERS
WILLHIDLL, JOHN	FRE	116	CREAGERS
WILLHISON, WILLIAM	FRE	408	JEFFERSO
WILLHORN, JOHN	BAL	250	2ND WARD
WILLIA, ROBERT	CEC	046	1ST E DI
WILLIAM, ANN	BAL	135	2ND DIST
WILLIAM, ELIZABETH A.	BAL	286	1ST DIST
WILLIAM, EMILA	BAL	352	1ST DIST
WILLIAM, FRANCIS	CHA	282	BOJANTOW
WILLIAM, GEORGE	CEC	152	PORT DUP
WILLIAM, GEORGE	BAL	455	14TH WAR
WILLIAM, GEORGE	BAL	166	1ST WARD
WILLIAM, HELEN M.	ANN	471	HOWARD D
WILLIAM, HENRY	BAL	211	2ND WARD
WILLIAM, HENRY	HAR	191	3RD DIST

Name	Co.	No.	District
WILLIAM, HONOR	CAR	360	9TH DIST
WILLIAM, JOHN	HAR	181	3RD DIST
WILLIAM, LEWIS W.	MGM	393	ROCKERLE
WILLIAM, MARGARET	CAR	359	9TH DIST
WILLIAM, MARY	BAL	351	1ST DIST
WILLIAM, MARY A.	CHA	225	ALLENS F
WILLIAM, RICHARD	HAR	191	3RD DIST
WILLIAM, WILLIAM	CAR	363	9TH DIST
WILLIAM, WILLIAM	ANN	285	ANNAPOLI
WILLIAMS, W.E.	BAL	209	19TH WAR
WILLIAMS, A.	BAL	295	3RD WARD
WILLIAMS, A. J.	BAL	153	1ST WARD
WILLIAMS, AARON	WAS	157	HAGERSTO
WILLIAMS, ABBOT	BAL	311	3RD WARD
WILLIAMS, ABBOTT	BAL	172	1ST WARD
WILLIAMS, ABIGAL	HAR	146	3RD DIST
WILLIAMS, ABNER	BAL	075	15TH WAR
WILLIAMS, ABRAM	BAL	136	2ND DIST
WILLIAMS, ABRAM	BAL	037	2ND DIST
WILLIAMS, ADAM	TAL	036	EASTON D
WILLIAMS, ADLE	BAL	207	2ND WARD
WILLIAMS, AGNES	BAL	212	11TH WAR
WILLIAMS, AGNESS	BAL	268	7TH WARD
WILLIAMS, ALEXANDER	BAL	002	EASTERN
WILLIAMS, ALEXANDER	BAL	369	1ST DIST
WILLIAMS, ALEXANDER	BAL	310	1ST DIST
WILLIAMS, ALEXANDER M.	BAL	100	15TH WAR
WILLIAMS, ALFRED	BAL	132	1ST WARD
WILLIAMS, ALICARIA*	BAL	382	3RD WARD
WILLIAMS, ALICE	BAL	131	16TH WAR
WILLIAMS, ALLEN	BAL	122	1ST WARD
WILLIAMS, AMANDA	BAL	218	6TH DIST
WILLIAMS, AMELIA	BAL	286	1ST DIST
WILLIAMS, AMELIA	BAL	107	10TH WAR
WILLIAMS, AMOS A.	BAL	065	10TH WAR
WILLIAMS, AMUS	ANN	270	ANNAPOLI
WILLIAMS, AMY	BAL	232	12TH WAR
WILLIAMS, AMY	BAL	101	18TH WAR
WILLIAMS, ANDREW	BAL	311	20TH WAR
WILLIAMS, ANDREW	BAL	129	1ST WARD
WILLIAMS, ANN	BAL	379	8TH WARD
WILLIAMS, ANN	BAL	358	8TH WARD
WILLIAMS, ANN	BAL	195	11TH WAR
WILLIAMS, ANN	BAL	194	11TH WAR
WILLIAMS, ANN	ALL	074	5TH E.D.
WILLIAMS, ANN	BAL	095	15TH WAR
WILLIAMS, ANN	BAL	461	1ST DIST
WILLIAMS, ANN	BAL	459	1ST DIST
WILLIAMS, ANN	BAL	157	6TH WARD
WILLIAMS, ANN	BAL	208	6TH WARD
WILLIAMS, ANN	BAL	166	19TH WAR
WILLIAMS, ANN	BAL	138	18TH WAR
WILLIAMS, ANN	BAL	269	20TH WAR
WILLIAMS, ANN	BAL	321	20TH WAR
WILLIAMS, ANN	SOM	426	PRINCESS
WILLIAMS, ANN	SOM	426	PRINCESS
WILLIAMS, ANN	CAL	007	1ST DIST
WILLIAMS, ANN	BAL	144	11TH WAR
WILLIAMS, ANN	SOM	361	BRINKLEY
WILLIAMS, ANN	SOM	480	TRAPP DI
WILLIAMS, ANN D.	BAL	010	4TH WARD
WILLIAMS, ANN E.	CAR	079	NO TWP L
WILLIAMS, ANN E.	BAL	430	8TH WARD
WILLIAMS, ANN M.	BAL	094	5TH WARD
WILLIAMS, ANN M.	BAL	333	3RD WARD
WILLIAMS, ANN M.	BAL	414	8TH WARD
WILLIAMS, ANN M.	CAL	038	2ND DIST
WILLIAMS, ANN M.	BAL	052	18TH WAR
WILLIAMS, ANN P.	ST	282	3RD E DI
WILLIAMS, ANN-BLACK	FRE	200	5TH E DI
WILLIAMS, ANNA	CAR	362	9TH DIST
WILLIAMS, ANNA	BAL	119	15TH WAR
WILLIAMS, ANTHONY	BAL	095	15TH WAR
WILLIAMS, ARCHIBALD	BAL	263	1ST DIST
WILLIAMS, ARNOLD	HAR	079	2ND DIST
WILLIAMS, ASBERY	WOR	244	1ST CENS
WILLIAMS, AUGUSTUS	MGM	327	CRACKLIN
WILLIAMS, AUSTIN	ANN	391	4TH DIST
WILLIAMS, B.	BAL	131	1ST WARD
WILLIAMS, B.	BAL	149	1ST WARD
WILLIAMS, B.	ANN	336	3RD DIST
WILLIAMS, BARBARA	FRE	410	8TH E DI
WILLIAMS, BARBARA J.	BAL	073	15TH WAR
WILLIAMS, BARNET	HAR	019	1ST DIST
WILLIAMS, BASIL	ANN	387	4TH DIST
WILLIAMS, BASIL E.	MGM	335	CRACKLIN
WILLIAMS, BAYNARD	CAR	143	NO TWP L
WILLIAMS, BELLY	BAL	046	18TH WAR
WILLIAMS, BEN	ANN	438	HOWARD D
WILLIAMS, BENJAMIN	ANN	323	2ND DIST
WILLIAMS, BENJAMIN	BAL	095	15TH WAR
WILLIAMS, BENJAMIN	BAL	452	1ST DIST
WILLIAMS, BENJAMIN	ANN	507	HOWARD D
WILLIAMS, BENJAMIN	BAL	051	4TH WARD
WILLIAMS, BENJAMIN	CAL	037	2ND DIST
WILLIAMS, BENJAMIN	HAR	123	2ND DIST
WILLIAMS, BENJAMIN	BAL	253	20TH WAR
WILLIAMS, BENJAMIN	BAL	297	20TH WAR
WILLIAMS, BENJAMIN	CHA	246	HILLTOP
WILLIAMS, BENJAMIN	CAR	372	9TH DIST
WILLIAMS, BENJAMIN	CAR	182	8TH DIST
WILLIAMS, BENJAMIN	BAL	416	3RD WARD
WILLIAMS, BENJAMIN	FRE	343	MIDDLETO
WILLIAMS, BENJAMIN	SOM	371	BRINKLEY
WILLIAMS, BENJAMIN	SOM	361	BRINKLEY
WILLIAMS, BENJAMIN B.	HAR	153	3RD DIST
WILLIAMS, BENJAMIN JR.	SOM	361	BRINKLEY
WILLIAMS, BENNET S.	BAL	189	2ND WARD
WILLIAMS, BETSY	BAL	212	6TH DIST
WILLIAMS, BETSY	BAL	340	13TH WAR
WILLIAMS, BETTY	CHA	271	ALLENS F
WILLIAMS, BRIDGETT	BAL	059	4TH WARD
WILLIAMS, BROTHER	BAL	216	11TH WAR
WILLIAMS, C. S.	WOR	264	BERLIN 1
WILLIAMS, CAESAR	CAL	056	3RD DIST
WILLIAMS, CAHRLES	BAL	092	2ND DIST
WILLIAMS, CALEB	HAR	091	2ND DIST
WILLIAMS, CALEB E.	CEC	139	6TH E DI
WILLIAMS, CAROLAN	FRE	247	NEW MARK
WILLIAMS, CAROLINE	CEC	026	ELKTON 3
WILLIAMS, CAROLINE	SOM	492	SALISBUR
WILLIAMS, CASEY-BLACK	BAL	218	2ND WARD
WILLIAMS, CASSA	ANN	379	4TH DIST
WILLIAMS, CATHARINE	BAL	151	5TH WARD
WILLIAMS, CATHARINE	BAL	458	1ST DIST
WILLIAMS, CATHARINE	BAL	249	2ND WARD
WILLIAMS, CATHARINE	BAL	300	17TH WAR
WILLIAMS, CATHARINE A.	WAS	230	1ST DIST
WILLIAMS, CATHERINE	BAL	011	9TH WARD
WILLIAMS, CATHERINE A.	BAL	270	7TH WARD

WILLIAMS, CATHERINE M. BAL 414 8TH WARD
WILLIAMS, CHARITY SOM 366 BRINKLEY
WILLIAMS, CHARLE BAL 117 1ST WARD
WILLIAMS, CHARLES BAL 137 1ST WARD
WILLIAMS, CHARLES BAL 038 15TH WAR
WILLIAMS, CHARLES BAL 051 15TH WAR
WILLIAMS, CHARLES BAL 338 3RD WARD
WILLIAMS, CHARLES BAL 169 1ST WARD
WILLIAMS, CHARLES BAL 176 6TH WARD
WILLIAMS, CHARLES BAL 121 16TH WAR
WILLIAMS, CHARLES ALL 097 5TH E.D.
WILLIAMS, CHARLES TAL 061 EASTON D
WILLIAMS, CHARLES BAL 072 18TH WAR
WILLIAMS, CHARLES BAL 012 18TH WAR
WILLIAMS, CHARLES CAR 182 8TH DIST
WILLIAMS, CHARLES BAL 166 19TH WAR
WILLIAMS, CHARLES HAR 194 3RD DIST
WILLIAMS, CHARLES BAL 220 17TH WAR
WILLIAMS, CHARLES HAR 185 3RD DIST
WILLIAMS, CHARLES BAL 251 20TH WAR
WILLIAMS, CHARLES H. BAL 122 16TH WAR
WILLIAMS, CHARLES S. CHA 264 HILLTOP
WILLIAMS, CHARLES T. BAL 190 17TH WAR
WILLIAMS, CHARLES T. BAL 415 1ST DIST
WILLIAMS, CHARLOTT BAL 334 1ST DIST
WILLIAMS, CHARLOTTE BAL 108 15TH WAR
WILLIAMS, CHARLOTTE BAL 047 15TH WAR
WILLIAMS, CHARLOTTE BAL 377 3RD WARD
WILLIAMS, CHARLOTTE ANN 337 3RD DIST
WILLIAMS, CHARLOTTE BAL 057 4TH WARD
WILLIAMS, CHARLOTTE BAL 150 11TH WAR
WILLIAMS, CHARLOTTE SOM 487 SALISBUR
WILLIAMS, CHARLOTTEE DOR 297 1ST DIST
WILLIAMS, CHRIST. BAL 286 1ST DIST
WILLIAMS, CHRISTIAN BAL 116 1ST WARD
WILLIAMS, CITY BAL 312 3RD WARD
WILLIAMS, CLARISSA BAL 439 8TH WARD
WILLIAMS, COLMORE MGM 413 MEDLEY 3
WILLIAMS, CORNELIA PRI 084 QUEEN AN
WILLIAMS, CORNELIUS S. BAL 116 11TH WAR
WILLIAMS, CRITTY BAL 192 17TH WAR
WILLIAMS, CYAR WOR 247 1ST CENS
WILLIAMS, CYRUS WOR 239 6TH E DI
WILLIAMS, DANIEL PRI 083 QUEEN AN
WILLIAMS, DANIEL BAL 452 8TH WARD
WILLIAMS, DANIEL BAL 402 1ST DIST
WILLIAMS, DANIEL BAL 023 2ND DIST
WILLIAMS, DANIEL BAL 471 14TH WAR
WILLIAMS, DAVID HAR 018 1ST DIST
WILLIAMS, DAVID BAL 304 17TH WAR
WILLIAMS, DAVID BAL 145 2ND DIST
WILLIAMS, DAVID BAL 142 2ND DIST
WILLIAMS, DAVID BAL 375 1ST DIST
WILLIAMS, DAVID BAL 033 15TH WAR
WILLIAMS, DAVID ALL 074 5TH E.D.
WILLIAMS, DAVID BAL 137 5TH WARD
WILLIAMS, DAVID BAL 238 2ND WARD
WILLIAMS, DAVID SOM 543 TYASKIN
WILLIAMS, DAVID PRI 084 QUEEN AN
WILLIAMS, DAVID WAS 237 CAVETOWN
WILLIAMS, DAVID P. BAL 130 1ST WARD
WILLIAMS, DEBORAH ALL 089 5TH E.D.
WILLIAMS, DENARD WOR 299 SNOW HIL
WILLIAMS, DENNIS ANN 293 ANNAPOLI
WILLIAMS, DENNIS ANN 379 4TH DIST
WILLIAMS, DIANA BAL 365 3RD WARD
WILLIAMS, DOROTHY BAL 424 14TH WAR
WILLIAMS, DOROTHY MGM 325 CRACKLIN
WILLIAMS, E. J. BAL 333 1ST DIST
WILLIAMS, EDWARD BAL 109 5TH WARD
WILLIAMS, EDWARD ANN 416 HOWARD D
WILLIAMS, EDWARD BAL 308 12TH WAR
WILLIAMS, EDWARD BAL 469 14TH WAR
WILLIAMS, EDWARD BAL 138 11TH WAR
WILLIAMS, EDWARD CEC 192 5TH E DI
WILLIAMS, EDWARD WOR 266 BERLIN 1
WILLIAMS, EDWARD SOM 364 BRINKLEY
WILLIAMS, EDWARD ST 261 3RD E DI
WILLIAMS, EDWARD F. BAL 163 6TH WARD
WILLIAMS, EDWARD H. ANN 433 HOWARD D
WILLIAMS, EDWARC-BLACK FRE 028 FREDERIC
WILLIAMS, EDWARDS BAL 103 18TH WAR
WILLIAMS, ELEANOR MGM 391 ROCKERLE
WILLIAMS, ELEANOR SOM 551 TYASKIN
WILLIAMS, ELENORA BAL 371 3RD WARD
WILLIAMS, ELI BAL 437 1ST DIST
WILLIAMS, ELI FRE 136 CREAGERS
WILLIAMS, ELIAS BAL 344 3RD WARD
WILLIAMS, ELIAS BAL 161 1ST WARD
WILLIAMS, ELIAS BAL 163 1ST WARD
WILLIAMS, ELIAS BAL 140 1ST WARD
WILLIAMS, ELIAS PRI 032 VANSVILL
WILLIAMS, ELIE WAS 173 FUNKSTOW
WILLIAMS, ELIEANORA BAL 250 6TH WARD
WILLIAMS, ELIJAH ANN 357 3RD DIST
WILLIAMS, ELIJAH WAS 173 FUNKSTOW
WILLIAMS, ELIJAH SOM 443 DAMES QU
WILLIAMS, ELIJAH CEC 009 ELKTON 3
WILLIAMS, ELISA BAL 302 3RD WARD
WILLIAMS, ELISABETH ANN 331 2ND DIST
WILLIAMS, ELISHA CEC 038 CHESAPEA
WILLIAMS, ELISHA BAL 419 3RD WARD
WILLIAMS, ELISHA W. MGM 406 MEDLEY 3
WILLIAMS, ELIZA CEC 014 ELKTON 3
WILLIAMS, ELIZA FRE 111 CREAGERS
WILLIAMS, ELIZA CHA 278 BOJANTOW
WILLIAMS, ELIZA BAL 149 11TH WAR
WILLIAMS, ELIZA BAL 374 13TH WAR
WILLIAMS, ELIZA DOR 392 1ST DIST
WILLIAMS, ELIZA BAL 290 3RD WARD
WILLIAMS, ELIZA BAL 383 1ST DIST
WILLIAMS, ELIZA BAL 213 6TH DIST
WILLIAMS, ELIZA BAL 204 2ND WARD
WILLIAMS, ELIZA BAL 205 2ND WARD
WILLIAMS, ELIZA BAL 132 16TH WAR
WILLIAMS, ELIZA BAL 150 16TH WAR
WILLIAMS, ELIZA WAS 156 HAGERSTO
WILLIAMS, ELIZA A. BAL 310 3RD WARD
WILLIAMS, ELIZABETH BAL 452 1ST DIST
WILLIAMS, ELIZABETH BAL 318 12TH WAR
WILLIAMS, ELIZABETH BAL 177 16TH WAR
WILLIAMS, ELIZABETH BAL 079 15TH WAR
WILLIAMS, ELIZABETH BAL 322 7TH WARD
WILLIAMS, ELIZABETH BAL 095 10TH WAR
WILLIAMS, ELIZABETH BAL 043 9TH WARD
WILLIAMS, ELIZABETH ANN 478 HOWARD D
WILLIAMS, ELIZABETH BAL 272 7TH WARD
WILLIAMS, ELIZABETH BAL 440 9TH WARD
WILLIAMS, ELIZABETH BAL 014 9TH WARD
WILLIAMS, ELIZABETH BAL 075 15TH WAR
WILLIAMS, ELIZABETH ST 275 3RD E DI
WILLIAMS, ELIZABETH SOM 533 QUANTICO
WILLIAMS, ELIZABETH TAL 017 EASTON D
WILLIAMS, ELIZABETH QUE 206 3RD E DI
WILLIAMS, ELIZABETH BAL 367 13TH WAR
WILLIAMS, ELIZABETH BAL 381 13TH WAR
WILLIAMS, ELIZABETH DOR 308 1ST DIST
WILLIAMS, ELIZABETH CEC 129 6TH E DI
WILLIAMS, ELIZABETH BAL 263 17TH WAR
WILLIAMS, ELIZABETH BAL 048 18TH WAR
WILLIAMS, ELIZABETH CAL 034 2ND DIST
WILLIAMS, ELIZABETH BAL 300 17TH WAR
WILLIAMS, ELIZABETH A. BAL 110 18TH WAR
WILLIAMS, ELIZABETH D. BAL 195 6TH WARD
WILLIAMS, ELLEANOR ANN 450 HOWARD D
WILLIAMS, ELLEN BAL 326 7TH WARD
WILLIAMS, ELLEN BAL 461 1ST DIST
WILLIAMS, ELLEN ALL 196 CUMBERLA
WILLIAMS, ELLEN WAS 171 FUNKSTOW
WILLIAMS, ELLINOR BAL 118 5TH WARD
WILLIAMS, ELRY BAL 269 20TH WAR
WILLIAMS, EMER BAL 252 5TH WARD
WILLIAMS, EMILY J. BAL 312 3RD WARD
WILLIAMS, EMMELINE BAL 422 14TH WAR
WILLIAMS, ENOCH CEC 091 4TH E DI
WILLIAMS, ENUCK HAR 095 2ND DIST
WILLIAMS, EPHRAIM BAL 162 1ST WARD
WILLIAMS, EPHRAIM BAL 160 1ST WARD
WILLIAMS, EPHRAIM BAL 153 5TH WARD
WILLIAMS, EPHRAIM BAL 171 6TH WARD
WILLIAMS, EPHRAIM WOR 257 1ST CENS
WILLIAMS, EZEKIEL BAL 158 6TH WARD
WILLIAMS, EZEKIEL DOR 315 1ST DIST
WILLIAMS, F. BAL 137 1ST WARD
WILLIAMS, FENWICK * BAL 202 6TH WARD
WILLIAMS, FERDINAND BAL 293 7TH WARD
WILLIAMS, FRANCES BAL 318 3RD WARD
WILLIAMS, FRANCES BAL 037 4TH WARD
WILLIAMS, FRANCES SOM 539 TYASKIN
WILLIAMS, FRANCIS CAR 404 2ND DIST
WILLIAMS, FRANCIS BAL 125 11TH WAR
WILLIAMS, FRANCIS ANN 456 HOWARD D
WILLIAMS, FRANCIS* BAL 378 3RD WARD
WILLIAMS, FRANKLIN HAR 074 1ST DIST
WILLIAMS, FREDERICK W. BAL 454 14TH WAR
WILLIAMS, G. ANN 338 3RD DIST
WILLIAMS, G. ANN 338 3RD DIST
WILLIAMS, G. BAL 131 1ST WARD
WILLIAMS, G.H. BAL 451 1ST DIST
WILLIAMS, GABRIAL TAL 032 EASTON D
WILLIAMS, GEN O.H. WAS 141 HAGERSTO
WILLIAMS, GEORGE ST 268 3RD E DI
WILLIAMS, GEORGE SOM 385 BRINKLEY
WILLIAMS, GEORGE TAL 016 EASTON D
WILLIAMS, GEORGE WOR 184 6TH E DI
WILLIAMS, GEORGE KEN 275 1ST DIST
WILLIAMS, GEORGE ST 311 1ST E DI
WILLIAMS, GEORGE BAL 127 1ST WARD
WILLIAMS, GEORGE BAL 142 1ST WARD
WILLIAMS, GEORGE BAL 007 EASTERN
WILLIAMS, GEORGE ANN 376 4TH DIST
WILLIAMS, GEORGE BAL 026 9TH WARD
WILLIAMS, GEORGE BAL 175 6TH WARD
WILLIAMS, GEORGE BAL 305 12TH WAR
WILLIAMS, GEORGE BAL 048 15TH WAR
WILLIAMS, GEORGE HAR 099 2ND DIST
WILLIAMS, GEORGE BAL 321 20TH WAR
WILLIAMS, GEORGE CEC 016 ELKTON 3
WILLIAMS, GEORGE CEC 014 ELKTON 3
WILLIAMS, GEORGE CEC 016 ELKTON 3
WILLIAMS, GEORGE CEC 033 CHESAPEA
WILLIAMS, GEORGE CAR 191 4TH DIST
WILLIAMS, GEORGE CEC 065 1ST E DI
WILLIAMS, GEORGE BAL 440 14TH WAR
WILLIAMS, GEORGE MGM 326 CRACKLIN
WILLIAMS, GEORGE HAR 175 3RD DIST
WILLIAMS, GEORGE A. BAL 136 11TH WAR
WILLIAMS, GEORGE HENRY BAL 295 17TH WAR
WILLIAMS, GEORGE P. BAL 121 1ST WARD
WILLIAMS, GEORGE R. CAL 003 1ST DIST
WILLIAMS, GEORGE W. FRE 225 BUCKEYST
WILLIAMS, GEORGE W. BAL 286 20TH WAR
WILLIAMS, GEORGE* SOM 394 BRINKLEY
WILLIAMS, GEORGE-BLACK WOR 327 1ST E DI
WILLIAMS, GEORGE-BLACK FRE 008 FREDERIC
WILLIAMS, GREENBURY CAR 194 4TH DIST
WILLIAMS, H. BAL 148 1ST WARD
WILLIAMS, H. A. ANN 347 3RD DIST
WILLIAMS, HADEL BAL 131 11TH WAR
WILLIAMS, HAMPDEN J. BAL 152 11TH WAR
WILLIAMS, HANDA WOR 315 2ND E DI
WILLIAMS, HANNAH WAS 151 HAGERSTO
WILLIAMS, HANNAH BAL 138 11TH WAR
WILLIAMS, HANNAH HAR 026 1ST DIST
WILLIAMS, HANNAH BAL 023 2ND DIST
WILLIAMS, HANNAH BAL 108 1ST WARD
WILLIAMS, HANNAH A. BAL 126 18TH WAR
WILLIAMS, HARRIET FRE 164 EMMITTSB
WILLIAMS, HARRIET BAL 126 5TH WARD
WILLIAMS, HARRIET A. HAR 139 2ND DIST
WILLIAMS, HARRY BAL 244 6TH WARD
WILLIAMS, HAZAND BAL 176 2ND DIST
WILLIAMS, HEATHER* BAL 045 4TH WARD
WILLIAMS, HELEN M. BAL 109 1ST WARD
WILLIAMS, HENRIETTA BAL 077 15TH WAR
WILLIAMS, HENRIETTA BAL 106 15TH WAR
WILLIAMS, HENRIETTA BAL 060 4TH WARD
WILLIAMS, HENRIETTA BAL 336 13TH WAR
WILLIAMS, HENRIETTA WOR 263 BERLIN 1
WILLIAMS, HENRIETTA PRI 042 VANSVILL
WILLIAMS, HENRY WOR 183 6TH E DI
WILLIAMS, HENRY WOR 213 4TH E DI
WILLIAMS, HENRY SOM 533 QUANTICO
WILLIAMS, HENRY WAS 162 2ND DIST
WILLIAMS, HENRY KEN 256 1ST DIST
WILLIAMS, HENRY BAL 085 4TH WARD
WILLIAMS, HENRY BAL 309 20TH WAR
WILLIAMS, HENRY HAR 156 3RD DIST
WILLIAMS, HENRY FRE 136 CREAGERS
WILLIAMS, HENRY HAR 195 3RD DIST
WILLIAMS, HENRY MGM 408 MEDLEY 3
WILLIAMS, HENRY CAL 043 3RD DIST
WILLIAMS, HENRY BAL 279 20TH WAR
WILLIAMS, HENRY BAL 300 17TH WAR
WILLIAMS, HENRY CAR 337 6TH DIST
WILLIAMS, HENRY CAR 276 7TH DIST
WILLIAMS, HENRY BAL 101 15TH WAR
WILLIAMS, HENRY BAL 166 16TH WAR
WILLIAMS, HENRY BAL 121 1ST WARD
WILLIAMS, HENRY BAL 377 3RD WARD
WILLIAMS, HENRY BAL 066 2ND DIST
WILLIAMS, HENRY BAL 123 2ND DIST
WILLIAMS, HENRY BAL 145 1ST WARD
WILLIAMS, HENRY BAL 055 15TH WAR
WILLIAMS, HENRY BAL 463 1ST DIST
WILLIAMS, HENRY L. BAL 128 1ST WARD
WILLIAMS, HENRY-MULATTO FRE 049 FREDERIC
WILLIAMS, HESTER ANN 454 HOWARD D
WILLIAMS, HESTER BAL 097 15TH WAR
WILLIAMS, HESTER WOR 185 6TH E DI
WILLIAMS, HETTY SOM 503 SALISBUR
WILLIAMS, HETTY BAL 175 16TH WAR
WILLIAMS, HEZEKIAH CHA 284 BOJANTOW
WILLIAMS, HEZIAH ANN 439 HOWARD D
WILLIAMS, HILLARY ST 321 4TH E DI
WILLIAMS, HNERY BAL 144 1ST WARD
WILLIAMS, HUGH HAR 046 1ST DIST
WILLIAMS, ISAAC HAR 095 2ND DIST
WILLIAMS, ISAAC QUE 129 1ST E DI
WILLIAMS, ISAAC HAR 191 3RD DIST
WILLIAMS, ISAAC BAL 425 8TH WARD
WILLIAMS, ISAAC ANN 439 HOWARD D
WILLIAMS, ISAAC ANN 445 HOWARD D
WILLIAMS, ISAAC BAL 279 12TH WAR
WILLIAMS, ISAAC BAL 430 8TH WARD
WILLIAMS, ISAAC BAL 159 6TH WARD
WILLIAMS, ISAAC SOM 395 BRINKLEY
WILLIAMS, ISAAC WOR 274 BERLIN 1
WILLIAMS, ISAAC S. WOR 286 BERLIN 1
WILLIAMS, ISAAC-MULATTO CAR 398 2ND DIST
WILLIAMS, ISABEL BAL 298 20TH WAR
WILLIAMS, ISABELL WOR 258 1ST CENS
WILLIAMS, ISHMAEL WOR 262 BERLIN 1
WILLIAMS, J. BAL 148 1ST WARD
WILLIAMS, J. BAL 150 1ST WARD
WILLIAMS, J. BAL 162 1ST WARD
WILLIAMS, J. BAL 159 1ST WARD
WILLIAMS, J. BAL 165 1ST WARD
WILLIAMS, J. BAL 168 1ST WARD
WILLIAMS, J. BAL 173 1ST WARD
WILLIAMS, J. BAL 286 2ND WARD
WILLIAMS, J. BAL 310 12TH WAR
WILLIAMS, J. A. BAL 332 1ST DIST
WILLIAMS, J. S. BAL 154 1ST WARD
WILLIAMS, J. W. BAL 153 1ST WARD
WILLIAMS, J.H. BAL 164 1ST WARD
WILLIAMS, J.P. BAL 159 1ST WARD
WILLIAMS, J.P. BAL 166 1ST WARD
WILLIAMS, J.S. BAL 169 1ST WARD
WILLIAMS, J.W.H. BAL 162 1ST WARD
WILLIAMS, JACK ANN 321 2ND DIST
WILLIAMS, JACK WOR 284 BERLIN 1
WILLIAMS, JACOB QUE 219 3RD E DI
WILLIAMS, JACOB SOM 496 SALISBUR
WILLIAMS, JACOB ALL 090 5TH E.D.
WILLIAMS, JACOB BAL 012 1ST WARD
WILLIAMS, JACOB FRE 361 CATOCTIN
WILLIAMS, JACOB BAL 025 4TH WARD
WILLIAMS, JAEMS TAL 098 ST MICHA
WILLIAMS, JAMES SOM 400 BRINKLEY
WILLIAMS, JAMES ST 283 3RD E DI
WILLIAMS, JAMES SOM 529 QUANTICO
WILLIAMS, JAMES SOM 480 TRAPP DI
WILLIAMS, JAMES WOR 244 1ST CENS
WILLIAMS, JAMES KEN 261 1ST DIST
WILLIAMS, JAMES QUE 185 3RD E DI
WILLIAMS, JAMES WOR 284 BERLIN 1
WILLIAMS, JAMES TAL 002 EASTON D
WILLIAMS, JAMES TAL 032 EASTON D
WILLIAMS, JAMES TAL 032 EASTON D
WILLIAMS, JAMES PRI 006 BLADENSB
WILLIAMS, JAMES CAR 204 4TH DIST
WILLIAMS, JAMES CAR 195 4TH DIST
WILLIAMS, JAMES CEC 024 ELKTON 3
WILLIAMS, JAMES BAL 243 20TH WAR
WILLIAMS, JAMES BAL 125 18TH WAR
WILLIAMS, JAMES SOM 406 DUBLIN D
WILLIAMS, JAMES BAL 320 20TH WAR
WILLIAMS, JAMES CEC 107 3RD E DI
WILLIAMS, JAMES CAL 035 2ND DIST
WILLIAMS, JAMES CAL 001 1ST DIST
WILLIAMS, JAMES CAL 001 1ST DIST
WILLIAMS, JAMES CAR 124 NO TWP L
WILLIAMS, JAMES BAL 396 14TH WAR
WILLIAMS, JAMES BAL 345 13TH WAR
WILLIAMS, JAMES BAL 238 17TH WAR
WILLIAMS, JAMES BAL 235 17TH WAR
WILLIAMS, JAMES BAL 121 1ST WARD
WILLIAMS, JAMES BAL 121 1ST WARD
WILLIAMS, JAMES BAL 114 1ST WARD
WILLIAMS, JAMES BAL 312 1ST DIST
WILLIAMS, JAMES ALL 177 7TH E.D.
WILLIAMS, JAMES BAL 166 1ST WARD
WILLIAMS, JAMES BAL 165 1ST WARD
WILLIAMS, JAMES BAL 151 1ST WARD
WILLIAMS, JAMES BAL 129 5TH WARD
WILLIAMS, JAMES BAL 461 1ST DIST
WILLIAMS, JAMES BAL 110 10TH WAR
WILLIAMS, JAMES BAL 440 8TH WARD
WILLIAMS, JAMES BAL 052 15TH WAR
WILLIAMS, JAMES ANN 458 HOWARD D
WILLIAMS, JAMES ANN 434 HOWARD D
WILLIAMS, JAMES ALL 234 CUMBERLA
WILLIAMS, JAMES BAL 424 8TH WARD
WILLIAMS, JAMES BAL 128 1ST WARD
WILLIAMS, JAMES A. BAL 183 16TH WAR
WILLIAMS, JAMES A. BAL 017 18TH WAR
WILLIAMS, JAMES H. WAS 227 1ST DIST
WILLIAMS, JAMES L. PRI 053 AQUASCO
WILLIAMS, JAMES N. BAL 244 6TH WARD
WILLIAMS, JAMES R. ANN 424 HOWARD D
WILLIAMS, JAMES W. BAL 153 1ST WARD
WILLIAMS, JAMES W. BAL 301 17TH WAR
WILLIAMS, JANE BAL 001 18TH WAR
WILLIAMS, JANE BAL 001 18TH WAR
WILLIAMS, JANE BAL 071 4TH WARD
WILLIAMS, JANE BAL 009 4TH WARD
WILLIAMS, JANE CAR 319 1ST DIST
WILLIAMS, JANE CHA 271 ALLENS F
WILLIAMS, JANE FRE 174 5TH E DI
WILLIAMS, JANE BAL 004 EASTERN
WILLIAMS, JANE BAL 259 6TH WARD
WILLIAMS, JANE ALL 211 CUMBERLA
WILLIAMS, JANE BAL 360 3RD WARD
WILLIAMS, JANE SOM 360 BRINKLEY
WILLIAMS, JANE R. CAR 194 4TH DIST
WILLIAMS, JANE-MULATTO FRE 033 FREDERIC
WILLIAMS, JANNETT BAL 025 4TH WARD
WILLIAMS, JEFFERSON BAL 337 3RD WARD
WILLIAMS, JEHU BAL 042 2ND DIST

Name	County	Page	District
WILLIAMS, JENKINS	WOR	272	BERLIN 1
WILLIAMS, JEREMIAH	SOM	538	TYASKIN
WILLIAMS, JEREMIAH	ANN	487	HOWARD D
WILLIAMS, JEREMIAH	BAL	044	9TH WARD
WILLIAMS, JESSE	TAL	039	EASTON D
WILLIAMS, JESSE	BAL	086	18TH WAR
WILLIAMS, JESSE N.	CAR	372	9TH DIST
WILLIAMS, JHN	WOR	295	9TH E DI
WILLIAMS, JOHN	WOR	285	BERLIN 1
WILLIAMS, JOHN	PRI	006	BLADENSB
WILLIAMS, JOHN	WAS	029	2ND SUBD
WILLIAMS, JOHN	PRI	083	QUEEN AN
WILLIAMS, JOHN	WOR	180	6TH E DI
WILLIAMS, JOHN	SOM	489	SALISBUR
WILLIAMS, JOHN	WOR	249	1ST CENS
WILLIAMS, JOHN	SOM	508	BARREN C
WILLIAMS, JOHN	SOM	498	SALISBUR
WILLIAMS, JOHN	WAS	120	2ND DIST
WILLIAMS, JOHN	SOM	391	BRINKLEY
WILLIAMS, JOHN	SOM	399	BRINKLEY
WILLIAMS, JOHN	WAS	135	2ND DIST
WILLIAMS, JOHN	QUE	219	3RD E DI
WILLIAMS, JOHN	CAR	353	6TH DIST
WILLIAMS, JOHN	BAL	197	19TH WAR
WILLIAMS, JOHN	CAR	232	5TH DIST
WILLIAMS, JOHN	CAR	214	5TH DIST
WILLIAMS, JOHN	DOR	327	3RD DIVI
WILLIAMS, JOHN	CEC	191	5TH E DI
WILLIAMS, JOHN	FRE	383	PETERSVI
WILLIAMS, JOHN	DOR	333	3RD DIVI
WILLIAMS, JOHN	CHA	279	BOJANTOW
WILLIAMS, JOHN	FRE	180	5TH E DI
WILLIAMS, JOHN	DOR	302	1ST DIST
WILLIAMS, JOHN	BAL	268	17TH WAR
WILLIAMS, JOHN	BAL	362	13TH WAR
WILLIAMS, JOHN	BAL	398	14TH WAR
WILLIAMS, JOHN	BAL	472	14TH WAR
WILLIAMS, JOHN	BAL	147	11TH WAR
WILLIAMS, JOHN	BAL	151	11TH WAR
WILLIAMS, JOHN	CAR	067	NO TWP L
WILLIAMS, JOHN	HAR	022	1ST DIST
WILLIAMS, JOHN	SOM	408	DUBLIN D
WILLIAMS, JOHN	HAR	206	3RD DIST
WILLIAMS, JOHN	BAL	158	1ST WARD
WILLIAMS, JOHN	BAL	129	5TH WARD
WILLIAMS, JOHN	BAL	322	3RD WARD
WILLIAMS, JOHN	BAL	215	6TH DIST
WILLIAMS, JOHN	BAL	394	1ST DIST
WILLIAMS, JOHN	BAL	392	1ST DIST
WILLIAMS, JOHN	ANN	431	HOWARD D
WILLIAMS, JOHN	ANN	463	HOWARD D
WILLIAMS, JOHN	BAL	365	3RD WARD
WILLIAMS, JOHN	BAL	119	1ST WARD
WILLIAMS, JOHN	BAL	105	1ST WARD
WILLIAMS, JOHN	BAL	122	1ST WARD
WILLIAMS, JOHN	BAL	115	1ST WARD
WILLIAMS, JOHN	BAL	086	1ST WARD
WILLIAMS, JOHN	BAL	066	1ST WARD
WILLIAMS, JOHN	ANN	332	2ND DIST
WILLIAMS, JOHN	ANN	337	3RD DIST
WILLIAMS, JOHN	BAL	318	1ST DIST
WILLIAMS, JOHN	ANN	315	1ST DIST
WILLIAMS, JOHN	ALL	089	5TH E.D.
WILLIAMS, JOHN	ALL	127	4TH E.D.
WILLIAMS, JOHN	ALL	046	10TH E.D
WILLIAMS, JOHN	BAL	130	1ST WARD
WILLIAMS, JOHN	BAL	128	1ST WARD
WILLIAMS, JOHN	BAL	126	1ST WARD
WILLIAMS, JOHN	BAL	147	1ST WARD
WILLIAMS, JOHN	BAL	139	1ST WARD
WILLIAMS, JOHN	BAL	144	1ST WARD
WILLIAMS, JOHN	BAL	390	3RD WARD
WILLIAMS, JOHN	BAL	301	7TH WARD
WILLIAMS, JOHN	BAL	227	2ND WARD
WILLIAMS, JOHN	BAL	280	2ND WARD
WILLIAMS, JOHN	BAL	279	2ND WARD
WILLIAMS, JOHN	BAL	280	2ND WARD
WILLIAMS, JOHN	BAL	282	2ND WARD
WILLIAMS, JOHN	BAL	330	7TH WARD
WILLIAMS, JOHN	BAL	277	12TH WAR
WILLIAMS, JOHN	BAL	062	15TH WAR
WILLIAMS, JOHN	BAL	457	8TH WARD
WILLIAMS, JOHN	BAL	459	8TH WARD
WILLIAMS, JOHN	BAL	351	7TH WARD
WILLIAMS, JOHN	BAL	008	15TH WAR
WILLIAMS, JOHN B.	CAR	235	UNION TO
WILLIAMS, JOHN C.	CAL	006	1ST DIST
WILLIAMS, JOHN C.	MGM	377	ROCKERLE
WILLIAMS, JOHN D.	DOR	324	1ST DIST
WILLIAMS, JOHN D.	BAL	038	2ND DIST
WILLIAMS, JOHN F.	BAL	156	1ST WARD
WILLIAMS, JOHN G.	BAL	140	1ST WARD
WILLIAMS, JOHN H.	ANN	448	HOWARD D
WILLIAMS, JOHN H.	DOR	317	1ST DIST
WILLIAMS, JOHN H.	FRE	012	FREDERIC
WILLIAMS, JOHN H.	FRE	447	8TH E DI
WILLIAMS, JOHN H.	ST	346	5TH E DI
WILLIAMS, JOHN H.	PRI	054	AQUASCO
WILLIAMS, JOHN M.	CAL	006	1ST DIST
WILLIAMS, JOHN M.	BAL	009	4TH WARD
WILLIAMS, JOHN S.	BAL	291	12TH WAR
WILLIAMS, JOHN SR.	WOR	240	6TH E DI
WILLIAMS, JOHN T.	MGM	411	MEDLEY 3
WILLIAMS, JOHN W.	BAL	058	4TH WARD
WILLIAMS, JOHN W.	BAL	131	16TH WAR
WILLIAMS, JOHN W.	BAL	143	16TH WAR
WILLIAMS, JOHN W.	BAL	024	2ND DIST
WILLIAMS, JOHN W.	BAL	277	2ND WARD
WILLIAMS, JOHN W.	BAL	457	8TH WARD
WILLIAMS, JOHN W.	BAL	356	3RD WARD
WILLIAMS, JOHN WILBER	BAL	029	18TH WAR
WILLIAMS, JOHN-BLACK	FRE	044	FREDERIC
WILLIAMS, JOHN-BLACK	FRE	028	FREDERIC
WILLIAMS, JOHNB	BAL	114	1ST WARD
WILLIAMS, JOHNSY	BAL	212	6TH DIST
WILLIAMS, JOP B.	ANN	438	HOWARD D
WILLIAMS, JOSEPH	ANN	438	HOWARD D
WILLIAMS, JOSEPH	ALL	239	CUMBERLA
WILLIAMS, JOSEPH	BAL	136	2ND DIST
WILLIAMS, JOSEPH	BAL	117	1ST WARD
WILLIAMS, JOSEPH	BAL	055	1ST WARD
WILLIAMS, JOSEPH	BAL	005	1ST WARD
WILLIAMS, JOSEPH	BAL	185	11TH WAR
WILLIAMS, JOSEPH	BAL	301	12TH WAR
WILLIAMS, JOSEPH	BAL	277	12TH WAR
WILLIAMS, JOSEPH	ALL	111	5TH E.D.
WILLIAMS, JOSEPH	BAL	362	13TH WAR
WILLIAMS, JOSEPH	BAL	184	19TH WAR
WILLIAMS, JOSEPH	WOR	214	4TH E DI
WILLIAMS, JOSEPH	TAL	010	EASTON D
WILLIAMS, JOSEPH-BLACK	BAL	218	2ND WARD
WILLIAMS, JOSEPHIEN	BAL	321	1ST DIST
WILLIAMS, JOSEPHINE	BAL	029	9TH WARD
WILLIAMS, JOSEPHINE	BAL	195	11TH WAR
WILLIAMS, JOSHUA	BAL	301	12TH WAR
WILLIAMS, JOSHUA	BAL	116	2ND DIST
WILLIAMS, JOSHUA	BAL	118	2ND DIST
WILLIAMS, JOSHUA	ANN	369	4TH DIST
WILLIAMS, JOSHUA	BAL	093	2ND DIST
WILLIAMS, JOSHUA	BAL	414	3RD WARD
WILLIAMS, JOSHUA	SOM	407	DUBLIN D
WILLIAMS, JSEOPH	BAL	131	16TH WAR
WILLIAMS, JUDY	SOM	392	BRINKLEY
WILLIAMS, JULIA	BAL	110	10TH WAR
WILLIAMS, JULIA	BAL	375	13TH WAR
WILLIAMS, JULIA A.	ANN	446	HOWARD D
WILLIAMS, JULIA ANN	SOM	541	TYASKIN
WILLIAMS, JULIANA	QUE	248	5TH E DI
WILLIAMS, JULIET	BAL	308	3RD WARD
WILLIAMS, KETTY	BAL	026	2ND DIST
WILLIAMS, KIRTES*	DOR	327	3RD DIVI
WILLIAMS, L.	BAL	168	1ST WARD
WILLIAMS, LAUANDA-BLACK	BAL	219	2ND WARD
WILLIAMS, LAURA A.	BAL	058	10TH WAR
WILLIAMS, LEAH	BAL	349	13TH WAR
WILLIAMS, LEAH	SOM	421	PRINCESS
WILLIAMS, LEAH	WOR	298	9TH E DI
WILLIAMS, LEATH	BAL	010	EASTERN
WILLIAMS, LETTY	PRI	034	VANSVILL
WILLIAMS, LEURGUS *	BAL	415	1ST DIST
WILLIAMS, LEVI	BAL	418	1ST DIST
WILLIAMS, LEVI	WOR	247	1ST CENS
WILLIAMS, LEVIN	SOM	504	SALISBUR
WILLIAMS, LEVIN	CAR	195	4TH DIST
WILLIAMS, LEWIS	BAL	027	9TH WARD
WILLIAMS, LEWIS	BAL	143	5TH WARD
WILLIAMS, LEWIS	BAL	123	5TH WARD
WILLIAMS, LEWIS	BAL	401	8TH WARD
WILLIAMS, LEWIS J.	HAR	139	2ND DIST
WILLIAMS, LIDIA	BAL	381	1ST DIST
WILLIAMS, LITTLETON	BAL	300	3RD WARD
WILLIAMS, LITTLETON-MULAT	BAL	136	1ST WARD
WILLIAMS, LORTON	BAL	293	17TH WAR
WILLIAMS, LOUIE	SOM	413	DUBLIN D
WILLIAMS, LOUIS H.	BAL	116	11TH WAR
WILLIAMS, LOUISA	BAL	378	13TH WAR
WILLIAMS, LOUISA	BAL	048	18TH WAR
WILLIAMS, LOUISA	FRE	452	8TH E DI
WILLIAMS, LOUISA	BAL	425	8TH WARD
WILLIAMS, LOUISA	BAL	207	6TH WARD
WILLIAMS, LOUISA	ANN	357	3RD DIST
WILLIAMS, LOUISA	BAL	231	12TH WAR
WILLIAMS, LOUISA	ANN	270	ANNAPOLI
WILLIAMS, LOUISA	BAL	077	1ST WARD
WILLIAMS, LOUISA M.	CAL	033	2ND DIST
WILLIAMS, LOYD	BAL	286	1ST DIST
WILLIAMS, LOYD W.	BAL	007	EASTERN
WILLIAMS, LUCULIA	CEC	194	7TH E DI
WILLIAMS, LUCURGUS *	BAL	415	1ST DIST
WILLIAMS, LUCY	ANN	506	HOWARD D
WILLIAMS, LUTHER	BAL	218	6TH DIST
WILLIAMS, LYDIA	BAL	006	9TH WARD
WILLIAMS, LYDIA	BAL	090	15TH WAR
WILLIAMS, LYDIA	BAL	122	16TH WAR
WILLIAMS, MADALINE R.	BAL	260	2ND WARD
WILLIAMS, MADISON	CAR	160	NO TWP L
WILLIAMS, MADISON A.	FRE	234	BUCKEYST
WILLIAMS, MAGER	WOR	312	2ND E DI
WILLIAMS, MANA	BAL	221	12TH WAR
WILLIAMS, MANUEL	HAR	184	3RD DIST
WILLIAMS, MARGARET	FRE	162	EMMITTSB
WILLIAMS, MARGARET	HAR	154	3RD DIST
WILLIAMS, MARGARET	BAL	273	20TH WAR
WILLIAMS, MARGARET	DOR	296	1ST DIST
WILLIAMS, MARGARET	BAL	004	9TH WARD
WILLIAMS, MARGARET	BAL	277	2ND WARD
WILLIAMS, MARGARET	BAL	121	16TH WAR
WILLIAMS, MARGARET	BAL	094	2ND DIST
WILLIAMS, MARGARET	BAL	059	1ST WARD
WILLIAMS, MARGARET	ALL	177	7TH E.D.
WILLIAMS, MARGARET	WOR	264	BERLIN 1
WILLIAMS, MARGARET	PRI	121	PISCATAW
WILLIAMS, MARGARET	SOM	384	BRINKLEY
WILLIAMS, MARGARET A.	KEN	250	2ND DIST
WILLIAMS, MARGARETT	BAL	082	4TH WARD
WILLIAMS, MARIA	BAL	232	17TH WAR
WILLIAMS, MARIA	BAL	256	20TH WAR
WILLIAMS, MARIA	BAL	156	11TH WAR
WILLIAMS, MARIA	FRE	043	FREDERIC
WILLIAMS, MARIA	HAR	076	BEL AIR
WILLIAMS, MARIA	BAL	004	EASTERN
WILLIAMS, MARIA	ALL	217	CUMBERLA
WILLIAMS, MARIA	BAL	108	15TH WAR
WILLIAMS, MARIA	BAL	286	12TH WAR
WILLIAMS, MARIA	BAL	261	6TH WARD
WILLIAMS, MARIA	BAL	256	12TH WAR
WILLIAMS, MARIA	BAL	205	11TH WAR
WILLIAMS, MARIA	BAL	175	11TH WAR
WILLIAMS, MARIA C.	BAL	323	12TH WAR
WILLIAMS, MARIA-BLACK	FRE	046	FREDERIC
WILLIAMS, MARIAH	CAR	206	4TH DIST
WILLIAMS, MARIAH	SOM	400	BRINKLEY
WILLIAMS, MARIAH	WOR	321	1ST E DI
WILLIAMS, MARIAH	TAL	017	EASTON D
WILLIAMS, MARIAH-BLACK	CAR	096	NO TWP L
WILLIAMS, MARTHA	CAR	233	5TH DIST
WILLIAMS, MARTHA	HAR	041	1ST DIST
WILLIAMS, MARTHA	WOR	303	SNOW HIL
WILLIAMS, MARTHA	TAL	001	EASTON D
WILLIAMS, MARTHA	BAL	254	12TH WAR
WILLIAMS, MARTHA H.	WOR	262	BERLIN 1
WILLIAMS, MARY	WOR	262	BERLIN 1
WILLIAMS, MARY	SOM	360	BRINKLEY
WILLIAMS, MARY	SOM	386	BRINKLEY
WILLIAMS, MARY	ST	290	2ND E DI
WILLIAMS, MARY	WAS	192	1ST DIST
WILLIAMS, MARY	BAL	247	12TH WAR
WILLIAMS, MARY	BAL	167	11TH WAR
WILLIAMS, MARY	BAL	197	11TH WAR
WILLIAMS, MARY	BAL	011	9TH WARD
WILLIAMS, MARY	BAL	111	15TH WAR
WILLIAMS, MARY	BAL	174	16TH WAR
WILLIAMS, MARY	BAL	255	6TH WARD
WILLIAMS, MARY	BAL	377	8TH WARD
WILLIAMS, MARY	BAL	304	7TH WARD
WILLIAMS, MARY	BAL	389	3RD WARD
WILLIAMS, MARY	BAL	095	2ND DIST
WILLIAMS, MARY	BAL	044	2ND DIST
WILLIAMS, MARY	ALL	089	5TH E.D.
WILLIAMS, MARY	BAL	434	1ST DIST
WILLIAMS, MARY	BAL	288	3RD WARD
WILLIAMS, MARY	BAL	134	5TH WARD
WILLIAMS, MARY	BAL	245	6TH WARD
WILLIAMS, MARY	SOM	421	PRINCESS
WILLIAMS, MARY	HAR	022	1ST DIST
WILLIAMS, MARY	HAR	092	2ND DIST
WILLIAMS, MARY	BAL	412	3RD WARD
WILLIAMS, MARY	CEC	003	ELKTON 3
WILLIAMS, MARY	CEC	003	ELKTON 3
WILLIAMS, MARY	BAL	471	14TH WAR
WILLIAMS, MARY	BAL	453	14TH WAR
WILLIAMS, MARY	CEC	197	7TH E DI
WILLIAMS, MARY	BAL	071	4TH WARD
WILLIAMS, MARY	CEC	146	PORT DUP
WILLIAMS, MARY	HAR	147	3RD DIST
WILLIAMS, MARY	BAL	082	18TH WAR
WILLIAMS, MARY A.	BAL	311	7TH WARD
WILLIAMS, MARY A.	BAL	440	8TH WARD
WILLIAMS, MARY E.	BAL	151	5TH WARD
WILLIAMS, MARY E.	CHA	251	MIDDLETO
WILLIAMS, MARY E.	WOR	282	BERLIN 1
WILLIAMS, MARY F.	WAS	219	1ST DIST
WILLIAMS, MARY J.	BAL	064	4TH WARD
WILLIAMS, MARY J.	BAL	411	3RD WARD
WILLIAMS, MARY J.	ANN	454	HOWARD D
WILLIAMS, MARY L.-BLACK	BAL	215	2ND WARD
WILLIAMS, MARY LOUISA	BAL	125	11TH WAR
WILLIAMS, MARY V.	BAL	338	7TH WARD
WILLIAMS, MARY W.	CAR	068	NO TWP L
WILLIAMS, MARY-BLACK	FRE	036	FREDERIC
WILLIAMS, MARY-BLACK	WOR	324	1ST E DI
WILLIAMS, MARY-MULATTO	BAL	233	2ND WARD
WILLIAMS, MATILDA	BAL	239	12TH WAR
WILLIAMS, MATILDA	PRI	029	VANSVILL
WILLIAMS, MATILDA	SOM	444	DAMES QU
WILLIAMS, MATILDA	BAL	032	4TH WARD
WILLIAMS, MATILDA J.	BAL	100	15TH WAR
WILLIAMS, MICAJAH	BAL	024	2ND DIST
WILLIAMS, MICHAEL	ANN	453	HOWARD D
WILLIAMS, MILBY	WOR	295	9TH E DI
WILLIAMS, MILLY	BAL	227	19TH WAR
WILLIAMS, MILLY	BAL	340	13TH WAR
WILLIAMS, MINTY	BAL	084	15TH WAR
WILLIAMS, MISS	ANN	268	ANNAPOLI
WILLIAMS, MONICHA	ST	307	1ST E DI
WILLIAMS, MORZILLA	WOR	328	1ST E DI
WILLIAMS, N.	BAL	157	1ST WARD
WILLIAMS, NANCY	BAL	106	10TH WAR
WILLIAMS, NANCY	BAL	279	12TH WAR
WILLIAMS, NARON	WOR	284	BERLIN 1
WILLIAMS, NATHAN	KEN	274	1ST DIST
WILLIAMS, NATHAN	BAL	279	12TH WAR
WILLIAMS, NATHAN	DOR	324	1ST DIST
WILLIAMS, NATHAN-BLACK	CAR	169	NO TWP L
WILLIAMS, NATHANEL	WAS	116	2ND DIST
WILLIAMS, NATHANIEL	WAS	229	1ST DIST
WILLIAMS, NATHANIEL	BAL	241	20TH WAR
WILLIAMS, NATHANIEL Y.	BAL	148	11TH WAR
WILLIAMS, NED	ANN	322	2ND DIST
WILLIAMS, NELLY	BAL	195	17TH WAR
WILLIAMS, NELSON	BAL	196	11TH WAR
WILLIAMS, NELSON	BAL	185	11TH WAR
WILLIAMS, NELSON	BAL	185	11TH WAR
WILLIAMS, NELSON	BAL	456	1ST DIST
WILLIAMS, NELSON	BAL	170	2ND DIST
WILLIAMS, NOAH	BAL	282	17TH WAR
WILLIAMS, NOAH	SOM	365	BRINKLEY
WILLIAMS, NOAH	SOM	479	TRAPP DI
WILLIAMS, OCTAVIA	SOM	498	SALISBUR
WILLIAMS, OSCAR	BAL	312	12TH WAR
WILLIAMS, OTHO	WAS	027	2ND SUBD
WILLIAMS, OWEN	WAS	141	HAGERSTO
WILLIAMS, OWEN	BAL	041	9TH WARD
WILLIAMS, OWEN	BAL	417	14TH WAR
WILLIAMS, P.	BAL	141	1ST WARD
WILLIAMS, PALPH	HAR	202	3RD DIST
WILLIAMS, PAUL	BAL	006	9TH WARD
WILLIAMS, PEMBROKE	BAL	050	4TH WARD
WILLIAMS, PERRY	TAL	100	ST MICHA
WILLIAMS, PETER	WOR	301	SNOW HIL
WILLIAMS, PETER	FRE	318	MIDDLETO
WILLIAMS, PETER	CHA	235	HILLTOP
WILLIAMS, PETER	BAL	139	1ST WARD
WILLIAMS, PETER	BAL	269	2ND WARD
WILLIAMS, PETER	BAL	126	1ST WARD
WILLIAMS, PETER	BAL	013	1ST WARD
WILLIAMS, PHENIES	WAS	198	1ST DIST
WILLIAMS, PHILLIP	BAL	167	6TH WARD
WILLIAMS, PHILLIP	BAL	194	17TH WAR
WILLIAMS, PHOEBE	BAL	401	8TH WARD
WILLIAMS, POLLY	SOM	539	TYASKIN
WILLIAMS, POLLY	BAL	422	14TH WAR
WILLIAMS, POLLY	BAL	354	13TH WAR
WILLIAMS, POMPEY	BAL	075	4TH WARD
WILLIAMS, PRICELLA	SOM	393	BRINKLEY
WILLIAMS, R.	BAL	229	12TH WAR
WILLIAMS, R.	ANN	392	4TH DIST
WILLIAMS, RACHAEL	BAL	433	14TH WAR
WILLIAMS, RACHAEL	HAR	130	2ND DIST
WILLIAMS, RACHEL	BAL	293	20TH WAR
WILLIAMS, RACHEL	ANN	364	4TH DIST
WILLIAMS, RACHEL	ANN	357	3RD DIST
WILLIAMS, RACHEL	ANN	456	HOWARD D
WILLIAMS, RACHEL	BAL	249	12TH WAR
WILLIAMS, RACHEL	BAL	147	16TH WAR
WILLIAMS, RACHEL	BAL	168	6TH WARD
WILLIAMS, RACHEL	ANN	298	1ST DIST
WILLIAMS, RACHEL	QUE	205	3RD E DI
WILLIAMS, RACHEL A.	BAL	121	16TH WAR
WILLIAMS, RACHELL	BAL	126	5TH WARD
WILLIAMS, REBEC	BAL	314	12TH WAR
WILLIAMS, REBECCA	ANN	415	HOWARD D
WILLIAMS, REBECCA	BAL	026	15TH WAR
WILLIAMS, REBECCA	BAL	313	3RD WARD
WILLIAMS, REBECCA	TAL	017	EASTON D
WILLIAMS, REBECCA	CEC	200	7TH E DI
WILLIAMS, REBECCA	BAL	087	4TH WARD
WILLIAMS, REBECCA	BAL	030	18TH WAR
WILLIAMS, REBECCA	CAL	033	2ND DIST
WILLIAMS, REBECCA	BAL	472	14TH WAR
WILLIAMS, REBECCA S.	BAL	070	10TH WAR
WILLIAMS, REVERDY	BAL	149	1ST WARD
WILLIAMS, RHODA	BAL	278	12TH WAR
WILLIAMS, RHUBEN	BAL	266	1ST DIST
WILLIAMS, RICHARD	BAL	247	1ST DIST
WILLIAMS, RICHARD	BAL	458	8TH WARD
WILLIAMS, RICHARD	BAL	133	2ND DIST
WILLIAMS, RICHARD	BAL	124	11TH WAR
WILLIAMS, RICHARD	BAL	003	18TH WAR
WILLIAMS, RICHARD	BAL	207	17TH WAR

WILLIAMS, RICHARD CHA 251 MIDDLETO
WILLIAMS, RICHARD CEC 041 CHESAPEA
WILLIAMS, RICHARD HAR 046 1ST DIST
WILLIAMS, RICHARD FRE 090 FREDERIC
WILLIAMS, RICHARD FRE 098 FREDERIC
WILLIAMS, RICHARD MGM 392 ROCKERLE
WILLIAMS, RICHARD QUE 219 3RD E DI
WILLIAMS, RICHARD QUE 209 3RD E DI
WILLIAMS, RICHARD H. MGM 315 CRACKLIN
WILLIAMS, RICHARD T. CAR 365 9TH DIST
WILLIAMS, RICHARD W. MGM 410 MEDLEY 3
WILLIAMS, ROBERT CEC 019 ELKTON 3
WILLIAMS, ROBERT CEC 196 6TH E DI
WILLIAMS, ROBERT BAL 269 20TH WAR
WILLIAMS, ROBERT ST 290 2ND E DI
WILLIAMS, ROBERT SOM 504 SALISBUR
WILLIAMS, ROBERT BAL 355 3RD WARD
WILLIAMS, ROBERT BAL 106 15TH WAR
WILLIAMS, ROBERT BAL 106 15TH WAR
WILLIAMS, ROBERT BAL 201 6TH WARD
WILLIAMS, ROBERT BAL 170 1ST WARD
WILLIAMS, ROBERT ALL 089 5TH E.D.
WILLIAMS, ROBERT ALL 089 5TH E.D.
WILLIAMS, ROBERT A. ST 260 3RD E DI
WILLIAMS, ROBERT M. MGM 406 MEDLEY 3
WILLIAMS, ROBERT-BLACK WOR 339 1ST E DI
WILLIAMS, ROBERT-BLCK CAR 381 2ND DIST
WILLIAMS, ROBERT-MULATTO FRE 174 5TH E DI
WILLIAMS, ROBERTA E. MGM 393 ROCKERLE
WILLIAMS, RODNEY BAL 234 20TH WAR
WILLIAMS, ROSEANA BAL 334 1ST DIST
WILLIAMS, RUTH ANN MGM 390 ROCKERLE
WILLIAMS, RUTH E. HAR 122 2ND DIST
WILLIAMS, S. BAL 235 20TH WAR
WILLIAMS, S. BAL 216 11TH WAR
WILLIAMS, S. BAL 130 1ST WARD
WILLIAMS, SALEM BAL 213 6TH DIST
WILLIAMS, SALLY WOR 246 1ST CENS
WILLIAMS, SAMPSON WOR 179 6TH E DI
WILLIAMS, SAMUEL PRI 114 PISCATAW
WILLIAMS, SAMUEL WOR 190 8TH E DI
WILLIAMS, SAMUEL WOR 193 8TH E DI
WILLIAMS, SAMUEL WAS 115 2ND DIST
WILLIAMS, SAMUEL SOM 366 BRINKLEY
WILLIAMS, SAMUEL SOM 470 TRAPPE D
WILLIAMS, SAMUEL SOM 467 HANGARY
WILLIAMS, SAMUEL MGM 440 CLARKSTR
WILLIAMS, SAMUEL WAS 114 2ND DIST
WILLIAMS, SAMUEL WAS 094 2ND SUBD
WILLIAMS, SAMUEL BAL 313 7TH WARD
WILLIAMS, SAMUEL ALL 186 9TH E.D.
WILLIAMS, SAMUEL ALL 045 10TH E.D
WILLIAMS, SAMUEL BAL 239 6TH WARD
WILLIAMS, SAMUEL BAL 191 5TH DIST
WILLIAMS, SAMUEL CEC 019 ELKTON 3
WILLIAMS, SAMUEL BAL 257 17TH WAR
WILLIAMS, SAMUEL DOR 306 1ST DIST
WILLIAMS, SAMUEL BAL 128 11TH WAR
WILLIAMS, SAMUEL C. BAL 217 6TH DIST
WILLIAMS, SAMUEL N.S. MGM 418 MEDLEY 3
WILLIAMS, SAMUEL T. SOM 507 BARREN C
WILLIAMS, SARAH WOR 313 2ND E DI
WILLIAMS, SARAH WOR 300 SNOW HIL
WILLIAMS, SARAH WAS 217 1ST DIST
WILLIAMS, SARAH WAS 268 1ST DIST
WILLIAMS, SARAH MGM 391 ROCKERLE
WILLIAMS, SARAH SOM 434 PRINCESS
WILLIAMS, SARAH SOM 444 DAMES QU
WILLIAMS, SARAH BAL 135 11TH WAR
WILLIAMS, SARAH BAL 140 11TH WAR
WILLIAMS, SARAH CEC 127 5TH E DI
WILLIAMS, SARAH BAL 380 13TH WAR
WILLIAMS, SARAH BAL 381 13TH WAR
WILLIAMS, SARAH BAL 379 13TH WAR
WILLIAMS, SARAH CAR 222 5TH DIST
WILLIAMS, SARAH CEC 197 7TH E DI
WILLIAMS, SARAH BAL 303 3RD WARD
WILLIAMS, SARAH BAL 156 2ND DIST
WILLIAMS, SARAH BAL 216 6TH WARD
WILLIAMS, SARAH BAL 152 5TH WARD
WILLIAMS, SARAH BAL 032 9TH WARD
WILLIAMS, SARAH BAL 401 8TH WARD
WILLIAMS, SARAH BAL 293 12TH WAR
WILLIAMS, SARAH BAL 187 16TH WAR
WILLIAMS, SARAH BAL 110 2ND DIST
WILLIAMS, SARAH ANN 434 HOWARD D
WILLIAMS, SARAH A. ANN 369 4TH DIST
WILLIAMS, SARAH A. CAL 038 2ND DIST
WILLIAMS, SARAH A. CAL 052 3RD DIST
WILLIAMS, SARAH E. CAL 030 2ND DIST
WILLIAMS, SARAH J. SOM 488 SALISBUR
WILLIAMS, SARAH K. BAL 335 13TH WAR
WILLIAMS, SETH PRI 107 PISCATAW
WILLIAMS, SEWALL CEC 016 ELKTON 3
WILLIAMS, SHADRICK BAL 168 1ST WARD
WILLIAMS, SIDNEY CAL 035 2ND DIST
WILLIAMS, SIMON SOM 479 TRAPP DI
WILLIAMS, SOLOMON HAR 183 3RD DIST
WILLIAMS, SOLOMON BAL 341 7TH WARD
WILLIAMS, SOPHIA BAL 200 6TH WARD
WILLIAMS, SOPHIA BAL 098 10TH WAR
WILLIAMS, SOPHIA BAL 130 11TH WAR
WILLIAMS, SOTHA-BLACK WOR 343 1ST E DI
WILLIAMS, SPENCER ALL 196 CUMBERLA
WILLIAMS, STEPHEN BAL 179 2ND DIST
WILLIAMS, STEPHEN WOR 245 1ST CENS
WILLIAMS, STEPHEN BAL 042 4TH WARD
WILLIAMS, SUSAN BAL 044 18TH WAR
WILLIAMS, SUSAN BAL 474 14TH WAR
WILLIAMS, SUSAN CEC 045 1ST E DI
WILLIAMS, SUSAN BAL 234 20TH WAR
WILLIAMS, SUSAN ANN 486 HOWARD D
WILLIAMS, SUSAN T. BAL 194 11TH WAR
WILLIAMS, SUSANNAH BAL 089 15TH WAR
WILLIAMS, T. R. A. BAL 340 13TH WAR
WILLIAMS, TEAGLE WOR 185 7TH E DI
WILLIAMS, THEODORE PRI 084 QUEEN AN
WILLIAMS, THEODORE WOR 300 SNOW HIL
WILLIAMS, THOMAS WAS 036 2ND SUBD
WILLIAMS, THOMAS WOR 285 BERLIN 1
WILLIAMS, THOMAS PRI 079 QUEEN AN
WILLIAMS, THOMAS PRI 091 MARLBROU
WILLIAMS, THOMAS SOM 501 SALISBUR
WILLIAMS, THOMAS WOR 339 1ST E DI
WILLIAMS, THOMAS BAL 267 17TH WAR
WILLIAMS, THOMAS BAL 419 14TH WAR
WILLIAMS, THOMAS BAL 206 19TH WAR
WILLIAMS, THOMAS BAL 207 19TH WAR
WILLIAMS, THOMAS HAR 138 2ND DIST
WILLIAMS, THOMAS CEC 211 7TH E DI
WILLIAMS, THOMAS DOR 417 1ST DIST
WILLIAMS, THOMAS BAL 280 12TH WAR
WILLIAMS, THOMAS BAL 255 12TH WAR
WILLIAMS, THOMAS BAL 024 9TH WARD
WILLIAMS, THOMAS BAL 024 9TH WARD
WILLIAMS, THOMAS BAL 175 6TH WARD
WILLIAMS, THOMAS BAL 025 2ND DIST
WILLIAMS, THOMAS BAL 133 1ST WARD
WILLIAMS, THOMAS BAL 260 2ND WARD
WILLIAMS, THOMAS H. BAL 134 11TH WAR
WILLIAMS, THOMAS L. BAL 312 7TH WARD
WILLIAMS, THOMAS P. FRE 412 8TH E DI
WILLIAMS, THOMAS P. TAL 025 EASTON D
WILLIAMS, THOMAS S. ANN 367 4TH DIST
WILLIAMS, THOMAS-BLACK BAL 219 2ND WARD
WILLIAMS, THOMS ALL 142 6TH E.D.
WILLIAMS, TIMOTHY HAR 096 2ND DIST
WILLIAMS, URIAH FRE 388 PETERSVI
WILLIAMS, VALENTINE ANN 480 HOWARD D
WILLIAMS, W.H.H. BAL 174 1ST WARD
WILLIAMS, W.J. BAL 161 1ST WARD
WILLIAMS, WALTER BAL 242 6TH WARD
WILLIAMS, WALTER BAL 456 8TH WARD
WILLIAMS, WALTER BAL 368 3RD WARD
WILLIAMS, WASHINGTON DOR 435 1ST DIST
WILLIAMS, WESLEY BAL 395 14TH WAR
WILLIAMS, WESLEY BAL 072 1ST WARD
WILLIAMS, WESLEY ANN 370 4TH DIST
WILLIAMS, WESLEY ANN 415 HOWARD D
WILLIAMS, WHITINTON* DOR 323 1ST DIST
WILLIAMS, WILIAM CAR 231 5TH DIST
WILLIAMS, WILIAM CAR 283 7TH DIST
WILLIAMS, WILLIAM BAL 301 17TH WAR
WILLIAMS, WILLIAM BAL 304 17TH WAR
WILLIAMS, WILLIAM CEC 091 4TH E DI
WILLIAMS, WILLIAM BAL 082 18TH WAR
WILLIAMS, WILLIAM BAL 236 20TH WAR
WILLIAMS, WILLIAM CEC 014 ELKTON 3
WILLIAMS, WILLIAM CAR 167 NO TWP L
WILLIAMS, WILLIAM BAL 292 20TH WAR
WILLIAMS, WILLIAM BAL 128 18TH WAR
WILLIAMS, WILLIAM FRE 044 FREDERIC
WILLIAMS, WILLIAM MGM 342 CLARKSBU
WILLIAMS, WILLIAM HAR 132 2ND DIST
WILLIAMS, WILLIAM HAR 162 3RD DIST
WILLIAMS, WILLIAM BAL 205 17TH WAR
WILLIAMS, WILLIAM BAL 270 17TH WAR
WILLIAMS, WILLIAM BAL 355 13TH WAR
WILLIAMS, WILLIAM ANN 414 HOWARD D
WILLIAMS, WILLIAM BAL 310 1ST DIST
WILLIAMS, WILLIAM ANN 375 4TH DIST
WILLIAMS, WILLIAM ANN 346 3RD DIST
WILLIAMS, WILLIAM BAL 012 2ND DIST
WILLIAMS, WILLIAM BAL 062 2ND DIST
WILLIAMS, WILLIAM BAL 042 2ND DIST
WILLIAMS, WILLIAM ANN 416 HOWARD D
WILLIAMS, WILLIAM BAL 137 2ND DIST
WILLIAMS, WILLIAM BAL 144 2ND DIST
WILLIAMS, WILLIAM BAL 176 2ND DIST
WILLIAMS, WILLIAM BAL 266 1ST DIST
WILLIAMS, WILLIAM BAL 113 1ST WARD
WILLIAMS, WILLIAM BAL 235 12TH WAR
WILLIAMS, WILLIAM BAL 156 1ST WARD
WILLIAMS, WILLIAM BAL 160 1ST WARD
WILLIAMS, WILLIAM BAL 311 7TH WARD
WILLIAMS, WILLIAM BAL 232 2ND WARD
WILLIAMS, WILLIAM BAL 279 2ND WARD
WILLIAMS, WILLIAM BAL 146 1ST WARD
WILLIAMS, WILLIAM BAL 130 16TH WAR
WILLIAMS, WILLIAM BAL 192 17TH WAR
WILLIAMS, WILLIAM BAL 120 16TH WAR
WILLIAMS, WILLIAM BAL 148 16TH WAR
WILLIAMS, WILLIAM BAL 337 7TH WARD
WILLIAMS, WILLIAM BAL 211 6TH DIST
WILLIAMS, WILLIAM WOR 285 BERLIN 1
WILLIAMS, WILLIAM PRI 021 VANSVILL
WILLIAMS, WILLIAM QUE 242 5TH E DI
WILLIAMS, WILLIAM QUE 239 5TH E DI
WILLIAMS, WILLIAM SOM 497 SALISBUR
WILLIAMS, WILLIAM TAL 103 ST MICHA
WILLIAMS, WILLIAM SOM 487 SALISBUR
WILLIAMS, WILLIAM WAS 243 CAVETOWN
WILLIAMS, WILLIAM SOM 468 TRAPPE D
WILLIAMS, WILLIAM A. DOR 308 1ST DIST
WILLIAMS, WILLIAM A. FRE 276 NEW MARK
WILLIAMS, WILLIAM C. BAL 379 3RD WARD
WILLIAMS, WILLIAM H. BAL 104 1ST WARD
WILLIAMS, WILLIAM H. BAL 320 3RD WARD
WILLIAMS, WILLIAM H. BAL 174 16TH WAR
WILLIAMS, WILLIAM H. CAR 399 2ND DIST
WILLIAMS, WILLIAM H. BAL 267 17TH WAR
WILLIAMS, WILLIAM J. BAL 096 5TH WARD
WILLIAMS, WILLIAM J. BAL 160 1ST WARD
WILLIAMS, WILLIAM J. BAL 167 1ST WARD
WILLIAMS, WILLIAM J. BAL 171 1ST WARD
WILLIAMS, WILLIAM J. SOM 539 TYASKIN
WILLIAMS, WILLIAM L. BAL 311 7TH WARD
WILLIAMS, WILLIAM M. CEC 147 PORT DUP
WILLIAMS, WILLIAM N. CAR 081 NO TWP L
WILLIAMS, WILLIAM P. SOM 363 BRINKLEY
WILLIAMS, WILLIAM S. BAL 145 16TH WAR
WILLIAMS, WILLIAM SR.* SOM 363 BRINKLEY
WILLIAMS, ZACARIAH BAL 070 4TH WARD
WILLIAMS, ZACHARIAH MGM 417 MEDLEY 3
WILLIAMS, ZEDEKIAH SOM 403 BRINKLEY
WILLIAMS.A NN CAR 095 NO TWP L
WILLIAMS.E DWARD BAL 115 1ST WARD
WILLIAMS.ELIAS BAL 133 1ST WARD
WILLIAMS.HAMILTON FRE 202 5TH E DI
WILLIAMS.J. BAL 135 1ST WARD
WILLIAMS.J.G. BAL 161 1ST WARD
WILLIAMS.JOHN BAL 126 1ST WARD
WILLIAMS.JOHN J. FRE 442 8TH E DI
WILLIAMS.MORRIS BAL 134 1ST WARD
WILLIAMS.P. BAL 116 1ST WARD
WILLIAMS.WILLIAM BAL 124 1ST WARD
WILLIAMS.WILLIAM BAL 162 1ST WARD
WILLIAMSON, AARON CAR 151 NO TWP L
WILLIAMSON, ALEXANDER S. BAL 015 1ST WARD
WILLIAMSON, ALEXANDER BAL 261 6TH WARD
WILLIAMSON, ANDREW BAL 259 20TH WAR
WILLIAMSON, ARIANA QUE 171 2ND E DI
WILLIAMSON, CATHARINE E. WAS 151 HAGERSTO
WILLIAMSON, CHARLES QUE 150 1ST E DI
WILLIAMSON, CHARLES BAL 371 8TH WARD
WILLIAMSON, CHARLES BAL 421 8TH WARD
WILLIAMSON, CHARLES A. BAL 104 10TH WAR
WILLIAMSON, DAVID WAS 146 HAGERSTO
WILLIAMSON, ELIJAH CAR 153 NO TWP L
WILLIAMSON, ELIZA BAL 031 9TH WARD
WILLIAMSON, ELIZA H. HAR 008 1ST DIST
WILLIAMSON, ELIZABETH BAL 364 8TH WARD
WILLIAMSON, FRANCIS BAL 116 11TH WAR
WILLIAMSON, GEORGE QUE 172 2ND E DI
WILLIAMSON, HARRIET BAL 363 3RD WARD
WILLIAMSON, HENRY H. BAL 257 1ST DIST
WILLIAMSON, ISAAC BAL 050 18TH WAR
WILLIAMSON, JAMES FRE 316 MIDDLETO
WILLIAMSON, JAMES A. BAL 251 6TH WARD
WILLIAMSON, JAMES G. BAL 096 5TH WARD
WILLIAMSON, JOHN BAL 142 1ST WARD
WILLIAMSON, JOHN ALL 088 5TH E.D.
WILLIAMSON, JOHN ALL 095 5TH E.D.
WILLIAMSON, JOHN BAL 275 20TH WAR
WILLIAMSON, JOHN TAL 014 EASTON D
WILLIAMSON, JOHN C. MGM 319 CRACKLIN
WILLIAMSON, JOHN D. BAL 018 18TH WAR
WILLIAMSON, JOHN S. HAR 007 1ST DIST
WILLIAMSON, JOHN Y. DOR 317 1ST DIST
WILLIAMSON, JONATHAN QUE 156 2ND E DI
WILLIAMSON, LETTY WAS 143 HAGERSTO
WILLIAMSON, M. PRI 106 PISCATAW
WILLIAMSON, MARGARET CEC 197 7TH E DI
WILLIAMSON, MARGARETT BAL 210 11TH WAR
WILLIAMSON, MARIA BAL 294 1ST DIST
WILLIAMSON, MARY L. BAL 432 8TH WARD
WILLIAMSON, MARY W. BAL 366 3RD WARD
WILLIAMSON, MILKY CAR 121 NO TWP L
WILLIAMSON, MITCHELL CAR 128 NO TWP L
WILLIAMSON, PAUL D. BAL 311 3RD WARD
WILLIAMSON, RULY BAL 204 19TH WAR
WILLIAMSON, SAMUEL BAL 218 6TH WARD
WILLIAMSON, THOAMS HAR 032 1ST DIST
WILLIAMSON, THOMAS BAL 309 12TH WAR
WILLIAMSON, VIRGINIA BAL 295 1ST DIST
WILLIAMSON, W. BAL 160 1ST WARD
WILLIAMSON, WARNER CAR 138 NO TWP L
WILLIAMSON, WARREN R. FRE 311 MIDDLETO
WILLIAMSON, WILIAM BAL 158 1ST WARD
WILLIAMSON, WILLIAM BAL 082 10TH WAR
WILLIAMSON, WILLIAM CAR 112 NO TWP L
WILLIAMSON, WILLIAM WAS 150 HAGERSTO
WILLIAMSON, WILLIAM ST 341 5TH E DI
WILLIAMSON, WILLIAM A. CAR 107 NO TWP L
WILLIAMSON, WILLIAM F. BAL 271 20TH WAR
WILLIAMSON, WILLIAM W. CAR 158 NO TWP L
WILLIAMSON.JAMES CAR 398 2ND DIST
WILLIAMSON.REUBIN CAR 114 NO TWP L
WILLIANS, L. BAL 172 1ST WARD
WILLIANS, VACHEL ANN 370 4TH DIST
WILLIAR, GEORGE * BAL 419 14TH WAR
WILLIAR, JACOB FRE 149 10TH E D
WILLIARD, ABRAHAM FRE 324 MIDDLETO
WILLIARD, ADAM FRE 416 8TH E DI
WILLIARD, AMANDA J. FRE 157 10TH E D
WILLIARD, CHARLES FRE 157 10TH E D
WILLIARD, DEWALT FRE 392 PETERSVI
WILLIARD, ELIZABETH WAS 164 HAGERSTO
WILLIARD, ELLENORA BAL 255 17TH WAR
WILLIARD, EZRA FRE 146 10TH E D
WILLIARD, EZRA FRE 156 10TH E D
WILLIARD, GEORGE FRE 157 10TH E D
WILLIARD, HENRY FRE 408 JEFFERSO
WILLIARD, JOHN FRE 146 10TH E D
WILLIARD, JOHN WAS 162 HAGERSTO
WILLIARD, JOSIAH FRE 195 5TH E DI
WILLIARD, LEWIS E. FRE 144 10TH E D
WILLIARD, MARY FRE 396 PETERSVI
WILLIARD, PETER FRE 324 MIDDLETO
WILLIAS, NATHANIEL F. BAL 263 1ST DIST
WILLIAS, PETGER WOR 285 BERLIN 1
WILLIASM, CHARLES BAL 229 17TH WAR
WILLIASM, KISSY ANN 285 ANNAPOLI
WILLIASM, RICAHRD BAL 351 13TH WAR
WILLIASM, SALLY BAL 343 13TH WAR
WILLIASM, SOLOMON FRE 343 MIDDLETO
WILLIASM, TOBIAS BAL 102 2ND DIST
WILLIASM, WILLIAM J. BAL 164 1ST WARD
WILLIG, CHARLES BAL 080 1ST WARD
WILLIG, GEORGE BAL 193 11TH WAR
WILLIG, JAMES A. BAL 102 5TH WARD
WILLIGMAN, CHARITY BAL 205 11TH WAR
WILLIGMAN, SARAH E. BAL 205 11TH WAR
WILLIMAS, BENJAMIN H. CAL 027 2ND DIST
WILLIMAS, C. S. WOR 261 BERLIN 1
WILLIMAS, COLLIER HAR 183 3RD DIST
WILLIMAS, F. A. WOR 260 BERLIN 1
WILLIMAS, GEORGE BAL 155 5TH WARD
WILLIMAS, HARRIETT BAL 099 5TH WARD
WILLIMAS, HOOPER BAL 152 16TH WAR
WILLIMAS, J. H. B. BAL 151 1ST WARD
WILLIMAS, JOHN CAR 248 3RD DIST
WILLIMAS, JOSEPH BAL 280 2ND WARD
WILLIMAS, JOSHAWAY HAR 152 3RD DIST
WILLIMAS, JULIA BAL 204 11TH WAR
WILLIMAS, LAWRENCE BAL 142 5TH WARD
WILLIMAS, MARIA BAL 139 5TH WARD
WILLIMAS, MARIA BAL 311 12TH WAR
WILLIMAS, MARTHA BAL 415 8TH WARD
WILLIMAS, MARTHA BAL 227 1ST DIST
WILLIMAS, MARY BAL 160 16TH WAR
WILLIMAS, ROBERT W. WOR 300 SNOW HIL
WILLIMAS, WILLIAM H. BAL 122 12TH WAR
WILLIMSON, ANGUS BAL 018 18TH WAR
WILLIN, BETSEY SOM 480 TRAPE DI
WILLIN, DAVID TAL 081 ST MICHA
WILLIN, ELIZABETH SOM 443 DAMES QU
WILLIN, HENRY DOR 299 1ST DIST
WILLIN, ISAAC SOM 446 DAMES QU
WILLIN, THOAMS SOM 443 DAMES QU
WILLIN, THOMAS DOR 298 1ST DIST
WILLIN, ZADOC DOR 297 1ST DIST
WILLING, CHARLES SOM 476 TRAPPE D
WILLING, DAVID FRE 232 BUCKEYST
WILLING, EDWARD DOR 341 3RD DIVI
WILLING, EDWARD BAL 034 15TH WAR
WILLING, GEORGE* SOM 539 TYASKIN
WILLING, JAMES SOM 539 TYASKIN
WILLING, JAMES JR. SOM 539 TYASKIN
WILLING, JOHN BAL 140 1ST WARD
WILLING, LEVIN SOM 547 TYASKIN
WILLING, LITTLETON SOM 538 TYASKIN
WILLING, MARGARET CEC 189 7TH E DI
WILLING, MARTHA E. SOM 446 DAMES QU
WILLING, MARY SOM 474 TRAPPE D
WILLING, MATTHIAS SOM 539 TYASKIN
WILLING, NANCY SOM 448 DAMES QU
WILLING, SARRAH SOM 547 TYASKIN
WILLING, SUSAN SOM 543 TYASKIN
WILLING, SUSAN DOR 363 3RD DIVI

Name	County	Page	District
WILLING, TERRESA*	DOR	363	3RD DIVI
WILLING, WARE*	SOM	548	TYASKIN
WILLING, WILLIAM	SOM	546	TYASKIN
WILLING, WILLIAM	DOR	341	3RD DIVI
WILLING, ZACHEUS	SOM	539	TYASKIN
WILLING, ZEPORA	SOM	449	DAMES QU
WILLINGHAM, ANN	BAL	083	2ND DIST
WILLINGHAM, BENJAMIN	BAL	004	EASTERN
WILLINGHAM, CHARLES A.	BAL	217	6TH WARD
WILLINGHAM, JAMES	BAL	004	EASTERN
WILLINGTON, JAMES C.	CAR	149	NO TWP L
WILLINGTON, JOHN	BAL	041	1ST WARD
WILLIS, ADAM W.	CAR	208	5TH DIST
WILLIS, ARRA	WOR	283	BERLIN 1
WILLIS, ARULLA	BAL	100	2ND DIST
WILLIS, AUTHOR J.	CAR	164	NO TWP L
WILLIS, BAYNARD	CAR	144	NO TWP L
WILLIS, BENJAMIN	BAL	382	3RD WARD
WILLIS, BENJAMIN F.	BAL	130	5TH WARD
WILLIS, CATHERINE A.*	TAL	032	EASTON D
WILLIS, CHARLES	CAR	125	NO TWP L
WILLIS, CHARLES T.	DOR	319	1ST DIST
WILLIS, CORDELIA	BAL	419	3RD WARD
WILLIS, CORNELIUS L.*	BAL	406	3RD WARD
WILLIS, DAVID T.	CEC	093	4TH E DI
WILLIS, DENWOOD	CAR	140	NO TWP L
WILLIS, DRUSELLA	WOR	296	9TH E DI
WILLIS, E.	ANN	343	3RD DIST
WILLIS, EASTER	CAR	130	NO TWP L
WILLIS, ELIZABETH	CAR	124	NO TWP L
WILLIS, ELIZABETH	BAL	364	3RD WARD
WILLIS, ELIZABETH E.	CAR	168	NO TWP L
WILLIS, EZEKIEL	CAR	116	NO TWP L
WILLIS, FRANCIS	BAL	364	3RD WARD
WILLIS, FRANCIS	BAL	322	3RD WARD
WILLIS, FRANSIS	TAL	040	EASTON D
WILLIS, G.	BAL	225	19TH WAR
WILLIS, GEORGE	BAL	225	17TH WAR
WILLIS, H.	BAL	157	1ST WARD
WILLIS, HENRY	BAL	009	EASTERN
WILLIS, HENRY	ANN	435	HOWARD D
WILLIS, HENRY	BAL	413	3RD WARD
WILLIS, HENRY	BAL	115	11TH WAR
WILLIS, HENRY	PRI	033	VANSVILL
WILLIS, HENRY N. *	BAL	477	14TH WAR
WILLIS, HIRAM	ALL	215	CUMBERLA
WILLIS, HYRAM	SOM	350	BRINKLEY
WILLIS, JAMES	KEN	294	3RD DIST
WILLIS, JAMES	CAR	125	NO TWP L
WILLIS, JAMES	CAR	067	NO TWP L
WILLIS, JAMES	CEC	093	4TH E DI
WILLIS, JAMES	DOR	323	1ST DIST
WILLIS, JAMES E.	TAL	010	EASTON D
WILLIS, JAMES H.*	TAL	030	EASTON D
WILLIS, JAMES P.	TAL	012	EASTON D
WILLIS, JANE*	DOR	380	1ST DIST
WILLIS, JOHN	BAL	135	18TH WAR
WILLIS, JOHN	DOR	445	1ST DIST
WILLIS, JOHN	CEC	091	4TH E DI
WILLIS, JOHN	CAR	324	1ST DIST
WILLIS, JOHN F.	CAR	157	NO TWP L
WILLIS, JOHN G.	CAR	168	NO TWP L
WILLIS, JOHN H.	SOM	550	TYASKIN
WILLIS, JOHN R.	CAR	142	NO TWP L
WILLIS, JOHN*	DOR	418	1ST DIST
WILLIS, JONATHAN	FRE	137	CREAGERS
WILLIS, JONATHAN S.	TAL	092	ST MICHA
WILLIS, JOSEPH	CAR	144	NO TWP L
WILLIS, JOSEPH C.*	TAL	056	EASTON D
WILLIS, JULIA A.	WOR	330	1ST E DI
WILLIS, LEVIN	BAL	100	2ND DIST
WILLIS, LUIS*	TAL	011	EASTON D
WILLIS, MARGARET	TAL	040	EASTON D
WILLIS, MARGARET	BAL	419	3RD WARD
WILLIS, MARGARET*	TAL	010	EASTON D
WILLIS, MARGRETT	CAR	148	NO TWP L
WILLIS, MARTHA A.	KEN	232	2ND DIST
WILLIS, MARTIN	TAL	034	EASTON D
WILLIS, MARY	WAS	296	1ST DIST
WILLIS, MARY	CAR	157	NO TWP L
WILLIS, MARY	BAL	226	19TH WAR
WILLIS, MARY	BAL	145	19TH WAR
WILLIS, MARY	BAL	417	14TH WAR
WILLIS, MARY ANN	BAL	129	5TH WARD
WILLIS, MATILDA	BAL	272	7TH WARD
WILLIS, NANCY	CAR	211	5TH DIST
WILLIS, PERMELIA	BAL	408	14TH WAR
WILLIS, PETER	CAR	138	NO TWP L
WILLIS, PHILIMON	TAL	040	EASTON D
WILLIS, PURNAL *	WOR	282	BERLIN 1
WILLIS, RICHARD	CAR	159	NO TWP L
WILLIS, RICHARD	BAL	050	18TH WAR
WILLIS, RICHARD B.	TAL	039	EASTON D
WILLIS, ROBERT	BAL	468	14TH WAR
WILLIS, ROSAN	CAR	209	5TH DIST
WILLIS, SALESBERRY	BAL	085	18TH WAR
WILLIS, SAMUEL	BAL	425	1ST DIST
WILLIS, SHORT A.	CAR	142	NO TWP L
WILLIS, SOPHIA	BAL	351	13TH WAR
WILLIS, SUSAN	BAL	184	19TH WAR
WILLIS, THEADORE	BAL	448	8TH WARD
WILLIS, THOAMS	KEN	238	2ND DIST
WILLIS, THOMAS A.	BAL	397	3RD WARD
WILLIS, THOMAS N.	KEN	239	2ND DIST
WILLIS, THOMAS*	DOR	418	1ST DIST
WILLIS, THOMAS*	DOR	325	1ST DIST
WILLIS, WILLIAM	FRE	006	FREDERIC
WILLIS, WILLIAM	CAR	145	NO TWP L
WILLIS, WILLIAM	CAR	149	NO TWP L
WILLIS, WILLIAM B.	TAL	041	EASTON D
WILLIS, WILLIAM H.	BAL	296	20TH WAR
WILLIS, WILLIAM T.	TAL	012	EASTON D
WILLISHOUSEN, JOHN	BAL	209	2ND WARD
WILLISMS, ISAAC	BAL	167	11TH WAR
WILLISON, AMOS	ALL	219	CUMBERLA
WILLISON, AMOS	ALL	096	5TH E.D.
WILLISON, ASHFORD	ALL	190	9TH E.D.
WILLISON, BENJAMIN	CEC	082	CHARLEST
WILLISON, CAROLINE	HAR	186	3RD DIST
WILLISON, GEORGE	CEC	042	CHESAPEA
WILLISON, HAINS	CEC	055	1ST E DI
WILLISON, HARY	ALL	219	CUMBERLA
WILLISON, ISAAC	CEC	061	1ST E DI
WILLISON, ISAAC	CEC	045	1ST E DI
WILLISON, JANE	HAR	151	3RD DIST
WILLISON, JOHN	CEC	042	CHESAPEA
WILLISON, JOHN	CEC	042	CHESAPEA
WILLISON, JOHN	CEC	044	CHESAPEA
WILLISON, JOHN	CEC	043	CHESAPEA
WILLISON, JOHN L.	HAR	153	3RD DIST
WILLISON, JULIA	CEC	051	1ST E DI
WILLISON, MILLICENT	CEC	057	1ST E DI
WILLISON, MOSES	ALL	193	9TH E.D.
WILLISON, SAMUEL	CEC	048	1ST E DI
WILLISON, SARAH	ALL	234	CUMBERLA
WILLISON, WILLIAM	BAL	436	14TH WAR
WILLISS, JOHN K.	QUE	226	4TH E DI
WILLIT, SOLOMON	CHA	253	MIDDLETO
WILLIT, THEODORE	PRI	104	PISCATAW
WILLIT, THOMAS	CHA	255	MIDDLETO
WILLITT, WILLLIAM	BAL	191	17TH WAR
WILLIXON, ELISHA	ALL	185	9TH E.D.
WILLKISON, PETER	WOR	253	1ST CENS
WILLMER, CHARLES	BAL	429	14TH WAR
WILLMER, MARGARET	BAL	174	16TH WAR
WILLMER, NICHOLAS	BAL	206	11TH WAR
WILLMORE, H.	BAL	172	1ST WARD
WILLMORE, HARRIETT	BAL	111	5TH WARD
WILLMORE, RACHEL	HAR	182	3RD DIST
WILLMYER, JOSEPH H.	BAL	106	18TH WAR
WILLNER, JAOCB	BAL	413	14TH WAR
WILLOSN, EDWARD	CAR	105	NO TWP L
WILLOUGHBY, ELIZABETH	CAR	143	NO TWP L
WILLOUGHBY, HARRIET	BAL	182	6TH WARD
WILLOUGHBY, HENRY	DOR	313	1ST DIST
WILLOUGHBY, HESTER	TAL	066	EASTON T
WILLOUGHBY, JANE	CAR	163	NO TWP L
WILLOUGHBY, JOBE	DOR	312	1ST DIST
WILLOUGHBY, JOHN	CAR	164	NO TWP L
WILLOUGHBY, JOHN	CAR	161	NO TWP L
WILLOUGHBY, JOHN	DOR	461	1ST DIST
WILLOUGHBY, JOSIAH	BAL	026	9TH WARD
WILLOUGHBY, MARGRETT	CAR	140	NO TWP L
WILLOUGHBY, MARY	TAL	037	EASTON D
WILLOUGHBY, MARY E.	QUE	134	1ST E DI
WILLOUGHBY, PHILADELPHIA	CAR	137	NO TWP L
WILLOUGHBY, RICHARD	CAR	130	NO TWP L
WILLOUGHBY, RICHARD	CAR	140	NO TWP L
WILLOUGHBY, SALLY	CAR	139	NO TWP L
WILLOUGHBY, SAMUEL	QUE	213	3RD E DI
WILLOUGHBY, SARAH	CAR	139	NO TWP L
WILLOUGHBY, SARAH C.	TAL	051	EASTON D
WILLOUGHBY, THOMAS	CAR	114	NO TWP L
WILLOUGHBY, THOMAS	DOR	309	1ST DIST
WILLOUGHBY, WILLIAM	CAR	140	NO TWP L
WILLOUGHBY, WILLIAM	CAR	137	NO TWP L
WILLOUGHBY, WILLIAM	BAL	199	19TH WAR
WILLOUGHBY, WILLIAM	DOR	454	1ST DIST
WILLOUGHBY,MARGRETT	CAR	151	NO TWP L
WILLS, ANDREW	BAL	230	12TH WAR
WILLS, ANN	CHA	217	ALLENS F
WILLS, BUCHANAN	BAL	111	10TH WAR
WILLS, CHARLES	CHA	260	MIDDLETO
WILLS, CHARLOTTA	CEC	119	3RD E DI
WILLS, ELIZA	CAL	041	3RD DIST
WILLS, F. TED *	CHA	255	MIDDLETO
WILLS, FRANCIS	CHA	220	ALLENS F
WILLS, FRANCIS	CHA	278	BOJANTOW
WILLS, FRANCIS R.	CHA	218	ALLENS F
WILLS, IWILLIAM	CAL	047	3RD DIST
WILLS, JOHN	BAL	292	20TH WAR
WILLS, JOHN	HAR	107	2ND DIST
WILLS, JOHN	ANN	302	1ST DIST
WILLS, JOHN B.	FRE	044	FREDERIC
WILLS, JOSEPH T.	CHA	264	HILLTOP
WILLS, JOSHUA	BAL	005	1ST WARD
WILLS, MARY	MGM	335	CRACKLIN
WILLS, MARY A.	BAL	356	8TH WARD
WILLS, MARY C.	BAL	046	15TH WAR
WILLS, MARY*	BAL	405	3RD WARD
WILLS, REBECCA	CAL	041	3RD DIST
WILLS, RICHARD C.*	BAL	415	3RD WARD
WILLS, ROSE A.	BAL	106	1ST WARD
WILLS, SARAH C.	BAL	215	11TH WAR
WILLS, SOPHIA	FRE	055	FREDERIC
WILLS, THOMAS	BAL	100	10TH WAR
WILLS, THOMAS B.	BAL	075	10TH WAR
WILLS, THOMAS B.	BAL	226	6TH WARD
WILLS, WALTER	CHA	269	ALLENS F
WILLS, WASHINGTON	FRE	073	FREDERIC
WILLS, WILLIAM	HAR	147	3RD DIST
WILLS, WILLIAM	FRE	167	EMMITTSB
WILLSON, AARON	CAR	168	NO TWP L
WILLSON, AARON	CAR	127	NO TWP L
WILLSON, ALCANY	CAR	113	NO TWP L
WILLSON, ANN	CAR	133	NO TWP L
WILLSON, ANN	TAL	066	EASTON T
WILLSON, ANN M.	FRE	449	8TH E DI
WILLSON, CATHARINE	TAL	085	ST MICHA
WILLSON, CHARLES	WAS	060	2ND SUBD
WILLSON, COLUMBUS	FRE	238	NEW MARK
WILLSON, DANIEL	CAR	116	NO TWP L
WILLSON, EDWARD	CAR	094	NO TWP L
WILLSON, ELENOR	WAS	003	WILLIAMS
WILLSON, ELIZABETH-BLACK	CAR	093	NO TWP L
WILLSON, ELLEN	WOR	304	SNOW HIL
WILLSON, EMILY J.	TAL	032	EASTON D
WILLSON, FRANCES	CAR	142	NO TWP L
WILLSON, GEORGE W.	CAR	167	NO TWP L
WILLSON, GEORGEINIA	BAL	364	13TH WAR
WILLSON, HENRIETTA	FRE	060	FREDERIC
WILLSON, HENRY	CAR	168	NO TWP L
WILLSON, HENRY	CAR	134	NO TWP L
WILLSON, HENRY	CAR	131	NO TWP L
WILLSON, HENRY	TAL	018	EASTON D
WILLSON, HENRY	WOR	301	SNOW HIL
WILLSON, HESTER-BLACK	CAR	156	NO TWP L
WILLSON, HUDENCH-BLACK	FRE	244	NEW MARK
WILLSON, ISAAC	WAS	060	2ND SUBD
WILLSON, JACOB C.	CAR	159	NO TWP L
WILLSON, JAMES	CAR	131	NO TWP L
WILLSON, JAMES	HAR	146	3RD DIST
WILLSON, JAMES H.	QUE	244	5TH E DI
WILLSON, JAMES-BLACK	CAR	100	NO TWP L
WILLSON, JANE	BAL	273	17TH WAR
WILLSON, JANE	WAS	094	2ND SUBD
WILLSON, JEFFERSON-MULATT	CAR	157	NO TWP L
WILLSON, JESE-BLACK	CAR	085	NO TWP L
WILLSON, JOHN	CAR	130	NO TWP L
WILLSON, JOHN	CAR	327	1ST DIST
WILLSON, JOHN	QUE	239	5TH E DI
WILLSON, JOHN	TAL	080	ST MICHA
WILLSON, JOHN	TAL	060	EASTON D
WILLSON, JOHN B.	BAL	060	10TH WAR
WILLSON, JOHN J.	FRE	045	FREDERIC
WILLSON, JOHN-BLACK	CAR	101	NO TWP L
WILLSON, JONATHAN	CAR	113	NO TWP L
WILLSON, JONATHAN	CAR	093	NO TWP L
WILLSON, JONATHAN	CAR	170	NO TWP L
WILLSON, JOSHUA	WAS	143	HAGERSTO
WILLSON, JULIAN	QUE	252	5TH E DI
WILLSON, LEEVY	HAR	152	3RD DIST
WILLSON, LUESA	HAR	161	3RD DIST
WILLSON, MARGARET	TAL	066	EASTON T
WILLSON, MARY	TAL	033	EASTON D
WILLSON, MARY	CAR	150	NO TWP L
WILLSON, NANCY*	TAL	020	EASTON D
WILLSON, NICHOLAS	HAR	192	3RD DIST
WILLSON, PEGGY C.	TAL	039	EASTON D
WILLSON, PERRY	TAL	062	EASTON D
WILLSON, RICHAD	TAL	070	EASTON T
WILLSON, RICHARD	QUE	239	5TH E DI
WILLSON, RICHARD	CAR	092	NO TWP L
WILLSON, ROBERT	TAL	025	EASTON D
WILLSON, ROBERT	WAS	088	2ND SUBD
WILLSON, ROBERT	WAS	046	2ND SUBD
WILLSON, ROBERT M.	TAL	078	EASTON T
WILLSON, ROBERT-BLACK	CAR	089	NO TWP L
WILLSON, SALLY	TAL	042	EASTON D
WILLSON, SAMUEL	TAL	079	ST MICHA
WILLSON, SAMUEL	TAL	104	ST MICHA
WILLSON, SARAH	TAL	045	EASTON T
WILLSON, SARAH	WAS	005	WILLIAMS
WILLSON, SARAH	CAR	120	NO TWP L
WILLSON, SARAH	CAR	129	NO TWP L
WILLSON, SEARE	TAL	077	EASTON T
WILLSON, SIDNY A.	FRE	238	NEW MARK
WILLSON, SOLOMON	CAR	165	NO TWP L
WILLSON, SOLOMON-MULATTO	CAR	106	NO TWP L
WILLSON, SUSAN	TAL	073	EASTON T
WILLSON, SUSAN J.	FRE	382	PETERSVI
WILLSON, THOMAS	CAR	066	NO TWP L
WILLSON, THOMAS	TAL	052	EASTON D
WILLSON, THOMAS	WAS	034	2ND SUBD
WILLSON, THOMAS H.	CAR	095	NO TWP L
WILLSON, THOMAS S. DR.	QUE	239	5TH E DI
WILLSON, VANCE-BLACK	CAR	151	NO TWP L
WILLSON, WESLY	HAR	206	3RD DIST
WILLSON, WILLIAM	CAR	075	NO TWP L
WILLSON, WILLIAM	TAL	097	ST MICHA
WILLSON, WILLIAM	TAL	017	EASTON D
WILLSON, WILLIAM	MGM	443	CLARKSTR
WILLSON, WILLIAM G. G.	TAL	041	EASTON D
WILLSON, WILLIAM H.	CAR	148	NO TWP L
WILLSON, WILLIAM-BLACK	CAR	107	NO TWP L
WILLSON,AMO E.	CAR	083	NO TWP L
WILLSON,ELISHA	CAR	167	NO TWP L
WILLSON,NATHAN	CAR	084	NO TWP L
WILLSON,ROBERT	CAR	098	NO TWP L
WILLSON,SUSAN	CAR	169	NO TWP L
WILLY, CHARLES L.	HAR	165	3RD DIST
WILLY, CHARLES W.	TAL	120	ST MICHA
WILLY, EDWARD	TAL	087	ST MICHA
WILLY, HUGH	CEC	169	6TH E DI
WILLY, ISAAC	HAR	165	3RD DIST
WILLY, ROBERT	ALL	143	6TH E.D.
WILMA, FRANCIS	BAL	328	13TH WAR
WILMAN, HENRY	BAL	181	2ND WARD
WILMAN, LEWIS	BAL	309	20TH WAR
WILMER, AMY	BAL	395	14TH WAR
WILMER, ANNE	BAL	212	19TH WAR
WILMER, BENJAMIN	QUE	242	5TH E DI
WILMER, BENJAMIN	KEN	297	3RD DIST
WILMER, BENJAMIN-BLACK	QUE	131	1ST E DI
WILMER, CHARLOTTE	KEN	307	3RD DIST
WILMER, EDWIN M.	CEC	149	PORT DUP
WILMER, EMORY	ALL	200	CUMBERLA
WILMER, GEORGE	BAL	320	7TH WARD
WILMER, GEORGE	BAL	256	17TH WAR
WILMER, HENRY	CEC	017	ELKTON 3
WILMER, HENRY	CEC	057	1ST E DI
WILMER, HENRY	BAL	305	3RD WARD
WILMER, HENRY	KEN	287	3RD DIST
WILMER, ISAAC	CEC	018	ELKTON 3
WILMER, JACOB	KEN	247	2ND DIST
WILMER, JACOB-BLACK	QUE	199	3RD E DI
WILMER, JAMES	KEN	287	3RD DIST
WILMER, JAMES	KEN	263	1ST DIST
WILMER, JAMES	KEN	260	1ST DIST
WILMER, JAMES	KEN	241	2ND DIST
WILMER, JAMES	KEN	221	2ND DIST
WILMER, JAMES C.	BAL	433	8TH WARD
WILMER, JANE H.	CHA	251	MIDDLETO
WILMER, JOHN	CEC	060	1ST E DI
WILMER, JOHN	BAL	413	1ST DIST
WILMER, JOHN L.	WAS	276	RIDGEVIL
WILMER, JOHN W.	QUE	184	3RD E DI
WILMER, JOHN W.	BAL	068	15TH WAR
WILMER, JOSEPH	KEN	257	1ST DIST
WILMER, LAMBERT	KEN	304	3RD DIST
WILMER, LEMUEL	CHA	251	MIDDLETO
WILMER, MARGARETT	KEN	307	3RD DIST
WILMER, MARY	BAL	243	6TH WARD
WILMER, MARY H.	BAL	354	7TH WARD
WILMER, MARY J.	CHA	252	BOJANTOW
WILMER, MARY J.-BLACK	QUE	131	1ST E DI
WILMER, MOSES	CEC	024	ELKTON 3
WILMER, NATHANIEL	KEN	236	2ND DIST
WILMER, PERE-SR.	QUE	203	3RD E DI
WILMER, PERRY	TAL	021	EASTON D
WILMER, PERRY	CHA	228	BOJANTOW
WILMER, PHILIP-BLACK	QUE	167	2ND E DI
WILMER, ROBERT-BLACK	CAR	138	NO TWP L
WILMER, S.	CEC	064	1ST E DI
WILMER, SAMPSON	CEC	098	3RD E DI
WILMER, SAMUEL-BLACK	QUE	199	3RD E DI
WILMER, SARAH R.	KEN	210	2ND DIST
WILMER, SCINT	KEN	226	2ND DIST
WILMER, SOLONA	QUE	157	2ND E DI
WILMER, STEPHEN	KEN	308	3RD DIST
WILMER, THOMAS	KEN	251	2ND DIST
WILMER, THOMAS	HAR	119	2ND DIST
WILMER, THOMAS S.	KEN	226	2ND DIST
WILMER, WILLIAM B.	KEN	235	2ND DIST
WILMER, WILLIAM B.	KEN	209	2ND DIST
WILMER, WILLIAM H.	BAL	067	10TH WAR
WILMER, WILLIAM R.	BAL	472	14TH WAR
WILMER, WILLIAM R.	BAL	375	13TH WAR
WILMER, WILLIAM R.	KEN	302	3RD DIST
WILMER, YILLEY	BAL	458	8TH WARD
WILMINGTON, LUCY ANN	BAL	364	13TH WAR
WILMIR, EDWIN	CEC	149	PORT DUP
WILMON, CHARLOTTE	FRE	144	10TH E D
WILMON, JULIUS	FRE	146	10TH E D
WILMORE, ABRAHAM	HAR	122	2ND DIST
WILMORE, EDWARD	BAL	472	14TH WAR
WILMORE, HARRIET A.	BAL	348	3RD WARD
WILMORE, JACOB	HAR	027	1ST DIST
WILMORE, JOHN	HAR	204	3RD DIST
WILMORE, JOHN H. E.	BAL	121	16TH WAR

Name	County	Page	District
WILMORE, SAMUEL	BAL	176	6TH WARD
WILMOT, ADAM	BAL	433	14TH WAR
WILMOT, ELIZABETH	BAL	145	5TH WARD
WILMOT, MRS.	ANN	280	ANNAPOLI
WILMOTH, AQUILLA	BAL	329	1ST DIST
WILMOTH, SARAH J.	BAL	358	1ST DIST
WILMRE, EMALINE	CEC	105	3RD E DI
WILMS, F.C.B.	WAS	268	1ST DIST
WILNDER, HICKS	BAL	083	2ND DIST
WILNOT, JOHN G.	BAL	145	5TH WARD
WILPAN, JOHN	BAL	244	2ND WARD
WILS, SIDNEY	HAR	153	3RD DIST
WILSEY, CAREY	BAL	185	11TH WAR
WILSN, HARRIET	ALL	259	CUMBERLA
WILSON, AAMON	ALL	190	9TH E.D.
WILSON, AARON	SOM	369	BRINKLEY
WILSON, ABRAHAM	KEN	285	3RD DIST
WILSON, ABSOLOM	BAL	404	1ST DIST
WILSON, ADAM	KEN	309	3RD DIST
WILSON, ADAM	DOR	405	1ST DIST
WILSON, ADAM	FRE	300	WOODSBOR
WILSON, ADAM	DOR	309	1ST DIST
WILSON, ADEL	BAL	354	7TH WARD
WILSON, ADELINE	BAL	309	7TH WARD
WILSON, ALEXANDER	DOR	393	1ST DIST
WILSON, ALEXANDER	KEN	249	2ND DIST
WILSON, ALEXANDER	CEC	085	5TH E DI
WILSON, ALEXANDER	CEC	070	5TH E DI
WILSON, ALEXANDER *	KEN	221	2ND DIST
WILSON, ALFRED	DOR	436	1ST DIST
WILSON, ALLEN	WAS	202	1ST DIST
WILSON, AMAN	BAL	398	1ST DIST
WILSON, AMAN	BAL	243	1ST DIST
WILSON, AMELIA	FRE	163	EMMITTSB
WILSON, AMELIA	BAL	152	11TH WAR
WILSON, AMY	BAL	037	4TH WARD
WILSON, ANDREW	BAL	187	19TH WAR
WILSON, ANDREW	CEC	074	NORTHEAS
WILSON, ANDREW	BAL	233	17TH WAR
WILSON, ANDREW F.	BAL	171	19TH WAR
WILSON, ANGELINA	QUE	236	4TH E DI
WILSON, ANGLEINE	BAL	015	2ND DIST
WILSON, ANN	BAL	014	1ST WARD
WILSON, ANN	BAL	008	1ST WARD
WILSON, ANN	BAL	297	1ST DIST
WILSON, ANN	BAL	454	8TH WARD
WILSON, ANN	BAL	321	12TH WAR
WILSON, ANN	KEN	290	3RD DIST
WILSON, ANN	PRI	036	VANSVILL
WILSON, ANN	BAL	259	17TH WAR
WILSON, ANN	CEC	181	7TH E DI
WILSON, ANN	CEC	179	7TH E DI
WILSON, ANN	BAL	065	18TH WAR
WILSON, ANN	BAL	001	18TH WAR
WILSON, ANN	BAL	117	11TH WAR
WILSON, ANN	DOR	437	1ST DIST
WILSON, ANN	BAL	129	18TH WAR
WILSON, ANN	BAL	279	20TH WAR
WILSON, ANN E.	FRE	431	8TH E DI
WILSON, ANN E.	MGM	405	ROCKERLE
WILSON, ANN M.	BAL	176	6TH WARD
WILSON, ANN N.	BAL	085	1ST WARD
WILSON, ANNA	BAL	411	1ST DIST
WILSON, ANNE	BAL	078	18TH WAR
WILSON, ANTHONY	BAL	152	5TH WARD
WILSON, AQUILLA	BAL	434	1ST DIST
WILSON, AQUILLA	BAL	433	1ST DIST
WILSON, ARCHIBALD	BAL	017	4TH WARD
WILSON, ARIAN	ALL	192	9TH E.D.
WILSON, ARRON	BAL	021	18TH WAR
WILSON, ARTHUR	BAL	223	17TH WAR
WILSON, ASEL	BAL	083	2ND DIST
WILSON, AUGUST S.	BAL	064	10TH WAR
WILSON, BARBARA	BAL	204	2ND WARD
WILSON, BENJAMIN	BAL	090	2ND DIST
WILSON, BENJAMIN	BAL	414	8TH WARD
WILSON, BENJAMIN	QUE	148	1ST E DI
WILSON, BENJAMIN	QUE	146	1ST E DI
WILSON, BENJAMIN	SOM	537	TYASKIN
WILSON, BENJAMIN H.	BAL	116	11TH WAR
WILSON, BENJAMIN-BLACK	QUE	148	1ST E DI
WILSON, BENNETT	KEN	231	2ND DIST
WILSON, BERNARD-BLACK	ST	329	4TH E DI
WILSON, CAROLINE	HAR	077	BEL AIR
WILSON, CATHARINE	KEN	230	2ND DIST
WILSON, CATHARINE	BAL	160	11TH WAR
WILSON, CATHARINE	CEC	001	ELKTON 3
WILSON, CATHARINE	BAL	193	2ND WARD
WILSON, CATHARINE	BAL	172	16TH WAR
WILSON, CATHARINE	BAL	273	12TH WAR
WILSON, CATHARINE A.	CAR	234	UNION TO
WILSON, CATHERINE	BAL	100	18TH WAR
WILSON, CATHERINE	BAL	281	7TH WARD
WILSON, CATHERINE	MGM	443	CLARKSTR
WILSON, CATHINE	BAL	067	18TH WAR
WILSON, CATHRINE A.	BAL	034	18TH WAR
WILSON, CHARELS	QUE	214	3RD E DI
WILSON, CHARELS	BAL	281	2ND WARD
WILSON, CHARELS	BAL	147	1ST WARD
WILSON, CHARLES	BAL	147	1ST WARD
WILSON, CHARLES	BAL	125	1ST WARD
WILSON, CHARLES	BAL	131	1ST WARD
WILSON, CHARLES	BAL	171	11TH WAR
WILSON, CHARLES	BAL	155	5TH WARD
WILSON, CHARLES	BAL	172	1ST WARD
WILSON, CHARLES	BAL	090	2ND DIST
WILSON, CHARLES	BAL	122	1ST WARD
WILSON, CHARLES	QUE	207	3RD E DI
WILSON, CHARLES	WAS	301	1ST DIST
WILSON, CHARLES	WAS	011	WILLIAMS
WILSON, CHARLES	WOR	299	SNOW HIL
WILSON, CHARLES	BAL	202	17TH WAR
WILSON, CHARLES	DOR	434	1ST DIST
WILSON, CHARLES A.	CAR	385	2ND DIST
WILSON, CHARLES H.	HAR	092	2ND DIST
WILSON, CHARLES-BLACK	QUE	158	2ND E DI
WILSON, CHARLES-MULATTO	BAL	212	2ND WARD
WILSON, CHARLOTTE	BAL	003	9TH WARD
WILSON, CHARLOTTE	HAR	120	2ND DIST
WILSON, CHARLOTTE	BAL	024	18TH WAR
WILSON, CHARLOTTE	BAL	243	20TH WAR
WILSON, CHRISTIANA	BAL	072	15TH WAR
WILSON, CHRISTINA	BAL	116	15TH WAR
WILSON, CHRISTOPHER	HAR	029	1ST DIST
WILSON, CHRISTOPHER	HAR	001	1ST DIST
WILSON, CHRISTOPHER	HAR	047	1ST DIST
WILSON, CLARA	CEC	206	7TH E DI
WILSON, CLARISA	CAL	004	1ST DIST
WILSON, CLEM-BLACK	QUE	180	2ND E DI
WILSON, COLLAMBIA	CHA	257	MIDDLETO
WILSON, COMFORT B.	BAL	302	7TH WARD
WILSON, CORDELIA	BAL	304	7TH WARD
WILSON, CORNEALOUS	CAR	212	5TH DIST
WILSON, COSMORE-BLACK	WOR	170	6TH E DI
WILSON, D.	BAL	173	1ST WARD
WILSON, DANIEL	BAL	398	3RD WARD
WILSON, DANIEL	BAL	009	1ST WARD
WILSON, DANIEL	WAS	134	HAGERSTO
WILSON, DANIEL	DOR	360	3RD DIVI
WILSON, DANIEL	BAL	376	13TH WAR
WILSON, DAVID	BAL	070	4TH WARD
WILSON, DAVID	CEC	117	4TH E DI
WILSON, DAVID	BAL	384	8TH WARD
WILSON, DAVID	BAL	455	8TH WARD
WILSON, DAVID	BAL	036	2ND DIST
WILSON, DAVID	BAL	345	1ST DIST
WILSON, DAVID	BAL	108	5TH WARD
WILSON, DAVID S.	BAL	109	10TH WAR
WILSON, DAVID S.	WAS	127	2ND DIST
WILSON, DAVIE	BAL	387	1ST DIST
WILSON, DEBORAH	BAL	093	15TH WAR
WILSON, DELIA	BAL	201	11TH WAR
WILSON, DENARD	SOM	375	BRINKLEY
WILSON, DIANA	PRI	039	VANSVILL
WILSON, DIXON	BAL	108	2ND DIST
WILSON, DOROTHEA	BAL	116	15TH WAR
WILSON, DURAM	BAL	149	11TH WAR
WILSON, DURHAM	BAL	189	11TH WAR
WILSON, DURHAM	BAL	188	11TH WAR
WILSON, E.	BAL	103	10TH WAR
WILSON, E.A.	PRI	051	AQUASCO
WILSON, E.H.	BAL	173	1ST WARD
WILSON, EDWARD	BAL	346	3RD WARD
WILSON, EDWARD	BAL	275	7TH WARD
WILSON, EDWARD	BAL	355	3RD WARD
WILSON, EDWARD	ALL	189	9TH E.D.
WILSON, EDWARD	BAL	059	18TH WAR
WILSON, EDWARD	CEC	009	ELKTON 3
WILSON, EDWARD H.	BAL	142	1ST WARD
WILSON, EDWARD W.	BAL	093	18TH WAR
WILSON, EDWARD-BLACK	QUE	182	3RD E DI
WILSON, ELEANOR	MGM	407	MEDLEY 3
WILSON, ELEANOR	BAL	157	16TH WAR
WILSON, ELI	ALL	193	9TH E.D.
WILSON, ELI	DOR	429	1ST DIST
WILSON, ELIAS	ALL	192	9TH E.D.
WILSON, ELIJAH	SOM	385	BRINKLEY
WILSON, ELIJAH	SOM	384	BRINKLEY
WILSON, ELIJAH	WOR	300	SNOW HIL
WILSON, ELIJAH	PRI	004	BLADENSB
WILSON, ELIJAH-BLACK	QUE	185	3RD E DI
WILSON, ELIZA	TAL	074	EASTON T
WILSON, ELIZA	BAL	169	11TH WAR
WILSON, ELIZA	BAL	054	2ND DIST
WILSON, ELIZA	BAL	108	18TH WAR
WILSON, ELIZA	CAL	018	1ST DIST
WILSON, ELIZA	CEC	173	6TH E DI
WILSON, ELIZA	QUE	132	1ST E DI
WILSON, ELIZA J.	BAL	080	4TH WARD
WILSON, ELIZA R.	BAL	056	15TH WAR
WILSON, ELIZA-BLACK	BAL	242	2ND WARD
WILSON, ELIZABETH	BAL	006	9TH WARD
WILSON, ELIZABETH	ANN	478	HOWARD D
WILSON, ELIZABETH	BAL	105	10TH WAR
WILSON, ELIZABETH	BAL	107	10TH WAR
WILSON, ELIZABETH	BAL	285	12TH WAR
WILSON, ELIZABETH	BAL	061	1ST WARD
WILSON, ELIZABETH	BAL	155	2ND DIST
WILSON, ELIZABETH	BAL	333	3RD WARD
WILSON, ELIZABETH	BAL	216	6TH DIST
WILSON, ELIZABETH	BAL	237	6TH WARD
WILSON, ELIZABETH	BAL	032	9TH WARD
WILSON, ELIZABETH	BAL	248	17TH WAR
WILSON, ELIZABETH	BAL	140	11TH WAR
WILSON, ELIZABETH	CAR	388	2ND DIST
WILSON, ELIZABETH	BAL	017	4TH WARD
WILSON, ELIZABETH	KEN	306	3RD DIST
WILSON, ELIZABETH	WAS	204	1ST DIST
WILSON, ELIZABETH	PRI	037	VANSVILL
WILSON, ELIZABETH-BLACK	ST	320	4TH E DI
WILSON, ELLEN	SOM	520	BARREN C
WILSON, ELLEN	BAL	143	11TH WAR
WILSON, ELLEN	BAL	404	14TH WAR
WILSON, ELLEN	CAL	002	1ST DIST
WILSON, ELLEN	BAL	442	14TH WAR
WILSON, ELLEN	BAL	373	13TH WAR
WILSON, ELLEN	MGM	366	BERRYS D
WILSON, ELLEN	BAL	129	5TH WARD
WILSON, ELLEN	BAL	005	1ST WARD
WILSON, ELLEN	BAL	139	16TH WAR
WILSON, ELLEN	BAL	347	7TH WARD
WILSON, ELLEN ANN	BAL	396	14TH WAR
WILSON, ELLEN J.	ALL	238	CUMBERLA
WILSON, ELLENORA-BLACK	FRE	015	FREDERIC
WILSON, ELLIOTT C.	BAL	119	1ST WARD
WILSON, ELVIRA A.	BAL	304	7TH WARD
WILSON, EMANDA	BAL	458	1ST DIST
WILSON, EMANUEL	BAL	218	6TH DIST
WILSON, EMELINE	KEN	220	2ND DIST
WILSON, EMILY	ANN	287	ANNAPOLI
WILSON, EMILY J.	BAL	017	2ND DIST
WILSON, EMILY M.	BAL	214	11TH WAR
WILSON, EMMA J.	BAL	341	7TH WARD
WILSON, EMORY-BLACK	QUE	167	2ND E DI
WILSON, ENOCK	DOR	436	1ST DIST
WILSON, ENOS	PRI	003	BLADENSB
WILSON, EPHRIAM	BAL	407	1ST DIST
WILSON, ESTHER	QUE	229	4TH E DI
WILSON, FIELDER	ANN	444	HOWARD D
WILSON, FORRESTER	BAL	129	2ND DIST
WILSON, FRANCES A.	BAL	124	16TH WAR
WILSON, FRANCIS	BAL	003	1ST WARD
WILSON, FRANCIS	BAL	350	13TH WAR
WILSON, FRANCIS W.	BAL	360	3RD WARD
WILSON, FRANKLIN	MGM	370	BERRYS D
WILSON, FRANKLIN REV.	BAL	109	10TH WAR
WILSON, FREDERIC	BAL	245	6TH WARD
WILSON, FREDERICK	BAL	049	15TH WAR
WILSON, FREDERICK	BAL	107	18TH WAR
WILSON, FREDERICK	BAL	117	11TH WAR
WILSON, FREDERICK	KEN	289	3RD DIST
WILSON, G.	BAL	166	1ST WARD
WILSON, G. B.	BAL	063	10TH WAR
WILSON, G. F.	BAL	155	1ST WARD
WILSON, GEORGE	BAL	155	1ST WARD
WILSON, GEORGE	BAL	155	5TH WARD
WILSON, GEORGE	BAL	141	5TH WARD
WILSON, GEORGE	BAL	345	7TH WARD
WILSON, GEORGE	BAL	347	7TH WARD
WILSON, GEORGE	BAL	419	8TH WARD
WILSON, GEORGE	BAL	086	2ND DIST
WILSON, GEORGE	ANN	343	3RD DIST
WILSON, GEORGE	BAL	285	7TH WARD
WILSON, GEORGE	BAL	134	1ST WARD
WILSON, GEORGE	BAL	127	1ST WARD
WILSON, GEORGE	BAL	131	1ST WARD
WILSON, GEORGE	KEN	306	3RD DIST
WILSON, GEORGE	KEN	293	3RD DIST
WILSON, GEORGE	PRI	030	VANSVILL
WILSON, GEORGE	SOM	540	TYASKIN
WILSON, GEORGE	WOR	237	6TH E DI
WILSON, GEORGE	HAR	205	3RD DIST
WILSON, GEORGE	MGM	378	ROCKERLE
WILSON, GEORGE	BAL	244	20TH WAR
WILSON, GEORGE	BAL	304	20TH WAR
WILSON, GEORGE	CAR	384	2ND DIST
WILSON, GEORGE	BAL	077	18TH WAR
WILSON, GEORGE	CEC	077	NORTHEAS
WILSON, GEORGE	CEC	054	1ST E DI
WILSON, GEORGE	KEN	231	2ND DIST
WILSON, GEORGE A.	BAL	071	4TH WARD
WILSON, GEORGE E.	BAL	312	7TH WARD
WILSON, GEORGE G.	BAL	164	1ST WARD
WILSON, GEORGE H.	CAL	039	2ND DIST
WILSON, GEORGE W.	BAL	195	6TH WARD
WILSON, GEORGE W.	ANN	344	3RD DIST
WILSON, GEORGE W.	BAL	322	7TH WARD
WILSON, GEORGE W.	PRI	074	MARLBROU
WILSON, GEORGE W.	KEN	290	3RD DIST
WILSON, GEORGIANA	BAL	402	3RD WARD
WILSON, GREENBERRY	FRE	446	8TH E DI
WILSON, GREENBURY	CAR	210	5TH DIST
WILSON, H.	BAL	156	1ST WARD
WILSON, H.	BAL	158	1ST WARD
WILSON, H.	BAL	150	1ST WARD
WILSON, H. S.	ANN	344	3RD DIST
WILSON, H.C.	BAL	158	19TH WAR
WILSON, HANAH	BAL	354	7TH WARD
WILSON, HANNAH	BAL	170	11TH WAR
WILSON, HANNAH	BAL	221	12TH WAR
WILSON, HANNAH	BAL	249	12TH WAR
WILSON, HANNAH	BAL	254	6TH WARD
WILSON, HANNAH	BAL	393	14TH WAR
WILSON, HANNAH	CEC	182	7TH E DI
WILSON, HANNAH	BAL	274	17TH WAR
WILSON, HANNAH	CEC	114	3RD E DI
WILSON, HANNAH	KEN	301	3RD DIST
WILSON, HANNAH	SOM	485	TRAPP DI
WILSON, HANNAH-BLACK	QUE	170	2ND E DI
WILSON, HARLES	BAL	329	7TH WARD
WILSON, HARRIET	BAL	056	2ND DIST
WILSON, HARRIET	BAL	173	6TH WARD
WILSON, HARRIET	WAS	180	BOONSBOR
WILSON, HENRIETTA M.	CEC	132	6TH E DI
WILSON, HENRY	CEC	145	PORT DUP
WILSON, HENRY	CAR	388	2ND DIST
WILSON, HENRY	BAL	401	14TH WAR
WILSON, HENRY	BAL	129	11TH WAR
WILSON, HENRY	BAL	152	11TH WAR
WILSON, HENRY	CEC	002	ELKTON 3
WILSON, HENRY	HAR	030	1ST DIST
WILSON, HENRY	QUE	231	4TH E DI
WILSON, HENRY	TAL	075	EASTON T
WILSON, HENRY	SOM	360	BRINKLEY
WILSON, HENRY	TAL	060	EASTON D
WILSON, HENRY	QUE	207	3RD E DI
WILSON, HENRY	QUE	210	3RD E DI
WILSON, HENRY	SOM	534	QUANTICO
WILSON, HENRY	TAL	001	EASTON D
WILSON, HENRY	BAL	220	6TH WARD
WILSON, HENRY	BAL	030	9TH WARD
WILSON, HENRY	BAL	040	2ND DIST
WILSON, HENRY	BAL	061	2ND DIST
WILSON, HENRY	ANN	352	3RD DIST
WILSON, HENRY	ANN	452	HOWARD D
WILSON, HENRY	ALL	234	CUMBERLA
WILSON, HENRY	BAL	106	10TH WAR
WILSON, HENRY	BAL	382	3RD WARD
WILSON, HENRY	BAL	186	11TH WAR
WILSON, HENRY	ANN	329	2ND DIST
WILSON, HENRY	ALL	127	4TH E.D.
WILSON, HENRY M.	HAR	069	1ST DIST
WILSON, HENRY R.	BAL	152	11TH WAR
WILSON, HENRY S.	HAR	033	1ST DIST
WILSON, HENRY-BLACK	FRE	040	FREDERIC
WILSON, HERNY	CAR	347	6TH DIST
WILSON, HESTER-BLACK	QUE	152	1ST E DI
WILSON, HEZEKIAH	SOM	371	BRINKLEY
WILSON, HILEARY	MGM	422	MEDLEY 3
WILSON, HIRAM	WAS	204	1ST DIST
WILSON, HNERY CLAY	BAL	001	1ST WARD
WILSON, HORACE	BAL	460	8TH WARD
WILSON, HUBBORD	BAL	382	8TH WARD
WILSON, HUMPHRY	HAR	090	2ND DIST
WILSON, ICHABOD	CEC	107	3RD E DI
WILSON, ISAAC	CEC	099	3RD E DI
WILSON, ISAAC	BAL	295	17TH WAR
WILSON, ISAAC	SOM	440	DAMES QU
WILSON, ISAAC	HAR	122	2ND DIST
WILSON, ISAAC	CEC	003	ELKTON 3
WILSON, ISAAC	BAL	096	10TH WAR
WILSON, ISAAC	BAL	113	2ND DIST
WILSON, ISAAC	SOM	454	DAMES QU
WILSON, ISAAC	KEN	290	3RD DIST
WILSON, ISAAC	SOM	515	BARREN C
WILSON, ISAAC C.	ALL	192	9TH E.D.
WILSON, ISABEL	BAL	242	1ST DIST
WILSON, ISABELLA	BAL	320	7TH WARD
WILSON, J.	BAL	135	1ST WARD
WILSON, J.	BAL	163	1ST WARD
WILSON, J.	BAL	090	5TH WARD
WILSON, J.	KEN	259	1ST DIST
WILSON, JACKSON	BAL	050	2ND DIST
WILSON, JACOB	BAL	453	1ST DIST
WILSON, JACOB	BAL	156	1ST WARD
WILSON, JACOB	BAL	246	6TH WARD
WILSON, JACOB	BAL	101	15TH WAR
WILSON, JACOB	BAL	055	15TH WAR
WILSON, JACOB	CAR	389	2ND DIST
WILSON, JACOB	DOR	305	1ST DIST
WILSON, JAMES	CEC	155	PORT DUP
WILSON, JAMES	BAL	345	13TH WAR
WILSON, JAMES	CEC	172	6TH E DI
WILSON, JAMES	BAL	104	18TH WAR
WILSON, JAMES	BAL	021	18TH WAR
WILSON, JAMES	CHA	288	BOJANTOW
WILSON, JAMES	KEN	233	2ND DIST
WILSON, JAMES	HAR	179	3RD DIST
WILSON, JAMES	SOM	434	PRINCESS
WILSON, JAMES	SOM	440	DAMES QU

WILSON, JAMES HAR 045 1ST DIST
WILSON, JAMES MGM 368 BERRYS D
WILSON, JAMES HAR 005 1ST DIST
WILSON, JAMES BAL 129 11TH WAR
WILSON, JAMES BAL 122 11TH WAR
WILSON, JAMES BAL 453 14TH WAR
WILSON, JAMES BAL 152 19TH WAR
WILSON, JAMES HAR 196 3RD DIST
WILSON, JAMES BAL 131 18TH WAR
WILSON, JAMES CAR 399 2ND DIST
WILSON, JAMES BAL 265 20TH WAR
WILSON, JAMES BAL 262 12TH WAR
WILSON, JAMES BAL 430 8TH WARD
WILSON, JAMES BAL 322 7TH WARD
WILSON, JAMES BAL 078 10TH WAR
WILSON, JAMES BAL 073 10TH WAR
WILSON, JAMES BAL 299 12TH WAR
WILSON, JAMES BAL 302 12TH WAR
WILSON, JAMES BAL 239 6TH WARD
WILSON, JAMES BAL 040 9TH WARD
WILSON, JAMES BAL 167 1ST WARD
WILSON, JAMES BAL 174 1ST WARD
WILSON, JAMES ANN 505 HOWARD D
WILSON, JAMES BAL 100 5TH WARD
WILSON, JAMES BAL 016 2ND DIST
WILSON, JAMES BAL 039 2ND DIST
WILSON, JAMES BAL 114 2ND DIST
WILSON, JAMES BAL 149 2ND DIST
WILSON, JAMES BAL 127 1ST WARD
WILSON, JAMES BAL 280 2ND WARD
WILSON, JAMES BAL 281 2ND WARD
WILSON, JAMES BAL 142 1ST WARD
WILSON, JAMES BAL 007 1ST WARD
WILSON, JAMES BAL 152 2ND DIST
WILSON, JAMES ALL 190 9TH E.D.
WILSON, JAMES ALL 065 10TH E.D
WILSON, JAMES KEN 293 3RD DIST
WILSON, JAMES SOM 534 QUANTICO
WILSON, JAMES SOM 501 SALISBUR
WILSON, JAMES PRI 050 AQUASCO
WILSON, JAMES TAL 066 EASTON T
WILSON, JAMES B. BAL 101 2ND DIST
WILSON, JAMES C. BAL 131 11TH WAR
WILSON, JAMES H. BAL 081 4TH WARD
WILSON, JAMES H. BAL 211 11TH WAR
WILSON, JAMES J. CAL 002 1ST DIST
WILSON, JAMES J. BAL 090 18TH WAR
WILSON, JAMES M. CEC 157 PORT DUP
WILSON, JAMES P. KEN 231 2ND DIST
WILSON, JAMES S. ANN 356 3RD DIST
WILSON, JAMES S. KEN 293 3RD DIST
WILSON, JAMES W. SOM 527 QUANTICO
WILSON, JAMES W. PRI 003 BLADENSB
WILSON, JAMES-BLACK ST 316 4TH E DI
WILSON, JAMSE BAL 044 15TH WAR
WILSON, JANE BAL 006 1ST WARD
WILSON, JANE BAL 258 6TH WARD
WILSON, JANE BAL 413 1ST DIST
WILSON, JANE BAL 026 9TH WARD
WILSON, JANE SOM 548 TYASKIN
WILSON, JANE SOM 522 BARREN C
WILSON, JANE QUE 234 4TH E DI
WILSON, JANE WAS 162 HAGERSTO
WILSON, JANE BAL 340 13TH WAR
WILSON, JANE BAL 210 17TH WAR
WILSON, JANE BAL 039 4TH WARD
WILSON, JANE BAL 014 4TH WARD
WILSON, JANE M. BAL 389 13TH WAR
WILSON, JEMIMA SOM 379 BRINKLEY
WILSON, JEREMIAH BAL 057 15TH WAR
WILSON, JEREMIAH ALL 125 4TH E.D.
WILSON, JESSE BAL 190 17TH WAR
WILSON, JESSE WAS 175 FUNKSTOW
WILSON, JESSE KEN 225 2ND DIST
WILSON, JESSEN BAL 167 2ND DIST
WILSON, JOHN BAL 022 1ST WARD
WILSON, JOHN BAL 100 10TH WAR
WILSON, JOHN BAL 093 10TH WAR
WILSON, JOHN BAL 318 12TH WAR
WILSON, JOHN ALL 106 5TH E.D.
WILSON, JOHN ALL 065 10TH E.D
WILSON, JOHN ANN 332 2ND DIST
WILSON, JOHN BAL 168 11TH WAR
WILSON, JOHN BAL 185 2ND WARD
WILSON, JOHN BAL 170 1ST WARD
WILSON, JOHN BAL 170 1ST WARD
WILSON, JOHN BAL 158 1ST WARD
WILSON, JOHN BAL 150 1ST WARD
WILSON, JOHN BAL 404 1ST DIST
WILSON, JOHN BAL 139 1ST WARD
WILSON, JOHN BAL 130 1ST WARD
WILSON, JOHN BAL 129 1ST WARD
WILSON, JOHN BAL 133 1ST WARD
WILSON, JOHN BAL 410 8TH WARD
WILSON, JOHN BAL 248 6TH WARD
WILSON, JOHN BAL 112 2ND DIST
WILSON, JOHN BAL 042 2ND DIST
WILSON, JOHN FRE 122 CREAGERS
WILSON, JOHN FRE 105 CREAGERS
WILSON, JOHN CAL 016 1ST DIST
WILSON, JOHN BAL 160 11TH WAR
WILSON, JOHN CEC 012 ELKTON 3
WILSON, JOHN CEC 042 CHESAPEA
WILSON, JOHN CEC 032 CHESAPEA
WILSON, JOHN CEC 126 5TH E DI
WILSON, JOHN CEC 178 7TH E DI
WILSON, JOHN CEC 071 5TH E DI
WILSON, JOHN CEC 059 1ST E DI
WILSON, JOHN CEC 190 5TH E DI
WILSON, JOHN KEN 221 2ND DIST
WILSON, JOHN HAR 026 1ST DIST
WILSON, JOHN MGM 395 ROCKERLE
WILSON, JOHN SOM 450 DAMES QU
WILSON, JOHN HAR 069 1ST DIST
WILSON, JOHN MGM 420 MEDLEY 3
WILSON, JOHN SOM 373 BRINKLEY
WILSON, JOHN SOM 383 BRINKLEY
WILSON, JOHN SOM 370 BRINKLEY
WILSON, JOHN QUE 236 4TH E DI
WILSON, JOHN QUE 235 4TH E DI
WILSON, JOHN TAL 061 EASTON D
WILSON, JOHN TAL 059 EASTON D
WILSON, JOHN WOR 329 1ST E DI
WILSON, JOHN SOM 520 BARREN C
WILSON, JOHN TAL 017 EASTON D
WILSON, JOHN KEN 306 3RD DIST
WILSON, JOHN A. BAL 022 1ST WARD
WILSON, JOHN B. BAL 270 7TH WARD
WILSON, JOHN C. KEN 265 1ST DIST
WILSON, JOHN C. MGM 319 CRACKLIN
WILSON, JOHN D. BAL 250 12TH WAR
WILSON, JOHN E. BAL 010 1ST WARD
WILSON, JOHN F. ANN 401 8TH DIST
WILSON, JOHN F.* DOR 377 1ST DIST
WILSON, JOHN G. WAS 156 2ND DIST
WILSON, JOHN H. HAR 137 2ND DIST
WILSON, JOHN H. BAL 067 4TH WARD
WILSON, JOHN H. BAL 311 1ST DIST
WILSON, JOHN J. PRI 048 AQUASCO
WILSON, JOHN KELLY BAL 140 11TH WAR
WILSON, JOHN L. BAL 253 1ST DIST
WILSON, JOHN R. DOR 377 1ST DIST
WILSON, JOHN S. BAL 369 1ST DIST
WILSON, JOHN S. BAL 169 1ST WARD
WILSON, JOHN S. BAL 169 1ST WARD
WILSON, JOHN S. BAL 061 10TH WAR
WILSON, JOHN T. BAL 215 6TH DIST
WILSON, JOHN T. BAL 034 2ND DIST
WILSON, JOHN T. FRE 382 PETERSVI
WILSON, JOHN T. CAR 384 2ND DIST
WILSON, JOHN T. J. CAL 015 1ST DIST
WILSON, JOHN W. BAL 038 18TH WAR
WILSON, JOHN W. BAL 035 18TH WAR
WILSON, JOHN W. BAL 415 8TH WARD
WILSON, JOHN-BLACK QUE 125 1ST E DI
WILSON, JOHN-BLACK QUE 197 3RD E DI
WILSON, JONATHAN ALL 052 10TH E.D
WILSON, JONATHAN M. BAL 066 15TH WAR
WILSON, JONATHANJ. FRE 033 FREDERIC
WILSON, JOSEPH DOR 359 3RD DIVI
WILSON, JOSEPH CAR 391 2ND DIST
WILSON, JOSEPH BAL 094 18TH WAR
WILSON, JOSEPH BAL 302 17TH WAR
WILSON, JOSEPH HAR 115 2ND DIST
WILSON, JOSEPH BAL 341 7TH WARD
WILSON, JOSEPH BAL 415 8TH WARD
WILSON, JOSEPH ANN 481 HOWARD D
WILSON, JOSEPH BAL 148 2ND DIST
WILSON, JOSEPH BAL 402 1ST DIST
WILSON, JOSEPH BAL 155 1ST WARD
WILSON, JOSEPH C. BAL 109 10TH WAR
WILSON, JOSEPH E. BAL 276 20TH WAR
WILSON, JOSEPH H. PRI 013 BLADENSB
WILSON, JOSEPH L. CAL 015 1ST DIST
WILSON, JCSHUA HAR 141 2ND DIST
WILSON, JOSHUA BAL 061 4TH WARD
WILSON, JOSHUA CAR 212 5TH DIST
WILSON, JOSHUA BAL 451 1ST DIST
WILSON, JOSHUA ALL 192 9TH E.D.
WILSON, JSOHUA ST 297 2ND E DI
WILSON, JULIA BAL 125 5TH WARD
WILSON, KESIAH BAL 437 8TH WARD
WILSON, KITTY BAL 107 15TH WAR
WILSON, LAURA BAL 128 5TH WARD
WILSON, LAZARUS SOM 452 DAMES QU
WILSON, LEAH SOM 548 TYASKIN
WILSON, LEMUEL D. WOR 328 1ST E DI
WILSON, LEONARD PRI 067 NOTTINGH
WILSON, LETECIA FRE 217 BUCKEYST
WILSON, LETITIA SOM 363 BRINKLEY
WILSON, LEVI BAL 166 19TH WAR
WILSON, LEVIN SOM 525 QUANTICO
WILSON, LEVIN J. WOR 187 7TH E DI
WILSON, LEVIN M. SOM 525 BARREN C
WILSON, LEWIS BAL 173 1ST WARD
WILSON, LORENZO D. ANN 480 HOWARD D
WILSON, LOTTY SOM 373 BRINKLEY
WILSON, LOUIS BAL 403 1ST DIST
WILSON, LOUISA BAL 387 1ST DIST
WILSON, LOUISA SOM 459 HANGARY
WILSON, LUCRECE ANN 521 HOWARD D
WILSON, LUCY PRI 066 NOTTINGH
WILSON, LUTHER BAL 067 18TH WAR
WILSON, LUTHER H. BAL 457 8TH WARD
WILSON, LUTHER M. SOM 515 BARREN C
WILSON, LYDIA BAL 100 10TH WAR
WILSON, LYDIA HAR 156 3RD DIST
WILSON, M. ELIZABETH BAL 140 11TH WAR
WILSON, M. H. BAL 333 1ST DIST
WILSON, M.A. ANN 272 ANNAPOLI
WILSON, MACLEENY MGM 354 BERRYS D
WILSON, MALVINA BAL 165 16TH WAR
WILSON, MARGARET BAL 127 16TH WAR
WILSON, MARGARET BAL 427 1ST DIST
WILSON, MARGARET BAL 158 6TH WARD
WILSON, MARGARET BAL 237 6TH WARD
WILSON, MARGARET BAL 252 6TH WARD
WILSON, MARGARET MGM 384 ROCKERLE
WILSON, MARGARET HAR 002 1ST DIST
WILSON, MARGARET CAR 390 2ND DIST
WILSON, MARGARET DOR 379 1ST DIST
WILSON, MARGARET J. BAL 288 7TH WARD
WILSON, MARGARET M. PRI 026 VANSVILL
WILSON, MARGARET-BLACK QUE 125 1ST E DI
WILSON, MARGARETT DOR 305 1ST DIST
WILSON, MARGARETT DOR 305 1ST DIST
WILSON, MARGARETT KEN 288 3RD DIST
WILSON, MARGARETT KEN 293 3RD DIST
WILSON, MARGARETT KEN 300 3RD DIST
WILSON, MARGARETT KEN 311 3RD DIST
WILSON, MARGARETT A. KEN 286 3RD DIST
WILSON, MARGARETT J. BAL 135 18TH WAR
WILSON, MARGRETT HAR 207 3RD DIST
WILSON, MARIA BAL 344 3RD WARD
WILSON, MARIA ALL 190 9TH E.D.
WILSON, MARIA BAL 140 2ND DIST
WILSON, MARIA BAL 356 3RD WARD
WILSON, MARIAH SOM 355 BRINKLEY
WILSON, MARTA KEN 287 3RD DIST
WILSON, MARTH A.J. BAL 209 2ND WARD
WILSON, MARTHA BAL 001 15TH WAR
WILSON, MARTHA BAL 190 11TH WAR
WILSON, MARTHA BAL 088 4TH WARD
WILSON, MARTHA BAL 148 11TH WAR
WILSON, MARTHA CAL 028 2ND DIST
WILSON, MARTHA E. BAL 401 14TH WAR
WILSON, MARTHA-BLACK FRE 051 FREDERIC
WILSON, MARTHEY DOR 357 3RD DIVI
WILSON, MARY DOR 309 1ST DIST
WILSON, MARY CHA 223 ALLENS F
WILSON, MARY HAR 037 1ST DIST
WILSON, MARY HAR 080 2ND DIST
WILSON, MARY HAR 088 2ND DIST
WILSON, MARY CEC 148 PORT DUP
WILSON, MARY BAL 046 18TH WAR
WILSON, MARY BAL 361 13TH WAR
WILSON, MARY BAL 113 18TH WAR
WILSON, MARY BAL 139 19TH WAR
WILSON, MARY BAL 108 18TH WAR
WILSON, MARY CEC 078 NORTHEAS
WILSON, MARY BAL 184 11TH WAR
WILSON, MARY BAL 245 12TH WAR
WILSON, MARY BAL 204 2ND WARD
WILSON, MARY BAL 137 5TH WARD
WILSON, MARY BAL 027 9TH WARD
WILSON, MARY BAL 014 1ST WARD
WILSON, MARY BAL 122 2ND DIST
WILSON, MARY BAL 040 2ND DIST
WILSON, MARY ANN 450 HOWARD D
WILSON, MARY BAL 336 1ST DIST
WILSON, MARY BAL 279 7TH WARD
WILSON, MARY BAL 127 16TH WAR
WILSON, MARY BAL 058 10TH WAR
WILSON, MARY BAL 077 10TH WAR
WILSON, MARY SOM 388 BRINKLEY
WILSON, MARY QUE 228 4TH E DI
WILSON, MARY WAS 162 HAGERSTO
WILSON, MARY A. BAL 094 15TH WAR
WILSON, MARY A. BAL 379 8TH WARD
WILSON, MARY A. DOR 394 1ST DIST
WILSON, MARY A. SOM 413 DUBLIN D
WILSON, MARY A. CAL 007 1ST DIST
WILSON, MARY A. HAR 122 2ND DIST
WILSON, MARY A.-MULATTO BAL 212 2ND WARD
WILSON, MARY D. CAL 011 1ST DIST
WILSON, MARY E. CAR 385 2ND DIST
WILSON, MARY E. BAL 361 3RD WARD
WILSON, MARY F. CAL 016 1ST DIST
WILSON, MARY H. KEN 287 3RD DIST
WILSON, MARY J. BAL 039 9TH WARD
WILSON, MARY J. BAL 092 10TH WAR
WILSON, MARY J. ANN 440 HOWARD D
WILSON, MARY J. BAL 196 11TH WAR
WILSON, MARY JANE SOM 520 BARREN C
WILSON, MARY L. ANN 452 HOWARD D
WILSON, MARY T. BAL 203 17TH WAR
WILSON, MARY-BLACK QUE 191 3RD E DI
WILSON, MARY-MULATTO FRE 051 FREDERIC
WILSON, MATELDA FRE 100 FREDERIC
WILSON, MATILDA BAL 243 20TH WAR
WILSON, MATILDA BAL 026 15TH WAR
WILSON, MATILDA BAL 096 5TH WARD
WILSON, MICHAEL ALL 154 6TH E.D.
WILSON, MICHAEL MGM 360 BERRYS D
WILSON, MICHE BAL 407 1ST DIST
WILSON, MILLY SOM 515 BARREN C
WILSON, MINEY CEC 060 1ST E DI
WILSON, MINTA QUE 227 4TH E DI
WILSON, MIRANDA BAL 100 10TH WAR
WILSON, MITELDA BAL 187 11TH WAR
WILSON, MORTIMER L. PRI 013 BLADENSB
WILSON, NACKY ANN 435 HOWARD D
WILSON, NANCY BAL 058 10TH WAR
WILSON, NANCY BAL 007 1ST WARD
WILSON, NANCY TAL 074 EASTON T
WILSON, NANCY PRI 051 AQUASCO
WILSON, NANCY BAL 145 11TH WAR
WILSON, NATHAN KEN 212 2ND DIST
WILSON, NATHAN BAL 270 1ST DIST
WILSON, NATHANIEL CAL 015 1ST DIST
WILSON, NICHOLAS ANN 481 HOWARD D
WILSON, OFFA E. PRI 070 MARLBROU
WILSON, OLIVA BAL 148 11TH WAR
WILSON, OSBORN S. MGM 400 ROCKERLE
WILSON, P. CEC 009 ELKTON 3
WILSON, PEGGY BAL 251 1ST DIST
WILSON, PERE QUE 208 3RD E DI
WILSON, PEREGRINE T. BAL 080 15TH WAR
WILSON, PERRY BAL 081 15TH WAR
WILSON, PERRY BAL 262 6TH WARD
WILSON, PERRY BAL 039 4TH WARD
WILSON, PETER BAL 463 1ST DIST
WILSON, PETER BAL 175 6TH WARD
WILSON, PETER L. ALL 242 CUMBERLA
WILSON, PHILIP BAL 313 1ST DIST
WILSON, PHILIP BAL 453 14TH WAR
WILSON, PRINDY ANN 292 ANNAPOLI
WILSON, PRISCILLA HAR 104 2ND DIST
WILSON, R. ANN 352 3RD DIST
WILSON, R. C. BAL 149 1ST WARD
WILSON, R. O. BAL 154 1ST WARD
WILSON, RACHAEL ALL 052 10TH E.D
WILSON, RACHAEL BAL 296 1ST DIST
WILSON, RACHAEL BAL 144 11TH WAR
WILSON, RACHAEL WAS 130 HAGERSTO
WILSON, RACHEL CEC 089 4TH E DI
WILSON, RACHEL HAR 122 2ND DIST
WILSON, RACHEL HAR 139 2ND DIST
WILSON, RACHEL MGM 335 CRACKLIN
WILSON, RACHEL BAL 318 7TH WARD
WILSON, RACHEL BAL 190 11TH WAR
WILSON, RACHEL A. ANN 431 HOWARD D
WILSON, RACHELL BAL 135 5TH WARD
WILSON, REBECA BAL 446 8TH WARD
WILSON, REBECCA BAL 013 1ST WARD
WILSON, REBECCA BAL 410 1ST DIST
WILSON, REBECCA BAL 359 1ST DIST
WILSON, REBECCA BAL 357 1ST DIST
WILSON, REBECCA BAL 345 3RD WARD
WILSON, REBECCA QUE 143 1ST E DI
WILSON, REBECCA BAL 087 18TH WAR
WILSON, REBECCA MGM 382 ROCKERLE
WILSON, RICHARD HAR 023 1ST DIST
WILSON, RICHARD BAL 463 14TH WAR
WILSON, RICHARD BAL 422 14TH WAR
WILSON, RICHARD BAL 463 1ST DIST
WILSON, RICHARD BAL 201 11TH WAR
WILSON, RICHARD BAL 041 2ND DIST
WILSON, RICHARD QUE 225 4TH E DI
WILSON, RIDER W. SOM 519 BARREN C
WILSON, ROBERT TAL 062 EASTON D
WILSON, ROBERT BAL 033 2ND DIST
WILSON, ROBERT BAL 054 2ND DIST
WILSON, ROBERT ANN 459 HOWARD D
WILSON, ROBERT BAL 422 8TH WARD
WILSON, ROBERT BAL 161 2ND DIST
WILSON, ROBERT BAL 120 1ST WARD
WILSON, ROBERT BAL 114 1ST WARD
WILSON, ROBERT BAL 163 1ST WARD
WILSON, ROBERT BAL 218 6TH WARD
WILSON, ROBERT BAL 377 8TH WARD
WILSON, ROBERT BAL 131 11TH WAR
WILSON, ROBERT SOM 447 DAMES QU
WILSON, ROBERT CEC 097 4TH E DI
WILSON, ROBERT BAL 302 17TH WAR
WILSON, ROBERT KEN 255 1ST DIST
WILSON, ROBERT KEN 247 2ND DIST
WILSON, ROBERT KEN 253 1ST DIST
WILSON, ROBERT CAR 207 4TH DIST
WILSON, ROBERT HAR 205 3RD DIST

WILSON, ROBERT HAR 205 3RD DIST
WILSON, ROBERT DOR 402 1ST DIST
WILSON, ROBERT BAL 147 19TH WAR
WILSON, ROBERT BAL 243 20TH WAR
WILSON, ROBERT FRE 019 FREDERIC
WILSON, ROBERT R. QUE 180 2ND E DI
WILSON, ROBERT Y. BAL 463 14TH WAR
WILSON, ROSE HAR 109 2ND DIST
WILSON, ROSEAN BAL 334 1ST DIST
WILSON, ROSEANN TAL 009 EASTON D
WILSON, ROSETTA BAL 014 4TH WARD
WILSON, ROSINA BAL 176 2ND DIST
WILSON, RUFUS H. WAS 130 2ND DIST
WILSON, RUTH HAR 120 2ND DIST
WILSON, RYAN BAL 059 1ST WARD
WILSON, SALEY DOR 412 1ST DIST
WILSON, SALLY SOM 440 DAMES QU
WILSON, SALLY A. BAL 063 15TH WAR
WILSON, SAMUEL BAL 202 11TH WAR
WILSON, SAMUEL BAL 010 1ST WARD
WILSON, SAMUEL BAL 124 1ST WARD
WILSON, SAMUEL BAL 344 1ST DIST
WILSON, SAMUEL BAL 143 1ST WARD
WILSON, SAMUEL BAL 242 2ND WARD
WILSON, SAMUEL BAL 162 1ST WARD
WILSON, SAMUEL BAL 169 1ST WARD
WILSON, SAMUEL BAL 083 2ND DIST
WILSON, SAMUEL SOM 419 PRINCESS
WILSON, SAMUEL MGM 385 ROCKERLE
WILSON, SAMUEL HAR 030 1ST DIST
WILSON, SAMUEL BAL 471 14TH WAR
WILSON, SAMUEL DOR 362 3RD DIVI
WILSON, SAMUEL CEC 089 4TH E DI
WILSON, SAMUEL CEC 089 4TH E DI
WILSON, SAMUEL BAL 424 14TH WAR
WILSON, SAMUEL CEC 178 7TH E DI
WILSON, SAMUEL WAS 158 2ND DIST
WILSON, SAMUEL SOM 388 BRINKLEY
WILSON, SAMUEL SOM 521 BARREN C
WILSON, SAMUEL SOM 494 SALISBUR
WILSON, SAMUEL B. CEC 141 6TH E DI
WILSON, SAMUEL B. CAL 016 1ST DIST
WILSON, SAMUEL H. HAR 079 2ND DIST
WILSON, SAMUEL P. BAL 249 6TH WARD
WILSON, SARA CHA 225 ALLENS F
WILSON, SARAH FRE 377 PETERSVI
WILSON, SARAH BAL 134 11TH WAR
WILSON, SARAH BAL 153 11TH WAR
WILSON, SARAH CEC 122 4TH E DI
WILSON, SARAH BAL 077 4TH WARD
WILSON, SARAH BAL 070 4TH WARD
WILSON, SARAH DOR 403 1ST DIST
WILSON, SARAH CEC 002 ELKTON 3
WILSON, SARAH KEN 230 2ND DIST
WILSON, SARAH ALL 233 CUMBERLA
WILSON, SARAH BAL 008 EASTERN
WILSON, SARAH BAL 218 6TH WARD
WILSON, SARAH BAL 179 6TH WARD
WILSON, SARAH BAL 201 6TH DIST
WILSON, SARAH BAL 002 1ST WARD
WILSON, SARAH BAL 054 15TH WAR
WILSON, SARAH BAL 230 12TH WAR
WILSON, SARAH BAL 303 12TH WAR
WILSON, SARAH BAL 126 16TH WAR
WILSON, SARAH SOM 373 BRINKLEY
WILSON, SARAH A. SOM 373 BRINKLEY
WILSON, SARAH A. BAL 116 11TH WAR
WILSON, SARAH C. BAL 102 1ST WARD
WILSON, SARAH E. ANN 515 HOWARD D
WILSON, SARAH E. SOM 428 PRINCESS
WILSON, SARAH S. SOM 426 PRINCESS
WILSON, SAUL SOM 419 PRINCESS
WILSON, SHADRACK BAL 253 1ST DIST
WILSON, SHEM HAR 015 1ST DIST
WILSON, SHERRY BAL 225 17TH WAR
WILSON, SOLOMON DOR 408 1ST DIST
WILSON, SOLOMON BAL 069 10TH WAR
WILSON, SOLOMON BAL 072 15TH WAR
WILSON, SOLOMON W. PRI 004 BLADENSB
WILSON, SOPHIA BAL 085 15TH WAR
WILSON, SOPHIA BAL 242 2ND WARD
WILSON, SOPHIA BAL 047 18TH WAR
WILSON, SPEDDON ANN 292 ANNAPOLI
WILSON, SPELLER ANN 272 ANNAPOLI
WILSON, SPENCER-BLACK QUE 135 1ST E DI
WILSON, SPHRAIM CAR 234 UNION TO
WILSON, SRAH BAL 215 6TH DIST
WILSON, SUSAN BAL 279 12TH WAR
WILSON, SUSAN BAL 168 11TH WAR
WILSON, SUSAN CEC 090 4TH E DI
WILSON, SUSAN-BLACK QUE 181 2ND E DI
WILSON, SUSANNAH BAL 117 15TH WAR
WILSON, SUSANNAH BAL 329 13TH WAR
WILSON, SUTTON A.* TAL 001 EASTON D
WILSON, SYSANDRA-BLACK MGM 433 CLARKSTR
WILSON, TABITHA* BAL 039 4TH WARD
WILSON, TAMER SOM 350 BRINKLEY
WILSON, THOAMS KEN 274 1ST DIST
WILSON, THOAMS BAL 033 18TH WAR
WILSON, THOAMS BAL 150 1ST WARD
WILSON, THOMAS BAL 019 9TH WARD
WILSON, THOMAS BAL 170 1ST WARD
WILSON, THOMAS BAL 175 2ND WARD
WILSON, THOMAS BAL 167 1ST WARD
WILSON, THOMAS BAL 169 1ST WARD
WILSON, THOMAS BAL 167 1ST WARD
WILSON, THOMAS BAL 174 1ST WARD
WILSON, THOMAS BAL 172 1ST WARD
WILSON, THOMAS BAL 128 5TH WARD
WILSON, THOMAS BAL 081 15TH WAR
WILSON, THOMAS BAL 065 10TH WAR
WILSON, THOMAS BAL 340 7TH WARD
WILSON, THOMAS BAL 337 3RD WARD
WILSON, THOMAS BAL 399 1ST DIST
WILSON, THOMAS BAL 434 1ST DIST
WILSON, THOMAS ALL 066 10TH E.D
WILSON, THOMAS ALL 260 CUMBERLA
WILSON, THOMAS ANN 438 HOWARD D
WILSON, THOMAS BAL 145 2ND DIST
WILSON, THOMAS BAL 128 2ND DIST
WILSON, THOMAS CEC 106 3RD E DI
WILSON, THOMAS BAL 412 3RD WARD
WILSON, THOMAS KEN 250 2ND DIST
WILSON, THOMAS KEN 231 2ND DIST
WILSON, THOMAS KEN 248 2ND DIST
WILSON, THOMAS HAR 127 2ND DIST
WILSON, THOMAS HAR 138 2ND DIST
WILSON, THOMAS CEC 188 7TH E DI
WILSON, THOMAS CEC 149 PORT DUP
WILSON, THOMAS KEN 216 2ND DIST
WILSON, THOMAS DOR 326 3RD DIVI
WILSON, THOMAS DOR 326 3RD DIVI
WILSON, THOMAS KEN 296 3RD DIST
WILSON, THOMAS KEN 257 1ST DIST
WILSON, THOMAS WAS 246 SMITHSBU
WILSON, THOMAS A. BAL 077 10TH WAR
WILSON, THOMAS C. BAL 263 17TH WAR
WILSON, THOMAS C. CEC 015 ELKTON 3
WILSON, THOMAS G. SOM 386 BRINKLEY
WILSON, THOMAS J. PRI 082 QUEEN AN
WILSON, THOMAS J. BAL 152 11TH WAR
WILSON, THOMAS J. BAL 179 16TH WAR
WILSON, THOMAS K. BAL 028 15TH WAR
WILSON, THOMAS N. MGM 358 BERRYS D
WILSON, THOMAS O. MGM 358 BERRYS D
WILSON, THOMAS-BLACK QUE 134 1ST E DI
WILSON, TIBATHA* BAL 039 4TH WARD
WILSON, TRACY SOM 549 TYASKIN
WILSON, TRAVER BAL 121 2ND DIST
WILSON, VIENA BAL 213 11TH WAR
WILSON, VIRGINIA BAL 081 15TH WAR
WILSON, W.H. ANN 276 ANNAPOLI
WILSON, WALTER BAL 117 18TH WAR
WILSON, WALTER PRI 030 VANSVILL
WILSON, WASHINGTON SOM 541 TYASKIN
WILSON, WASHINGTON HAR 055 1ST DIST
WILSON, WESLEY CAR 389 2ND DIST
WILSON, WESLEY BAL 002 9TH WARD
WILSON, WESLEY BAL 152 2ND DIST
WILSON, WILLAIM BAL 185 16TH WAR
WILSON, WILLAM BAL 462 14TH WAR
WILSON, WILLAM BAL 193 19TH WAR
WILSON, WILLIAM BAL 186 19TH WAR
WILSON, WILLIAM BAL 472 14TH WAR
WILSON, WILLIAM BAL 140 11TH WAR
WILSON, WILLIAM BAL 396 14TH WAR
WILSON, WILLIAM CEC 107 3RD E DI
WILSON, WILLIAM CEC 082 CHARLEST
WILSON, WILLIAM BAL 016 18TH WAR
WILSON, WILLIAM BAL 078 18TH WAR
WILSON, WILLIAM SOM 413 DUBLIN D
WILSON, WILLIAM HAR 048 1ST DIST
WILSON, WILLIAM HAR 092 2ND DIST
WILSON, WILLIAM BAL 117 18TH WAR
WILSON, WILLIAM HAR 124 2ND DIST
WILSON, WILLIAM KEN 229 2ND DIST
WILSON, WILLIAM KEN 224 2ND DIST
WILSON, WILLIAM MGM 336 CRACKLIN
WILSON, WILLIAM FRE 103 FREDERIC
WILSON, WILLIAM BAL 264 17TH WAR
WILSON, WILLIAM CEC 146 PORT DUP
WILSON, WILLIAM CEC 178 7TH E DI
WILSON, WILLIAM CEC 166 6TH E DI
WILSON, WILLIAM BAL 055 4TH WARD
WILSON, WILLIAM CEC 192 5TH E DI
WILSON, WILLIAM FRE 442 8TH E DI
WILSON, WILLIAM BAL 093 15TH WAR
WILSON, WILLIAM BAL 110 15TH WAR
WILSON, WILLIAM BAL 322 7TH WARD
WILSON, WILLIAM BAL 166 2ND DIST
WILSON, WILLIAM BAL 165 2ND DIST
WILSON, WILLIAM BAL 094 1ST WARD
WILSON, WILLIAM BAL 368 3RD WARD
WILSON, WILLIAM BAL 456 8TH WARD
WILSON, WILLIAM BAL 263 12TH WAR
WILSON, WILLIAM BAL 222 12TH WAR
WILSON, WILLIAM BAL 286 2ND WARD
WILSON, WILLIAM BAL 249 12TH WAR
WILSON, WILLIAM BAL 185 11TH WAR
WILSON, WILLIAM BAL 026 2ND DIST
WILSON, WILLIAM BAL 411 1ST DIST
WILSON, WILLIAM BAL 180 6TH WARD
WILSON, WILLIAM BAL 165 1ST WARD
WILSON, WILLIAM BAL 025 9TH WARD
WILSON, WILLIAM BAL 402 3RD WARD
WILSON, WILLIAM BAL 137 1ST WARD
WILSON, WILLIAM BAL 417 8TH WARD
WILSON, WILLIAM BAL 133 1ST WARD
WILSON, WILLIAM BAL 282 2ND WARD
WILSON, WILLIAM PRI 036 VANSVILL
WILSON, WILLIAM SOM 382 BRINKLEY
WILSON, WILLIAM SOM 352 BRINKLEY
WILSON, WILLIAM QUE 228 4TH E DI
WILSON, WILLIAM SOM 397 BRINKLEY
WILSON, WILLIAM TAL 070 EASTON T
WILSON, WILLIAM KEN 307 3RD DIST
WILSON, WILLIAM WAS 123 HAGERSTO
WILSON, WILLIAM B. CHA 259 MIDDLETO
WILSON, WILLIAM C. HAR 127 2ND DIST
WILSON, WILLIAM E. QUE 216 3RD E DI
WILSON, WILLIAM F. SOM 515 BARREN C
WILSON, WILLIAM F. DOR 382 1ST DIST
WILSON, WILLIAM G. FRE 442 8TH E DI
WILSON, WILLIAM G. KEN 295 3RD DIST
WILSON, WILLIAM H. PRI 044 VANSVILL
WILSON, WILLIAM H. PRI 070 MARLBROU
WILSON, WILLIAM H. WOR 187 7TH E DI
WILSON, WILLIAM H. HAR 206 3RD DIST
WILSON, WILLIAM H. BAL 255 6TH WARD
WILSON, WILLIAM H. BAL 157 1ST WARD
WILSON, WILLIAM K. HAR 126 2ND DIST
WILSON, WILLIAM M. BAL 094 18TH WAR
WILSON, WILLIAM R. ALL 058 10TH E.D
WILSON, WILLIAM S. MGM 363 BERRYS D
WILSON, WILLIAM T. CAL 023 2ND DIST
WILSON, WILLIAM W. BAL 037 9TH WARD
WILSON, WILLIAM W. BAL 115 1ST WARD
WILSON, WILLIAM-BLACK QUE 197 3RD E DI
WILSON, WILLIAMW. QUE 148 1ST E DI
WILSON, YOUNG O. BAL 138 16TH WAR
WILSON, ZACHARIAH BAL 015 4TH WARD
WILSON, ZADOK MGM 394 ROCKERLE
WILSON,ALLEN BAL 054 2ND DIST
WILSON,ALLY ALL 192 9TH E.D.
WILSON,AMICHAEL CAR 350 6TH DIST
WILSON,ANNE-BLACK BAL 179 2ND WARD
WILSON,ELIAS BAL 170 1ST WARD
WILSON,ELIZA BAL 005 EASTERN
WILSON,J. BAL 141 1ST WARD
WILSON,JACOB BAL 163 1ST WARD
WILSON,JAMES BAL 170 1ST WARD
WILSON,JAMES BAL 133 1ST WARD
WILSON,JAMES-BLACK QUE 191 3RD E DI
WILSON,JEMIMA BAL 034 2ND DIST
WILSON,LAWRENCE ALL 192 9TH E.D.
WILSON,MAINACE BAL 105 1ST WARD
WILSON,MARANDA BAL 026 2ND DIST
WILSON,MARY BAL 297 1ST DIST
WILSON,MARY ALL 046 10TH E.D
WILSON,MARY CAR 380 2ND DIST
WILSON,MARY E. FRE 024 FREDERIC
WILSON,MATILDA BAL 351 1ST DIST
WILSON,THOMAS BAL 080 1ST WARD
WILSON,THOMAS BAL 129 1ST WARD
WILSON,WASHINGTON CAR 388 2ND DIST
WILSOP, DAVID ANN 471 HOWARD D
WILSOT, AQUILLA PRI 116 PISCATAW
WILSTER, JOSEPH HAR 179 3RD DIST
WILT, CHRISTIA WAS 132 2ND DIST
WILT, GEORGE CAR 358 9TH DIST
WILT, GEORGE CAR 310 1ST DIST
WILT, GEORGE ALL 144 6TH E.D.
WILT, JACOB CAR 360 9TH DIST
WILT, JACOB BAL 413 14TH WAR
WILT, JOHN ALL 046 10TH E.D
WILT, MARY A. BAL 123 16TH WAR
WILT, MARY ELLEN ALL 245 CUMBERLA
WILT, SAMUEL HAR 146 3RD DIST
WILT, SARAH E. ALL 046 10TH E.D
WILT, THOMAS ALL 125 4TH E.D.
WILTBECKER, W. BAL 303 12TH WAR
WILTE, LEVI ALL 231 CUMBERLA
WILTON, AQUILLA * KEN 218 2ND DIST
WILTON, EMMA BAL 031 9TH WARD
WILTON, JOHN N. * KEN 212 2ND DIST
WILTON, LEWIS * KEN 240 2ND DIST
WILTON, ROBERT KEN 242 2ND DIST
WILTON, ROBERT JR. * KEN 242 2ND DIST
WILTON, SARAH * WAS 067 2ND SUBD
WILTY, FRANKLIN FRE 129 CREAGERS
WILWORTH, GEORGE CEC 080 NORTHEAS
WILXRON, SARAH M. * ALL 132 4TH E.D.
WILY, LOUISA BAL 472 14TH WAR
WILY, MARY BAL 302 3RD WARD
WILZBACKER, AUGUSTUS BAL 202 6TH WARD
WIMAN, ROSS BAL 011 18TH WAR
WIMANS, JACOB BAL 163 19TH WAR
WIMBACH, AUGUST BAL 204 6TH WARD
WIMBER, JAEMS WOR 302 SNOW HIL
WIMBRE, EZEKIEL WOR 347 1ST E DI
WIMBRON, JOHN T. WOR 168 6TH E DI
WIMBROW, LOUISA C. WOR 169 6TH E DI
WIMBROW, LOUISA C. WOR 168 6TH E DI
WIMBROW, PETER WOR 236 5TH E DI
WIMBROW, WILLIAM WOR 221 4TH E DI
WIMBROW, WILLIAM J. WOR 168 6TH E DI
WIMEL, G. C. BAL 307 3RD WARD
WIMERT, MAGADALENA CAR 260 3RD DIST
WIMHOFF, MARGARET BAL 214 19TH WAR
WIMLER, JOHN CAR 297 7TH DIST
WIMMEL, JOHN BAL 127 16TH WAR
WIMMEL, JOSEPH BAL 422 8TH WARD
WIMMELL, FREDERICK BAL 265 7TH WARD
WIMMEN, PETER BAL 128 11TH WAR
WIMMER, EMILY BAL 136 18TH WAR
WIMMER, GEORGE BAL 141 19TH WAR
WIMMER, GEORGE BAL 248 20TH WAR
WIMPA, ENGLE BAL 111 2ND DIST
WIMSATT, ROBERT W. BAL 133 18TH WAR
WIMSETT, ELLEN BAL 310 3RD WARD
WIN, JACOB CAR 299 1ST DIST
WINAR, MARY BAL 246 2ND WARD
WINBLAST, GEORGE * BAL 277 2ND WARD
WINBRENNER, MORRIS ALL 113 5TH E.D.
WINBRENNER, WILLIAM ALL 113 5TH E.D.
WINBRINNER, HORACE ALL 097 5TH E.D.
WINCH, JACOB BAL 269 12TH WAR
WINCH, JOHN CEC 177 7TH E DI
WINCH, JOHN CEC 177 7TH E DI
WINCH, MARY KEN 248 2ND DIST
WINCH, WILLIAM BAL 317 20TH WAR
WINCHELL, TRUEMAN MGM 324 CRACKLIN
WINCHESTER, ALEXANDER BAL 194 11TH WAR
WINCHESTER, ALLEN KEN 262 1ST DIST
WINCHESTER, ALMIRA QUE 208 3RD E DI
WINCHESTER, ANN BAL 257 17TH WAR
WINCHESTER, AUGUSTA A. BAL 058 10TH WAR
WINCHESTER, E.C. BAL 204 11TH WAR
WINCHESTER, EDWARD BAL 374 3RD WARD
WINCHESTER, ELIZA KEN 262 1ST DIST
WINCHESTER, ELIZAR CEC 179 7TH E DI
WINCHESTER, FREDERICK BAL 357 8TH WARD
WINCHESTER, GEORGE CEC 189 7TH E DI
WINCHESTER, HENRY BAL 179 19TH WAR
WINCHESTER, HIRAM FRE 065 FREDERIC
WINCHESTER, ISAAC QUE 236 4TH E DI
WINCHESTER, J.M. BAL 205 11TH WAR
WINCHESTER, JACOB BAL 134 1ST WARD
WINCHESTER, JACOB BAL 124 1ST WARD
WINCHESTER, JACOB BAL 121 1ST WARD
WINCHESTER, JACOB ANN 353 3RD DIST
WINCHESTER, JAMES KEN 258 1ST DIST
WINCHESTER, JOHN CAR 081 NO TWP L
WINCHESTER, JOHN CEC 084 CHARLEST
WINCHESTER, JOSEPH BAL 212 19TH WAR
WINCHESTER, LONDON-BLACK CAR 088 NO TWP L
WINCHESTER, MADDIAN-BLACK CAR 087 NO TWP L
WINCHESTER, MARIA BAL 290 1ST DIST
WINCHESTER, MARIA BAL 204 11TH WAR
WINCHESTER, MARTHA BAL 050 4TH WARD
WINCHESTER, PERE QUE 222 4TH E DI
WINCHESTER, RICHARD FRE 20 5TH E DI
WINCHESTER, SAMUEL BAL 106 10TH WAR
WINCHESTER, SAMUEL C. BAL 053 9TH WARD
WINCHESTER, SARAH QUE 208 3RD E DI
WINCHESTER, WILLIAM WOR 246 1ST CENS
WINCHESTER, WILLIAM BAL 195 11TH WAR
WINCHESTER, WILLIAM BAL 039 1ST WARD
WINCKELMAN, FREDERICK BAL 151 16TH WAR
WINCKELMAN, FREDERICK BAL 145 16TH WAR
WINCKER, HENRY BAL 248 2ND WARD
WINCKER, HENRY BAL 272 2ND WARD
WINCKNAUR, WILLIAM BAL 268 12TH WAR
WINDER, ABRAHAM BAL 087 1ST WARD
WINDER, BENJAMIN BAL 086 2ND DIST
WINDER, CHARLES BAL 121 16TH WAR
WINDER, CHRISTIAN BAL 154 19TH WAR
WINDER, ELIZABETH BAL 425 14TH WAR
WINDER, ELIZABETH TAL 026 EASTON D
WINDER, EMILY BAL 214 11TH WAR
WINDER, GEORGE BAL 181 2ND WARD
WINDER, HANNAH SOM 514 BARREN C
WINDER, HENRY BAL 092 2ND DIST
WINDER, ISRAEL BAL 110 10TH WAR
WINDER, J. BAL 149 1ST WARD
WINDER, JANE BAL 363 13TH WAR
WINDER, JOHN BAL 054 2ND DIST
WINDER, JOHN BAL 252 12TH WAR
WINDER, JOHN BAL 269 7TH WARD
WINDER, JOHN SOM 535 QUANTICO

Name	County	Page	District
WINDER, JOHN*	BAL	352	3RD WARD
WINDER, LENNEY	BAL	378	1ST DIST
WINDER, LIDIA	BAL	378	1ST DIST
WINDER, LOUISA	BAL	106	15TH WAR
WINDER, MARTHA	BAL	458	8TH WARD
WINDER, REVELL	SOM	548	TYASKIN
WINDER, RIDER H.	WOR	300	SNOW HIL
WINDER, SALLY	SOM	525	QUANTICO
WINDER, SAMUEL	SOM	521	BARREN C
WINDER, SARAH	SOM	530	QUANTICO
WINDER, SARAH	BAL	083	2ND DIST
WINDER, SOPHIA	SOM	553	TYASKIN
WINDER, SUSAN	BAL	425	14TH WAR
WINDER, WILLIAM	SOM	533	QUANTICO
WINDERS, HENRY	WAS	226	1ST DIST
WINDERS, JACOB	WAS	222	1ST DIST
WINDERS, JANE	WAS	217	1ST DIST
WINDERS, JOHN	WAS	172	FUNKSTOW
WINDERS, SAMUEL	WAS	131	2ND DIST
WINDERS, SARAH	BAL	103	10TH WAR
WINDFIELD, S.	PRI	068	NOTTINGH
WINDHAM, ELIZABETH	MGM	360	BERRYS D
WINDHAM, JAMES	MGM	360	BERRYS D
WINDHAM, JAMES M.	MGM	427	MEDLEY 3
WINDHAM, WILLIAM	MGM	361	BERRYS D
WINDLE, JACOB	CAR	354	6TH DIST
WINDLE, JOHN	ALL	208	CUMBERLA
WINDLE, WILLIAM	CEC	178	7TH E DI
WINDOBORN, AUGUST	BAL	035	18TH WAR
WINDOURS, MARY J.	BAL	010	4TH WARD
WINDSOR, ALEXANDER	MGM	439	CLARKSTR
WINDSOR, CASSEY	PRI	074	MARLBROU
WINDSOR, COLUMBUS	FRE	012	FREDERIC
WINDSOR, JOHN H.	MGM	323	CRACKLIN
WINDSOR, MARGARET M.	BAL	366	3RD WARD
WINDSOR, MARY	BAL	059	4TH WARD
WINDSOR, SAMUEL	CHA	223	ALLENS F
WINDSOR, ZACHARIAH T.	FRE	226	BUCKEYST
WINDSOR, ZADOCK	FRE	232	BUCKEYST
WINDWARD, CHARLES H.	BAL	132	1ST WARD
WINEBERG, ROSE	BAL	073	4TH WARD
WINEBERRY, BETTSY	FRE	251	NEW MARK
WINEBERRY, DENNSI	FRE	056	FREDERIC
WINEBERRY, JOHN	MGM	351	BERRYS D
WINEBRENNEN, JOSEPH	ALL	114	5TH E.D.
WINEBRENNER, ELLEN	FRE	031	FREDERIC
WINEBRENNER, JACOB	ALL	113	5TH E.D.
WINEBRENNER, PETER	ALL	097	5TH E.D.
WINEBRUNER, ELIZA	FRE	285	WOODSBOR
WINEBRUNER, GEORGE L.	FRE	283	WOODSBOR
WINEBRUNER, WILLIAM	FRE	284	WOODSBOR
WINEBRUNNER, GEORGE A.	FRE	310	WOODSBOR
WINECUM, JOHN	BAL	132	11TH WAR
WINEFIELD, J. H. D.	BAL	332	1ST DIST
WINEGARDEN, PHILIP	WAS	164	2ND DIST
WINEHAD, MARTIN	BAL	253	2ND WARD
WINEHART, ANN E.	BAL	280	7TH WARD
WINEMARD, CHARLOTT	BAL	193	2ND WARD
WINEMILLER, JOHN H.	MGM	442	CLARKSTR
WINEMILLER, RACHEL	CAR	256	3RD DIST
WINENGER, JOSEPH	BAL	296	7TH WARD
WINEON, DANIEL	ALL	197	CUMBERLA
WINEOUT, HENRY D.	ALL	212	CUMBERLA
WINEOW, HENRY	ALL	220	CUMBERLA
WINER, HENRY	BAL	303	7TH WARD
WINETER, MARY	CAR	355	6TH DIST
WINEY, PHIL	QUE	206	3RD E DI
WINFIELD, GEORGE	FRE	371	CATOCTIN
WINFIELD, JOHN	ALL	098	5TH E.D.
WINFIELD, MARY	BAL	181	19TH WAR
WINFIELD, SUSAN	BAL	181	19TH WAR
WINFIELD, WILLIAM	BAL	181	19TH WAR
WINFIELD, WILLIAM	PRI	118	PISCATAW
WINFORD, H.	BAL	151	1ST WARD
WINFRED, THOMAS	BAL	041	1ST WARD
WING, ANN	BAL	322	12TH WAR
WING, CHARLES	TAL	049	EASTON T
WING, CHARLES	DOR	397	1ST DIST
WING, CHARLES-BLACK	BAL	217	2ND WARD
WING, DAVID	BAL	207	17TH WAR
WING, EBENEZER	BAL	146	1ST WARD
WING, EDWIN	TAL	021	EASTON D
WING, ELLEN*	TAL	010	EASTON D
WING, GEORGE	DOR	397	1ST DIST
WING, GRACE	TAL	070	EASTON T
WING, JANE R.	BAL	323	12TH WAR
WING, JOHN	BAL	352	13TH WAR
WING, JOHN W.	TAL	017	EASTON D
WING, JOSEPH T.*	TAL	042	EASTON D
WING, NANCY	BAL	199	11TH WAR
WING, SUSAN C.	TAL	049	EASTON T
WING, WARTE *	TAL	075	EASTON T
WING, ZACHARIAH	BAL	201	6TH WARD
WINGAR, CASPER	BAL	051	18TH WAR
WINGARD, JOHN P.	PRI	009	BLADENSB
WINGATE, CANE	DOR	345	3RD DIVI
WINGATE, CASSANDRA	CAL	045	3RD DIST
WINGATE, CATHARINE	BAL	176	19TH WAR
WINGATE, CLARA	DOR	376	1ST DIST
WINGATE, EDWARD	BAL	047	18TH WAR
WINGATE, ELIZABETH	DOR	340	3RD DIVI
WINGATE, EMILEY	DOR	336	3RD DIVI
WINGATE, EMILY	DOR	381	1ST DIST
WINGATE, EMILY V.	DOR	373	1ST DIST
WINGATE, FANNY	BAL	237	2ND WARD
WINGATE, GARRETTSON	DOR	338	3RD DIVI
WINGATE, GEORGE	BAL	273	17TH WAR
WINGATE, GEORGE E.	SOM	536	TYASKIN
WINGATE, GEORGE W.	DOR	373	1ST DIST
WINGATE, GILBERT	DOR	342	3RD DIVI
WINGATE, HENRY	CHA	224	ALLENS F
WINGATE, HENRY*	DOR	381	1ST DIST
WINGATE, HICKSON	DOR	340	3RD DIVI
WINGATE, ISAAC	CAR	115	NO TWP L
WINGATE, JACOB	CEC	085	5TH E DI
WINGATE, JAMES E.	CHA	219	ALLENS F
WINGATE, JOHN H.	BAL	136	16TH WAR
WINGATE, JOHN H. D.	CHA	237	HILLTOP
WINGATE, JOSEPH	CEC	072	5TH E DI
WINGATE, LEWIS*	DOR	376	1ST DIST
WINGATE, LOUIZA	CAR	115	NO TWP L
WINGATE, MARGARET	DOR	377	1ST DIST
WINGATE, MARY C.	DOR	374	1ST DIST
WINGATE, MAYJOR C. R.	BAL	325	3RD WARD
WINGATE, NELLY	SOM	422	PRINCESS
WINGATE, REBECCA	CEC	115	3RD E DI
WINGATE, RICHRD	CEC	029	CHESAPEA
WINGATE, ROBERT	DOR	346	3RD DIVI
WINGATE, SAMUEL	SOM	537	TYASKIN
WINGATE, SARAH	BAL	176	19TH WAR
WINGATE, SHADRACK	DOR	340	3RD DIVI
WINGATE, STANLEY	DOR	430	1ST DIST
WINGATE, SUSAN	BAL	449	8TH WARD
WINGATE, THOMAS	DOR	427	1ST DIST
WINGATE, THOMAS T.*	BAL	379	3RD WARD
WINGATE, W. HENRY	BAL	019	15TH WAR
WINGATE, WALLACE	DOR	340	3RD DIVI
WINGATE, WILLIAM	DOR	374	1ST DIST
WINGATE, WILLIAM	CEC	027	CHESAPEA
WINGATE, WILLIAM	CEC	147	PORT DUP
WINGATE, WILLIAM	BAL	389	3RD WARD
WINGATE, WILLIAM	PRI	030	VANSVILL
WINGATE, WILLIAM L.	DOR	316	1ST DIST
WINGATE, ZEBELON	TAL	082	ST MICHA
WINGERT, JOHN	ALL	145	6TH E.D.
WINGERT, PHILIP H.	WAS	138	HAGERSTO
WINGFIELD, R. C. M.	BAL	333	1ST DIST
WINGLE, WOLFGANG	BAL	138	2ND DIST
WINGMAN, FREDERICK	BAL	162	11TH WAR
WINGMAN, R.	BAL	191	11TH WAR
WINGS, MARIA	ANN	285	ANNAPOLI
WINGS, SUSAN	ANN	349	3RD DIST
WINIGER, HENRY	BAL	220	17TH WAR
WINIHON, SAMUEL P.	WOR	168	6TH E DI
WINK, A.	BAL	140	1ST WARD
WINK, ADAM	CAR	206	4TH DIST
WINK, GEORGE	CAR	172	8TH DIST
WINK, JOHN	CAR	172	8TH DIST
WINK, JOHN	BAL	014	1ST WARD
WINK, LANER	CAR	172	8TH DIST
WINK, SAMUEL	CAR	171	8TH DIST
WINK, WILLIAM	CAR	172	8TH DIST
WINK, WILLIAM	BAL	357	1ST DIST
WINKELMAN, JOHN	BAL	141	16TH WAR
WINKELMAN, JOHN	BAL	342	13TH WAR
WINKELMANN, HARMAN	BAL	165	16TH WAR
WINKELMANN, HENRY	BAL	149	16TH WAR
WINKERSON, MARY E.	CHA	278	BOJANTOW
WINKFIELD, JOHN	WAS	170	FUNKSTOW
WINKFIELD, MARIAH	WAS	025	2ND SUBD
WINKFIELD, WILLAIM	WAS	019	2ND SUBD
WINKINGTON, JOHN	BAL	005	1ST WARD
WINKLE, BEN	PRI	099	SPALDING
WINKLE, HENRY	BAL	170	16TH WAR
WINKLE, JOHN	PRI	045	VANSVILL
WINKLE, THOMAS	PRI	045	VANSVILL
WINKLE, WILLAIM	PRI	102	SPALDING
WINKLEMAN, WILLIAM	BAL	371	13TH WAR
WINKLEMAN, WILLIAM	BAL	055	4TH WARD
WINKLEMARD, ANTON	BAL	216	2ND WARD
WINKLER, CATHARINE	BAL	367	13TH WAR
WINKLER, GEORGE	PRI	039	VANSVILL
WINKLER, JOHN	PRI	091	MARLBROU
WINKLER, JOHN	BAL	364	13TH WAR
WINKLER, JOSEPH	BAL	294	1ST DIST
WINKLER, MARY	BAL	189	6TH WARD
WINKLER, RUTH L.	HAR	124	2ND DIST
WINKLEY, MARY J.	BAL	107	10TH WAR
WINKS, JOSEPHINE	BAL	315	1ST DIST
WINKS, JOSEPHUS	WAS	086	2ND SUBD
WINKS, ROBERT	BAL	158	1ST WARD
WINKS, ROBERT	BAL	028	1ST WARD
WINKS, SAMUEL M.	FRE	213	BUCKEYST
WINKS, SAMUEL*	BAL	394	3RD WARD
WINKS, THOMAS	WAS	046	2ND SUBD
WINKS,ROBERT	BAL	126	1ST WARD
WINLEY, WASH	BAL	219	12TH WAR
WINMAN, MARY	BAL	341	7TH WARD
WINN, ACHSAH C.	BAL	474	14TH WAR
WINN, ANN M.	WAS	174	FUNKSTOW
WINN, ARCHIBALD	BAL	192	6TH WARD
WINN, CHARLOTT B.	BAL	106	18TH WAR
WINN, CHRISTOPHER	BAL	327	13TH WAR
WINN, ELISHA T.	BAL	397	8TH WARD
WINN, ELIZABETH	FRE	271	NEW MARK
WINN, JOHN	BAL	254	12TH WAR
WINN, JOHN	BAL	177	2ND DIST
WINN, JOHN W.	BAL	423	8TH WARD
WINN, JOSEPH	BAL	174	19TH WAR
WINN, LEWIS	BAL	156	19TH WAR
WINN, MARY	FRE	203	5TH E DI
WINN, MARY ANN	BAL	097	5TH WARD
WINN, PRUDENCE G.	BAL	474	14TH WAR
WINN, WILLIAM	BAL	106	18TH WAR
WINN, WILLIAM	BAL	100	18TH WAR
WINNEBERGER, JANE	BAL	349	13TH WAR
WINNEKEY, JOHN	BAL	330	7TH WARD
WINNER, EDWARD	CEC	191	5TH E DI
WINNER, GEORGE	ALL	042	10TH E.D
WINNER, JACOB	ALL	042	10TH E.D
WINNER, JESSE	ALL	042	10TH E.D
WINNER, W.H.	BAL	013	18TH WAR
WINNEY, FRANCES	BAL	230	12TH WAR
WINNITT, JOSEPH	BAL	147	19TH WAR
WINNMILLA, MARY	BAL	252	2ND WARD
WINNUME, ANN C.	BAL	120	11TH WAR
WINPENHY, THOMAS	BAL	392	1ST DIST
WINPIGLER, ELIZABETH	FRE	257	NEW MARK
WINPIGLER, JOHN	FRE	262	NEW MARK
WINPIGLER, WILLIAM	FRE	346	MIDDLETO
WINRA, MARY DENNIS SIS- *	BAL	316	20TH WAR
WINROD, HENRY	FRE	244	NEW MARK
WINRODE, CATHERINE	MGM	436	CLARKSTR
WINRODE, JAMES E.	MGM	435	CLARKSTR
WINROTT, LEVI T.	CAR	334	6TH DIST
WINROW, ANN E.	HAR	134	2ND DIST
WINROW, CAHRLES B.	HAR	133	2ND DIST
WINSEIT, A.	BAL	303	20TH WAR
WINSETT, CHARLES	BAL	416	1ST DIST
WINSETT, JOHN G.	BAL	100	15TH WAR
WINSEY, WILLIAM	BAL	138	5TH WARD
WINSLOW, ALEXA	BAL	118	1ST WARD
WINSLOW, ALEXANDER	BAL	337	3RD WARD
WINSLOW, ANDREW	BAL	126	1ST WARD
WINSLOW, HARRIET	BAL	337	3RD WARD
WINSLOW, ISAAC	BAL	159	1ST WARD
WINSLOW, ROBERT	BAL	033	9TH WARD
WINSLOW,A.A.	BAL	142	1ST WARD
WINSON, ANN	PRI	061	NOTTINGH
WINSON, JOHN	PRI	063	NOTTINGH
WINSON, JOHN H.	PRI	056	AQUASCO
WINSON, LAVINIA	WOR	193	8TH E DI
WINSON, MARY A.	BAL	094	5TH WARD
WINSON, SARAH	PRI	058	NOTTINGH
WINSON, SUSAN	PRI	056	AQUASCO
WINSON, THOMAS	BAL	219	12TH WAR
WINSOR, ALFRED	SOM	510	BARREN C
WINSOR, CHARLOTTE	SOM	496	SALISBUR
WINSOR, ELEANOR	SOM	519	BARREN C
WINSOR, ELIJAH	SOM	488	SALISBUR
WINSOR, HAMILTON	SOM	439	DAMES QU
WINSOR, MARY J.	DOR	452	1ST DIST
WINSOR, HENRY	SOM	457	DAMES QU
WINSOR, HENRY	MGM	341	CLARKSBU
WINSOR, ISAAC	SOM	515	BARREN C
WINSOR, ISAAC J.	SOM	439	DAMES QU
WINSOR, JAMES	DOR	376	1ST DIST
WINSOR, JAMES H.	SOM	510	BARREN C
WINSOR, JAMES W.	SOM	447	DAMES QU
WINSOR, JOHN	DOR	346	3RD DIVI
WINSOR, JOHN	DOR	350	3RD DIVI
WINSOR, JOHN	SOM	491	SALISBUR
WINSOR, JOHN	SOM	457	DAMES QU
WINSOR, JOHN	SOM	355	BRINKLEY
WINSOR, JOSEPH	SOM	516	BARREN C
WINSOR, LUKE	PRI	061	NOTTINGH
WINSOR, MARGARET A.	SOM	447	DAMES QU
WINSOR, MARTHA	SOM	496	SALISBUR
WINSOR, MARTHA	SOM	550	TYASKIN
WINSOR, MARY A.	DOR	346	3RD DIVI
WINSOR, MARY E.	SOM	458	DAMES QU
WINSOR, MATILDA T.	SOM	439	DAMES QU
WINSOR, ROBERT	SOM	510	BARREN C
WINSOR, ROBERT B.	FRE	399	JEFFERSO
WINSOR, SARAH	SOM	448	DAMES QU
WINSOR, SEVERN	SOM	439	DAMES QU
WINSOR, STEPHEN	SOM	438	DAMES QU
WINSOR, THOMAS D.	PRI	062	NOTTINGH
WINSOR, WILLIAM	SOM	489	SALISBUR
WINSOR, WILLIAM	SOM	458	DAMES QU
WINTER, ABRAHAM	BAL	416	14TH WAR
WINTER, ADAM	BAL	208	19TH WAR
WINTER, ANDREW	BAL	121	2ND DIST
WINTER, CARHARINE	BAL	442	14TH WAR
WINTER, CHRISTIAN	BAL	368	1ST DIST
WINTER, DAVID	CAR	353	6TH DIST
WINTER, EVE	CAR	348	6TH DIST
WINTER, FLORENCE	BAL	406	14TH WAR
WINTER, FRANCIS	BAL	029	18TH WAR
WINTER, FRANCIS	BAL	141	5TH WARD
WINTER, FREDERICK	FRE	006	FREDERIC
WINTER, FREDERICK	CAR	397	2ND DIST
WINTER, FREDERICK-BLACK	QUE	136	1ST E DI
WINTER, GEORGE	ALL	098	5TH E.D.
WINTER, HENRY	BAL	104	5TH WARD
WINTER, HENRY	FRE	160	EMMITTSB
WINTER, HENRY	CAR	335	6TH DIST
WINTER, HENRY	BAL	406	14TH WAR
WINTER, HENRY	BAL	470	14TH WAR
WINTER, HENRY	BAL	267	17TH WAR
WINTER, JACOB	ALL	116	5TH E.D.
WINTER, JACOB	ALL	119	5TH E.D.
WINTER, JACOB	WAS	269	1ST DIST
WINTER, JOHN	ALL	112	5TH E.D.
WINTER, JOHN	ALL	073	5TH E.D.
WINTER, JOHN	BAL	029	15TH WAR
WINTER, JOHN	BAL	139	1ST WARD
WINTER, JOHN	BAL	421	14TH WAR
WINTER, JOHN	BAL	408	3RD WARD
WINTER, JOHN D.	WAS	271	1ST DIST
WINTER, JOHN S.	ALL	116	5TH E.D.
WINTER, JOSEPH	BAL	169	2ND DIST
WINTER, JOSEPH	CAR	411	2ND DIST
WINTER, LOUIS	BAL	103	5TH WARD
WINTER, MARTHA	FRE	163	EMMITTSB
WINTER, MARTIN	CAR	340	6TH DIST
WINTER, MARTIN	BAL	255	2ND WARD
WINTER, MARY	BAL	269	12TH WAR
WINTER, MARY	BAL	421	14TH WAR
WINTER, RODNEY	WAS	095	2ND SUBD
WINTER, SAMUEL	BAL	209	17TH WAR
WINTER, SAMUEL	CAR	390	2ND DIST
WINTER, SARAH	BAL	122	11TH WAR
WINTER, THOMAS	FRE	380	PETERSVI
WINTER,ELIZABETH	CAR	389	2ND DIST
WINTERBOTTOM, HARRISON	DOR	382	1ST DIST
WINTERBOTTOM, SAMUEL	DOR	377	1ST DIST
WINTERBOTTOM, THOMAS	BAL	367	3RD WARD
WINTERBOTUM, JOHN*	TAL	001	EASTON D
WINTERFIELD, MARY ANN	BAL	149	5TH WARD
WINTERLING, JOHN	BAL	004	9TH WARD
WINTERNIGHT, HENRY	BAL	209	17TH WAR
WINTERNITZ, CHARLES	BAL	087	10TH WAR
WINTERNITZ, LOUIS	BAL	087	10TH WAR
WINTERS, BENJAMIN	BAL	322	1ST DIST
WINTERS, BERY	BAL	272	12TH WAR
WINTERS, CATHARINE	CAR	269	WESTMINS
WINTERS, CHARLES	BAL	129	1ST WARD
WINTERS, CHRISTIAN	WAS	132	HAGERSTO
WINTERS, DIVID	WAS	235	1ST DIST
WINTERS, ELIZABETH	WAS	235	1ST DIST
WINTERS, ELIZABETH	CAR	275	7TH DIST
WINTERS, FARTZ	BAL	444	8TH WARD
WINTERS, GEORGE	CAR	319	1ST DIST
WINTERS, GEORGE-BLACK	CAR	100	NO TWP L
WINTERS, JAMES	BAL	123	11TH WAR
WINTERS, JAMES	BAL	314	3RD WARD
WINTERS, JAMES JR.-BLACK	CAR	103	NO TWP L
WINTERS, JAMES-BLACK	CAR	102	NO TWP L
WINTERS, JOHN	BAL	417	3RD WARD
WINTERS, JOHN	BAL	315	1ST DIST
WINTERS, JOHN	WAS	235	1ST DIST
WINTERS, JOHN REV.	CAR	270	WESTMINS
WINTERS, JOHN T.	ST	293	2ND E DI
WINTERS, JOHN-BLACK	CAR	099	NO TWP L
WINTERS, JOSEPH	WAS	235	1ST DIST
WINTERS, LEWIS	CAR	268	WESTMINS
WINTERS, LOUISA S.	CAR	279	7TH DIST
WINTERS, SAMUEL	BAL	309	1ST DIST
WINTERS, WILLIAM	BAL	044	15TH WAR
WINTERS, WILLIAM	WAS	098	2ND DIST
WINTERS, WILLIAM	WAS	095	2ND SUBD
WINTERS,DAVID	FRE	420	8TH E DI
WINTERSON, ELIZA A.	BAL	342	7TH WARD
WINTERSON, GASSAWAY	ANN	305	1ST DIST
WINTERSTINE, JOHN	ALL	240	CUMBERLA
WINTERSY, MARY	CEC	184	7TH E DI
WINTHROP, GEORGE	DOR	454	1ST DIST
WINTKLE, WASHINGTON*	BAL	325	3RD WARD
WINTON, HORACE B.	FRE	347	MIDDLETO
WINTRY, JOHN	BAL	107	2ND DIST
WINYARD, HY	BAL	461	1ST DIST
WIPLE, FREDERICK	BAL	317	1ST DIST
WIPPEY, J.	BAL	171	1ST WARD
WIPPLE, JAMES	BAL	114	11TH WAR
WIRALAND, SAMUEL	KEN	287	3RD DIST
WIRDER, SARAH	BAL	050	2ND DIST
WIRE, BARBARA	BAL	282	1ST DIST
WIRE, DAVID	CEC	170	6TH E DI
WIRE, HENRY *	KEN	243	2ND DIST

WIRE, JAMES ALL 085 5TH E.D.
WIRE, JAMES * KEN 232 2ND DIST
WIREMAN, DANIEL * FRE 128 CREAGERS
WIREMAN, GEORGE WAS 282 1ST DIST
WIRGHT, PETER L. CAR 121 NO TWP L
WIRMAR, VALENTINE BAL 212 19TH WAR
WIRNS, HENRY-BLACK FRE 388 PETERSVI
WIRST, GEORGE BAL 171 19TH WAR
WIRT, BENJAMIN CEC 094 4TH E DI
WIRT, JAMES ANN 384 4TH DIST
WIRT, JOHN W. CEC 079 NORTHEAS
WIRT, SAMUEL H. CEC 028 CHESAPEA
WIRTEBERGER, JOHN FRE 147 10TH E D
WIRTEBERGER, LEWIS FRE 147 10TH E D
WIRTER, PHILIPEONA BAL 367 1ST DIST
WIRTS, GEORGE BAL 255 17TH WAR
WIRTS, JACOB FRE 220 BUCKEYST
WIRTS, JOHN BAL 008 15TH WAR
WIRTS, JOHN BAL 142 16TH WAR
WIRTS, MICHAEL BAL 255 17TH WAR
WIRTS, SARAH C. BAL 122 16TH WAR
WIRTS, WILLIAM FRE 215 BUCKEYST
WIRY, SAMUEL TAL 004 EASTON D
WISE, ADALINE BAL 128 11TH WAR
WISE, AMELIA FRE 350 MIDDLETO
WISE, ANDREW BAL 221 19TH WAR
WISE, ANDREW KEN 259 1ST DIST
WISE, ANN BAL 291 7TH WARD
WISE, ANN B. CAR 355 6TH DIST
WISE, ANTONY BAL 102 2ND DIST
WISE, BANDAET BAL 031 1ST WARD
WISE, CAROLINE-BLACK WOR 325 1ST E DI
WISE, CHARLES B. ST 274 3RD E DI
WISE, CHARLES L. ST 292 2ND E DI
WISE, DANIEL FRE 325 MIDDLETO
WISE, EDWARD BAL 107 2ND DIST
WISE, EDWARD BAL 225 12TH WAR
WISE, ELIZA FRE 160 EMMITTSB
WISE, ELIZABETH BAL 061 10TH WAR
WISE, ELIZABETH BAL 206 2ND WARD
WISE, ELKANAH ST 291 2ND E DI
WISE, EUGENE FRE 161 EMMITTSB
WISE, G.B. ALL 251 CUMBERLA
WISE, GEORGE BAL 081 4TH WARD
WISE, GEORGE L. ST 300 2ND E DI
WISE, GEORGE M. FRE 164 EMMITTSB
WISE, GEORGE-BLACK WOR 327 1ST E DI
WISE, HENERETTA BAL 126 18TH WAR
WISE, HENRY BAL 381 3RD WARD
WISE, HENRY* BAL 403 3RD WARD
WISE, JACOB ALL 233 CUMBERLA
WISE, JACOB WAS 012 WILLIAMS
WISE, JAEMS C. ST 282 3RD E DI
WISE, JAEMS E. WOR 259 BERLIN 1
WISE, JAMES L. FRE 165 EMMITTSB
WISE, JEHU FRE 403 JEFFERSO
WISE, JOHN CAR 355 6TH DIST
WISE, JOHN CAR 279 7TH DIST
WISE, JOHN FRE 040 FREDERIC
WISE, JOHN ST 302 2ND E DI
WISE, JOHN BAL 040 2ND DIST
WISE, JOHN BAL 035 2ND DIST
WISE, JOHN BAL 131 1ST WARD
WISE, JOHN BAL 363 8TH WARD
WISE, JOHN BAL 148 16TH WAR
WISE, JOHN BAL 298 3RD WARD
WISE, JOHN BAL 399 1ST DIST
WISE, JOHN ALL 091 5TH E.D.
WISE, JOHN A. ST 329 4TH E DI
WISE, JOHN F. ST 299 2ND E DI
WISE, JOHN H. ST 299 2ND E DI
WISE, JOHN H. ST 256 3RD E DI
WISE, JOHN J. BAL 038 9TH WARD
WISE, JOHN S. TAL 117 ST MICHA
WISE, JOSEPH BAL 043 15TH WAR
WISE, JOSEPH FRE 314 MIDDLETO
WISE, JOSEPHUS W. FRE 331 MIDDLETO
WISE, JOSHUA FRE 407 JEFFERSO
WISE, LAWRENCE BAL 282 1ST DIST
WISE, LEWIS BAL 416 14TH WAR
WISE, LEWIS BAL 210 19TH WAR
WISE, LEWIS O. FRE 333 MIDDLETO
WISE, LYDIA FRE 316 MIDDLETO
WISE, MADELINE BAL 126 18TH WAR
WISE, MARGARET CAR 180 8TH DIST
WISE, MARGARET BAL 255 2ND WARD
WISE, MARGARET WAS 133 HAGERSTO
WISE, MITCHEL-BLACK WOR 348 1ST E DI
WISE, MOSES-BLACK WOR 328 1ST E DI
WISE, NICHOLAS BAL 044 2ND DIST
WISE, PETER ALL 204 CUMBERLA
WISE, PETER FRE 333 MIDDLETO
WISE, QUITOL BAL 353 13TH WAR
WISE, SAMUEL ST 257 3RD E DI
WISE, SARAH F. TAL 118 ST MICHA
WISE, SISTER M.B. FRE 198 5TH E DI
WISE, TULLY R. BAL 410 3RD WARD
WISE, WILLIAM BAL 261 20TH WAR
WISE, WILLIAM SOM 426 PRINCESS
WISE, WILLIAM WAS 141 HAGERSTO
WISE, WILLIAM ALL 165 6TH E.D.
WISE, WILLIAM BAL 254 2ND WARD
WISE, WILLIAM H. WAS 121 HAGERSTO
WISE, WILLIAM H. HAR 038 1ST DIST
WISE, WILLIAM-BLACK WOR 326 1ST E DI
WISE, WILLIAM-BLACK WOR 328 1ST E DI
WISEAL, GEORGE BAL 285 1ST DIST
WISEBAUGH, BENJAMIN BAL 328 7TH WARD
WISEBAUGH, MARTIN BAL 311 7TH WARD
WISEHIERN, ADAM FRE 080 FREDERIC
WISEKETTLE, AUGUST ALL 199 CUMBERLA
WISEL, JOHN BAL 223 12TH WAR
WISEL, MOLLENA FRE 012 FREDERIC
WISEMAN, ANN BAL 037 18TH WAR
WISEMAN, CATHERINE BAL 316 20TH WAR
WISEMAN, CHALRES BAL 037 18TH WAR
WISEMAN, DANIEL FRE 330 MIDDLETO
WISEMAN, ELIZABETH BAL 298 20TH WAR
WISEMAN, HENRY BAL 431 8TH WARD
WISEMAN, JACOB BAL 095 18TH WAR
WISEMAN, JOHN R. PRI 035 VANSVILL
WISEMAN, JOSEPH FRE 124 CREAGERS
WISEMAN, M. ANN BAL 126 18TH WAR
WISEMAN, MARY A. FRE 330 MIDDLETO
WISEMAN, NEALE PRI 068 NOTTINGH
WISEMAN, SAMUEL FRE 340 MIDDLETO
WISEMAN, SOPHIA FRE 124 CREAGERS
WISEMAN, WILLIAM BAL 402 3RD WARD
WISEMILLER, LOUIS BAL 066 15TH WAR
WISEMUT, THEODORE * BAL 309 20TH WAR
WISENALL, JACOB BAL 196 6TH WARD
WISENBON, PAMELIA BAL 165 2ND DIST
WISENSILL, GEORGE BAL 017 9TH WARD
WISER, GEORGE CEC 122 4TH E DI
WISER, JACOB CEC 098 3RD E DI
WISER, MARGARET CEC 120 3RD E DI
WISER, TELL BAL 002 4TH WARD
WISER, WILLIAM CEC 112 4TH E DI
WISER, WILLIAM CEC 068 5TH E DI
WISETH, SARAH BAL 149 11TH WAR
WISGNER, AUMENT* BAL 354 3RD WARD
WISHA, ANNA BAL 196 17TH WAR
WISHARD, AMANDA WAS 026 2ND SUBD
WISHARD, ANN WAS 124 HAGERSTO
WISHARD, EDWARD WAS 026 2ND SUBD
WISHARD, JACOB WAS 284 1ST DIST
WISHARD, JAMES WAS 026 2ND SUBD
WISHARD, JOHN D. WAS 215 1ST DIST
WISHBACK, HENRY BAL 329 13TH WAR
WISHER, ANN QUE 209 3RD E DI
WISHER, ANNA BAL 080 15TH WAR
WISHER, AUGUSTA CAR 065 NO TWP L
WISHER, CHARLOTTE BAL 054 15TH WAR
WISHER, DANIEL BAL 226 17TH WAR
WISHER, HARRETT HAR 171 3RD DIST
WISHER, HENRY BAL 143 5TH WARD
WISHER, JAMES-BLACK QUE 160 2ND E DI
WISHER, JAOCB CAR 065 NO TWP L
WISHER, LEAR-BLACK CAR 166 NO TWP L
WISHER, MARGARET HAR 165 3RD DIST
WISHER, MARTHY A. HAR 165 3RD DIST
WISHER, RACHELL BAL 253 17TH WAR
WISHER, RICHARD BAL 041 15TH WAR
WISHER, VIOLETT-BLACK CAR 142 NO TWP L
WISHERD, ELIZABETH WAS 132 2ND DIST
WISHERD, JACOB WAS 132 2ND DIST
WISHERD, SUSAN WAS 132 2ND DIST
WISHINGER, LEO BAL 264 20TH WAR
WISHMIRE, CHARLES ALL 217 CUMBERLA
WISING, ISAAC FRE 035 FREDERIC
WISLON, GREENBERRY CAR 267 WESTMINS
WISLON, HENRY QUE 211 3RD E DI
WISLON, THOMAS FRE 415 8TH E DI
WISNARE, JACOB BAL 289 12TH WAR
WISNER, ABRAHAM BAL 189 5TH DIST
WISNER, ABRAHAM BAL 183 5TH DIST
WISNER, ABRAHAM BAL 190 5TH DIST
WISNER, ABRAHAM WAS 301 1ST DIST
WISNER, ADAM BAL 169 2ND DIST
WISNER, CATHARINE BAL 188 5TH DIST
WISNER, CHRISTOPHER CAR 249 3RD DIST
WISNER, CLINES BAL 191 5TH DIST
WISNER, DINAH BAL 186 5TH DIST
WISNER, ELIZABETH BAL 190 5TH DIST
WISNER, ELLEN WAS 123 HAGERSTO
WISNER, GEORGE BAL 191 5TH DIST
WISNER, GEORGE BAL 440 1ST DIST
WISNER, GEORGHE BAL 198 5TH DIST
WISNER, ISAAC BAL 184 5TH DIST
WISNER, JACOB BAL 169 2ND DIST
WISNER, JHN BAL 011 2ND DIST
WISNER, JOHN BAL 219 6TH DIST
WISNER, JOHN BAL 201 6TH DIST
WISNER, JOSHUA CAR 278 7TH DIST
WISNER, JULIANN BAL 202 6TH DIST
WISNER, LOUISA BAL 291 20TH WAR
WISNER, MARY BAL 432 1ST DIST
WISNER, PHILIP WAS 287 1ST DIST
WISNER, SAMUEL BAL 191 5TH DIST
WISNER, SARAH BAL 184 5TH DIST
WISNER, SUSAN BAL 184 5TH DIST
WISNER, URIAH CAR 249 3RD DIST
WISNER, WILLIAM BAL 441 1ST DIST
WISON, JOSEPH PRI 104 PISCATAW
WISONG, THOMAS J. ALL 259 CUMBERLA
WISS, EDWARD DR. BAL 371 13TH WAR
WISSEL, CATHARINE BAL 193 19TH WAR
WISSIGAR, JOSEPH J. ST 291 2ND E DI
WISSIGER, PETER * FRE 340 MIDDLETO
WISSILL, FRONEY BAL 443 14TH WAR
WISSINGER, LEONARD FRE 350 MIDDLETO
WISSMAN, MARY BAL 119 15TH WAR
WISTLER, ABRAHAM HAR 066 1ST DIST
WISWARE, MARGARET CEC 008 ELKTON 3
WISZEBERGER, JOSEPH WAS 152 2ND DIST
WITACRE, JAMES BAL 228 1ST DIST
WITAKER, LOYD BAL 431 8TH WARD
WITCHER, GEORGE BAL 154 1ST WARD
WITCHRISSON, ELIZABETH BAL 175 16TH WAR
WITCOME, MARY BAL 265 1ST DIST
WITEMARSH, HENRY BAL 116 11TH WAR
WITERMAN, ALEXANDER BAL 044 4TH WARD
WITERMARSH, JOHN BAL 116 11TH WAR
WITFIELD, ABRAHAM BAL 268 2ND WARD
WITFIELD, ELENORA BAL 268 2ND WARD
WITFIELD, LEVI BAL 042 15TH WAR
WITHAM, ROBERT BAL 153 1ST WARD
WITHERALD, SAMUEL BAL 035 9TH WARD
WITHERDD, GEORGE BAL 457 8TH WARD
WITHEROW, JOHN FRE 181 5TH E DI
WITHEROW, KATE FRE 065 FREDERIC
WITHEROW, ROSS FRE 186 5TH E DI
WITHERS, JOSEPH BAL 312 1ST DIST
WITHERS, MICHAEL BAL 033 2ND DIST
WITHERSTEIN, HAMILTON BAL 206 6TH WARD
WITHERSTINE, MARY BAL 445 8TH WARD
WITHERSTON, HESTER QUE 204 3RD E DI
WITHERTON, PRISCILLA WAS 097 2ND DIST
WITHINGTON, HENRY BAL 106 10TH WAR
WITHINGTON, JOHN BAL 385 13TH WAR
WITHINGTON, MARY A. BAL 126 16TH WAR
WITHRIDE, ISAAC CAR 321 1ST DIST
WITHUM, CHARLES BAL 129 1ST WARD
WITIGIAN, HUTCHADON WAS 021 2ND SUBD
WITLOE, ELLEN CEC 160 6TH E DI
WITMAN, GEORGE BAL 114 15TH WAR
WITMAN, MARGARET BAL 131 16TH WAR
WITMAN, MARY BAL 350 7TH WARD
WITMAN, SOPHIA L. BAL 114 15TH WAR
WITMER, ANNA WAS 295 1ST DIST
WITMER, BENJAMIN WAS 223 1ST DIST
WITMER, CALVIN WAS 150 HAGERSTO
WITMER, DANIEL WAS 224 1ST DIST
WITMER, DANIEL CAR 309 1ST DIST
WITMER, DANIEL D. WAS 105 2ND DIST
WITMER, DAVID WAS 226 1ST DIST
WITMER, ELIZABETH CAR 309 1ST DIST
WITMER, FRANCIS BAL 298 3RD WARD
WITMER, GEORGE FRE 365 CATOCTIN
WITMER, HENRY B. WAS 105 2ND DIST
WITMER, JACOB WAS 296 1ST DIST
WITMER, JOHN WAS 295 1ST DIST
WITMER, JOHN WAS 223 1ST DIST
WITMER, JOSEPH CAR 320 1ST DIST
WITMER, ROSANA WAS 105 2ND DIST
WITMER, WILHELMINA FRE 345 MIDDLETO
WITMEYER, LYDIA CAR 411 2ND DIST
WITMORE, ELEANORA BAL 365 3RD WARD
WITMORE, MARTIN FRE 165 EMMITTSB
WITMORE, WILLIAM FRE 183 5TH E DI
WITMYER, BARBARA CAR 255 3RD DIST
WITMYER, LYDIA CAR 408 2ND DIST
WITMYER, REBECCA CAR 255 3RD DIST
WITNER, CAROLINE E. BAL 298 3RD WARD
WITNEY, AMANDA BAL 266 20TH WAR
WITNEY, AMANDA BAL 266 20TH WAR
WITNEY, JOHN ALL 094 5TH E.D.
WITNEY, PATERICK WAS 116 2ND DIST
WITRIGHT, P. W. ANN 329 2ND DIST
WITSEL, ALBERT WAS 230 1ST DIST
WITSON, JAMES BAL 281 2ND WARD
WITT, FRANCIS BAL 165 11TH WAR
WITT, JOHNATHAN ALL 250 CUMBERLA
WITT, MARTIN WAS 266 1ST DIST
WITT, WILLIAM ALL 250 CUMBERLA
WITTAKER, WILLIAM BAL 129 1ST WARD
WITTEL, JOHN BAL 093 15TH WAR
WITTER, EMANUEL WAS 185 BOONSBOR
WITTER, HANSON BAL 229 1ST DIST
WITTER, SAMUEL CAR 355 6TH DIST
WITTER, SOPHIA WAS 185 BOONSBOR
WITTERKIND, HENRY BAL 123 16TH WAR
WITTERS, CATHARINE WAS 180 BOONSBOR
WITTERS, JAMES BAL 289 3RD WARD
WITTERS, LILIA WAS 235 1ST DIST
WITTERS, WILLIAM* BAL 397 3RD WARD
WITTERSPOON, CHRISTOPH BAL 273 7TH WARD
WITTETTS, ISAAC BAL 142 1ST WARD
WITTICH, HENRY BAL 081 10TH WAR
WITTICH, LOUISA BAL 252 12TH WAR
WITTIG, CATHERINE C. BAL 023 4TH WARD
WITTIG, FREDERICK BAL 119 15TH WAR
WITTIG, FREDERICK W. BAL 023 4TH WARD
WITTINGTON, R. BAL 144 5TH WARD
WITTLE, ELIZABETH BAL 456 1ST DIST
WITTLING, ANDREW BAL 128 11TH WAR
WITTS, CHARLES BAL 225 6TH WARD
WITTS, HENRY BAL 208 6TH WARD
WITTY, WILLIAM BAL 164 2ND DIST
WITZ, DANIEL BAL 274 7TH WARD
WITZ, HENRY BAL 098 5TH WARD
WITZ, PHILIP BAL 308 7TH WARD
WIVEL, HENRY C. CAR 312 1ST DIST
WIVEL, JAMES CAR 311 1ST DIST
WIVEL, JOSEPH CAR 312 1ST DIST
WIVLE, DAVID BAL 294 3RD WARD
WMITH, MARY BAL 317 20TH WAR
WOCKLICK, GEORGE BAL 070 1ST WARD
WODARD, GEORGE WAS 094 2ND SUBD
WODARD, JAMES WAS 124 2ND DIST
WODE, MAGDALENA BAL 132 16TH WAR
WODE, WILLIMA BAL 161 16TH WAR
WODETSKY, GOTLEIB E. BAL 037 15TH WAR
WOEE, CHRISTOPHER ALL 113 5TH E.D.
WOESNER, LOUISA WAS 151 HAGERSTO
WOFEL, ADAM BAL 328 7TH WARD
WOFFLAN, JOHN A. BAL 028 2ND DIST
WOHLENBACH, FRANCES BAL 081 10TH WAR
WOHLWEVER, JACOB BAL 254 12TH WAR
WOINGS, HENRY CAL 043 3RD DIST
WOLBB, JAMES BAL 117 2ND DIST
WOLBERT, JOHN BAL 004 15TH WAR
WOLCOTT, AMELIA J. BAL 060 15TH WAR
WOLCOTT, MARY BAL 176 2ND DIST
WOLD, WILLIAM CAR 264 WESTMINS
WOLDER, JOHN BAL 275 20TH WAR
WOLDMAN, ELIZA* BAL 001 4TH WARD
WOLDMANN, ELIZA BAL 113 15TH WAR
WOLDNAR, SARAH BAL 066 4TH WARD
WOLEIN, WILLIAM* DOR 437 1ST DIST
WOLES, PRISILLA CAL 015 1ST DIST
WOLES, SHADE * KEN 225 2ND DIST
WOLF, AARON BAL 373 8TH WARD
WOLF, ADAM BAL 092 10TH WAR
WOLF, ADAM BAL 313 12TH WAR
WOLF, ADAM BAL 005 EASTERN
WOLF, ADAM FRE 029 FREDERIC
WOLF, ALEXANDER BAL 064 15TH WAR
WOLF, ANN E. CAR 307 1ST DIST
WOLF, ANNY BAL 053 4TH WARD
WOLF, ANTHONY BAL 129 11TH WAR
WOLF, BARNHARD BAL 458 14TH WAR
WOLF, C. A. S. BAL 475 14TH WAR
WOLF, CATHARINE BAL 284 1ST DIST
WOLF, CATHARINE WAS 175 1ST DIST
WOLF, CATHERINE BAL 051 9TH WARD
WOLF, CONA D CAR 329 MANCHEST
WOLF, CONRAD BAL 212 17TH WAR
WOLF, CONRAD BAL 215 17TH WAR
WOLF, DANIEL CAR 319 1ST DIST
WOLF, DANIEL CAR 179 8TH DIST
WOLF, DANIEL WAS 232 1ST DIST
WOLF, DAVID WAS 230 1ST DIST
WOLF, DAVID WAS 030 2ND SUBD
WOLF, DAVID CAR 186 8TH DIST
WOLF, ELBERT BAL 032 1ST WARD
WOLF, ELIZABETH WAS 215 1ST DIST
WOLF, ELIZABETH WAS 174 FUNKSTOW
WOLF, EMILY V. BAL 032 1ST WARD
WOLF, EPHRAIM WAS 011 WILLIAMS
WOLF, EUGENE ALL 044 10TH E.D
WOLF, FANNY BAL 292 12TH WAR
WOLF, FERDINAND CAR 180 8TH DIST
WOLF, FERDINAND CAR 397 2ND DIST
WOLF, GEORGE BAL 115 18TH WAR
WOLF, GEORGE CAR 256 3RD DIST
WOLF, GEORGE ALL 030 2ND E.D.
WOLF, GEORGE ALL 036 2ND E.D.
WOLF, GEORGE WAS 301 1ST DIST
WOLF, GEORGE WAS 271 1ST DIST
WOLF, GEORGE MGM 433 CLARKSTR
WOLF, GEORGE W. BAL 033 1ST WARD
WOLF, GOERGE WAS 004 WILLIAMS
WOLF, HARRIET FRE 042 FREDERIC
WOLF, HENRY CAR 277 7TH DIST
WOLF, HENRY BAL 191 19TH WAR
WOLF, HENRY WAS 130 2ND DIST
WOLF, HENRY ALL 062 10TH E.D
WOLF, HENRY BAL 042 9TH WARD
WOLF, J.B. ALL 239 CUMBERLA

Name	County	Page	District
WOLF, JACOB	BAL	117	15TH WAR
WOLF, JACOB	BAL	384	1ST DIST
WOLF, JACOB	FRE	362	CATOCTIN
WOLF, JACOB	FRE	362	CATOCTIN
WOLF, JAMES	WAS	187	BOONSBOR
WOLF, JAMES	WAS	070	2ND SUBD
WOLF, JAMES	WAS	232	1ST DIST
WOLF, JAMES M.	WAS	232	1ST DIST
WOLF, JEAB	WAS	208	1ST DIST
WOLF, JESSE	BAL	293	1ST DIST
WOLF, JOH	FRE	124	CREAGERS
WOLF, JOHN	BAL	216	19TH WAR
WOLF, JOHN	CAR	247	3RD DIST
WOLF, JOHN	CAR	399	2ND DIST
WOLF, JOHN	ALL	240	CUMBERLA
WOLF, JOHN	BAL	083	2ND DIST
WOLF, JOHN	BAL	042	9TH WARD
WOLF, JOHN	BAL	453	8TH WARD
WOLF, JOHN	WAS	198	1ST DIST
WOLF, JOHN	WAS	228	1ST DIST
WOLF, JOHN	WAS	062	2ND SUBD
WOLF, JOHN	WAS	004	WILLIAMS
WOLF, JOHN	WAS	298	1ST DIST
WOLF, JOHN G.	WAS	233	1ST DIST
WOLF, JOHN G.	CAR	243	TANEYTOW
WOLF, JOHN T.	BAL	399	8TH WARD
WOLF, JOSEPH	FRE	126	CREAGERS
WOLF, JOSEPH	FRE	406	JEFFERSO
WOLF, JOSEPH	WAS	002	WILLIAMS
WOLF, JOSEPHINE C.	CAR	265	WESTMINS
WOLF, JULIAN	WAS	300	1ST DIST
WOLF, LANSON	BAL	417	3RD WARD
WOLF, LAURAN	DOR	396	1ST DIST
WOLF, LEONIA	WAS	131	2ND DIST
WOLF, LEVI	ALL	030	2ND E.D.
WOLF, MAGDALENA	CAR	244	3RD DIST
WOLF, MARCUS	BAL	444	8TH WARD
WOLF, MARTIN	ALL	224	CUMBERLA
WOLF, MARTIN	CAR	380	2ND DIST
WOLF, MARTIN	WAS	230	1ST DIST
WOLF, MARY	CAR	313	1ST DIST
WOLF, MICHAEL	BAL	009	15TH WAR
WOLF, MICHAEL L.	BAL	165	6TH WARD
WOLF, MINNA	BAL	213	19TH WAR
WOLF, MINNA	BAL	371	13TH WAR
WOLF, MOLLY	BAL	236	1ST DIST
WOLF, PETER	BAL	370	1ST DIST
WOLF, PETER	WAS	003	WILLIAMS
WOLF, POWELL	BAL	165	6TH WARD
WOLF, RACHEAL	WAS	176	1ST DIST
WOLF, SALEY	DOR	396	1ST DIST
WOLF, SAMUEL	FRE	366	CATOCTIN
WOLF, SAMUEL	WAS	255	1ST DIST
WOLF, SAMUEL	BAL	287	7TH WARD
WOLF, SARAH	WAS	132	HAGERSTO
WOLF, SARAH	WAS	063	2ND SUBD
WOLF, SARAH	CAR	390	2ND DIST
WOLF, SARAH C.	ALL	240	CUMBERLA
WOLF, SIMON	WAS	210	1ST DIST
WOLF, SUSAN	WAS	001	WILLIAMS
WOLF, SYLVESTER	BAL	056	18TH WAR
WOLF, THOMAS J.	BAL	254	1ST DIST
WOLF, UPTON	CAR	385	2ND DIST
WOLF, UPTON	WAS	230	1ST DIST
WOLF, VIRGINIA	BAL	113	18TH WAR
WOLF, WILLIAM A.	BAL	111	1ST WARD
WOLF, WILLIAM H.	BAL	287	3RD WARD
WOLF, WILLIAM S.	BAL	028	1ST WARD
WOLF.ABRAHAM	CAR	383	2ND DIST
WOLF.MOSES	BAL	052	1ST WARD
WOLFAS, LOUIS	BAL	368	13TH WAR
WOLFE, A. J.	FRE	153	10TH E D
WOLFE, ALCAEUS B.	BAL	324	12TH WAR
WOLFE, ANN L.	MGM	438	CLARKSTR
WOLFE, B.	BAL	271	12TH WAR
WOLFE, CHARLOTTE	FRE	174	5TH E DI
WOLFE, DANIEL	BAL	182	19TH WAR
WOLFE, DAVID	FRE	151	10TH E D
WOLFE, DAVID	FRE	155	10TH E D
WOLFE, ELI	BAL	258	20TH WAR
WOLFE, ELI	MGM	437	CLARKSTR
WOLFE, ELIZABETH	BAL	210	19TH WAR
WOLFE, ELIZABETH	BAL	033	4TH WARD
WOLFE, ELLEN	BAL	312	12TH WAR
WOLFE, FERDINAND	BAL	328	13TH WAR
WOLFE, GARRET	FRE	148	10TH E D
WOLFE, GEORGE	FRE	182	5TH E DI
WOLFE, GEORGE	BAL	238	20TH WAR
WOLFE, GEORGE	MGM	393	ROCKERLE
WOLFE, GEORGE	BAL	049	9TH WARD
WOLFE, GEORGE	BAL	283	1ST DIST
WOLFE, HANNAH	FRE	155	10TH E D
WOLFE, HENRY	FRE	154	10TH E D
WOLFE, HENRY	BAL	010	15TH WAR
WOLFE, HIRAM A.	FRE	151	10TH E D
WOLFE, HIRAM B.	ALL	211	CUMBERLA
WOLFE, ISAIAH	FRE	244	NEW MARK
WOLFE, JACKSON	FRE	146	10TH E D
WOLFE, JAMES	FRE	120	CREAGERS
WOLFE, JAMES	FRE	119	CREAGERS
WOLFE, JOHN	FRE	176	5TH E DI
WOLFE, JOHN	FRE	150	10TH E D
WOLFE, JOHN	FRE	410	8TH E DI
WOLFE, JOHN JR.	FRE	433	8TH E DI
WOLFE, LOUISA	FRE	161	EMMITTSB
WOLFE, MARY C.	BAL	183	19TH WAR
WOLFE, MICHALA	FRE	426	8TH E DI
WOLFE, PETER	FRE	148	10TH E D
WOLFE, PETER	FRE	149	10TH E D
WOLFE, SAMUEL	FRE	153	10TH E D
WOLFE, SAMUEL	BAL	258	20TH WAR
WOLFE, SARAH	FRE	172	5TH E DI
WOLFE, SUSAN T.	MGM	393	ROCKERLE
WOLFE, SYLVESTER	BAL	171	2ND DIST
WOLFE, THOMAS	FRE	156	10TH E D
WOLFE, WILLIAM	FRE	176	5TH E DI
WOLFE, WILLIAM	FRE	244	NEW MARK
WOLFELDER, JACOB	BAL	091	10TH WAR
WOLFENDEN, JAMES	BAL	397	1ST DIST
WOLFENDEN, JAMES T.	BAL	389	1ST DIST
WOLFENDEN, JOHN	BAL	397	1ST DIST
WOLFENDEN, LIDIA	BAL	397	1ST DIST
WOLFENDEN, THOMAS	BAL	340	1ST DIST
WOLFENTON, GEORGE	BAL	251	6TH WARD
WOLFESBERGER, BARBARA	WAS	149	HAGERSTO
WOLFESBERGER, FRANCIS	WAS	222	1ST DIST
WOLFESBERGER, JACOB	WAS	252	1ST DIST
WOLFESBERGER, JOHN P.	WAS	236	CAVETOWN
WOLFESBERGER, JOSIAH	WAS	182	BOONSBOR
WOLFESBERGER, MARY A.	WAS	236	CAVETOWN
WOLFF, AUGUST	BAL	103	1ST WARD
WOLFF, DUSEY	BAL	143	19TH WAR
WOLFF, ELIZABETH	BAL	231	2ND WARD
WOLFF, JOHN	BAL	177	2ND WARD
WOLFF, JOHN	BAL	177	2ND WARD
WOLFF, JOSEPH	BAL	235	2ND WARD
WOLFF, MOSES	BAL	063	15TH WAR
WOLFF, N.	BAL	281	2ND WARD
WOLFF, WOLFF S.	BAL	012	9TH WARD
WOLFFENSBERGER, GEORGE	WAS	110	2ND DIST
WOLFGANG, ANN	CAR	350	6TH DIST
WOLFGANG, DANIEL	CAR	344	6TH DIST
WOLFGANG, ESAN	CAR	341	6TH DIST
WOLFGANG, JACOB	CAR	342	6TH DIST
WOLFGANG, LYDIA	BAL	047	2ND DIST
WOLFGANG, MARY	CAR	352	6TH DIST
WOLFGANG, SOLOMON	BAL	198	5TH DIST
WOLFGANGER, AUGUSTUS	BAL	183	19TH WAR
WOLFINBERGER, JOHN	WAS	090	2ND SUBD
WOLFINBERGER, LOUISA	WAS	089	2ND SUBD
WOLFINGELCN, MARGARET	BAL	164	16TH WAR
WOLFINGER, DANIEL G.	WAS	287	1ST DIST
WOLFINGER, DANIEL G.	WAS	280	LEITERSB
WOLFINGER, ELIZABETH	WAS	286	1ST DIST
WOLFINGER, JACOB	WAS	279	LEITERSB
WOLFINGER, JOHN	WAS	274	RIDGEVIL
WOLFINGER, MICHAEL	WAS	285	1ST DIST
WOLFKILL, JACOB	WAS	215	1ST DIST
WOLFKILL, JOHN	WAS	216	1ST DIST
WOLFKILL, LAWSON	WAS	183	BOONSBOR
WOLFKILL, MARIA	WAS	216	1ST DIST
WOLFMAN, ELIZABETH	BAL	255	1ST DIST
WOLFORD, CATHARINE	WAS	168	FUNKSTOW
WOLFORD, CRESTA	SOM	434	PRINCESS
WOLFORD, DANIEL	WAS	131	2ND DIST
WOLFORD, DANIEL	WAS	301	1ST DIST
WOLFORD, DANIEL	ALL	188	9TH E.D.
WOLFORD, DAVID	WAS	297	1ST DIST
WOLFORD, DELY-BLACK	CAR	079	NO TWP L
WOLFORD, ELIZABETH	WAS	128	2ND DIST
WOLFORD, HARRIET-BLACK	CAR	085	NO TWP L
WOLFORD, HENRY-BLACK	CAR	076	NO TWP L
WOLFORD, HENRY-BLACK	CAR	068	NO TWP L
WOLFORD, HIRAM	ALL	162	6TH E.D.
WOLFORD, JOHN	WAS	129	2ND DIST
WOLFORD, JOHN	WAS	135	2ND DIST
WOLFORD, JONOTHAN	WAS	296	1ST DIST
WOLFORD, LOUISA	BAL	119	15TH WAR
WOLFORD, MARY	WAS	293	1ST DIST
WOLFORD, MARY	CAR	067	NO TWP L
WOLFORD, MARY	DOR	370	3RD DIVI
WOLFORD, NOAH-BLACK	CAR	121	NO TWP L
WOLFORD, ROBERT	CAR	065	NO TWP L
WOLFORD, SAMUEL	WAS	129	2ND DIST
WOLFORD, SARAH	FRE	379	PETERSVI
WOLFORD, SHARLOTT	CAR	066	NO TWP L
WOLFORD, SHARLOTT	CAR	067	NO TWP L
WOLFORD, THOMAS	WAS	173	FUNKSTOW
WOLFORD, WILLIAM	WAS	129	2ND DIST
WOLFORD, WILLIAM	DOR	370	3RD DIVI
WOLFORT, JOHN	WAS	109	2ND DIST
WOLFRAM, BENEDICT*	BAL	400	3RD WARD
WOLFRED, JOE	BAL	458	8TH WARD
WOLLARD, WILLIAMS	FRE	120	CREAGERS
WOLLEN, RICHARD H.	BAL	014	2ND DIST
WOLLERING, CHRISTENA	BAL	368	8TH WARD
WOLLET, J. P.	BAL	045	4TH WARD
WOLLETT, GEORGE	BAL	042	18TH WAR
WOLLYHAND, HYNSON	QUE	123	1ST E DI
WOLLYHAND, JOHN	QUE	123	1ST E DI
WOLTERS, JOHN	BAL	236	6TH WARD
WOLTON, A.F.	BAL	140	1ST WARD
WOLTZ, ELIE	WAS	204	1ST DIST
WOLTZ, JOHN	WAS	004	WILLIAMS
WOLTZ, SAMUEL A.	WAS	004	WILLIAMS
WOLVERTCN, ISAAC	ALL	035	2ND E.D.
WOLVINGTON, JAMES	ALL	212	CUMBERLA
WOLVINGTCN,HAMILTON	ALL	212	CUMBERLA
WOLVINGTON,W ILLIAM	ALL	206	CUMBERLA
WOLY, MARGARET	ALL	205	CUMBERLA
WOLZ, MICHAEL	ALL	204	CUMBERLA
WOMBLE, PEMBROKE M.	BAL	162	16TH WAR
WOMBLE, SUSAN M.	BAL	097	10TH WAR
WOMBLEY, BENJAMIN	BAL	229	6TH WARD
WONDELL, JAMES	BAL	271	20TH WAR
WONDER, JOHN	BAL	423	8TH WARD
WONDERLY, DAVID	ALL	046	10TH E.D
WONDERLY, DAVID	ALL	067	10TH E.D
WONDERLY, ELIZA	BAL	091	5TH WARD
WONDERLY, JOHN	BAL	035	9TH WARD
WONDERLY, LUCY	ALL	067	10TH E.D
WONDERLY, WILLIAM S.	BAL	091	5TH WARD
WONN, DANIEL	BAL	298	20TH WAR
WONN, HORATIO	PRI	028	VANSVILL
WONN, JOHN	BAL	475	14TH WAR
WONN, MARY	BAL	118	15TH WAR
WONN, MARY A.	BAL	040	9TH WARD
WONNELL, JAMES	WOR	180	6TH E DI
WONNER, CHARELS	BAL	311	12TH WAR
WONNER, JOHN	BAL	025	4TH WARD
WONST, ANDREW	BAL	350	7TH WARD
WONTER, CATHERINE	ALL	207	CUMBERLA
WOOCDCOCK, ASBURY B.	BAL	059	10TH WAR
WOOD, A.	BAL	316	20TH WAR
WOOD, A.L.C.	WAS	003	WILLIAMS
WOOD, ACAM	BAL	257	20TH WAR
WOOD, ADELA	CEC	028	CHESAPEA
WOOD, ALBERT H.	BAL	361	3RD WARD
WOOD, ALEXANDER	BAL	306	12TH WAR
WOOD, ALEXANDER	ST	259	3RD E DI
WOOD, ALICE	BAL	283	20TH WAR
WOOD, ANDREW	MGM	369	BERRYS D
WOOD, ANN	BAL	336	1ST DIST
WOOD, BASIL	FRE	110	CREAGERS
WOOD, BASIL	FRE	277	NEW MARK
WOOD, BENJAMIN	CAL	023	2ND DIST
WOOD, BENJAMIN	BAL	168	2ND DIST
WOOD, CAROLINE	SOM	498	SALISBUR
WOOD, CARROLL H.	FRE	260	NEW MARK
WOOD, CATHARINE	ST	262	3RD E DI
WOOD, CATHARINE	BAL	157	2ND DIST
WOOD, CATHARINE	ANN	521	HOWARD D
WOOD, CATHARINE	ANN	418	HOWARD D
WOOD, CECIL	HAR	068	1ST DIST
WOOD, CHARLES	FRE	296	WOODSBOR
WOOD, CHARLES	CHA	222	ALLENS F
WOOD, CHARLES	BAL	160	2ND DIST
WOOD, CHARLES	BAL	199	11TH WAR
WOOD, CHARLES	BAL	185	6TH WARD
WOOD, CHARLES	ST	311	1ST E DI
WOOD, CHARLES J.	ST	346	5TH E DI
WOOD, CHARLESWORTH	MGM	412	MEDLEY 3
WOOD, CHRISTIANA	HAR	049	1ST DIST
WOOD, CLEMENT	ST	346	5TH E DI
WOOD, DANIEL	BAL	060	10TH WAR
WOOD, DORCAS	CAL	056	3RD DIST
WOOD, E.	PRI	121	PISCATAW
WOOD, ELIAS	BAL	178	6TH WARD
WOOD, ELISA	BAL	124	2ND DIST
WOOD, ELIZA J.	BAL	337	7TH WARD
WOOD, ELIZABETH	BAL	305	12TH WAR
WOOD, ELIZABETH	ST	346	5TH E DI
WOOD, ELIZABETH	BAL	344	13TH WAR
WOOD, EMELIA	BAL	357	1ST DIST
WOOD, EMMA	ANN	521	HOWARD D
WOOD, EMORY	ANN	400	8TH DIST
WOOD, ENOCH	BAL	108	10TH WAR
WOOD, FRANCIS	CEC	114	3RD E DI
WOOD, GEORGE	BAL	319	12TH WAR
WOOD, GEORGE C.	PRI	019	VANSVILL
WOOD, GEORGE H.	ANN	400	8TH DIST
WOOD, GEORGE W.	CAL	003	1ST DIST
WOOD, GEORGE W.	HAR	068	1ST DIST
WOOD, GILBERT	KEN	229	2ND DIST
WOOD, GUSTAVUS	CAL	058	3RD DIST
WOOD, HENRY	CAL	047	3RD DIST
WOOD, HENRY	MGM	384	ROCKERLE
WOOD, HERTSON	HAR	176	3RD DIST
WOOD, HUGH	ALL	105	5TH E.D.
WOOD, ISAAC	BAL	013	2ND DIST
WOOD, ISAAC	BAL	015	2ND DIST
WOOD, JACOB D.	CAR	315	1ST DIST
WOOD, JAMES	KEN	250	2ND DIST
WOOD, JAMES	FRE	410	8TH E DI
WOOD, JAMES	ANN	402	8TH DIST
WOOD, JAMES A.	FRE	292	WOODSBOR
WOOD, JAMES H.	BAL	298	17TH WAR
WOOD, JAMES H.	BAL	048	15TH WAR
WOOD, JAMES R.	CAL	048	3RD DIST
WOOD, JANE	ST	259	3RD E DI
WOOD, JEREMIAH R.	ST	263	3RD E DI
WOOD, JOEL	FRE	424	8TH E DI
WOOD, JOHN	CHA	256	MIDDLETO
WOOD, JOHN	FRE	440	8TH E DI
WOOD, JOHN	CAL	042	3RD DIST
WOOD, JOHN	CAL	028	2ND DIST
WOOD, JOHN	CAL	018	1ST DIST
WOOD, JOHN	CEC	108	3RD E DI
WOOD, JOHN	FRE	309	WOODSBOR
WOOD, JOHN	HAR	009	1ST DIST
WOOD, JOHN	QUE	243	5TH E DI
WOOD, JOHN	BAL	125	2ND DIST
WOOD, JOHN A.	PRI	106	PISCATAW
WOOD, JOHN F.	BAL	054	15TH WAR
WOOD, JOHN G.	BAL	025	9TH WARD
WOOD, JOHN H.	ANN	343	3RD DIST
WOOD, JOHN H.	FRE	244	NEW MARK
WOOD, JOHN JR.	CAR	362	9TH DIST
WOOD, JOHN L.R.	FRE	244	NEW MARK
WOOD, JOHN P.	HAR	189	3RD DIST
WOOD, JOHN P.	CAL	055	3RD DIST
WOOD, JOHN P.	BAL	295	7TH WARD
WOOD, JOHN S.	ST	320	4TH E DI
WOOD, JOHN T.	CAR	284	7TH DIST
WOOD, JOHN W.	CAR	074	NO TWP L
WOOD, JOSEPH	FRE	238	NEW MARK
WOOD, JOSEPH	BAL	256	20TH WAR
WOOD, JOSEPHEEN	BAL	422	1ST DIST
WOOD, JOSHUA	BAL	413	1ST DIST
WOOD, JOSHUA	BAL	211	6TH WARD
WOOD, JOSHUA	FRE	238	NEW MARK
WOOD, JOSHUA	FRE	296	WOODSBOR
WOOD, JULIA	BAL	388	13TH WAR
WOOD, LAVINA	BAL	346	1ST DIST
WOOD, LEWIS	ANN	375	4TH DIST
WOOD, LEWIS	CAL	008	1ST DIST
WOOD, MARGARET	CEC	074	NORTHEAS
WOOD, MARGARET T.	CHA	232	HILLTOP
WOOD, MARGARET T.	CHA	232	HILLTOP
WOOD, MARGARET-MULATTO	MGM	399	ROCKERLE
WOOD, MARTHA	ALL	263	CUMBERLA
WOOD, MARTHA	BAL	077	15TH WAR
WOOD, MARTHA	ST	316	4TH E DI
WOOD, MARTHA	WAS	044	2ND SUBD
WOOD, MARY	ST	346	5TH E DI
WOOD, MARY	BAL	307	12TH WAR
WOOD, MARY	BAL	137	2ND DIST
WOOD, MARY	ANN	403	8TH DIST
WOOD, MARY	FRE	283	WOODSBOR
WOOD, MARY	FRE	254	NEW MARK
WOOD, MARY	BAL	154	19TH WAR
WOOD, MARY A.	ST	340	5TH E DI
WOOD, MARY E.	FRE	381	PETERSVI
WOOD, MARY E.	CAL	028	2ND DIST
WOOD, MARY E.-BLACK	QUE	150	1ST E DI
WOOD, MATILDA	BAL	288	20TH WAR
WOOD, MISS R.	FRE	199	5TH E DI
WOOD, MISS S.	FRE	199	5TH E DI
WOOD, MISS V.	FRE	199	5TH E DI
WOOD, MRS-	ANN	328	2ND DIST
WOOD, NANCY	FRE	286	WOODSBOR
WOOD, NICHOLAS L.	BAL	475	14TH WAR
WOOD, ORLANDO	BAL	260	6TH WARD
WOOD, PERRY	CAL	042	3RD DIST
WOOD, PETER	CHA	285	BOJANTOW
WOOD, PHILIP	ANN	467	HOWARD D
WOOD, RACHEL	CAL	054	3RD DIST
WOOD, REBECCA	CAL	033	2ND DIST
WOOD, REBECCA	ANN	446	HOWARD D
WOOD, REBECCA J.	CAL	058	3RD DIST
WOOD, RICHARD	BAL	047	18TH WAR
WOOD, RICHARD	ST	342	5TH E DI
WOOD, RICHARD A.	ST	311	1ST E DI
WOOD, RICHARD-BLACK	FRE	387	PETERSVI
WOOD, ROBERT	CAL	004	1ST DIST
WOOD, ROBERT	WAS	034	2ND SUBD
WOOD, ROBERT	PRI	114	PISCATAW
WOOD, ROBERT	BAL	102	2ND DIST
WOOD, ROBERT B.	MGM	347	BERRYS D
WOOD, ROBERT H.	CAL	054	3RD DIST
WOOD, RUTH H.	FRE	243	NEW MARK
WOOD, SALLY	CHA	276	ALLENS F
WOOD, SAMUEL	CAL	054	3RD DIST
WOOD, SAMUEL	BAL	172	16TH WAR
WOOD, SARA	CHA	222	ALLENS F
WOOD, SARAH	CAL	054	3RD DIST
WOOD, SARAH	CAL	033	2ND DIST
WOOD, SARAH	ANN	401	8TH DIST
WOOD, SARAH A.	FRE	389	PETERSVI
WOOD, SARAH A.	PRI	019	VANSVILL

Name	County	Page	District
WOOD, SARAH K.	BAL	295	3RD WARD
WOOD, SARAH MRS-	BAL	315	20TH WAR
WOOD, SELIN	CEC	048	1ST E DI
WOOD, SIMONS	KEN	307	3RD DIST
WOOD, SUSAN	CAL	051	3RD DIST
WOOD, SUSAN M.	ST	342	5TH E DI
WOOD, THOAMS	CAL	007	1ST DIST
WOOD, THOMAS	CAL	020	2ND DIST
WOOD, THOMAS	BAL	050	4TH WARD
WOOD, THOMAS	MGM	369	BERRYS D
WOOD, THOMAS	PRI	046	AQUASCO
WOOD, THOMAS	BAL	034	15TH WAR
WOOD, THOMAS H.	BAL	034	15TH WAR
WOOD, THOMAS W.	CAR	070	NO TWP L
WOOD, W.P.	ALL	219	CUMBERLA
WOOD, WESLY	ANN	399	8TH DIST
WOOD, WILILAM	BAL	279	2ND WARD
WOOD, WILILAM	CAL	032	2ND DIST
WOOD, WILLIAM	CAL	020	2ND DIST
WOOD, WILLIAM	CAL	002	1ST DIST
WOOD, WILLIAM	BAL	411	3RD WARD
WOOD, WILLIAM	CHA	282	BOJANTOW
WOOD, WILLIAM	ANN	341	3RD DIST
WOOD, WILLIAM	KEN	307	3RD DIST
WOOD, WILLIAM	QUE	241	5TH E DI
WOOD, WILLIAM H.	BAL	072	15TH WAR
WOOD, WILLIAM T.	SOM	497	SALISBUR
WOOD, WILLIAM W.	ST	262	3RD E DI
WOOD, WILLIAM W.	KEN	286	3RD DIST
WOOD, WILLIAM W.	KEN	298	3RD DIST
WOOD, WILLIAM W.	CHA	221	ALLENS F
WOOD, ZACHARIAH	PRI	041	VANSVILL
WOOD,W ILLIAM	ST	311	1ST E DI
WOODALE, THOMAS	KEN	303	3RD DIST
WOODALL, ALLICE	BAL	113	18TH WAR
WOODALL, ANDREW	KEN	289	3RD DIST
WOODALL, ANN R.	KEN	213	2ND DIST
WOODALL, FREEMOND B.	BAL	069	18TH WAR
WOODALL, JANE	BAL	241	17TH WAR
WOODALL, JESSEY	KEN	300	3RD DIST
WOODALL, JOHN	BAL	143	1ST WARD
WOODALL, SAMUEL	KEN	225	2ND DIST
WOODALL, SIMON	KEN	289	3RD DIST
WOODALL, THEODORE	BAL	153	16TH WAR
WOODALL, WALTER W.	BAL	100	18TH WAR
WOODALL, WILLIAM	KEN	225	2ND DIST
WOODALL, WILLIAM	BAL	254	6TH WARD
WOODARD, CORA	ST	318	4TH E DI
WOODARD, HIRAM	ANN	507	HOWARD D
WOODARD, MARY	CAL	056	3RD DIST
WOODARD, RICHARD	CAL	062	3RD DIST
WOODARD, SINGLETON	ANN	498	HOWARD D
WOODARD, SUSANNA	BAL	004	9TH WARD
WOODARD, WILLIAM J.O.	ALL	216	CUMBERLA
WOODBURN, ELIZA	BAL	143	11TH WAR
WOODBURN, HEZEKIAH	ST	345	5TH E DI
WOODBURN, JOHN	BAL	233	6TH WARD
WOODBURN, LEONARD	ST	341	5TH E DI
WOODBURN, MICHAEL	ST	343	5TH E DI
WOODBURN, SARAH	BAL	081	1ST WARD
WOODBURN, WILLAIM	ANN	469	HOWARD D
WOODBURN, WILLIAM	CHA	281	BOJANTOW
WOODBURY, THOMAS	BAL	123	1ST WARD
WOODCOCK, REBECCA A.	BAL	156	16TH WAR
WOODCOCK, WILLIAM	BAL	061	15TH WAR
WOODDAL, JAMES JR.	QUE	179	2ND E DI
WOODDAL, LEVIN	QUE	177	2ND E DI
WOODDALL, AMOS	QUE	143	1ST E DI
WOODDALL, CATHERINE	QUE	172	2ND E DI
WOODDALL, JAMES	QUE	171	2ND E DI
WOODDALL, JOHN	QUE	154	1ST E DI
WOODDALL, LEVIN JR.	QUE	171	2ND E DI
WOODDALL, MARY M.	QUE	168	2ND E DI
WOODDALL, ROCHES	QUE	167	2ND E DI
WOODDALL,MARY	QUE	167	2ND E DI
WOODDEN, GLEN	BAL	230	12TH WAR
WOODDEN, WILLIAM H.	BAL	245	20TH WAR
WOODDIN, JULIA	BAL	164	19TH WAR
WOODE, CHARLES	BAL	123	16TH WAR
WOODE, FERDINAND	BAL	153	16TH WAR
WOODEN, ALMIRA	BAL	400	8TH WARD
WOODEN, BENJAMIN	BAL	234	1ST DIST
WOODEN, CALVEN	BAL	234	1ST DIST
WOODEN, ELIJAH	CAR	194	4TH DIST
WOODEN, ELLEN	BAL	069	18TH WAR
WOODEN, HARRIETT	BAL	124	11TH WAR
WOODEN, JOHN	BAL	402	1ST DIST
WOODEN, JOHN	BAL	426	8TH WARD
WOODEN, LEAH	BAL	157	6TH WARD
WOODEN, MARY A.	BAL	035	15TH WAR
WOODEN, MORDICA	BAL	439	1ST DIST
WOODEN, OEADIAH	BAL	127	1ST WARD
WOODEN, RICHARD	QUE	193	3RD E DI
WOODEN, SAMUEL	BAL	311	3RD WARD
WOODEN, SOLOMON	CEC	076	NORTHEAS
WOODEN, STEPHEN	BAL	269	1ST DIST
WOODEN, THOMAS	BAL	376	1ST DIST
WOODEN, THOMAS	BAL	234	1ST DIST
WOODEN, THOMAS	BAL	196	6TH WARD
WOODEN, WILLIAM	BAL	450	1ST DIST
WOODEN, WILLIAM	BAL	425	8TH WARD
WOODEN, WILLIAM	BAL	024	2ND DIST
WOODFIELD, EDWARD	MGM	341	CLARKSBU
WOODFIELD, JOHN F.	BAL	021	1ST WARD
WOODFIELD, JOSEPH	MGM	343	CLARKSBU
WOODFIELD, THOMAS	BAL	306	1ST DIST
WOODFORD, JAMES	CEC	006	ELKTON 3
WOODHOUSE, WILLIAM	HAR	147	3RD DIST
WOODHULL, HANNAH	BAL	225	6TH WARD
WOODIN, MARTHA	BAL	318	3RD WARD
WOODLAND, A.	BAL	164	1ST WARD
WOODLAND, ABRAHAM	BAL	166	16TH WAR
WOODLAND, ABRAHAM	KEN	225	2ND DIST
WOODLAND, ABRAHAM	KEN	296	3RD DIST
WOODLAND, ANNA	KEN	299	3RD DIST
WOODLAND, CHARLOTTE	BAL	055	15TH WAR
WOODLAND, ELIZABETH	BAL	034	15TH WAR
WOODLAND, ELIZABETH	ST	338	4TH E DI
WOODLAND, EMILY	BAL	028	15TH WAR
WOODLAND, EMORY	KEN	306	3RD DIST
WOODLAND, FRANCIS	CEC	154	PORT DUP
WOODLAND, HENRY	ST	268	3RD E DI
WOODLAND, HENRY-BLACK	QUE	175	2ND E DI
WOODLAND, IGNATIUS	ST	267	3RD E DI
WOODLAND, IGNATIUS-BLACK	ST	323	4TH E DI
WOODLAND, ISAAC	KEN	313	3RD DIST
WOODLAND, ISAAC-BLACK	QUE	150	1ST E DI
WOODLAND, JACOB	KEN	266	1ST DIST
WOODLAND, JAMES F.	KEN	295	3RD DIST
WOODLAND, JAMES-BLACK	ST	320	4TH E DI
WOODLAND, JAMES-BLACK	QUE	168	2ND E DI
WOODLAND, JANE	ST	273	3RD E DI
WOODLAND, JANE-BLACK	ST	328	4TH E DI
WOODLAND, JOHN	BAL	114	2ND DIST
WOODLAND, JOHN H.	ST	270	3RD E DI
WOODLAND, JOHN T.	ST	259	3RD E DI
WOODLAND, JOHN-BLACK	ST	329	4TH E DI
WOODLAND, JOSEPH	KEN	299	3RD DIST
WOODLAND, JULIA-BLACK	QUE	177	2ND E DI
WOODLAND, LAVINIA	BAL	034	15TH WAR
WOODLAND, LOUISA	BAL	194	19TH WAR
WOODLAND, MARIA	KEN	255	1ST DIST
WOODLAND, MARY E.	ST	281	3RD E DI
WOODLAND, MARY-BLACK	ST	323	4TH E DI
WOODLAND, SAMUEL	KEN	299	3RD DIST
WOODLAND, SARAH	BAL	021	4TH WARD
WOODLAND, SARAH	BAL	118	5TH WARD
WOODLAND, SOLOMON	KEN	263	1ST DIST
WOODLAND, SOPHIA-BLACK	ST	301	2ND E DI
WOODLAND, SUSAN	ST	261	3RD E DI
WOODLAND, THOMAS	ST	267	3RD E DI
WOODLAND, THOMAS	BAL	034	15TH WAR
WOODLAND, WILLIAM-BLACK	QUE	164	2ND E DI
WOODLEY, ELIZABETH	BAL	095	10TH WAR
WOODLEY, HARRIET	BAL	381	13TH WAR
WOODLEY, ROBERT D.	ST	276	3RD E DI
WOODLIN, WESLEY	BAL	120	1ST WARD
WOODLING, EDWARD	DOR	331	3RD DIVI
WOODLING, JOHN	DOR	343	3RD DIVI
WOODLING, JOHN A. M.	DOR	338	3RD DIVI
WOODLING, MARIAH E.	DOR	328	3RD DIVI
WOODLING, SILAS	DOR	364	3RD DIVI
WOODLING, WILLIAM	DOR	331	3RD DIVI
WOODLY, LUCY	BAL	460	1ST DIST
WOODMAN, JOHN	BAL	109	15TH WAR
WOODPECKEN, FRANCIS	BAL	156	2ND DIST
WOODRED, WILLIAM	HAR	182	3RD DIST
WOODRO, GEORGE W.	BAL	162	16TH WAR
WOODROUGH, ROSA	PRI	033	VANSVILL
WOODROW, ANN	CEC	165	6TH E DI
WOODROW, BENJAMIN	CEC	107	3RD E DI
WOODROW, CAHTERINE	CEC	209	7TH E DI
WOODROW, HENRY	CEC	201	6TH E DI
WOODROW, HENRY	CEC	172	6TH E DI
WOODROW, JACOB	CEC	165	6TH E DI
WOODROW, JACOB	CEC	197	7TH E DI
WOODROW, JACOB H.	CEC	166	6TH E DI
WOODROW, JEMIMA	HAR	180	3RD DIST
WOODROW, JOSIAH	CEC	171	6TH E DI
WOODROW, LEVI	CEC	121	4TH E DI
WOODROW, LYDIA	CEC	171	6TH E DI
WOODROW, MARY	CEC	206	7TH E DI
WOODROW, NANCY	CEC	201	6TH E DI
WOODROW, REBECCA	CEC	165	6TH E DI
WOODROW, SAMUEL	CEC	212	7TH E DI
WOODROW, SARAH	CEC	198	7TH E DI
WOODROW, STEPHEN	CEC	203	6TH E DI
WOODROW, STEPHEN J.	BAL	159	16TH WAR
WOODRUFF, ALBERT P.	BAL	437	1ST DIST
WOODS, ANN	BAL	379	1ST DIST
WOODS, ANN B.	ANN	437	HOWARD D
WOODS, ANNA	BAL	394	14TH WAR
WOODS, BERY	BAL	231	12TH WAR
WOODS, BRIDGET	BAL	098	18TH WAR
WOODS, CATHARINE	BAL	213	2ND WARD
WOODS, CHARLES	BAL	065	1ST WARD
WOODS, CHARLES	BAL	201	17TH WAR
WOODS, CHARLOTT	BAL	284	17TH WAR
WOODS, DANIEL	CEC	100	3RD E DI
WOODS, DAVID	BAL	240	1ST DIST
WOODS, DAVID	BAL	087	2ND DIST
WOODS, DAVID	ALL	087	5TH E.D.
WOODS, DELIA A.	BAL	395	14TH WAR
WOODS, DENNIS	BAL	124	1ST WARD
WOODS, DENNIS	BAL	138	1ST WARD
WOODS, EDWARD	BAL	256	17TH WAR
WOODS, EDWARD	BAL	194	19TH WAR
WOODS, ELIAS	CAR	394	2ND DIST
WOODS, ELIZA	FRE	164	EMMITTSB
WOODS, ELIZA	BAL	093	2ND DIST
WOODS, ELIZA	BAL	077	10TH WAR
WOODS, ELIZABETH	BAL	389	3RD WARD
WOODS, ELIZABETH	BAL	392	14TH WAR
WOODS, ELIZABETH	BAL	157	11TH WAR
WOODS, ELLEN	BAL	260	6TH WARD
WOODS, FRANCES	BAL	356	8TH WARD
WOODS, GEORGE	BAL	140	1ST WARD
WOODS, GEORGE	BAL	123	1ST WARD
WOODS, GEORGE	BAL	164	11TH WAR
WOODS, GEORGE H.	BAL	088	18TH WAR
WOODS, GEROGE	BAL	402	1ST DIST
WOODS, HANNAH	BAL	426	1ST DIST
WOODS, HENRIETTA	BAL	395	14TH WAR
WOODS, HENRY	BAL	171	1ST WARD
WOODS, HENRY B.	FRE	396	PETERSVI
WOODS, HENRY H.	BAL	458	1ST DIST
WOODS, HESTER	BAL	106	10TH WAR
WOODS, HESTER	BAL	010	18TH WAR
WOODS, HIRAM	BAL	280	20TH WAR
WOODS, HIRAM	BAL	103	15TH WAR
WOODS, J.	BAL	136	1ST WARD
WOODS, JAMES	BAL	124	16TH WAR
WOODS, JAMES	BAL	010	18TH WAR
WOODS, JAMES	BAL	393	14TH WAR
WOODS, JAMES	CEC	010	ELKTON 3
WOODS, JAMES	FRE	286	WOODSBOR
WOODS, JAMES	HAR	091	2ND DIST
WOODS, JESSE	CAR	401	2ND DIST
WOODS, JOHN	BAL	318	20TH WAR
WOODS, JOHN	BAL	017	18TH WAR
WOODS, JOHN	BAL	137	1ST WARD
WOODS, JOHN	BAL	346	3RD WARD
WOODS, JOHN	BAL	167	1ST WARD
WOODS, JOHN	BAL	178	2ND WARD
WOODS, JOHN	BAL	198	2ND WARD
WOODS, JOHN	BAL	212	2ND WARD
WOODS, JOHN	BAL	020	9TH WARD
WOODS, JOHN	BAL	151	1ST WARD
WOODS, JOHN	BAL	120	1ST WARD
WOODS, JOHN	BAL	137	2ND DIST
WOODS, JOHN	ANN	427	HOWARD D
WOODS, JOHN	ALL	021	2ND E.D.
WOODS, JOHN L.	BAL	274	17TH WAR
WOODS, JOHN THOMAS	BAL	397	14TH WAR
WOODS, JOHN W.	BAL	357	13TH WAR
WOODS, JOSEPH	CAR	287	7TH DIST
WOODS, JOSEPH-BLACK	FRE	182	5TH E DI
WOODS, JOSEPH-BLACK	FRE	188	5TH E DI
WOODS, JOSHUA	BAL	236	17TH WAR
WOODS, LAURA	BAL	356	3RD WARD
WOODS, LAURA J.	BAL	165	11TH WAR
WOODS, LYDIA	BAL	018	2ND DIST
WOODS, MARGARET	BAL	336	7TH WARD
WOODS, MARGARET	BAL	415	3RD WARD
WOODS, MARIA	MGM	395	ROCKERLE
WOODS, MARY	BAL	154	19TH WAR
WOODS, MARY	BAL	256	12TH WAR
WOODS, MARY-BLACK	BAL	217	2ND WARD
WOODS, MATHEW	BAL	235	17TH WAR
WOODS, MATILDA	BAL	077	4TH WARD
WOODS, MATTHEW	CEC	176	7TH E DI
WOODS, MICHAEL	BAL	197	2ND WARD
WOODS, MINTA	BAL	425	1ST DIST
WOODS, OLIVER	BAL	095	1ST WARD
WOODS, PETER	BAL	433	8TH WARD
WOODS, PETER	BAL	159	19TH WAR
WOODS, PETER	CAR	297	7TH DIST
WOODS, PHILIP	BAL	015	2ND DIST
WOODS, RICHARD	BAL	172	2ND DIST
WOODS, ROBERT	BAL	160	2ND DIST
WOODS, RUFUS	CAR	290	7TH DIST
WOODS, SALLY	CAR	380	2ND DIST
WOODS, SAMUEL	BAL	017	18TH WAR
WOODS, SAMUEL	CAR	401	2ND DIST
WOODS, SAMUEL	BAL	133	18TH WAR
WOODS, SARAH	BAL	379	1ST DIST
WOODS, SARAH	BAL	129	5TH WARD
WOODS, STEPHEN	BAL	142	5TH WARD
WOODS, SUSAN	BAL	171	16TH WAR
WOODS, SUSAN	BAL	384	3RD WARD
WOODS, SUSAN S.	CAR	391	2ND DIST
WOODS, T.	BAL	117	1ST WARD
WOODS, THOMAS	BAL	065	1ST WARD
WOODS, W.H.	BAL	173	1ST WARD
WOODS, WESLEY	BAL	394	14TH WAR
WOODS, WILLIAM	CAR	389	2ND DIST
WOODS, WILLIAM	BAL	071	1ST WARD
WOODS, WILLIAM	BAL	364	3RD WARD
WOODS, WILLIAM	BAL	321	12TH WAR
WOODS, WILLIAM	ANN	476	HOWARD D
WOODS, WILLIAM	ANN	406	8TH DIST
WOODS, WILLIAM H.	BAL	118	18TH WAR
WOODS, WILLIAM M.	BAL	160	19TH WAR
WOODS, ZEPHANIAH	BAL	132	16TH WAR
WOODSBARKER, JOHN	BAL	318	3RD WARD
WOODSIDE, JAMES	BAL	151	1ST WARD
WOODSIDE, WILLIAM S.	BAL	083	15TH WAR
WOODVILL, WILLIAM	BAL	251	1ST DIST
WOODVILLE, ANN	BAL	251	1ST DIST
WOODVILLE, ELIZABETH	BAL	156	11TH WAR
WOODVILLE, MARY	BAL	106	10TH WAR
WOODVILLE, WILLIAM	BAL	157	11TH WAR
WOODWARD, ALEXANDER	FRE	050	FREDERIC
WOODWARD, ANN	BAL	068	18TH WAR
WOODWARD, BENJAMIN	DOR	407	1ST DIST
WOODWARD, C.H.	BAL	140	1ST WARD
WOODWARD, CHARLES	BAL	180	2ND WARD
WOODWARD, CHARLES H.	BAL	279	2ND WARD
WOODWARD, DAVID A.	BAL	339	13TH WAR
WOODWARD, ELI	FRE	305	WOODSBOR
WOODWARD, ELISABETH	ANN	331	2ND DIST
WOODWARD, EMANUEL	BAL	064	2ND DIST
WOODWARD, EMILY W.	BAL	174	16TH WAR
WOODWARD, EMOS	HAR	059	1ST DIST
WOODWARD, EUGENIA	BAL	055	15TH WAR
WOODWARD, G. B.	BAL	282	2ND WARD
WOODWARD, GARRETT	BAL	460	8TH WARD
WOODWARD, GEORGE	BAL	238	1ST DIST
WOODWARD, GEORGE H.	ST	284	2ND E DI
WOODWARD, GEORGE H.	ST	285	2ND E DI
WOODWARD, GEORGE P.	BAL	389	8TH WARD
WOODWARD, GEORGE W.	FRE	050	FREDERIC
WOODWARD, HARRIET	FRE	050	FREDERIC
WOODWARD, HENRY	HAR	049	1ST DIST
WOODWARD, HENSON	MGM	322	CRACKLIN
WOODWARD, HORSAIC	FRE	035	FREDERIC
WOODWARD, JAMES	ANN	269	ANNAPOLI
WOODWARD, JOHN	BAL	171	2ND DIST
WOODWARD, JOHN	FRE	006	FREDERIC
WOODWARD, JOSEPH	MGM	328	CRACKLIN
WOODWARD, LEWIS	TAL	017	EASTON D
WOODWARD, LYDIA	FRE	024	FREDERIC
WOODWARD, MARY	BAL	213	19TH WAR
WOODWARD, MARY A.	BAL	004	18TH WAR
WOODWARD, MARY J.	FRE	051	FREDERIC
WOODWARD, NICHOLAS	ANN	364	4TH DIST
WOODWARD, NICHOLAS R.	BAL	075	10TH WAR
WOODWARD, PHILIPPY	ST	290	2ND E DI
WOODWARD, RIGNALD D.	ANN	323	2ND DIST
WOODWARD, ROBERT B.	BAL	352	7TH WARD
WOODWARD, SAMUEL-MULATTO	BAL	208	2ND WARD
WOODWARD, SARAH A.	ANN	487	HOWARD D
WOODWARD, THOMAS	BAL	204	19TH WAR
WOODWARD, WILLIAM	BAL	366	13TH WAR
WOODWARD, WILLIAM	BAL	393	14TH WAR
WOODWARD, WILLIAM	BAL	262	1ST DIST
WOODWARD, WILLIAM T.	BAL	108	5TH WARD
WOODWARD, WILLIAM T.	ALL	162	6TH E.D.
WOODWARD, WILLIAM W.	BAL	455	14TH WAR
WOODWELL, ELLEN	BAL	136	11TH WAR
WOODWORTH, FRED B.	BAL	237	12TH WAR
WOODWORTH, FREDERICK	BAL	236	12TH WAR
WOODY, LEWIS	BAL	459	14TH WAR
WOODY, WILLIAM	BAL	410	14TH WAR
WOODYARD, ANDREW	CAR	394	2ND DIST
WOODYARD, ANDREW	CAR	399	2ND DIST
WOODYARD, ANDREW-BLACK	CAR	399	2ND DIST
WOODYARD, DANIEL	FRE	301	WOODSBOR
WOODYARD, DANIEL	CAR	358	9TH DIST
WOODYARD, DANIEL-BLACK	CAR	394	2ND DIST
WOODYARD, DAVID-BLACK	CAR	402	2ND DIST
WOODYARD, HENRIETTA	BAL	323	1ST DIST
WOODYARD, JEREMIAH	BAL	364	13TH WAR
WOODYARD, JOHN-BLACK	CAR	398	2ND DIST
WOODYARD, JULIA A.	CAR	286	7TH DIST
WOODYARD, MARIA	CAR	394	2ND DIST
WOODYARD, NATHAN	BAL	269	1ST DIST
WOODYEAR, CALEB	BAL	280	12TH WAR
WOODYEAR, ELIZABETH	BAL	072	15TH WAR
WOODYEAR, ELLEN	BAL	461	1ST DIST
WOODYEAR, WILLIAM H.	BAL	206	17TH WAR
WOOK, ELIZABETH	TAL	076	EASTON T
WOOK, ELIZABETH	TAL	076	EASTON T
WOOLDRIDGE, JOHN B.	BAL	379	13TH WAR
WOOLEHAM, JACOB	CEC	017	ELKTON 3
WOOLEIN, LEVIN*	DOR	445	1ST DIST
WOOLEN, ELIZA	BAL	145	5TH WARD
WOOLEN, ELIZABETH	BAL	008	18TH WAR
WOOLEN, LEONARD R.	BAL	413	14TH WAR
WOOLEN, MARGARETT	HAR	096	2ND DIST

Name	County	Page	District
WOOLEN, MISSOUIR	BAL	413	14TH WAR
WOOLEN, PROVIDENCE	BAL	138	2ND DIST
WOOLEN, RICHARD	HAR	076	BEL AIR
WOOLEN, ROSANA	ANN	275	ANNAPOLI
WOOLEN, TYLATHA	BAL	221	17TH WAR
WOOLENHAM, MARY S.	BAL	009	18TH WAR
WOOLENTON, WILLIAM	BAL	106	18TH WAR
WOOLERY, ELIJAH	CAR	197	4TH DIST
WOOLERY, FERDINAND	CAR	245	3RD DIST
WOOLERY, HELLEN	CAR	279	7TH DIST
WOOLERY, JOHN C.	CAR	196	4TH DIST
WOOLERY, NOAH	CAR	178	8TH DIST
WOOLESY, SUSANNAH	BAL	170	2ND DIST
WOOLEY, GEORGE E.	CEC	138	6TH E DI
WOOLEY, TABITHA	CEC	033	CHESAPEA
WOOLF, CHARLES	CHA	228	BOJANTOW
WOOLF, CHARLES W.	CAL	001	1ST DIST
WOOLF, JOSEPH	BAL	432	8TH WARD
WOOLFE, MARY	FRE	438	8TH E DI
WOOLFENDEN, CAROLINE	BAL	358	1ST DIST
WOOLFENDEN, ELI G.	BAL	321	1ST DIST
WOOLFORD, ALEXANDER	BAL	300	3RD WARD
WOOLFORD, ALEXANDER	BAL	030	15TH WAR
WOOLFORD, ANN	DOR	366	3RD DIVI
WOOLFORD, ARTHER	HAR	156	3RD DIST
WOOLFORD, BARTHOLOMEW	BAL	196	17TH WAR
WOOLFORD, BENJAMIN	ALL	163	6TH E.D.
WOOLFORD, CASEY	DOR	324	1ST DIST
WOOLFORD, CATHARINE	DOR	424	1ST DIST
WOOLFORD, CHARLES	DOR	367	3RD DIVI
WOOLFORD, CHARLOTT	BAL	316	3RD WARD
WOOLFORD, CLARA	SOM	517	BARREN C
WOOLFORD, DANIEL	ALL	162	6TH E.D.
WOOLFORD, DANIEL	ALL	162	6TH E.D.
WOOLFORD, E.	BAL	141	5TH WARD
WOOLFORD, EDWARD*	DOR	414	1ST DIST
WOOLFORD, EMORY	BAL	206	17TH WAR
WOOLFORD, FANNY	BAL	309	3RD WARD
WOOLFORD, GEORGE	ALL	162	6TH E.D.
WOOLFORD, GEORGE	DOR	393	1ST DIST
WOOLFORD, GEORGE	DOR	324	1ST DIST
WOOLFORD, GEORGE	BAL	009	4TH WARD
WOOLFORD, GEORGE	DOR	454	1ST DIST
WOOLFORD, GEORGE L. H.	SOM	554	TYASKIN
WOOLFORD, HENRY-BLACK	CAR	079	NO TWP L
WOOLFORD, HIRAM	DOR	467	1ST DIST
WOOLFORD, JAMES	DOR	380	1ST DIST
WOOLFORD, JAMES	DOR	404	1ST DIST
WOOLFORD, JAMES*	DOR	393	1ST DIST
WOOLFORD, JETHERO	DOR	364	3RD DIVI
WOOLFORD, JOHN	DOR	412	1ST DIST
WOOLFORD, JOHN	SOM	430	PRINCESS
WOOLFORD, JOHN H.	BAL	060	4TH WARD
WOOLFORD, JOHN W.	DOR	366	3RD DIVI
WOOLFORD, JOSEPH	BAL	094	10TH WAR
WOOLFORD, LEVEN	DOR	364	3RD DIVI
WOOLFORD, LEVI	DOR	434	1ST DIST
WOOLFORD, LEVIN	SOM	430	PRINCESS
WOOLFORD, LITTLETON	DOR	433	1ST DIST
WOOLFORD, NELEY*	DOR	428	1ST DIST
WOOLFORD, NOAH	DOR	408	1ST DIST
WOOLFORD, SARAH	DOR	414	1ST DIST
WOOLFORD, SARAH	DOR	325	1ST DIST
WOOLFORD, SIDONA	BAL	191	17TH WAR
WOOLFORD, STEPHEN	BAL	191	17TH WAR
WOOLFORD, STEPHEN B.	DOR	468	1ST DIST
WOOLFORD, STEPHEN B. B.	DOR	468	1ST DIST
WOOLFORD, THEODORE T.	BAL	062	15TH WAR
WOOLFORD, THOMAS	DOR	418	1ST DIST
WOOLFORD, THOMAS	DOR	413	1ST DIST
WOOLFORD, THOMAS	DOR	394	1ST DIST
WOOLFORD, WASHINGTON	DOR	414	1ST DIST
WOOLFORD, WHITEFIELD	DOR	467	1ST DIST
WOOLFORD, WILLIAM	DOR	468	1ST DIST
WOOLFORD, WILLIAM	DOR	447	1ST DIST
WOOLFORD, WILLIAM	SOM	430	PRINCESS
WOOLFORD, WILLIS	BAL	146	16TH WAR
WOOLFORK, A.	BAL	333	1ST DIST
WOOLFORK, J. B.	BAL	332	1ST DIST
WOOLFROM, JONATHAN	BAL	237	1ST DIST
WOOLFSCHAGAR, ADOLF	BAL	265	1ST DIST
WOOLHOUS, H.	BAL	319	12TH WAR
WOOLIN, JAMES	BAL	020	2ND DIST
WOOLIN, JOHN	DOR	308	1ST DIST
WOOLIN, JOHN	DOR	315	1ST DIST
WOOLIN, WHEATLEY	DOR	320	1ST DIST
WOOLLEN, ELIZABETH	FRE	273	NEW MARK
WOOLLEN, MARTHA	BAL	006	18TH WAR
WOOLLEN, MARY E.	BAL	014	2ND DIST
WOOLLEN, THOMAS	BAL	022	4TH WARD
WOOLLEN, WILLIAM	BAL	377	3RD WARD
WOOLLET, ELIZABETH A.	BAL	173	19TH WAR
WOOLLET, JAMES	BAL	244	12TH WAR
WOOLLET, SARAH A.	BAL	173	19TH WAR
WOOLLSLELEGER, FREDERICK*	BAL	071	2ND DIST
WOOLLY, CATHERINE	BAL	076	4TH WARD
WOOLLYHAND, JAMES	QUE	133	1ST E DI
WOOLMAN, DANIEL	TAL	044	EASTON T
WOOLPER, BENJAMIN	BAL	410	3RD WARD
WOOLSEY, ARMELIA	HAR	093	2ND DIST
WOOLSEY, HENRY	HAR	083	2ND DIST
WOOLSEY, HENRY JR.	HAR	084	2ND DIST
WOOLSEY, MARTIN	BAL	170	2ND DIST
WOOLSEY, RICHARD	HAR	049	1ST DIST
WOOLSEY, SAMUEL	BAL	114	5TH WARD
WOOLSEY, WILLIAM	HAR	117	2ND DIST
WOOLTON, CORNELIUS	ST	288	2ND E DI
WOOLTON, MARGARET	PRI	080	QUEEN AN
WOOLTON, THOMAS	ST	287	2ND E DI
WOOLTZ, CATHARINE	BAL	120	5TH WARD
WOOMLEY, VIRGINIA	BAL	106	15TH WAR
WOOSTER, MARY	BAL	230	2ND WARD
WOOTEN, POLLY	SOM	420	PRINCESS
WOOTEN, ZEPORA	SOM	385	BRINKLEY
WOOTERS, DAVID*	TAL	031	EASTON D
WOOTERS, JAMES	QUE	184	3RD E DI
WOOTERS, JAMES*	TAL	005	EASTON D
WOOTERS, JANES	QUE	125	1ST E DI
WOOTERS, LEVISA	CAR	108	NO TWP L
WOOTERS, MARY	TAL	032	EASTON D
WOOTERS, MARY E.	QUE	211	3RD E DI
WOOTERS, SARAH A.	QUE	215	3RD E DI
WOOTHENS, JOHN	CAR	111	NO TWP L
WOOTHERS, LEVIN	CAR	114	NO TWP L
WOOTON, LEWIS	DOR	330	3RD DIVI
WOOTON, RETSON	DOR	330	3RD DIVI
WOOTTEN, EDWARD	ANN	307	1ST DIST
WOOTTEN, JAMES	ANN	307	1ST DIST
WOOTTEN, THOMAS R.	BAL	077	18TH WAR
WOOTTERS, GEORGE	CAR	134	NO TWP L
WOOTTERS, JAMES	CAR	148	NO TWP L
WOOTTERS, JOHN W.	CAR	108	NO TWP L
WOOTTERS, MATHEN	CAR	115	NO TWP L
WOOTTON, ANN	ST	309	1ST E DI
WOOTTON, EDWARD	ANN	310	1ST DIST
WOOTTON, EDWARD SR.	ANN	310	1ST DIST
WOOTTON, ELIZABETH S.	MGM	375	ROCKERLE
WOOTTON, FRANK	BAL	059	10TH WAR
WOOTTON, JOHN	ANN	409	8TH DIST
WOOTTON, JOSEPH S.	ST	308	1ST E DI
WOOTTON, MARY	ST	279	3RD E DI
WOOTTON, RACHEL	MGM	325	CRACKLIN
WOOTTON, REBECCA	ANN	310	1ST DIST
WOOTTON, SWINE	MGM	404	ROCKERLE
WOOTTON, WILLIAM T.	MGM	442	CLARKSTR
WOOTTON, WILLIAM THOMAS	BAL	381	1ST DIST
WOOTTUS, ELIZABETH	CAR	103	NO TWP L
WOOTUS, DAVID*	TAL	031	EASTON D
WOOTUS, JOHN C.*	TAL	022	EASTON D
WORBURTON, JAMES	CEC	123	3RD E DI
WORBURTON, WILLIAM	CEC	122	4TH E DI
WORCESTER, EDWARD B.	MGM	442	CLARKSTR
WORD, HESTER	BAL	234	12TH WAR
WORD, JAMES A.	CAL	014	1ST DIST
WORD, SARAH	CAL	015	1ST DIST
WORDEL, JOHN	BAL	054	2ND DIST
WORDEN, MARGARET	BAL	433	1ST DIST
WORDLE, CHARLES	CEC	096	4TH E DI
WORDS, DAVID	BAL	061	2ND DIST
WORHT, JOHN	CEC	211	7TH E DI
WORHTINGTON, MARY	BAL	024	9TH WARD
WORICK, JOHN	SOM	360	BRINKLEY
WORICK, JOSEPH	SOM	417	PRINCESS
WORK, ANN E.	CEC	105	3RD E DI
WORK, CHALOTTE	BAL	012	2ND DIST
WORK, CLEMENT V.	BAL	140	16TH WAR
WORK, ELISABETH	ALL	250	CUMBERLA
WORK, ELIZABETH	BAL	232	1ST DIST
WORK, ISABELL	CEC	106	3RD E DI
WORK, RACHEL	CEC	105	3RD E DI
WORKAMO, ECHARD	ALL	245	CUMBERLA
WORKING, GEORGE	FRE	310	WOODSBOR
WORKING, HENRY	BAL	111	15TH WAR
WORKING, NATHANIEL	FRE	174	5TH E DI
WORKING, WILLIAM	FRE	395	PETERSVI
WORKING, WILLIAM	BAL	187	11TH WAR
WORKINGER, ATHALINDA	FRE	143	10TH E D
WORKINGER, HENRY	FRE	284	WOODSBOR
WORKINGER, HENRY	FRE	287	WOODSBOR
WORKINGER, NATHANIEL	FRE	187	5TH E DI
WORKMAN, ANN	ALL	086	5TH E.D.
WORKMAN, ELI	WOR	233	6TH E DI
WORKMAN, ELISABETH	ALL	086	5TH E.D.
WORKMAN, ELIZA JANE	BAL	192	17TH WAR
WORKMAN, JOHN	ALL	086	5TH E.D.
WORKMAN, JOHN	ALL	096	5TH E.D.
WORKMAN, JOHN	ALL	146	6TH E.D.
WORKMAN, JOHN	BAL	282	7TH WARD
WORKMAN, WINGATE	WOR	213	4TH E DI
WORKS, CLARA	BAL	374	13TH WAR
WORKS, MAHELA	BAL	374	13TH WAR
WORLAN, MARY	WAS	184	BOONSBOR
WORLEY, ADAM	BAL	408	14TH WAR
WORLEY, ALEXANDER	BAL	102	5TH WARD
WORLEY, AMANDA	WAS	130	2ND DIST
WORLEY, BRIDGET	BAL	462	14TH WAR
WORLEY, ELIZABETH	BAL	267	12TH WAR
WORLEY, HARRIETT	CAR	299	1ST DIST
WORLEY, JACOB	BAL	455	8TH WARD
WORLEY, JACOB	WAS	131	2ND DIST
WORLEY, JOSEPH D.	BAL	079	15TH WAR
WORLEY, MARGARET	BAL	057	1ST WARD
WORLEY, MARY A.	BAL	409	14TH WAR
WORLEY, RACHEL	CEC	017	ELKTON 3
WORLEY, REBECA	WAS	107	2ND DIST
WORLEY, SUSAN	BAL	418	14TH WAR
WORLEY, WILLIAM	CAR	284	7TH DIST
WORLEY, WILLIAM R.	FRE	014	FREDERIC
WORLY, WILLAIM	WAS	124	2ND DIST
WORMAN, HENRY C.	FRE	442	8TH E DI
WORMAN, JOHN	CAR	100	NO TWP L
WORMAN, MOSES	FRE	092	FREDERIC
WORMAN, NOAH	CAR	391	2ND DIST
WORMWOOD, MICHAEL	ALL	250	CUMBERLA
WORNER, JOHN	BAL	282	2ND WARD
WORNICK, PHILIP	BAL	427	8TH WARD
WORREL, SARAH	PRI	064	NOTTINGH
WORRELL, ANN C.	TAL	041	EASTON D
WORRELL, CLARISSA	KEN	229	2ND DIST
WORRELL, HENRY	KEN	242	2ND DIST
WORRELL, HIRAM	MGM	337	CRACKLIN
WORRELL, JAKE	KEN	240	2ND DIST
WORRELL, JAMES	CEC	135	6TH E DI
WORRELL, JAMES J.	BAL	211	2ND WARD
WORRELL, JOHN	BAL	104	15TH WAR
WORRELL, JOHN	KEN	242	2ND DIST
WORRELL, THOMAS	BAL	248	1ST DIST
WORRELL, WILLIAM H. P.	KEN	245	2ND DIST
WORREN, ELIZA	WOR	283	BERLIN 1
WORREN, GERTRUDE	WOR	281	BERLIN 1
WORREN, JOSIAH	WOR	266	BERLIN 1
WORREN, MARTHA	WOR	261	BERLIN 1
WORREN, MORGAN J.	WOR	281	BERLIN 1
WORREN, ROBERT	WOR	283	BERLIN 1
WORREN, SARAH P.	WOR	269	BERLIN 1
WORRER, ISAAC	WOR	260	BERLIN 1
WORRER, JOHN	WOR	256	1ST CENS
WORRER, MARTHA	WOR	254	1ST CENS
WORRER, PIERCY ANN	WOR	267	BERLIN 1
WORRICK, JOHN	BAL	273	2ND WARD
WORRICK, NACKEY	BAL	450	1ST DIST
WORRINGTON, JAMES	WOR	270	BERLIN 1
WORROLL, BENJAIN	KEN	229	2ND DIST
WORSBER, FREDERICK	WAS	150	HAGERSTO
WORSLY, WILLIAM G.	BAL	125	1ST WARD
WORST, MARTIN	BAL	124	16TH WAR
WORT, CASPER	BAL	354	3RD WARD
WORT, JONAH	CEC	036	CHESAPEA
WORTEMBAKER, PHILIP	FRE	351	MIDDLETO
WORTES, JACOB	CEC	023	ELKTON 3
WORTH, ANDREW	BAL	366	8TH WARD
WORTH, ANN R.	BAL	337	7TH WARD
WORTH, CHARLES	ANN	376	4TH DIST
WORTH, FRANCIS J.	BAL	164	16TH WAR
WORTH, GEORGE*	BAL	307	3RD WARD
WORTH, JAMES	ANN	376	4TH DIST
WORTH, JAMES W.	CEC	054	1ST E DI
WORTH, JANE W.	CEC	016	ELKTON 3
WORTH, MARGARET	CEC	080	NORTHEAS
WORTH, RICHARD	TAL	036	EASTON D
WORTH, SAMUEL	BAL	335	1ST DIST
WORTH, THUSHBAZZAR	CEC	098	4TH E DI
WORTHAN, HENRY	FRE	177	5TH E DI
WORTHAN, JOSEPH	FRE	188	5TH E DI
WORTHAN, R.	FRE	200	5TH E DI
WORTHEYLEN, DORSEY	FRE	274	NEW MARK
WORTHEYTER, JOHN H.	FRE	274	NEW MARK
WORTHEYTON, THOMAS	FRE	276	NEW MARK
WORTHING, ANN	BAL	279	12TH WAR
WORTHING, QUCHE	BAL	229	12TH WAR
WORTHINGONT, CHARELS	BAL	178	2ND DIST
WORTHINGOTN, THOAMS Q.	BAL	334	13TH WAR
WORTHINGTON, ABRAHAM	HAR	001	1ST DIST
WORTHINGTON, ABRAHAM	BAL	348	7TH WARD
WORTHINGTON, AMOS D.	ANN	434	HOWARD D
WORTHINGTON, ANN	ANN	447	HOWARD D
WORTHINGTON, ANN D.	PRI	085	QUEEN AN
WORTHINGTON, B.T.	BAL	243	1ST DIST
WORTHINGTON, B.T.B.	ANN	259	ANNAPOLI
WORTHINGTON, BRICE	BAL	126	11TH WAR
WORTHINGTON, CASANDER	HAR	033	1ST DIST
WORTHINGTON, CHARLES	HAR	002	1ST DIST
WORTHINGTON, CHARLES	FRE	126	CREAGERS
WORTHINGTON, CHARLES	ANN	416	HOWARD D
WORTHINGTON, CHARLES	BAL	052	15TH WAR
WORTHINGTON, CHARLES G.	ANN	449	HOWARD D
WORTHINGTON, CHARLES T.	ANN	321	2ND DIST
WORTHINGTON, COMFORT	BAL	331	1ST DIST
WORTHINGTON, DEYE W.	BAL	374	1ST DIST
WORTHINGTON, EDWARD	BAL	243	1ST DIST
WORTHINGTON, ELIZABETH	ANN	521	HOWARD D
WORTHINGTON, GEORGE G.	ANN	415	HOWARD D
WORTHINGTON, GRACEY A.	BAL	173	16TH WAR
WORTHINGTON, H.P.	ANN	418	HOWARD D
WORTHINGTON, HARRIATT	HAR	124	2ND DIST
WORTHINGTON, HENRY	PRI	068	NOTTINGH
WORTHINGTON, J.	BAL	222	12TH WAR
WORTHINGTON, JAMES	BAL	349	3RD WARD
WORTHINGTON, JAMES	HAR	116	2ND DIST
WORTHINGTON, JAMES	FRE	276	NEW MARK
WORTHINGTON, JAMES C.	HAR	123	2ND DIST
WORTHINGTON, JAMES C. DR.	BAL	382	13TH WAR
WORTHINGTON, JOHN	BAL	330	1ST DIST
WORTHINGTON, JOHN	BAL	133	1ST WARD
WORTHINGTON, JOHN H.	HAR	030	1ST DIST
WORTHINGTON, JOHN T.	BAL	242	1ST DIST
WORTHINGTON, JOHN Y.	ANN	418	HOWARD D
WORTHINGTON, JOSEPH	BAL	425	1ST DIST
WORTHINGTON, JSOEPH F.	BAL	157	6TH WARD
WORTHINGTON, KINSEY	BAL	242	1ST DIST
WORTHINGTON, MARGARET	HAR	125	2ND DIST
WORTHINGTON, MARY A.	BAL	403	1ST DIST
WORTHINGTON, N. J.	ANN	320	2ND DIST
WORTHINGTON, NICHOLAS B.	ANN	281	ANNAPOLI
WORTHINGTON, NICHOLAS D.	BAL	374	1ST DIST
WORTHINGTON, NICHOLAS	MGM	344	CLARKSBU
WORTHINGTON, NOAH	BAL	372	1ST DIST
WORTHINGTON, NOAH	BAL	330	1ST DIST
WORTHINGTON, NOAH H.	ANN	460	HOWARD D
WORTHINGTON, RACHAEL A.	BAL	126	11TH WAR
WORTHINGTON, RACHEL	BAL	400	8TH WARD
WORTHINGTON, RESIN H.	BAL	374	1ST DIST
WORTHINGTON, RESIN H. JR.	BAL	374	1ST DIST
WORTHINGTON, REUBEN	ALL	238	CUMBERLA
WORTHINGTON, RICHARD	BAL	242	1ST DIST
WORTHINGTON, RUBEN	BAL	107	18TH WAR
WORTHINGTON, SALLY H.	BAL	249	1ST DIST
WORTHINGTON, SAMUEL	BAL	418	1ST DIST
WORTHINGTON, SAMUEL	BAL	440	1ST DIST
WORTHINGTON, SAMUEL	HAR	123	2ND DIST
WORTHINGTON, SARAH	BAL	425	1ST DIST
WORTHINGTON, SARAH	PRI	068	NOTTINGH
WORTHINGTON, THOMAS	BAL	058	2ND DIST
WORTHINGTON, THOMAS	HAR	125	2ND DIST
WORTHINGTON, THOMAS	MGM	315	CRACKLIN
WORTHINGTON, THOMAS C.	ANN	447	HOWARD D
WORTHINGTON, THOMAS C.	BAL	328	1ST DIST
WORTHINGTON, THOMAS C.	PRI	062	NOTTINGH
WORTHINGTON, UPTON	FRE	271	NEW MARK
WORTHINGTON, WILLIAM	HAR	123	2ND DIST
WORTHINGTON, WILLIAM	HAR	033	1ST DIST
WORTHINGTON, WILLIAM G.	BAL	475	14TH WAR
WORTHINGTON, WILLIAM H.	ANN	449	HOWARD D
WORTHINGTON, WILLIAM L.	BAL	033	1ST WARD
WORTHINGTON, WILSON	BAL	078	15TH WAR
WORTHINGTON, ZACHARIAH H.	MGM	365	BERRYS D
WORTHINGTON, BENJAMIN	BAL	079	2ND DIST
WORTHUGTON, SUSAN *	FRE	276	NEW MARK
WORTHUYTEN, CHARLES	FRE	273	NEW MARK
WORTLE, JAMES	CAR	408	2ND DIST
WORTMAN, FREDERICK	BAL	063	4TH WARD
WORTS, GEORGE	BAL	203	6TH DIST
WORTS, SARHA	BAL	197	5TH DIST
WORTSCHA, HENRY	BAL	193	2ND WARD
WORWICK, WILLIAM	SOM	360	BRINKLEY
WOSLEY, IRA	BAL	230	12TH WAR
WOSSELFROSS, GEORGE S.	BAL	114	1ST WARD
WOTHERED, LEVIN *	BAL	389	13TH WAR
WOTTLEN, RICHARD	FRE	067	FREDERIC
WOTTON, ANN	ST	330	4TH E DI
WOULRATH, JOHN	BAL	213	2ND WARD
WOUN, WILLIAM	BAL	079	2ND DIST
WOUSIDER, FRANCIS	BAL	179	2ND WARD
WOVLFORD, SARAH	DOR	373	1ST DIST
WOWALING, PETER	BAL	001	9TH WARD
WOZENCRAFT, HANNAH	BAL	134	16TH WAR
WQALTEN, MARY L.	BAL	423	3RD WARD
WRALEN, JOHN	BAL	054	9TH WARD
WRANER, WENSON	BAL	252	12TH WAR
WRANICK, WENZEL	BAL	090	10TH WAR
WRAY, MARY	BAL	051	9TH WARD
WRD, JOSHUA	CEC	084	CHARLEST
WREN, B. R.	BAL	361	13TH WAR
WREN, CATHARINE	FRE	210	BUCKEYST
WREN, CORD	BAL	425	14TH WAR
WREN, JOHN	ANN	470	HOWARD D
WREN, MRS.	QUE	248	5TH E DI
WREN, SOPIA	BAL	425	14TH WAR
WRENCHER, ELIZABETH	SOM	553	TYASKIN
WRENCHER, GEORGE H.	SOM	433	PRINCESS
WRENCHER, GEORGE T.	SOM	461	HANGARY
WRENCHER, MATILDA	SOM	461	HANGARY
WRIGHT, A.	BAL	286	2ND WARD
WRIGHT, ABIGAL	CEC	091	4TH E DI
WRIGHT, ADAM	BAL	194	2ND WARD
WRIGHT, ALEXANDER	BAL	046	15TH WAR
WRIGHT, ALEXANDER	QUE	191	3RD E DI
WRIGHT, ALFRED	BAL	213	17TH WAR
WRIGHT, ALICE	BAL	089	2ND DIST
WRIGHT, ALLISON	DOR	299	1ST DIST

Name	County	Page	District
WRIGHT, ALLISON	CEC	041	CHESAPEA
WRIGHT, ALMON	BAL	187	16TH WAR
WRIGHT, ALPHONGO P.	QUE	189	3RD E DI
WRIGHT, ANN	BAL	124	16TH WAR
WRIGHT, ANN	BAL	228	12TH WAR
WRIGHT, ANN	BAL	376	3RD WARD
WRIGHT, ANN	BAL	249	6TH WARD
WRIGHT, ANN	DOR	305	1ST DIST
WRIGHT, ANN R.	FRE	448	8TH E DI
WRIGHT, ANN-BLACK	CAR	070	NO TWP L
WRIGHT, ANTHONY	FRE	394	PETERSVI
WRIGHT, BARBARA	FRE	425	8TH E DI
WRIGHT, BARETENA	BAL	308	7TH WARD
WRIGHT, BATHIA	SOM	552	TYASKIN
WRIGHT, BEACHAM	SOM	506	BARREN C
WRIGHT, BENJAMIN	QUE	238	5TH E DI
WRIGHT, BENJAMIN	BAL	224	19TH WAR
WRIGHT, BENNONA	CEC	198	7TH E DI
WRIGHT, BETSEY	SOM	507	BARREN C
WRIGHT, BILL-BLACK	QUE	186	3RD E DI
WRIGHT, BOYCE	SOM	553	TYASKIN
WRIGHT, CALEB	CEC	213	7TH E DI
WRIGHT, CALEB	CAR	120	NO TWP L
WRIGHT, CALOB	HAR	019	1ST DIST
WRIGHT, CAROLINE	BAL	162	19TH WAR
WRIGHT, CAROLINE	BAL	144	5TH WARD
WRIGHT, CAROLINE A.	FRE	065	FREDERIC
WRIGHT, CASSANDRIA	BAL	414	8TH WARD
WRIGHT, CASSEY	BAL	039	4TH WARD
WRIGHT, CASSY	ANN	505	HOWARD D
WRIGHT, CATHARINE	BAL	258	2ND WARD
WRIGHT, CATHARINE	KEN	267	1ST DIST
WRIGHT, CATHERINE	QUE	206	3RD E DI
WRIGHT, CATHERINE L.	CEC	149	PORT DUP
WRIGHT, CATHRINE	PRI	090	MARLBROU
WRIGHT, CECILIA	BAL	053	15TH WAR
WRIGHT, CHARELS	BAL	123	5TH WARD
WRIGHT, CHARELS	QUE	209	3RD E DI
WRIGHT, CHARELS B.	BAL	144	1ST WARD
WRIGHT, CHARLES	BAL	273	7TH WARD
WRIGHT, CHARLES	BAL	114	1ST WARD
WRIGHT, CHARLES	BAL	024	1ST WARD
WRIGHT, CHARLES	CEC	138	6TH E DI
WRIGHT, CHARLES	CAR	123	NO TWP L
WRIGHT, CHARLES	CAR	109	NO TWP L
WRIGHT, CHARLES	CEC	055	1ST E DI
WRIGHT, CHARLES F.	ANN	286	ANNAPOLI
WRIGHT, CHARLES-BLACK	CAR	163	NO TWP L
WRIGHT, CHARLOTTE	ALL	221	CUMBERLA
WRIGHT, CHARLOTTE R.	BAL	077	15TH WAR
WRIGHT, CHRISTEY A.	BAL	302	7TH WARD
WRIGHT, CHRISTIANA	BAL	393	14TH WAR
WRIGHT, CLAYTON	BAL	063	10TH WAR
WRIGHT, CLEMENT	SOM	506	BARREN C
WRIGHT, CLINTON	QUE	199	3RD E DI
WRIGHT, CLINTONIA	BAL	417	3RD WARD
WRIGHT, COMZEY	BAL	253	20TH WAR
WRIGHT, CORNELIOUS	CAR	152	NO TWP L
WRIGHT, DANIEL	BAL	312	7TH WARD
WRIGHT, DANIEL	BAL	169	1ST WARD
WRIGHT, DANIEL	BAL	163	1ST WARD
WRIGHT, DANIEL R.	CAR	126	NO TWP L
WRIGHT, DANIEL*	TAL	051	EASTON D
WRIGHT, DANIEL-BLACK	BAL	217	2ND WARD
WRIGHT, DARCUS	DOR	319	1ST DIST
WRIGHT, DAVID	HAR	046	1ST DIST
WRIGHT, DAVID	ANN	267	ANNAPOLI
WRIGHT, DAVID C.	BAL	195	6TH WARD
WRIGHT, DAVID-BLACK	CAR	114	NO TWP L
WRIGHT, DEBORA	SOM	494	SALISBUR
WRIGHT, DEBORAH	CAR	121	NO TWP L
WRIGHT, DENARD	SOM	483	TRAPP DI
WRIGHT, DENTON	ANN	504	HOWARD D
WRIGHT, DERIAH*	DOR	455	1ST DIST
WRIGHT, E.	BAL	103	10TH WAR
WRIGHT, EBENEASOR	BAL	308	1ST DIST
WRIGHT, EDWARD	BAL	057	15TH WAR
WRIGHT, EDWARD	CHA	233	HILLTOP
WRIGHT, EDWARD	DOR	305	1ST DIST
WRIGHT, EDWARD L.	BAL	121	11TH WAR
WRIGHT, EDWARD M.	BAL	120	11TH WAR
WRIGHT, EDWARD-BLACK	QUE	155	2ND E DI
WRIGHT, EDWIN B.	CEC	003	ELKTON 3
WRIGHT, ELI	CEC	002	ELKTON 3
WRIGHT, ELISABETH	ANN	350	3RD DIST
WRIGHT, ELISHA	CAR	129	NO TWP L
WRIGHT, ELIZA	KEN	246	2ND DIST
WRIGHT, ELIZA	BAL	100	2ND DIST
WRIGHT, ELIZA	BAL	445	1ST DIST
WRIGHT, ELIZA	TAL	030	EASTON D
WRIGHT, ELIZA A.	TAL	015	EASTON D
WRIGHT, ELIZA J.	HAR	127	2ND DIST
WRIGHT, ELIZA J.	CEC	105	3RD E DI
WRIGHT, ELIZA J.	BAL	102	18TH WAR
WRIGHT, ELIZA-BLACK	QUE	167	2ND E DI
WRIGHT, ELIZABETH	SOM	473	TRAPPE D
WRIGHT, ELIZABETH	CAR	383	2ND DIST
WRIGHT, ELIZABETH	BAL	007	18TH WAR
WRIGHT, ELIZABETH	CHA	277	BOJANTOW
WRIGHT, ELIZABETH	CAR	129	NO TWP L
WRIGHT, ELIZABETH	CAR	235	UNION TO
WRIGHT, ELIZABETH	BAL	155	16TH WAR
WRIGHT, ELIZABETH	BAL	411	8TH WARD
WRIGHT, ELLEN	BAL	462	1ST DIST
WRIGHT, ELLEN	KEN	256	1ST DIST
WRIGHT, EMELINE	BAL	305	7TH WARD
WRIGHT, EMELINE S.	ANN	499	HOWARD D
WRIGHT, EMILY	BAL	030	4TH WARD
WRIGHT, EMILY	DOR	296	1ST DIST
WRIGHT, EMILY MISS-	BAL	315	20TH WAR
WRIGHT, EMORY	CEC	055	1ST E DI
WRIGHT, ESAU	SOM	472	TRAPPE D
WRIGHT, FRANCES	BAL	042	15TH WAR
WRIGHT, FRANCES T.	BAL	219	6TH WARD
WRIGHT, GEORGE	BAL	448	8TH WARD
WRIGHT, GEORGE	QUE	213	3RD E DI
WRIGHT, GEORGE	TAL	012	EASTON D
WRIGHT, GEORGE	SOM	514	BARREN C
WRIGHT, GEORGE	BAL	093	18TH WAR
WRIGHT, GEORGE	CEC	107	3RD E DI
WRIGHT, GEORGE	CHA	276	ALLENS F
WRIGHT, GEORGE	KEN	243	2ND DIST
WRIGHT, GEORGE B.	BAL	168	1ST WARD
WRIGHT, GEORGE W.	BAL	426	14TH WAR
WRIGHT, GEORGE W.	WOR	195	8TH E DI
WRIGHT, GEORGE-BLACK	CAR	167	NO TWP L
WRIGHT, GEROGE	KEN	261	1ST DIST
WRIGHT, GHEORGE	BAL	022	18TH WAR
WRIGHT, GIBSON W.	TAL	060	EASTON D
WRIGHT, GRACE R.	BAL	041	4TH WARD
WRIGHT, GUSTAVUS	BAL	402	1ST DIST
WRIGHT, GUSTAVUS A.T.	QUE	178	2ND E DI
WRIGHT, H.	BAL	117	1ST WARD
WRIGHT, HANNAH	QUE	233	4TH E DI
WRIGHT, HARRIET	BAL	077	15TH WAR
WRIGHT, HARRIET	FRE	448	8TH E DI
WRIGHT, HARRIETT E.	BAL	095	5TH WARD
WRIGHT, HARRISON	BAL	315	3RD WARD
WRIGHT, HENRY	BAL	091	15TH WAR
WRIGHT, HENRY	BAL	121	1ST WARD
WRIGHT, HENRY	BAL	114	1ST WARD
WRIGHT, HENRY	BAL	056	1ST WARD
WRIGHT, HENRY	ANN	355	3RD DIST
WRIGHT, HENRY	CEC	032	CHESAPEA
WRIGHT, HENRY	MGM	331	CRACKLIN
WRIGHT, HENRY	MGM	390	ROCKERLE
WRIGHT, HENRY	DOR	401	1ST DIST
WRIGHT, HENRY	DOR	400	1ST DIST
WRIGHT, HENRY D.	DOR	310	1ST DIST
WRIGHT, HENRY E.	QUE	203	3RD E DI
WRIGHT, HENRY J.	DOR	448	1ST DIST
WRIGHT, HENRY S.	PRI	052	AQUASCO
WRIGHT, HENRY-BLACK	CAR	167	NO TWP L
WRIGHT, HERTCE	BAL	057	1ST WARD
WRIGHT, HESTER	WOR	239	6TH E DI
WRIGHT, HETTY	SOM	518	BARREN C
WRIGHT, HETTY	SOM	447	DAMES QU
WRIGHT, HJENRYH	BAL	159	2ND DIST
WRIGHT, HORATIO	CAR	131	NO TWP L
WRIGHT, HUGH	CEC	208	7TH E DI
WRIGHT, HULDAH H.	BAL	385	8TH WARD
WRIGHT, ISAAC	BAL	362	8TH WARD
WRIGHT, ISAAC	DOR	325	1ST DIST
WRIGHT, ISAAC	BAL	204	19TH WAR
WRIGHT, ISAAC	FRE	162	EMMITTSB
WRIGHT, ISAAC	QUE	225	4TH E DI
WRIGHT, ISAAC K.	SOM	515	BARREN C
WRIGHT, J.	ANN	272	ANNAPOLI
WRIGHT, J. H.	ANN	291	ANNAPOLI
WRIGHT, J. H.	BAL	332	1ST DIST
WRIGHT, J. J.	BAL	156	1ST WARD
WRIGHT, J. N. J. S.	BAL	143	1ST WARD
WRIGHT, JABEZ	DOR	309	1ST DIST
WRIGHT, JACOB	KEN	253	1ST DIST
WRIGHT, JACOB	BAL	062	1ST WARD
WRIGHT, JACOB	BAL	458	8TH WARD
WRIGHT, JACOB	QUE	235	4TH E DI
WRIGHT, JACOB	TAL	011	EASTON D
WRIGHT, JACOB W.	BAL	046	9TH WARD
WRIGHT, JAMES	BAL	162	1ST WARD
WRIGHT, JAMES	BAL	217	6TH WARD
WRIGHT, JAMES	BAL	151	1ST WARD
WRIGHT, JAMES	BAL	410	8TH WARD
WRIGHT, JAMES	ALL	220	CUMBERLA
WRIGHT, JAMES	WAS	017	2ND SUBD
WRIGHT, JAMES	QUE	224	4TH E DI
WRIGHT, JAMES	QUE	159	2ND E DI
WRIGHT, JAMES	CEC	191	5TH E DI
WRIGHT, JAMES	CAR	124	NO TWP L
WRIGHT, JAMES	DOR	447	1ST DIST
WRIGHT, JAMES	BAL	432	14TH WAR
WRIGHT, JAMES A.S.T.	BAL	110	1ST WARD
WRIGHT, JAMES B.	BAL	312	3RD WARD
WRIGHT, JAMES B.	WOR	329	1ST E DI
WRIGHT, JAMES E.	BAL	157	1ST WARD
WRIGHT, JAMES M.	BAL	308	7TH WARD
WRIGHT, JAMES M.	BAL	052	15TH WAR
WRIGHT, JAMES N.	DOR	401	1ST DIST
WRIGHT, JAMES P.	BAL	324	7TH WARD
WRIGHT, JANE	CHA	263	MIDDLETO
WRIGHT, JANE	QUE	233	4TH E DI
WRIGHT, JANE	QUE	236	4TH E DI
WRIGHT, JANE	WAS	149	HAGERSTO
WRIGHT, JANE	WAS	138	HAGERSTO
WRIGHT, JANE	WAS	113	2ND DIST
WRIGHT, JANE L.	BAL	352	7TH WARD
WRIGHT, JERO	BAL	402	1ST DIST
WRIGHT, JERRY	ANN	342	3RD DIST
WRIGHT, JERVIS-BLACK	QUE	169	2ND E DI
WRIGHT, JESE C.*	DOR	421	1ST DIST
WRIGHT, JESSE	FRE	239	NEW MARK
WRIGHT, JESSE	SOM	482	TRAPP DI
WRIGHT, JESSE H.	SOM	554	TYASKIN
WRIGHT, JESSEE	DOR	296	1ST DIST
WRIGHT, JOEL	BAL	419	14TH WAR
WRIGHT, JOHN	CEC	154	PORT DUP
WRIGHT, JOHN	DOR	400	1ST DIST
WRIGHT, JOHN	CAR	122	NO TWP L
WRIGHT, JOHN	CAR	115	NO TWP L
WRIGHT, JOHN	BAL	448	14TH WAR
WRIGHT, JOHN	DOR	318	1ST DIST
WRIGHT, JOHN	FRE	448	8TH E DI
WRIGHT, JOHN	BAL	002	4TH WARD
WRIGHT, JOHN	FRE	056	FREDERIC
WRIGHT, JOHN	CEC	114	3RD E DI
WRIGHT, JOHN	BAL	093	18TH WAR
WRIGHT, JOHN	BAL	073	18TH WAR
WRIGHT, JOHN	SOM	524	BARREN C
WRIGHT, JOHN	PRI	041	VANSVILL
WRIGHT, JOHN	QUE	244	5TH E DI
WRIGHT, JOHN	ALL	251	CUMBERLA
WRIGHT, JOHN	BAL	412	1ST DIST
WRIGHT, JOHN	BAL	024	15TH WAR
WRIGHT, JOHN	BAL	244	12TH WAR
WRIGHT, JOHN	BAL	300	12TH WAR
WRIGHT, JOHN	BAL	399	8TH WARD
WRIGHT, JOHN	BAL	163	1ST WARD
WRIGHT, JOHN	BAL	090	1ST WARD
WRIGHT, JOHN	ANN	268	ANNAPOLI
WRIGHT, JOHN	ALL	010	3RD E.D.
WRIGHT, JOHN N.	DOR	305	1ST DIST
WRIGHT, JOHN O.	HAR	053	1ST DIST
WRIGHT, JOHN S.	BAL	204	11TH WAR
WRIGHT, JOHN W.	BAL	277	7TH WARD
WRIGHT, JOHN W.	BAL	400	3RD WARD
WRIGHT, JOHN W.	FRE	435	8TH E DI
WRIGHT, JOHN-BLACK	CAR	146	NO TWP L
WRIGHT, JOHN-BLACK	WOR	322	1ST E DI
WRIGHT, JOSEPH	SOM	524	BARREN C
WRIGHT, JOSEPH	PRI	017	BLADENSB
WRIGHT, JOSEPH	KEN	267	1ST DIST
WRIGHT, JOSEPH	CEC	091	4TH E DI
WRIGHT, JOSEPH	CEC	088	4TH E DI
WRIGHT, JOSEPH	CEC	059	1ST E DI
WRIGHT, JOSEPH	CHA	278	BOJANTOW
WRIGHT, JOSEPH	BAL	415	1ST DIST
WRIGHT, JOSEPH	ANN	360	3RD DIST
WRIGHT, JOSEPH A.	KEN	312	3RD DIST
WRIGHT, JOSEPH H.	BAL	372	1ST DIST
WRIGHT, JOSEPH-BLACK	CAR	097	NO TWP L
WRIGHT, JOSHUA	BAL	299	20TH WAR
WRIGHT, JOSHUA	BAL	425	1ST DIST
WRIGHT, JOSHUA	ANN	512	HOWARD D
WRIGHT, JOSHUA	BAL	096	2ND DIST
WRIGHT, JOSHUA	BAL	095	2ND DIST
WRIGHT, JULIA	BAL	170	11TH WAR
WRIGHT, JULIA	ANN	272	ANNAPOLI
WRIGHT, JULIA A.	BAL	023	4TH WARD
WRIGHT, KENNELLY	DOR	312	1ST DIST
WRIGHT, LANE	SOM	459	HANGARY
WRIGHT, LEAH	BAL	387	13TH WAR
WRIGHT, LEVICA*	DOR	325	1ST DIST
WRIGHT, LEVIN	SOM	514	BARREN C
WRIGHT, LEVIN	SOM	511	BARREN C
WRIGHT, LEVIN W.	SOM	507	BARREN C
WRIGHT, LEWIS	WAS	046	2ND SUBD
WRIGHT, LORENZO D.	BAL	312	7TH WARD
WRIGHT, LOUISA	ANN	499	HOWARD D
WRIGHT, LOUISA	BAL	234	6TH WARD
WRIGHT, LOUISA	BAL	339	13TH WAR
WRIGHT, LUKEY	BAL	225	19TH WAR
WRIGHT, LUTHER	BAL	140	5TH WARD
WRIGHT, MADELLA	DOR	296	1ST DIST
WRIGHT, MAGDALENE	WAS	144	HAGERSTO
WRIGHT, MARGARET	BAL	338	13TH WAR
WRIGHT, MARGARET	BAL	037	2ND DIST
WRIGHT, MARGARET	BAL	105	10TH WAR
WRIGHT, MARGARET	BAL	053	9TH WARD
WRIGHT, MARGARET J.	SOM	511	BARREN C
WRIGHT, MARIA	BAL	129	11TH WAR
WRIGHT, MARTHA	QUE	235	4TH E DI
WRIGHT, MARTHA	BAL	323	3RD WARD
WRIGHT, MARTHA	BAL	326	3RD WARD
WRIGHT, MARTHA A.	BAL	324	7TH WARD
WRIGHT, MARTIN L.	DOR	377	1ST DIST
WRIGHT, MARY	BAL	125	11TH WAR
WRIGHT, MARY	BAL	245	17TH WAR
WRIGHT, MARY	SOM	435	PRINCESS
WRIGHT, MARY	BAL	332	7TH WARD
WRIGHT, MARY	BAL	165	6TH WARD
WRIGHT, MARY	BAL	379	8TH WARD
WRIGHT, MARY	BAL	009	9TH WARD
WRIGHT, MARY	BAL	157	2ND DIST
WRIGHT, MARY A.	BAL	218	6TH WARD
WRIGHT, MARY A.	BAL	324	12TH WAR
WRIGHT, MARY A.	KEN	261	1ST DIST
WRIGHT, MARY E.	DOR	318	1ST DIST
WRIGHT, MARY-BLACK	CAR	169	NO TWP L
WRIGHT, MATIELA	BAL	180	2ND WARD
WRIGHT, MATILDA A.	BAL	079	10TH WAR
WRIGHT, MILTON	CAR	220	5TH DIST
WRIGHT, MINGO	SOM	447	DAMES QU
WRIGHT, MINTY*	TAL	008	EASTON D
WRIGHT, MOSES S.	CAR	388	2ND DIST
WRIGHT, MOSES-BLACK	WOR	323	1ST E DI
WRIGHT, NANCY	SOM	519	BARREN C
WRIGHT, NANCY	CAR	234	UNION TO
WRIGHT, NATHANIEL	DOR	466	1ST DIST
WRIGHT, NATHANIEL	DOR	461	1ST DIST
WRIGHT, NELSON	BAL	021	18TH WAR
WRIGHT, NICOLS	DOR	320	1ST DIST
WRIGHT, NOAH	SOM	435	PRINCESS
WRIGHT, NOBLE	DOR	413	1ST DIST
WRIGHT, OLOVER	BAL	403	1ST DIST
WRIGHT, PERRY	BAL	084	15TH WAR
WRIGHT, PERRY	ANN	354	3RD DIST
WRIGHT, PERRY	KEN	258	1ST DIST
WRIGHT, PERRY-BLACK	SOM	458	DAMES QU
WRIGHT, PETER	CAR	086	NO TWP L
WRIGHT, PETER	CAR	129	NO TWP L
WRIGHT, PETER	CAR	128	NO TWP L
WRIGHT, PETER	CEC	041	CHESAPEA
WRIGHT, PETER	BAL	307	20TH WAR
WRIGHT, PETER	WAS	139	HAGERSTO
WRIGHT, PETER	BAL	445	1ST DIST
WRIGHT, PHEBE	BAL	119	5TH WARD
WRIGHT, PHILIP	ANN	508	HOWARD D
WRIGHT, POLLARD	CEC	109	3RD E DI
WRIGHT, PRESCILLA	MGM	385	ROCKERLE
WRIGHT, PRICILLE	CAR	120	NO TWP L
WRIGHT, PRISCILLA	BAL	425	1ST DIST
WRIGHT, RACHAEL-BLACK	FRE	030	FREDERIC
WRIGHT, RACHEL	BAL	265	20TH WAR
WRIGHT, RACHEL	QUE	217	3RD E DI
WRIGHT, RACHIEL	HAR	046	1ST DIST
WRIGHT, RACHIEL	HAR	022	1ST DIST
WRIGHT, REBECCA	BAL	370	13TH WAR
WRIGHT, REGINOLD W. DR.	BAL	341	13TH WAR
WRIGHT, RICHARD	BAL	089	1ST WARD
WRIGHT, RICHARD A.	QUE	219	3RD E DI
WRIGHT, RICHARD H.	CAR	126	NO TWP L
WRIGHT, RIDGEWAY	ANN	347	3RD DIST
WRIGHT, ROBERT	BAL	121	1ST WARD
WRIGHT, ROBERT	BAL	403	1ST DIST
WRIGHT, ROBERT	BAL	219	6TH DIST
WRIGHT, ROBERT	BAL	202	6TH DIST
WRIGHT, ROBERT	BAL	165	1ST WARD
WRIGHT, ROBERT	BAL	200	6TH WARD
WRIGHT, ROBERT	BAL	238	2ND WARD
WRIGHT, ROBERT	BAL	066	4TH WARD
WRIGHT, ROBERT	SOM	438	DAMES QU
WRIGHT, ROBERT	KEN	253	1ST DIST
WRIGHT, ROBERT	QUE	240	5TH E DI
WRIGHT, ROBERT	PRI	003	BLADENSB
WRIGHT, ROBINSON	BAL	328	7TH WARD
WRIGHT, SAIGN	BAL	244	12TH WAR
WRIGHT, SALLY	CEC	099	3RD E DI
WRIGHT, SAMUEL	BAL	248	1ST DIST
WRIGHT, SAMUEL	PRI	072	MARLBROU
WRIGHT, SAMUEL	PRI	072	MARLBROU
WRIGHT, SAMUEL L.	QUE	196	3RD E DI
WRIGHT, SAMUEL T.	BAL	268	17TH WAR
WRIGHT, SAMUEL-BLACK	QUE	159	2ND E DI
WRIGHT, SARAH	DOR	464	1ST DIST
WRIGHT, SARAH	CEC	061	1ST E DI
WRIGHT, SARAH	DOR	374	1ST DIST
WRIGHT, SARAH	DOR	387	1ST DIST
WRIGHT, SARAH	KEN	211	2ND DIST
WRIGHT, SARAH	BAL	154	5TH WARD
WRIGHT, SARAH A.	BAL	415	1ST DIST
WRIGHT, SARAH A.	DOR	452	1ST DIST
WRIGHT, SARAH E.	BAL	403	1ST DIST
WRIGHT, SARAH J.	DOR	319	1ST DIST
WRIGHT, SCIPIO	SOM	431	PRINCESS
WRIGHT, SILAS	TAL	116	ST MICHA
WRIGHT, SOLOMON E.	BAL	321	7TH WARD
WRIGHT, STEPHEN	BAL	010	EASTERN
WRIGHT, STEPHEN L.	QUE	191	3RD E DI
WRIGHT, SUSAN	QUE	204	3RD E DI
WRIGHT, SUSAN	ALL	112	5TH E.D.

WRIGHT, SUSAN	DOR	400	1ST DIST
WRIGHT, SUSAN	DOR	398	1ST DIST
WRIGHT, SUSAN	CEC	015	ELKTON 3
WRIGHT, SUSAN S.	BAL	157	16TH WAR
WRIGHT, SUSAN-BLACK	CAR	133	NO TWP L
WRIGHT, SUSANNAH	BAL	058	15TH WAR
WRIGHT, SYLVESTER H.	BAL	367	3RD WARD
WRIGHT, TEMPERENCE	BAL	106	15TH WAR
WRIGHT, TENPY-BLACK	QUE	194	3RD E DI
WRIGHT, THOAMS	BAL	149	1ST WARD
WRIGHT, THOMAS	BAL	024	1ST WARD
WRIGHT, THOMAS	ALL	115	5TH E.D.
WRIGHT, THOMAS	ALL	006	3RD E.D.
WRIGHT, THOMAS	BAL	412	1ST DIST
WRIGHT, THOMAS	BAL	134	1ST WARD
WRIGHT, THOMAS	QUE	204	3RD E DI
WRIGHT, THOMAS	KEN	258	1ST DIST
WRIGHT, THOMAS	PRI	092	MARLBROU
WRIGHT, THOMAS	DOR	401	1ST DIST
WRIGHT, THOMAS	HAR	042	1ST DIST
WRIGHT, THOMAS	HAR	081	2ND DIST
WRIGHT, THOMAS	HAR	053	1ST DIST
WRIGHT, THOMAS	MGM	426	MEDLEY 3
WRIGHT, THOMAS	BAL	268	20TH WAR
WRIGHT, THOMAS	BAL	265	20TH WAR
WRIGHT, THOMAS	BAL	295	20TH WAR
WRIGHT, THOMAS	CHA	243	HILLTOP
WRIGHT, THOMAS	CAR	365	9TH DIST
WRIGHT, THOMAS	QUE	125	1ST E DI
WRIGHT, THOMAS H. DR.	BAL	337	13TH WAR
WRIGHT, THOMAS L.	CAR	132	NO TWP L
WRIGHT, THOMAS 3RD	QUE	206	3RD E DI
WRIGHT, THOMAS-BLACK	CAR	163	NO TWP L
WRIGHT, TURPIN	DOR	451	1ST DIST
WRIGHT, URIAH	CAR	366	9TH DIST
WRIGHT, VIOLET	SOM	448	DAMES QU
WRIGHT, VIRGINIA	BAL	083	18TH WAR
WRIGHT, WASHINGTON	ANN	286	ANNAPOLI
WRIGHT, WILLIAM	ALL	112	5TH E.D.
WRIGHT, WILLIAM	BAL	273	7TH WARD
WRIGHT, WILLIAM	BAL	124	5TH WARD
WRIGHT, WILLIAM	BAL	113	1ST WARD
WRIGHT, WILLIAM	BAL	157	2ND DIST
WRIGHT, WILLIAM	BAL	036	1ST WARD
WRIGHT, WILLIAM	BAL	153	1ST WARD
WRIGHT, WILLIAM	BAL	160	1ST WARD
WRIGHT, WILLIAM	BAL	239	6TH WARD
WRIGHT, WILLIAM	BAL	170	16TH WAR
WRIGHT, WILLIAM	BAL	258	12TH WAR
WRIGHT, WILLIAM	BAL	001	9TH WARD
WRIGHT, WILLIAM	BAL	018	15TH WAR
WRIGHT, WILLIAM	BAL	292	17TH WAR
WRIGHT, WILLIAM	HAR	023	1ST DIST
WRIGHT, WILLIAM	HAR	115	2ND DIST
WRIGHT, WILLIAM	KEN	255	1ST DIST
WRIGHT, WILLIAM	MGM	331	CRACKLIN
WRIGHT, WILLIAM	DOR	310	1ST DIST
WRIGHT, WILLIAM	FRE	253	NEW MARK
WRIGHT, WILLIAM	QUE	209	3RD E DI
WRIGHT, WILLIAM	KEN	257	1ST DIST
WRIGHT, WILLIAM C.	BAL	035	4TH WARD
WRIGHT, WILLIAM D.	BAL	107	15TH WAR
WRIGHT, WILLIAM E.	BAL	096	5TH WARD
WRIGHT, WILLIAM H.	BAL	415	1ST DIST
WRIGHT, WILLIAM F.	BAL	024	15TH WAR
WRIGHT, WILLIAM H.	CAR	123	NO TWP L
WRIGHT, WILLIAM T.	BAL	454	8TH WARD
WRIGHT, WILLIS	CAR	132	NO TWP L
WRIGHT, WILSON	KEN	221	2ND DIST
WRIGHT, WILSON	CEC	118	4TH E DI
WRIGHT, Y.	BAL	302	12TH WAR
WRIGHT,ELLENORE	FRE	436	8TH E DI
WRIGHT,IGNATIUS	CAR	373	9TH DIST
WRIGHT,LEVIN	CAR	163	NO TWP L
WRIGHT,RACHE	BAL	236	12TH WAR
WRIGHT,ROBERT	CAR	124	NO TWP L
WRIGHT,THOMAS	CAR	362	9TH DIST
WRIGHT,WILLIAM	CAR	128	NO TWP L
WRIGHTLY, CLEMINS	ALL	096	5TH E.D.
WRIGHTON, FRANCIS A.	TAL	103	ST MICHA
WRIGHTON, WILLIAM	TAL	109	ST MICHA
WRIGHTS, JOHN	BAL	051	4TH WARD
WRIGHTSON, BETSEY	TAL	071	EASTON T
WRIGHTSON, EMILY	TAL	066	EASTON T
WRIGHTSON, HUGH S.	TAL	083	ST MICHA
WRIGHTSON, JAMES	DOR	433	1ST DIST
WRIGHTSON, JAMES R.	TAL	110	ST MICHA
WRIGHTSON, JAMES S.	TAL	104	ST MICHA
WRIGHTSON, JEREMIAH	TAL	014	EASTON D
WRIGHTSON, JHN E.	TAL	103	ST MICHA
WRIGHTSON, JOHN F. S.	TAL	117	ST MICHA
WRIGHTSON, JOHN S.	DOR	434	1ST DIST
WRIGHTSON, JOSHUA	DOR	397	1ST DIST
WRIGHTSON, JOSIAH	TAL	071	EASTON T
WRIGHTSON, LIDIA	TAL	109	ST MICHA
WRIGHTSON, LYDIA	DOR	392	1ST DIST
WRIGHTSON, MARY	DOR	451	1ST DIST
WRIGHTSON, MARY H.	BAL	098	1ST WARD
WRIGHTSON, SALEY	DOR	432	1ST DIST
WRIGHTSON, SAMUEL H.	TAL	101	ST MICHA
WRIGHTSON, THOMAS	DOR	433	1ST DIST
WRIGHTSON, WILLIAM	TAL	109	ST MICHA
WRIN, CAROLINE V.	ANN	518	HOWARD D
WRITE, JOHN-BLACK	WOR	346	1ST E DI
WRITE, WILLIAM W.*	BAL	406	3RD WARD
WRITELINK, HENRIETTA*	BAL	313	3RD WARD
WRITH, CHARLES	BAL	133	1ST WARD
WRITH, MARY	BAL	442	14TH WAR
WROCH, E. W. *	BAL	302	20TH WAR
WROE, JOHN A.	FRE	391	PETERSVI
WROIN, JOHN	TAL	033	EASTON D
WRONER, J. T.	BAL	314	12TH WAR
WROPH, JAMES O.	BAL	097	15TH WAR
WROTEN, COLUMBIA C.	BAL	325	3RD WARD
WROTEN, THOMAS H.	SOM	488	SALISBUR
WROTH, BENJAMIN B. *	KEN	245	2ND DIST
WROTH, EDWARD T.	KEN	284	3RD DIST
WROTH, LEVI	KEN	245	2ND DIST
WROTH, LOUISA	KEN	253	1ST DIST
WROTH, MARY	KEN	245	2ND DIST
WROTH, PEREGRINE	KEN	211	2ND DIST
WROTH, W. G.	BAL	046	9TH WARD
WROTIN, P.H.	BAL	130	1ST WARD
WROTON, ANN	DOR	348	3RD DIVI
WROTON, ANN	DOR	337	3RD DIVI
WROTON, ANN	DOR	338	3RD DIVI
WROTON, APSAY	DOR	355	3RD DIVI
WROTON, DANIEL	DOR	349	3RD DIVI
WROTON, GEORGE	DOR	349	3RD DIVI
WROTON, GEORGE	DOR	348	3RD DIVI

WROTON, GEORGE	DOR	330	3RD DIVI
WROTON, JOSEPH	DOR	331	3RD DIVI
WROTON, JOSEPH	DOR	334	3RD DIVI
WROTON, LEVEN	DOR	348	3RD DIVI
WROTON, LITTELTON	DOR	355	3RD DIVI
WROTON, LITTLETON	DOR	348	3RD DIVI
WROTON, MARCELUS	DOR	354	3RD DIVI
WROTON, MARY A.	DOR	354	3RD DIVI
WROTON, ROBERT	DOR	337	3RD DIVI
WROTON, SOLOMON	DOR	346	3RD DIVI
WROTON, THOMAS	DOR	338	3RD DIVI
WROTON, THOMAS	DOR	330	3RD DIVI
WRRENFELTZ, MARY	FRE	374	CATOCTIN
WUEEN, JOHN	CHA	278	BOJANTOW
WUETER, JOHN *	BAL	285	20TH WAR
WUGANT, PETER	BAL	063	2ND DIST
WUGHTSON, THOMAS H.	DOR	397	1ST DIST
WUNTERLING, JULIUS	BAL	063	15TH WAR
WURNCH, XAVIER	BAL	302	17TH WAR
WURTZ, MARCIANIA SIS- *	BAL	316	20TH WAR
WUSENY, GEORGE	BAL	221	19TH WAR
WUSHIEM, JOHN E.	BAL	089	1ST WARD
WUYMEYER, MARY	BAL	454	14TH WAR
WVANS, JONATHAN	QUE	217	3RD E DI
WWOOD, J. F.	BAL	147	1ST WARD
WYANT, DAVID	CAR	328	MANCHEST
WYANT, JACOB	CAR	350	6TH DIST
WYANT, JACOB	CAR	329	MANCHEST
WYANT, JOHN G.	BAL	002	9TH WARD
WYANT, SUSAN	CAR	350	6TH DIST
WYART, R.H.	BAL	255	12TH WAR
WYAT, GEORGE	ALL	211	CUMBERLA
WYATT, ABSALOM	WOR	203	4TH E DI
WYATT, ACDAIDE	BAL	360	13TH WAR
WYATT, ALEXANDER H.	BAL	184	2ND WARD
WYATT, ANN	SOM	377	BRINKLEY
WYATT, ANN M.	BAL	394	14TH WAR
WYATT, EDWARD	SOM	391	BRINKLEY
WYATT, EDWARD	BAL	275	12TH WAR
WYATT, FANNY C.	HAR	111	2ND DIST
WYATT, GEORGE	BAL	071	4TH WARD
WYATT, JOHN	WOR	204	4TH E DI
WYATT, JOHN	TAL	028	EASTON D
WYATT, JOSEPH L.	BAL	260	17TH WAR
WYATT, LEMUEL	SOM	387	BRINKLEY
WYATT, ROBERT	WOR	207	4TH E DI
WYATT, THOMAS	BAL	022	1ST WARD
WYATT, WILLIAM	BAL	142	1ST WARD
WYATT, WILLIAM C.	BAL	204	11TH WAR
WYBELL, LEWIS	MGM	344	CLARKSBU
WYCOFF, EMMA	BAL	388	13TH WAR
WYE, ABE	BAL	039	2ND DIST
WYE, BENJAMIN	BAL	114	1ST WARD
WYE, CATHARINE	BAL	109	5TH WARD
WYE, FRISBY-BLACK	QUE	169	2ND E DI
WYE, GEORGE	BAL	041	2ND DIST
WYE, GEORGE	BAL	042	2ND DIST
WYE, HETTY-MULATO	QUE	189	3RD E DI
WYE, JOHN	BAL	280	12TH WAR
WYE, JOHN	BAL	141	19TH WAR
WYE, JOSEPHINE	BAL	010	4TH WAR
WYE, JOSHUA	BAL	015	2ND DIST
WYE, PHILLIP	BAL	238	2ND WARD
WYETH, CHARLES	BAL	152	11TH WAR
WYETH, NATHAN	BAL	152	11TH WAR
WYETT, BENEDICT-MULATTO	CAR	085	NO TWP L
WYETT, CHARLES T.	CAR	082	NO TWP L
WYETT, ELIZABETH-MULATTO	CAR	077	NO TWP L
WYETT, JAMES	CAR	170	NO TWP L
WYETT, JOHN-MULATTO	CAR	083	NO TWP L
WYETT, SMAUEL	CAR	078	NO TWP L
WYETT,W ILLIAM-MULATTO	CAR	098	NO TWP L
WYFORD, GEORGE	BAL	258	6TH WARD
WYGER, EMMA R.	BAL	434	8TH WARD
WYHE, HENRY-BLACK	QUE	190	3RD E DI
WYKOFF, ELIAS	CEC	139	6TH E DI
WYL, G.C.	BAL	183	2ND WARD
WYLAND, OTIS	BAL	320	7TH WARD
WYLAND, PETER	BAL	293	17TH WAR
WYLE, AUGUST	BAL	275	17TH WAR
WYLIE, SAMUEL F.	BAL	346	13TH WAR
WYLIE, WILLIAM	BAL	125	1ST WARD
WYLLIE, ABRAHAM	BAL	116	1ST WARD
WYM, JOHN	PRI	101	SPALDING
WYMAN, ANN	BAL	175	2ND WARD
WYMAN, BARNET	HAR	109	2ND DIST
WYMAN, CATHARINE	BAL	247	2ND WARD
WYMAN, EDWARD	BAL	226	6TH WARD
WYMAN, ELIZABETH	BAL	318	7TH WARD
WYMAN, ELIZABETH	BAL	412	1ST DIST
WYMAN, EMANUEL	BAL	234	2ND WARD
WYMAN, EMANUEL	BAL	235	2ND WARD
WYMAN, JACKSON	BAL	412	1ST DIST
WYMAN, JESSE	BAL	209	11TH WAR
WYMAN, JOHN	BAL	399	1ST DIST
WYMAN, JOHN H.	BAL	108	10TH WAR
WYMAN, JOSEPH	BAL	227	6TH WARD
WYMAN, MARK	BAL	399	1ST DIST
WYMAN, MARY A.-BLACK	BAL	219	2ND WARD
WYMAN, NICHOLAS	BAL	161	19TH WAR
WYMAN, SAMUEL	BAL	165	2ND DIST
WYMAN, SAMUEL C.	BAL	187	11TH WAR
WYMAN, SAMUEL JR.	BAL	108	10TH WAR
WYMERT, JOSEPH	CAR	278	7TH DIST
WYMERT, WILLIAM	CAR	273	WESTMINS
WYNDER, JOHN	BAL	242	2ND WARD
WYNEHOLT, ANDREW	BAL	339	7TH WARD
WYNN, CATHERINE	BAL	362	3RD WARD
WYNN, EMILY	BAL	134	5TH WARD
WYNN, JOHN	BAL	134	5TH WARD
WYNN, THOMAS	BAL	148	16TH WAR
WYNN, WILLIAM	BAL	338	3RD WARD
WYNN, WILLIAM G.	BAL	377	3RD WARD
WYNNE, JAMES	BAL	104	10TH WAR
WYNNE, MARY EL. AP G.*	BAL	104	10TH WAR
WYOE, ROBERT	CAL	037	2ND DIST
WYON, CHRISTIAN	BAL	188	2ND WARD
WYOTT, EBENEZER	CAR	167	NO TWP L
WYRELL, SAMUEL	PRI	064	NOTTINGH
WYRICK, JOHN P.	HAR	063	1ST DIST
WYROUGH, JOHN W.	BAL	390	8TH WARD
WYRTS, JULIA	BAL	158	11TH WAR
WYSE, FRANCIS A.	BAL	404	1ST DIST
WYSE, JOHN M.	BAL	404	1ST DIST
WYSHAM, E. C.	BAL	333	1ST DIST
WYSHAM, EVERLINE	BAL	378	1ST DIST
WYSHAM, EZEKIEL C.	BAL	445	14TH WAR
WYSHAM, EZEKIEL C.	BAL	445	14TH WAR
WYSHAM, EZEKLE	BAL	270	1ST DIST
WYSHAM, ISABEL	BAL	270	1ST DIST

WYSHAM, JOHN	BAL	203	19TH WAR
WYSHAM, WILLIAM E.	BAL	471	14TH WAR
WYSHAM, WILLIAM E.	BAL	287	1ST DIST
WYSONG, THOMAS	HAR	121	2ND DIST
WYVELL, EDWARD H.	PRI	111	PISCATAW
WYVELL, GEORGE	BAL	301	20TH WAR
WYVIL, M. D.	BAL	073	10TH WAR
WYVILL, WILLIAM	BAL	318	20TH WAR
WYVILLE, EDWARD H.	MGM	430	CLARKSTR
XAUPI, HONORATUS X.	FRE	20	5TH E DI
XAVIAR, FRANCIS	BAL	127	5TH WARD
YADES, HENRY	CEC	046	1ST E DI
YAFRAINE, SEMARD G. *	BAL	262	2ND WARD
YAGER, ARTHUR	BAL	199	2ND WARD
YAGER, CASPER	BAL	277	2ND WARD
YAGER, CATHARINE	BAL	306	7TH WARD
YAGER, CHARLES	BAL	001	9TH WARD
YAGER, DAVID	WAS	133	2ND DIST
YAGER, ELIZABETH	BAL	268	2ND WARD
YAGER, HENRY	BAL	248	2ND WARD
YAGER, HENRY	ANN	486	HOWARD D
YAGER, HENRY R.	ANN	485	HOWARD D
YAGER, JOHN	WAS	122	2ND DIST
YAGER, LAURA	BAL	165	6TH WARD
YAGER, MICHAEL	BAL	256	2ND WARD
YAGER, PHILLIP	BAL	105	1ST WARD
YAGER, SAMUEL	WAS	133	2ND DIST
YAGGARD, G.	BAL	165	1ST WARD
YAGLE, JOHN	ALL	258	CUMBERLA
YAHN, HENRY	CAR	264	WESTMINS
YAKELY, ELIRA	BAL	291	3RD WARD
YAKIN, JOHN	BAL	210	2ND WARD
YAKLE, CONRAD	BAL	008	9TH WARD
YAN, DOLLY	BAL	049	1ST WARD
YANCE, BRADLEY	PRI	107	PISCATAW
YANCE, MARY	PRI	109	PISCATAW
YANER, JOWHER	HAR	196	3RD DIST
YANEY, GEORGE	CAR	264	WESTMINS
YANEY, WILLIAM	BAL	307	12TH WAR
YANFAN, GEORGE-BLACK	FRE	245	NEW MARK
YANG, DAVID	CAR	225	5TH DIST
YANGBLUIST, C. *	BAL	295	20TH WAR
YANGEY, ARTHUR	FRE	241	NEW MARK
YANKANING, JACOB	BAL	285	2ND WARD
YANKER, JONATHAN *	WAS	154	2ND DIST
YANKMAN, JOHN J.	BAL	273	2ND WARD
YANSEY, BERNARD	BAL	285	20TH WAR
YANSLEY, THOMAS	BAL	214	11TH WAR
YANTES, SUSAN	FRE	285	WOODSBOR
YANTIS, DAVID F.	FRE	285	WOODSBOR
YANTZ, HENRY	ALL	186	9TH E.D.
YANTZ, LOUISA	ALL	164	6TH E.D.
YAP, JOHN D.	BAL	142	11TH WAR
YAR, SARAH E.	BAL	214	11TH WAR
YARAL, JOHN	BAL	183	19TH WAR
YARD, CHARLES D.	WAS	130	HAGERSTO
YARDLEY, CHARLES F.	BAL	166	16TH WAR
YARDLEY, JOSEPH	FRE	377	PETERSVI
YARDSTICKER, JOHN	BAL	235	20TH WAR
YARE, JOHN	BAL	314	12TH WAR
YARFIN, SUSAN	BAL	259	20TH WAR
YARKER, CHARLES	BAL	340	1ST DIST
YARKER, HENRY	BAL	339	1ST DIST
YARN, FANNY	BAL	181	19TH WAR
YARNAL, ELIZABETH	HAR	153	3RD DIST
YARNALL, MORDECAI	CEC	170	6TH E DI
YARNELL, JOHN B.	CEC	153	PORT DEP
YARRINGTON, EUNICE	BAL	353	7TH WARD
YARRINGTON, JOHN	BAL	109	5TH WARD
YARRO, MARRY	WAS	088	2ND SUBD
YASE, CHARLES	FRE	069	FREDERIC
YASEN, THOMS	BAL	128	1ST WARD
YASTE, GEORGE	FRE	326	MIDDLETO
YASTE, JONAHTAN	FRE	346	MIDDLETO
YATE,S JOHN	MGM	379	ROCKERLE
YATEM, MARY J.	BAL	145	11TH WAR
YATER, HARRIET	FRE	153	10TH E D
YATER, HENRY	BAL	450	8TH WARD
YATERN, WILLIAM A.	CAR	148	NO TWP L
YATERS, SARH J.	ST	277	3RD E DI
YATES, BRIDGET	BAL	125	5TH WARD
YATES, C.	BAL	165	1ST WARD
YATES, CATHARINE	FRE	381	PETERSVI
YATES, ELI	BAL	287	12TH WAR
YATES, ELIZABETH	BAL	168	6TH WARD
YATES, GEORGE A.	ST	319	4TH E DI
YATES, HARIET*	SOM	546	TYASKIN
YATES, HENRY P.P.	BAL	140	5TH WARD
YATES, HIRAM	BAL	145	5TH WARD
YATES, JAMES	BAL	151	1ST WARD
YATES, JAMES	KEN	306	3RD DIST
YATES, JAMES	WAS	092	2ND SUBD
YATES, JAMES L.	ST	285	2ND E DI
YATES, JAMES TG.	ST	284	2ND E DI
YATES, JANE	BAL	211	11TH WAR
YATES, JANE	CHA	259	MIDDLETO
YATES, JOHN	FRE	382	PETERSVI
YATES, JOHN	HAR	004	1ST DIST
YATES, JOHN	BAL	253	1ST DIST
YATES, JOHN	ST	265	3RD E DI
YATES, JOHN L.	BAL	125	5TH WARD
YATES, JOHN R.	BAL	140	16TH WAR
YATES, JOSEPH	WAS	163	2ND DIST
YATES, JOSEPHINE	FRE	389	PETERSVI
YATES, MARTYIN	ST	265	3RD E DI
YATES, MATHEW	BAL	408	1ST DIST
YATES, MATILDA	ST	280	3RD E DI
YATES, SARAH P.	ST	285	2ND E DI
YATES, STEPHEN	ANN	496	HOWARD D
YATES, WILLIAM	CAR	290	7TH DIST
YAWBE, J.	BAL	156	1ST WARD
YAWCOM, JOHN	BAL	203	2ND WARD
YAZER, CASPER	BAL	004	4TH WARD
YEA, JAMES M.	BAL	149	1ST WARD
YEADER, ALEXANDER	BAL	248	12TH WAR
YEAGAR, ADAM	BAL	034	18TH WAR
YEAGEL, CONRAD	BAL	287	20TH WAR
YEAGER, ANDREW	BAL	023	18TH WAR
YEAGER, ANDREW	BAL	022	18TH WAR
YEAGER, ANDREW	BAL	001	18TH WAR
YEAGER, ANDREW	BAL	018	9TH WARD
YEAGER, CATHARINE	BAL	193	19TH WAR
YEAGER, CHARLES	BAL	163	2ND DIST
YEAGER, CONRADT	BAL	332	7TH WARD
YEAGER, J.	BAL	259	12TH WAR
YEAGER, JACOB	BAL	192	19TH WAR
YEAGER, JOHN	BAL	162	2ND DIST
YEAGER, JOSEPH	BAL	162	2ND DIST
YEAGER, MARY	BAL	001	18TH WAR
YEAGER, THOMAS	BAL	162	2ND DIST

Name	County	Page	District
YEAGERS, JOSIAH	BAL	130	2ND DIST
YEAGLE, CONRADT	BAL	209	17TH WAR
YEAGLE, MARTIN *	BAL	095	15TH WAR
YEAGLE, WILLIAM	BAL	102	15TH WAR
YEAGLER, JOHN	BAL	157	19TH WAR
YEAKLE, AQUILLA R.	FRE	026	FREDERIC
YEAKLE, CATHARINE	WAS	242	CAVETOWN
YEAKLE, DAVID	WAS	188	1ST DIST
YEAKLE, ELIZABETH	BAL	278	17TH WAR
YEAKLE, GECRGE	WAS	237	CAVETOWN
YEAKLE, JACOB	WAS	237	CAVETOWN
YEAKLE, JACOB	WAS	034	2ND SUBD
YEAKLE, JACOB	FRE	043	FREDERIC
YEAKLE, JOHN	BAL	277	17TH WAR
YEAKLE, JOHN	WAS	242	CAVETOWN
YEAKLE, LAURA	WAS	134	HAGERSTO
YEAKLE, MARY A.	WAS	149	HAGERSTO
YEAKLE, SAMUEL	WAS	146	HAGERSTO
YEAKLE, SARAH A.C.	FRE	043	FREDERIC
YEAKLE, WILLIAM	FRE	025	FREDERIC
YEAKLES, CHRISTIAN	WAS	051	2ND SUBD
YEAKLEY, E.M.M.	BAL	012	18TH WAR
YEAL, HENRY	BAL	230	12TH WAR
YEALDALL, SIDNEY	BAL	361	1ST DIST
YEALDHALL, E.	ANN	342	3RD DIST
YEALDHALL, E. B.	ANN	342	3RD DIST
YEALDHALL, HENRY	ANN	342	3RD DIST
YEALDHALL, JOHN	ANN	346	3RD DIST
YEALDHALL, RICHARD	ANN	342	3RD DIST
YEALDHALL, SAMUEL	BAL	025	18TH WAR
YEALDHALL, THOMAS	BAL	184	16TH WAR
YEALHALL, ANN R.	BAL	163	16TH WAR
YEARBY, JOHN	BAL	153	1ST WARD
YEARGER, HENRY	BAL	041	18TH WAR
YEARLEY, FRAZIER	KEN	238	2ND DIST
YEARLEY, JOHN	BAL	173	1ST WARD
YEARLEY, JOHN	BAL	336	7TH WARD
YEARLEY, RICHARD	KEN	295	3RD DIST
YEARLOY, RUTH	BAL	170	11TH WAR
YEARLY, ANN	BAL	197	11TH WAR
YEARLY, COTH E.G.	BAL	229	2ND WARD
YEARLY, J.	BAL	164	1ST WARD
YEARLY, JOHN S.*	BAL	334	3RD WARD
YEARLY, M.F.	PRI	057	NOTTINGH
YEARNBULL, JOSEPH	BAL	166	1ST WARD
YEARNEY, ROBERT	BAL	174	11TH WAR
YEARWICKER, MARY	BAL	375	3RD WARD
YEAST, CATHARINE	FRE	186	5TH E DI
YEAST, MICHAEL	ALL	009	3RD E.D.
YEAST, PETER	ALL	008	3RD E.D.
YEAST, PETER	ALL	008	3RD E.D.
YEAST, WILLIAM	ALL	017	3RD E.D.
YEATES, ANN	BAL	158	16TH WAR
YEATES, GEORGE W.	BAL	219	6TH WARD
YEATES, HENRIETTA	BAL	181	16TH WAR
YEATES, JOHN C. C.	BAL	007	9TH WARD
YEATES, JOSEPH C.	BAL	026	9TH WARD
YEATES, JOSIAH	CEC	045	1ST E DI
YEATES, MARTHA	BAL	156	11TH WAR
YEATES, SAMUEL	CEC	054	1ST E DI
YEATES, WILLIAM	CEC	046	1ST E DI
YEATMAN, GEORGE E.	BAL	385	13TH WAR
YEATMAN, JOHN	BAL	135	5TH WARD
YEATS, JOHN R.	BAL	456	14TH WAR
YEATS, MARY S.	KEN	271	1ST DIST
YEDIER, JACOB	BAL	231	12TH WAR
YEDINGS, ENOCH	BAL	301	12TH WAR
YEGE, M.	BAL	160	19TH WAR
YEGELY, JOHN	BAL	156	19TH WAR
YEHLING, HENRY	BAL	147	11TH WAR
YEIGER, NANCY	WAS	260	1ST DIST
YEIGHTER, WILLIAM H.	BAL	146	11TH WAR
YEISER, DANILL	CAR	252	3RD DIST
YEISER, DAVID	CAR	248	3RD DIST
YELLER, HENRY	WAS	005	WILLIAMS
YELLMAKER, FREDERICK	BAL	288	1ST DIST
YELLMAN, HENNA	BAL	104	2ND DIST
YELLOTT, COLEMAN	BAL	059	10TH WAR
YELLOTT, JOHN	BAL	087	2ND DIST
YELLOTT, REBECCA	HAR	106	2ND DIST
YELLOTT, WASHINGTON*	BAL	108	10TH WAR
YELTER, MARVIN	BAL	035	9TH WARD
YELTZ, PHILIP	BAL	313	12TH WAR
YEMAN, HENRY	BAL	322	7TH WARD
YEMELL, JOHN	BAL	236	17TH WAR
YEMER, JOSEPH	BAL	176	19TH WAR
YEMMERSON, SARAH	CAR	100	NO TWP L
YEMPKINS, ANN	BAL	226	12TH WAR
YENDER, AUGUSTUS	BAL	357	8TH WARD
YENDY, EMILY O. *	BAL	299	12TH WAR
YENER, MARY	BAL	322	12TH WAR
YENERICK, SARAH	BAL	374	8TH WARD
YENGLE, BARBARA	BAL	412	14TH WAR
YENRICK, HENRIETTA	BAL	252	6TH WARD
YEO, ALEXANDER	BAL	384	3RD WARD
YEO, THOMAS B.*	TAL	008	EASTON D
YERBA, HY.	BAL	288	1ST DIST
YERBY, WILLIAM	BAL	207	17TH WAR
YERDEN, HENRY	BAL	383	1ST DIST
YERGAN, REGINA	BAL	214	19TH WAR
YERHART, MARGARET	BAL	249	20TH WAR
YERK, CATHARINE	FRE	184	5TH E DI
YERKER, JERRY	KEN	255	1ST DIST
YERKER, STEPHEN *	KEN	255	1ST DIST
YERKES, ANDREW	CEC	121	4TH E DI
YERKES, CAVID A.	BAL	084	4TH WARD
YERKES, STEPHEN	BAL	058	2ND DIST
YERLEY, THOMAS	BAL	374	8TH WARD
YERNTEY, PHILIP	BAL	159	11TH WAR
YERST, JACOB	BAL	429	8TH WARD
YERTY, AARCN	WAS	086	2ND SUBD
YERTY, ABRAHAM	WAS	086	2ND SUBD
YERTY, GEORGE	WAS	089	2ND SUBD
YERTY, JACOB	WAS	067	2ND SUBD
YERTY, JOHN	WAS	088	2ND SUBD
YESLER, JOHN	WAS	229	1ST DIST
YESLER, SARAH E.	WAS	229	1ST DIST
YEST, MATILDA	BAL	260	20TH WAR
YET, PHILLIP	BAL	298	17TH WAR
YETTER, HENRY	BAL	248	20TH WAR
YETTOW, JEREMIAH	BAL	086	2ND DIST
YEUETT, CHARLES C.	BAL	171	11TH WAR
YEVENTY, JOHN *	FRE	083	FREDERIC
YEWELL, FRANCES J.	ANN	354	3RD DIST
YEWELL, JOHANNA R.	MGM	376	ROCKERLE
YEWELL, JOHN	ANN	413	HOWARD D
YEWELL, MARGARET	ANN	314	1ST DIST
YEWELL, MATILDA	ANN	310	1ST DIST
YEWELL, THOMAS	ANN	310	1ST DIST
YEWELL, THMAS	ANN	355	3RD DIST
YEWEN, GEORGE	ANN	371	4TH DIST
YEYSMIRE, ANN	BAL	250	20TH WAR
YHEEBALD, E. W.	BAL	143	11TH WAR
YICKEL, FRANCIS	FRE	254	NEW MARK
YIEGER, JOHN *	BAL	313	20TH WAR
YIERMAN, ANN	CEC	143	7TH E DI
YIESLEY, JACOB*	BAL	379	3RD WARD
YIFFAMY, O.	BAL	145	11TH WAR
YIGHLMAN, MARY	BAL	392	8TH WARD
YILGHMAN, ELIZA	BAL	144	11TH WAR
YILGHMAN, R. LYOD	BAL	149	11TH WAR
YILGLEMAN, MARY A.	BAL	151	11TH WAR
YINGER, GEORGE	FRE	051	FREDERIC
YINGLING, ABDIEL	CAR	355	6TH DIST
YINGLING, ABSCLUM	BAL	252	1ST DIST
YINGLING, ADAM	CAR	246	3RD DIST
YINGLING, ADAM	MGM	408	MEDLEY 3
YINGLING, ANN	CAR	346	6TH DIST
YINGLING, ANN E.	CAR	405	2ND DIST
YINGLING, BENJAMIN	CAR	379	2ND DIST
YINGLING, CHRISTAIN	CAR	246	3RD DIST
YINGLING, CHRISTIAN	CAR	262	3RD DIST
YINGLING, DAVID	CAR	403	2ND DIST
YINGLING, DAVID	BAL	225	1ST DIST
YINGLING, EPHRAIM	CAR	246	3RD DIST
YINGLING, FERDINAN	CAR	267	WESTMINS
YINGLING, FRANCIS	MGM	421	MEDLEY 3
YINGLING, FREDERICK	CAR	262	3RD DIST
YINGLING, FREDERICK JR.	CAR	262	3RD DIST
YINGLING, GEORGE C.	CAR	356	6TH DIST
YINGLING, HANNAH	CAR	403	2ND DIST
YINGLING, HENRY	CAR	353	6TH DIST
YINGLING, JACOB	CAR	253	3RD DIST
YINGLING, JAOCB	CAR	174	8TH DIST
YINGLING, JERCME *	CAR	266	WESTMINS
YINGLING, JESSE	CAR	266	WESTMINS
YINGLING, JESSE R.	BAL	220	1ST DIST
YINGLING, JOHN	BAL	220	1ST DIST
YINGLING, JOHN	CAR	266	WESTMINS
YINGLING, JOHN	CAR	353	6TH DIST
YINGLING, JOHN T.	FRE	448	8TH E DI
YINGLING, JOSHUA	CAR	385	2ND DIST
YINGLING, JOSHUA	CAR	268	WESTMINS
YINGLING, LEWIS	CAR	253	3RD DIST
YINGLING, MARGARET	CAR	264	WESTMINS
YINGLING, MARTHA	CAR	254	3RD DIST
YINGLING, MARTIN	CAR	192	4TH DIST
YINGLING, MARY	CAR	264	WESTMINS
YINGLING, MICHAEL	CAR	357	6TH DIST
YINGLING, NIMROD	BAL	225	1ST DIST
YINGLING, OLIVER P.	CAR	264	WESTMINS
YINGLING, PETER	CAR	244	3RD DIST
YINGLING, REBECCA	CAR	251	3RD DIST
YINGLING, RODGER, N.	CAR	265	WESTMINS
YINGLING, SAMUEL	CAR	346	6TH DIST
YINGLING, SARAH	CAR	182	8TH DIST
YINGLING, SOPHIA	CAR	237	UNION TO
YINGLING, SYLVESTER	CAR	244	3RD DIST
YINGLING, WASHINGTON	MGM	424	MEDLEY 3
YINGLING, WILLIAM	CAR	246	3RD DIST
YINGLING, WILLIAM	CAR	174	8TH DIST
YINGLING, WILLIAM G.	FRE	233	BUCKEYST
YINGLING, WILLIAM H.	CAR	194	4TH DIST
YINGLING, WILLIAM W.	FRE	430	8TH E DI
YINGLING,JAOCB	CAR	406	2ND DIST
YINGLING,RACHAEL	CAR	386	2ND DIST
YINHLING, HEZEKIAH	CAR	236	UNION TO
YINKING, JACOB	BAL	255	2ND WARD
YINKING, MARY	BAL	255	2ND WARD
YITTETT, WILLIAM	BAL	168	1ST WARD
YOCHEN, WILLIAM H. *	BAL	284	20TH WAR
YODER, JOSEPH	ALL	040	2ND E.D.
YOE, BENJAMIN F.*	BAL	312	3RD WARD
YOE, JAMES F.	CAL	038	2ND DIST
YOE, SAMUEL	TAL	072	EASTON T
YOGLE, CHRISTOPHER	BAL	309	7TH WARD
YOIST, FREDERICK	BAL	268	2ND WARD
YOKE, HOLLYDAY	ANN	283	ANNAPOLI
YOLINAN, F. M.	BAL	157	11TH WAR
YOLLERDT, CARL E.	BAL	031	9TH WARD
YOLLERT, JOHN	BAL	031	9TH WARD
YOLLEY, HENRY*	DOR	329	3RD DIVI
YOMNER, WILLIAM	BAL	168	11TH WAR
YONCE, JOHN P. *	BAL	273	7TH WARD
YONER, GEORGE	BAL	177	19TH WAR
YONER, HARRIET	FRE	011	FREDERIC
YONER, JOHN	BAL	376	8TH WARD
YONER, MARY A.	BAL	398	8TH WARD
YONETTA, THOMAS-MULATTO	BAL	212	2ND WARD
YONG, ABIJAH	CAR	212	5TH DIST
YONG, HANAH	BAL	448	8TH WARD
YONG, JANE	WOR	344	1ST E DI
YONG, JOSEPH	BAL	344	7TH WARD
YONG, RICHARD	BAL	328	7TH WARD
YONG, SUSAN	HAR	150	3RD DIST
YONG, WILLIAM H.	BAL	268	7TH WARD
YONG, WILLIAM S.	HAR	193	3RD DIST
YONGER, HENRY	BAL	457	1ST DIST
YONGER, WILLIAM	BAL	309	20TH WAR
YONKER, ----- *	BAL	382	8TH WARD
YONKER, ALBERT	BAL	268	7TH WARD
YONKER, ELIZABETH	BAL	308	7TH WARD
YONKER, HENRY	WAS	021	2ND SUBD
YONKER, MARCELENA W.	BAL	308	7TH WARD
YONKER, MARTHA	BAL	298	7TH WARD
YONKINS, JOHN	FRE	330	MIDDLETO
YONN, WILLIAM	CAR	374	9TH DIST
YONNER, FREDERICK	BAL	235	20TH WAR
YONNEY, JAMES	BAL	202	19TH WAR
YONSOULER, GEORGE *	BAL	312	20TH WAR
YONTZ, SUSANNA	FRE	119	CREAGERS
YORBACK, JAMES-BLACK	BAL	202	2ND WARD
YORDSON, CHARLES *	BAL	293	20TH WAR
YORK, ABAGAIL	CEC	120	4TH E DI
YORK, BENJAMIN	CEC	024	ELKTON 3
YORK, BENJAMIN	BAL	142	2ND DIST
YORK, FRANCIS A.	BAL	364	3RD WARD
YORK, G. W.	BAL	148	1ST WARD
YORK, HENRY	CEC	153	PORT DUP
YORK, JOHN	BAL	353	3RD WARD
YORK, JOHN	BAL	142	2ND DIST
YORK, JOHN	BAL	142	2ND DIST
YORK, JOHN W.	BAL	143	1ST WARD
YORK, JOHN WOOD	MGM	412	MEDLEY 3
YORK, MARY E. *	BAL	043	18TH WAR
YORK, RACHEL	BAL	244	20TH WAR
YORK, WILLIAM	BAL	142	2ND DIST
YORK, WILLIAM	BAL	158	1ST WARD
YORKER, AARON	KEN	276	1ST DIST
YORKER, GEROGE	KEN	236	2ND DIST
YORKER, JACOB	KEN	275	1ST DIST
YORKES, JOHN	BAL	281	2ND WARD
YORKMAN, LEWISA	BAL	094	18TH WAR
YORMAN, JAMES	BAL	123	1ST WARD
YORNOLYON, JESSE	BAL	218	12TH WAR
YORNEY, OTTO	BAL	261	12TH WAR
YORST, JEROME	BAL	231	19TH WAR
YORSUCH, RACHEL	BAL	362	3RD WARD
YOST, ABRAM	ALL	171	7TH E.D.
YOST, AMELIA	MGM	395	ROCKERLE
YOST, CHARLES *	BAL	313	1ST DIST
YOST, DANIEL	ALL	102	5TH E.D.
YOST, ELIZABETH	BAL	052	18TH WAR
YOST, ELIZABETH L.	WAS	121	HAGERSTO
YOST, JACOB	BAL	031	2ND DIST
YOST, JAOCB S.	CAR	348	6TH DIST
YOST, JOHN	BAL	052	18TH WAR
YOST, JOHN	CAR	253	3RD DIST
YOST, JOHN	BAL	157	19TH WAR
YOST, JOHN	BAL	009	9TH WARD
YOST, JOHN	BAL	009	9TH WARD
YOST, JOHN	BAL	221	1ST DIST
YOST, JOHN B.	BAL	228	2ND WARD
YOST, JOHN B.	BAL	228	2ND WARD
YOST, JOHN N.	ANN	463	HOWARD D
YOST, JOSEPH K.	BAL	029	2ND DIST
YOST, LOUISA	FRE	066	FREDERIC
YOST, MARIA	CEC	149	PORT DUP
YOST, MARY	BAL	029	2ND DIST
YOST, PHILIP	CAR	344	6TH DIST
YOST, PHILLIP	CAR	349	6TH DIST
YOST, PRISCILLA	FRE	066	FREDERIC
YOST, VALENTINE	CAR	344	6TH DIST
YOST, WILLIAM	BAL	101	18TH WAR
YOSTS, CHARLES	FRE	023	FREDERIC
YOUCE, JOHN P. *	BAL	273	7TH WARD
YOUG, MARY	CEC	044	CHESAPEA
YOULER, ANN R.	FRE	304	WOODSBOR
YOUMAN, FRANCIS	ALL	195	CUMBERLA
YOUNAN, JOHN	BAL	284	20TH WAR
YOUNG, A. J.	SOM	350	BRINKLEY
YOUNG, ABRAHAM	KEN	288	3RD DIST
YOUNG, ABRAHAM	QUE	241	5TH E DI
YOUNG, ABRAHAM	FRE	304	WOODSBOR
YOUNG, ABRAHAM	BAL	055	2ND DIST
YOUNG, ALBERT	ST	347	5TH E DI
YOUNG, ALESON	ALL	080	5TH E.D.
YOUNG, ALEXANDER	BAL	219	6TH WARD
YOUNG, ALEXANDER	BAL	008	4TH WARD
YOUNG, ALEXANDER	BAL	430	14TH WAR
YOUNG, ALFRED	DOR	432	1ST DIST
YOUNG, ALFRED	FRE	034	FREDERIC
YOUNG, ALFRED	ANN	346	3RD DIST
YOUNG, ALLEN M.	FRE	015	FREDERIC
YOUNG, ALVAH	BAL	266	20TH WAR
YOUNG, ALVAH	BAL	266	20TH WAR
YOUNG, AMELINE	TAL	100	ST MICHA
YOUNG, AMOS	WAS	154	HAGERSTO
YOUNG, ANN	TAL	074	EASTON T
YOUNG, ANN	BAL	228	19TH WAR
YOUNG, ANN	CAR	372	9TH DIST
YOUNG, ANN	CHA	267	BOJANTOW
YOUNG, ANN	BAL	017	2ND DIST
YOUNG, ANN	BAL	366	1ST DIST
YOUNG, ANN	BAL	413	1ST DIST
YOUNG, ANN E.	BAL	192	6TH WARD
YOUNG, ANNY	BAL	075	4TH WARD
YOUNG, ANTHONEY	BAL	380	8TH WARD
YOUNG, ARCHIBALD	ALL	170	6TH E.D.
YOUNG, ARCHIBALD	BAL	007	15TH WAR
YOUNG, AUTHER*	TAL	056	EASTON D
YOUNG, BARBARA A.	WAS	276	RIDGEVIL
YOUNG, BARNETT	WAS	194	1ST DIST
YOUNG, BENJAMIN	BAL	242	6TH WARD
YOUNG, BENJAMIN	ANN	346	3RD DIST
YOUNG, BENJAMIN	BAL	124	18TH WAR
YOUNG, BENJAMIN O.	HAR	098	2ND DIST
YOUNG, BETSEY	BAL	087	4TH WARD
YOUNG, CARLINE	QUE	157	2ND E DI
YOUNG, CAROLINE	BAL	057	18TH WAR
YOUNG, CATHARINE	FRE	306	WOODSBOR
YOUNG, CATHARINE	FRE	307	WOODSBOR
YOUNG, CATHARINE	QUE	241	5TH E DI
YOUNG, CELDIA *	BAL	369	13TH WAR
YOUNG, CHALRES	CAL	024	2ND DIST
YOUNG, CHARITY	CEC	008	ELKTON 3
YOUNG, CHARLES	KEN	292	3RD DIST
YOUNG, CHARLES	BAL	020	2ND DIST
YOUNG, CHARLES	BAL	023	9TH WARD
YOUNG, CHARLES	BAL	001	9TH WARD
YOUNG, CHARLES	ANN	301	1ST DIST
YOUNG, CHARLES	BAL	287	3RD WARD
YOUNG, CHARLES B.	CAL	030	2ND DIST
YOUNG, CHARLOTTE	BAL	304	20TH WAR
YOUNG, CHRISTOPHER	BAL	301	3RD WARD
YOUNG, CHRISTOPHER	BAL	059	15TH WAR
YOUNG, CHRISTOPHER	BAL	151	2ND DIST
YOUNG, CLARA	BAL	058	4TH WARD
YOUNG, CLEB	ANN	452	HOWARD D
YOUNG, CLEMENCY	HAR	158	3RD DIST
YOUNG, CLEMENT	DOR	455	1ST DIST
YOUNG, CONROD	FRE	026	FREDERIC
YOUNG, CORNELIUS W.	BAL	041	18TH WAR
YOUNG, DANIEL	FRE	288	WOODSBOR
YOUNG, DANIEL	FRE	329	MIDDLETO
YOUNG, DANIL	DOR	465	1ST DIST
YOUNG, DAVID	WAS	076	2ND SUBD
YOUNG, DAVID	TAL	048	EASTON T
YOUNG, DAVID	PRI	050	AQUASCO
YOUNG, DAVID	FRE	292	WOODSBOR
YOUNG, DAVID	FRE	114	CREAGERS
YOUNG, DAVID	BAL	079	4TH WARD
YOUNG, DAVID	BAL	067	4TH WARD
YOUNG, DAVID	MGM	414	MEDLEY 3
YOUNG, DAVID W.	CAR	352	6TH DIST
YOUNG, DEVAULT	WAS	079	2ND SUBD
YOUNG, DEWALD	FRE	334	MIDDLETO
YOUNG, DURAH	BAL	383	13TH WAR
YOUNG, E.M.	PRI	111	PISCATAW
YOUNG, EDMUND	FRE	067	FREDERIC
YOUNG, EDWARD	WOR	342	1ST E DI
YOUNG, EDWARD	ANN	424	HOWARD D
YOUNG, EDWARD	BAL	395	8TH WARD
YOUNG, EDWARD S.Y.	CAR	149	NO TWP L
YOUNG, ELIAS	WAS	029	2ND SUBD
YOUNG, ELIJA	BAL	058	4TH WARD
YOUNG, ELIJAH	BAL	077	10TH WAR
YOUNG, ELIJHA*	DOR	432	1ST DIST
YOUNG, ELIZA	BAL	106	15TH WAR
YOUNG, ELIZA	BAL	188	11TH WAR

Name	County	Page	District
YOUNG, ELIZA	BAL	379	1ST DIST
YOUNG, ELIZABETH	BAL	345	3RD WARD
YOUNG, ELIZABETH	BAL	055	9TH WARD
YOUNG, ELIZABETH	FRE	304	WOODSBOR
YOUNG, ELIZABETH	FRE	262	NEW MARK
YOUNG, ELIZABETH	BAL	042	4TH WARD
YOUNG, ELIZABETH	BAL	083	4TH WARD
YOUNG, ELIZABETH	CAR	358	9TH DIST
YOUNG, ELIZABETH	BAL	084	18TH WAR
YOUNG, ELIZABETH	FRE	363	CATOCTIN
YOUNG, ELIZABETH	CEC	047	1ST E DI
YOUNG, ELIZABETH	PRI	026	VANSVILL
YOUNG, ELLEN	BAL	394	8TH WARD
YOUNG, EMILY	BAL	251	6TH WARD
YOUNG, EZRA	FRE	185	5TH E DI
YOUNG, F.	WAS	144	HAGERSTO
YOUNG, FRANCIS	BAL	414	8TH WARD
YOUNG, FRANCIS	BAL	212	6TH WARD
YOUNG, FRANCIS-BLACK	ST	342	5TH E DI
YOUNG, FREDERICK	BAL	193	2ND WARD
YOUNG, FREDERICK	BAL	096	10TH WAR
YOUNG, FREDERICK	BAL	121	5TH WARD
YOUNG, FRISBY	BAL	136	1ST WARD
YOUNG, GEORGE	BAL	121	5TH WARD
YOUNG, GEORGE	BAL	274	12TH WAR
YOUNG, GEORGE	WAS	219	1ST DIST
YOUNG, GEORGE	CEC	027	CHESAPEA
YOUNG, GEORGE	BAL	063	18TH WAR
YOUNG, GEORGE	BAL	397	14TH WAR
YOUNG, GEORGE	DOR	325	1ST DIST
YOUNG, GEORGE D.	CAL	031	2ND DIST
YOUNG, GEORGE W.	BAL	317	12TH WAR
YOUNG, GIDEON	WAS	190	1ST DIST
YOUNG, GREENBERRY	WAS	188	1ST DIST
YOUNG, HAGER	HAR	019	1ST DIST
YOUNG, HANNAH	BAL	057	18TH WAR
YOUNG, HANNAH	CEC	045	1ST E DI
YOUNG, HANNAH	BAL	152	19TH WAR
YOUNG, HARRIET	BAL	186	5TH DIST
YOUNG, HENNIE	ANN	317	1ST DIST
YOUNG, HENRY	BAL	196	17TH WAR
YOUNG, HENRY	BAL	263	12TH WAR
YOUNG, HENRY	BAL	313	7TH WARD
YOUNG, HENRY	BAL	229	6TH WARD
YOUNG, HENRY	FRE	283	WOODSBOR
YOUNG, HENRY	FRE	349	MIDDLETO
YOUNG, HENRY	MGM	413	MEDLEY 3
YOUNG, HENRY	CAL	046	3RD DIST
YOUNG, HENRY	FRE	002	FREDERIC
YOUNG, HENRY	FRE	118	CREAGERS
YOUNG, HENRY	MGM	434	CLARKSTR
YOUNG, HENRY H.	MGM	374	ROCKERLE
YOUNG, HENRY JR.	FRE	353	MIDDLETO
YOUNG, HENRY L.	FRE	045	FREDERIC
YOUNG, HENRY N.	PRI	112	PISCATAW
YOUNG, HENRY SR.	FRE	353	MIDDLETO
YOUNG, HENRY-BLACK	ST	323	4TH E DI
YOUNG, HESTER	BAL	181	6TH WARD
YOUNG, HESTER	BAL	066	10TH WAR
YOUNG, HEZEKIAH	FRE	354	MIDDLETO
YOUNG, HIRAM	BAL	058	18TH WAR
YOUNG, HORIS*	DOR	435	1ST DIST
YOUNG, HOSEA	CEC	050	1ST E DI
YOUNG, HOWARD	MGM	441	CLARKSTR
YOUNG, IDA	BAL	430	14TH WAR
YOUNG, IRA	CAL	035	2ND DIST
YOUNG, ISAAC	MGM	407	MEDLEY 3
YOUNG, ISAAC	BAL	147	2ND DIST
YOUNG, ISABELLA	BAL	159	11TH WAR
YOUNG, ISABELLA	BAL	432	14TH WAR
YOUNG, J. W.	BAL	148	1ST WARD
YOUNG, JACOB	BAL	245	6TH WARD
YOUNG, JACOB	ALL	243	CUMBERLA
YOUNG, JACOB	BAL	259	12TH WAR
YOUNG, JACOB	ANN	490	HOWARD D
YOUNG, JACOB	BAL	326	3RD WARD
YOUNG, JACOB	FRE	287	WOODSBOR
YOUNG, JACOB	HAR	200	3RD DIST
YOUNG, JACOB	CAR	277	7TH DIST
YOUNG, JACOB	FRE	426	8TH E DI
YOUNG, JACOB	FRE	374	CATOCTIN
YOUNG, JACOB	FRE	392	PETERSVI
YOUNG, JACOB	WAS	193	1ST DIST
YOUNG, JAMES	TAL	068	EASTON T
YOUNG, JAMES	WAS	055	2ND SUBD
YOUNG, JAMES	CEC	085	5TH E DI
YOUNG, JAMES	CEC	054	1ST E DI
YOUNG, JAMES	DOR	444	1ST DIST
YOUNG, JAMES	HAR	020	1ST DIST
YOUNG, JAMES	HAR	098	2ND DIST
YOUNG, JAMES	BAL	320	3RD WARD
YOUNG, JAMES	BAL	309	3RD WARD
YOUNG, JAMES	ANN	424	HOWARD D
YOUNG, JAMES	ANN	356	3RD DIST
YOUNG, JAMES	BAL	244	6TH WARD
YOUNG, JAMES	BAL	136	1ST WARD
YOUNG, JAMES	ANN	310	1ST DIST
YOUNG, JAMES	ALL	079	5TH E.D.
YOUNG, JAMES	BAL	051	1ST WARD
YOUNG, JAMES C.	MGM	354	BERRYS D
YOUNG, JAMES E.	BAL	226	6TH WARD
YOUNG, JAMES H.	WOR	340	1ST E DI
YOUNG, JAMES L.	BAL	069	4TH WARD
YOUNG, JAMES M	BAL	251	17TH WAR
YOUNG, JAMES-BLACK	ST	315	4TH E DI
YOUNG, JAMES-BLACK	ST	332	4TH E DI
YOUNG, JANE	TAL	104	ST MICHA
YOUNG, JANE	BAL	306	3RD WARD
YOUNG, JASON	ANN	466	HOWARD D
YOUNG, JOE	DOR	429	1ST DIST
YOUNG, JOE*	DOR	448	1ST DIST
YOUNG, JOHN	FRE	314	MIDDLETO
YOUNG, JOHN	FRE	329	MIDDLETO
YOUNG, JOHN	BAL	106	18TH WAR
YOUNG, JOHN	BAL	338	13TH WAR
YOUNG, JOHN	BAL	070	4TH WARD
YOUNG, JOHN	CEC	147	PORT DUP
YOUNG, JOHN	MGM	413	MEDLEY 3
YOUNG, JOHN	CAR	290	7TH DIST
YOUNG, JOHN	CAR	373	9TH DIST
YOUNG, JOHN	BAL	444	14TH WAR
YOUNG, JOHN	CEC	046	1ST E DI
YOUNG, JOHN	FRE	355	MIDDLETO
YOUNG, JOHN	CAR	213	5TH DIST
YOUNG, JOHN	CAR	303	1ST DIST
YOUNG, JOHN	FRE	191	5TH E DI
YOUNG, JOHN	ANN	432	HOWARD D
YOUNG, JOHN	BAL	008	EASTERN
YOUNG, JOHN	ALL	259	CUMBERLA
YOUNG, JOHN	BAL	217	6TH DIST
YOUNG, JOHN	BAL	031	9TH WARD
YOUNG, JOHN	BAL	155	2ND DIST
YOUNG, JOHN	BAL	151	2ND DIST
YOUNG, JOHN	BAL	120	1ST WARD
YOUNG, JOHN	BAL	311	1ST DIST
YOUNG, JOHN	ANN	414	HOWARD D
YOUNG, JOHN	BAL	397	8TH WARD
YOUNG, JOHN	BAL	284	7TH WARD
YOUNG, JOHN	BAL	450	8TH WARD
YOUNG, JOHN	BAL	087	15TH WAR
YOUNG, JOHN	BAL	110	10TH WAR
YOUNG, JOHN	BAL	129	16TH WAR
YOUNG, JOHN	BAL	134	16TH WAR
YOUNG, JOHN	WAS	259	1ST DIST
YOUNG, JOHN	KEN	300	3RD DIST
YOUNG, JOHN	WAS	178	BOONSBOR
YOUNG, JOHN	WAS	154	HAGERSTO
YOUNG, JOHN	QUE	233	4TH E DI
YOUNG, JOHN	WAS	122	2ND DIST
YOUNG, JOHN	WAS	009	WILLIAMS
YOUNG, JOHN A.	PRI	101	SPALDING
YOUNG, JOHN A.	CAL	018	1ST DIST
YOUNG, JOHN A.	BAL	026	18TH WAR
YOUNG, JOHN B.	PRI	049	AQUASCO
YOUNG, JOHN B.	BAL	226	6TH WARD
YOUNG, JOHN E.	MGM	377	ROCKERLE
YOUNG, JOHN G.	BAL	044	1ST WARD
YOUNG, JOHN H.	ALL	238	CUMBERLA
YOUNG, JOHN H.	FRE	342	MIDDLETO
YOUNG, JOHN L.	BAL	416	14TH WAR
YOUNG, JOHN L.	ANN	443	HOWARD D
YOUNG, JOHN T.	PRI	048	AQUASCO
YOUNG, JOHN W.	BAL	155	1ST WARD
YOUNG, JOSEPH	BAL	015	1ST WARD
YOUNG, JOSEPH	BAL	132	16TH WAR
YOUNG, JOSEPH	BAL	053	9TH WARD
YOUNG, JOSEPH	BAL	117	15TH WAR
YOUNG, JOSEPH	BAL	233	1ST DIST
YOUNG, JOSEPH	TAL	033	EASTON D
YOUNG, JOSEPH	CAR	262	3RD DIST
YOUNG, JOSEPH	BAL	453	14TH WAR
YOUNG, JOSEPH	CHA	234	HILLTOP
YOUNG, JOSEPH E.	WAS	083	2ND SUBD
YOUNG, JOSHUA	MGM	411	MEDLEY 3
YOUNG, JOSHUA	FRE	306	WOODSBOR
YOUNG, JOSHUA	FRE	259	NEW MARK
YOUNG, JOSHUA	ANN	434	HOWARD D
YOUNG, JOSHUA A.	BAL	360	3RD WARD
YOUNG, JOSIAH	PRI	069	MARLBROU
YOUNG, KITTEY	BAL	388	8TH WARD
YOUNG, LARKIN	BAL	331	1ST DIST
YOUNG, LEAH	CAR	293	7TH DIST
YOUNG, LEMUEL	BAL	223	19TH WAR
YOUNG, LEVI	ANN	480	HOWARD D
YOUNG, LEVI G.	WAS	124	HAGERSTO
YOUNG, LEWIS	FRE	304	WOODSBOR
YOUNG, LEWIS	FRE	004	FREDERIC
YOUNG, LOUISA	BAL	089	1ST WARD
YOUNG, LOUISA	BAL	110	10TH WAR
YOUNG, LYDIA-BLACK	ST	334	4TH E DI
YOUNG, LYRUS	WAS	077	2ND SUBD
YOUNG, M. J.	BAL	136	1ST WARD
YOUNG, MALINDA	BAL	174	16TH WAR
YOUNG, MALINDA	WAS	211	1ST DIST
YOUNG, MARANDA	CAR	406	2ND DIST
YOUNG, MARGARET	CEC	026	ELKTON 3
YOUNG, MARGARET	BAL	082	1ST WARD
YOUNG, MARGARET A.	BAL	351	7TH WARD
YOUNG, MARGARET A.	BAL	121	11TH WAR
YOUNG, MARGRETT	BAL	053	18TH WAR
YOUNG, MARIA LOUISA	BAL	338	13TH WAR
YOUNG, MARINDA	BAL	317	3RD WARD
YOUNG, MARTHA	BAL	171	11TH WAR
YOUNG, MARTIN	BAL	181	19TH WAR
YOUNG, MARY	BAL	419	14TH WAR
YOUNG, MARY	BAL	355	13TH WAR
YOUNG, MARY	BAL	476	14TH WAR
YOUNG, MARY	FRE	426	8TH E DI
YOUNG, MARY	FRE	061	FREDERIC
YOUNG, MARY	BAL	223	12TH WAR
YOUNG, MARY	BAL	325	12TH WAR
YOUNG, MARY	ANN	475	HOWARD D
YOUNG, MARY	ALL	078	5TH E.D.
YOUNG, MARY	BAL	204	2ND WARD
YOUNG, MARY	QUE	175	2ND E DI
YOUNG, MARY	WAS	162	HAGERSTO
YOUNG, MARY A.	KEN	286	3RD DIST
YOUNG, MARY C.	CAR	134	NO TWP L
YOUNG, MARY CECELIA	BAL	387	13TH WAR
YOUNG, MARY F.	BAL	263	2ND WARD
YOUNG, MARY G.	FRE	439	8TH E DI
YOUNG, MARY J.	BAL	052	9TH WARD
YOUNG, MARY J.	TAL	073	EASTON T
YOUNG, MARY M.	BAL	380	8TH WARD
YOUNG, MARY-MULATTO	ST	330	4TH E DI
YOUNG, MC CLENTOCK	FRE	044	FREDERIC
YOUNG, MICHAEL	BAL	242	2ND WARD
YOUNG, MISS H.	FRE	198	5TH E DI
YOUNG, MISS M.	FRE	199	5TH E DI
YOUNG, MOSES	DOR	439	1ST DIST
YOUNG, MOSES	BAL	168	1ST WARD
YOUNG, MOSES	KEN	288	3RD DIST
YOUNG, MR-	BAL	059	15TH WAR
YOUNG, NANCY	BAL	364	1ST DIST
YOUNG, NANCY	WOR	340	1ST E DI
YOUNG, NANCY	TAL	038	EASTON D
YOUNG, NATHAN	ANN	485	HOWARD D
YOUNG, NATHAN	DOR	389	1ST DIST
YOUNG, NELLY	ANN	356	3RD DIST
YOUNG, OCTAVEUS	CAL	010	1ST DIST
YOUNG, ORPHY	ANN	420	HOWARD D
YOUNG, PERRY	BAL	130	11TH WAR
YOUNG, PERRY A.	FRE	061	FREDERIC
YOUNG, PETER	FRE	322	MIDDLETO
YOUNG, PETER	DOR	440	1ST DIST
YOUNG, PETER	FRE	268	NEW MARK
YOUNG, PETER	TAL	088	ST MICHA
YOUNG, PETER	WAS	266	1ST DIST
YOUNG, PETER F.	BAL	163	6TH WARD
YOUNG, PHILIP	CEC	050	1ST E DI
YOUNG, PHILIP-MULATTO	ST	315	4TH E DI
YOUNG, POLLY	ANN	351	3RD DIST
YOUNG, POMPEY	QUE	214	3RD E DI
YOUNG, RACHAEL A.	BAL	131	18TH WAR
YOUNG, RACHEAL	WAS	163	HAGERSTO
YOUNG, RACHEL	CAR	253	3RD DIST
YOUNG, RACHEL T.	BAL	381	3RD WARD
YOUNG, RALPH	HAR	200	3RD DIST
YOUNG, REBECCA	FRE	035	FREDERIC
YOUNG, REBECCA	BAL	347	13TH WAR
YOUNG, REBECCA	BAL	034	1ST WARD
YOUNG, RICHARD	BAL	135	18TH WAR
YOUNG, RICHARD	CAL	023	2ND DIST
YOUNG, RICHARD	MGM	341	CLARKSBU
YOUNG, RICHARD	PRI	102	SPALDING
YOUNG, ROBERT	ST	333	4TH E DI
YOUNG, ROBERT	HAR	021	1ST DIST
YOUNG, ROBERT	BAL	228	19TH WAR
YOUNG, ROBERT	CEC	010	ELKTON 3
YOUNG, ROBERT	CHA	234	HILLTOP
YOUNG, ROBERT	BAL	149	2ND DIST
YOUNG, ROBERT	BAL	161	1ST WARD
YOUNG, ROBERT	BAL	164	1ST WARD
YOUNG, ROBERT	BAL	152	16TH WAR
YOUNG, ROBERT	BAL	318	1ST DIST
YOUNG, ROBERT J.	PRI	067	NOTTINGH
YOUNG, ROBERT-BLACK	ST	332	4TH E DI
YOUNG, ROSA	WOR	341	1ST E DI
YOUNG, ROSETTA-BLACK	ST	299	2ND E DI
YOUNG, RUTH	MGM	342	CLARKSBU
YOUNG, SALLY-BLACK	ST	324	4TH E DI
YOUNG, SAMUEL	HAR	139	2ND DIST
YOUNG, SAMUEL	FRE	349	MIDDLETO
YOUNG, SAMUEL	BAL	016	4TH WARD
YOUNG, SAMUEL	MGM	414	MEDLEY 3
YOUNG, SAMUEL	SOM	413	DUBLIN D
YOUNG, SAMUEL	FRE	292	WOODSBOR
YOUNG, SAMUEL	CEC	143	7TH E DI
YOUNG, SAMUEL	BAL	081	18TH WAR
YOUNG, SAMUEL	CAR	293	7TH DIST
YOUNG, SAMUEL	CEC	059	1ST E DI
YOUNG, SAMUEL	CEC	055	1ST E DI
YOUNG, SAMUEL C.	MGM	414	MEDLEY 3
YOUNG, SARAH	BAL	181	19TH WAR
YOUNG, SARAH	WAS	150	2ND DIST
YOUNG, SARAH	BAL	092	1ST WARD
YOUNG, SARAH	BAL	298	1ST DIST
YOUNG, SARAH	ANN	490	HOWARD D
YOUNG, SARAH J.	BAL	039	1ST WARD
YOUNG, SARAH P.E.	BAL	013	15TH WAR
YOUNG, SARAH R.	BAL	069	4TH WARD
YOUNG, SAULSBURY	ANN	352	3RD DIST
YOUNG, SIDNEY	BAL	049	9TH WARD
YOUNG, SIDNEY	BAL	397	14TH WAR
YOUNG, SILLY	BAL	090	5TH WARD
YOUNG, SOLON	MGM	390	ROCKERLE
YOUNG, SPENCER	BAL	223	17TH WAR
YOUNG, STEPHEN	BAL	242	6TH WARD
YOUNG, STEWART	MGM	355	BERRYS D
YOUNG, SUSAN	BAL	435	14TH WAR
YOUNG, SUSAN	FRE	129	CREAGERS
YOUNG, SUSAN	PRI	065	NOTTINGH
YOUNG, SUSAN-BLACK	QUE	129	1ST E DI
YOUNG, T.	BAL	286	2ND WARD
YOUNG, T.J.	BAL	138	1ST WARD
YOUNG, TABITHA	WOR	336	1ST E DI
YOUNG, THOAMS	ANN	301	1ST DIST
YOUNG, THOMAS	BAL	281	2ND WARD
YOUNG, THOMAS	BAL	247	5TH WARD
YOUNG, THOMAS	ANN	443	HOWARD D
YOUNG, THOMAS	ANN	450	HOWARD D
YOUNG, THOMAS	MGM	342	CLARKSBU
YOUNG, THOMAS	HAR	151	3RD DIST
YOUNG, TILGHMAN	BAL	132	16TH WAR
YOUNG, TILGHMAN H.	FRE	015	FREDERIC
YOUNG, TILLY	BAL	305	3RD WARD
YOUNG, VALENTINE	BAL	211	6TH DIST
YOUNG, VERGINIA	BAL	317	20TH WAR
YOUNG, VIRIGNIA-BLACK	BAL	219	2ND WARD
YOUNG, W.	HAR	082	2ND DIST
YOUNG, W. S.	BAL	148	1ST WARD
YOUNG, WALTER	BAL	059	1ST WARD
YOUNG, WAPGARET*	BAL	058	1ST WARD
YOUNG, WASHINGTON	FRE	029	FREDERIC
YOUNG, WELLS	CEC	098	3RD E DI
YOUNG, WILEY	DOR	469	1ST DIST
YOUNG, WILLIAM	BAL	448	14TH WAR
YOUNG, WILLIAM	BAL	120	11TH WAR
YOUNG, WILLIAM	MGM	393	ROCKERLE
YOUNG, WILLIAM	BAL	239	17TH WAR
YOUNG, WILLIAM	BAL	383	13TH WAR
YOUNG, WILLIAM	BAL	132	18TH WAR
YOUNG, WILLIAM	BAL	139	19TH WAR
YOUNG, WILLIAM	FRE	248	NEW MARK
YOUNG, WILLIAM	SOM	546	TYASKIN
YOUNG, WILLIAM	TAL	022	EASTON D
YOUNG, WILLIAM	WAS	079	2ND SUBD
YOUNG, WILLIAM	BAL	092	1ST WARD
YOUNG, WILLIAM	BAL	152	1ST WARD
YOUNG, WILLIAM	BAL	240	6TH WARD
YOUNG, WILLIAM	BAL	453	1ST DIST
YOUNG, WILLIAM	BAL	425	1ST DIST
YOUNG, WILLIAM	BAL	299	12TH WAR
YOUNG, WILLIAM	BAL	250	6TH WARD
YOUNG, WILLIAM	BAL	125	1ST WARD
YOUNG, WILLIAM	BAL	233	2ND WARD
YOUNG, WILLIAM	ANN	319	2ND DIST
YOUNG, WILLIAM	ANN	267	ANNAPOLI
YOUNG, WILLIAM G.	BAL	047	15TH WAR
YOUNG, WILLIAM H.	BAL	130	1ST WARD
YOUNG, WILLIAM H.	BAL	118	1ST WARD
YOUNG, WILLIAM J.	BAL	001	1ST WARD
YOUNG, WILLIAM N.	MGM	414	MEDLEY 3
YOUNG, WILLIAM S.	ANN	424	HOWARD D
YOUNG,ADAM	FRE	406	JEFFERSO
YOUNG,EDWARD	BAL	018	2ND DIST
YOUNG,MARY A.	BAL	062	1ST WARD
YOUNG,THOMAS	BAL	135	1ST WARD
YOUNGAR, MARIA	BAL	268	1ST DIST
YOUNGER, CHARLES	BAL	462	1ST DIST
YOUNGER, DANIEL H.	BAL	379	3RD WARD
YOUNGER, ELIZABETH	CAL	035	2ND DIST
YOUNGER, EMILY	BAL	233	17TH WAR
YOUNGER, EVA	BAL	222	17TH WAR
YOUNGER, FRANCES	BAL	193	19TH WAR
YOUNGER, GEORGE	CAL	029	2ND DIST
YOUNGER, HENRY	BAL	162	2ND DIST
YOUNGER, HIRAM	BAL	297	20TH WAR
YOUNGER, JAMES	CAL	015	1ST DIST
YOUNGER, JASPER	BAL	206	11TH WAR
YOUNGER, JOHN	BAL	285	20TH WAR
YOUNGER, JOHN	BAL	147	19TH WAR
YOUNGER, NICHOLAS	BAL	197	2ND WARD
YOUNGER, ROBERT JAMES	BAL	279	17TH WAR
YOUNGERMAN, DANIEL	BAL	461	1ST DIST
YOUNGERMAN, WILLIAM	BAL	202	17TH WAR
YOUNGMAN, CHARLES	BAL	202	17TH WAR
YOUNGMAN, JOHN	BAL	028	18TH WAR
YOUNGMAN, JOHN	HAR	077	BEL AIR
YOUNGMAN, RICHARD	HAR	077	BEL AIR

YOUNGMAN, WILLIAM	BAL	259	20TH WAR
YOUNGMARE, GEORGE	BAL	106	2ND DIST
YOUNGS, HARRIET	BAL	148	19TH WAR
YOUNGS, SUSAN	BAL	301	12TH WAR
YOUNK, GEORGE	BAL	244	17TH WAR
YOUNKER, JOHN	BAL	225	17TH WAR
YOUNKER, JOSEPH	WAS	146	2ND DIST
YOUNKLE, MARY J.	BAL	250	17TH WAR
YOUR, WILLIAM B.	FRE	315	MIDDLETO
YOUSE, CATHARINE	BAL	368	13TH WAR
YOUSE, CHRISTIAN	BAL	202	17TH WAR
YOUSEN, EDWARD C.	BAL	188	19TH WAR
YOUSEN, JAMES A.	BAL	188	19TH WAR
YOUST, BENEDICT	PRI	005	BLADENSB
YOUST, CHARLES K.	HAR	020	1ST DIST
YOUST, EMILEY	BAL	009	18TH WAR
YOUST, JOHN	PRI	013	BLADENSB
YOUST, RACHAEL	PRI	002	BLADENSB
YOUST, STEPHEN	BAL	281	17TH WAR
YOWLER, ELIZABETH	WAS	230	1ST DIST
YOWNS, SYLVA-BLACK	FRE	241	NEW MARK
YOWSE, GEORGE	BAL	411	1ST DIST
YRASHEE, CHARLOTTE	BAL	143	11TH WAR
YREGASAR, GEORGE	BAL	412	8TH WARD
YROSE, ELIZABETH	BAL	370	8TH WARD
YRUSTEN, JOSEPH	BAL	373	8TH WARD
YUDOR, TOBIAS	ALL	017	3RD E.D.
YUNK, HENRY	BAL	137	1ST WARD
YUNKAR, HENRY	BAL	384	1ST DIST
YUNKAR, WILLIAM	BAL	385	1ST DIST
YUNKER, JONATHAN *	WAS	154	2ND DIST
YUNKMANN, WILLIAM	BAL	118	15TH WAR
YUNT, GEORGE A.	BAL	267	7TH WARD
YURMAN, PATRICK	BAL	143	11TH WAR
YURNER, GEORGE	BAL	212	11TH WAR
YUSTON, ISABEL	BAL	264	20TH WAR
YWMER, JOHN	BAL	141	11TH WAR
ZABLER, JAMES W.	MGM	438	CLARKSTR
ZACARY, ELIZA	BAL	405	3RD WARD
ZACHARIAH, DANIEL	FRE	039	FREDERIC
ZACHARIAS, ANNA	FRE	179	5TH E DI
ZACHARIAS, CHRISTIAN	FRE	178	5TH E DI
ZACHARIAS, JOHN	ALL	056	10TH E.D
ZACHARIAS, JOSEPH	FRE	179	5TH E DI
ZACHARY, CATHERINE	BAL	068	10TH WAR
ZACHARY, MARY J.	BAL	058	1ST WARD
ZACHARY, SARAH	BAL	010	1ST WARD
ZACHAURAS, EDWARD *	ALL	054	10TH E.D
ZACHERY, ROBERT	BAL	421	8TH WARD
ZACHES, JOHN*	FRE	329	MIDDLETO
ZACHO, HENRY	CAR	356	6TH DIST
ZACHTY, JACOB *	ALL	166	6TH E.D.
ZAHN, AUGUST	BAL	017	9TH WARD
ZAHOLT, AGUSTUS	WAS	182	BOONSBOR
ZAILLER, JOSEPH	BAL	050	18TH WAR
ZAINE, R.U.	BAL	121	1ST WARD
ZAKER, JOHN	HAR	197	3RD DIST
ZALER, ELLENNOIR	FRE	308	WOODSBOR
ZALLEMOND, CONRAD	BAL	018	4TH WARD
ZALLER, JACOB	BAL	139	16TH WAR
ZAMBRUM, MARIA	FRE	188	5TH E DI
ZANCK, CONRAD	BAL	390	3RD WARD
ZANE, ELIZA	BAL	362	13TH WAR
ZANE, ELIZABETH	BAL	324	3RD WARD
ZANE, JOHN A.	BAL	473	14TH WAR
ZANE, PETER	BAL	324	3RD WARD
ZANE, S. S.	BAL	312	12TH WAR
ZANE, SARAH	BAL	240	20TH WAR
ZANE, WILLIAM A.	MGM	352	BERRYS D
ZANGABACK, WOLF	BAL	235	2ND WARD
ZANKARD, D.	BAL	220	19TH WAR
ZANKARD, ELY	BAL	221	19TH WAR
ZANKARD, N.D.	BAL	221	19TH WAR
ZANT, CHARELS	BAL	370	13TH WAR
ZANWICK, LUKE	BAL	266	2ND WARD
ZAPP, FRANCIS	BAL	221	17TH WAR
ZATEMORE, WILLIAM	CHA	223	ALLENS F
ZEAGER, MARY	BAL	185	2ND WARD
ZEALOUS, GEORGE	BAL	217	2ND WARD
ZEBARYLE, ELIZABETH	ALL	009	3RD E.D.
ZEBAUGHLE, MARIA	ALL	010	3RD E.D.
ZEBE, MARY	BAL	271	1ST DIST
ZECK, DEITER	FRE	175	5TH E DI
ZEDEN, MC CANN	BAL	177	2ND WARD
ZEDLAR, MICHAEL	BAL	075	1ST WARD
ZEDRICK, HENRY	ALL	218	CUMBERLA
ZEDRICKS, DANIEL	FRE	088	FREDERIC
ZEDRICKS, HANSON	FRE	103	FREDERIC
ZEDRICKS, SUSAN-BLACK	FRE	039	FREDERIC
ZEEHEER, ONNA	BAL	126	18TH WAR
ZEH, CHARLES	BAL	038	15TH WAR
ZEH, MARTIN	BAL	318	7TH WARD
ZEIGBE, JACOB	FRE	329	MIDDLETO
ZEIGENHART, CASPAR	BAL	068	2ND DIST
ZEIGFRIED, JAMES	FRE	452	8TH E DI
ZEIGHER, MARY	FRE	099	FREDERIC
ZEIGHER, REBECCA	FRE	103	FREDERIC
ZEIGLER, ABRAHAM	WAS	193	1ST DIST
ZEIGLER, ALBRECK	BAL	105	2ND DIST
ZEIGLER, AMELIA	WAS	179	BOONSBOR
ZEIGLER, ANN	FRE	279	WOODSBOR
ZEIGLER, ARCHIBALD	WAS	264	1ST DIST
ZEIGLER, BARBARA	WAS	278	LEITERSB
ZEIGLER, CATHARINE	WAS	200	1ST DIST
ZEIGLER, CATHARINE E.	WAS	280	LEITERSB
ZEIGLER, DANIEL M.	WAS	247	SMITHSBU
ZEIGLER, ELIZA	BAL	053	2ND DIST
ZEIGLER, FREDERICK	WAS	287	1ST DIST
ZEIGLER, FREDERICK	BAL	219	19TH WAR
ZEIGLER, GEORGE	MGM	330	CRACKLIN
ZEIGLER, GEORGE	WAS	285	1ST DIST
ZEIGLER, GEORGE	WAS	247	SMITHSBU
ZEIGLER, GEORGE	WAS	245	SMITHSBU
ZEIGLER, GEORGE W.	BAL	044	4TH WARD
ZEIGLER, GOTLEIB	WAS	122	HAGERSTO
ZEIGLER, GRAFF	WAS	189	1ST DIST
ZEIGLER, HANNAH	FRE	328	MIDDLETO
ZEIGLER, HENRY	FRE	328	MIDDLETO
ZEIGLER, HENRY	FRE	328	MIDDLETO
ZEIGLER, HENRY L.	FRE	053	FREDERIC
ZEIGLER, IRIS	BAL	254	20TH WAR
ZEIGLER, JACOB	FRE	037	FREDERIC
ZEIGLER, JACOB	WAS	253	1ST DIST
ZEIGLER, JOHN	WAS	259	1ST DIST
ZEIGLER, JOHN	WAS	280	LEITERSB
ZEIGLER, JOHN	BAL	176	19TH WAR
ZEIGLER, JOHN	BAL	212	6TH WARD
ZEIGLER, JOSEPH	FRE	327	MIDDLETO
ZEIGLER, LEWIS	WAS	285	1ST DIST
ZEIGLER, MARGARET	FRE	329	MIDDLETO
ZEIGLER, MICAHEL	FRE	100	FREDERIC
ZEIGLER, MILTON	WAS	285	1ST DIST
ZEIGLER, NATHAN	BAL	150	16TH WAR
ZEIGLER, SAMUEL F.	WAS	280	LEITERSB
ZEIGLER, SARAH	BAL	217	6TH WARD
ZEIGLER, WILLIAM	BAL	278	20TH WAR
ZEIKEL, PETER	BAL	272	2ND WARD
ZEILE, JOHN	BAL	410	14TH WAR
ZEILER, DAVID	FRE	041	FREDERIC
ZELCH, HENRY	WAS	144	2ND DIST
ZELGIN, ANN	BAL	196	2ND WARD
ZELL, BERNARD A.	BAL	296	12TH WAR
ZELL, CHRISTIAN	BAL	202	19TH WAR
ZELL, DAVID	CAR	372	9TH DIST
ZELL, E. W.	BAL	319	12TH WAR
ZELL, JACOB	FRE	390	PETERSVI
ZELL, JOHN	BAL	227	19TH WAR
ZELL, JOHN	BAL	121	11TH WAR
ZELL, JOHN	HAR	157	3RD DIST
ZELL, JOHN	BAL	226	17TH WAR
ZELL, MARGARET	BAL	158	11TH WAR
ZELL, MICHAEL	BAL	016	15TH WAR
ZELL, PETER	BAL	318	1ST DIST
ZELL, PHILIP	BAL	050	4TH WARD
ZELLAR, JACOB	BAL	470	14TH WAR
ZELLER, CHRISTOPHER	BAL	243	2ND WARD
ZELLER, DANIEL	WAS	291	1ST DIST
ZELLER, FREDERICK	BAL	225	17TH WAR
ZELLER, HANNAH	WAS	291	1ST DIST
ZELLER, MATILDA	ALL	248	CUMBERLA
ZELLERS, DAVID	WAS	290	1ST DIST.
ZELLERS, DAVID	WAS	298	1ST DIST
ZELLERS, JOHN	WAS	127	2ND DIST
ZELLERS, JOHN	WAS	125	2ND DIST
ZELLERS, MICHAEL	WAS	125	2ND DIST
ZELLERS, OLOVER	WAS	127	2ND DIST
ZELLERS, SAMUEL	WAS	129	2ND DIST
ZELLERS, SAMUEL	WAS	292	1ST DIST
ZELLINGER, JACOB	WAS	290	1ST DIST
ZELLOTT, WASHINGTON*	BAL	108	10TH WAR
ZELLOUS, GEORGE	BAL	030	18TH WAR
ZELTMAN, FREDERIC	BAL	172	6TH WARD
ZEMERLA, SAMUEL	ALL	192	9TH E.D.
ZEMERLEE, FRANCES	ALL	157	6TH E.D.
ZEMERLER, GEORGE S.	ALL	158	6TH E.D.
ZEMERLY, SARAH	ALL	193	9TH E.D.
ZENBACK, CHARLES	BAL	083	1ST WARD
ZENIA, RICHARD	BAL	418	14TH WAR
ZENIFT, JOHN	BAL	009	9TH WARD
ZENKAN, ULRIC	WAS	139	HAGERSTO
ZENNEIT, LEVI H.*	BAL	268	20TH WAR
ZENNER, CHRISTIAN	BAL	239	2ND WARD
ZENNUT, LEVI H.*	BAL	268	20TH WAR
ZENT, MAHALA	FRE	427	8TH E DI
ZENTMINE, JACOB	FRE	375	CATOCTIN
ZENTMYER, JACOB	FRE	342	MIDDLETO
ZENTZ, ABRAHAM	CAR	312	1ST DIST
ZENTZ, SHANT	BAL	113	2ND DIST
ZEORG, CLARENCE *	BAL	099	18TH WAR
ZEP, JANE E.	FRE	026	FREDERIC
ZEPP, CATHARINE	CAR	250	3RD DIST
ZEPP, CATHARINE	CAR	179	8TH DIST
ZEPP, CHRISTOPHER	CAR	370	9TH DIST
ZEPP, DAVID	CAR	268	WESTMINS
ZEPP, ELIZABETH	CAR	182	8TH DIST
ZEPP, EPHRAIM	CAR	226	5TH DIST
ZEPP, GEORGE	CAR	349	6TH DIST
ZEPP, HENRY	CAR	348	6TH DIST
ZEPP, HENRY	CAR	176	8TH DIST
ZEPP, JACOB	CAR	357	6TH DIST
ZEPP, JOHN	CAR	370	9TH DIST
ZEPP, JULIAN	CAR	387	2ND DIST
ZEPP, MICHAEL	CAR	359	9TH DIST
ZEPP, PREISTLY	CAR	370	9TH DIST
ZEPP, SAMUEL	CAR	175	8TH DIST
ZEPP, SOLOMON	CAR	212	5TH DIST
ZEPP, SUSANNA	CAR	252	3RD DIST
ZEPP, WILLIAM	CAR	370	9TH DIST
ZEPP, WILLIAM	CAR	258	3RD DIST
ZERBACK, ANN	BAL	202	2ND WARD
ZERBACK, HENRY	BAL	202	2ND WARD
ZEREKELL, WILLIAM	BAL	051	1ST WARD
ZERGLIS, CHARLES	BAL	174	19TH WAR
ZEROLD, CHRIST.	WAS	185	BOONSBOR
ZERWEEK, DANIEL	BAL	040	15TH WAR
ZETTEL, MARY	BAL	256	17TH WAR
ZETZELL, CHRISTIAN	WAS	273	RIDGEVIL
ZETZELL, PHILIP	WAS	273	RIDGEVIL
ZETZNER, D.	BAL	227	19TH WAR
ZEULERF, HENRY	BAL	335	3RD WARD
ZEYER, JAMES M.	FRE	285	WOODSBOR
ZEYLER, JACOB	BAL	239	12TH WAR
ZIEGELMEIER, LEONARD	BAL	109	15TH WAR
ZIEGLER, JOHN L.	BAL	112	15TH WAR
ZIEGLER, MARY	BAL	209	17TH WAR
ZIEGLER, MR.	BAL	222	17TH WAR
ZIEGLER, SISTER ZIPHARINA	FRE	197	5TH E DI
ZIGLEFELTER, PETER	ANN	347	3RD DIST
ZIGLER, ELIZABETH	BAL	358	8TH WARD
ZIGLER, GOTLIEB	WAS	031	2ND SUBD
ZIGLER, JACOB W.	CAR	212	5TH DIST
ZIGLER, MARY	BAL	310	7TH WARD
ZIGLER, MARY	BAL	438	1ST DIST
ZIGLER, SARAH	CAR	212	5TH DIST
ZILE, EDWIN A.	CAR	372	9TH DIST
ZILES, ABRAHAM	CAR	209	5TH DIST
ZILL, DAVID	CAR	372	9TH DIST
ZILL, MARY	BAL	296	12TH WAR
ZILLER, ADAM	BAL	024	4TH WARD
ZILLINGER, ELLEN	FRE	147	10TH E D
ZIMERLY, MARINE F.	ALL	198	CUMBERLA
ZIMERMAN, DYORICK	BAL	096	1ST WARD
ZIMERMAN, EMILA J.	BAL	390	1ST DIST
ZIMERMAN, JOHN	BAL	096	1ST WARD
ZIMERMAN, JOHN	WAS	029	2ND SUBD
ZIMERMAN, JOSHUA	BAL	390	1ST DIST
ZIMINGER, SAMUEL	BAL	063	1ST WARD
ZIMMER, CHARLES	BAL	083	18TH WAR
ZIMMER, JOHN P.	BAL	377	8TH WARD
ZIMMER, JOHN W. P.	DOR	369	3RD DIVI
ZIMMER, MARTIN	BAL	082	18TH WAR
ZIMMER, PETER	WAS	015	2ND SUBD
ZIMMERICH, LUDWIG	BAL	042	9TH WARD
ZIMMERMAN, ADAM	BAL	040	1ST WARD
ZIMMERMAN, ADAM	CAR	175	8TH DIST
ZIMMERMAN, ALEXANDER	BAL	385	1ST DIST
ZIMMERMAN, ANGELUS	BAL	386	13TH WAR
ZIMMERMAN, ANN	BAL	172	6TH WARD
ZIMMERMAN, B. F.	BAL	296	20TH WAR
ZIMMERMAN, BENJAMIM	WAS	189	1ST DIST
ZIMMERMAN, BENJAMIN	WAS	141	2ND DIST
ZIMMERMAN, CATHARINE	CAR	317	1ST DIST
ZIMMERMAN, CATHERINE	BAL	176	11TH WAR
ZIMMERMAN, CHARLES	BAL	123	16TH WAR
ZIMMERMAN, CHARLES	FRE	057	FREDERIC
ZIMMERMAN, CHRISTIAN	BAL	084	10TH WAR
ZIMMERMAN, CHRISTIAN	BAL	283	7TH WARD
ZIMMERMAN, CHRISTOPHER	BAL	086	1ST WARD
ZIMMERMAN, DANIEL	FRE	210	BUCKEYST
ZIMMERMAN, DAVID C.	BAL	193	19TH WAR
ZIMMERMAN, DAVID M.	FRE	210	BUCKEYST
ZIMMERMAN, EDWARD D.	FRE	208	BUCKEYST
ZIMMERMAN, ELIAS	FRE	071	FREDERIC
ZIMMERMAN, ELIAS	WAS	189	1ST DIST
ZIMMERMAN, ELIZABETH	CAR	337	6TH DIST
ZIMMERMAN, EMMA J.	BAL	100	10TH WAR
ZIMMERMAN, FREDERICK	BAL	341	3RD WARD
ZIMMERMAN, FREDERICK	BAL	099	2ND DIST
ZIMMERMAN, FREDERICK	CAR	356	6TH DIST
ZIMMERMAN, GEORGE	FRE	071	FREDERIC
ZIMMERMAN, GEORGE	FRE	090	FREDERIC
ZIMMERMAN, GEORGE	BAL	398	14TH WAR
ZIMMERMAN, GEORGE	BAL	191	6TH WARD
ZIMMERMAN, GEORGE P.	BAL	238	12TH WAR
ZIMMERMAN, GEORGE T.	FRE	121	CREAGERS
ZIMMERMAN, GIDEON M.	FRE	213	BUCKEYST
ZIMMERMAN, GOTHERO	BAL	101	1ST WARD
ZIMMERMAN, HENRY	BAL	132	2ND DIST
ZIMMERMAN, HENRY	BAL	100	10TH WAR
ZIMMERMAN, HENRY	FRE	206	BUCKEYST
ZIMMERMAN, HENRY	FRE	234	BUCKEYST
ZIMMERMAN, HENRY	CAR	357	6TH DIST
ZIMMERMAN, HENRY	WAS	226	1ST DIST
ZIMMERMAN, ISAAC	BAL	384	1ST DIST
ZIMMERMAN, J. NICHOLAS	FRE	084	FREDERIC
ZIMMERMAN, JACOB	FRE	088	FREDERIC
ZIMMERMAN, JACOB	CAR	337	6TH DIST
ZIMMERMAN, JACOB	BAL	017	9TH WARD
ZIMMERMAN, JOHN	BAL	142	5TH WARD
ZIMMERMAN, JOHN	BAL	385	1ST DIST
ZIMMERMAN, JOHN	BAL	207	6TH DIST
ZIMMERMAN, JOHN	FRE	085	FREDERIC
ZIMMERMAN, JOHN	FRE	097	FREDERIC
ZIMMERMAN, JOHN	BAL	142	19TH WAR
ZIMMERMAN, JOHN	FRE	166	EMMITTSB
ZIMMERMAN, JOHN	CAR	316	1ST DIST
ZIMMERMAN, JOHN	BAL	225	19TH WAR
ZIMMERMAN, JOHN	WAS	226	1ST DIST
ZIMMERMAN, JOHN	WAS	036	2ND SUBD
ZIMMERMAN, JOHN K.	CAR	336	6TH DIST
ZIMMERMAN, JOHN P.	FRE	131	CREAGERS
ZIMMERMAN, JOSHUA J.	FRE	212	BUCKEYST
ZIMMERMAN, JOSIAH	FRE	085	FREDERIC
ZIMMERMAN, LAUDEN	FRE	128	CREAGERS
ZIMMERMAN, MARGARET	FRE	012	FREDERIC
ZIMMERMAN, MARTHA	FRE	106	CREAGERS
ZIMMERMAN, MARY	FRE	090	FREDERIC
ZIMMERMAN, MARY	CAR	337	6TH DIST
ZIMMERMAN, MARY	BAL	043	9TH WARD
ZIMMERMAN, MARY A.	FRE	085	FREDERIC
ZIMMERMAN, MATHIAS	BAL	427	14TH WAR
ZIMMERMAN, MICAHEL	FRE	131	CREAGERS
ZIMMERMAN, MICHAEL	FRE	084	FREDERIC
ZIMMERMAN, MICHAEL	FRE	210	BUCKEYST
ZIMMERMAN, OLIVER	FRE	138	CREAGERS
ZIMMERMAN, P.	BAL	043	9TH WARD
ZIMMERMAN, PERT	BAL	218	12TH WAR
ZIMMERMAN, ROSANNA	BAL	333	3RD WARD
ZIMMERMAN, SAMUEL	FRE	071	FREDERIC
ZIMMERMAN, SOLOMON	FRE	074	FREDERIC
ZIMMERMAN, SUSSANNA	FRE	297	WOODSBOR
ZIMMERMAN, TILLY A.	FRE	107	CREAGERS
ZIMMERMAN, WILLIAM	FRE	109	CREAGERS
ZIMMERMAN, WILLIAM	CAR	388	2ND DIST
ZIMMERMAN, WILLIAM H.	FRE	300	WOODSBOR
ZIMMERMAN, WILLIAM H.	FRE	208	BUCKEYST
ZIMMERMAN, WILLIAM S.	BAL	178	16TH WAR
ZIMMERMAN, WOLFKING	BAL	171	6TH WARD
ZIMMERMAN, PHILIP	BAL	071	2ND DIST
ZIMMES, MICHAEL	BAL	217	19TH WAR
ZIMMISCH, CHARLES	BAL	127	16TH WAR
ZIMMISCH, FREDERICK	BAL	118	15TH WAR
ZIMMISCH, WILLIAM	BAL	127	16TH WAR
ZIMMS, CHARLES*	BAL	105	10TH WAR
ZINC, WILLIAM	CEC	006	ELKTON 3
ZINCON, BALTZER	CAR	195	4TH DIST
ZINDER, JOSEPH	BAL	085	10TH WAR
ZINOKAN, ANDREW	WAS	138	HAGERSTO
ZINGER, FRANCIS	BAL	425	14TH WAR
ZINGLING, ELIAS	BAL	469	14TH WAR
ZINK, JOHN	BAL	451	1ST DIST
ZINK, MATHIAS	BAL	030	1ST WARD
ZINKARD, JOSEPH	BAL	002	1ST WARD
ZINKE, NICHOLAS	BAL	297	20TH WAR
ZINKHAND, ANN	BAL	034	9TH WARD
ZINKHAW, JOHN *	BAL	120	18TH WAR
ZINKINE, JOSHUA	BAL	382	3RD WARD
ZINZLEMAN, MATT	BAL	298	12TH WAR
ZIRKEIBLE, JAOCB	FRE	200	5TH E DI
ZITTLE, JACOB	FRE	333	MIDDLETO
ZITTLE, MARY E.	WAS	210	1ST DIST
ZITTLE, MICHAEL	WAS	209	1ST DIST
ZITTLE, PETER	WAS	209	1ST DIST
ZITTLE, SAMUEL	WAS	188	1ST DIST
ZITTLE, WILLIAM	FRE	312	MIDDLETO
ZITZNER, PETER	BAL	293	20TH WAR
ZIVERLY, A. S.	ALL	161	6TH E.D.
ZOLENGE, EMILY	BAL	237	12TH WAR
ZOLL, JACOB	WAS	146	HAGERSTO
ZOLL, JOHN	BAL	215	2ND WARD
ZOLLECKOFFER, ANN LOUISA	BAL	387	13TH WAR
ZOLLICKOFFELL, CAROLINE *	CAR	236	UNION TO
ZOLLICKOFFER, C.	BAL	073	10TH WAR
ZOLLICKOFFER, DANIEL	CAR	403	2ND DIST
ZOLLICKOFFER, DAVID	CAR	277	7TH DIST
ZOLLICKOFFER, HENRY L. *	CAR	234	UNION TO
ZOLLICKOFFER, WILLIAM	CAR	235	UNION TO
ZOLLICKOFFER, WILLIAM T.	CAR	234	UNION TO
ZOLLINGER, GEORGE	BAL	268	12TH WAR
ZOLLINGER, LEVI A.	FRE	147	10TH E D
ZOLLNHOFFER, ANN	BAL	092	10TH WAR
ZOLLNHOFFER, GEORGE	BAL	092	10TH WAR
ZOLLY, HARRIETT	KEN	289	3RD DIST
ZONG, PETER	BAL	112	2ND DIST
ZONTEEZE, WILLIAM	FRE	121	CREAGERS
ZOOK, BARBARA	WAS	152	HAGERSTO
ZORINSKI, JACOB	BAL	040	9TH WARD
ZOUNGER, ELIZABETH	CAL	035	2ND DIST
ZOYLER, JOSEPH A.	ALL	149	6TH E.D.
ZUBACK, CATHARINE	BAL	423	14TH WAR

ZUBY, CANIEL *	FRE	294	WOODSBOR
ZUCK, ENOCK	FRE	094	FREDERIC
ZUGBER, IDA	FRE	032	FREDERIC
ZUGLER, CAVID A.	MGM	437	CLARKSTR
ZUKUST, CHRISTIAN *	BAL	075	18TH WAR
ZULAUF, BALTHAZER	BAL	274	7TH WARD
ZULOFF, H.	BAL	241	20TH WAR
ZUMBREEN, JACOB	FRE	253	NEW MARK
ZUMBRIM, JACOB	CAR	302	1ST DIST
ZUMBROCK, WILLIAM	BAL	471	14TH WAR
ZUMBRUM, BENJAMIN C.	CAR	306	1ST DIST
ZUMSTEIN, FREDERICK	FRE	049	FREDERIC
ZUNDORF, ELIZA	BAL	276	12TH WAR
ZURHORST, FRED	BAL	456	1ST DIST
ZWANZGER, JOHN A.	BAL	165	16TH WAR
ZWISELEE, PIERS	BAL	226	6TH WARD